"You have, in a common cause, fought and triumphed together; the independence and liberty you possess, are the work of joint counsels, and joint efforts, of common dangers, suffering and successes."

G Washington

17 September 1796

DAR PATRIOT INDEX

National Society
of the
Daughters of the American Revolution
Diamond Jubilee Administration

Mrs. William Henry Sullivan, Jr.
President General

WASHINGTON: 1966

To the Patriots of the American
Revolution and the descendants
who kept their memory alive.

FOREWORD

This first edition of the DAR PATRIOT INDEX is published at a time when wide interest is being aroused in the history of the American Revolutionary War era, during which the patriots listed herein lived. Of particular note is the fact that on July 4, 1966, the President of the United States of America signed into law a bill establishing the American Revolution Bicentennial Commission, "to plan, encourage, develop and coordinate the commemoration of the American Revolution bicentennial."

For this DAR PATRIOT INDEX to be in print at the time of the 200th Anniversary of the American Revolution is a tribute to the memory of these patriotic men and women, and it is indeed fitting for it to be published by the Daughters of the American Revolution. One or more descendant "Daughters" of each of these patriots has joined the National Society, Daughters of the American Revolution. Through their membership and work in the Society, they have endeavored to maintain and preserve the ideals these patriots endorsed, and for which they fought.

Acknowledgment is made to Mrs. Frank L. Harris of Wisconsin and the members of the Patriot Index Committee, NSDAR, for their enthusiasm and hard work in making this publication possible not only for DAR members but for all researchers of genealogy and history.

This project represents another special Diamond Jubilee achievement honoring the National Society, Daughters of the American Revolution and its 75 years of service to the Nation. It is hoped that this Index will assist many more descendants of American Revolutionary patriots to join the NSDAR. May the Society continue to render ever greater service to future generations.

Adèle Erb Sullivan

Mrs. William Henry Sullivan, Jr.
President General,
National Society
Daughters of the American Revolution

October 11, 1966

NATIONAL SOCIETY
of the
DAUGHTERS OF THE AMERICAN REVOLUTION

Objects

The objects of this Society as stated in Article II of the Bylaws are:

1. To perpetuate the memory and spirit of the men and women who achieved American Independence; by the acquisition and protection of historical spots and the erection of monuments; by the encouragement of historical research in relation to the American Revolution and the publication of its results; by the preservation of documents and relics, and of the records of the individual services of Revolutionary soldiers and patriots; and by the promotion of celebrations of all patriotic anniversaries.

2. To carry out the injunction of Washington in his farewell address to the American people, "to promote, as an object of primary importance, institutions for the general diffusion of knowledge" thus developing an enlightened public opinion, and affording to young and old such advantages as shall develop in them the largest capacity for performing the duties of American citizens.

3. To cherish, maintain, and extend the institutions of American freedom, to foster true patriotism and love of country, and to aid in securing for mankind all the blessings of liberty.

PREFACE

This DAR PATRIOT INDEX contains the names of Revolutionary patriots, both men and women, whose service (between 1774-1783) and identity have been established by the National Society, Daughters of the American Revolution from its organization in October 1890 through the June 1966 meeting of the National Board of Management: over 105,000 names. Included with the alphabetically listed names are the dates of birth and death, name(s) of wife (wives) or husband(s), rank or type of service, and the State where the patriot lived or served. If pension papers are known to exist, this fact is indicated.

This Index has been compiled from data extracted from original applications of members of the Daughters of the American Revolution, from published references, and from exhibits of proof such as authenticated copies of unpublished documents which are on file with the Society. Full credit is given to the members and the staff of the Society for their persistence and skill in the difficult work of obtaining, compiling, and checking this data.

Omission from this volume of any name in the DAR ancestor index is due to conflicting data, received over the years, which raised some question about the patriot. As members or future applicants present substantiating information to satisfactorily prove the line and service of the patriot, the name will be included in a supplement to this Index. To the best of the knowledge of the Committee members the identity of each patriot listed herein has been established and the service accepted.

The files in the offices of the Registrar General are used only by the staff and are not available to those doing research or to the general membership. Frequent inquiries about Revolutionary ancestors are received in these offices and result in much correspondence. At the suggestion of Mrs. Albert Grover Peters, present Registrar General, a committee was appointed by Mrs. William Henry Sullivan, Jr., President General, to produce this book. Its main purpose is to assist genealogists in DAR Chapters who are working on application papers of prospective members and to eliminate the necessity for much correspondence. In addition, the Index could save many hours of research for all historians and genealogists compiling family histories.

To compile over 105,000 names and other data in one volume of usable size, it has been necessary to abbreviate all words other than names of patriots and spouses. When the patriot's service is military, the proven highest rank attained is given; other services have been classified as Patriotic Service or Civil Service. A guide to the use of this Index and a list of the symbols and abbreviations follow.

Members of the Patriot Index Committee have been happy and eager to do everything possible to aid in the production of this long-needed and highly useful reference book, but wish to give particular credit to the chairman, Mrs. Frank L. Harris, and to Miss Eunice B. Haden.

It is with pride that this DAR PATRIOT INDEX is published by the National Society, Daughters of the American Revolution to list in one volume our patriot ancestors and their vital data and to provide a means through which other descendants may more readily become members of a great and beloved patriotic society.

DAR Patriot Index Committee
Mrs. Frank L. Harris, Wisconsin, Chairman

Mrs. Howard Arnest, Oregon

Mrs. Adolphus B. Bennett, D.C.

Mrs. John G. Biel, Indiana

Mrs. John S. Devanny, Illinois

Miss Eunice B. Haden, D.C.

Mrs. Wilburn Walker, Kentucky

Key to Using DAR PATRIOT INDEX

The names of patriot ancestors are arranged alphabetically. A patriot will be found listed under the most commonly used spelling of the surname. All names which are pronounced similarly are grouped together. Should your ancestor not be listed under the name as you spell it, try other spellings. Remember that our vowels are often interchangeable in sound. For example there are eight known variations of spelling for the name "Bevans," but this Index uses "Bevans" only.

Men of the same name (and some with service in the same State) are identified by their birth and death dates, and by the wife's name. There may be instances when the researcher will desire information on the patriot's children. It was impossible to include that data here. The NSDAR requires proof *only* of the child through whom the member descends.

Study the pages containing the Symbols and Abbreviations for ease in understanding what the symbols denote. If the existence of pension papers is indicated by a star (★), a photocopy may be obtained from the National Archives and Records Service, Central Research Room Branch, Washington, D. C. 20408.

Questions regarding further data on these patriots cannot be answered by the Registrar General's Office. A photocopy of an application paper of a related member is available for a small fee. If the line is "closed" by request of an active member, notification will be sent and money refunded. If there is on file more than one application paper on the line of an ancestor, a copy of the most complete "open" paper will be sent.

A request for a photocopy should be mailed with check to the Treasurer General, NSDAR, 1776 D Street, N.W., Washington, D.C. 20006. Since the amount of the fee may change, consult the DAR Handbook. Current price is $2.00. The order *must* include the following information: (1) date of request; (2) name of DAR member or prospective member; (3) Chapter and location of Chapter; (4) name of ancestor and page number in the DAR PATRIOT INDEX; (5) name and complete address including zip code of individual to whom photocopy is to be sent, if other than the one placing the order:

Evelyn Cole Peters

Mrs. Albert Grover Peters
Registrar General, NSDAR

Symbols and Abbreviations

★ *means* the soldier was pensioned:

W ★ *means* the soldier's widow was pensioned:

Heirs ★ *means* the soldier's heirs were pensioned; etc;

SDI *means* a Signer of the Declaration of Independence;

CS *means* Civil Service, that is, the holding of a Civil office such as: Constable; Jailor; Judge; Juror; Justice of Peace; Legislator; Ordinary; Selectman; Sheriff; Surveyor of Highways; Tax Collector; Town Clerk; Town Treasurer; etc: (See page 33, DAR Handbook).

PS *means* Patriotic Service, such as: An Associator; Collector of Provisions; Defender of fort or frontier; Delegate to a Continental Congress or to a Provincial Congress; Express Rider; Fence Viewer; Furnishing a substitute; Gunsmith who gave his services; Inspector of provisions; Member of the Boston Tea Party, or the Cherokee Expedition, or the Galvez Expedition, or the Kaskaskia Campaign; Member of a Committee made necessary by the War; Minister who made patriotic sermons; Munitions maker; Nurse; Taking an oath of allegiance; Patroller; Prisoner of War or of the Indians; Ranger; Rendering aid to the wounded; Rendering material aid; Signer of an Association Test; Signer of a petition; Surgeon; Wheelwright: (See page 8, "NSDAR Requirements for and Preparation of Application Papers.")

Rank, when stated, is the highest rank attained which has been proven for the patriot.

Military Ranks
of the Revolutionary Period
(listed in descending order)

ARMY	NAVY
General (George Washington only)	Admiral
Lieutenant General	Vice-Admiral
Major General	Rear-Admiral
Brigadier General	Commodore
Colonel	Captain (of a ship of 40 guns or more)
County Lieutenant	
Lieutenant Colonel	Captain (of a ship of 20 to 40 guns)
Major	Captain (of a ship of 10 to 20 guns)
Captain	Lieutenant
Captain-Lieutenant	
1st Lieutenant	
2nd Lieutenant	
Ensign	

Alphabetical List of Symbols

A.

a . . . . before
ADC . . . . . Aide-de-camp
Adj . . . . Adjutant
AdvGen. . . . . . Advocate
General
ae . . . . age or aged
Arfr . . . . Artificer
Armr. . . . . . . Armorer
Artl. . . . . Artillery

B.

b. . . . . born
Bbd . . . . Bombadier
Bgd. . . . . Brigade
BgdMaj . . . Brigade Major
BGen or BG . . . . Brigadier
General
bpt. . . . . baptized
Btm . . . . boatman

C.

c. . . . . circa
Capt . . . . Captain
CaptLt . . . . Captain-
Lieutenant
Cav . . . . Cavalry
Cdr. . . . . . . Commander
CG. . . . . . . Coast Guard
Chn★ . . . . Children
received a pension
Chp . . . . Chaplain
CL . . . . . Continental Line
Cmdt . . . . . Commandant
CMman . . . . Court Martial
man
CMOF. . . . . Court Martial
Officer
Cmsry . . . . . Commissary
Cnt . . . . Cornet
Col . . . . Colonel
Commo . . . . Commodore
Cpl. . . . . Corporal
CS . . . . Civil Service
CT . . . . Connecticut
CtyLt . . County Lieutenant

D.

d. . . . . died
DE . . . . Delaware
Dep . . . . Deputy
Dr. . . Physician or Surgeon
Drm . . . . Drummer
DrmMaj . . . . Drum Major

E.

Ens . . . . Ensign

F.

Fif . . . . Fifer
FifMaj . . . . . Fife Major
FrA . . . . . . French Army
FrN . . . . . . French Navy

G.

GA . . . . Georgia
Gen . . . . General
Gnr . . . . Gunner
Grd. . . . . Guard
Grl . . . . Guerilla

H.

Heirs★ . . . Heirs Pensioned

I.

IL . . . Kaskaskia Campaign
(in now Illinois)
IN. . . . . Indiana
(at Vincennes)

K.

KY . . . . Kentucky

L.

LA . . . . Louisiana
(Galvez Expedition)
LCol . . . Lieutenant Colonel
LGen . . Lieutenant General
Lt . . . . Lieutenant
1Lt . . . . . 1st Lieutenant
2Lt . . . . . 2d Lieutenant

M.

m. . . . . married
MA . . . . . Massachusetts
Maj. . . . . Major
Mar. . . . . Marine
Matr . . . . Matross
MD . . . . Maryland
ME. . . . . Maine
MGen . . . . Major General
Mid . . . . . Midshipman
Mil . . . Militia or Militiaman
MilS. . . . Military service
(no details known)
MM . . . . . Minute Man
MO . . . . Missouri
Mrnr . . . . Mariner
MS . . . . . . Mississippi
Mstr . . . . Master of a Ship
Mte . . . . Mate on a ship
Mus. . . . . . . Musician

N.

N. . . . . Nurse
NC. . . . . . North Carolina
NCapt. . . . . Navy Captain
NGnr . . . . . Navy Gunner
NH. . . . . New Hampshire
NJ . . . . . . New Jersey
Noncom Non-Commissioned
Officer

O.

Of or O . . . . Officer (rank
unknown)
Ordl. . . . . Orderly
OrdlSgt . . Orderly Sergeant

P.

p. . . . . after
PA . . . . . Pennsylvania
PM . . . . . . Paymaster
PS . . . . . Patriotic Service
Pvt . . . . Private
Pvtr . . . . Privateer

Q.

QM . . . . . Quartermaster
QMSgt. . . . Quartermaster
Sergeant
QMGen . . . Quartermaster
General

R.

RI . . . . . . Rhode Island
RO . . . . Recruiting Officer

S.

SC. . . . . . South Carolina
Sct . . . . Scout
SDI . . . . . Signer of the
Declaration of
Independence
SeaCap. . . . . Sea Captain
Sgt . . . . Sergeant
Slr . . . . Sailor
Smn . . . . Seaman
Sol . . . . Soldier (no details
known)
SrgnMte . . Surgeon's Mate
Stl . . . . Sentinel
SurGen . . . . The Surgeon
General

T.

Tms. . . . . Teamster
TN. . . . . Tennessee
Trm . . . . . . Trumpeter

V.

VA . . . . Virginia
Vol . . . . Volunteer
VT . . . . Vermont

W.

W★ . . . Widow pensioned
Wgm . . . . Wagon Master
Wgn . . . . Wagoneer
Wm. . . . . William

X.

X or — means the name of
the wife is unknown

NS . . . . . . Naval Service
(no details known)
NY . . . . New York

DAR PATRIOT INDEX

AARON,
Abraham: b *c.* 1734 d *p.* 1785 m — PS VA
Jacob: b *c.* 1756 d 1824 m Judith Kearby Pvt PA
Obed: b 1761 d 4-22-1837 m — Pvt PA

ABBEY, (includes ABBE, ABBIE, & ABBY)
Aaron: b 9-20-1747 d *p.* 1800 m Anna — Lt MA
Abner: b 11-5-1758 d 12-13-1803 m Sarah Swetland Pvt CT
Daniel: b 11-7-1749 d 9-26-1815 m Sarah Pease CS CT
David: b 7- -1751 d 8-7-1799 m Sarah Preston Cpl MA
Jeduthan : b 8-14-1757 d 2-9-1821 m Lucretia Bement Sgt CT
John, Sr.: b 4-18-1717 d 8-1-1794 m Sarah Root Pvt CT
John, Jr.: b 11-27-1739 d 10-17-1805 m Charity Simonds Pvt CT
John: b 8-23-1747-8 d *p.* 1789 m Dorothy Bugbee Pvt CT
John: b 8-22-1743 d *p.* 1790 Abial Averill MM Sgt VT
Mason: b 4-17-1759 d 10-18-1849 m Sarah Frisell Pvt CT
Richard, Sr.: b 8-1-1735 d 9-28-1807 m Mary Bement Capt CT
Richard, Jr.: b 1760 d 8-9-1831 m Lydia Stevenson Pvt CT W ★
Richard: b 7-1-1730 d 2-17-1794 m Mary Huntington Sgt CT
Samuel: b 8-10-1806 m (1)Rachel Matson (2)Mrs
    Sarah Warren Leland Pvt CT
Samuel: b 1-7-1755 d 3-29-1824 m Miriam Hall Pvt CT
Solomon: b 5-29-1730 d 1799 m (1)Sarah Knight (2)Mrs
    Elizabeth Burnham Pvt CT
Stephen: b *c.* 1727 d 3-26-1798 m Mary — PS CT
Thomas: b 4-11-1731 d 6-13-1811 m Penlope Terry Capt CT

ABBOTT, (includes ABBETT, ABBIT, ABBOT, & ABOTT)
Aaron: b 11-3-1758 d 12-9-1854 m Betsey — Pvt Tms CT ★
Aaron: b 4-2-1746 d 1-15-1821 m Mary Ayers Cpl MA
Abel: b — d *p.* 1790 m Hannah Dibble Pvt CT
Abiel: b 4-19-1741 d 8-19-1809 m Dorcas Abbott Maj MA
Abiel: b 8-23-1749 d 12-5-1832 m Sarah Mann Pvt MA
Abijah: b 7-11-1756 d 4-10-1810 m Rachel Jennings Pvt MA
Amos, Jr.: b 7-15-1754 d 10-11-1834 m Judith Morse Cpl NH ★
Asa: b 1761 d 1823 m Eliz Pratt Pvt CT W ★
Asa: b 10-28-1721 d 12-23-1796 m Elizabeth (Abbot) PS MA
Bancroft: b 6-4-1757 d 10-29-1829 m Lydia White Pvt NH
Barachias: b 5-14-1707 d 10-2-1784 m Hannah Holt PS MA
Benjamin: b 1-26-1738 d 11-5-1778 m Joanna Barker Pvt MA
Benjamin, Sr.: b 4-6-1730 d 1-5-1776 m Elizabeth (Abbott) Pvt NH
Benjamin, Jr.: b 2-10-1750 d 12-11-1815 m Sarah Brown Sgt NH
Beriah: b 1757 d 3-13-1832 m (1)Mary Fairfeild (2)Mrs. Martha
    Griswold Pvt NH ★
Bixby: b 11-24-1750 d 1813 m (1)Hepzibah Ames (2)Mary Johnson
    Cpl MA
Caleb: b 10-8-1751 d 4-12-1837 m Lycy Lovejoy Sgt NH & MA ★
Daniel: b *a.* 1755 d *a.* 1785 m — Capt CT
Daniel: b 1-4-1725/26 d 1783/84 Lois Smith PS CT
Daniel: b 11-11-1748 d 12-4-1834 m (2)Hannah Hodsdon (3) Eliza-
    beth Workman Pvt MA
Daniel: b 7-25-1764 d 11-11-1809 m (1)Naomi Graves (2)Hannah
    Porter Pvt MA
David: b 3-28-1728 d 11-1-1788 m Prudence Sheldon Pvt MA
Edward: b 12-27-1730 d 9-15-1801 m Deborah Stevens PS NH
Enoch: b 1752 d 9-10-1823 m Molly Betts Pvt CT
Ephraim: b 5-27-1740 d 6-3-1815 m Sarah Curtis Pvt MA
Ephraim: b 3-19-1759 d 1-2-1834 m Esther Eastman Pvt MA ★
Ephraim: b 4-18-1718 d 1776-90 m (1)Mary (Abbot) (2)Hannah
    Kneeland PS NH
Ezra: b 8-24-1756 d 2-21-1837 m (1)Betty Andrews (2)Anner
    Choate (3)Jane Jackman Pvt NH
George: b 12-14-1724 d 12-26-1775 m Hannah Lovejoy QM MA
George: b 12-29-1755 d 9-15-1818 m Naomi Tuttle Pvt MA
George: b 11-6-1706 d 10-6-1785 m Sarah (Abbot) PS NH
Henry: b 6-16-1762 d 2-3-1776 m Mary Platt PS MA
Henry: b — d 6-9-1846 m Keziah — Pvt RI
Isaac: b 6-16-1762 d 6-23-1861 m Susanna Knight Cpl MA ★
Isaac: b 2-3-1744 d 5-21-1836 m Phebe Chandler Lt MA ★
Isaac: b 8-29-1732 d 1800 m Sarah Barker Pvt NH
Jabez: b 4-18-1731 d 1-7-1804 m (1)Phebe — (2)Hepzibah Stevens
    PS CS NH
Jacob: b 3-22-1746 d 3-5-1820 m Lydia Stevens CS NH
Jacob: b *c.* 1750 d *c.* 1840 m Prudence Mackay Pvt NJ
James: b 1747 d 1-26-1799 m Sarah — Lt CT
James: b 1-12-1717 d 1803 m Sarah (Lampson) Bancroft PS NH
James: b 3-9-1753 d 5-2-1830 m (1)Hannah Dennison (2)Phebe
    (Howe) Coray Sgt CT

James: b 1761 d 5-23-1837 m Martha Tarr Sol MA
James: b 10-18-1750 d 8-1-1815 m (1)Zylpha Smith (2)Mehit-
    able Hidden Pvt NH
Jeduthan: b 8-1-1749 d 12-26-1821 m Hannah Poor Sgt MA
Jeptha: b 1752 d 7-18-1826 m Mercy Ann Garrison Pvt NJ
Jeremiah: b 3-17-1744 d 11-8-1823 m Elizabeth Stickney Lt NH
Jeremiah: b 5-25-1743 d 11-2-1825 m Chloe (Abbot) PS NH
Jesse: b 3-30-1742 d 2-20-1827 m Sarah Wakefield Sgt MA
Joel: b 1-1-1732 d 1-23-1823 m Judith Steavens Pvt MA
Joel: b 12-4-1757 d 4-12-1806 m Lydia Cummings Pvt MA
John: b 7-30-1750 d 5-7-1814 m Temperance Baker Sol CT
John: b 3-1-1726 d 1-6-1804 m Elizabeth St. John PS CT
John: b 9-12-1735 d 4-24-1818 m Abigail — Capt MA
John: b 6-5-1738 d 5-23-1799 m Mary Gleason Allen 2Lt MA
John: b 12-2-1743 d 5-8-1804 m (1)Lucy Proctor (2)Mary Far-
    rar Lt PS MA
John: b 5-30-1762 d 1-10-1820 m Betsey Webb Cpl MA
John: b 2-7-1718/19 d 1803 m (2)Hannah Farnham Pvt MA
John: b 4-12-1741 d *a.* 11-6-1823 m Ann Hooper Pvt MA
John: b 8-3-1768 d 5- -1837 m Martha Twombley Pvt MA
John: b 8-23-1762 d 11-20-1818 m Anna Nichols Pvt MA
John: b 8-3-1704 d 11-10-1793 m Phebe Fiske PS MA
John: b 1-4-1759 d 7-26-1840 m Alce Akers Pvt Tms Wgm NJ ★
John: b 4-8-1758 d 4-3-1834 m (1)Rebecca Chattin (2)Eliza-
    beth Harding Pvt NJ
John: b 2-16-1755 d 1836 m — Pvt NC ★
John: b 8-9-1741 d 7-18-1778 m Alice Fuller Pvt PA
John, Sr.: b 4-2-1724 d 5-21-1814 m (1)Sarah Baker (2)Mrs
    Hawley Col VT
John, Jr.: b 7-17-1748 d 3-30-1835 m Susanna Meachman Pvt VT ★
Jonathan: b 4-12-1747 d 6-26-1833 m Ruth Bragg Capt MA
Jonathan: b 4-1-1723 d 1-26-1805 m Elizabeth Barnes Pvt MA
Jonathan: b 8-29-1740 d 12-26-1821 m (1)Mehitable — (2)Dorcas
    — Sgt MA
Joseph: b 2-14-1735 d 1-5-1814 m (1)Elizabeth Stedman (2)
    Olive Pearce Col CT
Joseph: b 8-28-1737 d *p.* 1790 m Rachael Brown Pvt CT
Joseph: b 7-10-1752 d 1834 m Ruth Buckman Sgt MA
Joseph: b 6-8-1727 d 6-23-1794 m Hannah White Sol MA
Joseph: b 4-2-1744 d 1792 m Mary Barker 2Lt NH & MA
Joseph: b 2-16-1758 d 5-3-1836 m Lucy King Pvt MA & NH ★
Joseph: b 8-5-1759 d 10-7-1837 m Molly Meloon Pvt NH ★
Joseph: b 10-23-1741 d 1-19-1832 m Phebe Lovejoy PS CS NH
Joseph: b 1739 d *p.* 1804 m Esther Osborn Sol VA CL
Joshua: b 6-15-1759 d 3-4-1837 m (1)Sally Brown (2)Ann Man-
    ning Pvt NH & MA
Joshua: b 11-5-1765 d *p.* 1797 m Huldah — Pvt NH
Joshua: b 2-24-1740 d 3-12-1815 m Elizabeth Chandler Capt
    NH
Josiah: b 12-29-1759 d 2-15-1837 m (1)Ruth Bodwell (2)Nancy
    Furbush Ens MA
Judd: b 7-7-1760 d 8-2-1827 m Sarah Weed Pvt CT
Moses: b 1-13-1727 d 5-22-1809 m Mary Hill Lt MA
Moses: b 8-9-1735 d 2-23-1827 m Elizabeth Holt Lt CS MA
Moses: b 5-19-1752 d 7-11-1837 m Mary Batchelder Pvt NJ ★
Nathan: b 9-9-1753 d 2-5-1801 m Sarah Ballard Pvt MA
Nathan: b 1743 d 10- -1812 m Lydia Hatch Pvt NH
Nathan: b *c.* 1753 d *p.* 1790 m Elizabeth Furman Pvt NH
Nathaniel: b 26-1751 d 3- -1791 m Sarah Stevens Pvt MA
Nathaniel: b 3-10-1726 d 2-4-1806 m Mirriam Chandler Pvt
    PS NH
Peter: b — d *p.* 3-1-1805 m — Pvt MA
Peter: b 7-27-1701 d 1785 m (1)Lydia Gilbert (2)Rachel Stevens
    Sol MA
Peter: b 7-28-1762 d *p.* 1805 m Abigail Farnum Pvt NH
Phillip: b 3-23-1751 d 3-8-1834 m (1)Anna Hewett (2)Mabiel
    Merritt Pvt CT
Reuben: b 1763 d 1843 m Mirabah Hodgkins Cpl MA
Reuben: b 4-4-1723 d 5-13-1822 m Rhoda Whittemore Pvt NH
Roger: b 1750 d 11-12-1809 m Alice (McClanahan) Vaugn Sgt
    VA
Roger: b 12-31-1743 d 2-11-1809 m Ann Ruffner Pvt VA
Samuel: b 10-1-1727 d *p.* 1790 m Miriam Stevens PS Pvt NH
Samuel: b 6-16-1736 d *p.* 1780 m Bethsebe Dustin Pvt NH
Samuel: b 1748 d 1837 m Desire Gibbs Pvt VT
Silas: b 1745 d 1837 m (1)Anes Hutchins (2)Lydia Cluff Sgt CL
    MA ★
Solomon: 5-7-1759 d 1-5-1842 m Rachael Bowers Pvt NH

ABBOTT, contd.
Solomon: b 3-6-1761 d 7-15-1856 m Phoebe Turner Pvt SC
Stephen: b 8-12-1749 d 8-12-1813 m Sarah Croel Capt MA
Thomas: b — d c. 1828 m Polly Day Sol PA
Timothy: b 1745 d 1826 m Sarah — 2Lt MA
Timothy: b 10-15-1762 d 9-8-1831 m Sarah Smith Pvt NH ★
Uriah: b 9-29-1735 d 1797 m (1) Sarah Wright (2)Sarah Perry Sgt NH
Walter: b 1-1-1749 d 1-15-1823 m Persis — Sgt VT
Wm: b 10-7-1745 d 7-25-1832 m (1)Mary Coy (2)Esther Green Ens CT
Wm: b 10-9-1724 d 1-2-1798 m Experience Bigsby Pvt MA
Wm: b 7-21-1746 d p. 1795 m Bridget Spaulding Pvt MA
Wm: b 4-24-1755 d 6-14-1807 m Mabel Whittlesey Sgt NH
Wm: b 1-14-1748 d 11-30-1793 m Phebe Ballard PS NH
Wm: b 1740 d 1820 m Sarah Dennard PS SC
Wm, Jr.: b 1753/54 d p. 1833 m Hannah Ann Pvt VA
Wm: b 1757 d 1-4-1848 m Mary Parker Pvt VA ★

ABEL, (includes ABEEL, ABELL, & ABLE)
Abel: b 9-14-1757 d 3-14-1841 m (1) Lucy Hubbard (2) Jemima Brainard Pvt NS CT ★
Azel: b 7-9-1764 d 9-17-1833 m (1)— Nichols (2) Mary Phipps Pvt VT ★
Conrad: b c. 1730 d a. 10-31-1794 m Maria Margaret Sturm Pvt PA
Cuthbert: b 2-1-1759 d 12-2-1794 m Mary M Simmonds Sgt MD
David: b 6-15-1750 d 1-25-1839 m Chloe Sackett Cpl CT
David: b 1-13-1763 d 10-31-1840 m Jane Hassert Mid NJ ★
David: b 1-1/2-5-1727 d 2-5-1813 m Neltje Van Bergen PS NY
Elijah: b 5-12-1758 d 1837 m Mary Cleveland Cpl CT ★
Enoch: b 1745 d 3- -1784 m Judith — 1Lt MD
Garrett: b 5-2-1734 d 9-23-1799 m Mary Byvank Maj NY
George, Sr.: b 1735 d a. 1786 m Maria Catharine Pvt MA
Jacob, Jr.: b 9-12-1744 d 7-12-1822 m Mary Maria Bentz Pvt PA
Jacob: b 1-21-1719 d 7-21-1807 m Maria Catherine PS PA
James: b 5-12-1731 d 4-25-1825 m Gertrude Neilson Dep Qm Gen NJ
John: b 3-8-1757 d 12-23-1836 m Mary Luce Cpl CT
John: b 1746 d 8- -1794 m Elizabeth — Lt MD
John: b c. 1724 d 12-1-1794 m Mary Knouts PS NY
John Barton: b c. 1755 d 2-1-1820 m (1)Eleanor Heard (2)Dorothy Wimsatt Capt MD
Joseph: b 1752 d 7-22-1846 m Catherine Hartley Pvt MD
Joshua: b c. 1760 d 4-10-1814 m Susannah Mills Pvt MD
Joshua: b 7-16-1731 d 8-29-1811 m (1)Elizabeth Lyon (2)Ruth Manning (3)Molly Lyon Cpl CS MA
Matthias: b 1754 d 1837 m Mary — Pvt NJ
Preserved: b — d 1-22-1828 m Lucy Brown Sgt RI
Robert: b 11-11-1721 d 9-22-1800 m Mary Thompson Pvt MA
Samuel, Sr.: b c. 1716/17 d 1777 m Ellinore O Brien PS CS 2Maj MD
Samuel, Jr.: b c. 1738/39 d 6-4-1795 m Ann — Sol MD
Simeon: b 6-22-1736 d p. 1784 m Martha Crocker Sgt CT
Simon, Sr.: b 9-15-1721 d 12-10-1778 m Parnal Willes Sgt CT
Simon, Jr.: b 2-28-1747 d 12-5-1816 m (1)Rachel Brewster (2)Betty Bigelow Ens CT
Thomas: b 10-9-1749 d 10-10-1814 m Eunice Griswold Sgt VT
Thomas: b 1759 d 8-30-1822 m Elizabeth — Pvt VA W ★
William: b 1-14-1749 d 3-17-1837 m Lois Merry Pvt CT W ★
William: b 1747 d 1820 m Catherine Ben or Berd Pvt NJ

ABENDSCHON,
Reinholt: b a. 1749 d p. 4-18-1783 m Anna — PS PA
Samuel: b 1-13-1754 d a. 7- -1824 m Phebe Daler Sol PS PA

ABERCROMBIE,
Charles: b 3-4-1742 d 1819 m Edwina Malinda Booth Capt CS NC
James: b 1754 d 12-14-1836 m Margarey Conkey Pvt MA
Robert, Sr.: b 1715 d c. 1779 Jane— CS NC
Robert, Jr.: b c. 1748 d c. 1814 m (1)Mary — (2)Mrs Nancy Moore 1Maj NC

ABERNATHY, (includes ABERNETHY)
Buckner: b 1745 d 1850 m Hulda Rivers Pvt VA
David: b 7-29-1759 d 4-14-1838 m Christina Forney Sol NC ★
David: b c. 1740 d 1814 m Ann Turner PS NC
James: b c. 1740-48 d 1785 m Elizabeth Cox PS NC
John: b 1753 d 6- -1816 m Susan M Forney Sol NC
John: b— d 12-17-1807 m Rhoda Davis PS SC
Laban: b c. 1748 d 1833 m (2)Elizabeth Drake PS VA
Miles: b c. 1728 d 1789 m Sarah Ann (Jones) Goode PS NC
Robert: b c. 1721-23 d 1792 m Sarah — Capt PS NC
Robert: b 1752 d p. 9-6-1845 m Sarah Nichols Pvt VA ★
William: b 4-4-1742 d 2-8-1832 m Elizabeth Clayton PS VA

ABNEY,
John: b c. 1745 d 1788 m Isabella Van Lear CS VA
Nathaniel: b 4-4-1734 d p. 7- -1806 m Isabella Madison Capt SC
Paul: b 1744 d c. 12-27-1820 m Eleanor Hamilton Pvt SC
Paul: b c. 1760 d 6-15-1815 m Rhoda Norman Pvt VA W ★
Samuel, Sr.: b 1715 d 1781 m Martha Collins Sgt SC

Samuel, Jr.: b c. 1746/47 d c. 1782 m Martha Harriet Hamilton Pvt SC
William: b 5-5-1736 d 1-4-1832 m (1)Mary Clark (2)Elizabeth Burnham Capt SC
William: b 1757 d 1-31-1845 m Judith Clark Pvt VA ★

ABORN, (includes EBORN)
Daniel: b 7-1-1749 d 1783 m Mary Arnold Capt NS RI
James: b 1747 d 9-28-1803 m Hannah Dove Sgt MA
James: b 9-28-1734 d 3-31-1801 m Hannah Westgate MM RI
John: b 1749 d 11-15-1796 m Arcadia Foreman Col NC
Samuel: b 1756 d 1827 m Dorothy Post Pvt NJ

ABRAHAMS, (includes ABRAHAM & ABRAMS)
Daniel: b c. 1747 d 1790 m Sarah Combs PS NY
Emanuel: b c. 1760 d 1802 m Judith Mordecai Pvt SC
Enoch: b a. 1744 d 8-6-1823 m Jean Hamilton CM man PA
Gabriel: b 10-11-1750 d 10-1-1841 m Rebekah Loveberry Pvt PA
Henry, Sr.: b 1720 d 1828 m Rhoda—CS PA
Henry, Jr.: b 1747 d c. 1828 m—Ens 2Lt PA
Isaac: b 4-28-1717 d 1785 m Dinah Harvard Pvt PA
James: b 9-23-1763 d 8-11-1839 m Elsie Suydam Pvt NJ ★
James: b 1755 d p. 1800 m Eleanor Brisbon Sgt PA
Mordecai: b 1735/40 d 1800 m Sarah Levy Capt VA

ACHE, see AUGHE

ACHENBACH, (includes ACHENBAUGH & AUGHENBAUGH)
Philip: b 1759 d 6-5-1844 m (1)Mary Ann Harter (2)Elizabeth — Pvt PA
Philip: b 2-17-1732 d 1-30-1800 m Anna Maria (Boyer) Engler Pvt PA

ACHESON, see ATCHISON

ACHORN, (includes ACORN & EICHORN)
Jacob, Sr.: b—d p. 1790 m Jane — PS ME
Jacob, Jr.: b 3-14-1741 d 9-19-1836 m Margaret Ulmer Pvt MA
Jacob: b 1724 d 8- -1805 m Rachel — Sol NY
Michael: b 1759 d 4-29-1823 m Margaret Smouse Pvt MA ★

ACKEN,
John(Jonathan): b 1730-5 d 1797 m Sarah De Camp MM NJ
Jonathan: b 9-19-1764 d 12-7-1807 m — Pvt NJ
Joseph: b 11-12-1733 d 8-22-1803 m Rebecca Crane Pvt NJ

ACKER, (includes AKER & AKERS)
Benjamin: b 8-17-1763 d 11-25-1851 m Mary Jones Pvt NY
Conrad: b 1- -1741 d 7-15-1815 m Barbara Rubel Ens PA
John: b 1758 d p. 1834 m Nannie Jeffs Pvt VA
Joseph: b c. 1758 d 1843 m Anna — Pvt VA
Peter: b c. 1745 d 1815 m Jane Southerland PS SC
Peter: b 11-9-1754 d 3-17-1845 m Jemima Benway Sgt NY ★
Solomon: b c. 1745 d p. 1806 m — Pvt VA
Stephen: b— d— m Nancy Ward Pvt NY
Thomas: b c. 1736 d p. 1815 m Mary — Sol KY
William: b 10-30-1730 d 7-29-1814 m Eleanor Lanning Cpl NJ
William: b 1755 d 1809 m Anna — Pvt PA
William: b 1-17-1735 d 11-21-1836 m Polly Blackburn Sgt VA

ACKERMAN, (includes AKERMAN)
Abram: b 1-2-1755 d 1-22-1796 m Elizabeth ver Wie Pvt NJ
Barnet: b 1-14-1749 d 3-27-1824 m Sarah March PS NH
Benjamin: b—d—m Elizabeth Mead CS NH
Gulian: bpt 8-26-1722 d p. 1790 m Annatje Westervelt PS NY
Jacobus: b 1-21-1758 d 1-28-1835 m Sarah Conklin Sol NY
Johannes: b 3-18-1760 d 12-25-1831 m Elizabeth Dierman Pvt NJ
John: b 1747 d p. 1790 m Mary Akerman Pvt NH
John: b 1758 d 9-8-1841 m (2)Mrs Amy (Barton) Roberts Pvt NJ ★
John: b 1745 d 1810 m Dorothy Montfort Ensign PS NY
Nahum: b 1-21-1736 d 1802 m (1)Ann— (2)Mrs Ann Hayes Sgt NH
Peter: b 12-28-1755 d 1804 m Margaret Dierman PS NJ
Peter: b 2-29-1748 d 5-22-1832 m (1)Rachel Foss (2)Charity (Foss)Locke Pvt NH ★
Robert: b 1763 d 5-7-1839 m Roxelane Child Cpl NY

ACKERT,
Martinus: b 1749 d 12-18-1842 m Salome Escher Pvt NY
Solomon: b 1753 d 2-5-1844 m Elizabeth Quackenbos Pvt NY

ACKISS,
John: b c. 1740 d p. 1-28-1797 m Jane Woodhouse PS VA

ACKLEY, (includes ACKLY)
Bezaleel: b 2-4-1723/24 d p. 1776 m Bridget Champion Maj CT
Daniel: b 1760 d 1815/16 m Sarah Price Parker Pvt NJ
Elijah: b 6-23-1745 d 7-25-1831 m Anna Osborn Ens CT
Gideon: b 4-14-1716 d 12-11-1805 m (1)Hannah Andrews (2) Deborah Rowley Ens CT
Hezekiah: b 1-1-1762 d 10-6-1816 m Jemima Whittlesey Pvt CT ★

Isaac Chalker: b 3-18-1760 d *p.* 1832 m Ruthy Burr Pvt CT ★
Jacob: b 1764 d 4-1-1840 m Phoeby Jenkins Pvt NY
John: b 12-14-1759 d *p.* 1803 m Hannah— Pvt NJ
Nathaniel: b 9-30-1763 d 9-5-1838 m Elizabeth Spencer Tms Grd CT
Samuel: b 7-17-1763 d 3-21-1861 m Elizabeth Hodgkins Moody Pvt MA ★
Silas: b *c.* 1760 d 1808 m Esther English Guinn Pvt NJ
Stephen, Sr.: b 9-9-1739 d 1-3-1823 m Thankful Watrous Pvt CT
Stephen, Jr.: b 1763 d 1836 m Mehitable Chamberlain Pvt CT ★

ACKLIN,
Joseph: b 12-2-1732 d 4-5-1836 m Nancy Kimber Pvt VA

ACOCK,
Robert: b 1753 d 1847 m Mary Blanchett Pvt NC ★

ACREE,
Wm.: b 8-16-1752 d 3-3-1833 m (1)Phoebe Acree (2)Edith Doss Pvt NC W ★

ACTON,
Henry: b *c.* 1755 d 7-10-1842 m Lucy — Pvt MD ★
Smallwood: b 9-14-1758 d 3-25-1844 m (1)Mary Wilson (2) Nancy Cave Pvt MD ★

ADAIR, (includes ADARE)
James: b *c.* 1742 d *c.* 1816 m Mary Cunningham Pvt SC
James: b 12- -1747 d 3-23-1831 m Rebecca Montgomery Sol SC
James: b 5-15-1752 d 8-18-1818 m Hannah — Wgm SC
James: b 5-8-1752 d 1835 m Hannah Netherton Vol SC
James, Jr.: b *a.* 1755 d 7- -1835 m Anna — Pvt SC
James Robert: b 1709 d *a.* 8- -1786 m (1)Clark Hobson Jr., Dr PS NC
John: b 1754 d *a.* 8-11-1843 m Mary — Pvt NC ★
John: b 1732 d 2-24-1827 m Eleanor Crawford Sol NC
John: b *c.* 1725 d *p.* 12-29-1806 m Sarah—Pvt PA
John: b 1-9-1757 d 5-19-1840 m Catherine Palmer Maj SC
John: b *c.* 1756-9 d 1812 m Jane Jones PS SC
Joseph, Sr.: b 1711 d 1801 m (1)Sarah Laferty (2)Susannah Long Cmsry SC
Joseph, Jr.: b 1733 d 10-17-1812 m Sarah Dillard Dep Cmsry SC
Mary: b *a.* 1730 d 1819 m William Adair PS SC
William: b *c.* 1760 d 5-15-1808 m Catherine Janes Lt SC ★
William: b 6-17-1761 d 8-25-1811 m Mary Montgomery Adj SC
William, Sr.: b *a.* 1730 d — m Mary Moore PS SC
William.: b *a.* 1755 d 1822-28 m Margaret — Lt SC

ADAMS (includes ADAM, ADDAMS, & ADDOMS)
Aaron: b 5-1-1758 d 2-21-1836 m (1)Rhoda Hanford (2)Hannah Morehouse Pvt CT
Aaron: b 1749 d 10-28-1843 m Sarah Dodge Sgt MA
Aaron: b 7-20-1761 d 7-24-1843 m Lydia Washburn Pvt MA VT ★
Aaron: b 12-21-1737/38 d 3-14-1819 m Betsey Adams Capt NH
Aaron: b 3-11-1747 d 12-13-1833 m Sarah Hard Sgt VT W ★
Abel: b 4-30-1756 d 3-25-1829 m Rosene Cosset Pvt CT
Abel: b 5-16-1746 d 9-21-1792 m Olive Richardson 2Lt MA
Abel: b 2-20-1757 d 10-22-1826 m Rebecca Jones Pvt MA
Abijah: b l2-1-1760 d 6-12-1843 m Dorcas Fassett Pvt RI
Abner: b 11-5-1735 d 8-5-1825 m Abagail Hubbard Capt CT
Abner: b 8-10-1733 d 1828/29 m Dorothy Murray Pvt MA
Abner: b 10-22-1749 d 2-13-1834 m (1)Moley Sawtell (2)Sarah Sartell Sgt MA ★
Abraham: b 12-2-1745 d *p.* 1833 m Sarah — Pvt CT ★
Abraham: b 9-3-1740 d 4-15-1803 m Lydia Giddings Pvt CT
Abraham: b 6-26-1737 d 1809 m Michel Belinger Sgt MA
Abraham: b 5-24-1748 d 5-4-1827 m Mary Bricket Drm MA
Abraham: b 1755 d 11-22-1822 m Susannah — Sgt NJ
Abraham: b *p.* 1-8-1732 d *a.* 9-26-1803 m Elizabeth McCormick Pvt PA
Alexander: b *c.* 1757 d *p.* 1777 m Nancy Williams Gnr NS PA
Amasa, Sr.: bpt 8-3-1708 d 7-6-1790 m Hannah Camp PS CT
Amasa, Jr.: b 3-15-1753 d 1-6-1819 m (1)Mary Sarah Deming Griswold (2)Mrs Caroline Delebe (3)Mrs Lydia Belden Pvt CT
Amos: b 6-29-1746 d 1844 m Sarah — Sgt MA ★
Amos: b 2-15-1746 d 3-6-1823 m Mary Lynde Sgt MA
Amos: b 9-1-1728 d 10-5-1775 m (1)Elizabeth Prentice (2)Abigail Mears (3)Sarah Chauncey PS MA
Andrew: b 12-11-1736 d 11-27-1797 m Eunice (Fairchild) Buel PS CS CT
Andrew: b 8-12-1735 d 1783 m Ruth Wadsworth Sgt MA W ★
Andrew: b 10-21-1751 d 8-25-1841 m Lucy Merriam Sgt MA
Anthony: b 1736 d 1809 m Rosena Dunkel Lesher Pvt PA
Asa: b 3-26-1757 d 2-20-1828 m Abigail Curtis Pvt MA
Asahel: b 9-13-1754 d 5-25-1818 m Olive Avery Pvt CT
Bartholomew: b 1754 d 1814 m Elizabeth Manlove Pvt DE ★
Benjamin: b 12-1-1735 d 11-27-1816 m Patience Blinn 2Lt CT
Benjamin: b 1-2-1738 d 1- -1816 m Hannah Dyer Lt CT
Benjamin: b 7-13-1764 d 1-1-1853 m Mary Williams Pvt CT
Benjamin: b 1745 d *p.* 1794 m (1)Chloe Hatch (2)Sarah Gridley PS CT

Benjamin: b 3-1-1747 d 1-10-1821 m (1)Sarah Spofford (2)Elizabeth Woodman Capt CS MA
Benjamin: b 11-20-1735 d 12-23-1817 m Mary Harriman Capt MA
Benjamin: b 10-20-1750 d 5-20-1843 m Mrs Elizabeth Adams Pvt MA
Benjamin, Jr.: b 4-9-1748 d 2-23-1829 m Eunice Hale Pvt PS MA
Benjamin: b 8-20-1752 d 2-25-1819 m Judith Adams Pvt MA
Benjamin: b 10-25-1754 d 8-23-1821 m Anne Holmes Pvt MA
Benjamin: b 10-7-1752 d 4-9-1830 m Mary Stone Pvt MA
Benjamin: b 8-6-1728 d 5-5-1815 m Priscilla — Sol MA
Benjamin: b 1-18-1728/29 d 3-29-1803 m (1)Abigail Pickering (2)Susanna Brown CS NH
Benoni: b 12-31-1754 d *p.* 1792 m Susanna Chamberlain Pvt MA
Bulkeley: b — d — m Persis Stone Sol MA
Camp: b 10-9-1739 d 3-20-1823 m Mehitabel Baxter PS CT
Charles: b 9-14-1757 d 3-14-1808 m Mary Hughlett Ens MD
Chester: b 1754 d 3-17-1829 m Elizabeth Sutherland Pvt NY
Daniel: b 10-7-1754/55 d 2—1829 m Alice Ensworth Pvt CT
Daniel, Sr.: b 1-18-1724 d 1809 m Elizabeth Balch Pvt MA
Daniel, Jr.: b 2-11-1755 d 11-11-1815 m (1)Lucinda Watkins (2)Mary Whiting Pvt MA
Daniel: b 1742 d 1820 m Hepzibah Batchelder Pvt MA
Daniel: b 4-20-1750 d 12-17-1832 m (1)Martha Watkins (2)Sarah Alden (3)Elizabeth Parmenter Pvt MA
Daniel: b 1720 d 10-10-1795 m Mehitabel Crosby PS MA
Daniel: b — d — m Hannah Middleton Pvt MA
Daniel: b 1751 d 2-23-1846 m Deborah Cooley Pvt NH ★
Daniel: b *a.* 1758 d *p.* 1815 m Eleanor (Jackson) Allen Sgt VT
Daniel Jenifer: b 1751 d 11-29-1796 m Nancy Hanson Maj MD
Davenport: b1751 d 2-15-1833 m Elizabeth Taney Pvt MA
David: b 3-22-1756 d 5-31-1833 m Abigail Carver 1Sgt CT ★
David: b 12-10-1754 d 1-24-1816 m Mary Woodman Sgt MA
David: b 1723 d 11-25-1783 m (2)Margaret Cain Matr MA
David, Jr.: b 11-6-1755 d 10-27-1824 m (1)Hannah Russell (2)Sophia — Cpl NH ★
David: b 3-7-1757 d 10-1-1844 m Alice Loveland Sgt NH
David: b 6-20-1747 d 11-17-1831 m Phoebe Spofford PS NH
David: b 12-25-1761 d 4-23-1835 m Elizabeth Fisher Pvt NJ ★
David: b 1762 d 5-1-1839 m Mary Kephart Pvt PA ★
David, Sr.: b 11-8-1753 d 8-24-1828 m (1)Ann Chaplin (2)Mary Lawrence Mil SC
David: b 1-28-1766 d 10-19-1834 m Betsy Brassfield Pvt SC
Drury: b *c.* 1755 d *p.* 12-19-1814 m (1)Elizabeth Fudge (2)Mrs Sarah Roper Pvt SC
Ebenezer: b 10-6-1749 d 1-31-1835 m (1)Mary Morse (2)Molly Merritt Pvt CT
Ebenezer: b 1751/2 d 1-31-1846 m Elizabeth Martin Cpl CT NY ★
Ebenezer: b 3-15-1737 d 1791 m Mehitable Spear PS MA
Ebenezer, Jr.: b 8-19-1746 d 4-19-1798 m Mary Carpenter Cpl MA
Ebenezer: b 6-20-1753 d 6-9-1832 m Lydia Hoyt Sgt NH ★
Ebenezer: b 2-22-1732 d 5-14-1799 m (1)Martha Taylor (2)Sarah (Fanning) Noyes Capt RI
Ebenezer Thomas: b 1-10-1762 d 8-6-1804 m Polly Goodwin Pvt MA
Edmund: b 1740 d 1825 m Hannah Thurston Pvt MA
Edward: b 1729 d 8-3-1808 m (1)Eliza — (2)Frances (Bowen) Rogers Slr CT
Edward: b 3-27-1753 d 2-23-1843 m Martha Barrett Cpl MA
Edward: b 3-16-1739 d 11- -1825 m (1)Dorothy Spear (2)Mrs Green Pvt MA
Edward: b 1750 d 3-22-1843 m Amelia Fish Pvt NY
Eleazer: b 3-31-1740/1 d 10-4-1823 m Elizabeth Corey Pvt MA
Eli: b 10-22-1748 d 1795 m Sophia Adams Sol MD
Eli: b 4-15-1759 d 8-10-1825 m Hepsibah Farley Pvt NH
Eliahib: b 7-28-1727 d 8- -1801 m (1)Betsey Phillips (2)Molley (Webb) Annable CS CT
Elihu: b 5-29-1741 d 3-18-1776 m Thankful White Capt MA
Elijah: b 1753 d 12-7-1843 m (2)Sarah Carol Vails Sgt CT ★
Elijah: b 11-14-1743 d 4-5-1823 m Abigail Chenery Pvt MA
Elijah: b 1-30-1753 d 12-7-1817 m Lizzie Morse Sol MA
Eliphalet: b 1-29-1756 d 7-2-1844 m Patience Rice Pvt CT & NH
Elisha: b 7-5-1733 d *p.* 1779 m Margaret (or Phoebe) — Cpl CT
Elisha: b 2-25-1751 d 2-23-1823 m Sarah Watkins Pvt MA
Elisha: b 1765 d 3-31-1827 m Lucinda Adley Pvt NH
Enoch: b 7-11-1752 d 8-19-1819 m (1)Sally Bragg (2)Lydia Moody Pvt MA
Enoch: b 11-29-1755 d 2-27-1842 m Elizabeth Russell Pvt MA ★
Ephraim: b 11-20-1727 d — m Sarah Granger Pvt CT
Ephraim: b *c.* 1748 d *a.* 4-8-1824 m Rebecca Sherwood Sol CT
Ephraim: b 13-1751 d 4-28-1823 m (1)Betty Pierce (2)Anna (Adams) Kinney CS Tms NH
Ephraim: b bpt 10-18-1724 d 3-26-1799 m (1)Lydia Kinsman (2) Rebecca Locke Pvt NH
Ephraim, Jr.: b 12-26-1749 d 4-15-1825 m (1)Elizabeth Stearns (2) Bridget — Pvt NH
Evi: b 12-21-1744 d 9-14-1828 m Jane Lewis Pvt NJ
Ezekiel: b 11-29-1757 d 5-30-1835 m Sally Rice Pvt VT
Ezekiel Gilman: b 11-17-1749 d 8-24-1831 m (1)Mary Hoyt (2) Drusilla Ewer PS NH
Ezra: b 1751 d 2-28-1837 m (1)Hannah Wilcox (2)Hannah Seymour Pvt CT
Feathergill: b 2-4-1755 d 11-9-1807 m Elizabeth — Wgn VA
Francis: b 5-6-1749 d 11-7-1802 m Abigail Taft Pvt MA

ADAMS, contd.

Francis: b 11-24-1763 d 9-12-1846 m (1)Margaret McKee (2)Mrs Mary Ryan Pvt SC .

Francis: b 2-7-1749 d 5-1-1811 m Ann Peake Ens VA

Freegrace: b 11-14-1723 d 1815 m Anna Kent PS VT

Freiderich: b 9-7-1757 d 5-10-1827 m Barbara Haushaltemn Pvt PA

Gawin: b 1748 d 1818 m Nancy Irwin Capt PA

George: b 5-17-1733 d 2-8-1814 m (1)Abigail Prentice (2)Elizabeth Crosby Pvt MA

George: b 10-26-1767 d 11-29-1832 m Elizabeth Ellis Drm PA

George: b 4-6-1747 d 9-16-1827 m Anna Turner Pvt VA

Gideon: b 1-19-1754 d 3-3-1835 m Rhoda Hanchett Pvt CT ★

Gideon: b 5-2-1743 d 1827 m Mary Leach PS CT

Gilbert: b 11-21-1760 d 7-13-1825 m Rachel — Pvt NY

Heman: b 6-11-1761 d 11-21-1848 m Lucy Cobb Pvt MA ★

Henry: b 3-7-1742 d 1806 m Edy Adams Pvt NH

Isaac: b 10-27-1746 d 4-11-1809 m Barbara Ruth Addams Capt PA

Israel: b 1753 d 5-30-1811 m (3)Joanna Dodge Pvt MA

Issacher: b 12-11-1754 d 6-18-1829 m Millicent Alden Pvt MA

Jacob: b 1-16-1758 d 10-16-1821 m Hannah Hammell Pvt NJ

Jacob: b 1762 d 8-7-1853 m Loretta Dischtimer Sgt PA

Jacob: b 9-23-1758 d 8-23-1803 m (1)Catherine Hoy (2)Mrs Catharine Lintner Wilson Pvt PA

Jacob: b a. 1760 d 11-11-1833 m Mrs Mary Stamper Pvt VA

James: b 2-17-1759 d 1843 m (2)— Stebbens (3)Edna Allen Pvt CT ★

James: b 6-15-1748 d 6-28-1805 m Jerusha Knight Lt. CT

James: b 1737 d 1795 m Jane Brinam Pvt MD

James: b 11-2-1741 d p. 1800 m Susanna (Dement) PS MD

James, Jr.: b 4-21-1737 d 1813 m (1)Submit Purchase (2)Mrs. Trescott Pvt MA

James: b 6-6-1721 d 12-26-1775 m Elizabeth (Johnson ?) Pvt MA

James: b c. 1740 d 5-28-1799 m Lydia (Benson) Crawley Pvt MA

James: b 11-5-1744 d 12-20-1836 m Susannah Jenkins Pvt MA

James: b 3-19-1732 d 3-10-1803 m Delia Adams ADC MA

James: b 10-30-1734 d 10-17-1824 m Isabella Weldon Capt MA

James: b c. 1740 d p. 2-10-1796 m Mary — Sol SC

James, Sr.: b c. 1730 d 1782 m Sarah — Pvt SC

James: b 6- -1712 d 5-22-1787 m Sarah Callender Pvt VT

James: b 10-18-1753 d 1835 m (1)Miss Wells (2)Jane Cunningham Sgt VA ★

James: b c. 1730 d 7-27-1809 m Mrs Ann Harper Pvt VA

James: b 1757 d 11-15-1813 m Sarah — Cpl VA

James: b c. 1754 d p. 1786 m Mary Ann Irvine Capt VA

Jedediah: b 1-1-1762 d 7-30-1840 m Betsey Gates Pvt CT ★

Jeremiah: b 3-1-1732 d 5-23-1816 m Rhoda — Pvt VT

Jesse: b 7-17-1757 d 1812 m Zerviah Cady Pvt CT

Jesse: b 1-20-1755 d 9-24-1827 m Miriam Richardson Pvt MA

Job: b 1765 d p. 1790 m Candace Adams Pvt VT

Joel: b 12-20-1729 d a. 3- -1820 m Elizabeth Fowler Lt CT

Joel: b 4-8-1752 d 11- -1837 m Joanna Hale Pvt MA

Joel: b 4-1-1749 d 1-17-1828 m (1)Lucy Whitney (2)Rebecca Stratton MM Pvt MA ★

Joel: b 12-31-1751 d 10-9-1821 m Lydia Drury Pvt MA

Joel: b 7-21-1753 d 10-22-1830 m Jemima Robbins Pvt MA

Joel: b 2-4-1750 d 7-9-1830 m Grace Weston Asst Cmsry SC

John (5): b 2-12-1745 d 12-10-1818 m (1)Mary Parker (2)Hannah Faucet Capt CT

John: b 2-17-1744 d 10-25-1810 m Submit Butts Lt CT

John: b 1746 d c. 1834 m (2)Mary Conorey Pvt CT

John: b 2-2-1751/2 d 4-4-1826 m (1)Sarah Bronson (2)Cynthia Fitch Pvt CT

John: b c. 1755 d p. 1808 m Mary Abigail Ellis Pvt GA

John: b 12-8-1760 d 3-29-1842 m Eleanor Worland Pvt MD ★

John: b 7-3-1735 d 6-27-1813 m (1)Hannah Osgood (2)Hannah Thurston (3)Mary Holt Capt MA

John: b 1732 d 1829 m Betsey Ward Capt MA

John: b 1-22-1744 d 2-26-1849 m (1)Joanna Munroe (2)Lucy (Simonds) Munroe Lt MA

John, Sr.: b 1738/9 d 8-30-1793 m Chloe — 2Lt MA

John: b c. 1750 d a. 2-14-1837 m Sarah Hunt Sgt MA

John: b 6-14-1714 d 4-15-1806 m Thankful Washburn Cpl MA

John: b 6-17-1727 d 2-16-1823 m Abigail Baxter Cpl MA

John: b 9-27-1746 d 4-7-1801 m Lydia Hayward Cpl MA

John: b 5-20-1747 d 12-31-1820 m (1)Molly Parker (2)Mary Lock Cpl CS MA

John, Sr.: b 9-13-1719 d 4-24-1796 m Mary Hunt Pvt MA

John, Jr.: b 11- -1746 d 6-22-1828 m Elizabeth Newton Pvt MA

John: b 10-27-1724 d 1802 m (1)Silence Clark (2)Zilphia Daniels Pvt MA

John: b 10-26-1744 d p. 1807 m Lucy Sibley Pvt MA

John: b 3-29-1746 d p. 1833 m Deborah Beals Pvt MA

John: b 1748 d 8- -1836 m (1)Naomi Pratt (2)Eunice Moulton (3)Elizabeth Stearns Pvt MA

John: b 10-5-1752 d 2- -1824 m Rhoda Lakin Pvt MA

John: b 7-25-1751 d 3-31-1819 m (1)Ruth Perry (2)Elizabeth Gardner (3)Hannah Phelps Pvt CS MA

John: b 3-25-1760 d 9-27-1849 m (1)Aner Hickox (2)Mrs Polly Grinel Pvt MA ★

John: b 1766 d 3-24-1845 m Prudence White Pvt MA

John: b c. 1730 d c. 1780 m Mary Pedrick Smn MA

John: b 2-22-17-6 d 10-30-1803 . (1)Mercy Sanderson (2)Mrs Abigail Faulkner MM MA

John: b 10-31-1735 d 7-4-1826 m Abigail Smith SDI MA

John: b 2-26-1709 d 6-11-1790 m Sarah Swift PS MA

John, Sr.: b 6-18-1715 d 5-30-1793 m Rachael Adams PS CS MA

John: b 11-11-1723 d 1-17-1809 m Lucy Hubbard PS MA

John: b 10-8-1758 d 8-28-1847 m Ann Folsom Ens Lt NH ★

John: b 6-5-1756 d 8-22-1838 m (1)Elizabeth Cochran (2)Mary Ann Morrison Pvt NH

John: b 6-19-1725 d 6-9-1792 m (1)Sarah Elizabeth Wheeler (2) Hannah Chesley PS NH

John: b 3-11-1752 d 1-13-1820 m Mary Rollins PS NH

John: b 1737 d 4-7-1798 m Margaret Garwood Ens NJ

John: b 10- -1759 d 1821 m Elizabeth Beesner Pvt NJ

John: b c. 1765 d 7-24-1823 m Easter Hawkins Drm CL

John: b 9-9-1737 d 6-8-1823 m (1)Charity Smith (2)Mary Townsend Maj NY ★

John: b 11-3-1759 d 12-12-1826 m Christina Klinker Pvt PA

John: b 4- -1765 d 8-2-1850 m Ann Beatty Pvt PA

John: b c. 1750 d 11-4-1822 m Sarah — QM SC

John: b c. 1730 d p. 1782 m Susan Wood Pvt VA

John Bradford: b 1-11-1750 d 6-30-1829 m Sarah Davenport Pvt CT

John Carroll: b 1747 d 5-1-1836 m Sarah — Sgt SC ★

Jonas: b 8-18-1758 d 2-19-1813 m Phoebe Hoar Cpl MA

Jonas: b 3-26-1753 d 7-16-1837 m Phebe Rose Lt PS NY

Jonathan: b 11-27-1753 d 1-13-1849 m Jemimah Hill Cpl MA ★

Jonathan: b 2-26-1748 d 3-30-1840 m Sarah Wood Pvt MA

Jonathan: b a. 1759 d p. 1795 m Hannah Parkhurst Pvt MA

Jonathan: b 3-5-1759 d 12-11-1843 m Elizabeth Gary Pvt MA ★

Jonathan: b 10-13-1757 d 3-8-1811 m Abigail Sperry Drm MA W ★

Jonathan: b 1709 d 11-4-1804 m Patience Clark PS MA

Jonathan: b 1729 d 3-20-1820 m Sarah Smith PS NH

Jonathan: b 1-6-1735 d 4-16-1808 m Mary Covenhoven Pvt NJ

Jonathan: b c. 1763 d 4-25-1835 m Margaret — Pvt NJ W ★

Jonathan: b 9-20-1765 d 10-29-1828 m Sally Daniels Pvt Sct NY

Jonathan: b 1740 d 1783 m Mary Robeson Pvt SC

Joseph: b 12-6-1715 d 12-6-1780 m Sarah Bradford Cpl CT

Joseph: b 4-2-1757 d 12-25-1835 m Abiah Edgerton Pvt CT

Joseph: b 11-29-1743 d 12-2-1824 m (1)Lucy Kent (2)Sally Tufts Sgt MA

Joseph: b 4-19-1745 d 1803 m Mary Currier Sgt MA

Joseph: b 7-3-1715 d 5-3-1794 m (1)Martha Frost (2)Hannah Hall Pvt MA

Joseph: b 11-27-1730 d p. 1790 m (1)Elizabeth Draper (2)Abigail Perrin Pvt MA

Joseph: b 3-10-1759 d 11-2-1830 m Betsey Davis Pvt MA

Joseph: b 10-2-1740 d 8-7-1815 m Eleanor Carney Sol CS MA

Joseph: b 1707 d 1799 m Mercy Fowle Pvt NH

Joseph, Sr.: b 1688 d 5-20-1783 m (1)Elizabeth Knight Janvrin (2) Elizabeth Brackett PS NH

Joseph, Jr.: b 1-17-1723 d 3-22-1801 m Joanna Gilman PS NH

Joseph: b 8-12-1723 d p. 1790 m (1)Prudence Pratt (2)Esther Grout (3)Mrs Dorcas Winship PS NH

Joseph: b 1749 d 1837 m Winifred Rowland Pvt NC

Joseph: b c. 1713 d 1800 m (1)Lydia — (2)Ann Allen Pvt PA

Joseph: b 12-19-1757 d 1-7-1835 m Hannah Cutler Cpl RI ★

Joseph: bpt 3-3-1749 d 2-15-1844 m (1)Jerusha Preston (2)Sarah Carey Pvt RI ★

Josiah: b 9-6-1729 d 10-24- — m Sarah Reed Pvt MA

Jude: b 3-1-1748 d 4- —1801 m Jemima (Adams) Cpl MA

Lemuel: b 5-29-1764 d 8-8-1852 m Betsey Kimball Sgn's Mte CT

Levi, Sr.: b 11-18-1728 d 1816 m Margaret Perkins Cpl CT

Levi, Jr.: b 2-14-1754 d 12-26-1833 m Hannah Pettingall Sgt CT & VT ★

Levi: b 12-30-1762 d 6-18-1831 m (1)Mercy Finch (2)Ruth Stevens Pvt CT W ★

Levi: b c. 1745 d 3-17-1801 m (2)Betty Potter (3)Anna — Pvt MD

Levi: b 4-2-1747 d 1-2-1835 m (1)Mary Abbecca Perry (2)Lydia Patch Sgt MA ★

Levi: b 8-1-1761 d 1-18-1832 m Dolly Houghton Sgt VT

Luke: b 3-8-1756 d 4-18-1831 m Lucy Nichols Cpl CT ★

Martin: b 2-5-1764 d 8-8-1839 m Mercy Ryder Drm VT ★

Mathew: b 1744 d 1823 m Janet Hebron Pvt PA

Matthew: b 4-9-1746 d 9-22-1776 m Keziah Moses Sgt CT

Matthew: b 1-1-1756 d 4-1-1838 m Mary (Fisher) Undersee Pvt NJ ★

Mayhew: b 12-22-1729 d 10-2-1823 m Rebecca Mayhew Maj MA

Micajah: b 1759 d 1842 m Elizabeth Holston Pvt NC ★

Moses: b 8-4-1731 d 9-5-1815 m Rachel Leland Capt MA

Moses: b 11-30-1748 d 8-26-1778 m Ann Willard Sgt MA

Moses: b 11-5-1737 d 3-7-1820 m Susanna Merrill Cpl MA

Moses: b 10-16-1749 d 10-13-1819 m Abigail Stone Chp MA

Moses: b 4-17-1726 d 6-4-1810 m (1)Hepzebah Death (2)Mary Swan PS CS MA

Nathan: b 1-9-1721 d 8-17-1782 m Mary Burr Lt CT

Nathan, Jr.: b 12-1-1757 d 4- -1830 m Betsey Poor Lt MA

Nathan: b 4-17-1760 d 6-5-1835 m (1)Ruth Kendrick (2)Polly Sterns Cpl MA

Nathan, Sr.: b 12-3-1723 d 1-26-1800 m Keziah Thompson Pvt MA

Nathan, Jr.: b 5-24-1751 d 6-8-1825 m Mary (Adams) Pvt MA

Nathan: b 5-16-1736 d 1-1-1832 m (1)Hannah Rood (2)Sybil Ward Pvt MA

Nathan: b c. 1755 d 3- -1830 m (1)Mary — (2)Sidney — PS NC

Nathan: b c. 1750 d p. 10-28-1801 m Ann — PS VA

Nathaniel: b 6-8-1739 d 9-6-1781 m Elizabeth Comstock Pvt CT

Nathaniel: b 12-20-1747 d 3-7-1806 m Anne Bolton CS GA

Nathaniel: b 1-19-1745 d 1822 m Rachel Chambers Pvt MD
Nathaniel: b 1-1-1756 d 1-24-1829 m Mary Harrington Cpl MA
Nipper, Sr.: b 1730 d *p*. 1820 m (1) Lucy McEndree (2)Mrs Obedience Farmer PS VA
Nipper, Jr.: b 1753 d 1830 m Mary Farmer Ens VA
Noah: b 8-27-1747 d 7-26-1819 m Elizabeth Fassett PS PA
Nudigate: b 6-13-1753 d 1-5-1798 m Frances Low Cpl RI
Obadiah: b 12-18-1721 d 1-2-1803 m Sarah Partridge Pvt MA
Oliver, Sr.: b 10-27-1729 d *p*. 1787 m Rachel Proctor Pvt MA
Paul: b 2-24-1727 d 9-19-1777 m Mary Hubbard Pvt CT
Paul: b 4-12-1758 d 9-9-1833 m Hannah Ilsley Cpl MA
Peter: b 11-2-1718 d 11-25-1806 m Priscilla Warren Sgt CT
Peter: b 2-2-1722 d 3-12-1802 m Esther Ward Sgt MA
Peter: b 2-6-1761 d 7-30-1832 m Lucy Gibson Pvt MA
Peter B. F.: b 3-11-1759 d 6-8-1845 m Jerusha Barlow Pvt VA ★
Peter Boylston: b 10-16-1738 d 6-2-1823 m Mary Crosby PS CS MA
Philemon: b 10-21-1760 d 9-11-1847 m Betsy Pond Pvt MA
Phineas: b 9-7-1726 d 1-7-1779 m Lydia Fitch Pvt CT
Phineas: b 7-18-1760 d 11-3-1800 m Patience Pond Pvt MA
Reuben: b 10-22-1761 d 8-30-1833 m Abigail Lovett Pvt CT
Reuben: b 7-9-1760 d 6-17-1848 m Azuba Jones Pvt MA ★
Richard: b 6-14-1719 d 8- -1795 m Mary Carver Capt MA
Richard: b 11-2-1726 d 11-6-1788 m Sarah Noyes PS MA
Richard: b 7-26-1740 d *a*. 2-18-1816 m Susanna — Pvt PA
Richard: b 1735 d 5- -1800 m Elizabeth Griffin 1Lt VA
Richard: b 5-17-1726 d 8-2-1800 m Elizabeth Griffin PS VA
Robert: b *c*. 1742 d 1806 m Elizabeth — 2Maj PA
Robert: b 1751 d 11-17-1816 m Rebecca Willy Sol SC
Robert 2nd.: b 1725 d 1785 m Penelope Flournoy Lynch PS VA
Robert 3rd.: b 1754 d *c*. 1790 m Mary Terrell Capt VA
Robert: b *c*. 1730 d 1783 m Mourning — PS CS VA
Roger: b 5-27-1753 d 4-10-1811 m (1)Hepseybeth Russell Pvt MA
Roswell: b 6-13-1753 d 3-23-1829 m Eunice Davenport Pvt CT
Sampson: b 8-25-1729 d 8-26-1785 m (1)Mary Burridge (2)Katherine (Davis) Bacon Sol MA
Samuel: b 5-16-1753 d 11-23-1827 m Betsey Litchfield Cpl CT ★
Samuel: b 6-11-1728 d 1-25-1798 m Phebe Pellet Pvt CT
Samuel: b 9-4-1736 d 3-24-1811 m (1)Dorcas Frost (2)Elizabeth Purchase Pvt CT
Samuel: b 1749 d 8-31-1818 m Eunice Adams Pvt CT
Samuel: b *c*. 1755 d *p*. 1795 m (1)Sallie Nelson (2)— Wright Pvt MD
Samuel: b 9-16-1722 d 10-2-1803 m (1)Elizabeth Checkley (2)Elizabeth Wells SDI MA
Samuel: b 6-30-1734 d 10-26-1829 m (2)Elizabeth Temple (3)Olive Jones Sgt Fif MA
Samuel: b 12-30-1752 d 2-12-1838 m (1)Elizabeth Newhall (2)Deborah Bishop Sgt MA ★
Samuel: b 4-19-1737 d 8-19-1809 m Sarah Clark Pvt MA
Samuel: b 4-2-1733 d 5-18-1818 m Sarah Reed Pvt MA
Samuel: b 9-28-1744 d 8-21-1822 m Rachel Burrill Pvt MA
Samuel: b 9-9-1747 d *p*. 1784 m Thankful Chamberlain Pvt MA
Samuel: b 11-7-1755 d 7-11-1840 m Mrs Chloe Legge Pvt MA
Samuel: b 5-24-1757 d 9-10-1835 m Ruth White Pvt MA ★
Samuel: b 1759 d 8-9-1840 m (1)Hannah Buker (2)Elizabeth Gardner Pvt MA
Samuel: b 4-21-1749 d 11-7-1845 m Catharine Hodges Pvt MA
Samuel: b 10-25-1760 d 1-7-1828 m Susanna Rist Pvt Drm MA ★
Samuel: b 6-24-1762 d 9-7-1847 m Anna Stone Mrnr Pvt MA ★
Samuel: bpt 5-16-1736 d 3-29-1814 m Mary Stickney PS MA
Samuel: b 1-28-1745 d 3-6-1819 m (1)Deborah Larned (2)Abigail Jordan (3)Sarah Preston (4)Abigail Dodge Dr MA ★
Samuel: b 6-6-1717 d 5-8-1791 m Mrs Mary Jewett Brown PS MA
Samuel: b — d — m Elizabeth Parker Lt NH
Samuel: b 8-11-1750 d 2-21-1813 m Lucy Peabody Spofford Pvt NH
Samuel: b 12- -1753 d 5-19-1832 m Sarah Felt Pvt NH ★
Samuel Calvin: b 2-16-1765 d 10-17-1842 m Susanna Walden Pvt CT ★
Seth: b 2-18-1747 d 11-18-1835 m (1)Elizabeth Lane (2)Joanna Fairman (3)Lydia Taylor Pvt MA
Silas: b 12-6-1741 d 11-15-1800 m Lucy Underwood Capt MA
Silas: b 6-8-1745 d 1812 m Susannah Woods Pvt NH
Simon: b 3-14-1748 d 2-22-1825 m (1)Dinah Spaulding (2)Hannah Taft Capt MA
Simon: b 1750 d 1809 m Catherine Wren Pvt VA
Smith: b 3-13-1757 d 3- -1812 m (1)Lucy Warren (2)Susanna Rice MM MA
Solomon: b *c*. 1745 d *p*. 1800 m (1)Mary Mix (2)Sarah Dolph Pvt CT
Solomon: b 12-7-1758 d 11-4-1833 m Hannah Butterfield Pvt MA ★
Solomon: b 3-4-1759 d *p*. 1799 m Mary Sargent Pvt MA
Stephen: b 12-27-1729 d 2-11-1795 m Mary Littlefield Pvt CS MA
Stephen: b 5-6-1743 d *p*. 3-29-1780 m Esther — Sol MA
Stephen: b 5-5-1760 d 2-8-1838 m Sarah Adams Pvt MA ★
Stephen: b 2-4-1715 d 8-3-1801 m Rebecca — Pvt NH
Sylvanus: b 1-22-1759 d *p*. 1791 m Sarah Hopkins Pvt CT
Sylvester: b *c*. 1760 d 3-2-1830 m Rebecca Boyd Pvt VA
Thomas: b 7-31-1734 d 4-22-1815 m Susannah Peck Capt CT
Thomas: b 1-14-1711/2 d 2-13-1780 m Deborah (Tracy) Adams PS CS CT
Thomas: b 11-8-1761 d *p*. 9-22-1831 m (2)Mary — Pvt MD
Thomas: b 3-31-1725 d 7-13-1812 m (1)Elizabeth Clark (2)Sarah Harris Sol MA

Thomas: b 4-5-1726 d 12-5-1783 m Mary Partridge Pvt MA
Thomas: bpt 9-18-1757 d 5-10-1799 m Mary Bright Pvt MA
Thomas: b 10-21-1758 d 4-14-1858 m Lucy Perkins Pvt MA
Thomas: b 11-16-1761 d 8-15-1844 m Mary White Pvt MA ★
Thomas: b 1761 d 2-12-1856 m Eunice Wheeler Pvt MA
Thomas: b 8-20-1713 d 11-9-1802 m (1)Anna Frost (2)Lydia Chadwick (3)Mrs Elizabeth Bowman PS CS MA
Thomas: b *a*. 1760 d 1809 m Elizabeth Nicholson Pvt SC
Thomas: b 1758 d 2-4-1836 m Sallie Ford Sgt VA ★
Thomas: b 1752 d 1- -1802 m Lucy Green Pvt VA
Thomas: b 2-10-1760 d 10-1-1828 m Rebecca Wood Pvt VA
Thomas: b *c*. 1750 d *p*. 3-4-1826 m. — Sol VA
Timothy: b 9-5-1742 d 8-25-1834 m Susanna Adams Pvt CT ★
Timothy: b 7-14-1758 d 9-1-1831 m Mary Plimpton Pvt MA
Timothy: b 8-14-1757 d 1824 m Joanna Keyes Pvt MA
Timothy: b 6-14-1762 d 5-23-1841 m Lydia Robbins Pvt Mar MA ★
Uriah: b *c*. 1733 d *p*. 1-11-1814 m — Ens NJ
William: b 10-17-1752 d 12-8-1840 m Phyllis Ensworth Sgt CT ★
William: b 11-2-1752 d 2-14-1811 m Rosabella Loomis Cpl CT
William: b *c*. 1723 d *p*. 1783 m Tabytha Addams Pvt MD
William: b 1-12-1725 d 9-10-1787 m Sarah Hill Capt CS MA
William: b 8-18-1750 d 10-19-1815 m Mary Porter Sgt MA
William: b 9-19-1719 d 2-15-1790 m Ruth — Pvt MA
William: b 1757 d 5-10-1819 m Persis Ware Pvt MA
William, Jr.: b 6-3-1756 d 8-5-1835 m Ester Parker Sol NH ★
William: b 4-13-1762 d 12-25-1840 m Mary Roby Pvt NH
William: b *c*. 1745 d *c*. 1806 m Sarah — Pvt NJ
William: b 1730 d 1833 m Margaret — Dr NY
William: b 12-25-1734 d 7-22-1824 m. Susan Godwin Dr NY
William: b *c*. 1750 d 1777 m Mary White Lt PA
William: b 1746 d 9- -1832 m Nancy — Pvt PA
William: b 12-25-1748 d 1832 m Martha Baird Pvt PA ★
William: b 1750 d 1818 m (2) — Flanigan Dr PA
William: b 1733 d 11-27-1799 m Margaret Ewart Pvt SC
William: b *c*. 1760 d *a*. 2-4-1809 m Jane — Pvt SC
William: b 1743 d 1795 m Mary — Sol SC
William: b 1756 d 9-10-1839 m Elizabeth Boyd Pvt VA
William: b *c*. 1723 d *p*. 7-29-1789 m Mary Walker CS VA
William: b — d *p*. 9-23-1807 m Anne — PS VA
Windborn: b — d 4-19-1777 m Sarah Bartlett Col NY
Zabdiel: b 11-5-1739 d 3-1-1801 m Elizabeth Stearns PS MA
Zebediah: b 7-5-1753 d 10-3-1837 m Abigail Taft Sgt MA ★
Zebulon: b 11-19-1744 d 1778 m Abigail Pennell Pvt MA

ADAMSON,
Basil: b 1728 d 11-17-1785 m Nancy Spiers PS Pvt MD

ADCOCK,
Leonard: b *c*. 1730 d 1797 m Mary — PS NC

ADDINGTON,
William: b 1759 d 9-7-1846 m Delila Duncan Lt SC ★

ADDIS,
John: b 1747 d 11-21-1810 m Elizabeth — Pvt PA
Simon: b 11-27-1745 d 6-23-1834 m (1)Eleanor — (2)Maria Van Cleef (3)Nelly Van Voorhees Capt NJ
Thomas: b 1739 d 4-14-1827 m Elizabeth Jones Cpl CT

ADDISON,
Arthur: b 1763 d 5- -1825 m (3)Rose Anna James Pvt VA
John: b 1751 d 1817 m Lucy (Belt) Watkins Col MD
John: b 1763(?) d 1827 m Amy — Pvt SC

ADDITON,
Thomas: b 3-2-1763 d 4-11-1835 m Bethiah Richmond Pvt MA

ADENOT,
Jean: b 6-17-1746 d 1-19-1815 m Maria-Anne Ersiny Sol FrA

ADERHOLD,
Frederick William: b *c*. 1740 d 1807 m Mary Elizabeth Pvt PA
Peter: b 1761 d 1829 m Eliza Newton Pvt PA

ADGATE,
John Hart: b 9-13-1759 d 5-23-1809 m Sally Fitch Dr CT
Matthew, Sr.: b 7-21-1706 d 1787 m (1)Hannah Hyde (2)Abigail Culverhouse Waterman PS CT
Matthew, Jr.: b 5-13-1737 d 3-1-1818 m (1)Lucy Waterman (2) Eunice Baldwin (3)Mrs Jane Williams (4)Mrs Norton PS NY

ADKISSON,
Ellis: b 1760 d *p*. 1832 m Nancy Prather Pvt VA ★
James: b 4-3-1747 d 1837 m (2)Mary Virginia Pvt VA ★
Michael: b 1725 d 1791 m Sarah Jane — Drm VA

ADLE,
John: b *c*. 1758 d *c*. 1819 m Lany Klock Pvt NY

ADLEY,
Peter: b 1750 d 1-29-1840 m Mary Watkins Pvt NY ★

ADLINGTON,
John: b 2-18-1766 d 4-10-1853 m Lydia Myrick Mid MA ★

ADRIANCE,
Albert: b c. 1747 d 1793 m Hannah Platt Pvt PS NY
Cornelius b 1750 d 1801 m Aaltje Swartout Pvt NY
Isaac: b 4-27-1722 d 4-15-1799 m Letitia Van Wyke Pvt NY
Rem: b 5-14-1748 d 4-3-1795 m Geerediena Hoogland Sol NY
Rem: b 9-21-1753 d 11-26-1839 m (1)Catharine Storm (2)Catharine Griffin Pvt NY
Theodore: b c. 1757 d p. 1808 m (1)Catherine Van Hook (2)Abigail (Evans) Allen Sgt NY
Theodorus: b 6-22-1751 d 5-14-1817 m Killetie or Hellicke Swartwout Sgt NY

ADSIT,
Benjamin: b 9-30-1729 d 7-2-1793 m Roda Cheddick Pvt NY
John, Sr.: b 1715 d 1786-90 m Abigail Graves Pvt NY
John, Jr.: b 1756 d 3-22-1827 m Tamar Holdridge Pvt NY
John: b 10-4-1751 d 1-20-1798 m Elizabeth Palmer Pvt NY
Martin: b 12-4-1762 d 1841 m Roba Haight Pvt NY
Samuel: b 10-30-1722 d 4-11-1806 m Abigail Kenyon Pvt NY
Silas: b 10-27-1757 d 3-13-1817 m Phoebe Smith Sgt NY
Stephen: b 8-20-1730 d 1796 m (1)Lucy Chadwick (2)Mary Purdy Lt NY

ADYE, (includes ADY)
John: b 5-18-1752 d 11-4-1833 m (2)Bathsheba Mix Cpl CT ★
Jonathan: b c. 1722 d p. 12-17-1800 m Rebecca Yorke Pvt PA
William: b 1745 d p. 1780 m Chloe Staniford Pvt PS MD

AFLERBACHE,
Henry: b c. 1739 d 1816 m Maria Renshimer: Pvt PA

AGARD,
Amos: b 6-25-1735 d p. 1783 m Alice Smith Pvt NY
Joseph: b 8-17-1746 d 8-25-1836 m Tabitha Leach Pvt NY
Joshua: b 1-31-1754 d 1-24-1830 m (1)Ruth Needham (2)Tryphena — Pvt CT
Noah: b 5-3-1756 d 7-26-1840 m Lucina Jones Pvt CT & NY ★

AGEE,
Jacob: b 1755 d 5- -1838 m Elizabeth Garrett Sol VA
James: b 1725 d 4-9-1821 m Mary Elizabeth Ford PS VA

AGENS,
James: b 1751 d 2-12-1825 m Phebe Force Pvt NY & MD ★

AGNEW,
David: b 7-17-1743 d 1-17-1797 m Mary Erwin Ens PS PA
James: b 5-1-1742 d 4-10-1825 m Mary Ramsey LCol PA
James: b 1740 d 1799 m Martha — Pvt PA
James: b 10-11-1707 d 12-22-1789 m Rebecca Scott Pvt PA
Robert: b 1757 d 1840 m Esther Carnegie Pvt PA
Samuel: b 1738 d p. 12-10-1790 m Elizabeth Seawright Sol SC

AGUR,
Judson: b 5-3-1750 d 1820 m Ann Mills Sgt CT

AHL,
John Peter: b 1750 d 1842 m — Sgn's Mte PA

AIKEN, (includes AKIN, & AKINS)
Arthur: b — d 1809 m (1)Elizabeth Pleasant (2)Nancy — Pvt VA
Benjamin, Jr.: b 1714 d 1800 m Mary Allen Pvt PA
Ezekiel: b 1750-60 d p. 1820 m Sarah McCravey Sol SC
James: b 6-1-1731 d 7-21-1817 m Molly McFarland PS Pvt NH
James: b a. 1736 d 7- -1780 m Molly McFarland PS Pvt NH
James: b 1732 d 5-13-1787 m Margaret Waugh Pvt PS NH
John: b c. 1750 d p. 1795 m Frances Alexander Pvt DE
John: b 2-15-1759 d 2-20-1811 m Mary McAfee Pvt NH
John: b p. 1725 d 1780-1797 m Elizabeth Hunter PS NH
Jonathan: b 11-22-1735 d 8-15-1782 m Margaret Jameson Pvt NH
Nathaniel: b 12-18-1753 d 2-21-1844 m Elizabeth Clark Pvt VT
Peter: b 5-8-1762 d 1-19-1828 m Elizabeth Goodhue Pvt VT
Phineas: b 12-16-1761 d 4-18-1836 m Elizabeth Patterson Pvt NH
Samuel Sr.: b 1702 d 1786 m — Young PS NH
Solomon: b 7-15-1758 d 6-1-1833 m Mary Warner Sgt MA ★
Solomon: b 1725 d 12-10-1805 m Dorcas Whitcomb CS VT
Thomas: b 10-5-1758 d 1-12-1846 m Betty Hyatt Pvt CT ★
Thomas: b 2-27-1747 d 1-10-1830 m Mary Anderson PS Pvt NH
Thomas: b c. 1735 d a. 7- -1811 m Avice — Sol PS VA
William: b 2-27-1743 d 2-19-1799 m Betsy Woodburn Pvt NH
William, Sr.: b — d p. 1-7-1783 m — Pvt PA ★
William Jr.: b 2- -1760 d 10-31-1844 m Hannah — Pvt SC

AIMEN,
George: b c. 1750 d 1818-20 m Barbara Hicks Pvt PA

AINGER,
Jesse: b 7-9-1763 d 1852 m Rebecca Harris Pvt MA ★

AINSWORTH,
Amariah: b 1760 d p. 1805 m Rebecca Skinner Pvt NH
Daniel, Sr.: b 10-21-1724 d 1810 m (1)Sarah Bugbee (2)Elizabeth Corbin Pvt PS CT
Daniel: b c. 1736 d a. 7- -1807 m Auzubah Green Sol MA
Daniel, Jr.: b 1758 d 10-4-1811 m Olive Sprague Pvt PS VT
Darius: b 9-18-1738 d 3-21-1818 m Mary Child Cpl CT
Edward: b 11-21-1729 d 2-10-1806 m (1)Keziah Cobrin (2)Sybil Childs Pvt NH
Edward: b 1758 d 1812 m Mary Ames Pvt NH
Henry: b 1-8-1753 d 7-11-1827 m Frances Throop Pvt VT
Jacob: b 1-21-1743 d 2-4-1828 m Marcy Abbott Pvt CT
John: b 1740 d 8-14-1812 m Margaret Mayes Pvt PA
Laban (Rev.): b 7-19-1757 d 3-17-1858 m Mary Minot PS NY
Moses: b 1741 d 1834 m Margaret McKnowland Pvt MA
Nathan: b 7-28-1740 d 1776/7 m Phebe Kinsley Pvt CT
Samuel: b 1716 d 5- -1783 m Margaret Young Pvt PA
William: b 7-12-1733/4 d 11-14-1815 m Mary Marcy Ens CT

AIREY,
Thomas Hill: b c 1740 d p 1790 m Mary Harris PS MD

AITKEN,
Andrew: b 2-18-1755 d 4-9-1809 m Elizabeth Houston Dr Army & NS
Robert: b 1-22-1735 d 7-13-1802 m Janet Skeoch PS PA

AKELEY,
Thomas: b 5-25-1755 d 2-28-1850 m Abigail Wilder Pvt VT & MA ★

AKERLY, (includes ACKERLY)
Benjamin: b 1754 d 1834 m Phebe Monroe 2Lt NJ
John: b 1742 d 1811 m Joanna — Pvt NY
Philip: b 9-29-1715 d 2-8-1785 m Joanna — PS NY
Stephen: b 8-19-1742 d 5-26-1819 m Dorothy Ackerly PS NY

ALBAN, (includes ALBIN, ALBION)
George: b 2-14-1758 d 1-27-1840 m Jane Green Pvt PS VA ★
James: b c 1757 d a 4-26-1827 m (2)Barbara Hoover Sol VA
William: b 1764 d 10-2-1849 m Jane — Ens PA

ALBARTY,
Frederick: b c 1741 d 8-29-1831 m Elizabeth Rapier Ens NC ★

ALBAUGH,
William: b 3-8-1723 d 1-13-1794 m Magdalene — PS MD
Zachariah: b 10-31-1758 d 11-8-1857 m X Pvt MD & PA ★

ALBEE, (includes ALBE, & ALLBEE)
Asa: b 7-24-1753 d 1843 m (1)Alice Hayward (2)Abigail Harrington Cpl MA ★
Benjamin: b 9-7-1729 d 7-2-1818 m Sarah Taft Pvt MA
Benjamin: b 6-28-1740 d 1844 m Abagail Clifford Pvt MA
Ebenezer: b 4-17-1734 d 5-23-1799 m (1)Esther Fish (2)Hannah — Pvt MA
Ebenezer: b 6-9-1743 d 8-18-1818 m Rachel Avery Pvt PS VT
Eleazer: b 2-20-1740 d 1808 m Dinah Hastings Pvt VT
Eleazer John: b 1758 d 3-3-1831 m Sarah Ballou Pvt MA ★
Ichabod: b 12-18-1755 d 7-3-1844 m Lona Hayward Pvt MA
James: b 3-11-1753 d 8-18-1814 m Ruth White Pvt MA
John: b 2-15-1720 d 3-25-1799 m Sarah Corbitt Capt MA
Jonathan: b 8-30-1743 d 8-21-1844 m Sarah Danforth Pvt MA ★
Nathan: b 8-14-1752 d 2-16-1792 m Elizabeth Wheelock Pvt MA
Peter: b 1746 d 5-30-1816 m Rhoda Penniman Pvt MA
Simeon: b 1760 d 10-8-1848 m (1)Rebecca Stoddard (2)Mrs Sabra Holbrook Drm Pvt MA
Stephen: b 7-20-1741 d p. 1795 m Mary Wood Pvt MA
Thomas: b 8-15-1762 d 1839 m Olive (Albee) Pvt MA
William: b 6-20-1743/46 d 6-26-1833 m Ellen Dillaway Lt MA

ALBERGOTTI,
Anthony: b a. 1740 d 1815 m Amy Reynolds Sol SC

ALBERT,
Abraham: b 5-4-1746 d 6-10-1811 m Maria Elizabeth Pvt PA
Adam: b a. 1748 d 7- -1807 m (1)Elizabeth Schepler (2)Clara — Pvt PA
Andrew: b 4-20-1753 d 10-12-1841 m Susanna Myers Pvt PA
George: b 1748 d 12-19-1804 m Catherine Brosius Pvt PA
John: b 2-27-1741 d p. 1792 m Anna Barbara Long Pvt PA
John: b 12-16-1759 d 5-4-1849 m Catherine Riehm Pvt PA
John: b c. 1742 d 1790 m Innocent Crandall Cpl RI
Wm.: b 8-29-1760 d p. 8- -1833 m (2)Hannah Clark Drm RI ★

ALBERTSON,
Abraham: b 2-16-1757 d — m Sarah Mannery Pvt NJ ★
Cornelius: b 1737 d p. 2-16-1813 m (1)Maru Robinson (2)Catherine Bogart PS NJ
Daniel: b 9-22-1745 d 6-22-1816 m Elizabeth — PS NY
Garret: b 9-15-1753 d 8-12-1813 m Elizabeth Reynolds 2Maj NJ
Jacob: b 1-31-1752 d 10-13-1832 m Lydia Rider QM Sgt RI ★
Josiah: b 1741 d 1827 m Ann Chew Pvt NJ

ALBRIGHT, (includes ALBRECHT)
Adam: b 8-5-1758 d 10-6-1839 m Margaret Minell Pvt PA ★
Andrew: b 4-2-1718 d 4-19-1802 m Elizabeth Orth PS PA
Bernard: b c. 1755 d p. 3-5-1818 m Anna Mary Pvt PA
Christian: b 1726 d 7- -1784 m Elizabeth Rick CMman PA
George: b 1720 d 3-20-1794 m Anna Maria — 1Lt PA
George: b — d c. 1822 m Barbara — Pvt PA
Hendrick: b 1716 d p. 1790 m Elizabeth Folent Pvt NY
Henry: b 12-10-1758 d 1-9-1840 m Mary Gibbs Sgt NC ★
Jacob: b 11-8-1758 d p. 11-22-1820 m Martha Elner Sol NC
Jacob: b 11-10-1763 d 3-20-1829 m (1)Hannah Arnold (2)Elizabeth
 Wheeler Pvt NY
Jacob: b c. 1728 d 1791/92 m Sophia Katharine Wilder Drm NC
Jacob: b 5-1-1759 d 5-18-1808 m Katherine Cope Drm PA
Johannes: b 7-13-1749 d p. 1790 m Rosina Buis Cpl NY
John: b 1760 d 3-2-1845 m Catherine Smith Cpl NY ★
John: b 2-17-1761 d 4- -1816 m Elizabeth Sharp (2)Mary Troxler
 Pvt NC
John: b 2-24-1745 d 8-15-1806 m Anna Maria Kohl Pvt PA
Joseph: b 1733 d 1790 m Susanna — Pvt PA
Ludwig: b 11-11-1731 d 11-16-1810 m Anna Maria Keller Sol NC
Michael: b 3- -1744 d 1817 m Catherine — Pvt PA
Philip: b 1734 d 4-2-1800 m Anna Maria Ursula Dinkel LCol PA
Theobald: b 1759 d 11- -1811 m Susanna Schmeyer Pvt PA

ALBRITTON, (includes ALLBRITTON)
John: b c. 1750 d 1815 m Abbie — Sol GA
John: b 12- -1747 d 12-19-1836 m Mary Manley Pvt Gd SC ★
Mathew: b — d p. 1782 m Susan — Capt PS NC
Richard: b c. 1745/6 d p. 3-30-1816 m Ann — PS NC

ALBRO,
Benjamin: b 10-24-1754 d — m Abigail Bill Pvt RI
Henry: b c. 1750 d 3-12-1823 m Abigail (Albro) Pvt MA
Job: b 1743 d 4- -1825 m Eunice Potter Pvt RI ★
Job: b 7-24-1743 d 1832 m Huldah Tallman Pvt RI
Robert: b 3-9-1760 d — m Innocent Taber Pvt RI
Stephen: bpt 3-14-1729/30 d — m Alice Albro Pvt RI
Stephen: b 1758 d 7-24-1802 m Hannah Bentley Pvt RI
Wait: b c. 1744 d c. 1798/99 m Ruth Albro Cpl RI

ALCORN,
James: b c. 1750-5 d 3-15-1781 m Jane Mills Pvt VA

ALCOTT, (includes ALCOCK, ALCOCKE, ALCOT, ALCOX, ALLCOTT & ALLCOX)
Asa: b 4-27-1760 d 1-18-1846 m Sabra Plumb Pvt CT
Daniel: b 3-25-1738 d 5-24-1805 m Elizabeth Dutton PS Lt CT
Jesse: b 3-23-1736 d 10-29-1829 m Patience Blakeslee PS CT
John: b 12-28-1731 d 9-27-1808 m Mary Chatfield Capt CT ★
Robert: b 8-1-1743 d 4-10-1830 m Elizabeth Marvin Pvt NH
Samuel: b 11-29-1761 d 6-9-1810 m Lydia Warner Pvt CT
Thomas: b 11-26-1744 d 5-10-1834 m Anne Roane Lt VA ★

ALDEN,
Austin: b 3-25-1729 d 3-23-1804 m (2)Salome Lombard (3)Hannah
 Battles 1Lt MA
Barnabas, Sr: b 9-10-1732 d 1792 m Elizabeth Patterson Pvt MA
Barnabas: b 12-16-1759 d 4-1-1830 m Mehetabel Gould Pvt MA
Benjamin: b 12-1-1757 d 12-13-1825 m Polly Judd Pvt MA ★
Briggs: b 6-8-1723 d 10-4-1796 m Mary Wadsworth PS MA
Caleb: b 10-26-1751 d 1-20-1802 m Susanna Dunbar Pvt MA
Daniel: b 9-5-1720 d 5-18-1790 m Jane Turner CS CT
Daniel: b 3-15-1753 d 1-27-1817 m Sarah Alden Pvt CT
David: b 1727 d 1807 m Lucy Thomas Pvt MA
David, Jr: b 1759 d 1842 m Susanna Ward Sol MA ★
Ebenezer: b 10-8-1720 d 2- -1810 m (1)Ann Whitaker (2)Rebecca
 Smith Pvt MA
Ebenezer: b c. 1760/1 d 1835 m Elizabeth Rogers Pvt MA
Eliab: b 1760 d 3-14-1844 m Mary Hathaway Pvt MA
Elijah: b — d 1843 m Rebecca Fuller Pvt MA
Elijah: b 6-13-1754 d 6-26-1826 m Mary Alden Pvt MA
Elisha: b 11-15-1745 d 3-3-1843 m Irene Markham 2Lt MA
Humphrey: b 1-21-1763 d 6-12-1844 m Mary Lord Pvt MA ★
Ichabod: b 8-11-1739 d 11-11-1778 m Mary Wakefield Col MA
Isaac: b 5-5-1755 d 3-5-1822 m Irene Smith Sgt MA
Isaiah: b 11-26-1758 d 3-15-1845 m Mercy Weston Pvt MA
Israel: b 5-18-1747 d 7-20-1817 m Lucy Markham Pvt MA
James: b 1751 d — m Esther York Cpl NH
Job: b 9-24-1737 d p. 1790 m Lucy Spooner Cpl MA
John: b 2-7-1740 d p. 1785 m Lois Southworth Pvt MA
John: b 10-8-1718 d 3-27-1821 m (1)Lydia Lazell (2)Rebecca Wes-
 ton CS MA
John Adams: b 7-11-1762 d 4-13-1843 m Hannah Daniels Pvt
 MA ★
Jonathan: b 1721 d 1801 m Experience Hayward Pvt MA
Jonathan: b 1733 d 1825 m (2)Hannah Green Pvt MA
Joseph: b 5-9-1753 d 1-1-1832 m Lydia Hyde Sgt CT
Joseph: b 1747 d 4-8-1803 m Bethiah Carver Cpl MA
Josiah: b 5-26-1738 d 1785 m Bathsheba Jones Pvt MA
Judah: b 10-31-1750 d 3-1-1845 m Welthea Wadsworth Capt MA
Mason Fitch: b 11-21-1750 d 6-14-1812 m Mary Thompson Hyde
 Sgt CT

Moses: b 1760 d 1833 m Elizabeth Whitney Pvt MA
Nathan, Sr: b 1727 d 1807 m (1)Mary Hudson (2)Lydia Richards
 Capt MA
Nathan, Jr: b 7-2-1751 d 11-6-1842 m Sarah Barrell Pvt MA
Nathan: b 8-22-1743 d 12-9-1820 m Priscilla Miller Sgt MA
Noah: b 5-30-1725 d 5-5-1797 m Joanna Vaughn Pvt PS MA
Prince: b 10-28-1718 d 5-22-1804 m Mary Mason Fitch Pvt PA
Samuel, Jr.: b 8-13-1737 d 2-29-1799 m Abigail Sylvester Pvt MA
Seth, Jr.: b c. 1749 d 7-30-1809 m Priscilla Cole Dr PS VT
Silas: b 10-23-1736 d 2-22-1826 m Margaret Capron 2Lt MA
Simeon: b 4-10-1740 d c. 1781 m Mary Packard Pvt MA
Solomon: b 11-21-1728 d 12-13-1813 m Sarah Hall 2Lt MA
Thomas: b 12-6-1744 d 2-22-1813 m Mary Cheney Sol NH
William: b — d — m Susannah Whitney Pvt MA & VT

ALDERDICE,
Abraham: b c. 1750 d a. 2-20-1802 m (1)Deborah — (2)Ruth —
 Pvt DE

ALDERMAN,
Daniel: b 3-11-1748 d 8-8-1824 m Sarah Newton Cpl NC W*
David: b 1749 d 10-23-1831 m Jemima Hall Sol NC
Egad: b 1-5-1765 d 7-19-1825 m Happy Buckley Pvt CT ★
Eli: b 8-13-1759 d 12-26-1814 m Eunice Laird Gd CT
John: b 1742 d 8- -1822 m Mary Cashwell Pvt NC
Timothy: b 1754 d 1- -1815 m Ruth Hart Pvt CT

ALDERSON,
George: b 8-30-1762 d 1811 m Sarah Osburn PS VA
James: b c. 1730 d p. 6-2-1782 m Sarah Ann — PS VA
John, Jr.: b 3-5-1738 d 3-2-1821 m Mary Carroll PS VA
John S: b 11-18-1766 d p. 1814 m Elizabeth Sydnor Coleman Pvt VA
Thomas: b 8-22-1744 d p. 3-5-1836 m (1)Hannah Davis (2)Sarah
 Bomd OrdlSgt QM VA ★

ALDRICH, (includes ALDRIDGE)
Aaron: b 9-29-1743 d 1838 m Marcy — Pvt MA
Abel: b 11-16-1749 d 4-7-1841 m Elizabeth Rawson Pvt MA
Abel: b 11-14-1741 d 8-31-1819 m Hannah Tilson Pvt RI
Abner: b — d — m Phebe Inman Pvt CT
Abner: b 11-17-1727 d 10-31-1815 m (1)Elizabeth Cook (2)Anna
 Brown Capt NH
Amasa: b 6-13-1760 d 12-2-1813 m Uranah Paine Sgt MA
Augustus(5): b 5-9-1760 d — m Bathsheba Arnold Pvt RI
Caleb, Sr.: b 1728 d 12-6-1799 m Deborah Niles Cpl PS NH
Caleb, Jr.: b 1758 d 1-4-1828 m Eunice Bullock Pvt NH
Caleb: b 1-14-1726 d 11-18-1809 m Mary Arnold PS RI
Ebenezer: b 6-5-1740 d 10-29-1818 m Deborah Pierce Pvt NH
Esek: b 9-9-1753 d 3-2-1830 m Amy Whipple Drm RI
Francis: b 1763 d 5-17-1845 m (1)Henrietta Prince (2)Margaret
 Cole (3)Mary — Pvt NC ★
George: b 10-19-1763 d 10-19-1845 m Polly Bowen Pvt MA
George: b 3-13-1738 d 7-17-1815 m Azubah How Capt NH
Henry: b 8-13-1746 d 10-4-1822 m Elizabeth Hunt Pvt MA ★
Jacob, Sr.: b 1723 d 8-3-1806 m (1)Mary — (2)Mrs Mary Reeve
 MM PS NY
Jacob, Jr.: bpt 2-9-1755 d 12-22-1840 m (1)Mary Owen (2)
 Jemima Cleaves OrdlSgt NY
James: b 11-7-1747 d 12-29-1821 m Alce Smith Lt RI
James: b 1759 d p. 1783 m Susan — Pvt VA
John: b 4-1-1760 d 2-22-1843 m Elizabeth Thurston Dr & Sol CT★
John: b 2-9-1761 d 11-17-1842 m Mary Lakin Pvt VA ★
Jonathan: b 8-3-1721 d p. 1790 m Patience Gaskill Sol RI
Joshua: b 9-28-1759 d 10-17-1849 m Ruth Evans Pvt RI ★
Levi: b 12-19-1729 d 12-22-1795 m Abigail Hunt Capt MA
Naaman: b 5-6-1756 d p. 1802 m Mercy Arnold Pvt RI
Nathaniel: b 5-9-1739 d 1-7-1831 m Hope Thayer Pvt MA
Nathaniel: b 1-10-1763 d 3-5-1834 m Mary Googins Pvt MA ★
Nathaniel: b 12-3-1755 d 1825 m Cleopatra Ramsdell Sol NH
Noah: b c. 1745 d 3-1-1825 m Huldah Whitaker Pvt MA
Peter: b 9-19-1722 d 3-17-1799 m (1)Esther Comstock (2)Isabel —
 Pvt MA
Robert: b 4-3-1752 d p. 1836 m (1)Mary Beetlebrunt (2)Mrs
 Ludia Breetlebrunt Divine Pvt NY
Rufus: b 12-19-1745 d 5-8-1833 m (1)Lois Lovett (2)Susannah
 Thompson (3)Mrs Susannah Benson (4)Sally Thompson Sgt MA
Samuel: b c. 1726 d 7-5-1814 m Huldah Hill PS MA
Samuel, Jr.: b 10-16-1748 d 8-13-1800 m Anne Aldrich Pvt RI
Seth: b 12-4-1739 d 12-26-1817 m Mary Aldrich CS MA
Silas: b 8-14-1734 d 2-24-1812 m Elizabeth Brown Pvt MA
Solomon: b 1752 d 12-5-1833 m Rebecca — Pvt NH ★
Stephen: b c. 1740 d a. 1-7-1795 m Mary Brown Sgt MA
Stephen: b 1741 d 3-15-1808 m Sarah — Pvt RI
Stephen: b 8-4-1747 d 10-18-1813 m (1)Keziah King (2)Jerusha
 Bartlett Pvt RI
William: b 1-13-1731 d 9-9-1803 m Dina Aldrich Sol NH
William: b 4-3-1752 d 1798 m Prusha Paine Maj RI
Ziba: b c. 1753 d 7-23-1840 m Hannah Webber Cpl VT

ALESHIRE, (includes ALESHITE)
John Conrad: b 1755/56 d 1847 m Susannah — Pvt VA ★

ALEXANDER,

Aaron: b 1737 d 11-2-1805 m Eleanor — PS NC VA & GA
Abraham: b 1-2-1743 d 2-21-1816 m (2)Ann Sarah (Huguenin) Irby Lt SC
Abraham: b 1718 d 4-23-1786 m Dorcas — CS PS NC
Abram: b 3-16-1760 d 12-17-1832 m Margaret Robinson Sgt MM NC ★
Adam: b 3-13-1758 d 3-3-1812 m (1)Esther Lawson (2)Louisa Frederika Schmidt Dr GA
Adam: b 9-28-1728 d 11-13-1798 m Mary Shelby Col PS NC
Alexander: b 1731 d 11-8-1815 m Mrs Agnes KellySmn Pvt PA
Alexander: b 1753 d 9-22-1806 m Anny — Pvt SC
Amos, Sr.: b 1729 d 1780 m Sarah Sharpe CS MD
Amos: b c. 1750 d p. 12-7-1813 m Susanna — Sol NC
Andrew: b c. 1714 d 9-11-1789 m Mrs Catherine Stewart Thompson Aiken Sol VA
Anthony: b 1715 d 1784 m Mary — Pvt NC
Archibald: b 2- -1756 d 9-12-1822 m Mary Enos Dr VA
Archibald: b 2-4-1708 d p. 1780 m (1)Margaret Parks (2)Jane McClure CS VA
Asa: b 1760 d 1847 m Faitha Wootten Pvt GA ★
Asa: b 10-17-1742 d 11-4-1811 m Mary Bond PS NH
Benjamin: b 1758 d p. 1818 m Mrs Rebecca Woodland McClure Pvt DE
Charles, Sr.: b 1-4-1730 d 1801 m Susan Polk PS NC
Charles: b 1744 d 12- -1800 m Mary Hopkins Pvt PA
Charles, Sr.: b 7-20-1737 d 1806 m Frances Brown PS VA
David: b c. 1740 d c. 1820 m Martha — Sol NC
Ebenezer: b 2-16-1716 d 7-29-1788 m Abigail Rockwood PS NH
Elias, Jr.: b 1749 d c. 1818 m Annie McCall Col NC
Elias: b 1750 d 1827 m — Taylor Pvt NC
Ezekiel: b 10-21-1754 d 8-18-1832 m Jemima Esther McCoy Pvt NC
Ezra, Sr.: b c. 1721 d p. 1798 m Mary — Sol PS NC
Francis: b c. 1710 d 1781 m (1)Abigail — (2)Eleanor Simonton PS DE
Francis: b a. 4-20-1743 d 7-2-1804 m Catharine — Cpl PA
George: b 1743 d 9-8-1814 m Margaret Harris Col NC
George: b a. 1762 d a. 9-4-1809 m Mary — PS VA
Hezekiah: b 1-13-1722 d 7-17-1801 m Mary Sample PS NC
Hugh: b 1747 d 1835 m Molly Woods Lt GA
Hugh: b 5-14-1756 d 9-6-1818 m (1)Agnes Clark (2)Elizabeth Alexander Pvt NH W ★
Hugh: b 2- -1728 d 3-20-1802 m (1)Abigail Stephenson (2)Agnes McClalland Pvt NY
Hugh: b 1724 d 3-30-1777 m (1)Martha Edmeston (2)Lettice Thompson CS PS PA
Hugh, Jr.: b 8-6-1765 d 1-5-1839 m Jemima Patterson Pvt PA
Isaac: b 1763 d 8-10-1838 m Chloe Ballard Pvt NC ★
Isaac: b 1736 d 5- -1780 m Zilpha Ann Norman Pvt NC
Isaac: b 1749 d 1-13-1812 m (1)Catharine Orr (2)Mrs Margaret Smith (3)Sarah Thornton Dr SC
Jabez: b 1755 d p. 1834 m (1)Lois Pool (2)Betsey Marston Pvt NH
James: b c. 1750 d 11-13-1826 m Esther Dewey Pvt CT ★
James: b 7-14-1761 d p. 1832 m Mary Babcock Pvt CT ★
James: b 1760 d 1798 m Tabith Wootten Capt GA
James: b c. 1690 d 1779 m (1)Margeret McKnitt (2)Abigail — PS MD
James: b 1739 d p. 1790 m Elizabeth Read Capt NC
James: b 4-8-1749 d 12-6-1835 m Elizabeth Sanborn Pvt PA & NC ★
James: b 12-23-1756 d 6-28-1844 m Rhoda Cunningham Pvt NC ★
James: b 1726 d 1791 m Rosa Reed Bgd QM PA
James: b 1760 d 1810 m Margaret Harper Pvt PA
James: b 5-9-1733 d 5-9-1817 m (1)Margaret Wilson (2)Mrs Margaret Clarke Ross Pvt PA
James, Jr.: b 1767 d 5-11-1852 m Isabella Ross Pvt PA
James: b 1725 d 1810 m Mary Peden Pvt SC
James: b 3-8-1761 d 6-12-1839 m Mary Miller Pvt SC ★
James: b 1761 d 4- -1812 m Elizabeth Long Sgt VA
James: b 1750 d a. 7- -1814 m Isabella Erskine Cpl VA
James: b 7-28-1723 d 1806-10 m — Pvt VA
James: b 1762 d p. 1818 m Mary — Pvt VA ★
John: b 1750 d p. 1786 m X Pvt NC
John: b 1745 d c. 1818 m Elizabeth Clark Pvt MA
John: b c. 1733 d 1814 m Agnes Craighead CS NC & TN
John: b 8-14-1753 d 8-4-1804 m Jean Byers Capt PA
John: b 1756 d 11-23-1816 m Margaret Clark Pvt PA
John: b c. 1755 d 5-29-1830 m (1)Elizabeth Williamson (2)Mrs Sarah Russell Maj SC
John: b 1738 d 7-8-1828 m Rachel — Lt VT
John: b 12-14-1741 d 10-17-1830 m Lucy Nunn Sgt VA
John: b 2-28-1756 d 3-3-1832 m Jennet Alexander Pvt VA
John McKnitt: b 6-6-1733 d 7-10-1817 m Jane Bain PS NC
Jonathan: b c. 1750 d p. 1803 m Bartheda — Ens VT & NY
Joseph: b c. 1733 d 1-29-1796 m Minah Norman PS NC
Joseph: b 1743 d p. 1799 m Martha McLean Pvt NC
Joseph: b 1756 d 11-19-1839 m Fannie Malone Capt PA
Joseph: b 1735 d 7-30-1809 m Esther Davies PS SC
Joshiah: b 3-19-1764 d 7-13-1828 m Hannah — Pvt NC
Josiah: b — d — m Mildred Orr Sol NC
Margaret Clarke Ross: b 1743 d 1809 m (1)James Ross (2)James Alexander PS PA

Matthew: b c. 1760 d p. 9-5-1823 m Elizabeth — Pvt NC
Matthew: b 1757 d 1-14-1841 m Elinor (McMillan) Pvt SC ★
Miles: b 1739 d 4-10-1803 m Mary Warner 2Lt MA
Morgan: b 1-10-1746 d 1783 m Sarah Snickers Col VA
Moses: b — d 1781 m Jane Taylor Pvt NC
Nathaniel: b 9-9-1743 d 2-16-1829 m Eunice Hitchcock Capt MA ★
Obidiah: b — d a. 10-8-1785 m Rachel — CS NC
Oliver: b 1732 d 1812/13 m Margaret Paul Sol CS VA
Peter: b 1757 d 2-14-1842 m Janet Steel Sol VA ★
Philip: b 9-29-1712 d — m Abigail — Pvt MA
Philip: b 10-26-1755 d 1830 m Olive Morgan Pvt NH ★
Quartus: b 6-10-1761 d 2-26-1848 m (1)Clarissa Taylor (2)Mary L Sargent Pvt MA & NJ
Reuben: b 2-17-1740 d 5-19-1811 m Sarah Foster Capt CS PS NH
Reynold: b c. 1712 d p. 1790 m Margaret McClellan PS PA
Robert: b 1743 d 1813 m Mary Jack Capt NC
Robert: b 11- -1746 d 11-20-1820 m Ann Austin CS Capt VA
Robert: b 10- -1766 d 8- -1843 m Elizabeth McClure Pvt PA
Roger: b 11-26-1762 d 5-31-1840 m Anna — Pvt RI
Samuel: b 6-25-1737 d 6-25-1835 m Mary Boynton CS PS NH
Samuel, Sr.: b c. 1733 d p. 1790 m Bethiah — Capt NC & GA
Samuel, Jr.: b 7-18-1757 d 12-3-1817 m Olivia Wooten Capt NC & GA
Samuel: b 1759 d 4-26-1842 m Jean Penland Pvt NC
Seth: b 1746 d 12-10-1780 m Hannah Oak Ensign Sgt NH
Simeon, Jr.: b 5-26-1722 d 2-19-1801 Sarah Howe Sol MA
Solomon: b 1753 d 2-22-1796 m (1)Rosalinda Burnham (2)Jerusa Brown Pvt MA
Stephen: b 6-16-1749 d 6-26-1831 m Martha Wilson Capt SC W ★
Stephen: b c. 1741 d p. 1816 m Mary King PS NC
Thomas: b 1760 d 1-16-1836 m Mabel Dorchester Pvt MA ★
Thomas: b 5-30-1727 d 3-23-1801 m Azubah Wright Capt MA
Thomas: b 1752 d 1844 m Jane Morrison Pvt NC ★
Thomas: b 7-6-1740 d 6-15-1802 m Agnes Mitchell Wgm PA
Wm., Sr.: b 1761 d 10-19-1847 m Elizabeth Campbell Pvt Smn MA
Wm.: b 12-27-1725/26 d 1-15-1783 m Sarah Livingston MGen NY
Wm.: b c. 1749/50 d p. 10-22-1836 m X Capt NC
Wm.: b 7-30-1739 d 5-7-1828 m Elizabeth King Capt NC
Wm.: b 1-30-1745 d 5-31-1820 m Mary Brown Lt NC
Wm., Sr.: b 1752 d 1824 m Margaret Ireland Pvt NC
Wm.: b c. 1760 d p. 11-18-1831 m Elizabeth Fish Mus NC
Wm.: b 1740 d 8- -1807 m Deborah Dicks PM Adj SubLt PA
Wm.: b 1737 d p. 11-18-1818 m (1)Isabel Alexander (2)Susanna — Pvt PA
Wm.: b 3-22-1738 d p. 1782 m Agnes Ann Reid CS PA
Wm.: b 3-3-1744 d 4-3-1814 m Segismunda Mary Massie LCol VA
Wm.: b 2-17-1757 d 9-4-1835 m Elizabeth McClelland Sgt VA ★
Wm.: b c. 1738 d 1819 m Margaret Hogue Pvt VA
Wm.: b 1744 d 1- -1829 m Susan McClung Pvt VA
Wm.: b 1758 d 1805/06 m (1)Frankey Rucker (2)Nancy — Sol VA
Wm. Lee: b — d — m Elizabeth Henderson PS NC
Wm. Locke: b 12-25-1746 d 8-4-1830 m Mary Brandon Capt NC SC ★
Wm.: b c. 1757/8 d 10-8-1804 m Sarah (Bruce) Casson Capt VA
Wm. S.: b 1752/3 d 10-20-1826 m (1)Elizabeth (Alexander) (2) Sarah Rogers (3)Martha — QM NC
Zebulon: b c. 1720 d 3- -1784 m — McClung Mil NC

ALFORD,

Alexander: b 6-25-1752 d 8-13-1836 m Elizabeth Lease Pvt CT ★
Asahel: b 11-22-1760 d 6-25-1853 m Lydia — Pvt MA
Benedict: b 2-27-1757 d 1838 m Hulda — Sgt CT VT MA ★
George: b 3-10-1764 d 4-16-1851 m Betsey Hulbert Pvt VT ★
Jacob: b 12-12-1737 d p. 7-4-1794 m Mary Pace Sol NC
Jacob: b a. 1759 d 6-3-1803 m Nancy Hunter Pvt VA W★
James: b 5-21-1741 d a. 2-7-1814 m Luraner Boykin Pvt NC
Job: b 7-3-1736 d p. 1790 m Jerusha Burnham Pvt CT
John: b 5-8-1760 d 4-24-1837 m Elizabeth Bibb Pvt VA ★
Joseph: b 7-6-1748 d 11-1-1826 m Lucy Griswold Pvt PS CT
Lodwich: b 1715 d 1789 m (1)Elizabeth — (2)Susannah — (3)Rebecca Ferrell PS NC
Nathaniel, Jr.: b 1- -1738 d 1-13-1818 m Abigail Hill Pvt CT ★
Pelatiah: b 4-14-1739 d 10-25-1804 m Anne Bacon Pvt CT

ALGER,

Abizer: b 7-25-1757 d 7-31-1830 m Hepsibah Keith Pvt MA
Daniel: b 12-10-1752 d 1-9-1826 m Sarah Howard Sgt MA
Israel: b 6-26-1755 d 10-7-1825 m Rachel Howard Cpl MA
James: b 1729 d 1800 m Martha Kingman Matross Cpl MA
Jonathan: b 9-21-1755 d 3-5-1837 m Dorothy Carpenter Pvt RI MA ★
Stoughton: b 3-8-1749/50 d 12-23-1822 m Ruth Taylor Pvt MA

ALKIRE,

Armonies: b 1730 d p. 5-29-1800 m Lydia Patten 1Lt VA

ALLAIRE,

Peter: b 1750 d 3-9-1839 m Frances Wilmot Pvt NY
Uytendale: b 5-8-1752 d 1-16-1826 m Sarah Simonds QM NY

ALLARD,

David: bpt 3-22-1746 d 11-23-1831 m Lydia Berry Pvt NH
Henry: b 1700 d p. 1784 m Sarah Rawlins PS NH

ALLD,
David: b 3-15-1742 d *a.* 1821 m Margaret Patten Lt PS NH

ALLEBACH, (includes ALLABOUGH)
Abraham: b 1747 d 1794 m Catherine Rosenberger Pvt PA
David: b 3-18-1762 d 10-31-1849 m Helena Gotschall Pvt PA
Michael: b 1757 d 6-12-1844 m Sebella Hall Pvt PA

ALLEE,
David: b 4-25-1762 d *a.* 1- -1835 m Charity Bibee Pvt Grd VA ★

ALLEGRE,
Matthew: b— d *p.* 11-7-1806 m (1)Elizabeth — (2)Mary — PS VA

ALLEMAN, (includes ALLIMANG)
Christian: b *c.* 1731 d *a.* 1784 m X PS PA
Christopher: b 1742 d 5-2-1806 m Barbara Sheetz Pvt PA
Henry: b 3-5-1759 d 2-28-1829 m (1)Juliana Long (2)Mrs Seibert Pvt PA
John: b 10-8-1753 d 10-11-1811 m Barbara Eschnauer Pvt PA
Nicholas: b 9- -1746 d 1803 m Mary Magdalena Snyder PS PA

ALLEN, (includes ALLAN, ALLIN, ALLING, ALLYN)
Aaron: b 5- -1752 d 1808 m Lucy Train Sgt MA
Aaron, Sr.: b 2-13-1715/16 d 5-3-1794 m (1)Hannah Mason (2)Deborah Plimpton PS MA
Abel: b 4-9-1747 d 7-29-1802 m Sarah Allen Pvt MA
Abel: b 4-26-1756 d 4- -1841 m Mary Symmonds Pvt MA
Abel, Sr.: b 8-14-1733 d 8-8-1808 m Elizabeth Chapin PS NH
Abel, Jr.: b 11-15-1756 d 2-5-1837 m Susanna Wilbur Pvt NH ★
Abijah: b 7-17-1754 d 2-23-1832 m Abigail Maxcy MM MA
Abner: b 12-30-1757 d 5-31-1831 m Roxalina Hibbard Sol CT
Abraham: b 1759 d 10-14-1823 m Susan Ridecut Pvt MA
Adam: b 1754 d 8-27-1851 m (1)Miss Kyger (2)Nancy Gardner Pvt PA ★
Amasa: b 3-7-1753 d 12-22-1820 m Alice Lord Pvt CT NY ★
Ambrose: b 3-17-1754 d — m Hannah Lee Smn MA
Amos: b 9-15-1734 d 1-26-1825 m Dinah Bishop Pvt MA
Amos: b 1749 d *p.* 1804 m Lydia Bryant Pvt MA
Amos: b 8-1-1753 d 1851 m Rebecca Thurston Pvt MA ★
Amos: b — d — m Abigail Smith Pvt MA
Ananias: b 1-4-1742 d 10-2-1825 m Rachael Harker Capt NJ
Ananias: b 1756 d 1840 m — Laxton Pvt NC
Appollos: b 12-14-1756 d 9-18-1807 m Deborah Parda Pvt MA
Archelaus: b 1749 d 1828 m Prudence Merriman Pvt CT
Archer: b 4-6-1741 d 1-26-1811 m Elizabeth Allen Maj VA
Archibald: b 2-7-1751 d 2-23-1846 m Anne McClehoe Sol VA
Asa: b 1751 d 4-20-1812 m Jemima Purdy Ens NY
Asa: b 2-18-1728 d *c.* 1786 m Anna — Pvt NY
Asahel: b 1741 d — m Patience Richardson Pvt MA
Asaph: b 10-22-1752 d 3-19-1841 m Persis Sheldon Cpl MA ★
Barnabas: b 1730 d 1815 m Elizabeth Fuller PS CT
Barnabas: b 4-28-1741 d 1811 m Amy (Perry) Camp Pvt MA
Benjamin: b 3-13-1736 d 12-30-1827 m (1)Sarah Eilsworth (2)Abigail — Lt CT
Benjamin: b 10-4-1743 d 3-27-1827 m (1)Rhoda Allen (2)Mary — Pvt CT
Benjamin: b 9-15-1763 d 10-5-1843 m Rheuama Buckley Pvt CT ★
Benjamin: b 8-3-1754 d — m Sarah Kirkland Pvt MA
Benjamin: b 12- -1724 d 1788 m Peggy Spafford , 'H
Benjamin: b 8-7-1755 d 12-8-1823 m Hannah — Pvt NJ
Benjamin: b 1735 d 1823 m Sarah Somers Cpl FrA
Benjamin: b 9-10-1748 d *a.* 1-25-1808 m Elizabeth Austin 2Lt VA
Benjamin: b 1758 d 1840 m Elizabeth Davis Cpl VA
Byram: bpt 6-5-1763 d 7-31-1833 m Elizabeth Childs Pvt MA
Caleb: b 9-17-1746 d 11-25-1823 m Lois Dorman Capt CT
Caleb: b 8-26-1748 d 12-12-1797 m Lydia Wheaton PS CT
Caleb: b 6-25-1755 d 27-22-1839 m Rhoda (Allen) OrdlSgt MA ★
Caleb: b 3-30-1737 d 11-26-1807 m Judith Hawkes PS CS MA
Charles, Sr.: b *c.* 1730 d *p.* 12-8-1807 m Nancy Ann Vincent Capt NC
Charles, Jr.: b 3-8-1758 d 1848 m Patty Jenkins Pvt NC
Charles, Jr.: b 5-3-1764 d 1-5-1856 m Susan Garner Pvt SC ★
Charles: b 9-10-1748 d 2-8-1816 m Mary Venable LCol VA
Charles: b *c.* 1752 d 2-5-1814 m Elizabeth Chambers Maj VA
Charles: b 1753 d 1830 m Elizabeth Mosby Lt VA
Charles: b 1764 d 9-15-1845 m Sallie Wilbourne Lt VA ★
Chester: b 2-28-1747 d 10-15-1808 m Anne Powell Pvt CT
Christopher: b *a.* 1755 d *p.* 1800 m Experience Slade Pvt CT
Daniel: b 10-22-1747 d 1-10-1828 m Mary Horton Capt CT
Daniel: b 8-28-1732 d 2-15-1793 m Huldah Clark Sgt CT
Daniel: b 6- -1744 d 1-13-1777 m Dorcas Dibble Pvt CT
Daniel: b 1754 d 1-7-1848 m Sarah Delano Sgt MA ★
Daniel: b 4-25-1757 d 2-3-1811 m (1)Harriet Bassett (2)Thankful Butler MM MA
Daniel: b *a.* 1759 d 7-30-1834 m Alathea Hale Ens NC W★ .
Daniel: b 9-12-1728 d 1807 m (1)— Harrison (2)Johanna Read Hill Pvt VA
David, Jr.: b 11-13-1743 d 1-20-1812 m Sarah Hull Lt PS CT
David: b 10-23-1759 d 3-15-1841 m Desire Tyler Sgt CT ★
David: b 10-17-1757 d *p.* 1792 m Sylvia Briggs Cpl CT

David: b 12-22-1752 d 8-11-1849 m Elizabeth Goff Pvt CT ★
David: b 1755 d *p.* 1827 m Eliza Caroline — Sol GA
David: b 2-11-1741/2 d 7-3-1812 m Betty Hatch Cpl MA
David: b 5-27-1763 d 7-15-1845 m Rachel Dunbar Pvt MA
David: b 8-18-1738 d 8-5-1799 m (1)Elizabeth Fisk (2)Lydia Woods PS MA
David: b *c.* 1745 d 1823 m Mary Camp Pvt NJ
David: b 1762 d 1823 m Nancy Dawson Pvt NC
David: b *c.* 1732 d 1821 m Susan White Pvt PS PA
David: b *c.* 1750 d 7- -1830 m (1)Ivea Fox (2)Elizabeth Wright Cpl VA
David: b 1754 d *c.* 1800 m Aphia Fauntleroy Lewis 1Lt VA
David: b 6-10-1738 d *a.* 11-16-1779 m Elizabeth (Allen) — Cpl PS VA
Diarca: b 4-2-1761 d 6-9-1850 m Rebecca Lane Howe Pvt NH ★
Drewry: b 12-1-1749 d 1-20-1826 m Elizabeth Yarbrough Pvt NC
Ebenezer: b 3-10-1740 d 11-11-1800 m Lydia Punderson Cpl CT
Ebenezer: b 7-21-1739 d *p.* 1793 m Sarah (Allen) Pvt CT
Ebenezer: b 12-27-1761 d 4-19-1845 m Hulda Stewart Cpl CT
Ebenezer: b 2-10-1711 d 1795 m Rebecca Bartlett PS CT
Ebenezer: b 2-5-1738 d 1816 m Elizabeth P(T)ousley PS CT
Ebenezer: b 5-24-1762 d 7-3-1824 m Phebe Healy Sgt MA
Ebenezer, Jr.: b 4-12-1751 d 8-24-1778 m Mary Henry 3Cpl MA W★
Ebenezer, Sr.: b 3-2-1726 d 3-31-1801 m Jerusha Graves Pvt MA
Ebenezer, Jr.: b 7-21-1754 d *p.* 1840 m (1)Sarah Bush (2)Anna Bennett Pvt MA ★
Ebenezer: b 10-17-1743 d 3-2b-;806 m Lydia Richards Col VT
Ebenezer: b 3-19-1758 d 12-16-1805 m Ester — Pvt MA
Ebenezer: b 10-31-1722 d 1-26-1812 m Tabitha Fulham PS MA
Edward: b 6-16-1763 d 9-26-1839 m Abigail Palmer Cpl CT ★
Eleazer: b 10-25-1754 d 7-29-1837 m Phoeba Cornell Pvt MA
Eleazer: b 8-20-1760 d — m Margaret Harwood Pvt MA
Eli: b 6-19-1756 d *p.* 1830 m Sarah Griffith Pvt PA
Elias: b 1-14-1762 d 7-11-1836 m Amy Atwood Pvt Smn CT
Elihu: b 5-4-1739 d 2-27-1820 m Abigail Dean Pvt MA
Elihu, Jr.: b 10-9-1764 d 12-16-1816 m (1)Ruth — (2)Mrs Orlena Fish Pvt VT W★
Elijah: b 12-19-1722 d 2-27-1792 m Sarah Morse Pvt MA
Elijah: b 1756 d 1830 m Keziah Wright Pvt MA
Elijah: b 11-19-1757 d 1789 m (1)Sarah Garfield (2)Elizabeth Phillips Pvt MA
Eliphalet: b 8-24-1727 d 11-20-1783 m Elizabeth Livermore Pvt MA
Elisha: b 9- -1751 d 2-5-1819 m Abigail Pardee Pvt CT
Elisha: b 12-10-1744 d 7-16-1793 m Miriam Goodale Sgt MA W★
Elisha: b 1752 d 1796 m Merab Clapp Pvt MA
Elisha: b 8-9-1753 d 10-31-1834 m Sarah Wing Pvt MA
Elisha: b — d *c.* 1809 m Tryphosia Vine Sgt VT
Elnathan: b 1752 d 10-21-1827 m Sarah Gribbs Pvt CT
Elnathan, Sr.: b 11-18-1728 d 10-2-1805 m Thankful Hastings Pvt MA
Elnathan, Jr.: b 5-13-1754 d 6-20-1830 m (1)Lydia Pratt (2)Lydia Roberts (3)Lois — Pvt VT
Enoch: b 11-27-1744 d 7-8-1789 m Mercy Belding Cpl MA
Enoch: b *c.* 1750 d 3-14-1834 m (1)Hannah Collins (2)Ann Kirby (widow) Sol NJ
Ephraim: b 6-18-1747 d 12-28-1816 m (1)Temperance Morgan (2)Mrs Rebecca Morgan Gallup Cpl CT
Ephraim: b 10-24-1731 d *p.* 1790 m Mrs Huldah Chestnut Pvt MA
Ephraim: b 1746 d 2-11-1820 m Sarah Evans Capt PA
Ephraim Wm.: b 4-10-1752 d 4-1-1816 m Huldah Brown QM MA
Ethan: b 1-10-1737/8 d 2-12-1789 m (1)Mary Brownson (2)Mrs Frances (Brush) Buchanan Col VT
Gabriel: b 1-23-1755 d 10-12-1838 m Sarah Churchill Pvt CT ★
Gabriel: b 1-23-1755 d 10-26-1810 m Salome Nott Cpl CT
George: b 1-15-1741 d 8-2-1824 m Lydia Perkins Pvt CT
George: b 7-18-1756 d 10-9-1835 m Sabra Case Matr CT ★
George: b 1743 d 1836 m Susanah Rieves Pvt NC ★
George: b *c.* 1720 d *p.* 3-2-1803 m X PS NC
George: b 1762 d 2-17-1815 m Jane Paull Pvt PA
George: b 1750 d 1800 m Mary Easts Pvt VA
Gideon: b 3-16-1754 d 8-16-1830 m Sarah Russell Mar CT
Gideon: b 10-30-1746 d 3-12-1841 m Phebe Beardsley Sgt VT ★
Gilbert: b 1736 d 1-6-1816 m Elizabeth Lindsley Pvt NJ
Grant: b *c.* 1751 d 1840 m (1)Tabitha Marshall (2)Mrs Nancy DeBow PS CS NC
Heber: b 10-4-1743 d 4-10-1782 m Sarah Owen Maj VT
Henry: b 1743 d — m Phoebe Blake Pvt NY
Henry: b 1764 d 8-11-1831 m Catherine McCouchie Pvt VA ★
Henry: b 1748 d *p.* 1788 m Eunice — Pvt VT
Hezekiah: b 10-30-1762 d *p.* 1840 m Polly — Pvt Fif CT ★
Hezekiah: b 10-8-1739 d 6-14-1807 m Abagail Bartlett PS CT
Hezekiah: b 4-15-1724 d 7-12-1798 m (1)Jemima Kingsbury (2)Mary Peters Pvt MA
Hudson: b 10-29-1745 d 4-4-1820 m Martha Harwood Capt VA
Hugh: b *a.* 1745 d 10-10-1774 m Jane Anderson Lt VA
Humphrey: b 7-14-1754 d 2-17-1842 m Phebe Burgess Pvt MA
Ichabod: b 1-1-1753 d 11-25-1828 m (2)Welthy Bill MM CT
Ichabod: b 10-24-1756 d 9-19-1809 m Rhoda Gilbert Pvt CT
Ira: b 4-12-1751 d 1-7-1814 m Jerusha Enos Col VT
Isaac: b 12-21-1755 d 10-8-1818 m Esther Alling Pvt CT
Isaac: bpt 8-3-1740 d *p.* 1776 m Abigail Burnham Cpl MA
Isaac: b 1719 d 2-21-1791 m Joanna Packard Pvt MA
Isaac: b 12-3-1756 d 5-21-1854 m Abigail Bradbury Pvt MA ★

ALLEN, contd.

Isaac: b 2-6-1758 d 9-26-1841 m (1)Rebecca Tewksbury (2)Mary Foster Wells Sol MA
Isaac: b c. 1735 d p. 8-22-1783 m Margaret Whiteside Capt PA
Isaac: b 12-18-1753 d 1-16-1825 m Betsy Miller Pvt NY
Isaac: b 3-15-1755 d 12-15-1831 m (1)Frances Pettit (2)Margaret Elizabeth Poplet Pvt VA
Isham: b c. 1764 d 10-24-1834 m Elizabeth Mosby Pvt VA ★
Israel: b 4-24-1743 d 7-17-1833 m Thankful Greenwood Pvt MA
Ithamar: b 9-25-1750 d 1830 m Chloe Risley Pvt MA
Jacob, Sr.: b 4-4-1739 d 9-19-1777 m Abigail Bailey Capt MA
Jacob, Jr.: b 12-18-1763 d 12-3-1836 m Susanna Alden Fif Sgt MA
Jacob, Sr.: b 2-24-1734 d 5-24-1824 m Lucy Howard Pvt MA
Jacob, Jr.: b 12-1-1760 d p. 8-14-1832 m Polly Corbin Pvt MA ★
Jacob: b 6-13-1721 d 3-23-1805 m Sarah Lee MM MA
Jacob: b 1-20-1755 d 8-22-1840 m Armenia Brown Pvt MA ★
Jacob: b 12-23-1754 d 10-23-1821 m Hephzibah Vinton Pvt MA
Jacob: b 6-22-1764 d 9-27-1846 m Phoebe Allen Pvt NJ
James, Jr.: b 1768/9 d 5-5-1867 m (1)Abigail Berry (2)Sarah Carver (3)Salome Carver Drm CT
James: b 7-17-1739 d 10-13-1825 m Anna Stanton PS CT
James: b 11-17-1740 d 11-28-1815 m Irene Scripture Pvt CT
James: b 8-31-1750 d 4-4-1835 m Frances Simons Pvt GA
James, Jr.: b — d — m Phebe Thayer Pvt MA
James, Jr.: b 12-5-1735 d 1-10-1789 m Martha Hayward Capt MA
James, Sr.: b a. 1727 d — m Ruth Wesson Pvt MA
James: b 3-20-1757 d 2-14-1844 m Polly Whitman Sol Drm MA
James: b 3-28-1732 d 11-3-1815 m Martha Athearn PS MA
James: b 1-28-1758 d 11-26-1837 m Susanah Wilcox Pvt NY ★
James: b c. 1720 d 1781 m Mary Elizabeth Col NC
James: b 2-19-1744 d 4-12-1811 m Martha Pierce Pvt RI
James: b c. 1764 d 1819 m Mary Phillips Pvt SC
James, Jr.: b c. 1750 d 11-28-1808 m (1)Judith — (2)Margaret Calhoun Ens VA
James: b c. 1720 d 1-4-1811 m Mary Kelsey Pvt VA
James: b 1733 d 5-10-1810 m Margaret Anderson Sol CS VA
James: b c. 1735 d p. 3-24-1789 m Mary — Sol VA
James, Sr.: b 7-7-1724 d 1793 m Elizabeth Sims PS VA
Japhet: b 1739 d 1791 m Elizabeth Thomas Pvt MA
Jared: b 6-3-1759 d 8-14-1836 m Anna Newell Pvt CT RI ★
Jason: b 11-4-1740 d 5- -1817 m Lydia (Allen) Pvt CT
Jeremiah: b 2-11-1753 d 10-28-1837 m Abagail Rogers Pvt MA
Jesse: b 12-10-1744 d 4-11-1816 m Abigail Willis Pvt MA
Jesse: b 1750 d 6-24-1824 m Elizabeth Eikler Pvt (NY or PA)
Job: b 11-24-1753 d 2-23-1828 m Abigail Mather Sgt CT
Job: b 8-27-1750 d 3-16-1798 m Mary Minton Capt PS NJ
Joel: b 9-21-1755 d 12-24-1825 m Diademia Newell Fif CT
John: b 5-20-1740 d 12-29-1825 m Ruth Burham Lt Capt CT
John: b 12-24-1727 d 6-15-1805 m Priscilla (Allyn) Pvt CT
John: b 11-28-1729 d 2-6-1796 m Elizabeth Mather Pvt CT
John: b 1753 d 12-31-1830 m Sarah Kendall Pvt CT
John: b 1756 d 11-28-1831 m Electa Peck Pvt CT ★
John: b 1758 d 10-5-1830 m Sarah Edmonds Arfr CT
John: b 4-27-1762 d 4-15-1824 m Tirzah Morgan Pvt CT
John: bpt 10-31-1714 d 12-30-1791 m Sarah Bennett CS CT
John: b 3-5-1760 d 8-12-1828 m Elizabeth Inman Pvt GA
John: b 1750 d 1825 m X Pvt MD
John: b 1-3-1746 d 2-7-1805 m Mary Patten Col MA
John: b 11-24-1729 d 4-29-1811 m Hannah Hopkins Paine Pvt MA
John: b 1732 d 7-6-1803 m Elizabeth (Allen) Pvt MA
John: b 7-1-1740 d 9-30-1809 m Eunice Gleason Pvt MA
John: b — d 1778 m Abigail Pierce Pvt MA
John: b 3-28-1754 d 10-20-1841 m Abiah Holloway Pvt MA
John: b 1-13-1759 d 1-15-1824 m Rachael Hendrick Pvt MA
John: b 3-1-1761 d 1834 m Cynthia Phillips Pvt MA
John: b 1751 d 8-5-1836 m Ruth Stephens Pvt MA
John: b 9- -1713 d 7-15-1790 m (1)Sarah Shepard (2)Elizabeth Trusdill PS MA
John: b 4-29-1739 d 1785 m Ann Kimball Capt NH
John: b 4-2-1746 d 12-2-1795 m Abigail Young Lt NJ
John: b 1760 d 1837 m (1)Rachel Wykoff (2)Sarah Jones (3)Mary Bruce Pvt NJ
John: b c. 1760 d 1786 m Mrs Ester (Bishop) Wright Pvt NJ
John: b 11-3-1760 d 1813 m Persis Clark Pvt NY W★
John: b 4- -1749 d 4-7-1836 m Mary Allen Pvt NY ★
John: b 11-29-1752 d 10-11-1825 m Phoebe Smith Deuel Pvt NY
John, Sr.: b 7-29-1734 d 8-8-1826 m Rhoda Allen PS NY
John: b 11- -1752 d p. 4-4-1834 m Myrick (Middleton) Wilson Ens NC ★
John: b 1756 d 1860 m Patty (Molly) Turner Pvt NC ★
John: b 1750 d p. 10-20-1812 m Janett Coleman PS NC
John: b 1747 d 9-8-1805 m Margaret Ann Hanawalt Pvt PA
John: b 6-24-1752 d 8-10-1829 m Martha Tribble Pvt PA
John: b 1757 d 1845 m Mary — Pvt PA ★
John: b 3-26-1747 d 8-5-1813 m (1)Mary Gould (2)Martha (Allen) PS RI
John: b. 1743 d p. 6-8-1822 m—Cpl SC
John, Sr.: b 3-23-1729 d p. 1800 m Sylvia Keen 1Lt VT
John: b 4-2-1762 d 12-14-1852 m Sarah Brown Pvt VA
John: b 1749 d 1815 m Jane Tandy Maj VA
John: b—d 1799 m—Capt PS VA
John: b 7-1-1757 d 11-1-1816 m Ann Sims Sgt VA

John: b c. 1732 d 1794 m Ann Pollock Sol PS VA
John: b 8-17-1759 d 5-30-1828 m Rebeckah Poage Pvt VA
John, B.: b 8-9-1763 d 3-22-1840 m Sarah Green Pvt MA
Jonas: b 1729 d 1-1-1822 m Ruth Jones Capt MA
Jonathan, Jr.: b 1754 d 11-1-1832 m (1)Hannah Bradley (2)Anna Case Pvt CT ★
Jonathan: b 6-23-1755 d 8-22-1803 m Sarah Adams Pvt CT
Jonathan: b 1732 d 2-9-1780 m Sarah Bass Lt MA
Jonathan: bpt 7-24-1763 d p. 1794 m (1)Margaret Fitzgerald (2) Phebe Norton Pvt MA
Joseph: b 6-3-1737 d 4-14-1831 m Elizabeth Filley Pvt CT
Joseph: b 3-10-1754 d— m Mary Spalding Pvt CT
Joseph: b 3-23-1762 d 11-9-1822 m Lucy Chapin Sol CT
Joseph: b 1739 d — m Mary Belton Sol CT
Joseph: b 7-30-1704 d 6-11-1777 m Mary Hewlett PS CT
Joseph: b 7-17-1723 d 1-5-1798 m Patience Nye Capt MA
Joseph: b 10-12-1735 d 7-17-1814 m Sarah Lyman Lt MA
Joseph: b c. 1762 d 1833 m Agnes Patterson Sol GA
Joseph: b 6-30-1719 d 11- -1799 m Mrs Sarah Butterworth Pvt MA
Joseph: b 3-29-1757 d 12-28-1828 m Eunice Kingsley Pvt MA
Joseph: b 11-14-1759 d 9-23-1838 m Prudence Earl MM Artl MA
Joseph: b 1709 d 8-18-1793 m (1)Mercy Livermore (2)Mrs. Sarah Knowlton PS MA
Joseph, Sr.: b 1-15-1719 d 3-21-1802 m Lydia Aldrich PS MA
Joseph: b 4-13-1738 d 12-4-1815 m Elizabeth Warner PS MA
Joseph: b 9-2-1749 d 9-1-1827 m Dorothy Kingsbury CS MA
Joseph: b 6-30-1754 d 1816 m Molly Barney Pvt MA
Joseph: b 1724 d 1796 m — Capt NJ
Joseph: b 2-24-1756 d 3-12-1828 m (2)Kesia Wesley Pvt NY
Joseph: b c. 1733 d p. 1790 m Sarah Crawford Sgt NC
Joseph: b 4-4-1728 d 3-24-1817 m Jane Riddle Pvt PA
Joseph: b c. 1750 d 1818 m Sarah Tilloston Thornburg Pvt PA
Joseph: b 6-5-1754 d 5-2-1837 m Phebe Green Capt RI ★
Joseph: b 2-4-1752 d 1-28-1842 m Mary Taggart Lt RI
Joseph: b 1753/6 d p. 1832 m (1)Mary Thurber (2)Hannah Clark (Brimmer) QM Sgt MA & RI
Joseph, Sr.: b 4-1-1737 d 12-20-1804 m Hepzibah Coffin Pvt RI
Joseph: b 6-30-1719 d 1816 m (1)Sarah Butterworth (2)Joanna Whitehorn Sol RI
Joseph: b 1737 d 2-16-1782 m Sara (Allen) Sol VA
Joseph: b 1746 d 1804 m Alice Tyler Pvt VA
Joseph: b 1730 d 1805 m Eunice — Pvt VA
Joshua: b 1-28-1743 d 9-30-1841 m Patience Ida Pvt MA
Joshua: b 1753 d 7- -1817 m Elizabeth — Pvt NJ
Joshua: b c. 1738 d 1799 m Jerusha — Sol NC
Josiah: b 5-25-1742 d 8- -1795 m Deborah Day Pvt MA
Josiah: b 1756 d 12-28-1830 m Elizabeth Shepherson Pvt MA
Josiah: b 5-31-1744 d 2- -1821 m Bathsheba Nelson Pvt PS NH
Josiah: b 1748 d 1786 m Martha — Pvt PA
Josiah: b 1-17-1761 d 12-28-1842 m Susannah Dickerson Pvt PA
Jude, Jr.: b 9-18-1743 d 9- -1828 m Mrs Sarah Philbrick PS NH
Lemuel: b 11-11-1746 d 3-26-1809 m Phebe Peck Cpl CT
Malcum: b 1736 d p. 1786 m Mary Cunningham Pvt VA
Maria: b 1758 d 3-1-1820 m David Smith PS MA
Marshall: b 1732 d 12-28-1804 m Abigail Brockett Pvt CT
Mary Patton: b 2-3-1746 d 6-8-1819 m John Allan PS ME
Mathew: b 1733 d 1799 m Hannah Dyer PS VA
Matthew: b 3-10-1708 d 1787 m Sarah Brett PS MA
Matthew: b 1750 d 1845 m Mary Brauner Cpl VA
Micah, II: b 2-20-1740 d 8-14-1823 m Catherine Everett Pvt MA
Moses: b 5-14-1746 d 9-26-1826 m (1)Mary Adams (2)Mrs. Mary Pease Sol CT
Moses: b 1745 d 1824 m Comfort Buffam Pvt NH
Moses: b 3-5-1764 d 1-12-1834 m Margaret Rauback Pvt Wgm NJ
Moses: b 1752 d 8-31-1833 m Sarah Whittaker Pvt NJ ★
Moses: b c. 1740 d p. 1796 m Chloe Ward Pvt NY
Moses: b 1753/54 d 8-22-1845 m — Sgt VA ★
Nathan: b 10-14-1729 d 6-2-1812 m Mary Hitchcock Pvt CT
Nathan: b 6-5-1740 d 6-2-1814 m Sarah Freeman Smn CT
Nathan: b 12-2-1764 d 7-29-1833 m Mary Putman Pvt CT
Nathan: b 1722 d 4-5-1800 m Rebekah Read Sgt MA
Nathan, Jr.: b 2-28-1749 d 9-26-1814 m Persis Gilbert Sgt MA
Nathan: b 6-1-1753 d 4-10-1848 m Ame (Amy) Smith Pvt MA ★
Nathan: b 2-4-1746 d— m Rachel Barton Pvt NJ
Nathan: b 3-13-1760 d 1-13-1834 m Lovinia Winslow PS VT
Nathaniel: b 8-1-1732 d 12-28-1804 m Abigail Brockett Pvt CT
Nathaniel: b 5-21-1762 d 9-18-1828 m Susanna Carpenter Pvt CT
Nathaniel: b 10-31-1759 d 9-10-1843 m Anna Dodge Pvt MA
Nathaniel: b 1761 d 2-10-1839 m Lydia Stevens Pvt NY
Nathaniel: b c. 1750 d 1812 m (1)Pamelia Hudson 2Lt VA ★
Nehemiah, Sr.: b 12-10-1733 d 12-28-1799 m Abiah Thomas Capt MA
Nehemiah, Jr.: b 3-12-1765 d 3-22-1852 m Moley Bothwell Pvt MA
Noah: b 5-15-1730 d 10-27-1776 m Anna Root Ens CT
Noah: b 12-21-1757 d p. 1790 m Mabel Cambee Pvt CT
Noah: b c. 1735 d 7-4-1822 m Sarah Knapp Maj MA & CT ★
Noah: b 11-8-1719 d 3-23-1804 m Miriam Fisher Lt MA
Noah: b 6-24-1727 d 2-17-1802 m Ruth Martindale Lt MA
Noah: b 10-8-1747 d 3- -1797 m Sarah Haskins 1Lt MA
Obadiah: b 1-4-1755 d 1800 m Mehetable — Pvt VT
Oliver: b 4-4-1752 d a. 1-20-1778 m Lavina Hopkins Pvt MA

DAR Patriot Index

11

Parley: b 1764 d 10-3-1839 m Catherine Ter Bush Pvt CT ★
Parmalee: b 1746 d 2-10-1806 m (1)Ann Wheeler (2)Mrs. Deborah Burroughs Carl Capt VT W ★
Pelatiah: b 2-5-1756 d 5-21-1815 m Mary Ann Gillett Pvt CT
Philemon: b 1762 d 3-26-1825 m Lydia Estey Pvt MA
Philip: b 1-26-1755 d 3-18-1809 m Esther Tisdale Pvt MA
Philip: b 7-9-1757 d 7-1-1845 m Sally Keys Pvt MA ★
Phillip: b c. 1755-9 d c. 1807/06 m Rebecca Wood Pvt MA
Philow: b 1754 d 4-7-1813 m Hannah Lines Pvt CT
Phineas: b 10-29-1758 d 9-6-1851 m Sibyl Bicknell Pvt CT ★
Phineas: b 10-3-1754 d 4-12-1840 m Rebecca (Allen) Pvt CT
Phineas: b 4-24-1764 d 8-13-1836 m Ruth Smith Pvt MA
Phineahas: b 4-6-1745 d 5-15-1830 m (1)Abigail Foster (2)Sarah Danford (3)Dolly Flagg Sol MA
Prince: b — d a. 1825 m (2)Experience King Pvt VT
Reuben: b 10-18-1762 d 7-20-1836 m Rebecca Rhodes Pvt CT Pvt NY
Reuben: b 6-1-1763 d 12-6-1848 m Betsey Sherwood Pvt NY
Richard, Sr.: b 11-26-1741 d 10-10-1832 m Nancy Lindsay Capt NC
Richard: b 1739 d 1830 m Susannah Gatewood Pvt VA
Richard: b 2-10-1738 d 6-28-1844 m Elizabeth Donaho Capt VA
Richard: b 2- -1757 d 1-22-1824 m Ann Wisdom Pvt VA
Robert: b 9-8-1728 d 11-11-1811 m Hannah Gallup CS CT
Robert, Jr.: b 11-4-1756 d 10-10-1811 m Rebecca Mumford Lt CT
Robert: b 1762 d p. 8-3-1829 m Nancy Ham Pvt SC
Robert: b — d p. 9-7-1815 m — Hannah PS SC
Robert: b 1760 d 9-9-1823 m Mary White Pvt VT
Robert: b 1736 d 1791 m Martha Allen Pvt VA
Robert: b — d 1789 m Jane Turk Pvt VA
Roger: b 1-15-1741 d 8-2-1824 m (1)Lucy Smith (2)Lydia Perkins Sol CT
Ruel: b 10-8-1748 d p. 1807 m (1)Hannah Knapp (2)Lucy Johnson Sgt MA
Rufus: b 4-13-1749 d 10-7-1813 m Emiliscent Seymour Capt CT
Samuel: b 11-21-1734 d 9-6-1781 m Mary Wood Capt PS CT
Samuel: b 12-9-1742 d 6-14-1813 m Mrs Marcy Otis Ross 2Lt NY & CT
Samuel: b 11-15-1759 d 6-7-1829 m Jerusha Bissell Cpl CT
Samuel: b 1-28-1716 d 4-4-1788 m Kezia Lines MM CT
Samuel: b 6-8-1736 d 10-10-1816 m (1)Elisabeth Wells (2)Sarah Booth (3)Lucy Alden Markham Pvt CT
Samuel: b a. 1755 d c. 1805 m Mary Roby Lt MA
Samuel: b 4-30-1738 d 2- -1833 m Zilpha Hawks Lt MA
Samuel: b 9-10-1733 d 7-7-1794 m Sarah Perry Pvt MA
Samuel: b 9-16-1737 d 4-12-1784 m Hannah Pratt Pvt MA
Samuel: b 9- -1757 d 8-31-1832 m Elizabeth Fleming Capt NJ
Samuel: b 11-27-1751 d 12-15-1828 m (1)— Smith (2)Hannah Beach Arfr Ens NJ ★
Samuel: b 1750 d 10-26-1832 m Nancy Anderson Pvt NJ ★
Samuel: b 1751 d 2-4-1810 m Pamelia Lowrey Sgt NY
Samuel: b 1756-8 d 4-4-1831 m Margaret MacKnight Pvt NY ★
Samuel: b 1739 d 11-12-1801 m (1)Lucy French (2)Jerusha Clark Lt VT
Samuel: b 12-30-1756 d 12-11-1841 m Nancy Hester Pvt VA & NC ★
Seth: b 12-1-1760 d 1854 m Lydia Martin Pvt CT ★
Seth: b 3-29-1726 d p. 1787 m (1)Elizabeth Guild (2)Mary Treadway Pvt MA
Seth: b 3-13-1746 d p. 1790 m Jemima Jordan Pvt MA
Seth: b 8-2-1755 d 1-14-1838 m Anna Gage Pvt MA ★
Seth: b 10-9-1750 d p. 1790 m Charlotte Moore Pvt VT
Silas: b 2-9-1754 d 9-7-1825 m Mary Cleveland Dr CT
Silas: b 11-20-1749 d 4-6-1834 m Priscilla Plimpton Pvt MA
Silas: b 5-16-1754 d 12-12-1841 m Esther Hastings Pvt MA
Simeon: b 5-27-1745 d 9-6-1781 m Esther Gallup Stoddard Capt CT
Simeon: b 12-21-1750 d 12-28-1805 m Candace Howe Sgt MA
Solomon: b 10-8-1732 d 11-16-1810 m (1)Abiah Stoughton (2) Rachel — (3)Sarah Burr 2Lt CT
Solomon: b 3-23-1743 d 1820 m Catherine Slack Pvt MD
Solomon: b 2-23-1751 d 1821 m Beulah Clapp Maj MA
Solomon: b 12-6-1737 d 6-6-1836 m Susan Riggs Pvt MA
Squire: b 11-9-1727 d 1808 m Ann — Pvt MA
Stephen: b 8-25-1730 d 7-30-1803 m Anna Fargo Pvt CT
Stephen: b 1760 d p. 1832 m — Pvt CT ★
Stephen: b 5-14-1764 d 5-4-1852 m Weighty Thorp Pvt CT ★
Stephen Oney: b 9-17-1758 d 4-17-1831 m Jemima Dodd Pvt NY
Sylvanus: b 3- -1735 d 8-16-1811 m (1)Abigail Kidder (2)Sarah Wood Pvt MA
Thomas: b 3-17-1749 d 7-4-1825 m Rhoda Cares Pvt MD
Thomas (Rev): b 1-7-1743 d 2-11-1810 m Elizabeth Lee PS MA
Thomas: b 1752 d 1826 m (1)Abagail Brown (2)Dolly Ricker PS MA
Thomas: b 12-9-1747 d 3-20-1803 m Elizabeth Wheaton Pvt NJ
Thomas: b 5-24-1757 d 6-26-1833 m Mary Jouett PS Comsry QM VA & NC ★
Thomas: b c. 1755 d p. 1780 m Winifred Armour Sol NC
Thomas: b 4-15-1742 d 5-30-1800 m Amy Drowne Capt RI
Thomas: b 1750 d 1780 m Rachel Hedrick Sgt VA
Thomas: b 1732 d 1822 m Deborah Montgomery Millar Pvt VA
Titus: b 1752 d 11- -1830 m (1)Thankful Goodwin (2)Mrs. Abigail Coolidge Thompson Pvt CT ★
Tryal: b 4-14-1744 d 1790 m Lizzie — PS CT

Valentine: b 1730 d 8-1-1797 m Ann Arnold Sol NC
Weston: b c. 1757 d 1809/10 m Thankful — Pvt MA
William: b c. 1740 d 1833 m Sybil — Pvt CT
William: b 5-28-1746 d p. 7-28-1790 m Deborah Clark Lt MA
William Sr.: b 6-9-1731 d p. 1790 m Abigail Hooper Smn MA
William Jr.: b 12-3-1752 d 1824 m (1)Anna Lee (2)Sally Edwards Pvt MA
William: b 4-11-1763 d — m Hannah Travis Pvt NY
William: b 1-5-1756 d 1842 m Love Coffin Pvt MA
William: b 8-17-1744 d 10-7-1805 m Janet Drummond Pvt NY
William: b c. 1755 d 1806 m Judith Smartt Sgt NC
William: b 8-17-1731 d 8- -1797 m Sarah De Witt Pvt NC
William: b c. 1700 d 1786 m (1)Mary Owen (2)Frances Grant PS NC
William: b 1744 d 10-16-1794 m Rebecca Green Lt PA
William: b 9-14-1750 d 7-7-1822 m Susana Ruckman Pvt PA
William, Sr.: b 2- -1709 d 12-26-1784 m Elizabeth — PS PA
William: b 3-27-1752 d 8-17-1815 m Sally Jones Maj RI
William: b 1743 d 10-12-1823 m (1)Martha — (2)Rebeckah Moss Capt VA
William: b c. 1740 d 12- -1815 m Mary — Lt VA
William, Sr.: b 1725 d 1789 m (1)Mary Lewis (2)— Beverly (3)Sarah Ann Smith Pvt PS VA
William: b 6-20-1756 d 1839 m Sallie Andrews Pvt VA
William, Davis: b 8-21-1749 d c. 1800 m Mary Jane Polk Whittington Strawbridge Pvt MD
Woodson: b 1750-1760 d p. 9-11-1834 m Annis Palmer Sol GA
Zachariah: b c. 1740 d p. 9-27-1789 m — Sol NC
Zadok: b 1755 d p. 1795 m Lucy Herrick Pvt MA
Zebadiah: b 3-12-1734 d 1-28-1797 m Hannah Grout Lt MA
Zebulon: b 10-23-1727 d 2-15-1786 m Freedom Cooley 1Lt MA
Zenas: b 12-5-1763 d 3-29-1811 m Eliphael Patridge Pvt MA
Zoheth: b 4-27-1760 d 9-14-1848 m Jane Harper Pvt RI ★

ALLENDER,
Joseph: b 1762/3 d 8-27-1846 m Maria Nagel Pvt PA
William: b 11-16-1763 d 3-14-1843 m Barbara — Pvt MD

ALLER, (includes OLLER)
John: b a. 1752 d 1817 m Heziah — PS NJ
Peter: b c. 1756 d p. 1-11-1823 m Catherine Welshans PS VA

ALLERTON,
Isaac: b 8-15-1725 d 12-26-1807 m Lucy Spaulding PS CT
John: b 3-10-1763 d 4-8-1851 m (2)Rachel Crage (3)Mrs Mary Fry Pvt NJ
Jonathan: b 9-15-1746 d 8-10-1806 m Bathsheba Mead PS NY or CT
Reuben: b 12-25-1753 d 10-13-1808 m Lois Atherton Dr NY

ALLEY,
Ephraim: b 1754 d 5-2-1821 m (1)Mehitable Hallowell (2)Hepzibah Lewis Pvt Matr MA
John: b 3-25-1738 d 3-10-1807 m Sarah Bassett Pvt MA
John: b c. 1760 d p. 1803 m Elizabeth Burge Pvt VA
Joseph, Sr. b 9-7-1728 d c. 1783 m Rebecca Hall Pvt MA
Joseph, Jr.: b c. 1758 d 2-10-1832 m Hannah Batchelder Slr MA
Joshua: b 4-4-1756 d p. 1790 m Hannah — Cpl MA
Nathan: b 2-29-1752 d 2-7-1832 m Mary Alley Pvt Gnr Matr MA
Samuel: b 1747 d 1836 m — Pvt VA ★
Samuel: b 6-25-1761 d 8-12-1847 m Mary Osborne Pvt VA ★
Shadrick: b 1751 d 3- -1835 m Mary Price Pvt VA & NC ★

ALLGAIER,
Sebastian A.: b 5-5-1757 d 2-27-1846 m Catherine Ruttner Pvt Grd PA ★

ALLGOOD,
John: b 5-12-1751 d p. 1831 m — Pvt VA

ALLINGTON,
John: b 1760 d 1827 m Martha — Pvt VA

ALLIS,
Eber: b 8-29-1745 d 6- -1821 m Sarah Mann Pvt MA
Eliphalet: b 12-9-1710 d 1794 m Mary Brook CS MA
John: b 12-15-1753 d 8- -1790 m Dollie West Pvt MA
Josiah: b 1754 d 4-17-1794 m Anna Hubbard PS CS MA
Julius: b 9-18-1732 d 8-16-1817 m Hannah Dickinson Pvt MA
Lucius: b 5-9-1737 d 3-12-1822 m (1)Jemima Bliss (2)Mary Wells (3)Mehitable Graves (4)Lois Graves Pvt MA
Moses: b 2-13-1756 d 3-30-1842 m Anna Newton Sgt MA ★
Nathaniel: b 2-27-1741/2 d 2-16-1825 m Hannah Norton Pvt Drm CT
Russell: b 4-2-1756 d 3-7-1835 m Sarah Edson Pvt MA
Stephen: b 3-4-1758 d 12-3-1848 m (2)Mary Munn (5)Mrs. Rachel Trow Pvt MA ★
William: b 2-6-1752 d 1802 m (2) Rachel Allis Pvt MA
Zebediah: b 7-2-1754 d — m (1)Martha Brooks (2)Lucy Tuttle Pvt MA

ALLISON, (includes ALISON)
Alexander: b 1740 d 7-12-1814 m Margaret Hope PS NC
Andrew: b c. 1755 d 2-17-1803 m Mary Bingham Cav DE
Andrew: b 1720 d 1779 m Margaret Allison Pvt NC
Andrew: b 6-30-1757 d 1-6-1815 m Sallie Barr Pvt PA
Archibald, Jr.: b 4-15-1761 d 5-3-1845 m Eleanor McCormick Pvt
    PA
Benjamin: b 1760 d 4- -1844 m Cassandra — PS MD
Benjamin: b c. 1749 d 1796 m Leah Ackerman Pvt NY
Benjamin: b 6-6-1759 d 10-12-1830 m Phobe Davidson Pvt NY
Burch: b 2-24-1764 d 1848 m — Pvt Grd MD ★
Charles: b c. 1728 d 1795-1810 m Barbara — PS MD
Francis: b 1751 d 5-11-1813 m Mary Mackey Dr PA
Gaius: b 1-28-1759 d 12-28-1838 m Mary Kountze Pvt PA & VA
Gavin: b c. 1730 d 1782 m Jean Wallace Pvt PS PA &MD
Henry: b 1739 d 1-23-1826 m Hannah Jackson Pvt NY
Holbert: b a. 1750 d 1813 m Agnes — Pvt VA
Isaac: b c. 1732 d 1793 m Anna — Pvt NY
Isaac: b 1762 d 1825 m Mary Davis Pvt NY
James: b 3-30-1741 d 3-27-1841 m Nancy — Lt PS MD
James: b 5-1-1748 d 6-10-1821 m Amy Knapp Pvt NY
James: b 1743 d 7-24-1820 m Mary Bradford Sub Lt PA
James: b 6-4-1765/6 d p. 1789 m — Pvt SC
John: b 1758 d 2-2-1832 m Martha Hodges Pvt TN ★
John, Jr.: b 1762 d 3-28-1842 m Sarah Tollar Pvt NC ★
John: b 12-23-1738 d 6-14-1795 m Elizabeth Wilkin Col PA
John: b 10-2-1764 d 8-16-1834 m Mary Herron Pvt Sct PA W ★
Joseph: b 8-3-1721 d 1-2-1796 m (1)Elizabeth Benson (2)Elsie Par-
    cells Pvt NY
Joseph: b c. 1750 d 1826 m — Donaldson Lt NC
Joseph: b 1752 d 1-11-1813 m Anne Cooper Pvt CS PA
Joseph, B: b 12-13-1761 d 12-20-1848 m Mary Storms Pvt NY
Matthew: b 1750 d 2-9-1828 m (1)Sarah Mehaffy (2)Catherine
    Lamb (3)Sarah Bane PS PA
Richard: b c. 1735 d 1808 m Sarah Cheshire Pvt PS MD
Richard: b — d 1810 m Anne — Pvt PS NY
Robert: b 9-25-1749 d 3-2-1826 m Martha McKinley Cpl PA
Robert: b 1750 d p. 1798 m Catherine Hodge Sol CS NC
Robert: b 1750 d 1804 m Sarah Graham Lt NC
Robert: b 1730 d 1811 m Elizabeth — Pvt VA
Robert: b 1725 d p. 2-8-1805 m Rebecca — Sol PA
Robert: b 8-31-1745 d 9-15-1812 m Elizabeth Phillips 2Lt PA
Robert: b 1734 d 11-21-1822 m Jane— Sol PA
Robert: b 1754 d 6-29-1827 m Sarah Turner Wgn Pvt SC
Robert: b 1750 d 1820 m Jane Moore Pvt TN
Samuel, Sr.: b 1722 d 6-5-1792 m Janet McFarland PS CS NH
Samuel, Jr.: b 4-27-1749 d 8-27-1800 m Mary Barr PS NH
Thomas: b a. 1761 d p. 1789 m Mary Kingsland Pvt PS NY
Thomas: b 1-18-1759 d 11- -1799 m Esther Neill Sol NC
Thomas: b 1755 d 1830 m (1)Ann Allison (2)Mary Pilson Pvt PA
William: b 1738 d 1804 m (1)Mary Jackson (2)Mrs Mary Everett
    Graham BGen NY
William: b c. 1745 d a. 2- -1818 m Lucy — Sol NC
William: b 1-14-1759 d 11-5-1825 m Nancy Gilchrist Pvt PA

ALLMAN, (includes ALMOND)
Edward: b c. 1764 d 1839 m Jennie Dutton Pvt NC ★
Thomas: b 8-18-1762 d 5-2-1845 m Nancy David Pvt GA

ALLNUTT,
James, Sr.: b 1713 d 1786 m (1)Sarah Lawrence (2)Jane Coberth
    PS MD
James, Jr.: b 1752 d 2-21-1838 m Verlinda Hawkins Dawson
    PS MD
Jesse: b 2-17-1745 d 8-7-1815 m Anne Newton Chiswell PS MD
Lawrence: b 1750 d 1825 m Eleanor Dawson PS MD
William: b 1711 d p. 1779 m Mary Talbot PS MD

ALLRED,
John: b c. 1764 d 1850-2 m Sarah — Pvt NC
William: b c. 1730 d 1825 m Elizabeth — Pvt NC

ALMY, (includes ALMEY)
John: b 4-18-1720 d 5-14-1808 m Hannah Cook PS RI
John: b c. 1720 d 1776-8 m Sarah Sherman PS RI
John, C: b 3-2-1752 d 1846 m (2)Sarah Dunham Pvt MA
Peleg: b 1-6-1761 d 4-5-1853 m Hannah Cory Pvt RI ★
Sanford: b 8-28-1759 d 9-18-1844 m Lydia Gray Sgt RI

ALPHINE,
Ransom: b 1758 d p. 1831 m Elizabeth Shelton Pvt VA ★

ALSDORF,
Lawrence: b 1757 d 1863 m — Pvt NY ★

ALSOP,
George, Sr.: b 1735 d 1797 m Delphia — PS VA
John: b 1720 d 11-22-1794 m Mary Frogat PS NY
Joseph: b 1743 d 1783 m Mary Freeman Pvt MD W ★

ALSPACH, (includes ALSPAUGH)
David: b 1757 d 1794 m (1)Mrs. Mary Smith Kraut (2)Barbara
    Thrush Pvt PA

Henry: b — d c. 1819 m Dolly — Pvt PA
Philip: b 12-15-1742 d 8-26-1808 m Maria Magdalena Heinkel Pvt
    PA

ALSTON, (includes ALLSTON & ALSTONE)
Isaac: b 11-12-1758 d 12-14-1832 m Elizabeth Johnstone Pvt NJ
James: b c. 1746 d 1815 m Grisel Yancey Sol NC
James: b 2-1-1754 d 2-27-1805 m (1)Sarah Kearney (2)Sarah Ma-
    con Hawkins MM PS NC
John: b c. 1740 d 1784 m Ann Hunt Macon*Capt NC
John: b 1750 d 1814 m Charity Jones Pvt NC
John: b c. 1740 d 6-3-1787 m Mary Boyd Capt PS SC
Joseph John: b 6-13-1763 d 1-10-1847 m Esther Wright Pvt NC
Joseph John: b 1702 d 1781 m (1)Betsey Chancey (2)Euphan Wilson
    PS NC
Philip: b c. 1740 d p. 1788 m Mary Drew Temple Col NC
Thomas: b 3-21-1753 d 3-23-1833 m Rebecca Brown Ens NJ
William: b 10-7-1747 d 7-15-1795 m Martha Hardee L Col PS NC
William: b 12-25-1736 d 1810 m Charity Lillington Alston L Col NC
William: b 1748 d 1789 m Sarah Yeargen CS NC
William: b 8-23-1756 d 6-26-1839 m (1)Mary Ashe (2)Mary Brewton
    Motte Capt SC
William: b 1735 d 7-31-1781 m (1)Ann Simons (2)Rachel Moore
    PS SC
Willis: b 1750 d 9- -1816 m Elizabeth Wright Col PS NC

ALTER, (includes ALDER)
Christopher: b c. 1750 d 1804 m Susanna — PS MD
George: b 1755/6 d 8-28-1824 m Lucy Ann Wynn Pvt MD ★
Henry: b c. 1720 d p. 1784 m Maria Magdalena — PS PA
Henry, Jr.: b c. 1750 d 1800 m Margaret — Pvt PA
Jacob: b 4-10-1754 d 3-13-1836 m Anna Jordan Pvt NY ★
Jacob: b 1742 d 4-18-1815 m Margaret Landis Pvt PA
James Latimer: b 2-13-1760 d 8-8-1852 m (1)Rebecca Atchison
    (2)Ellen Tippit Sol MD
John Jacob: b c. 1735 d 7- -1778 m Elizabeth Willerich Pvt PA

ALTHOUSE,
Christian: b 1718 d p. 6-14-1786 m — PS PA
Daniel: b 9-9-1750 d 9-8-1812 m Catherine Richstein Pvt PA
George: b 5-5-1744 d 1-7-1811 m Maria Barbara Herbein Pvt PA
Henry: b 2-8-1757 d 11-8-1836 m (1)Miss Truxel (2)Catherine —
    Fif PA ★

ALTIMUS, (includes ALTEMOSE)
John: b 1741 d 1815 m Sarah E — Pvt PA
Nicholas: b 5-20-1745 d 7-2-1836 m Schalona Altemonin Pvt PA

ALTIZERA,
Emera b p. 1736 d 10- -1819 m (1)Mary Pitzer (2)Mary Miller
    Sol VA

ALTLAND,
Philip: b 1-11-1738 d 7-12-1804 m Anna Maria Schneider Pvt PA

ALTMAN,
Anthony: b c. 1730 d p. 2-3-1809 m Anna Maria Tetoit PS PA
John Peter: b 1739 d 11- -1800 m (1)Chrisena — (2)Barbara —
    Pvt PS PA
Philip: b 12-26-1763 d 5-29-1813 m Louisa Keppel Pvt PA
William: b c. 1740 d 1798 m Maria Barbara — Sol PS PA

ALTON, (includes ALLTON)
Benjamin: b 1742 d 10-21-1808 m Susannah Blood Capt MA
John: b 5-22-1759 d 7-18-1823 m Catherine Adams Pvt PA

ALTZ, (includes ALTS, & AULTZ)
Adam: b c. 1756 d p. 1810 m Elizabeth — Pvt PA

ALVERSON,
Caleb: b 5-26-1755 d 4-30-1824 m Hannah A King Pvt RI
George: b c. 1750 d 9-24-1839 m Experience White Pvt MA ★
John: b 1757 d 2-2-1829 m Frances — Pvt Wgm VA
Uriah: b 4-7-1738 d 12-7-1835 m (1)Marcy Sayles (2)Amey Sayles
    CS PS RI

ALVIS,
Jesse: b 8- -1757 d p. 1840 m Mary Mallory Pvt VA ★

ALVORD, (includes ALFORD & ALVARD)
Azariah: b 1-20-1738 d 1-11-1819 m (1)Abigail Nash (2)Lucy Nash
    1Lt MA
Bela: b 8-31-1741- d 1-13-1793 m Sarah Welton Sol NY
Benjamin: b 5-1-1762 d 9-4-1830 m Katherine Davenport Pvt VT
Caleb: b 10-5-1751 d 12-22-1819 m Mary Murdock CS VT
Daniel: b 1-27-1742/3 d 1-14-1814 m Phebe Hamlin Pvt CT
Daniel: b 5-4-1758 d 6-20-1847 m (1)Susanna Judd (2)Anna Tower
    Pvt MA ★
Ebenezer: b 12-17-1720 d 8-7-1784 m Catherine Strong Sol MA
Elijah: b 1-17-1718 d 5-15-1788 m Hannah Huntington Pvt MA
Elijah: b 4-13-1757 d 4-11-1832 m Olive Adams Higley Pvt MA
Elisha: b 3-15-1731 d 11-23-1807 m Mary Hamilton Pvt MA
Elisha: b 3-17-1753 d 8-15-1825 m Sarah Danks Pvt MA

Gad, Sr.: b 1726 d 5-11-1810 m (1)Lydia Smith (2)Mrs. Thankful (Wells) Holland Pvt MA
Gad, Jr.: b 6-27-1759 d 8-29-1817 m Phebe White Pvt MA
Gideon: b 6-12-1734 d 5- -1808 m Sarah Montague Pvt MA
Jehiel: b 1-7-1756 d 10-21-1829 m Dorothy French Pvt MA
Job: b 1729 d 1-30-1789 m Rebecca Smith Capt MA
John: b 7-11-1750 d 7-3-1845 m (1)Sarah Wakeman (2)Abigail Banks Sgt CT ★
John: b 1750 d 1831 m Olive Cogswell Sol CT
John: bpt 9-22-1754 d 6-22-1833 m Maria Judd Cpl MA
John: b 1-21-1739 d 1813 m Relief Crosby Pvt MA
Moses: b 8-26-1735 d 1816 m Perces — Pvt MA
Nathan: b 1729-34 d p. 1784 m Lydia White Pvt MA
Obed: b 8-1-1744 d p. 1792 m Catherine Johnson Pvt CT
Phineas: b 7-14-1760 d 9- -1834 m Salome Judd Pvt MA ★
Reuel: b 1750 d 3-27-1810 m Hannah Hall Pvt CT
Samuel: b 1-27-1751 d 7-9-1814 m Miriam White Pvt MA
Saul, Sr.: b 4-23-1717 d 9-28-1793 m Martha Churchill PS CT
Saul, Jr.: b 9-7-1753 d 9- -1832 m (1)Eleanor Kellogg (2)Cynthia Olcott Cnt CT
Seth: b 7-18-1754 d 7-14-1836 m (1)Ruth Norcott (2)Sarah Sears Pvt CT ★
Seth: b 2-21-1762 d 9-18-1831 m Deborah Crouch Pvt MA
Stephen: b 8-18-1735 d 3- -1812 m Abigail Davis CS MA
Thomas Gould, Sr.: b 3-1-1742 d 5-18-1810 m (1)Keziah Orvis (2)Mrs. Hannah Byington Sgt CT NY
Thomas Gould, Jr.: b 3-23-1763 d 6-22-1835 m Nancy Scouton Gnr NY W ★
Zebadiah: b 2-14-1725 d 2-16-1806 m Rebecca Searl Pvt MA

ALWARD,
Benjamin: b 1751/2 d 10-24-1813 m Sarah Ayres Pvt NJ
Samuel: b 1732 d 6-24-1818 m Katy King Pvt NJ

ALWORTH,
James: b c. 1760 d 1847 m Margaret Strain Sol PA ★

AMASON,
Eli: b a. 1765 d a. 8- -1823 m Ellendor — PS NC

AMBERSON,
William: b 1755 d 1-4-1838 m (1)Elizabeth Smith (2)Mary — 1Lt PS Aide PA ★

AMBLER,
Abraham: b 6-27-1762 d 9-10-1839 m (1)Rhoda Keeler (2)Rowena Boland Pvt NY
David: b 4-29-1739 d 1-8-1808 m Olive Wildman PS Pvt CT
Ebenezer: b 4-22-1756 d 4-26-1826 m Elizabeth Brewster Pvt VT
James: b 1754 d 1839 m Theodora Seeley Pvt CT
Jaquelin: b 8- -1742 d 2-10-1798 m Rebecca Burwell NS PS VA
John: b 3-28-1733 d 10-21-1814 m Huldah Fairchild Sgt CT
John: b 9-23-1732 d 8-13-1802 m Sarah Weed Pvt NY
John: b 9-25-1762 d 4-8-1836 m (1)Frances Armistead (2)Lucy Marshall (3)Mrs. Katherine Bush Norton PS VA
Peter: b 9-20-1759 d 3-7-1836 m Hannah Shove Pvt CT
Squire: b 1763 d 1-14-1829 m (1)Elizabeth Pickett (2)Jerusha Hoyt Pvt NY ★

AMBROSE,
Frederick: b 5-4-1738 d 7-29-1821 m Margaret — CS PA
Henry: b — d a. 12-12-1811 m — Capt PS VA
Jacob: b c. 1734 d 4-22-1776/2-27-1779 m Katherine — Capt MD
Jonathan: b 4-24-1723 d p. 1790 m Abigail Goodhue Sol NH
Joseph: b 2- -1762 d 1847 m Elizabeth Rickets Pvt VA
Mathias: b c. 1742 d a. 12-31-1808 m Barbara — PS Pvt PA
Nathaniel: b 3-2-1741 d 7-20-1801 m Elizabeth Elkins Capt CS NH
Nathaniel: b 3- -1741 d 1835 m Phebe Lovejoy Pvt NH
Robert: b 3-6-1733 d 3-8-1816 m (1)Mary Etheredge (2)Mrs. Molly Stevens Thistle (3)Mrs Sarah Cleasby PS NH
Samuel: b 4-21-1753 d 12-2-1830 m Mary Goodhue Pvt NH

AMBURGEY,
John: b 1758 d 5-3-1831 m Elizabeth Hamon Vol NC

AMENT, (includes AMEND)
George: b 12-2-1758 d 12-11-1843 m Esther Markle Pvt PA ★
Jacob: b 1740 d 1820 m Mary Lee Pvt PA
Matthias: b 1-21-1753 d 1829 m Elizabeth Buschong Sol PA
Philip: b 1755 d 1836 m Margaret — Pvt PA ★

AMES, (includes AMIS, AMISS, & EAMES)
Aaron: b 3-11-1759 d 4-10-1824 m Elizabeth Boyd Pvt MA
Amos: b 18-1734 d 8-4-1817 m Abigail Bulkley Pvt MA
Barnabas: b 1-11-1763 d 9-23-1823 m Electa Noble Sol CT
Benjamin: b 6-6-1724 d 1-10-1809 m (1)Hepsibah Chandler (2) Dorcas Lovejoy Capt MA
Daniel: b 2-1-1755 d 4-29-1854 m Mercy Langdon Pvt CT ★
Daniel: b 2-8-1751 d p. 1785 m Mehitable Perkins Pvt MA
David: b 4-18-1727 d 4-11-1821 m Irenoi Waldo Pvt NH
David: b 5-30-1749 d p. 1799 m Anna Wright Pvt NH
Ebenezer: b 3-15-1739 d 1779 m Jane Howard 2Lt MA

Elijah: b 1-7-1743 d a. 3-21-1807 m Betty Johnson Lt MA
Elijah: b 3-27-1741 d 11-30-1821 m Sarah Blood MM MA
Elisha: b 1758 d 9-26-1845 m Elizabeth Cook Pvt MA ★
Jacob: b 1750 d 6-2-1818 m Jane — Pvt NH
James: b 1735 d 1821 m Elizabeth Hall Pvt MA
Job: b 10-28-1752 d 5-29-1827 m Mary Dike Pvt MA
John: b 4-7-1738 d 7-17-1805 m Susannah Howard Capt MA
John: b 1760 d 10-11-1844 m Sarah Fargo Sol Mar Capt CT ★
Jonathan: b 3-26-1759 d 12-14-1836 m Patience Sturtevant Pvt MA
Joseph: b 16-1757 d 11-13-1836 m Hannah Barnes Tyler Pvt CT ★
Joseph: b 5-6-1711 d 5-13-1790 m (1)Susanna Littlefield (2)Ruth Field Packard (3)Abihail Lathrop Alger Bosworth Pvt MA
Joseph: b 3-4-1746 d p. 1780 m Elizabeth Noyes Pvt MA
Joseph: b 1710-20 d p. 1-19-1801 m Constant — PS VA
Levin: b c. 1750 d 1825 m (1)Mary Hutchinson (2)Comfort Scott Smn VA
Mark: b 1742 d p. 1789 m Priscilla Howland PS MA
Moses: b 6-4-1763 d 6-24-1825 m Lydia Brigham Pvt MA
Nathaniel: b 4-25-1761 d 8-27-1863 m Sarah Hall Pvt CT
Noah: b 6-25-1748 d — m Ruhama French Hines Pvt MA
Phineas: b 10-26-1757 d 1839 m Mehitable Jewett Pvt CS NH
Prince: b 1759 d 4-21-1817 m Eunice Russ Pvt MA
Robert: b 1738 d 2-2-1821 m Lydia Harrington Pvt MA
Samuel: b c. 1725 d 7-23-1802 m (1)Sarah Ball (2)Lusaney Henry Pvt MA
Samuel, Sr.: b 2-13-1723 d 1-16-1803 m Hannah Dolloff PS NH
Samuel, Jr.: b 1745 d 9-1-1825 m Jane Gerrish Pvt PS NH
Samuel, Jr.: b 9-19-1746 d p. 7-15-1792 m Abigail Stevens Pvt NH
Simon: b 1740 d 11-15-1820 m Sarah (Mann) Wilson Sgt NH
Spofford: b 3-21-1752 d 9-14-1835 m Mary White Pvt MA
Stephen: b 9-1-1712 d 2-19-1801 m Jane Robbins CS PS NH
Sylvanus: b 1-20-1749 d 1777/8 m Huldah Johnson Chp, PA
Thomas: b 1-1-1744 d 12-4-1797 m (1)Alice Gale (2)Lucy Haynes PS Capt NC
Thomas: b c. 1741 d a. 7-15-1810 m — Hudson Sol VA
Thomas: b 3-24-1736 d 8-23-1812 m Deborah Brett Pvt MA

AMMARINE,
Abraham: b 1760 d 11-14-1849 m (1)Mary Wolford (2)Nancy Cook PS PA

AMMEN, (includes AMMON)
Christopher: b c. 1715 d 1783 m Mary Bristow PS VA
Thorst: b 1731 d 12- -1805 m Eva Rauck Pvt PA

AMMERMAN, (includes AMERMAN)
Albert: b 2-9-1733 d 9-1-1818 m Apolonia de la Montague Pvt NJ
Albert: b c. 1750 d c. 1819 m Jane Campbell Pvt NJ
Daniel: b 1-14-1743 d p. 1794 m Lena Nefews (Nevious) Brokaw Sgt NJ
Derick: b 9-28-1759 d 3-4-1826 m Mary Belknap Pvt NY
Derrick: b — d 2-27-1813 m Margaret Ranous Pvt NY W★

AMMIDOWN, (includes Amadon, Amidon, Ammedon)
Caleb: b 8- -1736 d 4-13-1799 m Hannah Sabine Sgt MA
Henry: b 5-3-1727 d p. 1800 m Sarah Doubleday Capt·CT
Jacob: b 3-5-1764 d 9-17-1838 m Hannah Pool Pvt CT ★
Jedediah: b 1753 d 11-5-1839 m Hannah Walker Capt CT ★
John: b 5-2-1765 d 4-21-1843 m Sarah Adams Pvt MA
Joseph: b 3-14-1741 d 5-14-1821 m Dorcas Carpenter Pvt MA
Moses: b 1756 d 1834 m Sally Davis Pvt CT ★
Philip: b 1-6-1748 d 2-2-1834 m Eunice Shumway Pvt MA
Reuben: b 12-13-1747 d 1-12-1802 m Olive Lyon Pvt MA
Roger: b 5-12-1747 d 5-31-1825 m (1)Elizabeth (Shepherd) Rider (2)Ruth Eddy Pvt MA
Samuel: b 10-13-1742 d p. 1783 m Ruth Wood Lt MA
Titus: b 7-18-1763 d 3-19-1846 m Sabra Gilbert Pvt MA

AMMONETT, (includes AMMONETTE, AMONET)
Charles: b 10-13-1758 d 4-14-1833 m Phebe Hall Pvt VA
John: b 1753 d 3-30-1833 m Bathsheba Rogers Pvt VA ★
William: b c. 1728 d 1810 m Elizabeth Badgett PS VA

AMMONS,
Joshua: b 1-22-1756 d 4-11-1833 m Frances Parker Pvt SC ★

AMOS,
Mordecai: b 1753 d 1842 m Margaret — 2Lt MD ★
Nicklos: b 9-19-1742 d 2-12-1799 m Christianna Ditto Ens MD
William: b 1717 d 1814 m — Mauldon PS MD

AMSDELL, (or AMSDILL)
Abner: b 8-27-1757 d 1851 m Susan Sirkin Pvt MA

AMSDEN,
Abel: b 9-1-1755 d 7-25-1828 m (1)Mary Fish (2)Sybil Hubbard (3)Susanna Story Pvt MA
Abraham: b 2-20-1752 d 3-20-1833 m Submit Morse Pvt MA ★
Adam: b 1762 d 1830 m Dolly Kidder Pvt MA
Isaac: b 1-10-1755 d 3-26-1841 m (1)Elizabeth Gates (2)Diadema — Sgt MA ★
Noah: b 1-19-1758 d 12-11-1843 m Prudence Cummings Pvt MA ★

AMSDEN, contd.
Simeon: b 4-20-1763 d 8-18-1832 m Abigail Whitney Pvt MA ★
Thomas: b 6-12-1752 d 1811 m Patience Miller PS VT
Uriah: b 6-19-1725 d 9-7-1794 m Abigail — PS NH

AMSPOKER,
Jonas: b c. 1758-60 d 7-6-1796 m Elizabeth Leeper Pvt PA

AMWEG,
Jacob: b. 1730 d 1790 m (1)Anna Elizabeth — (2)Catherine —
    Sol PA

AMY, (includes E IGHME)
Abraham: b 6-17-1732 d 1802 m Sarah Corliss Cpl PS NH
Daniel: b 6-13-1754 d c. 1840 m Catherine (Scott) Dymond Pvt
    Tms NY
Micah: b 11-30-1726 d p. 1785 m Elizabeth Middleton CS VT
William: b 1759 d 11-11-1837 m X Pvt NH ★

AMYX,
Andrew: b c. 1760 d p. 1-1-1830 m — Taylor Pvt VA

ANCIAUX,
Nicholas: b c. 1760 d 1805-1820 m Lydia Richardson QM FrA RI

ANCRUM, (includes ANKROM)
Jacob: b 1752 d 1823 m (1)Elizabeth Clark (2)Nancy — PS MD
John: b 1724 d 10-10-1779 m Mary Hasell PS NC

ANDERS,
Abraham: b 4-1-1739 d 4-19-1819 m Susanna Kriebel Pvt PA
John, Jr.: b c. 1755 d 1814 m X Lt NC

ANDERSON,
Abraham: b a. 1747 d p. 11-16-1805 m Sarah — Sol VA
Absolom: b — d 2- -1787 m (1)Mary — (2)Anne Waters Lt MD
Alexander: b 1765 d 1835 m Elizabeth Holmes Drm Fif NY
Andrew: b c. 1750 d p. 5-29-1821 m Martha Crawford Capt VA
Andrew: b — d — m Mary Crawford Pvt VA
Armstead: b 9-2-1756 d 1852 m (1)Ursula Allen (2)Sarah Davis
    Pvt VA ★
Augustine: b 1750 d 1-18-1834 m Hannah Edsel Lt NJ ★
Benjamin: b 9-13-1766 d 8-2-1830 m Charity Martin Pvt PA
Benjamin: b c. 1743 d p. 1787 m (1)Judith Mimms (2)Sarah
    Johnson 1Lt VA
Bailey: b 1754 d 1840 m D. (Anderson) Pvt Spy VA ★
Charles: b 8-3-1759 d 6-25-1836 m (1)Rebecca McKorkle (2)Eliza-
    beth George Drm PA
Charles: b c. 1720 d a. 2-27-1784 m (1) X (2)Elizabeth Chambers
    PS VA
Charles: b 5-5-1750 d 10-23-1829 m (1)Sallie Barker (2)Sarah
    Thornton (3)Nancy Richardson Sgt VA
Charles: b 1756 d 2-20-1832 m Betsy Snead Sgt VA
Cornelius: b 1749 d p. 1810 m Anna Redmond Pvt VA
Daniel: b a. 1760 d 4-15-1784 m Mary Carlisle Pvt MD
David: b 1730 d p. 4-12-1784 m (1)X (2)Mrs. Sarah (Melvin)
    Westbury (3)Mrs. Mary Copper McClelland PS GA
David: b 8-26-1741 d 5-31-1827 m Maria Mason Maj SC
David: b 4-9-1765 d 4-26-1836 m Rachel Wade Ens SC ★
David: b 7-15-1756 d p. 1832 m Margaret McHatton MM Grd VA
Denny: b 12-23-1763 d 12-19-1832 m Elizabeth Massey Pvt SC
Eli: b 6-17-1745 d 8- -1830 m Achsah Van Dyke Pvt NJ
Elijah: b c. 1750 d a. 1828 m (1)Elvina Brack (2)Sarah — Pvt GA
Elijah: b 7-15-1736 d p. 1781 m Jemima — Pvt NJ
Elijah: b a. 1765 d 1838 m (1) X (2)Miriam Anderson (3)Mary
    Priest Pvt VA
Enoch: b 1754 d 4-21-1824 m Eleanor McCalmont Capt DE
Enoch: b 5-5-1750 d 3-5-1820 m Jane Stroud Capt PA ★
Ezekiel: b — d p. 9-11-1793 m Elizabeth Laws CS DE
Ezekiel: b 12-28-1734 d 9-16-1820 m (2)Mary Combs (3)Ann
    Stover Pvt NJ
Francis: b 12-16-1759 d 1-6-1805 m Frances Spencer Pvt VA
Francis: b c. 1720 d 1787 m Edith Walden PS VA
Garland: b c. 1742 d 3-8-1811 m Marcia Elizabeth Burbidge PS VA
George: b 2-23-1726 d 1816 m Abigail Brown Pvt CT
George: b 1751 d 11-8-1839 m Sarah Skirm Capt NJ
George: b 1760 d 1822 m Elizabeth Cochran Pvt PA
George: b 5-17-1760 d 6-10-1848 m Elinor Sharp Pvt PA ★
George: b 1740 d 5-28-1808 m (1)Miss Anderson (2)Mary Lewis
    (3)Molly Saxon Sol SC
George: b 4-3-1745 d 3-10-1828 m Jane Presberry 2Lt VA
George: b c. 1715 d 1784-9 m Elizabeth Crawford Drm Fif VA
George: b a. 1765 d 6-29-1814 m Mary Breden Pvt VA ★
Henry: b 1731 d 10-3-1781 m Ruth — Capt SC
Henry: b 1755 d 1823 m Elizabeth Bass 1Lt VA
Henry: b 1753 d p. 1793 m Jane Grimsby Pvt VA
Isaac: b 11-23-1760 d 10-27-1838 m Mary Lane Lt PA
Isaac: b 9-15-1758 d 12-18-1839 m Euphemia Moorehead Lt PA
Isaac: b 1745 d p. 1787 m Sarah Holmes Freeman Pvt VA
Jacob: b c. 1722 d p. 1790 m Agnes Phiney CS ME
Jacob: b 3-2-1745 d 5-11-1837 m (1)Catherine — (2)Rebecca Lan-
    ning Capt NJ & NC ★
Jacob: b 11-8-1731 d 11-22-1822 m Mary Calloway Lt VA

James: b — d 9-26-1787 m Abigail Goodwin Pvt CT
James: b c. 1747 d 2-4-1813 m Margaret Boyd Pvt MD
James, Sr.: b 1725/6 d 10-1-1804 m Lydia Meek PS MD
James: b c. 1760 d 5-5-1836 m Elizabeth Wallace PS MD
James: b 10-3-1757 d 1-20-1836 m Marcy Stebbins Pvt MA W ★
James: b 1750 d 1825 m Helena Hankinson Capt NJ
James: b 3-9-1731 d 1802 m Elizabeth Mebane Pvt NC
James, Jr.: b 12-26-1741 d 12-13-1799 m (1)Jean Tate (2)Mar-
    garet Chambers Capt PA
James: b c. 1753 d c. 1830 m Martha Hook Capt PA
James: b 1762 d 3-29-1833 m Mary Stewart Lt PA
James: b 1750-60 d 10-26-1832 m Esther Thom Pvt PA
James: b 3-25-1763 d 9-6-1850 m Rachel Hopkins Pvt PA ★
James: b 5-14-1721 d 6-1-1790 m Ruth Bayley PS PA
James: b 3-6-1746 d 9-9-1813 m Agnes Craig Capt VA
James: b 12-13-1757 d 5-30-1831 m Hannah Wallace Sgt VA
James: b c. 1755 d 1814 m Susannah Daniels Cpl VA
James: b 10-22-1743 d 4- -1835 m Inez Lavarro Sgt VA ★
James: b c. 1736 d a. 12-6-1796 m Mrs. Sarah (Hall) Lynam Pvt
    VA
James: b 1749 d 1815 m Isabel King Pvt VA
James: b 1-24-1739 d 9- -1798 m Hannah Tyler PS VA
James: b c. 1750 d p. 10-15-1821 m Ann — PS VA
John: b a. 1730 d p. 1791 m Rebecca Patterson Sol MD
John: b 1728 d 12-22-1780 m Margaret (Stewart) Kately Pvt MA
John: b 1755 d 3-4-1822 m Phebe Barr Pvt MA
John: b 8-31-1757 d 10-22-1827 m Jane Archibald Sgt NH
John: b 1737 d 5-30-1816 m (1)Anna Davidson (2)Mrs. Mary Will-
    iams Pvt NH
John: b 4-5-1731 d 6-9-1797 m Anna Lloyd PS Capt NJ
John: b 1703 d 7-19-1793 m Sarah Craig PS NJ
John: b 5-2-1761 d 2-10-1840 m (1)Mary Smith (2)Charity Wood-
    ward Btm NY ★
John: b 1762 d 1834 m Sarah Mansfield Pvt NY ★
John: b 12-22-1759 d 9-20-1842 m Tarley Anderson Pvt NC ★
John: b 1728 d 1818 m Susanna Griffith Pvt PA
John: b c. 1737 d 1807 m Abigail Glasgoe Pvt PA
John: b 1737 d 12- -1814 m Jane Neely Capt SC
John: b c. 1732 d a. 1786 m Sarah — Sol SC
John: b c. 1740 d 1- -1798 m Elizabeth Pace Pvt SC
John: b c. 1755 d 4-19-1805 m (1)Elizabeth Conyers (2)Frances
    (Moore) McBride Sol SC
John: b 5-5-1750 d 10-13-1817 m Rebecca Maxwell Capt PS VA
John: b 1752 d 1814 m Mary Elizabeth — Capt VA
John: b 1757 d 1845 m Sarah Beck Capt VA
John: b — d p. 2-25-1814 m Susannah — Sol VA
John: b 1-13-1724 d 1796 m Ann Irvin Pvt VA
John: b 1741 d 1810 m Mary Southard Sol VA
John: b 12-25-1757 d 1834 m Louisa Poindexter Pvt VA ★
John: b c. 1710 d 1787 m Jane — PS VA
Joseph: b 1-2-1755 d 6-4-1839 m Hannah Packard Pvt MA ★
Joseph: b 10-28-1766 d 12-4-1853 m Lydia Smith Pvt NH
Joseph: b 11-5-1757 d 4-17-1837 m Only Patience Outlaw Brevet
    Maj NJ W ★
Joseph: b 1746-50 d 10- -1828 m (1) X (2)Sarah Bess Pvt VA ★
Joseph: b c. 1758 d 6- -1848 m Sarah — Pvt SC
Joseph: b 4-7-1764 d 10-23-1823 m Mary — Pvt SC
Joseph: b c. 1750 d 1806 m Mary — Sgt VA
Joshua: b a. 1740 d c. 4-27-1815 m (1)Elizabeth Brearley
    (2)Elizabeth Longshore LCol PS PA
Kenneth: b 6-8-1742 d 9-15-1820 m (1)Ruth Amanda Gordon
    (2)Ruth Scudder Adj NJ
Lemuel: b 1-7-1765 d 2-16-1845 m Rachel Hall Pvt CT
Lewis: b 1-22-1757 d 3-29-1838 Jane Gaston Mount MM NJ
Matthew: b 10-28-1755 d 8-29-1824 m Nancy Taylor Pvt NH
Nancy Stephenson: b c. 1750 d 1827 m (1)William Anderson
    (2)Daniel Green PS SC
Nathan: b — d c. 1819 m Martha Puryear Lt VA
Nathan: b 1-23-1764 d 10-31-1834 m Marianna Mayo Pvt VA ★
Nathaniel: b 1-26-1742 d 1-26-1812 m Sarah Anderson Lt VA
Nelson: b 1726 d 1819/1820 m (1)Frances Jackson (2Anne —
    Capt VA
Oliver: b 1742 d 1810 m (1)Elizabeth Martial (2)Sarah Kyle (3)Jane
    Humphreys Pvt PA
Patrick: b 7-24-1719 d 3-18-1793 m (1)Hannah Martin (2)Elizabeth
    Morris (3)Ann Beaton Capt CS PS PA
Presley: b c. 1750 d 1816 m Elizabeth Steele Pvt VA
Richard: b 12-2-1751 d 5-31-1831 m Katharine Love Capt MD
Richard: b 1-16-1752 d 6-22-1835 m Ann Wallace Capt MD
Richard: b 7-19-1761 d 5-12-1835 m Frances — Maj VA
Richard: b c. 1723 d 2-12-1796 m (2)Jane Foster Capt VA
Richard: b 1735 d 8-17-1819 m (1)Mary Johnson (2)Catherine Fox
    PS VA
Richard Clough: b 1-12-1750 d 10-16-1826 m (1)Elizabeth Clark
    (2)Sarah Marshall LCol VA
Robert: b 1755 d 2-4-1833 m Anna Hungerford Pvt CT ★
Robert: b 1753 d 9-2-1838 m Margaret Johnson Pvt MD
Robert: b 12-27-1761 d 3-27-1846 m Mary Darah Pvt NH ★
Robert: b 3-16-1734 d 12-7-1778 m Margaret Clark Pvt VA
Robert: b 1739 d 9- -1823 m Mary — Pvt VA
Robert: b 1748 d 12-17-1808 m X PS Lt SC
Robert: bpt 11-15-1741 d 1- -1813 m (1)Anne Thompson (2)Lydia
    (Turpin) Marverick (3)Jane (Harris) Reese LCol SC

Robert: b 8-10-1741 d 2-1-1805 m Elizabeth Shelton Capt VA
Samuel: b 10-2-1762 d 10-25-1828 m Ann Boggs Stl MA
Samuel: b 6-25-1757 d 4-4-1826 m Ann Dabney Sgt VA
Samuel: b 1746/7 d 7-18-1832 m Sarah Young PS VA
Thomas: b 2-18-1747 d 12-15-1822 m Mary Ely Lt QM CT ★
Thomas: b 6-24-1758 d 3-30-1834 m Alice Whitmore Pvt CT
Thomas: b 1-31-1762 d 4-6-1837 m (1)Susan Hosley (2)Eunice
   Lindsay Pvt MA ★
Thomas: b 1732 d c. 1804 m Jane Craige PS NH
Thomas: b a. 1760 d 1829 m Mary — Pvt NC
Thomas: b c. 1760 d p. 3-6-1841 m Ann — Pvt NC
Thomas: b 1749 d 8-17-1799 m Eleanor Stewart Pvt PA
Thomas: b 1733 d 10- -1806 m Mary (or Sarah) Bruce Pvt VA
Thomas: b 4-1-1762 d 5-13-1840 m (1)Elizabeth Owen (2)Didama
   Wimbush Pvt VA ★
Timothy: b 8-6-1762 d 10-31-1842 m Amy (Wade ?) Pvt Pvtr CT ★
Turner: b c. 1748 d 1-19-1814 m Susan Roane Daniel Lt VA
William: b 1-8-1763 d 5-6-1844 m (1)Sara Finch (2)Mary Hunnicott
   Pvt GA ★
William: b p. 1720 d a. 3-21-1805 m (1)Elizabeth Edwards (2)
   Sarah Edwards Pvt PS MD
William: b 1746 d 11- -1809 m Sarah Bealmear PS MD
William: b 8-18-1749 d 7- -1832 m Sarah Holmes Pvt MA
William: b 1748 d 11-11-1825 m Jane Rogers 2Lt PA
William: b c. 1740 d 12-25-1802 m Margaret McCord Pvt PA
William, Jr.: b 11-21-1763 d 4-22-1836 m Jane Bell Pvt PA
William Clark: b 10-6-1754 d 7- -1810 m Carry Brashear Pvt PS
   MD
William: b 1745 d p. 1809 m X Pvt SC
William: b c. 1750 d 1800 m (2)Eliza Ann Purvis Pvt SC
William: b c. 1750 d 1780 m Nancy Stinson Pvt SC
William: b 1706 d 1783 m Rebecca Denny PS SC
William: b 4-18-1744 d 7-22-1792 m Cecelia (Anderson) Capt VA
William: b 7- -1750 d 7- -1817 m (1)Mary Craig (2)Catherine Blair
   Capt VA
William: b 3-13-1756 d p. 1820 m Barbara Hendericks Pvt VA ★
William: b c. 1756 d 12-17-1830/31 m Nancy McCampbell Pvt
   Wgn VA
William: b 3-21-1763 d 10-25-1837 m Elizabeth Lewis Pvt VA ★
William: b 1760 d 1806 m Sarah Early Pvt VA
William: b 1693 d 1797 m (1)Rachel — (2)Margaret Barnett PS VA
William: b 6-2-1764 d 9-13-1839 m Anne Thomas Vol VA
William: b 7-7-1747 d 1821 m Mary Ann Cann Sgt PA

ANDREAS,
Jeremiah: b 2-11-1764 d 1-5-1847 m (1)Sarah How (2)Cynthia
   Hawley Pvt CT ★
Martin: b c. 1729 d p. 1783 m Anna Elizabeth Wotring (Vantrin)
   Pvt PA
Peter: b c. 1751 d p. 1818 m Thankful Washburn Sgt PA
William: bpt 8- -1757 d 1824 m Elizabeth — Pvt PA

ANDREW,
Benjamin: b 10-20-1713 d 11-7-1788 m Elizabeth Philbin PS GA
Benjamin: b 12-28-1757 d 4-5-1830 m Mary Kenyon Pvt RI ★
Charles: b 1-16-1726 d p. 1778 m Mary — Pvt RI
John: b 10-4-1746 d 10-1-1814 m (1)Rachel Chamberlain (2)Elizabeth
   McConnell Dr NJ
John: b 9-14-1758 d 3-10-1830 m (1)Ann Lambright (2)Mary Buer
   Andrew (3)Mary Overton Cosby QM Adj SC W ★
Sylvester: b 12-12-1760 d 11-25-1838 m Mary Weaver Pvt RI ★
William: b 9-14-1753 d 1826 m Hannah Holloday PS NC

**ANDREWS, (includes ANDDRES, ANDRE, ANDROSS,
   ANDRUS & ANDRUSS)**
Abel: b 1-28-1728 d p. 1783 m (1)Sarah — (2)Lettis Williams Pvt CT
Abel: b 5-6-1735 d 5-15-1811 m Eunice Stoddard Pvt CT
Abraham: b 9-6-1747 d 7-13-1823 m (1)Esther Stearns (2)Abigail
   Cross Carter Lt MA
Alexander: b 1758 d 1-15-1846 m Abigail Guthrie Pvt PA
Alexander: b c. 1760 d a. 3- -1807 m Abigail Redmond Pvt VA
Ammi: b 4-13-1737 d 3-30-1816 m (2)Molly Brown Lt NH
Ammi: b 5- -1738 d 10-10-1827 m Deborah Andrews 2Lt NH
Amos: b c. 1730 d p. 1797 m Anna Seavey 2Lt MA
Amos: b 5-31-1743 d 10-21-1827 m Joanna Burnham Pvt MA W ★
Andrew: b 8-16-1719 d 2-22-1792 m (1)Esther Royce (2)Elizabeth
   Dunbar PS CT
Andrew: b c. 1750 d a. 9- -1820 m Edney — Sol NC
Arthur: b 3-10-1753 d 5-6-1837 m Annes Cooper Lt PA ★
Asa: b c. 1749 d 2-25-1813 m Lucy Ackley Pvt CT
Asa: b 9-6-1746 d p. 1781 m Chloe (Andrews) Sgt CT
Asa: b 9-17-1758 d 2-28-1733 m Elizabeth Stone Pvt MA
Asahel: b 1742/3 d 11-1-1825 m Sarah Rowley Pvt CT
Benjamin: b 12-18-1755 d 2-21-1841 m Hannah Pierce Rowe Pvt
   CT ★
Benjamin: b 5-10-1758 d p. 6-1-1840 m Annice Case Pvt CT
Benjamin: b 3-20-1742 d 11-9-1821 m (Mary) Ellenor Russell Beal
   Cpl MA
Bildad: b 5-12-1719 d c. 1794 m Mary Stebbins CS PS VT
Charles, Sr.: b 10-3-1710 d 6-3-1790 m Elizabeth Strickland PS CT
Charles, Jr.: b 8-11-1744 d 11-2-1801 m Anne Fox Mil CT

Charles: b c. 1730 d p. 12-14-1780 m Elizabeth — PS MD
Daniel: b 5-12-1720 d 12-4-1799 m (1)Mrs. Eunice (Barnes) Kelsey
   (2)Mrs. Mary Mitchell Pvt CT
Daniel: b 6-4-1737 d 3-28-1814 m Sarah Clark Pvt CT
Daniel: b 1749 d 7-31-1828 m (1)Sarah Hall (2)Mrs. Jemima Copps
   Pvt CT
Daniel: b 1734 d 12-3-1818 m Anna Eddy PS CT
Daniel: b 1755 d 4-20-1818 m Susannah Choate Pvt MA
David: b 2-12-1756 d 2-14-1849 m Abigail McDonald Pvt CT ★
David: b c. 1745 d 6-12-1778 m Hannah Fuller Cpl MA
David: b 12-28-1757 d 9-1-1847 m Sarah Thaxter Fif Pvt MA
David, I: b 1766 d 8-22-1831 m Seely Ranney Fif Pvt CT ★
Deliverance: b 10-10-1754 d 3-23-1811 m Irene — Cpl NY
Ebenezer: b 1-10-1726 d 5-21-1808 m (1)Elizabeth Shaw (2)Mary
   Francis Sgt MA
Ebenezer: b 5-16-1756 d 10-28-1841 m (1)Sarah Dutton (2)Rhoda
   Dutton Pvt VT
Edmund: b 1-9-1741 d 5-17-1808 m Mellicent Barrett Pvt MA
Edmund: b c. 1725 d a. 1790 m Agnes Wallace PS NC
Eleazer: b 12-24-1747 d 12-4-1829 m Anna Clark Pvt MA
Elijah: b 12-6-1731 d 9-28-1803 m Sarah Thompson Pvt CT
Elijah, Jr.: b 10-16-1752 d 11-24-1839 m Rachel Gridley Pvt CT
Elijah: b 12-25-1758 d 6-19-1826 m Mabel Fox Pvt CT
Elisha, Jr.: b 5-4-1730 d 3-13-1813 m Jerusha Keeney Pvt CT
Elisha: b 12-12-1746 d 1840 m Sarah Moulthrop Pvt CT ★
Elkanah: b 3-4-1731/2 d 6-11-1787 m Alice Beal CS MA
Elnathan: b 2-22-1732 d 6-20-1824 m (1)Jane Greene (2)Mrs Ezekiel
   Johnson Pvt PS RI
Ely: b 1757 d 7- -1850 m Ruth Rockwell Pvt CT
Enos: b 4-13-1719 d 11-11-1790 m Content Curtiss Pvt CT
Ephraim: b 2-4-1720 d 1808 m Frances — Pvt VA
Ezekiel: b 1745 d 3-14-1828 m Martha Munson Pvt CT
Francis: b 7-8-1754 d 12-30-1825 m (2)Sabra Parsons Cpl CT
George: b 5-6-1755 d 6-11-1841 m Ruth Vaughan Ens RI ★
Gideon: b c. 1721 d p. 1785 m Abigail Potter Pvt CT
Gray: b c. 1740 d p. 8-25-1811 m Millie — PS NC
Hezekiah: b 8-14-1731 d 4-19-1796 m Anna Stedman Sol CT
Hugh: b 1754 d 7-6-1846 m Elizabeth Rebecca Blair Pvt NC ★
Isaac, Sr.: b 11-11-1728 d 12-30-1796 m Lucy Perkins Pvt MA
Isaac, Jr.: b 11-11-1755 d 5-4-1843 m (1)Rebecca Symonds (2)Mrs.
   Sarah Beard Pvt NH
Isaac: b 4-22-1731 d 6-30-1824 m (1)Elizabeth Tracy (2)Truelove
   Oatman (3)Mrs. Anna Spencer (4)Mrs. Freelove (Wilcox) Parks
   Capt VT
Isham: b — d c. 1788 m Rebecca Way Sol GA
Israel: bpt 3-22-1752 d 2-1-1810 m Mary Seavey Sgt MA
Issachar: b 12-25-1744 d 7-16-1796 m Rebecca Hodgman Lt MA
Jacob, Sr.: b 4-29-1734 d 4-5-1806 m Hulda — Pvt MA
Jacob: b 1738 d 1786 m Mary Holt Pvt MA
James: b 2-4-1752 d 5-5-1836 m (1)Ruth Mills (2)Mrs. Lois (Case)
   Norton 1Lt CT ★
James: b 1749 d 8-10-1821 m Susannah Atwood Pvt MA
James: b c. 1756 d 1786 m Elizabeth Ogle Pvt PS VA
Jeremiah: b 1-16-1732 d 6- -1782 m Sarah Bryant Pvt CT
Jeremiah: b 4-6-1757 d 1826 m Elizabeth Sawtelle Pvt NH
Joel: b 2-5-1753 d 6-25-1825 m Anna Moore Pvt NH ★
John: b 3-17-1734 d 11-19-1777 m Temperance Cable Capt CT
John: b 7-9-1746 d 10-25-1809 m Lucy Cone Ens CT
John, Jr.: b 9-11-1751 d 9-20-1825 m (1)Eunice Seeley (2)Mary
   Sperry Ens CT
John: b 1748 d 1817 m Miriam Matthews Pvt CT
John: b 7-20-1759 d 5-20-1825 m Lydia Gorham Pvt CT
John: b 8-20-1745 d 1804 m Sarah Kinsman Sgt MA
John: b 1755 d 1-23-1807 m Patience Hathoway N Capt MA
John: b 5-2-1744 d 1-26-1816 m Sarah Lewis Sgt MA
John: b 3-29-1757 d 2-13-1822 m Peggy Parker Cpl MA
John: b 8-20-1761 d 11-24-1840 m Esther Gray Pvt MA
John: b 1750 d p. 1790 m Deborah Sargent Pvt MA
John: b 1744 d 10-6-1817 m Grace Rude (or Rood) Pvt NH
John: b a. 1763 d 5-6-1814 m Nancy Briscoe Pvt NC W ★
John, Jr.: b — d 1803/4 m Hannah (Dixon ?) Capt PA
John: b 1746 d 8-23-1813 m Jane Cooper Ens PA
John: b 6-20-1749 d 10-10-1817 m Edith Strange Pvt PS VA
John: b 4-4-1764 d 7-4-1842 m — Tapley Pvt VA ★
John: b 5-4-1762 d 5-2-1816 m Ann Goode Sol VA
John: b c. 1750 d p. 5-30-1806 m Mary — PS VA
John Nicholas: b 1762 d 7-13-1835 m Cathrine Sober Pvt PA
Jonathan: b 2-1-1760 d 4-13-1837 m Sophia Lawrence Pvt CT
Johanthan: b 1730 d 1816 m Elizabeth Aldrich Pvt CT
Jonathan, Sr.: b 4-4-1715 d 12-2-1797 m Susannah Richards PS CT
Jonathan, Jr.: b 5-28-1756 d 12-27-1806 m Ruth Deming Sol CT
Jonathan: b 1745 d 1832 m Dorcas Stuart Capt MA
Jonathan, Sr.: b 7-17-1734 d p. 11-2-1784 m Anne Story Pvt MA
Jonathan, Jr.: bpt 7-22-1764 d 11-21-1826-8 m Mary Burnham Pvt
   MA
Jonathan: b 9-15-1758 d 3-27-1829 m Marcy Ames Pvt MA ★
Joseph: b 12-23-1751 d 11-23-1831 m (1)Lydia Judd (2)Amy Cowles
   Cpl CT
Joseph: b 4-17-1745 d 5-11-1837 m (1)Susannah Brooks (2)Prudence
   Williams Mil CT
Joseph: b 11-20-1757 d 4-23-1793 m Eunice Griste Matr MA

ANDREWS, contd.

Joseph: b 1-15-1719 d 1800 m Sarah Torrey Pvt MA
Joseph, Sr.: b 9-25-1729 d 4-15-1806 m Rachel Burnham Pvt MA
Joseph, Jr.: b 4-23-1757 d 10-18-1831-4 m Margaret Ober Smn MA
Joseph: b 2-16-1753 d 5-28-1833 m Betty Wise Pvt NY
Joshua: b 5-7-1720 d 1799 m Olive Emery Pvt MA
Josiah: b 10-27-1752 d *p.* 1832 m Abigail Gridley Sgt CT ★
Laban: b 4-25-1728 d 1-24-1813 m Prudence Stanley PS CS CT
Lemuel: b 5-4-1761 d — m Martha Anderson Pvt MA ★
Ludim: b 10-17-1756 d 1-7-1817 m Lois Davis Pvt MA
Ludwick: b 9-29-1734 d 4-9-1792 m Sophia Knauss Pvt PA
Mark: b 7-16-1760 d 5-16-1848 m Ruth Parris Pvt MA ★
Mark: b *c.* 1733 d *p.* 12-20-1820 m Winnifred Lyell Sol PS VA
Mary: b 5-20-1766 d 1-29-1853 m Joseph Blakeslee Jr. PS CT
Miles: b 5-22-1735 d 1810 m Phoebe Hulbert Cpl Pvt CT
Moses, Sr.: b 5-12-1722 d 5-17-1806 m Lydia Root PS CT
Moses C., Jr.: b 4-7-1755 d 7-20-1848 m Elizabeth Clark Sgt CT ★
Moses: b 10- -1760 d 10- -1800 m Catherine Brown Lt PA
Nathaniel: b 10-15-1762 d 8-27-1845 m Jerusha Sage Pvt CT ★
Nathaniel: b 5-20-1760 d 11-21-1836 m Lois Blakeslee Sol CT
Nathaniel: b 8-1-1745 d 8-20-1818 m Mehitable Mix MM NJ
Nehemiah: b 1745 d 1844 m Sophia Gillette Pvt CT
Nehemiah: b 5-28-1746 d 3-8-1813 m (1)Hannah Fox (2)Elizabeth Stott Pvt MA
Nehemiah: b *c.* 1740 d 4-17-1828 m (1)Phebe Benham (2)Sarah Goodwin Tms CT
Nehemiah: b 5-8-1722 d *p.* 1-6-1800 m Hannah Borden CS PS CT
Nehemiah: b 2-7-1753 d 2-10-1800 m Catherine Seymore Mstr Seacap MA
Ozias: b 3-20-1742 d 4-2-1812 m Ann Nott Pvt MA
Philarmon: b 5-7-1763 d 8-4-1830 m Phylinda Wilson Pvt CT
Richard: b 4-5-1755 d *p.* 12-19-1794 m Mary Lane PS VA
Robert: b 11-8-1722 d 11-11-1789 m Lucy Bradstreet Capt MA
Robert: b 6-19-1735 d 8-6-1811 m Delight Kellogg Ens MA
Robert, Jr.: b 12-28-1747 d 7-13-1835 m Dorothy Goodenow CS MA
Robert: b *c.* 1743 d 1-1-1804 m Elizabeth Ballard Cpl VA
Samuel: b 9-21-1744 d 11-21-1831 m Esther Cone Cpl CT
Samuel: b 10-26-1753 d 8-6-1832 m Elizabeth Barnes Cpl CT ★
Samuel: b 4-27-1741 d 3- -1808 m Mary Johnson Sol CT
Samuel: b 11-2-1749 d 9-20-1776 m Abigail Smith Pvt CT
Samuel: b 9-27-1755 d 9-16-1836 m (1)Hannah Smith (2)Prudence — Cpl MA ★
Samuel: b 1728 d 2-5-1799 m Abigal Cobb Pvt MA
Samuel: b 9-14-1750 d 4-15-1814 m (1)Judith Flagg (2)Annis Morse Pvt MA
Samuel: b 1753 d 12-30-1845 m (1)Ruth Blackmer (2)Asenath Moore Pvt MA ★
Samuel E: b *c.* 1763 d 1-1-1822 m Hannah E Elder Pvt NH
Seth: b 1737 d 10-24-1823 m Sarah Baldwin Pvt NY
Silas: b 3-27-1727 d 3-16-1803/4 m (1)Sarah — (2)Esther Strickland Pvt CT
Silas F.: b 6-8-1758 d 7-25-1820 m Patty Hancock Pvt CT
Solomon: b 9-4-1759 d 3-29-1840 m Sarah Bradford Pvt NH
Squire: b 4-15-1750 d 11-6-1828 m Sarah Bishop Pvt RI ★
Stephen: b 5-24-1722 d 4-19-1795 m (1)Mabel — (2)Mrs. Hannah (Hull) Tuttle PS CS CT
Stephen: b 8-26-1757 d 4-10-1805 m (1)Deborah Williams (2)Hannah Williams Smn MA
Stephen: b 5-10-1762 d — m Sally Millington Pvt NH
Theodore: b 1757 d 8-19-1805 m Lucinda Phelps Pvt CT ★
Theodore: b 9-18-1751 d 9- -1823 m Susannah Thompson Pvt MA
Thomas: b 5-17-1762 d *a.* 1815 m Abigail Stork Pvt CT
Thomas: b 5-1-1759 d 12-30-1845 m (1)Abigail Cutler (2)Sophia Sanford Vol Pvt PS CT ★
Thomas: b 1728 d 1-15-1815 m Elizabeth Davis Pvt MA
Thomas: b *c.* 1747 d 2-7-1815 m Elizabeth Pitts Sol VA
Thomas: b 4-4-1758 d 1-22-1833 m Margaret — Pvt VA ★
Thomas: b 12-12-1761 d 8-31-1853 m Tabitha Lee Pvt VA ★
Timothy, Sr.: b 4-1-1713 d 7-25-1793 m (1)Temperence Griswold (2)Rachel Atkins (3)Widow Anna Holt PS CT
Timothy, Jr.: b 4-4-1749 d 8-27-1789 m Mary Pierpont Pvt CT
Timothy: b 1- -1734 d 12- -1820 m (1)Rachel Eagles (2)Mrs — Neal Pvt NJ
Varney: b 1754 d *a.* 7-19-1847 m X Pvt Drm VA ★
Whipple: b 6-11-1760 d 1802 m Mary Cooke Pvt RI
William, Jr.: b 4-3-1745 d *p.* 1818 m Submit Frost Lt CT ★
William: b *c.* 1736 d 7-28-1823 m Ruth Humphrey Sgt CT
William: b 1749 d 3-14-1816 m Jane Hayes Lt MA
William: b 1750 d *p.* 2-15-1820 m X NC
William: b 2-25-1758 d 5-3-1821 m Mary Gaines Sgt VA ★
Zephaniah: b 1760 d *p.* 1804 m Hepsibah Luscomb Pvt MA
Zephaniah: b 2-9-1738 d 1-23-1816 m Elizabeth Eddy Capt RI

ANEWALT,

Valentine: b 1-12-1732 d 2-8-1802 m (1)Johanna Margaret Kurtz (2)Anna Barbara — Pvt PA

ANGELL, (includes ANGEL, & ANGLE)

Abiathar: b 12-13-1748 d 6-17-1830 m Lucy Bennett Capt MA
Abraham: b 7-23-1733 d 5- -1804 m Mary Hawkins Sgt RI
Abraham: b *c.* 1746 d 5-23-1831 m Ann Smith Pvt RI

Bartlett: b *c.* 1748 d 1839 m Sarah — PS VA
Benjamin: b 3-9-1760 d 9-28-1826 m Lydia Benchley Pvt RI
Daniel: b 1733/55 d 12-2-1840 m (2)Catherine Wolfe (3)Hannah — Pvt MA ★
Daniel: b 9-23-1741 d 5-9-1810 m Phoebe Olney Capt RI
Daniel: b 10-22-1744 d *p.* 1782 m Phebe Arnold Sol RI
David: b 8-23-1754 d — m Patience Smith Pvt RI
Elisha: b 2-22-1757 d 4-28-1838 m (1)Anna Fenner (2)Mary Deane (3)Catherine Pierce Pvt MA ★
Eseck: b 9-12-1752 d 11-14-1836 m (1)Martha Brown Pvt MA
Ezekiel: b 1722 d 9-27-1782 m Ruth Sprague Pvt RI
Ezekiel, Jr.: b 10-25-1762 d 1-15-1816 m Abigail Thornton Pvt RI
Fenner: b 6-25-1755 d 11-5-1851 m (1)Sarah Sprague (2)Mrs. Amey Johnson Sgt RI ★
Hope: b 3-28-1742 d 6-4-1819 m Avis Olney PS RI
Israel: b 8-24-1740 d 5-4-1832 m (1)Martha (Angell) (2)Susannah (Luther) Wright (3)Sarah Wood Col RI
Jacob: b *c.* 1720 d *p.* 5-11-1777 m Elizabeth — PS NJ
Jeremiah: b 1-29-1707 d 12-12-1785 m Mary Matthewson PS RI
Jesse: b 1-6-1745 d *p.* 11-24-1792 m Amy Hammond Ens RI
Job: b 1-9-1745 d 8-6-1811 m Amey Angell Capt RI
John: b *c.* 1725 d *p.* 5-1-1784 m Martha Burwell Pvt NJ
John: b 6- -1762/3 d 7-5-1843 m Mary Griner Sgt NC
John: b 7-16-1740 d 1-5-1817 m Martha Aldrich LCol RI
Joseph: b 1-9-1745 d 1808 m Phebe Edwards Pvt RI
Joshua: b 3-29-1760 d 2-10-1838 m Mehitable Manton Pvt RI
Nehemiah: b 9-3-1752 d 3-3-1828 m Anna Hill Ens RI
Pardon: b 10-4-1749 d 6-2-1838 m (1)Anna (Angell) (2)Susannah Wells Sgt RI ★
Samuel: b 10-24-1742 d 1-24-1795 m Lydia Medbury Capt RI
Stephen: b 10-9-1764 d 8-4-1853 m Abigail Moulton Pvt MA
William: b 3-30-1743 d 8- -1815 m Abigail — Pvt RI

ANGIER (includes ANGER)

Charles: b 1752 d 6-3-1816 m Elizabeth Newton Pvt MA
John: 7-12-1724 d 8-3-1793 m Bethia Liscomb Pvt MA
John: b 9-8-1744 d 9-5-1833 m Mary Hemingway Lt NH
Silas: b 10-9-1737 d 10-6-1808 m Elizabeth Drury Pvt NH

ANGLIN,

Adrian: b 1761 d 8-31-1839 m Mary McClung Pvt VA

ANGUS,

Jacob: b 5- -1760 d 11- -1848 m Susanna Mohler Pvt PS PA
James: b 1751 d *a.* 6-4-1806 m Mary Magdalene Baker Pvt NY

ANKENY, (includes ANGENY)

Christian: b 12-25-1751 d 3-17-1821 m (1)Elizabeth Shaffer (2)Mary Kooser 1Lt PA
Dewalt: b 1728 d *p.* 3-11-1781 m (1)Mary Jane Dormer (2)Mrs. Margaret Frederick PS MD
Peter: b 3-6-1751 d 12-23-1804 m Rosanna Bonnett Capt PA

ANNABLE, (includes ANABEL)

Ebenezer: b 7-16-1756 d 9-23-1842 m Ann Meriam Ordl Sgt Smn CT ★
Edward: b 6-22-1753 d 6-10-1836 m Jemima Smith Lt MA
John: b 4-18-1744 d 10-23-1815 m (1)Hannah Stewart (2)Deborah Spencer Pvt CT
Robert: b 1741 d 1832 m Sarah Whipple Cpl MA ★

ANNAN, (includes ANNIN)

Daniel: b 5-6-1753 d 3-29-1844 m (2)Elizabeth Allen 1Lt NY
Joseph: b 11- -1750 d 5-12-1841 m (1)Ellen Schenk (2)Ida (Vanarsdale) Gaston Pvt NJ ★
Robert: b 1742 d 12-5-1819 m (1)Margaret Cochran (2)Elizabeth Hawthorne (3)Philuthia — PS NY
Samuel: b 11- -1753 d 4-16-1837 m Lydia Cooper Lt NJ ★
William: b 1715 d 5- -1784 m (1)Sarah Ross (2)Sarah Davison PS NJ

ANNIS, (includes ANES)

Charles: b 3-10-1739 d 5-30-1823 m Sarah Emerson Pvt NH
Daniel Sr.: b 12-1-1711 d 1790 m Catherine Thomas PS CS NH
Ezra: b 3-25-1726 d *p.* 1782 m Sarah (Haggett) Long Pvt MA
John: b 7-1-1764 d 1-19-1834 m Sabre Closson Pvt MA ★
Phineas: b 5-22-1753 d 2-2-1801 m Hannah Griffin Drm MA
Samuel: b 1745 d 5-26-1828 m Sarah Stevens Pvt NH

ANSART,

Lewis (de Marasquelle): b 1741/2 d 5-22-1804 m Catherine Wimble Col MA

ANSLEY,

John: b 4- -1749 d *p.* 1839 m Catherine Royer Pvt NJ
Thomas, Sr.: b 1-14-1737 d 6-14-1809 m Mrs Rebecca Cocke Harrison CS GA

ANSPACH,

John: b 1750 d *p.* 1800 m Mary — Capt PA
John Adam: b 8-21-1754 d 2-25-1838 m Barbara Barrow Sgt NJ

ANSTINE,
George: b 11-24-1761 d 5-30-1846 m (1)Anna Barabara Sharer (2) Hester Newcomer Sol PA
Simon: b 8-4-1763 d 2-22-1849 m Catharine Blaser Pvt PA

ANTES,
John Henry Sr.: b 10-8-1736 d 5-13-1820 m (1)Anna Maria Paulin (2)Sophia Snyder LCol PS PA
John Henry Jr.: b 4-17-1757 d 3-27-1834 m Elizabeth Shoemaker Pvt PA
Philip Frederic: b 7-2-1730 d 9-20-1801 m (1)Barbara Tyson (2) Catherine Schuyler Col PA
William: b 11-18-1731 d 3-9-1810 m X Sub Lt PA

ANTHOINE,
Nicholas, Jr.: b 1760 d 12-30-1834 m Anna Pettingill Pvt MA

ANTHONY,
Allard: b 1-22-1760 d 11-21-1847 m Hannah Van Wyck Pvt NY
Bartholomew: b 1740 d p 1780 m Catherine Pik (or Peek) Pvt NY
Daniel: b 2-21-1740 d 8-16-1824 m Mary Bowen Pvt MA
David: b 5-6-1747 d 1831 m Judith Hicks Pvt MA
David: b 8-3-1760 d 1-20-1842 m Submit Wheeler Pvt MA
Gideon: b 10-10-1753 d 11- -1841 m Abigail Cornell Cpl RI ★
Israel: b 12-17-1760 d 10-22-1835 m Elizabeth Van Aernem Mus NY ★
Jacob: b 10-30-1759 d 7-18-1844 m Deborah — Pvt MA ★
Jacob: b 10-30-1759 d 1810 m Nancy Ann Johnson Pvt PA
James: b a 1763 d 1794 m — Corder Pvt NC
James: b 12-18-1752 d 1827 m Anne Tate PS VA
John: b 1756 d 8- -1836 m Sophia Briscoe Pvt MD
John: b c. 1734 d p. 5-9-1785 m Usley (or Ursula) — Cpl NC
John: b 1718 d 1796 m Nancy Hart PS Pvt NC
John: b 11-16-1708 d — m Lydia Luther Cpl RI
John: b 1744 d 1846 m Elizabeth Lochlane Pvt VA
John Jr.: b 1750 d 1825 m Susan Austin Pvt VA
Joseph, Sr.: b 5-2-1713 d 11-23-1785 m Elizabeth Clarke PS VA
Joseph Jr.: b 3-28-1750 d 1810 m Betty Ann Clark 2Lt VA
Martin: b c, 1759 d p, 8-2-1813 m Catherine — PS NC
Michael: b 1720 d 3-13-1816 m Catherina — Pvt PA
Nicholas N: b 1-4-1742 d 10-20-1824 m Susanna Roome Pvt NY
Peter Jr.: b 7-7-1752 d 12-25-1818 m Mrs. Arner Lt PA
Philip: b 7-21-1756 d 5-8-1850 m Mary Moore Pvt NJ
Philip: b 1- -1754 d 11-4-1838 m Mary Elizabeth — Pvt NC ★

ANTILL,
Edward: b 4-11-1742 d 5-21-1789 m Charlotte Riverin LCol NY
Jacob: b c. 1755 d 8-11-1800 m Dorcas Dawkins Pvt VA W★

ANTISEL, (includes ANTISDEL & ANTIZELL)
Pereas: b c. 1752 d 1816 m (1)Betsey West (2)Phoebe Crandall (3)Mrs Canfield Pvt MA VT
Silas: b 9-13-1749 d 9-13-1817 m Maria Bethiah Curtis Pvt CT
Simon: b 6-10-1740 d 8- -1815 m Martha Fuller Pvt VT

ANTONIDES,
Johannes: b 6-24-1733 d 1797 m Sarah Van Doren Sol PS NJ

ANTRIM,
John: b 9-4-1753 d 8-8-1833 m (1)Sarah Gibbs (2)Margaret Kerling Pvt PA ★

AORSON,
Aaron: b 1741 d c. 1790 m Altze Quackenboss Maj NY

APGAR,
Conrad, Sr.: b 1-3-1755 d 9- -1837 m (1)Mary Farley (2)Charity Sutton Pvt Wgn NJ ★
Peter: b 4-30-1758 d 4-23-1846 m (1)Mary A. Alpock (2)Christian Anderson Sgt NJ

APPELL, (includes APPEL, APPELLE & APPLE)
Andrew: b c, 1750 d 1817 m Ety — Sol PA
Conrad: b c. 1755 d a. 1801-8 m Martha Ann Vandervoort Pvt NY
George: b 5-26-1755 d a: 5- -1797 m Agnes or Nancy Zimmerman 2Lt PA
Jacob: b c. 1732 d p. 2-27-1789 m Ann Eva Eckert Pvt PA
John: b 18-1726 d 9-1-1805 m (1)Maria Bogert (2)Catherine Switz Pvt PA
John Martin: b c. 1733 d p. 9-2-1823 m Maria Catharina Hornecker Sgt PA
Peter: b 11-26-1743 d 10-6-1845 m Lois Baldwin Pvt FrN

APPERSON, (includes EPPERSON,)
David: b 5-27-1734 d p. 2-2-1799 m Hannah Thompson Pvt VA
Francis: b 11- -1750 d 11-18-1840 m Susanna Abernathy Pvt VA ★
Francis: b c. 1738 d 1806 m Betty Long PS VA
John: b 12-4-1753 d 9-30-1834 m Alcey Favor Pvt VA ★
John: b c. 1740 d a. 10-14-1817 m Elizabeth — Sol VA
John: b c. 1735 d 6-11-1785 m Margaret — PS VA
Peter: b c. 1730 d 7-21-1834 m Frances — Mar Pvt VA ★

Thomas: b 1760 d 1848 m Mary Cross Pvt NC ★
Thompson: b 1757 d 6-9-1836 m Mary —Pvt VA & NC
William: b 3-22-1757 d 3-22-1826 m Elizabeth Carr Pvt NC ★

APPLEBY, (includes APPLEBE & APPLEBEE)
Elnathan: b c. 1730 d c. 1800 m Mary — Pvt NY
James Jr.: b 10-2-1733 d 8-29-1813 m Ester Sayles PS RI
Simeon: b -- d 1844 m Bridget Lord Pvt Mar MA
William: b c. 1742 d p. 11-23-1807 m (1)Nannie Megehin (2)Nancy McCurdy Pvt PA

APPLEGATE,
Andrew: b 2-4-1756 d 10-4-1839 m (1)Lydia Perrine (2)Elizabeth Pew Pvt NJ ★
Anthony: b c. 1750-5 d 1776 m Abigail Davidson Pvt NJ
Asher: b 5-13-1762 d 3-27-1834 m Sarah Higby Pvt NJ
Bartholomew: b 5-5-1757 d 5-20-1846 m Mary Miller Pvt NJ ★
Benjamin: b 1725 d 5-21-1823 m Rebecca Wall Pvt PA
Daniel: b 1768 d 2-11-1826 m Rachel Lindsay Fif Drm NJ ★
Daniel: b c. 1740 d c. 1812 m Mrs Elizabeth Harvey Brown Pvt PA
Garret: b 11-2-1752 d 8-21-1837 m Mary Johnson Pvt PA ★
Henry: b 1758 d p. 12-16-1831 m Sarah — Pvt NJ
Joseph: b 1739 d 12-26-1823 m Ann Davidson Pvt NJ
Richard: b c. 1740 d 1800 m (1)— Wiggins (2)Rebecca— Pvt PA
Richard: b c. 1742 d p. 2-2-1791 m Amy Fenton PS PA
Stacey: b c. 1764-5 d 1800-1 m Mary McClayne Pvt Sct VA
William: b 1745 d 5-26-1823 m Catherine Wiggins Pvt NJ
William: b 1745 d 5-26-1823 m Elizabeth Rogers Pvt NJ W ★

APPLEMAN,
David: b 1757 d 1839 m Nancy Todd Pvt NJ

APPLETON,
Francis: b 1-29-1732 d 1-29-1816 m Mary Hubbard Pvt NH
Isaac: b 5-31-1731 d 2-25-1806 m Mary Adams Pvt PS NH
Nathaniel Sr.: b 12-9-1693 d 2-9-1784 m Margaret Gibbs PS MA
Nathaniel Jr.: b 10'5-1731 d 1798 m Mary Walker PS MA
Oliver: b 11-27-1757 d 1816 m Martha Patch Sgt MA
Samuel: b 10-22-1740 d 9-11-1784 m Sarah Anson Sgt MA
Thomas: bpt 10-5-1740 d 9-14-1830 m (1)Susanna Perkins (2)Mrs Lydia Dane Pvt MA
William: b 1747 d 1785 m Sarah Odiorne PS NH

APPLEWHITE,
Henry: b c. 1730 d 1783 m Ann Harris PS VA
John: b c. 1760 d — m Rebecca Moore Pvt VA

APPLING,
Joel: b c. 1758 d 1838 m Mary Strange Pvt VA

APPOLD,
Andrew: b c. 1755 d 10-31-1818 m (1)Elizabeth Odenbaugh (2)Nelly Decker (3)Margaret Hubbard Sol MD

APSLEY,
William: b 1746 d 1776-90 m Mary Simmonds Sol MD

ARBOGAST,
Adam: b 10-25-1760 d 1861 m Margaret Hull Sgt Spy VA ★
Michael: b 1734 d 1812 m Mary — Pvt VA

ARBUCKLE,
John: b 11- -1752 d 3-29-1839 m Racheal Barron Pvt NH
John: b 6-24-1734 d 12-1-1790 m Elizabeth Worrill Pvt PA
Matthew: b c. 1730 d 6-22-1781 m (1)Jane Lockhart (2)Frances (Hunter) Lawrence Capt VA
Thomas: b 5-2-1747 d 1843 m Elizabeth Lawrence Lt VA ★
William: b 3-3-1752 d 3-21-1836 m Katherine (Madison) McClannahan Page Pvt VA

ARCHDEACON,
Edmund: b c. 1740 d 1793 m Ann — Sol VA

ARCHER,
Abraham: b 1756 d a. 1801 m Sally Starling Capt VA
Benjamin: b 1719 d 5- -1784 m (1)Elizabeth Thayer (2)Mary Holbrook (3)Mrs Debora Hull PS MA
Benjamin, Sr.: b 6-22-1702 d 3-23-1781 m Rebecca Curtice PS NH
Benjamin, Jr.: b 4-14-1735 d 1786 m (1)Elizabeth Ellis (2)Lucy Sanders Sgt PS NH
Benjamin: b 1727 d 12-21-1780 m (1)Sarah — (2)Charity — Pvt NJ
Benjamin: b 1735 d 1807 m Rachel Devaux Pvt NY
David: b 2-8-1743 d a. 1800 m Mary Benson Pvt VA
Edward: b 1-16-1747 d 2-27-1807 m (1)Mary Cocke (2)Mrs (Silvester) Wirmington PS VA
James: b 1752 d 12-15-1830 m Nancy Vail 2Lt Guide NY
James: b 1746 d 1832 m (2)Jane Lincicome Lt VA
John: b 5-5-1741 d 9-28-1810 m Catharine PS Dr Maj MD
John: b 3-26-1712 d 3-26-1830 m (1)Elizabeth Tupper (2)Mrs Alice B Small Maj MA
John: b 1752 d 10-18-1793 m Elizabeth Calvert Lt VA ★
John: b 1- -1746 d 5- -1825 m Million Barrow 1Lt VA

ARCHER, contd.
John: b c. 1740 d 1815 -20 m Elizabeth — Pvt PS VA
John: b 4-2-1734 d 2-28-1784 m Eliza Trent PS VA
Jonathan: b a. 1748 d 5- -1821 m Mary Ann — Pvt NY
Joshua: b 1745 d 3- -1800 m Jane Hunter Lt VA
Peter Field: b 1756 d 4-25-1814 m Francis Tanner 1Lt VA
Robert: b 1748 d 1818 m Mary Steele Pvt SC
Sampson: b c. 1710 d 1791 m Rebecca Thompson Sol PS VA
Thomas: b c. 1729 d 3-14-1797 m Azuba Old Sol CT
William: b 1734 d 1790 m Margaret — Pvt PA
Zechariah: b 1752 d 7-5-1822 m Jane Kilgore Pvt PA

ARCHIBALD, (includes ARCHBOLD)
John: b 1726 d 10-22-1789 m Mary Hall PS NC
Thomas: b 1755 d 3-17-1837 m Mary Kent Pvt PA ★

ARDEN,
Jacob: b —d 1778-81 m Catharine Beekman Pvt NY

ARDERY,
James: b c. 1726 d 8- -1793 m Sarah — Pvt PA
John: b c. 1761 d 1827-30 m Mary Watts Pvt PA

ARDIS,
Mathias: b 10-29-1724 d 9-9-1781 m Christian — PS SC

ARENDALL,
Nathan: b c. 1760 d p. 10-28-1822 m Susannah Fannin Pvt NC

ARGABRITE,
Jacob: b 9-9-1760 d 11-9-1853 m Mary Shatel Pvt VA ★

ARGESINGER,
John: b 6-25-1757 d 4-10-1837 m (1)Eliza Ritts (2)Mary Carncross
Pvt NY

ARLINE,
John: b c. 1760 d c. 1813 m Phereby Pullen Pvt GA

ARMANTROUT, (includes ARMENTROUT, & ERMENTROUT)
Christopher: b — d p. 10-22-1804 m Susannah — PS VA
Frederick: b 1758 d 6- -1855 m Barbara Monger PS VA
John: b 1745 d c. 1831 m Catherine Miller PS VA
Peter: b 9-17-1751 d 1-9-1824 m (1)Catherine Ergebrecht (2)Margaret Wolf Sol VA

ARMEL,
Daniel: b c. 1755 d a. 8-24-1805 m Christena — PS PA

ARMFIELD,
William, Sr.: b 1720 d 1816 m (1)Mary Hamilton (2)Mrs Lydia Fields
PS NC

ARMINGTON, (includes ARMENTON)
John: b 6-12-1735 d 1818 m Ruth Kent Pvt MA
Joseph: b 2-12-1759 d 12-16-1832 m Deborah Kent Sgt MA
Joseph: b 6-4-1731 d 4-27-1817 m Esther Walker Pvt MA
William: b 11-14-1746 d p. 1792 m Lucy Brown Sgt RI

ARMISTEAD, (includes ARMSTEAD)
Ellison: b 1757 d 1- -1792 m Susanna Christian Capt VA
John: b a. 1733 d 5-2-1779 m (1)Agnes — (2)Mary Burbage
Col PS VA
John: b 4- -1751 d 9- -1798 m Elizabeth — Pvt PA
John: b 1741 d 4-10-1790 m Lucy Baylor PS VA
Robert: b 1745 d 1805 m Louisa Westwood PS VA
Robert: b 1730 d p. 1787 m (1)Mrs. Elizabeth (Burgess) Ball (2)
Ann Smith Pvt VA
Westwood: b 1735 d 1786 m Mary Jenkins PS VA
William: b 1762 d 3-1-1842 m (1)Rebecca Kimbell (2)Elizabeth
Westmoreland (Lewis) Morris Pvt VA ★
William: b c. 1750 d 1799 m (1)— Latimer (2)Mary Latham
Curle PS VA

ARMITAGE,
Caleb: b 1737 d 4- -1832 m Mary Striker Capt PA
Shubert: b 11-5-1756 d 12-27-1823 m Sallie Macomber Lt PA

ARMONT,
John: b 1736-8 d p. 1778 m Catherine Tiley Pvt DE

ARMOUR, (includes ARMOR)
Andrew: b c. 1750 d a. 10-29-1835 m Elizabeth — Sol GA
James, Sr.: b c. 1710 d 6-17-1787 m (1)Margaret Anderson (2)
Mrs Hannah McNeil Pvt CT
James: b 1740 d 11-11-1805 m Margaret Whitehill Lt PA
John: b c. 1752 d c. 1820 m Susanna Jenkins Pvt PA
Robert: b c. 1730 d a. 9-22-1784 m Margaret — PS PA
Thomas: b c. 1759 d 6- -1826 m Jane Moor Pvt PA
William: b 1758 d 9-18-1820 m Rachel Pontoni Pvt PA

ARMS,
Consider: b 10-14-1736 d 6-19-1792 m Mercy Catlin PS MA
Ebenezer: b 1-9-1720-1 d 6-13-1788 m Elizabeth Allen Capt MA
Jonathan: b 1-27-1735 d 2-13-1819 m Eunice Lyman Pvt MA
Josiah: b 3-17-1750 d 3-28-1803 m Cynthia Avery CS VT
Moses: b 10-12-1749 d 1-7-1818 m (1)Catherine Bardwell (2)Mary
Waite Swain Pvt MA
Susannah (Willard): b 6-4-1720 d 3-7-1793 m John Arms PS VT
Thomas: b 6-22-1729 d 8-7-1808 m Lydia Alvord Pvt MA

ARMSBURY,
John: b 7-3-1752 d 10-15-1845 m Priscilla Tompkins Pvt MA ★

ARMSBY,
Matthias: b 1757 d 6-3-1799 m Unity Boyden Pvt MA

ARMSTRONG,
Abel: b c. 1745 d p. 1799 m (1)Margaret Cowan (2)Mary Roseborough Capt NC
Abel: b 6-4-1758 d 8-26-1837 m Mary Wanless Pvt VA ★
Ambrose: b 1759 d 11-16-1841 m Elizabeth — Pvt VA ★
Andrew: b c. 1730 d p. 7-21-1795 m Margaret — Pvt PA
Andrew: b c. 1735 d 1778 m Sophia — PS PA
Archibald: b c. 1750 d 1789-92 m Nancy Sterling 2Lt NY
Bela: b 11-3-1754 d 4-27-1842 m Bethiah Sanford Pvt CT ★
Daniel: b c. 1750 d 1- -1815 m Nancy Malone Pvt PA
David: b 6-30-1742 d 1832 m Nancy Miller Pvt NY
David: b 1746 d 3-20-1811 m Sarah Harris Pvt PA
Edward: b 4-18-1757 d 10-19-1824 m Molly Bines Lt DE
Edward: b 1735 d 1784 m Mrs Milly House PS NC
Elijah: b 7-17-1755 d 2-281829 m (1)Lydia Cowen (2)Mercy
Hawks Lt RI ★
Francis: b 6-3-1735 d 9-1-1799 m Jane Borland Pvt NY
George: b a. 1760 d p. 1808 m Sarah Fair Pvt NY
George: b 1755 d 3-18-1842 m Elizabeth — Sgt PA ★
Hezekiah: b 10-22-1744 d 3-4-1816 m Miriam Haynes Capt VT
Hopestill: b 4-10-1746 d 1-28-1806 m Lydia Haynes Sol VT
Isaac: b c. 1750 d p. 9-11-1821 m (1) X (2)Mary — PS NC
James: b 5-11-1754 d 5-7-1816 m Miriam Mackay Pvt CT W ★
James: b 9-6-1754 d 11-17-1829 m Abigail Ladd Pvt CT
James: b 10-31-1762 d 7-9-1825 m Martha Halstead Pvt NY
James: b a. 1758 d p. 1821 m (1)Ruth Bennett (2)Debora Craig
Ens PA
James: b 2-18-1762 d 9-15-1853 m Margaret Martin Pvt PA
James: b 1749 d 5- -1828 m Mary Stevenson Dr VA
James: b p. 11- -1759 d p. 1816 m — Johnson Pvt SC ★
James: b 4-6-1764 d 11-11-1837 m Mary Agnes Frierson Pvt SC ★
James: b 3-17-1758 d 3-15-1819 m Nancy Lanier Sol PS VA
James Francis: b 4-3-1750 d 1-19-1816 m Susanna Livingston Pvt
Chp NJ & MD
Jane (Stewart): b c. 1760 d 1817 m William Stewart PS PA
John, Sr.: b 10-18-1711 d 1-3-1791 m Mary Durkee Pvt CT
John: b 1734 d a. 1-8-1807 m Mary Sprangler 2Lt PS DE
John: b 1729 d 1805 m Catherine McDonald Dep Adj Gen GA
John: b 1731 d 10-26-1822 m Lucy Cox Lt MA
John: b 1748 d 11-20-1794 m Elizabeth Williams Sgt MA
John: b 9- -1749 d 1-15-1816 m Elizabeth A — Capt SC ?
John: b 8-20-1749 d 5-7-1836 m Sarah Stinson 2Lt NJ
John: b 11-10-1727 d 9-8-1797 m (1)Polly McWhorter (2)Mrs
Sarah McWhorter Pvt PS NY
John: b c. 1735 d p. 9-8-1806 m Anne — LCol NC
John, Sr.: b 10-13-1717 d 3-9-1795 m Rebecca Lyon PS MGen PA
John, Jr.: b 11-25-1758 d 4-1-1843 m Alida Livingston Maj PS PA
John: b 4-20-1755 d 2-4-1816 m Tabitha Goforth Capt PA
John: b 4-25-1755 d 1812 m Sarah Jane Robeson 2Lt PA
John: b 3-29-1758 d 1843 m Sarah Richardson Lt PA
John: b 10-27-1737 d a. 3-30-1782 m Basmath — Pvt VT
John: b 1759 d 1821 m Agnes Ervine Pvt PA
Jonathan: b 10-1743 d 12-27-1826 m Abigail Haynes Vol VT
Joseph: b 4-22-1764 d p. 6-14-1839 m Frances Tinnin Pvt NC
Joshua: b 8-1-1756 d 9-25-1845 m Sarah Morris Pvt Arfr PA ★
Lebbeus: b 9-13-1738 d 10-17-1789 m Rebecca Hyde Lt VT
Martin: b c. 1748 d a. 2-5-1810 m Mary — Lt SC
Matthew: b 1762 d 6-21-1838 m Margaret Shipley Sloan Pvt NC ★
Nathan: b 2-7-1757 d 8-8-1839 m Hannah Coville Pvt NY ★
Rebecca Lyon: b 5-2-1719 d 11-16-1797 m John Armstrong PS PA
Richard: b 1730 d 1787 m Ann Lindsay Ens VA
Robert: b c. 1740 d p. 1788 m Rachel Springer Pvt PS DE
Robert: b 4-19-1730 d 1783 m Margaret Thompson Pvt NY
Robert: b 5-28-1760 d 9-9-1834 m Nancy Green Pvt NC & SC
Robert: b 1731 d 2-28-1796 m Margaret Cunningham Lt SC
Robert: b 1724 d 1811 m Jane Loudon Pvt VA
Samuel: b 8-10-1754 d 12-10-1810 m Nancy Allen Ens MA
Samuel: b 1739 d 9-28-1828 m Elizabeth Gibson Pvt PA
Solomon: b 10-12-1750 d 4-27-1843 m Fear Barlow PS OrdlSgt
NY ★
Thomas: b 8-3-1750 d 1-3-1833 m Martha Britton QM Maj NJ
Thomas: b 1734 d 9-26-1776 m Mary — Lt PA
Thomas: b 7-20-1755 d 4-23-1849 m X Pvt PA & NC ★
Timothy: b 6-14-1760 d 1-14-1856 m Dolly Crosby Pvt MA ★
William: b 10-11-1718 d 12-28-1807 m Mary Pitcher Pvt Fif CT
William: b 5-10-1737 d p. 1- -1783 m Jane Lapsley Capt NC
William: b c. 1752 d c. 1812 m Elizabeth House Pvt PA

William: b 1-20-1759 d 9-5-1841 m Sarah Ann Huston Pvt PA ★
William: b 12-12-1759 d 10-29-1853 m (1)Margaret Jamison (2) Margaret Kirkpatrick Pvt VA★
William: b 12-12-1760 d 10-29-1853 m Margaret McAfee Pvt VA

ARNAUD,
Jean Pierre: b 1751 d 9-4-1833 m Elizabeth Leland Pvt MD ★

ARNDT,
Abraham Jr.: b c. 1750 d 9-3-1825 m Anna Maria Van Der Werken 2Lt NY W ★
Abraham: b 8-3-1722 d c. 12-1-1795 m (1)Catherine Reed (2)Mary — Scl PS CS PA
Bernhard: b 8-7-1754 d 2-12-1827 m Anna Mary Frederick Pvt PA
Jacob: b 2-11-1758 d 9-18-1831 m Mary Morrison Ens PA
Jacob: b 3-24-1725 d 8-3-1805 m Elizabeth Geiger PS PA
John: b 6-5-1748 d 5-6-1814 m (1)Elizabeth Feit (2)Elizabeth Ihrie Capt PS PA
John Godfrey: b 12-12-1741 d 7-9-1807 m Hanna Rudisill PS NC
Philip: b 1-27-1754 d (living 1790) m Mary Little Lt PA

ARNER,
Henry: b 8-10-1742 d c. 1828 m Catherine Daubenspeck Sol PA
Martin: b 1752 d 1847 m (1)Magdalena Solt (2)Elizabeth Nagel Pvt PA ★

ARNETT, (includes ARNET)
Hannah White: b 1-15-1733 d 1-10-1824 m Isaac Arnett PS NJ
Henry: b 3-12-1762 d 5-21-1847 m Elizabeth Truesdale Pvt NY ★
Isaac: b 1726 d 9- -1801 m Hannah White PS NJ
James: b a. 1734 d 1781 m Susannah PS VA
Thomas: b 1758 d 1848 m Martha — Sol Spy PA ★
William: b a. 1761 d p. 1796 m (1)Sarah Reed (2)Molly Meriday Pvt MD

ARNOLD,
Abimelech: b 11- -1762 d 1833 m Prudence Bennett Pvt NY ★
Abraham: b 10-5-1761 d 10-25-1827 m Catherine Close Pvt PA
Alexander: b 1-27-1755 d 3-22-1844 m Avis Martin Pvt RI ★
Anne Hendricks: b c. 1731 d 1806 m Benjamin Arnold PS SC
Benedict: b 11-20-1752 d 4-30-1839 m Sarah Potter Pvt RI
Benjamin: b 3-4-1758 d p. 1793 m (1)Isabel Green (2)Rachel Harris Pvt RI
Benjamin, Sr.: b 1719 d p. 1-30-1796 m Ann Hendricks Capt SC
Bildad: b 9-30-1737 d p. 1776 m Mercy Seabury Capt MA
Caleb Sr.: b 5-26-1725 d 2-5-1784 m (1)Patience Brown (2)Anna (Arnold) PS RI
Caleb Jr.: b 7-5-1757 d 10-16-1838 m Mary Arnold Fif Maj RI ★
Caleb: b 3-17-1754 d 11-8-1844 m Hannah Taylor Pvt RI ★
Caleb: b 3-5-1759 d 11-1-1834 m Avis Stone Pvt RI ★
Christopher: b 1745 d 10-23-1833 m (1)Hulda Brown (2)Elizabeth Arnold Pvt RI
Conrad: b c. 1735 d 1791 m Margaretha Young PS PA
Daniel: b 6-9-1757 d 3- -1813 m Esther Fox Pvt VT
David: b 6-17-1749 d 4-11-1812 m Jerusha Thomas Pvt CT
David: b c. 1740 d p. 1783 m Mary — CS MA
David Sr.: b 7-23-1732 d 12- -1810 m Pheobe Pratt Lt MA
David Jr.: b 12-23-1757 d 1812 m Helen Andrews Pvt MA
David: b 11-11-1759 d 5-6-1825 m Elizabeth Hamilton Pvt NY
Ebenezer: b 9-26-1727 d 9-14-1807 m Anna Miller PS CT
Ebenezer: b 2-5-1744 d 3-12-1832 m Hannah Haviland Pvt NY
Edward: b 1761 d 10-28-1842 m Mercy Pettyplace Pvt Drm RI ★
Elisha: b 1756 d 5-27-1838 m Roba Ballou Pvt Arfr MA ★
Elisha: b 11-23-1731 d 1815 m Sarah — Sgt NY
Elisha: b 8-3-1758 d 1849 m Sally Marshall Pvt VA ★
Elizabeth Hitt: b 3-12-1751 d p. 8- -1848 m John Arnold PS VA KY
Ezra: b 7-30-1707 d 2-18-1780 m Rebecca Sprague PS MA
Fenner: b 7-17-1738 d 2-29-1836 m Hannah Turner Pvt CT & MA ★
Francis: b 1- -1758 d 2-5-1830/31 m Elizabeth Parker Pvt VA
George: b 1745 d — m Catherine — Pvt MD
George Sr.: b c. 1740 d c. 6-23-1783 m Philipina — Pvt PA
George: b c. 1752 d 6-21-1835 m (1) X (2)Eve Plumb Pvt PA ★
Hendrick: b c. 1755 d p. 7-15-1795 m Ruth Howard Cash PS VA
Isaac: b 5-27-1764 d 1-30-1841 m Sarah Howe Drm CT
Israel: b 11-1-1754 d 6-27-1840 m Deborah Olney Sgt Tms RI
Jabez: b 1738 d 7-4-1822 m Martha Freeman Pvt CT
Jabez: b 6-10-1755 d 6-9-1839 m Lucinda Hunter Pvt RI
Jacob: b 1745 d 1825 m Martha A. Norton Pvt CT
Jacob: b 12-14-1749 d 3-1-1827 m (1)Elizabeth Tuttle (2)Sarah H. Nixon Capt NJ
Jacob: b 10- -1763 d 12-2-1840 m Anna — Pvt PA
James: b 1760 d 1823 m (1)Martha Scott (2)Elizabeth Stroud Cpl VA
James F.: b 4-1-1754 d 1825 m Bethany Bailey Maj NC
Job: b 9-26-1736 d 1794 m Mary Wightman Cpl RI
Job: b 10-16-1760 d 4-14-1834 m Hannah Dexter Pvt RI ★
John: b 7-5-1720 d p. 2-21-1791 m Mary Hurlburt Pvt CT
John: b 7-20-1726 d 1807 m Bridget Cady Pvt CT
John: b 1753 d 1818 m Abigail Partridge Pvt MA
John: b 1750 d 1812 m Mary Pettis Pvt NC
John: b c. 1750 d p. 1799 m Martha — PS NC
John: b 6-24-1758 d 7-15-1840 m Mary Arnold Pvt VA ★

John: b 1-10-1754 d 5-4-1818 m Elizabeth Hitt PS Sgt VA
John: b c. 1735 d 6-16-1816 m Hannah — PS VA
Jonathan: b 5-21-1754 d 10-16-1828 m Lucy Smith Pvt CT ★
Jonathan: b 10-7-1758 d 3-31-1838 m (2)Mary Lester OrdlSgt CT NY ★
Jonathan: b 1748 d 4-21-1824 m Rachel Scott Pvt PA
Jonathan: b 12-3-1741 d 2-2-1793 m (1)Mary Burr (2)Alice Crawford (3)Cynthia Hastings PS Dr RI
Joseph: b 8-2-1738 d 1804 m Mary Crane Pvt CT
Joseph: b a. 1740 d 1796 m (1)Lydia — (2)Persis — 2Lt MA
Joseph: b 8-13-1755 d 7-30-1840 m (1)Sarah Stafford (2)Betsey Carpenter (3)Mary Collier (4)Rebecca Arnold Capt RI
Josiah: b 1755 d p. 1837 m Judith Dougherty Pvt VA ★
Mark: b — d a. 10-19-1784 m Grace — PS VA
Moses: b 1751 d 6-7-1788 m Sarah Vinton Cpl MA
Moses: b 8-13-1759 d 3-29-1829 m Sarah Greene Drm Maj RI W ★
Moses: b c. 1740 d 1796 m Molly — Pvt VA
Nathan: b 5-31-1761 d 3-31-1855 m Irene Hathaway Pvt MA
Nathan: b 10-18-1733 d 9-11-1778 m Lucy Cargill Capt RI
Nicholas: b c. 1734 d 1808 m (1)Margaret — (2)Sarah Champ Pvt VA
Oliver: b a. 1740 d a. 1790 m (1)Mary — (2)Almy Green Lt RI
Oliver: b 5-15-1746 d 1-9-1834 m Elnathan Rice Pvt VT ★
Owen: b 7-12-1750 d 1835 m Susan Wheeler Pvt RI ★
Patience Brown: b 3-3-1729 d 9-3-1780 m Caleb Arnold PS RI
Peleg: b 2-15-1749 d 1839 m Margaret Slocum Pvt RI
Peleg: b 10-18-1728 d 12-26-1801 m Patience Westgate PS RO RI
Peter: b 1750 d 10-10-1828 m Anna Marie Gilbert Pvt PA
Remington: b 8-25-1761 d 2-22-1841 m Jane Niles Drm RI ★
Richard: b 1743 d 7-24-1843 m Mary Blackmore Cpl PA
Samuel: b 1746 d 10-8-1805 m Elizabeth Smith Cpl CT
Samuel: b 11-21-1746 d 1-7-1829 m Lucy Pratt Pvt CT
Samuel: b c. 1750 d p. 3-17-1829 m Elizabeth Wright Pvt NC
Samuel: b 8-1-1728 d 8-3-1808 m Elizabeth — Pvt CT
Seth: b 9-3-1737 d 7-6-1849 m Esther Ranney Sgt CT
Solomon: b 1758 d 10-23-1844 m Mary Gurley Pvt NC ★
Stephen: b 6-12-1749 d 1825 m Lois Derbe Pvt CT
Stephen: b 4-20-1739 d 2-24-1810 m Martha Gardiner Pvt NY
Stephen: b 1738 d 10-1-1812 m Rhoda Rice Pvt CS VT
Sylvanus: b 9-21-1758 d 4-2-1796 m Phebe Harrison Pvt NJ
Temperance: b 1762 d 7-22-1849 m Thomas Hamilton PS SC
Thomas: b 3-4-1727 d 2-8-1795 m Abigail Arnold Capt MA
Thomas: b 10-5-1763 d 3-23-1844 m Mary Bedeston Pvt SC ★
Thomas: b 1727 d 1795 m Miss Wicke Capt VA
Thomas: of age 2-22-1758 d p. 4-18-1793 m Mary — PS VA
Welcome: b 2-25-1745 d 9-30-1798 m Patience Greene PS RI
William: b 5-1-1734 d 3-17-1809 m Elizabeth Willson Pvt NY
William: b c. 1750 d p. 1810 m X Pvt NC
William: b 1759 d p. 3-7-1825 m Elizabeth — Pvt NC ★
William: b 12-16-1739 d 1-16-1816 m Alice Wilcox LCol RI
William: b 1741 d 1816 m Alice Rhodes LCol RI
William: b 5-31-1751 d 5-9-1836 m Iscah Malavery QM Lt RI
Zibey: b 11-12-1756 d 12-6-1842 m (1)Mary Reeves (2)Polly Sweezy (3)Mahala (Smith)(Dudley)(Case) Pvt NJ ★

ARNOT, (includes ARNETT & ARNOTT)
Henry: b 3-12-1761 d 5-26-1847 m Elizabeth Trusdel Pvt NJ ★

ARRANTS,
Harmon: b 4-4-1746 d 1815 m Francina Price 2Lt PS MD
Nathan: b 8-23-1748 d a. 7- -1777 m Anne — Ens MD

ARRINGDALE,
Wm.: b c. 1755 d p. 4-14-1812 m X PS Pvt MD

ARRINGTON, (includes ARRANTON)
Adler: b 6- -1750 d c. 1840 m Patsy Wood Sol VA
Arthur, Sr.: b 1709-10 d 7- -1801 m Mary West CS NC
Arthur, Jr.: b — d 1795 m Mary Sandiford QM PS NC
John: b 1764 d 4-27-1844 m (1)Mrs. Elizabeth N. Mann (2)Mrs. Sarah Kerney Gardner Pvt NC
John: b 1-3-1757 d 11-26-1837 m Susannah Vaughan Pvt VA ★
Joseph: b c. 1757 d 1818-19 m Martha Crawford PS NC
Wm.: b 1748 d 9-17-1812 m (1)Ann Jackson Thomas (2)Mrs Mary Ann Williams Battle Capt NC

ARROWSMITH, (includes ARRASMITH)
Benjamin: b 6-3-1754 d 10-18-1824 m Mariah Hunt Pvt NJ
Nicholas: b 11-10-1756 d 4-21-1843 m Eleanor Sutphen Asst. Cmsry NJ
William: b 1-30-1762 d 11-15-1839 m Susan McBee Drm Fif VA

ARTHERS,
Richard: b c. 1758 d 1843 m Mary Ann Bowman Pvt PA

ARTHUR,
Barnabas: b c. 1725 d p. 3-2-1815 m (1)Martha Talbot (2)Nancy Williamson Lt VA
Bartholomew: b 1725 d p. 1781 m Mercy — Pvt CT
Benjamin: b 4-27-1737 d 3-27-1820 m Sarah Terrell Capt VA
James: b 5- -1764 d 7-29-1856 m Rachel Brown Pvt VA ★
John: b c. 1718 d a. 1-28-1793 m X Pvt VA

ARTHUR, contd.
John: b 1756 d 1848 m Eva Manke Pvt VA ★
John: b 1758 d 8-24-1850 m Elizabeth Adams Pvt VA ★
Richard: b 1745 d 1790 m Hannah Bradford Pvt CT
Robert: b — d 1816 m Susan Boone Lt PS PA
Thomas: b 1749 d 9-8-1883 m Sarah (Arthur) Mil VA
William: b 11-14-1762 d 7-9-1847 m Mary Henry Pvt VA ★

ARTMAN, (includes ERDMAN)
Andreas: b c. 1727 d p. 1790 m (1)Anna Dorothea — (2)Anna Mar-
garetha Frederick Pvt PA
John Justis: b 11-6-1757 d 2-12-1838 m Elizabeth Perry Tms CT &
NY ★

ARUNDELL,
John: b 1757 d 2-16-1822 m Jerminia Davis Pvt PA ★

ASBURY, (includes ASBERRY)
Daniel: b 2-18-1762 d 5-15-1825 m Nancy L. Morris Pvt VA
George: b c. 1755 d 10- -1816 m Mary Taylor Ens VA
Henry: b 1736 d p. 6-12-1813 m (1)Emily Reade (2)Ann — (3)
Mary Kelly (4)Sally Maulden Kelly PS VA
Joseph: b 1759 d 1815 m Hannah Talbot Sol VA
Richard: b 2-13-1761 d p. 2- -1845 m (1)Betty Thornton (2)Martha —
(3)Mrs Sarah Sherrell Watts 2Lt VA
William: b 1-20-1755 d 3-12-1814 m Susan Glascock Pvt VA W ★

ASH, (includes ASHE)
Adam: b 1744 d 5-1-1819 m Catherine Yost Pvt PA
James: b 12-9-1749 d 1-24-1830 m (1)Sarah Hinchman (2)Rachael
(Morgan) Douglas Lt PA
John: b 1720 d 10-24-1781 m Rebecca Moore BGen PS NC
John, Jr.: b 2-4-1762 d 7-13-1843 m Priscilla Frink Pvt & Mar RI ★
John: b c. 1745 d 1800 m Arrabellah — Lt VA
John Baptist: b 1748 d 11-27-1802 m Elizabeth Montfort Capt NC
Joseph: b 1739 d 1836 m Rachael Whitaker Pvt PA
Matthew: b 2-25-1758 d 8-5-1835 m Mary Gibbons Pvt PA
Michael: b 1740 d 11-8-1803 m Johanna Elliot PS CT
Michael: b — d 1810 m Catharen — Pvt PA
Phineas: b 1-11-1740-41 d a. 5- -1778 m Elizabeth —
Samuel, Jr.: b 12-3-1725 d 1813 m (1)Mary Porter (2)Mrs Elizabeth
Jones Merrick PS CS NC
Samuel, Jr.: b 2-1-1763 d 11-3-1835 m Elizabeth Shepperd Lt NC ★
Wm.: b c. 1757-60 d 10-15-1831 m Jane Fleming Pvt SC ★

ASHBRIDGE,
David: b 1744 d 1788 m (1)Mary Powell (2)Sarah Vernon Pvt PA
George: b 1-1-1732-3 d 10-25-1785 m Rebecca Garret Pvt PA
Joshua: b 9-17-1746 d 9-4-1820 m Mary Davis Pvt PA

ASHBROOK,
Levi: b c. 1738 d 1794 m (1)Mary Pentacost (2)Mary Chenoweth
PS VA
Thomas: b 1758 d 8-24-1848 m Agnes — Pvt VA ★

ASHBURN,
Luke: b 1749 d p. 8-5-1837 m (1)Elizabeth Wheeler (2)Susanna A.
Roberts Smn VA ★

ASHBY,
Bladen: b 1759 d 12-28-1828 m Katherine Vanmetre Spy Pvt VA
Jesse: b 1738 d 11-28-1823 m (1)Nancy Williams (2)Tamar Ruby
Pvt VA
John: b 6-16-1754 d 11-21-1802 m Esther Mackintire (McIntyre)
Cpl MA W ★
John: b 4-1-1740 d 4-4-1815 m Mary Turner Maj VA
John: b c. 1735 d 11 or 12-1776 m Sarah McCollough Sol VA
John: b a. 1743 d p. 1-16-1792 m Rachel Beech Sol VA
John, Sr.: b 1707 d 1797 m (1)Jean Combs (2)Catherine Huffman
PS VA
Joseph: b 1759 d c. 1847 m Rebecca McGinnis Pvt VA ★
Nathaniel: b 1-4-1750 d 5- -1812 m (1)Marguerite Mauzie (2)Anne
(Ashby) Lt VA
Peter: b 1751 d 1-29-1833 m Winifred Timmons Pvt VA
Silas: b 6-17-1765 d 9-24-1806 m Sarah Collette Pvt PS PA
Stephen: b c. 1745 d 12- -1830 m Susannah — Pvt PA
Stephen: b 1710 d 5-19-1797 m (1)Elizabeth — (2)X (3)Elizabeth —
Capt VA

ASHCRAFT,
Edward: b 11-26-1753 d 7-19-1819 m Sarah Strickland Pvt CT
Gibson: b 3-29-1749 d 10-9-1823 m Deborah Smith Pvt NJ
Jedediah: b 1-22-1727-8 d 3-6-1813 m Saranna Rhow Cpl CT
John: b c. 1740 d 12- -1816 m Rebecca — PS NC
Richard: b c. 1740 d 1792 m Elizabeth Carr Sct Spy PA

ASHEAD,
Amos: b 12-18-1742 d 6-5-1816 m Lydia Lippincott Sol NJ

ASHENFELTER,
Peter: b — d c. 1822 m Elizabeth — Pvt PA

ASHER,
Bartlett: b 2- -1763 d 6- -1841 m Margaret Curry Pvt IL ★
Wm.: b c. 1739 d 7-23-1780 m Anna — Ens VA

ASHFIELD,
John: b 2-20-1756 d 8-13-1818 m Mary Taylor Matr NY

ASHFORD,
George, Jr.: b 2-11-1758 d 4-25-1815 m Jemima Rabb Pvt SC

ASHLEY,
Abner: b 1-19-1754 d p. 11-17-1832 m Tryphena Abbot Pvt CT &
RI ★
Abner: b 3-5-1751 d 1-26-1838 m Lydia Churchill Pvt MA
Abraham: b 8-8-1743 d 12-20-1824 m (1)Phebe Tabor (2)Hannah
Crapo Pvt MA
Benjamin: b 11-14-1737 d 1-19-1828 m Ruth Weller Lt NH
Daniel: b 1-28-1758 d 12-16-1848 m (1)Elizabeth Smith (2)Mrs
Sarah Huntington Pvt CT & RI ★
Daniel: b 8-24-1759 d 6-13-1826 m (1)Olive Boardman (2)Polly
Benson Pvt MA
Daniel: b 9-22-1764 d 8-8-1812 m Sally Hunt Pvt MA
Daniel: b 1-15-1754 d 10-8-1810 m Mercy Pratt Lt CS PS NH
David: b 7-19-1735 d 3-28-1813 m Meribah Gaylord Lt MA
David: b 7-8-1731 d 7-15-1800 m Vashti Brook Pvt MA
David: b 9-27-1727 d 10-22-1813 m Mrs Hannah Leonard Miller
Pvt MA
Elisha: b c. 1757 d 5-30-1835 m Beulah Dewey Pvt VT ★
Elkanah: b 6-13-1744 d p. 1781 m Amy Wood Ens VT
Enoch: b 1-25-1750 d p. 1820 m Phebe Owen Pvt VT
Israel: b 6-15-1747 d 3-25-1814 m Mary Gelston Dr MA
James: b c. 1743 d 1828 m Annet Caswell MM Pvt MA
John, Sr.: b 12-2-1709 d 9-1-1802 m Hannah Hogeboom CS PS MA
John, Jr.: b 9-26-1736 d 11-5-1799 m (1)Movisa Ward (2)Mary
Ballantine MGen MA
John: b 7-8-1747 d 1-3-1833 m Mary Booth Bliss Pvt NH
John: b c. 1755 d c. 1810 m X Sgt Maj NC
John: b 8-30-1740 d p. 1811 m Desire Thatcher Sgt VT
Joseph, Jr.: b 1756 d 9-26-1846 m Elizabeth Reckard Pvt CT ★
Joseph: b 11-15-1721 d 1-7-1785 m (1)Hannah Sikes (2)Phebe
Markham Pvt MA
Joseph: b 9-18-1756 d 11-19-1823 m Catherine Day Pvt MA
Justin: b 7-27-1760 d 3-19-1829 m Freelove Davis Pvt MA
Martin, Sr.: b 9-17-1724 d 8- -1788 m Sarah Root Dr NH
Martin, Jr.: b 11-20-1758 d 6-14-1834 m Theodosia Kilbourn Pvt
NH W ★
Moses: b 7-22-1731 d 7-27-1792 m Sarah Rowe Pvt MA
Noah: b 12-2-1757 d 8-23-1839 m Abigail Hoar Pvt MA
Percival: b 1740 d 1-13-1822 m Anna Bishop Lt MA
Robert: b 1762 d 9-27-1829 m Sarah Rue Pvt NC
Samuel, Sr.: b 3-20-1720 d 2-18-1792 m Eunice Doolittle Col PS NH
Samuel, Jr.: b 9-29-1747 d 10- -1820 m Lydia Doolittle Lt NH
Stephen: b 9-4-1751 d 1776 m Charlotte Calkins Sgt MA
Stephen: b 4-28-1745 d 3-21-1820 m Hannah Cooley Pvt MA
Stephen: b 11-27-1740 d 2-20-1815 m Elizabeth Billings PS CS MA
Thomas: b 1-15-1737 d 7-9-1810 m (1)Zeruiah Richards Pvt PS VT
Thomas: b 1752 d 1826 m Mary Hart Pvt VA ★
Wm.: b c. 1742 d p. 1786 m Jane Dutcher Lt MA
Wm.: b 5-18-1752 d c. 1811 m Ruth Hubbard Fif MA
Wm.: b 5-7-1753 d 12-28-1828 m Phebe Howe Sgt VT
Wm Symmes: b 9-16-1757 d 6-10-1846 m (1)Clarissa Willard (2)
Aurelia Lathrop Pvt VT

ASHLINE,
John: b c. 1725 d p. 11-7-1795 m Frances Shepherd PS VA

ASHMAN, (includes ASHMUN)
George: b 1740-50 d 11-5-1811 m Eleanor Cromwell Col PA
John: b 12-26-1758 d 9-3-1793 m Hannah Hall Pvt MA
Samuel: b 2-5-1764 d 8-29-1846 m Parthenia Raymond Pvt NY ★

ASHMEAD,
Jacob: b 5-30-1712 d 7-10-1814 m Mary Naglee Capt PA
John: b 5-24-1757 d c. 1794 m Elizabeth — PS Capt MD
John: b 9-29-1738 d 6-6-1818 m Mary Mifflin Capt PA
Samuel, Sr.: b 3-4-1710 d 3-19-1794 m Esther Morgan CS PS PA
Samuel, Jr.: b 1-5-1731 d 12- -1778 m Ruth Robinson Sol PA

ASHMORE,
Hezekiah: b 1756 d 8-21-1822 m Elizabeth Kerr PS NC

ASHTON,
Benjamin: b — d 2-15-1810 m Mary Miservy 2Lt NS
Burditt: b 11-24-1747 d 3-8-1814 m (1)Ann Washington (2)Sharh
Blair (3)Mary Keene PS VA
Isaac: b 7-17-1742 d 9-8-1777 m Rebecca Powell 2Lt PA
James: b 1729 d 10-9-1802 m Elizabeth — Maj NY
John, Sr.: b c. 1740 d 1788 m (1)Mary Watts (2)Hannah West PS
VA
Joseph: b c. 1750 d a. 1817 m Mary — Capt PA ★
Joseph: b 7-25-1754 d 12-15-1793 m Elizabeth Parker CS PA
Samuel: bpt 3-30-1746 d 3-10-1818 m Elizabeth Malcom Pvt Matr
MA
Wm.: b 12- 1736 d 9-24-1800 m Catherine Easterly Pvt PA

ASHWAY, (includes ESHWAY)
Nicholas: b c. 1759 d 1813 m Catherine — Sgt PA

ASKEW,
Wm.: b c. 1755 d 5-6-1827 m Catherine Slaughter Sol DE

ASPELL,
James: b 1743 d 8-6-1827 m Christiana Johnson Pvt NY

ASPER,
George: b 9-18-1726 d 9-23-1804 m Elizabeth Bowman Pvt PA

ASPINWALL,
Aaron, Jr.: b 10-6-1743 d 5-1-1834 m Abigail Mathews Pvt CT ★
Caleb: b 1-15-1762 d 12-24-1808 m Elizabeth Freeman Pvt MA
John, Sr.: bpt 8-16-1736 d p. 1786 m Penelope Dwelly Pvt MA
John, Jr.: b 5-3-1764 d c. 1804 m Nancy Spurr Pvt MA
Thomas: b 1-15-1734 d 8-1-1799 m Lucy Sparhawk Col MA
Wm.: b 5-23-1743 d 4-16-1823 m Susanna Gardner Dr MA
Zalmon: b 2-15-1742 d 8-11-1824 m Hannah Conant Pvt CT

ASPLEY,
John: b 1756 d 1808 m Mrs — Porter Sgt NC

ASPRIL,
Joseph: b 2-2-1742 d 1-12-1802 m Mary Skeer PS DE

ASTON,
Alexander: b 2-17-1765 d p. 1841 m Ann Braly Sol VA ★

ATCHISON, (includes ACHESON)
Humphrey: b c. 1735 d c. 12-1-1814 m Rebecca Reed Pvt PA
Matthew: b 1734 d 11-26-1814 m (1)Elizabeth Baldidge (2)Jean
    Reed Pvt PA
Thomas: b 1756 d 1836 m (1)Catharine — (2)Annie Grinyard Pvt
    PA

ATCHLEY,
Thomas: b 5-3-1755 d c. 10-1836 m Lydia Richards Pvt NJ & VA ★

ATHEARN,
James: b 10-17-1724 d 11-10-1814 m Rebecca Scudder CS PS MA

ATHERTON,
Amos: b 10-5-1731 d 2-19-1801 m Lydia Gould Pvt MA
Cornelius: b 1736 d 12-4-1809 m (1)Mary Delano (2)Jane Johnston
    PS NY
David: b 9-17-1757 d 3-17-1830 m Esther Atherton Pvt MA
James, Jr.: b 9-19-1751 d 5-5-1828 m Lydia Washburn Pvt PA
James: b 1715 d 10-28-1798 m Elizabeth Borden PS PA
Jephthah: b a. 1735 d p. 1-19-1787 m (1)Penelope Pruden (2)Sarah
    Tynes (3)Mrs Elizabeth (Thorp) Jarrell LCol CS PS NC
Joel: b 1764 d 1844 m Nancy Crombie Pvt MA
John, Jr.: b 3-26-1762 d 6-17-1834 m Anna Shaw Cpl MA ★
John: b 2-22-1736 d 12- -1795 m Hannah Cole Pvt MA
Jonathan: b 11-14-1743 d 3-10-1813 m Susan Farrell MM MA
Jonathan: b 11-11-1759 d 3-21-1826 m Nancy Bridge Pvt MA
Jonathan: b c. 1740-50 d 2-23-1830 m Amy Saben PS NH
Joseph: b 4-28-1758 d 4-6-1834 m Miriam Scott Cpl MA
Joseph: b 1726 d 12-5-1787 m Sarah Hutchins Pvt MA
Joseph: b 8-5-1750 d 4-4-1839 m Hannah Farnsworth Pvt MA
Matthew: b 10-1-1760 d c. 1843 m (1)Elizabeth Adams (2)Jemima
    Pelton Pvt MA ★
Oliver: b 4-28-1738 d 9-29-1820 m Mary Severance Sgt MA
Oliver: b 8-1-1721 d 5-29-1813 m Rachel Godfrey PS MA

ATHEY, (includes ATHY)
James B.: b 1753 d 1825 m Rebecca McAtee Pvt VA
John: b 1730 d 1830 m Sarah Foster Cpl VA
Thomas: b 1746 d 9-18-1826 m Martha — Pvt VA
Thomas: b 1746 d c. 1820 m Scenna Ann Wilder Pvt VA

ATKINS, (includes ADKINS)
Ambrose: b 1754 d 12-11-1833 m Frankey Mansfield Pvt VA ★
Benjamin: b 8-20-1726 d p. 1781 m Sarah Harding Pvt MA
Benona: bpt 2-26-1748 d 10-31-1817 m Sarah Hitcock Pvt CL
Charles: b 9-2-1748 d 5-20-1817 m Ruth Kilburn Drm MA
Daniel: b 12-2-1755 d 1798 m Lucy Tyler Pvt CT
David: b 11-12-1759 d 11-21-1844 m Cornelia Cleaver Pvt CT ★
Edward: b 1756 d 2-4-1850 m Frances Wisdom Sgt VA ★
Hezekiah: b 9-20-1759 d p. 1-26-1835 m Mary Lafon Pvt VA
Ica Sr.: b c. 1740 d p. 1790 m Nancy Hutchens PS NC
Ica Jr.: b 3-7-1763 d 1-19-1832 m Mary Gordon Sol GA
Ica: b 1743 d 1802 m Polly — CS PS NC
Isaiah: b 9-24-1760 d 5-14-1842 m Rhoda Carey Cpl CT ★
Isaiah Sr.: b 1703 d 4-3-1782 m Hannah Cooke CS MA
John: b 1-28-1755 d 1-11-1806 m Lucretia Fosdick Pvt PS NH
John: b c. 1723 d 1792 m Elizabeth Hutchins PS NC
John: b a. 1743 d p. 2-18-1786 m Anne — Sgt VA
John: b 1760 d 1832 m — Wynne Pvt VA
John: b c. 1732 d 1811 m Susana Brockman PS VA
Joseph, Jr.: b 1743 d 4-5-1820 m Phebe Hall Pvt CT
Joseph: b — d a. 1-9-1816 m Jane — Sol VA

Josiah: b 11-4-1757 d 8-23-1828 m (1)Sarah Rogers (2)Mary Gillett
    Sol CT
Josiah: b 6- -1749 d 10-31-1781 m Sarah Rogers Sol CT W ★
Luther, Sr.: b 1718 d 8-31-1788 m Eunice Andrews Pvt CT
Nathaniel: bpt 8-15-1736 d p. 1781 m Mary Parker Pvt MA
Nimrod: b c. 1762 d p. 1-18-1825 m Elizabeth Parsons Sol MD
Samuel: b 1-17-1750 d 7-2-1830 m Eunice Wightman Pvt CT
Samuel: b 5-17-1757 d 12-5-1812 m (1)Olive Cady (2)Anna Jones
    Pvt NH
Silas, Jr.: b 10-25-1747 d c. 1835 m Martha Howland PS NS MA

ATKINSON,
Amos: b 3-20-1754 d p. 1778 m Anna Bailey Lt MA
Charles: b 1760 d 4-23-1834 m (1)Sarah McNight (2)Elizabeth
    Stevens Pvt PA
Cornelius: b 1732 d 4- -1815 m Mary Cross Lt PA
John: b c. 1750 d p. 8-22-1778 m Abigail Wharf Pvt MA
John: b 1760 d 8-14-1847 m (1)Nancy Altman (2)Phereba Ann
    Altman Sol NC
John: b 1720 d c. 1800 m Anne Atkinson Ponsomby Pvt VA
John: b a. 1736 d 1808 m Elizabeth Gardner Pvt VA
John: b 9-18-1755 d 4-2-1837 m Mary Armistead Pvt VA W ★
Joseph: b 11-28-1718 d 8-2-1801 m (1)Hannah Hale (2)Mrs Mary
    Couch PS NH
Joseph: b 4-28-1758 d 3-20-1830 m Anne Atkinson Pvt NH
Joseph: b 1753 d 1795 m Martha Johnson Pvt VA
Joshua: b 1750 d 1818 m Eliza Wilson Sgt VA
Moses: b 11-17-1747 d 11- -1813 m Rebecca Woodman Ens MA
Nathan: b — d p. 5-8-1813 m Martha Whitehead Sol NC
Nathaniel: b 3-19-1717 d 10-26-1794 m (1)Elizabeth Greenleaf (2)
    Sarah Morse PS NH
Nathaniel: b 12-12-1753 d 10-31-1834 m Abigail Bradley Cpl NH
Reuben: b 1736 d 1783 m Nancy Roberts Pvt VA
Richard Thomas: b 1744/45 d a. 6-28-1828 m X Pvt VA ★
Samuel: b 9-24-1748 d 10-4-1796 m Sarah Bamford Capt NH
Samuel: b c. 1750 d 1797-1801 m Sarah Washington Pvt VA
Thomas: b c. 1742 d p. 3-21-1803 m (1)Elizabeth Speed (2)Patience
    Chapin Pvt GA
Thomas: b 9-18-1741 d c. 1815 m (1)Ruth Cruze (2)Ruth Harvey PS
    NC
Thomas: b 1751 d 1794 m Salome Weidner 2Lt PA
Thomas: b 6-16-1735 d 9-9-1784 m Martha — Cpl VA
Wm.: b 8-12-1730 d 3-24-1778 m Hope Shinn Pvt NJ
Wm.: b 3-14-1749 d 12-2-1789 m Susan Meredith Pvt VA

ATLEE,
Samuel John: b 1739 d 11-25-1786 m Sarah Richardson Col PA
William Augustus: b 7-1-1735 d 9-9-1793 m Esther Bowes Sayre
    CS PS PA

ATSATT,
John: b 1725 d 1802 m Bathsheba — Pvt MA

ATWATER,
Abraham: b 11-10-1716 d 1-4-1786 m Mary Ball Sol CT
Amos: b 6-12-1752 d 5-8-1805 m (1)Martha Cowles (2)Mary Moss
    (3)Mehitable Brooks Pvt CT
Asaph: b 8-1-1745 d — m Lucy Ann Dibble Pvt CT
Benjamin: b 8-23-1756 d 5-6-1833 m Hannah Reynolds Pvt NY ★
Caleb: b 9-5-1741 d 12-19-1831 m Abigail Jones Ens CT
David: b 9-15-1723 d 3-4-1806 m (1)Elizabeth Bassett (2)Mrs Abiah
    Cooper PS CT
Elizabeth: b 6-2-1719 d 1-2-1783 m David Atwater PS CT
Enos: b 4-10-1750 d 12-22-1802 m Lois Alling Pvt CT
Isaac: b 6-15-1743 d 9-13-1776 m Eunice (Atwater) — Pvt CT
Isaac: b 12-4-1758 d 7-20-1839 m Lucy Merriam Pvt CT
Jeremiah: b 12-5-1734 d 11-12-1811 m (1)Anna Mix (2)Catherine
    Gale (3)Mary Saltonstall PS CT
John: b 12-24-1757 d 6-2-1838 m (1)Susanna Goodyear (2)Lucy
    Davis Pvt CT ★
Jonathan: b 10-12-1723 d 2-24-1794 m (1)Miriam — (2)Sarah
    Beach Pvt CT
Medad: b 3-23-1751 d 2-14-1832 m (2)Rhoda Dickerman Pvt Grl CT
Reuben: b 10-13-1728 d 8-19-1801 m (1)Sarah Hull (2)Mary Russ-
    ell Maj CT
Samuel: b 1757 d 1-12-1848 m Patience Peck Drm CT
Samuel: b 6-1-1718 d 5-9-1793 m Sarah Ball PS CS CT
Stephen: b 6-2-1751 d 3-4-1831 m Hannah Mead PS NY
Stephen: b 7-27-1758 d 1-28-1791 m (1)Rebecca Gorham
    (2)Elizabeth Gorham Pvt CT
Wm.: b 10-18-1745/6 d 8-8-1816 m (1)Mehitable Clark (2)Mrs
    Sarah (Atwater) Brintall (3)Mrs Esther (Northrop) Carrington PS
    CT
Zophar: b 6-28-1756 d c. 1849 m Lucy Osborn Pvt CT

ATWELL, (includes ATTWILL)
Benjamin: b 1735 d 5-12-1806 m Mary Ann Lee Ens CT
Francis: b c. 1750 d 1781 m Mary McDonald Capt VA
Jesse: b 1745 d 7-11-1781 m Mary — Sgt CT
John, Sr.: b 1736 d 1-31-1820 m Bridget Cummings Pvt NH
John, Jr.: b 6-6-1761 d 2-3-1831 m (1)Rebecca Lawrence (2)Dolly
    Whitcher Pvt MA & NH ★
Joseph: b 10-26-1754 d 11-30-1834 m (2)Chloe Pease Pvt NY

ATWELL, contd.
Wm.: b 1720 d 1806 m Lydia Dagget Pvt MA
Zachariah: b 10-9-1755 d 11-6-1836 m Elizabeth Breed Pvt MA

ATWOOD, (includes ATTWOOD)
Asa: b 12-30-1754 d 9-15-1778 m (1)Esther Atwood (2) X Sol CT
Benjamin: b 1730 d 9-5-1778 m Martha Hardy Pvt MA
Caleb: b 6-26-1749 d 6-4-1835 m Sarah Shaw Pvt MA
Caleb: b 1760 d 7-14-1833 m Mariam Walton Pvt MA
Charles: b c. 1752 d a. 11-30-1810 m Mary Brayton Pvt RI
David: b 8-24-1758 d 2-19-1817 m Susannah Newcomb Pvt MA
David: b 1747 d 1809 m Ruth Knight Cpl NH
Ebenezer: b 11-3-1729 d c. 1795 m Rachael Harding PS Pvt Cdr MA
Elijah, Sr.: b 1724 d 8-4-1806 m Anna Goodspeed PS CT
Elijah, Jr.: b 11-5-1760 d 6-9-1806 m Esther Whiting Lt CT
Elisha: b 4-27-1745 d 5-24-1825 m Mary Skilton Cpl PS CT
Ephraim: b 6-16-1737 d 1-21-1799 m Ruth Richmond Pvt MA
Hezekiah: b 4-13-1727 d 9-   -1809 m Abigail Hun Pvt MA
Ichabod: b 9-24-1744 d 8-24-1819 m Hannah Shaw Pvt MA
Isaac: b 7-17-1747 d 3-15-1836 m Hannah Chubbuck Pvt MA
Isaac: b 3-24-1760 d 3-14-1847 m Elizabeth Dodge Pvt CT & MA ★
James: b 10-29-1728 d p. 1790 m Thankful Young Pvt MA
James: b 2-10-1764 d 10-   -1806 m Mrs Mary (Shaw) Suther Pvt MA
Jedediah: b 1748 d 1852 m X Sol PA
Jesse: b 5-23-1752 d 10-14-1836 m Rachel Atwood Pvt MA ★
John: b 1728 d 12-31-1814 m Elizabeth Lawrence Pvt MA
John: b 7-27-1755 d 3-11-1829 m Candace Achley (Ackley) Pvt MA
John: b 1714 d 1812 m (1)Abigail Sanders (2)Ruth Whittaker PS CS NH
John: b 1747 d 10-   -1802 m Roby Kimball Sgt RI
Jonathan: b 9-29-1736 d 10-17-1816 m (1)Elizabeth Plummer (2) Dorothy Wells Capt PS NH
Jonathan: b 9-9-1710 d 5-4-1783 m Hannah Sherman PS CT
Joseph: b 8-1-1742 d 3-24-1824 m (1)Elizabeth Shaw (2)Content (Rickard) Pratt Sgt MA
Joseph: b 4-8-1756 d 4-9-1821 m (1)Ruth Cross (2)Polly Powers Pvt NH
Joshua: b c. 1725 d p. 1780 m (1)Esther Chamberlain (2)Mrs Martha Barrett Pvt MA
Joshua: b 4-17-1762 d 1829 m (1)Susan Cram (2)Mrs Anna Dresser Sgt NH ★
Joshua: b 12-3-1723/4 d 7-8-1809 m Mehitable Seavey Pvt NH
Moses: b 11-13-1761 d 5-9-1808 m Mary Tenney Pvt MA
Moses: b 2-25-1761 d 9-17-1842 m Judith Wadley Pvt NH ★
Nathan: b 2-20-1765 d p. 1799 m Betsey Stubbs Pvt MA
Nathaniel: b 12-11-1725 d 10-19-1804 m (1)Susanna Shurtleff (2) Lydia (Timberlake) Boult Pvt MA
Philip: b 1-4-1756 d 10-8-1841 m (1)Ruth Gates (2)Mrs Sophia Griffin Pvt MA ★
Samuel: b 8-24-1735 d p. 1789 m Bathsheba Crosby Sol MA
Samuel: b 7-6-1768 d 6-20-1816 m Hannah Boyden PS MA
Samuel: b 1724 d 12-23-1796 m (1)Peace Stewart (2)Sarah Smith Pvt VT
Solomon: b 1750 d 12-31-1843 m Hannah Rogers Sgt MA
Stephen: b 3-9-1748 d 1777 m Jennet Murdock Pvt MA
Timothy: b 9-9-1749 d 4-24-1837 m (1)Sarah Convers (2)Grace Pickett Pvt NY
Wait: b 12-15-1749 d 10-31-1836 m Susanna Marshall MM MA
Wm.: b 4-16-1740 d 4-30-1814 m Lydia Tilson Pvt MA
Wm.: b 6-20-1740 d 2-14-1809 m Jane Hardy Sgt MA
Zaccheus: b 1-10-1752 d 1-24-1833 m Chloe Hovey Pvt MA ★

AUBRY,
Frederick: b c. 1740 d c. 4-15-1818 m Sarah Hedden Pvt Dr NH

AUCHMUTY, (includes AUCHMOODY)
David: b 9-20-1738 d 1809 m Maria De Graff Sol NY
James: b — d p. 1790 m (1)Mary Deyo (2)Dorcas (Frederick) Eyverie PS NY
Samuel: b 6-25-1752 d 8-2-1834 m Ann McMahan Capt PA ★

AUDUBON,
— b 1740 d 1813 m Ann Moquette Commo (FrN)

AUGHE, (includes ACHE, ACHEY, ACHIA)
Harmon: b 8-8-1759 d 5-19-1846 m Mary Munger Pvt PA ★
Henry: b c. 1718 d 1786 m (1)Elizabeth — (2)Maria Catharine Philbert Pvt PA
Henry: b 1-26-1759 d 1-31-1825 m (1)Elizabeth Shuey (2)Mary Magdalene Felty Pvt PA
Herman: b 1724 d 6-   -1815 m Anna Maria— CS PA
John: b 1721 d 2-   -1808 (2)Elizabeth Venrick Sgt PS PA

AUGUR,
Abraham: b c. 1724 d 5-31-1798 m (1)Elizabeth Bradley (2)Mrs Sarah Allcock PS CS CT
Felix: b 6-2-1760 d 7-21-1839 m Esther Taylor Pvt CT ★
Hezekiah: b 1750 d 11-7-1818 m (1)Susan Minot (2)Lydia Atwater Pvt CT
John: b c. 6-11-1748 d 1-8-1827 m (1)Dinah Page (2)Mrs Deborah Hoadley Pvt CT

Philemon: b 5-20-1754 d 8-11-1826 m (1)Tabitha Perkins (2)Mary Shepard Cpl CT
Prosper: b 1-18-1756 d 12-16-1836 m (1)Thankful Miller (2)Mrs Mary Word Pvt CT

AULD, (includes AULL, AULLS, AWL, AWLL)
Hugh, Sr.: b 5-23-1745 d 12-7-1813 m Frances Harrison 1Lt MD
Jacob: b 8-6-1727 d 9-26-1793 m Sarah Sturgeon PS Pvt PA
James: b 1732 d 1799 m Harriet — Maj PS NC
Thomas: b 8-24-1758 d a. 7-4-1798 m Elizabeth Dawson Sgt MD
Wm.: b 1-21-1748 d 2-23-1816 m Elizabeth (Calhoun) Morris Pvt PA

AULT,
Frederick: b c. 1738-40 d 1815 m — Rebeak Pvt Lt PA
Henry: b 10-31-1745 d 9-14-1816 m (1)Anna Maria Walter Neas (2) Christiana Graybell Pvt PA
Michael: b c. 1750 d p. 3- 28-1816 m Mary — Pvt PA
Valentine: b 3-22-1750 d p. 1790 m Catherine Lau Ens PA

AUMACK, (includes AUMOCK)
William: b 7-23-1762 d 10-22-1833 m Christiana — Pvt NJ ★

AURANT, (includes AURAND, AURANDT)
Henry: b 1747/8 d p. 6-26-1818 m Rebecca Breisbach Pvt PA
John: b 9-5-1725 d 3-13-1804 m (1)Mary Elizabeth Pontius (2)Catherine Emerick PS CS PA
John Detrick: b 11-8-1761 d 4-24-1831 m Catherine Reiber Pvt PA ★

AUSPACH,
Peter: b a. 1750 d p. 1792 m Mary Williams 2Lt NY

AUSTIN, (includes AUSTEN)
Aaron, Sr.: b 2-25-1716 d 2-9-1802 m Elizabeth Spencer Kent PS CT
Aaron, Jr.: b 8-27-1745 d 7-15-1829 m Esther Kellogg Capt CT ★
Abiathar: b 4-28-1758 d 12-12-1833 m Tylie Smith Pvt MA
Amos: b 6-24-1752 d 5-15-1833 m (1)Mary Parker (2)Lydia — Pvt CT
Andrew D.: b 8-11-1751 d 12-11-1838 m Mary Griswold Pvt CT ★
Augustine: b 7-2-1738 d 3-5-1809 m Sarah Ashley Pvt MA
Benjamin: b 1763 d 11-6-1838 m Susanna Goodwin Pvt CT ★
Caleb: b 2-6-1719 d 5-9-1792 m Phoebe King Pvt CT
Caleb: b 5-25-1755 d 10-23-1822 m Martha Hopkins Dr CT ★
Caleb: b 1732 d 5-26-1806 m Hepzibah Jones Pvt VT
Daniel: b 4-28-1720 d 6-24-1804 m Abigail Phelps PS CT
David: b 5-6-1732 d 2-5-1801 m Mary Mix PS CT
David, Sr.: b 7-16-1734 d 7-7-1814 m Mary Harmon PS Pvt CT
David: b 11-1-1735 d 8-30-1822 m Sarah Wood Pvt MA
David: b 1752 d 3-23-1813 m Judith Hall Pvt RI ★
Elijah: bpt 2-3-1751/2 d 6-2-1794 m Esther Phelps Pvt CT
Elijah: b 3-27-1758 d p. 1832 m Elizabeth Harrington (or Eldridge) Pvt RI
Eliphalet, Sr.: b 1760 d 1-28-1838 m Sibell Dudley Sgt CT ★
Ellis: b 1727 d p. 1790 m Sarah Aylesworth Pvt RI
Eusebius: b 4-17-1758 d 1-20-1834 m Abigail Wood Pvt CT ★
Ezekiel: b 5-1-1759 d 7-19-1849 m Martha — Sol RI
Gideon: b 7-16-1731 d 1792 m Prudence Angell Pvt RI
Henry, Sr.: b 1736 d 2-   -1822 m Sarah — Lt VA
Henry, Jr.: b 1760 d 11-   -1809 m Nancy Watts Pvt VA
Isaac, Sr.: b 11-8-1723 d p. 1790 m Mehitable Harris Pvt MA
Isaac, Jr.: b 4-5-1755 d 7-26-1851 m Elizabeth Huse Pvt MA
Isaac: b 3-18-1737 d 11-21-1824 m Rhodinah Vaughan Pvt NY
Isaac: b 1746 d 10-14-1813 m Anne Currey Pvt NY
Jacob: b 1746 d 3-28-1828 m Prudence Dean PS CT
James: b 9-27-1751 d 9-13-1831 m Hannah Wilder Ens CT
Jeremiah: b 12-30-1760 d 5-20-1846 m Mrs. Esther Colgrove Pvt RI ★
Joab: b 7-29-1740 d 3-5-1820 m (1)Elizabeth Fox (2)Eleanor Kellogg Sgt MA
Job: b 3-31-1759 d 2-7-1847 m (1)Mary Nelson (2)Mrs Hannah Hazen Sgt NY
Joel: b 10-22-1747 d 10-30-1814 m Hannah Saxton Pvt CT
John: b 2-20-1758 d 4-20-1841 m Esther Herrick Pvt CT ★
John: b 8-1-1738 d 8-30-1823 m (1)Elizabeth Fox (2)Lois Chapman (Chipman) Pvt MA
John: b 1740 d 5-25-1820 m Rachel Lawrence Pvt MA
John: b 1-15-1754 d 4-   -1838 m Martha P. Messer Pvt NH ★
John: b 1757 d 7-7-1825 m Sarah Ellis Sgt NY
John: b 1760 d 10-28-1838 m Wadie West Sol NY
John: b c. 1760 d p. 1840 m Elizabeth — Pvt SC
John, Sr.: b 9-14-1726 d 12-12-1815 m Mary Crenshaw PS VA
John, Jr.: b 12-15-1761 d p. 6-9-1815 m (1)Lucy Shelton (2)Mary — Pvt VA
John: b 1736 d 10-5-1845 m (2)Elizabeth Lindsey Pvt VA
Jonah: b 7-29-1753 d 9-27-1833 m Sarah Foote Fairbanks Cpl MA ★
Jonathan: b c. 1755 d 10-13-1842 m Mary Goodspeed Matr Bbd RI ★
Joseph: b 1-28-1710 d p. 1- -1792 m Abigail Allen Pvt CT
Joseph: b c. 1730-35 d c. 1810 m (2)Welthy Prewett PS VA
Levi, Sr.: b 7-7-1743 d 10-4-1823 m Mary Gates Pvt MA

Moses: b 11-10-1751 d 7-17-1827 m Hannah Jaggers Pvt NJ
Nathan: b 6-11-1748 d 1840 m Phebe Barker Pvt NH
Nathaniel: b 11-28-1752 d 9-24-1844 m (1)Anna Bidwell (2)Margaret Bissell Pvt CT
Nathaniel: bpt 7-19-1741 d 3-5-1816 m Margaret Rand Pvt MA
Nathaniel: b 9-15-1764 d 5-6-1803 m Humilis Owen Pvt MA
Nathaniel: b 1760 d 1840 m Ann Merritt Pvt MA & VT ★
Phillip: b 11-28-1766 d 1814 m (1)Lucretia — (2)Chloe Rue Pvt MA
Phineas: b 1752 d 2-12-1812 m Hannah Germain Pvt NY
Richard, Jr.: b — d a. 1780/1 m Hannah Neal PS MD
Samuel: b 10-28-1747 d c. 2-20-1833 m Mary Bissell Pvt CT
Seth: b 9-13-1748 d 7-23-1819 m Hannah Smith Capt CT
Seth: b 12-14-1731 d 4-16-1806 m Mary Seymour PS CT
Smith: b 1753 d 9-17-1834 m Martha Brewer Pvt NY
Stephen: b — d 12-17-1807 m X Cpl MA
Thomas: b 8-29-1738 d 8-28-1816 m Lucy Rising Sgt CT
Wm.: b 5-6-1752 d 2-28-1846 m Hannah Clark Pvt MA
Wm.: b 12-9-1750 d 3-7-1819 m (1)Martha Rogers (2)Lucy Clossen Pvt RI
Wm.: b 1755 d 2- -1840 m Jane Collins Sct VA & SC
Zephaniah: b 4-16-1727 d p. 1790 m Sarah Egglestone 1Lt MA

AUSTRAW,
John: b c. 1760 d a. 2-26-1842 m Martha — Pvt PA

AUTEN, (includes ATEN, ATER, ATTEN, AUTER, & EATON)
Adrian: b 11-7-1737 d 1826 m Elizabeth Stryker Pvt PA
George: b 12-25-1745 d 6-18-1820 m Mary Boyer Pvt VA
John: b 12-22-1732 d 1790 m Elizabeth (Sutphan ?) Pvt NJ
Richard: b 4-22-1751 d 9-8-1809 m (1)Judith Van Fleet (2)Arianche Longstreet (3)Catherine Warner PS PA
Thomas: b 2-9-1746 d 4-3-1781 m Ann Probasco Pvt NJ
Thomas: b 1760 d 1847 m Elizabeth Vantuile Pvt NJ

AUTRY,
John: b 1735-40 d 2-2-1788 m Elizabeth Autry Capt GA

AUXIER, (includes OXER)
Christopher: b c. 1757 d 1803 m Catharine Danner Pvt PA
Samuel: b c. 1759 d c. 1800 m Sarah Brown Pvt VA W ★

AVANT, (includes AVENT)
John: b c. 1740 d 12-10-1821 m Mary — PS NC
Joseph: b 8-24-1720 d 8-24-1798 m Malinda Davis Pvt VA

AVEN,
James: b 1750 d 11- -1778 m Mary Eliza Stanford Pvt NC

AVERILL, (includes AVEREL & AVERELL)
Asa: b 1739 d 8-25-1825 m (1)Anna Chaffee (2)Mercy (Phippen) Lovejoy (3)Mrs Betsey Wall Ens VT
Daniel: b 1743 d 8-5-1842 m (1)Eunice Calhoun (2)Hannah Tyler Pvt Fif CT ★
Daniel: b 12-3-1730 d 3- -1801 m Johanna Hood Pvt MA
Daniel: b 1762 d 5- -1848 m (1)Mary Weston (2)Mrs Manning Pvt NH
David: b 4-1-1755 d 2-13-1812 m Mary Charlton Pvt NH
Ebenezer: b 1731 d 1795 m Mary Towne Pvt NH
Elijah: b 1756 d 1806 m Mehitable Bradford Pvt NH
Elisha: b 1-16-1754 d 8- -1821 m Mary Russell PS CT
Isaac: b 6-2-1740 d 6-23-1816 m Priscilla Peabody Pvt CS MA
Israel, Sr.: b 4-21-1713 d 1778 m (1)Mary Kenney (2)Mary Hilton CS ME
Israel, Jr.: b 1756 d 1-26-1833 m Jane Clark Pvt MA
James: b 2-23-1734 d 4- -1815 m X Capt CT
Jesse: b 4-13-1759 d 8-17-1843 m Elizabeth Mansfield (or Stoddard) Pvt VT ★
John, Sr.: b 6-2-1740 d 5-21-1815 m Mary Bradford Pvt NH
John: b 4-24-1711 d 9-2-1797 m Mary Phippen Capt PS VT
Jonathan: b 1756 d 8-16-1835 m Anna Watkins Dr CT ★
Joseph: b 8-29-1742 d 1822 m Sarah Stone Sgt MA
Joseph: b 1-17-1719/20 d p. 6-15-1780 m (1)Mary Symonds (2)Serah Mansfield Pvt VT
Josiah: b 10-12-1755 d 10-12-1819 m Catherine Canfield Sgt VT
Moses: b 3-6-1722/3 d 1-22-1784 m (1)Martha Cogswell (2)Sarah — CS CT
Moses: b 1761 d 1843 m (1)Nancy Parker (2)Mary Bridges (3)Eunice — Pvt NH ★
Nathaniel: b 12-15-1745 d 4-11-1820 m Rosanna Noble Pvt CT
Paul: b 12-7-1711 d 1805/6 m Zeruah Howe Pvt MA
Perry: b 9-18-1754 d 7-10-1842 m (1)Dorothy Whittlesey (2)Mrs Sarah Turrell Lt CT
Robert: bpt 1745 d 9-10-1828 m Anne — Sgt VT ★
Samuel: b 1742 d 9-27-1824 m Mary McLelland Lt MA
Samuel: b 1745-54 d c. 1825 m (1)Mary Barnes Pvt CT
Stephen: b 10-18-1730 d 5-9-1810 m (1)Sarah Hendee (2)Mehitable Allen Pvt CT
Thomas, Jr.: b 9-26-1747 d 1-25-1825 m Mary Dresser PS NH
Thomas: b 1745 d 4-22-1823 m Elizabeth Robinson Pvt VT
William: b 6-13-1748 d 2-27-1839 m (1)Abigail Gray (2)Eunice Mayhew Pvt MA

AVERY, (includes AVARY & AVERA)
Abel: b 8-30-1760 d 4-30-1846 m Elizabeth Gennings Pvt CT ★
Abner: b 5-1-1748 d 8-24-1836 m Elizabeth Shattuck MM CT
Abraham: b 5-20-1754 d 2- -1843 m Mercy Packer Sgt PS CT MA ★
Alexander: b c. 1735 d 11-15-1809 m Sarah Carraway CS Capt NC
Alexander, Sr.: b a. 1748 d 1794 m Salatheal Holton CS NC
Amos: bpt 4-18-1735 d 1823 m (1)Irene Kingsbury (2)Anna Edgerton 2Lt CT
Amos: b 2-1-1754 d 4-16-1831 m Mary — Pvt CT ★
Amos: b 5-22-1757 d 9-16-1837 m Abigail Loomis Sgt CT ★
Amos: bpt 3-6-1743 d c. 1792 m Prudence Williams Pvt CT W ★
Asa: b 1721 d 9-27-1789 m Lucretia Williams PS CT
Benajah: b 12-15-1743 d 6-26-1811 m Bridget Monroe Ens CT
Benjamin: b 3-4-1758 d 5-4-1843 m Anna Foote Pvt CT
Caleb: b 2-25-1763 d 4-6-1835 m Mary Avery Col CT
Daniel: b 11-14-1740 d 9-6-1781 m Deborah (Avery) Ens CT
Daniel: b c. 1757 d a. 12-22-1823 m Patience — Sol NC
David: b 11-5-1764 d 1842 m Hannah (Avery) Pvt CT
David: b 4-5-1746 d 2-16-1818 m Hannah Chaplin Chp MA
Ebenezer, Sr.: b 3-29-1704 d 7-11-1780 m (1)Lucy Latham (2)Mrs Rachael Denison LCol CT
Ebenezer, Jr.: b 3-7-1732 d 9-6-1781 m Phebe Denison Lt CS PS CT
Ebenezer: bpt 8-17-1746 d 1-11-1828 m (1)Elizabeth Green (2)Elizabeth (Smith) Avery (3)Elizabeth (Coleman) Latham (4)Mrs Elizabeth Eldrekin Ens CT
Ebenezer: b 10-10-1761 d 6-15-1856 m (1)Abigail Story (2)Mary Allen Pvt CT ★
Ebenezer Punderson: b 5-21-1765 d 9-10-1840 m Lovina Barnes PS CT
Edmond: b 12-3-1750 d 12-17-1805 m (1)Sarah Rice (2)Anne Barnes Scl CT
Edward: b 1750 d p. 1781 m Rachel Daniels Pvt CT
Elihu: b 4-6-1755 d 3-8-1779 m Thankful Avery Lt CT
Elijah: b 9-15-1734 d 9-6-1781 m Mrs Prudence Morgan Capt CT
Elisha: b 12-30-1756 d 2-10-1807 m Sybil Sanger Cpl CT
Enoch: b c. 1744 d 3-20-1832 m (1)Dorcas Woolsey (2)Abigail — PS Pvt NY
Ephraim: bpt 6-25-1727 d 4-1-1792 m Abigail Bill Pvt MA
Ezekiel: b 2-27-1764 d 1844 m Lucinda Rogers Pvt CT ★
Frederick: b 1763 d 1804 m Elizabeth Stoddard Pvt CT
Gardiner: bpt 9-22-1751 d 12-27-1831 m Amy Newell Pvt MA ★
George, Sr.: b 9-2-1724 d 2-16-1785 m Eunice (Avery) Pvt CT
George, Jr.: b 4-24-1759 d — m Mary Allyn Pvt CT
George: b 1-23-1759 d 1-21-1857 m Mary Sanborn Pvt CT MA & VT ★
George: b 1764 d 6-10-1853 m Elizabeth Allen Pvt NC ★
Griswold: b 9-15-1739 d 10-6-1812 m Anna Avery Capt CT
Humphrey: b 7-12-1750 d 10-30-1831 m Joanna Smith Pvt NY
Humphrey, Sr.: b 3-10-1725 d a. 1-29-1790 m Mary Baldwin PS NY
Isaac: b 8-23-1747 d 9-23-1827 m Lucy Swan Sol CT
Isaac: b 3-24-1743 d 6-17-1812 m Mercy Williams Sgt CT
Isaac: b 10-27-1743 d a. 12-24-1799 m Margaret Stringer MC VA
Jacob: b c. 1756 d b. 4-6-1757 d 7- -1810 m Mary Elizabeth Avery Pvt CT
James: b 12-27-1748 d p. 1790 m Martha Smith Pvt CT
James: b 2-28-1737 d 2-22-1822 m (1)Mary Comstock (2)Mrs Lydia Satterlee Sol PS CT
James: b 11-29-1758 d 3-18-1798 m Rebecca Edes QM Lt MA
Jasper: b 1743 d 9-6-1781 m Elizabeth Smith Sgt CT
Jeremiah: b 10-8-1762 d 9-13-1850 m Polly Coffin Pvt NH
John: b 1-24-1738 d 1-5-1826 m Sarah Belton Sgt CT
John: b 4-29-1727 d 9-11-1815 m Anna Miner Pvt Drm CT
John, Jr.: b 6-12-1732 d 7-23-1794 m (1)Mary Parke (2)Experience Stanton PS CT
John: b 1740 d 1817 m Mary Loggett Pvt GA
John: b 9-9-1758 d 9-1-1840 m (1)Mary Cushman (2)Beulah Briggs Pvt Matr MA ★
John, (4th): bpt 1-2-1731 d c. 1-8-1814 m Mehitable Buell RO MA
John, Jr.: b 9-2-1739 d 6-7-1806 m Mary Cushing CS MA
John: b 1735 d p. 1-15-1813 m Phoebe Archer PS VA
Jonas: b 7-15-1745 d 12-18-1776 m Mary (Avery) Pvt CT
Jonathan: b 9-10-1755 d 6-14-1847 m Pamela Fox Ordl Sgt CT ★
Jonathan: b 6-27-1737 d 2-7-1805 m Preserved Smith CS CT
Jonathan: b 9-15-1744 d 9- -1833 m (1)Sarah Farrington (2)Jerusha Neal Ens MA ★
Joseph: b 10-14-1751 d 3-5-1824 m Mary Adams Allen PS MA
Joshua: b 10-15-1740 d 11-24-1829 m Hannah Clarke PS NH
Josiah: b 10-24-1740 d a. 11-24-1801 m Anna — PS NH
Miles: b 9-5-1760 d 6-27-1850 m Malinda Pixley Sgt NH
Moses: b 1759 d 11-5-1825 m Elizabeth Colbath Pvt NH
Nathan: b 1754 d 5-3-1821 m Aliff Pearson Pvt CT ★
Nathan: b 3-31-1759 d 1-16-1841 m Anna Ayers Pvt CT ★
Nathan: b 5-2-1744 d 8-31-1832 m Rebecca Elderkin Pvt CT ★
Nathaniel: b 8-28-1751 d 8-30-1839 m (1)Desire Clark (2)Anna Littlefield (3)Amy Denison Sgt MA ★
Oliver: b 3-23-1729 d 6-27-1815 m (1)Sarah Corse (2)Abigail Gilman Capt CT
Parke, Sr.: b 12-9-1710 d 5-4-1797 m Mary Latham PS CT
Parke, Jr.: b 3-22-1741 d 12-20-1821 m Hannah Morgan Lt CT
Peter: b 5-10-1764 d 10-7-1845 m Hannah Avery Sol CT

AVERY, contd.
Ransford: b 1754 d 3-27-1849 m (1)Eunice Leffingwell (2)Mrs Mary Hutchinson Pvt MA ★
Richard: b 1763 d 5-4-1834 m Submit Maritta Ferguson Fif MA ★
Richardson: b 1-25-1718 d 1779 m Sara Plumb PS CT
Roger: b 4-14-1761 d 11-12-1841 m Elizabeth Foote Pvt CT ★
Rufus: b 11-15-1758 d 7-30-1842 m Hannah Lord Sgt CT ★
Samuel: b 11-15-1752 d 12-15-1844 m Candace Charlton PS CT
Samuel: b 10-17-1731 d 8-4-1806 m (1)Sybil Noyes (2)Mary Ann Rose Pvt VT
Simeon: b 10-20-1753 d 8-1-1796 m Lucy Swan Lt CT
Simeon: b 9-17-1759 d 1-16-1803 m Sarah Bump Pvt CT
Solomon: b 6-17-1729 d 12-23-1798 m Hannah Punderson PS CT
Stephen: b 5-10-1751 d 6-15-1827 m Fanny Barnes Pvt CT
Stephen: b 1-13-1756 d 4-1-1828 m (1)Anna Wheeler (2)Elizabeth Morgan Pvt CT
Stephen: b 7-17-1756 d 9-1-1838 m Mary Walker Pvt CT W ★
Stephen: b 8-13-1762 d 10- -1842 m (1)Sarah Bement (2)Renewey (Carpenter) Maxon (3)Anna (DeLapp) Reynolds Pvt CT
Thaddeus: b 10-19-1749 d 11-16-1836 m Elizabeth Underhill PMGen NY
Theophilus, Sr.: b 9-6-1708 d 9-30-1799 m Elizabeth Billings PS CT
Theophilus, Jr.: b 6-22-1753 d 2-10-1839 m Sabra Andrews Pvt CT
Thomas: b 2-10-1746 d 5-4-1825 m Hannah Smith 1Lt CT ★
Thomas: b 1727 d 1787 m Mary — Sol NC
Uriah: b 8-23-1760 d 8-25-1843 m Sybil Little Pvt CT ★
Waightstill: b 5-10-1741 d 3-13-1821 m Leah (Probart) Franks Col PS NC
Waitstill: b 12-31-1757 d 11-2-1807 m Amy Wheeler Pvt CT
Wm.: b c. 1750 d p. 1796 m Lucy Everett Ens CT
Wm.: b 1726 d 3-4-1787 m Mary Dolbeare CS CT
Wm.: b 9-2-1757 d 9-24-1822 m Sarah Dewey Pvt MA
Wm.: b a. 1725 d p. 1794 m Rachel — Pvt NC
Wm.: b c. 1755 d 1825 m (1)Nancy E. Ingram (2)Prudence Peoples Sol NC
Wm.: bpt 4-5-1724 d p. 1780 m Abigail (Avery) Williams Sgt CT
Wm. Halley: b 1739 d 12-28-1807 m — Mac Lannen Capt VA

AVIS,
John: b 1759 d c. 1835 m Susanna Downs Pvt MA
Joseph: b 3-31-1756 d 1802 m Sarah Riley Ens NJ
Robert: b 1755 d 6-15-1834 m Martha Dark Pvt VA ★

AX,
George: b c. 1745-50 d p. 1802 m (1)Rebecca Haas (2)Elizabeth Kupp Capt PA
Wm.: b 8-6-1762 d 3-5-1810 m Lydia Scriber Pvt PA

AXFORD,
John, Sr.: b 11-20-1735 d 1-7-1809 m Abigail Hunt Lt NJ

AXLINE, (includes EXLINE)
John: b 1739 d 2-19-1833 m Christena Mertz Sol PS VA
John: b 8-28-1761 d 1847 m X Pvt VA

AXSON,
Samuel Jacob: b c. 1751 d 10-6-1827 m (2)Mrs Ann Lambright Dix Dr GA

AXTELL,
Daniel: b 1-17-1734 d 9-1-1799 m Elizabeth Whittemore Pvt MA
Daniel: b 4-12-1748 d 6-27-1826 m Ruth Tuthill Pvt PA
Henry: b 3-16-1738 d 4-6-1818 m (1)Mary Beach (2)Phoebe (Condict) Day Maj NJ
Luther: b 4-22-1753 d 6-2-1822 m Hannah Condit Pvt NJ
Moses: b 1-11-1755 d 3-25-1813 m (1)Tamar Curtis (2)Bathsheba Peake Pvt MA
Thomas: b 9-15-1750 d 7-12-1808 m (1)Mary Tuthill (2)Ellen McLean Pvt PA

AYCOCK,
Jesse: b c. 1747 d p. 11-7-1822 m (1)Charity Barden (2)Mrs Patience Newsom PS NC
Richard: b c. 1740 d 1790 m (1)Rebecca Thurman (2)Mary — Pvt GA

AYER, (includes AYARS, AYERS, AYRES, AYRS, EYRE, & OYER)
Aaron: b 11-12-1744 d 4-9-1813 m (1)Lois Moody (2)Mary Hitchcock Pvt MA
Asa: b 6-5-1761 d p. 1810 m Mary Wait Pvt MA
Benjamin: b 11-23-1763 d 2-79-1844 m (1)Rachel Sanborn Pvt Drm MA★
Daniel: b 3-31-1763 d 2-12-1827 m Rhoda Holton Tms NJ
David: b 1741 d c. 1812 m (1)Betsey Barrister (2)Hannah Compton (3) X Pvt NJ
David: b 1743 d 6-7-1828 m Mary Amelia Perkins Pvt MA VT
David: b — d 1792 m Rachael Bailey Pvt PA
David: b 4-8-1744 d 1834/35 m Elizabeth (McDowell) McCollum Pvt PA
Ebenezer: b 5-20-1716 d 1- -1785 m Elizabeth Holly Pvt CT
Ebenezer: b 1754 d 5-31-1832 m Achsa Squires Pvt CT ★
Ebenezer: b 3-22-1727 d p. 1786 m Hannah (Plaisted) Scammon Scl ME

Eli: b 2-27-1761 d 2-2-1840 m Sarah Crawford Pvt MA
Elihu: b 1-26-1761 d 3-19-1844 m Lydia Owen Sgt NC
Elijah, Sr.: b 4-30-1727 d p. 1790 m (1)Content Wertner (2)Abigale Merrill PS MA
Elijah, Jr.: b 4-27-1753 d 4-12-1837 m (1)Elizabeth Hicks (2)Mary — Capt PS MA ★
Elisha: b 8-14-1721 d 6-13-1801 m Hannah — Pvt NJ
Ellis: b 3-26-1751 d 2-13-1831 m Sarah Munday Pvt NJ
Ezekiel, Sr.: b 2-23-1730 d 8-5-1796 m (1)Anna Stark (2)Mrs Euphemia (Van Why) Longstreet Pvt NJ
Ezekiel, Jr.: b 11-25-1754 d 8-21-1835 m Eleanor Pike Ens NJ ★
Ezekiel: b 12-6-1755 d 4-2-1814 m (1)Charlotte Freeman (2)Meribah Manning Pvt NJ
Frederick: b a. 1747 d 8-6-1777 m Elizabeth — Pvt NY
Hartwell: b c. 1755-60 d 1797 m (1)Jane Hicks (2)Mary Auld Pvt SC
Isaac: b 1-12-1742 d 1794 m (1)Joannah Coe (2)Mary Cooper Pvt NJ
Isaac: b 1740 d 10-23-1825 m (1)Ann Preston (2)Abigail Dicks Capt PS PA
Jabez, Jr.: b 4-26-1737 d 2-24-1824 m Persis Stewart Sgt MA
Jacob: b c. 1753/4 d 8-19-1836 m Eunice — Pvt NJ
James: b 1750 d 1798 m Pricilla — Sgt MD
James: b 1748 d 7-18-1821 m Mary Woodbridge Sgt MA
James: b 1749 d 7- -1816 m Mary Neal CS NH
James: b 5-2-1716 d p. 4- -1794 m Hope Bloomfield PS NJ
James, Sr.: b c. 1730 d 1797 m Hannah — PS VA
Jedediah: b 12-15-1760 d p. 1820 m Experience — Fif Grd MA ★
John: b 1-12-1757 d 9-12-1830 m Diantha Wells Pvt CT
John: b 4-2-1744 d p. 1811 m Elizabeth Pike Pvt MA
John: b c. 1730 d 7-23-1807 m Hannah Dana PS MA
John: b c. 1749 d c. 1810 m Abia — Sol NH
John: b 6-14-1719 d 4-29-1777 m (1)Joanna — (2)Sarah Bayles MM NJ
John: b a. 1731 d p. 1783 m Susanna Jarman Pvt NJ
John: b 2-9-1752 d 8-17-1825 m Jane Lytle PS PA
John: b c. 1752 d 11- -1828 m Jane Sally Pvt VA ★
Jonathan: b 1750 d 12-8-1826 m Deborah Schofield Cpl CT
Jonathan: b 2-14-1722 d 9-13-1792 m Phebe Bowen PS NJ
Joseph: b 12-5-1756 d 10-29-1843 m Lydia Knight Pvt Gnr MA ★
Joseph: b 11-28-1750 d 1-8-1808 m Elizabeth Brown Sgt NH
Levi: b 1730 d 1786 m Phoebe — Pvt NJ
Lewis: b 10-16-1761 d p. 9-4-1837 m Hanah — Pvt NJ ★
Mark: b c. 1740 d 12-2-1794 m Elizabeth Walker Sgt PS NH
Micajah: b 9-24-1729 d 1-27-1804 m Sarah Barnes Pvt MA
Moses: b 2-27-1747 d 2-28-1823 m Sarah — Pvt MA
Moses: b 12-3-1725 d 12-6-1796 m Sarah Converse Pvt MA
Moses, Jr.: b 1-30-1751 d p. 1788 m Lucy Cutting Pvt MA
Moses: b 3-17-1757 d 7-12-1815 m Mary Tyler Pvt MA
Moses: b 9-11-1747 d p. 10-6-1827 m (1) X (2)Abigail — Sol PS VA
Nathan: b 1-29-1744/5 d 6-24-1820 m Desire Tracy Sol CT
Nathan: b 1752 d 1-16-1822 m (1)Mary Christian Leake (2)Mary (Bondurant) Maxey PS VA
Nathaniel: b 1728 d 9-17-1806 m (1)Elizabeth Worth (2)Sarah — PS CS NJ
Noah: b 11-15-1762 d p. 1787 m Abigail Hahn Pvt NJ
Onesiphorus: b 4-7-1733 d 6-2-1809 m Anna Goodale MM PS MA
Perley: b 9-30-1732 d 4-11-1781 m (1)Sarah Mitchell (2)Lois Stevens PS MA
Phineas: b 6-25-1739 d 1-6-1790 m Sarah Barrett Pvt NJ
Phineas: b 1751 d 8-5-1789 m Hannah Rolfe Pvt NJ
Richard: b 1-23-1726 d 1780 m Martha Mitchell PS MA
Richard: b 5-12-1757 d 12-17-1831 m Susanna Sargeant Capt PS NH
Robert: b 7-4-1754 d 2-4-1846 m Johanna Margaret Wilson Pvt NJ ★
Robert: b 4-12-1765 d 4-30-1833 m Sarah Ashton Pvt NY W ★
Samuel: b a. 1747 d 1795 m Elizabeth Nesbitt Pvt PS CT
Samuel: b 1747 d 12-20-1823 m Mary Ann Drury Cpl MA
Samuel, Jr.: b 11-29-1742 d 4-6-1811 m Sarah Chase Pvt MA
Silas: b 12-29-1749 d 12-29-1826 m Mary Bryan MM NJ
Stephen: b 12-1-1744 d p. 1782 m Sarah Gray PS NH
Thomas: b 8-31-1755 d 1-28-1844 m Mary — Pvt Arfr NY ★
Thomas: b c. 1723 d 1781 m Frances Malone Sol SC
Timothy: b 10-15-1758 d 9-29-1814 m Elizabeth Hazen Pvt CT
William: b 4-9-1720 d p. 4-9-1803 m Susanah Mayes Capt GA
William: b 2-28-1724 d 12-31-1814 m Rachel Barns Lt MA
William: b 10-28-1753 d 6-5-1827 m Mary Runnels Pvt NH
William: b 1720 d 1784/5 m Mary Kean Pvt PA

AYLETT,
William: b 9-21-1743 d 5-20-1780 m Mary Macon Col PS VA

AYLSWORTH, (includes AILSWORTH, AYLESWORTH)
Abel: b 12-18-1745 d 5-14-1830 m Freelove Mattison Ens VT
Abraham: b 8-10-1755 d 5-8-1825 m (1)Catherine Crydenwise (2)Mrs. Mary Henry Pvt NY
Benjamin: b 2-5-1734 d 1810 m (1)Mary Parker (2)Molly Eldredge Capt NY
David: b 4-18-1752 d 1834 m Ruth Parker Pvt RI ★
George: b 1758 d 12-21-1841 m Susannah Harlow Pvt VA W ★

Jeremiah: b 1739 d 1-21-1827 m (1)Phoebe Allen Ens RI
Philip, Sr.: b c. 1710 d p. 11-14-1789 m Elizabeth — PS RI
Richard: b 2-5-1733/4 d p. 1790 m Lydia Straight Cpl RI

AYRAULT,
James: b 9-17-1730 d 6-21-1813 m Abigail Kilborn Pvt MA
Peter, Sr.: b 12-4-1702/3 d 10-28-1799 m Mary (Dodd) Francis PS CT

AYTON,
Henry: b 1755 d 1803 m (1)Ann Gaither (2)Eleanor Beale 1Lt MD

AZAM,
Jean Jacques: b 2-2-1756 d 9-5-1801 m Marie Reine Dolle Gnr FrA

BABB, (includes BAPP)
Benjamin: b 1764 d a. 1837 m Rachel Clark Pvt MA
Blanche (Mercer): b 6-14-1742 d 9-1-1821 m Thomas Babb PS VA
John: b c. 1755 d 1827 m Media Brown Pvt NC
John: b 4-20-1727 d 3-14-1811 m Anna Maria Riel Tms PA
Mary: b. 1737 d a. 12-30-1818 m Joseph Babb PS SC
Moses: b 1753 d 1837 m Meribah Locke Pvt NH ★
Peter: b c. 1735 d 1820 m Mary — Capt VA
Peter: b 3-14-1764 d 6-24-1842 m Thankful Bangs Pvt MA
Samson: b c. 1740 d 10-28-1814 m Anne Way Pvt PA
Seth: b 10-2-1760 d 8-26-1836 m Mary McClellan Pvt VA ★
Thomas: b 11-16-1729 d 11-26-1788 m Sarah Bishop Pvt DE
Thomas: b 6-14-1740 d p. 10-31-1779 m Blanch Mercer PS VA
William: b 1759 d a. 1827 m Elizabeth Yates Pvt NC
William: b 1742 d p. 1783 m Elizabeth Conant Cpl MA
William A: b 12-12-1745 d c. 1812 m Jemima — Lt PS NH

BABBIDGE, (includes BABIDGE)
Christopher: b 1-24-1741 d 8-26-1792 m (2)Martha Babbidge Ens Gnr Mstr MA
Courtney: b — d 10-9-1834 m Catherine Staples Pvt MA
John: b 1757 d 1851 m Sarah Becket Slr MA
Stephen: b 1759 d 1841 m (1)Hannah Staples (2)Mrs. Ann (Staples) Saunders (3)Mrs. (Sellers) Dow Pvt MA

BABBITT,
Abel: b 9-31-1740 d 1824 m (1)Elizabeth Hathaway (2)Patience — Capt MA
Asa: b 4-23-1756 d 2-23-1838 m Ruth Harriman Pvt MA
Daniel: b 1-7-1752 d 1-4-1817 m Sarah Beach Arfr NJ
Ebenezer: b 12-24-1740 d 11-7-1803 m Mary Ingell Sgt MA
Elijah: b 1750 d 11-1-1805 m Amey Tefft Lt Mrnr RI
Elkanah: b 8-14-1737 d 1815 m (1)Hannah Briggs (2)Mrs. Abigail Palmer Pvt MA
Elkanah: b 12-5-1737 d 2-9-1807 m Rachael — Pvt MA
Elkanah: b 1750 d 8- -1823 m X Pvt NJ
Gideon: b 1756 d 10-6-1832 m (1)Bathsheba Tobey (2)Mrs. Phoebe Nichols Pvt MA
Ira: b 1764 d 11-29-1833 m Sabra Vincent Fif MA ★
Isaac: b 2-6-1763 d 2-19-1844 m Miriam Hathaway Pvt MA ★
John: b c. 1750 d 8-30-1825 m Mercy Briggs Sgt MA
John: b 8-2-1733 d 3-8-1816 m (1)Elizabeth Dean (2)Lydia Myrick Pvt MA
Joy: b 9-26-1767 d 11-4-1849 m Esther Cook Pvt MA ★
Levi: b 8-31-1757 d 5-8-1795 m Betty (Babbitt) Pvt MA
Nathan: b 10-8-1730 d 8-31-1794 m Abigail Cobb Pvt MA
Nathan: b 3-6-1755 d 4- -1826 m Anna Newcomb SgnMte RI
Nathaniel: b 9-13-1728/9 d p. 1790 m (1)Mary Crane (2)Mary Mendall Pvt MA
Samuel: b 10-7-1760 d 3-18-1824 m Mary Haywood Sol MA
Snellum: b 12-11-1760 d 4-6-1854 m Betty Blanchard Pvt MA
Stephen: b 9-18-1764 d 1803 m Mary Beach Pvt NJ
Thomas: b 11-27-1761 d 2-7-1813 m Mary (Babson) Jackson Pvt MA
Uri: b 3-3-1760 d 1-5-1844 m Lydia Morrell Harris Pvt MA ★
William: b 2-9-1756 d 10-29-1831 m Rhoda Miller Pvt CT
Ziba: b 4-6-1764 d 2-2-1803 m Bathsheba Luscombe Pvt MA

BABCOCK, (includes BADCOCK)
Amos: b 1-21-1749 d — m Peggy Peabody Pvt PS NH
Amos: b — d 1804/5 m Zerviah — Cpl NY
Andrew: b 1-1-1731 d 1-16-1801 m Susanna White PS NY
Benjamin: b 6-17-1726 d 1809 m (1)Virtue Eastland (2)Ruth Potter PS MA
Charles: b c. 1757 d 1829 m Catherine Smith Pvt CT
Christopher: b 9-12-1734 d 3-15-1815 m Mehitable Chalker CS RI
Christopher A: b 1-26-1757 d 11-2-1780 m Mary Benedict SgnMte C1
Daniel: b 4-7-1761/2 d 8-11-1818 m (1)Jerusha Wales (2)Charlotte Lord Pvt CT
Daniel: b 8-31-1762 d 9-18-1846 m Content Potter Pvt RI
Daniel: b 1748 d 1850 m Sarah Ainsworth Sgt VT
David: b 2-2-1745 d 11-6-1820 m Mary Hinckley Pvt CT
Ebenezer: b 7-20-1758 d 3-24-1815 m Rhoda Woodard Drm MA

Elias: b 12-14-1757 d 5-12-1839 m Huldah Kinney Cpl MA ★
Elihu: b — d 1-24-1823 m Elizabeth Preston Pvt CT
Elijah: b 8-15-1739 d 9-12-1778 m (1)Sarah Brown Capt CT
Elkanah: b 8-21-1738 d 6-21-1821 m Esther Crandall Capt RI
George: b 7-27-1749 d 3-18-1816 m Susannah Sheldon Cpl MA
George: b 12-29-1727 d 10-22-1777 m Mehitable Wheeler Sgt RI
George: b 1760-3 d 8-22-1850 m (1)Glory — (2)Content Vowers Pvt MM RI & CT ★
Gershom: b 11-9-1752 d 2-17-1815 m Chloe Davis Sgt NY
Gideon: b 7-21-1744 d p. 1802 m Mary Cheeseborough Lt RI
Gideon: b 4-3-1757 d 3-7-1807 m Hannah Brown Sol RI
Henry: b 4-26-1736 d 10-7-1800 m Mary Stanton Col RI
Henry: b 6-23-1757 d p. 11-19-1833 m Prudence Gavitt Pvt RI ★
Hezekiah: b 5-30-1739 d p. 1790 m Martha Hoxsie PS RI
Ichabod, Sr.: b 12-12-1731 d 8-22-1801 m Esther Stanton Cnt RI
Ichabod, Jr.: b 1-15-1758 d 1852 m Dorcas Hoxey Pvt CT ★
Isaac: b 1-16-1754 d 8-31-1811 m Amy Gavitt Pvt RI ★
Isaiah, Sr.: b 1-29-1719 d 10-5-1814 m Elizabeth Plumb PS CT
Ithamar: b 2-8-1755 d 4-25-1803 m Mary Haley Pvt MA
James, Jr.: b 11-1-1734 d 9- -1781 m (1)Sarah Stanton (2)Joanna McDowell LCol CS RI
Jethro: b 8-25-1750 d 10-5-1798 m Phoebe Brownell 2Lt MA
John: b 8-26-1746 d 1-21-1815 m Lydia Woodward Pvt CT
John: b 11-13-1752 d p. 6-24-1800 m Eunice Rockwell Pvt MA
John: b 6-21-1760 d   1812 m Anna — Sol MA
John Prentice: b 10-14-1750 d 9-6-1781 m Ann Gavitt Sol CT
Jonas: b 5-14-1764 d 12-27-1847 m (1)Betsey Parker (2)Elizabeth Chester Sgt MA
Jonas: b 12-22-1748 d 8-24-1838 m Miriam Hudson Cpl MA
Jonathan: b 11-19-1735 d p. 1775 m Susanna Perry PS MA
Jonathan: b 12-8-1762 d 5-16-1842 m Rebecca Cutler Pvt NY
Jonathan: b 6-5-1764 d 2-10-1849 m Selinda Hanks Pvt NY
Jonathan: b 1765 d 1852 m X Pvt RI ★
Joseph: b 10-18-1726 d 1-24-1796 m Anna Harris Pvt CT
Joseph: b 7-14-1746 d 5-28-1813 m Hannah Howe Maj MA
Joseph: b 12-20-1757 d 1784 m Phoebe Mackey Pvt NJ
Joseph: b 2-3-1735/6 d 1804 m (1)Hannah Champlin (2)Hannah Ross Pvt RI
Joshua: b 6-5-1743 d 10-1-1810 m Elizabeth Palmer CS CT
Joshua: b 5-7-1707 d 4-1-1783 m (1)Hannah Stanton (2)Ann Maxson MGen CS RI
Malachi: b 9-22-1729 d 7-7-1806 m Mary Holbrook Pvt MA
Nathan: b 5-15-1716 d 4-25-1803 m Susanna Tucker Pvt MA
Nathan: b 11-25-1726 d 1-24-1804 m (1)Deborah Stafford (2)Elizabeth Brown (3)Nancy Lewis (4)Dorcas Babcock PS RI
Nathaniel, Jr.: b 1-24-1735 d 4-19-1813 m Mary Larrison Sgt CT
Nathaniel: b 1-24-1734/5 d 4-27-1793 m Irena Kingsley Sgt CT
Nathaniel: b 3-26-1765 d 7-4-1839 m Rachel Rodgers Pvt CT ★
Oliver: b 1741 d 1-25-1777 m Mercy Kinney Lt CT
Oliver, Sr.: b 9-16-1722 d 2-24-1806 m Patience Pendleton Pvt RI
Oliver: b 7-27-1738 d 2-13-1784 m Sylvia Belcher CS PS RI
Paul: b 3-30-1760 d 4-21-1845 m Charlotte Crandall Pvt Grd RI ★
Peleg: b 10-4-1748 d 11-12-1834 m (1)Lucy Maxson (2)Ruth Maxson (3)Mrs Phebe Denison CS MA
Reuben: b 3-2-1758 d 2-24-1849 m Hannah Hendricks Sgt CT ★
Reuben: b 1755 d 1-19-1844 m Hannah Goddard Pvt MA
Robert: b 7-5-1732 d 12-19-1819 m Jedidah Turner Smn CT
Roger: b 6-10-1758 d 5-11-1836 m Thankful — Pvt CT ★
Samuel: b 12-2-1761 d 9-26-1836 m Sylvinia Kinnie Pvt MA W ★
Samuel: b 2-18-1760 d 11-23-1813 m Elizabeth Swift Sol MA
Samuel: b 9-4-1747 d 1-27-1828 m Rachel Conklin Pvt RI
Sherman: b 10-19-1762 d c. 1845 m Electa Rich Pvt CT
Simeon: b 5-31-1745 d 9-21-1806 m Mary Percy Sgt RI
Solomon: b 12-27-1751 d 6-3-1831 m Ruth Woodbury Pvt NH
Timothy: b 10-12-1724 d 12-3-1795 m (1)Lois Billings (2)Thankful Read Pvt CT
William: b 5-22-1743 d 12-20-1816 m Sarah Tucker Capt MA
William Avery: b 3-31-1747 d 9-21-1829 m Lucretia Davis Sgt NY

BABENMEYER,
Frederick: b c. 1712 d 1782 m (1)Elizabeth — (2)Catherine — PS PA

BABER,
Edward: b c. 1756 d 1-31-1832 m Nancy Pleasant Sol VA
James: b 6-2-1762 d 7-17-1836 m Mildred Arthur Pvt VA ★
James: b 1742 d 10-6-1804 m Elizabeth — PS VA
Obadiah: b c. 1760 d 1-28-1822 m Hannah Martin Pvt VA
Robert: b c. 1725 d p. 1785 m Jane — PS VA
Thomas: b 1756/7 d p. 1800 m Sallie Oglesby Sgt VA
William: b 1758-60 d 1830 m Susannah Southern PS VA

BABSON,
Samuel: b 3-22-1740/41 d 10-8-1805 m Lydia Plummer N Capt MA
William: b 9-5-1749 d 12-30-1831 m Anne Rogers NLt MA

BACHE,
Richard: b 9-12-1737 d 7-29-1811 m Sarah Franklin PS PA
Sarah Franklin: b 9-11-1744 d 10-5-1808 m Richard Bache PS PA

BACHER,
Jacob: b a. 1762 d 1832-8 m Maria Barbara — Pvt PA
Jacob: b 1760 d 1846 m (2)Catherine — Pvt PA ★

BACHLOTT,
John: b 1760 d 6-6-1833 m Mary Conard Sol VA

BACHMAN, see BOWMAN

BACK,
Elisha: b 1760 d 1843 m Garusha — Pvt CT ★
John: b 6- -1760 d 4-14-1843 m Sarah — Pvt VA ★
Judah: b 7-10-1737 d 2-12-1821 m Priscilla Slate or Gates Lt CT
Lyman: b 4-6-1762 d 7-20-1842 m Eunice Bennett Pvt CT ★

BACKENSTOE, (includes BACISTOE, BACKESTOE)
John: b c. 1730 d p. 1790 m Magdalena — Pvt Lt PA

BACKUS, (includes BACKHOUSE, BACKKESS, BAKUS & BOCKUS)
Asa: b 5-3-1736 d 7-23-1788 m Esther Parkhurst Cpl CT
Benjamin: b 11-15-1735 d 4-18-1795 m Lydia Fish Pvt MA
Ebenezer: b 8-17-1747 d c. 1786 m Elizabeth Fitch PS NS CT
Ebenezer: b 3-21-1740 d 6- -1812 m Mercy Edwards PS Maj CT
Ebenezer: b 1-10-1743/4 d 1-28-1828 m (1)Elizabeth Waterman (2)Phebe Calkins (3)Elizabeth (Talcott) Crocker Pvt CT
Electus Mallory: b 10-27-1765 d 6-7-1813 m Sabra Judson Fif CT
Elijah: b 7-23-1755 d p. 1800 m Triphena Cross Pvt CT
Elijah: b 3-14-1726 d 9-4-1798 m (1)Lucy Griswold (2)Margaret Grant Tracy Capt CT
Elisha: b 1752 d 3-21-1801 m Betsy Johnson Vol CT
Ichabod: b 6- -1750 d 11-5-1827 m Deliverance Hamlin Pvt MA
Isaac: b 1-9-1724 d 11-20-1806 m Susanna Mason PS MA
Jacob: b c. 1762 d 7-4-1825 m Juda Murray Pvt NY
John: b 8-25-1747 d 2-11-1842 m (1)Jerusha Baker (2)Mrs Sally Dodge Sgt MA & NY ★
Joseph: b 9-18-1748 d 4-20-1830 m Oliva Parks PS Sol NY
Ozias: b 1762 d 5-27-1810 m Elizabeth Abell Pvt CT
Samuel: b 8-20-1764 d 7-20-1854 m Abigail — Pvt CT ★
Seth: b 6- -1741 d 3-21-1813 m Mary De Lapp CS MA
Solomon: b 12-11-1752 d 8-17-1807 m Mercy Hyde Pvt MA
Stephen: b 11-27-1759 d 8-31-1848 m Polly Shepherd Fif NS CT ★
Timothy: b 6-9-1754 d p. 1787 m Ruby Tracy Capt CT

BACON,
Abner: b 5-3-1758/9 d 8-21-1832 m (1)Eve Lewis (2)Dosha Kirby (3)Hannah Merriman Pvt MA
Andrew, Jr.: b 1731 d 5-25-1805 m Anna Moore Grd CT
Andrew: b 12-25-1736/7 d 12-27-1834 m Anna Simkins Pvt NJ ★
Benjamin: b 12-17-1726 d 7-14-1807 m Deborah Adams Capt CT
Benjamin: b 12-3-1737 d p. 1781 m Miriam Howlet PS CT
Benjamin: b 7-6-1741 d 1-19-1828 m Esther Davis Pvt MA
Daniel: b 12-1-1740 d 1776 m Mary Abernathy Pvt CT
Darius: b 8-29-1745 d 8-11-1815 m Sarah Sheffield Pvt CT
David: b 6-2-1752 d 6-25-1810 m Lucretia Simonds Pvt MA
David: b 8-24-1754 d 11-30-1849 m Abigail Sampson Pvt MA
David: b 10-26-1766 d 11-12-1831 m Hannah Tarbox Pvt NY
David: b 1745 d 1-18-1777 m (1)Elizabeth Ensworth (2)Freelove Carpenter Lt RI
Ebenezer, Jr.: b 9-2-1759 d 3-13-1817 m (1)Sarah Bement (2)Jane Berry Lewis Pvt CT
Ebenezer: b c. 1763 d 9- -1838 m (1)Eunice Hough ( )Polly Chandler Sgt CT ★
Ebenezer: b 2-2-1749 d 7-4-1825 m (1)Martha Dickenson (2)Sarah Baldwin Fowler Pvt CT
Ebenezer: b 9- -1756 d 12-31-1815 m (1)Eleanor Gay (2)Catey Gay Cpl MA
Ebenezer: b 10-12-1752 d 9-5-1817 m Sophia Dillingham Smn ME
Ebenezer: b 9-15-1736 d 2-12/8-2-1798 m Abigail (Farwell) Richardson PS MA
Edmund: b 6-5-1757 d 9-27-1828 m Tamma Durkee Pvt VT MA ★
Edward: b 1714/15 d 3-16-1783 m (1)Patience Marsten (2)Rachel Doane PS MA
Elias: b 2-6-1742 d 7-20-1828 m Beriah Ware 2Lt MA
Elijah: b 4-7-1736 d p. 3-3-1802 m Sarah Perry Pvt MA
Elijah: b 4-9-1760 d 12-10-1854 m Ruth Brockway Fif MA ★
George: b 2-5-1757 d 7-14-1834 m Hepzibah — Pvt MA
Hezekiah: b 2-8-1764 d 1-3-1799 m Mehitable Morse Pvt MA
Isaac: b 1-10-1754 d 1-24-1830 m Abigal Barnes Pvt PA
Jacob: b 11-17-1754 d 6-21-1844 m (1)Sarah Johnson (2)Martha Clark Pvt & NS CT ★
James: b 10-1-1733 d p. 1780 m Martha Jewell Sgt MA
Jarib: b 3-27-1749 d 4-9-1833 m Mary Jones Cpl MA
Jeremiah, Sr.: b 8-24-1729 d 9-5-1795 m Anna (Bullard) Whiting Sgt MA
Jeremiah, Jr.: b 8-30-1754 d 5-2-1816 m (1)Betsy Davis (2)Eunice Davis Sgt MA
John: b 11-20-1733 d 1785 m Obedience Hobson Capt GA
John: b 10-19-1721 d 4-19-1775 m Abigail Sawin Lt MA
John: b 1722 d 1-8-1797 m Susannah Shed Pvt MA
John: b 8-28-1760 d 9-12-1828 m Elizabeth Balch Adams Sol MA W ★
John: bpt 8-4-1751 d 3-22-1813 m Molly Bugbee Sgt PS CT VT
Jonathan, Sr.: b 1732 d 6-28-1815 m Martha Wood PS MA
Jonathan, Jr.: b 4-30-1759 d 10-11-1845 m Mary Adams Cpl MA ★
Jonathan: b 4-9-1760 d 2-18-1844 m Submit Bacon Pvt MA

Joseph, Jr.: b 10-26-1761 d 12- -1794 m Eleanor Loomis Pvt CT
Joseph: b c. 1747 d 11-27-1808 m Abigail Cole Capt MA
Joseph: b 5-24-1762 d 6-3-1852 m Lucy Conant Pvt MA ★
Josiah: b 10-18-1756 d 11-1-1840 m Abigail — Sgt CT ★
Josiah, Sr.: b 2-11-1719 d 6-17-1775 m Abigail Holden Sgt MA
Josiah, Jr.: b 7-11-1753 d 1841 m Mary Tlieston Pvt CL MA ★
Lyddall: b c. 1745 d p. 1785 m Anne Apperson Capt VA
Michael: b a. 1757 d 1818-24 m Isabella Bourland CS TN
Nathaniel: b 2-16-1706 d 1792 m (1)Esther Hubbard (2)Anne Harrison PS CT
Nathaniel, Jr.: b c. 1757 d 11-22-1843 m Betty Dyer Pvt MA
Nehemiah: b 9-6-1736 d 1832 m Ruth Adams Pvt CT ★
Oliver: b 10-19-1724 d 3-1-1803 m Sarah Hawes Pvt MA
Oliver: b 1740 d 5-25-1794 m Sarah Reed Drm MA
Oliver: b 10-28-1755 d 3-25-1835 m Rebecca Cummings Jewett 1Lt NH
Phineas: b 10-19-1744 d 2-20-1816 m Sarah Atkins Pvt PS CT
Richard: b 2-7-1757 d 11-2-1822 m Anna Fosdick Sgt CT
Richard: b 1727 d 1810 m Anna Hawes Pvt MA
Rufus: b 11-12-1758 d 9-23-1820 m Ellen Edwards Pvt Fif MA
Samuel: b 7-21-1721 d 2- -1786 m Eunice (Bacon) Pvt MA
Seth: b 11-24-1736 d 11-24-1822 m Abigail Whiting 1Lt MA
Silas: b 9-11-1758 d 7-31-1835 m Molly Draper Pvt MA ★
Simeon: b a. 1733 d 11-1-1778 m Esther Davis Pvt & NS MA
Solomon: b 9-13-1751 d 4-3-1836 m Margaret Forbes Pvt MA
Thomas: b 8-23-1726 d p. 1800 m Lydia Pond Capt MA
Thomas: b 10-23-1716 d p. 1785 m Desire Hallet Pvt MA
Thomas: b 1745-50 d 1812 m (1)Catherine Winn (2)Martha Wheeler Lt GA
Thomas: b 9-13-1721 d p. 1782 m Elizabeth Ditson Pvt MA
Thompson: b 3-5-1760 d 12-4-1833 m Martha Hosmer Sol MA ★
Timothy: b 4-12-1753 d 7- -1834 m Sybil Parker Pvt MA
Timothy: b 1762 d 10-24-1849 m Mary Irish Pvt MA ★
William: b 1758 d 11-4-1838 m Bathsheba Cook Pvt MM CT ★
William, Jr.: b 1745 d 2-17-1799 m Sarah Sumner PS GA
Winthrop: b 5-31-1760 d 2-8-1812 m Anna — Pvt NY

BACOT,
Samuel: b 3-3-1745 d 1797 m Sarah Margaret Allston 1Lt SC

BADDER,
Nicholas: b 1733 d p. 1-8-1820 m Eve — Pvt VA

BADGER,
Enoch, Jr.: b 7-5-1750 d p. 1811 m (1)Mary Lamphear (2)Susanne Tryon Sol CT
Ezra: b 2-25-1744 d p. 1793 m Hannah Carter Pvt & PS NH
Henry: b 1715 d p. 1790 m (1)Mary Langdon (2)Judith Coggswell (3)Mrs. Eunice Bottom Sgt PS MA
Jeremiah: b 12-13-1742 d p. 1788 m Zeruiah Peake Pvt CT
John: b 12-6-1723 d 3-31-1782 m Abigail — PS CT
Joseph: b 5-9-1751 d 11-6-1842 m Prudence Flint Sgt CT
Joseph: b 2-28-1757 d 4-5-1846 m (1)Lois Noble (2)Abigail Ely Pvt MA
Joseph, Sr.: b 1-11-1722 d 4-4-1803 m Hannah Pearson BGen NH
Joseph, Jr.: b 10-23-1746 d 1-15-1809 m Elizabeth Parsons Capt NH
Joshua: b — d — m Mary Hathaway Cpl NY
Lemuel: b 7-4-1755 d 8-30-1839 m Sabra Smith Sgt MA W ★
Obadiah: b 4-19-1727 d 12-29-1821 m Mary Martin Pvt MA
Stephen: b 4-17-1758 d 4-22-1852 m (1)Betsey Davis (2)Sarah Sawyer Pvt MA

BADGETT, (includes BADGET)
John: b c. 1740-2 d 11- -1810 m Priscilla Parker Pvt NC
Thomas: b 1760 d 1835 m Sarah Miller Pvt VA ★
William: b 7-23-1762 d p. 1832 m Miss Howard Pvt NC ★

BADGLEY,
Anthony: b — d a. 8-4-1804 m Ann Woodruff Tms PS NJ
George: b 1726 d 4-25-1794 m Charity Noe Pvt NJ
Ichabod: b c. 1760 d p. 1803 m Sarah Hathaway Pvt NJ
Jonathan: b 7-1759 d 5-2-1834 m (1)Lydia Scudder (2)Hannah Searing Pvt NJ ★
Robert: b 1726 d 5- -1783 m Rachel Vreeland Pvt NJ

BADLAM, (includes BADLUM)
Samuel: b 12-14-1720 d 11- -1787 m Deborah Ayers Lt MA
Stephen: b 5-7-1751 d 8-24-1815 m Mary (Adams) Maj MA
Stephen: b c. 3-10-1752 d 8-24-1815 m Mary Webb Maj MA

BADMAN,
David: b 1750 d 8-14-1824 m Catherine — Pvt NY

BAER, (includes BAIR, BARR, BEAR)
Abraham: b 9-7-1741 d 3-14-1828 m Catherine Horst Pvt PA
Adam: b 11-17-1740 d 11-28-1828 m (1)Annetje Spaan (2)Mrs. Catharine Fiero Russell Pvt PS NY
Adam: b 1761 d 1833 m Elizabeth Schnaveley Lt PA
Adam: b 9-24-1743 d 3-8-1835 m Catherine Speilman Pvt PA
Andrew: b 2-9-1768 d 6-17-1787 m Mary Showers PS PA
Andrew: b 1-3-1725 d 11-9-1815 m Anna Christine Behr Pvt PA
Daniel: b 1758 d 5-15-1805 m Julia A C John Pvt VA

Henry: b 1758 d 1849 m Elizabeth Shellman Pvt MD
Henry: b c. 1750 d c. 1810 m Atte— Pvt PA
Jacob: b 1745 d 2-24-1810 m Elizabeth Peter Pvt PA
Jacob: b 7-14-1747 d 7-14-1793 m Catherine Snyder Pvt PA
Jacob: b 1748 d 1822 m Elizabeth Amole Pvt PA
Jacob: b 1753 d 9-23-1827 m Eva Ziegler Pvt PA
Jacob: b 1763 d 1-21-1856 m Polly Sevitz Pvt PA
Jacob: b 6-12-1758 d 2-28-1837 m Catherine Roland Pvt PA ★
Jacob: b 1724 d 2-12-1792 m Istana Barbara Muller PS VA
Johannes: b 9-29-1749 d 11-1-1798 m Anna Marie Beistein Pvt PA
John: b 1755 d 4-10-1818 m Mary Thomas PS MD
Martin: b c. 1752 d 1785/6 m Eve—Pvt PA
Melchior: b 1751 d 1792 m Juliann — PS PA

BAGBY,
George: b a. 1751 d 7- -1807 m Miriam — Sol GA
John: b 5-25-1761 d 11-17-1834 m Matilda Davis Sgt VA★
William: b 5-1-1750 d 1806 m Drusilla Semmes Ens VA

BAGENT,
John: b 8-10-1761 d p. 4-26-1824 m Catherine Lewis Pvt VA ★

BAGG, (includes BAGGS)
Aaron: b 9-23-1757 d 8-16-1839 m Sarah Miller Pvt MA
Archibald: b 1753 d p. 1796 m Hannah Ester Dennison Spy GA
Daniel Jr.: b 1757 d 5-29-1829 m Thirza Ingram Pvt MA
John: b c. 1745-50 d 1808 m Eleanor White Pvt SC
Joseph: b 1-6-1740 d 5-28-1826 m Eunice Loomis Lt MA
Judah: b 4-2-1758 d 8-18-1812 m Anna Roberts Cpl MA
Martin: b 1745 d 1824 Olive Wright Sgt MA
Noble: b c. 1745 d 6-16-1814 m Mary — Pvt MA
Oliver: b 1-27-1754 d 11-17-1833 m Tryphena Day Pvt MA ★

BAGGERLY,
Henry: b 1748 d 1-14-1831 m (1)Elizabeth Tyson (2)Mary Bell Pvt MD

BAGGETT, (includes BADGET & BADGETT)
James: b 1744 d 1789 m (1)Ann — (2)Elizabeth — Pvt NC
John: b 1763 d p. 1-25-1792 m Mary Taylor Pvt VA
Joseph: b 1743 d 1789 m Sarah—Pvt NC

BAGLEY,
David: b 10- -1762 d 1- -1841 m Sophia Andrews Pvt NH
Edward: b 1750 d a. 7-29-1837 m Fanny — Pvt NY
Enoch: b 1758 d 1842 m Marian Hoyt Pvt MA
Jonathan: b 1736 d 1819 m Anna Faver Ens PS NH
Jonathan: b 2-13-1717 d 12-28-1780 m Dorothea Wells CS MA
Orlando: b 5-30-1755 d p. 1817 m Dorcas Taylor Pvt NH & MA
Samuel: b 8-29-1742 d 4-25-1805 m Mehitable — Pvt NH
Samuel: b 1754 d 9-12-1841 m (1)Naomi Curtis (2)Prudence Pvt VT ★
Sargent: b 1-8-1750 d p. 1795 m Rebecca Challis Sgt MA
Thomas: b c. 1750 d p. 1792 m Molley Wier Pvt MA
Thomas: b 2-26-1761 d 6-19-1838 m Olive Green Pvt MA & NH ★
Winthrop: b 8-19-1762 d 7-21-1850 m Maria Dudley Pvt NH ★

BAGNALL, (includes BAGNAL, BAGNELL)
Isaac: b 11-11-1760 d 10-14-1819 m Mary Belton Sol SC
Richard: b 5-9-1752 d 3-22-1809 m Bethiah West Lt MA
Robert: b 1750 d 7- -1789 m Mary Rhodes Wgm VA

BAGWELL,
Isaiah: b 9-13-1760 d 10-8-1839 m Christina Newton Pvt VA ★
John: b 1760 d c. 1852 m Chamblee — Pvt NC ★

BAHL,
John Philip: b 3-12-1739 d 3-23-1820 m Catherine Sewitz LCol PA

BAHN,
Adam: b 12-30-1748 d 7-26-1819 m (1)Elizabeth Herbach (2) Mrs. Catharine Morgan Pvt PA

BAIL,
Henry Calvin: b 1756 d 6- -1810 m Sarah Hotchkiss Pvt CT

BAILEY, (includes BAILY, BALEY, BAYLEY & BAYLY)
Aaron: b 4-12-1764 d 12-6-1841 m Hannah Ladd Cpl CT
Abijah: b c. 1722 d 1785 m Sarah Grover Pvt MA
Abijah: b 9-3-1758 d 3-5-1842 m Mary Sawyer Pvt NH ★
Abner: b 1752 d 2-7-1803 m Mrs. Sarah Bates Pvt MA
Abraham: b 1-25-1747 d 5-12-1838 m Ruth Kendall Sgt MA
Abraham: b 9-5-1760 d 8-13-1825 m Rachel Carpenter Dr PA
Abraham: b — d 5-15-1835 m X Pvt VA ★
Adams: b 1722 d 1797 m Sarah Howard PS & CS MA
Adams: b 1-27-1749 d 7-26-1824 m Mary Little Capt MA
Amos: b 1-27-1720 d 6-20-1800 m Sarah Cottle Pvt MA
Amos: b 3-9-1756 d p. 1795 m Zilpah Hardy Pvt NH
Asa: b 5-24-1745 d p. 1791 m Abigail Abbott Pvt NH
Benjamin: bpt 5-17-1747 d 9-11-1822 m Mrs. Mercy Bailey Sgt MA
Benjamin: b 2-23-1713 d 2-14-1790 m Sibella Howe Pvt MA

Benjamin: b 10-16-1747 d 10-21-1830 m (1)Mehitable Johnson (2)Mary Lowell PS MA
Benjamin: b 5-25-1760 d 12-10-1840 m (1)Polly McCauber (2)Mary Smith Drm VT
Benjamin: b 1755 d 1813 m Ann Elizabeth Watkins 1Lt VA
Benoni: b 12-15-1717 d a. 1790 m Elizabeth Witt Pvt MA
Caleb: b 8-9-1760 d 4-23-1828 m Elizabeth Tuells Pvt CT
Caleb: b 12-11-1738 d 5- -1786 m Philippa Peakes Pvt MA
Callum: b 1-1-1749 d 12-30-1842 m Judith Ann Gilliam Pvt VA ★
Carr, Jr.: b c. 1740 d 1825 /6 m (1)— Short (2)Mary — PS VA
Charles: b 8-27-1744 d 5-15-1835 m Abigail Safford Pvt VT NH
Cyrus: b 11-2-1748 d 5-29-1822 m Abigail Weeks Bedell Pvt NH
Daniel: b 3-17-1756 d 3-13-1817 m Susannah Blanchard Pvt MA
Daniel: b 11-28-1759 d 7-3-1826 m Molly Standley Pvt MA
Daniel Sr.: b 3-13-1728 d 1-15-1798 m Rebekah— Sgt NH
Daniel Jr.: b 12-8-1755 d 3-13-1847 m Elizabeth French Pvt NH ★
Daniel: b 9-5-1757 d 5-16-1848 m Mary Tuthill Sgt NY ★
David: b 7- -1758 d 2-22-1839 m Eunice Ward Pvt PS NY ★
David: b 3-21-1754 d p. 1809 m Dorothy Bailey Cpl MA
David Jr.: b 3-18-1717 d 12-23-1803 m Elizabeth Dole PS MA
David: b 1764 d 1844 m Phoebe Hatch Pvt NH
Dudley: b 12-16-1744 d 3-8-1812/13 m Ruhamah Dunster Pvt MA
Ebenezer: b c. 1750 d — m Anne Starr Pvt CT
Ebenezer: b 7-13-1740 d 1807 m Mehitable Eaton Lt PS NH
Ebenezer: b 4-30-1739 d 9- -1815 m Elizabeth Trull PS NH
Edmund: b 9-2-1741 d 2-11-1808 m Abigail West PS ME
Eli: b 4-6-1749 d c. 1797 m Ruth Taylor Pvt PA
Eliakim: b 9-29-1758 d 10-31-1838 m (1)Thankful Brainerd (2)Mary (Spencer) Treadwell Pvt CT ★
Elijah: b 3- -1762 d 8-11-1838 m Sarah Cleveland Pvt CT ★
Elijah: b 10-15-1757 d 3-9-1825 m Susanna Litchfield Pvt MA ★
Eliphalet: b 1747 d 1821 m Abigail Choate Pvt MA
Eliphalet: b 1758 d — m X Sol MA
Elisha: b — d p. 1783 Susanna — Pvt NY
Elisha: b — d 1811 m Pamelia Burnham Pvt VT
Elisha: b 11-20-1763 d 11-30-1841 m Hannah Gay Pvt VA ★
Enoch: b 3-1-1759 d 3-18-1842 m (1)Jerusha Beardsley (2)Elizabeth Rodgers Pvt & Fif CT ★
Ephraim: b 10-1-1746 d 7-2-1825 m (1)Hannah Fowler (2)Lucy Hodges Pvt VT
Esme: b 12-27-1740 d 11-10-1801 m Sinah — Maj MD
Ezekiel: bpt 5-14-1732 d 9-6-1781 m Elizabeth Williams Sgt CT
Ezekiel: b 1-5-1746 d p. 1783 m Lois Brocklebank Sgt MA
Francis: b 9-3-1744 d 11-1-1817 m Eleanor Millar PS PA
George: b 1750-55 d c. 1b26 m Nancy — Pvt MD
Gideon: b 11-17-1751 d 5-10-1806 m Lydia Spencer 2Lt CT
Gilbert: b 9-16-1759 d 11-20-1831 m Sarah Field Pvt NY
Henry: b 11-16-1745 d 5-3-1798 m Margaret Lossee QM Lt NY
Henry: b 9-6-1755 d 4-11-1837 m Agnes Keiser Pvt PA ★
Hudson: b a. 1764 d p. 1784 m Sarah Yeaton Ens ME
Isaac: b 8-8-1729 d 6-7-1812 m Mary Lovejoy Pvt MA
Isaac: b 6-29-1767 d 8-30-1850 m Betsey Johnson Grd VT
Israel: b 1748 d 5- -1833 m Abigail Tilden Sgt MA ★
Israel: b 11-18-1747 d 6-17-1843 m Ruth Fisher Drm MA
Jacob: b a. 1758 d 1829 m X Ens PA
Jacob Jr.: b 10-2-1755 d 6-26-1837 m (1)Ruth Bedell (2)Mary Ladd MM Sct NH
Jacob: b 1741 d 9-19-1797 m Rachel Steele Ens PA
James: b 8-22-1735 d 7-6-1812 m Lucy Gay Grd CT
James: b 1758 d 7-11-1828 m Bathenia Crawford Sgt MA
James: b 11-5-1756 d 8-15-1839 m Dorothy Worcester Pvt MA
James: b 2-11-1721/2 d 1808 m (1)Rachel Berry (2) Mary Kincaid 2Maj PS CS NH
James: b 10-8-1747 d 11-13-1826 m Anna Brown Pvt NY
James: b 1756 d 1847 m — Umphrey Pvt NY ★
James: b 1751 d 1831 m Elizabeth Canady Sol NC
James: b c. 1730 d p. 10-1-1793 m (1)— Boyd (2)Mrs Mary Cook CS PS PA
Jared: b 8-20-1757 d 8-26-1839 m Elizabeth — Cpl CT RI ★
Jeremiah: b 10-19-1758 d p. 1792 m Mary Freeman Sgt CT
Jeremiah: b c. 1740 d p. 1790 m Hannah Parke Smn CT
Jeremiah: b 8-14-1709 d 11-27-1802 m Mercy Burbank PS MA
Jeremiah: b 3-2-1761 d 11- -1798 m Roby Miller Pvt RI W ★
Jeremiah Garland: b c. 1745 d p. 3-25-1791 m Susanna Sydnor 2Lt VA
Jesse: b 5- -1750 d 9-5-1837 m Sarah Thurston Pvt NH W ★
Jesse: b 3-26-1752 d 1836 m Sarah Philbrick Pvt PS NH
Jethro: b 6-21-1741 d p. 1800 m Hannah Davis PS NH
Job: b 2-19-1750 d p. 1833 m Mehitable French Sgt MA
Joel: b 6-20-1746 d 12-1-1813 m Elizabeth Deming Pvt NH
Joel: b 12-16-1732 d 10-29-1797 m Elizabeth Marshall Pvt PA
John: b 1749 d 11- -1815 m Grace— Sol GA
John: b 10-30-1730 d 10-27-1810 m Ruth Randall Col MA
John: b 2-2-1737 d 7-29-1813 m Annie Memory Capt MA
John: b 7-15-1741 d— m Charity Dodge Pvt MA
John: b 7-9-1761 d 4-22-1828 m Mary Huling Smn NY
John: b 20-1765 d 7-26-1839 m (1)Betsey Bailey (2)Hannah Ladd Sct MA
John: b 12-4-1732 d 8-9-1806 m Attie Van Wyck LCol PS NY
John: b 11-29-1753 d 4-12-1824 m Magdalena Coutant Sol NY
John: b 1734 d 1-23-1815 m Ann Brickstock PS NY
John: b c. 1753 d 11-20-1840 m Penelope Joplin Pvt NC ★

BAILEY, contd.

John: b 1- -1763 d 11-22-1853 m (1)Elizabeth Cox (2)Elizabeth — Sol NC
John: b — d p. 10-20-1784 m Jean — Sol NC
John: b 3-23-1734 d 5-23-1789 m Hannah Pennock Pvt PA
John: b 2-12-1747 d 6-26-1806 m Isabella Simpson Pvt PA
John: b c. 1750 d 11-10-1837 m Sarah Butler Pvt PA
John: b a. 1760 d p. 1787 m Mary — Pvt PA
John: b 10-25-1724 d 5-2-1793 m (2)Hannah Clark PS PA
John: b a. 1745 d 7-21-1797 m Madaline Guerry Pvt SC
John: b 5-4-1748 d 7-3-1816 m Priscilla Townsend Capt VA
John: b c. 1740 d p. 10-3-1783 m Judith Brent Capt VA
John: b 1746 d 1817 m Sarah Ann Smith Pvt VA
John: b c. 1761 d p. 1784 m Sarah Tatum Ens VA
John G.: b a. 1744 d 1816/17 m Abigail Little Capt VT
Jonathan: b 9-1-1755 d 5-25-1827 m Sarah Street Pvt CT
Jonathan Jr.: b 3-4-1742 d 1-30-1823 m Mary Ames Pvt MA
Jonathan: b 11-24-1733 d 11-1-1814 m Eunice Houghton Pvt MA
Jonathan: b 6-28-1745 d 2-16-1814 m (1)Phebe Horton (2)Keturah (Conkling) Dunning Capt NY
Jonathan: b 10-11-1756 d 2-5-1821 m (1)Catherine Nichols (2)Ruth Budd Dr. Sgt NY
Joseph: b 5-4-1733 d 9-15-1802 m Jerusha Webster Pvt CT
Joseph: b 1744 d 9-24-1800 m Hannah Street Pvt CT
Joseph: b c. 1720 d. 1790 m Margaret Osborn Pvt MD
Joseph: b 1-21-1750 d 1839 m Abigail Packard Pvt MA ★
Joseph: b 9-15-1766 d p. 1803 m Mary Woodbury Drm NS MA
Joseph: b 11-1-1704 d 9-14-1782 m Elizabeth White PS MA
Joseph: b c. 1754 d p. 1788 m Abigail Walker Pvt NH
Joseph: b 1747 d 4-27-1830 m Rhoda Connor Pvt NY
Joseph: b c. 1760 d p. 1799 m X Sol NY
Joseph: b 1-28-1761 d 6-21-1850 m Eleanor Frum Sol PA ★
Joseph: b 9-1-1756 d 3-29-1841 m Elizabeth Hall Pvt RI ★
Joshua Sr.: b 173l d 9-1-1809 m Annie White Pvt CT
Joshua, Jr.: b bpt 5-6-1764 d 2-2-1852 m Ruth Sears Pvt & Tms CT ★
Joshua Jr.: b 9-29-1749 d 11-4-1827 m Sarah Webb Cpl MA
Joshua: b 5-11-1757 d 3-15-1809 m Sarah Chase Pvt MA
Joshua: b 12-22-1737 d 4-9-1806 m (1)Anna Putney (2)Sarah Celement Capt NH
Joshua Jr.: b 1-9-1763 d 4-8-1844 m Hannah Corey Pvt MA VT ★
Joshua: b 4-20-1747 d 1-26-1826 m Ann Jackson Pvt PA
Joshua: b 6-11-1753 d 7-3-1841 m Anna Fowler Sgt VT ★
Lewis: b 2-12-1754 d 1817 m Mary Barnard Pvt MA
Luther: b 4-11-1762 d 9-4-1839 m Anna Kincaid Pvt VT ★
Mary: b c. 1720 d p. 1782 m Carr Bailey Sr. PS VA
Moses: b 1-16-1744 d 3-14-1842 m Elizabeth Moar 1Lt MA
Moses: b c. 1750 d a. 11-27-1812 m Ann — PS VA
Nathan: b 1735 d 1819 m Sarah Pillsbury Sgt MA
Nathaniel: b 1743 d 2-2-1832 m Sarah Goodwin Pvt MA
Nathaniel: b 12-27-1730 d 12-17-1812 m (1)Tamar White (2)Mrs Deborah Pratt CS MA
Oliver: b 1738 d 10-4-1822 m Hannah Scoville Pvt CT
Paul: b 2-11-1743 d 4-19-1831 m Anna Holmes Pvt MA
Peter: b 2-26-1750 d 9-3-1820 m (1)Frances Winfrey (2)Miss— Precise Smn VA
Pierce: b 5-12-1742 d 10-7-1800 m Mary Payne CS PS VA
Richard: b 5-9-1745 d 1- -1828 m Hannah Burbank Pvt NH
Richard Sr.: b 5-9-1717 d c. 1815 m Rachel Page PS MA
Richard, Jr.: b 7-15-1746 d 6-14-1829 m Mehitable Emerson Sgt CS NH
Richard: b c. 1735 d c. 1811 m Mary — Pvt PA
Richard: b 1708 d 11-21-1780 m Abigail Woodmansee PS RI
Richard: b 1748 d 1818 m Annie Belcher PS VA
Robert: b 7-10-1761 d 4-17-1852 m Elizabeth Dixon Pvt GA NC ★
Robert: b 1706 d 3-15-1798 m Margaret McDill PS PA
Robert: b 11-16-1731 d 3-6-1814 m Phoebe Waite Sgt RI
Robert: b c. 1740 d a. 1820 m Hannah — PS VA
Samuel: b 7-18-1739 d 9-7-1824 m Abigail Gay Pvt CT
Samuel: b 11-25-1709 d 8-1-1796 m Jane Wyatt Fif MA
Samuel: b 5-11-1751-56 d 5-16-1829 m Eleanor Bird Mus MA ★
Samuel: b 11-14-1729 d 6-17-1775 m Hannah Kittredge Pvt MA
Samuel: b 11-3-1745 d 11-5-1824 m Hannah Clark Sol NH
Samuel: b 11-6-1754 d 8-2-1839 m Mary Terry Pvt NH ★
Samuel: b 4-24-1756 d 4-28-1815 m Phebe Reuck Pvt NJ
Samuel: b 3-19-1740 d 9-9-1827 m Ruth Clark Lt NY
Samuel: b 3-30-1759 d 4-7-1820 m (1)Susannah — (2)Hannah Wright Hazelton Pvt NY
Samuel: b 4-25-1750 d 7-12-1806 m Susanna Smith Pvt PA
Samuel: b 4-7-1720 d 8-17-1781 m Augusta Parks Capt VA
Samuel B.: b 1728 d — m Rebecca — Lt CT
Seth: b 12-13-1747 d c. 1810 m Deborah Packard Pvt PS MA
Seth: b 7-5-1739 d 10-12-1796 m (1)Lydia Basstor (2)Alice Neal Pvt MA
Shubael: b 6-6-1740 d 4-5-1824 m Hannah Whitmore Pvt MA W ★
Silas, Jr.: b 7-22-1756 d 10-3-1840 m Lavinia Bartlett Lt MA
Solomon: b 2-11-1755 d 10-12-1835 m Miriam Snow Pvt NH
Stephan: b c. 1760 d p. 1810 m Susanna Lunceford Pvt VA
Stephen: b 9-29-1753 d 2-12-1815 m Sally Crosby Pvt MA
Thaddeus: b 4-17-1737 d 5- -1803 m Lois Morgan Sol CT
Theodorus: b 10-12-1758 d 9-6-1828 m (1)Elizabeth Hoffman (2)Rebecca Tallmadge (3)Martha McWorter Adj NY
Thomas: b 2-14-1746 d 5-25-1795 m Elizabeth Kimball Lt MA

Thomas: b 2-9-1760 d 1840 m Sarah Dixon Pvt PA
Thomas: b 3-1-1715 d 2- -1793 m Mary Bennett PS RI
Thomas: b 4-17-1756 d 2-24-1841 m Mary Meredith Cpl VA
Thomas: b c. 1760 d 1813 m Nancy Gentry Pvt VA
Thomas: b 4- -1757 d 1820 m Elizabeth Ash Pvt VA
Thomas: b 4-8-1761 d p. 11-21-1832 m Rebecca — Pvt MA
Timothy: b 2-9-1749 d 12-6-1780 m Martha Rice Lt MA W ★
Timothy: b 1753 d 1826 m Anna — Pvt CT ★
Timothy: b 1749 d 9-19-1825 m Zeruiah Blodgett Ens NH ★
Timothy: b 2-20-1761 d 4-28-1841 m Thankful Curtis Pvt NY
Ward: b 12-23-1742 d 12-26-1823 m Mary Sargent Lt VT ★
William: b 1757/8 d 4-2-1823 m Rachel Bishop Pvt CT ★
Wiliam: b c. 1750 d p. 2-15-1808 m (2)Mary — Pvt GA NC
William, Jr.: b — d 1854 m Nancy Brewer PS MD
William: b 10-10-1719 d 8-23-1788 m Anna Lowell Pvt MA
William: b 2-13-1747 d 3-12-1836 m Rebecca Hildreth Pvt MA
William: b c. 1747 d 1-17-1781 m Margaret Kile Maj PA
William: b 4-28-1739 d c. 5-29-1813 m (1)Phebe Olin (2)Mary Straight (3)Patience Gorton Pvt RI
William C.: b 1754 d 1832 m Anne — Cpl VA ★
Yancey: b c. 1750 d p. 9-4-1804 m Sarah — PS NC

BAINBRIDGE,

John: b 9-2-1759 d 1826 m Elizabeth Dumont Pvt NJ

BAIRD, (includes BEARD)

Aaron: b 10-14-1733 d 10-4-1817 m Elizabeth — Pvt MA
Abijah: b 2-3-1757 d 7-26-1841 m Hannah Judd Pvt CT ★
Absalom: b 7-16-1755 d 10-27-1805 m Susanna Drm Dr PA
Adam: b 1745 d 11-17-1811 m Mary Adams Capt NC
Asa: b 4-4-1761 d 6-11-1825 m Abigail Birchard Pvt MA ★
Barzilla: b c. 1725 d c. 1805 m Mary Bullman Pvt NJ
Daniel: b 11-13-1742 d 12-9-1819 m Jane Smith Sgt MA
David: b 7-16-1754 d 12-25-1839 m (1)Rebekah Ely (2)Lydia Tapscott Gaston (3)Mary Edwards Capt NJ
David: b 3-4-1760 d 2-20-1837 m Elinor Barkelow Pvt NJ ★
David, Jr.: b 1755 d 1820 m Elizabeth Taylor Pvt GA
Francis: b 4-7-1759 d 6-27-1836 m Margaret Edams Pvt PA ★
James, Jr.: b a. 1760 d p. 1797 m Eleanor Knox Pvt MA
James: b a. 1750 d p. 10-9-1808 m Meney — Capt PS NC
James: b — d p. 1790 m Margaret Brown Pvt PA
John: b 5-15-1755 d 3-19-1834 m Catherine Dubois Capt NJ ★
John: b 5-26-1760 d 4-26-1808 m Mary — Pvt NJ
John: b c. 1763/64 d c. 1804 m Ann Ribble Pvt NJ
John: b 1737 d 1-4-1808 m Hannah — CS NC
John: b c. 1740 d 1812 m Mary — Pvt PA
John: b c. 1750 d p. 1790 m X Pvt PA
John: b 2-13-1760 d 12-24-1843 m Susan Frame Pvt PA ★
Kendall: b 9-16-1765 d 9-24-1828 m Catherine Hunter Pvt MA
Robert: b 12-26-1756 d 10-5-1835 m (1)Elizabeth Reeves (2)Sarah Hannah McClelland Pvt PA ★
Samuel: b 1758 d 6-26-1820 m Rebecca Potts Pvt PA
Thomas: b 2-14-1749 d 10-24-1834 m (1)Esther Kilgore (2)Jane Eliza Johnson Lt PA ★
William: b c. 1730 d 1794 m Margaret O'Riley Wgn NJ
William, Sr.: b 2-24-1704 d 12-17-1793 m Alice Van Cleef PS NJ
William, Jr.: b 12-22-1742 d 10-5-1830 m (1)Hannah Scott (2) Catalina Hoagland Maj NJ
William, Sr.: b 9- -1713 d 9-23-1792 m Tabitha — Tms NJ
William: b a. 1745 d 5-11-1791 m (1) X (2)Mrs Margaret Smith Reynolds PS MD
William, Jr.: b 1753 d 11-26-1813 m Mary Ogden Lt PA
William: b 1-26-1758 d 6-28-1828 m Nancy Moore Pvt PA
William: b 1762 d 6-30-1815 m Margaret Durborow Pvt PA
Zebulon: b 10-13-1720 d 1-28-1804 m Ann Smith PS NJ
Zebulon: b 8-22-1764 d 3- -1827 m Hannah Erwin Wgn NC

BAKE,

John: b 7- -1748 d 10- -1838 m Ellenor Slaught Pvt NJ ★
Peter: b c. 1760 d p. 9-9-1822 m Phebe Titus Pvt NJ

BAKEMAN,

Daniel Frederick: b 9-28-1759 d 4-5-1869 m Susan Brewer Pvt NY ★
John: b 1731 d 10-29-1800 m Christiana Smart PS ME

BAKER, (includes BACKER)

Aaron: b 1726 d 4-23-1802 m Jemima Clark Pvt MA
Aaron: b 1729 d 8- -1812 m Sarah Hayes Pvt PA
Abel: b 1752 d p. 1832 m Pruny Wilcox Pvt CT ★
Abner: b 8-27-1754 d 9-15-1845 m (1)Lois Waters (2)Mrs. Sophia Colyer Pvt MA ★
Abner: b c. 1754 d 6-8-1826 m Hannah Morton Pvt MA ★
Abraham: b 9-27-1748 d 5-28-1822 m Anna Baxter Mus MA
Allen: b 8-14-1748 d 4-7-1814 m Rebecca Porter Pvt MA
Amos: b c. 1760 d p. 1788 m Sarah Stevens SrgnMte CT
Amos: b 4-8-1756 d 7- -1850 m (?)Betsey Weston (?)Amy Prescott — Sgt MA ★
Andrew: b 1749 d 9-24-1815 m Elizabeth Avant Pvt VA
Arnold: b a. 1741 d 1791 m Barbara — Pvt PA
Beal: b 2-9-1756 d 8-31-1842 m Sarah Brown Pvt NC ★

Benajah: b 6-16-1747 d 5-10-1830 m Mary Manchester Sol RI
Benjamin: b 1717 d 12-1-1785 m (1)Susannah Osgood (2)Elizabeth Lax Sol & PS GA
Benjamin: b 1-21-1740 d 7-11-1818 m (1)Anna Parker (2)Abigail Robbins Sgt PA
Benjamin: b 1-15-1753 d 11-11-1830 m Mary George Pvt NH
Benjamin, Jr.: b 3-31-1755 d 2-22-1820 m Elizabeth Merrill Pvt NH
Benjamin: b 5-5-1727 d p. 1782 m Mary Brown PS NH
Benoni: b 1765 d 5-1-1838 m Abigail Snow Smn Pvt MA ★
Bethuel: b 11-28-1735 d 1813-16 m Hannah — Lt MA
Bolin: b 1763 d p. 1812 m Patsy Morris Pvt NC ★
Bradford: b 10-2-1756 d 10- -1834 m X Pvt MA ★
Caleb: b 1734 d 3-10-1824 m (1)Catherine Hadnitt (2)Mrs Catherine Baker Pvt PS VA
Charles: b 4-26-1741 d p. 1790 m Deborah Williamson PS CS MA
Conrad: b 1721 d 1-25-1795 m Catharina Lambert Pvt PA
Conrad, Sr.: b 12-8-1739 d 9-8-1808 m Anna Maria Boyne Pvt PA
Cornelius: b 11-27-1744 d 9-13-1808 m Mary Elliot Lt MA
Cornelius: b 1736 d 1815 m Susannah Lee Pvt NJ
Daniel: b 11-8-1763 d 12-19-1836 m Jerusha Parsons Pvt CT ★
Daniel: b 10-10-1752 d 5-6-1806 m Mary Doggett Sgt MA
Daniel: b 1751 d 12-12-1821 m Deborah Rand Pvt MA
Daniel: b 6-3-1753 d 7⁻10-1814 m Margaret Osborn Ens NJ
Daniel: b 1-6-1733 d 1-30-1805 m Abigail Miller Sol NJ
Daniel: b 10-3-1755 d 9-14-1845 m Hannah Halsey Pvt NJ ★
Daniel: b 1760 d 3-8-1813 m Anna Cummings Pvt VT
David: b 9-7-1756 d 2-9-1803 m Hannah Gookin Cpl MA
David: b 1746 d 10-22-1790 m Jane (Baker) Pvt MA
David: b 1750 d 3- -1833 m X Sol NJ
David: b 8-22-1733 d 10-27-1786 m Mary Conklin PS NY
David: b 6-3-1749 d 9-15-1838 m Dorothy Wiseman Cpl VA ★
Ebenezer: b 1741 d 4-22-1794 m Jemima Annable Pvt MA
Edey: b 10-22-1764 d 11- -1853 m (1)Sarah Campbell (2)Anna — Pvt NY
Edmund: b 1740 d 9-28-1804 m Mary King Capt NY
Edward: b 6-15-1755 d p. 1796 m (1)Hephzibah Fairbanks (2)Polly Fletcher (3)Submit Shurtluff Pvt MA
Elijah: b 5-16-1718 d 10-25-1804 m (1)Thankful Blakesley (2)Ruth — Pvt CT
Elijah: b 7-11-1744 d 5-17-1827 m Mary Whittemore Lt MA
Elijah: b 5-14-1720 d 11-8-1802 m Hannah Puffer Pvt MA
Elijah: b 1730 d 1811 m Rebecca Smith PS MA
Elisha: b 10- -1724 d 5-22-1797 m Phebe Nichols Sol PS MA
Elisha: b 4-5-1763 d p. 7-20-1790 m Mercy Paine Pvt MA
Ely: b 1750 d 3- -1836 m Keturak Baker Pvt MA ★
Enoch: b 1754 d p. 1840 m (1)Anne Caulkins (2)Mary Bailey Sgt CT
Enoch: b 4-30-1751 d 1792 m Huldah Ingham Pvt MA
Ernest: b c. 1732 d c. 1810 m Eva — PS MD
Ezekiel: b 1726 d 8-15-1800 m Elizabeth — Pvt CT
Ezra: b 1- -1762 d 5-19-1841 m (1)Sarah Tucker (2)Eliza Tucker Pvt MA
Ezra: b 8-2-1753 d 12-15-1826 m Dorcas Whitney Cpl MA
Francis, Jr.: b 1-1-1762 d 4-20-1846 m (1)Nancy Davis (2)Mary Magdelina Brandenburg Mil MD
Francis: b 1746 d 7-24-1808 m (1)Elizabeth Kelly (2)Anna Norton Pvt MA
Gardner: b 11-17-1761 d p. 1800 m Mary Wrighton PS NY
George: b 10-14-1759 d 5-13-1841 m Susannah Morris Capt Sct NC ★
George: b 2-6-1762 d 6-27-1844 m Elizabeth Norris Pvt PA
George: b 1730 d p. 3-17-1819 m Polly Brown Pvt VT
George: b c. 1751 d p. 1781 m Patsey Goddin Bbd Matr VA
George Adam: b 7-27-1736 d 12-8-1816 m Ann Katerine Kling Lt PA
Gideon: b 7-3-1738 d 12-20-1830 m Rhoda Crocker Cpl CT
Glover: b 1755 d 2-28-1827 m Mary Ferrell Pvt VA ★
Heman: b 8-4-1741 d 1-24-1821 m Temperance Baker Drm Pvt MA
Heman: b 1718 d 6-27-1805 m Lois Gilbert PS CT
Henry: b 1759 d a. 10- -1802 m (1)Susanna Putnam (2)— Ault Lt MD
Henry, Sr.: b c. 1727 d 5-13-1780 m Phoebe Hedges Sgt NJ
Henry, Jr.: b 5-27-1755 d 6- -1838 m Phoebe Clark Pvt NY
Henry: b 3-23-1750 d 2-7-1831 m Eve Keiffer Pvt PA
Hilary: b 2-21-1746 d 9-25-1798 m Anna Maria Kreider CS Mil PA
Ira: b 9-16-1764 d 4-9-1843 m Mary Burbank Pvt MA
Isaac: b 8-6-1758 d 9- -1849 m Phoebe Waddell Pvt MD
Isaac, Sr.: b 1726 d p. 1-12-1793 m (1)Catherine Choctlethwaite (2)Mary Head Sol VA
Isaiah: b 8-14-1739 d 9-25-1795 m Experience Crowell Pvt MA
Jacob: b c. 1752 d p. 1777 m Deborah Brown PS NY
Jacob: b 6-12-1742 d 9-9-1802 m Rachel Wheldon Pvt MA
Jacob: b 11- -1764 d 5-17-1822 m Hannah Lemon Drm PA
Jacob: b 1748 d 9-21-1821 m Magdalena — Pvt VA
James: b 3-17-1714 d 5-19-1795 m Dorothy Williams Pvt CT
James: b 1742 d 1804 m Elizabeth Foreman Pvt DE
James: b 5-24-1713 d 11-18-1776 m Priscilla Paul Pvt MA
James: b 1-20-1760 d 12-5-1841 m (1)Phoebe Brown (2)Margaret Crawford Pvt NY
James: b 4-28-1765 d 7-26-1840 m Ruth Post Pvt NY
James: b c. 1730 d 6-29-1804 m (1)Sarah Hewlitt (2)Elizabeth — Pvt NC
James: b 1759/60 d 1833 m Sarah Davis Sgt VA

Jeremiah: b 5-3-1747 d 12-23-1825 m Anna Stephens Pvt CT
Jeremiah: b 1743 d 5-16-1813 m (1)Hannah Thackery (2)Rebecca Mauldin Capt MD
Jeremiah: b 5-22-1762 d 9-14-1855 m (1)Fanny Whitney (2)Lucy Newell (3)Abagail Prentiss Pvt MA
Jethro: b c. 1701 d 6- -1777 m Anne Gonsen PS MD
Joel: b 1741 d 7-28-1817 m Sarah Graves PS MA
Joel: b 1765 d 11-5-1839 m Mary Todd Pvt NH ★
John: b 5-12-1729 d 4-12-1819 m (1)Rose Anna — (2)Anna Barbara — Pvt MD
John: b 5-12-1722 d 6-3-1792 m (1)Sarah — (2)Mrs. Mary Jones Lapine Col PS GA
John: b 8-14-1721 d 6-9-1785 m Eunice Pope Col MA
John: b 11-23-1733 d 11-11-1815 m Mary Emerson Capt MA
John: b 8-3-1749 d p. 1795 m Mary Hayden Pvt MA
John: b 5-16-1753 d 9-25-1807 m (1)Mary Flagg (2)Mrs Abigail Chase Sol MA
John, Jr.: b 4-14-1755 d 7-23-1830 m (1)Eunice Goodrich (2)Sarah Brewer (3)Rebecca Culver Pvt MA
John: b 7-16-1761 d 9-23-1842 m (1)Sarah Ann — (2)Marietta Jenkins (3)Clarissa Brewster Pvt MA VT & NY ★
John: b a. 1750 d c. 1830 m Ann Norfleet PM & Col NC
John: b 1747 d 1822 m Patty Harris SrgnMte NC
John: b p. 1716 d p. 1784 m Elizabeth Wilson PS NC
John: b 1730 d 1789 m Martha Weaver PS PA
John: b c. 1755 d p. 1830 m (1)Margaret — (2)Sarah Dunn Lt PA
John: b 6-10-1748 d 1808 m X Pvt PA
John: b c. 1752 d 1-22-1843 m X Pvt PA ★
John: b 6-3-1758 d 12-7-1806 m Ursula White Pvt PA
John: b c. 1740 d p. 9-30-1827 m Elizabeth King Pvt RI
John: b 1762 d 10-7-1835 m (1)Rachel Bandy (2)Mary McCoy (3) Chelly Esom PS & Pvt SC ★
John: b 10-31-1740 d 8- -1788 m Amy Legare Pvt SC
John: b 12-24-1750 d 9-4-1838 m X OrdlSgt VA ★
John: b c. 1740 d 1787 m Elizabeth Sullivan Sol VA
John (Wood): b 7-2-1756 d 9-2-1841 m (1)— White (2)Susannah Pennell Pvt MD
Jonas: b 8-29-1751 d — m Polly — Pvt CT
Jonathan: b 1744 d 3-19-1824 m (1)Keziah Clark (2)Charity Clark Pvt NJ
Jonathan: b 8-2-1756 d 3-28-1822 m Hannah Ball Pvt NJ ★
Jonathan: b 10-31-1734 d p. 1790 m Abigail Pears 2Maj NY
Jonathan: b 11-10-1736 d p. 1800 (1)Mary Papillion Barker (2)Sarah Morris Adj NY
Jonathan: b 1761 d 1807 m Rachel Kershaw Pvt PA
Joseph: b 12-17-1748 d 5-16-1804 m (1)Deborah Avery (2)Lucy De Votion Dr. CT
Joseph: b 1-22-1721/22 d 7-8-1776 m Sarah Wheeler Pvt MA
Joseph: b 1738 d 6-15-1796 m (1)Experience Martin (2)Mehitabel — Pvt MA
Joseph: b 12-13-1752 d 10-24-1840 m (1)Rosanna Mason (2)Mercy Luther Pvt MA
Joseph: b 1754 d 9-5-1826 m Elizabeth Sadler Pvt MA
Joseph: b 5-19-1736 d p. 1790 m Martha Death PS MA
Joseph: b 1744 d 1816 m Dorcas Smith PS ME
Joseph, Sr.: b 12-25-1714 d p. 1790 m (1)Hannah Lovewell (2) Mrs. Morrill PS MA
Joseph, Jr.: b 11-7-1740 d 2-27-1816 m Marion Moore Pvt NH
Joseph, 3rd b 5-29-1745 d 3-14-1827 m Mary Yarnell Pvt PA
Joseph: b 1-1-1719 d 7-17-1799 m Esther Head Pvt PA
Joseph: b c. 1758 d p. 1787 m X Pvt & CS VT
Joshua: b 1752 d 2-18-1836 m Mary Gates Pvt CT
Joshua: b 11-26-1762 d 7-27-1856 m Abigail — Pvt NH NY ★
Joshua: b 3-11-1763 d 4- -1816 m Susannah Lewis PS VA
Judah, Sr.: b 8-19-1705 d 4-14-1794 m Mercy Burgess Pvt MA
Judah: b 1763 d 5-7-1851 m Lydia Chase Pvt NY W ★
Lawrence: b 1745 d 1805 m (1)Anne Jones (2)Anna Maria Burgess Col PS NC
Lewis: b 12-28-1761 d 2-18-1834 m Lois Walker Pvt MA W ★
Lewis: b 1750 d 11-24-1830 m Elizabeth Sayre Pvt NJ
Lovewell: b 9-18-1843 d p. 1784 m Mary Worth Pvt PS NH
Marshall: b 3-5-1707/8 d p. 1776 m Thankful Ward PS MA
Martin: b 7-10-1750 d 7-13-1821 m Phebe Snodgrass Sol VA
Mashack: b 4-27-1733 d 1778-90 m Elizabeth — PS MD
Matthias: b 11-15-1742 d 4-9-1789 m Catherine Edgar PS NJ
Melyn: b 1-10-1760 d 1-20-1826 m Prudence Whitehead Pvt NJ ★
Michael: b a. 1760 d 11-19-1853 m Rosanna — PS PA
Michael, Sr.: b 1720 d 1779 m Mary Gull Pvt PA
Michael: b 1758 d 1834 m Jane Nice Lt PA
Michael: b a. 1750 d 12-6-1803 m Elizabeth Bok Capt VA
Michael M.: b 3-27-1753 d 9-13-1831 m Mrs. Mary McGahe Sgt PA ★
Moses: b 1758 d 8-18-1828 m Rachel Swett Sol Gnr MA
Moses: b 4-8-1738 d 4-6-1802 m Deborah Davis LCol PS NH
Nathan: b 4-14-1760 d 10-20-1836 m Lucy Norton Pvt CT ★
Nathan: b 1742 d 1811 m Margaret Hutchinson Pvt MA
Nathan: b 1758 d 5-4-1819 m Abigail Westcott Pvt MA ★
Nathan: b 1751 d 1803 m (1)Elizabeth Baker (2)Mrs Hannah Jordan Pvt PA
Nathaniel: b 9-23-1742 d p. 1788 m (2)Elizabeth (Woodward) Mills Sgt MA
Nathaniel: b 1755 d 1-17-1812 m Mehitable Hazeltine Pvt NH

BAKER, contd.

Noah: b 1719 d 12-29-1810 m Sarah Burt PS MA
Otis: b 1727 d 10-27-1801 m (1)Lydia Wentworth (2)Tamsen (Chesley) Twombly PS CS NH
Paul: b 2-17-1753 d 10-14-1829 m Elizabeth Pinkham Pvt MA
Peleg: b 1760 d 1830 m Susana — Pvt NY
Peter: b 8-5-1757 d 5-31-1838 m Mary Carpenter Lt Spy NY
Prince: b 7-18-1742 d 3-24-1829 m (1)Experience Gould (2)Thankful Mayhew 2Lt MA
Remember: b 6-26-1737-40 d 8-22-1775 m Desire Hurlburt Capt VT
Reuben: b 1718 d 3-5-1795 m Lydia — Pvt MA
Reuben: b 5-30-1758 d 10-19-1811 m Lydia Mason Pvt MA
Richard: b 1759 d 1806 m Catherine Quick Sol NY
Richard: b c. 1750 d 11-24-1800 m Elizabeth James Pvt PA
Richard Bohun: b 11- -1755 d 11-8-1837 m Harriet Hyrne Capt SC
Rufus: b 11-22-1751 d 9-4-1838 m Sybil — Pvt CT & VT
Salathiel: b c. 1750 d 5—1822 m Leah Evans Sol MD
Samuel: b 9-30-1740 d 5-6-1812 m (1)Lydia Smith (2)Chloe Silsby Sgt CT
Samuel: b 4-25-1742 d p. 1784 m Rhoda Weed Silliman Pvt CT
Samuel: b 7-25-1764 d 3-28-1852 m Esther Gustin Pvt NY CT ★
Samuel: b 8-27-1722 d 5-4-1795 m Susanna Taintor Sgt MA
Samuel: b c. 1732 d 4-9-1801 m (1)Mary Allen (2)Abigail Crocker Cpl MA
Samuel: b 1761 d 8-3-1826 m Mary Mason Pvt MA
Samuel: b 1751 d 6-17-1838 m Patience Jones Sol MA
Samuel: b 1740 d 8-19-1817 m (1)Mrs Sarah Richardson (2)Mrs Sarah Holland Pvt MA
Samuel: b 9-23-1764 d 11-27-1826 m (1)Huldah Green (2)Lucy Garlick Pvt MA
Samuel: b 2-14-1763 d 12-2-1842 m Elizabeth Daniels Pvt NY
Samuel: b 4-5-1733 d 10-5-1786 m (1)Joanna Dayton (2)Abigal Shaw PS NY
Samuel: b 1745 d 7-8-1818 m Mary Beatty Pvt PA
Seth: b 7-14-1735 d 1810 m Abigail Woodruff Pvt CT
Seth: b 5-12-1740 d p. 1790 m Thankful Crowell Capt MA
Seth: b 5-1-1744 d 7-2-1811 m Priscilla Taylor Pvt MA
Sherebiah: b 3-18-1747 d 5- -1823 m Clotilda Daniels Sgt MA
Shubael: b 11-11-1741 d 10-29-1814 m (1)Rebecca Chase (2)Elizabeth Chase 2Lt MA
Simeon: b 8-1-1754 d p. 3-11-1795 m Ruth Young Matr MA
Simeon: b 10-24-1735 d p. 1790 m Elizabeth Ingalls Pvt MA
Solomon: b 5-22-1752 d 11-20-1834 m Sarah Whitney Pvt MA W ★
Stephen, Sr.: b 6-22-1712 d 3-8-1787 m Mrs. Hannah Bacon MM CT
Stephen: b 11-19-1731 d 5- -1812 m Lucy King Pvt MA
Stephen: b c. 1749 d 1789 m Deborah Crossman Pvt RI
Sylvanus, Jr.: b 1760 d 9- -1812 m Phoebe Chase Pvt MA
Sylvanus, Sr.: b 3-10-1734/5 d 1777 m (1)Hannah Burgess (2)Jane Crowell Sgt MA
Sylvanus, Jr.: b 1760 d 9- -1812 m Phoebe Chase Pvt MA
Sylvester: b 6-16-1754 d p. 1840 m Experience — Pvt NC ★
Thaddeus: b 1761 d 8-21-1845 m (1)Phebe Silvester (2)Mrs Mary Watt Warner (Prentiss) Pvt MA
Thomas: b 1740 d 1783 m Mary Burton Lt CT
Thomas: b 10-29-1751 d 1-14 1840 m Mary Carswell Sgt MA ★
Thomas: b 12-31-1756 d 12-6-1842 m Sarah Temple Sgt MA W ★
Thomas: b 1757 d 1-31-1841 m Miriam Allard Sgt NH ★
Thomas, Sr.: b 3-5-1730 d 7-15-1806 m Sarah Hale PS CS NH
Thomas, Jr.: b 7-5-1752/3 d 4-2-1842 m Mrs. Betsey King Abbott PS NH
Thomas: b 7-24-1742 d 11-27-1825 m Joan Conklin Lt PS NY
Thomas: b — d 1798 m Sarah Wood Pvt NY
Thomas: b 4- -1759 d 3-7-1820 m Jane McCutcheon NS PS PA
Thomas: b 1764 d p. 1810 m (1)Ann Elliot (2)Elizabeth — Pvt VA
Thomas Marshall: b 1742 d 11-14-1809 m Susanna Whipple Capt MA
Timothy: b 11-4-1730 d p. 1785 m Mary Dakin Pvt MA
Timothy: b 4-21-1732 d p. 1790 m Keziah Davis Pvt MA
Timothy: b 12-2-1748 d 4-3-1836 m Abigail Kibbe Pvt MA
Timothy: b 1759 d 1844 m (1)Sally Gould Pvt MA
Timothy: b 12-8-1742 d 8- -1794 m Deborah — Pvt NJ
Timothy: b 1750 d 5-10-1812 m Prudence Brooks Pvt VT
Titus: b 6-18-1736 d p. 1790 m Eunice Badger Pvt CT
Wm.: b 1740 d 11- -1776 m Mercy Jewett Pvt CT
Wm.: b 1710 d 1788/89 m Margaret — PS MD
Wm.: b 1755 d 11-12-1827 m (2) Chloe Leland Ens MA ★
Wm.: b 4-6-1746 d 3-26-1815 m Sarah Fletcher Pvt MA
Wm.: b 9-10-1759 d 11-13-1832 m Abigail Low Pvt MA ★
Wm.: b c. 1754 d a. 1804 m X Pvt NC
Wm.: b 1740 d 1815 m Polly Kimbrough Cpl PA
Wm.: b 1760 d p. 1804 m Waitsel Heath Pvt PA
Wm.: b 1739 d 10-9-1823 m Mary Evans Pvt SC
Wm.: b 1753 d 1820 m Tempa Prescott Pvt SC
Wm.: b 9-14-1759 d 3-3-1829 m Barbara Sykes PS SC
Wm.: b 12-17-1764 d 1-30-1838 m Hannah Baker Pvt VA ★
Zachariah: b 1750 d 9-4-1808 m (1)Abigail Merrill (2)Mary Wells Pvt MA
Zebulon: b 1744 d 1806 m Abigail Ann — Sol VT

BALCH,

Amos: b 7-20-1758 d c. 1835 m Ann Patton Sgt NC
Andrew: b 2-27-1706/7 d 6-22-1779 m (1)Bethiah Lovitt (2)Ruth Woodbury PS NH

Barzillia: b 1765 d 2-23-1817 m Ruth Davis Pvt CT
Benjamin: b 2-12-1743 d 5-4-1815 m Joanna O'Brien Chp & Lt MA
Benjamin: b 1747/48 d p. 1800 m (1)Elizabeth Blake (2)Julia Ellis Pvt PS NH
Caleb: b 10-16-1740 d c. 1794 m Elizabeth M. — Pvt NH
Cyrus: b 7-14-1765 d 1805 m Judith Stone Pvt NH
Ebenezer: b 5-14-1723 d 4-28-1808 m (1)Sarah Belden (2)Lois Belden PS CT
Hart: b 11-9-1751 d 2-15-1846 m (1)Priscilla Holt (2)Dorcas Somers Pvt NH
Hezekiah James: b 1746 d 1776 m — Sconnell PS NC
Israel: b 1-26-1751 d 11-4-1798 m Sarah Arnold Pvt CT
Israel: b 4-1-1753 d 2-9-1825 m (1)Hannah Kimball (2)Mrs Mary Fletcher Sgt MA
James: b 12-25-1750 d 1-12-1821 m Susannah Lavinia Garrison PS NC
John: b 9—1759 d 11-10-1845 m Lucy Brown Pvt CT ★
John: b 11—1760 d 5-27-1849 m Barbara Patton Sol NC
John: b 10-12-1735 d 4-30-1808 m (1)Mary — (2)Safrona — Pvt NH
John: b 1-23-1715 d p. 11-27-1790 m Sarah — PS NC
Jonathan Belden: b 11-14-1754 d 2-16-1825 m (1)Hopeful Hurlburt (2)Eleanor Whitman Pvt CT
Joseph: b 2-16-1760 d 12-5-1855 m Mary Watson FifMaj CT ★
Joseph: b 2-10-1738 d 9-1-1826 m Abigail Andebert Capt MA
Nathaniel: b 9-18-1753 d 4- -1795 m Lydia Twombley Pvt PS NH
Robert: b 7-25-1745 d 8-3-1830 m Sarah Dodge Pvt MA
Roger: b 5-26-1755 d 1-6-1842 m Sarah Perley Pvt MA
Samuel: b 6-25-1739 d 2-11-1816 m Susan Aldrich Pvt MA
Stephen Bloomer: b 4-5-1747 d 9-22-1833 m (1)Elizabeth Beall (2)Mrs Elizabeth King (3)Mrs Jane Parrott Capt MD ★
Thomas: b 10-2-1765 d 1-8-1840 m (1)Elizabeth Kingman (2)Judith (Swain) Perkins Mar
Veren: b 5-22-1724 d 1797 m Sarah Taylor Pvt CT
Wm. Goodwin: b c. 1758 d 10-14-1822 m Elizabeth Rodgers PS NC

BALCOM, (includes BALCOME, BALCOMB, BOLKCOM)

Bezaleel: b 1758 d 3-4-1834 m Jemima Morse Cpl MA
Daniel: b 3-4-1739 d p. 1790 m Rebecca Cobb Pvt MA
David: b 1754 d 9-18-1844 m Mary Hayward Pvt MA ★
Henry: b 8-16-1740 d 10-28-1812 m Keziah Stow Pvt VT
John: b 3-8-1752 d 9-6-1838 m Millie Le Sure Pvt MA
Joseph: b 9-24-1728 d 1809 m Mary King PS CT
Joseph: b 4-16-1752 d 11-11-1827 m Catherine Haynes Lt MA
Micah, Jr.: b 1-16-1744/5 d 6-10-1811 m Catherine Harrington Pvt MA W★
Micah: b 7-31-1757 d 7-5-1858 m Betsey Cutler Pvt MA
Nathaniel: b 7- -1754 d 5-21-1834 m Lois McIntire Pvt CT ★
Samuel, Sr.: b 3-10-1727 d 1783 m Susannah Jeperson Pvt MA
Samuel, Jr.: b 11-10-1746 d p. 1784 m Thankful Griffith Sgt MA
Wm.: b 11-3-1734 d 6-4-1801 m Chickering Shepard Lt MA

BALDRIDGE,

Alexander, Sr.: b 1717 d 3-12-1805 m Jane Ramsey PS NC
John: b 9-28-1754 d 10-17-1823 m Isabella Luckey Capt NC W ★
John: b a. 1748 d p. 1785 m Mary McIntyre Pvt VT
Michael: b 5-19-1726 d 5-12-1812 m (1)Mabel Wilson (2)Margaret Rush Pvt PA
Wm.: b 2-26-1761 d 10-26-1830 m (1)Rebecca Agnew (2)Mary Logan Pvt NC

BALDWIN, (includes BAULDIN)

Aaron: b 9-3-1724 d 3-24-1800 m Sarah Frisbee Pvt CT
Aaron: b 12-27-1758 d 3-27-1805 m Sarah Baldwin PS NJ
Aaron: b 8-2-1762 d 3-25-1853 m (1)Mary Crane (2)Mrs Sarah Vanderpool Pvt NJ
Abel: b 1764 d 1813 m Susannah Coffeen Pvt VT
Abiel, Sr.: b 3-26-1730 d 8-11-1802 m Mehetable Johnson QM Cnt CT
Abiel, Jr.: b 8-28-1762 d 4-5-1847 m (1)Eunice Coe (2)Mrs Elizabeth Sanford Pvt CT ★
Amos: b 2-21-1744 d 11-20-1815 m (1)Martha Allen (2)Sally Hicks Sol CT
Amos: b 1742 d c. 1810 m Phoebe Wicks PS NY
Ananias: b 10-3-1764 d 10-21-1850 m Elizabeth Cooley Pvt NJ
Anthony: b 1733 d 1793/4 m Elizabeth Davis Pvt PA
Asa: b 12-12-1721 d 4-23-1811 m Abigail White Maj MA
Asa: b 1-25-1764 d 7-27-1827 m Chloe Underhill Pvt VT
Augustus: b 8-27-1764 d 5-23-1808 m Mrs Rebecca Cocke Pvt CT
Barnabas: b 8-31-1726 d 12-24-1804 m Mary Terrell Lt CT
Barnabas, Sr.: b 1-1-1698/9 d p. 10-25-1782 m Mrs Mehitable Beecher PS CT
Benjamin: b 4-9-1724 d p. 12- -1776 m Sarah Pollard Pvt MA
Benjamin, Jr.: b a. 1760 d — m Betty Davis Pvt MA
Benjamin: b 1-1-1761 d 1838 m Isabella Wright Mus NJ ★
Benjamin: b 7-15-1728 d 10-24-1808 m Lydia Goodsell Capt CT
Benjamin: b 5-26-1741 d 9-14-1827 m X Sgt VA
Brewen: b 1-17-1753 d 9-6-1833 m Hannah Foote Pvt CT ★
Caleb: b 12-13-1728 d 9-6-1804 m (1)Naomi Hard (2)Betty Betts (3)Anna Fabrique Maj CT
Caleb: b 5-2-1723 d 9-5-1823 m Jerusha Parmalee Capt CT
Caleb: b c. 1750 d 1807 m Rebecca Coleman Pvt NJ

Caleb: b 10-27-1757 d 1799 m Lydia Johnson Pvt NJ
Caleb: b 10-17-1752 d 2-19-1810 m Elizabeth Pitney Sol NJ
Cornelius: b 1751 d 1820 m (1)Mary Briscoe (2)Mildred Throgmorton (3)Susan Pritchard Dr VA
Daniel: b 1731 d 7-17-1810 m Theodocia Barker Pvt CT
Daniel: b 5-16-1725 d 1775-1790 m (1)Ann Towsey (2)Abigail Northrop PS CT
Daniel: b 9-28-1713 d 2-9-1800 m Mercy Eaton Pvt CT
Daniel: b 8-26-1750 d — m Lucy Hills Pvt CT
Daniel: b 1722 d 4-21-1792 m Hannah Havens Pvt NH
Daniel: b 11-14-1731 d 7-17-1810 m Anna Knight Pvt VT
David: b 5-8-1742 d 5-2-1826 m Esther Puffer Ens CT
David: b 11-10-1755 d 3-31-1831 m Martha Perkins Pvt CT
David: b 1739 d 9-1-1808 m Parnall Clark PS Pvt CT
David: b 1728 d 1781 m Sarah Owen Capt GA
David: b 8-20-1758 d 6-8-1839 m Olive Phelps QMSgt MA ★
David: b12-12-1747 d 4-28-1810 m Sarah Harrison Pvt NJ
David: b 1761 d 1847 m Hannah Bull Pvt NY ★
Ebenezer: b 2-5-1736 d 1818 m Abigal Blackman Pvt NH
Ebenezer: b c. 1741 d 12-25-1827 m Phoebe Baldwin Pvt CS MA
Ebenezer: b 1724 d 10-23-1801 m X Pvt NJ
Eleazer: b 10-21-1764 d p. 8-14-1832 m Jane Redfield Pvt CT ★
Elijah: b 5-16-1756 d 7-5-1841 m (1)Ascanath Allen (2)Polly Richardson (3)Sally Hall Sgt CT ★
Elisha: b 2-7-1750 d 10-19-1816 m Elizabeth Cornell Pvt NY
Elisha: b a. 1755 d c. 1820 m X Sol NC
Elizabeth Pitney: b 7-23-1760 d 5-19-1850 m (1)Caleb Baldwin (2)William Thorne PS NJ
Enoch: b 2-12-1754 d 12-29-1829 m Sybil Knapp Cpl MA
Enos: b 1723 d 12-21-1807 m (1)Phebe Williams (2)Sarah Woodruff (3)Phebe Tucker (4)Prudence Mulford Pvt NJ
Ethan: b 8-30-1760 d 2-18-1829 m (1)Rhoda — (2)Rachel — Pvt NJ
Ezekiel: b 12-19-1719 d 1-27-1805 m Sarah — Sol NJ
Ezra, Sr.: b 3—1706 d 3-26-1782 m Ruth Curtis PS CT
Ezra, Jr.: b 1737 d 1824 m Elizabeth Lyman Pvt MA
Ezra: b 3-15-1755 d 1-31-1837 m Abby Clark PS NJ
Francis: b a. 1728 d a. 3-9-1784 m Margaret Little Pvt DE
Francis: b 4-9-1743 d 11-23-1814 m Innocent— 2Lt VA
Henry: b 1752 d 1-15-1831 m Jane Shipman Pvt CT W ★
Henry: b 1794 m (1)Sarah Rawlings (2)Maria Graham Woodward Lt MD
Henry: b 2-27-1717 d 11-17-1789 m Abigail Butler Pvt MA
Hezekiah: b 8-24-1756 d 11-6-1831 m Elizabeth Hine CS CT
Hezekiah, Jr.: b 3-25-1762 d 1831 m Abiel Curtiss Pvt NY ★
Hezekiah, Sr.: b 9-26-1732 d 5-11-1803 m Abigal Peet Capt NY
Ichabod: b 1-25-1757 d 8-30-1839 m Joanna Dodd Pvt NJ
Isaac: b 1740 d 1799 m Philene Pardee Sgt CT
Isaac: b 3-17-1735 d 12-16-1811 m Hannah Davis Sol CT
Isaac: b 3-12-1759 d 3-7-1820 m Lucy Lewis Pvt CT
Isaac: b 12-11-1738 d 6-17-1775 m Eunice Jennison Capt NH
Isaac: b 6-12-1730 d 6-9-1791 m Patience Rathburn Pvt NY
Isaac, Jr.: b 1-8-1765 d 1815 m (1)Alice Hascall (or Mrs. McDowell) (2)Zerniah — Sol NY
Isaac: b 5-22-1760 d 10-4-1832 m Anne Coffeen Sgt VT
Israel: b 3-19-1736 d 3-16-1778 m Elizabeth Warner Lt CT
Israel: b 10-31-1718 d 7-1-1792 m Mrs Hannah Gunn PS CT
Jabez: b 1-1-1763 d 5-10-1844 m Hannah Tucker Pvt Drm CT MA ★
Jabez: b 1-11-1764 d 5-10-1825 m Nancy Tilden Pvt NH ★
Jacob: b 1760 d 10-13-1844 m Sarah Turner Sol MA
Jacob: b 10-2-1746 d 4—1798 m Lucy Sharpe PS MA
James: b 11-12-1758 d 5-24-1843 m Nabby Dickerson Pvt CT
James: b 1-29-1760 d 3-3-1839 m (1)Bettina Goodwell (2)Mary Rice Pvt CT
James: b c. 1750 d 1810 m Sarah Rawlings PS MD
James: b 1-17-1759 d 9-4-1843 m Sarah Davis Fitch Pvt MA
James: a. 1752 d p. 1791 m Elizabeth Ferrell Sol VA
Jared: b 3-10-1732 d 1817 m Damaris Booth Pvt CT
Jared: b 1744 d 1—1830 m Hannah Plant Pvt CT
Jeduthan: b 1-30-1730 d 6-4-1788 m Lucy Parkman Col MA
Jeremiah: b 1-23-1749 d p. 1780 m Rebecca Totman Pvt MA
Jeremiah: b 1728 d 1778 m Mehitable — Pvt NJ
Jesse: b 1757 d 8-17-1839 m Harriet Owen Ens 2Lt QM NJ W ★
Jesse: b 1750 d 1825 m Elizabeth Stringfellow Sol NC
Job: b 5-1-1738 d 12-1-1800 m (1)Phoebe — (2)Hannah — Pvt NJ
Joel: b 7-16-1759 d p. 10-1-1832 m Sarah Gorham Pvt CT
John: b 9-13-1750 d 1-3-1817 m Althea Hobart Pvt CT
John: b — d 7-4-1779 m X Pvt CT
John: b 1757 d 10-14-1848 m Mary Barker Pvt MD ★
John: b 5-3-1730 d 2-27-1809 m Ruth Way Pvt PA
John: b 4-1-1763 d 9-18-1838 m Jane House Pvt PA
John: b 2-21-1749 d 4-18-1820 m Hannah Simmons Capt VA
John P.: b 12-5-1762 d 4-19-1844 m Mary Crane Pvt NJ
Jonathan: b 9-15-1722 d 4-2-1802 m Mary Bronson LCol CT
Jonathan: b 6-6-1758 d 7-4-1843 m Submit Lord Pvt CT W ★
Jonathan: b 5-1-1753 d 6-4-1821 m Susanna Williams Pvt NJ
Joseph: b 12-26-1758 d 9-29-1825 m Rosana Meloy Sgt CT W ★
Joseph: b 1729 d 1782 m Mary Searles Pvt MA
Joseph: b c. 1760 d p. 1840 m Patsy Clendennin Pvt VA
Joshua: b 12-14-1726 d 12-21-1821 m Abigail Beard PS CT
Joshua: b 12-25-1735 d 2-15-1807 m Sarah — Capt MA

Judah: b 2-22-1733 d — m Deborah Royce Pvt CT
Levi: b 2-28-1755 d 2-25-1837 m (2)Lydia Haven Pvt MA
Linus: b 3-18-1760 d 12-16-1836 m Rhoda Crane Cpl NJ
Loammi: b 1-21-1744/5 d 10-20-1807 m (1)Mary Fowle (2)Margaret Fowle Col MA
Miles: b 4-22-1754 d 1854 m Elizabeth — Sol VT
Mordecai: b — d p. 8-24-1803 m Sarah Kimbrough 1Lt GA
Moses: b 1731 d — m Elizabeth — Pvt Drm CT
Moses: b 12-17-1749 d 2-27-1823 m (1)Lois Whedon (2)Mary Potter (3)Lucretia Drm Pvt CT
Moses: b 2-21-1757 d 6-6-1831 m Sarah Johnson Pvt NJ
Moses: b 1753 d 7-14-1837 m Elizabeth Ann — Pvt PA ★
Nahum Sr.: b 5-8-1734 d 5-7-1788 m Marth Lowe Col NH
Nahum Jr.: b 1-30-1762 d 8-30-1840 m (1)Sarah Hinckley (2)Huldah Stow Pvt NH ★
Nathan Sr.: b 9-21-1721 d 5-9-1804 m Eunice Mallett Lt CT
Nathan, Jr.: b 11-8-1755 d 3-25-1803 m Avis Durand Smn & PS CT W ★
Nathan: b 1721 d 1810 m (1)Joanna — (2)Elizabeth Hart Ball Sgt CL
Nicodemus: b 8-4-1755 d 6-9-1799 m Martha Harrison Pvt CT
Noah Sr.: b 3-20-1710 d 11-23-1799 m Rebecca Frisbie CS PS CT
Noah Jr.: b 11-18-1738 d 9-2-1776 m Abigail Frisbie Pvt NY
Peleg: b 2-13-1708 d 1797 m Abigail Camp Pvt CT
Peleg: b 1758-64 d 1-11-1845 m Ann Turrell Drm CT W ★
Philemon: b 1760 d 12-28-1851 m Sarah — Pvt CT ★
Richard: b 12-1-1745 d 4-2-1823 m (1)Alice Botsford (2)Abiah Botsford PS CT
Rufus: b 3-8-1754 d 6-30-1834 m Hannah Haskell Pvt PA & CT
Samuel: b 12-20-1749 d 8-31-1828 m Hannah Taylor Lt CT
Samuel Jr.: b 5-25-1715 d 6-6-1838 m Lucina Hill Pvt CT
Samuel: b 1758 d p. 4-1-1851 m Nancy — Pvt MD ★
Samuel: b 1755 d 12-16-1831 m Abigail Estey Pvt MA
Samuel: b 7-28-1743 d 7-9-1826 m (1)Millicent Cutler (2)Mercy P. — Capt PS MA
Seth C.: b 5- -1760 d 9-16-1835 m (1)Ruth White (2)Abigail Kellogg Pvt VT CT ★
Silas: b 4-4-1729 d 11- -1813 m Mrs Mary Plumb Dr Pvt CT
Silas: b 1749 d 9-14-1811 m Phebe Brown Pvt NJ
Simeon: b 7-24-1724 d 6-7-1808 m (1)Mercy Bronson (2)Rebecca Buck Cmsry PM CT
Solomon: b 2-19-1737 d 7-4-1798 m Philena Baldwin PS CT
Stephen: b 1747 d 8-29-1838 m Elizabeth Losee Capt NJ ★
Thaddeus: b 2-16-1735 d a. 7-27-1815 m Sarah — Pvt CT
Theophilus Jr.: b 11-17-1735 d 1-7-1826 m Sarah Strong Ens CT
Theophilus: b 6-16-1728 d 3-10-1804 m (1)Mrs. Mary Noble (2) Mrs. Eunice Noble (3)Mrs. Martha Sherwood Pvt CT
Theophilus: b 10-22-1699 d 8-1-1784 m Dorothy — PS CT
Thomas: b 2-23-1755 d 1-10-1810 m Mary Fuller Sgt CT
Thomas: b 2-22-1732 d 3-1-1794 m Abigail Pollard Pvt MA
Thomas, Jr.: b 10-16-1755 d 12-5-1834 m Mary Lovejoy Pvt MA & VT ★
Thomas: b 12-9-1746 d 10-28-1821 m (1)Sarah Camp (2)Mrs. Elizabeth Bailey Ens NJ
Thomas: b 2-12-1742 d p. 4-19-1797 m Nancy Bibb Pvt VA
Timothy: b 9-16-1750 d 3-15-1818 m (1)Olive Norton (2)Mrs. Sarah Fowler Woodward Pvt CT
Timothy: b 12-13-1722 d 12-22-1800 m Sarah Beecher PS CT
Tyler: b c. 1755 d 1795 m Tomsey Davidge PS MD
Waterman: b 1-8-1757 d 4-21-1810 m Clarinda Hazen Sol CT
William: b 5-22-1746 d 1819 m Elizabeth Kimbrough Sgt GA
William: b 4-12-1748 d a- -1802 m (2)Susanna Wilson Sgt Maj MA
William: b c. 1736 d 1796 m Erbenza — 1Lt VA
William: b 12-27-1750 d 1834 m Mary Webster Pvt VA ★
William: b c. 1721 d 1799 m Anne Wimbish PS VA
Zacheus: b 1754 d 1831 m (1)Sarah Bradfield (2)Hannah Rogers (3)Mrs. Welthian Jones Pvt CT
Zenas: b c. 1742 d p. 3-5-1809 m Dorcas Younglove Pvt NC
Ziba: b 2-16-1755 d 9-27-1803 m Anna Brown PS CT
Zophar: b 2-9-1740 d 2-4-1801 m Rebekah Ward Pvt NJ

BALDY,
Christopher: b 1752/3 d 1820 m (1)Susanna — (2)Mrs. Eva Metzger Capt PA
Paul: b 7-20-1757 d 3-19-1825 m Mary Catherine Ream Pvt PA

BALFOUR,
Andrew: b 9-3-1735 d 3-11-1783 m (1)Janet McCormick (2)Elizabeth Todd Dayton PS Col NC

BALL,
Aaron: b 1754 d 1835 m Patty Wade Pvt NJ
Abner: b 1-1-1760 d 5-21-1848 m Rachel Robertson Pvt NJ
Adonijah: b 12-5-1762 d 12-17-1833 m Mary Phillips Pvt MA
Benjamin: b 2-12-1752 d p. 1780 m Jerusha Woodbury Cpl MA
Benjamin: b c. 1749 d a. 4-1-1807 m Ann — PS VA
Benjamin Gott: b 5-6-1757 d 3-14-1824 m Huldah Hatfield Pvt MA ★
Burgess: b 7-28-1749 d 3-7-1800 m (1)Mary Chichester (2)Frances Thornton Washington PS & Col VA
Charles: b 8-3-1760 d 7-3-1838 m Merab Miller Sgt MA
Daniel: b 1769 d c. 1833 m Lucia Wells Pvt MA
Daniel Jr.: b 1756 d 2-23-1830 m Lydia Smith Pvt MA

BALL, contd.

Daniel: b 1737 d 10-12-1820 m Anna Carter Beach Pvt NJ
Daniel: b 8-7-1763 d 9-27-1844 m Ann — Sgt NC ★
David: b 1720 d 4-19-1789 m Joanna Watkins MM NJ
David: b 1-30-1756 d 7-24-1805 m Mary Baldwin Pvt NJ
David: b 1735 d 1811 m Hannah Haynie Sol VA
Davis: b 1759 d 3-27-1819 m Mary Hatfield MM NJ
Ebenezer Sr.: b 12-30-1721 d p. 1790 m Sarah Gookin Pvt NH
Ebenezer: b 6-22-1729 d 4-7-1797 m Rebecca Butterfield Pvt MA
Edward: b 11-8-1756 d 4-16-1815 m Esther Conklin MM NJ
Edward: b 2- -1745 d 1779 m Rebecca Baker Jones Lt PS GA
Eleazer: b 1-29-1760 d 4-4-1826 m Lucy Rozier Pvt MA
Eli: b 8-5-1766 d 12-11-1857 m X Pvt MA★
Elias: b 12-22-1709 d 8-8-1786 m Lidia Chicken PS SC
Elijah: b 2-1-1743 d p. 1792 m Joanna French Lt MA
Elijah: b 1748 d 11-10-1834 m Rebecca Moore Sgt MA ★
Eliphalet: b 1728 d 1797 m Elizabeth von Fleming PS NY
Eusebius: b 5-7-1761 d 9-6-1814 m Mary Burke Pvt MA
Ezekiel: b 1761 d 1812 m Elizabeth Peck Sol NJ
Farlin: b 1730 d p. 7-16-1796 m Mary— Capt VA
Flamen: b 1760 d 1816 m Ann Western Pvt NY
George: b 5-22-1748 d p.1790 m (1)Sarah Blew (2)Ann Kelly PS MD
George: b c. 1750 d 1835 m Elizabeth Tunnell Capt VA
Gideon: b 8-4-1762 d 11-27-1826 m Lydia Brockway Cpl MA ★
Henry: b 5-25-1753 d p. 1790 m Miss Condon PS MD
Isaac: b 8-16-1744 d 4- -1784 m Rachel Ball 2Lt MA
Isaac Jr.: b 12-31-1747 d p. 1790 m Hannah Cummings Pvt MA
Israel: b 10-10-1758 d 10-8-1807 m Mary Rice PS Bbd PA
Jacob: b 2-24-1749 d 11-29-1809 m Mary Vergason Pvt NJ
James: b 4-15-1754 d 9-9-1834 m Abigail Starr Pvt MA ★
James: b 10-19-1761 d 5-19-1802 m Mercy Thompson Pvt MA
James: b 1749 d 3-27-1830 m Margaret Bray Pvt VA
James: b 1753 d p. 1802 m Winifred — Pvt VA
James Sr.: b 12-31-1718 d 11-24-1789 m (2)Mildred — (3)Lettice Lee PS VA
James Jr.: b 2-20-1755 d 12-18-1825 m Frances Downman Capt VA
Jesse: b 1740 d 1778 m Aggatha Conway Col VA
Johannes: b 5-15-1724 d 1804 m (1)Maria Deitz (2)Gertrude Snyder PS NY
John: b c. 1755 d p. 1790 m Lucretia — Lt CT
John: b 1740 d c. 1815 m Miss Robinson Pvt GA
John: b 2-19-1757 d 9-3-1823 m (2)Rachel Chamberlin Sgt MA ★
John: b 12-16-1742/3 d 2-8-1814 m Lydia Ward OrdlSgt MA W★
John: b 6-16-1739 d p. 1790 m Lydia Pratt 4Sgt MA
John: b 7-18-1738 d 4-17-1801 m (1)Abigail Wilder (2)Mary Baker MM & Pvt MA
John: b 1747 d 9-4-1775 m Beulah Whitney Pvt MA
John: b 1753 d 8-28-1815 m Hannah Farley Pvt NH
John: b 2-14-1746 d 2-10-1838 m (1)Phebe Crane (2)Martha Howell Fairchild Ens NJ ★
John: b 1755/6 d 11-7-1838 m (1)Mary Collins (2)Anna Swart 1Lt NY★
John: b 10-2-1742 d 1806 m Sara Ellen Payne Ens VA
John: b 7-25-1746 d 12-14-1814 m Mary Thrift Ens VA
John: b c. 1749 d 1-9-1829 m Mary — Sol VA
Jonas: b 10-16-1748 d 11-21-1803 m Mehitable Latham PS MA
Jonathan Sr.: bpt 2-18-1728 d 1809 m Martha French Pvt MA
Jonathan Jr.: b 9-16-1751 d 1819 m Molly Pratt Sgt MA
Jonathan: b 1-7-1755 d 2-18-1829 m Abigail Childs Pvt MA
Jonathan: b 12-31-1759 d 1834 m Sarah Stiles Pvt NJ
Joseph: b c. 1740 d 8-6-1821 m X PS DE
Joseph: b 6-21-1750 d 10-5-1817 m (1)Esther — (2)Lucretia Stearns Drm MA
Joseph: b 7-29-1734 d 9-2-1805 m Anna Harrison Pvt NJ
Joseph: b c. 1742 d 1808 m (1)Rachel Thompson (2)Phoebe Hand Pvt NJ
Joseph: b c. 1730 d 2- -1779 m Hannah Haynie Bbd VA
Josiah: b 12-16-1742 d 7-26-1810 m Esther Ward Pvt MA
Josiah: b 3-2-1712/13 d 10-28-1791 m Rachel Corbett Pvt MA
Lebbeus: b 11-11-1739 d 1806 m Thankful Stowe Maj MA
Mary Reed: b 1762 d 10-3-1822 m Thomas Ball PS KY
Moses: b 7-23-1742 d 11-15-1820 m (1)Susanna Nutt (2)Relief Twichell Cpl MA
Moses: b 1733 d 1810 m Lucy King Pvt MA
Nathan: b 8-5-1762 d p. 1796 m Elizabeth Ball Pvt MA
Nathaniel Sr.: b 6-3-1717 d 8- -1814 m Mary Weston PS NH
Nathainel Jr.: b 1-24-1751 d 4-9-1805 m Martha Boynton Pvt NH
Nehemiah: b 12-1-1756 d 6- -1847 m Esther Sallee Sgt NJ ★
Noah: b 12-31-1755 d p. 1800 m Mary Seekins Pvt MA
Richard: b c. 1754 d 2-21-1807 m Eleanor — PS CS MD
Sampson: b c. 1754 d p. 1800 m (1)Lucy Gray (2)Mrs. Margaret Lawrence Pvt SC
Samuel: b 2-29-1742 d 3-17-1831 m Phebe Taylor Pvt MA
Samuel: b 7-10-1762 d 5-20-1839 m Hannah Ranger Sol NH
Samuel: b 7- -1734 d 1-12-1810 m (2)Sarah Plume Capt NJ
Samuel: b 7-28-1752 d 6-7-1780 m Hannah Gardner Pvt NJ
Silas: b 4-23-1754 d 7-15-1807 m Rhoda Griffin Dr MA
Stephen: b 2-12-1726/7 d 10-10-1799 m Abigail Atwater PS CT
Stephen: b 10-21-1749 d 12-22-1783 m Sarah Ross Dr NJ
Stephen: b 3-17-1751 d 1-29-1781 m Elizabeth Ford PS NJ
Thomas: b 1731 d 5-20-1806 m Mary Crane Sgt & QM NJ
Thomas: b c. 1737 d p. 5-14-1814 m Mildred Downman Sol VA

Thomas: b 1754 d 3-1-1820 m Mary Reed Sol VA
Thomond: b 1736 d 6-3-1779 m Margaret Denham PM PA
Timothy: b 9-28-1758 d 3-28-1828 m Mary Crowell Pvt NJ
Uzal: b 3-20-1747/8 d 4-9-1799 m Abigail Burnett Pvt NJ
William: b 1750 d 1805 m (1)Sarah Martin (2)Lillie Ann Hitt PS Sol GA
William: b 1760 d 1843 m Maria Weidman Pvt NY
William: b 1718 d 1783 m Martha Broomfield Capt VA
William: b 1738 d 1807 m Hannah Smith 2Lt VA
William: b 1759 d 7-7-1829 m Elizabeth Riley Mus VA ★
Williamson: b c. 1735-40 d c. 1798/99 m (2)Anne Beale (3)Priscilla Spann Capt VA
Zopher: b 1724 d 7-6-1803 m Elizabeth — Ens PA

BALLANCE,

Charles: b 11-10-174— d 5-13-1777 m Martha Lampton Pvt VA
Willis: b c. 1760 d 5-18-1824 m (1)Joyce Green (2)Mrs. Joanna Read Cpl VA

BALLANTINE, (includes BALENTINE)

Ebenezer:b 7-14-1756 d 10-7-1823 m Mary Osborn Dr's mate MA
William: b c. 1758 d p. 1-4-1803 m Susannah Marlin Pvt PA

BALLARD,

Bland: b 1735 d 3-31-1788 m (1)— Williams (2)— Tyler Sgt VA
Bland W. Jr.: b 10-16-1759 d 9-5-1853 m (1)Elizabeth Williamson (2)Diana Mathews ( )Mrs. Elizabeth Weaver Garrett Pvt VA ★
Dane: b 10-9-1753 d 4-15-1831 m (1) — Forbes (2)Anna Lindsay PS MA
Daniel: b 11-1-1754 d 11-14-1835 m (1)Freelove Kinney (2)Ruth Gaines Pvt CT ★
Daniel: b 5-1-1728 d 5-31-1808 m Ruth Holton Pvt MA
Ephraim: b 5-6-1725 d 1-7-1821 m Hannah Moore PS MA
Israel: b 2-4-1748 d 9-25-1810 m (1)Sarah Case (2)Alice Fuller (3) Susanna Rogers Pvt CT
James: b 6-4-1763 d 2-1-1856 m Isabella Montague Cpl VA★
Jeremiah: b 9-16-1726 d p. 1817 m Isabelle Pearce Capt MA
Jeremiah: b c. 1750 d c. 1813 m Rachel Clark Capt NJ
Jethro: b 1734 d 1801 m Elizabeth Sumner CS NC
John: b 1745 d 1829 m Elizabeth Thompson Pvt VA
John: b 4-19-1752 d 3-2-1824 m Mary Coates Pvt MA
John: b 10-10-1758 d 8-22-1821 m Polly Pierson Pvt MA
Joseph: b 7-25-1741 d 1-29-1777 m Sarah Simonds PS MA
Joseph: b 10-6-1732 d p. 1795 m Rebecca Southwick Pvt VT
Josiah: b 8-4-1721 d 8-6-1799 m Sarah Carter PS CS MA
Kedar: b 1747 d 6-28-1834 m (1)Theresa Sumner (2)Anne Benton Capt PM NC
Moses: b 4-14-1756 d 4-4-1833 m Ruth Morley Pvt MA★
Nathan: b 1745 d 1-14-1835 m Hannah Holt Lt NH ★
Philip: b 3-21-1747 d 8-28-1835 m Mary Yours Sgt MA
Sherebiah: b 9-24-1722 d 1802 m Keziah Osgood Pvt MA
Sherebiah: b 5-9-1745 d 9-29-1828 m Sarah Emerson Pvt MA★
Thomas: b 1720 d 1820 m Anna Davis Lt NY
Thomas: b 3- -1751 d 12-28-1843 m (1)Elizabeth Graham (2)Mary (Parks) Stafford Capt SC
Thomas: b 1717 d 1782 m Susanna — Pvt VA
Thomas: b 1717 d p. 9-3-1804 m Mary — Pvt VA
Uriah: b 10-7-1758 d 12-22-1840 m (1)Lois Lovejoy (2)Hannah F. Sargeant Drm Sgt NH ★
William: b 1732 d 9-14-1799 m Elizabeth Steppe Lt VA
William, Sr.: b 1715 d 1794 m (1)Mary Byron (2)Rachel Moorman PS VA
Wyatt: b 2- -1760 d p. 1820 m Diacy Ballard Pvt NC★
Zaccheus: b 3-21-1731 d 4- -1800 m Elizabeth Valentine Pvt MA

BALLIET,

Jacob: b 6-1-1751 d 11-6-1831 m (1)Anna Maria Ritter (2)Elizabeth Barabara Ritter Capt PA W ★
John: b 11-30-1761 d 11-2-1837 m Catherine Mickley Pvt PA
John: b 1746 d 12-25-1830 m (1)Maria Barbara Snyder (2) X (3) Catherine Stichle CS PA
Joseph, Sr.: b 5-11-1729 d a. 10-16-1804 m Maria Barbara — CMman PA
Leonard: b 1758 d p. 1802 m Hannah Beattie Pvt PA
Stephen: b 1753 d 8-4-1821 m Magdalena Burkhalter Col PA

BALLINGER, (includes BALLENGER)

James: b c. 1755-60 d p. 1782 m Dorcas Dodsen PS SC
John: b 1747 d 1829 m Nancy Eastham Pvt VA
Joseph: b a. 1733 d 1787 m (1)Sarah Hensley Franklin (2)Tabitha Ballow PS VA
Richard: b 3-30-1727 d 1808 m Elizabeth Franklin Capt VA

BALLMER, (includes BALMER)

Christian, Jr.: b 4-17-1737 d 1785 m Margaret Brown Pvt PA
Michael: b 12-28-1737 d 1817 m Mary — Pvt PA

BALLOU, (includes BALLEW, BILLEW)

Abraham: b 1717 d c. 1780 m Mary Sayles Ens RI
Abraham: b 1764 d 2—1844 m (1)Diana Mowry (2)Mrs Mary Blake Pvt RI
Ariel: b 2-21-1758 d 9-26-1839 m (1)Lucina Comstock (2)Edilda Tower Pvt RI

Asa: b 8-31-1762 d 8-4-1832 m Roba Williams Sgt RI
Benjamin: b 7-11-1747 d 3-26-1822 m Sarah Whipple Pvt RI
Charles: b 1722 d 1800 m Temperance Bailey Capt VA
Daniel: b 12-27-1722 d 6- -1801 m (1)Amie Brown (2)Martha Buxton Sgt RI
David: b c. 1742 d 1811 m Mary Smith Pvt RI
David: b 3-21-1756 d 7-11-1832 m Lucy Martin Sgt RI
Duty: b 4-22-1756 d 12-29-1783 m Waitstill Jilson Pvt RI Heirs ★
Edward: b 11-24-1756 d 2-22-1833 m Bethany Streeter Pvt RI
Eleazer: b 6-12-1730 d p. 1779 m Phebe Lapham Pvt RI
Elias: b 12-24-1752 d 1-2-1834 m Mary Parker Pvt MA
Ezekiel: b 1-5-1718/19 d 6-5-1789 m Joanna Cook Pvt RI
James: b 12-10-1723 d 1-21-1812 m (1)Tamasin Cook (2)Mrs Huldah Carpenter Pvt Fif NH
Jesse: b 3-30-1741 d 3-16-1800 m (1)Rhoda Salisbury (2)Lydia Mason (3)Elizabeth Pitts Pvt RI
Joseph: b 1-31-1749 d 2-9-1801 m Sarah Sweet Pvt RI
Leonard: b c. 1760 d p. 6-22-1852 m Sarah Wingfield PS VA
Levi: b 9-23-1744 d 7-13-1805 m Comfort Thompson Ens PS RI
Maturin: b 11-30-1722 d 11-3-1804 m (1)Lydia Harris (2)Mrs Lydia Bliss PS NH
Nathaniel: b 10-6-1750 d 7-17-1838 m (1)Jane Ware (2)Jane Pickering Pvt RI ★
Noah: b 8-31-1728 d 3-20-1807 m (1)Abigail Razee (2)Abigail Cook Lt RI
Oliver: b 1759 d 1-19-1818 m (1)— Tiffany (2)Mary Simonds Pvt RI
Reuben: b 1-26-1747 d 9-19-1803 m (1)Chloe Comstock (2)Freelove Whipple Maj RI
Seth: b 2-20-1748 d 9-15-1778 m Margaret Hilton Pvt NH
Silas: b 2-24-1753 d 5-27-1837 m Hannah Hilton Pvtr NH
Simeon: b 3-21-1740 d 5-3-1786 m Mary Cole Lt RI
Stephen: b 9-24-1756 d 5-22-1837 m (1) — McWhirter (2)Mary Richmond Pvt NC ★
Thomas: b 1-26-1734 d 9-25-1784 m Chloe Battersby Cpl VA
Thomas: b 3-31-1759 d 4-28-1809 m Frances Hobson Pvt VA

BALSBAUGH,
Valentine: b 2-14-1755 d 11-26-1851 m Elizabeth Miller Pvt PA

BALTZELL,
Jacob: b 9-7-1711 d 11-7-1791 m Eva Catharine Wirtz PS MD

BALTZER, (includes BALZAR)
Anthony: b c. 1754 d 2-19-1842 m Elizabeth Funk Pvt PA ★

BALTZLY, (includes BALSLEY, BALTZLE & BALTZLEY)
Andrew: b 10-16-1756 d 1842 m X Pvt NY ★
Christian: b 5-1-1756 d 6-22-1831 m Elizabeth Keinadt Ens PA ★
Christian: b 1728 d 1825 m X MM PA
John: b 10-13-1759 d 10-29-1814 m (2)Lucinda Clapper Pvt PA

BAMFORD,
Jacob: b 1754 d 6-28-1801 m Susan Shepherd PS NH

BANCROFT,
Abel: b 5-28-1752 d 10-30-1786 m Sarah Lawrence 2Lt MA
Benjamin: b 1701 d 7-21-1787 m Anna Lawrence PS MA
Caleb: b 6-27-1759 d — m Susannah Tay Pvt MA
Daniel: b 9-1-1762 d 6-5-1825 m Patience Marble Pvt MA
David: b 8-7-1718 d 4-16-1782 m Eunice — PS MA
Ebenezer: b 4-1-1738 d 9-20-1827 m Susannah Fletcher LCol MA
Edmund: b 4-23-1726 d 10-25-1806 m (1)Elizabeth Atherton (2)Rachel Barron (3)Phebe Bancroft Capt MA
Edmund: b 7-27-1751 d 8—1810 m Sarah Pool Pvt MA
Enoch: b 11-25-1753 d 3-9-1823 m Sarah Stowe Pvt MA
Ephraim: b 3-12-1718/19 d 1791 m Esther Gleason Lt CT
Isaac: b 8-17-1720 d 6-5-1808 m (1)Abigail Eggleston (2)Lydia Chapin PS CT
Isaac, Jr.: b 9-8-1742 d 4-22-1813 m (1)Ann — (2)Mary Barrett PS CT
James: b 5-9-1739 d 5-17-1831-m (1)Sarah Pearson (2)Sarah Parker Capt MA
James: b 10-27-1745 d 3-2-1832 m Lucy Whitney Sgt PS NH
John: b 9-18-1748 d 1837 m Anna Waters Sgt MA ★
Jonas: b 10-26-1744 d 1- -1821 m Sarah Blood 4Sgt MA
Jonathan: b 8-11-1750 d 7-11-1815 m Martha Green 2Lt MA
Jonathan: b 5-16-1761 d 12-10-1847 m Bathsheba Tarbell Sgt MA
Jonathan: b 5-25-1750 d 9-25-1826 m (1)Sarah Case (2)Mrs Elizabeth Bancroft Pvt MA
Joseph: b 11-10-1735 d 2-18-1825 m Elizabeth Temple Lt MA
Joseph: b 1-13-1756 d 4-23-1839 m (1)Hannah Taintor (2)Esther Bond (3)Anna Rice (4)Sarah Livermore Cpl MA ★
Joshua: b 1712 d 1791 m Mary Lampson Pvt MA
Kendall: b 1742 d 1806 m Susannah Ewers Pvt MA
Lemuel: b 7-25-1741 d 7-23-1800 m Comfort Munson Lt MA
Nathaniel: b 1748 d 1805 m Sarah Bancroft Capt MA
Oliver: b 7-20-1757 d 8-18-1840 m Sarah Hawley Sol CT
Robert: b 1755/56 d 10-30-1822 m Abigail Capen Pvt MA★
Samuel: b 10-29-1737 d 7-1-1830 m Jerusha Foote Lt CT
Samuel: b 7-21-1715 d 11-25-1782 m Lydia Parker PS MA
Samuel, Sr.: b 1-2-1711 d 7-6-1788 m Sarah White CS MA

Samuel, Jr.: b 4-22-1737 d 1-2-1820 m Elizabeth Spelman 2Lt MA
Thaddeus: b 8-13-1764 d 11-11-1840 m (1)Molly Houghton (2)Mrs Huldah Terry Pvt MA ★
Thomas: b 9-26-1746 d p. 1790 m Lydia Mason Pvt CT
Timothy: b 7-15-1759 d 1848 m Abigail Taylor Pvt MA ★
Wm.: b 1742 d 1835 m Mary Daniels Pvt MA ★

BANDFIELD,
James: b 5-1-1747 d 2-2-1832 m (1)Tabitha Jones (2)Malinda Owens Pvt MD ★

BANDY,
Lewis: b c. 1750 d p. 2-11-1827 m Mary Barnes Sol GA(?)
Thomas: b 6-22-1748/49 d 10-18-1835 m (1)Polly — (2)Nancy Burns Pvt VA ★

BANGHART,
Andrew, Sr.: b 2-19-1750 d 4-10-1819 m Catherine Summers PS NJ
Barney: b a. 1756 d c. 1784 m Mary Grimes Pvt NJ
George: b 1743 d 1806 m Mary Buskirk PS NJ

BANGS,
Allen: b 3-23-1734 d 9-14-1793 m Rebecca Howes Sol MA
Barnabas: b 3-11-1728 d 1-29-1808 m Loruhama Elwell Pvt MA
David, Sr.: b 3-29-1709 d 4- -1802 m Eunice Stone Pvt MA
Dean: b 5-31-1756 d 12-6-1845 m Eunice Sparrow Pvt MA
Elijah: b 5-5-1757 d 9-28-1828 m (1)Sarah — (2)Sally Knowlton Pvt MA
Elkanah: b 3-31-1732 d 7- -1777 m Susanna Dilligham Mar PS MA
James: b 1738 d 1810 m Susanna Hallett Sgt MA
John: b 12-30-1757/8 d 7-6-1814 m Content Smith Pvt MA
John: b 6-21-1764 d 3-31-1813 m Eunice Root Pvt MA
Jonathan: b 6-29-1746 d 1-29-1808 m (1)Deborah Hurd (2)Mrs Rebecca Babb Pvt MA
Joseph: b 7-5-1757 d 6-30-1809 m Desire Sears Cpl MA
Lemuel: b 1-1-1740 d 5-9-1824 m (1)Hannah Hall (2)Rebecca Keeler Lt CS CT
Nathan: b 5-2-1736 d 12-26-1793 m Abigail Wing Pvt MA
Reuben: b 12-9-1760 d 7-11-1822 m Lucy Thayer Pvt MA W ★
Solomon: b 5-23-1729 d 1-19-1797 m Experience Berry Pvt MA
Zenas: b 5-3-1763 d 3-16-1828 m (1)Ruth Hall (2)Abigail Crosby Pvt MA

BANKER, (includes BANCKER)
Abraham B.: b 9-20-1754 d 2-7-1806 m Arrietta Mancius 1Lt NY
Adolph: b 3-27-1754 d 1-22-1822 m Ruth Oakley Pvt NY
Adrian: b 7-25-1724 d 9-29-1792 m Anna Boelen PS NY
Evert: b 5-29-1721 d 1-13-1803 m Elizabeth Boelen PS NY
Floris: b 3-29-1741 d 8-30-1821 m Martha Young Maj NY
Gerrit: bpt 2-27-1737 d 8-8-1803 m Hester Van Arnhem Pvt NY
John: bpt 2-22-1738 d 9-2-1815 m (1)Alida Mesnard (2)Catharine Stevens (3)Margaret Garribrandt Capt NY
Thomas Brouwer: b 12-8-1729 d 5-25-1807 m Annie Mabie Capt NY
Wm. E.: b 2-9-1755 d 8-15-1832 m Ruth Soule Pvt NY

BANKHEAD,
James: b 1742 d 1798 m Elizabeth Black Pvt SC
James: b 1743 d p. 1808 m Christian Miller Lt VA

BANKS,
Daniel: b 12-5-1739 d 1-16-1839 m Hannah Thorp Ens PS CT
David: b 3-27-1751 d 1830 m Mary Mesnard Cpl CT
David: b 5-14-1743 d a. 1815 m Susan Crane Plum Capt QM NJ
Ebenezer, Sr.: b 11-27-1727 d 3-22-1777 m Sarah Hyde Lt CT
Ebenezer, Jr.: b 10-19-1753 d 7-1-1838 m Huldah Sherwood Lt CT
Elijah: b 8-7-1762 d 3-3-1816 m Mabel Ogden Pvt CT
Gershom, Sr.: b 5-1-1712 d 1787/9 m (1)Mary Bradley (2) Hannah Bradley (3)Mary Perry Sol CT
Gershom, Jr.: b 9-11-1753 d 1-11-1835 m Ruth Banks Pvt CT ★
Henry: b c. 1758 d 1829 m (2)Polly Messick Sol MD
Hezekiah: b 1748 d 3-31-1812 m Sarah Couch Sol CT
Hyatt: b 3-7-1764 d 4-16-1847 m Elizabeth Wakeman MM CT
Isaac: b 5-26-1766 d 12-24-1840 m Eleanor Sturges CG CT
James: b 8-31-1732 d 6- -1793 m Anna Small PS PA
Jesse, Jr.: b 10-14-1736 d 11-1-1820 m Mehitable Wheeler Pvt CT
John, Jr.: b 8-19-1755 d p. 3-26-1792 m Abigail Brundage Pvt CT
John: b 11-25-1757 d 8-30-1850 m (1)Deborah Cassel (2)Mary Adams Sgt NJ ★
John: b 1729 d p. 1822 m Deborah Newman Pvt NY
John: b 7-22-1735 d 7-17-1818 m Mary — DepCmsry NY
Jonathan: b 12-4-1759/60 d 11-29-1820 m Molly Wakeman PS CT
Jonathan: b 8-29-1759 d c. 4-15-1811 m Anne Murphy Sgt NY
Joseph: b c. 1750 d c. 1820 m Elizabeth Lyon Sgt CT
Joseph: b 1753 d 7-15-1830 m Esther Williams Pvt CT W ★
Joseph: b 4-12-1713 d 7-8-1802 m Johanna — PS CT
Joshua: b 2-23-1759 d 4-11-1843 m Ruth Smith Pvt CT
Linn: b c. 1745 d p. 12-27-1799 m Sarah — PS VA
Moses: b 7-24-1732 d 10-9-1823 m Phebe Curtis Lt & QM MA
Nathan: b 5-6-1760 d 3-10-1847 m Mabel Bradley Sgt CT ★
Nehemiah, Sr.: b 2-28-1722 d 11-16-1807 m Abigail Bradley Pvt CT

BANKS, contd.
Nehemiah, Jr.: b 10-20-1754 d 4-9-1835 m Sarah Sherwood Pvt CT ★
Ralph: b 10-21-1757 d 8-24-1824 m Rachael Alston Jones PS NC
Samuel, Jr.: b 9-1-1731 d 1787 m Phebe Stackpole PS MA
Samuel: b 4-18-1755 d 6-24-1826 m Charity Lyon Ens NY
Talkent: b 4-22-1759 d 6-24-1812 m Emma Chapman Pvt CT
Thaddeus: bpt 5—1740 d *p.* 1790 m Olive Bradley Pvt CT
Thomas: b 10-14-1747 d 7-1-1819 m Sarah Dean Pvt CT
Thomas: b 1709 d 6-28-1789 m (1)Sarah Chandler (2)Betty
   White (3)Susannah Hunt PS NC
Thomas: b c. 1750 d 2-23-1825 m X Sol VA
Tunstall: b c. 1730 d 1810 m X PS VA
Wm.: b 6-23-1762 d 9-5-1839 m Elizabeth Brown Sgt VA ★

BANKSTON,
Jacob: b c. 1733 d *p.* 1800 m X Pvt GA
John: b 6-11-1754 d 9-15-1823 m Henrietta Coates Pvt GA
Lawrence: b 1748 d 1840 m Nancy Henderson Pvt GA

BANNER,
Ephraim: b 5-20-1753 d 4-3-1838 m (2)Elizabeth Hartgrove Pvt
   NC ★
Joseph: b 12-28-1749 d 4-24-1838 m Sarah McAnally Pvt NC ★

BANNERMAN,
Geroge: b 2-18-1762 d 6-26-1841 m (1)Phebe Williams (2)Hester
   Player Pvt NC ★

BANNING,
Abner: b 1755 d *p.* 1780 m Annar Sparrow Pvt CT
Asa: b c. 1742 d 1818 m (1)Sabina — (2)Esther — Ens MD
Benoni: b 6-26-1744 d 2-25-1827 m Ann Frazier Pvt NC
John: b 1740 d 2-15-1791 m Mrs Elizabeth (Alford) Casson PS
   CS DE

BANNISTER, (includes BANISTER)
Aaron: b 2-15-1764 d 7-6-1848 m (1)Phebe Bemis (2)Mrs Fanny
   (Bemis) Howe Pvt MA
Andrew: b 5-30-1762 d 11-24-1840 m Bathiah Witt Fif MA ★
Barzillai: b 2-4-1750 d 1810 m (1)Deborah Cushman (2)Nancy
   Fairbank Cpl MA
Christopher: b 8-21-1737 d 4-29-1805 m Abial Manning Maj MA
Jesse: b 4-24-1754 d 4-1-1833 m (1)Mercy Phips (2)Louise Bumrill
   Pvt MA
John: b 12-26-1734 d 9-3-1788 m (1)Mary Bland (2)Anne Blair Col
   PS VA
Joseph: b 8-8-1711 d 1795 m Mary Hinds Pvt MA
Lemuel: b 1748 d 7-28-1821 m Elisabeth Hines Cpl MA
Levi: b 1753 d 12-31-1833 m Anna — Pvt Mus MA ★
Seth: b 12-7-1739 d 11-7-1819 m Marcy Wariner Bgd Maj MA
Silas: b 6-22-1751 d 4-29-1827 m Thankful Ely Pvt VT
Solomon: b 11-28-1739 d 7-2-1835 m (1)Patience — (2)Ruth
   Wesson Sgt MA ★
Thomas, Jr.: b 5-18-1759 d 4-6-1824 m Lydia Downer Pvt MA ★
Timothy: b c. 1759 d 1822 m Prudence Stewart Drm Fif VT
Wm. George: b c. 1735 d *p.* 1786 m Mary Ann Watts Sol SC

BANTA, (includes BONTA)
Abraham: b 7-7-1745 d *a.* 9-30-1793 m Margareta Monfort Pvt PA
Albert: b 8-8-1728 d 9-29-1810 m Madalena Van Vorhees PS NJ
Daniel: b 9-13-1762 d 9- -1837 m Mary Van Vorhees Pvt NJ ★
David: b 9-2-1723 d 10-8-1782 m Antjen Ackerman CS NJ
Dirck: b 2-5-1749 d 3-25-1820 m Elizabeth Benson Pvt NJ
Hendrick: b 6-10-1716 d *p.* 1808 m Elizabeth Benson PS NJ
Hendrick: b 6-30-1751 d 8-12-1817 m Elizabeth Lake PS NJ
Hendricks: b 1-31-1758 d — m Rachel Hopper Pvt NJ
Henry: b 4-5-1756 d 9-14-1824 m Engeltie Schermerhorn 1Lt NY
Henry: b 1-22-1762 d 10-17-1844 m Sally Shook Pvt PA
Henry, Sr.: b 1718 d 1805 m (1)Rachel Brower (2)Ann Demarest PS
   PA
Hildebrant: b 2-11-1763 d 9-4-1832 m Deborah Van Epps Pvt NY ★
John: b 6-3-1723 d *a.* 2-24-1786 m (1)Trintie Demarest (2)Cornelia
   (Huyler) Helm Pvt NJ
John: b 12-18-1737 d 10-29-1812 m Ann Demarest Sol NJ
John: b 1-17-1758 d 1-17-1812 m Jane Van Zile Pvt NJ
John: b 10-17-1760 d 1-7-1846 m Engeltie Vedder Sol NY
John: b 9—1756 d c. 1815 m Polly Riker Drm PA
Peter: b 5-17-1760 d 5-12-1829 m Rachel Van Clap Sct NJ
Samuel: b 11-25-1739 d c. 1776 m Eraetje Berdan Pvt NJ
Samuel: b 5-30-1741 d 1821-6 m Elizabeth Blauvelt Pvt NJ
Samuel: b 6-13-1753 d *p.* 5—1833 m Dyna Dorland Pvt PA
Thomas: b 4-13-1740 d 5-29-1824 m Gerritie Terhune PS NJ
Wiert: b 7-8-1753 d 1—1834 m Leah DeGroot Pvt NJ

BANTHAM,
John: b c. 1747 d 1824 m Mrs Rachel Riley Sgt MD ★

BANTZ,
Adam: b c. 1730 d *p.* 1790 m X PS MD

BARBEE, (includes BARBY)
Christopher, Sr.: b c. 1715 d 1777 m Margaret — CS NC
Christopher: b 1743 d c. 1834 m X Sol NC

Elias: b 6-14-1763 d 10-6-1843 m Elizabeth Slaughter Pvt VA ★
Gray: b c. 1747 d *a.* 8—1830 m Nancy Cain PS NC
John: b — d *p.* 5-5-1799 m Sarah — PS NC
John: b 11-12-1724 d 1801-05 m (1)Elizabeth Welsh (2)Phillis
   Duncan Capt VA
John: b c. 1757 d 9-23-1835 m Mary Dyson QM Sgt VA W ★
Joseph: b 2-7-1761 d 10-3-1826 m Sarah Trice Dragoon NC W ★
Wm.: b 9-14-1759 d 9-21-1813 m Mary Smith Pvt VA

BARBER,(includes BARBOUR)
Barnet White: b c. 1748 d 5-21-1802 m Elizabeth Story Briscoe
   Pvt MD
Benjamin: b 1758 d 1849 m Hannah Morse Pvt NY
Benjamin: b 1753 d 4-12-1797 m Desire Moore Pvt CT
Benjamin: b 2-7-1755 d 9-28-1834 m Susannah Boss Pvt RI
Bildad: b 1745 d 1816 m Lois Humphrey Pvt CT
Caleb: b 1724 d 1816 m (1)Elizabeth Niles (2)Hannah Green PS RI
Charles: b c. 1720 d 7-22-1806 m Elizabeth — PS MD
Daniel: b 11-23-1719 d 9-29-1775 m Naomi Barber Pvt CT
Daniel: b 1732 d 1799 m Martha Phelps Fif CT
Daniel: b 1759 d 4-17-1805 m Ruth Emily Hinman Pvt MA
Daniel: b 4-23-1733 d 1-31-1801 m (1)Sarah Parson (2)Anna Davis
   PS NH
Daniel, Jr.: b 1748 d 5-21-1842 m Charity Rathbun Capt RI ★
David: b 3-31-1733 d 10-30-1795 m Mary Brown Capt CT
David, Jr.: b 1-15-1755 d — m Jane Filley Sgt CT
David: b 1765 d 1857 m Deborah Adams Capt CT
David: b 2-17-1716 d 1-14-1801 m (1)Patience Case (2)Abigail
   (Newcomb) Horsford Pvt CT
David: b 1746 d 1783 m Sarah Lawrence Vol CT
David: b 1760 d 3-13-1839 m Lois Dutton Drm CT
David: b 4-6-1763 d 9-2-1843 m Hannah Baker Pvt NY ★
Ebenezer: b 1763 d 11-28-1855 m (1)Lovice — (2)Theoda — Pvt
   MA ★
Elijah: b 1-11-1745 d 5-22-1825 m Abigail Wood Pvt CT
Elijah: b 5-11-1746 d *p.* 1782 m Mary Hills Pvt CT
Elijah: b 7-25-1748 d 12-13-1820 m Sarah Pettibone Pvt CT
Elisha: b 8-21-1742 d 11-29-1833 m Elizabeth Adams Sgt CT
Elisha: b 5-31-1758 d 2-11-1814 m Martha Bullard Pvt MA
Ephraim: b 5-20-1748 d 11-14-1817 m Elizabeth Crosby 1Lt MA
Ezekiel: b 4-12-1750 d 1806 m Elizabeth Goddard Sol CT
Ezekiel: b 3-6-1710 d *p.* 1782 m Hannah Webster Ens RI
Francis: b 11-26-1750 d 1-11-1783 m (1)Mary Ogden (2)Anne
   Ogden LCol NJ
Geroge: b c. 1743 d 1822 m Margaret — Capt GA
George: b 12-21-1743 d 7-10-1832 m Bethia Jones Pvt MA
Isaac Pierce: b c. 1760 d *p.* 1795 m Lois Benedict Pvt MA
Jacob: b 9-23-1738 d 1817 m Patience Lawrence Cpl CT
James: b 2-13-1752 d 2—1832 m Pennina Barker PS NJ
James: b 1736 d 1-21-1824 m Rachel — Pvt NY
James: b 1736 d 1786 m Elizabeth Wright Capt PA
James: b 8—1726 d 10-10-1821 m (2)Margaret Wilcox Pvt RI ★
James, Sr.: b c. 1707 d 4-17-1775 m (1)Elizabeth Todd (2)Sarah
   Todd CS VA
James, Jr.: b 1734 d 1804 m Frances Throckmorton Col PS VA
James: b 10-16-1761 d 6-3-1842 m (1)Mary Rowland (2)Hannah
   Manning Pvt VA ★
James: b 6-2-1762 d 7-17-1836 m Melley — Pvt VA ★
James Noyes: b 1749 d 1-27-1795 m Zerviah Bushnell Pvt CT
Jerijah: bpt 12-31-1738 d 2-7-1792 m Loannah Filley Pvt CT
John: b 1748 d *p.* 1793 m Elizabeth Denison Sgt CT
John, Sr.: b 12-4-1719 d 12-27-1799 m Lydia Read Pvt CT
John, Jr.: b 11-29-1749 d 11-3-1825 m Elizabeth Case Pvt PS CT
John: b 10-23-1742 d 6-26-1777 m Abigail Fuller MM PS MA
John: b 9-19-1757 d 6-24-1840 m Azuba Warren Pvt MA ★
John: b 1761 d 12-8-1843 m Marriam Eastman Pvt NH ★
John: b 12-23-1731 d 7-27-1802 m Hannah Gray Pvt & PS CS NY
John: b *a.* 1745 d *p.* 1790 m Sarah Martin Capt NC
John: b 1738 d 1802 m Mary (Barber) PS CS NC
Jonathan: b 5-15-1745 d 6-28-1839 m Sebra Stanton Pvt RI ★
Joseph: b 4-23-1731 d 1-12-1812 m (1)Rebecca Clark (2)Hepzibah
   Hanen Pvt MA
Joseph: b 4-25-1738 d 6-29-1811 m Elizabeth Maclanathan Pvt MA
Joseph: b 6-3-1744 d 1-17-1824 m Lydia Miller Pvt MA
Joseph: b 8-12-1744 d 12-31-1806 m (1)Betsy Anderson (2)Leah
   Grover Sgt VT
Joseph Bane: b 1737 d 3-15-1795 m Elizabeth Goodridge Pvt MA
Matthew: b 8-8-1734 d 6-1-1809 m Hannah McFarland Pvt MA
Matthew: b 1753 d 1830 m Mary Anderson Pvt MA
Mordecai: b 10-21-1763 d 1-21-1846 m (1)Elizabeth Strode (2)
   Sally (Haskell) Byrne Lt VA ★
Moses: b c. 1745 d *p.* 1781 m Rachel Losee Lt NY
Nathan, Sr.: b 1733 d 6-2-1816 m Thankful Maxson Capt PS CS RI
Nathan, Jr.: b 1759 d 9-19-1835 m Mary Pendleton Lt RI
Nathaniel: b 1722 d 1797 m X Pvt CT
Nathaniel: b 2-19-1744 d 3-31-1782 m Mercy Spofford Pvt CT ★
Noah: b 5-8-1735 d 3-13-1822 m Sybil Booth Capt CT
Obadiah: b 1752 d 1833 m Wealthy Ann Phelps Sol CT
Peleg: b 1755-61 d 1836 m Isabel Sherman Pvt RI
Philip: b c. 1750 d 1790 m — Holt PS VA
Reuben: b 1-26-1728 d 12-28-1815 m Sarah Merriman Pvt CT
Reuben: b 12-7-1751 d 1825 m Elizabeth Case Pvt CT

Reynolds: b 3-29-1754 d 4-14-1837 m (1)Ruth Crandall (2)Alced Dawley (3)Sarah Lewis Sgt RI ★
Richard: b c. 1722 d 1792 m Hannah — PS NC
Robert: b 8-21-1759 d 5-9-1827 m Rebecca Johnson Pvt MA
Robert: b 1723 d c. 1808 m Sarah March Capt NH
Robert: b 10-10-1722 d 10-4-1782 m Sarah Taylor 1Lt PA
Samuel: b 6-16-1756 d 5-23-1847 m (1)Anna — (2)Mary Hoppock (3)Charity Wilson Pvt NJ
Samuel: b 5-1-1762 d 1843 m Thankful Kenyon Pvt RI
Simeon: b 5-12-1741 d 10-17-1808 m Lois Allen Pvt & PS CT
Simeon: b 8-13-1753 d 2-1-1847 m Sarah Peck Cpl CT ★
Simeon: b 4-6-1763 d 6-14-1849 m Catherine Moore Pvt MA
Simeon: b 1737 d 5—1817 m Susannah Skidmore Cpl NY
Solomon: b 1-15-1746/7 d 6-20-1827 m (1)Polly Pray (2)Deborah Faxon Pvt MA ★
Stephen: b 4-4-1724 d 7-22-1807 m Alice Cass Capt CT
Thomas: b 9-5-1728 d 1-8-1794 m Martha Case Pvt CT
Thomas: b 1716 d 1792 m Elizabeth Adams Pvt CT & NY
Thomas: b 1736 d 12-1-1816 m Margaret (Barber) Pvt NJ
Thomas, Sr.: b 6-5-1731 d 4-19-1796 m Mary Barney PS RI
Thomas, Jr.: b 4-28-1762 d 11-25-1837 m Elizabeth Greenold Pvt RI ★
Thomas b 1735 d 1825 m Mary Pendleton Thomas Col PS VA
Timothy: b 10-9-1748 d p. 1790 m (1)Anna Peck (2)Hannah Peck Sol CT
Uriah: b 1-3-1761 d 6-2-1846 m (1)Barbara Clingman (2)Rachel Beard Pvt PA
Wm.: b 5-16-1743 d 8-11-1789 m Margaret Knox 2Lt MA
Wm.: b c. 1756 d 1799 m Anne Crook Maj ADC NY
Wm.: b 1760 d 3-16-1834 m Sarah Coon Pvt RI
Zachariah: b 11-17-1752 d 1-1-1822 m Patience Whitney Pvt MA
Zachariah: b 6-17-1764 d 3-30-1860 m Mary Ellis Pvt MA

BARBIN, see DeBELLEVUE

BARCLAY,
Hugh: b 7-13-1747 d 11-24-1807 m Hester Fulton Cmsry PA
Hugh: b 1729 d 1806 m Mary Culbertson Adj PA
Hugh: b 2-18-1751 d 10-20-1834 m Sarah Culbertson PS VA
John: b 1768 d a. 3-4-1806 m Mary Jenkins Pvt GA
John: b 2-13-1763 d 7-3-1850 m Jane Knox Pvt NC ★
John, Jr.: b 9-15-1749 d 1824 m Esther Madina Capt PA
John: b c. 1752 d c. 1818 m Anne Tate Pvt PA
Robert: b 4-15-1756 d 9-29-1804 m Rhoda Way Pvt NH W ★
Samuel: b 11-5-1757 d 8-27-1822 m Grace Knowles Pvt PA
Thomas: b 3-1-1755 d 1804 m Catherine Williams Sol MD
Thomas: b 1728 d 1-20-1793 m Sarah Hoops PS PA

BARCO,
John: b 1759 d 1822 m Sallie Montfort Sol NC

BARCROFT,
John, Sr. b 1-6-1724 d 2—1795 m Hannah — PS PA
John, Jr.: b 2-19-1760 d 3-5-1829 m Lydia Lee Pvt PA

BARD, (includes BEARD)
Daniel: b 2-7-1748 d 12-18-1792 m Ann Margaret Grube Capt PA
George: b 6-2-1736 d 6-26-1793 m Margaret Kitzmiller PS PA
Jacob: b — d 4-25-1829 m Barbara — Lt PA
Richard: b 2-28-1738 d 2-22-1799 m Catherine Poe Pvt PA
Samuel: b 1-1-1742 d 1821 m Mary (Bard) Dr NY
Wm.: b 6-7-1738 d 7-31-1802 m Mary Kincaid Braxdale Pvt PA

BARDWELL, (includes BORDWELL)
Ebenezer, Sr.: b 9-10-1707 d 11-14-1789 m Elizabeth Gillett Lt MA
Ebenezer, Jr.: b 6-24-1733 d 12-31-1818 m Sarah Tute Pvt MA
Elijah: b 7-12-1755 d 5-12-1809 m Sarah Wentworth Smith Lt MA
Enoch: b 12-1-1748 d 12-18-1789 m Abigail Wells CS MA
John: b 4-7-1735 d 2-5-1814 m Mercy Sheldon Lt MA
Jonathan: b 12-17-1724 d 5-27-1781 m Violet Amsden Capt MA
John: b 2-17-1761 d 9-25-1845 m Mrs. Mary (Rogers) Edson Pvt MA
Joseph: b 1713 d 1-1-1791 m Lydia Morton Pvt MA
Martin: b 1740 d 1824 m Sybel Sikes Sgt MA
Noah: b 4-28-1748 d 3-13-1828 m Lucy Waite Lt CS MA
Obadiah: b c. 1757 d p. 10-10-1832 m Mehitable Smith Pvt MA ★
Perez: b 1737 d 1812 m Tobiatha Hastings Lt MA
Remembrance: b 1713 d 11-19-1779 m Hannah Dickenson PS MA
Reuben: b 3-30-1754 d 9-13-1840 m Susanna Wilson Pvt MA ★
Samuel: b 1739 d 1797 m Martha Belden Pvt MA
Samuel: b 1-18-1757 d 3-13-1848 m Editha Gunn Pvt MA ★
Samuel: b 8-25-1715 d 11-30-1795 m Anna Severance CS PS MA
Seth: b 12-22-1752 d 6-16-1795 m Hannah Dickenson Pvt MA
Simeon: b 1-21-1748 d 3-25-1837 m (1)Huldah Warner (2)Dolly Mills Cpl MA ★
Thomas: b 12-16-1744 d 9-20-1826 m Catherine Seekins Lt MA

BARFIELD,
Frederick: b c. 1758 d p. 1815 m Susannah Williams Sol NC
Jesse: b 1738 d 8-22-1780 m Sarah Castillo PS NC
Richard: b 1754 d c. 1812 m X Pvt GA

BARGE,
Lewis: b 1741 d 2-2-1809 m (1)Mary — (2)Christianna — Sol NC

BARGERHOFF,
Nicholas: b 1756 d p. 4-13-1832 m X Pvt PA ★

BARGES, (includes BARTGES)
Christopher: b c. 1745 d 1782 m X PS PA

BARHAM,
Charles: b a. 1711 d p. 9-17-1783 m (1) — Judkins (2)Mrs Ann Arrington PS VA
James: b 5-18-1764 d 1-8-1865 m Prudence Dunn Pvt VA

BARHYDT, (includes BARHEIT, BARHEET, BARHOUT, BARHUYDT)
Cornelius: bpt 12-21-1737 d p. 1790 m Rachel Yates Pvt NY
Johannes: b 1-7-1739 d p. 1790 m Helena Peek Pvt NY
Nicholas: b 11-12-1744 d 4-15-1827 m Susanna Van Antwerp 2Lt NY W ★
Teunis: b 10-3-1742 d p. 1795 m (1)Jacomyntje Van Vorst (2)Cornelia Bovie (3)Catherine Vrooman Pvt NY

BARILLE, (includes BARILL)
Louis: b 1755 d 6-22-1832 m Mary Beckwith Contremaitre FrN

BARKELOW, (includes BARKALOW, BARCKELOO, BUCKALEW & BUCKELEW)
Arthur: b 7-8-1740 d a. 4-20-1802 m Sarah Pohlemus Pvt NJ
Conrad: b 7-10-1742 d 4-10-1802 m Sarah Miller Pvt NJ
Cornelius: b 11-17-1717 d p. 2-18-1783 m Jannetje Amuck PS CS NJ
Frederick: b c. 1750-60 d p. 1830 m Ruth Gosling Sol GA
Frederick: b 2-14-1756 d p. 2-12-1825 m Phebe Messerole Pvt NJ ★
Harmanus: b 2-23-1745 d 11-10-1788 m Elizabeth Duryea 2Lt NY
John: b 1755 d 1845 m Susan Dudbridge Pvt NJ ★
John: b 1762 d 1815 m Ruth Stout Pvt NJ
John: b 4-14-1743 d 7-3-1833 m Mary McKinney PS PA
Peter: b 5-15-1760 d 9-10-1846 m (1)Elizabeth Hileman (2)Nancy Vorum Pvt NJ
Stephen: b 4-24-1748 d 3-15-1825 m (1)Ann Stout (2)Margaret — Pvt PS NJ

BARKER,
Abijah: b 2-6-1748 d p. 1790 m Delight Dewey Pvt MA
Asa: b 12-10-1748 d 9-10-1822 m Lucy Porter Pvt MA
Barnabas: b 4-13-1724 d 3-23-1797 m Sarah Green Pvt MA
Benjamin: b 11-12-1752 d 10-18-1802 m Sarah Beere Pvt CT
Benjamin: b 9-4-1755 d 3-14-1841 m (1)Lydia Foster (2)Dorcas Stevens Cpl MA ★
Carr: b c. 1745 d 12-25-1832 m Sarah Prible ILt MA
Charles: b 5-10-1763 d 8-29-1841 m Frances Chiles Sol VA
Daniel: b 5-30-1746 d — m Bathsheba Blanchard Sol NH
Daniel: b 4-22-1754 d 1820 m Anna Hill Pvt & PS NH
David, Sr.: b 6-1-1731 d 1815 m Sarah Barker Pvt MA
David: b 7-20-1749 d 9-8-1819 m Eunice Sherman Pvt MA
David Edward: b 3-23-1761 d 11-14-1839 m Sarah Cochrane Pvt NC ★
Ebenezer: b 8-3-1739 d 7-10-1781 m Priscilla Loring 1Lt MA
Ebenezer: b 11-5-1731 d 8-18-1805 m Hannah Bodwell Pvt MA
Ebenezer: b 3-31-1739 d 7-23-1826 m Dolly Sherburn Pvt NH
Ebenezer: b 5-4-1716 d p. 1784 m Sarah Stevens CS NH
Edward: b 1754 d c. 1835 m Mary Carson Pvt VA
Eleazer: b 5-1-1760 d — m Mahitabel — Pvt MA
Elihu: b 3-18-1744 d 1-4-1840 m Bethia Thomas Sgt NY
Elisha: b 6-27-1744 d 5-30-1827 m Phebe Peckman Ens RI
Ethan: b 1-1-1762 d 11-9-1838 m Jerusha Ellsworth Pvt CT
Ezra: b 11-4-1759 d 7-6-1818 m (1)Betsey Miner (2)Sally Brick Witt Cpl MA
George, Sr.: b — d a. 10—1788 m Susanna Perkins PS NC
George, Jr.: b 3-25-1759 d 3-4-1841 m Frankey Kerr Pvt NC
Gideon: b 12-4-1751 d 9-11-1834 m Elizabeth Croad PS RI
Hannaniah: b 4-4-1748 d 8-19-1825 m Sarah Hathorne Pvt CT
Henry: b 10-18-1754 d 1807 m Eleanor Caldwell Capt PA
Hezekiah: b 4-14-1757 d 7-5-1834 m Sarah Wood Pvt RI
Isaac: b 1750 d 1790 m Abigail Emerson Pvt MA
Isaac: b 11-16-1751 d 1806 m Jemima Davis Pvt NH
Isaac: b 5-21-1752 d 12-3-1834 m (1)Sarah Peckham (2)Wealthy Peckham PS Spy RI
Jacob: b 1764 d 1853 m Mary Price Pvt SC
James: b 12-12-1725 d 2-5-1796 m Annie Peckham CS MA
James: b 1727 d p. 1-7-1818 m Elizabeth Moore PS NY
James: b 1762 d p. 1785 m Mary Smith Pvt VA
Jeremiah: b 3-31-1752 d 10-4-1835 m Abigail Sturgis Goshom Pvt MA
Jesse, Jr.: b 4-21-1761 d 3-19-1804 m Prudence Paine MA W ★
Jessie: b 4-30-1762 d 11-16-1859 m Maamah Swan Pvt MA ★
John, Jr.: b 1742 d 1806 m Hannah Wilson Sgt MA
John: b 4-24-1753 d 10-6-1839 m Phebe Wood Sgt MA ★
John: b c. 1748 d 1-11-1818 m Prudence Gleason Sgt MA
John: b 12-18-1756 d 3-15-1834 m (1)Esther Richardson (2) Mrs Sally Guild Warren Sgt MA
John: b 8-13-1732 d 5-2-1736 m Lucretia Newhall Pvt MA
John: b 12-16-1764 d 12-19-1835 m Margaret Smith Pvt NY ★
John: b 1746 d 1795 m Nancy West Pvt VA

BARKER, contd.
John: b c. 1762 d 4-23-1835 m Lucy Irby Pvt VA
Jonathan: b 10-23-1728 d 4-29-1794 m Abigail Mitchell SgtMaj MA
Jonathan: b 9-6-1762 d 1812 m Abiah Parker Pvt MA
Joseph, Jr.: b 5-20-1744 d 2-14-1831 m Ruth Fletcher Pvt MA
Joseph, Jr.: b c. 1750 d p. 12-28-1782 m Catherine Carpenter Pvt PA
Joseph: b 4-8-1753 d 7-30-1827 m Martha Tuttle Pvt VT
Joshua: b c. 1719 d 1-16-1778 m Mary Throope Pvt CT
Josiah: b 11-16-1763 d 9-23-1847 m Penelope Hatch Pvt Mrnr MA ★
Josiah: b 3-30-1727 d 1808 m Mary Heard Pvt NH
Levi: b 1761 d 6-19-1835 m Lydia Benton Pvt NY
Moses: b 4-10-1737 d 10-16-1821 m Lydia Gutterson Lt MA
Nathan: b 6-8-1761 d 10-7-1849 m Hannah Grove Pvt MA
Nicholas: b 5-8-1737 d 3-24-1826 m Hannah Allen Sol NC
Papillion: b a. 1737 d 1813 m Abigail Foote CS CT
Paul: b 8-20-1762 d 9-27-1833 m Mary Biddlecome Cpl MA
Peter: b 5-26-1756 d 5-23-1829 m Sally Wood Pvt MA
Robert: b 11-5-1760 d 5-22-1839 m Mehitable Davis Armr Cdr MA
Russell: b 3-29-1757 d 4-15-1814 m Elizabeth Wilford Pvt CT
Samuel: b 8-6-1739 d 11-5-1807 m Lucy Graves Leete Capt CT
Samuel: b 2-9-1715 d 9-21-1781 m Esther Baker CS CT
Samuel: b 1-11-1742 d 12-5-1823 m Susanna Foster Sgt MA
Samuel: b 10-10-1714 d 11-11-1796 m Elizabeth Farnum PS MA
Samuel: b 1-21-1762 d 3-25-1831 m (1)Betsey Rodgers (2)Abigail Blanchard Pvt MA
Samuel: b — d p. 1790 m Dorcas Barton Pvt PS NY
Samuel: b 1739 d 10-27-1803 m (1)Margaret Greenfield (2)Rebecca Woolson Pvt NC
Samuel Still Augustus: b 10-19-1756 d 11-19-1819 m (1)Maria Delavan (2)Emily Conklin BgdMaj CT
Stephen: b 4-29-1756 d 5-8-1837 m Peggy Hyde Pvt MA
Stephen: b 1-21-1741 d 8-15-1834 m Rebecca Gibson Pvt MA
Stephen: b 8-2-1759 d 9-16-1843 m (1) X (2)Elizabeth Massey Pvt NY ★
Thomas: b 2-17-1713 d 12-10-1787 m (1)Mrs Ferebee Savage Pugh (2)Penelope Craven Hogdson PS NC
Thomas: b c. 1759 d a. 3-14-1845 m X Pvt VA
Timothy: b 4-5-1750 d 1833 m Irene Barker Pvt CT
Timothy: b 5-23-1723 d 1779 m Hannah Baker PS VT
Uriah: b 1761 d 7- -1847 m Polly Clingman Pvt PA
Uzal: b 11-19-1732 d 1-21-1817 m Desire Sanford Pvt MA
William: b - -1752 d 5-17-1826 m Betsey Armstrong Pvt CT ★
William: b 2-4-1763 d 1-13-1851 m Lydia Parmelee Pvt CT
William: b 1-1-1717 d 1-11-1796 m (1)Hannah Wood (2)Amy Wood Pvt MA
William, Sr.: b 4-10-1734 d 12-28-1821 m (1)Rhoda Wheeler (2)Anne Holden (3)Phebe Upton PS NH
William, Jr.: b 7-8-1759 d 2-19-1819 m (2)Lydia Morse Pvt MA
William: b 1750 d c. 1811 m Mrs — Williams Capt SC
William: b 1740 d 11-4-1820 m Chloe Bronson LCol NY
William: b 8-19-1762 d 10-6-1826 m Mary Ann Seal Markham Sgt VA
William: b c. 1747 d a. 8-14-1814 m Ann Evans Sol VA
Zebediah: b 11-25-1750 d 10-10-1819 m Susanna Messer OrdlSgt MA
Zenas: b 1-25-1765 d 7-2-1834 m Rhoda Andrews Pvt NY ★

BARKLEY,
James: b c. 1750 d 8-24-1826 m Catherine Crawford PS PA
John: b — d 1795 m Sarah Gellum Sol NY
John: b c. 1725 d 1785 m X Pvt PA
John: b 1743 d p. 1820 m Sarah Logan Pvt NJ
John: b 1743 d 1820 m Margaret Grey Cav Tms SC
John: b 3-8-1720 d 1-10-1796 m Agnes — PS SC
Joseph: b 1736 d — m X Pvt MD
Robert: b 4-15-1756 d 9-29-1804 m Rhoda Way Pvt NH
Robert: b 3-25-1753 d 1- -1813 m Eleanor Cathey Pvt NC W ★
Thomas: b 1749 d 3-10-1821 m Sarah Crawford Pvt NY
William: b c. 1748 d 1824-33 m Margaret Ramsey PS SC
William: b c. 1739 d a. 7- -1804 m Sarah — Pvt VA

BARKMAN,
Jacob: b 1749 d 1833 m X Pvt PA

BARKSDALE,
Beverly: b 1756 d 4- -1822 m (1)Anna Terry (2)Judith Womack PS VA
Claiborne: b 11-10-1738 d 1-12-1821 m (1)Sarah Goode (2)Mrs Jane Morton Carter Sol VA
Henry Hickerson: b 1758 d 11-27-1819 m Molly Bayne Wgn VA W ★
Hickerson: b c. 1740 d 1804 m X Sol SC
Jeffrey: b c. 1755 d 1836 m Phoebe — Sol GA
John: b c. 1746 d a. 8-31-1801 m Sarah — ILt VA
Joseph: b c. 1741 d p. 1800 m Hannah Ford Sol VA
Nathan: b 1743 d p. 9-8-1812 m Mary Allen PS SC
Nathaniel: b 9-9-1760 10- -1830 m Anne Garden Pvt VA
Peter: b 8-4-1760 d 1-15-1826 m (1)Elizabeth Watlington (2)Nancy — Ens VA
Samuel: b 10-25-1759 d 6-20-1842 m (1)Mary Hamner (2)Virginia Jermina Wingfield SgtMaj VA ★
William: b c. 1710-25 d 1796 m (1)Ann — (2)Anne — PS VA

BARLEY,
John: b — d a. 11-17-1808 m Elizabeth — PS VA

BARLOW,
Aaron: b 2-11-1750 d 8-1-1800 m Rebecca Sanford Lt CT
Aaron: b 4-13-1735 d 3-12-1822 m (1)Mary Nye (2)Mary (Winslow) Terry (3)Priscill Andrews Pvt PS CS MA
Abner: b 1750 d p. 1832 m X Pvt MA ★
Ambrose: b 7- -1755 d 8-13-1839 m Anna Smith Pvt VA
Benjamin: b 3-4-1758 d p. 1802 m Phoebe Doud Pvt MA
David, Sr.: bpt 3-1-1718/19 d 10-5-1795 m (1)Susannah Hubbart (2)Ester Sturgis Pvt CT
David, Jr.: b 1-10-1745 d 3-27-1817 m Sarah Bradley Pvt CT
Edmund: b 5-4-1749 d 1-18-1825 m Salome Middlebrook Pvt CT
Edmund: b 5-18-1732 d 11-21-1818 m Sybil Root ILt MA
Edmund, Jr.: b 3-18-1763 d 4-25-1842 m Tabitha Bancroft Lt MA
Elisha: b 2-23-1749 d 12-30-1828 m Sarah — Capt NY
Heman: b 8-13-1758 d 12-4-1788 m Diana Bancroft Pvt MA
James: b c. 1757 d 11-5-1827 m Lucy Edwards Pvt VA
Jesse: b 9-12-1749 d 12-10-1815 m Sarah Nye Sgt MA
John: b 3-5-1748 d 1833 m (1)Anna Caswell (2)Temperance Branch (3)Lucy Hatch Pvt CT ★
Lemuel: b 7-14-1758 d 3-10-1813 m Thankful Bassett Pvt MA
Lewis: b 1755 d p. 1830 m Judah Frances Smith Pvt VA ★
Moses: b 11-24-1728 d 3-17-1799 m Sarah Wing PS NY
Nathan: b 8-25-1726 d 8-26-1798 m Joanna Swift Pvt NY
Nathaniel: b 5-13-1745 d 12-26-1782 m Jane Bradley PS CT
Samuel: b 2-18-1748 d 3-31-1835 m X Sgt CT
Thomas: b 10-7-1764 d 8-10- 1853 m (1)Amy Delona (2)Lucy Allerton Pvt NY
Thomas: b 8-25-1760 d 1-30-1825 m Susan Childs Isbell Pvt VA
Thomas: b c. 1756 d 1811 m (1) X (2)Mary — Pvt NC

BARMORE,
James: b — d p. 6-8-1829 m (1)Judah — (2)Mary — Wgn VA

BARNABY,
Ambrose, Jr.: b 2-11-1745 d 6-8-1802 m (1)Elizabeth Wilbur (2)Philena Burt (3)Abigail Williams Pvt MA
Samuel: b 4-20-1735 d 10-25-1811 m Sylvia Winslow PS CS MA

BARNARD,
Benjamin, Sr.: b 2-14-1714/15 d 10-24-1794 m Lucy Bush Pvt PS MA
Benjamin, Jr.: b 1738 d p. 1790 m Mary Hunt Pvt MA
Benjamin: b 7-30-1735 d 12-22-1792 m Eunice Fitch NS MA
Benjamin: b 2-20-1750 d 6-11-1837 m Lucy Wood Pvt MA ★
Charles: b 7-14-1748 d p. 1781 m Sarah Foster Pvt NH
Dan: b 5-15-1730 d p. 1784 m Lydia Dodge Pvt CT
David: b 10-23-1747 d p. 1802 m Dolly Winchell Sgt CT
David: b 10-12-1756 d 6-6-1834 m Rhoda Allen Pvt MA
Dorus: b 12-10-1758 d 1-18-1818 m Abigail Dodd Pvt CT
Ebenezer: b 1727 d 1799 m Thankful Nichols Capt CT
Ebenezer: b 9-12-1757 d 3-17-1829 m Mary Pinney Pvt CT
Ebenezer: b 10-2-1752 d 12-8-1827 m Lydia Clark Cpl MA
Edmund: b 4-10-1756 d 10-24-1845 m Mrs Sarah Brown Pvt MA ★
Edward: b — d 1783 m Mabel Pinney PS CT
Elisha: b 7-28-1763 d 9- -1845 m Prudence Hunt Pvt MA
Francis: b 4-25-1740 d 3-18-1828 m Chloe Mills Capt CT
Francis: b 7-4-1747 d 3-15-1805 m Catharine Osborne PS NC
Isaac: b 4-19-1746 d p. 1793 m Mary Merrill Sgt MA
Jeremiah: b 3- -1751 d 1-15-1835 m Deborah Henchman Chp MA
Joel: b 7-14-1732 d 8-15-1775 m Lucy Stevens Pvt MA
John: b 12-25-1732 d 12-28-1813 m Hannah Bigelow Capt CT
John: b 11-12-1750 d 5-5-1825 m Lucy Turner CS & Maj GA
John: b 8-30-1743 d 5-10-1813 m Mary Gale Pvt MA
Jonathan: b 3-31-1732 d p. 1790 m Abigail Gould Pvt MA
Jonathan: b c. 1740 d 1807 m Molly — Pvt MA
Joseph, Jr.: b 4-25-1741 d 9-5-1803 m Rebecca Jones 2Lt PS MA
Joseph: b 1720 d 12-1-1800 m (1)Esther Church (2)Mrs Sarah Cummings MM MA
Joseph: b 2-25-1732 d p. 1790 m Mary Gardner PS MA
Jotham: b 2-24-1745 d 4-17-1808 m Lucy Wetherbee Pvt MA
Moses: b 1729 d 10-15-1776 m Ann Loomis Pvt CT
Moses: b 12-12-1750 d 1812 m Hannah Barnard Pvt CT
Nathan: b 12-8-1751 d 7-21-1830 m Sarah Wellington Pvt MA ★
Richard: b 1723 d 4-6-1813 m (1)Susanna Echoff (2)Lettice Baker PS PA
Robert: b 10-24-1748 d 12-29-1776 m Margaret Whitney Pvt MA
Rufus: b 9-5-1761 d 9-23-1851 m Mary Hale Pvt CT ★
Samuel: b 6-14-1737 d 8-8-1782 m Elizabeth Bond Maj MA
Samuel: b 9-25-1741 d 9- -1791m (1)Mary Kingsbury (2)Mrs Elizabeth Connor Pvt MA
Samuel: b 10-12-1752 d 11-3-1809 m Abigail Fisk Pvt MA
Samuel: b 11-24-1746 d 4-2-1819 m Abigail Upham PS MA
Stephen: b 11-7-1719 d 1797 m Mary Collins PS NH
Thomas: b 11-4-1709 d 1791 m Martha Henley CS MA
Thomas Webster: b 10-4-1743 d p. 1776 m Judith Jones Cpl MA
Timothy: b 3-8-1741 d 3-17-1798 m Elizabeth Fowler Capt MA
Timothy: b 6-19-1756 d 3-29-1847 m Phebe Dewey DrmMaj Sgt NY
Tristram: b 5-30-1721 d p. 1792 m Dorothy Currier Cdr MA

Tristram: b 3-5-1743 d 1807 m (1)Margaret Folger (2)Lovinia — PS NC
William: b 9-22-1764 d 4-16-1850 m Eunice Baker Pvt CT ★
William L.: b 1759 d 1845 m Sara Pigman Pvt MD ★

BARNCARD,
Peter: b 1755-60 d *p.* 1810 m Elizabeth — Pvt PA

BARNDT - see BARNHART

BARNES, (includes BARNS)
Abraham: b 11-22-1733 d 9-7-1816 m Mary Stevens Sgt MA
Abraham: b 1-17-1756 d 10-24-1819 m Margaret Stackpole Pvt MA
Abram: b *c.* 1730 d 1794 m Martha Fort Sol NC
Adam: b 1761/2 d 5-2-1809 m Ruth Shipley Sol & PS MD
Amos: b - -1732 d 2-20-1814 m (2)Abigail Brooks Capt CT
Amos: b 1-9-1755 d 12-18-1840 m Polly Eastman Sol NH
Asa: b 8-24-1745 d 2-15-1819 m Phebe Adkins Pvt CT
Asa: b 5-9-1736 d 3-21-1802 m Lois Yale Col MA
Asa: b 6-28-1754 d 1812 m Matilda Woods Pvt MA
Asa: b 9-23-1760 d 1-8-1824 m Mary Day Pvt MA
Asa: b 1746 d 1825 m Esther Richardson PS NH
Benjamin: b 10-6-1761 d 11-3-1805 m Abigail Goodsell Pvt CT
Benjamin: b 3-8-1741 d 6-13-1834 m (1)Mary Coe (2)Mrs Lucretia Day Miller Capt MA★
Benjamin: b 7-6-1726 d 6-13-1803 m (1)Hannah Beal (2)Ruth Loring (3)Mrs Hannah Leavitt Pvt MA
Benjamin, Jr.: b 6-7-1747 d 12-30-1833 m (1)Miriam Wilcutt (2)Polly Pritchard Pvt MA
Bill: b 2-11-1753 d 2-24-1842 m (1)Eunice — (2)Esther Spalding PS NH
Bradford: b 8-1-1747 d 4-5-1816 m Sarah Howard Pvt MA
Brinsley: b 1715 d *c.* 1795 m (1)Sarah — (2)Elizabeth — PS NC
Canterbury: b 4-13-1760 d 4-29-1833 m Hannah Burr Pvt MA
Charles: b 1-1-1751 d 3-26-1815 m Catherine — Sol VA
Chesley: b 1760 d 9-8-1840 m Mary Means Ens NC ★
Comfort: b 4-3-1737 d 2-8-1816 m Hannah Cooey Pvt MA
Cornelius: b 1720 d 11-3-1778 m Elizabeth Otis Lincoln PS MA
Cornelius, Jr.: b 7-10-1757 d 4-4-1790 m Sarah Clapp Pvt MA
Daniel: b 3-31-1752 d 2- -1814 m (1)Jerusha Webster (2)Sarah Webster Capt CT
Daniel: b 11- -1725 d 4-20-1809 m Sarah Sackett Pvt CT
Daniel: b 7-19-1736 d 10-21-1813 m (1)Martha Bridgman (2)Sarah Straten Capt MA
David: b *c.* 1735 d 3-9-1814 m Rebecca Clarke Sgt MA
David: b 3-24-1731 d 4-26-1811 m Rachel Leonard Pvt MA
David: b — d 7- -1788 m X Pvt NJ
Dimon, Sr.: b 6-14-1740 d 12-10-1815 m Hannah Paine Ens CT
Ebenezer: b 2-3-1759 d 5-17-1836 m Ruth — Sgt MA VT ★
Edward, Jr.: b 3-21-1744 d 11-16-1803 m Submit Forbush LCol MA
Elias: b *c.* 1735 d *a.* 2-1-1808 m Rebecca Turner Pvt NC
Elijah: b 1763 d 1-6-1855 m Eloise Taylor Cpl CT
Elijah: b *c.* 1755 d *p.* 1790 m Marcy Farnham Pvt CT
Elijah: b 1-21-1759 d 4-23-1839 m Lucy Hunter Pvt MA ★
Eliphalet: b 2-17-1756 d 7-27-1827 m X Pvt CT ★
Enos, Sr.: b 1-1-1723 d 3-2-1798 m Abigail Ludington Pvt CT
Enos, Jr.: b 9-27-1755 d 1-22-1837 m (1)Hannah Farnham Woodruff (2)Lucy Woodruff OrdlSgt CT W ★
Ezra: b 9-10-1730 d 7-20-1805 m Eunice Morgan PS CT
Fortunatus: b 9-25-1738 d 11-9-1807 m Persis Hosmer Sgt MA
Francis: b 10-2-1739 d *p.* 5-11-1820 m (1)Anne Brackett (2)Anne Osborne 2Lt VA
Gamaliel: b 1757 d 2-5-1853 m Hannah Harris Pvt NY
George: b 3-4-1732 d 2-28-1821 m Dorothy Vanderbeek PS NY
Hartwell: b 1748 d 9-11-1820 m Hannah Clark Pvt CT ★
Henry: bpt 3-7-1762 d 1818 m Ann Roby Lanham Pvt MD
Isaac: b 1749 d 2-20-1832 m X Pvt CT
Israel: b 10-11-1758 d 4-9-1841 m Susannah Hills Pvt CT ★
Ithiel: b 4-27-1763 d 4-23-1840 m Grizzel Hunt Mus CT ★
Jabez: b 1-15-1734/5 d 1780 m Martha Atkins Pvt CT
Jacob: b 1743 d 1-27-1821 m Rebecca Crowell Pvt NY
James: b *c.* 1742 d 1809 m Experience Wise Lt CT
James: b 1740 d 1850 m Tempy Parker Pvt NC
James: b 1757 d 4-11-1825 m Fanny — Pvt VA ★
Jeremiah: b 3-3-1751 d 8-28-1845 m Sarah Curtis Pvt MA
Jeremiah: b 1756 d 8-24-1840 m Phoebe Schellinger Pvt NY
John: b 1759 d 6-12-1834 m Lucretia Barnes Pvt Arfr CT ★
John: b 1-28-1745/6 d *p.* 2-12-1798 m Abigail Collins Pvt CT
John: b 11-6-1763 d 9-12-1834 m Sarah Howe Pvt MA ★
John, Sr.: b 1735 d 1804 m Elizabeth Hamilton Capt NY
John: b — d *p.* 9-9-1789 m Christian — PS NC
John: b — d 3- -1812 m Mary Lemen Lt VA
John: b 1740 d 1817 m Hannah Cartmell Ens VA
John C.: b 2-24-1761 d 7-12-1842 m (1)Joanna Malory (2)Abigail Barnes Pvt CT ★
Jonah: b 5-6-1763 d 11-21-1835 m Abigail Curtis Pvt Drm CT ★
Jonathan: b 3-2-1760 d 6- -1845 m Sybil Bartholomew Drm CT ★
Jonathan: b 4-21-1740 d 3-21-1797 m Dorothey How Capt MA
Jonathan: b 3-4-1752 d 9-9-1822 m Phebe Talmage Pvt NY
Joseph, Sr.: b 12-17-1726/27 d 2-13-1813 m Hannah Stowe Capt MA
Joseph, Jr.: b 5-2-1751 d 3-24-1819 m Sybel Buck Pvt MA
Joseph: b 11-21-1728-30 d 3-25-1826 m (1)Susanna Cannon (2)Elizabeth — Lt MA

Joseph: b 6-1-1751 d 9- -1814 m Elizabeth Wheeler Pvt MA
Joseph: b 1762 d 5-28-1838 m Lydia Thompson Pvt MA ★
Joseph, Sr.: b 7-6-1726 d 10-29-1781 m Joanna Sprague Dr NH
Joseph, Jr.: b 5-2-1754 d 8-24-1826 m Sarah Hills Pvt NH
Joshua: b 1-11-1723 d 1-7-1790 m Deborah Woodin Pvt CT
Joshua: b *c.* 1753 d 1806 m Delilah Williams 1Lt MD
Joshua: b 12-20-1756 d 2-21-1813 m Mary — Pvt Bbd MA
Josiah: b 9-6-1764 d 5-23-1835 m Olive Cornwell Cpl CT ★
Josiah: b 1752 d 7-28-1843 m Rebecca Kidder Pvt MA
Lemuel: bpt 1-30-1757 d *p.* 1801 m Rebecca Bement Pvt MA
Leven: b 1-25-1762 d 2-7-1836 m Hannah Slack PS MD
Levi: b 3-1-1753 d 6-8-1824 m Hannah Waterman Pvt RI
Moses: b 8-8-1732 d *p.* 1781 m Hepzibah Osborn Pvt CT
Moses: b 1741 d *p.* 1785 m Phebe Blakeslee Pvt CT
Moses: b 11-15-1760 d 12-12-1825 m Olive Barnes Pvt CT
Moses: b 12-14-1740 d 3-2-1781 m Sarah Banister Capt MA
Moses: b 3-27-1714 d 4-28-1802 m Hannah Olds Pvt MA
Nathan: b 12- -1758 d 6-13-1847 m Martha Judd Pvt CT
Nathaniel: b 1-11-1707 d 10-1-1798 m (1)Mary Russell (2)Abigail Hotchkiss (3)Abigail Howell Pvt CT
Nathaniel: bpt 5-1-1743 d 8-25-1808 m (1)Polly Dawson (2)Hannah Gray Pvt CT
Nathaniel: b 3-18-1740 d 1790-1800 m Elizabeth Brown SeaCap NY
Nehemiah: b 2-2-1761 d 10-10-1839 m Hannah Williams Pvt CL ★
Noah: b 1-12-1747 d *p.* 1782 m Hannah Parsons Pvt CT
Noah: b 12- -1703 d 12-27-1794 m Hannah Parsons CS NY
Oliver: b *c.* 1750 d — m Mary Negus Cpl MA
Peter: b 1-27-1744 d 4-29-1814 m Sophia Inman Pvt NY
Phineas: b 5-9-1756 d 9-3-1828 m Mary Lynch Pvt MA
Reuben: b 4-22-1756 d *p.* 1840 m X Pvt CT ★
Richard: b 3-16-1747 d 1813 m (1)Anna Bathrick (2)Mary Bennett Pvt MA
Richard: b 5-23-1762 d 1-23-1839 m Elizabeth Tappan Pvt NY
Robert: b *c.* 1750 d — m Sarah Curtis Cpl MA
Samuel: b 5-10-1758 d 1-27-1833 m Lydia Fowler Pvt MA ★
Samuel: b 11-12-1752 d 7-16-1844 m Priscilla Wilson Fif Pvt PA
Samuel: b 1760 d 3- -1812 m Mary Kellar Pvt VT
Shadrack: b *c.* 1752 d *c.* 1844 m Hannah Turner Sol NC
Shadrack: b 2-6-1764 d 12-31-1844 m Frau Mozingo Sgt VA ★
Silas: b 1-21-1735 d 1-6-1813 m Betty Bigelow Pvt PS MA
Stephen: b 1-2-1704 d 3-27-1777 m Martha Wheadon PS CT
Stephen: b 1736 d *c.* 1800 m Ezudia Kellogg Pvt CT
Theodore: b — d 1823 m Mary Sciester Pvt PA
Thomas: b 4-26-1744 d 12-7-1825 m Esther Wilcox Pvt CT
Thomas: b 1752 d 3-24-1821 m Hannah Driver Maj MA ★
Thomas: b 12-25-1743 d 11-20-1819 m Mary Whitemore Pvt MA
Thomas: b 1763 d 3-19-1851 m (1)Alice Bohannon (2)Mary Strien Ens NC
Thomas: b 1760 d 1826 m Margaret Caldo Pvt PA
Thomas: b 7-3-1753 d 1-8-1811 m Anna Ober Pvt VT W ★
Thomas: b 12-6-1750 d 10-19-1836 m Sarah Scott Sgt VA
Timothy: b 4-8-1749 d 11- -1825 m Eunice Munson Pvt CT
Timothy: b 4-1-1739 d 3-12-1831 m Marian Miller Pvt CT
Timothy: b *a.* 1750 d 6-17-1775 m Mercy Bucklin Pvt MA
Uz: b 9-24-1752 d 4-29-1833 m (1)Lydda — (2)Tabotha Ogden Pvt VA PA
Weavour: b *c.* 1720 d 2-27-1781 m Elizabeth — PS MD
William: b — d *p.* 1790 m Deborah Griswold Pvt CT
William, Jr.: b 9- -1747 d 1-24-1831 m (1)Lydia Hall (2)Esther Luddon Pvt MA
William: b 7-7-1751 d 9- -1828 m Lucy Pease Pvt MA
William: b *c.* 1740 d 9-22-1805 m Tabitha Meacham Pvt MA
William: b 3-5-1738 d 8-23 1807 m Catherine Storm MM Pvt NY
William, Sr.: b 8-16-1723 d 7-3-1814 m Jemima Scherrill PS NY
William: b 1746 d 5-2-1823 m Jane — PS PA
William: b 2-19-1754 d 10-23-1824 m Freelove Whipple Pvt MA VT
William: b 1735 d 1824 m Mary Marietta — Pvt VA MD

BARNETT, (includes BARNET)
Abraham: b 11740-2 d 1792 m Mary Brownfield CS NC
Alexander: b 8-3-1745 d 2-16-1819 m Jane — Pvt KY
Alexander: b 1754 d 1826 m Dorcas Long Pvt SC
Ann Spratt: b 1720 d *p.* 1781 m John Barnett PS NC
David: b 7-31-1755 d *a.* 9-4-1836 m Lucinda Dunahoo Pvt NC ★
David: b 5-29-1760 d 3-22-1845 m Mary Wallace Sol VA
George: b 1742 d 1810 m Sarah Ann — Mil VA
Hugh, Jr.: b *c.* 1760 d 1796 m Margaret McFarland Pvt NC
James: b 11-19-1748 d 11-10-1819 m Jerusha Hyde Sgt CT
James: b 1758 d 5-15-1824 m Martha Finney Pvt MD
James: b 1749 d 2-28-1821 m Martha Mills Sol NY
James: b 1756 d 5-1-1805 m Mary Allen Pvt PA
James: b 1742 d *p.* 1802 m Ann Rachel Clements Col VA
James: b 1703 d 1787 m Jane Miller Capt VA
James: b 1-16-1750 d 8-27-1835 m Marcy Hawkins Capt VA ★
James: b — d 1815 m Mrs Ann — Capt VA
James: b *c.* 1735 d *p.* 9-17-1781 m Mildred Neville Capt VA
James: b 1735 d 1798 m Jane Greenlee Pvt VA
Jesse: b 7-4-1749 d 1834 m (1)Elizabeth — (2)Elizabeth Terry Sol PS NC
Joel: b 10-13-1762 d 7-30-1851 m (1)Anna Crawford (2)Mildred Meriwether Sol GA
John: b 6-27-1762 d 3-10-1814 m Caroline Fleming Tindall Sol GA

BARNETT, contd.
John: b 1759 d 1835 m Hannah Morrison Pvt MA ★
John: b 6-26-1753 d 12-5-1837 m Tryphena (Spencer) Parker Chp MA
John: b 1749 d 7-16-1805 m Elizabeth Flinn Pvt PA
John: b 1755 d 7-7-1825 m Rachel Crosby Pvt PA
John: b 7-17-1760 d 7-7-1827 m Eleanor — Pvt PA
John: b c. 1740 d c. 5-11-1787 m Ann Bochet Capt PS SC
John: b 3-6-1752 d 11-24-1833 m (1)Lucy Medlock (2)Mary — Sgt VA
John: b 1714 d 1800 m Ann — Pvt VA
John: b c. 1738 d 1815 m — O'Connell Pvt VA
John Perry: b 7-23-1764 d 9-8-1828 m Elizabeth Self Fif VA ★
Joseph: b 1726 d 1808 m Elizabeth Graham Pvt PS PA
Joseph: b 1754 d 4-15-1838 m Elizabeth Scott Pvt PA
Joseph: b 5- -1760 d 6-19-1846 m Jane Smith Pvt PA ★
Joseph: b c. 1730 d p. 8-8-1795 m Abagail — Sol VA
Nathan: b 1729 d 1805 m Lucy Webb Sol GA
Nathaniel: b 2-9-1755 d 7-18-1846 m Esther Smith Pvt CT
Nathaniel: b c. 1727 d 1820 m Susannah Crawford Sol GA
Robert: b 1732 d 1797 m Rachel Barnett Sgt KY
Robert: b 4-14-1754 d 1827 m (1)Sarah Love (2)Sarah Boyd Pvt SC
Robert: b a. 1743 d 1787 m Mary Montgomery Pvt VA
Simon: b 1743 d 3-1-1837 m Margaret Seidell Smn NY
Thomas: b 1743 d 4-9-1813 m Margaret Pentz Pvt PA
Thomas: b 11-13-1761 d 3-28-1836 m Jane Finney Pvt PA
Thomas Spratt: b 1742 d 1829 m (1)Mary McKnight (2)Ann Graham Sol NC
William: b 3-4-1761 d 10-25-1834 m (1)Mary Meriwether (2)Mrs Sallie Bibb Pvt GA VA
William: b 1728 d 12-1-1790 m X Maj NJ
William: b 11-16-1747 d 10-25-1834 m Jean Jack Capt NC
William: b 5-15-1759 d 5-5-1839 m Nancy Richardson Pvt SC ★
William: b 4-14-1756 d 2-3-1831 m Frances Jones Pvt VA

BARNEY,
Aaron: b 4-12-1734 d 1817 m Susannah Carpenter 1Lt MA
Benjamin: b 1740 d 1831 m Amy Conklin Grant Pvt MA ★
Benjamin: b 8-8-1732 d 2-6-1803 m Jemima Jenkins PS MA
Benjamin: b 1760 d 7-24-1819 m Deborah Crapo Pvt MA ★
Christopher: b 28-1739 d 9-25-1823 m Experience Smith 1Lt MA
Constant: b 4-23-1731 d 8-4-1819 m Hannah Carpenter Pvt NH
Daniel, Jr.: b 1-24-1739 d p. 1785 m Elizabeth — Pvt PS NH
David: b 1-24-1739 d p. 1785 m Elizabeth — Pvt PS NH
Edward: b 8-18-1749 d 8-9-1835 m (1)Elizabeth Brown (2)Pheobe Bennett Pvt VT
Elisha: b 3-26-1730 d 10-9-1781 m Silence Eddy Capt PS MA
Jacob: b 1743 d 8-29-1821 m Mercy Burt Sgt MA
Jeffery Amherst: b 8-31-1760 d 10-19-1817 m Phila Aldrich Abner Pvt NH
John: b 7-24-1752 d 3-25-1840 m (1)Elizabeth — (2)Charity Stiles (3)Margaret Webster (4)Mary Miles PS MD
John, Sr.: b 5-1-1730 d 2-19-1807 m Rebecca Martin PS VT
John, Jr.: b 9-15-1753 d 5-6-1793 m (1)Sarah — (2)Ruth Shepardson Pvt VT
Jonathan: b 1751 d 1826 m Abigail Eddy Cpl MA
Jonathan: b 4-24-1758 d 12-4-1814 m Elizabeth Mason SgtMaj MA ★
Joseph: b c. 1735 d 1821 m Sybil Chapman Pvt CT
Joseph: b 11-28-1755 d 1836/7 m Experience Simmons Sgt MA ★
Joseph: b 3-15-1731 d 10-4-1821 m Lois Martin Pvt MA
Joshua: b 7-6-1759 d 12-1-1818 m (1)Ann Bedford (2)Harriet Cole Commo PA
Josiah, Jr.: b 8-10-1736 d 2-14-1819 m Mehitable Millerd Pvt MA
Luther: b 3-4-1757 d 9-20-1844 m (1)Abigail Winship (2)Ruth Garrison Pvt NS MA ★
Martin: b 1759 d p. 1789 m Betsey Bucklin Drm MA
Rufus: b 7-22-1754 d 2-28-1826 m Sarah Holmes Capt MA
Samuel: b 1753 d 7-17-1805 m Sarah Bassett Pvt CT
Thomas: b 1745 d 9-13-1828 m Mabel Chittenden Capt VT
William: b c. 1762 d — m Mercy Crapo Pvt MA

BARNHART, (includes BARNDT, BARNHARDT, BERNHARD & BERNHART)
Cornelius: b 7-25-1752 d p. 1832 m — Bellinger Pvt NY
Henry: b 10-26-1763 d 8-5-1805 m Elizabeth Shadick Pvt NY
Jacob: b c. 1750 d 1839 m Catharine — Cpl PA
Jeremiah: b 11-5-1758 d 9- -1834 m Hannah Winslow Pvt NY ★
John: b 1-21-1756 d 1-24-1827 m (1)Barbara Flury (2)Susanna Balsley (3)Elizabeth Balsley Pvt PA
John (or Wendell): b 1-6-1746 d 12-26-1813 m Catherine Ebling Pvt PA
John: b 6-13-1759 d 12-4-1829 m Rachel Heiser Pvt PA
John Christian: b 5-5-1719 d 8-10-1799 m Mary Elizabeth Barringer PS NC
Mathias: b 4-3-1752 d 6-6-1818 m Anne Margaret Boshart Sol NC
Mathias: b c. 1730 d 4-1-1794 m Anna Margaret Bugel Pvt PS PA
Peter: b 1751 d 8-13-1836 m Molly Boyer Pvt PA
Philip: b 7-24-1757 d 4-3-1843 m Elizabeth Antes Pvt PA
Stephen, Sr.: b c. 1714 d 9-29-1778 m (1)Maria Bertolet (2)Elizabeth Ely PS PA
Stephen, Jr.: b 3-7-1755 d 7-18-1826 m Magdalene Messerschmidt Pvt PS PA

BARNHILL,
Robert: b c. 1750 d p. 7-22-1818 m Rachael — PS NC
William: b c. 1720 d p. 9-23-1791 m Sarah — Sol NC
William, Sr.: b 5-4-1735 d 5-4-1810 m Isabella Barr Pvt CS NC

BARNHISER,
John: b c. 1753 d 6-2-1848 m (1)Mary — (2) X Pvt PA ★

BARNITZ,
Daniel: b 1755 d 12-13-1827 m (1)Susan Eichelberger (2)Mrs Decker Pvt PA
Jacob: b 1758 d 4-16-1828 m Anna Maria McClean Ens PA

BARNSAY,
William: b a. 1754 d a. 4-5-1825 m Margaret Wallace PS VA

BARNSLEY,
John: b 1736 d 2-2-1796 m Elizabeth Van Court Pvt Tms PA

BARNUM,
Abel: b 1757 d 1799 m Annis Turner Pvt CT
Abijah: b 1742 d 1824 m Orpha Hamilton PS CS CT
Ashbel D.: b c. 1766 d 6-3-1816 m Abigale — Pvt VT
Azor: b 1746 d 9-9-1807 m Anna Sweet Capt NY
Bethuel: b c. 12-25-1756 d p. 1811 m Sarah Molineaux Pvt NY
Caleb: b 6-30-1737 d 8-23-1776 m Priscilla Rice Chp MA
David: b 3-30-1733 d 1-28-1822 m (2)Mrs Jemima Stevens Pvt CT
David: b 1739 d 1795 m Rachel Benedict Sol CT
Ebenezer: b 11-16-1751 d 1-21-1830 m Mabel Booth Cpl CT
Elijah: b 2-1-1738 d 6-28-1807 m Hannah — Lt CT
Eliphalet: b 12-10-1750 d 2-2-1803 m Mary Benedict Sgt CT
Ephraim: b 8-28-1733 d 4-17-1817 m (1)Keziah Covill (2)Rachel Beebe (3)Anna Stow Capt CT
Ezbon: b 7-21-1753 d 1835 m X Pvt CT ★
Gideon: b c. 1720 d 1818 m (1)Mary Humphrey (2)Elizabeth Merry Sgt VT
Jabez: b 5-7-1760 d 3-3-1814 m (1)Susanna — (2)Mary Sanford Pvt MA
Jehiel: b 1751 d 4-23-1831 m Rachel — Sgt CT ★
John: b 4-2-1758 d 2-23-1819 m Sally Parish Pvt CT
Joseph: b a. 1739 d 4-13-1791 m (1)Keziah — (3)Mabel — Sol CT
Joshua, Sr.: b 1714 d p. 9-3-1777 m Emma Barnum 1Lt NY
Joshua, Jr.: b 1737 d 10-23-1822 m Adah Crane Capt NY
Joshua, 3rd: b 1-20-1763 d 1-14-1818 m Thankful Crosby Pvt NY
Justus: b c. 1753 d p. 1786 m Mary Benedict Pvt CT
Lazarus: b c. 1739 d 1-3-1814 m (1)Rachel — (2)Sarah — Pvt CT
Levi: b 1754 d 1796 m Joanna Stocker Pvt CT
Matthew: b 1736/37 d 5-13-1805 m Jane Dibble Cpl CT
Noah: b 6-27-1760 d 12- -1828 m Catharine Bishop Pvt CT
Samuel: b 4-18-1749 d 6-4-1815 m Rebecca Church Lt CT
Seth: b 11-3-1754 d 12-26-1809 m Abigail Bearss Pvt CT ★
Seth, Sr.: b a. 1754 d 1799 m Mary Cartwright Pvt CT
Stephen: b 1745 d 1819 m Ruth Strong Sgt CT ★
Stephen: b 2-17-1757 d 8-24-1834 m (1)Lucy Wolcott (2)Ruth North Pvt MA
Stephen: b 10-16-1762 d 6-21-1847 m Sarah Benedict Pvt CT ★
Thaddeus: b 1749 d 4-10-1816 m Lois Stevens Ens CT
Thomas: b 8-25-1749 d 9-28-1837 m (1)Achsah Benedict (2)Martha Berry Sgt NY ★
Thomas S: b 2-22-1752 d 2-17-1836 m Anna Skells Pvt Spy MA ★

BARNWELL,
Edward: b 11-16-1757 d 4-15-1808 m (1)Mary Bower Williamson (2)Mary Hutson Wigg LCol SC
James: b 10-10-1756 d 3-25-1825 m Susan Harper Pvt NC W ★
John: b 7-15-1748 d 1799 m (1)Elizabeth Fenwicke (2)Ann Hutson BGen SC
Robert: b 12-21-1761 d 10-24-1814 m Elizabeth Hayne Wigg Sol SC

BARR, (includes O'BARR; see also BARRE)
Adam: b 1-10-1761 d 11-10-1857 m Mary Claycomb Sol DE
Andrew: b c. 1740 d 1815 m Jane Hamilton Pvt PA
Daniel: b — d p. 8-19-1806 m Amy — Pvt NC
David: b 1705 d 7-2-1787 m (1)Anna More(?) (2)Elizabeth(?) — PS MD
David: b 8-15-1750 d 1835 m Sarah Thompson Pvt PA ★
George: b c. 1760 d 3- -1814 m Elizabeth Richards Pvt PA
Hugh: b 11-12-1760 d 3-5-1833 m (1)Sarah Stone (2)Sarah Collins Sgt & Fif MA ★
Hugh: b 1757/58 d 4-24-1842 m (1)Priscilla James (2) X Pvt NC ★
Isaac: b 12-14-1751 d 12-14-1832 m Anna Foster Pvt Trm VA ★
James: b 12-12-1752 d 3-7-1829 m Molly Cummings MM NH
James: b 9-24-1753 d 9- -1838 m Rachel Ross OrdlSgt NJ ★
James: b 1746 d 5-22-1788 m Elizabeth McCorkle Capt NC
James: b 1738 d 5-14-1823 m Elizabeth Kirk PS Pvt PA
John: b 1727 d 11-4-1815 m Damarias — Pvt MA
John: b c. 1750 d 1825 m Catherine Reiser Pvt PA
John: b c. 1750 d 1806 m Susanna Young 1Lt PA
John: b c. 1752 d 1811-21 m Mary Jane Bell Pvt PA
Joseph: b 1735 d 6-30-1801 m Ann Nye Pvt MA
Martin: b 1745 d 1821 m Barbara Anne — Pvt PA

Patrick: b 1740 d *p*. 1801 m Nancy Killpatrick Pvt NC
Paul: b 3-16-1747 d 12-7-1822 m Dorothea Heller Pvt PA
Philip: b 6-24-1749 d 8-7-1829 m Mary Bond Pvt VA ★
Robert: b 1748 d *p*. 1784 m Rebecca Tilton 2Lt PA
Robert: b 10- -1755 d 3-15-1857 m (2) X Pvt PA
Samuel: b 1754 d 9-25-1842 m Margaret Boies Pvt NH
Thomas: b *c*. 1750 d *p*. 3-18-1812 m Margaret Roan Capt PA
Thomas: b 1756 d *p*. 1781 m — Wilson Pvt PA

BARRACK,
William: b *c*. 1730 d *p*. 1803 m Elizabeth — PS NJ

BARRAS,
Vincent: b 8-5-1750 d *a*. 1834 m Marie Francoise Labbe PS LA

BARRAUD,
Philip: b 1760 d 1833 m Anne Hansford Dr VA

BARRE,
Jacob: b *c*. 1750 d 1800 m Mary Christiana Quattlebaum 1Lt SC

BARRELL,
Colburn: b 5-4-1738 d 11-30-1777 m Desiah Bowker Sgt MA
James, Sr.: b 12-29-1727 d 4-17-1827 m Deborah Bowker Pvt MA
James, Jr.: b 6-30-1751 d *p*. 1795 m Martha Farrow Pvt MA
Joseph: b 2-28-1739/40 d 10-13-1804 m Ann Pierce PS MA
Joshua: b 11-30-1746 d 5-25-1828 m Olive Bass Pvt MA
William: b 10-14-1753 d 3-7-1846 m Rebecca Wilder Pvt MA

BARRETT, (includes BARRATT BARRET & BERRITT)
Alexander: b *c*. 1756 d *p*. 1790 m Eleanor Caecil Pvt MD
Amos: b 4-23-1752 d 1-25-1829 m Mary Hubbard Pvt MA
Arthur: b 9-10-1742 d 3-7-1828 m Elizabeth Baldwin Pvt PA
Benjamin: b 9-19-1759 d 2-8-1845 m Clarinda Barnes Pvt MA
Benjamin: b 6-22-1760 d 12-12-1831 m Dorothy Day Pvt NH
Casper: b *a*. 1732 d 1796 m Elizabeth Magdalene Wannemaker Pvt PA
Daniel: b 4-30-1755 d 1830 m Rebekah Bosworth CS MA
Edward: b 1740 d 1829 m (1)Susan Griffith (2)Esther Wallace Burnsides Pvt VA CL
Elijah: b *c*. 1740 d *p*. 1-7-1785 m X Ens NJ
Ezekiel, Jr.: b 9-6-1740 d 2-10-1838 m (1)Sarah Lathrop (2)Sally Freeman Sgt CT
Francis: b 2-20-1762 d 1833 m Elizabeth Lowrey Sgt VA ★
Isaac: b 4-12-1753 d 12-10-1826 m Susan Page Pvt MA
Isaac: b 5-28-1744 d 6-28-1830 m Philena Whitemore Sol NH
Isaac: b 1755 d 3-7-1824 m Jemima Lockwood Pvt NY
Israel: b 3-21-1756 d 1828 m Lucy Mower Sol MA ★
Jacob: b 4-8-1764 d 10-15-1846 m Jane Stranahan Pvt CT ★
James, Sr.: b 7-31-1710 d 4-11-1779 m Rebecca Hubbard Col MA
James, Jr.: b 1-4-1733 d 10-30-1799 m Millicent Esterbrook Pvt PS MA
Joel: b 1762 d — m Eunice Barrett Pvt MA
John: b 2-14-1719/20 d 4-19-1790 m Lois Brooks MM MA
John: b 6-12-1708 d 9-9-1786 m Sarah Gerrish PS CS MA
John: b 1721 d 7-31-1802 m Elizabeth — Pvt NY
John: b 12-7-1731 d 12-3-1806 m Elizabeth Edwards LCol VT
John: b 5-19-1748 d 6-9-1830 m Mary Strachan Pvt VA
Jonas: b 9-24-1737 d 7-31-1803 m (1)Mary Fletcher (2)Uranah Locke Lt MA
Jonathan, Sr.: b 7-6-1731 d 1802/1803 m (1)Sarah Hascal (2)Mary — PS CT
Jonathan, 2nd: b 3-29-1760 d 5-13-1839 m (1)Elizabeth Murdock (2)Mrs. Bruce Pvt CT ★
Jonathan: b 10-27-1746 d 9-11-1818 m Abigail Raymond Pvt MA
Jonathan: b *c*. 1750 d *a*. 11-24-1830 m Amy Lowe NLt VA
Joseph: b 1-25-1735 d 1821 m Sarah Brooks Capt NH
Joseph, Jr.: b 4-15-1853 d 7-10-1809 m (1)Sarah — (2)Martha Carter Pvt MA
Lemuel: b 1722 d 1814 m Sarah Tittle Col CS PS MD
Lemuel: b 10-12-1761 d 10-4-1842 m Anna Chase Pvt MA
Lewis: b 6-7-1752 d 1835 m (1)Elizabeth Anderson (2)Jane Price (3)Mary Toombs (4)Mrs Patsey Coates Pvt VA ★
Moses: b 9-3-1751 d 4-30-1830 m (1)Hannah Fuller (2)Lydia Huntington Loomis Pvt CT
Nathan: b 12-30-1735 d 2-22-1791 m Miriam Hunt LCol MA
Nathaniel: b 1765 d 12-29-1853 m Sybil Spaulding Pvt NH
Ninian: b 1751 d 1806/7 m Mary James Pvt PS MD
Oliver, Sr.: b 1-17-1712 d 4-4-1788 m Hannah Hunt Sol MA
Oliver, Jr.: b 7-22-1746 d 5-11-1817 m Sarah Whitcomb Sgt MA
Oliver: b 1-9-1726 d 10-7-1777 m Anna Fiske MM Sol MA
Oliver: b 4-17-1755 d 3-13-1832 m Elizabeth High Ens NH ★
Philip: b 1729 d 10-26-1784 m Miriam Sipple CS DE
Reuben: b 1730 d 9-19-1800 m Sarah Fletcher PS CS NH
Reuben: b *c*. 1762 d 8-4-1830 m Elizabeth Knowlton Sol NY
Robert: b — d 6-9-1823 m Barbara Winston Capt VA
Robert: b 4-4-1716 d 1805 m (1)Elizabeth Lewis (2)Ann Lee PS VA
Samuel: b 1-17-1738 d 8-25-1798 m (1)Mary Clark (2)Elizabeth Salisbury PS CS MA
Samuel: b 4-4-1755 d 12-10-1844 m Abigail (Waterbury) Gray Pvt NY ★
Samuel: b 2-21-1758 d 1838 m Ellen Hanna Pvt VA ★

Simeon: b 11-2-1750 d 12-22-1832 m Ruth Wright Sgt MA
Smith: b 1766 d *p*. 1832 m Abigail White Pvt CT
Stephen: b 4-18-1720 d 4-25-1793 m Elizabeth Hubbard How Pvt MA
Thomas: b 1761/62 d 4-1-1844 m X Pvt CT
Thomas, Sr.: b 10-2-1707 d 6-20-1779 m Mary Jones CS MA
Thomas, Jr.: b 11-15-1737 d 3-16-1816 m (1)Dorcas Minott (2) Hannah Stone Capt MA
Thornton: b 5-2-1740 d 6- -1806 m Abigail Bowker Cpl MA
William: b 4-4-1755 d 11-5-1841 m Mary Lamplugh Cpl MD
William: b 1752 d — m Eunice Barrett Pvt NY
William: b 1-2-1760 d 2-16-1815 m Dorothy Winston Capt VA
William: b 1713 d 1789 m Mary — PS VA
Zadoc: b 1740 d 1819 m Mary — PS NH

BARRICK,
Nicholas: b — d *p*. 7- -1842 m Mary — Sol PA State ★

BARRICKLO,
Farrington: b 9-24-1756 d 10- -1817 m Mary Reed Lt NJ

BARRICKMAN, (includes BACKMAN)
Jacob: 2-17-1763 d 2-23-1842 m Jane Swan Pvt PA
Jacob: b *c*. 1750 d 1786 m Mary — Pvt VA

BARRINGER,
Henry: b 9-21-1714 d 11-2-1801 m Elizabeth Best PS NY
Jacob: b 9-30-1746 d 7-25-1828 m Katherine Haynes Pvt NY
John: b 11-26-1752 d 8-25-1817 m Christina Burlinger Capt NC
John Paul: b 6-4-1721 d 1-1-1807 m (1)Ann Eliza Eisemen (2)Catherine Blackwelder PS & CS NC
Matthias: b *a*. 1747 d 1776 m Margaret Bushart Capt NC
Peter: b 1749 d 11-28-1839 m Susan Kuhn Pvt NY ★

BARRON,
Archibald: b 1734 d 5-17-1817 m Elizabeth Ingram Wgm SC
Barnaba: b 4-26-1759 d 1803-8 m Constance Mercer Pvt NC
Benjamin: b 2-22-1755 d 1816 m Abigail Varnum Sgt MA
Daniel: b 1755 d 1810 m Mary Ann Wilson Pvt MD
Elias: b 1756 d 3-9-1822 m Lucy Handley Pvt MA
Eliseus: b 6-20-1728 d *p*. 1777 m Lydia Jefts PS Pvt MA
Ellis: b 1736 d 5-27-1807 m Sarah Stone Capt PS NJ
Isaac: b 1750 d 5-8-1820 m Anna Spalding Lt MA
Isaac: b *a*. 1753 d *p*. 1781 m Rachel Rich Lt MA
James: b 1740 d 5-14-1787 m Jane Cowper Commo VA
John: b 10-3-1749 d 3-14-1841 m Susanah McBee Pvt NC & VA ★
John: b 11- -1755 d 2-9-1820 m Susanna (Huston) Ferguson Pvt PA
John: b 1745 d 3-14-1814 m Mehitabel Rogers Maj VT
Jonathan: b 6-30-1760 d 12-2-1835 m Thankful Minor Pvt NH
Joseph: b *c*. 1763 d 5-9-1847 m Magdelaine Langdon Pvt CL W ★
Joseph: b *c*. 1750 d *p*. 8-2-1793 m Ann — Pvt CS VA
Joshua: b 6-30-1749 d 5-4-1828 m (1)Lavina Derby (3)Sarah (Wheeler) West Pvt MA
Jotham: b 12-1-1760 d 3-21-1814 m Mehitable Wood Cpl MA
Moses: b 1755 d 3-7-1841 m Mary Barron Pvt NH
Oliver: b 1-7-1733 d 11-11-1809 m Abagail Proctor Capt CS PS MA
Samuel: b 2-28-1757 d 10-3-1836 m Sybel Cummings Pvt NH
Samuel: b 1711 d 9-1-1801 m Elizabeth Frazee PS NJ
Timothy: b 1-20-1740 d 11-17-1797 m Olive (Moore) Russell Capt NH
William: b *c*. 1740 d 1788 m Prudence Davis Sol GA
William: b 1755 d 1836 m Sarah Brunette Pvt GA
William: b 1737 d 8-28-1805 m Olive Johnson Capt NH
William: b 7-2-1743 d 6-2-1813 m Rebecca Fassett Capt CS NH
William, Sr.: b *c*. 1730 d 5-19-1797 m (1)Isabel Larrabee (2)Tabitha Williams (3)Jemima — Pvt PS NH
William, Jr.: b 4-30-1765 d 8-24-1851 m (1)Janet McCurdy (2)Cynthia Metcalf Pvt PS NH★

BARROWS, (includes BARROW & BARRUS)
Andrew: b 11-30-1748 d 2-10-1809 m Sarah Perkins Pvt MA
Benjamin: b 1716 d 11-29-1800 m (1)Lois Tilson (2)Hannah Atwood Sol MA
Daniel: b 4-4-1729 d 4-9-1779 m Prudence Briggs Pvt MA
Daniel: b 12-6-1757 d 11-8-1837 m Hannah Stone Pvt VA & NC ★
David: b 12-22-1758 d *p*. 1790 m (1)Mary Walker (2)Rachael Parker Sol CT
Elisha: b 4-13-1730 d 3-10-1814 m Hannah Mayo PS CT
Ephraim: b 8-14-1762 d 5-2-1838 m Charlotte Churchill Pvt MA ★
Gershom: b 4-29-1730 d 10-14-1814 m Elizabeth Tuttle Capt CT
Isaac: b 4-1-1725 d 1779 m Elizabeth Palmer Lt CT
Isaac: b 12-30-1742 d 1833 m Rebecca Turner Pvt CT
Isaac: b 7-1-1750 d 7-12-1828 m Annie Blackmer Sgt MA
Isaac: b 1760 d 11-5-1794 m Elizabeth Miller Pvt MA
Jabez: b 7-27-1737 d 4-18-1811 m Martha Stow Lt CT
James: b 1-31-1757 d 1-20-1828 m Patience Crenshaw Pvt SC
Jeremiah: b 10-18-1756 d 10-25-1850 m Prudence Shafter Pvt NH
John: b 10-13-1743 d 3-30-1782 m Sarah Morton Capt MA
John: b 5-22-1740 d 1794 m Hannah Robinson Pvt NH
Joseph: b 11- -1748 d 2-13-1825 m Esther Wetherell Pvt MA

BARROWS, contd.

Lemuel: b 3-23-1762 d 8-1-1845 m Abigail Grant Pvt CT
Michael: b 7-2-1751 d 11-26-1834 m Elizabeth Simonds Sgt PS NH
Moses: b 1765 d a. 2-10-1813 m Elizabeth Colby Pvt MA W★
Moses: b 1755 d 1801 m Mildred Powell Pvt NC
Peleg: b 1708 d 5-24-1803 m Hopestill Darling Pvt MA
Peter: b 7-19-1755 d 1841 m Elizabeth Barrows Pvt RI
Philbrook: b 10-21-1754 d 11-28-1846 m (1)Celinda Bucklin (2)Mrs Hannah Wheaton (3)Mrs Phebe Warner Pvt Mar MA ★
Robert: b 5-8-1739 d 7-6-1826 m Joanna Porter PS CT
Samuel: b 3-8-1824 d 1775 m Desire Rogers Pvt MA
Samuel: b a. 4-14-1734 d 1-18-1791 m Barbara Anderson MM VT or MA
Thomas: b 9-13-1716 d 7-16-1802 m (1)Mehitabel Porter (2)Abigail Crane (3)Elizabeth Turner Cpl CT
Thomas: b 9-20-1742 d 5-4-1802 m (1)Eleanor Cross (2)Jerusha Robinson Ens CT
Thomas: b 7-27-1750 d 3-14-1844 m Martha Hall Cpl CT ★
Thomas: b 1-16-1760 d 8-11-1848 m Bethia Besse Pvt MA
William: b 1-22-1756 d 11-22-1837 m (1)Sarah Dunham (2)Catherine Pratt Macomber Pvt MA ★
Zadoc: b 8-17-1734 d p. 1790 m Jemima Doten Sol MA

BARRY, (includes BARRE)

Andrew: b 1746 d 6-17-1811 m Margaret Katherine Moore Capt SC
Jacob: b 1754 d 3- -1831 m (1)Susanna Hall (2)Mary Disney Pvt MD
James: b c. 1740 d p. 1781 m Ann Philips Sgt PA
James: b 1734 d 11- -1788 m Rachel Phillips LCol PA
John: b 5-6-1735 d 12-5-1784 m Mary Blake Pvt MA
Margaret Catharine Moore: b 1752 d 9-29-1823 m Andrew Barry Sct SC
Richard: b 1726 d 8-21-1801 m Annie Price PS NC
Standish: b 11-25-1763 d 11-27-1844 m Agnes Thompson Pvt MD
William: b 5-29-1734 d 2-12-1826 m (1)Catherine Polhemus (2)Ann Schenck Ens NY

BARSTOW,

Benjamin: b 1756 d 8-20-1821 m Susannah Hussey Pvt MA
Caleb: b c. 1749 d 3-17-1800 m Sylvanna Magoun Pvt MA
Ebenezer: b 9-17-1756 d 3-30-1834 m Esther Owen Pvt CT
Gideon: b 1- -1738 d 3-9-1826 m (1)Jane Wilson (2)Tamar Cushing Lt MA
Jacob: b 11-7-1762 d 1819 m Alice Barker Young Sgt MA
Jacob: b c. 1735 d 8-27-1796 m Keziah (Dezier) ? Pvt MA
James: b 7-15-1759 d 9-23-1815 m Sarah Leavitt Pvt MA
Job: b 3-5-1760 d 4-20-1813 m Lurania Curtis Pvt MA
John, Jr.: b 12-21-1752 d 12-9-1838 m Susannah Smith Pvt CT ★
Joseph: b 1725 d c. 1800 m Mrs Mary Bliss Webster Pvt CT
Joseph: b 7-10-1760 d p. 1797 m (1)Mary Hatch (2)Mrs Tufts Fif MA
Joseph: b 3-12-1725 d 7-29-1834 m Lydia Soule Pvt MA ★
Joshua: b 6-26-1749 d 12-22-1821 m Margaret Bonney Lt PS MA
Michael: b 5-24-1754 d 2-4-1849 m Ruth Abbott Pvt Gnr NH ★
Samuel: b 12-28-1749 d 7-17-1822 m (I)Mary Adams (2)Hannah Spaulding (3)Amy Fitch MM CT
Samuel: b 4-8-1760 d 2-27-1846 m Lucina Wright Pvt CT ★
Samuel, Jr.: b 7-28-1734 d 5-4-1826 m Huldah Hatch Lt MA
Samuel: b 2-7-1709 d 11-9-1801 m Margaret Stockbridge Pvt MA
Thomas: b 2-27-1732 d 3-27-1797 m Sarah Studley Pvt MA

BARTEAU, (includes BARTO BARTOO BARTOW)

Benjamin: b 10-13-1735 d 9-9-1825 m Mary Williams Pvt VT
Francis: b c. 1748 d a. 2-26-1810 m Jemima Turner Pvt NY
Jonah: b 12-15-1760 d p. 10-31-1820 m X Pvt NY ★
Morris: b 8-18-1758 d 2-6-1839 m Hannah Smith Pvt NY
Silas: b 5-31-1742 d 11-7-1831 m Ruth Luce Pvt CT

BARTEE,

William: b c. 1735 d p. 1786 m Mary — Pvt VA

BARTER,

Henry: b 1747 d 5-13-1829 m Jemima Pike Pvt NH ★

BARTH,

Peter: b 9-24-1760 d 3-22-1831 m Tabitha Loomis Pvt NY

BARTHOLOMEW,

Abigail Patchen: b 12-14-1755 d 1-10-1839 m Benjamin Bartholomew PS NY
Abraham, Sr.: b 6-28-1708 d c. 1798 m (1)Hannah Page (2)Deborah — Sol CT
Abraham, Jr.: b 1-28-1732 d 3-3-1785 m Eunice Orvis Pvt CT
Andrew: b 1-24-1744 d 7-17-1818 m (1)Rachel Royce (2)Sarah Hubbell Lt CT
Benjamin: b 6-23-1723 d 10-30-1801 m Martha Carpenter Pvt CT
Benjamin: b 1752 d 2-22-1797 m Abigail Patchen Pvt NY
Benjamin: b 2-16-1752 d 3-31-1812 m Rachel Dewees Capt PA
Charles: b 6-1-1760 d 3-19-1848 m Belinda Orvis Pvt CT
Daniel: b c. 1740 d 1779 m Anna Maria Singmaster Ens PA
Gardner: b 3-22-1748 d 1810 m Susana Dana Pvt CT
Henry: b c. 1745 d p. 1787 m Elizabeth Shofstall Sgt PA
Henry, Sr.: b 9-28-1728 d 9-7-1807 m Hanna Zimmerman Pvt PA
Henry, Jr.: b 9-23-1758 d 2-23-1829 m Catherine Hecker Pvt PA

Isaac: b 6-2-1761 d 2-11-1841 m Lydia (Deming) Crampton Cpl CT
Isaac: b 1754 d 1840 m Thankful Maltby Pvt CT
Jacob: b 1-9-1736 d 10-29-1805 m (1)Sarah Gridley (2)Mrs Eunice Cowles Pvt CT
Jepthai: b a. 1761 d 4-8-1813 m Sarah Earl Pvt CT
John: b 2-20-1741/2 d 7-8-1798 m Candice Ainsworth Sgt CT
John: b 11-17-1710 d 1798 m Dorothy — PS NY
John: b 1745 d 1782 m Elizabeth Heatherlin Wgm PA
John: b 9-6-1755 d 7-7-1802 m Mary Milne Bbd PA
Jonathan: b 11-5-1750 d 1-28-1846 m Anna Cook Pvt CT
Joseph, Sr.: b 5-6-1721 d 10-27-1791 m Mary Sexton MM CT
Joseph, Jr.: b 8-25-1752 d 5-21-1808 m Esther Cleveland Ens CT
Joseph: b 3-15-1766 d 11-3-1840 m (1)Christiana Pickenpaw (2)Elizabeth McNaught Sct PA
Lemma: b 1758/9 d 3-22-1789 m Anna Wilson Ens NY
Lemuel: b 1726/27 d 3-22-1801 m Mary Squire Ens NY
Luther: b 2-18-1758 d 5-5-1839 m Azubah Farnam Sgt CT ★
Moses: b 9-3-1751 d 2-11-1839 m Lydia Cook Sol MM VT
Oliver: b 10-20-1757 d 6-18-1850 m Anna Lacey Pvt & Arfr CT ★
Peter: b 1760 d 1802 m Rosina — Pvt PA
Philip: b 1762 d 4-16-1824 m Elizabeth Vroman Pvt NY
Reuben: b 9-17-1736 d 12- -1804 m Thankful Dewey Cpl CT
Samuel: b 1756 d 4-18-1833 m Irene Munson Pvt CT
Samuel: b 1762 d 12-12-1840 m Elizabeth Butler Pvt CT
Samuel: b 10-21-1762 d 1842 m Chloe Fancher Pvt CT
Theobald: b c. 1731 d 1827 m Elizabeth Brewer Pvt NY
Timothy: b 8-11-1745 d 2-20-1831 m Esther Grant Lt VT

BARTLE,

Andrew: b a. 1745 d p. 10-12-1811 m (1)Mary Magdalena — (2)Sophia Braun Pvt PA
John, Sr.: b 1736 d 5-17-1808 m Margaret — Pvt NY
John, Jr.: b 9-8-1761 d 4-2-1822 m (1)Harriet Duffy (2)Lydia Tuttle Sol NY
Peter, Sr.: b 1-1-1736 d 4-5-1796 m Elizabeth Ebblie Pvt NY
Peter, Jr.: b 6-10-1757 d 9-8-1797 m Pauline Herty Pvt NY

BARTLETT, (includes BARTLET)

Aaron: b 3-30-1753 d 4-22-1823 m Joanna Perkins Cpl MA ★
Aaron: b 3- -1753 d 10-16-1827 m Anna — Pvt MA
Abner: b 3-2-1735 d 10-28-1813 m Ann Hovey Cpl MA
Abner: b 4-18-1755 d 2-13-1792 m Martha Forbes Pvt MA
Abraham: bpt 9-19-1742 d p. 1790 m Lena Palmetier Pvt NY
Abraham: b 4-14-1759 d 3-16-1841 m Melinda Camp Pvt NY ★
Adam: b 7-27-1754 d 7-22-1828 m Persis Babcock Pvt MA
Andrew: b 1738 d 12-9-1808 m Lydia Churchill Sgt MA
Asa: b 9-2-1757 d 9-17-1839 m Patience Arnold Fif RI ★
Bailey: b 1-29-1750 d 9-9-1830 m Margaret White Pvt MA
Benjamin, Sr.: b 1-23-1707 d 4-23-1786 m Hannah Stevens Pvt MA
Benjamin, Jr.: b 1741 d 7-31-1799 m Susannah Hayden Pvt MA
Benjamin, 2d: bpt 10-5-1725 d 10-10-1812 m Mary Baker Pvt MA
Benjamin: b 1763 d 1824 m Mary Ann H — Pvt VA
Caleb: b 1756 d 6-14-1819 m Mary Cooper Pvt MA
Cornelius: b 8-10-1760 d 5-8-1829 m Sarah Fisher Pvt MA
Daniel: b 1-16-1757 d 1835 m Esther Read Pvt CT ★
Daniel: b 8-19-1754 d 3-12-1843 m (1)Elizabeth Smith (2)Deborah Fergerson Pvt MA ★
Daniel: b 4-11-1756 d p. 1810 m Phoebe Arnold Mar RI
David: b 3-7-1713 d 1792 m Priscilla Holgate Pvt MA
David: b 9-24-1761 d 8-29-1844 m Joanna Hazeltine Pvt MA
Diman: b 1759 d p. 1802 m (1)Lydia Barrows (2)Hannah Bagnall Pvt MA
Ebenezer: b 1711 d 3-2-1788 m (1)Ann Clark (2)Anna Ball PS MA
Ebenezer: b 8-28-1721 d 4-1-1791 m Rachel King CS PS MA
Ebenezer: b 10-4-1759 d 12-3-1838 m Jane Sairs Pvt NY ★
Edmund: b 3-3-1723 d 9-30-1804 m Mary Moody Marsh PS MA
Edmund: b 12-23-1759 d 1836 m Mary — Pvt VA
Edward: b 3-1-1745 d 8-4-1815 m (1)Elizabeth Bliss (2)Zilpha Cole Pvt MA
Eli: b 11-18-1753 d 4-30-1837 m Mary Hill Cpl MA
Elihu: b 8-11-1754 d 9-14-1827 m Rachel Edwards Pvt MA W ★
Elijah: b 3-6-1725 d 10-29-1788 m Bathsheba Gilbert Pvt MA
Elijah: b 3-5-1758 d 5-20-1844 m Jerusha Pomeroy Pvt MA ★
Elisha: b 2-15-1753 d 3-14-1834 m Sarah Beals Pvt MA
Elisha: b 12-16-1754 d 9-30-1855 m (1)Hannah Comstock (2)Elizabeth Stannard PvtMM VT MA ★
Enoch: b 9-27-1742 d 8-31-1825 m (1)Elizabeth Segar (2)Anna Hall Tms PS MA
Ezekiel: b 2-18-1749/50 d p. 1794 m Mitty Cutler Pvt MA
Gershom: b c. 1758 d p. 1790 m Hannah Burton Pvt VT
Harry, Sr.: b 1731 d 1822 m Sarah Crane Lt VA
Haynes: b 3-4-1757 d 10-16-1841 m Hannah Cooley Pvt NY ★
Ichabod: b 10-20-1723 d 12-10-1798 m Desire Otis PS CT
Ichabod: b 5-27-1753 d 2-1-1834 m Azubah Norton Pvt VT
Israel: b 5-8-1748 d 4-21-1838 m Tabitha Walker Capt MA
James: b 11-24-1759 d 10-30-1836 m Lois Hill Pvt MA
Jeremiah: b 5-15-1753 d p. 1808 m Lydia Blaisdell PS ME
Jermiah: b 8-16-1741 d 8-20-1800 m Rebecca Lapham PS RI
John: b 9-29-1754 d 9-6-1831 m Desire Loomis Pvt CT
John: b 1-18-1757 d 6-15-1797 m Deborah Hubbard Pvt CT
John: b 2-14-1736 d 4-29-1814 m Mary — Cpl MA
John: b a. 1760 d 4-1-1796 m Loruhmah Matthews Sgt MA

John: b 2-20-1750 d 10-17-1831 m Apphia Stevens Pvt MA
John: b 1- -1752 d 6-10-1847 m Molly Bonney Pvt MA ★
John: b 8-15-1730 d 10-10-1795 m (1)Susanna Southworth (2) Lucretia Stewart SurGen RI
John: b c. 1760 d 1816 m Anne Barkley Sol VA
John: b 1764 d p. 1822 m X Pvt VA ★
John Heard: b 4-8-1726 d 7-28-1805 m (1)Dorcas Moulton (2)Mrs Elizabeth Atkinson (3)Mrs Bertha Meriam PS MA
Jonathan: b 8-1-1716 d 3-29-1799 m Hannah Watson Bissell PS CT
Jonathan: b 9-18-1744 d 3-31-1786 m Annie Mixture Sgt MA
Jonathan: b 5-16-1757 d 2-20-1830 m Dorcas — Pvt MA
Jonathan: b 1753 d 1787 m Lydia Ellis Sgt MS ★
Joseph, Jr.: b 8-1-1739 d 1-15-1808 m Lydia Cobb Sgt MA
Joseph: b 9-13-1759 d 3-9-1840 m Lucretia Hamilton Sgt MA ★
Joseph: b 1-18-1759 d 2-5-1829 m Susanna Davis Cpl MA
Joseph: b 1738 d 1790 m Mary (Bartlett) — Pvt MA
Joseph: b 2-6-1763 d 12-15-1830 m Lucy Phelps Pvt MA
Joseph: b 2-22-1703/4 d 5-30-1783 m Sarah Morton PS MA
Joseph: b 1-14-1751 d 9-20-1800 m Hannah Colcord Sol PS NH
Joshua: b 1762 d 1817 m Martha Alice Phoenix Pvt MA
Joshua: b 3-29-1736 d 7-23-1823 m Sarah Badger PS NH
Josiah: b 4-8-1753 d p. 1800 m Martha Holmes Pvt MA
Josiah: b 8-1-1759 d 3-3-1820 m Elizabeth Call Dr MA
Josiah: b 11-21-1729 d 5-19-1795 m Mary (Bartlett) — Col SDI NH
Malachi: b 6-19-1758 d 2-29-1832 m Mary Noble Pvt MA ★
Mary: b 12-27-1730 d 7-14-1789 m Josiah Bartlett PS NH
Mathew: b 7-8-1728 d p. 1776 m Susannah (Hinds) Bell Pvt MA
Mathias: b 9-26-1742 d 1-10-1839 m (1)Elizabeth Davis (2)Tamesin Horbert Pvt NH
Moses: b 11-13-1756 d 1-16-1818 m (1)Mary Barbour (2)Esther Beall Pvt MA
Nathaniel: b 7-3-1734 d 1800 m Mercy Otis CG CT
Nathaniel: b 4-22-1727 d 1-11-1810 m Eunice Russell Chp CT
Nathaniel: b 1753 d 1-11-1831 m Sarah Bartlett Pvt NH ★
Nathaniel: b 1755 d 9-7-1838 m Anna Fitch Pvt NH
Nicholas: b 12-2-1751 d 4-17-1819 m Hannah Barker Capt NS MA
Obadiah: b 4-5-1730 d 11-19-1779 m Rebecca Adams Lt MA
Oliver: b c. 1740 d p. 1784 m Asenath Smith Pvt MA
Oliver: b 10- -1758 d p. 1790 m Rebecca Smith Fif MA
Reuben: b 11-5-1755 d 8-20-1831 m Amy Jenks Pvt MA ★
Richard: b 5-27-1755 d 10-11-1832 m Mary Currier Pvt MA
Samuel: b 4-27-1760 d 9-25-1841 m Cynthia Benton Pvt CG CT
Samuel: b 3-31-1736 d 7-31-1827 m Susanna Dunbar Sgt MA
Samuel: b 2-3-1748 d 2-4-1813 m (1)— Hix (2)Eleanor (Martin) Kimball PS ME
Samuel: b 1762 d 1847 m X Tms PS MS MA
Samuel: b 3-9-1732 d 1812 m Elizabeth Appleton Pvt NH
Samuel: b 1748 d 7-1-1810 m Hannah Meigs Capt Dep PM VT
Silas: b 7-2-1760 d 5-4-1840 m Hannah Parish Pvt MA ★
Silvanus: b 1751 d 2-1-1829 m Sarah Loring Pvt MA
Simeon: b 3-5-1737 d p. 1801 m (1)Lucy Searle (2)Elizabeth Burt Pvt MA
Solomon: b — d 8-20-1815 m Jerusha Richardson Sgt MA W ★
Solomon: b 2-12-1757 d 4-26-1838 m Huldah Washburn Pvt MA
Stephen: b 4-10-1745 d 5-16-1813 m Hannah Belknap Lt NH
Susanna: b c. 1700 d p. 2-23-1788 m William Bartlett PS VA
Sylvanus: b 11-26-1719 d 11-16-1811 m Martha Waite CS & PS MA
Thomas: b 1741/2 d 9-17-1808 m Elizabeth Bartlett Pvt MA
Thomas: b 4-16-1757 d 1836 m Sarah Rider Pvt MA
Thomas: b 10-22-1745 d 6-30-1805 m Sarah Cilley PS Col NH
Thomas: b 2-2-1734 d 1814 m Dolly Blaisdell Sgt NH CL
Thomas: b 1733 d 1809 m Mary Foster Capt VA
Uriah: b 11-19-1741 d 4-30-1818 m (1)Lois Washburn (2)Susanna Cooke PS MA
Wm.: b 2-23-1741 d 2-10-1823 m (1)Mary Raymond (2)Elizabeth (Mullett) Hickman Pvt MA
Wm.: b 9-12-1760 d 9-5-1840 m Azubah Gleason Pvt MA ★
Wm.: b 6-27-1741 d 12-30-1794 m Joanna Herrick PS MA
Wyman: b 4-15-1754 d 4-3-1815 m Elizabeth Smith Pvt MA
Zacheus: b 1-15-1725 d 3-6-1800 m Margaret Barnes Capt VA
Zadoc: b 4-10-1756 d 1-23-1837 m Hannah Sever Pvt MA ★

BARTLEY,
Elijah: b c. 1760 d 5-10-1791 m Rachael Pearshall Pvt PA
Henry: b 6-16-1746 d 1-17-1832 m Nancy Sherwood Pvt NY W ★
Hugh: b 1719 d 6-23-1803 m Elizabeth Kirkpatrick Pvt NJ
James: b 10-3-1746 d 2-15-1783 m Polly Redford Pvt NC
John: b 1743 d p. 1820 m Sarah Logan Pvt NJ
Joshua: b 1757 d 1804 m Elizabeth Allen Cpl VA
Thomas: b 1760 d a. 1854 m Margaret Birchett Pvt PA VA CL

BARTLING,
Conrad: b 8-9-1756 d 2-14-1839 m Mary Campbell Pvt PA

BARTOL,
Frederick: b 5-5-1760 d 9-12-1824 m Eliza Dreisbach Pvt PA
George: b 1750 d 8-16-1796 m Jane Soule Pvt PS MA
Samuel: b 8-12-1764 d 1-23-1835 m Mercy Northey Drm PA

BARTON,
Andrew: b c. 1706 d p. 1790 m Sarah Waterman PS RI
Benjamin: b 4-21-1758 d 7-9-1834 m Mehitable Fry Pvt MA ★
Benjamin: b 1750 d 10-27-1830 m Nancy Hetzel Pvt NJ

Benjamin: b 8-4-1744 d 3-20-1836 m Sarah Hall Pvt RI ★
Benjamin: b c. 1760 d 2-16-1818 m Dorcas Anderson Pvt SC ★
Bezaliel, Sr.: b 7-26-1722 d 7-12-1775 m Phebe Carlton Pvt MA
Caleb: b 1749 d 6-4-1833 m Margaret Congdon Pvt MA
David: b 2-6-1739 d 5-13-1833 m Hannah Breed (or Dickinson) Capt MA
David: b 12-9-1746 d p. 1790 m Rebecca Brightman Capt RI
David: b 3-15-1744 d p. 7-12-1815 m Hannah Hill Lt PS VA
David: b — d p. 1796 m Peggy — PS VA
Elisha: b 10-5-1729 d 3-31-1823 m Jemima Van Kirk Capt NJ
Elisha: b 6-21-1742 d 9-12-1816 m (1)Mary Simonton (2)Ann McCarter Pvt PA
Elisha: b 1757 d 1843 m Priscilla Witt Pvt VA
Elkanah, Sr.: b 10-10-1758 d 5-27-1829 m (1)Mary Grant (2)Annie Starkweather Pvt MA CL ★
Flint: b 12-3-1749 d 5-12-1833 m Lydia Crosby PS ME
Isaac: b 8-16-1746 d 11-10-1831 m Keziah Murphy Grd KY
Isaac: b 10-6-1760 d 2-6-1834 m Martha — Pvt NY
Jedediah: b 5-6-1747 d 9-15-1808 m Lydia Pierce Pvt MA
John: b 1752 d 5-12-1834 m Abigail Davis Cpl MA
John: b 10-12-1726 d 3-26-1810 m Abigail Dana Pvt MA
Jonathan: b 9-11-1754 d 2-5-1830 m Hannah Dix Cpl MA ★
Joshua: b 8-14-1718 d 1790 m (1)Jane Dubart (2)Susan Dodd PS NC
Kimber: b 1746 d 1800 m Elizabeth Lewis Pvt VA
Lewis, Sr.: b 1724 d 10-29-1813 m Sarah Hustis/Husted Pvt NY
Lewis, Jr.: b 7-19-1752 d 5-15-1819 m Abigail Bradford Pvt NY
Nathaniel: b 1748 d 3-22-1822 m Eunice Woodward Pvt MA
Peter: b 9-3-1763 d 9-24-1825 m Hepsibah Baker Sol CL MA
Phineas: b 5-9-1752 d 7-26-1827 m Elizabeth Hasey Pvt MA
Reuben: b — d 1-20-1838 m Olive Jennison 2Lt MA
Roger: b 1756 d 11-11-1835 m Sarah Canfield Pvt NY ★
Roger: b 7-9-1747 d 6-24-1826 m Margaret Gilbreath Pvt VA
Rufus: b a. 1751 d 6-10-1807 m Prudence Cole Lt RI ★
Seth: b 7-29-1755 d 12-29-1813 m (1)Sarah Emerson Maxwell (2) Mary Chew Lt RI
Stephen: b 6-10-1740 d 10-21-1804 m Dorothy Moore PS ME
Stukely: b 1744 d 6- -1813 m Alse Holden Pvt RI
Thomas: b 1746 d p. 3-27-1783 m Patience — Pvt NJ
Thomas: b c. 1750 d p. 1790 m Bethia Williamson Sol PS SC
Timothy: b 4- -1732 d 1796 m (1)Hepzibah Stow (2)Amma Allen Pvt MA
Timothy Stow: b 10- -1758 d 6-30-1844 m (1)Phoebe Stone (2)Mrs Susannah Grant Pvt MA ★
Titus: b 2-17-1765 d 11-31-1827 m Mrs Ruth Huse Wood Pvt PS MA
Wm., Sr.: b c. 1740 d 1793 m Sarah Sage Capt CT
Wm.: b 11-21-1762 d 7-15-1849 m Clarissa Betts Arfr CT ★
Wm.: b — d — m Mirabeau Lawrence Capt NJ
Wm.: b 1730 d 1817 m Frances Conway Fif PA
Wm.: b 3-22-1762 d 11-30-1826 m Hannah Roberts Pvt PA
Wm.: b 5-26-1748 d 10-22-1831 m Rhoda Carver Col RI
Wm.: b 10-26-1745 d 8-15-1809 m (2)Elizabeth Miller Pvt PS RI
Wm.: b c. 1720 d 1786-90 m Amy — Pvt SC
Wm. E.: b 10-25-1754 d 12-27-1829 m Margaret Henderson MM NJ
Willoughby: b 1750 d 1800 m Rebecca McCoy Pvt GA

BARTRAM,
Benjamin: b 7-6-1748 d 3-17-1826 m Elizabeth Hunt Pvt PA
Daniel: b 10-23-1745 d 5-17-1817 m Ann Merchant Pvt CT
Ebenezer: bpt 6-10-1732 d 1-3-1783 m Mary — Lt CT
Isaac: b 4-15-1758 d 9-13-1843 m Molly Hamilton Pvt CT CL ★
James: b 1736 d 1836 m Hannah Morehouse Pvt CT ★
Job: b 3-20-1735 d 10-17-1817 m Ruth — Pvt CT

BASCOM, (includes BASCOMB)
Elias: b 5-8-1738 d 11-29-1833 m (1)Eunice Allen (2)Thankful Graves Sol MA
Elisha: b 1739 d 9-18-1776 m Lucy Sheldon Lt MA
Moses: b 6-8-1736 d 9-19-1805 m Eunice Severance CS PS MA
Samuel: b 6-13-1723 d 9-16-1779 m Mary — Lt MA
Timothy: b 11-10-1748 d 2-7-1824 m (1)Abigail Atherton (2)Mary Patterson (3)Jemimah Booth Pvt MA

BASCOT,
Samuel: b 3-3-1745 d 1797 m Sarah Margaret Alston 1Lt SC

BASH,
Martin: b c. 1738 d 1824 m Catherine — Pvt PS PA

BASHAM,
Obediah: b 1760 d 5-28-1840 m Selia — Pvt VA ★
Wm.: b 1740-50 d p. 12-17-1824 m Molly — PS VA

BASHAW,
Peter: b 3-31-1763 d 5-20-1864 m Frances (Bashaw) Pvt VA ★

BASHFORD,
Ebenezer: b 9-10-1742-4 d 9-21-1816 m (1)Mary Richardson (2)Mrs Mehitable Young Pvt PS NH

BASHORE,
John: b 1750 d 7-1-1778 m Elizabeth Swartz PS PA

BASKERVILLE, (includes BASKERVILL)
George: b c. 1750 d 1804 m (1)— Scott (2)Fannie Cocke (3)Priscilla Cheshire Sol PS VA
George: b — d 1777 m Martha Minge PS VA
Samuel: b 12-24-1754 d 8-29-1830 m (1)Mary K Booker (2)Statira Bently 1Lt VA
Wm.: b 5-12-1756 d 11-8-1814 m Mary Eaton 2Lt VA

BASKETT, (includes BASKET)
James: b 1728 d 1789 m Yourrath McMillan Pvt NC
Martin: b 12-6-1761 d 5-26-1833 m Frances Shepherd Pvt VA W ★
Wm.: b 5-31-1715 d p. 1790 m Elizabeth — Pvt NC

BASKIN,
Andrew: b 1740 d 1810 m Mary Marshall Pvt SC
Charles: bpt 3-15-1741 d p. 1811 m Mary Craig Capt VA
George Washington: b 1760 d 1853 m Rachel Braddock Sol PA
James: b c. 1739 d 1790 m (1)Margaret Pickens (2)Mrs Prudence Reid Crawford Lt PS SC
Wm.: b 2-14-1737 d 4-9-1794 m Annie Reid Capt SC

BASON,
Jacob: b 1741 d a. 8- -1800 m — Sharpe PS NC

BASS,
Andrew: b c. 1740 d p. 1790 m Ann — CS PS NC
Benjamin: b 6-6-1741 d 3-17-1821 m (1)Mercy Tolman (2)Mary Eels PS MA
Benjamin: b 1735-40 d p. 2-20-1798 m Sarah Hicks PS VA
Burrell: b 1752 d 8-23-1831 m X PS VA
Ebenezer: b 10-26-1746 d 3-6-1814 m Ruth Waldo 1Lt CT
Edward: b 1749 d 9-29-1821 m Bathsheba Keith Sgt CL MA ★
Edward: b 8-15-1754 d 4-26-1834 m (1)Nancy Elam (2)Elizabeth Ann Jefferson (3)Rebecca (Moseley?) Sgt VA
Esau: b c. 1760 d p. 1830 m X Pvt NC
Gillam: b 4-9-1746 d — m Rebecca Wimble PS MA
Henry: b c. 4- -1758 d p. 1818 m X PS VA
Isaac: b c. 1745 d 2- -1801 m Nancy — Pvt NC
Jacob: b c. 1724 d a. 1795 m (1)Tabitha Bass (2) X Pvt NC
James: b 1761 d p. 1832 m Temperance Jordan Pvt VA ★
Jeremiah: b c. 1746 d — m Hannah Whitney Pvt MA
Jeriah: b 2-25-1759 d 1813 m Lucretia Savill Pvt MA
John: b 6-22-1761 d 5-3-1849 m Ann Vaughan Pvt VA ★
John Hicks: b 1763 d 1850 m (1)Rebecca Patilla (2)Mrs. Cleghorn Pvt VA
Jonathan: b 11-14-1733 d 5-12-1790 m Susannah Belcher LCol MA
Jonathan: b 1720 d 1800 m Susanna Byram Capt MA
Joseph: b 1750-60 d a. 2-17-1809 m Martha Jones PS SC
Josiah: b 1768 d p. 1809 m Ann Adams Smn MA
Moses, Jr.: bpt 7-20-1735 d 1-31-1817 m (1)Elizabeth Wimble (2) Margaret Sprague Pvt MA
Nathan: b 10-10-1740 d 9-10-1776 m Ann Rockwell Sgt CT
Obadiah: bpt 11-20-1748 d p. 1790 m Lucy Stevens Barnes Lt MA
Richard: b c. 1732 d p. 11-17-1791 m Sarah — PS NC
Samuel: b 10-4-1754 d a. 12-23-1802 m Mercy North Pvt CT
Samuel, Jr.: b 8-22-1747 d 2-23-1840 m Elizabeth Brackett 1Lt MA
Thomas: b c. 1725 d 1786 m Mary — PS VA

BASSETT, (includes BASSET)
Abel: b 2-29-1759 d 11-27-1842 m Hannah Chapin Pvt CT ★
Abraham: b 8-12-1733 d 9-9-1776 m Lydia Smith Pvt CT
Abraham, Sr.: b 2-27-1725 d 9-13-1805 m Phoebe Miles PS CT
Abraham, Jr.: b 3-20-1754 d 11-17-1833 m Mary Baldwin Sgt CT W ★
Amos: b 2-13-1757 d 12-31-1826 m (1)Hannah Goodyear (2)Anna (Smith) Hall Cpl CT
Benjamin: b c. 1740 d 3-25-1825 m Mary Hinman PS CT
Benjamin: b 8-1-1752 d 1-2-1830 m Abigail Nickerson Pvt MA
Burwell: b 3-3-1734 d 1-17-1793 m (1)Anne Chamberlayne (2)Anna Maria Dandridge PS VA
Cornelius: b 1754 d 11-21-1805 m Chloe A. Smith Pvt CT
Cornelius: b 6-24-1754 d 4-27-1841 m Abigail Bassett Pvt Smn MA ★
Daniel: b 8-7-1736 d p. 1790 m Hannah Bearse 1Lt MA
David: b 11-14-1749 d 5-21-1819 m Mabe Tomlinson PS CT
Ebenezer: b c. 1751/2 d p. 1799 m Abigail Adams Pvt MA
Elisha: b 2-11-1761 d 9-28-1814 m (1)Mercy Sherman (2)Keturah West (3)Abigail Dillingham Pvt MA
Elisha: b 2-15-1714 d 2-12-1793 m Ruhannah Jennings PS MA
Elisha, Jr.: b 12-15-1722 d p. 4-5-1777 m Mary Woodnut PS NJ
Fortunatus: b 1742 d 1778 m Sarah (Bassett) (cousin) 1Lt MA
Isaac: b 1750 d 2-28-1841 m Desire Hotchkiss Pvt CT
Isaac: b 12-18-1755 d 7-20-1852 m Mehitable Makepeace Pvt MA
Jeremiah: b 2-9-1751 d 4-4-1817 m Hannah Woodward Pvt MA
Jeremiah: b 1759 d 2- -1821 m Elizabeth Simpson Sol NJ
John, Sr.: b 2-15-1721 d 5-8-1804 m (1)Naomi Wooster (2)Sarah (Gunn) Thompson PS CT
John, Jr.: b 1758 d 5-14-1832 m Keziah Judson Pvt CT
Jonathan: b 5-24-1764 d 7-4-1833 m Temperance Crocker Pvt MA
Joseph: b 2-3-1731/32 d 5-6-1803 m (1)Phebe Cushman 1Lt MA
Joseph: b 3-6-1726 d Winter 1783/84 m Mary Burt Pvt MA
Joseph 2d: b 10-26-1748 d 3-13-1817 m Hannah Lathrop Pvt MA

Joseph: b 4-21-1763 d 7-7-1855 m (1)Zerviah Bearse (2)Nancy Howes Pvt MA ★
Joseph: b 4-26-1743 d 10-23-1826 m Mary Tilton Pvt MA
Joseph: b 10- -1747 d 2-8-1813 m (1)Mary Pittee (2)Tabitha (Burrill) Nye Pvt MA
Joseph: b 1759 d 9-8-1822 m Mary Milligin Pvt MA ★
Joseph: b 1-1-1760 d 11-5-1822 m Lydia Jones Pvt MA
Joshua, Jr.: b 1-22-1757 d 12-14-1836 m Lydia Lawrence Pvt Arfr CT
Jotham: b 5-29-1738 d p. 4-2-1803 m Naomi Newland Pvt MA
Lot: b 1-22-1755 d 7-23-1835 m Deborah Howes Pvt Cpl Ordl Sgt MA ★
Michael: bpt 10-25-1741 d — m Martyje Van Franken Pvt NY
Nathan: b 12-11-1751 d 4-8-1832 m Olive Clark Pvt CT
Nathan, Jr.: b 8-15-1751 d 10-10-1841 m (1)Martha (Bassett) (2)Lydia Norton Pvt Drm MA ★
Nathan: b 8-12-1763 d 4-23-1853 m Sarah Standish Pvt MA
Nathan, Sr.: b 1715 d 1791 m Thankful Fuller PS MA
Nathan, Jr.: b 12-30-1750 d 3-13-1836 m (1)Mary Bourne (2)Azubah Jones Pvt MA
Nathaniel, Sr.: b 10-15-1719 d 1814 m Hannah Hall Pvt MA
Nathaniel, Jr.: b 1-26-1758 d 5-6-1846 m Bethia Smith OrdlSgt Smn MA ★
Nathaniel: b 3-20-1755 d 1-4-1832 m (1)Mercy Phillips (2)Ruth Paine (3)Anna Davis Sol MA
Nehemiah: b 9-12-1743 d p. 1790 m Dorcas Cole Pvt MA
Rufus: b 4-6-1757 d p. 10-1-1796 m Jedidah Handy Sgt MA
Samuel: b 11-29-1719 d 1809 m Sarah Botsford PS CT
Samuel: b 3- -1754 d 11-8-1834 m Martha Belding Fif NH ★
Samuel: b c. 1740 d 1808 m Tabitha Waite Sgt RI
Thomas: b 6-19-1759 d 2-24-1833 m Lydia Mendall Pvt MA
Wm.: b 10-10-1743 d 10-9-1807 m Deriah Blakeslee Sgt CT
Wm.: b 4-18-1755 d 2-6-1840 m Peggy — Pvt VA ★

BASSFORD, (includes BASFORD)
Joseph: b 8-24-1750 d 1-11-1834 m Leah Harris Pvt NH
Stephen: b 1755 d 1814 m Susannah Stewart 2Lt MD

BASSLER, (includes BOSLER)
John: b c. 1730 d p. 1794 m — Longenecker Pvt PA
John: b 1733 d 12-18-1812 m Anna Huber Pvt PA
Simon: b 1734 d 1- -1802 m Eva Maria Illig Pvt PA
Thomas: b 1739 d 5- -1789 m Elizabeth Schmehl Pvt PA
Valentine: b 8-25-1738 d 1806 m X PS PA

BASTEDO,
Wm.: b 12-12-1754 d 11-10-1843 m Margaret Selover Pvt NJ ★

BOSTIAN, (includes BASTIAN)
George Michael: b 1732 d 1798 m Mary Magdalena Wenner Pvt & PS PA
Jacob: b 1757 d 5-3-1847 m Catherine — Pvt NC ★

BASTIAANSE,
Johannes: b 1-11-1754 d p. 1816 m Evah Van Schaick Pvt NY

BASTON,
Wm.: b 1752 d 8-6-1817 m Mercy Cheney Cpl MA
Winthrop: b 6- -1739 d 6-25-1817 m (1)Hannah Weare (2)Hannah Ludden Capt MA ★

BASYE,
Edmund: b 1750 d 1783 m Nancy Mauzy Pvt VA
Elizmond: b 1752 d 1824 m Nancy McClanahan Sol VA
Richard: b c. 1755 d 11-4-1822 m Nancy Taylor Pvt VA W★

BATCHELDER, (includes BACHELDER, BACHELLER, BATCHELER, & BATCHELLER)
Abner: b 9-1-1755 d 1827 m Prudence Leland Sgt MA
Abraham, Sr.: b 6-5-1722 d 1-31-1813 m (1)Sarah Newton (2)Elizabeth — Capt PS MA
Abraham, Jr.: b 3-17-1752 d 8-14-1832 m Rebecca Dwight Lt MA
Amos: b 4-6-1727 d 5-4-1809 m Lydia Kimball MM MA
Amos: b 1761 d 9-20-1843 m Huldah Batchelder Pvt NH ★
Benjamin: b 8-12-1720 d 9-9-1787 m Sarah Whipple Pvt Matr MA
Benjamin: b 7-16-1749 d 7-12-1826 m (1)Anna Burnap (2)Sarah Dinsmore Pvt MA
Benjamin: b 10-20-1735 d 1813 m Dorotha Prescott Sgt NH
Benjamin: b 9-25-1746 d 1818 m (1)Esther — (2)Mrs Thankful Weeks Ens NH
Benjamin: b 3-31-1726 d 3-9-1792 m Mary Dow PS NH
Carter: b 10-31-1736 d 7-16-1806 m (1)Huldah Moulton (2)Hannah Lane PS NH
Daniel: b 8-15-1750 d 1-17-1832 m (1)Judith Judkins (2)Zerviah Morrell PS NH
Daniel: b 1750 d 3-17-1832 m Rebecca Abbot Pvt NH
David: b 4-28-1742 d 5-6-1806 m (1)Lois Wood (2)Abigail Bacon Capt MA
David: b 11-4-1742 d 1-8-1829 m Sarah Prescott Sgt NH ★
David: b 1-13-1736 d 3-11-1811 m (1)Elizabeth Swett (2)Mary Emery CS NH
David: b 5-30-1744 d 6-10-1822 m Anna Page PS NH

Davis: bpt 9-1-1734 d 10-5-1816 m (1)Mary Taylor (2)Ruth Palmer (3)Mrs. Marston PS NH
Ebenezer: b 11-5-1750 d 4-24-1849 m Elizabeth Tompson Pvt MA
Elijah: b 2-28-1747 d 1820 m Elizabeth Munger Cpl MA
Enoch: b 11-14-1755 d 8-29-1846 m Jemima Fiske Cpl MA
Ephraim: b 5-15-1749 d 6-15-1815 m (1)Apphia Lowell (2)Lydia (Ball) Richardson Pvt MA
Henry: b 6-5-1755 d 12-10-1810 m Sally Randall Fif NH
Isaiah: b 1750 d 1833 m Mary Copp Pvt NH
Jacob: b 2-8-1752 d 12-10-1827 m Lois Rice Pvt MA
James: b 2-26-1756 d 12-13-1845 m Elizabeth Perkins Pvt MA
James: b 1760 d c. 1840 m (1)Elizabeth Marston (2)Hannah Southworth Pvt NH ★
Jeremiah: b 3-16-1761 d 12-13-1834 m Lydia Prentiss Pvt MA ★
Jeremiah: b 9-19-1740 d 2-1-1818 m Sarah Page 2Lt NH
Jethro: b 1747 d 11-24-1841 m Dorothy Mighals Pvt NH
Jethro, Jr.: b 7-7-1761 d 4-10-1849 m Deborah Leavitt Pvt NH
Jethro, Sr.: b 1723 d p. 1780 m Abigail Lovering PS NH
John: b 11-24-1759 d 3-6-1840 m Mary Eames Capt MA
John: b 8-11-1724 d 12-14-1806 m Mary Rea Sgt MA
John: b 10-9-1743 d 1-10-1819 m (1)Lydia Perkins (2)Mrs Lydia Boardman Pvt MA
John: b 8-16-1755 d 12-18-1848 m Elizabeth (Batchelder) Pvt MA
John: b 1-10-1762 d 7-31-1846 m Sally Herrick Pvt MA
John: b 3-13-1745 d 1817 m Margaret Swain CS MA
John: b 10-6-1757 d 8-6-1835 m (1)Molly Cotton (2)Martha (Lang) Fogg Pvt NH
John: b 9-7-1741 d 6-6-1812 m Sarah Murry CS PS NH
John: b 10-5-1719 d 9-25-1792 m Esther — PS NH
Jonathan: b 1720 d 10-19-1776 m Hepzibah Conant 1Lt MA
Jonathan: b 3-13-1746 d 12-12-1823 m Thankful Whitney Cpl MA
Jonathan: b 2-17-1757 d 5-4-1846 m Sarah Clifford Pvt MA ★
Joseph (1): b 3-6-1720 d 5-19-1816 m (1)Judith — (2)Judith Holt Sgt MA
Joseph (2): b 1748 d 1826 m Phebe Holt Pvt MA
Joseph: b 10-29-1743 d p. 1790 m Rachel Prescott Sgt NH
Joseph: b 12-28-1750 d 3-25-1827 m Sarah Ferrin Pvt NH
Josiah, Sr.: b 12-16-1709 d 3-14-1798 m Mary Leach CS MA
Josiah, Jr.: b 9-25-1736 d 12-10-1809 m Hannah Dodge PS MA
Josiah: b 1748 d 5-2-1827 m Ruth Fletcher Sgt MA W ★
Josiah: b 10-31-1753 d 2-19-1832 m Deborah Allen Pvt NH ★
Nathan: b 10-25-1734 d 1801 m Margaret Bean Maj NH
Nathan: b 10-11-1747 d 2-12-1832 m (1)Elizabeth Taylor (2)— Bryant Cpl NH
Nathaniel: b 3-8-1714 d p. 2-21-1783 m Mrs. Abigail Nichols Flint Pvt MA
Nathaniel: b 1742 d 12—1834 m (1)Lydia Leland (2)Elizabeth Waite (3)Hannah — Pvt MA
Nathaniel, Jr.: b 1763 d 1808 m (1)Mary Libby (2)Mary E. Perkins Cpl NH W ★
Nathaniel, Sr.: b 7-9-1732 d 3-28-1778 m Mary Longfellow Sgt MA
Nathaniel: b 5-20-1722 d 10-11-1784 m Hanna Butler PS CS NH
Nathaniel: b 6-4-1725/26 d 4- -1809 m Susanna Gale Adj PS CS NH
Nathaniel: b c. 1746 d 3- -1778 m X Pvt NH
Nathaniel: b 3-2-1731 d 2-22-1802 m Ruth Sanborn PS NH
Nehemiah: b 10-23-1741 d 8-29-1822 m Lucy Hayward Lt MA
Perrin: b 11-1-1737 d p. 1778 m Martha Fisk Ens MA
Rupee: b 8-7-1753 d 6-22-1842 m (1)Sarah Parsons (2)Mrs Tryfena Cameron Pvt RI ★
Samuel, Jr.: b 8-30-1757 d 3- -1817 m Nancy Low Pvt & Mus MA
Samuel: bpt 8-23-1741 d 1-7-1822 m Elizabeth Taylor Pvt NH
Samuel: b 1-1-1755 d 2-17-1814 m Elizabeth Woodbury Sgt MA
Samuel: b 4-1-1765 d 10-8-1819 m Anna Richardson Pvt MA
Simon: b 3-5-1758 d 3-10-1847 m Rachel Johnson Cpl NH ★
Stephen: b 12-11-1721 d 2-18-1796 m (1)Elizabeth Tucker (2)Fanny Mushaway Pvt NH
Stephen: b 1-19-1755 d 3-6-1847 m Sarah Cotton Pvt NH
Theophilus: b 6-11-1751 d 10-10-1833 m (1)Mehitable Breed (2)Zerviah Cornish Lt MA ★
Theophilus: b 1742 d 1807 m Ann Sleeper 2Lt MA
Thomas Freeman: b c. 1737 d p. 8-12-1785 m Sarah Parsons Pvt PA
Timothy: b 4-14-1753 d 10- -1809 m Esther Conant Pvt MA
Timothy: b 1744 d 7-16-1816 m Mary Hinckley Pvt NH
Uzziel: b 10-30-1755 d — m Sarah Blanchard Cpl MA
Wm.: b 2-24-1743 d 10-29-1821 m Lydia Warren Pvt MA
Wm.: b 2-13-1750 d 9- -1825 m Lydia Chase Dr. MA

BATEMAN,

Elisha: b 1753 d 1830 m — Crissey Pvt NY
Hector: b c. 1748 d 6-19-1785 m Susannah Nichols Pvt RI
Henry: b 1-19-1752 d 1801 m Elizabeth Linthicum Capt MD
John: b 1750 d 1825 m Hannah Wheaton Lt Adj NY
Jonas: b 6-17-1735 d 12-14-1806 m Elizabeth Fletcher MM MA NY
Levi: b 1750 d 1783 m X Cpi PA
Nathan: b — d p. 2-13-1790 m Jane — PS CS NC
Wm.: b 1740 d p. 1820 m Rachael — Lt Adj MA ★
Wm.: b 5-13-1749 d 12-18-1835 m (1)Sarah Smith (2)Elizabeth Trenchard (3)Mrs Abigail Howel Pvt NJ
Wm.: b 1757 d p. 1828 m (1)Mary O'Blains (2)Mrs. James Wilson Pvt VA ★
Zadock: b 8-17-1762 d 9-22-1842 m Lucy Wheet Pvt MA ★

BATES,

Abner: b 5-29-1735 d 5-8-1817 m Elizabeth Vinal Pvt MA
Abner C.: b 8-10-1740 d p. 1780 m Sarah Tower Sgt MA
Abraham: b 2-29-1724 d 8-7-1806 m Sarah Tower Sgt MA
Abraham, Jr.: b 4-28-1751 d — m Hannah Pratt Pvt MA
Alpheus: b 3-12-1758 d 4-18-1830 m Elizabeth Pratt Pvt MA
Amasa: bpt 6-4-1749 d 10-3-1834 m Jemima Randall Pvt MA ★
Ambrose: b 9-3-1758 d 4-30-1833 m Priscilla Lincoln Sgt MA
Asa: b 5-20-1745 d 2-22-1810 m (1)Mary — (2)Lydia Bond Pvt MA
Asa: b 6-10-1758 d 2-9-1841 m Elizabeth Jerusha Cranston Sol RI
Barnabas, Sr.: b 1-15-1719 d p. 1790 m Phoebe Gibbs PS MA
Barnabas, Jr.: b 1748 d 1835 m Silvia C. — Pvt MA
Benjamin: b 1745 d 2-17-1818 m Abigail Billings Capt MA
Benjamin, Jr.: b 2-9-1728 d 3-5-1800 m Betty Dyer Lt MA
Benjamin 3rd: b 1-11-1763 d 9-9-1817 m Susanna Reed Pvt MA
Benjamin: b 11-1-1762 d 3- -1853 m Martha Stetson Pvt MA
Benjamin: b 8-9-1733 d 5-3-1815 m Huldah Cudworth Pvt MA
Caleb: b 11-14-1763 d 4-29-1845 m Mary Wilbur Pvt MA
Charles: b 8-13-1752 d 7-28-1820 m Rachel Saint John Sol CT
Christopher: b 2-8-1761 d 5-27-1817 m Mary Brown Pvt MA
Clement: b 12-27-1707 d 3-14-1788 m Agatha Merritt Pvt MA
Clement: b 9-21-1755 d 11-30-1839 m Rebecca Stetson Pvt MA
Comfort: b 1756 d 1813 m Sarah Brown Sgt MA
Conrad: b 1743 d p. 1790 m Jane — Pvt PA
Cornelius: b 11-26-1761 d 1-2-1850 m Anna Mann Pvt MA ★
Daniel: b 2-17-1763 d 2-6-1845 m (1)Mary Kitchel (2)Sarah Osborn Pvt NJ ★
Daniel: b 17? d 12-1-1795 m Elizabeth Himes Pvt Drm RI W ★
David: b 3-4-1749 d 6-25-1799 m (1)Ruth Ward (2)Abigail Burt Sgt MA
David: b 3-5-1735 d p. 1787 m Mary — Capt NH ★
David: b 1725 d 9-7-1820 m Phebe Tappan Capt NJ
Eleazer: b 1749 d 1-16-1826 m Hannah Stocking Pvt CT ★
Elnathan: b 4-23-1736 d 2-27-1820 m Ruth Hunt Lt MA
Ephraim: b 1739 d 7-27-1829 m Rebecca Wiley PS PA
Ephraim: b 5-24-1743 d 1-3-1834 m Susannah — Sgt VA ★
Ezekiel: b 5-8-1738 d 9-5-1816 m Abigail Legg PS MA
Fleming: b 11-22-1747 d 6-22-1804 m Margaret McCarter Capt VA
Francis, Sr.: b 5-1-1727 d 3-28-1803 m Elizabeth Bissell PS VT
Gamaliel: b 1-31-1745 d 1-9-1823 m Mary Carver Pvt MA
Hinsdale: b 12-25-1757 d p. 9-20-1833 m Hannah — Pvt CT
Humphrey: b 1-13-1765 d 3-23-1853 m Rachel Mitchell Pvt NC
Isaac: b 3-20-1736 d 1-4-1804 m Temperance Kirkland Pvt MA
Isaac: b 3-3-1707/8 d 1787 m Martha Clark Pvt MA
Isaac: b c. 1752 d p. 1786 m X Sol VA
Isaiah: b 9-2-1739 d 10-3-1810 m (1)Rachel Joy (2)Mollie — Pvt MA
Israel: b 5-25-1749 d 1-11-1844 m Mary Cooper Pvt MA
Issachar: b 11-6-1735 d 8-29-1795 m Hannah Joy Pvt CT
Issachar: b 6-27-1758 d 3-17-1837 m — Day Fif Maj MA ★
Jabez: b 1760 d p. 1805 m Elizabeth Barker Pvt MA
Jacob: b 11-2-1746 d 10-22-1836 m Mrs Ruth Robinson Chapmen Lt MA ★
Jacob: b 11-9-1759 d 7-19-1850 m Lydia Gurney Pvt MA ★
James: b 5-19-1743 d p. 1790 m Abigail Litchfield Pvt MA
James: b 5-21-1747 d 6-3-1787 m Mary Spivey Pvt NC
James: b 1760 d p. 10-14-1833 m X Pvt NC & VA ★
James: b c. 1761 d 9-2-1847 m Lavina Frances Nance Ens VA ★
James: b 1762 d 3-24-1828 m Mehitable Sergeant Cpl VA
James: b 12-1-1760 d 1814 m Mary Murphy Sol VA
James: b 3-7-1721 d 11-9-1785 m Winnefred Hix PS VA
James: b 6-30-1734 d 1789 m Phebe Clark PS CT
John: b 6-30-1734 d 1789 m Phebe Clark PS CT
John, Jr.: bpt 11-20-1743 d p. 1792 m Chloe Graves Pvt CT
John: b 12-4-1748 d 12-12-1834 m Chloe Fuller Pvt MA
John: b c. 1742 d p. 1787 m Sarah Fern Capt VA
Jonathan: b 10-25-1721 d 6-17-1775 m Lucy (Susannah) Nichols Pvt MA
Jonathan: b 5-15-1757 d 3-13-1829 m Susa Orcutt Pvt MA
Joseph: b 5-4-1750 d 5-5-1828 m Deborah Nye Capt MA
Joseph: d 1725 d p. 10-3-1782 m Leah Matross Capt MA
Joseph, Sr.: b 3-18-1722 d 7-27-1789 m Eunice Tinkham Sgt MA
Joseph: b 8-29-1733 d 4-1-1793 m (1)Mrs Sarah Hayward (2)Martha Chilson Pvt MA
Joseph: b 11-3-1725 d 11-20-1792 m Phebe Powers PS Pvt NH
Joshua: b 12-1-1724 d 6-8-1816 m (1)Grace Lincoln (2)Mrs Hannah Cowing Pyncheon PS MA
Josiah: b 1-6-1756 d 11-22-1823 m Mary Tower Pvt MA
Laban: b 10-30-1749 d 4-7-1832 m Olive Wheelock Sgt MA
Leavitt: bpt 9-27-1747 d p. 1790 m Elizabeth Paine Pvt MA
Lebbeus: b 1-16-1760 d 9-6-1844 m (1)Mary Packard (2)Melatiah Robbins Sgt MA ★
Lemuel: bpt 6-15-1729 d a. 10-16-1820 m Dorothy Lewis Capt CT
Lemuel: b 8-30-1755 d 10-25-1842 m Lucy Wait Pvt MA★
Levi: b 8-15-1748 d 1-8-1813 m Hannah Litchfield Lt MA
Michael: b c. 1740 d 1- -1801 m Katie — PS SC
Moses: b 12-23-1740 d 3-31-1781 m Hannah Norton Pvt MA
Morwry: b 11-7-1763 d 8-23-1862 m (1)Hannah Lewis (2)Hannah Potter Pvt RI ★
Nathaniel: b 10-3-1733 d p. 3- -1777 m Mary Hamlen Pvt CS MA
Nehemiah: b 6-19-1740 d 5-20-1817 m Mehitable (Barber) Marble Pvt MA

BATES, contd.
Nehemiah: b 1-23-1764 d 2-25-1860 m Prudence Bigelow Sol MA
Oliver: b 3-4-1742 d 1786 m Abigail Taft Pvt RI
Phineas: b 7-26-1749 d 1829 m Esther Curtis Pvt CT
Reuben: b 2-4-1735 d 3-14-1835 m Mary Hayden Sgt MA
Reuben: b 1762 d 5-15-1835 m Abigail Bull Tms PS RI
Reuben: b 2-24-1764 d 2-11-1853 m Nancy Edmonds Pvt VA
Roger: b 11-9-1745 d 1825 m Hulda Stodder Cpl Tms VT
Samuel: b 5-25-1742 d 11-10-1815 m (1)Sarah Spellman (2) X Pvt CT
Samuel: b 3-19-1738 d *p.* 1801 m (1)Eunice Sherman (2)Keziah Burt Lt MA
Samuel: b 11-5-1754 d 2-14-1838 m Selah White Pvt MA ★
Samuel, Jr.: b 12-21-1760 d 12-3-1808 m Dorcas Shaw Pvt MA
Samuel, Sr.: b 3-25-1718 d 1789/90 m Mercy Beal PS MA
Samuel, Jr.: b 11-15-1744 d 11-3-1801 m Martha Beal Pvt Smn MA
Samuel: b 8-9-1760 d 8-21-1822 m Abigail Willard Pvt NH
Selleck: b 1-12-1745 d *a.* 1790 m Mary — Pvt CT
Seth: b 8- -1735 d 4-9-1820 m Anne Neal 2Lt MA
Silas: b 1737 d 1- -1801 m Dorcas Cordiner Pvt RI
Solomon: b 6-29-1741 d 1815 m Aquilla (Bates) — Cpl MA
Solomon, Jr.: b — d *p.* 1787 m Hannah Balcom Pvt MA
Thaddeus: b 10-8-1757 d 12-6-1840 m Hannah Humphrey Pvt MA
Theodore: b 10-11-1762 d 10-24-1846 m (1)Molly Shattuck (2) Abigail Wheeler Pvt MA ★
Thomas: b 1-6-1757 d 10-4-1846 m (1)Ruth Besse (2)Lorana Besse Fif & Sgt MA ★
Thomas: b 4-15-1755 d — m Ann Darrah Pvt PA
Thomas Fleming: b 1742 d 5-26-1805 m Carolina Matilda Woodson Capt VA
Urban: b 11-6-1739 d 4-13-1809 m Hannah Holbrook Pvt MA
Uzal: bpt 2-5-1749 d 1805 m Elizabeth — Pvt NJ
Wm.: b 10-27-1736 d 12-15-1808 m Sarah Webb Pvt MA
Wm.: b 12-15-1761 d 1-5-1852 m X Pvt MA ★
Wm.: b 8-23-1752 d 3-24-1828 m Mehitabel Sargent Ens CL VA
Wm.: b 1757 d 12-27-1843 m (3)Elizabeth — Bithy (last wife) Spy Pvt NC ★
Wm.: b 2-2-1737 d 5-6-1811 m Annabel Alexander PS NC
Wm.: b *c.* 1759 d 1831/32 m Mary Kay Sol VA
Zealous: b 3-12-1754 d 7-5-1831 m (1)Abigail Nichols (2)Lois Gilman Sgt MA

BATHHURST,
Lawrence: b 9-22-1757 d 7-17-1845 m Rebecca Archibald Pvt PA ★

BATHRICK,
Jason: b 1730 d 2-22-1828 m Sarah — Pvt MA
Tillabee: b 1745-50 d *p.* 5-25-1778 m X Pvt MA

BATSON,
Peter: b *c.* 1745 d 1822 m Mary — PS NC
Thomas: b 1749 d 1822 m Sarah Davis Sol PS NC

BATTAILLE,
Nicholas: b — d — m Mary Thornton Capt VA

BATTE,
John: b *c.* 1745 d *a.* 6-10-1811 m Elizabeth — PS VA
Wm.: b *c.* 1741 d 3-23-1789 m Sarah Parham Capt VA

BATTEN, (includes BATTON)
Henry: b 1750 d 1845 m Elizabeth — OrdlSgt PA ★
James: b 1741 d 3-6-1811 m Jane Russell 1Lt PA
John: b 4-8-1735 d 1781 m Mary Masury Sgt Smn MA
Richard: b 7-3-1737 d 8-25-1822 m Lydia Stylman Pvt NH
Wm.: b 1754 d *a.* 1811 m Elizabeth — Pvt MD

BATTERSHELL,
Freeman: b *c.* 1760 d 4-16-1818 m Nancy — Pvt VA W ★

BATTERSON,
Abijah: b 10-24-1763 d 1-24-1835 m Anna — Pvt CT
George Jr.: b 1758 d 5-11-1837 m Mary Seeley Pvt CT ★
John: b 1766 d 3-17-1831 m Sarah Allen Pvt CT W★
Joseph: b 1755 d 4-30-1838 m Rebecca Dodd Pvt NY ★
Stephen: b 1761 d 1847 m (1)Mary Wardwell (2)Anne — Pvt CT★

BATTERTON,
Samuel: b 1758 d 6-12-1833 m Lydia — Pvt VA

BATTEY,
William: b 9-2-1759 d 3-9-1842 m (1)Elizabeth Shelden (2)Lydia Hill (3)Lucy Peckham Smith Pvt RI ★

BATTLE, (includes BATTELLE, & BATTLES)
Asa: b — d — m Mary Pratt Pvt MA
Ebenezer: b 1-7-1727 d 2-18-1806 m (1)Hannah Allen (2)Lois (Adams) Draper Maj MA
Ebenezer Sr.: b 1-10-1729 d 11-6-1776 m Prudence Draper Lt MA
Ebenezer Jr.: b 2-4-1754 d 1815 m Anna Durant Capt MA
Elisha: b 1-9-1723 d 3-6-1799 m Elizabeth Ruth Sumner PS NC
Ephriam: b *c.* 1750 d *p.* 3-15-1798 m X Capt NC
Hezekiah: b 1758 d 3-22-1819 m Mary Mansell Fif & Drm MA

Ithiel: b *c.* 1751 d 10-18-1827 m Kezia Taylor Lt MA
James Jr.: b 3-12-1760 d 9-20-1858 m Ruhamie Mellen Pvt MA ★
James: b *c.* 1732 d *p.* 1804 m Anne — PS MA
Jeremiah: b 3-16-1720 d *p.* 1790 m Hannah — Sgt MA
Jesse: b 7-8-1738 d 8-25-1805 m Susanna Forsette Sol NC
John: b 4-30-1718 d 11-18-1800 m Mehitable Sherman 2Lt MA
John: b 1721 d *c.* 1792 m Hannah Curtis Pvt MA
Jonathan: b 11- -1755 d 1830 m Hannah Porter MM Lt MA
Josiah: b 7-15-1756 d 10-5-1834 m (1)Lucy Richards (2)Olive Turner Pvt MA
Samuel: b 9-1-1759 d 10-4-1817 m Dorothy Dyer Pvt MA
Samuel: b 1734 d *p.* 1790 m Alice Barnes PS CS MA
William: b 1758 d 12- -1802 m Mary Ann Williams Capt NC
William Sumner: b 10-26-1761 d 1828 m Sarah Whitehead Sol NC

BAUCOM,
John Sr.: b *c.* 1725 d *a.* 6- -1800 m Rachel — PS NC

BAUDER,
Elizabeth: b 4-2-1769 d 5-16-1848 m Peter J. Walrath PS NY
Melchert: b *c.* 1740 d *p.* 1781 m Barbara — Pvt NY
Melgert: b 3-25-1756 d 12-28-1822 m Elizabeth Cook Pvt NY

BAUGH,
Henry: b 4-12-1762 d 10-9-1836 m Margaret Phillipi Sol VA
John: b 4-9-1755 d 10-27-1819 m Catherine Grumbacher Pvt PA
Peter Jr.: b *c.* 1747 d 1817 m Mary Ann Elam PS VA

BAUM,
Charles: b *c.* 1744 d 1817 m Barbara (Youngken) Pvt PA
Frederick: b 10-24-1758 d 10-16-1843 m Elizabeth Helmer Pvt NY★
Frederick Sr.: b 1728 d 1831 m Barbara Ullman Pvt PA
John: b 1-23-1725 d 2-28-1808 m Maria Magdalena Reijjel CMman PA
Jonas: b 6-16-1734 d 1784 m Maria Eva Hurz Pvt PA

BAUSMAN,
William Sr.: b 6-1-1724 d 3-30-1784 m Elizabeth — PS PA
William Jr.: b 6-1-1759 d 4-25-1833 m Elizabeth Bier Lt PA

BAXLEY,
John: b 7-15-1743 d 12-2-1799 m Mary — Qm MD

BAXTER,
Aaron Sr.: b 10-9-1740 d 2-24-1822 m (1)Hannah Burroughs (2)Mary Mentor Pvt CT★
Aaron Jr.: b - -1766 d 12-6-1836 m Abigail Webster Pvt NY★
Andrew Sr.: b 1-31-1725 d 9-4-1781 m Francis — PS NC
Andrew Jr.: b 1750 d 1814 m Elizabeth Harris Lt NC
Andrew: b 1732 d 1799 m Mary Elizabeth — Sol SC
Barnabas: b 1-13-1758 d *p.* 1809 m Mercy Blatchford Pvt MA
Benjamin: b 2- -1757 d 7-7-1823 m (1)Mabel Brown (2)Hannah Hale Pvt CT
Benjamin: b 1757 d 10-17-1831 m (2)Margaret Hewett Pvt NH★
Daniel: b 1747 d 5-4-1851 m Elizabeth Carn Pvt SC
Edward Willard: b 4-11-1756 d 10-25-1823 m (1)Rhoda Field (2) Eunice Belcher Pvt MA
Francis: b 2-3-1742/43 d 1827 m Sarah Ellsworth MM Cpl CT ★
John: b 4-16-1754 d 10-31-1831 m Reliance Ewer Cpl MA★
John: b 1756 d 2-17-1847 m Eunice Beach Pvt MA★
John: b 8-19-1757 d 4-18-1847 m (1)Anna — (2)Candace Emerson Pvt Gnr MA★
John: b 5-2-1708 d 11-14-1788 m Rebecca Fisher CS MA
John: b 9-24-1760 d 11-28-1841 m Dorcas Whitlock Pvt NY★
John: b 2-17-1746 d 8-30-1783 m Elizabeth Sappington Pvt PA
John: b 7-23-1747 d *p.* 1785 m (1)Ann Ridgill (2)Mary Britton LCol SC
Jonathan: b 1732 d 3-3-1778 m Mary Lovejoy Pvt MA
Joseph: b 6-14-1731 d 5-17-1820 m (1)Ann Adams (2)Jerusha (Glover) Arnold Capt PS MA
Joseph: b 1-1-1748 d 2-22-1822 m Mary Ferebee PS NC
Malachi: b - -d 7-17-1835 m Rhoda Manter 3Cpl MA
Moses: b 2-29-1753 d 1845 m Comfort Chaffee Pvt MA
Nathan: b 5-17-1764 d *p.* 1835 m Anna Dodge Pvt Tms CT★
Pettit: b 12-16-1732 d 2-5-1809 m Sarah Brush Pvt NY
Reuben: b 5-2-1745 d 8-14-1813 m Betty Crowell Pvt MA
Samuel: b 1-6-1758 d 11-5-1839 m Sarah Chenoweth Pvt CS MD
Schuyler: b 4-10-1761 d 12-5-1843 m (1)Penelope Dodge (2) Magdalen Bogart Pvt NY
Simon: b 1747 d 4-17-1817 m Margaret — PS NH
Thomas: b 9-3-1755 d 1824 m Zilpha Nickerson Pvt MA
William: b 1755 d 8-25-1832 m Deborah Buel Pvt CT★
William: b 1761 d *p.* 1808 m Abigail Newcomb Pvt MA★
William: b 4-18-1757 d 3-20-1842 m Ruth Elson Sgt VA ★

BAY,
John: b 1743 d 1818 m Ann Williams PS NY
Robert: b 1760 d 2-21-1844 m Ann Gibson Sol PA★
Thomas Sr.: b 1745 d 2- -1827 m Elizabeth Blackburn Ensign PA

BAYARD,
John: b 8-11-1738 d 1-7-1807 m (1)Margaret Hodge (2)May (Grant) Hodgden Col PA

Marshall: b 10-26-1736 d 1826-30 m Mary Donaldson Pvt CT
Peter: b 6-16-1732 d 1817 m Sarah Frisby PS MD
Phoebe: b 1743 d 9-18-1818 m Arthur St. Clair PS PA
Stephen: b 1-23-1743/44 d 12-23-1815 m Elizabeth Mackay LCol PA

BAYER, see BOYER

BAYLESS, (includes BALES, BALIS, BAYLIES, BAYLES. BAYLIS)
Benjamin: b 5-26-1734 d 1782 m Deborah Austin Pvt MD
Benjamin: b 12-25-1752 d 7-27-1819 m Sarah Hayles Pvt PS NC
Daniel: b 10-9-1764 d- -1830 m Margaret Van Hyce Pvt NJ
David: b 7-9-1762 d c. 1849 m X Pvt VA & PA
Frederick: b 7-19-1741 d 3-22-1808 m (1)Lucy Andrews (2)Hannah Brown Pvt MA
Henry: b c. 1761 d p. 1835 m Sophia Edmonds Lt VA
Hodijah: b 9-17-1756 d 4-26-1843 m Elizabeth Lincoln Maj MA
Isaac: b 1752 d 6-4-1827 m Mary — Sol NY
John: b 4-26-1727 d p. 8-2-1784 m Susanna Burtis PS NJ
John: b 5-7-1752 d 12-17-1776 m Katharine Blume Cpl NY
John: b 1741 d 1789 m Hannah Dickenson Pvt NY
John: b 11-25-1746 d 2- -1823 m Anne Price Pvt VA
John: b c. 1760 d 1845 m Margaret Donnelly Pvt VA
Nathaniel: b 5-15-1748 d p. 1790 m Sarah — Lt MD
Nicholas Sr.: b 5-19-1719 d 7-26-1807 m Elizabeth Parker PS MA
Nicholas Jr.: b 11-15-1739 d 1-19-1831 m (1)Abigail Wood (2) Hannah Elliott (3)Mrs Abigail Adams (4)Mrs Olive Taft PS CS MA
Platt: b 1733 d 1778 m Phoebe Lewis Maj NJ
Platt: b 10- -1735 d 5- -1777 m Mary Lewis Qm Gen NJ
Samuel: b 1736 d 1808 m Elizabeth Bayless Capt MD
Thomas: b 1714 d 1795 m Elizabeth — Pvt PS NY
Thomas Sergeant: b 10-18-1748 d 10-30-1835 m (1)Bethiah Godfrey (2)Deborah Barnum Sol MA
Timothy: b 10-5-1763 d 12- -1853 m Hannah Wood Pvt MA
William Jr.: b 8-22-1752 d — m Rhoda Keyes Pvt NH
William: b 1759 d 6-17-1844 m Elizabeth Turner Capt PM VA ★

BAYLOR, (includes BAILOR)
George: b 1-12-1752 d 9-24-1784 m Lucy Page Col VA
Gregory: b 2-10-1710 d — m Mary Whiting PS VA
Jacob: b 1737 d 1804 m Catherine — Pvt PA
John: b 9-4-1750 d 2-5-1808 m Frances Norton PS VA
Martin: b 3-12-1761 d 8-13-1829 m Barbary Myer Pvt PA
Michael: b 5-8-1756 d 6-6-1833 m X Pvt NJ★
Walker: b 10-4-1760 d 1823 m Jane Bledsoe Capt CL

BAYMILLER,
Michael: b 1752 d 1818 m Ann Mary — Pvt PA

BAYNARD,
Daniel: b c. 1760 d 1817 m Nancy Parrott PS MD

BAYNE, (includes BAIN, BANE)
Ellis: b 10-1-1743 d 8-29-1838 m Elizabeth (Patton) Pvt PA ★
Henry: b c. 1760 d p. 1851 m Sophia Duvall Pvt MD
Isaac: b 1-3-1753 d 5-12-1844 m Sarah Ferguson Pvt PA
James: b 5-19-1729 d 11-26-1783 m Catherine Schutt Pvt NY
James: b a. 1755 d a. 8- -1808 m Margaret — PS NC
James, Jr.: b 1754 d 1- -1835 m Elizabeth Haven Pvt VA
Nathan: b 1750 d 1816 m Charity Nelson Pvt PA
Thomas: b 10-3-1744 d 1-23-1828 m Mary Tillyer Pvt PA
William: b c. 1730 d 11-9-1826 m Mary Fenley Lt MD

BAYTOP,
Thomas: b 10-11-1751 d 10-11-1812 m Sarah Booth Capt VA

BAZEMORE,
Thomas: b c. 1750 d p. 7-2-1836 m Sarah — Sol PS NC

BEACH,
Aaron: b 6-10-1761 d 6-17-1846 m Rachael Walker Pvt VT
Abel: b 9-29-1743 d 11-8-1800 m Sarah Edwards Pvt CT
Abel: b 2-9-1712 d 10-3-1796 m Margaret Pickett PS CT
Adna: b 11-10-1757 d 4-20-1820 m Mary Stanley PS CT
Agur: b — d a. 10-6-1794 m (1)Rachel — (2)Debra — (3)Mary — PS CT
Asa: b 8-1-1759 d 9-27-1832 m Elizabeth Benham Pvt CT
Barnids: b 6-15-1737 d 12- -1776 m Chloe Palmer Pvt CT
Benajah: b 3-24-1752 d 7-31-1816 m Annar Linas Sgt CT
Benjamin: b 5-21-1740 d 7-19-1825 m Jannetie Hoogtelen Pvt NY
Caleb: b 3-10-1732 d 1781 m Lois Preston PS MA
Chancy: b 10-31-1748 d 5-13-1825 m Catherine Alwood Sgt CT
David: b 11-25-1753 d 1830 m Anna Clark Lt CT
David: b 1-18-1761 d 1-31-1815 m Phoebe Daniels Pvt NJ
Ebenezer: b 1-6-1752 d 1819 m Eunice Beach Sgt CT
Edmund: b 9-4-1733 d c. 1804 m Eunice Edwards PS CT
Edmund, Sr.: b 2-18-1720 d 1804 m Mary Deming PS CT
Edmund, Jr.: b 1758 d 1837 m Susanna Stanley DrmMaj CT ★
Eliakim: b 7-13-1751 d 10-31-1821 m Abiah Summers PS CT
Elias: b 11-5-1745 d 1806 m Joanna Camp MM Sol NJ

Elihu: b 3-17-1758 d 8-9-1832 m Mercy Moses Pvt CT ★
Elijah: b 2-27-1731 d — m Prudence Wheeler Capt CT
Elisha: b 4-17-1737 d 3-15-1823 m Desire Taylor Ens CT
Elisha: b 1732 d 1815 m (1)Sarah Latham (2)Mrs Sibella Newton Clark PS NJ
Elnathan: b 12-10-1729 d 8-22-1799 m Lydia — PS CT
Enoch: b 1737 d 3-14-1814 m (1)Susan Darling (2)Hannah (Young) Wheeler Capt NJ
Ephraim: b 6-18-1742 d 7-4-1827 m Sarah Stone Pvt PS CT
Fisk: b 5-15-1742 d 3-16-1801 m Martha Carrington Pvt CT
Gershom: b 9-24-1729 d 1812 m (1)Mary Salter (2)Jane Keeler Armr & Sol VT
Isaac: b 4-16-1746 d 12-28-1775 m Mary — Pvt CT
Israel: b 7-6-1759 d 7-10-1836 m Polly Booth Pvt CT ★
Israel: b 5-3-1707 d - -1793 m Hannah Burritt PS CT
Jabez: b c. 1747 d 1-13-1815 m Anne Ayers Arfr NJ
james: b 1757 d 12-24-1824 m (1)Elizabeth Morehouse (2)Susannah Simpson Pvt NJ
James Eaton: b 9-20-1762 d 2-21-1838 m Huldah Sherman Sol CT
Jedediah: b - -1755 d 5- -1841 m Mary Post Pvt NJ
John: b 6-16-1734 d 3-25-1785 m Eunice Heaton PS & Ens CT
John: b 6-10-1748 d 9-16-1776 m Hannah Hoadley Sgt CT
John: b 5-2-1750 d 4-1-1824 m Mercy Bassett Pvt CT
John: b 2-6-1756 d 7-27-1836 m Rhoda Lacey Pvt CT
John: b 4-28-1757 d 1-28-1835 m (1)Sallie Burr (2)Avis Judd Pvt CT
John: b 9-5-1734 d 5-15-1791 m Phoebe Curtis CS CT
John: b 5-12-1757 d 1- -1801 m Jerusha Bonnell Pvt NJ
Jonathan: b 10-3-1760 d 4-26-1850 m (1)Lucy Baldwin (2)Ann Gilbert Buckingham Pvt CT
Joseph Sr.: b 6-10-1714 d 7-25-1795 m Experience Beecher PS CT
Joseph Jr.: b 11-21-1751 d 6- -1802 m Hannah Miles Drm & Ens CT W★
Joseph Jr.: b 7-26-1753 d 1798 m (1)Edie Cook (2)Jerusha Phelps Pvt CT
Joseph: b 10-5-1738 d 1800 m (1)Keziah Johnson (2)Eunice Johnson Capt NJ
Joseph: b 4-14-1753 d 4-13-1816 m Catherine Ogden Pvt NJ
Josiah: b 1705 d 1- -1779 m Annis Day PS NJ
Julius: b 1-19-1765 d 11-7-1848 m Eunice Oviatt Pvt CT ★
Landra: b 3-5-1727 d 2-26-1824 m Abigail Baldwin PS CT
Linus: b 11-22-1752 d 9-29-1828 m Elizabeth Abbott PS CT
Miles: b 11-14-1742/3 d 2-14-1818 m (1)Abigail Hopkins (2)Sarah Butler Maj CT
Moses: b — d 3-30-1838 m (2)Margaret Cooley Pvt VT
Nathan: b 7-16-1763 d 7-26-1847 m (1)Susan Thomas (2)Margaret Fryburg Sgt Wgm PA ★
Nathaniel: b 2-14-1741 d 12-1-1812 m Phebe Potter Pvt CT
Nathaniel: b 1758 d 10-5-1825 m Ruth Porter Pvt CT
Obil: b 12-25-1758 d 10-5-1846 m Elizabeth Kilbourne Pvt CT ★
Reuben: b 12-4-1757 d 7-4-1844 m Hannah Kimball Sgt CT ★
Rice: b 6-15-1762 d 2-22-1818 m Esther Willams Pvt CT
Robert: b 10-16-1760 d 7-4-1852 m Sarah Washburn Pvt VT ★
Samuel: b 12-26-1736 d 7-11-1805 m (1)Mary Hall (2)Esther Cook CS CT
Samuel: b 8-10-1729 d a. 1790 m Mary Nettleton PS CT
Samuel: b - -1752 d 4-10-1829 m Mary S — Lt VT
Stephen: b 9-14-1751 d 11-17-1821 m Miriam Parker Pvt CT
Stephen: b - -1732 d p. 4-26-1791 m Patience Bedford Pvt CT
Thaddeus: b 1765 d 1818 m Lucretia Goldsmith Mrnr CT ★
Wait: b 10-25-1747 d 12-28-1810 m Huldah Loomis Ens CT
Zerah: b - -1746 d p. 1790 m Lucy Stevens Qm CS PS CT
Zophar: b 2-10-1723 d 3-23-1799 m Elizabeth Wadhams Pvt CT

BEACKLEY, (includes BEAKLEY)
Christian: b 4-26-1754 d 1801-03 m Mary Stroud Lt PS PA

BEADLE, (includes BEDEL, BEDLE, & BEEDLE)
Joel: b 4-13-1727 d 2-2-1792 m Mary Walling Pvt NJ
John: b 1-31-1742 d 8-15-1798 m Eunice Barker Capt CT
John: b 10-6-1732 d 1820 m Alche Van Nostrand Pvt NY
John: b 1740 d p. 10-13-1792 m Rhoda Morris Lt VA
Joseph: b 1749 d 7-9-1826 m Mary Meeks Pvt PA
Moody: b 5-12-1764 d 1-13-1841 m (1)Ruth Hutchins (2)Mary Heit Pvt NH
Thomas: b 1-16-1752 d 3-5-1821 m Amy Herbert Pvt NJ

BEADLES,
John: b — d 1824 m Lurenna Miller Capt VA

BEAGLE, (includes BEEGLE)
Charles: b-1750 d 3-20-1808 m Catherine Holler Pvt PA
John: b 9-19-1745 d 11-6-1829 m Winche Van Nosdall Pvt NY

BEALL, (includes BEAL, BEALE, BEALS)
Aaron: b 4-3-1741 d 1820 m Catherine Snyder PS Pvt NH
Abel: b 10-20-1733 d 4-19-1805 m (1)Deborah Lambert (2)Mrs Susannah Humphrey Cpl MA
Adam, Sr.: b 8-20-1725 d 12-25-1796 m Jael Worrick Pvt MA
Adam, Jr.: b 11-3-1754 d 7-1-1834 m Lydia (Beal) Pvt MA ★
Archibald: b 10-4-1756 d 7-31-1840 m Pamilia Cruse Sol VA
Basil: b 1725 d 1818 m Harriet — Lt MD
Basil: b 3-19-1754 d 1824 m Anne Jourdan PS MD

BEALL, contd.

Basil: b 3-19-1751 d *c.* 1819 m Ariana — CS MD
Benjamin: b 4-19-1744 d 8-6-1814 m Martha Thaxter Capt MA
Benjamin, Sr.: b 12-9-1731 d 8-30-1805 m Mary Porter Lt MA
Benjamin, Jr.: b 10-30-1757 d *p.* 1792 m Mary Noyes Pvt MA
Brooke: b 1742 d 1798 m Margaret Johns PS CS MD
Charles: b *a.* 1750 d 12- -1789 m Tabitha Beall Pvt MD
Clement: b 1734 d *p.* 1790 m Pricilla Perry Pvt CS PS MD
Daniel: b 1-15-1762 d 1-14-1831 m Celia (Beall) Pvt MD
Daniel: b 9-2-1752 d 1811 m Martha Peyton Pvt VA
David: b 1730 d 1791 m Nancy — Capt PA
David: b 6-20-1745 d 2-6-1828 m Rachel McConnell Pvt PA
Edward: b 10-25-1743 d 12-7-1797 m Rachel Edmonston PS MD
Elijah, Sr.: b 7-7-1714 d 7-11-1789 m (1)Sarah Jones (2)Rachel
   Hobart Pvt MA
Elisha: b 1-4-1745 d 12-17-1837 m Jane Perry Capt MD
Elisha: b 5-11-1761 d 11- -1830 m Lydia Tower Pvt MA
Enoch: b 1-1-1760 d 8-29-1829 m Hannah Halbert Pvt MA ★
George: b 1695 d 1780 m Elizabeth (Brooke) Dent PS MD
Isaac: b — d *p.* 1797 m Marjorie White CS Maj VA ★
Jacob: b *c.* 1720 d 1792 m Elliner — CS GA
Jacob: b 2-1-1734 d *p.* 1775 m (1)Ruth Pool (2)Mary Tower Pvt
   MA
Jairus: b 7-21-1760 d 1-11-1787 m Susanna Lincoln PS MA
James: b 1728 d 2- -1804 m Mary Elizabeth Edmonson PS MD
Jedediah: b 9-8-1717 d — m Hannah — Slr MA
Jeremiah: b *c.* 1750 d *p.* 6-26-1841 m Delilah Gatrill Pvt PS MD
Jeremiah: b 7-24-1744 d 10-1-1832 m Mary French Sgt MA
John: b *c.* 1713 d *p.* 5-1-1792 m (2)Mary Magdalene Hacket PS MD
John: b 1-7-1743 d 2-20-1792 m Lydia Horton Pvt MA
John: b 12-12-1740 d 1-25-1777 m Lamar Bourgoyne PS PA
Jonathan, Sr.: b 3-22-1737 d *c.* 1825 m Mary Joy Smn
Jonathan: b 3-15-1758 d *p.* 8-15-1832 m Naomi Bates Pvt MA ★
Jonathan: b 7-20-1708 d *p.* 1777 m (1)Percilla Lincoln (2)Mrs
   Mercy Bates PS MA
Jonathan: b 1730 d 1813 m (1)Abigail Harlow (2)Abigail Egerton
   Pvt MA
Joseph: b 1708 d 1798 m Mrs Rachel Howard PS MD
Joseph: b 9-23-1743 d 7-23-1797 m Lilly Davis Lt MA
Joseph: b 9-11-1698 d 9- -1780 m Love Curtis Sol MA
Joseph: b 1752 d 1815 m Lydia Loring Porter Pvt MA
Joseph: b 10-1-1747 d 8-16-1809/10 m Hannah Russell Pvt PA
Joshua: b 9-22-1722 d 2-9-1804 m Priscilla Paine Sgt MA
Josiah: b 1715 d *p.* 1778 m Millicent B. Bradley PS MD
Josias: b 1725 d 1796 m Priscilla Clark Col PS &CS MD
Josias: b *c.* 1735 d *p.* 1790 m Millicent Beall Bradley PS MD
Lazarus Andrew: b 9-30-1753 d 11-23-1822 m Bethiah Lewis Pvt
   MA
Lloyd: b 8-19-1756 d 1817 m Elizabeth Jones Lt MD
Matthew: b — d *p.* 1797 m Mrs Hannah Swezey Pvt NJ
Menum: b 1738 d *p.* 1814 m Frances Lewis PS & Sol MD
Mordecai: b 1742 d 1777 m Elizabeth (Beall) Capt PS MD
Moses: b 8-31-1758 d 3-2-1810 m Sarah Brownwell Pvt MA
Nathan: b 1727 d 8-9-1798 m Bethsheba — Pvt MA
Nathaniel: b 1747 d 1781 m (1)Nancy Jackson (2)Nancy Weeks Sol
   GA
Nathaniel: b 4-17-1761 d 10-18-1832 m Agather Bostick Sol GA
Nathaniel: b *c.* 1760 d *c.* 11- -1813 m Nancy Head Trooper VA ★
Nicholas: b — d *p.* 6-26-1790 m Elizabeth — Pvt PA
Ninian: b 1751 d *a.* 1784 m Ann Sisell PS MD
Ninian: b 1761 d 6-13-1836 m Christina Stull Pvt VA ★
Ninian Edmonstone: b 1-16-1755 d 4-11-1831 m Anna Maria
   Stricker PS MD
Obadiah: b 11-9-1761 d *p.* 1806 m Rebecca Moody Pvt MA
Philip: b 1754 d 1810 m Elizabeth — Pvt PA
Rezin: b 1723 d 1809 m (1)Amelia Beall (2)Valinda Sheppard BGen
   MD
Richard: b *c.* 1740 d 12- -1799 m Rebecca Adamson Capt MD
Richard: b 1738 d 8-18-1778 m Sarah Brooke PS Ens MD
Richard: b 1-30-1759 d 1819 m Alice G. Colston SgtMaj VA
Richard Eustace: b 1760 d 1835 m (1)Margaret Bronaugh (2)Mrs
   Mary Elizabeth Grayson Adj VA ★
Robert: b 1700 d 1788 m Hannah Kinsey PS MD
Robert: b 1753 d 1819 m Polly — Pvt PA
Robert: b 1-30-1759 d 9-1-1843 m Martha Felicia Turberville Capt
   VA
Robert: b — d *c.* 1789 m Mrs Elizabeth Somers Stevenson Lt VA
Robert Lamar: b 3-4-1757 d 11-6-1851 m (1)Ann Aldridge (2)Mrs
   Ann Edmonston Nichols Pvt MD ★
Roger Brooke: b 1734 d 1790 m Ruth Hamilton PS MD
Samuel: b *c.* 1714 d 1- -1778 m Eleanor Brooke CS PS Col MD
Samuel, Sr.: b 1706 d *a.* 12-12-1780 m Jane Edmonston PS MD
Samuel, Jr.: b 9-12-1749 d 1825 m (1)Celina (Beall) (2)Elizabeth
   Perry PS MD
Samuel: b 3-7-1758 d 11-15-1795 m Rebecca Wilkerson Matr Pvt
   Bbd MA
Samuel: b 10-8-1761 d 7-7-1834 m (1)Susan Cobb (2)Sarah
   Remington (3)Eunice Boynton Pvt MA ★
Seth, Sr.: b 5-3-1710 d 12- -1786 m Abigail Clark Pvt MA
Seth, Jr.: b 12-20-1736 d 5-8-1803 m Leah Nash Pvt MA
Shadrack: b 1745 d *p.* 10-5-1820 m Agnes — PS MD
Taverner, Jr.: b 2-3-1742 d 6-5-1810 m Elizabeth Hite Lt VA
Thaddeus: b 1747 d 1815 m Jane Beall BgdMaj MD

Thomas: b — d *a.* 9-1-1818 m Lucy Beall Capt MD
Thomas: b 1743 d 11-16-1823 m Verlinda Beall Capt MD
Thomas: b 1727 d 1806 m Huldah Flagg Pvt MA
Thomas: b 8-6-1735 d 6-30-1803 m Sarah Todhunter Capt PA
Thomas, Sr.: b 1719 d 8-29-1801 m Sarah Antrim PS VA
Thomas Allen : b 10-12-1762 d *c.* 1826 m X Pvt MD
Thomas Brooke: b 1763 d 10-21-1801 m Margaret Heugh Cpl MD
William: b *c.* 1740 d 1805 m (2)Elizabeth Murphey Sol GA
William: b 11-16-1729 d 1796 m Lydia Bent PS NH
William: b *p.* 7-16-1749 d *p.* 1791 m Anna Woods Pvt VT
William Dent: b 11-8-1757 d 8-23-1829 m Sarah Ann (Magruder)
   Brooke Maj MD
Zachariah: b 7-17-1742 d 6-5-1817 m Rebecca Tyson Pvt MD
Zachariah: b 1761 d 9-10-1826 m Nancy Evans Pvt MD
Zechariah: b — d 11-8-1777 m Abigail Goodwin Capt NH
Zephaniah: b 2-15-1753 d 6-15-1809 m Anne — Capt MD
Zephaniah: b *c.* 1720 d 7- -1801 m Keziah White Pritchard Maj PA

BEALMEAR,

Francis: b *c.* 1740 d 10- -1782 m Elizabeth Brewer PS MD

BEAM, (includes BEEM, BEHM)

Abraham: b 1748 d 2-22-1814 m Esther — Pvt PA
Christopher: b 9-1-1761 d 6-15-1828 m Elizabeth Crise᾽ Pvt PA
Henry: b 1746 d 5-7-1830 m Rachael Roose Pvt PA
George: b 1756 d 2-6-1827 m Ann Eve Yoxhine Pvt PA
Jacob: b 1693 d 1780 m Barbara Kendig PS PA
John: b *a.* 1754 d 3-11-1843 m Catherine Pace Sol NJ
Michael: b 2-7-1755-8 d 9-12-1850 m Elizabeth Green Pvt VA ★
William: b 3-1-1724 d *p.* 3-26-1783 m Rebecca Freer PS NY
Yoost: b *c.* 1720 d *p.* 1-16-1797 m Catherine Sloat CS NJ

BEAMAN, (includes BEEMAN & BEMAN)

Aaron: b 11-25-1762 d 7-11-1843 m Phebe Gould Pvt MA
Daniel: b 1-18-1756 d 4-3-1844 m Mary Bliss Cpl CT ★
Daniel: b 8-29-1756 d *p.* 1784 m Abigail Ackley Sol CT
David: b *c.* 1746 d *p.* 1782 m Sarah Pierce Cpl MA
David: b *c.* 1735 d 1802/3 m (1)Mary Stanborrough (2)Anna
   (Jackson) Ayals PS NJ
Ebenezer: b 1-7-1761 d 2-9-1840 m Hannah Lum Cpl NY ★
Elijah: b 1743 d 1833 m — Hatch Lt CT
Ezra: b 10-16-1736 d 6-4-1811 m Persis Keyes Maj MA
Francis: b *c.* 1730-35 d *p.* 5-11-1785 m Mary — Pvt NC
Friend: b 2-6-1750 d 10-20-1838 m Mary Logan Pvt CT ★
Gideon: b 7-12-1764 d *p.* 1-14-1833 m Dolly Wilder Pvt MA ★
Jeremiah: b 5-17-1757 d 10-12-1836 m Ruth Barrow Pvt NC
Jethro: b 1752 d 5-15-1787 m Elizabeth Garlington Sol VA
John: b 1738 d 1820 m Mary Fuller Pvt MA
John: b 2-9-1755 d 3-1-1827 m Hannah Jennings Pvt MA
Joseph: b 7-29-1718 d 6-27-1784 m Mary Walker Sgt MA
Joseph: b 4-21-1756 d 10-20-1820 m (1)Sally Davis (2)Sene Ellis
   Pvt MA ★
Joseph: b 1725 d 3- -1814 m Catherine Durkee Pvt VT
Josiah: b 1756 d 11-6-1831 m Sarah Crane Pvt NJ ★
Moses: b 8-8-1757 d 7-1833-40 m Margaret Poland Pvt PA ★
Nathan: b 9-15-1755 d 12-20-1846 m Jemima Roberts Sgt NY ★
Nathaniel: b 10-5-1747 d 5-17-1817 m Thankful Farnsworth Capt
   MA W ★
Samuel: b 9-12-1755 d 1845 m Silence Douglass Sgt PS NY ★
Samuel, Sr.: b 7-30-1730 d 7-20-1821 m Sybil Thompson Sol VT
Thomas: b 7-6-1734 d 5-3-1804 m Lydia Roberts Lt CT
Thomas: bpt 10-9-1715 d 5-12-1790 m Bethiah Tracy Pvt CT
Tracy: b 5-20-1762 d 3-13-1850 m Polly Cogswell Pvt CT
William: b 5-2-1758 d 10-21-1837 m X Pvt CT ★

BEAN, (includes BEANS)

Alexander: b *c.* 1750 d *p.* 1788 m Christiana Massey Pvt SC
Benjamin: b 1758 d 4-17-1828 m Rebecca Evans PS MD
Benjamin: b 5-15-1727 d 1777 m Mary Baker Capt PS NH
Benjamin: b 1757 d 7-2-1835 m Susan Carr Capt VT
Curtis: b 1731 d 2-8-1833 m Apphia Bean Cpl NH
Daniel: b 10-20-1754 d 5-31-1809 m Abigail Beedle Pvt MA
Daniel: b 3-10-1757 d 3-16-1834 m Margaret Shaw Pvt MA ★
Ebenezer: b 1-20-1737 d 9- -1824 m Eliza Thomas Pvt RI ★
Ebenezer: b 9-5-1755 d 3-3-1846 m Catherine Kilgore Pvt NH ★
George: b 1723 d *a.* 9-26-1797 m (2)Ann — PS MD
Henry: b 11-21-1760 d 10- -1821 m Susanna Schrach Pvt PA
Isaac: b 1-17-1741 d 1820 m Christiana Johnson Pvt PA
James: b 1758 d *p.* 1792 m Hannah Ames Pvt NH
James: b 1754 d *p.* 1833 m Jane Carmicheal Pvt PA
Jeremiah: b 1753/4 d 12-17-1835 m Lydia Sanborn Pvt NH MA ★
Jeremiah: b 4-9-1707 d 12- -1796 m Sarah Blake PS NH
Jesse: b *c.* 1750 d *p.* 1800 m Elizabeth Mitchell Capt NC
John, Jr.: b 9-1-1756 d 11-9-1832 m Betsey Moody Lt MA
John: b 6-3-1757 d 3-17-1854 m Nancy Johnson Pvt MA
John: b 9-9-1752 d *p.* 1790 m Sarah Foster Ens PS NH
John: b 1751/2 d 5-7-1814 m Hannah Ames Sgt NH
John: b *c.* 1760 d *p.* 1811 m Sarah Jordan Pvt NC
John, Sr.: b 1723 d 3-3-1799 m Elizabeth Newberry Pvt PA
John, Jr.: b 9-16-1759 d 3-26-1847 m Catherine Hunsicker Pvt PA
John: b 1763 d 12-25-1849 m Eva Senseney Pvt VA

Jonathan: b 9-10-1736 d 1802 m (1)Mary Leavitt (2)Lydia Sleeper Pvt PS NH
Joseph: b 8-7-1744 d 6-1-1804 m Elizabeth — Pvt PS NH
Joshua, Jr.: b 5-2-1741 d 4-25-1814 m Mary Bean PS NH
Joshua: b 3-22-1761 d 8-4-1851 m Elizabeth Meredith Pvt PA
Josiah: b 4-27-1759 d 1-28-1835 m Lois Emerson Pvt NH ★
Moody: b 1745 d 1795 m X Sgt NH
Mordecai: b 3-28-1740 d 11-28-1814 m Judith Hammond PS VA
Nathan: b 9-21-1758 d 5-11-1827 m (1)Hannah Buswell (2)Elizabeth Towle Pvt NH
Nathaniel: b 11-21-1761 d 6-11-1829 m Mary — Pvt NH & MA ★
Nathaniel: b 4- -1750 d 11-6-1804 m Susannah Currier CS NH
Nicholas: b 3-16-1760 d 8-21-1838 m Ann Wilbourn Pvt PA ★
Phineas: b 9-11-1750 d 3-2-1825 m Judith Snow Pvt NH
Phineas: b 7-25-1763 d 10-16-1838 m Hannah Clifford Pvt NH
Robert: b 1750 d 10- -1824 m Martha Womack Sol NC
Samuel: b 1708 d 6- -1800 m Mary Buzzell PS NH
Sinkler: b c. 1715 d 2-31-1798 m Shuah Fifield Sol NH
Stephen: b 1742-47 d 1812-19 m Jemima — CS & PS NH
Thomas: b 1755 d p. 1805 m Mary Gwynne Pvt MD
Thomas Stacy: b 9-18-1757 d 7-2-1839 m Patience Andrews Pvt RI
Wm.: b 1747 d 8-17-1833 m (1)Martha Frost (2)Lydia Nutting Pvt MA
Wm.: b 6-25-1754 d 9-19-1837 m Sarah Barker Pvt Pvtr MA ★
Wm.: b 4-5-1752 d 1-15-1833 m Sarah Griffin Pvt NH
Wm.: b 1745 d c. 1825 m — Ball Capt NC
Wm.: b c. 1720 d a. 5- -1782 m Lydia Russell CS NC
Wm.: b 1730 d 1790 m X Pvt CL PA
Wm.: b 1756 d p. 11-26-1834 m Jane Sadler Pvt PA ★
Wm.: b 7-15-1740 d 12-14-1817 m Hannah Balderson Sol CL VA

BEARD, (includes BARD & BORD)

Aaron: b 11-25-1717 d 7-18-1796 m Susanna Frost Pvt CS PS MA
Adam: b 5-18-1753 d 11-7-1829 m Katherine Umstead Lt PA
Amos: b 1748 d 1822 m (1)Hannah Needham (2)Isabella — Pvt MA
Andrew: b 3-9-1752 d 1-3-1838 m Susan Rogers Pvt CT ★
Andrew, Jr.: b 9-27-1741 d 1-22-1831 m Elizabeth Burnap Pvt MA
Andrew: b c. 1738 d 7- -1781 m Sarah Heldridge Sgt NC
Christian: b c. 1760 d 1832-34 m Mary Grimm Pvt VA
David: b 6-7-1755 d 12-16-1840 m Mary Tomlinson Pvt CT
David: b 7-25-1746 d 1836 m Hannah Hayward Sgt MA
David: b c. 1746 d p. 1-16-1815 m (1)Isabel Carson (2)— Meek Capt VA
Ebenezer: b 4- -1759 d 2-14-1809 m Anne Thompson Pvt CT
Elizabeth: b 1710 d p. 1782 m John Beard PS VA
Frederick: b 9-30-1758 d 3-9-1842 m Magdalena Weigle Pvt MD ★
George: b 9-3-1759 d 5-15-1812 m Elizabeth — Pvt PA
James: b 8-28-1728 d 1812 m (1)Ruth Holbrook (2)Mrs. Hobart Pvt PS CT
James, Sr.: b 1730 d 3-5-1802 m Isabel — Pvt PA
John: b 4-7-1751 d 3-8-1836 m Ann Doughty Pvt MD
John: b 1753 d 2-15-1814 m Margaret Kirk Pvt MA
John: b c. 1745 d 11- -1788 m X Pvt PA
John: b 4-4-1766 d 8-28-1835 m (2)Watty Groves Pvt PA ★
John: b 1750 d 1805 m Mary Bartley Sol SC
John: b 1733 d 1808 m Jennet Wallace Capt VA
John: b c. 1705 d p. 4-26-1780 m Elizabeth — Sol VA
John Lewis: b 1715 d p. 12-13-1788 m Christina Snapp Capt CL PS NC
Joseph: b 6-27-1750 d 3-17-1813 m Susannah Hartshorn Cpl MA
Joseph: b c. 1760 d p. 1799 m Racheal McConoughey Pvt MA
Samuel: b 7-22-1734 d 4-4-1816 m Elizabeth Wheeler Sgt CT
Stephen: b c. 1750 d p. 12-25-1814 m (1)Elizabeth — (2)Susanna Rawlings Sol CL MD
Wm., Jr.: b 6-4-1758 d 8-11-1838 m Deliverence Heseltine Pvt MA ★
Wm.: b 10-20-1751 d 1-21-1832 m Jane Burns Ens NH
Wm.: b c. 1754 d a. 1835 m Martha Patterson Pvt VA

BEARDEN,

Benjamin: b 1748 d p. 12-16-1821 m Malley Harris PS NC
John: b 3-11-1744 d 1836 m X Pvt SC ★

BEARDSLEY, (includes BEARDSLEE)

Abijah: b 12-2-1755 d 3-13-1830 m Elizabeth Ann — Pvt CT
Abraham: b 9-28-1726 d 2-18-1815 m Bethia Curtiss Pvt CT
Austin: b 2-9-1726 d p. 1790 m Ann Canfield PS NY
Benaijah: b 9-27-1749 d 8- -1810 m Rebecca Taylor Sgt CT
Benjamin: b 2-28-1728 d — m Thankful — Ens CT
Benjamin: b 1-13-1754 d 6-6-1837 m Amelia Stevens Pvt CT
Charles: b 5-28-1739 d 11-20-1803 m (1)Mary — (2)Louisa — PS NJ
Curtis: b 8-9-1754 d 9-13-1796 m Mary Allen Pvt CT
David: b 1728 d 5-11-1802 m Mary Gregory Pvt CT
Elias: b 3-9-1761 d 1-19-1822 m Hannah Clark Pvt CT
Elijah: b 5-16-1760 d 10-22-1826 m Sarah Hubbell Pvt CT ★
Ephraim: b 3-30-1733 d 3-22-1806 m Martha Hatch Pvt Fif CT
Gershom: b 10-8-1753 d 11-13-1826 m Linda Rosetta Evans Srgn-Mte CL CT ★
Gideon: b 1738 d 5-28-1810 m Mary Bearss Capt CT
James: b 7-27-1758 d 1-26-1845 m Ruth Summers Pvt CT ★
Jared: b 1744 d 1802 m Grace Perry Cpl CT
John: b 1735 d 12-29-1815 m Rachel Smith Pvt CT

John: b 2-6-1757 d p. 1796 m Polly Binns CG CT
Jonathan: b 4-21-1746 d 4-17-1816 m Huldah Ferris Ens CT
Josiah: b 2-6-1756 d 8-6-1842 m Abigail Bulkely Pvt CT ★
Lemuel: b 1743 d 12-23-1806 m Deborah Hyde Laborie Lt CT
Nehemiah: b 12- -1731 d 3-31-1811 m Sarah — Col CT
Philo: b 11-21-1755 d 3-11-1826 m Esther Curtis Pvt CT
Phineas: b 3-5-1733 d 1-20-1812 m Ruth Fairchild Capt CT
Salmon W.: b 11-15-1759 d 5-16-1825 m Abigail Penfield Pvt CT ★
Samuel: b 6-30-1719 d 6-20-1790 m (1)Ann French (2)Thankful (Moss) Doolittle Capt CT
Stephen: b 4-5-1740 d 2-16-1804 m Mehitable — Cpl CT
Thomas: b 11-17-1757 d 3-28-1842 m Mabel Thompson Pvt CT ★
Whitmore: b 1759 d 2-8-1833 m Dolly Beard Pvt CT ★

BEARMORE,

Lewis: b 10-28-1749 d 8-21-1836 m X Ens NJ ★

BEARSE, (includes BEARCE, BIERCE, BEARSS)

Asa: b 5-13-1740 d 7-15-1829 m Mary Randall 2Lt MA
Benjamin: b 3-28-1758 d 8-25-1843 m Lydia Bisbee Pvt MA
Hezekiah: b 5-25-1730 d p. 1790 m Deborah Sturtevant Pvt CT
Jonathan: b 8-25-1754 d p. 1793 m Salome Bridgeman Pvt MA
Joseph: b 1-8-1756 d 11-4-1835 m Jemima Beebe Sgt CT ★
Josiah: b 8-17-1755 d 5-30-1845 m Freelove Canfield Pvt CT ★
Newcomb: b 1759 d 7-13-1804 m Martha Pickett Sol CT
Wm.: b 3-26-1753 d 1-18-1835 m Abigail Bell OrdlSgt CT ★

BEARSTICKER,

Andrew: b 7-20-1747 d 8-26-1796 m Mary Gravel Sgt CL PA

BEASLEY, (includes BEAZLEY, BEESLEY)

Ann: b c. 1730 d p. 1781 m William Beasley PS VA
Benjamin: b 2- -1760 d 4-24-1841 m Rachel Prather Pvt VA ★
Edward: b c. 1745 d p. 1790 m (1)Elizabeth Beazley (2)Ann — PS MD
Ephraim: b c. 1741 d 1823 m Winifred Pleasants Sol VA
Isaac: b 1753 d p. 1833 m Mary Bee Pvt & Spy VA
Isham: b 1-11-1760 d 5-20-1855 m Polly Andrews Pvt NC ★
James: b c. 1739 d 8-12-1803 m Ann — Pvt VA
John: b 1717 d 1792 m Jane Cagwell Sol VA
John: b 1757 d 1829/30 m Susan Hubbard Pvt VA
John Baptist: b c. 1746 d 1790/91 m Elizabeth Blount PS & CS NC
Leonard: b 4-11-1764 d 9- -1844 m (2)Nancy Clark Pvt VA ★
Richard: b — d p. 11-5-1810 m Jane Yarbrough Pvt GA
Stephen: b 5-26-1742 d 11-16-1814 m Abagail Harrison Capt PA
Wm.: b — d a. 9-12-1806 m Ann — PS VA

BEASTON,

Wm.: b 4-18-1757 d 1839 m Sophia Williams (or Silvia Steelman) Pvt NJ

BEATH,

John: b 1710 d 12-9-1798 m Margaret Fullerton NS MA
Joseph: b 12-29-1740 d 8-1-1828 m Mary Pelham NS ME

BEATTY, (includes BATEY, BEATTIE, & BEATY)

Alexander: b a. 1757 d p. 1790 m Hannah Welling Lt NY
Andrew: b 1753 d 9-8-1823 m Judith Carter Pvt PA
Benjamin: b 1745 d 1834 m Martha Chamberlain Ens PA
David: b c. 1744 d 4-25-1814 m Mary Beattie (cousin) CS Capt VA
Edward, Jr.: b 1756 d 12-27-1845 m Nancy Umstead Sol PA ★
Francis: b c. 1759 d 8-13-1826 m Jane Hall Pvt NY
George: b c. 1735 d p. 1784 m Anne Cullens Pvt VA
George: b 1758 d 11- -1798/1799 m Sarah — Pvt VA W ★
Henry: b 9-23-1760 d 4-23-1840 m Sara Hening Pvt VA MD ★
Isaac: b 1755 d 3-12-1834 m Sarah Sutton Capt Wgm NJ
James: b 1742 d 1820 m Elizabeth Von Raymer 2Lt MD
James: b 1753 d 11-25-1827 m Catherine — Cpl PA
James: b 1747 d 1839 m Catherine Smith Pvt PA
James: b 1752 d 1-11-1838 m Mary Quigley Pvt PA
John: b 1738 d 1821 m Sarah Parkinson PS MD
John: b 11-15-1719 d p. 12-3-1799 m (1)Mary Brink (2)Martha Pemberton Pvt NY
John: b 1751 d 4-17-1840 m Elizabeth Goldsmith Pvt NY
John: b c. 1740 d 5-20-1817 m Grizzy McRabert Pvt NY
John: b 12-10-1749 d 5-31-1826 m Mary Longstreet Col PA
John: b 1749 d 5-30-1826 m (1)Jane Banks (2)Elizabeth Gray Lt PA
John, Sr.: b 1730 d 1787 m Catherine — Pvt PA
John, Jr.: b 1755 d 1815 m Anna — Pvt PA
John: b 1755 d 7-17-1829 m Jane Lowry Pvt PA ★
John: b 1762 d 8- -1837 m Elizabeth Prince PS SC
John: b 1756 d 6-9-1839 m Mrs Sarah Beatty Sgt VA ★
John: b c. 1730 d p. 8-18-1790 m Elenor — CS VA
Reading: b 12-23-1757 d 10-29-1831 m Christina Wynkoop Lt Dr PA
Thomas: b 1759 d 2-20-1815 m Ann Harrison Lt MD
Thomas: b 1731 d 1787 m Mary Abernethy Col NC
Wm., 3rd: b 1-17-1739 d 4-25-1801 m Mary Dorothea Grosh Col MD
Wm.: b 1726 d 1799 m Mary Frazer Pvt PA
Wm.: b 1737 d 2-7-1814 m X Pvt PA
Wm.: b 5-1-1760 d 1-11-1835 m (1)Mary — (2)Anne Bass Capt VA
Wm.: b 4-4-1760 d 4-4-1860 m Mary Allison Pvt VA

BEAUCHAMP,
Fountain: b 1727 d 8-6-1782 m Rhoda Adams Pvt MD
Newell: b 5-8-1743 d 8-10-1825 m Annis Downham Capt MD DE
Wm.: b c. 1760 d p. 1795 m Nancy Parker Pvt MD

BEAUJEAN, (includes BENJEAN)
Charles: b 1754 d 1799 m Anna Kimberly Sgt MA W ★

BEAUMONT,
Deodate: b 1735 d p. 1832 m Mary Parsons Pvt PA ★
Isaiah: b 5-23-1757 d 7-23-1837 m Fear Alden Pvt CT ★
Samuel: b 2-23-1734 d 8-9-1789 m Thankful Towner Sol CT
Samuel: b 1755 d 1836 m Seabrid Towner Sgt CT ★
Wm.: b 5-25-1753 d 10- -1807 m Mary Wright Lt Qm CT

BEAUREGARD, (includes BOUREGARD)
Elie Toutant: b 6-17-1759 d 12-3-1809 m Marie Felecite Durel PS LA

BEAUVAIS,
Jean Baptiste Ste. Beme: b 3-21-1746 d 7-9-1833 m Marie Therese Boucher de Mombruem de La Soudray PS ILL
Vital: b 1751 d p. 1789 m Felicite Janis PS VA

BEAVER, (includes BEIBER, BIEBER)
Adam: b 7-7-1754 d 3-16-1842 m Magdalene Reber Pvt PA ★
Anthony: b 1-26-1761 d 9-7-1839 m (1)Mary Clapper (2)Susanna Clapper Pvt PA
Benjamin: b 1763 d 1830 m Caroline Snyder Pvt PA ★
Dewalt: b 10-16-1729 d 2-6-1808 m Sibylla Steinbrenner Pvt PA
Dietrich: b 1719 d 1787 m Elizabeth Kieffer Pvt PA
George: b 5-1-1755 d 1-16-1836 m Katherine Kieffer Pvt PA ★
Jacob: b 10-13-1761 d 11-8-1835 m Esther Lesher Pvt PA
Jacob: b 12-24-1731 d 10-16-1798 m Christina Steinbrenner PS PA
John, Sr.: bpt 5-11-1740 d p. 5-5-1794 m (1)Cornelia Decker (2) Catherine Wold Pvt NY
John, Sr.: b 4-21-1722 d 12-15-1777 m Margaret Barbara Steinbrenner Pvt PA
John, Jr.: b 5-2-1748 d 4-17-1844 m Elizabeth Schaeffer CMman PA
John: b 3-11-1761 d 2-28-1846 m Margaret Julia Dimner Pvt PA
Margaretta Barbara Steinbrenner: b 8-25-1725 d 3-19-1816 m John Beaver PS PA
Mathias: b c. 1750 d c. 1827 m Nancy Ann (Coon?) PS VA
Michael: b 2-11-1740 d 10-26-1832 m Anna Maria Fenstermacher Pvt PA
Nicholas: b 3-8-1739 d 3-29-1812 m (1)Mary Wathkim (2)Catherine Simmer Pvt PA
Nicholas: b 9-12-1751 d 12-26-1827 m Elizabeth Dimner Sol PA

BEAVERS,
George: b 4-1-1758 d 9-2-1820 m Sarah Lanning Pvt NJ
Joseph: b 1728 d 12-20-1816 m (1)Mary White (2)Ann Clifford Col PS NJ
Robert: b c. 1740 d 1- -1805 m Jane Little Sol GA
Robert: b 1747 d 10-11-1822 m (1)Mary Armstrong (2)Catherine Kerr Capt NJ W ★
Wm.: b a. 1743 d 1781/1782 m Mary Wyckoff Drm VA

BEAZELL,
Matthew: b 1729 d 5-17-1788 m Ann Catherine Smith PS PA
Wm.: b 1759 d 8-1-1851 m Rebecca Fell PS PA

BEBOUT,
Benjamin: b 12-4-1758 d 11-8-1857 m Hannah Marlett Pvt NJ
John, Sr.: b 8-25-1729 d 6-21-1803 m Mary Thurmah Pvt NJ
John, Jr.: b 1-20-1752 d 3-8-1836 m Mary Agnew Pvt NJ ★
Peter: b 8-16-1731 d 6-13-1782 m (1)Sarah Jewell (2)Sarah Darling Pvt NJ

BECHAM,
Allen: b c. 1755 d 10-25-1809 m Charlotte Newsome Sol GA

BECHLE,
Conrad: b 1737 d 11-18-1824 m (1)Marghrette Wiles (2)Susan Wiles Pvt PA

BECHT,
Frederick: b c. 1758 d c. 1796 m Eve Stiel Cpl PA

BECHTEL,
Christian: b 1-12-1752 d 11- -1814 m Catherine Bohlman Lt PA
Frederick: b 1746 d 9-10-1812 m Sarah Holm Pvt PA
Isaac: b 6-23-1751 d 4-3-1820 m (1)Esther Stauffer (2)Barbara Bitz Pvt PA
Jacob: b 5-9-1720 d 1-2-1803 m Mary Elizabeth — Pvt PA
John: b 1729 d 3-28-1814 m Christina Romig PS PA

BECK,
Andrew: b — d c. 1823 m Rachel Veil Sgt PA
Charles: b — d p. 2-25-1823 m Sarah — Sol SC
Conrad: b c. 1750 d 1802 m Elizabeth Dorothea Gosaler PS PA
George: b 1757 d 1837 m Catherine Elizabeth Holsopple Pvt PA

George: b c. 1738 d 1792 m Christiana — PS PA
Henry: b 1748 d 1824 m Margaret Wolfgang Pvt PA
Henry: b 4-7-1758 d 6-18-1822 m Catherine Wolf Pvt PS PA
Jacob: b a. 1761 d 1785 m Catherine Van Aken Pvt PA
Jeffrey: b 11-25-1752 d 4-12-1838 m Mary McDonald Pvt Sct PS NC ★
Jesse: b 9- -1758 d 5-8-1841 m Ann Hughes Pvt Sgt VA ★
Johan Jacob: b c. 1736 d 1819 m Anna Marie Weidman Matr PA
John: b 1730 d 1790 m (1)Elizabeth Whitfield (2)Mrs Taylor Lt NC
John: b 12-17-1761 d 12-14-1853 m (1)Annie Maria Diffendofer (2) Margaret Wilhelm Drm Pvt PA
John (Peter): b 1746 d 1802 m Elizabeth Walter Pvt PA
John: b 1746 d 8-29-1816 m Rebecca Miller Lt VA W ★
John: b 1756 d 1821 m Sarah Wansley Ens VA
John Diehlman: b 4-5-1730 d 6-14-1789 m Elizabeth Katharina Reinthaler Sgt PA
John Philip: b 1751 d 10- -1811 m (1)Anna Maria Laucks (2)Barbara Bashor Pvt PA
Jonathan, Jr.: b 5-7-1757 d 6-30-1838 m (1)Sarah Bass (2)Mary Sawyer Pvt MA
Leonard: b 1759 d 3-14-1831 m Susanna Deeter Pvt PA
Samuel: b 1738 d 1818 m Sarah Davis Lt MD
Thomas: b 1763 d 11-10-1840 m Ann Vickers Drm MD ★
Wm.: b 1722 d 1777 m X PS PA

BECKEL,
Frederick: b 3-19-1716 d 10-21-1780 m (1)Anna Elizabeth Rohrbach (2)Catherine Barbara Gump PS PA

BECKER, (includes BACCHUS & BECKES)
Abraham: bpt 5-20-1733 d 5-3-1815 m Elizabeth (Becker) Pvt PS NY
Albertus: b 4-28-1731 d 9-7-1790 m Magdalina (Becker) Pvt NY
Benjamin: b 1753 d p. 3-26-1822 m (1)Mary — (2)Mrs Sarah Browning Sol PA
Christian: b 2-19-1759 d 8-10-1837 m Anna Brubaker Pvt PA
David, Sr.: b 9-6-1728 d 11-13-1803 m Gertrude Zeiley Pvt NY
David, Jr.: b 12-5-1757 d 3-15-1796 m Elizabeth Van Vechten Pvt NY
Frederick: b 1740 d 1809 m Annatge Hager Pvt NY
Frederick: b c. 1744 d 1840 m Margaret — Pvt NY
George: b 10-16-1735 d p. 1775 m Maria Elizabeth Zimmer Pvt NY
Hendrick P.: b 6-26-1746 d 12-28-1829 m Agnes Eckerson Pvt NY
Henry: bpt 4-27-1743 d p. 6-10-1792 m (1)Magdalena Warner (2) Maria Zimmer Pvt NY
Jacob: b 8-1-1726 d 11-4-1829 m Elizabeth Ludwig Pvt PA
Jacob: b c. 1724 d c. 1780 m X Sol NY
Johannes: b 1-7-1736 d 1781 m Justina Fischer Pvt NY
Johannes H.: b 1719 d 1794 m Anna Maria Sherz Pvt NY
Johannes S.: b 1740 d 1815 m (1)Christina Vrooman (2)Engeltje Zielle Pvt NY
John A: b 8-5-1744 d 4-15-1804 m Sara Van Hoesen Pvt NY
John P.: b 1763 d 9-20-1837 m Margaret Van Buren Sgt NY ★
Lodowick: b 10-16-1760 d 3-15-1839 m Eva Hagedorn Pvt NY
Martinus: b 5-31-1749 d 1-28-1843 m (1)Lena Boskirk (2)Jane Morlatt Pvt NY ★
Matthias: b 3-24-1761 d 1-12-1833 m Esther Holder Sol PA
Peter: b 1721 d 1809 m (1)Gezina Vroman (2)Maria Vrooman PS NY
Peter: b 1740 d 1805 m Anna Eckerson Cmsry NY
Peter: b 4-21-1753 d 3-28-1833 m Catherine Carper Pvt PA
Philip: b 1763 d 12-18-1846 m Christine Loucks Sol NY ★
Philip: b 1761 d 11-3-1826 m (1)Maria Feek (2)Catherine Wagher Pvt NY
Storm, Sr.: b 1-18-1724 d 11-6-1790 m Gertrude Vroman Capt NY
Storm, Sr.: b 1-18-1715 d p. 1790 m Geertruy Kleyn Pvt PS NY
Storm, Jr: b 2-5-1748 d p. 1790 m Cornelia (Becker) Ens NY

BECKETT,
Humphrey: b 6-24-1761 d 4-2-1830 m Mary Shreves SgtMaj Srgn-Mte MD ★
Humphrey: b 4-19-1758 d 9-16-1839 m Susannah Blann Battott Pvt VA ★
James: b c. 1753 d a. 1821 m Sarah Taylor Pvt PA
John: b 9-15-1755 d 4-22-1843 m Mary — Pvt PA ★
Joseph: b 1744 d 7-22-1816 m Lucy — Capt PA

BECKHAM, (includes BICKHAM)
Abner: b 7-26-1755 d 1-29-1834 m Dicy E.— Capt GA ★
James: b 1735 d 1800 m Hannah Bohon Pvt VA
Samuel: b 11-24-1760 d 11-2-1825 m (2)Elizabeth Haughton Capt GA
Sherwood: b 1762 d 1- -1837 m Mary Stephens Sol GA
Simon: b c. 1728-30 d p. 12-29-1785 m Susannah McMillan Sol PS GA
Solomon: b c. 1764 d 3-25-1838 m Susannah Stacy Wealters Pvt GA
Stephen: b 1755 d p. 9-20-1820 m (1)Rachel — (2)Catherine Merritt PS NC

BECKLER,
Daniel: b 1749 d 3-25-1830 m Elizabeth Miller Pvt MA ★

BECKLEY,
Daniel: b 6-11-1758 d 11-9-1843 m Levia Lewis Pvt Matr CT ★

Elias: b 2-27-1735 d 2-14-1816 m Lois Parsons Capt CT
John: b 1732 d 2-14-1776 m Ruth Hubbard Lt CT
Joseph, Jr.: b 5-3-1749 d 11-10-1813 m Jane Bosworth Pvt CT
Richard: b 1759-62 d 5-2-1841 m Susannah Wilcox Pvt CT
Theodore: b 1-17-1744 d 1-26-1806 m Lucy Kirby Norton PS CT
Zebedee: b 12-31-1753-1763 d 2-5-1851 m Elizabeth Belding Pvt CT ★

BECKWITH,
Amos: b 4-17-1754 d 12-6-1823 m Susannah Truman Pvt CT
Barzillai: b 1736 d 2- -1818 m Mary Butler Sgt CT
Basil: b 4-9-1703 d 1780 m Volinda Claggett PS MD
Benjamin: b c. 1752 d 4-3-1839 m (1)Lavina Crum (2)Martha Rogers Pvt MD ★
Cyrus: b 10-18-1743 d 1816 m Sara Berger Capt NJ
David: b 6-12-1761 d 6-27-1827 m Mabel Lane Pvt CT
David: b 2-16-1752 d 1834 m Abigail Whitney Pvt MA ★
Elisha: b 1718 d 10-28-1776 m Adelaide Carpenter Pvt CT
George: b 9-17-1702 d 12-16-1794 m Sarah Brown PS CT
George: b 5-16-1760 d 12-13-1849 m Ann Clarkson Sgt MD ★
Jabez: b 8-18-1745 d p. 1800 m Elizabeth Hurd Ens NH
Jason: b 1-5-1764 d 2-18-1821 m Elizabeth Crocker Pvt CT
Jennings: b 1764 d 1836 m Catherine Miskell Capt VA
Jesse: b 1753 d 1840 m Esther Smith Pvt CT ★.
John: b 4-7-1752 d 9-12-1834 m Chloe Bosworth QM CT ★
John: b — d 11-28-1793 m Elizabeth Dart CS CT
John: b 10-20-1752 d 8-18-1824 m Martha Williams PS MD
Jonathan: b 11-14-1720 d 12- -1796 m Rebecca Barnes PS VA
Lemuel: b 10-9-1765 d c. 1842 m Orra Gray Pvt CT ★
Marmaduke: b 1687 d 1780 m Elizabeth (Brokenbrough) Dickenson CS VA
Marvin: b 1-10-1737 d 1812 m Abigail Clark Ens CT
Miles: b 1753 d 2-20-1821 m Jemima Wedge Cpl NH ★
Nathan: b 1747 d p. 1834 m Patience — Pvt CT
Nehemiah: b 1762 d 6-20-1844 m Cornelia Mitchell Cpl Smn MD ★
Nehemiah: b 1721 d — m Mary Thomas Slr MD
Reynold Sr.: b 2-15-1706/7 d 12-27-1796 m (1)Martha Marvin (2)Dorothy Sawyer PS CT
Roswell: b 10-21-1753 d 2-2-1836 m Lydia Dorr Pvt CT
Silas: b 1746 d 10-13-1835 m (1)Anna Reeves (2)Anna Smith Pvt Tms NY & CT ★
Sylvanus: b 5-22-1742 d 5-30-1839 m Amy Sutherland Pvt NY
Zachariah: b 2-14-1761 d 5-20-1811 m Eunice Gaylord Pvt CT

BECRAFT,
Benjamin: b 9-16-1710 d 1800 m (1)Deborah— (2)Harriott — Pvt PS MD
Peter: b 11-5-1740 d 11-5-1811 m Mary Nixon Pvt MD

BECTON,
Frederick: b a. 1740 d a. 12-13-1775 m Fruza Speight Maj NC
George: b 7-20-1740 d 5- -1834 m Dorcas Slade PS NC
Michael: b c. 1743 d 1799 m Mary Blackman CS NC

BEDDO,
Absolum: b c. 1754 d 1807 m Mary — Pvt PS MD

BEDELL, (includes BEDEL)
Abraham: b 1756 d 1805 m Mary Osborn Pvt NJ
Absolom: b c. 1740 d 11-6-1802 m Ruth Jackson Maj CS GA
Benjamin: b 1731 d 12-13-1793 m Sarah Harriman Sgt NJ
Daniel: b 1735 d 11- -1807 m Elizabeth — Pvt NY
David: b 4- -1761 d 3-24-1840 m Ruth Fairchild Pvt PA ★
Elisha: b c. 1735 d c. 1795 m Phoebe — Pvt NY
Ephraim: b 1-24-1727 d 9-16-1809 m Philena Frost Pvt NY
Isaac: b 1763 d p. 1842 m Mary Kinnan Fif & Sgt NJ ★
Jacob: b 1746 d 2-16-1777 m Eleanor Powers Pvt NJ
John: b 3-12-1752 d 5-12-1821 m Abigail Cleveland Pvt NH
John: b — d p. 8-5-1808 m Deborah Mulford Pvt NJ
Reuben: b 1759 d 1825 m Dorothy — Pvt NY
Timothy: b 1736/7 d 2- -1787 m (1)(Elizabeth) Merrill (2)Mary Johnson Col PS NH

BEDFORD,
Daniel: b c. 1740 d 7- -1804 m (1)Phoebe Kip Hedden (2)Sarah — Cpl NJ
David: b c. 1747 d 6-3-1815 m Rebecca Hopping Lt NJ
David: b 1-1-1740 d 9-26-1815 m (1)Hannah Hallock (2)Hannah — (3)Sarah Haight Pvt NY
Gunning: b 1720 d 3-25-1802 m Susanna Jaquet PS PA
Mercy: b — d p. 12-26-1785 m Jonas Bedford PS NC
Peter: b 3-28-1759 d a. 12-15-1818 m Mary Van Solengin PS PA
Raymond: b c. 1758 d p. 5-5-1820 m Martha Hawkins PS NC
Stephen: b 7-30-1761 d 2-26-1835 m Lydia Drake Pvt NJ ★
Thomas: b 1725 d p. 2-3-1785 m (1)Mary Ligon Coleman (2)Drucilla Williamson PS VA
Thomas,Jr.: b 6- -1751 d 4- -1804 m Anne Robertson Sol VA

BEDIENT,
Mordecai: b 10-7-1737 d 11-16-1777 m Abigail Raymond Pvt CT
Mordica, Jr.: b 8-16-1762 d 10-12-1855 m (1)Mary Rockwell (2)Polly Canfield Pvt CT ★

BEDINGER,
Daniel: b 3-27-1760 d 3- -1818 m Sarah Rutherford Lt VA
George Michael: b 12-10-1757 d 12-8-1843 m (1)Nancy Keene (2)Henrietta Clay Maj VA ★
Henry, Jr.: b 10-16-1753 d 5-14-1843 m Rachel Strode Capt VA ★
William: b 1761 d p. 1787 m Polly — Sol VA

BEDLOW,
William: b 10-28-1747 d 3-12-1833 m Elizabeth Cook Sgt MA W★

BEDORTHA, (includes BODURTHA)
Joseph: b 2-21-1730 d 4-8-1813 m Mary Smith Pvt MA
Stephen: b 3-22-1746 d 1-22-1803 m Eleanor Worthington Pvt MA

BEDSAUL,
John: b c. 1753 d p. 1803 m Sarah Brown Sol VA

BEDWELL,
Robert: b 2-10-1759 d 9-13-1842 m Elender Black Pvt NC ★

BEEBE,
Abner: b 1725 d 10-6-1801 m Apphia Sparrow Sol CT
Alexander: b 10-29-1759 d 1-30-1841 m Sarah Bowker Cpl MA ★
Asa, Sr.: b 1728 d 12-5-1813 m Lydia Day PS CT
Asa, Jr.: b 5-2-1764 d 7-4-1851 m Sarah Day PS CT
Asahel: b 3-5-1763 d 4-26-1848 m Amarilla Parmalee Arfr CT ★
Azariah: b 1-20-1755 d 11-20-1826 m Diadamy Marvin Sol CT
Bezalleel: b 4-27-1741 d 5-24-1824 m Elizabeth Marsh Col CT
David: b 4-12-1747 d 11-11-1840 m Lydia Terrill QMSgt CT ★
David: b 1-22-1755 d 4-7-1830 m Lydia Paine Pvt CT
Ezekiel: b 1754 d 1844 m Agnes Loomis Pvt MA ★
Ezra: b 1761 d 3-16-1832 m Naomi Huntley Pvt NY
Gideon: b — d — m Thankful Cook Pvt MA ★
Hopson: b 2-28-1749 d 1836 m Deliverance Curtis Capt MA ★
Ira: b 7-20-1735 d 12-29-1792 m Jemima Hickox Capt CT
Jabez: b 9-18-1729 d 5-30-1814 m (1)Eunice Newburry (2)Patience Beebe Capt CT
James: b 1718 d 9-8-1785 m Ruth Curtice PS CS CT
Jeduthan: b 9-10-1734 d 1798 m Lucretia Daton Sol CT
Jethro: b 6-20-1756 d 8-12-1822 m Martha Stewart Pvt CT
John: b 8-10-1758 d p. 1780 m Hannah Rodgers Pvt NY
John, Jr.: b 5-25-1727 d p. 1783 m Mary Hill PS NY
Joseph: b 1748 d 3-17-1835 m Tameson Terrell MM Sgt CT ★
Joseph: b c. 1750 d 1844 m Rebecca Benedict PS CT
Levi: b 4-25-1743 d 2-13-1817 m Martha Cone Cpl CT
Paul: b 11-26-1760 d 3-13-1834 m Mary Rogers Pvt CT ★
Peter: b 2- -1754 d 1834 m Hannah Bigelow Pvt NY ★
Reuben: b 8-28-1751 d 12-15-1834 m (1)Xena Matthews (2)Hannah — Pvt Drm CT ★
Roderick: b 3-1-1753 d 1-2-1836 m Anna Vaughan Sgt NY W★
Seba: b 4-15-1749 d 2-26-1837 m Sarah Davis Sgt VT ★
Solomon: b 1755 d p. 1818 m Rebecca Bowker Pvt MA ★
Steward: b c. 1754 d 6-13-1825 m (1)Hannah Butler (2)Huldah Beebe (3)Dorothy Colton Pvt MA
Thomas T.: b 9-7-1743 d 2-24-1792 m Olive Hall Ens NY
Zadock: b 11-29-1745 d 1843 m Sarah Lash Pvt MA

BEECHER, (includes BEACHER, BECHER)
Abraham: b 9-17-1745 d 10-11-1823 m Desire Tolls PS CT
Amos: b 6-10-1743 d 9-8-1818 m (1)Lucy (Beecher) (2)Rebecca Abbott Capt CT
Burr: b 10-5-1757 d 11-10-1823 m Anna Eunice Smith Pvt CT
David: b 8-16-1743 d 11-17-1780 m Hannah Perkins Capt CT
Eli: b 1748 d 5-15-1789 m Susannah Kimberly Pvt CT
Hezekiah: b 10-8-1752 d 12-11-1797 m Lydia Hotchkiss Pvt CT
Hezekiah: b 1-1-1753 d 5-22-1820 m Dorcas Strong MM CT
Hezekiah: b 7-29-1755 d 2-3-1828 m Hannah Philena Johnson Pvt CT
Isaac, Sr.: b 7-15-1716 d 10-28-1801 m Mabel Hotchkiss PS CT
Isaac, Jr.: b 3-23-1748 d 9-24-1789 m Hannah Ball Capt CT
Isaac, Jr.: b 1-8-1726/7 d 10-26-1814 m Esther Hodges CS CT
Jesse: b 4-20-1741 d 4-7-1813 m Abigail Sperry Lt CT
John: b 1762 d 3-22-1819 m Mary Ann Albert Pvt PA ★
Jonathan: b 3-27-1726 d 3-27-1779 m Lois Hull Pvt Matr CT
Jonathan: b 4-8-1757 d 1-29-1826 m Annie Baldwin Sol CT
Joseph: b 2-9-1730 d 5-3-1821 m Esther Potter Capt CT
Moses: b 1-1-1766 d 2-7-1852 m Dorcas Lord Sol Slr CT
Thomas: 4-20-1722 d 11-23-1787 m Elizabeth Terrell PS CT
Wheeler: b 9-30-1754 d 1838 m Polly Hotchkiss Pvt CT ★

BEEDY, (includes BEEDE)
Daniel: b 7-21-1729 d 4-7-1799 m (1)Patience Prescott (2)Mrs Dorothy Eldridge PS CS NH
John: b 1758 d 11-15-1841 m Sarah Sleeper Pvt NH
Phineas: b 9-24-1749 d 1-1-1806 m Sarah Bachelder Pvt NH
Reziah: b 7-6-1764 d 11-24-1841 m Mary Ann Stroud Pvt NH ★
Thomas: b 6-1-1732 d 1806 m Elizabeth Ewing PS NH

BEEKMAN,
Christopher: b 1730 d 11-16-1829 m Martha Veghte PS NJ
Cornelius, Sr.: b 9-3-1733 d — m Catherine Schoonmacher Lt NY
Gerard G.: b 9-19-1746 d 6-22-1822 m Cornelia Van Cortlandt 1Lt NY

BEEKMAN, contd.
Gerardus: b 8-6-1707 d *p.* 8-4-1777 m Cathrine Van Dyke PS NJ
James: b 1732 d 1807 m Jane Ketellas PS NY
John: b 11-5-1741 d 3-17-1789 m Arrientje Tunnison Pvt NJ
Samuel: b 11-26-1729 d 10-19-1808 m Elizabeth Waldron Pvt NJ
Samuel: b *c.* 1755 d 1-28-1812 m Anne Lee Lt SC W★
Tjerck: b 12-30-1754 d 12-25-1791 m Rachel Dumont Ens NY
William: b 8-27-1755 d 6-13-1834 m Sarah Firman Capt NJ W★
William: b 6- -1767 d 11-26-1845 m Joanna Lowe PS NY

BEEKS,
Christopher: b *c.* 1756 d 1818 m Catherine Barnes Pvt VA

BEELER,
Joseph: b *c.* 1762 d *p.* 8-22-1845 m (1)Katey Petre (2)Anna — Sol NC
Samuel, Sr.: b 1743 d *p.* 6-13-1824 m Amelia — Capt VA
Samuel, Jr.: b 1-27-1760 d 1-14-1840 m Mary Graves Pvt PA

BEERS, (includes BEARS, BEER)
Abner: b 1736 d 1-3-1816 m Hannah Beardslee Pvt CT
Benjamin: b *c.* 1752 d 1813 m Sarah (Bristol?) Pvt Grd VT
Daniel: b 6-24-1757 d 10-13-1839 m Mrs Elizabeth Dykeman Fif CT ★
Daniel: b 1726 d 1-4-1801 m Abigail Dykeman Sol CT
Daniel: b 1747 d 1782 m Abigail Martin Lt RI
David: b 1753 d 5-3-1835 m Hannah Porter Pvt CT ★
David: b 4-27-1756 d 7-11-1838 m (1)Eunice Burr (2)Molly Ogden Pvt CT ★
Elnathan: b 8-15-1740 d 12-29-1818 m Mehitable Booth Pvt CT
Enoch: b 1744 d 1806 m Mary Gloria Dieter 1Lt PA
Fanton: b 1-11-1756 d 9-26-1847 m Mrs Sarah Fairchild Pvt CT
Foard: b 1752 d 10-24-1819 m Rosanna Gray Pvt MA W★
Gershum: b *c.* 1761 d 1832 m Sarah White Pvt CT
Hezekiah: b 4-16-1754 d 4-28-1778 m X Cpl CT
Isaac: b 1764 d 1829 m Jemima Rowell Pvt CT ★
Joel: b *c.* 1765 d 9-11-1801 m Phoebe Osborne Pvt CT W★
John: b 5-5-1759 d 4-22-1848 m Elizabeth Ann Clinton Cpl CT
Matthew: b 1758 d 11-25-1837 m Sarah Curtis Pvt CT ★
Nathan, Sr.: b 8-23-1718 d 7-10-1779 m (1)Hannah Nichols (2) Abigail Alling PS CT
Nathan,Jr.: b 2-24-1753 d 2-10-1849 m Mary Phelps Lt PM CT
Nathan: b 6- -1757 d 12- -1836 m Mehitable Perry Pvt CT ★
Nathan: b 2-10-1718 d 6-18-1805 m Lydia Hawley PS CT
Nehemiah: b *c.* 1730 d 1793 m Eunice Fanton Sgt CT
Robert: b 4-21-1750 d 3-26-1842 m Nancy Quinn Ens PA ★
Samuel: b 11-18-1759 d 2-21-1843 m (1)Lydia Fellows (2)Anna Raymond (3)Anna Tuttle Pvt CT
Stephen: b 12-9-1734 d 6-19-1815 m Anna Benjamin PS CT
Thomas: b 3-23-1756 d 1-26-1809 m Addy Auten Pvt PA W★
Timothy: b 9-26-1749 d 11-17-1825 m Susanna Randall Pvt NY
Zachariah: b 6-3-1758 d 2-3-1842 m Mary Hurd OrdlSgt CT

BEESON,
Benjamin, Sr.: b *c.* 1716 d 6-14-1794 m Elizabeth Hunter PS NC
Edward: b 1-1-1757 d 1-16-1837 m (1)Betty Lamb (2)Ann Pennington (3)Dicy Mullen Capt NC ★
Henry: b 5-19-1743 d 2-23-1819 m Mary Martin PS PA
Isaac: b 12-26-1739 d 9-21-1811 m Isabell Parsons PS NC
Jacob: b 6-1-1741 d 12-16-1818 m Elizabeth Hedges PS VA
Mercer: b *c.* 1744 d 1777/8 m Catherine — Pvt VA
Richard: b 11-3-1747 d 1817 m Abigail — PS NC
Richard: b *c.* 1710 d *p.* 1785 m Anne Brown PS VA

BEETHAM,
George: b *c.* 1720 d 1805/6 m Sarah — PS PA

BEETLE,
James: b 11-23-1754 d 10-26-1801 m Mary Butler Pvt MA

BEGEANT,
John: b 8-10-1761 d *c.* 1832 m Catherine Whitenack Pvt VA★

BEIBELHEIMER,
Conrad: b 5-17-1760 d 2-26-1860 m Susanna Zimmerman Cpl PA

BEIDLEMAN, (includes BEIDELMAN)
Jacob: b 9-26-1737 d 11-14-1805 m Elizabeth Margaret Pvt PA
Jacob: b *c.* 1756 d *p.* 1790 m Sarah — Pvt PA
Leonard: b *a.* 1760 d 1789 m X Pvt PA
Leonard,Sr.: b *c.* 1720 d *p.* 12-23-1788 m Anna Maria PS PA
Samuel: b 10-9-1750 d 4-16-1836 m Elizabeth Hess Pvt PA
Simon: b — d - -1815 m Ann Crouse Pvt NY

BEIDLER,
Conrad: b 4-3-1730 d 4-17-1800 m Barbara — Pvt PS PA
John: b 11-15-1757 d 7-16-1811 m (1)Susannah High (Hoch) (2)Hannah Hottenstein Pvt PA

BEINHAUER,
Peter: b 2-22-1744 d 12-4-1818 m Christiana — Pvt PA

BEISECKER, (includes BIESECKER)
Abraham: b *a.* 1745 d 1794 m Elizabeth — Pvt PA
Jacob: b 1-31-1746 d 10-17-1793 m Catharine Geres Pvt PA

BEISEL,
Jacob: b 6-8-1758 d 9-12-1824 m Gertrude Wagner Pvt PA
Jacob: b 1762 d 1842 m Sarah — Pvt PA
Peter, Sr.:b 1725 d 1783 m (1)Catharine — (2)Anna Margaret Pvt PS PA
Peter, Jr.: b 9-6-1754 d 10-10-1829 m Gertrude Griesemer Sgt PA

BEITEL, (includes BEUTEL)
Frederick: b 7-9-1752 d 6-3-1833 m Maria Salome Vetter Wgm PA
Johann Renatus: b 12-21-1740 d 9-27-1840 m Julianna Schmidt Pvt PA

BEITENMAN,
Frederick: b 8-17-1754 d 9-16-1826 m Anna Maria Richards Capt PA

BELCHER, (includes BELSHER)
Abraham: b *c.* 1750 d *p.* 1815 m X PS NC
Adam: b 6-30-1756 d 5-30-1819 m (1)Elizabeth Bennett (2)Sarah Bennett PS NY
Edmund: b *c.* 1725 d *p.* 1782 m Mary — Pvt VA
Edward: b 3-3-1729 d 10- -1781 m Priscilla Mann Pvt VA
Eleazer: b 9-1-1745 d 12-24-1818 m Elizabeth Morse Pvt Drm MA
Elisha: b 3-7-1756/57 d 12-25-1825 m Lydia Reynolds Dr CT
John: b 9-26-1740 d *p.*1778 m Abigail Bracket Pvt MA
John: b 1-20-1744 d 3-11-1825 m (1)Hannah Rawson (2)Susannah Hazeltine Pvt MA
Jonathan: b 2-27-1718 d 10-17-1785 m Elizabeth Floyd Tuttle Grd MA
Jonathan: b 3-18-1753 d 2-14-1826 m (1)Abigail Corthrell (2)Sarah Drake Pvt MA ★
Joseph: b 8-5-1734 d 10-14-1818 m Susannah Baxter Pvt MA
Joseph: b 5-13-1749 d 5-27-1814 m Mary Baker Pvt MA
Joseph: b 5-10-1751 d *p.* 1782 m Rachel Shute Pvt MA
Nathaniel,Sr.: b 1729/30 d 9-2-1810 m Ann Dowse Capt MA
Nathaniel,Jr.: b 8-30-1756 d 9-29-1797 m Martha Humphry Pvt MA
Robert: b 1758 d 1845 m Nancy Hopkins Sol SC ★
Robert: b *c.* 1740 d *a.* 10-12-1789 m Mrs Susannah Winn 2Lt VA
Samuel: b 10-24-1743 d 8-8-1812 m Deborah Thompson Capt MA
Sarson: b 6-21-1741 d 12-24-1794 m Fanny Hill Capt MA
Supply: b 3-29-1751 d 6-9-1836 m Margaret More Pvt OrdlSgt MA ★
Wm.: b 8-29-1731 d 6-27-1801 m Desire Morgan Capt CT
Wm.: b — d — m X Pvt MD

BELDING, (includes BELDEN)
Augustus: b 1-13-1753 d 8-20-1831 m Desire Dennison Pvt MA
Azor: b 9- -1749 d 11-27-1828 m (1)Hannah Smith (2)Hannah Fitch Capt CT W★
Bartholomew: b 12-16-1762 d 10-31-1831 m (2)Speedy — Pvt CT
Benjamin: b 10-25-1757 d 2-5-1839 m Sylvia Culver Pvt CT ★
David: b 6-17-1758 d *p.* 1834 m Lois Wolcott Pvt CT
David Sr.: b 2-4-1718 d 8-4-1804 m Thankful Graves PS NH
Elijah: b 2-5-1749 d 1-19-1813 m (1)Rhoda Carr (2)Submit Graves (3)Mrs Elizabeth Warner Pvt NH
Hezekiah: b 7-2-1728 d 6-22-1813 m (1)Mary Dickinson (2)Abigail Nash (3)Martha Field (4)Martha Smith Pvt MA
James: b 3-6-1751 d 5-22-1840 m (1)Dorcas — (2)Mindwell — Pvt MA
Joab: b 7-5-1757 d 1-12-1814 m Betsy Stevens Cpl MA
John: b 3-1-1715/6 d 12-20-1785 m Sarah Kellogg PS CT
John: b 12-17-1756 d 3-25-1839 m Priscilla Wait Pvt MA
Jonathan: b 11-16-1737 d 1-9-1778 m Sarah (Belding) Lt CT
Joseph Jr.: b 10-31-1735 d *p.* 1796 m Lydia Silvey Sgt MA
Joshua: b 10-29-1733 d 9-20-1805 m Anna Fitch Pvt MA
Moses: b 10-25-1740 d 7-4-1811 m Rachel Hayes Lt NH
Oliver: b 11-17-1732 d 9-16-1811 m (1)Abigail Merrill (2)Anna Woodruff Capt MA
Othniel: b 3-27-1755 d 12-19-1834 m Sarah Lindsay Pvt CT ★
Richard: b 1762 d 1-31-1848 m Mercy Collins Fif Cpl CT ★
Selah: b 5-11-1758 d 7-3-1838 m Esther Gates Cpl MA
Silas Sr.: b 11-13-1717 d 4-9-1784 m Jane Knickerbocker Lt NY
Silas Jr.: b 3-9-1745 d 9-30-1789 m Dorcas Gillett Pvt NY
William: b 1-29-1741 d 2- -1824 m Priscilla Rider Pvt CT

BELFIELD,
John: b 6-23-1725 d 8-19-1805 m Ruth Sydor Lt VA

BELFORD,
John: b 1-7-1741 d 8-7-1802 m Catharine Kent Pvt PA

BELK,
John Sr.: b 1742 d 1-13-1822 m Hannah — Pvt NC

BELKNAP, (includes BELNAP)
Abel: b 9-15-1736 d 10-15-1810 m (1)Elizabeth Stevens (2)Anna White Lt NY

Abel, Sr.: b 1-13-1739 d 11-15-1804 m (1)Mollie Richardson (2)Hannah Williams (3)Hannah Williams PS CS Sol NY
Abel: b 5-24-1754 d 4-3-1838 m Bathiah Newhall Pvt MA★
Abraham: b 1736 d 6-12-1805 m X MM MA
David: b 1-14-1744 d 3-11-1831 m Sarah Case PS Sol NY
Ezekiel: b 11-15-1735 d 1- -1837 m Katherine Sawyer Lt NH ★
Francis: b 6-22-1755 d 11-22-1838 m Roxana Bingham Pvt CT
Isaac: b 12-14-1733 d 4-29-1815 m (1)Bridget Richardson (2) Deborah (Alden) Coffin Capt NY
Jeremy D.D.: b 6-4-1744 d 6-20-1798 m Ruth Elliot PS MA
Jesse: b 8-3-1760 d 10-11-1854 m Eunice Hall Arfr CT★
Jesse: b 4-9-1739 d p. 1790 m (1)Eunice — (2)Deborah Hatheway Pvt CS VT
John: b 1-25-1734 d 10-25-1825 m Dorcas Phinney Capt NY ★
Jonas: b 1759 d p. 1791 m Esther Parker Sgt MA
Joseph: b 1745 d 8- -1817 m Esther Snow Pvt MA
Moses: b 9-7-1754 d 9-21-1836 m Sarah Kibbee Pvt VT
Nathaniel: b 10-3-1748 d 1826 m Hannah Ayers OrdlSgt NH
Samuel: b 10-13-1735 d 3-31-1821 m Abigail Flagg Capt NY
Simeon: b 4-17-1758 d 1-11-1841 m (1)Mary Gibbs (2)Miriam Edson PS VT
Stephen: b 1-19-1757 d - - m Eunice Warren Drm Pvt MA
William: b 2-21-1751 d 7-18-1831 m Martha Carscadden Lt NY★

BELL,
Andrew: b 6-30-1755 d 10-25-1845 m Hannah Bell Pvt CT ★
Andrew: b 1757 d p. 1-9-1832 m (1)Martha McKinley (2)Mrs Winnie Knox Sol GA
Andrew: b 3-15-1729 d 1-3-1791 m Elizabeth Lovick Wgm NC
Andrew: b 1747 d 1822 m Elizabeth — Pvt PA
Arthur: b 8-1-1761 d 1-9-1833 m Mary Elizabeth Greenwood Pvt PA
Arthur: b 1-11-1753 d 8-6-1834 m Eleanor Montgomery Sgt PA★
Benjamin: b 1761 d 2-9-1843 m Elizabeth Ledbetter Pvt NC★
Benjamin: b 1762 d 2-10-1853 m Elizabeth Enoch Pvt PA
Caleb: b c. 1737 d p. 1785 m Eadye Brickhouse PS NC
David: b 1722 d c. 1780 m Florence Henderson Capt VA
Dorothy: b c. 1752 d p. 1778 m Frederic Bell Jr. PS NY
Francis: b 1750 d Aug. o r Nov. 1839 m Esther Montgomery Sol NC
Frederic Sr.: b c. 1725 d 7-18-1778 m Anna Mary — PS NY
Frederic Jr.: b c. 1748 d 7-18-1778 m Dorothy Crim Sol NY
George: b c. 1734 d 3- -1816 m Mary (Bell) — Capt PA
George: b a. 1760 d 11-3-1825 m Sarah — 2Lt PA
George: b 1755 d p. 9-10-1828 m Elizabeth Catlett Lt VA
George: b 3-11-1760 d 4-25-1834 m Susan (Bell) Cpl VA
George: b c. 1756 d 1839 m Sarah Shaw CS VA
George Henry: b c. 1730 d 4-20-1807 m Catherine Herkimer Capt CS NY
Hendrick: b 1740 d 4-9-1814 m Margrietje Christie Pvt NY
Henry: b 1750 d c. 1816 m Elizabeth Garrett Alcocke Capt NC
Henry: b 11-17-1745 d 1811 m Rebecca Harrison Lt VA
Hugh Ferguson: b 1753 d 1849 m Margaret Montgomery Pvt PA
Jacob: b 1-1-1747 d 1-8-1838 m Elizabeth Weber Pvt NY
James: b 1755 d 9-17-1831 m Michal Johnson Pvt MD★
James: b 1740 d 5-12-1806 m Mary Kierley Sol NY
James: b c. 1746 d 5-19-1801 m Rebekah Quince Cpl NC
James: b 10-4-1747 d 10-23-1809 m Olive Moseley Sol NC
James: b 1749 d 1791 m X 3Sgt PA
James: b 1750 d 1821 m Mary (Bell) Pvt PA
James: b 1750 d 12-4-1836 m Mary Newkirk Pvt PA
James: b c. 1750 d p. 12-24-1835 m Mary Ford Matr PA
James: b 4-20-1759 d 12-30-1851 m Rebecca Horner Pvt PA
James: b 1750 d 1805 m Esther — Capt VA
James R.: b 1761 d 1-16-1839 m Jane McIntire Lt DE★
Jason: b 10-26-1762 d 10-22-1843 m Lydia Hill Pvt CT
Jesse: b 3-6-1745 d 10-20-1834 m (1)Comfort Guernsey (2)Mary Scofield Capt CT ★
John: b 1738 d 3-7-1824 m (2)Mary Kerr Lt MD
John: b 1753 d 8-11-1826 m Catherine Doyle Pvt MD W★
John: b — d 3-4-1808 m Hannah White Pvt MA
John: b 8-15-1730 d 11-30-1825 m Mary Anne Gilmore PS Col NH
John: b 1732 d 1778 m (1)Jane Carr (2)Sarah Bell Pvt PS NH
John: b 1753 d 2-23-1834 m Keziah Mapes Cpl NY★
John: b 1758 d 1834 m Ann Bradford Pvt NC & SC★
John: b c. 1745 d p. 4-4-1813 m Martha Gilchrist Pvt PA
John: b 1732 d 8- -1810 m Elizabeth Boyd Pvt PA
John: b c. 1755 d 11-2-1800 m Sopha — Pvt SC
John: b c. 1747 d 3-10-1831 m (1)Anna Lilly (2)Anne Tunstall (3)Mary Henderson Lt VA
John: b c. 1755 d 10-17-1842 m (1)Widow Young (2)Esther Gamble (3)Elizabeth Griffith Ens VA
John: b1737/8 d 1805 m Elizabeth — Pvt VA
John: b c. 1740 d 8- -1804 m Frances Chapman Pvt VA
John Briggs: b 4-7-1731 d 1-29-1819 m Mary Robbins Fif MA
John Sprig: b 1745 d 1797 m Margaret — Capt MD
Jonathan: b 10-22-1717 d p. 1776 m Lydia Hoyt Capt CT
Jonathan: b 6-8-1755 d 6-10-1844 m Deborah Butterfield Pvt NH
Jonathan: b a. 1755 d p. 12-2-1815 m Mary Randolph Sol SC
Joseph: b 10-4-1747 d 4- -1818 m Elizabeth Mosely Sol GA
Joseph: b 4-17-1757 d 1828 m Mary Houston PS NH
Joseph: b 1761 d 1-27-1851 m Anna — Pvt PA
Joseph: b c. 1760 d — m X Sol PS PA
Joseph: b 5- 25-1742 d 3-4-1823 m Elizabeth Henderson Capt VA
Joseph: b c. 1746 d p. 3-13-1822 m Rebecca Worrell PS VA

Malachi: b c. 1745 d p. 9-22-1803 m (1)Elizabeth Coale (2)Sarah (Fulford) Robertson LCol PS CS NC
Martha: b 1735 d 9-9-1820 m (1)John Mc Gee (2)William Bell PS NC
Mathew: b 9-28-1750 d 1-28-1792 m Dorothy Watkins PS NH
Nathan: b c. 1750 d a. 1822 m X Pvt NC
Nathaniel: b 3-15-1755 d 1-17-1835 m X Pvt NC★
Nathaniel: b 1757 d 3- -1845 m Mary Timmons Sgt PA
Nathaniel: b c. 1726 d p. 2-19-1800 m Hannah — Sol VA
Oliver: b -- d - - m — Allen Pvt NY & VT
Onesimus: b 6-12-1738 d 1827 m Anna Cosart Sol NJ
Peter: b c. 1744 d 5-15-1778 m Elizabeth Leiter Capt MD
Phineas: b 3-1-1761 d 5-13-1845 m Elizabeth Rockwell Pvt NJ
Robert: b 1731 d 2- -1816 m (1)Catherine Walker (2)Mary Boyd Capt NC
Robert: b 1763 d 10-17-1849 m Rachel Espy Pvt PA
Robert: b 1728 d c. 1784 m Mary — Capt VA
Robert: b 9-6-1744 d a. 1790 m Mary Jarvis Sgt VA
Robert: b c. 1750 d p. 7- -1796 m Ann — PS VA
Samuel: b 3-16-1750 d 10-29-1836 m Susan Moore Sol KY
Samuel: b 1-26-1752 d 4-24-1829 m Elizabeth Campbell Pvt MA
Samuel: b 12-12-1742 d 12-28-1802 m Mary McKee Pvt PA
Samuel: b p. 1756 d p. 1794 m Ann Berryhill Pvt PA
Samuel: b 1757 d 3-28-1828 m Lucetta Pope Lt VA
Samuel: b 2- -1759 d 5-15-1838 m (1)Nancy Bell (2)— Cunningham (3)Rebecca Hays Pvt VA W★
Solomon: b 9-25-1738 d 12-3-1825 m Dorcas Carter Sgt MA
Stephen: b 7-28-1755 d p. 4-26-1834 m Lea ı S. ıfk. Pvt CT ★
Sylva: b c. 1745 d 1784 m Michael Bell PS NC
Thaddeus Sr.: b 3-31-1728 d 1806 m Mary Leeds PS ıT
Thaddeus Jr.: b 3-18-1759 d 10-31-1851 m Elizabeth Howe Sgt CT
Thomas: b 1745 d 1835 m Euphania McCotter Capt MD
Thomas: b 1717 d 9-1-1789 m Esther Bell PS MA
Thomas: b 1743 d 2-14-1825 m (1)Jane Montgomery (2)Jane McGuire Pvt Wgn NC
Thomas: b 2-2-1745 d 6-19-1830 m Rachael Ewart Pvt PS NC
Thomas: b 1754 d p. 5-14-1827 m Mary Lassiter PS NC
Thomas Jr.: b 1737 d 6-23-1815 m Ann Graham CM man PA
Thomas: b 1758 d 4-7-1821 m Nancy Steele Pvt SC
Thomas Sr.: b - - d p. 9-9-1791 m Elizabeth Weir Capt VA
Thomas Jr.: b 6-6-1754 d - -1816 m Judith Thomson Sgt VA
Thomas: b 2-25-1756 d 3-30-1837 m Mary Edwards Pvt VA
Thomas: b 1727 d p. 1803 m (1)Mary Linnon (2)Elizabeth Taylor PS VA
Walter: b 5-18-1759 d 12-12-1851 m Sarah Crouch Pvt MA★
William, Jr.: b 4-6-1744 d 12-20-1798 m Eve — PS MD
William: b 4-7-1731 d 11-20-1804 m (1)Abigail — (2)Martha Hill Capt MA
William: b 1738 d 11-22-1825 m (1)— McFarland (2)Hannah Stone Ens MA
William, Sr.: b 12- -1740 d 1794 m Ann — Pvt NJ
William, Jr.: b 5-28-1761 d 11-18-1801 m Mary Brady Pvt NJ
William: b 12-12-1757 d 1793 m Susan Sneeden Pvt NY
William: b 12-25-1759 d 6-5-1845 m Sarah McGuire Pvt NC
William Sr.: b 1744 d 9- -1813 m Dorcas Forster Capt PA
William, Sr.: b c. 1705 d p. 8-18-1783 m Jane Lea PS PA
William Jr.: b 1728 d 11-17-1783 m Dorcas Dorens Pvt PA
William: b 5-1-1732 d 4-19-1819 m Elizabeth Stewart Pvt PA
William: b a. 1750 d p. 1786 m Louisa Rustin Pvt PA
William: b 1755 d 11-28-1828 m Mrs. Rosannah Bell Pvt PA
William: b p. 1740 d 1784 m Rosanna Bell PS PA
William: b 1754 d 9-3-1825 m Ann Montgomery Sol Cav SC
William: b c. 1749 d 12-12-1838 m Martha Waters Pvt SC
William: b 1751 d 1802 m Elizabeth Savage Drm VA
William: b c. 1740 d 1801 m Mary Foster. PS VA

BELLAH,
Samuel: b 1-2-1752 d a. 5-5-1828 m (1)— Hanna (2)Jane Morgan Pvt NC

BELLAMY,
Abram: b 1752 d 3-18-1828 m Claramond — Lt SC
John: b 10-9-1734 d 12-22-1810 m Mary Burnham Sgt MA
Justus: b 1755 d 9-2-1840 m Lidia Hall Pvt CT

BELLESFELT,
Peter: b 2-10-1756 d 12- -1844 m Jane Van Horn Pvt PA★

BELLINGER,
Adam: b 1-2-1740 d 1-2-1824 m Marie Elizabeth Petrie Lt NY
Adam: b 12-14-1757 d 9- -1822 m Lena G. Zimmerman Pvt NY
Christian: b 1-15-1764 d 5-2-1838 m Barbara Diefendorf Pvt NY★
Edmund: b 4-9-1719 d 9-12-1787 m Mary Lucia Bull CS PS SC
Frederick: b c. 1735 d 1803 m Catherine Weber LCol NY
Frederick: b 11-12-1752 d 7-14-1833 m Magdalena Wohlenben Cpl NY ★
Frederick: b c. 1747 d 7-12-1781 m Catharina Putnam Pvt NY
Henry: b 6-30-1764 d 4-3-1836 m Margretha Nellis Pvt NY
John: b c. 1719 d 8-6-1777 m Maria Lena Klock Lt NY
John: b 11-28-1745 d 1-13-1809 m Rebecca D'Oyley Pvt PS SC
John P.: b 4-28-1743 d 2-26-1820 m (1)Maria Dygert (2)Catherine Petrie Ens NY
Johannes : b 3-3-1738 d 11-17-1820 m Anna Maria Reckert Pvt NY
Markus: b 2-19-1742 d 2-4-1822 m Maria Borst Cpl NY

BELLINGER, contd.
Peter: b 3- -1726 d 3-25-1813 m Adelia Herkimer Col NY
Peter P.: b 4-24-1758 d 1851 m Christina Tenbrook Pvt NY
Wm.: b 10-6-1759 d 6-13-1833 m Hannah Mattice Cpl NY ★
Wm.: b 1758 d 7- -1826 m (1)Sarah Pinckney (2)Harriet Field Pvt SC

BELLIS, (includes BELLES)
Adam: b 7-4-1753 d *p.* 1788 m Mary Rockafeller Pvt NJ
Adam: b 1- -1752 d 12-18-1841 m Katrina Dilts Pvt NJ
John: b 7-4-1753 d 7-11-1838 m Nellie Williamson Sgt NJ★

BELLOWS,
Benjamin, Sr.: b 5-26-1712 d 7-10-1777 m (1)Abigail Stearns (2)Mrs
    Mary Jennison PS NH
Benjamin Jr.: b 10-6-1740 d 6-4-1802 m Phoebe Strong Col NH
Charles: b 6-5-1754 d 3-10-1839 m Eleanor Bellows Pvt MA★
Daniel: b 12-8-1723 d *c.* 1791 m Deborah Rix Pvt MA
Ebenezer: b 12-21-1756 d 10-14-1828 m Lydia — Cpl MA
Elihu: b 12-19-1754 d 11-1-1826 m Sarah Phelps Pvt MA★
Ezekiel: b 1-23-1739 d 1-23-1807 m Mercy Davis 1Lt MA
Hezekiah: b 3-16-1734 d *p.* 1779 m Mary Newell PS MA
Isaac: b 1-18-1727 d 5-22-1811 m Eunice Stone Pvt MA
James: b 1756 d 9-10-1813 m Tryphena Chandler Pvt CT
John: b 11-3-1742 d 8-9-1812 m Rebecca Hubbard Maj NH
John: b 1750 d 8-18-1831 m Mary Smith Pvt NY
Joseph: b 5-26-1744 d 5-22-1817 m Lois Whitney Maj MA
Jotham: b 8-7-1731 d 7-13-1817 m (1)Abigail Knight (2)Abigail
    Ward Pvt MA
Peter: b 12-26-1738 d 4-5-1825 m Mary Chase Pvt NH
Theodore: b 8-13-1760 d 5-6-1835 m Sarah Hutchins Sgt NH
Thomas: b 6-16-1753 d 10-15-1833 m Deliverance Button Ens VT★

BELLUNE,
William: b 6-5-1755 d 3-28-1830 m Frances Rebecca Port Pvt SC

BELOTE,
Jonas: b 12-8-1760 d 5-7-1857 m Mrs Susannah Holt Moore Pvt
    VA ★
Noah: b *c.* 1755 d *p.* 1806 m (1)Elizabeth Wise (2)Elinor — (3)Tabitha
    — Sgt VA
William: b *c.* 1752 d *p.* 7-7-1804 m Sarah — Pvt VA

BELSER,
Christian: b 1753 d 4-3-1812 m Mary Bromiller Sgt SC W★

BELT,
Carlton: b 1744 d 1802 m (1)Mary Watson (2)Anne Campbell Ens
    PS MD
Higginson Sr.: b *c.* 1708 d *p.* 7-15-1786 m Sarah — PS MD
Jeremiah: b *c.* 1750 d 12-31-1819 m (1)Eliza Skinner (2)Susan
    Magruder (3)Priscilla Gantt (4)Ann West PS MD
John: b *c.* 1743 d 1-4-1814 m X CS PS MD
Joseph: b 1716 d 6-16-1793 m Esther Smith PS MD
Joseph Sprigg: b 1752 d *p.* 1793 m Sarah Burgess Pvt PS MD
Marsham: b *c.* 1735 d 10-8-1802 m Elizabeth — PS MD
Middleton: b 1747 d 1-15-1807 m Mary Ann Dyer CS MD
Thomas: b *a.* 1740 d *p.* 2-21-1810 m Priscilla — Pvt MD
Tobias: b 8-20-1720 d 1785 m Mary Gordon PS MD

BELTON,
Abraham: b 1748 d 1826 m Elizabeth Alexander PS SC
James: b 1728 d 3-18-1803 m Elizabeth Dickey CS NH

BELVIN,
Aron: b 1-4-1759 d 11-29-1822 m Elizabeth Dobson Pvt VA

BEMENSDERFER,
John: b *a.* 1755 d 1-24-1836 m Elizabeth Eherman Ens PA

BEMENT, (includes BEAMONT)
Asa: b 2-4-1739 d *p.* 1790 m Ruth Neal CS MA
Benjamin: b 6-28-1754 d *p.* 7-31-1832 m Keziah Winters Pvt CT ★
Consider: b 1762 d 1848 m Mary Olcott Pvt MA★
David: b 12-18-1734 d 8-8-1806 m Rhoda Wright Lt CT
Edmund: b 9-13-1739 d 9-11-1808 m Mary Sheldon Pvt CT
John: b 5-5-1734 d 9-10-1810 m Mary Wait CS MA
Jonathan: b 3-8-1732 d 6-1-1795 m Lois Sikes Pvt PS CT
Samuel: b 12-25-1742 d — m Martha Bingham Pvt CT

BEMIS, (includes BEMAS, BEMUS)
Abijah: b 1753 d 12-9-1829 m Mary Pike Pvt MA
Abijah: b 3-16-1722/3 d 6-19-1790 m Dinah Hagar CS MA
Amasa: b 10-10-1757 d 11-21-1842 m (1)Persis Bemis (2)Nancy
    Dunbar Sgt MA ★
Amos: b 11-24-1762 d 10- -1835 m Lydia Goodnow Pvt MA
Benjamin: b 1-29-1744 d 3-9-1828 m Rebecca Draper Sgt MA
Daniel: b 3-5-1758 d 1-4-1832 m Patty Winch Pvt MA ★
David: b 7-30-1727 d 1813 m Mary Dunston Pvt MA
Edmund: bpt 10-22-1732 d 12-1-1807 m (1)Elizabeth Rand
    (2) Mrs Phebe Spring Capt MA
Edmund: b 11-1-1720 d 12- -1810 m Eunice Chadwick Capt
    MA

Edmund: b 1740 d 7-16-1829 m Mrs Abigail Gilbert Sgt MA ★
Isaac: b 3-7-1756 d 12-28-1839 m Mary E. Stevens Arfr MA ★
Isaac: b 12-22-1753 d 7-25-1834 m (1)Elizabeth Green (2)
    Abigail Biglow Ens MA
James: b 9-7-1757 d 12-15-1832 m (1)Hannah Frost (2)Lois Walker
    Pvt NH W★
Jeduthan: b 6-10-1753 d 8-5-1828 m (1)Polley Stapels (2)Statira
    Squires Pvt MA ★
John: b *c.* 1755 d 8- -1828 m Lucy Bates Cpl MA W★
John: b 8-28-1732 d 7-20-1820 m Abigail Sanders PS MA
John: b 6-13-1753 d 1835 m (1)Abigail Stevens (2)Jemima
    Whipple Pvt VT
Jonas, Sr.: b 3-25-1737 d 5-7-1790 m Dorothy Wood Lt MA
Jonas, Jr.: b 6-29-1760 d 3-25-1846 m Judith Bemis Sgt MA
Jonas: b 1757 d 1831 m Catherine Tower Pvt MA ★
Jonathan: b 1-24-1724/5 d *p.* 12-31-1779 m Hulda Livermore Pvt
    MA
Joseph: b 11-20-1752 d 1-17-1823 m Jemima Craig Pvt MA
Joseph: b 2-1-1758 d 8-16-1837 m Jemima Stoddard Pvt VT
Joshua: b 3-19-1761 d 1827 m Joanna Frost Pvt MA
Josiah, Sr.: b 2-29-1715/16 d *p.* 1790 m Elizabeth Warren PS MA
Josiah, Jr.: b 3-14-1755 d *c.* 1821 m Joanna Fish Pvt MA
Jotham, Jr.: b 1756 d 3-24-1813 m Asenath Andrus Pvt RI
Nathaniel: b 3-12-1745 d 10-10-1819 m Esther Cox Pvt MA
Phineas: b 8-19-1749 d 4-25-1834 m Sarah Childs Pvt MA
Reuben: b 6-10-1752 d 1-18-1779 m (1)Abigail Smith
    (2) Sibbilah Bemis Pvt MA
Silas: b 10-4-1760/61 d 6-18-1850 m (1)Olive Spencer
    (2) Beulah Sartwell (3)Judith Mamual Pvt MA
Thaddeus: b 4-22-1759 d 1845 m Judith Day Pvt MA ★
Timothy: b 3-6-1734 d 1806 m Martha Wesson PS NH
William: b 11-1-1722 d 3-23-1801 m Rebekah White CS MA
William: b 2-25-1762 d 1-30-1830 m Mary Prendergast Pvt NY
Zaccheus: b 7-25-1736 d 1805-11 m Elizabeth Lyon Pvt MA

BENBOW,
Edward: b 8-22-1761 d 4-12-1829 m Mary — Pvt PS SC

BENBROOKS,
Ezekiel G.: b 12- -1748 d 1840 m Mary — Capt NC

BENBURY,
Thomas: b 11-28-1736 d 2-5-1793 m Thamir Howcott Maj PS NC

BENDER, (includes BENNER, BINDER)
Christian: b 1731/2 d 6-6-1808 m Elizabeth Cramer Sgt NY
Conrad: b *c.* 1755 d 1- -1823 m Elizabeth — Pvt PA
David: b 7-26-1741 d 4-20-1824 m Margret Gonder Sol PA
George: b 1752 d 12-6-1843 m Eunice Belknap Pvt MA ★
Heinrich: b 1759 d 1817 m Catharina Pitcher PS NY
Jacob: b 1-19-1736 d 3-18-1804 m Mary Weisbach 1Lt PA
Jacob: b 2-13-1722 d 7-10-1786 m Catherine Schneider Pvt PA
Jacob: b 12-6-1740 d 2-15-1820 m Elisabeth Catherine Schaefer
    2Lt PA
Johannes: b *c.* 1700 d *p.* 1778 m Magdalena Streid PS NY
John: b 4-11-1855 d 7-5-1818 m Julianna Margaret Altemus
    Pvt PA W★
Martin: b 6-12-1730 d 1-12-1797 m Magdalena — Pvt PA
Peter: b 10-11-1737 d 9-2-1820 m (1)Catherine Babb (2)Christina —
    Pvt & PS PA

BENEDICT,
Aaron: b 1-17-1745 d 12-16-1841 m Esther Trowbridge Lt CT ★
Aaron: b 12-5-1740 d 1816 m Elizabeth Knowles Sol NY
Abel: b 10-1-1748 d 12-20-1819 m Hannah (Benedict) Sgt MA
Abijah: b *a.* 1760 d 1823 m Betsey Stuart Sgt CT
Abner: b 11-9-1740 d 11-19-1818 m (1)Rebecca Benedict
    (2) Lois Northrup (3) — (4)Mrs. Sawyer Chp CT
Abraham: b 5-27-1746 d 9-7-1846 m Lydia Hoyt Pvt CT
Amos: b 11-30-1756 d 1-14-1848 m (1)Tabitha Ferry (2)Mary
    Munn Pvt CT★
Amos: b 9-17-1722 d 7-29-1809 m Martha Sturtevant Pvt NY
Benajah: b 1747 d 2-7-1831 m Hannah Seeley Sgt CT
Benjamin: b 9-27-1740 d 9-27-1823 m Mary Bowton Capt PS CT
Benjamin: b 12-28-1757 d 9-25-1839 m Mary Moses Pvt CT
Benjamin: b 10-21-1755 d 10-17-1832 m Elizabeth Gilbert Ens
    NY
Caleb: bpt 12-28-1740 d 5-6-1812 m Deborah St. John Pvt NH
Daniel: b *c.* 172- d *c.* 1777 m Phebe — Capt CT
Daniel: b 4-22-1741/2 d 12-23-1822 m Mary Wood Pvt CT
Ebenezer: b 9-4-1764 d 8-28-1833 m Asenath Abbott Pvt CT ★
Elisha: b 4-2-1736 d 8-26-1798 m (2)Jerusha Barnum Capt NY
Elisha Jr.: b 7-5-1760 d 8-17-1845 m Thankful Gregory Sgt NY ★
Ezra: b 5-30-1746 d 9-11-1832 m Mary — 2Lt CT
Felix: b 5-13-1767 d 10-29-1828 m Clarissa Hubbell Pvt NY
George: b *c.* 1757 d 7-27-1817 m Susannah (Intlea) Schelter Pvt
    PA W★
Gilbert: b 1745 d *p.* 1787 m Mercy Weed Pvt CT
Hezekiah: b 3-16-1754 d 3-16-1831 m Huldah Hall Pvt CT
Ichabod: b 1-15-1756 d 3-21-1822 m (1)Lois Mitchell (2)Esther
    Burritt Pvt VT

Isaac: b 1-25-1751 d 5-17-1840 m (1)Jane Raymond (2)Mary Davenport Cpl CT ★

Isaac Oliver: b 8-14-1764 d 10-24-1845 m (1)Asenath Beach (2)Amy Reed (3)Mary Huntington Pvt MA

Jacob: b 3- -1756 d 4-17-1811 m Dorcas Roscoe Pvt NY

James: b 12-18-1743 d 6-17-1838 m Thankful G. Lockwood Pvt CT

James: b 8-12-1762 d 7-18-1849 m (1)Sylvia Reed (2)Mrs Sarah Hall Pvt MA NY ★

James: b 5-5-1745 d 11-9-1822 m Mary Wood Pvt NY

James: b 2-19-1719/20 d 9-9-1792 m (1)Mary Blackman (2)Joanna — PS PA

Jesse: b 2-2-1735 d 9-2-1805 m Mehitable Northrop Sgt CT

John: b — d — 1789 m Elizabeth — Pvt CT

John: b 1719 d 3-17-1792 m Lydia Gregory PS CT

John: b 10-3-1726 d 7-9-1814 m Esther Stebbins PS CT

John: b 4-24-1747 d 1810 m Hannah Wisner Ens NY

Jonas: b 9-21-1742 d 10-30-1820 m Mercy Boughton Pvt CT

Jonathan: b 4-12-1744 d 7-20-1834 m (1) X (2)Huldah Seelye OrdlSgt CT ★

Joseph: b 1728 d 12-15-1815 m Elizabeth Hall PS CS CT

Joseph: b 5-20-1730 d 8-24-1785 m Keziah Wood LCol NY

Joseph: b 7-29-1708 d 7-17-1793 m Susannah — CS NY

Joshua: b 4-2-1753 d 3-16-1825 m Ruth Westcott Pvt PS CT

Lemuel: b 8-10-1734 d 3-28-1804 m Sarah Trowbridge 1Lt CT

Levi: b 3-25-1755 d 9-20-1803 m Hannah Hurlbut Pvt CT

Lewis: b 6-25-1754 d 7-21-1827 m Jemima Newman Pvt NY

Moses: b 175- d 1832 m Lucy Peck Pvt CT

Nathan: b 3-9-1753 d 2-13-1802 m Deborah Todd Pvt NY

Nathaniel Jr.: b 3-24-1744 d 2-24-1833 m (1)Anah Raymond (2)Hannah Selleck Sgt CT ★

Nathaniel: b 1721/3 d p. 10-26-1805 m (1)Hannah — (2)Hannah Keeler CS CT

Nathaniel Sr.: b 1716 d 1806 m (1)Mary Lockwood (2)Hannah Hawley PS CT

Oliver: b 11-17-1748 d 10-28-1827/8 m Mary Starr Sgt CT

Peter: b 3-4-1753 d 5-20-1830 m Susannah Norton 2Lt NY★

Peter: b c. 1738-40 d 1797 m Elizabeth Lanckster Pvt PA

Robin: b 1744 d 1828 m Sarah Ketchum Pvt CT

Samuel: b 7-29-1753 d 6-28-1845 m Sarah Weed Pvt Tms CT ★

Samuel: b 1722 d 5-19-1792 m Phebe (Benedict) PS CT

Stephen: b 3-28-1743 d 3-10-1828 m (1)Abigail Howes (2)—Kellogg (3)Lydia Betts 1Lt NY

Thaddeus: b 9-2-1758 d 8- -1812 m Ruth Lockwood Pvt CT

Thaddeus: b 11-1-1728 d 1-20-1805 m (1)Abigail Starr (2)Mrs Catharine Dibble CS CT

Theophilus: b 1738 d 7-30-1810 m Mary — Ens CT

Thomas: b 1727 d 3-14-1821 m Mercy Knapp Pvt CT

Thomas: b 11-9-1694 d 7-4-1776 m Abigail Hoyt CS CT

Thomas: b 2-25-1725 d 2-21-1802 m Hannah Raymond PS CT

Thomas: b 9-28-1758 d 10-28-1839 m (1)Martha Scudder (2)Elizabeth Seelye (3)Mrs Selote Sweet Sol CT

Thomas: b 2-27-1753 d 1-9-1841 m (1)Miss Strong (2)— (3)Miss Wallace (4)Susan Swift Pvt MA ★

Thomas: b 10-3-1726 d p. 1785 m Jane Gunn PS VT

Uriah: b 2-15-1745 d 2-25-1800 m Mary Howes Pvt NY

William: b c. 1748 d— m Anna Andrews Ens CT

William: b 11-16-1757 d 2-4-1836 m Ruth Peck Pvt CT

William: b 7-14-1755 d 5-24-1827 m Jane Vance Sgt NY

BENEFIEL,
John: b c. 1760 d p. 6-26-1821 m Rebeckah — Pvt PS PA

BENEFIELD, (includes BENFIELD)
George: b 12-25-1759 d 4-1-1832 m Mary Buchanan Pvt PA
Samuel: b 1-12-1742 d 12-7-1831 m Ana Maria Smith Pvt PA

BENEZET,
Daniel: b 12-26-1723 d 4-25-1797 m Elizabeth North Pvt PA
James: b 8-26-1721 d 5-16-1794 m Ana Hasell Pvt PS PA

BENFORD, (includes BENEFORD, BENFER)
George: b 3-21-1745 d 4-23-1818 m (1)— Scharf (2)Maria Magdalene Miller Pvt PA
James: b c. 1740 d c. 1801 m Mary — CM Ofr PA

BENHAM, (includes BENNEM, & BENNUM)
Cornelius: b 11-6-1736 d 8-22-1805 m Charity Carter Pvt NY
Elihu: b 4-21-1748 d 2-28-1836 m Mehitable Smith Pvt CT
Enos: b 11-5-1761 d c. 1830 m — Raymond Pvt Fif CT
Isaac: b 8-29-1737 d c. 1818 m Lucy Cook Lt CT
Isaac: b 10-21-1760 d 12-7-1853 m Thankful Reed Pvt CT
James: b 2-6-1746 d p. 1790 m Elizabeth Prindle Cpl CT
James Sr.: b 2-10-1735 d 5-6-1830 m Huldah Kellogg Pvt CT
James Jr.: b 8-14-1764 d 1-6-1809 m Sarah Sedgwick Pvt CT
James: b 10-26-1753 d 9-4-1831 m X PS CT
Jared: b 6- -1756 d 5-8-1829 m Elizabeth Merriman SgtMaj CT
Jehiel Sr.: bpt 3-29- 1751 d p. 1793 m Lydia Cadwill Pvt CT
John: b 10- -1723 d 5-24-1811 m Mary Curtis Ens CT
John: b 1761 d 11-8-1804 m Elizabeth Welch Cpl CT★
John: b 12-13-1737 d 12-30-1794 m (2)Joanna Stoothoff Ens NY
Joseph: b 7-13-1750 d 1-25-1836 m Elizabeth Bunnell Pvt CT ★
Lyman: b 5-6-1759 d 2-16-1831 m Lois Hall Pvt CT

Peter: b 1-1-1725 d a. 6-12-1780 m (1)Anne James (2)Catherine Wessel Ens VA

Richard: b 2-24-1755 d 1819 m Lydia — Pvt NJ

Thomas: b 5-28-1759 d 1-27-1842 m Desire Beecher Pvt CT★

Uri: b 12-15-1739 d 4-21-1832 m Lois Doolittle Sol PS CT

BENJAMIN,
Abiel: b 12-16-1716 d 12-20-1820 m Judith Ford Pvt CT
Amaziah: b 11-18-1741 d 1812 m Patty Howell Pvt PS NY
Asa: b 3-20-1762 d 4-25-1834 m Mary Roath Pvt CT★
Asa: b 10-7-1753 d 12-28-1825 m Polly Brumley Sol MA
Caleb: b 5-26-1729 d 1818 m Martha Bodman 1Lt MA
Chester: b 2-9-1752 d 1830 m Ann Harp Pvt NY
Cyrus: b 7-7-1762 d 7-19-1817 m Rhoda Dibble Pvt NY
Darius: b 1-17-1758 d 2-12-1850 m Charity Rice Pvt NY★
David: b 4-11-1743 d 9-1-1785 m (1)Esther Wibourn (2)Lucy Park Pvt CT
Ebenezer: b 1734 d 12-22-1789 m Phoebe Benjamin Capt NY
Elijah: b 12-27-1755 d 6-17-1819 m Elizabeth Paddock Pvt NY
Ezra: b 12-13-1742 d 9-29-1819 m (1)Prudence Main (2)Jeane Eames (3)Mrs Amy Stanton Pvt CT
George: b 9-28-1734 d p. 1779 m Mary Howes Capt CT
James: b c. 1753 d p. 1777 m Mary Phillips PS Pvt CT
James: b 1758 d 5-28-1821 m Eunice Worthington Pvt MA
Jesse: b 10-28-1758 d 12-6-1851 m Rachel Bunn (Burns?) Cpl Mus CT
Joel: b 4-9-1760 d 12-4-1839 m Sarah Anderson Pvt MA
John Jr.: b 8-28-1731 d 9-14-1796 m Lucretia Backus Maj CT
John Jr.: b 12-25-1751 d 6-24-1781 m Grace — Sol CT
Jonas: b 4-6-1762 d 6-6-1854 m (1)Mercy Salter (2)Mrs. Polly — Pvt MA W★
Jonathan: b 1725 d 12-29-1787 m Elizabeth — Pvt PS NY
Jonathan: b 10-14-1738 d 8-26-1842 m Margaret Brown Pvt PA ★
Joseph: b 1748 d 10-7-1825 m Elizabeth Grace Winchester Pvt VA ★
Judah: b 7-8-1755 d 8-16-1834 m X Joanna — Pvt NH ★
Nathan: b 4-19-1737 d 7-1-1785 m (1)Abigail Dibble (2)Hannah Wells Pvt MA
Nathan Sr.: b 1733 d 5-14-1805 m Jemima Aldrich Lt PS NY
Nathan Jr.: b 1760 d 7-30-1838 m Johanna Sweezey Sol NY
Phineas: b 1759 d 1845 m Mehitable Chapman Pvt CT
Richard: b 1757 d 12-8-1808 m Nancy Fanning PS Pvt NY
Samuel: b 1757 d 1840 m Elizabeth Bostwick Pvt CT★
Samuel: b 2-5-1753 d 4-14-1824 m Tabitha Livermore Lt MA
Sarah Mathews: b 11-17-1745 d 4-6-1861 m (1)William Reid (2)Aaron Osborn (3)John Benjamin PS NY
William: b 1-16-1737/8 d p. 1787 m Sarah Child Pvt MA

BENNEFIELD,
John: b 1731 d 1779 m Martha — PS GA

BENNER,
Abraham Sr.: b 1734 d 1822 m Barbara — Pvt PA
Abraham Jr.: b 1756 d 1829 m Sarah Markley Pvt PA
Christopher: b c. 1756 d p. 1820 m Thankful Gardner Pvt MA ★
Henry Jr.: b 7-31-1758 d 9-4-1818 m Elizabeth Hauge Cpl PA ★
Isaac: b — d 1823 m Catherine — Pvt PA
Peter: b 8-28-1761 d 9-9-1835 m Abigail Hunt Cpl MA ★
Philip: b 5-19-1762 d 7-27-1832 m Ruth Roberts Sol PA

BENNETSH,
Johannes: b 1756 d 1787 m Magdalene — PS PA

⌣ BENNETT, (includes BENNET)
Aaron: b 10-25-1748 d p. 1803 m (1)Hannah Holdredge (2)Abigale Smith Pvt CT
Aaron: b 1751 d 12-5-1834 m Margaret Bennett Sgt NJ
Abraham: b 1739 d 7-25-1835 m Sarah Goodnow Pvt MA
Abraham: b 11- -1747 d 5-26-1839 m Mary Smith OrdlSgt NJ ★
Abraham: b 1735 d 1804 m Levice Stevens PS N Capt NJ
Abraham: b c. 1744 d p. 1-18-1817 m Jennetje — Pvt NJ
Abraham Sr.: b 6-26-1715 d p. 1790 m Silence Hickox Pvt NY
Abraham Jr.: b 1742 d c. 1795 m Jerusha Wanzer Pvt NY
Abraham: b 1764 d 5-12-1852 m Liddy Bentley Pvt NY★
Abraham: b 3-23-1745/6 d 1-29-1824 m Catherine Roberts Pvt PA
Abraham: b 1-17-1753 d — m Margaret Craig Cpl PA
Amos: b 1758 d 4-18-1840 m Wealthy Safford Pvt CT★
Amos: b 3-26-1739 d 11-1-1828 m (1)Jane Shaw (2)Mary Keyes Pvt NY
Andrew: b 3-2-1760 d 2-4-1837 m Mary Folsom Cpl MA
Andrew: b 1-13-1764 d 11-20-1821 m (2)Abigail Kelly Pvt PA
Arthur: b 7-2-1756 d 4-22-1829 m Elizabeth Cox Pvt MA
Asa: b 6-9-1752 d 8-21-1827 m Mary Barrows Pvt CT
Asher: b 9-16-1753 d 3-2-1837 m Mary Harrington Sgt RI
Asahel P.: b 2-20-1754 d 6-11-1840 m Sarah Ensign Pvt MA
Bartlett: b c. 1740-45 d p. 1797 m Sarah — PS VA
Batchelder: b 1743 d 3-10-1820 m Mary Sampson Cpl MA
Benjamin, Jr.: b 5-22-1753 d 8-25-1832 m Mary Brownell Pvt CT ★
Benjamin: b — d — m Abigail Clark Sgt CT
Benjamin: b 1741 d 7-22-1779 m Mary Hosier Pvt MA
Caleb: b 10-21-1758 d 1848 m Freelove Chapman Pvt CT

BENNETT, contd.

Caleb Prew.: b 11-11-1758 d 5-9-1836 m Catherine Britton Lt DE
Charles: b c. 1750 d 8- -1818 m Mary — Pvt CT
Charles: b 1759 d 6-27-1855 m Achsah — Pvt NY★
Charles: b 1745 d 1820 m Duanna Sydnor Capt VA
Daniel: b 4-1-1754 d 12-22-1822 m Mary Monroe Drm CT★
Daniel Jr.: b 7-13-1752 d 1812 m Hannah Read Pvt CT
Daniel, Sr.: b 2-2-1722 d 11-2-1815 m Mercy Simmons PS RI
David: bpt 4-30-1732 d bet 1776-1781 m Bethia Burton Sgt CT
David: b 1751 d 4-30-1825 m Martha Smith Pvt MA W★
Deliverance: b 4-7-1738 d 3-7-1808 m Mary Bennett Pvt CT
Ebenezer: b 9-26-1743 d 3- -1821 m Grace Ensworth Pvt CT
Ebenezer: b 9-15-1751 d 2-8-1844 m (1)Ruth — (2)Elizabeth — Pvt CT ★
Ebenezer: b 1-31-1747 d 11-10-1778 m Elizabeth Ellis Pvt MA
Edward: b 7-1-1739 d 10-4-1812 m Elizabeth Akin Pvt MA
Edward: b 1742 d 2-26-1818 m Ann Bolesberry Pvt NJ
Edward: b 6-2-1739 d 8-3-1789 m Mary Lester Pvt NY
Edward: b c. 1760 d c. 1820 m X Pvt VA
Elias: b 5-10-1752 d 2-17-1842 m (1)Abigail Crossman (2) Elizabeth Squires Pvt CT★
Elias: b 4- -1763 d 2-24-1829 m Lydia Justin Pvt Fif CT ★
Elisha: b 8-8-1758 d 1819 m Lucy Raymond Pvt MA
Ephraim: b 1714 d 10-7-1779 m (1)Ann Baldwin (2)Johanna Stilson Pvt CT
Ephraim Sr.: b 1742 d 1826 m Mary Stafford Sgt NY
Ephraim Jr.: b 5-1-1762 d 10-26-1843 m Hannah Bentley Pvt NY★
Ezekiel: b 8-3-1762 d 10-25-1846 m Sarah Perry Pvt CT★
Frances: b c. 1733 d p. 1794 m Peter Bennett PS VA
Gamaliel: b 1751 d 1815 m Anna King Pvt PS NY
George: b 1739 d 12-21-1811 m Charity Bishop Lt PA
Godfrey Durfee: b 9- -1759 d 2-15-1834 m Abigail — Pvt RI ★
Henry: b 5-14-1746 d p. 4-28-1806 m X Pvt NY
Henry: b 8- -1762 d 1-8-1841 m Harriett Clute Pvt NY ★
Isaac: b 3-14-1738 d 7-17-1817 m Sarah Cady Pvt CT
Isaac: b 1747 d p. 1780 m Catherine Dayton Sgt MA
Issac: b 6-8-1741 d p. 1790 m Dorcas Wharff 2Sgt MA
Ishmael: b c. 1730 d 1820 m (1)Martha — (2)Abigail Weeks Pvt PA
Jabez: b 9-11-1754 d 1-16-1849 m (1)Abigail Thomas (2)Mrs Dinah Richardson Pvt VT
Jacob: b 6-10-1752 d 3-21-1825 m Barbara Ann Brower Pvt NY ★
James: b 5-22-1749 d 12-21-1819 m Lydia Williams Pvt CT
James: b 12-5-1736 d 8-9-1808 m (1)Hannah — (2)Olive Shattuck Capt MA
James, Sr.: b 5-4-1727 d 1809 m Sarah Dodge Pvt MA
James, Jr.: b 1758 d 9-4-1842 m Mary Walker Ens MA ★
James: b 3-12-1756 d 7-24-1799 m Elizabeth Slade Pvt NC
James: b 5-27-1758 d 1-2-1841 m Patience Shreeve Pvt Smn RI★
Jeremiah: b c. 1760 d 1834 m Anne Randolph Pvt NJ ★
Jeremiah: b 2-20-1760 d 8-24-1811 m Phoebe Lain Pvt NY
John: b c. 1720 d c. 1806 m Mary Baldwin Pvt CT
John: b 11-11-1740 d 2-27-1824 m Mary (Bennett) — Pvt NH
John: b 5-9-1721 d p. 1790 m Abigail Roberts CS NH
John: b 3-2-1761 d 4-2-1847 m (1)Elizabeth McArthur (2)Diana McDuffey Pvt NJ
John: b 1750 d 1798 m Elizabeth Sadler PS VA
John L.: b 2-28-1757 d 11-27-1843 m Sarah Logan Sgt NJ ★
John Nobel: b 5-3-1755 d 11-24-1821 m Polly — Pvt VT
Jonathan: b 1-25-1756 d 1832 m (1) — Bateman (2)Judith Buck Pvt NJ
Jordon: b — d 10-4-1822/23 m Ann Murphy Pvt VA W★
Joseph: b 10-9-1719 d 1802-08 m (1)Deborah Boone (2)Elizabeth Prew PS DE
Joseph: b 1752 d 2-12-1816 m Mary Swift Pvt MA
Joseph: b 1765 d 10-19-1825 m Susanna Simmons Pvt MA ★
Joseph: b 5-20-1744 d 6-5-1835 m Mary Remington Pvt RI ★
Joseph: b 1758 d 12-19-1838 m Esther Green Pvt RI ★
Joseph: b 1745 d 1810 m Hannah Starnes Sol VA
Joseph: b 1757 d p. 1840 m Mary — Pvt DrmMaj VA ★
Joseph Davenport: b 5-13-1763 d 6-17-1841 m Elizabeth Sprague Pvt RI ★
Martha Jackson: b 11-25-1731 d 9-10-1810 m Thomas Bennett PS PA
Matthew: b c. 1762 d 9-19-1834 m Rebecca — Pvt NY
Matthew: b - - d - - m Sarah Scattergood Lt PA
Matthew: b c. 1750 d 8-15-1800 m (1) X (2)Mary Osgood Sol SC
Miles: b 11-13-1763 d 9-10-1853 m Lucina Byington Pvt CT ★
Moses: b 4-3-1755 d 2-12-1832 m Judith Norwood Plummer Pvt MA ★
Najah: b 9-30-1742 d 8-26-1821 m (1)Sarah Gilbert (2)Mary — Capt CT
Nathan: b 3-28-1755 d 4-8-1831 m Hulda Barlow Ens CT
Nathan: b 2- -1741 d 6-11-1800 m Elizabeth Lewis PS CT
Nathan: b 1743 d 6-29-1804 m (1) X (2)Lydia Hyde Pvt VT NY
Nathan: b 6-10-1756 d 9-24-1837 m Mary Harrindeen Pvt RI ★
Nathaniel: b 7-8-1721 d 10-18-1800 m Mary Smith Pvt CT
Nathaniel: b 11-15-1741 d 1-25-1804 m Catherine Tripp Lt MA
Nathaniel: b 6-30-1744 d 1-1-1810 m Hannah — 1Lt MA
Nehemiah: b 3-25-1753 d 12-4-1809 m (2)Polly E. Edwards Pvt MA
Nehemiah: b 4-15-1758 d 1812 m Hester Oliver Pvt MA

Oliver Cromwell: b 1759 d 6-3-1832 m (1)Huldah Bushnell (3)Zeurah Pratt Pvt CT
Peter: b 1750 d 4-9-1822 m Elizabeth Pomfrett Capt NC
Phineas: b 1756 d 7-14-1823 m Rachel Grover Pvt VT
Reuben: b c. 1755 d 1808 m Elizabeth — Pvt GA
Reuben: b 1757 d 11-14-1847 m Elizabeth Beckham Pvt NC SC ★
Richard: b c. 1752 d a. 1820 m Sylvia Smart Sol NC
Richard: b 1758 d 1830 m Mary Cook Sol NC
Richard: b c. 1720 d 1786 m Anne — PS NC
Robert: b - - d - - m X Pvt NY ★
Robert: b c. 1753 d p. 10-5-1781 m Anne Enroughty Sol VA
Rufus: b 1754 d 4-20-1842 m Martha — Pvt CT ★
Samuel: b10-17-1755 d 8-28-1819 m Pauline Jennings Pvt CT
Samuel: b 12-14-1707 d p. 5-3-1779 m Hannah Wade PS CT
Samuel: b 3-26-1736 d 1-11-1778/9 m Anna — Pvt MA
Samuel: b 10-5-1757 d 2-27-1846 m Phoebe Paul Pvt NJ ★
Samuel: b 1758 d 5-23-1841 m Rebecca Shaw Drm Maj RI ★
Silas: b- -d- -m Sarah Scofield Pvt VT
Solomon: b 1750 d 10-23-1823 m Mrs. Sarah Upson Pvt PA
Stephen: b 8-1-1757 d 12-15-1845 m Louisa Abigail Johnson Pvt CT ★
Stephen: b 5-28-1761 d 10-21-1831 m Mary Gates Pvt CT ★
Stephen: b 5-8-1758 d 3-26-1837 m Hannah Wakefield MM Sgt MA ★
Thaddeus, Sr.: b 1725 d 1-21-1777 m Elizabeth — Capt CT
Thaddeus, Jr.: b 8-23-1758 d 1-8-1831 m Martha Hall Pvt CT W★
Thaddeus: b 1764 d 1834 m (1)Eunice Bentley (2)— (3)Mrs. Meade Pvt NY
Thomas: b 1754 d 1824 m Anna Tillett Pvt MD
Thomas: b - - d a. 7-4-1784 m Lydia — Sgt MA
Thomas: b 8-21-1757 d 3-18-1822 m Mary Smith Pvt MA
Thomas: b 1-14-1761 d p. 1806 m Sarah Davis PS NH
Thomas: b 1721 d 1796 m Martha Jackson Sol PA
Thomas: b 2-11-1754 d p. 1790 m Anna Warnock Capt SC
Thomas: b a. 1746 d a. 6- -1807 m Elizabeth Dodson Sol VA
Timothy: b 1748 d 11-21-1823 m Martha Titus Sgt NY
Timothy: b 1742 d 1800 m Hannah Darling Pvt RI
Trowbridge: b c. 1745 d 9-4-1804 m Sarah Hine Cpl CT
Walter': b 5-22-1745 d 12-21-1812 m Jenny Wyatt Dr. VA
William: b 1763 d 1850 m Lucy Lee Pvt CT
William: b 1742 d p. 6-13-1824 m Adria Ann Britton Lt PA
William: b - - d 1789 m Hilda Chase Pvt NY
William : b 1-18-1746 d 2-20-1843 m Ann Hunt Pvt NY ★
William: b 1717 d 9-21-1815 m (1)Nancy Huckston (2)— Cheers (3)Rachel — Capt SC
William: b 3-25-1737 d 7-28-1802 m Luranah Swearingen Pvt VA
William: b c. 1736 d a. 1796 m Sarah,Oldham Pvt VA
William: b c. 1762 d 7-17-1826 m Mary Edwards Pvt VA
William: b 1765 d 4-17-1825 m Rachel — Pvt VA
William: b c. 1720 d p. 1783 m Hannah — PS VA
Wolcott: b a. 1757 d 12-6-1831 m Johanna Patchen Sgt CT W★

BENNING,
John: b 12-10-1737 d 3-6-1809 m Sally Cobb Capt VA

BENSINGER,
Frederick: b 1747 d 1831 m Hannah — Pvt PA

BENSLEY, (includes BENCHLEY)
David: b 2-14-1755 d 11-9-1847 m (1)Elizabeth Rushton (2)Mehitable Eaton (3)Abigail Putnam Haskins Pvt MA ★
Joseph: b 8-23-1758 d 12-18-1834 m Lucinia Brown Ens RI
William: b 1725 d 9-29-1811 m Deborah Arnold PS RI

BENSON, (includes BENSEN)
Aaron: b 10-28-1753 d 7-8-1827 m Lydia Fairbanks Capt MA
Asa: b 3-7-1754 d p. 8-13-1833 m (1)Betsey Perry (2)Mrs. Drucilla Ward Pvt MA★
Benjamin: b 3-3-1742 d 3-29-1802 m Martha McNamara Pvt MA
Benjamin: b 2-13-1732 d 8-20-1779 m Catherine De Ronde Pvt NY
Benjamin: b 8-29-1749 d 9-5-1812 m Hannah Scott Pvt PA
Benoni: b 7-18-1724 d 1-10-1806 m (1)Abigail White (2)Abigail Staples LT PS MA
Consider: b 4-16-1730 d 1-16-1802 m Elizabeth Washburn Lt MA
Daniel: b 6-1-1761 d 10-9-1854 m Phoebe Bugbee Pvt MA
Dirck: b c. 1745 d p. 1786 m Marytje Wyngaart Sol PS NY
Elihu: b c. 1756/7 d c. 1804 m Hulda Brown Pvt NY
Elkanah: b 2-21-1766 d 5-6-1844 m Deborah Wheelock Pvt MA
Elnathan: b 2-15-1745 d 8-10-1814 m Sarah Gibbs Pvt MA
Enoch: b 12- -1756 d p. 9-25-1832 m X Pvt VA ★
Henry: b 12-5-1743 d 4-7-1777 m Susanna Thayer Sgt CS MA
Henry: b a. 1755 d 11-1-1828 m Nancy Jones Sol PS VA ★
Ichabod: b 1740 d 1833 m Mrs. Abigail Griffith Pvt MA
Isaac: b 11-26-1739 d 1818 m (1)Martha Cass (2)Deborah Cass Pvt PS NH
Jacob: b 1743 d p. 1818 m (1)Jane Morrell (2)Mary Meach Pvt MA
James: b 1753 d 1795 m Mollie Taylor Pvt PA
James: b c.1740 d p. 6-5-1797 m X PS VA
Jephtha: b 5-14-1757 d 3-2-1858 m (2)Mrs. Mary A Ross Pvt ME W★
Job: b c. 1722 d 7-22-1801 m Mary Richardson Pvt NY
Joel: b 10- -1749 d 3-17-1837 m Mary Shaw Pvt NY

Johannes: b 10-14-1759 d 5-8-1828 m Mary Lydecker Pvt NJ
John: b 7-22-1751 d 5-5-1819 m Mary Holbrook Lt MA
John: b 6-29-1759 d 12-25-1799 m Maria Westervelt Sol NJ
John: b 1-27-1730 d 6-16-1804 m Rebecca Demorest CS NJ
John: b 6-20-1744 d 12-28-1818 m Mercy Casey Pvt RI
Jonathan: b 1718 d 12-16-1788 m Martha Snell Pvt MA
Joseph: b 12-6-1744 d p. 1781 m Susana Clap Sgt MA
Joseph: b c. 1737 d p. 1790 m Hannah Swift Pvt NY
Matthew: b 4-7-1764 d 9-11-1843 m Johannah Davis Pvt NY
Perry: b 1751 d 1814 m Anne Bromwell Ens MD
Peter: b 7-16-1763 d p. 1806 m Azubah Marsh Pvt MA & CL
Samuel: b 7-17-1762 d 5-26-1848 m Rebecca Hunt Pvt MA
Samuel: b 1733 d 11-22-1825 m Rebecca Dykman Capt NY
Samuel: b c. 1760 d p. 1814 m Rachel Darling Pvt NY
Seth: b 1753 d 2-16-1834 m Mrs. Lydia Morgan Pvt MA ★
Stephen: b 7-13-1742 d 7-30-1823 m Mary Holbrook Cpl MA
Stutson: b 3-2-1741 d 3-1-1820 m Bursheba Lewis Sol VT
Thomas: b 3-7-1762 d 3- -1843 m (1)Martha Prince (2)Elizabeth —
    Pvt SC
William: b c. 1730 d a. 11-8-1783 m Ann — PS MD
William: b 1745 d 8- -1796 m Eleanor Key Adj PS SC
William: b 4-19-1761 d 10-9-1778 m Syntze Elmendorf Pvt NY
William: b 9-17-1759 d 4-14-1834 m Sarah Seale Pvt VA

BENT,
David, Sr.: b 3-30-1730 d 1-15-1794 m (1)Lucy Moore (2)Martha
    Browning Capt MA
David, Jr.: b 4-3-1756 d 1-1-1832 m Phebe Whittemore Pvt MA
Ebenezer: b 8-22-1737 d 9-10-1796 m (1)Hannah Shepherd (2)Mrs
    Ruth Crouch Pvt MA
Jason: b 7-25-1749 d 10-1-1786 m Anna Glover Pvt MA
Joel: b 2-22-1750 d 11-25-1812 m Mary Mason Pvt MA
John: b 5-4-1730 d 9-14-1818 m Molly Stacey Lt MA
John: b 7-10-1746 d 1-12-1817 m Hannah Coller Pvt MA
John: b 2-2-1763 d 9-14-1853 m (1)Elizabeth Murdock (2)Polly Shaw
    Pvt MA
Jonathan: b 4-22-1758 d 4-11-1826 m (1)Experience Smith (2)Ruth
    Haynes Rice Pvt MA
Peter: b 3-20-1707 d 3-11-1798 m Mary — PS MA
Rufus: b 2-13-1755 d 11-28-1821 m Mary Wyman Pvt MA
Samuel: b 6-1-1755 d 4-22-1833 m Molly Hunt Pvt MA
Silas: b 4-14-1744 d 4-4-1818 m Mary Carter Lt MA
William: b 11-13-1737 d 10-17-1806 m Chloe Blackman Capt MA
William: b 6-8-1741 d 4-26-1829 m Abigail Bruce 1Lt MA

BENTHAM,
James: b 9-7-1749 d 10-20-1811 m (2)Mary Hardy Lt SC

BENTLEY, (includes BENTLY)
Caleb: b 5-20-1742 d 3-2-1827 m (1)Mary Gardner (2)Mary Hewitt
    Capt NY W★
Caleb: b 1739 d 1809 m Martha Foster Pvt RI
Caleb: b 8-25-1739 d p. 1790 m Leah Spencer Pvt RI
Charles: b 1750 d 10-16-1833 m (1)Polly Ransford (2)Polly Button
    (3)Hannah Wilson Pvt & Arfr CT ★
Daniel: b c. 1752 d 1834 m Rebecca Purcell Sol NC
Efford: b 11- -1759 d 7-3-1837 m (1)Lucy Markham (2)Elizabeth Gay
    Sgt VA★
Eli: b 2-16-1752 d 8-13-1822 m Mary Hunter 1Lt PA
Ezekiel: b 1738 d 2-2-1834 m (1)Alice Sabin (2)Anna Chapman Pvt
    RI W★
Gardner: b 10-1-1744 d p. 1822 m Sarah — Pvt MA
George: b 6-26-1756 d 5-3-1831 m Lucy Gardner Pvt CT W★
Gideon: b 8-12-1750 d 2- -1857 m Isabel Gardner Pvt Slr MM RI ★
Green: b 3-23-1735 d 1823 m Dinah Straight Pvt NY
Henry: b 6- -1738 d 5-21-1819 m Jane Nicholson Pvt PA ★
James: b 6-6-1739 d 1829 m Mary — Capt VT
John: b 12-3-1756 d 7-20-1830 m (1)Mary — (2)Thankful Ballou
    Pvt NY
John: b c. 1755 d 1845 m Susannah Sweet Pvt PA
Joseph: b c. 1725 d 1810 m Jane — Sol NY
Joseph: b 1765 d 9-22-1840 m Lucy Daly Sgt PA
Joshua: b 1-18-1727 d 4-15-1819 m Elizabeth Paine Capt MA
Samuel: b c. 1752 d p. 1782 m Elizabeth Younger PS VA
Solomon: b 3-16-1754 d 11-2-1838 m Rebecca Wood 2Lt MD
Tillinghast: b 6-2-1735 d 8-3-1820 m Sarah Thomas 1Lt PS NY
William, Sr.: b 1710 d 9-25-1800 m (1)Elizabeth Tillinghast (2)Alice
    — Pvt NY
William: b 4-25-1765 d 5-2-1850 m (1)Anna Mathews (2)Mrs. Diana
    Paddock Cpl MA ★
William, Sr.: b c. 1720 d p. 1782 m Mary Sweet Pvt RI
William: b c. 1729 d 1802 m Mary Elliot Lt Capt VA
William: b c. 1755 d p. 1818 m (1)Judith Archer (2)Lucy Harris Capt
    VA★
William: b 1728 d 1- -1803 m Margaret — Sgt VA

BENTON,
Abijah: b 2-25-1752 d 5-26-1823 m Rebecca Field Pvt NH ★
Amos: b 11-10-1732 d 2-20-1797 m (1)Elizabeth White (2)Jerusha
    Bull Pvt CT
Bethel: b 12-14-1750 d 1-27-1838 m (1)Esther Saddler (2)Bula Rice
    Pvt MA
Caleb: b 1-28-1722 d 1783 m Lydia — Sgt MA

Daniel 3d: b 4-9-1748 d 1805 m Betty Richardson Pvt CT
David., Jr.: b 12-2-1763 d 3-7-1845 m (1)Sarah Bingham (2)Thankful
    (Reynolds) McKane Sol Slr MA
Ebenezer: b 1728 d 10-31-1813 m Anna Hosford CS CT
Elihu: b 1734 d 2-19-1798 m Sarah Lyman Pvt CT
Elihu Stanley: b 12-8-1762 d 12-13-1829 m Anna Filley Pvt CT
Felix: b 4-3-1762 d 4-19-1851 m Tamer Leicester Pvt MA ★
Jabez: b 7-12-1743 d 2-8-1829 m Mary Bartholomew PS CT
Jacob: b 1-2-1728/9 d 1-13-1807 m Hannah Slade Pvt CT
Jacob: b 4-22-1754 d 6-9-1843 m (1)Sarah Weston (2)Sarah Ladd
    Dragoon CT
Jesse: b c. 1747 d 1793 m Ann Gooch Pvt PS NC
John: b 3-13-1746 d 2-6-1808 m Mary Blinn Sgt CT
Jonathan: b 9-17-1747 d 9-4-1832 m X Pvt CT ★
Joseph: b c. 1730 d 1807 m (1)Elizabeth — (2)Rachel — PS MD
Josiah: b 6-16-1705 d 11-9-1783 m Hannah House PS CT
Lemuel: b 10-23-1754 d 5-18-1818 m Elizabeth Kimbrough Col SC
Medad: b 3-19-1732 d 9-10-1810 m Abigail—Lt VT
Nathan: b 4-10-1764 d 7- -1826 m (1)Susannah Crawford (2)Nancy
    Tinley Pvt NC
Nathaniel: b 8-25-1726 d 9-30-1800 m Abigail Gillett Pvt CT
Noah, Jr.: b 1763 d 1847 m Phoebe Davis Pvt CT
Samuel: b 5-9-1757 d 4-18-1816 m Mary Tupper Pvt Tms MA W★
Samuel: b 6-18-1749 d 4-23-1803 m Prudence Seymour PS CT
Selah: b 1740 d 5-10-1832 m Mary Jones Capt CT
Stephen: b 3-6-1742 d p. 1790 m Molly West Cpl NH
Timothy: b 12-15-1732 d 11-27-1807 m (1)Rachel Fowler (2)Mrs
    Desire Stevens Pvt CT
Timothy, Jr.: b 8-2-1755 d 4-18-1816 m Sarah West Pvt CT
William: b c. 1750 d 3- -1824 m Sarah Austin Dragoon MD
William: b c. 1750 d p. 7-19-1820 m Sarah Davis PS NC
Zadock: b 3-7-1761 d 11-3-1845 m Lydia Day Pvt CT
Zebulon: b c. 1758-60 d 11-16-1842 m (1)— (2)Lois Avery (3)Lois
    Abigail Burt Dinsmore Pvt CT

BENTZ, (includes PENTZ)
George: b c. 1740 d 1805 m Anna Maria Holtzinger Pvt PA
Henry: b 4-27-1755 d 2-25-1810 m Catherine Rothrock Pvt PS PA
Henry: b c. 1740 d 3-1-1824 m Mary Blimly Pvt VA

BERCAN,
Peter: b 1-18-1753 d 10-15-1823 m X Pvt NJ

BERDAN,
Jacob: b 3-28-1746 d 10-25-1829 m Rebecca Ryerson PS NJ

BERGEN, (includes BERGAN, BURGAN)
Christopher: b 5-20-1760 d 2-20-1846 m Jemima Bayley MM NY
Daniel P.: b c. 1750 d c. 1827 m Mary Clymer Pvt PA
George, Sr.: b 10-9-1712 d 10-13-1784 m (1)Griete Du Mont
    (2) 'Maria — (3)Mrs Mareya Van Aersdalen PS NJ
George, Jr.: b 2-14-1743 d 9-14-1785 m Helena Hoogland PM NJ
Jacob: b 7-19-1719 d 1-7-1781 m Margaret Lane PS NJ
Jacob G.: b 7-8-1745 d 12-7-1805 m (1)Margaret Van Arsdale
    (2) Elizabeth Cowenhoven Lt NJ
John: b 7-23-1740 d p. 1775 m Margaret Van Duersen PS NY
John B.: b 3-27-1739 d 6-2-1808 m Sarah Stryker Pvt NJ
Simon: b 10-13-1746 d 2-22-1777 m Geshe De Hart Lt NY

BERGEY, (includes BERGY)
Christian: b 6-13-1741 d 5-24-1819 m Mary — Pvt PA
Isaac: b 1734 d 1805 m (1)Susanna Landis (2)Susanna Hunsberger
    Pvt PA
Jacob: b c. 1731 d p. 1794 m Catharine— Pvt PA
Jacob: b 3-31-1758 d 2-8-1836 m (1)Susanna Freed (2) — Kaufman
    Pvt PA
John: b 9-5-1762 d 8-28-1839 m Elizabeth Keck Pvt PA

BERGH, (includes BERTSCH, BERGE)
Abram: b 10-17-1759 d 4-31-1835 m Helena Schaeffer Pvt NY★
Christian: b 8-17-1753 d 7-8-1819 m Julianna Seiberling Pvt PA
Christian: b 6-13-1741 d 3-24-1819 m Mary — Pvt PA
Philip: b 10-16-1724 d 2-9-1790 m Christina Fuchson Pvt NY

BERGMAN,
John: b c. 1754 d p. 1800 m Eliza Buddy Capt PA

BERGSTRASER,
Phillip: b c. 1725 d p. 1807 m Lena Heller Pvt PA

BERKEY,
John, Jr.: b 5- -1745 d 1815 m Sarah Schmidt Pvt PA
Peter: b 8-24-1744 d 9-18-1826 m Elizabeth Jennings Pvt PA

BERKLEY, (includes BERKELEY)
George: b c. 1760 d a. 12-8-1817 m Sarah Wheeler Pvt VA W★
Nelson: b 5-16-1733 d 1-24-1794 m Elizabeth Wormeley PS VA
Scarlett: b c. 1755 d a. 8-5-1808 m Ann Keen Lt VA

BERKSTRESSER,
Valentine: b 11-1-1737 d 10-1-1780 m Elizabeth Negley Pvt PA

BERLET,
Paul: b 8-29-1714 d 9-12-1796 m (1)Catharine Werth (2)Anna Marsteller PS PA

BERLIN,
Isaac: b 9-16-1745 d 6-16-1831 m Maria Cost Pvt PA ★

BERNARD,
John: b 11-16-1736 d 9-9-1825 m Elizabeth Barnett Sol VA
Luke: b 3-10-1755 d 2-12-1816 m Catherine Pinkley Pvt MD
Richard: b 4-10-1758 d 1-22-1785 m Ann Thornton Capt VA
Thomas: b 3-   -1756 d 6-11-1833 m Mary Hicks Pvt VA ★
Walter: b 2-13-1758 d 2-5-1841 m Ruth Hill Pvt VA ★
Will: b c. 1725 d 1779 m Mary Fleming Lt VA
William: b 9-6-1730 d 4-27-1776 m (1) — (2)Sarah Sevigue Lt VA

BERNER,
Joseph: b 6-9-1759 d 5-17-1833 m Cathrin Borst Pvt NY ★

BERNHEISEL, (includes BERNHEISLE)
John: b 5-12-1765 d 9-21-1825 m Catherine Loy Pvt PA
Martin: b 5-19-1727 d 6-29-1802 m Christina Margretha Shatto PS PA

BERRAY,
Seth: b 8-29-1765 d 5-14-1846 m Anna Goodrich Pvt CT ★

BERRIEN,
Cornelius: b 1-30-1735 d p. 1800 m Jane Warner Pvt NY
John: b c. 1760 d 11-7-1815 m (1)Margaret Macpherson (2)Williaminia Sarah Eliza Moore Lt GA
Margaret Eaton: b c. 1730 d 6-   -1819 m John Berrien PS NJ

BERRINGER,
Jacob: b c. 1718/19 d p. 11-1778 m Gertrout Schneider PS NY

BERRY, (includes BEERY)
Abraham: b c. 1736 d 5-26-1799 m Elizabeth Gochenour Pvt PA
Bazil: b a. 1750 d 1823 m X Signer of Patriot's Oath MD
Benjamin: b c. 1755 d p. 7-2-1802 m Chloe — Pvt MD
Benjamin: b 1-10-1738 d 2-7-1790 m Mercy Birge Capt MA
Benjamin, Jr.: b 8-22-1739 d p. 1787 m Phoebe Perkins Pvt MA
Benjamin: b 3-15-1762 d 3-29-1860 m Mary Foss Pvt NH ★
Benjamin: b 2-21-1755 d 10-14-1838 m (1)Mary Allen (2)Nancy Blanton Pvt VA
Benjamin: b 1756 d p. 1830 m Sarah Mathews Pvt VA
Cyrus: b 12-30-1758 d 2-15-1815 m Sybil Mudge Pvt CT
David: b 10-4-1755 d 6-6-1815 m Hannah Pickering Cpl VA
Divan, Jr.: b 5-2-1735 d 12-3-1783 m Lydia Yale Capt CT
Francis: b 1754 d 1816 m Sarah Sharp Pvt VA
Francis: b 1745 d p. 1800 m Isabell — Capt VA
George: b 1754 d 8-1-1838 m Sarah Conway Lt VA
George: b c. 1729 d 6-   -1804 m X Sol PS VA
Hudson: b 9-10-1752 d 1-13-1840 m Sarah Anthony Sol NC
Isaac: b 8-15-1728 d 5-6-1803 m Sarah Crowell Pvt MA
Jabez, Sr.: b 2-1-1720/1 d p. 1790 m Rebecca Gray Pvt NY
James: b 1740/1 d — m Mary Stocker Sgt MA
James: b c. 1749 d 12-4-1836 m Margaret — Pvt PA
James: b c. 1750 d 12-4-1836 m Mary Montgomery Pvt PA
James: b 2-26-1764 d 8-20-1825 m Hannah Williams Sol PA
James: b 1757 d 11-28-1808 m Jane Doak Pvt VA
James: b 1752 d 2-l2-1822 m Sarah Grubbs Pvt VA
Jeremiah: b 5-1-1751 d 1-24-1829 m Elizabeth Marchant Pvt MA
Jeremiah: b 1721 d 1785 m (1)Hannah Locke (2)Eleanor Brackett Cpl & PS NH
Joel: b 1754 d 2-28-1843 m Ann Holsworth MM PS Pvt VA ★
John: b 1762 d 1817 m Mary Reisser Pvt CA
John: b 1741 d 12-25-1803 m Rhoda Mitchell Capt MA
John: b 2-14-1736 d p. 1790 m Sarah Libby Pvt MA
John: b 1733 d 1821 m Lucy Rice Pvt MA
John: b 1759 d 2-13-1833 m Frances Baird PS NC
John: b 1753 d 6-7-1809 m Elizabeth Gilmore Pvt MA
John: b c. 1759 d c. 1821 m Elizabeth Merritt Pvt PA
John: b 1760 d 1828 m Jane Campbell Lt VA
John: b 1735 d 1798 m Susannah Smith Pvt VA
John: b 12-27-1760 d 8-12-1838 m (1)— (2)— (3)Elizabeth Claypole Pvt VA
John: b 12-27-1764 d 11-9-1816 m Janet Given Pvt VA
John: b — d p. 8-10-1789 m Hannah — Pvt VA
Jonathan: b 12-27-1743 d 8-4-1830 m Hannah Snow Sgt MA
Jonathan: b 5-18-1737 d 5-6-1822 m Joanna Ridden Pvt MA
Jonathan: b 1754 d 2-13-1838 m Hannah Knight Pvt MA
Joseph: b 11-11-1752 d 10-9-1815 m Betsey Allard Pvt NH
Joshua: b 9-27-1755 d 9-27-1826 m Mary Cate Pvt NH
Jotham: b c. 1711 d   p. 1790 m (1)Mary Bates (2)Tryphene Sanders PS NH
Martin: b 7-26-1756 d 1852 m Elizabeth Mandeville Sol NJ
Nathaniel, Jr.: b 12-22-1755 d 8-20-1850 m Lydia — Pvt MA
Peleg: b 5-30-1746 d 6-30-1796 m Mary Kinyon Lt RI VA ★
Peter: b c. 1735 d a. 8-29-1795 m (1)Margaret Kublings (2)Maria Margaret Noacre 2Lt PA
Richard: b — d 1798 m (1) — (2)Sarah Rachel Shipley CS VA
Samuel: b 2-10-1737 d 11-23-1809 m Sarah Thorne Lt MA

Samuel: b 4-20-1741 d p. 1790 m (1)Mary Foss (2)Elizabeth Marden Pvt NH
Samuel: b 1748 d 7-20-1831 m Abigail Hall Pvt PS NH
Samuel: b 11-1-1755 d 1805 m Susannah Courter PS NJ
Samuel: b 9-27-1744 d 5-29-1811 m Molly Foster PS RI
Scottow: b 10-20-1745 d 6-12-1832 m (1)Hannah Mayo (2)Bethia — Pvt MA
Shears: b 12-25-1725 d p. 1788 m Esther Woodward Pvt MA
Sidney: b 5-20-1745 d 8-3-1820 m Catherine Waldron Maj QM NY
Stephen: b 4-21-1724 d 4-4-1820 m Mary Allen Sgt NH
Thomas: b 1745 d 1-27-1828 m Abigail Coombs Adj Lt MA
Thomas: b 2-27-1731 d 3-14-1799 m Abigail Lane Capt NH
Thomas: b 2-29-1756 d 9-15-1832 m (1)Tamson Stanton (2)Mary Jenness Pvt &MM NH ★
Thomas: b 7-   -1735 d 12-18-1818 m Frances Ann Kendall Capt VA
Thomas, Jr.: b 1750 d 1805 m Elizabeth Walker Ens VA
Thomas: b 1763 d 1835 m Hester Grey Pvt VA ★
Thomas: b 6-8-1757 d 8-7-1839 m Mildred — Pvt VA ★
William: b 8-24-1753 d 8-24-1820 m Joanna Doane Sgt MA
William: b 2-29-1720 d 9-3-1775 m Elizabeth Hobbs PS NH
Wm., Sr.: b 6-30-1723 d 11-24-1820 m Elizabeth Roseboom Pvt NY
Wm., Jr.: b 5-29-1761 d 5-   -1787 m Maria Vrooman Pvt NY
William: b 11-25-1753 d p. 1832 m Ruth — Pvt NY ★
William: b 10-10-1755 d 12-19-1838 m (1)Rebecca McCleary (2) Margaret Collins Sgt VA ★
Zachariah: b 7-11-1749 d 3-27-1845 m Mary Williams Lt MD
Zebulon: b 1760 d p. 1793 m X Pvt MA ★

BERRYHILL,
Alexander: b 1738 d 9-7-1798 m Matilda — Pvt PA
Alexander: b 1764 d 10-8-1823 m Rachel Thompson Pvt SC
Andrew, Sr.: b 1730 d 1805 m Eleanor — Ens PA
John: b c. 1742 d 1778 m Elizabeth Downs Pvt NY
Samuel: b 12-1-1759 d 5-20-1816 m Mary Brunson Ens PA
William: b 1739 d 10-28-1799 m Elizabeth — Lt NC
William: b c. 1750 d 9-2-1804 m Ruth McLean Capt PA

BERRYMAN, (includes BEREMAN)
Sarah Dishman: b 4-5-1733 d 4-19-1812 m James Berryman PS VA
Thomas: b 1761 d 1845 m Rebecca Reeves Pvt NJ ★
William: b 1713 d p. 8-21-1783 m Rebecca Vowels PS VA

BERTHOLF, (includes BARTHOLF)
Crineus: b 4-20-1750 d 12-3-1834 m Willempe Bogart Capt NJ
Henry: b 8-12-1750 d 1-24-1818 m Anna Vandervoort Ens NY
Jacobus: b 3-2-1760 d 7-26-1845 m Leah Dobbs Gnr & PS NJ
John S.: b 12-20-1760 d 1-5-1846 m Susannah Storms Pvt NJ ★
Peter: b 12-7-1746 d 12-14-1801 m Agnes Van der Bogart Capt NY
Samuel: b 4-27-1745 d 5-4-1813 m (1)Hannah Hopper (2)Elsie Alyea Pvt NY

BERTINE,
John: b 5-11-1744 d 1786/7 m (1)Mary Rodman (2)Mary Hicks Pvt NY

BERTOLET,
Daniel DeTurk: b 5-9-1741 d 11-19-1797 m Mary Yoder Pvt PS PA
John: b 1760 d 1784/1785 m Miss — Shenkle Pvt PA
John Frederick: b 8-2-1752 d 10-21-1803 m Susanna Alstadt Pvt PA
Samuel: b 9-14-1743 d 1-1-1805 m (1)Esther Frey (2)Elizabeth Frey Sol PA

BERTRON,
Abraham: b 1730 d p. 1786 m Rebecca Moses Cpl NJ
David: b 1763 d 8-4-1826 m Deborah Reading Fif NJ

BERWICK,
John: b c. 1730 d 2-7-1784 m Ann Ash PS SC
Robert: b c. 1752 d 1797 m Mary Vandervort Sol NY

BESANT, (includes BISANT)
Randolph: b — d 9-11-1777 m Catherine Lansden Pvt VA

BESOM,
Philip: b 1731 d 9-4-1797 m (1)Sarah Bubier (2)Ruth Collier Sol Slr MA

BESORE, (includes BESHORE)
Daniel: b 7-31-1732 d 1-21-1811 m Catharine Rudy Pvt PA
David: b 4-6-1760 d 7-9-1844 m Barbara Schnoderle Pvt PA
Johannes: b 10-11-1732 d 4-16-1814 m (1)Anna Maria — (2)Rosina — PS PA

BESSAC,
John William: b 2-4-1760 d 3-25-1824 m Annah Nichols Dr NJ

BESSE, (includes BESSEE, BESSEY)
Ebenezer: b 1753 d 10-24-1846 m (1)— Doughty (2)Lucy Kent Pvt MA ★
Ephraim: b c. 1740 d p. 1807 m Elizabeth — Pvt NY
Jabez, Sr: b 11-7-1738 d p. 1808 m Ruth Besse Pvt MA

Jonas: b 1760 d 1856 m Sarah Washburn Pvt MA
Joshua: b — d 1837 m Mercy Morton Drm MA

BESSON, (includes BISSON)
Charles: b 3-8-1752 d 3-28-1826 m Elizabeth Eliza Roberts Pvt PA
John: b 4-17-1750 d 6-24-1842 m Margaret Opdyke Ens NJ ★

BESSONETTE,
John: b c. 1710 d c. 1778 m (1)Mary — (2)Mrs Joyce Brelsford PS CS PA

BEST, (includes BEAST)
Christian: b 5-10-1746 d 11-28-1813 m Catherine — Sgt PA
George: b 5- -1753 d 8-19-1811 m Maria Mesick Pvt NY
Harmanus: b c. 1730 d p. 1790 m Mareitje Rivick Pvt NY
Jacob: b — d — m Annatje Tact 2Lt PS NY
John, Sr.: b c. 1720 d 3- -1788 m Eve Lounart Pvt NY
John, Jr.: b 4-24-1751 d 10-25-1820 m Margaret Mesick Lt NY
John: b 1725 d 1805 m Betsy — Lt NC
John: b 1751 d p. 1790 m X Sol NC
John I; b 3-7-1756 d 5-10-1835 m Christina Ham Pvt NY ★
Nicholas: b 5-6-1762 d 4-24-1844 m Eva Catherine Reeg Pvt PA
Nicholas: b c. 1720 d 1- -1779 m Elizabeth Catharine ——— PS PA
Peter: b c. 1758 d 2-17-1832 m (1)Christina Whittenbury (2)Elizabeth Forney (3)Leanna Van Dyke Jenkins PS NC
Thomas: b 1762 d 6-3-1807 m Elonor McClarety Pvt PA
William: b 1733 d 1823 m (1) — (2)Catharine Dorn CMman PA

BESTPITCH, (includes BESPICH)
Levin: b 1745 d a. 5-17-1802 m Dolly Jones 1Lt MD

BETHEA,
Goodman: b 1754 d 1-7-1798 m Mary — Lt SC
Jesse: b 1736 d 4- -1812 m (1)— Long (2)Mrs Elizabeth Breeden Thomas Sol SC
John: b 1740 d 8-12-1821 m (1)Absala Parker (2)Lucy — PS SC
John: b 10-20-1752 d 3-4-1812 m Mary Henagan PS Sol SC
William: b 11- -1725 d 1783-5 m Sarah Goodman PS SC

BETHEL, (includes BETHELL)
Wm.: b c. 1744 d 1804 m Nancy Stubblefield Capt NC
Wm.: b 1746 d 1813 m Rebecca Trueman Sol VA

BETSINGER,
John: b 1760 d 5-29-1848 m (2)Elizabeth Ochsen (3)Hannah — Sol NY

BETSON,
Samuel: b 1738-40 d p. 1-12-1814 m X PS NJ

BETTERLY,
Thomas, Jr.: b 4-28-1751 d 6-25-1836 m Lyda Warren Pvt MA ★
Wm.: b 11-17-1758 d 11-20-1841 m Anna Marshall Pvt MA ★

BETTERTON,
Benjamin: b 1737 d 4-18-1786 m Rebecca Harvey PS PA

BETTINGER,
Martin: b 1734 d p. 1789 m Magdalena Keller Pvt NY

BETTISWORTH,
Charles: b 11-4-1761 d 6-12-1842 m X Cpl VA ★

BETTON,
James: b 1728 d 3-18-1803 m Elizabeth Dickey PS NH
Thomas: b c. 1750 d a. 1793 m — Seth PS MD

BETTS, (includes BETTES, BETTIS, BETZ, BETZER, BITZER, BOYTS)
Aaron: b 9-16-1757 d 4-3-1833 m Clarinda Ward Pvt MA ★
Abraham: b 8-14-1743 d 1-3-1821 m (1)Elizabeth Geiger (2)Mrs Eve Bower Harvey Maj PA
Andrew: b 7-12-1749 d p. 9-2-1805 m X Pvt PA
Benjamin: b 10-20-1747 d p. 1783 m Jane Cameron Pvt CT
Elijah: b 6-5-1745 d 8- -1800 m Adah Taylor Pvt CT
Gideon: b 6-8-1730 d 9-19-1801 m Rachel St John Pvt CT
Hezekiah: b 7-31-1760 d 5-31-1837 m Grace Hanford Sol CT
Isaiah: b 1- -1758 d 6- -1844 m Hannah Thacher Ens CT
James, Jr: b 1759 d 9-17-1843 m Viletta Murdock Cpl NY W★
John: b c. 1738 d c. 1782 m Mary Wilson Pvt SC
Justus: b 9-20-1749 d 7-26-1826 m Elizabeth Darrow Pvt CT
Leonard: b 9-17-1766 d 9-21-1854 m Susannah Couch Pvt MA
Matthew: b c. 1754 d a. 9-28-1833 m Winifred — Pvt NC
Moses: b 11-22-1754 d 2-19-1818 m Mary Gregory Pvt CT
Moses: b 4-5-1751 d 6-3-1821 m Ann Sturges Pvt CT
Nathaniel: b 1752 d 1-13-1840 m (1)Hannah Mills (2)Candace Ives Ens MA ★
Samuel Comstock: b 3-2-1732 d 5-16-1823 m Mary Taylor Cpl CT
Silas: b 9-1-1752 d 9- -1789 m Sarah — Pvt CT
Silas: b 10-27-1753 d 11-2-1840 m Hannah Smith Pvt CT
Solomon: b 1755 d 10-23-1837 m Rosina Dunkel Pvt PA
Spencer: b 4-6-1759 d 11-2-1837 m (1)Nancy Fowlkes Sol VA

Stephen: b 7-16-1756 d 11-28-1832 m Ruth Church Capt CT ★
Thomas: b 3-14-1753 d 1-17-1813 m Elizabeth Smith Sgt CT
Timothy: b 5-8-1743 d c. 1818 m Mehetable Huntington Sgt CT
Urban: b 4-11-1748 d 11-2-1820 m Dorothy Baker Pvt PA
Uriah: b 2-25-1761 d 8-10-1841 m (1)Sarah Rosseter (2)Rebecca Rossiter (3)Lucy Betts Pvt CT
Wilhelmus: b 1743 d 11-9-1823 m Maria Fronica Pvt NY
Wm.: b c. 1757 d 11- -1835 m Caroline Davidson Pvt PA
Zophar, Jr.: b 1-1-1761 d 3-10-1842 m Jane Warren Pvt CT ★

BEVANS, (includes BEAVAN, BEVAN, BEVIN, BEVINS, BIBBENS, BIBBINS, BIVINS)
Benjamin: b c. 1750 d p. 6-27-1820 m Casanna — Lt MD
Charles: b 4-11-1756 d 1829 m Anne Jenkins Lt MD ★
Davis: b 8-16-1738 d 3-30-1818 m Agnes Coupland Capt PA
Ebenezer: b 2-11-1747 d 1792 m Huldah Sedgwick Pvt CT
Edward: b 1741 d 1815 m Eunice — Cpl NH
Edward, Jr.: b 4-8-1759 d 1-8-1821 m Mary — Pvt NH
Evan: b 12-22-1762 d 4-27-1849 m (1)Hannah Culver (2)Catherine Carmer Pvt NJ
Isaac: b 1-12-1746 d 12-25-1791 m Sarah Clark Sol PS CT
John: b 9-15-1760 d 2-24-1839 m Hannah Owen Pvt Fif MA NY ★
Rowland: b 5-10-1740 d 1809 m Tabitha Dennis 1Lt MD
Samuel: b 12-12-1742 d p. 1793 m Deborah — Pvt MA
Wm.: b 1714 d 12-17-1797 m (1)Sarah Parke (2)Mary — Pvt CT
Wm.: b 4-2-1746 d 12-11-1828 m (2)Polly (Melson) Hall Sol GA
Wm.: b c. 1754 d p. 11-22-1830 m (1) X (2)Eliza W. Harriss Sol SC

BEVARD,
James: b 11-29-1762 d p. 1809 m Mary Shidle Pvt MD

BEVERLY,
John: b 1753 d 1842 m Frances Morris Sol NC
Robert: b 8-21-1740 d 4-12-1800 m Maria Carter PS VA

BEVIER,
Abraham: b 1-1-1713 d 1796 m Margaret Elting Pvt NY
Abraham: b 11-18-1746 d p. 1808 m (1)Maria DuBois (2)Margrietje LeFevre (3)Naeltje Vanderbilt Pvt NY
Andries: b 4-14-1742 d 1800 m Jacomyntje DuBois Capt PS NY
Benjamin, Jr.: b 6-10-1762 d 12-13-1822 m Leah Roosa Sgt NY
David: b 11-27-1746 d 6-17-1822 m Marie Hasbrouck Adj PS NY
David: b 3-5-1764 d 1829 m Sally Ann Gear Pvt NY W★
Jacob: b 2-1-1747 d 9- -1834 m Marie York Pvt NY
Jacobus: b 8-18-1717 d 7-17-1800 m Anna Vernooy PS NY
Jesse: b 5-11-1729 d 1803 m Elizabeth Hoffman Pvt NY
Johannis: b 1-29-1724 d 1797 m (1)Rachel Lefever (2)Elizabeth Van Capt NY
Jonas: bpt 7-26-1758 d 10-4-1819 m Maria DeWitt Pvt NY
Philip Du Bois: b 12-28-1751 d 4-18-1802 m Anne De Witt Capt NY
Samuel: b 11-9-1740 d p. 1791 m Rachel Auchmaogty Lt PS NY
Solomon: b 12-4-1748 d 11-10-1810 m Nellie Griffin PS NY

BEVILLE,
James: b 11-15-1748 d 5-7-1785 m Susannah Woodley PS VA
Paul: b c. 1756 d 1- -1836 m Sarah Scruggs Pvt GA
Robert: b c. 1753 d p. 1838 m Sarah Hudson Sol GA

BEVINGTON, (includes BEAVINGTON, BEVERINGTON)
John: b 2-2-1750 d 6-10-1810 m Ruth McKinnion Pvt PA
Thomas: b 11-19-1757 d 5-9-1839 m Elizabeth Johnson Pvt PA ★

BEY,
Hugh: b c. 1755 d p. 1781 m Elizabeth Bell Gnr Bbd PA

BEYEA,
Peter: b 1735 d p. 1790 m Miss Banks Pvt NY

BEYL,
John: b 1747 d 1826 m Dorothea — CS PA

BEYMER,
Conrad: b 1740 d 1-22-1801 m Juliana — 1Lt PA

BIAYS,
Joseph: b 1753 d 1822 m Elizabeth May Capt MD

BIBB,
Benjamin: b 1746 d 1-14-1835 m Agnes Tate Sgt VA ★
Henry: b 11-11-1750 d 11- -1803 m Sarah Meade PS VA
James: b 12-28-1745 d 11- -1820 m Sallie Farrar 1Lt VA
James: b 1754 d 11-23-1846 m Nancy Fleming Sgt VA ★
John: b 9-10-1743 d p. 5-25-1790 m Elizabeth Holcombe Capt VA
Richard: b 4-13-1752 d 1-25-1839 m Lucy Booker Maj VA
Sarah Martin: b c. 1718 d 1781 m Thomas Bibb PS VA
Susannah Bigger: b 1711 d 12-22-1786 m John Bibb PS VA
Wm.: b 10-1-1735 d 1796 m (1)Hannah (Clark) Booker (2)Sarah S. Wyatt Capt PS VA
Wm.: b 1750 d 1817 m Elizabeth Atkins Pvt VA

BIBBER,
James: b 1756 d 1-29-1846 m Joanna Bailey Pvt MA

BICE, (includes BUYS)
Abraham: b 1-12-1756 d 10-14-1830 m Clarissa Scammehorn Pvt NY
Dennis: b 12-1-1745 d 7-18-1835 m Annie Ceburn 1Lt NJ ★
Simon: b c. 1717 d p. 1775 m Elizabeth Brower PS NY

BICKEL,
Adam: b 7-16-1754 d 1798 m Mary Hughes Pvt PA
Henry: b c. 1745 d c. 1779 m Esther Regina Pvt PA
Jacob: b 12-15-1754 d 12-16-1822 m Elizabeth Schidtler Pvt PA
John: b 1748 d 1840 m X Ens PA
Simon: b 2- -1750 d 1824 m Catherine Elizabeth Buchtel Pvt PA

BICKER, (includes BEKKER)
Henry: b c. 1750 d 1820 m X Col PA
Victor: b 1-1-1716 d c. 1799 m Antje Turck PS NY
Walter: b 1747 d 4-6-1821 m Wilemina Marie Welp Capt NY

BICKERS,
Nicholas: b 1744 d c. 6- -1836 m Jane — Pvt VA ★

BICKETT,
Wm.: b c. 1742 d p. 1824 m X PS MD

BICKFORD, (includes BECKFORD)
Benjamin: b 1743 d a. 1-2-1835 m Lydia Stanton Pvt MA ★
Daniel: b 1-19-1760 d 3-28-1815 m X Pvt NH
Dennis: b 1741 d 1825 m Lydia Akers Pvt NH
Eli: b 9-29-1754 d 5-5-1856 m Abigail Rand Pvt NH
George: b 7-13-1729 d 10-7-1799 m Eunice Cook Gnr MA
John: b 1759 d 4-27-1837 m Elizabeth Pearl Pvt Mar NH ★
John: b 1-4-1762 d 11-15-1827 m Joan Brown Pvt NH
Jonathan, Jr.: b 1-2-1730 d 5-11-1818 m Sarah Wilmot Cpl NH
Paul: b 4-25-1757 d 11-2-1838 m Elizabeth Kendall Pvt MA
Pierce: b 5-11-1744 d 12-18-1816 m Olive Milberg Pvt MA
Wm.: b 1743 d 1832 m Tabitha Parker 2Lt MA

BICKING,
Frederick: b 3-29-1730 d 11-4-1809 m (1)Mary Catherine Ungervast (2)Dorothea Jarrett PS PA

BICKLEY,
Charles Wesley: b 7-23-1753 d 6-1-1839 m (1)Mary Hatler (2)Delila Wingfield Pvt VA ★
Henry: b 7-1-1746 d 10-4-1807 m Margaret Heyer Arfr PA
John: b 12-7-1713 d p. 11-25-1792 m Mary Hurt PS VA
John James: b 1757 d 4-8-1807 m Mary — CS VA

BICKNELL, (includes BICKNAL)
Asa: b 4-13-1747 d 6-14-1799 m Elizabeth — Pvt RI
Benjamin: b 6-24-1727 d 3-14-1806 m (1)Mary Kingman (2)Hannah Gardner (3)Mrs Temperance Whitmarsh Pvt MA
Daniel: b 6-3-1761 d 6-1-1833 m Hannah Reed Pvt MA
Jacob: b 6-13-1751 d 4-20-1821 m Anna Hardin Fif Sgt MA
John: b 3-14-1744 d 1-25-1825 m (1)Prudence White (2)Rebecca Nash (3)Mrs Susanna Sturtevant 2Lt MA
Joseph, Jr.: b 3-20-1754 d 8-11-1826 m Abigail Turner Pvt MA
Joshua: b 1-14-1759 d 12-16-1837 m Amy Brown Pvt RI ★
Josiah: b 12-4-1760 d 5-17-1824 m (1)Penelope Abbie (2)Submit — Pvt CT ★
Lemuel: b 6-25-1739 d 2-24-1788 m Ruth Vining Pvt MA
Luke: b 10-22-1749 d 8-22-1814 m Olive Gurney Capt MA
Moses: b 11-18-1744 d 10-21-1807 m Huldah Field Pvt CT
Nathan: b 2-8-1737 d 1807 m Beulah Metcalf Pvt PS NH
Nathaniel: b 1725 d 1804 m Elizabeth Lincoln Pvt MA
Samuel: b 2-11-1752 d 1820 m (2)Elizabeth Fitchpatrick PS NC
Thomas: b 2-19-1749 d 1815 m Sabra Dexter Pvt RI
Zachariah, Sr.: b 7-25-1728 d 1802 m Patience Gardner Tower Pvt MA
Zachariah, Jr.: b 10-21-1756 d 6-29-1805 m Molly Lovell Pratt Pvt MA

BICKSLER,
Christian: b 3- -1734 d p. 10-4-1795 m Magdalena — Pvt PA
Joseph: b c. 1748 d 1801 m Mary Stettler Pvt PA

BIDDLE, (includes BITTLE)
Aaron: b 7-29-1736 d 10-19-1797 m Elizabeth Stoumez Capt NJ
Andrew: b 1740 d 1812 m Christina Cover 1Lt MD
Charles: b 12-24-1745 d 4-4-1821 m Hannah Shepard Capt PA
Clement: b 5-10-1740 d 7-14-1814 m (1)Mary Richardson (2) Rebecca Cornell Col Dep QM Gen PA
George: b 1759 d 1845 m Anna Maria Elizabeth Beale Pvt PA
Owen: b 1737 d 3-10-1799 m Sarah Parke PS PA

BIDDLECOME, (includes BIDDLECOMB)
Richard: b 2-15-1750 d 8-22-1835 m Ruth Hendricks Pvt VT ★
Thomas: b 1726 d 1813 m (1)Mary Burlingame (2)Sarah Burlingame Pvt PS MA

BIDLACK,
James, Sr.: b 10-28-1728 d 1800 m (1)Mehitable Durkee (2)Mrs Esther Lawrence Ransom Capt PA

James, Jr.: b 11-28-1750 d 7-3-1778 m Abigail Fuller Capt PA
Philemon: b 1763 d 7-8-1844 m Sarah Fleming Pvt PA

BIDWELL,
Adonijah: b 8-6-1761 d 2-14-1837 m Milicent Dench Pvt MA
Allen: b 1759 d 8-2-1823 m Anna Wood Pvt CT ★
Ashbel: b 8-23-1751 d 3-17-1830 m Prudence Roberts Pvt CT
Ashbel: b 6-20-1757 d 6-7-1825 m Mary Whiting Pvt CT
Benjamin: b 5-9-1744 d 10-31-1831 m (1)Anner Lane (2)Eunice — Capt CT
Eleazer: b 8-2-1752 d 11-2-1840 m Ruth Bidwell Sgt CT
Elisha: b 7-11-1750 d 3-14-1834 m Lydia Loomis Pvt CT ★
Ephraim: b 1759 d 6-25-1831 m Sarah Wright Pvt CT
Ephraim: b 1761 d 7-23-1830 m Dorcas Andrews Pvt CT
George: b 10-7-1756 d 4-17-1840 m Sarah Sedgwick Pvt CT
Isaac: b 8-16-1723 d 11-14-1793 m Anna Porter CS PS CT
Isaac: b 3-31-1755 d 3-9-1813 m Rhoda Beckley Pvt CT
John: b 12-28-1750 d 11- -1825 m Sarah Penfield OrdlSgt Asst Cmsry CT ★
Jonathan, Jr.: b 2-6-1745 d 5-12-1811 m Abigail Eggleston Pvt CT
Jonathan: b 1739 d 11-25-1810 m Hannah Matson PS CT
Joseph: b 7-30-1750 d c. 1824 m Theodosia Holcomb Pvt CT
Josiah: b 3-8-1760 d 9-5-1790 m (1)Denniss Giddings (2)Lucinda Kneeland Arfr CT
Nathaniel: b 1750 d 4- -1812 m (1)Martha Bixby Pvt CT
Ozias: b 1745 d 3-30-1821 m (1)Penelope Beckwith (2)Esther (Brainerd) Brooks (3)— (Butler) Smith Sgt CT ★
Phineas: b 7-9-1758 d 11-5-1835 m Mary Williams Pvt CT
Samuel: b 1720 d 4-14-1799 m Sarah Sparks Sgt PS CT
Samuel: b 3-15-1730 d 10-22-1782 m Isanak Hubbard Pvt CT
Thomas: b 1738 d 12-3-1802 m Esther Orton Capt CT
Thomas: b c. 1759 d 10-14-1826 m Elizabeth Brooks Pvt CT ★
Zebulon: b 1743 d 1777 m Mary Burnham Ens CT

BIERBOWER, (includes BEERBOWER, BIERBRAUER)
Casper: b 1736 d 1822 m Elizabeth Ashenfelter Pvt PA
Herman: b 7-16-1741 d 12-29-1801 m Christiana Hoffman Pvt PA
Philip: b 12-29-1749 d p. 12- -1811 m Elizabeth Stough Sol PA

BIERY, (includes BIERRY)
Henry: b 3-25-1741 d 5-1-1804 m Mary Salome Newhard Pvt PA
Michael: b 8-2-1739 d 9-5-1800 m Mary Eva Smith Drm PA

BIFFLE,
Jacob: b 3-2-1763 d 2-16-1844 m Mary Deaver Pvt NC ★

BIGELAR,
Nicholas: b 1747 d p. 9-4-1846 m Margaret Wiedman Pvt PA ★

BIGELOW, (includes BIGLO)
Abel: b 1-27-1755 d 10-14-1821 m Martha Bigelow Pvt MA
Abijah: b 4-16-1756 d 10-22-1848 m Mercy Amelia Spring Pvt MA
Alpheus: b 1750 d 10-13-1847 m Eunice Mixter Sgt MA ★
Amasa: b 7-10-1765 d p. 1806 m Hannah Bathrick Pvt MA
Anna Fiske: b 12-18-1731 d 10-23-1810 m Abraham Bigelow PS MA
Asa: b 5-12-1755 d 7-28-1830 m Lydia Newton Sgt Cmsry CT
Asa: b 9-13-1738 d 9-22-1807 m Rebecca Richardson Pvt MA
Asaph: b 1-27-1745 d 1-29-1824 m Martha Gleason Lt MA
Ashael: b 5-11-1755 d 3- -1806 m Martha Hall Pvt MA
Barna: b 9-11-1762 d 4-3-1840 m (1)Nabby Pride (2)Lois Griswold Pvt MA
Charles: b 4-22-1729 d 11-11-1782 m Lucy Bennett Pvt MA
Converse: b — d — m Anna Parks Cpl MA
Daniel: b 7-16-1732 d p. 1799 m Martha Pratt Pvt MA
David: b 9-19-1730 d 5-10-1810 m (1)Sarah Eaton (2)Deborah Heywood PS MA
David: b 5-7-1732 d 10-6-1820 m Patience Foote Pvt CT
Eli: b 5-29-1756 d 1830-35 m Anna Freeman Sgt CT
Elisha, Sr.: b 4-14-1731 d c. 1793 m (1)Mary Kilborn (2)Deborah Chapman (3)Thankful Beebe Pvt CT
Elisha, Jr.: b 1-7-1752 d 11-15-1826 m (1)Weltha Gorton (2)Susanna Townsend Sol CT
Elisha: b 1-11-1728 d 2-1-1814 m Sarah Goodridge Pvt MA
Ephraim: b 1761 d p. 1803 m Lydia Johnson Pvt MA
Humphrey: b 9-4-1761 d 10-2-1842 m Hannah Whipple Pvt MA ★
Ira: b 1763 d p. 1805 m Rachel Allen Pvt CT
Ithamar: b 7-30-1745 d 3-10-1807 m Persis Barrett Pvt MA
Ivory: b 10-7-1741 d 2-14-1804 m Sophia Banister Lt MA
Jabez: b 12-19-1736 d 8-13-1822 m Deborah Knowlton Lt MA
Jabez, Jr.: b 8-30-1760 d 5-30-1829 m (1)Almy Gardiner (2)Mary Sedgwick Pvt MA
James: b 1-26-1742 d 1-27-1829 m Mary Sawyer Sgt MA
James: b 6-7-1762 d 1842 m Mary Graham Pvt MA
Jedidiah: b 2-8-1714 d a. 1780 m (1)Thamesine Nurse (2)Jane Wheeler Cpl MA
Joel: b 1-9-1761 d 2-12-1849 m Lucretia Lathrop Pvt CT ★
Joel: b 6-30-1752 d 1830 m Sarah Stowell Adj VT
Joel: b 6-10-1747 d 3- -1815 m Abigail McCall Pvt VT NY
John: b 11-20-1739 d 6-23-1780 m Hannah Wadsworth Maj CT
John: b 8-24-1757 d 4-25-1843 m Persis Wright Pvt MA
John: b 11-8-1743 d 2-14-1822 m Molly Melvin Pvt MA
John: b 1765 d p. 1800 m Lydia Spring Pvt MA
Joseph: b 12-6-1759 d p. 1819 m Nancy Cheyney Pvt MA

Joshua: b 4-12-1733 d *p.* 1790 m Margery Knowlton Pvt MA
Joseph: b 1-1-1703 d 1-24-1783 m Martha Brigham PS MA
Joshua: b 2-5-1702 d 1792 m Lydia Hastings CS MA
Timothy, Sr.: b 8-2-1739 d 3-31-1790 m Anna Andrews Col MA
Josiah: b 7-30-1730 d 7-15-1810 m Mary Harrington Lt MA
Jotham, Sr.: b 9-1-1717 d 4-8-1786 m (1)Percis Temple (2)Mary Richardson PS VT
Jotham, Jr.: b 12-12-1745 d 6-18-1821 m Mary Powers Pvt MA
Noah: b 9-9-1742 d 1819 m Catherine Shay Pvt MA
Otis: b 1-4-1747 d 9-10-1832 m (1)Lydia Loomis (2)Betty Bartlett Sgt CT
Paul: b 1-21-1741 d 3-1-1806 m Hannah Ober Drm & Pvt MA
Roger: b 1755 d 2-10-1829 m Elizabeth Russel Pvt MA
Russell: b 9-26-1765 d 6-13-1838 m Lucy Sanger Pvt VT
Samuel: b 4-2-1763 d 9-4-1841 m Elizabeth Fuller Pvt NY ★
Simeon: b 4-12-1752 d 7-13-1837 m (1)Sarah Foster (2)Elizabeth Avery (3)Mrs Sarah Avery Pvt Arfr MA ★
Solomon: b 7-1-1742 d 9-12-1808 m (1)Sarah Newton (2)Hannah Sanderson Cpl & PS MA
Stephen: b 6-1-1760 d 4-3-1839 m Rachel Pike Pvt MA
Thomas: b 8-14-1753 d 3-14-1837 m Hannah Chase Cpl MA
Timothy, Jr.: b 4-30-1767 d 5-18-1821 m Lucy Prescott PS MA
Timothy: b 11-18-1739 d 9-15-1818 m Rhoda Williams 1Lt MA
Timothy: b 11-1-1738 d 11-6-1817 m Miriam How Pvt MA
Timothy: b 7-6-1764 d 4-28-1847 m Hannah Ogden Meeker Pvt NJ W★
Wm.: b 4-10-1727 d 2-15-1815 m Margaret Gates Pvt MA
Wm.: b 1-8-1764 d 12-30-1807 m Catherine Brigham Pvt MA

BIGFORD,
Samuel: b 1755 d 9-13-1848 m (1)Margret McDonald (2)Anna Reynolds Pvt NY ★

BIGGER, (includes BIGGERS, BIGGERT)
James: b — d 1827/28 m Jane Hurst Pvt PA
James: b 7-11-1761 d 5-14-1800 m Edith Wilson Sol SC
John: b 1760 d 12-30-1831 m Mary — Pvt PA
Samuel: b 1735 d 1820 m (1)Abigail Wilson (2)Mrs Mary Shannan McCune Pvt PA
Thomas: b 1750 d 2-7-1839 m Elizabeth Moore Pvt PA
Wm.: b *c.* 1720 d — m Martha Pollard PS VA

BIGGERSTAFF, (includes BICKERSTOFF)
Benjamin: b *c.* 1740 d 1780 m Mary Van Zant Sol NC
John: b 1720 d 1800 m Cynthia Pollard Adj NC

BIGGS, (includes BAGGS, BEGGS)
Benjamin: b 7-29-1760 d 5-5-1819 m Elizabeth Ohler Pvt MD
Benjamin: b 3-1-1753 d 12-2-1823 m Priscilla Metcalf Capt VA ★
John: b 5-11-1758 d 10-8-1823 m Priscilla Wilson Pvt MD
John: b 1727 d 1778 m Rebecca — Sol NC
John: b *a.* 1733 d *p.* 8-12-1789 m Bethiah — PS NC
John: b 1752 d 6-7-1782 m Abigail — Capt PA VA
John: b 1752 d 12-1-1833 m Isabella Wilson Pvt PA ★
Joseph: b 1755 d 2-1-1833 m Mary Daily Ens VA
Robert: b 1753 d 11- -1831 m Jane Miller Pvt PA ★
Thomas: b *c.* 1730 d 1780 m Sarah McDowell Barnes Capt VA
William: b 1753-55 d 1827 m Nancy — Lt MD VA
William: b 1759 d 6-28-1828 m (1)Sarah Burr (2)Nancy (Russell) Rhodes 2Lt NJ

BIGLER,
Jacob: b *c.* 1740 d *p.* 1829 m Hannah Booher Pvt MD

BIGNALL,
Robert: b 1735 d 1786 m Peggy Parrish PS NC

BIGONY,
Francis: bpt 5-19-1754 d 1-15-1827 m Marie Magdalene Brandt Pvt PA

BILDERBACK,
Charles: b 1744 d 1789 m Elizabeth — Capt PA
Jacob: b *a.* 1760 d *p.* 1-16-1832 m Mary Guthrie Pvt PA

BILES,
Daniel: b 1755 d 1835 m Jean Conger Pvt NC
Henry: b 2-29-1748 d 1-14-1811 m Eleanor Patterson Pvt PA
Thomas: b 1752 d 12-31-1844 m Tabitha Marbury Pvt NC ★

BILISOLI,
Antonio Sylvestre: b 12-17-1758 d 10-6-1845 m Marie Adelaide Accinelli Mstr FrN

BILL, (includes BILLS)
Benajah: b 6-29-1760 d 5-22-1842 m Content Park Pvt CT
Benjamin: b 1740 d 3-17-1813 m Sarah Holmes Sol CT
Daniel: b 9-23-1740 d 3-18-1829 m Deborah Denmon PS NC
Ebenezer: b 3-25-1760 d 3-13-1822 m Hannah Bullard Matr MA CL
Ebenezer: b 1-19-1751 d 2-15-1815 m Rachel Root Cpl NH
Eleazer: b 2-24-1758 d 4-4-1851 m Elizabeth Cole Pvt CT ★
Eliphalet: b 8-25-1750 d 9- -1825 m Dorothy Marsh Sol CT
Ephraim: b 8-15-1719 d 11-24-1802 m Lydia Huntington Capt CT

Jabez: b 1743 d 10-22-1832 m Olive — Lt & QM MA ★
James: b 2-20-1736 d 7-25-1823 m Asenath Norton PS CT
John E.: b 12-17-1760 d 7-9-1852 m (1)Ruth — (2)Mary Reel Pvt VA W★
Jonathan: b 4-23-1756 d 1-13-1843 m Asenath (Bill) — Sgt CT ★
Joshua: b 5-14-176? d 12-20-1841 m Abigail Miner Sol Pvtr CT
Nathaniel: b — d 4-7-1839 m Jane Damon Pvt Matr MA
Oliver: b 10-27-1737 d 5-23-1828 m Martha Skinner Sgt CT ★
Roswell: b 12-29-1753 d 10-13-1830 m Rebecca Burgess Pvt CT ★
Wm.: b 7-7-1751 d 3-19-1838 m Esther — Pvt NJ ★
Wm.: b 7-1-1758 d 11-15-1819 m Polly — Sgt VA ★

BILLHEIMER,
Christian: b 1742 d 7-19-1826 m (1)Margaretha Rath (2)Mrs Beers Pvt PA

BILLIGER,
Michael: b 1750 d 2-13-1836 m Catherine Carscadden Sgt NY

BILLINGS, (includes BILLING)
Abraham: b 7-14-1745 d 9-28-1830 m Lydia Morton 1Lt MA
Andrew: b 1743 d 4-23-1808 m Cornelia Livingston Maj NY
Benjamin: b 9-23-1753 d 1-13-1838 m (1)Mary Hewitt (2)Eunice Tracy (3)Welthea Allyn Ens CT
Benjamin: b 11-5-1744 d 3- -1829 m Rahama Palmer Pvt CT
Christopher: b 11-4-1748 d *p.* 1778 m X Pvt CT
Daniel: b 2-11-1748 d 1-15-1797 m Rebecca Battles Pvt MA
Daniel: b 2-23-1750 d 2-3-1801 m Katherine (Eldridge) Geer Ens CT
Daniel: b 11-21-1731 d 12-23-1778 m Mary Ruggles Pvt MA
Daniel, Jr.: b 12-25-1753 d 2-28-1805 m (1)Anna Hunt (2)Lydia Wheeler Pvt MA
Edmund: b 1731 d 1798 m Theodora Dyer LCol MA
Elijah, Jr.: b 2-26-1750 d 3-28-1810 m Huldah Cobb Pvt MA
Elkanah: b 4-17-1747 d 1828 m Joanna Rogers Pvt MA
Gideon: b 1-5-1759 d 10-9-1835 m Mary — Pvt MA
Jacob: b 7-1-1732 d *p.* 1795 m Rachel White Pvt MA
James: b 10-11-1751 d 11- -1829 m Sarah — Pvt CT ★
Jesse: b 1742 d 1801 m Sarah Bardwell PS MA
Jesse: b 5-8-1765 d 3-19-1849 m (1)Eleanor Wright (2)Lucy Wright (3)Olive Edwards Pvt MA ★
John: b 11-10-1751 d 8-22-1832 m Olive Noble Cpl CT
John: b 12-15-1732 d 9-6-1781 m Eunice Gallup Pvt CT
John: b 7-8-1725 d 8-31-1813 m (1)Jerusha Waite (2)Sarah Matthews MM PS MA
Jonathan, Jr.: b 1749 d 11-2-1827 m (2)Mary Fisher Pvt MA
Jonathan: b 8-3-1709 d 3-11-1783 m Dorothy Brooks PS MA
Joseph: b 4-6-1759 d 10-30-1836 m Sarah (Belcher?) Sgt CT ★
Joseph: b 11-4-1732 d 1809 m Abigail Crowfoot Cpl MA
Kane: b 1766 d 1846 m Nellie Fisher PS CT
Lemuel: b 3-26-1757 d *p.* 1832 m Hannah Whiting Sgt MA ★
Lemuel: b 7-24-1757 d 10-14-1797 m Mary Rawson Cpl MA
Nathan: b 1750 d 8-27-1818 m Myra — Sgt VT
Oliver: b 10-14-1733 d 3-23-1815 m Mehitabel Davenport Capt MA
Peleg: b 1-26-1738 d 1779 m Mary Stanton Pvt CT
Roger: b 3-19-1708 d 2- -1792 m Abigail Denison Pvt CT
Roger: b 3-15-1729 d 1-29-1802 m Sarah Billings Pvt MA
Samuel: b 1718 d 9-6-1781 m Grace Minor Pvt CT
Samuel, Jr.: b 10-29-1733 d 12-28-1817 m (1)Mary — (2)Hannah — Pvt CT
Samuel: b 1739 d 6-23-1789 m Beulah Fay Capt MA
Samuel: b 1747 d 9-12-1777 m Sarah Keech Pvt PA
Sanford: b 4-23-1736 d 4-25-1806 m Lucy Geer Capt CT
Silvanus: b 2-10-1745 d *p.* 1790 m Keturah Fosgate PS MA
Stephen, Sr.: b 3-27-1723 d 4-11-1814 m (1)Bridget Grant (2)Mrs Martha Avery Ledyard (3)Mrs Martha Wheeler Denison Capt CT
Stephen, Jr.: b 12-8-1750 d 1-29-1798 m (1)Cynthia Hewitt (2)Anne Raymond Ens CT
Stephen: b 2-23-1725 d 11-20-1805 m Elizabeth Kenny Pvt MA
Thaddeus: b 2-13-1735 d 8-2-1830 m Eunice Tiffany Pvt CT
Thomas: b *c.* 1716 d *p.* 1790 m Sarah — PS MA
Wm., Jr.: b 11-14-1742 d 2-18-1816 m Mary Leonard Capt MA
Wm.: b 8-5-1731 d 5- -1777 m Sarah Nason Pvt MA

BILLINGSLEY,
Charles: b *a.* 1765 d *a.* 1-10-1810 m Rachel — Ofr VA
Francis: b 1734/5 d *a.* 1800 m Asenath Howell PS MD
James: b 10- -1749 d 1809/10 m Ann Rea Capt NC
James, Sr.: b 1726 d 4- -1776 m Elizabeth Crabtree PS NC
John, Jr.: b 1753 d *p.* 1822 m (1)Charity Chandler Ford (2)Elizabeth Billingsley Lilly Pvt MD
John: b 12-17-1754 d 9-19-1844 m Jean Millsap Pvt NC ★
Samuel: b 1747 d 1816 m Mary — Pvt NC
Sias: b 11- -1737/38 d 12- -1819 m Hannah Webster PS MD
Walter: b 1744 d *c.* 1805 m Ruth Clark 1Cpl & PS MD
Zachariah: b 1743/4 d *c.* 1802 m Elizabeth Ashcum PS VA

BILLINGTON,
Ezekiel: b 3- -1759 d 9-29-1848 m (1)Elizabeth Penny (2)Esther Sargent Pvt NJ ★
Francis: b 1-15-1761 d *p.* 1791 m Jededial Wood Pvt MA
Isaac: b 12-10-1758 d 12-16-1829 m Rebecca West Pvt MA
John: b 11-24-1760 d 2-20-1826 m (1)Lurania Horton (2)Mercy — Pvt MA

BILLMAN, (includes BILLMANN)
Conrad: b *c.* 1740 d 1798 m Catherine Grimm Pvt PA
Jacob: b *c.* 1740 d *c.* 5- -1799 m (1)Maria Eva Ruprecht (2)Elizabeth — PS PA

BILLMEYER,
Andrew: b 11-22-1756 d 2-2-1825 m Frances Bruner Pvt PA
Jacob: b 3-14-1733 d 9-17-1812 m Hellena — Pvt PA

BILLUPS,
Edward: b 1735 d *p.* 9-9-1820 m Sarah Casey LCol VA
John: b 1743 d 7-18-1815 m Ann — Capt VA
John: b 3-17-1755 d 10-23-1814 m Susannah Cox PS VA
Joseph: b 1723 d *p.* 1780 m Ann — Capt VA
Joseph, Jr.: b 9-28-1760 d 4-5-1815 m Joice Respass Sgt VA
Richard: b 1744 d 1823 m Lucy Lilly Capt VA
Richard, Sr.: b 1750 d 2-3-1786 m Ann — Capt VA

BINEGAR,
George: b 8-28-1763 d 3-27-1837 m Mary Bennett Pvt VA

BINFORD,
Peter, Sr.: b 1701 d 1782 m Rebecca Chappell PS VA
Wm: b 4-3-1755 d 11- -1827 m Dorcas Richardson Sgt MA

BING,
John: b 10-25-1747 d 6-7-1824 m Martha Young Pvt PA
Samuel: b 9-3-1755 d 12-27-1827 m Mary Fulton Pvt MD

BINGEMAN,
Frederick: b 1-13-1755 d 10-30-1845 m Maria Christina Hufnagle Sol PA

BINGHAM, (includes BIGHAM)
Abisha: b 1730 d 1813 m Ann Sawyer Sgt CT
Alvin: b 12-20-1754 d 2-11-1841 m Elizabeth Jones Cpl CT
Benjamin: b 10-1-1730 d 5-17-1788 m (1)Sarah Stewart (2)Lois Dunbar Pvt MA
Calvin: b 10-8-1750 d 2-23-1831 m Lydia Denton Pvt VT
Charles: b 8-29-1756 d 2-5-1818 m Sarah Earle Pvt & PS PA
Ebenezer: b 1-30-1732/33 d 1-31-1811 m Amy Wood Ens CT
Eleazer: b 7-7-1745 d 2-8-1828 m Esther Loomis Sol CT
Elias: b 9-28-1753 d 5-17-1829 m (1)Vashti Elderkin (2)Hannah T. — Sol CT
Elijah: b 6-1-1719 d 1798 m (1)Theody Crane (2)Sarah Jackson PS NH
Elisha: b 7-13-1740 d 12-21-1821 m Hannah Slapp Cpl NH
Ithamar: b 9-7-1724 d 4-27-1791 m Sarah Kellogg PS CT
Jeremiah: b 8-24-1748 d 12-30-1835 m Esther Palmer Pvt CT
Jeremiah: b 6-25-1748 d 1-24-1842 m Abigail Hawks Sgt VT ★
John: b 11-26-1755 d 2-21-1808 m Eunice Warner Sgt CT
John, Jr.: b 2-2-1756 d 3-6-1836 m Talitha Waldo Pvt CT
John Clark: b 2-22-1765 d 3-11-1826 m (1)Caroline Charity Brock-way (2)Silence Harlow Pvt VT
Johnson: b 3-22-1764 d 6-8-1843 m Anna Johnson Pvt CT ★
Jonathan: b 2-20-1734/5 d 3-9-1812 m (1)Rachel Mudge (2)Elizabeth Warner (3)Abigail Ames PS NH
Joseph: b 6- -1708 d 11-4-1787 m Ruth Post PS VT
Lemuel: b 9-20-1713 d 11-3-1788 m Hannah Perkins 2Lt CT
Luther: b 5-10-1760 d 8-1-1831 m Abagail Johnson Drm CT
Nathan: b 3-24-1752 d 11-6-1812 m Zerniah Sabin Sgt CT
Nathaniel: b 5-16-1725 d 4-26-1802 m Joanna Read Pvt & PS NH
Ozias: b 6-11-1750 d 2-9-1845 m (2)Martha Rutty Pvt CT
Rial: b 6-20-1755 d 1830 m (1)Elizabeth Dockstader (2)Katherine Tyler Lt CT NY
Ripley: b 1757 d *c.* 1819 m Elizabeth Mack Sgt NH ★
Silas: b 7-29-1738 d 5-15-1840 m (1)Irene Rice (2)Mrs Lucy Kingsbury (3)Mrs Davis (4)Mrs Martha Cable Herrold Pvt VT ★
Stephen: b 11-30-1740 d 2-19-1835 m (1)Sarah Long (2)Jerusha Sprague Ens CT
Theodorius: b 1750 d 1807 m Tamar Fuller Pvt NH
Thomas: b 7-14-1742 d 9-23-1823 m Marcy House 1Lt CT ★
Thomas: b 6-20-1727 d 2-9-1807 m Amy Smith Sgt CT
Wm.: b 3-6-1737/38 d 3-19-1790 m Mrs Mary Nevins Cnt CT
Wm.: b 2-19-1756 d 6-24-1842 m Sarah Brawly Pvt NC ★
Wm.: b 1752 d *p.* 1797 m Mary Reed Ens PA
Wm.: b 4-8-1748 d 2-2-1816 m Anne Wilson Sgt PA

BINGLEY,
Lewis: b *c.* 1760 d 10-13-1799 m Elizabeth Morris Pvt VA W★

BININGER,
Isaac: b 9-12-1760 d 7-30-1827 m Elizabeth Merritt Pvt NY W★

BINKLEY,
John: b *c.*1720 d 8-8-1797 m Susanna — Pvt PA

BINNEY, (includes BENNY)
Benjamin: b 10-19-1749 d 7-16-1783 m Jane Loring Pvt MA
Elkman: b 4-27-1742 d 10-10-1809 m Olive Pittee Cpl MA
John: b 12-21-1727 d 1-23-1784 m (1)Elizabeth Ward (2)Dinah Beaman Pvt MA

Thomas: b 7-24-1738/9 d 9-19-1805 m Elizabeth Chadwick Dr MA
Wm.: b 5-3-1753 d *p.* 4-30-1797 m Sarah Neal Ens MD

BINNS,
Charles: b *a.* 1757 d *p.* 1800 m Anne Alexander CS VA
Thomas: b 11-13-1735 d *p.* 1785 m Frances Watson Pearson PS VA

BIOREN,
Benjamin: b — d 1780 m Mary Lykins Pvt PA

BIRCHARD, (includes BURCHARD)
David: b *a.* 1754 d *p.* 1800 m Mercy Mapsey Pvt MA
Elias: b 1730 d — m Sarah Jacobs Pvt CT
Elias: b 9-27-1763 d 6-1-1840 m Betsy Moore Pvt NY ★
Elisha: b 1757 d *p.* 1805 m Gerusha Butler Pvt MA
Jabez: b 5-16-1765 d 1-2-1844 m Lucina Barton Pvt MA
James: b 1731 d 7-27-1820 m Abigail King PS MA
Jesse: b 9-1-1736 d 7- -1809 m (1)Lydia Backus (2)Mrs Ruth Kennedy Pvt CT
Jonathan: b 11-14-1763 d 3-4-1839 m Beulah Ely Arfr MA ★
Joseph: b 1-1-1755/6 d 8-28-1830 m Deborah Waring Pvt PS CT
Roger: b 1758 d — m Drusilla Austin Pvt CT

BIRCKHEAD, (includes BIRKHEAD)
Christopher: b 1730 d 1788 m (1)Anne Edmondson (2)Henrietta Trippe Col MD
Francis: b *c.* 1752 d *a.* 6-7-1830 m Elizabeth Ward Pvt MD
John: b *c.* 1750 d 11-7-1821 m Mary Deborah Simmons Pvt MD
Nehemiah: b 12-29-1746 d *p.* 1816 m Elizabeth Anne Harrison Pvt PS MD

BIRD, (includes BYRD)
Aaron, Sr.: b 1-17-1732 d 11-21-1807/8 m Ann — 1Lt MA
Aaron, Jr.: b 4-7-1756 d 11-12-1822 m Johanna Glover Drm MA
Abraham: b 1737 d *p.* 8-11-1808 m Rachael Ziegler PS VA
Andrew: b 11-30-1754 d 11-30-1838 m Ann — Capt VA ★
Ebenezer: b 5-12-1761 d *p.* 9-24-1816 m Ruby Howard Drm MA
Edmund R.: b 1-26-1759 d 10-28-1835 m Eve Brewer Pvt MA ★
Edward: b 6-21-1725 d 6-2-1793 m Mary Star Pvt MA
Elijah: b 1753 d 11-20-1821 m Sarah Pratt Pvt MA
Elisha: b 5-8-1753 d 4-10-1829 m Rachel Osmun CS NJ
Empsom: b 3-25-1745 d 1-27-1802 m Mary Whitted Pvt NC
Francis Otway: b 1756 d 1804 m Anne Munford Pvt VA
George: b 7-12-1757 d 1840 m Deborah Thomas Pvt PA
George: b 1730 d 1817 m Sarah Commander Lt VA
Henry: b 1764 d *p.* 9-4-1858 m Nancy Baldwin Pvt VA ★
Isaac: b 5-5-1757 d 1-16-1829 m Rhoda Selleck Pvt CT
Isaac: b 1-18-1723/4 d 8- -1804 m Elizabeth Searle Pvt MA
Isaac: b 12-25-1746 d 5-28-1829 m Mary French Pvt MA
Jacob: b 1-9-1754 d 9-16-1799 m Sarah Mellish 2Cpl MA
James: b 6-30-1722 d 9-28-1794 m Abigail Gridley PS CT
James: b 1755 d 1830 m Cynthia — MM NJ
Jeremiah: b 1745 d *p.* 1788 m Elizabeth Marsh Pvt NJ
Jesse: b 1764 d 1847 m X Sol NC
John: b 4-4-1750 d 3-10-1777 m Joanna Esty Pvt Fif & Drm MA
John: b 3-21-1757 d 3-5-1839 m Rebecca Mantanye Pvt NJ ★
John: b 1750 d *a.* 10-25-1830 m Mary — Pvt NC
John: b 1748 d *p.* 1813 m Miss — Hamilton PS VA
Jonathan: b 1743 d 12-17-1786 m Amy Humphrey Dr CT
Joseph, Sr.: b 6-18-1733 d 6-23-1811 m Huldah Sprague Lt MA
Joseph, Jr.: b 8-8-1759 d 1840 m Cynthia Binney Pvt MA
Levin: b *c.* 1755 d 1799 m Nancy Bird Pilot in VA Navy
Mark: b 1- -1739 d *p.* 1790 m Mary Ross CS PS Col PA
Mounce: b *c.* 1729 d 1793 m Clara Ruddle Sol VA
Peter: b 1758 d 1803 m Penelope — Pvt NC
Philemon: b *c.* 1740 d *p.* 11-21-1809 m Mary Lee PS VA
Samuel: b 3-27-1724 d 5-3-1784 m (1)Mabel Jenner (2)Sarah Prout Chp CT
Samuel: b 4-26-1759 d 4-14-1824 m Susannah — Pvt MA
Samuel: b 7-27-1726 d 1787 m Anna Atherton Pvt MA
Thomas: b 1750-5 d *p.* 1827 m Judith May Sol GA
Thomas: b 1753 d 1822 m Elizabeth Hearn Sol MD
Wm.: b 1763 d 9-10-1847 m Martha — Pvt NC & VA ★
Wm.: b *a.* 1758 d *p.* 1-13-1800 m Mary — Sol NC
Williamson: b 1728 d 7-23-1806 m Phoebie Price Capt VA

BIRDSALL,
Benjamin: b 8-4-1743 d 10-8-1828 m Elizabeth Aiken LCol NY
Benjamin: b 9-17-1736 d 7-20-1798 m Freelove Jones LCol PS NY
Daniel: b 1-17-1734 d 10-29-1800 m Hannah Mandeville 2Lt NY
John: b 8-11-1727 d 9-17-1815 m (1)— Tripp (2)Rebecca Elwell PS NY
Nathan: b 1-12-1732 d 1803 m (1)Content Soule (2)Susannah Shippon (3)Ann Britt (4)Mary Cary Stevens Pvt NY
Zadock: b 8-30-1733 d 8-17-1819 m Lavinia Purdy PS NY

BIRDSEY,
Jonas A: b 9-8-1750 d 1797 m Mary — Pvt CT
Nathan: b 8-12-1714 d 1-18-1818 m Dorothy Hawley PS CT

BIRDSEYE,
Joseph: b 2-4-1740 d 5-26-1817 m Dinah Blakeman Capt CT
Thaddeus: b 4-18-1753 d 2-23-1800 m Helen Lewis Sgt CT ★

BIRDSONG, (includes FOGLESONG)
John, Sr.: b 1725 d p. 9-21-1790 m Mary — Maj PS NC
John, Jr.: b c. 1750 d 1832 m Elizabeth — Sol NC
John: b 1758 d 1848 m (1)— Ewing (2)Ruth Nail Pvt PA

BIRELY,
Lodwick: b — d p. 8-15-1803 m (1)Eva Maria Hefner (2)Rosina Schneider PS MD

BIRGE, (includes BURDGE)
Asahel: b 11-15-1731 d 11-12-1815 m Clarinda King 2Lt MA
David: b 12-11-1753 d 4-14-1836 m Abigail Howland Sgt CT
James: b10-16-1758 d 2-10-1850 m Sallie Palmer Pvt CT ★
John: b 6-9-1755 d 5-17-1838 m Ruhama Foote Pvt CT
Jonathan: b 8-10-1734 d 11-10-1776 m Priscilla Hammond Capt NY
Michael: b 5-6-1762 d 4-10-1842 m (1)Hannah Risher (2)Mrs — Quigg Sgt NY ★
Samuel: b 8-21-1756 d 11-21-1844 m (1)Nancy McCartney (2)Agnes Ann Johnson Pvt PA
Simeon: b 10- -1756 d 6-8-1854 m Experience Hamlin Pvt CT
Simeon: b 11-3-1736 d 6-8-1816 m Lois Kentfield Pvt MA

BIRNEY, (includes BURNEY)
Henry: b 1732 d 1814 m Rachel Shears Sgt PA
James: b c. 1757 d 6-13-1814 m Elizabeth — Pvt PA
John: b c. 1725 d 1794 m Catherine — PS NC
William: b c. 1740 d a. 1819 m X Pvt NC
William: b c. 1750 d 1823 m (1) X (2)Mary Maiben PS NC

BISBEE, (includes BISBY)
Aaron: b 8-20-1724 d p. 1777 m Sarah Soule Pvt MA
Abner: b 7-31-1734 d 9-28-1805 m Mary Hall Capt VT
Charles: b 1726 d 6-7-1807 m Beulah Howland Pvt MA
Ebenezer: b 1754 d 1-12-1837 m X Pvt MA ★
Ebenezer: b 2-10-1722 d p. 1790 m (1)Bethsheba Whitmarsh (2) Mehitable Shaw CS MA
Elijah: b 9-4-1746 d 4-24-1831 m Susannah Ripley 1Lt MA
Elisha: b 3-4-1757 d 12-1-1826 m Mary Pettingill Pvt MA
Hopestill: b 5-28-1741 d p. 1783 m Abigail Churchill Pvt MA
Issachor: b 4-22-1744 d 1827 m Mary Harlow Cpl MA
Joseph: b 6-16-1734 d p. 10-2-1856 m Zibiah Cook Pvt CT ★
Luther Jarvis: b 11-18-1762 d 1854 m Sarah Foster Pvt MA ★
Noah: b 5-23-1752 d 1-28-1839 m Jane Bradford Pvt MA ★
Samuel: b 3-29-1757 d ?-28-1846 m Jerusha Merchant Pvt MA

BISBING,
Bernard: b 5-21-1726 d 4-10-1799 m Margaret Heileger PS PA
George: b c. 1737 d 1808 m Elizabeth — Pvt PA

BISCOE,
James: b c. 1730 d 3- -1796 m Ann — Pvt PS MD
James: b 7-3-1760 d 12-11-1853 m (1)Elizabeth — (2)Mary Kendall NS VA W★

BISER, (includes BYSER)
Daniel: b c. 1750 d 9-29-1817 m Elizabeth Staley Sgt PS MD

BISHOP, (includes BISHOFF)
Asa: b 1-1-1750 d 1813 m Rebecca Winchell PS NY
Austin: b 5-25-1764 d 9-25-1833 m Anna Stalker Pvt CT W★
Benjamin: b 4-5-1759 d 1838 m Anna Hawkins Pvt NJ
Caleb: b 4-25-1752 d 5-20-1845 m Catherine Phillips Pvt NY
David, Sr.: b 4-20-1728 d 6-25-1792 m Andrea Fowler PS CT
David, Jr.: b 5-10-1757 d 4-19-1833 m Deborah Fowler Pvt CT
David: b c. 1750-5 d 1814/15 m Ann Schenck Maj NJ
Ebenezer: b 1-19-1746 d p. 1781 m Hannah Andrus Pvt CT
Ebenezer: b 10-14-1752 d 5-2-1820 m Lydia Grant Pvt RI
Elijah: b 2- -1763 d 3-11-1839 m Tabitha Holcomb Sgt Spy VT ★
Elkanah: b 6-2-1743 d p. 1789 m (1)Lydia Leonard Robinson (2) Lydia Paine Pvt MA
Enos: b 1-31-1724 d 8-8-1778 m (1)Elizabeth Bellamy (2)Anna — Pvt NH
Ezekiel: b 5-12-1762 d 1847 m Hannah Aldrich Pvt RI
Gabriel: b 8-26-1755 d 7-30-1811 m Sarah Every Matr & Gnr NY W★
Henry: b 4- -1757 d 6-2-1839 m Fanny Simpkins Pvt VA ★
Ichabod: b c. 1750 d 1812 m Elizabeth — PS NJ
Isaac: b 3-18-1735 d 10-9-1776 m Sarah Macomber Pvt CT
Isaac: b 12-9-1758 d 5-18-1845 m (2)Mrs Sarah Lockwood Pvt MA
Israel: b 8-27-1743 d 8-11-1821 m Hannah Peck 1Lt CT
Jacob: b 10-6-1759 d 4-10-1813 m Mary Powel Pvt PA W★
James: b 1-3-1745 d 6-16-1832 m (1)Elizabeth Wetmore (2)Mary Johnson Sgt CT ★
James: b 4-30-1751 d 8-13-1827 m Mary DeCamp Pvt NJ
James: b 1759 d 11- -1833 m Katherine Warn Pvt NY ★
Jared: b 4-2-1752 d 4-13-1818 m Sarah Goodsell Pvt CT W★
Jared: b 8-17-1753 d 11-24-1839 m Vashti Adams Pvt MA
Joel: b 10-2-1759 d 4-17-1839 m Phoebe Avery Pvt CT
John: b 9-3-1756 d 10-23-1848 m Irene Bartlett Pvt CT
John Jr.: b 10-13-1731 d - -1814 m Ruth Parker Cpl CT
John: b — d 1812 m Susanna Keim Capt PA
John: b 1736 d —m Martha Allen Sgt PA

John: b 1739 d 8-11-1828 m (1)Mary Ann Claypool (2)Catherine Iden Sol PS VA
John, Sr.: b 12-31-1730 d p. 1790 m Rachel Ruggles Pvt VT
Jonathan: b 6-24-1754 d 4-18-1840 m Anne Allen Pvt CT
Joseph: b 8-14-1758 d — m Dezire Gilbert Pvt CT
Joseph: b 3-9-1760 d 3-18-1845 m Ruth Merriman Pvt CT ★
Joshua: b 7-4-1753 d 8-15-1822 m Hannah Davis Matr NY
Josiah: b 10-7-1750 d 1-17-1821 m (2)Esther Aldrich Pvt NH
Joy, Jr.: b 10-11-1745 d 6- -1837 m Abigail Tuttle Pvt CT
Lawrence: b 5-12-1763 d 1850 m (1)— Sousley Pvt & Grd PA ★
Levi: b 12-9-1760 d 2-8-1849 m Nancy Hunt Artl NY
Levi: b 9-17-1759 d 3-26-1837 m (1)Elizabeth Grandey (2)Mrs Hannah Train Sct Cpl VT
Linus: b 5-10-1749 d 9-14-1829 m Sarah Hill Chapman Sol CT
Luman: b 8-25-1757 d p. 1784 m Lucretia Bradley Sol CT
Mathew: b c. 1747 d 1810 m Martha — Pvt VA
Moses: b a. 1761 d a. 1-15-1816 m Mary Griffin Sgt NC
Naaman: b 1-24-1746 d 2-9-1816 m Hannah Grant Cpl RI
Nathaniel: b 8-17-1739 d p. 5-1-1795 m Lydia Perkins 2Lt CT
Nathaniel: b 6-2-1751 d 2-1-1826 m (1)Ruth Bartlett (2)Nancy Pomeroy (3)Sally Reed PS MA
Newman: b 12-24-1759 d 1855 m Mary Tuttle Pvt CT
Nicholas: b 1-22-1723 d 7-21-1780 m Hannah Douglass Capt CT
Nicholas: b 1760 d 11-20-1843 m Jane Dickson Pvt SC ★
Phanuel: b 9-3-1739 d 1-6-1812 m Elizabeth Hunt Capt MA
Philip: b a. 1753 d a. 1-18-1832 m (1)Barbara — (2)Mary — Pvt PA
Reuben: b 11-2-1740 d 9-24-1775 m Hannah (Bishop)Sgt MA
Richard: b 1759 d 6-5-1829 m Mercy Gillett Pvt CT W★
Richard: b 8-9-1732 d 4-30-1806 m (1)Sarah King (2)Rachel Lee (3) Peggy Goodwell Pvt MA
Risdon: b c. 1745 d 1792 m Mrs Mary Lewis PS DE
Samuel, Jr.: b 1731 d p. 1809 m (1)Hannah Page (2)Lois Gaylord Sgt CT
Samuel: b 9-27-1730 d 5-6-1813 m Patience Cox Pvt CT
Samuel: b 1765 d 12- -1850 m Hannah Forbes Pvt CT
Samuel, Sr.: b 3-14-1699 d 6-25-1778 m Mehitable Spencer PS CT
Samuel: b 7-18-1698 d 10-2-1779 m Abigail Atwater PS CT
Seth: b 3-7-1761 d p. 9- -1842 m Prudence Dare Pvt NJ
Shotwell: b 2-10-1755 d 10-29-1827 m Anna Harned Pvt NJ
Smith: b — d 1783 m X PS Dr. MD
Solomon: b 4-20-1758 d 10-17-1843 m Elizabeth Fuller Pvt MA ★
Solomon: b c. 1755 d 12-3-1834 m Catherine — Pvt VA ★
Stephen: b 12-3-1722 d p. 1791 m Sarah Slason PS CT
Sylvanus: b 4-16-1765 d 6-1-1860 m Rachel Spicer Pvt MA ★
Thomas: b 8-1-1752 d 2-29-1801 m Amy Fargo Pvt CT W★
Thomas Fitch: b 10-20-1763 d 7-30-1851 m Lucy Foote Vol CT
Timothy: b 1-23-1771 d p. 1801 m Hannah — Pvt NH
William: b c.1748 d p. 1791 m Rebecca Leeds Pvt NJ
William: b 1731 d 1-24-1815 m Elizabeth McKallor Pvt NY
William: b 1740 d 1783 m Sarah — Pvt NC
William: b c. 1766 d 3- -1783 m Anna — Pvt PA
William: b 10-10-1737 d 11-2-1812 m (1)Mary Keech (2)Keturah Leonard Pvt RI
Zadock: b 4-24-1749 d 1840 m (1)Molly Rawson (2)Elizabeth Hale Pvt MA & RI
Zephaniah: b 6-19-1745 d 8-25-1835 m Sarah Stone Sgt MA

BISPHAM,
Benjamin: b c.1760 d p. 1789 m Hope Fortune Pvt NJ

BISSELL, (includes BIZZELL, BIZZELLE)
Benjamin: b 1-15-1754 d 2-28-1825 m Esther Benton Sgt CT
Benjamin: b 12-12-1743 d 12-12-1821 m Mabel Griswold Pvt CT ★
Benjamin: b 7-6-1764 d 12-8-1850 m Tryphena Little Pvt CT ★
Benjamin, Sr.: b 3- -1719 d 2-20-1790 m Mary Strong PS CT
Calvin: b 4-21-1753 d 10-28-1837 m Elizabeth Killbourne Pvt CT ★
Daniel: b 12-30-1754 d 8-5-1824 m (1)Rhoda Hulbert Sgt Spy CT ★
Daniel: bpt 7-20-1768/69 d 12-15-1833 m Debora Sebor OrdlSgt CT ★
Daniel, Jr.: b 4-2-1748 d 4-28-1813 m Sarah Wattles Fif CT
Daniel: b 5-3-1741 d 12-7-1823 m Bulah Rockwell Pvt MM CT
Daniel: b 2-2-1724 d a. 1824 m (1)Elizabeth Newbury (2)Elizabeth Loomis CS CT
Daniel: b c. 1726 d 1-30-1809 m Lydia Munsell PS CT
David: b 4-27-1732 d 12-16-1799 m Elizabeth Backus Pvt CT
Ebenezer: b 10-25-1743 d 11-8-1820 m Lucy Roberts Pvt CT
Ebenezer Fitch: b 1736 d 1814 m Esther Hayden Capt CT
Elias: b 6-10-1759 d 1813 m Dorothy Leavitt Cpl CT
Elijah: b 6-16-1750 d 12-3-1790 m Kesia Ellsworth Pvt CT
Elijah: b 1762 d 2-23-1825 m Rachel Cook Pvt CT
Eliphaz: b 10-11-1744 d p. 1791 m Elizabeth Birge Pvt CT
Elisha: b 5-9-1728 d 12- -1776 m (1)Mary Roberts (2)Sarah Thomas Pvt CT
Enos: b. 1742 d 10-22-1783 m X Pvt NC
Ezekiel, Jr.: b 3- -1746 d 10-1-1832 m Lucretia Spencer Pvt CT
George: b 8-6-1763 d 11-5-1838 m Lois Cone Pvt CT
George: b 1750 d 3-18-1834 m Abigail Diego Pvt CT ★
Hezekiah: b 5-20-1737 d 11-14-1831 m (1)Sabra Trumbull (2)Hannah Blodgett (3)Elizabeth Bartlett Capt CT
Isaac: b 5-8-1747 d 6-19-1823 m Alithea Way Pvt CT
Isaac: b 7-25-1749 d 7-28-1822 m Amelia Leavitt Sgt CT
Israel: b c. 1725 d 1776 m Hannah — Pvt CT

BISSELL, contd.
John Partridge: b 3-9-1759 d 3-11-1811 m Temperance Stark Pvt CT
Jonathan Marsh: b 1762 d 1850 m Submit Cushman Sol MA
Joseph: b 8-2-1730 d 1814 m Hannah Partridge Pvt CT
Josiah: b 11-17-1714 d — m Ruth Bissell PS CT
Leverett: bpt 2-1-1861 d 3-25-1813 m Sarah Newton Cpl VT CT W★
Levi: b 3-22-1747 d 12-10-1828 m Abilena Mann Pvt CT
Oliver: b 10-13-1753 d 4-7-1849 m Catherine Van Horn Pvt CT ★
Ozias: b 5-13-1731 d 11-16-1822 m (1)Mabel Roberts (2)Anner (Weston) Miller Bivins (?)Sarah Hoffman Capt CT
Russell: b 1-11-1756 d 12-18-1807 m Eunice Rockwell Ens CT
Samuel: b 3-19-1755 d 2-28-1825 m (1)Sarah Allen (2)Ann Spink Lt RI ★
Samuel: b 3-15-1755 d 3- -1820 m Sarah — Pvt RI ★
Thomas: b 12-2-1757 d 12-31-1855 m Eleanor Mills Pvt CT W★
William: b c. 1735 d p. 8-6-1800 m Hannah — Pvt NC
Zebulon: b 1724 d 12- -1777 m Abigail Smith Pvt CT

BISSETT,
Asher: b 1755 d 1805 m — Slover Pvt NJ

BITELEY,
John: b 1752 d 7-16-1840 m Martha Ellis Sgt NY ★

BITER,
Peter: b 1758 d 3-4-1827 m Eunice Strout Cpl MA ★

BITGOOD,
John: b 6-26-1761 d 10-6-1833 m Lydia Mitchell Pvt CT ★

BITTENBENDER,
Christopher: b 1750-4 d p. 1778 m Anne Miller Pvt PA
Christopher: b 1750 d p. 6-3-1791 m Maria Magdalena Fetterolf Pvt PA
Conrad: b 12- -1755 d 3-6-1824 m Elizabeth Barnett Pvt PA
Jacob: b 3-2-1752 d 2-26-1844 m Dorothy — Ens PA

BITTING,
Anthony: b 10-17-1738 d 6-27-1804 m Martha LePeau LCol PA
Joseph: b 5-19-1758 d 12-9-1844 m Catharine Graef Ordl Sgt PA

BITTINGER, (includes BETTINGER)
Michael: b 1730 d 5-29-1812 m Elizabeth — Pvt PA
Nicholas: b 6-26-1725 d 5-2-1804 m Maria Christina Reinboldt Capt PS PA

BITTNER,
Andrew: b 10-10-1759 d 1-19-1831 m Maria Schneider Pvt PA
Mathias: b 8-20-1749 d p. 1792 m Margaret Wiest Pvt PA

BITZELL,
Henry: b 1718 d 1821 m Margaret Alexander PS MD

BIXBY, (includes BYXBEE)
Aaron: b 12-23-1761 d 12-24-1841 m Mary Burrill Pvt CT
Adonijah: b 1743 d p. 1809 m Mary Brown Drm Sgt MA
Asa: b 2-24-1735 d 2-24-1809 m (1)Susanna Howard (2)Elizabeth Wilkinson Pvt MA
Asa: b 1-29-1748/9 d 6-6-1825 m Elizabeth Dane Sol NH
Benjamin: b 5-2-1759 d 2- -1829 m Margaret Walker Pvt MA CT ★
Daniel: b 8-31-1746 d 6-29-1803 m Lydia Parker Pvt NH
David: b 1757 d 12-8-1838 m Nancy Parker Pvt NH
Edward: b 9-8-1744 d 10-22-1816 m Lucy Barnes Pvt NH
Ephraim: b 4-11-1754 d 1817 m (1)Pheobe Wilder (2)Susanna Wood Cpl MA
Hull: b 1758 d a. 1825 m Mercy Bagley Pvt NY
Jacob: b 7-23-1754 d 8-26-1831 m Martha Hardy Pvt MA W★
John, Sr.: b 3-2-1736/7 d c. 1810 m Elizabeth Waring Ens CT
John: b 3-5-1747 d p. 1819 m Mary Floyd Pvt MA ★
John: b 1761 d 12-31-1830 m (1)Rebecca Goodell (2)Sally Goodell Pvt NH
Jonathan: b 5-4-1760 d 2-12-1834 m Esther Newton Cpl MA W★
Jonathan: b 9-29-1728 d 1-20-1802 m (1)Eliza — (2)Keziah Allen Pvt MA
Jonathan: b 12-15-1744 d a. 2-6-1816 m Esther Gale Sgt NH
Jonathan: b 1730 d 1-20-1812 m (1)Martha Hull (2)Elizabeth — Capt NY
Joseph: b 8-13-1758 d p. 1802 m Nancy Slawson Pvt CT
Manassah: b 1743 d 12-19-1828 m Elizabeth Dunsmore Sgt VT
Moses: b 5-4-1756 d 9-9-1826 m Dorothy Witter Pvt MA
Nathan: b 11-25-1745 d 9-15-1818 m Martha Twitchell Pvt NH
Pelatiah: b 8-9-1731 d 10-17-1822 m Ann Stone PS MA
Sampson, Jr.: b 5-3-1759 d 2-11-1847 m Sarah Richardson Pvt MA ★
Sampson: b 3-3-1731 d 1785 m Mary Bullard Pvt RI
Samuel: b 9-9-1721 d 3-3-1809 m (1)Lydia Bond (2)Rebeckah Bartlett Pvt MA
Samuel: b 5-30-1754 d 7-4-1843 m (1)Elizabeth Strong (2)Sarah Nelson Pvt NH ★
Samuel: b 1740 d 1825 m Hannah Powers Sgt VT
Solomon: b 9-30-1761 d 9-2-1835 m Lucy Taylor Pvt MA
Thomas, Jr.: b 1-28-1729 d p. 1781 m Lois Walker CS MA
Thomas: b 7-5-1752 d 1-3-1827 m (1)Rebecca Holmes (2)Rhoda Downes Ens NH

BLACHLY, (includes BLATCHLEY)
Daniel: b 1722 d 1781 m Prudence Wiser Pvt PS NY
Ebenezer: b 1735 d 4-19-1805 m Mary Wickham Dr NJ
Joshua: b 2-15-1724 d 9-2-1816 m Abigail Dudley PS CT
Moses: b 8-28-1722 d 11-16-1791 m Huldah Munger PS CT
Oliver: b 6-24-1747 d 4- -1830 m Polly Pinney Pvt CT

BLACK,
Adam: b c. 1750 d 7-16-1816 m Sarah Boyd Capt PA HEIRS ★
Alexander: b c.1761 d 3-18-1812 m Isabella Wilson Sol SC
David: b 8-4-1763 d 10-18-1832 m Catharine Cramer Pvt NY W★
Edmund: bpt 10-9-1737 d p. 1790 m Sarah Lufkin Pvt NH
Edward: c. 1725-30 d 2- -1797 m Rebecca — Pvt GA
Edward: b c. 1743 d 5-1-1793 m Elizabeth Eddy Pvt PA
George: b c. 1752 d 3-2-1831 m Betty Henry Pvt MA
George: b c. 1755 d p. 8-9-1815 m X PS NC
Hans: b c. 1728 d p. 3-10-1806 m Agness — PS NC
Henry: b 10-6-1739 d 6-15-1817 m Sarah Stowers 2Lt MA
Henry: b 1753 d 1789 m Sarah — PS NC
Henry: b 1753 d 4-19-1836 m Mary Weems Capt PA ★
Henry: b c.1735 d 9-23-1795 m Margaret — Pvt PA
Hugh: b 9-19-1759 d 11-10-1849 m (2)Martha Alexander Pvt PA
Isaac: b 1745 d 12-27-1826 m Mehetable Brown Pvt MA
Jacob: b 8-21-1763 d 10-24-1829 m (1)Margaret Grinstaff (2)Jerusha — Pvt PA
Jacob: b 7-15-1758 d 1842 m Mary — Pvt SC ★
James: b — d 1813 m Mary Moore Capt MA
James: b 1731 d 12-15-1824 m Elizabeth Black 2Lt MA
James: b 1728 d 1818 m Elizabeth Russell Pvt NC
James: b c. 1745 d 1808/9 m — Robinson Cpl PA
James, Sr.: b 1733 d 1- -1806 m Jane Thomas Pvt PA
James, Jr.: b 1760 d 1826 m Elizabeth Harrison Pvt PA
James: b 1756 d 1846 m Jane Stewart Pvt PA
James: b 1743 d p. 10-28-1803 m Jane McDonough CMman PA
James: b 3-14-1740 d 8-8-1780 m Rachel Adams Pvt PS SC
John: b 1754 d p. 1789 m Anna — Pvt GA
John: b 9-11-1737 d 1-7-1797 m Elizabeth Caldwell Capt MA
John: b a. 1753 d p. 1799 m Jeannette McNarrin Pvt NY
John: b 5-15-1737 d 11-29-1809 m Margaret Hamilton Lt NC
John, Sr.: b c. 1723 d 9-28-1790 m Abigail — Pvt PA
John: b 12-21-1755 d 7-14-1849 m (1)Jane Alexander (2)Mary Breeden CS VA
Joseph: b 1-17-1763 d 11-7-1843 m Mary Burnette Pvt NC SC ★
Joseph: b a. 2-22-1747 d a. 3-25-1825 m Jane — Lt VA
Josiah: b 1750 d 7-4-1840 Martha Cookson Pvt MA ★
Peter: b 5-15-1756 d 5-19-1820 m Lydia Dewey Cpl NY
Robert: b 1725 d 1781 m Elizabeth — Pvt PS NC
Robert: b c.1750 d 1805 m Sarah Latimore PS NC
Robert: b 1742-52 d 1790/1 m Mary Hosack Lt PA
Robert: b 10-12-1750 d 7-18-1837 m Ann Spears Pvt VA
Samuel: b 1762 d 3-16-1838 m Catharine Van Leer Pvt PA
Samuel: b 1727 d 12-28-1782 m Jane Porter 2Lt VA
Steward: b c.1753 d p. 1792 m Anna Parmenter Ens MA
Thomas: b 1747 d 4-27-1807 m Frances Howell Pvt PA
Thomas: b 1743 d 6-27-1811 m (1)Margaret — (2)Mary — Sol PS SC
Thomas: c. 1745 d c. 1814 m (1)— Skipwith (2)Susannah — Capt PS VA
Thomas Osborn: b a. 1750 d 1831 m — Springs Pvt NC
William: b 12- -1753 d 4-2-1837 m Elizabeth — Pvt NC & GA ★
William: b 6-5-1762 d 8-10-1837 m Mary Jane Cooper Pvt NC & SC ★
William: b 1754 d 2-22-1823 m Elizabeth — Pvt PA
William: b c. 1735 d 2-14-1811 m Sarah Hickling Lt VA

BLACKBURN, (includes BLACKROURNE)
Ambrose: b 1750 d 1820 m Francis Jones Halbert Capt SC
Andrew: b 1728 d 1785 m Virginia Anne Wilson PS VA
Clement: b 2-11-1760 d 2-7-1843 m Mary Lewis Pvt VA ★
Edward: b c. 1729 d 1800 m Margaret Harrison PS VA
Ephraim: b 1754 d 12-19-1802 m Prudence Rich Capt PA
James: b c.1745 d p. 8-8-1810 m Jane — Pvt VA
John: b 6-21-1751 d 1825/6 m Jane Armstrong Lt PA
John: b c. 1745 d p. 1790 m Nancy Maxwell Pvt PA
John: b 1752 d 1- -1835 m (1)Mary — (2)Elizabeth Henderson 1Lt PA ★
John: b. 1-27-1741 d 2-8-1808 m Janet Mathes Sol VA
John: b c. 1736 d 1814 m Mary — Pvt PS VA
Joseph: b 5-28-1757 d 7-30-1831 m (1) X (2)Martha Brookins Pvt PA
Julius: b 9-14-1756 d 3-3-1822 m Betsy Scruggs Sgt VA
Moses: b 1753 d p. 8-8-1833 m Margaret McKnight Pvt MA ★
Robert: b 1742 d 2-9-1808 m Sarah Richie Pvt VA
Samuel: b c. 1745 d p. 1810 m Mary Hinman Pvt VA
Thomas: b 1742 d 10-27-1807 m Christian Scott Lt VA
William: b c. 1748 d 10-7-1780 m Elizabeth Black Lt PA
William: b 2-12-1757 d 3-13-1841 m Sally Baird Sgt VA ★

BLACKERBY,
Jeduthan: b c. 1750 d 8-29-1829 m Mary Ann Chamberlayne Pvt VA
Thomas, Jr.: b 1725 d 12-28-1776 m Susan Watson Pvt VA

BLACKFORD,
Ephraim: b 1-20-1760 d 1-9-1820 m Mary Burnett Pvt NJ
Jacob: b 1759 d 5-1-1847 m (3)Margaret Zimmerman Pvt PA ★

Jeremiah: b 10-10-1752 d 1825 m Mary Kelly Pvt NJ
John: b 2-23-1713 d 1786 m Hannah — Pvt NJ
Nathan: b 7-14-1756 d 8-21-1851 m Rachel Runyon Pvt NJ ★

BLACKINTON,
Benjamin: b 1-4-1746/47 d 9-6-1812 m Eunice Woodcock Sgt MA
George: b 9-15-1744 d c. 1816 m Marcy Wolcott Pvt MA
Oliver: b 1734 d 12-16-1811 m Mary Whipple Pvt MA
Peter: b 5-13-1761 d 2-27-1802 m Hepsibah — Pvt MA
William: b 11-2-1758 d 1-30-1816 m Elizabeth Babcock Pvt MA

BLACKLEDGE, (includes BLACKLIDGE)
Ichabod: b 1-1-1745 d 6-15-1829 m Susan Woodruff Pvt NJ
John: b c. 1756 d c. 1800 m Phoebe Winans Pvt NJ
Richard: b —d p. 2-20-1776 m Ann Bass PS NC

BLACKLER,
William: b 1740 d 6-9-1818 m (1)Mary Ingalls (2)Rebecca Chipman CS Capt MA
William: bpt 3-1-1752 d 11-17-1786 m Elizabeth Jackson Pvt Drm MA

BLACKMAN, (includes BLACKMON, BLAKEMAN)
Charles: b 2-3-1760 d p. 1830 m Ruth Crane Pvt CT
Daniel: b 6-17-1748 d 8-1-1833 m Mary Hubbell Ens CT ★
David: b 12-18-1746 d 6-22-1821 m Mary Scull MM NJ
Elijah: b 2-21-1739/40 d 5-15-1822 m Elizabeth Hall Capt MA
Elisha: b 9-22-1760 d 12-17-1787 m Ruth Blackman Pvt CT
Elisha, Sr.: b 9-19-1717 d 9- -1804 m Mrs Lucy Polly Smith 2LT CT
Elisha, Jr.: b 4-4-1760 d 12-5-1845 m Anna Hurlbut Pvt PA ★
Enoch: b 9-15-1762 d c. 1846 m Abigail — Sgt CT
George Sr.: b 7-31-1728 d 7-24-1798 m (1)Amee Dwelley (2)Ruth Morse 2Lt MA
George Jr.: b 1761 d 3-20-1807 m Phebe Strong Pvt MA
Ichabod: b 3-24-1762 d 4- -1798 m Elizabeth Franklin Pvt PA
James: b 4-17-1747 d 5-7-1835 m (1)Sarah Frost (2)Ann Curtis Pvt CT W★
Jonas: b 1730 d c. 1785 m Elizabeth Smith Lt CT
Moses: b 12-30-1753 d 8-15-1798 m Mrs Prudence Tileston Pvt MA
Nathaniel: b 7-24-1738 d 1815 m Huldah Wells Lt CT
Nehemiah: b c. 1742 d p. 1790 m Abiah Booth Sol CT
Samuel: b 9-12-1726 d11-21-1826 m Mehetabell Curtis PS CT
Samuel, Jr.: b 1758 d 1826 m Phoebe Beardsley Pvt CT
Samuel: b 10-18-1759 d 4-4-1837 m Abigail Wentworth Pvt MA
Samuel, Jr.: b 1762 d 1855 m Jerusha Babcock Pvt MA ★
William: b 11-10-1745 d 3-10-1832 m Martha Babcock Pvt CT
William: b c. 1740 d p. 1795 m Elizabeth Bryan Pvt NC
Zachariah: b 7-14-1720 d 7-11-1779 m Elizabeth Hull Sol CT
Zachariah, Jr.: b c. 1753 d 4-23-1835 m (1)Anne Hawley (2)Sarah Beard Pvt CT
Zachariah: b 7-12-1760 d 6-5-1851 m Alice Swift Pvt CT ★

BLACKMORE, (includes BLACKMAR)
Abner: b c. 1754 d p. 1783 m Anne — Sol RI
Amaziah: b 3-16-1755 d p. 1802 m Candace Simmons Sgt RI
Ephraim: b 7-20-1755 d 2-27-1796 m Mary Jones Pvt MA
George: b 2-20-1760 d 9-27-1833 m Mrs. Elizabeth Montgomery Pvt MD ★
George: b 5-14-1763 d 8-24-1837 m Sarah Thompson Drm VA ★
Jacob: b 4-12-1760 d 4-17-1853 m (1)Phebe Ann Green (2)Zeruah Brown Pvt RI ★
John: b c. 1720 d p. 1790 m Mary Mitchell Cpl RI
Joseph: b 4-6-1729 d 2-12-1795 m Mary Corbit Pvt MA
Samuel: b 1736 d a. 8-27-1787 m Abrilla Dowden Capt MD & PA
Samuel: b 6-14-1740 d 4-5-1813 m Abigail Brunson Pvt VT
Solomon: b 5-4-1730 d 1805 m Janet Thompson Pvt MA
Stephen: b 1-2-1749 d p. 1790 m Lydia A. White Pvt CT
William: b 1745 d c. 1811 m Sarah Dawson Capt MD
William: b 1736 d 5-16-1822 m Lydia Record Pvt MA

BLACKSHEAR, (includes BLACKSHIRE)
Alexander: b c.1705-8 d p. 10-3-1785 m Agnes — PS NC
David: b 1-31-1764 d 7-4-1837 m (1)Mrs Catherine Bush (2)Frances Hamilton Pvt GA
Ebenezer: b 12-15-1750 d p. 3-31-1831 m (1)X (2)X (3)Elizabeth — Pvt DE ★
Edward: b 1-20-1762 d 9-3-1829 m Emily Goodwin Mitchell Sct NC
James, Sr.: b — d 1788 m Catherine Bush Lt NC

BLACKSTOCK,
William, Jr.: b 1750 d 5- -1841 m Mary Yarbrough Sol SC

BLACKSTONE,
John, Sr.: b 7-18-1699 d 1-3-1785 m (1)Elizabeth Foote (2)Rebecca Harrison (3)Sarah Huggins PS CT
John, Jr.: b 5-7-1733 d 8-18-1818 m Rebecca Baldwin PS CT
John, 3rd: b 4-24-1763 d 7-29-1841 m Rebekah Foote Pvt CT ★
Nehemiah Herbert: b c. 1740 d 1816 m (1)Mary Cheseldein (2) Eleanor Gardiner Hebb PS MD
Prideaux: b c. 1751 d 2-20-1778 m Bridget Shrader Pvt VA

BLACKWELDER,
Caleb: b 11-8-1722 d 9-26-1794 m Betsey Phifer PS NC

Isaac: b 11-17-1757 d 1843 m (1)Mary Phifer (2)Mary Redling Sgt NC ★
Mary Decker: b c. 1705 d 1785 m Caleb Blackwelder PS NC

BLACKWELL, (includes BLACKWALL)
Benjamin: b 4-29-1756 d 6-2-1831 m Parmelia Drake Pvt NJ W★
Elijah: b 3-7-1761 d p. 9-3-1832 m Martha Lanning Pvt NJ ★
Jacob: b 11-20-1717 d 10-23-1780 m (1)Frances Sackett (2)Lydia Hallett PS Col NY
James: b 1750 d p. 5-12-1810 m Temperance Pope Pvt NC
John Eustace: b 3-22-1755 d 1808 m (1)Agatha Ann Eustace (2) Judith Peachy (3)Nancy Blackwell Capt VA
Joseph: b c. 1746 d 1806 m Sally Chandler Banks Sol GA
Joseph: b 8- -1757 d 9-15-1823 m (1)Ann Greyson Gibson (2)Mary Waddy Brent Capt VA ★
Joseph, Sr.: b 7-9-1715 d 5-30-1787 m Lucy Steptoe PS VA
Joseph, Jr.: b 1750 d 10- -1826 m Mrs Ann Eustace Hull Lt QM VA W★
Joshua: b 1747 d 1-15-1822 m Bathsheba— Pvt MA
Micah: b 12-28-1741 d 9-20-1781 m Lydia Tobey Pvt QM MA
Robert: b 1730 d 5-1-1789 m Elizabeth Goodwin Capt VA
Robert: b 5-2-1766 d p. 8-25-1856 m Mary White Pvt VA
Samuel: b a. 1735 d p. 1791 m Elizabeth Dozier PS SC
Samuel, Jr.: b 11-20-1731 d c. 1781 m Sarah — Capt VA
Stephen: b 1756 d 12-3-1831 m Rachel Hunt Pvt NJ
Thomas: b c. 1775 d 8-20-1830 m Elizabeth Burgess Pvt MA
Thomas: b 1751/52 d 4-28-1831 m Judith Grant Capt VA ★
Thomas: b 1760 d 1837 m (1)Mary Debuam (2)Polly Kittrell Pvt VA

BLACKWOOD,
James: b 1744 d 12-16-1836 m Nancy — Matr Cpl MA ★
William: b 1706 d 1790 m Elizabeth Craig PM NC

BLADES,
Samuel: b c. 1727 d p. 1-29-1825 m (1)Amelia Barnes (2)Mary Pilchard Pvt PS MD

BLAGGE,
Benjamin: bpt 7-3-1709 d c. 1709 m Sarah Browne PS NY

BLAGROVE,
Benjamin: b — d p. 1784 m (2)Sarah Pelham PS VA

BLAINE, (includes BLAIN, BLEAN)
Alaim: b 1758 d 11-22-1846 m Catherine Reed Pvt CL ★
Alexander: b 1735 d 1798 m Miss — Hoge Pvt PA
David: b 1725 d 1804 m Isabella F. Hill Almoner PA
Ephraim: b 5-26-1741 d 2-18-1804 m (1)Rebecca Galbraith Cmsry Gen PA
George: b c. 1735 d p. 1-13-1805 m (1) X (2)Lucy — PS VA
Jacob: b c. 1763 d 12-18-1813 m (1)— Hoagland (2)— Dickinson (3)Nancy Robinson Pvt NJ
James, Sr.: b c. 1718 d 7- -1792 m (1)Isabella — (2)Elizabeth Carscaddon Lt PA
James: b 1763 d p. 3-27-1815 m Deborah Baird Cpl VA
John: b a. 1731 d 1817 m Jane — Pvt NY
Thomas: b 1744 d p. 1797 m X 2Lt NY
Thomas: b 3-23-1765 d 4-26-1839 m Esther Scott Pvt NY
Thomas: b — d 4- -1807 m Sarah Wilson Pvt PA
William: b c. 1722 d 10- -1779 m Hannah — Maj NY

BLAIR,
Abraham: b 6-15-1756 d 10-2-1846 m Elizabeth Leech Pvt NJ ★
Absalom: b 12-2-1742 d 4-28-1811 m Martha Young 2Lt MA
Alexander: b 9-22-1739 d p. 1838 m Elizabeth Marr Pvt MA
Allen: b 7-8-1754 d 4-23-1835 m Mary Ann Staples Pvt VA ★
Archibald: b 1753 d 10-7-1824 m Mary Whiting PS CS VA
Charles: b 1753 d 12-12-1810 m Mary Smyth Pvt PA
David: b 3-30-1749 d p. 1779 m Miriam Boise Lt MA
Jacob: b 4-13-1735 d 11-18-1815 m Martha Gilmore Pvt CS MA
James: bpt 10-23-1748 d 4-13-1832 m (1)Sally Josslyn (2)Mrs Ann Hager Sgt MA
James: b 1753 d 4-28-1838 m (1)Mehitabel Robinson (2)Mrs Mary Monroe Pvt MA ★
James: b 1763 d 1848 m Molly Chaffee Pvt Grd NH
James: b 3-6-1761 d 10-16-1839 m (1)Elizabeth Powell (2)Elizabeth Cleveland Ens Spy NC ★
James: b 1738 d 4- -1828 m Martha Elliott Pvt PA
James: b 1753 d p. 1796 m Margaret Jenkins Cav & Sol SC
James: b 7-16-1752 d 8-26-1824 m (2)Amelia Hagerman Pvt VA
Joel: b 5-31-1757 d 2-17-1839 m Polly Lawson Pvt MA ★
John: b 4-23-1743 d 9-28-1814 m Elisabeth Halbert Sgt PS MA
John: b 1755 d 1779-85 m Jane Miller Pvt MA
John: b c.1723 d 3-9-1780 m (1)Nancy Brown (2)Mary Freeman Pvt PS NH
John, Jr.: b 1758 d 7-13-1818 m Susanna Kelsey 1Lt NJ ★
John, Sr.: b 1720-4 d 3-7-1789 m Sarah — Col NY
John, Jr: b 2-25-1754 d 12-9-1826 m Jean Rogers Pvt NY
John: b 4-28-1750 d 12-17-1819 m (1)Jean Gamble (2)Hannah Caruthers Sol NC
John: b 1754 d 1818 m Susanna Ewing Lt PA
John, Sr: b c. 1737 d 1799 m Martha Laird Pvt PA

BLAIR, contd.

John: b 1764 d 1846 m Frances Hill Pvt SC
John: b 1728 d 1808 m Jane Robertson Capt VA
Johnson: b — d c. 1818 m Martha Ann Roberson Sol GA
Reuben: b 1755 d 1-14-1834 m Susan Shepard Cpl MA
Reuben: b 2-12-1763 d 7-16-1856 m (1)Tryphena Moses (2)Hannah Nobel Pvt MA
Robert: b 3-26-1756 d 9-20-1837 m Elizabeth Harrington Pvtr MA
Robert: b 6-10-1720 d 6-22-1801 m Hannah Thompson PS MA
Robert: b 1762 d 3-11-1841 m Mary Osborne Pvt NJ ★
Robert: b 8-10-1744 d 10-18-1794 m Lydia House Pvt NY
Rufus: b 2-24-1758 d 10-7-1800 m Dolly Boise Pvt MA
Samuel: b 1743 d 4-15-1827 m (1)Margaret Smith (2)Mary — 3Sgt MA
Samuel: b 6-14-1759 d 1836 m Elizabeth Tinder Pvt NC ★
Samuel: b 1758 d 5-8-1825 m Rebecca Hetherington Pvt Sct PA W★
Seth: b 11-29-1760 d 5-6-1852 m Hannah McAllister Pvt MA
Sibbiah Earl: b 1754 d 1815 m William Blair PS GA
Thomas: b c. 1740 d 1825 m X 2Maj NC
Thomas: c. 1760 d 9-10-1808 m X Capt PA
Thomas: b 1756 d 9-15-1800 m Sarah Wolf Pvt PA
Thomas: b 1762 d 12-29-1840 m (1)Margaret — (2)Rachel — Sol SC
William: b c. 1748 d — m Sibbiah Earle Pvt GA
William: b 5-20-1750 d 10-12-1825 m Elizabeth Little Pvt NH
William: b 4-4-1754 d 12-28-1829 m Jane Mason Pvt NJ
William, Sr.: b 1729 d 12-7-1802 m Mary Cowan Lt PA
William, Jr.: b 10-14-1760 d 3-21-1792 m Sarah Holmes Pvt PA
William: b c. 1748 d p. 1790 m X Pvt PA
William: b c. 1750 d 1- -1789 m Sarah Sutter Pvt PS PA
William: b 12- -1760 d 4- -1840 m Catherine Evans Pvt PA ★
William: b 1731 d 1799 m Phoebe Harris Sol PA
William: bpt 7-5-1741 d 1788 m Elizabeth Downey Capt VA

BLAISDELL, (includes BLASDEL, BLASDELL)

Daniel: b 2-13-1739 d p. 1780 m Mary Allen Pvt MA
Daniel: b 1-25-1762 d 11-10-1833 m Sally Springer Pvt NH ★
David: b 2-21-1736 d 1794 m Judith Jewell Pvt PS MA
Ebenezer: b 4-9-1715 d p. 10-12-1798 m (1)Lydia Webber (2)Sarah Johnson (3)Sarah Stover Pvt MA
Enoch: b 7-9-1714 d 2-12-1790 m Mary Satterly Pvt MA
Ephraim: b 6-15-1740 d 3-9-1814 m Susanna Barnard Sgt MA
Ephraim: b 9-23-1717 d p. 10-9-1786 m Thankful Webber CS ME
Ezra: b 2-22-1757 d 2-15-1840 m Deborah Batchelor Pvt MA ★
Henry, Jr.: b 1740 d 10-11-1831 m (1)Elizabeth Foot (2)Sarah Foster Pvt NH
Henry: b 9- -1736 d 8- -1828 m (1)Mary Currier (2)Sarah Dolloffe (3)Mrs Hannah Ross (4)Hannah Nicholson PS NH
Isaac, Sr.: b 3-27-1738 d 10-9-1791 m Mary Currier CS PS NH
Isaac, Jr.: b 6-2-1760 d 3-11-1817 m (1)Elizabeth Green (2)Sabra Green (3)Abigail Pettingill Cpl NH
Jacob: b 7-23-1735 d 10-16-1818 m (1)Judith Currier (2)Lydia Morrill (3)Mrs Elizabeth Sanborn Lt PS NH
Jacob: b 4-8-1754 d 4-25-1831 m Ruth Morse Pvt NH
Jedediah: b 5-4-1754 d 1-13-1844 m Lydia Trafton Pvt MA
Jeremiah: b 2-11-1749 d 1794 m Elizabeth Ross Pvt MA
John: b 1733 d 11-28-1799 m Judith Shepard Cpl & PS NH
John: b 5-9-1760 d 2-4-1835 m Dorothy Carter Pvt NH ★
John: b 9-15-1765 d 11-8-1848 m (1)Anna Smith (2)Laney Baldwin Pvt NH ★
Jonathan: b 10-17-1748 d 1781 m Hannah Elliott Armr MA
John: b 8-15-1756 d 8-30-1823 m (1)Abigail LeGro (2)Mrs Sarah Horne Sgt MA
Johathan: b 8-15-1709 d 1782 m Hannah Jones PS NH
Levi: b 9-20-1757 d 6-1-1833 m Mary Cronk Sgt MA
Nathaniel: b 4-6-1721 d 12-22-1786 m Mary Blay PS Pvt NH
Oliver: b 6-16-1744 d 12-17-1796 m Catherine Sargent PS NH
Parrit: b 1-11-1759 d 8-3-1836 m Ruth Folsom Ball Pvt MA & NH
William: b 11-30-1756 d 1818-20 m Lydia Robbins Pvt MA ★

BLAKE,

Aaron: b 4-24-1730 d 4-10-1796 m Mehitable Ellis Pvt PS MA
Abraham, Sr.: b 8-17-1732 d 3-15-1790 m Silence Whiting Bbd MA
Ariel: b 6-30-1756 d 10-9-1827 m (1)Hannah Metcalf (2)Phyllis Jillson Pvt NH
Benjamin: b 5-9-1739 d 10-12-1809 m Elizabeth Harris Pvt MA
Benjamin, Jr.: b c. 1765 d 3- -1837 m Phebe Lombard Pvt MA
Benjamin: b 2-3-1731 d 2-12-1824 m Molly Connor Pvt PS MA
David: b 2-25-1762 d 10- -1843 m (1)Hannah Messer (2)Lovicey Evans Pvt NH
Ebenezer: b 1-15-1750 d 6-3-1801 m Keziah Munroe Sgt CT
Ebenezer: b 1761 d 8-14-1843 m (1)Dorcas Worcester (2)Chloe Bond Sgt MA
Edward: b 7-4-1736 d 11-9-1818 m Mercy Thayer Capt MA
Edward: b 12-22-1742 d 4-21-1824 m (1)Rebecca True (2)Mrs Sarah Smith Underwood Pvt MA
Eleazer: b 4-1-1757 d 9-27-1852 m Jerusha Gerould Sgt MA ★
Elijah : b 6-18-1756 d 10-2-1833 m Sarah Hamlin Pvt CT ★
Ezekiel: b 8-26-1735 d 11-10-1775 m Rachel Bent Lt MA
Ezra: b 1-11-1746/7 d 5-25-1838 m (1)Abigail Read (2)Melatiah Ray Cpl MA
Francis: b c. 1756-8 d 1827-9 m Susan Wanamaker Pvt NH

Freelove: b 7-29-1745 d 4-1-1825 m (1)Sarah — (2)Rachel — (3)Olive — Pvt CT
Freelove: b 8-11-1751 d 1815 m Louis Louisa Spencer Pvt CT
George: b 10-3-1758 d 12-17-1851 m Huldah Leonard Drm MA ★
Henry, Jr.: b 11-22-1755 d 7-12-1833 m Molly Colby Fif NH
Hezekiah: bpt 6-25-1751 d 5-19-1821 m Hannah — Sgt PS NH
Increase: b 10-28-1726 d 2-28-1795 m (1)Anne Crafts (2)Elizabeth Bridge PS MA
Isham: b 6-21-1755 d 1830 m (1)Mary Macy Clifton Pvt Fif NC
Jacob: b 3-17-1747 d 1-30-1837 m Mary Bowker Pvt MA
James: b 1746 d 9-4-1802 m (1)Sarah Fillebrown (2)Thankful Babcock (3)Sarah Rawson Pvt MA
Jethro: b 1747 d 4-11-1831 m Dolly Stordley Sgt NH
John: b 8-29-1753 d 1-12-1842 m Mary Dupee Lt MA ★
John: b 10-30-1716 d 6-23-1812 m Elizabeth Bragg Pvt MA
John: b c. 1760 d 3- -1827 m Deborah Tuckerman Pvt ME ★
John, Sr.: b 4-5-1736 d p. 1790 m Jane Webber PS ME
John: b 1733 d 1-28-1818 m Mary Norris Pvt NY
John: b 7-3-1746 d 8-7-1828 m Mary T. Smith Pvt CL
John: b 1752 d 7-2-1810 m Margaret Mercier 1Lt SC
John: bpt 2-21-1737/8 d p. 6-11-1784 m Alice Hackney Pvt VA
Jonathan: b 1-1-1749 d 10-8-1836 m Sarah Pierce Adj MA
Jonathan: b 6-12-1742 d 5-24-1817 m Mary Brown PS NH
Joseph: b 6-17-1760 d 12-11-1843 m Elizabeth Benson Blake Ens MD
Joseph: b 1757 d 1-27-1840 m Hannah Hopkins 2Sgt MA & CL
Josiah: b 12-30-1759 d 7-14-1840 m (2)Betsey Lyon (3)Sarah Ferguson Sol MA ★
Josiah: b 1-5-1725 d 11-9-1790 m Elizabeth Brown Sgt NH
Michael: b 3-22-1748 d 7-3-1794 m Eliza Buller Pvt PA
Nathan: b 3-13-1712 d 8-4-1811 m (1)Elizabeth Graves (2)Mrs Mary Brinton PS NH
Nathan, Jr.: b 5-1-1752 d 1-10-1813 m Bathsheba Day Pvt NH
Nathan: b 1756 d 5-5-1799 m Mary Cross Pvt NH
Nathan: b 6-4-1705 d 3-5-1783 m Judith Batchelder PS NH
Nathaniel: b 12-19-1758 d 5-14-1806 m Anna Robinson Pvt MA
Nathaniel: b 10-1-1753 d 2-28-1843 m Mary Fogg Sol MA
Nicholas: b c. 1756 d 9-5-1831 m Dorcas Freeland Pvt PA
Oliver Smith: b 11-6-1742 d 2-16-1823 m Deborah Ingalls PS Sgt NH
Paul: b 1758 d 1-22-1806 m Abigail Giles Ordl Sgt NH
Payne: b. 1740 d p. 1790 m (1)Dorothy Sanborn (2)Polly Leach PS NH
Philemon: b 3-12-1706 d 1789 m Lydia Boulter PS NH
Philemon: b 7-30-1738/9 d 1-10-1826 m Tabitha Tuck Sgt NH
Philip: b 3-6-1746 d 12-16-1836 m (1)Sarah Allen (2)Beriah Lawrence (3)Mrs Olive Whiting Sgt CS MA
Reuben: b 1765 d 11-7-1831 m Eunice Baldwin Sol CT
Richard: b 10-7-1747 d 9-17-1807 m Damaris Smedley Pvt CT
Robert: b 3-25-1739 d 9-12-1800 m Martha Hancock Pvt MA
Robert: b 1752 d p. 1783 m Martha Dudley Pvt NH
Samuel: b 4-3-1747 d 1-11-1802 m Abigail Record Sgt MA
Samuel: b 12-31-1759 d 11-6-1813 m (1)Eunice Rockwood (2)Lois Partridge (3)Mary Phillips Matr MA
Samuel: b 8-17-1718 d 8-19-1801 m (1)Sarah Libby (2)Sarah Bickford PS NH
Samuel: b 7-14-1732 d 10-31-1817 m Mary Garland PS NH
Samuel: b 1725 d 4-14-1797 m Molly Baird PS NH
Seth: b 2-19-1752 d 3-4-1829 m Ruexbe Marshall Pvt Matr MA ★
Solomon, Sr.: b 10-10-1737 d 1-5-1824 m Sybil Richardson Cpl MA
Solomon: b 10-8-1734 d 2-8-1825 m Abial Pond Pvt MA
Thomas: b 10-7-1752 d 2-16-1840 m Mary Barnard Pvt MA
Thomas: b a. 1740 d p. 1790 m Mary Gordan Lt PM NH
Thomas: b c. 1746 d a. 9- -1846 m Eva Westbrook Pvt VA ★
Warner: b c. 1763 d a. 11-23-1812 m Elizabeth — PS VA
William: b 1757/58 d 2-23-1813 m Deborah Willson Pvt PS MD
William, Sr.: b 1741 d 2-24-1825 m Sarah Taylor Sgt NH
William: b c. 1745 d p. 10-8-1796 m (2)Mrs Lucy Mobley Pvt NC
William: b 1703 d 1798 m (2)Rachel Williams Pvt VA

BLAKEMORE,

George: b 5-23-1759 d 7-23-1833 m Elizabeth Mauzey Lt VA
John: b 1762 d 4-18-1856 m Sallie Keene Pvt VA ★
Thomas: b 6-19-1718 d 10-26-1808 m Ann Neville Pvt VA

BLAKENEY,

John, Sr.: b c. 1732 d 8-8-1832 m Mary E. — Capt SC
John, Jr.: b 1-14-1758 d 3-30-1848 m (1)Nancy Lowry (2)Nancy May Adj QM SC NC ★

BLAKER,

Echylus: b c. 1752 d 11-19-1822 m (2)Sarah Buckman PS PA

BLAKESLEE, (includes BLAKELY, BLAKESLY, BLAKSLEE, BLAKSLEY)

David: b 11-2-1722 d 2-11-1781 m (1)Phebe Todd (2)Abigail How Pvt CT
David: b 7-25-1749 d 7-10-1821 m Phoebe Hall Pvt CT
David: b 4-30-1741 d 2-28-1823 m Sarah Ann Woodworth Capt NY
Enos: b 1756 d 8- -1842 m Sara Northrup Pvt CT
Enos: b 9-8-1758 d 2-10-1812 m Hannah Sperry Pvt CT
Isaac: b 2-26-1733/4 d 11-16-1814 m Lydia Alcott Lt CT

James: bpt 10-26-1760 d 3-4-1836 m Ruth Root Pvt CT ★
James: b 5-29-1763 d 1852 m Ann Travers Pvt NY ★
James: b 2-3-1736 d 12- -1781 m Anna Bradley Capt VT
James: b c. 1730 d 1799 m Rebecca — PS VA
Jared: b 1760 d 9-27-1833 m Rhoda Belcher Sgt CT ★
John: b a. 1730 d 1798 m Rachel Orr Pvt SC
Joseph: b 4-1-1732 d 1804 m Lois Ives PS CT
Jotham: b 7-14-1736 d 2-18-1792 m (1)Hannah Todd (2)Mary—(3)Mary Wooding Sol CT
Laban: b 9-12-1754 d 11-25-1819 m Ann — Pvt CT
Obed: b 8-29-1754 d 1779/80 m Sarah Gilbert CL CT
Reuben: b 1-18-1725/6 d 1-4-1813 m Rhoda Griswold PM CT
Samuel: b 11-23-1759 d 7-12-1834 m (1)Phoebe Curtis (2)—Pearson Pvt CT ★
Samuel: b 1760 d — m Silence Church Pvt CT
Seth: b 12-10-1738 d 4-17-1799 m Jemima Tuttle Lt CT
William: b 5-12-1760 d 5-12-1847 m Nancy Boyd Pvt SC

BLAKEY,
Churchill: b 1750-60 d p. 10-22-1829 m Agnes Anthony Sol PS VA
George: b 11-22-1749 d 9-8-1842 m Margaret Whitsitt Pvt VA W★
John:b 12-14-1718 d 1781 m Jean — Sol VA

BLALOCK,
John: b 9-4-1762 d 3-10-1846 m Polly Dorman Lt VA ★
Lewis: b 1749 d 1828 m Eleanor — PS SC

BLANCH,
Ezekiel Alfred: b 6-10-1757 d 1832 m (1)Sarah White (2)Mildred Cook Pvt VA
Thomas: b 2-22-1740 d 6-3-1823 m Effie Johns Mabie Capt NJ

BLANCHARD,
Aaron: b 5-1-1722 d 1-7-1787 m (1)Rebecca Hall (2)Tabitha Floyd Pvt MA
Aaron: b 7-27-1740 d 10-28-1801 m (1)Nellie Holt (2)Mrs Mehitable Chase Pvt MA
Abel: b 2-17-1761 d 1827 m Mary Elizabeth Eastman Pvt NH
Abiel: b 10-4-1748 d p. 1792 m Elizabeth Church Pvt MA
Amos: b 2-15-1766 d 5-25-1842 m Lavinia Hopkins Mus MA ★
Augustus: b 7-29-1746 d 2-27-1809 m Bridget Lovewell Capt NH
Azariel: b 6-13-1740 d 3-27-1818 m Abigail Mason Sct Sgt VT & NY
Caleb: b 4-8-1759 d 1-1-1836 m Zylphia Slye Pvt VT
Calvin: b 2-27-1754 d 1-2-1800 m Abigail Reed Sgt MA
Daniel: b 3-5-1755 d 5-10-1833 m Mary Vinson Sgt MA
David, Sr.: b 1-1-1731 d 3-6-1788 m (1)Mary Walker (2)Ann Humphrey CS MA
David, Jr.: b 12-10-1759 d 7-3-1824 m Mary Humphrey Pvt MA
David: b 1756 d 2-5-1845 m Azubah Heath Sgt NH
Edward: b 1740 d 4-13-1814 m Isabelle Wasson Capt MA
Elias: b 3-28-1753-5 d 11-8-1822 m Anna — Ens RI ★
Hezekiah: b 1-4-1727/28 d 8-24-1803 m (1)Susanna Dexter (2)Sarah Hall Pvt MA
Isaac: b 1762 d 4-26-1826 m Olive Hopkins Pvt NH
Isaac: b 1746 d 11- -1816 m Rosanna Green Lt RI
Jeremiah: b 1733 d 1-27-1826 m (1)Dorothy Smith (2)Susanna Martin Lt MA
Jeremiah: b 1738 d 5-26-1807 m (1)Phoebe Bates (2)Phoebe Stevens (3)Abigail Steward Capt PA
John: b 1740 d 3- -1814 m Sara Carrill Pvt MA
John, Sr.: b 1743 d 1821 m Lovey Adams Brevet-Maj MA ★
John, Jr.: b 1767 d 1847 m Sarah Blanchard Drm MA
John: b 7-19-1737 d p. 1819 m Eleanor Stevens Pvt NH
John: b 9-11-1763 d 9- -1844 m Hannah Perrin Pvt NH ★
Joseph: b 8- -1756 d 12-28-1857 m Relief Osgood Fif MA ★
Joseph: b 11-24-1761 d 2-19-1839 m Phoebe Abbott Pvt NH ★
Joseph: b 2-18-1762 d 4-5-1824 m Jemima — Pvt PA ★
Joseph: b c. 1762 d p. 3- -1829 m Mary Parke Pvt PA
Jotham: b 3-6-1751 d 2-16-1832 m Abigal Crosby Pvt MA
Justus: b 11-22-1759 d 9-9-1831 m Chloe Marshall Pvt MA
Lemuel: b 1749 d 6-9-1811 m Mary Littlefield Pvt MA
Lemuel: b 1-23-1763 d 9-2-1855 m (1)Phoebe Mayo (2)Margaret Witherspoon Davidson Pvt MA
Nathaniel: b 5-29-1760 d p. 1800 m Anna Green Pvt MA
Nathaniel: b 1760 d 7- -1829 m Eunice Root Drm MA ★
Ozias: b 7-31-1742 d 9-2-1826 m (1)Mercy Soule (2)Mrs Martha Anderson 2Lt MA
Peter: b 1746 d 2-1-1823 m Martha Brock Pvt CL FrA ★
Reuben: b 1750 d — m Sarah Cartledge Pvt GA
Richard: b 1721 d 4-9-1814 m Mary Hancock Pvt PS NH
Samuel: b 4-1-1749 d p. 1799 m Susan Tenney Pvt MA
Samuel: b 1-14-1716 d 5-24-1807 m Ruth Tenney Pvt MA
Samuel: b 2-21-1732 d 3-5-1812 m (1)Dorothy Thayer (2)Mrs Esther Holbrook Pvt CS PS MA
Simon: b 10-8-1759 d 10-18-1820 m Jemima Chapman Pvt NH
Simon, Jr.: b 12-23-1749 d 10-2-1831 m Catherine Wyman Pvt NH
Solomon: b 8-18-1763 d 2-25-1853 m Ardra Robinson Pvt Artl MA ★
Stephen, Sr.: b 8-20-1726 d p. 1786 m (1)Hannah Abbott (2)Mrs Elizabeth Potter Lancy Pvt NH
Sylvanus: b 4-11-1738 d 8-5-1800 m Sarah Grover Pvt MA
Thomas: b 10-30-1754 d 12-29-1831 m Ruth White Drm MA
Thomas: b 1-15-1700 d 11-25-1779 m Elizabeth Johnson PS MA

Timothy: b 10-16-1755 d 2-3-1840 m Mercy Kidder Sgt RI ★
William: b 1-1-1750 d 12-14-1836 m Sarah Smith Lt CT ★
William: b 3-21-1750 d 1-8-1833 m Mary Kidder Lt RI & CL ★
William: b 8-31-1747 d 1-21-1814 m (1)Rachel Spear (2)Betsy Mann Cpl MA

BLANCHER,
Jacob: b 2-5-1752 d 3-19-1831 m Elizabeth Weed Pvt CT ★

BLAND,
John: b 1766 d p. 7-3-1846 m Fanney Drummond Sol VA
Richard: b 5-6-1710 d 10-26-1776 m (1)Anne Poythress (2)Elizabeth Harrison PS VA
Robert: b 3-8-1732 d 3-27-1787 m Ann Wormley Pvt SC
Theodoric: b 12-2-1708 d p. 5-8-1784 m (1)Frances Bolling (2)Elizabeth Yates PS VA
Thomas: b a. 1748 d 1788 m Jane — Sgt VA
Thomas: b — d a. 6-6-1807 m X PS VA
William: b c. 1749 d p. 1816 m Rachel — Sol NC

BLANDING, (includes BLANDEN, BLANDIN)
Benjamin: b 8-13-1751 d 9-2-1820 m Susanna Wetherell Pvt MA
Christopher: b 10-1-1756 d 1-1-1828 m Martha Wheeler Martin Cpl MA
Ebenezer: b 2-26-1754 d 1844 m (1)Nancy Wheeler (2)Elizabeth Ingalls Pvt MA
Francis: b 10-19-1718 d 5-22-1775 m (1)Susanna Bailey (2)Abigail Toser Pvt MA
Jonathan: b 1753 d 8-6-1849 m Submit Cook Pvt Wgn CT
Lamech: b 7-28-1759 d 3-18-1839 m Lydia Lambert Sgt MA
Noah: b 9-12-1721 d 1-19-1785 m Bridget French Pvt MA
Samuel: b 1760 d 9-1-1841 m Elizabeth Granger Pvt MA CT
William: b 2-27-1747 d 6-12-1830 m Lydia Ormsbee Capt & QM MA

BLANK, (includes BLANCK)
Adam: b 5-6-1767 d 3-26-1830 m Mary Magdalene Krautzer Lt PA
George: b 12-27-1729 d 5-7-1799 m Eva Elizabeth Steinmetz PS PA

BLANKENBAKER,
Michael: b — d p. 1783 m Elizabeth Barbara Gaar PS VA
Nicholas: b 10-6-1758 d 7-17-1849 m Fannie Wilhoyt Pvt VA ★
Samuel: b 7-31-1754 d 1827 m Amy Yager Sol VA
Thomas: b c. 1763 d 1835 m Jemima — PS VA

BLANKENSHIP, (includes BLANKINSHIP)
Benjamin: b 1760 d 1844 m Patience Jackson Pvt VA ★
Daniel: b 1738 d 1807 m Sallie Clay Sol VA
Henry: b 1742 d 1812 m Rhoda Leggon Sol VA
William: b 1720 d 1788 m Nancy Henry Sol VA

BLANTON,
Burwell: b 1762 d 1860 m (1)Margaret Bridges (2)Pollie Wiley Pvt NC
Charles: b c. 1743 d a. 1799 m X PS NC
James: b 3-15-1764/65 d p. 1833 m X Pvt NC
Thomas: b 1724 d p. 1810 m Jane — Pvt VA
Thomas: b 1758 d 5-27-1846 m Scilly Auglea Pvt VA ★
William: b c. 1740 d p. 1804 m Rebecca Hobbs Pvt VA

BLASER,
Peter: b 1746 d 3-10-1839 m Elizabeth — Cpl PA

BLASHFIELD,
John: b 1722 d 11-8-1802 m Marcy — Pvt MA
Ozem: b 4-5-1757 d 4-11-1808 m (1)Eunice Brown (2)Mrs. Bathsheba Burt Pvt MA
William: b 2-16-1748 d 2-19-1791 m Lois Lombard Pvt MA

BLASIER,
Lawrence: b 10-7-1766 d p. 2-4-1833 m Evae Wererin Pvt NY

BLASSINGAME,
James: b a. 1760 d a. 6-23-1821 m Mary Gowan Capt SC
John: b c. 1735 d 1809 m Rachel Westfield PS Pvt SC

BLATCHFORD,
Benjamin: b 6-11-1738 d 3-9-1778 m Sarah Godfrey Sgt MA
John, Jr.: b 1762 d 1794 m Anna Grover Slr MA

BLATTENBERGER,
John: b 10-14-1744 d 6-14-1813 m (1)Christiana Haines (2)Anna Maria Brandon Pvt PA

BLAUVELT,
Abraham J.: b 10-4-1738 d 7-3-1798 m Maria A — Capt NJ
Abram: b 6-29-1740 d 1797 m Maria Flierboom 2Maj NY
Auri: bpt 9-12-1758 d 3-8-1804 m Altie Smith Capt NY
Cornelius: b 3-1-1750 d p. 1790 m (1)Rebecca Nagel (2)Maria Smith Lt NY
Gerrit J.: b 1-4-1731 d 7-28-1810 m Elizabeth Mebie Pvt NY
Harman: b 5-9-1761 d p. 1832 m Krisje Haring Pvt NJ ★
Harmanus: b 4-16-1741 d 2-28-1833 m Rachel Van Orden Pvt PS NY

BLAUVELT, contd.
Hendrick: b 6-26-1732 d 11-24-1816 m (1)Marretye — (2)Lena Yorks Pvt NY
Isaac: b 11-8-1761 d *p*. 6-8-1813 m Sara Johnston Pvt NJ
Isaac: b 8-9-1755 d 12-3-1798 m Eleanor Cornelison Cpl NY W★
Jacobus: b 3-17-1728 d 4- -1803 m Geertje Vervelen Sgt NY
James: b 1-31-1756 d 12-25-1819 m Agnes Graham Pvt NY
James J.: b *c*. 1763 d 5-30-1842 m Rachel Hogencamp Pvt NY NJ ★
Johannes J.: b 3-6-1752 d 9-17-1848 m Margrietje Smith Pvt PS NY
Johannes Joseph: b 11-9-1714 d 10-2-1789 m Margaritie Smith Maj NY
Joseph: b 9-9-1740 d 3-15-1789 m Johanna Demorest Pvt NY

BLEAKNEY,
William: b *c*. 1730 d 2- -1798 m Jenat McKnight PS PA

BLEDSOE,
Aaron: b 1760 d 1805 m Belara Jackson Sol NC
Anthony: b 1733 d 7-20-1788 m Mary Ramsey Col CS VA
Bartley: b *c*. 1760 d *c*. 1811 m Martha Schaeffer Pvt SC
Benjamin: b 7-7-1763 d 5-7-1845 m Sarah Bledsoe Pvt NC ★
Isaac: b *c*. 1735 d 4-9-1793 m Katherine Montgomery 1Maj CS PS NC
Jacob, Sr.: b 1730 d 5-1-1817 m X PS NC
Jacob, Jr.: b 3-28-1762 d 1835 m Ruth — Lt NC ★
John: b *c*. 1758 d 11/12-24-1829 m Sarah Beckham Pvt NC
Mary Ramsey: b 1-6-1734 d 3-23-1808 m Anthony Bledsoe PS TN
Miller: b 10-7-1761 d 1841 m Jean Elizabeth Bolling Pvt VA ★
William: b *c*. 1760 d *c*. 1820 m Sally Morton Pvt VA
William Miller: b 4-13-1761 d *p*. 1792 m Patience Ousley Pvt VA

BLEECKER,
Anthony Lespenard: b 6-13-1741 d 4-26-1816 m Mary Noel Maj NY
John: b 1763 d 1833 m (1)Jane Gilliland (2)Elizabeth Van R Schuyler Sol NY
John R.: bpt 2-8-1713 d 1800 m Elizabeth Staats PS NY
Leonard: b 12-21-1755 d 3-9-1844 m Joanna Abeel Maj NY

BLESSING,
Jacob: b *c*. 1728 d *a*. 4-30-1790 m Elizabeth — Sol VA
Michael: b 2-24 1739 d 12-29-1819 m Mary Magdalena Pvt PA

BELVINS,
John: b *c*. 1760 d 1816 m Catherine Cox Pvt VA
William, Jr.: b 1760 d *p*. 6-7-1832 m Mary Thompson Pvt VA

BLEWETT,
William: b *c*. 1729 d 6-15-1813 m (1)Sarah Garton (2)Miss White (3)Elizabeth Morris CS NC

BLICKENSDERFER,
Christian: b 10-6-1753 d 3-8-1820 m Barbara Born Pvt PA

BLIFFIN,
Increase: b 5-15-1758 d 1837 m Isabella Whitney Cpl MA

BLINN,
Billy: b *c*. 1730 d 1803 m Hannah Hurlbut Pvt CT
James: b 1755 d 11-16-1831 m Abigail Delano Pvt MA
Silas: b 11-14-1756 d 3-15-1821 m Tryphena Hewett Sgt MA ★
Solomon: b 3-26-1734 d *a*. 1-18-1808 m Desire Andrus PS CT
William: b 9-14-1742 d 8-1-1822 m Nancy Lucas Pvt CT

BLISH,
David, Sr.: b 10-26-1732 d 10-26-1817 m Zerviah Skinner PS CT
David, Jr.: b 9-16-1752/3 d 12-5-1817 m Lucy Wilcox Sgt CT
John: b 9-9-1717 d *p*. 1790 m Mary Goodspeed PS MA

BLISS,
Aaron: b *c*. 1738 d *a*.1-12-1786 m Elizabeth Lilley Pvt MA
Aaron: b 3-20-1752 d 5-11-1812 m Lucy Shaw Pvt MA
Abdiel: b 12-15-1740 d 6-10-1805 m Lydia Smith Lt MA
Abel: b 4-27-1763 d 11-3-1852 m (1)Betsy Barrows (2)Lucy Carpenter Pvt MA
Abner: b 11-29-1752 d 5-29-1812 m Naomi Loveland Pvt PS CT
Abraham: b 10-11-1743 d 1-29-1795 m (1)Lydia Hebard (2)Sarah Hall Young Sol & QM CT
Asa: b 11-5-1760 d 9-23-1851 m Molly Emmerson Pvt MA ★
Azariah: b 4-7-1714 d 6-6-1803 m (1)Mary Tilden (2)Lydia Southworth Storrs PS CT
Benjamin: b 8-7-1761 d 4-11-1823 m Amy Bowen Pvt MA
Beriah: b 7-28-1765/6 d 8-30-1827 m (1)Temperance Rogers (2)Mehitable Hubbell Pvt CT
Calvin: b 9-23-1753 d 2-2-1814 m Lucy Hale Pvt MA
Calvin: b 5-14-1754 d 10- -1849 m Ruth Janes Pvt MA ★
Daniel: b 11-16-1726 d 6-30-1815 m Sarah Allen Pvt MA
David: b 6-17-1763 d 3-18-1835 m (1)Bathsheba Cole (2)Jane McDuffee Pvt CT ★
David: b 4-10-1756 d 1809 m Susannah Walker Cpl MA
David: b 2-21-1737 d 5-16-1813 m Sarah Porter Pvt VT
Ebenezer: b 4-7-1724 d 10-20-1787 m Sarah Cooley Pvt MA
Ebenezer: b 12-7-1725 d 3-2-1808 m (1)Mary Booth (2)Abigail Cooley Pvt MA

Ebenezer: b 4-15-1749 d 7-12-1839 m Abigail Parsons Pvt MA
Eleazer: b 5-7-1745 d 9- -1833 m (1)Betsy Ingalls (2)Mrs Sally Tuttle Pvt MA
Elijah: b 1732 d 1796 m Abigail — Sgt PA
Elisha, Jr.: b 7-17-1732 d 12-13-1777 m Ruth Thomas Pvt MA
Ellis: b 4-5-1759 d 8-22-1829 m Abigail Taylor Sgt VT
Ephraim, Sr.: b 6-3-1726 d 7-2-1804 m (1)Mary Moulton (2)Sarah Read (3)Huldah Smith Pvt MA
Gad: b 7-29-1762 d 11-21-1845 m Deborah Olcott Pvt MA
Gaius: b 5-17-1761 d 12-24-1843 m (1)Eunice Robinson (2)Flavia Keep Pvt MA ★
Henry: b 1760 d 1821 m Mary — Pvt PA
Henry: b 1722 d 5-10-1808 m Mary Clark CS RI
Isaac: b 8-10-1760 d 6-19-1845 m Welthea Butler Pvt MA ★
Israel: b 4-17-1739 d 1-26-1829 m Mary Stiles Pvt CT
Jacob: b 3-12-1763 d 3-27-1829 m Mary Collins Pvt MA
James: b 1-18-1762 d 8-12-1831 m Mehetabel Johnson Pvt CT ★
James: b 4-19-1757 d 9-29-1834 m (1)Hannah Guild (2)Mrs. Sarah Deane Srgn Mte MA
John: b 5-26-1726 d *p*. 1800 m Mary Throop PS CT
John: b 2-1-1727 d 11-3-1809 m (1)Abiel Pease Colton (2)Mrs. Sarah Chaffee Morris Col MA
John: b 1-7-1760 d 4-28-1845 m Reliance Babcock Sgt CT RI ★
Jonathan: b 1-26-1739 d 1-24-1800 m Lydia Wheeler Smn MA
Jonathan, Sr.: b 1-4-1712 d 4- -1799 m Sybil Fox PS NH
Jonathan, Jr.: b 1745 d 10-14-1799 m Sarah — PS NH
Joseph: b 5-3-1742 d *p*. 3-28-1804 m (1)Anne Simeon (2)Susannah Sweeting (3)Amy Bowen 2 Lt MA
Joshua: b 1-1-1757 d 6- -1831 m Sybil Peck Pvt MA
Josiah: b 3-17-1725 d 2- -1805 m Sarah Frost Pvt MA
Levi: b 1747 d 1819 m Elizabeth Bullock Pvt RI
Luther: b 9-9-1760 d 8- -1830 m Lovice Stebbins Pvt MA
Moses: b 1- -1753 d 3-1-1842 m Abiah Chapin Pvt MA & CL ★
Nathan, Sr.: b 12-9-1736 d 12-3-1820 m Joanna Bowen Sgt MA
Nathan: b 12-19-1761 d 1-31-1852 m Ruth Briggs Pvt MA
Nathan: b 9- -1744 d 7-27-1813 m Submit White Jr. Pvt MA ★
Nathaniel: b 11-26-1741 d 11-5-1782 m Miriam Bartlett Pvt MA
Neziah: b 3-21-1736/7 d 8-31-1787 m Martha H. Shipman Lt & PS CT
Noah, Jr.: b 11-30-1759 d 2-28-1840 m (1)Mary Carpenter (2)Elizabeth Martin Sgt MA ★
Pelatiah: b 12-12-1748 d 10-29-1828 m (1)Ruth Woolworth (2)Mary Sheldon Fif Pvt MA
Pelatiah, Jr.: b 4-3-1749 d 1797/98 m Ruth Lowell Sct MM NH VT
Reuben: b 12-14-1726 d 9-18-1806 m Elizabeth Hitchcock PS MA
Samuel, Sr.: b 1730 d 4-17-1816 m (1)Hannah Carpenter (2)Keziah Carpenter (3)Lydia Perry Capt MA
Samuel, Jr.: b 11-4-1761 d 3-15-1837 m Anna Mason Pvt MA
Samuel: b 2-17-1734 d 1786 m Mary Gleason Pvt MM MA
Samuel: b 2-13-1752 d 1836 m Olive Pinnock Pvt OrdlSgt NY ★
Solomon: b 1-16-1737 d 5-24-1803 m (1)Martha Young (2)Margaret Smith Pvt MA
Stephen: b 2-26-1732 d 2-13-1806 m Catherine Burt Pvt MA
Thomas: b 10-26-1742 d 8-15-1806 m Sarah King Sgt MA
Thomas: b 11-25-1747 d 1830 m Temperance Colton Cpl MA
Thomas Theodore: b 5-21-1745 d 9-1-1802 m (1)Elizabeth Barrett Bartlett (2)Hannah Delano Capt MA
Timothy: b 1-17-1741 d *a*. 4-8-1791 m (1)Thankful Merrick (2)Elizabeth —Capt MA
Timothy: b 3-22-1745 d 5-3-1817 m Zeriah Williams Pvt & QM VT
William, Sr.: b 2-5-1728 d 5-4-1808 m (1)Barbara Phillips (2)Elizabeth Ward PS RI
William, Jr.: b 11-22-1746 d 11-16-1782 m Eleanor Sikes Pvt MA
William, Jr.: b 7-15-1758 d 7-31-1846 m Abigail Lyndon Ens CT RI ★
Zadock: b 7-3-1755 d 12-7-1813 m Sarah Cushman Pvt MA
Zenas: b 8-13-1767 d 4-1-1853 m (1)Sarah Anton (2)Hannah Thomas Pvt VT
Zenas: b 2-3-1756 d 5-26-1822 m Mary Babcock Pvt MA
Zephaniah: b 7-8-1753 d 8-7-1827 m Temperance Lord Sgt CT

BLITCH,
Thomas: b *c*. 1740 d 9-11-1777 m Ann Hodges Pvt GA

BLIVEN,
Edward: b 5-30-1722 d *p*. 1781 m Ann Ross Capt RI
James: b 3-22-1735 d 3-10-1801 m Sarah Stetson Pvt RI
John: b 9-22-1730 d *a*. 10-10-1805 m Elizabeth Hern Pvt RI
Samuel: b 3-12-1744 d 12-23-1816 m Ruth Greene PS RI
Samuel: b 1763 d 1826 m Polly Worden Pvt RI
William: b 12-15-1745 d 1-13-1834 m Eleanor Maxson Capt RI ★

BLIZZARD,
Burton: b 1757 d 3-17-1837 m Sarah Keister Pvt VA ★

BLOCKER,
John: b 7-11-1748 d 9-18-1814 m (1)Pearcy Mayson (2)Juliana Johnston Pvt SC

BLODGETT, (includes BLODETT, BLODGET, BLOGETT, BLOGGET)
Abisha: b 11-24-1763 d 4-15-1840 m Hannah Ensley Pvt CT ★

Admantha: b 12-15-1758 d 2-22-1855 m Eunice Merrick Pvt MA
Archippus: b 8-16-1733 d 1785-90 m Mary Lamkin Pvt NH
Archippus: b 12-29-1755 d *p.* 1790 m X Sgt VT
Asa: b 1720 d 1806 m Irene Owen PS CS VT
Asahel: b 6-19-1755 d 6-2-1842 m (1)Catherine Pollard (2)Lois Pollard Pvt NH
Benjamin: b 5-17-1717 d 1781 m (1)Mary Satterlee (2)Abigail Swan Dr CT
Benjamin: b 6-9-1744 d 12-24 1832 m Miriam Thompson Ens CT
Benjamin: b 5-18-1759 d 12-12-1842 m Mary Riddle Pvt CT
Caleb: b 9-20-1751 d 10-23-1813 m Charity Walbridge Pvt CT
Daniel: b 10-13-1738 d 11-12-1776 m Lydia Robinson Sgt CT
David: b 4-14-1735 d 3-6-1800 m Jerusha Dickinson Pvt MA
Elijah: b 10-25-1751 d 3- -1839 m (1)Mary Branch (2)Mrs Cleveland Pvt CL
Ephraim: b 1764 d *p.* 1796 m Sibyl Roberts Pvt MA
Henry: b 7-25-1759 d 12-6-1843 Pvt MA
Isaac: b 2-28-1748 d 1- -1824 m Persis Whitcomb Pvt MA
Jacob: b 7-4-1755 d 3-30-1836 m Lucy Tarbox Ens NH
James: b 2-13-1734 d 1813 m (1)Sarah Snow (2)Esther Wyman Pvt NH
James: b 12-21-1723 d 3-20-1817 m Theoda Walbridge Ens MA
Jonas: b 1764 d *p.* 1796 m (1)Rhoda Dady (2)Mrs Hannah Bugbee Cpl MA
Jonas: b 8-4-1757 d 8-19-1826 m Sarah Fletcher Pvt MA ★
Jonathan: b 3-6-1758 d 12-10-1850 m (1)Susan Tenney (2)Parney Goodnow Pvt NH W★
Joseph: b 5-19-1745 d 4- -1818 m Lucy Munger Pvt MA W★
Joshua: b 1-10-1722 d 10-31-1816 m Hannah Alden Drm MA
Joshua: b 1744 d 10-22-1834 m Ruth Merrill Pvt NH ★
Josiah: b 1752 d 12-19-1823 m Theodosia Crane Pvt CT
Josiah: b 7-27-1709 d 2-9-1792 m Jemima Nutting PS MA
Luden: b 4-25-1764 d 7-26-1849 m (1)Annis Hitchcock (2)Submit Eames Pvt MA ★
Nathan: 10-25-1741 d 4-17-1789 m Abigail Cushman Pvt CT
Nathan: b 11-3-1756 d 7-12-1845 m Abigail Bliss Drm Sgt MA ★
Paul: b 5- -1737 d *p.* 1807 m Phillis — Capt CT
Phineas: b 1756 d 8-29-1810 m Damaris Loomis Pvt CT
Roswell: b 1749 d 5-28-1781 m Hannah Bartlett Pvt CT
Rufus: b 7-19-1761 d 1-8-1828 m Bathsheba Hubbard Pvt MA
Samuel, Sr.: b 4-1-1724 d 9-1-1807 m Hannah White PS NH
Samuel, Jr.: b 8-28-1757 d 1814 m Rebecca Smith Capt NH
Samuel: b 5-26-1751 d 8-5-1838 m (1)Mary Palmer (2)Mrs. Dickenson Sgt VT ★
Sardius: b 5-25-1754 d 9-26-1828 m Sabra Wheeler Pvt VT
Silas: b 1-22-1731/2 d 8-27-1824 m Abigail Stocking Lt CT MA ★
Solomon: b 4-4-1756 d *p.* 1802 m (1)Hepzibah Brown (2)Thankful Blair Pvt MA
Thomas: b 12-29-1717 d 2-4-1800 m (1)Charity Raymond (2)Mrs Mary Bruce Pvt MA
Thomas: b 9-26-1734 d *p.* 1784 m Margaret Weber Pvt MA
Timothy: b 8-7-1740 d 1-13-1831 m Millicent Perry MM MA
William: b 6-8-1754 d 10-10-1809 m Ann Phillis Chace Maj CL
William: b 3-3-1762 d 11-15-1852 m Mary Cheney Cpl MA

BLOOD,
Abel: b 1758 d 8-19-1852 m Hannah Hale Pvt MA ★
Asa: b 11-19-1758 d 5-17-1825 m Betsey Follet Pvt MA
Caleb: b 11-23-1734 d 12-9-1804 m (1)Hannah Holden (2)Elizabeth Farnsworth PS MA
Daniel: b 7-23-1749 d 1786 m Sarah Putnam Pvt NH
David: b 11-5-1751 d 10-26-1829 m Mrs Hannah Coburn Pvt MA
David: b 9-28-1718 d 12-6-1788 m Abigail Farnsworth CS MA
Edmund: b 7-26-1764 d 11-26-1842 m (1)Lucy Taylor (2)Phebe Ball Pvt & Pvtr MA
Elijah: b 10-10-1748 d 1-31-1817 m (1)Annis Ward (2)Eunice Sleeman Pvt MA
Francis: b 3-18-1735/6 d 1814 m Elizabeth Spaulding PS NH
Isaiah: b 11-19-1720/1 d *p.* 1790 m (1)Martha Thomas (2)Thamazin Hudson Pvt PS MA
John: b 11-19-1744 d *p.* 1790 m Mrs Mary Chamberlin Trm MA
John: b 1759 d 9-5-1848 m (1)Asenath Powers (2)Piercy Barker Pvt MA ★
Joseph, Jr.: b 5-5-1747 d 1826 m Betty Bruce Cpl MA
Joseph: bpt 5-8-1709 d 1-5-1794 m Hannah Blood CS MA
Joshua: b 6-6-1744 d 4-17-1823 m Kezia Jewett CS MA
Josiah: b *a.* 1747 d *p.* 1786 m Tabitha Corey Sgt MA
Josiah, Sr.: bpt 9-7-1717 d 9-16-1776 m (1)Sarah Farley (2)Sarah Heywood Pvt NH
Josiah, Jr: b 7-18-1743 d 1-15-1816 m (1)Abigail Pierce (2)Sarah French Pvt NH
Lemuel: b 1761 d 4-20-1834 m Lucy Hale Pvt MA ★
Nathan: b 4-4-1747 d 6-17-1775 m Elizabeth Noyes 1Sgt MA
Nathaniel, Sr.: b — d *p.* 1790 m Ruth Hall CS & PS MA
Nathaniel: b 1754 d 4-4-1838 m Polly Allen Pvt MA
Nathaniel: b 9-1-1714 d 11-11-1782 m Sarah — Pvt NH
Phineas: b *c.* 1763 d 9-19-1821 m Lois Ingalls Pvt MA
Richard: b 1746 d 4-10-1820 m Mary Thompson Lt MA
Sewell: b 5-24-1765 d 12-16-1814 m Mary Kendall Sol MA
Simeon: b *c.* 1760 d *c.* 1835 m (1)Rhoda Youngman (2)Mrs Mary Hutchins Pvt MA
Simon: b 8-4-1729 d *a.* 1-28-1800 m Anna Shattuck Pvt MA

Stephen: b 2-12-1731 d 2-20-1789 m (1)Mary — (2)Frances Hutchings PS MA
Timothy: b 10-15-1754 d *p.* 1796 m Sarah Dix Pvt NH

BLOODGOOD,
James: b 1735 d 5-4-1799 m Lydia Van Valkinburg Pvt NY
William: b 1761 d 1817 m Mary Bengle Pvt NJ

BLOODWORTH,
John: b 1730 d 1808 m (1)Tamsie Axson (2)Susan Lee Lt NC
Thomas: b 6-24-1755 d 1-23-1836 m Tamsie Proctor Col PS CS NC
Timothy: b 1736 d-8-24-1814 m Priscilla — PS NC

BLOOM,
Abraham: b 2-24-1759 d 5-24-1832 m Mary Sophia Pickle Pvt NJ
Benjamin: b 3-15-1744 d 3-25-1817 m Helen Dubois Pvt NY
Ephraim: b 11-13-1728 d 11-17-1828 m (1)Catharine — (2)Elizabeth — Pvt PA
George: b 1758 d *p.* 1801 m Mary Ater Pvt PA
Stephen: b 10-11-1734 d 3-25-1795 m Mary Levering Capt PA
William: b 2-26-1752 d 5-4-1828 m Mary Metter Sol NJ

BLOOMER,
Abraham: b 4-19-1758 d 1849 m Abbie Bugbee Pvt NY
Gilbert: b — d 1784 m (1)Phebe Sherwood (2)Hannah Theil Pvt NY
Reuben: b 10-10-1736 d 5-9-1824 m Susannah Paddock Ens VT
Robert: b 12-18-1725 d-10-5-1776 m Elizabeth Purdy Capt PS NY
William: b 5-11-1749 d 10-31-1824 m Rachel Cosman Pvt NY

BLOOMFIELD,
Aaron: b 1762 d 7-30-1833 m Keziah Bloodgood Pvt NJ
Ellis: b 11-17-1752 d 4-3-1802 m Hulda Kent Pvt NJ
Jonathan: b 8-25-1735 d 1810 m (1)Elizabeth Wood (2)Anna — PS NJ
Jonathan: b 8-8-1759 d 1828 m Eunice — Pvt NJ
Moses: b 7-6-1755 d 8- -1807 m Mary Moss Pvt NJ
Thomas: b 11-23-1746 d 9-30-1830 m Elizabeth Morris Pvt NJ & CL
Timothy: b 1729 d 1-24-1803 m (1)Sarah Ford (2)Margaretta — PS NJ

BLOOMINGDALE, (includes BLOOMINDALE)
Albertus: b 12- -1735 d 7-4-1818 m (1)Maria Ostrander (2)Anne Harssen Pvt NY
John: b 9- -1759 d 2-1-1833 m Mary Sharpe Sgt NY

BLOSS, (includes BLOSE)
Conrad: b *c.* 1720 d 1776 m Anna Magdalena Pvt PA
Daniel: b *c.* 1752 d 1803 m Elizabeth Brazil Pvt PA
Hendrick P.: b 1733 d 1803 m Eva Link Pvt NY
Joseph: b 9-29-1759 d 2-15-1838 m Amy Wentworth Kennedy Sgt CT ★
Michael: b 4- -1759 d 7-5-1837 m Elizabeth Shultis Fif Pvt NY ★
Samuel: b 1751 d 11-15-1841 m Hannah — Pvt MA W★
Valentine: b 8-1-1757 d 9-4-1850 m Margaret Smith Pvt VA ★
Walter: b 7-20-1760 d 8-8-1817 m Hannah Wilder Pvt NH

BLOSSER, (includes BLOSER)
Jacob: b 1-13-1758 d 10-6-1842 m Barbara Beery Pvt PA
Peter: b 1746 d 3-10-1839 m Elizabeth Schlobacher Cpl PA

BLOSSOM,
Benjamin, Jr.: b 8-18-1753 d 8-9-1837 m Rebekah Toby Sgt MA
Benjamin: b 11-14-1746 d 2-12-1831 m Molly Ripley Pvt MA ★
Churchill: b 10-15-1749 d 11-26-1841 m Hannah Davis Pvt MA
David: b 1-12-1755 d 1833 m (1)Thankful Bodfish (2)Desire Denison (3)Mrs Rhoda Birch Day Pvt MA
James: b 2-9-1731 d 6-16-1811 m Bethia Smith Lt MA
Peter: b 12-4-1756 d 1841 m Hanna Goodspeed Pvt MA

BLOUGH, (includes BLAUCH)
Christian: b 9-9-1757 d 1830 m Sarah Cable Pvt PA
Christian: b *c.* 1722 d *p.* 2-24-1783 m (1)X (2)Mrs Rosanna Steck Pvt PA
Jacob: b 1736 d 1811 m Annie Kauffman Pvt PA

BLOUIN,
Daniel: b *c.* 1740 d *a.* 2-23-1782 m Helene Charleville Pvt VA

BLOUNT, (includes BLUNT)
Asher: b 1-22-1759 d 11-29-1847 m Sarah Gates Pvt CT ★
Benjamin: b 1720 d 1800 m Affie Smithwick Col PS NC
Charles: b 10-31-1721 d 3-11-1785 m (1)Mary Clayton (2)Martha — LCol PS NC
Ebenezer: b 5-29-1745 d 1-13-1824 m Katherine Kaler PS ME
Edmund: b 8-27-1745 d 2-20-1792 m Mary Hoskins Pvt CS NC
Edmund: b 1755 d 10-16-1822 m Judith Rhodes Pvt PS NC
Frederick: b *c.* 1734 d *c.* 1800 m Rachel Heritage Pvt NC
Henry: b *c.* 1760 d *p.* 1810 m Regina Krum Sol NY
Jacob: b 1726 d 8-17-1789 m (1)Barbara Gray (2)Hannah Baker (3)Mrs Mary Adams PS & Dep PMGen NC
James: b 1750 d 8-4-1824 m Anne Hall Capt NC
Jesse: b 4-6-1752 d *p.* 1786 m Abigail Salter PM & Cmsry NC

BLOUNT, contd.
John: b 10-6-1736 d 5-18-1804 m Rebecca Streeter Capt MA
John: b 1-31-1756 d 11-27-1836 m Sarah Eames Pvt MA W★
John: b 1734 d 6-17-1798 m Hannah Sherburne Pvt PS CS NH
John: b c. 1718 d p. 12-17-1790 m Elizabeth — PS NC
John Gray: b 1752 d 1833 m Mary Harvey PS NC
Joseph, Sr.: b 2-15-1715 d 11-9-1777 m (1)Sarah Durant (2)Mrs Elizabeth H. Scarborough (3)Mrs Sarah Haskins PS NC
Joseph, Jr.: b 8-17-1755 d 12-1-1794 m (1)Lydia Bonner (2)Ann Gray Sol NC
Page: b c. 1730 d c. 1802/3 m Ann — PS VA
Phillip: b c. 1740 d p. 5-17-1801 m Margaret — 2Lt NC
Reading: b 2-22-1757 d 10-13-1807 m Lucy Harvey Maj NC
Stephen: b c. 1760 d 10- -1804 m (1)Judith Hull (2)Eliza Hull (3) Charlotte Praylon Lt GA
Thomas: b 6-24-1737 d 10-10-1777 m Anne Gray PS VA
Walter: b 5-21-1764 d 9-15-1832 m Deborah Herrick Sol CT
Warren: b c. 1760 d 1790-1800 m prob Anne — Pvt NC
Whitmel: b — d 10-4-1777 m Amelia Bryan Lt NC
Wm.: b — d 10-1-1831 m Mary Furnald Slr NH ★
Wm.: b 11-15-1742 d 11-10-1836 m Hannah Thompson Lt NY ★
Wm.: b 3-26-1749 d 3-21-1800 m Mary Granger PM & PS NC
Wm.: b — d p. 11-6-1792 m (1)Martha Peete (2)Frances Jones PS Col VA
Wm.: b 1756 d 2-24-1825 m X Pvt VA ★

BLOW,
Benjamin: b — d a. 8-10-1785 m Priscilla — Pvt NC
Michael: b a. 1738 d 1799 m Priscilla Drew PS VA
Richard: b 10-17-1746 d 2-3-1833 m Fanny Wright Lt VA

BLUE, (includes BLEW)
David: b 6-9-1760 d p. 1838 m Phoebe Murphy Tms VA
Isaac: b 1-20-1758 d 1833 m Anna Sortore Pvt NJ
John: b 1756 d p. 1-11-1809 m Jerusha — Pvt NJ
John: b 1750 d 1834 m X Pvt & PS PA ★
John, Sr.: b 1713 d 4- -1791 m Margaret — PS VA
John, Jr.: b 1740 d 1826 m (1)— Williams (2)Sallie Herriott Pvt VA
Michael: b c. 1748 d 1787 m Mary Stout Sol NJ
Michael: b 11-7-1749 d 2-14-1833 m Phoebia Voris Pvt NJ ★
Michael: b 1742 d 8-25-1821 m Mary — Pvt VA
Uriah: b 12-2-1746 d 4-14-1814 m Susannah Williams PS VA
Uriah: b 8-8-1752 d 3-2-1839 m Ruth — Pvt VA

BLUM,
Johann Heinrich: b 4-19-1752 d 1-19-1824 m Catharine Claus Pvt PA ★

BLUMER,
Abraham: b 12-14-1736 d 4-23-1822 m Susanne M. Frary Chp PA

BLUNDON,
Elijah: b 1740 d 1829 m Mary Colter Pvt VA ★

BLY,
Clark: b 12- -1761 d 7-18-1849 m Barbary Lampshire Sgt NY
John: b 8-9-1757 d 3-23-1845 m Hannah Ray Sgt RI ★
Jonathan: b c. 1735 d — m Margaret Spencer Pvt NY
Moses: b 6-19-1752 d 9-1-1844 m Betsey — Pvt NH

BLYDENBURGH,
Joseph: b 1-30-1732 d 1-25-1833 m Nancy Smith PS NY

BLYTHE,
Benjamin: b c. 1728 d 4- -1807 m Abigail Arthur Col PA
David: b 3-22-1740 d 2-10-1831 m Elizabeth Finley Lt PA
Samuel: b 1727 d p. 1791 m Elizabeth Patten Lt NC
Wm.: b 1728 d 1785 m X PS PA
Wm., Jr.: b 1755 d 1800 m Mrs Ona Gentry Martin Pvt VA

BOAL,
David: b 1755 d 1824 m Nancy Boal Pvt PA
Robert: b — d p. 1-27-1803 m (1)Frances Rogers (2)Mary Wilson (3)Mrs Martha Crain Ens PA

BOARD,
David: b 3-24-1727 d 1-19-1799 m (1)Hannah Kingsland ( )Mary Ford PM PS NJ
James: b — d a. 1760 m Hannah — Sol NC & SC
James, Jr.: b 1720 d 1803 m Jane Ann Schuyler PS NJ
James, Jr.: b 6-1-1763 d 10-2-1801 m Nancy Heard Pvt NJ
John: b 1-3-1754 d 1821 m Jane Harwood PS VA
Joseph: b 8-2-1737 d 12-31-1831 m Pheobe Beach Capt NJ
Patrick: b 6-12-1750 d 11-6-1839 m Mary Keezer Pvt NJ ★
Phillip: b 8-17-1760 d 6-3-1850 m (1)Aliner Thompson (2)Mary Mitchler Pvt NJ ★

BOARDMAN, (includes BORDMAN)
Amos: b 11-17-1764 d 7-21-1854 m Prudence Chapman Pvt CT ★
Amos: b 5-15-1755 d 8-12-1823 m Mary Lewis Pvt MA ★
Benajah: b 5-14-1749 d 2-27-1813 m (1)Lucy Price (2)Martha Churchill Sgt CT
Benjamin: b 10-27-1757 d 7-7-1846 m Hepzibah Martin Sgt MA ★

Charles: b 9-4-1725 d 8-12-1793 m Abigail Stillman PS CT
Daniel: b 1-18-1756 d 5-11-1823 m (1)Mary Hodgkins (2)Bethiah Burnham Pvt MA
David: b 9-8-1749 d 4-10-1833 m Jemima Kinne Cpl CT
Elias: b 10-27-1757 d 5-16-1841 m Hannah Lewis Cpl MA W★
Elijah: b 3-31-1752 d 7-26-1814 m Nancy Deming Ens CT
Elijah: b 1756 d 9-4-1808 m Mercy Nott Sgt CT
Elijah: b 3-7-1760 d 8-18-1823 m Mary Anna Whiting Pvt CT
Ephraim: b 1738 d 7-24-1813 m Rhoda Andrews Pvt NY
Hezekiah: b 10-9-1756 d 11-6-1827 m Hannah Cook Pvt CT
Jehiel: b 9-30-1761 d 7-27-1834 m Sarah Hatch Pvt VT ★
John: b 12-21-1716 d 4-7-1780 m Elizabeth Kegwin Sgt MA
Jonathan: bpt 3-9-1734/5 d 5-18-1813 m Rebecca Moody Mrnr MA
Joseph: b 10-20-1722 d 9-23-1796 m Rachel Killam Capt CT
Joshua: b c. 1739 d c. 1820 m Dorothy Case Pvt MA
Josiah, Sr.: b 6-30-1705 d 1-29-1781 m Rachel Cole CT
Josiah, Jr.: b 8-26-1740 d 9-17-1776 m Hannah Rice Sol CT
Levi: b 5-6-1739 d 3-22-1782 m Esther — Pvt CS PS CT
Moses: b 1763 d 9-29-1816 m Abigail Mead Pvt CT
Nathaniel: b 3-14-1731 d 11-11-1814 m Esther Carver Capt VT
Offin: b 2-18-1748 d 1-8-1811 m (1)Sarah Greenleaf (2)Sarah Tappan Capt MA
Oliver: b 8-2-1758 d 7-28-1826 m Sarah Danforth Pvt CT
Samuel: b 3-9-1751/2 d 1780 m Katherine Thorp Pvt CT
Seth: b 4-21-1742 d 2-25-1831 m Abigail Fosdick Pvt CT ★
Sherman: b 8-2-1725 d 7-29-1814 m Sarah Bostwick PS CT
Wm.: b 3-31-1762 d 1793 m Mary Short Pvt MA

BOAS, (includes BOAZ, BOOS)
Henry: b 10-30-1760 d 3-4-1838 m Dorotha Baumgartner Pvt PA ★
James: b 5-30-1749 d 11-12-1850 m (1)Anna Russell (2)Milly Boaz QM Sgt VA ★
John Wm.: b 1739 d 11-28-1814 m Barbara Epler PS PA
Thomas: b 9-27-1721 d 9-13-1791 m Agnes — PS VA

BOATMAN,
Claudius, Sr.: b c. 1724 d 1802 m Esther — Pvt PA
Claudius, Jr.: b 1759 d 2-15-1794 m Marie Reed Pvt PA

BOATWRIGHT, (includes BOOTWRIGHT)
James: b — d p. 1-10-1814 m (1)Elizabeth Kidd (2)Mary Kidd PS VA
Samuel: b 1764 d 5-4-1834 m Nancy Weathers Pvt VA ★

BOBB,
John Conrad: b 2-5-1740 d 2-5-1808 m Eve — PS & Sol PA
Peter: b 1760 d p. 1814 m Mena Hassinger Pvt PA

BOBBENMEIER,
Gabriel: b 4-2-1749 d 4-4-1817 m Christenah Walter Pvt PA

BOBBITT,
Isham: b 3-3-1754 d 1836 m Elizabeth — Sgt NC ★
Lewis: b — d p. 1-16-1816 m Mary — PS NC

BOBO,
Lewis: b c. 1736 d 1805-8 m Sarah — PS SC
Sampson: b c. 1738 d 1804 m Sarah Simpson Pvt SC

BOCK,
Baltzer: b 3-30-1746 d 6-17-1827 m Susanna M. Bolick Sol PA
Michael: b 1756/7 d 1838 m Margaret Crowser Pvt VA ★

BOCKEE,
Jacob: b 10-18-1757 d 10-16-1819 m Catharine Smith Lt NY

BOCKIUS,
Francis Wm.: b 3-12-1754 d 5-31-1837 m Susanna Miller Pvt PA

BOCKOVEN, (includes BOCKOVER)
George: b 9-17-1734/5 d 6-8-1814 m Mary Whitenack Lt NJ
Jacob: b 1735 d 3-19-1819 m Elizabeth Whitenac Capt NJ

BODDIE,
Bennett: b 9-9-1763 d 2-21-1809 m Sarah Smith Sol NC
John: b a. 1753 d a. 1808 m Hannah — Sol NC & SC
Nathan: b 2-22-1732 d 12-7-1797 m Chloe Crudup PS NC
Wm.: b 5-10-1749 d 1-6-1817 m Martha Jones PS NC

BODE,
Johannas Peter: b 3-12-1732 d 12-14-1808 m Catherine Barbara Schoeffer Pvt PA

BODFISH,
Jonathan: b 8-10-1727 d 1- -1818 m Desire Howland Pvt MA

BODGE,
Benjamin: b 1-18-1746 d 8-18-1822 m Susanna Pecker Pvt MA
Benjamin: b 1-6-1755/6 d 8-21-1831 m (1)Susannah Hunnewell (2) Elizabeth Gammon Pvt MA
Benjamin: b c. 1755 d 1802 m Meribah Hall Sgt NH
Samuel: b 1743 d 1796 m Margaret Osborn Pvt MA

BODINE,
Cornelius: b 10-12-1755 d 6-12-1820 m Margaret Sutphen MM NJ
John: b 1746 d 3-26-1826 m (1)Mary Roundtree (2)Ann Taylor Ens NJ
John: b 4-15-1743 d c. 1790 m Lementje Cozine MM NJ
John: b 1744 d 9-2-1822 m Jane Marlatt Sgt VA ★

BODLE,
Samuel: b 1751 d p. 1790 m Katie Van Tyle Sgt NY
Wm.: b 3-31-1746 d 1-23-1838 m Sarah Owen Pvt CS CT

BODLEY,
John: b 9-15-1733 d 4-9-1801 m Jannitje De Witt Pvt NY
Thomas: b 9-13-1757 d 3- -1847 m Mrs Margaretta Davis Pvt PA ★
Wm.: b 1746 d 12-4-1780 m Isabella Parker Maj PA

BODMAN,
Samuel: b 1711 d 7-8-1803 m Martha Warner PS & CS MA

BODWELL,
Benjamin: b 8-22-1741 d 4-7-1787 m Mary Griswold Woodbridge Sgt CT
Daniel, Sr.: b 1-22-1721/22 d p. 2- -1804 m Abigail Ladd Pvt MA
Daniel, Jr.: b 10-14-1748 d p. 1795 m Allice Messer Pvt MA
Eliphalet: b 7-8-1739 d p. 1778 m Hannah Barker Capt MA
Henry: b 7-26-1729 d 4-9-1816 m Ann Pottelle Capt MA
John: b 1-16-1752 d 11-19-1811 m Miriam White Capt MA
John: b 12-27-1723 d p. 4-26-1788 m (1)Elizabeth Messer (2)Elizabeth Powers PS MA
Joshua: b 10-4-1736 d p. 1787 m Pricilla Barker Pvt MA
Parker: b 10-29-1750 d 8-7-1795 m Hannah Abbot Pvt MA

BOEHM,
Philip, 3rd: b 12-14-1747 d 1-10-1816 m Anna B. Schreiber LCol PM PA

BOGARDUS,
Cornelius: b 4-26-1726 d 11-23-1794 m Catherine M. Phillips Pvt NY
Cornelius: b 1-22-1758 d 7-6-1811 m Elizabeth Van Voorhis Pvt NY
Ephraim: b 8-7-1726 d 1813 m Annetje Hallenbeck Sgt NY
Evert: b 5-28-1732 d 6-13-1810 m Arietta Kiersted Capt NY
Evert: b 6- -1733 d 1808 m Catherine Dubois Pvt NY
Francis: b 7-4-1731 d 9-25-1830 m Mariann Losee Pvt NY
Hendrick: bpt 12-17-1755 d p. 1845 m Eleanor McCayg (McKeg) Sgt NY
Jacob: b 9-15-1750 d 4-24-1839 m Marie Vandenberg Sol NY
James: b c. 1760 d p. 1818 m Mary Lent Pvt NY
James C.: b 7-18-1764 d 10-13-1836 m Mary Scott Pvt NY ★
Lewis: b 10-9-1738 d 1-12-1808 m Annie Mills Sgt NY
Lewis: b 1753 d — m Annetjie Knoxen Pvt NY
Nanning: b 5-11-1761 d 10-24-1828 m Neeltje Goes Pvt NY
Peter: b 1748 d 12-20-1820 m Anna De Witt Pvt NY
Peter: b 1-15-1756 d 4-3-1826 m (1)Martha Van Tassel Medler (2) Silvy Frink (3)Sally Mooney Pvt NY
Petrus: b 4-24-1699 d 8-8-1775 m Rebecca DuBois PS NY

BOGART, (includes BOGAERT, BOGERT)
Adrain: b 12-1-1720 d 1-7-1799 m Magdalena Schenck PS NY
Cornelius: b 8-26-1744 d 9-30-1825 m Sitchy Demarest Pvt NJ
Cornelius: b 4-13-1755 d p. 1810 m Agnes Still Pvt NJ
Cornelius: b 1-15-1730 d 7-22-1811 m (1)Sarah Outwater (2)Sarah Frier Pvt PS NY W★
Cornelius: bpt 8-3-1760 d 7-22-1811 m Sarah Freer Pvt NY W★
David: b 5-14-1747 d 10-23-1805 m Cornelia Ryckman Pvt NY
Guilliam: bpt 10-12-1746 d p. 1795 m Catlyntje Ackerman 2Lt NJ
Hendrich Isaac: b 10-26-1729 d 6-27-1821 m ( )Henchichie Outhout ( )Belitje Westervelt Capt NY
Hendrick: b 5-23-1760 d 8-11-1822 m Catherine Coons Pvt NY
Henry: b 8-20-1761 d 1-25-1834 m Prudence Keeler Pvt NY ★
Isaac: b 6-13-1741 d 9-25-1818 m Cathalyna Hun Lt NY
Jan: b 1-28-1748 d 2-21-1781 m Philandera Forbes Sgt NY
Johannis: b 8-30-1755 d 4-2-1850 m Catherine Mebie Pvt NY
John: b 1734 d 1780 m Mary Vredenberg Pvt NY
John: b 9-5-1761 d 5-22-1853 m (2)Christiana Vought NCapt NY ★
Matthew: b 4-24-1749 d 1784-90 m Sara Bogert Pvt NJ
Nicholas C.: bpt 12-22-1734 d 9-23-1794 m (1)Cornelia Bradus (2) Anne Myndert Schuyler Adj NY
Ort: b c. 1730 d p. 1790 m Catrina Pele Pvt NY
Peter: bpt 4-12-1736 d 1841 m Rachel Banta Pvt & MM NJ

BOGER, (includes BOGARD)
Christian: b 12-29-1747 d 7-29-1779 m Barbara — Pvt PA
Cornelius: b — d p. 4-21-1795 m X Pvt VA
Matthias: b p. 1716 d p. 3-27-1784 m Anna Magdalena Wampsler PS PA
Valentine: b 11-16-1758 d 7-24-1826 m Juliana Imboden Pvt PA

BOGGAN, (includes BOGAN)
Isaac: b c. 1745 d p. 10- -1805 m Easter Farrar Sgt SC
Patrick: b 1725 d 1817 m Mary Dabbs PS NC

BOGGESS, (includes BOGGASS)
Henry: b 1740 d 1813 m Abigail — Ens VA
Samuel: b 9-20-1742 d 12-30-1825 m Elizabeth Dorsey 1Lt MD

BOGGS,
Aaron: b 10-10-1750 d 3-26-1832 m Elisabeth Hamilton Sgt SC
Alexander: b 10-7-1755 d 3-30-1839 m Ann Alricks Capt PA
Andrew: b a. 1743 d c. 1784 m Marjorie Harris Sgt PA
Francis: b 6-24-1742 d 2-8-1826 m Jane Morrison Campbell Pvt PA
James: b 7-21-1730 d 1805 m (1)Hannah Reese (2)Sarah Brown Capt PA
James: b 1745 d p. 9-30-1783 m Martha — Sol PA
John: b 1-11-1759 d 4-5-1847 m Elizabeth Pearson Pvt DE
John: b c. 1750 d 10-25-1788 m Eve Springer Pvt NC W★
John: b 1731 d 12- -1796 m Elizabeth Johnston Maj PM PA
John: b 3-3-1739 d 2-6-1826 m Jane Irwin PS PA & VA
Joseph: b c. 1750 d p. 8-24-1794 m Jane Renwick PS SC
Joseph: b 10- -1749 d 1- -1843 m Sarah Riddle Lt PA
Moses: b 11-12-1756 d 2-22-1833 m Margaret Donnall PS DE
Robert: b 9-9-1748 d 8-25-1827 m Sarah Huston Capt VA
Samuel, Jr.: b 1759 d 10-1-1834 m Susanna Annis Cpl MA ★
Samuel: b c. 1725 d 1779 m Mary Giffin Sol MA
Thomas: b 7-10-1732 d 1790 m Catherine — Lt NY
Wm.: b 1755 d 6-22-1841 m Margaret Boggs Pvt PA
Wm.: b c. 1767 d 9-1-1821 m Margaret Sara Wrenshall Pvt PA

BOGLE,
Andrew: b 4-20-1753 d 11-29-1813 m Elizabeth Campbell Pvt PA VA
Joseph: b c. 1730 d 9-6-1790 m Jane McIntire Pvt PA
Robert: b c. 1760 d p. 9-10-1802 m Jennet — PS NC
Rowand: b 5-9-1736 d 2-20-1822 m Elizabeth Goodnow Lt MA

BOGMAN,
Charles Laurens: b 5- -1747 d 8-10-1821 m Mary Scudder Cpl RI

BOGNER,
Tobias: b 1730 d 7-22-1822 m X Sol PA

BOGUE,
Jeffery: b 8-21-1759 d 8-31-1828 m Freedom Barnard Pvt CT W★
Oliver: b 4-13-1757 d 2-2-1828 m Lucy Dervin Pvt CT W★
Publius Virgilius: b 3-30-1764 d 8-28-1836 m Catherine Robinson Pvt CT ★
Samuel Cook: b 8-7-1755 d 6-10-1829 m Triphena Thompson Pvt CT
Wm.: b c. 1760 d a. 1787 m Penelope Pettis Pvt VT

BOHANON, (includes BOHANNON, BOHONAN, BOHONNON)
Ananiah: b 7-22-1743 d 1818 m Shuah Fifield Sgt NH
Andrew, Sr.: b 1709 d 1803 m Tabitha Flanders PS NH
Andrew, Jr.: b 8-11-1737 d 5-24-1826 m (1)Susannah Webster (2) Betsey Garvin Lt NH
Elliott, Jr.: b 1753 d 1824 m (2)Mary — PS VA
George: b 6-23-1738 d 1797 m Elizabeth — Pvt MD
John: b 1753 d 7-10-1832 m Helen Cook Pvt VA
Joseph: b 1755 d 1825 m Patty Snead Pvt VA
Stephen: b 10-10-1763 d 1-26-1831 m Olive Elliott Cpl Stl NH ★
Wm.: b c. 1730 d 3-13-1816 m X PS VA
Wm.: b 1740 d 1796 m Mary Gordon PS VA

BOHON,
John: b 12-25-1756 d p. 1832 m Sarah Johnson Pvt VA ★

BOHRER,
Peter: b c. 1745 d p. 1790 m Magdalena Schenkmayer PS MD

BOILER,
David: b 1743 d 1-13-1824 m Nancy Fisher PS PA

BOLAND,
David, Jr.: b 7-23-1748 d 6-8-1795 m Betty Keeler Lt CT
Wm.: b 1742 d p. 1800 m X Capt CT

BOLDEN,
John: b — 1745 d 10-23-1826 m Sybil Tarr Pvt VA ★

BOLENDER,
Adam, Jr.: b c. 1745 d 5-21-1829 m Barbara Moyer Pvt PA
Stephen: b 10-9-1756 d 2-25-1820 m (1)Margreta Schenckel (2) Mrs Elizabeth Fitterman Pvt PA

BOLEY,
Pressley Mountford: b 12-15-1766 d 5-20-1838 m Polly A. — Pvt CL ★

BOLICH, (includes BLACH)
Andreas, Sr.: b c. 1730 d 4- -1780 m Christina — PS PA
Andreas, Jr.: b 10-20-1757 d 1843 m Margaretha Elizabeth Kimmel Pvt PA

BOLLEN,
John: b 7-5-1756 d 11-7-1846 m Mrs Ann Hoge 1Sgt NJ ★

BOLLING, (includes BOLING, BOWLING)
Anne: b 1718 d c. 1800 m James Murray PS VA
James: b 1752 d 11-12-1836 m Letitia More Gillespie Pvt VA ★
Jarret: b 1-18-1762 d 1856 m Winnie Gryson Pvt VA ★
Jesse: b 5-22-1758 d p. 1832 m Polly Greene Sgt NC ★
Jesse: b 6-1-1758 d 8-15-1841 m Mary Pennington Pvt VA
Jesse: b 1759 d 1815 m Sarah Robinson Pvt VA
Jesse: b c. 1745-50 d 11-1-1793 m Sally — PS VA
John: b 1761 d p. 12-25-1845 m Naomi Ray Pvt VA
Mary Marshall : b 6-12-1737/8 d 2-24-1814 m Robert Bolling PS VA
Robert, Jr.: b 3-3-1759 d 1-26-1839 m (1)Mary Augusta Burton Bolling (2)Catherine Stith (3)Sally Washington (4)Anne Dade Capt VA
Robert: b 3-24-1751 d 1791 m Clara Yates NLt VA
Robert: b 8-17-1738 d 9-29-1775 m (1)Mary Burton (2)Susan Watson PS VA
Samuel: b c. 1752 d p. 5-9-1808 m Abigail Choice Ens VA
Wm.: b 1731 d a. 4- -1778 m Amelia Randolph Sol VA
Wm.: b c. 1730 d a. 8-20-1778 m Mary Randolph Pvt VA

BOLLINGER,
Abraham: b 1756 d 1837 m Barbara Catherine — Pvt PA
Henry: b 1744 d 1776 m Miss Cline Sol NC

BOLLMAN,
Abraham: b— d 5-7-1786 m Catherine Young Pvt PA
John: b 1-11-1755 d 12-4-1836 m Anna Maria Phillipi Pvt PA

BOLSINGER,
George: b 4-26-1752 d 6-19-1832 m Elizabeth — PS MD

BOLSTER,
Baruch: b 8-3-1763 d p. 3-14-1846 m Anna Loveland Pvt MA ★
Isaac: b 4-28-1737 d 4-27-1825 m Mary Dwinnell Capt MA
Nathan: b 4-28-1756 d 2-23-1823 m Chloe Keith Sol MA

BOLTER,
Lemuel: b 1760 d 1840 m Sarah Jane Rose Pvt MA ★

BOLTON,
Aaron: b 2-12-1753 d 4-29-1837 m Dorcas Winship Sgt MA ★
Charles: b c. 1735 d p. 2-15-1803 m Elizabeth — PS NC
James: b c. 1756 d c. 1798 m Mary — PS PA
John: b— d 1799 m Kitty (Christian)Wynne Sol GA
John: b 6-20-1726 d 3-2-1784 m Eleanor Dougherty Cmsry MD
John: b 1740 d 1807 m Martha McGee Lt MA
John: b 6-8-1757 d 10-27-1838 m. (2)Mary Lancaster Sol NC
John: b 1738 d 1810 m Mary Bolton Pvt PA
Matthew: b 6-9-1763 m 9-4-1824 m Mary Chapman Sol VA
Richard: b c. 1736 d 8- -1820 m Tabitha Wheatley Sgt NC
Robert: b 12-1-1757 d 12-4-1802 m Sarah Jackson Pvt GA
Solomon: b 1756 d 1-4-1840 m Elizabeth Pratt Pvt MA
Thomas: b 2-25-1758 d 6-18-1793 m Hannah Crockett Pvt MA
Thomas: b c. 1760 d p. 9-2-1807 m Phebe Waller Pvt NC
Timothy: b 5-5-1759 d 3-4-1826 m Sybil Bennett Pvt MA
Wm.: b 4-13-1731 d 10-12-1787 m Rachel Haskell Pvt MA
Wm., Jr.: b 1-21-1744 d 5-7-1780 m Mrs Abigail Sheldon Drm MA

BOLTWOOD,
John: b 10-3-1759 d 2-5-1803 m Sarah Hayze Pvt MA
Solomon: b 12-26-1727 d 5-17-1777 m Mary Strong Pvt MA

BOLTZ,
Jacob: b c. 1730 d 1795 m Catherine Madern PS PA
John Michael, Sr.: b 1731 d 4- -1806 m Veronica — Pvt PA
John Michael, Jr.: b 1-22-1758 d a. 1-26-1806 m Eve Zombro Pvt PA

BOMAR,
John: b 7-31-1757 d p. 10-7-1845 m X Pvt VA ★
John: b — d p. 1-17-1799 m Barbary Bush PS VA

BOMBAUGH,
Conrad: b 1751 d 2-4-1821 m Esther Zell Pvt PA

BOMBERGER, (includes BOMBARGER)
Jacob: b 1760 d 1828 m Maria Ellamoker Pvt PA
John: b 1-31-1739 d 5-6-1798 m Catharine Flora Pvt PA

BOND, (includes BONDE)
Abner: b 9-24-1760 d 10-24-1846 m Mary — Pvt NJ
Asa: b 8-25-1757 d 4-20-1835 m Sarah Humphrey Pvt MA
Bethuel: b 1-1-1762 d 8-3-1818 m Ruth Herrick Pvt CT
Bethuel: b 1763 d 8-15-1841 m Lydia Dolph Pvt MA
Dudley: b a. 1755 d p. 4-14-1815 m Frances — Sol SC
Elihu: b 1746 d 3-29-1819 m Eleanor Abbot Pvt MA
Ephraim: b 1746 d 3-29-1819 m Eleanor Abbot Pvt MA
Henry: b 2-4-1741/2 d 1828 m Mary Fletcher Sgt MA
Henry: b 9-6-1712 d p. 1781 m Mary Cutting PS CS NH
Israel: b 11-27-1760 d 1-31-1836 m Mary Morgan Sgt MA ★
John: b — d 1808 m Elizabeth — Cpl MD
John: b 4- -1730 d 12- -1786 m Alice Anna Webster Pvt MD

John: b 3-16-1724 d 6-30-1808 m Silence King Pvt MA
Jonas: b 8-5-1723 d p. 1790 m Abigail Dewey Pvt CT
Jonathan: b 4-30-1750 d 7-26-1810 m Sarah Crossman Cpl MA
Jonathan: b 11-7-1710 d 1-11-1789 m Mary Harrington Pvt MA
Joshua: b 11-20-1720 d 2-18-1790 m Millicent Russell PS MA
Josiah, Jr.: b 6-21-1724 m 1-17-1809 m Sarah Melondy Pvt MA
Nathaniel: b 1759 d p. 1789 m Elizabeth Dickinson Pvt NJ
Nathaniel: b 12-10-1762 d 1-20-1855 m Rachel Potter Pvt NJ
Richard, Sr.: b 10-4-1728 d 1-14-1819 m (1)Mary Wells (2) Mary Booth PS CS MD
Richard: b c. 1742 d p. 1800 m Susannah Gardiner Key PS MD
Richard: b c. 1756 d p. 9-11-1823 m (1)Mary Blanchard (2)Libey Speight (3)Nancy Hinton Sgt NC
Richard, Jr.: b 3-9-1756 d 2-14-1820 m (1)Tamar Davis (2)Mary Brumfield (3)Mary Lewis 1Lt MD
Robert: b 9-19-1743 d 5-28-1806 m Eunice — Pvt MA
Samuel: b — d 9-11-1777 m Mary Bethel Gen DE
Sarah Carruthers: b c. 1730 d p. 1790 m Vinyard Bond PS NC
Thaddeus: b 11-16-1751 d 10-27-1831 m Relief Damon Cpl MA
Thomas: b c. 1739 d p. 1791 m Rebecca Stansbury PS MD
Thomas: b 6-31-1739 d p. 1787 m Lydia Newton Lt MA
Thomas: b 6-3-1712 d 3-26-1784 m Susannah Roberts Dr PA
Wm.: b 1746 d p. 3-25-1783 m Sarah Wrongs CS MD
Wm.: b 2-17-1734 d 8-30-1776 m Lucy Brown Col MA
Wm.: b 3- -1757 d 10-22-1851 m Sarah Parks Pvt MA ★
Wm.: b 1740 d 3-20-1827 m (1)Frances Ballou (2)Sarah Cranson Pvt VA ★
Wright: b 4-13-1759 d 2-10-1843 m (1) — Hubbard (2)Martha Brown Sgt VA ★

BONDURANT,
John, Jr.: b 8-1-1737 d a. 1810 m X PS VA
Joseph: b c. 1719 d p. 11-26-1803 m Agnes Redford PS VA

BONEAUX, (includes BONNEAU)
Charles: b c. 1730 d a. 8-2-1784 m Genevieve Du Devoire PS VA
Pierre: b 2-4-1761 d 1832 m (1) — Vanderburgh (2)Mary Anne De Noyon Cmsry VA

BONEBRAKE,
De Walt: b 10-1-1755 d 8-29-1824 m Christiana Wolfe Pvt PA

BONES, (includes BONE)
John: b c. 1760 d p. 1-8-1824 m Elizabeth Winstead Drm Pvt VA
Thomas: b c. 1740 d p. 1796 m Mary McCreary Pvt NC
Thomas: b 1753 d 4-2-1830 m Susannah Rowland Pvt PA

BONESTEEL,
David: b 1-27-1766 d 10-15-1854 m Hannah Rowley Pvt NY
Nicholas: b 11-21-1753 d — m Margaret Staats Pvt NY
Philip: b 1753 d 9-17-1848 m Elizabeth Ray Pvt NY

BONEY,
John: b 1-17-1766 d 10-3-1831 m Mary Wells PS NC
Wimbeck: b c. 1730 d p. 9-18-1801 m Catharine — Pvt NC

BONFOY, (includes BONFOEY)
Benanuel: b 12-13-1755 d 8-14-1825 m Concurrence Smith Pvt CT ★
Henry: b 1752/3 d 6-8-1837 m Sarah — Pvt CT ★

BONHAM,
Absolom: b 1739 d 10-4-1794 m (1)Jemima Harker (2)Mrs Rebecca (Morris)Cox Brevet Capt NJ
Benjamin: b c. 1754 d — m Elizabeth Ransom Capt NJ
Ephriam: b 1716 d 1785 m (1)Elizabeth Morris (2)Susannah Jones Pvt NJ
Jacob: b— d 6- -1782 m X Sgt PA
Jacob: b 1726 d 1798 m Polly Warford Pvt PA
James: b 1766 d 1815 m Sophie Butler Smith Pvt MD
Moses: b 1750 d 11- -1782 m Rebecca Park Pvt PA
Zedekiah: b 2-24-1762 d 4-22-1835 m Prudence Heth Pvt NJ W★

BONIFACE,
Wm.: b 1748 d 10-2-1820 m Amillea — Sgt VA

BONIFANTE, (includes BONNIFIELD)
Samuel: b 4-11-1752 d 2- -1848 m Dorcas James Pvt VA
Samuel: b 6-3-1731 d 1-6-1810 m Sarah Townshend Pvt MD

BONINE,
Daniel: b 1-11-1736 d 7- -1817 m (1)Elizabeth — (2)Sarah Miller (3)Mary Copeland Pvt PA
Thomas: b 1753 d 8-1-1785 m Mary — Pvt PA

BONNELL,
Aaron: b 3-4-1759 d 10-4-1837 m Rachael Clark Pvt Arfr MM NJ
Abraham: b 8-4-1732 d 11-1-1797 m Elizabeth Foster LCol NJ
Anthony: b c. 1752 d 1805 m Mary Ann — Lt GA
Benjamin, Sr.: b 1723 d 1798 m (2)Rachel Van Winkle Pvt NJ
Benjamin, Jr.: b 1756 d 10-9-1808 m (1)Hannah Ward (2)Hannah Golden Sol NJ

Jacob: b *c.* 1740 d *a.* 4- -1797 m Mary Schooley Pvt NJ
James: b 1754 d 1808 m Elizabeth Shimer Capt NJ W★
John: b 9-26-1737 d 12-15-1817 m Sarah Carter Pvt NJ
John: b *c.* 1757 d *c.* 1845 m Nancy Pandy Sgt PA
Nathaniel: b 12-29-1731 d 7-23-1809 m (1)Elizabeth Allen (2)Mary Simpson Pvt NJ
Paul: b 11-7-1762 d 8-26-1820 m X Pvt PA ★

BONNER, (includes BONAR, BUNNER)
Andrew: b 3-17-1740 d 12-19-1791 m Sarah Fisher PS PA
Benjamin: b 2-4-1750 d 1-1-1815 m Frances — 1Lt NC
Charles: b 1744 d 3-20-1833 m Nancy Galbraith Capt PA
David: b — d 11-5-1804 m Mercy Hancock Pvt MA
Frederick: b 11-4-1758 d 1830 m Elizabeth Smith PS VA
Henry: b 1734 d 1-1-1822 m Ann Cate Capt VA
Henry: b *c.* 1732 d *p.* 1779 m Elizabeth Ann Snoad 2Maj NC
James, Sr.: b *c.* 1719 d *p.* 1782 m Mary Snode Col NC
James, Jr.: b 1753 d 1791 m Sarah Wilson Sol NC
James: b 1753 d 11-1-1825 m Mary Laird Sol SC
John: b 8-20-1764 d 9-4-1842 m Sarah Love Pvt VA ★
John: b *c.* 1760 d *p.* 10-20-1824 m Rebecca Calhoun Sol VA
John: b 8-13-1755 d 3-13-1835 m Jean Thompson SgtMaj PA ★
John: b — d 1784/85 m Sarah — Pvt PA
Joseph: b 1752 d *p.* 11-10-1828 m X Pvt PA ★
Joseph: b *c.* 1760 d 1-6-1825 m Susannah — Sol VA
Thomas: b *a.* 1720 d 1787 m Sarah Peyton Col NC
Thomas: b *c.* 1744 d 12- -1804 m X Sol SC
Wm.: b 12-29-1759 d 4-9-1847 m Hannah — Pvt PA ★
Wm.: b *c.* 1755 d *a.* 3-4-1814 m Sarah — Pvt PA
Wm.: b 1756 d 12-29-1834 m Elizabeth Richards Pvt NC ★

BONNETHEAU,
Peter: b 12-7-1742 d 11-19-1798 m (1)Ann Anderson (2)Elizabeth Weyman 1Lt SC

BONNETT,
John: b 1731 d 8- -1793 m Dorothy Bickley CS PA
John: b 2-7-1761 d 3-1-1840 m Margaret Marchand Pvt PA
Joseph: b 5-18-1757 d 9-28-1824 m Tamma Johnson Sgt CT ★
Lewis: b 1737 d 8-9-1808 m Elizabeth Waggoner Pvt VA

BONNEY,
Benjamin: bpt 5-6-1739 d 9-4-1803 m (1)Silence White (2)Hannah Day LCol PS MA W★
Ebenezer: b 3-2-1735 d 7-13-1802 m Deborah Drew Sgt MA
Ezekiel: b 12-20-1762 d 10-29-1845 m Zerviah Perry Fif MA
Ichabod: b — d — m X Officer ME
Ichabod, Jr.: b 12-14-1762 d — m Anna Merrill Pvt MA
Isaac: b 10-14-1765 d 2-11-1809 m Sarah Stephens Cpl MA
James: b 11-27-1737 d 11-5-1802 m Anne — Capt NJ
Jarius: b 2-14-1747 d 1820 m Anne Brown Pvt CT
Joseph: b 6-24-1736 d 4-30-1825 m Elizabeth Delano Pvt MA
Levi: b 1743 d 5-24-1824 m Mary May PS CT
Noah: b 11-7-1748 d 2-13-1826 m Ann Torrey 2Lt MA
Perez: b 7-13-1742 d 3-4-1813 m Priscilla Pierce Pvt CT
Samuel: b 4-21-1742 d *p.* 1782 m Mary Soper Pvt MA
Simeon: b 1730 d 9-29-1781 m Thankful Whitin Pvt MA

BONSALL,
Benjamin: b 9-6-1756-9 d 6-6-1845 m (1)Rachel — (2)Catherine Egler Pvt PA ★
Caleb: b 2-25-1764 d 4-2-1833 m Mary Noblitt Sol PA
Jonathan: b 9-3-1738 d 4-4-1814 m (1)Elizabeth Evans (2)Margaret Crozier Sol PA

BONT,
Jacob: bpt 2-2-1739 d *p.* 3-13-1785 m (1)Geesje Jansen (2)Janetje Schutt Pvt NY

BONWELL,
James: b 1-12-1750 d 3-4-1820 m May Robin Pvt VA ★

BOODY, (includes BOODEY)
Azariah: b 8-15-1720 d 2-26-1803 m Bridget Bushbie PS NH
John: b 6-23-1749 d 4-23-1815 m Susan Langley Pvt NH

BOOGHER,
Jacob: b 1756 d 1804 m Elizabeth Christ Matr MD

BOOK, (includes BUCH)
George: b 1758 d 1823 m Isabella Vogan Pvt PA
Jacob: b 12-27-1761 d 9-20-1852 m Mary Book Pvt PA
Michael: b — d 1813 m Barbara — Pvt PA

BOOKER, (includes BUCHER)
Aaron: b 8-29-1758 d *p.* 1779 m Anne Ellingwood Pvt MA
Daniel: b 2-25-1760 d 11-8-1856 m Mary Douglass Pvt MA
Edmund: b 6-17-1741 d 9-24-1795 m Mary Pride LCol VA
Edmund: b — d *p.* 9-26-1792 m Edith Cobbs CS VA
Edward (4th): b 10-8-1740 d 6-22-1812 m Mary Bentley Capt VA
Edward: b 1761 d 1- -1800 m Edith Cobbs Anderson Pvt VA
George, Jr.: b 1729 d 1791 m Sarah Richardson PS VA

Jacob: b — d 1799/1800 m Mary Ann Witzell Pvt VA
James: b *c.* 1725 d *p.* 5-3-1790 m (1) X (2)Ann Camm (3)Mrs Elizabeth Wright PS VA
John: b 5-16-1736 d *p.* 7-5-1799 m Omai — Pvt NC
John: b 6-23-1751 d 6-18-1803 m Ann Elizabeth Giles Cmsry VA
John Eaton: b *c.* 1757 d *c.* 1820 m Elizabeth Ford Pvt VA
Lewis: b 5-21-1754 d 12-23-1814 m Judith Dudley CaptLt VA & MD
Lewis: b *c.* 1750 d 1806 m Jane Wyatt 1Lt VA
Richard Marot: b 1751 d 4- -1805 m Elizabeth Palmer PS VA
Samuel: b 8-9-1758 d 12-22-1847 m (1)Rachel Jones (2)Nancy A. Nantz Pvt & QM VA W★
William: b *c.* 1720 d 1783 m Mary Flournoy PS VA
William Marshall: b *c.* 1750 d 3-19-1802 m Elizabeth — PS VA

BOOKMAN,
Jacob: b 1730 d *a.* 1790 m Anna — PS SC

BOOKSTAVER,
Jacob, Sr.: b — d 1798 m Anna Medgar Pvt NY
William: bpt 8-9-1750 d 3-19-1807 m Maria Sensebach Pvt NY

BOOMER,
Daniel: b *c.* 1746 d *p.* 6-2-1801 m Hannah Church Pvt MA
Ephraim: b 4-3-1763 d 3-29-1856 m Abigail Crocker Sgt MA
James: b 5-26-1759 d *p.* 2-20-1837 m Susanna Borden Pvt MA
Martin: b 12-25-1732 d 6- -1802 m (1)Jemima Elsbree (2)Sarah Stillwell Pvt MA
Nathaniel: b 8-6-1762 d 1-18-1842 m Sarah Borden Pvt MA

BOONE, (includes BOHN, BOON)
Andrew: b 11-17-1737 d *p.* 1783 m Martha Gunion Sol PA
Benjamin: b 1754 d 1823 m Mary Wilson Sol NC
Benjamin: b 8-13-1741 d 9-25-1824 m Eve Lofter Pvt PA
Daniel: b 10-22-1734 d 9-26-1820 m Rebecca Bryan Col PS VA & KY
David: b *c.* 1759 d *c.* 1802 m Ann Davis Pvt PA
Edward: b 11-30-1740 d 10-6-1780 m Martha Bryan Sol VA
George: b *c.* 1759 d 6-30-1824 m Margaret Mayberry PS PA
George: b 11-2-1739 d 11-14-1820 m Nancy Linville Pvt VA
Hugh: b *c.* 1735 d 1805 m (1)Catherine — (2)Frances Millard Pvt PA
Ignatius: b *a.* 1750 d 1785-90 m Jean Gardiner Sgt MD
Isaac: b 7-27-1739 d 7- -1794 m Sarah — Pvt PA
Jacob: b 1744 d 1814 m Catherine — PS & Pvt VA CL
Jacob: b 8-15-1754 d 5-4-1827 m Mary De Hart Pvt & PS PA
James: b 1735 d 1805 m Elizabeth Bryan Pvt NC
James: b *c.* 1758 d 5-20-1822 m Mary Whiteman Lt RI
Jeremiah: b 2-29-1760 d 6-10-1832 m Joyce Nevel Pvt VA
John: b 3-27-1736 d 1790-1802 m Elizabeth Williams Capt MD
John: b 7-16-1755 d 1-27-1837 m (1)— Starns (2)Elizabeth Barringer (3)Anne Montgomery Pvt NC ★
John: b 1755 d 1835 m Elizabeth Alford Pvt PA ★
Joseph: b 1752 d 1836 m Sarah Bass CS NC
Josiah, Sr.: b 3-6-1726 d *c.* 1814 m Hannah Hite Pvt & Grd VA
Josiah, Jr.: b *c.* 1758 d *c.* 1822 m (1)Percis Hinton (2)Ellenor Adams Pvt VA
Nicholas: b *c.* 1736 d *p.* 1823 m (1)Anna Maria — (2)Barbara — PS MD
Nicholas: b *c.* 1731 d 4-10-1804 m Anna Elizabeth — Pvt PA
Raiford: b 11-8-1763 d 12-19-1834 m Polly Simmons Pvt NC
Ratliff: b — d *a.* 2-4-1799 m Patience — PS VA
Rebecca Bryan: b 1-9-1739 d 3-18-1813 m Daniel Boone PS VA & KY
Samuel: b 2-22-1736 d *c.* 1805 m (1)Rachel Coles (2)Jane Hughes PS MD
Samuel: b 5-31-1728 d 1808 m Sarah Day Sol PS KY & VA
Squire: b 10-13-1760 d 6-28-1817 m Annie Grubbs Sgt SC W★
Squire, Jr.: b 10-5-1744 d 8-5-1815 m Jane Van Cleft CS Capt PS VA
Thomas: b 8-21-1759 d 2-6-1831 m Susanna Brumfield Pvt PA
Wm.: b 1735 d 1799 m Rebecca — Pvt NC
Wm.: b *c.* 1740 d *a.* 2-17-1792 m Keziah Green Pvt VA

BOOR,
Michael: b 2-19-1716 d 9-1-1778 m Margaret — Pvt PA
Nicholas: b 1754/55 d *p.* 1804 m X Pvt PA

BOORUM, (includes BOERUM, BOORAEM, BURMAN)
Henry: b — d 8-22-1823 m Mary Miller Pvt & Wgn PA
Jacob: b 1756 d 1-17-1836 m Christiann — Pvt NJ W★
Nicholas: b *c.* 1750 d 1825 m (2)Mercy Rolfe Pvt NJ

BOOSER,
Henry: b 1756 d 3-2-1837 m Elizabeth Senn Sgt SC

BOOTH (includes BOOTHE)
Abijah: b 1-12-1745 d 9- -1802 m Ruth Leavenworth Cpl CT
Andrew: b 1744 d *p.* 1800 m Jerusha Kirby Pvt MA
Beverly: b *c.* 1752 d *p.* 7-30-1830 m (1) X (2)Mary Cornwell Pvt VA ★
Caleb, (3): b 8-22-1751 d 9-10-1830 m Anna Bartlett MM & Pvt CT

BOOTH, contd.
Daniel: b 2-6-1724 d 5-8-1801 m Polly Judson Pvt CT
Daniel: b 1729 d 1802 m Priscilla — PS NC
Daniel: b c. 1735 d 11-17-1812 m Ruth Terry PS NY
Daniel: b 1738 d a. 5- -1795 m Jane Houston PS VA
Edwin: b 3-26-1753 d 10-11-1836 m Rachel Reynolds Pvt MD ★
Epaphras: b 1- -1757 d 2-13-1852 m (1)Ede Roundy (2)Mrs
　　Elizabeth Emmerson Pvt NH
Ephraim: b 8- -1719 d 1790 m (1)Sarah Fairchild (2)Phebe
　　Fairchild Pvt CT
George: b 1717 d 1-20-1800 m Elizabeth Rapier Sol PS NH
George: b 4-11-1727 d 9-28-1804 m Pamela Carroll Cpl VA
George: b 10-6-1758 d 1844 m (3)Anna Nelms Pvt VA
Henry: b 11-17-1745 d 3-1-1792 m Dorothy Fish Sgt CT
Isaac: b 3-9-1739 d 1-13-1798 m Deborah Hurlbut Pvt CS CT
Isaac: b 4-27-1758 d p. 7-19-1839 m (1)— Frelove (2)Mary
　　Ferguson Sol VA
Jas.: b 10-1-1734 d 3-19-1809 m Abigail Ann Paterson Capt CT
James: b 3- -1747/48 d 9-18-1830 m Thankful Winchell Pvt CT
James: b 1755 d — m Ellen Booth OrdlSgt VA ★
James: b 1709 d 6-17-1778 m Nancy Stalnaker Capt VA
John: b 12-19-1755 d 9-7-1833 m Sarah Mattoon Pvt CT ★
John, Sr.: b 8- -1736 d 12-2-1822 m Lucy Curtis Pvt CT
John: b 10-25-1728 d 8-22-1802 m Hannah Phelps PS CT
John: b 7-21-1729 d 11-30-1802 m Lydia Richmond MM MA
John: b c. 1730 d 9- -1804 m Mary — Pvt NC
John: b 1726 d 7- -1779 m Mary — Pvt SC
John: b 1737 d 1807 m X 2Lt & CS VA
John: b c. 1750 d 1798 m Winifred — PS VA
Joseph: b 10-28-1736 d 2-4-1810 m Mary Hale Capt CT
Joseph: b 10-1-1751 d 6-10-1835 m Elizabeth Francis Pvt CT
Joseph: b 1750 d p. 9-7-1824 m Sarah — Pvt & PS NC
Joshua: b — d 12-17-1816 m Mehitable Slader Pvt NH
Nathan: b 2-27-1720 d 12-27-1800 m Comfort Thompson PS CT
Nathaniel: b 5-14-1755 d 12-16-1836 m Martha Hinman Ens CT ★
Oliver, Sr.: b 12-29-1725 d 8-25-1807 m (1)Ruth Ingham (2)Mrs
　　Anna Way PS NH
Oliver, Jr: bpt 9-6-1761 d 6-25-1825 m Mary Story PS NH
Reuben: bpt 6-22-1739 d 7-22-1800 m Sarah Hine PS CT
Robert: b 6-20-1758 d 1796 m Abigail Barton Pvt CT
Solomon: b 1740 d 1-21-1821 m Naomia Mallett Lt CT
Stoughton: b 1761 d 1836 m Almy Allen Pvt MA
Walter: b 2-16-1761 d 1-3-1825 m Mary Newton Sgt CT
Wheelock: b 4-2-1742 d 12-6-1824 m Elithea Overton Sgt NY
William: b c. 1750 d p. 1770 m X Sol VA
William Aylett: b 12-29-1754 d 1820 m Rebecca Hite PS VA

BOOTON,
Travis: b a. 1768 d 4- -1814 m Ruth Estill Sol VA W★

BOPP,
Adam: b c. 1760 d 1837 m Sarah — Pvt PA
Matthias: b 1733 d 1793 m X Ens PA

BORAH,
Jacob: b 1765 d 1838 m (1)Abigail Aumiller (2)Betsey Lawrence
　　(3)Elizabeth Forsythe (4)Mrs Nancy Waggoner Pvt PA ★

BORDEAUX, (includes BOURDEAUX)
Daniel, 2nd: b 1745 d 1815 m Elizabeth Miller MM NC
Daniel: b c. 1746-48 d p. 1790 m Elizabeth Martha Smith PS SC

BORDELEAU,
Antoine: b 1725 d 10-29-1793 m Catherine Caron PS VA

BORDEN,
Benjamin: b 1750 d p. 1790 m Lovice Cook Capt RI
Benjamin: b 1743 d 1816 m Rachel Cobb CS RI
Elijah: b 5-25-1737 d 5-25-1822 m Sarah Baker Pvt MA
Elizabeth Rogers: b 7-10-1725 d 9-2-1807 m Joseph Borden PS NJ
Job: b 1760 d 1-30-1839 m Mary — Pvt NJ ★
John: b 1737 d 1833 m Lydia Worthley Pvt NJ
Joseph, Sr.: b 8-1-1719 d 4-9-1791 m Elizabeth — Col NJ
Joseph, Jr.: b 1755 d 10-16-1788 m Mary Biles Capt NJ
Joseph: b 1733/34 d p. 4-29-1803 m Mrs Jane Ferguson PS NC
Joseph: b 8-12-1733 d 1809 m Peace Borden PS RI
Nathan: b 3-4-1756 d 1-18-1851 m Susannah Read Pvt NY
Richard: b 1722 d 7-4-1795 m Hope Cook CS & PS MA
Stephen: b c. 1742 d p. 1779 m Mary Church PS MA
Thomas: b -20-1750 d 11-29-1831 m Mary Hathaway Pvt MA
William: b 2-26-1736 d 1-21-1813 m Ruhama Jennings Pvt MA
William, 2nd: b 2-6-1731 d 11-2-1799 m Mrs Comfort Small PS MA
William: b a. 1751 d p. 1792 m Ann Sherman CS RI

BORDERS,
Christopher: b 1763 d p. 5-12-1834 m Sarah Blizzard Pvt VA ★
Michael: b c. 1749 d p. 9-7-1804 m Mary — Sol NC

BORDLEY,
William: b 9-18-1741 d 1784 m (1)Mrs Elizabeth Tilden (2)Mary —
　　Col MD

BORDNER, (includes BOATNER, BORTNER)
George, Sr.: b 1731 d p. 1802 m Appolona Floucher Pvt PA
Jacob, Sr.: b 1722 d 1792 m Sarah Bolt PS PA
Jacob, Jr.: b 11-15-1754 d 1-6-1837 m Anna Maria Brosz Ens PA
John: b 1755 d 1816 m Anna Maria Groh Capt PA
Lewis: b 4-12-1758 d 12-6-1849 m (1)Polly Lashley (2)Martha
　　Sieber PS SC

BORELAND, (includes BORLAND)
Andrew: b 12-22-1744 d 4-30-1827 m Mary Evans Pvt PA
John: b — d 1815 m Catharine Montgomery Pvt PA CL
Samuel: b 1748 d 7-15-1811 m Lydia Gregg Lt PA

BOREMAN, (includes BOARMAN,
John: b c. 1745 d 9-11-1814 m Sarah Kenner Seaton Dep PMGen
　　PA
Joseph: b c. 1755 d 11-21-1825 m Sarah Jameson Pvt MD

BORGA, (includes BERCAW)
Abraham: b c. 1762 d 1824 m Maria Cosine Pvt PA

BORING,
Isaac: b 3-8-1762 d 5-18-1831 m Phoebe Browning Pvt NC

BORK,
George Christian Frederick: b 3-11-1758 d 9- -1823 m Tabitha
　　Chisholm OrdlSgt NY

BORNHEIMER,
Godfrey: b 1732 d 1819 m Catherine Elizabeth Ludwig Sgt MA

BOROWAY, (includes BORROWAY)
Isaac: b 9-28-1754 d 10-6-1801 m Anna Johanna Uhrich Pvt PA
John Abraham: b 12-13-1750 d p. 1804 m Elizabeth Uhrich Pvt PA

BORROR,
Charles: b 1761 d 1843 m Sidney Wees Pvt VA ★

BORST,
Baltus: b 6-4-1720 d 9-7-1789 m Maria Borst Pvt NY
Hendrick: b 12-9-1735 d 3-7-1808 m Maria Margaret Bouck 1Lt
　　NY
Jacob: b 10-3-1748 d 11-6-1823 m Catharine Schaeffer Lt NY
John: b 9-14-1735 d 10-7-1810 m Catherine Rickert Pvt NY
Joost: b 1-14-1730 d 7-30-1784 m (1)Margaret Sternburgh
　　(2)Catharine Fox Pvt NY
Joseph: b a. 1750 d 1- -1812 m Betsy Hager Pvt & PS NY
Martinus: b 9-9-1763 d 1-2-1843 m Elizabeth Lemm Pvt NY ★
Michal: b 9-28-1728 d 1-4-1810 m Ann Eliza Lewiston Pvt NY
Peter: b 11-28-1751 d p. 1789 m (1)Catherine Loucks
　　(2)Catherine Ostrander Pvt NY
Philip: b 12-10-1755 d 1-14-1830 m Nellie Loucks Pvt NY

BORTHWICK,
James: b 1738 d 1821 m Margaret Byres PS NY

BORTLE,
Philip H.: b 1750 d 8-24-1844 m (1)Elberta Michel (2)Margaretha
　　Bonstiel (3)Helen Van Deusen Pvt NY

BOSANG,
John: b 1750-60 d 1792 m Elizabeth Burk Pvt VA

BOSE,
Peter: b c. 1759 d p. 1808 m Mary Sluthour Pvt PA

BOSEMAN, (includes BOZEMAN)
Jacob: b c. 1763 d 1837 m (1)Fannie Allen (2)Sarah Patrick Pvt NC
Meeda: b 1745 d 1809 m Chloe Nelson PS NC
Samuel: b 1730 d 1795 m Ann Richardson Pvt NC

BOSHART,
Jacob: b c. 1731 d p. 1791 m Margareit Koch Pvt NY
John: b 3-1-1757 d 1-14-1789 m Hannah Sponenburgh Pvt NY
Rudolph: b c. 1759 d 10-12-1846 m X Sol SC

BOSLEY,
Gideon: b — d p. 1810 m Sarah Cole PS MD
James: b 1736 d 1806 m Temperance Marsh PS MD
John: b 1756 d 1795 m Ann Cole PS MD
John: b a. 1750 d 1800 m Hannah Bull PS PA
Zebulon: b 1756 d c. 3-30-1791 m Elizabeth Bond Ens MD

BOSS, (includes BOST)
Benjamin, Jr.: b 2-2-1757 d 6-1-1848 m (1)Mary Hopkins (2)Sarah
　　Peckham (3)Amy Taylor Sgt RI ★
Elias: b 6- -1748 d 10-12-1822 m Katharine — Pvt NC
Jabez: b 3-23-1759 d 7-17-1828 m Sarah Brayman Pvt RI
Jacob: b 1-1-1753 d 9-25-1830 m Catharine Cress Pvt NC
Jacob: b 1760 d 1829 m Mary Aron Pvt PA
John Linscom: b 5-6-1757 d 8-7-1824 m Sarah — Ens RI W★

Obadiah: b 1745 d 10-20-1820 m Lucy Stevens Barnes 2Lt MA
Samuel: b 11-22-1749 d 11-24-1836 m Lydia Lincoln Lt MA

BOSSART, (includes BUZARD, BUZZARD)
George: b c. 1750 d p. 1802 m Rachel Godschalk Pvt PA
John: b c. 1762 d 1810 m Mary High Pvt PA
John: b a. 1725 d 3- -1803 m Catherine La Rue Pvt PA
Melchior: b 12-8-1745 d 2-9-1830 m Margaretha Catharina — Pvt PA

BOSSERMAN,
Christian: b — d a. 1- -1828 m Susanna — Pvt VA

BOSSON,
Jonathan Davis: b 6-14-1762 d p. 1790 m Martha Young Pvt MA
William, Jr.: b 4-28-1753 d 8-15-1824 m (1)Prudence Mayo (2)Susanna Mayo Pvt MA

BOSTON, (includes BOSTEYON)
Adam: b 1-18-1764 d 3-5-1832 m Juliet How Pvt VA ★
Esau: b a. 1753 d 2-4-1846 m Leah — Sol MD
John: b 1737 d 5-8-1810 m Rebecca Randle Maj NC
Levin: b 6-22-1747 d p. 1782 m Gertrude Benton Pvt MD
Reuben: b 1750 d 1842 m Sarah Hawkins Pvt VA ★

BOSTWICK, (includes BOSTICT)
Absolom: b c. 1738 d p. 6-20-1798 m Bethenia Perkins Capt NC
Amos: b 1743 d 11-19-1829 m (1)Sarah Grant (2)Sarah Hayes Ens CT
Andrew: b 4-20-1754 d 3-9-1830 m Abigail Welton Cpl CT
Arthur: b 6-28-1729 d 1-10-1802 m Eunice Warriner Pvt VT
Benjamin: b 2-13-1745 d 11-30-1815 m Olive Judson Pvt CT
Bushnell: b 11-16-1712 d 1-31-1793 m Miriam Skeeles PS & CS CT
Chesley: b c. 1740-45 d p. 1804 m (1)Jane Gervais (2)Ann Matilda Hargreaves Capt GA
David: b 4-24-1752 d 6-12-1818 m Currence Hard Pvt CT
Ebenezer: b 6-22-1751 d 3-16-1840 m Rebecca Northrop Sgt CT
Edmund: b 9-13-1732 d 2-20-1826 m Mercy Ruggles PS CT
Elijah: b 6-8-1740 d 1-18-1825 m Rebecca Warner Capt NY
Elizur: b 1-13-1757 d 8-13-1851 m Mercy — Pvt CT
Isaac: b 9-6-1730 d 4-21-1808 m Prudence Warner Capt CT
Israel: b 8-7-1749 d 7-11-1826 m Elizabeth Mallory Pvt VT
James: b c. 1750 d n 9-20-1823 m Comfort — Sol NC
John, Sr.: b 3-24-1715 d 12-17-1806 m X Pvt CT
John: b 1753 d 1820 m (1)Patience Hubbell (2)Samantha Lilley Pvt CT
John: b 1746 d 1822 m Mary Wilson Pvt NY
John: b 5-26-1755 d 11-12-1801 m Sarah Holmes Capt NY
John: b 6-18-1763 d 9-20-1850 m Mary Garvis Capt NC
John Warriner: b 10-18-1761 d 1-27-1835 m Anna Collins Pvt VT
Jonathan: b 7-7-1762 d 6-29-1843 m Abigail Trowbridge Sol CT
Jonathan: bpt 9-3-1749 d a. 12-26-1814 m Margaret Hawkins PS SC
Levi: b c. 1756/57 d 5-3-1826 m Anna Smith Pvt CT
Littlebery: b 7-18-1751 d 9-10-1823 m (1)Rebecca Beale (2)Mary Phillips Capt GA
Medad: b 1760 d 3-15-1841 m (1)Comfort Oviatt (2)Mary W Craig Fif CT
Nathan: b 11-16-1746 d 8-10-1829 m Elizabeth Coggeswell Ens CT
Nathan: b 1-26-1746 d 2-14-1818 m Martha Guinn Pvt GA
Nathaniel: b 2-7-1757 d 2-10-1807 m Miriam Baker Pvt VT
Reuben: b 9-2-1734 d 7-16-1813 m Mabel Ruggles Capt CT
Robert: b 1752 d 1828 m Mary Miller Sgt NY
Samuel: b 12- -1748 d 8-13-1798 m Mrs Dorcas Rockwell Pvt NY

BOSWELL,
George: b 11- -1748 d 3-9-1803 m Nancy Taylor PS & CS VA
George: b — d 4-1-1817 m Judith Swann Fauntleroy CS VA
Jesse: b 1755 d 11-23-1828 m (1)Elizabeth Carrington (2)Mary Kelough Sgt MD
John: b 3-10-1750 d 1815 m Mary Robey PS MD
John: b 1760 d 1832 m Lydia Slusher Sgt VA
John Iverson: b 1761 d 1792 m Mary Coleman Pvt VA
Joseph C.: b c. 1730 d 1794 m Elizabeth Elliott PS VA
Machen: b c. 1740 d c. 1784 m Mellicent Marriott Capt VA
Wm.: b c. 1760 d p. 7-14-1829 m Alvira Randall Pvt RI

BOSWORTH,
Aaron: b 1-15-1744/45 d a. 7-5-1814 m Sarah Ames Sol CT
Allen: b 11-7-1758 d 3-18-1830 m (1)Mary Peabody (2)Sarah Harwood Pvt CT
Amaziah: b 1725/26 d 2-26-1805 m Tabitha Hartshorn PS CT
Benjamin: b 2-23-1757 d 2-17-1830 m Barbara Lindley OrdlSgt MA
Benjamin: b 1-9-1733 d 11-7-1810 m (1)Mrs Frances Bennett Nichols (2)Mrs Mary Church (3)Abigail Potter Munroe Maj RI
Benjamin: b 1752/53 d 7-1-1825 m (1)Hannah Martin (2)Sarah — Lt RI
Constant: b 8-19-1736 d 6-21-1826 m (1)Mary Ward Mather (2)Thankful — Sgt MA
David: b 4-25-1750 d 9-12-1809 m Mindwell Fitch Cpl CT

David: b 1750 d 1840 m Elizabeth Curtis Pvt CT
Frederic: b 1760 d 12-25-1797 m Hannah Couch Pvt MA
Hezekiah: b 1-30-1741 d 5-4-1820 m Mary Giddings Pvt NY
Ichabod: b 3-1-1748 d 12-8-1818 m Abigail Chappel 1Lt CT
Ichabod: b 2-17-1748/49 d 11-18-1820 m (1)Mrs Chloe Cook (2) Ruth Braley Pvt MA ★
Ichabod: b 10-14-1739 d 5-15-1820 m Hannah Horton Sgt MA
Isaac: b 10-1-1760 d 11-7-1842 m Joanna Cushman Pvt MA
Jabez: b 3-12-1742 d 8-2-1827 m Rebecca Moody Sgt MA
Jabin: b 4-8-1752 d c. 1792 m Luna West Pvt NY
John: b 9-23-1751 d 2-8-1832 m Hannah Smith Sgt MA
John: b 12-29-1729 d c. 2-1-1802 m Sarah Jackson Pvt MA
John: b 9-20-1760 d 9-13-1831 m Chloe Seymour Sol MA
John: b 2-20-1762 d 5-8-1831 m Silence Maxham Pvt RI MA ★
John: b 6-1-1759 d 12-25-1845 m (1)Rosanna Blackman (2)Hannah Luther PS RI
Jonathan: b 1757 d 3-7-1833 m Abigail Williams Pvt MA
Jonathan: b 9-1-1748 d 12-1-1818 m Mary Holt Pvt PS NH
Joseph: b 11-15-1756 d 5-6-1830 m Mary Winslow Pvt MA
Nathaniel: b 4-12-1753 d 3-12-1844 m Mary Ranney Cpl CT VT ★
Nathaniel: b 6-16-1767 d 4-6-1853 m Serviah Mason Wgn RI
Nehemiah: b 4-3-1731 d c. 1806 m Sarah Goodspeed Cpl MA
Peleg: b 5-6-1754 d p. 1781 m Mary Smith Pvt MA
Peter: b 2-20-1764 d 8-16-1822 m Deborah Smith Pvt MA
Richard: b 1-27-1750 d p. 1800 m Hanna Chipman Sgt MA
Salah: b 3-11-1764/65 d 10-12-1823 m Rebecca Perkins Pvt MA
Samuel: b 5-19-1744 d 5-4-1824 m Elizabeth Joy Capt RI
Timothy: b 2-22-1759 d 8-17-1838 m Nancy Monroe Pvt Slr RI MA ★
Zadoc, Sr.: b 10-14-1735 d 7-5-1810 m Joanna Raymond PS MA
Zadoc, Jr.: b 1761 d 4-28-1840 m (1)Deborah Bundy (2)Mrs Lucretia Moore Pvt MA ★

BOTELER,
Edward: b c. 1740 d p. 2-21-1818 m Elizabeth DeLashmutt PS MD
Henry: b 10-15-1728 d 1814 m Sallie Elsby Capt MD

BOTHWELL,
Alexander: b 1-7-1744 d 5-1-1813 m Mary — 1Lt MA

BOTKIN, (includes BODKIN)
Charles: b 10-8-1738 d 3-1-1820 m (1)Jemima Kahrl (2)Rebecca Richards (3)Sarah Elsworth Pvt VA
Hugh: b c. 1740 d 1801 m Hester — Pvt VA
John: b c. 1758 d p. 3-6-1829 m Polly — Pvt VA

BOTSFORD,
Aaron: b 2-29-1764 d 6-17-1842 m Comfort Seaton Pvt CT
Clement: b 8-4-1751 d 7-25-1824 m Mary Baldwin Ens CT
David: b 1712 d 1796 m Hannah Skeels Pvt CT
Edmund: b 11-1-1745 d 12-26-1819 m (1)Susanna Nunn (2) Catherine Evans (3)Ann Deliesline (4)Hannah Goff Chp SC
Elnathan: b 1739 d 2- -1827 m X Pvt CT
Ephraim, Sr.: b 6-25-1720 d 12-5-1795 m Sarah Hawley Pvt CT
Jared: b 2-9-1745 d 4-18-1828 m Ann Sherman Lt CT
John: b 4-23-1734 d c. 1- -1802 m (1)Dorcas Warren (2)Rachel Murray Pvt & PS CT
John: b 3-28-1710 d 11-9-1794 m Anna Bennet Pvt CT

BOTT,
Jonas: b 1733 d 1793 m Ann Catharine Joseph Pvt PA
Rhinardt: b c. 1730 d 1790 m Mary Elizabeth Capt PA
Thomas: b 1750 d p. 4-8-1783 m Mary Bland Capt VA

BOTTOM,
Wm.: b c. 1748-50 d 1825 m Mary — PS VA

BOTTOMER,
Jacob: b c. 1758 d 1820 m X Pvt PA

BOTTORFF, (includes BATDORF, BATTURFF)
Christian: b 6-1-1748 d a. 5-15-1797 m (1)Maria Elizabeth Schneider (2)Rosina Schaeffer Pvt PA
Henry: b 10-17-1754 d 5-10-1806 m Sophia Frieker Ens PA
John Adam: b c. 1724 d p. 1781 m Elizabeth Ann Zeller Sol PA
Martin: b 8-30-1748 d p. 1792 m Maria Barbara Hautz PS MD
Martin: b a. 1712 d c. 1782 m Maria Elizabeth PS PA

BOTTUM,
David, Jr.: b 11-16-1746 d — m X Pvt CT

BOUCHILLON,
Joseph: b 1729 d 1799 m Marie Majinnett Capt SC

BOUCK,
Christian: b 2-9-1723 d 4-13-1786 m Eliza Rickert Sol NY
Christian: b 1753 d 1836 m Margaret Pvt NY
John, Sr.: b 4-7-1726 d 9-4-1784 m Elizabeth Bellinger Pvt NY
John, Jr.: b 1-8-1747 d 11-9-1826 m Catherine Lawyer Lt NY
John William: b 4-7-1720 d 9-23-1784 m Anna Crysler 2Lt NY
Lawrence: b 7-26-1763 d 11-19-1840 m Eva Snyder Pvt NY
Nicholas: b 11-24-1749 d 11-14-1804 m Catharine Sidney Pvt NY
Wm.: b 9-1-1728 d 12-8-1807 m Elizabeth Matice Pvt NY

BOUDEMAN,
Isaac: b 7-5-1728 d 4-3-1818 m Mary Hilborn Pvt PA

BOUDINOT,
Elisha: b 1749 d 1819 m Catherine Smith PS NJ
John: b 1-10-1734 d 1789 m Rachen (Catherine) Van Norden Dr NJ

BOUGHER,
Abraham: b 1748 d 2-2-1833 m Frances McElroy Pvt VA ★

BOUGHNER,
Martin: b c. 1762/63 d 1838 m Anne Rittenhouse Pvt PA

BOUGHTON, (includes BANTON, BAUTON, BOUTEN, BOUTON, BOUTUN)
Asa: b 7-28-1766 d 9-20-1843 m Polly Richtmyer PS CT
Azor: b 11-5-1761 d 3-21-1848 m Betsey Nickerson Pvt CT
Daniel: b 10-24-1740 d 2-12-1821 m Mary Mead Capt CT
Daniel: b 6-20-1743 d 1820 m Sarah Andros Capt NY
David: b 11-15-1757 d 12-11-1834 m Dinah Hanford Pvt CT
David: b 1748 d 1830 m Esther Belden Sgt NY
Ebenezer: b 3- -1744 d p. 1790 m Martha Gilbert Pvt NY
Gould: b 1-24-1733 d 6-22-1811 m Elizabeth Gilbert Capt NY
Hezekiah, Sr.: b 11-2-1725 d 1793 m Abigail Penoyer Pvt MA
Hezekiah, Jr.: b 12-29-1752 d 1793 m Huldah Wilson Pvt MA
Jehiel, Sr.: b 2-17-1732 d 1800 m Anna Finch Ens NY
Jehiel, Jr.: b 7-27-1755 d 1830 m Lois Dixon Pvt NY
Jesse: b 10-23-1748 d c. 1823 m Rachel Ferris Sol NY
John: b 8-19-1759 d 2-12-1831 m Elizabeth Roberts Pvt NY
Joseph, Sr.: b c. 1740-45 d 12-25-1783 m X Pvt PS CT
Joshua: b 10-18-1759 d 2-8-1812 m Margaret McLean Fif CT
Matthew: b 4-25-1758 d 9-13-1847 m Elizabeth Stringham Ellen — Pvt CT
Miles: b 1740 d 1783 m Mary Benedict Sgt CT
Nathan: b 3-4-1745 d p. 1790 m (1)Dorothy — (2)Rhoda Curtis Pvt MA
Noah: b 11-17-1743 d 7-12-1812 m Deborah Hoyt Capt NY
Seth: b 3-7-1754 d 12-10-1840 m Sarah Pvt CT
Shubael: b 12-29-1740 d p. 1785 m Mary Hodge Pvt NY
Timothy: b 6-1-1746 d 10-27-1806 m Martha Scott Pvt NY
Wm.: b 1-16-1749 d 5-30-1828 m Sarah Benedict Sgt CT ★
Wm.: b 1760 d 1820 m (1)Ann Smith (2)Polly Glover Sol VA

BOULDIN, (includes BOULDEN)
James: b 9-4-1712 d p. 1-4-1783 m Elizabeth PS DE
James: b 8-10-1734 d 5-13-1801 m Sally Watkins PS VA
Nathan: b 2-22-1737 d 9-28-1802 m Sara — PS DE
Richard: b 1744 d 1806-11 m Betsey Mosely Pvt VA
Thomas: b 4-1-1728 d 1783 m Augustina Boulding Capt MD
Thomas: b 1-15-1706 d a. 6-2-1783 m Nancy Clark PS VA
Wood: b 1742 d 3-13-1800 m Joanna Tyler Lt VA

BOULIGNY,
Francisco: b 1735/36 d 11-25-1800 m Marie Louise Le Senechal D'Auberville PS LA

BOULWARE,
Mark: b 1748 d 1813 m Louisa Lee Pvt VA
Mark: b c. 1755 d 3-15-1811 m (1)Milly — (2)Agatha Saunders Pvt VA
Muscoe: b c. 1758 d p. 12-15-1824 m Nancy Pickett Pvt VA
Samuel: b 1723 d 1791 m Polly Mark Pvt VA

BOUNDS,
James: b c. 1718 d p. 1790 m Elizabeth — Sol NC

BOURDETTE,
Peter: b 5-12-1735 d 5-21-1826 m Rachel Bush PS NJ

BOURGIGNON,
Joseph: b 12-24-1760 d 7-16-1832 m Marie A Rodet PS LA

BOURNE, (includes BOURN)
Abel: b 12-18-1751 d 1-16-1822 m Deborah Bourne Pvt MA
Abner: b 10-23-1747 d 5-25-1806 m Mary Torrey Capt MA
Andrew: b 11-7-1746 d 9-3-1814 m Sarah Comins Sgt MA
Andrew: b 1740 d 1795 m Christy Pvt VA
Andrew, Jr.: b a. 1762 d p. 12-12-1809 m (1)Elizabeth Robertson (2)Eleanor Bowrne Sol VA
Andrew: b 1716 d p. 8-22-1788 m Jane Morton PS VA
Asa: b — d p. 1787 m Abigail Bourne Pvt MA
Barnet: b 1-13-1756 d 1-13-1821 m Elizabeth Lewis Pvt VT
Benjamin: b 1-25-1760 d 3-14-1829 m Hannah Perry Pvt MA
Benjamin: b 9-9-1755 d 9-17-1808 m Hope Childs QM RI
Ebenezer: b 6-10-1755 d 5-9-1802 m (1)Deborah Tobey (2)Lydia Freeman (3)Ruth Briggs Sgt MA
Francis: b 1730 d 1792 m Elizabeth Sterns Sol MA
Francis: b 7-5-1727 d 7-20-1803 m Frances Christopher Cpl VA
James: b 7-12-1737 d 7-27-1810 m Lydia Allen Pvt MA
James: b 1757 d 6- -1847 m Elizabeth Gore Pvt VA
John: b 1750 d 10-30-1820 m Lovisa Bourne Pvt MA
John: b 4-10-1759 d 10-6-1859 m Martha Sampson Pvt MA

John: b — d 3- -1792 m Mary Brock Pvt VA W★
Moses: b 6-20-1757 d 11-4-1824 m Huldah Reed Pvt MA
Nathan: b 5-6-1756 d 1835 m Patience Jones Pvt MA
Nathaniel: b 1735 d 11-20-1840 m Mehitable Tobey Pvt MA ★
Nathaniel: b 1725 d 12-11-1798 m Freelove Haile Pvt VT
Newcomb: b 1-19-1745 d 4-25-1829 m Abigail Joy 2Cpl MA
Shearjashub, Sr.: b 4-18-1721 d 2-9-1781 m Ruth Church PS RI
Shearjashub, Jr.: b 12-4-1751 d 11-24-1821 m (1)Ruth Waldron (2) Rachel Kent QM RI W★
Stephen: b 6-24-1757 d 11-5-1822 m Deborah Bourn Sgt MA
Stephen: b 6-5-1752 d 10-21-1814 m (1)Mary Dryer (2)Susan Ormsbee Pvt MA
Thomas: b 1-4-1716 d 2-3-1804 m May Randall 2Lt MA
Wm.: b 8-23-1743 d 6-8-1836 m Rosamond Jones Pvt VA

BOURQUIN,
David Francis: b 5-18-1757 d 1-11-1825 m (1)Elizabeth Fox (2)Ann Semms (3)Margaret Thornton Maj GA

BOUSH,
Arthur: b 1742 d 1782 m Anne Sweeney PS VA
Charles, S.: b 1755 d 2- -1809 m Martha Sweeney NLt VA
Frederick: b c. 1745 d 1805 m (1)Jacamine Wilson (2)Elizabeth Smith Capt PS VA
Robert: b 1753 d 1809 m Catherine Ballard PM &Ens VA
Samuel: b c. 1720 d a. 5-20-1784 m — CS VA

BOUTELLE, (includes BOUTELL, BOUTELLS)
Ebenezer: b 9-10-1735 d 1828 m Anne Seaver Pvt MA
Jacob: b 8-23-1740 d 1-23-1789 m (1)Eunice Drew (2)Jerusha Follet Cpl CT
James: b 6-26-1736 d 2-6-1804 m Mary Johnson PS NH
John: b 5-17-1739 d 3-30-1825 m Ruth Bryant Pvt MA
John: b 8-8-1762 d 9-12-1847 m Betsy Eaton Pvt NH ★
Joseph: b 3-6-1757 d 7-4-1840 m Abigail Farmer Pvt MA ★
Kendall: b 4-1-1737 d 10-19-1819 m Mary Wilder Lt MA
Kendall: b 8-12-1736 d 8-12-1820 m Sarah Boutelle PS NH
Reuben: b 1760 d 3- -1816 m Olive Bradford Pvt NH
Samuel: b 11-20-1761 d 1-18-1822 m Elizabeth Hale Pvt MA
Timothy: b 1740 d 5-25-1810 m Rachel Lincoln 2Lt MA
Wm.: b 5-4-1728 d 4-8-1779 m Persis Hubbard Pvt MA
Wm.: b 7-7-1755 d 7- -1835 m Rachel Wood Pvt MA

BOVARD,
James: b a. 1756 d 1-8-1808 m Hannah Beaty Lt PA
John: b 1745 d 10-11-1817 m Frances Johnston Pvt PA CL

BOVEE, (includes BOVIE)
Jacob: b 7-5-1763 d 8-27-1853 m Lydia Hall Pvt NY
John: b 10-3-1759 d 12-22-1830 m X Sgt NY
Nicholas: b 1761 d p. 1840 m Sarah Jane Taylor Pvt NY
Philip: b 10-13-1732 d p. 9-22-1783 m Geertruy Vandenburgh Pvt NY

BOW, (includes BOWE)
Edward: b 1757 d 4-24-1842 m Ruth Hubbard Pvt CT ★
Thaddeus: b 12-17-1760 d 9-7-1828 m Mehetabel Stowe Pvt MA ★
William: b c. 1750 d c. 1800 m — Winston Sgt VA

BOWCOCK,
Jason: b c. 1750 d 1816 m Judith — PS VA

BOWDISH,
Abraham: b 9-30-1723 d 3-3-1814 m Hannah Reynolds Sol VT
John: b 4-3-1752 d — m Phebe Aylsworth Pvt NY

BOWDLE,
Henry, Jr.: b 1756 d 1816 m Ruth Mullikin Pvt MD

BOWDOIN, (includes BODEN, BOWDEN)
John: b c. 1750 d p. 10-15-1825 m Molly — PS NC
Martha: b 1756 d 11- -1800 m Isaac Odell PS NC
Samuel: bpt 10-23-1743 d 7-25-1813 m Priscilla Proctor Sol MA
Twisden: bpt 3-17-1744/45 d a. 1794 m Sarah Orne Sgt MA
Wm.: b 1746 d 10-27-1807 m Experience Dowing Drm Pvt MA
Wm.: b c. 1745 d 1831/32 m Martha PS NC
Wm.: b 1759 d 1814 m Sarah Owen Pvt VA

BOWDRY, (includes BOWDRE)
Elisha: b — d a. 1791 m Milly — PS NC
James: b c. 1759 d 1808 m Lettice (Letitia) Perrin Sol VA
Lewis: b a. 1765 d p. 2-7-1821 m Lucy — Matr VA
Samuel: b c. 1740 d 1790 m Elizabeth — Pvt VA

BOWEN,
Aaron: b 5-3-1759 d 3-8-1839 m Abigail Smith Pvt MA
Aaron: b 9-2-1730 d 10-7-1816 m Elnathan Gorton CS RI
Anthony: b — d p. 9-11-1787 m Ellia PS VA
Arthur: b 1744 d p. 1-17-1816 m Mary Mc Murray Capt VA
Benjamin: b 1756 d 11-5-1836 m Mary Hindley Pvt NC ★
Christopher: b 12-17-1750 d 11-29-1836 m (1)Elizabeth Chaffee (2) Mrs Betsey Leland Sgt CT

Clifton: b c. 1736 d a. 8-3-1789 m Martha — Lt NC
Consider: b 9-16-1757 d 3-24-1838 m (2)Sabra Hosmer Pvt RI ★
Danforth: b 1755 d 12-6-1803 m Mary — Pvt CT
Daniel: b 10-21-1750 d 4-13-1829 m Mehetible Packard Pvt CT
Daniel: b 1731 d 1801 m Lydia Tapp Pvt NJ
David: b 2-24-1740 d 7- -1820 m Hopestill Aldrich CS MA
David: b c. 1740 d 1815 m (1)Sarah James (2)Anna Powell Pvt PA
Edward: b c. 1720 d 1796 m Sarah Smith Pvt NJ
Eleazer: b 6-10-1753 d — m Olive Shaw Pvt MA
Eleazer: b 2-10-1722 d 7-13-1810 m (1)Lydia Wood (2)Martha Ballou Pvt RI
Eleazer: b 10-5-1755 d 2-14-1841 m Jane — Pvt RI ★
Elijah: b 11-10-1756 d 1807 m Patty Cody Pvt MA
Henry: b 3-9-1749 d 12-8-1830 m Lydia Fowler Pvt CT
Hezekiah: b 6-20-1715 d 5-16-1785 m (1)Mary Amsby (2)Zerviah — Pvt RI
Ichabod: b 8-21-1727 d 2-27-1816 m Mary Bucklin Pvt RI
Isaac: b 4-12-1740 d 8-10-1823 m Sarah Whitaker Lt RI
Jabesh: b 7-4-1735 d p. 1790 m Patience Millard Cpl MA
Jabez: b 6-2-1739 d 5-8-1816 m Sarah Brown Col RI
James: b 12- -1759 d 7-29-1850 m Martha Pvt RI ★
James: b 1745 d p. 1787 m Mary Hanslow Pvt VA
James: b 6-7-1750 d 2-26-1815 m Rachel Bower Pvt VA
Jeremiah: b 1750 d 1840-50 m Hannah Webster Pvt NH
Jesse: b 1757 d 1781 m Susannah Whann Ens DE
Joel: b 12-22-1761 d 4-1-1848 m Susanna Armington Pvt MA
John: b 1734 d 1789 m (1)Jane Oliver (2)Mrs — David PS DE
John: b 4-28-1756 d 6- -1831 m (1)Sarah Briggs Pvt MA
John: b 5-29-1744 d 9-2-1832 m Catherine French Pvt NH
John: b a. 1740 d 1-11-1800 m (1)Sarah Shaw (2)Martha Carey Pvt RI
John: b 4-16-1757 d 12-8-1841 m Phoebe Congdon Pvt RI
John: b 1762 d 1812 m (1)— (2)Rebecca Withers Pvt SC
John: b 9-18-1758 d 9-8-1790 m Rachael Clarke Lt VA
John: b c. 1760 d 7-12-1789 m Nancy Gillespie Pvt VA
John: b 1766 d 1819 m Sarah Bean Pvt VA
Jonathan: b 1751 d 1822 m Ann Blackburn Pvt PA
Joseph: b 1755 d 1779 m Anne Reves Ens RI
Joseph: b 1755 d 8-12-1832 m Hannah Robinson Simons Dr RI
Joshua: b 4-14-1740 d p. 1790 m Abigail Smith Smn MA
Josiah: b c. 1752 d 4-27-1831 m (1)Ann Smith (2)Margaret Steelman Pvt NJ
Lemuel: b 3-9-1755 d 4-25-1832 m Hulda Bowen Pvt MA
Lilly McIlhaney: b c. 1705 d 4-1-1780 m John Bowen PS VA
Louisa Smith: b c. 1741 d 2-16-1834 m Rees Bowen PS VA
Matthew: b 10-22-1724 d 2-16-1806 m Mary Dana Capt CT
Moses: b 3-12-1752 d 6- -1830 m Martha Ball Pvt MA
Nathan: b 1740 d 11- -1825 m Hannah Cook Pvt MA
Nathan: b 1-5-1755 d 2-10-1842 m Annie Lockwood Pvt MA
Nathan: b 1-5-1763 d 4-5-1853 m Patience Lindley Pvt MA
Noah: b 5-18-1755 d 2-17-1830 m Elizabeth Brown Cpl MA
Peleg: b 9-17-1761 d p. 1811 m Usebe Presbury Pvt MA
Reese: b c. 1737 d 10-7-1780 m Louisa Margaret Smith Lt VA
Richard: b c. 1750 d 9- -1808 m Mrs Sarah (Bowen) Murphy Pvt VA
Robert: b 1740 d 8-25-1817 m Mary Gillespie Capt VA
Samuel: b 3-9-1760 d 5-25-1840 m Polly Holmes Pvt MA ★
Samuel: b 2-28-1701/02 d 10-23-1784 m (1)Sarah Smith (2)Martha Fowler PS RI
Seth: b 1748 d 1815 m Elizabeth Wood Lt NJ
Simeon: b 1-2-1730 d 12-4-1809 m Mary Newman Pvt MA
Smith: b 1738 d 3-19-1827 m Mary Warren Lt RI
Thomas: b 1743 d p. 1795 m Araminta Gardner PS MD
Thomas: b 12-21-1743 d 7-12-1834 m Penelope Aldrich PS NH
Thomas: b 1747 d 1810 m (1)Agnes Crea (2)Elizabeth (Spicer) Daugherty Pvt PA
Thomas Bartholomew: b 1742 d 10-12-1805 m X Capt PA
Uriah: b 6-6-1740 d p. 1790 m Esther Ide Pvt MA
Valentine: b 11-25-1722 d 1-20-1799 m Jemima Martin Lt MA
Wm., Jr.: b 3-17-1761 d 2-6-1844 m Mary Hathaway Sol MA
Wm.: b 1755 d 10-28-1848 m Deborah Pvt NH ★
Wm. Sr.: b 12-17-1731 d 4-3-1808 m (1)Ann Jennings (2)Mary Turpin Ens RI
Wm.: b 9-25-1760 d 2-14-1854 m Lydia Pearce Pvt RI ★
Wm.: b 1742 d 12-15-1804 m Mary Henley Russell Capt VA
Wm.: b 1762 d 10-1-1832 m Betsy Brannon Cpl VA ★

BOWERS, (includes BAUER, BOWER)
Andrew: b 1744 d 1824 m Barbara Klages Pvt PA
Andrew: b — d a. 3-1-1813 m X PS SC
Balaam: b 10- -1752 d 1834 m Mary — Pvt VA ★
Benjamin: b 2-11-1754 d 11-26-1835 m Silence Stickney Pvt MA
Benjamin: b 8-1-1761 d 7-8-1834 m Sabrina Wright Pvt MA
Benjamin: bpt 7-19-1741 d 5-6-1781 m Sally Russell Lt NH
Christopher: b 6-19-1759 d 1-10-1826 m Cathrine E Pvt PA
David, Jr.: b 8-13-1755 d 2-7-1805 m Hannah Bowers NCapt MA
David: b c. 1730 d p. 2-20-1793 m Ann — Mil SC
Dielman, Sr.: b c. 1718/19 d c. 1796 m Elizabeth Smith PS PA
George: b 1740 d 1782 m Christiana PS MD
George: b 9-1-1763 d p. 1837 m Elizabeth Lewis Pvt PA
George Michael: b c. 1738 d 2-26-1820 m Hannah Martha Hill Pvt PA

Giles: b c. 1740 d 1800 m Sarah — Pvt NC
Giles: b c. 1747 d c. 1783 m Ann Lee Pvt SC
Isaac: b 6-26-1741 d 9-14-1808 m Priscilla Dodge Pvt MA
Jacob: b 11-30-1747 d 12-24-1797 m Anna Maria Lieder 1Lt PA
Jacob: b 9- -1757 d 3-6-1818 m Rebecca Wood Capt PA
Jacob: b 10-11-1754 d 9-28-1825 m Anna Rohrer Pvt MD PA ★
James: b 1761 d 1827 m Elizabeth Freeman Pvt NJ
John: b 1737 d 3-23-1825 m (1)Hepzibah Strong (2)Catherine — Cpl CT
John: b 9-2-1757 d 8-10-1808 m Elizabeth Boutelle Pvt MA
John: b 2-13-1760 d 3-22-1845 m Hannah Bonnell Drm NJ
John: b c. 1728 d a. 11-26-1803 m Elizabeth — Pvt PA
John: b 4-6-1753 d 2-27-1791 m Catrina Heller Pvt PA
Joseph: b 1760 d 1827 m Sarah Slaymaker Sol PA
Josiah: b 1-10-1719 d 4-20-1794 m (1)Abigail Thomson (2)Sarah Trowbridge Capt MA
Leonard: b 1760 d 10-5-1840 m Rebecca Nave Pvt MD ★
Luke: b 2-25-1763 d 1818 m Anne Pratt Sol MA
Martin: b 12-27-1741 d 8-5-1832 m Elizabeth Shobe PS VA
Michael: b 1720-22 d 1784 m Fronica Landis PS PA
Morris: b c. 1735 d 12-30-1781 m Esther Bonner Pvt VA
Nehemiah: b 2-26-1752 d 4-26-1828 m Sarah Sawin Pvt MA
Sampson: b 9-26-1755 d 6-21-1797 m Azubah Robbins Pvt MA
Samuel: b 4-17-1754 d 3-23-1823 m (1)Becca Nichols (2)Phebe Piper Pvt MA
Samuel: b 3-1754 d 1828 m Mary Sutter Artl PA
Samuel: b 5-22-1760 d 12-10-1834 m Ann Mary Sutter Pvt PA
Sebastian: b 1-21-1757 d 10-16-1840 m Magdalena Bear Pvt PA
Thomas: b 1750 d 1820-22 m Sarah Yerkes Pvt PA
Tillman: b 1744 d 8-29-1810 m Maria Eva Pvt PA
Wm.: b 10-15-1736 d 11-25-1812 m Hannah Kidder Pvt MA
Wm.: b 12-1-1750 d 12-21-1804 m Sarah Farmer Maj PA

BOWERSOX,
George Adam: b 4-1-1744 d 3-8-1817 m Magdalene Rausenzaner Sgt MD
Paul: b 1750 d 1806 m X Pvt PA

BOWES,
Robert: b c. 1740 d 6-4-1800 m Frances Scott PS VA
Wm. G.: b 1764 d 1828 m Mary Jones Fif VA

BOWIE, (includes BOWEY)
Allen, Sr.: b 1709 d 1- -1783 m (1)Mrs Priscilla Finch (2)Anne Fraser PS MD
Allen, Jr.: b 1736/37 d 5-28-1803 m Ruth Cramphin 1Lt MD
Fielder: b 1745 d 9- -1794 m Elizabeth Clagett Eversfield Capt MD
George: b a. 1775 d 1793 m Rachel Strout Pvt MA
John: b 5-21-1740 d 9-20-1827 m Rosa Reid Maj SC
Rezin: b 9- -1756 d 10-3-1819 m Elve ap Catesby ap Jones Sol GA
Rhoda: b 1752 d 8-8-1814 m Ann Price Pvt MD
Robert (Gov): b 3-6-1750 d 1-5-1818 m Priscilla Mackall Capt MD
Walter, Sr.: b 1748 d 11-9-1810 m Mary Brooks Lt MD
Wm., 3rd.: b a. 1752 d 9-17-1809 m (1)Ursula Burgess (2)Ursula Burgess Lt MD
Wm.: b 1721 d 1791 m Margaret Sprigg PS MD

BOWKER, (includes BOUKER, BUKER)
Asa: b 11-12-1755 d 10-5-1825 m Hannah Hero Pvt MA W★
Bartlett: b 2-22-1749 d 1-16-1829 m (1)Christiana Webb (2)Mrs Susanna Wellington (3)Mrs Jemima (Knowlton) Wright Pvt MA
Benjamin: b 2-14-1738 d 6-28-1820 m Anna (Brooks) Silvester Pvt MA
Charles: b 8-17-1725 d 3-11-1781 m Eunice Stone Pvt MA
Daniel: bpt 4-11-1731 d 1-21-1822 m Sarah Brigham Capt MA
Edmund: b 8-20-1732 d 2-9-1827 m Lydia Lambert Pvt MA
Edmund: b 1757 d 1841 m Hannah Stearns Pvt MA ★
Gideon: b 3-9-1760 d 8-3-1815 m Hannah Fletcher Pvt MA
Israel H.: b 4-17-1763 d 11-5-1848 m (1)Bathsheba Carver (2)Sarah Black Sgt MA ★
Ithamar: b 11-27-1750 d 4-26-1820 m Miriam Bartlett Pvt MA ★
John, Sr.: b 10-3-1724 d 2-17-1807 m Anna Rite PS MA
Joseph: b 12-28-1725 d 7-11-1784 m Sarah Taintor PS VT
Josiah: b 1701 d 4-27-1781 m Hazadiah Eager PS MA
Lazarus, Jr.: bpt 3-11-1743 d 5-26-1832 m Mary Collier Sgt MA
Levi: b 7-25-1763 d 8-28-1850 m Betsey Watts Pvt MA ★
Luke: b c. 1730 d p. 1790 m Mrs Joanna Dunbar Pvt MA
Silas, Sr.: b 5-29-1733 d 4-1-1820 m Bethia Ward Pvt PS NY
Silas, Jr.: b 4-26-1763 d 10-14-1834 m Amy Harding Pvt PS NY ★
Zebulon: b 10-23-1751 d 10-23-1839 m (1)Deborah Randall (2)Grace Rice Pvt MA ★

BOWLER,
Charles: b 1754 d 8-31-1802 m Rebecca Irish PS RI
Metcalf: b 5-30-1726 d 9-24-1789 m Anne Fairchild PS CS RI

BOWLES, (includes BOLLES)
Benjamin: b 1764 d 10-5-1844 m Elizabeth Wells Pvt NC ★
David: b 2-27-1729 d p. 1790 m Lydia Kirby Pvt MA
David: b c. 1730 d 2-20-1806 m Winnie Minerva Rice Capt VA
Ebenezer: b 10-14-1750 d 5-10-1825 m Anna Clifton Pvt MA

BOWLES, contd.
John: b 3-2-1759 d 9-24-1808 m Deidamia Sims Sgt MA W★
John: b 1748 d — m Parmelia — Sgt RI
John: b 6-8-1743 d 8-5-1836 m Betsy Curd Sol VA
John C.: b 1752 d 6-26-1831 m X Sol NC
Knight: b 1746 d 2-14-1820 m (2)Mrs Patsy (Wood) Ellis Sol VA
Lemuel: b 1757 d 6-16-1825 m Lucy Perkins Pvt CT
Martin: b c. 1760 d c. 1819 m Peggy — Pvt MD
Ralph Hart: b 3-10-1757 d 10-30-1813 m Hannah Crocker Lt MA
Samuel: b 5-10-1744 d 8-10-1842 m Margaret Moore Pvt CT
Thomas: b c. 1743 d p. 9-7-1787 m Eleanor Price PS MD
Thomas: b 1763 d 1-22-1847 m Anne Davis Pvt NC ★
Thomas: b 2-9-1761 d 12-7-1839 m Sarah Holman Sgt VA
Thomas: b c. 1730 d p. 11-19-1783 m X PS VA
Thomas Philip: b a. 1749 d 1783 m Sarah Bacon Lt VA

BOWLSBY,
Samuel: b 1730 d 1810 m Betsey Duran Pvt NJ
Thomas: b 4-2-1744 d 1-8-1827 m Sarah Cowell Pvt NJ

BOWMAN, (includes BACHMAN, BAUGHMAN)
Abiather: b c. 1759 d 4-2-1833 m Thankful Rice Pvt NH ★
Abraham: b 10-16-1749 d 11-17-1837 m Mrs Sarah Henry Bryan Col VA
Abraham: b a. 1753 d c. 1794 m Christine Pvt PA
Adam: b 12-14-1758 d 10-14-1834 m Barbara Herter Pvt NY ★
Benjamin: b 7-4-1742 d 6-29-1822 m Elizabeth Ferree Pvt PA
Bernard: b 1749 d 12- -1824 m Catherine Drysbaugh Lt PA
Christian: b 5-19-1727 d 8-23-1783 m Barbara — Sol PA
Christian: b 6-18-1758 d 7-14-1838 m Maria Snyder Sol PA
Christian b 1761 d 1831 m Rebecca Dotson Pvt PA
Christopher: b 1733 d 1806 m Susan Banks Ens PA
Conrad: b c. 1730 d p. 2-10-1792 m Catharine Magdalena Kuntz Cpl PA
Ebenezer: b 7-3-1757 d 3-1-1829 m Esther Ann Watson Pvt MA
Frederick: b 1750 d 1823 m Delia Folts Pvt NY
George: b 9-11-1758 d 1820 m Catherine Zinn Capt PA
George, Jr.: b — d 4- -1806 m Ester 1Lt PA
George: b 10-14-1755 d 4-13-1834 m Barbara Steele Pvt PA
George: b 1750 d 4-4-1820 m Polly Sigurfost Wgm PA
Grace Greenlee: b 6-23-1750 d 5-18-1823 m (1)John Bowman (2)Charles McDowell PS NC
Henry: b 9-21-1751 d 11-27-1824 m Catherine Driesbach Capt PA
Henry: b c. 1742 d 1816 m Catherine Conkle Pvt PA
Henry: b 9-23-1743 d 1832 m Ann Whitmore Sol PA
Hugh: b c. 1728 d 1791 m Margaret — PS CS NC
Isaac: b 4-24-1757 d 9-9-1826 m (1)Elizabeth Gatewood (2)Mary Chinn Lt & QM IL
Jacob, Sr.: b 7-25-1704 d 1788 m (2)Mrs Catharine Schmetter Pvt PA
Jacob: b 1751 d p. 1782 m Maria Fohantzer Pvt PA
Jacob: b c. 1748 d p. 1803 m (1)Anna Hunsaker (2)Elizabeth — PS VA
James: b 12-25-1738 d 9-29-1816 m Mary Gashit Lt MA
James: b 1751 d 1-2-1820 m Catherine Mc Cormack Ens PA
Johannes: b 1729 d 4- -1785 m X Pvt PA
John: b 7-3-1759 d 10-22-1846 m Hannah Frye Pvt MA ★
John: b c. 1748 d p. 1802 m X Capt NY
John, 2d.: b c. 1759 d 1830 m Catherine Stuart Sol NY
John: b 4-14-1752 d 10-14-1797 m Margaret Countryman Pvt PA
John: b 1755 d 11/10/1813 m Eve Breneman Pvt PA
John: b c. 1763 d 1843 m Mary Magdalina Sol PA
John: b 1743 d 3-7-1813 m Hannah Elliot Pvt VT
John: b 12-2-1733 d 6-20-1780 m Grace Greenlea Capt VA
John: b 1752 d 5-25-1841 m Bashaba Hooker Pvt VA ★
John: b 1750 d 3- -1816 m Mary Magdalene Zervus PS VA
Jonas: b 7-19-1739 d 3-29-1807 m (1)Susannah Gregory (2)Mrs Prudence (Hardy) Rice PS Capt NH
Joseph: b 2-18-1740 d 1-5-1818 m Catherine (Mason) Monroe Maj MA
Joseph: b 5-1-1744 d 2-5-1831 m Nancy Pvt PA
Joseph: b c. 1730 d p. 1784 m Easter — Pvt PA
Joshua: b 2- -1746 d 3-30-1780 m Abigail Towle Capt SC
Martin: b c. 1730 d 10- -1816 m Elizabeth — Capt PA
Matthew: b 1757 d 2-21-1827 m Elizabeth Drose PS SC
Nicholas: b 1735 d p. 3-14-1802 m Maria Magdalena Pvt PA
Paul: b 1735 d 8- -1823 m Anna Margaret Pvt PA
Peter: b c. 1759 d 11-24-1818 m Eve — Pvt PA
Peter, Sr.: b c. 1730 d 1782 m Mary Kauffman Pvt PA
Peter, Jr.: b 1-31-1762 d 8-23-1823 m Elizabeth Huber Pvt PA
Philip: b 10-25-1755 d 1-17-1845 m Katy Fast Ens MD ★
Samuel: b 11-1-1749 d 12-21-1819 m Hannah Davenport Lt MA
Samuel: b c. 1746 d p. 1790 m Catherine Landis Pvt PA
Sebastian: b 4-6-1739 d 10-19-1803 m Anna Wetzell Maj NY
Solomon: b 6-2-1745 d 6-28-1778 m Abigail Brown Lt MA
Thaddeus, Sr.: b 3-10-1723 d 5-26-1806 m (1)Sarah (Fisk) Loring (2)Sybil (Roper) Woolson PS MA
Thaddeus, Jr.: b 2-10-1743 d 4-14-1815 m Elizabeth Lawrence Lt MA
Walter: b 11-25-1750 d 3-30-1831 m Annie Litchfield Pvt CT
Wm.: b 3-5-1742 d 1808/09 m Susanna Hinds Pvt MA
Wm.: b c. 1760 d 1814 m Elizabeth Mc Pherson Pvt & PS NC

Wm.: b 1749 d 1843 m — Shockley Pvt VA
Zadock: b 12-28-1760 d 5-22-1832 m Susan How Pvt NH

BOWMAR,
Robert: b — d p. 5-17-1826 m Chloe Collins Ens VA

BOWNE,
David Holmes: b 11-9-1747 d 12-9-1820 m Mary Nichols MM NJ
George: b 1748 d p. 1790 m Abigail Smith PS NY
Henry: b 1749 d 12-25-1829 m Charity Huff Cpl NJ ★
John: b 2-9-1751 d 9-20-1797 m Johanna Rynders Provost Pvt NJ
Joseph: b 5-17-1735 d 10-8-1812 m Hannah Anderson Cpl NJ
Samuel: b 1722 d 3-11-1799 m Patience Conover Pvt NJ

BOWSER,
John: b 1740 d a. 10-1-1813 m Mary — Pvt PA
Noah: b 1750 d 1830 m Eunice Ditto Pvt PA

BOWSHER, (includes BOORSE, BOUCHER)
Anthony: b 6-12-1755 d 1835 m Christine Reigeldoerfer Pvt PA ★
Arnold: b 8-30-1743 d 1- -1795 m Susanna Heistler Pvt PA
Daniel: b c. 1730 d c. 1792 m X PS PA
Henry: b 3-10-1759 d 11-19-1834 m Maria Shumaker PS PA

BOX,
Edward: b 1754 d 5-17-1857 m Nancy — Pvt SC

BOXLEY,
Benjamin: b c. 1745 d c. 1814 m Tibitha Irby PS VA
Joseph: b c. 1735 d p. 6-27-1787 m Catherine Spiller PS VA

BOY,
Jacob: b 4-17-1752 d 5-20-1833 m Mary Drummond Pvt VA ★

BOYCE, (includes BOICE, BOIES, & BOYS)
Abraham: b 1753 d 1819 m Mary — Pvt NY
Benjamin: b c. 1730 d p. 1790 m (1)Sarah Atwater (2)Marion Husted Sgt NY
Boaz: b 1729 d p. 1805 m Sarah — Pvt DE
Cornelius: bpt 12-9-1739 d a. 1782 m Jane Coriell Ens NJ
David: b 1-15-1750 d 2-6-1839 m Dolly Blaire Pvt MA
Joel: b 6-18-1753 d 3-28-1809 m Betsy Blaire Pvt MA
John: b 9-27-1760 d 3-17-1833 m Mary Parker Pvt NH
John: b 1734 d 1802 m Mary Tiffany Pvt NY
John: b 1758 d p. 1802 m Margaret Allison Pvt PA
John: b 1734 d 4-25-1818 m Susannah — Pvt SC
John: b 1745 d 4-3-1806 m Elizabeth Miller Pvt SC
Nathan: b c. 1740 d 1803 m Mary Reynolds N Commo NJ
Peter: b c. 1760 d 2-9-1817 m Abigail Brown Pvt NY W★
Samuel: b 6-6-1724 d 9-14-1804 m Elizabeth Crooks PS & CS MA
Samuel: b 1755 d p. 1800 m (2)Martha Hood Cpl PA
Thomas: b 3-20-1746 d 6-7-1826 m (1)Mary Van Wart (2)Catharine See Ens NY ★
Wm.: b 1722 d 7-9-1804 m Mary Hamilton CS MA
Wm.: b c. 1740 d c. 1805 m Sarah Anderson Capt NH
Wm.: b 2-8-1743 d 8-12-1813 m Priscilla Price Pvt VA
Wm.: b 1745 d p. 2-1-1795 m (1) X (2)Judith Lamb Pvt NC
Wm.: b c. 1755 d 1804 m Elizabeth Nance Pvt NC
Wm.: b 7-29-1749 d 1-5-1812 m (1)Martha Adams (2)Elizabeth McKenney Capt VA

BOYD,
Abram: b c. 1746 d p. 1790 m Hannah Hill Pvt MA
Adam: b 3-21-1746 d 8-15-1835 m Elsie Van Cleve PS NJ
Alexander: b 8-16-1743 d 8-11-1801 m Matilda Ann Swepson PS VA
Andrew: b 1740 d 3-23-1786 m Jane Whitehill Col PA
Andrew: b 1747 d 8-5-1828 m Sarah Ross Adj PA
Andrew: b c. 1745 d a. 6-6-1820 m Mary Buchannan Pvt & PS VA
Benjamin: b 1734 d 1784 m Eleanor Taylor Pvt MD
Benjamin: b 1738 d 5-8-1803 m Jinnet Elliott Pvt PA
David: b 3-23-1743 d 7-16-1831 m Elizabeth Henderson Pvt PA
David: b 1758 d 12-5-1833 m Eleanor Crosson Pvt SC
David: b 1737/38 d 5-11-1815 m Margaret — PS SC
Ebenezer: b 1735 d 6-29-1792 m Sarah Merrett Capt NY
Francis: b 1758 d 12-7-1824 m Ann Worsham Pvt VA ★
George: b a. 1748 d 1803 m Amy — Col VA
Hugh: b c. 1730 d a. 1800 m Jane — MD NC
Hugh: b a. 1754 d a. 3-3-1799 m — Jennett PS SC
James: b 1752 d 10-14-1824 m Janet Bell Cpl MA
James: b 2-1-1762 d 2-2-1839 m Alida Conde Pvt NY
James: b 1743 d 10-9-1813 m Nancy Brown Maj PA
James: b 1738 d — m Martha Burns Sol SC
John: b c. 1738 d 1817 m Ann Adamson PS MD
John: b 8-17-1731 d 7-27-1828 m Hannah Dean Col MA
John: b 8-3-1758 d 12-2-1814 m Ann Bone Sgt NC W★
John: b 1-21-1739 d 9-18-1798 m (2)Christina Van Deusen Pvt NY
John: b — d 1-9-1823 m Mary Cowen Maj PA
John: b 7-27-1750 d 2-13-1831 m Rebecca Bull Capt PA
John: b c. 1740 d 5-6-1817 m Mary Fulton PM PA
John: b 1715 d c. 1789 m Nancy Urie Sol PA
John: b 1730 d a. 1-4-1799 m Agnes Cooper Pvt PA

John: b c. 1735 d p. 11-3-1810 m Martha — Pvt PA
John: b 11-21-1740 d 12-2-1802 m Jane Bernardoe Pvt SC
John: b c. 1745 d 4-5-1805 m Irma R. — Pvt VA
John: b 1762 d 10-15-1824 m Elizabeth Davis PS VA
John: b 175— d 179— m Martha — Pvt VA
John: b 1-9-1760 d 1829 m Nancy Martin Pvt VA
Matthew: b 1737 d 1782 m Hannah — LCol PA
Patrick: b 1759 d 3-1-1835 m Ann McDowell Pvt VA ★
Robert: b 1762 d 1811 m Sarah Clements Pvt GA
Robert: b 1757 d 3-14-1853 m (1)Mrs Young Silverthorn (2)Sarah
    Cox Longshore Tms MD
Robert: b 1-10-1740 d p. 1792 m Jane Smith Pvt & PS NY
Robert, Jr.: b 1734 d 10-29-1804 m — Smith PS NY
Robert: b 1762 d 2-19-1849 m Elizabeth Larimer Pvt PA
Roland: b c. 1740 d 1821 m Nancy — Pvt PA
Samuel: b 1-3-1736 d 4-28-1828 m Frances Fletcher Pvt & Drm ME
Samuel: b 1734 d 5-27-1801 m Elizabeth McDoel PS NY
Samuel: b 6-7-1754 d 8-21-1831 m Mehetable Tuthill Pvt NY
Samuel: b 5-20-1763 d 11-27-1835 m Isabella Higgins Pvt SC
Thomas: b 9-14-1734 d 1796/97 m (1)Charity Duckett (2)—
    Landsdale Lt MD
Thomas: b 1-28-1748 d 6-9-1803 m Catherine Wylie PS ME
Thomas: b 8-18-1761 d 8-19-1851 m Margaret Huggins Pvt NY ★
Thomas: b 3-10-1761 d 10-12-1847 m Grezelda Allen Pvt NC
Thomas: b 1754 d 11-14-1814 m Ann Martin 2Lt PA
Thomas: b 7-23-1734 d 9-22-1778 m Catherine Wallace QM PA
Thomas Duckett: b 3-11-1761 d 7-21-1820 m Mary Magruder 2Lt
    MD
Wm.: b 10-8-1731 d 4-2-1821 m Sarah Johnson PS DE
Wm.: b c. 1736 d p. 1790 m Charity Tolbert PS MD
Wm.: b 3-15-1750 d 6- -1839 m Margarey Taylor Cpl MA
Wm.: b 2-25-1735 d 8-5-1817 m Lydia Morse Pvt & QM MA
Wm.: b 1719 d 11-24-1789 m Alice Hunter Pvt NH
Wm.: b 1736 d 10-10-1825 m Martha Dickey Pvt NH
Wm.: b c. 1750 d p. 6-12-1797 m Esther Parkinson Pvt NJ
Wm.: b 1758 d 1831 m Rhoda Davenport Pvt NC
Wm.: b 3-15-1761 d 2-14-1847 m (1)Mary Wasson (2)Nancy Small
    Pvt NC ★
Wm.: b c. 1730-34 d 1805 m Elizabeth McTeer PS NC
Wm.: b 1733 d 5-17-1808 m Gennet Brisban Pvt PA
Wm.: b 1751/52 d 5-10-1846 m (1)Margaret — (2)Martha Bales
    Sgt PA
Wm.: b 1766 d 1-18-1838 m Keziah Porter Pvt SC ★
Wm.: b c. 1710 d p. 1-29-1791 m (1)— (2)Martha Wood PS VA
Wm.: b 1752 d 2-28-1812 m Ann Jack (Jacques) Sol VA
Wm. Blanton: b 3-14-1739 d 12-10-1809 m Margaret Evaline
    Cochran Pvt SC

BOYDEN,
Amos: b 12-21-1749 d 2-3-1823 m (1)Mary Paine (2)Ama Morse
    Pvt MA
Amos: b 4-15-1763 d 4-1-1837 m Abigail Wood Pvt MA
Benjamin: b 11-6-1733 d 2-5-1806 m (1)Huldah Armsby (2)Mrs
    Hannah Jackson Pvt MA
Daniel: b 1746 d 11-23-1800 m Margery Foster 2Lt MA
Daniel, Jr.: b 10-20-1741 d 8-29-1813 m Rebecca Barber Pvt MA
Darius: b 12-6-1743 d 3-16-1783 m Lavinia Brown Pvt MA
David: b 2-9-1732 d p. 4- -1775 m (1)Margery Foster (2)Abigail
    Carrel Pvt MA
Ezekiel: b 11-30-1741 d 2-2-1808 m Leah Richardson Pvt MA
Jacob: b 3-26-1744 d 3-10-1818 m Sarah Patten Pvt MA
Jairus: b 8-2-1759 d — m Caroline Lawrence Pvt MA
James: b 11-20-1758 d 11-20-1816 m Susanna Norton Cpl MA
John: b 1-22-1717 d 1808 m Thankful Morse Lt MA
John: b 1-7-1748 d 2-22-1795 m Abigail (Hobbs) Brown Sgt MA
John: b 1-29-1764 d 10-2-1857 m (1)Eunice Hayden (2)Mary Jones
    Pvt MA ★
John: b 10-4-1734 d 4-25-1813 m (1)Hannah Hartshorn (2)Sarah
    Foster Pvt MA
Jonathan: b 12-4-1729 d 5-31-1795 m Hannah Carroll Sol MA
Jonathan: b 2-24-1737 d — m Freelove Smith Pvt MA
Jonathan: b a. 1744 d c. 1799 m Esther Rhodes Pvt VT
Jonathan: b 12-6-1741 d c. 1833 m Elizabeth Sawtelle Pvt MA
Joseph: b 8-6-1741 d 3-19-1812 m Miriam Clark Lt MA
Joseph: b 9-23-1757 d 5-27-1840 m Polly Knowlton Pvt MA ★
Josiah: b 11-19-1761 d 4-4-1845 m (1)Anna Gates (2)Mrs Sophia
    Pulsipher Pvt MA
Justis: b 3-4-1765 d 2-11-1840 m Polly Boyden Pvt MA
Phineas: b 11-2-1760 d 4-29-1828 m Lydia Boyden Pvt MA
Seth: b 4-19-1715 d 3-28-1777 m (1)Elizabeth Turner (2)Mary
    Patten Pvt MA
Thomas: b 11-7-1733 d p. 1775/76 m Hepsibah Fisher PS MA

BOYDSTON, (includes BOIDSTONE)
David: b 5-2-1726 d 8-3-1811 m Mehitable Snow Pvt VA
James: b 9-23-1747 d 2-6-1814 m Mary Bruitt (Pruitt) Sol NC
Samuel: b 1762 d 10-2-1847 m Sarah Reed Pvt NC ★
Wm.: b 3-24-1753 d 3- -1835 m Elizabeth Christian Pvt VA ★

BOYER, (includes BAYER, BEYER, BOWYER, & BOYERS)
Abraham: b c. 2-6-1722 d 3-6-1796 m Barbara Heystand Pvt PA
Anthony: b c. 1755 d 1831 m Salome Reinhart Pvt PA

Casper: b 6-17-1732 d 5-23-1793 m (1)— (2)Elizabeth Lambert
    Lt PA
Charles: b 1763 d 1828 m Maria Magdalena Reitnour Pvt PA
Christian: b 3-16-1759 d 11-16-1839 m (1)Christina Boyer (2)Hannah
    Nagle Sol PA
Christopher: b 5-20-1752 d 2-10-1832 m Mary Ann Youst Pvt PA
Christopher: b 11-4-1743 d 5-15-1817 m Catharine Reifschneider
    PS PA
Conrad: b 3-14-1744 d 1-2-1806 m Margaret Riel PS PA
Conrad: b 10- -1748 d 4-13-1827 m Elizabeth Seidel Pvt PA
Daniel: b 11-6-1765 d 8-2-1852 m Rebecca Woodward Pvt PA
Frederick: b 12-20-1732 d 2-19-1801 m Ann Margaret Moyer Sol
    MD
Frederick: b 12-31-1732 d 10-31-1832 m Susanna Mehrkam Pvt PA
Frederick: b 1742 d 1-7-1806 m Catherine Frey Pvt PA
Frederick: b 5-31-1746 d 2-3-1825 m Anna Martha Nowlane Pvt PA
Frederick: b 6-20-1756 d 12-4-1840 m Maria Elizabeth Scholl Sol
    PA ★
George: b 3-3-1734 d 3-29-1806 m Elizabeth — Pvt PA
George: b 10-31-1760 d 5-24-1831 m (1)Anna Maria (2)Susanna —
    Pvt PA
George: b 7-15-1762 d 2-10-1828 m Mary Zieber Pvt PA
George Philip: b 1-30-1750 d 9-18-1824 m Catherine Pvt PA
Henry: b 1760 d 6-13-1832 m Agatha Madison Lt VA
Jacob: b 1760 d c. 1851 m Elizabeth Lorah Pvt PA
Jacob: b 8- -1754 d 2-11-1796 m Catherine Schantz Cpl PA
Jacob: b 1728 d 1808 m Lucy Ludwig Pvt PA
Jacob: b 6-24-1763 d p. 1817 m Margaret Huffman Sol VA
James: b 11-3-1760 d 7-13-1837 m Anne Rees PS PA
Johannes Frederick: b 4-25-1718 d 9-11-1804 m Anna Maria PS PA
Johannes Nicholas: b 2- -1753 d 6- -1823 m (1)— (2)Amelia
    Catharine Wentzel Sgt PA
John, Jr.: b 10-17-1760 d 10-14-1836 m (1)Margaret Ritter (2)Kate
    Bateman Kramer Pvt NY ★
John: b c. 1740 d p. 10-7-1808 m Elizabeth — Pvt PA
John: b 1720 d 1805 m Margaret Mary Becker Col VA
Joseph: b c. 1750 d p. 1800 m Mary Hall PS MD
Leonard: b 1758 d 1830 m Catherine Trout Sgt PA
Leonard: b 5-1-1737 d p. 1790 m Margaret — Pvt PA
Leonard: b 11-24-1758 d 4-7-1823 m Hannah — Pvt PA
Lewis: b 1756 d 9-19-1843 m Rosetta Walters Kerns Pvt PA ★
Michael: b 8-9-1750 d 8-9-1810 m (1)Margaret Clapper (2)Dorothy
    Wolf Noch Capt MD
Michael: b 1752-55 d 1788 m Annie Mary — 1Lt PA
Michael: b 12-25-1746 d 8-3-1820 m Margaret Freyman Pvt PA
Michael: b c. 1730 d 1809 m Frances Carpenter Capt & CS VA
Michael: b 1755 d 1835 m X Pvt VA & PA
Oziel: b 1730 d c. 1781 m Maria Eva Speiler Pvt PA
Peter: b 11-2-1731 d 7-20-1790 m (1)Susannah Buckley
    (2)Catherine Wells (3)Charlotte Johonnot PS MA
Peter: b 1753 d 4-18-1797 m Ann Castner Capt NJ
Peter: b a. 1748 d 8-27-1776 m Anna Marie Shultz Pvt PA
Peter: b 1760 d 10-10-1850 m (1)Eva — (2)Catharine Shellman
    PS PA
Philip: b 1746 d 12-24-1832 m Elizabeth Mungesser Pvt PA
Philip: b 12- -1750 d 1823 m Catherine Metz Pvt PA
Philip: b 12-14-1754 d 7-31-1832 m Anna Christina Pvt PA
Samuel: b 2-5-1751 d 1-20-1822 m Catherine Kuzer Pvt PA
Samuel: b 11-16-1758 d 11-1-1829 m Anne Pvt PA
Thomas: b c. 1751 d 11-5-1778 m Mary Montgomery Lt MD
Valentine, Sr.: b 3-2-1734 d p. 1790 m Maria Christina Winckie Pvt
    PA
Valentine, Jr.: b 7- -1760 d 1850 m Elizabeth Kuehn Pvt PS PA
Wm.: b 1738 d 1808 m (1)Elizabeth Christian (2)Margaret Ann
    (Lewis) McClanahan Col VA

BOYKIN,
Burwell: b 1751 d 8-17-1817 m (1)Elizabeth Whitaker (2)Mary
    Whitaker Lt SC
Byus (Tobias): b 1757 d 11-22-1812 m Sarah Peebles Lt VA
Francis: b 1754 d p. 10-7-1803 m Ann Marshall Maj VA
Francis: b c. 1745 d 1821 m Catherine Whitaker Maj SC
John: b c. 1756 d 1798 m (1)Miss Starke (2)Francis Brown Col SC
Samuel: b 1748 d 12- -1791 m Elizabeth Brown Capt SC
Simon: b c. 1750 d 4- -1824 m (1)Mary Saunders (2)Virginia
    Saunders (3)Sally Chalmers (4)Annie Clinch Capt VA

BOYLAN,
Aaron: b 5-15-1749 d 9-20-1824 m Sarah McDade Pvt NJ W★
James: b 8-14-1743 d 5-10-1823 m Ann Dunlop PS Dr NJ
John: b 1746 d 3-4-1793 m Eleanor Hodge Lt NJ

BOYLE, (includes BOYLL)
Charles: b c. 1760 d 3-15-1859 m — Pvt PA ★
Daniel: b 1748 d 3-4-1831 m — Pvt PA
Henry: b 3-27-1764 d 9-24-1839 m (1)Sarah Park (2)Elizabeth Sol
    VA
Hugh: b 1755 d 12-4-1832 m Ann Gilmore Pvt PA
James: b 1754 d 6-28-1825 m Martha Williams Capt PA
John: b 1750 d 9-1-1824 m (1)Jane Black (2)Mrs Ruth Wright Capt
    VA
Robert: b 1751 d 2-28-1834 m Jemimah Pvt VA ★

BOYLES,
David: b 1747 d 6-17-1845 m Polly Sappongton Matr CL ★

BOYLSTON,
Edward: b 1-21-1737 d 12-21-1814 m (1)Catherine Bourdette (2)Lydia Worthington Capt MA

BOYNTON,
Abiel: b 12-23-1753 d 12-17-1810 m Lois Raymond Pvt MA
Abijah: b 3-25-1740 d 12-26-1821 m Sarah Chamberlain 1Lt MA
Abraham: b — d 1829 m Mary Hartshorn Pvt MA
Amos: b 4-26-1742 d 11- -1810 m Sarah Snow Sgt NH
Amos: b 9-20-1744 d p. 1800 m Mary Parker Pvt NH
Amos: b 2-2-1745 d p. 1792 m (1)Polly Libby (2)Lucy Loring 1Lt MA
Asa: b 3-4-1760 d 2-21-1837 m Mary Frye Edmunds Pvt MA
Benoni: b 1726 d — m Mary Buttrick Pvt MA
Caleb: b a. 1755 d p. 1788 m Sarah Flagg Pvt MA
Caleb: b 7-14-1751 d — m Rachel Boynton Sol MA
David: b c. 1740-50 d 1815 m Anna Batchelder Pvt NH
Elias: b 2-24-1755 d 1-20-1842 m Elizabeth Blood Cpl NH
Ephraim: b 3-9-1734/35 d 2- -1826 m Abigail Emery 2Lt MA
Isaac: b 4-3-1755 d 1824 m (1)Mary Brooks (2)Lydia Masher (3)Judith Macomber Pvt NH ★
James: b 3-5-1739 d 6-17-1775 m Mary Wood Pvt MA
Job: b 1-6-1748 d p. 1815 m Mary Joslyn Pvt NH
Joel: b 3-22-1759 d p. 1835 m Elizabeth Wallis Sol NH
John: b 9-8-1736 d 3-21-1825 m (1)Elizabeth Jewett (2)Elizabeth Beaman (3)Mrs Phebe (Jewett) Grayes Col MA
John: b 8-30-1713 d 1777 m Mary Hancock Pvt MA
John: b 5-22-1723 d a. 1790 m Martha Atwood Pvt MA
John: b 6-4-1754 d 1-28-1842 m Marget Hatfield Fif Maj NH
John: b 5-4-1756 d 1841 m Lydia Dow Pvt NH
Jonathan: b 2-11-1745 d 1814 m (1)Elizabeth Dival (2)Mrs Molly Hodskins Pvt MA
Joseph: b 6-24-1738 d 1820 m Zerviah Wilder Lt MA
Joseph: b 6-3-1731 d 10-14-1787 m Sarah Tarbell MM MA
Joseph: b 1-17-1755 d 6-24-1830 m Rebecca Thurston 1Lt NH
Joseph: b 8-16-1749 d 3-13-1813 m Annie Cummings Pvt PS NH
Joshua: b 11-28-1743 d p. 1788 m Mary Parker Sgt NH
Joshua: b 1726 d 1796 m Elizabeth Rand Pvt NH
Moses: b 1752 d 1823 m Lucy Howe Pvt MA
Moses: b — d 12-10-1836 m Mary Osgood Cpl MA
Nathan: b 10-16-1757 d a. 1801 m Beulah Eaton Pvt MA
Oliver: b 4-30-1747 d 10-3-1801-06 m Mary Brown Sol CT
Richard: b 3-22-1741 d 1814 m Rebecca Abbot Pvt NH
Samuel: b 5-5-1743 d 5-20-1806 m Ruth Hardy Pvt MA
Samuel: bpt 7-14-1751 d 1793 m Mary Robinson Pvt MA
Samuel: b 1-17-1755 d 2-18-1837 m Mary Dearing Pvt NH
Solomon: b 5-14-1754 d 12-24-1830 m Abigail Warren Pvt MA
Thomas: b 11-29-1747 d 3-10-1833 m Hannah Ames Sgt MA
Thomas: b 9-2-1752 d 9-24-1823 m Elizabeth Keezer Tms NH
Wm.: b 12-5-1744 d p. 1785 m Mary McLucas Pvt MA

BOZARTH,
John: b c. 1740 d c. 1794 m X Sol VA
Jonathan: b 12-13-1754 d 9-14-1830 m Mary Hargis Pvt PA W★

BRABROOK,
Benjamin: b 7-12-1741 d 1-14-1827 m Lydia Taylor Lt MA

BRACE,
Abel: b 10-6-1740 d 7-20-1832 m Kezia Woodruff Capt CS CT
Ariel: bpt 8-7-1748 d p. 5-12-1810 m Deborah Loomis Cpl CT
David: b 2-1-1757 d 8-27-1840 m Eunice Comptom Pvt CT ★
Elijah: b 2-25-1750 d 9-11-1824 m Catharine Calkins Pvt CT
Henry: b 1744 d 3-17-1814 m Abigail Hooker Pvt CT
Joseph: b c. 1757 d 1820 m Lucy Jackson Sgt CT
Joseph: bpt 1-31-1742 d 8-21-1812 m Jemima Pvt MA
Nathaniel: b 6-10-1741 d p. 5-20-1777 m Elizabeth Crandall Pvt CT
Wm.: b a. 1756 d 1820 m (1)Hannah Mills (2)Ruth — Lt NY
Zenas: b 9- -1729 d 7-30-1791 m (1)Deliverance Goodwin (2)Mary Skinner Pvt CT

BRACK,
Benjamin: b 3-12-1763 d 4- -1827 m Christiana Fields Pvt GA
Eleazer: b c. 1730 d a. 4- -1802 m Esther — Pvt GA

BRACKEN,
Samuel: b 1742 d 1812 m (1)Martha Ector (2)Rebecca Reed Pvt NC
Wm.: b c. 1730 d a. 3-15-1792 m Sarah Garritt PS DE

BRACKETT, (includes BRACKET, BROCKETT)
Anthony: b 1749 d c. 1821 m Mary Coffey Pvt MA
Christopher: b a. 1748 d c. 1823 m (1)Elizabeth Tuttle (2)Elsa — Pvt VT
Ebenezer: b 11-23-1743 d 4-13-1826 m Abigail Clark Pvt NH
Enos: b 9-17-1755 d 11-13-1828 m (1)Hannah Jacobs (2)Mrs Lucy Eunice Tuttle Pvt CT
Giles: b 4-30-1761 d 6-2-1842 m Sarah Smith Pvt CT ★
James, Jr.: b 1736 d 8-16-1825 m Mary Spear Pvt MA

James, Jr.: b 3-12-1748 d 3-27-1831 m Anna Stillings Pvt MA
James: b 4-10-1726 d 1-3-1825 m Margarey Lord PS ME
James: b 5-5-1764 d 3-22-1845 m Mary Lunt PS MA ★
James: b 1-3-1714 d 11-13-1803 m (1)Martha Cate (2)Mrs Lucy (Cutts) Gerrish PS NH
Jeremiah: b 2-6-1754 d p. 1820 m Sarah Gooding Pvt MA
Joel: b 7-28-1750 d 7-6-1798 m (1)Hannah Clark (2)Esther Wightman Pvt CT
Joel: b 8-11-1760 d 7-4-1846 m Elizabeth — Pvt CT ★
John: b 10-5-1734 d 9-24-1775 m (1)Mary Fabyan (2)Pelatish March Capt MA
John: b 6-29-1720 d 2-18-1814 m Miriam Thompson Cpl MA
John: b 4-11-1761 d 2-22-1844 m Mary Walker Pvt MA ★
John Snow: b 11-23-1749 d 1801 m Betsy Berry Pvt MA
Joseph: b 5-17-1758 d 7-27-1838 m Sarah Bangs Sgt MA
Joseph: b 6-6-1751 d 5-3-1816 m (1)Jemima Roberts (2)Anna Winchell Pvt MA
Joseph: b 7-14-1740 d 1813 m Mary (Weeks) Nye Lt NH
Joshua, Sr.: b 6-7-1723 d 1816 m Esther Cox Pvt MA
Joshua, Jr.: b 7-31-1762 d 6-10-1849 m Lydia Hasty Pvt MA
Joshua: b — d — m Mrs Mary Nye PS NH
Nathan: b 8-26-1754 d 2-17-1837 m Mary Hurd Pvt MA ★
Nathaniel: b 1-13-1751 d 4-10-1842 m Sarah Chadbourne Pvt MA
Peter: b 11-7-1756 d 10-27-1834 m Sarah Sawyer Pvt MA ★
Samuel: b 11-30-1741 d 3-16-1826 m Rebecca Hayward Pvt MA
Samuel, Sr.: b 9-3-1724 d 5-9-1794 m Elizabeth — Pvt MA
Samuel: b 8-8-1757 d 10-31-1850 m Mary Wentworth Pvt MA
Thomas: b 1742 d 5-7-1788 m Margaret Sproul Capt MA
Thomas: b c. 1756 d 4-14-1785 m Martha Folsom Lt NH
Wm.: b 8-9-1752 d 1848 m (1)Betsy Walker (2)Judith Smith Sgt MA

BRACY, (includes BRACEY)
Sackfield McLynn: b 2- -1757 d 10-11-1807 m Lucy Hicks 2Lt VA
Thomas: b 1730-35 d p. 4-10-1802 m Mary Floyd PS VA
Wm.: b c. 1760 d 11-12-1825 m (1)Eugenia Singleton (2)Mrs Aider (3)M. Rudolph Pvt VA

BRADBURY,
Ammi Ruhamah: b 3-11-1762 d 3-5-1830 m Sarah Lewis Pvt MA ★
Benjamin: b 1744 d 9- -1834 m Mary Elden Sgt MA
David: b 10-13-1760 d 5-7-1824 m Susanna Craig Pvt NJ
Elijah: b 1737 d 1795 m Sarah Lane Sgt MA
Jabez: bpt 7-28-1752 d p. 1811 m (1)Sarah Atkinson (2)Mrs Mary Billings Pvt MA
Jacob: b 1729 d 1801 m Abigail Cole Capt MA
Jacob, Jr.: b 10-30-1743 d 10-30-1811 m (1)Mary Goodwin (2)Catherine (Simonton) Morris Sgt MA
John: b 9-9-1697 d 12-3-1778 m Abigail Young CS ME
Moses: b 2-4-1731 d p. 1790 m Mary Page 2Sgt MA
Moses: b 11-3-1715 d p. 1790 m Abigail Fogg Pvt MA
Samuel: b 1757 d 5-1-1796 m (1)Bethulah Haskell (2)Hannah Noyes Pvt MA
Sanders: b 11-29-1737 d 11-15-1779 m Sarah Colby Pvt NH
Thomas: b 1-10-1736 d 11-9-1803 m Ruth Page 2Lt MA
Wm.: b 5-5-1738 d p. 1784 m Susannah Hopkins Sgt MA

BRADDOCK,
Francis: b c. 1746 d 7-6-1800 m Elizabeth Martin Pvt PA
John: b 5-23-1731 d 6-16-1797 m Lucy Ann Cook Capt GA
John: b 1744/45 d 5-18-1818 m Sarah — Pvt PA
Raphael: b 1730 d 1803 m Minerva Williams Pvt MD

BRADEEN,
Robert: b 8-26-1745 d 1-4-1833 m Sarah Welch Pvt MA ★

BRADEN,
Andrew: b 2-4-1765 d 11-19-1842 m Dorothy McNeely Pvt NC W★
Jacob: b 1755 d 6-25-1829 m Rebecca Cooley Pvt PA
John: b 5-1-1759 d 5-19-1827 m Susan Jansen Cpl NY

BRADFORD, (includes BRADFORT)
Alexander: b 1728 d 1808 m Jamima Jones 1Lt VA
Andrew: b 6-11-1763 d 1-31-1836 m Lucy Parker Pvt NH ★
Andrew: b 11-1-1717 d 1798 m (1)Rebecca Cole (2)Hannah (Goffe) Chandler PS NH
Benjamin: b 1750 d p. 1810 m (1)Mary Read (2)Mary McAdams Lt PS NH
Calvin: b 7-25-1754 d 4-24-1835 m Lucy Pratt Pvt MA
Carpenter: b 2-7-1739 d 1-27-1823 m (1)Mary Gay (2)Mrs. Steel Pvt MA
Cornelius: b 12-10-1737 d 2-10-1790 m Patience Davis Capt MA
Daniel: b 1721 d 7-22-1810 m (1)Mrs Mary (Reynolds) Church (2)Susan Jarvis PS RI
David: b 1747 d 1800 m Elizabeth Pvt NC
Ebenezer: b 5-29-1746 d 1-3-1801 m Elizabeth Green Chp NJ
Elisha: b 10-15-1755 d 9-3-1835 m Lucy Rossetter Pvt CT ★
Elisha: b 1720 d — m Hannah Cole Cpl MA
Elisha: b 5-10-1753 d 5-31-1809 m Eunice Bennett Pvt MA
Ezekiel, Sr.: b 11- -1728 d 9- -1816 m Betsey Chandler Pvt MA

Ezekiel, Jr.: b 12-15-1759 d 10-26-1829 m Mary House Pvt MA W★

Gamaliel, Sr.: b 9-2-1731 d 1-9-1807 m (1)Sarah Alden (2)Mary Cooper Col MA

Gamaliel, Jr.: b 11-4-1763 d 3-7-1824 m Elizabeth Hickling Lt MA

George: b 5-19-1757 d 5-11-1823 m Susannah Hopkins Pvt RI W★

Gideon: b 5-30-1752 d 4-5-1805 m Abigail Sampson Pvt MA

Henry: b 1758 d 1815 m Elizabeth (Payne) Blakemore Sgt VA

Henry Swift: b 9-21-1736 d p. 8-8-1812 m Prudence Glover Sol CT

Israel: b 10-26-1766 d 1-5-1855 m (1)Hannah Everson (2)Mrs Olive Jeffers Pvt MA

James: b 1749 d 1833 m Sarah Ellis Cpl MA ★

James: b 1762 d 11-29-1844 m Rachel Robinson Pvt NC ★

James: b 1758 d 1-20-1837 m Elizabeth Bradford Pvt NJ RI ★

James: b 1754 d 4-18-1822 m (1)Barbara — (2)Catherine — Pvt PA

James D.: b 1744 d 2-8-1821 m (1) Jannett McMillen (2)Isabel Sterling Pvt NY

Jeremiah: b a. 1729 d 1817 m Rebecca Dart PS CT

Jesse: b 3-7-1758 d 5-20-1829 m Judith Weston Pvt MA

Joel: b 1758 d 7-12-1836 m Alsa Mosier Pvt & QM RI ★

John: b 12-7-1739 d 6-5-1818 m Mary Fitch Cpl CT

John: b 7-27-1750 d 10-9-1827 m Elizabeth Bond Pvt CT

John: b 7-29-1748 d 6-11-1807 m Eunice Loring Capt MA

John: b 8-24-1723 d 5-18-1784 m Margaret Barton PS MA

John: b 1744 d 6-27-1836 m Sarah Putnam Capt NH

John: b 1708 d 10-31-1787 m (1)Patience Reed (2)Dorothy Miriam Burgess (3)Elizabeth Smith Col NC

John: b 3-30-1759 d 3-22-1820 m (1)Mary Gillespie (2)Rachel Retenhous Pvt PS PA

John: b 10-28-1758 d 3-17-1837 m Mary James Sol SC

John: b 8-12-1754 d 4-30-1832 m (1)Bethiah Bond (2)Sally Williamson Cpl VT

John: b 4-17-1717 d 1789 m M. Timberlake Pvt VA

John: b 1745 d 1830 m — Strouse Pvt VA

John: b 1749 d 3- -1830 m Eliza James Pvt VA

John: b c. 1760 d 2-18-1821 m Ann Calvin Pvt VA

John Angel: b 9-16-1764 d 12-5-1829 m Mary Mitchell Pvt SC

Joseph: b 6-17-1742 d 3-21-1815 m Eunice Maples Lt CT

Joseph Bennett: b 11-14-1738 d 7-30-1822 m (1)— George (2)Margaret Wilson (3)Susannah (Bush) Jones Ordl NC

Joshua: b 10-17-1751 d 6-11-1819 m Anne Cleveland Pvt CT

Lemuel: b 2-20-1751 d 5-22-1828 m (1)Mary Sampson (2)Lydia Holmes Capt MA

Nathaniel: b 7-26-1748 d 11-24-1837 m Rebecca Holmes Pvt MA ★

Oliver: b 1-10-1759 d 11-14-1835 m Sarah Chipman Pvt MA ★

Peabody: b 1758 d 1-17-1852 m Hannah (Bradbury) Freeman Cpl MA

Peleg: b 3-9-1727 d 5-13-1809 m Lydia Sturtevant Pvt MA

Peres: b 7-25-1764 d 8-2-1847 m Polly Nickerson Pvt CT

Perez: b 10-11-1746 d 5-8-1817 m Betsy Rogers Ens CT

Perez: b 11-10-1752 d 3-15-1834 m (1)Sarah Prince (2)Lydia Cushman Pvt MA

Peter: b 6-6-1745/6 d 12- -1833 m Abigail Loring Sgt MA ★

Philemon: b 1757 d 1824 m Susanna Clopton PS NC

Robert: b 7-21-1739 d 1-20-1808 m Penelope (Bonfoey) Rich Ens CT

Robert: b 7-11-1750 d 9-11-1823 m Keziah Little Capt MA

Robert: b 8-28-1755 d 11-27-1836 m Hannah Eaton Sol NH

Samuel: b 7-27-1748 d 11-3-1811 m Lydia Dean PS CT

Samuel: b 1738 d 1810 m (1)Sarah Fitzgerald (2)Tabitha — Pvt MD

Samuel: b 1-2-1729 d 2-17-1777 m Grace Ring Capt MA

Samuel: b 1764 d 6-30-1812 m Lucy Churchill Smn MA

Samuel: b 1738 d 2-5-1813 m (1)Annie Washer (2)Mary Flint Lt NH

Samuel: bpt 5-8-1720 d 8- -1776 m Mary Taylor PS NH

Seth: b 9-14-1733 d 2-8-1823 m Lydia Southworth Pvt MA

Shubal: b 10- -1762 d 3-26-1837 m Anna Hadlock Pvt MA

Simeon: b 8-28-1729 d 10-7-1793 m Phebe (Whiton) Whiting PS VT

Thomas: b 11-14-1712 d a. 11-29-1788 m Eunice Adams Pvt CT

Thomas, Jr.: b 1-29-1751 d 6-8-1807 m Philena Davison Pvt CT W★

Thomas, Sr.: b c. 1720 d 1786 m Mary Lavet PS NC

Thomas: b 1757 d 3-15-1830 m Mary — Sol SC

Thomas: b 1760 d 1847 m Martha — Sol SC

Timothy: b 9-17-1745 d 1833 m Edith Howe PS Ens CS NH

Walt: b 1731 d p. 1783 m Weltha Bassett Pvt MA

Wm.: b 4-13-1734 d c. 1778/79 m Sarah Rich Sol CT

Wm.: b 7-1-1718 d p. 4-13-1799 m (1)Zeriah Lathrop (2)Mary Cleveland (3)Martha Warren PS CT

Wm.: b c. 1735 d a. 1798 m Sarah McComas Capt MD

Wm.: b a. 1763 d p. 1783 m Margaret Hill Richardson 1Lt MD

Wm.: b 11-25-1755 d 3-24-1811 m Hannah Parker Sgt MA

Wm.: b Sol d 1-10-1840 m Anna Cross Pvt NH ★

Wm., Sr.: b 10-25-1715 d 1791 m (1)Mary Lambert (2)Rachel Small PS NH

Wm. Jr.: b 1753 d 10-23-1816 m (1)Hannah Hopking (2)Mrs Lois Bruce Lt NH

Wm.: b 1-19-1719-21 d 9-25-1791 m Rachel Budd Col PA

Wm., Sr.: b 11-4-1729 d 7-6-1808 m Mary Le Baron PS RI

Wm.: b 8-4-1760 d 7-30-1834 m (1)Mary Ellen Steele (2)Catherine Morgan (3)Nancy Bayles Pvt VA ★

Wm., Jr.: b 9-15-1752 d 12-22-1811 m Elizabeth Bloom James Maj RI

BRADISH,

Daniel: b 4-30-1760 d 11-4-1855 m Phoebe Jones Pvt PS MA ★

David: b 1745 d 1818 m Abiah Merrill Capt MA

James: b 10-21-1752 d 9-18-1813 m Irene (Townsend) Clark Dr MA

John: b 1750 d 1825 m Hannah Warner Pvt MA

John: b 8-30-1719 d 4-2-1781 m Mary Green PS MA

Samuel: b 9-20-1750 d 12-24-1812 m Hannah Dunton Pvt MA

BRADLEY, (includes BRADLEE)

Aaron: b 3-27-1762 d 10-24-1843 m Loren Abernathy Pvt CT

Abijah: b 10-31-1751 d 1779 m Sarah Thompson Pvt CT

Abraham: b 12-3-1731 d 8-23-1824 m Hannah Baldwin Capt CT

Abraham: b 1746 d 1-28-1825 m Mary Punchard PS CT

Amos, Sr.: b 1736 d 10-11-1813 m Elizabeth Page PS MA

Amos, Jr.: b 5-30-1759 d 5-6-1817 m Lydia Jones Pvt MA

Aner: b 3-5-1753 d 3-13-1824 m Ann Guernsey 1Lt CT

Ariel: b 12-30-1768 d 3-25-1857 m Chloe Lane Spy CT

Asa: b 5-9-1746 d 1780 m Amy Morris Slr CT

Ashbel: b 1756 d 10-6-1817 m Chloe Graves Pvt CT

Benjamin: b 9-16-1760 d 8-2-1847 m Sally Brownson MM VT

Benjamin: b 1761 d 6-24-1840 m (1)Betty Quimby (2)Judith Morse Pvt NH ★

Cornelius: b 1755 d 8-26-1840 m Mary Hogan Pvt MD ★

Daniel: b 1750 d 1818 m Esther Ives Pvt CT

Daniel: b 2-13-1757 d 12-8-1837 m Elizabeth (Stratton) Winton Pvt 1Lt CT ★

Daniel: b 1-17-1756 d 4-14-1825 m Eunice Ives Sgt CT★

Daniel: b c. 1752/53 d 1802 m Mary — Capt PS PA

Demas: b 1731/32 d 1784 m Lydia Blakeslee Sol CT

Diamon: b 3-1-1757 d 7-1-1828 m Beulah Turner Pvt CT ★

Ebenezer: b 10-5-1723 d c. 1786 m Sarah Hull Pvt CT

Eber: b 3-4-1761 d 8-13-1841 m Diantha Judson Pvt & Fif VT ★

Edmund: b 9-24-1757 d 2-10-1828 m Lydia Chedsey Pvt CT

Eli: b 5-3-1762 d 12-29-1833 m Phebe Bartholomew Pvt MA

Elihu: b 10-2-1756 d 2-22-1842 m Sybil Grannis Pvt CT

Elijah: b 10-10-1759 d 5-29-1844 m Hester Thompson Pvt CT

Elisha: b 5-20-1745 d c. 1811 m Eunice Banks Pvt CT

Elisha: b 11-3-1732 d 3-5-1815 m Mary Ives Pvt MA

Elizabeth (Gordon): b 5-4-1730 d 11-24-1804 m Samuel Bradley PS SC

Elizabeth Pelham: b 1724 d 1788 m James Bradley PS NC

Elnathan: b 1-21-1729/30 d 1-31-1805 m (1)Sarah Goodsell (2)Hannah Bartram Sol CT

Enoch: b 6-22-1749 d 5-29-1834 m Mary Low Sgt MA

Enos: bpt 9-14-1739 d 7-23-1814 m Mary Merwin Pvt CT

Filo: b c. 1752 d p. 1790 m Rhoda Wattles Pvt CT

Francis: b 1743 d 11-14-1780 m Abigail Alexander Pvt PS NC

George: b 6-2-1753 d 9-28-1832 m Mary Gilpin Taylor Pvt PA

George: b c. 1750 d 1820 m Lucy Rice Pvt VA

Gershom, Sr.: b 1712 d 1-15-1795 m (1)Sarah Sherwood (2)Eliza-beth Osborn (3)Jane Dimon (4)Deborah Dimon PS CT

Gilbert: b 9-9-1757 d 1800 m Anna Meigs Sgt VT

Gurdon: b 1738 d 11-16-1821 m Mary Woodward Pvt CT

Isaac: b 11-30-1717 d 9-19-1783 m Hannah Hemingway Pvt CT

Isaac: b 11-7-1722 d 11-21-1784 m (1)Sarah Mix (2)Lois Bishop Pvt CT

James: b 6-17-1756 d 3-3-1817 m Asenath Bird Sgt CT

James: b 5-2-1759 d 4-27-1834 m (1)Leah Stone (2)Parnell Stone Pvt CT

James: b 1712 d 7-10-1786 m Abigail Sanford Pvt CT

James: b 3-19-1763 d 2- -14-1830 m Dolly Burton Lt NC

James: b 1759 d 1822 m (2)Jane Davidson Pvt NC

James: b 6-6-1720 d 1796 m Elizabeth Pelham PS NC

James: b 1761 d 7-20-1831 m (1)Deborah Stetson (2)Sylvia Woodcock Pvt VT

James, Jr.: b 12-4-1752 d 1-3-1816 m Mary Wilson Sol SC

James: b 1753 d 1828 m Caroline Everett Capt VA

James: b c. 1750 d p. 4-20-1797 m Margaret Beasley Pvt VA

Jared: b 5-30-1749 d 6-18-1832 m Sarah Smith Lt CT

Jared: b 8-25-1760 d 3-14-1814 m (1)Charity — (2)Phebe Munson Pvt MA

Jesse: b 5-4-1736 d 7-26-1812 m Mamry Ives Capt MA

Joel: b 12-6-1738 d 9-18-1801 m Abigail Tuttle 2Lt CT

Joel: b 12-23-1722 d 1-27-1797 m Miriam Robinson MM CT

John: b 1-19-1755 d 1782 m Mary Ardis PS GA

John: b 2-13-1743 d 7-6-1815 m Hannah Ayer Lt NH

John: b 1736 d 1833 m Mollie — Sol NC

John: b a. 1748 d p. 1779 m Sarah Lillard Pvt VA

Jonathan: b 2-14-1744 d 2-22-1818 m (1)Sarah Osgood (2)Sarah Ayer 2Lt MA

Jonathan: b 1748 d p. 1794 m Hannah Hazeltine Pvt PS NH

Jonathan: b 1754 d p. 1796 m (1)Susan Emery (2)Lucretia — Pvt NH

Joseph: b 10-19-1746 d 1-24-1828 m Martha Bates Pvt CT

Joseph: b — d 10-11-1847 m Naomi Taylor Pvt CT

Joseph: b 6-24-1720 d 6-12-1810 m Sibyl Meigs Lt VT

Josiah: b 9-17-1743 d 9-30-1827 m Comfort Hitchcock Capt CT

Lemuel: b 1759 d 6-19-1832 m (1)Eunice Durand (2)Mrs Lois McCoy Pvt CT

Lemuel: b 2-26-1750 d 12-11-1800 m (1)Lucy Baker (2)Mercy Washburn Capt VT

BRADLEY, contd.

Lent: b 6-14-1751 d 12-20-1840 m (1)Mary Ann Bristol (2)Roxada — Cpl MA ★
Leonard Keeling: b c. 1756 d 12-2-1834 m Polly Boone Lt NC
Moses: b 1721 d 4-17-1804 m Mary Rowe PS CT
Moses: b 2-14-1748 d p. 1782 m Thankful Eaton Pvt NH
Nathan: b 7-20-1740 d c. 1808 m Mary Meeker Pvt CT ★
Nathaniel: b 2-17-1746 d 5-8-1813 m Ann Dunlap 2Lt MA
Philip Burr: b 3-26-1738 d 1-4-1821 m (1)Mary Bostwick (2)Ruth Smith Col CT
Richard: b 1-16-1747 d p. 1790 m Olive Root MM CT
Richard: b 1734 d 1782 m Elizabeth Ashbridge Sharpless PM NC
Richard: b 1765 d 4- -1838 m Abadiah Thompkins Pvt GA
Samuel, 2d: b 5-24-1764 d 1851 m Abigail Pike Pvt & Slr MA
Samuel, Sr.: b c. 1730 d c. 9-13-1778 m Elizabeth Gordon PS SC
Samuel, Jr.: b 6-18-1760 d p. 1804 m Mary Bradley Pvt SC
Seth: b 5-5-1735 d 5-29-1798 m (1)Eunice Hull (2)Dorothy Treadwell Ens CT
Stephen, Jr.: b 9-15-1760 d 11-23-1839 m Mehitable Luddington Pvt CT ★
Stephen Rowe: b 2-20-1754 d 12-9-1830 m Merab Atwater Capt CT
Sturgis: b 5-10-1765 d 1849 m Rhoda Nash Pvt CT
Thaddeus: b 3-15-1756 d 11-10-1840 m Parnell Whitney Pvt CT ★
Thomas: b c. 1750 d 5- -1817 m Esther — Pvt DE
Thomas: b 1753 d 1828 m Elizabeth Ann Cpl PA
Thomas: b 3-5-1761 d 6- -1824 m Philadelphia Ficklin PS VA
Thomas: b c. 1750 d c. 1826 m Mary Haslett Pvt PA
Timothy: b 4-30-1721 d 1803 m Mercy Baldwin PS CT
Timothy, Sr.: b 6-16-1711 d p. 5-3-1779 m Abiah Stevens PS NH
Timothy, Jr.: b 10-13-1743 d 7-31-1811 m (3)Sarah Foster Pvt NH
Wm.: b 4-22-1756 d 10-26-1829 m Sally Swazey Cpl MA
Wm.: b 10-26-1730 d 12-18-1809 m Lois Beach Pvt MA
Wm.: b 7-6-1717 d 2-28-1780 m Mehitable Emerson PS MA
Wm.: b 1761 d 1810 m Aspasia Spriggs Pvt NC W★
Wm.: b 1740 d p. 1-12-1799 m (1)— Dancy (2)Lucy Drury (3)Elizabeth Christian Sgt VA
Wm.: b c. 1750 d 2-5-1819 m Elizabeth Whitman Sgt VA

BRADNER,

Benoni: b 1733 d 1-29-1804 m Rebecca Bridges Pvt NY
Colvill, Sr.: b 1719 d c. 1799 m X Pvt NY
John: b c. 1725 d 7-1-1790 m X Pvt NY

BRADSHAW,

Benjamin: b 5-28-1758 d p. 12-10-1834 m Fanny Melton Pvt VA★
Edward: b 1763 d 9-11-1830 m Frances Summers Sol VA
James: b 1-3-1742 d 2-19-1809 m Martha Watson CS NC
John: b 12-18-1743 d 12-25-1818 m Nancy Agnes Clendennen Sol NC
John: b 1760 d 1825 m Mary Harvey Pvt NC
John: b 1759 d 12- -1834 m Nancy McKamie Spy VA ★
John: b 2-1-1721/22 d p. 3-28-1787 m Margaret Clemons PS VA
Jonas: b 1759 d 2-6-1840 m Elizabeth Ratley Pvt NC ★
Richard: b — d p. 4-15-1783 m Patience — PS VA
Robert: b 11-14-1760 d 2-20-1832 m (1)Elizabeth Haden (2)Mrs Elizabeth Pearson Foard OrdlSgt VA ★
Thomas: b 7-8-1743 d 9-1-1802 m Martha Tufts Pvt MA
Wm.: b c. 1727 d 1811 m Susannah Robinson Pvt VA

BRADSTREET,

Andrew: b 4-1-1722 d 5-1-1804 m (1)Mary Hill (2)Joanna Hill Pvt MA
Henry: b 11-30-1741 d 9-2-1818 m Abigail Porter Pvt MA
John: b 6-26-1748 d 8-5-1833 m (1)Judith Hale (2)Abigail Glidden Pvt MA ★
Samuel: b 3-8-1729 d 7-6-1777 m Ruth Lamson Sgt MA
Simon: b 4-21-1714 d 1-25-1788 m Anne Flint Pvt MA

BRADT, (includes BRATT)

Cornelius: b 9-22-1765 d 7-15-1828 m Annatje Peterson Pvt NY ★
Gerrit: bpt 7-30-1749 d p. 9-20-1795 m Maria Van Antweip Pvt NY
Gerrit Tunis: b 2-16-1748 d 10-1-1834 m Sarah O'Conner Capt NY
Jacobus A.: b 1730 d 3-26-1801 m Elizabeth Delmont Pvt NY
Peter A.: b 10-19-1744 d 11-22-1826 m (1)Miss Eiedman (2)Jane Hunderman Sol NY
Peter B.: bpt 5-22-1754 d a. 3-9-1810 m Maria — Sol NY

BRADY,

Archibald, Sr.: b 5-27-1746 d 11-27-1829 m Margaret Ervin Pvt NC
Benjamin: b 4-14-1761 d 1839 m Barbara Miller Pvt VA ★
Ebenezer: b 1751 d 1804 m Jane Irvine Pvt PA
Hugh: b c. 1739 d p. 5-16-1782 m Jane Young Pvt PA
James: b 1743 d 1818 m Rebecca Young Pvt PA
John: b a. 1750 d p. 1780 m Mary Diamond 2Lt NY
John, Sr.: b 1733 d 4-11-1779 m Mary Quigley Capt PA
John, Jr.: b 1761 d 12-10-1809 m Jane McCall Pvt PA
John: b 5-13-1762 d 1796 m Jane Kemp Pvt PA
Joseph: b 1735 d 1787 m Mary Carnahan Capt PA
Mary Quigley: b 1735 d 1783 m John Brady PS PA
Samuel: b 1756 d 12- -1795 m Drusilla Van Swearingen Capt PA

Samuel: b 1734 d 1811 m Jane Simonton Pvt PA
Simeon: b 9-13-1737 d 9-22-1806 m Mary Brundage Pvt NY
Thomas: b 10-17-1762 d 1833 m Frances Murphy Pvt VA

BRAGDON,

Daniel: b 6-7-1707 d 3-6-1791 m Mary Banks PS MA
Ebenezer: b — d p. 5-28-1806 m Jane Willson Pvt MA
James: b 1762 d 8-10-1839 m (1)Tabitha Littlefield (2)Ruth Sargent Pvt MA
Joshua: b 6-11-1743 d p. 1785 m Mehitable Littlefield Capt MA
Samuel: b 8-3-1762 d 11-22-1852 m (2)Mehitable Hanscom (3)Olive Sampson Pvt MA ★
Thomas, Jr.: b c. 1738 d 1811 m (1)Sarah Ware (2)Elizabeth Hodge Capt MA

BRAGG,

Ariel: b 1749 d 1780 m Sarah Fisher Pvt MA
Elijah: b c. 1760 d 1838 m Sophia McCord Sol VA
Joab: b 4-29-1760 d 4-9-1832 m Mrs Lydia Bran Pvt MA ★
John: b 1755 d 1804 m Mary Tucker Smn MA
Luther: b c. 1740 d 8-18-1804 m Hannah Foster Pvt NH
Nathaniel: b 2-19-1743 d — m Hannah Moore Sgt MA
Nicholas: b 8-5-1759 d 1-22-1836 m Abigal Browne Pvt NH
Peter Newport: b 3-4-1763 d 5-21-1841 m Abagail Brutain Sol VA
Thomas: b 3-2-1720/21 d 8-21-1788 m Dorothy Ingalls Pvt MA
Thomas: b 1754 d 1819 m Lucy Neville Blakemore Capt VA
Wm.: b 2-28-1757 d 1-25-1833 m Elizabeth Crabtree Pvt MA ★

BRAIDFOOT,

John: b a. 1753 d 1784/85 m Blandinah Moseley Chp VA

BRAINE, (includes BRAINARD)

Abijah: b 11-26-1705 d 9- -1782 m (1)Esther Smith (2)Thankful Fuller PS CT
Abner: b 5-1-1731 d 10-17-1786 m (1)Elizabeth Champion (2)Elizabeth Burr Lt CT
Ansel: b 4-7-1765 d 6-12-1855 m Mary Warren Pvt CT ★
Asahel: b 6-20-1740 d 5-23-1822 m Experience Ackley Pvt CT
Bezaleel: b 1737 d 6-25-1827 m Lydia Deming Lt CT
Chileab: b 10-21-1741 d c. 1816 m Jemima Worcester Pvt NH
Daniel: b 1-9-1752 d 12-2-1809 m (1)Susannah Clark (2)Abigail Fowler Capt CT
Daniel: b 6-13-1755 d 12-31-1837 m Damaris Chamberlain Pvt CT
Daniel: b 2-24-1721 d 1-9-1777 m Hannah Selden PS CT
Daniel: b 9-10-1734 d 5-3-1798 m (1)Esther (Brainerd) (2)Mrs. Eunice Brooks Hubbard PS CT
Daniel: b 7-17-1715 d p. 1798 m (1)Esther Spencer (2)Susannah Cotton CS NH
David: b 11-27-1748 d 1828 m Hannah Willard Cpl CT
Eliakim: b 3-17-1730/31 d 1-18-1815 m (1)Eunice Doane (2)Lucy Smith Capt CT
Elijah: b 9-7-1734 d 1-27-1806 m Lucy Smith Lt CT
Elijah: b 10-25-1757 d 5-23-1828 m Parthena Marsh Pvt CT ★
Enoch: b 9-9-1749 d 4-12-1796 m (1)Prudence Hungerford (2)Esther Southward MM & Sgt CT
Ezra: b 8-17-1744 d 4-7-1837 m (1)Jerusha Smith (2)Bethia (Higgins)(Post) Wilder (3)Lucretia (Post) Post CS CT
Gideon: b 3-2-1728/29 d 12-25-1801 m Sarah Richardson Pvt CT
Heman: b 1754 d 7-8-1803 m (1)Deborah Hopson (2)Ruth (Stocking) Brainerd Pvt CT
Israel: b 2-10-1748/49 d 1818 m Deborah Hoyt Cpl NH
Jabez: b 2-19-1714 d 8-20-1778 m Hannah Clark CS CT
Jeptha: b 11-16-1749 d a. 1781 m Anna Fisk Pvt CT
Jeptha: b 1754 d 1825 m Abigail Mack PS CT
Jepthai: b 3-2-1746 d p. 1790 m Anna Markham Pvt CT
John: b 8-2-1754 d 10-3-1820 m Hannah Hubbard Sgt CT
Joshua: b 5-31-1738 d 1-22-1811 m Susanna Chapman 2Lt CT
Josiah, Sr.: b 5-4-1711 d 7-8-1792 m (1)Sarah Smith (2)Hannah Spencer CS CT
Josiah, Jr.: b 8-17-1739 d 11-6-1805 m Lois Hurlburt Ens CT
Nathaniel: b 7-3-1742 d 1-17-1815 m Ann Johnson Pvt CT
Nehemiah: b 1742 d 11-8-1807 m Sarah — Capt CS CT
Othniel: b 6-5-1728 d 12-9-1815 m (1)Lucia Swaddle (2)Jerusha Kilborn Pvt CT
Phineas: b 10-17-1720 d 3-8-1803 m Jerusha Towner CS CT
Reuben: b 9-11-1763 d 3-15-1798 m Hannah Mack Sgt NY W★
Reuben: b 4-13-1752 d 5-31-1824 m Panny Allen Pvt CT
Shubael: b 1-12-1751/52 d c. 6-4-1782 m Ruth Stocking 1Lt CT
Simon, Sr.: b 10-7-1730 d p. 9- -1806 m Hepzebah Spencer Pvt NH
Simon: b 11-9-1752 d 5-18-1843 m Abigail Hulburt Pvt CT
Stephen: b 3-24-1742 d 12-9-1820 m Rachel Day Capt CT W★
Timothy: b 4-2-1754 d 9-29-1834 m Sarah Wilson Pvt CT ★
Timothy: b 8-6-1758 d 1801 m Mehitable Metcalf Sgt MA
Timothy: b 4-22-1740 d 5-8-1823 m (1)Margaret Dolph (2)Elizabeth Spencer Sol NY
Wm.: b 8-27-1746 d 1-26-1820 m Lucy Day Capt CT
Zachariah: b 2-6-1741/42 d 12-26-1826 m Mehitable Clark Sol CT
Zachariah: b 11-28-1757 d c. 1780 m Dorothy Thomas Pvt CT

BRAITHWAITE,

Wm.: b c. 1751 d 7-13-1831 m Catherine Brookover Pvt MD W★

BRAKE,
Jacob: b c. 1746 d 1831 m Mary Slaughter Lt VA

BRAKEBILL,
Peter: b 4-16-1769 d 1-22-1844 m Catherine — Pvt PA ★

BRALEY, (includes BRAILEY, BRAWLEY)
Gideon: b 9-5-1758 d 9-4-1840 m Anna McCloud Pvt MA ★
John, Sr.: b 1720 d 1-18-1798 m Sarah Carruth CS NC
Nathaniel: b 5-6-1755 d 6-25-1802 m Cynthia Carpenter Lt MA
Neil: b 1751 d 10-19-1834 m Mary Mosmon Sol SC
Samuel: b c. 1751 d p. 1829 m (1)Sarah Gifford (2)Mrs Maria Rollins Cpl RI

BRAMAN,
James: b 1758 d 7-4-1849 m Abigail Dewey Pvt CT ★
Nathaniel: b 3-29-1740 d 10-15-1817 m Anne Brace Pvt CT
Sylvanus: b 6-17-1753 d 1-16-1842 m Sally Andrews Pvt MA
Wm.: b 6-4-1758 d 4-9-1804 m Anna Austin Pvt RI

BRAMBLE,
John: b c. 1730 d p. 1795 m Mary — 1Lt MD
Wm.: b 1741 d 2- -1827 m Elizabeth Buel Capt VT

BRAMBLEE,
Wm.: b 1747 d 1843 m Gertrude Kidder Lt NY ★

BRAMHALL,
Joseph: b 1-4-1751 d 1805 m Experience Blackman Pvt NY
Sylvanus: b 4-30-1712 d 3-14-1779 m (1)Mary Bennett (2)Mercy Warren PS CS MA

BRAMLETTE,
James: b 1762/63 d 1849 m Milly Shrewsbury Pvt VA ★
Reuben: b 3-15-1757 d 9-11-1844 m Elizabeth Brown Pvt VA ★

BRAMMER,
Burgess: b c. 1760 d p. 1813 m Milly — Pvt VA

BRANCH,
Asa: b 4-1-1744 d p. 1790 m Elizabeth Tracy Pvt MA
Benjamin: b 1732 d 1786/87 m (1)Anne Bass (2)Mary (Goode) — Capt CS VA
Edward: b 1736 d 1781 m Lucy Finney 1Lt VA
Edward: b c. 1745 d 1814 m Tabitha — PS VA
Elijah: b 1752 d 1816 m Polly — Pvt & Fif VT
Henry: b c. 1740 d 1797/8 m Tabitha — PS VA
Job: b 1760 d a. 6-5-1802 m Rachel Bratten Cpl NC
John, Sr.: b 10-7-1729 d 3-5-1812 m Priscilla Drury Pvt MA
John: b c. 1750 d 3-14-1806 m (1)Rebecca Bradford (2)Elizabeth Norwood LtCol CS NC
Nathan: b 6-26-1745 d 11-14-1823 m Polly — Pvt MA
Nicholas: b 1756 d 1811 m Thankful — Pvt RI
Peter: b 8-8-1743 d p. 1790 m Ruth Partridge Sgt CT
Rufus: b 2-5-1739/40 d 3-10-1821 m Abigail Mason Lt VT
Samuel: b 5-7-1768 d 1-21-1843 m Ruth Chidsey Matr CT ★
Samuel, 1st: b c. 1730 d 1789 m Sarah Holman PS VA
Samuel, 2nd: b c. 1755 d a. 12-1-1789 m Jane Martin PS VA
Stephen: b 4-1-1744 d 2-7-1828 m Hannah Starkweather Cpl CT
Wm.: b 9-3-1760 d 4-13-1849 m Lucretia Tracy Pvt CT ★
Wm.: b c. 1760 d a. 1830 m Hester — Sol NC
Wm.: b 1719 d 1794 m Elizabeth — CS NC
Wm. Scott: b c. 1760 d p. 1838 m Dicy Jane Calicutt Pvt GA

BRAND,
Adam, Jr.: b c. 1752 d p. 1805 m Sarah Beshore Pvt PA
James: b 1754 d a. 2-25-1836 m Alice Elliott Pvt PA
John: b 1752 d 1-12-1834 m Jane McCray Pvt PA
Joseph: b c. 1757 d c. 1814 m Frances Whitlock Pvt VA

BRANDEGEE,
Elishama: b 4-17-1754 d 2-26-1832 m Lucy (Plumb) Weston Pvt CT

BRANDENBURG,
Mathias: b c. 1740 d 1806/07 m Esther — PS VA
Samuel: b 4-6-1756 d 10-30-1833 m Madelaine Hargerhymer PS MD

BRANDON, (includes BRANNAN, BRANNON)
Alexander: b 3-13-1748 d 3-17-1813 m Elizabeth Mabinette Sgt PA
Benjamin: b 4- -1759 d 5-5-1837 m Mary Knox Pvt NC
Benjamin: b 9-23-1739 d 4-9-1825 m Eunice Esty LCol PA
Charles: b 3-19-1751 d 11-11-1813 m Mrs Mary McFarlan Pvt PA
Francis: b 6-18-1756 d 8-9-1842 m Sarah Scott Pvt VA
Francis: b c. 1745 d 1804 m Mary Asher Pvt VA
George: b c. 1745 d c. 1832 m (1) X (2)Rebecca Neely (3)Mary Luckey Wgm NC
James: b c. 1741/42 d p. 6-17-1790 m Rebecca — Sgt NC
James: b c. 1755 d 1820 m Esther Horah 1Maj & PS NC
John: b 1761 d 1850 m (1)Annie Woods (2)Martha Jenkins Sol GA
John: b 12-5-1753 d 11-27-1823 m Mary Hall Lt PA W★
John: b 4- -1744 d 1835 m Elizabeth Haborn Pvt PA ★

John: b c. 1745 d 1804 m Rebecca — Sol VA
Josiah: b 6-26-1761 d 11-5-1842 m Rachel Brown Pvt NC W★
Matthew: b 1-13-1752 d 9-9-1819 m Jane Armstrong Pvt NC
Michael: b c. 1760 d p. 1813 m Bridget O'Reilly Pvt PA
Thomas: b 1741 d 2-5-1802 m (1)Elizabeth McCool (2)Mrs Rebecca Harland Col SC
Wm.: b 5-13-1748 d 9-17-1836 m X Lt NC ★
Wm.: b 1753 d 1791 m Sarah Livingston Ens PA

BRANDOW,
John: b 2-18-1712 d p. 1-11-1786 m Jannetje Van Schaack PS NY

BRANDT, (includes BRANT)
Abraham: b 1748-50 d 1799 m Mary — Pvt PA
Adam: b 11-23-1751 d 8-13-1838 m Eva Metzler Pvt PA
Christian: b 1740 d p. 1800 m X Pvt PA
Johan Christian A.: b 1752 d 1831 m Margaret Brown Pvt NY ★
John, Jr.: b 10-19-1752 d 11-20-1844 m Eva Elizabeth Heil Pvt PA
John: b 3- -1754 d 1-1-1844 m (1)Elizabeth Taylor (2)Hannah — Pvt PA
John: b 1-10-1763 d 6-25-1833 m Margaret Brandt Pvt PA
Lewis: b 8-14-1734 d 3-28-1796 m Annie Morse Capt NJ
Samuel: b 1763 d 6-11-1823 m (1)Judith Burdit (2)Abigail Muchmore Pvt NJ

BRANHAM, (includes BRAMHAM)
Benjamin: b 12-1-1728 d a. 3-7-1814 m — Murrah PS VA
John, Sr.: b 1763 d 9-5-1824 m Letitia — Cpl VA
Spencer: b c. 1751 d 6-5-1803 m Elizabeth Richardson Pvt VA
Wm. Bourne: b 12-2-1763 d 1-9-1845 m (1)Mrs Frances Vivian Webb (2)Mrs Mollie Burris Cpl VA

BRANK,
Peter: b 1737 d 10-7-1781 m Ruby Alexander Sol NC
Robert: b 3-17-1757 d 4-10-1846 m Margaret McLean Pvt NC ★

BRANNER,
Casper: b 6-18-1724 d a. 1792 m Catherine — Pvt VA
John: b 8-28-1752 d 4-30-1837 m Catharine Harpine Pvt VA

BRANSFORD,
John, Jr.: b 1725 d p. 1785 m (1)Sally Easter (2)Judith Amonett PS VA
Wm.: b 1761 d 1812 m Patsey Moseley Pvt VA

BRANTLEY,
Amos: b 9-11-1759 d 3- -1828 m X Pvt NC ★
John: b c. 1750 d p. 11-15-1811 m Elizabeth Marsh Pvt NC
Joseph: b — d. 3-27-1807 m (1)Ann — (2)Mrs. Jane Mathis PS NC
Malachi: b 1-3-1760 d 6-14-1827 m Mary Thomas PS NC
Phillip: b c. 1750 d p. 3-18-1819 m Polly — Pvt NC
Thomas: b 1754 d p. 7-27-1822 m Rachel Hill Sol GA
Wm.: b 4-19-1742 d 10-15-1823 m (2)Mary Tomlinson Pvt NC

BRASEE,
Andreas: b 1737 d 7-12-1825 m — Pvt NY

BRASELTON,
Jacob: b 6-27-1749 d 9-22-1835 m Hannah Greene Pvt PS MD

BRASHEAR, (includes BRASHEARS)
Ignatius: b 4-10-1734 d 1807 m Frances — Pvt MD
Marsham: b — d 1807 m Lucy Phelps CS VA
Nathan: b — d p. 9-22-1791 m Mrs Ester Sappington PS MD
Otho: b c. 1739 d 1792 m Ruth Brown Pvt PA
Rezin: b 11-6-1736 d a. 1833 m (1)Catharine — (4)Mary Johnston 2Lt MD
Samuel: b 8-6-1763 d 12-25-1829 m Margaret Eakins Pvt NC W★
Tobias: b c. 1756 d 12- -1807 m Martha Brookes Capt IL
Wm.: b c. 1756 d a. 8-7-1781 m Anne — Lt VA
Zadock: b 1756 d p. 12-18-1816 m Susanna Vaughan Sol MD

BRASHER, (includes BRASIER)
Abraham: b 12-4-1734 d 1782 m Helen Kortright PS NY
Henry: bpt 11-3-1742 d 1824 m Lucy Clark Capt NY ★
John: b 5-15-1764 d 1840 m Keziah Brown Pvt CT & NY ★

BRASINGTON,
Samuel: b 10-5-1752 d 6-30-1838 m Miriam Cobb Tms NY ★

BRASS,
Garrit: b 1764/65 d 11-25-1837 m Lucy Mathews Pvt MA ★

BRASSELL,
Brittan: b c. 1747 d 9- -1827 m Dicy Davis Sol GA

BRASTOW,
Thomas: b 11-13-1740 d 6-15-1799 m Susanna Fisher Lt MA

BRASWELL,
Benjamin: b 1-10-1744 d 1-25-1792 m Mary Ida Mercer Sol NC
Jacob: b 3-7-1763 d 7-25-1837 m Nancy Cotton Pvt NC
Richard: b 7- -1755 d 8-20-1839 m Penelope Blow Pvt NC ★

BRATNEY,
Robert: b 11-4-1746 d 1-1-1824 m Mrs Henrietta J Madole Pvt NC

BRATTLE,
Wm. 2nd: b 9-9-1745 d 11-6-1826 m (1)Abigail Fairfield (2)Lucy Leffingwell Lt MA ★
Wm.: b c. 1710 d p. 6-5-1784 m Mary Wright Pvt MA

BRATTON, (includes BRATTEN)
Adam: b 2-1-1745 d 6-26-1820 m Ann Gillespie Lt PA
Adam: b c. 1750 d a. 12-22-1800 m Elizabeth Feamster Sol & CS VA
James: b c. 1760 d 4-22-1792 m Mary Polk Lt DE
James: b c. 1748 d 1786 m Isabella — Pvt PA
James: b 4- -1757 d 10-6-1844 m Bathsheba Riley Pvt PA ★
James: b 6-30-1746 d 6-29-1828 m Rebecca Hogset Capt VA
Martha Robertson: b 1750 d 1- -1816 m William Bratton PS SC
Robert: b 5-20-1712 d a. 10-18-1785 m Ann Dunlap Capt VA
Samuel: b c.1762 d 12- -1799 m Margaret Robertson Pvt PA
Wm.: b 1740 d 1815 m Martha Robertson Col SC

BRAUCHER,
Christian: b 9-21-1758 d 6-27-1842 m Susannah — Pvt PA
Christopher: b 12-15-1729 d 4-19-1793 m Anna Margaretta Schissler Pvt PA

BRAUNMILLER,
Luttwick: b c.1753 d 11- -1801 m Maria Magdalena — Pvt PA

BRAWNER,
Henry, Sr.: b c. 1755 d p. 10-16-1817 m (1) X (2)Esther — PS MD
Richard: b 1736 d 3- -1783 m Elizabeth Elder PS MD

BRAXTON,
Carter: b 9-10-1736 d 10-10-1797 m (1)Judith Robinson (2)Elizabeth Corbin SDI VA

BRAY,
Andrew: b 2-18-1760 d 6-30-1846 m Cornelia Traphagen Pvt NJ
Asa: b 6-22-1741 d 10-21-1815 m (1)Lydia Andrews (2)Hannah Hull Capt CT
Daniel: b 10-12-1751 d 12-5-1818 m Mary Wolverton Capt NJ
Ebenezer: b 4-18-1732 d 2-24-1817 m Judith Bennett Smn MA
Edmund: b 8-21-1740 d 7-27-1821 m Data Crowell Pvt PS MA
Henry: b c. 1738 d p. 3-2-1798 m Cathryn — PS MD
Henry: b 1742 d p. 2- -1812 m Sarah Yokley PS & CS NC
Humphrey, Jr.: b 10-18-1756 d p. 1792 m Mrs Molley Bray Cpl MA
John, Sr.: b 9- -1714 d p. 1776 m Jean Elkins Lt MA
John, Jr.: b 1740 d — m Rebecca Thompson Lt MA
John: b 11-13-1738 d 7-7-1806 m Susan Bray Cmsry NJ
John: b 4-28-1761 d 6-10-1832 m (1) X (2)Elizabeth Coonies Pvt VA ★
Joseph: b 12-25-1762 d 1-21-1841 m Annah Gott Pvt MA ★
Nathaniel: b 3-2-1737 d p. 1786 m Lucy Nason Pvt MA
Nicholas: bpt 3-15-1752 d 2-5-1843 m Polly Bray Pvt MA ★
Thomas: b c. 1748 d a. 2-16-1814 m Elizabeth Bowlby Pvt NJ

BRAYTON,
Borden: b 5-25-1760 d 12-10-1849 m Mary Remington Pvt & Pvtr MA ★
Freeborn: b 9-12-1748 d 1-1-1813 m Marcy Colvin Pvt RI W★
James Wheaton: b 10-8-1757 d 9-23-1832 m Ruby Easterbrooks Pvt & Pvtr RI ★
John: b 4-12-1762 d 3-12-1829 m Sarah Bowers Pvt MA
Joseph: b 3-3-1757 d 7-27-1821 m (2)Mrs Elizabeth Reead Capt RI
Matthew: b 7-24-1759 d p. 1787 m — Carey Pvt NY
Stephen: b 11-10-1741 d — m Amy Arnold PS RI
Thomas: b 5-22-1759 d 8-7-1814 m Mrs Patience Burlingame Pvt RI W★

BRAZEAU,
Louis: b c. 1745 d 12-15-1828 m Marie Francoise de Lisle CS VA

BRAZIER, (includes BRAZER)
Christopher: b 1747 d 10-12-1803 m Margaret Corbett Pvt MA
Harrison: b 3-12-1734 d 8-10-1782 m Sarah Gustine Pvt MA

BREADING,
Nathaniel: b 3-16-1751 d 4-22-1821 m Mary Ewing Pvt PA

BREADY,
Thomas: b 1755 d 2-9-1818 m Elizabeth Hamilton Pvt PA

BREARLEY,
David: b 6-11-1745 d 8-16-1790 m (1)Elizabeth Mullen (2)Elizabeth Higbee CS Col NJ
Joseph: b 8-6-1742 d 1-12-1805 m Rachel McClary Maj NJ

BREAUX,
Firmin: b 1748 d 10-1-1808 m Marguerite Braud Sol LA

BRECHALL,
Martin: b 1757 d 2-13-1831 m Catharine Lonferrin Pvt PA ★

BRECHBIEL,
Peter: b c. 1739/40 d p. 5-30-1788 m Catherine Maria Barbara Franck PS PA

BRECK, (includes BRICK)
Daniel: b 8-18-1748 d 8- -1845 m Hannah Porter Chp MA ★
John: b 12-1-1735 d 3-18-1824 m Mary Hill MM MA
John: b 1760 d 1832 m (1)Mercy Hartley (2)Bathsheba Hartley Pvt NJ
Jonathan: b 5-19-1762 d 12-19-1830 m Patience Dunton Pvt MA W★

BRECKENRIDGE, (includes BRACKENRIDGE, BRAKENAGE)
Alexander: b 5-16-1743 d 1813 m (1)Magdalen Gamble (2)Mary Chadd Pvt VA
David: b a. 1740 d p. 1781 m Ellen Brown Pvt PA
George: b 7-24-1768 d 11-13-1852 m Elizabeth Cowan Pvt VA
George: b c. 1714 d p. 2-3-1790 m (1)Ann Doak (2)Agnes Watson PS & CS VA
Hugh Henry: b 1748 d 6-25-1816 m Sabina Wolff Chp PA
James: b 5-28-1721 d 4-16-1783 m Mary Moore Lt VT
James: b 9-20-1759 d 8-21-1826 m Eunice Shaw Mar MA
James: b 3-7-1763 d 5-13-1833 m Anna Cary Selden Pvt VA
John: b 12-2-1760 d 12-14-1806 m Mary Hopkins Cabell CS VA
Robert: b c. 1743 d p. 1-26-1814 m Mary Doak PS & CS VA
Samuel: b 1750 d 9-17-1797 m Susanna Cooker Pvt PA
Samuel: b — d 1793 m Martha Culbertson Pvt PA
William, Sr.: b 9-17-1723 d 2-16-1807 m (1)Agnes Sinclair (2)Ro'salla Ann Page Capt MA
William: b 1750 d 1833 m Thankful Marsh Pvt MA

BREED,
Aaron: b 3-7-1761 d 12-23 1817 m (1)Sarah Atwell (2)Mary Kemp Fillebrown Pvt MA
Allen: b 8-29-1714 d p. 2-7-1789 m (1)Ann Cole (2)Hannah Dewey Pvt CT
Allen: b 7-14-1759 d 4-2-1842 m Lucy Taylor Cpl NH ★
Allen: b 4-19-1744 d 4-16-1806 m Lydia Mansfield Pvt NH
Amos: b 12-23-1744 d 3-20-1785 m Lucy Randall Sol CT
Amos: b 8-14-1728 d 5-5-1776 m Ruth Newhall Pvt MA
Ephraim: b 5-26-1736 d 4-4-1812 m Susannah Mansfield Pvt MA
Frederick: b 8-20-1755 d — m (1)Hepsebah Cox (2)Sarah Mansfield (3)Mary Richardson Pvt MA
Gershom: b 4-29-1756 d 9-15-1815 m Hannah Palmer Cpl NY
John, Sr.: b 1-26-1700 d 1-24-1781 m Mary Prentice PS CT
John. Jr.: b 9-5-1729 d 1780 m (1)Silence Grant (2)Grace Palmer PS CS Capt CT
John: b 10-15-1757 d 4-29-1846 m Sarah Felt Pvt NH & MA ★
Joseph: b 7-9-1758 d 1-23-1839 m Mercy Holmes Sgt Smn RI W★
Joseph: b 1761 d 7-12-1850 m Anna Hutchinson Pvt MA ★
Josiah: b 12-16-1731 d 12-12-1790 m (1)Mary — (2)Hannah Bachelor Pvt MA
Nathan: b 12-13-1731 d c. 1816 m Lucy Babcock Cpl CT
Nathaniel, Sr.: b 7-22-1728 d 11-5-1810 m Ann Knowles PS CS NH
Nathaniel, Jr.: b 6-4-1753 d 10-30-1831 m (1)Thankful Day (2)Elizabeth Whitcomb Pvt MA
Oliver: b 2-6-1757 d 7-13-1834 m Grace Green Sgt CT
Thomas Knowles: b 4-10-1761 d 2-9-1847 m Polly Keyes Pvt NH ★

BREEDEN,
Charles: b 4-16-1753 d p. 2-26-1836 m Joana Starrett Sgt NC ★
Enoch: b 1- -1759 d 10- -1832 m Mary Brooker Pvt VA ★

BREEDLOVE,
James: b — d 11- -1795 m Mrs Kindness Shorter Sol VA
John: b 12-13-1749 d 8-20-1833 m (1)X (2)Nancy Parker Pvt VA
William: b 1762 d 2-28-1838 m Mary Watts Pvt VA ★

BREESE, (includes BREES, BREEZE, & BRIES)
Anthony: bpt 6-3-1734 d 1809/10 m Catharyntie Yates Capt NY
Azeriah: b c. 1743 d 11-27-1820 m Susannah Gildersleeve Sol NJ
Henry: b 8-29-1752 d 6-3-1835 m Ruth Pierson Pvt NJ ★
Henry: b 1-1-1755 d 2-10-1835 m Eliza Ann Vunck Pvt NJ ★
James: b 1750 d 3-10-1809 m Euphemia Freeman Cpl NJ
John, Sr.: b 1713 d 3-4-1803 m Dorothy Riggs Pvt NJ
John, Jr.: b 11-8-1738 d 3-24-1829 m Hannah Gildersleeve Pvt NJ
John: b 1755 d 5-27-1827 m (1) X (2) Sophia Breeze Pvt PA ★
John: b 9-15-1750 d p. 1832 m Susan Cooper Tms NJ
Samuel: b 5-23-1737 d 4-16-1800 m (1)Rebecca Finley (2)Elizabeth Anderson Col NJ
Samuel: b 4-17-1758 d 7-21-1837 m (1)Hannah Pierson Pvt NJ ★
Stephen: b 1755-8 d 10-23-1833 m Nancy Bayles Pvt NJ
Timothy: b 1758 d p. 9-5-1846 m Miss Doty Pvt NJ ★

BREIDINGER,
Peter: b 4-15-1756 d 11-3-1806 m Anna Maria Klase Sgt PA

BREINIG,
George Ludwig: b 1-31-1733 d 5-12-1812 m Christiana — Col PA
Mark: b c. 1725 d p. 1777 m Marie Catherine — PS PA

BREITIGAM,
John: b 1-17-1755 d 10-28-1832 m Elizabeth — Pvt PA ★

BREMNER,
John: b 4-2-1737 d 1-31-1807 m Barbara Nesbitt Pvt NY

BRENDLINGER,
Joseph: b 3-21-1738 d 4-5-1825 m Anna Rosina Lober Pvt PA

BRENNEMAN,
Abraham: b 12-3-1744 d 3-8-1815 m (1)Maria Reiff (2)Magdalena
   Shenk Mil VA
Benjamin: b c. 1737 d 8- -1804 m Barbara — Pvt PA
Christian: b 12-25-1758 d 6-4-1842 m Mary Cresner Pvt PA ★
Christian: b 1755 d 1817/18 m Catherine — Pvt PA
Daniel: b c. 1747/48 d p. 1810 m (1)— Mennard (2)Mrs. Barbara
   Shank (3)Chriatiana — Pvt PA
Isaac: b c. 1746 d p. 1800 m Anna Herr Pvt PA
Jacob: b 1761 d 1808 m Catherine Wolfe Pvt PA
John: b 3-10-1763 d 10-14-1827 m Catharine Bergthold Pvt PA
John: b 3-10-1763 d 9-2-1843 m Elizabeth Bossier Pvt PA
Melchior: b 5-10-1726 d 12-6-1809 m Ann Snavely PS PA

BRENNER,
George: bpt 12-2-1752 d 6- -1795 m Anna Maria — Pvt PA
Jacob: b c. 1730 d 6-18-1825 m Elizabeth Catherine — Pvt PA
John: b 10-3-1738 d 11-28-1815 m Catharine — Pvt PA

BRENNERMAN,
 Peter: b c. 1739 d 1783 m Anna Kauffman Pvt PA

BRENNISON, (includes BRENEISER)
Conrad: b c. 1740 d 1825 m Maria Elizabeth — Pvt PA
Martin: b 1737 d 1813 m Mary Brennison Cpl PA

BRENT, (includes BRUNT)
George, Sr.: b c. 1726 d 1778 m Margaret Simmons Sgt VA
George: b 1703 d 1778 m Catherine Trimmingham PS VA
Hugh: b 11-3-1739 d 9- -1813 m Elizabeth Baxter Capt VA
Hugh: b 12-8 d 2-7-1778 m (1)Susannah Payne (2)Easther
   Sherman (3)Judith (Newton) Kenner CS VA
James: b c. 1736 d 1815 m Sarah (Doggett) Cammell Pvt VA
John: b 1739 d 1781 m Margaret Caldwell Maj PS VA
John: b 1762/63 d p. 9-8-1786 m Hannah — Sol VA
Newton: b c. 1758 d p. 1-31-1795 m Ann Steptoe Lawson Lt VA
Wm: b 5-19-1742 d p. 1810 m Hannah Neale Capt VA
Wm: b 1730-33 d 1782 m Eleanor Carroll PS VA

BRENTON,
James: b 12-16-1747 d 1812 m Mary Woodfield Maj VA
James: b 1764 d 6-15-1836 m (1)Ellen — (2)Mrs. Mary Ansley Pvt
   VA ★
Joseph: b 4-28-1747 d 1825 m Elizabeth Litten Lt PA
Wm: b 1760 d 11-21-1838 m Fannie — Spy & Pvt VA ★

BRENTZINGER, (includes BRENSINGER)
Casper: b 1756 d 6-4-1848 m Catherine Rothchild Pvt PA

BRERETON,
Wm: b c. 1734 d p. 1805 m (1)Nancy Parsons (2)Sarah Vance Pvt
   MD

BRESSLER,
George: b 10-10-1738 d 8-16-1806 m Fannie Herr Pvt PA

BRETT,
Amzi: b — d — m Phebe Packard Pvt MA
George: b 2-7-1752 d p. 1800 m Mary Cooper Pvt & PS NY
John: b c. 1740 d p.3-22-1791 m Esther — Sol VA
Joshua: b 7-10-1751 d 12-2-1822 m Anne Dunbar PS RI
Rufus: b 8-2-1751 d 11-4-1812 m Susanna Cary Pvt MA
Samuel: b 8-22-1714 d 1807 m Hannah Packard Pvt MA
Silas: b 2-28-1715/16 d 4-17-1795 m Thankful Howard PS MA
Simeon, Sr.: b 1-8-1720 d 8-18-1792 m Mehitabel Packard Pvt MA
Simeon, Jr.: b 10-12-1753 d 1-20-1786 m Susanna Perkins Pvt MA
Theodorus: b 10-2-1755 d 2-9-1822 m Mary Wiltse Ens NY
Thomas: b 1740 d 1792 m (1)Elizabeth Horry Sol SC
Wm: b 4-7-1758 d 2- -1840 m (1)Mollie Allen (2)Betty Phillips
   Pvt MA

BRETZ, (includes BRITTZ)
Adam: b 1747 d a. 10- -1832 m Margaret Stover Sol PA
Ludwig: b c. 1737 d 1807 m (1)Susan Margaret Bishop (2)Elizabeth
   — Sgt PA

BREVARD,
Adam: b c. 1750 d — m Sally Winslow Sol NC
Alexander: b 4- -1755 d 11-1-1829 m Rebecca Davidson Capt NC

Hugh: b 1748 d a. 6-30-1781 m Jane Young PS & Col NC
Jean McWhorter: b c. 1723 d c. 1800 m John Brevard PS NC
John: b c. 1740 d a. 7-27-1799 m Sarah Campbell 2Lt MD
John, Jr.: b 2-18-1751 d 11-9-1826 m Hannah Thompson Lt NC
John, Sr.: b 1716 d 9-15-1790 m Jean McWhorter PS NC
Robert: b 1-10-1718 d 10-20-1800 m Sarah Craig Capt NC
Robert: b 7-17-1763 d 1-2-1847 m Nancy — Pvt NC
Zebulon: b 3-29-1724 d p. 1790 m Ann Templeton Sol NC

BREVITT,
John: b 1760 d 7-24-1824 m — Swoop Lt VA & MD

BREVOORT,
Elias: b 12-15-1749 d 12-9-1830 m Maria Stoutenburgh QM NJ
Henry: b 12-9-1711 d 1782 m Catharine DeLamatre PS NY

BREWER, (includes BRUA, BRUER, BRUERE, BROWER)
Abraham: b c.1745 d 7- -1828 m (1)Sara Van Orden (2)Mary Wells
   Pvt PA
Benjamin: b 4-24-1755 d 5-6-1834 m Caty Mellenger Pvt PA ★
Charles: b 12-18-1748 m Anna Chatterton Pvt MA
Daniel: b 5-3-1731 d p. 1818 m (1)Anna Van Sant (2)Ruth
   Strickland Sgt CT
Daniel: b 6-12-1725 d 12-11-1820 m Abigail — Pvt CT
Daniel, Jr.: b 2-12-1765 d 5-19-1826 m Mary Slate Pvt CT W★
Daniel: b 11-11-1753 d 11-26-1831 m Hannah Dill Pvt MA
David b 12-24-1731 d p. 1775 m Mary Smith Col MA
David, Jr.: b 1-30-1758 d 12-17-1834 m Comfort Wheeler Capt MA
Ebenezer: b — d — m Mary Chase Pvt MA
Edward: b 10-19-1762 d 3-24-1845 m Mary Strickland Pvt NC
Eliab: b 4-6-1760 d 9-24-1835 m Sally Rice Pvt MA
Elisha: b 1754 d 7-23-1827 m Martha Livermore Capt MA
Gaius: b 8-28-1753 d 12-7-1843 m Lucretia Babcock Sgt MA
George: b c. 1750 d 1820-5 m Naomi Woolworth Pvt MA
Harmonus: b 1-6-1723 d p. 1793 m (1)Margrita Akker
   (2)Margaret Van Epps Lt NY
Isaac: b 8-1-1763 d 1-8-1841 m Esther Tyrell Pvt MA ★
Isaac: b 8-17-1742 d 7- -1788 m Sybill Miller CS MA
Jacob: b 8-22-1744 d p. 3-1-1815 m Abigail Yerks Pvt NY
James: b 10-28-1746 d 11-21-1832 m Mary Hoar Lt NH
James: b 3-18-1742 d 10-15-1806 m Jean Black Capt MA
James: b 2-9-1751 d 7-2-1807 m Sarah Horsful Capt NJ
John: b 5-7-1709 d 7-17-1782 m Eleanor McCubbin PS MD
John: b 6-27-1743 d 7-31-1825 m (1)Martha Graves (2)Ruth
   Prescott (3)Abigail White Capt MA
John: b 12-18-1753 d p. 1784 m Esther Doud Lt MA
John: b 7-4-1749 d 12-12-1822 m Hannah Timpson Pvt NJ ★
John: b 3-26-1733 d p. 1790 m Elsie — Pvt NY
John: b 8-23-1764 d 11-29-1846 m Mary Twist Pvt NY ★
John: b c. 1753 d 1783-1800 m Catherina — Pvt PA
John: b 1727 d 1793 m Rachel — PS VA
Jonathan: b 2-3-1725 d 1-4-1784 m Fanny Buckminster Col MA
Joseph: b c. 2-15-1738/39 d p. 12-10-1782 m Jane — Cpl MA
Joseph: b 2-14-1722/23 d 6-26-1777 m Rebecca Weld Capt MA
Josiah: b 8-17-1744 d 6-12-1830 m Mary Hall Col MA
Lewis: b c. 1760 d 1839 m Agatha Holland Pvt NC
Mathew: b 8-7-1743 d p. 1789 m (1)Hannah Onderkirk (2)Sarah
   West Lt NY
Nathan: b 1746/47 d 10-19-1832 m Sarah Crosby CS MA
Oliver: b — d a.1792 m Rebecca PS NC
Peter: b 1-31-1756 d 9-5-1834 m Mary Grove Capt PS MD
Peter: b 4-1-1740 d 3-22-1804 m Elizabeth Stone Pvt NY
Peter: b — d 2-6-1839 m Moriah Harden Pvt NY ★
Peter: b 2-2-1729 d 10-1-1808 m Maria Pvt MA
Sackfield: b — d p. 6-2-1810 m X PS NC
Samuel: b 1-1-1732/33 d 1810 m Mehitable Upham Lt MA
Samuel: b 1755 d p. 1782 m Anna Horn Pvt NJ
Samuel: b c. 1730 d c. 1778 m Hannah Mabie Pvt NY
Solomon: b 6-4-1746 d 3-18-1824 m (1)Martha Smith (2)Rene
   Benton Lt MA
Thomas Stockett: b 2-6-1753 d 4-1-1823 m Susannah Lampley
   Sgt MD
Wm: b 11-8-1744 d 6-11-1830 m (1)Mercy Ely (2)Jemima Boltwood
   Grd MA
Wm: b 1752 d 3- -1835 m X Pvt NC ★
Wm: b 1758 d p.1818 m (1)Elizabeth Holmen (2)Sarah Doggett
   Lt SC
Wm: b 3-22-1744 d c.1841 m Sarah — Pvt VA ★

BREWSTER, (includes BRUSSTAR)
Agnes: b 4-25-1763 d 8-25-1830 m Wm Alexander PS VA
Amos: b 6-22-1735 d 11- -1777 m Jerusha Knight Pvt CT
Asa: b 10-11-1739 d 3-10-1811 m Ruth Badger Pvt CT
Asher: b 7-22-1745 d p. 1784 m Elizabeth Prentice Pvt CT
Benjamin, Sr.: b 1713 d 1782 m Mehetable — PS NY
Benjamin, Jr.: b 7-15-1731 d 12- -1819 m Peninah Jones Pvt NY
Caleb: b 1747 d 2-13-1827 m Anne Lewis Pvt NY
Charles, Sr.: b 4-4-1724 d c. 1790 m Keziah Owens Pvt PS VT
Charles, Jr.: b 6-8-1755 d 3-13-1809 m Anna Turner Pvt VT
Comfort: b 8-21-1745 d 5-27-1822 m Elizabeth Abell Pvt CT
Daniel: b 1735 d 11-7-1815 m Abiah Flagg PS NH
Daniel: bpt 11-1-1747 d 2-9-1784 m Mary Tracy Pvt MA

BREWSTER, contd.

Daniel: b 8-16-1734 d 1788 m Prudence Reeves Pvt NJ
Elias: b 9-11-1759 d 3-12-1834 m Margery Morgan Pvt CT
Elijah: b 9-3-1724 d 10-10-1803 m Elizabeth Fitch Capt CT
Eliphaz: b 1-25-1747 d 6-28-1828 m (1) — Owens (2)Temperance Yaw Pvt VT
Elisha, Sr.: b 10-29-1715 d 3-26-1789 m (1)Lucy Yeomans (2)Jane — PS CT
Elisha, Jr.: b 7-8-1751 d at sea 1798 m Margaret Curtis 2Lt CT
Elisha: b 10-29-1755 d 9-25-1833 m Sarah Huntington Sgt CT ★
Ephraim: b 8-20-1731 d 5-10-1810 m Margery Parks PS VT
Francis: b 2-28-1744 d p. 1802 m Mary Strong Ens &PS NY
Frederick: b 6-7-1763 d 2-19-1845 m Anna Frink Sgt CT ★
Henry, Sr.: b 1- -1722 d — m Mary — Pvt CT
Henry, Jr.: b 5-2-1751 d 3-15-1830 m Martha Halsey Lt NY ★
Hezekiah: b 8-17-1749 d 1820 m Eunice Brown Pvt CT ★
Ichabod, Jr.: b 3-6-1753 d 7-27-1841 m Lucy Clark Pvt CT
Ichabod: b 1-15-1710/11 d 7-27-1797 m Lydia Barstow PS CT
Jabez: b 3-16-1747 d 5-12-1802 m (1)Sara Avery (2)Dorothy Brewster Park Ens PS CT
James: b 12-29-1747 d 5-27-1835 m Anna Foster Pvt NY ★
James: b 1755 d 3-29-1804 m Mildred Downs Sol NC
James: b 1720 d 1808 m Elinor Williamson PS VA
Jedediah: b 6-7-1754 d 7- -1827 m (1)Prudence Robinson (2)Aisenath Bushnell Pvt CT
John: b 1749 d 1-28-1827 m Elizabeth Knight Capt NH
John: b 12-5-1705 d 8-23-1778 m Charity Goldsmith PS NY
John: b 1728 d 1816 m Elizabeth Sheriff Pvt NC
Jonah: b 9-1-1750 d 1833 m Sarah Robinson Pvt VT
Jonathan: b 9-13-1735 d 3-2-1805 m Mary Williams Capt CT
Jonathan: b 6-8-1734 d 4-13-1800 m Zipporah Smith PS CS MA
Jonathan: b 8-25-1744 d 4-29-1820 m Eunice Kingsley CS CT
Joseph, Jr: b 8-20-1726 d 7-19-1775 m Deborah — Pvt CT
Joseph: b 2-10-1735 d 3-17-1819 m Rebecca Mills PS NY
Joseph: b 1759 d 8- -1850 m Sarah Geer Pvt & Arfr RI ★
Joseph, Jr.: b c. 1747 d 6-19-1807 m Deborah Hunt Pvt MA
Joseph Wadsworth: b 12-13-1764 d 9-4-1849 m Lovisa Badger Pvt MA
Joshua: b 5-2-1761 d 9-22-1832 m Ruth Chandler Pvt MA
Joshua: b 7-9-1763 d 4-2-1851 m Lydia Western Pvt MA
Martin: b 11-16-1758 d 8-22-1833 m Sarah Nye Drew Pvt & Cdr MA
Nathan: b 12-21-1724 d 11-3-1808 m (1) Rachel Partridge (2) Hannah Kent (3)Diadema Dawes Pvt MA
Nathaniel: b 7-4-1755 d 10-2-1827 m Ruth Dimmock Pvt MA
Nathaniel: b 1743 d 9-30-1825 m Experience — Ens NY
Oliver: b 4-2-1760 d 2-15-1812 m Jerusha Badger Dr MA
Ozem: b 3-13-1751 d 4-27-1809 m (2)Huldah Chandler Pvt VT
Peter: b c. 1760 d 1793/94 m Sarah Bentley Pvt & Drm CT
Samuel, Sr.: b 7-18-1718 d 2-9-1802 m (1)Mary Hawkins (2)Mary Wood PS NY
Samuel, Jr: b 1740 d 11-29-1824 m (1)Phoebe Rose (2)Freelove Williams (3)Mary Gardner PS NY
Samuel: b 5-15-1738 d 8-18-1824 m Rebecca Tabor PS PA
Seabury: b 10-21-1754 d 7-27-1847 m (1)Sallie Bradford (2)Lucy Lefingwell (3)Mrs. Sarah Lefingwell Star Baker Pvt MA
Simon, Sr: b 6-10-1720 d 6-29-1801 m Anne Andruss PS CT
Stephen: b 3-4-1744 d 2-21-1821 m Hepsibah Rudd Ens CT
Timothy: b 11-3-1746 d 1816/17 m (1)Phebe Wood (2)Sarah Youngs Pvt NY
Timothy: b 9-12-1759 d 6-28-1848 m Temperance Andrus Pvt VT
Wadsworth: b 4-14-1737 d 3-30-1812 m Jerusha Newcomb Cpl CT
Wm: b 1732 d 5-18-1793 m Temperance Sweezy Capt & PS NY
Wm: b 4-19-1757 d 1845 m Margaret Dempsey Pvt NC ★
Wrestling: b 8-29-1724 d 2-8-1810 m Deborah Wiswell Seabury Pvt MA
Zadock: b 3-15-1742 d 5-21-1811 m (1) Lois Brewster (2)Lucy Knight NLt CT ★

BREYFOGEL,

George: b 2-4-1747 d 10-6-1827 m Catharine Ely Pvt PA
Jacob: b 1-26-1748 d 1840 m Maria — Pvt PA

BRICE,

James: b 10-11-1751 d 12-22-1832 m (1)Alice Smith (2)Anne Grant Capt MD
James: b c. 1746 d 1800 m Jane Marshall Pvt PA
John: b 9-22-1738 d 7-20-1820 m Mary Clare Maccubbin Capt MD
Samuel: b 1-6-1743 d p. 1810 m Rachel Boone Pvt PA
Samuel: b c. 1760 d p. 9-8-1795 m Joan — Pvt SC
Wm.: b 6-10-1743 d p. 1-27-1794 m Rachel Jones Capt PA

BRICKELL,

Matthias: b 3-23-1725 d 10-17-1788 m (1)Rachiel Noailles (2)Mrs Nannie Jones LCol NC

BRICKER,

Christian: b c. 1740 d 1782 m Barbara Kissinger Pvt PA
David: b 2-3-1755 d 4-8-1833 m Molly Erbe Pvt PA
Jacob: b 4-2-1759 d 1841 m Barbara Kissinger Pvt PA

John: b c. 1750 d 10- -1818 m Nancy Boyer Cpl MD
Peter: b 4-1-1735 d 8-1-1804 m Mary Baer Pvt PA

BRICKETT,

Barnard: b 10-7-1742 d p. 1782 m Mary Hall PS NH
James: b 2-16-1738 d 12-10-1818 m Edna Merrill BGen PS MA
James: b 1-15-1765 d 1-21-1851 m (1)Anna Wheeler (2)Ruth (Chase) Smith Pvt MA
John: b 3-13-1740 d 2-1-1825 m Prudence Adams Lt MA
Moses: b 5-4-1742 d 12-20-1813 m Sarah Chase Ens MA
Nathaniel: b 5- -1731 d 2-15-1805 m Anna Woodman Pvt MA

BRICKEY,

Jarrett: b 4-10-1760 d 1841 m Amy Compton Sol VA
Peter: b 4-10-1761 d p. 4-13-1836 m (1)Elizabeth Brickey (2)Elizabeth Dunn Pvt VA
Peter: b c. 1715 d p. 9-16-1786 m Winnifred Lucas PS VA
Wm.: b 1-9-1756 d 1832 m Sarah Elizabeth — Fif CS VA ★

BRIDENBECKER,

Baltis: b 1746 d 1827 m Eva Sneck Pvt NY

BRIDGE, (includes BRIDGEO, BRIDGERS, BRIDGES)

Benjamin: b 11-26-1739 d 1-26-1814 m Esther Parker Sgt MA
Benjamin: b 10-13-1748 d 4-17-1843 m Elizabeth Hathaway Pvt MA
Benjamin: b 7-7-1751 d 9-8-1821 m Chloe Drake Pvt NC
Caleb: b 1-22-1738 d 8-6-1812 m Lucy Tucker Pvt MA
Ebenezer: b 2-3-1742 d 2-13-1823 m Mahitable Wood LtCol MA
Edmund: b 8-10-1762 d 9-14-1851 m Elizabeth Avery Pvt MA ★
George: b 2-12-1762 d p. 10-20-1834 m Nancy Edwards Drm Pvt NC ★
Hackaliah: b 10-11-1737 d 4-22-1792 m Elizabeth Underwood Cpl MA
Isaac: b 1734 d 1-14-1821 m Mary Mixter Pvt MA
James: b a. 1755 d p. 2-10-1812 m Susannah — Spy GA
James: b 1-24-1756 d 12-14-1819 m Mary Montgomery Pvt MA
Jesse: b 1-13-1763 d 5- -1823 m Kesiah Cutting Pvt MA
John: b c. 1750 d p. 1790 m X Sol SC
John: b 9-1-1700 d 5-7-1776 m (1)Anna Herrick (2)Sarah Tidd (3) Mrs. Mary Porter PS MA
John: b 1742 d 8-14-1836 m X Pvt VA ★
Jonathan: b 10-12-1753 d 10-25-1818 m Prudence Simonds Pvt CT
Jonathan: b 9-20-1758 d 2-16-1850 m (1)Phoebe Bowman (2)Mrs Phoebe Wait Pvt MA
Joseph: b 6-18-1752 d 1831 m (1)Sarah Crosset (2)Mrs. Elizabeth Torrey Sol MA
Joseph: b 2-1-1750 d 3-22-1837 m Frances Davis Lt VA ★
Nathaniel: b 7-8-1725 d 12-19-1794 m Mary Fiske Pvt MA
Philip: b 6-28-1759 d 10-31-1820 m Hannah Knight Pvt & Smn MA
Richard: b 4-8-1752 d 3-4-1824 m (2)Ann Johnson Norment Sgt VA
Richard Perkins: b 11-3-1756 d 8-22-1797 m Anna Harrington PS MA
Robert: b 11-18-1739 d 1-18-1800 m Jemima Shepherd Sol &PS PA
Samuel: b 1730 d 12-22-1788 m Anna Foote CS & PS CT
Samuel: b c. 5-2-1705 d 6-3-1791 m (1)Susannah Paige (2)Martha Bowman PS MA
Samuel, Jr: b 1-6-1735 d p. 1802 m Hannah Townsend Pvt MA
William: b 4-19-1741 d 2-9-1804 m Mary Porter Adj MA
Wm.: b a. 1751 d 1805 m Elizabeth Bass Sol NC

BRIDGEWATER,

Samuel: b 4-10-1749 d 5-11-1827 m Mary Ann Caughman Pvt VA ★

BRIDGFORTH,

James: b c. 1765 d 6- -1798 m Elizabeth Greenhill PS VA

BRIDGHAM,

John, Sr.: b 8-27-1729 d p. 1815 m Joanna Comer Capt MA
John, Jr: b 5-16-1754 d 7-31-1840 m Sibella Shaw Sgt Ens MA ★
Joseph: b 11-22-1732 d 12-4-1789 m Martha Bucklin PS MA

BRIDGMAN, (includes BRIDGMANN)

Abel: b 4-15-1759 d 9-23-1800 m Anna Fowler Pvt NH
Erastus: b 2-24-1762 d 4-21-1805 m Rhoda Hulbert Pvt MA
Gideon: b 5-21-1753 d p. 1840 m Fanny Nevens Pvt NH ★
Isaac: b 1718 d 2-25-1781 m Elizabeth Hatch PS & CS NH
John: b 1-26-1747 d 10-23-1800 m Mary Dorman Sol NH
Joseph: b 1-4-1745 d 3-10-1826 m Ruth Wright Pvt MA
Noah: b 12-1-1731 d 11-9-1820 m Mercy Clark Pvt MA
Orlando: b 1743 d 3-14-1813 m Martha Wait CS NH

BRIER,

John: b c. 1748 d p. 1790 m Joanna Morgan Pvt NH
Nathaniel: b 1763 d 1835 m Nancy Baumback Pvt PA

BRIESLER,

John: b 12-14-1756 d 4-28-1836 m Esther Field Pvt MA ★

BRIGGS,
Abiel: b 12-16-1752 d 7-11-1832 m Dier Paul Pvt MA
Abiel: b 1760 d 10-23-1844 m Elizabeth Chase Cpl RI
Abiezer: 3-27-1753 d 5-5-1849 m Pamela Palmer Pvt RI
Abner: b 7-18-1754 d 4-23-1827 m Sarah Phillips Pvt Matr MA W★
Abner: b 2-16-1764 d 2-4-1839 m Sarah Flagg Pvt MA ★
Abraham: b 6-17-1744 d 9-15-1827 m Abigail Shreefe Pvt NY
Allen: b 4-27-1756 d 4-29-1826 m Nancy Brown Pvt MA
Amos: b 9-24-1748 d 4-24-1833 m Hannah Cobb Pvt MA
Amos: b 2-22-1762 d 6-3-1828 m Thankful Brown Pvt RI
Asa: b 6-22-1755 d 1834 m Elizabeth Paul OrdlSgt RI MA VT NS ★
Benjamin: b 10-19-1735 d c. 7-3-1805 m Elizabeth Saunders Cpl MA
Benjamin: b 1745 d p. 1787 m X Capt PA
Benjamin: b 4-3-1760 d 1-7-1841 m Elizabeth Gay Pvt VA
Benjamin, Sr.: b c. 1715 d 1819 m Rebecca Welch Pvt PA
Benjamin, Jr.: b 8-28-1752 d 1802 m (2)Mary Davis Pvt MA
Benjamin Franklin: b 1-22-1752 d 1833 m Naomi Wells Pvt MA
Caleb: b 1753 d 6- -1836 m Sarah Smith Pvt CT
Charles: b c. 1755 d 1800 m Elizabeth Jones Sol NC
Charles: b 12-6-1732 d 1-22-1801 m (1)Elizabeth Blow (2)Sarah Andrews CS VA
Daniel: b 1737/38 d 8-17-1809 m Silence Hart Sgt & PS MA
Darius: b — d — m Elizabeth Gilmore Pvt MA
Ebenezer: b 3-24-1731 d 10-26-1808 m Elizabeth Smith Pvt MA
Edward: b 1-28-1741 d 8-14-1824 m (1)Mary Lynch (2)Euphemia Honeywell CS Pvt NY
Elijah: b 9-2-1730 d 1795 m Jemima Dean Pvt MA
Eliphalet, Sr.: b 1713 d 1780 m Abigail Gay PS NH
Eliphalet, Jr.: b 1734 d 1776 m Mary Cobb CS PS NH
Elisha: b 8-10-1761 d 9- -1843 m Abigail Foster Sgt MA ★
Elisha: b 12-21-1750 d 9-10-1836 m Laurentia Hall Cpl MA
Ephraim, Sr.: b 10-19-1744 d p. 5-15-1790 m Lettis Hill Cpl MA
Ephraim: b 4-19-1736 d 12-22-1799 m Rebecca Waterman PS MA
Ephraim: b 6-30-1756 d 8-10-1829 m Rhoda Whitcomb Pvt RI ★
Ephraim: b 5-13-1753 d 1-13-1843 m Nancy Burlingame Pvt RI ★
Ezra, Sr.: b 1732/33 d p. 1790 m Abigail Allen Pvt MA
Ezra, Jr.: b 1760 d 1824 m (1)Polly Jones (2)Miriam Macomber Pvt MA
Ezra: b c. 1758 d 11-2-1815 m (2)Lydia Southworth Pvt MA
George: b 4-4-1734 d 1816 m (1)Hannah Wightman (2)Sarah Wells (3)Lydia — Ens RI
George: b 1756 d p. 1790 m Frances Dyer Pvt RI
Godfrey: b 2-24-1756 d 1815 m Sarah Paul Smn MA
Henry: b 8-22-1729 d 1782 m Elizabeth — Capt & PS VA
Isaac: b 7-29-1748 d p. 1790 m Sarah Gorton Pvt RI
Isaac: b 11-25-1764 d 10-15-1836 m Dorothy Fowler Pvt NY
Jabez, Sr.: b 6-29-1723 d p. 1790 m Tabatha Babbit Pvt MA
Jabez, Jr.: b 3-8-1760 d p. 5-8-1818 m Lucy Batchelder Pvt MA ★
Jacob: b 4-20-1739 d 12-25-1821 m Esther Skinner Cpl MA
James: b 6-18-1760 d 7-26-1841 m Phoebe Bowen Pvt CT
James: b 2-27-1719 d 5-9-1804 m Hannah Barker PS MA
James: b 1-17-1745 d 12-7-1825 m Ann Wiswall PS MA
Jedediah: b 4-21-1738 d p. 1802 m Bathsheba Paull Lt MA
Jesse: b 1741 d 1790-1800 m Mary Parmenter Pvt MA
Joel: b 4-15-1757 d 1-18-1828 m Hannah Sprague Cpl MA
John: b 9-18-1721 d 5-23-1791 m Abigail Burt Pvt MA
John: b 1742 d 2-20-1822 m Abigail Chase Pvt MA
John: b 8-31-1753 d 11-22-1842 m (1)Hannah Redding (2)Loraine — Pvt MA
John: b — d 2- -1802 m Mary Brown Pvt PA
John: b 11-5-1758 d 2-11-1837 m Mary Tucker Sgt RI ★
Jonathan: b 2-25-1757 d 12-23-1837 m Abigail Greene Pvt Cpl RI
Jonathan: b 9-3-1752 d 1818 m Elizabeth Bird Sgt MA
Joseph: b 6-22-1757 d 2-16-1850 m Molly Chaddock Pvt MA ★
Joseph: b 6-9-1749 d 10-5-1830 m Mary Spooner Pvt RI
Joseph: b 12-2-1757 d 5-15-1851 m Annie Essex Pvt RI ★
Joseph: b 12-5-1749 d 3-29-1832 m Patience Barlow Capt VT ★
Joshua: b 9-30-1754 d 5-27-1841 m Tryphena Austin Pvt CT ★
Josiah L.: b c. 1760 d 12-17-1840 m Lois Vaughan Pvt MA
Leonard: b 2-26-1750 d 11-13-1844 m Hope Wood Pvt MA
Michael: b 9-16-1751 d 2-10-1828 m Sarah Greene Lt VT
Nathan: b 1728 d 4-9-1813 m Mary Talbot Ens MA
Nathan: b 10-7-1748 d 5-25-1817 m Mary Hammond Pvt MA
Nathan: b 12-31-1748 d 1805-26 m (1)Hopestill Paull (2)Abigail Henry Pvt MA
Nathaniel: b 1747 d a. 11- -1776 m Prudence Smith Pvt CT
Nathaniel, Jr.: b c. 1733 d 7-26-1821 m Betsy Dean Pvt MA
Owen: b 11-24-1758 d 4-24-1844 m Margery Brown Pvt MA ★
Peter: b 9-30-1764 d 8-16-1842 m Abigail Dyer Pvt RI
Peter: b 5-13-1749 d 7-28-1825 m (1)Prudence Thomas (2)Rebecca Pullen Sgt PS VT
Philip: b 6-21-1730 d 9-12-1787 m Sarah Finch Pvt NY
Richard: b c. 1735 d p. 1790 m Susannah Baker Pvt RI
Richard: b 1753 d 4-11-1835 m Huldah Reed Dr MA
Robert: b 1735 d 2- -1810 m Judith Rose Sgt NC
Robert: b — d 7-15-1814 m Dinah Walling Pvt RI
Samuel: b 2- -1732 d 1821 m Susannah Nye Capt MA
Samuel: b 1721 d 2-25-1807 m Mary Pigsley Pvt MA
Samuel: b 7-29-1745 d 1790-1816 m Ruth Paul Pvt MA

Samuel: b 2-14-1747/48 d 10-18-1839 m Sarah Blackmer Pvt MA
Samuel: b c. 1730 d c. 1795 m Mary Sarah Logan Sol VA
Seth: b 11-8-1748 d 6-17-1781 m Deborah Barker Sgt MA
Seth: b 11-7-1760 d 3-21-1824 m Hannah Merrick Pvt MA
Solomon: b 5-30-1737 d 1-7-1812 m Mary Lincoln Sgt MA
Sweet: b 1754 d 1844 m Martha Tanner Pvt RI ★
Thomas: b 6-4-1717 d 11-10-1779 m Thankful Axtell Pvt MA
Thomas: b 7-18-1757 d 4- -1822 m Lucy Shaw Pvt RI
Thomas: b 10-13-1728 d 1797 m Abigail Cole Pvt RI
William: b 10-5-1748 d 1-22-1840 m (1)Elizabeth Gallup (2) Hannah Stevens Sgt CT ★
Wm.: b 1737 d 8-11-1819 m Mary — Capt MA ★
Wm: b 12-22-1752 d p. 2-9-1804 m Frances Smith Sol CT
Wm: b 5-14-1758/59 d 7-6-1838 m Catharine E. Boss Sgt RI ★
Wm: b 4-24-1718 d 7-16-1802 m Abishag Records Pvt RI
Wm: b 1-14-1725 d p. 12-9-1800 m Judith Wroe Lt VA
Zadock: b 1759 d 9-16-1823 m (1)Harriet Seymour (2)Widow Parmetier Sol MA
Zebedee: b 2-6-1763 d 1833 m Prudence Hill Pvt MA
Zephaniah: b 5-3-1736 d 1837 m Patience Newton Lt CT ★

BRIGHAM,
Aaron: b 11-22-1762 d 3-23-1831 m Elizabeth R. Barnes Pvt MA
Abijah: b 8-26-1737 d 4-2-1814 m Eunice Willis Lt MA
Antipas: b 5-25-1740 d 6-20-1791 m Catharine Woods Sgt MA
Artemas: b 9-29-1739 d 11-25-1802 m Keziah Rice Sgt MA
Artemas: b a. 1760 d c. 1802 m Mary Cornish Cpl MA
Asa: b 11-9-1737 d 1-18-1806 m Elizabeth Warren Pvt MA
Asa: b 12-2-1721 d 11-6-1777 m Mary Newton 2Maj CS PS NH
Carlos: b 2-21-1763 d 3-27-1843 m Polly Greenleaf Pvt CT
Charles: b 12-30-1700 d 3-17-1781 m Mary Peters CS MA
Daniel: b 12-25-1760 d 10-11-1818 m Thankful — Pvt MA
Daniel: b 6-12-1760 d 6-12-1837 m Anna Monroe Pvt MA
Daniel: b 11-15-1760 d 3-7-1807 m Anna Beaman Pvt MA
Edmund, Sr.: b 8-12-1733 d 6-29-1806 Capt MA
Edmund, Jr.: b 10-19-1758 d 4-22-1840 m Mary Martin Pvt MA
Edward: b 5-21-1754 d 5-5-1838 m Sally Miller Sgt MA ★
Elijah: b 9-5-1742 d 1-8-1804 m Ruth Taylor Lt MA
George: b 3-17-1730 d 3-27-1808 m Mary Bragg Pvt PS MA
Gershom: b 6-27-1750 d 10-22-1817 m Sarah Allen MM MA
Henry: b 10-26-1752 d 1-16-1829 m Anna Phillips Ens MA W★
Ithamer: b 10-6-1729 d 5-3-1784 m (1)Ruth Ward (2)Mary Beaman Lt & CS MA
James: b 10-2-1717 d 3-15-1794 m Hannah Rice Pvt MA
James: b 1735 d 1818 m Louisa Looney Pvt NC
Joel: b 3-5-1756 d 6-25-1813 m Elizabeth Maynard Sgt MA W★
Joel, Sr.: b 10-2-1714 d 4-7-1797 m Mary Church Pvt MA
Joel, Jr.: b 4-5-1751 d 1-20-1820 m Catherine Howe Sol MA
John: b 4-16-1758 d 2-20-1828 m Abigail Williams Pvt MA
John: b 8-8-1758 d 4-2-1841 m Lydia Howe Pvt NH
Jonas, Sr.: b 2-25-1718 d 9-25-1789 m Persis Baker PS MA
Jonas, Jr.: b 10-29-1748 d 1826 m Anna Draper Capt MA
Jonathan: b 10-29-1754 d 7-26-1848 m (1)Lydia Stevens (2)Sarah Brigham Pvt MA
Joseph: b 9-27-1743 d 8-25-1810 m Lydia Barnes Lt MA
Levi, Sr.: b 8-21-1717 d 2-1-1787 m Susanna Grout Lt MA
Levi, Jr.: b 8-26-1746 d 4-26-1821 m Tabitha Hardy Lt PS NH
Lewis: b 3-24-1756 d 2-22-1803 m Mary Rice Cpl MA
Lovewell: b 12-1-1754 d 4- -1824 m Betty Rice Pvt MA
Paul: b 1-6-1746 d 6-15-1824 m Lydia Sawyer Capt CT
Paul: b 3-26-1737 d 6-4-1777 m Sarah Stratton Capt MA
Paul: b 6-17-1761 d 11-17-1838 m Fanny — Pvt MA
Phineas: b 7-23-1755 d p. 1793 m Lydia Batherick Sgt MA
Phineas: b 10-7-1757 d 3-17-1813 m Susanna Howe Pvt MA
Samuel: 8-23-1756 d 6-24-1830 m Mary Ball Pvt MA
Samuel: 12-3-1760 d 3-2-1813 m Phebe Davis Pvt MA
Stephen: b 4-5-1756 d 5-7-1816 m (1)Eunice Hide (2)Hannah Field Lt CT
Stephen: b 5-13-1754 d 10-11-1849 m Sarah Harrington Pvt NH ★
Uriah: b 11-3-1722 d 1-25-1777 m (1)Lydia Ward (2)Anne Richardson PS CT
Wm.: b 3-25-1742 d 6- -1813 m Betty Stratton Capt MA
Wm.: b 4-8-1735 d 4-20-1793 m (1)Rebecca Ball (2)Lydia Chamberlain Capt MA
Wm: b 3-26-1739 d 8-1-1833 m Sarah Prentice PS MA
Winslow: b 8-30-1736 d 8-29-1791 m Elizabeth Harrington PS MA

BRIGHT, (includes BRECHT, BRITE)
Albertus: b 10-7-1732 d 3-12-1824 m Patience Hopkins PS SC
Charles: b 7-16-1728 d a. 11- -1816 m Jemima — Pvt PS VA
Christian: b 9-8-1755 d p. 3-3-1823 m Mary — Pvt PA
David: b 9-6-1719 d 9-22-1783 m Sarah — Pvt PA
David: b 8-9-1740 d 1808 m Mary Grout PS PA
Jacob: b 1729 d 9-17-1802 m Susanna Rittenhouse Capt PA
James: b 1752 d 7-3-1837 m Sarah — Pvt MD ★
Jesse: b c. 1755 d a. 4- -1824 Cpl NC
John: b 2-5-1754 d 12-31-1840 m Elizabeth Brown Pvt MA
John: b 2-20-1736 d 1817 m Margaret Shaeffer Pvt PA
John: b 6-2-1747 d 2-9-1834 m Anna Maria Leiss Pvt PA
John: b 4-8-1753 d 10-8-1826 m (2)Jane Ann Faucett Pvt VA

BRIGHT, contd.
John: b *a*. 1762 d 1828 m Susanah Kleiner Sol VA
Joseph: b 8-23-1760 d 2-12-1816 m Hannah Smith Pvt MA
Michael, Sr.: b 5-28-1706 d 9-13-1794 m Margareta Simone PS PA
Michael, Jr.: b 3-24-1732 d 8-1-1814 m (1)Sarah Stoner (2)Catherine Bowers PS PA
Peter: b 5-5-1738 d 9-25-1793 m Catharine — PS PA
Simon, Jr: b *c*. 1738 d *c*. 1799 m Elizabeth Graves Capt PS NC

BRIGHTBILL,
Peter: b 2-7-1730 d 8-21-1809 m Christina 1Lt PA

BRIGHTMAN,
George: b 9-26-1721 d 1-5-1786 m Hannah — Pvt MA
Henry: b 12-20-1749 d 9-3-1835 m Hannah Paddock Capt CT
Israel: b — d — m Bethana Palmer Pvt MA
John: b 1753 d *p*. 1790 m Elizabeth Ann Taylor Pvt RI
Joseph: b 1750-4 d 1803 m Elizabeth Hill Pvt MA
Peleg: b 3-3-1762 d 2-21-1844 m Parthany Hill Pvt MA
Thomas: b 8-4-1751 d 8-24-1843 m Thankful Nye Pvt RI ★

BRIGHTWELL,
Charles: b 1756/57 d *p*. 1840 m Mary — Pvt VA ★

BRILL,
John, Jr.: b 7-30-1756 d 9-6-1832 m Hannah Cornell Pvt NY

BRILLHART,
Christian: b *a*. 1755 d *p*. 1810 m Anna Weber Pvt PA

BRIMHALL,
Gideon: b 1764 d *p*. 1835 m Mary Brimhall Pvt MA ★
Sylvanus: b 3-15-1758 d 9-18-1839 m (1)Tryphena Johnson (2) Lucy Lincoln Pvt MA ★
Sylvanus: b 1742 d 2-24-1821 m (1)Esther — (2)Sarah — Pvt MA ★

BRIMIJION,
Thomas: b 1754 d 12-17-1843 m Ruth — Pvt MA ★

BRINCKERHOFF, (includes BRINKERHOFF)
Adrian Martense: b 9-12-1753 d 1-13-1835 m ( )Adrianna Van de Linde ( )Elizabeth Schuyler QM NY
Derick: b 1720 d 1789 m Geertie Wyckoff Col PS NY
Derick: b 4-9-1750 d 1822 m Catharine Van Vlack Sol NY
Dirck: b 5-21-1739 d 11-17-1780 m Rachel Van Ranst Pvt NY
Garrett: b 3-18-1762 d 5-7-1840 m Margaret Goetschins Pvt NJ W★
George: b 10-17-1744 d *c*. 1780 m Magdalena Banta 1Lt NJ
George: b 10-17-1726 d 12-5-1797 m Catherine Herring Capt NY
Guylbert: b 2-22-1753 d *p*. 1794 m Elizabeth Ackerman Pvt PA
Henry: b 1-22-1755 d 4- -1826 m Annatje Vreeland Pvt NJ
Jacob: b 2-25-1756 d 11-13-1829 m Annatie Demarest Ens PA
James: b 11-23-1746 d 5- -1813 m Catherine Voorhees Pvt PA
John: b 4-6-1749 d *p*. 1789 m Sara Van Ardolen Capt NJ
John: b 1701 d 3-26-1785 m Jannetje Van Voorhees PS NY
John: b *c*. 1738 d *c*. 1775 m Elizabeth Brinckerhoff PS 1Lt NY
John G.: b 5-13-1733 d *p*.1780 m — Capt NY
John J.: b 4-6-1759 d 5-13-1838 m Sarah Van Arsdale Pvt NY
Joris: b 10-9-1719 d 1-3-1810 m Martina Bogart PS PA
Roeliff: b 11-10-1748 d 2-28-1830 m Baeltie Demarest Pvt PA

BRINDLE,
Lawrence: b — d *p*. 12-10-1809 m Veronica Freany Pvt PA
Samuel: b *c*. 1754 d *p*. 7-31-1804 m Elizabeth Stambaugh Pvt PA

BRINEGAR,
Adam: b *c*. 1755 d 10- -1816 m Margaret — PS NC

BRINGHURST,
George: b 6-20-1755 d 12-29-1829 m Ann Clarkson 2Lt PA

BRINGMAN,
Martin: b *c*. 1750 d *p*. 1810 m Martha Margueritta — Pvt MD

BRINK,
Adam: b 2-5-1761 d 6-30-1843 m Catherine Snyder Pvt NY
Benjamin: bpt 12-10-1752 d *p*. 4-10-1794 m Sarah Gonsolis Sgt PA
Benjamin: b 8-29-1763 d 12-31-1845 m Elizabeth Horton Pvt PA ★
Cornelius: b *c*. 3-4-1722 d 2-15-1791 m Marretjen Beatty Mil NY
Jacob: b 3-25-1760 d 12-30-1849 m Christina Longyear Pvt NY
John, Jr.: b 10-1-1744 d 6-9-1814 m Margaret Burhans Sol NY
Peter: b 5-29-1739 d *p*. 8- -1784 m Catharina Davids Cpl NJ

BRINKER,
Henry: b 4-18-1757 d 1-6-1845 m Margaret Wise Pvt PA ★
Jacob: b 11-9-1727 d 10- -1798 m Susanna Hinkle Pvt PA
Ulrick: b 4-14-1726 d 6-20-1785 m Apollonia Bayer Pvt PA

BRINLEY,
Wm.: b 7-4-1754 d 1-16-1840 m (1)Rebecca White (2)Rachel Chamberlain Pvt NJ ★

BRINSMADE,
Abraham: b 2-27-1726 d 11-17-1801 m Mary Wheeler Capt CT
Cyrus: b 12-19-1762 d 1-26-1833 m (1)Anna — (2)Joanna Banks (3)Sally Jerrills Pvt CT ★
Daniel Nathaniel: b 1750 d 1826 m Abigail Farrand Adj CT
Zachariah: bpt 5- -1745 d 1778 m Johannah Prindle Vol CT

BRINSON,
Adam: b 6-10-1751 d 11-23-1825 m Mary Sheppard Pvt NC
Hilary: b 4- -1758 d 2-27-1834 m Elizabeth Barfield Pvt NC W★
John: b 2-21-1767 d *p*. 1840 m (1)Susannah Slade (2)Martha — Sol NC
Matthew: b 9-16-1763 d *p*. 1803 m Sabra Heidelburg Sol NC
Moses: b 2-3-1763 d 1830 m (1)Mrs Agnes Wright Underwood (2)Mrs Apsabeth Purvis Parker Pvt GA

BRINTLE,
Jacob: b *c*. 1744 d *p*. 2-24-1815 m Drusilla — PS VA

BRINTNALL,
Jonathan: b 9-21-1756 d 1-31-1836 m Mary Williams Pvt MA
Thomas: b 8-10-1744 d 8-18-1830 m Lucy Bullard Sgt MA

BRINTON,
Amos: b 12-22-1754 d 11-28-1823 m Sarah Darlington Pvt PA
George: b 10-27-1739 d 1798 m Christiana Hill PS PA
Joseph: b 7-21-1754 d 2-4-1826 m Mary Martin Pvt PA
Moses: b 8-10-1761 d 11-23-1846 m (1)Elizabeth Whitson (2)Hannah Chamberlin Sol PA

BRISBANE, (includes BRISBAN, BRISBEN, BRISBIN)
Adam Fowler: b 1754 d 7-1-1797 m Mary Camber PS SC
John: b 12-25-1730 d 3-13-1822 m Isabella Simmons McNab Capt PA ★
Wm.: b 4- -1728 d 1811 m Elizabeth Watson Capt PA
Wm.: b 1758 d 12-20-1836 m Jannet Moore Pvt PA

BRISCOE, (includes BRISCO)
George: b 1733 d 6-7-1805 m Frances McMillan PS VA
Gerard: b 8-17-1737 d *p*. 1790 m (1)Ruth McMillan (2)Margaret Baker LCol CS MD
Hanson: b 1749 d 9-12-1817 m Mary A Jordan PS CS MD
Henry: b 2-3-1763 d 9-26-1839 m Katharina Brookhart Pvt MD ★
Jeremiah: b *c*. 1760 d *a*. 1-13-1827 m Elizabeth Harlan Pvt VA
John: b 1755 d 1830 m Cevilla DeLashmutt QM MD
John, Sr.: b 3- -1717 d 12-7-1788 m (1)Elizabeth McMillian (2)Ann Lamar Dr CS VA
John, Jr.: b 7-2-1752 d 5-12-1818 m Eleanor Magruder PS VA
John Hanson: b 1752 d 9-26-1796 m Mary Elizabeth Attaway Bond Maj Dr MD
Nathaniel: b 6-12-1762 d 10-4-1848 m Olive Prindle Fif CT ★
Philip: b *c*. 1758 d *p*. 1832 m Elizabeth Mason Pvt PS MD ★
Phillip: b 1729 d *p*. 1778 m Chloe Hanson Pvt MD
Reuben: b 1752 d 1810 m Nancy Lawson Capt VA
Wm.: b 6-2-1719 d 6-2-1797 m Dianah — CS Pvt VT
Wm.: b 1750 d *p*. 10-7-1829 m Elizabeth Wallace Capt PS VA

BRISTOL,
Aaron: b 5-7-1743 d 7-21-1823 m Sybil Scovil Pvt CT
Abel: b 6- -1755 d 5-11-1827 m Mary Norton Pvt NY
Abel: b 5-5-1755 d 1820 m Anna Pearl Cpl VT
Amos: b 2-22-1713 d 4-15-1799 m (1)Joanna Parker (2)Ruth Beach PS CT
Amos: b 1-20-1759 d 12-8-1848 m Jarusha Pratt Pvt MA
Benjamin, Sr.: b 7-24-1721 d *p*. 1790 m Thankful Trowbridge PS NY
Benjamin, Jr.: b 1-24-1750 d 9-25-1839 m Abigail Warner Sgt NY
Bezalee: b 3-30-1749 d 6-20-1828 m Mary Redfield Capt CT
Eli: b 9-27-1755 d 9-28-1843 m Sara Peck Pvt CT ★
Eliphalet: b 4-7-1751 d 7-16-1833 m Sarah Scovill Pvt CT
Gideon: b 6-11-1755 d 10-19-1837 m Abigail Badger Fif Cpl CT ★
Job: b 2-13-1744 d *p*. 1809 m (1)Ada Sherman (2)Hanah Pvt VT
John, Jr.: b 1739 d 1823 m Sarah Nearing Pvt CT W★
John: b 10-21-1759 d 10-28-1849 m Elsey Aylsworth Sol NY
Justus: b 12-31-1736 d 1-13-1820 m Sarah Hawkins Sgt CT
Nathan: b 2-5-1751 d 4-2-1826 m Annie Lambert Sgt CT CL
Nathaniel: b 1755 d 1843/4 m Annis Stiles Pvt CT
Reuben: b 10-20-1755 d 12-21-1851 m Catharine Galbraith Pvt Tms CT ★
Samuel: b 1- -1757 d 8-2-1834 m X Pvt VT ★
Thomas: b 3-28-1741 d 10- -1608 m Eunice Parker Pvt CT ★

BRISTOW, (includes BRISTOE)
Benjamin: b 4-15-1741 d 7-28-1788 m (1)Elizabeth Saunders (2) Sarah Lester Pvt VA
Benjamin: b *c*. 1760 d *a*. 1-9-1815 m Sarah Miles Sol VA

James, Jr.: b 9-28-1751 d *p.* 3-12-1804 m Margaret (Clopton) Peasley Pvt NC
James: b 1752 d 6- -1818 m (1)Delilah Elkins (2)Elizabeth Clevenger Pvt VA
John: b 1753 d *a.* 2-14-1825 m Rachel Thackery PS MD
John: b 11-7-1748 d 12-11-1820 m Susannah Parrish Pvt NC

BRITELL,
Claudius: b 6-8-1733 d *p.* 1790 m Ellathea Owen PS VT

BRITT,
Charles: b 6-2-1762 d 10-7-1837 m Mary Langel Pvt SC ★
Frederick: b 5-2-1745 d 9-25-1811 m Helena Burhause Pvt NY
John: b *c.* 1750 d *p.* 1788 m Susan Holeman Ens VA
Lemuel: b *c.* 1719 d *p.* 11-20-1795 m Mary Taylor Sol NC
Obediah: b 2-12-1759 d 3-20-1834 m Mary Elizabeth Smith Sgt VA ★
Samuel: b 10-17-1760 d 3-18-1848 m Dorcas Baggett PS NC
Seth, Sr.: b 1722 d *p.* 1776 m Patience Curtis PS NH
Seth, Jr.: b 1746 d *p.* 1790 m Susanna Latham Pvt NH
Wm. Sr.: b *c.* 1725 d 1-4-1787 m (1) — Randolph (2)Hannah Conolly PS VA
Wm. Jr.: b 8-9-1766 d *p.* 9- -1830 m Sarah Poor Pvt VA

BRITTON, (includes BRITTAIN, BRITTEN, BRITTIN)
Abraham: b 1754 d 5-21-1824 m Lanaoh Fredericks Pvt NJ
Benjamin: b 8-27-1740 d 1821 m Abigail Hoff Pvt MA
Charity (Tucker) Bellergean: b — d 4- -1790 m (1) — Bellergea₁ (2)Abraham Brittain PS NJ
David: b 6-14-1741 d 11-20-1833 m Lydia Leonard Pvt NH
Ebenezer: b 6-1-1715 d 1-21-1788 m (1)Tabitha Leonard (2) Sarah Bullock PS SC NH
Elijah: b 1780 d 1816 m Jane Evans Pvt PA
Francis: b *c.* 1735 d *p.* 2-2-1780 m Ann Goddard PS CS SC
Isaac: b 1752 d *p.* 1803 m Margaret Hering PS NJ
Jacob: b 1744 d 8-18-1784 m Elizabeth Van Sickle Pvt NJ
James: b *c.* 1740 d *c.* 1823 m — Stringfield PS NC
Job: b 2-20-1755 d 12-15-1804 m Abagail Chamberlin Pvt NH
John: b 6-19-1749 d *p.* 1785 m (1)Phebe Hewett (2)Jerusha Thompson Pvt MA
John: b 5- -1749 d 5-30-1836 m Jerusha Thompson (?) Pvt MA
John: b *c.* 1730 d 1811 m (1)Phoebe Pettit (2)Martha Gray Lt NJ
John: b — d *p.* 2-1-1798 m Catherine — Pvt NJ
John: b 1755 d 5-20-1846 m (1)Isabel Rice (2)Lydia Pitts Harris Pvt NJ ★
John: b 1755-60 d *p.* 1820 m Mary — PS NC
John: b 7-15-1758 d 5-21-1834 m Hannah Lott Pvt NJ ★
Joseph: b 1756 d 8-8-1823 m Dorothy Horner Pvt NC
Joseph: b 3-7-1755 d 9-26-1830 m Hannah Frain Pvt PA ★
Nathan: b 1740 d 10-17-1776 m Elizabeth Parks Pvt VA
Nathaniel: b 3-12-1744 d 10-2-1817 m Jane Simanton Pvt PA
Nicholas: b *c.* 1755 d 5- -1828 m (2)Mary (Messler) Wetherill Pvt NJ
Pendleton: b 1722 d 1806 m Hannah Selee Pvt MA
Samuel: b 1761 d 4-19-1835 m Mindwell Butterfield Sgt NH
Seth: b 1742 d 8-2-1823 m (1)Hannah (Merrifield) Ranstead Sgt PS NH
Wm.: b 4-10-1744 d 3-23-1814 m Lydia Whitney Pvt MA
Wm.: b 10-15-1756-9 d 2-5-1840 m Mrs Mary Britton Pvt MA ★
Wm.: b *c.* 1740 d 6- -1778 m Mary Latham Pvt PS NH
Wm. Jr.: b 1738 d 7-22-1783 m Mary Pierson Capt NJ
Wm.: b 4-25-1755 d 4-1-1828 m Sarah Clark Pvt NJ
Wm: b 2-7-1762 d 1846 m Rachel Brank 2Sgt NC ★
Zeboeth: b 1746 d 7-11-1790 m Elizabeth Mars Pvt PA

BRITZIUS,
Adam: b *c.* 1728-30 d *p.* 4-21-1814 m Catharine — Pvt PA

BRIZENDINE,
Leroy: b 5-26-1761 d 3-23-1839 Lucy Barnes Pvt VA ★
Wm.: b 1743 d *p.* 7-17-1833 m Mary Dupree Pvt VA ★

BROAD, (includes BROD)
Paul: b *a.* 1749 d 12- -1783 m Maria Barbara Miller Pvt PA
Timothy: b 12-2-1745 d 12-13-1811 m Dorothy Colburn Pvt MA

BROADBROOKS,
Ebenezer: b 1717 d 4-20-1802 m Lydia Smalley Pvt MA

BROADFIELD,
Charles: b 7-25-1749 d 1809 m Catherine Penny Pvt MA

BROADNAX, (includes BRODNAX)
Stephen Edward: b 1754 d 1840 m Rebecca Danzee Capt CS VA
Wm.: b 3-3-1762 d *p.* 1799 m Mary Walker 2Lt VA

BROADSTREET,
James: b 1762 d 1809 m (1)Cloey — Cpl NC

BROADUS, (includes BROADDUS)
Edward: b *c.* 1735 d *p.* 1826 m (1)Mary Pritchett (2)Margaret Ham Pvt VA

Edward: b *c.* 1745 d *p.* 1790 m (1) — Brown (2)Mrs Elizabeth Hickman Mitchel Pvt VA
James: b 12-27-1756 d 3-19-1839 m (1)Mary Ann Ferguson (2) Betty — Ens VA
John: b *a.* 1740 d 1799 m Frances Pryor Cmsry VA
John: b 5-7-1764 d 1837 m (1)America(Broaddus) (2)Martha Richerson (3)Catherine Gatewood Pvt VA
Richard: b *c.* 1759/60 d *c.* 1814 m Amenia (Ellerson) Jeter Pvt VA
Thomas: b *c.* 1717 d 5- -1787 m Ann Redd 1Lt VA
Wm., Jr.: b 1755 d 10-7-1830 m (1)Martha Jones (2)Martha Richardson Lt VA

BROADWATER,
Charles: b *c.* 1730 d 5-8-1806 m Ann Amelia (Markham) Pierson PS VA
Charles Lewis: b 1752 d 1841 m Behethelund Sebastian Lt VA

BROADWELL,
David: b 1748 d 3-9-1816 m (1)Mary Howell (2)Salura Wilcox (3)Elizabeth Carroll Sgt NJ
David: b *c.* 1760 d *p.* 1809 m X Pvt NC
Jacob: b 1766 d 8-20-1836 m Jane Williams Pvt NJ ★
Moses: b 11-14-1764 d 4-10-1827 m Jane Broadwell Pvt NJ

BROBST, (includes PROBST)
George: b *c.* 1740 d 11-21-1795 m (1)Catharina Stambach (2) Anna Mary — Cpl PS PA
Matthias: b 3- -1736 d 12- -1792 m (1)Magdalena Stambach (2) Anna Elizabeth Stambach Capt CS PA
Michael: b *c.* 1750 d 1814 m Magdelene Everett LCol PA
John: b 10-15-1759 d 8-19-1834 m Catherine Stumpfund Pvt Sct PA

BROCK,
Barnet: b 6-23-1746 d 7-15-1781 m Mary Ann Brosard Lt NC
George: b 8- -1762 d *a.* 2-12-1839 m Catherine Zink Sol VA
Henry: b *c.* 1730 d *p.* 2-28-1801 m Christena — Sol VA
Jesse: b *c.* 12-8-1751 d *p.* 10-16-1833 m Rebecca Hoard Pvt NC ★
John: b 4-13-1755 d 3-26-1830 m Hannah Taber Pvt Mus CT
John: b 5-25-1750 d 1816 m Lydia Reese 1Lt VA
John: b 1751 d 12-4-1792 m Ann Curtis Sol VA
Joseph: b 1750 d 1800 m Elizabeth Clayton Capt VA
Nathaniel: b 2-2-1757 d 6-21-1815 m (1)Mary Huddlestine (2)Sarah (Eaton) Danly Pvt VA
Reuben: b 1754 d 1842 m Elizabeth Kemp Pvt VA ★
Thomas: b 1745 d 6-16-1811 m Judith Abbott Cpl MA
Uriah: b 1763 d 1843-48 m Elizabeth Brock Pvt VA ★
Walter: b 1743 d 11-8-1825 m (1)Janet Stuart (2)Martha Chamberlain Pvt VT

BROCKENBROUGH,
John: b 1741 d 11-20-1801 m Sarah Roane Dr NS VA
Moore Fauntleroy: b *c.* 1742 d *a.* 1793 m Lucy (Roane) Barnes Capt VA
Wm.: b 6-15-1715 d *a.* 1778 m Elizabeth Fauntleroy Cty Lt VA

BROCKETT, (includes BRACKET)
Abel: b 8-11-1725 d 8-4-1815 m Hannah Pierpont Pvt CT
Hezekiah: b 12-31-1727 d 4-17-1797 m Mary Beecher Pvt CT
Isaiah: b 12-4-1753 d 2-3-1840 m Sarah Cooper Pvt CT
Jacob: b 4-12-1727 d *a.* 1792 m (1)Mary Tuttle (2)Sarah Munson Capt CT
Richard: b 9-11-1727 d 2-22-1813 m (1)Mary Pierpont (2) Mrs Jemima Jacobs MM CT
Samuel: b 4-4-1751 d *p.* 1804 m Sarah Bullard Pvt MA
Wm.: b 6-26-1748 d 5-3-1821 m Patsey Ives Capt SC W★

BROCKLEBANK,
John: b 12-31-1738 d 1-21-1819 m Sarah Fowler Pvt MA
Joseph: b 1759 d 12-25-1838 m Mary Ellsworth Pvt MA ★
Samuel: b 12-19-1741 d *p.* 1786 m Jane Dickenson Lt NH

BROCKMAN,
John: b *c.* 1735 d 8-13-1825 m Amelia Martin PS NC
John: b — d *p.* 9-25-1823 m Elizabeth (Burris) PS VA
John: b 1745-9 d *a.* 7- -1796 m Elizabeth — PS VA
Samuel: b *c.* 1733 d *p.* 1798 m (1)Mary Bell (2)Christian Bibb Woolfolk VA
Thomas: b 1759 d *c.* 1838 m Elizabeth Burress Pvt VA
Wm.: b 10-23-1740 d 1812 m Elizabeth Smith PS Pvt VA

BROCKWAY,
Asa: b 6-18-1759 d 5-29-1838 m Sarah Chapman Pvt CT ★
Asa: b 4-23-1758 d *p.* 1799 m Hepsibeth Hodgman Pvt NH
Consider: b 3-22-1762 d 7-3-1847 m (1)Hannah Maine (2)Keziah Ferry Pvt NY
Ebenezer: b 10-15-1731 d 5-9-1812 m Mary Butler PS CT
Edward: b 1736 d 3-4-1813 m (1)Abigail Palmer (2)Martha Hoadley (3)Hannah Parmer (4)Sarah (Morris) Scott Sgt CT
Edward: b 7-21-1737 d 10-25-1828 m (1)Mary Ely (2)Martha (Downer) Morgan Sgt CT
Gideon, Sr.: b *c.* 1720 d 1783 m Lois Beman Pvt CT
Isaiah: b 1749 d 12-13-1829 m Elizabeth Comstock Pvt CT

88 — DAR Patriot Index

BROCKWAY, contd.
John: b 10-1-1757 d 11-29-1841 m Irena Reed Sgt CT W★
Jonathan: b 5-28-1738 d 1- -1829 m (1)Phebe Smith (2)Rebecca Jones Capt NH
Justus: bpt 11-30-1746 d 1827 m Alse Gardner Pvt NY
Martin: b 12-3-1761 d 8-21-1844 m Besy Hidreth Pvt NH ★
Thomas: b 1-20-1745 d 7-5-1807 m Eunice Lathrop Chp CT
Timothy: b c. 1756 d p. 1790 m Hannah Boland Cpl CT
Timothy: b — d 3-17-1812 m Hannah Green Pvt CT
Woolston: b 12-25-1711 d 10-23-1789 m Esther — CS VT

BRODERICK, (includes BRODRICK)
James: b a. 1752 d 1813 m Sarah — Capt NJ
James: b 5-2-1749 d 10-10-1790 m (1)Sarah Butler (2)Mary Rickey Maj NJ
Wm.: b c. 1757 d p. 1792 m Esther — Sgt NJ

BRODHEAD,
Charles W.: b 6-15-1734 d 11-6-1821 m Ann Peck Capt NY
Charles Wessel: bpt 12-12-1742 d 9- -1799 m Sarah Hardenbergh Capt NY
Daniel, Jr.: b 2-10-1755 d 8-10-1831 m Blandina Edmendorf Ens NY
Daniel: b 9-17-1736 d 11-15-1809 m (1)Elizabeth Depue (2)Rebecca Mifflin BGen PA
Garret: b 1-21-1733 d 1804 m Jane Davis Ens PA
Garret: b 1755 d 9-21-1835 m Affy Decker Sgt NJ
John: b 1727 d p. 2-2-1811 m (1)Mary Davis (2)Mary Effnor Capt NY
Luke: b 1737 d 6-19-1806 m (1)Elizabeth Harrison (2)Elizabeth Wills Capt PA
Richard: b 5-19-1739 d 1812 m Jannetje Newkirk 1Lt NY
Samuel: b 1758 d 8-17-1842 m Blandina Dubois Sgt NY ★

BRODIE,
John: b 10-18-1753 d 5- -1830 m Mary Taylor Dr VA

BROGA,
Andrew: b 3- -1759 d 3- -1841 m Huldah Waite Pvt CT

BROGNARD,
John Baptiste: b 1761 d 4-17-1823 m (1)Sarah Smith (2)Mary Herd Dr FrA or N

BROHAWN,
John: b 4-17-1761 d 1820 m Mary Edmonson Ens MD

BROKAW,
Abraham, Sr.: b 6-19-1728 d 1-20-1810 m Judith Davis PS NJ
Abraham, Jr.: b 1756 d 5-25-1825 m (1)Seletie Westbrook (2)Margaret — Pvt NJ
Caleb: b 7-12-1746 d 5-8-1814 m Jane Brokaw Pvt NJ
Evert: bpt 1- -1741 d p. 7- -1784 m Cornelia Stryker Sgt NJ
George: b 3-29-1755 d 6-27-1842 m Jane Custard Pvt NJ
Isaac: b 4-12-1759 d 7-29-1838 m Mariah Van Nortwick Pvt NJ ★
Jasper: b 10-19-1752 d 10- -1833 m (1)Neeltje — (2)Catherine Brokaw Ens NJ ★
John: bpt 5-23-1754 d p. 5-12-1808 m Arriantje Van Nortwick Cpl NJ
John, Sr.: b 10-26-1709 d p. 7-6-1803 m (1)Maria Van Cleef (2)Catherine — Pvt NJ
John, Jr.: b c. 1735 d 10-4-1777 m (2)Maria Van Der Veer Lt NJ
Peter: b 4-29-1754 d 8-23-1826 m Elizabeth Low Pvt NJ ★
Simon: b 12-19-1756 d 4-11-1789 m Mary Maclow Pvt NJ

BROMLEY, (includes BRUMLEY)
Adin: b 1764 d 12-14-1846 m (1)Thirza Rix (2)Sally Rix Pvt CT
Bethuel: b 12-22-1737 d 1808 m (1)Arabella Herrick (2)Susanna Weller (3)Lydia McCleveland Cpl Drm VT
Daniel: b c. 1750 d p. 1796 m Elizabeth Hallock Sgt VT
John: b 1734 d 8-24-1818 m (2)Eliza Beekman Pvt VA
Preserved: b 9-15-1740 d 1804 m Lucy Safford Sgt CT
Simeon: b 2-17-1752 d p. 1832 m Anna Burdick Pvt RI ★
Wm.: b 3-4-1766 d 3-11-1848 m Robah Smith Pvt VT
Wm.: b 5-1-1721 d 1804 m (1)Mary Charles (2)Hannah Palmer PS CS VT

BROMMETT,
Lambert: b 9-13-1737 d p. 1791 m Susannah Griffin Pvt MA

BROMWELL,
Wm.: b 9-14-1751 d 12-31-1820 m (1)Mary Forster (2)Beulah Hall Pvt PS PA

BRONAUGH,
Thomas: b a. 1741 d p. 12-28-1794 m X Capt VA
Wm.: b 1-16-1730 d 3- -1800 m (1)Mrs Margaret Murdock (2) Mrs Mary Doniphan Cooke (3)Rebecca Craine Col VA
Wm.: b c. 1740 d p. 10-20-1810 m Mary Grant Capt VA

BRONK, (includes BRONCK)
Ephraim: b 3-1-1755 d 9-15-1832 m Annatje Knott Pvt NY
Philip: b 10-2-1726 d 1790 m Catrina Conyn Capt NY
Richard: bpt 4-21-1745 d p. 3-29-1814 m Judikje Bronck Pvt PS NY

BRONNER,
Christian: b 6-7-1764 d 5-26-1826 m Hannah Fetterly Pvt NY
Jacob: b a. 1740 d 1800 m Elizabeth Strawbeck Pvt NY

BRONSDON,
John Box: b 5-21-1751 d 2-22-1823 m Abigail Baker Pvt MA

BRONSON, (includes BROWNSON, BRUNSON)
Abraham, Sr.: b 1729 d 1802 m Abigail Hawley PS CT
Abraham, Jr.: b 1-21-1759 d 4-1-1837 m Rhoda Warner Sgt VT
Amos, Sr.: b 5-4-1760 d 11-8-1835 m Lucy Lewis Pvt MA W★
Amos: b 1-20-1732 d 6-28-1815 m Dorcas Strong Pvt NH
Asa: b 10-25-1733 d 2-27-1778 m Achsa Curtiss Pvt CT
Asa: b 8-24-1742 d p. 1-2-1813 m (1)Mary Winchell (2)Atheldred Parker CS CT
Asa: b 1760 d 1823 m Sallie Tinker Pvt CT ★
Asa: b 5-3-1746 d 1-2-1831 m Mary Harkins Pvt VT
Asahel: b 11-28-1759 d 4-23-1850 m Esther Upson Pvt CT
Benjamin: b 11-1-1735 d 5-9-1803 m Mary Arnold Capt CT
Beriah: b 8-3-1742 d 4-8-1794 m Mary MacLean Pvt CT
Daniel: b 3-8-1738/9 d 11-2-1824 m Esther Bronson Sgt CT
Daniel: b c. 1760 d p. 1-31-1831 m Frances Stanton Pvt SC
Eli: b 6-30-1743 d 9-30-1816 m Mahitabel Atwater PS CT
Eli: b 5-31-1748 d 3-29-1830 m Abi Jewel Capt PS VT
Elijah: b 5-15-1756 d 3-17-1822 m Lois — Pvt CT
Ezra: b 4-24-1732 d 9-1-1795 m Susanna Judd CS Cmsry CT
George: b 1752 d 1822 m X Pvt SC
Gideon: b 10-4-1739 d 10-9-1796 m Cornelia White Maj VT
Isaac, 3d.: b 3-27-1707 d 12-7-1799 m (1)Eunice Richards (2)Abigail Brockett PS CT
Isaac, Sr.. 4th.: b 10-2-1736 d 4-15-1826 m Mary Brocket Capt CT
Isaac, Jr.5th.: b 3-17-1760 d 5-19-1838 m Ann Alcott SrgnMte CT ★
Isaac: b 7-27-1758 d 8-23-1853 m Joanna Beardslee Pvt CT ★
Isaac: b 7-19-1761 d 4-28-1845 m Thankful Clark Pvt CT ★
Isaac: b c. 1745-9 d 1827 m Susannah — Pvt PS SC
James: b 10-22-1727 d p. 1791 m Sarah Brocket Pvt CT
Joel: b 3-9-1759 d 7-29-1839 m Cynthia Minerva Squire Pvt CT
Joel: b 5-12-1762 d 5-22-1843 m Betty Lee Sgt VT
Jonathan: b 1-6-1758 d 2-14-1822 m Hannah Willing Pvt PA
Joseph: b 3-1-1764 d 1851 m Hannah Porter Pvt CT
Josiah, Sr.: b 6-6-1713 d 2-20-1804 m (1)Dinah Sutliff (2)Sarah Leavenworth (3)Rebecca Hurlburt (4)Mrs Huldah Williams Pvt CT
Josiah: b 9-7-1749 d a. 1808 m Miss Comfort Sol PS SC
Levi: b 6-24-1765 d 1- -1800 m Sarah Prindle Pvt CT
Lionel: b 2-17-1753 d 3-21-1810 m Rebekah Millar Ens VA
Luman: b 11-15-1757 d 8-31-1829 m Clarissa Pingra Pvt CT ★
Matthew: b a. 1758 d 1- -1781 m Ann Brown Pvt SC
Michael: b 3-25-1754 d 7-25-1822 m Eunice Nichols Lt CT
Moses: b 6-19-1736 d p. 1790 m Mary Hatch Pvt MA
Noah: b 10-15-1739 d 3-19-1812 m Elizabeth Oviatt Drm CT
Ozias: b 9-3-1742 d 3-12-1810 m Abigail Peck Capt CT
Phineas: b 11-9-1764 d 10-25-1844 m Isabel Wright Pvt CT ★
Reuben: b 6-10-1761 d 9-29-1835 m Huldah Beardsley OrdlSgt CT ★
Richard: b 5-3-1737 d 3-25-1790 m Mary McDowell Dr PA
Roswell: b 9-9-1751 d 3- -1836 m Susannah Adams Pvt CT
Samuel: b 10-12-1742 d 7-21-1813 m (1)Temperance Spencer (2) Huldah Willians Capt CT
Seba: b 9-23-1740 d 1-25-1816 m Mary Hickox PS CT
Selah: b 1763 d 1-27-1843 m (1)X (2)Ann Daily (3)Anna Hopkins Pvt CT ★
Stephen: b 6-30-1735 d 12-15-1809 m Sarah Humaston CS PS CT
Timothy, Jr.: b 8-26-1734 d 8-11-1798 m (1)Hannah Vallance (2)Elizabeth Nash Col PS VT
Titus: b 10-15-1751 d 5-26-1820 m Hannah Cook Pvt CT ★
Wm.: b 12-29-1756 d 5-11-1803 m Elizabeth Powell Pvt SC
Wm.: b 5-30-1734 d 11-5-1801 m Esther Kelsey PS Capt MA
Zadock: b 8-7-1745 d — m Eunice Dutton Ens CT

BROOKBANK,
John: b - -1752 d 1-22-1820 m Ann Adams Pvt MD

BROOKE,
Basil: b 12-13-1738 d 8-22-1794 m Elizabeth Hopkins Sol MD
Benjamin: b 9-24-1753 d 7-22-1834 m Anna Davis Capt PA
Dudley: b 7-22-1762 d 10-25-1844 m Martha Childress Pvt VA★
Francis Taliaferro: b 8-27-1763 d 3-3-1851 m (1)Mary Randolph Spottswood ( )Mary Champe Carter Lt QM VA
George: b a. 9-28-1728 d 4-7-1782 m Hannah Tunstall Col VA
Henry: b 1730 d 6- -1784 m Mary Carroll CS MD
Humphrey: b 9-18-1760 d 1840 m Sarah Walker Page Pvt VA
Humphrey: b 9-28-1730 d 4-7-1802 m (1)Ann Whiting (2)Mrs Mildred Thompkins CS VA
Isaac: b 3-21-1759 d 1785 m Sarah Ann Magruder PS MD
James: b 4-8-1760 d 10-10-1823 m Hannah Stetler Ens PA
John: b 1753 d 1790 m Mrs Mary (Wheeler) Bond Capt MD
John: b 3-27-1740 d 6-21-1813 m (1)Elizabeth May (2)Mrs Mary Brant Keppner Capt PA

Matthew: b 1719 d 10-10-1806 m Sarah Rees PS PA
Nicholas: b a. 2-13-1752 d p. 12-14-1797 m — Hill 2Lt PS MD
Roger: b 8-9-1734 d 7-9-1790 m Mary Matthews PS MD
Samuel: b 6-25-1752 d 12-31-1791 m Elizabeth — PS PA
Thomas: b 1734 d 1789 m Elizabeth — PS CS MD
Walter: b 1- -1735 d 1- -1798 m Anne Darrell Commo VA
Wm.: b c. 1760 d p. 1793 m X Pvt PA
Wm.: b 5-12-1746 d 9-2-1829 m Margaret Moore Maj PA

BROOKER,
Abraham: b 8-17-1736 d 10-28-1813 m Tamar Murray Pvt CT
Samuel: b 10-10-1761 d 11-5-1848 m Polly Stewart Pvt CT ★

BROOKFIELD,
Benjamin: b 1723 d 7-12-1819 m Abigail Ruhl Pvt NJ
Brown: b 3-5-1760 d 4- -1845 m Mary Vanderbilt Pvt NJ
Jacob: b 1722 d 6-4-1782 m Abigail Sayre Capt NJ
Jacob: b 7-20-1764 d 2-28-1838 m Huldah Anderson Pvt NJ ★
John: b 1715 d 6-11-1795 m Esther — CS NJ

BROOKHOUSE,
Robert: b 10-9-1757 d a. 12-8-1779 m Elizabeth Reeves Mstr MA

BROOKHOUSER,
Adam: b 1722 d 2-2-1818 m Mary — Lt PA
John Adam: b 6-1-1747 d 11-4-1811 m Mary Ann Howchin Pvt PA

BROOKING,
John: b 9-10-1764 d 10-24-1817 m Lavinia — Pvt VA
Samuel, Sr.: b c. 1730-40 d c. 1792/3 m Sarah — Pvt VA
Vivian: b 1738 d 12-8-1808 m Elizabeth Hall Broadnax Col VA
Wm.: b 1764 d 1829 m Elizabeth Barrett Ens VA

BROOKINS, (includes BROOKINGS)
Artemas b 1757 d a. 1845 m Lois Johnson Pvt MA
James: b 5-29-1747 d 7-20-1826 m Mary Taft Capt VT
Reuben: b 5-10-1763 d 2-16-1834 m Lois — Pvt MA ★
Samuel, Jr.: bpt 8-10-1745 d p. 1779 m Elizabeth Mighill Smn MA
Silas: b 1759 d 12-16-1832 m Lucy Mott Sgt VT

BROOKS, (includes BROOKES)
Abijah: b 4-29-1752 d 4-4-1829 m Sarah Salina Wetmore Pvt CT
Abijah: bpt 8- -1759 d 11-5-1812 m Nancy Strode Pvt MA
Abraham: b 9-16-1750 d 3-27-1850 m Martha — Pvt CT
Adonijah: b 10-13-1738 d 10-3-1809 m Olive Harrington Pvt VT
Almarin: b 9-7-1756 d 1-25-1824 m Sarah Champney Ens NJ ★
Asa: b 4-30-1761 d p. 1789 m Rebecca Sawyer Pvt MA
Benjamin, Jr.: b 9-4-1752 d 1- -1800 m Margaret Sprigg Bowie Maj MD
Benjamin: b 1729 d 6-7-1790 m Elizabeth Green Pvt MA
Benjamin: b 3-11-1753 d 12-21-1838 m (1)Elizabeth Harkins (2)Mary Wood Sgt PA
Castleton: b c. 1749 d 1777 m Elizabeth — CS VA
Charles: b — d — m Rachel Atwood Church Slr
Charles: b 4-6-1732 d 3-8-1798 m Mary Hapgood Pvt MA
Cornelius: b 3-17-1758 d 5-9-1837 m Mary Hyndshaw Fif MM PA★
Daniel: b 9-6-1764 d 9-20-1839 m Bathsheba Dakin Pvt MA
Daniel: b 12-20-1751 d 11-4-1816 m Patty — Pvt NY
David: b 8-14-1744 d 1802 m Elizabeth Doolittle CS Pvt CT
David: b 3-29-1749 d 9-7-1840 m Patience White Pvt MA
David: b 10-22-1754/5 d 3-5-1841 m Waity Blanchard Pvt MA ★
Ebenezer: b 1-27-1723 d p. 1790 m Mary Glazier Pvt CT
Ebenezer: b 1763 d 3-8-1847 m Eda Wheeler Pvt MA ★
Edward: b 3-16-1728 d 1- -1776 m Anna Hayward Lt MA
Edward: b 11-4-1743 d 5-6-1781 m Abigail Brown Chp MA
Edward: b 6-10-1758 d 6- -1827 m Margaret Garretson Pvt PA
Eleazer: b 9-10-1726 d 11-9-1806 m Mrs Elizabeth Greenough BGen MA
Elijah: b 1-21-1757 d 11-18-1843 m Mary Hall Pvt MA
Elisha: b 4-16-1761 d 1806-12 m Nancy Butler 1Lt SC
Enoch: b 3-16-1741/2 d 9-18-1825 m Hannah Jones CS Lt MA
Enos: b 4-11-1735 d 9-27-1798 m Lois Williams Cpl CT
Ephraim, Sr.: b 7-13-1725 d 7-16-1792 m Sarah Heywood Pvt CS PS MA
Ephraim, Jr.: b 4-27-1753 d 3-29-1799 m Susannah Eastabrook Pvt MA
Esau: b c. 1745 d 4-7-1797 m (1)Mary — (2)Mary Hawkins Pvt MD
Francis: b 1751 d 3-20-1819 m Susanna Stuart Pvt MA ★
Hannahhah: b 1752 d 7-4-1849 m Elizabeth Spooner Pvt MA ★
Isaac: b 8-24-1745 d 1797 m Jemima Wright Pvt CT
Isaac: b 1735 d 1825 m (1)Ruth Terrell (2)Mrs Hannah Harper Pvt CS NC
Jabez: b 5-4-1729 d 5-11-1817 m Sarah Smith Capt CT
Jacob: b 1740 d 1786 m Mary — Sol SC
James: b 1758 d 12-30-1832 m Lydia King Pvt CT
James: b 1758/9 d 1828 m Elizabeth Traylor Sol GA
James: b 8-6-1723 d 1801 m Elizabeth Bathrick Pvt MA
James: b 11-10-1760 d 1-22-1814 m Phebe Collar Pvt MA
James: b 1-7-1729 d 1-7-1812 m Mary Johnson Pvt NJ
James: b c. 1725 d 1812 m (1)Elizabeth Smith (2)Margaret Thomason (3)Eunity — Pvt SC
James: b a. 1750 d 1800 m Susan Price Sgt VA

James: b 4-24-1750 d 1815 m Elizabeth Woods Pvt VA
Jehiel: b 1735 d 1789 m Susanna Whitney Pvt MA
Joab: b 1753 d 1803 m Catherine Campbell Sol GA
Joab, Sr.: b c. 1735 d 11- -1775 m Katharine Dimmaux CS NC
Job: b 2-11-1757 d p. 1832 m Sarah Hildreth Pvt MA ★
Joel, Sr.: b 7-25-1721 d 5-11-1811 m (1)Sarah Drury (2)Mrs Mary Hall Pvt MA
Joel, Jr.: b 2-19-1760 d 1- -1859 m (1)Lydia Baker (2)Patty Jackson Pvt MA
John, Sr.: b 10-9-1739 d 1788 m Dorothy Birdseye PS CT
John, Jr.: b 11-3-1763 d 1861 m Mary Coe Pvt CT ★
John: b 5- -1752 d 3-1-1825 m Lucy Smith LCol MA
John: b 12-17-1728 d 1784 m Eunice Derby Pvt MA
John: b 2-8-1753 d 3-8-1820 m Rachel Taylor Pvt MA
John: b c. 1755 d 5-8-1813 m Remember Proctor Mate MA
John: b 8-11-1757 d 4-2-1832 m Martha Prentice Matr MA
John: b 2-24-1760 d 6-12-1851 m Betsey Woods Pvt NH
John: b 12-4-1755 d 9-22-1846 m (1)Rachel Blizzard (2)Mrs Orilla Hancock Lt NY ★
John: b 2-22-1741 d 12-31-1834 m Anne Paul Pvt NY
John: b 11-10-1755 d p. 1804 m Mary Potter PS NY
John: b 1760 d 1835 m Mary Polk Pvt NC
John: b c. 1750 d 1811 m Sarah — Sol NC
John: b c. 1745 d a. 10- -1815 m Lilly Ann — Pvt SC
John, Jr.: b 1-18-1750 d 1-22-1835 m Nancy — Pvt VA MD
John: b 1- -1730 d 1793 m Annie Irvin Pvt VA
John: b 1750 d 1826 m Sarah Adams Pvt VA
John: b 11-16-1748 d 3-12-1840 m (1) X (2)Sarah Faulkner Pvt PS VA
Jonathan: b 3-25-1743 d c. 1815 m Chloe Bradley Pvt CT
Jonathan: b 5-13-1738 d 4-3-1829 m Elizabeth Bradt Pvt NY
Joseph: b 1753 d 8-17-1808 m Amanda Collins Pvt CT
Joseph: b 1716 d 12- -1796 m Rebecca — PS CT
Joseph: b 8-27-1747 d 12-20-1820 m Lydia Stetson Pvt MA
Joseph: b 12-28-1759 d 1-18-1810 m (2)Rebecca Wyman Pvt MA
Joshua: b 2-11-1755 d 11-8-1825 m (1)Martha Barrett (2)Sarah Davis Pvt MA
Josiah: b 10-25-1759 d 2-9-1838 m Abigail Goslee Cpl CT ★
Josiah: b c. 1745 d 6-17-1775 m Rebecca Smith Pvt MA
Lemuel: b 3-13-1742 d 10-27-1815 m Hannah Raymond PS Pvt CT
Lemuel: b 2-20-1748 d 1831 m (1)Kezia Haskill (2)Esther Sprague Sol CT
Levi: b 7-24-1758 d 1831 m Bettsa Flint Pvt MA ★
Luke: b 8-10-1731 d 1-7-1817 m Lucy Whaler Pvt MA
Luther: b 1763 d 4-30-1826 m (1)Thankful Huxley (2)Miriam Gleason Pvt MA
Matthew: b 1744 d 1-13-1825 m (1)Ruth Hunt (2)Mrs Dolly Kimbel Sgt MA
Micajah: b 12-25-1761 d 6-15-1862 m (1)Mary Hunter (2)Margaret T. Carter Pvt SC GA ★
Middleton: b 1759 d 11-15-1851 m Sallie Smith Pvt VA ★
Moses: b 4-1-1760 d 1-25-1830 m Agnes (Gamble)Fowler Lt VA
Nathan: b c. 7-2-1761 d 8-11-1848 m Lucy Jones Pvt MA ★
Oliver: b 1759 d 1-14-1849 m (1)Anne Wetherell (2)Rachel Bacon Pvt NJ ★
Peter: b 1732 d 3-8-1825 m Francynje Wendell Pvt NY
Porter: b 9-12-1755 d p. 1790 m Elizabeth Clarke Pvt CT
Reuben: b 10-19-1763 d 10-21-1843 m (1)Rocksa — (2)Esther Clark Pvt CT ★
Reuben: b 1-8-1744 d 6- -1776 m Abigail Cleaveland Slr MA
Richard: b 6-7-1758 d 7-13-1783 m Rachel Gantt PS MD
Robert: bpt 6-23-1754 d p. 1806 m Rebecca Hopkinson Pvt MA
Robert, R: b 1723 d a. 6-9-1806 m Abigail — Pvt PS VA
Ruben: b 6-15-1763 d 1-15-1843 m Anna — Pvt MA ★
Samuel: b 4-4-1738 d 1812 m Ruth Doolittle Capt CT
Samuel: b 1-20-1745 d p. 1788 m (1)Rachel Brainard (2)Jemima Stocking Brooks Capt CT
Samuel: b 5-14-1730 d 3-12-1816 m Dorothy Smith Lt CT
Samuel: bpt 6-18-1749 d 4-22-1826 m Olive Knight Sgt MA ★
Samuel: b 8-24-1729 d 3-21-1807 m (1)Elizabeth Pike (2)Tirzah James PS CS NH
Samuel: b 1-29-1758 d 9-26-1839 m Sarah Wallace Ens PA
Samuel: b c. 1755 d a. 1830 m Sarah Van Tromp Pvt PA
Samuel: b 1- -1750 d a. 9-22-1806 m Mary Penrose Pvt VA
Samuel Lewis: b 1760 d 1-23-1846 m Phebe Beers Gnr CT ★
Sarah Boone: b 11-24-1763 d 12-31-1848 m (1)Thomas Brooks (2)David Montgomery PS KY
Seth: b 1740 d 1-9-1831 m Molly Conant Pvt MA
Shadrach: b 1758 d 1834 m Esther Brown Pvt MM MA ★
Silas: b 1760 d 1-23-1849 m Elizabeth — Pvt CT ★
Simeon: b 1740 d 5-9-1815 m (2)Lois Church Sol CT
Simon: b 9-21-1722 d 1806 m Rachael Drury Pvt CS MA
Simon: b 11-27-1760 d 5-31-1836 m Hannah Owen Grd MA
Solomon: b 5-5-1754 d 2-8-1836 m Lois (Brooks) Cpl MA
Stephen: b 12-1-1756 d 5- -1836 m Prudence Whitcomb Pvt MA
Stephen: b 3-22-1719 d 1-29-1848 m Rachel Taylor Pvt MA
Thomas: b 1-10-1761 d 6-12-1839 m Zurviah Collins Pvt CT ★
Thomas: b 11-22-1763 d 5-24-1835 m Esther Beers Pvt CT W★
Thomas: b 1-6-1732 d 3-7-1799 m Anna Hall CS MA
Thomas: b 1728 d 3-3-1803 m Katherine Smith PS NJ
Thomas, Sr.: b c. 1720 d 1796 m Mary — PS NC
Thomas, Jr.: b c. 1743 d 7-31-1812 m Martha Temple Pvt NC
Thomas: b 12-2-1750 d 11-29-1790 m Mary Richardson Pvt PA
Thomas: b c. 1738 d a. 1823 m Hannah Anderson Pvt PA

BROOKS, contd.
Thomas: b *a*. 1760 d 4-15-1800 m Sarah Boone Pvt VA
Thomas: b *c*. 1745 d 10-4-1795 m (2)Elizabeth — PS VA
Wm.: b 1761 d 1842 m Elizabeth — Pvt GA
Wm.: b 2-19-1752 d 1821 m (1)Bettey Stodder (2)Lucy Stodder Sgt MA
Wm, Sr.: b 3-3-1737 d 10-11-1804 m Abigail Kemp 2Lt NH
Wm, Jr.: b 5-1-1760 d 9-5-1843 m Deborah Parker Sgt NH
Wm.: b 1750 d 1827 m Hannah Jones Pvt NY
Wm.: b 2-3-1752 d 1-24-1841 m Nancy — Pvt VA ★
Wm, T.: b *c*. 1744 d 3- -1825 m Mary Gilliam Pvt VA
Zachariah: b 4-20-1742 d 2-5-1792 m (1)Hannah Wild (2)Susanna Watts Lt MA
Zachariah Smith: b 5-18-1765 d 4-6-1849 m Elizabeth Butler Pvt SC

BROOKSHIRE,
Manring: b 1754 d 12-23-1843 m Prudence — Lt NC ★

BROOME, (includes BROOM)
Jacob: b 1752 d 4-25-1810 m Rachel Pierce MilS CS DE
John: b 1726 d 1797 m Mary Mackall PS MD
John: b 1738 d 8-8-1810 m Rebecca Lloyd LCol PS NY
John: b — d *p*. 1784 m Sarah Isdall Pvt PA
Samuel: b *c*. 1735 d 6-29-1810 m Phoebe Platt Capt PS NY

BROOMHALL,
John: b 6-10-1752 d 3-17-1835 m X Pvt PA

BROSIUS,
Abraham, Jr.: b 1754 d 1-6-1833 m Rosanna Grau — Pvt PA ★
Henry: b 1768 d 12-28-1816 m Mary Roberts Cpl PA
Jacob: b 1744 d 12-6-1822 m Kathrine Newman Pvt PA
Nicholas: b 12-23-1754 d 12-13-1833 m Anna Maria Reitz Pvt PA

BROSS, (includes BROST)
Hermanus: b 2-21-1746 d 11-20-1834 m (1)Jennie Smith (2)Caty Smith (3)Elizabeth Ann Aller Pvt NJ ★
Michael: b *c*. 1730 d *p*. 1779 m X PS PA

BROTHERS,
Jacob: b 1749 d 1822 m Barbara Little (Klein) Sgt PA
John: b 1755 d 1820 m Lydia Berry Pvt NC
Mathias: b 1758 d 9-5-1828 m X Sol PA

BROTHERTON,
James: b — d *c*. 1785 m Jane Pownall Pvt PA
James, Sr.: b 8-28-1726 d *p*. 1790 m Alice Schooley Lt PA
James, Jr.: b 12-20-1761 d 1800 m Martha Caldwell Pvt PA
James: b — d 3-30-1809 m Jane Henry Pvt PA

BROTHWELL,
Benjamin: b 11-3-1760 d 6-18-1845 m Anna Beach Cpl CT ★
Joseph: b 1727 d 1-27-1811 m Hannah Fairweather Lt CT
Joseph Fayerweather: b 3-30-1758 d *p*. 1833 m (1)Molly Lacy Sgt CT ★
Thomas: b 8-17-1766 d 4-14-1842 m (2)Nancy Webb Pvt CT ★

BROTZMAN, (includes BRAKEMAN, PROTZMAN)
Lawrence: b 8-4-1751 d 9- -1823 m Elizabeth Miller Sgt MD
Ludovic: b 1735 d 1814 m Eva Bleecker Capt NY
Nicholas: b 1746 d 1824/5 m Gertrund Hertzel Pvt PA

BROUGH, (includes BROACH, BRUCH)
Daniel: b 7-19-1762 d 12-26-1825 m Elizabeth — Sol PA
Herman, Jr.: b *a*. 1752 d *a*. 6- -1796 m Christina Deardorff PS PA
Hermanus: b 1722 d *p*. 8-13-1794 m Catharine — PS PA
Jacob: b 7-5-1752 d 9-25-1828 m Sophia Trimmer Pvt PA
Jones: b *c*. 1755 d 1-5-1809 m Elizabeth — Pvt NC

BROUGHT,
Daniel: b 1-10-1760 d 2-7-1820 m Ann Pyle Pvt PA

BROUGHTON,
Charles: b 8-14-1737 d 11-6-1790 m Elizabeth Greene PS VA
Ebenezer: b 1760 d 10- -1832 m Lois Sargeant Mus CT
John: b 2-9-1744 d 9-26-1805 m Hannah — Pvt CT W★
John, Sr.: b 6-16-1717 d *p*. 10- -1777 m Anna Ainsworth Pvt CT
John, Jr.: b 9-10-1754 d 5-31-1811 m Lucy Perkins Pvt VT
Michael: b 1763 d 12-15-1815 m Sarah Richards Sol CT
Nathan: b 6- -1752-60 d — m Elizabeth Clark Pvt CT
Nickolson, Sr.: b 9-13-1724 d 8-3-1798 m Sarah Martin Pedrick Maj MA
Nickolson, Jr.: b 10-29-1764 d 6-21-1804 m Susanna Glover Sol MA
Thomas: b 4-18-1760 d 2-14-1835 m Mary Wallace Lt SC ★
Wm.: b 1725 d 6-12-1798 m Hannah — Sgt Maj VA

BROUILLETTE,
Michael: b *c*. 1745 d 1-6-1796 m Mary Louise Bonneau Lt PS VA

BROUSE, (includes BRAUSE, BRAUSS)
Adam: b *c*. 1750 d 1802 m Catherine — Pvt PA
Henry: b *c*. 1740 d *c*. 1821 m Anna Craven Pvt PA
Michael: b 4-3-1755 d 11-6-1854 m — Duck Pvt PA ★

BROUSSARD,
Augustine: b 1747-50 d *a*. 7-30-1811 m Anne Lendrie — Sol LA
Pierre: b 1753 d 12-12-1828 m (1)Marie Malancon (2)Marguerite Guidry PS LA

BROWDER,
Edmund: b *c*. 1725 d 1784 m X Sol NC
Isham: b 6-12-1762 d 2-19-1830 m (1)Rachel Slayton (2)Elizabeth Scarce Pvt VA W★

BROWER, (includes BROUWER)
Abraham: b 9-4-1763 d 3- -1826 m Phebe Maybee Pvt NJ
Adolphus: b *c*. 1740 d *p*. 3-13-1825 m Altie Hulst Pvt NY
Cornelius: b 11-9-1730 d 10-22-1805 m Mary Archer Pvt NY
Daniel: bpt 1718 d *a*. 2-22-1791 m Marytin Konig Pvt PA
David: b 9-18-1728 d 8-18-1814 m Ariantje Stymets Pvt NJ
David: b 1758 d *p*. 1782 m Ann Morris Pvt NJ
Elias: b 3-22-1741 d 4-5-1812 m Phebe Lucas Pvt NY
Garret: b 1749 d 3-24-1832 m Anna Seger Pvt NY
Hendricks: b 3- -1765 d 2-20-1829 m Anne Hawk Pvt VA ★
Jacob: b 4-7-1726 d 8-26-1784 m Jannetje Vanderbeck Pvt NJ
Jacob: bpt 1-7-1721 d 1806 m Elsie Hickock Pvt NY
Jacob: b 3-6-1740 d *p*. 1790 m Margaret Vreeland Pvt NY
John: b 3-26-1733 d 1801 m Rachel Van Bruckle Pvt NJ
John: b 9-12-1759 d 8-8-1846 m Elizabeth Gause Pvt NY
John: b *c*. 1755 d *c*. 1841 m Elizabeth Duryee PS NY
John: b *c*. 1738 d *p*. 1792 m X Sgt PA
Nazareth: b 10-26-1756 d 11-9-1817 m (1)Jane Brower (2)Deborah Wiltsie Sol NY
Nicholas: b 3-8-1747 d — m Mary Birdsall Capt NY
Peter: b 1745 d 2-28-1799 m Magadelena Snyder Pvt PA
Wm.: b 1745 d *p*. 1784 m Elizabeth Rendell Pvt NY

BROWN, (includes BROUN, BROWNE)
Aaron: b 12-17-1758 d 1838 m Elizabeth Gillette Pvt NY
Aaron: b 2-28-1757 d 1-25-1830 m (1)Nancy Harwell (2)Elizabeth Melton (3)Mrs Susan Stockett Pvt VA PA
Abel: b 2-19-1756 d 3-1-1823 m Mary Parlin Pvt MA
Abel: b 1764 d 2-22-1837 d Sally Stoddard Pvt MA ★
Abia: b 9-2-1743 d 4-15-1785 m Margaret Sharp PS NJ
Abial: b 4-25-1755 d 4-11-1839 m (1)Hopestill Brown (2)Lucy Taylor Adj MA RI ★
Abial: b 3-26-1727 d 8-18-1821 m Abigail Bucklin Lt RI
Abijah: b 11-27-1736 d 5-25-1818 m Sarah Sterns LCol MA
Abishai: b 5-2-1746 d 4-13-1799 m Jerusha (Brown) Maj MA
Abner: b *c*. 1727 d *p*. 1790 m (1)Dorcas Greenwood (2)Mrs Mehitabel Russell Pvt MA
Abraham: b 7-1-1740 d 1-8-1777 m Beulah Patterson Sol MA
Abraham: b 5-8-1753 d 3-8-1824 m Mary Butler Ens NH W★
Abraham: b 4-23-1730 d *p*. 4-17-1794 m Mary Trotter Pvt PA
Absalom: b 12-16-1760 d 7-13-1837 m Abigail Bean Pvt VT
Adam: b — d 1840 m Priscilla Putnam Sgt NH
Adam: b 5-8-1738 d 3-4-1806 m Juliana Catharine — Pvt PA
Adam: b 10-28-1742 d 8-23-1828 m Catherine (Brown) Pvt PA
Adam: b 11-1-1760 d 10-1-1820 m Christina Statler Pvt PA
Adley: b *c*. 1750 d *p*. 3-28-1814 m Tamer Forrester Pvt PA
Alexander: b 1720 d *c*. 4-9-1801 m Amitta Smith Pvt CT
Alexander: b 10-3-1745 d 7- -1795 m Rebekah Hutchinson PS NC
Alexander: b *c*. 1763 d 1791 m Jane Alexander LCol PA
Alexander: b *c*. 1755 d 7-1-1823 m Anna Horton Pvt PA ★
Alexander: b 1759 d *p*. 1820 m Jane — Pvt PA ★
Allan: b 1729 d 10-14-1808 m (1)Mary Brotherton (2)Margaret Oliver Pvt PA
Alpheus, Sr.: b 3-25-1762 d 1-12-1842 m Abigail Pierce Pvt MA
Amasa: b 4-27-1754 d 1-21-1830 m (1)Mary — (2)Deborah Carr Pvt MA
Ambrose: b 3-8-1767 d 4-26-1841 m Susanna — Pvt MA ★
Amos: b 10-28-1730 d 1-12-1817 m Eunice Turner Pvt CS CT
Amos: b 9-18-1738 d 2-3-1812 m Anna Sanderson Lt MA
Amos: b 8-18-1741 d *p*. 1790 m Rachael Reed Sgt MA
Amos: b 3-3-1752 d 1824/5 m (1)Sarah Cilley (2)Hannah Proctor Pvt MA
Andrew: b 11-22-1748 d 1-28-1813 m Sarah Cobb Grd CT
Andrew: b 1723 d 11-26-1789 m Ann — CS MA
Andrew: b 1760 d 6-8-1842 m Mary Webber Pvt MA
Andrew: b 1759 d 3-27-1823 m Jane Bigham Pvt PA
Andrew: b 9-20-1706 d 2-12-1783 m Mary Knowlton PS RI
Andrew: b — d *p*. 1783 m X Sol NC
Andrew: b *c*. 1760 d 1804 m Mary — Pvt VA
Angus: b 1745 d 9-10-1820 m Mary McFarland Sol NC
Anthony: b 10-1-1758 d 1-7-1845 m Esther Bailey Pvt RI
Arabia: b 11-27-1755 d 3-13-1844 m Elizabeth Dooley Pvt VA ★
Archibald: b *p*. 1739 d *p*. 1790 m Rebecka — Pvt NY
Archibald: b 1-7-1753 d 12-14-1797 m Mary Deas Capt SC W ★
Arthur: b *c*. 1746 d *c*. 9-16-1783 m Mary — 2Maj NC
Asa: b 7-29-1740 d 1-15-1818 m Deborah Grant Pvt CT
Asa: b 1-14-1746 d 11-8-1812 m Mrs Sarah (Trow) Trask Sgt MA
Austin: b 7-31-1762 d 4-26-1837 m Anna Fox Cpl CT
Azariah: b 8-16-1745 d 5-4-1807 m Amy Post Pvt CT
Barnabus: b 1-3-1762 d 12-6-1855 m Nancy Medbury Pvt MA
Barron: b *c*. 1753 d *p*. 1790 m Elizabeth Snow Pvt MA
Bartholomew: b 7-3-1752 d 11-2-1829 m Lucy Chubb Pvt MA
Bartlett, Sr.: b 1731 d 1789 m Katherine Holcomb Sol SC

Bartlett, Jr.: b 1-15-1755 d 12-6-1822 m Patience Overstreet Pvt SC
Bazaleel: b 7-29-1754 d 1-4-1829 m Mary Thompson Capt VA
Bazil: b 10-25-1732 d 2-10-1807 m Elizabeth Brashear Pvt MD
Benjamin: b c. 1734 d 1792 m Hannah Benjamin PS CT
Benjamin: b 9-16-1740 d 3-27-1809 m Sarah Keeney PS CT
Benjamin: b 3-13-1770 d 9-1-1865 m (1)Ann Beebe PS CT
Benjamin: b 2-17-1763 d 2-27-1846 m Nancy Brown Sol GA
Benjamin: b 10-17-1745 d 10-1-1821 m Jean Thomas Capt MA ★
Benjamin, Sr.: b 6-30-1720 d 3-4-1802 m Sarah Reed Pvt PS MA
Benjamin, Jr.: b 1-1-1744 d 10-20-1792 m Esther Whittemore Pvt MA
Benjamin: b 1746 d 1828 m Sarah Pillsbury Pvt MA
Benjamin: b 5-31-1757 d — m Nanny Merrill Pvt MA
Benjamin: b 4-4-1762 d 1807 m Catharine Stuart Pvt MA
Benjamin: b 9-23-1756 d 9-7-1831 m Susannah Wells Dr MA
Benjamin: b 4-14-1713 d 5-7-1797 m Submit Ward Pvt PS NH
Benjamin: b 10-14-1755 d 4-13-1818 m (1)Prudence Kelley (2)Mary Lunt Pvt NH
Benjamin: b 1721 d 7-12-1807 m Abigail Longfellow PS NH
Benjamin: b 5- -1763 d 1-4-1838 m Rebecca Wright Pvt Smn NJ ★
Benjamin: b 2- -1750 d 2-7-1838 m Christina Sherwood Lt NY
Benjamin: b 11-11-1741 d 12-22-1822 m Sarah Case Pvt NY
Benjamin: b 1751 d a. 1790 m Susanna Westcott Pvt NY
Benjamin: b c. 1730 d 2- -1778 m Ruth Langston Cpl NC
Benjamin, Sr.: b c. 1735 d 1778-90 m Sapphira — PS NC
Benjamin, Jr.: b 1764 d 9-28-1822 m Elizabeth Mooring Pvt NC
Benjamin: b 10-17-1756 d 1-29-1815 m Patience Devol Pvt RI
Benjamin: b 10-1-1751 d 1842 m Mary Jarman Pvt VA
Beriah: b 1-16-1715 d 7-8-1792 m (1)Elizabeth Smith (2)Elizabeth Babcock CS RI
Bernard: b 1-28-1750 d 2-26-1800 m Elizabeth Dabney PS VA
Bernis: b c. 1747 d 1815 m Henrietta Rodes PS VA
Berryman: b 6- -1742 d 7-9-1793 m Mary Noell Smn VA
Brightberry: b 1762 d 1-26-1846 m Susan Thompson Sgt Maj VA
Bowman: b 7-1-1738 d 7-30-1806 m Abigail Page Lt VT
Caleb: b 8-11-1760 d 3-7-1842 m Annie Sweat Cpl MA NH ★
Caleb: b 4-2-1754 d 5-22-1827 m Amy Mason Pvt MA
Caleb: b 1742 d 1822 m Mary Lyford Pvt NH
Caleb: b 12-29-1753 d 1-8-1817 m Sarah Elwell Pvt NY
Chad: b 4-28-1729 d 9-19-1814 m Zerviah Evans Col PS RI
Charles: b 8-6-1759 d 5-21-1837 m Hannah Palmer Pvt CT ★
Charles: b 5-9-1762 d 4-20-1819 m Susannah C Tennent Lt SC
Charles: b c. 1755 d 1831 m Mary Snead Pvt VA
Charles Benjamin: b 1742 d 12-20-1816 m Sarah Gorton Cpl CT
Christian: b 1-30-1741 d p. 1781 m Elizabeth Hager Capt NY
Christian, 2d.: b 12-8-1740 d 9-27-1821 m Anna Maria Lawall Pvt PA
Christopher: b 3-12-1736 d 10-20-1820 m Margaret Holmes Capt CT
Christopher: b c. 1764 d 9-9-1807 m Eunice Lee Pvt CT
Christopher: b 4-30-1745 d p. 1832 m Hannah Terry PS NY
Christopher: b 7-16-1751 d 7-16-1816 m Maria Mason Pvt PA
Clarke: b 3-14-1748 d 1-30-1819 m Mary Mott 2Lt QM RI
Clement: b c. 1750 d 1836 m X Sol VA
Cornelius: b c. 1747 d a. 8-2-1795 m (1)Elizabeth Schesnut (2)Maria Magdalena Haffner Pvt PA
Cornelius: b 6-11-1759 d — m Jane Rowland CS VA
Daniel: b 1-15-1746 d 6-1-1832 m Anna Phelps QM Sgt CT
Daniel: b 11-3-1743 d 10-7-1788 m Hannah English Pvt CT
Daniel: b 1-24-1752 d 10-11-1842 m Lydia Rogers Pvt Mar CT ★
Daniel: b 1759 d 4-4-1842 m Amy — Pvt CT ★
Daniel: b 8-16-1747 d 12-31-1840 m Chloe Bucklen Capt MA
Daniel, Jr.: b 12-10-1750 d 9-14-1818 m Margaret Elliott Pvt MA
Daniel: b 12-17-1761 d 6-12-1826 m Jennet Moore Pvt MA
Daniel: b 1747 d 11-9-1776 m Eunice Baldwin 2Lt NJ
Daniel: b 7-1-1742 d 10-6-1822 m Hannah Brown Maj NJ
Daniel: b 11-9-1759 d 9-3-1831 m Margaret Warne Pvt NJ
Daniel: b 1744 d 12-13-1806 m Sarah — Pvt PS NY
Daniel: b 7-18-1753 d 10-24-1837 m Martha Rogers Pvt NY
Daniel: b 6-25-1753 d 3-25-1795 m Polly Calloway Dr VA
Daniel: b 5-6-1737 d 1789 m Mary Miller PS NC
Daniel: b 12-1-1748 d 7-14-1833 m Elizabeth Hill Pvt QM Sgt VA ★
Daniel: b 6- -1755 d 2- -1839 m Mary Pemberton Sol VA
David: b 1748 d 1833 m Catherine Avery Pvt CT ★
David: b 7-2-1758 d 9-14-1825 m Lydia Minor Sol CT
David: b 3-12-1732 d 5-22-1802 m Abigail Munroe Capt MA
David: b 6-3-1744 d — m Hannah Alden Lt MA
David: b 3-22-1746 d 1824 m Mercy Jackson 2Lt MA
David: b 1740 d p. 1790 m Mary Emerson Pvt MA
David: b 10-2-1741 d — m Eunice Hinckley Pvt MA
David: b 6-18-1756 d — m Rachel Cahoon Pvt MA
David: b 5-1-1758 d 1826 m Sybil Chamberlin Pvt MA
David: b 1727 d 11-18-1778 m Isabelle McClintock Pvt NC
David: b 1717 d 1791 m Ameriah — 1Lt PA
David: b 1752 d 1816-18 m X Pvt PA
David: b 1757 d 1820 m Salina Stuthern Pvt PA
David: b 7-13-1757 d 1-23-1841 m Margaret Oliver Pvt PA
David: b 9-5-1757 d 10-18-1849 m Chloe Carpenter Lt RI ★
David: b 1744 d 11-20-1828 m Letitia Cruce Sgt SC
David: b 1744 d 12-26-1799 m (1)Sarah Hite (2)Naomi Hurford PS Wgn VA
Ebenezer: b 11-10-1751 d 11-15-1847 m (1) X (2)Sarah Gee (3)Abigail Baldwin Cpl CT

Ebenezer: b 1725 d 9-15-1803 m Sarah — Pvt CT
Ebenezer: b 1752 d 1-3-1833 m Molly Redway Pvt CT
Ebenezer: b 10-14-1744 d — m Elizabeth Perkins Pvt MA
Ebenezer: b 2-12-1757 d p. 1785 m Bridget Bryant Pvt MA
Ebenezer: b 8-15-1752 d 4-1-1834 m (1)Rebecca Witt (2)Lydia Coggeswell Sgt MA ★
Ebenezer: b c. 1758 d 1-19-1839 m Pamelia Ferris Ens NY
Ebenezer: b 6-23-1745 d 4-30-1787 m Susannah Bradford Pvt NY
Ebenezer: b 9-20-1716 d 1-2-1792/3 m Mary Congdon Pvt RI
Edward: b 3-16-1734 d 8-14-1823 m (1)Margaret Durbin Pvt MD
Edward: b 1716 d 6-2-1803 m Hannah Thomas Pvt CS MA
Eleazer: b 7-4-1758 d 3-21-1818 m Edith Palmer Pvt CT
Eleazer: b 12-31-1736 d a. 3-23-1822 m Sarah Scott CS MA
Eliada: b 7-30-1761 d 1-23-1855 m (1)Phebe Stevens (2)Nancy Brown Pvt NH
Elias: b 3-16-1758 d 1-18-1843 m (1)Prudence Fitch (2)Mrs Nancy Hart Fif Maj CT
Elias: b 2-24-1744 d 9-15-1806 m Sabra Billings PS CT
Elias: b 1-30-1762 d 1-29-1836 m Hepsibeth White Pvt RI ★
Elihu: b 8-16-1761 d 10-25-1840 m Mercy Thwing Pvt MA ★
Elihu: b 4-30-1750 d 2-29-1832 m Sarah Arnold Pvt RI
Elijah: b 1758 d 1-8-1835 m Phebe — Ens CT
Elijah: b 1760 d 1800 m Sarah Adams Pvt CT
Elijah: b 8-4-1730 d 12-18-1819 m (1)Sarah Whittlesey (2)Phebe Nash PS MA
Elijah: b 4-10-1752 d 4-13-1801 m Anna Ballou Pvt PS RI
Elisha: b 1731 d 9-28-1813 m Content Leeds Pvt CT
Elisha: b c. 1751 d p. 5-25-1836 m Nancy — Pvt GA
Elisha, Sr.: b 1737 d 4- -1799 m Mrs Elizabeth Roberts Lt MA
Elisha: b 8-8-1748 d 9-10-1827 m Merrial Bates Cpl MA ★
Ephraim: b 1-23-1748/9 d 6-27-1815 m (1)Rachel Carpenter (2)Mercy Atkinson Cpl MA
Ephraim: b 11-7-1710 d 10-9-1788 m Abigail Wheeler Pvt MA
Ephraim: b 6-19-1717 d p. 1780 m Anna Twist MM MA
Ephraim: b 1753 d 1833 m Mabel Nason Pvt MA
Ephraim: b 3-27-1758 d 1-20-1839 m Sibyl Wright Fif Pvt MA
Ephraim: b 12-20-1742 d 1-16-1812 m Sybil Patterson Pvt PS NH
Eseck: b 11-1-1755 d 5-12-1843 m Mary Bowen Sgt RI ★
Esek: b 9-7-1757 d 10-22-1839 m Mary Sayles Ens RI
Ezekiel: b 8-10-1755 d — m Elizabeth Mallet Pvt Drm MA
Ezekiel: b 3-13-1760 d 4-23-1841 m Jane Smith Pvt Spy PA ★
Ezekiel: b 10-11-1749 d 2-15-1801 m Ruth Winsor Lt RI
Ezra: b 11-2-1750 d 2-19-1829 m Jane Stocker Pvt Drm MA
Francis: b c. 1728 d 12-12-1796 m (1)Mary Guerin (2)Mary Boone Capt CS PS GA
Francis: b 1-22-1737 d 4-21-1800 m Mary Buckman MM Capt MA
Francis: b 4-16-1755 d 3-18-1827 m Anna Brown Ens MA
Frederick: b 1743 d 1803 m Polly Steagall Mil VA
Frederick Ferdinand: b 11-8-1761 d 4-3-1851 m (1)Ruth Eames (2)Mrs Mary Burrill Chandler Pvt MA
George: b 1765 d 12-10-1846 m (1)Barbara Wasnbouoy (2)Mrs Margaret Sowers Pvt NC ★
George, Jr.: b c. 1755 d 2-1-1826 m Susan Harvey 2Lt PA
George: b c. 1750 d 2-20-1840 m Mary Glass Pvt PA
George: b 1746 d 6-19-1836 m Hannah Robinson PS RI
George: b 6-22-1760 d 9-21-1825 m (1)Margaret Conrad (2)Hannah John Sgt VA
Gershom: b 12-8-1760 d 12-3-1843 m Eunice Parke Fif CT
Gershom: b 1-28-1747 d 9-22-1801 m Mary — PS NY
Gideon: b — d p. 4-19-1806 m (1)Ruth — (2)Sarah — Pvt RI
Gustavus Richard: b 10-17-1747 d 9-30-1804 m Margaret Graham Dr PS MD
Henry: b — d 5-20-1822 m Lydia Humphreys Sgt CT
Henry: b 12-2-1730 d p. 2- -1815 m Rachel Burger Pvt NJ
Henry: b 1756 d 1824 m Mary Smith Pvt NC
Henry: b 9-11-1757 d 4-28-1801 m Julianna Rose Lt PA
Henry: b c. 1745 d p. 1812 m X Ens VA
Hope: b 7-22-1742 d 4-10-1812 m Ruth Hosmer Cpl MA
Hugh: b 4-21-1730 d 6-4-1815 m Olive Sage Pvt CT
Hugh: b 2-16-1755 d 7-11-1811 m Ruth Barney PS MD
Hugh: b 1717/8 d 10-8-1794 m (1) X (2)Mary Bine Sol NC
Hugh: b 6-20-1745 d 9-23-1816 m Isabel Gilkerson Pvt VA
Humphrey: b 1760 d 2-23-1843 m Oliver Mallason Pvt Fif ★
Ichabod: b 2-14-1732 d 5-25-1797 m Thankful Baldwin Capt CT
Ichabod: b 3-23-1753 d 5-31-1850 m Submit Millard Pvt CT ★
Ichabod: b 1745 d 1829 m Hannah Ballou Ens RI
Isaac: b 1749 d 2-25-1816 m Hannah Hills Pvt CT W ★
Isaac: b c. 1740 d a. 1814 m — Brasilton Cpl MD
Isaac: b 11- -1753 d 12-22-1848 m (1)Hannah — (2)Lydia Ingalls Pvt NH ★
Isaac: b 12-16-1739 d p. 1790 m Agnes Fifield PS NH
Isaac: b 2-4-1752 d 1-28-1837 m Esther Barrington PS Sgt NY RI ★
Isaac: b 2-2-1758 d 3-25-1838 m Sarah Shute Cpl NY
Isaac: b c. 1755 d a. 10-14-1793 m Elizabeth — Pvt NC
Isaac: b 10-17-1756 d 7-22-1836 m Hannah Cook Pvt RI
Isaac: b 4-15-1756 d 10-26-1825 m Hester Williams Pvt VA ★
Isaiah: b 6-10-1745 d p. 1803 m (1)Phebe How (2)Abigail — Lt MA
Isham: b 1749 d 1846 m Martha Still Pvt VA ★
Israel: b 2-12-1754 d 1839 m Mariam — Pvt NY
Issacher: b 10-14-1760 d 6-17-1840 m Hannah Craven Pvt PA
Jabez: b 1-14-1748 d 11-22-1834 m Rebecca Smith Pvt CT

BROWN, contd.

Jacob: b 8-14-1755 d 3-16-1820 m Kerzia Ward Pvt CT
Jacob: b 12-7-1755 d 1-19-1834 m (1)Mehitable Morrill (2)Ruth Hoyt Ens MA
Jacob: b 7-24-1720 d 1-10-1789 m Lydia Weare Maj MA
Jacob: b 10-5-1728 d 1776 m Anna — Capt MA
Jacob: b 1731 d 4-26-1812 m Eunice Eaton Pvt MA
Jacob: b 2-12-1763 d 2-29-1844 m Mary Welds Pvt MA
Jacob: b 2-1-1747 d 1-21-1833 m Sophia — Pvt NJ ★
Jacob, Sr.: b 12-4-1736 d 6-28-1785 m Ruth Gordon Col NC
Jacob, Jr.: b 8-3-1761 d 8-23-1838 m Elizabeth Bird Ens SC NC ★
Jacob: b 1750 d 10-5-1841 m (1)Elizabeth Artmire (2)Mary Salts Pvt NC
Jacob: b 1-14-1755 d 6-9-1831 m (1)Mary Armfield (2)Mary — Sol NC
Jacob Roberts (M.D.): b 11-7-1731 d 11-10-1805 m Christina Neely Lt SC
James: b 8-3-1753 d 12-4-1822 m Deborah Tarbox Cpl CT W ★
James: b 1-23-1715 d p. 1775 m Rebecca Perry Pvt CT
James: b 12-24-1762 d 11-3-1813 m Prudence Ladd Pvt CT
James: b 8-4-1753 d 11-24-1843 m Silence Bates Pvt CT W ★
James: b 3- -1753 d 1781 m Catherine McCormick Pvt MD
James: b c. 1754 d 12- -1780 m Mary Elwell Pvt MA
James 2nd.: b 9-5-1760 d 11-28-1836 m (1)Anna — (2)Mary Clark Pvt MA ★
James: b 3-11-1762 d 7-31-1834 m Katherine Barry Pvt MA
James: b 2-21-1744 d 3-6-1813 m Hannah Lembkin Pvt Cmsry NH
James: b 2-7-1743 d p. 1787 m Sarah Aldrich Pvt NH
James: b 1720 d 9-8-1785 m Dorothy — Pvt NY
James: b 1738 d 5-9-1788 m Jane Gillespie Pvt NC
James: b 5- -1742 d 11-6-1830 m (1)X (2)Mary Meach Noncom PA ★
James: b 2-1-1750 d 12-7-1826 m Elizabeth Thompson Pvt PA
James, Sr.: b 3-30-1724 d 5-29-1780 m (1)Eleanor Mordah (2)Mary McClelland (3)Susannah Simons PS PA
James, Sr.: b 1-2-1706 d 5-4-1777 m Ruth Pierce CS RI
James, Jr.: b 9-19-1731 d 2-2-1805 m Mary Anthony Ens RI
James: b 11-2-1763 d 1-18-1830 m Nancy Burdine Pvt SC
James: b — d a. 11-12-1805 m Susanna — Lt VA
James: b 1723 d 1804 m Elizabeth Poole Sgt VA
James: b 1760 d 12- -1829 m (2)Martha Venable Pvt VA
James: b c. 1720 d 12- -1793 m Sophia (Brown) Pvt VA
James: b 4-19-1742 d 6-24-1825 m (1)Anne Davis (2)Mrs Frances Dobbins Pvt VA
James M.: b 1752 d 1820 m Elizabeth Jones Sol VA
Jedediah: b 3-14-1729 d 10-31-1791 m Anna Holmes Pvt CT
Jedediah: b 9-10-1743 d 1815 Mary Lockwood Pvt CT
Jehu: b 4-28-1753 d p. 3-11-1840 m Sarah Gartrill Pvt PA
Jehu: b 6-11-1753 d 9-9-1817 m Abigail Rhodes Pvt VA
Jeremiah: bpt 11-9-1746 d — m Lucy Potter Pvt MA
Jeremiah: b a. 1749 d 1787 m Heart Allen Pvt MA
Jeremiah: b 3-16-1756 d 3-13-1813 m Abigail Lincoln Ens MA
Jeremiah: b 4-3-1762 d 12-28-1840 m Sarah Dalton Pvt NH
Jeremiah: b 10- -1757 d 1846 m Jane Kirk Pvt VA ★
Jesse: b — d 1818 m Anne Rudd CS PS CT
Jesse: b 4-1-1745 d 6-19-1822 m Mary Palmer Sgt CT
Jesse: b 2-11-1759 d 3-16-1835 m Delaney Alston Pvt GA
Jesse: b 12-3-1734 d 1814 m Lydia Smith Pvt MA
Jesse: b 6-8-1740 d 1824 m Hannah Gore Pvt MM MA
Jesse: b 3- -1763 d p. 2-27-1833 m Arabella Middleton Pvt NC ★
Jesse: b 1739 d 4-13-1813 m Mary — Pvt RI
Job: b 1756 d 1814 m Huldah Page Pvt PS NH
Job: b — d p. 1799 m Elizabeth Hopkins Pvt NJ
Job: b 7-1-1752 d 1-5-1826 m Jane Tompkins Pvt NJ
Joel: b 10-31-1754 d 4-3-1831 m Tryphena Ordway Sgt NH
John, 3d: b 11-4-1728 d 9-2-1776 m Hannah Owen Capt CT
John: b 4-2-1755 d 6-22-1835 m Phoebe Brown FifMaj CT
John: b 1757-8 d 1831 m Elizabeth — Pvt CT ★
John: b 10-25-1760 d 1-6-1837 m Elizabeth Dorman Pvt CT ★
John, Jr.: b 7-25-1735 d 7-25-1777 m Mary Holmes PS CT
John: b 6-18-1742 d 12- -1824 m Sybil Barrows PS CT
John: b 5-5-1754 d 8-12-1846 m Achsa Russel Pvt DE
John: b 1729 d 1786 m Rebeckah Yates Pvt GA
John: b 1760 d 1827 m Elizabeth Gaston Sgt MD
John: b 10-19-1744 d 10-19-1780 m Huldah Kilburn Col MA
John: b 1747-49 d 8-29-1815 m Elizabeth Boardman Maj MA
John: b 1737 d 12-18-1820 m (1)Amy Blood (2)Dorothy Bigelow Sgt MA
John: b 1747 d 1813 m Abigail Reed Sgt MA
John: b 2-19-1755 d 1809 m Lovina Lyon Sgt MA W ★
John: b 5-7-1758 d 9-1-1855 m Mary Grow Sgt MA ★
John: b c. 1740 d p. 1784-7 m Ann Greenman Pvt MA
John, Sr.: b 1703 d 1791 m (1)Lydia Newhall (2)Mary Jones PS MA
John, Jr.: b 1734 d 9-23-1821 m (1)Rebekah Baldwin (2)Elizabeth Devoe Sgt MA ★
John: b c. 1750 d 7-14-1804 m Sarah Gibson Cpl MA
John, Sr.: b 5-5-1727 d 3-8-1810 m Lucy Underwood Pvt MA
John: b 2-7-1739 d 2-21-1826 m Lydia Hersey Pvt MA
John: b 6-24-1752 d 2- -1812 m Sarah Gilson Pvt MA
John: b 1754 d 8-10-1803 m Abigail Brown Pvt MA
John: b 1754 d 11-4-1818 m Lydia — Pvt MA
John, Jr.: b 7-1-1724 d 1803 m Elizabeth Bateman Pvt MA

John: bpt 7-30-1732 d p. 1780 m Amy Peach Pvt MA
John: b 1741 d 1831 m Mrs Hannah Marr Smn ME
John: b 9-5-1744 d 7- -1828 m Lucy Rugg Pvt MA
John: b 7-10-1745 d p. 1784 m Esther Carpenter Pvt MA
John: b 4-10-1755 d 2-15-1837 m Alice Howe Pvt MA
John: b 1-1-1761 d 2-21-1838 m (1)Sally Morgridge (2)Mrs Sarah Young Sol ME
John, Sr.: b 1732 d 5-13-1817 m Sally Gilmore PS MA
John: b 9-5-1756 d 4-17-1852 m Betsey Burgin Pvt NH
John: b 1-27-1747 d 1806 m Abigail Phillips CS NH
John, Sr.: b 1736 d 12-31-1822 m Alice Coward Lt NJ
John: b c. 1754 d 1845 m Mary Brown Lt NJ
John: b c. 1754 d 6 or 7- -1797 m Elizabeth — Sgt NJ
John: b c. 1750 d 7-31-1778 m Deborah Claypole Pvt NJ
John, Jr.: b 1762 d 10-29-1820 m Susan Stevenson Cnt NJ
John: b 6-25-1746 d 9-24-1819 m (1)Mary M. Brugler (2)Mrs Margaret Haines Pvt NJ
John: b 11-1-1752 d 1-15-1828 m Sarah Cutter Pvt NJ
John: b 5-15-1761 d 1-2-1827 m (1)Anna — (2)Elizabeth Sims (3)Hannah — Sol NJ
John: b 1723-8 d 7- -1801 m Charity Duncan Pvt NY
John, Jr.: b 1757 d 10-14-1795 m Mary Bosson Matr NY
John: b 12-4-1731 d 2-10-1810 m Margaret Keyser Sol NY
John: b 10-31-1738 d 2-3-1812 m Jane McDowell Capt NC
John: b c. 1754 d c. 1792 m Mary Little Tarver Capt NC
John: b 12-28-1751 d 1-16-1794 m Ala Bennett Sgt NC
John: b 1760 d 1822 m (1)Alice Nodding (2)Martha Elkins Pvt NC
John: b 5-21-1746 d 12-8-1827 m Barbara Lawall Capt PA
John: b 4-14-1739 d 6-20-1825 m Mary Arell Lt PA
John: b 1758 d p. 1784 m Mary — Sol PA
John: b 11-12-1756 d 12-13-1838 m X Sol PA
John: b c. 1760 d 10-30-1822 m Hannah — Sol PA
John: b 9-10-1752 d 6-10-1842 m Margaret Truesdale PS PA
John: b 8-29-1725 d 1-1-1802 m Ann Field PS PA
John: b 7-9-1761 d 11-18-1841 m Lois Taylor Pvt RI
John: b 1764 d 1826 m Sarah — Smn RI ★
John: b 1-27-1736 d 9-20-1803 m Sarah Smith PS RI
John: b 1740 d 1822 m Martha — Pvt SC
John: b 4-7-1755 d 12-16-1826 m Sarah Weeks Pvt SC
John: b 6-15-1763 d 12-11-1842 m Mary McCullouch Sol SC
John: b 5- -1765 d 8-8-1847 m (1)Betty Crawford (2)Jincey Stephenson Pvt SC ★
John: b c. 1745 d 12- -1793 m Sarah Cooper Cmsry Gen VA
John: b 2-15-1743 d 2-16-1830 m Mary Donnally Capt VA
John: b c. 1765 d 9-13-1835 m Margaret Carpenter Spy Ens VA ★
John: b — d 8-20-1822 m (1)Rachel — (2)Nancy Glenn Sgt VA ★
John: b 10-15-1759 d 12-31-1834 m Lucy Doggett Pvt VA ★
John: b 9-12-1757 d 8-28-1837 m Margaretta Mason Pvt VA
John: b 2-16-1763 d 1-5-1819 m Mary Taylor Trm VA
John: b 1725 d 1803 m Margaret Preston PS VA
John M.: b 11-5-1745 d 11-1-1838 m Gitty Hager Capt NY
John Wood: b a. 1755 d p. 1787 m Mary Richards Pvt MA
Jonas: b 12-15-1752 d 7-31-1834 m Hannah Heald MM Ens MA ★
Jonathan: b 1730-7 d — m Esther Parsels Capt CT
Jonathan: b 6-13-1748 d 5-15-1841 m X Pvt CT ★
Jonathan: b 12-20-1757 d 8-11-1830 m (1)Esther Moon (2)Esther Byington Pvt CT ★
Jonathan: b 2-26-1735 d 12-18-1822 m (1)Lydia Osgood (2)Mary French Brown Col MA
Jonathan: b 9-22-1755 d 8-29-1822 m Sarah Twist 2Lt CT ★
Jonathan, Jr.: b 1740-2 d 3-14-1820 m Huldah Hawkes Sgt MA
Jonathan, Sr.: b 12-31-1716 d 9-26-1799 m Abigail Russell Sol CS PS MA
Jonathan, Jr.: b 3-16-1744 d 3-14-1813 m (2)Abigail Sargent Lt MA
Jonathan, Jr.: b 7- -1738 d p. 1779 m Mary Cowing Pvt MA
Jonathan: bpt 8-29-1714 d p. 1776 m Susanna Garnet Pvt PS MA
Jonathan: b 8-24-1724 d 11-25-1797 m Esther Mason Cmsry MA
Jonathan: b 1-22-1741 d 9-25-1775 m Hannah Gove Pvt NH
Jonathan: b 6-7-1764 d 12-1-1829 m Anna Sanborn Pvt NH
Jonathan: b 2-13-1737 d 8-18-1830 m Sarah Brown Lt NH
Jonathan: b 12-20-1753 d 6-11-1836 m Lucy Douglas Maj CS NY
Jonathan: b 1-30-1760 d p. 1832 m Achsah Arnold Sol RI ★
Joseph: b 1749 d 1812 m Elizabeth Gary Ens CT
Joseph: b 3-23-1752 d 1825 m Charlotte Tinges Sgt MA
Joseph: b 4-28-1747 d 7-15-1843 m Mary Longley MM MA
Joseph: b 1751 d 1813 m Abigail Putnam Pvt MA
Joseph: bpt 9-29-1751 d p. 1814 m (1)Elizabeth Perkins (2)Martha Perkins Pvt MA
Joseph: b 4-28-1733 d 4-6-1812 m Elizabeth Sawyer Pvt NH
Joseph: b a. 1739 d 1796 m Ann Otterson Pvt NH
Joseph: b 1748 d 2-27-1808 m Elizabeth Curry Pvt NH
Joseph: b 1731 d p. 1790 m Ann Brown PS NH
Joseph: b 1748 d 1849 m Jennie Brown Pvt NH
Joseph: b 2-23-1758 d 12-13-1802 m Lydia Mace Pvt NH W ★
Joseph: b 1-15-1753 d 12-23-1826 m Susanna Ridgway Capt NJ
Joseph: b 4-13-1760 d 6-29-1847 m Elizabeth Olmstead Pvt NY ★
Joseph: b 9-21-1763 d 12-22-1847 m Catherine Whitney Lawyer Pvt NY ★
Joseph, Jr.: b 11-30-1760 d 10-28-1800 m Jemima Broyles Pvt NC W★
Joseph: b 11-15-1763 d — m Mary Gordon Pvt NC

Joseph: b 1-18-1757 d 9-20-1849 m Abigail Wells Sol Spy Tms PA
Joseph: b 6-19-1759 d 5-15-1843 m (1)Mary Harbison (2)Mary Kelsey Pvt PA W★
Joseph: b 1-18-1757 d 9-20-1849 m X Wgn Sol PA VA
Joseph: b 1758 d 1- -1810 m Catherine De Visme Dr PA
Joseph: b 2-19-1727 d 1-9-1807 m Hopestill (Dexter)Peck PS CS RI
Joseph: b 8-29-1743 d 3-1-1831 m Roby Burlingame Sgt RI
Joseph, Sr.: b 1-1-1731 d 10-15-1815 m Mary Porter Pvt SC
Joseph: b 7-2-1759 d 5-5-1839 m Jane Duncan Pvt NC
Joseph: b c. 1749 d — m Lucy Brown PS VA
Joshua: b 4-8-1740 d 9-26-1824 m (1)Joannah Rogers (2)Lydia Stanton Lt CT
Joshua: b 7-22-1754 d 12-21-1820 m Margaret Mansel Sol MD
Joshua: b 3-20-1751 d 10-6-1819 m Hannah Hamilton Pvt MD
Joshua: 6-24-1742 d 6-27-1817 m Elisabeth Gates Capt MA
Josiah: b 1-13-1758 d 3-19-1830 m Mary Kingsbury Sgt CT
Josiah: b 9- -1736 d 10-19-1796 m (1)Lydia Stevens (2)Sarah Bradbury Sgt MA
Josiah: b 1-26-1752 d p. 1804 m Sally Mahan Cpl MA
Josiah: b 1756 d 12-25-1827 m Mrs Elizabeth Dodge Olmstead Pvt MA ★
Josiah: b 1-30-1742 d 3-18-1831 m Sarah Wright Capt NH
Josiah, Jr.: b 1-31-1759 d p. 1807 m Rachel Fellows Lt NH
Josiah: b 1741 d 5-12-1818 m Lois Chapman Pvt NY
Josias: b 1744 d 3-27-1821 m Hannah Mitchell Pvt PA
Jotham: b 9-17-1708 d 2-25-1798 m Hepzibah Robbins Pvt MA
Judah: b 11-15-1750 d 11-16-1856 m Polly Fuller Lt CT
Justus: b c. 1760 d 184- m Thirza Brown Pvt CT
Kingsley: b — d 3-29-1806 m Mary Warner Pvt RI ★
Knight: b 1749 d 1820 m Lydia Beals Pvt MA
Lewis: b 12-25-1761 d 4- -1830 m (1)Margaret Blue (2)Rebecca Owen Pvt NJ
Lewis: b 1735 d p. 12-3-1804 m (1)Anna Lovett (2)Martha Richardson (3)Fannie Dugger PS VA
Libbius: b 1758 d 9-4-1841 m Hannah Godfrey Pvt CT ★
Lowe: b 1756 d 1-28-1841 m Jane Davidson Pvt Spy VA ★
Luther: b 7-27-1764 d 1-29-1837 m Hannah Miner Pvt CT
Lyndon: b 2-4-1739 d 4-14-1790 m (1)Margaret Jones (2)Ruth Garwood (3)Sarah Hood PS NJ
Mahlon: b a. 1755 d 7-25-1812 m Letitia Henry Pvt PA
Manuel: b c. 1738 d c. 1799 m (1)— (2)Susannah Power Pvt VA
Martin: b 10-10-1764 d 8-24-1850 m Hannah Post Pvt NJ
Matthew: b 10-17-1742 d 3-19-1831 m Mary Blair 2Lt MA
Matthew: b 6-18-1751 d 6-1-1832 m Elizabeth Dick Pvt MA
Matthew: b 7-15-1732 d 4-22-1777 m Eleanor Lyttle PS PA
Matthew: b 1733 d 1837 m Mary Throckmorton Pvt PA
Matthew: b 1752 d 1839 m Jane Jones Pvt SC
Meredith: b 1764 d 2- -1837 m Mary Glover Pvt GA
Michael: b 12-4-1731 d 1-22-1810 m Anna Matthes Pvt NY
Michael: b 1730 d p. 10-12-1807 m (1)Margareta — (2)Mrs Eleanor Reaves CS NC
Morgan: b 1-13-1753 d 2-23-1840 m Elizabeth Little 1Lt PS NC SC ★
Morgan: b 1715 d 1-28-1808 m Elizabeth Brown CS NC
Moses: b 1-23-1742 d 1-2-1804 m Mrs Sarah Coffin NCapt MA
Nathan: b 1735 d 3-21-1787 m (1)Sarah Kent(2)Lovel Kent 1Lt MD
Nathan: b 7-22-1761 d 11-25-1842 m Tamar Sammons Pvt NY ★
Nathan: b 1753 d p. 4-15-1837 m Margaret — Sol VT
Nathaniel: b 1756 d — m Polly — Pvt CT ★
Nathaniel: b 7-1-1737 d 7-30-1806 m Abigail Page 2Lt MA
Nathaniel: b 8-13-1741 d p. 1786 m Eleanor Hayden Pvt MA
Nathaniel: b 1760 d p. 1796 m Rebecca Ide Pvt MA
Nathaniel: b 10-7-1755 d p. 1826 m Polly Gee Pvt NH
Nathaniel: b 1745 d 3-15-1829 m Hannah Ayer PS NH
Nathaniel: b 4-7-1765 d 9-2-1852 m Abigail Alger Pvt VT ★
Nehemiah: b 7- -1745 d 6- -1812 m Mary Choate Adj MA
Nehemiah: b 11-28-1717 d 7-12-1793 m Anna Longfellow PS NH
Nehemiah: b a. 1765 d p. 1790 m Hannah Pratt Pvt NY
Nicholas: b 10-17-1765 d 6-29-1858 m Sarah Whitaker Ens PA
Nicholas: b 7-28-1729 d 5-29-1791 m Rhoda Jencker PS RI
Noah: b 8-21-1752 d 5-13-1821 m Judith Short Cpl MA
Noah, Jr.: b 8-24-1762 d 5-11-1841 m Lois Mills Pvt NY
Obadiah: b 6-2-1756 d 2-23-1836 m Penelope Swazey Lt NJ ★
Oliver: b c. 2- -1760 d 6-5-1845 m (1)Mrs Gracie Welch (2)Mrs Beardsley Pvt CT ★
Oliver: b 6-25-1753 d 2-17-1846 m Abigail Richardson CaptLt MA ★
Oliver: b 12-25-1754 d 7-17-1850 m Susanna Law Pvt Drm MA ★
Oliver: b 1747 d 1843 m Mary Alexander Pvt PA
Orlando: b 4-2-1753 d p. 2-8-1779 m Mary Hodgkins Pvt MA
Othniel: b 4-20-1759 d 9-28-1843 m (1)Sibyle Olney (2)Nancy Lyon Pvt Mar RI W ★
Paul: b 1747 d 1802 m Mary Wheeler Pvt MA
Pelatiah: b 1735 d 2-14-1830 m Hannah — Capt MA
Peleg: b 9-26-1746 d 1-26-1814 m Experience Morgan Pvt CT
Peleg: b 4-28-1757 d 11-26-1831 m Mary Coggeshall Pvt RI
Peres: b 6-30-1753 d 6-20-1807 m Betsey — Pvt MA
Perley: b 5-27-1737 d 10-28-1776 m Elizabeth Wilson Pvt MA
Peter: b 1753 d 10-20-1802 m Mercy Eliot Pvt CT W★
Peter: b c. 1738 d c. 1815 m X Lt MD
Peter: b 1-21-1748 d 1831 m Elizabeth Beall Lt MD
Peter: b c. 1750 d 1823 m Susan — Sgt MD
Peter: b 1765 d 1796 m Mary Oneal DrmMaj NJ

Peter: b 1-24-1735 d 9- -1798 m (1)Hannah Scobey (2)Frances Sayre Pvt NJ
Peter: b c. 1740 d p. 1790 m X Capt PA
Peter: b 1756 d p. 1831 m Susannah — Pvt PA
Philemon: b 2-11-1742 d 1811 m Nancy Rice Pvt MA
Phineas: b 1756 d 1-31-1842 m Huldah Paine Sgt MA ★
Phineas: b 5-30-1747 d 6-6-1818 m (1)Sarah Patterson (2)Elizabeth Rossiter Pvt MA
Phineas: b c. 1750 d 7-23-1801 m Esther — Pvt NJ
Phinehas: b 1742 d 6-20-1821 m Lydia Badcock Sgt MA
Prentice: b 11-17-1743 d 10-20-1813 m Luphina Earl Capt NY
Reuben: b 1765 d 8-9-1824 m Ruth Park Fif CT
Reuben: b 5-28-1748 d 8-25-1832 m Mollie Howe PS MA
Richard: b 12-2-1725 d 1789 m (1)Helen Bailey (2)Mrs — Key (3)Mrs — Hawkins Pvt MD
Richard: b 11-11-1760 d 10-18-1832 m Frances Moss Pvt MD
Richard: b 1745 d 1782 m Margra Foote QM NH
Richard: b 5-18-1739 d 2-8-1811 m Honour Holmes Capt PA
Richard: b 2-28-1712 d 3-16-1812 m Mary Boone Pvt RI
Richard: b c. 1730 d a. 7-20-1784 m Sarah — 1Lt VA
Robert: b 3-8-1736 d 9-8-1807 m (1)Sarah Huggins (2)Mary Law Capt CT W★
Robert: b 6-5-1764 d 2-13-1849 m (1)Lydia Dewey (2)Lorinda Green Pvt CT
Robert: b 1-4-1757 d 8-19-1833 m Dinah Bowen Pvt MD
Robert: b 8-3-1738 d p. 1790 m Catherine Jacklin Pvt NY
Robert: b 12-25-1744 d 2-26-1823 m Catherine Snyder 1Lt PA W★
Robert: b — d a. 1786 m Martha — PS PA
Robert: b 4-9-1735 d 8-2-1794 m Elizabeth Cooke Col RI
Robert: b 1759 d 1-20-1840 m Jane — Pvt VA ★
Roger: b 1734 d 1820 m (2)Rebecca Wallace Pvt SC
Roswell: b — d — m Ruth Kellogg Pvt MA
Rowland: b 1750 d 7-4-1801 m (1)Hannah Babcock (2)Polly Wicks Ens RI
Rufus: b 7-5-1736 d 11-8-1801 m Jerusha Alexander Pvt MA
Samuel: b 6-1-1753 d — m Annie J. Clark Cpl CT
Samuel: b 2-14-1761 d 4-8-1833 m Mary Kellogg Mus CT CHN ★
Samuel: b 1750/1 d 12-13-1836 m — Day Pvt CT
Samuel: b 2-14-1761 d 4-8-1833 m Mary Kellogg Mus CT CHN ★
Samuel: b 1750/1 d 12-13-1836 m — Day Pvt CT
Samuel: b 1740-1750 d 9- -1837 m Mary Mooney Sol GA
Samuel 2nd: b 1-9-1747 d 10-6-1833 m Achsah Riggs Lt MD
Samuel: b 11-10-1737 d 1787 m Deborah Torrey 1Lt MA
Samuel: b 10-12-1749 d 1-16-1828 m (1)Elizabeth Fletcher (2)Polly Newkirk Lt MA
Samuel: b 3-25-1740 d 10-19-1816 m (1)Esther Bucklin (2)Hulda Hunt 1Lt MA
Samuel, Jr.: b 1735/6 d 1775 m (1)Mary Glene (2)Mary Wheeler Lt MA
Samuel: b 5-14-1740 d p. 1780 m Bridget Bryant Pvt MA
Samuel: b 5-1-1758 d 1-15-1841 m Lydia Thayer Pvt MA
Samuel: b 12-27-1759 d 6-20-1816 m Abagail Darby Pvt MA
Samuel: b 7-22-1761 d 11-29-1836 m Mary Dorr Pvt Matr MA ★
Samuel: b 2-18-1752 d 10-29-1819 m Elizabeth (Brown) Pvt MA
Samuel: b 7-2-1703 d 3-2-1784 m Mercy Paterson PS MA
Samuel: b 11-20-1720 d 5- -1794 m Susanna Knowles PS NH
Samuel: b c. 1738 d p. 1790 m Jean Gibson PS NH
Samuel: b c. 1755 d p. 10-11-1836 m Rebecca Chamberlain Sol PS NJ
Samuel: b 11-28-1740 d 5-8-1804 m Eleanor Cutler Pvt NJ
Samuel: b 11-14-1760 d 1804 m Mary Davis Pvt NJ
Samuel: b 6-30-1759 d 4-1-1814 m Catherine Green Pvt NY
Samuel: b c. 1760 d p. 1-26-1804 m Christian McMillan Sol NC
Samuel: b 1755 d c. 1813 m Nancy Williams Pvt NC
Samuel: b 1745 d 1812 m Ruth Wheeler Pvt RI
Samuel: b 1739 d p. 1800 m (1)Harriet Whitten (2)X Pvt SC
Samuel: b a. 1754 d 7-5-1793 m (2)Olive Smalley Gaines Pvt VT
Samuel: b 1761 d 1843 m Lucinda Coy Pvt VT ★
Samuel: b a. 1764 d 1828 m Elizabeth Grattan Col VA
Samuel: b a. 1754 d p. 1785 m Sarah Truby Pvt VA
Samuel: b c. 1755 d a. 1829 m Susan Bacon Pvt VA
Samuel: b 4- -1764 d p. 3-29-1850 m Pheby Clark Pvt VA ★
Seth Ingersoll: b 7-28-1750 d 3-9-1809 m (2)Sarah Godding MM MA
Shubel: b 3-12-1761 d 9-3-1836 m Nancy Murdock Pvt CT
Silas, Sr.: b 6-21-1729 d 8-4-1804 m Catharine Searle Lt MA
Silas: b 10-17-1754 d 1-9-1813 m Mrs Mary Larrabee Pvt MA
Simms: b 1760 d 10-5-1822 m Mary Baldreck Pvt SC
Simon: b 6-14-1756 d a. 11-23-1810 m Elizabeth Topliff Cpl MA
Simon: b 8-13-1744 d 7-20-1831 m Mary Leavitt Sgt NH
Solomon: b — 1761 d 12-3-1850 m Betty Wheston Drm CT
Solomon: b 1756 d 1837 m Patty — Sgt MA ★
Solomon: b 1-15-1756 d 6-6-1837 m (1)Mariana Barnet (2)Eunice Bigelow Sgt MA ★
Solomon: b c. 1750 d c. 11-1821 m Sarah Slauson Pvt NY
Solomon: b 1-24-1757 d 7-2-1815 m (1)Hannah Olmstead (2)Sarah Nash Sol NY
Stephen: b 8-27-1735 d a. 1-27-1814 m Mary Shattuck PS CT
Stephen, Sr.: bpt 3-7-1717 d 1797 m Anne Starte Cpl MA
Stephen, Jr.: bpt 6-14-1747 d — m Elizabeth Potter Pvt MA
Stephen: b 9-3-1756 d 4-22-1834 m Phoebe Williams Pvt NJ ★
Stephen, Jr: b 1-31-1746 d 7-23-1787 m Huldah Dexter Pvt RI
Stephen, Richard: b 12-10-1759 d 8-28-1833 m Catherine King Pvt NY
Sylvanus: b 3-2-1736 d a. 1808 m Rebecca Newman Capt CT

BROWN, contd.
Sylvanus: b 8-5-1737 d 1-24-1805 m Hannah Rackett PS NY
Sylvanus: b 3-14-1749 d 7-6-1822 m Kesia Cushman Sgt VT
Tarleton: b 4-5-1757 d 9-8-1845 m (1)Almedia Mathews (2)Judith Cook Capt SC ★
Thaddeus: b 1756 d 8-20-1830 m X Pvt CT ★
Thaddeus: b 10-25-1760 d 6-15-1842 m Mary Pollard Pvt MA ★
Theodore: b 10-30-1757 d 9-10-1830 m Sarah Gile Pvt NH
Thomas: b 4-28-1754 d 2-27-1848 m Catherine Cooper Pvt CT
Thomas, Jr: b 1755 d 1836 m Hannah Spencer Pvt CT ★
Thomas: b 4-16-1733 d 3-11-1814 m (1)Ruth — (2)Hannah Jones Sgt MA
Thomas: b 2-20-1723/4 d 10-14-1818 m (1)Esther — (2)Lucy Kemp Pvt MA
Thomas: b 3-19-1758 d 3-22-1822 m Hannah Lovell Pvt MA
Thomas: b 3-4-1703 d p. 1785 m (1)Abigail Ockillee (2)Elizabeth Dorne (3)Mercy Mayo (4)Mary Hopkins PS MA
Thomas: b 1717 d 10-23-1782 m (1)Anna Van Boskirk (2)Maritje Ten Eyck PS NJ
Thomas: b 2-14-1726 d 10-28-1781 m Frances Moores PS NJ
Thomas: b 1-7-1733 d 12-31-1820 m Lydia Barclay Capt NY
Thomas: b 1-7-1744 d 11-22-1814 m (1)Lucy Bradley LCol NC
Thomas, Jr: b 1738 d 3-8-1797 m Ruth Brashear LCol PA VA
Thomas: b c. 1746 d 1796 m (2)Eleanor Searight Pvt PA
Thomas: b 4-5-1717 d 6-25-1791 m (1)Hannah Spooner (2)Patience Brockway PS PA
Thomas: b 5-29-1730 d 9-27-1818 m Mary Osborn Ball Pvt VA CL
Thomas: b c. 1740 d 4- -1809 m Betsy Ann (Wyatt or Wyant) Pvt VA GA
Thomas: b 9-7-1760 d 8- -1844 m Anna Ash Pvt VA ★
Thomas: b— d p. 12-8-1793 m Mary — PS VA
Thomas, C: b 8- -1761 d 4-17-1857 m (1)Mary — (2)Mary Brown Cnt VA ★
Timothy: b 3-30-1742 d p. 8-5-1807 m Sarah Paine Pvt PS MA
Timothy: b 5-30-1762 d 5-3-1852 m Sarah — Pvt NJ ★
Titus: b 11-11-1714 d 2- -1802 m Rachel Marshall Sol CT
Valentine: b 3-8-1755 d 1817 m Bethana Briggs Sol NY
Valentine: b 7- -1742 d 1-16-1787 m Regina Heimberg Pvt PA
Waldo: b 3-25-1759 d 7-24-1835 m Abigail Fish Fif CT ★
Waller: b 1749 d 9-30-1833 m Frances Watkins Pvt NC ★
Walter, Sr: b 2-1-1728 d 9-14-1808 m (1)Elizabeth Wilbur (2)Mary Frink Pvt PS CT
Walter: b 1725 d 1784 m Margaret Brown PS SC
White: b 3-23-1749 d 3-25-1842 m (1)Lucretia Clarkson (2)Anna Withgott (3)Sarah Thomas Lt DE
William: b 1760 d 1805 m Ruth Hanford Sgt CT
William: b 10-4-1758 d 4-25-1834 m Mary Cheseboro Pvt FifMaj CT ★
William: b 1750 d 9-8-1793 m Amy Brown Pvt CT
William: b 10-11-1752 d 7-3-1832 m Patience Marvel Pvt DE
William: b 1763 d 10-23-1853 m Mrs — (Shackelford) Pvt GA
William: b 3-23-1753 d 6-4-1828 m Elizabeth Lacey PS MD
William: b 8-30-1724 d 8-23-1808 m (1)Elizabeth Shortridge (2)Rachael French Lt MA
William: b 12-15-1761 d 1847 m Betsy Clements Lt MA
William: b c. 1710 d 12- -1780 m Ruth Walker Pvt MA
William: b 4-8-1731 d 4-13-1808 m Martha King Pvt MA
William, Jr: b 3-28-1760 d 3-31-1831 m (2)Hannah Lucas Pvt MA
William: bpt 4-28-1723 d 12-23-1793 m Elizabeth Conant PS MA
William: b 2-24-1730 d 10-5-1817 m Mary Osgood PS MA
William: b 4- -1761 d 8- -1855 m Sarah Campbell Pvt NH
William: b 7-25-1756 d 7-3-1803 m Phebe Bond Arfr NJ
William: b 5-19-1749 d 3-31-1782 m Elizabeth Dunham Sol NJ
William: b 11-24-1755 d 1828 m Mary Campbell Col NC
William: b 8-27-1760 d 1853 m Sarah Elizabeth Barton Pvt NC ★
William, Jr: b c. 1760 d 1839 m Ruth Piper Pvt NC
William: b 1-14-1751 d 12- -1794 m Mary Gray PS NC
William: b 1734 d 9-6-1808 m Mary Coren (Knight) Capt PA
William: b 9-10-1734 d 9-11-1777 m Elizabeth Bouradail Lt PA
William: b 3-4-1736 d 12-14-1825 m Mary Scott Lt PS PA
William: b 12-25-1753 d 3-9-1839 m Anna McSweney 1Lt PA
William: b 9-19-1738 d 3-1-1833 m Mary — Pvt PA VA ★
William: b c. 1738 d p. 1800 m Hannah — Sol PA
William: b c. 1748 d 4- -1779 m Mary Dailey Pvt PA
William: b 1751 d 3-2-1828 m Sarah McMillan Pvt PA
William: b 1754 d 1813 m Polly Melawn Pvt PA W ★
William: b 5-23-1757 d 11-29-1789 m Frances Lamond Pvt PA
William: b 2-3-1755 d 1-20-1831 m Jean Brown Pvt PA
William: b 8-30-1757 d 4-30-1853 m Ruth Lane Pvt PA ★
William: b 1732 d c. 1782 m Anne Rebecca Marshall Capt SC
William: b 1720 d 1780 m — Duke Sol SC
William: b 5-20-1730 d 12-5-1803 m Jenny Doke Pvt VA
William: b 1752 d 1-11-1792 m Katherine Scott Dr SurGen VA
William: b 1722 d 1- -1807 m Elizabeth Buckner Capt VA
William: b 9-13-1724 d 7-24-1801 m Elizabeth Shepherd Pvt VA
William: b 1759 d 10- -1825 m Hannah Street Pvt VA
William: b 1760 d a. 2-3-1840 m Elizabeth Scott Pvt VA ★
Woodbridge: b 9-18-1714 d 11-28-1783 m Anne Emery PS CS MA
Zaccheus: b 10-23-1744 d 6-29-1791 m Elizabeth Goodspeed Cpl CT
Zebulon: b 11-20-1730 d 7-14-1814 m Anna Main Pvt CT
Zebulon: b c. 1760 d 2-23-1811 m Sarah Bolston Sgt NJ
Zephaniah: b 6-13-1739 d 7-25-1810 m Dinah Westcott Capt RI

BROWNELL, (includes BROWNEWELL)
Benjamin: b 6-13-1734 d 12-3-1816 m Phebe Potter Pvt MA
Benjamin: b 9-4-1759 d 11-30-1833 m Hannah Whipple Pvt NY
Casper: b 1730 d 1833 m Marie Magdelena Rappoldt Pvt PA
Charles: b 4-13-1745 d 1-28-1811 m Content Shaw Pvt RI
Edward: b 1-10-1746 d 1824 m Susannah Wells Capt PS CT
Elijah: b 1736 d 7-29-1812 m Sarah Fish Pvt MA
George: b 12-9-1746 d p. 1789 m Rhoda Milk Sgt MA
George: b 3-31-1744 d 1817 m Lucy Richmond CS RI
Gideon: b 1746 d 9-27-1818 m Phoebe Brown Sgt RI W ★
Isaac: b 10-2-1742 d 10-10-1775 m Anna Nearing PS CT
Israel: b 1738 d 5-23-1808 m Rachel Potter Pvt RI
Jonathan: b 5-30-1746 d 5-8-1821 m Patience Boomer Capt RI
Joseph: b 4-6-1761 d 3-4-1843 m Polly Draper Pvt NY
Joseph: b 2-21-1754 d p. 1806 m (1)Elizabeth Chase (2)Elizabeth Borden PS RI
Joseph: b 4-26-1720 d p. 5-3-1795 m Rebecca Tripp PS CS RI
Nathan: b 2-7-1747 d p. 1780 m Elizabeth Fish PS RI
Nathaniel: b c. 1747 d p. 1810 m Susannah Bennett Pvt MA
Pardon: b 7-6-1745 d 1-24-1799 m Prudence Shaw Lt MA
Pearce: b 3-30-1715 d p. 1799 m Ruth Thurston Grd RI
Robert: b 1756 d 7-20-1801 m Deborah Pattee Pvt MA
Samuel: b 7-13-1738 d 1817 m (1)Ruth Briggs (2)Phebe Thompkins Pvt RI
Stephen: b 3-17-1762 d 1855 m Mary Coggshall Pvt RI ★
Sylvester: b 11-20-1757 d 3-21-1840 m Mercy Church OrdlSgt MA ★
Thomas: b 3-18-1724 d c. 1788 m Sarah Brownell Pvt MA
William A: b 4-8-1752 d 1-14-1827 m (1)Amey Harris (2)Amey Aldrich Lt RI

BROWNELLER,
Henry: b c. 1750 d p. 4-9-1802 m Margaret — Pvt PA

BROWNFIELD, (includes BROMFIELD, BRUMFIELD)
Benjamin: b 10-5-1755 d 12-21-1823 m Mary — Pvt VA
John: b c. 1742 d p. 9-15-1788 m Elizabeth Clark Pvt PA
Robert, Sr: b 1733 d 1821 m Elloner Sutton Pvt PA
Robert, Jr: b 10-10-1760 d 2-6-1815 m Mary Bowel Pvt PA
Robert: b 6-4-1760 d 6-17-1841 m — Ramsey Sol PA
Solomon: b c. 1733 d 1797 m Sarah Evans Pvt PA

BROWNING,
Charles: b 1757 d 1821 m Martha Hazelwood Sol SC
Charles: b c. 1754 d 1821 m Frances Wright PS VA
Charles: b 1746 d 1839 m Mary Wade Strother Capt VA
Edward, Sr: b c. 1717 d 1788 m Elizabeth — PS MD
Enos: b 1751 d 1815 m Jane Trim Pvt VA W★
Francis: b 11-24-1753 d 7-18-1855 m Elizabeth Vermillion Pvt NC ★
James: b 2-15-1757 d 7-20-1821 m Elizabeth Easterbrook Lt MA
James: b 5-5-1727 d 7-20-1820 m Rebecca Scott MM VA
James: b c. 1745 d 1812 m Susannah Hickman Pvt VA
John: b 1-1-1761 d 1797 m Mary Clark Pvt RI
John: b 7-19-1758 d 11-4-1809 m Clara Sherman Pvt VA
John: b 1-15-1742 d 2-24-1832 m (1)Mary Davis (2)Eunice Williams (3) — X — Sgt RI
John: b c. 1728 d 12- -1803 m Elizabeth Demarest Sol VA
John: b 4-16-1749 d 9-25-1818 m Elizabeth Strother PS VA
John Radford: b 5-17-1757 d 1844 m (1)S E Culberson (2)Nancy Peebles Pvt VA
Joseph: b 11-22-1733 d 12-26-1813 m (1)Lois Sherman (2)Lucy Sherman (3)Louisa Barnaby Capt MA
Joshua: b c. 1756/57 d c. 1812 m Mary Briscoe Cpl MD
Joshua: b c. 1733 d p. 1-10-1807 m Margaret — Sol NC
Levi: b 4-16-1758 d 1- -1839 m Margaret Purnell Pvt NC ★
Phillip Jacob: b 7-25-1753 d 10-22-1794 m Margaret Lawrence Capt NJ
Reuben: b 3-31-1750 d 9-21-1844 m Sallie Duncan Sol VA
Robert: b 1757 d 1829 m (1)Mary Allen (2)Susannah Wells Mrnr RI
Samuel: b 1754 d 6-3-1845 m Lucy Kingsley Pvt RI ★
William: b 8-20-1723 d 10-16-1806 m Rebecca McFarland PS MA
William: b c. 1760 d 9- -1820 m Isabella McAlpin Pvt NC
William: b 7-21-1754 d 4-5-1820 m Sarah Cole 1Cpl PA
William: b 1747 d p. 1809 m Mildred Roberts Pvt VA

BROWNLEE,
Alexander: b 1755 d 1820 m Florence Duncan Ens VA
George: b 1756 d 9-17-1836 m Sara Caldwell PS Pvt SC
James: b 1745 d 1828 m Jean Rankin Pvt PA
James: b 1-4-1745 d 1822 m Jane Lemen Pvt PA
John, Sr: b 1715 d 1800 m Sarah Wilson Sol VA
John: b 9-10-1747 d 8-17-1811 m Elizabeth Baldridge SrgnMte VA
Thomas: b 12-2-1751 d 7-29-1816 m (1)Martha Shearer (2)Mrs Elizabeth Muncey Pvt VA
William: b 1749 d 2-5-1829 m Margaret Leman Pvt PA
William: b 1730 d 1799 m Sarah Goen Lt VA

BROWNLOW,
John: b c. 1760 d p. 1820 m — X — Pvt NC

BROWNRIGG,
George: b 1754 d 1810 m(1)—Bloomfield(2)Obedience Tartt Pvt NC

BROWNSBERRY,
Lewis: b 1757 d 1825 m (1)Kate Wyning Cpl PA

BROYLES, (includes BROILS)
Daniel: b 5-1-1763 d 2-12-1848 m Mary — Pvt VA ★
Lewis: b c. 1763 d 8-22-1804 m Mary Cain (McCain) PS NC

BRUBAKER, (includes BREWBACKER, BRUBACHER)
Abraham: b 12- -1762 d 12- -1818 m Maria Errisman Pvt PA
Christian: b 10-18-1757 d 1788 m — Hershey Pvt PA
Conrad: b 1728 d a. 2-16-1810 m Eva Crone Pvt PA
Jacob: b 7-25-1751 d 10-25-1832 m Anna — Pvt PA
John: b 1752 d 1803 m Anna Musser Pvt PA
Peter, Sr: b 2-15-1725 d 7-15-1811 m Barbara — Pvt PA
Peter, Jr: b 1760 d 1820 m Anna Frick Pvt PA

BRUCE,
Abner: b 5-7-1754 d p. 1790 m Abigail Rowlee Sgt MA
Arnold: b 1759 d 1817 m Elizabeth — Pvt NC
Asa: b 1759 d 2-20-1833 m Hannah Wilder Sgt VT
Benjamin, Jr: b 8-19-1759 d 9-11-1839 m Philadelphia Wheeler
  Pvt MA
Benjamin: b c. 1750 d p. 1810 m Mildred Watts Pvt VA
Charles: b 7-15-1754 d 2-11-1785 m Mercy Gilbert Sgt PS MA
Charles: b 2-1-1733 d 1832 m Betty Benton PS NC
Charles: b c. 1738 d p. 1-17-1802 m — X — Pvt PA
Charles: b 1740-5 d 1820 m Margaret Ramsey Sol SC
Charles: b c. 1735 d 1792 m (1)Diana Banks (2)Frances Stubble-
  field Capt VA
Daniel, Sr: b 2-22-1701 d c. 1790 m Bathsheba Bowker Pvt MA
Daniel, Jr: b 9-21-1752 d p. 1805 m Mary Bruce Cpl PA
Donald: b 1742 d 1795 m (1)Jane Lockhart (2)Margaret Lockhart
  PS SC
Elijah: b 1-20-1760 d 5-16-1835 m Abigail Whitney Pvt VT MA
George: b 1765 d 1855 m Sarah Cole Pvt NC
George: b c. 1758 d 1808 m Temperance — Cpl VA
Jesse: b 2-16-1749/50 d 1-31-1826 m Anne Benton Pvt MA ★
John: b 3-12-1729 d 6-4-1779 m Mary Joslyn Sgt MA
John: b 3- -1744 d 1- -1844 m Martha Moore MM MA
John: b 11-30-1745/6 d 10-13-1824 m Temperance Packard Pvt MA
John: b 4-30-1748 d 4-3-1827 m Elizabeth Clay Sgt VA
John, Sr.: b — d p. 3-16-1816 m — X — PS VA
Joseph: b 8-19-1759 d 9-13-1849 m Ruth Lowell Sgt MA ★
Moses: b 9-24-1744 d p. 1787 m Sarah — MM MA
Norman: b 1740 d 4-25-1811 m Susanna Gardiner Key Col CS MD
Reuben: b 5-8-1751 d 7-31-1839 m Lucy Rice MM Pvt MA ★
Robert: b c. 1750 d 10-16-1795 m Elizabeth — PS NC
Thomas: b 3-10-1757 d 5-2-1819 m Susanna Wyman Sgt MA
Thomas: b 1759 d 3-8-1822 m Lucy Gaines Pvt NC
Timothy: b a. 1732 d 1-3-1787 m Susannah Joslin Pvt MA
Timothy, Jr.: b 8- -1752 d 1-24-1843 m Mathilda Wheeler Pvt MA
  W★
William: b 6-10-1759 d 3-5-1842 m (1)Hannah Morgan (2)Catherine
  Gaines Pvt NC ★
William: b 2-14-1745 d 8-20-1818 m Polly Lucas Perciful Lt PA
William: b 9-20-1762 d 1832 m Frances Lewis Pvt PA
William: b 1752 d p. 10-13-1811 m Annie Ballard Sgt VA

BRUCKMAN, (includes BROOKMAN)
Godfrid: b 9-28-1734 d 4-2-1813 m Anna Stever Pvt NY
John: b 9-8-1764 d 3-28-1833 m Anna Sanders Pvt NY
John: b 1756 d 1820 m Lucy — Pvt CL

BRUEN, (includes BRUIN)
Elias: b 11-6-1748 d 4-9-1806 m Elizabeth Burnet Pvt NJ
Jabez: b 7-24-1750 d 11-27-1814 m Abagail Spinning Pvt NJ
Jonathan: b 5-5-1757 d 8-26-1807 m Lydia Ward Pvt NJ
Joseph: b 8-15-1746 d 1-11-1822 m Rachael Carter Pvt NJ
Peter Bryan: b 1754-6 d 1-27-1827 m Elizabeth Edmunds Maj VA
Timothy, Jr: b 1735/6 d 8-21-1797 m Lydia Crane Pvt NJ

BRUFF,
Christopher: b 1760 d 11-17-1805 m Mary Berry Pvt MD
James: b 1734 d 11-15-1815 m Henrietta Bruff Capt MD
John: b 12-4-1740 d 11-12-1819 m Lucy Hopkins PS Pvt MD

BRUGLER,
Peter: b 3- -1755 d 12-5-1843 m — X — Sol NJ

BRUMBACK, (includes BRUBACH, BRUMBAUGH)
Conrad: b 1735 d 1791 m — X — Pvt PA
Henry: b 2-18-1733 d 7-30-1804 m Mary Magdalin Paul Ens PA
Henry: b 4-14-1739 d 1799 m (1)Anna Kauffmann (2)Anna Strickler
  PS VA
Hermanus Emanuel: b 1751 d 2- -1803 m Maria Catherine Pott Pvt
  PA
Jacob, Sr: b 1728 d 4-10-1799 m Mary Elizabeth Angle PS MD
Peter: b 1754 d 4-6-1846 m Elizabeth Lee Simpson Pvt GA ★

BRUNDAGE, (includes BRUNDIGE, & BRUNGAGE)
Gilbert: b 11-29-1759 d 4-22-1847 m Jane Ryer Pvt NY
Hackaliah: b 1748 d 1842 m (1)Esther Brown (2)Deborah — Pvt NY

Israel: b 9-17-1757 d 10-11-1835 m (1)Elizabeth Williams (2)Kezia
  Perry Cpl NY W ★
Jesse: b c. 1752 d 5-18-1828 m Hannah — Pvt NY
John: b 2-28-1733 d 2-9-1796 m Martha Ogden Pvt NY
Martin: b c. 1763 d c. 1832 m Rachel Golden Pvt NY
Nathaniel W: b 1-12-1756 d 8-31-1827 m Rebecca Smith Pvt NY
William: b 1741 d 11-12-1825 m Anna Perkins Pvt NY

BRUNER, (includes BRUNNER)
Abraham: b 1762 d 12-16-1844 m Catherine — Pvt PA
Adam: b 1763 d 10-19-1846 m Elizabeth Rice Pvt PA
Andrew: b 2-12-1758 d 4-28-1820 m Christina Gangware Pvt PA
Casper: b 6-20-1730 d 5-27-1783 m Ursula Shellenberger Pvt PA
Elias: b 10-14-1756 d 6-28-1826 m (2)Maria Elizabeth Zimmerman
  Ens PS MD
Frederick: b 1751 d 1836 m Mary Hummel Pvt PA
George: b c. 1758 d a. 3-24-1818 m — X — 2Lt PA
Henry: b 1745-50 d 1813 m Magdalena Putman Pvt PA
Henry: b 12- -1754 d 10-4-1828 m Margaret Keyser Pvt PA
Jacob: b 4-12-1764 d 8-10-1847 m Margaret Cline Pvt MD ★
John: b c. 1720 d 2-15-1776 m Ann Mary — PS MD
John: b 1730 d 1820 m Elizabeth Krugger Pvt PA
Leonard: bpt 6-10-1753 d p. 1830 m Charlotte Claycomb Pvt PA
Peter: b 1724 d 10-2-1821 m Anna Maria — PS MD
Peter: b c. 1730 d a. 7- -1801 m — X — CS NJ
Peter: b 1760 d 7- -1850 m Sarah — Pvt PA
Peter: b 9-17-1763 d 9-23-1851 m Catherine Sims Pvt PA ★
Peter: b 1733 d p. 1801 m Elizabeth — PS PA
Ulrich Owen: b 6-4-1730 d 2-19-1821 m Fronica Gross Pvt PS PA

BRUNTHAVER, (includes BRANDHOEFER & BRUNTHAFER)
Adam: b 12-21-1748 d 7-29-1834 m (1)Anna Maria Frolick
  (2)Magdalena Kunkle Pvt PA ★

BRUSH,
Alexander: b 1-21-1755 d 7-15-1815 m Ruth Fay Lt VT
Ananias: b 1721 d 3-3-1794 m Mary Kelsey PS NY
Benjamin: b 1749 d 11-22-1822 m (1)Rebecca Finch Lt CT
Daniel: b 5-10-1744 d 1805 m Hannah Phillips PS NY
Dorothea Platt: b 7-27-1751 d 12-16-1835 m Jesse Brush PS NY
Eliphalet: b 12-4-1748 d 6-8-1847 m (1)Hannah Hamilton (2)Abigail
  Dunning (3)Mrs Eunice Hull Lee Capt CT
Israel: b 1727 d 1779 m Tapthath Saxton Pvt NJ
James: b c. 1750 d a. 1- -1794 m Elizabeth — Sgt VA
John: b 1726 d 11-5-1795 m Hannah Wickes Pvt NY
Jonas: b 4-20-1755 d 1-30-1831 m Tamar Ann Ruggles Ens CT W ★
Joshua: b 9-13-1743 d a. 3-28-1781 m Margaret Ireland PS NY
Josiah: b 10-6-1746 d 8-11-1832 m Elizabeth — Cpl PS W ★
Nathaniel: b 4-22-1741 d 7- -1804 m Semantha Parker Col VT
Nehemiah, Sr: b 9-6-1713 d 1786 m Bathsheba (Brush) — Pvt NY
Nehemiah, Jr: b 9-5-1756 d 3-16-1822 m Mary Jarvis Pvt NY
Timothy: b c. 1745 d 8-6-1806 m Catherine Lain Ens NJ
William: b 1750 d p. 1783 m Sarah Thompson Lt VT

BRUTON,
George: b 6-5-1762 d p. 1840 m Sally A — Pvt SC ★

BRUYN,
Cornelius: b 1-7-1711 d 12-21-1777 m Ida Hoffman Pvt NY
Jacobus: b 1-5-1707 d 4-26-1781 m Jeannie Graham PS NY
Jacobus, Jr: bpt 3-7-1749 d 5-25-1823 m Jeneke Dewitt QM NY
Jacobus Severyn: b 10-27-1751 d 7-12-1825 m Blandina Elmendorf
  LtCol NY
Severyn Ten Hout: b 3-27-1749 d 8-30-1794 m Margaret Anderson
  2Lt NY

BRYAN, (includes BRIAN, BRYON)
Alexander: b 2-4-1733 d 4-9-1825 m Martha Tallmadge Sct NY
Alexander: b — d p. 5-9-1778 m — X — Pvt PA
Andrew: b 11-12-1756 d 11-10-1808 m Delphia Garnett Jones
  Pvt PA
Blake: b 6-12-1757 d c. 1820 m Elizabeth Blackshear Ens NC
Charles: b 6-10-1752 d 5-15-1838 m Catharine Stone Pvt MD
Cornelius: b 1760 d 1820 m (2)Sarah Danford Pvt VA
Daniel Boone: b 2-11-1758 d 2-28-1845 m Elizabeth Turner Sol NC
David: b 1-3-1760 d 11-12-1826 m Dorcas Stokes Pvt GA
David: b 10-29-1757 d 3-20-1837 m Mary Poor Pvt NC
Edward: b 10-2-1759 d 12-2-1813 m Susannah Blackshear Sol NC
Elijah: b 9-6-1760 d 1-12-1844 m Content Fowler Pvt CT
George: b 2-15-1758 d 11-22-1845 m (1)Elizabeth Ragan
  (2)Cassandra (Wright) Miller Pvt Spy NC ★
George: b 11-17-1740 d 10-10-1801 m Elizabeth Hinely Pvt PA
George: b 8-11-1731 d 1-27-1791 m Elizabeth Smith NOf CS PA
Hardy: b 5-20-1755 d 7-31-1813 m Jemima Morgan Pvt NC SC
Isaac: b 1734 d 12- -1790 m — X — PM NC
James: b 9-22-1752 d 12-20-1832 m Elizabeth Langley Lt GA
James: b 1755 d 8-20-1815 m Mary Yeoman Pvt PA
James: b 1760 d 11-28-1840 m (2)Mary Jane — Pvt SC
James: b 4-3-1723 d 8-14-1807 m Rebecca Enocks Pvt VA
James: b 6-3-1762 d 5-29-1837 m Elizabeth Vineyard Pvt VA
Jehiel, Sr: b 6-15-1728 d 9-8-1807 m Esther Buckingham Capt CT
Jehiel, Jr: b 10-15-1754 d 4-12-1837 m Mary Treat Sgt CT

BRYAN, contd.
Jesse: b 1-3-1744 d 1-15-1794 m Mary Carney Lt NC
John: b 1754 d 1840 m Mable Clark Pvt CT W ★
John: b 1734 d 5-25-1801 m Rebecca Martin PS Col NC
John: b *c.* 1730 d 3-12-1782 m Elizabeth Oliver Col PS NC
John: b 4-9-1730 d 3-12-1782 m Elizabeth Frances Battle Capt NC
John: b 11-2-1753 d 1-31-1842 m Nancy Robbins Capt PA ★
John: b 12-5-1752 d 11-10-1803 m (1)Rachel Simons (2)Mrs Lidia (Ball) Simons PS SC
John: b 1735 d *p.* 1790 m Biotha Farren Cpl VA
John: b 12-19-1756 d 9- -1825 m Catherine Evans Pvt VA W ★
John: b 10-22-1760 d *p.* 12-18-1806 m (1)Mary — (2)Dorcas Allen Pvt VA
John Council: b 1-3-1742 d 3-14-1807 m (1)Ann — (2)Mary Ann Fulford QM PS NC
John Hill: b 9-30-1761 d 1826 m Elizabeth Harrison Pvt NC
Jonathan: b 9-12-1708 d 3-8-1788 m Mary Williamson PS GA
Joseph: b 9-23-1742 d 7-10-1807 m Mary Hunter PS NC
Joseph, Jr: b *c.* 1743 d *.* 1835 m Susan Calloway Pvt NC
Joseph, Sr: b 1720 d 1805 m(1)Hester Hampdon(2)Aylee—PS KY
Joseph, Jr: b *c.* 1750 d 1833/4 m Elizabeth — Sol VA
Kedar: b 1750 d 1807 m (2)Mary Whitfield CS NC
Lewis: b 1750-2 d *a.* 5- -1796 m (1)Elizabeth (Bryan) Sasser (2)Mary (Swann) Bryan Pvt NC
Mary, Boone: b 11-14-1736 d 1819 m William Bryan PS KY
Morgan: b 1710 d 1779 m Penelope Whitmell PS NC
Nathan: b 1750 d 1798 m (1)Winnifred Bryan (2)Nancy Reynolds Col PS NC
Nathan: b 1756 d *a.* 9-17-1835 m Rebecca Little Sol NC GA
Needham, Jr: b 1750 d *p.* 1785 m Sallie Hinton PS NC
Needham, Sr: b 1725 d 1784 m (1)Nancy Smith (2)Charlotte Moore PS Col NC
Oliver: b 6-3-1756 d 12-15-1832 m Esther (Bryan) Sgt CT W ★
Richard: b 4-30-1759 d 3-19-1826 m Elizabeth Harper PS SC
Robert, Jr.: b 2-6-1751 d 10-23-1802 m Ingebur Stidham Ens DE
Samuel: b 1756 d 3-4-1837 m Mary Hunt Pvt VA W ★
Simon: b *c.* 1751 d *p.* 1792 m Ann Moore Pvt SC
William: b 1728 d 1795 m Mary Ann — Pvt MD
William: b *p.* 1746 d *a.* 3- -1831 m (1)Catherine Lowe (2)Elizabeth Carville Pvt MD
William: b 2-12-1761 d 1845 m Mary Sutphen Pvt NJ
William: b 1730 d 1810 m (1)Susan Green (2) X (3) X BGen PS NC
William: b 10-23-1724 d 11-28-1781 m Elizabeth Smith Col PS NC
William: b 3-6-1733 d 5-30-1780 m Mary Boone Pvt NC
William: b 1-1-1767 d 9-22-1840 m Sarah Price Pvt PA
William: b 5-2-1735 d 1808 m Jane (Williamson) Crocker Pvt SC
William: b *c.* 1746/7 d *p.* 9-19-1808 m Elizabeth Moore Pvt SC
William: b *c.* 1752 d *p.* 3-9-1806 m Letty — Lt VA
William: b 1746 d 1835 m Martha (Love) Lewis Ens VA
Zephaniah: b 1752 d 5-9-1838 m (1)Elizabeth De Vorce (2)Mrs Mary Jane Wade Pvt VA ★

BRYANT, (includes BRIANT)
Alexander: b 11-6-1761 d 9-20-1844 m Susan McAllister Halbert Pvt MA
Alexander: b 3-4-1749 d *p.* 9-28-1816 m Elizabeth — Sol VA
Amos: b 1753 d 8-12-1833 m (1)Eleanor Morse (2)Martha (Barker) Pvt MA ★
Bartholomew: bpt 7-11-1737 d *p.* 1810 m Ellen Brookins Sgt MA
Benjamin: b *c.* 1760 d 1796 m Sarah Whitfield Pvt GA
Benjamin: b 10-17-1734 d 8-3-1788 m Ruxby Perry Pvt MA
Billa: b 10-29-1759 d 1838 m Abigail — Pvt MA ★
Daniel, Sr: b 4-4-1732 d 3-9-1779 m Keziah Richardson MM 2Lt MA
Daniel, Jr: b 4-28-1761 d *c.* 1782 m Mary Bucknam MM Pvt MA
Daniel: b 12-26-1758 d 10-20-1839 m Sarah Merrill Pvt MA ★
Daniel Chandler: b 11-18-1761 d 4-27-1840 m Susanna Byam Sgt NH ★
Daniel Damon: b 11-25-1755 d 8-27-1805 m Bethia Newton Pvt CT W ★
David: b 7-10-1761 d 10-7-1841 m Abigail Eddy Pvt MA
David: b 7-16-1755 d *c.* 1830 m Mary Gilman Lt NH
David: b 5-22-1756 d 8- -1835 m Catharine Woodruff Woolley Pvt NJ ★
David: b *c.* 1760 d — m Kesiah Dawson Sol NC
Ebenezer: b 9-19-1744 d 1-6-1839 m Mrs Lois Sweetland Foster Pvt CT ★
Edmund: b 6-3-1744 d 9-28-1786 m (1)Abigail Fletcher (2)Hannah Sprague Capt NH
Elias: b 7-12-1756 d 5-25-1834 m Mary Boardman Pvt MA ★
Ephraim: b 7-10-1739 d 4-12-1831 m (1)Hepzibah Sawyer (2)Lydia Hovey Sgt MA
George: b 12-3-1693 d 10-21-1779 m Sarah Ripley PS NJ
Hannah Searing: b 1718 d 4-7-1785 m Simeon Bryant PS NJ
James: b *c.* 1753 d 3- -1816 m Hannah — Pvt NH
James: b 1-1-1739 d *p.* 1782 m (1)Jane Guerrant (2)Jane Forsee Pvt VA
Jarathmell: b *c.* 1737 d *p.* 1796 m Sarah McClucas 2Lt MA
Jeremy: b 8-7-1743 d 5-25-1785 m Mary — Pvt PS NH
Job: b *a.* 1744 d *p.* 1786 m Mary Turner Ens MA
John: b — d *p.* 2- -1793 m Sarah Durkee Pvt CT
John: b 5-11-1743 d 5-1-1816 m Hannah Mason CaptLt MA
John: b 1744 d 9-21-1830 m Elizabeth Fly Pvt MA

John: b 4-23-1716 d 10-20-1793 m Abigail Stockbridge Benson PS MA
John: b 1-1-1760 d 7-4-1833 m Mary Owsley Sgt VA ★
Joseph: b 3-8-1729 d 4-14-1810 m Abigail Osgood Maj MA
Joshua: b 2-16-1744/5 d 4-24-1799 m (1)Lucana Randall (2) X (3)Dorcas Hayward Pvt MA
Josiah: b 1748 d 4-17-1798 m Lydia Green Pvt MA
Levi: b 9-23-1756 d 8-31-1823 m Lydia Bradford Sol Fif MA W ★
Micah, Jr.: b 4-2-1744 d *p.* 1790 m Margaret Paddock Pvt MA
Peter: b 1755 d *c.* 1810 m Betty Hubbard Lt VA
Peter: b 1760 d 1819 m Elizabeth Jennings Pvt VA
Robert: b — d 11-23-1830 m Johanna Stevens Ens NH W ★
Samuel: b — d 9- -1785 m Phoebe Dicerson Pvt CT
Samuel: b — d — m Sarah Robertson Pvt NJ
Seth: b 1742/3 d 1-15-1807 m Elizabeth French MM SgtMaj MA
Simeon: b 1710 d 6-25-1784 m Hannah Searing PS NJ
Stephen: b 3-8-1742/3 d *p.* 1804 m Rebecca Bearce Pvt MA
Stephen: b 4-14-1759 d 3-18-1823 m Miriam Davis Pvt MA ★
Sylvanus, Jr: b 5-5-1758 d 10-12-1832 m Judith Chase Pvt MA
Thomas: b 2-25-1742 d — m Elizabeth Chandler Pvt MA
Thomas: b 1789 m Martha Hunt Dr VA
Timothy: b 8-15-1750 d 2-17-1794 m Sarah Flint Pvt CT
Walter, Sr: b 2-10-1710 d 1807 m Elizabeth Folsom CS PS NH
William: b 1739 d 10- -1834 m (1)Rachel Wilcoxon (2)Nancy Wood Pvt NC
William: b — d *p.* 5- -1835 m Mary Owen Sgt VA
Zebulon: b 4-16-1741 d 10-25-1828 m (1)Mary Conant (2)Mary West Lt MA
Zenas: b 7-12-1753 d 6-28-1835 m Mary Ruggles Drm MA ★

BRYDIA,
David: b 1750/1 d 6- -1831 m Olive Marks Pvt CT NH VT ★

BRYER,
Samuel: b 1743 d 1-24-1824 m (1)Huldah — (2)Hannah Booker Pvt MA

BRYNER, (includes BRINER)
Jacob: b 1746 d 12-18-1790 m Barbara Mayer Sgt PA
John: b *c.* 1750 d *a.* 1-31-1837 m Elizabeth — Pvt PA

BRYSON, (includes BRISON)
Hugh: b 1759 d 1835 m Sarah — Pvt PS PA
James: b 6-17-1744 d 11-20-1813 m Mary Miller PS 1Lt PA
John: b 1-1-1758 d 8-3-1855 m Jane Montgomery Pvt PA ★
John: b *c.* 1740 d 11-13-1822 m Priscilla LeFevre 1Lt PA

BUB, (includes BUBB)
George: b 1745 d *p.* 10-12-1825 m Maria Margaret — Pvt PA

BUBIER,
John: b 1760 d 1793 m Hannah Jarvis Cpl Matr MA W ★

BUCHANAN,
Alexander: b 12-4-1752 d 1827 m Rachael Van Schaick Sol NJ
Andrew: b 1740 d 1794 m Joanna Hay Capt VA
Andrew: b 10-22-1734 d 3-12-1786 m Susan Lawson BGen CS MD
Archibald: b *c.* 1738 d 1806 m Mrs Agnes Bowen McFerrin Pvt VA
Benjamin: b *c.* 1757 d *p.* 8-23-1798 m Judith May Sol NC
Benjamin: b 1754 d 8- -1821 m Mary Wood Cpl SC
David: b 1754 d 2-7-1818 m Jane Young Pvt PA
David: b 1749 d 1818 m Susanna Wares Lt VA
George: b 1721 d 1818 m Esther Campbell Pvt PA
George: b 1745 d *p.* 8-17-1811 m Margaret McAfee CS VA
James: b *c.* 1745 d 1810 m (1)Susanna — (2)Hannah — Pvt PA
James: b 11- -1755 d *p.* 1818 m Agnes Turner Pvt PA ★
James: b 5-23-1761 d 11-25-1823 m Margaret Ross Pvt PA
James: bpt 2-5-1749 d *c.* 1797 m Isabel Hall Capt VA
John: b 1736 d 1801 m Anne — Sol GA
John: b 1-5-1743 d 10-19-1795 m Deborah Ann Areson Capt NY
John: b *a.* 1760 d 1806 m Miriam Eager Sgt NY
John: b 1730 d 7-3-1795 m Mary Ross Capt PA
John: b 1725 d 1-25-1810 m (2)Jane Rowan Pvt PA
John: b 1750 d *p.* 1802 m Margaret Wilson Capt SC
John: b 1753 d 1801 m Elizabeth Miott Capt SC
John, Jr: b 1-12-1759 d 11-17-1832 m (1)Margaret Kennedy (2)Sarah Ridley PS SC
John: b 1724 d 1783 m Martha Buchanan Capt VA
Joseph: b 1761 d 1811 m Mary — Sol GA
Robert: b 3-26-1729 d 1818 m Elizabeth Falls Sgt NY
Robert: b *c.* 1750 d 1813 m Mary — Pvt PA
Robert: b 1741 d 1831/2 m (2)Mary Jameson Capt VA
Samuel, Sr: b 1718 d 1783 m Martha Keys CS VA
Samuel, Jr: b *c.* 1742 d *p.* 1788 m Elizabeth Kennedy Ens VA
William: b 1732 d 9-19-1804 m Esther Smith PS MD
William: b 1754/5 d *c.* 1830 m Cathrine McClabe Cpl PA
William: b 1762 d 5-15-1836 m — X — Pvt SC
William: b 1743 d *a.* 9-2-1805 m Isabelle Montgomery Ens VA

BUCHER,
Henry: b 4-16-1764 d 2-3-1824 m Catherine Epley Ens PA
John Conrad: b 7-13-1730 d 8-15-1780 m Mary Magdalena Hooke Chp PA

BUCK,
Aaron: b *c.* 1738 d *a.* 3-7-1787 m Margaret Dillon Pvt PS NJ
Aholiab: b 4-14-1751 d 7-3-1778 m Lucretia York Capt CT
Amasa: b 6-6-1756 d 11-17-1840 m Sybil Hubbard Fif Pvt CT ★
Asahel: b 1743 d 2-23-1779 m Mehetabel — 2 Lt CT
Benjamin: b 10-10-1744 d 12-24-1807 m Dorcas Sutton Capt MD
Benjamin: b 11-21-1752 d 2-4-1851 m Phebe — Pvt NY
Christian: b 1754 d 2-18-1829 m Catherine — Pvt PA
Daniel: b *c.* 1766 d 8-14-1816 m Content Ashley 3Sgt MA ★
Daniel: b 1762 d 1843 m Marietta Heyford Pvt MA
Daniel: b *c.* 2-27-1737 d 4-13-1814 m (1)Ann Denton (2)Olive Stephens 2Maj NY
David: b 4-6-1738 d 7-1-1810 m (1)Anne Russell (2)Sarah Roberts 1Lt CT
Ebenezer: b 4-25-1752 d 8-20-1824 m Mary Brown Capt ME
Ebenezer: b 3-8-1750 d 7-16-1831 m Anna Tallcott Sgt MA
Elijah: b 1749 d 7-26-1830 m Margaret Foster Pvt CT
Elijah: b 4-14-1760 d 8-24-1852 m Lois Buck Pvt CT MA ★
Ephraim: b *c.* 1742-4 d 1829 m Mary Wainwright Lt NJ
Francis: b 5-13-1758 d 8-5-1829 m Lucretia Thayer Pvt Drm MA
George: b 9-20-1760 d 1-9-1845 m Agnes Simonds Pvt CT ★
George: b 11-17-1766 d *p.* 1802 m Lucy Hard Pvt VT
Ichabod: b 11-25-1757 d 3-19-1849 m (1)Lucy Boardman (2)Sybil Dayton Pvt NY ★
Isaac: b 1745 d 2-6-1825 m Abigail Randall Pvt CT
Isaac: b 9-27-1757 d *p.* 1840 m Patty Phillips Cpl MA ★
Isaac: b 11-11-1750 d 8-20-1830 m Sarah Hayward Pvt MA
Isaac: b 1764 d *p.* 1833 m Submit Willson Pvt NH
Isaac, Sr.: b 1729-35 d 1-20-1776 m Elizabeth Waters Sgt VT
Isaac, Jr: b 5-23-1763 d 1841 m Sarah Hall Pvt VT
Israel: b 5-7-1762 d 2-3-1807 m Phebe Benedict Cav CT
Jacob: b 7-27-1752 d — m Hannah Ames Cpl MA
James: b 3-24-1726 d 1-28-1793 m Elizabeth Sherman Capt CT
Joel: b 6-4-1758 d 5-31-1831 m Huldah Bostwick Pvt CT
John: b 7-26-1731 d 1798 m Elizabeth Judd Pvt CT
John: b *c.* 1754 d 3-4-1828 m Abigail Irish Ens MA
John: b 1746 d 3-18-1839 m (1)Mary —(2)— (3)Priscilla Pvt VT
John: b 1748 d 9- -1816 m Miriam Richardson CS LCol VA
Jonathan: b 1751 d *p.* 4-15-1833 m Mary Brecenbridge Pvt CT ★
Jonathan, Sr: b 2-20-1719 d 3-18-1795 m Lydia Morse Col MA
Jonathan, Jr: b 1740 d 3-27-1824 m Hannah Gale Maj MA
Joseph: b 5-13-1753 d 5-15-1803 m Ruth Seeley Capt NJ
Josiah: b 1-25-1756 d 7-15-1813 m Mary Towner Ens CT
Justus: b 3-11-1726 d *p.* 1794 m Rosamond Parmalee Capt CT
Lemuel, Sr: b 9-6-1732 d *p.* 1790 m Bertha McEwen PS VT
Lemuel, Jr: b 4-8-1753 d 6-29-1823 m Phebe Buck Pvt VT
Moses: b *c.* 1747 d 1809 m Pollie Adams Pvt MA
Moses: b 11-26-1760 d 8-24-1826 m Hannah Chubb Pvt MA
Nathan: b 2-16-1744 d 3-9-1830 m Elizabeth Thompson Pvt MA
Nicholas: b *c.* 1730 d 11-13-1786 m Elizabeth Hartman Pvt PA
Perrigriene: b 1769 d 12- -1822 m Abigail Brown Pvt NY
Reuben: b 6-27-1759 d 11-30-1805 m Esther Harnden Pvt MA
Robert: b *c.* 1745 d *a.* 11-1-1805 m Margaret — PS PA
Samuel: b 12-17-1734 d 9-10-1810 m Martha Bloss Pvt CT
Samuel: b 1730 d 1785-90 m (2)Hannah Wright Pvt CT
Samuel: b 3-22-1747 d 7-26-1833 m Susannah Palmer Pvt MA ★
Samuel: b 2-25-1758 d 3-18-1852 m Jerusha Greenough Baker Pvt MA
Samuel Beebe: b 1751 d 3-26-1834 m Hannah Fairchild PS CT
Stephen: b *c.* 1755 d 1820 m — X — Ens NC
Thomas: b 9-2-1762 d 1-6-1840 m Abigail Carpenter Pvt Mrnr CT
Thomas: b 10-1-1752 d 7-27-1818 m Silence Brett Pvt MA
Thomas: b 1-9-1756 d 6-4-1842 m Anne Richardson Capt VA
William: b 3-23-1723 d 3-13-1800 m Deborah Farman PS CT
William: b 4-2-1755 d 4-1-1839 m Sarah Maxwell Sgt MA
William: b 1765 d 10-8-1805 m Elizabeth Murray Pvt VT
Zebediah: b 3-29-1719 d *a.* 3-10-1788 m (1)Lydia Carter (2)Mary Butters PS CS MA

BUCKBEE,
John: b 1-20-1742 d 6-14-1809 m Sophia — Pvt NY
Russell: b 1-28-1715 d 9-22-1795 m Marcy — Pvt NY

BUCKHOLTZ,
Abraham: b 1729 d 1812 m Sarah (Hodge) Malone Maj SC

BUCKHOUT,
Jacob: bpt 11-1-1720 d *p.* 9-5-1787 m Maritie Acker Sol NY

BUCKINGHAM,
David: b 3-14-1760 d 2-5-1832 m Chloe Merrell Pvt CT
Ebenezer: b 12-10-1727 d 10-6-1798 m Abigail Andrus Capt CT
Ebenezer: b 11-1-1748 d 10-24-1824 m Esther Bradley Pvt NY
Hezekiah: b 3-22-1727 d — m Elizabeth Chatfield Pvt CT
Jared: b 10-22-1732 d *c.* 1812 m Lucy Mather Pvt CT
John: b 9-2-1735 d 11-2-1802 m Sarah (Buckingham) Ens CT
John: b 9-27-1744 d 9-15-1809 m Sarah Green Pvt CT
John: b 11-10-1741 d 12-1-1794 m Mary Bell CS PA
Nathan: b 8-20-1735 d 1815 m Esther Osborn PS CT
Richard: b 11-19-1757 d 1-17-1841 m Mary Rice Gilpin Pvt DE
Stephen: b 5-12-1763 d 2-26-1814 m (1)Mary Dorrance (2)Polly Brewster Pvt CT
William: b 6-2-1734 d 6-23-1829 m Jane Jones PS Pvt PA

BUCKLES,
Robert: b 10-10-1740 d 1809 m Rachel Van Meter 2Lt VA
Robert, Sr: b 6-15-1702 d *a.* 12-21-1790 m Ann Brown PS VA
William: b 1743 d 7- -1824 m Priscilla Hendricks Lt VA

BUCKLIN, (includes BUCKLAN, BUCKLAND, & BUCKLYN)
Darius: b 6-25-1751 d 8-25-1814 m Hannah Brown Pvt MA
David: b 9-5-1726 d 1-22-1820 m Abigail Waldo PS RI
Elijah: b 10-27-1733 d 4-30-1820 m (1)Mercy Ballou (2)Beebe Newell Pvt MA
George: b 9-25-1757 d 12-12-1843 m Elizabeth — Pvt CT ★
James: b 11-30-1743 d 4-4-1780 m Hannah Shaw Pvt MA
Jeremiah: b 1745 d 5-13-1837 m Rhoda Eaton Pvt MA
John: b 2-12-1732 d 4-2-1790 m Jemima Peck Ens MA
John: b 3-23-1718 d 12-5-1803 m Jerusha Eaton Pvt MA
John: b 1754 d 5-12-1838 m Leah Scott Ens RI
Jonathan: b *c.* 1716 d *c.* 1812 m (1)Sybil Burnham Pvt CT
Jonathan: b 6-8-1764 d 4-22-1855 m Laura Lad Pvt CT MA
Nathaniel: b 1741 d 9-18-1829 m Margaret Gamble PS MA
Oliver: b 6-11-1736 d *p.* 3-11-1787 m Sarah Newman Pvt MA
Rufus: b 1757 d 1841 m (1)Lucinda Barrows (2)Mrs Buckmaster MA ★
Squire, Jr: b 10-3-1756 d 11-21-1814 m Amy Pray Pvt RI
Stephen: b 8- -1742 d 1782 m Mary Olmsted Capt CT

BUCKMINSTER,
Job: b *c.* 1720-2 d *c.* 1787/8 m Sarah Colborn Pvt MA
Joseph, Sr.: b 6-18-1697 d 5-15-1780 m (1)Sarah Lawson (2)Mrs Hannah Kiggell CS MA
Lawson: b 4-8-1742 d 2-26-1832 m Mary Jones Capt MA
Thomas: b 8-18-1751 d 7-7-1826 m (1)Hannah (Winch) Rice (2)Keziah (Perry) Bacon SgtMaj MA

BUCKNAM, (includes BUCKMAN)
Aaron: b 2-23-1728/9 d 1778 m (1)Alice Skinner (2)Joanna Floyd Pvt MA
Benjamin: b 4-16-1759 d 10-1-1842 m Mrs Eunice Judd Mather OrdlSgt MA
Benjamin: b 7-26-1756 d 10-28-1808 m Ann Janney Ens PA
Daniel: b 1722 d 1808 m (1)Phebe Gould (2)Rebeckah Boyden Capt MA
Edwards: b 6-21-1741 d 3-29-1813 m (1)Susannah Page (2)Mrs Nancy (Daggett) Hartwell Sct PS CS NH
Jacob: b 8-16-1759 d 2-19-1839 m Elizabeth Munroe Pvt MA
John: b 9-19-1730 d 8-2-1808 m Anna Wright 1Lt MA
John: b 7-2-1746 d 4-22-1792 m Mary Wilson Pvt MA
Joses: b 1744 d *p.* 1786 m Nabby Hay Pvt MA
Nathan: b 11-11-1756 d 5-11-1824 m Anna Pote 2Lt MA
Nathan: b 11-2-1703 d 2-6-1795 m Margaret Fiske Sol MA
Nathan: b 1751 d 9-4-1807 m Elizabeth Stower Pvt MA
Reuben: b 5-3-1759 d 3-16-1842 m Mercy Blackmer Pvt MA ★
Thomas: b 7-15-1754 d 10-22-1837 m Mary Harding Pvt PA

BUCKNER,
Aylett: b 3-3-1745 d 1811 m Judith Presley Thornton Maj VA
Bernard: b 1-19-1759 d 7-30-1792 m Sarah Heape Sol CS SC
Horace: b 1754 d 1821 m Fanny Thornton Dr VA
Jesse: b *c.* 1740 d *p.* 3- -1826 m Martha — PS NC
Mordecai: b 1721 d 1800 m Elizabeth Beverly (Chew) Standard Col VA
Philip: b 5-13-1747 d 10-24-1820 m Tabitha Ann Daniel Capt VA
Richard: b *c.* 1720 d 12- -1777 m Elizabeth Aylett Maj VA
Richard: b 1730-5 d *p.* 10-15-1793 m Eliza Ariss PS VA
Thomas, Sr: b 5-13-1728 d 1795 m (1)Judith Presley Thornton (2)Elizabeth Taliaferro Capt VA
Thomas, Jr: b 8-21-1755 d 1804 m Elizabeth Hawes Ens VA
Thomas: b *c.* 1754 d *p.* 1785 m Elizabeth Throckmorton Lt VA
Thomas: b 1765/6 d 1827 m Hanna Burton Pvt VA
William: b 10-1-1753 d *p.* 1787 m Elizabeth Monroe Capt VA
William: b *c.* 1730 d *p.* 3-5-1783 m (1)Lucy Thornton (2)Mary (Madison—) Capt VA
William: b 1750 d 2-13-1804 m — X — Mstr VA

BUCKWALTER,
Abraham: b 2-28-1761 d 1-2-1837 m Barbara — Pvt PA
Daniel: b 1751 d 12-18-1830 m Ruth Shainholtz Pvt PA
David: b 3-19-1753 d 3-27-1819 m Barbara Ziegler Pvt PA
Jacob: b 1-4-1754 d 2-9-1818 m Mary M Aker Pvt PA
Jacob: b 3-26-1757 d 7-4-1838 m Maria Essig Pvt PA

BUDD,
Berne: b 1738 d 12-14-1777 m Phebe Wheeler Dr NJ
Daniel: b 7-27-1722 d 12-24-1806 m Mary Purdy Capt NJ
Daniel: b 1-5-1751 d 3-15-1815 m Rebecca Lawyer Dr NY
Gilbert: b 1736 d *p.* 1781 m Deborah Searles Lt NY
Gilbert: b 12-25-1758 d 10-13-1825 m Frances Jevoe Pvt NY
John, Sr.: b *c.* 1730 d *p.* 1790 m Mrs Susannah Robson PS MD
John, Jr.: b *c.* 1755 d *p.* 1815 m (1)Rebecca Tolley (2)Barbara Brooke PS 1Lt MD
John: b 1756 d 6-12-1804 m Mary — Sol MA
John: b 10-10-1730 d 10-1-1813 m Mary Merritt Pvt Adj NY
John: b 1-8-1760 d 6-19-1845 m Mary Russell Pvt NY ★
John: b 10-23-1750 d 11-13-1832 m — X — Pvt PA ★
John: b *c.* 1732 d 10-8-1791 m Rosannah Shivers Dr SC

BUDD, contd.
Joseph: b 9-21-1755 d 7-21-1821 m Mary Fox Maj NJ
Joseph: b *a.* 1763 d *p.* 1796 m —X— Pvt NY
Joshua: b 10-21-1759 d 4-22-1823 m Elizabeth Fitch Sol PA
Thomas: b *c.* 1724 d 3-7-1778 m Ann Hawkhurst Mstr Pvtr NJ

BUDDINGTON,
Walter: b 1732 d 4-8-1800 m Ruth Waterman Sol CT
Walter: bpt 8-26-1744 d 7-22-1826 m Ruth Couch Pvt PS CT

BUDDY, (includes BUDDEN)
James: b *a.* 1760 d 1-7-1788 m Frances Bisphon Lt PA
Peter: b 1734 d 7-23-1787 m Margarita Barbara Fischer Pvt PA

BUDLONG,
Samuel, Sr: b 1735/6 d 12-16-1816 m Katharine Rhodes Sol RI
Samuel, Jr: b 11-2-1764 d 5-1-1836 m Waite Salisbury Pvt Drm RI
Stephen: b 8-17-1761 d 10-13-1850 m (2)Isabella Lippitt Pvt RI

BUEHLER,
Henry: b 1-24-1740 d 8-2-1801 m Jane Trotter 3Lt PA

BUELL, (includes BUEL)
Aaron: b 9-21-1730 d 11-11-1807 m (1)Hannah Post (2)Amy Park Pvt NH
Abraham: b 2-19-1734 d 1815 m Sarah Stone Pvt NH
Archelaus: b 4-14-1737 d 8-13-1811 m Mary Langdon Capt CT
Asa: b 1-10-1760 d 5-24-1827 m Mercy Porter Pvt CT
Bela: b 5-1-1747 d 2-15-1848 m Temperance Griswold Sgt CT
Daniel: b 12-8-1760 d 8-26-1839 m Eunice Bascom Pvt CT
David: b 7-21-1757 d 9-10-1841 m Chloe Fischer Pvt CT ★
Ebenezer: b 3-26-1747 d 5-26-1823 m Hannah Plumb PS CT
Elias: b 10-8-1737 d 5-17-1824 m Sarah Turner Maj CT
Ephraim: b 8-21-1742 d 1-4-1820 m Priscilla Holmes Capt VT
Gordon: b 2-21-1752 d 3-24-1819 m Martha Whittlesey Pvt CT
Ira: b 2-20-1744/5 d 3-4-1778 m Prudence Deming PS CT
Isaac: b 11-18-1757 d 1-4-1845 m (1)Prudence Sprague (2)Mary — Pvt PM Arfr CT ★
Jedediah, Jr.: b 9-2-1739 d 10-5-1818 m Esther Wilcox Lt CT
Jeremiah, Jr.: b 7-24-1742 d *p.* 1789 m (1)Dinah Kelsey (2)Jerusha Pvt CT
Jesse: b 4-10-1748 d 5- -1818 m Lydia Beach Ens CT
Job, Sr.: b 2-10-1725 d 3-2-1791 m (1)Lois Bradley (2)Sarah Murray Pvt CT
Job, Jr.: b 4-9-1758 d 9-2-1819 m Ruth Redfield Pvt CT
John: b 5-1-1750 d 3-29-1842 m Ruth Wellman Pvt CT ★
John Hutchinson: b 11-21-1753 d 9-19-1813 m (1)Phebe Hubbell (2)Sarah Taylor Metcalf Capt CT
Jonathan, Sr: b 12-13-1717 d 8-2-1796 m Lydia Landon PS CT
Jonathan: b 3-7-1745 d 4-13-1823 m Hannah Bailey Sgt CT
Joseph: b 5-29-1749 d 7-24-1828 m Hope Loveland Pvt CT
Joseph: b 8- -1758 d 6-19-1832 m (2)Lucy Pickett Pvt CT
Joseph: b 9-1-1738 d 1-1-1801 m Jane Chalker Pvt NH
Joseph: b 8-24-1710 d *p.* 1790 m (1)Anna Submit Colton (2)— Lane PS NH
Josiah: b 10-28-1757 d 1838 m Lois Clark Pvt CT
Martin: b 6-1-1759 d 9-15-1844 m Aseneth Dibble Sol CT
Matthew, Sr.: b 3-10-1734 d 11-2-1804 m Mary Kibbie Lt CT W ★
Matthew: b 2-25-1758 d 5- -1840 m Mary Nevers Sol NH
Nathaniel: b 10-26-1734 d 11-27-1808 m Hannah Lee LCol CT
Nathan: b 4-4-1763 d *p.* 1850 m Hannah Turner Pvt CT ★
Orange: b 12-18-1763 d 12-13-1838 m Sarah — Pvt Tms CT
Peter, Jr.: b 10-12-1739/8 d 1-30-1797 m Abigail Seymour Lt CT
Samuel, Sr: b 6-22-1713 d 3-9-1790 m Lydia Wilcox Pvt CT
Samuel: b 9-1-1716 d 7-19-1798 m Mary Mulford Chp CT
Samuel, Jr.: b 1742 d 9-14-1819 m Clarinda Hoadley Lt MA
Solomon, Sr: b 8-22-1734 d 3-23-1793 m Lydia Case Capt CT
Solomon, Jr: b 2-1-1757 d 1-17-1835 m Abiah Wells Pvt CT ★
Solomon: b 4-12-1760 d 10-18-1837 m Sophia Root QM CT ★
Solomon: b 8-30-1715 d 3-22-1795 m (1)Eunice Griswold (2)Jerusha (Jewett) Gillett PS CT
Timothy: b 5-3-1757 d 1-26-1849 m (1)Olive Norton Sol CT

BUFFETT,
John: b 1728 d 12-7-1807 m Rebecca Ketcham Capt NY
Joseph, Jr: b 1733 d 1781 m Sarah Smith PS NY
Josiah: bpt 3-28-1736 d 1786 m Rachel Wickes PS NY
Nathaniel: b 7-2-1742 d 6-14-1826 m Zeruiah Platt Ens NY

BUFFINGTON,
Benjamin: b 2-2-1730 d 2-11-1814 m (1)Mary Frissell (2)Mrs Catharine Deibler Pvt PA
David: b 1762 d 10-6-1836 m Margaret — Pvt VA ★
George: b 2-8-1759 d 5-26-1830 m Barbara Hoffman Pvt PA
Isaac: b 6-7-1753 d *p.* 1796 m Ann — Pvt PA
Joel: b — d *a.* 2-18-1834 m Elizabeth — Tms VA
Joseph: b 1742 d *p.* 1819 m Sarah Young Pvt PA
Joseph: b 7-20-1737 d 8-12-1798 m Mary Aston Few Pvt SC
Preserved: b 12-20-1759 d 7-23-1843 m Sarah Howard Pvt RI ★
Robert: b *c.* 1740 d 6-1-1807 m Elizabeth — Pvt VA
Thomas: b 1756 d 2-23-1814 m Elizabeth Slaymaker Lt PA
Thomas: b — d 1796 m (2)Lydia Brinton PS PA

BUFFUM,
Jedediah: b 8-17-1737 d 1808 m Sarah Taft CS & PS NH

BUFORD,
Abraham: b 7-31-1749 d 6-30-1833 m Martha McDowell Col VA
Henry: b 9-19-1751 d 12-31-1814 m (1)Mildred Blackburn (2)Jane Kent Quirk Capt VA
James: b 1740 d *p.* 11-5-1792 m Elizabeth Bramblett Capt VA
James: b 7-5-1746 d *p.* 1803 m Priscilla Ragsdale Sol VA
James: b 1712 d *p.* 1789 m Mary — CS VA
John: b *c.* 1760 d *p.* 1831 m (1)Mary Green (2)— Blackshear (3)— Crosby Pvt SC
John: b 10-13-1757 d 2-14-1852 m Rhoda Shrewsbury Sgt Spy VA ★
John: b 1764 d 1854 m Frances Turpin Banton Pvt VA
Leroy: b 4-29-1751 d 1810 m Frances Ragsdale PS VA
Simeon: b 12-19-1757 d 1840 m Margaret Kirtley Capt VA ★
Thomas: b 1736 d 10-10-1774 m Anna Watts Capt VA
William: b 2-1-1747 d 1810 m Francis June Maj NC
William: b *c.* 1760 d *c.* 1817 m Martha — Maj SC
William: b 1745 d 1814 m Mary Welsh Pvt VA

BUGBEE,
Abial: b 2-27-1746 d 1-17-1824 m Hannah Harwood Pvt CT
Amos: b 11-3-1749 d 2-15-1804 m Martha Woodward Pvt CT
Benjamin: b 1729 d *p.* 1790 m Susannah Morse PS VT
Ebenezer: b 1-28-1751 d 1-12-1834 m Mary White Pvt MA
Elijah: b 10-9-1755 d 11-13-1827 m Sarah Bacon Pvt CT ★
Hezekiah: b 2-19-1746 d 8-4-1826 m Bathshua Holmes Ens CT
Isaiah: b 12-9-1729 d 8-3-1806 m Hulda Ainsworth Sol CT
Jedediah: b 5-6-1741/2 d 10-24-1776 m Molly Hiscox Pvt CT
Jedediah: b 1-22-1746 d *p.* 1793 m Sarah Dodge Pvt CT
John: b 4-9-1752 d 3-18-1838 m Hannah Peters Pvt CT ★
Peter: b 6-11-1762 d 2-18-1835 m Isabel Root Pvt CT ★
Samuel: b 8-29-1753 d 2-23-1818 m (1)Eunice Everett (2)Betsey Reed Pvt MA
William: b 4-24-1737 d 11-18-1815 m Elizabeth Franklin Cpl CT
William: b 5-19-1741 d *p.* 1816 m Hannah Maxfield Pvt MA

BUGG,
Anselm: b 1742/3 d 1815/20 m Lucy Morgan 1Lt PA
Edmund: b *c.* 1730 d 1-17-1782 m Obedience Hobson PS GA
Elizabeth Hobson: b 172- d 1799 m Sherwood Bugg PS GA
John: b 2-1-1731 d 1818 m Elizabeth — Sol GA
John: b 1745 d 1825 m Ruth C Hicks Pvt GA
Joseph: b *c.* 1720 d *a.* 7-3-1781 m (2)Deborah Hudson Pvt NY
Sherwood: b 7-8-1720 d *p.* 1-20-1783 m Elizabeth Hobson Capt GA
Wm.: b 1712 d 1798 m(1)Mary Bacon(2)Susanna Woodson CS VA

BUGH,
Peter: b 12-21-1753 d 10-11-1819 m Catherine Haverstock Pvt PA

BULFINCH,
John: b 7-17-1727 d 2-4-1812 m Anna Breed CS MA
Thomas: b 1728 d 2-13-1802 m Susan Apthorp CS MA

BULFORD,
John: b 5-17-1762 d 2-27-1831 m (1)Eunice — (2)Sarah Barney (3)Olive — Pvt CT

BULKLEY, (includes BUCKLEY, BULKELEY)
Benjamin: b 8-1-1731 d 8- -1822 m (1)Susannah Kirby (2)Elizabeth Brownell Lt PS CT
Butler: b *c.* 1710 d *c.* 1819/20 m Elizabeth Story PS VA
Charles, Jr: b 3-9-1760 d 1-15-1799 m Eunice Robbins Pvt CT
Charles: b 5-22-1752 d 2-12-1824 m (1)Betsy Taintor (2)Prudence Wells Lt CT
Chauncey: b 1743 d 5-10-1818 m Mary Bowers Pvt CT
Daniel: b 5-13-1744 d 7-20-1810 m (1)Dorothy Olmsted (2)Mary Clark Lt CT
Daniel: b 9-14-1751 d 11-2-1830 m (1)Mary Parsons (2)Anna Howard (3)Rhoda Preston Pvt CT ★
Edward: b 1741 d 6-30-1737 m (1)Rachel Lyman Pomeroy (2)Prudence Welles BgdMaj CT
Eleazer: b 2-2-1763 d 2-5-1843 m Mary Ogden Pvt & Mar CT
Eliphalet: b 8-8-1746 d 1-11-1816 m Anna (Bulkeiey) LCol CT
Francis: b 7-31-1757 d 4-26-1813 m (1)Rhoda Griswold (2)Elizabeth Fosdick Pvt CT
Fred: b — d *p.* 9-15-1776 m Elizabeth Somers Pvt CT
Giles: b 12-14-1729 d 8-4-1785 m — X — Pvt CT
Isaac: b 1743 d 8-1-1822 m Elizabeth Lacey Pvt PA
Israel: b 1-22-1762 d 12-18-1828 m Lucy Chapin Pvt CT
Job: b 2-23-1719 d 9-6-1786 m Dorcas Conklin Pvt CT
John: b 10-16-1719 d 7-19-1799 m (1)Hannah Clemson (2)Alice Williamson Lownes PS Sol DE
Joseph: b 8-21-1759 d 10-17-1859 m Ellen Hubbell Pvt CT ★
Joseph: b 5-1-1755 d 6-4-1813 m Grizzel Thorp Sgt CT W ★
Joshua: b 1750 d 7-26-1821 m — X — Pvt CT
Nathan: b 2-16-1757 d 6-9-1837 m (1)Sarah Jennings (2)Ann Jerusha Bulkley Pvt CT
Roger: b 9-14-1751 d 8-1-1819 m (1)Jerusha Root (2)Rhoda Loomis (3)Mrs Polly (Champion) Bulkley Lt CT
Solomon: b 3-21-1747 d 3-4-1790 m Martha Williams Pvt CT

Stephen: b 11-19-1749 d 5- -1813 m Martha Marsh Sgt CT
Turney: b 6-9-1755 d 12-2-1826 m — Ens CT W★
William, Sr.: b c. 1725 d 1789 m Elizabeth — Pvt VA
William: b c. 1752 d 9-16-1776 m — X — Pvt VA

BULL,
Abraham: b 3-9-1740 d 9-13-1820 m Abigail Payne Sol NY
Ambrose: b c. 1750 d p. 3-27-1789 m Elizabeth — Pvt NC
Asa: b 9-4-1752 d 4-16-1805 m Tamar Little Pvt CT
Asher: b — d 1816 m Hannah Hopkins Sgt CT
Caleb: b 3-13/18-1717/18 d 2-14-1789 m Martha Cadwell PS & Mil CT
Crispin: b 1740 d 3-24-1810 m Mary Carpenter CS VT
Daniel: b 10-23-1763 d 3-4-1845 m Elizabeth Durand Lt CT
Daniel: b 8-14-1762 d 11-14-1849 m Catharine Miller Pvt NY
Edmund: b 1-13-1729/30 d p. 3-8-1776 m Susana Lyon Pvt MD
Epaphras: b 2-3-1748 d 9-30-1781 m Deborah Coleman Maj CT
Gurdon: b 5-9-1767 d 1-26-1841 m Mary Ann Harper Pvt CT
Henry: b 1749 d 10-29-1816 m Grace Brown Pvt PA
Isaac: b 11-27-1729 d 8-11-1794 m Sarah Mulliner Pvt NY
Jacob: b a. 1733 d p. 1776 m Rennis Bussey PS MD
John: b 12-4-1759 d 8-14-1837 m Martha Rodgers Cpl CT ★
John: b 2-11-1749 d 11-14-1839 m Dorcas Smith 2Lt MA
John: b 1750 d 1817 m Sarah Meredith Lt PA
John: b 6-1-1731 d 8-9-1826 m Mary Phillips Col PS PA
Jonathan: b 1718 d c. 1800 m Abigail — QM CT
Mary Phillips: b 8-3-1731 d 2-23-1811 m John Bull PS PA
Nathaniel: b 8-30-1740 d 6-14-1807 m Sarah Bartholomew Lt CS CT
Richard: b 9-21-1757 d 8-20-1840 m Ann Anderson Pvt PA
Roger: b 1743 d 5-23-1783 m Ruth Russell Ens CT
Samuel, Sr: b 2-26-1722 d 10-27-1794 m Jerusha Hopkins PS CT
Samuel: b 11-12-1758 d 3-30-1840 m Margaret Gale Pvt NY
Stephen: b 3-18-1734 d 1779/80 m Anne Barnwell BGen SC
Thomas: b 3-15-1729 d 2-24-1804 m (1)Elizabeth Curtiss (2) Amaryllis Prindle Maj CT
Thomas: b 1746 d p. 1779 m Sarah Gronow Capt PA
Thomas: b c. 1728-1744 d 7-13-1837 m (1)Ann Hunter (2)Mrs Lydia Crowell LCol PA ★
Thomas: b 1738 d 1787 m Sarah — PS PA
Thomas, Sr.: b c. 1740 d p. 1790 m Mrs Martha Hart Capt VT
Thomas, Jr.: b 11-17-1762 d 10-16-1823 m Sylvia Benedict Pvt VT
William: b 9-25-1762 d 4-6-1842 m Elizabeth Hager Pvt Fif MA
William: b 9-28-1751 d 10-7-1817 m Bethiah Reeve Capt NY
William: b 4-5-1758 d 3-23-1828 m Sarah Darlington Pvt PA
William: b 1740 d 10-31-1811 m — X — PS Pvt VA

BULLARD,
Adam: b 8-10-1752 d 3-8-1843 m Lois Richardson Pvt MA
Asa: b 7-10-1730 d 5-1-1803 m (1)Hannah Jones (2)Hannah Cook Pvt MA
Baruch: b 12-16-1758 d p. 1788 m Juletta Messenger Cpl MA
Benjamin: b 1730 d 8- -1778 m Judith Lewis Pvt MA
David: b 8-30-1761 d 2-8-1831 m Elizabeth Hadley Pvt & Fif MA
Ebenezer: b 9-16-1737 d 1792 m Elizabeth Haven Pvt MA
Eleazer: b 3-11-1737 d 10-25-1825 m Hannah Rawson Pvt MA
Elijah: b 1-11-1750/51 d p. 1804 m Milcah Pond Pvt MA
Elisha: b 4-6-1752 d 3-14-1834 m Rachel Rockwood Sgt MA ★
Henry, Jr.: b 4-29-1749 d 5-11-1821mRebecca Richardson Pvt MA
Isaac: b 7-9-1744 d 3-18-1810 m Mrs Mary Fisher Sgt MA
Isaac: b 7-10-1744 d 6-8-1808 m Patience Baker Ens MA
Isaac: b 10-9-1726 d 1-12-1814 m Beulah Leland Pvt MA
Isaac: b 4-2-1749 d 1846 m Catherine Tyler Pvt MA ★
James: b 1750 d 4- -1832 m Sarah Pittman Pvt NC W ★
John: b 8-21-1744 d p. 1790 m Mrs Johanna Thare Cpl MA
Jonathan, Jr: b 10-21-1734 d 9-30-1824 m Polly Barbour Pvt MA
Jonathan: b 3-29-1727 d 11-26-1796 m (1)Anna Harrington (2) Lydia Foster PS MA
Malachi: b d 12- -1793 m Bethiah Fisher Pvt MA
Moses: b 3-9-1734 d 11-21-1793 m Sarah Newell Capt MA
Nathan: b 5- -1746 d 5-5-1822 m Bathsheba Hill Cpl MA
Nathan: b 1-15-1754 d 12-25-1836 m Rebecca Fenton Pvt MA ★
Nathaniel: b 3-11-1759 d 11-27-1816 m Sarah Saunders Drm MA
Peter: b 9-23-1734 d 6-11-1809 m Elizabeth Ware PS MA
Samuel: b 8-2-1729 d 3-5-1807 m (1)Martha Perry (2)Mary Coolidge Ware Col PS MA
Samuel, Sr: b 1-11-1715 d 5-27-1793 m Deborah Morse CS MA
Samuel, Jr: b 9-5-1740 d 1-27-1816 m Lydia Partridge Cpl MA
Seth: b 1-6-1736 d 8-1-1811 m Joanna Lewis Maj MA
Silas: b 5-24-1746 d 2-9-1826 m Mary Furnis Cpl MA
Silas: b 4-2-1752 d 5-15-1835 m Avis Keyes Pvt NH
Thomas: b 12-13-1759 d 3-26-1837 m Jemima Hall Pvt NC ★
William: b 9-4-1741 d 1824 m Hannah Sumner Pvt MA

BULLEN,
David: b 3-10-1733 d 11-5-1801 m Isabel — Cpl CT
Jeduthan: b 1-30-1751 d 3-5-1830 m (1)Dolly Clark (2)Bathsheba Daniels Lt MA
John: b c. 1748 d 6-17-1824 m Mary Winslow (or Green) Pvt MA
Joseph: b 1753 d 3-26-1825 m Hannah Morse PS VT
Michael, Sr.: b c. 1727 d p. 3-10-1807 m (1)X (2)Margaret Miller Sol NC
Michael, Jr.: b 1750 d a. 11-2-1830 m — X — Cpl NC
Samuel: b 7-29-1733 d p. 1800 m Elizabeth Legg Sgt MA

Samuel, Sr.: b 4- -1735 d 11-10-1810 m Anna Brown CS PS MA
Samuel, Jr.: b 3-30-1761 d p. 1808 m (1)Sarah Fletcher (2)Jane Smith Pvt MA

BULLINGTON,
Robert: b c. 1740 d 1821 m (1)Elizabeth — (2)Nancy Harvey 2Lt VA

BULLIS,
Charles: b 1723 d 7-6-1809 m Elizabeth Bulles Sol VT

BULLITT,
Cuthbert: b 1740 d 8-27-1791 m —X — PS VA

BULLMAN,
Joseph: b — d — m Margaret Doty Ens NJ

BULLOCK, (includes BULLOCH)
Aaron: b 8-27-1748 d 7-24-1811 m Mehitable Hix Cpl MA
Archibald: b 1731 d 2-22-1777 m Mary De Veaux PS CS GA
Barak: b 12-9-1744 d c. 1823 m Zillah Caswell Pvt MA
Caleb: b 10-12-1751 d 1832 m Nancy Rowland Sgt MA
Comfort: b 3-9-1762 d 7-23-1851 m (1)Sibble Pearce (2)Bethiah Bowen Pvt MA
Daniel: b 1757 d 1809 m Mary Whitehurst Sgt NC
Darius: b 10-21-1761 d 10-28-1833 m Chloe Pierce Pvt MA W ★
David: d c. 1740-50 d p. 1830 m Frances Killebrew Sol NC
David: b 5-25-1740 d p. 1778 m Mary Ballou Cpl RI
David: b 1761 d 7-30-1838 m Jane Terry Pvt VA ★
Ebenezer: b 6-30-1739 d 1804 m Ruth Round Sgt MA
Edward: b c. 1736 d 1783 m Agnes Wingfield Capt VA
Hawkins: b 3-19-1764 d 11-1-1833 m Frances R Gordon Pvt SC ★
Hezekiah: b 11-12-1754 d p. 1802 m Abigail Aldrich Pvt NH
Israel: b 1756 d 3-6-1837 m Freelove Davenport Pvt MA ★
Jabez: b 4-19-1741 d 5-3-1806 m Mary Richmond Capt MA
James: b 3- -1701 d 10-25-1780 m (1)Jean Stobo (2)Mrs Anne Barker Ferguson (3)Mary Jones (4)Mrs Annie Cuthbert Graham CS GA
James, Sr: b 2-23-1735 d 6-29-1813 m (1)Rebecca Wingfield (2)Ann Waller PS VA
James, Jr: b 12-18-1760 d 3-10-1836 m Anne Waller Sgt VA ★
John: b 4-16-1752 d p. 1787 m Elizabeth Railey Sgt VA
John: b c. 1725 d p. 9-27-1784 m Anne Rice PS VA
Joseph: b 1753 d c. 1830 m Ann Edwards Pvt VA
Micajah: b 1745 d 3-10-1829 m (1)Frances Pryor (2)Susanna Pryor PS NC
Nathaniel: b c. 1735 d p. 1815 m (1)Mary Hawkins (2)Elizabeth Brantley Pvt VA
Obediah: b c. 1759 d c. 1813 m Chloe — Pvt VA
Shubel: b 2-11-1746 d p. 1790 m Mary E Richardson Cpl VT
Stephen: b 10-10-1735 d 2-2-1816 m Mary Horton Capt MA
William: b 10-7-1760 d 6-28-1837 m (1)Kezia — (2)Margaret Ferry Pvt MA ★
Wm., Sr.: b 4-29-1716 d 12-10-1810 m Susanna Kent PS CS MA
Wm., Jr.: b 3-26-1743 d 8-19-1785 m Mirriam Whitney PS CS VT
Wm.: b c. 1730 d 1796 m (1)Unity Wright (2)Elizabeth Lewis Sol NC

BULSEN,
John: b 7-8-1744 d 6-2-1834 m — X — Pvt NY

BUMGARDNER, (includes BUMGARNER)
Christian: b — d — m Mary Bumgardner Pvt VA
David: b 5-7-1758 d 10-9-1835 m Catharine Burner Pvt VA ★
Jacob: b — d — m Mary Bumgardner Pvt PS MA
Leonard: b c. 1755 d 3-24-1839 m Margaretha — Pvt PA

BUMM,
Jacob: b c. 1720 d c. 1780 m Mary Elizabeth — PS PA

BUMP, (includes BUMPAS, BUMPUS, BUMPUSS, BYMPUS)
Asa: b 6-2-1758 d 3-4-1837 m Achsah Churbuck Pvt MA ★
Edward: b 1755 d p. 1816 m Jerusha Wheat Pvt VT
Jacob: b 1738 d 12-17-1829 m Dinah Slew PS NH
Jeremiah, Sr: b 1724 d 2-28-1806 m Judith Randall PS MA
Jeremiah, Jr: b 9-8-1752 d 9-4-1828 m Elizabeth Savery Lt MA
John: b 7-11-1761 d 4-19-1846 m (1)Penelope Beckwith (2)Rebecca Beckwith Cpl CT ★
John: b c. 1730 d p. 1781 m Annie (Bumpas) Pvt NC
Joseph: b 10-28-1749 d 2-17-1817 m Mercy Barden Pvt MA
Lot: b 7-6-1763 d 1-9-1835 m (1)Abigail Avery (2)Susannah Perry (3)Bethiah Stone Pvt MA
Salathiel: b 11-2-1760 d 5-4-1842 m (1)Mary Strong (2)Lovisa Tinkham Pvt NY
Shebael: b 8-18-1759 d 1841/42 m — X — Pvt Fif MA ★
Simeon: b 8-31-1739 d p. 1798 m Experience Gladding Pvt CT

BUNBURY,
William: b 2-13-1750 d 1804 m Elizabeth Short Sgt VA

BUNCE,
Asa: b 1756 d 1813 m Sally Abbey Cpl CT
John: b c. 1745 d p. 9- -1775 m Annie Beach Pvt CT
John: b 8-8-1725 d 1798 m Phoebe Smith PS NY

BUNCE, contd.
Joseph: b 2-27-1739 d 9-13-1785 m Elizabeth Clapp Ens CT
Lodewick: b 1763 d 1847 m Christine Warn Pvt NY
Rora: b 1-9-1758 d 6-27-1812 m Elizabeth Olcott Cpl CT
Timothy: b 1743 d 4-5-1842 m Rachel Turner QMSgt CT

BUNCH,
Winston: b 1759 d 1830 m Eliza — Pvt VA

BUNCOMBE,
Edward: b 1742 d 1778 m Elizabeth Dawson Taylor Col NC

BUNDY, (includes BUNDA)
Asahel: b 1747 d 11-29-1816 m (1)Hannah — (2)Esther Eastman
  Pvt NH
Christopher: b 1759 d 1834 m Margaret Hill Pvt NC
Elisha: b 10-6-1760 d 10-5-1826 m Abigail French Pvt MA W ★
Peter: b 9-11-1754 d 4-7-1822 m Bershabah Avery Pvt MA
Simeon: b 1752 d 1832 m Elizabeth Galloup Pvt CT

BUNKER,
Benjamin: b 6-5-1731/2 d 1810 m Hannah Gibson Frothingham
  Armr Smn MA
Dodavah: b 11-3-1744 d 12-12-1828 m Martha Smith PS NH
Eli: b 4-22-1760 d 8-3-1842 m Anna Gordan PS NH
Enoch: b 1731/2 d p. 1802 m Dolly Bunker Cpl NH
Isaac: b c. 1740 d 1828 m Esther Ives PS MA
John: b c. 1730 d p. 6-19-1805 m (1)Abigail Young (2)Hannah
  Hadlock PS MA
Jonathan, Sr.: b 1729 d 9- -1796 m Sarah Runnels PS NH
Jonathan, Jr: b 1-9-1764 d 3-23-1814 m Elizabeth Rand Pvt NH
Joseph: b 10-1-1738 d 6-26-1826 m Sarah Noble Pvt NH
Richard: b 1758/9 d 8-23-1834 m (1)Susanna Roberts (2)— Davis
  Pvt MA ★
Samuel: b 9-4-1711 d 9-3-1786 m Pricilla Coleman PS MA
Silas: b 1746 d 2-15-1829 m Mrs Mary Smith Pvt MA
Thomas: b 5-1-1719 d 5-13-1785 m Anna Swain CS MA
William: b c. 1760 d p. 3-25-1803 m (1)Ann — (2)Tamer Biddle
  Scott Sol PS DE
Zachariah: b 11-13-1744 d 10-11-1816 m Mary Bean Pvt NH

BUNN,
Barron: b c. 1755 d 1823 m Mary — Pvt NJ ★
Benjamin: b 1740 d 1813 m — Burwell Lt NC
Edward: b — d 1796 m Catharine — CS NJ
John: b 1754 d — m Bethiah Fields Cpl CT
John: b 1753 d c. 1813 m Temperance French Pvt NY
Jonathan: b 1-28-1744 d 1-3-1815 m Mary Shinn Pvt NJ
Nathaniel, Jr.: b 10-8-1765 d 1802 m Lydia Wheeler Pvt MA W ★

BUNNELL, (includes BONNELL, BUNNEL, & BUNNELLE)
Abner: b 3-24-1721 d 2-3-1810 m Elizabeth Preston PS CT
Amos: b 5-9-1761 d 11-5-1834 m Katherine Merriman Pvt CT ★
Benjamin: b 11-10-1742 d 3-24-1814 m Catharine Berry Pvt PA
Enos: b 5-15-1753 d 3-19-1834 m Naomi Atwater Pvt CT
Daniel: b 3-30-1751 d 9- -1798 m Martha Hughes Pvt NJ
Issac, Sr.: b 6-12-1734 d 3-4-1822 m Ann Collins Pvt CT
Issac: b 7-13-1738 d p. 9- -1812 m Lena Barcalow Pvt NJ
Jacob: b 4-6-1734 d 1-19-1828 m Mary Kimberly 2Lt CT
Joel: b 11-12-1758 d p. 1840 m Martha — Pvt CT
Joseph: b 12-3-1733 d 5-7-1807 m Abia Kirby Pvt CT
Joseph: b 1-17-1723 d 10-1-1799 m Hannah Hotchkiss Pvt CT
Nathaniel, 2nd: b 5-9-1758 d 8-22-1828 m (?)Rhoda (Bates) Hotch-
  kiss Capt PS CT W ★
Noah: b 1-18-1741 d a. 12-18-1790 m Mary Beardsley Sgt CT
Solomon: b 10-27-1705 d 1779 m Mary Holdren PS PA
Titus: b 1735 d 11-29-1820 m Sibyl Yale Lt CT

BUNTING, (includes BUNTAIN, BUNTEN, BUNTIN, BUNTON)
Andrew: b 1736 d 10-28-1776 m Janet Otterson Capt NH
Andrew: b c. 1733 d 4- -1823 m Elizabeth — Sol VA
James: b 1744 d 1793 m Mary — Pvt VA
John: b 11-25-1756 d 5-26-1833 m Elizabeth Webster Pvt NH ★
John: b 1741 d p. 2-18-1792 m Patience Tilton Sol NJ
Joseph, Jr: b c. 1752 d 1830 m Phoebe Moon Pvt PA
Joshua: b 7-23-1738 d 10-8-1808 m (1)Amy Nutt (2)Mary Large
  CS NJ
Robert: b — d 1814 m Margaret Hayes Pvt PA
William: b 1742 d 7-26-1786 m Billy Drew Andrew Pvt MD
William: b 1764 d 3-10-1841 m (1)Elizabeth — (2)Mrs NancySmoot
  Pvt VA ★
William Black: b c. 1745 d p. 3-8-1818 m Sally Cropper Ens VA

BUNTZ,
Margaret: b c. 1735 d p. 1782 m Urban Buntz PS GA

BURBACH,
Philip: b c. 1747 d 1812 m Anna Catherine Elizabeth Ilgenfritz Pvt PA

BURBANK,
Abijah: b 3-26-1736 d 9-23-1813 m (1)Mary Spring (2)Mary Pierce
  Capt MA

Abraham: b 2-24-1738/9 d 8-5-1808 m (1)Bethia Cushing (2)Sarah
  Pomeroy PS & CS MA
Asa: b c. 1731 d 2-7-1824 m (1)Eunice Hutchins (2)Esther Emery
  (3)Hannah Foster PS MA
Daniel: b 4-4-1736 d 9-27-1802 m Mary Marks Lt MA
David: b 7-4-1754 d 11-4-1815 m (1)Mary Little (2)Dorothy Lowell
  Cpl NH
David: b 1750 d 1840 m Hannah Johnson Pvt NH ★
Ebenezer: b 1741 d 11-8-1803 m Eunice King Pvt CT
Eleazer: b 10-14-1764 d 8-31-1840 m Mary Brackett Fif MA
Eliphalet: b 6-22-1760 d 7-4-1816 m Susanna Jackman Pvt MA
Ezra: b 2-20-1738 d 1800 m Priscilla Savory PS MA
Gershom: b 8-23-1734 d 5-14-1817 m Anna Pearsons Lt NH
Isaac: b 1733 d 5-18-1815 m Mary Marble Pvt MA
John: b 3-20-1752 d 10-13-1843 m Mrs Anna English Sgt MA
John: b c. 1755 d 12-23-1831 m Dorcas Welch Pvt MA W ★
Moses, Sr: b 2-6-1716/7 d 3-15-1804 m Sarah Emery PS NH
Moses, Jr: b 6-26-1741 d p. 1780 m Sarah Danforth Pvt & PS NH
Nathaniel: b 12-25-1747 d 10-31-1831 m Molly Durgin Pvt NH
Samuel, Jr.: b 6-24-1734 d 2-26-1808 m (1) — (2)Eunice Kendall
  Lt MA W ★
Samuel: b 10-2-1746 d 1- -1777 m Mehitable Ruhamah Foster Sgt
  MA W ★
Samuel: b 11-4-1715 d p. 1792 m (1)Eunice Hardy (2)Sarah Hardy
  PS NH
Silas: b 1738 d 9-14-1814 m Hannah Beard Capt MA
Thomas: b 9-27-1757 d 4-20-1794 m Abigail Woodbury Pvt MA
Timothy: b c. 1747 d p. 1825 m Hannah Ripley Sgt MA
Wells: b 8-8-1756 d 8-12-1823 m(1)Mary—(2)Mercy Hooker Pvt NH

BURBECK,
Edward: b a. 1741 d 6-23-1782 m Jane Milk Capt MA
Henry: b 6-8-1754 d 10-2-1848 m Lucy Elizabeth Rudd Capt CT
William: b 7-22-1716 d 7-22-1785 m (1)Abigail Tuttle (2)Jerusha
  Glover Col MA

BURBEE,
Peter: b 1729/30 d 6-12-1778 m Margaret Currica Pvt NH

BURBRIDGE,
John: b 1740 d 3- -1782 m Mary Brown Pvt VA
Roland: b 1745 d 1842 m Jane Wells Pvt VA

BURCH, (includes BIRCH, BURCHE, BURTCH)
Benjamin: b 5-2-1729 d 11-3-1783 m Elizabeth Taylor Sgt MD
Benjamin: b 5-9-1761 d 5-5-1832 m Rebecca Barron Sgt MD W ★
Benjamin: b — d — m Anna Davis Pvt VT
Beverly: b 5-3-1753 d p. 1799 m Rachel Earl Pvt NY
Billings: b 1746 d c. 10-3-1836 m (1)Susannah Bentley (2)Ellen
  J Clark Lt RI ★
Ebenezer: b 10-5-1749 d 11-22-1834 m Phebe Doty Pvt CT ★
Edy: b 1760 d 10-15-1848 m Elizabeth — Pvt VT ★
Ezra: b — d 1821 m Jedidah Lacey Capt CT
Henry: b 6-6-1744 d 4-6-1813 m Mary Irish PS CT
John, Jr: b 12-13-1738 d p. 1790 m Patty Ralph Sol NY
John: b 1755-60 d p. 8-1-1827 m Frances — Mus NC
John: b c. 1758 d 5- -1849 m — X — Pvt VA
John: b 1-18-1759 d 3-1-1834 m Elizabeth Benham Pvt VA ★
Jonathan: b 9-16-1740 d p. 1790 m Eunice — Pvt VT
Joseph: b 6-27-1763 d 12-29-1843 m (1)Mary Rodes (2)Ann J
  Hawkins Pvt VA ★
Joseph: b 1758 d 3-3-1818 m (1)Edith Hargrove (2)— Wilcox
  Cpl NC
Justinian: b c. 1742 d c. 1806 m Behethland Dade PS MD
Oliver: b c. 1713 d p. 1793 m Ann — PS MD
Robert: b 9-15-1762 d 6-26-1830 m (1)Mary Felshaw (2)Polly
  Spaulding Pvt CT
Thomas: b 2-25-1756 d 8-3-1837 m Susanna — Pvt NY ★
Thomas: b 1-20-1757 d 1-24-1828 m Sarah Jones Sol VA
Thomas: b 5-9-1751 d 10-5-1841 m (1)— Clark (2)Susannah Tolbert
  (3)Verlinda Harvey Pvt VA
Thomas Erskine: b 1-15-1756 d 1-3-1821 m (1)Mary Clay Murry
  (2)Mary Magdalen Miller N Ens VA
William: b c. 1755 d 1-2-1844 m Judith Winfrey Cpl NC
William: b 1759 d 6-10-1835 m (?)Rebecca Keys Pvt VA ★
Zachariah: b 1757 d 11-19-1844 m Mildred Robey Pvt MD ★

BURCHAM,
David: b 5-17-1754 d 9- -1847 m Rebecca Vanvactor Pvt PS PA

BURCHFIELD,
James: b 1758 d 1-21-1831 m Margaret — Pvt PA
Robert: b 12-18-1759 d 10-29-1844 m Elizabeth Hill Pvt NC ★

BURCHINAL,
Joseph: b 10-25-1744 d 1786 m Elizabeth Cunningham Pvt MD

BURCHSTEAD,
Benjamin Braeme: b 3-6-1733 d 1785 m Mrs Elizabeth Skillin Pvt MA

BURD,
James: b 3-10-1726 d 10-5-1793 m Sarah Shippen Col PA

BURDANE,
Samuel: b 7-23-1759 d — m — X — Pvt CT

BURDEN, (includes BARDEEN, BARDEN, BARDIN, BARDON, BOURDON)
Henry: b 8-27-1752 d 3- -1847 m Else — Lt NJ ★
James: b 1730 d 1805 m Mary — PS Cpl NC
John: b 9-3-1747 d 9-20-1837 m Lucy Sibley Cpl MA
John: b 2-14-1740 d 11-18-1815 m Hannah Chamberlain Pvt MA
Jonathan: b 11-13-1761 d 5-8-1817 m Bilote Bartlett Pvt MA
Lemuel: b 10-11-1758 d 3-7-1839 m Sarah Reed Cpl MA ★
Moses: b 7-15-1756 d 1837 m Catherine Cook Pvt MA ★
Nathaniel: b 4-8-1753 d p. 1787 m Susanna Saunders Cpl MA
Nicholas Joseph: b c. 1750 d 1- -1813 m (1)Martha Dennis (2)Jane Dennis Dr VA
Noah: b 1721 d 8-20-1819 m Remember Avis Thayer Pvt MA
Philip: b 11-10-1724 d 11-3-1802 m Mary Hill Pvt MA
Thomas, Sr: b 1735 d p. 1799 m Susanna Riggs Pvt MA
Thomas, Jr: b 1-24-1764 d 6-11-1813 m Olive Benton Sol MA

BURDETT, (includes BURDETTE & BURDITT)
Ebenezer: b 1761 d 1830 m Ruth Loveland Pvt MA
Frederick: b c. 1732 d 4- -1808 m (1)Dorothy Kemple (2)Mary Smith PS VA
John: b 10-20-1746 d 12-19-1843 m Abagail Sargent Pvt MA
Samuel: b 9-12-1735 d 6-15-1790 m Esther Pratt Lt MA

BURDICK,
Abel: b 1752 d 1815 m (1)Comfort Palmer (2)— (Burdick) PS RI
Abraham: b 1-16-1737 d 1787 m Amy Brown Pvt NY
Adam: b 12-28-1759 d 2-20-1845 m (1)Hannah Burdick (2)Lodema Lee Pvt MA ★
Clarke, Sr: b 2-25-1748 d 8-29-1778 m Amy Sisson Pvt RI
David: b 2-24-1710 d p. 4-17-1776 m Mary Thompson PS RI
Elijah: b 1758 d 12-17-1833 m Avis Robinson Pvt CT
Elisha: b 2-24-1760 d 12-10-1828 m Hannah Greene Pvt NY ★
Elnathan: b 4-11-1743 d 7-25-1832 m Anne Sisson Pvt RI
Gideon: b 11-6-1762 d 4-5-1846 m (1)Catharine Robertson (2)Jane Brown Pvt NY ★
Gideon: b 1759 d 1834 m Keturah Cottrell Drm Mus RI
Hazard: b 1-25-1759 d 1-25-1841 m Esther Shirley Pvt RI ★
Hubbard: b 11-24-1716 d 1784 m Avis Lewis Pvt RI
Ichabod: b 1740 d 6-16-1821 m (1)Bethsheba McKee (2)Mary Chapman Capt RI
Isaiah: b 11-17-1761 d 11-15-1847 m Abby Cottrell Pvt RI ★
James: b 3-7-1744 d 11-29-1807 m Phebe Smith Pvt MA
John: b 5-19-1721 d 1780 m Elizabeth Babcock Sol CT
John: b c. 1744 d 1798 m (1)Martha Hitchcock (2)Mehitable — Pvt PS CS MA
John: b 12-27-1753 d 10-24-1844 m Hannah Carpenter Pvt RI ★
Jonathan: b c. 1708 d 1791 m Judith Clarke PS RI
Joshua: b 1730 d 1790 m Mary Lamb Pvt RI
Lucas: b 4-25-1749 d 1-5-1825 m Sarah Haskell Pvt RI
Nathan: b 1746 d — m Mary Keeler Ens NY
Oliver, Sr: b 3-27-1735 d p. 1790 m Lydia Elderton Pvt PS RI
Oliver: b 2-7-1760 d 8-23-1806 m Olive Brown Pvt RI
Peter, Jr: b 5-12-1730 d 2-7-1828 m Esther Gavitt Pvt CT
Robert: b 1701 d 1-12-1784 m Susannah Clark PS RI
Robert: b 1731 d 12-24-1807 m Hannah Hall PS CS RI
Robert, Jr: b 1763 d 9-7-1841 m Sarah Williams PS RI
Robert: b 1747-50 d p. 1-26-1804 m Sarah Remington PS RI
Simeon: b 1723-27 d 1802 m Isabel Saunders (2)Mary Davis Pvt PS RI
Thompson: b 9-1-1753 d 10-5-1830 m Tabitha Wilcox Pvt RI ★
Walter: b 8-11-1756 d 8-11-1831 m Elizabeth Franklin Pvt RI ★
Zaccheus: b 2-28-1734 d 4-7-1809 m Elizabeth Smith Pvt MA

BURFOOT,
Thomas: b — d 11-13-1820 m Francis — Sgt VA

BURFORD,
Daniel, Sr: b 5-20-1714 d a. 7-2-1787 m Mary — PS VA
Daniel, Jr: b c. 1737 d 1811 m Sarah — Capt PS VA
James: b c. 1755-60 d a. 10-14-1811 m Mary Rucker Pvt VA
John: b 11- -1758 d 5- -1835 m — Kitchens Sgt NC ★
John William: b 6-21-1756 d 7-19-1788 m Nancy Hastings Pvt VA
Philip Terrel: b 6-29-1763 d 6-14-1834 m Rebecca Clack Lt NC ★
Thomas: b 5-20-1750 d 9-26-1838 m Mary Wade Lt QM VA
William: b c. 1755 d p. 8-8-1834 m — X — Sol GA
William: b c. 1735 d 1795 m Grissell — Pvt VA
William: b 1759 d a. 6-17-1833 m Susan — Pvt VA

BURGAMY,
John: b c. 1755 d 9-18-1780 m Elizabeth — Sol GA
William: b 1739 d 1819 m Susan Hawkins Pvt GA

BURGER, (includes BARGER, BERGER, BERRIER, & BOURGER)
Casper: b 6- -1732 d 11-8-1815 m (1)Ann — (2)Jane Sutphen Sol NJ
George: b 2-13-1755 d 4-20-1839 m Catherine Smith Pvt NY
George Henry: b 1-30-1734 d 3-30-1820 m (1) X (2)Catharine Casper PS CS NC

George Henry: b 1739 d 1810 m Susanna Letterman LCol NC
Herber: b 6-10-1735 d 2-11-1815 m Catharine — Pvt PA
Isaac: b c. 1734 d 1805 m (1)Susanna Landis (2)Susanna Hunsberger Pvt PA
Jacob: b 6-4-1760 d 11-28-1828 m Catharine Cooper Pvt PA
Jacob: b 10-24-1749 d 8-24-1794 m Elizabeth Hadrick CS VA
John: b 1748 d 1818 m Martha Thompkins Pvt NY
John: b 1752 d 6-27-1836 m Catherine — Pvt PA
John: b c. 1764 d 1820 m Polly — Pvt VA
Martyn: b c. 1700 d p. 1785 m Ursula Fraleigh PS NY
Michael: b 12-25-1763 d 8-5-1869 m Marguerite Leedgwood Sol PA
Nicholas: b 10-20-1736 d 9-20-1828 m Ann Maria Burger Cpl PA
Nicholas: b 1761 d 1841 m Fannie Harding Pvt VA ★
Peter: b 1-8-1738 d p. 2-28-1803 m Catharine Deyo Pvt NY

BURGESS, (includes BURGE, BURGES)
Bangs: b 1746 d 4- -1822/3 m (1)Eunice Russell (2)Phebe Lillie Pvt MA ★
Basil: b 1734/35 d p. 4-11-1780 m Anna — Capt MD
Benjamin: b 2-5-1731 d 4-5-1793 m Agnes Battee PS MD
Benjamin: b 1737 d 1807 m Susannah Manter Sol PS MA
Benjamin: b 1-25-1749 d 1829 m Elizabeth Paine Pvt MA ★
Benjamin: b 11-1-1732 d 1806 m Rebecca Parker Pvt MA
Benjamin: b 3-17-1751/2 d 6-13-1852 m Fear Wing Pvt MA
Covill: b c. 1750 d p. 1794 m Lydia Crowell Pvt MA
Dempsey: b c. 1750 d p. 1820 m — X — Col PS NC
Depsay: b 1736 d 1792 m Dora Fayme PS NC
Ebenezer: b — d 1-1-1829 m Anna Fairbanks Sgt MA
Ebenezer: b 1715 d 12-21-1807 m Rachel Farnsworth Pvt MA
Ebenezer: b 6-14-1743 d 2-28-1829 m Hannah Gibbs Pvt MA
Edward: b c. 1740 d 12-5-1809 m (1)Margaret Magruder (2)Mary Davis Capt PS MD
Edward: b c. 1744 d 1835 m Ann Francis Pvt Spy VA
Ephraim: b 1735 d 11-10-1818 m Sarah Bacon Pvt MA
Ephraim: b 4-7-1738 d 7-20-1784 m Anna Abbot Sgt NH
Frederick: b c. 1750 d p. 7-28-1814 m Frances Brown PS VA
Gideon: b 1-25-1743 d 3-22-1803 m (1)— Spink (2)Dorcas Thornton PS Pvt RI
Henry John: b 11-28-1744 d 1797 m (1)Ann Geddy (2)Judith Driver (3)Sarah Jones PS VA
Ichabod: b 1753 d 12-17-1834 m Keziah Handy Cpl MA ★
Ichabod: b 2-5-1742 d 10-18-1821 m Hannah Simmons Sgt RI
Isaac: b 1-10-1758 d 4-30-1858 m Elizabeth Layton Pvt NJ ★
James: b 10-25-1736 d 12-9-1812 m (1)Sarah Sturtevant (2)Eunice Doane Parker Sgt MA
Jeremiah: b 1739 d p. 1817 m Reliance Crosby 2Lt NY
John: b 3-19-1736 d 11-9-1791 m Abigail Chase Lt MA
John: b 5-12-1736 d 12-2-1827 m Sarah Rogers Pvt MA
John: b 1753 d 4-24-1827 m Urania Morey QM RI
John: b 1754 d 1-20-1840 m Sallie Miller Pvt MA
Jonathan: b 1761 d 1853 m Meribah Tilton SgtMaj MA
Joseph, 3rd: b 3-8-1734 d 5-20-1820 m Mehitable Shephard Lt CT
Joseph: b 1-27-1727 d 11-17-1778 m Elizabeth Dorsey Capt MD
Joshua: b 1760 d 1831 m Sallie Dorsey Lt MD
Josiah: b 1758 d 3-12-1834 m — X — Pvt MD ★
Josiah: b 7-16-1736 d 12-12-1828 m Dorcas Hinckley 1Lt MA
Lovatt: b 1-31-1762 d 10-10-1807 m (1)Elizabeth Irwin (2)Pricilla Maney (3)Sarah Black Sol NC
Micheal: b 1754 d p. 1795 m Sarah Warfield Ens MD
Nathaniel: b 5-17-1729 d 1-13-1798 m Ruth Chandler Pvt MA
Nathaniel: b 3-4-1758 d 4-15-1839 m Lucretia Scott Pvt MA ★
Philip: b 1756 d 10-7-1794 m Temperance Vrowell Pvt MA
Prince: b 5-24-1749 d 11-17-1832 m (1)Mercy Nye (2)Martha Crowell Lt MA
Samuel: b 8-28-1747 d 5-15-1783 m Hannah Sturtevant Pvt MA
Stephen: b 1753 d 4-14-1839 m Temperance Wing 3Lt MA
Thomas: b 5-23-1741 d 1820 m Annis Fuller Pvt MA
Thomas: b 2-27-1744 d 1786 m Mercy Ransom Pvt NY
Thomas: b 1-15-1757 d 11-10-1812 m Mary Guyre Pvt MA
William: b 5-8-1762 d 1-25-1836 m Lucy Sampson Pvt MA ★

BURGIN,
Ede Hall: b 1741 d 5- -1813 m Elizabeth Bryant PS NH
John: b 1735 d 1793 m Elizabeth Abel 2Lt NJ

BURGNER,
Peter: b c. 1755 d 1824 m — X — Pvt PA

BURGWINE, (includes BURGWIN)
John: b 2-25-1731 d p. 3- -1803 m (1)Margaret Haynes (2)Eliza Bush PS NC
John: b 1748-52 d 10-4-1843 m Mary Walton Pvt PA

BURHANS,
Abraham: b 1-16-1747 d 11-24-1827 m Leah Miller Sgt NY
Barrent: b 10-2-1757 d p. 1799 m Margaretha Eignaar Pvt NY
Benjamin: bpt 10-5-1763 d 10-5-1829 m Johanna Davis Pvt NY
Cornelius: b 8-15-1746 d 9-8-1821 m (1)Margaret Van Leuven (2)Hannah Legg Sgt NY
Cornelius: b 9-1765 d 11-27-1831 m Maria TenBroeck Sgt NY
Edward: b 11-28-1752 d 9-3-1832 m Bretje Blanchant Pvt NY ★
Henry: b 6-22-1766 d 9-18-1848 m Lydia Churchill Pvt NY
Isaac: b 5-20-1737 d 1811 m Susanna Foland Lt NY

BURHANS, contd.
Jacob: b 5-16-1725 d 6- -1810 m Elizabeth Whitaker Pvt NY
Jan: b 1-1-1727 d 4-25-1787 m (1)Catharine Whittaker (2)Sarah Van Aken Pvt PS NY
Johannes: b 2-18-1709 d 1794 m Jannetje Newkirk PS NY
Petrus: b c.1730 d p.5-21-1802 m Johanna VonSteenburg Pvt PS NY
Samuel: bpt11-16-1755 d 9-17-1793m Margaret Jeralemon Pvt NY
Tjerck: b 10-12-1757 d 11-25-1832 m Catherine Dedrick Pvt NY

BURKAM,
Stephen: b 1-27-1752 d 7-5-1850 m Sarah Henthorne Pvt PA

BURKE, (includes BURK & BURKS)
Henry: b 8-8-1758 d 5-18-1840 m (1)X (2)Mary McKinney Sol VA
Isham: b 1759 d 8-22-1839 m Elizabeth Rowland Sol VA
James: b c. 1750 d p. 1822 m (1)Catherine — (2)Chloe — Pvt VA
Jesse: b 4-8-1738 d 1-20-1810 m Leah Rice Capt VT
John: b 11-28-1717 d 10-27-1784 m Sarah Hoyt CS PS MA
John: b 2-12-1757 d 3-12-1836 m Kate Marshall Lt GA
John: b 7-23-1760 d 2-1-1836 m Mrs Alcy Robinson Sebastian Pvt NC ★
John: b 1757 d 1832 m Mary Porter Capt VA
Jonathan, Jr.: b 2-2-1733/4 d p. 1790 m (1)Sarah Abbott (2)Sarah Gould Pvt PS VT
Joseph: b 12-12-1753 d 1-7-1828 m (2)Fortune — MM GA
Joseph: b 4-27-1758 d p. 7-11-1820 m Judith Barrell Sgt NH
Samuel: b c. 1750 d 11-29-1829 m Elizabeth — Pvt NJ W ★
Samuel: b 1758 d 3-16-1841 m Mary Hurley Pvt VA ★
Seth: b 1740 d 1785 m Rebecca Stearns Pvt MA
Silas: b 4-10-1765 d 8-21-1843 m Martha Millington Pvt MA ★
Simeon: b 5-3-1736 d 4-15-1781 m Martha Strong Sgt VT
Solomon: b 12-2-1742 d 2-8-1819 m Keziah Benjamin Pvt VT
Sylvanus: b c. 1763 d 7-4-1825 m Achsa Webster Pvt Drm MA ★
Thomas: b 1740/41 d 1808 m Clara Fries Capt CS VA
Wm.: b 1752 d 5-24-1836 m (1)Lettice Maynard (2)Olive Arnold Sgt CT
Wm.: b 1736 d 6-2-1809 m Lydia Chase Pvt RI
Wm.: b 1732 d 1826 m Sallie Scott Pvt VA
Wm.: b c. 1730/3 d 1782 m Ann — PS VA

BURKETT, (includes BURKET)
Henry: b 1761 d 12-11-1838 m — Musser Pvt VA ★
John: b 4-4-1756 d 9-20-1845 m Elizabeth Roush Pvt PA
John: b 1744 d 12-   - m X Pvt SC
Joseph: b c. 1755 d 1823 m Anna — Pvt SC
Thomas: b 1749 d 6-2-1817 m Margret Moody Pvt SC

BURKHALTER, (includes BURCKHOLDER, BURKHOLDER)
Christian: b c. 1754 d 7-25-1784 m Fronica Binkley Pvt PA
David: b 1759 d 6-25-1846 m — Moseley Pvt SC
Henry: b 1760 d 1828 m Sarah — Pvt PA
Jacob: b 1755 d 1848 m Mary Lawson Sol GA
John: b 1760 d 3-23-1861 m Sarah Hardin Loyless Pvt GA
John: b 1723 d a. 1- -1784 m Sarah M — Sol GA
John: b 1735/36 d 1800 m Ann Brenneman Pvt PA
John Peter, Sr.: b 12-2-1731 d 10-22-1803/5 m Eva Catherine Deshler Capt PA
John Peter, Jr.: b 1760 d 1814 m Dorothea Steckel Ens PA
Martin: b c. 1730 d c. 10- -1811 m Anna Eva — 1Lt PA
Michael: b 1725 d 1828 m Martha Newsome Pvt GA

BURKHART, (includes BURCKARTT, BURGHARDT, BURKHARD, BURKHARDT, BURGHERT)
Christian: b 11-30-1751 d 6-1-1840 m Barbara Haines Pvt PA
Christopher, Sr.: b c. 1735 d 1799 m X PS MD
Christopher, Jr.: b 12-19-1756 d 10-14-1827 m Elizabeth Hobbs PS MD
Frederick: b 7-13-1761 d 1-2-1844 m Mary — Pvt PA ★
Hendrick: b 1749 d 3-27-1826 m Hannah Spoor PS MA
Jacob: b 5-8-1758 d p. 10-26-1840 m Elizabeth — Cpl PA
Jehu: b c. 1735 d a. 10-13-1823 m Motlene Croll PS NC
John: b 8-21-1753 d 1-2-1847 m (1)Barbara Fox (2)Catherine Fox Sol PA
Wm.: b 2-28-1755 d 8-24-1793 m Sarah Miller Pvt PA

BURLEIGH, (includes BOWLEY, BURLEY)
Daniel: b 6-6-1745 d 11-12-1807 m Ann Stewart Ens PS MD
Gordon: b 4-10-1763 d 1-30-1823 m Elizabeth Dow Pvt NH ★
Jacob: b 6-5-1756 d p. 1804 m Lucy McLaughlin Pvt CT ★
Jacob, Sr.: b 1-23-1720 d p. 7-17-1776 m Abigail — PS NH
Jacob, Jr.: b 6-23-1756 d 2-13-1828 m Sarah Burley Pvt NH
James: b 2-11-1753 d 4-3-1812 m Susanna Swasey Pvt MA
James: b 10-20-1720 d 9-6-1788 m Sarah Foss PS NH
John: b 10-8-1731 d 1784 m Persis Harwood Pvt CT
John: b 12-18-1717 d 11-18-1776 m (1)Sarah Hall (2)Elizabeth Chesley (3)Mehitable Sheafe PS NH
John: b 5-22-1754 d 6-7-1827 m (1)Hannah Hardy (2)Abigail Smith PS NH
John: b 9-1-1759 d 12-8-1841 m X Pvt NH ★
John: b 1739 d 1-23-1800 m Jane Spear PS PA
Jonathan: b 1757 d 5-24-1814 m Sarah Haley Pvt NH

Joseph: b 8-7-1755 d 8-6-1838 m Mary Hilton Pvt NH
Josiah: b 11-8-1742 d 11-13-1790 m Hannah Hiscock Cpl CT
Josiah: b 1728 d 11-20-1808 m Judith Tuttle Sol PS NH
Samuel: b 9-22-1745 d 4-9-1826 m Rachel Roberts Pvt CT
Samuel: b a. 1740 d 1800 m Martha Low Pvt NH
Stephen: b 12-25-1755 d 12-31-1829 m Abigail Taylor Pvt NH
Thomas: b 7-2-1723 d 6-1-1805 m Sarah Haley PS NH
Wm.: b 1722 d 6-28-1801 m Hannah Smith MM Pvt NH
Wm.: b 3-28-1760 d 12-28-1796 m Sarah Ames Pvt NH

BURLESON, (includes BURLASON)
Aaron: b 1749 d p. 11-16-1781 m X Pvt NC
David: b c. 1755 d 1832 m Ursula — Pvt NC
Jesse: b 1751 d 1822 m Elizabeth Clifton Pvt NC

BURLING,
Benjamin: b 1745 d 3-28-1825 m Sybil Sands Pvt NY
Ebenezer: b 6-10-1741 d 9-12-1831 m Keziah Hunt Pvt NY

BURLINGAME, (includes BURLINGHAM, BURLINGHAME)
Benedict, Jr.: b 6-18-1759 d 10-17-1836 m Rachel Bicknell Pvt RI ★
Christopher: b 1753 d 7-12-1841 m Susanna Putnam FifMaj Sgt MA ★
David: b 10-26-1736 d p. 1790 m Mehitable Bishop Capt RI
Eleazer: b a. 1749 d 9-17-1810 m Rhoda Briggs Lt RI
Elisha: b 9-6-1749 d 6-12-1823 m Hannah Plummer Sol RI
Eseck: b 3-24-1765 d 2-17-1855 m (1)Waity Mowry (2)Mary Thornton (3)Asenath Robbins MM RI
Hopkins: b 1759 d 8-31-1833 m Margaret — Pvt RI
Israel: b 1738/9 d 2-9-1814 m Eunice Crandall Lt PS VT
James, Jr.: b 1740 d 7-8-1802 m Abigail Knight Ens RI
Jeremiah: b 7-19-1752 d 4-15-1826 m Leah Ide Pvt CT
Jeremiah: b 1-27-1755 d 1- -1811 m Ruth (Grinnell)Palmer Sgt RI
Nathan: b 2- -1761 d 6-15-1839 m (1) X (2)Mary Hill Pvt RI ★
Nathan: b 1-13-1746 d 1821-23 m Mary Kinyon Pvt RI
Nathan: b 2-24-1762 d 8-7-1856 m Sarah Bartlett Pvt RI ★
Pardon: b 4-12-1756 d 1832 m Patience Edmunds Lt RI
Peter: b c. 1730 d p. 10-26-1784 m Patience Potter Capt RI
Philip: b 1759 d 9-5-1804 m Elizabeth Downey Pvt NY
Roger: b c. 1744 d p. 1790 m Ruth Field Cpl RI
Silas: b 5-20-1739 d 11-5-1829 m Mehitable Fisk Pvt NY
Stephen: b 3-13-1742 d 4-10-1808 m Ruth King Ens RI
Wanton: b 2-19-1762 d 9-9-1853 m Lucy Stone Pvt VT ★
Wm.: b 6-11-1759 d p.10-5-1833 m Sawyer Avis Seacap RI

BURNAP,
Ebenezer, Sr.: b 6-10-1723 d 4-12-1804 m Mary Wyman Pvt MA
Ebenezer, Jr.: b 10-13-1756 d 3-12-1820 m (1)Thankful Singletary (2)Ruth Tucker MM Pvt MA
Isaac: b 1-31-1713 d 12-26-1821 m Susanna Emerson Pvt MA
Isaac: b 2-17-1751 d 3-18-1816 m (1)Beulah Jones (2)Hannah Thayer Pvt MA
Jacob: b 10-4-1761 d 6-14-1807 m Hannah Parker Pvt MA
John: b 4-23-1762 d 9-1-1812 m Candace Bliss Pvt MA
John: b 2-8-1753 d 10-10-1824 m Nancy Stevens Pvt NC
John, Sr.: b 1726 d 1804 m Susanna — Pvt VT
John, Jr.: b 1752 d 1837-39 m (1)— Bartlett (2)Eleanor Freeman (3)Polly Holbrook (4)Polly Peck Pvt VT ★
Samuel: b 7-17-1747 d 1-2-1832 m Betsey Howard MM NH
Thomas: b 1-19-1758 d 9-13-1819 m Abigal Willington Pvt MA
Timothy: b 12-25-1753 d 10-26-1828 m Bethiah Waite Pvt MA

BURNELL,
John: b 3-16-1750 d 7-15-1837 m Mary Bannister Pvt MA
Joseph, Sr.: b 12-19-1725 d 9-23-1807 m Hannah Tucker PS MA
Joseph, Jr.: b 12-13-1756 d 11-14-1841 m Marhta Gilbert Pvt MA ★
Samuel: b 10-4-1758 d 7-5-1838 m Sophia Tucker Cpl CT

BURNER,
Abraham: b 8-15-1757 d 6-18-1827 m Mary Magdalene Hull Pvt VA ★

BURNETT, (includes BURNET)
Andrew: b 2-13-1762 d 1841 m Catherine Lyon Smn RI ★
Daniel: b 9-17-1758 d 7-12-1824 m Mary Parcells Pvt NJ
David: b 2-9-1736 d 11-26-1800 m Martha Cooper Pvt NJ
Ebenezer: b — d p. 1840 m Lydia Estel Sgt NY
Edmund: b 1-1-1756 d 1840 m Sarah Smith Pvt NJ ★
Henry: b c. 1755 d p. 1817 m X Capt VA
Isaac: b 2-11-1746 d 10-18-1816 m (1)Esther Merriam (2)Lydia Eddy Pvt MA
James: b 4-5-1756 d 1-27-1840 m Chloe Martin Sgt CT ★
James: b 1-1-1732 d 12-23-1807 m Mary Nicholson Lt NY
James: b 1741 d 1810 m Margaret Robinson Lt VA
Jeremiah: b 1749 d 6-28-1848 m (1)Sarah Hicks (2)Diana Davie (3)Patsy Hughes (4)Jane Turner Pvt PS VA
John: b c. 1735 d c. 1788 m Sarah — Capt GA
John: b 1750 d 1823 m Winnifred Wilson Pvt GA
John: b 10-25-1742 d 5-9-1826 m Mehitable Dickerson Pvt MA
John: b 1739 d 1824 m Charity Vandermark Capt NY
John: b c. 1760-65 d 4-17-1826 m Molsy Sheppard Pvt NC
John: b — d a. 6-21-1827 m (1)Elizabeth — (2)Nancy — Pvt VA

John: b c. 1760 d 5-22-1809 m Sarah Johnson Pvt VA
Josiah: b c. 1750 d 1813 m Hannah Ball Ens NJ
Matthias: b 1722 d 10- -1783 m Mary Linsley PS NJ
Matthias: b 11-15-1739 d 5-29-1805 m Dorcas — Pvt NJ
Patrick: b c. 1750 d 3-27-1825 m Keziah Cook Pvt NY
Peter: b c. 1760 d c. 1837/8 m Mary Strail Pvt NY
Robert: b 2-22-1762 d 11-24-1854 m Rachel De Witt Lt NY ★
Robert: b 1755 d 2-2-1820 m Susannah Hollingsworth Pvt PA
Samuel: b 11-8-1753 d 6-4-1819 m Ruth Hedges Pvt NJ
Squire: b 12-30-1749 d 1812 m Rhoda — Pvt NJ
Stephen: bpt 1726/7 d p. 1778 m Hannah Merry PS NY
Wm.: b 1-28-1744 d 3-24-1835 m Lucy Gleason Pvt MA ★
Wm.: b 12-2-1730 d 10-7-1791 m (1)Mary Camp (2)Gertrude
    Rutger SurGen NJ
Wm.: b c. 1725 d 1805/6 m Mary Miller Pvt NJ CL
Wm.: b c. 1725 d 1819 m Rebecca Morse PS NJ
Wm.: b c. 1759 d 7-4-1844 m (1)Martha Jeffries (2)Lettie — Pvt
    VA ★
Wm.: b 1749 d 1799 m Eliza Correll Pvt VA

BURNHAM, (includes BURNAM)
Aaron, Jr.: b 5-23-1756 d 9-15-1832 m (1)Mabel Brown (2)Lucy
    Williams MM CT
Abner: b 8-15-1753 d 5-27-1843 m Elizabeth Rockwell Pvt CT ★
Abraham: b 5-24-1742 d 7-13-1814 m Mary Perkins PS NH
Ammi: b 3-24-1734 d 3-16-1785 m Martha Foster Sol MA
Asa: b 5-28-1753 d 1-1-1849 m Lucy Huntington Sgt CT
Asahel: b 9- -1737 d 8-13-1820 m Hannah Wadsworth Pvt CT ★
Augustus: b 8-4-1751 d 8-27-1823 m Mary Stedman Pvt CT
Benjamin: b 10-7-1753 d p. 1807 m Tabitha Perkins Capt PS CT
Benjamin: b c. 1758 d — m Elizabeth Gordon Pvt NH
Charles: b 12-19-1753 d p. 1822 m Rachel Winchell Sgt MA
Daniel: b 3-21-1753 d 8-16-1823 m Martha Smith Pvt CT
Daniel: b 1745 d 10-11-1785 m Jemima — Pvt MA
David: b 8-4-1740 d 1834 m Anna Grover Pvt MA
David: b 1-31-1741/2 d — m (Olive) Berry Pvt MA
David: b 8-25-1765 d 9-16-1830 m Martha Perkins Pvt MA W★
Ebenezer: b 9-25-1758 d 4-9-1828 m Abigail Low Pvt MA
Elisha: b 2-12-1730 d 5-28-1815 m Jerusha Lee Pvt MA
George: b 10-5-1735 d 5-1-1812 m Bathsheba Dart PS CT
Gurdon: b 2-20-1757 d 1791 m Martha Cahoon Pvt CT
Isaac: b 1730 d 10-14-1808 m Eunice Holt Sgt CT
James: b 8-21-1759 d 5-5-1836 m Tamma Holt Sgt CT ★
James, Sr.: b 9-24-1710 d 11-25-1787 m Grace Dalzell PS MA
James, Jr.: b 10-17-1737 d 8-8-1782 m ()Hannah Merrill (2) Mrs
    Jane Wildes Capt VA
James: b 1-4-1761 d 7-15-1835 m Eunice Allen Pvt MA ★
Jedediah: b 4-3-1755 d 3-11-1840 m Lydia Kent PS CT
Job: b 5-10-1745 d p. 1790 m Mary O'Brien PS ME
John: b 12-20-1749 d 1-8-1833 m Trypena Robinson Sgt CT ★
John: b 1754 d 10-24-1820 m (1)Sally Snow (2) — Chapman
    (3)Bridget Hubbard Pvt CT ★
John: b 10-15-1758 d 10-7-1837 m Barbara G. McCarty Sol CT
John: b 12-10-1749 d 6-8-1843 m Nabby Collins Maj MA ★
John: b 1760 d 1827 m (2)Roxana Burnham Pvt MA W ★
John: b 1738 d 7-29-1798 m Abigail Stickney PS MA
John: b 10-29-1762 d 6-9-1831 m Mary Ann Fort Pvt CL SC NC
John, Jr.: b 1742 d 8-1-1829 m Abigail Clark Pvt PS VT
John: b c. 1755 d p. 1840 m Patsey — Lt VA
John, Sr.: b 1714 d 1811 m Bethiah Marshall PS VT
Jonathan: b 1716 d 3-29-1802 m Elizabeth Proctor Pvt MA
Jonathan: b 11-30-1758 d 2-5-1839 m Rachel Holt Pvt NH ★
Joseph: b 4- -1752 d 4- -1839 m Elizabeth Durkee Pvt PS CT
Joshua: b 3-8-1746 d 1813 m Miria Symons Pvt CT
Joshua: b 1-26-1754 d 1-7-1835 m Jemima Wyman Pvt NH ★
Josiah: b 3-21-1751-3 d 7-5-1838 m (1)Sally Hovey (2)Roxana
    Elderkin Sgt CT ★
Mark: bpt 3-11-1739 d 6-9-1791 m Hannah Goodhue Pvt MA
Nathan: b 1759 d 10-28-1849 m Mary Fuller Pvt CT ★
Nathaniel: b 3-19-1747 d 3-17-1838 m Mary Burnham Pvt NH
Oliver: b 11-11-1760 d 4-30-1846 m Sarah Rogers Sgt MA
Seth: b 3-9-1760 d 11-17-1846 m Lydia Lassell Pvt ME
Solomon: b 1762 d 5- -1824 m Anna Wheeler Pvt MA
Stephen: b 1749 d 4-19-1826 m Elizabeth Cole Pvt CT
Thomas: b 5-4-1732 d 5-6-1808 m Elizabeth Harmon Lt MA
Thomas: b 1732 d 10-19-1820 m Mary Howe Capt MA
Wesley, Sr.: b 10- -1719 d 6-28-1797 m (1)Joanna Thornton
    (2)Deborah Story Pvt MA
Wesley, Jr.: b 8-27-1747 d 9-1-1835 m Molly Woodbury Pvt MA
Wm.: b 9-9-1760 d 1-19-1822 m Marcey Dwelly Pvt CT ★
Wolcott: b 4-19-1762 d 1-24-1849 m Hannah Sturdevant Pvt CT
Zenas: b 1-29-1762 d 4-25-1822 m Thankful — Pvt CT

BURNLEY,
Garland: b 1-12-1753 d 8-17-1793 m Frances Taylor Capt VA
Henry: b 1755/6 d 1- -1835 m (1)Lucy Davenport (2)Polly Lockie
    Lt VA ★
Israel: b 1725 d 2- -1793 m Ann Terrell Sol PS VA
James, Sr.: b 1731 d 2. 6-3-1819 m Elizabeth Mills PS VA

BURNS, (includes BURN, BURNES, BYRNE, & BYRNES)
Adam: b 1736 d 5-15-1799 m Sarah — PS MD
Alexander: b 1740 d 6-20-1821 m Nancy Ann Barnes Pvt PA

Alexander: b 1739 d 1-12-1826 m Jane Carroll Pvt PA
Andrew: b 1736 d 1793 m Mary Johnson PS GA
Edward: b 1754 d 1814 m Abigail Amy Pvt CT
Edward: b — d 1803 m Sarah Milligan Ens NY
Ignatius: b 1750 d 5-19-1810 m (1)Mary — (2)Eleanor — Capt VA
Isaac: b 7-4-1753 d 7-4-1831 m (1)Margaret Green (2)Elizabeth
    Vernon Pvt PA
James: b 1740 d 1799 m Mary Orme Sgt PS MD
James: b 12-2-1755 d 6-10-1835 m Margaret — Sgt MD ★
Jeremiah: b 10-26-1752 d 10-31-1824 m Elizabeth Rowland Pvt VA ★
John: b 8-17-1751 d 5-7-1852 m Mrs Sarah McMarston Pvt
    NH ★
John, Sr.: b c. 1700 d 8-4-1782 m X PS NH
John, Jr.: b 3-28-1732 d 2-17-1825 m Elizabeth Jones PS NH
John: b 1762 d 1843 m Sara Glaze Pvt NC ★
John: b c. 1753 d 8-24-1781 m Agnes — Pvt PA
John: b 8-10-1750 d 5-4-1827 m Catherine Gray Pvt PA ★
John: b — d 4-20-1802 m Esther Morrow Pvt PA
John: b c. 1740 d p. 1790 m Mary McCoy Sol SC
John: b c. 1745 d 1782 m Mary — Sol PS SC
John: b 5-20-1748 d 6-30-1821 m Catherine Cameron Gnr SC
John: b 1750 d 5-2-1846 m Ann — Pvt VA
Lawrence: b 1756 d 7-15-1832 m Elizabeth Baker Pvt VA
Mary: b c. 1750 d p. 1785 m John Burns PS SC
Otway: b c. 1750 d p. 8-14-1797 m X Sol PS NC
Owen: b p. 1740-45 d 1795 m Sarah — PS NC
Phillip: b 1759 d 1-28-1849 m (1) X (2)Catherine — Pvt NC★
Thomas: b 1740 d 3- -1811 m Elizabeth Harkness PS NH
Thomas: b c. 1761 d 1846 m Margaret Montgomery Pvt PA
Walter: b 1739 d 9-15-1822 m Hannah Turner Pvt RI
Wm.: b — d — m Welthy Hutchinson Pvt CT
Wm.: b 2-12-1752 d 7-22-1827 m Margaret Mitchel Sol NC
Wm.: b 1743 d 12-4-1814 m (1)Rachel — (2)Hannah Kerlin McKee
    Pvt PA

BURNSIDE,
James: b — d 1781-85 m (1)Debora Janse (2)Catherine Warren
    1Lt NY
James: b 1761 d 1833 m Rebecca Lawhead Mus PS ★
James, Sr.: b 1727 d 1812 m Isabella Patterson Pvt VA
John, Jr.: b c. 1760-65 d 12- -1817 m Deliah Sheffield Pvt GA
John: b 9-10-1766 d 2-17-1838 m Mary Denton Pvt NC ★
Thomas: b 7-30-1750 d 1827 m Ariaantie Ten Eyck Pvt NY
Walter: b 1713 d 1804/5 m Mary — Pvt NC

BURPEE,
Ebenezer: b 1-31-1760 d 2-4-1832 m Elizabeth Weston Pvt Matr
    MA W ★
Edward: b 6-2-1756 d 3-28-1840 m Hannah Gallop Pvt MA
Elijah: b 1761 d 6-17-1836 m Hannah Waite Pvt MA ★
Jeremiah: b 1744 d p. 1792 m Elizabeth Maxfield PS NH
Moses: b 8-11-1750 d 11-20-1827 m Elizabeth Kendall Cpl MA
Moses: b 12-9-1733 d 11-11-1826 m Margaret Harriman Pvt MA
Nathan: b 12-13-1758 d 1-5-1836 m (1)Mrs Eunice (Farrer) Rice
    (2)Lucinda Pearson Pvt MA
Nathan: b 7-8-1756 d 12-13-1846 m Anna — Pvt NH ★
Nathaniel, Jr.: b 2-19-1753 d p. 1832 m Dorothy Currier Pvt MA
Nathaniel, Sr.: b 2-7-1721 d 1815 m Esther Rolfe PS NH

BURR,
Adonijah, Sr.: b 1727 d 1799 m Thankful Holcomb Capt CT
Adonijah, Jr.: bpt 1-21-1750 d p. 1790 m Phebe — Pvt CT
Asa: b 11-2-1753 d 9-22-1836 m Malinda Hoskins Cpl CT
Charles: b 8-31-1759 d 8-7-1820 m (Polly) Holyoke Pvt CT
Daniel: b 7-2-1730 d p. 12-31-1780 m Ann Silliman Pvt Bgd Armr CT
Daniel: b 1761 d 3- -1834 m Susanna Danforth Pvt MA ★
Daniel, Jr.: b 12-2-1759 d 1-6-1827 m Sarah Underhill Sol Sct NY
David: b 10-16-1745 d 11-3-1814 m Mary Yearing Cpl MA
Ebenezer: bpt 3-18-1732 d 1821 m (1)Sarah Sherwood (2)Abigail
    Thorp Pvt CT
Ebenezer: bpt 2- -1761 d 2-2-1819 m Amelia Goodsell Pvt CT
Ebenezer: b 3- -1749 d 9-15-1829 m Elizabeth Dorchester Sol NH
Elisha: b 5-5-1738 d 5-15-1804 m Lucretia Bates Sgt MA
Ephraim: b 3-5-1736 d 11-19-1779 m Eunice Wilson Sol CT
Ezekiel: b 3-23-1755 d p. 1792 m Huldah Merchant Cpl CT
George: b 5-26-1736 d 6- -1813 m Mable Wakeman Capt CT
Henry: b 5-12-1731 d p. 4-13-1786 m Elizabeth Foster PS NJ
Ichabod: b 5-1-1736 d 3-10-1805 m Rachel Bradley Pvt CT
Increase: b 12-26-1726 d 12-24-1793 m (1)Jane Bradley
    (2)Rhoda Burritt Sol CT
Increase, Jr.: b 4-22-1759 d 11-17-1841 m Annie Bulkley Pvt CT
Isaac, Jr.: b 1760 d 4-27-1827 m Irene Orcott Sol VT
Isaac: b 4-11-1744 d 3- -1813 m Abigail Beardsley Pvt CT
Isaac: b 9-8-1729 d 2-3-1776 m Rachel Bliss Capt MA
Isaac: b 1736 d 1826 m Mary Baldwin PS NJ
Israel: b 1755 d 1826 m Hannah Ames Cpl MA
Jabez: b 8-20-1752 d 6-28-1825 m Mary Bartram Pvt CT
Jehiel: b 4-11-1757 d 11-24-1814 m Mabel — Pvt CT
Jehu: b 3-15-1752 d 8-4-1833 m Mary Hawley Ens CT
Jesse: b 12-30-1755 d 6- -1813 m Sarah Wilson Pvt CT
Joel: b 8-23-1758 d 9-6-1841 m Elizabeth Gould Pvt CT
John, Jr.: b 5- -1726 d 8-6-1788 m Tabitha Loomis Sgt CT
John: b 4-6-1729 d 2-15-1790 m Emma Cushing Pvt MA

BURR, contd.
Jonathan: b 4-11-1756 d 2-10-1804 m Lydia Bailey Cpl CT
Jonathan: b 12-28-1726 d 12-17-1804 m Hannah Bates Pvt MA
Jonathan: b 4-16-1731 d 1797 m (1)Martha Cudworth (2)Lydia Kingsley Pvt MA
Joseph: b 9-25-1732 d 1796 m Rachel Coate Pvt NJ
Joshua: b 8-12-1741 d 10-27-1824 m Betsey Thayer Pvt MA
Luther: b 4-7-1764 d 1840 m Jane Howard Pvt MA
Nathan: b 9-17-1733 d p. 1777 m Ruth Jennings Pvt CT
Nathan: b 1-1-1745 d 1818 m Phoebe Yoing Pvt CT
Nathaniel: b c. 1742 d 9-21-1822 m Abigail Strong Sol CT
Nathaniel, Sr.: b 3-23-1717 d 9-12-1802 m (2)Sarah Porter PS CT
Nathaniel, Jr.: b 4-27-1752 d 9-4-1836 m (1)Jemima Stevens (2)Hannah Clark Pvt CT ★
Nehemiah: b 4-18-1734 d 2-21-1815 m Sarah Osborn Pvt CT
Noadiah: b 4-29-1732 d 6-28-1793 m Abigail Pease Pvt CT
Ozias: b 5-19-1760 d 9-25-1815 m Margaret Tredwell Pvt NY
Peter: b 11-2-1754 d 4-7-1816 m Esther Jennings PS CT
Reuben: b 1-13-1752 d 12-20-1827 m (1)Mehitable Stark (2)Martha Willson Pvt PS CT
Roger: b 1765 d — m X Pvt CT
Samuel: b 4-2-1730 d 10-18-1782 m Susannah Wooley Sgt CT
Samuel: b 1732 d 8-13-1815 m Christain Cadwell Pvt CT
Samuel: b 8-27-1741 d p. 1782 m Jerusa Stevens Pvt CT
Samuel: b 7-19-1740 d 1822 m Mary Cheshire Sgt NY
Stephen: b 1698 m 1778 m (1)Elizabeth Hull (2)Abigail Hall PS CT
Thomas: b 8-17-1735 d 9-23-1812 m Margaret Fearing Lt MA
Timothy, Sr.: b 1749 d 8-19-1799 m Susan M Hinsdale Pvt CT
Timothy: b 1757 d 12-22-1835 m Naomi Walden Cpl MA
Wakeman: b 10-3-1743 d 5-9-1799 m Mary Davis 1Lt CT
Wm.: b 6-29-1762 d 6-28-1841 m Sarah Hubbell Sgt CT
Wm.: b 1761/2 d — m Eunice Thorpe Sol CT

BURRIDGE, (includes BURRAGE)
John: b 8-29-1755 d 7-22-1822 m Lois Barthrick Sgt MA ★
John: b c. 1750 d 6-28-1815 m Mary Spear Pvt MA ★
Thomas: b 1731 d 1799 m Abigail Fisher Pvt MA
Wm.: b 12-9-1731 d 9-23-1820 m Phoebe Barrett Pvt MA

BURRILL, (includes BURRALL, BURRELL)
Abraham: b 4-1-1729 d 11-18-1798 m Mary Austin Pvt MA
Benjamin: b 1-17-1760 d 3-27-1844 m (1)Mary Damon (2)Esther Twist Pvt NY ★
Benoni: b 9-7-1756 d 4-27-1814 m Lydia Ripley Pvt Drm MA
Charles: b 3-3-1720 d 10-7-1803 m (1)Joanna Seger (2)Abigail Kellogg Col CT
Ebenezer: b 2-6-1703 d 5-20-1778 m Mary Mansfield PS CS MA
Francis: b 9- -1760 d 2-4-1852 m X Pvt Spy VA
John: b 8-29-1726 d 12-14-1793 m Ann Thompson Pvt MA
John: b 10-5-1752 d 9-11-1842 m (1)Betsy Brooks (2)Elenor Craig Pvt MA ★
Jonathan: b 2-10-1757 d 12-30-1835 m (1)Lucy Wright (2)Lucina Wright Sol MA
Joseph: b 2-13-1756 d 5-31-1837 m (1)Lydia Mulliken (2)Susanna Mulliken Pvt MA ★
Joseph: b 1761/2 d 7-23-1818 m Sarah Belcher Pvt MA
Nathaniel, Jr.: b 5-17-1761 d 10-18-1842 m Rachel Springer Pvt Fif MA
Samuel: b 4-1-1717 d 5-3-1797 m Anna Alden PS MA
Sylvanus: b 9-4-1757 d 10-2-1824 m Mary Williams Pvt MA W★
Theophilus: b 10-30-1740 d — m Martha Newhall Pvt MA
Thomas: b 1739 d 9-25-1794 m Grace Garnett Pvt MA

BURRITT,
Andrew: b 5-28-1741 d 8-5-1836 m Eunice Welles Tms CT
Anthony: b 12-4-1752 d 4-12-1839 m (1)Anna Curtiss (2)Mrs Abigail Hinman Srgn Mte CT
Blackleach: b 1740 d 8-27-1794 m (1)Martha Wells (2)Deborah Wells PS CT
Eben: b 4-19-1762 d 10-10-1840 m Sarah Fairchild Pvt CT ★
Elihu: b 12-24-1732 d 3-19-1793 m Eunice Wakeman Pvt CT
Israel: b 4-24-1726 d 3-28-1778 m Mary Salter Pvt CT
Israel: b 1744 d 1-17-1833 m Hester Holabird Capt VT ★
John: b 1745 d 7-21-1818 m Elizabeth Hall Blakeman Cpl CT
Joseph: b 8-9-1758 d 10-3-1830 m Sally Ufford Pvt CT
Phillip: b a. 1753 d 1804 m Rachel Read Sgt CT
Samuel: b 11- -1729 d 1798 m Mercy Burton Pvt CT

BURROUGHS, (includes BORROUGHS, BURRIS, BURRISS, BURRUS, BURROUGH, BURROWS, BURROWES)
Benjamin: b 1742 d p. 1-20-1799 m Mary Van Horn Pvt NJ
Benjamin: b 1745 d c. 1820 m (1)Elizabeth Buyce (3)Dorcas — Sgt NY
Caleb: b 2-13-1765 d 11-6-1853 m Rebecca Madison Pvt CT
Charles: b c. 1750 d 2-4-1819 m (1)Elizabeth Dickinson (2)Susannah Ballard (3)Jean Owen Pvt VA
Daniel: b 1756 d 1843 m (1)Mary Crane (2)Olive Carpenter Pvt PS NH
David: b 3-10-1747 d 2-2-1838 m Hannah Blogget Pvt MA
Ebenezer: b 7-1-1753 d 10-27-1828 m Anne Easton Pvt MA
Eden: b a. 1760 d 2-26-1825 m Hannah — Lt NJ
Elisha: b 1754 d 9-18-1830 m (1)Susan Fish (2)Sarah Fish Pvt CT
Greene: b 1760 d 2-28-1838 m Sarah Tilley Cabin Boy RI

Henry: b c. 1748 d 1813 m Mary Burroughs Pvt MD
Hubbard Daniel: b 6-26-1739 d 9-6-1781 m (1)Priscilla Baldwin (2)Sarah Avery Capt CT
Jacob: b 1755 d 10-1-1832 m Susannah Martin Sgt MD ★
James: b 1735 d 1784 m Mary Jones NJ
Joel: b 8-7-1748 d 1807 m Phoebe Messer Pvt PS NH
John: b 10-9-1734 d 1784 m Hannah Wilbur Pvt CT
John, Sr.: b 4-16-1711 d 2-21-1798 m Sarah Abbey PS NH
John, Jr.: b a. 1747 d 1828 m Mehitable Carlton Sgt NH
John: b 10-27-1753 d 1799 m Margaret Forman Maj NJ
John: b 1-13-1754 d 4-27-1842 m Rhoda Hendrickson Sgt NJ
John: b 1754 d 2-4-1824 m Elizabeth Miller Pvt NJ
John, Jr.: b 5-15-1760 d 8-22-1837 m (1)Jane Torbert (2)Mary McCormick Pvt PA ★
John: b 1718 d 1804-06 m Lydia Baker Pvt PA
John: b c. 1740 d p. 1807 m Esther Terry Pvt NC
Jonathan: b 5-13-1752 d p. 1790 m Lucy Avery Pvt CT
Jonathan: b 1- -1755 d 1-2-1817 m Elizabeth Witherell OrdlSgt NH W★
Joseph: b 7-26-1762 d 1-14-1821 m Sophia Rucker Pvt VA
Matthew: b 1760/61 d 11-11-1819 m Ruth Scott Sol VA
Nathan: b 5-17-1746 d 8-18-1808 m (1)Amy Williams (2)Sarah Williams Pvt CT
Nathan: b 11-13-1758 d 3-24-1825 m Elizabeth Lane Pvt NY
Nathaniel: b 1762 d 1-26-1855 m Mary Thrailcal Pvt VA ★
Peleg: b 6-14-1748 d 12-22-1799 m Keziah Burdick PS RI
Phillip: b 2-6-1745 d 4-18-1794 m Sarah Brower Pvt NY
Solomon: b 1752 d 5-21-1845 m Judith Taylor Sol NC SC ★
Stephen, Sr. b 10-4-1729 d 8-21-1817 m (1)Elizabeth Browne (2)Huldah Pixlee Capt CT
Stephen: b 1-27-1712 d p. 9-8-1790 m (1)Mary Moore (2)Sarah Temple PS NJ
Thomas: b a. 1752 d 1-8-1825 m Rebecca Fish Pvt NJ
Thomas: b 1748 d 1790 m Hannah Ashton PS NJ
Thomas: b c. 1722 d p. 10-3-1788 m Frances Tandy Cpl VA
Timothy: b 8-20-1751 d 1-2-1829 m Esther Hulburd Pvt PS NH
Waters: b 8-3-1746 d 7-5-1815 m Frances Meeker Pvt NJ
Wm.: b 1-25-1728 d 1825 m Mercy Farrar Lt MA ★
Wm.: b 1738 d 7-30-1811 m Mary Ashe Pvt SC
William Ward: b 1-16-1758 d 4-5-1805 m Mary Bond MarOf SC
Zebulon: b 9-3-1758 d 11-13-1845 m Hannah Rust Pvt CT ★

BURSIEL,
Moses: b — d — m Mary Colby Pvt MA ★

BURSON,
Isaac: b c. 1740-50 d c. 1829 m Sarah — Sol GA
James: b 9-28-1763 d p. 1790 m Jane Orlton Capt PA
James: b c. 1735 d 1814 m Mary — PS VA
John: b 1739 d 1799 m Jane Whinery Ens PA

BURT, (includes BURTT)
Abel: b 11-21-1753 d 7-8-1788 m Bathsheba Thompson Pvt MA
Alvin: b 5-15-1761 d 7-19-1841 m Wealthy Austin Pvt MA
Benjamin: b 6-3-1761 d 3-1-1849 m (1)Mehetabelle — (2)Mrs Mary Crull Pvt Art NJ ★
Benjamin: b 3-7-1750 d 5-10-1826 m Johanna Parshall Pvt NY
Benjamin: b 5-10-1740 d 6-9-1835 m Mary Root CS VT
Caleb: b 3-10-1765 d 9-19-1847 m Anne Murry Pvt MA
Daniel: b 9-16-1729 d 9-22-1812 m Mary Burt Frizzell Pvt MA
Daniel, Sr.: b 7-8-1716 d 3-18-1805 m Hannah Benedict Sct NY
Daniel, Jr.: b 10-20-1740 d 7-5-1823 m Martha Bradner Pvt NY
David: b 3- -1760 d 6-20-1828 m Hannah Bennett Pvt NY
David: b 6-1-1733 d 11-14-1822 m (1)Mary Colton (2)Mrs Eunice Hall Capt MA
David: b 1758/9 d 3-8-1832 m Silence Burt Sgt MA
Ebenezer: b 2-12-1755 d 1831 m Lydia Stanley Pvt MA
Elijah: b 1740 d 3-3-1817 m Sarah Williams 2Lt MA
Elijah: b 10-3-1742 d 4-5-1820 m (1)Deborah Colton (2)Mrs Dorothy Fish Booth Pvt MA
Elisha: b 12-14-1764 d 2-11-1833 m (1)Chloe Wales (2)Electa Ellis Pvt MA
Enos: b 9-4-1745 d 1836 m Sarah Sawyer Pvt NH
Enos: b 9-3-1760 d 4-4-1822 m Hannah Haskins Pvt RI
George: b 1741 d 5-24-1787 m Dinah Witherell Pvt MA
Gideon: b 7-30-1743 d 6-12-1825 m (1)Lydia Hale (2)Celia Sabin Col MA
Ithamar: b 12-16-1755 d 9-25-1841 m Prudence Dickinson Pvt MA
James: b 10-25-1760 d 3-17-1852 m Abigail Coe Sgt NY
Joel: b 5-24-1759 d 11-21-1841 m Martha Lyman Pvt MA ★
John: b 11-9-1720 d p. 3-31-1801 m — Smith Mus NJ
John, Jr.: b 1756 d 1826 m Priscilla Senter Pvt NC
Jonathan: b 2-9-1739 d 4-18-1794 m Hannah Cooley Adj MA
Joseph: b 1726 d 12-29-1810 m Abiah Moore Pvt MA
Joseph: b c. 1730 d 1788 m Elizabeth — PS NC
Martin: b 11-10-1745 d 6-6-1803 m Dorcas Clark Sgt MA
Noah: b 8-30-1734 d 4-27-1800 m Hannah Loomis Pvt MA
Oliver: b 6-3-1738 d 10-6-1807 m Jerusha Kingsley MM MA
Reuben: b 9-10-1761 d 8-8-1860 m Bathsheba Wright Cpl MA ★
Samuel: b 9-15-1715 d 11-7-1799 m Hannah King PS MA
Stephen: b 10-7-1747 d 3-21-1803 m Hannah Pitts Pvt MA
Thomas: b 1733 d 7-28-1800 m (1)Molly Tisdale (2)Zilpha Haskins Pvt MA

Thomas: b 5-26-1752 d 7-24-1842 m (1)— Welling (2)— Hathorn Pvt NY ★
Wm.: b 6-28-1745 d 11-17-1832 m Prudence Lincoln Pvt MA
Wm.: b *c.* 1754 d 7-8-1823 m (1)— Turner (2)Salome Ballard Pvt VA
Wm, Sr.: b *c.* 1725 d 1783 m X PS VA

BURTIS,
John, Jr.: b 2-26-1749 d 1-3-1827 m Sarah Foster Pvt NY

BURTON,
Abel: b *c.* 1734 d 11- -1804 m Ann Cousins Pvt·VA
Abraham: b 6-10-1743 d 11-15-1830 m (1)Mary Kenney (2)Betsey Dale Pvt NH
Abraham: b 1-28-1727 d *p.* 9-13-1810 m X PS VA
Basil: b *a.* 1762 d *a.* 1-27-1823 m Alice — PS Pvt MD
Benjamin: b 6-26-1748 d 9-5-1811 m Hannah Hawley Pvt CT
Benjamin: b 1-28-1718 d 11-5-1783 m (1)Ann — (2)Hester Cord PS DE
Benjamin: b 12-9-1749 d 5-24-1835 m Hannah Church Maj MA
Benjamin: b 12-1-1756 d 9-12-1847 m Hannah Griswold Pvt VT ★
David: bpt 10-25-1761 d 8-28-1822 m Abigail Greely Pvt NH
Elijah: b 2-22-1760 d 1-17-1849 m (1)Rachel Smith (2)Hannah Taylor Cpl VT
Ephriam: b 11-30-1727 d 1806 m Betty Wells Pvt CT
George: b 9-11-1751 d *p.* 1778 m Rosannah Potter Pvt RI
Henry: b 7-16-1759 d 9-1-1841 m Ann Hazen Pvt VT W ★
Henry, Sr.: b *c.* 1730 d *c.* 1801 m Judith — PS VA
Isaac: b 1750 d 1813 m Rachel — Pvt NY
Jacob: b 1-17-1762 d 8-7-1819 m Keturah Palmer Pvt CT
Jacob: b 2-29-1762 d 1-16-1844 m Mary Swearingen Pvt MD
Jacob: b 9-14-1715 d 6-12-1798 m (1)Rachel Benton (2)Elizabeth — PS VT
James: bpt 8- -1745 d 6-16-1818 m Naomi Burch Capt CT W ★
James: b *c.* 1750 d 8-21-1829 m (1)Mary White (2)Elisabeth Goodridge Capt VA W ★
Jeremiah: b 4-12-1724 d 1-13-1812 m (1)Miriam Huse (2)Asenath Clark Pvt CT
Jesse: b 1750 d 1795 m Anne Maria Hudson PS VA
John: b 1738 d 11-18-1816 m Rebecca Gage Cpl PS NH
John: b *c.* 1750 d 1801 m Elizabeth — Pvt CS NC
John: b *c.* 1730 d *p.* 1-10-1801 m — Ware PS VA
John: b 7-8-1758 d 7-4-1836 m Susannah Stamper Pvt VA
John: b *a.* 1760 d *a.* 9-3-1822 m Martha Cocke Farley Smn VA
Jonathan: b 9-18-1741 d 4-30-1811 m Huldah Nichols Lt NH
Joseph: b 8-19-1722 d 11-7-1801 m Rebecca Booth Cmsry CT
Joseph: b *c.* 1731 d 1811 m X PS SC
Josiah: b 9-18-1741 d 1-1-1803 m Susan Winans Capt NY
Josiah: b 6-6-1732 d 5-28-1793 m Sarah Howes Pvt VT
Judah: b 6-9-1739 d 3-18-1813 m (1)Huldah Stanton (2)Eunice Morgan Lt NY
Judson: b 9-14-1730 d 1805 m Comfort Keeney Ens CT
Martin: b *c.* 1728 d 1792 m Mollie East PS VA
May: b *c.* 1725 d 1801 m Hannah Medley PS VA
May, Jr.: b 1752 d 5-13-1829 m Sarah Head Capt VA Heirs ★
Nathan: b 11-30-1754 d 3-19-1834 m Sarah Wilcox Sgt CT ★
Richard: b 1735 d 1800 m Nancy Hamilton Pvt GA
Robert: b 10-20-1747 d 5-31-1825 m Agatha Williams QMGen NC
Robert: b 3-7-1751 d 1819 m Mary Lewis Pvt VA
Rufus: b 1754 d 6-14-1828 m Abigail Snell Ens RI
Samuel: b 12-12-1750 d 1820 m Martha Clarke Pvt CT
Thomas: b *c.* 1755 d 1810 m Rhoda Hubbard Pvt GA
Thomas: b 1741 d 1821 m Sinah Roberts Ens VA
Thomas: b 1757 d 3-13-1835 m Lucy Stith Bradley Pvt VA
Thomas: b 1-26-1761 d 3-26-1845 m Frances Phillips Pvt VA ★
Thomas, Sr.: b *c.* 1721 d 8-19-1800 m Sarah Thompson PS VA
Thomas, Jr.: b — d *p.* 10-31-1827 m Nancy Nunnelee Sol GA
Thomas: b 1743 d *p.* 5-4-1802 m (1)Nanney Perrin (2)Lillian — PS VA
Wm.: b 8-15-1759 d 9-23-1841 m Mary Ross Cpl MA ★
Wm.: b 10-14-1757 d 3-12-1842 m (1)Jane Robinson (2)Chloe Davis Pvt MA ★
Wm., Sr.: b 3-15-1735 d 4-26-1826 m Phoebe Douglas Pvt SC
Wm.: b 1755 d 1810 m Mary Smith Sol SC

BURVINGER,
Leonard: b 1-8-1727 d 7-21-1792 m Mary Bucher Pvt PA

BURWELL,
Daniel: b 2-19-1754 d 12-1-1839 m Abigal Pardee Pvt CT ★
Jerre: b 5-4-1756 d 3-7-1835 m Lucy Pardee Pvt CT ★
John: b — d — m Lyons Pvt NJ
John: b 11-13-1746 d 2-26-1788 m Anne Powell Pvt VA
Lewis: b 9-26-1745 d 7-2-1800 m (1)Ann Spottswood (2)Elizabeth R Harrison Col VA
Lewis: b 1737 d 3- -1779 m Judith Page PS VA
Nathaniel: b 4-15-1750 d 3-29-1814 m (1)Susan Grymes (2)Lucy Baylor Col VA
Nathaniel: b 10-4-1750 d 3-20-1801 m Martha Digges Maj ADC VA
Nicholas: b — d — m Sarah Day Pvt MA
Robert: b 6-3-1720 d 1777 m (1)Sarah Nelson (2)Mary Braxton PS VA
Samuel: b 12-12-1729 d 1816 m Abigail Arnold PS CS CT
Thacker: b 1746 d 1780 m Mary Armstead LCol VA

BUSBY,
James: b 5-2-1754/5 d 7-20-1838 m Elizabeth Shackleford Pvt VA ★
Wm.: b 2-27-1758 d 1794 m Sarah Burrough CS Lt NJ

BUSEY, (includes BUSSEY)
John: b 1751 d 6-24-1807 m (2)— Lansdale 1Sgt MD
Joshua: b 1711 d *c.* 1786-90 m Eleanor — PS MD
Thomas: b *c.* 1762 d *p.* 9-25-1822 m Judith — Pvt GA

BUSH, (includes BUSCH)
Aaron: b 5-30-1725 d 1805 m Mary Ashley Pvt CT
Aaron: b 8-18-1717 m Alice French CS CT
Abiel: b 9-15-1759 d 12-1-1813 m Barbara — Pvt MA
Benjamin: b 4-27-1745 d 10-30-1830 m Sarah — Pvt MA
Caleb: b 10-3-1756 d 11-6-1822 m Susanna Maria Wilcox Cpl MA
Conrad: b 11-13-1759 d 8-15-1832 m Catherine Vischer Cpl NY
Conrad: b 10-29-1753 d 12-19-1854 m Mary Watson Matr NY ★
Daniel: b 1718 d 2 -17-1792 m Dorothy — MM MA
Daniel: b 1750 d 2-2-1836 m Catherine — Pvt PA ★
Daniel: b *c.* 1739/40 d 1800 m Elizabeth Freeman Pvt SC
David: b *c.* 1760 d 5-5-1797 m (1)Sarah Isaacs (2)Mrs Sarah Isaacs Pvt CT
David, Sr.: b 12-7-1721 d 1801 m Thankful Pettibone PS MA
David, Jr.: b 10-29-1762 d 11-12-1836 m Anna Bush Pvt MA
Ebenezer: b 1745 d 1-18-1791 m (1)Tabitha Taylor (2)Sarah Cary Sgt MA
Francis: b 2-20-1750 d *c.* 1824 m (1)Lucy Davis (2)Rachel Martin Pvt VA
George: b 6-11-1756 d 3-3-1843 m Prudence Churchill Drm CT
George: b 6- -1745 d 1838 m Margretha Stansler Pvt VA ★
George: b 1755 d 1830 m Catherine Marshall Pvt VA KY
Gilbert: b 8-18-1734 d 1809 m (1)Hester Ryke (2)Titia — Pvt NY
Henry: b. 1747 d 10- -1805 m Rachel DeGraw Sol NY
Henry: b 11-25-1760 d 4-6-1839 m Catharine Dolson Ens PA
Henry: b 7-9-1754 d 7-7-1832 m Eve Elizabeth Hoffman Pvt PA
Isaac: b 6-18-1763 d 1- -1835 m (1)Charlott Costelo (2)Zelpeter Bryant Sol SC
Jacob: b 1759 d 1838 m (2)Catherine — Pvt PA
Jacob: b 1756 d 11-28-1832 m Margaret Swan Sol Spy VA ★
James: bpt 10-26-1740 d *p.* 2-19-1809 m Eva Brink Pvt PA
James: b 9-26-1759 d *a.* 2-5-1849 m (1)Lydia — (2)Polly Plunkett Pvt VA ★
John: b *c.* 1735-38 d *c.* 1815 m Mary — Pvt NY
John: b 5-4-1760 d 12-17-1843 m Jane Vosburgh Pvt NY ★
John: b 6-21-1752 d 4- -1805 m Susannah Bryan Lt NC
John: b 2-7-1755 d 5-2-1806 m Mary Sharp Capt PA
John: b 11-26-1747 d *p.* 1823 m Catharine Leinbach Lt PA
John: b 8-18-1736 d 5-27-1816 m Sarah Richards Lt PA
John: b 1750 d *p.* 4-4-1802 m Mary Miley Pvt SC
John: b 1754 d 4-10-1816 m Lydia Arms Pvt VT
John: b 2-2-1742 d *a.* 3- -1798 m (1)Elizabeth Watson (2)Mary Tillman Sol VA
Jonathan: b 6-17-1745 d 7-2-1828 m Esther Warner Capt CT
Jonathan: b 3-2-1747 d 2-23-1816 m Patience Killam Sgt CT
Joseph: b 9-11-1741 d 10-18-1828 m (1)Dorothy How (2)Mary Watson 2Lt MA
Leonard: b 3-5-1755 d 7-6-1832 m Catherine Stingley Pvt VA
Michael: b 1-10-1750 d 8-10-1825 m Magdalene — Sol VA
Moses: b 12-8-1714 d 9-23-1803 m (1)Susannah Johnson (2)Luch Warren PS CT
Moses: b 5-23-1756 d *p.* 11-11-1790 m Lucretia Ensign Pvt MA
Peter: b 2-22-1753 d 2-16-1826 m Maria Elizabeth — Pvt PA
Philip, Jr.: b 2-26-1737 d 6-21-1819 m Frances Vivian Pvt VA
Philip: b 10-12-1733 d 12-8-1812 m Catherine Slough CS VA
Prescott: b 1758 d 6-23-1846 m Susan Hinds Pvt SC
Richard: b *c.* 2-28-1755 d 7-4-1829 m Ann Vanderbeek Sol NY
Richard: b 11-23-1754 d 11-4-1835 m (1)Hannah Hazard (2)Eunice T. Champlin Sgt RI
Richard: b — d *a.* 2-18-1803 m Mary Prescott PS NC
Samuel: b 1-7-1760 d 11-24-1826 m Anna Hubbard Pvt CT
Samuel: b 12-27-1747 d 1830 m Anne McKee PS DE
Stephen: b 8-7-1759 d 5-16-1842 m Zilpha Thrasher Pvt CT MA ★
Wm.: b *c.* 1755 d 1821 m Mourning Sheffield Capt NC
Wm.: b 10-29-1744 d 7-15-1815 m Frances Tandy Burris Lt VA
Wm.: b 1758 d 1843 m Elizabeth Shearer Collester Pvt VA
Wm.: b 1760-2 d 1835 m Joicy King Sol VA
Wm. Martin: b *c.* 1750 d *a.* 2- -1799 m Penelope Lane Capt NC
Zachariah, Jr.: b 10-25-1742 d 11-20-1811 m Mary Falley Lt MA
Zita: b — d 8-25-1844 m (2)Mary Smith Pvt MA ★

BUSHEE,
Consider: b 5-10-1763 d 7-8-1846 m Patience Carter Cpl RI
Jonathan: b 2-5-1761 d 6-9-1835 m Anstees Sisson Pvt RI ★

BUSHMAN,
John: b *c.* 1755 d *p.* 1810 m — Stockalager Pvt PA

BUSHNELL,
Alexander: b 12-2-1739 d 3-8-1818 m Chloe Waite Lt CT
Banajah: b 3-21-1744 d 1814 m Lucy Abel Lt CT
Constant: b 5-12-1751 d 7-18-1805 m Temperance Kelsey Pvt CT
Daniel: b 1740 d 12-12-1818 m Hannah — Pvt CT
Doud: b 5-15-1762 d 8-12-1845 m Lucy Joyce Pvt CT ★

BUSHNELL, contd

Ebenezer, Sr.: b 12-9-1730 d *p.* 1792 m Elizabeth Tiffany PS CT
Elijah: b 3-20-1746/47 d 4- -1843 m Eunice Pratt Cpl CT
Ephriam: b 8-24-1760 d 9-24-1836 m Mary Stevens Pvt CT ★
Ezra: b 6-29-1746 d 2-16-1786 m Patience Lord Sgt CT
Gideon: b 1756 d 1-8-1830 m Nancy Hurd Pvt CT
Handley: b *c.* 1730 d 1-10-1811 m Chloe Bishop PS CT
Ira, Sr.: b 10-19-1727 d 8-16-1794 m (1)Patience Bushnell (2)Mable Chapman CS PS CT
Jabez: b 1-26-1744/5 d 11-8-1810 m Lydia Wells Pvt CT
James: b 11-21-1762 d 12-3-1858 m Electa Munson Pvt CT
Jason: b 11- -1763 d 9- -1847 m (1)Hannah Kirkland (2)Sarah Smith Pvt CT
John Handley: b 12-2-1744 d 2-5-1828 m Sarah Willard Pvt CT
Jordan: b *c.* 1750 d 6-30-1787 m Sarah Pratt Pvt CT
Joseph: b 6-20-1716 d 1795/6 m (1)Abigail Bushnell (2)Elizabeth French (3)Sarah — PS CT
Josiah: b 3-10-1757 d *p.* 1808 m Ann Young Pvt MA
Josiah: b 6-14-1737 d 1-20-1809 m Mary Barnett Pvt MA
Nathan: b 7-18-1753 d *p.* 2-18-1777 m Esther Lord Pvt CT
Phineas: b 4-23-1718 d 1783 m Priscilla Clark Sgt CT
Thomas: b 1-11-1762 d 4-10-1817 m Rebecca Andrews Pvt CT

BUSHONG, (includes BUSHUNG)

Jacob: b 1754 d *p.* 1818 m Eva Bossert Pvt VA ★
John: b 8-30-1732 d 12-8-1808 m Elizabeth Black 1Lt PA
Philip: b 1722 d 5-19-1785 m Anna Eve Hergard Almonar Mil PA

BUSS,

Ebenezer: b 11-9-1756 d 3-5-1833 m (1)Ruhamah Mason Pvt MA
John: b 4-23-1759 d 10-31-1845 m Sarah Richardson Pvt MA ★

BUSSEY,

Benjamin, Jr.: b 3-1-1757 d *p.* 1780 m Judeth Gay Pvt MA
Bennett: b 11-8-1745 d 12-25-1827 m (1)Ann Green (2)Mrs Elizabeth Slade Maj MD
Edward: b 1740 d 1782 m Ruth Colgate 1Lt MA
Edward: b 1718 d 1782 m X Pvt MD
Hezekiah: b *c.* 1750 d 1796 m Amie — Sol GA
Isaiah: b 6-12-1741 d 178-1 m Bathsheba Wentworth CaptLt MA
John: b 6-12-1751 d 3-8-1841 m Mrs Polly Davenport Capt MA
Thomas: b *a.* 1744 d *p.* 1792 m Anna — Capt MA

BUSSIER,

Bartholomew: b *c.* 1733 d *a.* 5-18-1805 m Judith Raybolt PS PA

BUSSING,

Harman: b 12-19-1759 d 5-28-1845 m Alida Fort Pvt NY
Peter, Jr.: b 10-1-1735 d 7-9-1790 m Charity Williams Pvt NY

BUSTARD,

Claudius: b 1753 d 1807 m Dorcas Sumpter PS VA

BUSTER,

Claudius: b 11-24-1763 d 11-20-1843 m (1)Elizabeth — (2)Elenor Paul Pvt VA ★
John: b 1737 d 1820 m Elizabeth Woods Sol VA

BUSTIN,

Christopher: b *c.* 1740 d 1784 m (1)Elizabeth Dunn (2)Martha Pitts PS VA

BUSWELL,

Benjamin: b 5-8-1733 d *p.* 1775 m Judith Moody Drm MA
Caleb: b 1740 d 8-31-1803 m Mary Badger PS NH
Daniel: b 5-10-1735 d 8-12-1813 m (1)Mary Reynolds (2)Abigail West Pvt MA
Daniel: b 4-2-1763 d 1859 m Ede Bodwell Pvt MA
John: b 9-4-1748 d 2-6-1828 m Rebecca Demary Pvt NH
John: b 1-26-1752 d 1839 m Mary Smith Pvt NH
Nicholas Colby: b 1-17-1762 d 8-6-1841 m Elizabeth Chamberlain Cpl NH
Samuel: b 4-14-1729 d 10-26-1781 m Mary Winslow PS NH
Thomas: b — d — m Thankful Fox Pvt CT

BUTCHER,

Paulser: b 1748 d *p.* 1829 m Elizabeth Bush Pvt VA
Samuel, Jr.: b 3-28-1756 d 5-2-1847 m Hannah Drake Lt VA
Wm.: b 1750 d 1800 m Jane — Pvt VA

BUTLER,

Abel: b 1760-2 d 8-21-1829 m Rebecca Lawton Pvt VT
Abigail: b 1-25-1750 d 3-11-1845 m Jasper Pratt PS CT
Abijah: b 7-2-1750 d 1-19-1822 m (1)Mary Putnam (2)Beulah Fairbanks 2Lt MA
Allen: b 4-14-1754 d 2- -1839 m Elizabeth — Pvt MA ★
Benjamin: b 1749 d 2- -1828 m Amy Daggett Pvt MA
Benjamin: b 5-5-1729 d 12-26-1804 m Dorcas Abbott CS PS NH
Benjamin: b 1750 d 10-7-1805 m Mary Reese Pvt PA
Benjamin: b 8-21-1762 d 8-8-1828 m Hannah Webster Pvt PA
Benjamin: b 12-18-1727 d 1800 m Susanna Whiting Pvt VT
Caleb: b 7-25-1741 d 9-8-1813 m Rebecca Frost CS NH
Charles: b 7-18-1732 d 6-18-1782 m Azubah Rawney Lt CT

Charles: b 1747 d 10-17-1819 m Mary Cooper Pvt NC
Charles: b *a.* 1746 d *p.* 1-12-1811 m Elizabeth — Sol NC
Comfort: b 11-16-1743 d 2-19-1826 m Mary Berry Sgt CT
Cornelius: b 9-17-1738 d 1794 m Jane Coffin Mstr MA
Curry: b 1760 d 12-7-1822 m (1)Elizabeth Folk (2)Mary Crickett Pvt NC
Daniel: b 10-13-1751 d *p.* 1786 m Hannah Reed Pvt CT
Daniel: b 10-23-1748 d 11-29-1831 m Molly Tenney Sol NH
David: b 6-17-1760/1 d 1815 m Olive Henry Cpl CT
David: b 1762 d 7-11-1842 m Chloe Jones Pvt CT
Ebenezer, Sr.: b 12-9-1733 d 1829 m X Pvt CT
Ebenezer, Jr.: b 1761 d 1829 m Rebecca Davis Pvt CT
Ebenezer: b 9-14-1723 d 2- -1808 m (1)Mehitable Norton (2)Bethiah Gould (3)Jerusha Butler Pvt MA
Edmund: b 1755 d 1802 m Fannie Garrett Pvt GA
Edmund: b *a.* 1747 d *p.* 4-27-1801 m Mary — Sol PS GA
Edward: b 3-20-1762 d 5-6-1803 m Isabelle Fowler Lt PA
Edward: b 2-10-1748 d 12-15-1809 m Elizabeth Wingfield Pvt VA
Eleazer: b 6-22-1763 d 3-24-1857 m Joanna Ellenwood Pvt CT
Eli: b 1-26-1740 d 4-19-1802 m Rachel Stocking Capt CT
Elijah: b 5-16-1713 d 4-6-1789 m Thankful Smith PS MA
Elisha: b 1757 d *a.* 10- -1829 m Ann — Pvt VA
Ephraim Gould: b 12-9-1758 d 4-3-1832 m Lovey Sherman Pease Mate MA
Ezekiel 1st.: b 4-12-1734 d 7-26-1781 m Mabel Jones PS CT
Ezekiel: b 1755 d *p.* 1790 m — Munn Pvt CT
Ezekiel, Jr.: b 11-3-1761 d 6-15-1830 m Lydia Elizabeth Frisbie Pvt CT W ★
George: b 3-15-1749 d 8-19-1837 m Chloe Bidwell Pvt CT
Henry: b 4-27-1754 d 7-20-1813 m Isabella Fisk Capt NH
Hezekiah: b 4-29-1708 d 12-17-1786 m Rebecca Standish PS CT
Ignatius: b 10-2-1755 d *p.* 5-20-1810 m Delilah — Matr PS VA
Isaac: b 6-15-1752 d 1-16-1833 m Hannah Hull Pvt CT ★
Isaac: b *c.* 1750 d 1812 m Mary Pomfret Pvt NC
Isaiah: b 10-23-1750 d 1820-30 m (1)Elizabeth Barber (2)Lora Hix Sol CT
Israel: b 7-14-1759 d 4-10-1846 m Mercy Covill Pvt RI ★
James: b 9-8-1754 d 11-12-1813 m Esther Wadsworth Sol CT
James: b 12-15-1736 d *p.* 1790 m Puella Luce Pvt MA
James: b 2-15-1740 d 12-20-1827 m Mary Sigourney PS MA
James: b 1-8-1766 d 4-10-1826 m Mary Hood Drm PA ★
James, Sr.: b 1737 d 11-7-1781 m Mary Simpson Capt SC
James: b *c.* 1745 d 5-16-1811 m Winnifred Brooks Pvt SC
James: b 1755 d *p.* 4-11-1829 m Unis Kinsley Sgt VT
Jethro: b 9-20-1750 d *c.* 6- -1839 m Rebecca Dunham Pvt MA
Joel: b 3-20-1752 d 9-13-1822 m Mabel Thompson Pvt VT
John: b *c.* 1759 d *p.* 9-4-1819 m Anna Easton Ens CT ★
John: b 5-9-1763 d 1-11-1838 m Martha Eells Cpl W★
John: b 1-18-1744 d *p.* 1783 m Elizabeth Lindsley Pvt CT
John: b 3-28-1729 d 3-20-1795 m Hannah Drury Adj MA
John: b 5-9-1734 d *p.* 1790 m Mary Morgaridge Pvt MA
John: b 1750/1 d 8-4-1834 m Abigail Brown Pvt Smn MA ★
John, Jr.: b 1-16-1741 d 1824 m Chloe Norton Pvt NY
John: b 1761 d 1836 m Nellie Walden Pvt MA
John George: b 1754 d 12-12-1816 m Catherine Miller Pvt PA
Jonathan: b 5-23-1740 d 11-5-1830 m Ruth Benton Pvt CT
Jonathan: b 11-2-1752 d 12-5-1844 m Lois Kidder Sgt MA ★
Joseph: b *c.* 1750 d 1785-1794 m Mary Ogle Pvt MD
Joseph: b 8-15-1734 d *p.* 1778 m Sarah — Capt MA
Joseph: b *c.* 1730 d *c.* 1792 m Anna Carter Sol VA
Joseph: b *c.* 1742 d 3-18-1811 m Elizabeth — Sol VA
Joseph: b 1758 d 8-3-1843 m Francis Oliver Pvt VA ★
Joshua: b 1761-3 d 1829 m Susan Green PS NC
Josiah, Sr.: b 1764 d — m Hannah Hull Cpl CT
Josiah: b 7-8-1745 d 11-18-1806 m Martha Riley Pvt CT
Matthew: b 8-1-1748 d 11-28-1836 m Hannah Palmer Cpl CT ★
Mathew: b 1753 d 12-6-1832 m (1)Anna Merry (2)Sarah Butler (3)Mary Hubby Pvt NH
Moses, Sr.: b 2-22-1731 d 9-8-1817 m Sarah Goodwin Pvt MA
Moses, Jr.: b 2- -1756 d 4-25-1839 m Mary Moon Pvt MA ★
Moses: b 2-28-1741 d 9-21-1823 m Keziah Nason Pvt MA
Nancy: b 9-27-1765 d 1854 m Elisha Brooks PS SC
Nathaniel: b 7-5-1762 d 11-25-1841 m Tabatha Joy Pvt MA
Patrick: b 3-1-1760 d 1838/39 m Elizabeth Fannin Pvt VA ★
Patrick: b 1730 d 8-7-1813 m Mercy Bartlett CS CT
Percival: b 4-4-1760 d 9-9-1821 m Mildred Hawkins 1Lt PA
Peter: b 3-1-1748 d 4-2-1836 m (2)Anna Bass Cpl NH
Philip: b 12-30-1760 d 8-12-1813 m Ruth Dole Pvt MA
Phineas, Sr.: b 6-3-1732 d 1-16-1806 m Bathsheba Graves Cpl MA
Phineas, Jr.: b 4-8-1758 d 9-25-1852 m Milea Robbins Cpl MA ★
Pierce: b 1744 d 1822 m Mary Middleton Maj SC
Reuben: b 2-24-1757 d 1- -1829 m Ann Lisle Lt VA W★
Richard: b 7-1-1743 d 11-4-1791 m Mary Smith MGen PA
Robert, Sr.: b *c.* 1728/9 d *a.* 3-26-1802 m Delilah Rhodes Maj NC
Robert: b 1756 d 1819 m Mary E Jones Sol VA
Samuel: b 1747 d 11- -1807 n Hester Buckingham Sgt CT
Samuel, Jr.: b 3-6-1743 d 8-27-1810 m Prudence — Pvt CT
Samuel: b 5-19-1734 d 7-15-1799 m Lydia Kimball Pvt ME
Samuel: b 1749 d 1777 m Betty — Pvt VA
Shebael: b *c.* 1761 d 1790 m (1)Susanna Folger (2)Mrs Hepsibah Jones (3)Hannah Garnet Pvt MA
Silas: b 1746 d 10-19-1828 m Mary Neal Pvt MA
Stephen: b 12-10-1758 d 4-25-1822 m Phebe Graves Sgt CT ★

Stephen: b 10-3-1759 d 3-29-1846 m Thankful Bishop Pvt CT
Thomas: bpt 5-27-1733 d 8-24-1809 m Bridget Vaughan Gerrish Lt MA
Thomas: b 2-18-1754 d 2-18-1818 m Margaret Rogers Ens MA
Thomas: b 1732 d 1-2-1816 m Abigail West Pvt MA
Thomas, Jr.: b c. 1753 d p. 1790 m Catherine Stewart Pvt MA
Thomas: b 5-28-1748 d 9-7-1805 m Sarah Jane Semple Capt PA
Thomas: b 1-2-1740 d 8- -1832 m Ann Dalrymple Pvt PA
Thomas: b 4-6-1720 d 1789 m Eleanor Parker PS PA
Thomas: b 11-4-1763 d. 3-6-1816 m Elizabeth Grigsby Sgt SC
Tobias: b 1747 d 4-15-1815 m (2)Sarah Tool (3)Elizabeth Smith PS MD
Wm.: b 4-16-1752 d 4-7-1839 m Sarah Hull Pvt CT
Wm.: b 1-1-1759 d a. 1815 m Frances Poindexter Sol GA
Wm.: b c. 1735 d 1820 m Elizabeth Goodhue Pvt MA
Wm.: b 1-6-1745 d 5-16-1789 m Jane Carmichael LCol PA
Wm.: b 7- -1743 d 3-4-1837 m Eliner Douglas Pvt PA ★
Wm.: b 2-27-1730 d 5-27-1838 m Ann Griffin Pvt PA ★
Wm.: b 1759 d 12-17-1821 m Behethand Foote Moore Capt SC
Wm.: b c. 1735 d 1810 m Mary — Sol PS VA
Wm.: b 1758 d p. 1785 m Zilpha — Sol VA
Zachariah: b 1736 d 12-4-1792 m Mary Edwards Pvt VA
Zachariah Dingle: b 6-28-1754 d 1-22-1836 m (1)Elizabeth Driskil (2)Rachel Garrison Pvt NC ★
Zebulon: b 1-23-1731 d 7-28-1795 m (1)Anna Lord (2)Lydia Johnson (3)Phoebe Haight Col CT
Zephaniah: b 1728 d 1800 m Abigail Cilley Pvt NH
Zephaniah: bpt 1750 d 7-19-1816 m Hannah Ripley Pvt MA

BUTMAN,
Richard: b 2-22-1739 d a. 1-12-1803 m Mary Woodbury Sgt MA

BUTT,
Epaphroditus: b 1755 d 8-23-1829 m Sophia Etheridge Pvt VA
John: b c. 1759 d 5- -1808 m Catherine — Pvt PA
John: b 1758 d 3- -1805 m Abiah Wilson Lt VA
Josiah: b a. 1741 d p. 1811 m Mary Boush Pvt VA
Solomon: b 1763 d p. 9-21-1810 m Dorcas Williamson Pvt VA
Thomas: b 9-18-1763 d 3-1-1833 m Mary Taylor Mus MD W ★
Wm.: b 1745 d 1805 m Susan Eldridge Ross Pvt NC

BUTTERFIELD,
Abel: b 2-1-1742 d p. 1790 m Mercy — Sol MA
Abraham: b 11-1-1750 d 2-18-1833 m Ruth Averill Pvt NH
Benjamin: b 5-25-1759 d 8-31-1837 m Sarah Chamberlain Pvt MA
Benjamin: b 5-14-1726 d 12-7-1804 m (1)Susanna Spaulding (2)Lois Herrick PS VT
Charles: b 9-25-1735 d a. 11-29-1777 m Hannah — Pvt NH
Ebenezer: b 7-13-1706 d 1795 m (1)Sarah — (2)Alice Taylor PS MA
Elijah: b 8-14-1763 d 9-16-1851 m Hannah Campbell Pvt MA
Ephraim: b 1734 d 3-16-1814 m Mary Snow Pvt MA
Isaac: b 11-1-1702 d 10-12-1812 m (1)Ruth Spalding (2)Mrs Ruth Fletcher Sol MA
Isaac: b 3-5-1749 d 1-6-1844 m Sarah Sherwin Capt NH
James: b c. 1755 d 10-13-1818 m Catherine Runyon Capt NH ★
James: b 4-23-1753 d p. 1790 m Susan Brockway Lt VT
Jesse: b 4-28-1752 d 2-6-1842 m Lydia Blodgett Sgt MA ★
John, Jr.: b 9-7-1753 d 10-10-1823 m Naomy Stevens Sgt NH
Jonas: b 4-27-1740 d 3-18-1795 m Fanny Jane Hazeltine 1Lt NH
Jonas: b 9-12-1742 d 6-22-1826 m Esther Cummings Cpl MA
Jonathan: b 1-3-1721 d 4-6-1793 m Lydia Proctor Pvt MA
Nathaniel: b 1-22-1732/33 d 9-24-1809 m Elizabeth Stewart Campbell Cpl MA
Peter: b 6-16-1739 d 12-31-1811 m Harriet Butterick 1Lt MA
Peter: b 1-6-1755 d 10-22-1838 m (1)Hannah Guy (2)Rachel Grear Cpl NY ★
Philip: b 10-8-1757 d p. 1802 m (1)Mary Parkhurst (2)Mrs Polly Foster Pvt MA
Reuben: b 10- -1727 d 2-22-1816 m Mary Richardson Capt MA
Robert: b 11-16-1756 d 2-26-1841 m Elizabeth Chamberlain Pvt NH
Samuel: b 4-9-1750 d 3-18-1816 m Elizabeth Bemis 2Lt MA
Samuel: b 2-24-1738 d 7-29-1808 m Hannah Chandler Pvt MA
Simeon: b 11-11-1740 d 1824 m Sarah Coburn Pvt NH
Stephen: b 2-29-1736 d — m (1)Hannah — (2)Sarah Sawyer PS NH
Thomas: b 6-6-1746 d 2-17-1823 m Esther Hawley Lt VT
Timothy: b 3-23-1730 d 4-10-1819 m Lucretia Adams Sgt NH
Wm.: b 8- -1757 d 6-12-1835 m (3)Esther Hale (4)Chloe Randall Pvt NH ★

BUTTERS,
Benjamin: b 1754 d 8-19-1820 m Elizabeth Stimpson Pvt MA
Jacob: b 1754 d 1816 m Rachel Smith Pvt NY
James: b 2-22-1746 d 3-21-1838 m (1)Abigal Butterfield (2)Mrs Esther Reed Pvt MA
Jesse: b 11-21-1761 d 11- -1796 m (1)Rebecca — (2)Betsey Cutler Pvt MA
John: b 4-26-1732 d 6-4-1793 m Mary Killam Pvt MA
Reuben: b 11-17-1729 d 10- -1794 m (1)Rachel Thomson (2)Mrs Catherine Beard Pvt MA
Samuel, Sr.: b 11-30-1728 d 5-7-1793 m (1)Keziah Dana PS MA
Samuel, Jr.: b 11-15-1749 d 6-14-1812 m (1)Tabitha Nichols (2)Elizabeth Eastman Pvt MA

Simeon: b 8-23-1759 d 4-3-1827 m Betsey Eames Sgt MA
Wm., Jr.: b 2-27-1736 d 7-5-1814 m (1)Elizabeth Boutwell (2)Esther Wesson Pvt MA

BUTTERWORTH,
Benjamin: b 1740 d 1818 m Elizabeth — Lt VA
Benjamin: b 2-4-1736 d a. 9- -1801 m (1)Elizabeth Clement (2)Sarah Hoskins CS VA
Hezekiah: b 1742 d 9-22-1808 m Elizabeth Cole Pvt RI
Nathaniel: b 12-4-1735 d 7-13-1796 m Elizabeth Hayward Pvt MA
Noah: b 10-19-1761 d 4-3-1850 m Rachel Ray Pvt RI

BUTTOLPH, (includes BUTTLES)
Abijah: b 12-4-1751 d 8-30-1814/15 m Olive Waters Pvt CT W ★
George: b 1726 d 4-26-1826 m (1)Mary Collins (2)Anna Baker Pvt CT
Joel: b 1749 d 1786 m Hannah Hayden Pvt CT
Jonathan, Sr.: b 3-8-1724 d c. 1776/77 m (1)Jerusha Dibble (2)Mrs Martha Phelps Capt CT
Jonathan, Jr.: b 5-12-1749 d 1823 m Lois Vietz Lt CT
Roger: b 10-4-1734 d — m Mary Gardner Pvt MA
Seba: b 1763 d p. 1796 m Thankful Mosier Pvt NY

BUTTON,
Benjamin: b 12-31-1759 d 1847 m Clarissa Hamblin Pvt CT ★
Benjamin: bpt 2-11-1759 d 12- -1784 m Esther Chapman Pvt CT
Charles: b 4-17-1739 d 6-27-1790 m Anna Wilcox Pvt VT
Daniel: b 1746 d p. 1783 m Elizabeth Button Pvt CT
Elias: b 1747 d 1830 m Sarah Bluit Sgt CT ★
Harman: b c. 1753 d 5-5-1822 m Sarah Fishback Pvt VA
John: b 1749 d 1841 m Anna Coon Pvt RI ★
Jonathan: b 5-16-1750 d 6-18-1837 m Naomi Munsell Pvt CT ★
Joseph: b 1762 d 6-4-1842 m (1)Olive Prentice (2)Racheal Read Pvt CT
Joseph: b 1-16-1753 d 10-5-1826 m (1)Sarah Glass (2)Mrs Betsey Park Pvt CS CT VT
Newbury: b 3-25-1766 d 12-18-1843 m Bedotha Pierpont Fif CT

BUTTRICK, (includes BUTRICK & BUTTERICK)
Abel: b 6-21-1751 d 2-15-1830 m Abia Coburn Pvt MA
Abiel: b 6-1-1752 d 6-7-1821 m Eunice Haywood Cpl MA
Daniel: b 5-13-1748 d 5-16-1848 m Eunice Buttrick Pvt MA
Edward: b — d p. 5-28-1819 m Abigail Kilbourn Sgt RI ★
Francis: b 4-17-1748 d 1-5-1829 m Lydia Howe Cpl MA
John: b 7-20-1731 d 5-16-1791 m Abigail Jones Maj LCol MA
Joseph: b 1-9-1723 d 12-29-1803 m Sarah Brown Pvt MA
Nathan: b 9-27-1725 d 12-25-1812 m Grace Wheeler Pvt MA
Oliver: b 1748 d c. 1840 m (1) X (2)Patty Sabin Pvt MA ★
Samuel: b 11-16-1718 d 1-14-1814 m Lucy Wheeler Pvt MA
Tilly: b 4-26-1754 d 2- -1837 m Abagail Brown Sgt MA
Willard: b 11-11-1746 d 1-3-1813 m Esther Blood MM MA

BUTTRILL,
Wm.: b 2-20-1763 d 1-3-1857 m Mary Williams Pvt GA

BUTTS, (includes BUTT & BUTZ)
Christian: b 11-18-1756 d 10-10-1821 m Mary Wagener Pvt PA
Gideon: b 8-8-1758 d 2-21-1830 m Amy Knight Pvt CT
James: b 3-11-1757 d 2-17-1835 m (1)Keziah Simmons (2)Fannie Lewis (3)Sallie Simmons Sol VA
John: b 11-20-1747 d 1-7-1827 m Maria Elizabeth Miller Pvt PA
Josiah: b 9-18-1753 d 5-5-1814 m Eunice Knight Pvt CT W ★
Michael: b 1728 d 7- -1779 m Elizabeth Weaver PS PA
Peter: b 4-8-1754 d 1-26-1831 m Magdalina Romig Pvt PA
Rufus: b 8-14-1755 d 2-13-1828 m Abigail Thayer Sgt MA
Samuel: b 8-10-1750 d 8-17-1821 m Anna Marie Romig Pvt PA
Samuel: b¹ 12-20-1742 d p. 1790 m Phoebe Brown Pvt VT
Sherabiah: b 3-25-1733 d 11-27-1807 m Deboah Knight Capt CT
Thomas: b c. 1746 d p. 3-25-1826 m Mary Edwards Capt VA
Wm.: b 6-20-1755 d 3-20-1841 m Rachel Rice Lockwood Sgt NY ★

BUXTON,
Benjamin: b 1753 d 1813 m Hannah Flint Pvt MA
Ebenezer: b 6-9-1755 d 10-17-1835 m Susannah Damon Sgt MA ★
Enos: b 7-24-1752 d 12-10-1838 m (1)Mary Dodge (2)Mary Chase Cpl MA
James: b 1745 d 1817 m Esther Southwick Capt MA
Jarvis: b 11-22-1737 d 8- -1811 m Sarah Berry Pvt NC
John: b 5-8-1757 d 4- -1781 m Rachel Lounsbury Pvt CT
John: b 3-7-1746 d 6-23-1840 m Elmira C— Cpl CT ★
John: b 1730 d 1821 m Elizabeth Burnap Cpl NH
John: b c. -1752 d 1845 m Betsey Kelley Sol RI
Stephen, Sr.: b 1720 d 1795 m Mary Damon Capt MA
Wm., Sr.: b 2-19-1726 d p. 1790 m Lydia Jones Pvt MA
Wm., Jr.: b - -1763 d p. 7-30-1832 m Catherine Loring Pvt MA ★
Wm.: b 1747 d p. 1790 m Mary Mahan Pvt MA

BUZZELL, (includes BUSSELL)
Isaac: b 1-23-1756 d c. 1840 m X Pvt MA ★
James: b 1735 d 1800 m Abigail Clough Pvt NH
James: b 6-2-1759 d 8-23-1838 m Tabitha Allen Drm NH
Jonathan: b 1755 d 7-1-1842 m Susanna Goodale Pvt MA ★
Jonathan: b 1-13-1761 d 2-13-1826 m Martha Pike Pvt NH ★
Joseph: b 8-12-1733 d p. 1782 m Sarah — Pvt PS NH

BUZZELL, contd.
Matthew: b 1756 d 1-30-1844 m Frances Reynolds Smn Pvt VA ★
Samuel: b 3-3-1733 d 1817 m Lydia Evans PS NH
Solomon: b 1-5-1761 d 9-4-1813 m (1)Mrs Elizabeth Burnham (2)Susannah Clark Pvt NH
Stephen: b 5-20-1746 d 5-17-1815 m Lucy Grant Pvt ME
Wm.: b 12-8-1720 d 1792 m Elizabeth Winslow PS NH
Wm.: b 9- -1759 d 10-13-1840 m Sarah Ann Wyatt Pvt VA ★

BYAM,
John: b 6-8-1761 d 6-6-1835 m Sarah Haywood Drm Pvt MA ★
John, Sr.: b 2-7-1731 d 7-3-1813 m Sarah Blanchard CS MA
Samuel: b 1737 d 10-5-1821 m Bulah — Pvt MA

BYBEE,
Cornelius: b 1763 d 11- -1841 m (1)Mary Norman (2)Mildred Wright Pvt VA ★

BYERLY, (includes BEYERLE, BEYERLY)
Beatrice Gulden: b c. 1727/28 d p. 1801 m (1)Andrew Byerly, Sr. (2)Benjamin Lord PS PA
Casper: b 8-24-1727 d 11-7-1794 m Catherine — PS PA
Francis: b 1755 d p. 1797 m Magdalene Harmon Pvt PA
Jacob: b 5- -1760 d 7-7-1858 m Anna Elizabeth Harmon Pvt PA ★
Ludwig: b — d 3-26-1778 m Anna Maria Jeder PS PA
Micheal: b 1746 d 7-22-1829 m Anna Maria Harmon PS MD
Michael: b 7- -1758 d 8-20-1844 m Rebecca Pitcock Pvt VA ★

BYERS, (includes BYARS & BYER)
Andrew: b c. 1737 d p. 6-18-1789 m Martha — PS PA
Charles: b 2-10-1757 d 9-13-1830 m Polly Heilman Pvt PA CL
David: b 2-13-1755 d 5-11-1831 m Esther Baer Pvt PA
David: b 1748 d 1814 m Rosannah — Ens PA
Edward: b c. 1730 d p. 1790 m Elizabeth Walton Capt SC
Jacob: b c. 1745 d 5-1-1810 m Nancy — Pvt PA
James: b c. 1760 d a. 9- -1828 m (1) X (2)Elizabeth Watson PS PA
James: b 1713 d 1792 m Rachel Mathews PS VA
Jeremiah: b c. 1755 d 11-18-1796 m Elizabeth Hendricks PS VA
John: b 3-9-1759 d 8-16-1834 m Margaret Rahm Sgt PA
John: b 3-16-1734 d 11-23-1781 m Elizabeth Thompson Capt VA
John: b c. 1745 d — m Elizabeth — Pvt & Grd PA
Robert: b 4-25-1746 d 6-30-1809 m Jean Armour Capt PA
Thomas: b 9-7-1757 d 8-30-1825 m Margaret Shannon Pvt PA
Wm.: b — d p. 12-25-1797 m Elizabeth — PS SC
Wm.: b 1735 d 6-3-1811 m Anne — Pvt VA

BYINGTON,
Benjamin: b 1742 d p. 1782 m Phebe Harrison Pvt CT
Daniel, Jr.: b 1738 d 1824 m Elizabeth Hall 2Lt CT
Isaac: b 1-24-1761 d 7-6-1828 m Elizabeth Byington Pvt MA ★
Jared: b 8-20-1758 d 2-22-1827 m Rebecca Porter Pvt CT
John: b 1741 d 1-6-1834 m Sarah Saint John Pvt CT ★
Joseph: b 9-23-1736 d 8-25-1798 m (1)Jemima Hungerford (2)Hannah Spencer (3)Hannah Warren Lt PS CT
Justus: b 4-7-1763 d 4-28-1839 m Lucy Hinsdale Pvt CT ★
Samuel: b 3-21-1751 d 1823 m Olive Warren Pvt CT W ★

BYNUM,
Britton: b 1762 d 10-8-1834 m Virgina Dupree Pvt NC
Gray: b 12-20-1737 d 2-22-1814 m Margaret Hampton PS NC
Luke: b c. 1735 d a. 5- -1810 m Martha Patterson PS NC
Tapley: b 3-6-1761 d 1847 m Anne — Sol NC ★
Turner: b 1756 d 1831 m Elizabeth — Capt NC
Turner: b 1753 d 9-12-1820 m Mary Atherton Capt VA

BYRAM,
Benjamin: b 1731 d 12-28-1813 m (1)Anne Holman (2)Rachel Bailey Pvt VT
Ebenezer: b 12-5-1754 d 11-27-1833 m Margaret Gay Pvt MA
Ebenezer: b 6-24-1743 d c. 1827 m Lydia Guerin Sol NC
Edward: b 6-11-1742 d 8-25-1824 m Phoebe Ann Coe Pvt PA
Japhet: b 1721 d 1798 m (1)Sarah Allen (2) — Conklin (3)Elizabeth Tappan Pvt NJ
Joseph: b 5-22-1753 d 4-27-1829 m Esther Douglass Pvt NJ
Naphtali: b 3-13-1749 d 6- -1812 m Amy Hedges Pvt NJ

BYROD,
Frederick: b 6-16-1762 d 5-16-1840 m Christiana Brown Pvt PA ★

CABANESS, (includes CABANISS, & CABINESS)
George: b 1744 d 1815 m Palatier Harrison Pvt NC or VA
Matthew, Sr.: b 1712 d 1789 m Hannah Clay PS VA

CABBAGE,
John: b 2-24-1758 d 12- -1848 m X Pvt VA ★

CABEEN,
Thomas: b 1752-54 d 12-9-1801 m Euphemia Graham Sct SC

CABELL,
John: b 1742 d p. 4-22-1815 m (1)Paulina Jordan (2)Elizabeth Brierton Jones PS Cty Lt VA
Joseph, Sr.: b 9-19-1732 d 3-1-1798 m Mary Hopkins Cty Lt VA
Joseph, Jr.: b c. 1750 d 8-31-1831 m Pocahontas Rebecca Bolling Pvt VA
Nicholas: b 10-29-1750 d 8-18-1803 m Hannah Carrington Col VA
Samuel Jordan: b 12-15-1756 d 8-4-1818 m Sarah Syme LCol PS VA
Wm.: b 3-13-1730 d 3-23-1798 m Margaret Jordan PS VA
Wm., Jr.: b 3-25-1759 d 11-22-1822 m Ann Carrington Maj VA

CABLE, (includes CABLES, See also COBLE)
Abner: b 1760 d 2-21-1840 m Ann Scott Pvt CT
Abraham: b — d 1805 m Mary Magdalena — Sub-Lt PA
Gershum: b 6-24-1753 d 4- -1800 m (1) — Foot (2)Biah Meeker Pvt CT
Phillip: b 1754 d 1834 m Matilda Walker Capt PA

CABOT,
Francis: b 11-16-1752 d 2-20-1831 m Marcy Hodgman PS VT
Samuel: b 5-21-1753 d 3-12-1818 m Sarah Barrett PS MA
Sebastian: b 5-26-1737 d 6-30-1797 m Alice Corbin Sgt CT

CACKLER,
Christian: b 6-27-1756 d 9-28-1830 m Julia Ann — Pvt PA ★

CADDELL,
Samuel: b 1759 d p. 8-7-1832 m Nancy Cecil Sol VA

CADE,
Drury: b 10-15-1740 d 8-20-1838 m Winefred — Capt GA
John: b 1738-42 d p. 3-11-1793 m Elizabeth Hobson Adair Pvt NC
Richardson, Sr.: b c. 1740 d p. 1796 m Priscilla Dorman PS DE
Stephen: b 1715 d p. 1783 m Mary — PS NC
Wm.: b 8-24-1735 d p. 1787 m Elizabeth Smith Pvt SC

CADMAN,
Edward: b 5-28-1725 d 1816 m Sarah Seabury PS NY
George: b 10-7-1760 d 1-10-1839 m Desire Beebe Pvt NY ★
John: b 1755 d 1803 m Phoebe De Wolfe Drm Pvt NY

CADMUS,
Andries: b 10-28-1733 d c. 1805 m (1)Phoebe Van Tuyl (2)Deborah Bradt Pvt NJ
Henry: b 1751 d 1809 m(1)Margrietje Wauterse (2)Aaltje Keen Pvt NJ
John: b 12-20-1761 d 7-16-1828 m (1)Phebe Crane (2)Rebecca Wright Pvt NJ
Peter: b 6-2-1739 d 6-30-1810 m Blendina Kip MM NJ
Thomas: b 1-16-1736 d 11-2-1821 m Peterchie Cadmus LCol NJ

CADWALLADER, (includes CADWALADER)
Charles: b c. 1740 d 1800 m (1) — Mendenhall (2)Ann Miller Pvt PA
Isaac: b 1741 d p. 1790 m Elizabeth Mitchener PS PA
John: b 1-10-1742 d 2-11-1786 m Elizabeth Lloyd BGen PA
Thomas: b 1705 d 11-14-1779 m Hannah Lambert CS Dr PA

CADWELL,
Abel: b 11-27-1703 d 1780 m Anna Dwight Pvt MA
Daniel, Sr.: b 5-18-1710 d 1791 m Mary Warriner PS MA
Daniel: b 11-15-1735 d 3-16-1799 m Abigail Phelps Pvt PS MA
Daniel, Jr.: b 1-15-1733 d 3-27-1777 m Eunice Burt Capt MA
Ebenezer: b 3-3-1737 d — m Tabitha Day Lt MA
Hezekiah: b — d — m Tamar Lilly Pvt CT
John: b 1-9-1758 d 3-3-1834 m Annar — Sgt CT ★
Joseph: b 1745 d 3-7-1798 m Thankful Segdwick Drm CT
Phineas: b 2-28-1757 d 2-11-1857 m Eleanor Haydon Cpl CT ★
Reuben: b 6-28-1763 d 9-23-1842 m Rebecca Keeney Sol NY
Timothy: b 8-28-1747 d 1-13-1787 m Rhoda Kellogg Cpl CT

CADY,
Abijah: b 9-3-1729 d 5-6-1819 m Lucy Adams Pvt CT ★
Abner: b 3-23-1760 d 10-16-1835 m Molly Holmes Pvt CT ★
Amasa: b 4-10-1765 d 1842 m Ann Palmer Pvt VT
Daniel: b 3-30-1738 d 1-11-1807 m Mary Spalding Pvt CT
David, Sr.: b 9-17-1703 d 11-1-1788 m Hannah Whitmore PS CS CT
David, Jr.: b 2-10-1743 d 4-17-1807 m (1)Mary Sprague (2)Lois Cleveland (3)Lydia Young Capt CT
David: b 10-17-1764 d 4-25-1845 m (1)Zilpah Waterman (2)Irena Pratt Pvt NY ★
Ebenezer: b 1-20-1743 d 9-11-1816 m Chloe Beebe Capt NY
Eleazer: b 10-15-1749 d 10-28-1830 m (1)Mary Converse (2)Elizabeth Curtiss Pvt MA
Elias: b 9-7-1759 d 3-31-1853 m Olive Baker Pvt RI
Elijah: b 3-17-1720/21 d 10-12-1812 m Dinah Spaulding Lt NH
Elijah: b 3-8-1747 d 8-10-1833 m Isabel Jackson Ens NY
Elisha: b 6-8-1750 d 8-24-1827 m Ruth Waterman Ens NY
Isaac: b 1-24-1741 d 1777 m Sabra Green Pvt CT
Isaac, Sr.: b 12-25-1739 d p. 1790 m Sarah Hendrick Pvt NH
Isaac, Jr.: b 1765 d 1-18-1851 m Eunice Houghton Pvt NH ★
Isaiah: b 4-22-1732 d 10-30-1815 m Mary Nelson Pvt CT
Jedediah: b 11- -1759 d 1-10-1831 m Rhoda Holmes Ens CT

DAR Patriot Index

Jeremiah: b 7-17-1752 d 6-1-1848 m Hannah Warner Pvt MA
Jesse: b 4-10-1752 d — m Eunice Ward CS CT
John: b c. 1758 d c. 1845 m Catherine Spore Pvt NY
John: b 11-28-1736 d 2-25-1824 m Hannah Miles Sol VT
Jonathan: b 6-14-1748 d 7-12-1834 m Rebecca Cady Capt CT
Joseph: b 6-25-1727 d 1794 m Zerviah Hosmer LCol CT
Manasseh: b 6-21-1758 d 9-26-1833 m Elizabeth Hutchins Pvt VT
Nedebiah: b 12-18-1750 d 3-26-1838 m (1)May O. Buck (2)Sarah Washburn Pvt VT
Nicholas: b 1743 d p. 1794 m (1)Ruth Chase (2)Thankful Higbee (3)Betty Gile Pvt NH
Oliver: b 1741 d 1813 m Betsey Berchard Pvt NY
Palmer: b 7-4-1748 d p. 1780 m Rebecca Reed LCol NY
Reuben: b 9-3-1755 d 1826 m Lydia Wood Pvt CT
Rufus: b 4-22-1755 d 4-9-1821 m Lydia — Sgt MA
Samuel, Sr.: b 2-24-1724 d 4-8-1799 m Elizabeth Winter Pvt MA
Samuel, Jr.: b 11-20-1759 d 9-16-1813 m Keziah Richardson Pvt MA
Squire: b 10-28-1754 d 6-3-1841 m (1)Thankful Cutler (2)Abiah Spalding Sgt CT ★
Stephen: b 9-12-1750 d 7-31-1829 m (1)Jane Patrick (2)Esther Parker Sgt NH

CAFFEY,
John: b 1752 d 8-19-1826 m Mary Buchannan Pvt MD

CAGE,
Wm.: b 1746 d 3-12-1811 m (1)Elizabeth Douglas (2)Ann Morgan Maj NC

CAHILL,
James: b 1-27-1749 d 2-5-1851 m Ellender — Pvt MD ★
John: b c. 1738 d a. 1809 m Sarah — Pvt PA

CAHOON,
Benjamin: b 1761 d p. 1800 m Mary Auburn Pvt RI
Daniel: b 7-1-1737 d 9-13-1811 m Mrs Lillis (Dyer) Thomas PS RI
Jesse: b 3-10-1763 d 6-21-1830 m (1)Thankful Bassett (2)Anna Phillips Cahoon Pvt MA
John: b 1736 d 1800 m Sophia Van Gesel Pvt DE
Nathaniel, Jr.: b 1752 d 5-24-1827 m Abia Stuart Pvt MA

CAIN, (includes CAINE, KAIN, KANE)
Abner: b 1762 d 2-14-1832 m Sarah Townsend Pvt Cav SC
Daniel: b 5-28-1758 d 1818-26 m Hannah Holmes Pvt MA ★
Daniel: b c. 1751/52 d 1797 m Priscilla — Pvt PA
Edward: b 1753 d 12-10-1832 m Mary — Pvt MD ★
Hugh: b c. 1740 d p. 6-21-1781 m X Sol NC
James: b 9- -1752 d 7-18-1835 m Mary Meaks Sgt NC ★
James, Jr.: b 2-13-1749 d 4-10-1815 m Catherine — Sgt PA
James: b c. 1725 d p. 12-17-1782 m Lucretia — PS VA
John: b 6-25-1745 d 11-18-1814 m Elizabeth Kain Sol GA
John: b 3-6-1760 d 3-15-1810 m Ann Smith Pvt MD
John: b 12-10-1762 d 6-7-1840 m Sophia Frederick Sgt NY W ★
John: b 12-12-1734 d 3-15-1808 m Sybil Kent PS NY
John: b 6-24-1764 d 11-19-1838 m (1)Agnes — (2)Martha—Pvt PA
John: b 1745 d 1792 m Mary Busheba Drm SC
John: b 6-22-1760 d 4- -1835 m (1)— Pearson (2)Susanna Henley Pvt SC ★
John: b 1741 d 1816 m (2)Mrs Celia Jane Mabry Hobbs Pvt VA
Nathaniel: b 3-4-1752 d c. 3-2-1832 m Mary — Pvt NJ W ★
Patrick: b c. 1735 d 1779 m Mary Griffith 1Lt SC
Patrick: b 1762 d 1805 m Susan Crawford Pvt SC
Thomas: b c. 1755 d 8-10-1780 m Elizabeth Peake Pvt MA
Wm: b — d p. 2-10-1781 m Olive — PS NC
Wm.: b 1749 d 1794 m (1)Basheba — (2)Sarah Linam Sgt SC

CAKE,
David: b c. 1760 d 12- -1826 m (1) X (2)Sarah Royal Cpl NJ
Henry: b c. 1750-52 d 1817 m Catherine Miller Pvt PA
John: b c. 1740 d 2- -1804 m Anna — Pvt PA

CALCOTT, (includes CALLECOTE)
Harwood: b c. 1760 d 1793 m Flora — Ens VA

CALDER,
James: b 2-21-1755 d 11-2-1843 m Agnes Boise Pvt RI
John: b 8-15-1761 d 1-24-1845 m (1)Phebe Houghton (2)Winewood F. Richey Pvt SC GA ★
Robert: b 12-11-1757 d 3-16-1826 m Lydia Brock Mrnr MA ★
Wm.: b 1735 d 9-15-1802 m Anne Estabrook Capt MA

CALDERWOOD,
John: b 2-15-1725 d 1808 m Elizabeth McCurdy Sol NH

CALDWELL,
Alexander: b 2-6-1748 d 5-8-1823 m Jane Glover Pvt NH
Alexander: b 6-22-1752 d 5-31-1821 m Elizabeth Stephenson Pvt PA
Andrew: b c. 1753 d 1828 m Ruth Reese Sharpe Capt NC
Andrew: b c. 1759/60 d 3-2-1797 m Elizabeth Barker Lt Dr PA
Anthony: b 10- -1764 d 7- -1832 m Elizabeth Aiken Pvt VA
Charles: b a. 1760 d 1796 m Jane Browne Pvt PA

David: b 1752 d 4-7-1843 m (2)Mary Wilson Pvt NC ★
David: b 3-22-1725 d 8-25-1824 m Rachel Craighead Chp PS NC
David: b 5-8-1762 d 4-28-1813 m Rebecca Dean Pvt PS PA
David: b c. 1750 d 1840 m Phoebe Mann Sol VA
Ebenezer: b 1744 d 11-22-1827 m Sarah Price Pvt MA
Ebenezer: b 9-21-1745 d 12-16-1821 m Mercy Dodge Pvt MA
Elizabeth: b c. 10-15-1757 d 12-29-1851 m Robert Gillam Jr. PS VA
George: b 2-15-1760 d 5-20-1835 m Sarah — Pvt VA ★
Hugh, Jr.: b 2-7-1759 d 10-20-1829 m Jane Boyd Pvt PA
Hugh: b 1740 d p. 1815 m Ruth Hostein Pvt VA
Jacob: b 4-11-1748 d 1823 m Patience Sanderson Pvt MA
James: b 4-13-1742 d 2-18-1813 m Mary Clyde Cpl NH
James: b 1741 d 2-25-1824 m (1)Anna — (2)Martha — Sgt PS NH
James: b 4-14-1734 d 11-24-1781 m Hannah Ogden Chp Dep Qm Gen NJ
James: b 1759 d 12-19-1836 m (1)Fannie — (2)Betsy — Pvt PA
James: b c. 1760 d a. 1816 m Jane — Pvt PA
James: b 7-8-1755 d 1-11-1813 m Mary Forest Capt SC
James: b — d p. 4-15-1804 m Elizabeth — Capt SC
James: b 1724 d 4-22-1804 m Elizabeth Alexander CS VA
John: b 12-21-1755 d 5-26-1838 m Mrs Rachel Bishop Brown Sol CT
John: b 5-13-1743 d 10-8-1786 m Sarah Trask Sgt MA
John: b 1715 d 3-17-1807 m Jain — Pvt MA
John: b 7-11-1717 d 10- -1801 m (1)Abigail Hovey (2)Mrs Ruth Andrews Wells PS MA
John: b 5-28-1737 d 3-19-1812 m Letitia — Pvt NH
John: b 5-15-1757 d 11-15-1840 m Elizabeth Swan Pvt NH ★
John: b 8-23-1755 d 9-10-1801 m Hannah Rutan Pvt NJ
John: b 12-20-1760 d 1-9-1832 m Elizabeth — Pvt NY ★
John, Jr.: b 12-25-1754 d 11-24-1834 m Rebecca Bird Pvt PA
John: b — d 1775 m Mary Davis Capt SC
John: b 1740 d 1795 m Elizabeth Huggins Capt PS SC
John: b 1720 d 1790 m Mary Caldwell Capt VA
John: b 1750 d 1841 m Louisa Wetzel Sgt VA
John: b 1747 d 6-11-1829 m (1)Dicey Mann (2)Jean Neely Walker Pvt VA
John: b 1-22-1753 d 1842 m Jane Boggs Pvt VA ★
Joseph, Jr.: b 1-23-1752 d 9-9-1828 m Rachel McGee Pvt MA
Joseph: b 1-15-1724 d 12-22-1811 m Ann Gilmore LCol NY
Joseph: b 1729 d 4- -1802 m Jane McGrew Pvt PA
Matthew: b 4-3-1757 d 10-25-1810 m Mary Pinkerton Ens PA
Rachel Craighead: b 1739 d 6-3-1825 m David Caldwell PS NC
Rebecca Parks: b 1707/08 d 1806 m William Caldwell PS SC
Robert: b 7-21-1721 d 10- -1799 m Margaret — PS Sol PA
Robert: b 1722 d c. 1790 m Margaret — Pvt PA
Robert: b 6-1-1757 d 7-31-1845 m Sarah Ann Fryer Pvt PA ★
Robert: b 1732 d 7-30-1806 m Mary Logan Pvt PA
Samuel: b 1728 d 11-26-1798 m Martha Rounds PM PA
Samuel: b 1756 d 1835 m Elenor Paige Pvt NH ★
Thomas: b 1747 d p. 1786 m (1)Lucy Henderson (2)Mrs Mary Sweet Pvt MA
Thomas: b 7-7-1757 d 5-25-1824 m Elizabeth (Glover) Greenwood Pvt MA
Thomas: b 1733 d 2-20-1816 m Elizabeth Holmes PS NH
Thomas: b c. 1740 d 8-27-1804 m Delphia Ballard CS Capt NC
Wm.: b 10-5-1726 d 11-4-1791 m Margaret McCune Pvt PA
Wm.: b 5-18-1763 d 3- -1849 m Mary Brown Capt SC
Wm.: b 3- -1748 d 12-10-1814 m Elizabeth Williams Lt SC
Wm.: b 1760 d 4-20-1840 m Margaret Crawford Pvt SC ★
Wm.: b 1754 d 1806 m Esther Buchanan Pvt VA
Wm.: b 1754 d 1829 m Ann Sutherland Sgt KY

CALE, (includes KAIL)
Jacob: b — d 1790-1800 m Rebecca — Pvt NC
John: b 1745 d p. 8-30-1803 m Selah Brodgen Pvt NC
John: b 4-19-1726 d 7-26-1798 m Elizabeth Pugh Pvt VA

CALEF, (includes CALFE, CALIF)
James: b 1749 d 8- -1811 m Sarah Calef Cmsry CT
John: b 6-13-1741 d 10-30-1808 m Lois — Maj PS CS NH
John: b c. 1740 d 10- -1816 m Sarah — Pvt PS VA
John: b — d — m Judith Chellis Capt NH
Joseph: b 10-31-1718 d 12-21-1793 m Elizabeth Jewell Pvt NH
Oliver: b 1747 d 4-18-1826 m Elizabeth Melcher Cpl NH
Stephen: b 3-15-1734 d 1814 m Anna Stearns Sgt MA
Wm.: b 6- -1737 d 6-10-1812 m Anna Rowell Pvt NH
Wm.: b 1706 d 1784 m Lois Sawyer PS NH

CALHOUN, (includes CALHOON & COLHOUN)
Andrew: b 3-11-1760 d 1824 m Naomi Hawley Pvt MA
Andrew: b — d 5-8-1794 m Esther McDowell Lt PA
Andrew: b c. 1761 d 1804 m Anna Maria Ford Pvt PA
David: b 1736 d 8-23-1805 m Lois Chittenden Lt CT
David: b 1757 d 8-18-1834 m Eleanor King Pvt PA
George: b 2-1-1754 d 10-20-1835 m Susan Cotton Lt PA ★
James: b 4-15-1764 d 2-1-1848 m (1)Susa Hines (2)Mary Perry (3)Mrs Isabella Smith Pvt MA W ★
James: b c. 1750 d p. 1790 m (1)Eleanor Templeton (2)Mrs Mary (Abram) Walker Lt PA
John: b 8-15-1738 d 7-8-1788 m Tabitha Clark PS CT
John: b c. 1760 d p. 1791 m Mary — PS NC
John, Jr.: b 1752 d 1-10-1822 m (1)Agnes Thomson (2)Mrs Mary Thompson Pvt PA

CALHOUN, contd.
John: b 1740 d 12-22-1782 m Ruhamah Chambers PS PA
John: b 8-10-1757 d 9-29-1838 m (1)— Stephens (2)— Byrd (3)Sarah Cemp Pvt SC ★
John Ewing: b 1750 d 10-26-1802 m Floride Bonneau Pvt SC
Joseph: b 1730 d c. 1795 m Miss Ewing Capt SC
Patrick: b 6-10-1727 d 1-15-1796 m (1)Miss Craighead (2)Martha Caldwell PS SC
Samuel: b 10-25-1761 d 1-17-1844 m Lucy Gibbs Pvt MA ★
Samuel: b 1740 d 4-6-1833 m Nancy Neely PS NC
Samuel: b 7-29-1755 d p. 9-4-1847 m X Pvt PA
Thomas: b 1735 d 1-17-1823 m X Pvt PS PA
Wm.: b c. 1726 d p. 1790 m Agnes Long Pvt CS SC

CALK,
Wm.: b 3-7-1740 d 10-18-1823 m Sarah Basnett PS KY

CALKINS, (includes CALKIN & CAULKINS)
Abram: b 1761 d 1833 m Elizabeth Freeman Pvt MA
Amos: b 7-12-1755 d p. 1802 m Elizabeth Torrey Pvt CT
Caleb: c. 1757 d 4-5-1831 m (1)Mary Beckwith (2)Elizabeth (Calkins) Doane Pvt MA
Eleazer: b 1762 d 2-22-1836 m Polly Disbrow Pvt NY
Elijah: b 4-15-1740 d 7-3-1813 m Mehitable Heath Pvt PS NY
Frederick: b a. 1752 d 11-21-1815 m Annis Huntington Mate CT W ★
Israel: b 6-8-1731 d 3-18-1783 m Sarah Hoadley Pvt CT
Joel: b 1-27-1760 d 2-7-1848 m Bethiah Barras Pvt CT ★
John: b 5-16-1761 d 12-17-1844 m Catherine Dustin Pvt MA ★
John, Jr.: b 3-14-1748 d 10-7-1811 m Rebecca Jewett Pvt NY
John Prentiss: b 8-22-1753 d 4- -1836 m Sarah Hubbard Harris Sol CT NH
Jonathan: b 1736 d 9-21-1787 m Lydia Smith Capt CT
Moses: b 2-8-1757 d 5-25-1837 m Thankful Stevens Pvt Tms NY ★
Oliver, Jr.: b 1750 d 9-18-1787 m Hannah Thomas Pvt NY
Roswell: b 10-6-1761 d 11-15-1823 m Eunice Hine Pvt CT ★
Simon: b 3-9-1737 d 2- -1820 m (1)Selah — (2)Abigail Hall Pvt NY
Simeon: b 6-10-1738 d p. 1790 m Ruth Alger Pvt NY
Solomon: b 1747 d 4-12-1840 m Annie Crandall Ens VT
Stephen, Jr.: b 1737-35 d 12-15-1803 m (1)Mary Calkin (2)Mrs Dillie Jewett Pvt CT
Stephen, Jr.: b 3-13-1731 d 1814 m Rebecca Rowland Capt VT
Wm.: b 4-18-1724 d 1782 m Mary Prentiss Lt CT
Wm.: b 8-28-1749 d 10-9-1833 m Hannah Douglas Lt NY

CALL,
Amos: b 12-9-1759 d 1-27-1787 m Joanna Temple Cpl MA
Asa: b c. 1758 d p. 1816 m Azubeth — Pvt VT
Asa: b 6- -1752 d 1806 m Phebe White Pvt NH
Caleb: b 11-16-1718 d 8-7-1780 m (1)Rebecca Stimpson (2)Mrs Lydia (Saley)(Stephens) Greenleaf PS MA
Ebenezer: b 1723 d 1-4-1793 m Margaret Thompson Pvt PA
James, Sr.: b 9-2-1728 d 1807 m (1)Sarah Barret (2)Hannah Masters (3)Anna Powers Pvt VT
John: b 8-17-1760 d 1814 m Betsey Harwood Cpl CT
John: b 4-16-1739 d 1808 m (1)Lucy Chaffee (2)Martha Safford Pvt MA
John: b 11- -1758 d 4-10-1838 m Letitia Middleton Cpl PA
Joseph: b 2-11-1725 d 1815 m Mary Sanderson Pvt VT
Nathaniel: b a. 1750 d p. 1784 m Elizabeth Green Lt MA
Silas: b c. 175- d 11-8-1814 m Mary Corser Lt PS NH
Wm.: b 12-5-1735 d 7-19-1815 m Elizabeth Taylor Col VA

CALLAHAN, (includes CALLAGHAN)
Daniel: b 1724-6 d 4-11-1826 m Rebecca (English) Campbell Pvt PA ★
George: b 12-27-1765 d 1-25-1839 m Mary Wells Sol MD
James: b 1763 d p. 1790 m Elizabeth — Lt NC
James: b 1754 d 1825 m Mary Wasson Pvt DE
Joel: b 1738 d c. 1790 m Elizabeth Scott Lt NC
John: b 1-15-1746 d 9- -1837 m Jane Templeton Pvt NC
Robert: b 1745 d p. 11-25-1775 m Lydia Gardner Pvt MA

CALLENDER,
Amos: b 9-13-1744 d 9-15-1831 m Joanna Dewey Sol VT
John: b 3-28-1740 d 2-26-1810 m X Lt NY
Philip: b 1746 d 3-18-1818 m Abigail Franklin Pvt MA
Robert: b 1726 d a. 11-4-1776 m (1)Mary Scull (2)Frances Gibson Col PS PA
Samuel: b 4-10-1756 d 3-12-1830 m Martha Slawson Pvt VA ★
Silas: b 7-11-1755 d p. 12- -1820 m Electa Downing Pvt MA ★

CALLER,
John: b c. 1756 d p. 3- -1816 m Sarah Wood PS NC

CALLEY,
Josiah: b c. 1758 d — m (1)Anna Fullington (2)Eleanor Weeks Pvt NH

CALLIHAM,
David, Sr.: b c. 1726 d p. 8-18-1785 m Elizabeth — PS SC

CALLIN,
James: b 1750 d p. 1816 m X Pvt PA VA

CALLIS,
Wm. Overton: b 3-4-1756 d 3-14-1814 m (1)Martha Winston (2)Anne Price Maj VA

CALLOWAY, (includes CALLAWAY)
Charles: b 6-18-1754 d 6-3-1827 m Judith Early (Mrs Pate) Capt VA
Chesley: b 5-6-1760 d 9-15-1845 m Mary Walters Pvt VA ★
Elijah: b 1769 d 1847 m Mary Cutbirth Sol NC
Elizabeth: b 1760 d c. 1793 m Samuel Henderson PS KY
Flanders: b 12-9-1752 d 8-19-1828 m Jemima Boone PS VA
Frances: b 1762 d 1805 m (1)John Holder (2)— McGuire PS KY
Jacob: b 1760 d p. 1833 m Lucy — Sol NC
James: b 12-21-1736 d 11-1-1809 m (1)Sarah Tate (2)Elizabeth Early (3Mrs Mary (Langhorne) Turpin PS Cty Lt VA
James: b 1756 d 1835 m Susanah White Pvt VA ★
Job: b 1741 d 2/3- -1804 m Mary — Sol NC
John: b 1745 d 4-13-1819 m Bethany Arnold Sol NC
John: b 6-10-1738 d 1-28-1820 m (1)Tabitha Tate (2)Agatha Ward LCol CS VA
Joseph: b 9-21-1754 d 11-13-1821 m Sabrina Morgan Sol NC
Joseph: b 12-10-1756 d 1838 m X Lt VA
Richard: b 6- -1722 d 3-8-1780 m (1)Frances Walton (2)Mrs Elizabeth Hoy Col PS VA
Thomas, Sr.: b 10-12-1700 d 2- -1800 m Mary Baker PS NC
Thomas, Jr: b 1737 d 3-25-1819 m Jude (Callaway) Sol NC
William, Sr: b 1714 d 1777 m (1)Elizabeth Tilley (2)Elizabeth Crawford CtyLt VA
William, Jr: b 1748 d 1821 m Ann Bowker Smith LCol VA
Zachariah: b c. 1756/7 d 1816 m Ellenor (Ellender) Sol VA

CALMES,
Marquis: b 2-26-1755 d 2-27-1834 m Priscilla Hale Capt VA
William, Jr: b 1761 d 1-8-1836 m Nancy Elizabeth Berry Lt VA

CALVERT,
Basil: b c. 1755 d 12- -1831 m Mary Ewell Pvt VA
Christopher: b 9-26-1736 d 1791 m Peggy Boush NCapt PS VA
Cornelius: b 3-13-1725 d 1804 m Elizabeth Thoroughgood PS VA
George, Sr: b 1712 d 5-19-1782 m (1)Anne Crupper (2)Mary Strother Deathridge Capt VA
George, Jr.: b 2-6-1744 d 5-22-1821 m Lydia Beck Ralls Sol PS VA
George: b 1700 d 1782 m (1)Sytha Elizabeth Harrison (2)Mrs Esther Stone PS VA
Jesse: b c. 1742 d 1802 m (1)Mollica Brown (2)Susanna — PS VA
John: b c. 1750 d p.1802 m Ann — PS SC
John: b 1742 d 1790 m (1)Sarah Bailey (2)Helen Bailey Capt VA
John: b 1759 d 1783 m Mary (Calvert) Pvt VA
Obed: b 1743 d1809 m Mary — PS VA
Obediah, Sr: b c. 1719 d a. 5-6-1805 m (1)Mary — PS VA
Wm.: b 2-26-1757 d 5-31-1834 m Elizabeth Nodding Pvt MD

CALVIN,
Luther: b 1747 d 10- -1831 m (1)Priscilla LaFarge (2)Mrs Ruth Corwine Pvt PA

CALVIT,
Frederick: b 3-23-1747 d 9-22-1790 m Mary — PS NC
Wm.: b c. 1740 d 1816 m (1)Miss Holmes (2)Phoebe Crawford PS NC

CAMBRIDGE,
John: b 1752 d 1835 m Sylvie Sheldon Sgt MA ★
John: b — d 1829 m — Knox Sgt NH

CAMBRON,
John Baptist: b c. 1725 d 5-8-1815 m X PS MD   [wash, Ky]

CAMBURN,
Joseph: b c. 10-27-1745 d 1-11-1831 m Frances Bogart Pvt NJ

CAMDEN,
John: b c. 1755 d 1827 m Oney Wright Pvt VA
William: b c. 1740 d 5- -1813 m Sybil Dent Sgt VA

CAMERON,
Alexander: b 1763 d p. 1834 m Elizabeth Simmerman Pvt PA
Charles: b 2-22-1753 d 7-14-1829 m (1)Nancy Miller (2)Rachel Primrose Warwick Capt VA
Daniel: b 1734 d 1781 m Mary Stuart Pvt NY
Daniel: b 10- -1753 d c. 1805 m Susan Clinton Mil VA
James: b 4-24-1761 d 4-17-1840 m Sarah Brown Pvt SC
James: b c. 1749 d 1830 m Jennett (Cameron) Sol NC
John C.: b c. 1760 d p. 1792 m X Non-Com VA
Lewis: b 1743 d 1818 m Frances Sutter Pvt PA
Simon: b 1725 d 1789 m X Pvt PS PA

CAMMETT,
John: b a. 1754 d 10-19-1834 m Miriam — Pvt PS NH

CAMP,
Aaron: b 1-24-1765 d 4-15-1850 m Rebecca Bruen Pvt NJ
Abel, Sr: b 1-21-1729 d 4-20-1820 m Abigail Gould Ens CT

Abel, Jr.: b 3-17-1756 d 10- -1839 m Anna Manning Tms OrdlSgt CT ★

Abel, Jr.: b 7-11-1748 d 5-8-1825 m Sabra Marsh PS CT

Amos: b 9-29-1759 d 2-17-1822 m Jemima Hart Pvt NH

Asa: b 9-14-1759 d 7- -1848 m Rachael Parker Cpl MA ★

Benjamin: b 1757 d 1832 m Elizabeth Dykes Pvt NC

Caleb: b 1736 d 1816 m Lydia — PS NJ

David: b 7-17-1752 d p. 1790 m Sibyl Smith Sgt CT

Edward: b c. 1715 d 2-6-1795 m (1)Mary — (2)Esther — PS CT

Elah: b 5-5-1729 d 10-17-1787 m Phebe Baldwin PS CT

Elnathan: b 1-24-1734 d 5-12-1807 m Eunice Talcott Cmsry CT

Ephraim: b 6-8-1755 d p. 1832 m (1)Mabel Ludington (2)Sarah Moss (3)Mabel Pardy Pvt CT ★

Ephraim: b 1734 d 1811 m Rachel Wheeler Pvt NJ

Ezra: b 3-7-1763 d 12-23-1838 m Anna Coe Guardsman CT

Goold: b 7-22-1760 d 6-5-1852 m Elizabeth Knox Pvt VT

Hardin: b a. 1760 d p. 1812 m Sarah Hawkins Pvt SC

Heth: b 3-2-1735 d p. 1784 m Mary Tibbals Cav PS CT

Ichabod: b 2-20-1726 d 4-20-1786 m (1)Content Ward (2)Anne Oliver PS VA

Isaac, Jr: b 9-9-1740 d 4-3-1793 m Jane Baldwin Pvt CT

Israel: b 1756 d 4-24-1840 m Bettie Hurlbut Pvt CT ★

Israel: b 1722 d 1804 m Anna Hine PS CT

Israel: b 2-16-1723 d c. 1778 m (1)Ann Talcott (2)Mary Guernsey PS CT

James: b 11-30-1746 d 6-22-1782 m Elizabeth Kilborn Pvt CT

James: b 7-6-1758 d 5-26-1793 m Mary — Pvt MA

Job: b 11-16-1747 d 1-17-1822 m Anna Oviatt Capt LCol CT

Job: b — d 1796 m Sarah — Pvt NJ

John: b 12-23-1761 d 2-8-1846 m Annis Clark Pvt CT ★

John: b 12- -1747 d 2-19-1777 m Hannah Tinkham Sol MA

John: b a. 1755 d 1801 m Sarah Pollard Capt VA

John: b 1743 d 1813 m Mary Tarpley Pvt VA

Joseph: b 1762 d 1831 m Ann Halsted Pvt NJ

Mary Banks: b 6-5-1754 d c. 1799 m Samuel Camp PS VA

Moses: b 8-26-1747 d 7-13-1828 m Thankful Gaylord Pvt CT

Nathan: b 1- -1746 d 10-26-1792 m Esther Bostwick Pvt CT

Nathaniel, Sr: b 1707 d 1789 m Elizabeth — PS NJ

Nathaniel, Jr.: b 12-28-1739 d 7- -1827 m Rachel Crane Capt NJ

Nicholas: b 5-19-1722 d c. 1798 m Amy Perry Pvt MA

Richard: b 1746 d 1813 m Ann Coe Sgt CT

Samuel: b 10-6-1746 d 3-24-1826 m (1)Betty Record (2)Lydia Royce Cpl CT

Samuel: b 5-14-1753 d 8-18-1827 m Mary Banks QM VA

Stephen: b 1770 d 1828 m Annie Alexander PS SC

Talcott: b 3-4-1762 d 9-25-1832 m Nancy Hale Cmsry NY

Thomas, Sr: b 2-8-1717 d 1798 m (1)Winifred Starling (2)Margaret Corney PS NC

Thomas: b 6-15-1757 d 10- -1825 m Martha Wester Pvt VA ★

CAMPBELL, (includes CAMBELL, CAMBLE)

Aaron: b 1765 d 1843 m Nancy — Pvt NC

Aeneas: b 1730 d 2-21-1812 m (1)Lydia — (2)Margaret Hickman Capt MD

Alexander: b 4-13-1740 d 6-3-1803 m Delia Williams Dr CT

Alexander: b 9-16-1731 d 1807 m Elizabeth Nichols LCol MA

Alexander: b c. 1755 d 2-15-1827 m Mary Dennen Pvt CS MA ★

Alexander: b 2-12-1732 d 12-28-1782 m Lydia Sterne PS Dr MA

Alexander: b 11-14-1764 d 1-1-1813 m Charity Sincox Pvt NJ

Alexander: b 1760 d 9-7-1816 m Mary Lockhart Sol NC

Alexander: b 1764 d 2-21-1815 m Catherine Byford Edwards Mrnr PS PA

Alexander: b 1750 d 7-26-1806 m Janet Smith Lt VA

Alexander: b 1744 d 1786/7 m Joana Nelson Pvt VA

Allen: b c. 1764 d 1820-28 m Mary Dickey Pvt VA

Allen: b 2-24-1749 d 3-6-1829 m Sarah Kinne Pvt Dr CT

Ambrose: b 1740 d 1811/12 m Margaret — Sol PS VA

Andrew: b 4-11-1747 d 9- -1833 m (2)Sarah Bunn Pvt NY ★

Andrew: b a. 1740 d 3- -1789 m Esther — Pvt PA

Andrew: b c. 1727 d p. 7-27-1792 m Rachel Hubbs Capt PA

Angus: b — d 1809 m Mildred Llewellyn Sol PS SC

Annas: b c. 1744 d — m Elizabeth Webster Sol NH

Archibald: b 2-16-1760 d 5-5-1844 m Mary Wylie Pvt CT

Archibald: b 1730 d 12-28-1798 m Catharine Wier PS NJ

Archibald: b 5-15-1761 d 6-17-1852 m Abigail — Sol NJ

Archibald: b c. 1745 d 4-29-1793 m Christina Sternberg Pvt NY

Archibald: b — d 1778 m X Lt PA

Archibald: b 1760 d 8-15-1844 m Jane Smith Pvt PA ★

Archibald: b c. 1760 d p. 7-11-1826 m Hannah Flinn Lt VA

Archibald: b — d p. 9-28-1801 m Elizabeth — PS VA

Arthur: b 11-3-1743 d 8-8-1811 m Margaret Campbell Col VA

Charles: b 1746 d 1828 m (1)Margaret Clark (2)Elizabeth Porter Ramsey Col PA

Charles: b 1741 d 1826 m Mary Ann Downey Capt VA

Cleary: b c. 1740 d 8- -1809 m Anna Gamble Lt PA

Colin: b 1-27-1749 d 1-30-1834 m Jean McPherson Adj VA

Daniel: b 1750-4 d 2-25-1829 m Ann Houston Pvt NH

Daniel: b 1755 d p. 1-16-1832 m Mary Lee Pvt NJ

Daniel: b 1738 d 1834 m Rachel Howe Pvt PA

David: b 4-30-1758 d 2-27-1836 m Lucy Laflin Pvt MA

David: b 2-19-1746 d 2-4-1803 m Sarah Patterson Lt NH

David: b 7-29-1757 d 3-11-1830 m Rachel Elizabeth Dickey Pvt NH ★

David: b 11-30-1738 d 6-17-1835 m Hannah Ackerman Pvt NJ

David: b 7-11-1767 d 12-15-1848 m Polly Miller Pvt NY ★

David: b c. 1762 d 4- -1813 m Janet Lockhart Sol NC

David: b 1-31-1760 d 4-15-1846 m (1) X (2)Lucinda Cooper Pvt SC ★

David: b 8- -1763 d 8- -1832 m (1)Margaret Campbell (2)Jane Montgomery Cowen Capt VA

David: b 1750 d 1812 m Elizabeth Outlaw Maj CS VA

David: b 3-8-1706 d 10-19-1790 m Mary Hamilton CS VA

Dugel: b 9- -1732 d 3-5-1809 m Sarah Bloomfield Pvt NJ

Edward: b 2-10-1759 d 6-10-1828 m Ann Russell Pvt NY

Elias: b c. 1733 d 1794 m X PS VA

Ellis: b 1756 d 2-10-1814 m Nancy Clawson Sgt NJ

Enos: b 1753 d 6-2-1838 m Damarius Nowe Pvt NJ ★

Farquahard: b — d p. 1790 m (1)Isabella McAllister (2)Mrs Elizabeth Smith PS NC

Francis: b 1724 d 3-9-1791 m (1) X (2)Elizabeth Parker Pvt PA

Francis Lee: b 1760 d 10-15-1840 m Ann Barnett Capt VA

George: b 3-13-1758 d 1836 m Martha — Pvt NC ★

George: b 1730 d 1810 m Helen Donaldson Pvt PS PA

George C.: b 2-14-1753-5 d 8-9-1841 m Frances Harris Pvt NC

Henry: b 1754 d 10-6-1825 m Isabel Gregg CS Sol NH

Henry: b 1697 d 10- -1782 m Martha Black PS NH

Hugh: b 7-2-1744 d 2-4-1810 m Mary Smith SgtMaj NH

Hugh: b c. 1720 d 1791 m Margaret Kelso PS NH

Hugh: b 1740 d p. 1790 m Eliza Reilly FifMaj SC

Hugh: b c. 1750 d p. 1-10-1807 m Jane Alexander Pvt VA

Isaac: b 3-2-1763 d 3-31-1841 m Elizabeth Edmunds Pvt CT

Jacob: b 2-4-1760 d 6-27-1845 m Martha Hoag Pvt RI

James: b 7-18-1721 d 3-2-1788 m Agnes Kennedy Pvt CT

James: b 7-5-1724 d 7-2-1812 m Dinah Main Pvt CT

James: b c. 1745 d 3-18-1821 m (1)Leah —(2)Kitty Cahale Capt MD

James, Sr: b c. 1738 d 12-28-1813 m Jane Knox 2Lt PA

James, 2d: b 12-3-1753 d 8-7-1835 m Sabra Ingalls Pvt MA ★

James: b 1-8-1745 d 3-18-1838 m Isabel Elder Pvt MA

James: b 1756 d — m Lucy Johnson DrmMaj NH

James: b 1759 d p. 1832 m Anna Blood Sol NH

James: b 5-1-1754 d 1834 m (1)Rachel Gregg (2)Agnes Patrick Pvt NH

James: b 6-23-1759 d 10-12-1825 m Desire Slader Pvt NH

James, Jr: b 4-16-1763 d 1848 m Mahetable McPherson Pvt NY ★

James: b 1750 d 1780 m Sarah James Mil NY

James: b 1746 d 11-10-1807 m Isabella Ochiltre Capt NC W★

James: b 3-3-1752 d 1822 m Lida — Capt NC

James: b 1740 d 6-20-1779 m Lucy Morehead Capt NC

James: b 12-25-1754 d c. 1840 m Jane Sample Pvt Spy NC ★

James: b c. 1750 d p. 2-6-1813 m Susana — Pvt NC

James: b c. 1756 d 7-19-1842 m (1)Katherine Lamon (2)Isabella Clark Pvt NC

James: b — d p. 1810 m Mary — PS PA

James: b 8-23-1745 d 4-23-1817 m Sarah — PS PA

James: b 5-12-1760 d 9-27-1827 m Elizabeth Wylie Pvt RI ★

James: b 1753 d 1-5-1825 m Ann Brandon Lt VA

James: b 1754 d 8- -1827 m Elizabeth Reed OrdlSgt VA ★

James: b c. 1760/1 d 1826 m Jane Means Pvt VA

Jeremiah: b 12-15-1762 d 10-4-1843 m (1)Sarah Marr (2)Hannah Stone Pvt NC ★

Joel: b c. 1745 d p. 4-7-1832 m Pattey — PS VA

John: b 11-22-1760 d 1-26-1840 m Jean Campbell Pvt CT ★

John: b 1750 d 1810 m Mary Jackson Pvt DE

John: b 1761 d p. 1840 m Mrs Ruth Edwards Davis Pvt MD

John: b 9-15-1727 d 11-4-1791 m Hannah Rogers Nickless Pvt MA

John: b 11-13-1744 d 1833 m Elizabeth Stone Sgt MA

John: b 11-2-1752 d 4-25-1833 m Lydia Kent Pvt MA ★

John: b 8- -1754 d 1-17-1820 m Martha E. Stephens Pvt MA

John: b 9-5-1747 d 5-2-1823 m Molly Campbell Pvt PS NH

John: b 1758 d 3-27-1820 m Betsey Moore Pvt NH

John: b 11-6-1719 m 3-21-1804 m (1)Rachel Walker (2)Hendrika Covenhoven QM NJ

John: b 1756 d 11-5-1836 m Katharine Row Pvt NY ★

John, Jr: b a. 1757 d p. 1791 m Mollie McKeown Lt NY

John: b 5-11-1762 d 10-18-1846 m Lydia Whiting Pvt NY ★

John: b 1755 d 1790 m Janet Breckenridge Capt NC

John: b a. 1725 d p. 7-6-1777 m (1)Mary Elizabeth Hill (2)Mrs Martha (Curle ?) PS NC

John: b 5-5-1758 d 5-18-1840 m Nancy Hughes 2Lt PA

John: b c. 1734 d p. 3-12-1812 m Letitia Alexander Pvt PA

John: b c. 1755 d 4-12-1812 m Jane Cluggage Capt PA

John: b 1732 d 6-1-1781 m Jane Stewart Pvt PA

John: b c. 1750 d 6-4-1782 m Rosannah Petticrew Pvt PA

John: b 4-3-1742 d 3-18-1824 m Hester Clark Pvt SC

John: b 4-20-1741 d 12-17-1825 m Elizabeth McDonald Capt VA

John: b — d 1781 m X Capt VA

John: b 1748 d 5- -1808 m Ruth Edwards Capt VA

John: b 2-6-1761 d 5-14-1847 m Sarah Vance Pvt VA ★

John: b 5-31-1765 d p. 1833 m Sarah Taylor Pvt VA ★

John: b 3-7-1756 d 12-18-1838 m Isabelle Blakely Pvt VA

John: b c. 1760 d c. 1818 m Elizabeth Newman Sol VA

Joseph: b 3-3-1752 d 3-13-1801 m Catherine Elizabeth Miller 1Lt PA

Joseph, Jr: b 1762 d 1-9-1841 m Sarah Givens Ens VA ★

Joseph: b c. 1740 d 1794 m Elizabeth — PS VA

Lawrence: b c. 1735 d 1814 m Henrietta Catlett Sol VA

CAMPBELL, contd.

Matthew: b 1-7-1747 d 2-15-1816 m (1)Sarah Mars (2)Sarah Bell Pvt MA
Matthew: b *a.* 1750 d 1-18-1819 m Mary Shelby Pvt PA
McDonald: b 2-12-1754 d 3-20-1845 m (1)Margaret Tingley (2) Nancy Stout (3)Widow Valentine Lt PS NJ ★
Moses: b 4-14-1737 d 4-18-1827 m Sarah Dixon Capt CT
Moses: b 2-15-1754 d 8-25-1821 m Esther Gillett Sgt MA
Nathan: b 8-14-1761 d 12-18-1829 m Martha — Sol NJ
Neil: b 1745 d 1815 m Sarah — Pvt CT
Noble: b 1745 d 1815 m Sarah — Pvt CT
Patrick: b 1750-2 d 1796 m Catharine — Ens NY
Patrick: b *c.* 1732 d 7-2-1804 m (1)Jane — (2)Mary Studebaker Capt PA
Robert: b 1730 d 1799 m Margaret Muir Adj MD
Robert: b *c.* 1745 d 2-12-1795 m Elizabeth — Pvt MA
Robert: b 1761 d 9-20-1839 m Sarah White Pvt MA ★
Robert: b 6-4-1742 d 1-18-1827 m Elizabeth Waugh OrdlSgt NH ★
Robert: b 1725 d 1796 m Mary Ayres Pvt NJ
Robert: b 8-20-1735 d 8-6-1777 m Margaret Shannon 1Lt NY
Robert: b 1-3-1759-61 d 12-29-1841 m Mary Young Sct Spy NC ★
Robert: b 1729 d 6-30-1813 m Martha Sinclair Capt PS PA
Robert: b *c.* 1740 d *p.* 1790 m Jane Montgomery Lt PA
Robert: b 10-1-1728 d 7-10-1822 m Jane Campbell Pvt PA
Robert: b 1751 d 2-23-1843 m Martha Paxton Pvt PA ★
Robert: b 1760 d 7-20-1829 m Rachel Morrison Pvt PA ★
Robert: b 5-25-1755 d 12-25-1831 m Rebecca McDonald Col PA
Robert: b 1724 d *p.* 8-6-1804 m Rebecca Wallace 1Lt VA
Samuel: b 1722 d 2-1-1797 m Mary Robinson Pvt NH
Samuel: b 4-25-1738 d 9-12-1824 m Jane Cannon Col NY
Samuel: b 1724 d 1825 m Mary Graham Pvt PA
Samuel: b 1761 d 3-8-1841 m Sarah Colter Vol PA
Samuel: b 1731 d 11-3-1819 m Esther — Lt VT
Samuel: b 10-8-1762 d 11-8-1844 m Grace Plum Pvt VT
Samuel: b 1743 d 3-18-1821 m Mary Anderson Kennedy Lt VA
Simeon: b 1759 d *p.* 1800 m Hannah — Pvt NY
Solomon: b 6-13-1749 d 12-30-1823 m Sarah Andrews Sgt NY
Spencer: b 7-29-1756 d 1-26-1794 m Sarah Willett Pvt NJ
Thomas, Sr.: b 7-10-1737 d 10-18-1803 m Margaret Dunning Capt MA
Thomas: b 12-6-1747 d 1834 m (2)Keziah Owen Pvt MA
Thomas: b 12-25-1747 d 1833 m Eunice Noble Pvt MA
Thomas: b 5-16-1759 d 8-11-1840 m (1)Rachel Chase (2)Mrs Rebecca Cunningham Stl MA
Thomas: b — d — m Jemima Oakley Pvt NY
Thomas: b 8- -1757 d 8-10-1787 m Mary Moore Pvt NC
Thomas: b 1738 d 1794 m X Pvt PA
Thomas: b 1759 d 1849 m Ella MacPherson Pvt PA ★
Thomas: b 11-18-1748 d 6-27-1827 m Mary Church PS VA
Whitaker: b 1727 d 1814 m (1)Jane Hill (2)Marth De Shazo Capt VA
William: b 4-2-1734 d 2-14-1808 m Mary Stone Capt PS MA
William: b 1725 d 1-14-1798 m Sarah — Cpl MA
William: b 1745 d 9-4-1822 m Mary Young 2Lt MA
William: b 1719 d 1-8-1776 m Mary Gregg PS NH
William: b 1748 d 11-13-1830 m Anna Christie PS NH
William: b 1-20-1765 d 1847 m Margaret Cook DrmMaj NJ
William: b *c.* 1740 d *p.* 1783 m Katharine Reid Pvt NY
William: b 1757 d 1836 m Jane Harvey Sgt PA
William, Sr: b *c.* 1735 d *p.* 1-25-1803 m Jane — Pvt PA
William: b 1759 d 12-13-1837 m Mary Gouldy Pvt PA
William: b 1760 d 6-13-1834 m Rachel Robinson Pvt PA ★
William: b 1761 d 12-26-1836 m Martha Baird Sol PA
William: b 1759 d 4-27-1837 m Elizabeth Bogan Pvt SC ★
William: b 1732 d 11-29-1826 m Elizabeth Weller Sol VT
William: b 1745 d 8-22-1781 m Elizabeth Henry BGen VA
William: b 1-12-1757 d 10-29-1825 m Susan Pierce Capt VA
William: b 1753 d *p.* 1831 m X Pvt VA ★
William: b 1754 d 1822 m Elizabeth Wilson Pvt VA
William: b 1750 d 12-22-1831 m Elizabeth Crump Cmsry Pvt VA
Zuriel: b 10-13-1743 d 9-2-1811 m Lydia Barrows Cpl CT

CAMPERNELL,
William: b 5-27-1739 d *p.* 12-5-1803 m Betsey Hodgkins Pvt MA

CAMPFIELD, (includes CAMFIELD)
Abiel: b 8-30-1744 d 8-7-1805 m Mary — QM NJ
Jabez: b 12-24-1737 d 5-20-1821 m Sarah Ward Dr NJ
John: b 7-9-1755 d 9-25-1845 m (1)Mary Dixon (2)Affa Cory Pvt NJ
Williams: b 4-13-1752 d 8-24-1824 m Sarah Squires Capt NJ

CANAN,
John: b 10- -1746 d 10- -1831 m Margery Dean Lt PA

CANBY,
Samuel: b 8-6-1751 d 3-18-1832 m Frances Lea Sol DE

CANDEE,
Caleb: b 1743 d 12-1-1828 m Anna Sperry Pvt CT
Daniel: b 2-19-1760-2 d 8-9-1831 m Lydia Wilmot Sgt CT
Job: b 4-20-1760 d 12-2-1845 m Sarah Benham Sgt CT ★
Nehemiah: b 4-14-1758 d 8-17-1834 m Content Woodruff Pvt CT
Samuel: b 12-15-1753 d 1-3-1841 m Mabel Bradley Sgt CT ★
Theophilus: b 8-2-1736 d — m (1)Rebecca Churchill (2)Mary Converse Pvt CT

CANDLER,
Daniel: b *c.* 1750 d 6-18-1810 m Rosanna Benson PS MD
William: b 4-21-1736 d 7- -1784 m Elizabeth Anthony Col GA

CANFIELD,
Abiel: b 4-6-1753 d 12-6-1812 m Mary Barlow Mus CT
Abraham: b 1732 d 7-29-1789 m Sarah Sealey PS NJ
Andrew: b 2-3-1760/1 d 6-13-1843 m Eunice Fairchild Pvt CT ★
Daniel: b 6-27-1754 d 7-30-1819 m Comfort Newton Pvt CT
Daniel: b 5-1-1761 d 12-25-1818 m Anna Hurd Sol CT
Daniel: b 5-19-1761 d 1841 m Ruth Stevens Pvt Arfr MA or CT
Daniel: b 2-10-1757 d 10-31-1832 m Elizabeth Nettleton Pvt NY W ★
David: b 3-9-1757 d 3-9-1804 m Sarah Collard Pvt NY
Dennis: b 5-20-1763 d 5-29-1846 m (1)Polly Lobdell (2)Mrs Ruth Bull McDaniels (3)Polly Walton Mix Pvt NY ★
Ebenezer: b 1761 d 9-8-1831 m Rhoda Baldwin Pvt NJ
Elijah: b 3- -1758 d 4- -1841 m Anna Read Pvt CT
Ezekiel: b *c.* 1750 d 6-23-1831 m Ann Jecox Pvt CT
Gideon: b *c.* 1717 d 1784 m Anne Robinson PS CT
Isaiah: b 2-11-1750 d 6-11-1820 m Anne Leete Lt CT
Israel: b 3-13-1733 d 3-20-1818 m Mary Sackett Sgt VT
James: b *a.* 1743 d *p.* 1785 m Dinah Keeler Pvt NY
James, Jr: b 7-16-1752 d 8-15-1830 m Ann Brower Pvt NY
Jeremiah: b 8-20-1737 d 3-31-1791 m (1)Mary Everton (2)Mrs Abigail Oviatt PS CT
John: b 11-30-1740 d 10-26-1786 m Dorcas Bull BgdMaj CT
John: b 1760 d 2-21-1814 m (1)Phebe Treat (2)Mrs Polly (Treat) Betts Pvt CT
Nathan: b 1760 d 1803 m Hannah Sutherland Lt NY
Philo: b 6-13-1762 d 3-11-1827 m Mary Parsons Clark Sgt CT
Phineas: b 4-10-1753 d 5-13-1800 m Anne Newton Pvt CT
Samuel: b 4-5-1726 d 8-17-1799 m Elizabeth Judson LCol CT
Samuel: b 1734 d *p.* 1790 m Mehitabel Stillson Pvt CT
Thomas: b 1748 d 1808 m Lucy Burr Pvt MA
Thomas: b 1717 d 6-27-1791 m Elizabeth Baldwin PS NJ

CANN,
John: b 1757 d 7-22-1846 m (1)Hannah Tice (2)Mrs Sarah Harvey (3)Amy Peterson Sgt NJ
William: b 1758 d 1834 m (1)Sarah McMullen (2)Ann (Reynolds) Reed Pvt DE

CANNON, (includes CANON)
Abraham: b 5-7-1751 d 1809 m Susanna Wortman Sol NY
Andrew: b *c.* 1744 d 10- -1828 m Deborah Campbell Pvt NY
Cornelius: b 5-31-1748 d — m Molly Weeks Pvt MA
Daniel: b 1744 d 2-5-1797 m Agnes McClellan Capt PA
Daniel: b 7-10-1726 d 10- -1802 m Martha Winn PS SC
Elanor McKinney: b 1717 d 11-12-1778 m Matthew Cannon PS NY
Elijah: b *c.* 1730 d *p.* 1800 m Tabitha — PS DE
Ephraim: b *c.* 1737 d *c.* 1803 m Eleanor Ulmer PS SC
Henry: b 1758 d 1803 m Mary Ervin Pvt SC
Isaac: b — d *p.* 1847 m Mary Bathurst Pvt DE
Isaac: b 6-8-1759 d 8-9-1808 m Sarah Speake Pvt SC
James: b *c.* 1727 d *p.* 12-29-1788 m Mary — Sol DE
James, Sr: b 3- -1731 d 9-8-1784 m Margaret Alexander PS NC
James: b 12-1-1762 d 4-20-1842 m Rachel Stark Pvt SC ★
Jesse: b *c.* 1761 d *c.* 1834 m Frances Hardesty 2Lt VA
Jane: b 1743 d 1836 m Samuel Campbell PS NY
John: b 5-22-1758 d 10-17-1792 m Mary Butler Pvt NC
John: b 1730 d 1-19-1794 m Martha A. — Sol PS NC
John: b 1709 d 1782 m — Elison Pvt SC
John: b 1740 d 11-6-1798 m (1)Polly — (2)Mrs Janet Mercer Col PS VA
Joseph: b 12-14-1745 d 3- -1807 m Abigail Dexter Pvt MA
Matthew: b 1717 d 1792 m Eleanor McKinney Pvt PS NY
Minos: b 1756 d 5-10-1829 m Letitia Thompson Sol NC
Nathaniel: b 1763 d 1837/38 m Frances — Pvt SC ★
Roger: b *c.* 1760 d *p.* 1808 m Nancy Ann (Spaulding) McPherson Sol SC
Samuel: b — d *p.* 5-16-1791 m Lydia Pennington PS SC
Thomas: b 1757 d 12-6-1839 m Abigail Sloat Sgt NY ★
William: b *a.* 11-18-1794 d 1820 m (1)Sarah Mosby (2)Martha Cocke Capt PS VA
Wingate: b 3-8-1751 d 7-8-1793 m Sally Calloway Pvt DE

CANTERBURY,
Jacob: b *a.* 1746 d *p.* 1797 m Azubah Canterbury Pvt MA

CANTEY,
James: b 1755 d 11-9-1817 m Martha Whitaker Capt SC
Samuel: b 1760 d 1826 m Judith Wilburn Pvt SC
Samuel: b 6-7-1731 d 12-16-1776 m (1)Anne — (2)Martha Brown PS Maj SC

CANTINE,
Abraham: b 12-8-1727 d 12-26-1814 m Elizabeth DeLaMater Lt PS NY
John: b 10-20-1735 d 4-30-1808 m Mary Brodhead Col NY
Matthew: b 9-10-1721 d 1789 m Catherine Nottingham PS NY
Peter, Jr: b 7-23-1747 d 4-14-1820 m Eleanor Hermanse Pvt NY
Peter: b 12-28-1729 d *p.* 1813 m Magdalena Le Fever PS NY

CANTRELL, (includes CANTRELLE, CANTRILL)
Abraham: b 1744 d 1814 m (1) X (2) — Watson PS NC
Benjamin: b c. 1750 d p. 1817 m — Parvin Pvt MA
Isaac: b c. 1745 d 1804 m Nancy — Pvt NC
Jacob: b 1744 d 1790 m Mary — Pvt NC
John: b c. 1751 d 10-17-1825 m Elizabeth Cantrill Sol NC
Joshua: b 8-8-1748 d 9-9-1800 m Ann Graham PS VA
Miguel: b 3-24-1762 d 10-24-1814 m (1)Magdaline Croizat (2)Celeste Andry Capt LA
Stephen: b 6-28-1758 d 2-5-1827 m Mary Ann Blakemore Sol CS NC VA
Thomas: b 1-3-1761 d 9-25-1830 m Elizabeth Norris Pvt NC

CANTWELL,
John: b 6-24-1745 d 9-20-1836 m Jane Barnett Pvt VA
Wm.: b 1750-5 d p. 1801 m Margaret Obrien Pvt MD

CAPELLE,
Joseph Eugene Philippe : b 1758 d 11-5-1796 m Mary Pearce Dr DE

CAPEN,
Abijah: b 9-23-1762 d 4-30-1840 m Rachel Bartlett Pvt MA
Andrew: b 11-22-1757 d 6-1-1846 m Hannah Richards Sol MA
Barnard: b 3-13-1728/9 d 4-8-1796 m Hannah White Pvt MA
Benjamin: b a. 1760 d p. 1798 m (1)Elizabeth Greenwood (2)Lucinda Sears Pvt MA
Christopher: b 5-1-1730 d 10-30-1809 m Abigail Thayer Pvt MA
Edward: b 4-25-1731 d 6-8-1819 m (1)Susannah Clap (2)Elizabeth Paul Pvt MA
Ephraim: b 3-24-1745 d c. 1820 m Dorothy Thayer Pvt MA
Ezekiel: b 7-27-1745 d 2-16-1836 m Mary — Pvt MA
James: b 8-13-1756 d 2-23-1853 m Elizabeth Comins Pvt MA ★
John: b 5-23-1745 d 3-15-1829 m Patience Davis Pvt Adj MA
John: b 2-13-1755 d 2-8-1837 m Patience Drake Pvt MA ★
Jonathan, Jr: b 9-22-1752 d 1-1-1841 m Hannah Glover Pvt MA
Josiah: b 6-7-1748 d p. 1790 m Rebekah Gridley Lt MA
Robert: b 5-30-1724 d 12-20-1788 m Jane Lyon Lt MA
Samuel: b 1727 d 1801 m Sarah Bailey MM MA
Samuel: b 11-20-1760 d 6-28-1843 m Miriam Childs Pvt MA

CAPERS,
Wm.: b 10-13-1758 d 12-12-1812 m (1)Mary Singletary (2)Mary Wragg (3)Mrs Hannah Coachman Postell Capt SC

CAPERTON,
Adam: b a. 1755 d 3-22-1782 m Elizabeth Miller Pvt KY
Hugh: b c. 1754 d 1816 m (2)Rhoda Stodgill Lt VA

CAPLINGER,
George: b 8-23-1744 d 1-15-1829 m Elizabeth Dice PS VA

CAPP (includes CAPE, CAPPS & KAPP)
Anthony: b 3-16-1751 d 2-13-1818 m Margaret Zeller Pvt PA
Christopher: b 10-5-1738 d 5-13-1806 m Anna Faber Pvt PS PA
Demsey: b 9-7-1760 d 3-16-1839 m Sarah (Pool) Overman Pvt NC ★
John: b 3 - -1745 d 6-18-1836 m Sarah — Lt VA ★
John: b c. 1730 d p. 8-12-1784 m Margaret — PS VA
Michael: b 1748 d 5 - - 1815 m Catherine — Pvt PA
Peter: b 3-26-1757 d 4-23-1835 m Elizabeth — Pvt PA

CAPPER,
Thomas: b — d 11-7-1780 m — X — Pvt NC

CAPRON,
Comfort: b 3-18-1743 d 6- -1800 m Martha Metcalf Dr MA
Elijah: b 6-27-1742 d 10-17-1813 m Abigail Stanley 2Lt MA
Elisha: b 7-19-1737 d 10-18-1808 m Abigail Makepeace Pvt MA
Elisha Jr: b 1754 d 4-8-1845 m Abigail — Pvt MA ★
Ephraim: b 8-30-1761 d 10-13-1827 m (1)Mrs Sally Fairbanks (2)Lucy Garfield (3)Hannah Sanders Pvt MA ★
Giles: b 1748 d 1826 m Lucy Andrews Ens CT
Greene: b 8-19-1758 d 3-27-1843 m (1)Rebecca Bailey (2)Mrs Lydia Carpenter Sgt RI SC ★
John: b 7-28-1757 d 7-11-1836 m Asenath Cargill Capt MA
Jonathan: b 9-5-1755 d 5-22-1837 m Lois Porter Pvt MA
Joseph: b 11-1-1722 d 8-1-1784 m (1)Sarah Robeson (2)Sarah Foster Pvt MA
Joseph: b 9-14-1750 d 3-7-1843 m (1)Sally Arnold (2)Ester (Darling) Arnold Pvt RI ★
Nathan: b 4-24-1758 d 2- 1804 m Dorothy Whitcomb Pvt VT
Oliver: b 7-20-1736 d 7-31-1816 m Esther Freeman Capt NH
Philip: b 5-9-1745 d 7-21-1821 m Priscilla Tillson Pvt CS RI
Seth: b 9-23-1762 d 9-4-1835 m Eunice Mann Sgt MA ★
Welcome: b 3-7-1766 d 1841 m Cynthia Wilkinson Pvt MA

CAPWELL,
James: b 1756 d 4-30-1848 m Anna Johnson Pvt RI ★
Stephen Sr: b 3 - -1718 d 3-26-1801 m Abigail Colvin Sol PS RI
Stephen Jr: b 1755 d 2-17-1817 m Hannah Whitford Pvt RI
William: b 10-18-1750 d 6- -1842 m Mary Wall Sgt RI ★

CARBAUGH,
Peter: b 1756 d 2-4-1844 m Mary — Pvt PA ★

CARBEE,
Joel: b 4-3-1764 d 2-19-1834 m Lois Downer Pvt MA ★

CARBERRY,
Joseph: b 7-20-1753 d 1819 m Mary Elizabeth — Pvt PA

CARD,
Bowen: b 1758 d 11-30-1793 m Margaret Hefferron Ens RI
Edward: b 6-17-1713 d 1780 m Dorcas Evans Pvt PS NH
Elisha: b 2-8-1763 d 9-6-1832 m Hannah Yarrington Vol CT
Elisha: b 7-16-1738 d p. 1784 m Martha Williams Pvt VT
Jonathan: b c. 1725 d 5-30-1802 m Renewed Sweet Pvt RI
Joshua: b 11-13-1747 d 11- -1833 m Sarah Pittis Pvt RI
Peleg: b 3-13-1755 d 10-19-1846 m Alce Dorley Pvt MA RI & VT ★
Thomas: b 7-20-1762 d 1856 m Rebecca Briggs Pvt VT ★
William: b 8-27-1752 d 7-29-1842 m Abigail Carpenter NS RI

CARDER,
John: b 2-15-1744 d p. 11-29-1815 m Hannah Carver Pvt CT
Sanford: b 9-16-1760 d 8-7-1845 m (1)Nancy Hoffman (2)Sarah David Pvt VA ★

CARDIN,
Charles: b 1765 d 11- -1815 m Milly — Pvt NC

CARDINAL,
Nicholas: b c. 1729 d 8-23-1789 m Marie Joseph Girard PS VA

CARDOZA,
David Menez: b 7-27-1754 d 7-13-1835 m Sarah — Of SC

CARDWELL,
Perrin: b 7-12-1764 d 12-2-1854 m Elizabeth Worsham Pvt VA ★
Thomas: b c. 1734 d 8- -1789 m Sarah Crouch Sol VA
William: b 4-6-1751 d 10-24-1825 m Sibel Griswold Pvt CT
Wm.: b 1760 d 3-1-1836 m Famariah Hughes Pvt VA ★

CAREW,
Palmer: b 12-9-1739 d 8-22-1792 m Sarah Chapman PS CT
Simeon Chapman: b 1762 d 12-14-1831 m Prudence Maples Sol CT

CARGILL, (includes CARGYLE)
Henry: b 5-14-1757 d p. 10-14-1792 m Rachel Sherwood Pvt NY
James: b 10-24-1725 d 6-18-1812 m (1)Agnes Kennedy (2)Mrs Margaret Hatch Col MA
James, Sr.: b 2-27-1729 d 11-21-1808 m Dorcas Arnold Pvt RI
James, Jr.: b 4-22-1762 d 1-25-1848 m Chloe Chaffee Pvt RI
John: b 1719 d p. 1794 m Catherine Reneau Pvt VA
John: b c. 1742 d a. 12-2-1777 m (1)— (2)Lucy Binns (3)Anne —PS VA

CARHART, (includes CARHARTT)
Cornelius, Sr.: b 9-6-1729 d 6-3-1810 m Willimpia Coleman Maj NJ
John: b 7-13-1756 d 1816 m — X— Pvt NJ ★
John: b 12-15-1752 d 2-6-1836 m Hannah Merritt Pvt NY ★
Thomas: b 10-1-1760 d 2-26-1811 m Mary Walling Pvt NJ

CARKIN,
John: b 1736/7 d 3-2-1799 m Elizabeth Cram Pvt NH

CARL, (includes CARLE, CARLL)
Ananias: b 4-25-1733 d 8-22-1801 m Jerusha Scudder PS NY
Ephraim Taylor: b 12-23-1757 d 12- -1837 m X Pvt NJ ★
George Frederick: b c. 1740 d p. 1-20-1787 m Maria Dederick Pvt PS NY
Israel: b 10-1-1757 d 7-7-1822 m Lydia Green Capt NJ
John: b 9-26-1759 d 9-20-1833 m Mary Morrill Pvt MA ★
John: b 1733 d 8-23-1815 m Providence Layton PS NJ
Joseph: b 8-5-1753 d p. 10-2-1798 m Margery Deering Pvt MA
Loudon: b 1762 d 2-28-1821 m Eleanor Wood Pvt NJ
Nathaniel: b 3-11-1747 d 1-11-1828 m Sarah Burbank Sgt ME
Samuel: b 1710-15 d 5-13-1785 m Esther Burbank CS ME
Timothy: b 5-16-1729 d 1-28-1805 m Hannah Scudder PS NY

CARLETON, (includes CARLTON)
Ambrose: b 3-29-1763 d 12-23-1832 m Jean Montgomery Sgt NC GA ★
Amos: b 5-21-1754 d 5-14-1832 m Sarah Dole Pvt MA
Caleb: b 1758 d 10-3-1823 m Margaret Day Pvt CT
Christopher, Jr.: b 5-2-1751 d 12-30-1822 m Mary Farnham Pvt MA
Daniel: b 3-6-1736/7 d 12-9-1801 m Mary Kimball Pvt MA
Darius: b 1785 d p. 1810 m Anna Spencer Pvt CT
David: b 1762 d 3-21-1846 m (1)Martha Currier (2)Rachel Clough Pvt MA ★
David: b a. 1753 d 10-22-1820 m Ruth Stevens Ens NH ★
David: b 5-10-1757 d 9-14-1845 m Beneter Porter Pvt NC ★
Dean: b — d — m Thankful Byam Pvt NH
Dudley: b 5-16-1748 d 4-21-1825 m Mehetable Barker Pvt VT
Ebenezer: b 10-13-1739 d 3-30-1818 m Mehitable — Lt MA
Ebenezer: b 4-2-1754 d 12-8-1836 m Rebecca Farrar Pvt NH
Edmund: b 7-3-1758 d 10-6-1792 m Abigail Hutchins Pvt MA
Edward: b c. 1729 d 1835 m Jane Stafford Pvt PA
Elijah: b 10-20-1746 d 1816 m Rebekah Webster Cpl MA ★
Enos: b 1-1-1756 d p. 1798 m Elizabeth Burbank Pvt MA

CARLETON, contd.
Ezra: b 1764/5 d p. 6- -1841 m Susan Whitney Drm Pvt NH ★
Francis: b 1756 d 1813 m Priscilla Cravath Pvt NJ
Jeremiah: b 4-13-1743 d 3-16-1814 m Lois Hoyt Pvt NH
Jesse: b 1-15-1762 d 8-1-1827 m Nancy Agnes Harriman Pvt MA
John: b 12-19-1719 d 7-3-1786 m Lydia Ladd MM CT
John: b 5-10-1738 d 12-5-1807 m Tabitha French Pvt MA
John: b 1759 d 1834 m Elizabeth Littlefield Pvt MA
John: b 10-16-1762 d 12-20-1838 m Judith Weston Pvt NH
John: b 12-11-1748 d 4-2-1787 m Mary Hunt Pvt NC
John: b 1760 d 1838 m Anna — Pvt NC
Jonathan: b 7-19-1760 d 7-23-1844 m Eunice Lufkin Pvt MA
Jonathan: b 1731 d 1785 m Miss Mainerd Pvt MA
Joseph: b 1-2-1754 d 11-2-1826 m Sarah Wood Pvt MA
Kimball: b 1744-6 d p. 1783/4 m Sarah Kingsbury Capt NH
Kimball: b 1747 d 5-22-1830 m Elizabeth Spillman Pvt PS NH
Lewis: b 9-12-1758 d 3-13-1827 m Elizabeth Eve — Pvt VA NC
Moses: b 2-17-1759 d 10-1-1838 m Mary Webster Sol MA
Nehemiah: b 12-15-1730 d 3-1-1778 m Sarah Gage Pvt MA
Oliver: b 9-11-1732 d 1801 m Amy Washer PS NH
Osgood: b 1740 d 1816 m Lydia Johnson Lt MA
Peter: b 9-9-1755 d 8-26-1828 m (1)Abigail Hazeltine (2)Azubah Taylor Stone SgtMaj MA W ★
Robert: b c. 1730 d p. 3-11-1796 m Rebecca Wofford PS VA
Samuel, Jr.: b 9-23-1750 d 3-18-1843 m Susannah Morse Pvt MA
Samuel, Sr.: b 1-22-1726 d 3-1-1803 m Rebecca Goodrich LCol MA
Samuel: b 3-23-1753 d 11-25-1839 m Sarah Bartlett Pvt MA
Thomas: b 5-10-1747 d 10-3-1795 m Martha — Pvt NC
Thomas, Jr.: b 2-15-1752 d 6-20-1818 m (1)Elizabeth Hyde (2)Martha Finch 2Lt VA
Timothy: b 1753 d 4-9-1834 m Rebecca Fields Pvt MA ★
William: b 1735 d 1808 m Eunice Laws Pvt NH
William: b 1735 d p. 12-3-1806 m Esther Brown Pvt VA
Woodman: b 1755 d 2-13-1837 m Rebecca Rogers Pvt NH

CARLEY,
Abraham: b 1711 d 9- -1790 m Susanna — Pvt NY
Ichabod: b 1738 d 9-17-1818 m Mary — Sgt VT
Johnathan: b 1757 d p. 1832 m Jenny Gray Sgt NY ★
Jonathan: b 3-16-1760 d 8-21-1841 m Elizabeth Kentfield Pvt MA

CARLIN,
John: b 1740 d p. 1776 m — X — Ens VA
Joseph: b 1754 d p. 4-10-1803 m Frances Lange PS LA

CARLISLE, (includes CARLYLE, CARLILE)
Daniel: b 8-15-1739 d 10-29-1794 m (1)Lydia Conant (2)Lydia Pierce Capt NH
David: b 2-20-1740 d 12-7-1797 m Sarah Cummings Capt MA
Edmund: b c. 1760 d p. 4-13-1828 m Elizabeth Whatley Sol GA
George: b 5-30-1756 d 5-27-1827 m Margaret Crockett Pvt VA
James: b 1762 d 1-11-1839 m Elizabeth Cate Pvt NC
James: b c. 1725 d 1802 m Rachel Campbell Pvt PS VA
John: b 2-6-1720 d p. 4-5-1780 m (1)Sarah Fairfax (2)Sybil West PS VA
Joseph: b 1761 d 10-15-1843 m (1)Elizabeth Merry (2)Phebe Alley (3)Sarah White Pvt MA ★
Robert: b c. 1740 d p. 9-26-1786 m Sarah Coleman PS NC
William: b 5-25-1757 d 6-2-1837 m Deborah Studley Pvt MA
William: b 9-29-1738 d 10-24-1808 m Hannah Taylor Pvt NJ
William Jr: b 1757 d 4-11-1840 m Mary Taylor Pvt PA

CARLOCK,
George: b 1740 d 1815 m — X — Pvt NC
Hanchrist: b 1715 d 1803 m (1)Susan Witmer (2)Sarah Whitman Pvt VA

CARLOS,
III King of Spain: b 1-20-1716 d 12-13-1789 m Maria of Saxony PS

CARMACK, (includes CAMMACK)
Evan: b 2-25-1740 d 1830 m Mary Wolf PS MD
John: b — d p. 12-26-1831 m Margaret — Sol SC
William: b 11-10-1738 d 5-16-1825 m — X — Capt MD
William: b 1-5-1761 d 10- -1849 m Elizabeth Walker Pvt VA ★

CARMAN, (includes KARMAN)
Caleb: b 6-28-1708 d 7-30-1807 m Elizabeth Wood PS NJ
John: b 6-15-1760 d 5-19-1840 m Barbara Wonderlich Pvt PA
Joseph: b 10-7-1759 d 1831 m Ruth Mott Pvt NY
Joseph: b 10- -1745 d 1786 m Mary LaRue Pvt VA
Moses: b 1730 d 1-26-1778 m Abigail Acken Pvt NJ
Phineas: b 9-9-1762 d 2-25-1827 m Huldah Ayers Pvt NJ
Samuel: b 3-26-1749 d 4-21-1817 m Mary DeMott Pvt PS NY
Silas: b 3-14-1709 d 1-3-1797 m Hannah Smith PS NY

CARMER,
Abraham: b 1-1-1760 d 9-11-1848 m (1)Sarah Alword (2)Sarah Carter Pvt NJ ★

CARMICHAEL,
Alexander: b 9-12-1734 d 1-25-1808 m Mary Elizabeth Odgen Lt NJ
Archibald: b — d 1814 m Elizabeth Nix Pvt NC

Daniel: b 1743 d 12- -1778 m Mary Duncan Ens PA
Duncan: b c. 1750 d p. 1784 m — X — Pvt NC
Ichabod: b a. 1745 d 1829 m Phebe Clark Sgt NJ
James: b c. 1747 d p. 1790 m Jane Moore Maj PA
John: b 5-5-1740 d 11-19-1806 m Esther Canfield Pvt NY
John: b c. 1740 d 2-20-1799 m (2)Isabella Pomeroy Pvt PA
John: b 10-17-1728 d 11-15-1785 m Catherine Mustard PS PA
John: b a. 1757 d 1808 m Nancy Graham Pvt PA
John: b 8-7-1757 d 1848 m — X — Pvt PA ★

CARNAGEY,
Wm.: b 2-28-1755 d 10-26-1841 m Mary Swem Pvt PA ★

CARNAHAN, (includes CARNAGHAN)
Adam: b 1743 d 11-7-1815 m Sarah — Pvt PA
David: b 9-17-1747 d p. 1800 m Agnes McGahey Pvt PA
James: b c. 1750 d 1815 m Jane Freyer Capt PA
James: b 1-13-1754 d 5-31-1788 m Hannah Mahon Capt PA
John: b 1756 d 1840 m (1)Jennie Billingsley (2)Mary Pyeatte Lt PA
John: b 1745 d 3-24-1825 m Rebecca Caruthers 2Lt PA
Nathan: b 12-3-1759 d 1846 m Elizabeth Gilmore PS MA
Robert: b a. 1765 d c. 1801 m Judith McDowell Pvt PA

CARNALL,
Patrick: b c. 1756 d c. 1835 m — X — Pvt VA ★

CARNER,
Anthony: b 1752 d 6-17-1834 m Catherine Stiembeck Sgt NC ★

CARNEY,
John: b — d 7-24-1826 m (1)—(2)Mary Eve Bittenbender 1Lt PA W★
John: b 4-15-1757 d p. 8-29-1832 m Margaret Floyd Pvt VA ★
Mark: b c. 1740 d 10-16-1782 m Susanne Goux Pvtr MA
Thomas: b c. 1732 d p. 1795 m Mary Carroll PS VA
Timothy: b c. 1758 d p. 1800 m Margaret — Pvt PA

CARNINE, (includes CARNAN)
Andrew: b 10-22-1761 d 6-11-1836 m Lydia Bice Pvt VA W ★
Charles Ridgely: b 12-6-1760 d 7-17-1829 m Priscilla Dorsey Lt MD
John: b 8-3-1745 d 9-6-1823 m Rebecca Ellis Hynson PS MD
Peter: b 11-16-1752 d 2-2-1841 m (1)Caterdienty Sebring (2)Christina Sebring (3)Hanna Sebring OrdlSgt NJ ★
Robert North: b 8-8-1756 d 5-12-1837 m (1)Katherine Risteau (2)Mrs Sarah Goldsborough Ennals Cav PS MD

CAROTHERS, (includes CARRUTHERS, CARUTHERS, CROTHERS, CROWTHERS)
Andrew: b c. 1756 d a. 3-14-1817 m Mary — Pvt PA
Andrew: b 3-10-1739 d 6-25-1826 m Margaret Neely Lt NC
Armstrong: b c. 1762 d 1837 m — X — Pvt PA
Benjamin: b c. 1759 d 7-9-1800 m Susanna Lockhart Pvt KY
James: b 1753 d 11-11-1835 m Mary Smith Cpl NC ★
James: b 4-17-1750 d 12-7-1836 m (1)Mary — (2)Agnes Woods Pvt NC
James: b 1738 d 11-26-1826 m (1)Nancy Neely (2)Abigail Henderson Sol PA
James: b 4-5-1760 d 1-13-1846 m Margaret Jackson Pvt PA
John: b 1743 d 1822 m Miss — Rogers Sol NC
John: b 1739 d 2-26-1798 m Mary Armstrong Col PA
John: b- -1744 d 1-11-1782 m Ailsie McTeer Capt PA
John: b 7-12-1746 d 9- -1841 m Sarah — Pvt SC ★
John: b 10- -1740 d 10-4-1822 m Mary — Capt PA
John: b 1750 d 1779 m Rebecca Moffett Lt VA
Nathan: b 1750 d 1797 m Polly — Pvt PA
Richard: b 12-28-1740 d 2-9-1790 m (1)Philathea Mills (2)Mary Ewing Adj NJ
Robert: b 5-3-1753 d 10-4-1826 m Elizabeth Patillo Pvt NC
Roger: b c. 1750 d p. 2-27-1794 m Sarah Pennwell Pvt PA
William: b 1736 d 8-19-1811 m Sarah Harvey Pvt NC
William: b 4-12-1754 d 8-23-1826 m Mary McGowan Pvt SC W★

CARPENTER,
Abel: b 1747 d 11-16-1804 m Sarah Phippin Pvt VT
Abiel: b 6-20-1759 d 10-30-1840 m Mary Sherman Pvt MA
Adam: b 4-20-1760 d 6-11-1806 m Mrs Catherine Spears Fry Sol VA
Amos: b 2-12-1715/16 d 9-13-1787 m (1)Polly Gould (2)Phebe Gould Sol VT
Amos: b 2-14-1754 d 3-31-1837 m (1) —Bickel (2)Margaret McLaughlin Pvt Spy VA ★
Andrew: b 1745 d 1778 m Mercy Reynolds Pvt CT
Andrew: b c. 1727 d a. 9-24-1795 m Barbara Weber PS VA
Asaph: b 7-22-1746 d 1830 m Mary — Pvt VT
Ashman: b 1762 d 10-5-1839 m Ann Wood Pvt NJ
Barlow: b 9-12-1747 d 6-7-1818 m Sarah Goss Pvt VT
Benjamin: b 1756 d 1776 m Mary Seaver Vol CT
Benjamin: b 1725 d p. 7-27-1780 m Lucy Allen Pvt MA
Benjamin, Sr.: b 9-8-1729 d p. 1777 m Joanna Hayward Sol VT
Benjamin: b 5-17-1725 d 3-29-1804 m Amie Carpenter LCol PS VT
Benjamin: b 1737 d 1813 m Jane Edmonds Pvt NY

Benjamin: b 1756 d 2-26-1820 m Margaret Decker Pvt NY W ★
Benjamin: b 1730 d 9-2-1793 m Jane Leonard PS NY
Benjamin: b 4-13-1750 d 1-21-1837 m Mary Ferrier Ens PA
Benjamin: b 1763 d 2-25-1847 m (1)Mary Burk (2)Lucy Bennett Pvt RI
Benjamin, Jr.: b 10-21-1760 d 2- -1838 m Ruth Hayward Pvt NH
Caleb: b 3-13-1730 d 10-10-1801 m Hannah French Pvt MA
Caleb: b 9-21-1736 d 8-30-1785 m Elizabeth Bullock Pvt MA
Caleb: b 3-10-1740 d 3-22-1810 m Lucy Carpenter Pvt MA
Caleb: b 9-25-1736 d 12-20-1826 m Amy — PS NY
Caleb: b 9-26-1742 d 3-22-1810 m (1)Deborah — (2) — Carpenter Sgt VT
Cephas: b 3-2-1754 d 2-26-1829 m (1)Phoebe Collins (2)Mehitable Ormsby Ens VT
Cornelius: b c. 1757 d 3- -1847 m Mary Utz Sol VA
Cyril: b 9-7-1743 d 11-23-1811 m (1)Lucy Lane (2)Mrs Mary Andrews Pvt MA
Cyril: b 7-25-1758 d 6-1-1832 m Jemima Culiver Pvt VT
Daniel: b 7-17-1730 d 1804 m Abiah Porter Pvt CT
Daniel: b 9-29-1744 d 4-14-1803 m Elizabeth Tyler Cpl MA
Daniel: b c.1752/3 d 1811 m Lucy Nichols Pvt MA
Daniel: b 12-29-1761 d 8-18-1840 m Mary Thompson Pvt MA W ★
Daniel: b 7-27-1738 d 4-18-1823 m (1)Anna Lyon (2)Olive Ide PS MA
Daniel: b 10-10-1730 d 3-10-1790 m Susannah Thompson Pvt NY
Daniel: b 1750 d 1828 m Mary Lease Capt PA
David: b 1-28-1759 d 4-3-1845 m Azubah Allin Pvt NH
Ebenezer: b 7-21-1708 d 8-31-1807 m Suzanna Perrin Pvt MA
Ebenezer: b 4-22-1745 d 8-24-1833 m Prudence Carter Sgt PS NH
Elias: b 10-7-1761 d 2-16-1851 m Sarah Prescott Pvt CT
Elihu: b 12-18-1752 d 7-5-1827 m Martha Hutchins Sgt MA
Elijah: b 8-9-1762 d 5-5-1795 m Sarah Younglove Cpl CT
Elijah: b 4-16-1758 d 8-29-1814 m Sarah Wing Sgt MA
Elijah: b 5-3-1732 d p. 1790 m Patience Brewster Pvt CT
Eliphalet, Jr.: b 11-9-1747 d 12-21-1820 m Esther Gurley Pvt CT
Elisha: b 8-17-1745 d 8-21-1825 m Anna Freeman Pvt MA
Elisha: b 4-27-1725 d 7-14-1816 m Deliverance Marough PS MA
Elisha: b 6-18-1728 d 3-25-1813 m Esther Greenwood PS MA
Emanuel, Sr.: b 1702 d 4- -1780 m Caroline Line PS PA
Emanuel, Jr.: b 1744 d 1822 m Mary Maria Smith Pvt PS NH
Ephraim: b 7-24-1735 d 8-21-1809 m Tabitha Chaffee Capt CT
Ezekiel: b 8-17-1734 d 10-9-1822 m Betsey Bucklin Pvt MA
Ezra: b 2-11-1741 d 8-7-1815 m Esther Read Pvt MA
Ezra: b 3-21-1753 d 7-1-1841 m Margaret Daniels MM MA
Gabrill: b 1757 d 4-18-1808 m Elizabeth Byer Pvt PA
Gardner: b 3-16-1749 d 4-22-1815 m Mary Huntington PM CT
George: b 8-7-1726 d 5-27-1811 m Amy Dean Adj NY
George: b 1755 d 9- -1830 m Eve Rose Baker Pvt PA
Gideon: b 5-24-1725 d 11-28-1805 m (1)Mary — (2)Jemima Jenney PS MA
Greenwood: b 3-31-1733 d 2-3-1809 m (1)Sarah Leathers (2)Susanna Hammond Pvt NH
Hezekiah: b 12-8-1736 d 5-7-1822 m (1)Joanna Aldrich (2)Lois Corbin Pvt CT VT
Hope: b 3-16-1757 d 5-4-1840 m Phebe Yost Pvt NJ ★
Increase: b 8-20-1736 d 4-20-1807 m Mary Bailey Lt NY
Isaac: b 3-24-1740 d 4-8-1818 m (1)Mrs Susanna (Horton)Little (2)Mrs Susanna (McKinney) Thompson Sol NY
Isaac: b 1764 d 7-23-1837 m Martha Allen Pvt NC ★
Isaiah: b 1-8-1735 d 1-17-1809 m Miriam Sleigh Sgt VT
Jabez: b 4-26-1731 d p. 1800 m (1)Abigal Dyer (2)Mary Lawrence Pvt MA
Jacob: b 3-16-1745 d 8-28-1830 m Rachel Davenport Pvt NY
Jacob: b 1734 d 5-3-1807 m Catherine Ramsour PS NC
Jacob: b 6-30-1741 d 12-6-1797 m Maria Forney LCol PA
James: b 4-4-1741 d 11-4-1813 m Irene Ladd Pvt CT
James: b 2-16-1738 d 11-4-1829 m Bethia Hyde Pvt MA
Jedediah: b 10-8-1742 d 1816 m (1)Hannah — (2)Mary Peck PS NH
Jesse: b 7-9-1749 d 1843 m (1)Ruth Streeter (2)Dorcas Cooper Pvt MA ★
Jesse: b 5-3-1756 d 3-27-1832 m Marian Fairfield Pvt CT NH
Jesse: b 9-27-1760 d 2-23-1838 m (1)Anne Cutter (2)Sarah Andrews Pvt NH
Jesse: b 9-19-1755 d 1-17-1815 m Sally Seely Pvt NY
John: b 1-4-1728 d 10-3-1816 m Mary Loomis Pvt CT
John: b 1735 d 2-25-1803 m Susannah Turner Pvt MD
John: b 2-22-1739/40 d 11-2-1805 m Mercy Morgan Capt MA
John, Sr.: b 4-6-1733 d 4-1-1821 m (1)Bethia French (2)Mary Woodward (3)Mrs Mary Ide Pvt MA
John, Jr.: b 4-6-1756 d 2-1-1843 m (1)Cynthia Brown (2)Azubah Perham Pvt MA
John: b 3-29-1752 d p. 1786 m Elizabeth Brown Pvt MA
John: b 10-25-1743 d 11-10-1819 m Mary Carpenter Adj PS NY
John: b 1725 d p. 11-28-1786 m Amy Jennings PS NY
John: b 2- -1745 d 2- -1800 m (1)Frances — (2)Abigail Moore PS NY
John: b 1735 d 1-15-1807 m Elizabeth Sherer Lt PA
John: b 3-1-1737 d 6-13-1798 m (1)Mary Ferree (2)Susan Hartman 1Lt PA
John: b 12-14-1752 d 5-10-1842 m (1)Sarah Weathers (2)Margaret Vaughn Drm RI ★
John: b — d c. 1800 m Nancy — QM Sgt VA
John: b 1725 d 1785 m Elizabeth Spears Pvt VA

John: b a. 1750 d a. 12-12-1803 m Mary — Pvt VA
Jonah: b 11-7-1742 d 1-31-1805 m Zeruiah Whitmore Pvt CT
Jonathan, Sr.: b 4-25-1732 d 5-17-1810 m Abigail Walker Pvt MA
Jonathan, Jr.: b 6-19-1757 d 3-19-1837 m Olive Sessions Cpl MA ★
Jonathan: b — d — m Lucy Johnson PS RI
Jonathan: b 11-1-1743 d 5- -1815 m Elizabeth Pratt CS VT
Joseph: b 7-19-1764 d 4-17-1834 m Sarah Buell Pvt CT
Joseph: b 5-6-1751 d 7-26-1813 m Persis Rawson Pvt MA
Joseph: b 2-1-1753 d 1-20-1839 m Susannah Eakers Pvt NC
Joseph: b 6-22-1736 d 8-29-1796 m Sarah Greenman 1Lt RI
Joseph: b 4-2-1756 d 6-14-1842 m Esther Knight Pvt RI ★
Joshua: b 1740 d p. 1791 m (1)Hannah Ludham (2)Sarah Burt Pvt NY
Josiah: b 10-6-1762 d 3-1-1851 m Hannah Morrill Pvt PS CT
Josiah: b 1-5-1747 d 1-20-1821 m Hepsibah Wilmarth Pvt MA
Jotham: b 8-1-1708 d 5-10-1777 m (1)Mehitabel Thompson (2)Freelove Kingsley PS RI
Jotham: b 11-28-1750 d p. 1784 m Hannah Gulley Pvt MA
Lewis: b 5-9-1762 d 3-11-1843 m Mary Ann Bliss Cpl MA ★
Matthew: b 9-26-1759 d 10-6-1839 m Catherine Matthews Pvt MA
Michael: b c. 1735 d p. 9- -1782 m Maria Crisler PS VA
Michael: b 1758 d 1818 m Rebecca Delph 1Lt VA
Miles: b c. 1725 d 11-4-1791 m Mary — Drm Maj PA
Moses: b c. 1750 d 7-20-1799 m (1)Elizabeth Bunyan (2)Hannah Smith Pvt NY
Nathan: b 4-12-1757 d 9-19-1814 m (1)Irene Reid (2)Naomi Cornell Pvt CT
Nathan: b 2-6-1748 d 2-11-1842 m (1)Anna Cox (2)Mrs Hannah Lurvey Andrews Pvt MA
Nathaniel: b 4-6-1736 d 6- -1816 m Susanna Read LCol MA
Nathaniel: b 1-13-1743 d 1826 m Elizabeth — Pvt VT
Nathaniel: b c. 1755 d 1829 m (2)Lydia — Cpl VA
Nehemiah: b 10- -1731 d 5-14-1799 m (1)Elizabeth Sweet (2)Sarah Harthorn Capt MA
Nehemiah, Sr.: b 3-11-1731 d 4-25-1821 m Elizabeth Van Vliet Pvt NY
Nehemiah, Jr.: b 6-29-1757 d 2-24-1832 m Ann Bookhout Pvt NY
Obadiah: b 9-2-1742 d 12-6-1810 m Amie Lee Sgt MA
Oliver: b 9-26-1756 d 2-21-1845 m Prudence Alexander Pvt CT
Oliver: b 11-15-1753 d 7-13-1845 m Joanna Ballou Cpl MA
Peter: b 12-31-1747 d 10-9-1806 m Patience Bullock Pvt MA
Peter: b 1736 d 1817 m Barbara Deppen PS NC
Reuben: b 2-22-1757 d 10-5-1802 m (1)Sarah Miller (2)Hannah Cook Pvt MA
Richard: b 2-1-1746 d 1-6-1781 m Elizabeth Brackett PS MA
Richard: b 4- -1750 d 4-27-1813 m Abigail — Lt NY
Robert: b 3-5-1722 d p.1777 m (1)Charity Roberts (2)Mercy — Cpl CL
Rufus: b 1746 d 6-6-1816 m Olive Whitcomb Pvt VT
Samuel: b 5-24-1757 d 4-26-1798 m (1)Dolly Alton (2)Sibyl Alton Pvt CT
Samuel: b 3-27-1741 d p. 1800 m Sarah Hix Pvt PS NH
Samuel: b 1753 d 3- -1834 m (1)Sarah Smith (2)Anna Hillard Ens PA W ★
Samuel: b 1754 d p. 9-23-1822 m Esther Hopkins Pvt NY
Samuel: b 1734 d 1800 m Betsey Allison CS NY
Simeon: b 5-13-1759 d 1847 m Sallie Blanchard Pvt MA
Simeon: b 3-23-1740 d 10-21-1830 m Anna Burton Pvt VT
Solomon: b c. 1701 d a. 8-8-1794 m Elinor — PS NY
Stephen: b 10-15-1740 d 2-13-1815 m (1)Amy Field (2)Ruth Fisk (3)Mrs Esther Newhall Green MM MA
Thomas: b 10-24-1733 d 4-26-1807 m Elizabeth Moulton Col MA
Thomas: b 7-15-1725 d 1-22-1809 m Dorothy Bosworth Pvt MA
Thomas, Jr.: b 3-6-1758 d 10-29-1822 m (1)Olive Wheaton (2)Chloe Bliss (3)Rebecca Bliss Pvt MA
Thomas: b 11-21-1752 d 7-7-1747 m Mary Tonkins Ens PM NJ
Thomas: b 1747 d 2-26-1817 m Elizabeth Haviland 2Lt NY
Thomas: b 3-29-1760 d 9-9-1805 m Martha Avery Pvt NY W ★
Thomas: b 6-25-1710 d 8-24-1784 m Martha Clement Pvt NY
Thomas: b 2-1-1739 d 2-1-1815 m Esther Squarel Capt PA
Uriah: b 1-6-1741 d 1- -1821 m (1)Lucy Wyman (2)Martha Bartlett Sgt MA
Uriah: b 1762 d 1-3-1816 m Eliphal Briggs Pvt CT W ★
Wait: b 1754 d 1797 m Elizabeth (?) Clark Pvt NY
Walter: b 8-8-1740 d 2-25-1816 m (1)Maria Huic (2)Sybil (Ludding-ton)Dawson Pvt NY
William: b 10-16-1742 d 12-24-1814 m Rachel Badger MM CT
William: b 9-24-1721 d 1809 m Hannah Needham Sgt PS MA
William: b 1-21-1736/37 d 3-30-1784 m (1)Elizabeth Briggs (2)Sarah Fuller Pvt MA
William: b 7-25-1757 d 4-5-1816 m Sarah Sherman Pvt MA
William: b 9-25-1752 d 7-24-1843 m Lucina Sumner Pvt NH ★
William: b 1757 d 9-26-1803 m Elizabeth Ware Pvt NJ
William: b 4-5-1731 d 7-6-1814 m Sarah Seaman Ens NY
William: b 3-13-1725 d 1-1-1815 m Mary French Cpl RI
William, Sr.: b 1728 d p. 6-14-1809 m Mary Wilhoite Sol PS VA
William, Jr.: b 5-20-1762 d 2-13-1833 m Polly Aylor Pvt VA
William: b 3-19-1765 d 9-14-1835 m Mary Strickling Pvt VA
Zacariah: b 2-27-1734/5 d 10-1-1775 m Hannah — Pvt VA

CARPENTIER,
Henri: b 1727 d 5-14-1777 m Marie Aubuchon PS IL

CARPER,
Nicholas: b c. 1749 d p. 2-12-1811 m Elizabeth — CS VA

CARR, (includes KARR)
Andrew: b 1744 d 7-31-1828 m Katherine Wilson Pvt PA
Benjamin: b 1746 d 1838 m Margaret McIntire Pvt MA
Bradbury: b 7-27-1713 d c. 1777 m Anna Richardson PS NH
Caleb: b 8-17-1750 d 6-19-1837 m Roba Hopkins Pvt CT
Caleb, Jr.: b 6-19-1744 d 1793 m Abigail Very Cpl MA NY
Caleb, Sr.: b 1720 d 12-30-1783 m Elizabeth Phillips Capt RI
Caleb, Jr.: b 5-7-1744 d 2-1-1818 m Margaret Adams Pvt NY
Caleb: b 9-4-1743 d 4-3-1829 m Lillis Barton Capt RI ★
Christian Frederick: b 1742 d 7-30-1814 m (2)Anna Eva Whitsell Pvt SC
Christopher: b 6-10-1742 d 12-14-1845 m Joanna — Pvt PA
Conrad: b 1-3-1755 d 11-14-1814 m Magdaline — Sol VA
Daniel: b 7-13-1734 d 4-12-1822 m Elizabeth Chase Ens MA
David: b 7-14-1751 d 5-3-1826 m Cornelia Chamberlain Pvt PA
Edward, Sr.: b 11-6-1723 d 9-25-1781 m Sarah Weeden PS RI
Eleazer: b 4-22-1746 d 7-19-1816 m Eleanor Stafford Capt RI
Elliott: b 7-5-1742 d — m Joanna Dow Pvt MA
Eseck: b 1738 d p. 1790 m Ann Clarke Cpl RI
Ezekiel: b 2-12-1750 d p. 1793 m Mary Winch PS NH
Francis: b 12-6-1751 d 10-5-1821 m Mary Eliot Capt MA
George: b 8-20-1764 d 6-8-1829 m Mary Marden Slr NH
George: b 1740 d 2-12-1815 m Mary Waugh PS PA
Gideon: b 1750 d 1847 m Anne — Pvt VA
Gideon: b 11-5-1752 d 3-21-1844 m Ann Sandridge Pvt VA ★
Henry: b 1758 d 1822 m Elizabeth Alexander Pvt VA
Isaac: b 8-13-1742 d 4-2-1824 m Phoebe Carr Sea Cap RI
James: b 10-20-1727 d 1809 m Sarah Follinsbee Capt MA
James: b 4-22-1748 d 3-11-1829 m Susanna Wentworth Col NH
James: b 6-10-1763 d 5-3-1839 m Margaret Morrell Pvt NY ★
James: b 1754 d 3-13-1823 m Mary Kerr Capt NC ★
James: b 1763 d 8-5-1796 m Susan Powell Sgt NC
John: b 1709 d 10-22-1782 m Elizabeth Wilson PS NH
John, Sr.: b 6-4-1711 d 5-2-1786 m (1)Ann Moody (2)Abigail Perley PS NH
John, Jr.: b 5-18-1739 d 1-12-1825 m Ruth Morse PS NH
John: b 1759 d 12-16-1840 m Marcy Lee Pvt NJ ★
John: b 5-5-1758 d p. 1789 m Amy Armstrong Pvt NY
John: b 1759 d 9-3-1823 m (1)Susan Sloan (2)Elizabeth Brook Sol NC
John: b c. 1737 d 1792 m Elizabeth — 2Lt PA
John: b c. 1755 d p. 1783 m Margaret Ewing Sgt PA
John: b c. 1745 d 4-22-1780 m Mary — Pvt PA
John: b 10-6-1738 d 3-25-1814 m Mary Arnold Capt RI
John: b 6-5-1761 d 7-7-1842 m Mary Wilbor Pvt RI
John: b 8-28-1738 d 11-13-1807 m — X — Ens VA
John, Sr.: b 1735 d 1798 m Ann Eliza Thomas Pvt VA
John, Jr.: b 1760 d 1832 m Margaret Crow Pvt VA
John: b 1746 d 1809 m Mary Elizabeth Downer PS VA
John Baxter: b c. 1760 d 12-12-1814 m Susanna Currier Pvt Smn MA W★
John Fendall: b 12-11-1765 d p. 1833 m Elizabeth Dalton Pvt VA ★
Joseph: b 4-3-1757 d 3-15-1848 m Rebecca — Cpl RI
Joseph: b 3-21-1752 d 3-6-1817 m Priscilla Mary — Cpl VA
Levi: b 1762 d 8-10-1849 m (1)Ruth Goodrich (2)Betsey Holmes Sgt MA ★
MacCrest: b 5-2-1731 d 1779 m Elizabeth Waite Capt MA
Mark: b 1743 d 7-26-1789 m Elizabeth Gilchrist PS NH
Matthew: b a. 1734 d 6-16-1791 m Margaret — Pvt PA
Mathew: b c. 1748 d 1803 m Elizabeth Wilkerson Pvt VA
Nathan: b a. 1754 d 12-16-1842 m Elizabeth Smith Ens NH
Nicholas: b 12-25-1732 d 3-13-1813 m Mary Eldred PS RI
Parker: b 5-29-1750 d 11-26-1809 m Judith Preston PS NH
Peleg, Sr.: b 8-19-1741 d 4-20-1821 m Ruth Tew PS RI
Peter: b 1747 d 4-30-1835 m Hester Schuyler Pvt NJ ★
Peter: b 1740 d 2-28-1812 m (1) — X — (2)Mrs Mary Wilson PS VA
Robert: b 5-23-1742 d 10-20-1823 m Prudence Wheeler Capt CT
Robert: b 7-27-1763 d 9-8-1821 m Mary Green Pvt NY
Robert: b 12- -1750 d 1849 m — X — Pvt PA
Robert: b 1754 d 1823 m Mary Levering Pvt SC
Robert: b 5-5-1741 d 8-15-1789 m Lydia Turner Maj RI
Robert: b 1738 d c. 1778 m Isabella Irwin Sgt VA
Samuel: b — d p. 10-7-1780 m Emma Chase Bgd Maj MA
Samuel: b 1748 d 1809 m Ann — PS PA
Samuel, Jr.: b 9-26-1756 d 3-21-1814 m Damaris Underwood Ens RI
Samuel: b 1750-2 d 8-27-1819 m Frances Eldred Pvt RI
Sanders: b 8-27-1734 d 1809 m Miss Maxwell Sgt NH
Stephen: b a. 1763 d 10-5-1797 m Juliana De Bruhl Pvt SC W ★
Thomas, Jr.: b 12-20-1742 d 6-14-1807 m Abigail Lovering Pvt MA
Thomas, Sr.: b 8-5-1725 d 4-22-1797 m Hannah Carr PS NH
Thomas, Jr.: b a. 1757 d 7-27-1838 m Elizabeth Jones Pvt NH ★
Thomas: b 1-17-1755 d 3-4-1828 m Bethiah — Pvt NH ★
Thomas: b 6-23-1755 d 10-26-1822 m Hannah Coombs Capt PA
Thomas: b 10-4-1758 d 10-5-1820 m Frances Bacon Col VA
Thomas: b 11-25-1735 d 1807 m Mary Clarkson Capt VA
Thomas: b 5-15-1742 d 5-5-1821 m Anne Sanders Sgt VA
Thomas: b 1762 d 3-11-1838 m Ann Gates Sol VA
Thomas: 1733 d 10-15-1796 m Mary Cumming Wgn VA
Walter Childs: b 11-1-1753 d 12-5-1838 m Elisabeth Chiles Pvt VA
Wm : b 1745 d 1814 m (1)Rebecca Whirley (2)Susan Brandenburg Pvt PA

Wm.: b 5-29-1754 d 6-10-1841 m Margaret Greer Pvt NC ★
Wm.: b 1728 d 1788 m Mary Robinson Pvt PA

CARRAWAY,
Thomas: b c. 1750 d 1800 m Sarah — Pvt NC
William: b 1754 d 2-1-1834 m Elizabeth Averea Sgt SC

CARRICK, (includes KERRICK)
James: b c. 1760 d — m — X — Pvt VA
Mareen: b a. 1751 d 1793 m (1) —X—(2)Elizabeth Jones PS MD
Thomas: b c. 1755 d p. 1787 m Henrietta Monroe Pvt NJ

CARRIEL, (includes CARYL)
John: b 4-14-1756 d 9-5-1791 m Eunice Willard SrgnMte MA W★
Jonathan: b 5-28-1734 d p. 1777 m Elizabeth Greenwood Capt MA
Jonathan: b 3-1-1730 d 7-22-1806 m Anne Clark Pvt MA
Nathaniel: b 1-23-1724 d 6-8-1816 m Jane Dwight PS MA

CARRIER,
Amaziah: b 7-17-1754 d 12-25-1832 m Abia Churchill Pvt NY ★
David: b 12-5-1756 d 6-28-1828 m Rebecca Huxford Pvt CT
Titus: b 8-23-1733 d 7-25-1795 m Mercy Cook Ens CT

CARRIGAN,
William: b 1760 d 11-24-1844 m Cathrine Adams Pvt NC ★

CARRIGER,
Godfrey: b 3-7-1732 d 10-8-1811 m Margaret Hanchpaugh Sol NC

CARRINGER,
Martin: b 1759 d 1-25-1835 m Mary Hoat Pvt PA

CARRINGTON,
Aaron: b 2-6-1747 d 11-21-1805 m Patience Bartholomew Pvt NY
Abraham: bpt 11-11-1733 d 1785 m Rebecca Johnson Cdr of Grds CT
Clement: b 11-22-1762 d 11-28-1847 m Jane (Watkins)Poage Ens VA
Elias: b 5-17-1734 d 8-6-1800 m Esther Northrop Dr CT
George: b 7-1-1711 d 2-7-1785 m Anne Mayo Col PS VA
John: bpt 11-6-1743 d 1783 m Mabel Beach Pvt CT
Joseph: b 2-6-1741 d 11-23-1802 m Theodosia Mosby Capt PS VA
Mayo: b 4-1-1753 d 12-28-1803 m Anne Adams DepQM Gen VA
Paul: b 3-5-1735 d 6-23-1818 m (1)Margaret Read (2)Pricilla Sims PS VA
Riverius: b 6-13-1757 d 5-29-1823 m Lola Wheeler Pvt CT
Samuel: b 1754 d 5-6-1818 m Milly McDonald Pvt MD
Solomon: b 12-18-1747 d 2-15-1788 m Rebecca Sackett Pvt CT

CARROLL, (includes CARRELL, CARRIL, CARRILL, CARROL, CARRYL)
Amos: b 1-23-1728 d 1-28-1792 m (1)Mary Smith (2)Mrs Lucy Hosmer Barrett Lt CT
Barthomew: b 1722 d 12-7-1827 m Catherine — Pvt VA ★
Benjamin: b 8-25-1755 d p. 1793 m Permelia Proctor Pvt PA
Charles: b 1751 d 10-9-1836 m Elizabeth Warfield PS MD
Douglas: b — d — m — X — Pvt NC
Hugh: b c. 1760 d 1815 m Marcial Willis Pvt PA
Jacob: b 4-27-1735 d 7-3-1817 m Elizabeth Jamison Pvt PA
Jacob: b 1748 d 6- -1815 m Elizabeth Fair Pvt SC
James: b 1765 d 5-16-1834 m Rhoda Stevens Pvt NC ★
James: b 3-26-1730 d 3-18-1804 m Sarah — Pvt PA
James: b 1756 d 1829 m Delphia Gualtney Sol VA
Jesse: b c. 1750 d p. 3-10-1802 m Mary Rachel Gavin Sol NC
John: b c. 1754 d p. 1840 m Frances Hamilton Sol MD
John : b 3-17-1728 d 1-19-1781 m Mary King Bbd MA
John: b 4-13-1736 d — m Tamer King Pvt MA
John: b 3-7-1756 d 9-15-1855 m Maria Van Alstyne Pvt NY
John: b c. 1745 d p. 8-13-1825 m Rhoda Niblak Pvt PA
Joseph, Jr.: b 8-26-1755 d 8-8-1785 m Esther Pond Pvt MA
Joseph: b 1746 d 2-17-1803 m Martha Swansey QMSgt SC
Patrick: b c. 1760 d p. 5-14-1819 m Jemima Hayes Pvt MD
Samuel: b a. 1740 d p. 1790 m Margaret Leslie Sol SC
Thomas: b c. 1762 d 1823 m Mary Montgomery Sgt PA
William: b 4-10-1755 d 3-16-1845 m Elizabeth Fee Pvt MD
Wm.: b 8-22-1755 d 1-21-1824 m Phoebe Wortman Pvt NJ ★
William: b 1755 d 12-8-1815 m Elizabeth Hicks Pvt NY
William: b 1745 d p. 6-13-1830 m Joanna Wakefield Pvt PA

CARRUTH,
James: b 10-2-1737 d 12-6-1812 m Lucy Gary Pvt MA
John: b 6-9-1734 d 12-28-1814 m Miriam Maynard Ens PS MA
John: b 1750 d 6-8-1828 m Elizabeth Cathey Maj NC
Robert: b 1749 d 4-6-1817 m Margaret Knox Pvt NC
Walter: b 1750-2 d c. 1827 m Nancy — CS Capt NC

CARSKADEN, (includes CARSKADDEN)
James: b 1757 d 8-15-1830 m Christiana Murphy Sol PA
William: b 1760 d 3-7-1810 m Susanna — Sol NY

CARSON,
Adam: b 1765 d 1841-43 m Sarah McGovie OrdlSgt GA

Andrew: b 3-1-1756 d 1-25-1841 m Temperance Young Pvt NC ★
Benjamin: b 1750 d *p.* 1830 m — X — Pvt PA ★
David: b *c.* 1750 d *c.* 1804 m Elizabeth Dysart CS PS VA
James: b 1756 d *p.* 1804 m Sarah Abney Lt SC
John: b 5-24-1760 d *p.* 1805 m Isabella McGough Sol GA
John: b 3-5-1737 d 10- -1817 m Margaret Duncan Sol CS PA
John: b 5-3-1761 d 1845 m Hester Lewis Pvt VA ★
Richard: b *c.* 1710 d 1782 m (1)—X—(2)Martha Rumford PS DE
Robert: b 5-7-1762 d 11-10-1837 m Margaret — Pvt PA
Thomas: b — d 1817 m Mary Smith Pvt PA
Thomas: b 1740-45 d *p.* 1-16-1816 m — X — Pvt PA
Thomas: b 2-18-1760 d 1-18-1840 m Ann Porter Pvt VA ★
Walter: b *a.* 1755 d *p.* 1780 m (1)Margaret Galaspie (2)Nancy Hare Capt DE
Walter: b 1758 d 3- -1834 m Mary— Capt SC ★
William, Jr.: b 1745 d 1829 m Isabella Gilmore Pvt PA
William: b 8-15-1748 d *c.* 1838 m Sally — Pvt VA

CARSTARPHEN,
James: b *a.* 1760 d 1816 m (1)— X— (2)Mary Powell Lt CL

CARSWELL,
Abner: b 5- -1755 d 1836 m (2)Jane Stewart Sgt MA NY ★
Alexander, Sr.: b 1727 d 1803 m Isabella Brown Pvt GA
David: b 3-6-1764 d 2-26-1844 m Martha Simpson Sol CL
John: b 1- -1760 d 3- -1817 m Sarah Wright Ens GA
Nathaniel: b 1729 d 3-23-1807 m Esther Henry Pvt NY

CART,
William: b 1749 d *p.* 1829 m Catharine — Pvt PA ★

CARTER, (includes CARTIER)
Aaron: b 4-30-1744 d 9-12-1804 m Elizabeth Davis Pvt NJ
Abijah: b 9-5-1761 d *p.* 1832 m Nancy Warner MA ★
Abraham: b *c.* 1760 d 11- -1817 m Mary Harriss Pvt NC
Anthony: b 2-24-1765 d 10-10-1836 m Mary Wilcox Pvt NY ★
Barnabas: b *c.* 1760 d 8-24-1841 m (1)Sarah Clayton (2)Rebecca Davis Pvt VA
Benjamin: b 9-10-1737 d 2-16-1832 m Pheba Spencer Pvt CT
Benjamin: b 6-5-1757 d 1827 m Lois Whittemore Pvt MA
Benjamin: b 10-3-1754 d 11-1-1814 m Elizabeth Blasdell Pvt NH
Benjamin: b 1755 d *p.* 1796 m (1)Sibbie Chocke (2)Mary — Capt NC
Benjamin: b — d 1789 m — X — PS SC
Benoni: b 7-10-1745 d 4-11-1812 m Anna Comstock Sgt CT
Charles: b 4-19-1752 d *p.* 4-12-1842 m — X — Pvt NC ★
Charles: b 1757 d *p.* 10-29-1838 m Catherine — Pvt VA ★
Charles: b 1760 d 2-8-1828 m Jean Carlisle Anderson Pvt VA
Charles: b 10-10-1743 d *a.* 12-29-1781 m — X — Sol PS VA
Charles: b 1732 d 1806 m(1)Mary Walker(2)Ann Butler Moore PS VA
Churchill: b 10-10-1746 d 10-4-1820 m Leah — Pvt SC
Dale: b 1708-10 d *p.* 12-11-1776 m (1) — Edwards (2)Mrs Elizabeth Stradford PS VA
Daniel: b 5-29-1744 d *p.* 1797 m Jemima Merriman PS Cpl CT
Daniel: b 9-19-1749 d 1834 m Mary Runnells Sgt NH
Daniel: b 4-8-1719 d *p.* 1782 m Hannah Fowler PS NH
Daniel: b *c.* 1745 d *a.*5-20-1789 m Elizabeth Stiles Pvt NJ
Daniel: b 1757 d 7-7-1802 m Annie Lawrence Pvt NY
Daniel: b 11-27-1761 d 6-22-1844 m Sarah Conyers Lt SC ★
David: b 12-30-1746 d 10-8-1790 m Thankful — Pvt CT
David: b 10-5-1744 d 1-2-1812 m Mary Garrigues Cpl NJ
David: b 1758 d 12-16-1849 m Mehitable Cobb Pvt NC ★
Edward: b 1743 d *p.* 7-24-1820 m Esther Powers Pvt NH
Edward: b 5-29-1761 d 3-11-1838 m Mary Brown Sgt NC
Edward: b *c.* 1710 d *p.* 4-1-1783 m Catherine Brent PS VA
Edward: b 1726 d 1792 m Sarah Champ PS VA
Eleazer: b 8-23-1740 d 2-7-1777 m Elizabeth Buell Lt CT
Elias: b 11-24-1737 d 12-21-1821 m Deborah White Sol MA
Elihu: b 1-20-1759 d 5-22-1844 m (2)Sarah Hopkins Pvt CT
Elijah: b 2-26-1742/3 d 12-19-1813 m Jane Goodridge CS MA
Elijah: b 1-16-1762 d 6-20-1834 m Sarah Ballard Sol NY
Enoch: b 3-1-1757 d 5-14-1831 m Olive Woodward Pvt CT
Enoch: b *c.* 1741 d 1792 m Sarah Rivers Sol PS NY
Ephraim: b 11-14-1748 d 5-7-1817 m Joanna Wheelock Ens MA
Ephraim: b 1742 d 1-8-1826 m Mary Waterhouse Pvt MA
Ephraim: b 10-21-1746 d 1796 m Dorcas Hall Pvt NH
Ezekiel: b 5-4-1734 d 10-2-1804 m Eleanor Eastman 2Lt PS NH
Ezekiel: b 3-31-1763 d 10-17-1833 m Ann Brookover Sol VA
Ezra: b 2-26-1746 d 2-11-1827 m Hannah — Pvt MA
Frederick: b 1752 d *p.* 1790 m Annis Carter Pvt CT
George: b 1742 d 1822 m — X — Pvt SC
George: b 1740-46 d *p.* 1807 m Mary — Capt CS VA
George: b 12-18-1728 d 1788 m Frances Diana Goodloe Pvt VA
Hannah Benedict: b 1733 d 1780 m John Carter PS CT
Heman: b 1-1763 d 6-15-1847 m Marion Cass Sgt CT
Henry: b 1751 d 5-23-1843 m Nancy Edwards Pvt VA ★
Isaac: b 1756 d 7-8-1792 m Ruth — Capt NC
Isaac: b 1764 d 3-24-1834 m Ann Elizabeth Young Pvt NC ★
Israel: b 3-28-1742 d *p.* 1786 m Jerusha Rust Lt CT
Ithiel: b 8-1-1753 d 10-8-1827 m Lois Deming Arfr Pvt CT W ★
Jabez: b 4-10-1757 d 10-22-1845 m Mary Bennett Pvt NY
Jacob, Sr.: b 11-26-1716 d 7-6-1796 m Mary Barnes PS CS CT

Jacob, Jr.: b 5-1-1745 d 1-24-1831 m Mary Hitchcock Pvt CT
Jacob: b 1755 d 1-7-1805 m Sarah Eastman Drm NH
James: b 1750 d 9-18-1780 m Mary Martin Maj GA
James: b 11-2-1758 d *p.* 1833 m Eleanor Knott Pvt MD ★
James: b 2-11-1740 d 6-20-1818 m Lydia Day Pvt MA
James: b 6-8-1757 d 10-16-1847 m (1)Hannah Buck (2)Mehitable Straw (3)Abi Wheeler Pvt MA
James: b 10-14-1750 d 8-15-1817 m Ann Bowen Sol PA
James: b 8-19-1732 d 10-25-1798 m Ann — PS VA
Jesse: b 1746 d *p.* 1786 m Lydia Skipper Pvt SC
Jesse, Sr.: b 1737 d 1811 m (1)Susan Saterwhite (2)Mary Chattin Pvt VA
Jesse, Jr.: b 1762 d 1815 m (3)Sarah Brown Pvt VA
Jesse D.: b *c.* 1760 d 4-24-1853 m (1)Mary D. Haines (2)Sarah Dyehouse (3)Mary Sword (4)Mrs Anna S. White Pvt VA
Jiles: b 1760 d 5-2-1846 m (1)Mary Dubose (2)Mary Ingram Pvt NC
Joel: b 5-9-1749 d — m Sarah Jenkins Pvt MA
Joel: b 12-19-1764 d 10-10-1845 m Sarah Hyde Pvt MA
John: b 6-18-1736 d 12-29-1816 m (1)Bethiah Tiffany (2)Mary Curtis Capt CT
John: b 2-22-1730 d 1-2-1819 m Hannah Benedict Capt CT
John: b 1758 d 9-11-1834 m Lucinda Pratt Pvt CT
John: b 12- -1759 d 9-18-1843 m Susanna Bliss Sgt CT ★
John: b 3-14-1757 d *c.* 1823 m Hannah Scarborough Cpl MD
John, Sr.: b 9-13-1748 d 3-2-1824 m (1)Lydia Nichols (2)Sarah Cooper CS MA
John: b 6- -1759 d 11-7-1847 m (1)Betsey Brown (2)Lucy (Cavis) Wells Pvt NH ★
John: b 1730 d 1785 m Elizabeth Taylor CS Col VA
John, Jr.: b 1740/41 d *p.* 1806 m Mary St John Capt VA
John: b 12- -1760 d 8-28-1820 m Anna Matilda Wray Capt VA
John: b 8-26-1737 d *p.* 6-18-1781 m Mary — Sol VA
John: b 1-11-1760 d 5-3-1806 m Elizabeth Nash Pvt VA
John: b *c.* 1715 d 1783 m (1)Elizabeth Armistead (2)Hannah Chew PS VA
John: b 1740 d 1792 m Jane Michel PS VA
John B.: b 2-10-1768 d 2-2.1839 m Elizabeth Mosby Wgm VA ★
John C: b 1764 d 1-3-1838 m Nancy Thomas Sol VA
John Champ: b 7-25-1758 d 4-5-1826 m Apphia Fauntleroy Capt VA
Jonah: b *c.* 1763 d 2-1-1839 m (1)Charlotte De Angelis (2)Tempa (Hitchcock) Allen Pvt CT ★
Jonas: b 1762 d 9-20-1837 m Rachel Wadsworth Pvt MA ★
Jonathan: b 5-20-1751 d 8-6-1817 m Abigal Multhrop Pvt CT
Jonathan, Sr.: b 2-17-1715 d 3-12-1793 m (1)Susanna Curtis (2)Eunice Kendall (3)Deborah Hunt Lt MA
Jonathan, Jr.: b 10-15-1744 d 6-12-1819 m (1)Deborah Hunt (2)Hannah Stevens Pvt MA
Jonathan: b 12-16-1739 d 5-20-1790 m Sybil Johnson Pvt MA
Joseph, Sr.: b 9-13-1731 d 8-26-1824 m Ruth Curtice Capt CT
Joseph: b 7-18-1736 d 8-5-1796 m Patience Pellet QM CT
Joseph: b 8-7-1740 d 1-17-1823 m Sarah — 2Lt MA
Joseph: b 11-17-1745 d 6-17-1804 m (1)Beulah Carter (2)Anna Smith PS MA
Joseph: b 12-19-1747 d 8-4-1818 m Mary(Carroll)Scott Pvt CL VA
Joseph: b 9-4-1736 d *a.* 8-1-1809 m Elizabeth Presley Pvt VA
Joseph: b 1760 d 9-18-1833 m Elizabeth Pierce Pvt VA
Joseph: b *c.* 1760 d *p.* 2-25-1845 m Madgalen Chastain Pvt VA
Joseph: b 12-20-1760 d 8-20-1846 m (1)Jane Shelton (2)Anne Winlock Pvt VA ★
Joshua: b 5-28-1759 d 6-6-1846 m (1)Rachel Putnam (2)Sarah Putnam Sgt MA
Josiah: b 1735 d *p.* 1827 m Mary Anthony Pvt GA
Josiah, Sr.: b1-26-1762 d 2-13/14-1812 m Tabitha Hough Col MA
Josiah, Jr.: b 1-29-1749 d 7-19-1827 m Elizabeth Graves Sgt MA
Josiah: b 3-14-1738 d 7-19-1827 m Sarah Williams Lt MA
Landon: b 1-29-1760 d 6-5-1800 m Elizabeth Maclin Capt SC
Landon, Sr.: b 6-7-1709 d 8-10-1778 m(1)Elizabeth Wormley (2)Maria Byrd (3)Elizabeth Beale PS VA
Landon, Jr.: b 8- -1737/8 d *a.* 7-6-1801 m Judith Fauntleroy Sol PS VA
Levi: b 3-28-1748 d *p.* 1782 m Silence Beaman Pvt MA
Matthew: b *c.* 1750 d 4-2-1812 m Casandra Barber Pvt NC
Merryman: b *c.* 1736 d 1816-18 m Frances Leftwich PS VA
Nathan: b 4-16-1748 d 5-21-1810 m Mary Squires Pvt CT
Nathan, Sr.: b 1-2-1728 d 7-21-1807 m Martha Jones Pvt MA
Nathan, Jr.: b 11-15-1753 d 2-18-1835 m Beulah Butters Pvt MA
Obadiah: b *c.* 1750 d 7-28-1820 m Judiath (Carter) Sgt VA
Oliver: b 10-5-1763 d 4-5-1812 m Jane Stuart Pvt MA
Peter: b 5-23-1706 d 12- -1789 m Judith Norris PS VA
Peter: b 3-9-1743 d *c.* 1- -1791 m Mary Anne Ellis Pvt VA
Philip: b 3-16-1766 d *p.* 10-15-1832 m Dicie Coats Pvt VA ★
Phineas: b 12-5-1727 d 12-16-1809 m Mary Sawyer 2Lt MA
Povall: b 1762 d *p.* 11-2-1826 m Martha Davis Pvt VA ★
Raleigh: b 1764 d *p.* 5-18-1820 m (1)Sarah Sharpe (2)Lucy Ann Crenshaw PS VA
Rebecca Cutter Hill: b 7-13-1712 d 2-1-1797 m (1)Zachariah Hill (2)Capt Samuel Carter PS MA
Richard, Sr.: b *c.* 1735 d *p.* 1782 m Frances — CS PS MD
Richard, Jr.: b 9-6-1759 d 10- -1835 m Mary Beall Pvt Ordl MD
Richard: b *c.* 1750 d *p.* 1- -1796 m Susannah — PS VA
Richard: b — d 12-1-1806 m Catherine — Pvt VA
Robert: b 8-12-1735 d 1784 m X Pvt NC
Robert: b *c.* 1745 d *p.* 2-19-1829 m Susannah — Sol VA

CARTER, contd.
Robert: b 2- -1728 d 3- -1804 m Frances Tasker PS VA
Robert William: b 1757 d 1824 m Jane Thomas Sol SC
Samuel, Sr.: b 5-31-1734 d 4-1-1822 m Martha Buell Lt CT
Samuel, Jr.: b 4-5-1760 d 3-22-1813 m Sarah Newcomb Pvt CT
Samuel: b 1730 d 12-8-1796 m Mary Irons Sgt MD
Samuel: b 1-7-1737 d 7-15-1808 m (1)Charity Van Norstrand
    Carter (2)Mary Briggs Pvt MA
Samuel: b 3-19-1753 d 1818 m Sarah Rand Pvt MA
Samuel: b 10-22-1752 d 4-25-1813 m Elizabeth Holley Keene Cpl NC
Samuel: b 1740 d 1812 m Lettia — PS NC
Silas: b 1-16-1740 d 1-4-1820 m (1)Lucy Sawyer (2)Mary May Pvt MA
Solomon: b 9-25-1739 d 9-28-1786 m Mary Ann Bickley PS VA
Stanton: b 2-5-1738 d 10- -1823 m Peninah Albert Pvt MA
Stephen: b 7-12-1741 d 1826/7 m Mehitable Davison 2Lt CS NH
Stephen: b c. 1755 d 1790 m Elizabeth Gerard Pvt NJ
Theodric: b a. 1747 d a. 7-13-1805 m (1)Miss Townes (2) Judith
    Cunningham PS VA
Thomas: 1750 d 1810 m Mary — Pvt SC & GA
Thomas: b 1752 d 1851 m (1)Sally Calhoun (3)Margaret Oraninger
    Pvt PA★
Thomas: b 1752 d 1817 m Susanna Gaines Capt PS VA
Thomas: b 3-20-1758 d 6-6-1792 m Ann Betts Gr VA & MD
Thomas: b 11-27-1734 d 7-15-1817 m Winifred Hobson Sol VA
Thomas: b 1759 d 1800 m Ann Brodnax Dr. VA
Thomas: b 4-24-1731 d 1803 m Elizabeth Morgan PS CS VA
Thomas A.: b 1750 d 1811 m (1)Lucy Faris(2)Elizabeth Stubbs Pvt VA
William: b c. 1717 d p. 12-21-1781 m Ann Haile Pvt MD
William, Sr.: b 3-28-1729 d 12-21-1783 m Abigail Bacon Capt MA
Wm., Jr.: b 11-5-1752 d 10-15-1842 m Hannah Mayhew Pvt MA ★
William: b 5-2-1748 d 9-21-1840 m X Pvt Tms PA ★
William: b 1732 d 6-12-1799 m Rebecca Edloe Dr. VA
Wm.: b 8-21-1760 d 10-14-1842 m Sarah(Evans)Williams Pvt VA ★
William: b 1750 d 1807 m Elizabeth Hobson Lt VA
Winthrop: b 1736 d 6-8-1808 m Susannah Eastman Lt PS NH
Wormley: b 1762 d 1815 m Sarah Edwards PS VA

CARTLEDGE,
Samuel, Sr.: b c. 1750 d 1843 m (1) X (2) X Pvt GA

CARTMELL, (includes CARTMILL)
Henry: b 1754 d p. 11-14-1838 m Sarah Anderson 1Lt VA
John: b c. 1750 d c. 1824 m X Capt VA
Nathaniel: b c. 1725 d 10-6-1795 m Sarah — Pvt PS VA
Thomas: b — d 1808 m Ann Hite Pvt VA

CARTWRIGHT, (includes CUTRIGHT)
Benjamin: b c. 1735 d 1790 m Mary — PS VA
Christopher: b 1763 d 3-7-1838 m Sarah — Pvt NY★
Cyrus: b 1759 d 2-27-1825 m Mary Varnis Pvt CT ★
Hezekiah: b 10-11-1761 d 8-5-1818 m (1)Hannah Lavender
    (2)Elizabeth Maholland Pvt NC
John: b 8- -1754 d 3-8-1850 m Rebecca Truby Pvt VA ★
John: b 1760 d p. 12-27-1830 m Elizabeth Subre Pvt VA
Justinian: b 2-22-1752 d 12-27-1832 m Frances Gillaspie Sgt VA ★
Matthew: b 2-20-1754 d 2-21-1812 m Polly Ginnes PS NC
Peter: b 1748 d 1808 m Christian Garbin Sol VA
Robert: b 2-22-1722 d 12-24-1809 m (1)Anne Huggins (2)Mary
    Hunter (3)Anne Pembroke Hunter Sol PS NC
Samuel: b 1741 d 1-17-1819 m Abiel — Pvt CT
Samuel: b 1745 d p. 4- -1828 m Rachel — Sol VA
Thomas: b 1755 d 1805 m Mary — Pvt NC

CARTY,
Henry: b — d a. 6- -1809 m Frances — Sol VA
John, 3d: b 1-13-1764 d 11-25-1845 m Mary Ayers Sol KY

CARVELL,
Henry: b 1755 d 7-12-1823 m Mercy Dyer Pvt MA ★

CARVER,
Aldric: b 7-4-1761 d 11-26-1828 m Asenath Tarbox Pvt CT ★
Caspar: b c. 1740 d 4- -1802 m X Pvt PA
Christian: b 1759 d 3-14-1836 m (1)Magdalina Ziegler (2)Mary
    Siegler Pvt NC ★
David: b — d — m Hannah Dyer Pvt CT
Eleazer: b — d — m Sarah Keith Adj Dr MA
Gideon: b c. 1750 d 3-1-1831 m Abigail Hovey Pvt CT
Job: b 10-1-1749 d 1-30-1799 m Elizabeth Jennings PS CS NC
John: b 11-30-1738 d 8-3-1803 m (2)Bathsheba Edson Fif Pvt MA
John: b 6-4-1753 d 1809 m Ann Carver Pvt PA
John: b 1758 d 1840 m Tilitha Mitchell Pvt VA
Jonathan: b 7-30-1729 d 1-13-1807 m Abigail Robins Capt MA
Joseph: b 3-23-1727 d 1-6-1787 m Sarah Hartwell Ens MA
Joseph: b 1720 d 1797 m (1)Martha Lowther (2)Hannah
    Worthington Pvt PA
Nathaniel: b 8-19-1752 d 4-14-1805 m Lydia Edgerton Pvt CT
Rufus: b 12-13-1755 d 3-20-1840 m Priscilla Cummings Pvt MA ★
Sampson: b c. 1750 -60 d a. 1840 m Rhoda Edmondson Pvt NC
Samuel: bc. 1730 d 9-8-1817 m Rachel Loomis 2Lt CT
Timothy, Jr.: b 10-30-1753 d 11-3-1824 m (1)Phebe Baldwin
    (2)Hannah Baldwin Pvt NY
Wm.: b 4- -1753 d 3-29-1836 m Elizabeth Carver Pvt MM NC ★

CARWILE,
Zachariah: b 9-11-1750 d 8-4-1841 m Mary McMahan Pvt NC SC ★

CARY, (includes CAREY)
Abel: b 1744 d 1815 m Elizabeth — Pvt NJ
Abraham: b 1762 d 1816 m —X— Pvt NJ
Absalom: b 4-9-1766 d 12-30-1841 m Temperance Cooley Pvt NY ★
Alpheus: b 4-21-1761 d 11-1-1816 m Ruby Perkins Pvt MA
Anson: b 3-15-1762 d 5-3-1842 m Hannah Cary Pvt CT ★
Archibald: b 2-4-1721 d 2-26-1787 m Mary Randolph PS VA
Barnabas: b 1733 d 1795 m Mary Short Sol NH
Benjamin: b 1763 d 8-3-1830 m Mercy Abbott Grd PA
Christopher: b 2-25-1763 d 2-6-1837 m (1)Elsie Terril (2)Leah
    Brakaw (3)Margaret McCarty Pvt NH
Daniel: b 6-11-1758 d 1820 m Mehitable Brett Pvt MA
Daniel: b 1762 d 1791 m Phebe Doty Sol MA
Dudley: b 1756 d a. 1-27-1804 m Lucy Tabb Lt VA
Ebenezer: b 2-28-1745 d 5-18-1815 m (1)Mary Bentley (2)Delight
    Champlin Dr PS NY
Edward: b 10-13-1737 d 6-6-1782 m Susanna Brown Pvt MD
Eleazer: b 3-5-1718/9 d c. 1779 m Charity Sturdevant PS PA
Elihu: b c. 1740 d p. 1790 m Catharine North Pvt NY
Ephraim: b 7-7-1748 m Jane Holman Pvt MA
Ezra: b 4-7-1749 d 2-28-1847 m Cynthia Tolman Sgt MA
Henry: b 6-6-1711 d 1801 m Abigail Paul PS NY
Isaac: b 2-1-1742 d 1791 m Eunice Beardsley Sol NJ
Jabez, Sr.: b 7-30-1727 d p. 1790 m Martha Gilbert Pvt CT
James: b 11-27-1750 d 2-28-1827 m (1)Abigail Kingsley (2)Anna
    (Spaulding) Bradford Sgt CT
James: b 1752 d 1816 m Sarah Roberts 1 Lt MA
James: b 9-29-1728 d p. 5-28-1785 m Annie Taplin Drm NY
James: b 1762 d 10- -1855 m (2)Mary Hendricks Pvt SC
John: b 2-28-1755 d 4-2-1823 m Mary Rude Sgt CT
John: b 5-7-1756 d 9-15-1844 m (1)Susannah (Greene) Mann
    (2)Mrs Catherine Christman Pvt CT ★
John: b 7-25-1757 d 11-29-1824 m Joanna Lyon PS NJ
John: b 4-25-1753 d 11-20-1839 m Mary Reed Cpl PA ★
John: b 4-29-1753 d 1-8-1828 m Lucy McKay Pvt PA
John: b c. 1760 d 1826 m —X— PS PA
John: b 1745 d 1795 m (1)Sally Sclater (2)Susanna Armistead Capt
    PS VA
John: b 5-9-1760 d a. 2-8-1823 m Eliza Williams Sol VA
John: b 1722 d c. 1800 m Dorothea Dudley Lt VA
Jonathan: b 6-5-1749 d p. 1793 m Martha Hurlburt Sgt CT
Jonathan: b 4-30-1717 d 12-29-1801 m Elizabeth Procter Capt MA
Jonathan: b 3-26-1723 d 2-2-1813 m Mary Curtis Pvt MA
Jonathan: b 2-14-1757 d 12-25-1852 m Abigail Perkins Pvt MA ★
Joseph: b 1736 d 1818 m (1)Ruth Carew (2)Zeruiah Hutchins Pvt CT
Joseph: b 5-6-1760 d 11-19-1841 m Sarah Bostwick Pvt CT ★
Joseph: b 3-7-1757 d 2-3-1848 m Rachel Thompson Pvt MA ★
Joseph: b 2-22-1732 d 1814 m (1)Abigail Hebard (2)—X— Pvt NY
Josiah, Jr.: b 1761 d 1807 m Lydia Clark Pvt CT
Levi: b 2-26-1756 d 2-6-1845 m Ruth Goodrich Pvt Arfr CT
Lewis: b 10-23-1742 d 9-27-1817 m (1)X (2)Isabella Carson
    Matr NJ
Luther: b 1761 d 1848 m Abigail King Fif MA
Luther: b 7-8-1752 d 10-8-1834 m Rhoda Leonard Pvt PA
Michael: b 1756 d 1832 m —X— Pvt MD ★
Nathan: b 10- -1751 d 3-18-1835 m Jane Mann Pvt MA
Nathaniel, Sr.: b 10-23-1729 d p. 1786 m (1)Dorcas Marcy
    (2)Sarah Sargent (3)Mrs Tabitha Root Sgt CT
Nathaniel: b 11-1-1731 d 11-22-1776 m Jerusha Downer Pvt CT
Peter: b 1760 d 4-23-1832 m Beulah Pratt Pvt MA ★
Phineas: b 10-7-1746 d 10-29-1824 m Mary Hurlburt Mar CT
Reuben: b 1744 d 1819 m — Smith Cpl MA
Richard: b 1-15-1759 d 12- -1841 m (1)Susanna Ford (2)Mrs Lucy
    Doolittle Pvt CT
Richard: b 1-13-1747 d 12-15-1806 m (1)Anna Phillips (2)Anne
    Louise Low ADC LCol NY
Richard: b 1739 d 11-3-1789 m Mary Cole Capt PS VA
Robert Philipson: b 1763 d p. 2-13-1819 m Martha North Pvt VA
Samuel: b 4-2-1752 d 9-26-1823 m Rachel Doane Pvt PA
Samuel: b 8-12-1758 d 4-23-1843 m (1) Mrs Rosanna Cary Slocum
    (2)Theresa (Gore)Clark Pvt PA
Seth: b 4-3-1747 d 12-31-1829 m Lydia — Pvt MA ★
Simeon: b 12-6-1719 d 1802 m Mary Howard Col MA
Thomas: b 1734 d 1790-92 (1) — Whitaker (2)Frances Godwyn
    Capt VA
Wm.: b 6-19-1760 d 10-12-1806 m Maria Barbara Fritchie Pvt MD
William: b 1723 d p. 1799 m Esther Frost Pvt MA
William: b 10-28-1729 d 5-7-1808 m Eunice Webb Capt PS NH
Wilson: b 1760 d 1793 m Jean Barbra Carr 2Lt VA
Wilson Miles: b 1734 d 12-1-1817 m (1)Sarah Blair (2)Rebecca
    Dawson PS Col VA

CASE, (includes KAAS, KEHS)
Aaron: b 6-6-1755 d 3-24-1811 m Margaret Meacham Pvt CT
Abel, Sr.: b 1748 d 1834 m Huldah Higley Pvt CT
Abner: b 8-14-1752 d 10-6-1807 m Hannah — Pvt CT
Absalom: b 6-16-1759 d 6-21-1828 m Sarah Elizabeth Dunn Pvt MA
Adam: b 3-6-1760 d 8-19-1832 m (1)Alcie Cornell (2)Hannah
    Wickham Pvt MA

Amasa, Sr.: b 10-18-1731 d 8-8-1824 m (1)Elizabeth Hoskins
  (2)Elizabeth Viets (3)Abigail (Phelps) Griswold (4)Charity (Pettibone)
  Cornish (5)Sarah (Humphrey) Graham Pvt CT
Amasa, Jr.: b 10-29-1753 d 6-23-1834 m Mercy Hillger Pvt CT
Asa: b 12-9-1758 d 2-26-1837 m (1)Lois Dill (2)Mrs Thede (Case)
  Humphrey Pvt CT
Asahel: b 3-23-1729 d 1809 m Dorothy Phelps Pvt CS CT
Augustus: b 7-17-1759 d 3-24-1852 m Elizabeth Bell Pvt NJ ★
Benajah: b 8-10-1738 d p. 1790 m Lydia Woodruff Pvt CT
Benjamin: b 2-25-1734 d 3-27-1801 m Abigail Richardson Sgt CT
Caleb: b 1754 d — m (1)Sarah Case (2)Rhoda (Mills) Case Pvt CT
Charles, Sr.: b 7-1-1723 d 10-17-1808 m Phebe Holcomb Sol CT
Charles 2d: b 7-19-1754 d 1828 m Deborah Veits Cnt CT
Daniel: b 1-30-1720 d 5-24-1801 m Mary Watson Pvt CT
Darius: b 1756 d 1801 m Mary Giddings Pvt CT
Darius: b 7-9-1757 d 5-23-1797 m Hepzibah Foote Pvt CT
Dudley: b 1722 d 1792 m Dorcas Humphrey Sgt CT
Edward: b 4-15-1748 d 12-2-1822 m Jeruah Lawrence Pvt CT
Elisha: b 12-10-1747 d 1808 m Judith Humphrey Pvt CT
Ezra: b 9-15-1757 d 1-24-1815 m Mehitable — Pvt CT
Fithen: b 9-17-1758 d 8-25-1829 m Amarilla Humphrey Pvt CT
Giles: b 5-24-1757 d 10-5-1831 m Dorcas Humphrey Cpl CT ★
Hosea: b 8-6-1756 d 10-11-1834 m (1)Rhoda Case (2)Sarah Buell
  Pvt CT ★
Ichabod: b 3-29-1752 d p. 7-17-1801 m (1)Sarah Smith (2)Mary
  Corwin Pvt NY
Immanuel, Jr.: b 11-8-1739 d p. 1782 m (1)Ann Rathbun (2)Lydia
  Allen CS RI
Isaac, Sr.: b 10-16-1717 d 1-3-1796 m Bathsheba Humphrey Pvt CT
Isaac: b 2-25-1762 d 11-3-1852 m Joanna Snow Pvt MA
Israel: b 11-14-1757 d p. 1815 m Joanna Case Pvt CT
James: b 4-2-1744 d 1-7-1822 m Lydia Case Lt MA
Jedediah, Sr.: b 3-30-1733 d 1-11-1818 m Mercy Hart Pvt NY
Jeremiah, Jr.: b 3-18-1747 d c.1805 m Sarah Phelps Pvt CT
Jesse: b 5-19-1738 d 10-3-1807 m Sarah Humphrey Cpl CT
Job: b 6-3-1737 d 5-6-1798 m Joanna Wilcox Capt CT
John: b 1754 d 10-12-1838 m Nancy — Pvt NJ
John M.: b 3-13-1763 d 6-28-1847 m Abigail Wadsworth Pvt CT
  W ★
Joseph: b 1731 d 3-28-1809 m (1)Vashti Morton(2)Susanna —PS CT
Joseph: b 1747 d 2-5-1811 m Esther Budd 2Lt NY
Joshua: b 1722 d 7-9-1777 m Elizabeth Dickerson Pvt NJ
Martin: b 3-27-1730 d 4-18-1827 m Lucy Adams Pvt CT
Micah: b 7-10-1759 d 6-22-1834 m Catherine — Pvt CT ★
Moses: b 9-9-1723 d 9-25-1814 m Mary Hutchinson PS NY
Nathan, Jr.: b 1740 d 1796 m Elizabeth Mussey Pvt NY
Nathaniel: b 10-31-1748 d 3-13-1831 m Sarah Carr Pvt PS CS RI
Oliver: b 6-1-1761 d 2-12-1836 m Amy Case Pvt CT ★
Peter: b c. 1731 d p. 10-13-1793 m Anna Margaret Fues Pvt PA
Philip: b 2-12-1731/2 d 1814 m Lydia Soveril Pvt MA
Richard: b 6-7-1734 d 4-7-1805 m (1)Ruth Case (2)Mary Case Ens CT
Roger: b 8-3-1734 d p. 1790 m Mindwell Buel Lt CT
Roger: b 5-25-1745 d 11-11-1827 m Molly Owen Pvt CT
Simeon: b 7-4-1739 d 10-19-1823 m Mary — Pvt CT
Solomon: b 3-11-1735 d 7-3-1811 m Anna Case Sgt CT
Stephen: b 6-21-1746 d 11-26-1794 m Glorianna — Capt NY
Timothy: b 9-28-1759 d 7-30-1844 m (1)Dernis — (2)Annry Curtis
  Pvt MA ★
Uriah: b 1-16-1744 d 12-23-1826 m (1)Susannah Lawrence
  (2)Eunice Dill QM CT
William: b 5-23-1751 d 1807 m Sarah Hickox Pvt CT
William: b 8-14-1744 d 10-29-1836 m Mary Pease Lt MA
William: b 1753 d 11-1-1827 m Rebecca Glover Pvt VA PA CT ★
Zaccheus: b 1728 d 1812 m Abigail Barber Capt CT
Zenas: b 9-10-1751 d — m Margaret Peters Pvt NH

CASEY, (includes CAYCE)
Archibald: b c. 1756 d 3-16-1820 m Phebe Farmer Pvt VA
Benjamin: b 1-21-1731 d 4-4-1779 m Julia Carson Capt VA
Christopher: b 1755 d 8-2-1840 m Sarah Smith Lt SC ★
Edward: b 9-8-1757 d 5-23-1817 m Martha Stearns Pvt RI
Joseph: b 1763 d 1846 m — Blackwood Sgt PA ★
Levi: b 1749 d 2-1-1807 m Elizabeth Duckett LCol PS SC
Nicholas: b 1-7-1745 d 5-10-1833 m Grace Forman Pvt VA
Peter: b c. 1759 d 1828 m Nancy Waggener CS KY
Peter, Sr.: b c. 1715 d 1787 m (1)Mary Magdalin Depew (2)Mrs
  Mary Williams PS VA
Randolph: b 1738 d 1813 m Mary Jane Pennington Sgt SC
Shadrack: b c. 1754 d p. 1794 m Ann — CS VA
Silas: b 6-5-1734 d 9-22-1814 m Abigail Coggeshall PS RI
Thomas: b 1741 d 11-18-1823 m Elizabeth Wightman Sol NY
Wanton: b 2-24-1760 d 12-17-1842 m Elizabeth Goodale Pvt RI
William: b 1759 d 1843 m Margaret — Pvt SC NC ★
William: b 1761 d 12-1-1820 m Jane Montgomery Sgt VA

CASH,
Howard: b — d p. 7-6-1843 m (1)Lucy — (2)Easter — Pvt VA
John: b a. 1726 d 1805 m Rachel Dawson Pvt VA
John: b 4-5-1757 d 8-13-1836 m Lucy Campbell Pvt VA ★
Warren: b 4-4-1760 d 9-15-1850 m Susanna Basket Pvt VA ★
William: b 1756 d c. 1855 m Nancy Cash Pvt MD ★
William: b 1752 d 6-14-1837 m Dorothy Irwin Pvt VA ★

CASHELL,
George: b 1748 d 1802 m Mary Wade PS Pvt MD

CASHION,
Burrel: b 1758 d 9- -1843 m Judy— Pvt VA ★

CASHO,
Jacob: b 1750 d 3-18-1823 m Elizabeth Critzen Interpreter for La
  Fayette DE

CASKY,
Joseph: b 1749 d 2-15-1847 m Lucy Lewis Sgt PA

CASLER, (includes KESLAER, KESLER & KESSLER)
Conrad: b 3-21-1747 d 8-6-1818 m Maria Catharine Crim Cpl NY
George: b 1746 d 2-21-1813 m (1) —X—(2)Barbara Braucher Pvt PA
Jacob: b 1737 d 1830 m Mary Catherine Petre Pvt NY
Jacob: b 1753 d 4-1-1822 m Elizabeth Miller Pvt NY
Jacob: 7-14-1757 d 8-12-1843 m Katherine — Pvt NC ★
Johannes: b c. 1741 d p. 3-24-1795 m Gertrude Helmer Pvt NY
John, Sr.: b 3-8-1728 d 3-24-1823 m Dorothea Leyman PS MD
John: b 3-20-1755 d 1816 m Catherine Shoemaker Pvt NY
John, Jr.: b 2-2-1761 d p. 2-15-1840 m Elizabeth — Pvt MD
John: b 9-21-1761 d 3-17-1840 m (1)Abigail Anderson (2)Mrs
  Martha Berrill Shriver Mid Pvt PA
Mathias: b c. 1760-2 d a. 3-28-1818 m (2)Barbary Neff Pvt PA
Richard: b 4-14-1767 d 9-15-1855 m Margaret — Pvt NY ★

CASON, (includes CASSON)
James: b 7-23-1758 d 1840 m Rebecca Smith Pvt VA
James, Sr.: b — d p. 9-4-1783 m Dinah — PS VA
Miers: b 1741 d 9- -1844 m (1)Annaka Marim (2)Rebecca
  Derborough (3)Sarah Barber Sol CS DE
William: b 4-10-1749 d 1-1-1847 m (1)Nancy Roberts (2)Janette
  Rodgers Pvt SC ★
William: b 1760 d 1- -1846 m Lucy McGehee Pvt VA ★

CASPER,
John: b 1745 d 1820 m Martha Biddle Pvt PA ★
Lawrence: b c. 1740 d p. 10-18-1809 m Margaret Halder PS NJ

CASS,
Aaron: b 12-25-1761 d 1812 m Ruth Bull Pvt CT
Benjamin: b 1-30-1738 d 1-14-1804 m Elizabeth — 2Lt NH
Daniel: b 11-29-1724 d 10- -1798 m Mary Cook Pvt PS NH
Daniel: b 1747 d 10-11-1801 m Abigail Fogg Sgt NH
John: b 12-30-1761 d c. 1835 m Joanna Hunt Pvt MA
Jonathan: b 10-9-1753 d 8-9-1830 m (1)X (2)Mary Gilman Capt NH
Jonathan: b 1737 d 2-14-1816 m Sarah Eastman PS NH
Joseph: b 8-21-1731 d 1807 m (1)Sarah Flanders (2)Miriam
  Flanders (3)Hannah Sanborn Sgt CS NH
Moses: b 6-6-1749 d 9- -1776 m Abia Sturtevant Pvt CT
Moses: b 3-16-1729 d 5-9-1817 m (1)Molly French (2)Hannah
  Cinlley (3)Mrs Sarah (Ring) Berry Pvt NH
Nason: b 5-24-1751 d 9-22-1819 m Sarah Hoyt Cpl NH
Theophilus: b 3-18-1756 d 11-6-1845 m Susanna Libbee Sgt NH ★

CASSELL, (includes CASSEL, CASSELS)
Abram: b 9-25-1756 d 5-26-1844 m Catherine Lingenfelder Pvt MD ★
Benjamin: b 1754 d p. 3-23-1852 m — Porter Pvt SC
Hupert: b 8-13-1751 d 1840 m Magdalena Johnson Pvt PA
Isreal: b 1728/9 d 9-20-1799 m Rebecca Atkinson Pvt PA
Jacob: b 10- -1734 d 2-12-1818 m Margaret Burkhart PS MD
Johannes: b 3-17-1732 d 4-17-1815 m Maria Gertraud PS PA
John: b 1725 d p. 1803 m Rebecca — PS MD

CASSIDY, (includes CASSADA, CASSADY)
James: b 1757-60 d 6-15-1852 m Mary Willard Pvt VA ★
John: b — d 8-1-1805 m Margaret Van Antwerp Pvt NY W★
Michael: b 10-20-1755 d 3-22-1829 m Mary Ann (Evans) Givens
  Pvt VA W★
Patrick: b 1744 d 1828 m — Mooney Pvt PA
Thomas: b p. 1757 d 9-6-1825 m Margaret McGriff Hale Pvt VA
William: b 3- -1761 d 7-12-1847 m Hannah Dees Pvt VA

CASSIN, (includes CASSAN)
John: b 1758 d 3-24-1822 m Ann Wilcox NS & Pvt PA
Samuel: b 1745 d 1803 m Hannah Price Cdr NS PA

CASSLE,
Jacob: b 6- -1760 d 9-29-1845 m Elizabeth Johnson Pvt PA

CASTAING,
Peter: b c. 1740 d 1800 m Maria — Lt ADC MA

CASTEEL,
Samuel: b 1741 d c. 1820 m Nancy — Pvt PA ★

CASTELLOW,
James: b c. 1745 d p. 8-10-1785 m Priscilla — Pvt SC

CASTERER,
John: b 7-16-1748 d 3-4-1835 m Anna Calkins Ens NY ★

CASTERLINE,
Benjamin: b 6-4-1749 d 1-4-1828 m Ruth Mathers Pvt NJ
Loammi: b 4-14-1763 d 12-14-1835 m Charlotte Fairchild Pvt NJ ★

CASTLE,
Abel: b 2-25-1749 d 6-15-1843 m (1)— Hurlburt (2)Desire Hawley (3)Sarah Woodworth Aubrey (4)Esther Smith Pvt VT
Amasa: b 4-6-1755 d 6-21-1826 m Mary H. Stanley Pvt CT
Daniel: b 1743 d 1809 m Lydia Ann Pitcher MM NY
David: b 1725 d 1823 m Phoebe Sanford Pvt VT
Gideon: b 6-23-1746 d 6-9-1836 m Abigail Hurd Pvt NY
Lemuel: b 2-17-1740 d p. 1806 m Charity Hurd Pvt NY
Phineas: b 3-25-1731 d 9-25-1815 m (1)Mehitable Munson (2)Mary Dickerman Capt CT
Thomas: b 1750-5 d 8-31-1838 m Elizabeth Colter Pvt NC ★
Timothy: b 4-22-1747 d p. 1803 m Mary Hunt Lt CT

CASTLEBERRY,
John: b c. 1738 d p. 4-21-1801 m Mary — Sol GA
Paul: b 3-1-1761 d 6-16-1841 m (1) X (2)Nancy Gillespie Pvt GA ★
Richard: b c. 1740 d a. 1815 m Anna Trice Sol GA

CASTLEMAN, (includes CASSELMAN)
Andrew: b 8-22-1760 d 8-11-1844 m Margaret Ewing Sct TN
David: b 1734 d 2-13-1826 m Margaret Johnston PS VA
Johannes: b c. 1724 d p. 1782 m Maria Eva Siebel Sol NY

CASTLIO, (includes COSTLIO)
John: b 1764 d 11-23-1830 m Ellen Harrison Lowe Pvt KY

CASTNER, (includes KASTNER)
Daniel: b 1757 d 2-12-1839 m (1)Elizabeth Souers (2)Elizabeth Moore Sol NJ
Johann Anton: b 11-29-1743 d 2-17-1817 m (1)Gottliebe Isel (2)Maria Magdalena Spach (3)Jacobina Schneider (4)Catharine Krumm Pvt NC
Samuel: b 6-11-1737 d 11-30-1833 m Mary Linderman Pvt PA

CASTO,
Azariah: b c. 1754 d 1824 m Hannah Goulder Pvt NJ

CASTON,
Glass: b c. 1730-40 d 1804 m Elizabeth — Wgm SC

CASTOR, (includes KESTER)
Benjamin: b c. 1741 d 1-28-1826 m Ruth — Pvt PA
Frederick: b 4-27-1739 d 5-25-1800 m Elizabeth Rohrer Lt PA
George: b 12-14-1736 d 5-25-1811 m Margaretha Shuterle Pvt PA
Jacob: b 1742 d 1815 m (1)Sophy Rorer (2)Catherine Fox Ens PA
Peter: b c. 1759 d p. 3-23-1842 m Magdalena — Pvt PA
Philip: b 1749 d p. 1781 m Sally Elic Pvt PA

CASWELL,
Beal: b 1-21-1738 d 11-22-1826 m Priscilla Newland Sgt MA
David: b 1744 d 8-2-1807 m Elizabeth — Sgt NY
Elijah, Jr.: b 12-13-1745 d 11-17-1836 m Mary Chubbuck Pvt MA
Gilbert: b 2-9-1755 d 11-10-1812 m (2)Hannah Foster Sgt NH
James: b 3-10-1763 d p. 1815 m Elizabeth — Pvt NY
Joseph: b 1758 d 2-9-1846 m Lydia Evans Pvt NH ★
Joshua: b 3-22-1749 d 3-3-1832 m (1)Elie Reynolds (2)Lydia — Pvt MA ★
Lemuel: b 9-2-1749 d 11-15-1833 m Deliverance Chubbuck Sgt MA
Nathan, Sr.: b 3-8-1740 d 6-13-1824 m Hannah Bingham Capt NH
Nathan, Jr.: b 1765 d — m (2)Sarah Bishop Pvt NH
Richard: b 8-3-1729 d 11-10-1789 m (1)Mary McElwain (2)Sarah Herritage BGen CS NC
Samuel: bpt 9-27-1747 d 4-6-1819 m Sarah Hutchinson Cpl MA
Samuel: b 8-24-1760 d 1-3-1851 m Polly Seaver Pvt MA
Simeon: b 1-19-1763 d 10-21-1844 m Rachel Staples Pvt MA ★
William: b 11-16-1760 d 5-6-1825 m Hannah Andrews Vincent Pvt MA ★
William: b 1731 d 1805 m Mary — Ens NC
William: b 9-24-1754 d 1786 m Garathy Mackilwean BGen NC

CATCHINGS,
Benjamin: b 10-31-1748 d 7-31-1798 m Mildred Criddle Maj GA
Joseph: b 1762 d 1806 m Martha Townsend Pvt VA

CATER,
John: b 1737 d 1-26-1801 m Susan Johnson PS NH
Thomas: b 12-17-1751 d 4-20-1803 m Rachel Miles Capt CS SC

CATES, (includes CATE, KATES)
Andrew: b 4-14-1760 d 2- -1829 m Ann Wiggin Pvt NH ★
Enoch: b 1760 d 5-16-1834 m Susan Page Cpl NH
James, Sr.: b 1728 d 6-10-1813 m Elizabeth Mason CS NH
James, Jr.: b 1747 d p. 1791 m Lucy Sanborn Pvt PS NH
John: b 6-14-1741 d 3- -1816 m Mary Garland PS NH
John: b — d 1827/28 m X PS NC
Joseph: b 6-9-1759 d 4-21-1808 m (1)Prudence Marden (2)Susanna Caverno Sgt PS NH
Joseph: b — d 1796 m Ann — Pvt NC
Joseph: b c. 1730 d p. 1790 m Margaret Bell Pvt SC

Neal: b 9-6-1760 d 6-14-1846 m (1)Jane Thompson (2)Sally — Pvt NH
Robert: b c. 1754 d 6-7-1801 m Mary Holmes Cpl MA
Samuel: b 6-2-1724 d 4-9-1816 m Abigail Neal PS NH
Stephen: b c. 1755 d p. 1789 m Ann Griffin PS NH
Thomas: b a. 1763 d p. 12-17-1811 m Martha — PS NC
William, Jr.: b 1727 d p. 1790 m Sarah Norton PS CS NH
Zachariah: b 1720 d 1796 m Polly — PS CS NC

CATHCART, (includes KITHCART)
James Leander: b 6-1-1765 d 10-6-1843 m Jane Bancker NS PA ★
John: b 1737 d 10-26-1812 m Sarah White Pvt PA
Joseph: b c. 1818 m Mary (Manifold) Payne Pvt PA
Thomas: b 5-7-1758/9 d 8-22-1842/3 m Jane Gates Pvt MA

CATHELL, (includes CATHEL)
James Walker: b — d a. 1790 m Betsey Reed Sgt MA
Jonathan: b c. 1759 d a. 4-29-1801 m Betty Collins Ens PS MD
Levi: b 9-18-1754 d 11-26-1815 m Rebecca Porter Pvt MD

CATHER,
Jasper: b 1740 d 7-30-1812 m (1)Catherine — (2)Barbara Lawrence (3)Sarah Moore Sol VA

CATHERS,
William: b c. 1737 d c. 1815 m Elizabeth Inghram Pvt PA

CATHEY,
Alexander: b 9-11-1759 d 11-9-1839 m Margaret — Pvt NC
George: b 1- -1755 d 12-14-1840 m Margaret Chamberlain Pvt NC ★
George: b 1724 d 5-25-1801 m Frances Henry PS NC
James: b c. 1750 d 1791 m Jane Rutherford Capt NC
John: b — d p. 3-4-1788 m Mary Henry CS NC
William: b 1747 d 1827 m Alice Hagin CS NC

CATLAND,
John: b 7- -1744/5 d 12-18-1818 m Lydia Winslow Sgt MA

CATLETT,
David: b 1753 d 9-11-1834 m Ann Morgan Pvt VA ★
George: b 5-6-1743 d 9-13-1814 m (1)Eleanor Johnson (2)Lucy Beverley Buckner NLt VA
John: b 9-30-1749 d 2-5-1826 m Allie T King Capt VA

CATLIN,
Abel: b 2-25-1746 d 12-23-1831 m Dorothy Seymour Dr CT
Abijah: b 7-17-1747 d 9-27-1813 m Huldah Wiard Pvt CT
Abraham: b 8-13-1720 d 12- -1802 m Mindwell Griswold Pvt CT
Alexander: b 1-6-1739 d p. 1780 m Abigail Goodman Capt PS CT
Benjamin: b 7-21-1748 d 2- -1782 m Anna W. Deming Cpl QM CT
David: b 1747 d 10-13-1839 m (1)Ann Peck (2)Ann Parmalee Sgt CT ★
Eli: b 1-22-1733/4 d 3-13-1820 m Elizabeth Way Capt CT
Elisha: b 1745 d 5-30-1826 m (2)Roxanna Dewey Pvt CT
George: b 12-22-1731 d 12-6-1812 m Mindwell Phelps Pvt CT
Hezekiah: b 8- -1764 d 4-26-1837 m Sarah Stone Cpl CT ★
Isaac: b 1-23-1757 d 6-12-1833 m Ruth Carter Pvt CT ★
Jacob: b 6-3-1727 d 7-1-1802 m Hannah Phelps Pvt CT
Joel: b 2-16-1721 d 7-27-1797 m Sophia Holcomb PS CS CT
Lewis: b 6-3-1758 d 1-7-1839 m Candace Catlin Pvt CS CT ★
Nathan: b 1760 d 6-24-1830 m Eleanor Decker Pvt CT
Phineas: b 10-22-1760 d 1-30-1827 m Sally Ross Cpl CT
Putnam: b 4-5-1764 d 3-12-1842 m Polly Sutton FifMaj CT
Theodore: b 10-16-1734/5 d 2-19-1824 m Mary Goodwin Capt CT
Thomas: b 6-18-1737 d 12-9-1829 m Avis Buel 2Lt CT
Timothy: b 11-5-1753 d p. 8-16-1832 m Silence Bartlett Cpl MA ★

CATO,
William: b 1754 d 1800 m Amanda — Pvt GA

CATON,
John: b 1751 d 1830 m Deborah Barton Pvt NY

CATRON, (includes KETTERING)
Christopher: b 1725 d 1793 m X PS VA
Jacob: b 1749 d p. 4-23-1817 m Elizabeth Gose CS VA
Peter: b 11-8-1754 d 7-7-1836 m (1)Elizabeth Lilland (2)Barbara Houch Pvt VA ★

CATT,
George: b c. 1748 d 10- -1816 m X Pvt VA

CATTELL,
Benjamin: b 7- -1749 d 1782 m Mary McCall Capt SC
Elijah: b 7-27-1751 d p. 1793 m Hannah Ware Capt NJ
Jonas: b 12-12-1740 d 2-2-1828 m Elizabeth Roberts Pvt NJ
Jonas: b 11-3-1758 d 7-25-1854 m (1)Amy Pearce (2)Mary Stockton Pvt Sct NJ ★

CATTERLIN,
Joseph: b c. 1750 d p. 1780 m Mary Ann Mercer Lt NJ

CAUGHEY,
Andrew: b 1756 d 1828 m Elizabeth Caughey Pvt PA
John: b 1752 d 5-26-1833 m Elizabeth Kerr Ens PA
John: b c. 1747 d 1820 m X Pvt PA
John: b 1747 d a. 4-30-1833 m Sarah A. — Pvt PA ★
Samuel: b 1751 d 1826 m Ellen Moore Pvt PA

CAUSEY,
Ezekiel: b 1759 d a. 1821 m Elizabeth Clary Sol GA
Patrick: b 1746 d 1812 m Unicy (Fooks) Lingo Pvt MD
William: b 6- -1744 d p. 7-3-1828 m (2)Susannah Jackson Ens MD

CAUSTEN, (includes COUSTEN)
Isaac: b 1758 d 5-10-1833 m Mrs Jane Kinnicut Capt NY ★

CAUTHEN,
Thomas: b c. 1750 d a. 1-19-1824 m X PS NC

CAUTHORN, (includes CAUTHON, CAWTHON)
Richard: b a. 1750 d 1790 m Catherine Fisher Pvt VA
William: b a. 1764 d 1816-18 m Judah — Sol GA
William, Sr.: b c. 1725 d p. 7-11-1801 m Elizabeth — PS NC

CAVAN,
Miles: b 11-7-1734 d 9-27-1796 m Mary — Pvt NY

CAVANAUGH, (includes KAVANAUGH)
Charles, Sr.: b c. 1726 d 1796 m Ann Coleman Sol VA
Edward: b 1750 d 12- -1842 m Mary Spencer Pvt PA
William: b c. 1755 d 1829 m (1)Hannah Woods (2)Ruth Booten Sol VA

CAVE,
Benjamin: b 6-15-1760 d 2-16-1842 m Keziah — Pvt VA ★
Elizabeth Craig: b c. 1752 d 1827 m Richard Cave PS KY
John: b. 1757 d 1812 m Sarah Brown PS SC
John: b 1725 d p. 5-26-1809 m X PS VA
Richard: b 1750 d 1816 m Elizabeth Craig PS KY
Thomas: b a. 1768 d 5-11-1817 m (1)Ellen Meyer (2)Lydia Matlock Mrnr PA
William: b 1749 d 9-4-1839 m Rachel — Pvt NC ★

CAVENDER,
Charles: b 1736 d 1824 m Elanor Addison Cpl NH

CAVENDISH,
William Hunter: b c. 1750 d 1828 m (1)Jane Murphy (2)Alice Mann Commissary VA

CAVERLY,
Charles: b 12-15-1760 d p. 1811 m Molly Danielson Pvt NH
John: b 11-24-1731 d 8-23-1825 m Mary Swan Capt PS CT
John: b 5-11-1752 d 4-27-1842 m Betsey Boodey PS NH
Philip: b 3-23-1745 d 4-1-1813 m Bridget Pendergast PS Pvt NH

CAVITT, (includes CAVETT)
James: b c. 1747 d 1798 m Mary Forster PS PA
John: b 11-3-1742 d 9-7-1812 m Margaret — Pvt PA
Patrick: b 1735 d 1835 m (2)Mary Porter Pvt PA

CAWOOD, (includes CAYWOOD)
Berry: b 1758 d p. 1834 m Nancy Scott Pvt VA NC ★
John: b 1755 d 9-15-1833 m Catherine Gano Pvt NJ W★

CAZIER,
Jacob: b 1754 d 5-2-1807 m Charity Benson McCoy PS DE
John: b c. 1730 d — m (1)Rebecca Van Bibber (2)Rachel — SgtMaj DE

CAZOTTE,
Scevole de: b 1-31-1764 d 6-20-1853 m Therese Amiel NS FR

CEBRA,
William: b 3-5-1750 d p. 1790 m Rebecca Yates Lt NY

CECIL, (includes CISSELL, SISSELL)
John: b c. 1750 d p. 1790 m Elizabeth — Pvt MD
John: b 1721 d a. 8-22-1778 m Mrs — Brightwell Wilson PS MD
Joshua: b a. 1733 d p. 2-28-1801 m Mary — Pvt MD
Leonard: b 5-5-1751 d 9-25-1792 m Harriet Browning PS GA
Sabret: b 1723 d p. 4-12-1805 m Mary Beall PS MD
Samuel: b 3-23-1719 d 3-23-1786 m Rebecca White Sol VA
William: b 5-28-1750 d 12-11-1836 m Nancy Witten Spy VA
Zacheriah: b c. 1758 d p. 1804 m Nancy Ingram Pvt VA

CENTER,
Abel: b 12-16-1758 d 11-14-1835 m Sarah Nichols Pvt NH
John Sheldon: b 1758 d 1811 m Phoebe Tay Pvt MA

CERRÉ,
Gabriele: b 8-17-1734 d 4-4-1805 m Catherine Giard PS MO

CESSNA, (includes CISSNA, CISNEY)
Charles: b 3-2-1744 d 7-30-1837 m Elizabeth Culbertson LCol PA

John: b 1-26-1726 d 3-31-1802 m (1)Sarah Rose (2)Elizabeth Hall Maj PA
Jonathan: b c. 1752 d c. 1781 m Mary Friend PS PA
Stephen: b 1755 d 8-14-1823 m (1)Elizabeth Barnhill (2)Margaret — Pvt PA ★
Theophilus: b 1760 d 1867 m — Richardson Ens PA

CHADBOURN, (includes CHADBOURNE)
Eleaser: b 1754 d 1814 m Anne Har PS ME
Humphrey: b 5-24-1744 d 3-21-1792 m Elizabeth Libby Pvt MA
James: b 2-4-1758 d 5-18-1839 m Deborah Harmon Pvt MA
Joseph: bpt 6-26-1748 d p. 1790 m Martha Hamilton 2Lt MA
Levi: b 4-18-1754 d c. 1840 m Martha Hodgkins Pvt MA
Samuel: b 1750 d 1810 m Mehitable Hatch Cpl MA
Silas: b 8-8-1752 d 1-14-1823 m (1)Abigaile Crockett (2)Mrs Lucy (Roberts) (Seiver) Crockett QM MA
Simeon: b 5-16-1750 d 10-29-1846 m (2)Elizabeth Yeaton Sgt MA ★
William: b 9-9-1734 d 4-23-1816 m Sarah Weymouth Pvt MA

CHADEAYNE,
Henry: b c. 1734 d p. 1781 m Ruth Conklaine Pvt NY

CHADSEY,
Jabez: b 1-31-1754 d 9-30-1820 m Hannah Greene Pvt RI ★
William, Jr.: b 6-1-1730 d 1798 m (1)Lucy — (2)Barbara Eldred Smn RI

CHADWELL,
David: b 1733 d 1833 m (1)Elizabeth Turner (2)Susannah — Capt PS VA
Harris: b 3-14-1746 d 8-16-1834 m Ruth Witt 1Lt MA

CHADWICK, (includes CHADDOCK)
Archelaus: b 3-1-1757 d 9-8-1807 m Sarah Goodspeed Cpl MA
David: Jr.: b 1-9-1752 d 12-30-1817 m Hannah Mower Pvt MA
Edmund: b 4-1-1754 d 8-20-1819 m Susannah Atkinson Pvt PS NH
Edmund: b 3-10-1751 d 12-8-1826 m Elizabeth Gookin Dr NH
Elihu: b 5-27-1759 d 8-30-1837 m (1)Mary Jeffries (2)Rebecca Wall Jeffries Lt NJ ★
Gayer: b 2-10-1735 d p. 4-27-1804 m (1)Elizabeth — (2)Sarah Piner CS NC
James, Sr.: b 7-5-1725 d 9-6-1786 m Ruth Hatch Pvt MA
James, Jr.: b 2-25-1753 d 10-25-1826 m Rhoda Weeks Pvt & Mid MA
John: b 7-9-1744 d 5-8-1821 m Nancy Jane Allen 1Lt MA
John, Sr.: b 1-4-1720 d 4-2-1797 m Susannah Peabody Pvt MA
John, Jr.: b 3-18-1743 d 11-30-1804 m Mary Swan Pvt MA
John: b 4-28-1717 d p. 1790 m Abigail — CS MA
John: b 1760 d 1825 m Abigail Currier Pvt NH
John: b 3-12-1713 d 4-18-1783 m Martha Ann Jackson PS NJ
John: b 1760 d 4-4-1850 m (1)Keran Elizabeth Shortridge (2)Lucinda Bartram Ens NC ★
John: b 1750 d 11-10-1794 m Annie — Pvt PA
Joseph: b 1760 d 6-26-1812 m (1)Sarah Bruce (2)Elizabeth Wilson PS CS Capt MA
Joseph: b 1747 d p. 1788 m Anna Hatch Pvt MA
Nathan: b 10-22-1764 d 1-18-1844 m Thankful Downer Pvt CT VT ★
Nathan: b 4-24-1734 d 11-17-1801 m Jerusha Gleason Pvt MA
Richard, Sr.: b 1709 d 2-4-1784 m Deborah Swain PS MA
Thomas: b 11-12-1760 d 12-3-1835 m Persis Smith Pvt MA
Thomas: b 7-6-1750 d 9-3-1791 m Elizabeth Woolley Capt NJ
Thomas: b 3-25-1730 d 2- -1802 m Rachel — Col CS NC
William: b 1730 d — m Eunice Goss Pvt MA
Wm.: b 9-25-1745 d p. 4-23-1810 m Elizabeth Goodwin Pvt CS NH

CHAFFEE, (includes CHAFEE, CHAFEY, CHAFFE)
Abiel: b 8-13-1761 d 4-26-1847 m Hannah Sargent Pvt CT
Amos: b 8-9-1744 d 2-3-1815 m Anna Brown Pvt MA
Amos: b 12-11-1750 d 3- -1793 m Sarah Monroe PS RI
Asa, Sr.: b 6-5-1734 d 12- -1801 m Mary Howlett Pvt MA
Asa, Jr: b 1754 d 1818 m (1)Anne Elmer (2)Frances Elmer Pvt MA
Braddock: b 11-1-1756 d a. 5-10-1813 m Sarah Brown Sgt MA
Calvin: b 2-3-1760 d 1-6-1817 m Ruth Eviden Pvt CT W★
Chester: b 4-6-1755 d 9-17-1841 m Carolin Walker Pvt CT
Clifford: b 1-20-1757 d 8-25-1802 m Anna Burke Sgt VT
Comfort: b 3-20-1738 d 6-4-1811 m Mary Bliss Pvt MA
Comfort: b 3-9-1756 d 2-23-1828 m Mrs Lucy (Stow) Hoyt Pvt MA ★
Cyril: b 5-3-1758 d 12-11-1837 m Patience Sexton Arfr CT ★
David, Jr.: b 10-28-1733 d 10-3-1814 m Priscilla Robbins Ens CT
Ephraim, Jr.: b 4-25-1760 d 8-6-1825 m Elizabeth Whittaker Pvt MA
Ezra: b 4-9-1742 d 7-16-1815 m Jerusha Hurlburt Capt VT
Francis Green: b 4-6-1745 d 7-3-1786 m Dorcas Chafee Pvt CT
Frederick: b 3-6-1767 d 1-1-1837 m (1)Elizabeth Knowlton (2)Betsey Shurtliff Matr Pvt CT ★
Henry: b 6-6-1747 d 11-19-1818 m Rachel Plank Pvt CT
Hezekiah: b 12-6-1731 d 3-4-1819 m Lydia Griswold Phelps Dr CT
Joel: b 7-2-1759 d 2-18-1844 m (1)Rachel Booth (2)Dolly Hyde (3)Eleanor Stuart Brown Pvt CT ★
Jonathan: b 5-11-1746 d 3-8-1826 m Lucy Allen Pvt CS CT
Joseph: b 9-17-1752 d 10-26-1842 m (1)Lois Barney (2)Huldah Walker Cpl MA
Joseph: b 10-2-1761 d 3-10-1846 m Mercy White Pvt MA ★
Joshua: b 1733 d 1789 m Mary St John Pvt CT
Josiah: b 9-1-1731 d 10-10-1802 m Sarah Cady Pvt CT

CHAFFEE, contd.

Josiah, Jr.: b 4-26-1765 d 9-17-1839 m Mrs Joanne Parker Pvt CT
    W★
Nathan: b 11-17-1750 d 8-13-1815 m Pricella Wedge Pvt VT
Nathaniel, Jr.: b 3-5-1735 d 7-3-1822 m (1)Ruth Mansfield
    (2)Susannah Carpenter Pvt MA
Noah: b 2-22-1745/6 d 1-3-1816 m Susanna Esterbrook Pvt MA
Otis: b — d 5-29-1813/14 m Abigail Abby Pvt VT
Samuel: b 6-9-1760 d 10-20-1813 m Azubah Sanger Sol CT
Stephen: b 1-23-1757 d 1-23-1819 m Patience Mason Pvt MA
Thomas: b 2-22-1756 d 6-28-1826 m Mary — Pvt CT
Thomas: b 4-8-1731 d 12-5-1810 m Hannah Reed CS CT
Thomas, Sr.: b 12-10-1712 d a. 3-27-1792 m Rebecca Hunt Pvt MA
Thomas: b 1756-60 d 1828 m Sarah H. Horner Pvt NJ ★
William: b 1756 d 10-27-1834 m Mary Whipple Pvt CT ★

CHAFFIN,

David: b 7-18-1757 d 8-31-1828 m Betty Chamberlain Pvt MA
Ephraim: b 9-24-1760 d p. 1804 m Sarah Hill Pvt MA
Francis: b 1-25-1730 d 1-28-1778 m Rebecca Cummings Cpl MA
Isham: b c. 1757 d 5-23-1822 m (1)Betsy Holcomb (2)Patience —
    Sol VA
Jonathan: b 10-12-1754 d 6-6-1790 m Sara Darby Pvt MA
Joshua: b 10-22-1748 d 4- -1824 m (1)Bettie Tinsley (2)Pattie
    Giles 1Lt VA
Joshua: b c. 1730 d p. 10-1-1804 m X Fif VA
Robert: b 7-8-1752 d 9-7-1828 m Hannah Tenney Pvt MA
Samuel, Sr.: b 5-3-1732 d 11-20-1811 m (1)Sarah Hubbard (2)Lucy
    (Darby) Ball Sgt MA
Samuel, Jr.: b 12-1-1760 d 1838 m Abigail Hemenway 1Pvt MA
Simon: b 9-27-1764 d 8-8-1837 m Mercy Sanderson Pvt MM MA
Tilla: b 5-14-1762 d 9-1-1838 m Hannah Mirick Pvt MA
Timothy: b 3-7-1734 d 7-25-1838 m Sarah Forbush Pvt MA

CHAILLE,

Peter: b 1740 d 1802 m Comfort Houston Col MD

CHALFANT, (includes CHALFFIN)

Evan: b 4-4-1757 d 1830 m Ruth Buffington Pvt PA
Mordecai: b 4-8-1757 d 12-18-1823 m Margaret Forsythe Pvt PA
Robert: b c. 1746 d 1811 m Phebe — Pvt PA
Solomon: b 1-25-1753 d 2-26-1837 m (1)Jemima Eaton (2)Mrs
    Achsa Cotton Pvt Wgn VA ★

CHALK,

William: b c. 1758 d 1810 m Peggy Askew Sgt NC

CHALKER,

Isaac: b 6-1-1736 d 8-24-1803 m Sarah Stair SrgnMte CT
Jabez: b 1757 d 3-25-1841 m Hannah Pickett Pvt CT ★
Oliver: b 8-12-1760 d 7-19-1846 m Lydia Chapman Pvt CT ★

CHALLIS, (includes CHELLIS)

Enos: b 11-25-1752 d 6- -1815 m Joannah Chase Sgt NH
Hugh: b 1734 d p. 8-5-1786 m Marta Wimbish PS NC
John: b 1746 d c. 1800 m — Harvey PS NH
Nathaniel: b 3-4-1761 d 1-16-1855 m Dolly Dole Pvt MA ★
Thomas: b 7-6-1749 d 2-1-1835 m Mary French Sgt NH ★

CHALMERS,

Andrew: b c. 1754 d 11-25-1833 m Alice Beasley Pvt PA ★

CHALONER,

Walter, Jr.: b 10-2-1748 d 1808 m Hope Durfee PS MA
William: b 7-17-1749 d 8-31-1802 m Mary Eliza Dillaway Lt PS MA

CHAMBERLAIN, (includes CHAMBERLAYNE, CHAMBERLIN, CHAMBLEN)

Aaron: b 1-19-1758 d 8-25-1825 m (1)Catherine Waters (2)Wealthy
    Root Pvt CT
Aaron: b 6-12-1757 d 1-21-1848 m Mary — NJ ★
Abiel: b 12-20-1737 d 1-12-1818 m Grace Ainsworth CS CT
Abiel: b 3-22-1739 d 5-14-1787 m Elinor Johnson Lt VT
Abiel: b 10-6-1734 d 2-27-1823 m Lois Whitney Vol NH
Abner: b 10-4-1745 d 8- -1832 m Lucretia — Lt VT
Amasa: b 6-1-1748 d 4-18-1826 m Molly Briscoe Pvt NH
Amos: b 1-3-1748 d p. 1796 m (1)Martha — (2)Anna Alger Lt VT
Asa: b 3-26-1765 d 9-16-1823 m Prudence Dresser Sol NH
Benjamin: b 9-3-1750 d 2-21-1824 m Lucy Day Lt MA
Benjamin, Sr.: b 9-7-1724 d 3-29-1803 m Hannah Snell Cpl MA
Benjamin, 3rd.: b 10-23-1733 d 12-26-1812 m Susanna Barron
    Sol MA
Benjamin: b 3-31-1758 d 4-26-1844 m Martha Wheelock Pvt MA ★
Benjamin: b 5-25-1758 d 2-4-1847 m (1)Tryphena Tibbets (2)Sally
    Keys Pvt MA
Benjamin, Jr.: b 6-19-1762 d 1822 m Olive Wilkinson Cpl RI
Benjamin: b 12-15-1747 d 6-11-1832 m Hannah Eaton Lt VT
Benjamin: b 10-5-1742 d 3-7-1810 m Jerusha Green Pvt VT
Byrd: b — d 12-1-1800 m Elizabeth Dandridge 1Lt VA
Charles: b 5-18-1727 d c. 3- -1814 m Marlena — Pvt PA
Colbe: b 12-13-1739 d 9-11-1796 m Catharine Winegar Capt NY
Daniel: b 3-12-1753 d 7-14-1825 m Lydia Harrington Pvt MA
David: b 11- -1746 d 1-16-1821 m Chloe Conant Pvt MA ★

Ebenezer, Jr.: b 10-10-1740 d 9-17-1806 m (1)Esther Fay
    (2)Mehitable Walker Sgt MA
Ebenezer: bpt 5-25-1729 d p. 11-6-1790 m Lucretia Rogers 1Lt NH
Ebenezer: b 1754 d 1843 m Patty Howe Pvt NH
Edmund: b 3-27-1743 d 10-24-1824 m Elizabeth Kingsley Sgt CT
Edmund: b 8-20-1742 d 5-28-1819 m Ruth Pratt 2Lt MA
Edmund: b 10-11-1730 d c. 1795 m Mary Caryl CS MA
Edward: b 2-20-1723 d 10-18-1810 m Hannah Edmunds Capt MA
Edward Pye: b 1753 d 6-4-1806 m (1)Agnes Dandridge (2)Mary
    Bickerton Webb NLt VA
Eleazer: b 8-11-1737 d 3-28-1805 m Eleanor Pratt Sgt CT
Eliakim: b c. 1752 d 1832 m Anna Stowe Pvt MA
Elias: b 1750 d 1-20-1835 m Betsey Gillett Ens VT
Elisha: b 4-16-1736 d 6-26-1805 m Damaris Bugbee Pvt CT
Elisha: b 9-2-1763 d 6-11-1840 m Susan Brown Pvt MA ★
Enoch: b 11-18-1737 d 9-20-1812 m Elizabeth Doane Pvt MA
Ephraim: b 9-28-1725 d p. 1790 m Esther Boynton CS MA
Err: b 6-24-1744 d 1831 m (1)— Fowler (2)Mercy Wright Sgt VT
Freedom: b 10-21-1730 d 2-23-1821 m Deborah Turner Capt MA
Freegift: b 10-20-1758 d 1- -1838 m Elizabeth Whitaker Pvt Spy PA
Godfrey: b 1755 d 1828 m Mercy Moore Pvt NJ
Green: bpt 7-13-1755 d 4- -1813 m Dimmis Bigelow Pvt CT
Gurden: b 1-27-1755 d 12-10-1810 m Hannah Lawrence Pvt NY
Henry: b 1747 d 5-14-1828 m (1)Abigail Chamberlain (2)Mrs Jemima
    Smith Pvt NH ★
Ichabod: b a. 1747 d p. 1788 m Sarah Gale Pvt MA
Increase: b 1741 d 8-24-1813 m Rachel Davis Pvt NH
Isaac: b 10-29-1756 d 7-14-1833 m (1)Elisabeth Sprague (2)Huldah
    — Sgt CT ★
Jacob: b 3-18-1716 d 9-5-1780 m Phebe Vinton PS MA
Jacob, Jr.: b 8-9-1746 d 1-27-1791 m Molly Vinton Sgt MA
Jacob: b 1756 d 1819 m Mary Woy (Waugh) PS PA
James: b 2-11-1734 d 4-28-1812 m Mrs Abigail Palmer Capt CS CT
James: b 1740 d 1-24-1826 m Hannah Adams Pvt NH ★
James: b 5-27-1745 d 1-18-1819 m Ann Sample LCol PA
James: b 1756 d 1819 m Mary — Pvt PA
Jason: b 2-9-1756 d 1-29-1833 m Mary Brewster Pvt NS NH
Jeremiah: b 1740 d 1830 m Margaret Carmichael Sol NC
Jireh: b 11-29-1762 d p. 1832 m Joanna Morgan Pvt CT
Joel: b 7-1-1759 d 1-3-1834 m Mercy Everett Ens CT
John: b 3-30-1735 d 1-24-1817 m (1)Lydia Wells (2)Sarah—CS CT
John: b 3-21-1720 d 1-20-1806 m (1)Rachel Lawrence (2)Mary
    Patch Pvt MA
John: b 1-22-1755 d 9-14-1834 m Patience Whitton Pvt MA
John: b — d — m Mary Lee CS Ens MA
John: b 1-15-1742 d 1-15-1847 m Ann Sylvester Pvt NJ ★
John: b 1742 d p. 2-4-1793 m Hannah Lackey Pvt NC
John: b 11-9-1764 d 4-11-1843 m Lydia Hosford Pvt VT ★
John: b c. 1716 d 3-17-1802 m (1)Mehetible Fuller (2)Susannah
    Green CS VT
Jonathan, Sr.: b 2-11-1711 d 1-19-1795 m Elizabeth Cram Pvt NH
Jonathan, Jr.: b 2-26-1743/4 d 4-26-1815 m Margaret Cram Pvt NH
Jonathan: b 2-15-1747 d 9-12-1823 m Rachel Ford Pvt NY
Joseph: b 2-14-1741/2 d 8-12-1810 m (1)Abiah Wells (2)Mrs
    Phoebe Worthington Sgt MA
Joseph: b 12-27-1762 d 8-21-1800 m Lucy Whitney Pvt MA
Joseph: b 5-5-1738 d 9-5-1815 m Ruth Preston Lt VT
Joseph: b 7-12-1755 d c. 1848 m (1)Deborah Nye (2)Rosamond
    (Cady) Gates Pvt VT
Joshua: b 6-14-1735 d 2-27-1801 m Mary Powel Pvt PA
Leander: b 1-25-1766 d 6-16-1822 m Mercy Berry Pvt CT ★
Lemuel: b 11-13-1754 d 2-14-1829 m (1)Lucretia Newton
    (2)Mehitable Bacon Pvt MA
Lewis: b 2-25-1750 d 6-30-1813 m (3)Anna Fisher Pvt NJ
Moses: b 7-30-1735 d 4-4-1777 m Sarah Partrige Pvt MA
Moses: b 12-15-1761 d 12-9-1833 m Mary Baker Pvt MA ★
Moses, Jr.: b 12-10-1749 d 2-14-1832 m Abigail Stevens Lt NH ★
Moses: b 9-1-1748 d 1-30-1803 m Hepsibah Nurse PS NH
Moses, Sr.: b 3-30-1716 d 6-25-1796 m Jemima Wright Pvt VT
Nathaniel: b 1748 d 4-12-1836 m (1)Amee Porter (2)Mrs Ann Banks
    Punchard SgtMaj MA
Nathaniel: b 9-3-1760 d 11-6-1859 m Permelia Comee Pvt MA
Ninian: b 1718/19 d 1798 m Jannet — Sgt NC
Ninian: b 10-1-1751 d 12-20-1833 m Elizabeth Ewing Pvt PA
Oliver: b 3-13-1738 d 10-18-1821 m Mary Jones Pvt CT
Peleg: b 5-12-1736 d 1808 m (1)Abigail Swift (2)Jane Baldwin
    Lt CT
Phineas: b 9-17-1760 d 3-22-1847 m Rebecca Dalrymple Pvt MA ★
Remembrance: b 12-19-1747 d 1-10-1813 m Elizabeth (Elliott)
    Johnson Lt VT
Richard: b 1730 d 12-12-1789 m Mary Dickenson Pvt PS CT
Richard, Sr.: b 7-9-1714 d a. 12-16-1784 m Abigail Wright Pvt VT
Samuel: b 9-9-1743 d 5-18-1821 m Sybil (Thompson) Denslow Pvt
    CT ★
Samuel: b 10-26-1723 d p. 1777 m Sarah Tenney Pvt MA
Samuel, Sr.: b 3-18-1734 d p. 1792 m Mrs Margaret (Atwood)
    Ballard Pvt MA
Samuel, Sr.: b 6-7-1724 d 6-3-1802 m Martha Mellen PS CS NH
Samuel, Jr.: b 5-2-1750 d 9-23-1812 m Abigail Townsend Lt NH
Simeon: b c. 1731 d 11-21-1816 m Elizabeth Dodge PS NH
Swift: b 10-15-1764 d 1828 m (1)Sarah Sherwood (2)Mary Tuttle
    Pvt CT W★
Thomas: b 1758 d 10-8-1836 m Mary Whitman Sgt MA

Thomas: b 2-17-1753 d 4-4-1815 m Judith Burleigh Pvt NH
Thomas: b a. 1754 d 1792 m Mary — Pvt NJ
William: b 5-31-1755 d 1-2-1834 m Mary Wilcox Pvt CT ★
William: b 11-23-1753 d 8-25-1842 m (1)Loas Ingersoll (2)Elizabeth Winslow (3)Meribah Stevens (4)Margaret — Pvt MA ★
William: b 7-6-1725 d 12-13-1815 m (1)Eleanor Horne (2)Mrs Hannah Wentworth PS NH
William: b 4-27-1755 d 9-28-1828 m Jane Eastman Lt NH
William: b 9-25-1736 d 8-21-1817 m (1)Elizabeth Ten Broeck (2)Anne Park (3)Margaret Park (4)Mary Ann Kimble LCol NJ
William: b 1-25-1745 d 11-27-1810 m Abigail Hatch Capt NY
William: b 10-4-1740 d 10-4-1777 m Esther — Pvt NY
William: b 11-24-1724 d 1810 m Martha Palmer Ens PA
William: b c. 1756 d c. 11-16-1836 m (1)Sara Post (2)Ann Hampton Pvt PA
Wilson: b 9-24-1724 d 6-23-1791 m Elizabeth Austin Pvt MA
Wright: b 5-16-1758 d 7- -1841 m (1)Hannah Heath (2)Sally Holdridge (3)Mary Billings Sgt VT

CHAMBERS,
Alexander, Sr.: b 1716 d 9-16-1798 m Rose Crage PS NJ
Alexander, Jr.: b a. 1765 d 1824 m (1)Miss Hunt (2)Elizabeth Eyre (3)Margaret Mott Pvt NJ
Alexander: b 1752 d 1834 m Polly — Pvt VA ★
Alexander: b 5-15-1756 d 6-29-1857 m Rachel Ann Monroe Sol VA
Benjamin: b 10-16-1749 d 1-10-1816 m Elizabeth Forman Col MD
Benjamin: b 1755 d 12-29-1813 m Sallie Brown Capt PA
Benjamin: b 1-4-1764 d 8-27-1850 m Sarah Lawson Kemper Lt PA ★
David: b 9-25-1748 d 9-15-1842 m Ruth Clark Capt NJ ★
David: b a. 1757 d 4-1-1809 m Isabella Vachub Pvt VA ★
Edward: b c. 1746 d p. 1790 m — Fish Pvt PA
Elijah: b 11-17-1758/9 d 11-30-1853 m Mary Lindaberry Pvt PA
Henry: b 1753 d 7-17-1822 m Elizabeth Fox Sgt NJ
Jacob: b 10-6-1747 d 10-15-1823 m Hester Davis Ens NY
James: b 1755 d 1818 m Sarah — Pvt NC
James: b 4-5-1744 d 4-25-1805 m Catherine Hamilton Col PA
John: b 1-26-1730 d a. 11-7-1807 m Sarah Black Pvt DE
John: b 1749 d 1802 m Mary Irwin Pvt GA
John: b — d p. 1830 m Mary Ball Ricketts PS MD
John: b c. 1712 d 12-4-1778 m Susannah Carter PS NJ
John: b 1747 d 1837 m Esther Beam Pvt PA ★
John: b 1742 d 1802 m Elizabeth Rutter Sol SC
John: b 1739 d 12-30-1841 m Elizabeth Thompson Pvt VA
John: b 5- -1757 d 8-7-1842 m X Pvt VA ★
John: b 1760 d 1817 m Martha Allen Capt VA
Josiah: b 1727 d a. 9-19-1785 m Mary Watson Capt VA
Josiah: b 8-28-1747 d 12-21-1818 m Martha Strange PS VA
Nathaniel: b 1741 d 1848 m Mary — Pvt NC ★
Robert: b 7-28-1758 d 1-25-1813 m Francina Reeder Pvt NJ
Robert: b 1703 d 1782 m (2)Mary Caldwell Pvt PA
Robert: b 1-23-1756 d 1825 m (1)Mary Culbertson (2)Catharine Campbell (3)Elizabeth Sprinkle Dunnhoeffer Pvt PA
Robert: b 9-15-1756 d 9-23-1836 m Hannah — OrdlSgt VA ★
Rowland: b 1744 d 10- -1821 m Phoebe Mullican Pvt PS NJ
Thomas: b 1731 d 1815 m (1)Rachel Gallup (2)Mary Gore Lt VA
Thomas: b c. 1730 d 1798 m X Sgt VA
William: b c. 1760 d p. 1828 m Dorcas — PS MD
William: b a. 1760 d 9-4-1791 m Lydia Loring Lt PS NH
William: b 6-19-1753 d 2- -1807 m Rachel Scudder 2Lt NJ
William: b 1744 d 10-5-1809 m Eleanor Talbot Col PA

CHAMBLISS,
Christopher: b 4-4-1746 d 1843 m Mary Taylor Pvt GA
Joel: b — d 12-12-1816 m Mary — Sol NC
Peter: b c. 1755 d p. 1820 m (1)— (2)Elizabeth Corbin (3)Mary (Rutledge) Rife Sgt SC

CHAMPE,
John: b 1752 d 1798 m Phebe Barnard SgtMaj Spy VA W★

CHAMPION,
Daniel: b — d c. 1805 m Ruhame — Pvt NJ
Daniel: b 5-23-1763 d 5-23-1856 m (1)Lucena Harris (2)Asenath — (3)Mary Betsey Hubbell Pvt VT ★
Deborah: b 5-3-1753 d 11-30-1845 m Judge Samuel Gilbert PS CT
Elisha: b 3-7-1758 d 4-23-1815 m Phebe Miller Pvt CT
Ezra: b 8-28-1763 d 10-3-1837 m (1)Lucretia Tubbs (2)Lucy Tubbs Pvt CT ★
Henry, Sr.: b 1-19-1723 d 7-23-1797 m (1)Deborah Brainard (2)Mrs Sarah Lewis CmsryGen CT
Henry, Jr.: b 3-27-1757 d 7-13-1856 m Abigail Tinker Maj CT ★
Henry: b 3-20-1729 d 5-17-1791 m Sarah Peck Capt CT
Israel: b 12-20-1726 d 3-6-1815 m Mehitable Fuller PS CT
Jacob: b — d 6-12-1832 m Anne — Sol SC
Joel: b 3-4-1755 d 2-22-1846 m Thankful Champion Pvt NY
Judah: b 8-20-1729 d 10-10-1810 m Elizabeth Welch Chp CT
Medes: b 8-18-1764 d 12-4-1834 m Lydia Farnum Sol MA
Reuben, Sr.: b 9-4-1727 d 3-29-1777 m Lydia Ingram Duncan Dr NY
Reuben, Jr.: b 7-30-1760 d 5-26-1832 m Silence Morgan Ely Pvt MA
Reuben: b 2-16-1757 d 12-10-1848 m Esther Chadwick Pvt CT ★
Stephen: b 3-16-1755 d 2-1-1810 m Phebe Moshier Smn CT

CHAMPLIN, (includes CHAMPLAIN)
Adam Babcock: b 7-24-1762 d 3-25-1844 m Henrietta Coggeshall Pvt RI ★
Asa: b 6-27-1741 d p. 1778 m Mollie Thompson Pvt RI
Caleb: b 2-20-1759 d 3-22-1840 m Anna Ely Pvt CT
Charles: b 3-24-1754 d 1-29-1838 m Mary Woodburn Pvt CT
Christopher: b 11-30-1707 d 7- -1781 m Hannah Hill PS RI
Christopher: b 10-13-1739 d 5-26-1801 m Mary Cottrell 2Lt RI
George: b 12-21-1765 d 3-15-1848 m Nancy Bentley Pvt RI
Jeffery: b 3-10-1757 d p. 1832 m Ann Card Pvt RI ★
Jeffery: b 3-21-1743-5 d 5-17-1797 m Mary Gardner PS RI
John, Sr.: b 7-10-1759 d 9-25-1796 m Hannah Congdon Ens RI
Jonathan: b 10-6-1755 d 1842 m Mary Moon 2Sgt RI ★
Joseph: b 8-4-1709 d 12-20-1792 m (1)Rebecca Chesebrough (2)Mary Noyes Of RI
Joseph: b 1756 d 6-17-1850 m Nancy Kenyon Pvt RI ★
Joshua: b 1710 d p. 1778 m Bridget Thompson PS Capt NY
Lodowick: b 1745 d 3-20-1786 m Mary Richard Ely NCapt CT
Nathan: b 10-8-1749 d c. 1816 m Sarah Foster Sgt RI
Robert: b 4-12-1747 d 9-25-1809 m Mary Browning PS RI
Samuel: b c. 1726 d 11-25-1811 m Mary — Capt RI
Samuel: b 7-17-1746 d 11-1-1818 m Alice Reynolds Lt RI
Samuel: b 9-18-1758 d p. 1800 m Freelove Ross PS RI
Stephen: b 8-3-1763 d 12-25-1848 m Elizabeth Raymond Perry Sgt RI
William: b 1757 d 3-2-1848 m Content Leeds Brown Capt RI ★

CHAMPNEY,
Nathaniel: b 12-28-1756 d 11-12-1826 m Susanna — Pvt MA
Samuel: bpt 10-2-1748 d 1-16-1809 m Hannah Corey Pvt MA

CHANCE,
Simpson: b 1761 d 1850 m Elizabeth Reeves Pvt GA
Vinson: b 3-17-1758 d p. 1783 m Sarah Taylor Drm NC

CHANCELLOR,
John: b 1726 d 3-10-1815 m Jane Monroe PS VA
Thomas: b 1745 d c. 1823 m (3)Judith Gaines Pvt VA

CHANDLER,
Aaron: b 1722 d 7-24-1819 m Ruth Butterfield PS NH
Abial: b 5-11-1744 d 8-27-1776 m Judith Walker Capt NH
Abiel: b 10-20-1765 d 1872/3 m Abigail Thomas Pvt NH ★
Abner: b 2-6-1731 d p. 1790 m Sarah Hill Pvt NH
Asa: b 8-25-1742 d 10-1-1825 m Martha Delano Pvt MA
Benjamin: b 1721 d 8-16-1777 m Elizabeth Geoffrey Pvt VT
Benjamin: b 1718 d 1798 m Hannah Dutton Drm MA
Benjamin: b c. 1721 d p. 1790 m Mary — Sgt PS NH
Christopher: b 3-10-1744 d 4-9-1809 m (1)Prudence Grubb (2)Phoebe Kirk Sol DE
Daniel, Sr.: b 3-21-1729 d 1-7-1790 m Violet Burnham Pvt CT
Daniel, Jr.: b 5-2-1764 d 1-1-1853 m Polly Ayers Pvt CT
Daniel: b 3-29-1748 d 1844 m Mary Galucia Pvt CT
Daniel: b 2-15-1735 d 10-25-1795 m (1)Sarah Eastman (2)Sarah Merrill PS Pvt NH
David: b 9-24-1747 d 9-2-1816 m Miriam Simons Cpl CT
David: b 3-12-1751 d 10-18-1832 m Miriam Pierce PS DE
David, Sr.: b 12-17-1724 d 2-11-1776 m Mary Ballard Capt MA
David: b 3-7-1743 d 8-17-1822 m Mary Parks Pvt NH
David: b 11-22-1765 d p. 11-7-1832 m Anne Stovall Sol NC
Ebenezer: b 5-14-1749 d 9-25-1823 m (1)Mary Burnap (2)Mrs Sarah Hutchinson (3)Mrs Remembrance Pierce Pvt NH
Ebenezer: bpt 11-16-1755 d 6-12-1842 m Sally Sargent Pvt NH ★
Enos: b 7-3-1742 d 5-23-1785 m Elizabeth Soule Lt MA
George: b 6-11-1733 d 7-10-1809 m Jane McConnell Pvt PA
Hill: b 5-14-1761 d 7-8-1825 m Rhoda Squier Pvt NH
Isaac, Sr.: b 1717 d 6-5-1787 m Abigail Hale CS CT
Isaac, Jr.: b 6-24-1743 d 7-10-1791 m Anna Loomis Pvt CT
Isaac: b 12-7-1730 d a. 1781 m Betty Proctor Pvt MA
Isaac: b 4-8-1732 d 3-6-1817 m Hannah Ballard Pvt MA
Isaac: b 10-30-1732 d 9-4-1802 m Esther Chandler Pvt PA
Jacob: b 12-22-1725 d 1800 m Ann Taylor PS SC
James: b 11-28-1761 d 12-2-1835 m Phoebe Dane Dmr MA
James, Sr.: b 2-22-1713 d 12-8-1793 m (1)Mary Wright (2)Mary Flagg PS MA
James, Jr.: b 12-24-1740 d 5-9-1824 m (1)Mary Melvin (2)Deliverance Heald Pvt MA
James, Sr.: b 12-18-1717 d 4-20-1791 m Jemima Meeker Pvt NJ
Joel: b 10-24-1748 d 8-20-1825 m Abigail Simmons PS NH
John: b 1-4-1736 d 3-15-1796 m Mary — Col CT
John, Sr.: b 9-7-1725 d 1-10-1812 m Lydia Taylor 2Lt PS ME
John, Jr.: b 11-27-1754 d 11-7-1837 m Hannah Streeter Pvt MA ★
John: b 8-15-1730 d 3-1-1807 m Mary Carter PS Lt NH
John, Jr.: b 12-31-1758 d 10-19-1804 m Margaret Mack MM Smn MA W★
John: b 7-18-1750 d 3-26-1832 m (1)Katy Holman (2)Mary Jackson Pvt MA
John: b 12-26-1727 d 4-25-1800 m Elizabeth Wells PS MA
John, Sr.: b 11-26-1731 d 11-22-1810 m Beulah Merriam Pvt PS CS MA
John: b 10-15-1758 d 6-13-1825 m Olive Jane Stevens Pvt NH

CHANDLER, contd.

John: b 2-1-1762 d 9-26-1841 m Mary Whittier Pvt NH
John: b 1728 d a. 8-21-1800 m Mary — MM NJ
John: b c. 1744 d 6-13-1835 m Anna Jones Pvt PA
John: b 1755 d p. 1832 m Miss Nance Pvt SC
John: b 4-28-1757 d 5-12-1829 m Mary Royce Sol VT
John: b 3-4-1737 d 1-21-1820 m (1)Esther Painter (2)Olive Archer PS VT
Jonathan: b 1731 d p. 1807 m Rebecca Packard Pvt MA
Jonathan: b 2-17-1731 d 1-28-1839 m (1)Hannah Brooks (2)Rachel Wilson Pvt NH
Jonathan: b 1735 d 5-24-1799 m Sarah Pierce Capt NH
Jonathan: b 5-23-1762 d 2-9-1837 m Mary Jewell Pvt NY NJ ★
Joseph: b 9-10-1753 d 11-7-1844 m Patience Mary Andrews Pvt CT ★
Joseph: b 4-28-1738 d 9-16-1816 m Mary Chapin Pvt CT
Joseph: b 8-30-1745 d 10-11-1831 m Olive Backus Pvt PS CT
Joseph: b 3-12-1756 d 1-17-1838 m Mary Felt Pvt MA
Joseph: b 1-6-1753 d 1-2-1833 m Elizabeth Dobson Pvt MA ★
Joseph: b 1725 d 1776 m Lydia Eastman Capt PS NH
Joseph: b 11-18-1760 d 4-23-1826 m Hannah Farrington Pvt NH
Joseph: b 4-23-1740 d 7-17-1815 m Betsey Jewett PS NH
Joseph: b 1757 d 5-5-1817 m Eleanor Caples Pvt PA
Joseph: b 10-20-1747 d 6-13-1835 m Margaret Gunnison PS NH
Joshua: b 10-31-1757 d 11-19-1853 m (1)Sarah Parker (2)Lydia Cobb Pvt MA
Josiah: b 1-9-1755 d 10-30-1840 m Eunice Dana Sgt PA ★
Josiah: b 10-2-1724 d 12-12-1798 m (1)Freelove Carpenter (2)Lydia Richardson (3)Mary Blanchard Pvt MA
Josiah: b 9-8-1738 d 12-15-1834 m Rachel Magoon Drm MA
Lewis: b 8-4-1761 d 9-19-1847 m Sarah Bailey Pvt MA
Matthew: b 1-5-1764 d 8-13-1852 m Ruth Easten Pvt CT ★
Mordecai: b 1758 d 1835 m Nancy — Pvt SC
Mordecai: b 5-15-1762 d 5- -1846 m Elizabeth Musgrove Pvt SC ★
Moses: b 5-19-1720 d 3-15-1800 m (1)Dorothy Marble (2)Elizabeth Kimball PS MA
Moses, Jr.: b 8-27-1757 d 4-27-1828 m Sarah Berry Pvt MA
Moses: b 11-23-1765 d 4-10-1822 m (1)Sarah Goodwin (2)Mary Langdon Pvt NH
Nathan, Sr.: b 6-3-1708 d 7-31-1784 m Priscilla Holt PS MA
Nathan, Jr.: b 2-19-1730 d 4-30-1786 m Phebe Abbott Pvt MA
Nathan, 3d: b 6-16-1756 d 1-27-1837 m Lucy Ballard Cpl MA
Nathan: b 8-23-1758 d 5-19-1835 m Lucy Wing Pvt MA ★
Nathaniel: b 1760 d 6-4-1854 m Ruth Fish Pvt MA ★
Peleg: b 5-27-1735 d 8-24-1819 m Sarah Winslow PS ME
Perez: b 7-10-1730 d 1-28-1800 m Rhoda Wadsworth PS MA
Peter: b 6-23-1733 d 10-25-1816 m (1)Mary Hodges (2)Abigail Wales CS PS CT
Philemon: b 4-30-1754 d 5-9-1834 m Mary Sabin Sol CT
Robert: b 1760 d 1831 m Sarah Walker Pvt CT ★
Robert: b 8-25-1729 d a. 7-22-1792 m Mary Hamblen PS VA
Samuel: b 3-8-1762 d 11-4-1809 m Dorcas Terry Pvt CT
Samuel: b 1-25-1764 d 1-12-1842 m Sarah Jaques Pvt MA
Samuel: b 10-11-1737 d 1-26-1784 m Margaret Thompson Pvt NH
Samuel, Sr.: b 8-7-1745 d p. 2-8-1793 m Rebecca Walton PS NH
Samuel: b 1735 d 2-12-1804 m Elizabeth Price Pvt NJ
Seth: b 5-8-1738 d 3-3-1818 m Eunice Durkee Sgt CT
Shadrack: b 8- -1757 d c. 1840 m X Pvt SC ★
Stephen: b 2-2-1730/1 d 9-10-1804 m (2)Hephsibah Warrener PS CT
Stephen: b 8-23-1753 d 8-25-1842 m (1)Meribah Nye (2)Catharine Lampson Harwood Pvt MA ★
Stephen: b 1740-6 d p. 1784 m Elizabeth McMinn Pvt PA
Swithin: b 10-1-1715 d p. 1785 m Ann Wilson PS DE
Thomas, Jr.: b 9-23-1740 d p. 5-22-1791 m Sarah Lord PS CS VT
Timothy: b 4-5-1738 d p. 1790 m Mary Walker Pvt MA
William: b 4-29-1723 d 6-29-1800 m (1)Mary Ballard (2)Rebekah Lovejoy Sgt MA
William: b 1751 d 1826 m Joanna Read Pvt MA
William: b 11-22-1761 d 1841 m Lovisa Shumeray Pvt MA
William: b 6-9-1754 d 4-21-1844 m (1)Mary Grosvenor (2)Patty Hill (3)Eunice Tenney Pvt NH
Zachariah: b 5-28-1751 d 4-20-1830 m Sarah Patten Pvt NH
Zebadiah: b 11-11-1752 d 2-5-1835 m Lucy Chandler Pvt MA
Zebedee: b 1712 d 12-2-1777 m (1)Lydia (Gray) Loring (2)Repentence (Lucas) Bennett Lt MA

CHANNELL, (includes CHANEL)

Abraham Fitz John: b 11-24-1748 d 1-9-1858 m (1)Abigail Burnham (2)Wealthy Cox Pvt MA
Joseph: b c. 1750 d p. 1830 m Mary Sea Pvt VA
Lewis: b 1740 d 10-17-1780 m Susanna Marston Cpl MA

CHAPEZE,

Henry: b 1759 d 1810 m Sarah Kenny Dr FrA

CHAPIN,

Aaron: b 4-20-1753 d 12-25-1838 m Mary King Pvt CT
Abel: b 4-5-1756 d 10-10-1831 m Dorcas (Chapin) Pvt MA
Abner, 2d: b 5-29-1749 d 4-1-1814 m Rhoda Kibbe Pvt MA
Adams: b 1750 d 10-23-1832 m Olive Sumner MM QMMaj MA
Amos: b 1752 d 11-13-1833 m (1)Tamar Church (2)Trifernia Sheldon Cpl MA
Asahel: b 2-2-1748 d 1-20-1828 m Sarah Frink Pvt MA

Benjamin: b 5-24-1736 d 1781 m Margaret Colton Dr VA
Caleb: b a. 7-13-1736 d 11-10-1815 m Rebecca Bascom Capt PS MA
Calvin: b 1-5-1755 d 3-3-1834 m Huldah Whittemore Sgt MA
Charles: b 12-26-1720 d 1-21-1813 m (1)Ann Camp (2)Anne — PS CT
Charles: b 8-22-1742 d 4-22-1813 m (1)Silence Kellogg (2)Mary Smith 1Lt MA
Daniel: b 1-3-1758 d 9-14-1831 m (2)Ruth Lane Pvt CT
David: b 8-1-1762 d 1-4-1858 m Ruth Seymour Pvt CT
David, Jr.: b 9-19-1746 d 2-15-1826 m Lydia Cook Pvt MA
Ebenezer: b 10-4-1735 d 4-23-1822 m Mehitabel Bartlett Sol CS CT MA
Eli: b 6-9-1754 d 3-7-1830 m Margaret Taft Pvt MA
Elias: b 2-15-1751 d 2-4-1839 m (1)Alice Collins (2)Dimis Chapman Pvt CT
Elijah: b 1760 d 3-22-1830 m Lavina Phillips Pvt MA
Enoch: b 9-16-1740 d 10-8-1802 m Eunice Nash Capt MA
Ephraim: b 10-29-1729 d 10-12-1805 m Jemima Chapin Capt MA
Frederick: b 5-12-1760 d 6-12-1802 m Lucretia Morton Pvt CT
Gad: b 8-11-1726 d 8-18-1813 m Abigail Case Pvt MA
Gad: b 11-3-1748 d 5-26-1836 m Sarah Browne Pvt MA ★
Gershom: b 5-27-1734 d 8-23-1801 m (1)Elizabeth Johnson (2)Mrs Deborah Torrey (3)Mrs Mary Sherwood Pvt MA
Gideon: b 4-16-1754 d 3-10-1838 m Lydia Potwine Arfr CT ★
Gideon: b 2-24-1742 d 11-10-1820 m Elizabeth Thomas Capt MA
Henry: b 6-7-1721 d p. 1790 m Mary Butler Sol MA
Hiram: b 8-19-1747 d 3-15-1783 m Sarah Bartlet Ens NH
Ichabod: b 9-26-1760 d 5-16-1843 m (1)Asenath Smith (2)Jerusha Bruce Pvt CT ★
Isaac: b 11-10-1756 d 3-26-1835 m (1)Rachel Wheaton (2)Huldah— (3)Martha Stone Pvt MA CL ★
Israel: b 12-4-1741 d 3-7-1795 m Elizabeth Marsh Col MA
Israel: b 9-18-1751 d 4-25-1810 m (1)Chloe Lombard (2)Mary Booth 2Lt MA
Ithamar: b 10-15-1759 d c. 1825 m (1)Mary — (2)Mrs Lucy Van Horn Pvt MA
Japhet: b 8-8-1760 d 10-6-1822 m Lovina Wright Pvt MA
Japheth: b 7-13-1726 d 7-25-1797 m Patience Hayward Pvt MA
Jehiel: b 12-19-1761 d — m Ursula Beament Pvt MA
Jeremiah: b 4-16-1734 d 2-17-1814 m Caroline Fowler 1Lt MA
Jesse: b 8-27-1761 d 3-4-1834 m Eunice Wheelock Sgt MA ★
Joel: b 4-22-1732 d 3-17-1803-5 m (1)Sarah Burke (2)Mrs Rhoda Scott PS Sgt MA
John: b 4-6-1743 d 11-19-1839 m Mary Simmons (2)Elizabeth Bur Pvt CT ★
John: b 10-7-1730 d 7-17-1815 m Rhoda Albee PS MA
Jonathan: b 10-22-1738 d 2-8-1819 m Abigail Munn 2Lt MA
Jonathan: b 4-13-1754 d 10-15-1826 m Rebecca Hall Pvt MA
Joseph: b 9-8-1749 d 2-11-1832 m (1)Lucy Morgan (2)Mrs Abigail Chapman Pvt MA
Joseph, Jr.: b 10-28-1758 d 1-14-1851 m Mary Stoughton Pvt MA
Joseph: b 6-11-1718 d 6-11-1803 m Jane Allen Wolcott CS PS MA
Joshua: b c. 1730 d a. 10-2-1801 m Mary Hayward Pvt MA
Josiah: b 1-28-1719 d p. 1787 m (1)Rachel Albee (2)Mary Corbitt Pvt MA
Judah: b 4-17-1756 d 11-14-1821 m Lois Stebbins Pvt MA
Justus: b 1-30-1753 d 7-15-1825 m (1)Joannah Fuller (2)Martha Taylor Pvt PS NH
Levi: b 8-23-1751 d 8-19-1834 m Sarah Richardson Pvt PA ★
Lucius: b 4-25-1760 d 12-24-1842 m Susannah Rousseau Fif MA ★
Martin: b 10-6-1738 d 4-24-1793 m Bathsheba Cooper Sgt MA
Moses: b c. 1736 d 6-9-1802 m Lydia Atwood Sgt MA
Nathan: b 2-3-1735 d 2-13-1830 m Mary Smith Sgt MA
Nathaniel: b 12-31-1738 d 2-11-1831 m (1)Sibyl Terry (2)Zeriah Parsons Ens CT
Noah, Sr.: b 10-25-1707 d 8-23-1787 m Mary Wright Ens CT
Noah, Jr.: b 7-20-1748 d 5-5-1790 m Mary Williams Cnt MM CT
Paul: b 11-11-1760 d 1845 m Mary Stillman Pvt MA
Perez: b 9-3-1752 d 4-26-1839 m Elizabeth Smith Dr Srgnmte MA
Peter: b 9-23-1756 d 9-23-1839 m Elizabeth Austin Pvt MA
Phineas, Sr.: b 9-23-1715 d 10-11-1788 m Bethiah Chapin CS MA
Phineas, Jr.: b 3-7-1747 d 3-2-1821 m Sabrina Wright Lt MA
Phinehas: b 12-15-1755 d 1-21-1849 m Mary Lane Sgt CT NH ★
Samuel: b 10-29-1736 d 9- -1803 m Beulah Taft Cpl MA
Samuel: b 7-4-1758 d 5-28-1833 m Sibyl Joclyn Pvt MA
Samuel: b 9-24-1760 d 2-13-1842 m Susannah Walbridge Pvt VT ★
Selah: b 8-29-1751 d 5-30-1830 m Jerusha Burnham Pvt MA
Seth: b 3-3-1746 d 11-15-1833 m (1)Ruth Bullard (2)Elizabeth Rawson (3)Eunice Thompson 1Lt MA
Seth: b 8-17-1758 d 4-13-1832 m Sybel Lombard Pvt MA
Shadrack: b 9-16-1753 d 12-12-1819 m Abigail — Cpl MA
Simeon: b 8-20-1739 d 5-20-1799 m Lucy Doolittle Lt MA
Stephen: b 12-27-1744 d 3-31-1816 m (1)Sarah Hill (2)Rachel Rawson Cpl MA
Stephen: b 5-29-1718 d 1-22-1800 m Zebiah Ely PS CS MA
Thaddeus: b 4-7-1756 d 3-14-1835 m Lucy Whitney Cpl MA
Timothy: b 2-10-1760 d 12- -1844 m Tiercy Frink Pvt CT W★
William: b 4-12-1729 d 11-10-1777 m Martha — Pvt MA
Zebulon: b 11-11-1741 d 10-27-1823 m Lydia Ely Pvt MA

CHAPLIN, (includes CHAPLINE)

Abraham: b 1755 d 1-19-1824 m (1)Elizabeth Higgins (2)Hannah (Smith) Moore Capt VA

Asa: b 2-8-1739 d 4-11-1807 m Mary Bailey Pvt MA
Ebenezer: b 9-4-1751 d 2-23-1845 m (1)Ruth Copley (2)Lucy Hathaway Pvt CT ★
Ebenezer: bpt 7-3-1720 d 1781-90 m (1)Rebecca Poor (2)Mary — Ens PS NH
Isaac: b 1-17-1755 d 10-30-1810 m Elender Wallace Shenton PS VA
Jeremiah: b 1756 d 3- -1809 m Elizabeth Nourse Pvt MD
John: b 1-22-1758 d 8-3-1837 m Margaret Chaplin Pvt MA
Joseph: b 1-23-1741/2 d p. 1790 m Lois Hastings Pvt MA
Micah: b 10-3-1745 d 10-10-1819/20 m Betsey Philbrick Sgt NH
Moses: b 10-20-1754 d 2-10-1812 m Mary Caldwell Capt MD
Moses: b 1755 d p. 1782 m Elizabeth Hopkinson Pvt MA
Moses: b 6-22-1760 d 11-18-1840 m Mary Platts Pvt NH
Samuel: b 5-14-1758 d 1833 m Mrs Rozoba Blood Pvt NH
Thomas: b 3-26-1742 d 10-8-1835 m (1)Elizabeth Fripp (2)Mary — PS SC
William, Sr.: b 1714 d 1784 m Sarah Reynolds Pvt SC
William, Jr.: b 6-8-1744 d 1808 m Martha Fripp Pvt SC

CHAPMAN.
Abner: b c. 1745 d 1828-31 m Elizabeth — Sol NC
Albert: b 8-19-1745 d 12-27-1820 m Lydia Ketchum Maj CT
Allen: b 1751 d 1821 m (1)Rachel Powe (2)Eleanor De Witt Sol VA
Alpheus: b c. 1743 d a. 1-2-1824 m Martha — 1Lt CT
Amos: b 9-7-1763 d p. 1803 m Abigail Burdick Pvt CT
Andrew, Sr.: b 3-3-1719 d 4-13-1794 m Hannah Smith Pvt CT
Andrew, Jr.: b 5-10-1754 d 8-22-1827 m Anna York Pvt CT
Asa: b 2-12-1753 d 2-17-1805 m (1)Mary Williams (2)Elizabeth Brainard Sgt CT W★
Benjamin: bpt 5-26-1751 d 10-9-1808 m Loas Hill Pvt CT
Benjamin: b 2-26-1763 d 3-7-1824 m (1)Polly Clark (2)Sylvia Upson Pvt CT
Benjamin: b c. 1753 d 1791-1800 m Abigail — Capt QM NY
Benjamin, Sr.: b 6-28-1736 d 1-20-1802 m Jemima Gates CS NH
Benjamin, Jr.: b 8-29-1759 d 7-13-1804 m Caroline Matilda Fuller Pvt NH
Caleb: b 7-23-1764 d 10-5-1837 m Lydia Sheather Pvt CT ★
Caleb: b 4-19-1732 d 1805 m (1)Elizabeth Clark (2)Hanna Brown Pvt CT
Caleb: b 12-19-1735 d 10-19-1827 m Freelove Lamb Pvt MA
Constant: b 12-27-1761 d 9-24-1847 m Jemima Kelsey SgtMaj CT ★
Daniel: b 3-12-1753 d 11-23-1842 m Lucy Talcott Pvt CT
Daniel: b 1755 d — m X Capt CT NY
Daniel, Jr.: b 12-21-1740 d 7-6-1799 m Hepzibeth Howe Pvt MA
Daniel: b 7-25-1763 d 2-8-1841 m Lucretia Finch 2Sgt NY ★
Daniel: b 8-29-1743 d 9-6-1777 m Mary Andrews Sol CT
David: b 7-22-1734 d 3-12-1814 m Abigail Willett PS MA
David: b 3-23-1761 d a. 9- -1826 m Mary Lyman Pvt MA
Ebenezer: b 1763 d 2-9-1830 m Mary Calkins Pvt CT ★
Ebenezer: b 1764 d 12- -1850 m Lydia Wilson Pvt MA
Edward: b 7-1-1760 d 10-18-1849 m (2)Rebecca Tainter Pvt NY ★
Elijah, Sr.: b 1726 d 2-17-1808 m Sarah Steele PS CT
Elijah, Jr.: b 2-12-1753 d 12-17-1825 m Sarah Keeler Pvt CT
Elijah: b 12-3-1753 d 5-31-1804 m (1)Jennie Chaffee (2)Esther Jennings Cpl CT W★
Elisha: b 11-10-1740 d 6-17-1825 m Huldah Lord Capt CT
Elisha: b 9-2-1750 d 11-10-1819 m (1)Rebecca Bellamy (2)Mary Bristol (3)Phoebe Gates Dr Capt CT
Enoch: b 6-8-1755 d 11-12-1837 m Chloe Gage Pvt NY
Erastus: b 8-25-1760 d 10-26-1821 m Mary Huntington Pvt VT
Ezra: b 8-10-1749 d 8-31-1778 m Mary Dewey Ens CT
George: bpt 7-26-1741 d 3-21-1824 m Lydia Henfield Pvt QM MA
George: b 1756 d 5-20-1833 m Mariah Ann Hall Pvt PA ★
George: b c. 1757 d p. 1-1-1807 m Joanna LeMaster Fif Drm VA
George: b c. 1755 d 4-9-1836 m Sarah Reynolds Sol PS VA
Giles: b 6-21-1748 d 4-12-1819 m Mary Summers Pvt SC
Henry, H.: b 1-9-1764 d 12-5-1821 m Mary Davidson Lt MD
Hosea: b 3-8-1755 d 1812 m (1)Mary McKinney (2)Martha Converse Sgt CT
Isaac: b 1-3-1739 d 2-14-1811 m (1)Tabitha Chapman (2)Abigail Brooks Drm CT
Isaac: b 1-29-1736 d 1777 m Rebecca Harris 1Lt MA
Isaac: b 5-9-1747 d 11- -1776 m Ruth Robinson Sol MA
Jabez: b 1731 d 1-27-1820 m Sarah Olmstead LCol CT
James, Sr.: b 1734 d 9-15-1776 m (1)Sarah Birch (2)Abigail Coit Maj CT
James, Jr.: b 1759 d 1841 m Mary Holt Capt CT
James: b 4-8-1750 d 9-6-1822 m (1)Abigail Sherwood Lt CT
James: b 1735 d 3-31-1822 m Mary Ogden PS NJ
James: b 11-2-1747 d 5-26-1800 m Martha Kirkpatrick Sol PA
James: b 3-25-1743 d a. 1783 m Betty Allen Pvt VA
James: b 11-10-1760 d 5-14-1839 m Phoebe — Pvt VA
Jason: b 2- -1762 d 7-28-1841 m Mary Baker Pvt CT
Jedediah: b 15-1726 d 2-29-1816 m Mary Grinnell Capt CT
Jedediah: b 8-19-1759 d 11-5-1848 m Jane Sherril Sgt CT ★
Jedediah: b 1741 d 5-22-1813 m (1)Blanche Smith (2)Margaretta Le Conte Chp NJ
John: b 1746 d 1818 m Mary Thompson Sgt GA
John: b c. 1750 d 1814 m (1)Rachel Jackson (2)Dorcas — Pvt MA
John: b 6-1-1764 d 1829 m Ruth Berri Pvt NH
John: b 10-18-1740 d 1-27-1800 m Mercy Beaumont PS Dr PA
John: b a. 1747 d — m (1)Susan Leith (2)Katharine Ten Eyck Pvt PA

John: b 1-18-1740 d 1813 m Sallie Abbott 2Lt VA
Jonah: b 1748 d 7-13-1831 m Abigail Blaisdell Lt NH
Jonathan: b 9-25-1729 d 12-19-1813 m Mary Steward Pvt CT
Jonathan: b 1760 d 6-17-1813 m Anna Sweet Pvt MA
Joseph: b 5-2-1731 d 8-9-1822 m Anna Kendrick Capt CT
Joseph: b 3-31-1741 d 8-9-1822 m (1)Lois Burchard (2)Elizabeth Abel Lt QM CT
Joseph: b 6-2-1749 d p. 7-11-1809 m (1)Prudence Lewis (2)Mary Main Sol CT
Joseph: b 6-10-1713 d 1795 m (1)Mary Winn PS NH
Joseph: b 2-28-1743 d 2-5-1830 m Allice Potter Pvt NH
Joseph: b 12-25-1745 d 1-18-1836 m Jemima Caswell Capt NC ★
Joseph: b c. 1745 d p. 12-19-1808 m Catherine — Pvt VA
Joshua: b 3-14-1755 d 7-22-1837 m Mary Lee Pvt MA ★
Josiah: b 10-14-1757 d 4-24-1813 m Bethiah Pease Sol NY
Lebbeus: b 11-21-1752 d 10-16-1833 m (1)Sybil Kirtland (2)Jemima Grinnel Lt CT
Lemuel: b 9-1-1757 d 9-17-1847 m Annie Brayman Pvt CT ★
Levi: b 10-21-1747 d 6-21-1828 m Elizabeth Stoddard Pvt CT
Levi: b 10-9-1740 d p. 1794 m Elizabeth Hull PS CT
Levi: b 1753 d 7-24-1825 m Sarah Barber Pvt NH
Micah: b 7-18-1735 d 10-29-1792 m Elizabeth Howes LCol MA
Michael: b 1758 d 1839 m Keziah Hawley Pvt CT
Nathan: b 10-17-1760 d 2-14-1824 m Abigail Peabody Pvt CT
Nathan: b 5-3-1761 d 1-29-1828/9 m Elizabeth Coleman Pvt VA W★
Nathaniel: b 10- -1714 d — m Mary Denison Capt CT
Nathaniel: b 9-13-1746 d 2-18-1807 m (1)Elizabeth Symonds (2)Lucy Cooley Capt MA
Nathaniel: b 11-5-1758 d 1-2-1819 m Sally Gott Pvt MA ★
Nicholas: b 1746 d 1-21-1821 m (1)Rachel Wallace (2)Jennet McCartney Pvt PA
Obadiah: b 1752 d 1812 m Elizabeth Northrup Pvt NY
Peleg: b 1730 d 1784 m Mary Young Pvtr RI
Phineas: b 5-15-1716 d 11-20-1782 m Sarah Hulbert Ketchum PS CT
Reuben: b 12-8-1749 d 10-25-1776 m Mary Cobb Pvt CT
Reuben: b 1746 d 6-16-1824 m Ann Reynolds Capt VA
Reuben Rowley: b 10-15-1758 d 8-3-1846 m Mary Doane Pvt CT
Richard: b 1736 d 9-6-1781 m Esther Richards Lt CT
Richard: b 9-20-1741 d 12-1-1789 m (1)Mary Massom Curtis (2)Elizabeth Masson Reynolds Pvt VA
Robert, Jr.: b 11-19-1763 d 1-18-1842 m Judith Whitten MM Pvt CT ★
Robert, Sr.: b 1707/8 d p. 1785-7 m Margaret — PS MD
Samuel: b 1722 d 3- -1803 m Sarah White Col CT
Samuel: b 7-12-1755 d p. 1792 m Zilphia Gates Pvt CT
Samuel: b 2-13-1743 d 8-7-1799 m Mary Edwards Smn MA
Samuel, Sr.: b 12-7-1706 d 1796 m (1)— York (2) X PS NH
Samuel, Jr.: b 3-9-1734 d 4-9-1809 m Mary Barber Pvt NH
Samuel: b 12-13-1748 d 12-29-1826 m Rebecca Barnum Pvt NY
Simon: b 12-28-1736 d 7-26-1823 m (1)Eunice Preston (2)Lydia Carlton PS CT
Simon: b 4-22-1723 d 1792 m (1)Rebeccah De Wolf (2)Alice Rouse CS VT
Smith: b 10-28-1756 d 1-16-1840 m Sarah Foss Burleigh Pvt NH ★
Stephen: b c. 1756 d 1838 m Susanna Call Pvt CT
Sumner: b 2-1-1725 d 12-12-1812 m Elizabeth Herrick PS RI
Thomas: b 7-20-1749 d 3-2-1793 m Lydia Harding Pvt CT
Thomas: b 1721 d 12-11-1797 m Mary Beeman CS CT
Thomas: b 6-8-1725 d 1804 m Margaret Mitchell CS NC
Thomas: b 1753 d 1795 m Sarah Bell Pvt VA
Thomas: b 5-28-1758 d 1814 m Rebecca Todd Sol VA
Throop: b 3-25-1739 d p. 3-17-1794 m (1)Susan Barrey (2)Deborah Wilson Pvt MA
Timothy: b 6-3-1752 d 7-28-1828 m Avis Curtis Sgt CT ★
Timothy: b 10-3-1736 d 11-4-1819 m Sarah Fuller Pvt CT
Titus: b 9-30-1744 d 10- -1808 m Elizabeth Kelsey Grd CT
Uriah, Sr.: b 6-1-1731 d 4-22-1816 m Sibyl Olmstead CS PS PA CT
William: b 8-12-1745 d 9-9-1828 m Lydia Ingham Pvt CT
William: b 7- -1725 d 3-22-1808 m Sarah Jones Pvt CT
William: b 6-26-1745 d 12-30-1823 m Ann Rogers Pvt GA
William: b 1-19-1748 d 6-16-1800 m Mary Gosnell Pvt MD
William: b 1752 d c. 1823 m Hannah Smith Pvt NJ
William: b 1760 d 3-13-1813 m Elizabeth Cowan Pvt SC
William: b a. 1755 d 1-15-1796 m Cattran — Sol VA
William: b c. 1750 d p. 12-24-1804 m Mary Crocker PS VA
Zachariah: b 8-2-1740 d 1825 m Isabella Stanton Mil CT

CHAPOTON,
Jean Baptiste: b 6-17-1721 d 1-22-1803 m (1)Genevive Elizabeth Godfroy (2)Felicite Cesire PS MI

CHAPPELEAR,
Elias: b 1730-41 d c. 1795/6 m Ann Brammell Sol MD

CHAPPELL, (includes CHAPEL, SCHAPPELLE)
Abner: b 4-13-1763 d p. 2-15-1833 m Susannah Moore Pvt VA
Amaziah: b 8-14-1753 d 5-18-1829 m Jerusha Jones Pvt CT ★
Amos: b 3-27-1738 d 3-3-1777 m Sarah Slosson Capt CT
Daniel: b c. 1729 d 4-21-1825 m Anna Chapel Pvt CT ★
Ezekial: b 1744 d 10-3-1832 m Sarah Gardner Sol CT
Frederick: b c. 1746 d 1789 m Patience Bills NCapt CT
Hicks: b 3-5-1757 d 3-11-1836 m Elizabeth Threewiets Capt SC ★
Isaac: b 2-28-1761 d 5-1-1817 m Tamasin Wilcox Pvt MA
Jacob: b 2-2-1744 d 9-11-1826 m Susanna — Capt PA

CHAPPELL, contd.
James: b 1-21-1755 d 12-12-1829 m Abigail Hempstead Pvt RI ★
James: b 1740 d c. 1781 m Mary Harris Pvt SC
James, Sr.: b 1722 d p. 9-14-1776 m (1)Susan Hudson (2)Phoebe Archer Pvt VA
James, Jr.: b 1755 d 1-2-1826 m Lucy Woodson PS VA
James, Sr.: b 1717 d 1778 m (1)Elizabeth Briggs (2)Judith Rives (3)Mary Briggs PS VA
James, Jr.: b 3-5-1746/7 d 1818 m Sally Hines Pvt PS VA
James: b 1754 d c. 1830 m Martha Wooding QM VA
John: b 1755 d 9-10-1825 m (1)Dorothy Ford (2)Elizabeth Craddock Ens VA
John: b 1752 d 7-5-1812 m (1)Sarah Dickie (2)Ann de Graffenried Sol VA
John: b 1756 d 4-9-1835 m Mary Yayman Sol VA
Jonathan: b 1717 d 8-29-1783 m Elizabeth Comstock CS PS CT
Joshua: b 1735 d 7-3-1775 m Bathsheba Brewster Cpl CT
Laban: b 1762 d 11- -1829 m Margaret (Spigner) Adams Pvt SC
Noah: b 3-6-1760 d 3-23-1849 m Tarzah Chappell Pvt CT
Robert: b 4-2-1732 d p. 6-14-1798 m (1)Agnes Cross (2)Nancy Chappell Sol SC
Robert: b 1746 d 3- -1829 m Mary Tucker Pvt VA
Thomas: b 1763 d 1820 m Delia Hazel PS SC
William: b 6-20-1763 d 12-20-1850 m Anna Maples Cpl CT ★

CHARD,
Barce: b 1- -1764 d 8-6-1842 m Catharine Rosebush Sgt NY ★

CHARLES,
Aaron: b 1724 d 11-18-1802 m Elizabeth Burt Capt MA
Elisha: b c. 1750 d a. 1831 m Elizabeth Moore PS NC
Jacob: b 10-27-1742 d 8-16-1840 m Elizabeth — Pvt PA
James: b 1739 d p. 12-5-1777 m Sarah — PS NC
John: b 2-28-1746 d 6-8-1831 m Phoebe Russell Pvt MA
John: b 1739 d c. 1830 m X Pvt PA
Joseph: b 1749 d 9- -1828 m Elizabeth Fisher Pvt PA
Michael: b c. 1730 d 1813 m X PS NC
Samuel: b 9-6-1755 d 1840 m Susan Abbott Pvt MA

CHARLESWORTH,
John Miles: b 12-21-1760 d 4-28-1816 m Margaret Lipe Sgt NY W ★

CHARLOCK,
Henry: b 4-13-1749 d 4-29-1833 m Hannah Jewell Pvt NY ★

CHARLTON, (includes CHARLETON)
Francis: b 2-2-1759 d 11-25-1851 m Susanna Akers Pvt VA ★
Jacob: b 4-25-1743 d p. 5-12-1834 m Susan — Pvt VA ★
James: b 6-3-1752 d 1825 m (1)Abigail Bowles (2)Hannah Sigler Pvt VA
John, 2d.: b 11-1-1754 d 9-14-1823 m Nancy Carter Pvt VA
John: b 4-12-1761 d 5-19-1839 m Ann — Pvt VA ★
John Usher: b 6-21-1753 d 12-8-1806 m Elizabeth Beatty Capt MD
Thomas: b 11-21-1745 d 1795 m Lucy Kenan Lt Dr SC

CHARTER,
James: b 1742 d 4-22-1821 m (3)Phebe Phillips Sgt VT
John: b c. 1721 d 11-3-1807 m Mary Chase Lt CT
John, Jr.: b 1750 d p. 1790 m Sarah Russell Pvt CT

CHASE, (includes CHACE)
Aaron: b 1-3-1761 d 10-3-1828 m Priscilla Harrington Pvt MA
Abel: b 4-15-1739 d 12-29-1828 m Mrs Hannah Morse Campbell Pvt MA
Abel: b 8-9-1750 d 1- -1806 m Elizabeth Elliott PS MA
Abel: b 8- -1746 d c. 1810 m Hannah Bedell Pvt NH
Abner: b 6-22-1729 d p. 1790 m Deborah Baker Pvt MA
Abner: b 7-18-1742 d 1812 m Hannah Lawson Pvt MA
Abner: b 11-18-1746 d 3- -1838 m Joanna Moody Sgt NH
Abraham: b 12-9-1756 d 10-16-1832 m Elizabeth Bourne Pvt Smn MA
Abraham: b 10- -1734 d 1795 m (1)Jane McGonegal (2)Martha Spencer Pvt NY
Amos: b 1-9-1719 d 3-2-1818 m (1)Sarah Cole (2)Deborah — PS ME
Amos: b 5-19-1760 d 1-25-1850 m (1)Rebecca Hart (2)Joanna Lannam Lt NH
Amos: b 1747 d 5-11-1803 m Abigail Miller Cpl RI
Aquila: b 5-10-1715 d 1789 m (1)Hannah Davis (2)Mary Boley Pvt MA
Aquila, Jr.: b 9-26-1757 d 1-13-1835 m Anna Moulton Pvt MA
Benjamin: b 4-28-1747 d 10-3-1821 m Mary Chamberlain Pvt CT
Benjamin: bpt 7-15-1759 d 12-31-1826 m Alice Bartlett Pvt MA
Benjamin: b 2-3-1736/7 d 5-9-1802 m Catharine Campbell CS 1Lt MA ME
Benjamin: b 1-29-1737 d 3-20-1826 m (1)Elizabeth Durfee (2)Mrs Mehitable Thurston Cpl RI
Benjamin: b 5-21-1753 d 5-19-1822 m Martha Earle CS VT
Berry: b 7-23-1742 d 3-8-1815 m Mercy Baker Sgt MA
Berry: b 1750-5 d 1810 m Phoebe Wixon Sgt NY
Beverly: b 2-22-1759 d 1817 m Lucy Van Tress Pvt NY
Caleb: b 7-28-1746 d 2-13-1810 m Joanna Whitney CS ME

Caleb: b 11-21-1722 d 10-2-1808 m Sarah Prince Pvt MA
Caleb: b 4- -1761 d 1835 m (1)— Challis (2)Joanna Babb (3)Mary Straw Cpl NH
Charles: b 1753 d 1-21-1822 m Hannah Stewart Smn ME
Daniel: b 10-24-1744 d a. 2-16-1802 m Mary Downs Sol MA
Daniel: b 8-28-1762 d 9-1-1827 m Elizabeth Tappan Pvt MA
Daniel: b c. 3-23-1753 d 8-13-1841 m Mehitabel Kimball Lt NH
Daniel, Jr.: b 11-12-1751 d 8-7-1793 m Susannah Wilson Sgt MA
Daniel, Sr.: b 10-15-1728 d 7-31-1789 m Mary Pratt PS NH
Daniel: b 1-9-1720 d p. 1790 m Hannah Cook PS NY
David: b 4-15-1752 d 10-20-1841 m Jemima Humes Pvt MA
David: b 1721 d p. 1798 m (1)Elizabeth Asten (2)Mary Chase Pvt MA
David Prince: b 1-15-1753 d 3-22-1828 m (1)Sarah Greenwood (2)Judith Brown Sgt MA
Dudley: b 8-29-1730 d 4-13-1814 m Alice Corbett Pvt NH
Dudley: b c. 1745 d 1826 m Alice Abbot Pvt NH
Dudley Leavitt: b c. 6-4-1751 d p. 1790 m Mrs Mary (Ayers) Davis Lt QM NH
Ebenezer: b 9-25-1722 d p. 1790 m Susanna Berry Pvt MA
Ebenezer: b 3-27-1729 d 1802 m Hepsibeth Sargent Pvt MA
Ebenezer: b 1744 d 1-26-1823 m Hannah Barney Pvt MA W ★
Ebenezer: b 9-6-1760 d 9-5-1847 m (1)Sarah Snow (2)Mary Skinner Pvt MA ★
Ebenezer: b 1-31-1766/7 d 6-22-1855 m Jane Adams Pvt MA
Edmund: b 6-21-1748 d c. 1822 m Esther Merrill Pvt MA
Edward: b 4-27-1742 d 5-29-1815 m Abigail (Strange) Paine Pvt MA
Edward: b 11-24-1754 d 6-19-1814 m Mary Moore Pvt NH
Eleazer: b 7-25-1722 d 1808 m (1)Jeannette Elder (2)Mrs Mary (Booby) Brown Pvt MA
Enoch: b 9-16-1750 d 10-7-1819 m Sarah Sawyer Pvt MA
Ephraim: b 6-1-1744 d 4-17-1836 m Lydia Hathaway Capt MA
Ezekiel, Sr.: b 5-24-1727 d 1810 m Annie Spalding Pvt MA
Ezekiel, Jr.: b 7-9-1761 d 9-14-1843 m Betsy Goodwin Pvt MA
Ezekiel: b 10-20-1760 d 11-22-1845 m Lydia Wilbur Pvt MA
Ezra: b 5-25-1720 d 2-16-1799 m Abigail Low Pvt MA
Ezra: b 7-2-1717 d 3-3-1792 m Johanna Davis PS MA
Ezra: b 4-20-1758 d 11-18-1836 m Jerusha Gilbert Pvt RI ★
Francis: b c. 1726 d 1-16-1791 m Mary Perkins 2Lt MA
Francis: b 9-10-1738 d 9-21-1802 m Naomi Gardner CS MA
Gadeliah: b 11-28-1761 d 7-4-1832 m Rebecca Dewey Pvt NY W ★
Gowell: b 10-27-1744 d 1787 m Jerusha Higgins Cpl MA
Greenfield: b 1753 d 3-29-1810 m Sarah Briggs Pvt MA
Grindall: b 11-1-1757 d 6-10-1843 m (1)Susannah West (2)Sarah Peck Sgt MA
Henry: b 1746 d 12-12-1831 m Hepsibah Walker Pvt MA
Holder: b 8-24-1733 d 2- -1820 m Freeborn Dennis PS RI
Isaac: b 12-15-1757 d 11-12-1840 m Lois Smith Pvt MA
Isaac: b 9-12-1761 d 1-9-1833 m Sarah Bond Sol MA
Isaac: b 1756 d 1836 m Susan Smith Pvt NY
Jacob: b 8-4-1754 d 1818 m Content Sanders Pvt MA
Jacob: b 12-25-1727 d 12-12-1803 m Prudence Hills Pvt PS NH
Jacob: b 3-4-1744 d 1815 m Mary Hardy PS NH
James: b 7-9-1749 d 10-15-1832 m Abigail Bickford Sgt MA
James: b 6-16-1746 d 4-4-1821 m Susanna Perry Pvt MA
James: b c. 1754 d c. 1809 m Mercy Godfrey Smn MA
James, Jr.: b 3-6-1751 d p. 18-4 m Elizabeth Haseltine Pvt MA
James: b 1761 d 12-3-1804 m Mercy Eldridge Pvt MA
James, Sr.: b 2-19-1705 d 4-20-1782 m (1)Alice Anthony (2)Lydia (Goddard) Thurston PS RI
Jeremiah Townly: b 5-23-1748 d 5-11-1828 m Hester Baldwin PS MD
John: b 6-15-1749 d 5-10-1826 m Hannah Dennett Sgt MA
John: b 7-27-1731 d 1-11-1804 m Hannah Plummer Pvt MA
John: b 1733 d 10-5-1787 m Rachel Gove Pvt MA
John: b c. 1756 d 1796 m Edie Hutchins Pvt MA
John: b 1760 d 1842 m Elizabeth Parker Pvt MA
John: b 2-18-1760 d 4-6-1838 m Martha Thurston Pvt NH
John: b 10-3-1743 d 5-12-1817 m (1)Deborah Wing (2)Mrs Shepherd (3)Margaret Crandell Pvt NY
Jonathan: b 8-18-1723 d 10-6-1799 m Joanna Morss MM MA
Jonathan: b 12-5-1751 d 4-13-1825 m Hannah Merrill Capt MA
Jonathan: b 12-6-1732 d 1-14-1800 m (1)Thankful Sherman (2)Sarah Hall Col NH
Jonathan: b 2-22-1740 d 3-21-1835 m (1)Abigail Wilson (2)Abigail Meserve Sgt NH ★
Jonathan: b 3-1-1732/3 d 2-6-1815 m Sarah Stickney Pvt CS NH
Joseph, Jr.: b 4-11-1732 d 3-26-1804 m Susanna Bancroft Pvt MA
Joseph: b 2-25-1745 d 6-13-1829 m Elizabeth Darrah Sgt NH
Joseph: b 4-25-1753 d 6-17-1844 m (1)Judith Cooper (2)Sarah Doolittle (3)Mary (Whitman) Goit Pvt NH ★
Joshua: b 11-5-1756 d p. 1799 m Anne Saunders Pvt MA
Joshua: b 5-27-1740 d 12-7-1822 m Mary Hadley Pvt NH
Josiah: b 4-16-1746 d 9-21-1824 m Hannah Grow Lt QM MA
Josiah: b 2-20-1748 d 8-2-1813 m (1)Sarah Allen (2)Hannah Goddard (3)Sarah Bodwell Sgt MA
Josiah: b 9- -1735 d 1782 m (1)Margaret Gill (2)Hannah Sanborn Sgt PS NH
Josiah: b 9-15-1741 d 10-19-1796 m Mehitable Frye Dr NH
Leonard: b 1745 d 1815 m Hannah Bodfish Pvt MA
Lot: b 6-30-1750 d c. 1797 m Lydia Chase Pvt MA
Lott: b 12-14-1758 d 2-10-1836 m Rhoda Peck Sgt PS NY CT ★
Lowery: b 11-23-1759 d p. 1798 m Mary Wightman Cpl RI

Macheson: b 5-9-1752 d 9- -1776 m Rebecca Pendleton Lmn RI
Moody: b 9-23-1723 d 4-27-1815 m Elizabeth Hale Pvt MA
Moody: b 10-7-1744 d 7-27-1808 m (1)Anna Webster (2)Abigail (Worth) Rogers PS NH
Moses: b 8-20-1738 d 2-5-1797 m Elizabeth Whittier Pvt MA
Moses: b 7-1-1713 d 10-9-1789 m Judith Bartlett MM MA
Moses: b 3-16-1727 d 10-18-1799 m Hannah Brown Capt NH
Moses: b 3-23-1759 d 8-8-1831 m (1)Hannah Spalding (2)Eunice — Pvt NH ★
Moses: b 9-21-1741 d p. 1790 m Susannah Kelly PS CS NH
Nathan: b 8-2-1701 d 4-29-1781 m Ruth Peaslee Pvt MA
Nathan: b 1-10-1756 d p. 1799 m Mercy Robbins Pvt MA
Nathan: b 1723-6 d 1806 m (1)Abigail Milk (2)Ruth Then Pvt NY
Nathaniel: b 9-2-1761 d 4-20-1853 m (2)Jemima Haskell Pvt ME
Nathaniel: b 8-21-1752 d 1-12-1836 m Lydia Dustin Drm Pvt MA
Nathaniel: bpt 2-8-1756 d 12-18-1826 m (1)Rachel Pierce (2)Naomi Kelley PS NH
Nehemiah: b 2-8-1751 d 10-5-1808 m Vashti Batcheller Cpl MA
Obadiah: b 1743 d 7-4-1799 m Susan Berry Ens NY
Oliver: b 6-14-1761 d 5-15-1843 m Phebe — Pvt MA RI ★
Parker: b 8-22-1765 d 7-22-1851 m (1)Sarah Evans (2)Mary Hayes Sgt NH
Parker: b 2-28-1745 d p. 1779 m Elizabeth Turner Pvt MA
Paul: b 7-17-1744 d 7-1-1824 m Betty Kennicut PS CS VT
Perley: b 1-2-1758 d 4- -1832 m Mary Ingalls Pvt NH
Peter: b 1756 d 7-17-1792 m Sarah Cady Pvt NH
Phineas: b 1756 d 1826 m Rebecca Mosher Pvt NH
Reuben: b 6-23-1754 d 11-18-1824 m Judith Gardner Mid MA
Richard: b 7-21-1745 d p. 1790 m Mary Chase Drm MA
Richard: b 10-29-1759 d 5-14-1845 m Roba Briggs Pvt RI ★
Robert: bpt 3-23-1766 d 2-18-1841 m Abigail Poor Pvt NH ★
Robert: b 1758 d a. 5-2-1831 m Sarah Revel Pvt NY
Roger: b 9-15-1749 d 6-25-1822 m Mary Smith Spear Pvt MA
Rogers: b 6-20-1734 d 9-11-1814 m (1)Sarah Walker (2)Susanna Burbank Pvt MA
Rufus: b 9-29-1746 d 8-24-1815 m Sarah Kingsley Pvt MA
Samuel: b 4- -1741 d 6-19-1811 m (1)Ann Baldwin (2)Hannah (Giles) SDI MD
Samuel: b 8-26-1754 d 2-22-1834 m Priscilla Merrill Cpl MA
Samuel: b 10-23-1739 d 5-17-1816 m Mary Stewart Maj NH
Samuel, Sr.: b 9-28-1707 d 8-11-1800 m (1)Mary Dudley (2)Ester — PS NH
Samuel, Jr.: b 11-28-1728 d 7-10-1790 m Silence Stowe Pvt NH
Samuel, 3d.: b 1754 d 10- -1838 m (1)Elizabeth Leet (2)Damaris Sabin Sgt NH
Samuel: b 1-21-1747-50 d c. 1821 m (1)Mary Connor (2)Sarah Bowley Pvt NH ★
Seth: b 11-21-1715 d 9-24-1791 m (1)Elizabeth Bartlett (2)Abigail March Pvt MA
Seth: b 12-26-1742 d 2-6-1814 m Mary Slade Pvt MA
Seth: b 1-1-1743/4 d 3-18-1826 m (1)Catharine Stafford (2)Mary Kenney Sgt NH
Simeon: b 1762 d c. 1805 m Eunice Bailey Pvt MA
Solomon: b 9-8-1743 d 8- -1828 m (1)Rebecca Chamberlin (2)Mercy Oldbridge Pvt MA
Solomon: b 9-1-1742 d 11-1-1828 m Sarah March Capt Dr NH
Somerby: b 1740 d 3-16-1822 m Sarah Jaques Pvt MA
Stephen: b 6-22-1742 d 3-31-1805 m Mary Frost PS NH
Stephen: b 7- -1728 d 12- -1792 m Hannah Blodgett Pvt VT
Thomas: b 9-30-1755 d 4-3-1844 m Desire Luce Slr MA ME
Thomas: b 3-24-1746 d 7-1-1839 m Deborah Killum Pvt MA
Thomas: b 1750 d 1807 m Temperance Crocker Pvt MA
Timothy: b 6-23-1745 d 4-28-1818 m Rebecca Bassett 1Lt MA
Walter Perry: b c. 1730 d 1788 m (1)Lucy Barker (2)Sarah Hale PS MD
Wells, Sr.: b 10-10-1710 d 12-2-1785 m (1)Martha Morse (2)Mary Currier Lt MA
Wells: b 9-9-1737 d 12-28-1824 m Sarah Hovey PS NH
William: b 5-29-1751 d 5-8-1800 m Hannah Ackerman Sol MA
William: b 6-13-1742 d 8-25-1806 m Phebe Hunt Lt PS NH
William: b 6-5-1736 d 9-4-1818 m Anna Green PS NH
Zephaniah: b 3-25-1748 d 5-30-1828 m (1)Abigail Skiff (2)Love West (Skiff) Pvt MA

CHASTAIN,
Peter: b 9-9-1736 d 1786 m Sarah — Pvt SC

CHATARD,
Jean Baptiste: b 1758 d — m Elizabeth Bon NS FrN

CHATFIELD,
Daniel: b 8-31-1735 d 7-11-1818 m Prudence Baldwin Capt CT
Henry: b 1-17-1750 d 1-8-1839 m Annie — Pvt PS NY
Isaac: b 10-13-1751 d 9-25-1837 m Sarah Whitmore Arfr CT ★
Joel: b 2-21-1757 d 6-14-1836 m Ruth Stoddard Sol CT
John, Sr.: b 3-5-1729 d 8-24-1786 m Ruth Buel Pvt CT
John, Jr.: b 1754 d 1-13-1832 m Sebrah Jones Pvt CT ★
John: b 3-8-1716 d c. 1802 m Jane Mulford PS NY
Levi: b 8-26-1756 d p. 1792 m Sarah Bradley Pvt CT
Oliver: b 7-23-1730 d p. 6-30-1788 m (1)Abiah — (2)Zerviah Tomlinson Pvt CT
Samuel, Jr.: b a. 7-29-1733 d p. 1778 m Joanna Gunn Pvt CT
Thomas: b 1743 d p. 1785 m Esther Huntting Pvt NY

CHATHAM,
William: b 1761 d 8-21-1854 m Nancy Shade Pvt PA ★

CHATTERTON,
Nathaniel: b 4-27-1755 d 8-2-1835 m Mary Manning Stonn Pvt Matr NY
Wait: b 3-2-1757 d 4-16-1837 m Susanna Dickerman Cpl VT ★

CHATTIN,
James: b 3-3-1755 d c. 1817 m Rebecca Nicholson Wgm NJ

CHATTLE,
Thomas: b a. 1750 d c. 1790 m Mrs Judith (Gilman) Jackson PS NH

CHAUDOIN,
Louis: b 3-25-1753 d 1-4-1845 m Kitty Mims Pvt VA ★

CHAUVIN,
Paul: b c. 1750 d p. 1799 m Charlotte Toups PS LA

CHEATHAM,
Eppes: b a. 1760 d a. 5- -1816 m Sarah — Sol VA
Thomas: b c. 1720 d 1795 m Prudence — PS VA

CHEATWOOD,
William: b — d 1787 m Jean — PS VA

CHEEDLE, (includes CHEADLE, CHEDLE)
Asa, Sr.: b 10-6-1734 d p. 1782 m Martha Paddock Sct CS VT
Asa, Jr.: b 5-1762 d 9-16-1836 m (1)Sarah Gray (2)Mrs Nancy Hersey (3)Sarah Divens Pvt VT ★
Elijah: b 1762 d 1849 m Anne Wilson Cpl CT ★
John: b 8-26-1732 d 10-20-1805 m (1)Mary Bosworth (2)Rachael Allen Pvt VT

CHEEKE, (includes CHEEK)
Randolph: b a. 1735 d 2-1-1816 m X PS NC
William: b 1723 d p. 10-14-1797 m Sarah — Pvt NC
William: b 9-29-1752 d 4-16-1845 m (1)Mary Vines (2)Mrs Sinthia Coker Pvt SC ★

CHEERS,
Thomas: b 1743 d 1786 m Mary Ann — 1Lt DE

CHEESMAN, (includes CHEESEMAN)
Abel: b 2-22-1758 d 5-15-1826 m Mary Mack MM Pvt MA
Anson: b 7-14-1752 d 2-14-1813 m Elizabeth Cary Cpl MA ★
Joseph: b 12-23-1744 d 9-15-1800 m Elizabeth Crawford Lt NY
Matthias: b 3-17-1730 d p. 3-10-1783 m Miriam Shaw Ens NJ
Richard: b 1749 d 11-3-1799 m Rachel Williams Capt NJ
Samuel, Sr.: b 3-15-1722 d 2- -1808 m Mary Tower Sgt MA
Samuel, Jr.: b 5-6-1752 d 2-28-1846 m Martha French Sgt MA
Thomas: b c. 1725 d 6- -1785 m Elizabeth Furman PS NY

CHEEVER, (includes CHEVER)
Abijah: b 3-23-1760 d 4-21-1843 m Elizabeth Scott Dr NS MA
Daniel: b 11-2-1735 d 4-10-1788 m Sarah Hathorn 2Sgt Gnr MA
Daniel: b 9-5-1757 d 9-9-1822 m Elizabeth Keyes Pvt MA
Ezekiel: bpt 5-15-1720 d a. 1793 m (1)Sarah Phillips (2)Sarah (Weaver) Gooch CmsryGen MA
Ezekiel: b 1743 d 1806 m Martha Hall Pvt MA
John: b 1740 d 8-25-1802 m Rosanna Read Pvt MA
Joseph: b 12-14-1752 d 11-23-1830 m Sarah Low Capt MA W ★
Joshua: b 10-10-1740 d 1-15-1813 m Abigaile Eustace Pvt MA
Richard: b 3-23-1753 d 1784/5 m Mary Toazer Pvt MA
Thomas: b 2-20-1733/4 d 1-28-1823 m Mary — Pvt MA

CHENAULT,
Benjamin: b 1760 d 5-4-1847 m Susan — Pvt VA W ★
John: b 11-22-1754 d — m (1)Ann Barbara Burke (2)Nancy — Pvt VA
William: b 12-30-1749 d 12-30-1813 m Elizabeth Mullins Pvt PS VA

CHENERY, (includes CHINREY)
Ephraim: b 1735 d 6-18-1816 m Dinah Hamant Capt CS MA
Isaac: b 11-20-1742 d 10-20-1822 m Susannah Pierce Dr MA
John: b 10-4-1739 d p. 1784 m Phebe Sargent Pvt MA
William: b 7-24-1742 d p. 1780 m Sibyl Cox Pvt MA

CHENEY, (includes CHANEY, CHEYNEY)
Abraham: b 1760 d 12-25-1848 m (1)Mary Cheatham (2)Nancy Donalson PS Pvt VA ★
Aquila: b 1761 d p. 1790 m Julia Benson Sol MA
Artemus: b 10-12-1760 d 12-29-1804 m Rachel Albee Fif Pvt MA
Benjamin: b 5-9-1763 d p. 1798 m Eunice Hubbard Pvt ME
Benjamin: b 4-13-1725 d p. 1776 m Judith Holman PS NH
Caleb: b 1-12-1738 d 7-5-1800 m Mary Wheelock Lt PS CS MA
Daniel: b 3-10-1737 d p. 1790 m Elizabeth Davis Pvt MA
Daniel: b 10-30-1749 d 12-27-1831 m Mary — Pvt MA
Ebenezer: b 5-23-1740 d 9-21-1800 m Priscilla Lyon Cpl CT
Ebenezer, Sr.: b 7-10-1741 d 11-14-1828 m (1)Abigail Thompson (2)Hannah Gould Pvt CS MA
Ebenezer, Jr.: b 9-7-1761 d 8-12-1828 m Anna Nelson Pvt MA
Ebenezer: b 5-22-1759 d 2-27-1853 m (2)Abagail Wood Pvt MA

CHENEY, contd.
Edward: b 12-5-1752 d 1-24-1813 m Abagail Hale Pvt MA
Elias: b 2-20-1741/2 d 3- -1832 m (1)Jane Plumer (2)Ruth Jackman (3)Hannah Pike Pvt MA
Elias: b 10-14-1760 d 12- -1816 m Lucy Blanchard Pvt NH
Eliphalet: b 12-5-1756 d 9-11-1822 m Mary Ela Pvt MA ★
Ephraim: b 8-1-1741 d 12-22-1815 m (1)Elizabeth Wild (2)Bathsheba Segur Pvt MA
Ezekiel: b c. 1750 d 1815 m Letty Dodson PS VA
Isaac: b 6-3-1744 d 1-6-1830 m Abiah Hunkins PS NH
James: b 7-19-1740 d 12-28-1810 m Joanna Williams Pvt MA
Jesse: b 10-13-1754 d 9-20-1827 m Anna Nichols Pvt NH
John: b 8-3-1765 d 10-19-1838 m (1)Rachel Benson (2)Catherine Evans Owens Pvt MD
John, Sr.: b 8-26-1740 d 2-23-1831 m (1)Susannah Farwell (2)Elizabeth Blodgett (3)Elizabeth Swallow Lt MA
John, Jr.: b 7-29-1763 d 7-2-1847 m Abigail Blodgett Sol MA
John: b 4-6-1755 d p. 1800 m Hannah Adams Cpl MA
John: b 4-29-1749 d p. 1805 m Abigail Corkin PS NH
John: b 1732 d 1- -1811 m Martha Fendin Pvt SC
Joseph: b 3-21-1762 d c. 1830 m Seelah Tyler Pvt CT ★
Joseph: b 7-1-1759 d 11-14-1815 m Isabella Littlefield Cpl MA
Joseph: b 2-7-1726 d p. 1779 m Dorcas Stewart Pvt MA
Joseph: b 10- -1755 d 1-22-1827 m Elizabeth — Pvt MA ★
Joseph: b 3-23-1761 d 6- -1834 m Susannah Wadsworth Pvt MA ★
Joseph: b 1-18-1735 d 8-10-1794 m Edith Mendenhall Pvt PA
Levi: b 1-21-1729/30 d 1782-95 m Mehitable Morse Pvt MA
Levi: b 11-23-1756 d 4-11-1847 m Mary Hill Pvt MA
Moses: b 10-20-1715 d p. 1782 m (1)Abigail Whitmore (2)Hannah Woodward Pvt MA
Nathan: b 8-18-1709 d 10-3-1779 m Lavina Shumway Pvt MA
Nathaniel: b 10-1-1758 d 10-31-1844 m (1)Elizabeth Hudson (2)Hannah Read Cpl Mrnr MA
Nathaniel: b 10-7-1747 d 8-3-1833 m Elizabeth Ela Pvt MA ★
Nathaniel: b c. 1754 d 3-6-1847 m Mary Stevens Pvt MA & NH ★
Ralph: b 10-4-1750 d 8-10-1826 m (1)Lydia Grover (2)Anna Jarvis Oliver Pvt MA
Reuben: b 3- -1744 d p. 1790 m Olive Day Cpl MA
Richard: b 3-23-1739 d 6-17-1791 m Mary Hannum Pvt PA
Samuel: bpt 12-19-1762 d 10-5-1841 m Abigail Joseph Pvt MA ★
Solomon Clark: b 6-27-1758 d 4-26-1826 m Molly — Pvt MA
Thomas: b 7-10-1742 d 1828 m Keturah Owen Pvt CT
Thomas: b 9-29-1758 d 1-18-1838 m Hannah Danforth Pvt NH
Thomas: b 12-12-1731 d 1-12-1811 m (1)Mary Riley Taylor (2)Mary (Bennett) Vernon SubLt PS PA
Timothy: b 5-10-1731 d 9-27-1795 m (1)Mary Olcott (2)Martha White Capt CT
Timothy: b 10-18-1745 d 2-19-1807 m Sussana Cook Pvt MA
Tristram: b 10-14-1726 d 12- -1816 m Margaret Joyner PS NH
Waldo: b 7-7-1748 d 7-31-1834 m Priscilla Bowen Sgt CT ★
Wm.: b 4-22-1766 d 6-13-1851 m (1)Delilah Shipman (2)Sarah Crayton Pvt CT
Wm., 4th: b 1718 d 6-17-1775 m (1)Ruth Eastman (2)Mehitabel Chubb Pvt CT
Wm.: b 9-8-1741 d 4- -1803 m Elizabeth Sweet Lt MA
Wm.: b 1733 d 1815 m — Norris Pvt VA
Wm.: b 2-1-1750 d 7-15-1802 m Rebecca —Pvt NH

CHENOWETH, (includes CHENOWITH)
Arthur, Sr: b 1716 d 4- -1802 m Mary Smith CS MD
Arthur, Jr: b 7-16-1752 d p. 1793 m Elspa Lawrence Cpl MD
Arthur: b 1737 d 1802 m (1)Ann Beaseman (2)Deliah Bosley Helms 1Lt PS MD
John: b 5-15-1751 d 3-3-1820 m (1)Rachel Kerr (2)Mary Buskirk Sgt MD
John: b 7-1-1745 d 1820 m Hannah Cromwell PS VA
John: b 1735 d p. 4-19-1811 m Eleanor — Pvt VA
John: b 11-15-1755 d 6-15-1831 m Mary Pugh Pvt VA ★
Jonathon: b 1757 d 1834 m Chlora— Pvt VA
Richard: b 1734 d 1796 m Margaret McCarthy Capt VA
Richard: b c. 1755 d p. 1815 m Elinor Askew — 2Lt MD
Thomas: b 1720 d p. 1787 m Mary Pritchett PS MD
Wm.: b 1758 d 7-20-1820 m Sarah Baxter PS MD
Wm.: b 6-10-1760 d 4-16-1828 m Mary Van Meter Henton Pvt VA

CHERRY,
Aaron: b — d p. 1821 m Mary — Pvt PS PA
Aaron: b 9-22-1746 d 10-2-1856 m Sarah — Pvt PA
George: b 1755 d 1798 m (1) X (2)Mrs Susanna McTyre Pvt SC
George: b c. 1755 d 1799 m Jane Chesnut PS SC
Henry: b 1758 d 3-5-1820 m Abigail — Pvt NJ ★
Lemuel: b 1744 d 1821 m Nancy Moring Pvt PS NC
Moses: b c. 1750 d a. 12-17-1782 m Elizabeth Talbert Sol SC
Ralph: b 7-10-1744 d 7-22-1820 m Ann Meek PS Pvt PA
Samuel: b 1756 d 10-27-1825 m Ann Wallace Capt NH
Samuel: b 1736 d 1813 m (1)Mary Williams (2)Clara — PS Lt NC
Solomon: b a. 1750 d p. 1800 m Mary Eason Capt NC
Thomas: b c. 1740 d p. 1788 m Mary — PS Pvt PA
Thomas Perrin: b 6-19-1759 d 1829 m Elizabeth Hurst Ens PA
Wm.: b 6-26-1743 d 9-22-1804 m Mary Ann Hollenback PM Cmsry Capt VA
William: b a. 1755 d p. 12-15-1802 m Susanna — CS NC

CHESEBROUGH, (includes CHESEBRA, CHESBRO, CHESEBOROUGH)
Amos: b 12-21-1730 d p. 1790 m (1)Mary Christopher (2)Anna (York) Gavitt CS CT
Charles: b 6-6-1736 d 1780 m Bridget Chesebrough(Cousin) QM CT
Christopher: b 11-16-1754 d 3-3-1835 m Abigail Williams Pvt CT
Elijah: b 10-1-1759 d 5-6-1807 m Thankful Williams Matr CT
Jabez: b 9-26-1756 d 10-29-1814 m Rhoda Woodworth Cpl CT
James, Sr.: b 6-27-1736 d a. 1818 m Lucy Pendleton Artl RI
James, Jr.: b 1-1-1761 d 3-17-1849 m Nancy Larkin Pvt RI ★
Jedediah: bpt 4-30-1738 d p. 1790 m Rebecca Slack Pvt CT
Naboth: b 4-1-1751 d 8-27-1804 m Phebe Palmer PS CT
Nathaniel: b 1-6-1734 d 2-24-1804 m (2)Mary Hallam Ens CT
Peleg: b 2-3-1737 d — m X Pvt CT
Perez: b 3-2-1762 d 1-10-1850 m Priscilla Thompson Pvt CT ★
Samuel: b 3-25-1743 d 9-9-1811 m Submit Palmer PS CT
Thomas: b 1-19-1754 d 4-4-1807 m Joanna Tyler Sgt CT
William: b 1-7-1745 d 12-21-1840 m Esther Williams PS CT
Zebulon: b 11-25-1750 d 7-16-1825 m Zerviah Hobart Cpl CT

CHESHIRE,
John: b c. 1705 d p. 12-19-1789 m Jane — PS MD
John: b 1745 d 2-2-1832 m Catherine Graves Pvt NC

CHESLEY,
Benjamin: b 1-24-1743 d 2-5-1831 m Deborah Randall PS NH
George: b 1720 d 1785 m Sarah Sampson PS NH
James: b 5-23-1751 d 2-6-1836 m Elizabeth Hill Pvt Mrnr NH
John, Jr.: b c. 1754 d 9- -1806 m Mary Ashcorn Parran Lt MD
John: b 1-13-1762 d 1-30-1852 m Magdalena Land Pvt NY ★
Jonathan: b 1736 d 10-20-1826 m Elizabeth Emerson QM Capt NH
Joseph: b c. 1740 d 1825 m (1)Abigail Graffam (2)Sarah Gilpatrick Sol MA
Philip: b 1754 d 8-26-1825 m Abigail Hayes Cpl NH
Samuel: b 1725 d 7- -1799 m Sarah Hicks Lt NH
Samuel: b c. 1743 d p. 1801 m X Pvt PS NH
Thomas: b c. 1720 d 1778 m Mary Hill PS NH

CHESTER,
Christoper: b 10-26-1757 d 1-6-1831 m Martha Chase Pvt CT NH
Elisha: b 12-12-1767 d 7-19-1847 m Mary Walworth PS CT
John: b 1-18-1849 d 11-4-1809 m Elizabeth Huntington Col CT
John: b 8-28-1761 d 8-30-1804 m Frances— Pvt CT
John: b c. 1748 d 8-3-1842 m X Pvt NC ★
Joseph: b 1730/1 d 8-4-1803 m (1)Rachel Hillhouse (2)Elizabeth Otis CS CT
Simeon, Sr.: b 3-20-1733 d p. 2-21-1811 m Elizabeth Bent Sol CT
Thomas: b 8-18-1721 d 1801 m Sarah Eldredge PS CT

CHESTNUT, (includes CHESNUT)
Benjamin: b 8-2-1759 d p. 1832 m Ann McKinney Pvt PA ★
James: b 1752 d 9-1-1822 m Esther Starmont Pvt SC
John: b 6-18-1743 d 4-1-1818 m Sarah Cantey PM Capt SC
John: b c. 1749 d 5-5-1805 m Patience — Pvt VA
Thomas: b 1762 d 1830 m Patience Milan Mil PA

CHESTON,
John: b a. 1749 d 1-31-1792 m Amy Walker Pvt NJ

CHESWELL,
Wentworth: b 4-11-1746 d 3-8-1817 m Mary Davis Pvt NH

CHETWOOD,
John: b 1736 d 2-20-1807 m Mary Emott PS NJ

CHEUVRONT,
Joseph: b 2-2-1757 d 8-12-1832 m (1)Elizabeth Ellsworth (2)Sara Bollin Pvt VA

CHEVALIER, (includes CHEVELIER)
Anthony: b 1753 d p. 1820 m Rachel Scott Nelson Pvt VA ★
Peter: b 3-25-1730/1 d 10-19-1778 m Mary Renaudet Pvt PS PA

CHEW,
Aaron: b 12-19-1751 d 9-23-1805 m (1)Elizabeth Wood (2)Hannah (Clark) Gardner 2Lt NJ
James: b c. 1745 d a. 1-27-1783 m Mary Caldwell Maj VA
John: b c. 1739/40 d 5-26-1785 m X Ens MD
John: b c. 1740 d 1789 m Ann Fox Lt VA
John: b c. 1753 d p. 5-19-1805 m Elizabeth Smith Lt VA
John: b 3-31-1749 d 5-22-1838 m Margaret Reeder 1Lt VA
Richard: b 4-10-1753 d 6-6-1801 m (1)Margaret Mackall (2)Frances Holland Pvt MD
Richard: b 1740 d 1841 m (1)Ann Albertson (2)Susannah (Money) Tomlinson Pvt NJ
Robert Beverly: b 1750 d 1814 m Molly Perrott 1Lt VA
Samuel: b 1737-9 d 2-20-1790 m (1)Sarah Weems (2)Priscilla Claggett CS MD
Samuel: b — d 3-4-1778 m Lucy Miller NCapt CT
Samuel Loyd: b 12-9-1755 d 2-1-1785 m Dorothy Harrison 1Lt MD
William: b 1740 d 4-9-1801 m Elizabeth Reynolds PS MD

CHEWNING,
Hardin: b c. 1759 d p. 1810 m Elizabeth Holland Pvt VA
Samuel: b 1-21-1723 d a. 1-16-1816 m — Garrett PS VA

CHICHESTER,
Abraham: b 8-5-1725 d 10-25-1807 m Jerusha Stevens PS CT
David: b 8-25-1757 d 11-17-1803 m Mary Nichols Pvt CT W★
Eliphalet: b 1737 d 2-7-1804 m (1)Mary Prime (2)Margaret (Carman) Oakley Pvt PS NY
Henry: b 1762 d 9-25-1849 m Deborah Hoyt Pvt CT ★
Richard: b 1736 d 8-22-1796 m (1)Anne Gordon (2)Sarah McCarty Col CS VA

CHICK,
Aaron: b 3-23-1742 d p. 1779 m Molly Keyes 1Lt MA
James: b 5-14-1760 d 11- -1845 m X Cpl VA

CHICKERING,
John: b c. 1745 d p. 1779 m Lois Marsh Sgt MA
John: b 10-22-1745 d 4-5-1805 m Ruth Dale Sgt MA
Nathaniel: b 3-24-1750 d 2-5-1837 m Esther Dewing Pvt MA
Oliver: b 1753 d 2-21-1831 m Tabitha Hooker Lt MA ★
Timothy: b 3-10-1750 d 1-10-1829 m Rhoda Wheelock Pvt MA

CHIDESTER,
Phineas: b 7-13-1757 d 4-22-1814 m Rebecca Byram Pvt NJ
Wm.: b 1757 d 2-26-1813 m (2)Martha Dean Pvt CT ★

CHIDSEY,
Ebenezer: b c. 1737 d 7-9-1806 m Elizabeth Grannis Pvt CT
Ephraim: b 3-19-1752 d 9-26-1832 m (1)Desire Denison (2)Hannah Barnes Sgt CT ★
Isaac: b 11-7-1731 d 7-30-1814 m Sarah Bradley Pvt CT
John, Sr.: b 9-15-1720 d 9-17-1783 m Sarah Shepard Matr CT
John, Jr.: b 12-16-1749 d 5-6-1816 m Annie Luddington Pvt CT
Levi: b 2-1-1745 d 8-4-1825 m Hannah Potter Cpl CT

CHILCOT,
Elihu: b 1757 d 5-25-1831 m Lydia Payne Pvt VA W★

CHILDRESS, (includes CHILDERS)
Abraham: b 11-15-1752 d 5-6-1849 m Elizabeth — Pvt VA
Benjamin: b 4-3-1764 d 3-25-1857 m Ann Key Johnson Pvt VA
David: b 1760/1 d 2-7-1849 m Lucy Gaines Pvt GA ★
Goolsbury: b 1-1-1757 d 3-4-1842 m Nancy Swinney Pvt VA ★
Isham: b 1766 d p. 1841 m Patience — Pvt NC
John: b 5-5-1755 d 1-9-1844 m Martha Calhoun Pvt Wgn PS NC ★
John: b 12-2-1759 d 1-11-1849 m X Pvt VA ★
Mosby: b c. 1763 d 8-3-1843 m Elizabeth Jeffries Pvt VA ★
Pleasant: b 1761-3 d 4-25-1839 m Sarah Jeffries Pvt NC
Richard: b 1750-60 d 1830 m Martha Spann Sol GA
Thomas: b a. 1760 d p. 1789 m Lottie Brewer Sgt GA
Wm.: b 12-25-1762 d 1-14-1839 m Charity — Pvt SC NC ★
Wm.: b 1740 d p. 2- -1803 m Martha Lowther Sol VA

CHILDS, (includes CHILD)
Aaron: b 9-14-1736 d 6-7-1778 m Phoebe Jackson Pvt MA
Aaron: b 8-6-1741 d 8-8-1795 m Susannah Gridley MM MA
Abel: b 10-18-1752 d 11-12-1807 m Rebecca Allard Cpl CT
Abel: b 11-9-1757 d 5-17-1807 m Hannah Eaton Pvt MA
Abijah: b 12-7-1748 d 1-31-1834 m Lois Davis Sgt MA
Abijah: b 1-12-1734 d 1823 m (1)Beulah Harrington (2)Ann Bemis Capt MA
Abijah, Jr.: b 9-3-1749 d p. 1794 m Sarah Mascraft Pvt MA
Abraham: b 8-12-1741 d 1-3-1834 m Rebecca Stowell Capt MA
Amasa: b 1-13-1745 d 9-8-1820 m Joanna Carpenter Sol CT
Caleb: b 9-20-1721 d p. 1781 m (1)Lucy Underwood (2)Esther Wheeler Pvt MA
Cephas: b 9-7-1756 d 7-13-1836 m Martha Child Pvt CT
Charles: b 11-22-1751 d 3-7-1838 m Elizabeth May Sol CT
Cromwell: b 1716 d p. 1790 m Abigail Turner PS RI
Daniel, Sr.: b 1-1-1712 d 5- -1776 m Ruth Curtis Amidown Pvt MA
Daniel, Jr: b 10-8-1747 d 1802 m Rebeckah Howland Pvt MA
David: b 1-30-1744/5 d 3-17-1812 m Lydia Stearns Cpl MA
David: b 2-7-1735 d — m Hannah Davis Pvt MA
David: b 1754 d 1810 m Elenor Gay Pvt MA
Ebenezer: b 4-17-1727 d 6-7-1791 m (1)Charity Bugbee (2)Alice Cobb Sol CT
Eliphaz: b 10-1-1752 d a. 3-3-1795 m Ruth Gibbs Pvt MA
Elisha: b 12-11-1725 d 11-22-1796 m Alice Manning Capt PS CT
Haile: b 1-23-1759 d 2-10-1815 m Amy Kennicutt Pvt RI
Henry: b 5-28-1717 d 1-17-1795 m Rebecca Bacon PS CT
Hezekiah: b c. 1760/1 d 8-28-1834 m X Pvt NC ★
Hezekiah: b 8-3-1734 d 12-4-1798 m Patience Barton Pvt RI
Increase: b 12-13-1740 d 6-10-1810 m Olive Pease Capt NY
Issac: b 5-1-1722 d 5-23-1794 m Elizabeth Weld Pvt MA
Jacob: b 4-23-1756 d 7-20-1822 m (1)Sybil Summer (2)Miletiah Curtis Pvt CT
James: b 1760/1 d 1840-52 m X Pvt VA ★
John: b 3-10-1753 d 5-31-1804 m Mary Gragg MM NJ
John: b 7-16-1743 d 8-4-1777 m Frances Filkins 2Lt Cmsry NY
John: b 1-20-1733 d 9-19-1819 m Rosabillar Cole CS RI

Jonas: b 1762 d 2-14-1815 m (1)Peggy Wilcott (2)Anna Hayden Pvt MA
Jonathan: b 10-24-1756 d 7-31-1819 m (1)Deliverance Freeman (2)Anna Thompson Pvt MA
Jonathan: b 12-17-1731 d 4-5-1814 m Dinah Bacon Col VT
Moses: b 4-6-1731 d 2-8-1793 m Sarah Styles Lt MA
Moses: b 1752 d 10- -1776 m Triphenia — Pvt MA
Nathaniel: b 4-13-1717 d 6-19-1791 m (1)Jemima Bugbee (2)Mrs Elinor Fox PS CT
Penuel: b 5-7-1757 d 8-22-1843 m (1)Charlotte Loomis (2)Mrs Sabra Cannon Henry Sgt CT ★
Salmon: b 9-19-1765 d 1-28-1856 m Olive Rose Vol NY
Samuel, Jr.: b 5-1-1733 d 5-1-1783 m (2)Elizabeth Weld Pvt CT
Samuel: b 2-7-1719 d 12-18-1803 m (1)Mary Ball (2)Esther — (3)Mrs Elizabeth Stimson Pvt MA
Shubael: b 8-13-1735 d 6-7-1811 m Abigail Bowen Sol CT
Stephen: b 4-5-1762 d 11-22-1820 m Zilpha Brooks Pvt CT ★
Stephen: b 11-27-1749 d 5-24-1831 m Mercy Chase Cpl NH
Sylvester: b 3-16-1730 d p. 1780 m Abigail Miller (3)Priscilla Bradford Col RI
Thomas: b 1731 d 12-25-1787 m Mary Freeman NOf MA
Timothy: b 3-17-1760 d 2-5-1825 m Amy Parish Pvt CT
Timothy, Sr.: b 9-18-1720 d 1781 m Mary Wells Capt MA
Timothy, Jr.: b 4-9-1748 d 2-25-1821 m Rachel Easton Lt Dr MA
Willard: b 5-7-1758 d 11-1-1844 m (1)Lydia Morse (2)Sylvia — Pvt CT ★
Wm.: b 6-16-1759 d 8-13-1836 m Bethiah Howard Pvt MA
Wm.: b 12-10-1757 d 8-27-1843 m Mary Heaton Pvt Sct VT
Zachariah: b 11-18-1763 d 9-19-1845 m Lydia Bigelow Pvt MA ★

CHILES,
Henry: b 12-18-1762 d 1834 m Sarah Cheadle Sgt VA ★
John: b c. 1760 d p. 11-22-1824 m X Sol GA
John: b c. 1755 d 1838 m Sarah Ballenger Pvt VA
John: b 1730 d 1803 m Mary Ann White PS VA
Micajah: b 1720 d 1799 m Anna — PS VA
Walter: b c. 1740 d p. 1796 m Phebe Carr Sol VA
William: b 1- -1736 d 9- -1804 m Agnes (White) Pvt VA

CHILLSON, (includes CHILSON)
John: b 2-3-1754 d 12-5-1830 m Mrs Abigail Draper Pvt MA
Joseph: bpt 2-12-1758 d 1821-32 m Mary — Pvt MA
Waters: b 10-14-1748 d p. 1794 m Parateen Field Sgt MA

CHILTON,
Andrew: b c. 1760 d 11-15-1819 m Elizabeth Davis Pvt VA
Charles: b 10-1-1741 d 9-5-1793 m Elizabeth Blackwell Capt VA
Charles: b c. 1739 d p. 7-26-1795 m Ann — Sol VA
John: b 8-29-1739 d 9-11-1777 m Letitia Blackwell Capt VA
Richard: b c. 1740 d p. 6-17-1815 m Judith Arms PS VA
Stephen: b 1731 d p. 1785 m Judith Hobson PS VA
Sturman: b 1725-30 d 1784 m Mary — Pvt PS MD VA
Thomas: b c. 1740 d a. 1-4-1807 m Sapphira Pierce Ens PS MD
William: b 9-14-1730 d 6-18-1774 m Sarah Orrick PS VA

CHINA,
John: b 12-8-1764 d 8-24-1847 m Agnes O'Dell Pvt SC ★

CHINN,
Charles: b 1723/4 d a. 2-25-1788 m Sythe Davis CS VA
John: b 1739 d p. 1-18-1791 m Sarah Yates PS CS VA
Perry: b 1763 d 3-7-1847 m (1)Elizabeth Evans (2)Elizabeth Carr Pvt VA ★
Rawleigh: b 1735 d p. 10-15-1815 m (1)Frances Tarpley (2)Elizabeth Shearman CS VA

CHIPLEY,
Joshua: b c. 1755 d 5-18-1798 m Mary Hunter 1Lt MD
William: b 1739 d 5-8-1811 m Sarah Bell Capt MD

CHIPMAN,
Ammi: b 2-7-1764 d 12-10-1808 m Sarah Evarts Pvt VT
Amos: b 3-1727 d p. 1790 m (1)Sarah Daggett (2)Mrs Boardman CS VT
Amos, Jr.: b 12-21-1751 d 11-12-1833 m Sarah Boardman Pvt VT
Anthony: b c. 1754 d p. 1790 m Anna Lurvey Pvt MA
Barnabas Lathrop: b 11-5-1762 d 1847 m Beulah Evarts Pvt VT
Benjamin: b 5-23-1729 d 5- -1787 m Hannah Wadsworth Pvt MA
Benjamin: b 2-4-1752 d 6-18-1838 m Abigail Milliken Matr MA
Cyrus: b 12-3-1751 d 9-17-1840 m Anna Fitch Pvt VT
Darius: b 8-17-1756 d 3-22-1832 m Lydia Dickenson Pvt VT
Jacob: b 5- -1733 d 12-9-1777 m Anna Waterman Pvt MA
Jesse: b 2-2-1755 d 6-4-1841 m Mary White Sgt VT MA ★
John: b 1755 d 1843 m (1)Eliza — (2) X Drm CT
John: b 9-8-1746 d 12-25-1819 m (1)Hannah Moses (2)Elizabeth Tozer Armr NS MA
John: b 1745 d 1829 m Sarah Washburn Lt VT
Jonathan: b 10-24-1729 d 1819/20 m Catherine Reed Pvt CT
Joseph: b 8-5-1761 d 3-25-1826 m Amy Reed Pvt VT
Lemuel: b 7-25-1754 d 4-28-1831 m Assenath Fitch Dr VT
Nathaniel: b 11-27-1752 d 2-15-1843 m Sarah Hill 1Lt CT
Perez: b c. 1730 d 3-13-1801 m Margaret Manlove PS NC
Samuel: b 12-10-1763 d 3-24-1839 m Hannah Spofford Sgt VT ★

CHIPMAN, contd.

Samuel: b 3-22-1721 d 1812 m Hannah Austin Pvt VT
Thomas: b 3-8-1755 d 1-25-1830 m Martha Whittlesey Sgt CT ★
Thomas: b 1735 d 7-6-1792 m Bethia Fuller Pvt MA
Timothy Fuller: b 2-1-1761 d 5-7-1830 m Polly Smith Pvt MA
William: b 1752 d 1836 m (1)Prudence Williams (2)Abigail Chester
    Pvt CT
William: b 5-6-1731 d 1795 m (1)Martha Treat (2)Betty Mayo Pvt
    Matr MA
William: b 8-14-1765 d 3-30-1849 m (1)Ester Lane (2)Jane
    Sampson Pvt MA ★

CHIPS,

Morris: b c. 1760 d 5-1-1818 m Sarah — Pvt NJ W★

CHISM, (includes CHISHOLM, CHISUM)

Elijah: b 1744 d p. 1-28-1818 m Lucy — PS NC
James: b 1754 d 1819 m Mary Howard Pvt VA
John: b c. 1737-42 d p. 1797 m Elizabeth Muse CS NC

CHISWELL,

Stephen Newton: b 1715 d 1800 m Sarah Newton PS MD

CHITTENDEN,

Abraham: b 8-10-1751 d 3-4-1848 m (1)Diana Ward (2)Lydia
    (Baldwin) Rose BdgMaj CT
Benjamin: b 11-23-1749 d 9-1-1820 m (1)Mabel Dudley (2)Lucy
    Fowler Sol CT
Cornelius: b 4-6-1766 d 12-24-1858 m Rachel Porter Pvt CT ★
Daniel: b 3-15-1700 d 5-18-1781 m Abigail Downs Sol CT
Jairus: b 10-17-1745 d 3-9-1828 m Rebecca Hall Pvt CT
Jared: b 8-20-1734 d 2-12-1824 m (1)Deborah Stone (2)Elizabeth
    (Dudley) Ward Pvt CT
Jared: b 5-3-1756 d 4-2-1828 m (1)Elizabeth Lusk (2)Asena
    Douglas Sgt CT
Moses: b 9-29-1748 d 1802 m Hannah Ingraham Sgt NY
Nathaniel: b 6-21-1731 d 1-11-1820 m Mehitable Beebe Pvt CT
Reuben: bpt 5-21-1758 d 6-16-1849 m Sarah Johnson Pvt CT
Simeon, Sr.: b 12-28-1714 d 4-12-1789 m SubmitScranton Pvt CT
Simeon, Jr.: b 4-13-1742 d 9-22-1812 m Sarah Dudley Pvt CT
Solomon: b 9-14-1761 d 2-9-1855 m Susannah Sanford Pvt CT ★
Thomas: b 1-6-1730 d 8-25-1797 m Elizabeth Meigs CS VT

CHITTIM,

Thomas: b c. 1750 d 1781 m X Pvt NC

CHIVVIS,

William: b 1748 d 1823 m Jane Doty Pvt Gnr VA ★

CHOATE,

Abraham: b 3-24-1732 d 4-23-1800 m Sarah Potter Pvt MA
David, Jr.: b 2-27-1763 d 1851 m Miriam — Pvt MA ★
Ebenezer: b 4-16-1748 d 11-2-1801 m Anna Pillsbury Pvt MA
Ebenezer: b 4-21-1765 d 4-30-1852 m Elizabeth — Sol MA
Humphrey: b 11-9-1720 d 8-25-1795 m (1)Abigail Burnham
    (2)Ruth Lufkin Ens MA
Isaac: b 1-31-1734 d 5-30-1813 m Elizabeth Low Sgt MA
Jacob: b 10-11-1746 d 10- -1828 m Hannah Burnham Pvt NH
James: b 4-23-1761 d 7-23-1846 m Abigail Perkins Pvt MA
Jeremiah, Sr.: b 1725 d 1798 m (1)Eunice Giddings (2)Mary
    Story Sgt MA
Jeremiah, Jr.: b 1755 d 10- -1799 m Ruth Choate Pvt MA
John: b 12-27-1745 d 11- -1779 m Abigail Tyler Pvt MA
Joseph: b 1742 d 1-27-1802 m Mary — Pvt MA
Nehemiah: b 12-6-1730 d 1-24-1797 m Susanna Brown Cpl MA
Samuel: b 1731 d 1789 m Abigail — Lt MA
Simeon: b 1-14-1748 d 9-22-1829 m (1)Ruth Thompson (2)Hannah
    Norton Sgt MA ★
Stephen: b 11-1-1727 d 10-19-1815 m (1)Mary Low (2)Mrs
    Elizabeth Potter PS MA
Thomas: b 10-8-1718 d 10-20-1798 m (1)Abigail Haskell (2)Dorothy
    Proctor Capt MA
Wm. Sr.: b 9-5-1730 d 4-23-1785 m Mary Giddings Pvt MA
Wm.: b 8-10-1759 d 1-2-1835 m Susanna — Pvt MA

CHOICE,

Tully, Sr.: b 1706 d p. 11-2-1777 m Ann — PS VA
Tully, Jr.: b 6-17-1753 d 12-19-1837 m Rebecca Sims Pvt VA ★
Wm.: b 1-30-1756 d 9-30-1843 m Mary McDonald 1Lt VA ★

CHOWNING,

John: b c. 1750 d p. 7-24-1811 m Catharine — PS 2Lt VA
William: b 2-22-1742 d a. 6-6-1827 m Tomazin Sharpe Capt VA
William: b 2-21-1727 d p. 5- -1808 m Elizabeth — Dr VA

CHRISTIAN,

Anthony, Jr.:b 1760 d p. 1796 m Rebecca — Sol VA
Charles: b c. 1715 d 1784 m X PS VA
Daniel: b 1762 d 12-26-1847 m Elizabeth Nikirk Pvt PA
George: b 9-26-1762 d 2-22-1831 m Martha Walton PS VA
Gilbert: b 1734 d 11- -1793 m Margaret Anderson Maj VA
Henry: b c. 1738 d 6- -1805 m Martha Patterson Capt VA
Israel: b 1720 d 1784 m Elizabeth Starke PS VA

John: b a. 1750 d 1805 m Mary Maynard Capt VA
John: b c. 1755 d 2-15-1808 m Elizabeth Hunt Dillard Capt VA
John: b c. 1750 d 1-20-1792 m Judith Pate PS Sgt VA
John: b 1755 d 3-25-1824 m Mary Wilson FifMaj NC ★
John: b 1752 d 1834 m Judith Leek Pvt VA★
Joseph: b 9-4-1757 d 4- -1825 m Elizabeth Ashfield Graves Lt VA
Michael: b c. 1752 d p. 1792 m — Miller Pvt VA
Michael, Sr.: b — d — m Rose Yeardley PS VA
Patrick: bpt 7-29-1744 d 1808-11 m (1) — Robertson (2)
    Elizabeth Bradford Hays Pvt VA
Phillip: b c. 1755/6 d a. 1-8-1827 m Barbara — Pvt PS PA
Rawleigh Chinn: b 1754 d 7-4-1828 m Mrs Elizabeth Pope Pvt
    PS VA ★
Robert, Sr.: b c. 1730 d p. 6-8-1785 m Mary — Sol PS VA
Robert: b 2-28-1764 d 8- -1846 m Mary Huston Pvt VA ★
Turner: b 7-13-1750 d 4-7-1832 m Anne Payne 1Lt VA
Turner: b 1759 d 12- -1833 m (1)Susan Walker (2)Fontaine —
    (3)Polly Dancy Asst Cmsry Gen VA
Wm.: b 1743 d 4-18-1786 m Anne Henry Col VA
Wm.: b 1725 d 1779 m Mary Campbell Maj VA
Wm.: b 1758 d 1828 m X Pvt VA ★
William 2d: b 1739 d 1814 m (1)Elizabeth Collier (2)Sally Atkins
    PS VA

CHRISTIANCE,

Cornelius: bpt 5-20-1760 d p. 1790 m Elizabeth Bratt Pvt NY

CHRISTLIEB,

Charles: b 6-1-1751 d 6-27-1837 m Catherine Umberger Pvt PA

CHRISTMAS,

John: b 1700-1703 d p. 1789 m X PS NC
Richard: b 1-4-1764 d p. 12-2-1847 m (1)Anne Butler (2)Mary
    Roberson Pvt NC ★

CHRISTOPHER,

John: b 1745 d 1816 m Mary Christopher Pvt NJ
John: b c. 1750 d p. 6-29-1832 m Aaltje Zabriskie PS Wgn NJ
Joseph: b 8-8-1736 d 1832 m Charity Houghwout PS NY
Morton: b c. 1740 d p. 1795 m Elizabeth Wayland Pvt VA
William: b — d 1784 m Sarah Paine Seacap

CHRISTY, (includes CHRISTIE)

Andrew: b a. 1750 d p. 1790 m Marjorie Cole Pvt NY
Archibald: b 1760 d 10-21-1838 m Mary Maryland Pvt PA
Daniel: b c. 1755 d 1848 m Rebecca — Pvt PA
Gabriel: b 11-29-1756 d 4-1-1808 m Priscilla Hall Pvt MD
George: b 10-1-1731 d 4-22-1790 m Margaret Kelso Capt PS NH
James: b a. 1758 d 1790 m Hannah Cristie Lt NH
James: b 8-20-1744 d 7-3-1817 m Maria Banta Capt NJ
James: b 1-13-1750 d 6- -1807 m Mary Weygand Capt PA
James: b 1751 d 8-22-1822 m Elizabeth McFee Pvt PA
James: b 1-19-1751/2 d 11-5-1832 m (1)Mary Campbell (2)Mary
    McCall PS PA
James: b 4-16-1758 d 3-8-1837 m Sally Lemen Pvt VA★
Jesse: b — -1736 d 1-22-1824 m Mary Gregg Lt NH
John: b 11-25-1748 d 11-23-1836 m Elizabeth Laroe Pvt NJ
John: b 9-29-1755 d 3-19-1833 m Anne Tripp Cpl NY
John: b c. 1740 d a. 1790 m Elizabeth — Capt PA
John: b c. 1744 d 1829 m Sarah Dunbar Ens PA
John W.: b 5-7-1754 d 9-11-1815 m Annatje Brinkerhoff Pvt NJ
Peter: b 9-1-1746 d 5-14-1838 m Margaret Frazier Pvt NH
Robert: b 1750 d 4-3-1801 m Ann Elizabeth Marshall 1Lt SC
William: b 8-3-1720 d 9-28-1809 m Catalyntjen De Maree
    Asst QM NJ

CHUBB,

Alexander: b 6-1-1761 d 1812 m Mindwell Wheeler Pvt CT
David: b 1-9-1760 d 10-21-1813 m Molly Peck Pvt VT
Gideon: b 1760 d 1828 m Jane Doane Pvt MA
John: b 1745 d 1800 m Amanda Smith Pvt NJ
Samuel, Jr.: b 1761 d 4-30-1817 m Relief Frisbie Pvt MA

CHUBBUCK,

David: b 3-23-1760 d p. 1782 m Ruth Gardner Pvt MA
Ebenezer, Sr.: b 1725 d 1810 m (1)Mary Burgess (2)Tabitha
    Fowler Lt MA
Ebenezer, Jr.: b 1762 d 7-26-1841 m Lucina Craw Pvt CT ★
Ensign: b 11-1-1741 d 1790 m Sarah Terrill Pvt MA
Levi: b 1761 d 1-16-1832 m Mary — Fif MA ★
Simeon: b 8-25-1754 d 1843 m Lydia Pratt Pvt MA ★
Thomas: b 2-7-1732 d 3-11-1802 m Patience Garnet PS MA
Timothy: b 8-10-1750 d — m Lurana Barrows Pvt MA

CHUNN,

Launcelot, Sr.: b 1723 d 1809 m Judith Cartwright PS MD
Launcelot, Jr.: b 10-27-1764 d 12-29-1830 m Martha Ridgley Pvt
    MD

CHURCH,

Abner: b 6-8-1738 d 1834 m Sarah Lindsay Coye Cpl CT
Amasa: b 1-23-1755 d 10-10-1839 m Mnetriphantham Allen Pvt
    CT ★

Anthony: b 2-18-1761 d 8-28-1848 m Deliverance Chaffee Pvt RI★

Asa: b 6-25-1738 d 7-21-1823 m Abiah Pease PS CT

Asa: b 1749 d 2-15-1809 m Rachel Newton Sgt MA

Benjamin: b 11-27-1756 d 11-24-1833 m (1)Mehitable Triby (2)Eliza Phillips Pvt Smn MA

Benjamin: b 6-5-1740 d 12-6-1831 m Joanna Wilber Pvt NY

Benjamin: b 12-3-1754 d 1791 m Elizabeth Barney PS RI

Caleb: b 3-1-1754 d 8-2-1842 m Mercy Braman Lt RI ★

Charles: b 3-16-1757 d 11-3-1836 m (1)Betsey Wheeler (2)Rebecca Knight Pvt MA

Charles: b 8-18-1761 d 11-4-1858 m Dorcas Fischer Pvt MA W ★

Constant: b 12-30-1758 d 6-23-1835 m Deborah Wheeler Pvt NY W ★

Ebenezer: b 1-9-1742/3 d 7-23-1810 m Sarah Winslow CS ME

Ebenezer: b 12-14-1752 d 9-29-1808 m Abigail Holdridge PS NH

Elias: bpt 7-9-1732 d p. 1778 m Elizabeth Berry Sgt PA

Gideon: b c. 1755 d 1792 m Abigail Harris Pvt CT

Giles: b 8-20-1754 d 2-14-1807 m Louise Billings Pvt MM MA

Henry: b 1745 d p. 1790 m Mary Head Pvt NY

Issac: b 1-31-1742 d p. 5-5-1836 m Eleanor Daniels Lt MA★

Jabez: b 1747 d 6-30-1826 m Dorothy Bartlett Pvt NH ★

James Cady: b 9-6-1765 d 3-28-1855 m Mary Porter Pvt CT★

Joel Winter: b 5-27-1760 d 4-10-1834 m Beulah Barnum Pvt Arfr CT★

John: b 8-3-1755 d 12-6-1834 m Deborah Spencer Cpl NH MA CT ★

John: b 1753 d 3-12-1838 m Susanna Cony Cpl Drm MA

John: b 11-5-1745 d 12-27-1842 m Hannah Ambrose PS NH

John Barker: b 1750 d 1818 m Angelica Schuyler Cmsry FrA

Jonathan: b 1763 d 8-11-1804 m Dosha Morley Slr MA

Jonathan: b 4-17-1747 d 12-23-1827 m Perone Whipple 2Lt VT

Joseph: b 1-14-1726 d 1-28-1798 m Phoebe Sterling PS CT

Joseph: b 1-28-1752 d 9-7-1819 m Abigail Smith Pvt MA

Joseph: b 1742 d 1816 m Sarah Brightman Pvt MA

Joseph: b 3-27-1764 d 4-27-1840 m (1)Elizabeth Taylor (2)Lydia (Palmer) Dring Pvt RI

Joshua: b 8-6-1743 d p. 4-10-1818 m Keziah Goss QM 2Lt NH VT ★

Joshua: b 1756 d 5-10-1841 m (1)Deborah Brown (2)Jane Smith Pvt NH

Josiah: b 7-9-1744 d 1-27-1826 m Elizabeth Alvord Sol MA

Malachi, Sr.: b 6-24-1732 d c. 1785 m Elizabeth Miller PS NY

Moses: b 1736 d 10-10-1810 m Anne Brewer Asst Cmsry PS MA

Moses: b 1749 d 5- -1814 m Esther Montague Pvt VT

Nathaniel: b 11-16-1756 d 11-10-1837 m (1)Lois Ensign (2)Dorcas Nickerson (3)Ruth Hamlin Sol CT

Nathaniel: b 5-27-1755 d p. 1802 m Rebecca Barstow Pvt MA

Nathaniel, Sr.: b 5- -1721 d p. 1790 m Sarah Austin Lt RI

Nathaniel, Jr.: b 8-30-1748 d 10-30-1844 m (1)Ruth Stafford (2)Dorcas Austin 2Sgt RI ★

Noah: b 9-18-1712 d p. 1790 m Lydia Barnard Sol MA

Peleg: b 1738 d 1804 m Elizabeth Congdon Sol CT

Perley: b 5-7-1764 d 4-5-1853 m Zerviah Jacobs Pvt CT

Peter: b 12-1-1737 d 10-21-1821 m (1)Mrs Sarah Fales (2)Hannah Gay Col RI

Philemon: b 1-6-1752 d 11-19-1842 m Sarah Tryon Pvt CT ★

Reuben: b 3-23-1757 d 9-18-1834 m Elizabeth Whipple Lt VT

Richard: b 1-23-1741/2 d 11-12-1807 m Rebecca Warner CS MA

Robert: b 1752 d 1815 m Margaret Campbell Pvt VA

Samuel: b 10-27-1759 d 3-30-1842 m Lydia Nichols QMSgt CT

Samuel: b 9-7-1752 d 5-18-1817 m Mary Jones Pvt CT

Samuel: b 1757 d 6-11-1840 m Ruby Pettingill Pvt MA

Samuel: b 1730 d 2-5-1794 m Ann Davis PS RI

Samuel: b 1745 d 1838 m Pheobe Knapp Pvt VT ★

Seth: b 3-1-1749 d 2-16-1797 m Elizabeth Palmer Pvt MA

Simeon: b 8-11-1750 d 6-4-1841 m Theodora Beebe Pvt Grd CT ★

Thomas: b 1749 d 4- -1835 m Sarah — Sgt NY ★

Thomas: b 1743 d 9- -1812 m Ann Lane Maj PA

Thomas: b 9-1-1727 d a. 7-4-1797 m (1)Ruth Bailey (2)Huldah Soule Col MA

Thomas: b c. 2-17-1761 d 5-16-1842/3 m Mary Tripp Sol RI

Timothy: b 5-12-1736 d 11-13-1823 m Abigail — LCol VT

Uriah, Sr.: b 2-20-1740 d 3-8-1822 m Deborah Hungerford Lt CT ★

Uriah: bpt 5-11-1755 d 4-10-1832 m Phebe Dickson Sgt CT ★

Willard: b 9-7-1758 d 9-17-1846 m Sally Davis Pvt Smn CT ★

William, Sr.: b 3-3-1730 d p. 1790 m Jane Wood Pvt PS MA

William, Jr.: b 1-26-1753 d 8-20-1829 m Molly Pitts Sgt MA

William: b 3-10-1724 d 6-23-1814 m Parnel Southworth Pvt RI

CHURCHILL, (includes CHURCHELL, CHURCHWELL)

Amos: b 3-5-1743 d p. 1784 m Lydia Cowles Capt CT

Armistead: b 11-25-1733 d 9-13-1795 m Elizabeth Blackwell Col VA

Benjamin: b 8-19-1725 d 8-22-1798 m Ruth Delano Pvt MA

Caleb: b 4-4-1757 d 9-15-1856 m Sarah Hawley Pvt MA

Charles, Sr.: b 12-31-1723 d 10-29-1802 m Lydia Belding Capt CT

Charles, Jr.: b 5-3-1755 d 9-16-1818 m Mary McClure Pvt CT

Charles: b 4-25-1733 d 10-10-1797 m Sarah (Gobb) Churchill Pvt MA

Daniel: b 10-2-1749 d 12-12-1812 m Eunice Saxton Pvt CT

David: b 8-4-1729 d 2-23-1812 m (1)Jane Ellis (2)Lura McFarland Pvt MA

Ebenezer: b 11-9-1732 d p. 1775 m Jean Fisher Pvt MA

Ebenezer: b 3-1-1744 d 5-19-1822 m Lucy Palmer Pvt MA

Elijah: b 9-5-1755 d 4-11-1841 m Elinor Nooney QMSgt CT

Ephraim: b 7-2-1738 d 12-13-1817 m Jemima Bryant Sgt MA

Francis: b 1- -1762 d 10-27-1841 m Phebe Leathers Fif MA

George: b 4-18-1761 d 9-14-1796 m Elizabeth Harlow Pvt MA

Hezekiah: b 2-2-1752 d 12-19-1792 m Reliance Byington Pvt CT

Ichabod 2d: b 1751 d 5-7-1813 m Abigail Doten Pvt MA

Ichabod: b 8-9-1746 d 8-7-1826 m (1)Sarah Tinkham (2)Hannah Bennet Sgt VT

Isaac: b 2-11-1735/6 d 2-25-1826 m Melitiah Bradford Pvt MA

Isaac: b 6-28-1758 d 6-14-1843 m Nancy Phillips Pvt NY ★

Jabez: b 1759 d 8-16-1843 m Mariah Benson Pvt MA ★

Jacob: b 11- -1744 d 10-16-1815 m Lillis Reed Pvt CT W ★

James: b 5-29-1746 d 3-12-1803 m Priscilla Soule Capt QM MA

Janna: b 2-20-1739 d 1815 m Sarah Foster 1Lt MA

Jesse, Sr.: b 8-31-1726 d 5-7-1806 m (1)Jerusha Gaylord (2)Sarah (Boardman) Cady (3)Elizabeth Belden PS VT CT

Jesse, Jr.: b 3-18-1757 d 9-29-1838 m (1)Hannah Boardman (2)Olive Tilden (3)Mrs Anna Eggleston Pvt CT

John: b 6-2-1744 d 11-15 1815 m (1) — Allen (2)Sarah — Pvt CT

John: b 5-9-1739 d 3-18-1819 m Molly Bradford Sgt MA

John: b 11-14-1731 d 2-24-1826 m Joanna Bisbee Pvt MA

John: b 6-23-1763 d 6-8-1849 m Mehitabel Hubbard Pvt MA

John: b 1718 d 1798 m (1)Hannah Hincke (2)Rebecca Sudrea Pvt NY

John: b 1743 d 1802 m Hannah Smith Pvt NY

John: b 3-12-1758 d 9-27-1817 m Martha Baldwin Pvt NY

Jonas: b 8-25-1760 d 11-10-1848 m Maria Tottem Pvt NY

Jonathan: b 11-25-1749 d 2-26-1829 m (1)Sarah Burgess (2)Comfort Woodcock Sol CT

Joseph: bpt 1-27-1734 d 12-19-1797 m Prudence Tryon Capt CT

Joseph: b 2-3-1738 d 3-20-1821 m Amy Styles Pvt MA

Joseph: b c. 1757 d p. 1802 m — Williams Pvt MA

Joseph: b 3-25-1744 d — m Elizabeth Cotton Lt NH

Joseph: b c. 1758 d p. 1811 m Abigail Hanley Pvt NY

Joshua: b 2-23-1742 d 10-17-1831 m Elizabeth Bonney Pvt MA ★

Moses: b 12-1-1759 d 1810/11 m Mary Crosby DrmMaj CT

Nathaniel, Sr.: b 6-25-1731 d p. 1802 m (1)Elizabeth Sage (2)Jane Bushnell Capt CT

Nathaniel, Jr.: b 3-2-1756 d 3-22-1835 m (1)Eunice Woolcutt (2)Mrs Lydia Osgood Pvt CT ★

Nathaniel, Sr.: b 5-11-1718 d 6-22-1785 m (1)Susanna McFarland (2)Mrs Lydia Sampson Pvt MA

Oliver: b 4-15-1762-4 d 1-27-1847 m (1)Eunice Barnes (2)Lydia Goodrich Pvt CT ★

Perez, Sr.: b 10-15-1722 d 10-22-1797 m Deborah Thayer Capt MA

Perez, Jr.: b — d — m Priscilla Wood Sgt MA

Richard: b c. 1750 d 1836 m (1)Nancy Napier (2)Sallie McBride Pvt VA

Samuel, Jr.: b 1733 d p. 1790 m Elizabeth Curtis Pvt CT

Samuel: b 7-10-1754 d 12-15-1810 m Elizabeth — Pvt MA

Samuel: b 4-27-1721 d 1- -1801 m Thankful (Hewit) Seager PS MA

Solomon: b 7-27-1762 d 4-10-1835 m Elizabeth Bartlett Pvt MA ★

Stephen: b 6-7-1743 d p. 1817 m Lucy Burbank Capt MA

Thomas: b 1762 d 1807 m Alice Creighton Pvt NH

Wm.: b 11-25-1739 d 3-7-1824 m Sarah Rider Pvt MA

Wm.: b 11-6-1732 d p. 1782 m (1)Ruth Tryon (2)Abiah Wildman Pvt NY

William: b 1754 d 1859 m Mary Elizabeth Williams Sol NY

Wilson: b 7-23-1747 d p. 1780 m Lydia Darling Pvt MA

CHUTE,

Daniel: b 5-6-1722 d 1-6-1805 m Hannah Adams Capt MA

James: b 2-6-1751 d 4-8-1825 m Mehitable Thurston Pvt MA

Thomas: b 2-19-1762 d 9-4-1816 m Mary Mayberry Pvt MA

CILLEY, (includes CELLEY)

Aaron: b 1746 d 3-11-1805 m Elizabeth Dodge PS NH

Benjamin: b 1758-61 d 9-18-1846 m (2)Sally Newt Pvt MA ★

Cutting: b 1738 d 1825 m Martha Morrill Capt PS NH

John: b 1739 d p. 1790 m Abigail Clark PS NH

Jonathan: b 3-8-1762 d 3-21-1807 m Dorcas Butler Lt NH ★

Jonathan: b 9-14-1745 d 9-11-1825 m (1)Deborah Dearborn (2)Mary Fellis (3)Mrs May Williams Pvt NH

Joseph, Sr.: b 10-6-1701 d 1786 m Alice Rawlings PS NH

Joseph, Jr.: b 1734 d 8-25-1799 m Sarah Longfellow Col NH

Samuel: b 4-13-1753 d 12-10-1842 m Elizabeth Eastman Pvt NH ★

Wm.: b — d 1818 m Anna Clark Smn MA

CINNEY,

John: b 1749 d 1819 m Rebecca Davis Pvt PA

CISNA,

James: b 1751 d p. 4-15-1832 m Mary — Pvt PA

CISSEL,

Samuel: b 1750 d 1824 m Susan Gartrell Belt Pvt PS MD

CITY,

Jacob: b 6-28-1760 d 5-6-1836 m Elizabeth Runion Pvt MD VA ★

CLACK,

Moses, Jr.: b 1764 d 1842 m Ann Dedman Pvt VA ★

Spencer: b 3-28-1740 d 7-9-1832 m Mary Beavers 1Lt VA

Sterling: b 11-17-1759 d 11-6-1837 m Mary Wood Pvt VA ★

CLADER,
Jacob: b 2-8-1751 d 3-25-1832 m (1)Salome Sherer (2)Margaret Kulp Capt PA

CLAFLIN, (includes CLAFLEN)
Abner: b 8-31-1738 d 1791 m (1)Hannah Rockwood (2)Perces Merriam Sgt MA
Allen: b 11-6-1754 d 4- -1841 m Mary Tyler Pvt MA
Cornelius: b 3-13-1733 d 7-25-1818 m Deborah How 1 Lt MA
Daniel: b 9-8-1749 d p. 1799 m Submit Page Drm MA
Ebenezer: b 9-14-1742 d 1-8-1797 m Sarah Tilton Sol MA
Ebenezer: b 11-26-1751/2 d 3-28-1831 m Cynthia Stanley Pvt MA ★
Increase: b 11-13-1757 d 1832 m Sarah Stimpson Sgt MA
James: b 5-6-1746 d a. 1814 m Mary Amsden Drm MA
John: b 7-5-1750 d 1-18-1835 m Mary Sheffield Sol MA
John: b 4-8-1754 d 3-17-1822 m Henrietta Stimpson Pvt MA
Nathaniel: b 10-26-1751 d 1830 m Kezia Hodges Pvt MA
Nehemiah: b 1743 d 1820 m Mehitable Starkey Cpl MA
Phineas: b 7-30-1738 d 3-27-1817 m Mercy Fuller Pvt MA
Samuel: b 6-7-1743 d 2-3-1782 m Mary — 1 Lt MA
Thomas: b 4-8-1760 d c. 1790 m Lucy Wood Cpl MA
Timothy, Sr.: b 3-4-1729 d p. 1784 m Mary Gould Cpl MA
Timothy, Jr.: b 5-31-1754 d 2-20-1821 m Molly Nelson Pvt MA ★

CLAGGETT, (includes CLAGETT)
Alexander: b 1745 d 6-11-1821 m (1)Elizabeth Perry (2)Eleanor Beall 1 Lt MD
Charles: b 8-23-1729 d 2-21-1791 m Mary — PS MD
Henry: b 3-18-1755 d 1823/4 m Elizabeth Hayse PS Sol MD
Henry: b 1730 d 1- -1778 m Ann Magruder Pvt MD
John: b 1733 d 1781 m Cassandra White Pvt MD
Ninnian: b 1750 d 1805 m Euphron Wilson PS MD
Samuel: b c. 1750 d 3-29-1821 m Annie Jane Ramey SrgnMte MD W ★
Thomas: b 6-17-1750 d 8- -1790 m Sarah White CS PS MD
Wyseman: b 8- -1721 d 12-4-1784 m Lettice Mitchell PS NH

CLAGHORN,
George: b 7-6-1748 d 2-6-1824 m Deborah Brownell Maj MA
James: b 6-25-1751 d 8-1-1810 m (1)Salome Cottle (2)Mary Wilde (3)Asenath Strong Miller Pvt MA
James: b 7-30-1739 d 1-12-1813 m Anne Hutchinson Col VT
William: b 1733/4 d 2-24-1793 m Thankful Dexter NCdr MA

CLAIBORNE, (includes CLAYBORN)
Augustine: b 1721 d 5-3-1787 m Mary Herbert PS VA
Buller: b 10-27-1755 d p. 1804 m Patsy Ruffin BgdMaj ADC VA
John: b 1760 d 9-5-1840 m Elizabeth Smith Pvt VA★
John Herbert: b 5-3-1763 d p. 1790 m Mary Gregory Pvt VA
Leonard: b 1759 d 1839 m Francis Tanner Pvt VA
Richard, Sr.: b c. 1720 d 1776 m (1)Miss Dudley (2)Mary Glenn PS VA
Richard, Jr.: b c. 1760 d p. 1791 m Mary Cook 1 Lt VA
Thomas: b 1735 d 1777 m Anne Robinson PS VA
Wm.: b 1743 d 9-29-1809 m Mary Leigh Sol VA

CLAMPITT,
John: b 1750 d p. 1778 m Suffiah — Pvt DE

CLANAHAN,
Robert: b 1755 d p. 1820 m Anna — Pvt MD ★

CLANCY,
David: b 4-1-1752 d 4- -1849 m Bethiah Call Pvt MA
John: b 1754 d c. 1841 m Betty Huston Cpl MD

CLANEY,
James: b — d 1-5-1820 m Mrs Jane (Smith) Rowland Pvt PA

CLANTON,
John, Jr.: b c. 1750 d p. 7-29-1790 m Sarah Holt PS VA

CLAPP, (includes CLAP)
Aaron: b 4-16-1748 d p. 1798 m Phebe Dauks Cpl MA
Abiel: b 2-7-1728 d 5-20-1780 m (1)Bathsheba Pratt (2)Susa Caswell Capt MA
Abner: b 1737 d 12-5-1800 m Mercy Rust Cpl MA
Asa: b 3-15-1762 d 4-17-1848 m Elizabeth Wendell Quincy Sol NOf MA
Asahel: b c. 1745/6 d 1-5-1804 m Esther — Sgt MA
Asahel: b 3-12-1730 d 11-15-1808 m (1)Rebecca Baker (2)Elizabeth Gilbert CS MA
Barney: b 1-17-1764 d 9-27-1844 m Judith Foust Sol NC
Bela: b 6-2-1760 d 7-12-1812 m (1)Sarah Warland (2)Elizabeth Gilbert Fif Pvt MA
Benjamin: b 12-16-1738 d 11-8-1815 m Phebe Boynton QM MA
Benjamin: b 10-11-1762 d 6-26-1840 m Mary Dean Pvt MA★
Caleb: b 2-9-1752 d 6-5-1812 m Elizabeth Stone Capt MA
Daniel: b 8-7-1743 d 9-23-1802 m Abigail Root Pvt MA
David: b 8-20-1744 d 9-5-1832 m Hannah King Lt MA
David: b 11-30-1759 d 5-15-1846 m (1)Susannah Humphries (2)Auzubah Capen Pvt MA
Dwelly: b 8-2-1763 d 6-22-1819 m Rachel — Pvt MA W ★

Earl: b 4-21-1741 d 6-22-1836 m (1)Sarah Howes (2)Mrs Phebe Dutch Maj MA ★
Ebenezer, Sr.: b 4-23-1732 d 1-29-1802 m Mary Glover LCol MA
Ebenezer: b 1745 d p. 1807 m Comfort Durfey Pvt MA
Eleazer: b 2- -1731 d 1801 m Sylvia Fobes Gushee PS MA
Eliakim: b 7-31-1758 d 2-14-1839 m Parmelia Wright Pvt MA
Elias: b 1747 d 1840 m Mary Dorland Pvt NY
Elijah: b 5-3-1736 d 2-27-1806 m Submit Clark Lt PS MA
Eliphalet: b 3-6-1736 d p. 1783 m Hannah Billings Pvt MA
Elkanah: b 10-2-1739 d 10-13-1805 m Abigail Partridge 2Maj MA
Ezekiel: b 3-14-1756 d 11-4-1823 m Lydia Pratt Cpl MA
Galen: b 2-25-1733 d 2-23-1776 m Patience Brooks Capt MA
George: b 4-17-1739 d 12-18-1806 m Elizabeth Albright PS NC
Increase: b 2-27-1740 d 5-24-1801 m Bethiah Winslow Sgt MA
Isaac: b 1761 d 1848 m Jane McCracken Pvt MA
Jacob: b 3-13-1749 d 5-9-1832 m Hannah Fairbanks Pvt MA
Jeremiah: b 4-20-1762 d 11-11-1817 m Polly Briggs Cpl MA
Joel: b 1737 d 4-9-1829 m (1)Mercy Pomeroy (2)Mrs Abigail Barns Pvt CS MA
John: b 7-5-1734 d 2-13-1810 m Chloe Stowers Capt MA
John: b 10-1-1714 d 1796 m Jerusha Day Pvt MA
John: b 1752 d 5-7-1832 m Sarah Pomeroy Pvt MA
John: b 5-1-1754 d 9-19-1817 m Anna Waterman Pvt RI
Jonathan: b 9-2-1713 d 5-10-1782 m Submit Strong 2Maj MA
Jonathan: b 10-1-1714 d 1800 m Sarah Hewes PS MA
Joseph: b 11-3-1736 d 1797 m Hannah Lyman Capt MA
Joshua: b 2-9-1752 d 11-5-1810 m Nabby Barnard Lt QM MA
Joshua, Sr.: b 1707 d 5-6-1802 m (1)Abigail Bullard (2)Mrs Deborah Hewins PS MA
Joshua, Jr.: b 9-7-1729 d p. 1790 m Margaret Guild Sgt MA
Lemuel: b 4-9-1735 d 12-29-1819 m (1)Susanna Capen (2)Rebecca Dexter Capt MA
Leodwick: b 1742 d 1-20-1834 m Sophia Albright Pvt NC ★
Levi, Sr.: b 1760 d 3-12-1825 m Phebe — Pvt MA
Noah: b 4-28-1747 d 11-10-1820 m Olive Shepard Pvt MA
Noah: b 1-25-1718 d 4-10-1799 m Ann — CS MA
Norman: b 1761 d 5-6-1830 m Huldah Wright Pvt CT
Paul: b 6-24-1752 d 4-24-1845 m (1)Hepsibah Guilford (2)Mrs. Johnson Pvt MA★
Perez: b 6-14-1757 d 4-14-1818 m Mary Strong Sgt MA
Preserved: b 5-6-1731 d 1-24-1811 m Eunice Atherton PS MA
Reuben: b 10- -1755 d 2-10-1835 m Celinda Hyde Pvt VT
Roger: b 1721 d 1807 m Susanna Wales MM MA
Roger: b 8-20-1747 d 1816 m Zeriah — Pvt MA
Roswell: b 1766 d 3-11-1842 m Rachel Stevens Pvt NH VT ★
Samuel: b 12-23-1744 d 8-1-1828 m Anna Stacy Sgt MA★
Samuel: b 7-25-1725 d 2-2-1809 m Lucy Dwelly Pvt MA
Samuel: b 11-8-1742 d 5-10-1781 m Sarah Parsons Pvt MA
Samuel: b 7-13-1745 d 1-22-1823 m (1)Elizabeth Foster (2)Hannah Pierce Pvt MA
Selah: b 5-16-1744 d 5-12-1794 m Abigail Clark Pvt MA
Seth: b 3-3-1746 d 4-13-1814 m Esther Rust Pvt MA
Seth, Sr.: b 1-4-1722 d 9-10-1788 m (1)Mary Bullard (2)Elizabeth (Everett) Wetherbee Pvt MA
Seth, Jr.: b 12-17-1747 d 9-1-1825 m Hannah Blake Pvt MA
Simeon: b 1758 d 2-25-1812 m Sarah Clark Capt MA
Simeon: b 11-7-1759 d 5-31-1851 m Patty Root Pvt MA
Solomom: b 1751 d 1838 m (1)Lois Bardwell (2)Widow Anna Allen Pvt MA
Stephen: b 8-10-1752 d 5-3-1829 m Katharine Wheeler Lt MA ★
Sylvanus: b 1-20-1742 d 4-29-1811 m X Pvt MA
Thomas: b 7-5-1713 d 8-11-1798 m Elizabeth Preston Pvt MA
Thomas: b 2- -1763 d 6-23-1857 m (2)Aurelia Allen Dedham Pvt MA
Timothy: b 8-16-1740 d 1786 m Rachael Bascom Sgt CS MA
Timothy: b 12-24-1733 d 8-18-1811 m Rhoda Witherell Pvt MA
William: b 8-8-1745 d 3-8-1778 m Sarah Tileston Pvt MA
William: b 9-17-1757 d p. 1777 m Mary Rhodes Pvt MA
William: b 12-3-1733 d c. 1807 m Priscilla Otis Sol MA

CLAPPER,
George: b 1757 d 8-11-1837 m Elizabeth Souders Pvt PA ★
John: b 11-19-1759 d 12-29-1848 m Elizabeth Murphy Pvt NY ★
William: b 1760 d 1803 m X Pvt NY

CLAPSADDLE, (includes CLAPSATTLE)
Enos: b 1727 d 8-6-1777 m Barbara Wentz Maj NY
Wm.: b 1762 d 1830 m (1)Maria Haner (2)Mariah Elizabeth Emphie Pvt NY

CLARIDGE,
Levin: b 1755 d c. 11-11-1811 m (1) X (2)Catherine McDowell Pvt MD

CLARK, (includes CLARKE, DE CLARK)
Aaron: b 9-13-1758 d 5-7-1848 m Elizabeth Fowler Cpl CT
Aaron: b 4-14-1750 d 5-26-1803 m Anphillis Jencks Pvt MA
Abraham: b 9-9-1741 d p. 1781 m Rachel Goodeal Pvt NY
Abraham: b — d a. 1808 m Sarah Badgley Sol VA
Abram: b 1753 d 9-9-1820 m Jenette Pratt Sgt CT ★
Alexander: b 1740 d 1794 m Sarah Lafferty Sol PS VA
Amasa: b 8-11-1764 d 7-12-1847 m Eleanor Fuller Pvt CT

Ambrose: b *a.* 1765 d *p.* 6-19-1825 m Mary Thomas PS VA
Amos: b 10-12-1754 d 3-12-1843 m Anna Sears Sgt CT
Amos: b 4-25-1736 d 8-3-1795 m Patience Williams Cpl CT
Andrew: b 1750-5 d 4-7-1819 m Mary Robinson Pvt CT
Andrew: b 11-12-1752 d 10-17-1835 m Anna — QM CT ★
Andrew: b *c.* 1762 d 9- -1827 m Ann Davis PS Matr PA
Andrew: b 7-10-1761 d 1836 m Polly MacClenethon Cpl CT VT NY ★
Anthony: b 1759 d 7-23-1833 m Katie Pentsinger Sgt MD VA ★
Asa: b 6-26-1753 d 2-6-1820 m Rebecca Allen Pvt CT ★
Asa: b 1-8-1755 d *p.* 9-4-1834 m Jemima Case Pvt CT ★
Asa: b 1731 d 12-23-1810 m Elizabeth Barstow 2Lt MA
Asa: b *a.* 1755 d 3-20-1821 m Mary Clemmon Cpl MA
Asahel: b 2-17-1737 d 2-17-1822 m Submit Clapp Lt MA
Asahel: b 9-5-1744 d 11-11-1796 m (1)Dorothy — (2)Mary
    Bugbee Ens CT
Atkins: b 1751 d 4-14-1801 m Ruth Chessman Cpl MA
Barnabas: b 3-9-1743 d 12-13-1831 m Mehitable Hall Sgt MA
Barnabas: b 11-12-1749 d 12-25-1828 m Bethiah— Drm Pvt MA
Barnabas: b *c.* 1750 d 1804 m Polly Manley Pvt NY
Bazel: b 1750 d 9-23-1840 m Nancy Wells Pvt PA
Beaumont: b 12-27-1739 d 9-10-1827 m Hannah Bull Pvt CT
Belcher: b 1742 d 10-17-1826 m (1)Ann Wade (2)Mrs Sarah
    (Josselyn) Perry Sgt MA
Benjamin: b *c.* 1725 d 1796 m Ruth Jerrard PS DE
Benjamin: b 1758 d 4-25-1827 m Thankful Watkins Sgt MA
Benjamin: b 5-16-1738 d 1810 m (1)Susanna Adams (2)Thankful
    — Lt MA
Benjamin: b 1750 d 4-1-1815 m Mehetabel Edson MM Cpl MA W★
Benjamin: b 6-13-1727 d 3-29-1783 m Ann Loring Pvt MA
Benjamin: b 12-24-1729 d 6-14-1798 m (1)Elizabeth Lyman (2)Mary
    Hunt Pvt PS MA
Benjamin, Jr.: b 10-19-1748 d 12-4-1834 m Sarah Brooks Pvt MA
Benjamin: b 8-12-1758 d 2-28-1842 m Olive Skinner Sgt NH ★
Benjamin: b 10-15-1744 d 8-2-1830 m (1)Mary Elizabeth Leonard
    (2)Mary — Pvt NJ
Benjamin: b 4-20-1742 d 5-23-1818 m Hannah Lawrie Tms Wgm
    NJ
Benjamin, Sr.: b 1731 d 11-25-1785 m Elizabeth Mershon PS NJ
Benjamin: b 1- -1758 d 2- -1838 m Huldah Kathern Anthony Pvt
    QM NC
Benjamin: b *c.* 1750 d 1825 m Nancy — Sol NC
Benjamin: b 1747 d 8-9-1834 m (1)Nabby — (2)Keziah Gose Cpl
    PA ★
Benjamin: b 1745 d 1800 m (2)Nancy Finley Pvt PA
Benjamin, Sr.: b *c.* 1730 d 1-9-1778 m Susanna Ellis Pvt VA
Benjamin: b 1730 d 1-9-1806 m Elizabeth Lee Pvt VA
Benoni: b 11-26-1760 d 7-4-1842 m Sally Lewis Pvt CT ★
Benoni: b 1700 d 1804 m Abigail Beaver Pvt NY
Beverly: b *c.* 1747 d *p.* 12-15-1795 m Carey — PS NC
Brice: b 1739/40 d 11-7-1820 m (1)Mary Crawford (2)Margaret
    (Clark) Anderson Pvt PA
Caleb: b 11-28-1744 d 3-8-1790 m Esther Sabin Capt CT
Caleb: b 2-27-1724 d 11-1-1792 m Hannah Parsons Capt MA
Caleb: b 9-22-1758 d 5-17-1837 m Lodama Gage Cpl NH ★
Caleb: b 9-5-1764 d 1847 m Susannah Wilson Pvt RI
Caleb: b 1761 d 4-8-1794 m Hope Ann Jackson Pvt VT
Cary: b 1765 d *p.* 1850 m(1)Dorcas Moon(2)Mrs—Williams Pvt NY
Cephas: b 1-7-1745 d *p.* 1790 m Jemina Griggs Pvt NH
Charles: b *c.* 1755 d *a.* 9-30-1793 m Ann Lovett Sol GA
Charles, Jr.: b 9-21-1752 d 9-8-1821 m (1)Anna Yoemans
    (2)Elizabeth — Lt NJ
Charles, Jr.: b 1752 d 1828 m Nancy Martin Sol VA
Christopher, Sr: b 2-20-1737 d *p.* 9-12-1800 m Mildred Terrell
    Sol VA
Christopher, Jr.: b 1-6-1760 d 9-19-1819 m Rebecca Davis Pvt VA
Christopher: b 4-5-1763 d 2-1-1851 m Elizabeth Hope Pvt VA ★
Clement: b *c.* 1750 d 1852 m Chloe Andrews Pvt VT
Comfort: b 5-27-1764 d 2-17-1839 m Esther Babb Pvt CT
Cornelius: b *c.* 1723 d 3-24-1791 m Patience Carter Armr RI
Cutting: b 2-24-1754 d 1825 m Lucy Carver Pvt MA
Daniel: b 10-13-1752 d 4-12-1854 m Lydia Davison Pvt CT ★
Daniel: b 12-24-1760 d 4-24-1843 m (1)Lucy Pardee (2)Betsey
    Hurlbut (3)Mary Wood (4)Lodima Berry Cpl CT ★
Daniel: b 5-6-1756 d 1811 m Rebecca Davis Fif CT
Daniel: b 10-28-1750 d 3-22-1837 m Mehitable Slaight Pvt CT
Daniel: b 6-17-1764 d 8-31-1847 m Abigail Northrop Pvt CT
Daniel: b 4-27-1743 d 11-5-1826 m Bethiah Lewis Pvt PS NH
Daniel: b 7-30-1737 d 10-14-1813 m Hannah Miller Pvt NJ
Daniel: b 1726 d 3-10-1792 m Hannah Dearborn PS NH
Daniel: b 10-29-1760 d 11-10-1832 m Lydia Towne Sol VT
David: b 1751 d 7-17-1831 m (1)Anna Clark (2)Martha (Hine) Peck
    Pvt CT
David: b 8-6-1754 d 2-9-1829 m Sarah Hawley Pvt CT W★
David: b 11-20-1750 d 1813 m Abigail Hazleton Sol CT
David: b 5-23-1760 d 1-8-1829 m (1)Jerusha Hall (2)Eunice Griffith
    (3)Mehitable Hubbard Pvt Tms CT
David: b 1761 d 12-28-1827 m Susannah Sadd Pvt CT
David: b 7-17-1725 d 10-26-1819 m Rachel Moore Pvt CT
David: b 5-18-1748 d 5-17-1811 m Elizabeth Nodine PS CT
David: b 9-24-1729 d 11-13-1810 m (1)Eunice Bartlett (2)Mrs Mary
    Wood Pvt MA
David: b 9-27-1737 d *p.* 1783 m Sarah Bacon Pvt MA
David: b 6-25-1739 d 1784 m Sarah Taylor Pvt MA

David: b 8-24-1742 d 11-27-1806 m (1)Kezia Fisher (2)Thankful
    Turner Pvt MA
David: b 4-6-1754 d 3-9-1806 m Margaret Branch MM Pvt VT MA
David, Sr.: b 3-18-1755 d 12-20-1842 m Matilda — Pvt MA ★
David: b 11-27-1755 d 3-16-1833 m Anna Woodman Sol MA
David: b 10-14-1756 d 1-29-1820 m Mrs Mary Clarke Cross Sol
    MA
David: b 1724 d 1803 m Elizabeth Betts Pvt NJ
David: b 1739 d 11-24-1802 m Elizabeth Moore Pvt NJ
David: bpt 9-29-1742 d 3- -1778 m Hannah Johnson Sgt NY
David: b 4-8-1762 d 1846 m Mary Ann Cobb Pvt VA
Diamond: b *c.* 1750 d 5-27-1839 m Sybil Tuttle Pvt CT
Ebenezer, Sr.: b 7-12-1711 d 4-5-1800 m (1)Abigail Wetmore
    (2)Ann Warner PS CT
Ebenezer, Jr.: b 2-28-1742 d 1813 m Hannah Tenney Cpl CT
Ebenezer: b 10-19-1717 d 3-1-1792 m Ann Dimmock Pvt CT
Ebenezer: b 10-3-1747 d 7-7-1834 m (1)Eunice Pomeroy (2)Mindwell
    (Pomroy) Marsh (3)Elizabeth (Pomeroy) Lyman Cpl MA
Ebenezer: b 5-5-1745 d 2-20-1810 m Abigail Ellis 2Lt MA
Ebenezer: b 1754 d 11-24-1835 m Ruth Wilde Pvt MA
Ebenezer: b 1754 d 2-10-1826 m Elizabeth Nesbitt Capt NY
Edmund: b 10-12-1741 d 10-26-1795 m Charity Stilson Pvt MA
Edmund: b 1750 d 9-17-1828 m Lois Jackson Cpl VT
Edward: b 11-9-1759 d 1-9-1840 m Elizabeth Wesson Pvt NH
Edward: b 8-4-1761 d 4-12-1803 m Phebe Baker Pvt NJ
Edward: b 2-14-1759 d 1816/7 m Mary — Sol VA
Eleazer: b 1756 d 1831 m Sarah Jones Pvt MA
Eleazer: b 1756 d 6-27-1842 m Sibil Reynolds Pvt RI ★
Eli: b 1751 d 12-26-1817 m Lois Stone Cpl MA
Eliakim: b 6-2-1762 d 4-21-1828 m (1)Lydia Kingsley (2)Jerusha
    Barlett Pvt MA
Elias: b 10-10-1752 d 7-17-1817 m Abigail Clark Pvt QM CT
Elijah: b 6-14-1730 d 4-12-1791 m Experience Field PS 1Lt MA
Elijah, Sr.: b 9-9-1727 d 10-7-1801 m Bathsheba Harding Pvt MA
Elijah, Jr.: b 8-30-1756 d 5-30-1805 m Julia Bullard Sgt MA W★
Elijah: b 1730 d 12-9-1795 m Jane Lardner LCol NJ
Elijah: b 1733 d 12-15-1799 m Hannah Arrington Col GA
Elijah: b 1759 d 7-15-1835 m Elizabeth White OrdlSgt VT ★
Eliphalet: b 6-2-1761 d 6-23-1840 m (1)Hepsabeth Fay (2)Abigail
    Gardner Sgt CT
Eliphalet: b 11-12-1750 d *p.* 3-2-1837 m Mrs Lydia (Warren) Thomas
    Pvt CT
Elisha: b 10-19-1758 d 5-30-1840 m Sarah Beach Cpl CT
Elisha: b 1757 d 5-17-1835 m (1)Hannah Sherwood (2)Martha
    Woodruff Pvt CT
Elisha: b 5-14-1734 d 9-11-1811 m Hannah Hopkins Pvt MA
Elisha: b 11-17-1718 d 8-21-1796 m Mary Potter Pvt RI
Elisha: b 1738 d 1785 m Desire Gardiner Pvt RI
Elisha: b 9-22-1752 d 12-12-1838 m (1)Mary Stuart (2)Betty
    (Jewell) Spafford (3)Edna Mattocks Adj Cmsry VT ★
Enoch: b 5-4-1736 d 1800 m Mercy Kingsley Pvt MA
Enos: b 1745 d 1-21-1826 m Elizabeth — Pvt MA
Ephraim: b 10-18-1748 d 7-12-1828 m Druzilla Blakeslee Pvt CT
Ephraim: b 8-14-1756 d 8-12-1847 m Lucy Small Slr Cpl MA
Ethan: b 3-7-1745 d 1833 m Anna Ward Capt RI
Ezra, Sr.: b 4-4-1716 d 7-19-1788 m Martha Phelps PS MA
Ezra, Jr.: b 2-26-1745 d 8-14-1805 m Sarah How Sol MA
Ezra: b 1761 d 1844 m Hulda Richmond Pvt MA
Francis, Sr.: b 2-8-1713/14 d *c.* 11-9-1796 m (1)Mary Lee (2)Else
    Smith PS CT
Francis, Jr.: b 10-22-1757 d 1810/11 m Mary Johnston Pvt CT
George: b 6-13-1752 d 11-21-1841 m Lydia Osborn Cpl CT ★
George: b 8-25-1763 d 7-14-1845 m Ruth Doane Sgt CT ★
George: b 5-12-1722 d 8-17-1790 m Alice Harroun PS MA
George: b 9-26-1723 d 12-12-1810 m Mary Wilson Pvt NH
George: b — d *a.* 7-1-1812 m Margaret — Pvt PA
George: b 1755 d 9-22-1831 m Keziah Maxson Pvt RI
George: b *c.* 1750 d 1806 m Jean Hope Sol PS VA
George Hill b *c.* 1760 d 1819 m Sarah Oatman Pvt VT
Gersham: b *a.* 1755 d 6- -1813 m Abigail — PS NY
Gershom: b 4-29-1753 d 2-3-1813 m Lavinia Wright Pvt CT W★
Gershom: b 9-6-1755 d 3-10-1840 m Lucretia Thatcher Pvt Drm
    CT ★
Gideon: b 4-16-1759 d 1-2-1835 m Jemima Newcomb Pvt CT
Gideon: b 4-25-1757 d 12-7-1814 m Russell Gardner Pvt NY
Gideon: b 10-15-1738 d 4-4-1817 m Eunice Browning CS RI
Giles: b 8-24-1746 d 4-5-1824 m Eliphal Johnson Pvt CT
Giles: b 1758 d 11-28-1801 m Huldah Pomeroy Pvt MA
Greenleaf: b 12-17-1748 d 12-5-1836 m Eleanor White Capt MA
Greenleaf: b 2-26-1736 d 1-11-1776 m Mary Moody Capt NH
Hannah: b 1737 d 8-26-1827 m Elijah Clark PS GA
Henry: b 1754 d 1777 m Anna Rowe Pvt MA
Henry: b 4-23-1717 d 2-27-1804 m (1)Kezia Brickett (2)Catherine
    Bean (3)Abigail Frances PS NH
Henry, Jr.: b 6-3-1731 d 1-10-1797 m (1)Massa Ferguson (2)Sibillia
    (Newton) Loree Pvt NJ
Henry: b 9-11-1761 d 5-22-1848 m (1)Elizabeth Newman (2)Rachel
    — Pvt NY
Henry: b 4-23-1750 d 7-20-1815 m (1)Dorcas Hinton (2)Nancy Sin-
    nicks (3)Mary Ryan OrdlSgt NY
Henry: b 1754 d 1830 m Sarah Jones Sgt VA
Henry A: b 1748 d 9-18-1838 m Sarah — Pvt NY
Hezekiah: b 10-19-1752 d *p.* 1803 m Abigail Hutchins Pvt CT

CLARK, contd.

Hezekiah: bpt 9-1-1723 d *a.* 11- -1776 m Mary Peck Sol CT
Hezekiah Ward: b 9-11-1761 d 11-19-1829 m Judy Hoyt Pvt NH W★
Hosea: b *c.* 1732/3 d 1-7-1799 m Mary Skinner Sgt CT
Ichabod: b 2-1-1745 d 2-22-1827 m Phebe Sprange Seacap MA
Ignatius: b 1750 d *a.* 1789 m Frances Leigh Pvt MD
Ira: b 3-13-1757 d 1-26-1836 m (1)Bede Barnes (2)Eliza Chaucer Pvt CT ★
Isaac, Sr.: b 2-21-1727 d 7-12-1787 m (1)Elizabeth Andrew (2)Hannah Fowler (3)Mrs Hannah Curtis PS CT
Isaac: bpt 3-30-1760 d 6-11-1836 m (1)Martha Clark (2)Polly Gates Lt MA
Isaac, Jr.: b 11-24-1746 d 8-18-1814 m Patience Stearns MM MA
Isaac: b 2-27-1760 d 11-2-1831 m Nancy Edwards Pvt MA
Isaac: b 10-10-1761 d 2-11-1819 m Temperance Sears Pvtr
Isaac: b 9-6-1721 d 12-24-1804 m Content Weeks CS MA
Isaac: b 1712 d 11-8-1784 m Sarah — PS NJ
Isaac: b 1749 d 1-31-1822 m Hannah Chittenden LCol VT
Israel: b 1751 d 2-5-1827 m (1)Mary Stedman (2)Mary Kendall (3)Rhoda — (4)Margaret Dye Pvt CT
Ithamar: b 8-27-1716 d 1-1-1802 m (1)Martha Alexander (2)Elizabeth Alvord(3)Sarah (Janes)Parsons(4)Mary(Montague) Brown Pvt MA
Jacob: b 10-13-1755 d *c.* 1833 m Tabitha Dennis Sgt MD ★
Jacob: b 12-24-1755 d 7-16-1832 m Susanna Jones Pvt MA
Jacob: b 4-15-1749 d 7-4-1830 m Mary Ricker Lt NH ★
Jacob: b *c.* 1735 d *c.* 1802 m Temperance — Pvt NJ
Jacob: b 4-16-1742 d 8-11-1793 m Elizabeth Dann Pvt NY
Jacob: b 1-12-1761 d 9-18-1841 m Lucy — Pvt NC
Jacob: b 8-6-1745 d 10-16-1809 m Anne Livingston Pvt SC
Jacobus: b 11-16-1745 d 9- -1808 m (1)Antje Van Oostrant (2)Catherine — Pvt PS NY
Jahleel: b 3-6-1732 d 6-5-1827 m Esther Law Pvt MA
James: b 1737-40 d 5-16-1787 m Rhoda Gibbs Lt CT
James: b 12-15-1751 d 12-3-1816 m Jerusha Marcy Sgt CT W★
James: bpt 6-28-1747 d *p.* 1788 m Jemima Robbins Sol CT
James: b 9-24-1750 d 6-14-1840 m Mrs Anne Nadenbouch Gnr MD
James: b 1-28-1728 d 11-3-1799 m Mary — Lt PS MA
James: b 7-14-1734 d 4-22-1792 m Sarah Scott 2Lt PS MA
James: b 1-6-1747 d 3-5-1819 m Desire Hawes Pvt MA
James, Jr.: b 8-11-1758 d 7-22-1832 m (1)Hannah Given (2)Patience Jones Pvt MA
James: b 1735 d 6-3-1789 m Sarah Harris Pvt NJ
James: b 1745 d 9-23-1794 m Esther Marsh Pvt NJ
James: b 2-22-1762 d 1838 m Rachel Cole Pvt NJ
James: b 9-27-1760 d 6-29-1843 m Susan Clark Cpl NC
James: b 1740 d 1783 m Hannah Pickens Sol NC
James: b 1718 d 5-1-1821 m (1)Nancy Reed (2)Esther Rennick Capt PA
James: b 1742 d 1824 m Barbara Sanderson Capt PA
James: b 1756 d 1841 m (1) X (2) X Ens PA★
James: b *c.* 1750-5 d *p.* 5-18-1815 m Jean McCullock Sgt PA
James: b 5-13-1740 d 3-28-1808 m Hannah Hayes Pvt PA
James: b 1751 d 1833 m Jane Jack Pvt PA
James: b 1-22-1752 d 1-20-1815 m (1)Barbara Tillinghast (2)Hannah — Sgt RI
James: b 10-16-1744 d 4-7-1790 m Elizabeth Grimball Lt SC
James: b 1737 d *p.* 6-2-1789 m Mary Marston Capt VA
James: b 1742 d *p.* 1814 m Miranda West Sgt VA
James: b 1750 d 2-9-1840 m Barbara Rock Pvt VA ★
James: b 1753 d 1806 m Alice Arbuckle Sol VA
James: b 4-30-1759 d 6-6-1810 m Susannah Ellis Pvt VA
Jared: b 1-28-1718 d 5-2-1787 m Martha Baldwin PS CT
Jared: b 2-13-1742 d 6-5-1803 m Mehitabel Dimmock Cpl CT
Jedediah: b 3-25-1726 d 8-9-1800 m Sarah Russell PS MA
Jehiel: b *c.* 1710 d *p.* 1775 m X PS NY
Jephthah: b 4-4-1760 d 8-25-1815 m Tamar Sanders Sol MA
Jeremiah, Jr.: b 3-25-1751 d *p.* 1795 m Hannah Flint Pvt CT
Jeremiah: b 1737 d 12-25-1797 m Agnes Oliver Lt NJ
Jeremiah: b 7-15-1760 d 1-15-1846 m Margaret Ritchie Pvt PA
Jeremiah: b 1730 d 5-30-1808 m Martha Newman PS NY
Jeremiah: b 5-3-1734 d 9-12-1815 m Sarah Wanton Lt RI
Jeremiah: b 9-14-1740 d 6- -1783 m Elizabeth Howland PS RI
Jeremiah, Sr.: b 1733 d 10-17-1818 m (1)Susannah Clark Maj CS VT
Jeremiah, Jr.: b 11-3-1760 d 6-1-1845 m Sarah Millington Pvt VT
Jerome: b 1757 d 5-16-1850 m (1)Anna Penneo (2)Nancy (Ripley) Waldo Lt CT ★
Jesse: b 1-5-1758 d 11-30-1838 m Sarah Foote Sgt MA
Jesse: b 1738 d 12-24-1815 m Charity Scudder Wgm NJ
Jesse: b 11-29-1756 d 9-25-1832 m Deborah Alexander Sol NC
Job: b 9-10-1743 d 3-27-1817 m Eunice Strong Pvt MA
Joel: b 7-20-1728 d 12-19-1776 m Lois — LCol CL CT
Joel: b 1752 d 11-6-1844 m Chloe Reed Sol CT
Joel: b 1-17-1746/7 d 1-29-1809 m Martha Pinney Sol CT
Joel: b 10-10-1767 d 11-8-1847 m Susannah Richardson Mus CT ★
Joel, Sr.: b 2-9-1731 d 7-13-1806 m Martha Kingsley Pvt MA
Joel, Jr.: b 1763 d 1837 m Achsah Stearns Pvt MA
John: b 2-15-1752 d 1-5-1847 m Lucy Hammond Sgt CT ★
John: b 1754 d 1-7-1833 m (1)Phebe Russell (2)Eunice Staples(3)(3)Hannah Mosley Fif CT ★
John: b 3-16-1756 d 7-9-1818 m Phebe Curtis Cpl CT W★
John: b 1748 d 9-6-1781 m Elizabeth Worthylake Vol CT

John: b 1-7-1728 d 12-23-1822 m Jerusha Huntington PS Dr CT
John: b 10-12-1737 d 5-16-1791 m Mary Adams Capt DE
John: b 1725 d 1785 m Elizabeth — CS DE
John: b 1766 d 1836 m Nancy Williamson Capt GA
John: b 1743 d *c.* 1830 m Jane — Sgt MD ★
John: b 11-18-1731 d 6- -1834 m Maria Theresa Lark Capt MA
John: b 10-8-1738 d 1-29-1829 m Margaret Farrand 1Lt MA
John, Sr.: b 3-1-1723/4 d 2-15-1793 m Epiphany Dexter Pvt MA
John, Jr.: b 8-25-1752 d 4-2-1831 m Bethiah Haskell Sgt MA★
John: b — d 7-1-1778 m Thankful Wing Pvt MA
John: b 2-10-1718 d 1804 m Susanna Maynard Pvt MA
John: b 1745 d 11-1-1828 m Jane Montgomery MM MA
John: b 11-22-1756 d 12-25-1825 m Silence Barbour Pvt MA
John, Jr.: b 3-27-1753 d 6- -1837 m Relief Barnum Pvt MA
John: b 1754 d *p.* 1781 m Lusina Smedly Pvt CT
John: b 1758 d 10- -1842 m Abigail Bryant Pvt MA
John: b *c.* 1756 d 1847 m Sarah Duncan Pvt MA
John: b 12-14-1757 d 1-26-1852 m Sarah Chamberlain Pvt MA★
John 3d: b 8-11-1760 d 1-12-1837 m (1)Keziah Smith (2)Elizabeth Prouty Pvt MA ★
John: b 7-21-1730 d 1816 m Elizabeth Norcross PS CS MA
John: b *c.* 1745 d 1790 m Betsey Folsom Lt NH
John: b 1-21-1741 d 1799 m Betsy Batchelder Sgt NH
John: b 10-15-1751 d 1-23-1827 m Sarah Wadleigh Pvt NH
John: b 1756 d 10-14-1811 m Mehitable Hutchins Pvt NH W★
John: b 1759 d 4-8-1841 m Eunice Jewett Pvt NH
John: b *c.* 1738/9 d 9-14-1824 m Abigail Harriman Pvt NJ
John: b 1750 d 7-30-1806 m Rachel Corson Pvt NJ
John: b 7-8-1740 d 1818 m (1)Martha Westcott (2)Polly Robinson Pvt NY
John: b 1745 d 11-11-1825 m Gertrude Swart Pvt NY
John: b 1759 d 1825 m Eleanor — Pvt NY
John: b 1749 d 1822 m Maria Dyckman PS NY
John: b 1751 d 12-27-1819 m Elizabeth Kenby Maj PA
John: b 1736 d 10-22-1809 m Florence Watson Capt PA
John, Jr.: b 8-4-1734 d 4-9-1798 m (1)Mercy Case (2)Mary Peckham Pvt RI
John: b 7-8-1738 d 2-22-1836 m Sarah Gardner Capt RI ★
John: b 1748 d 9-9-1822 m (1)Ann Tobler (2)Helena Zubly Sol SC
John: b 1746 d 10-25-1836 m Persis Clark Pvt VT
John: b 1757 d *p.* 1794 m Nancy Hobson Capt VA
John: b 1761 d 5- -1827 m(1)Marie Sims(2)Priscilla Sims Capt VA
John: b 12-26-1743 d 1819 m Mary Moore Capt PS VA
John: b 5-28-1749 d 4-13-1844 m (1)— Carr (2)X (3)Polly Eubank (4)— Fogg (5)Lucy Smither Ens VA ★
John: b *a.* 1745 d 3-31-1779 m Rebecca — Cpl VA
John: b 2-19-1741 d 10-28-1831 m Mary Towles Sol VA
John: b 1743 d 1825 m (1)Letitia — (2)Mrs Letitia (Sharp) Sharp Pvt VA ★
John: b 2-27-1764 d 1-25-1839 m Ann Whitten Pvt VA ★
John: b 5-20-1767 d 11-7-1844 m (1)Mildred Gibbs (2)Mary Gaines Pvt VA
John, Sr.: b *c.* 1720 d 1786 m Ann Paulett PS VA
John: b *c.* 1756 d 1786 m Ann — PS VA
John Scott: b 4-1-1762 d 3-1-1850 m Selah Anderson Pvt MA ★
Jonas: b 1833 d 8-27-1833 m Abigail Morton Pvt MA
Jonas: b 12-14-1730 d 11-15-1805 m Lucy Hancock Bowes PS MA
Jonas: b 5-16-1749 d 2-28-1846 m Ann Alexander Lt NC ★
Jonathan: b 3-28-1747 d 12-23-1821 m Esther Parker Lt MA ★
Jonathan: b 2-3-1747 d 7-17-1827 m Hannah Gloyd Sgt MA
Jonathan: bpt 11-8-1733 d *p.* 3-15-1786 m Mercy Dana Pvt MA
Jonathan: b 1753 d 1-5-1846 m (1)Susanna French (2)Elizabeth (Dickey) Davidson Pvt MA★
Jonathan: b 1758/9 d 1-1-1840 m Mary Mattoon Pvt MA
Jonathan: b 4-20-1756 d 12-24-1843 m Mariam Champney Pvt NH ★
Jonathan: b *c.* 1740 d *p.* 1792 m Susanna — Pvt NY
Jonathan: b 5-20-1759 d 3-12-1850 m Jane Rogers Lt NC★
Jonathan: b 1757 d 1810 m 11-25-1811 m Sarah Hite LCol VA
Joseph: b 9-17-1753 d 5-29-1831 m Sarah Harmon Dudley Sgt CT
Joseph: b 5-30-1750 d 2-24-1832 m Mabel Bartholomew Pvt CT
Joseph: b 3-9-1759 d 12-21-1838 m Anna Hilton Burleigh Pvt CT
Joseph: b *c.* 1717 d *c.* 1782 m Annie Coffin Mil CT
Joseph: b 1739/40 d 4-22-1816 m Sarah — Sgt MA
Joseph: b 1717 d 1787 m Phoebe Crosby Pvt MA
Joseph: b 1743 d 1817 m Sarah Frost Pvt MA
Joseph: b 12- -1755 d 10-7-1843 m Rebecca Jacocks Dr MA
Joseph: b 1719 d 12-26-1807 m Abigail — Pvt MA
Joseph: b 8-7-1751 d 12-3-1835 m Sarah Muzzy Lt NH VT ★
Joseph: b 1754 d 1847 m Bettie Allard Pvt NH
Joseph: b 10-21-1751 d 10-20-1813 m Margaret Imlay Adj NJ
Joseph, Sr.: b 3- -1713 d 4-18-1791 m Sarah Smith Lt NY
Joseph, Jr.: b 1753 d 1821 m Hannah Clock Sgt NY
Joseph: b 10-6-1728 d 5-6-1793 m Debora Pendleton Capt PS RI
Joseph: b 1735 d 5-8-1822/3 m Dorcas Helme Sheffield Sol RI
Joseph: b 3-5-1728 d *p.* 1780 m Hannah Perry CS RI
Joseph: b 1753 d 1838 m Ruth Alexander Pvt SC
Joseph: b 4-12-1752 d 2-15-1839 m (1)Ann Haynes (2)Catharine Cannady Pvt VA Heirs ★
Joseph: b 1732 d 1800 m Hannah Hutchinson PS VA
Joshua: b 1750 d *p.* 1823 m Mary Thompson Sol MD

Joshua: b 2-19-1749 d 7-7-1796 m Elizabeth Dodge Pvt RI
Joshua: b 6-20-1759 d 12-15-1842 m Wealtha Stillman Pvt RI ★
Joshua, Sr.: b 4-26-1717 d 3-8-1793 m Hannah Cottrell PS RI
Josiah: bpt 12-5-1735 d 5-12-1818 m Martha Benton Pvt CT
Josiah: b 1757 d 6-17-1835 m Lucy Bull Pvt CT
Josiah: bpt 2-17-1739/40 d 12-22-1830 m Sarah Nute Pvt MA
Josiah: b 10-25-1749 d 4-15-1826 m Hannah Coe MM MA
Josiah, Sr.: b 6-11-1697 d 4-9-1789 m Thankful Sheldon PS MA
Josiah: b 1758 d 6-7-1851 m Pernal Barber Pvt NH
Josiah: b c 1750 d p. 1802 m Jerusha Burt Sgt VT
Lamberton: b 8-24-1731 d 3-25-1797 m (1)Rebecca Jones
   (2)Sarah Foster Pvt CT
Larkin: b 9-18-1760 d 9- -1843 m (1)Rebecca Bell (2)Lucy
   (Simpson) Welch Sol GA
Lemuel: b 11-24-1731 d 6-25-1801 m (1)Mercy Bridges
   (2)Jerusha Bill Sgt CT
Lemuel: b 1743 d 12-3-1825 m Lois Averill Pvt CT
Lemuel: b 8-8-1753 d 1831 m Ruth Baldwin Pvt CT
Lemuel: b 3-24-1755 d 8-22-1840 m Keziah Hubbard Sgt MA
Lemuel: b 4-11-1760 d 5-30-1838 m Susannah — Pvt MA ★
Luther: b 3-31-1761 d 9-16-1826 m Relief Bellows Pvt MA
Lyman: b 1751 d 1849 m Ursula Winchell Sol CT
Major: b 10-31-1727 d 2-23-1786 m (1) X (2)Mary (Vines)Wilkinson
   PS NC
Malatiah: b 2-25-1761 d 3-12-1849 m Hannah Snow Pvt MA
Malcomb: b c. 1729 d c. 1779 m Mary —CS CT
Mary: b 6-30-1766 d 11-31-1862 m Mark Whitten PS ME
Matthew: b 6- -1758 d 10-20-1839 m Nancy Wright Pvt MA ★
Matthew: b 1750 d 8-19-1798 m Abigail Rand PS MA
Matthew: b 11-16-1758 d c. 1831 m Ellen Stubblefield Brown Cpl PA
Matthew: b 2-7-1763 d 6-2-1841 m (1)Abigail Baldwin (2)Martha
   Baldwin (3)Mrs Jane Morris Pvt VA
Matthias: b 3-8-1754 d 6-7-1808 m Charity Woodruff 1Lt NY
Matthias: b 1742 d 12-14-1814 m Immetje Page PS NY
Mervin: b 11-26-1746 d 8-17-1825 m Sarah Woodruff MM CT
Micajah: b 12-5-1749 d c. 12-22-1838 m Lurany Johnson Capt
   VA
Micajah, Sr.: b 9-16-1718 d p. 1800 m Judith Adams PS VA
Moses: b — d 10-1-1784 m Ursula Phelps Pvt CT
Moses: b 9-24-1761 d 1-2-1844 m Patty Bill Fif CT
Moses: b 7-7-1747 d 1-11-1833 m (1)Rebecca Dickinson (2)Sarah
   Ayers Sgt MA ★
Moses: b 6-7-1716 d 3-7-1785 m (1)Sarah Parsons (2)Lydia Root
   (3)Martha Henderson (4)Rebecca Dickenson PS MA
Moses: b 1754 d 1-28-1839 m Mary Hale Pvt MA
Moses: b 10-24-1737 d 1819 m Mehitable French PS NH
Nathan: b 9-13-1736 d a. 9-13-1775 m Abigail Abell Ens CT
Nathan: b 2-5-1747 d 9-17-1834 m Eunice Rust Cpl CT
Nathan: b 5-9-1756 d p. 8- -1832 m Sarah Maxson Pvt MA RI ★
Nathan: b 7-21-1718 d 4-8-1792 m Abigail Satterlee PS VT
Nathaniel, Sr.: b 1728 d 11-7-1805 m Mary Hardy Pvt PS MA
Nathaniel, Jr.: b 1762 d 3-19-1846 m Abigail Woodman Cpl MA
Nathaniel: b 1731 d 1-12-1814 m Alice Healy Pvt MA
Nathaniel: b 2-17-1730 d 10-20-1821 m Bethiah Crosby Pvt MA
Nathaniel: b 1743 d 1790 m Mehetible Winslow Pvt MA
Nathaniel: b 9-2-1749 d 11-2-1823 m Abigail Warner Pvt MA
Nathaniel: b 4-6-1757 d — m Mary Sturtevant Pvt MA
Nathaniel: b 1761 d 6-10-1836 m (1)Rebecca Byrd (2)Louisa Beal
   Pvt NC ★
Noah: b 4-14-1764 d 7-28-1851 m Suze Phelps Tms CT
Noah: b 2-26-1719 d 12-20-1789 m Rachel Phelps Pvt MA
Noah: b 3-5-1763 d 5-14-1847 m Crissia Ann Ross Pvt NJ
Norman: b 12-12-1743 d 5-25-1842 m (1)Sarah Hammond
   (2)Joanna Sprague (3)Elizabeth Gleason Reed Lt NY
Oliver: b 10-5-1760 d 2-25-1837 m Betty Starr Pvt CT
Oliver: b 8-16-1748 d 9-23-1825 m Elizabeth Fish Sgt CT W★
Oliver: b 1-18-1756 d 5-27-1824 m Phebe Parsons Pvt MA
Oliver: b 1742 d 1832 m Mary — Pvt MA
Oliver: b 11-21-1743 d p. 1797 m (1)Mary Wells (2)Louise
   Babcock Capt RI
Othaniel: b 1730 d 1792 m Tabitha — Pvt VT
Parker: b — d 1742 d 1-3-1844 m Martha Leak Pvt NJ
Paul: b 4-15-1744 d p. 1780 m Elizabeth Nash Sgt MA
Paul: b 5-30-1754 d 1-27-1835 m Submit Phelps Pvt MA ★
Paul: b 1-3-1757 d 8-9-1850 m Elizabeth Wright Sgt RI ★
Pease: b 1703 d 1- -1782 m Abigail Wedge PS ME
Peter: b 1-10-1762 d 4-22-1818 m Elizabeth Wilson Sgt MA
Peter: b 8-8-1761 d 10-20-1839 m Mary Cole Sol MA
Peter: b 2-4-1743 d 10-14-1826 m Hannah Eppes Capt CS NH
Phineas: b 7-2-1759 d 2-15-1817 m Elizabeth White Pvt MA
Phineas: b 2-23-1740 d 11-6-1793 m Mary Babcock Pvt RI
Pitt: b 1-15-1763 d 2-13-1833 m Mary Jones Stimson Sol MA
Reuben: b 1734 d 12-13-1812 m (1)Elizabeth Truby (2)Prudence
   Jones Ens CT W★
Reuben: bpt 11-23-1745 d p. 1790 m Dorothy Josselyn Sgt MA
Reuben: b 1759 d 12-8-1844 m Lucy Shepardson Pvt MA ★
Reuben: b 11-14-1743 d 12-8-1813 m Mary Peppard PM NY
Richard: bpt 7-16-1732 d 2-24-1809 m Elizabeth — Pvt PS CS MA
Richard: b 1752 d 10-29-1822 m Nancy Miller Pvt PA
Richard: b 5-12-1752 d 4-21-1837 m Elizabeth Dunham Pvt NJ
Robert: b 12-16-1745 d 12-9-1826 m Phebe Higgins Pvt CT ★
Robert: b 1757 d c. 1820 m Rebecca Sledge Pvt GA
Robert, Jr.: b 1761 d 2-22-1815 m Mary — Tms QM NJ

Robert: b 1-2-1740 d 1-20-1821 m Sarah Hutchinson LCol PA
Robert: b 1752 d 1799 m Jane Gebby Pvt PA
Robert: b 6-13-1738 d 10-3-1816 m Susannah Henderson Capt VA
Robert: b c. 1745 d 1- -1801 m Agnes Gay Lt VA
Robert: b 7-20-1761 d 9-25-1837 m Sarah Burchard Sgt VA
Robert: b c. 1756 d 1830-40 m Mary — Pvt VA
Roswell: b 6-5-1761 d 9-19-1837 m (1)Thankful Hotchkiss
   (2)Susanna Cook Pvt CT
Roswell: b 1744 d 1820 m Mrs Parnell Peck Pvt CT
Rufus: b 10-3-1765 d 9-6-1849 m Lydia Bushnell Pvt CT ★
Russell: b 9-12-1753 d 1828 m (1)Phebe Thayer (2)Dorothy Hill
   Pvt MA
Samuel: b 2-7-1750 d 2-14-1834 m Jane — Sgt CS CT ★
Samuel: b 11-13-1729 d 11- -1807 m Sarah Cushman Pvt CT
Samuel: b 1750 d 5-18-1813 m Susannah Thomas Pvt CT
Samuel: b 9-10-1754 d 11-23-1786 m Ruth Cooper Pvt CT
Samuel: b 9-12-1727 d 9-30-1803 m Experience Tyler CS CT
Samuel: b 7-31-1747 d 11-9-1822 m Mary Cooper Pvt CT
Samuel: b — d 4-21-1798 m Sophia — Pvt MD
Samuel: b c. 1740 d p. 1781 m Ama — Capt MA
Samuel: b 5-20-1743 d 5-22-1830 m Mary Stone 1Lt MA
Samuel, Jr.: b 5-29-1748 d 11-6-1824 m Sarah Clark Ens MA
Samuel: b 1729 d 1-16-1812 m Mercy Town Pvt Matr MA
Samuel: b 8-7-1749 d 12-14-1839 m (1)Elizabeth Learned (2)Mary
   Breck Pvt MA ★
Samuel: b 11-20-1750 d 2-1-1804 m Ursula F. Church Pvt MA
Samuel: b 1750 d p. 1775 m Mary Sharpe Pvt MA
Samuel: b 1753 d 4-6-1831 m Submit Warner Pvt MA
Samuel: b 5-13-1764 d 2-12-1855 m Abigail Hanson Pvt MA ★
Samuel: b 12-15-1720 d 6-14-1807 m Eunice Lyman PS MA
Samuel, Jr.: b 7-2-1758 d 8-18-1837 m (1)Jerusha Phillips
   (2)Lucretia Sheldon Pvt MA
Samuel: b 6-11-1722 d 3-14-1795 m (1)Mary Morse (2)Sarah
   Harrington CS MA
Samuel: b — d 8-31-1841 m Sarah Wheeler Lt NH
Samuel: b 5-18-1746 d 4-15-1821 m Mary Folsom Pvt NH
Samuel: b 12-9-1752 d 2-23-1822 m (1)Jane Osborn (2)Damaris
   Day Sgt NJ
Samuel: b c. 1750 d — m (1)Chloe Clouse (2)Rachel — Pvt NJ
Samuel: b 2-17-1741 d 7-27-1823 m Elizabeth Fowler Maj NY
Samuel: b 10- -1748 d 10-30-1817 m Rachel Bratten Sol NC
Samuel: b c. 1738 d p. 1784 m Mrs Nellie (Violette) Littleton Pvt
   PA
Samuel: b 11-10-1754 d 10-15-1780 m Martha Curtis Maj RI
Samuel: b c. 1719 d 8-20-1783 m (1)Rachel — (2)Mrs Elizabeth
   (Barney) Streeter Pvt RI
Samuel: b 12-11-1754 d 2-13-1830 m Chloe Maxon SgtMaj RI ★
Samuel: b 4-18-1764 d 1-27-1857 m Mary Margaret Handley Pvt
   VA ★
Sarah Barnard: b 1738 d 7-19-1811 m Seth Clark PS MA
Satchel: b 3- -1736 d 5-4-1809 m Rachel Cate Pvt NH
Scotto: b 9-22-1746 d 3-28-1823 m Sarah Griffith Sgt MA
Scotto: b 11-8-1709 d 8-30-1795 m Thankful Crosby CS MA
Seth: b 1736 d 2-23-1787 m Sarah Barnard Morrill Seacap MA
Seth, Sr.: b 4-29-1723 d p. 1790 m Mary Edwards Pvt MA
Seth, Jr.: b c. 7-15-1753 d 7-8-1837 m Eleanor Burr Pvt MA ★
Seth: b 5-20-1760 d 5-20-1844 m Lucinda Shattuck Pvt MA ★
Shadrack: b 1759/60 d 12- -1810 m Rebecca — Sol VA
Silas: b 6-20-1724 d 4-16-1809 m (2)Abagail White PS CT
Silas: b 1745-50 d 8-13-1800 m X Capt MA
Silas: b 2-12-1729 d 4-14-1813 m Elizabeth Strong Pvt MA
Simeon: b 9-17-1736 d 1-17-1813 m Mary Newman Pvt MA
Simeon, Sr.: b 10-20-1720 d 10-28-1801 m Rebecca Strong PS MA
Simeon, Sr.: b 1720 d 12-9-1793 m Betty — PS CS NH
Simeon, Jr.: b c. 1755 d p. 1795 m Rebecca Goss Pvt NH
Simeon, Jr.: b 8-22-1742 d p. 1786 m Hannah Champlin Capt CS
   RI
Solomon: b 1-10-1759 d 2-4-1826 m Sarah Turner Lt MA
Solomon: bpt 6-28-1740 d p. 1790 m Judith Norton Sgt MA
Solomon: b 9-2-1744 d 11-4-1821 m Eleanor Wright Pvt MA
Stephen: b 3-3-1745 d 8-29-1834 m (1)Mary — (2)Anne — Lt CT
Stephen: b 5-12-1751 d 1839 m Hannah — Pvt MA
Stephen: b 1724 d 12-22-1801 m Sarah Barton Maj NH
Stephen: b 1750 d 1825 m Mrs Lydia (Gillison) Strickland MM NY
Stephen: b 5-13-1753 d 5-17-1810 m Susanna Potter Pvt RI
Sylvanus: b 4-10-1753 d 7-18-1838 m Dorothy Smith Cpl CT
Sylvanus: b 5-19-1760 d 2-21-1846 m Mary Graves Pvt MA ★
Theophilus: b 6-18-1766 d 11-24-1859 m Susannah Ellis Pvt MA
Thomas: b 1729 d 4-5-1811 m Susannah — PS Capt CT
Thomas: b 1725 d 1788 m X Pvt CT
Thomas: b 12-2-1743 d 6-9-1823 m Lydia Fletcher Lt MA
Thomas: b 6-27-1742 d 1818 m Mary Fuller Pvt MA
Thomas: b 1746 d 12-20-1799 m (1)Lydia Ellis (2)Ruth Hovey Pvt
   MA
Thomas: b 10-25-1750 d 12-10-1802 m Lois Williams Pvt MA
Thomas: bpt 3-27-1745 d 2-19-1814 m Mary Lewis Pvt MA
Thomas: b 1-12-1736 d 5- -1810 m Betty Spencer Capt NJ
Thomas: b 2-18-1737 d 10-29-1809 m Christian Vanneman Capt CS
   PS NJ
Thomas: b 10-7-1758 d 3-28-1827 m Mary Giberson Pvt NJ
Thomas: b 11-27-1742 d a. 9-22-1804 m Deborah Denny PS NJ
Thomas: b c. 1735 d 1780/81 m Susanna — Capt NC

CLARK, contd.
Thomas: b 3-1-1747 d 7- -1844 m Nancy Hammond Cpl PA
Thomas: b *c.* 1764 d *p.* 3-3-1804 m Margaret — Pvt PA
Thomas: b 9-4-1764 d 8-7-1743 m Mary — Pvt Tms PA
Thomas: b 1712 d 5-11-1802 m Martha Dunlap PS PA
Thomas: b 8-7-1743 d 4-20-1813 m Sarah Case Maj RI
Thomas: b 1752 d 1-14-1830 m Fanny Brown Pvt RI
Thomas: b 1748 d 5- -1828 m X Pvt VT
Thomas: b 9-12-1745 d 1-26-1836 m Catherine Ward PS VT
Thomas: b 8-10-1759 d 3-9-1831 m X 1Lt VA
Thomas: b 8-28-1755 d 2-7-1842 m Jane Ford Sgt VA ★
Timothy: b *a.* 1790 m Ruth Warner Capt CT
Timothy: b 11-2-1725 d 7-1-1798 m Submit Williams Lt CT
Timothy: b 5-17-1732 d 9-18-1824 m (1)Sarah Hopkins (2)Hannah
   Bronson (3)Elizabeth Porter Ens PS CT
Timothy, Sr.: b 1-26-1720 d 10-21-1805 m (1)Freedom Edwards
   (2)Priscilla Bundy Capt MA
Timothy, Jr.: b 3-25-1753 d 11-22-1823 m (1)Lovinia Parks
   (2)Sarah Judd Pvt MA
Timothy: b 12-26-1745 d 2- -1813 m Amy Woodworth Ens VT
Turner, Jr.: b 12-27-1759 d 5-7-1828 m Elizabeth Anne Cragwell
   Pvt VA
Uzziel: b 9-15-1737 d 10-5-1801 m Abigail Whitmore Capt NS CT
Walter: b 1738 d 12-17-1803 m Eunice McClure PS PA
Walter: b 1737 d 1813 m Mary Cathcart Pvt PA
Walter: b 1738 d 4-6-1822 m Abigail Phillips Capt RI
Watrous: b 1-29-1740 d *p.* 1818 m Lucy Hill Ens CT ★
William: b 4-19-1730 d 8-3-1792 m (1)Any Baldwin (2)Mrs Lucy
   (Newton) Pond 2Lt CT
William: b 8-25-1752 d 7-9-1839 m Patience Robbins Sgt CT ★
William: b 8-31-1713 d 9-26-1812 m Mary Wright Pvt CT
Wm., Jr.: b *c.* 1755/6 d *p.* 4-28-1820 m Christian Bailey Pvt CT ★
William: b 5-30-1762 d *p.* 1820 m (1)Eunice Wetherby (2)Mrs Esther
   Clough Pvt CT ★
William: b *c.* 1740 d — m Jane — Capt DE
William: b 1763 d 1-16-1831 m Mary Harvey Sol GA
William: b 9-28-1752 d 6-4-1807 m (1)Mary Newman (2)Elizabeth
   Wilkinson (3)Margaret Redgrave Glascow Ens MD
William: b 1750 d 12-20-1820 m (1)— Taylor (2)— Simms
   (3)Catherine McDaniel (4)Mary Johnson Pvt MD
William 5th: b 5-27-1742 d 11-11-1825 m (1)Mary Palmer
   Bingham (2)Mary Warner Mower LCol MA
William: bpt 7-16-1624 d *p.* 1790 m (1)Ruth — (2)Mrs Mary
   Goodwin Smn QM MA
Wm., Sr.: b 12-10-1716 d 3-24-1801 m Mary Marean Pvt MA
Wm., Jr.: b 4- -1753 d 3-6-1812 m Hannah Smith Pvt MA
Wm., Jr.: b 12-2-1753 d 5-17-1837 m (2)Thankful Rogers Pvt MA
William: b 10-21-1753 d 4-15-1846 m Elizabeth Whitney Pvt MA
William: b 1757 d 2-19-1849 m Sarah Lesly Pvt MA ★
William: b 3-5-1764 d 12-31-1842 m (1)Jerusha Wright (2)Mary
   Clapp Pvt MA
William: b 6-10-1753 d *p.* 1813 m Hannah Horne PS MA
William: b 1735 d 3-9-1808 m Anne Wallace PS NH
William: b 6-17-1756 d 9-28-1835 m Sarah Hatfield Pvt NJ ★
William: b 10-29-1736 d 1-3-1802 m Ann — PS NJ
William, Jr.: b 9-15-1746 d 7-18-1779 m Phebe Dabis Lt NY
William: b *c.* 1740 d 7-13-1828 m Hester Leavens Cpl NY
William, Sr.: b — d 1-12-1789 m Mary (Reeve) Benjamin PS NY
William: b 1753 d 7-21-1836 m Eleanor Dugan Capt NC W★
William: b *c.* 1740 d *a.* 10-15-1831 m Sarah — Sol NC
William: b 4-7-1757 d 6-14-1843 m (1)Elizabeth Hawkins Sevier
   (2)Ruth Goodwin Pvt NC ★
William: b *c.* 1750 d *p.* 11-19-1795 m Mary — Sol NC
William: b — d *p.* 11-25-1790 m Susannah — Sol NC
William: b *c.* 1722 d 1808 m Ann Love PM LCol PA
William: b 2-20-1744 d 3-14-1838 m Susan Anna Cowsard Capt PA
William, Sr.: b 12-25-1757 d 6-11-1827 m Mary Gardner Pvt RI
William: b *c.* 1740 d 1791 m Mary — Lt PS CS SC
William: b 1755 d 4-16-1834 m Rosey Cunningham Lt SC ★
William: b 1-28-1762 d 9-20-1846 m Martha Rowlett Lt VA
William: b 9-4-1760 d 10-27-1800 m Judith W. Cheadle Pvt VA
William: b 1760 d 7-23-1841 m Barbara Helmick Pvt VA ★
William: b 7-3-1759 d 1827 m Jane Hamilton White Pvt VA
William: b 4-26-1716 d 1787 m (1)Ann (Christopher) James
   (2)Martha Foster PS VA
Zachariah: b 1734 d 4-9-1814 m Ann Bushnell Lt CT
Zachariah: b 5- -1739 d 8-12-1831 m Mary Bacon PS CT
Zelotus: b 1747 d 12-5-1834 m (1) X (2)Elizabeth Harris Pvt
   CT

CLARKSON,
Anselm: b *c.* 1730 d *p.* 1810 m Ann or Nancy — PS VA
Constantine: b 12-18-1762 d 3- -1836 m Rhoda Johnson Pvt VA ★
David: b 6- -1761 d 11-13-1833 m Phoebe Smith Pvt VA ★
David: b 1737 d 1822 m Ann Perkins PS VA
Gerardus: bpt 12-26-1738 d 9-19-1790 m Mary Flower Dr PA
Jeremiah: b *c.* 1750 d *p.* 3-23-1813 m Mary — Pvt NJ
John: b 1745 d 8-1-1801 m (1)Maryan Noe (2)Margaret Hudson
   Ens NJ
John: b 1-9-1758 d 1793-1811 m Mary — Pvt PA
Julius: b 5-11-1749 d 4-22-1831 m (1)Elizabeth Sandidge
   (2)Margaret Bell Pvt VA

Matthew: b 4-15-1733-5 d 10-5-1800 m Mary Bonde QM CS PA
Randolph: b 8-4-1759 d 3-13-1833 m Catherine Low Pvt NS NJ ★
William: b 1760 d 1-29-1832 m Molly Smith Sol VA

CLARY,
Benjamin: b *c.* 1725 d *p.* 6-1-1782 m Elinor — PS MD
Daniel: b 1730 m Catherine Taggart Pvt NH
Daniel: b — d *c.* 1795 m (2)Sarah Nesbitt PS NC
David: b 1754 d — m X PS MD
Joseph: b 6-24-1737 d 8-22-1780 m Sarah Ward 1Lt MA

CLASON, (includes CLAUSON & CLAWSON)
Garret: b 12-25-1759 d 4-14-1830 m Kezia (Sturgis) Pvt VA W★
Jacob: b 7-7-1758 d *p.* 1833 m Pheobe Fuller Pvt NY
Jonathan: b *c.* 1734 d *p.* 1-13-1796 m Mary Barron PS NJ
Jonathan: b 6-17-1747 d 10- -1821 m Ruth Rood Pvt VT
Samuel: b 12-21-1740 d *p.* 1782 m Hannah Briggs Pvt CT
Stephen, Jr.: b 12-1-1736 d 10-24-1809 m Martha Whelpley
   Pvt CT

CLATTERBUCK,
Reuben: b 12-31-1755 d 10-12-1838 m Martha Griffin Pvt VA ★

CLAUSEL,
Clausel B.: b *c.* 1750 d *p.* 1- -1808 m Susannah — 2Lt VA

CLAUSER,
Philip Adam: b *c.* 1730 d *p.* 1795 m Anna Maria Althouse
   Ens PA

CLAUSS,
George: b *c.* 1751 d 4-4-1806 m Elizabeth Clewell Mil PA

CLAWGES, (includes KLAUGH)
John: b 1752 d 7-20-1836 m Roseanna Stahl Pvt PA

CLAY,
Abia: b *c.* 1744 d 1814/15 m Elizabeth 1Lt VA
Charles, Sr.: b 6-31-1716 d 2-25-1789 m Martha Green PS VA
Charles, Jr.: b 12-24-1745 d 2-8-1820 m Editha Davies PS VA
Daniel: b 7-12-1745 d 1810 m Jerusha Elwell Pvt ME
David: b *c.* 1761 d 8- -1818 m Eve Hardin Pvt NC W★
David: d 5-5-1813 m Mary — Pvt PA
Greene: b 8-14-1757 d 10-31-1826 m Sally Lewis PS KY
Henry: b 9-19-1736 d 1-17-1820 m Rachel Povall PS VA
James, Sr.: b 4-18-1718 d 8-3-1798 m Lydia Walker PS VT
James, Jr.: b 1751 d *p.* 1790 m Elizabeth Warner Capt VT
James: b *c.* 1737 d 1790 m Margaret Muse Of PS VA
John, Sr.: b *c.* 1730 d 8-16-1804 m (1)Mary Robie (2)Mrs Ludia
   (Robbie) Ordway PS NH
John: b *a.* 1726 d *a.* 10-12-1782 m Sarah Chappell PS VA
John, Jr.: b 4-7-1757 d 6-28-1832 m (1)Lydia Ordway (2)Abigail
   Brown (3)Mrs Deborah Lang Pvt NH ★
John: b 2-29-1757 d 1814 m Martha Ingram Cadet VA
John: b 1755 d 5-12-1835 m Melison Eppes Pvt VA
John: b 1745 d 10-12-1782 m Sarah Stratton Cadet Pvt VA
Joseph: b 10-11-1741 d 11-15-1804 m Anne Le Gardere LCol PS
   GA
Marston: b 1746 d *p.* 12-29-1804 m (1)Elizabeth Williams (2)Sarah
   — Cmsry VA
Matthew: b 3-25-1754 d 1815 m (1)Mary Williams (2)Mrs Saunders
   1Lt QM VA
Mitchel: b 1736 d 1811 m Phoebe Belcher Pvt VA
Sallie: b 11-16-1765 d 1-2-1842 m Matthew Martin PS VA
Samuel: b 6-30-1760 d 5-25-1840 m Elizabeth Karr Pvt NH MA ★
Samuel: b 5-10-1761 d 4-9-1810 m Nancy Winn Pvt VA
Slater: b 10-1-1754 d 9-25-1821 m Hannah (Holstein) Hughes
   CS PS DE
Thomas: b 7-31-1750 d 1824 m (2)Mrs Mary Jane Dawson Callahan
   Capt VA
Timothy: b 11-1-1761 d 8-6-1831 m Rhoda Lawson Pvt NH
William: b 8-11-1760 d 8-4-1841 m Rebecca Comer Sgt VA

CLAYCOMB,
Frederick: b 1758 d *c.* 1840 m Eliza — Pvt VA ★

CLAYES, (includes CLOYES)
Elijah: b 9-5-1744 d 9-10-1776 m Abigail Pepper Capt NH
James: b 2-13-1742 d 12-9-1809 m Mehitable Gates Pvt PS
   CS MA
John, Jr.: b 3-22-1735 d 6-3-1777 m Desire Perry Sgt MA

CLAYPOOLE, (includes CLAYPOLE, CLAYPOOL)
Abraham George: b 1756 d 2-10-1827 m (1)Elizabeth Poppelwell
   Falconer (2)Elizabeth Steele Capt PA
Elizabeth (Griscom): b 1-1-1752 d 1-30-1836 m (1)John Ross
   (2) Joseph Ashburn (3)John Claypole "Betsey Ross" PA
James, Sr.: b 2-14-1701 d 10-9-1789 m Jane — PS VA
James, Jr.: b 12-1-1730 d 8-11-1811 m Margaret Dunbar Sol VA
James: b 1744 d *p.* 1818 m Sibbie — PS VA
John: b 8-15-1752 d 8-3-1817 m Elizabeth (Betsey Ross) Ashburn
   2Lt PA
John: b 1-15-1758 d 1848 m Rebecca Osborne PS Sol VA

CLAYTON, (includes CLAYTOR)
Elijah: b 12-11-1757 d 3-20-1837 m Leah McIntyre Pvt NJ
Elisha: b 12-11-1757 d 3-31-1845 m (1)Elizabeth King (2)Elizabeth
	Little Pvt NJ ★
Henry: b 1750 d 2-10-1808 m Anna Speer Pvt PA
Jasper; b *c.* 1725 d 1779 m X — CS VA
John: b 3-10-1764 d 8- -1837 m Sarah Smith Pvt NJ ★
John: b 1763 d 2-10-1797 m Elizabeth Miller Pvt PA
John: b 1725 d 1826 m Elizabeth Willis Lt VA
John: b 1-12-1755 d 6-15-1826 m Mrs Margret (Wandless) Rice
	Lt VA
John: b *c.* 1733 d 1815 m Mary Holleman Ens PS VA
Jonathan: b *c.* 1745 d *p.* 1799 m Susannah Watkins Pvt VT
Jonathan Ives: b 4-17-1759 d 4-16-1840 m Anna Anderson Ens
	NJ ★
Joshua: b 7-20-1744 d 8-11-1798 m Rachel (Bassett) McCleary Dr
	LCol DE MD
Lambert: b 7-22-1755 d 7-12-1828 m Sarah Davidson Sgt SC W ★
Peter: b 1764 d 10-11-1838 m (1)Mary Lyon (2)Rachel Abby Pvt
	PA
Philip, Jr.: b 1746/47 d 9-13-1807 m (1)Mildred Dixon (2)Elizabeth
	(Wirt) Carnes Lt VA
Samuel: b *c.* 1740 d 1815 m (1)Ann Rogers (2)Martha Ann
	Mitchell Sgt VA
Thomas: b 1767 *p.* 1820 m X Pvt PA
William: b *a.* 1739 d *p.* 6-10-1797 m Elvira — PS VA
Zebulon: b 4-11-1761 d 10-27-1836 m Mary Gorden Pvt NJ

CLEARMAN,
John: b 3-10-1764 d 3-9-1857 m Nancy Vandeveer Drm Pvt NJ

CLEARWATER, (includes KLAARWATER, CLEARWATERS)
Abraham: b 6-26-1699 d 12-27-1782 m Elizabeth Schoonmaker
	PS NY
Benjamin: b — d 3-7-1848 m Elender Robins Pvt VA
Daniel: b 1750 d *p.* 1788 m Maria Sheley Pvt NY
Jacob: b — d *p.* 1800 m Elizabeth — Pvt NC
Matthias: b 8-28-1756 d 1-16-1840 m Elizabeth Trumpbour Pvt NY
Thomas: b 1757 d 1830 m (1)Leah Wood (2)Elizabeth Gray Pvt PS
	NY

CLEASBY,
Joseph: b 7-8-1741 d 9-25-1805 m Sarah Williams Sgt MA W ★

CLEAVES,
Joshua: b 2-2-1723/4 d *a.* 1778-90 m (1)Elizabeth Putnam (2)Hulda
	Perly PS Pvt MA

CLECKNER, (includes KLECKNER)
Frederick: b 8-17-1737 d 10-6-1804 m Elizabeth Maria Rothermel
	Pvt PA
John: b *c.* 1738 d 1787 m Anna Elizabeth — Pvt PA
John: b 8-12-1750 d 9-21-1839 m Anna Barbara Koch Pvt PS PA
John Nicholas: b — d *p.* 8-2-1794 m Anna Catherine Ritter Pvt PA

CLEGG,
Alexander: b — d 1829 m Margaret Farmer Lt PS PA
Alexander: b 1743 d 1822 m Susan Marion — Pvt PA

CLELLAND,
John: b 2-16-1758 d 2-16-1827 m Thankful Eaton Pvt CT ★

CLEM, (includes KLEMM)
Michael: b *c.* 1757 d 3-12-1827 m (1)Margaret Rudy (2)Rebecca
	— Pvt VA

CLEMENT, (includes CLEMENTS, CLEMENCE, CLEMENS)
Abel: b 9-4-1749 d 10-10-1820 m Elizabeth Wills Pvt NJ
Adam: b 4-22-1738 d 10-17-1811 m Agnes Johnson Capt PS VA
Benjamin: b 3-19-1717 d 12-22-1786 m Mary Bartlett PS MA
Benjamin: b 12- -1765 d 3-23-1835 m (1)Susan — (2)Mildred —
	Sol VA ★
Benjamin: b *c.* 1700 d 1780 m Susanna Hill PS VA
Benjamin, Jr.: b *c.* 1735 d *a.* 1782 m Elizabeth Williams PS VA
Benjamin Moody: b 9-9-1763 d 3-17-1842 m Rachael Herrick
	Drm Pvt NH
Casper: b 4-30-1753 d 5-25-1813 m Mary Caldwell 1Lt VA
Charles: b 8-24-1745 d *p.* 1797 m Sarah Titus Pvt NY
Christopher: b 4-6-1751 d 12-30-1820 m Hannah Carlton Cpl MA
Clement: b *c.* 1764 d 11-11-1851 m X Pvt SC ★
Daniel: b 12-18-1748 d 4-12-1820 m Catherine Moffat Pvt NY
Gabriel: b 12-25-1749 d 10-20-1825 m Mary Watts Capt SC W★
Garrett: b 1-2-1745 d 5-1-1820 m Catharine Hunsicker Pvt PA
Henry: b 6-16-1749 d 9-20-1830 m (1)Hannah Emerson (2)Mrs Mary
	Treadwell Pvt NH
Isaac: b 1756 d 3-22-1836 m Hannah Sicles Sgt MA
Isaac: b 1758 d 3-9-1846 m Dorothy McHorn Sgt NH ★
Isaac: b 1727 d 12-7-1816 m Ann Denham Capt PS VA
Jacob: b 1-14-1760 d 1840 m — Stienwax Pvt NY ★
Jacob: b 4-12-1749 d 1-17-1823 m Anna Updegraffe Pvt PA
James: b 1759 d 1810 m (1)Elizabeth Baggs (2)Ann Swift Cpl MD
James, Jr.: b 3-4-1746 d 1795 m Mary Moore Pvt MA
James: b 1736 d 12- -1789 m Catherine — Pvt VA

Jeremiah: b 6-5-1724 d 9-23-1784 m Mary Moseley PS CT
Job: b 11-19-1722 d 11-13-1799 m Elizabeth Rollins PS NH
John: b 7-13-1746 d 11-20-1804 m Mary Stanley PS NH
John: b 1-10-1755 d — m X Pvt MA
John: b 1732 d 1822 m Jane Bradt Sol NY
John: b 7- -1743 d 7-4-1807 m Mary Irwin Pvt NC
John: b 8-17-1753 d 8-20-1834 m Elizabeth Eckle Pvt VA ★
Jonathan: b 1-29-1754-56 d 6-21-1827 m Sarah Grushé Sgt PS NH
Jonathan: b 8-2-1708 d *p.* 8-27-1784 m Sarah Watts PS NH
Lambert: b 6-4-1757 d 3-31-1842 m Mary Vedder Cpl NY ★
Moses: b 9-24-1758 d 1-27-1837 m Rachel Perham Pvt MA
Moses, Sr.: b 3-26-1713 d 1788 m Phebe Willson PS MA
Moses, Jr.: b 9-4-1747 d 4-8-1815 m Sarah Bailey Pvt MA
Nathaniel: b 1726 d 12-5-1809 m Mary Hill Adams Drm NH
Nathaniel: b 10-2-1742 d 4-4-1825 m Abigail Rowand Pvt NJ
Obediah: b 2-19-1743 d 7-27-1829 m (1)Sarah Bachiler (2)Sarah
	Baker Capt NH
Philip: b 3-15-1744 d 11-10-1817 m (1)Phebe Sawyer (2)Sally Gage
	Pvt MA
Richard: b 8-5-1760 d 12-23-1815 m (1)Mehitable Runnels (2)Mrs
	Hannah (Morrill) Noyes Pvt NH W★
Roger: b 1-1-1762 d 7-31-1835 m Hannah Hathaway Pvt NC ★
Samuel: b 5-2-1730 d 12-24-1803 m Anna Gage 1Lt MA
Samuel: b 3-20-1744 d 5-8-1804 m (1)Sarah Austin (2)Judith
	Knox Pvt MA
Samuel: b 4-3-1726 d 1801 m Elizabeth Carlton PS NH
Samuel: b 3-16-1755 d 2-16-1809 m Elizabeth Doane Pvt NJ
Simeon: b 1759 d 10-24-1833 m (1)Abigail Emerson (2)Betsey
	Young Pvt NH ★
Simon: b *c.* 1740 d 1800 m Mary P. Wright Pvt NC
Susanna (Hill): b *c.* 1700 d *p.* 1785 m Benjamin Clement PS VA
Thomas: b — d *c.* 1825 m Betsey — Pvt MA
Thomas: b 2-1-1737 d 3-2-1824 m Charity Koonz Pvt NY
Thomas: b 3- -1752 d 1823 m Mary — Pvt SC
Timothy: b 5-9-1728 d 8-26-1819 m Jemima Chandler Capt NH
Tobias: b 1738 d 8- -1827 m Elizabeth Rogers PS NY
Wm.: b 1742 d 1-4-1823 m Mary Hoyt QM NH
Wm.: b 11-24-1757 d 8-24-1833 m (1)Alice Shepard (2)Abigail
	Hill Pvt NH
Wm.: b 1759 d 1834 m Elizabeth Daniel 1Lt NC
Wm.: b *c.* 1750 d 1790/91 m Ann — Sol PS VA
Wm.: b 8-9-1760 d 12-12-1804 m Sigis — Pvt VA

CLEMONS, (includes CLEMMENS)
Edward: b 1724 d 1791 m X Pvt MA
John: b 6-4-1763 d 3-5-1845 m Mary McLellan Sol MA
Jonathan: b 1732 d 8-12-1807 m Hannah Woodward Pvt MA
Jonathan: b 1-19-1754 d 4-18-1841 m Rachel — Pvt MA ★
Michael: b 8-28-1761 d *p.* 1790 m Eunice Howe Pvt MA
Nicholas: b 3-17-1749 d *p.* 7-1-1828 m Elizabeth Getts Pvt PA

CLEMSON,
James: b 12-5-1730 d 7-13-1792 m Margaret Heard PS PA

CLENDENIN, (includes CLENDENEN & CLENDENNIN)
Alexander: b *c.* 1754 d *p.* 8-28-1829 m Catherine Spencer Pvt VA
James: b 4-3-1737 d 11-16-1795 m Mrs Mary Fullerton PS MD
James: b 1752 d 12-5-1834 m Jane McCamus Pvt PA ★
John: b 1-2-1756 d 5-3-1837 m Ann Webb BrevetCapt NC
John: b *a.* 1755 d 8- -1802 m Elizabeth Caldwell Lt PA
John: b 6-7-1748 d 1- -1813 m Rebecca De France Sgt PA W★
John: b 1733 d 1-12-1796 m Margaret Steele Cpl PA
John: b *c.* 1758 d *p.* 5-9-1809 m Mary Simpson Sgt VA
Robert: b 1747 d *p.* 1785 m Mary — Pvt VA
Thomas: b 1744 d 4-20-1817 m (1)Lydia Hastlett (2)Nancy
	(McNeece) Armstrong (3)Margaret — Sol SC
Wm.: b 5-23-1753 d 9-18-1828 m Margaret Handley Lt VA

CLEVELAND, (includes CLEAVELAND)
Aaron, Sr.: b 11-27-1727 d 4-14-1785 m Thankful Paine Capt CT
Aaron, Jr.: b 6-18-1750 d 9-19-1818 m Jemima Robinson Lt CT
Aaron: b 2-3-1744 d 9-21-1815 m (1)Abiah Hyde (2)Elizabeth
	Clement Breed CS Capt CT
Alexander, 3d: b 1736 d 1829 m (1)Sarah Ann Harrison (2)Bridget
	Harrison Capt VA
Amasa: b 6-16-1756 d 7-1-1833 m Naomi Warner Sgt MA ★
Benjamin: b 4-10-1755 d 9- -1803 m Sarah Stratton Pvt MA W★
Benjamin: b *c.* 1744 d 4-19-1806 m Margaret Hopkins Pvt NY
Benjamin: b 5-20-1714 d 1797 m Rachel (Hall?) Pvt VT
Benjamin: b 5-26-1738 d 10-15-1806 m Mary Graves Col NC
Chester: b 3-8-1762 d 2-8-1840 m Elizabeth Hutchings Pvt CT W★
Curtis: b 7-5-1734 d 1795 m Elizabeth Lord Pvt CT
David: b 5-1-1744 d 4-11-1820 m (1)Rachel Allen (2)Keziah
	(Mason) Allen Pvt MA
Ebenezer: b 1-5-1725 d 7-4-1805 m Abigail Stevens Chp MA
Edward: b 7-4-1737 d 2-15-1776 m Sabra Hosmer Pvt CT
Edward: b 12-30-1738 d 12-14-1830 m (1)Deborah Adams (2)Mrs
	Elizabeth Perry Pvt MA
Elijah: b 1-5-1720/21 d 9-28-1794 m Alice Lawrence Sol NY
Elijah Phillips: b 8-5-1765 d 2-26-1845 m Mary Kinney Sol CT
Elisha: b 1-7-1716 d 9- -1783 m (1)Esther Morse (2)Ruth Paine Sct
	Pvt NH
Ephraim: b 8-20-1740 d *a.* 1820-27 m Mary Griffin Capt MA

CLEVELAND, contd.
Ephraim: b 2-3-1711 d *p.* 1781 m (1)Abigail Curtiss (2)Ruth Nichols (3)Mrs Hannah (Paige) Hayward CS MA
Ezra: b 4-5-1746 d 10-27-1822 m Abiah Neal 2Lt MA
Ezra: b 4-17-1726 d 1-7-1802 m Jerusha Bradford Newcomb Pvt MA
Frederick: b 11-28-1756 d 3-7-1827 m Susannah Hill Sol Tms CT W★
Gardiner: b 9-25-1763 d 4-22-1851 m (1)Mary Holmes (2)Huldah Demming Pvt CT ★
Gardiner: b 4-16-1764 d 8-26-1826 m Annis Durkee Cpl VT
George: b 1762 d *c.* 1805 m Sarah Mabee Pvt MA
Henry: b 5-11-1746 d 1-6-1841 m Elizabeth Royce Pvt MA
Ichabod: b 6-28-1765 d 8-12-1844 m Katurah Baldwin Pvt NJ ★
Isaac, Sr.: b 5-13-1735 d 3-19-1819 m (1)Sarah — (2)Mary — Pvt CT
Isaac, Jr.: b 1-22-1755 d 5-14-1838 m Mamre Matthews Pvt CT★
Jabez: b 1737 d 6-17-1775 m Jane Trumbull Fif MA
Jacob: b 5-31-1760 d 10-5-1821 m Lucy Vaughn Sgt CT
James: b — d *c.* 1791 m Frances Johnstone Capt VA
Jedediah: b 9-5-1758 d 9-28-1831 m (1)Lydia Merrill (2)Mrs Polly Johnson (3)Prudence Van Kirk Sgt MA
Jeremiah: b 8-12-1757 d *p.* 1839 m (1)Nancy Helen Clark (2)Martha Smith Sol GA
Job Wm.: b 3-27-1757 d 4-5-1826 m Hannah Clark Pvt NY
John: b 2-28-1735 d 2-15-1818 m Betsey Downer Ens CT
John: b — d *p.* 1818 m Sarah Scofield Pvt Sol CT
John: b 4-11-1722 d 4-22-1799 m Mary Dodge Chp MA
John: b 11-30-1768 d 4-22-1828 m Rhoda Kidd Sol GA
John: b 1756 d 6-25-1826 m Mrs Annah Taft Pvt CT
John: b 1738 d 3- -1825 m Mollie McCann Sol SC
John: b 1755 d 8-5-1832 m Elizabeth Robertson Pvt VA ★
Jonas: b 10-16-1718 d *c.* 1788 m Prudence Phillips Pvt CT
Joseph: b 4-29-1749 d 4-9-1844 m (1)Elizabeth Wheeler (2)Mrs — Pvt MA
Josiah: b 4-4-1713 d 5-7-1793 m (1)Sarah Lawrence (2)Mrs Joanna (Waldo) Brewster 1Lt CT
Josiah: b 1758 d 12-26-1831 m Delight Utley Pvt MA ★
Josiah, Jr.: b 5-7-1742 d 8-23-1825 m (1)Ruth Johnson (2)Sybil — Pvt CT ★
Larkin: b 4- -1748 d 7-9-1814 m Frances — Lt SC
Lemuel: b *c.* 1744 d *c.* 1820 m Margaret Burgett Cpl MA
Lemuel: b 9-23-1761 d 9-26-1807 m Sybil Johnsen Cpl VT
Moses: b 7-20-1736 d 1790/91 m Tabitha Spencer Capt CT
Moses: b 5-23-1745 d 11-16-1818 m Phoebe Fargo Lt CT
Nehemiah, Sr.: b 7-30-1721 d 10-29-1792 m Dinah Brown Pvt CT
Nehemiah, Jr.: b 4-5-1753 d 10-25-1843 m Hannah Parsons SgtMaj MA
Noahdiah: b 6-6-1756 d *p.* 1791 m (1)Jemima White (2)Sarah Hamilton Pvt CT
Oliver: b 10- -1733 d 9-5-1803 m Azubah Smith Sgt NY
Robert: b 1-8-1744 d *p.* 2-26-1812 m (1)Aley Mathis (2)Sallie Johnson Capt NC
Roswell: b 7-2-1759 d 6-9-1848 m Temperance Finney Pvt MA
Rufus: b 6-14-1754 d 2-22-1838 m (1)Mary Chamberlain (2)Mrs Alice (Jenkins) Kent Cpl CT
Samuel: b 6-7-1730 d 9- -1809 m (1)Ruth Darby (2)Anna Welch Pvt CT
Samuel: bpt 9-4-1759 d 6-6-1829 m (1)Betsey Allen (2)Mrs Lucy (Comstock) Jones Pvt CT
Samuel: b 7-14-1753 d 5-30-1839 m Mercy Wilbur Cpl MA
Samuel: b *c.* 1747 d *c.* 1816 m Mary Daniels Pvt MA
Seth: b 11-9-1742 d 5-20-1809 m Jedediah Claghorn Sgt MA
Silas, Jr.: b 3-17-1766 d 9-24-1840 m Lois Sharpe Cpl NS CT ★
Solomon: b 6-14-1754 d 5-10-1823 m Hannah Dana Sharpe Pvt CT
Solomon: b 2-26-1754 d 6-16-1844 m Martha Rathbone Pvt Matr CT★
Solomon: b 12-13-1747 d 1797 m Lucretia Owen Pvt NH
Solomon: b 9-17-1756 d 1836 m Esther Knight Pvt MA
Squire: b 7-17-1764 d 6-14-1834 m Pamelia Green Pvt CT ★
Stephen: b 10-9-1746 d 5-17-1835 m Hannah Huntington Pvt CT ★
Stephen: b 8-27-1754 d 8-3-1843 m Polly Goodin Pvt VT
Stephen Sewell: b 10-8-1742 d 10-8-1801 m Margaret Jeffry Capt MA
Timothy, Jr.: b 2-18-1735 d 11-3-1803/4 m Esther Fish Pvt MA
Tracy: b 5-8-1751 d 2-27-1836 m Phebe Hyde Pvt CT ★
Tyxhall: b 4-26-1750 d *p.* 1789 m Abigail Crane PS NH
Waitstill: b 10-22-1764 d 2-17-1815 m Martha Taber Pvt NY
Wm.: b 1752 d 1778 m Mary Arnold Lt CT
Wm.: b 2-24-1765 d 12-4-1835 m Amy Tourtellotte Pvt CT
Wm., Sr.: b 1719 d 1791 m Rachel Warren Pvt MA
Wm., Jr.: b 1746 d 12-28-1799 m Sarah (Pelton) Tozer Pvt MA
Wm.: b 12-24-1757 d 6-18-1842 m Margaret Wilson Pvt VA ★
Zimri: b 8-22-1760 d 5-19-1827 m Eunice Clark Pvt MA

CLEVENGER, (includes CLEAVENGER)
Abraham: b 8-1-1834 d 9-1724 m Mary Pitman Pvt NJ
Eden: b 1755 d 1-14-1830 m X Pvt VA ★
Isaiah: b 1756 d 10-14-1838 m Catherine — Pvt NJ ★

CLEWELL,
Daniel: b 2-14-1756 d 4-29-1844 m Susanna M. Klein Pvt PA
Jacob: b 9-21-1751 d 6-22-1824 m Anna C. Rohrig Pvt PA
John: b 9-12-1754 d 6-30-1827 m (1)Christina Weinland (2)Leah Heil Pvt PA

CLEWLEY,
Isaac, Sr.: b 12-15-1729 d 11-4-1800 m (1)Sarah Burditt (2)Sarah Stimson Lt MA
Isaac, Jr.: b 7-11-1755 d 2-3-1839 m Abiah Hawes Pvt Gnr Bbd MA

CLIFFORD,
Charles: b 11-10-1730 d 1-1-1815 m Jane Gordon Pvt PA
David: b 11-28-1761 d 4-4-1837 m (1)Lydia Jones (2)Mehitable Hansen Pvt NH ★
Ebenezer: b 10-29-1746 d 3-19-1833 m Rhoda Elliott CS NH
Edward: b 10-16-1733 d 4-14-1824 m Abigail Winslow PS MA
Isaac, Sr.: b 5-1-1721 d *p.* 1790 m Sarah Healey Pvt NH
Isaac, Jr.: bpt 3-30-1746 d *p.* 1790 m (1)Ruth Young (2)Alice Follinsby Pvt NH
Isaac: b 1748 d 12-4-1833 m Rachel Decker Pvt ME
James: b *c.* 1758 d *p.* 2-25-1801 m Mary Norris Pvt PA
John: b 3-18-1737 d *p.* 1790 m Mary Worthen Pvt NH
Joseph: b 1723 d *p.* 1790 m Eleanor — PS NH
Nathan: b 7-16-1758 d 1854 m Urana — Pvt MA
Samuel: b 11-9-1716 d 3-3-1797 m Elizabeth Gove PS NH
Samuel: b 9-3-1756 d 12-12-1812 m Mehitable — Sol NH
Zachariah: b *c.* 1735 d 9- -1814 m Elce — Sgt NH
Zacharias: b 1760/61 d *p.* 1783 m Elizabeth Lucas Pvt NH ★

CLIFT,
Adna Winslow: b 1754 d 1825 m Bethiah Orr Lt MA
Amos: b 9-20-1737 d 7-29-1806 m (1)Mary Coit (2)Mrs Anna Denison Avery CS CT
Hezekiah: b 12-4-1761 d 10-10-1822 m Lucy Walton Pvt CT
Joseph: b 6-22-1736 d 11-21-1828 m Mary Hatch Capt MA
Lemuel: b 10-10-1755 d 9-13-1821 m Sarah Hall Capt CT
Samuel: b 10-22-1709 d 8-22-1794 m Lydia Doggett Capt CT
Thomas: b 6-22-1736 d 11-21-1828 m Mollie Hatch Capt MA
Waterman: b 12-28-1741 d 9-17-1828 m (2)Keziah Bradford Maj CT

CLIFTON,
Absalom: b 10-12-1718 d *a.* 10-14-1783 m Nancy Marmaduke Pvt NC
Burdette, Jr.: b 2-3-1736 d *a.* 1-1-1799 m Rebecca Kenner Ens VA
George: b 1761 d 6-11-1840 m (1)Elizabeth Dickinson (2)Milly Brown Pvt DE ★
Howson: b 1762 d 1794 m Nancy Brashears Pvt PS PA
John: b 3-25-1750 d 12-2-1802 m Tabitha — Pvt DE
John: b 1751 d 3-4-1846 m Penelope Ward Pvt NC
Joseph: b 1732 d 1804 m Abigail Richardson Hadley Pvt PS MA
Nathan: b 12-26-1759 d 3-8-1864 m (2)Elizabeth Davis Pvt NC
Thomas: b *c.* 1745 d 1832 m Nancy Wells Pvt MD ★

CLINGAN,
Thomas: b 1723 d 10-14-1788 m Margaret McFarland Pvt PA
Wm.: b 5-3-1753 d 5-24-1822 m Jean Roan Lt PA

CLINGMAN, (includes KLINGMAN)
John Michael: b 10- -1734 d 1-26-1816 m Anna Elizabeth Miller Capt PA
Peter: b 12-23-1762 d 4-27-1848 m Margaret Englehart Pvt PA State ★

CLINKINBEARD,
Wm.: b 10-10-1761 d 1844 m Mary Mooney Pvt VA

CLINKSCALES,
Frances: b *c.* 1748 d 1837 m (1)Mary Franklin (2)Mary Carpenter PS Sgt MD

CLINTON,
Charles: b *c.* 1750 d 1828 m (1)Margaret — (2)Elenor Gapen Capt PS MD
George: b 7-26-1739 d 4-20-1812 m Cornelia Tappan CS BGen NY
James: b 7-29-1736 d 12-27-1812 m (1)Mary De Witt (2)Mary Little Gray MGen NY
James: b 8-11-1761 d 3-2-1847 m Ann Armstrong Capt SC ★
John, Sr.: b 11-8-1721 d 6-12-1788 m Elizabeth Beecher PS NY
John, Jr.: b 5-4-1752 d 1832 m (1)Mary Scribner (2)Mrs Elizabeth Darby Sgt NY
Joseph Benedict: b 5-28-1762 d 6-8-1828 m (1)Abigail Camp Cpl CT
Lawrence: b 1-1-1737 d 9-9-1804 m Elizabeth Todd Capt CT
Peter: b 4- -1745 d 3- -1780 m Frances Bradner Capt SC ★
Richard: b — d 1794 m Penelope Kenan PS NC
Richard: b 1755 d 8-18-1839 m Marcella Turbeville Pvt SC ★
Thomas: b 1760 d 1-7-1847 m Maria Simpson Pvt Fif MD ★

CLIPPINGER, (includes KLEPPINGER)
Anthony: b 1753 d *c.* 1805 m Anna Margaretha Heckman Sgt PA
Anthony: b 1765 d 11- -1846 m Margaret Miller Pvt PA
Frederick: b 2-4-1749 d 3-16-1802 m Maria Barbara Best Pvt PA
John: b 8-1-1743 d *c.* 1790 m Anna Margaretha — Pvt PA
Ludwig: b 9-16-1741 d 11-11-1827 m Anna Maria Best Pvt PA

CLISBY, (includes CLISBE)
Joseph: b *a.* 1758 d 1-9-1796 m Lois Eaton Slr MA
Joseph: b 6-27-1756 d 1-20-1840 m Hannah Robards Pvt NJ ★

CLOAK, (includes CLOKE)
Ebenezer: b c. 1740 d 1781 m Elizabeth Cook Seacap Pvtr

CLOGSTONE,
John, Jr.: b 1741 d 2-3-1803 m Mrs Anna Glassford Pvt NH

CLOPTON,
John: b 9-25-1753 d 9-11-1816 m Sarah Bacon Capt VA
Wm.: b 2-2-1721/22 d 8-3-1796 m Elizabeth Dorrall (Ford) Jones Capt VA
Wm.: b 11-19-1714 d p. 1785 m Cassandra — PS VA

CLORE,
John, Sr.: b c. 1726 d p. 12-2-1779 m (1)Dorothy Cafer (2)Catherine — PS Sol VA
John, Jr.: b 1-22-1749 d 12- -1824 m Margaret Blankenbaker PS VA
Michael: b 12-4-1746 d 12-7-1817 m Margaret Weaver PS Sol VA
Peter: b c. 1750 d c. 1827 m Maria Fray Pvt VA

CLOSE, (includes CLOES, CLOSS, CLOUSE, KLOSS)
Abraham: b 1-9-1762 d 3-9-1841 m Mary Hubbard Pvt CT ★
Benjamin: b 9-10-1760 d 10-11-1836 m Sarah Mead Pvt CT
Benjamin: b 12-15-1743 d 4-29-1812 m Theodosia Mead Pvt NY
Charles: b 8-10-1756 d 9-10-1838 m (1)Sarah — (2)Hannah Whitney Pvt MD
Christian: b 1-1-1758 d 9-26-1825 m Catharine Grunt Pvt MD
Christopher: b c. 1745 d a. 1821 m — Pvt PA
Ernst: b 1738 d 1805 m Catherine Suter Pvt PA
Jabez: b 1755 d 1791 m Abigail Smith Pvt NY
Jacob: b c. 1765 d p. 1790 m (1)Catherine Troutman Pvt PA
John: b 1758 d 12-26-1822 m Catherine Cananyer Pvt MD
John: b 1752 d 1800 m Mary Bell Sgt PA
John: b 1737 d 1813 m Mary Wickes Pvt Chp NY
Odle: b 10-22-1738 d 4-26-1812 m Bethia Reynolds PS Capt CT
Solomon: b 11-28-1759 d 1-28-1840 m Prewy Peck Pvt CT ★

CLOSSON,
Ichabod: b 1764 d 5-9-1807 m Sally Safford Pvt VT
John: b c. 1744 d 7-17-1776 m Sabra Alger Pvt NH
John: b 12-6-1764 d 5-18-1815 m Elizabeth Oden Graeff Pvt PA
Nehemiah: b 12-13-1758 d 4-16-1839 m Mary Crosman Pvt VT
Timothy: b 1721/22 d 8-9-1807 m Eunice Poppleton PS VT
Wilbert: b c. 1754 d 5-18-1830 m Mrs Elizabeth (Daily) Brown Pvt NY

CLOTHIER,
Ambrose: b 1738 d 1-4-1825 m Mercy May Pvt CT
Jesse: b 1760 d 1850 m X Pvt MA ★

CLOUD,
Abner: b c. 1738 d p. 1783 m Amy Pyle Pvt PA
Daniel: b 1755 d 2- -1815 m Elizabeth — Sol VA
Ezekiel: b- 14-1762 d 5-30-1850 m Elizabeth Jones Pvt GA ★
James: b 1755 d c. d p. 7-21-1819 m Janet McKoun Sol SC
Jeremiah, Sr.: b c. 1721 d 1787 m Ann Bailey Pvt GA
Jeremiah: b 11-23-1723 d 1817 m Lydia Harlan 2Lt PA
Jesse: b 9-13-1742 d 1821 m Mary Allen Pvt PA
John: b 2-5-1740 d 1840 m Elizabeth Lacy Pvt NC ★
Robert, Sr.: b 2-2-1723 d 4-2-1801 m Magdalen Peterson Pvt DE
Robert, Jr.: b 8-21-1755 d 6-5-1833 m Rachel Matson PS DE
Wm.: b — d 1811 m Ruth Buckingham Sol PS DE
Wm.: b 9-17-1750 d 2-8-1842 m (1)Adeline Martin (2)Mary Morgan (3)Nancy Vaughn Lt VA ★
Wm.: b c. 1745 d 1795 m Jane Jones Pvt VA

CLOUGH, (includes CLUFF, KLUG)
Amasa: b c. 1755 d 1814/15 m Tryphena Cowles Pvt MA
Amos: b 1742 d p. 1833 m Bethia Baker Pvt MA
Benjamin: b 10-7-1761 d p. 1836 m Mollie Marston Ens MA
Daniel: b 3-11-1763 d 7-1-1840 m Abigail Atwood Pvt MA
Daniel: b 6-6-1754 d 1835 m (1)Deborah Mason (2)Mrs Rachel Williams PS NH
Ephraim: b 1-12-1724 d p. 1790 m Mary — Pvt MA
Isaac: b 4-23-1753 d p. 1779 m Hannah Page Pvt NH
Ithamer: b 1750 d 5-7-1843 m Betty Heath Pvt CT
James: b c. 1744 d p. 1790 m Ruth Webster PS NH
Jeremiah, Sr.: b 4-4-1710 d 1792 m (1)Deliverance Leavitt (2)Sarah Elkins MA
Jeremiah, Jr.: b 11-2-1738 d 12-11-1815 m (1)Abigail Keizer (2)Patty Hoyt Capt NH
John: b 2-7-1719 d 3-15-1798 m (1)Lydia Goodville (2)Abigal Edes Sgt MA
John: b 1758 d 2-17-1847 m (1)Mehitable Coffin (2)Susanne Brown (3)Mrs Mehitable Whitehouse Pvt MA ★
John: b c. 1760 d 5-7-1847 m Elizabeth Savage Pvt NH ★
John: b 1763 d 7-18-1836 m Dolly Lawrence Pvt NH W★
John: b 1760 d 1841 m Elizabeth Frampton Cpl PA
Jonathan: b 7-30-1744 d 1835 m Keziah Abigail Walker Pvt CT
Jonathan: b 1749 d 3-4-1823 m Elizabeth Philbrick Pvt MA W★
Jonathan: b 2-17-1734 d 8-12-1816 m Elizabeth Thompson PS NH
Josiah: b 10-13-1747 d 7-1-1811 m Martha Currier PS NH
Michael: b c. 1742 d p. 4-17-1812 m Elizabeth Fisher Sol PS VA

Nehemiah: b 7-3-1741 d 1825 m Sally Clough Sol CS PS NH
Obadiah: b 8-24-1753 d 11-29-1823 m Sarah Clough Pvt NH
Obediah: b 2-18-1731 d 1803 m Elizabeth Whitmore Lt CT
Oliver: b — d 9-25-1847 m Sally Hurvey Pvt NH
Philip: b a. 1747 d p. 1795 m (1)Veronica — (2)Christianna Hinkle Sgt PA
Reuben: bpt 4-22-1756 d 9- -1817 m Hannah Sargent Pvt NH
Samuel: b 4-28-1738 d 12-31-1811 m Miriam Satterlee PS NH
Simon: b 11-3-1758 d 4-28-1843 m Mary Avery Sgt NH ★
Thomas: b 1-28-1717 d 1793 m Mary Call CS NH
Wm.: b 1750 d 5-15-1843 m Mrs Juda Rowell Pvt PA ★
Wm., Jr.: b 2-10-1754 d 12-16-1829 m Hannah (Clough) Pvt PS NH
Wyman: b 10-4-1726 d 1796 m Sarah Hall PS NH
Zaccheus: b 3-6-1725 d 1810 m Love Meader 2Lt MA

CLOUSER,
John: b c. 1754 d 1844 m Christina Crips Pvt PA

CLOUTMAN,
Stephen: b 11-23-1755 d 10-26-1804 m Hannah Smith Pvt MA

CLOVER, (includes CLOWER)
Daniel: b 7-18-1762 d 30-1847 m Nancy Wilson Pvt NC ★
John: b 1755 d 4-28-1832 m Elizabeth Shimer Capt PS PA
Jonathan: b 12-3-1763 d 9-18-1836 m Mary Shuler Pvt NC ★
Philip: b 6-12-1758 d 5-19-1830 m Mary Cooper Pvt PA

CLOWES,
John: b 11-5-1730 d 2-24-1790 m Mary Draper PS CS DE

CLOWNEY,
Samuel: b 1742 d 9-19-1824 m (1)Esther Leiper (2)Elizabeth Kennedy Pvt SC ★

CLOYD,
David: b 3-25-1738 d 8-20-1820 m Ann Boyd Pvt PA
James: b 10-29-1731 d 1817 m Jean Lapsley Sol VA
James: b 2-21-1762 d 3-26-1836 m Rachel Tilford Spy VA
John: b c. 1738 d c. 1799 m Margrett Scott Pvt VA
Joseph: b 6-10-1742 d 8-3-1833 m Mary Gordon Col VA
Michael: b 1735 d 1807 m Elizabeth Neely Pvt CS VA
Ninian: b c. 1730 d p. 1807 m Mary Kinkaid Pvt VA
Wm.: b 1751 d 4-7-1837 m Jeanette Barr Pvt PA ★

CLUGGAGE,
Thomas: b 1750 d 1-2-1832 m Miss Curlett Capt PA

CLUGSTON,
John: b c. 1750 d c. 1806 m X Pvt PA
Robert: b 1747 d 1833 m Margaret Young Pvt PA

CLUNG, (includes KLUNCK)
Henry: b 1760 d 6-26-1833 m Elizabeth — Pvt VA ★

CLUNN,
Joseph: b 1735 d 5-8-1816 m Maria Pearson Capt NJ

CLUP,
George: b 1758 d 6-3-1836 m Tanneke Spyker Pvt PA

CLUTCH,
John: b 5-3-1758 d 5-6-1849 m (1)Rebecca Hughes (2)Mrs Hannah Sinclair Pvt NJ ★

CLUTE,
Bartholomew: b 1-6-1765 d 9-16-1841 m Margretye Peck Pvt NY
Daniel Toll: b 11-29-1754 d 7-25-1815 m Annetie Bancker Pvt NY
Gerardus: bpt 10-19-1735 d 12-12-1803 m Sarah Visscher Capt NY
Isaac: b 1750 d 6-27-1833 m Helen Barheydt Pvt NY W★
Jacob: bpt 6-28-1729(?) d 1790-96 m (Maayke) Mordicai Lansing Pvt CS NY
Jacob P.: bpt 3-14-1759 d 1-16-1848 m (1)Maria Houck (2)Maria Van Schoonhoven Pvt NY ★
John: b 6-12-1739 d 4-20-1817 m Gizzenah Vrooman Capt NY
John B.: b 5-24-1762 d 1814 m (1)Catlyntje Van Vorst (2)Elizaveth Skiff Pvt NY
Nicholas: b 5-30-1725 d 11-30-1812 m Claartje Heemstraat Cpl NY
Peter: b 10-31-1731 d 1785 m Catharine Marselis Pvt PS NY

CLUTTER,
John: b c. 1747 d 1828 m Lucy — Pvt NJ

CLYDE,
Joseph: b 1722 d 6-7-1805 m Margaret Moffett Capt NH
Samuel: b 3-20-1732 d 10-10-1790 m Catharine Wasson PS CS LCol NY

CLYMER, (includes CLEMMER)
Daniel Cunyngham: b 4-6-1748 d 1-25-1810 m Mary Weidner LCol CS PA
George: b 6-1-1739 d 1-24-1813 m Elizabeth Meredith SDI PA
Henry: b c. 1753 d 1802 m Mary Hendricks Pvt PA
Henry: b 6-15-1734 d 6-8-1800 m Jane Lüeder Slr PA

COAKLEY,
Benjamin: b 10-13-1750 d 7-6-1815 m Sarah Dale Lt VA

COAPMAN,
Abraham: b c. 1748 d p. 2-12-1829 m Adelia Roesner Maj NY

COAS,
Wm., Sr.: b 1703 d 1781 m Mary Gardner Pvt MA
Wm., Jr.: b 9-20-1725 d p. 1780 m Susanna Parsons Capt Pvtr MA

COATS, (includes COATE, COATES)
Benjamin: b 1-17-1744 d p. 1783 m Esther Mash Pvt CT
Edward: b 1-15-1753 d 1840 m Eunice Brown Sgt CT
Elizabeth (Avery)(Evans): b 1724 d 1790 m Moses Coates PS PA
John: b 1748 d 1-19-1824 m Mehitable Way Pvt MA
John: b — d 7- -1777 m Sarah Smith PS CS PA
John: b 7-11-1751 d 11-30-1810 m Sarah Murray Capt PA
John: b c. 1740 d 5- -1803 m Mary — PS SC
John: b 11-24-1762 d p. 1835 m Sallie Ann Thompson Pvt VA ★
Joseph: b 11-12-1760 d 3-31-1828 m Sarah — Pvt NY
Marmaduke: b 6-13-1738 d 9-25-1822 m Mary (Jane) Coppock PS SC
Moses: b 11-25-1719 d 1785 m (1)Priscilla Hutchinson (2)Elizabeth (Avery) Evans PS Pvt PA
Moses: b 11-4-1746 d 8-4-1816 m (1)Hannah Musgrave (2)Mary Knight Vickers Pvt PA
Robert: b 4-14-1757 d p. 8- -1832 m Miriam Blodgett Pvt CT
Timothy: b c. 1750 d p. 1804 m Content Stuart Pvt CT
Warwick: b a. 1717 d 2-15-1782 m Rebecca — Capt PA

COBB, (includes COBBS)
Andrew, Sr.: b 3-27-1734 d 7-22-1822 m (1)Hannah Green (2)Hannah (Whitney) Fowler Pvt MA
Asa: b 1750 d 3-24-1828 m Sarah Stephens Pvt NY
Benjamin: b 1-9-1742 d 3- -1817 m Mary Tobie Pvt MA
Binney: b 1737 d 6-28-1817 m Azubah Shaw Cpl MA
Charles: b 1735 d p. 3-3-1798 m Anne Walton Capt VA
Daniel: b 1749 d 7-12-1827 m Hannah Hodges PS NH
David: b 9-14-1748 d 4-17-1830 m Eleanor Bradish Dr LCol MA
David: b 8-2-1735 d 1-26-1821 m (1)Huldah Ford (2)Hannah Orcutt (3)Mrs Hannah Reed Lt MA
Ebenezer: b 1724 d 11-10-1782 m (1)Jerusha Cushman (2)Martha (Harlow) Cole Sgt MA
Ebenezer, Sr.: b 8-24-1731 d 8-22-1811 m Lydia Churchill Cpl MA
Ebenezer, Jr.: b 3-17-1759 d 5-9-1826 m Elizabeth Cobb Pvt MA ★
Ebenezer: b 3-15-1752 d — m Elizabeth Lathrop Pvt NY
Edward: b 8-2-1732 d 8-9-1797 m Abigail Shaw Capt MA
Edward: b 11-6-1752 d 10-27-1819 m Hannah Hallett Pvt MA W★
Eleazer: b 1-5-1734 d 8-23-1813 m Keziah Crosby Pvt MA
Elisha: b 10-29-1730 d 1-29-1802 m (1)Dorcas Doane (2)Mehitable (Walker) Drane Col MA
Elisha: b 6-6-1736 d 6-11-1794 m Elizabeth Murch Pvt MA
Elisha: b 3-20-1757 d 11-6-1804 m (1)Sarah Braman (2)Lynda Fish Pvt MA
Elkanah: b 10-10-1757 d 9-23-1837 m Jerusha Foster Pvt MA
Farrar: b 9-14-1752 d 2-22-1841 m Barsheba Whitehead Sgt NC ★
Francis: b 11-2-1753 d 2-5-1845 m Phebe Hobbs Pvt MA ★
George: b 1756 d — m Tamour Burt Pvt MA CL
Isaac: bpt 4-1-1753 d 2-1-1823 m Deborah Lovett Seacap MA
James: b c. 1735 d p. 1798 m Barbara Bibb Capt VA
Jedediah: b 5-4-1752 d 6-16-1816 m Abigail Jordan Pvt CS MA
Jedediah: b 8-8-1742 d 8-21-1833 m (1)Reliance Paine (2)Mrs Sarah (Purington) Ross Sgt MA
Jeremiah: b 5-30-1742 d 12-19-1802 m Sarah Smith Pvt MA
Jesse: b 1742 d 9-3-1807 m Elizabeth Heritage Capt NC
John: b 11-25-1743 d 12-16-1815 m Mary Fuller 1Cpl CT
John: b 7-14-1748 d p. 1791 m Margaret Collins Pvt MA
John: b 1-2-1760 d 11-20-1814 m Anna White Pvt MA
Jonathan: b 1748 d 2-28-1801 m Hannah Beal Pvt MA
Joseph: b 8-22-1726 d 7-21-1807 m Rachael (Treat) Mulford Pvt Gnr MA
Matthias: b 1-6-1760/61 d 7-2-1832 m Elizabeth Brady Pvt NJ ★
Melatiah: b 4-1-1755 d 3-22-1835 m Rebecca Brewster Sgt MA
Nathan, Jr.: b 11-13-1737 d 2-16-1823 m Abigail Shores Sgt MA
Nathan: b 8-13-1763 d 3-24-1845 m Lydia Bliss Pvt MA
Nehemiah: b 2-29-1752 d 1-15-1841 m Mehitable Rickard Lt MA ★
Nicholas: b 4-30-1758 d 1-18-1830 m (1)Abigail Chick (2)Desire Rogers Pvt MA
Peter: b 12-18-1754 d 4- -1827 m Margaret Crandall Cpl MA
Robert: b 3-2-1754 d 8-2-1829 m Ann Gizaage Poindexter Capt VA ★
Roland: b 7-12-1757 d 11-12-1842 m Jerusha Bartlett Pvt MA
Samuel, Sr.: b 3-20-1717 d 4-6-1781 m (1)Mary Hinckley (2)Hannah Bicknell PS Dr CT
Samuel, Jr.: b 8-2-1746 d 3-15-1806 m (1)Esther Grant (2)Ann Steele CS PS CT
Samuel: b 9-3-1753 d 12-19-1839 m Silence Barney PS NH ★
Samuel: b — d 8- -1800 m (2)— Peak Pvt SC
Samuel: b 1745 d 1784/85 m Elizabeth Mumford Lt VA
Seth: b 3-6-1743 d 1-8-1799 m (1)Katherine — (2)Huldah Bond Pvt PS NH

Silas: b 9-4-1743 d 1833 m Deliverance Hodges 2Maj MA ★
Sylvanne: b 6-15-1741 d 6-9-1834 m Molly Ellis 2Lt MA
Sylvanus: b 10-3-1747 d 1831 m (2)Mary Oakes Pvt MA
Sylvanus: b 8-13-1747 d 2-23-1813 m Elizabeth Warren Pvt MA
Sylvester: bpt 7-28-1762 d 7-28-1840 m Mercy Hodges SgtMaj MA VT ★
Thomas: b 1762 d 1841 m Lucy Smith Pvt MA
Thomas: b 1-16-1760 d 1-19-1845 m (1)Hannah Price (2)Clara Rosina de Taberai Capt NJ
Thomas: b 1744 d 1780 m Judith — Sgt SC
Thomas: b 1722 d 1832 m Sarah — Capt VA
Wm.: b 9-11-1751 d 11-7-1802 m (2)Elizabeth Ripley BGen MA
Wm.: b 1710 d 3-1-1802 m Anna Williams PS MA
Wm.: b 1730 d 1797 m Sarah Stansall Lt NC
Wm., Sr.: b 1723 d 1803 m Bathsheba Whitehead CS NC
Wm., Jr.: b 1746 d 1796 m Martha Boone Pvt VA

COBEAN,
Samuel: b c. 1740-45 d a. 12-22-1808 m X Capt PA

COBIA,
Francis: b 6-11-1757 d 8-29-1792 m Christina Elizabeth — Cpl SC

COBLE, (includes KOBBLE)
David: b 12-3-1758 d 5-25-1841 m Barbara Witmer Pvt PA
Frederick: b — d 5- -1837 m Sophia Daniel Pvt PA
George: b 5-10-1733 d 6-21-1816 m Barbara Glass Sol NC

COBLEIGH,
Eleazer: b 1753/54 d 6-15-1847 m Tabatha Farr Pvt NH ★
John: b 1753 d 6-8-1825 m Deborah Harris PS NH
Jonathan: b 9-21-1748 d p. 1791 m Esther — Pvt NH
Oliver: b 1732 d 1807 m Margaret Peacock Capt NH

COBLER,
Frederick: b 8-14-1758 d 9-21-1840 m (1)Barbara — (2)Anna Threlkeld Pvt NC ★

COCHRAN, (includes COCHRANE, COCHRUN)
Abner: b 6-6-1758 d 12-17-1819 m Elizabeth — Pvt MA W★
Alexander: b 1760 d 1817 m Hannah — Pvt PA
Andrew: b c. 1749-54 d 1814 m Sarah Baird Btm NY
Charles: b 1755 d 1-8-1829 m Mary Murray Cpl PA
Isaac: b 4-23-1742 d 8-21-1825 m Ruth Hopkins Lt NH
James: b 1763 d 6-2-1835 m Mary — Sol GA
James: b 1743 d 1-23-1815 m Mary McDaniell Capt NH
James: b 2-14-1748 d 5-11-1837 m (2)Elizabeth Stone Sgt NH ★
James: b 10-6-1752 d 4-1-1837 m Salone Knowlton Cpl NH ★
James: b 3-28-1748 d 9-20-1822 m Elizabeth Nesmith PS NH
James: b c. 1740 d 1817 m Mrs Annis Lea McNeill Pvt NC
James: b 7-8-1732 d 12-8-1810 m Jane — Pvt PA
James: b 1751 d 11-13-1830 m Temperance Morgan Ens VA ★
James: b 2-15-1756 d c. 1820 m Magdalen Moffett Ens VA
James Henry: b 7-4-1763 d 7-12-1840 m Anna Mary Ahalt Pvt MD ★
John: b 1741 d 3-25-1784 m Sarah Miller Pvt MD
John: b 6-24-1749 d 10- -1839 m Mary Adams Pvt MA
John: b 1759 d 6-13-1823 m Elizabeth Greenslit Smn NY ★
John: b 1704 d 2-26-1788 m Jennie McKean PS NH
John, Sr.: b 1711 d 7-22-1799 m (1)Mary McHard (2)Margaret Owens PS NH
John, Jr: b 1739 d 11-22-1822 m (1)Margaret McDaniel (2)Mrs Elizabeth (Gorden) Burnham Pvt PS NH
John: b 1751 d 1804 m Sarah — Sgt PA
John: b 9-1-1730 d 4-6-1807 m Gertrude Schuyler SurGen NY
John: b 1762 d 7-23-1828 m Margaret McClanahan Cpl SC
John, Sr.: b c. 1727 d p. 1787 m X Pvt SC
Joseph: b 1740 d 3-20-1816 m Margaret Murray Sol PS NH
Nathaniel: b 2-29-1757 d 4-19-1808 m Elizabeth Ford PS VA
Phoebe Gray: b c. 1754 d 1807 m (1)Daniel Cochran (2)Maj. John Hearst PS SC
Robert: b c. 1740 d 7-3-1812 m Mary Miller LCol NY
Robert: b 9-18-1749 d 8-1-1835 m Susanna Elton Pvt PA
Robert: b 1735 d 1-22-1824 m Mary Elliott Seacap SC
Robert: b 7-24-1730 d 9-20-1807 m (1)Mary — (2)Thankful Rice Lt VT W★
Samuel: b 1731 d 1-24-1802 m Sarah Duncan Capt NH
Samuel: b 8-24-1750 d 7-2-1837 m (1)Esther John (2)Mrs Agnes McWhirter Robinson Sgt PA
Samuel: b 1763 d 5-3-1829 m (1)Rebecca — (2)Hannah Slaymaker Drm PA
Samuel: b 4-24-1760 d 1-7-1842 m Sarah Norcutt 2Sgt VA★
Samuel: b — d p. 10-27-1791 m Marah — PS VA
Simon: b 7- -1755 d 6-9-1845 m (2)Margaret — (3)Sarah Clark Pvt VA
Stephen: b 11-17-1732 d 11-1-1790 m Jane Young Pvt PA
Thomas: b 7-2-1746 d 4-15-1818 m (1)Lucretia Council (2)Louise Griffin (3)Mrs Elizabeth Hunter Lt SC
Wm.: b 1737 d 1778 m Experience Weeks Lt Pilot MA
Wm.: b 1722 d 3- -1814 m Elizabeth Booth Pvt PA
Wm. Sr.: b 5-15-1753 d 4-21-1821 m Margaret Gamble Pvt SC
Wm.: b 1740 d 10-10-1826 m (1)Mary Logan (2)Elizabeth Fulton Pvt VA
Wm.: b c. 1735 d 9-11-1782 m Jane — PS VA

COCKER,
Wm.: b 6- -1747 d 3-14-1787 m Dorothy Green Pvt NJ

COCKERHAM,
Wm. Winn: b *c.* 1743 d *a.* 1811 m (1)Edith Levina Stone (2)Nancy Estes PS VA

COCKEY,
Edward: b 12-20-1731 d 2-1-1795 m Eleanor Pindell Col MD
John: b 6-24-1743 d 2-8-1808 m Chloe Cromwell Capt PS MD
Thomas: b 4-15-1754 d 11-10-1813 m Ruth Brown 2Lt PS MD

COCKLEY,
John: b 2-14-1756 d 3-21-1847 m Dorcas — Pvt NY ★
John: b 7-30-1741 d 4-23-1823 m Elizabeth Whitman Sol PA
John: b 2-11-1742 d 7-5-1801 m Frances Bricker Pvt PA

COCKRILL, (includes COCKRELL, COCKERILL)
Ann Robertson Johnson: b 2-10-1757 d 10-13-1821 m John Cockrill PS NC
Jeremiah: b *c.* 1761 d 6-20-1815 m Jemimah Elizabeth Rhoden Pvt SC
Jeremiah: b 1733 d *p.* 10-6-1807 m (2)Katey—PS VA
John, Jr.: b 12-19-1757 d 4-11-1837 m Ann (Robertson) Johnson Noncom NC
Joshua Nelms: b *c.* 1760 d 3-3-1812 m (1)Mrs Sally Harcum Gill (2)Mrs Milly Kent (3)Sally Sebree Pvt VA
Littleton: b *c.* 1745-50 d 1813 m (2)Mary Tracey Pvt VA
Moses: b *c.* 1725 d 1798 m Jane — PS SC
Peter: b 1758 d 1834 m Sarah Smithers Pvt VA★
Thomas: b 1760 d 7-9-1842 m Amelia Lucas Pvt VA
Wm.: b 12-13-1756 d *p.* 1820 m Rebecca Brown Pvt SC★

CODDING,
Abijah: b 9-30-1757 d 2-14-1839 m Sarah Peirce Pvt MA
Elisha: b *c.* 1742 d 9-23-1784 m Anna Williams Pvt MA
George, Sr.: b 1709 d 4-20-1794 m Elizabeth Luscomb PS MA
George, Jr.: b 1734 d 3-28-1816 m Sarah Thayer Pvt NY
James: b 9-29-1755 d 10-2-1836 m Joanna Eddy Cpl MA
John: b 1763 d 1-21-1813 m Nancy Trafton MM RI
Samuel: b 4-3-1758 d 11-29-1821 m Sarah Hill Sgt MA
Samuel, 2nd: b 4-17-1742 d 12-7-1812 m Mercy Cobb Pvt MA

CODDINGTON, (includes CORRINGTON)
Archibald: b 1756 d 4-19-1822 m Mary Coon Pvt NY
Benjamin: b 1756 d 8-28-1836 m Hannah Coon Pvt NJ
Benjamin: b 11-10-1759 d *p.* 12-22-1838 m Anna Crane Pvt Slr NJ ★
Benjamin:b 10-8-1761 d 1848 m Mary Denton Pvt NY
David: b 1730 d 1787 m Ann Stone Pvt NJ
James: b 1754 d 3-21-1816 m Experience Inslee Randolph Pvt NJ
John: b 6-17-1761 d 8-20-1844 m Mary Coon Pvt NJ★
Joseph: b 1754 d *p.* 2-10-1806 m Elizabeth Inslee Pvt NJ
Robert: b 10-6-1760 d 8-15-1833 m Margaret Inslee Pvt NJ W ★
Wm.: b 7-11-1754 d 1839 m Mary Vincent Pvt NY

CODILL, (includes CAUDILL)
James: b 1753 d 5-30-1840 m X Pvt NC ★
Stephen: b 1763 d 7-26-1839 m Sarah Adams Pvt NC

CODMAN,
Henry: b 1743 d 3- -1812 m Agnes — Dr NH
Richard: b 6-23-1730 d 9-12-1793 m (1)Ann Jones (2)Sarah Smith Pvt MA
Wm.: b 5-13-1750 d 11-9-1813 m (1)Sarah Maria Abbot (2)Phillis — PS NH

CODWISE,
George: b 1732 d 10-10-1814 m Mary Van Raust Sol NY

CODY, (includes COADY)
Isaac: b 5-10-1793 d 4-30-1827 m Martha Caryl Pvt MA
James: b *c.* 1718 d 1795 m Sarah Womack Sol NC
John: b 8-17-1755 d 8-15-1828 m Mary Chamberlain Sgt MA W★
Joseph: b 5-2-1736 d 2-10-1787 m Mary Parmenter 1Lt CS MA
Nahum: b 7-14-1721 d 11-24-1815 m Mary Tucker Pvt CT
Samuel: b 5-13-1760 d 5-7-1854 m Susanna Armstrong Cpl MA★

COE,
Aaron: b 2-16-1731 d 10-20-1794 m (1)Phoebe Parsons (2)Mary Seward Capt MA
Abel: bpt 7-30-1727 d 1-10-1798 m Prudence Rossiter PS CT
Abner: b 4-12-1763 d 8-15-1846 m (1)Mary Ledyard Pvt CT
Benjamin: b 12-28-1738 d 10-14-1818 m Bethia Grummon MM NJ
Benjamin: b 6-11-1741 d 3-9-1821 m Phebe Horton Capt NY
Benjamin: b 11-13-1746 d 5-14-1831 m Sarah Johnson Capt NY
Benjamin, Sr.: b 1790 m Rachel Prudden Pvt PA
Benjamin, Jr.: b 11-6-1748 d 3-15-1833 m Margaret Biegle Lt PA
Benjamin: b 5-3-1753 d 1-21-1818 m Sarah Simmons Capt RI
Charles: b 7-12-1760 d *p.* 1817 m Hannah Bates Sol CT
Daniel: b 11-25-1759 d 2-6-1823 m Sarah Halstead Ens NY
Daniel: b 2-19-1731 d 1782 m Sarah Palmer Pvt NY
Daniel S.: b 2-4-1753 d— m Abigail Sniffen Pvt NY

David, Sr.: b 2-18-1716 d 1-14-1807 m Hannah Camp PS CT
David, Jr.: b 7-21-1747 d 4-15-1816 m Jerusha Miller Pvt CT
David Lyman: b 3-3-1761 d 7-24-1824 m Sarah Pratt Pvt MA
Denman: b 5-26-1759 d *p.* 1807 m Mary Northup Pvt CT
Ebenezer: b 7-4-1835 d 8-1-1820 m Sarah (Benjamin) Backus Capt CT
Ebenezer: b 7-19-1755 d 1-28-1839 m Cleopatra Conklin Sgt CT★
Ebenezer: b 1736 d 7-25-1827 m Eunice Jagger Lt PA★
Elijah: b *c.* 1751 d *p.* 12-1-1809 m Ann Smallwood PS Pvt MD
Elijah: b 1743 d 1827 m Margaret Hutchins Pvt CT ★
Halsted: b 3-20-1759 d 8-19-1832 m (2)Abby Ward Pvt NY
Isaac, S.: b 1-3-1746 d *p.* 1790 m Rachel Archer Pvt PS NY
Israel: b 7-22-1756 d 9-21-1821 m (1)Artemisia Wright (2)Asenath Fowler Sgt MA
Ithamar: b 9-10-1755 d 8-26-1826 m Sarah Ball Pvt MA
James: b 2-3-1741 d 7-31-1790 m Huldah Wilcoxson Pvt CT
James: b 11-19-1740 d 10-3-1794 m Rachel Benton Cpl MA
Jedediah: b 9-3-1761 d 12-19-1847 m Anna Pvt CT★
Joel: b 5-17-1758 d 9-23-1846 m Huldah Horton Pvt CT
John: b 9-20-1757 d 2-19-1846 m Lois Johnson Pvt Tms CT★
John: b 9-18-1729 d 12-10-1783 m Hannah Chatfield PS CT
John, Sr.: b 12-7-1719 d 5-11-1782 m Hannah Halstead PS NY
John, Jr.: b 8-28-1749 d 5-2-1839 m Mary Halstead Pvt NY ★
John Daniel: b 5-26-1755 d 5-3-1824 m Sarah (Coe) Pvt NY
Jonathan, Sr.: b 2- -1710/11 d 4-23-1795 m Elizabeth Elmer CS PS CT
Jonathan, Jr.: b 8-20-1742 d 8-1-1824 m (1)Eunice Cook (2)Mrs Sarah (Cook) Hurlbut Sgt CT
Joseph: b 3-18-1748/49 d 12-22-1824 m (1)Sarah Bell (2)Sarah Spellman (3)Ludia Ackley Bruce Pvt MA
Levi: b 7-3-1760 d 2-28-1832 m (1)Deborah McCall (2)Olive Marsh Pvt CT
Matthew D.: b 10-15-1757 d 12-12-1838 m Martha Gurnee Sol NY
Moses: b 8-18-1750 d 3-28-1813 m Sarah Howell Ens PA
Oliver: b 9-3-1738 d 12-31-1775 m Mary Agard Pvt CT
Peter: bpt 1-21-1753 d 10- -1836 m Mary (Shearer) Allen Sgt PA ★
Philip: b 1740 d 5-8-1818 m (1)Barbara Neston (2)Abigail Connor Pvt NY
Phineas: b 1753 d 9-30-1832 m Rhoda Banning Pvt QM CT
Robert: b 3-28-1740 d 1830 m Chloe Thrall Pvt CT
Robert Ebenezer: b 1755 d 1838 m Cleopatra Conklin Sol NJ
Samuel: b 8-5-1726 d 7-27-1790 m (1)Dorcas Allen (2)Hope Hubbard CS MA
Samuel: b 3-20-1746 d 8-16-1831 m Deborah Church Lt RI
Samuel: b 4-2-1760 d 1-20-1822 m Elizabeth Dusinberre OrdSgt NY
Seth: b 12-21-1757 d 11-15-1839 m (1)Lucina Hopkins (2)Sarah Elmer (3)Dorcas Kies Pvt CT★
Simeon, Sr.: b 3-22-1720/21 d 9-23-1782 m Anna Morris PS CT
Simeon, Jr.: b 2-12-1755 d 10-25-1838 m (1)Eunice Strong (2)Sarah Coe PS CT
Thomas: b 1759 d 7-7-1827 m Submit Griswold Pvt CT
Timothy: b 9-16-1760 d 2-26-1841 m (1)Mary Hall (2)Abigail Bates Pvt CT★
Wm.: b 11-19-1757 d 1834 m Mary Sears Cpl MD★
Wm.: b 2-17-1748 d 7-18-1814 m Sarah Ellis Ens RI
Wm. S.: b 1-25-1748 d 1828 m Martha Connelly Pvt NY
Zachariah: b 9-29-1732 d 8-8-1805 m Lavina Nichols Capt CT

COFER, (includes COPHER)
George: b 9-1-1757 d *p.* 11-25-1830 m (1)Francis Dawson (2)Mrs Mary A. Cobbs Cpl VA
Jesse: b 1760 d 1822 m Elizabeth Boone Sol KY
Wm.: b 1750 d 1819 m Mary Elizabeth — Pvt VA

COFFEEN, (includes COFFREN)
Henry: b 4-6-1738 d 1785 m (1)Lucy Hale (2)Mehitable Smith Capt PS NH
John: b 7-28-1727 d 11-29-1802 m Susannah Goldsmith Capt PS VT
Lake: b *c.* 1758 d 8-5-1818 m Zilpah Baldwin Sgt MA
Michael: b 3-2-1753 d 1814 m Sarah Preston Pvt MA
Robert: b 11-1-1764 d 1-1-1844 m (1)Elizabeth Merrill (2)Sarah Gower Pvt NH

COFFEY, (includes COFFEE)
James: b 1728 d *p.* 9- -1786 m Elizabeth Cleveland PS NC
James: b 8-17-1759 d 12-20-1836 m Mary Leeper Pvt PA
Joel: b 1730 d 1789 m Martha Sealey PS NC
Joshua: b 1745 d 9-8-1797 m Elizabeth Graves Capt NC
Nathan: b 1760 d 1823 m Mary Saunders Pvt NC
Osborn: b 7-29-1759 d 3-31-1840 m Mary Nightingale Sgt VA ★
Peter: b *c.* 1750 d *p.* 10-18-1803 m Sarah Smith Pvt VA
Reuben: b 9-16-1759 d *p.* 3-24-1842 m Sally Scott Pvt NC★

COFFIELD,
John: b 5- -1751 d 3- -1818 m Sarah Robison Pvt NC
John: b *c.* 1736 d 2- -1816 d 11-25-1787 m Elizabeth Hoskins PS NC

COFFIN,
Abner: b 4-15-1737 d — m Keziah Cromwell Pvt NH
Alexander: b 9-21-1740 d 2-11-1839 m Eunice Bunker Mstr PS MA
Amos: b 6-22-1723 d 5-18-1811 m Sarah Hook PS NH

COFFIN, contd.

Benjamin: b 9-6-1735/36 d 11-1-1818 m (1)Mary — (2)Anna Kincaid Pvt MA
Benjamin: b 4-3-1705 d 11-3-1780 m (1)Jedidiah Hussey (2)Deborah Macy PS MA
Daniel: b 1-23-1720/21 d 7-23-1789 m (1)Mary Harlock (2)Sarah Ripley Pvt MA
David: b 1718 d 6-7-1804 m Ruth Coleman CS MA
Edmund: b 3-19-1708 d 1-29-1789 m Shuah Barlett PS MA
Elias, Jr.: b 8-3-1741 d 1780 m Abigail CS MA
Eliphalet: b 9-8-1738 d 4-9-1812 m Lydia Emery CS MA
Eliphalet: b 9-11-1742 d 8-4-1808 m Patience Evans Pvt NH
Enoch: b 3-1-1712 d 3-23-1802 m Jane (Claghorn) Whellen PS MA
George: b 2-13-1761 d 9-14-1852 m Abigail Raymond Pvt MA
Isaac: b 1756 d *p.* 1840 m X Pvt NH ★
Isaac: b 1745 d 9-8-1778 m Sarah Nichols Cmsry NY
James: b 7-11-1745 d 11-26-1830 m Martha McLellan PS MA
James: b 3-20-1744 d 5-2-1820 m Jeannette Coffin Smn MA
John: b 8-12-1757 d *p.* 1787 m Mary Palmer PS MA
Josiah: b 1750 d 3- -1778 m Eunice Gardner Sol MA
Matthew: b 6-17-1756 d 1-17-1830 m Jane Wass Pvt MA
Micajah: b 8-12-1734 d 5-17-1827 m Abigail Coleman PS MA
Moses: b 6-2-1711 d 2-22-1793 m Anna Dole PS NH
Nathan: b 8-28-1749 d *p.* 1782 m (1)Martha Bowen (2)Dorcas Bartlett Sgt MA
Nathaniel: b 8-25-1738 d 7-23-1823 m Mary Norton Lt MA★
Nathaniel: b 7-19-1711 d 6-10-1800 m Mary Sheffield PS CS MA
Peter: b 8-10-1723 d 4-14-1796 m Mary Currier PS CS MA
Peter: b 5-21-1722 d 12-15-1789 m Rebecca Hazeltine Capt PS NH
Ruth: b *c.* 1700 d 1-14-1779 m Richard Coffin PS MA
Shubael: b 2-13-1754 d 11-7-1821 m (1)Margaret Pinkham (2)Priscilla Bunker PS MA
Thomas: b 1754 d 1796 m Sally— Pvt GA
Tristram: b 9-5-1733 d 9-30-1806 m Anne Davis Pvt MA
Uriah: b 8-3-1751 d 2-14-1830 m Mary — Pvt NY
Wm.: b 6-30-1756 d 6-20-1826 m Mary Langdon Dr MA
Wm.: b 11-4-1720 d 11-10-1803 m Priscilla Paddock PS NC
Wm.: b *c.* 1750 d *p.* 1779 m —Potts Clerk PA

COFFINBERRY,

George Lewis: b 2-10-1760 d 8-13-1851 m Elizabeth Little (Klein) Pvt VA W★

COFFROTH,

Conrad: b 8-19-1762 d 2-26-1831 m Mary Magdalene Snoterly Fif PA

COGBILL,

Charles: b *c.* 1750 d *p.* 1783 m Lucy Christian PS VA
George: b *c.* 1750 d *p.* 2-3-1803 m X PS VA
Wm.: b *c.* 1740 d 1805 m Tabitha Bass PS VA

COGBURN, (includes COCKBURN)

George: b 1746 d 1834 m Elizabeth — Sol GA
John: b 1745 d 1810 m Hannah — Sol PS SC

COGDELL,

George: b 1736 d 3-15-1792 m (1)Hannah (White) Scriven (2)Mary Elizabeth Stevens Capt SC
Richard: b 7-8-1724 d 5-10-1787 m Lydia Duncan Col CS NC

COGGESHALL,

Benjamin: b 9-6-1734 d 10- -1791 m Sarah Gould Pvt RI
George: b 2-8-1752 d 7-18-1812 m (1)Sarah Throop (2)Lucy Bowen NS Pvt RI
Gideon: b 8-25-1766 d 4-20-1821 m Mary East Pvt RI W★
John: b 10-5-1757 d 7-19-1830 m Abigail Hayden Sgt MA
Jonathan: b 12-4-1748 d 7-26-1796 m Sarah Wilcox Pvt Matr RI
Joseph: b 8-16-1754 d 10-7-1830 m Elizabeth Horswell Pvt RI
Joseph: b — 13-1734 d *p.* 1804 m Elizabeth Phillips PS RI
Newby: b 8-17-1726 d 8- -1814 m — Pvt RI
Peleg: b 9-29-1734 d 3-4-1813 m (1)Anna Folger (2)Sarah Fish CS RI
Thomas: b 8-26-1728 d 1-7-1803 m Hannah Corvell Ens RI
Wm.: b 1-28-1754 d 5-10-1823 m (1)Mary Finney (2)Hannah Fales OrdlSgt RI
Wm.: b 6-3-1758 d 10-29-1800 m Mehetable Smith Sol Slr NY CT

COGGIN,

Joseph: b 3-26-1740 d *p.* 1793 m Ruth Hopkins PS NH

COGHILL,

James: b 1758 d 1-11-1841 m Elizabeth Long Sol VA★
Thomas: b 5-9-1763 d *p.* 1850 m Sarah Atwell Pvt VA★
Wm.: b 1754 d 1826 m (1)Barbara Goodwin (2)Miss Coleman PS VA

COGLEY,

John: b 1754 d 1786 m Jane Price Pvt PS PA

COGSWELL, (includes COGSSWELL)

Amos: b 2-19-1754 d 1-4-1845 m Rebecca Chamberlain Pvt CT
Amos: b 10-2-1752 d 1-28-1826 m Lydia(Baker)Wallingford Maj MA
Emerson: b 2- -1743 d 5-13-1808 m (1)Eunice Robinson (2)Anna Learned (3)Elizabeth Batemen 1Lt MA

Ferris: b 5-3-1767 d 1836 m Phebe (Hawley) Bristol Pvt VT
Isaac: bpt 6-30-1745 d *p.* 1785 m Molly Loomis Pvt MA
James: bpt 1755 d 8-19-1837 m (1)Mrs Rebecca (Cotton) Baldwin (2)Lucy Hardy Cpl MA
James: b 7-31-1746 d 11-20-1792 m (1)Elizabeth Davenport (2)Abigail Lloyd Dr CL
Jeremiah: b 7-12-1743 d 4-20-1802 m Mehitable Clement PS CS NH
John: b 6-17-1738 d 1832 m X Sgt CT
John: b 12-28-1747 d 7-21-1829 m (1)Hannah Gallup (2)Elizabeth Brown Cpl CT
John: b 9-1-1759 d 6-18-1837 m Hanah Roys Pvt CT ★
John, Jr.: b 2-17-1728 d 3-31-1818 m (1)Abigail White (2)Sarah Bartlett PS MA
Jonathan: b 4-'-1736 d 3-20-1782 m Ruth Wyer Dr MA
Moses: b 9-22-1757 d 9-16-1811 m Hannah Foster NLt NH
Nathaniel: b 2-13-1716 d 11-4-1810 m (1)Huldah Kinney (2)Bridget (Cleveland) Wedge (3)Mrs Eunice Williams Sol CT
Nathaniel: b 5-9-1739 d 5-25-1822 m — Sol MA
Nathaniel: b 1-19-1707 d 3-23-1783 m Judith Badger PS NH
Nathaniel Peaslee: b 7-10-1755 d 1-10-1798 m Susanna Lakeman Cpl MA
Nehemiah: b 1749 d 11-5-1840 m Rachel Choate MM MA
Reuben: b 3-20-1756 d 6-12-1837 m Sarah Olmsted Pvt MA ★
Samuel: b 5-23-1754 d 8-29-1790 m Mary Backus Brevet Capt CL
Samuel: b 3-14-1742 d 12-8-1834 m Elizabeth Perkins Pvt MA
Samuel: b 5-23-1713 d 1790 m Mary Langdon Pvt MA
Solomon: b 3-26-1743 d 5-26-1806 m Sarah Cowles Pvt MA
Thomas: b 8-4-1746 d 9-3-1810 m Ruth Badger LCol MA
Wm.: b 12-22-1734 d 2-19-1786 m Anna Whittlesey Maj CT
Wm.: b 7-11-1760 d 1-1-1831 m Judith Badger SrgnMte NH W★

COHEN,

Jacob: b *c.* 1750 d 1798 m Margaret — Capt VA
Moses: b 1754 d 6-30-1789 m Judith deLion Sol SC VA

COIT,

Benjamin, Sr.: b 3-28-1731 d 4-21-1812 m Abigail Billings CS CT
Benjamin, Jr.: b 12-21-1759 d 12-8-1841 m Sarah — NCapt CT
Daniel: b 1-28-1757 d 10-1790 m (2)Mercy Brewster Cpl CT
Daniel: b 6-4-1760 d 7-4-1832 m Ruth Eastman MM Dr MA
Isaac: b 10-25-1743 d 2-28-1842 m Ruhamah Hall SGT CT ★
John: b 6-4-1741 d 3-3-1808 m Mehitable Tyler Pvt MA
Joshua: b 10-7-1758 d 9-5-1798 m Ann Boradil Hallam Sol CT
Samuel, Sr.: b 1708 d 10-4-1792 m (1)Sarah Spaulding (2)Mrs Jemima Hall CS Col CT
Samuel, Sr.: b 10-14-1726 d 12-3-1792 m Elizabeth Ely Pvt CT
Wm.: b 2-13-1735 d 11-16-1821 m Sarah Lathrop Capt CT
Wm.: b 11-26-1724 d 9-15-1802 m Sarah Prentiss Capt CT

COKER,

Thomas: b —d *p.* 1804 m X PS Lt SC
Thomas: b *c.* 1755 d 1818 m Sarah — PS SC
Wm.: b *c.* 1720 d *p.* 9-4-1816 m X Pvt SC
Wm.: b 1750 d 1823 m Mary Sweet Cpl NH

COLBREATH, (includes COLBATH)

Dependence: b 1761 d 7-26-1840 m Rachel — Cpl NH ★
Thomas: b — d 5-20-1798 m Susannah Finch Sol NY W ★

COLBURN, (includes COLBUN, COBURN, COUBURN)

Abraham: b 6-17-1729 m (1)Mercy Richardson (2)Mrs Mary Massey Coburn 2Lt MA
Alpheus: b 12-16-1759 d 2-17-1813 m Joanna Edwards Cpl MA
Amos: b 9-17-1744 d 1795 m Sarah Dodge 2Lt NH
Asa: b 10-20-1750 d 5-11-1834 m Jane Wood Pvt NH
Asa: b 9-14-1741 d 1789 m Mary McClure Capt MA
Asa: b 10-20-1755 d 12-2-1841 m Lettice Neven Sgt NH ★
Benjamin: b 5-31-1747 d 4-18-1814 m Joanna Tibbetts Lt MA
Benjamin: b 10-31-1747 d — m Allice Hardy Sol MA
Benjamin: b 5-5-1755 d 1-21-1847 m Esther Wheeler MM NH
Clement: b 9-19-1749 d 10-17-1814 m Dorothy Edwards Pvt MA
Daniel: b 1758 d 3-1-1830 m Elizabeth Moulton Pvt CT
Daniel: b 5-19-1759 d 12-12-1836 m Foxelena Phelps Pvt CT ★
Daniel: b 9-22-1759 d 5-20-1809 m Sarah Johnson Pvt MA W ★
Daniel: b 3-18-1722 d 7-9-1802 m Lydia — Maj NH
David: b 3-26-1747 d *p.* 1790 m Rebecca Richards Cpl MA
David: b 1729 d *p.* 7- -1776 m Abigail Green PS NH
Ebenezer: b 9-17-1731 d 10-3-1792 m (1)Prudence Carter (2)Mrs Dorthy Brewer Lt MA
Ebenezer: b 9-18-1747 d 3-2-1814 m Dorcas Shumway 1Lt MA
Edward: b 12-29-1721 d 1-26-1809 m Hannah Butterfield Pvt MA
Eleazer: b 3-4-1734 d 5-7-1810 m Bridget Hildreth Pvt MA
Eliphalet: b 1-2-1758 d *c.* 1818 m Lois Tracy Pvt CT
Ezra: b 4-19-1734 d 3-22-1811 m Phoebe Winn Pvt MA
George: b 9-5-1737 d 1-25-1812 m Mary Adams Cpl NH
Henry: b 1-5-1744 d 5-21-1829 m Sarah Richardson Pvt MA
Hezekiah: b 3-29-1748 d 3-13-1817 m Lydia Parker Pvt MA
Isaac: b 2-26-1725 d 1817 m Mrs Hepzibah Pond Sol PS MA
Jacob: b 2-10-1729 d 2-2-1809 m Lydia Hall Pvt MA
James: b 10-21-1757 d 10-21-1803 m Rebecca Wheeler Pvt MA
James: b — d 1797 m Fannie Wishard Pvt VA
Jeremiah: b 1736 d 1808 m Frances Hodgkins Lt MA
Job: b 9-29-1753 d 9-29-1814 m Hannah Hildreth Pvt MA

John: b c. 1750 d 1798 m Rachel Laws Pvt PS MD
John: b 8-3-1738 d 2-6-1827 m Anna Darby Sgt MA
John: b 1718 d 11-7-1826 m Sarah Dresser Pvt MA
John: b 11-10-1739 d 8-21-1803 m Sarah Richardson Pvt MA
John, Sr.: b 2-9-1746 d 12-20-1827 m (2)Theoda Dunham Sgt NH
John: b 1724 d 1808 m Hannah Monroe PS PA
Jonathan: b 10-24-1735 d 9-25-1808 m Mary Ellis Lt MA
Jonathan: b 7-10-1736 d 9-5-1826 m Sarah Harvey MM Pvt MA
Jonathan: b 1720-25 d p. 1790 m Catherine — PS VA
Joseph: b 7-17-1718 d 3-18-1776 m (1)Dorothy Draper (2)Elizabeth
  Clark Pvt MA
Josiah, Sr.: b 12-6-1765 d a. 3- -1836 m (1)Kezia Hedges (2)Polly
  Whiting (3)Mrs Parthena Rhodes Pvt CT ★
.Lewis: b 1-5-1752 d 6-14-1843 m Mary Onion OrdlSgt MA ★
Lemuel: b 9-12-1758 d 6-3-1839 m Sarah Russ Pvt MA
Merrill: b 5-17-1753 d 11-8-1842 m Abigail Bradford Cpl NH W ★
Moses: b 9-6-1751 d p. 1791 m Mary — Pvt MA
Moses: b 11-24-1759 d 5-4-1848 m Esther Spaulding Pvt MA
Nathan: b 11-18-1744 d 12-1-1835 m Betsey Fuller Cpl MA
Nathan: b 11-6-1752 d 2-17-1831 m Abigail Shattuck Pvt NH
Nathaniel: b 1760 d 4-6-1844 m Ann Coburn Fif PA ★
Oliver: b 1744 d 1-10-1788 m Margaret Capt MA
Peter: b 11-5-1737 d 5-8-1813 m Dolly Varnum Capt MA
Peter, Jr.: b 12-18-1764 d 2-12-1832 m Elizabeth Poor Pvt MA
Reuben: b 8-16-1761 d 5-6-1813 m (1)Rachel Coburn (2)Jane
  Austin Pvt MA
Reuben: b 1740 d 9-16-1818 m Elizabeth Lewis PS MA
Robert: b 1717 d 7-9-1783 m Elizabeth Smith Pvt MM NH
Robert, Jr.: b 4-9-1748 d 3-28-1819 m Dorcas Upton Pvt NH
Robert: b 1-11-1753 d 5-16-1836 m Effie Wortman Pvt NJ ★
Samuel: b c. 1720 d 1776 m — PS KY
Samuel, Sr.: b 3-6-1714 d 10-18-1804 m (1)Mary Fairbanks
  (2)Mercy Dean PS Pvt MA
Samuel, Jr.: b 4-3-1743 d 6-21-1794 m Mehitable Lewis Pvt MA
Saul: b 8-29-1757 d 6-15-1836 m Hannah Jones Pvt MA
Silas: b 11-14-1742 d 5- -1831 m Esther Keyes Pvt MA
Simeon: b 1733 d 1802 m (1)Elizabeth—(2)Abigail Bunnell Pvt CT
Simeon: b 10-29-1755 m Abigail Vose Pvt MA
Sylvanus: b 7-22-1757 d 7-19-1848 m X Pvt CT
Willard: b 10-28-1734 d 6-11-1809 m Mehitable — PS MA
Wm.: b 12-20-1731 d p. 1783 m (1)Mrs Mary (Barron) Fox (2)Hannah
  Jones Pvt MA
Wm., Sr.: b 10-2-1760 d 4-6-1847 m Abigail Whittemore Pvt MA ★

COLBY, (includes COLBEY)
Abraham. b c. 1715 d 1809 m Elizabeth Blaisdell PS NH
Barzillai: b 10-22-1731 d 11-21-1811 m (1)Elizabeth Plummer
  (2)Merriam Worthen Pvt MA
Benjamin, Jr.: b 1751 d p. 1833 m Betsey Foye Sgt ME
Benjamin: b 7-14-1750 d 11-9-1816 m Elizabeth Hunkins PS NH
Chase: b 9-4-1753 d 5-19-1837 m Esther Hardy Pvt MA
Daniel: b 11-23-1752 d 7-23-1851 m Mary Folsom Pvt MA
Daniel: b — d 11-10-1815 m Sarah Trussell Pvt NH W ★
David: b 10-15-1711 d p. 1780 m (1)Elizabeth — (2)Maria
  Emmons PS NH
David, Jr.: b 10-15-1745 d 8- -1821 m (1)Polly Randall (2)Margaret
  Craig PS Pvt NH
Ebenezer, Sr.: b 1-25-1717 d 8-13-1795 m (1)Mary Chase (2)Mrs
  Elizabeth Smith Quinby Capt PS MA
Ebenezer, Jr.: b 10-20-1761 d 6-25-1840 m Anna Hoyt Pvt MA ★
Eliphalet: b 10-28-1728 d 4-8-1812 m Mary Rogers PS NH
Eliphalet, Jr.: b 9-22-1751 d 1824 m Apphia Flanders PS NH
Elliott: b 5-22-1735 d 2-20-1811 m (1)Judith Sargent (2)Hannah
  Smith Pvt NH
Enoch: b 11-27-1756 d 12-8-1833 m Lydia Worthen Pvt NH ★
Ephraim: b 5-6-1747 d 5-7-1823 m Mary Merrill Pvt PS NH
Ezekiel, Sr.: b 7-15-1739 d 12-7-1791 m Sarah Fowler Capt VT
Ezekiel, Jr.: b 7-15-1763 d 3-24-1848 m Ruth Davis Pvt MA
Ichabod: b 9-10-1760 d 7-5-1840 m Ruth Rowell Pvt NH ★
Isaac: b 1760 d 1813 m Ruth Stevens Sgt NH
John: b 4-18-1760 d 8-29-1829 m (1)Sarah Hale (2)Eunice Dane
  Pvt NH
Joseph: b 12-1-1740 d 1828 m Sarah Thurlow Pvt MA
Levi: b 1757 d 12-10-1827 m Catherine Smith Sol NH
Moses: b 1751 d a. 1800 m Abigail Eastman Sgt NH
Nehemiah: b 1739 d p. 1790 m Dorothy Flanders PS NH
Nicholas: b 7-12-1754/55 d 3-30-1836 m Lois — Pvt NH
Obadiah: b 12-29-1731 d 12-29-1814 m Mary Merrill PS MA
Philbrook: b 3-16-1734/35 d p. 1793 m (1)Susanna Bradley (2)Ruth
  Lufkin Pvt MA
Roger: b 1736 d p. 1778 m Eleanor Challis Pvt MA
Rowell: b 11-22-1758 d 1-27-1832 m Lydia Pettingill Sol NH
Samuel: b 1763 d 2-1-1847 m Mary Swim Cpl Arfr MA ★
Sylvanus: b 1758 d 2-2-1833 m Dorcas Greenleaf Pvt MA
Thomas: b 6-22-1756 d 12-25-1848 m Susanna Colby Pvt NH
Thomas: b 1757 d 6-12-1842 m Lydia Webster Pvt MA NH
Valentine: b 3-29-1728 d 1812 m (1)Hannah Kimball (2)Elizabeth
  Lowell Lt MA
Willaby: b 2-28-1745 d 10-30-1829 m (1)Sarah Sergeant (2)Molly
  Sargent Pvt PS NH
Wm.: b 1760 d 8-5-1847 m Eleanor Lord Cpl NH ★

COLCOCK,
John, Jr.: b 6-6-1744 d 8-21-1782 m Mellicent Jones PS SC

COLCORD,
David: b 1745 d p. 1790 m Eunice Parsons Pvt NH
John: b 1746 d 7-27-1821 m Helena Carpenter 1Lt NH ★
John: b 11-7-1760 d 1-7-1825 m Lydia Morrill Pvt NH ★
Jonathan: b 9-26-1743 d 2-21-1804 m Elizabeth Boardman PS NH
Joseph: b 1754 d 10-30-1839 m Frances Russell Pvt NH

COLDING,
Blanchard: b 11- -1756 d 6- -1816 m Ann Colding Pvt SC

COLDRON, (includes COLDREN, COULDRON)
John: b 1738 d 1807 m Elizabeth Schwab PS PA
Mathias: b 8-15-1756 d 11-24-1819 m Nancy Golding Pvt PA

COLE, (includes COALE, COOL)
Aaron: b 3-5-1728/29 d 4- -1799 m (1)Huldah Butterworth
  (2)Susanna Smith Pvt MA
Abiel: b 2-6-1733 d 8-23-1781 m Anna Pierce Pvt MA
Abijah: b 12-9-1762 d 6-17-1845 m Nancy Williams Pvt MA ★
Abner: b 1754 d c. 1830 m Lydia Freeman SgtMaj CT ★
Abraham, Sr.: b c. 1735 d p. 6-12-1818 m — PS MD
Abraham: b 12-25-1736 d 4-23-1815 m Abigail Johnson Pvt NJ
Abraham: bpt 2-19-1744 d p. 5-12-1794 m Catherine Barringer PS NY
Adam: b c. 1750-55 d 1788 m Elizabeth — Pvt NH
Allen: b 10-16-1747 d 8-27-1797 m Patience Hill Ens PS RI
Amos: b 11-16-1759 d 2-14-1852 m (1) Dinah Croford (2)Naomi
  Orton (3)Stattira Hunt (4)Lucy Clark Pvt CT ★
Andrew: b 1743 d 1-1-1788 m Lois Butterworth Pvt MA
Archippus: b c. 1738 d p. 1-4-1817 m Drusilla Howland Lt MA
Asa: b 9-16-1759 d 5-17-1840 m Susan Wilcox Pvt MA
Azor: b 8-3-1744 d 4-4-1839 m Dorinda Clinton Sgt NY
Barnabas: b 1760 d p. 1805 m Mehitable West Pvt NY
Barnabas: b 3-20-1751 d 2-25-1839 m Sarah Alworth Pvt PA ★
Benjamin: b 1761 d 4-10-1842 m (1)Eunice Pierce (1)Jemima
  (Poor) Latham Pvt CT
Benjamin: b 8-1-1754 d 1-2-1834 m Rachel Salisbury Pvt CT
Benjamin: b 1750 d 7-12-1832 m Elizabeth Long Pvt MD ★
Benjamin: b 1760 d 1840 m Deborah — Pvt ME (?)
Benjamin: b 1750 d 1828 m — Kimball Pvt MA
Benjamin: b 9- -1751 d 4-20-1835 m (1)Sabra Brown (2)Iscah Keep
  Sgt MA
Benjamin: b 3-11-1763 d 12-31-1851 m (1)Elizabeth Gorham
  (2)Mahitable Vraft Matr Pvt NY ★
Benjamin: b 11-17-1751 d p. 1788 m Martha — Pvt RI
Benjamin: b 12-3-1759 d 12-16-1836 m (1)Sarah Luther (2)Patience
  Cole Pvtr RI
Benjamin: b 6-30-1750 d 10-25-1822 m Prudence Hard Pvt VT
Constant: b 2-21-1748/49 d p. 1790 m Mary Kelton Pvt MA
Curtis: b 4-4-1742 d 8-2-1830 m (1)Sarah Eddy (2)Mary Briggs Maj RI
Daniel: b 9-19-1758 d 6-20-1842 m Edith Wilbur Sgt CT ★
Daniel: b 10-26-1749 d 12-10-1834 m Susannah Ogden Pvt NY
Daniel, Sr.: b 8-26-1727 d 5-5-1819 m Amey Bowen Pvt RI
Daniel, Jr.: b 8-8-1757 d 5-6-1840 m Zilpha Lovgood Pvt RI
Daniel: b 2-20-1763 d 7-17-1851 m (1)Elizabeth Whitehead (2)Mary
  Ann Kelley Pvt VA ★
David, Jr.: b 11-29-1756 d 5-19-1810 m Abigail Van Zandt Capt NJ
David: b 4-15-1749 d 4-29-1845 m (1)Zeruah Huntington (2)Roxanna
  Barber Pvt VT
Ebenezer: b 10-28-1832 d 11-2-1808 m Elizabeth Wheeler Pvt CT
Ebenezer: b 1732 d p. 1790 m Elizabeth Hall Pvt MA
Ebenezer: b 1754 d 8-18-1815 m (1)Mary Ogden (2)Mrs Mary Ogden
  Wilson Sol NY
Ebenezer, Sr.: b 10-27-1715 d 7-9-1798 m (1)Prudence Miller
  (2)Lillis (Turner) Barton PS RI
Ebenezer, Jr.: b — d 10-16-1818 m Patty Ingraham Pvt RI
Edward, Jr.: b c. 1735 d 1802 m (1)Deborah Cobb (2)Elizabeth —
  Pvt MA
Eleazer: b 4-8-1747 d 8-7-1833 m Lucy Shurtleff Drm Sgt MA
Eli: b 1757 d 12-16-1822 m Olive Wilson Sgt MA ★
Elijah: b 1764 d 3-18-1825 m Deborah Dammon Sol MA
Elisha, Sr.: b 1-26-1719 d p. 1801 m (1)Priscilla Smalley (2)Hannah
  Smalley Pvt NY
Elisha, Jr.: b 2-16-1743 d 2-3-1826 m Charity Hazen Pvt NY
Ephraim: b 1750 d 1822 m Sophia Ada Mitchell Pvt MD
Ephraim: b 1724 d 1812 m Ruth Arnold Pvt MA
Ephraim: b 1731 d 1775 m Hannah Pratt Sol MA
Esau: b 1-15-1732 d 7-18-1830 m Susanna Chase Sol MA
Ezekiel: b 5-25-1756 d 6-10-1829 m Elizabeth Hess Pvt PA
Francis: b 1724 d 1788 m Abigail Clark Pvt MA
Freegift: b 1-10-1743 d 4-4-1814 m Mary Gardner PS VT
George: b 1759 d p. 1790 m Hannah Bounds Pvt NC
Gideon: b 5-15-1757 d 9-2-1826 m Chloe Beckley Ens NY
Hamolin: b 1757 d 7-24-1837 m — SgtMaj VA
Henry: b 9-28-1732 d 3-2-1827 m Christianna Althaus Pvt MA
Isaac: b c. 1755 d 6-8-1828 m Mary Corle Sgt NJ
Isaac: b 1-21-1741 d 10-23-1800 m Catharine Serven Pvt NY
Isaac: b 1743 d p. 1790 m Esther Yates Pvt NY
Israel: b 9-26-1735 d 7-6-1830 m Susannah Wood Pvt MA
Jacob: b 3-26-1726 d p. 12-26-1787 m Sara DeMaree PS NJ
Jacob: b 1740 d 1827 m Dinchy — Capt NY
James: b 6-18-1761 d 3- -1834 m Annah Stillson Pvt CT ★
James: b 7-29-1751 d p. 1776 m Sophia Hanson Pvt MD
James: b 9-26-1751 d 1818 m Fanny Chisman Wills 1Lt VA

COLE, contd.

Jesse: b 3-27-1752 d 1-20-1828 m Eunice Wilkinson Pvt CT
Job: b 3-28-1753 d p. 1820 m (1)Esther Martin (2)X Pvt MA
John: b 10-24-1725 d a. 5-6-1806 m Hannah Newman PS CT
John: b 4-19-1740 d 2-15-1814 m Abigail Gowen Capt MA
John, Sr.: b c. 1730 d p. 1798 m Elizabeth Elwell Cpl CG MA
John, Jr.: b a. 1760 d p. 1804 m Lucretia Woodsum Pvt MA
John: b 9-12-1742 d 10-12-1826 m (1)Mercy Wood (2)Susannah Salisbury Pvt MA
John: b 4-5-1756 d 10-5-1845 m Abigail Pattee Pvt MA
John: b 6-20-1741 d 8-15-1786 m Lois Davis Capt NH
John: b a. 1750 d c. 1815 m Keziah Dore Sgt NH ★
John: b c. 1720 d p. 1780 m Eunice Spofford Pvt NH
John: b 2-28-1752/3 d 9-25-1840 m Margaret Van Nest Sol Tms NJ ★
John: b 10-21-1749 d 5-3-1825 m Rachel Lewis Pvt PS NY
John: b 1750 d 1836 m Janetje Shufelt Pvt NY
John: b 7-6-1749 d 3-15-1825 m Virtue Davis Capt RI
John: b 1715 d 10-25-1777 m Mary Updike AdvGen RI
John: b 11-9-1728 d 1797 m Jane Bounds Lt VA
John: b 12-17-1752 d 1842-44 m Anna Hynes Pvt VA ★
Jonathan: b 5-11-1718 d 11-7-1791 m (1)Susannah Horton (2)Rhoda Snow PS MA
Jonathan: b 1730 d 9-13-1813 m Edith Davis PS NH
Joseph: b 1734 d p. 1783 m Elizabeth Southworth Capt PS MA
Joseph: b 1723 d 1- -1786 m Ruth Sampson 2Lt MA
Joseph: b 3-25-1743 d 9-28-1842 m (2)Chloe Jones Pvt MA
Joseph: b 1-11-1746 d 2-24-1814 m (1)Rebecca Berry (2)Susan Chase Pvt NY
Joseph, Jr.: b 1750 d 1826 m (1)Remember Cole (2)Margaret Leaper Capt VA
Justin: b 1751 d 1829 m Elizabeth Spofford Pvt MA
Levi: b 1753 d p. 1839 m X Pvt CT ★
Marcus: b 1733 d 2-8-1811 m Phoebe Scoville 1Lt CT
Matthew: b 1735 d 8-28-1807 m Mary Norton PvtrCapt CT
Matthew: b 1745/46 d 1826 m Lois Tyler Capt Cmsry CT
Moses: b 12-22-1757 d p. 1797 m Mary Seeley Pvt CT
Nathan: b 2-23-1750 d 1834 m Molly Flint Pvt NH ★
Nathaniel: b 2-15-1758 d 7-29-1824 m (1)Elizabeth Horton (2)Hulda Kent Cpl MA
Nathaniel: b 1747 d p. 1832 m Abigail Oviatt Sgt CT ★
Nathaniel: b 1759 d 1846 m Nancy Anthony Pvt MA ★
Nehemiah: b 1750 d 5-21-1812 m Judith Pierce Pvt RI
Parker: b 1-13-1756 d 4-25-1839 m Lois Martin Sgt MA ★
Parker: b 11-29-1746 d 8-13-1806 m Mary Marsh Pvt VT
Phillip: b 5-29-1730 d 1794 m Susannah Egle Col PA
Phineas: b 11-20-1744 d p. 1813 m (1)Abiah Hazeltine (2)Catherine Hudson 1Lt MA
Remick: b c. 1740 d — m Martha Rankin Cpl MA
Reuben: b 1765 d 10-30-1840 m Elizabeth King Pvt NY
Richard: b c. 1740 d 5- -1805 m Rebecca Carter Pvt MD
Richard: b 1745 d p. 1782 m Abigail Walker Ens RI
Richard: b 3-8-1750 d p. 1833 m Mary Richie Pvt VA ★
Richard: b 1717 d 2- -1781 m Lydia Hansford PS VA
Robert: b 1760 d 1813 m Nancy Carter Sgt VA
Royal: b 1-8-1760 d 7-4-1849 m Hannah Wheaton Stevens Pvt RI
Samuel: b 11-17-1726/27 d 1-29-1798 m (1)Sarah Brown (2)Abigail (Herrick) Morgan 1Lt MA
Samuel: b 1717 d 4-3-1805 m (1)Bethia Hardy (2)Abigail Currier Sol MA
Samuel: b 3-3-1755 d 4-13-1849 m Sarah Hartshorn Sgt NH ★
Samuel: b 12-8-1758 d 6-15-1833 m Catharine Oakley Capt NY
Samuel: b 1717 d 1797 m Margaret Horton Pvt PA
Samuel: b 5-9-1752 d 2-15-1840 m Rebecca Tillinghast Sgt Ri ★
Seth: b 1756 d a. 1812 m Celia Sanford Pvt MA
Silas: b 10-8-1762 d 1820 m Louisa Wattles 3Sgt CT
Simeon, Sr.: b 8-17-1726 d 1801 m Hannah Daggett Capt MA
Simon, Sr.: bpt 4-4-1697 d p. 9-21-1780 m Margaret Schot PS NY
Simon, Jr.: b c. 1759 d 6-12-1794 m Catherine Bernhard PS NY
Sisson: b 1-20-1746 d 3-18-1845 m Elizabeth Hunter Pvt RI ★
Solomon: b 1764 d 6-2-1840 m (1)Martha Wiard (2)Lydia Kilby Pvt CT ★
Solomon: b 4-1-1743 d 6-17-1836 m Mehitable Baker Sol NH
Southworth: b 6-20-1762 d p. 1797 m Rukesby Bryant Pvt MA
Stephen: b 4-8-1760 d 5-13-1816 m Hannah Hewett Pvt MA ★
Stephen: b 1760 d p. 7-4-1839 m Eliy T. — Capt NC
Stephen: b — d p. 5-9-1798 m X PS NC
Thomas: bpt 6-3-1753 d 12-10-1830 m Mary Ressique Pvt CT W ★
Thomas: b c. 1760 d 1815 m X Pvt PA
Thomas: b 8-25-1733 d 10-25-1825 m Miriam Kinnee Capt RI
Thomas: b 7-1-1758 d p. 1787 m Anna Vose Pvt RI W ★
Thomas Herrick: b 10-6-1757 d 9-25-1819 m Susanna Cleaves Sgt MA W ★
Timothy, Sr.: b 5-22-1723 d 1778 m Hannah Finch Pvt MA
Timothy, Jr.: b 2-3-1750/51 d 1815 m Deliverance Ide Pvt MA
Timothy: bpt 1-12-1718 d 11-2-1783 m (1)Delilah — (2)Rebekah Dibbel Pvt CT
Tobias: b 1758 d 1833 m Sarah Hack Pvt NY W ★
Walter King: b c. 1745 d 2-7-1794 m Sally Mitchell Dr VA
Wm.: b 8-5-1740 d p. 1829 m Sarah Webster Lt MD
Wm.: b 11-22-1740 d 11-26-1824 m Elizabeth Hill Lt PS MA
Wm.: b 1764 d 1856 m Jane Gunn Pvt NY
Wm.: b 1741 d p. 1783 m Lucy (Winston) Dabney Pvt VA

Wm.: b c. 1742 d 1820 m Elizabeth Simmons Pvt VA
Wm.: b c. 1745 d p. 1815 m Nellie Freeman Pvt VA
Wm.: b c. 1742 d 1795 m Eleanor Bibb PS VA

COLEMAN, (includes COLMAN)

Abner: b 9-29-1759 d 6-17-1834 m Ruth Tuthill Pvt NY
Abraham: b c. 1745-46 d a. 1-21-1801 m Elizabeth — Pvt VA
Asaph: b 9-27-1747 d 11-15-1820 m Eunice Hollister Dr CT
Benjamin: bpt 2-26-1720 d 1- -1797 m Anne Brown Pvt MA
Benjamin: bpt 8-3-1749 d 10-12-1826 m Susannah Martin Pvt MA
Benjamin, Jr.: b 1757 d 6- -1843 m Adaline Smith Pvt NJ (?)
Benjamin, Sr.: b c. 1725 d 6-1-1802 m Hannah Wood Pvt NY
Benjamin, Jr.: b 4-16-1755 d 8-5-1832 m Hannah Finch Pvt NY
Benjamin: b c. 1753 d 5-17-1813 m Elizabeth Goodman Capt NC
Caleb: b 4-22-1745 d p. 1789 m Desire Clark Pvt PS NY
Charles: b 1-25-1763 d 2- -1827 m Elizabeth Early Pvt MD
Charles: b c. 1750-55 d p. 12-16-1823 m Mary Roundtree QM NC
Charles: b 1762 d 4- -1842 m Eliza Gibson Armr SC
Christopher: b 5-25-1758 d p. 1819 m Ruth Simpson Drm Pvt PA
Daniel: b 5-24-1731 d 5-7-1794 m Susannah Harris Sol GA
Daniel: b 1-21-1753 d 1817 m (1)Mary Childs (2)Martha Cocke Col VA
Daniel: b 6-7-1768 d 4-8-1860 m Anna Payne Harrison PS VA
Daniel, Jr.: b c. 1746 d 1819 m X PS VA
Daniel: b — d a. 2-6-1789 m X PS VA
David: b 1762 d 1840 m Jane Hawkins Pvt NJ
Dudley: b 8-24-1745 d 11-16-1797 m Mary Jones LCol MA
Ebenezer, Jr.: b 10-20-1751 d 4-13-1827 m Phebe Carpenter Cpl CT
Ebenezer: b — d p. 1785 m X Sol Tms CT
Elijah: b 3-10-1745 d 1-19-1818 m Tabitha Meekins Sgt MA
Elliott Glenn: b c. 1764 d a. 3-24-1823 m Elizabeth Daniel Pvt VA
Francis: b 8-16-1744 d 8-13-1823 m Margaret — Sol GA
George: b 174- d 12- -1831 m Deborah Brown Pvt NY
Gideon: b 1753 d 4-11-1813 m Catherine Bull Pvt NY
Henry: b — d 1807/08 m Mary Ann Hutchison Pvt VA
Isham: b 9-17-1758 d 11-1-1825 m Ann Roper Pvt VA
Jacob: b 1764 d a. 6-20-1835 m Deborah — Pvt NJ ★
Jacob: b 1748 d 1828 m Sarah McCulloch Pvt Lt VA
James: b c. 1745 d 10- -1814 m Rachel Kobb Sol SC
James: b c. 1739 d 1817 m Jeane Critcher Col VA
James: b c. 1755 d 1825 m Sarah Taylor Pvt VA
James: b c. 1740 d 3-2-1796 m Anna Cocke PS VA
Job: b 10-25-1741 d 9-2-1805 m Elizabeth Martin Sol PS MA
Joel: b 8-23-1758 d 10-20-1840 m Mary Dunning Pvt NY
John: b 1748 d 8-16-1846 m Mary Mahon Pvt NJ ★
John: b 8- -1761 d 3-12-1845 m Rachel Barden Sgt NY ★
John: b 1735 d 5-7-1811 m Sarah (Coleman) Pvt NY
John: b 1-1-1747 d 2-19-1806 m Bathsheba Ryder Pvt PS Pvt NY
John: b 1760 d 1803 m Martha Smith Sol (Artl) NY
John: b 4-21-1759 d 6-13-1829 m Margaret — Pvt PA ★
John: b 1720 d p. 1779 m Sarah Embry Lt VA
John: b a. 1760 d p. 1786 m Mary Wells Ens VA
John: b 1758 d 1-20-1816 m Pleasance Goodwin SgtMaj VA
Jonathan: b 10-9-1750 d 1-13-1825 m Milly Pittman Sol GA
Joseph: b 1750 d 1777 m Elizabeth Denton Pvt NY
Joseph: b 1718 d 11-15-1800 m (2)Mary Salmon PS NY
Joseph: b c. 1757 d 1806 m Sithey Glenn Sgt VA W ★
Lemuel: b 1752 d 2-11-1824 m Catharine Edwards Cpl MA
Leonard: b 4-14-1745 d 3-28-1839 m Eunice Pierson OrdlSgt NJ ★
Moses: b 11-19-1755 d 1837 m Dorothy Pearson PS MA
Nathan: b 12-27-1755 d 4-26-1829 m Deborah Turner Pvt CT ★
Nathaniel: b c. 1742 d 9-14-1816 m Anna Dickinson Pvt MA
Nathaniel: b 1754 d 5-17-1837 m (1)Rachel Damon (2)Rebecca Damon Sol MA ★
Nicholas: b 10-14-1748 d 8-16-1816 m (1)Elizabeth Hicks (2)Fredreca — Pvt PA
Nicholas: b 9-8-1731 d p. 1795 m Jane McClelland Pvt PA
Phineas: bpt 8-22-1719 d a. 1783/84 m Abigail Huntress PS NH
Richard: b 1-18-1761 d p. 1798 m (1)Lucy Sydnor (2)Nancy Ann Stubbs Pvt VA
Robert: b 11-4-1748 d 8-14-1825 m Ann Old Lt PA
Robert: b — d 6-18-1823 m Trecy (Thresa) — Pvt SC
Robert: b 1748 d 1-9-1834 m Catharine Robinson Pvt VA ★
Samuel: b 1753 d 5-12-1837 m (1)Mary Dyar (2)Sarah Evans PS VA
Samuel: b — d 1797 m Sarah — Capt VA
Samuel: b 7-21-1755 d 3-8-1811 m Susanna Storrs 1Lt VA
Samuel: b 1752 d 7-23-1824 m (1)Millie Coffee (2)Ann — Pvt VA
Spencer: b 2-15-1752 d p. 1834 m Lucy — Pvt VA ★
Stephen: b 3-17-1739 d 1798 m Sarah Watson Capt CS PS VA
Theophilus: b 1760 d p. 1812 m Abigail Robertson Lt NC
Thomas: b 1748 d 2-2-1837 m Pheby Gray Sgt Ens PA ★
Thomas: b c. 1736 d p. 1825 m X Sol (Bbd) VA
Thomas: b 1738 d 3-29-1810 m Elizabeth — PS CS VA
Thompson: b c. 1760 d 1831 m (1)Elizabeth McFarlin (2)Mrs Sarah West Sol GA
Timothy: b 1752 d 8-18-1831 m Elizabeth DeWitt Lt NY
Valentine: b c. 1755 d 8-24-1845 m (1)Magdalena — (2)Anna Maria Shull Pvt PA
Wm., Sr.: b 1724 d 1785 m Ann Hester Pvt SC
Wm., Jr.: b 1754 d 1820 m Mary Gray Pvt SC

COLES,

Benjamin: b 2-6-1738 d 8-6-1810 m Mary Albertson Matr NY
Henrietta Maria: b 3-13-1763 d 2-17-1854 m Philip Fishburn PS PA

Isaac: b 2-25-1747 d 6-2-1813 m (1)Eliza Lightfoot (2)Katherine Thompson PS VA
James: b 10-16-1751 d 12- -1836 m Deborah Smith Pvt RI
Jesse: b 9-15-1757 d 1-11-1839 m (1)Deborah Carpenter (2)Freelove (Carpenter) Searing Sgt NY
John: b 1745 d 1808 m Rebecca Elizabeth Tucker Col VA
Wm.: b 8-1-1744 d 10-26-1810 m Sarah Cleveland Pvt MA
Wm.: b Temple: b c. 1725 d c. 1787 m Mrs Sarah Wilson Capt CS NC

COLESBERRY,
Jacob: b 1734 d 8-28-1797 m Catherine Greavenseal Pvt DE

COLESWORTHY,
Nathaniel: b 8-21-1748 d 9-6-1802 m Lydia Minot Pvt MA
Samuel: b 4- -1733 d 2-10-1806 m Mary G. — Pvt MA

COLFAX,
Ebenezer: b 9-15-1753 d 1782/83 m Lucretia Hempstead CG Mid CT
Robert: b 12-26-1761 d 1829 m (1)Sarah Wilson (2)Elizabeth (Wilson) Colfax Pvt CT
Wm.: b 6-3-1760 d 9-7-1838 m Hester Schuyler Capt CT

COLGAN,
John: b c. 1740 d p. 1791 m X Sgt PA
John: b c. 1750 d c. 1805 m Elizabeth Harwood Pvt VA

COLGLAZIER,
David: b 1764 d 1855 m Cynthia May Lt VA

COLGROVE, (includes COLEGROVE)
Benjamin: b 1729 d 1820 m Sarah — Sol CT
Christopher: b a. 1755 d p. 1789 m Eleanor Lewis Pvt CT
James: b 6-29-1746 d p. 1810 m Anne Bentley Sol NY
Jeremiah: b 1758 d 8-26-1837 m Lydia Waterman Sol RI
John: b 1750 d 1841 m Susan Bard Pvt CT
Jonathan: b 1745 d 10-8-1812 m Jemima Parks PS CT
Stephen: b 6-30-1763 d 3-4-1855 m Elizabeth Davis Pvt RI
Wm.: b 12-20-1763 d 6-21-1844 m Theodosia Smith Tms NY
Wm.: b 8-20-1760 d 2-12-1840 m X Pvt RI ★

COLLADAY,
Jacob, Sr.: b c. 1734 d p. 1777 m Frances Walters Sgt PA
Jacob, Jr.: b 1757 d 1826 m (1)Sarah Sands (2)Sophia Wonderly PS PA

COLLAMORE, (includes COLLAMER)
Anthony, Sr.: b 7-15-1735 d 12-15-1819 m Mercy Barker Pvt MA
Anthony, Jr.: b 1-19-1759 d 6-16-1823 m Tryphena Herrick Sgt MA★
Enoch: b 6-27-1745 d 4-22-1824 m Hannah Cushing Sgt CS MA
Joshua: b 11-16-1740 d 6-18-1827 m Abiah (Wadsworth) Morton CS ME
Peter: b 10-8-1734 d 1786 m Elizabeth Farrar Cpl MA

COLLARD, (includes COLLERD)
James: b c. 1762 d p. 1791 m Mary Tremper Pvt NY
Joseph: b c. 1750 d 1812 m Margaret — Sol VA

COLLES,
Christopher: b 5-9-1738/39 d 10-4-1824 m Ann Keough PS PA NY

COLLESTER,
John: b 4-22-1757 d 10-14-1855 m Mary Ferguson Cpl MA

COLLETT,
Daniel: b 2-10-1752 d 6-28-1835 m Mary Haines Pvt VA

COLLEY,
John: b 9-14-1752 d p. 5-30-1815 m Sarah France Pvt VA
Thomas: b c. 1750 d a. 10-28-1800 m (1)Rhoda — (2)Judith—Pvt VA Pvt VA
Wm.: b 1754 d 1844 m Martha — Pvt VA

COLLIER, (includes COLLAR, COLLIA, COLLYER & COLYER)
Aaron: b 1-15-1750 d 6- -1842 m Elizabeth — Sol VA
Cornelius: b 11-16-1720 d 3-9-1810 m Elizabeth Wyatt Capt VA
Gershom: b 1-13-1765 d 6-19-1830 m (1)Sally Hovey (2)Hannah Locke (3)Margaret Dickey Pvt MA
Isaac: b 7- -1745 d 6-3-1814 m Sarah Courtis Lt MA
Isaac: b 6-13-1750 d 12-5-1813 m Tamsin Hayden Pvt MA
Jacob: b c. 1740 d — m Maria Van Alstine Pvt NY
James, Jr.: b 5-1-1752 d 1-3-1844 m Martha Rutherford Capt PA ★
James: b 10-13-1757 d 8-20-1832 m (1)Elizabeth Bouldin (2)Elizabeth Littlepage Sgt VA
Jason: b 1-5-1744 d 10-14-1840 m (1)Sarah Bogel (2)Hannah Farrinton Pvt MA
John: b 3-9-1740 d 12-22-1806 m Ruthy Blackler Pvt MA
John: b 12-14-1732 d p. 1792 m Margaret Regart Col PS NC
John: b 1742 d 1820 m (2)Hannah — Pvt VA
John: b c. 1742 d 1821 m Mildred — Pvt VA ★
John: b 1744 d 3-31-1826 m Griselda Taylor Pvt VA W ★
Joseph: b 1754 d a. 1787 m Mary Marx PS PA
Joseph: b 1749 d 1819 m Amy Mosely 1Lt VA
Michael: b 8-31-1751 d 1817 m (1)Ann — (2)Mary — Drm Fif PA

Peter: b c. 1738 d 12-12-1804 m Margaretta Debevoise 2Lt PS NY
Richard: b 9-30-1760 d 12-22-1850 m Mary Haight Matr NY
Thomas: b 1744 d 8-24-1834 m Mrs Mary McAdams 1Lt NJ ★
Thomas: b 1-17-1740 d 1787 m Frances Dabney Capt VA
Vines: b c. 1735 d p. 9-7-1795 m Sara Elizabeth Williamson PS VA
Wm.: b c. 1725 d a. 1-1-1794 m Sarah — PS MD
Wm.: b c. 1760 d 1814 m Comfort — Pvt MD
Wm.: b 1724 d 1794 m Judith Briggs Pvt MA

COLLINS, (includes COLLINGS)
Abijah: b 1750 d 8-7-1783 m Abial — NS CT
Ambrose: b 5-28-1756 d 9-3-1839 m Mary Baldwin Pvt CT ★
Amos: b 7-16-1749 d 5-22-1796 m Thankful Clarke Pvt CT
Asael: b 11-5-1761 d 10-1-1832 m (2)Sarah Whipple Slr Pvt RI ★
Augustus: b 8-7-1843 d 4-30-1813 m Mary Chittendon Maj MA
Benjamin: b 1740 d — m Anne — Pvt NH
Benjamin: b 9-16-1751 d 4-3-1840 m Elizabeth Foster Pvt NY ★
Benoni: b 1754 d 1823 m Lydia Wilmarth Sgt MA
Charles: b 2-11-1745 d 6-8-1818 m Hannah Turner NCapt RI
Charles: b 8-5-1727 d 8-17-1796 m Ann Huntington Pvt CT
Charles: b 1755 d 1818 m Elizabeth Field Pvt VT
Chedor L.: b 7-9-1764 d 1-24-1831 m Sarah Severance Pvt MA ★
Cyprian: b 3-4-1733 d 1-9-1809 m Azuba Gibbs Lt PS CT
Cyreneus: b 1753 d 1-2-1798 m Hannah Williams Pvt CT
Daniel: b 2-16-1741 d 11-9-1819 m Susannah Lyman Capt CT
Daniel, Jr.: b 3-10-1732 d 11-6-1819 m (1)Dorothy Wells (2)Mrs Ann (Potter) Hillard 1Lt CT
Daniel: b 8-17-1743 d 8- -1810 m (1)Lucy Elwell (2)Polly Tuffts (3)Mrs Hannah Babson Lt MA
Daniel: b 1758 d 1851 m Mary Tewkesbury Cpl MA ★
Daniel: b 11-10-1755 d 8-3-1845 m Thankful Ashley Mrnr RI
Ebenezer: b 7-23-1762 d p. 3-5-1845 m Annie Stowe Pvt MA ★
Edward: b 11-26-1713 d 10-10-1796 m (1)Tabitha Geer (2)Rebecca Hale CS PS CT
Edward: b 7-25-1736 d 1803 m Ruth Blakeslee Lt CT
Edward: b 3-5-1757 d 3-25-1819 m Phoebe Matlack Pvt NJ
Eli: b 3-26-1759 d 2-4-1844 m Mary — Pvt NC ★
Eliphalet: b 7-11-1744 d 5-22-1815 m Abigail Abbe Pvt CT
Elisha: b 11-30-1759 d p. 4-18-1838 m Frances Madison Pvt VA ★
Ephraim: b 2-2-1715 d 6-1-1776 m Abigail Dow Sol NH
Ezekiel: b 5-1-1749 d 2-8-1808 m (1)Abigail Woods (2)Anna — Sgt MA
Gamaliel: b 1742 d a. 6-18-1786 m Rachel Rich CS PS MA
Henry: b 4-11-1764 d 4-10-1847 m (1)Minerva Bacon (2)Ruth Fifield Pvt MA ★
Hezekiah: b 12-1-1739 d 3-12-1828 m Rhoda Ricketson 1Lt NY
Isaac: b 2-16-1746 d 3-21-1817 m Rachel Budd CS NJ
Jabez: b 12-3-1744 d 10-5-1839 m Mary Gleason Sgt MA
James: b 5-7-1755 d 6-8-1828 m (1)Sarah Chambers Anderson (2)Mrs Charity Dew Sgt MD
James: b 1754 d 1802 m Christiana Davis Pvt MD
James: b 11-26-1742 d p. 1778 m (1)Rebeka Elwell (2)Mrs Abigail Warner Col MA
James: b 1730 d 1801 m Elizabeth Kelly Pvt PA
James: b 1759 d 9-26-1836 m Mary Halsey Pvt NC
James: b c. 1730 d 1788 m Mary Kirtley Cmsry VA
James Potter: b 11-22-1764 d 4-14-1840 m (1)— Neil (2)Mary Anderson Sol SC
John: b 9-14-1749 d 3-19-1818 m Mehetable Chapin Pvt CT
John: b 9-1-1738 d 1804 m Sarah Houston Capt DE
John: b c. 1750 d a. 7-7-1787 m (2)Betty Scrogin Sol DE
John: b 1758 d 1838 m Elizabeth Stubbs Sol GA
John: b 5-2-1754 d 8-11-1806 m Mary Baldwin Pvt NJ
John: b 1741 d 11-3-1813 m Mary — Pvt PA
John: b 6-8-1717 d 3-8-1795 m Mrs Mary (Avery) Collins PS RI
John: b 1754 d 4-4-1841 m Elizabeth Brown Capt SC ★
John: b 12-9-1760 d 3-8-1852 m Phebe Sailors Capt SC ★
John: b 9-10-1748 d 6-17-1836 m Judith Word Pvt VA
John: b 8-26-1757 d 1-21-1828 m Margaret — Pvt VA
John: b c. 1725 d 11- -1797 m Mary Carr PS VA
Jonathan: b 5-3-1755 d 4-6-1845 m Sarah Couch Sgt CT ★
Jonathan: b 4-28-1728 d p. 1790 m Elizabeth Prescott PS NH
Joseph: b 12-25-1747 d 3-2-1826 m (1)Grace Brown (2)Abiah Chapin Ens CT
Joseph: b 3-23-1760 d 12-6-1848 m (1)Sarah Bradbury (2)Mrs Betsy (Bradbury) Shaw Pvt MA
Joseph: b 2-20-1736/37 d p. 1790 m Sarah Bagley PS NH
Joseph: b 1746 d 1-1-1829 m Elsie Onderdonk Pvt NJ
Joseph, Sr.: b a. 1737 d 1802 m Sallie — PS NC
Joseph: b 6-18-1738 d 9-26-1827 m Bathsheba Hoxie Pvt RI
Joseph: b 2-10-1763 d 8-24-1847 m Elizabeth B. Fleming Pvt SC
Joseph: b c. 1755 d a. 1826 m Lucy — Pvt VA
Joseph: b c. 1760 d 1831 m Susannah — Pvt VA
Joshua: b 12-5-1741 d p. 1788 m Mary White Sol NY
Josiah: b 5-2-1757 d c. 1847 m Julietta Bohannan Pvt VA ★
Lemuel: b 2-28-1757 d 9-28-1841 m Mercy Garrin Pvt Matr MA ★
Levi: b 1-1-1760 d 4-10-1837 m Abigail Stanton Sol NH
Levin: b c. 1750 d a. 1813 m Catherine Odom Lt SC
Nathaniel: b 6-9-1763 d 1832 m Olive Stebbins Pvt VT
Nathaniel: b 1-9-1749 d 1-18-1825 m Mabel Richardson CS VT
Oliver: b 8-21-1762 d 8-14-1838 m (1)Lois Cowls (2)Betsy Wyman (3)Malinda Peirce (4)Keturah Kellogg Cpl CT
Philemon: b 5-1-1762 d c. 1836 m Betsey Osborn Pvt MA ★

COLLINS, contd.
Reuben: b a. 1760 d 10-8-1830 m Monaca — Lt SC
Richard: b 1753 d 8-31-1834 m Mary Fickett Pvt MA
Richard: b 6-8-1724 d 10-3-1782 m Esther Zane Pvt NJ
Richard: b 5-1-1725 d 6-17-1808 m (2)Sarah Griffiths Pvt NJ
Richard: b 1755 d p. 1810 m X Sol VA CL
Robert: b — d c. 12- -1777 m — Capt NH
Robert: b c. 1750 d 4-2-1816 m Mildred — Pvt VA
Rufus: b 2-15-1751 d 7-20-1808 m (1)Miss Parsons (2)Miss Kingsbury Drm CT
Samuel: b 8-11-1763/64 d 7-4-1840 m Betsey Bishop Pvt CT W ★
Samuel: b 8-23-1764 d 9-6-1852 m (1)Deborah Goodhue (2)Sarah Haines Pvt NH
Samuel: b 1753 d 4-15-1825 m Agnes Thompson Drm Fif PA
Solomon: b 9-15-1762 d 2-15-1848 m Jerusha Ryder Pvt MA ★
Spencer: b c. 1750 d p. 7-12-1815 m Jane — Sol VA
Stephen: b 1754 d 1842 m Dolly Olmstead Pvt CT
Stephen: b 1-23-1740 d 2-11-1819 m Sarah Keep Sgt MA
Stephen: b 8-28-1733 d 1794 m Mary Parrish PS PA
Stephen: b 8-2-1744 d 8-6-1825 m Catherine McIntosh Pvt VA KY
Thaddeus: b 1762 d 9-4-1828 m Esther Foster Pvt MA W ★
Thomas: b 1732 d 3-29-1789 m Sarah Cook BGen PS DE
Thomas: b 3-16-1752 d 12-24-1831 m Sarah Henderson Pvt DE
Thomas: b c. 1755 d p. 1796 m Elizabeth Pulate Sgt PA
Thomas: b 1729 d 9-11-1796 m Rosannah Dodd Sol PS SC
Thomas: b 8-17-1725 d 3-25-1793 m Lydia Hopkins Capt VT
Thomas: b a. 1765 d p. 1820 m X Pvt VA KY
Thomas: b c. 1754 d c. 1820 m Mary Wallace PS VA
Timothy: b 4-13-1699 d 2-7-1777 m Elizabeth Hyde CS CT
Timothy: b 9-23-1754 d 12-24-1833 m Elizabeth (Franklin) McFee Sgt MD ★
Tyrannies: b 1742 d — m Abigail Peck Capt NY
Wm.: b 10-9-1759 d 9-23-1850 m Polly Ross Pvt CT ★
Wm.: b 10-9-1760 d 4-19-1849 m Esther Morris Pvt CT ★
Wm.: b 2-24-1762 d 4-15-1809 m Olive Collins Pvt MA
Wm.: b 1751 d p. 10-14-1783 m Anna Head Pvt NC
Wm.: b 1760 d 8-27-1838 m Sabrina Loveland Pvt PA ★
Wm.: b c. 1755 d p. 1830 m (1)— Wright (2)Nancy Moore Dyer Sol SC
Wm.: b 1747 d 1786 m X Lt VA
Wm.: b c. 1754 d a. 1797 m Patty Snell PS VA
Wm. B.: b c. 1759 d p. 10-12-1844 m X PS VA

COLLINSWORTH,
John: b 1763 d 9-6-1838 m X Pvt Mar VA ★

COLLIS,
John: b c. 1748 d p. 1790 m Lois Smith Pvt MA

COLLOM,
Jonathan: b 12-10-1760 d 2-20-1842 m Martha — Drm Mil PA

COLOMBE,
Phillipe Louis de La: b 1750 d 1825 m Margaret Moore Ransteid Capt ADC FrA

COLONNA,
Major: b 7-22-1736 d 11-3-1811 m (1)Joice Hutchinson (2)Peggy Watson Lt VA

COLQUITT,
John: b c. 1735 d 6- -1800 m Elizabeth Hendrick Sol VA
John Terry: b c. 1760 d p. 1813 m Mrs Alice (Townes) Dickie Sol VA
Robert: b 10-9-1759 d 1834 m Susan Hubbard Sol VA

COLSON, (includes COULSON)
Abiah: b 12-7-1762 d c. 1812 m Sarah Colson Pvt MA ★
Bolter: b 1-6-1743/44 d p. 1794 m Sarah Holbrook Pvt MA
Christopher: b 5-10-1765 d 1828 m (1)Hannah Robinson (2)Patty Brown Fif MA ★
Ebenezer: b 3-14-1715/16 d 4-19-1801 m Hannah White PS CS MA
Jacob: b c. 1740 d p. 11-5-1777 m (1)Sara — Capt GA
Joseph, Jr.: b 8- -1750 d 11- -1835 m Ann Clark Sgt MA
Josiah: b 1-24-1727 d 6-11-1811 m Leah Beal Lt MA
Samuel: b c. 1745 d 3-5-1810 m Charity Dearth Pvt PA
Thomas: b 1-27-1713 d 6-6-1799 m Mary Bolter Pvt MA

COLSTON, (includes COULSTON)
Edward: b c. 1734 d 8- -1803 m Jane David Pvt PA
James: b 4-30-1746 d 2-8-1810 m Mary Shannahan Pvt MD
John: b a. 1758 d 12-1-1815 m Elizabeth Wentz Pvt PA
Rawleigh: b 5-10-1749 d 7-26-1823 m Elizabeth Marshall PS VA
Wm.: b c. 1750 d 9-23-1826 m (1)Rhoda Kerr (2)Hannah Underwood Capt PA
Wm.: b 10-10-1744 d 1781 m Lucy Landon Carter PS VA

COLT, (includes COULT)
Amherst: b 7-27-1759 d 1-25-1830 m Miram Giddings OMSgt Dr CT
Benjamin: b 1738 d 8-30-1781 m Lucretia Ely Pvt MA
Elisha: b 2-26-1758 d 8-23-1827 m Lucretia Ann Davis Pvt CT
James: b 4-4-1740 d 8-29-1809 m (1)Phebe Ely (2)Miriam Williams Capt PS MA

COLTMAN,
Robert: b 3-21-1739 d 6-27-1816 m Sarah Holl Capt PA

COLTON,
Aaron: b 6-13-1718 d 6-28-1778 m Mary Ely Cpl MA
Alpheus: b 1766 d 1820 m Lois Spencer Sol MA
Benjamin: b 2-1-1722 d 6-20-1808 m (1)Abiah Cooley (2)Mrs Rose Bond Sol MA
Caleb: b 1740 d 1820 m Keziah Pierce Pvt NH
Charles: b 3-8-1724 d 3- -1809 m Mary Sikes Capt MA
Charles: b 8-2-1736 d 1-31-1817 m Lucy Parsons Pvt MA
David: b 8-3-1756 d 1836 m Dolly Powers Pvt MA
Ebenezer: b 3-20-1743 d 9-2-1793 m Miriam Colton 1Lt MA
Eli: b 7-24-1750 d p. 1815 m Mary Crane Pvt MA
Enoch: b 11-30-1761 d 6-22-1842 m Sarah Colton Pvt MA
Festus: b 3-31-1743 d 1788 m Eunice Keep Pvt MA
Gad: b 3-12-1754 d 12-28-1831 m (1)Nancy — (2)Mrs Miriam (Colton) Hale Pvt MA
George: b 6-23-1747 d 7- -1812 m (2)Tabitha Cooley Pvt MA
Gideon: b 5-10-1763 d 4-21-1850 m Lucretia Walworth Sol MA
Henry: b 6-8-1738 d 11-11-1787 m Mary Burt Pvt MA
Isaac: b 8-9-1720 d 8-20-1800 m (2)Mercy — Capt MA
Ithamar: b 11-15-1744 d 6-15-1806 m (1)Alinda Wells (2)Andrus — (3)Miriam Benton Pvt CT
Jabez: b 3-20-1747 d 4-2-1819 m Mary Baldwin QM MA
John, Sr.: b 2-21-1729 d 1-25-1813 m Penelope Wolcott Pvt MA
John, Jr.: b 1-9-1756 d 4-21-1833 m Hannah Pomeroy Pvt MA ★
John Gunn: b 10-22-1747 d 1-16-1822 m Martha Warriner Lt MA
Jonathan: b 2-28-1758 d p. 1790 m Elizabeth Strong Pvt CT
Joseph: b 1-25-1745 d 6-15-1817 m Eleanor Bartlett Cpl MA
Julius: b 3-4-1763 d 1-3-1830 m Sybil Post Pvt MA
Lemuel: b 1751 d 4-29-1789 m Achsah Sheldon Pvt CT
Luther: b 11-15-1756 d 10-14-1803 m (1)Thankful Woolworth (2)Mehitabel Boardman MM MA
Moses: b 5-22-1724 d 2-23-1777 m Hannah Hitchcock Pvt MA
Moses: b 3-13-1748 d 6-18-1819 m Dorcas Winslow Pvt MA
Samuel: b 10- -1754 d 10-22-1823 m Lois Brown Pvt CT
Simeon: b 1-21-1755 d 1-5-1834 m Elizabeth (Colton) Pvt MA
Simon: b 1709 d 5-29-1796 m (1)Abigail Burt (2)Rebecca Hale PS MA
Thomas: b 10-6-1719 d 3-17-1808 m Deborah Dudley Pvt MA
Wm.: b 1-6-1754 d 5-6-1825 m Hannah Colton Fif MA

COLTRANE,
Wm.: b c. 1741 d 11-17-1835 m Rachel Worthington PS NC

COLTRIDER,
Henry: b 1745 d 5-5-1819 m Christina — Pvt PA

COLVILLE,
Andrew: b 1739 d 1797 m Mary Craig Capt VA

COLVIN,
Amos: b c. 1760 d p. 1829 m Mary — Pvt VT
Benjamin: b 1759 d p. 1832 m Nancy Coleman Pvt VA ★
Daniel: b 1737 d p. 2-13-1806 m Elizabeth Hansbrough Pvt VA
George: b 12-25-1744 d 12-13-1807 m Mary Sheldon Lt RI W ★
Henry: b 6-17-1762 d 1-31-1839 m (1)Susannah — (2)Catherine Williams Pvt VA ★
John: b 1752 d 1- -1814 m Sarah Fuller Pvt PS NY
John: b a. 1747 d 5-12-1777 m Hannah Nichols PS RI
John: b 3-16-1758 d 5-29-1832 m Sarah Dillard Pvt VA W ★
Joseph: b 9-18-1750 d 3-1-1832 m Ruth — Pvt RI
Joseph: b 1721 d a. 10-6-1792 m Phebe — PS RI
Josiah: b c. 1730 d 5-14-1791 m Freelove Ralph PS RI
Levi: b c. 1754 d 12-21-1834 m Lydia Jenks Ens VT ★
Peter: b 5-29-1749 d 7-21-1832 m Mercy Burlingame Sgt RI W★
Philip: b 4-11-1758 d 4-19-1832 m Sarah Berry Pvt RI ★
Reubin: b 1742/43 d 7-23-1812 m Sarah Mattison Cpl VT
Richard: b c. 1745 d c. 1815 m Rosannah Russell Cpl VT
Wm.: b 1762 d 1835 m Martha Feaster Pvt SC

COLWELL, (includes CALWELL)
John: b 10-11-176- d 10-28-1829 m Elizabeth Spell Pvt NC
Samuel: b c. 1750 d 1800 m Ann Richardson Capt MD
Stephen: b 4-22-1759 d 3-26-1834 m Martha Keach Pvt RI
Wm.: b 12-7-1741 d 7-27-1793 m Lucia Arnold Pvt RI

COMAN,
Daniel: b 1752 d 1-22-1839 m Hannah Angel Pvt MA

COMEGYS,
Abraham: b c. 1749 d p. 1800 m X Pvt MD
Jesse: b 10-30-1749 d p. 1790 m Mary Everett 2Lt MD
Samuel: b 8-29-1758 d 2-29-1812 m (1)Mary Gleaves (2)Mary Freeman 1Lt MD
William: b 1734 d 1832 m (1)Mrs Harrington (2)Martha Hooper Sol MD

COMER,
Hugh Moss: b c. 1760 d 1836 m Anne Trippe Pvt VA
James Thomas: b 1729 d 1837 m (3)Nancy Harper Pvt GA

COMEY, (includes COMEE)
David: b 4-21-1744 d 3-8-1826 m (1)Christianna Maltman (2)Hannah Maltman Pvt MA
Ezra: b 10-27-1751 d 11-19-1832 m Anna Porter Sol MA
John: b 1-14-1753 d 5-24-1830 m Betsey Carpenter Cpl MA
Jonathan: b 4-4-1746 d p. 1780 m Elizabeth Wells Pvt MA
Oliver: b 6-11-1757 d 1-4-1842 m Elizabeth Belcher Pvt MA ★

COMFORT,
John: b 1725 d 10- -1795 m Hannah Mould Pvt NY
Richard: b 8-15-1745 d 3-6-1824 m Charity Young Pvt NY
Samuel: b 1760 d 9-25-1802 m Anna Maria Youngblood Pvt NY

COMINGO, (includes COMINGORE)
Henry: b 1747 d 1-29-1836 m (1)Rachel Brewer (2)Tiny Rinearson Pvt PA ★
John: b 1749 d 10-6-1845 m Anntie Mattees Pvt PA ★

COMLY,
John: b 1753 d 4-28-1828 m Hannah Vaughn Pvt PA

COMPSON,
Thomas: b 1740/41 d 2-27-1797 m Mrs Hannah Sandford Pvt NJ

COMPTON, (includes CRUMPTON)
Abraham: b c. 1747 d 1779 m Mary Compton Pvt VA
Archibald: b 1760 d 4- -1826 m Sally Carpenter Sol VA ★
Edmund H.: b 6-10-1759 d 3-26-1836 m (1)Susannah — (2)Sarah Read Foster Lt MD ★
Gabriel: b 8-17-1735 d 3-30-1782 m Mary (Fitz Randolph) Coddington Pvt NJ
Jacob: b 5-21-1760 d 10-1-1821 m Orriminah (Miner) Hyde Pvt NJ
Jacob: b 1761 d 1808 m Rachel Robbins Pvt NJ
James: b c. 1751 d c. 3-10-1832 m Francis — Sol MD ★
John: b 2-28-1747 d 1-10-1803 m Elizabeth Briscoe Pvt MD
John: b 1726 d a. 1-16-1797 m Elizabeth — PS VA
John: b c. 1750 d p. 5-10-1807 m Ann Cross PS VA
Joseph: b 12-29-1759 d 3-13-1841 m (2)Rebecca Appleton (3)Nancy Tapscott Pvt NJ ★
Richard: b 6-1-1759 d 8-23-1828 m Mary Van Arsdale Pvt NJ
Robert: b c. 1764 d p. 2-13-1857 m Lydia Brown Messenger NJ
Samuel: b 1758 d 1856 m Catherine Bruer Pvt NJ
Wm.: b 1733 d 12-5-1807 m Susanna (Wilson) Briscoe PS MD
Zachariah: b 1745 d 1788/89 m Mary Middleton Sol VA

COMRIE,
Alexander: bpt 4-10-1743 d 1813 m Christina MacIntyre Pvt NY

COMSTOCK,
Aaron: b 10-20-1752 d 1-24-1834 m Ann Hanford Sgt CT W ★
Abel: b 1721 d 1814 m Judith Payne Pvt CT
Abijah: b 11-19-1721 d 6- -1797 m Deborah Benedict PS CT
Abner: b 12- -1727 d 3-22-1811 m Eunice Goodspeed Pvt CT
Adam: b 1-27-1740 d 4-10-1819 m Margaret McGregor LCol CS RI
Ansel: b 8-25-1762 d 7-28-1845 m Betsy Jewett Pvt CT
Anson: b 6-13-1764 d 9-5-1841 m Lorraine Bailey Pvt CT
Azariah: b 1714 d 1791 m Zeruiah Sprague PS NH
Caleb: b 4-12-1760 d 5-17-1834 m Lucy Mead Pvt CT
Daniel: b 1-6-1745 d 1816 m (1)Patience Jenckes (2)Sarah Fuller Pvt RI
Daniel: b 7-6-1742 d 1-11-1816 m Mary Bishop Capt VT
David: b 1-25-1754 d 5-11-1827 m (1)Rebecca Briggs (2)Hannah Parris Sol NY
Elisha: b 5-13-1737 d 9-24-1808 m Anna Fox Pvt CT
Enoch: b 7-29-1749 d 9-2-1807 m Anna Weed Sol CT
Gideon: b 11-4-1709 d 1801 m Ruth Arnold PS RI
Ichabod: b 3-17-1727 d 11-10-1800 m (1)Margaret Sackett (2)Catherine Smith Sgt MA
James: b 6-16-1712 d 9-6-1781 m Hannah Allen Lt CT
John: b 6-24-1734 d 10-23-1776 m Eunice Stoddard Lt CT
John: b 10-20-1722 d p. 12-17-1782 m Margaret Vibber Ens PS CT PA
John: b 4-9-1754 d 8-1-1834 m Charlotte Tinker Sgt CT
John: b 1722 d 1798 m Deborah Welch PS CT
Jonathan: b 9-7-1737 d 12-4-1784 m (1)Hannah Cass (2)Mary Angell (3)Hannah Reed Pvt PS CS RI
Jonathan: b 1730 d 1800 m (1)Sarah — (2)Susanna Matteson CS PS RI
Medad: b 8-11-1763 d 12-28-1842 m Elizabeth Lamb Pvt MA ★
Moses, Jr.: b 5-15-1749 d 3-14-1824 m (1)Betty Seymour (2)Lois Hoyt Pvt CT
Moses: b 11-9-1737 d 1802 m Bethia DuBois Pvt PS NH
Nathaniel: b 7-5-1740 d 12-23-1829 m (1)Sarah Bradford (2)Anna Stark Capt CT
Noah: b 1757 d 2-5-1825 m (1)Mary — (2)Hannah Lord Pvt CT
Oliver: b 9-15-1756 d 6-25-1820 m Amy — Cpl CT ★
Peregrine: b 11-11-1757 d 2-2-1849 m Polly Fox Sol CT
Peter: b 6-11-1731 d 4-30-1803 m (1)Elizabeth Fitch (2)Sarah Mirick Capt CT
Raynsford: b 3-6-1737 d 2-8-1814 m (1)Catherine Vibber (2)Aziba Davis Ens CT
Rufus: b 1727 d 4-17-1821 m (2)Mary Fargo Pvt MA
Samuel: b 1734 d 1823 m Laura Merritt Pvt CT

Samuel: b 7-7-1756 d 1852 m Hester Royce Pvt CT ★
Samuel: b 1725 d 9-3-1817 m Elizabeth Baldwin PS CT
Samuel: b 1738 d 1800 m Hannah Dwinell Pvt MA
Serajah: b 10-17-1758 d 2-23-1826 m (1)Ann Benedict (2)Clemina Austin Pvt CT
Simeon: b 1756 d p. 1820 m Amy — Cpl CT ★
Steven: b 4-13-1750 d 1833 m (1)Ruth Disbrow (2)Mary Benedict Pvt CT ★
Strong: b 1755 d 1-16-1814 m (1)Abigail Wescott (2)Betty Betts Pvt CT
Theophilus: b 10-5-1753 d 4-10-1829 m Lucinda (Comstock) Sgt CT ★
Thomas: b 1-26-1747 d 4-14-1812 m Phebe Sellack Pvt CT
Thomas: bpt 6-3-1739 d 8-16-1777 m Sarah (Comstock) Capt VT
Thomas: b 9-11-1745 d p. 1815 m Martha Matteson Lt RI
Wm.: b c. 1716/17 d 1787 m Ann Spink 1Lt RI

CONANT,
Abel: b 10-3-1755 d 5-2-1844 m (1)Margaret Jewett (2)Lydia Thurston Pvt MA ★
Amos: b 1-8-1753 d 6-21-1847 m Elizabeth Erskine Cpl PS NH
Andrew: b 8-22-1725 d 9-17-1805 m (1)Ruth Brooks (2)Mary — Capt PS MA
Benjamin: b 10-20-1740 d p. 1785 m Mary Davis 2Lt MA
Benjamin: b 8-29-1756 d 5-24-1836 m Elizabeth Hooper Pvt MA ★
Daniel: b 1740 d 7-20-1808 m Martha Cole Sgt MA ★
David: b 5-10-1759 d p. 1790 m — Drm Pvt MA
Ebenezer: b 8-11-1743 d 8-3-1783 m Lydia Oakes Lt MA
Ebenezer: b 10-12-1762 d p. 2-17-1846 m Eleanor — Pvt CT ★
Eleazer: b 6-29-1751 d 9-13-1819 m (1)Eunice Storrs (2)Betsey Cummins Sol CT
Eli: b 3-16-1741 d 5-26-1801 m (1)Elizabeth Gardner Lt MA
Elias: b 1749 d 1834 m Joanna Conant Pvt MA
Ephraim: b 1-4-1754 d 1-22-1836 m Rebecca Howard Pvt MA
Ezra: b 3-5-1723 d 12-7-1804 m (1)Millicent Newell (2)Mrs Anna Fiske Sol MA
Ezra: b 9-19-1730 d 1-20-1806 m Lucy Russell Pvt MA
Ezra: b 6-22-1750 d 2-2-1840 m Mary — Pvt MA
George, Sr.: b 1-13-1723 d 3-3-1792 m (1)Sarah Goodspeed (2)Susanna Crocker (3)Elizabeth Crocker (4)Lydia Freeman Pvt MA
George, Jr.: b 7-27-1762 d 2-22-1832 m Hannah Walden Pvt MA
James: b 9-3-1755 d 9-12-1842 m Dorothy Bullard Sgt MA ★
Jeremiah: b 1-28-1758 m (1)Mary Leonard (2)Chloe Pratt Sgt MA
John: b c. 1741 d 1797 m Sarah Farrar Sgt MA
John: b 1-25-1749/50 d 5-4-1844 m Deborah Perkins Pvt MA ★
John: b 8-29-1758 d p. 1793 m Sarah Leonard Pvt MA
John: b 1-3-1758 d 12-28-1829 m (1)Hulda Hubbard (2)Mrs Maria Goldsmith Pvt MA
Jonathan: b 10-25-1734 d 1820 m Jane Latham Sgt MA ★
Jonathan: b 2-3-1732/3 d p. 1-4-1790 m Eunice Farwell Pvt MA
Jonathan: b 8-9-1737 d 1787 m Mercy Lovett Clerk PM MA
Jonathan: b 4-16-1761 d 10-23-1810 m Irene Bennett Pvt NH
Joshua: b 2-6-1749 d 9-10-1777 m Mary Henderson Pvt PS NH
Josiah: b 9-15-1754 d 1804 m Ruth — Pvt CT
Josiah: b 11-19-1758 d 6-28-1835 m Annis Darby Pvt MA
Josiah: b 10-17-1746 d 8-21-1807 m (1)Elizabeth Elliot (2)Zeriah Fox Sgt NH
Lot: b 10-2-1735 d p. 1790 m Abigail Perkins Pvt MA
Luther: b 1-7-1758 d 5-13-1830 m Susannah Allen Sgt MA
Moses: bpt 2-22-1756 d — ,m Mary Wildes Pvt MA
Nathan: b 2-4-1743 d 6-26-1820 m (1)Betty Stevens (2)Esther Emory (3)Mrs Hannah (Pitts) Potter Cpl MA
Oliver: b 6-29-1754 d 9-16-1843 m Thankful Walker Cpl MA
Peter: b 8-3-1753 d 5-22-1825 m Jane Conant Sgt MA W ★
Peter, Sr.: bpt 10-29-1727 d 1785 m Sarah Gibson Sol MA
Peter, Jr.: b 5-26-1756 d 9-22-1833 m Elizabeth Fairbanks Cpl MA
Phineas: b 1-25-1759 d 1-23-1838 m Joanna Washburn Pvt MA ★
Roger: b 6-22-1748 d 1821 m Rhoda Randall Pvt MA
Rufus: b 3-27-1757 d p. 8-27-1832 m Thankful Leonard Pvt MA NH ★
Shebuel: b 12-23-1756 d 1829 m Anna Farley Sgt MA
Shubael: b 7-15-1710/11 d 9-16-1775 m (2)Ruth (Conant) PS CT
Silvanus: b 5-23-1741 d 6-22-1828 m Silvia Conant Sgt MA
Simeon: b 8-27-1762 d 6-3-1736 m Betsey Johnson Pvt MA
Solomon: b 3-12-1756 d 1-3-1825 m Lois Conant Sgt MA ★
Sylvanus: b 2-10-1750/51 d 9-5-1843 m Anna Royce Sgt CT ★
Timothy: b 11-21-1732 d 4-15-1777 m Hannah Blackman Pvt MA W★
Timothy: b 1752 d 3-5-1826 m Sarah Perry Sol MA
William: b 1746 d 7-28-1827 m Bethiah Lothrop Pvt MA ★
William: b 9-3-1747 d 5-8-1826 m Mary Perkins Pvt MA
Zebulon: b 10-29-1749 d — m Mary Wright Pvt MA

CONDÉ,
Adam: b 9-25-1748 d 9-22-1824 m Catelyntje Truax Pvt NY

CONDIT, (includes CONDICT)
Abner: b 8-1-1749 d 4-30-1837 m Martha Leonard Pvt NJ
Daniel: b 2-27-1723 d 11-11-1785 m Ruth Harrison Pvt NJ
Daniel: b 10-13-1756 d 9-23-1839 m Mary Dodd Pvt NJ ★
David: b 3-17-1734 d 4-24-1777 m Joanna Williams LCol NJ
Ebenezer: b 1736 d 4-3-1777 m Huldah Byram Capt NJ

CONDIT, contd.
Jabez: b 2-8-1739 d 11-22-1804 m Phebe Smith PS NJ
Isaac: b 7-19-1759 d 2-25-1829 m Phebe Baldwin Pvt NJ
Japhia: b 9-27-1763 d 4-5-1849 m (1)Dorcas Dodd (2)Phoebe
    Ogden Harrison Pvt NJ
Joel: b 1754 d 3-11-1833 m Sarah Wheeler Sgt NJ
John: b 1734 d 4-24-1777 m Joanna Williams LCol NJ
John: b 7-8-1755 d 5-4-1834 m (1)Abigail Halsey (2)Rhoda Halsey
    Dr NJ
Jonathan: b 10-18-1736 d 8-29-1823 m Jemima (Condit) Capt NJ
Joseph: b c. 1728 d 8-8-1776 m Rhoda Lindsley Lt NJ
Moses: b 1760 d 6-8-1838 m Hannah Smith Pvt NJ
Nathaniel: b 9-3-1746 d 10-2-1805 m Rhoda — Cpl NJ
Philip, Sr.: b 4- -1709 d 12-23-1801 m Mary Day PS NJ
Philip, Jr.: b 5-6-1753 d 9-22-1784 m Mary (Condit) Pvt NJ
Samuel: b 1761 d 8-31-1822 m Hannah Harrison Pvt NJ
Silas: b 3-7-1738 d 9-6-1801 m (1)Phoebe Day (2)Abigail Bryam
    PS NJ
Timothy: b 12-15-1740 d 9-9-1791 m Elizabeth Linsley Pvt NJ
Zenas: b 1739 d 12-20-1776 m Phebe Johnson Capt NJ
Zenos: b 1757 d 3-20-1829 m Hannah Pierson Pvt NJ

CONDON,
Benjamin: b 1751 d 11-30-1846 m Ruth Thomas Sol ME
Redmond: b c. 1753 d 1-8-1830 m Nancy — Pvt PA ★

CONDREY, (includes CONDRE)
Timothy: b 1731 d 4- -1815 m Elizabeth Beckett Pvt MA

CONDY,
Thomas Hollis: b 1757 d 8-29-1833 m Mary Aborn Capt MA

CONE,
Cephas: b 10-10-1756 d 2-27-1834 m (1)Sarah Gates (2)''Falla''
    Roberts Pvt CT
Conant: b 7-6-1760 d 1799 m Alice Houghton Pvt CT
Cyrus: b 7-28-1761 d 10-14-1825 m Rhoda Beebe Pvt CT
Daniel: b 7-7-1759 d 6-28-1843 m Olive Ackley Pvt CT ★
Daniel Hurlburt: b 7-16-1753 d 4-16-1841 m Elizabeth Atkins Pvt CT
Elijah, Sr.: b 8-11-1723 d 9-16-1793 m Elizabeth Cone Pvt CT
Elisha: b 12-1-1726 d 1-10-1783 m Abigail Olmsted Pvt CT
George, Jr.: b 6-3-1738 d 1-3-1801 m (1)Elizabeth Brainard
    (2)Demaris Saxton Lt CT
Giles: b 1741 d 10-25-1786 m Margaret — Sol Slr CT
Henry: b 1744 d 12-15-1827 m Waitstill Champion Pvt CT ★
Ichabod: b 1757 d 10-9-1831 m Anna Holmes Pvt CT
Israel: b 12-21-1749 d 11-4-1825 m (1)Lucy Ackley (2)Sarah
    Holmes Sgt PM CT
James: b 8-3-1729 d 10-31-1814 m Deborah Smith Sol CT
James, Jr.: b 9-4-1842 d 1-24-1897 m Alice Crocker Pvt CT
Jared, Sr.: b 12-31-1733 d 4-11-1807 m Christiana Loomis Capt CT
Jared, Jr.: b 6-24-1760 d 3-7-1842 m (1)Elizabeth Wells (2)Caroline
    Wales Webb Pvt NH
John: b 5-26-1746 d 10-5-1777 m Patience Strickland Pvt CT
Jonah: b 3-7-1721 d 7-24-1809 m Elizabeth Gates MM MA
Jonathan: b 9-27-1729 d p. 1781 m Elizabeth Smith Pvt NH
Joseph;: b 3-20-1711 d 2-1-1804 m Mary Smith PS CT
Joseph: b 1-26-1704 d 1779 m Susanna Wells PS CT
Joseph, Jr.: b 11-2-1735 d 1779 m Martha Brainard Spencer Pvt NS CT
Joshua: b 9-1-1757 d 7-22-1807 m Mehitable Blinn Sgt CT W★
Nathaniel: b 6-22-1748 d 6-27-1826 m Margery Adams Pvt CT ★
Oliver: b 12-2-1755 d 12-4-1844 m Anna Sterling Pvt CT ★
Oliver: b 1765 d 4-2-1829 m Esther Wellman Sol CT
Ozias: b 5-8-1747 d 3-6-1823 m Mary Doane Pvt CT ★
Phineas: b 9-27-1752 d 1833 m Azubah Stocking Cpl CT
Robert: b 1758 d 10-20-1821 m Sarah Cook Pvt CT W★
Robert: b 2-15-1759 d 5-19-1804 m Margaret Paget Pvt CT
Roswell: b 10-29-1753 d 6-27-1830 m Lydia Hungerford Pvt CT
Rufus: b 10-10-1737 d 8-27-1776 m Esther Stewart Pvt CT
Samuel: b 2-20-1748 d 4-22-1825 m Betsey Wadsworth Pvt CT
Solomon: b 1757 d 1816 m Sally Richmond Sgt CT
Solomon: b 9-2-1745 d 3-27-1805 m Mary Spencer Pvt CT
Sylvanus: b 1-21-1734 d 5-3-1812 m (1)Hannah Ackley (2)Mary
    Elizabeth Graves (3)Eunice Spencer Cpl CT
Timothy: b 5-25-1735 d 12-19-1800 m Abigail Dickson Sgt CT
William: b 3-14-1723 d 4-22-1793 m Elizabeth Bailey Capt CT
William: b 4-6-1755 d 1834 m Abia Atkins Pvt CT
William: b c. 1745 d p. 6-24-1816 m Keziah Barber Pvt GA
William: b c. 1758 d p. 1820 m — Beacham Pvt GA
William: b c. 1734 d p. 1796 m (1)Elizabeth Morris (2)Mrs. Hirst
    Pvt NC
Zachariah: b 6-23-1739 d c. 1802 m Mary Gilbert Pvt PS CT

CONEN,
William: b 1749 d 1779 m Mary Almond Fif VA

CONEY, (includes CONY)
Daniel: b 8-3-1752 d 1-21-1842 m Susanna Curtis 2Lt MA
John: b 3-26-1755 d 12-26-1838 m Lovina Patterson Sgt MA ★
John: b 7-6-1741 d 3-12-1797 m Keziah Holmes Pvt MA
Oliver: b 6-12-1749 d 12-13-1830 m Jane Adams Capt CS MA
William: b 3-29-1726 d 11-1-1805 m (1)Mehetable Ellis (2)Mary
    (Carr) Robbins Pvt MA

CONGDON,
James: b 1748 d 5- -1803 m (2)Rebecca Rider PS CS RI
James: b 11-23-1753 d 7-7-1839 m Hannah Nichols Pvt RI ★
James: b 3-28-1741 d 2-16-1829 m (1)Ruth Chase (2)Lydia
    Hedley PS RI
Job: b 8-1-1760 d 12-25-1820 m Freelove Matteson Pvt VT
John: b 3-17-1750 d 3-17-1832 m (1)Eunice Tillotson (2)Dorcas
    Huntly Sgt CT ★
John: b 2-28-1736 d 1-31-1827 m Abigail Rose Pvt RI
John: b 1760 d 4-22-1838 m Mary Bowers Pvt RI
Joseph; b 4-20-1733 d 6-16-1805 m Susanna Cross Capt RI
Samuel: b c. 1728 d p. 1785 m X PS RI
Stephen: b — d — m Martha Greenman Pvt RI
Thomas: b 3-25-1743 d 9-16-1828 m Miss Wescot Capt RI

CONGER,
David, Sr.: b c. 1740 d 1778 m Mary (Darby) Green Pvt NJ
David: b 9-7-1760 d 1-20-1807 m Elizabeth Ayres Pvt NJ
David: b 10-8-1740 d 7- -1827 m Mary Ellison Pvt NY
Enoch: b 1742 d 12-12-1801 m Susanna Whitehead Sol NJ
James: b 1-11-1760 d 11-11-1813 m Elizabeth McNab Pvt NY
Job: b 1755 d 11-8-1827 m Rahab Potter Pvt VT
John: b 1743 d 9-13-1797 m Mary Dunham Pvt NJ
John, Sr.: b c. 1710 d p. 2-7-1784 m Zipporah — PS NC
John, Jr.: b 1751 d 1793 m Mary Ross Ens NC
Jonathan: b 1-22-1732 d 5-7-1793 m Euphemia Ross QMSgt NC
Joseph: b 3-7-1758 d 12-8-1842 m Phebe Eggleston Pvt CT
Joseph: b 12-11-1748 d 1820 m (1)Rhoda — (2)Sarah Lampson
    PS NJ
Reuben: b 4-4-1756 d 4-7-1820 m Magdalen Devoe Sgt NY
Stephen W..: b c. 1750 d 4-18-1806 m Perina Bower Pvt NJ
Uzziah: b 1-14-1758 d 6-21-1841 m Mary Hungerford Cpl NY

CONGLETON,
Moses: b 10-4-1763 d 11-6-1838 m Mary Grimes Mus PA ★
William: b 1741/42 d a. 1811 m Jean — Sol NC

CONKEY,
Alexander: b 1754 d 1-17-1847 m Mary Pebels Pvt MA ★
Asa: b — d 8- -1804 m Margaret Hamilton Cpl NY
Dinah Dick: b 12-1-1738 d 6-2-1792 m Joshua Conkey PS NY
James: b 1771 d 5-4-1795 m Isabel McLancton Pvt MA
Jonas: b 7-14-1754 d 4-3-1817 m Ruth Bridge Sgt MA
Joshua: b 3- -1760 d 1840 m Millicent Bridge Sol MA
Joshua: b 1735 d 11-30-1814 m (1)Dinah Dick (2)Sarah Sears QM
    Capt NY

CONKLIN, (includes CONCKLIN, CONKCLYN, CONKLING)
Abraham: bpt 5-15-1739 d p. 1806 m (1)Sarah Carpenter
    (2)Charlotte Tappan Pvt NY
Benjamin: b 10-25-1743 d 4-8-1808 m Bethiah Reeves Pvt PS NY
Benjamin: b 1757 d 10-13-1832 m Esther Hand Sol PS NY
Cornelius: b 4-7-1727 d 9-11-1791 m Elizabeth Rogers Capt NY
Daniel: b 4-24-1737 d 9-25-1816 m (1)Abigail Parsons (2)Hannah
    Hutchinson Ens NY
Daniel: bpt 1718 d 10-26-1800 m Abegail Davis PS Pvt NY
Daniel: b 11-26-1751 d 1819 m (1)Susannah Roe (2)Hannah Brooks
    Pvt NY
David: b 6-1-1750 d 1854 m Mary Hays Lt NY ★
David: b 8-24-1744 d 12-3-1787 m Sybil Wheeler PS NY
Edward: b 9-29-1745 d 1779 m Elizabeth — Capt Pvtr CT
Edward: b 7-24-1732 d 6-7-1805 m Deborah Dayton PS NY
Elias: b 9-15-1758 d 2-20-1839 m Charlotte — Pvt NJ NY ★
Elias: b — d a. 6-26-1785 m Elizabeth Hedges PS NY
Elisha: b 3-4-1720 d 1-17-1804 m (2)Elizabeth Dayton Pvt NY
Ezekiel: b 11-17-1740 d 10-23-1820 m Mary Titus PS NY
Ezra: b 10-31-1756 d 2-17-1815 m Sarah Platt Cpl NY
Francis: b 1756 d 7-11-1846 m Hester Brown Pvt NY ★
Isaac: b 5-27-1739 d 2-25-1809 m Caroline Van Benschoten Capt NY
Isaac: b 8-1-1736 d 9-16-1814 m Mary Lockwood Pvt NY
Isaac: b 6-8-1753 d 9-13-1840 m (2)Phoebe Briggs Pvt NY ★
Jacob: bpt 5-26-1741 d 1813 m (1)Katrina Van Benschoten
    (2)Margaret Rump Capt NY
Jacob: b 6-13-1724 d 7-24-1809 m Sarah — PS Ens NY
Jeremiah: b 3-11-1722 d 1784 m Mary Dayton Sgt PS NY
Jeremiah: b 12-14-1758 d 9-13-1840 m Tamar Tompkins Pvt NY
John: b 1758 d 1822 m Mary Parvin MM NJ
John: b 5-8-1756 d 4-23-1846 m Ursula Van Noy Sgt NY ★
John, Jr.: b 3-14-1755 d p. 1803 m Elizabeth Rohrback Pvt NY
John: b 8-20-1700 d 1785 m Annatje Storm PS NY
John: b 11-9-1727 d 1789 m Jane Drake Pvt NY
John: b 4-14-1759 d 6-13-1832 m (1)Elizabeth Barmore (2)Vasti
    — Sol NY
John: b 1720 d 8-4-1796 m (1)Anna Young (2)Desire — PS NY
Jonathan: b 10-4-1726 d p. 1785 m Elizabeth Hempsted PS NY
Joseph: b 1729 d 2-24-1779 m Mary Cory Pvt NJ
Joshua, Sr.: b 3-10-1727 d 1-20-1806 m Sarah Halsey Pvt Tms NJ
Joshua, Jr.: b 5-5-1759 d 2-16-1815 m Polly Johnson Pvt NJ
Laurence: b — d a. 4-10-1813 m Annatie Shurrie Pvt NY
Lemuel: b 8-27-1739 d 11-20-1810 m (1)Susannah Hains (2)Mary
    — Pvt NY
Matthew: b 3-17-1747 d p. 1795 m Sarah Valentine Sol PS NY
Nathan: b 4-26-1758 d 1-12-1843 m Amy Mulford Pvt NY

Nathaniel, Sr.: b 1739/40 d 12-6-1815 m Martha — Sgt PS NJ NY
Nicholas: bpt 9-13-1724 d 1815 m Elizabeth Van Ditman Pvt NY
Samuel: b 2-19-1726 d 5-15-1802 m Abigail Datan Lt PS NY
Stephen, Sr.: b 9-2-1721 d 9-8-1791 m Deborah Dimon Mil NJ
Stephen, Jr.: b 5-10-1751 d 8-31-1788 m Rachel Lindsley Pvt NJ
Thomas: b 4-1-1730 d 3-26-1802 m Mary (Conklin) Pvt NY
Thomas: b 1753 d 1831 m Anna Hallock Pvt NY
Thomas, Jr.: b 1756 d 6-7-1834 m Anna Kelsey Pvt NY
Thomas, Jr.: b 1733 d 2-4-1783 m Phebe Glover PS NY
Timothy: b 1754 d 10-17-1831 m Mary Platt Lt NY
William: b a. 1739 d 1777 m Anna Case Ens NJ
William: b c. 1750 d 1830 m Elizabeth Brink Ens NY
William: b 7-18-1752 d p. 1799 m Susannah Wood Sgt NY

CONN,
George: b c. 1716 d 2-21-1796 m Mary — Pvt MA
James: b 10-16-1725 d 3-26-1798 m (1)Mary — (2)Ruth — PS MD
John: b 1740 d 6-3-1803 m Ruth Davis Lt CS MA
Robert: b — d 1798 m Elizabeth Cain Pvt MD
Samuel: b 1760 d 1841 m — Pvt VA ★
Thomas: b 1733 d a. 5- -1815 m Sarah Mattox Capt VA
Wm.: b 1760 d 9-18-1836 m Elizabeth Alexander Pvt Grd NC SC W★

CONNELL, (includes CONNAL)
Giles: b c. 1744 d a. 6-2-1804 m Elizabeth Gibbs PS SC
Jesse: b 1747 d 8-15-1826 m Nancy Ann Lawson Pvt SC
John: b 1737 d p. 1787 m Barbara Neile Pvt NY
Zachariah: b 1741 d a. 8-26-1813 m (1)Ann Crawford (2)Margaret Wallace Pvt PA

CONNELLY, (Includes CONERLY, CONLEY, CONNALLY)
Arthur, Sr.: b c. 1730 d p. 9-12-1804 m Jean — Pvt CS VA
Cullen: b c. 1745 d p. 11-11-1811 m Felisa — Sol NC
Daniel: b c. 1763 d 1-3-1851 m Sarah O'Brien Cpl MD
Henry: b c. 1748 d 5-7-1840 m (1)Ann MacGregor (2)Temperance Hitchcock Capt NC ★
John: b 1762 d 4-3-1849 m Elizabeth Turner Pvt MD ★
John: b 1737 d 7-16-1826 m Jane Ballew Capt NC W★
John: b 1749 d p. 1790 m Elizabeth Donaldson Pvt NC
John: b 12-25-1755 d 2-23-1827 m Ann Little CaptLt PA
John: b c. 1750 d a. 7-12-1778 m Rachel Morris Cpl VA
John: b 8-22-1757 d p. 1-14-1848 m — Pvt VA ★
John: b a. 1765 d a. 9-7-1807 m Sicily Moore Mus VA
John Wm.: b 12-5-1765 d p. 1819 m Obedience — Sgt GA
Michael: b 1750 d 12-19-1841 m (1)Peggy Green (2)Rebecca Braddock Pvt MD
Michael: b c. 1745 d 1806 m Naomi — Pvt NY
Patrick: b 1749 d 10-27-1817 m Elizabeth Allen PS PA
Thomas: b a. 1745 d 2-3-1794 m Hannah — Pvt PA
Thomas: b c. 1725 d 1783 m Mary Van Horlinger Pvt SC
Thomas: b a. 1750 d c. 1835 m Polly Price Fif VA
Thomas: b 1740 d c. 1785 m Mary Dunlevy Sol VA

CONNETT,
Wm.: b c. 1750 d c. 1790 m Ann Smith Pvt NJ

CONNOR, (includes CONNER)
Benjamin: b 4-8-1748 d 12-29-1835 m (1)Miss Griffin (2)Abigal Warner NCapt MA
Cornelius, Sr.: b c. 1730 d a. 1806 m Mrs Margaret Nolan Lt PA
Edward: b — d 12- -1836 m Sarah Wingate Lt SC
James: b c. 1755 d 1806 m Martha Marley Pvt MD
James: b 1766 d 1846 m Polly Barker Pvt SC
James: b c. 1737 d a.1-7-1807 m Eleanor Lucas Pvt PS NH
James: b 1751-53 d 4-11-1836 m Lillis Wilson Sol NC
John: b 7-23-1758 d p. 12-20-1815 m Sarah Lankford Pvt MD
John: b 10-14-1753 d 3-2-1836 m (1)Elizabeth Wiltse (2)Desire Hall OrdlSgt NY ★
John: b c. 1740 d p. 12-27-1790 m Elizabeth Jennings Sgt VA
John: b 1755 d p. 1800 m Mary Brothers Pvt VA
John: b c. 1748 d 1807 m Mary Ann — Pvt VA
John: b c. 1700 d 1796 m Rebecca — CS PS VA
John Thing: b 7-16-1745 d 6-20-1808 m Susanna Kimball Cpl NH
Joseph: b 12-1-1743 d p. 1781 m Hannah Chase Pvt MA
Lewis: b 1757 d 1794 m Catherine — Pvt SC
Lewis: b 11- -1746 d 6-1-1832 m (1)Mrs Susan Mallory Davis (2)Mrs Farrow Mil VA
Maximilian: b 10-14-1762 d 11-27-1834 m Phebe Bishop Pvt SC ★
Moses: b — d c. 7-3-1801 m Sarah — Cpl PS NH
Philip: b 11-1-1754 d 2-13-1834 m X Pvt VA ★
Phillip: b 9-25-1733 d p. 1790 m Patience Fiske Pvt PS NH
Richard: b 1718 d 4-17-1808 m Margaret — Sol VA
Richard: b 1753 d 1824 m Henrietta Hennar Pvt VA
Samuel: b 5-3-1704 d 1787 m Sarah Gilman PS Dr NH
Terence: b 1752 d 12-16-1841 m Sarah J. Speaks Pvt VA ★
Thomas: b 1738 d c. 1800 m Esther Ann Fakes Sgt PA
Thomas: b c. 1760 d a. 1844 m (1)Catharine Harris (2)Miss Vansant Pvt PA
Thomas: b 1727 d 9-12-1802 m Ann — PS SC
Timothy: b 1751 d 8-29-1815 m Geraldine — Pvt PA

CONOVER, (includes CONNOVER, COUWENHOVEN, COVENOVER)
Cornelius: b 7-29-1740 d 7-12-1796 m Jane Denise Pvt NJ
David: b c. 1750 d a. 11-7-1809 m — Pvt NJ
Garret: b 11-5-1716 d 12-9-1797 m Eleanor H. Schenck PS NJ
Garret: b 1756 d 3-26-1826 m Lydia Tilton Pvt NJ
Garret B.: b 12-31-1760 d 12-18-1824 m Lydia Forman Pvt NJ
John: b c. 1740 d a. 5-5-1781 m (1)Catherine — (2)Loetitia Covenover Pvt NJ
John: b 1746/47 d 5-20-1832 m Catherine Covert Pvt PA
Joseph: b 1739 d 4-6-1814 m Mary — Sgt NJ
Levi: b 10-10-1757 d 1-18-1837 m (1)Catherine dye (2)Mrs Jane Gilbraith Turnbow Pvt NJ ★
Lewis: b 9-1-1752 d 5-27-1843 m Rachel Scott Sgt NJ ★
Micajah: b a. 1730 d 2-3-1797 m Deborah Stanton Pvt NJ
William: b 1743 d 1832 m Mary Covert Pvt NJ
Wm.: b 3-13-1726 d p. 1790 m Elizabeth Amack PS NJ

CONRAD, (includes COONROD)
Adam: b 5-2-1744/45 d 12-25-1835 m Sarah Runyon Pvt Tms NJ ★
Charles: b 1757 d 1805 m — Matr PA
Daniel: b 1740 d 5-12-1812 m Barbara — Pvt PA
Frederick: b 1759 d 8-3-1827 m (1)Cathrina Schneider (2)Catherine Anslee Ens PA
George: b 1743 d 1797 m Catherine — ILt PA
Jacob: b 1753 d 1827 m Barbara Keller Ens PA
Jacob: b 2-3-1717 d 9-5-1798 m Maria Catherina — PS PA
Jacob, Jr.: b 5-11-1744 d 1-26-1829 m (1)Hannah Bogart (2)Barbara Propst Pvt VA
John: b c. 1760 d 1840-50 m Catherine Adams Pvt MD
John: b 9-5-1757 d p. 5-6-1836 m — Pvt PA ★
John: b 1762 d 9-7-1844 m Hannah Hackett Pvt PA
Joseph: b 6- -1759 d 1822 m Anna Maria Seitzinger Cpl PA
Matthew: b 7-4-1733 d 11-23-1793 m Mary Roberts Cpl PA
Peter: b 8-16-1737 d 11-22-1789 m Veronica Heller Lt PA
Rudolph: b — d p. 7-6-1782 m (1)— Schuford (2)— Shell (3)Christina Stockinger PS NC
Stephen: b a. 1760 d 8-12-1822 m Mary Margaret Moyers Capt VA
Woollery, Sr.: b c. 1710 d p. 1782 m Margaret — PS VA
Woolery, Jr.: b a. 1756 d p. 2-15-1814 m Elizabeth Drestern Pvt VA

CONREY,
John: b 4-22-1760 d 9-12-1834 m Sarah Calvin Pvt NY ★
Samuel: b 4-24-1754 d 5-31-1826 m Alice Blood Pvt NH

CONROW,
Darling: b 10-28-1746 d 3-24-1788 m Sarah Elkinton CS NJ

CONSAUL,
David: b c. 1763 d a. 5-7-1818 m Tanneke Clute Pvt NY

CONSER,
George: b 1752 d 1828 m Elizabeth Miller Pvt PA

CONSOLVER,
Charles: b 1732 d 1-17-1781 m Mary Ann — Pvt VA

CONSTABLE,
William K.: b 1-1-1752 d 5-22-1803 m Anna White ADC FrA

CONSTANT,
John, Sr.: b c. 1725-30 d 12- -1810 m (1)Sarah — (2)Elizabeth — Sol VA
John, Jr.: b c. 1750 d 1788 m Abagail — Capt VA

CONSTANTIN,
Pierre: b 1-5-1736 d 1-8-1811 m Marie Louise Bidot Sol FrA

CONTEE,
John: b 1722 d 1-2-1796 m Margaret Snowden PS MD
Richard Alexander: b c. 1750 d 11- -1818 m (1)Mary Crawford (2)Mrs Elizabeth Gassaway Rawlings Sanders Ens MD
Thomas: b c. 1729 d 1- -1811 m Sarah Fendall Col PS MD

CONTURIER,
John: b c. 1750 d 1783 m Martha — Capt SC

CONVEAR,
Jacob: b 5-12-1760 d 3-19-1827 m Elizabeth Reed Pvt PA

CONVERSE, (includes CONVERS)
Alpheus: bpt 8-23-1752 d 3-5-1817 m Jerusha Elliot Pvt CT
Amasa: b 6-8-1750 d 3-9-1826 m (1)Olive — (2)Mrs Sarah Cleveland Sgt MA
Benjamin: b 10-14-1732 d 3-6-1824 m Sarah Wright Pvt MA
Chester: b 12-7-1755 d 10-24-1815 m Esther Green Pvt MA
Damon Reed: b 3-18-1764 d 7-3-1834 m Sarah Lee Pvt CT
Edward, Sr.: b 11- -1720 d 12-9-1800 m Mary Davis CS MA
Edward, Jr.: b 6-6-1747 d 4-9-1816 m Phebe Perrin Drm Pvt MA
Elijah: b 6-20-1745 d 6-14-1820 m Experience Hibbard Pvt MA

CONVERSE, contd.

Elisha: b 3-13-1758 d 2-15-1843 m (1)Mary Bishop (2)Mary Wells Pvt CT
Israel: b 8-17-1743 d 3-28-1806 m (1)Sarah Lewis (2)Hannah Walbridge Capt CT
James: b 1757 d 4-26-1817 m (1)— Whiteman (2)Sally Larrabee Wheeler Pvt CT
James: b 9-2-1725 d 7-16-1811 m Dorothy Carter Col MA
Jeremiah: b 8-4-1761 d 6-26-1837 m Rhoda (Converse) Pvt MA
Jesse: b 9-1-1745 d 7-8-1805 m Mary Moulton Pvt CT
Joel: b 9-12-1750 d 6-29-1822 m (1)Demaris Wilson (2)Elizabeth Bixby Sol CT
Jonathan: b 1-27-1760 d 10-25-1845 m Esther Whipple Pvt CT
Joseph: b 11-13-1739 d 2-16-1828 m Elizabeth Davis Sgt MA
Joshua: b 1760-62 d p. 1810 m Mary Trask Pvt CT
Josiah, Sr.: b 3-2-1710 d 9-11-1775 m Eleanor Reed Richardson PS CT
Josiah, Jr.: b 6-4-1737 d 10-25-1814 m Elizabeth Lewis Capt CT
Josiah, Sr.: b 1-27-1733 d 1810 m Hepsibah Brooks Pvt MA
Josiah, Jr.: b 3-14-1759 d — m Martha Tidd Pvt MA
Jude: b 6-11-1750 d 10-23-1816 m Abigail Alden Drm Pvt CT
Pain, Sr.: b 11-25-1706 d 9-10-1781 m Mary Halford PS CT
Pain, Jr.: b 10-28-1739 d 3-29-1800 m Mary Lee Capt CT
Robert: b 3-20-1737 d p. 1800 m Sarah Newton Pvt NH
Samuel Davis: b 2-1-1741 d c. 1820 m Elizabeth Harris Pvt NH
Solvin: b 4- -1758 d 5-3-1813 m Sarah Holmes Pvt CT W★
Stephen: b 8-16-1745 d 10-2-1823 m (1)Zurviah Sanger (2)Sarah Kimbal OrdsSgt MA W★
Thomas: b 11-5-1738 d 1809 m (1)Mary Morse (2)Abigail Colton (3)Sabrina Smedley (4)Mary Colton Capt CT
Zebulon: b 3-21-1744 d 11-10-1805 m Sarah Merriam PS NH

CONVIS,

James: b c. 1735 d a. 1810 m Lucy — Pvt RI

CONWAY, (includes CONAWAY)

Catlett: b 12-25-1751 d 9-14-1827 m Susannah Fitzhugh Capt VA
Elizabeth Bridgewater: b — d 7-30-1809 m John Conway, Sr. PS VA KY
Francis: b 3-7-1748 d 2-13-1794 m Elizabeth Fitzhugh Capt VA
Henry: b 1745 d 5- -l812 m Sara Hundley Capt VA
James: b a. 1756 d 12-28-1776 m Mary — Lt VA
John: b c. 1749 d a. 4-1-1800 m (1)Sarah Kelley (2)Sarah Laskin (3)Mrs Mary (Cole) Burns (4)Mrs Martha Bowen Pvt Cdr MA
John: b 1-23-1742 d 1- -1802 m Jane Compton LCol NJ
John, Sr.: b c. 1730 d 12-4-1801 m Elizabeth Bridgewater PS VA
John: b 10-6-1762 d 10-25-1841 m Rachel Willison Sol VA
John: b 9-12-1757 d 4- -1842 m Mary Berry Pvt VA
John Spann: b c. 1740 d 8- -1803 m Susannah Chapline Capt CS MD
Joseph: b 12-14-1763 d 12-27-1830 m Elizabeth Caldwell PS VA
Michael: b 1-27-1738 d p. 1803 m Elizabeth Davis Smn MD
Miles Withers: b 1753 d 1822 m Susanna — Sol VA
Richard: b 1762 d p. 5-15-1855 m Polly — Pvt VA ★
Robert: b c. 1753 d 12-8-1823 m (1)Juliana Easton (2)Mrs. Susannah Beaty Crowson Sol SC
Robert: b 5-10-1749 d p. 1790/91 m — Lt CL NCapt VA
Samuel: b 4-30-1748 d 8-20-1833 m Rebecca Smith Pvt MD ★
Samuel: b 10-23-1756 d 9-17-1830 m (1)Elizabeth Clemmons (2)Mrs Margery Miller Cpl VA
Thomas: b 3-1-1755 d 2-14-1824 m Sarah Duh Pvt PS PA
William: bpt 2-27-1742 d 7-8-1823 m Ruth Adams Pvt MD
William: b 1742 d p. 1810 m Jane — Lt VA

CONWELL,

Jehu: b 2-15-1748 d 12-14-1834 m Elizabeth Stokely PS PA
William: b 1-13-1760 d 1-13-1831 m Nancy King Pvt DE
William: b 7-12-1746 d 1820 m Comfort Coulter Capt PA

CONYERS,

Charles: b 1757 d 3-15-1843 m (1)Ann McConnico (2)Elizabeth Dukes Pvt SC
Daniel: b c. 1748 d 1809 m Mary Witherspoon Capt SC
James, Sr.: b 5-24-1718 d a. 1784 m Mary McIntosh Sol SC
James, Jr.: b c. 1748 d 9- -1781 m Susanna Nelson Maj SC
John: b c. 1725 d 1814 m Sarah Miller Capt GA
John: b 1732 d 1808 m Rebecca Bowen CS GA
John: b 4- -1750 d c. 1812 m Sarah Barnard Sol NC
Richard: b 1730 d 1792 m Margaret Arrendal Sol NC

CONYN,

Casparus: b 2-19-1725 d 2-24-1805 m Tryntjie Van Wie Capt NY

CONYNE,

Peter: b 1753 d 5-6-1832 m Susan Mabee Adj NY

CONYNGHAM,

David Hayfield: b 3-21-1756 d 3-5-1834 m Mary West Sol PA

COOCH,

Thomas: b c. 1700 d 11- -1788 m Sarah Lowen Col DE

COODE,

John: b 1756 d p. 1795 m Drayden Hebb PS MD

COOK, (includes COOKE)

Aaron: b 10-1-1745 d 5-19-1804 m Lydia Preston Pvt CT
Aaron: b 2-21-1728 d 1-24-1800 m Ann Sheldon Pvt MA
Aaron: b 12-3-1746 d 4-1-1836 m Rachel Clark Pvt MA
Abel: b c. 1755 d 1790/1 m Catharine Bailey Pvt PA
Abial: b 1763 d 7-28-1849 m (1)Margaret Crego (2)Julia Anna Barras Pvt NY ★
Abner: b 1736 d 4-23-1817 m Rhoda Thompson Pvt MA
Abraham: b 6-1-1754 d 12-3-1843 m (1)Isabelle Rowe (2)Elizabeth Carpenter Pvt CT ★
Abram: b 1721 d 1800 m (3)Elizabeth — PS NC
Ambrose: b 3-17-1744 d 3- -1824 m Esther Peck Pvt CT
Ananias: b 1-12-1761 d 4-15-1852 m Sarah Butler Pvt RI
Andrew: b 1-1-1736 d 3-3-1814 m — Pvt MA
Andrew: b 1730 d 1783 m Ann Cook Pvt PA
Anthony: b 4-8-1742 d 7-8-1812 m Sarah Alloway Pvt PA
Ariel: b 10-15-1749 d 6-18-1803 m Dorcas Whipple Pvt RI
Arthur: b 11-30-1760 d 10-6-1846 m Philena Ballou Sol MA
Arthur: b c. 1725 d 1794 m Martha — Pvt NC
Asaph, Sr.: b 6-22-1720 d 1792 m Sarah Parker Capt CS VT
Asaph, Jr.: b 3-6-1748 d 1826 m Thankful Parker Capt NY
Atwater: b 11-3-1758 d 6-29-1839 m Mary Bartholomew Pvt CT
Barton: b 1-7-1732/3 d 12-4-1818 m Hannah Tracy Lt CT
Benajah: b 12-19-1759 d 11-8-1839 m Cassandra Fanning Pvt CT
Benjamin: b c. 1742 d 8-8-1800 m Effy — Pvt GA
Benjamin: b 1760 d 2-27-1846 m Nancy Dixon Pvt GA ★
Benjamin: b 8-16-1742 d 12-2-1790 m Lydia Hammond Sol MM MA
Benjamin: b 3-24-1760 d p. 1790 m (1)Tabitha Lake (2)Naomy Shrieve Pvt NJ
Benjamin: b 4-3-1739 d 12- -1785 m Sibbel Tyler PS SC
Benjamin: b 5-20-1740 d 1-5-1820 m Anne Slaughter Pvt VA
Benjamin: b 1758 d 1824 m Sallie Fuqua Sol VA
Burrell: b c. 1760 d p. 1798 m Mary Pope Sol SC
Caleb: b 11-14-1741 d 1821 m Abigail Finch MM MA
Casper: b — d p. 2-29-1828 m Catharina Lauchs Pvt NY
Charles: b 9-24-1747 d 1-14-1817 m Anna Greene Pvt RI
Charles: b 6-13-1741 d p. 1776 m Sybil Munson MM CT
Christopher: b 1756 d p. 1790 m — Lt PA
Colman: b 8-3-1747 d 12-20-1835 m Hannah Smith Pvt MA
Daniel: b 8-19-1720 d 1778 m Elizabeth Pond PS CT
Daniel: b 9-12-1722 d 11-11-1795 m Elizabeth Scott Pvt MA
Daniel: b 10-22-1763 d 1806 m Rebecca Pomeroy Pvt MA
Daniel: b 6-7-1732 d c. 1794 m Abigail Blackman Pvt MA
Daniel: b 5-29-1740 d 2-4-1811 m Sallie Morse Pvt MA
Daniel: b12-10-1739 d 1791 m Rebecca Owen Maj NJ
Daniel: b 1760 d 1846 m Nancy McNeeley Sol NC
Darius: b 1756 d 1845 m Elizabeth — Pvt NY ★
David: b 10-1-1752 d 3-9-1841 m(1)Mary—(2)Alice Butler Ens NJ
David: b 2-25-1756 d p. 3-13-1798 m Sarah — PS Ens KY
David: b 1720 d 12-15-1814 m Hannah Topping Pvt PS NY
David:b10-12-1731d3-16-1816 mAlice Bradford(Cook) Ens Lt RI
David: b 3-17-1753 d 1844 m Elizabeth Arnold Sgt Fif RI ★
Ebenezer, Jr.: b 10-12-1746 d 3-20-1813 m (1)Abigail West (2)Abigail Meeks 1Lt MA
Edward: b 3-22-1760 d 2-7-1842 m Ann Thomas Pvt NC ★
Edward: b 1740 d c. 1805 m (1)Ann — Pvt PA
Edward: b 1738 d 11-27-1808 m Martha Crawford Col PA
Edward Patterson: b 5-24-1733 d 7-26-1826 m Lydia Chandler Pvt NJ
Eli: b 1758 d 8-7-1836/7 m Hannah Houston Pvt NY
Eliakim: b 12-21-1745 d 3-5-1808 m Mary Colburn Cpl MA
Elihu: b 1-16-1753 d 4-5-1801 m Cynthia Frink Cpl MA
Elijah: b 9-11-1759 d 6-30-1839 m Charity Lockwood Pvt CT ★
Elisha: b 2-22-1715 d 3-7-1794 m Sarah (Cook) Pvt MA
Elisha: b 3-10-1717 d 1799 m (1)Rebecca Egerton (2)Sarah Jackson Doty (3)Mary Brown (4)Abigail Brown Pvt NJ
Ellis: b 3-7-1732 d 4-17-1797 m (1)Margaret Griswold Crocker (2)Lucy (Ely) Perkins Col NJ
Ellis: b c. 1740 d c. 1830 m Isabel Davis Wgm NJ
Enoch: b 1-4-1744 d 5-3-1827 m Mary Foster Sgt MA
Ephraim: b 5-7-1730 d 1-18-1789 m — Capt CT
Ephraim: b 1744 d 2-12-1826 m Phebe Tyler Capt CT
Ephraim: b 4-17-1756 d 4-30-1824 m Hannah Crosby Sgt MA
Ezekiel: b 6-19-1744 d 6- -1821 m Jerusha Ballou 2Lt MA
Francis: b 7-26-1758 d — m Sarah Berce Pvt MA
George: b c. 1752 d c. 1800 m Elizabeth Johnson NCapt MD
George: b 11-18-1764 d 9-4-1837 m X Pvt NC
George: b 10-23-1751 d 9-24-1842 m Rebecca Ankeny Pvt PA
George: b 1-10-1760 d 3-7-1850 m (1)Elizabeth Barkley (2)Rachael Troutman Pvt MA
George: b 5-22-1762 d c. 1835 m Mary M Groat Pvt PA
Harmon, Sr.: b c. 1730 d 5-10-1810 m Mary Agness CS VA
Henry: b 1742-7 d 1803 /4 m Mary — Capt VA
Henry, 1st: b 1754 d 1810 m (2)Margaret Bennett Pvt MD
Isaac, 1st: b 7-22-1710 d 3-16-1780 m Jerusha Sexton Capt CT
Isaac, 2d: b 7-28-1739 d 6-24-1810 m Martha (Cook) LCol CT
Isaac, 3d: b 7-16-1768 d 1-22-1842 m Margaret Scott Sct CT
Isaac: b 1761 d 1837 m Mrs. Ann (Stephens) Masterson Sgt PA
Isaac: b 6-21-1745 d 4-18-1826 m Lydia Gray Capt RI
Israel: b 12-4-1750 d 12- -1822 m Phebe Vinton Lt MA
Jacob: b — d 1736 d 2-8-1786 m (1)Katherine Camp (2)Rhoda — Capt MA
Jacob: b 10-23-1744 d 3-2-1806 m Joanna Williams Sol NJ

Jacob: b a. 1743 d 11-12-1789 m Rosetta Hall LCol PA
Jacob: b c. 1730 d a. 2-9-1792 m Susannah Road Pvt PA
Jacob: b c. 1746 d 1791 m Elizabeth Small Pvt PA
Jacob: b 4-19-1725 d 4-12-1808 m (1)Phebe Lindley (2)Margaret — PS CS VA
James: b 1755 d 1797 m Lucy Hall Drm MA
James: b 3-25-1760 d 3-26-1836 m (1)Elizabeth Phebe Condict (2)Ruth Woodbridge Pierson (3)Susan — Pvt NJ
James: b 1763 d 4-19-1851 m (1) X (2)Diana Brown Pvt NY ★
James, Jr.: b 8-17-1753 d 10- -1831 m (1)Esther Galbraith (2)Martha McCombs Lt Capt PA
James: b 12-14-1750 d 11-23-1804 m Susan Angell CS VA
Jesse: b 2-1-1739 d 6-22-1784 m Amanda Cook Capt CT
Jesse: b 1718 d 6-11-1792 m Submit Root Pvt CT
Jesse: b 17-8-1732 d p. 1790 m Prudence Johnson Pvt CT
Joel:: b 10-12-1760 d 12-8-1851 m Rebecca Hart Cpl CT ★
Joel: b 9-5-1746 d 10-15-1836 m Dinah Dunbar Pvt CT ★
Joel: b 1764 d 1795 m Kiturah Miers Sgt NJ
John, Jr.: b 5-16-1758 d 2-25-1847 m Thankful Eccleston Sol CT
John: b 6-4-1719 d 4-8-1779 m Rachel Wilson CS CT
John: b 1730 d 1789 m Elizabeth — CS Capt DE
John: b 3-12-1758 d 8-11-1822 m (1)Ida Van Liew (2)Rachel Bryson Pvt MD
John: b 9-13-1735 d 2-10-1810 m Molly Godfrey Ens MA
John: b 4-11-1726 d 2- -1805 m Mrs. Elizabeth (Smith) Smith Pvt MA
John: bpt 9-2-1754 d 8-5-1833 m Sarah Edwards Pvt MA
John: b 8-23-1730 d — m Mary (Downs 7) Pvt MA
John: b 1740 d 3-23-1804 m Magdalen Dillenbeck Sgt NY
John, Jr.: b 11-14-1748 d 3- -1810 m (1)Abigail — (2)Dorothy Parker Pvt NY
John: b 10- -1744 d 12-17-1812 m Sarah Gray Col RI
John: b 11-16-1756 d 1-4-1841 m Thankful Tripp Pvt RI ★
John: b c. 1740 d 1799 m (1)Betty Brown (2)Martha Ann Pearson Capt SC VA NC
John: b 1754 d 11-21-1832 m (1)Nellie Pemberton (2)Ann Keatley Pvt VA
John: b 1755 d 1824 m Elizabeth Drewry Pvt VA
John Conrad: b 1746 d 1-11-1837 m Phoebe Bunker Pvt VT
John Wanton: b 2-25-1762 d 5-22-1846 m (1)Lois Seaman (2)Phoebe (Cook) (3)Diantha Herrabel Pvt RI
Jonathan: b 1-17-1722 d p. 1775 m Ruth Goodman MM MA
Jonathan: b 2-3-1738 d 1- -1821 m Lydia Bacon Pvt MA
Jonathan: b 7-22-1753 d p. 1790 m Marcy Tilton Pvt MA
Jonathan: b 1754 d p. 1781 m Mary Howell Pvt NJ
Jonathan: b 8-7-1754 d 10-5-1837 m (1)Eunice Chappel (2)Eunice Kruger Cpl NY ★
Joseph, Sr.: b 2-3-1735 d 5-5-1821 m Lucretia Post CS CT
Joseph, Jr.: b 12-18-1762 d 2-19-1822 m Marcia Gillett Sol CT
Joseph: b 1726 d 6-23-1786 m Lydia Miller Capt MA
Joseph: b 4-19-1751 d 8-3-1823 m Elizabeth Barker NCdr Mstr MA
Joseph: b 9-15-1759 d 1-4-1845 m Abigail Wright Pvt MA
Joseph: b 4-13-1758 d 8-28-1845 m Rachel Langdon Pvt MA VT NY ★
Joseph Platt: b 12-24-1729 d 2-3-1816 m Sarah Benedict Col CT
Joshua: b 4-12-1740 d 3-21-1790 m Mary Cook Ens CT
Josiah: b 11-26-1746 d 11-12-1817 m Miriam Shepard Pvt MA
Josiah: b 1739 d 7-2-1807 m (1)Hulda Bassett, (2)Lucy Desmond PS Cpl NH
Lemuel: b 9-10-1759 d 5-20-1866 m Hannah Curtis Pvt CT ★
Lemuel: b 1762 d — m Betsey Bates Pvt CT
Levi: b 9-8-1757 d 8-24-1830 m Sarah Pool Pvt MA
Levi: b 1761 d 12-24-1843 m Achsah Smith Pvt MA
Marimon: b 11-12-1761 d 8-25-1858 m (1)Loly Bradley (2)Betsey Hulburt Pvt CT ★
Merriman: b 10-1-1748 d 9-27-1827 m Mary Osborn Pvt CT
Miles: b 1765 d 7-10-1846 m Susan Griffin Pvt Mus CT ★
Moody, Jr.: b 11-20-1750 d 12-30-1834 m (1)Sarah Elliot (2)Hannah Worcester (3)Mary Church Pvt MA ★
Mordecai: b — d 1810 m (1)Elizabeth Scrosby (2)Sarah Smith Cooke Lt VA
Moses: b 9-23-1742 d 5-15-1818 m (1)Elizabeth Cone (2)Ede (Clark) Norton PS CT
Moses, Jr.: b 5-30-1744 d 12-28-1831 m Jemima Upsom Pvt Drm CT
Moses, Sr.: b 5-26-1726 d 1812 m Hannah Smith Sgt MA
Moses, Jr.: b 7-21-1751 d p. 1790 m Susanna Henderson Pvt MA
Moses Bassett: b 4-6-1762 d 8-9-1839 m Phoebe Perkins Pvt NY ★
Nathan: b 5-14-1756 d 5-12-1838 m Martha Worden Sgt NY ★
Nathaniel: bpt 2-8-1756 d 10-18-1816 m Annis Sears Sgt CT
Nathaniel: b 9-25-1735 d 11-27-1822 m Martha Scott Pvt CT
Nathaniel: b 1-11-1754 d 7-2-1825 m Mrs. Elizabeth Rollins PS NH
Nathaniel: b 4-10-1728 d 1-10-1812 m Margaret Rollins Cpl NY
Nathaniel: b 4-4-1748 d 9-27-1846 m Amey Whipple Pvt Slr RI
Nicholas: b 2-3-1717 d 11-14-1782 m Hannah Sabin CS RI
Noah: b 2-12-1730 d 4-8-1796 m Kezia Parson Lt MA
Noah: b 8-9-1758 d 12-30-1834 m (1)Armanala Miller (2)Sarah Baldwin Sgt PA ★
Oliver: b 10-3-1750 d 12-30-1838 m Submit Cogsdell Pvt CT
Peter: b c. 1745 d p. 1813 m Catherine Fritcher Pvt NY
Peter: b 8-26-1720 d 1-5-1811 m (1)Elizabeth Bates (2)Mercy Wanton PS RI
Phillip: b c. 1758 d 1816 m Thankful — Pvt MA

Phineas: b 6-7-1736 d 1-12-1784 m Abigail Durant Capt MA
Raphael: bpt 4-27-1755 d 1822 m Mrs. Anna Merwin Pvt MA
Reuben: b 1739 d 1820 m Mollie Daniel Pvt GA
Reuben: b 8-25-1747 d 6-25-1829 m Sarah Cole Pvt PA
Reuben E.: b 1760 d a. 7-21-1856 m Mrs. Elizabeth Harrison Pvt NC ★
Richard: b 1751 d 8-13-1833 m (1)Mary Rowley (2)Susanna — Pvt CT ★
Richard Donaldson: b 3-3-1749 d 1811 m (1)Priscilla Bullock (2)Elizabeth — Capt NC
Robert: b 7-28-1729 d 4-27-1808 m Elizabeth Parker Capt MA
Robert: b 9-25-1743 d 1825 m Lydia Adams 1Lt MA
Robert, Jr.: b 1757 d 3-18-1831 m Judith Damon Vol MA
Robert: b 3-28-1752 d 11-12-1841 m (1)Susannah Watson (2)Mrs Sarah Sayers Pvt VA
Roswell: b 12-6-1764 d 12-27-1827 m Rachel Newell Drm CT
Samuel: b 7-6-1726 d 3-21-1815 m Dorothea Gillette Sgt CT
Samuel: b 12-31-1758 d 1-19-1819 m Mary Wright Pvt CT W ★
Samuel: b 2-18-1754 d 2-24-1842 m — Pvt CT ★
Samuel: b 4-19-1758 d 9-27-1824 m Mary Kirtland Pvt CT
Samuel: b 3-18-1755 d 12-7-1834 m Mehitable Marsh Pvt MA
Samuel: b 1753 d 1-16-1816 m Prudence Lanning Pvt NJ
Samuel: b a. 1750 d 1783 m Temperance (Hedges ?) Dr NY CT
Sarah Simpson: b 1742 d 7-29-1822 m William Cooke PS PA
Saul: b 5-27-1757 d 1-8-1846 m Elizabeth Snow Pvt MA ★
Sears: b 5-4-1746 d 9-1-1816 m Abigail Crosby Lt MA
Shubel: b 1758 d 6-11-1830 m Sarah Bangs Pvt CT
Silas: b 3-23-1753 d 2-12-1842 m (1)Joanna Darling (2)Mrs Sina Ballou Rawson Pvt MA ★
Silas, Jr.: b c. 1754/5 d p. 1787 m Ann Lechmere PS NC
Simeon: b 1726 d 12-17-1811 m Mary Lord Maj NY
Solomon: b 1750 d 12-23-1835 m (1)Selina Blandin (2)Hannah Shattuck Sgt MA ★
Solomon: b 9-12-1737 d 1819 m (1)Betsey — (2)Catherine Stafford Pvt MA
Solomon: b 1761 d 2-21-1823 m Elizabeth Peck Pvt MA ★
Stephen: b 12-16-1727 d 1-2-1800 m (1)Anna Culver (2)Thankful Preston (3)Anna Tyler PS CT
Stephen: b c. 1742 d p. 1795 m Johanna Scott Pvt MA
Stephen: b 3-21-1751 d 8-7-1829 m Sarah McFarland Pvt PA
Stephen: b 1751 d 3- -1816 m Catherine Esten NDr
Sylvanus: b 5-1-1738 d 11-12-1814 m (1)Sarah Barstow (2)Mary (Godfrey) Adams Pvt MA
Sylvanus (5th): b 2-10-1743 d 2-10-1831 m Martha Hopkins Pvt RI W ★
Thaddeus: b 9-10-1728 d 2-27-1800 m (1)Lois Beach (2)Sarah Hall (3)Abigal — Col CT
Thaddeus: b 11-18-1721 d 10-4-1785 m (2)Zerviah Hinkley CS PS CT
Theophilus: b 10-27-1761 d 6-16-1842 m Phebe Hedges Slr PA
Thomas: b 1751 d 1850 m Mary Ann Seward Pvt MD
Thomas: b 12-26-1747 d 2-19-1789 m Mary Ann Mahon Pvt NY
Thomas: b 1749 d 3-29-1812 m Catherine Coleman Pvt NY
Thomas: b 5-15-1752 d 3-5-1841 m Elizabeth Reagan Capt NC ★
Thomas: b 1756 d 1844 m Jane Hallowell Sgt NC
Thomas: b c. 1758 d 11-23-1831 m Elizabeth Bowen Pvt NC
Thomas: b c. 1761 d 9-7-1819 m Martha Vaughan Pvt VA W★
Thomas B.: b 9-4-1749 d 11-5-1831 m Elizabeth Smith Capt PA ★
Timothy: b 1749 d p. 1792 m Hannah Mahon Pvt NC
Uriah: b 6-27-1760 d 3-21-1830 m Mary Cumstock Pvt NH
Valentine: b c. 1740 d 1797 m Susannah — PS Sol VA
Waitstill: b 1-28-1727 d 1- -1780 m Elizabeth — Sol CT
Walter: b 1-19-1730 d p. 1808 m Elizabeth Hall CS RI
William: b 1759 d 9-7-1820 m Kaziah Matson Pvt CT
William: b 7-1-1753 d 1834 m Betsey Cope Pvt MD & PA ★
William: b 1735 d 1814 m Achsah Middleton MM NJ
William, Jr.: b 1758 d 11-5-1841 m (1)Elizabeth Bedford (2)Eleanor T. Johnson Pvt Tms NJ ★
William: b c. 1760 d p. 10-6-1818 m Rebecca Green Sol NJ'
Wm.: b 1732 d 4-22-1804 m Sarah Simpson Col PA
Wm.: b 2-27-1732 d 1-15-1820 m Elizabeth Slocum Pvt RI W★
Wm.: b 6-19-1722 d p. 1799 m (1)Rose — (2)Ruth Brown CS PS RI
William: b 11-7-1755 d 5-4-1843 m Ruth Taber Pvt RI
Wm.: b 1740 d 1821 m (2)Ann Nelson (3)Louisa Burton Sgt Bbd VA
William: b c. 1720 d a. 1797 m (1)Margaret (Green) (2)Ann Nelson Sgt VA
William: b c. 1751 d 1791 m Ann Kidley Chamberlayne NGnr VA
William: b 1715 d 1791 m Susanna Clinton CS VA
Wilson: b 10-21-1730 d 1801 m Judith Read Lt SC
Zachariah: b 1-15-1751 d 11-30-1836 m Martha Andrick Pvt VA ★

COOKENDORFER,
Leonard: b 1753 d 9-3-1823 m Susan Krusse Pvt MD

COOKINGHAM (includes GUGENHEIM)
John Michael: b 7-2-1757 d 11-6-1840 m (1)Maria Agenest Marquart (2)Mrs Elizabeth (Ackert) Nichols Pvt NY

COOKSEY,
Charles: b 6- -1762 d p. 1850 m Sarah King Pvt VA ★
Hezekiah: b c. 1750 d p. 1820 m (2)Elizabeth Grey Pvt MD

COOKSON,
Reuben: b 1745 d p. 4-28-1818 m Mary York Pvt MA ★

COOLBAUGH,
John: b 9-14-1760 d 9-25-1842 m (1)Susannah Van Campen (2)Mrs Mary (Wills) Field Pvt NJ ★
Moses: b 1752 d 2-22-1814 m Hannah Shoemaker Lt PA
William: b c. 1720 d 1801 m Sarah Johnson CS NJ

COOLEY, (includes COLEY)
Aaron: b 9-28-1753 d 6-7-1834 m (1)Persis Cleveland (2)Susan Parker Pvt MA
Abel: b 4-12-1717 d 6-13-1778 m Mercy — MM MA
Abner: b 7-3-1748 d 10-19-1824 m Martha Russell CS PS MA
Abner: b 8-17-1752 d 4-30-1832 m Marie Chapin Pvt MA W ★
Asahel: b 4-5-1753 d 9-11-1828 m Esther Warriner Pvt MA
Azariah, Sr.: b 3-7-1731 d 2-28-1778 m Eleanor Warriner Sol MA
Azariah, Jr.: b 1-26-1760 d 3-9-1829 m Mercy Belding Pvt MA ★
Benjamin: b 4-30-1747 d 2-27-1810 m Ruth Beach Capt VT
Caleb: b 6-4-1722 d 5-16-1793 m (1)Ann Clark (2)Mary Burt CS MA
Caleb: b 2-12-1762 d 2-13-1813 m Elizabeth Sanford Pvt VT
Daniel: b 1-17-1754 d 4-5-1821 m Hepsibah Stiles Pvt MA
Ebenezer: b 10-19-1741 d 11-2-1811 m (1)Abigail Morehouse Capt CT
George: b 10-15-1756 d 12-13-1819 m Penelope Rumrill Pvt MA
Gideon: b 1-31-1763 d 11-24-1838 m Dinah Sikes Pvt MA
Isaac: b 5-30-1745 d 3-5-1824 m (1)Eunice Bodurtha (2)Huldah Worthington (3)Abigail Gottier CS MA
Jabez: b 1729 d c. 1800 m Abigail Hancock Pvt MA
James: b 4-16-1758 d 1834/5 m Penelope Gargus Pvt NC ★
Joel: b 7-11-1735 d 9-22-1818 m Sarah Olcott Pvt MA
John: b 2-16-1737/8 d 11-29-1828 m (1)Ann Hosford (2)Mrs Phebe Pratt Cpl MA
John: b 1735 d 3-6-1823 m (1)Deborah Tibbetts (2)Dorothy French Cpl NH ★
John: b 5-24-1731 d 1-17-1801 m Sarah — Pvt VA
Jonathan: b 8-16-1744 d 5-22-1823 m Lucy Stebbins Pvt MA
Josiah: b 11-30-1749 d 2-13-1824 m Abiah Bliss Cpl MA
Nathan: b — d 4-18-1781 m Mabel Bixby Sgt CT
Nathaniel: b 1741 d 1826 m Sarah — PS NY
Noah: b 1744 d 9-18-1830 m Lois Holcomb Pvt CT
Noah: b 8-21-1741 d 3-19-1810 m Esther Hyde Pvt MA
Oliver: b c. 1740 d 5-2-1778 m Sarah Ingram Pvt VT
Roger, Jr.: b 1760 d 1843 m Electa Smith Pvt MA NY
Roger, Sr.: b 9-21-1719 d 6-6-1802 m Mary Stebbins Lt MA NY
Solomon: b 1-15-1753 d 7-11-1833 m Lucy Stephenson Pvt MA
Thomas, Jr.: b 3-30-1764 d 8-20-1847 m (1)Eunice — (2)Elizabeth Pvt CT ★
William: b 3-17-1736 d 3-4-1825 m Sarah Mather Capt MA
William: b 6-24-1758 d 11-30-1843 m Sybil — CS Pvt NY ★

COOLIDGE, (includes COOLEDGE)
Daniel: b 1752 d 1840 m Beulah Smith Sgt MA
Daniel: b 10-23-1741 d 2-23-1822 m (1)Lydia Hagar (2)Anna Shepard Pvt MA
Elisha: b 7-9-1720 d 8-29-1807 m Sarah Boutell CS MA
Isaac: b 8-29-1747 d 3-5-1822 m Abigail Bacon Pvt MA
Joel: b 7-19-1759 d 10-5-1841 m Martha Ware Cpl MA
John: b 1749 d 2-6-1798 m Lydia Dawes 2Lt MA
John: b 4-22-1752 d 5-29-1835 m Eunice Eames Pvt MA
John: b 1756 d 3-23-1822 m Hannah Lawrence Priest Pvt MA
Jonas: b 2-1-1744 d 8- -1776 m Ann Harrington Pvt MA
Jonathan: b 9-16-1761 d 9-25-1822 m Anna Burdick Pvt MA
Joseph, Sr.: b 6-18-1730 d 4-19-1775 m Eunice Stratton MM MA
Joseph, Jr.: b 10-4-1761 d 10-17-1843 m Mary Adams Pvt MA
Joseph: b 1-16-1757 d 3-15-1829 m Martha Daniels Pvt MA
Joseph, II: b 7-27-1747 d 10-6-1820 m (1)Elizabeth Boyer (2)Katherine Boyer PS MA
Josiah, Jr.: b 7-6-1744 d p. 9-9-1814 m Tabetha Fulham CS MA
Nathaniel: b 10-20-1724 d 1807 m Sarah Parker Sol PS NH
Paul: b 10-20-1751 d 1835 m Martha Jones Sgt MA
Samuel: b 8-13-1753 d p. 1779 m Hannah Russell Pvt MA
Samuel: b 8-31-1756 d 12-4-1800 m Mary Bemis Pvt MA
Silas: b 11-14-1756 d 5-23-1834 m Elizabeth Freeman Pvt NH ★
Thomas: b 4-8-1755 d 9-2-1830 m Molly Felch Cpl MA

COOMBS, (includes COMBS, COOMES)
Anthony: b 2-14-1739 d 1-13-1818 m Mercy Snow Lt MA
Anthony: b 1754 d 10-20-1843 m Annie Stimson Pvt MA
Asa: b 6-20-1759 d 4-10-1830 m (1)Abagail Thomas (2)Mary Pratt Pvt MA ★
Benjamin: b 1749 d 12-10-1838 m Sarah Richardson Lt VA
Cuthbert: b c. 1745 d 6-25-1815 m Sallie — Sol PS VA
Ebenezer: b 1746/7 d 10-5-1783 m Abigail Thompson Seacap MA
Elnathan: b 6-10-1732 d 1-4-1788 m Mary Taylor Sgt MA
Francis: b 1726 d 4-3-1822 m Charity — Pvt VA
Hezekiah: b 1-15-1755 d 8-4-1839 m Margaret Ewing Pvt MA
Ignatius: b 11-24-1740 d 8-30-1790 m Mary Fenwick 2Lt MD
Isaac: b 1751 d 1846 m Euphemea Rogers Pvt NJ
John, Sr.: b 1-26-1730 d 9-13-1811 m Mindwell Prior Sol CT
John, Jr.: b 12-22-1762 d 1851 m Joanna Colton Pvt CT
John: b 1758 d 3-26-1839 m Concurrence Southworth Pvt CT
John: b c. 1764 d a. 1806 m MrsHannah(Whitaker)Cole Pvt GA
John: b 11-11-1748 d 4-20-1836 m (1)Savia Brown (2)Charlotte Tarr Pvt MA

John: b 7-27-1757 d 9-16-1848 m Eunice Shepard Pvt MA
John: b 2- -1746 d 6-19-1824 m Lydia — Sgt NJ
John: b 1720 d 10-23-1803 m Sarah Abrahams PS NJ
John: b 11-5-1753 d p. 1840 m Rachel Pindell Pvt PA
John: b 1754 d 1-16-1849 m Nancy Vinander Sol VA
John: b 2-7-1761 d p. 5-13-1825 m Margaret — Pvt VA ★
John: b c. 1725 d p. 5-11-1785 m Seth Bullitt PS VA
Jonathan, Sr.: b 1720 d 10-29-1800 m Elizabeth — PS NJ
Jonathan, Jr.: b 11-1-1748 d p. 8-20-1803 m Catherine — Capt NJ
Joseph: b 3-25-1752 d 11-23-1817 m Elizabeth Gamble Sgt ME
Joshua: b 1764 d p. 12-26-1846 m Anna Loveland Pvt MA ★
Mahlon: b 1759 d 11-25-1834 m (1)Rebecca Norton (2)Sarah — Pvt VA ★
Moses Newell: b 1-2-1754 d 4-12-1834 m Mary Hayes Sgt Arfr NJ
Nathan: b 8-25-1751 d 11-18-1828 m Sarah Ewing Cpl ME
Nicholas: bpt 11-12-1738 d 7-10-1811 m Mary Girdler Pvt MA
Peter: b 10-1-1760 d 8-20-1820 m Rachel Walrad Pvt NY
Phields: b 1759 d p. 1815 m (1)Phoebe Holbrook (2)Martha Veazie Pvt MA
Philip: b c. 1762 d p. 1828 m Elizabeth Eidson Sol GA
Robert: b 1753 d 1846 m (1)Nancy Sears (2)Lucinda Seelock Sol VA
Robert: b 1753 d p. 1840 m Sarah Linton Pvt VA ★
Samuel: b 1-26-1730 d p. 1782 m Miriam Hale Pvt MA
Samuel Cotton: b 1756 d 10-31-1826 m Rachel Gardiner Pvt MA ★
Simeon: b 1760 d 11-14-1819 m Experience Miller Pvt MA
Stephen: b 4-1-1739 d 11-27-1808 m Jemima Dow Lt MA
Thomas: b 11-2-1732 d 12-22-1819 m Martha — Pvt NJ
William, Sr.: b p. 1734 d p. 8-7-1820 m Catherine Lancaster PS MD
William, Jr.: b a. 1740 d c. 1788 m Milburn Hager Pvt MD
William: b 1736 d 5-28-1814 m Jane Greenleaf PS MA
William: b c. 1757 d 3-8-1840 m Mill Cloud Ordl Sgt VA

COOMER,
Benjamin: b 3-8-1748 d 10-26-1817 m Ruth Goff Pvt MA
John: b 5-8-1755 d 2-27-1834 m Mahala Coggeshall Pvt Tms PS RI ★
Thomas K.: b 7-11-1757 d 10-22-1834 m Mary Coggeshall Pvt RI ★

COON, (includes KUHN)
Aaron: b 1760 d 10-27-1844 m Susanna Kelly Pvt NJ
Adam Simon: b 12-23-1714 d 1-23-1780 m Maria Sabina Schrack PS PA
Conrod: b 1751 d 1817 m Anna Barbara Stauffer Pvt PA
Daniel: b 1750 d 10-9-1834 m Elizabeth Spaulding Sgt CT ★
Henry, Jr.: b 1-9-1759 d 4-4-1834 m (1)Margaret Schneider (2)Catharina Kohl Pvt NY
Henry: b 7-6-1738 d 1783 m Eliserbeth Ersula Shealy 2Lt SC
Israel: b 1758 d 8-7-1809 m Sarah Sutton Cpl NJ
Jacob: bpt 12- -1759 d p. 6- -1850 m Maria Seifert Pvt NY ★
Jacob: b 1752 d 1813 m (2)Eve Ann Berger Pvt PA
Jeremiah: b 1754 d — m Ruth Mosher Pvt NY
John: b 1749 d 1825 m Elsie Ham Pvt NY
Joseph: b 4-4-1720 d p. 4-6-1798 m Kathrine Cunraed PS Sol VA
Joseph: b 5-2-1752 d p. 1803 m (1)Elizabeth Snider (2)Elizabeth Daniels Pvt VA
Levi: b c. 1750 d 8-7-1826 m Margaret Compton Pvt MA
Marcus: b 3-13-1748 d 3- -1820 m Abagail Loomis 2Lt NY
Michael: b 4-6-1747 d 1-30-1820 m Catharine McClarty PS PA
Peter: b 1748 d a. 4-2-1804 m Catherine Appler Pvt PA
Samuel: b c. 1742 d p. 1790 m Esther Saunders Pvt CT
Samuel: bpt 4-16-1745 d 1793 m Egji Schut Sgt NY
Thomas: b 1723 d 8-14-1785 m Hannah — Pvt NJ
Thomas: b 12-24-1737 d 1820 m Anne Crandall Cpl RI
William H.: b 1748-51 d a. 3-13-1813 m (1)Elizabeth Elich (2)Elsjen Schneider Pvt NY

COONER,
Jacob: b 6-21-1754 d 8-5-1824 m Mary Wolf Pvt SC

COONEY,
James: b — d 5-25-1818 m Hannah Reed Pvt PA

COONS,
Abraham: b 5-3-1748 d 7-24-1841 m (1)Anne Hegeman (2)Elizabeth Richard Cpl NY ★
Frederick: b 1762 d 1831 m Mary Ann Mathews Pvt VA ★
Jacob: b c. 1740 d 9-22-1807 m (1)Elizabeth Hanback (2)Letitia Kemper Lt VA
John: b 1-13-1742 d 1-16-1839 m — Pvt VA
Matthias: b 1746 d 10-6-1819 m Elizabeth Legg Pvt NY
Philip: b 10-13-1747 d 12-25-1842 m Elizabeth Wheeler Pvt NY

COOP,
Horatio: b 1758 d 1843 m — Pvt Wgn MD ★

COOPER,
Abel: b 10-15-1748 d p. 2-20-1835 m Tamar Bowen Sgt MA VT ★
Abraham: b 7-31-1754 d 2-9-1828 m Rebecca Potter Pvt CT ★
Abraham: bpt 2-21-1728 d p. 1813 m Catharina Ostrander Pvt NY
Adam: a. 1760 d 4-27-1830 m Elizabeth Foybeson Pvt NC ★
Albert: b 3-6-1733 d 4-4-1808 m Phoebe Palmer Pvt NY

Alexander: b 1-28-1754 d 2-9-1844 m Mary — Pvt NC ★
Ananias: b 1752 d 8-1-1803 m Mrs. Brigatta (Burke) Dwire Cpl NJ
Apollos: b c. 1750 d 9-11-1777 m Mary Reed Lt VA
Archibald: b 1724 d 6-26-1790 m Nancy — Pvt PA
Barney (Barnett): b 1742 d 1800 m Jane Patterson Sol VA
Benjamin A.: b 1-25-1756 d 11-5-1841 m Anne Fullerton Lt VA ★
Caleb: b 1745 d 4-16-1834 m Abigail Huntting PS NY
Charles: b c. 1755 d 1819 m — Pvt VA
Christian: b 11-7-1739 d 9-16-1809 m Anna Margaret Coen Pvt NY
Cornelius, Sr.: b 9-27-1724 d 1794 m Martha Van Dieu Pvt NJ
Cornelius, Jr.: b 4-8-1756 d 3-3-1832 m Nelly Stoutenburgh Pvt NJ
Cornelius: b 4-17-1722 d 12-27-1776 m Annetje Haring Sgt NY
Cornelius: b 12-21-1735 d 4-9-1824 m (1)Elizabeth Vanamborough (2)Mrs. Ranche Van Vorhis Sgt NY
Cornelius: b c. 1730 d p. 1-8-1805 m — PS NC
Dabney: b 11-22-1758 d 5-4-1842 m Henrietta Watt Sgt VA ★
Daniel, Sr.: b 5-1-1695 d 5-2-1795 m (1)Grace Runyon (2)Jane Westbrook (3)Grace Manning (4)Mrs Fanny Jones (5)Barbara M. Gibbs (6)Mrs Hannah Martin CS NJ
David: b c. 1756 d c. 1805 m Ann Wooley Pvt NJ
David: b 1-13-1724/25 d 11-5-1795 m Sybil Matlack CS PS NJ
David: b 1738 d 5-7-1792 m — Pvt PA
Elias: b 9-30-1734 d 3-19-1777 m Ruth Rogers PS NY
Elijah: b c. 1750 d p. 1790 m Abiah Leonard Pvt NY
Enoch: b 9-15-1739 d 4-2-1814 m Susannah Granger Lt MA
Eustacy: b 3- -1750 d 1821 m Margaret — Pvt SC
Ezekiel: b 10-7-1745 d p. 1783 m Hannah Smith Capt MA
Ezekiel: b 1761 d 1828 m Sarah Martha Magby Sol SC
Fleet, Sr.: b 1722 d p. 7-2-1795 m Margaret Coan PS NC
Frederick: b 1759 d 10-27-1841 m Dorothy Call Cpl NC PA ★
George: b 1751 d 11-11-1824 m Phoebe Billings Sol PA
George: b 1759 d 2-20-1829 m (1)Isabella Bradley (2)Mrs Howell (3)Jane Dubose Law Lt SC
Gilbert: b 4-28-1741 d 4-1-1815 m Elizabeth Vandervoort LCol NY
Henry, Sr.: b 10-26-1733 d 3- -1819 m (1)Barbara Dickinson Pvt NJ
Henry: b 1739-44 d 1842-47 m Francis Perry Sol NY
Henry: b 1761 d 1840 m Mary Green Sol PA
Ichabod: b 1740 d 11-27-1809 m (1)Phebe — (2)Hannah Morris Pvt MM NJ
Isaac: b 1760 d 12-5-1837 m Lydia Cooper Bbd CT
Isaac: b 6-8-1751 d 1783/84 m Ann Bolton Capt PA
Jacob: b. 1-9-1762 d p. 1819 m Rebecca Cooper Pvt MA ★
Jacob: b 4-17-1726 d p. 1790 m Josina Orchard Pvt NY
Jacob: b 1734 d p. 1805 m — Kennedy Spy NC ★
Jacob: b c. 1750 d 5- -1805 m Rebecca McKinney Capt SC
Jacob: b 3-24-1727 d 9-8-1781 m Lydia Clark Pvt SC
James: b 1752 d p. 1800 m Margaret Douglass 2Lt MA
James: b 1757 d 1789 m Phoebe Cary Pvt NJ
James: b 1760-70 d a. 1839 m Mary Renne Pvt NY
James: b 3-6-1753 d 5-3-1849 m Sarah Comly Pvt Smn PA
James: b 1755 d 1825 m Molly Hicks Sgt SC
James: b 1756 d 1833 m Rachel Powers Pvt PA
James B.: b 10-4-1761 d 2-5-1854 m (1)Rebecca Morgan (2)Elizabeth Clement Pvt NJ
James W.: b c. 1751 d p. 1789 m Elizabeth Douglas Pvt NY
John Adam: b 7-1-1759 d 11-11-1823 m Christiana Shott Pvt PA
John Martin: b 3-7-1749 d 7- -1829 m Anna Maria Deneg Pvt PA
Jonathan: b 1758 d 9-10-1845 m (2)Eleanor English Pvt PA ★
Joseph: b 1-12-1760 d 9-5-1843 m Suzannah Halsy Pvt NJ
Joseph: b 3-13-1757 d 12-19-1844 m Dolly Page Pvt MA ★
Joseph: b 1757 d 1-22-1819 m Mattie Lewis Pvt VA
Joseph: b 1-27-1758 d 6-16-1831 m (2)Mary Mills Pvt VA SC
Lamberton: b 1749 d 8-13-1821 m Dorcas Jennings Sgt MA
Leighton: b 1757 d 1848 m Grizzell Covington Pvt VA ★
Leonard: b c. 1740 d 1807 m Mary Tyler Sol VA
Leonard: b 1753/54 d 5-21-1821 m Christina Troenberger Capt VA
Leven: b 2-11-1754 d 7-24-1842 m Elizabeth Calloway Pvt VA PA
Malachi: b 4-4-1762 d c. 1843/44 m Ann Wilkerson PS NC
Matthew: b 5-14-1757 d 2-13-1842 m Lucretia Havens Pvt NY
Moses: b 3-14-1754 d 4-16-1831 m Sarah Griffith Sgt PA
Nathaniel, Jr.: b 7-4-1748 d 7-16-1851 m (1)Mary Aldrich (2)Mrs Abigail Chase Pvt MA
Nicholas: b c. 1734 d 1799 m (1)Sarah Gill (2)Elizabeth — Pvt PA
Obadiah A.: b 9-30-1762 d 7-24-1831 m Elizabeth Ostrander Pvt NY
Price: b c. 1756 d 7-16-1827 m (1) — (2)Elizabeth — Pvt CT ★
Reuben: b c. 1760 d p. 6-17-1824 m Elizabeth Cooper Sgt VA

Richard: b c. 1720 d p. 1786 m Miss — Merion PS GA
Richard: b 1739 d 9-10-1819 m Hannah Sampson Lt MA
Richard: b 1758 d 1836 m Lourene Howard Pvt NC
Richard Wibird: b 10-27-1761 d 1810 m Pricilla English Mid MA
Robert: b — d 11-23-1820 m Elizabeth Sherer Pvt NY W ★
Robert: b a. 1765 d 8-22-1843 m Alcy Bledsoe CS NC
Robert: b 1750 d 1820 m Catherine Harlin Lt PA
Robert: b 1732 d 4-12-1805 m Elizabeth Kearsley PS PA
Robert: b 1747 d 1794 m Jane Hamilton Capt SC
Samuel: b 9-10-1750 d 10-23-1823 m Jane McClure Pvt MD
Samuel: b 6-13-1757 d 8-19-1840 m Mary Horton 2Lt QM Adj MA
Samuel: b 3-28-1725 d 12-29-1783 m Judith Bulfinch PS Chp MA
Samuel: b 6-25-1744 d 9-22-1812 m Prudence Browne PS NJ
Samuel: b 1-6-1736 d 11-3-1807 m Elizabeth Post PS NY
Samuel: b c. 1759 d 1841 m Mary Bishop Pvt SC
Sherman: b 4-3-1761 d 8-3-1851 m Mary Powers Cpl NH ★
Spencer: b 1740 d 5-17-1809 m Nancy Crain Pvt VA ★
Stephen: b 5-19-1752 d 1831 m (1)Esther Evans (2)Roda Steere Pvt RI
Tacey: b 12-10-1764 d 5- -1834 m Jane Orr Mid PA ★
Thomas: b 3-23-1731 d 9-18-1798 m Mary Abercrombie Pvt PA
Thomas: b 1738 d 5-15-1813 m Peace Dean Pvt Sct VT
Thomas: b c. 1733-35 d p. 8-20-1793 m Sarah Anthony Capt VA
Thuenis: b 7-3-1733 d 10-15-1790 m Margrietje Talama Sol NY
Valentine: b c. 1745 d p. 12-24-1799 m Elizabeth — Sol VA
William: b c. 1748 d 1780-88 m — Pvt MD
William: b 1750 d 7-3-1836 m Polly — Pvt MD W ★
William: b 10-1-1721 d 11-28-1809 m Katharine Wendall PS CS MA
William: b a. 1760 d p. 1812 m Elizabeth Richmond Pvt NJ
William: b 1752 d 12- -1821 m (1) — (2)Martha Thames Sol NC
William: b 7-24-1738 d 10-30-1815 m Nancy Newberry Pvt PA
William: b 1747 d 2-1-1813 m Rachel Cooper Ens PA
William: b 2-28-1749 d 2-28-1790 m Margaret McVey Pvt PA
William: b 4-24-1756 d 8-18-1837 m Mary Hunter Cav SC
Zebulon: b 1-13-1752 d 12-22-1835 m Mary White Pvt NY

COOR,
Thomas: b c. 1753 d c. 1800 m X Sol NC

COOSARD,
Valentine: b 1745 d 1846 m — Riefsnyder Pvt NJ

COPE, (includes COPES)
John: b 1730 d 1812 m (1)Grace Cloud (2)Mary Dickinson Pvt PA
Lewis: b c. 1740 d 3-27-1787 m Rosannah — CS GA
Nathan: b 1733 d 12-3-1820 m Amy Bane Pvt PA
Parker: b 1763 d 1-11-1849 m (2)Margaret Warrington Elliott Pvt VA ★
Southy: b 1761 d 1-9-1834 m Ruth Hutton Sgt VA ★

COPELAND, (includes COWLAND)
Aaron: b 1762 d 5-9-1839 m Polly Melton Pvt SC
Alexander: b c. 1754 d 3-1-1836 m Rebecca Gillmore Pvt SC W ★
Amasa: b 4-22-1758 d 8-12-1852 m Tryphene Liscomb Pvt CT ★
Andrew: b c. 1759 d p. 1792 m Nancy Bennett PS VA
Asa: b 5-8-1752 d 12-14-1829 m (1)Rachel Briggs (2)Abigail Newcomb Pvt MA
Benjamin: b 3-28-1752 d 9-5-1834 m Deborah Shinn Pvt VA ★
David: b 5-14-1738 d p. 1790 m (1)Elizabeth Clapp (2)Martha Putnam Pvt MA
David: b c. 1750 d p. 7-24-1817 m Jane Craig Sol NC
Elijah: b 6-3-1739 d 9-8-1817 m Rhoda Snell Pvt Drm MA
Isaac: b 3-3-1726 d 6-19-1795 m Lydia (Copeland) Thayer Pvt MA
Isaac: b 10-17-1753 d 12-29-1833 m Rebecca Pierce Pvt MA ★
Jacob: b 7-10-1746 d 2-7-1837 m (1)Rachel Adams (2)Mary Daniels (3)Experience White Pvt NH
James: b 8-1-1759 d 6-15-1838 m Sarah Akers Pvt VA
John: b 2-12-1748 d 9-7-1826 m Margaret Blakeley Pvt SC
Jonathan: b 9-29-1757 d 6-11-1839 m Esther Chapman Pvt CT
Jonathan: b 1755 d 5-11-1837 m Deborah Otis Sgt MA
Jonathan: b 11-11-1724/25 d 1786 m Mary Nicholas Capt PA
Joseph: b 4-28-1734 d 1-9-1811 m Rebecca Hooper Lt MA
Joseph: b 8-22-1749 d 8-1-1841 m Celia Loring Pvt MA
Joshua: b c. 1750 d p. 1800 m Susanna — PS NC
Josiah: b 1729 d 1791 m Sarah — PS NC
Moses: b 11-16-1745 d 9-24-1840 m Hannah Stone Pvt MA
Moses: b 4-6-1741 d 6-2-1817 m Patience Sweet CS MA
Nathaniel: b 3-29-1762 d 5-5-1806 m Barbara Blackington Pvt MA
Phineas: b 5-14-1756 d 8-20-1813 m Rachel Prince Pvt CT
Richard: b 1750 d p. 1820 m X Pvt PA
Samuel: b 6-15-1758 d 11-3-1839 m Ruth Whitmarsh Pvt MA
Samuel: b c. 1756 d 11-6-1828 m (1)Lucy Proctor (2)Emma Parker Pvt NH
William: b 3-20-1748 d 3-24-1840 m Martha White Lt MA
William: b c. 1750 d 1843 m Jane Parkson Matr CS PA
William: b 1753 d 1838 m Sarah — Capt SC ★
William: b c. 1754 d 1822 m X Cpl VA

COPENHAVER, (includes COPPENHAVER, COPPENHEFFER, KOPPENHAVER, KOPPENHEFFER)
John Michael: b c. 1750 d a. 1798 m Elizabeth Wentz Pvt PA
Michael: b 1733 d a. 11-5-1823 m Eva — Pvt PA
Simon: b 1726 d 8-23-1802 m Maria Elizabeth — Capt CS PA

COPENHAVER, contd.
Thomas, Jr.: b 1761 d c. 1838 m Barbara Staley Pvt NC
Thomas: b c. 1739 d a. 1- -1806 m (1)Catharina Mosser (2)Elizabeth
M Niess (3)Juliana Seek Capt PS PA

COPLEY,
Daniel: b 3-7-1756 d c. 1840 m Theoda — Sol PS CT ★
Joseph: b c. 1750 d 1792/93 m Sara Boe Pvt MA

COPP,
David: b 11- -1750 d 6-6-1833 m (1)Mary Spaulding (2)Elizabeth
Torrey Sgt CT
David: b 12-13-1738 d 3-13-1817 m Margaret Palmer LCol NH
Joseph: b 11-28-1732 d 11- -1815 m Rachel Denison DrmMaj CT
Joshua: b 5-11-1741 d 1804 m Sally Poor Pvt PS NH
Samuel: b 4-6-1742 d 4-3-1818 m (1)Hannah Hayes (2)Mrs Sarah
(Scotes) Knox Wentworth Lt CS MA
Thomas: b 1754 d 7-3-1824 m Alice Kimball Pvt NH
Timothy: b 12-30-1755 d 3-24-1836 m Patience Earl Pvt MA
Tristram: b 1735 d p. 1790 m Martha Horn CS ME

COPPAGE, (includes COPPEDGE)
Charles: b 1735 d p. 1800 m Elizabeth Basye PS VA
John: b 1754 d c. 1823-25 m Mary — Pvt VA
Thomas: b 1752 d 5-15-1843 m Elizabeth Haden Pvt VA

COPPERNOLL, (includes COPPERNAEL)
Adam: b 8-6-1754 d 8-16-1826 m Elizabeth Van Sice Cpl NY
Richard: b 4-23-1748 d 7-14-1822 m Elizabeth Loucks Lt NY W ★
William: b — d 11-18-1830 m Sophia Kiehl Pvt NY

COPPINGER,
Higgins: b 1738 d 1-4-1832 m Anna Smith Pvt VA ★

COQUILLETTE,
Daniel: b 9-20-1750 d 1-29-1835 m Maria Stevens Pvt NY ★

CORAM,
Robert: b 5-2-1761 d 3-9-1796 m Rhoda Cleneay 4Lt NS SC

CORBETT, (includes CORBITT)
Brinkley: b 4-7-1745 d 12-10-1816 m Margaret — PS SC
Daniel: b c. 1755 d p. 1-7-1800 m Martha — Pvt SC
John: b 11-22-1761 d 12-8-1833 m Lydia Cheney Pvt MA
Joseph: b c. 1745 d 6- -1810 m Agnes — Pvt PA
Nathaniel: b 1741 d 4-9-1812 m Lucy Thayer Sol MA
Peter: b 8-23-1748 d 1816 m Keziah Dewey Cpl MA
Robert: b 2-10-1745 d 5-6-1823 m Elizabeth Daniels Pvt MA
Samuel: b 10-17-1759 d 1849 m "Beadie" Bird English Pvt VA ★
William: b 1-16-1751 d 1831 m Sarah Clover Pvt PA

CORBIN,
Abraham: b 9-7-1722 d 1798 m Rachel Marshall PS MD
Anderson: b 2-17-1765 d 3-1-1845 m Elizabeth Haines Pvt VA ★
Asa: b 3-6-1742 d 1-6-1808 m Mercy Harlow Pvt CT
Asahel: b 3-5-1740 d 3-31-1814 m Jerusha Morse Pvt CT
Clement, Sr.: b 5-1-1733 d 1825 m (1)Rachel Bacon (2)Mary
Fillebrown Sgt CT
Clement, Jr.: b 2-15-1764 d 6-2-1853 m Sabra Chamberlain Pvt
CT ★
David: b c. 1757 d 9-1-1846 m (1)Margaret Briggs (2)Sarah Knowles
Cpl NY
Elijah: b 12-1-1738 d 1780 m Elizabeth Prince Sgt CT
Elkanah: b 10-23-1752 d p. 1821 m Hannah Harlow Pvt MA
Isaiah: b — d 5-1-1822 m Lydia — Pvt VA ★
James: b 1-18-1735/36 d 5-12-1792 m Ann Tucker Pvt MA
James: b 1-2-1762 d 1-26-1826 m Lois Kibbe Pvt Dr MA
John: b 2-2-1750 d c. 1837 m Sarah Morris Pvt VA ★
John: b c. 1728 d p. 1-10-1786 m Frances Fant PS VA
John Tayloe: b c. 1746 d 7- -1791 m Mary Waller PS VA
Joseph: b 5-31-1751 d 10-3-1838 m Mary Tallmadge Pvt CT ★
Joshua: b 7-16-1757 d 1-11-1851 m Rhoda Wood Pvt MA ★
Lemuel: b 2-19-1740 d 5-7-1825 m Rebecca Davis Capt MA
Lewis: b 4-4-1754 d 4-1-1840 m Elizabeth Reed OrdlSgt VA ★
Nathaniel: b 9-29-1753 d 1838 m Keziah Loring Cpl MA
Peleg: b 9-7-1749 d p. 5-6-1811 m (1)Lavinia Lyon (2)Rebecca Day
Pvt CT
Samuel: b 8-27-1751 d 6-9-1785 m (1)Mehitable Lyon (2)Lucy
Larned Capt MA
Stephen: b 8-5-1760 d 10-19-1842 m Patience Martha Vinton Pvt
MA ★
Timothy: b 6-24-1750 d 10-26-1831 m Abigail Vinton Pvt MA
William: b 3-28-1746 d 11-16-1826 m Dorothy Perrin Pvt CT
William: b 3-30-1754 d p. 1807 m (1)Elizabeth Fletcher Pvt VA
William: b 11-10-1749 d 1812-15 m Sally Hill Sol VA
William: b 1757 d 1821 m Sarah Pollitt NS VA

CORBLEY,
John: b 2-25-1733 d 6-9-1803 m (1)Abigail Bull (2)Elizabeth Tyler
(3)Nancy Ann Lynn Sct PS Chp VA

CORDELL,
George Edwards: b 2-17-1742 d 7-25-1826 m Catherine Basye PS VA

John Sr.: b 1720 d 1800 m Elizabeth Edwards Sol VA
John, Jr.: b 4-29-1749 d 4- -1800 m Mrs Judith (Blackwell)Price
Capt Chp VA

CORDER,
John: b 1761 d 1-24-1849 m Hannah Way Pvt VA ★
Lewis: b 1760 d 1833 m Mary Garner Sol NC

CORE,
Henry: b 2-23-1763 d 1-17-1834 m Sarah Barrickman Pvt PA
Michael: b 1-23-1764 d 12-25-1815 m Catherine Rich PS VA

COREY, (includes CORY)
Abner: b 6-3-1748 d 12-10-1786 m Naomi Freeman Pvt NJ
Benjamin: b 5-8-1751 d p. 1786 m Mehetable Heath Pvt NY
Benjamin, Jr.: b c. 1764 d a. 12- -1831 m Abigail — Ens VT
Daniel: b 1733 d 6-6-1815 m Martha Bedell Pvt NJ
Daniel: b 6-20-1764 d 5-9-1850 m (1)Jemima Mayberry (2)Mrs
Margaret Cartwright Sol NJ
David: b 7-31-1750 d 3-18-1809 m Jemima Ross Pvt NJ
Ebenezer: b 11-15-1754 d 7-2-1833 m Jane Fletcher Pvt MA ★
Ebenezer: b 1730 d 4-14-1784 m (1)Hannah Mills (2)Mary Mills
Sol CT
Elnathan: b 2-14-1759 d 2-14-1838 m Sarah Walker Pvt NJ★
Ephraim: b 3-13-1736 d 1820 m (1)Susanna Stevens (2)Lois
Chase Capt MA
Gideon: b 3-21-1757 d 7-14-1822 m Ruth Niles Pvt RI
Hezekiah: b 6-22-1736 d 10-18-1818 m Sarah Fletcher Ens NH
Isaac, Sr.: b c. 1-9-1739 d 3-8-1817 m Ruhamah Comey Cpl MA
Isaac, Jr.: b 1763/4 d p. 1840 m (1)Loruhama Prentice (2)Eunice
Johnson Pvt MA ★
Isaac: b 8-12-1755 d 4-9-1817 m Anna Smith Pvt MM NY
Jacob: b 1759 d 9-21-1809 m Sarah (Hedges) Pvt NJ
Jeremiah: b 1740 d 9- -1805 m (1)Mary Wood (2)Mary Bishop Pvt
NJ
John: b 3-5-1762 d 7-16-1834 m (2)Phoebe Rutman Pvt NJ
John: b 1742 d 1785 m Eiizabeth Chase Lt NY
John: b 9-7-1731 d 7-13-1818 m Ruth Dennis Pvt RI
Jonathan: b 1732 d 3-30-1793 m Martha — PS NJ
Jonathan, Jr.: b c. 1736 d a. 4-19-1796 m Lucy Knapp Buchanan Mil
NY
Jonathan: b c. 1750 d p. 1790 m — X — Pvt VT
Joseph: b 1760 d p. 1797 m Martha (or Sarah) Parks Pvt CT PA
Joseph: b 1-23-1757 d 7-13-1802 m Margaret Darby Cpl NJ
Joseph: b 10-9-1737 d 6-23-1780 m Phebe Simpson Pvt NJ
Joseph: b 12-7-1756 d 12-17-1844 m Sarah Briggs Pvt RI ★
Nathan: b 5-18-1748 d 4-8-1820 m Molly Green Pvt MA
Nicholas: b 1751 d 8-15-1843 m Sarah Creight (Searight) QM Pvt
SC NC ★
Oliver Jr: b 3-15-1764 d 1-3-1858 m Hannah York Fif MA ★
Paris: b 4-7-1757 d 12-11-1844 m Lydia Pratt Pvt RI ★
Peleg: b 7-12-1754 d 10-6-1847 m Mercy Warner Pvt RI
Philip: b 11-23-1741 d 10-23-1802 m Comfort Hix Capt RI
Phillip: b 12-6-1761 d 12-9-1833 m (1)Patience Lees (2)Mrs Mercy
Frary Carr Ens MA ★
Reuben: b - -1746 d 2-11-1824 m Cathrine Clark Pvt MA
Samuel: b 1-18-1758 d 8-21-1841 m Mrs Jemima Walden Cory Pvt
RI ★
Thomas: b 7-10-1731 d - - m Deborah Almy Cpl NJ
Timothy: b 4-2-1742 d 4-19-1811 m Elizabeth Griggs Capt MA
Wm.: b 5-6-1743 d 5-18-1821 m (1)Sarah Dyer Clark (2)Mary Allen
2 Lt RI
Wm.: b 1754 d 9-26-1838 m Meribah Sawdy Pvt RI
Wm.: b 10-28-1764 d 7-31-1822 m Hope Almy Pvt RI

CORL, (includes CORLE)
John: b 3-6-1757 d 4-24-1842 m Susanna Van Vorst Pvt NY
Leonard: b 1755 d 8-4-1847 m Mary Magdalene Carbaugh Pvt
PA ★
Samuel: b 4-21-1745 d 1834 m Catherine de Reimer Pvt NJ ★
Wm.: b 11-16-1760 d 3-19-1848 m Marytje Springer Pvt NY

CORLEY,
Austin: b 4-28-1757 d 7-26-1841 m (1)X (2)Mildred — Pvt VA ★
Catlett: b 1758 d p. 11-27-1807 m Elizabeth Jennings Sol SC
Lawrence: b 1742 d 12-18-1815 m (1)Christine Blaken (2)Anna
Barbara Drafts Sol SC
Richard: b c. 1754 d p. 1805 m (1)X (2)— Pope (3)X (4)X Pvt SC
Wm.: b 3-2-1752 d 4-15-1853 m Louisa Sharp Pvt VA ★
Zaccaeus: b 1762 d a. 1-30-1843 m Elizabeth — Pvt SC

CORLISS, (includes CORLIS, CURLISS)
Asa: b 1732 d 1-17-1814 m Rebecca Woodbury PS NH
Bliss: b 5-10-1754 d 3-13-1839 m Phebe (Wright)Kibbe Pvt CT ★
Daniel: b 5-20-1762 d 5- -1842 m Rachel Bailey Pvt NH
Emerson: b 3-27-1758 d 12-29-1843 m Mehitable Poole Mitchell
Pvt NH
James: b 1754 d 1817 m Sarah Sherman Pvt NJ
Jonathan: b 10-8-1724 d 1811 m (1)— Mitchell (2)Mrs Rachel
Rowell (3)— Sanborn PS NH
Jonathan: b 2-25-1730 d 6-18-1776 m Lydia Emerson Sol VT

Joseph: b 11-27-1747 d 9-20-1820 m (1)Miriam Emerson (2)Betsey Utinox Pvt NH
Joshua: b 1-19-1723 d 12-17-1821 m (1)Abigail Marsh (2)Mrs Molly Wells Colby Sol NH
Samuel: b 1748 d 1828-33 m Hannah Silver Pvt MA
Samuel: b 5-1-1766 d 5-20-1833 m (1)Catherine Woolley (2)Elizabeth — Pvt NJ

CORN,
George: b 1740 d 1833 m Dolly — Pvt PS VA
Jesse: b 10-31-1753 d 3-5-1809 m Nancy Hancock 2Lt VA W ★
John Peter: b 3-15-1752 d 10-14-1843 m Elizabeth Parr Pvt VA ★
Timothy: b c. 1760 d 8-21-1848 m Nancy Douglass Pvt PS VA ★

CORNELISON,
Conrad: b 5-28-1763 d 1-26-1846 m Susanna Strange Pvt NC ★
John: b 1755 d 12-10-1815 m Elizabeth Bartlett 2Lt VA
Michael: b 6-5-1729 d 2-25-1804 m Margaret Tallman Pvt NY

CORNELIUS,
Charles: b 1762 d 1843 m Elizabeth Jennings Cpl VA
Elias: b 10-17-1758 d 6-13-1823 m Rachel Stalker SrgnMte RI
Isaac: b 1758 d 5-3-1836 m Mary McCormac MM MD
Moses: b 1-4-1743 d 9- -1796 m Anna Carman PS NY
Wm.: b 1754 d 7-27-1842 m Lettice Cargile Matr NC

CORNELL,
Benjamin: b 11-4-1750 d 2-6-1838 m Martha Elizabeth Wilbur Ens RI
Ebenezer: b 7-18-1738 d p 1811 m Peace Macomber Pvt MA
George: b 5-21-1729 d p 1780 m Rebecca Preston CS RI
Gideon: b 2-5-1746 d 6-21-1825 m Elizabeth Tucker Pvt RI
Gideon: b 12-1-1745 d 12-16-1830 m (1)Prudence Winslow (2)Mrs Martha Thornton Capt RI W ★
James: b 7-2-1751 d 1-12-1829 m Rachel Dennis Pvt NY
James: b 1-1-1753 d 1839 m (1)Elizabeth Chadeayne (2)Phoebe Smith Pvt NY
Joseph: b c 1720 d p 3-3-1775 m Jannetje — Sol NJ
Joseph: b 1759 d 4-2-1825 m Roxiant Preston Ens RI ★
Latham: b 1755 d 1-20-1803 m Susannah Wood Pvt RI
Lewis: b c 1755 d 2-8-1837 m Jane — Sgt NY
Matthew: b 11-11-1745 d 3-4-1807 m Elizabeth Shrieve PS MA
Rem: b 6-9-1744 d 7-18-1825 m Peter Neelitie Hegeman Pvt PA
Samuel: b 9-1-1761 d 9-26-1812 m Eleanor Hunt Sol NY
Thomas: b 1742 d 5-29-1807 m Ann Gale Pvt NY
Timothy: b p. 1735 d 1804 m Lititia Everett Capt CS NY
Wm.: b 10-17-1750 d 6-11-1825 m Hannah Finch Ens NY
Wm.: b 2-25-1762 d 11-3-1850 m Mary — Pvt NY ★
Wm.: b 7-13-1722 d 10-14-1783 m Elshe Kroesen Pvt PA
Zebulon: b 11-25-1751 d 3-13-1834 m Ruth Allen Sol NY

CORNETT,
Jean: b 1750 d 1792 m Margaret — Pvt MA
Nathaniel: b 1760 d a. 1-4-1838 m Mildred Hensley Pvt VA
Wm.: b 1762 d 11-26-1836 m (1)Rhoda Gilliam (2)Mary Everage Pvt VA ★

CORNING,
Benjamin: b 6-4-1738 d 1780-3 m Anna Corning Pvt MA
Bliss: b 10-30-1763 d 2-10-1846 m Lucinda Smith Pvt CT
John: b 10-20-1729 d 2-30-1807 m Miriam Crowell PS NH
Uriah: b 3-20-1758 d 5-5-1851 m Elizabeth Willett Pvt CT

CORNISH,
Andrew Hillard: b 7-15-1751 d 11-5-1791 m Huldah Shepherd Sgt MA
Benjamin: b 4-6-1744 d 2-15-1816 m Elizabeth — Sgt VT
Benjamin: b 11-4-1749 d p 1790 m Freelove Miller Pvt NY
Elisha Sr.: b 6-5-1722 d 4-27-1794 m (1)Hepzibah Humphrey (2)Mary Dyer (3)Charity Pettibone Humphrey Pvt CT
Elisha Jr.: b 12-7-1748 d 3-21-1826 m Sarah Case Pvt CT
Gabriel: b 5-1-1758 d 3-27-1841 m (1)Electa Moses (2)Anna Crooks Cpl MA
George: b 8-10-1760 d 11-21-1841 m (1)Anna Gillett (2)Susannah Mitchelson Pvt CT ★
Jabez Sr.: b 1726 d 1790 m (1)Dorothy Dibble (2)Sarah Whiting 1Lt MA
Jabez, Jr.: b c. 1754 d 1794 m (1)Rebecca Congdon (2)Mrs Kate Phillips Pvt MA
Joel: b 3-22-1763 d 7-28-1851 m Susannah L. Pettibone Pvt CT ★
John: b 1734 d p 1783 m (1)Lydia Shurtleff (2)Sarah Bartlett (3)Phebe (Spooner) Pope (4)Elizabeth Clark Sgt MA
John: b a.1753 d 1805 m Elizabeth Harriot Capt PA
Joseph: b 6-13-1729 d 12-29-1776 m Elizabeth Morton Lt CT
Joseph: b c 1744 d 8-24-1777 m Phebe — Pvt CT
Josiah: b 10-15-1760 d 10-10-1844 m Abigal Clark Pvt MA
Wm.: b 3-3-1757 d 2-21-1836 m (1)Mercy Swift (2)Mehitable Bates Sol MA

CORNUE,
Daniel: b 12-21-1740 d 11-27-1818 m (1)Sarah Wessels (2)Marjorie Brown Pvt NY

CORNWALL, (includes CORNWELL)
Andrew: b 1759 d 11-3-1799 m Mary Bartlett Pvt CT
Ashbel: b 2-9-1754 d 1-2-1835 m Susanna Gaylord Pvt CT
Benjamin Sr: b 2-16-1736 d 8- -1807 m Hannah Williams Sgt CT
Benjamin, Jr.: b 11-20-1759 d 6-1-1835 m (1)Esther Carrington (2)Submit Keep Pvt CT ★
Charles: b c 1760 d 1824 m Betty Thornton PS VA
Daniel: b 12-28-1760 d 12-24-1843 m (1)Zerviah Wise (2)Rachel Hale Pvt MA
Edmund: b c 1735 d p 1800 m Frances Wolfe Pvt VA
Elijah: b c 1760 d 11-18-1827 m Catherine Cavenaugh Pvt VA
Elisha: bpt 10-18-1721 d 2-17-1781 m Ann Johnson Pvt CT
Hewlett: b 12-31-1750 d 6-3-1828 m Elizabeth Willis LCol NY
Isaac: b 6-30-1747 d 1812 m Hannah Roberts Pvt CT
Isaac: b 9-17-1750 d 1837 m Candace Smith Pvt CT ★
John: b 5-6-1759 d 11-25-1841 m Lucy Joice Pvt CT ★
John: b 10-26-1715/6 d 1-8-1790 m (1)Martha Hewlett (2)Phebe Hewlett PS NY
Joseph: b 4-7-1711 d 2-16-1787 m (1)Abigail Candee (2)Mindwell Lane PS CT
Nathaniel: b 8-3-1753 d 1838 m Anna Plumb Pvt CT
Ozias: b 1762 d 3-13-1831 m (1)Susannah Robinson (2)Lydia — Pvt MA
Thomas: b 4-13-1740 d 12-12-1815 m Mary Beers CG CT
Wm.: b 1746 d p. 1794 m — X — Sgt MD

CORPE,
Caleb: b 6-23-1754 d 3-6-1837 m Anna Burgess Sgt RI ★
Joseph: b 9-15-1758 d 11-24-1823 m Sarah Toms Pvt NY

CORPMAN, (includes KORBMAN)
Christian: b c.1750 d a.11-11-1802 m Elizabeth Funk Pvt PA

CORRELL,
Philip: b 3-4-1736 d 4-5-1805 m Maria Engle Schug Pvt PA
Philip: b 2-18-1759 d 2-1-1843 m Catherine Fries Sol PA

CORRIGAN,
Patrick: b 1760 d 1838 m Polly Singleton Pvt PA

CORSA,
Andrew: b 1-24-1762 d 11-21-1852 m (1)Mary Poole (2)Helena Bussing (3)Mary Bussing Guide NY
Isaac: b 1735 d 8-9-1822 m Mary Gibbs Pvt NY

CORSER, (includes COURSER, COURSEY)
David: b 1-27-1754 d 8-23-1827 m Ruth Blasdell Pvt VT
James: b c. 1741 d p. 4-17-1814 m (1)Winifred Riddle (2)Mary Gay Dunlap CS VA
John Sr.: b 1678 d 1776 m Tabitha Kenney PS NH
John Jr.: b 1718 d 1791 m Jane Nichols PS NH
Jonathan: b c 1747 d 1831 m Lucy Foster Pvt NH
Samuel: b c 1746 d 11-1-1826 m (1)Sarah Fitz Gerald (2)Betsey Colby Cpl PA NH
Thomas: b 1743 d 12-11-1829 m (1)Ann Dunlap (2)Mary Downing Pvt PS NH
Wm.: b c. 1758 d 1812 m Abigail Gordon Pvt NH

CORSON, (includes CORSEN, COURSEN)
Abner: b 6-25-1729 d p.9-20-1798 m Jane Cresse PS NJ
Abraham: b c. 1760 d p. 5-22-1814 m Jemima Van Deren Pvt NJ
Benjamin: b 3-6-1743 d 10-2-1811 m Sarah Dungan Pvt PA
Cornelius Jr: b 1755 d p.1806 m Margaret Robinson Pvt PA
Daniel: bpt 3-9-1735 d 5-22-1801 m Elizabeth Bogart PS NY
Daniel: b 1- -1754 d 5-9-1816 m Prudence Carter Pvt PA
David: b 1-9-1761 d 7-6-1843 m Mary McDuffee Pvt Smn NH ★
Ichabod: b c. 1726 d p. 1807 m (1)Mary Allen (2)Joanna Twombly PS CS NH
Jacob: b a. 1737 d 1- -1803 m Charity Stillwell Pvt NJ
Jesse: b 5-6-1742 d p.1793 m Martha Somers Pvt NJ
John: b a.4-4-1739 d a.10-7-1803 m Martha (Corson) — Pvt NJ
John, Jr.: b c. 1739/40 d p. 1784 m Mary Goff Pvt NJ
Joshua: bpt 2-7-1754 d c.1790 m Kesiah — Sgt NH
Levi: b 11-17-1737 d 1777/8 m Margaret Hand Pvt NJ
Parmenas: b 1-23-1760 d 2-22-1843 m (1)Rachel Willets (2)Roxanna (Griffing) Benezett (3)Rachel Corson Pvt NJ
Rem: b a. 5-31-1730 d a. 5- -1797 m Hannah Stillwell Pvt NJ

CORSS, (includes CORSE)
Dan: b 12-18-1739 d p.1781 m Chloe Severance Sgt MA
Gad: b 1723 d 7-31-1788 m Mary Wright PS MA
John: b 10-17-1749 d 9- -1823 m (1)Elizabeth Roe (2)Mary Mannering Capt DE ★

CORTELYOU, (includes CORTELYOU)
Harman: b 1-28-1747 d 10- -1816 m Catherine Van Dyke Pvt NJ
Hendrick: b 8-8-1761 d 3-14-1841 m (1)Ann Dehart (2)Mrs Elizabeth Nevius Voorhees Pvt NJ
Hendrick Sr.: b 10-10-1736 d 10-31-1800 m Johanna Stoothoof PS NJ
Henry: b 7-1-1760 d 1- -1825 m Elizabeth Stulz MM Pvt NJ
Isaac: b 8-11-1736 d 10-3-1811 m Alotta Lott PS NY
Ruliff: b 7-6-1758 d 4-14-1802 m Gitty Van Arsdall Pvt NJ

CORTHELL,
Robert: b 6-1-1756 d 5-22-1833 m Elizabeth Hersey Cpl MA PA ★
Sherebiah: b 4-20-1760 d 10-22-1836 m Lydia Whiton Pvt MA

CORTNER,
George: b 5- -1738 d 2-5-1819 m — X — PS NC

CORTRIGHT, (includes CORTWRIGHT, COURTWRIGHT, KORTRIGHT)
Abraham: b 7-8-1748 d 1-12-1825 m Effie Drake Pvt PA
Benjamin: b a. 1743 d 12-3-1830 m Catherine Cudabee Capt NY
Benjamin: b 1731 d a.1787 m Catherine Hover Pvt PA
Cornelius: b 3-7-1764 d 5-25-1848 m Catherine Kennedy Sol PA
Daniel: b 5-3-1743 d p 1784 m Antje Westbrook PS NY
Daniel: bpt 4-13-1729 d 1788 m Russie Van Auken Pvt PA
John Sr: bpt 8-15-1714 d a. 5-14-1783 m Margaret Dennemerken Maj NJ
John: b a.1754 d 7-3-1778 m Margaret Yokee Sol PA
Lawrence: b 12-21-1758 d 2-11-1843 m Mary Cox Vol NY
Moses: bpt 3-24-1745 d 6-26-1824 m (1)Anna Vanetten (2)Mrs Mariah Cortright Capt PS NY
Solomon: b 7-8-1752 d 1844 m Hannah Ayers 2Sgt NJ ★
Wm Ennes: bpt 10-31-1739 d p 1804 m Sarah Hyndshaw Pvt NY

CORWIN, (includes CORWINE, CURRAN,CURRIN)
Benjamin: b 1750 d 4- -1821 m Hannah — Arfr NJ
David Jr: b 1733 d p. 10-16-1795 m (1)Mary Wells (2)Abigail Davis PS NY
Edward: b 2-13-1759 d 9-15-1849 m (1)Esther Barstow (2)Olive Colegrove Pvt NY ★
Eli: b 4-1-1757 d 3-16-1833 m Dorothy Horton Pvt NY
George: b 11-17-1759 d 12-19-1787 m Ruth Corwine Cpl NJ
Gilbert: b c 2- -1745 d 4-11-1810 m Amy Knapp Pvt NY
Henry: b 6-10-1752 d 1-28-1833 m Bethea Reeve PS NY
Isaac: b 4-7-1759 d 11-1-1830 m Experience Reeves Tms NJ
Jacob: b 10- -1747 d 9-20-1834 m (1)Sarah Howell (2)Mrs Mehitable Davis Pvt PS NY
Jedediah: b 1728 d 5-7-1799 m Abiah Swezy CS NY
Jeremiah: b 1735 d 10-22-1821 m (1)Mary — (2)Abigail — Sol PS NY
Jesse: b 1736 d 1791 m Keziah Case PS NJ
John, Sr.: b 1735 d 12-22-1817 m (1)Sarah Hubbard (2)Deborah Brown 1Lt NY
John: b 1732 d 11-8-1815 m (1)Elizabeth Wells (2)Anna Wells PS NY
Jonathan: bpt 1-28-1754 d 1-4-1785 m (1)Elizabeth Corwin (2)Hannah Reeve Pvt CT
Joseph: b 4-28-1753 d 1823 m Mary Wortman Pvt NJ
Joshua: b 3-25-1735 d 7-6-1812 m (1)Annie Paine (2)Rhoda (Davis) Emerson Pvt NY
Richard: b 1756 d 10-27-1848 m (1)Elizabeth Marthers (2)Hannah Hallock Pvt NJ PA ★
Richard: b 12-29-1748 d 11-19-1813 m Sarah Snyder LT NJ
Robert: b 1761 d 11-18-1819 m Nancy Chilcote Pvt MD
Samuel: b 1706 d 3-18-1784 m Phebe Howell PS NY
Selah: bpt 1-16-1757 d p 1792 m Johanna Halleck Pvt NY
Silas: b 1731 d 3-1-1806 m Elizabeth Halleck PS NY
Theophilus: b 1726 d 6-10-1777 m Anna Jaynes Pvt NY
Thomas: b 1752 d 2-18-1827 m Elizabeth Clark MM NY
Timothy: b 1750 d 10-18-1777 m Amy Jane — Sgt NY
Timothy: b c.1720 d 8-22-1792 m Mary Webb PS NY
Wm.: b 2-21-1744 d 12-1-1818 m Hannah Reeves Lt NJ

CORWITHE,
Caleb: b 7-31-1752 d 1-21-1813 m Mary Halsey Pvt NY

CORYELL, (includes CORIELL)
Abraham: b 8-29-1738 d 9-22-1828 m (1)Esther Heth (2)Deborah (Clark) Runyon Pvt NJ
Abraham: b 4-3-1738 d 5- -1828 m Sarah Davis Pvt NJ
Elias: b 8-22-1741 d 1-6-1820 m Sarah Runyon PS NJ
Elisha: b 9-19-1756 d 10-3-1847 m (1)Mary Covert (2)Nancy Dunn Pvt NJ W★
Emanuel: b 10-24-1754 d 1-7-1835 m Frances Caldwell Dep QM PS PA★
George: b 4-28-1761 d 4- -1836 m Charity Van Buskirk Pvt PA
John: b 6-12-1730 d 12-13-1799 m Elizabeth Harvey Maj PA

COSART, (includes CASSATT, CORSAT, COSAD, COSSART)
Anthony: b 1740 d 1790 m Catherine Coon Pvt NJ
David: b 4-11-1743 d 12-29-1823 m Sarah Van Duyn Pvt PA
Francis: b c. 1713 d p. 1795 m Margaretta Van Nest PS PA
Jacob: b 4-21-1751 d 5-14-1815 m Mary Montfort 1Lt PA
John: b 3-17-1761 d 3-10-1821 m Susannah Bird Le Ferre Sol NJ

COSBY, (includes COZBY)
Charles: b 1746 d 1795 m Barbara Byers Ens VA
Charles, Sr.: b 1726 d p. 8-2-1800 m (1)Elizabeth Wingfield (2)Elizabeth Sydnor Pvt VA
Charles, Jr.: b 1745 d 1795 m Rebecca Wood Pvt VA
Charles: b 10-21-1754 d p. 11-3-1802 m Mary Minter PS VA
David: b c. 1730 d p. 7-20-1803 m (1)Mary Johnson (2)Susanna Witte PS VA
Garland: b 1749 d 11-28-1839 m Lucy Poindexter OrdlSgt PS VA ★
Hickerson: b c. 1759 d 1804-21 m Ann Harris Sgt VA

James, Sr.: b 1715 d 3- -1789 m Sarah Nelson PS VA
James, Jr.: b 1753 d 1831 m Isabella Woods Cpl Dr VA
John: b 1732 d 1788 m Martha Baptist Pvt VA
John: b c. 1759 d p. 1788 m Jemima Yancey Sol VA
John: b 9-19-1741 d 1827 m Susanna Wingfield Pvt VA
Thomas: b c. 1760 d 12- -1806 m Elizabeth Watkins Pvt VA
Wingfield: b 1746 d 9- -1814 m (1)Mary Morris (2)Anne Baker PS VA
Zacheus: b 1753 d 5-27-1834 m Susan Dabney MM VA

COSDEN,
Samuel: b 10-23-1748 d 11-6-1811 m Martha — 3Sgt MD

COSGROVE,
Joseph: b c. 1739 d p. 1790 m (1)Mary North (2)Eliza — 2Lt NJ

COSMAN, (includes KAUTZMAN)
Bernhardt: b c. 1750 d 1822 m Margaret Annie Sweigart Pvt PA
Johannes: b 1721 d 9-15-1810 m Barbara — Pvt NY

COSNAHAN,
Joseph: b 3-25-1758 d 1840 m Henrietta McGee Pvt NC ★

COSSITT, (includes COSSIT)
Ambrose: b 9-17-1749 d 7-9-1809 m Anne Cathrine Cole Pvt CT
Asa: b 3-22-1754 d 1-30-1838 m Mary Cole Fif CT
Rene: b 9-3-1722 d 4-25-1810 m (1)Phebe Hillyer (2)Martha Holcomb (3)Martha Barbour Pvt CT
Roswell: b 5-22-1763 d — m — Ingalls Pvt VT
Timothy: b 10-9-1754 d 10-10-1836 m Chloe Battles Lt CT

COST,
Francis: b c. 1720 d 1- -1782 m Catherine Mullendore PS MD
Jacob: b 1745 d 2-22-1827 m Mariana — PS MD

COSTELLO,
John: b 1755 d 9-19-1825 m Mary Duane Sol MA

COSTIGAN,
Francis: b c. 1744 d 7-29-1821 m Jane Carr 1Lt NJ ★

COSTNER,
Jacob: b 1732 d 1-16-1779 m Mrs Elizabeth Brooks Hoyle Maj NC
Thomas: b 1747 d 7-2-1835 m Catherine — Pvt NC ★

COSTON, (includes COSTIN)
Bishop: b 1759 d 1847 m Elizabeth Pelhim Pvt NH ★
Ebenezer: b 9-10-1765 d 2-17-1814 m Sarah J. Hale Pvt NH
Francis: b c. 1740 d a. 12-14-1807 m Susanna Elliot Lt VA
Stephen: b 1755 d p. 9-13-1832 m Abigail Burns Pvt NC ★

COTHEAL,
Isaac: b 10-13-1743 d 5-1-1812 m Elizabeth Evans Pvt NJ

COTTER,
Wm.: b 1762 d p. 1789 m Catherine Vance Pvt VA

COTTINGHAM,
David: b 3-17-1742/3 d p. 1785 m Mary Gunby Pvt MD
John: b 6-24-1754 d 1-6-1829 m Priscilla Fleming Pvt MD
Thomas: b 1718 d c. 1783 m Mary Long PS MD

COTTLE,
Isaac: b c. 1751 d 1-31-1814 m Rhoda Manchester Pvt MA
Jabez: b c. 1747 d 6-4-1820 m Sarah Arnold CS VT
Joseph: b 7-28-1753 d p.1787 m Azubah Power Pvt VT
Robert: b 8-6-1758 d 9-4-1845 m Lydia Luce Sgt MA ★
Shubael: b 1723 d 10-16-1808 m Amy Allen PS CS MA
Silas: b 1752 d 1824 m (1)Jerusha Tilton (2)Jemima Tilton Cpl MA
Warren: b 1755 d p. 2-8-1811 m Relief Farnsworth Capt PS VT

COTTON, (includes COTTEN)
Arthur: b 1712 d 1786 m Elizabeth Rutland PS NC
Benjamin: b 5-14-1758 d 7-13-1846 m Dolly Smith Sgt NH ★
BybeLake: b 1763 d 3- -1846 m Alice Chase Pvt CT
Elihu: b 1-8-1734 d 8-16-1820 m (1)Jane Gilbert (2)Rebecca Hurlburt Grd CT
James: b 12-25-1749 d 2-20-1806 m Achsah Holloway Drm NJ
James, Jr.: b 10- -1765 d 2-18-1838 m Nancy Johnston OrdlSgt PS VA ★
John: b 1-7-1719 d 1785 m Bathsheba Sage CS CT
John: b 1-10-1746 d 2-1-1831 m Lucy Little QM Lt MA ★
John: b 4-5-1712 d 4-19-1789 m Hannah Sturtevant PS MA
John: b 10-28-1750 d 8-14-1820 m (1)Abigail Taylor (2)Hannah Lane Pvt NH
John: b 2-13-1748 d p. 1793 m Lydia Griffin Pvt NH
Josiah: b 4-14-1748 d 4- -1819 m (1)Lydia Parker (2)Rachel Barnes Sgt MA
Melvin: b 12-10-1759 d 12-16-1846 m (1)Joanna Dennis (2)Hannah Estabrook Pvt MA
Michael: b 3-15-1758 d 1833 m Mindwell Thrall Pvt MA
Nathaniel: b 8-3-1740 d 2- -1785 m (1)Elizabeth Berry (2)Hannah Elkins (Beck) PS NH
Ralph: b 1-10-1742 d 1817 m Elizabeth Kitchen Pvt PA

Rowland: b 3-22-1759 d 6-13-1848 m Kezia Holt Sgt CT ★
Samuel: b 11-7-1759 d 7-18-1836 m Sarah Banks Pvt CT
Theophilus: b 3-31-1716 d 2-18-1782 m Martha Saunders Col MA
Thomas, Jr.: b 4-30-1730 d 9-28-1808 m (1)Sarah Holbrook (2)Mary Bingham Pvt CT
Thomas: bpt 4-19-1724 d 12-29-1781 m Agnes (Smith) Hinckley PS ME
Thomas: b 11-4-1748 d 6-5-1795 m Priscilla Knight Capt NC
Thomas: b 1763 d p. 1830 m Anne Boylen Sol NC
Thomas: b — d a. 5-8-1816 m Anne — Pvt PS SC
Willard: b 2-4-1757 d 11-19-1828 m Mercy Gallop Pvt VT
Wm.: b 10-5-1751 d 3-28-1814 m Ruth Cram Pvt NH
Wm.: b 2-24-1738 d 9-8-1821 m (1)Mary Clark (2)Ruth Page PS NH
Wm.: b 1748 d — m Sibbel Peirce Pvt RI
Wm.: b c. 1720 d 1788 m Mary Taylor CS PS VA

COTTRELL, (includes COTTERAL, COTTEREL)
Asa: b 11- -1746 d 6-15-1833 m Lucinda Otis Clapp Pvt MA ★
Benjamin: b 9-14-1742 d c. 1820 m Mary Cheney Pvt MA
Eber: b 3-1-1756 d 7-31-1833 m Elizabeth Crandall Pvt NY
George: b c. 1759 d p. 1815 m — X — Pvt NJ
John: b 1724 d 10-31-1778 m Lois Boardman PS RI
Lebbeus: b 1755 d 8-15-1794 m Sarah — Lt RI
Nicholas: b 1754 d 6-19-1842 m Lydia Kinne Pvt MA ★
Richard: b 1712 d 3-12-1792 m (1)Judith Smith (2)Mary Alley PS VA
Thomas: b 7-16-1750 d 3-27-1836 m Nancy Gerance Spy Sgt VA ★

COTTRILL,
John: b c. 1763/64 d 7-9-1850 m Elizabeth Aior Pvt VA★

COUCH,
Abraham: bpt 7-10-1763 d 8-29-1841 m Abigail — Pvt Fif CT ★
Benjamin: b 6-25-1753 d 4-26-1816 m Rachel Heath Pvt NH
Daniel: b 7-29-1739 d 4-6-1818 m Sarah House Pvt CT
Ebenezer, Sr.: b 1709 d 3-23-1797 m (1)Ann Crane (2)Eunice — PS CT
Ebenezer, Jr.: b 1-20-1733 d p. 9-16-1800 m (1)Elizabeth McCarty (2)Sarah Kinney Bostwick Capt CT
Gideon: b 9-12-1757 d 9-21-1817 m Eleanor Wakeman Pvt CT
John: b 10- -1760 d 4-1-1824 m Rhoda Bennett Fif Pvt CT
John: b 8-6-1725 d 4-11-1806 m (1)Azubah Andrews (2)Sarah (Moss) Royce Capt CT
John: b 1762 d 3-14-1830 m Jane Hinckley Pvt MA
Jonathan: b 7-16-1736 d a. 8-3-1786 m (1)Eunice Griffin (2)Mabel (Cole) Meeker PS CT
Joshua: bpt 6-11-1758 d 10-13-1841 m Patty Patchen Pvt CT
Nathan: b c. 1725/26 d 1802 m Abigail — Pvt PA
Samuel: b 8-28-1758 d 4-16-1813 m — Ferris Pvt MA
Samuel: b 1755 d 8-14-1849 m Huldah Granger Pvt (MA or CT)
Simon: b 1729 d 4-25-1809 m Rebecca Nash PS CT
Stephen: b 9-18-1752 d 8-9-1833 m Poliphemia Carrington Pvt CT ★
Thomas: b 2-12-1751 d 3-16-1817 m Sarah Nash Sgt QM CT
Thomas: b 1757 d 8-30-1839 m Rachel Miller Pvt
Thomas Nash: b 4-18-1758 d 1-3-1821 m Abigail Stebbins Pvt CG CT CT
Timothy: b 1748 d p. 1779 m Eunice Perkins Pvt MA
Wm.: bpt 5-13-1759 d 1845 m Abigail Adams Pvt MA ★
Wm.: b a. 1748 d p. 1788 m Abegal Lane Pvt PA

COUCHMAN,
Henry: b 1761 d 11-29-1826 m Christina — Sol NY

COUGHLAN,
Richard: b — d 3-11-1801 m Sarah Peacock SgtMaj NH

COUILLARD,
John: b 11- -1728 d a. 1790 m Mary Mock Sol MA

COULTER, (includes COALTER)
Alexander: b 1760 d 10-3-1828 m Esther Mifflin McCaskey Pvt MD
James: b 1748 d 5-7-1783 m Eleanor Green Pvt NY
James: b 6-8-1751 d 5-14-1814 m Margaret — Pvt PA
John: b 1751 d 5-24-1823 m Mary McCaskey Dr NS
John: b c. 1740 d 1789 m Abigail Parshall Sgt NJ
John: b 1738 d 3-26-1831 m X Pvt PA ★
John, Sr.: b 1729 d 7-7-1789 m Issabella — CS VA
John, Jr.: b 1748 d 1809/10 m Olive — Lt VA
Martin: b 2-11-1759 d 7-7-1847 m Elizabeth Aydelotte Pvt NC
Matthew: b 1759 d 1843 m Mary Pendergrass Pvt NC
Michael: b 1736 d 1795 m Elizabeth Moore Lt VA
Nathaniel: b 1759 d 1825 m Isabella — Pvt PA
Robert S.: b 1760 d 1821 m Margaret Fleming Pvt SC
Samuel: b 12-30-1743 d 10-15-1820 m Mary Black Ens PA
Samuel: b 1744 d p. 1825 m Betty — Lt PA ★
Samuel: b c. 1742 d 5-6-1794 m Margaret Thompson Pvt PA
Thomas: b 12-18-1757 d 4-20-1805 m Hester Mustard Pvt DE
Wm.: b 12- -1760 d 1830 m X Pvt PA

COUNCIL, (includes COUNCILL)
Charles: b 1727 d 7-6-1805 m Eurydice — Sol NC
Henry: b 1712 d 1792 m Elizabeth Pledger Capt SC

James: b 1716 d 1804 m (1)Sallie Kitchen (2)Joanna Willis PS NC
Joshua: b c. 1712 d a. 9-2-1793 m X PS VA

COUNCILMAN,
George: b c. 1735 d 10-15-1794 m Ruth — PS MD

COUNTRYMAN, (includes CONTREMAN)
Adam: b 1755 d 9-5-1851 m Elizabeth Diefendorf PS Sol NY
Conrad: b 3-2-1736 d p. 1823 m X Sgt NY
George: b c. 1735 d 6-13-1779 m Rachel Milhaus CS PA
George: b c. 1728 d 1808/9 m Elizabeth Christina Diefendorf Lt NY
John: b 3-2-1736 d 4- -1789 m Rachel Richards Ens NY
John: b 2-14-1748 d 7-10-1839 m Katherine Horning Pvt NY

COURAIN,
Lazare: b 6-8-1743 d 1819 m Mary Ann Bouchillon Pvt SC

COURTER,
Peter: b 2-9-1748 d 8-20-1809 m Jannetje Jacobus Pvt NJ

COURTNEY, (includes COURTENAY, COURTENEY)
Hercules: b 10-1736 d 8-20-1816 m Sarah Drury PS MD
Hugh: b 1759 d 6-10-1802 m Jane Little Pvt PA
John: b 3-4-1759 d 10-26-1831 m (1)Mary Kincaid (2)Lucinda Martin Pvt PA
Luke: b 3-8-1757 d 10-28-1802 m Zipporah Crane Pvt NJ
Thomas: b 1741 d 1795 m Fannie Pines Sgt VA
Thomas: b 1759 d 1825 m Susan — Pvt VA
Wm.: b 1756 d 6-2-1817 m Mary Chamberlain Pvt PA
Wm.: b c. 1745 d p. 1795 m X Capt VA

COURTS,
George: b 5-6-1761 d 5-25-1847 m (1)Zippora Cooper (2)Chloe Tolson (3)Hannah Hudnall Sol VA

COURVOISIER,
John Francis William: b 1751 d 11-8-1811 m Mary Fox PS GA

COUSE,
Henry: b 8-4-1735 d 12-11-1804 m Mrs Margaret Kanoph PS NJ
John: b 9-3-1759 d 3-24-1845 m Mary Rarick Pvt NJ

COUSINS, (includes COZZENS, COUZENS)
Benjamin, Jr.: b 11-28-1755 d 7-21-1825 m Anne Wheaton 2Lt RI
Elisha: b 11-20-1735 d 1-18-1816 m Bathsheba Hamor Sgt MA
Henry: b 7-22-1758 d 6-5-1824 m Margaret — Matr VA
Issacher: b 8-24-1754 d 1-18-1840 m (1)Mary Daniels (2)Susanna Greene Sgt RI
John: b a. 1750 d p. 1792 m Eliza Clark Pvt VA
Joseph: b 2-2-1726 d 12-27-1787 m (1)Susanna Eames (2)Abigail Jones CS MA
Matthew: b 11-23-1762 d 9-17-1810 m Isabella Coddington Pvt NY
Nathaniel: b 1745 d 8-13-1832 m Catharine Lassell Maj MA
Wm.: b a. 1755 d 4- -1825 m Mary Ann — Pvt PA

COVELL, (includes COVEL, COVIL)
Benjamin: b 1762 d 11-22-1822 m Sybil Durkee Pvt MA ★
Ebenezer 2nd: b 1-11-1759 d 1840 m Saberina Childs Pvt RI ★
Elijah: b 5-12-1752 d 4-21-1821 m Lydia Hodge Pvt CT
Eliphalet: b 3-29-1756 d 4-2-1834 m Betsy Watson Pvt Mar MA
Ezra: bpt 9-21-1746 d 1793 m Hannah Hollister Pvt MA
Henry: b c. 1747 d p. 9- -1832 m Polly Reed Pvt CT MA ★
James: b 9-9-1742 d 4-20-1850 m (1)Mary — (2)Margaret Sluyter Pvt CT ★
James, Sr.: b 1701-8 d 6-14-1781 m (1)Mehitable Nickerson (2)Mrs Ruth Crowell Kelly CS MA
James, Jr.: b 6-28-1742 d p. 6-2-1781 m Sarah Hall PS NY
Jeremiah: b 11-23-1757 d 1-4-1825 m Margaret Ann — PS MD
Jonathan: b 1750 d 7-24-1831 m Mary — Pvt NY
Philip: b 9-18-1748 d 1787 m Mercy Fox PS CT
Richard: b 10- -1765 d 12-3-1853 m (1)Penelope West (2)Mercy Pratt Pvt RI
Sampson: b 4-4-1754 d 6-4-1840 m Mary Smith Pvt CT
Solomon: b 10-7-1745 d p. 1798 m Mary Baker Pvt MA

COVENHOVEN, (includes COWENHOVEN, KOUWENHOVEN)
Adrain: b 12-19-1753 d 3-28-1843 m Barbara DuBois Pvt MM NY
Albert: b 10-24-1743 d 3-6-1826 m Patience Covenhoven Pvt NJ
Albert: bpt 6-7-1756 d 5-12-1835 m (1)Sarah Bonham (2)Frances (Golden) Drake (3)Elizabeth La Rue Pvt NJ★
Albert: b 1721 d 1778 m Sarah — Pvt PA
Dominicus: b c. 1730 d 1778 m Mary Updike Pvt NJ
Edward: b 1730 d 2-26-1786 m Annatie Koeme Pvt NY
Gerrit: b 5-29-1744 d 7-23-1810 m Hannah White Pvt NJ
Harmen: b 6- -1740 d 1-4-1804 m Phoebe Bailey Sol NJ
Jacob: b 6-19-1746 d 11-18-1825 m Mary Schenck PS NJ
Johannes: b 10-4-1746 d 9-13-1823 m (1)Greta Ammerman (2)Elizabeth VanPelt (3)Catherine Stellerwerf PS NY
John: b 3-8-1734 d 4-21-1734 m Eleanor Wikoff Col NJ
John: b 2-6-1740 d 12-24-1811 m Jane McGaillard Pvt NJ
Peter: b 10-18-1743 d 8-20-1831 m Phoebe Dye Sgt NJ
Peter: b 10-12-1716 d 10-5-1784 m Williampie Voorhees PM NJ
Peter: b 12-4-1732 d 1800 (?) m Hannah Forman PS NJ

COVENHOVEN, contd.
Peter: b 9-25-1753 d 5-27-1787 m Lammettie Lott Pvt NY
Robert: b 12-7-1755 d 10-29-1846 m Mercy Kelsy Cutter Pvt PA ★
Ruliff: b 1706 d 1786 m Sarah Van Voorhees PS NJ
Ruliff: b 12-18-1767 d 12-18-1854 m Amy Lake Tms NJ
Thomas Davis: b c. 1763 d 12-19-1819 m Abigail Cook Pvt NJ W ★
Wm.: b 4-1-1753 d 10-11-1823 m Elizabeth Schenck Pvt NJ
Wm. P.: b 8-13-1735 d 2-13-1823 m Altia Jewell Pvt NJ

COVENTRY,
John: b 1750 d 5-2-1845 m Martha Brown Pvt PA
Wm.: b c. 1760 d 1820 m Elizabeth Cully Pvt NY

COVER, (includes KOBAR)
George: b 1-27-1741 d 1820 m Elizabeth Mohler Pvt PA
Gideon: b 12-17-1738 d 3-15-1810 m Frances Stahle Pvt PA
Jacob: b — d a. 1820 m Elizabeth Woods Pvt PA

COVERT,
Abraham: b c. 1741 d 6-17-1815 m Ara Ann Coshun Ens NJ
Daniel: b 1757 d 3-17-1849 m Jane Mannoth Pvt NJ ★
Daniel: b a. 1756 d 1803 m Catherine — Pvt NJ
Eder: b 5-15-1760 d 3-28-1826 m Rachel Ann Harris MM NJ
Isaac: b 12-1-1755 d 9-14-1825 m Anna Vanarsdell FifMaj NJ ★
Isaac, II: b 4-14-1745 d p. 1840 m Isabella Hull Sol PA
John: b 1761 d 3-17-1831 m Jane — Pvt NJ
Luke, Sr.: b 1713 d 1-22-1778 m (1)Femmite — (2)Hermte — (3)Hormpye — (4)Hovpie — PS NJ
Luke, Jr.: b 8-6-1732 d 1-26-1828 m (1)Anna Marselis (2)Delilah — (3)Mrs Jane Harris Pvt MM NJ
Peter: b 1-4-1759 d 1849 m Amy Parker Pvt NJ VA ★
Samuel: b 4-4-1760 d 1-27-1803 m Hannah Atwater Pvt CT
Tunis: b 3-25-1745 d c. 2-9-1825 m Magdalen Hoagland Pvt NJ

COVEY,
Wm.: b 6-18-1765 d 10-19-1844 m (1)Esther Yarns (2)Betsey Coon (3)Nancy Smith Pvt NY

COVIN, (includes COVVAIN)
Lazarus: b 6-8-1743 d 1819 m (1)X(2)Mrs Mary Anne LeRoy Bouchillon Pvt SC

COVINGTON,
Benjamin: b c. 1746 d 1813 m Frances — Pvt NC
Francis: b 1754 d 7-21-1823 m Lucy Strother Capt VA
John: b 1752 d c. 1808 m (1)Hannah Dockery (2)Nancy Love PS NC
John, Sr.: b 1735 d 1809 m Anne Dockary Pvt NC
John, Jr.: b 1757 d 2-28-1797 m Elizabeth Thomas Pvt NC
Matthew Dockery: b 1-24-1760 d 1837 m (1)— Dockery (2)Martha Yates Pvt NC
Robert: b 1-3-1760 d 8-10-1847 m (1)Mary Duncan (2)Amy Burk Pvt VA ★
Thomas: b 6-10-1725 d 8-25-1817 m Mary Hicks Lt NC
Wm.: b 1726 d 4-13-1778 m Mary Wall Adj NC
Wm.: b c. 1753 d 7- -1816 m Molly — Pvt SC
Wm.: b a. 1740 d 2-11-1785 m Frances Kavanaugh Sgt VA

COVODE,
Garrett: b 1735 d 2-21-1826 m Mary Maggee Sol PA

COWART, (includes COWARD, COWHERD)
John: b 10-7-1756 d p. 1821 m Michael Williams 2Lt NJ
Joseph, Jr.: b 1-9-1758 d 3-20-1826 m Nancy Kilpatrick Pvt NJ
Reuben: b 1744 d a. 5- -1830 m Susan Rucker Pvt VA
Samuel: b 11-2-1759 d 10-23-1811 m Elizabeth Walton Pvt NJ★

COWDEN, (includes COWDIN, COWDON)
David: b c. 1728 d p. 1790 m Frain — Capt PS MA
James: b 6-16-1737 d 10-10-1810 m Mary Crouch LCol PA
John: b 1-6-1735 d p. 5-29-1777 m Jane Brown PS NC
John: b 1758 d 6-15-1827 m (1)Anne Sloan (2)Esther Strothers (3)Margaret Nelson Pvt PA
Robert: b 1-20-1754 d 1841 m Mary Alcorn Lt NC SC ★
Robert, Sr.: b c. 1725 d 7- -1817 m Jennet McChesney Pvt PA
Samuel: b c. 1730 d p. 1783 m Mary Cowden Pvt PA
Thomas, Sr.: b 12-25-1721 d 4-22-1792 m (1)Experience Gray (2)Hannah Craige Capt MA
Thomas, Jr.: b 3-7-1754 d 4-3-1825 m Mary Farrington Cpl MA
Wm.: b 5-28-1747 d 10-10-1815 m Sarah Crawford Pvt MA

COWDRY, (includes COWDERY, COWDREY)
Ambrose: b 1762 d 1-2-1838 m (1)Mary Jane Reed (2)Lucretia Wright (3)Chlorsis Ursula Hitchcock Pvt CT ★
Asa: b 2-19-1758 d 4-21-1843 m Abigail Ensign Pvt CT ★
Jabez: b 5-29-1741 d 9-7-1826 m (1)Ruth Wickham (2)Jedida Sebury (3)Mrs Hannah Palmer Sgt MA
Jacob, Jr.: b 12-18-1762 d 4-5-1846 m Abigail Olmstead Beckwith Sol CT
John: b 12-5-1759 d 1-31-1835 m Christina Thompson Lt MA
Jonathan: b 10-26-1753 d 9-3-1816 m Sally Hait Pvt MA
Moses: b 11-1-1731 d 12-17-1813 m Martha Bushnell Sol CT
Nathaniel, Sr.: b 4-19-1737 d 6-30-1807 m Sarah Parker Capt MA

Nathaniel, Jr.: b 9-4-1759 d 9-27-1841 m Jerusha Emerson Slr Sgt MA
Thomas: bpt 9-14-1729 d 1791 m (1)Mary Anderson (2)Margaret PS CT

COWDRICK,
John: b 1740/1 d 2-22-1818 m Sarah — Ens NJ

COWELL,
Ebenezer: b 12-7-1716 d 5-4-1799 m Sarah — PS NJ
Isaac: b 4-22-1757 d 1841 m Sarah — Pvt NJ ★
John: b 3-12-1760 d 1-30-1789 m Mary Cash Dr NJ
Samuel: b 1-16-1737 d 2-23-1824 m (1)Jemima Metcalf (2)Mary — Capt MA

COWEY, (includes COWEE)
James: b 2-21-1765 d p. 1809 m Susannah Baldwin Pvt MA
Wm.: b 8-10-1746 d 4-13-1837 m (2)Sage Josselyn Lt MA

COWGER,
Michael: b c. 1740 d p. 1782 m X Capt VA

COWHERD,
Francis: b 1-9-1753 d 3-25-1833 m Lucy Scott Capt VA ★
James: b 1-16-1759 d a. 4-10-1841 m Ann Young Sgt VA ★
Jonathan: b 1-7-1727 d 2-10-1806 m Sarah Kirtley PS VA
Jonathan, Jr.: b 10- -1755 d 7-20-1844 m Elizabeth Henry Kirtley Lt VA ★

COWING, (includes COWAN, COWEN)
Andrew: b 6-22-1751 d 12-22-1834 m Mary Snoddy Pvt SC
Andrew: b c. 1742 d a. 5-1-1789 m Ann — Sol PS SC
Andrew: b c. 1755 d p. 3-14-1814 m (1)Mary — (2)Anne Moore Pvt VA
Andrew Matthew: b 1760 d 1815 m Martha Evans Pvt NC
Calvin: b 1752 d 2-16-1843 m (1)Mehitable Coombs (2)Dolly Smith Pvt MA ★
David: b 1764 d 7-24-1851 m Esther Smith Pvt RI
Gathelus: b 9-4-1745 d 4-1-1830 m Lucy Hatch Cpl MA ★
George: b 9-4-1763 d 11-26-1855 m Marjory Scott Pvt NC
Henry: b 1734 d 1830 m Temperance (Armistead) Robinson Pvt VA
James: b 5-16-1740 d 4-8-1829 m (1)Mary Cottle (2)Sarah Randall Cpl MA
James: b 1734 d 3-24-1816 m Elizabeth — Pvt NY
James: b 1745 d 1828 m Mary Russell Pvt VA
John: b 4- -1757 d 8-11-1833 m (1)Mary Wallace (2)Martha Marshall (3)Mary Caldwell Sgt PA
John: b 1748 d 1-5-1823 m Mary Craig Capt VA
John: b c. 1762 d p. 9-15-1804 m (1) X (2)Mary — Pvt VA
Joseph: b c. 1760 d 10-26-1836 m Mary Thomson Pvt PA
Joseph: b 2-24-1729 d 5- -1777 m Mary Scott PS PA
Joseph: b 9-28-1758 d 2-22-1843 m Phebe Sprague Pvt RI ★
Mathias: b 1735 d 2-25-1819 m Rachel Gray PS PA
Prince: b 8-26-1735 d 7-15-1788 m Margaret Kirkland Pvt MA
Robert: b 1742/3 d 2- -1789 m Joanna Rogers Pvt NY
Robert: b 1746 d p. 7-24-1784 m Susan Woods Cpl NC
Thomas: b 1-23-1748 d 12-4-1817 m Mary (Barkley) Capt NC
Wm.: b 1762/3 d 3-27-1816 m Jane Matthews Pvt NY W★
Wm.: b 12-25-1749 d 9-26-1838 m (1)Isabel Henderson (2)Mrs Mary Wilson Capt PA
Wm.: b 1-18-1755 d 1834 m Barbara Pelser Lt PA ★
Wm.: b 1-17-1742 d 5-7-1814 m Sarah — Pvt PA
Wm.: b 1750 d 1809 m Jane Walker CS Capt VA

COWLES, (includes COWLS)
Amasa: b 2-13-1744/5 d 1832 m Lucy North Pvt Wgn CT
Asa: b 6-11-1747 d 1838 m Molly Russell Sgt MA NY
Asahel: b 7-18-1728 d 4-7-1807 m (1)Esther Hooker (2)Rachel Bell Pvt CT
Benjamin, Jr.: b 5-21-1743 d 1828 m (1)Catharine — (2)Hannah (Boardman) Holcomb Sgt MA
Calvin: b 11-13-1749 d 12-19-1801 m Miriam Atwater CS CT
Daniel: b 2-12-1744 d 12-24-1809 m Esther Rhodes Pvt CT
David: b 10-31-1760 d 1- -1829 m Eunice Paine Pvt CT
David: b 8-11-1741 d 11-18-1817 m Sarah Eastman Pvt MA
Ebenezer: b 2-26-1718 d 8-12-1800 m (1)Lydia Royce (2)Mercy Johnson (3)Eunice (Tuttle) Ives PS CT
Eleazer: b 10-18-1746 d p. 7-19-1795 m Hannah (Cowles)—Pvt MA
Eli: b 6-29-1739 d p. 1779 m Abigail — Pvt MA
Elisha: b 6-24-1750 d 11-23-1799 m (1)Rebekah Merriam (2)Rebecca Parker (3)Mrs Lydia Watrous Pvt CT
Gamaliel: b 7-12-1742 d 6-26-1787 m Anna Carter Sgt CT
George: b 9-27-1761 d 1827 m Naomi Barnes Pvt CT
Gideon: b 9-14-1749 d 10-1-1802 m Eunice Thomas Lt NY
Isaac: b 7-31-1756 d 6-5-1831 m Lucina Hooker Pvt CT
Jabez: b 11-13-1755 d 9-20-1846 m Betsey Scoville Pvt CT
James: b 12-20-1723 d 6-21-1789 m (1)Abigail Hooker (2)Mrs Mary Lewis Pvt CT
John: b 3-1-1731 d 3- -1802 m Abigail Cole Lt CT
John, Jr.: b 7-28-1731 d 9-18-1811 m Hannah Bardwell Capt MA
John, Jr.: b 11-31-1757 d 6-24-1830 m Elizabeth Smith Cpl MA
John: b 5-9-1745 d c. 1793 m (1)Anna — (2)Amy — Sgt MA

Joseph: b c. 1755 d p. 1783 m Jerusha Frisbie Cpl CT
Joseph: b 1726 d 8-17-1777 m Sarah Williams PS CT
Josiah: b 11-20-1716 d 6-6-1793 m (1)Jemima Dickinson (2)Mary Pynchon Scott PS CT
Moses: b 6-15-1745 d 1845 m (2)Phoebe Alexander Pvt NY
Nathaniel: b 10-18-1755 d p. 3-8-1836 m Lydia Allis Pvt MA ★
Nathaniel: b 5-5-1730 d p. 1-7-1792 m Ruth Sedgwick Pvt MA
Noah: b 10-17-1759 d 1-14-1839 m (1)Ollie Mills (2)Abigail — Pvt Mar CT
Noah: b 12-9-1733 d 12-21-1820 m Anna Powell PS CT
Oliver: b 7-15-1735 d 1-13-1799 m Irene Dickinson Pvt MA
Ozias: b 1760 d 12-3-1813 m (1)Lucy Gridley (2)Sarah Belden PS CT
Phineas: b 1729 d 5-30-1811 m Sarah Hawley Pvt CT
Reuben: b 7-22-1749 d 3-13-1824 m Betsy Rice Pvt MA
Samuel: b 7-30-1735 d 10- -1815 m Sibil North Ens PS CT
Samuel: b 1753 d 1836 m Eleanor Cole Pvt CT
Samuel: b 12-31-1759 d 11-9-1825 m (1)Anne Rivers (2)Judith Haraway Sol VA
Selah: b 1755 d 12-15-1827 m (1)Zeruiah Riley (2)Lucy Smith (3)Cynthia Cole Root Pvt CT
Simeon: b 10-24-1755 d 7-8-1831 m Sarah Dickinson Pvt MA
Thomas: b 9-27-1753 d 7-29-1807 m (1)Theodosia Webster (2)Tamar Hitchcock Ens CT
Timothy: b 4-22-1746 d 3-13-1831 m Anna Hatch Pvt MA ★
Timothy: b 2-19-1754 d 11-29-1832 m Sarah Stillson Pvt NH
Zeba: bpt 8-9-1761 d 9- -1814 m Mabel Leete Pvt CT

COWLEY,
St. Leger: b 1735 d 1797 m Mary Reed Adj NY

COWNE,
Robert: b c. 1754 d 3-4-1829 m Sarah Whiting CaptLt VA

COWPER,
Edward: b 1736 d 1810 m Ann Latimer PS VA
John: b 1740 d 1780 m — Roe NCapt VA
Wm.: b c. 1735 d 1783/4 m Mary Godwin PS CS VA

COWPERTHWAITE,
Joseph: b 1735 d 9-12-1809 m Susannah Hulings Col PA

COWSERT,
John: b a. 1755 d 1817 m Margaret — PS SC

COX, (COCK, COCKE, COKE, COXE)
Abraham: b 1736 d 1799 m Sally — Sol GA
Abraham: b 1-1-1752 d 3-24-1834 m Elizabeth Clark 2Lt MD
Agnes: b c. 1730 d p. 1785 m George Cock PS VA
Andrew: b 3-22-1761 d 3-20-1852 m Rebecca — Pvt VA ★
Anthony: b c. 1754 d 1813 m (1)Leannah Murphy (2)Mary Kirkpatrick Pvt GA
Asher: b 11-8-1746 d 3-17-1812 m Rebecca Holmes Pvt NJ
Bartlett: b 1752 d 9-26-1842 m Polly Hopper Pvt VA ★
Benjamin: b c. 1755 d -4-1796 m Pembrouck — Pvt VA
Benjamin: b 1788 d 1784 m Margaret — Pvt NJ
Benjamin, Sr.: b 11-3-1740 d 9-25-1788 m Jerusha George Capt VT
Benjamin, Jr.: b 8-13-1766 d 5-15-1847 m Lucy Larnard Pvt Fif VT
Cary: b c. 1736 d 3-24-1814 m Mary Horn Sol NC
Christopher: b c. 1740 d 3- -1822 m Margaret — Pvt PA
Cornelius: b 1750 d 3-2-1803 m Mary Forster Maj CS PA
Curd: b 1762 d p. 9-11-1852 m Susan Overton Pvt VA ★
Daniel: b 3-26-1747 d 10-22-1804 m Rosannah Townsend PS NY
David: b 10-24-1756 d 2-14-1833 m Sarah Stevenson Vol NY
David: b 1745 d 12- -1820 m (1)Margaret Bruce (2)Susannah—Lt VA
David: b c. 1735 d p. 1-8-1818 m Anna McGowan Sol PS VA
Ebenezer: b 2-19-1758 d 1835 m Lillah Bates Pvt MA
Ebenezer: b 3-19-1762 d 7-10-1849 m Margaret Fling Pvt MA
Ebenezer: b a. 1754 d 8-3-1777 m Margaret Klock Col NY
Edward: b 1759 d 11-30-1850 m Sarah Meredith Lt NC ★
Edward: b c. 1746 d 1791 m Diana Holloway 1Lt VA
Elisha: b 1722 d 6-25-1776 m Anna Warren Ens MA
Enoch: b c. 1757 d 3-29-1840 m (1)Mary Mackey (2)Sally Stoneman Pvt VA
Fesser: b 1744 d 2-5-1822 m Margaret Jeans Pvt NY
Francis, Jr.: b 1742 d 1782 m Mercy Deadman Lt MA
Francis: b c. 1735 d p. 1-17-1816 m Mary — PS VA
Gabriel: b a. 1750 d 6- -1806 m Sarah Enoch LCol VA
George: b 7-31-1762 d 8-6-1843 m Sarah Chamberlin Pvt VT ★
George: b 1749 d 12-13-1837 m Susanna Decker Ens VA ★
George, Sr.: b c. 1725 d p. 12-24-1801 m Agnes — PS VA
Henry: bpt 1-18-1756 d 12-2-1817 m June — Pvt VA
Henry: b 11-13-1737 d 8-8-1817 m Elizabeth Chappell Pvt VA
Henry, Jr.: b c. 1740 d 2-20-1781 m Anne Harris Pvt VA
Isaac, Jr.: b 1759 d 1795 m Rebecca — Pvt MD
Isaac: b 6-25-1743 d 1838 m (1)Nancy Gray (2)Sarah Sutton Sgt NJ ★
Isaac: b c. 1716 d 1783 m Susan Tomlinson CS VA
Israel: b 10-5-1755 d 4-3-1850 m Jane Given Pvt MA
Jacob: b 7-7-1725 d 1798 m (1)Elizabeth Gain (2)Casiah Perego PS MD
Jacob: b 9-29-1754 d p. 1798 m Mary Harding Pvt NJ
Jacob: b 1743 d 1809 m Lucretia Chappel Pvt PA
Jacob: b c. 1744 d p. 1790 m Mary Daily Pvt VA
James: b 2-22-1739 d 9-11-1777 m Mary Alexander Maj MD

James: b 1765 d 12-22-1825 m Mary Moore Pvt MA
James: b 10-16-1753 d 9-12-1810 m Anne Borden Potts BGen NJ
James: b 1745 d 10-21-1801 m Hannah Howe Maj NY
James: b 2-24-1763 d 4-17-1842 m Mrs Elizabeth Terrell (2)Sally Fielder Vol Spy NC VA
James: b 1755 d 1840 m Elizabeth — Pvt PS VA
James: b c. 1751 d p. 7-7-1810 m Martha Holland Parrish Pvt VA
James: b 1762 d 9-10-1846 m Rebecca Ann — Pvt VA ★
Jesse: b c. 1758 d c. 1848 m Lucrecia Allen Sgt NC
John: b 1760 d 1832 m Mary Elizabeth — Sol GA
John, Sr.: b 10-3-1713 d a. 6-23-1785 m Rebecca — Capt MD
John: b 2-23-1765 d 12-20-1840 m Experience — Pvt NJ
John: b 9- -1732 d 4-28-1793 m (1)Mrs Sarah Edgil (2)Esther Bowes PS LCol NJ
John: b 2-10-1747 d 5-6-1820 m Keziah Thompson Pvt NY
John: b 11-1-1727 d p. 1782 m Margaret Morris PS NC
John: b 1750 d 1828 m Elizabeth Marlow PS PA
John: b 1750 d 1828 m Abigail — Pvt PA
John: b 1753 d 9-8-1829 m Mrs Mary McCormick Pvt VT
John: b 1744 d 1814 m Sarah — Capt PS VA
John: b 7-25-1739 d 12-24-1818 m Margaret Davis Capt CS VA
John, Jr.: b 1737 d 10-1-1793 m Francina Bouldin Pvt VA
John: b 1758 d p. 1833 m Mary Bryson Pvt VA ★
John: b 1760 d p. 10-23-1850 m Ealcey Harris Pvt VA
John: b c. 1740 d 1800 m Mary Seay PS VA
John: b c. 1740 d p. 5-22-1821 m Polly — PS VA
John Catesby: b 1730-40 d p. 1807-10 m (1)Mary Brackner (2)Winifred Thornton NCapt VA
John Hartwell: b 11-26-1749 d 2-9-1791 m Elizabeth Kennon Sol VA
John Hawkins: b 1754 d 6-24-1836 m Rebecca Jane Skeen Pvt NC
Joseph: b c. 1742 d c. 10- -1777 m Susan Ann Haywood Johnson 2Lt NY
Judith: b c. 1722 d c. 1785 m Henry Cox PS VA
Marmaduke: b c. 1735 d a. 11-18-1806 m X PS NC
Matthew: b 6-4-1754 d 2-28-1831 m (1)Mrs Margaret Lockwood (2)Mrs Hetty (Rash) Caldwell Pvt DE
Michael: b 8-27-1759 d 1-14-1832 m(2)Jeruthea Ann Brooks Pvt PA
Moses: b 10-20-1742 d 1808 m Hannah Evenson PS PA
Nathaniel: b c. 1746 d p. 1813 m Rebecca Thompson LCol VA
Nicholas: b 3-24-1742 d a. 4-7-1826 m Rebecca Potts Chp NJ
Peter: b c. 1738 d p. 9-4-1803 m Mary Whitehead PS NC
Philip: b 1763 d 1855 m Christianna Stelle Pvt NJ
Philip: b 9- -1755 d 3-24-1834 m Jemima Taylor Pvt NC ★
Phineas: b 10-10-1764 d 5-18-1842 m Barbara Stump Pvt VA
Richard: b 1-3-1755 d 3-9-1816 m Jane Ross Maj NJ
Richard: b 1760 d a. 4-3-1851 m — X — Pvt NC ★
Richard: b 1745 d 1798 m Mary Ann Thomas Pvt PA
Richard: b 6-20-1748 d 1-24-1816 m (1)Anne Claiborne (2)Theodosia Cowley White PS VA
Samuel: bpt 9-28-1746 d 1776 m (1)Lydia Cooper (2)Jemima Hussey Pvt MA
Samuel: b 3-24-1726 d 8-30-1806 m (1)Sarah Rogers (2)Mrs Elizabeth Bird Sol MA
Samuel: b 6-1-1755 d 4-12-1834 m (1)Mary McComb (2)Annie Peebles Pvt PA
Samuel: b 11-24-1759 d 1842 m Elizabeth Brown Pvt SC ★
Samuel: b 1740 d 1807 m Agnes Bridgewater Capt VA
Samuel: b 1755 d 7-12-1828 m Elizabeth — Pvt VA
Solomon: b — d p. 1814 m Naomi Hussey PS NC
Stephen: b 3-31-1740 d 12-27-1792 m Amy Jones CS VA
Thomas: b 1749 d 2-27-1801 m Ann Peterson Pvt DE
Thomas, Sr.: b — d a. 5- -1822 m (1)X (2)Elizabeth Hussey Sol NC
Thomas: b 1750 d 1853 m Elizabeth Husey Pvt NC
Thomas: b 10-26-1752 d 3-9-1824 m Elizabeth Willis Capt CS VA
Unite: b 11-14-1752 d 11- -1816 m Hannah Sprague Sgt MA
Valentine: b c. 1750 d c. 1812 m Nancy Dawson PS VA
Wm.: b c. 1740 d p. 1790 m — Adams Pvt MD
Wm., Jr.: b 9- -1817 m Mary Josselyn Pvt MA
Wm.: b 4-19-1750 d 7-27-1838 m Mary Sarvin PS MA
Wm.: b c. 1750 d 2-14-1832 m Mary Hoff Pvt NJ
Wm.: b 3-22-1757 d 2-3-1817 m Amy O'Neil Pvt NY
Wm.: b 1749 d 1792 m Anne Bright Pvt NC
Wm.: b 1762 d 3-21-1848 m (1)— X — (2)Katherine (Cox) Pvt NC ★
Wm.: b 12-21-1751 d 12-2-1846 m Lydia Garrett Pvt PA
Wm.: b 6-13-1749 d p. 1790 m Sarah Willard Pvt PA
Wm.: b a. 1739 d 10-28-1801 m Beulah Batt Pvt VT
Wm.: b 1747 d 8-22-1828 m Mary Maclin Capt VA
Wm.: b 1759 d c. 1839 m Rebecca Francis Pvt VA ★
Wm.: b 1755 d . 1788 m Melinda Madden PS NC
Zebulon: b — d 1-12-1816 m (2)Sarah Perry Sol GA

COY,
Archibald: b 5-6-1741 d 4-1-1794 m Elizabeth Badger Sgt CT
Benjamin: b 7-4-1756 d 2-22-1825 m Hannah Allen Cpl VT
Christopher: b a. 1753 d 10-12-1839 m Elizabeth — Pvt MD ★
David: b 5-19-1759 d 12-15-1854 m — Potter Pvt CT ★
Edee: b 10-14-1760 d 8-21-1830 m Flavia Gipson Cpl CT ★
John: b c. 1750 d — m Molly Millett Pvt MA
Jonathan: b 10-30-1730 d 9-7-1815 m Deborah Barker Lt MA
Joseph: b 1738 d 5-17-1823 m Jerusha Sawyer Sgt CT ★
Nathaniel: b 5-18-1733 d 5-14-1814 m Bridgett Goodell Pvt CT
Wm.: b 3-10-1756 d 7-10-1833 m Mary Ann Dennis Pvt MD

COYLE,
James: b c. 1740 d 1780 m Judith Pickett Sol VA
Patrick: b 1753 d 2-21-1845 m Lucinda — Pvt VA ★

COZART, (includes COZAD)
Anthony: b 2-4-1739 d 1817 m Winnefred Bumpass PS NC
Samuel: b c. 1725/6 d 2-20-1811 m (1)Anna Clark (2)Mrs Priscilla (Burt) Fairchild Capt NJ

COZIER,
Benjamin: b 9-12-1745 d 5- -1827 m Sarah — Pvt CT

CRABB, (includes CRAB, CRABBE, CRABBS)
Henry: b c. 1735 d p. 1790 m Sarah Keller Pvt PA
Jeremiah: b 1760 d 1800 m Elizabeth Ridgely Griffith 1Lt MD
John: b 4-10-1753 d p. 1802 m Anne — Pvt NY
John: b c. 1725 d 1779 m Elizabeth — NGnr VA
Philip: b 1762 d 1846 m (1) — X — (2)Elizabeth House Pvt PA
Wm. Augustus: b 6-14-1747 d 4-10-1813 m Jean Minshall Pvt PA

CRABTREE,
Agreen: b 12-15-1735 d 6-10-1808 m (1)Sarah Ingraham (2)Mary Dyer NCapt MA
Isaac: b 1757 d p. 1840 m Miss Pike Pvt VA ★
James: b c. 1750 d p. 2-11-1823 m Judah — Capt VA
John: b 6-20-1725 d 9-28-1815 m Abigail Rice Pvt MA
John: b 5-3-1763 d 10-24-1835 m Mida — Sol NC
Wm.: b 12-25-1758 d 12- -1836 m Mary Spearman Pvt MD ★
Wm.: b 1734 d 1818 m (1)Hannah — Lt VA

CRACROFT,
Charles: b 1748 d 3-10-1824 m Eleanor Atkinson Maj PS PA
Thomas: b c. 1745 d c. 1825 m Rebecca — PS VA

CRADDOCK, (includes CRADDOCK)
John: b 1-25-1749 d 10-4-1794 m Ann Worthington Maj MD
Richard: b c. 1740 d p. 2-18-1785 m Elizabeth Hill 2Lt VA
Wm. C.: b c. 1735 d 1795 m Obedience Hill Col VA

CRADY,
David: b c. 1762 d a. 12-2-1840 m Polly Edlin Fif Pvt MD

CRAFTS, (includes CRAFT)
Aaron: b 5-22-1754 d 1820 m Abigail Craft Pvt MA
Abner: b 2-28-1740 d 1-10-1810 m Hannah Childs Capt MA
Benjamin: b 8-20-1738 d 2-27-1823 m Anna Lee 2Lt MA
Ebenezer: b 9-22-1740 d 5-24-1810 m Mehitable Chandler Capt CT
Edward: b 10-12-1746 d 4-11-1806 m Eliot Winship Capt MA
Eleazer: b 7-31-1743 d 9-20-1793 m Elizabeth (Allen) Samples LCol MA
Eliot Winship: b 1-28-1745 d 12-17-1842 m Edward Crafts PS MA
Francis: b 4-16-1741 d 1-28-1794 m Joanna Orsmont Sgt MA
Griffin: b 7-18-1748 d 12-1-1835 m Hannah May PS CT
James: b 12-1-1743 d 1808 m Sara Cathrall PS NJ
John: b 1-7-1743 d 5-3-1826 m (1)Thankful Atkins (2)Martha Warner Sgt MA
John: b 1-15-1764 d 12-24-1857 m Rebecca Mandeville Pvt NY ★
John: b 1759 d 1821 m Lucinda Holt Pvt VA
John: b 4-17-1761 d p. 1812 m Sarah Crawford Pvt VA
Joseph, Sr.: b 3-8-1732 d c. 5- -1777 m Sarah Goodell Cpl CT
Joseph, Jr.: b 5-15-1763 d 10-12-1844 m Mary Sykes Pvt CT ★
Joseph: b 6-12-1736 d 4-21-1821 m Elizabeth Davis Lt MA
Joseph: b 11-6-1745 d 10-18-1815 m Roxcellany (Warner) White Pvt MA
Lawrence: b 1740 d 7- -1832 m Anne Thompson PS PA
Moses: b 8-17-1754 d 3-15-1812 m Hadessa Mills Pvt MA
Moses: b 5-6-1750 d 1-8-1826 m Abigail Kellogg Pvt MA
Reuben: b 3-25-1759 d 2-14-1814 m Henrietta Graves Pvt MA
Samuel: b 7-15-1722 d 11-20-1791 m Judith Payson CS CT
Samuel: b 11-23-1729 d 4-1-1803 m Rebecca Parker PS MA
Samuel: b 1747 d 1809 m Esther Jewett Pvt MM MA
Stephen Charles: b 1756 d 1792 m Esther Farnall Pvt NC
Thomas, Sr.: b 4-8-1706 d 11-17-1789 m Ann White PS CS MA
Thomas: b 7-13-1740 d 1-14-1799 m Frances Pinkney Gore Col MA

CRAGIN,
Amos: b 1-4-1741 d 1777 m Ruth Staples Pvt MA
Benjamin: b 7-8-1740 d 4-20-1816 m Mercy Robbins Lt NH
Francis: b 3-2-1742 d 8-26-1826 m (1)Elizabeth Law (2)Sybil Piper (3)Rebecca Minot Sgt NH
John, Sr.: b 3-24-1701 d 1-28-1794 m Judith Barker PS CS NH
John, Jr.: b 1-8-1728 d 5-16-1797 m (1)Sarah Barrett (2) Sarah Spaulding Pvt PS CS NH
Samuel: b 11-5-1739 d 1825 m Mercy Chapin LCol MA

CRAIG, (includes CRAGE, CRAIGE, CRAIGUE)
Absolum: b c. 1740 d a. 3-26-1793 m (1) — (2)Letty Feagan Pvt VA
Alexander: b 2-22-1741 d 1823 m Molly Stevens 2Maj NH
Alexander: b 11-20-1755 d 10-29-1832 m Jane Clark Lt PA
Alexander: b — d p. 1774 m Sarah — Pvt PA
Andrew: b 1729 d 11-17-1833 m Mary — Pvt PA
Daniel Terrill: b 7- -1760 d 1-16-1812 m Hannah Clark Cpl NJ
David: b — d c. 1795 m Abigail — PS NH

David: b 11-3-1755 d 5-2-1821 m (1)Hannah Bowne (2)Eleanor — Sgt NJ
David: b 1731-33 d 11-2-1785 m Eleanor Johnston Capt NC
David: b c. 1756 d c. 1841 m Catherine Dye Pvt NJ ★
Edward: b c. 1750 d p. 1-10-1788 m (1)Mary Lewis (2)Sarah (Simonton) Shankland Sol DE
Elias: b 9-27-1756 d 5-7-1837 m (1)Hannah McKecknie (2)Olive Hamlin Pvt MA ★
Elias: bpt 10-28-1750 d 8- -1786 m Mary Dunlap Pvt NJ
Elizabeth Johson: b c. 1735 d — m Tolliver Craig II PS VA
Enoch: b 9-11-1758 d 12-10-1835 m Dorothy Starling Pvt MA
George: b 1-4-1749 d 11-26-1801 m Elizabeth Evans Pvt VA
Henry: b 1729 d 2-29-1807 m Mary — Pvt SC
Isaac: b 5-14-1746 d 5-14-1826 m Amelia Neville Maj PA
Jacob: b 2-27-1749/50 d 1800 m Mary West Pvt PA
James: b 2-8-1754 d 9-28-1839 m Esther Rhea Capt NJ ★
James Jr.: b 1745 d 4-6-1790 m (1)Mary Jennings (2)Mary Bird Ens NJ
James: b c. 1745 d 1795 m Maria — Pvt NY
James Jr.: b 1735 d 9-29-1800 m Elizabeth Wilkenson Mstr PA
James: b 1745 d 1802 m Martha Miller Capt SC
James: b 3-17-1754 d 12-20-1820 m (1)Jinny Bell (2)Margaret McInnis Capt SC
James: b 9-23-1762 d 2-8-1834 m Anne Montgomery Pvt NC
James Sr.: b 12- -1715 d 2-7-1791 m Mary Laird Pvt VA
James Jr.: b 7-23-1745 d p. 4-19-1807 m Jane Stuart Pvt VA
James: b — d a. 9-10-1795 m Mary Tarry PS VA
John: b c. 1762 d p. 11-29-1807 m Phebe Johnston Pvt MD
John: b 10-1-1752 d p. 1800 m Content Daggett Pvt MA
John: b 7-17-1733 d 3-24-1838 m Mary (Craig) — Pvt NH ★
John: b 7-17-1733 d 7-11-1821 m (2)Jane (Robinson) English Capt NJ
John: b 5-8-1762 d 12-4-1840 m Lydia Baird Pvt NJ ★
John: b 1731 d p. 8-5-1816 m Mary Blackwood Pvt NC
John: b 1750 d 11-29-1829 m Elizabeth (Craig) Capt PA
John: b 4-23-1753 d 3-3-1850 m Martha Clark Pvt PA ★
John: b — d 1801 m Jean Boyd Pvt PA
John: b a. 1740 d p. 1790 m Ellen — Pvt SC
John: b 1761 d 2-10-1842 m (1) —Clarke (2)Catherine Wilson Pvt SC ★
John: b 1731 d a. 3-8-1808 m Molly Cox Capt VA
John: b 1732 d 1814 m Sarah Page Capt KY
John: b 1729 d 1802 m Sarah Laird Pvt VA
John: b 1754 d 1813 m (1)Elizabeth Hole (2)Elizabeth Scott Pvt VA
Joseph: b 6-11-1741 d 5-6-1819 m Sarah Wisdom PS VA
Lewis: b 1740 d 1825 m Elizabeth Sanders Sol VA
Mary: b 1765 d 1828 m Francis Dunlevy PS VA
Moses, Jr.: b 1743 d 2-14-1811 m (1)Sarah Graham Pvt NJ
Nathan: b 6-11-1754 d 4-6-1832 m Sarah Choate Lt MA
Polly Hawkins: b 1716 d 1804 m Tolliver Craig Sr. PS VA KY
Robert: b 12-28-1744 d 2-4-1834 m (1)Margaret Whitehill (2)Jane Denny Capt PA
Robert Sr.: b 9- -1720 d c. 1788 m Grizel Crawford Pvt VA
Robert Jr.: b 6-30-1755 d c. 1806 m Susannah Woods Pvt VA
Roderick: b 1750 d a. 10- -1854 m Becky — Sol NC
Sally Page: b c. 1746 d p. 1817 m John Craig PS VA
Samuel: b a. 1760 d 7- -1807 m Jane Innes Burnes Capt PA ★
Samuel Sr.: b c. 1732 d c. 11-1-1777 m (1)Elizabeth McDonald (2)Jane Boyd CS Lt PA
Samuel, Jr.: b 1755 d 8-28-1808 m Elizabeth Shields Lt PA W ★
Samuel: b c. 1741 d 9-21-1790 m Mary Johnston Sgt PA
Samuel: b — d c. 1795 m Mary Masterson Pvt PS VA
Thomas: b 1754 d 8-24-1832 m Elizabeth Fleming Sgt MD ★
Thomas: b 1-10-1740 d 1-20-1832 m (2)Dorothy Brineir Col PA ★
Thomas: b 2-27-1739 d 4-22-1813 m Jean Jamison Capt CS PA
Tolliver, Sr.: b 1704/5 d 1795 m Polly Hawkins PS VA KY
Tolliver Jr.: b 1738 d 3-20-1819 m Elizabeth Johnson Lt VA
Whitfield: b — d — m Charlotte Lampkin Pvt KY
Wm.: b 4-17-1754 d 12- -1847 m Esther Adams Cpl MA
Wm.: b 1731 d 1823 m Jane (Anderson) Allen Pvt VA
Wm.: b 1-8-1750 d 9-8-1829 m Jean Allen Pvt VA
Wm.: b 9-3-1759 d 1-27-1808 m Deborah Holmes Sol CS VA

CRAIGHEAD,
George: b 5-10-1733 d 2-21-1811 m Ann Brattain Col DE
Robert: b 6-27-1751 d 5-7-1821 m Hannah Clark Pvt NC ★
Robert: b 1742 d p. 1786 m Mary Davidson Pvt PA
Thomas: b 3-15-1737 d 11-13-1807 m Margaret Gilson Pvt PA
Wm.: b 6-13-1731 d a. 2-10-1803 m Mildred Thompson PS VA

CRAIK,
James: b 1730 d 2-6-1814 m Marianne Ewell Dr VA

CRALLE,
John: b c. 1740 d p. 1810 m (1)Sarah Harding (2)Mary (Leeland) Haynie Capt PS VA

CRAM,
Benjamin: b 1740 d 4-10-1837 m Abigail Blake Pvt NH
Benjamin: b 1754 d 7-31-1836 m Olive Chamberlain Pvt NH
Benjamin: b 3-10-1721 d 1821 m Elizabeth — PS NH
Daniel: bpt 3-28-1725 d 3-13-1815 m Sarah Green Pvt MA
Dudley: b 10-9-1760 d 9-13-1825 m Mary Rundlett Pvt NH

Ezekiel: b 1-18-1751 d 4-14-1821 m Mary Kinsor Pvt NH
James: bpt 4-12-1730 d 12-29-1809 m Mary Folsom PS CS NH
Joel: b 8-12-1749 d 8-13-1828 m (1)Betsey Batchelder (2)Sarah Hoyt PS NH
John: b 11-12-1730 d 8-30-1803 m Abigail Sanborn Capt CS NH
John: bpt 8-4-1717 d p. 1790 m Sarah Harwood PS NH
John Stanyan: b 1755 d 1-23-1824 m (1)Peace Nasson (2)Jerusha Hale (3)Sarah Coffin Pvt Drm MA ★
Jonathan: b 1-29-1737 d 10-14-1806 m Mary (Cram) — Maj NH
Jonathan: b 2-21-1708 d 1-23-1790 m Mary Chamberlain Pvt PS NH
Nathan: b 4-5-1752 d 1-21-1851 m Rachel Dutton Sol NH
Nathan: b 6-5-1720 d p. 1810 m Mary Carr PS NH
Reuben: b 4-8-1758 d 3-1-1818 m Susannah Sargent Pvt NH
Samuel Tilton: b 6-25-1760 d 10-28-1834 m Betsey Philbrick Pvt NH ★
Smith: b 1762 d 1857 m Jane Harriman Pvt NH
Thomas: b 1755 d p. 1800 m Sarah Mudgett Pvt NH
Tristram: b 3-6-1756 d 3-24-1831 m Anna Simpson Pvt NH ★

CRAMPHIN,
Thomas: b 1735 d 7-30-1819 m Maria Sabboth PS MD

CRAMPTON,
Elon: b 1760 d 5-27-1837 m Avis Webster Pvt CT
Jonathan: b 3-20-1764 d 5-29-1843 m Elizabeth Hubbard Pvt CT ★
Josiah: b 11-14-1750 d 9-26-1828 m Lydia (Post) Crampton Pvt CT
Neri: b 1743 d 9-20-1827 m Abigail Field Pvt VT

CRANCH,
Richard: b 10- -1726 d 10-16-1811 m Mary Smith PS MA

CRANDALL,
Abel: b 7-25-1757 d 9-2-1826 m Elizabeth Crocker Sgt VT
Abner: b 7-13-1762 d 12-12-1840 m Mary Wilcox Pvt RI ★
Adam: b 1756 d 4-14-1796 m (1)Eunice Blodgett (2)Charlotte Willard Sgt RI
Amariah: b 4-2-1759 d 1-18-1861 m Prudence Avery Pvt CT
Amos: b 4-5-1747 d 10-26-1812 m Elizabeth Brown 1Lt RI
Asa: b 9-13-1759 d — m (1)Phebe Taylor (2)Sarah Tefft 2Lt RI
Azariah: b 5-18-1739 d 2-11-1808 m (1)Rebecca Reynolds (2)Sarah (Carey) Stark Pvt NY
Benajah: b 1729/30 d 1809 m (1)Elizabeth Slack (2)Thankful—Sol RI
Benjamin: b c. 1750 d p. 1815 m (1)Ann Porter (2)Martha Ann Thorn Pvt NY
Benjamin: b 11-29-1736 d 11-29-1793 m Alice Kenyon Pvt RI
Caleb: b 4-7-1747 d 11-11-1822 m Patience Potter Ens RI
David: b 1-22-1740 d 2-24-1819 m (1)Sarah Sherman (2)Jemima Coon Pvt RI
Edward: b 2-17-1750 d 3-4-1834 m Anna Palmer Pvt CT ★
Elijah: b 1-7-1748 d p. 1783 m (1)Eunice Broughton (2)Mercy Kenyon Pvt RI ★
Ethan: b 9-17-1757 d 11-8-1847 m Sarah Burdick Pvt RI ★
Ezekiel: b 10-11-1746 d 1843 m Mary Pendleton Pvt RI ★
George: b 5-29-1739 d 9-5-1832 m Tacy Tanner Sol NY ★
Gideon: b 2-25-1762 d 3-10-1841 m Esther Rix Pvt RI ★
Henry: b 1-7-1754 d 7-24-1827 m Mary Greenman Sgt RI
James: b 5-12-1719 d. 1789 m (1)Damaria Kenyon (2)Elizabeth Chase Saunders Pvt RI
John: b 6-18-1716 d 1790 m Hannah Case Pvt RI
Jonathan: b 1764 d 3-4-1850 m Cynthia Waters Pvt RI
Joseph: b 1-21-1717 d 1- -1792 m (1)Elizabeth — (2)Martha — CS PS RI
Luke: b 1754 d 8-1-1832 m Rachel Richards Pvt NY W ★
Nathaniel: bpt 6-10-1733 d 4-10-1821 m Sarah Wilcox Pvt RI
Peleg: b 1755 d 1803 m (1)Eleanor Lewis (2)— Coon (3)Lucy Bumbley Pvt RI
Peter: b 8-1-1762 d 10-12-1838 m (1)Nancy Bliven Pvt RI ★
Phineas: b 4-7-1743 d 4-27-1821 m (1)Ruth Rogers (2)Hopestill Beebe Cpl RI
Robert: b 2-21-1735 d 8-29-1778 m Mary Havens CS RI
Samuel: b 1736 d 1836 m — X — Lt NY
Simeon, Jr.: b 9-23-1760 d 6-8-1834 m Catherine Welch Pvt RI ★
Thomas: b 5-8-1747 d p. 1790 m Ruth Rogers Smn CT
Thomas: b — d 3-8-1828 m Ann Tophan Ens NY
Thomas: b 1-10-1734 d p. 1783 m Mary Stoddard Pvt RI
Wm.: b 8-6-1721 d 1785 m Deborah Crandall Pvt RI

CRANDON,
Thomas: b 12-15-1728 d 1-9-1821 m Ruth Howland Capt MA

CRANE, (includes CRAIN)
Aaron: b 3-5-1750 d 2-7-1836 m Tabatha Baldwin Pvt NJ
Abel: b 1718 d 2-9-1801 m Jemima Burt PS RI
Abijah: b 8-26-1742 d 1817 m Abigail Woods Pvt MA
Abner: b 5-27-1737 d 1-23-1819 m (1)Hannah Fenno (2)Mrs Lydia Merion Capt MA
Amariah: b 10-16-1759 d 8-17-1836 m Tryphena Coburn Fif CT ★
Andrew: b 2-3-1741 d 1829 m Glory Ann Burrough Pvt NJ
Asa: b 7-15-1758 d 9-23-1848 m Abigail Young Pvt NJ
Benjamin: b 3-20-1740 d p. 1790 m Tryphena Hathaway Pvt MA
Benjamin: b 5-3-1741 d 12-15-1825 m Eunice Washburn Pvt MA
Benjamin: b 1740 d 1813 m Phebe Meeker Pvt NJ
Benjamin: b 11-29-1761 d 5-23-1844 m Sarah Thompson Pvt Mus NJ

Bernice: b 1-19-1743 d 11-20-1828 m Joanna Axtill Cpl MA ★
Caleb: b 1748 d p. 1798 m X Lt NJ ★
Curtis: b 3-27-1747 d 10-10-1828 m Elizabeth Palmer Cpl CT
Daniel: b 5-15-1756 d 4-2-1813 m Sylvia Marrium Pvt CT
Daniel: b 4-14-1752 d 1832 m Esther Fuller Pvt Trm CT
David: b 10-1-1748 d 1-8-1840 m (1)Theodocia Pitkin (2)Jerusha Smith Cpl CT
David: b 9-19-1743 d 3-2-1816 m Mary Reed Capt MD
David: b 1721 d 3-6-1794 m (1)Sarah A Dodd (2)Abigail Ogden Pvt NJ
David D.: b 9-17-1763 d 9-11-1838 m Martha Banks Pvt Mus NJ
Ebenezer: b 7-3-1750 d p. 1787 m (1)Jemima Tiffany (2)Mrs Eunice (Neff) Crandall SgtMaj CT
Eleazer: b c. 1749 d 8-27-1776 m Susan Day Pvt PA
Elias: b 1730 d 1789 m Elizabeth Johnson Pvt NJ
Elias: b 4-10-1753 d 3-13-1809 m Phoebe Brown Pvt NJ
Elihu, Sr.: bpt 6-27-1735 d c. 1778 m Mary Fowler PS CT
Elihu, Jr.: b 1761/2 d p. 9-21-1846 m Ruth Park Sgt CT ★
Elijah: b 1-9-1744 d 8-30-1806 m Martha Bush Cpl MA CT
Elijah: b 1-29-1728 d 9-5-1781 m Sarah Houghton Pvt MA
Elijah: b 2-22-1746 d 1-15-1818 m Sarah Hill Pvt MA
Elisha: b 8-28-1728 d 12-28-1805 m Elizabeth Stevens Pvt CT
Ezekiel: b 10-9-1747 d 3-15-1813 m Eunice Hayward Capt NJ
Ezra: b 3-6-1735 d 1819 m Prudence Leigh Pvt CT
George: b 1761 d 1798 m Martha Ritchey Pvt PA
Henry: b 2- -1753 d 1829 m Elizabeth Thompson Pvt MA
Hezekiah, Sr.: b 3-21-1721 d 1-5-1805 m Rachel Rockwell PS CT
Hezekiah, Jr.: b 8-7-1747 d 1794 m Sybil Lamphere Pvt CT
Hezekiah: b 3-4-1751 d 1813 m Rachel Hall Pvt CT
Ira: b 8-10-1761 d 8- -1828 m Elizabeth Brush Pvt Drm NY
Isaac: b 3-17-1745 d 1825 m Thankful Putnam Pvt CT (?)
Isaac: b 1-26-1753 d 3-6-1810 m Ann Sears Lt NY
Israel, Jr.: b 1755 d 1795 m Mary Cooper Cpl NJ
Israel: b c. 1713 d 3-27-1785 m Abigail — PS CS NJ
Jacob: b — d p. 1794 m Joanna Marsh LCol NJ
Jacob: b 1745 d 7-25-1811 m Phoebe (Crane) Capt NJ
James: b 1761 d 4-30-1845 m Lydia Squares Cpl CT
James: b 10-11-1763 d 8-17-1829 m (1)Sally Hallock (2)Clarinda Hallock Pvt NY
Jesse: b 8-29-1760 d 3- -1824 m Mary Mulford Pvt NJ
John, Sr.: b 3-21-1720 d p. 1779 m Hannah Griswold Lt CT ★
John: b 9- -1739 d a. 9- -1777 m Ruth — Pvt CT
John: b 7-1-1741 d 1784 m Abigail Camp Pvt CT
John: b 12-2-1744 d 8-21-1805 m Mehitable Wheeler BGen MA
John: b 1730 d 6-1-1800 m Rachel Terry Sgt MA
John: b 3-8-1751 d 4-17-1812 m Sarah Myer Lt NJ
John, 2d.: b 4-20-1723 d 9-12-1807 m (1)Huldah Grant (2)Hannah Pierson (3)Abigail — 2Lt NJ
John, 3d.: b 6-17-1755 d 5-14-1837 m Phebe Ross Pvt NJ ★
John: b 1-24-1749 d 1790 m Mary — Pvt NJ
John: b 11-24-1742 d 6-9-1827 m Tamer Carpenter Capt NY
John: b 2-6-1759 d 3-23-1836 m Mildred Walton Pvt NC ★
John, Sr.: b 1725 d 1781 m Ann — Pvt PA
John, Jr.: b 1746 d 1828 m Jane Souder Pvt PA
Jonas, Jr.: b 1766 d c. 1840 m (2)Elizabeth Kitchell CS NJ
Jonathan: b 8-20-1757 d 4-13-1820 m Sibbel Ranney Pvt CT ★
Jonathan: b 8-20-1757 d 1805 m Mary Ward Pvt NJ
Jonathan: b 3-17-1743 d 2-18-1805 m Rachel Clisby Ens NJ
Jonathan: b 5-8-1747 d 8-27-1834 m Bethia Baldwin Lt NY
Joseph: b 9-4-1737 d 8-1-1810 m Mary Savil Sgt MA
Joseph, Jr.: b 6-8-1757 d 1-30-1841 m Deliverance Mills Pvt MA
Joseph: b 1741 d 6-7-1778 m Ruth Miller 2Lt NJ
Joseph: b 5-20-1752 d p. 1785 m Susannah Ross Pvt NJ
Joseph: b 1752 d a. 5-5-1794 m Sarah Cook Arfr NJ
Joseph: b 1732 d 11-21-1789 m Patience (Crane) CS NJ
Joseph: b 10-2-1722 d 10-14-1800 m Esther Belden CaptLt .NY
Joseph: b 5-17-1696 d 8-18-1781 m Mary Couch PS NY
Joseph: b c. 1735 d 2-11-1789 m Mary Moore Capt PS PA
Joshua: b c. 1743 d p. 5-25-1816 m (1)Mary Brown (2)Mrs Miriam Ladd PS CT
Josiah: b 6-25-1745 d 7-10-1822 m (1)Abigail Hathaway (2)—Kitchell Capt NJ
Josiah: b c. 1740 d c. 1785 m Abigail (?) — Pvt NJ
Josiah, Sr.: b — d p. 1790 m Sara Ewoutse PS NY
Josiah, Jr.: b c. 1750 d a. 1800 m Caroline Walters Pvt NY
Louis: b 1762 d 9-7-1827 m Mary Lindsay Pvt TN
Matthias: b 1743 d 9-14-1786 m Elizabeth (Crane) MM NJ
Moses: b 1731 d 2-12-1795 m (1)Susannah Brant (2)Catherine (Little) Rogers Pvt NJ
Nathan: b 11-27-1748 d 12-10-1837 m Esther Damon Cpl MA
Nathaniel: b 11-24-1762 d 8-31-1825 m (1)Mary Woodruff (2)Sarah Miller Pvt NJ
Noah: b c. 1745 d p. 1-6-1836 m Phebe — PS NJ
Peter: b 12-22-1752 d 12-6-1821 m Elizabeth Wiser Ens MA ★
Phineas: b 2-6-1755 d 11-14-1840 m Abigail Baldwin Pvt NJ
Roger: b 5-4-1762 d 6-3-1841 m Sarah Whiton Pvt MA W ★
Rufus: b 1755 d 11-20-1820 m Rachel Grant Pvt CT
Rufus: b 1744 d 1814 m (1)— Lyon (2)Charity Campbell Pvt NJ
Samuel: b 5-29-1752 d 7-28-1818 m Charity Higley Pvt MA
Samuel: b 10-9-1746 d 2-28-1811 m Mary Baldwin Pvt NJ
Samuel: b 3-10-1744 d 3-25-1830 m X PS VA
Seth: b 7-22-1732 d 4-4-1803 m (1)Hannah Coplan (2)Susannah Bent Pvt MA

CRANE, contd.
Silas: b 5-16-1729 d 3-8-1781 m Jemima Kinney MM Sgt MA
Silas: b 12-9-1759 d 1-21-1829 m Sipporia Haywood Pvt NJ W ★
Stephen: b 5-19-1734 d 5-10-1814 m Mary Chapman CS CT
Stephen: b *c.* 1750 d — m Mary (Miner) Wheeler Pvt MA
Stephen, Sr.: b 7- -1709 d 6-23-1780 m Phoebe — PS NJ
Stephen, Jr.: b 10-14-1737 d 2-11-1796 m (1)Phebe Morse (2)Jane Haines Sol NJ
Stephen: b *c.* 1731 d 1794 m Rhoda Halloway Pvt NJ
Thaddeus: b 3-24-1728 d 9-1-1803 m (1)Sarah Paddock (2)Lydia Reed Baxter Col NY
Thomas: b 1-6-1726 d 10-7-1804 m Mary Fenno PS MA
Vose: b 1730 d 11-22-1804 m Jane Vose Pvt MA
Wm., Sr.: b *c.* 1717 d 8-15-1784 m (1)—Wheeler (2)Mercy—Capt NJ
Wm.: b 10-12-1747 d 7-9-1814 m (2)Abigail Miller Capt NJ
Wm. Jr.: b 1758 d 11-16-1832 m Lydia Baldwin Pvt NJ ★
Wm.: b *c.* 1755 d 1816 m Lucretia — Pvt SC
Zebulon: b 8-7-1746 d 12-31-1814 m (1)— Holmes (2)Elizabeth (Wood) Townsend PS NY

CRANFORD,
David: b — d 8- -1801 m Sarah Offutt PS MD

CRANMER,
Caleb, Sr.: b *c.* 1735 d *p.* 10-11-1810 m (2)Mary Baker (3)Phoebe (Leake) Mathis PS NJ
Isaac: b *c.* 1740 d *c.* 1798 m (1)Rebecca Jones (2)Eunice Devinney Pvt NJ
Jeremiah: b 1762 d 7-17-1832 m Hannah Cole Peck Pvt NJ
Noadiah: b 8-26-1736 d 2-14-1829 m Catherine — Pvt Tms NJ

CRANNELL,
John: b 1731 d 1813 m Florinda — Pvt NY
Wm. Winslow: bpt 9-26-1749 d 12-27-1828 m Marie Eman Pvt NY

CRANS, (includes CRANSE)
John: b 3-1-1763 d 10-2-1833-5 m Christeen Trumpour Pvt NY
Peter: b 3-7-1747 d 3-15-1813 m Margaret Murray QM NY

CRANSON,
Amasa: b 10-21-1730 d 4-23-1808 m Mary Harthorne Maj MA
Asa: b 3-16-1760 d 1-5-1841 m Zillah Fuller Pvt MA W ★
Elisha: b 1720 d 4-18-1804 m (1)Abigail Baldwin (2)Hannah (Burnell) Stearns Capt MA

CRANSTON,
Caleb: b 1730 d 10-12-1800 m Mary Gould Pvt RI
James: b 6-1-1764 d 6-21-1833 m Ruth Austin Pvt RI
John: b 4-7-1757 d 1-10-1828 m Abigail Tisdale Pvt NY
John: b 11-3-1755 d 8-29-1825 m (1)Phebe Ann Edwards (2)Cynthia Cook Pvt RI
Peleg: b 4-22-1757 d 2-6-1822 m Elizabeth Babcock Pvt RI W ★
Samuel: b 4-12-1752 d 4-19-1830 m Zilpha King Sgt RI ★
Samuel: b 3-7-1757 d 4-28-1841 m (1)Elizabeth West (2)Eunice Whipple Sgt MA RI ★
Wm.: b 1764 d 1860 m (1)Abigail Congdon (2)Olive Hoor Sol RI

CRAPO,
Consider: b 8-26-1735 d *p.* 1797 m Mercy West Sgt MA
Francis: b 4/5-14-1738 d *p.* 1779 m Margaret Beale Pvt MA
Jonathan: b 3-19-1763 d 10-22-1846 m Celia Clark Pvt MA ★
Joshua: b 1-28-1746 d 5- -1834 m Jane Haskins Cpl RI
Peter: b 12-4-1743 d 3-3-1822 m (1)Sarah West (2)Mrs Content Hathaway Pvt MA
Peter: b 1758 d 9-1-1836 m Elizabeth James Pvt NY ★
Seth: b 5- -1724 d 7-11-1810 m Abigail Paymer Pvt MA
Wm.: b 2-7-1750 d 5-22-1822 m Alice (Crapo) Sgt MA

CRARY,
Archibald: b 11-24-1748 d 3-16-1812 m Anne Robbins Col RI
Benjamin: b 1725 d 5-8-1798 m (1)Amy Stanton (2)Abigail Stanton 1Lt CT
Christopher: b 6-24-1759 d 6-2-1846 m Polly Witter Pvt CT
Elias: b 1764 d 1847 m Elizabeth Palmer Pvt VT
Joseph: b 1-25-1757 d 10-31-1840 m Lucy Bentley Sgt CT RI ★
Nathan, Sr.: b 10-7-1717 d 3-24-1798 m (1)Dorothy Wheeler (2)Ruth Searles PS CT
Nathan, Jr.: b 3-17-1747 d 3- -1813 m Keturah Ayer Capt CT
Nathan: b 3-9-1762 d 3-21-1852 m Lydia Arnold Pvt VT CT ★
Robert: b 1717 d 1-30-1790 m Sarah Tracy PS CT
Robert: b 9-3-1760 d 3-24-1805 m (1)Cynthia Lamb Cpl CT
Wm.: b *c.* 1759/60 d *p.* 1806 m Anna Davis Sgt CT
Wm.: b 1719 d 4-30-1796 m Elizabeth Campbell Pvt CT

CRATIN,
John: b *c.* 1755 d 9-8-1826 m Marcia Ann Lanham Lt MD

CRATTY,
Thomas: b *c.* 1730 d *p.* 1786 m Jane McKinney Pvt PA

CRAVEN,
Elisha: b 1755 d 1820 m Sarah Frances Dawkins Pvt PA
Gershom: b 2-2-1745 d 5-3-1819 m Rebecca Quick Dr NJ

James: b 10-15-1752 d 2-19-1824 m Adrianna Kroesen Pvt PA
John: b 7-3-1741 d 11-5-1829 m (1)Ann Stewart (2)Nancy Richardson QM DE
John: b 9-11-1760 d 1-29-1840 m (1)— Adams (2)Mary McCoy (3)Jean Irvin Pvt PA ★
Thomas: b 10-24-1756 d 6- -1832 m (1)Eleanor Adams (2)Charity Simpson Pvt PA
Thomas: b 6-4-1739 d 2-8-1795 m Eleanor Hough Pvt VA
William: b 1- -1750 d *p.* 4-20-1819 m Cornelia Cornell Sol PA

CRAVENS,
James: b 1750 d *p.* 11-25-1797 m Mary — Sol NC
Margaret Hiatt: b 1727 d 1826 m (1)William Dyer (2)John Cravens (3)Denis Lanaham PS VA
Mary Harrison: b 5-25-1696 d *a.* 5-28-1781 m Robert Cravens PS VA
Robert, Jr.: b *c.* 1733 d 3- -1784 m Hester Harrison Maj VA

CRAW, (includes CRAWE)
David: b 1757 d *p.* 1832 m Sally Bingham Pvt CT ★
Reuben: b 1742 d 1828 m (1)Mary Towner (2)Zeruiah Louis Sunderlin Pvt CT ★

CRAWFORD,
Alexander: b 4-5-1710 d 10-11-1793 m Elizabeth — Pvt MA
Alexander: b 2-12-1765 d 6-1-1845 m Bethiah Willis Pvt MA
Alexander: b 10-15-1750 d 2- -1839 m Elizabeth Craighead Sol SC
Alexander: b 1751 d 6-19-1830 m (1)Miss Hopkins (2)Mrs McClure Pvt VA
Andrew: b *c.* 1755 d *p.* 2-19-1795 m Ann Speer Pvt PA
Ann: b 1708 d *p.* 8-28-1802 m David Crawford 3d PS VA
Benjamin: b *c.* 1755 d *p.* 1836 m Mary (Teeney) Anderson Hone Sgt PA
Charles: b 1738 d 3-23-1808 m Marie Delzelle Capt NC
Charles: b 12-23-1738 d 10-23-1813 m Jane Maxwell Capt NC
Daniel: b 4-1-1760 d 3-27-1837 m Eleanor Mackey Pvt NY ★
David: b *c.* 1740 d 3-16-1812 m Lydia Lloyd Capt MD
David: b 1740 d 1- -1801 m Sarah Offutt PS MD
David: b 7-1-1764 d 5-26-1835 m (1)— Kidd (2)— Kidd Pvt PA ★
David: b 2-2-1734 d 9- -1802 m Elizabeth Henderson PS CS VA
Edward: b 8-23-1743 d 4-23-1801 m Elizabeth Reynolds Pvt PA
Edward, Sr.: b *c.* 1720 d 1792 m Elizabeth Sterritt PS PA
Edward, Jr.: b 1-10-1757 d 3-6-1833 m (1)Elizabeth C Hostiger (2)Rebecca Colhoun Lt CS PA ★
Eleazer: b 11-4-1759 d 4-18-1796 m Ruth Yates Smn NJ
Elijah: b 4-25-1756 d 2-4-1830 m Polly — Cpl PA
George, Jr.: b 1748 d 1790 m Florence Henderson Pvt VA
Hugh: b 2-18-1762 d 1-17-1832 m Hannah Gamble Pvt PA
Isaac: b 3-9-1758 d 6-4-1833 m Kathrin Selfridge Pvt MA
James: b 10- -1762 d 1810 m Hannah Brown CG CT W★
James: b 1757 d 8-16-1825 m Margaret Rivers Pvt MA
James: b 4-10-1751 d 6-14-1838 m Martha Dickey Pvt Mrnr MA ★
James: b 1719 d 2-23-1802 m Jane — Sgt NY
James: b 3-22-1741 d 1-4-1825 m Ann McCausland Cpl PA
James: b 1730 d 1817 m (1)Rosanna Allison (2)Agnes MacDonald Maj PA
James: b *c.* 1742 d *p.* 1790 m Margaret — Pvt PA
James: b *c.* 1740 d 1817 m (1)Jenny Hutchinson Sol SC
James: b 1- -1733 d 1-1-1807 m Grace Carpenter Cpl VT
James: b *c.* 1755 d *a.* 4- -1804 m Elizabeth English Pvt VA
James: b 1757 d 5-16-1836 m Sarah Van Sandt Pvt VA ★
James: b 1758 d 1836 m Rebecca Anderson Pvt VA
James, Jr.: b 1755-58 d 3- -1816 m Christina White Lt SC
Joel, Sr.: b 10-16-1736 d 10- -1788 m Fanny Harris PS SC
John: b 2-14-1731 d 1813 m (1)Sarah Smith (2)Elizabeth Moore Sol NC
John: b 7-16-1759 d 10-19-1836 m Rebecca Snyder Pvt GA NC ★
John: b 1-7-1739 d 10-16-1824 m (1)Rachel Henderson (2)Phebe Green (3)Mary (Ford) Perkins Capt MA
John: b 9-22-1722 d *p.* 1790 m Susanna Kelso Pvt MA
John: b 1717 d 11-10-1797 m Sarah Fisher PS ME
John: b 9-21-1760 d 11-21-1844 m (2)Ann Wood Pvt NY
John: b 2-21-1761 d 3-7-1851 m Catherine Trumpbour Pvt NY ★
John: b 6-20-1761 d 11-19-1834 m Sarah Barclay Pvt NY
John: b 1765 d 11-5-1831 m (1)Purthena — (2)Linda — Pvt NY
John: b 1731 d 1802 m (1)— Mastin (2)Mrs Clark Pvt NC
John, Jr.: b 1763 d 1808 m Eleanor Price Pvt NC
John: b 10-28-1762 d 1-31-1841 m Mary Vernon Pvt NC ★
John: b 1734 d 1835 m Hannah Robb Capt PA ★
John: b 8-11-1745 d 2-13-1827 m Anna Holmes 2Lt PA
John: b 11-1-1748 d 2-12-1812 m Isabella Parker Pvt PA
John: b *c.* 1752 d 7-21-1820 m Margaret — Pvt PA
John, Sr.: b 1730-55 d *p.* 1778 m Margaret Thompson PS PA
John: b *c.* 1740 d *c.* 1804 m X Pvt PA
John: b 2-16-1747 d *p.* 1800 m X Pvt SC
John: b 1760 d 1834 m Agnes Glass Pvt SC
John: b 1741 d 1-13-1832 m (1)Margaret Crawford (2)Mary Craig (3)Sally Newman Lt QM VA
John: b 1756 d *c.* 1831 m Jane Lauderdale Pvt VA
John: b 3-29-1764 d 12-17-1846 m Rebecca Allen Pvt VA
Jonathan: b 1746 d *p.* 1817 m Mary Heath Pvt NH
Joseph: b 9-9-1761 d 7-28-1829 m Margaret Shankland Sgt NY
Josiah: b 5-6-1767 d 12-15-1834 m Elizabeth Ruth Ricks Pvt PA

Josiah: b 1736 d 1-1-1819 m X Pvt PA
Moses: b 1759 d 12-17-1826 m (1)Sarah Ann Singleton (2)Nancy
    Dorsey Pvt VA
Nathan: b 10-16-1744 d 3-4-1833 m Judith Anderson PS VA
Oliver: b 11-5-1757 d 7-5-1829 m Nancy Ann Fauqua Pvt MA
Patrick: b 1750 d 1783 m Mary Cowan Pvt SC
Patrick: b 1723 d 12-1-1787 m Sally Wilson Sol PS VA
Peter: b 1764 d 2- -1842 m Hannah Christy Pvt VA W★
Peter: b 2-7-1765 d 10- -1830 m Mary (Crawford) Pvt VA
Robert: b 6-19-1731 d 10-16-1777 m (1) — Wood (2)Elizabeth
    Armstrong Pvt NY
Robert: b 1728 d 10-5-1801 m Jean White Maj PS SC
Samuel: b 7-22-1748 d 5-11-1824 m (1)Sarah Work (2)Olive Eddy
    Pvt CT
Samuel: b 6-16-1741 d p. 1791 m Elizabeth Barrett Pvt NJ
Samuel: b 10-12-1736 d 11-18-1777 m Jane Milage Capt PS NY
Samuel: b 12-18-1750 d 10-17-1828 m Janet McCurdy Pvt NY
Samuel: b 7-4-1763 d 10-19-1841 m Margaret Gillaspy Pvt NY
Samuel: b 6-2-1758 d 5-14-1822 m Nancy Forgey Sol PA
Samuel: b 1750 d p. 1798 m Elizabeth Roy Pvt SC
Thomas: b 8-23-1756 d 4-11-1837 m Fanny Grace Pvt MA ★
Thomas: b 1751 d 1789 m Rebecca Covington PS CS NC
Thomas: b 9-3-1729 d p. 1794 m Mary Smith Pvt VA
William: b 8-6-1744 d 1826 m Alice Kennedy LCol PA
William: b c. 1750 d 1803 m Ann Hines Capt PA
William: b c. 1760 d 6-6-1782 m Sarah — Ens PA
William: b 10-23-1745 d 6-30-1833 m Mary Henderson Sgt RI
William: b 9-2-1722 d 6-11-1782 m Hannah Vance Col VA
William: b 10-6-1759 d 4-29-1810 m Isabel McClure Lt VA
William: b 6-1-1744 d 10-15-1792 m Rachel Sawyers Pvt PS VA
William: b c. 1735 d 1783 m Mary — Pvt VA
William: b c. 1745 d 12-30-1826 m Martha Cooper Pvt VA
William: b 2-21-1762 d 1-9-1839 m Margaret Dean Pvt VA
William: b 1735 d 2-15-1835 m Mary McRoberts Pvt VA
William: b 1740 d 1814 m Margaret Henderson Pvt VA
William G.: b 10-1-1757 d 12-16-1837 m Martha Beadle Pvt NJ

CRAWLEY,
Abraham: b 10-22-1757 d 1830 m Margaret Gay Pvtr MA
Samuel: b 12-22-1761 d c. 1793 m Hannah (2)Armistead) Selden
    Capt VA

CRAY,
William: b 1726 d 11-29-1778 m Mary Gignilliatt PS NC

CREAL, (includes CRAIL, CURRELL)
George: b 1745 d 1825 m Mary Athey Mid VA
John: b 5-3-1745 d 7-3-1839 m Allethia Ervin Pvt VA ★
Philip: b c. 1750 d 1793 m Margaret Hill Spencer Pvt MD

CREASE,
Richard: b 3-14-1732 d 4-13-1792 m Hepzibah Cook Arfr MA

CREECH,
Richard: b 1751 d 6-13-1819 m Elizabeth Blish Drm Mus MA W★
William: b c. 1755 d 1834 m Susan — Sol SC

CREEKBAUM,
Philip: b 1758 d 3-2-1826 m Catherine Jolly Pvt MD ★

CREEKMORE,
William: b 1757 d c. 1824 m— Owen Pvt VA

**CREGAR, (includes CREAGER, KREAGER, KREEGER,
    KREIGER)**
Adam: b — d a. 11-2-1805 m X Ens MD
Conrad: b c. 1730 d 3- -1808 m Anna Maria — PS MD
George: b 1763 d 11-26-1838 m Elizabeth Kettering Pvt VA
George: b 7-12-1759 d 9-14-1841 m (1)Catharine Ludwig (2)Sally
    Hunter Pvt NC ★
Jacob: b 11-17-1753 d 1844 m Elizabeth — Sgt NJ ★
John: b 1741 d 8-24-1833 m Ann Rodenback Pvt Tms NJ
Michael, Sr.: b c. 1721 d 1807 m (1) X (2)Mary — Pvt VA
Nicholas: b 1709 d 1-26-1804 m Maria C Borger Krieper PS NC

CREGO,
Abraham: b 10-6-1757 d 3-27-1843 m Polly Strahanan Pvt NY ★

CREIGH, (includes CREE)
John: b 8-25-1741 d 2-17-1813 m (1)Jane Houston (2)Isabella
    Mateer Capt PS CS PA
Robert: b 1755 d 1832 m Mary — Pvt PA
William: b 1752 d 4-6-1835 m Jane Villers Pvt PA

CREIGHTON,
James: b c. 1743 d p. 1778 m X Cpl NH
James: b 3-3-1731 d 11-27-1818 m (2)Rebecca Ingles Pvt PA
Robert: b 1750-55 d 2-9-1820 m Mary — Pvt PS NH

CRENSHAW,
Daniel: b c. 1760 d p. 8-20-1794 m Nancy Dupree Pvt VA
Robert: b c. 1735 d 1811 m (1)Elizabeth Beauford (2)Mary — PS VA
William: b c. 1750 d c. 1829 m Sarah Baker PS VA

CREQUE,
Peter M.: b 4-3-1740 d 9-3-1821 m Elizabeth Nelson Lt MA

CRESAP,
Daniel, Sr.: b 2-29-1728 d 7- 1798 m (2)Ruth VanSwearingen CS
    PS MD
Daniel, Jr.: b 1753 d 12-11-1794 m Elizabeth VanSwearingen Lt MD
Joseph: b 1755 d 1827 m (1)Deborah Whitehead (2)Sarah
    Whitehead (3)Sidney Sanford (4)Margaret Eunce Lt MD
Michael: b 6-29-1742 d 10-18-1775 m Mary Whitehead Capt PS
    MD VA
Michael: b 1750 d 9-30-1788 m Elizabeth Whitehead Capt MD VA
Thomas: b 1694 d 1- -1790 m (1)Hannah Johnson (2)Mrs Milburn
    PS MD

CRESSMAN,
George: b 5- -1746 d 8-26-1794 m Anna Maria Hoffman Pvt PA

CRESSY, (includes CRESSE, CRESSEY)
Andrew: b 1745 d 12-1-1822 m Mary Woodbury Pvt NH
Benjamin: b 6-27-1756 d 7-16-1799 m Abigail Trask Pvt MA
Benjamin: b 6-1761 d 3-25-1835 m (1)Wealthy Ann Gillett (2)Annah
    (Robinson) Huse Pvt NH ★
Daniel: b 10-11-1730 d 1817 m (1)Eunice S Morgan (2)Abigail
    (Bowers) Allen Pvt NH
Daniel, Sr.: b — d 8-2-1829 m Rhoda — PS NJ
Jacob: b 5-14-1742 d 2-4-1816 m Pamelia Edwards Ens NJ
Jonathan: b 1764 d 8- -1825 m Prudence Brown Pvt CT ★
Jonathan: b 5-14-1732 d 4-26-1824 m Anna Davis Pvt NH
Joseph: b 10-26-1753 d 7-22-1832 m Hannah Ashley Pvt ME
Nathan: bpt 7-31-1743 d p. 1790 m Phebe Kimball Pvt MA
Nathaniel: b 1724 d 9-27-1809 m (1)Sarah Ober (2)Elizabeth Conant
    (3)Hitty Haskell Pvt MA
Richard: b 9-5-1737 d 9-9-1797 m Susan Eaton Armr NH

CRESWELL, (includes CRESSWELL, CRISWELL)
Andrew: b 1-12-1757 d 7-16-1838 m Dorothy Evins Pvt VA ★
James: b 5-12-1743 d 9-13-1816 m Mary Johnson Pvt PA
James: b a. 1740 d 1776 m Mary Elizabeth Garlington PS SC
John: b 1737 d 12-2-1790 m Martha Ann Rutherford Pvt PA
Robert, Jr.: b 1743 d 1790 m Martha Buyers Pvt PA
Robert: b — d 9-6-1810 m Martha Stevenson PS PA
Samuel: b 1751 d 4-15-1839 m(1)Jemima Bennet (2)Ally—Pvt VA

CREVELING,
Andrew: b 2-28-1743 d 2- -1814 m (1)Margaret Patrick (2)Hannah
    Waters Pvt NJ

CREW,
Edward: b 9-14-1757 d p. 1804 m (1)Margaret Crane (2)Elizabeth
    Crew Pvt MD

CREWS, (includes CREWES)
David: b 3-2-1740 d 11-2-1821 m (1)Annie Magee (2)Mildred
    Williford Kerlew Pvt VA
Gideon: b 1730 d 1815 m Jemima Wicker PS Sol NC
Gideon D.: b a. 1742 d 1790 m Anna McQueen Pvt VA
John: b c. 1750 d p. 6-1-1792 m — Monroe Pvt VA
Richard: b 1748 d p. 1-23-1835 m Ester Puckett Sol VA

CRIGLER,
Christopher: b c. 1720 d 1810 m Catharine — PS VA

CRIM, (includes CREM, GREM, GRIM)
Heinrick: b 1-12-1762 d 4-6-1845 m (1)Mary Margaret Casler Sol
    NY ★
Henry: b 8-1-1733 d 12-4-1804 m Anna Maria — Pvt PA
Jacob: b 1751 d 1830 m Elizabeth Frank Pvt NY
Jacob: b 6-17-1754 d 6-24-1833 m Catherine Hottenstine Lt PA
Johan George: b 1-22-1750 d 1827 m Anna Catharine Greenawalt
    Fif Pvt PA
John: b 10-15-1753 d p. 2-5-1833 m (1)Julianna Mainzer (2)Mrs
    Phoebe Drake Pvt VA ★
Lena Steele: b 1733 d 1802 m Paul Crim PS NY
Paul: b c. 1723/24 d 1813 m Lana Steele PS NY

CRIPPEN,
Alpheus: b 1760 d 9-23-1834 m Pheobe Wilcox Pvt MA ★
Ezra: b c. 2-10-1745 d 3-5-1813 m Tabitha — Sgt MA
Ichabod: b 8-3-1765 d 5-4-1828 m Mary Whiting Pvt NY W★
Roswell: b c. 1755 d p. 1810 m Sarah Griffis Pvt NY
Samuel: b c. 1743 d 1783 m(1)Esther Wheeler(2)—Shelden Pvt VT
Silas: b 7-29-1758 d 3-7-1831 m Elizabeth Waterman Pvt NY CT W★

CRIPPS, (includes CRIPS)
Mathew: b 1-21-1743 d 1-28-1805 m Elizabeth Stedham Sol DE
Whitten: b 1740 d 4-15-1796 m Martha Huddy LCol NJ

CRISE, (includes KRISE, KRISS)
Barnet: b 1757 d 6-26-1848 m Elizabeth Cool Sgt NY ★
Conrad: b 1762 d 10-24-1844 m Mary Iddings Pvt PA ★
Henry, Sr.: b a. 1735 d 1810 m Maria Eiserin Sol MD

CRISLER,
Henry: b 1737 d 1811 m Elizabeth Weaver PS VA

CRISPELL, (includes CRISPEL)
Johannes: b 11-8-1724 d 1810 m Annatje Rutsen Sol NY
Peter: bpt 10-8-1743 d p. 1790 m Sarah Dubois Pvt PS NY
Petrus: b 9- -1736 d — m Garretje DuBois Sol NY

CRISPIN,
Jacob: b 3- -1752 d 3-19-1848 m (1)Anne Chubb (2)Eliza Graham Pvt PA
Joseph: b 1761 d 2-18-1828 m Elizabeth Rickey Pvt Matr PA

CRISSEY,
Ebenezer: b — d 3-8-1793 m Sarah Smith Pvt NY
Gould: b 2-10-1760 d 10-20-1838 m Eunice Morse Pvt CT ★
John: b 12-26-1757 d 11-8-1842 m Luthena Dutton Pvt Arfr CT ★

CRIST, (includes CHRIST)
Adam: b 1742 d 5-17-1808 m Elizabeth Follmer Sgt PA ★
Christian: b 1747/48 d 1814 m Elizabeth Weller Pvt NY
David: b 12-10-1758 d 6-10-1811 m Cate Bodine Pvt NY
George: b 2-12-1753 d 3-19-1828 m Catharine Andress Pvt PA
Henry: b 10- -1738 d a. 9-17-1783 m (1)Elizabeth Youngblood (2)Anna (Bodine) Crist Pvt NY
Henry, Sr.: b 1-27-1721 d 8-13-1789 m Appelonia Richert Capt CS PA
Henry: b 10-20-1764 d 8-11-1844 m Rachel Cartmell Sol PA
Jacob: b c. 1716 d 7- -1793 m Anna Catherine — CS MD
Michael: b 4-26-1711 d 11-22-1779 m Elizabeth Stinsman Pvt PA
Philip: b 1759 d p. 10-2-1843 m Elizabeth Burger Pvt PA ★

CRISTMAN,
Felix, Sr.: b — d 6-18-1795 m X Pvt PA
Frederick: b 8- -1748 d 10-26-1823 m Eva Myers Pvt NY
George: b 1742 d 8-27-1816 m Hannah McDowell Capt VA
Henry: b 12-25-1744 d 9-16-1823 m Susanna Keely Pvt PA
Henry: b 1744 d 1838 m Mary — Pvt PA
Henry: b 1747 d 1808 m Mary Elizabeth McDowell Pvt VA
Jacob: b 1758 d 4- -1832 m (1)Elizabeth Lauffer (2)Mrs Elizabeth Albright Pvt PA
John: b 1763 d 1830 m Jane Bear Pvt PA
Paul: b c. 1730 d 10-20-1805 m Magdalene— PS MD
Susanna Keely: b 2-25-1750 d 9-19-1823 m Henry Christman PS PA

CRITCHET
Richard Peacock: b 7-13-1756 d 6-22-1837 m Mary Cook Pvt NH

CRITCHFIELD,
John: b 1758 d 1851 m Rachel Swimpling Pvt VA ★
Joshua: b 5-27-1753 d 6-8-1842 m Margaret — Arfr Pvt MD VA ★
William: b 1758 d 2-19-1845 m Phoebe Jellison Pvt VA ★

CRITES,
Adam: b 1740 d p. 1790 m Anna Catherine Schmidt Pvt PA
Jacob: b c. 1740 d p. 6- -1820 m Elizabeth — Pvt PA
Jacob: b c. 1755/60 d p. 8-25-1837 m Elizabeth Henkel Pvt VA

CRITTENDEN, (includes CRUTTENDEN)
Amos: b 9-26-1753/54 d 6-27-1838 m Phoebe McIntire Pvt MA ★
Daniel: b 7-19-1744 d 2-4-1824 m Rhoda Tryon Pvt MA
Ebenezer: b 10-25-1757 d 1-25-1846 m Love Booth Pvt NH ★
Jason: b 3-30-1761 d 4-17-1813 m Keziah Brown Pvt CT
John: b 1756 d 1806 m Judith Harris Maj VA
Levi: b 11-20-1757 d 4-25-1845 m Clarissa Fanning Pvt MA
Medad: b 1764 d 8-13-1856 m Mary Boyden Pvt MA
Nathan: b 8-6-1721 d 10-2-1793 m Mary Parmelee Pvt CT
Nathaniel: b 8-21-1752 d 5-22-1828 m Jerusha Lewis 2Lt MA ★
Osee: b 1-18-1760 d p. 1784 m X Pvt MA
Richard Hazelwood: b 3-6-1761 d 6-22-1841 m Sally Tanner Pvt VA
Salmon: b 8- -1749/50 d 2-15-1816 m (1)Lucy Griswold (2)Rebecca Bert Pvt CT
Samuel, Sr.: b 2-7-1733/44 d 1816 m Sarah — CS MA
Samuel, Jr.: b 9-27-1755 d 9-2-1839 m Elizabeth Rice Cpl MA
Samuel: b 11-22-1755 d 6-9-1796 m Sarah Jocelyn Pvt CT
Seymour: b — d 7-17-1828 m Sybil Kenney Sgt MA
Simeon: b 1-28-1762 d 8-12-1832 m Lucretia Chilson Pvt MA
Timothy: b 1-27-1747 d 9-22-1832 m (1)Huldah Adams (2)Lucy Thompson Mus OrdlSgt MA ★
William Sumner: b 5- -1754 d 3-19-1842 m Mary Brayman Pvt Matr Smn MA ★

CRITZ,
Hamon: b a. 1760 d 8-5-1828 m Nancy Dalton Capt VA ★

CRITZER,
Leonard: b 11-25-1758 d 3-17-1852 m Elizabeth McKnight Pvt NJ ★

CROASDALE,
John: b c. 1757 d p. 1790 m Martha Gilbert 2Lt PA

CROCKER,
Benjamin: b 9-17-1749 d 1804 m Deliverance Child Pvt MA
Benjamin: b 10- -1763 d 7-27-1824 m Hannah Wheeler Pvt MA ★
Champion: b c. 1740 d 11- -1815 m Joanna Davis Sol MA
Daniel: b 3-1-1725/26 d 11- -1788 m (1)Elizabeth Childs (2)Phebe Winslow (3)Bathsheba Jenkins Capt MA
Ebenezer: b 6- -1752 d 4-15-1806 m Sarah Langdon Pvt NY
Eleazer: b 4-10-1754 d 9-10-1820 m Susannah Hinckley Pvt PS CT
Elisha: b 3-18-1750 d 1-13-1834 m Lucy Higbe Pvt MA
Ezekiel: b 1732-39 d 12-25-1824 m Lydia Arnold Capt MA
James: b 8-4-1747 d p. 1811 m (1)Prudence Lothrop (2)Prudence Robbins MM Sol CT
Jedediah: b 6-24-1761 d 7-8-1841 m Sarah Gifford Sgt MA
Job: b 3-29-1724 d 1-3-1809 m Mercy (Freeman) Knowles 2Maj MA
Job: b 4-15-1748 d 5-7-1831 m Elizabeth — Pvt MA
John: b 1-12-1734 d p. 1802 m (1)Anne Camp (2)Thankful Hubbard Cpl CT
John: b c. 1740 d p. 1787 m (1)X (2)Mrs Jane Berry Pvt MA
Jonathan: b 3-16-1738 d p. 1793 m Rachel Skinner Pvt CT
Joseph: b 3-4-1720/21 d 3-2-1802 m Ann Fenton PS CT
Joseph: b 2-24-1749 d 11-13-1797 m Hannah Mather Lt MA
Joseph: b 4-15-1748 d 7-2-1825 m Mary Hinckley Cpl MA
Josiah: b 10-30-1742 d 2-24-1808 m Abigal Leonard Capt MA
Nathaniel: b 5-7-1736 d 11-1-1824 m Katharine Bridgham Pvt MA
Peter: b 1-11-1758 d 2-7-1846 m Hannah Young Pvt MA ★
Roland: b 4-8-1757 d 2-8-1838 m Mehitable Merrill Arfr Cpl NS MA ★
Seth: b 3-27-1746 d 11-20-1809 m Mary Hinckley Capt CT
Simeon C.: b 9-16-1752 d p. 1-22-1824 m Hannah Williams Sgt CT
Thomas: b 6-8-1735 d 7-5-1796 m Mercy Hamblen Lt RI
William, Jr.: b 12-8-1730 d 5-3-1819 m (1)Lydia Knowles (2)Mary Cobb Pvt MA
Winslow: b 12-31-1755 d 12-16-1821 m Mercy Blish Smn MA

CROCKETT, (includes CROCK IT)
Andrew: b c. 1742 d p. 10-15-1791 m Elizabeth — Pvt PA
Andrew: b 1745 d 5-28-1821 m Sallie Elliott 2Lt VA
Anthony: b 11-19-1756 d 12-6-1838 m Mary Margaret Roberson 1Lt VA IL ★
Asher: b 9- -1760 d 1-16-1845 m Sarah Blankinship Pvt VA ★
Daniel: b c. 1740 d p. 1790 m Mary Noyes Pvt MA
David: b 3-28-1745 d p. 1790 m Sarah Thompson PS NH
Ephraim: b 7-12-1755 d p. 1802 m Rebecca Stanford Sol MA
Hugh: b 1730 d 1816 m Rebecca Lorton Col VA
James: b 1750 d 1826 m Mary Drake Ens CS VA
John: b 1730 d 12-10-1800 m Margaret McCorkell PS SC
John: b 1754 d 1794 m Rebecca Hawkins Pvt NC
John: b 1737 d 1- -1799 m Elizabeth Montgomery 1Lt CS VA
Jonathan: b 7-2-1741 d 4-20-1829 m Elionai Robbins Pvt MA
Joseph: b 5-7-1742 d 10-7-1829 m Elizabeth (Moore) Woodson LCol VA
Joshua: b c. 1735 d 1-6-1809 m Hannah Babb Lt MA
Nathaniel: b 4-25-1750 d p. 1796 m Eunice Cooper CS ME
Richard: b c. 1711 d p. 1786 m Mary — Pvt PA
Robert: b 1760 d 1812 m Jane Lewis Stuart Capt VA
Robert: b 1755 d 2-26-1836 m X Pvt VA ★
Samuel: b 9-6-1752 d 3-8-1830 m (1)Tabitha Hamblen (2)Elizabeth Fickett Sgt MA
Samuel: b 12-14-1759 d 4-21-1841 m Sarah Wilson Pvt PA
Samuel: b 1761 d c. 1846 m Abbie Skillings Pvt MA
Samuel: b 1735 d 1795 m (1)Jane Steele (2)Mrs Elizabeth Young Pvt VA
Thomas B.: b 9-9-1757 d 4-27-1823 m Esther — Sol PA
Walter: b c. 1735 d 11- -1811 m Margaret Stelle Caldwell Col VA
William: b c. 1745 d 9-15-1816 m Agnes Ritchie Pvt VA

CROES,
John: b 6-1-1762 d 7-26-1832 m Martha Crane SgtMaj NJ

CROFT,
George: b c. 1760 d 1827 m Sarah — Pvt PA
George: b 7-6-1741 d 1780 m Elizabeth Legere PS SC
James: b 1755 d 3-9-1839 m Esther Vought Cpl NY
John: b c. 1760 d 12- -1796 m Christiana — Pvt MD W★
John: b 8-2-1741 d 1820 m Elizabeth Simonds Cpl MA
Thomas: b 1725 d 12-31-1796 m Elizabeth (Lanier) Burch Sol VA

CROFUT, (includes CROFOOT)
Mark: b 1755 d 1818 m Mehitable — Pvt MA
Seth: b 3-28-1755 d 10-11-1825 m Sarah Peck Sgt CT ★

CROGHAN,
William: b 1752 d 1822 m Lucy Clark Maj VA

CROLIUS,
John: b 12-26-1755 d 10-15-1841 m Jane Morgan Pvt NJ
John: b 12-16-1733 d 4-2-1812 m Mary Clarkson Sgt NY
William: b 12-12-1753 d 4-21-1830 m Mary Dobbs Pvt CS NY ★

CROMAN,
Michael: b 1-6-1734 d 1-11-1808 m Eva— Pvt PA

CROMARTIE,
William: b 5-1-1731 d 9-21-1807 m (2)Ruamiah Doane Pvt NC

CROMBIE,
James: b a. 1746 d 1-7-1814 m Jane Clark PS NH

CROMER,
George: b 1750 d 1826 m Mrs Elizabeth Gray Raff Sol SC
John: b 1758 d 1825 m Catherine Brubaker Mil PA
Martin: b c. 1760 d 1823 m Mary — Pvt SC

CROMWELL,
Francis: b 10-2-1752 d p. 12-20-1810 m (1)Elizabeth Gray (2)Patience Stansbury Capt MD
John: b 12-5-1727 d 1804 m (1)Anna Hopkins (2)Hannah — PS Tms NY
Joseph: b c. 1745 d 5-12-1831 m Mary — Pvt MA ★
Richard: b 11-30-1749 d 12-25-1802 m Rachel Cockey Capt MD
Richard, Sr.: b 1751 d 1804 m Elizabeth Waters Lt MD
Stephen: b 10-30-1747 d 4-10-1793 m Elizabeth Murray Maj PS MD
Thomas: b — d a. 2-1-1799 m Hannah Henrietta Smith Capt MD

CRONEY,
John: b c. 1740 d 4-6-1804 m Sybel Marsh Pvt MA

CRONINGER,
Joseph: b 1753 d 5-16-1842 m Elizabeth Hill Pvt PA ★
Leonard: b 1758 d 9-12-1831 m Barbara May Pvt PA

CRONISE,
Henry: b 9-10-1758 d 3-13-1815 m Barbara Wort Pvt MD
John: b 11-25-1748 d 9-29-1803 m Mary Fey PS MD

CRONK,
Cornelius: b 7-7-1755 d p. 10-29-1799 m Fanny Drake Pvt NY
Garret: b 1- -1759 d 4-29-1844 m Susannah Requa Pvt NJ ★
John: b 8-27-1756 d 1-20-1839 m Barbara — Pvt PA ★
John: b c. 1758 d 9- -1816 m Lois Gifford Cpl NY W★

CRONKHITE, (includes KRONKHYHT)
Aury: b 7-4-1757 d 8-5-1815 m Phebe Cronkhite Pvt NY
Cornelius: b 5-8-1760 d 5-8-1805 m Hannah Overacker Pvt NY
George: b 1740 d 7-27-1796 m Ester Adzih Pvt NY
Henry, Sr.: b 1720 d 1810 m Mary — Pvt NY
James: b 10-18-1737 d p. 1- -1804 m (1)Hester Lent (2)Naomi Baker Capt NY
James: b 1756 d p. 1813 m Hannah Martin Pvt NY

CRONKLETON,
Joseph: b 7- -1760 d 10-17-1824 m (1)X (2)Mary — Pvt PA

CRONMILLER,
Martin: b 1-31-1762 d 1-26-1838 m Elizabeth King Pvt PA ★
Thomas: b 1760 d 1838 m Catherine Kaylor Pvt PA

CROOK, (includes CROOKE, CROOKS)
Charles: b 9-19-1754 d 1838 m Polly Chandler Pvt NH ★
Charles: b 3-7-1759 d 11-4-1854 m Deborah Baker Pvt VA
James: b a. 1743 d p. 1817 m Elizabeth Warford Pvt VA
James, Jr.: b 5-29-1746 d 9-7-1823 m Mary Williams Pvt VA
John: b 2-10-1766 d 3-17-1849 m Ann D Reeves Pvt VA ★
Joseph: b 1758 d 1826 m Catherine — Pvt MD
Joseph: b 10-25-1742 d 12- -1790 m Edith Linekin Sgt VA
Joseph: b c. 1730 d p. 6-28-1804 m (1)X (2)Elizabeth Berry PS VA
Martin: b 3-4-1758 d 3-31-1832 m Mrs Sara Toffield Ploeg Pvt NY
Samuel: b 10-6-1757 d 4-12-1813 m Anna Chandler Pvt NH
William: b 1763 d a. 10-19-1812 m Martha Edwards PS VA

CROOKER,
Abner: b 2-20-1736 d 1776 m Jerusha Hatch Pvt MA
Benjamin: b 12-6-1756 d 10-26-1835 m (1)Deborah Vaughn (2)Jane Bisbee Pvt Smn MA ★
Daniel: b 7-13-1740 d 2-6-1818 m (1)Abigail — (2)Hannah White Cpl MA
Elijah: b 4-8-1731 d 12-28-1812 m Agatha Hatch Capt MA
Isaiah: b 1730 d 9-15-1795 m (1)Betsey Philbrook (2)Hannah Harding McKenney PS MA
James: b 9-10-1755 d 1835 m Joanna Cushman Pvt MA
Jonathan: b 4-30-1717 d 1793 m Bethia Lowden Pvt MA
Lemuel: b 1-20-1752 d 1812 m Rachel Foster Cpl MA
Lemuel: b 1-10-1727 d 9-7-1795 m Margaret Foster Pvt MA
Noah: b 5-5-1761 d 5-24-1847 m Faith Randall Drm MA W★

CROOKS,
Henry: b 1743 d 3-10-1831 m Jane — Pvt PA
Richard: b 8-10-1745 d 1818/19 m Lavina Wilson Pvt PA
Thomas: b 1735 d 2-25-1815 m Judith Parr Col PA
William: b 4-17-1756 d 4- -1835 m X Cpl PA

CROOM,
Jesse: b 1-12-1740 d 2-18-1827 m (1)Anne Grady (2)Sarah Ramsey Sol NC

Jesse: b c. 1730 d p. 6-2-1812 m Mary — Sol NC
Lott: b 1761 d 1830 m Elizabeth Rasberry Sol NC
Major, Sr.: b 1723 d p. 1790 m (1)Olief Avery (2)Susan Enloe Hardy PS NC

CROPPER,
John: b 12-23-1755 d 1-15-1821 m (1)Margaret Pettit (2)Catherine Bayley Col VA
Sebastian: b — d 1776 m Sabra Corbin Capt VA

CROPSEY, (includes CASPARSE, CRAPSER, & CRAPSEY)
Casper: b — d p. 1800 m Margretje Barkaloo PS NY
Harmanus: b 9-2-1753 d 10-7-1830 m (1)Anne Covenhoven (2)Elizabeth Lawrence (3)Elizabeth Rezeau Lt NY
John, Sr.: b 1719 d 4-27-1804 m Catherine (Schryver) Van Dyne Pvt NY
John, Jr.: b 5-20-1750 d 2-23-1824 m Charity Ostrom Sol NY
Matthew: b 12-11-1756 d 7-25-1845 m Rachel Kniffin Pvt NY

CROSBY,
Abner: b 12-25-1744 d 5-5-1813 m Ruth Foster Pvt NY
Alpheus: b 11-16-1762 d 4-23-1842 m Elizabeth Gilmore Pvt NH ★
Charles: b 6-10-1754 d 12-17-1835 m (1)Mary Daily (2)Mary Ann Dexter Pvt RI ★
David: b 9-18-1737 d 11-16-1816 m Rebekah Pvt NY
Ebenezer: b 4-12-1759 d 1838 m Bathsheba Nevers Pvt MA
Eleazer: b 1761 d 5-28-1828 m Jemima — Pvt NY
Elijah: b 5-13-1764 d 7-30-1835 m Phoebe Church Pvt CT
Elijah: b 5-9-1756 d 8-6-1831 m Celia Bates Pvt MA
Elkanah: b 5-10-1761 d 4-30-1806 m Mercy Cobb Smn MA
Increase: b 2-23-1731/2 d 1-19-1802 m Rachel Graves PS CT
Isaac: b 1719 d 182- m Mercy Foster Pvt NY
Isaac: b 5-15-1744 d 9-14-1812 m Mercy Hopkins Lt VT
Jeremiah: b 3-20-1760 d 10-19-1821 m (1)Abigail Jaquith (2)Mrs Lucy (Learned) Winship Pvt MA
Jesse: b 3-18-1732/33 d 2-24-1804 m Ruth Goodspeed Pvt MA
John: b 8-24-1735 d 8-22-1820 m Martha Goodspeed Pvt MA
John: b 1760 d 1847 m Polly White Pvt MA ★
John: b 3-12-1747 d 2-19-1826 m (1)Elizabeth Culin (2)Ann Pierce Capt PA
John: b 1739 d 1824 m Sarah Crosby Sgt PA
John: b 5-10-1755 d 7-17-1853 m Nancy Peters Sol VA
Jonah: b p. 1732 d 1813 m Lydia Chandler CS PS MA
Jonathan, Sr.: b 8-1-1719 d p. 1788 m (1)Rebecca Coburn (2)Mrs Elizabeth Gordon Sol MA
Jonathan, Jr.: b 8-5-1744 d 10-20-1813 m (1)Mrs Hannah Goodhue (2)Dolly Parker Pvt MA
Jonathan: b 1762/63 d 5-26-1822 m Anna Morse Pvt MA ★
Joseph: b 10-15-1753 d 10-9-1842 m Sarah Richardson Pvt MA
Joseph: b 7-13-1756 d 7-13-1805 m Abigail Paddock Pvt MA
Joshua: b 6-12-1761 d 9-24-1838 m Lydia Terry Pvt Smn SC MA ★
Josiah, Sr.: b 11-24-1730 d 10-15-1793 m Sarah Fitch Capt NH
Levi: b 1729 d 1804 m Ruth Comstock Pvt CT
Moses: b 1726 d 4-24-1816 m Abigail Sparrow Pvt MA
Moses: b 1755 d 7-2-1821 m (1)Polly — (2)Abigail Foster (3)Mary — Pvt NY
Oliver: b 9-17-1744 d 9-17-1825 m Rachel Stickney Lt MA
Peter: b c. 1763 d 11-9-1831 m Ruth Waring Sol NY
Reuben: b 1-1-1735/36 d 1810 m Sarah Sears QM NY
Richard: b 9-27-1741 d 5-24-1790 m Esther Phipps Pvt PA
Robert: b 1734 d p. 4-18-1792 m Susannah — PS CS ME
Samuel: b 1740/50 d 9- -1824 m Lydia — Sol NY
Samuel: b 2-2-1732 d 12-11-1814 m Azuba Howe Dr MA
Simon: b c. 1759 d 1-25-1837 m Huldah Gibbs Pvt CT ★
Stephen: b 1-5-1734 d 9-15-1776 m Hannah Carrol Capt CT
Stephen: b 3-19-1761 d 10-26-1831 m Hannah Layton Pvt MA ★
Thomas: b a. 1760 d 7-28-1827 m (1)Elizabeth Patterson (2)Diantha Orcutt Cpl CT NY W★
Thomas: bpt 2-2-1752 d 8-4-1832/33 m Rebecca Bishop Pvt PS NY
Thomas: b c. 1751 d 3-4-1791 m Margaret Dennis Sol SC
Timothy: b 3- -1761 d 2-23-1813 m Cornelia Sibley Pvt CT
William: b 1-29-1758 d 5-12-1831 m Sarah Shepard Pvt NH

CROSE,
Michael: b c. 1764/65 d 6-21-1819 m Mary Ross Sol VA

CROSKEY, (includes CROSKEYS)
Robert: b c. 1751 d 1836 m Catharine Ringland Pvt PA
William: b c. 1748 d c. 2- -1797 m Ruth — PS SC

CROSLAND,
Edward: b 1740 d 1821/22 m Ann Temperance Snead PS SC

CROSLEY, (includes CROSSLEY)
Jesse: b 6-8-1741 d 10-22-1791 m Elizabeth Fullmer Capt PA
Moses: b 1-2-1764 d 3-13-1843 m Rachel Powell Pvt MD
Thomas: b 9-13-1710 d 1-11-1791 m Caroline Chapman Sol PA

CROSS,
Abijah: b 7-6-1758 d 2-21-1848 m (1)Elizabeth Parker (2)Hannah Foster (3)Deborah Spofford Pvt MA
Charles: b 1747 d 1785 m Phoebe Tomlinson Pvt VA
Daniel: b 12-18-1742 d p. 1790 m Betty Tyler Pvt MA

CROSS, contd.
David: b *c.* 1745 d 1801 m Margaret Moore Sgt DE
Elijah: b 1758 d *p.* 8-21-1832 m Ann Looney Sgt NC
Ephraim: b 3-22-1744 d *p.* 1790 m Elizabeth Andrews Pvt NH
Ichabod: b 6-16-1736 d 1-6-1827 m (1)Jemima Cobb (2)Olive — Pvt VT
John: b 5-6-1764 d 1-13-1836 m Abigail (Sadler) Collins Pvt MA ★
John: b 1735 d 12-17-1816 m Elizabeth Dakin Ens NH
John: b *c.* 1745 d — m Elizabeth Cocke Pvt VA
John: b 1756 d *p.* 5-25-1811 m Mary Reid Pvt VA
John: b 3-2-1761 d 4-22-1847 m Elizabeth Hardwick Pvt VA ★
Jonathan: b 7-18-1706 d 2-19-1797 m Lydia Hall PS CT
Joseph: b 1753 d 1-20-1855 m — Pvt CT
Joseph: b 1759 d 1-10-1855 m Persis Wheeler Pvt CT ★
Joseph: b 4-13-1747 d *p.* 2-13-1776 m Sarah Tyler Pvt MA
Joseph: b 1758 d 9-21-1815 m Hannah Olcott Pvt NH
Joseph John: b 1-2-1758 d 12-1-1818 m Mary England Pvt VA
Joshua: b 3-22-1752 d 5-24-1829 m Lidia Derby Smn MA
Michael: b 12-16-1739 d 4-8-1784 m Mary Rea Pvt MA
Moses: b 10-27-1763 d 5-4-1842 m Sarah Merrill Pvt MA ★
Parker: b 6-8-1756 d 1-10-1815 m Abigail Marston Sol NH
Peleg: b 12-6-1723 d 12-27-1812 m Mary — CS RI
Peter: b 9-28-1729 d 4-27-1810 m Sarah Hale Capt NH
Ralph: b 1-5-1737/38 d 9-4-1811 m Miriam Atkinson Col MA
Richard: b 1750 d 11- -1802 m (1)Anna Maclin (2)— Compton Cpl VA
Richard: b 10-8-1750 d 6-14-1800 m Ann Reid Cpl VA
Robert: b 1-20-1754 d 2-27-1801 m Mary Sly Pvt NY
Ruben: b 1- -1765 d 10-22-1837 m Esther — Pvt NY ★
Samuel: b 1724 d *p.* 1790 m Ann Clark Pvt RI
Samuel: b 1759 d *p.* 2- -1828 m Elizabeth Findly Pvt SC
Simeon: b 3-10-1745 d 2-22-1837 m Abigail Corliss Cpl MA
Thomas: b 10-30-1711 d 3-23-1793 m Sophia — PS MD
Thomas: b 1760 d 4- -1788 m Mary Goolsby Pvt VA
Uriah: b 4-3-1760 d 4-4-1835 m Anna Payne Sgt CT ★
William: b 6-25-1748 d *p.* 1808 m Polly Wheeler Capt NY
Zachariah: b 3-25-1761 d 2-27-1838 m Easter Hetty Johnston Pvt NC ★

CROSSETT,
Jacob: b 12-19-1749 d *p.* 1794 m (2)Fanny Savage Pvt MA
John: b *a.* 1765 d 1820 m Olive — Pvt MA
Samuel: b 12-25-1750 d 11-3-1803 m Abigail Cady Pvt MA

CROSSMAN, (includes CROSMAN)
Asahel: b 5-15-1756 d 1-30-1837 m (1)Olive Bliss (2)Lydia Payne Cpl MA
Benjamin: b 1-8-1708 d 5-24-1792 m Bethia Haskins Pvt MA
Daniel: b 5-2-1757 d *p.* 1784 m Alice Brett Pvt MA
Elijah: b *c.* 1755/56 d 10-17-1835 m (1)Rebecca Marsh (2)Ruth Thayer (3)Elizabeth Hewit 3Sgt MA ★
Gabriel, Jr.: b 6-25-1750 d *p.* 1790 m Phoebe Richmond Pvt RI
George: b 1737 d 9-25-1805 m Sarah — CS MA
John: b 3-7-1739 d 4-26-1812 m Ann Allen Sgt CT
Joseph A.: b 2-8-1737 d 7-22-1831 m (1)Catherine Wells (2)Elizabeth Hutchings Mrnr MA ★
Noah: b — d *p.* 1793 m Huldah — Cpl MA
Otis: b 1759 d 7-21-1806 m Prudence Williams Pvt MA
Peleg: b 10-31-1754 d 2-22-1825 m Margaret Ferguson Pvt MA
Phineas: b — d *p.* 1778 m Ellis — Pvt CT
Robert: b 1734 d 12-15-1823 m Lydia Leonard Maj MA
Samuel: b 1760 d 10-30-1831 m Elizabeth Cole Pvt MA
Simeon: b 6-14-1749 d 11-1-1830 m Sarah Smith Pvt NY
Theophilus: b 8-6-1742 d 8-15-1826 m Priscilla Witherell Cpl MA ★
William: b 9-24-1757 d 9-20-1812 m Martha Workman Pvt NJ
William: b 7-29-1751 d 11-8-1837 m Susannah Gates Pvt VT MA ★

CROSSWELL,
Gilbert: b *c.* 1760 d 1810 m Mrs Lucy Atkinson Fort Sol SC

CROSTHWAIT,
William: b *c.* 1740 d *p.* 1781 m Ann Shelton PS VA

CROUCH,
Aaron: b 1728 d 1795 m (1)Hepzebah — (2)Martha Leech Cpl CT
Christopher, Sr.: b 1740 d 8-3-1826 m Rebecca Buell Sgt CT
Christopher, Jr.: b 1765 d 10-24-1842 m Lydia — Pvt CT ★
David: b 2-9-1752 d 3-3-1829 m Johanna Jordan Mrmr Mstr MA
James: b 1728 d 5-24-1794 m Hannah Brown Capt PA
Jonathan, Jr.: b 2-4-1745 d *p.* 1783 m (1)Dorothy Laws (2)Anna Hill Pvt MA
Robert: b *c.* 1746 d *p.* 4-27-1798 m Sarah —Pvt PA
William: b 11-15-1762 d *a.* 10-15-1832 m Sally Downer Redford Pvt VA

CROUNSE,
Frederick, Sr.: b 8-19-1717 d 11-11-1778 m Elizabeth Livingston PS NY
Frederick, Jr.: b 12-14-1746 d 4-16-1828 m Anna Barbara Weber Ens NY
Philip: b 11-18-1743 d *p.* 10-9-1806 m Anna Maria Swartz Sgt NY

CROUSE, (includes CRAUS, CROWS, KRAUS, KRAUSE, KRAUSS)
Balthasar: b 11-28-1743 d 10-14-1805 m Susanna Yeakle Pvt PA
Carl: b 4-4-1739 d 9-9-1807 m Susanna Kemp Capt PA
Charles Michael: b 6-14-1745 d 7-18-1827 m Hannah Connor Capt PA
David, Sr.: b 8-30-1752 d 12-22-1820 m Regina Orth Capt PA
George: b 8-5-1740 d 9-28-1824 m Katherine Klock Pvt NY
Jacob: b *c.* 1742 d 1807 m Mary — Pvt PA
John, Sr.: b 1-13-1759 d 9-5-1847 m Catharine Umsted Pvt MD
John: b *a.* 1754 d *p.* 1800 m X Lt NC
Leonard: b 1750 d *p.* 1790 m Magdalena Klock Pvt NY
Peter: b 10-17-1747 d 3-15-1813 m (2)Margaret Murray QM NY

CROUTER,
Anthony: b *c.* 1732 d 1788 m (1)Catharine Parleman (2)Maria Stevenson Pvt PS NY

CROUTHAMEL,
Henry: b 1744 d *a.* 8-25-1816 m Catherine — Pvt PA

CROW,
Benjamin: b *c.* 1760 d *p.* 1840 m Sallie Morris Sgt VA
Benjamin: b 1756/57 d *p.* 1802 m Ann Gregg Sol VA
Edward, Sr.: b — d *p.* 1783 m Priscilla Farmer PS MD
Edward: b 1757 d 1836 m Jane Crow Pvt VA
Jacob: b 1732 d 1822 m Susannah Secris Pvt PA
Jacob: b 4-3-1740 d *p.* 4-17-1820 m Nellie Miller Pvt VA
James: b *c.* 1728 d *p.* 7-16-1792 m Grace — Sol NC
John: b *c.* 1740 d 1830 m (1)Ruth Holland (2)Elizabeth Clark Pvt NC
John: b *c.* 1760 d 1-21-1797 m Martha Morton Pvt PA
Peter: b 1763 d 11-15-1826 m Susan Earlewine Sct PA
Robert: b 1-1-1761 d 1850 m Margaret Killinger Pvt VA
Samuel: b 1-1-1756-59 d 1-16-1819 m Elizabeth (Brashear) Crepps Pvt 1Lt PS MD
Samuel: b 1741 d 3-15-1801 m Elizabeth Potter LCol VA
Stephen: b 2-28-1750 d 8-6-1830 m Margaret Stroud Sol GA
Thomas: b 2-20-1761/62 d 1835 m Nancy Donnelly Pvt VA
Walter: b — d 1789 m Ann — PS VA
William: b 1731 d 1813 m Lucretia — Pvt SC
William: b 3-8-1755 d 1-30-1821 m (1)Sarah Lawrence (2)Patience — Ens VA
William: b 1757 d *c.* 1837 m Racheal Rickebaugh Pvt VA ★

CROWDER,
Philip: b 4-7-1760 d 2- -1844 m (1)Susan Parish (2)Rachel Saunders (3)Sally Chandler Sgt VA ★
Sterling: b 1759/60 d 1-18-1834 m (2)Mary Jemima McCarty Pvt VA ★
Wm.: b 1737/38 d 11-2-1839 m (1)Phoebe Elder (3)Lucy Thompson Pvt Cmsry VA
William: b *c.* 1740 d *p.* 10-30-1802 m Ann Marshall Lt VA

CROWDUS,
William: b 1754 d 7-9-1825 m Dorotha Arnold Pvt VA

CROWELL,
Aaron: b 1735 d — m — Sgt NJ
Aaron: b 1750 d 4-12-1814 m Abigail Brown Pvt NJ
Abner: b 1-20-1736 d 4-24-1799 m (1)Hannah Crowell (2)Sarah Lewis Sgt MA
Barzillai: b 3-1-1754 d 7-17-1821 m (1)Mrs Rhoda (Burgess) Look (2)Keziah Butler Cpl MA
Christopher: b 4-7-1737 d 11-26-1835 m Deborah Sears Pvt MA
Daniel: b 5-20-1734 d 10-26-1807 m Thankful — Pvt MA
David: b *c.* 1757 d 11-14-1846 m Elizabeth Emerson Pvt MA ★
Ebenezer: b 8-1-1756 d 2-21-1831 m Phebe Bangs Pvt MA
Edward: b 3-26-1718 d 8-10-1813 m Betsey Baker Pvt MA
Edward: b 4-13-1761 d 11-1-1800 m Sara Martin Pvt NJ
Elisha: b 12-16-1757 d 7-9-1836 m Sarah Nickerson Pvt MA
George: b 7- -1747 d *a.* 10-23-1837 m Jemima Sherrin Pvt NC ★
Heman: b 4-15-1748 d *p.* 1795 m Deborah (Crowell) Hedge Pvt MA
Henry: b *c.* 1732 d *p.* 9-6-1784 m Margaret — PS MD
Henry: b 1758 d 1833 m Catharine — Pvt PA
Jeremiah: b 6-8-1756 d 1-20-1827 m Mary Hallet Pvt MA
John: b *c.* 1727 d *p.* 5-21-1788 m (1)Mary Howes (2)Eunice Turner Pvt CT
John: b 1-17-1734 d 6-3-1830 m Anna White MM MA
Jonathan: b 3-20-1728 d *p.* 1788 m Phoebe Snow Capt MA
Joseph: b 4-27-1752 d 7-20-1831 m Azuba Smith 2Lt MA
Joseph: b 2-21-1725 d 4-22-1798 m Temperance Crowell PS MA
Joseph: b 12-8-1759 d 3-18-1834 m Eunice Bloomfield Pvt NJ
Levi: b 10-12-1746 d 1-13-1807 m Deborah Baxter Sgt MA
Lot: b 4-8-1730 d 3-20-1809 m (1)Hannah Hamblin (2)Hannah Berry Capt MA
Michael: b 9-27-1756 d 11-10-1842 m Annie Parker Pvt MD W★
Nathaniel: b 10-12-1728 d 10- -1793 m Thankful Weldon Pvt MA
Paul: b 5-20-1751 d 9-28-1830 m Jerusha Aikens Pvt MA
Samuel: b 1742 d 1-19-1811 m Jerusha Tracy Pvt CT
Samuel: b 6-5-1755 d 1810 m Lydia Woodbury Commo MA
Samuel: b 10- -1741 d 11- -1785 m Thankful Earl Pvt NJ

Shubael: b 3-10-1754 d 10-21-1815 m Abigail Parker Pvt MA
Solomon: b 5- -1750 d *p.* 1790 m (1)Sarah — (2)Thankful Pvt MA
Solomon: b 10-19-1761 d 10-20-1807 m Lucy Butler Pvt MA
Sylvanus: b 10-25-1760 d 4-24-1833 m Mary Pierson Pvt NJ

CROWL,
John: b 5-10-1733 d *p.* 1790 m Sarah (Chaflin) Merriam Capt MA

CROWLEY,
Benjamin: b 1730 d *p.* 10-15-1817 m Sarah — PS VA
Florence: b *c.* 1758 d 2-6-1810 m Elizabeth Milledoller 1Lt MA W★
James: b 5-20-1764/65 d *a.* 9-4-1840 m Mary McClain Pvt PA
Miles: b 1746 d 6-6-1822 m Ann Porter Pvt PA ★
Royal: b 4-8-1765 d 5-8-1856 m X Pvt MA ★

CROWN,
Lancelot: b *c.* 1750 d *p.* 1800 m Mary — Pvt PS MD

CROWNINSHIELD,
Benjamin: b 1757 d 11-22-1836 m Mary Lambert Lt NS MA W★

CROWSON,
William: b *c.* 1740 d *a.* 9- -1814 m Mary Thomas Pvt NC

CROXALL,
Charles Moale: b 10-7-1756 d 11-6-1831 m Mary Morris Capt PA ★

CROXFORD,
John: b 1750 d 12-25-1821 m Wilmot Foster Sgt MA ★

CROXTON,
Carter: b 3-16-1761 d 4-29-1848 m (2)Fannie (Cole) Faulconer Pvt VA

CROZIER, (includes CROZER)
John: b 1750 d 4-23-1823 m (1)Fanny Whiting (2)Drucilla Gleason (3)Mrs Sally Beemis 2Lt MA ★
John: b 3-20-1755 d 6-8-1846 m Eleanor Bradfield Sgt PA ★
John: b — d 1- -1816 m Sarah Price Pvt PA
Robert: b 1-1-1745 d 11- -1805 m Rosamund (Park) Green Pvt PA

CRUDUP,
Josiah: b *c.* 1746 d 2- -1819 m Elizabeth Battle PS NC

CRUGER,
Nicholas: b 3-15-1743 d 3-11-1800 m (1)Ann de Nully (2)Anne Markoo PS NY

CRUIKSHANK,
Andrew: b — d 1813 m Mrs Jane Miller Pvt PA

CRUM, (includes CRUMB, CRUME, KROM, KRUM)
Adam: b 10-5-1756 d 10-10-1851 m Barberry Horn Pvt Spy NC VA ★
Arnold: b 1756 d 7-15-1847 m (2)Susannah Cross Pvt RI ★
Daniel: b 8-19-1737 d 1816 m (2)Elizabeth Kenyon Pvt RI
David: b 7-18-1749 d 4- -1821 m Hannah Dennison Pvt RI
Hendrick W.: b 2-28-1755 d 2-2-1827 m Jennike Phoenix Pvt NY
John: b 3-6-1761 d 2-8-1837 m Mary (Crum) Pvt MD ★
John: b 3-11-1758 d 1-10-1841 m Catherine Shaverman Pvt NY
John: b 11-11-1740 d 10-10-1821 m (1)Elizabeth Allhands (2)Elizabeth King Pvt VA
John: b *c.* 1740 d *p.* 1787 m Amelia — Pvt VA
Philip: b 9-8-1724 d 4-20-1801 m (1)Sarah Weathers (2)Anna Barrett PS VA
Richard: b 2-4-1763 d 9-19-1847 m (1)Elizabeth Gardner (2)Mary Brooks Matr NY ★
Simeon: b 1752 d 1827 m Harriet Pendleton Sgt RI ★
William: b 3- -1729 d 7-23-1810 m Amelia Wise PS MD

CRUMBLEY, (includes CRUMBLY)
Anthony: b *c.* 1760 d *p.* 1-8-1844 m X Sol GA

CRUMBLISS,
Thomas: b *c.* 1750 d *c.* 1833 m Fanny Bogardis Pvt VA

CRUMMETT,
Frederick: b *c.* 1760 d *c.* 1825 m Catherine Snider Pvt VA

CRUMMEY,
Stephen: b *c.* 1760 d *c.* 1830 m Rebecca Carter Pvt SC

CRUMP,
Benjamin: b 1729 d 5-26-1816 m (1)Mary Barbour Price (2)— Moore Pvt VA
James: b 1758 d 1800 m Isabella Monroe Capt NC
John: b 1740-50 d *p.* 1830 m Mary — Pvt PS VA
Joseph: b *c.* 1745 d *p.* 12-10-1795 m Martha — Capt NC
Joshua: b 5- -1765 d 1848 m Judith Tompkins Pvt VA ★
Josias: b 6-24-1734 d 1812 m Mary — StaffOfr PS NC
Richard: b *c.* 1759 d 4-13-1799 m Mary — Capt VA
Robert: b *c.* 1740-50 d *p.* 1811 m Mary Parr PS NC
Thomas: b — d 3-10-1816 m Peggy Gearton Pvt VA

CRUMRINE,
Stephen: b 1737 d 4-10-1812 m Catherine Roth Capt PA

CRUTCHER,
Henry: b *c.* 1740 d 1807 m (1)Susanna — (2)Martha Beazley Pvt QM VA
James: b 3-23-1755 d 1823 m Ann Poor Pvt VA
Samuel: b *c.* 1750 d *p.* 1786 m Elizabeth Lee Pvt VA
Thomas, Sr.: b *c.* 1708 d 6- -1786 m Sarah — PS VA

CRUTCHFIELD,
George: b *c.* 1750 d *p.* 7-22-1805 m "E" or Dicey — PS VA
John: b 1754 d 12-31-1841 m Silvia Nichols Pvt NC ★
John: b 2-17-1748 d 4-3-1811 m (1)Mary Barret (2)Jane W Jelks Lt QM VA
John: b *c.* 1740 d *c.* 1819 m Mrs Frances Johnson Holliday Pvt VA ★
Stapleton: b 9-20-1758 d 3-4-1820 m Elizabeth Lewis Pvt VA ★

CRUTCHLOW, (includes CRITCHLOW)
David: b 1-12-1735 d 3-2-1811 m Martha — Pvt PA
James: b 1756 d 3-3-1834 m Mary Leach Pvt PA ★
William: b 2-7-1760 d 4-3-1830 m (1)Mary Burnsides (2)Mary Mann (3)Margaret Horton Pvt PS PA

CRUTE,
John L.: b *c.* 1755 d 10-6-1840 m Rebecca Smith Lt VA ★

CRUZAN,
Benjamin: b *c.* 1758 d 6-5-1848 m Serena Milton Boyd Pvt VA ★

CRYDER, (includes CRIDER, KREIDER, KREITER, & KRIDER)
Christian: b 1-22-1757 d 12-23-1847 m (1)Anna Ellenberger (2)Susannah Brandt Pvt PA
Conrad: b 9-7-1736 d 9-14-1828 m Regina Bastian Wgm PA
David: b 3-5-1749 d 7-13-1829 m Catherine — Trm PA ★
Jacob: b 9-25-1755 d 9-25-1837 m (1)Elizabeth Gromley (2)Harriet Weaver Ens PA ★
John, Sr.: b 1739 d 3-10-1803 m Angelia Fox Lt PA
Martin: b 2-14-1740 d 11-14-1826 m Catharine Schmutz Pvt PA
Michael: b 1742 d 1816 m (1)Susanna Carpenter (2)Salome Carpenter Pvt PA
Michael: b 11-2-1764 d 9-24-1835 m Anna Regina Buehler Pvt PA

CRYER,
Morgan, Sr.: b 2-22-1756 d 11- -1833 m X Sol SC ★

CUBBERLY,
James: b *c.* 1735 d *p.* 1783 m X PS VA

CUDDEBACK, (includes CAUDEBEC)
Abraham: bpt 10-31-1738 d 8-25-1817 m Esther Gumaer Capt NY
Benjamin: b 6-21-1747 d *c.* 1787 m Catharine Van Vliet Pvt PS NY
William: bpt 6-21-1704 d 1778 m Jacomyntje Eltinge PS NY

CUDDY,
James: b 6-15-1754 d 1-9-1839 m Alcey Dunlap Arfr MD SC PA

CUDWORTH,
David: b 8-23-1735 d *p.* 1775 m Phoebe Drinkwater Pvt MA
James: b *c.* 1737 d *c.* 1814 m Mrs Anne Bryant Cpl MA
John, Jr.: b *c.* 1750 d 2-10-1827 m Elizabeth Clap Pvt MA
Nathaniel: b 1745 d 1-21-1826 m Mary March Maj MA ★
Zephaniah: b 2-13-1752 d 12-16-1827 m Elizabeth Studley Lt MA

CULBERHOUSE,
Thomas Welman: b 1750 d 1789 m Ann Gilmore Sol PS NC

CULBERTSON, (includes CUTHBERTSON)
Alexander: b 1750 d 12-13-1822 m Mary Sharp Pvt PA
Alexander, Sr.: b *c.* 1760 d *p.* 6-9-1829 m Ruth Brice Pvt PA
Andrew: b 12-23-1731 d 3-14-1797 m Jeanette Boyd Pvt PA
David: b 1761/62 d 1796 m Clara Browning Sol NC
James: b 1748 d 12- -1805 m Ann Culbertson Capt PA
James: b 1750 d 9- -1812 m Margaret Smith Cnt PA
John: b *c.* 1740 d *c.* 1797 m Margaret — Pvt PA
John: b *c.* 1740 d *c.* 1808 m X Sol NC
John: b 3-3-1739 d 9-12-1794 m Sarah Denny Maj PA
Joseph: b 1738 d 1805 m Agnes — Sol NC
Joseph: b *a.* 1758 d 11-18-1818 m — Wylie Capt PA
Josiah: b 1742 d 9-27-1839 m Martha Thomas Pvt SC ★
Robert: b 1758 d 1835 m (1) X (2)Mary — Pvt DE
Robert: b 1750 d 1840 m (1)Elizabeth Porter (2)Dolly Pleasant Pvt NC ★
Robert: b 1742-44 d *p.* 1802 m (1)— (2)— Maj PA
Robert: b 1738 d 1820 m (1)— (2)Mrs Elizabeth Davis Jameson Irwin Maj PA
Robert: b 7-23-1755 d 7-26-1801 m Anne Duncan LCol PA
Robert: b — d 1778 m Elizabeth Lindsay Pvt PA
Samuel: b 12-17-1741 d 2-19-1817 m (1)Margaret Henderson (2)Elizabeth McClay Col PA
Samuel: b 1743 d 1801 m Martha McClay Col PA
Samuel: b *c.* 1747 d 1789 m Margaret Cloyd Capt PA

CULBERTSON, contd
Samuel: b *c.* 1738/39 d 2-16-1814 m (1)Martha — (2)Mary Wiley Pvt PA
Samuel, Sr.: b *c.* 1718 d *a.* 10-15-1789 m (1)Jennet Shields (2)Mrs Eleanor McKean PS PA
Thomas: b 1754 d 8-12-1823 m Nancy Ogle PS DE
William: b 2-17-1746 d 9-2-1786 m Nancy Thornton Pvt DE
William: b 3-17-1740 d 4-7-1838 m Rachel — Pvt NC ★
William: b 1760 d 5-18-1798 m Agnes Bell Pvt PA

CULLEN,
John: b 1748 d 8-17-1827 m Nancy Foster Cpl VA
Thomas: b 1753 d 1828 m Margaret Woods Pvt PA

CULLER,
Benjamin: b 12-14-1746 d *p.* 1780 m Elizabeth Utsey Pvt SC
Michael: b 12-11-1745 d 2-13-1818 m Lenora Smith PS MD

CULLEY, (includes CULLY)
Armistead: b 1758 d 2-17-1839 m Mary — Sgt VA ★
David: b 1-12-1756 d *p.* 1790 m Abigail — Pvt NJ
John: b 1760 d 9- -1805 m Elizabeth Chapman Pvt NJ
Thomas: b *c.* 1750 d 5-30-1798 m (1)X (2)Isabel — Pvt PA

CULLUM,
Francis: — d *p.* 3-10-1810 m Susannah Northcraft Pvt PS MD

CULPEPPER,
Benjamin: b 1750 d 1-10-1829 m Joyce Powel Sheppard Pvt SC
Joseph: b *c.* 1765 d 1816 m Nancy — Sol GA
Sampson: b 1740 d 1820 m Eleanor Gilbert Pvt GA

CULVER, (includes COLVER)
Amos: b 1748 d 1830 m (1)Sarah Hopkins (2)Sarah (Rogers) Atkins Pvt CT
Amos: b 8-7-1763 d 4-27-1828 m (2)Esther Moxley Pvt CT
Benjamin: b 7-28-1747 d 8-8-1827 m (1)Abigail Ellsworth (2)Tamar Brown Pvt NY MA
Bezaliel: b 12-24-1755 d 8-29-1821 m Ann Caldwell Pvt NY
Charles: b 1741 d 1817 m Anne Heil Pvt CT
Christopher: b 9-13-1752 d 5-31-1843 m Phebe Holt Sgt CT
Daniel: b 9-31-1723 d 3-2-1786 m Patience Johnson Capt VT
David, Jr.: b 9-1-1758 d 3-4-1848 m (1)Abigail Elizabeth Mary Curtis (2)Lucy Clark (3)Mary French Sgt CT ★
David, Sr.: b 1738 d 8-3-1814 m Mary Youngs PS CT
David: b 6-25-1764 d 10-24-1847 m Katharine Callendar Pvt NY ★
David: b *c.* 1730 d 1801 m Margaret — Pvt PS VT
Ebenezer: b 6-13-1722 d 7-7-1777 m (1)Mary Stone (2)Ada Gray Sgt MA
Eliakim: b 8-13-1754 d 2-28-1841 m Theodosia Belden Pvt CT
Jeremiah: b 12-7-1735 d 4- -1818 m (1)Susannah — (2)Dorothy — Cpl Gnr CT
John: b 10-3-1760 d 4-16-1852 m Dinah Post Pvt CT ★
Jonathan: b 3-15-1726 d 6- -1808 m Sarah Hinman Pvt NY
Joseph: b 5-6-1761 d 8-28-1849 m Rebecca Root Pvt MA ★
Joshua: b 6-13-1722 d *p.* 1790 m (1)Hannah Cook (2)Avis Webster Pvt CT
Joshua: b 10-30-1746 d *p.* 1775 m — Pvt NY
Joshua: b *c.* 1755 d *p.* 1809 m Elizabeth Allen Cpl VT
Joshua: b 5-20-1729 d 1817 m Jerusha Holcomb Sgt VT
Moses: b 4-11-1747 d 9- -1795 m Lucy Turner Cpl CT
Nathaniel: b 6-29-1728 d 2-1-1808 m Ruth Kilborn PS NY
Peter: b *c.* 1712 d *p.* 2-11-1788 m Mercy — Pvt CT
Samuel, Sr.: b 9-25-1728 d 3-2-1781 m Ann Miles Ens CT
Samuel, Jr.: b *c.* 1755 d *p.* 1796 m Sarah Hall Pvt CT
Samuel: b 5-24-1747 d 3-2-1831 m Anna Hall Sgt VT
Solomon: b 8-18-1760 d 4-2-1835 m Lodamia Burr Pvt NY ★
Timothy: b 12-29-1741 d 2-1-1829 m (1)Rebecca Clark (2)Mary Brink Sgt PA
William: b 1-1-1749/50 d — m (1)Hannah Bishop (2)Jane White Pvt CT
William: b — d 7-25-1788 m Esther Grant Pvt CT

CUMBERSON,
Thomas: b 1736 d 1784 m Elizabeth Cornish PS NY

CUMMINGS, (includes COMINGS, COMINS, COMMINS, COMMONS, & CUMMINS)
Abraham: b 7-9-1755 d 6-30-1840 m Mary Bourne Pvt MA
Alexander: b 2-1-1750 d 1-9-1842 m Jane Livingstone Pvt MA
Alexander: b *c.* 1750 d 9- -1811 m Elizabeth Starke Capt VA
Andrew: b 1759 d 11-27-1834 m Jane Paxton Pvt PA ★
Asa: b 9-1-1762 d 9-5-1836 m Kataline Conley Pvt CT ★
Asa: b 9-18-1759 d 2-22-1845 m (1)Hannah Peabody (2)Mrs Lydia Holt Town Pvt MA ★
Benjamin: b 11-25-1757 d 3-8-1804 m (1)Bridget Poole (2)Sarah Holden Lt NH
Benjamin: b 3-29-1755 d 4-14-1813 m Mary Cooper Col NH
Benoni: b 1763 d *p.* 1799 m Susanna Farrington Pvt MA
Charles: b 1744 d 1821 m (1)Elizabeth — (2)Jean — Pvt PA
Charles: b *a.* 1746 d 3- -1812 m Millicent Carter PS Pvt VA
Daniel: b 10-17-1743 d 5-16-1792 m Rachel Hayden Pvt MA
Daniel: b *c.* 1760 d *p.* 1806 m X Sol VA
David: b 3-26-1729 d 10-8-1799 m (1)Joanna Jones (2)Chloe Harrington Pvt MA

David: b 5-20-1738 d 2-28-1803 m Elizabeth Butterfield Pvt NH
Ebenezer: b 9-21-1749 d 6-4-1821 m (1)Jemima Hartwell (2)Lydia Tay Pvt MA
Ebenezer: b 4-17-1735 d 3-7-1788 m Elizabeth Abbot Pvt NH
Ebenezer: b 1-29-1730 d *p.* 4- -1803 m (1)Sarah Chase (2)Sarah Stevens Pvt PS NH
Eleazer: b 12-15-1740 d 8-4-1815 m (1)Sarah Reed (2)Mrs Mary (Reed) Hildreth Capt NH
Eleazer: b 10-2-1737 d 2-3-1779 m Hannah Whitney PS NH
Elisha: b 8-2-1719 d *p.* 1790 m (1)Mary Andrews (2)Mrs Jemima Marsten Pvt NH
Ephraim: b 4-19-1743 d 5-22-1803 m Mrs Betty Bradstreet Merrill Pvt NH
Francis: b 1751 d 10-25-1809 m Johanna Freer Pvt NY
Francis: b 1752 d 2-22-1832 m (1)Sarah Davis (2)Sarah Thompson Sol NC
Free: b 8-3-1751 d 5-3-1832 m (1)Ruth Stockwell (2)Alice Gould (3)Rachel Williams Cpl MA
George: b 1742/43 d *c.* 1808 m Sarah Collins Sgt NC
Gershom: b 1759 d — m Rhoda Newton Pvt MA
Isaac: b 12-25-1758 d 10-1-1842 m Elisabeth Bryant Drm MA
Isaac: b 4-24-1751 d *p.* 1790 m Betsey Boynton Pvt NH
Jacob: b 5-12-1717 d 10-13-1814 m Mary Marble CS MA
James: b 1748 d 12-21-1818 m Margaret — Ens MD
James: b 5-26-1759 d 9-26-1839 m (1)Charlotte French (2)Sarah Wright Cpl MA ★
James: b 1755 d 1835 m Margaret Armstrong Pvt PA
Jerathmel: b 9-23-1749/50 d *p.* 1789 m Deborah Kendall Lt VT
Jesse: b 11-6-1745 d 10-19-1835 m Mary Fitz Pvt MA
John: b 9-10-1755 d 4-28-1852 m Araminta Short Pvt MD ★
John, Sr.: b 1710 d 9-20-1789 m Sarah Lawrence Cpl MA
John, Jr.: b 3-16-1737 d 10-5-1805 m Rebecca Reed Lt NH
John: b 1754 d 1834 m Elizabeth Church Capt PA
John: b 1752 d 4-17-1813 m Amelia Forman Lt PA
John Noble: b 1-19-1752 d 7-6-1821 m Sarah Canfield Hedden LCol CT
Jonathan: b 10-14-1743 d 5- -1805 m (1)Mary Eastman (2)Mary (Lovejoy) Parker Pvt MA
Jonathan: bpt 11-9-1755 d 2-28-1846 m (1)Elizabeth White (2)Lydia Kimball Pvt MA
Jonathan: b 6-5-1729 d 7-10-1787 m Deborah Russell Pvt NH
Joseph: b 2-5-1733 d 2-23-1818 m Elizabeth Allard Cpl MA
Joseph: b 4-8-1753 d 6-29-1826 m Temperance Nye Pvt MA
Joseph: b 2-11-1762 d 12-8-1853 m Rose Colyar Sellars Pvt VA ★
Josiah: b 1-12-1763 d 9-12-1834 m (1)Sarah Taylor (2)Olive Taylor Pvt MA
Jotham: b 12-29-1741 d 4-1-1808 m Anna Brown 2Lt CS NH
Oliver: b 4-10-1728 d 8-15-1810 m Sybil Bailey Capt MA
Parker: b 5-23-1756 d 3-13-1825 m Patty Flynn Pvt CT
Peter: b — d *p.* 12-16-1814 m X Lt VA
Philip: b 11-26-1745 d 3-26-1826 m Mary McCaster Pvt MA
Reuben: b 12-4-1737 d 9-28-1808 m Mary Parker Sgt MA
Robert: b 1754 d 1825 m Mary Allen Coates Capt MD
Robert: b *c.* 1750 d *p.* 1808 m (1)Delpha Ballard (2)Dicea Gibson Ens PA
Robert: b 1748 d 12-19-1837 m Ruth Hayes Pvt PA
Robert: b 1751 d 7-4-1837 m Rebecca Jane Kilgore Pvt PA ★
Samuel: b 2-28-1732 d 3-19-1796 m Eunice Bradstreet Lt MA
Samuel, Sr.: b 2-14-1709 d 12-11-1804 m Susanna Hood Pvt MA
Samuel, Jr.: b 9-12-1734 d 9-23-1811 m Elizabeth Fisher Pvt MA
Samuel: b 11-18-1742 d 1-16-1826 m Sarah Butterfield Pvt NH
Samuel: b 1751/52 d 1790-99 m Mary Sheels CS NC
Simeon: b 1738 d 1-18-1810 m (1)Hannah Bowers (2)Mrs Smith Pvt CS NH
Thomas: b 2-12-1740/41 d 3-27-1806 m (1)Lois Boardman (2)Elizabeth Perkins Sgt MA
Thomas, Sr.: b 8-1-1714 d 11-11-1787 m Sarah Fassett PS MA
Thomas, Jr.: b 5-29-1734 d 11-17-1818 m Lucy Lawrence 1Lt PS MA
Thomas, 3rd: b 6-16-1757 d 1845 m Elizabeth Hildreth Fif MA ★
Thomas: b *c.* 1756 d 1- -1808 m Abigail Mason Pvt PA W★
Thomas: b *c.* 1754 d 1814 m Sarah Henry Pvt VA
William: b 1725 d 3- -1793 m Sarah Coppage Pvt MD
William: b 2-15-1734 d 1784 m Margaret Hammond Lt MA
William: b 10-12-1741 d 10-2-1831 m (1)Mehitable Eastman (2)Mrs Martha Johnson CS Pvt NH
William: b 10-10-1743 d *p.* 1790 m (1)Rhodea — (2)Huldah — Lt NY
William: b 1-18-1759 d 4-18-1849 m Annis Leigh QM Lt NY ★
William: b 1762 d *p.* 1793 m Mary McCain Pvt PA
William: b 5- -1758 d 10-19-1828 m X Pvt RI ★

CUMP, (includes KUMP)
Henry: b 1757 d 1849 m X Pvt VA ★

CUNARD, (includes CONARD, CUNNARD)
Edward: b 3-23-1750 d 1-12-1829 m Judith Hirst Pvt VA
Henry: b 5-17-1742 d 1786 m Elizabeth Streeper Sol PA
John: b 2-20-1738 d 4-9-1803 m Betty Potts Pvt VA

CUNDIFF,
John: b 1-14-1757 d 9-18-1837 m Sallie — Pvt VA ★
Richard: b *c.* 1750 d 1803 m Susannah — Pvt PS VA

CUNNABELL, (includes CONNABLE)
John: b 1749 d 8-26-1813 m (1)Amy Edwards (2)Sarah Dewey (3)Mrs Abigail Congdon Sol PS MA
John: b 8-10-1725 d 1-30-1801 m Sarah Crafts Pvt MA
Samuel, Sr.: b 4-7-1717 d 12-3-1796 m (1)Hannah Blanchard (2)Mary English Pvt MA
Samuel, Jr.: b 11-11-1743 d 4-29-1794 m Rebecca Ryther CS MA
Samuel: b 3-22-1762 d 2-2-1845 m Susannah Frizzle Pvt MA ★

CUNNING,
Robert: b 1758 d 11-8-1836 m (1)Nancy Young (2)Catharine Geho Pvt PA

CUNNINGHAM, (includes CUNNYNGHAM)
Adam: b c. 1740 d 1806 m X Pvt PA
Allan: b 1738 d 5-15-1801 m Rachel Menough Capt PA
Ansel: b 7-27-1763 d 1837 m (2)Mary — Pvt VA
Arthur: b c. 1725 d 8-25-1828 m (1)Jane Ellender Cunningham (2)Mrs Mary Twaddle PS SC
Arthur: b 1734 d 7-12-1825 m Mary Jones Pvt SC
Barnett: b 6-29-1736 d 9-13-1808 m Anna Wilson Pvt PA
Christopher, Sr.: b c. 1720 d p. 11-10-1782 m (1)Sussannah Patton (2)Mary Musgroves PS NC
David: b 1765 d p. 1816 m Unity Ryan Sol PA
Edward: b c. 1746 d 5-4-1804 m Sarah Price PS VA
George: b 4-7-1753 d 8-3-1837 m Mary McCarty Pvt Wgn SC ★
Hugh: b 1760 d 9-20-1824 m Mary Kent Pvt NC W★
Hugh: b 1741 d 3-25-1817 m Agnes Cunningham PS Pvt PA
Hugh: b 1708 d 1782 m Nancy O'Neil Pvt VA
James: b 1740 d 6- -1812 m Janette Park Col PS PA
James: b 3-31-1750 d 11- -1857 m (1)Agnes Moore (2)Pury L — Pvt VA ★
James: b c. 1758 d p. 1840 m Elizabeth Gillespie Pvt VA
James: b 1738 d 1785 m Arabella Goode PS VA
James: b c. 1720 d 1780 m Anne Thomson PS VA
John: b c. 1750 d 3-12-1829 m Ann Davis Col GA W★
John: b 1743 d 1814 m Priscilla Taber Capt MA
John: bpt 10-27-1745 d 8-20-1829 m Anne Thomson Lt MA
John: b 11- -1709 d 2-9-1789 m Ann Sinclair PS MA
John: b — d 11-1-1809 m Rebecca Taylor Pvt NJ ★
John: b 1754 d 1820 m Elizabeth Nicholson Bbd NY
John: b c. 1730 d. 6-20-1803 m Mary — Lt PA
John: b c. 1759/60 d 4-19-1797 m Elizabeth Stoteler Pvt PA
John: b — d p. 1778 m Elizabeth — Ens VA
John: b c. 6- -1758 d 12-17-1844 m Margaret Hill Cpl VA ★
John: b 1749 d 8- -1808 m Elizabeth — Pvt VA
John: b 2-10-1748 d 12-18-1842 m (1)Mary Hill Pettipool (2)Kigiah Chandler Pvt VA ★
Joseph: b c. 1732-35 d p. 1-29-1801 m Annie Buntin Lt NC
Joseph: b 1752 d 8-14-1836 m Margaret John Sgt PA ★
Nathaniel: b 1754 d 8-16-1832 m Betsey Sneed Sgt VA
Peter: b 8-14-1750 d p. 1790 m Elizabeth Pierpont 1Lt NS MA
Robert, Jr.: b 3-25-1740 d 9-3-1809 m Martha Blair Pvt MA
Robert: b 1735 d 1801 m Margaret — Pvt VA
Robert: b 1742 d 9-14-1823 m Martha Watt Lt PA
Robert John: b 1772 d 1775 m Martha St Julien PS SC
Robert Moore: b 9-10-1760 d 7-10-1839 m (1)Elizabeth Moore (2)Betsey Ann Parks (3)Catherine Emily Byrd OrdlSgt NC ★
Samuel: b 7-9-1738 d 3-16-1827 m Susan M Carter Capt CS NH
Samuel: b 1732 d 6-26-1806 m Sarah Smith Lt PA
Sarah Price: b — d p. 12-24-1800 m Edward Cunningham PS VA
Shubel: b c. 1744 d a. 1790 m Phebe Mosier Pvt NY
Thomas: b 1755 d p. 1796 m Nancy Cargill Pvt NH ★
Thomas: b — d 1813 m Ann Adams Pvt PA
Thomas: b — d 6-2-1826 m Phebe Tucker Pvt VA W★
Valentine: b c. 1755 d 10-7-1832 m (1)Mary LaPrad (2)Mrs Francis Lahon Pvt VA ★
Walter: b c. 1730 d c. 1809 m Jane Steele Sol VA
William: b 11-6-1746 d 9-7-1794 m (1)Mary Moore (2)Elizabeth Barrett Pvt MA
William: b 5-6-1747 d p. 1777 m Martha Peck Pvt MA
William: b c. 1739 d 7-12-1832 m (1)Dorothy — (2)Mrs Elizabeth Huff PS MA
William: b 2-2-1748 d 4- -1842 m Martha Blair Pvt NC ★
William: b 4-10-1741 d 1806 m Elizabeth Watkins Maj VA
William: b c. 1756 d 1795-97 m Elizabeth Whiddon NLt VA
William: b 7-24-1764 d 12-21-1862 m Susannah Barbara Handyshel Pvt VA★
William: b c. 1742 d 11-13-1833 m Susan Wood Sol VA
William Roe: b 1740 d 1829 m Nellie Mossam 1Lt NS Pilot VA

CUNNIUS,
John: b 2-17-1733 d 2-20-1808 m Catherine Elizabeth Griesemer LCol PA

CUP,
Michael: b 1740 d 1821 m Barbara Lagle Pvt GA

CUPP, (includes COPE)
Jacob: b c. 1737 d p. 1813 m (1)Maria Elizabeth — (2)Mrs Mary Eve Leedy Pvt PA
Leonard, Sr.: b 1-17-1755 d 8-17-1834 m Susannah — Pvt PA ★

CUPPLES,
James: b 5-21-1758 d 7-7-1843 m Mary Ann — Sol PA

CURD,
John, Jr.: b 11-29-1751 d 3-8-1819 m Ann Underwood Col VA
John: b 11-23-1760 d 9-10-1838 m Nancy Williams Curd Pvt VA ★
John: b 1726 d a. 8-29-1800 m Lucy Brent Sol PS VA
Joseph: b 1732 d 1811/12 m (1)Mary Warren (2)Mary Truehart Lt VA
William: b 1730 d p. 1788 m (1)Mary Watkins (2)Ann — Capt VA

CURETON, (includes CURTAINE)
James: b c. 1739 d p. 1809 m Betsey Heath Pvt VA
John: b 9-27-1731 d p. 8-31-1802 m (1)Winifred Heath (2)Hannah Davis Ens VA
Wm.: b c. 1760 d 3- -1833 m (1)Polly — (2)Celis Banister Sol GA
William, Jr.: b 6-10-1762 d 9-18-1827 m Margaret Crawl Pvt GA
William, Sr.: b 3-27-1737 d p. 5-10-1810 m Martha Baugh Lt SC

CURLE,
William: b 9- -1754 d 1-19-1841 m Sarah Brown Pvt VA

CURLEE,
John: b 1761 d 4- -1812 m Mary Barber Pvt NC

CURLING,
Thomas: b 4-17-1742 d p. 1-20-1797 m X 2Lt NS SC

CURRENCE,
William: b 1715 d 10-8-1780 m Lydia Steele PS VA

CURRIER,
Abner: b 9- -1744 d 11- -1792 m Sarah Ann Chase Sgt PS NH
Abraham: b 3-25-1759 d 3-24-1846 m Lydia Kimball Pvt MA
Asa: b 5-12-1734 d 12-24-1780 m Rebecca Plummer Cpl MA
Asa: b 9-4-1747 d 11-17-1818 m Gene Gilmore Pvt MA
Barnard: b 4-15-1719 d 6-14-1793 m Mary Emery PS NH
Benjamin: b 9-18-1740 d 1816 m Abigail Prescott Pvt NH
Challis: b 12-21-1724 d 7-25-1796 m Mary Clough PS NH
Daniel: b 1-5-1714/15 d 8-19-1801 m Electa Currier CS MA
David: b 9-16-1756 d 10-31-1843 m Elizabeth Peabody Pvt MA
David: b 1756 d 4-1-1840 m Mary Dinsmore Sgt NH
David: b 8-30-1737 d c. 1786 m Martha Ladd Sol PS NH
Dudley: b 4-17-1745 d 1-23-1816 m Sarah Ordway Pvt NH
Ebenezer: b 3-18-1716 d p. 11-6-1791 m Anna Jones Pvt MA
Edmund: b 5-27-1733 d p. 1778 m Susanna Kimball 1Lt MA
Edward: b 7-15-1761 d 11-29-1846 m Sarah Batchelor Pvt NH ★
Ezra: b 3-5-1745 d 4-27-1813 m Mehitabel Eaton Capt NH
Gideon: b 8-13-1754 d 10-1-1835 m (2)Anna Richardson Pvt NH
Jacob: b 1747 d p. 1793 m Hannah Morill PS Cpl NH MA
Jacob Bagley: b 4-4-1753 d 8-17-1831 m Elizabeth Johnson Pvt MA
John: b 11-17-1726 d 12-22-1806 m Mary Wells Capt MA
John: b 1748 d 11-19-1834 m Mary Poor Pvt MM MA★
Jonathan: b 1757/58 d 11-6-1829 m Nancy Sargent Pvt MA NH ★
Jonathan: b 11-27-1737 d 3- -1778 m Sarah Searles Sgt NH
Levi: b 5-22-1745 d a. 2- -1831 m Mary — Pvt MA
Moses: b 1746 d 1804 m Mehitable Barnard Pvt NH
Nathaniel: b 11-10-1724 d 12-23-1776 m Susanna Morrill PS MA
Nathaniel: b 8-18-1740 d 11-21-1826 m Sarah Wise PS NH
Reuben: b c. 1730 d p. 1790 m Susanna Day Pvt PS NH
Richard: b 6-2-1749 d 6-24-1821 m Molly Clough 2Lt MA
Richard: b 10-5-1755 d 1837 m Mary Currier Pvt NH ★
Samuel: b 1-5-1747 d 5-5-1802 m (1)Mary Rowell (2)Mrs Abigail Dearborn McClure Pvt PS NH
Seth: b 3-10-1734/35 d 3- -1792 m Ellis Sargent CS MA
Theophilius: b 12-22-1752 d 9-28-1837 m Elizabeth Follansbee Pvt NH ★
Thomas: b 12-7-1757 d 2-3-1834 m Ednah Bailey Pvt NH
William: b 1752 d p. 1778 m Abigal Beechum Cpl MA
William: b 5-12-1737 d 1809 m Mary Carter PS CS NH

CURRY, (includes CURRIE)
Alexander: b 1756 d 1819 m Mary Elizabeth — Pvt VA
Archibald: b 1-1-1728 d 12-26-1816 m Sarah McDonald Pvt PA
Cary: b — d p. 7- -1819 m Mary — Pvt GA
David: b 1752 d 1826 m Sarah Wells Pvt NC
David: b — d p. 7-5-1784 m (1)Ann Corbin (2)— Carter (3)Elizabeth Armistead PS VA
James, Sr.: b 1737 d 1790 m (1)Mary Catherine Armstrong (2)Sarah Wilson Pvt NC
James, Jr.: b 1765 d 1842 m Sarah Black Sol NC
James: b 1760 d 1- -1828 m Sarah — Sol GA
James: b 4-7-1756 d 11-18-1832 m Martha Crooks Pvt PA
James: b 12-26-1756 d 5-14-1819 m Elizabeth Butler Sol GA
James: b 1-29-1752 d 7-5-1834 m Mary Magdalene Burns Capt VA ★
James, Sr.: b c. 1728 d p. 1794 m — Warwick PS VA
John: b 1730 d 2 28-1826 m Cornelia Post Pvt NY
John: b 6-4-1762 d 8-22-1847 m Elizabeth Rainey Pvt NC
John: b 4-27-1750 d 8-27-1835 m Mary Catharine Baldwin Pvt PA ★
John: b p. 1757 d p. 6-17-1822 m (1)Margaret Adams (2)Sarah Ingle Pvt VA
John: b 1755 d 1822-25 m Kaziah — Pvt SC
Mathew, Sr.: b c. 1729 d c. 1809 m Hannah — Pvt PA
Moses: b 1739 d 3-16-1822 m Sarah Moore Pvt PA

CURRY, contd.
Peter: b c. 1740 d a. 11-2-1827 m Lucy Pope Sol GA
Richard: b 1750 d 9-16-1776 m Hannah Potts Pvt PA
Robert: b 12-31-1741 d 6-10-1780 m Jane McWilliams Lt PA
Robert: b 1754 d 6-25-1838 m Isabell McKenzie Pvt PA
Robert: b 1759 d 9-19-1804 m Phebe Sample Pvt VA
Robert: b 11-10-1717 d p. 12-29-1803 m Ann (Curry) CS VA
Stephen: b 1742 d 6-6-1829 m Frances Moore Pvt NY
Thomas: b 1762 d p. 1833 m Alsie Gordon Pvt VA ★
William: b 6-29-1748 d 5-6-1844 m Charity Lockwood Pvt NY ★
William: b 12-28-1739 d 1820 m Margaret Gray Lt PA
William: b 1730 d 2- -1808 m Frances — Pvt VA
William: b c. 1715 d 1791 m — McAfee PS VA

CURSER,
Benjamin: b 1746 d 11-1-1832 m Sarah Cox Pvt NY

CURTENIUS,
Peter Theobald: b 1734 d 9-8-1796 m Catharine Goelet Col NY

CURTIS, (includes CURTICE, CURTISS)
Aaron: b 9-9-1737 d 5-30-1801 m Hannah Griswold Sgt MA
Abel: b 12-22-1729 d 11-1-1797 m (1)Hannah Foster (2)Mrs Patience Wickham Pvt CT
Abel: b 3-25-1722 d 11-7-1790 m Freelove Bartholomew PS CT
Abel: b 1741/42 d 3-21-1823 m Anna Alcott PS Sol CT
Abel: b 2-17-1741 d 7-31-1829 m Sarah Neal Pvt MA
Abel: b 8-10-1752 d 6-21-1804 m Desire Cutis Pvt MA
Abijah: b 3-2-1750 d 9-8-1825 m Ann Bishop Pvt CT
Abner: b 1-27-1719 d 1799 m (1)Mary Chapman (2)Mrs Mary Whiting Lt CT
Abner: b 10-11-1732 d 12-19-1779 m X Pvt CT
Abner, Sr.: b 8-5-1727 d 9-18-1799 m (1)Deborah Mann (2)Sally Ford (3)Mrs Phoebe Dunbar 2Lt MA
Abner, Jr.: b 1754 d 2-2-1838 m Lydia Bowker Pvt MA
Abner: b 11-8-1733 d — m Ruth Hale Pvt MA
Abraham: b 2-6-1754 d 9-4-1776 m Anne Curtis Pvt CT
Agur: b 9-11-1730 d 2-8-1784 m Mercy Hinman Capt CT ★
Agur: b 3-28-1755 d 11-10-1838 m Mercy Blakeman Pvt CT ★
Amasa: b 7-19-1743 d 11-17-1822 m Lucy Garfield Sgt MA
Andrew: b 7-18-1756 d 7-20-1840 m Patience Nichols Pvt NY
Asa: bpt 8-3-1746 d 9-1-1794 m Eunice Woodward Pvt CT
Ashley, Jr.: b 4-20-1746 d 8-25-1831 m Susannah Fuller Pvt MA
Augustine: b 11-8-1761 d 9-16-1832 m Lodema Sackett Pvt CT ★
Benjamin, Jr.: b 2-13-1735/36 d 2-20-1817 m (1)Phidema Nichols (2)Mary Devine Pvt CT
Benjamin, Jr.: b 7-5-1755 d 9-27-1825 m (1)Content Pond (2)Aurelia Sterne Pvt CT ★
Benjamin: b 10-27-1735 d 7-1-1829 m Mindwell Hough CS CT
Benjamin: b 1752 d 1784 m Elizabeth Billings Dr NY
Caleb: b 1757 d 1820 m Abigal Winthrop Pvt MA
Caleb: b 4-1-1727 d 1781 m Phoebe St John Capt CT
Caleb, Jr.: b 5-22-1758 d 6-20-1850 m (1)Hannah Seavy (2)Anna Given (4)Mrs Susan Mitchell Cpl MA
Caleb: b 2-3-1727 d 3-21-1802 m (1)Charity Combs (2)Lucy Putney Pvt PS MA
Coleman: b 1738 d 1791 m Hannah Corwin Pvt PS NY
Daniel: b 4-29-1715 d 1783 m Rebecca Smith Pvt CT
Daniel, Sr.: b 1-23-1735 d p. 4-29-1802 m Mary Goodale Pvt MA
Daniel, Jr.: b 1761 d 8-4-1828 m Kezia Smith Pvt MA
Daniel: b 1739 d 2- -1782 m Tabitha Raymond Sol MA
Daniel: b 6-5-1755 d 4-27-1831 m (1)Hepzibah Burr (2)Huldah Burr CG CT
David: b 3 10-1739/40 d 11- -1819 m Sarah Frost Pvt CT
Ebenezer: b 1-31-1760 d 3-21-1819 m Rebecca Latimer Pvt CT
Ebenezer: bpt 8-31-1707 d p. 1790 m Elizabeth Palmer Pvt MA
Ebenezer: b 11-11-1759 d — m Elizabeth Streeter Pvt MA ★
Ebenezer: b 6-9-1760 d 8-22-1832 m Sarah Parker Pvt NH
Edmund: b 8- -1725 d p. 1790 m Sarah Welles Sgt CT
Eldad: b 11-13-1732 d 6-23-1823 m (2)Clotilda Meeks Pvt VT
Eleazer, Sr.: b 1711 d 1784 m Mary Dunham CS CT
Eleazer, Jr.: b 9-23-1736 d 10-1-1788 m Mary Carter Maj CT
Eleazer, 3rd: b 10-20-1759 d 9-7-1801 m Eunice Starr Sgt CT
Eleazer: b 9-3-1754 d 7-19-1796 m Hannah Gridley Pvt CT
Eli: b 2-23-1733 d 1-26-1818 m (1)Desire Turner (2)Elizabeth Bailey Pvt MA
Elias, Sr.: b 10-16-1747 d 10-16-1827 m Sarah Hutchinson Pvt VT
Elihu: b 5-10-1741 d 8-9-1820 m Phebe Burritt Sgt CT
Elijah: b 12-31-1761 d 3-23-1842 m (1)Content Wheeler (2)Mrs Pulling Pvt CT ★
Elijah: b 1747 d 1817 m Jane Moss Ens CT
Eliphalet, Sr.: b 2- -1735 d 1806 m Margaret Dyer Capt CT
Eliphalet, Jr.: b 1758 d 1816 m Mary Wilcox Pvt Fif CT
Elnathan: b 1-4-1726/27 d p. 1790 m Sarah Ufford PS CT
Elnathan, Sr.: b 4-10-1712 d 7-20-1781 m Rose Weller Maj MM MA
Elnathan, Jr.: b 10-16-1754 d 1828/29 m Violet Brown Pvt MA
Enoch: b 1-26-1745 d 1-11-1834 m Sarah Felton Pvt MA ★
Enos: b 3-15-1708 d 3-4-1788 m Mary Yale Sgt MA
Ephraim: b 3-27-1739 d 4-30-1794 m Ann Curtis Capt CT
Ezra St John: b 8-26-1758 d p. 1800 m — Ryan Pvt CT
Fleix: b 12-9-1761 d 4-8-1828 m Patience Hull Pvt CT ★
Francis: b 1743 d 8-27-1826 m Elizabeth Robbins Pvt MA
Frederick: b 1760/61 d 2-3-1830 m Persis Brown Pvt CT ★

Gideon: b 11-19-1767 d 7-7-1843 m Rebecca Hardy Pvt CT ★
Gideon: b 1752 d 6-8-1789 m Elizabeth Mills Pvt CT
Gideon: b 1-25-1726 d 1779-90 m Mirriam Hotchkiss PS CT
Giles: b 3-22-1764 d 5-28-1832 m Hannah Westover Cpl CT ★
Henry: b c. 1744 d p. 1820 m Elizabeth Merilla Swingle Pvt NY ★
Henry: b 8-17-1750 d 1833 m Elizabeth Davison Pvt CT
Hezekiah: b 12-23-1747 d 5-5-1822 m (1)X (2)Sarah Thompson Pvt CT
Hull: b 7-2-1753 d 1-23-1840 m Rhoda Titus Pvt CT
Isaac: b 6-4-1749 d 2-27-1831 m Hannah Higbee Sgt MA
Israel, Jr.: b 4-24-1742 d 1802 m Abigail Mallory Pvt CT
Israel, Sr.: b 6-14-1719 d a. 4- -1776 m Abigail Putnam Pvt MA
Israel: b 10-20-1754 d 10-20-1806 m Elizabeth Wilkins Pvt MA
Jacob, Jr.: b 4-10-1746 d 12-14-1786 m Mehitable Walker Ens MA
Jacob: b 3-10-1730/31 d 2-22-1797 m Mary Stiles PS NH
James: b 10-10-1716 d 12-3-1802 m (1)Elizabeth Burroughs (2) Keziah — Pvt CT
James, Jr.: b 1758 d 1-19-1811 m Sarah Fosdick Sol Slr CT
James: b c. 1714 d a. 2-8-1790 m Hannah Buel PS CT
James: b 10- -1762 d 7-22-1835 m Amy Seymour Pvt MA ★
James: b 2-10-1746 d 2-24-1818 m Jemima Alger Sol NY
James: b 1755 d 1845 m Elizabeth Coffinbery Pvt VA
Jeremiah: b 12-30-1752/53 d 10-27-1824 m (1)Mary Waterbury (2)Abigail — (3)Deborah — Pvt CT
Jesse: b 1735 d 5-25-1821 m Sarah Curtiss Maj CT
Jesse: b 3-27-1744 d 12-13-1811 m (1)Hannah Peterson (2)Lucy Morton Pvt MA
John: b 5-1-1745 d 8-31-1825 m Mary Shelton Lt CT
John: b 10-9-1721 d 4-18-1820 m Hannah Moseley Pvt CT
John: b 2-3-1735 d a. 12- -1805 m (1)Anna Ives (2)Louisa — Pvt CT
John: b c. 1740 d 8-27-1776 m Mrs Hannah (Merrill) Miller Pvt CT
John: b 1-20-1739/40 d 3-25-1801 m Mary Lewis PS CT
John: b 6-6-1750 d 7-27-1843 m Elsie Wilkins Sgt MD ★
John: b 4-20-1741 d 7-12-1783 m Ruth Peabody Sgt CS MA
John: b 10-30-1746 d 3-2-1837 m (1)Phebe Keith (2)Lydia Keith 4Sgt MA
John: b 4-19-1743 d 4-3-1826 m Mary Parker Pvt MA
John: b 1710 d 1800 m Hepzibah Hale PS MA
John: b 1-6-1760 d 8-16-1816 m (1)Mary Shaw (2)Elizabeth — PS NC
John: b 1758 d 1825 m Susan — Pvt PA
John: b c. 1730 d 1813 m Nancy — Sgt VA
John Thomas: b 1759 d 1818 m Agnes Johnston Sol GA
Jonathan, Sr.: b 4-13-1715 d 1789 m (1)Deborah Mix (2)Hannah Waples Pvt CT
Jonathan, Jr.: b 10-28-1747 d 4-7-1829 m (1)Mary Jacob (2)Prudence — Pvt MA
Jonathan: b 1757 d 1-15-1829 m Rhoda Hawes Cpl MA
Jonathan, Jr.: b 6-17-1754 d p. 1830 m Sybil Haven Pvt MA
Jonathan: b 1755 d 1830 m Mary Jones Pvt MA
Jonathan: b c. 1730 d — m Dorothy — Pvt NH
Joseph: b 10-20-1753 d 7-15-1839 m Lydia Marsh Pvt CT ★
Joseph: b 4-12-1756 d 5-16-1810 m Rebeckah Deming Pvt CT
Joseph: b 8- -1745 d p. 1790 m Mary Thompson Pvt CT
Joseph: b 3-28-1721 d 3-15-1801 m (1)Martha Judson (2)Esther Blakeman PS CT
Joseph: b 12-22-1721 d 10- -1791 m Abigail Baldwin Maj MA
Joseph: b 4-3-1747 d 12-11-1823 m Hannah Benson Pvt MA
Joseph: b 1-19-1751 d 12-20-1834 m (1)Phoebe Davis (2)Polly Williams (3)Sarah Davis Pvt NH
Joseph: b 1-28-1759 d 12-27-1833 m Adelia Mead Sgt VT W★
Joshua, Sr.: b 9-22-1733 d 11-2-1791 m Abigail House Sgt MA
Joshua, Jr.: b c. 1761 d 6-5-1823 m Nancy Ridyard Pvt MA
Joshua: b 10-30-1742 d 8-2-1795 m Jemina Wilbur Pvt NY
Josiah: b 12-17-1721 d 10-4-1800 m Mary Kilburn Pvt CT
Josiah: b 6-7-1752 d 1819 m Ann Ford Pvt CT
Jotham: b 5-2-1726 d 9-23-1785 m (1)Mary Yale (2)Esther Merriam Hull Capt CT
Jotham: b 8-22-1759 d 6-22-1848 m Elizabeth Mallison Pvt CT ★
Jotham W.: b 1-28-1765 d 9-20-1823 m Susannah Rexford Pvt NY
Lemuel: b 1755 d 6-23-1827 m Mary Smith Pvt NH ★
Mark: b 9-5-1761 d p. 1800 m Ellen Bulkley Sol CT
Matthew, Sr.: b 12-1-1712 d 11-29-1796 m (1)Phebe Judson (2)Abigail Gold Thompson CS PS CT
Matthew, Jr.: b 2-4-1746 d 6-3-1824 m (1)Hannah Ford (2)Ann Judson Lt CT
Michael, Sr.: b 4-30-1739 d 3-7-1800 m Bathshua Barstow PS MA
Moses: b 2-21-1747 d 1806 m Mary Mecham Cpl MA
Moses: b 3-2-1722 d 2-16-1808 m (1)Mary Vinson (2)Hannah Belcher (3)Experience White Colson Pvt MA
Nathaniel: b 8-6-1738 d 8- -1806 m Elizabeth Curtis PS MA
Nehemiah: b 1740 d 5-13-1810 m (1)Phebe Wells (2)Sarah (Lewis) Booth Pvt CT
Nehemiah: b 1-3-1733 d 12-26-1816 m (1)Hannah Roduck (2)Margaret Ewing Capt PS ME
Obadiah: b 1724 d 11-8-1811 m Martha Buckminster PS MA
Paul: b 5-29-1737 d 3-13-1836 m Deborah Webber PS MA
Peleg, Jr.: b 1754/55 d 6- -1834 m Ruth Bowker Cpl MA
Peter: b 1740 d 5-19-1797 m Ruth — Capt CT
Peter Burr: b 4-30-1755 d 3-25-1837 m Phoebe Sherman Pvt MA
Reuben: b 5-13-1757 d 1816 m Silence Allen Pvt CT
Richard, Sr.: b — d 11-20-1784 m Mrs Phoebe Jones PS SC

Robert: b 8-13-1727 d 1- -1797 m Amy Judson Pvt CT
Robert Welles: b 3-12-1757 d 1854 m Phoebe Curtis Pvt CT ★
Ruth Peabody: b 1744 d 1829 m (1)John Curtis (2)Bartholomew Trask PS MA
Samuel: b 3-30-1744 d 1810 m Mehitable Goodrich Ens CT
Samuel: b *c.* 1731 d *p.* 1790 m Sarah Barber Pvt CT
Samuel: b 11-15-1737 d 5-15-1801 m (1)Margaret Root (2)Mary Ann Day Pvt CT
Samuel: b 1757 d 4-30-1829 m Zipporah Morgan Smn CT ★
Samuel: b 12-23-1716 d 2-4-1802 m Dinah Clarke PS CT
Samuel: b 1736 d 1798 m Priscilla Williams Pvt MD
Samuel: b 2-26-1728 d 6-2-1777 m Mary Town Capt MA
Samuel: b *c.* 1760 d *p.* 1790 m Amy Chandler Sol VT
Silas: b 1766 d 7-3-1841 m Ruth Birdsey Pvt NY ★
Simeon: b 11-10-1760 d 12-13-1809 m Elizabeth Sled Tms CT
Simeon: b 2-29-1760 d 11-24-1831 m (1)Prudence French (2)Mrs Thirza (Poola) Lyon Pvt MA ★
Simeon: b 6-19-1746 d 8-24-1805 m Abigail Rood Pvt CT
Snow: b 8-10-1755 d 12-31-1823 m Bathsheba Hatch Sgt MA
Solomon: b 1762 d 1826 m Hannah Taylor Pvt CT MA W★
Solomon: b 2-19-1755 d 7-28-1838 m (1)Sarah Landers (2)Mary — (3)Aner — Pvt NY
Stephen: b 6-4-1727 d 5-8-1806 m (1)Tabitha Beardsley (2)Sarah Judson Pvt CT
Stephen: b 8- -1755 d 2-20-1832 m (1)Abigail Small (2)Bridget Smith Pvt MA W★
Stiles: b 2-3-1761 d 11-8-1827 m (1)Clara Adams (2)Betsy Hitchcock Pvt CT
Stiles: b 3-18-1708 d 4-22-1785 m Rebecca Judson PS CT
Thaddeus: b 4-24-1726 d 1811 m Mary Stoddard CS VT
Theophilus: b 7-15-1710 d *p.* 1790 m Elizabeth Thayer PS MA
Thomas: b 1740 d 10-18-1776 m Martha Cowles Cpl CT
Thomas: b 1-25-1737 d 2-26-1794 m Alice Beck Sol NJ
Thomas: b 6- -1756 d 12- -1830 m Azuba Hartwell Pvt NY
Thomas: b 5-6-1761 d 4-16-1843 m Thankful Crandall Pvt NY ★
William: b 7-17-1758 d 1-1-1841 m Charity Lewis Pvt NH CT ★
William: b 5-1-1720 d 11-20-1779 m (1)Sarah — (2)Mrs Elizabeth Breed Maj MA
William: b 8-28-1742 d 10-11-1821 m Hannah Tinkham Lt MA
William: b 12-4-1748 d 1-26-1793 m Debo Curtis Sgt MA
William, Jr.: b 3-3-1753 d 8-27-1844 m Hannah Lynfield Pvt MA
William: b 1730 d 1794 m Ruth — Pvt PA
Zachariah, Sr.: b 1726 d 1804 m — Pvt MA
Zachariah, Jr.: b 1762 d 1838 m Elizabeth Tompkins Pvt MA ★
Zadoc: b 1752 d 11-9-1830 m Rosy Bacheldor Pvt CT ★
Zarah: b 5-6-1762 d 6-9-1849 m Phalley Yale Cpl CT ★

CURTS, (includes KURTZ)

Henry: b *c.* 1750 d 1795 m Elizabeth Stetzer Sgt PA
Thomas: b 1755 d 9-28-1833 m Sarah — Pvt VA★

CUSHING,

Abel: b 10-27-1763 d 1834 m Sarah Wilder Cpl MA
Anna Wainwright: b 2-11-1712/13 d 12-2-1810 m James Cushing PS MA
Benjamin: b 1-20-1739 d 9-18-1810 m Hannah Hazeltine Pvt MA
Benjamin: b 7-16-1739 d 12-4-1792 m (1)Susanna Salter (2)Mary Colesworthy Pvt MA
Benjamin: b 7-18-1758 d 7-24-1847 m Lydia Beal Pvt MA
Benjamin, Jr.: b 7-18-1725 d 8-8-1812 m Ruth Croade CS MA
Benjamin, Jr.: b 9-28-1735 d 6-5-1786 m Hannah Cooke CS RI
Caleb: b 10-10-1703 d 12-27-1787 m Mary Newmarch Col MA
Caleb, Sr.: b 5-28-1737 d 1-16-1806 m Sarah Sawyer Bgd QM 1Lt MA
Caleb, Jr.: b 9-4-1767 d 8-22-1853 m Mary Church Fif MA
Charles: b 1734 d 11-17-1810 m Elizabeth Sumner BGen MA
Charles: b 7-13-1744 d 1809 m Hannah Croade Capt MA
Charles: b 5-23-1764 d *p.* 8-20-1832 m Chloe Carpenter Pvt MA★
Daniel: b 6-4-1752 d *p.* 1792 m Tamsen Hayes Pvt NH★
Daniel: b 11-5-1744 d *p.* 1796 m Patience Fairbrother Lt NY
David, Sr.: b 9-7-1727 d 2-15-1800 m (1)Ruth Lincoln (2)Mabel Gardner Col MA
David, Jr.: b 2-7-1754 d 5-3-1827 m Hannah Cushing 4Lt MA
Ebenezer: b 4-15-1724 d 12-30-1803 m Sarah Lincoln Pvt MA
Elijah: b 10-8-1725 d 9-13-1807 m (1)Tamer (Cushing) (2)Anna Thomas Capt MA
Err: bpt 9-22-1751 d 1824 m Mary Burrill Ens MA ★
Ezekiel: b 1751 d 2-10-1825 m Frances McCobb Pvt MA
Ezra: b 1748 d 5-5-1820 m Susannah Shaw Pvt MA
Francis: b 10-21-1745 d 3-24-1840 m (1)Temperance Foster (2)Lucy Dyer Capt MA
Frederic: b 2-1-1729 d 7-23-1824 m Grace Bates Pvt MA
Hawke: b 2-3-1745 d 2-16-1825 m (1)Ruth Cushing (2)Mrs Abigail Clapp Pvt MA
Jacob: b 9-26-1749 d 9-13-1825 m Elizabeth Cushing Cpl MA
James: b 1-9-1739 d 5-3-1812 m Sarah Towle Pvt MA
Job: b 1-1-1728 d 4-16-1808 m (1)Lucy Stone (2)Mrs Sarah Goulding Col MA
Job: b 4-17-1744 d 7-2-1816 m (1)Martha Nichols (2)Mrs Abigail Pierce Capt MA
Joel: b 1-17-1735 d 6-29-1796 m Susanna Neat PS MA
John: b 3-12-1722 d 3-1-1802 m Olive Lincoln Pvt Mstr MA
John: b 8-16-1722 d 6-1-1798 m (1)Deborah Barker (2)Mary Jacob Pvt MA

John: b 8-22-1744 d 4-27-1823 m Sarah Parkman PS MA
Jonathan: b 4-13-1759 d 1-29-1347 m Sarah Simmons Smn MA
Joseph: b 3-1-1731 d 12-19-1791 m Ruth Stockbridge PS LCol MA
Joseph: b 2-7-1757 d 4-28-1811 m (1) X (2) X Pvt VT
Joshua: b 1734 d 1822 m Mary Freeman Pvt MA
Leavitt: b 10-1-1734 d *p.* 1794 m (1)Silence Tower (2)Deborah (Scranton) Carpenter Pvt MA
Loring: b 8-10-1721 d 10-9-1777 m Mary Parker Pvt MA
Mathew: b 7-29-1730 d 12- -1813 m (1)Priscilla Smith (2)Abigail Titus Pvt VT
Matthew: b 10-1-1750 d 2-12-1846 m Mary Dexter Pvt MA
Moses: b 7-15-1745 d 12-31-1827 m Elizabeth Jackman Pvt MA
Nathaniel: b 4-8-1753 d 8- -1814 m Elizabeth Heath Brevet Maj MA
Nathaniel: b 9- -1752 d 5-29-1824 m (1)Phoebe Snow (2)Phebe Pease Pvt MA★
Nathaniel, Sr.: b 2-22-1730 d 12-3-1790 m Lucy Turner Pvt MA
Nathaniel, Jr.: b 6-24-1762 d 8-28-1845 m Mehitabel Dodge Fif MA
Nathaniel: b 3-30-1753 d 1795 m Alice Cushing Pvt Drm MA
Nathaniel: b 1-19-1724 d 11-13-1788 m (1)Jemima Ford (2)Anna Turner (3)Lydia Cook PS MA
Peter: b 5-3-1741 d 7-12-1783 m Silence Burr Capt MA
Pickels: b 2-18-1744 d 3-15-1819 m Abigail Hatch Ens MA
Pyam: b 8-8-1725 d 8-21-1776 m Hannah Lincoln Capt MA
Seth: b 1732 d 6-28-1810 m Lydia Everson 1Maj MA
Solomon: b 4-1-1742 d 1815 m Mary Burr Fif MA
Stephen: b 1749 d *p.* 1793 m Rachel Foster Pvt MA
Theophilus, Sr.: b 6-16-1703 d 6-15-1779 m Hannah Waterman PS CS MA
Theophilus, Jr.: b 12-5-1740 d 3-11-1820 m Patience Dunbar PS CS Sgt MA
Theophilus: b 10-22-1719 d 6-8-1788 m Hannah Lewis Pvt MA
Thomas: b 3-24-1725 d 2-28-1788 m Deborah Fletcher Cmsry Gen CS MA
Thomas: b 3-21-1747 d 12-15-1823 m Elizabeth Turner Pvt MA
Thomas: b 1745 d 1-15-1831 m (1)Sarah Hanson (2)Anna Tuttle Pvt NH
Timothy: b 2- -1738 d 12-26-1806 m Desire Jenkins Cpl MA
Wareham: b 8-27-1754 d 6-11-1804 m Lucy Harrington Pvt MA

CUSHMAN,

Allerton: b 5-3-1740 d 2-11-1801 m Harmony Allen Sgt CT
Amaziah: b 10-17-1752 d 6-1-1800 m Martha Smith Sgt MA
Andrew: b 1-6-1761 d 2-6-1844 m Bathsheba Jennings Pvt MA ★
Artemas: b 7-28-1752 d 10-18-1841 m Sarah Williams Capt MA
Barnabus: b 12-7-1751 d 6-7-1812 m Deliverance Lawrence Pvt MA
Benjamin: b 1-8-1753 d 12-24-1832 m (1)Lucy Lee (2)Elizabeth Cummings Pvt CT
Benjamin: b 5-25-1722 d 3-5-1813 m Zeruiah Sampson Pvt MA
Caleb: b 10-21-1749 d 1-3-1809 m Bathsheba Spalding Pvt MA
Caleb: b 7- -1757 d 1-17-1835 m Charlotte Packard Pvt Fif MA★
Cephas: b 11-20-1745 d 2-12-1808 m Judith Clark Pvt MA
Charles, Sr.: b — d 9-1-1791 m Mary Harvey Pvt VT
Charles, Jr.: b 1758 d 1-13-1810 m Desiah Branch Sol VT
Consider: b 7-6-1740 d 4-4-1819 m Submit Newcomb Pvt MA
Consider: b 4-12-1755 d 7-14-1818 m Phebe Townsend Pvt NY
Daniel: b 1755 d 4-12-1845 m Mary Bowman Cpl CT★
Desiah Branch: b 1752 d 8-3-1849 m Charles Cushman PS VT
Eleazur: b 1-17-1758 d 11-24-1813 m Elizabeth Plumley Pvt VT
Ephraim: b 2-20-1754 d 2-26-1832 m Mary Hackett Pvt MA
Frederick: b 7-7-1758 d 10-22-1852 m Alice Caswell Pvt MM VT CT ★
George: b 1-7-1759 d 1-17-1832 m Annie Perry Mar MA★
Gideon: b 11-21-1750 d 5-7-1845 m Ruth Shaw Pvt MA★
Holmes: b 10-22-1759 d 8-31-1833 m Mary Paddock Pvt MA★
Ichabod, Jr.: b 3-28-1757 d 10-14-1805 m Molly Morton Pvt MA
Issac: b 10-21-1734 d 1813 m X Pvt CT
Isaac: b 3-31-1759 d 6-2-1842 m Sarah Paine Sgt CT
Isaac: b 8-12-1730 d 8-1-1820 m Sarah Miller Pvt MA
Isaac: b 6-13-1748 d 6-14-1822 m Esther Gibbs Pvt MA
Isaac: b 7-16-1752 d *p.* 7-4-1837 m Deborah Frazee Sct Pvt PA ★
Isaac: b 6-5-1745 d 5-26-1783 m Lois — Ens VT
Isaiah, Sr.: b 2-21-1730/31 d 11-2-1818 m Sarah Ring PS MA
Isaiah, Jr.: b 2-6-1757 d 1-8-1841 m Sarah Ripley Sol MA
Jabez, Jr.: b 7-9-1756 d 6-3-1827 m Ursula Bearce Pvt MA
Jacob: b 2-29-1747 d 7-11-1842 m Sylvia Sampson Pvt MA
James: b 12-22-1756 d 11-24-1832 m Mercy Morton Cpl MA
Jonathan: b 10-26-1754 d 4-24-1834 m (1)Mary Spooner (2)Anna (Norton) Hervey NCdr MA
Joseph: b 2-23-1759 d 4-5-1843 m Tabitha Johnson Pvt CT ★
Joseph: b 1-19-1736/37 d 11-5-1800 m Deborah Barrows Pvt MA
Joseph: b 6-21-1755 d 6-5-1845 m Nancy Robinson Sheldon Pvt MA
Joshua: b 11-1764 d 1-27-1834 m Lucy Jones Pvt MA★
Josiah: b 2-9-1752 d 1809 m Patience Perkins Pvt MA
Mial: b 5-23-1753 d 1-27-1817 m Salome Atwood Pvt MA
Nathaniel,1st: b 5-28-1712 d 10-1-1793 m (1)Sarah Coomer (2)Temperance Sims CS MA
Nathaniel, 2nd: b 9-2-1738 d 8-17-1817 m (1)Phebe Newcomb (2)Hannah Hawkins Pvt CT
Nathaniel, 3rd: b 10-9-1771 d 12- -1832 m Sarah Bennett Pvt CT★
Noah: b 5-14-1745 d 3-29-1818 m (1)Mercy Soule (2)Zilpah Thompson (3)Zerviah Thomas Pvt MA
Robert: b 10-27-1738 d 1799 m Martha Delano Pvt MA

CUSHMAN, contd.
Robert: b 4-24-1761 d 1-18-1819 m Lucy Thomas Lt MA W★
Samuel: b 4-6-1742 d *p.* 1782 m Lydia Gano Pvt MA
Solomon: b 2-17 1733 d 2- -1814 m Esther Cross Pvt CT
Solomon: b 8-2-1745 d 1799 m Sarah Curtiss Capt VT
Thomas: b 10-11-1730 d 10-30-1777 m Anna Chipman CS Cpl MA
Thomas: b 6-25-1736 d 10-15-1820 m Bethiah Thompson Sgt MA
Thomas: b 12-19-1739 d*p.* 4-11-1787 m Mary Frazee Pvt NJ
William: b 7-5-1738 d 10-31-1818 m Abi Parker Pvt CT
William: b 1-29-1746 d*p.* 1785 m Jemima La Due Pvt NY
Zebulon: b 7-25-1763 d*p.* 1819 m (1)Deborah Wood (2)Nancy Hall Pvt MA

CUSHWA,
John: b 1731 d 1805 m Elizabeth — Pvt PS PA

CUSTARD,
Jacob: b 2- -1750 d 8-17-1833 m Margaret Lear Pvt VA ★
William: b 1760 d 1835 m Patience Rush Sgt PA

CUSTER,
Arnold: b 4-29-1756 d 5-14-1840 m — Schull Pvt VA
Conrad: b 1742 d*p.* 2-10-1826 m Elizabeth — Sol VA
Emanuel: b 1754 d*c.* 1854 m Mary Fadley Sgt PA
George: b 12-3-1744 d 12-17-1829 m (1)Susannah Long (2)Catherine Letherman Ens PA
Jonathan: b 1734 d 1823 m Mrs Hannah (Peters) Kendall Pvt PS PA
Paul: b 1720 d 11-10-1783 m Sarah Martha Ball Pvt PA
Paul: b*c.* 1737 d*a.* 7-31-1800 m Elizabeth — Pvt PA
Wm.: b 2-12-1753 d 9-22-1828 m Margaret — Pvt PA
William: b*c.* l755 d 2-28-1828 m Anna Smith Pvt VA

CUSTIS,
John: b*c.* 1740 d 2- -1808 m (1)Esther Savage (of John) (2)Esther Savage (of Griffith) Capt VA
John: b 2-23-1750 d 3-3-1809 m Catherine Parker Capt VA
John Parke: b 1753 d 1781 m Eleanor Calvert ADC VA

CUTBIRTH,
Benjamin: b 1740 d 1817 m Elizabeth Wilcoxsen Sol VA

CUTHBERT,
Anthony: b 3-4-1751 d 11-14-1832 m Mary Ogden Capt PA
Benjamin: b 1749 d 3-28-1844 m Mary Trencher Pvt Pvtr NY ★
Thomas: b 1713 d 1-11-1781 m Ann Wilkinson CS PA

CUTLER,
Abijah: b 3-25-1730 d 11-5-1795 m (1)Elizabeth Abbott (2)Sarah — Lt MA
Abijah: b 10-27-1747 d 8-9-1788 m Dinah Lee Pvt NJ
Amos: b 5-6-1741 d 12-14-1819 m (1)Priscilla Leonard (2)Lucy Green Pvt CT
Anthony: b 6-6-1763 d 1-1-1831 m (1)Jemima McConkey (2)Mrs Mary (Frisbie) Clark Pvt MA
Asher: b 9-8-1713 d 9-8-1811 m Rebecca — Pvt MA
Azariah: b 2-1-1744/45 d 5-4-1816 m Sarah Fulshaw Pvt CT
Benjamin: b 9-4-1725 d 1814 m (1)Elizabeth Burtick (2)Mrs Mary (Cozad) Coon Sgt MA
Benjamin: b 8-6-1747 d 11-5-1828 m (2)Mary Dunlap Cpl NY
Benoni: b 8-17-1737 d 1807 m Laurana Leavens Capt CT
Charles: b 8-26-1760 d 1- -1833 m Mary Kendrick Pvt Smn MA ★
Daniel: b 1-22-1743 d 3-27-1829 m Betsey Fitch Sgt CT
David, Sr.: b 10-7-1721 d 4-4-1783 m (1)Mehitable Whitney (2)Mrs Joanna (Cheney) Atwood Sol MA
Ebenezer: b 4-30-1747 d 10-29-1814 m Abigal Stone Pvt MA
Ebenezer: b 9-9-1760 d 7-22-1843 m (1)Phebe Wyman (2)Sally Brewster Pvt MA ★
Ebenezer, Sr.: b 1729 d 1819 m Meriam Bennett Pvt MA
Ebenezer, Jr.: b 9-28-1765 d 8-23-1819 m Elizabeth Brown Pvt MA ★
Elisha: b 4-30-1725 d*p.* 1779 m (1)Sarah Munroe (2)Mrs Mary Cutler Pvt CS MA
Elisha: b 12-11-1736 d 3-28-1806 m Mary Pond Pvt MA
Hezekiah: b 4- -1707 d 10-4-1792 m Susanna Clark Pvt CT
Hodges: b 7-27-1752 d 2-4-1857 m Mehitable Blunt Pvt NH
Joel: b 3-19-1738 d 6-5-1821 m Betsey Nicols Pvt CS VT
John: b*c.* 1746 d 1827 m Elizabeth — Cpl MA
John: b 7-14-1751 d 8-21-1821 m Dorothy Converse Capt VT
Jonathan: b 10-3-1737 d 8- -1826 m Elizabeth Holman Pvt MA
Joseph: b 12-16-1748 d 1827 m Dorothea Judd Sgt CT ★
Joseph: b 5-31-1733 d 2-7-1816 m (1)Rebecca Hoar (2)Mary Reed Capt MA
Joseph: b 8-9-1739 d 8-20-1825 m Martha Brown Pvt MA
Manassah: b 5-13-1742 d 7-28-1823 m Mary Balch Chp MA
Nathan: b 1756-58 d 1840 m Elizabeth Traves Sgt NY ★
Nathan: b 2-25-1755 d 11-8-1827 m Ruth Nelson Pvt MA
Nathaniel, Sr.: b 5-26-1724 d 5-16-1808 m Mary Wyman MM MA
Nathaniel, Jr.: b 1748 d 10-17-1813 m Elizabeth Bennett Sgt MA
Peter: b 3-5-1734/35 d 10-12-1802 m Rebecca — CS CT
Simeon: b 7-9-1749 d 7-30-1799 m Elizabeth Rockwood Lt MA
Simon: b 4-23-1738 d 8-3-1826 m Silence Clark Pvt MA
Solomon: b 5-10-1740 d*p.* 1781 m Rebecca Page Capt MA
Thomas: b 5-5-1742 d 7-3-1812 m (1)Abigail Reed (2)Elizabeth (Harrington) White Pvt MA
William: b 8-4-1760 d 4-9-1831 m Betsey Richardson Pvt MA

William: b 3-24-1726/7 d 2-21-1802 m (1)Susanna Shepard (2)Mrs — Cutler Sol MM MA

CUTTER,
Abraham: b*c.* 1745 d 11- -1811 m Huldah Bachelder Sgt MA
Ammi: b 10-27-1733 d 4-19-1795 m (1)Esther Pierce (2)Abigail Holden (3)Hannah Holden Pvt MA
Ammi Ruhamah: b 3-15-1735 d 12-8-1820 m Hannah Treadwell Dr ME
Andrew: b 2-9-1757 d 1-8-1794 m Rebecca Crosby Pvt MA
Benjamin: b 4-29-1762 d 3-5-1846 m Elizabeth Washburn Pvt Drm MA ★
Benjamin: b 12-3-1743 d 3-16-1821 m Hannah Andrews Ens NH
Campyon: b 1752 d 4-28-1832 m Frances Moores Pvt NJ
Daniel: b 4-24-1733 d 1804 m Patience Hall Pvt MA
Ford: b 1754 d 12-20-1815 m Elizabeth Smith SgtMaj NY
Gershom: b 11-6-17 d 8-20-1799 m (1)Hannah Newell (2)Catherine Sumner (3)Deborah Torrey Pvt MA
James: b 12-14-1759 d 12-15-1823 m Annie Russell Pvt MA
John: b 9-26-1737 d 10-16-1788 m Rebecca Hill Pvt MA
John: b 6-14-1737 d 1793 m Martha Richardson Pvt MA
John: b 8-25-1750 d 5-1-1812 m Rebecca Browning Pvt NH
Joseph: b 7-7-1761 d 9- -1807 m Prudence Wright DrmMaj MA
Joseph: b 5-13-1752 d 6-25-1840 m Rachel Hobart Lt NH ★
Kelsey: b 8-21-1750 d 3-28-1798 m Hannah Marsh Pvt MA
Moses: b 3-26-1760 d 4-17-1817 m Rachel Turner Pvt NH W★
Nathan: b 1733 d 1813 m Hannah Hastings Pvt NH
Nathaniel: b 8-6-1739 d 12-14-1783 m Sarah Wyman Lt MA
Nathaniel: b 7-27-1760 d 9-14-1841 m Sarah Hunter PS Sol MA
Richard: b 3-9-1725 d 4-8-1795 m (1)Keziah Pierce (2)Ruth Hadley Pvt NH
Samuel: b 8-7-1739 d 4-7-1824 m Amelia Loring 1Lt MA
Samuel, Sr.: b 1-21-1736 d 4-7-1791 m Susanna Francis Ens MA
Samuel, Jr.: b 1-30-1758 d 4- -1820 m Rebecca Hill Pvt MA
Seth: b 8-25-1760 d 1805 m Louisana Reed Pvt MA
Seth: b 4-14-1758 d 9-20-1853 m Abiah Tallant Fif Sgt NH ★
Solomon: b 5-30-1756 d 9-4-1827 m Sarah Southard Cpl MA
Stephen: b 1745 d 6-21-1823 m Tabitha FitzRandolph Pvt NJ
Thomas: b 5-29-1748 d 12-17-1825 m Betsy Sands NS Pvt MA NH ★
William: b 2-24-1759 d 7-27-1800 m Rebecca (Cutter) MM MA
William: b 5-28-1737 d 6-28-1776 m Mehitable Gray PS MA

CUTTING,
Aaron: b 11-23-1749 d*p.* 1820 m Margaret Claflen Pvt MA ★
Benjamin: b 1760 d 2-15-1848 m Annah Bemis Pvt MA ★
Eliphalet: b 7-2-1767 d 10-2-1843 m Tirzah Thompson Pvt MA ★
Francis: b 9-22-1728 d 1-16-1802 m Thankful Warren Matr MA
George: b*a.* 1738 d 1-6-1778 m Judith — Sgt MA
John: b 1750 d 9-8-1828 m Ann Gale Pvt MA
Jonah: b*c.* 1763 d 11- -1842 m Sarah Stow Pvt MA
Jonas, Jr.: b 1-14-1765 d 8-5-1834 m Sarah Baker Pvt MA ★
Jonathan: b 8-13-1747 d 1-18-1834 m (1)Pierces Hoar (2)Eunice (Prescott) Whitcomb Cpl MA ★
Josiah: b — d*a.* 1832 m Percis Glazier Pvt MA
Samuel: b 11-20-1720 d 3-24-1780 m Eunice Moore Pvt MA
Samuel: b 10-19-1747 d 12-31-1794 m Eunice Cooledge Sgt MA
Silas: b*a.* 1750 d 12-23-1777 m Sarah — Pvt MA
William: b 1747 d 9-11-1806 m Mary Eliza Coon Sol CS SC
Zebadee: b 10-18-1759 d 4-30-1833 m Phebe Strong Pvt CT ★
Zebulon: b 12-1-1751 d 12- -1797 m Abigail Bemis Pvt MA

CUTTS,
Edward: b 10-19-1728 d 1-24-1818 m Elizabeth Gerrish PS CS MA
John: b 1-26-1724 d 8- -1788 m Hannah — Fif NH
Joseph: b 8-2-1736 d 1808 m Mary Stevenson CS ME
Noah: b 12-30-1754 d*p.* 1820 m Mary Wilson Cpl MA
Samuel: b 12-8-1726 d 5-29-1801 m Anna Holyoke PS MA
Samuel: b 9-20-1744 d 11-16-1820 m Sarah Hall PS NH
Thomas: b 4-5-1736 d 1-10-1821 m Elizabeth Scammon Col MA
Thomas: b 11-23-1732 d 11-29-1800 m Elizabeth Donnell Capt MA

CUYLER,
Aaron: b*p.* 1755 d*p.* 11-14-1807 m Sarah — Pvt NY
Harmanus: bpt 5-3-1730 d 12-4-1811 m (1)Mary Marselis (2)Barbara Marselis (3)Elizabeth Van Bergen CS NY
Henry: b 1754 d 4-16-1781 m Dorothy Martin Capt GA
Jacob: b 9-28-1741 d 6-8-1802 m Lydia VanVeghten PS NY
Jeanne Latouche: b 7-30-1738 d 9- -1799 m Telemon Cuyler PS GA

CYPERT,
Francis, Jr.: b*c.* 1750-3 d*p.* 1790 m Abigail Johnson PS NC

CYRUS,
Jesse: b*c.* 1750 d*a.* 1814 m Frances — Pvt NC

DABBS,
Nathaniel: b*c.* 1740 d 7-12-1810 m X PS NC

DABNEY,
Benjamin: b 1750 d*p.* 1791 m (1)Martha Burwell Armistead (2)Sarah Smith Pvt VA

Cornelius: b 1756 d 10-13-1821 m Elizabeth S. Winstern Lt VA
George: b 1740 d 1824 m Elizabeth Price PS VA
Isaac: b c. 1748 d p. 1784 m Ann Hill Col VA
James: b 1-6-1735 d 11-13-1803 m Judith Anderson Capt PS VA
John, Jr.: b 5-3-1749 d 1831 m (2)Margaret Smith Lt VA
John Quarles: b 1762 d 1833 m (2)Sarah Bell Hartman Pvt VA ★
Richard: b c. 1753 d p. 1803 m Diana Gwathmey PS VA

DABOLL,
Benjamin: b 1757 d 8-26-1848 m Elizabeth Moxley Pvt CT
John: b 2-13-1751 d 5-7-1825 m (1)Sarah Luther (2)Sarah (Miner)
     Halsey Pvt CT★

DA COSTA,
Isaac: b 1721 d 11-23-1783 m Sarah — PS SC
Joseph: bpt 7-28-1740 d 2-26-1782 m Katharine Adams Sgt MA

DACUS,
Nathaniel: b 1749 d 3-25-1835 m (1)Mrs. Dupre (2)Elizabeth Glenn
     Pvt VA ★

DADA,
William: b 1743 d 4- -1776 m Jerusha Burt Pvt MA

DADE,
Baldwin: b 10-13-1716 d p. 8-11-1782 m ((1)Sarah Alexander (2)
     (2)Verlinda — PS VA
Baldwin, Jr.: b 1740 d p. 1797 m Catherine West Cadet VA
Francis: b 1757 d 5-28-1791 m Sarah Taliaferro Capt VA
Horatio: b c. 1720 d a. 4-4-1782 m (1)Frances Richardson (2)Mrs
     Mary Stuart Massie PS VA
Townshend, Sr.: b 1707 d 1781 m Parthenia (Alexander) Massey
     PS VA
Townshend, Jr.: b 1-15-1742 d 2-6-1822 m Mary Simmons PS VA

DADMUN,
Elijah: bpt 10-19-1755 d p. 1786 m Bathsheba Parmenter Pvt MA
Nathan: b 6-16-1747 d 2-16-1827 m Hannah Sanger Cpl MA
Samuel: b a. 1722 d 1794 m Lois Pratt Pvt MA
Timothy: b 3-28-1750 d 2- -1832 m Sybilla Winch Pvt MA

DAFFRON,
Rody: b c. 1757 d 10-17-1834 m Millie Gibbs Pvt NC

DAGGER,
Peter: b 1760 d p. 10-21-1822 m Mary Zollman OrdlSgt VA ★

DAGGETT, (includes DOGGETT)
Abner: b 8-5-1755 d 8-25-1832 m Mary Holmes Pvt MA
Arthur: b 1-30-1729 d 8-23-1755 m Mehitable Marsh Capt MA
Benjamin: b c. 1744 d a. 3-13-1778 m Ann — Pvt VA
Benjamin: b c. 1735 d a. 1-24-1735 m Hannah Webb PS VA
Brotherton: b 1744 d 5-13-1783 m (1)Mary Tucker (2)Jerusha
     (Pease) Bunker Maj MA
Bushrod: b c. 1759 d 7-25-1829 m Susannah Davis Pvt NC
Coleman: b 2-7-1736 d 3-11-1782 m Mary King PS VA
Daniel: b 2-1-1738 d 12-3-1796 m Margaret Woodcock 2Lt MA
Daniel: b c. 11-29-1731 d 9-23-1799 m Bebe Perry Pvt MA
Darius: b 7-17-1760 d 1-19-1853 m Hepspah Dean Pvt MA ★
David: b c. 1748 d 5-14-1777 m Azubah Wheelock Cpl MA
Elihu: b 12-4-1745 d 4-16-1823 m Charity Galusha Adj MA
Elmour: b c. 1758 d 1804-6 m Elizabeth Roberts Smn VA
Henry: b 2-27-1758 d 6-20-1843 m Anna Ball Lt CT ★
Ichabod: b 12-7-1736 d 9-3-1781 m Lucy Heddon Pvt MA
James William: b a. 1759 d p. 1797 m Ann Brown Sol VA
Joab: b 10-19-1754 d 3-7-1816 m Cloe Blackington Sgt MA
John: b 9-11-1754 d 2-12-1837 m (1)Sarah Hawkins (2)Polly Smith
     (3)Nancy Smith Sgt CT ★
John: b 9-2-1724 d 1-20-1803 m (1)Mercy Shepard (2)Mary Tucker
     Col PS MA
John: b 9-15-1748 d 1816 m Mary Stevens Sgt MA
John: b 1728 d 10-26-1810 m (1)Rachel Coffin (2)Thankful Vinson
     Pvt MA
John: b 11-6-1723 d 8-7-1799 m Penelope Wood Pvt MA
John: b c. 1732 d p. 5-22-1804 PS VA
Joseph: b 2-14-1758 d 9-9-1856 m Militiah Mehitable Clark
     QMSgt MA ★
Naphtali: b 9-6-1727 d 11-25-1780 m Sarah Smith Vol CT
Nathan: b 1750 d p. 1818 m Ann Wilkins Pilot Smn MA CT
Nathaniel: b 4-29-1747 d 1-18-1828 m Beulah Dryer Pvt NH
Prince: b 1723 d 1- -1795 m (1)Sarah Norton (2)Eleanor Cottle Pvt
     MA
Reuben: b 11-11-1755 d 2-8-1835 m (1)Esther Cobb (2)Keziah Darby
     (3)Abigail Woodward Pvt MA
Reuben: b 1739 d 1826 m Mary Brown Smn MA
Samuel, Jr.: b 10-5-1751 d 11-19-1831 m Elisabeth Badlam Lt MA
Samuel: b 5-19-1753 d 10-2-1835 m Jedidah Butler PS MA
Samuel, Sr.: b 5-9-1745 d 5-30-1835 m Sarah Butler PS MA
Samuel, Jr.: b 7-11-1764 d 9-23-1860 m Rebecca Daggett Fif MA
Samuel: b 1-3-1730/31 d 8- -1806 m Abial Kingsbury Sgt CS MA
Samuel, Jr.: b 2-22-1754 d 4-13-1824 m (1)Hannah McIntier (2)
     Hannah Murphy Pvt MA
Silas: b 5-24-1757 d 11-3-1825 m Deborah Butler Pvt MA

Tristram: b 8-22-1758 d 1-27-1848 m (1)Jane Merry (2)Mrs Nancy
     Norton Pvt MA ★
William: b 1747 d 6-8-1834 m Mary Stuart Pvt MA

DAGLEY,
Thomas: b c. 1755 d p. 1812 m X PS NC

DAGUE,
Frederick: b 1736 d 10-12-1796 m (1)Sophia Schmitt (2)Maria
     Guyslar Pvt PA
Mathias: b 6-25-1761 d 2-16-1847 m Elizabeth — Pvt PA ★
Michael: b 1758 d p. 11-14-1821 m Margaret — Pvt PA

DAICEY,
John: b 1748 d 7-4-1831 m Mehitable Tuttle Pvt MA ★

DAINS,
Asa: b 1760 d 5-4-1843 m Jane Kasson Pvt CT ★
Ephraim: b 7-4-1752 d 7-7-1836 m Irene Stedman Pvt CT ★

DAKIN,
Amos, Sr.: b 1-29-1732 d 4-23-1789 m Sarah Thankful Minot PS NH
Amos, Jr.: b 5-13-1760 d 10-29-1842 m Mary Kingsley Pvt NH
Jonathan: b 1761 d 5-11-1848 m X OrdlSgt DE ★
Joshua: b 4-22-1744 d 10-24-1813 m (1)Isabel Close (2)Ruth Craw
     (3)Waitstill Holley (4)Hannah Hathaway Pvt NY
Preserved: b 3-12-1749 d 7-27-1835 m Deborah Akin Pvt NY
Samuel: b 5-17-1731 d 1-23-1807 m (1)Ann Wheeler (2)Mehitable
     Eaton Sgt MA
Samuel, Jr.: b 6-21-1744 d 6-17-1811 m Elizabeth Billings Sgt MA
Wooster: b 8-17-1751 d p. 1806 m X Pvt PS NY

DALBY,
Abel: b 1754/55 d 1844 m Clarissa Miller Pvt PA

DALE,
Abraham: b 7-30-1753 d 11- -1831 m Mary Weakley Cpl VA W★
Adam: b 7-14-1768 d 10-14-1851 m Mary Hall Vol MD
Archalaus: b 9-7-1720 d 2-27-1797 m Margaret Elliot Ens MA
Ebenezer: b 12-25-1755 d p. 1781 m Abigail Cutler Pvt MA
George: b c. 1754 d 1833 m Hannah Dale PS VA
Henry: b 8-28-1758 d 5-11-1844 m (1)Rebecca Mabin (2)Phillena
     Letterman Pvt PA
James: b c. 1740 d 1795 m Margaret Read Pvt MD
James: b 1730 d 1- -1777 m Katherine — Pvt VA
John: b c. 1740 d p. 9-29-1785 m Tabitha — Pvt MD
John: b 7-26-1748 d 7-11-1809 m (1)Rhoda Holt (2)Lydia — Pvt
     NH
John: b 1755 d 1829 m Martha — Pvt VA
Mathew: b c. 1762 d a. 7-25-1814 m Keaty — PS MD
Samuel: b 9- -1735 d 9-27-1804 m Ann Futhey PS Capt PA
Thomas: b 3-5-1744 d 1-6-1812 m Elizabeth Evans 2Lt MD
William: b 1757 d 6-7-1822 m (1)Elizabeth Heth (2)Elizabeth Booth
     Pvt VA

DALES,
John: b a. 1751 d 9-6-1795 m Jane Ballagh Sgt NY

DALEY, (includes DAILEY, DAILY)
David: b 4-11-1746 d 3-28-1816 m Mary Harris Pvt MA
Dennis: b 1761 d p. 1820 m Mary Hanks Trm VA ★
Ebenezer: b 1735-40 d p. 1790 m Margaret Bates Sgt NY
James Farrell O'Neill: b 5-4-1757 d 4-20-1820 m Nancy McFadden
     Sgt PS VA ★
Jesse: b 12-7-1760 d 11-9-1845 m Mary Turner Pvt VA
John: b 7-20-1712 d 9-12-1792 m Martha Fobes Pvt MA
John: b 5-7-1-1820 m Nancy McGill Pvt VA
John: b c. 1758 d p. 4-11-1820 m Rachael Holiday Pvt PS PA
Lewis: b 1757 d 6-23-1823 m Rebecca Dickerman Pvt MA
Philip, Jr.: b 1762 d 1830 m Mary Wise Pvt MD
Philip: b c. 1730 d 1787 m Mercy — Pvt PA
Solomon: b 1748 d 1814 m — Butler Pvt RI
William Johnson: b 9-27-1759 d 12-15-1833 m (2)Lydia (Knox)
     Robinson Pvt CT ★

DALLAM,
Francis: b 1755 d — m Martha S. Dallam Gov Auditor MD
Josias William: b 11-5-1747 d 12-9-1820 m (1)Sarah Smith
     (2)Henrietta Jones PS MD
Richard: b c. 1714 d 3- -1805 m Frances Wallace DepPMGen PS
     MD

DALLAS,
John: b 1748 d 1815 m Mary Walker Pvt VA

DALLY,
Samuel: b 1732 d 3-11-1784 m Mary Jones Pvt NJ

DALRYMPLE, (includes DALRUMPLE)
Andrew: b 1723 d 3-5-1803 m Anna Winslow 1Lt MA
Archibald: b 1761 d 10- -1836 m Mary (Gaston) McClellan Pvt NC
David: b 3-12-1762 d 8-22-1840 m (1)Mary Corning (2)Polly
     Richardson Fairbanks (3)Jennette Clark Pvt MA

DALRYMPLE, contd.
James: b 3-4-1757 d 7-5-1847 m Azubah Parmenter Drm MA ★
John: b a. 1744 d p. 1795 m Susanna Dalrymple Pvt SC
William: b 6-4-1751 d p. 1796 m (1)Mary Straight (2)Mary Fairbanks Stacy Sgt MA

DALTON, (includes DAULTON)
David: b 1742 d c. 1810 m Susan Davis Sol PS VA
Isaac: b 3-2-1761 d 8-13-1838 m Eleanor Merrill Pvt NH
James: b a. 1720 d 1783 m Mrs Abigail (Roe) Alden CS PS MA
John: b 1761/62 d 10-7-1835 m Elizabeth Cooker Pvt PA
John: b 10-3-1758 d 9-15-1838 m Mary Ann Simms Sgt VA ★
Michael: b 11-13-1753 d 10-6-1846 m Mercy Philbrick Pvt Fif NH
Moses: b 8-12-1760 d 10-27-1819 m Mary Fristoe Sgt VA ★
Reuben: b — d p. 1-27-1822 m Elizabeth — Pvt VA
Samuel, Sr.:b c. 1710 d p. 11-24-1803 m Anne — PS NC
Samuel: b 7-29-1757 d 1-31-1837 m (1)Polly Merrick (2)Mrs Rachel Gile Wadleigh Pvt NH
Tristram: b 5-28-1738 d 5-10-1817 m Ruth Hooper CS MA
Valentine Thomas: b c. 1754 d c. 1806 m (1)X (2)Jane Catherine Yarrow Lt VA ★

DAME, (includes DAM)
Eliphalet: b 12-22-1719 d 1783 m Abigail — PS NH
George: b c. 1752 d p. 10-16-1805 m Mary Green PS Sol VA
Hatevil: b 8-26-1753 d 1822 m Jerusha Witham Pvt NH
Jabez: b 8-14-1732 d 11-14-1813 m (1)Miss Tibbetts (2)Meribah Emery CS NH
Joseph: b 5-16-1718 d 4- -1807 m Mehitable Hall PS NH
Samuel: b c. 1752 d a. 10- -1810 m Anna Nelson Pvt NH

DAMERON, (includes DAMRON)
Bartholomew: b 1730 d 1792 m Anne Moorehead PS VA
Christopher: b c. 1748 d a. 1808 m Sarah — PS VA
George: b 1733 d 1801 m Mary Ann Jones Fif Pvt VA
George: b c. 1760 d a. 9-28-1797 m Susannah — Pvt Fif VA
John: b 1-12-1757 d 4-15-1835 m (1)Anna Ladd (2)Cynthia Thompson Sol VA
Joseph, Sr.: b — d 1818 m X Pvt NS VA

DAMON, (includes DAMOND)
Aaron: b 3-1-1761 d 7-2-1828 m Rachel Griffin Matr MA
Abiah: b 9-3-1761 d 4-11-1836 m Lucretia Gardner Pvt MA
Amos: b 8-1-1729 d p. 1790 m Abigail Farrow Sol MA
Benjamin: b 6-4-1760 d 11-11-1846 m Polly Hosea Pvt MA
Daniel: b 4-23-1716 d 2-27-1733 m Judith Litchfield CS MA
Ebenezer: b 2-24-1737 d 7-14-1812 m Sussnnah Hartshorne Lt MA
Ichabod: b 11-9-1724 d 2-13-1805 m Ruth Studley CS MA
Isaac: b 10-7-1739 d 3-1-1829 m Lucy Cutting Pvt MA
Jabez: b 11-16-1722 d 9-5-1775 m (1)Elizabeth Gould (2)Lucy Wyman Pvt MA
Jason: b 7-30-1763 d 5-30-1835 m Lucy Owen Pvt MA ★
Jonathan: bpt 6-5-1726 d 1-31-1810 m Sarah Gowing Pvt CT
Jonathan: b 5-3-1754 d 1823 m Rachel French Pvt MA
Joseph: b 6-27-1759 d 2-17-1843 m Patience Richardson Pvt MA ★
Josiah, Jr.: bpt 6-20-1756 d 6- -1830 m Lucy Doane Pvt MA
Noah: b 8-25-1760 d 7-2-1853 m (2)Esther Sumner Pvt MA W★
Oliver: b 8-4-1758 d 11-7-1837 m Lois Maynard Sol MA
Peter: b 1740 d 11-27-1818 m Lydia Putnam Cpl MA
Reuben: b 2-13-1759 d 12-26-1837 m Lydia Ellms Fif MA
Samuel: b 2-20-1715/16 d 12-27-1798 m Anas Gowing Pvt MA
Samuel: b 4-16-1749 d 8-10-1807 m Anne Booker Pvt MA
Simeon: b 8-15-1751 d 8-21-1811 m Lucy Bowker Sgt MA
Stephen: b 2-16-1757 d 11-18-1842 m Rhoda Thayer Pvt MA ★
Thomas, Sr.: b 12-25-1703 d 3-6-1796 m Abigail Rice Pvt MA
Thomas, Jr.: b 9-5-1731 d 11-25-1813 m (1)Elizabeth Stowe (2)Margaret Rice Pvt MA
Thomas: b 3-6-1747 d 8-9-1830 m (3)Lydia — Pvt MA
Zadok: b 1-13-1754 d 5-25-1815 m Thankful Wade Cpl MA

DAMPF,
Frederick: b 5-14-1744 d 2-14-1843 m (1)Marie Eva — ( )Susan Chase Pvt NY

DAMPIER,
Daniel: b 7-2-1757 d 1847 m(1)X (2)Elizabeth Pitts Sgt GA

DAMUTH,
George: b — d 4-19-1844 m Catherine Cristman Adj NY

DANA,
Amariah: b 5-20-1736 d 10-29-1830 m (1)Dorothy May (2) Ruth Williams Pvt MA
Anderson, Sr.: b 10-26-1735 d 7-3-1778 m Susanna Huntington CS Vol PA
Asa: b 9-10-1754 d 10-12-1845 m Eunice Town Pvt MA
Danial: b 9-16-1760 d 11-8-1839 m Dorothy Kibby Pvt NY ★
David: b 2-26-1760 d 5-6-1812 m Rebecca Richards Pvt MA ★
Ephraim: b 9-26-1744 d 11-19-1782 m (1)Rebecca Leland (2)Tabitha Jones 1Lt MA
Francis: b 6-13-1743 d 4-25-1811 m Elizabeth Ellery PS MA
Francis: b 2-6-1737 d 2-6-1813 m Eleanor Foster Pvt NH
George: bpt 10-10-1742 d 4-11-1787 m (1)Margaret Clark (2)Elizabeth Parks Sgt MA

James: b 10-10-1732 d 10-16-1817 m Elizabeth Whittemore Capt CT
Joseph: b 11-2-1742 d 11-16-1827 m Mary Staniford PS MA
Joseph: b 2-21-1699/1700 d 1788 m (1)Rebecca Hamblett (2)Mrs Mary Moore PS NH
Josiah: b 8-22-1742 d 10-1-1801 m (1)Mercy Bridgham (2)Mrs Sarah Caldwell PS MA
Nathaniel: b 11-14-1740 d 12-16-1822 m Elizabeth Payton Ens RI
Samuel: b 11-23-1749 d 12-8-1830 m Martha Holland Pvt MA
Susannah Huntington: b 6-23-1730 d — m Anderson Dana PS CT
Thomas, Sr.: b 8-8-1723 d 8-31-1817 m Martha Williams Pvt MA
Thomas, Jr.: b 3-3-1753 d 6-30-1737 m Hannah Williams Pvt MA
William: b 9-29-1745 d 10-30-1809 m Mary Bancroft Capt MA
William: b 8-9-1737 d 12-11-1805 m Joanna Sessions Lt PS NH

DANAKER,
Christian: b c. 1762 d 2-29-1824 m Catharine Haynes Sgt PA

DANCE,
Ezekiel: b c. 1760 d 11-5-1819 m Asenath Hatcher 2Lt VA
Matthew: b 9-9-1750 d 8-13-1826 m Sara Hill PS VA

DANCER,
John: b 1740-50 d 1779 m (2) — Simmons Btm MD

DANCEY,
Benjamin: b c. 1745 d p. 8-3-1830 m (1)Sarah — (2)Mrs Sarah Thompson PS VA

DANDLEY,
John: b 1759/60 d 11-26-1808 m Rebecca Shed Sgt MA

DANDRIDGE,
Alexander Spotswood: b 8-1-1753 d 1785 m Anne Stephen Capt VA
Bartholomew: b 12-25-1737 d 4-18-1785 m (1)Elizabeth Macon (2)Mary Burbridge PS CS VA
John: b 4-6-1756 d 7-20-1804 m Elizabeth Booth Capt VA W★
Nathaniel West: b 9-7-1729 d 1-16-1786 m (1)Dorothea Spotswood (2)Jane Pollard PS VA
Robert Ambler: b 6-21-1760 d 9-20-1799 m Mildred Aylet Allen Lt VA
William: b 4-6-1750 d 1801 m Anne Bolling Col VA
William: b c. 1732 d 1784/85 m Agnes West PS VA

DANE, (includes DAIN)
Daniel: b 11-10-1735 d — m Prudence Phelps Pvt MA
Daniel: b 8-14-1743 d 8-7-1819 m Sarah Goodhue Sgt MA
Francis: b 2-18-1850/51 d 2-27-1832 m Abiah Burt Pvt MA
John: b 5-8-1747 d 8-7-1837 m Elizabeth Proctor Sgt MA
John, Jr.: b 1738 d 1777 m Mary Moody Vol MA
Joseph: b 8-16-1723 d 9-19-1807 m Elizabeth Abbott Pvt MA

DANENHOWER,
John: b 2-26-1751 d 179- m Eve Riter Pvt PA

DANFORTH, (includes DANFORD)
Abner: b 1760 d 1841 m Christina Eaton Pvt MA ★
Asa: b 7-6-1746 d 9-2-1818 m Hannah Wheeler Capt MA W★
Benjamin: b 12-8-1724 d 10-10-1816 m Mary Frost Pvt MA
David: b 1749 d 3-13-1827 m Mary Young Pvt MA
David:, Jr.: b 11-26-1752 d 7-4-1827 m Elizabeth Pierce Pvt MA
David: b 1-24-1747 d 3-1-1815 m Hannah Proctor Pvt NH
Edward: b c. 1758 d 8-5-1816 m Mary Chatman Pvt NH W★
Elijah: b 3-20-1733 d 2-12-1809 m Susannah Copeland Pvt MA
Elkanah: b 8-5-1750 d 2-16-1813 m Sibyl Tisdale Cpl MA
Enoch: b a. 1728 d p. 1783 m Dorcas Hurchins Mrnr MA
Jesse: b 1762 d 1827 m Martha Allison Pvt PA
Job: b 4-10-1745 d 11-23-1838 m Sarah Coy Ens RI ★
John: b 2-11-1736 d p. 1798 m Rhoda Dean Sgt MA
John: b 7-23-1756 d 8-16-1796 m Hannah Bancroft Pvt MA
Jonathan, Sr.: b- 6-14-1736 d 2- -1802 m (1)Lydia Reed (2)Miriam Cowie Capt MA
Jonathan, Jr.: b 3-2-1761 d 1- -1847 m Abigail Johnson Pvt MA
Jonathan: b 12-21-1752 d 2-4-1807 m Judith Spaulding Pvt MA
Jonathan: b 12-23-1751 d 8- -1811 m Jane — Pvt NH
Jonathan: b 7-20-1754 d 10-10-1816 m Sarah Chandler Pvt NH
Joseph: b 6-30-1720 d 3-30-1795 m Mary A. Richardson Lt PS MA
Joseph: b 10-31-1738 d 8-9-1807 m (1)Rebecca Brown (2)Anna Quimby Lt MA
Joseph: b 5-19-1754 d 3-9-1776 m Susanna French Pvt MA
Joseph: b 10-6-1763 d 2-12-1846 m Elizabeth Barker Pvt MA ★
Joshua: b 11-26-1759 d 1-30-1837 m Solame A. Noble SrgnMte Col MA
Joshua: b 1757 d 2-22-1815 m Lucretia Palmer Sgt NH
Nathaniel: b 1703 d 1799/1800 m Priscilla Wycom CS NH
Nicholas: b 12-8-1734 d c. 1810 m Elizabeth Jacquith Pvt MA
Oliver: b 7-6-1743 d 11-27-1828 m Hannah Pratt Lt MA
Peter: b 5-25-1761 d 1-12-1843 m Elizabeth Stevens Pvt MA
Peter: b 3-9-1757 d 8-22-1827 m (1)Sarah Morris (2)Mercy Ewing (3)Margaret DeLancy Pvt NJ
Samuel: b 5-11-1759 d 4-15-1838 m Sarah Ingraham Lt MA
Samuel, Jr.: b 2-24-1756 d 4-6-1815 m Anna Trull Pvt MA
Simeon: b 3-9-1745 d 2-23-1824 m (1)Jemima — (2)Judith Stickney Cpl NH

Solomon: b 1-12-1756 d 5-31-1833 m Sarah Cummings Pvt NH
Thomas: b 6-2-1756 d 1-13-1840 m Elizabeth Tallman PS CT
Thomas, Jr.: b 2-20-1745 d 4-23-1794 m Lydia Abbot Cpl MA
Thomas: b 1762 d 1845 m (2)Betsey Haskins (3)Mary Ann Perkins DrmMaj MA
Timothy: b 1⁴-11-1729 d 6-26-1792 m Sarah Patton PS Dr MA
William: b 7-31-1757 d 7-21-1804 m (1)Lucy Pollard (2)Sarah Smith Drm Cpl MA
William: b 7-31-1761 d 7- -1830 m Priscilla Hoadly Sol MA
William: b 8-18-1748 d 10-13-1838 m Olive Elliot Sgt PS NH

DANGERFIELD, (includes DAINGERFIELD)
John: b c. 1755 d 1814 m Elizabeth Townley Pvt VA
Leroy: b 1738 d 1823 m (1)Elizabeth Henley (2)Elizabeth Parker CS VA
William: b 1750 d 12- -1780 m Elizabeth Owen Drm VA

DANIELS, (includes DANIEL, DANIELL)
Aaron: b 1739 d p. 1790 m Betsey Whitfield Ens PS SC
Abram: b 3-15-1762 d 10-20-1832 m Jane Moore Pvt VA
Allen: b c. 1738 d c. 1814 m Mary Allen Capt VA
Amariah: b 1767-70 d 2- -1841 m Olive Rider Fif MA ★
Andrew: b 7-29-1753 d 4-22-1802 m Hannah Downing Pvt PA
Benjamin: b c. 1760 d 1- -1818 m Lucretia Bergamont Pvt GA
Benjamin Woodson: b 1747 d 2- -1849 m Elizabeth Moor Pvt Cmsry NC ★
Beverly: b 2-11-1762 d p. 9-18-1851 m Jane Hiatt Sgt VA ★
Campbell: b 1760 d 2-19-1816 m Elizabeth Sublett Pvt VA W★
Charles: b 1708 d p. 11- -1796 m Jane Mickelborough PS VA
Dan: b 1794 d 5-22-1846 m Zeruiah Herrick Pvt MA
Daniel: b - d 1-3-1812 m Mary Wicks Pvt CT
Daniel: bpt 10-9-1743 d 12-6-1819 m Mary Atwood Pvt MA
Daniel: b 11-23-1763 d 9-4-1849 m Catherine Clevenger Pvt PA
David: b 1759 d 7-13-1813 m Lucina Meigs Cpl CT W★
David: b 9-4-1710 d 3-21-1776 m Huldah Arnold Taft PS MA
Edward: b c. 1740 d 1814 m Thankful — Pvt PA
Eleazer: b 7-4-1761 d 5-1-1848 m Mary Burrell Pvt MA ★
Ephraim: b 1750 d 5-13-1819 m Anna Bruce Pvt NH ★
Frederick: b 3-2-1755 d p. 1837 m Elizabeth Powell Pvt NC
Henry: b 7-6-1755 d 11-7-1841 m Mary Magdalena Miller Pvt PS PA
Increase: b 1-18-1752 d 3-1-1806 m Elona Thayer Pvt MA
Isaac: b 1760 d p. 1835 m Mary Jane Maner Lt GA
Isaac: b 5-20-1760 d 6-28-1864 m (1) X (2) X (3) X Pvt NY
Isaiah: b 4-18-1745 d p. 1778 m Abigail Hill Pvt MA
James: b c. 1725 d p. 10-10-1785 m Sarah — 2Lt NC
James: b c. 1755 d 2-11-1817 m Mrs Rebecca Travis Adderton PS NC
James: b 4-8-1748 d 9-15-1826 m Martha Jones Pvt SC
James: b c. 1741 d 1798 m (1)X (2)Nancy — PS SC
James: b 6-18-1739 d 12-14-1835 m Elizabeth Montague PS VA
James: b 1758 d 1836 m Sarah Elmo Pvt VA
James, Sr.: b c. 1740 d a. 11-5-1821 m Elizabeth Cunningham Pvt VA
Japheth: b 2-17-1738 d 3-3-1805 m Meletiah Hayward Capt MA
Jeremiah: b 10-17-1744 d 4-21-1784 m Abigail Fisher Cpl MA
John: b 7-17-1757 d 3- -1788 m Mary Mason Sol GA
John: b 12-13-1756 d 2-8-1833 m (1)Zipporah Pierce (2)Mary — Pvt MA NH ★
John: b 6-17-1735 d 5-5-1814 m Mary Newcomb Capt NJ
John: b 1760 d 1830 m Rebecca Stevens Sol NY
John: b 5-23-1762 d 6-13-1841 m Marguriete Meanes Capt NC ★
John: b 12-26-1747 d p. 1796 m Susanna Quaintance Pvt PA
John: b c. 1755 d 1832 m (1)Mary Vereen (2)Lucy Bishop Sgt SC
John, Sr.: b c. 1740 d 5- -1803 m Lydia — Ens VA
John: b c. 1766 d 8- -1830 m Sarah Cunningham Ens VA
John: b 10-19-1760 d 5-30-1799 m Elizabeth Street Pvt VA W★
John: b 1751 d 8- -1802 m Elizabeth Morton Cmsry VA
John: b c. 1755 d 1809 m (1)Lucy Marshall (2)Martha Terrell PS VA
Johnathan: b c. 1724 d 1804 m Johanna Kinsey Pvt NJ
Joseph: b 4-12-1724 d 6-12-1779 m Margaret French 1Maj PS CS MA
Joseph: b 2-29-1758 d 6-10-1833 m Susanna Eames Pvt MA ★
Joseph: b 6-25-1736 d 10-16-1823 m Deborah Keith Capt MA
Joshua: b - d 9-23-1810 m Jane M. Hamilton CS VA
Josiah: b 1745 d p. 4-3-1811 m Elizabeth Jordan Pvt VA
Leonard: b 1763 d 1855 m Polly Spears Pvt VA
Littleton: b 10-8-1758 d 2-8-1835 m Elizabeth Minds Sol NC
Moses: b 2-25-1753 d 12-29-1830 m Abigail Aldrich Pvt MA
Moses: b 2-8-1736 d 10-20-1800 m Abigail Adams Pvt MA
Nathan: b 1760 d 1845 m — Dart Pvt CT
Nathan, Jr.: b 7-12-1748 d 11-25-1841 m (1)Elizabeth Partridge (2) Sarah Smith Pvt MA
Nathan: b 1747 d p. 1833 m — Tuttle Lt VT ★
Nathaniel, Sr.: b 7-17-1741 d 12-31-1777 m Hannah Wadsworth Pvt MA
Nathaniel, Sr.: b 8-23-1719/20 d p. 1780 m Ann Grosvenor Pvt CS PS MA
Nathaniel, Jr.: b 2-21-1742/43 d 9-15-1830 m Esther Lee Pvt MA
Pelatiah: b 1725 d 2-21-1808 m Abigail Daniels Pvt CT
Pelatiah: b 5-23-1734 d 3-5-1818 m Abigail Williams Pvt NH
Peter: b 9-29-1706 d p. 1782 m Sarah Travers PS CS VA
Randolph: b 2-20-1758 d 8-11-1829 m Effiah Mundy Pvt NJ
Reuben: b - d p. 5-27-1828 m Elizabeth Harrison PS NC

Reuben: b 6-20-1757 d 10-23-1839 m (1)Sarah Meeker (2)Anna Cowdery Pvt CT
Reuben: b 4-22-1721 d p. 1-2-1778 m (2)Elizabeth Montague (3) Elizabeth Stevens Merry Capt VA
Robert Campbell: b a. 1760 d 2-19-1816 m Elizabeth Sublett Pvt VA W★
Robert Howe: b 1735 d 1789 m Anna Verin Capt NC
Samuel: b 4-2-1762 d 2-20-1842 m Lydia Shipman Pvt CT ★
Samuel: b 9-4-1745 d 1810 m Sarah — Lt PS NH
Samuel, Jr.: b 10-21-1759 d 12-10-1832 m Abigail Pinkham Cpl NH ★
Samuel: b 6-21-1732 d 3-12-1778 m Elizabeth Wiswall Pvt VT
Samuel: b - d 4-19-1823 m Mary — Pvt VA
Simon: b 1758 d 1830 m Elizabeth Reddick Pvt NC
Starling: b 1742 d 1-24-1834 m Charity (Johnson) Sperry Pvt MA
Stephen: b 5-6-1757-59 d 1- -1832 m Lydia Palmer Pvt MA
Stephen: b c. 1759 d 3-28-1840 m Huldah Smock Lt NC
Stephen: b 10-10-1733 d 1785 m Adeline Verin Ens PS NC
Thomas: b c. 1740 d p. 4-7-1813 m Sarah — Sol GA
Timothy: b 9-22-1722 d 1802 m Ruth Lealand CS MA
Travers: b 5-26-1741 d 6-28-1824 m Frances Moncure PS VA
Verin: b 2-15-1737 d 2-1-1776 m Ruth Billings Pvt MA
Vivian: b 7-1-1726 d p. 6-21-1802 m (1)Elizabeth Vivian (2)Mrs Nancy Vaughan PS VA
Wm.: b 1745 d 1836 m Elizabeth Skinner Pvt GA
Wm.: b c. 1746 d 1788 m Bethiah Pratt Pvt MA
Wm.: b 7-27-1753-55 d 1817 m (1)Rachel Bacon (2)Lydia Hancock (3)Mrs Sarah Finlaw Pvt NJ
Wm.: b 11-25-1743 d 5-9-1840 m (1)Rachel — (2)Mary Melton Sol NC
Wm., Sr.: b 1747 d 1807 m Lucretia Bell Sol SC
Wm.: b c. 1740 d p. 1780 m Martha Allen Ens VA
Wm.: b 5-12-1761 d 4-13-1855 m Mollie Pendleton Gaines Pvt VA ★
Wm.: b 1-8-1762 d 5-15-1845 m Mary Thomas Pvt VA ★
Wm.: b c. 1750 d p. 6-20-1816 m X Sol VA CL
Wm.: b 1754 d a. 3-16-1816 m (1)Hannah Cunningham (2)Sarah Pettus PS VA
Wm. Powell: b c. 1755 d 6- -1841 m (2)Elizabeth Short Pvt VA
Woodson: b c. 1736/7 d 1791 m Nancy — Pvt NC

DANIELSON,
Calvin: b 1755 d 1845 m Katy McMaster Cpl MA
John: b 12-8-1727 d p. 1779 m Ruth Blodgett Pvt MA
Levi: b 6-24-1739 d p. 1790 m Hannah Foss Pvt PS NH
Samuel, Jr.: b 10-8-1740 d 6-13-1817 m (1)Hannah Whitman (2)Elizabeth Spaulding Capt CT
Wm.: b 8-11-1729 d 8-19-1798 m Sarah Williams Col CT

DANKE,
Frederick: b 8-19-1745 d 4-18-1793 m Anna Maria Clewell Pvt PA

DANKS,
Asahel: b 5-29-1739 d p. 1790 m Hannah Bartlett Pvt MA
John: b 11-26-1761 d p. 10-15-1832 m (2)Nancy Gilbert Pvt VA ★
Samuel, Jr.: b 1-18-1753 d 1-14-1834 m Abigail Rogers Pvt MA W★

DANN,
Squire: b 5-8-1755 d 3-25-1839 m (1)Rachel Lockwood (2)Mrs Rhoda Northrop Pvt CT ★

DANNER,
Abraham: b 2-5-1753 d 7-2-1833 m Charlotte — Pvt PA

D'ANTIGNAC,
Lois Jean Baptist Chamberon: b 1749 d 4- -1827 m Hannah Dubose Capt NY

DANTZLER,
Jacob: b 7-5-1742 d 1790 m Barbara Carn Pvt SC

DARBY, (includes DABY, DARBE, DARBEE, DERBY)
Andrew: b 1-26-1706/07 d 3-27-1783 m Elizabeth Patch Pvt MA
Asa: b 4-13-1756 d 12-30-1833 m Dorcas Goar Sol PS MD
Azariah: b 1762 d 8-19-1851 m Susannah Phelps Pvt VT
Basil: b 6-28-1758 d p. 1798 m (1)Rebecca Allnutt (2)Jane A Coberth Pvt MD
Benjamin: b c. 1760 d 5-18-1830 m Constant Hamilton Pvt CT W★
Benjamin: b 2-6-1762 d 11-14-1829 m Esther Finley Fif CT W★
Benjamin: b 1745 d 12-25-1787 m Sarah Twiford Sol MD
Benjamin: b 2-8-1748 d 1835/36 m Mary McRae Pvt SC ★
Caleb: b 3-17-1762 d 3- -1802 m (1)Elizabeth Ray (2)Sarah Gartrell 3Cpl MD
Daniel: b c. 1752 d 10-28-1776 m X Pvt PS NY
Eliab: b 3-8-1750 d 5-29-1812 m Bethiah Clark Cpl MA
George: b 6-12-1726 d 3-29-1788 m Ann — PS MD
Jedediah: b 1-20-1757 d 10-9-1828 m Elizabeth Avery Gore Pvt CT
John, Sr.: b 1-17-1736 d 6-28-1820 m (1)Rachel Squier (2)Mrs Margaret Stanbury Capt NJ
John, Jr.: b 5-29-1762 d 11-17-1829 m Nancy Stansbury Pvt NJ
John, Jr.: b 1736 d 1792 m Nancy Voorhies Pvt NJ
John: b 1725 d 12- -1805 m Mahetabel White Dr "Rebel Parson" NJ

DARBY, contd.
John: b 1-16-1763 d c. 1823 m Elizabeth McDaniel Pvt NC
Jonathan: b 7-26-1734 d 4-2-1819 m Elizabeth Pratt Lt MA
Jonathan, Sr.: b 7-4-1726 d 1-19-1794 m Abigail Dewey Lt NH
Jonathan: b 10-8-1753 d 10-6-1838 m Sarah Strong Ens NH VT ★
Joseph, Sr.: b 12-15-1716 d 9-7-1792 m Elizabeth Nourse Pvt MA
Joseph, Jr.: b 1745 d 9-13-1825 m Abigail Bennett Cpl MA
Josiah: b c. 1734 d p. 1820 m Drusilla — Pvt PS MD
Moses: b 10-1-1759 d 9-14-1834 m Dorothy Tiffany Pvt CT ★
Nathan: b 8-2-1737 d p.1818 m Abagail Pierce Pvt MA
Richard: b 9-16-1712 d 11-9-1783 m Mary Hodges PS MA
Samuel: b 3-29-1760 d 2-15-1822 m (1)Verlin Carr (2)Hesse Irwin Sgt MD
Samuel: b 9-15-1757 d 3-13-1839 m Hannah Minot Pvt MA ★
Samuel: bpt 2-14-1719/20 d 1783 m (1)Bridget Newhall (2)Ann Williams Pvt MA
Samuel: b 6-2-1758 d 4-20-1826 m Hannah Kimball Sol MA
Thomas: b 1-12-1731 d 10-24-1776 m Lucy Brewer Cpl MA
Thomas: b 9-22-1739 d p. 1790 m (1)Mary Holt (2)Orpah Jillson PS Pvt NH
Wm.: b 1759/60 d 4-30-1836 m (1)Signet Rushton (2)Hannah Andrews Drm PA ★

DARCY,
Joel: b c. 1765 d 1838 m (1) X (2)Catherine Wright Pvt GA
John: b 10-11-1760 d 1822 m (1)Phebe Johnes (2)Phebe Miller SrgnMte NJ

DARDEN, (includes DURDAN, DURDEN)
George, Sr.: b 1739 d p. 10- -1800 m Martha Burch Sol GA
George, Jr.: b 1-21-1763 d 5-30-1844 m Elizabeth Strosier Pvt GA SC ★
Jacob: b 8-3-1755 d 4-26-1845 m Mollie Hilliard Sol NC
James Madison: b 1748 d 1820 m Drucella Burche Pvt VA
John, Sr.: b 1710 d p.1781 m Mary — Capt VA
John, Jr.: b 1734 d 1800 m Sara Newton Sol NC
Stephen: b 1750 d 1810 m Ann Darden PS NC

DARE,
James A: b c. 1737 d 11-30-1791 m (1)Elizabeth Blackwood (2)Mary Ann Blackwood Pvt NJ
Reuben: b c. 1731 d 1777 m (1)Mrs Rhoda Stevens (2)Rebekah Carll Ens NJ

DARKE,
Wm.: b 5-6-1736 d 11-26-1801 m Sarah (DeLange) Deleyea LCol VA

DARLAND,
Lambert: b 4-5-1763 d 10-22-1852 m Martha Thenosdol Pvt PA

DARLING, (includes DARLON)
Benjamin: b 4-13-1738 d 9-26-1820 m Mary Chapman PS CT
Benjamin: b 6-19-1734 d 11-29-1807 m Hannah Harris Lt MA
Benjamin: b 7-4-1761 d 3-21-1814 m (2)Selina (Cook) Clark Pvt MA
David: b 1747 d 1823 m Melia Veazie Pvt MA
David: b 4-14-1753 d 3-15-1835 m (1)Esther Metcalf (2)Molly Woods (3)Matilda Bowditch Pvt MA
David: b 10-21-1761 d 8-24-1839 m (1)Elizabeth Goldthwaite (2)Marcy Phillips Pvt MA ★
Ebenezer: b 1758 d p. 1775 m Lydia Bowen Pvt CT
Eli: b c.1760 d — m Rebeckah Pond Pvt MA
Jacobus: b 12-2-1751 d 2-1-1822 m Sarah Cutler Pvt NY
John: b 12-1-1717 d 2-2-1800 m Hannah Healey Sgt MA
John: b 1727 d 1820 m Mary Loop Pvt MA
John: b 3-30-1758 d 5-25-1848 m Mary Wood Pvt MA
John: b 1-29-1744 d 1830 m Phebe Robert Pvt PS NH
John: b 7-11-1760 d 9-25-1831 m Asenath Vaughan Cpl VT W★
Jonathan: b a. 1758 d p. 1805 m Abigal Emey Pvt NY
Joseph: bpt 10-17-1743 d p. 5-3-1780 m Mary Street Sol CT
Joseph: b 7-5-1759 d 11-15-1850 m Aurelia Mills Slr CT
Joseph: b 10-29-1746 d 11- -1824 m (1)Eunice Flagg (2)Sarah Houghton Pvt MA
Joseph: b 9-22-1764 d 1841 m Huldah Darling Pvt MA ★
Joseph: b 1-27-1736 d 3-13-1809 m Huldah Thomas Sct VT
Levi: b 1761 d 7-12-1843 m Charlotte B — Pvt VT ★
Moses: b 1756 d 3-3-1822 m Judith French Pvt VT ★
Pelatian: b 4-2-1760 d 4-3-1839 m Phila Taft Pvt MA
Peter: b 1725 d 5-16-1818 m Amy Winkinson Pvt RI
Seth: b 3-21-1764 d 3-27-1825 m Chloe Marsh Pvt MA
Thomas: b 2-21-1720 d 11-30-1789 m Abigal Noyes CS CT
Thomas: b 5-7-1730 d 10-22-1778 m Rachel White Pvt MA
Timothy: b 10-29-1750 d 10-19-1837 m Minnie Chase Pvt NH
Wm.: b 1-15-1730 d 7-26-1819 m Rachel White 2Lt MA
Wm.: b 1730 d 1786 m Sofia — PS VA

DARLINGTON,
John: b c. 1727 d 2-2-1813 m Esther Dicks Pvt PA
John: b 8-20-1756 d 1-29-1833 m Elizabeth Irwin Pvt PA
John: b c.1750 d 1807 m Eleanor Armstrong Pvt PS SC
Meredith: b 1730 d 8-18-1783 m Sarah Davis PS VA
Robert: b 1740 d p. 1781 m Catharine Henderson Lt PA

DARNABY,
John: b 6-27-1760 d 9-21-1833 m Elizabeth Alsop Pvt VA

DARNELL, (includes DARNALL, DARNEILLE)
Aaron: b 1-28-1761 d 8-6-1816 m Jane Railey Drm VA
Isaac: b 1745 d 1824 m Stacy McDonald Pvt PA
John: b 1736 d p. 12-17-1797 m Marion McDonald PS Pvt PA MD
John: b c. 1755 d 8-16-1780 m Rachel — Sol NC
Joseph: b 1750 d p. 3-13-1834 m Winifred Perry Pvt NC ★
Thomas, Sr.: b 1735 d 7-1-1825 m (1)Susanna Soper (2)Elizabeth Nicholas Pvt VA
Thomas, Jr.: b c. 1760 d p. 1825 m Elizabeth Robey Pvt MD

DARON,
Adam: b c. 1740 d p. 11-20-1810 m (1)Annie Maria Schafer (2)Barbara — Pvt PA

DARRAH, (includes DARRAGH)
Henry: b c. 1726 d 6- -1782 m Ann Jamison Capt PA
Lydia Barrington: b 1728 d 12-28-1789 m William Darragh PS PA
Thomas: b 1730 d 8- -1799 m Agnes Thomson Pvt PA
William: b 1735 d 12-17-1808 m Rebecca Thomson Lt PA

DARRIN,
Daniel: b 12-8-1756 d 11-4-1838 m (1)Rhoda — (2)Martha Travis Pvt CT NY W★

DARROW,
Ammiras: b 3-20-1761 d 3-8-1824 m Sarah Fisher Melona Pvt NY
Benjamin: b 1759 d 1827 m Grace Stratton Pvt CT
Christopher: b — d p. 7- -1783 m Sarah Gorton Maj CT
Daniel: b 4-15-1754 d 8-5-1821 m Hannah Downes Pvt CT★
Daniel: b 3-26-1763 d 7-24-1858 m Tryphena Cady Pvt NY ★
Ebenezer: b 11-6-1754 d 4-29-1841 m Zurviah Lester Pvt CT★
Ebenezer, Jr.: b 1757 d 8-8-1834 m Esther Williams Cpl CT
Ebenezer: b 1719 d 7-5-1800 m Lydia Austin Cpl MA
George: b 1760 d 1816 m Abigail Littlefield Capt MA
George: b c. 1736 d p. 1790 m X Pvt Adj NY
Jedediah: b 1-1-1762 d 10-30-1835 m Alche Teachout Pvt NY
John: b 6-5-1755 d 3-22-1813 m (3)Eunice Eggleston Pvt NY
John: b 12-9-1763 d 7-4-1854 m Martha Herrick Sol NY★
Jonathan: b — d p. 10- -1779 m (1)Abigail Jackson (2)Mrs Grace (Barlow) Lines (3)Mrs Elizabeth Bulkley NS CT
Jonathan, Jr.: b 3-30-1746 d 1780 m (1)Elizabeth Bulkley (2)Molly Thorp Pvt CT
Nathan: b 1759 d p. 1832 m Anna Perkins Sgt CT ★
Nicholas: b 7-16-1750 d 4-1-1792 m Sarah Rogers Pvt CT
William: b 12- -1759/60 d 2-16-1835/6 m Sarah Smith Pvt CT★

DARST,
David: b 12-17-1757 d 12-2-1826 m Rosetta Holman Sol VA

DART, (includes DARTT, DORT)
Caleb: b 9-16-1756 d 8-10-1810 m Margaret Braddock Pvt CT
Cyrus: b 1764 d 6-29-1817 m Ann Harris Pvt CT
David: b 2-5-1761 d p. 7-31-1832 m (1)Mary Fargo (2)Mercy Ann Mynard Pvt CT ★
Ebenezer: b 10-26-1736 d p. 1790 m Elizabeth Miner PS CT
Ebenezer: b 12-3-1748 d 7-30-1825 m (1)Dorcas — (2)Hannah Pratt Pvt CT★
Elias: b 5-7-1759 d 8-27-1828 m Ruth Morley Gnr CT
Eliphalet: b 2-27-1740/41 d 11-9-1821 m Anna Field PS NH
Joseph: b 8-1-1737 d 5-5-1791 m Abigail Brainerd Capt CT
Joshua: b 8-14-1727 d p. 1790 m Deborah Spencer Pvt CS PS NH
Josiah: b 5-3-1759 d 8-26-1829 m Betsey Delano Pvt NH
Justus: b 5-28-1757 d 7-3-1838 m Hannah Gleason Pvt Mus NH VT★
Roger: b 6-18-1756 d 5-26-1812 m (1)Elizabeth Newton (2)Anna Nichols Drm Pvt MA NH
Thomas: b 4-25-1724 d 4-9-1791 m Sarah Belden Sol CS NH
Timothy: b 11-15-1756 d 6-27-1814 m Margaret Taylor Pvt CT

DARWIN,
John: b 3-19-1755 d 7-13-1837 m Jane Bland Lt VA

DARY,
John: b 10-28-1757 d 5-31-1824 m Rebecca Blondin Pvt MA

DASHER,
Christian: b c. 1733 d 1775-83 m Ann Christina Meyer Sol GA
Christian: b 1749 d p. 1800 m Elizabeth — Pvt GA
John Martin: b 1738 d 11-9-1802 m (1)Susannah Schaffer (2)Hannah Huxson Pvt GA

DASHIELL,
Arthur: b 7-29-1734 d 9- -1802 m (1)Rachel Cordray (2)Elizabeth Phillips 1Lt MD
Benjamin: b 1736 d 9-30-1799 m (1) X (2)Ann Yoe NCdr MD
George: b 1740 d 1825 m Priscilla Jones Pvt MD
James: b 8-20-1740 d a. 2-9-1796 m Sarah Evans Pvt MD
John: b 8-5-1757 d 3-25-1818 m (1)Anne (Dashiell) (2)Eleanor (Dashiell) Lt MD
John: b 4-17-1751 d 12-15-1816 m Sarah (Killam) Handy Cpl MD
William Francis: b 1-26-1750 d 1790 m Priscilla Evans Pvt MD

DASKAM, (includes DASCOMB)
Jacob: b 8-15-1760 d 7-4-1827 m Rachel Dale Pvt MA
James: b 1732 d 6-6-1807 m Elizabeth Farrington CS Pvt NH
John: b 6-4-1759 d 9-11-1834 m Louisa Bunce Pvt CT NY★

DAUBENSPECK,
George: b 1751 d *p.* 1797 m Barbara Geiger Pvt PA
John Jacob: b 1714 d *p.* 8-7-1777 m Juliana — PS PA

DAUCHY,
Jeremiah: b 11-1-1755 d 9-20-1823 m Sarah Hull Pvt MA
Nathan: b 1746 d 4-14-1824 m Mary Smith Lt CT

DAUGE, (includes DOZIER)
James J.: b 1740 d 1792 m Martha — Pvt VA
James S.: b 1739 d 1-2-1808 m Mary Dinwoody Sgt VA
John: b 12-2-1741 d 12-22-1807 m Elizabeth Giles Capt SC
John: b 1767 d 9-1-1838 m (2)Mrs Milly Reno Kinchelow Sol VA
Peter: b 12- -1739 d 9-1-1801 m (1)Elizabeth Williams (2)Margaret (Sawyer) Lamb Maj NC
Peter: b 11-2-1762 d 8-6-1838 m Alley Pritchett Pvt VA ★
William, Sr.: b 1-23-1723 d 2-19-1782 m Availrah Connell Pvt NC
William: b 1728 d 1797 m Elizabeth — Pvt VA

DAUGHERTY, (includes DOUGHERTY)
Charles: b *c.* 1735 d *p.* 1800 m Hannah Hemingway 1Lt QM MA ★
Edward: b 1764 d *c.* 1855 m Elizabeth — Pvt PA
James: b 1757 d 1825 m Anne Hammond Pvt PA
James: b *c.* 1740 d 1805 m Susanna — Capt VA
James: b *c.* 1737 d 12- -1812 m Rebecca Cunningham NLt VA
James: b 1740 d 1799 m Hannah — PS VA
Jarvis: b 1721/22 d *p.* 7-11-1812 m Elizabeth Morgan Pvt VA
John: b 1756 d 5-15-1833 m Deborah Boone Capt PA
John: b 1750-60 d *p.* 1830 m X Pvt PA
John: b 5- -1757 d *a.* 2-14-1848 m Margaret — Pvt PA ★
Joseph: b 1762 d *a.* 4-5-1847 m Mary Lanier Sol GA
Patrick: b *c.* 1760 d *c.* 1810 m — Davis Pvt PA
Patrick: b 1760 d *p.* 1812 m X Pvt VA
Thomas: b 1746 d 1836 m Margaret DeFoe Pvt NY
William: b 1754 d 9-1-1841 m Lydia Cox Pvt PA ★
William: b 3-10-1755 d 1834 m Mary Watson Pvt SC ★
William: b 1750-60 d 1834 m Mary Bridger Pvt VA
William: b 3-17-1763 d *p.* 1805 m Elizabeth Ramsey Pvt VA

DAUPHIN,
Jean: b *c.* 1758 d 12-12-1810 m Jane Jackson FrN

DAVANT,
Charles: b 1748 d 1781 m Elizabeth Fendin Pvt SC

DAVENPORT,
Abner: b 10-1-1760 d 3-22-1831 m Eunice Burnham Pvt MA
Abraham: b 6-6-1715 d 11-20-1789 m (1)Elizabeth Huntington (2)Mrs Martha Fitch PS CT
Abram, Jr.: b 2-9-1752 d 4-17-1825 m Frances Williams Sgt VA
Abram, Sr.: b 5-17-1714 d 10- -1789 m Mary Sims PS VA
Adrian: b 4-9-1759 d 5-2-1841 m (1)Nutty Chapman (2)Ann Ashby Pvt VA ★
Anthony Sims: b 5-19-1757 d 6-19-1835 m (1)Elizabeth — (2)Mary Bazil Sgt VA ★
Bedford: b *c.* 1745 d *p.* 8-22-1832 m Annie Comer 2Lt VA
Benjamin: b 1761-63 d 1800/1 m Elizabeth Rice Pvt CT W★
Benjamin: b 6-16-1743 d 12-28-1833 m Sarah Wilson Pvt MA
Birkett: b 10-25-1730 d 8-26-1817 m Eleanor Brown PS VA
Charles: b 7-2-1717 d 3-15-1779 m Miss Waitstill — Pvt CT
Charles: b 4-15-1751 d 12-12-1812 m Elizabeth Taylor Sgt NY
Charles, Sr.: b 3-5-1730 d 4-25-1805 m Mary Hart Pvt VT
Charles, Jr.: b 5-4-1761 d *p.* 1808 m Polly Wood Pvt VT
Clayborn: b 1759 d 8-18-1842 m Mary Lee Pvt VA ★
Cornelius: bpt 11-14-1739 d *a.* 11-29-1815 m Rachel — Pvt NJ
Ebenezer: b 7-9-1745 d 2-21-1819 m Mary Crane CS ME
Eliphalet: b 10-14-1751 d 12-17-1835 m Elizabeth Williams Pvt CT ★
Francis: b 1718 d *p.* 7-23-1798 m Mary Turner PS SC
Gould: b 10-5-1762 d *p.* 1840 m Rachel — Sea Coast Grd CT
Hezekiah: b 1-14-1738 d 4-27-1777 m Ruth Ketchams Lt CT
Isaac: b 5-24-1730 d 3-29-1799 m Mary Pray Cpl MA
James: b 8- -1759 d 4-9-1857 m Maria Moule Pvt NY ★
James: b 4-29-1759 d 6-8-1824 m Dicey Kennedy Pvt VA
James Madison: b 1742 d 7-23-1824 m Elizabeth Gilliam Pvt VA
John: b 1-16-1752 d 11-28-1830 m Mary Wells Maj CT
John: b 11-1-1737 d 4-25-1776 m Lois Badlam Pvt MA
John: b 12-14-1753 d 1-19-1815 m Eleanor Harris Cpl VA
John: b 1747 d 3-15-1781 m Lucy Barksdale Pvt VA
John: b 1742 d 1820 m Elizabeth Carter Pvt VA
Jonathan: b 5-7-1748 d 1785 m Sarah Thurston Pvt RI
Joseph: b 8-15-1748 d 10-26-1798 m Alice Bennett Sgt CT
Joseph: b 5-22-1756 d 7-23-1831 m Mary Crocker Cpl MA ★
Joseph: b 8-10-1747 d *c.* 1784 m Mary White Pvt MM MA
Joseph: b 9-30-1753 d 1-18-1815 m Elinor Harris Capt PA
Joseph: b 9-7-1759 d — m Frances Dobyns 1Lt VA
Noah: b 8-17-1758 d 8-13-1840 m Lydia Metcalf Pvt CT ★
Oliver: b *c.* 1726 d *p.* 7-9-1801 m Hannah Seeley Sol PS NY

Peter: b *c.* 1750 d 3-6-1816 m Alida Lent 1Lt NY
Robert: b 5-10-1757 d 1840 m Susan — Pvt NY PS ★
Samuel: b 9-1-1720 d 12-6-1793 m (1)Sarah Whiten (2)Mrs Sarah Tucker Pvt MA
Thomas: b *c.* 1754 d *a.* 9- -1808 m X Capt GA
Thomas: b 4-19-1736 d 3- -1818 m (1)Abigail Wilder (2)Relief Wilder Sgt MA
Thomas: b 11-27-1764 d 11-19-1845 m Mary Wilson Pvt MA
Thomas: b 4-11-1750 d 1789 m Martha — Pvt NY
Thomas: b 6-4-1749 d 5-4-1812 m Charity Lammereau PS NY
Thomas: b *c.* 1761/62 d 2- -1849 m Permelia Davenport Pvt VA
William: b 1700 d 3-11-1796 m Sarah Richards Pvt MA
William, Jr.: b 6-23-1737 d 3-3-1805 m Thomasin Bigelow Pvt MA
William: b 3-5-1763 d 10-29-1843 m Pheby — Sgt NC
William: b 9-20-1746 d 4-3-1790 m Mary Hunley Capt VA
William: b 1757 d 1828 m Mary Bullock Lt VA
William: b 1756 d 1814 m Mary Nullaly Pvt VA

DAVES,
John: b 1748 d 10-12-1804 m (1)Sally Bryan (2)Mary Eaton Haynes QM Capt NC

DAVID, (includes DAVIDE)
Enoch: b 3-6-1715 d 11-28-1793 m (1)Catolina Van Bebber (2)Rebecca Ayers (3)— (4)Elizabeth Harrison PS PA
Isaac: b *c.* 1760 d 1839 m Lucy White Pvt GA
John: b 6-20-1721 d 6-26-1797 m Elizabeth Wyngaart Pvt PS NY
John: b 1745 d *p.* 1820 m (1)Sarah Booth (2)Mary Jones (3)Isabella Allison (4)Sarah Stephens (5)Mary Bridges Stubbs Lt SC
Joshua: b 1756 d 1822 m Lucy Hodge Pvt SC
Michael: b 1763 d 6-4-1833 m Cecelah Thorpe Pvt VA ★
Peter: b 8-21-1764 d 1832 m Elizabeth Caldwell Pvt NY

DAVIDS,
William: b 11-6-1707 d 9-11/12-1787 m Petronella Storm CS NY

DAVIDSON, (includes DAVISON, DAVISSON)
Alexander: b 1-6-1751 d 1840 m (1) — Mears (2)Elizabeth Clark Pvt MA
Alexander: b *a.* 1755 d 1818 m Henrietta Clayton Capt NC
Asa: b 9-1-1736 d 1- -1824 m Sarah Pride Pvt CT
Benjamin: b 9-21-1756 d 8-23-1815 m Mary King Pvt MA
Benjamin: b 10-19-1761 d 2-16-1813 m Roxy Norton Matr MA
Benjamin: b 1743 d 1825 m Anne — Pvt NC
Daniel: bpt 6-4-1734 d *p.* 1798 m Margaret Searls Pvt CT
Daniel: b 1749 d 1- -1830 m Catharine Davis Pvt CT
Daniel, Sr.: b 1733 d 6-6-1828 m (1)Abigail Sumner (2)Martha Harrington Sgt MA ★
Daniel, Jr.: b 1764 d 1854 m Elizabeth Thayer Nelson Cpl MA ★
Daniel: b 1748 d 1819 m Prudence Izard Maj VA
David: b 1751 d 2- -1836 m Agnes Moore Sgt VA
David: b 1764 d 12-15-1822 m Maza Phillios Pvt VA ★
Douglas: b 11-3-1746 d 1-1-1825 m Aseneth Ives Pvt CT
Edward: b 1750 d 8- -1827 m (1)Eliza Stevenson (2)Elizabeth Ikes Pvt VA
Elias: b 1736 d *a.* 4-23-1806 m Agnes McDowell Capt PA
Ezra: b 8-12-1765 d 4-29-1834 m Diadamia Smith Matr CT
Francis: b 3- -1752 d 2-16-1827 m (1)Rebecca Richardson (2)Janet Eayers Pvt MA
George: b 1722 d 3-11-1801 m (1)Susanna Christie (2)Mary McCartney PS NY
George: b *c.* 1735 d 1811 m (1)Sarah Atkins (2)Barzilla Atkins Maj PS NC
George: b 8-27-1738 d 7-10-1826 m Mary Woods Lt VA
Giles: b 1762 d 1848 m X Sol VA ★
Hezekiah: b *a.* 1757 d 1794 m Ann — Ens QM VA
Hugh: b 1752 d *p.* 4-6-1814 m Catherine McDowell PS LCol PA
Isaac: b *c.* 1746 d 10- -1847 m Isabella Anderson OrdlSgt VA ★
James: b 8-24-1737 d 4-6-1826 m Ann Hine Sgt CT
James: b 11-11-1751 d 1819 m Betsey — Pvt PS DE
James: b 11-5-1760 d 11-28-1841 m Amelia Reed Pvt MD
James: b 1-9-1745/46 d *p.* 1809 m (1)Lydia Wetherbe (2)Hannah Loomis Pvt MA
James: b 1-12-1752 d 7-3-1837 m (1)Hannah Hemphill (2)Mrs. — Loomis 1Sgt NH
James: b 5-9-1730 d 9-10-1793 m Elinor Stinson Wgm NJ
James: b 1734 d 1780 m Elizabeth Anderson Pvt NJ
James: b 1742 d 1836 m Jane Hudson Pvt PA
Jesse: b 10-19-1758 d 8-18-1806 m Mary Dinsmore Pvt NH
John: b 11-20-1763 d 9-17-1842 m Lydia Wood Pvt CT'MA ★
John: b 1733 d 1788 m Elizabeth — Lt MD
John: b — d 1735 m X Pvt MA
John: b 8-10-1720 d 9-27-1799 m Sarah McNutt PS NH
John: b 1750 d 1818-22 m Lydia — Pvt NJ
John: b 11-18-1758 d 9-10-1834 m Elizabeth Fitchet Pvt NY ★
John: b 12-15-1735 d 1-10-1832 m Violet Winslow Wilson Maj PS NC
John: b 2-15-1750 d 2-28-1825 m (1)Ruth Clement (2)Frances Bateman Pvt NC
John: b 3-15-1752 d 1-19-1797 m Margaret Wilson Pvt NC
John: b 10-4-1764 d *p.* 9-13-1845 m Martha (Davidson) Pvt NC ★
John: b *c.* 1715 d *p.* 1790 m Widow Morrison PS Pack-Horse Master NC

DAVIDSON, contd.
John: b 1743 d 3-8-1823 m Tacy Laughlin Ens PA
John: b 1742 d 1-6-1808 m Sarah Armstrong Pvt PA
John: b c. 1725 d 1783 m Martha Draper Sol CS VA
John: b 10-20-1757 d 1835 m Mary Thompson Pvt VA ★
John Andrew: b 1746 d 3-4-1782 m Ann Copeland Capt MD
Joseph: bpt 5-11-1743 d — m X Lt of Guards CT
Joseph: b 12-26-1730 d 8-31-1808 m Lydia Goodell Pvt CT
Joseph: b 1750 d 1846 m Winifred May Pvt GA
Joseph: b c. 1725 d p. 9-15-1795 m Sarah — Pvt NC
Joseph: b 1-9-1754 d 5-13-1842 m (1)Margaret Brown (2)Margaret Robinson Pvt PA
Joseph: b 7-9-1754 d p. 1810 m Mary Burns Pvt VA
Joseph: b 1759 d 1851 m Matilda Patton Pvt VA
Joshua: b 1753 d 8-18-1844 m Mary Green Ens PA ★
Josiah: b 12-1-1743 d 9-9-1825 m (2)Nancy Ann Williams Pvt VA
Josiah: b 10-15-1759 d 9-7-1838 m Martha — Pvt Spy VA ★
Nathaniel: b 5-2-1750 d 1793 m Lydia Eaton Pvt NH
Patrick: b c. 1754 d c. 12-10-1816 m Martha Darro Pvt PA
Paul: b c. 1760 d 2-19-1805 m Sarah Gould Fif CT W★
Peter: b 5-15-1739 d 5-4-1800 m (1)Abigail Woodward (2)Mrs Susannah Weaver Lt CT
Robert: b 1755 d 12-17-1823 m Nancy DeMott Smn CT
Samuel: b 1736 d 1784 m Mary Smith Capt NC
Samuel: b 10-2-1738 d p. 1782 m Catharine Ferguson Capt Commo PA
Samuel: b 1748 d 6-11-1803 m Margery Ellen Thompson Capt PA
Thomas: b 1727 d 4-11-1813 m Anna Wright PS NH
William: b c. 1755 d a. 11-21-1805 m Mary Pennington PS MD
William: b 4-1-1758 d 12-23-1832 m Cathrine Holman Pvt NJ W★
William: b 10- -1736 d 5-16-1814 m Margaret McConnel Capt NC
William: b 7- -1760 d 7-29-1831 m (1)Sarah Oldon (2)Catherine Beaver Sgt PA ★
William: b 11-20-1747 d 11-16-1811 m (1)Rosanna Hutchinson (2)Barbara McDowell Pvt PA
William: b 1746 d 4-15-1833 m Elizabeth — Lt VA
William: b 1753 d 1849 m — Childreth Sol NC
William Lee: b 1746 d 2-1-1781 m Mary Brevard BGen NC

DAVIE, (includes DAVEY, DAVY)
Gabriel: b c. 1735 d p. 10-5-1791 m Elizabeth Bumpass Pvt PS NC
Robert: b 1757/58 d 10-7-1846 m (1)Miss — Wellborn (2)Levice Wellborn Sol NC
Thomas: b c. 1745 d 8-6-1777 m Mary — Pvt NY
William: b c. 1763 d p. 9-11-1813 m Margaret Jones Pvt NC
William Richardson: b 6-20-1756 d 11-18-1820 m Sarah Jones Col PS NC

DAVIS, (includes DAVES, DAVIES)
Aaron: b 7- -1729 d p. 1780 m Hannah Pond Pvt MA
Aaron: b 5-19-1737 d 1-5-1812 m Mary Knapp Pvt MA
Aaron: b 5-31-1741 d 5-29-1812 m Hannah Richards Pvt MA
Aaron: b 9-9-1757 d 3-1-1852 m Prudence Brightman Pvt MA
Aaron: b 4-26-1709 d 7-29-1777 m Mary Perrin PS MA
Aaron: b 1723 d 1-26-1803 m Janet Rhea Wgn NJ
Aaron: b 4- -1757 d 9- -1824 m Sarah Chase Cpl NH
Aaron: b 3-6-1759 d p. 1801 m Dorcas Larkin Pvt RI
Abel: b 12-25-1755 d 7-27-1841 m Lavinia Hosmer MM MA
Abel: b 7-26-1755 d 9-30-1839 m Sarah — Pvt VT ★
Abner: b 2-4-1754 d 12-25-1841 m Esther Young Pvt NH ★
Abraham: b — d 1816 m Mary Smith Pvt CT
Absolom: b c. 1730 d 1807 m X Pvt SC
Absolom: b c. 1744 d p. 1816 m Nancy — PS NC
Alexander: b 1-5-1749 d c. 1839 m Abigail Gregory Pvt MA
Alpheus: b 1747 d 8-20-1818 m Thankful Johnson Ens NY
Amasa: b 8-17-1744 d 1-30-1825 m Sarah Whitney QM PS MA
Amos: b 5-12-1741 d 3-20-1815 m Alice Merzervy Cpl MA
Amos: b 5-24-1752 d 12-3-1834 m Lucy Weston Cpl MA
Amos: b 9-2-1732 d 8-1-1794 m Sarah Metcalf Pvt NH
Amos: b 9-6-1757 d 3-3-1840 m Mary Album Capt SC
Andrew: b 5-9-1762 d 1853 m Mary Ketcham Pvt NY
Andrew: b 12-24-1756 d p. 1832 m Elizabeth Roe Pvt NC SC ★
Andries: b 12-22-1759 d 12-1-1850 m Sarah Bogart Pvt NY ★
Ann Simpson: b 12-29-1764 d 6-6-1851 m John Davis PS PA
Aquila: b 6-27-1760 d 2-27-1835 m Abigail Stevens Pvt NH
Aquilla: b 1756 d 8-23-1832 m Isabell Briggs Pvt VA ★
Archabald: b 4-4-1762 d 2-22-1821 m Elizabeth Hilliard Drm NC
Archibald: b a. 1754 d 1808 m (2)Nancy — Pvt NC
Asa: b 10-17-1743 d 7- -1798 m Mary Smith Pvt MA
Asa: b 10-6-1757 d p. 1806 m Frances Lipscomb Pvt VA
Avery: b 8-20-1757 d 2-25-1826 m Amy Lillibridge Pvt CT
Azariah: b 2-12-1756 d 9-22-1838/39 m (1)Elsie Van Meter (2)Mary Harrington Smith Ens PA
Barnabas: b 2-9-1750 d 11-12-1830 m Hannah Wright Cpl CT
Barnabas: b 9-14-1733 d 8- -1775 m (1)Ruth Gilson (2)Olive Farwell Pvt MA
Bartholomew: b -c. 1733 d p. 1800 m Jane Fowler Pvt PS PA
Bela: b 4-12-1753 d 10- -1800 m Ruth Rugg Pvt MA
Benajah: b 6-27-1734 d p. 8-10-1782 m Elizabeth Snow Pvt MA
Benajor: b 1751 d 8-26-1816 m Welthan Slocum Sgt RI ★
Benjamin: b 9-1-1728 d 1814 m Lydia Nichols Sol MA
Benjamin: b 3-18-1759 d 1-8-1837 m Anna Parker Pvt MA ★

Benjamin: b 4-8-1744 d 8-28-1823 m Annah Farnsworth Ens CS NH
Benjamin: b 1724 d 11-28-1822 m (1)Eunice — (2)Mrs Susannah Fisk Pvt NH
Benjamin: b 1749 d 8-28-1823 m (1)Anna Green Farnsworth (2)— (3)Brigget Robbins PS NH
Benjamin: b a. 1760 d 1816 m Elizabeth Daniel Pvt NC W★
Benjamin: b c. 1755 d p. 10-26-1824 m Priscilla Jones Sol NC
Benjamin: b 12-24-1731 d 1802 m Rebecca — PS Lt NC
Benjamin: b a. 1750 d 1813 m X CS NC
Benjamin: b 3-15-1742 d 8-2-1814 m Catherine Pugh Pvt PA
Benjamin: b1730 d a. 10-8-1792 m Phebe Cooper PS RI
Benjamin: b 7-17-1719 d 9-27-1797 m Rachel Port PS CS SC
Benjamin: b 1735 d a. 7-24-1797 m Mary Bush Pvt VA
Benjamin Franklin: b 1735 d 1817 m Tabiatha — Pvt VA
Caleb: b 1717 d 10-12-1780 m Ruth Bruen Pvt NJ
Caleb: b 1748 d 7-26-1826 m Deborah Tooker Pvt NY
Chapman: b 1-1-1759 d 8-24-1837 m (2)Elisabeth Corwin (3)Lydia — Pvt NY ★
Charles: b c. 1740 d 2-1-1807 m (1)Sarah Moreland (2)Anne Dent Pvt MD ★
Charles: b 1758 d 2-1-1807 m (1)Rosannah Ellis (2)Susannah Ragland Sol VA
Chesley: b c. 1763 d p. 8-6-1827 m X Sol SC
Clement: b 3-27-1755 d 10-29-1838 m Elizabeth Fleming Pvt SC
Cornelius: b c. 1750 d 8- -1782 m Eleanor — PS KY
Daniel: b 10-12-1742 d 11-4-1807 m Elizabeth Whittemore Capt CT
Daniel: b 2-1-1718 d 6-24-1786 m (1)Tamar Towne (2)Elizabeth Shurtleif CS CT
Daniel: b 7-8-1749 d 12-17-1816 m Rebecca White Capt MA
Daniel: b 4-28-1757 d 12-27-1830 m Ruth Head Pvt MA
Daniel: b 9-28-1713 d 4-22-1799 m (1)Mahitable Lothrop (2)Mehitable Sturgis PS CS MA
Daniel: b 6-18-1740 d 12-1-1826 m Jenica Westbrook Pvt NJ
Daniel: b 1-2-1742/43 d 12-6-1805 m (1)Hannah Foster (2)Susanna Leake Pvt NJ
Daniel: b a. 1726 d 5-5-1775/6-2-1777 m (1)Joanna — (2)Abigail Overton PS NY
Daniel: b 12-25-1746 d 11- -1846-48 m Sarah Elizabeth Albright Pvt PA
Daniel: b 1734 d 11-30-1826 m Mary — Pvt VT
Daniel: b a. 1755 d p. 1782 m Miss — Raglan Pvt VA
Daniel: b 2-11-1759 d 1838 m Betsy Thompson Pvt VA ★
David: b 3-18-1759 d 8-27-1837 m Olive Mayhew Pvt MA
David: b 1-30-1739 d 2-11-1824 m (1)Lucy Bucknam (2)Abigail Brown PS MA
David: b 11-3-1760 d 7-1-1844 m Noami Dunn Pvt NJ
David: b 10-31-1730 d 9-7-1806 m Martha Coles Wgm PS NJ
David: b 5-6-1737 d 3-10-1825 m Anna Norton Sgt NY
David: b 10-20-1729 d — m Rebecca Pennington Pvt PA
David: b 4-22-1749 d 11-29-1822 m (1)Eleanor Brooke (2)Mrs Elizabeth Garrett Brooke Pvt PA
David: b 7- -1756 d 10-16-1798 m Rebecca Keziah Godfrey 1Lt SC
David: b 6-21-1748 d p. 1796 m Eleanor — Cpl VT
David: b c. 1725 d p. 12-24-1789 m Margaret — Pvt VA
David Ward: b 9-10-1762 d 8-19-1837 m Elizabeth Brandenburg Sol MD
Devotion, Sr.: b c. 1725 d 1800 m X PS NC
Dolphin: b 1759 d 11-8-1819 m Ann Stevenson Pvt NC
Dudley: b 1764 d 9-14-1826 m Mercy Greenwood Cpl MA ★
Ebenezer: b 1753 d 11-14-1799 m Mehitable Griffin LCol MA
Ebenezer: b 2-14-1765 d 4-20-1818 m Mary Paine Pvt MA
Ebenezer: b 9-18-1737 d 8-12-1816 m (1)Deborah Davis (2)Mrs Sarah Allen (3)Mrs Hannah Ammidon PS MA
Edmund: b 7-8-1759 d 6-22-1832 m Eunice Hubbard Pvt MA
Edward: b c. 1745 d 1786-90 m Rebecca Lloyd PS GA
Edward, Sr.: b 1-23-1714 d 8-30-1784 m Abigail (Haynes) Learned PS MA
Edward, Jr.: b 9-5-1739 d 10-3-1796 m (1)Elizabeth — (2)Mrs Abigail Watson CS Pvt MA
Edward: b — d p. 1797 m Mary — Sol VA
Eleazer: b 1725 d p. 1776 m Sarah Ward Pvt MA
Eleazer: b 5-30-1734 d 3-13-1819 m Rebecca Putnam Lt MA
Eleazer: b 1-23-1742 d p. 1799 m Sarah Cook CS NH
Eli: b 10- -1760 d 12-12-1829 m Lucy Sims Mus VA
Eliakim: b c. 1745 d 1776 m Hannah Benedict PS CT
Eliakim: b 3-28-1761 d p. 5-7-1833 m Dorothy Hunt Pvt MA ★
Elias: b 3-10-1742/43 d c. 1790 m Phebe Woodman Capt MA
Elias: b 12-18-1763 d 6-17-1851 m Freelove — Pvt NY
Elijah: b a. 1731 d 9-10-1778 m Lydia V. Barns Pvt MA
Elijah: b 1726 d 1802 m Mary — PS NY
Elijah: b 10-2-1762 d 6-20-1823 m Desire Little Pvt PA
Elijah: b 7-27-1760 d 6-29-1829 m Mary G. Garrettson Dr PA
Eliphalet: b 9-27-1756 d 9-7-1804 m Hannah Somes Drm Pvt MA
Elisha: b 12-20-1759 d 9-1-1848 m Elizabeth Fiske Pvt CT ★
Elisha: b 1741 d 1-23-1816 m Rebecca Weyman Matr MA
Elisha: b 2-16-1722 d 10-22-1796 m Mary Harris PS MA
Elnathan: b 12-13-1735 d 12-14-1802 m Susannah Bond PS NJ
Enoch: b 2-14-1740 d 3- -1837 m Elizabeth Hawkins Capt NC
Enos: b 1761 d 2-26-1841 m Mary — Pvt MD ★
Ephraim: b 1-2-1737 d 11-18-1813 m Sarah Farnsworth Capt MA
Ephraim: b c. 1760 d 1825 m Elizabeth Holman Sol NC

Ezekiel: b 6-8-1753 d 2-18-1820 m Susanna Chaffin Sgt MA W★
Ezra, Jr.: b 2-27-1745 d 1-7-1832 m Sarah Mayo Sgt MA
Ezra: b 3-25-1755 d 9-28-1835 m Elizabeth Lord Pvt NY ★
Francis, Sr.: b 10-26-1723 d 11-26-1784 m Elizabeth Ferrin PS NH
Francis, Jr.: b 5-7-1757 d 10-30-1840 m Phelina Thurber Pvt NH ★
Francis: b 1756 d 1847 m Tabitha DeVane Capt. SC ★
Francis: b 1761 d 1800 m Abigail Boatright Pvt SC
Francis: b c. 1760 d a. 6-2-1818 m Mildred Dollins Pvt VA ★
Frederick: b 9-21-1701 d 1778 m Margerie VanLeuven PS NY
Frederick: b 9-22-1748 d 10-17-1831 m Fanny Grieves Pvt NC
Gabriel: b 1728 d 1813 m Jean Douglas PS PA
Gardner: b c. 1763 d p. 1797 m Lydia — Pvt MA
George: b 1736 d 1-31-1807 m Hannah — Sol NC
George: b c. 1745 d 3-3-1803 m Sarah Trickey Pvt PA
George: b 12- -1762 d 3-1839 m Ann Eakin Pvt NC
Gideon,: b 12-15-1748 d 7-2-1834 m Martha Patten Cpl NH
Goldsmith: b 1755 d 1826 m Elizabeth — Pvt NY
Henry: b 11-17-1758 d 2-9-1827 m Mary Tuttle Pvt NH
Henry: b c. 1735 d 1804 m Jean Bryan 1Lt VA
Henry Landon: b c. 1745 d p. 1795 m (1)Anne Clayton (2)Lucy (Clayton) Whiting Manson PS VA
Hezekiah: b 1733 d p. 1790 m Elizabeth Jennifer Pvt MD
Hezekiah: b 11-22-1747 d 12-27-1837 m Anna Schenck Lt PA
Hugh: b 11- -1755 d 2-26-1843 m Jennie Selectman Sgt VA ★
Increase: b 3-22-1761 d 11-28-1830 m Rachel Dana Pvt MA W★
Isaac: b 2-23-1745 d 4-19-1775 m Hannah Brown Capt MA
Isaac: b 1749 d 1826 m Anna Brigham 1Lt MA
Isaac: b 11-15-1752 d 8-17-1820 m Rachel Adams Pvt MA
Isaac: b 3-26-1758 d 11-11-1846 m Dorcas Chandler Pvt MA
Isaac: b 3-27-1728 d 1808 m Keturah Woodward Pvt NH
Isaac: b 9-25-1743 d 1816 m Mary Anna David Pvt NJ
Isaac: b 1724 d 11-30-1796 m Sarah — Wgn NJ
Isaac: b 10-4-1741 d 4-20-1814 m Hannah Roe Lt NY
Isaac: b 1-11-1740 d 1789 m Molsey Dunbar Sol NC
Isaac: b c. 1712 d 1778 m Elizabeth Bartholomew CS PA
Isaac, Sr.: b 1730 d 8-20-1805 m Elizabeth Winston Vol PS CS VA
Isaac, Jr.: b 1732 d p. 1805 m Harriet Garth PS VA
Isaac, 3rd: b 6-9-1754 d 8-8-1835 m Elizabeth Kirtley Capt VA ★
Isaac: b 1753 d c. 1800 m Winnifred — Pvt VA
Isaiah: b 10-18-1756 d 10-26-1823 m Sophia Koplin Capt PA
Isham: b 1-6-1758 d 12-30-1835 m Mrs Winifred Woodward Sgt SC ★
Isom: b c. 1761 d 1837 m Elizabeth Ingram Pvt SC
Israel: b c. 1730 d p. 1783 m Sarah McFarland Capt CS ME
Israel, Jr.: b 6- -1743 d 2-4-1811 m Rebeccah Hubbard Pvt MA
Israel: b 5-7-1744 d p. 1-21-1811 m (1)Elizabeth Wicks (2)Mary Wicks PS NY
Jacob: b 9-14-1741 d 9-14-1814 m Rebecca (Baker) Col MA
Jacob: b 9-17-1742 d 7-1-1809 m Dorothy Baker Lt MA
Jacob: b 9-9-1758 d 12-24-1843 m Deborah Tuttle Cpl NH
Jacob: b 2-6-1758 d 2-22-1843 m Mary Littell Pvt NJ ★
Jacob, Sr.: b 1748 d 7-17-1793 m Mary — Chp NJ
Jacob, Jr.: b 1769 d 12- -1827 m (1)Prudence Maxson (2)Sarah Hoffman Tms NJ
Jacobus: bpt 2-26-1744 d a. 5-19-1826 m Elizabeth Bosch Pvt NY
James, Sr.: b 5-28-1726 d 4-4-1814 m Mary Bailey Pvt CT
James, Jr.: b 3-25-1765 d 3-12-1852 m Ruth Griswold Pvt CT ★
James: b 6-2-1727 d 5-9-1796 m Jean Bacon Capt MA
James: b 7-17-1734 d 9-15-1821 m (1)Mary Wheeler (2)Mrs Abigail Wheaton Capt MA
James: b 12-27-1742 d 1812 m Irene Ticknor Lt MA
James: b 2-9-1746 d 3-12-1828 m Amy Haskins Pvt MA
James: b 4-27-1761 d 4-8-1835 m Chloe Wiley Pvt MA ★
James: b c. 1755 d 1- -1803 m (1)Susannah Chase (2)Lydia Brown Matr Pvt MA
James: b 1761 d 6-26-1827 m Mary Taylor Pvt NJ
James: b 1732 d 10-19-1802 m Johanna Roe 2Lt NY
James: b 3-3-1741 d 1791 m X Pvt Drm Fif NC
James: b 1743 d c. 1808 m (1)Margaret — (2) Jane — Pvt NC
James, Jr.: b 1767 d 1854 m Mary Winnford Sol NC
James: b 1-10-1758 d 4-2-1805 m Mary Meng 1Lt PA
James: b 1761 d 9-10-1850 m Keziah Phillips Sol PA
James: b 12-16-1747 d 1-5-1818 m Susannah Fryson 2Lt SC
James: b 8-28-1736 d 12- -1819 m Sarah Landlow Capt PS VA
James: b 1735 d 1808 m (1)Mrs Frances (Berry) Dobbins (2)Mrs Cathrine (Muse) Shropshire Lt PS VA
James: b 6-19-1758 d 7-12-1816 m Martha Reid 2Lt VA
James: b 1750 d p. 1782 m Elizabeth Edwards Pvt VA
James: b 4- -1755 d 3-29-1797 m — Ferguson Pvt VA
James: b 7-8-1761 d 1843 m X Pvt VA
James: b 1750 d 1823 m Naomi — Cmsry VA
James: b 1736 d 1816 m Mary McBride CS VA
James: b c. 1752 d p. 1782 m Margaret Dozier PS KY
James Hovey: b 7-27-1751 d 1-3-1797 m Mary Streeter Pvt MA
Jehu: b 6-25-1745 d p. 1791 m (1)Rhoda Lewis (2)Melissa Douglas CS DE
Jenifer: b — d 1825 m Ann Adams Pvt MD
Jesse: b 1754 d p. 1808 m Nancy Moran Pvt MD
Jesse: b 1754 d 1812 m Sarah — Pvt MD
Jesse: b 7-16-1757 d 1792 m (1)Elizabeth Wilson (2)Hannah Crutis Pvt MA
Jesse: b 11-14-1758 d 11-28-1830 m Sarah Stewart Pvt MA
Jesse: b 1764 d 4-1-1842 m Sarah Lawrence Pvt NH
Jesse: b c. 1755 d 10-23-1818 m Nancy Milton Capt VA W★

Jesse: b 1762 d 11-12-1857 m Elizabeth Hougham Pvt VA ★
Job: b 2-28-1759 d 1808 m (2)Sarah Johnson Pvt CT
Joel: b 7-31-1755 d 3-7-1841 m Chary — MM Pvt MA ★
Joel: b 10-1-1763 d 2-12-1841 m Rebecca Coats Pvt NC ★
John: b 4-12-1764 d 10-19-1840 m Mary Deming Pvt CT
John: b 3-5-1749 d 11-23-1832 m (1)Esther Austin (2)Anne Bissel (3)Polly — Pvt CT
John: b 9-28-1755 d 11-27-1848 m Mehitable Thomas PS CT
John: b 1740 d 1780/81 m Elizabeth Boyer Pvt DE
John: b 7-22-1751 d 1841 m Ann Furbee Pvt DE
John: b 1761 d 1-15-1840 m Elizabeth — Sol GA
John: b 1757 d 8-29-1810 m Mary Hodge Capt MD
John: b c. 1745 d 1789 m Clear Tower 2Lt MD
John: b 3-30-1732 d 11-17-1815 m Hannah Cross Capt MA
John: b 1-4-1734 d 12-19-1794 m Johanna Hicks 1Lt MA
John: b 1737 d 1790 m Sarah Bradford 1Lt ME
John: b 6-1-1735 d 5- -1808 m Hulda Thayer Sgt MA
John, Jr.: b 1759 d 2-8-1827 m Anne Holden Pvt MA ★
John: b 7-6-1754 d 10-29-1798 m Sarah Cutter Pvt MA
John: b c. 1758-60 d 2-20-1838 m Susanna Hatch Pvt MA
John: b 1761 d 8-26-1844 m (1)Molly Harper (2)Patience Irish Pvt MA
John: b — d p. 1- -1782 m — Drm Maj MA ★
John: b 1759 d 2-11-1831 m Elizabeth Mar Capt NH
John: b c. 1740 d p. 1797 m Abigail — PS NH
John: b 1756 d 2-12-1842 m Debora Roseberry Pvt NJ ★
John: b — d 1-10-1782 m Sarah Parsons Maj NY
John: b 1739 d 6-15-1817 m (1)Sarah Beebe (2)Dorcas (Ackerman) Capt NY
John: b 1721 d 7-15-1816 m — 1Lt NY
John: b 1760 d 1821 m Ketura Taylor Sgt NY
John, Sr.: b 1723-28 d a. 1-7-1800 m Edi Loree Pvt NY
John, Jr.: b 12-17-1743 d 3-11-1801 m Eleanor Mather Pvt NY
John: b 4-26-1740 d 12-13-1841 m Eleanor Ferris Pvt NY
John: b 10-18-1750 d 12-10-1803 m Elsie Terwiliger Pvt NY
John: b 1740/41 d 5- -1778 m Mary Henderson Pvt NC
John: b 1759 d 1827 m Sinah — Pvt NC
John: b 1759 d 1818 m Nancy Patterson Pvt NC
John: b 1759 d 1-5-1859 m Polly Taylor Pvt NC ★
John: b 1755 d 11-9-1831 m Mourning Pilkinton Pvt NC W★
John: b 8-19-1757/58 d 5-31-1844 m X Pvt Wgn NC ★
John: b 2-28-1753 d 7-11-1827 m (1)Ann Morton (2)Joanna McLean Capt PA
John: b 10-7-1732 d 1785-1804 m Mary Cornog Lt PA
John: b 10-8-1746 d 4-6-1810 m Lydia Keimer Adj PA
John: b 8-25-1764 d 2-27-1839 m Mary McGunneigle PS PA
John: b 9-6-1760 d 1-25-1833 m Ann Simpson Ens PA
John: b 12-13-1745 d 2-13-1816 m Ann Evans Dr PA
John: b 1754 d 6-8-1830 m Margaret — Pvt PA ★
John: b c. 1750 d a. 1-15-1802 m Katherine Foster Pvt PA
John: b 1757 d 1823 m Catharine Lewis Pvt PA
John: b 9-7-1760 d 3-20-1823 m Ellisif de Haas Pvt PA
John: b 9-1-1762 d 4-28-1847 m Margaret Jones Pvt Grd PA
John: b 5-21-1756 d 5-1-1846 m (1)Bathsheba Ellis (2)Theady Scarborough Maj RI★
John: b 1754 d 1791-1800 m Mary White Sgt SC
John: b 3-3-1746 d 5- -1780 m Jane Barkley PS SC
John: b 10-14-1743 d 1810 m (1)Mary Allison (2)Mrs Mary Curry Capt VA
John, Sr.: b a. 1747 d 1780 m — (Frost) McCormick Pvt VA
John: b 2-22-1730 d 10-18-1823 m Mary Glazebrook Sol VA
John: b c. 1749 d 3- -1823 m Mary Wigginton Sol VA
John: b c. 1750 d 4- -1800 m Jane Clendenin Pvt PS VA
John: b c. 1750 d 1797 m Mary Hutsell Pvt VA
John: b 7-2-1754 d 1843 m Sallie — Pvt VA ★
John: b 12-12-1758 d 9-30-1841 m Mornin Guffey Pvt VA ★
John: b c. 1760 d 1820 m Elizabeth — Pvt VA
John: b 3-19-1755 d 3-19-1834 m Margaret Barton Sol VA
John: b 8-19-1758 d 2-24-1842 m (1)Jane — (2)Nancy Lane Sol VA
John Dabney: b 1-20-1743 d 1817 m Ann Ragland Tinsley Sgt VA
John L.: b 1765 d 1844 m (1)Mary Edgerton (2)Elizabeth — Pvt NC ★
John Lane: b 11-8-1757 d 12-29-1839 m Susannah Lusher Pvt MA ★
John Marion: b 10-9-1750 d 1-25-1818 m Jemima Barnhill Sol Wgn VA
John Phelps: b 1-29-1760 d 11-23-1832 m Polly Brooks Pvt MA W★
Jonathan: b 4-6-1732 d p. 1808 m Rebecca Parker Sol CT
Jonathan: b 9-21-1751 d 3-31-1832 m Sarah Smith Pvt MA
Jonathan: b 2-4-1724 d 4-5-1801 m Hannah Stevenson PS NH
Jonathan: b 7-7-1743 d 7-23-1785 m Margaret Bond Pvt NJ
Jonathan: b c. 1730 d c. 1818 m Lucy Gibbs Sol VA
Joseph: b 2-5-1723 d p. 1786 m Lucretia Strickland Pvt CT
Joseph: b 4-6-1761 d 9-16-1831 m Rebecca Dent Pvt MD
Joseph: b 3-7-1725 d p. 1790 m Sarah Davis Pvt MA
Joseph: b 5-20-1738 d p. 1792 m (1)Elizabeth Foster (2)Sarah Campbell Pvt MA
Joseph: b 3-26-1747 d 8- -1803 m Hannah Akers Pvt MA
Joseph: b 12-13-1761 d 6-10-1847 m Elizabeth — Pvt MA ★
Joseph: b 4-11-1761 d 2-20-1821 m Mercy M Hammond Pvt MA
Joseph: b 11-24-1753 d 6-5-1827 m (1)Abby Farrand (2)Anna Crane Wgm NJ
Joseph: b c. 1750 d 1840 m Sarah — Pvt NJ
Joseph: b 10-24-1763 d 5-17-1821 m Sylvia Treat Pvt NY
Joseph: b 3-22-1702 d 9-26-1790 m Elizabeth Parshall PS NY
Joseph: b c. 1733 d 1792 m Mary Shepard Pvt NC

DAVIS, contd.

Joseph: b 1759 d *p.* 1-26-1820 m Susannah Stanton Pvt NC
Joseph: b 1-12-1761 d *p.* 1810 m Hannah Doane Pvt NY
Joseph: b 1758 d 1811 m Sarah Shock Pvt PA
Joseph: b 1760 d 12-21-1832 m Azubah Morton Mus RI
Joseph: b 1760 d 11-13-1833 m Annie Keene Lt SC ★
Joseph: b 8-4-1745 d 9-6-1795 m Jean Hamilton 2Lt VA
Joshua: b 12-28-1743 d 12-3-1806 m Betsey Parker 2Lt MA
Joshua: b 3-5-1730 d 9-22-1789 m Elizabeth Waters Pvt MA
Joshua: b — d — m Betsey Cole Pvt MA
Joshua, Sr.: b 10-20-1714 d 1-18-1777 m Hannah Jaquith PS MA
Joshua, Jr.: b 10-25-1743 d 2-11-1792 m (1)Betty Blood (2)Elizabeth
 — (3)Catherine Simpkins Pvt MA
Joshua: b 5-29-1744 d 10-16-1840 m Dorothy Wheeler Pvt NH
Joshua: b 9-15-1760 d 10-23-1839 m Jemima La Boiteaux Pvt NJ ★
Joshua: b 5-19-1734 d 9-14-1806 m Azubah Tusten Pvt PS NY
Joshua: b 4-5-1757 d 1-24-1833 m Abigail Redfield Pvt NY ★
Joshua: b *c.* 1755 d 1828 m Sarah Lincoln Pvt PA
Joshua: b 1765 d 1842 m Hannah Walton PS PA
Joshua: b 11-10-1742 d 9-12-1829 m (2)Sybil Dean Maj RI
Josiah: b 4-25-1738 d 2-8-1824 m (1)Thankful Matthews (2)Thankful
 Gorham (3)Mrs Martha Hill Lt MA
Josiah: b 1758 d 4-18-1848 m (1)Meriam Isbell (2)Annis — Pvt CT ★
Josiah: b 3-10-1761 d *p.* 1790 m Louisa Pierce Fif CT
Josiah: b 7-9-1713 d 1808 m Elizabeth Raymond Pvt MA
Josiah: b 3-20-1750 d 5-26-1834 m Mehitable Littlefield Pvt MA
Josiah: b 8-24-1753 d 12-31-1837 m Sarah Sawtelle Pvt MA ★
Josiah: b 6-14-1755 d 1798 m Sarah Billings Pvt MA
Josiah: b 10-3-1754 d 9-8-1794 m Susannah MacDonald Pvt MA
Josiah: b 5-29-1750 d 2-17-1815 m Abigail Hubbard Pvt NH
Josiah: b *c.* 1750 d *p.* 1820 m Priscilla Robinson CaptLt PA
Kitteridge: b 7-14-1760 d 2-27-1840 m Lucy Ann — Pvt MA ★
Lathrop: b 7-17-1756 d 4-16-1820 m Mary Swift Sgt CT ★
Lemuel: b 2-8-1755 d 4-4-1826 m Bethiah Lord Pvt NY
Levi: b 9-13-1755 d 1-31-1810 m Elizabeth Rammage Pvt MD
Levi: b 11-11-1752 d 7-5-1807 m Deborah Moore Lt MA
Levi: b 1760 d 1848 m Mrs Mary Holiday Pvt PS VT
Lewis C.: b 1756 d 2-3-1835 m (1)Sarah Anderson Pvt VA ★
Llewellyn: b 1755 d 6- -1809 m Martha Jones Lt VA
Llewellyn: b 5-1-1759 d 7-23-1803 m Rebekah Shannon Ens PA
Lodowick: b 2- -1764 d 8-13-1841 m Dolly Ann — Pvt MD ★
Margaret Dozier: b *c.* 1754 d *p.* 1782 m James Davis PS KY
Marmaducke S.: b 3-11-1760 d 3-13-1855 m (2)Eleanor Wilson Pvt
 MD ★
Mathew: b 1736 d *p.* 1790 m Elizabeth — Pvt NC
Matthew: b 11-5-1752 d *a.* 2- -1829 m — Madre Pvt NC
Matthias: b 10-14-1760 d 12-12-1849 m Frances Havens Pvt NY
Melatiah, Sr.: b 10-19-1716 d 5-9-1795 m Jemima Dunham Lt MA
Melatiah: b 5-13-1750 d 10-15-1821 m Mary Cousins Davis Lt
 MA
Micajah: b *c.* 1760 d 3-4-1802 m Martha Richards Fif Pvt NC
Michael: b — d — m Sarah Libby Pvt MA
Moses: b 3-20-1741 d 6-2-1806 m Lydia Johnson Pvt MA
Moses: b 1761 d 4-22-1829 m Sarah Sawyer Pvt MA W★
Moses: b 4-29-1744 d 6-2-1823 m (?)Rebecca Sharp (?)Hannah
 Pierpont Pvt MA
Moses: b 9-23-1748 d 11-18-1824 m Sarah Rolfe PS CS MA
Moses: b *c.* 1750 d 2-15-1807 m Anna Folsom PS NH
Moses: b 4-10-1762 d 5-3-1839 m Rachel Custard Pvt PA W★
Mumford: b 4-23-1757 d *p.* 1793 m Almy Rhodes Lt RI
Myrick: b *a.* 1742 d 12-11-1781 m Martha Emanuel PS GA
Naomi: b 1-27-1762 d 8- -1844 m Thomas North PS PA
Nathan: b *c.* 1712 d *p.* 1787 m Eunice Tomlinson CS CT
Nathan: b 8-10-1735 d 1811-12 m Zerviah Smith PS CT
Nathan: b 5-1-1744 d *p.* 1790 m Mary Blood Lt MA
Nathan: b 5-23-1736 d *p.* 1784 m Mary Nurse Pvt MA
Nathan: b 1740 d 2-1-1823 m Abigail Rogers Pvt MA ★
Nathan: b 1758 d 1-1-1834/35 m Mary — Pvt NJ
Nathan: b 12-1-1752 d 10-15-1843 m Betsey Howell Pvt PS NY
Nathaniel: b 1721 d *a.* 11-1-1779 m Elizabeth Atkins Sol VA
Nathaniel: b 1754 d 6-10-1835 m Lydia Harwood Pvt VT
 (2)Esther Slack PS VT
Nathaniel, Jr.: b 11-3-1715 d 10-26-1802 m (1)Susanna Lane
 (2)Esther Slack PS VT
Nehemiah: b 1709 d *p.* 4-13-1789 m (1)Mary Manlove (2)Susannah
 Hart PS DE
Nehemiah: b 4-23-1728 d 3-10-1782 m Dorothy Heald Pvt PS MA
Nehemiah: b 4-22-1755 d 8-23-1823 m (1)Elizabeth Marston
 (2)Phebe Doane Pvt NH
Nehemiah: b *a.* 1755 d *p.* 1793 m Catherine Dudley Pvt MA
Nicholas: b 1750 d *p.* 8-20-1818 m Lucy — Lt VA
Nicholas: b *c.* 1690 d *p.* 1790 m (1)Judith (Fleming) Randolph
 (2)Catherine Whiting PS VA
Noah: b 4-29-1741 d 10-30-1828 m Anna Ladd Cpl CT
Obadiah: b *c.* 1720 d *p.* 11-16-1778 m X PS NY
Oliver, Sr.: b 4-16-1732 d 1-25-1803 m Mary Read Pvt MA
Oliver: b 8-12-1744 d 8-29-1812 m Annie Boyington Pvt MA
Owen: b *c.* 1740 d 1806 m Mary — Sol VA
Paul: b 11-10-1760 d 12-28-1826 m Rachel Chapin Pvt MA
Peter: b 11-14-1732 d 1-2-1781 m Mary Howe Lt MA
Peter: b — d — m Jane TenEyck Sgt NJ
Peter: b 2-3-1752 d 9-3-1849 m Theodosia Ferris Pvt NY
Philip: b 1753 d 8-8-1831 m X Pvt VA
Phineas: b 9-14-1754 d 7-2-1848 m Sybel — Pvt NY

Reuben: b 6-5-1748 d 1826 m Sarah Jewell PS NH
Reuben: b 5-17-1749 d 10-9-1781 m Sarah Learned Moore Capt MA
Reuben: b 6-3-1754 d 9-4-1830 m Elizabeth Tuttle Pvt MA
Richard: b — d — m Mary — Capt MD
Richard, Sr.: b 10-6-1734 d 7-24-1814 m (1)Frances Lewis
 (2)Margaret — PS NY
Richard: b 7-14-1751 d 4-6-1817 m Isabella Grant Pvt NC
Richard: b 8-17-1740 d *p.* 1794 m Lucy Hackney Lt VA
Richard: b 1746 d 10-8-1812 m Ann Chiles Sgt VA
Richard: b 6-15-1725 d 10-7-1809 m Sabina Harrison Pvt VA
Robert: b 1723 d *p.* 1-11-1763 m (1)Mary Toogood Collins (2)Ruth
 Gaither Pvt MD
Robert: b 1-24-1747 d 11-8-1798 m (1)Ann Ruggles (2)Mary
 Farrington Maj MA
Robert: b — d 11-13-1814 m Cornelia Blake Pvt MA
Robert: b 1-9-1733/34 d 8-6-1823 m Sarah Walker PS NH
Robert: b 12-22-1739 d *a.* 5-25-1799 m Margaret — Pvt NC
Robert: b *c.* 1750 d 7-8-1835 m (1)— McElroy (2)Lucinda Malone
 Pvt NC
Robert L.: b *a.* 1744 d 1818 m Sarah Dyer Hawes Capt VA
Robert: b 1724 d 1816 m Mary Watson Ens VA
Robert: b 1752 d 9-20-1804 m Nancy Agnes Caldwell Sol VA
Samson: b 1739 d 1809 m Margaret Ploeg Sgt NY
Samuel: b 1738 d 1787 m Mary — Pvt CT
Samuel: b 2-28-1759 d 4-11-1826 m Lucy Dewey Pvt CT
Samuel: b 1756 d 7-4-1824 m Jane (Cook) Simpson Sol GA
Samuel: b 3-17-1768 d 10-15-1834 m Margaret Barrett Drm Fif MD
Samuel: b 3-5-1746 d 1798 m Rebecca Williams Lt MA
Samuel: b 1-13-1751 d 7-12-1817 m (1)Katherine Smith (2)Mary
 Osborn Sgt MA
Samuel, Sr.: b 9-13-1734 d *p.* 1776 m Mary Gorham Pvt MA
Samuel: b 6-4-1718 d *p.* 1790 m (1)Abigail George (2)Mary Erving
 Pvt MA
Samuel: b 1711 d 7-4-1800 m Sarah — Pvt MA
Samuel: b 1756 d 12-26-1834 m Ruth Holly DrmMaj MA
Samuel: b 4-1-1752 d 10-18-1833 m Deborah Chapin MM Pvt MA
Samuel: b 1-15-1762 d 5-3-1849 m Elizabeth Smith Pvt MA ★
Samuel: b 3-13-1765 d 8-14-1855 m (2)Mary Cogswell (Buttrick)
 Pvt MA
Samuel: b 3-25-1721 d *c.* 1797 m Dorothy Hadley Pvt NH
Samuel: b *c.* 1755 d 1804 m Abigail Drake Sgt NH
Samuel: b 4-17-1759 d 5-19-1848 m Lydia Merrill Cpl NH ★
Samuel, Jr.: b 5-10-1753 d 1848 m (1)Sarah Wyman (2)Deborah
 Tarbox Pvt NH ★
Samuel: b 1750 d *c.* 1820 m Cathrina Summers Pvt NJ
Samuel: b 11-5-1752 d 2-18-1834 m Hannah Smalley Pvt NJ
Samuel: b 8-3-1734 d *p.* 1787 m Mary — Pvt PA
Samuel: b 1735 d *p.* 1800 m Martha Williams Pvt PA
Samuel: b 6-16-1754 d 4-6-1826 m Elizabeth — Pvt PA
Samuel: b 9-28-1750 d 10-9-1804 m Amelia Holt Col VA
Samuel: b 1740-45 d *a.* 12-10-1794 m Jane Marshall Lt VA
Samuel: b 8-28-1741 d 4-4-1823 m Sarah — Pvt VA
Samuel: b 1753 d 1812 m Sarah Davis Pvt VA
Samuel: b 12-24-1755 d 8-31-1842 m Jane — Pvt VA ★
Samuel: b 10-10-1762 d 7-29-1849 m Francis Tinsley Pvt VA
Samuel Barker: b 1757 d 4-16-1840 m (1)Rebecca Bussey (2)Ann
 Bogle Pvt VA ★
Samuel D.: b 12-19-1764 d 1860 m (2)Nancy Crowder Pvt PA ★
Sanford: b 11-3-1763 d 10-3-1831 m Deborah Coffin Pvt MA ★
Septimus: b 12-11-1755 d 2-6-1836 m Mary Clark Lt PA ★
Silas: b 4-16-1748 d 1836 m (1)Mary Clark (2)Lydia Brooks (3)Mary
 Preston Pvt NH
Simon: b 1756 d 5-29-1818 m Margaret Drummond Sgt NH
Simon: b 1714 d 1779 m Silence Bulkley PS NH
Simon, Sr.: b 1724 d *p.* 1790 m Mary Powers Pvt VT
Simon, Jr.: b 9-15-1759 d 3-26-1842 m Mary Fuller Pvt NY VT ★
Solomon: b 1753 d *p.* 1790 m Elizabeth Veal Pvt VA
Squire: b 1-21-1762 d 8-6-1854 m Althea Bullock Pvt MA
Stephen: b 1736 d 1805 m Mary Thatcher Pvt CT
Stephen: b *c.* 1736 d 1802 m Rebecca Young Pvt MA
Stephen: b 11-6-1715 d 7-22-1787 m Elizabeth Brown CS MA
Stephen: b *c.* 1750 d — m Elizabeth Bowe Pvt VA
Steven: b *c.* 1734 d *c.* 12-14-1822 m (1)Peace Macomber (2)Mary
 (Bennett) Smith (3)Rebecca Russell Pvt MA
Surrey: b 12-22-1764 d 10- -1853 m (1)Sarah Maudlin (2)Margaret
 Maudlin Pvt SC
Thaddeus: b 2-8-1754 d 9-12-1830 m Sarah Stearns Pvt MA
Thomas: b 1-9-1757 d 11-12-1832 m Rebecca Brackett Sgt CT ★
Thomas: bpt 6-25-1764 d 7-18-1827 m Abigail Wakeman Pvt CT W★
Thomas: b 8-18-1726 d 9-19-1805 m Martha Squire PS CT
Thomas: b 11-8-1753 d 9-22-1840 m Joanna Whitter Pvt MD ★
Thomas: b 1753 d 5-14-1840 m Lettice Rice Pvt MA
Thomas: b 9-25-1755 d 4-2-1786 m Lydia Greenleaf Slr MA
Thomas: b 11-25-1705 d 11-18-1786 m Sarah Jones PS MA
Thomas: b 6-10-1732 d 1802 m (1)Elizabeth Roberts (2)Abigail
 Jones Pvt NH
Thomas: b *c.* 1711 d *p.* 12-31-1799 m (1)Hannah Washburn (2)Mary
 (Remey) Bush PS NH
Thomas: b 1723 d *c.* 7-18-1802 m Elizabeth Bassett Pvt NJ
Thomas: b 1746 d 1814 m Elizabeth Eagle LCol NC
Thomas: b *c.* 1760 d *p.* 9-15-1798 m Mary Clark Barnes Lt NC
Thomas: b 1748 d *p.* 3-28-1820 m Mary Newell Sol NC
Thomas: b *a.* 1736 d 1803 m Rachel — PS NC

Thomas: b 1755 d 1828 m Grace John Pvt PA
Thomas: b 1755 d p. 1819 m Jane Jenkins Pvt PA
Thomas: b 3-22-1760 d 3-20-1845 m Nancy Rivers Pvt SC ★
Thomas: b 1- -1756/57 d 2-17-1842 m Elizabeth Fritz Sgt VA W★
Thomas: b c. 1757 d p. 11-20-1840 m Sally Meadows Pvt VA
Thomas: b c. 1740 d 1810 m Elizabeth — Chp VA
Thomas: b c. 1730 d p. 2-16-1801 m — PS VA
Thomas Nicholas: b 1741/42 d 1805 m Rebecca Ward Pvt MD
Thomas W.: b 11-30-1761 d 11-8-1839 m Susannah Hyatt Sgt VA W★
Timothy: b c. 1722 d 1800 m Hannah Smith Pvt MA
Timothy: b 1729 d p. 1790 m Bethia White Pvt Drm MA
Timothy: b 4-9-1730 d 7-13-1798 m Hepsabah Hathaway Pvt MA
Timothy, Jr.: b 12-25-1733 d 10-5-1807 m Marcy Granville Pvt NH
Valentine: b 2-26-1764 d 10-18-1839 m Sarah Hoffman Pvt NY
Walter: b 3-9-1754 d 1-8-1844 m Mary Davis Pvt MA
Walter: b c. 1730 d 1803 m Martha Cunningham CS VA
Wm.: b 1761 d 1830 m Mary Collins Pvt CT ★
Wm.: b 10-16-1756 d 1843 m (1)Rebecca Bannister (2)Mary — Pvt MD ★
Wm.: b 1765 d 1840 m Rebecca — Pvt Matr MD
Wm.: b 4-19-1738 d 10-1-1814 m Mrs Sarah Newman Sgt MA
Wm., Sr.: b 11-17-1758 d 1850 m Abigail Fletcher Cpl MA
Wm.: b 1- -1743 d 1-10-1835 m Sarah Boardman Pvt Smn MA ★
Wm.: b c. 1730 d p. 1778 m Rhoda (Goodwin) Benefield Pvt MA
Wm.: b 10-25-1760 d 4-9-1825 m Hannah Buck Pvt MA ★
Wm.: b 3-28-1761 d 7-22-1833 m Rebecca Tuttle Pvt MA
Wm.: b 9-5-1753 d 8-28-1819 m Betsey Jones Pvt NH
Wm., Sr.: b 1719/20 d 7-15-1791 m Tacy Crandall Capt NJ
Wm.: b 3-11-1754 d 1834 m Elizabeth Havens Pvt PS NJ ★
Wm.: b 3-21-1758 d 1-6-1845 m Elizabeth Johnson Pvt NJ ★
Wm.: b 9-6-1739 d 6-1-1801 m (1)Elizabeth — (2)Dorothy — Sol NY
Wm.: b 9-11-1762 d p. 1821 m Jannetje Relyea Pvt NY
Wm.: b 1724 d 1780 m Kathrin Pickens LCol NC
Wm.: b c. 1741 d 10-5-1841 m Frankie Weatherman Cpl NC
Wm.: b a. 1749 d 1826 m Lucy Caroline Winston Cpl NC
Wm.: b 10-24-1763 d p. 1805 m Ann Marshall Pvt NC
Wm.: b c. 1735 d 4-13-1799 m Elizabeth — PS NC
Wm.: b 1756 d 2-10-1834 m Isabella Scott Cpl PA ★
Wm.: b 1720 d 1806 m Mary Evans Pvt PA
Wm.: b 5-15-1730 d 9-20-1824 m Mary Means Pvt PA
Wm.: b —d 1799 m Sarah Burley Pvt PA
Wm.: b 1759 d 5-2-1826 m Mary Rathburn Fif RI ★
Wm.: b c. 1737 d 1801 m (1)Anne McLeod (2)Rebecca Weakley Col PS SC
Wm.: b 3- -1750 d p. 4-5-1824 m Susan Mary Dunham Capt SC
Wm.: b c. 1738 d p. 1790 m Mary Westcott Capt SC
Wm.: b 2-21-1750 d 11-24-1820 m Martha Spence Capt SC
Wm.: b 1747 d 5-14-1818 m Agnes Lanier Maj VA
Wm.: b 1753 d 8-19-1848 m Mary Ann (Black) Pogue Pvt VA ★
Wm.: b 1752 d 9-4-1833 m — Pvt VA ★
Wm.: b 1755 d 4-26-1791 m Martha Clough Pvt VA
Wm.: b 1760 d 2-4-1837 m (1)— Windsor (2)Jane King Pvt VA
Wm.: b 1765 d p. 1851 m (1)Mary Holmes (2)Annis Reeves Cadwell Pvt VA
Wm.: b c. 1745 d a. 6-20-1791 m — PS VA
Wm.: b c. 1710 d p. 6-4-1790 m Susanna — PS VA
Wm.: b 1761 d 7-4-1849 m Ann Wright Cpl VA ★
Wm.: b c. 1740 d p. 1791 m Jean — Sgt VA
Wm.: b 8-3-1749 d 1821-30 m Mary (Murray) Gordon Col VA
Wm. L.: b 1-7-1765 d 10-31-1731 m Nancy Easton Sol VA
Wm. Ransom: b 1755 d 12-19-1799 m (1)Eleanora De Nerville (2)Martha Cantey Capt SC
Winthrop: b 1767 d 8-8-1842 m Sarah Evans Pvt NH ★
Zaccheus: b 2-20-1710 d 1787/88 m Jane Edwards PS PA
Zachariah: b 2-6-1760 d p. 1841 m Diana Abernathy Pvt PA ★
Zebulon: b 1733 d 1820 m (1)Mary Bray (2)Hannah Sawyer Marble Capt MA
Zebulon: b c. 1755 d — m Polly Emery Pvt NH

DAVOL,
Pardon: b 3-16-1743 d 11-22-1808 m Priscilla Read Pvt MA

DAWES, (includes DAWS)
Benjamin: b 2-6-1716 d 1893 m Hannah Mears Cpl MA
Ebenezer: b 1750 d 5-2-1822 m Priscilla Bassett Pvt MA
Elisha: b c. 1750 d p. 1788 m Mary Morgan Pvt MD
Robert: b 6-13-1747 d 10-14-1793 m Lydia Tirrell Lt MA
Thomas, Sr.: b 8-5-1731 d 1-2-1809 m Hannah Blake Col MA
Thomas, Jr.: b 7-8-1757 d 7-22-1825 m Margaret Greenleaf PS MA
Wm., Jr.: b 4-6-1745 d 2-25-1799 m (1)Mehitable May (2)Lydia Gendall 2Maj MA

DAWKINS,
John: b 1750 d 10-29-1837 m Susannah Barber MM NC ★
Wm.: b c. 1730 d p. 12-7-1800 m Jane — Capt SC

DAWLEY,
Daniel: b 1749 d 7-23-1832 m Elizabeth Card Pvt RI W★
David: b c. 1760 d p. 7-30-1810 m Mary Dudley Sol VA
Dennis: b a. 5-23-1728 d p. 2-18-1778 m Elizabeth Bonney PS VA
Nathan: b c. 1750 d 4-1-1785 m Elizabeth Dimond Pvt RI W★

DAWSON,
Benjamin: b c. 1762 d p. 11-4-1825 m (2)Ann (Pope) Roy Pvt VA
Benoni: b 1742 d 5-6-1806 m Rebecca Mackall PS MD
Edward: b 1755 d 8-28-1833 m Hannah Dawson Pvt PA
Elijah: b 1742 d 10-14-1777 m Rebecca Perkins Pvt VA
George: b 1760 d 1824 m Mrs Ruth Skidmore Pvt MD
George: b a. 1765 d p. 1810 m Nancy — Pvt VA
Henry: b 1748/49 d 10-11-1815 m Maria Wells Lt QM VA
Isaac: b c. 1750 d a. 3- -1812 m Sibell — PS VA
James: b c. 1760 d 1824 m Lydia Dexter Slr MA
James: b c. 1754 d 6-30-1838 m (1)Jane Kitchen (2)Mrs Jane Shoemaker Pvt NC ★
James: b 1747 d 9-15-1834 m Catharine Morrow Pvt PA
Jeremiah: b 5-30-1763 d 2-10-1846 m Nancy Dollard Pvt VA
John: b 1751 d 7-17-1826 m (1)Christian — (2)Elizabeth — Pvt NJ
John: b 1750 d p. 1782 m Prudence Martin Pvt PA
John: b 1734 d 1804 m Sarah Carroll Capt VA
John: b 4-14-1735/36 d 5-7-1812 m Joanna Broughton Monck PS SC
John: b 7-28-1750 d 12-7-1839 m Susan Taylor Pvt VA ★
John: b c. 1733 d a. 1805 m (1)Elizabeth Douglass (2)Mollie Hall PS VA
Joseph: b c. 1730 d 1822 m Judith Dudley Pvt VA
Joseph Harrington: b c. 1750 d 10-3-1822 m (1)Mary Haddaway (2)Deborah — Pvt MD
Levi: b —d p. 12-3-1790 m Mary Elizabeth Waters LCol NC
Martin: b c. 1730 d 1812 m (1)Priscilla Sorrell (2)Elizabeth Carter PS VA
Nicholas: b 6-14-1750 d 3-18-1806 m Elizabeth Bayne PS MD
Nicholas: b 4-3-1745 d 5-31-1789 m Violet Littleton Pvt PA & VA
Nicholas Lowe: b 1751 d 1831 m Mary Mackall PS MD
Pleasant: b 5-17-1756 d 1830 m Henrietta M Garland Pvt VA
Richard, Jr.: b 1758 d 5-19-1835 m — Breeland Pvt SC
Robert: b c. 1735 d p. 1790 m Sarah Lowe Cpl MD
Robert Boyne: b 5-29-1754 d 8-13-1824 m (1)Sarah Newton Chiswell (2)Henrietta Lane PS MD
Robert Dudley: b c. 1755 d c. 1825 m Mary Lightfoot Slaughter Sgt VA
Thomas: b 1708 d 8- -1800 m Elizabeth Lowe PS MD
Thomas: b c. 1760/61 d 2-1-1832 m (1)Barbara — (2)Anna Kopp (3)Catherine — Drm VA
Thomas: b 1759 d 1829 m Mary Ann Clay Pvt VA
Timothy: b 4-18-1743 d 6-17-1828 m (1)Anna Holt (2)Abagail Winston (3)Lucina Marsh Pvt CT
Titus: b 1-13-1748 d 3-14-1840 m (2)Sybil Dennison Pvt CT
Wm.: b 1759 d 1841 m— (Gibson) McElvin Pvt SC NC GA ★
Wm.: b c. 1738 d 1802 m Elizabeth — PS MD
Wm.: b 1749 d 1785 m Mary (Hamilton ?) Pvt SC

DAY,
Aaron: b 8-11-1715 d 9-9-1778 m (1)Sybil Munson (2)Susanna Stanley PS CT
Aaron: bpt 12-18-1728 d 8-24-1790 m Sarah Goodhue Pvt MA
Aaron: b c. 1750 d — m Mary Jelf Lt QM NJ
Abraham: b 1745 d 9-9-1797 m Irene Jackson Sgt MA
Abraham: b 8-29-1763 d 6-1-1842 m Mary Sprague Pvt MA W★
Abraham: b 3-17-1712 d 3-18-1792 m Irene Foot Drm PS MA
Adonijah: b 7-16-1733 d 10-1-1799 m Sarah Loomis Pvt CT
Amos: b 12-11-1760 d 3-17-1830 m Mary Genung Pvt NJ
Andrew: b 8-8-1743 d 10-21-1805 m Christianna — Pvt PA
Anthony: b 9-3-1762 d 10-22-1849 m Hannah Vine Pvt PS VT ★
Artemas: b 6-16-1745 d 4-18-1802 m Bethany Axtell Capt NJ W★
Asa: b 8-12-1761 d 10- -1841 m Anne Marvin Pvt CT
Asa: b 8-25-1760 d 8-23-1853 m Esther Chapin Sol MA
Benjamin: b 12-7-1735 d 1-28-1813 m Martha Knights Pvt MA
Benjamin: b 10-27-1710 d 5-10-1808 m (1)Eunice Morgan (2)Lucy Sheldon PS CS MA
Benjamin: b 1730 d 9- -1783 m (1)Abigail Darling (2)Elizabeth Roberts Sol NJ
Benjamin: b 9-13-1731 d 1-26-1811 m (1)Abigail Day (2)Eunice (Rood) Young Pvt VT
Comfort: b 1741 d 1799 m Esther (Day) Lt CT ★
Daniel: b 7-8-1749 d 8-19-1825 m (1)Anna Vanhorn (2)Abi Granger Cpl MA
Daniel: b 10-7-1721 d 11-7-1800 m Susanna Hutchinson Pvt MA
Daniel: b 11-14-1746 d 1830 m Martha Isham Pvt MA
David: b 5-2-1758 d 8-6-1845 m Asenath Childs Sgt MA ★
David: b 1745 d p. 1785 m Elizabeth Lyon Pvt NJ
Ebenezer: b 1736 d 11-3-1805 m Martha Ingraham Pvt MA
Edward: b 1760 d 4-11-1837 m Ursula Sublette Pvt VA ★
Elijah: b 1-1754 d 4-22-1798 m Dorothy Olmstead Pvt CT
Elijah: b 6-6-1754 d 12-14-1792 m Mary (Leonard) Lt MA W★
Eliphalet: b 2-11-1754 d 8-5-1826 m Thirza French Pvt MA
Eliphaz: b 3-2-1744 d 2-19-1820 m (1)Anna Peck (2)Eunice Weld Lt MA
Elisha: b 4-27-1755 d 11-16-1821 m Racheal Barnes Pvt PA
Elkanah: b 1-29-1733 d 3- -1803 m Lavinah Merell Capt NY
Enos: b —d — m Betsey Ann Watrous Pvt NH
Ephraim: b 7-10-1741 d 8-23-1825 m Sara Ackley Sgt CT
Ezra: b 4-21-1744 d 11-21-1823 m Hannah Kendall PS MA
Francis: b a. 1734 d 10-27-1778 m Avis — Cpl MD
George: b 1750 d 3-5-1738 m Sarah Catharine Rodgers Capt MD
Heman: b 1-27-1755 d 1-9-1837 m Lois Ely QMSgt MA

DAY, contd.

Isaac: b 11-3-1754 d 7-15-1838 m (1)Lucina May (2)Sarah May Cpl CT
Jacob: b 8-4-1753 d 9-5-1816 m Abigail Leonard 2Lt MA
James: b 9-8-1762 d 2-19-1842 m (2)Sarah — (3)Sarah Mark Pvt MD
Jedediah: b 3-7-1755 d 12-26-1839 m Phebe (Day) Pvt MA
Jeremiah: b 1752 d p. 8-14-1820 m Sarah Dodd Pvt NJ ★
Joel: b 4-6-1730 d 2-14-1803 m Eunice (Day) Pvt MA
Joel: b 8-16-1761 d 3-10-1835 m Martha Murray Pvt MA ★
John: b 3-12-1756 d 3-10-1836 m Annis Bowman Pvt CT
John: b 3-4-1754 d 1794 m Mary Maxwell Capt MD
John: b 10-14-1755 d 10-1-1791 m Mary Goldsmith Presbury Cpl MD
John: b 9-11-1750 d 4-12-1841 m Elizabeth Joslin Sgt PS MA ★
John: b 12-30-1751 d 12- -1840 m Rebecca George Pvt MA ★
John: b 12-14-1748 d 4-4-1814 m Abiah Bennett Sol MA
John: b 1-12-1749 d — m Betty — Pvt NH
John: b c. 1740 d 1-14-1778 m Abigail Poe Pvt NC
John: b c. 1730 d 1776 m Bettie Wentworth Capt VA
John: b 6-30-1742 d 12-4-1833 m Polly Susan — Ens Spy VA ★
John: b 6-28-1760 d 7-16-1837 m Rebecca Howe Pvt Spy VA W★
Jonathan: b 5-4-1744 d 5-10-1819 m Mary Mayo Cnt MA
Joseph: b 12-8-1750 d p. 1795 m (1)Rebecca Bacon (2)Elizabeth Gay Cpl MA
Joseph: b 1737 d a. 4-11-1777 m Deborah Taft Pvt MA
Joseph, Jr.: b 11-20-1745 d 3-19-1813 m (1)Azubah Adams (2)Lois Lyman Pvt MA
Joseph: b 4-16-1756 d 3-29-1840 m (1)Lucy Ellis (2)Susan Gould Pvt MA ★
Josiah: b c. 1742 d 1837 m Wealthy Blethen PS ME
Justin: b 1-10-1757 d 3-6-1828 m (1)Abigail Morgan (2)Rhoda Day Cpl MA ★
Lewis: b 7-19-1754 d 2-17-1847 m Sebra Ward Sgt MA ★
Loammi: b 8-13-1750 d 1827 m (1)Mrs Mary Jencks Pvt MA
Luke, Jr.: b 7-21-1743 d 6-1-1801 m Lydia Kelsey Capt MA
Moses: b 1755 d 5-24-1830 m — Darling Pvt NJ ★
Moses: b 7-28-1762 d 9- -1822 m Joanna Bonnel Pvt NJ
Nathaniel: b 10-14-1737 d 7-5-1806 m Adah Marshall Sgt MA
Nathaniel, Jr.: b 4-24-1740 d 2-15-1805 m Mary Davis Cpl MA
Nathaniel: b 7-26-1762 d 1842 m Achsah Strong Pvt MA
Nehemiah: b 8-10-1748 d 4-1-1837 m Phebe Loree Sgt NJ ★
Nicholas: b c. 1750 d p. 7-2-1815 m (2)Mrs Grace Angelly Pvt MD
Noah: b 6-10-1740 d 4-22-1813 m Ann Loomis Sgt CT
Noah: b 2-14-1757 d 1-10-1841 m Alice Whitney Sgt CT
Orion: b 8-5-1762 d 9-26-1835 m Joanna Everett Pvt MA
Othneil: b 11-2-1740 d 6-10-1820 m Rebecca — Pvt MA NH
Paul: b 1724 d 10-30-1802 m (1)Elizabeth Thompson (2)Elizabeth Crane (3)Patty Wilcox PS NJ
Ralph: b 6-19-1717 d 3-25-1795 m (1)Mary Ellis (2)Mercy Leland Winship Pvt MA
Robert: b c. 1745 d p. 1796 m — Eltonhead Pvt MD
Robert: b 1749 d p. 1786 m Mary — Cpl MA
Robert: b 10-11-1755 d 12-11-1836 m Keziah Turner Pvt MA
Samuel, Sr.: b 6-10-1713 d 3-15-1787 m Sarah Man Lt MA
Samuel: b 1743 d 10-12-1812 m Sally Bates Ens MA W★
Samuel, Jr.: b 2-3-1752 d 1-22-1821 m Jerusha Fisher Sgt MA
Samuel: b 7-15-1715 d 3-25-1777 m (1)Elizabeth — (2)Mrs Zervia Winans Lt NJ
Samuel: b 1757 d 5-11-1820 m Margaret Cohegan Pvt VA
Solomon: b 11-10-1762 d 12- -1840 m Eunice Lockwood Pvt CT NY ★
Stephen: b 2-20-1746 d 4-11-1820 m Demmis Ransom Capt CT
Stephen: b 1742 d 2- -1821 m Margaret — Sol GA
Stephen: b 1733 d 4-9-1815 m (1)Demaris Foster (2)Jemima Ogden Capt PS CS NJ
Thomas: b 6-9-1755 d 7-15-1830 m Susannah Buck Pvt CT W★
Thomas: b 10-27-1745 d — m Joanna Noble Cpl MA
Timothy: b 9-5-1720 d 9-29-1797 m Sarah Munn PS MA
Wm.: b — d 10-20-1783 m Abigail Woodward Pvt CT
Wm.: b 10-23-1715 d 3-22-1797 m (1)Polly Day (2)Eunice Ingersoll (3)Rhoda Hubbell CS MA
Wm.: b 8- -1759 d 1-17-1815 m Nancy Bonnel PS NJ
Wm.: b 8- -1754 d p. 3-12-1836 m (1)Frances — (2)Rutha — Pvt SC ★
Wm.: b c. 1730 d p. 1785 m Anna Harris Pvt VA
Wm.: b c. 1756 d p. 1820 m Miss Munday Pvt VA ★

DAYTON,

Benedict: b 1751 d 10-3-1804 m Deborah Cleveland Pvt RI
Caleb: b 1734 d 3-31-1813 m Sarah Taylor Sgt VT
Daniel: b 1741 d 2-19-1808 m Hannah — Pvt NJ
David: b 6-14-1731 d 3-21-1777 m Hannah — Dr NY
Elias: b 2-4-1737 d 10-22-1807 m Hannah Rolph BGen NJ
Henry: bpt 10-19-1718 d 9-4-1792 m Hannah Parsons CS PS NY
Henry: b 1751 d 4-5-1792 m Mary (Dayton) Capt RI
Hezekiah: b 12-20-1756 d 12-1-1818 m Phebe Crawford Pvt NY
Hezekiah: b 9-2-1749 d 5-30-1823 m Ruth Smith Lt RI
Isaac: b 5-30-1761 d 11- -1812 m Tabitha Welton Pvt CT
Israel: b 3-30-1744 d c. 1809 m Mary — Pvt CT
John: b 1728 d 2-19-1825 m (1)Mary Mulford (2)Amy — Capt NY
Jonah: b 7-21-1752 d 4-20-1837 m Jane Tyarall Pvt CT ★
Jonathan: b 1-31-1726 d 7-31-1804 m (1)Mary Yale (2)Bede (Cooper) Andrews Capt CT
Jonathan: b 10-16-1760 d 10-9-1824 m Susanna Williamson Capt PS NJ

Jonathan: b 1701 d 10-5-1776 m (1)Mary — (2)Patience — PS NY
Joseph: b 5-25-1763 d p. 1834 m Elizabeth Price Pvt Tms NY ★
Justus: b 6-30-1754 d 1825 m Hannah Titus Pvt CT
Michael: b 6-4-1722 d 9-22-1776 m Mahitable Doolittle Capt CT
Nathan: b 1758 d 10-26-1842 m Mehetable Hutchinson Pvt NY ★
Nathaniel: b 9-30-1758 d 8-13-1838 m Mabel Cooper Pvt CT ★

DEACON,

George: b 1726 d 6-4-1787 m (1)Anne Burr (2)Susanna Norcross Pvt NJ

DEADMAN,

Wm.: b 5-20-1760 d 1789/90 m Mary Green Pvt MA

DEADWYLER,

Joseph: b 1760 d 11-10-1830 m Alice Duncan Sol NC

DEAKE, (includes DAKE)

Benjamin: b 11-27-1753 d 3-1-1837 m Elizabeth Reynolds Pvt RI
Charles, Sr.: b 4-15-1738 d 11-11-1803 m Anna Gould Pvt NY
Charles, Jr.: b 3-26-1763 d 7-1-1843 m Abigail (Waite) Sherman Pvt NY
George: b 1735 d 3-8-1821 m Mary Woodbury PS Lt MA
Wm., Gould: b 3-5-1761 d 8-1-1843 m Margaret Mosher Pvt NY

DEAKINS,

James: b 11-14-1754 d 7-20-1834 m Martha Brand Pvt VA ★
Leonard: b 3-9-1746 d 6-8-1824 m (1)Ruth Orme (2)Deborah Mandit Duke Capt MD
Wm.: b 1739 d 1-5-1834 m Fannie — Sol MD ★

DEAL,

Daniel: b 4- -1759 d 7-4-1839/40 m Catherine Shake Pvt PA ★
George: b 1758 d 1832 m Mary Anna Meyers 2Sgt MD ★
John: b 1754 d 3-11-1838 m Elizabeth Bridges Pvt MA ★
John: b 1746 d 1788 m Elizabeth Gardener Sol PA
Martin: b 1-14-1721 d 12-12-1792 m (1)Fraulein Bunsinger (2)Anna Catherine Zerkiebel Pvt PA
Wm.: b 12- -1721 d 2- -1811 m Johanna Reisley Pvt NY

DEALEN, (includes DELAND)

Daniel: b 1744 d 1840 m Mary Starbird Pvt NH

DEAN, (includes DEANE, DEANS)

Aaron: b 8-16-1767 d 9-18-1854 m Eunice Gallup Pvt CT ★
Abel: b 1744 d 1835 m Mary Thayer Sgt MA
Abiel: b c. 1740 d 1810 m Zibiah Field Pvt MA
Abiezer: b 12-21-1759 d 2-11-1826 m Mary Leonard Cpl MA
Abraham: b 7- -1752 d 3-25-1816 m Isabel McDowell Pvt NJ
Abraham: b 1763/64 d 5-10-1806 m (1)Kate — (2)Sarah Stewart Pvt PA
Amos: b c. 1744 d 4-10-1821 m (1)Lydia Hills (2)Sybil Gates Pvt CT
Asa: b 1759 d 12-27-1815 m (1)Phebe Wilmarth (2)Chloe Bourne Pvt MA
Ashbel (Archibald): b 5-18-1764 d 5-5-1823 m Rachel Barnum Matr NY W★
Benjamin: b 7-17-1717 d 2-4-1810 m Mary Withington Cpl MA
Benjamin: b 5-26-1736 d 10-24-1799 m Mary Turner Pvt MA
Benjamin: b c. 1750 d 11-19-1815 m (1)Zilpha Harrington (2)Mrs Martha Blake Pvt NY
Charles: b c. 1750 d p. 1830 m Elizabeth — Pvt GA
Christopher: b 1-26-1756 d 8-22-1838 m (1)Rebecca Palmer (2)Prudence — Sol CT
Daniel: b c. 1750 d p. 1797 m Sarah — Sgt VA
David: b 1759 d 1832 m Phoebe — Pvt CT ★
David: b 11-5-1737 d 7- -1816 m Lydia Jones Pvt MA
David: b 3-31-1763 d 9-23-1838 m Phoebe Sweezey Pvt NY ★
Ebenezer: b 1731 d 1-6-1819 m Prudence King Capt MA
Ebenezer: b 11-5-1758 d 6-24-1857 m Jane Green Drm MA ★
Ebenezer 2d: b c. 1750 d — m Lydia Reed MM MA
Ebenezer: b 5-31-1741 d 1808 m Hannah Whitman Smn MA
Edmund: b 2-27-1757 d 10-24-1844 m (1)Ruby Chase (2)Rebecca Faunce Pvt MA
Edward: b 1717 d 4-9-1791 m Mercy Pratt Pvt MA
Elijah: b 4-17-1747 d 1782 m Susanna Bass Sgt MA
Elijah: b 2-19-1738/39 d 2-1-1830 m Eunice Shepard Lt MA
Elijah: b 2-21-1755 d 2-21-1836 m Anne Dedrick Ens NY
Elisha: b 1738 d 1822 m Hannah Hall Pvt MA
Enos: b 12-12-1751 d 4-16-1822 m Lydia Codding Sgt MA
Ephraim: b 1747 d 8-10-1759 m Martha Balcom Pvt MA
Ephraim: b 7-5-1759 d 1804 m Phebe Prosser Pvt NY
Evans: b 10-1-1744 d 8-1-1836 m Margaret Maxfield Pvt NY
Ezra: b 1756 d 1842 m Mary Ann Savage Arfr NY
George: b 1731 d 2-19-1814 m Tabitha Crossman Pvt MA
George Roger: b c. 1740 d 1832 m (1)Mary Campbell (2)Rebecca — Sgt PA
Gideon: b 7-23-1757 d 6-15-1842 m Mary Vicory Lancey Pvt MA ★
Gilbert: b 1735 d 1810 m Effie Drake Capt NY
Ichabod: b 10-11-1754 d 9-26-1820 m Chloe Pond Sgt MA
Isaac: b 1735 d 1-15-1824 m Rachel Staples Sgt MA
Jacob: b 5-3-1755 d 12-22-1833 m Lydia Parcells Pvt NJ ★
James: b 1758 d 9-29-1816 m Abigail Barker Pvt NH W★
James: b 8-20-1743 d 9-10-1823 m (1)Lydia Camp (2)Mrs Cynthia Phelps PS Maj NY

James Luddington: b 2-29-1763 d 1-14-1860 m (1)Ruth — (2)Sally (Edgarton) Copeland Pvt CT ★
Jesse: b 2-17-1754 d 11- -1834 m Mary Johnson Ens MA
Job: b 1756 d 10-10-1836 m Mercy Werden Pvt MA
Joel: b — d p. 1790 m Hannah Weston Pvt CT MA
Joel: b 2-16-1755 d 2-5-1842 m Mary Brockman Pvt NC
John: b 4-14-1707 d 3-3-1788 m Martha Black PS CT
John: b 3-21-1740 d 1-22-1808 m Abigail White Capt MA
John: b 1758 d 3-28-1842 m Delphos Harris Matr Cpl MA ★
John: b 1747 d 1796 m Prudence Page Pvt NH
John: b c. 1740 d c. 1816 m Mary (Stevens) Palmer Pvt NJ
John: b 1755 d 9-1-1831 m Mary Hart Pvt NJ
John: b 9-15-1755 d 4-6-1817 m Mary Storms QM Sgt NY
John: b 1740/41 d c. 1823 m (1)Mary Niles Pvt NY
John: b 1713 d 1795 m (2)Mrs Rhoda Parsons Ashley Pvt NY
John: b 1757 d 1846 m Hannah Marshall Pvt NC
John: b 7-5-1759 d 6-13-1837 m Elizabeth Minton Sgt VA
John: b 1750-60 d a. 1822 m Mary Niceley Sol VA
Jonathan: b 1745 d 8-17-1825 m Eunice Lee Ens CT ★
Jonathan: b 9- -1730 d 9-8-1805 m Elizabeth Balch Pvt MA
Jonathan: b 7-9-1741 d 8-2-1822 m (2)Mary Davis CS RI
Joseph: b 1-1-1751 d 9-7-1838 m Anna Strobridge Pvt MA
Joseph: b 1743 d 4-21-1818 m Hannah Boyd Pvt VA
Joseph: b c. 1755 d 1822 m (1)Margaret Higginbotham (2)Sarah Graham Pvt VA
Josiah: b 1-10-1747 d 12-3-1824 m Mariam Tracey Pvt CT
Josiah: b 3-6-1748 d 10-14-1818 m Sarah Byram Pvt MA
Levi: b 1758 d 9-16-1807 m Esther Wales Pvt CT
Lot: b 10-9-1757 d 1824 m — Pvt MA
Luke: b 2-9-1750 d 3-18-1825 m Rebecca Russell Cpl MA
Matthew: b c. 1731 d 4-22-1781 m Rebecca — PS Sol PA
Micajah: b 1753 d 3-17-1838 m Cornelia Anny Coykendall Pvt NJ ★
Michael: b c. 1738 d p. 1820 m — Pvt VA
Moses: b 1735 d 11-11-1814 m Hannah Tanner Sgt NY
Nathan: b 3- -1755 d 3-3-1799 m Lois Snow Sgt MA
Nathan: b 6-25-1740 d 1-23-1809 m Zipporah Cobb Pvt MA
Nathaniel: b 7-1-1721 d 11-17-1794 m Abigail Ellis Pvt MA
Nathaniel: b 1755 d p. 1832 m Mary Atchley Pvt NJ ★
Noah: b 1730 d 8-24-1794 m Elizabeth Hathaway 1Lt MA
Paul: b 12-23-1746 d 9-25-1828 m Elizabeth Ruggles Pvt MA
Philip, Sr.: b 1734 d 11-28-1780 m Abigail Shaw Cpl MA
Philip, Jr.: b 1762 d 1823 m Abigail Macomber Pvt MA
Phineas: b 1758 d 1843 m Ruth Hall Pvt CT ★
Richard: b 1730 d 12-14-1787 m Mary Odlum Capt NY
Richard: b 1736 d 7-16-1779 m Susan Ward Pvt NY
Robert: b 10-20-1757 d 2-28-1828 m Eunice Billings Cpl MA
Rufus: b 1739 d 2-24-1800 m Lydia Hodges Pvt MA
Samuel: b 1762 d 7-30-1845 m Hannah Buxton Pvt CT
Samuel: b 2-24-1717 d 6-17-1799 m Susanna Butters Sgt MA
Samuel: b 3-8-1748 d 2-26-1827 m Bethia Robinson Pvt MA
Samuel: b 8-4-1755 d 4-2-1840 m Mary Weller Pvt MA ★
Samuel: b c. 1758 d 4- -1818 m Wilhelmina vonBuhl Cpl PA ★
Samuel: b 1751 d p. 5-22-1826 m Gwendolyn James Pvt PA
Samuel: b 12-5-1760 d 1856 m Martha Camp Pvt PA
Seth: b 1-7-1757 d 4-28-1848 m Mercy Shaw Cpl Mrnr MA ★
Seth: b 10-3-1755 d 11-22-1851 m (1)Mary Bicknell (2)Ruth Wright Pvt VT & MA
Seth: b 10-5-1760 d 6-5-1834 m Edena Pond Pvt MA
Seth: b 8-7-1715 d 4-25-1782 m Mercy Fenner PS NH
Solomon: b a. 1752 d p. 1785 m Elizabeth Brown Arfr NY
Stewart: b 7-4-1747 d 8-5-1836 m (1)Pietezlje Bratt (2)Margaret Wheaton NCapt PS NY
Sylvester: b 2- -1757 d 12- -1817 m Abigail Holly Cpl MA
Thomas: b 8-6-1853 d 3- -1780 m Martha Low Cpl MA
Thomas: b 8-8-1733 d 5-2-1811 m Sarah (Leonard) Byram 2Lt MA
Thomas: b 4-19-1830 d 1-20-1800 m (1)Abigail Horton (2)Thankful (Atwood) Arey PS MA
Thomas: b c. 1760 d 1830 m Lucy Ezell Sol NC
Timothy: b 2-6-1747 d 11-13-1839 m (1)Sarah Potter (2)Hannah Pattey (3)Mrs Mary Matthewson Lt RI ★
Walter: b 9-5-1751 d 1-19-1814 m Abigail Adams Capt MA
Walter: b 1764 d 10-7-1833 m (1)Aletha Hathewy (2)Olive Gallup Pvt MA
Wm.: b c. 1754 d a. 8-7-1820 m Jane — Sgt GA
Wm.: b 1729 d 4-8-1825 m Lydia Leonard Pvt MA
Wm.: b 12-7-1736 d 5-12-1808 m Abigail Harlow Pvt MA
Wm.: b — d p. 1792 m — Pvt NY
Wm.: b 3-15-1753 d 1-21-1784 m Mary Johnson Pvt NY
Wm.: b 1740 d 9-4-1807 m Mary Cook Col PA

DE ANGELIS,
Pascal Charles Joseph: b 1-14-1763 d 9-8-1839 m Elizabeth Webb Smn Pvt CT ★

DEAR,
George: b c. 1732 d 1776 m Abigail Wheaton Pvt CT
John: b 1757 d a. 2-27-1823 m Mary Spiller Pvt VA
John Elijah: b c. 1730 d 1781 m Susanna Major Pvt VA
Jonathan: b 3-4-1766 d 7-14-1833 m Mary Reed Pvt CT ★

DEARBORN,
Asa: b 7-25-1756 d 10-16-1831 m Anna Emerson Pvt NH ★
Ebenezer: b 1-27-1705 d 1-10-1790 m (1)Huldah Nason (2)Elizabeth Hills Pvt NH

Edward: b 2-13-1749 d 5-16-1792 m Susanna Longfellow Brown Pvt PS NH
Henry: b 2-23-1751 d 6-6-1829 m (1)Mary Bartlett (2)Dorcas (Osgood) Marble (3)Sarah (Bowdoin) Bowdoin Col NH
James, Jr.: b 1755 d 11-29-1843 m Judith Tuttle Pvt NH
Jeremiah: b 11-30-1741 d 4-18-1816 m Hannah Locke Cpl NH
John: b 7-21-1740 d 10-19-1794 m Zipporah Towle Capt PS NH
John: b 10-3-1738 d 1-18-1830 m (2)Bethia Fogg Sgt NH
Jonathan: b 12-26-1746 d 11-22-1826 m Delia Robie Pvt NH
Jonathan: b c. 1740 d — m Abigail Leavitt CS NH
Josiah: b 1-11-1738 d 9-15-1814 m Sarah Freese Lt NH
Josiah: b 11-6-1751 d 4-28-1830 m Susanna Emerson Pvt NH
Micheal: b 1755 d 2-12-1809 m Martha Harriman Pvt NH
Nathaniel: b 5-25-1757 d 7-27-1850 m (1)Betsy Hill (2)Polly Bacon Pvt NH
Nathaniel: b 3-24-1751 d 1818 m Hannah Godfrey Pvt NH
Peter: b 11-14-1710 d 10-28-1781 m Margaret Fifield PS NH
Phineas: b 4-24-1749 d p. 1779 m Anna Neal PS NH
Reuben: b 8-10-1707 d 1790 m (1)Anna Page (2)Esther Hobbs PS NH
Samuel: b 10-6-1738 d 8-19-1823 m (1)Mary Brown (2)Sarah (Young) West Capt NH
Samuel: b 11-20-1754 d 11-15-1838 m Hannah Philbrook PS NH
Samuel: b 4-15-1745 d 7-22-1833 m (1)Sarah Clough (2)Abigail Ward PS NH
Shubael, Sr.: b 1-30-1719 d p. 1793 m Sarah Fogg PS Pvt NH
Shubael, Jr.: b 7-12-1753 d 2-19-1802 m Ruth Leavitt Pvt NH
Simon: b 11-27-1760/61 d 7-17-1853 m Mehitable Marston Pvt NH
Thomas: b 3-11-1745 d 8-28-1778 m Mary Morrison Lt NH

DEARDORFF, (includes DIERDORFF)
Abraham: b c. 1725 d 1805 m Catherine — Sol PA
Henry: b 1761 d a. 2-26-1827 m Susannah — Pvt PA
Jacob: b 8-15-1764 d 2-12-1838 m Catharine Zug Pvt PA
Peter: b 8-12-1709 d 11-6-1786 m Mary — Pvt PA

DEARINGTON,
Robert: b 5-28-1738 d 10-11-1793 m Anne Rees Pvt SC

DE ARMAS Y ARCILA,
Christobel: b 4-16-1754 d 1828 m Maris Manette Armirault Duplessis PS LA

DE ARMOND,
John: b c. 1738 d p. 5-25-1809 m Esther Flenniken Sol NC
Michael: b 1748 d 1839 m Hester McMahon Pvt PA ★
Thomas: b c. 1732 d p. 1811 m (2)Peggy King Pvt PA

DEARTH,
Henry: b 6-6-1741 d 1-24-1804 m Ruth Thayer Cpl MA

DEATH,
Benjamin: b 12-23-1751 d 8-31-1821 m Huldah Edson Cpl MA

DEATLY,
James: b 1750 d 12- -1843 m (2)Elizabeth Fegitt (3)Lucy Edwards Sol VA ★

DEAVER, (includes DEAVOR, DEVER,)
Henry: b c. 1745 d p. 9-21-1806 m Elizabeth Miles Pvt PA
John: b 4-13-1758 d 1812 m (3)Sarah Hunt Capt MD
John: b 10-20-1746 d 11-10-1827 m Hannah Coberly Pvt VA
Wm.: b 1761 d 2-9-1832 m Phebe Deaver Pvt MD
Wm.: b 9-22-1763 d p. 1853 m Susanah Smith Pvt VA ★

DE BAUN,
Joseph: b c. 1741 d p. 1796 m Charity Duree Sol VA

DEBELL,
John: b c. 1745 d p. 1786 m Mary — 2Lt VA
Wm.: b 1748 d 1- -1815 m Mary — 1Lt VA

DE BELLER IVE,
Louis Baury: b 9-16-1753 d 9-20-1807 m Mary Clark Maj SC

DE BELLEVILLE,
Nicholas J. E.: b 11-19-1753 d 12-17-1831 m Nancy Britton FrA MD NJ

DE BELLEVUE,
Prospero Casimir Barbin: b c. 1757 d p. 1804 m Helen Modeste Guinault PS LA

DE BERRY,
Henry: b 1758 d 1818 m Sallie — Sol NC

DE BLANC,
Louis Charles: b 4-29-1753 d c. 1825 m Elizabeth Pouponne D'Erneville PS LA

DE BOLT,
George: b c. 1720 d a. 10- -1788 m Elizabeth — Pvt PA

DEBORA,
Jacobus: b a. 1753 d 1805 m Bertrana — Fif Pvt MD

DE BOW,
Isaac: b *c.* 1740 d *a.* 12-30-1799 m (2)Mary Morgan Pvt NJ
John: b 1-13-1740 d 4-25-1817 m Jeneatte Van Ness Capt NJ

DE BROGLIE,
Charles Louis Victor: b 9-22-1756 d 7-10-1794 m Sophie de Rosen Col FrA

DE BUSSY,
Jean Baptiste Le Droit: b 1745 d 12-14-1812 m Maria Howard Maj SC

DE CAMP,
James: b 1749 d 3-26-1814 m Elizabeth — Ens NJ
John: b 10-18-1760 d 10-24-1844 m (1)Susan Grandin (2)Elizabeth Scott PS Pvt NJ ★
Moses: b 9-28-1735 d 10-5-1827 m Sarah Ross Vol NJ

DE CARTERET,
John: b 5-19-1745 d 1-23-1821 m (1)Mary Crosby (2)Hannah Alley (3)Nancy Smith Arfr MA

DECATUR,
Stephen: b 11- -1752 d 11-14-1808 m Ann Pine Commo NS RI

DECH,
Jacob: b 1-26-1746 d 2-26-1833 m Christina Best Pvt PA

DE CICATY,
Auguste Berode: b 1757 d 1789 m Holly Sablon Lt PA

DECK,
Frederick: b 10-2-1740 d 6-9-1820 m Maria Veronica — Sol PA
Henry: b 1752 d 1832 m — Yerdon Pvt NY
Michael: b 2-7-1759 d 4-3-1843 m Susan Monger Pvt VA ★

DECKER,
Abraham: bpt 6-19-1720 d 3-24-1792 m (1)Elizabeth Schut (2)Catharine — Pvt NY
Cornelius: b 1744 d 10-2-1802 m Charity — Lt PA
Daniel: b 4-22-1737 d 3-1-1813 m Blandina Vredenburgh PS NJ
Elisha: b 5-29-1739 d *p.* 1790 m Eva Dingman Pvt PA
Evert: bpt 10-28-1753 d 8-11-1832 m (1)Catrina — (2)Maria Terwilliger Pvt NY
Hendricus: bpt 2-4-1728 d *p.* 1788 m Hannah Kermer Pvt PA
Henry: bpt 8-2-1761 d *a.* 7-26-1826 m Margery Westbrook Ens NJ
Isaiah: b *c.* 1760 d 10-1-1797 m Maria Van Etten Pvt NY
Jacob: b 5-15-1753 d — m Annatje Sisabaugh Pvt NY
Jacob: b 8-17-1759 d 2-19-1849 m Mary Terwilliger Pvt NY ★
Jacob: b 4-19-1756 d 2-24-1843 m (1)Barbara Zehring (2)Catherine Zehring Sgt Wgn PA ★
Johannes: b 8-26-1735 d 1804 m (1)Margaret Gumear (2)Sarah Hornbeck Maj NY
Johannes: b 4-16-1741 d 9-27-1829 m Annatje Hasbrouck Pvt NY
Johannes: b 1703 d *p.* 1793 m Marytje Janez PS NY
Johannes: b *c.* 1729-31 d *p.* 1790 m Maria Van Tilburgh Pvt PA
John, Jr.: b 1760 d 12- -1817 m Hannah Kuykendall PS VA
John, Sr.: bpt 6-7-1719 d 1791 m Diana Kuykendall PS VA
Jacobus: bpt 11-11-1738 d *p.* 6-8-1777 m Jane Williams Pvt NY
Jonathan: b 8-30-1728 d 2- -1790 m (1)Catharina Terwilliger (2)Maria Van Steenberger Pvt NY
Josiah: bpt 6-17-1740 d *p.* 1-3-1814 m (1)Sarah Tietsoort (2)Elizabeth — PS NJ
Luke: b *c.* 1760 d *p.* 1825 m (1)Sarah Kuykendall (2)Trenny Claypool Ens PA
Martinus: b 12-14-1733 d 4-24-1802 m (2)Mary Penneton Sol NY
Moses: b *c.* 1759 d 1814 m Christine — Pvt PA
Peter, Jr.: b 2-3-1759 d 7-28-1840 m Annatje Decker Pvt NY
Petrus: b 12- -1748 d 2-20-1834 m Annatye — 1Lt NY ★
Reuben: b 4-17-1753 d 4-30-1826 m Ann Robinson Sol NY
Samuel: bpt 9-27-1749 d 9-7-1829 m Jennetje Kortright Pvt NJ
Solomon: b *c.* 1720-25 d *p.* 1778 m Lena Quick PS NY
Thomas: bpt 9-3-1704 d 1780 m Jenneke Van Inwegen PS NJ
Thomas: b 1756 d *p.* 1800 m Catherine Fullerton Pvt MA

DE COU,
John: b *c.* 1745 d 4-25-1813 m Sarah Antrim Pvt NJ

DE DAMAS (d' ANTIGNY)
Charles Francois, Le Duc d'Antigny: b 1758 d 1829 m — de Longeron ADC FrA

DEE,
Elijah: b 1740 d 12-24-1827 m Miriam Jones Pvt CT

DEEDS,
Andrew: b 1-1-1760 d 12-5-1831 m Mary Miller PS NJ
George M.: b 1755 d 2-3-1812 m Phebe Ball Pvt NJ W★

DEEMER,
Peter: b 8- -1761 d 1837 m Mary Hile Pvt PA
Philip: b 1762 d 1847 m Anna Maria — Pvt PA ★

DEEMS, (includes DEEMES)
Frederick: b 1740 d 1791 m — PS Capt MD
Mark: b *c.* 1750 d 4-14-1814 m — Pvt PA

DEERING, (includes DEARIN, DEARING, DERING, DERINGER)
Anthony: b *c.* 1750 d *p.* 1790 m — PS VA
Henry, Sr.: b 1733 d 4-8-1800 m Anna Maria Schmal Pvt PA
Henry, Jr.: b 6-30-1760 d 10-8-1807 m Rebecca Musser Pvt PA
James: b 7-3-1750 d 10-13-1811 m Elizabeth Adams Ens VA
James: b 1758 d 10-8-1800 m Elizabeth Hankins Pvt VA
John: b *c.* 1730 d *p.* 8-19-1789 m Miram Boothby Pvt MA
John: b 8-2-1755 d 3-16-1823 m Annie Maria Lawson Pvt NY
John: b 1763 d 1843 m Ruhamah Davis PS NC
John: b 3-24-1746 d 12-9-1822 m Anne Jett Lt VA
Joseph: b 10-6-1753 d 9-25-1834 m Hannah Jameson Pvt Fif MA
Thomas: b 5-16-1720 d 9-26-1785 m Mary Sylvester PS MA
Thomas: b 5-25-1747 d 11-5-1828 m Lucretia Townsend PS MA
Wm.: b 7-20-1760 d 1-16-1824 m Mary Hunter Pvt VA

DEES,
Benjamin: b *c.* 1745 d *a.* 11-26-1821 m — PS NC

DE FONTBONNE,
Louis Alexandre: b 6-13-1750 d *p.* 7-8-1892 m Marie-Anne V de Bonnefons Capt FrA

DE FORD,
John: b 1753 d 1794 m Annie (Marie) Marchant Pvt MD

DE FOREST,
Abraham: b 3-4-1749 d 12-11-1847 m Margaret Vandenburg Ens NJ ★
Davis: bpt 7-1-1733 d 1788 m Sarah Olmstead Pvt CT
David: b 7-9-1745 d 6-2-1783 m Hannah Lum PS CT
Gideon: b 9-14-1765 d 12-9-1840 m Hannah Birdsey Sol CT
Isaac: b 12-16-1758 d 1-24-1813 m Mary Gregary Pvt CT
Isaac: b 6-16-1734 d *a.* 10-15-1811 m Rachel Bostwick Lt PS CT
Jacob: bpt 3-3-1737 d 5-18-1804 m Trymtie Bratt Capt NY
Jesse: b 8-22-1756 d 1800 m Rebeccah Van Zandt Pvt NY
Joseph: b 1758 d 12-30-1855 m Aner Lamson Grd CT
Martin: b 5-14-1724 d *p.* 1790 m Tenneke Winne Pvt NY
Nehemiah: b 1-24-1743 d 12-9-1801 m (1)Mary Lockwood (2)Eleanor Hickock PS CT

DE FRANCE,
James: b 1763 d 1837 m Elizabeth Arthur Sgt PA
John: b 1761 d 7-20-1838 m (1)Jane Caldwell (2)Martha Ramsey Pvt PA ★

DE FREES,
Joseph Hutton: b 1753 d 8- -1826 m Mary Start Pvt PS PA

DE FREEST,
Philipp: b 4-14-1720 d 9-6-1790 m Maria Bloemendaal Maj NY

DE GARMO,
Mathew: bpt 4-6-1761 d *p.* 1839 m Margaret Vander Welker Pvt NY ★

DE GOLYER, (includes DE GOLIER)
James, Sr.: b 1725 d *p.* 6-1-1790 m Jane Hatch Pvt NY

DE GRAFF, (includes DE GRAAF)
Abraham N: b 4-20-1754 d 6-1-1810 m Margretta Schermerhorn Pvt NY
Cornelius: b 11-23-1738 d 7-11-1830 m Rebecca Van Patten Pvt NY
Daniel: b 5-26-1708 d 3-12-1790 m Gazena Swits Wgn NY
Emanuel: b 1-20-1751 d 11-10-1824 m Rebecca Gonzelus Capt NY
Frederick: b 1729 d 11-24-1800 m Sarah G Marselis Pvt NY
Hendrick: b 2-8-1741 d 1792 m Ossltje Eckert Pvt NY
Isaac: b 11-16-1757 d 12-21-1844 m Susan Van Epps PS NY ★
Jeremiah: b 10-21-1727 d *a.* 7-20-1809 m Annatje Quackenbush Pvt NY
Johannes: bpt 8-14-1720 d 1789 m (1)Magdolena Peesher (2)Mrs Maritje (Wust) Ekkert Pvt PS NY
Johannes: b 9-3-1754 d 10-23-1842 m Eva Van Driesen Sol NY
Moses: bpt 5-6-1724 d 10-11-1800 m Antoinette Van Kleeck Pvt NY
Simon: b 4-6-1753 d 3-31-1842 m Jannetie Bratt Pvt NY

DE GRAFFENREID,
Francis: b 2-24-1747 d 10- -1815 m (1)Ermine Boswell (2)Mary Walton Capt VA
Tscharner: b 11-28-1722 d 1794 m (1)Mary Baker (2)Sarah Lowry (3)Eliza Embrey (4)Lucretia Roberson PS VA
Wm.: b 3-22-1749 d 1809 m Elizabeth Robertson PS VA

DE GRASSE,
Francois Joseph Paul: b 9-13-1722 d 1-1-1788 m Antoinette R Accaron Adm Fr

DE GRAW,
John: b 1747 d 11-5-1817 m Aletta Ackerman PS NJ

DE GROOT, (includes DE GROAT)
Jacob: b 10-24-1749 d 7-22-1843 m Rachel Castner Capt NJ ★
Joseph: b 1746 d 1-7-1830 m Hannah Writer Sol NY
Wm.: b 7-6-1751 d 8-28-1841 m Anne La Tourette Lt NJ ★

DE GROVE,
Adolph, Sr.: b 1720 d 11-29-1796 m (1)Sarah Lawrence (2)Mary Carter PS NY
Adolph, Jr.: b c. 1750-55 d p. 1800 m Rhoda Cowles PS NY
Wm.: b 2-5-1759 d 9-8-1798 m Elizabeth Ellsworth Pvt NY

DE GRUY,
Jean Baptiste: b 8-3-1751 d 1-3-1838 m (2)Melanie Gaudin Tr PS LA

DE HAAS,
John Philip, Sr.: b 1735 d 6-3-1786 m Eleanor Bingham BGen PA
John Philip, Jr.: b 1762 d 8-23-1826 m Ann Shippin 2Lt PA

DE HART,
Abraham: b 1755 d p. 1820 m Christina Ensminger Pvt PA ★
Hendrick: b c. 1735 d 6-18-1816 m Maria Van Deripe Pvt NJ
James: b 12-12-1745 d 6-18-1822 m Ann De Hart Pvt NJ ★
John: b 1742 d 1811 m (1)Mary Van Name (2)Lydia Mercereau (3)Mary Dey Pvt NJ
John: b 1729 d 6-1-1795 m Sarah Dogwothy PS NJ
John: b 1750 d a. 9-26-1805 m Elizabeth Weidner Pvt PA
Peter: b 5- -1740 d p. 1811 m (1)Gertrude Veghte (2)Sarah Van Zandt Pvt NJ

DE HAVEN,
Andrew: b 2-19-1745 d 1788 m Elizabeth McGlathery Pvt PA
David: b 1748 d 9-20-1815 m Magdalane Zimmerman Pvt PA
Edward: b 1757 d 9-10-1849 m (1)Rebecca Johnston (2)Mollie Mathews Pvt VA ★
Jacob: b a. 1750 d 1826 m (1)Mary Sinclair (2)Nancy Bell PS VA
Moses: b 1765 d p. 1808 m Margaret Bisbing Pvt PA
Peter: b 1719 d a. 1-26-1816 m (1)Sarah Hughes (2)Elizabeth Knight PS PA
Peter: b 1-31-1741 d 1-4-1822 m Abigail West Pvt PA
Samuel: b 1752-54 d d. 7-24-1821 m Catherine Ramey Pvt PA
Samuel: b 5-3-1724 d 2-19-1815 m Susanna Spaulding Pvt PS PA

DE HAY,
John: b 10-14-1731 d p. 9-13-1804 m Elizabeth Cockfield PS SC
Zachariah: b 1760 d a. 3-29-1809 m Mary Lindsay Pvt PS SC

DE HUFF,
Abraham: b 2-13-1735 d 3-11-1821 m (1)Mary Finch (2)Charlotte Wolf Capt PA
George: b 9-2-1734 d 4-3-1810 m Anna Elizabeth Kislin Sol PA
George P.: b 11-5-1761 d 1832 m (1)Margaretha — (2)Louisa — Pvt PA
Mathias: b 8-27-1740 d 6-14-1803 m Cathrina Kraemer Pvt PA

DEIBERT, (includes DAUBERT)
Charles: b 8-5-1763 d a. 6-8-1844 m Mary Steel Pvt PS PA
Heinrich: b 2-21-1758 d 7-5-1820 m Maria Engel Pvt PA
John: b 1747 d p. 4-12-1807 m (1)Ene Ickes (2)Mary Ernst Pvt PA
Michael: b c. 1734 d p. 1806 m Maria Barbara LCol PA
Michael: b 1724 d 1788 m Anna Catherine Ublin PS PA
Wm.: b 11-3-1751 d 4-20-1832 m (1)Margaretha Renschler (2)Anna Maria Wagner PS PA

DEIBLER,
Matthias: b 12-14-1763 d 3-10-1837 m Catharine Etzweiler Lt PA

DEILEY, (includes DEILY)
Daniel: b 1755 d 2-12-1825 m Catherine Deiley Pvt PA ★
Frederick: b 1709 d 9-11-1790 m Anna Maria — PS PA
Philip: b 4-12-1754 d 6-22-1843 m (1)Elizabeth — (2)Anna Maria Breidinger Pvt PA

DEININGER,
Adam: b 4-23-1722 d 2- -1803 m (1)Rosina Diller (2)Maria Elizabeth Nast Pvt PA

DEISINGER,
Nicholas: b 1753 d 1840 m Catherine Eva Cere Cpl PA-

DEITSH,
Hartman: b 1750 d 1815 m Catherine Huebner Pvt PA

DE JARNETTE,
James Pemberton: b c. 1740 d 1826 m (1)Edna George (2)Mrs Mary Saunders (3)Elizabeth Pillar Capt VA
John: b 6-28-1748 d 12-21-1799 m Jemima Owen PS NC
John Thomas: b a. 1747 d 1788-89 m Millasant Hall PS VA

DE JUMECOURT,
Charles Arnould Ignace Hanus: b 7-30-1749 d 12-1-1798 m Marie Madeline Mathieu Descloches Capt Fr A

DEKALB,
John: b c. 1750 d p. 1783 m Sarah Otis Pvt NY

DE KAY,
Thomas: b 1732 d 2-12-1810 m Mary Roe Pvt NY

DE LA GRANGE, (includes LA GRANGE)
Conradt: b 4-9-1739 d 1803 m Annetje (de) LaGrange Sol NY
Issac: b 9-24-1735 d p. 1784 m Jacomyntje Knoll Pvt NY
Jacob O: b 1764 d 5-20-1839 m Elizabeth — Pvt NY
Jellis: b 4-3-1728 d 1- -1777 m Annetj — 1Lt NY
Myndert: b 1744 d 9-12-1778 m Helena A Switz 2Lt NY
Omie: bpt 4-10-1726 d p. 1809 m Eytie (de la Grange) Sol NY

DE LA HAUSSAYE,
Louis Le Pelletier: b 1760 d p. 1800 m Louise Charlotte Pellerin PS FrA

DE LA HUNTE,
John: b 12-8-1728 d 2-9-1816 m Hannah Neal PS NC

DELAMAR, (includes DE LAMAR)
Francis: b 1730-34 d p. 12-14-1797 m (1)Miriam Barclift (2) — Hasty Capt NC
Francis: b c. 1759 d c. 1825 m (1Elizabeth Dawson (2)Mrs Elizabeth Brooks Morris Pvt NC

DELAMATER, (includes DE LA MATER)
Benjamin: b 1750 d 1800 m Hannah Row Pvt NY
Benjamin: b 6-1-1762 d 4-26-1832 m Isabel Beverly Pvt NY
Cornelius: b 10-28-1744 d 5-7-1812 m Rachel Sleight Pvt NY
Henry: b 1-14-1739 d 3-30-1783 m Cathrine Kipp Pvt NY
Isaac: b 12-13-1752 d 3-12-1830 m Hannah Barlow Pvt NY
John: bpt 10-9-1754 d 12-28-1819 m Catherine Van Aken Pvt NY
John: b 4-9-1720 d 10-30-1792 m Maria Kip PS NY
Martin: bpt 9-19-1731 d 1805 m Anna Marsh PS Pvt NY
Samuel, Sr.: b 10-3-1725 d p. 6-18-1781 m Catalina Waldron Pvt NY
Samuel, Jr.: b 3-28-1759 d 6-8-1843 m Hannah Vandenburg Pvt NY

DE LANCE,
Delevan: b 8- -1747 d 11-25-1811 m Hepsibah Marvin Sgt NH

DE LAND, (includes DELAND)
Benjamin: b 9-21-1729 d 10-15-1810 m Hannah Cook PS MA
Daniel: b 5-10-1736 d p. 1790 m (1)Elizabeth Martha Hatfield (2)Elizabeth Anderson Pvt MA
Jedediah: b 12-19-1762 d 12-12-1826 m Persis Gregory Pvt MA
John: b — d c. 1776 m Judith Upham Pvt MA
Obadiah: b 4-28-1733 d 8-24-1824 m (1)Martha Jones (2)Mary Jones Pvt MA

DELANO, (includes DE LANO)
Aaron: b 11-12-1756 d 4-23-1782 m Anna Slosson Pvt CT ★
Abisha: b 1746 d 8-25-1802 m Hannah Hovey Pvt NH
Alpheus: b 10-2-1744 d 1826 m Margaret Sides Sgt MA
Amasa: b 2-18-1738 d 7-11-1816 m Sarah Shaw Pvt VT
Amaziah: b 1758 d 6-22-1851 m (1)Margaret Austin (2)Elizabeth Thompson Pvt MA
Amos: b 8-2-1747 d 11-4-1828 m Lydia Hubbard Sgt MA
Barzilla: b 12-11-1755 d 7-19-1835 m Elizabeth Delano Pvt MA
Benjamin: b 6-24-1746 d 6-19-1816 m Mary Brooks Sgt MA
Calvin Timothy: b 11-10-1756 d 1-18-1832 m Margary Knickerbocker Dr NY
Cornelius: b 10-10-1742 d 4-24-1801 m Sarah Peterson Sgt MA
Ebenezer: b 11-21-1761 d 11-27-1836 m Susanna Webb Pvt MA
Ephraim: b 8-25-1733 d 11-24-1809 m Elizabeth Cushman Pvt MA
Gideon: b 11-27-1742 d 7-4-1809 m (1)Mary — (2)Lois Benson Pvt NH
Ichabod, Sr.: b 4-28-1728 d 5-8-1778 m Huldah Sampson Pvt MA
Isaac, Jr.: b 1759 d 9-11-1833 m Elizabeth White Ripley Pvt MA ★
Jabez: b 6-15-1758 d 1817 m Rhoda Blankenship Sgt MA
Jeptha: b 10-29-1758 d 12-23-1843 m Rebecca Chandler Sgt MA
Jethro: b 10-29-1732 d 7-17-1787 m Elizabeth Lathrop Pvt CT
Jethro, Jr.: b 8-10-1707 d c. 1784 m Abigail Eldredge Pvt MA
Jonathan: b 8-7-1763 d 4-16-1835 m (2)Lois Strong (3)Mrs Lois Coats Pvt CT ★
Jonathan: b 12-2-1715 d 9-28-1811 m Anna Ladd PS CT
Jonathan: b 10-28-1756 d 3-17-1825 m Lydia Briggs Cpl MA
Joseph, Jr.: b 8-31-1755 d 1780-81 m Mary Thomas Cpl MA
Joshua: b 9-30-1744 d 7-22-1816 m Mary Chandler Pvt MA
Judah, Jr.: b 5-1-1751 d 9-9-1801 m Penelope Sampson Pvt MA
Lemuel: b 9-24-1741 d 12-21-1792 m Mary Eames Sgt MA
Nathan: b 1-5-1739 d 9-20-1794 m (1)Mrs Sarah Ellis (2)Hulda — Capt VT
Nathan: b 11-16-1764 d 4-3-1841 m (2)Phila Wilson Pvt NY ★
Nathaniel: b 1752/53 d 1812 m Deborah Sprague Pvt MA
Nathaniel: b 12-23-1728 d p. 1783 m (1)Mary Taber (2)Dinah Allen PS MA
Oliver: b 1-14-1759 d 1-7-1846 m Mary Chandler Pvt MA ★
Philip: b 1-4-1761 d p. 1790 m Esther Boardman Pvt CT
Philip: b 4-12-1760 d — m Sarah Bowman Pvt MA
Philip: b 5-24-1761 d 4-29-1836 m Mary Fuller Pvt MA
Reuben: b 1755 d — m Joanne Sackett Pvt CT
Samuel: b 5-11-1739 d 11-6-1814 m Abigail Drew PS MA

DELANO, contd.
Seth, Sr.: b 11-13-1751 d 9-27-1838 m Rebecca Fish Sgt MA W ★
Thomas, Sr.: b 12-24-1726 d 9-8-1803 m Lois — Pvt CT
Thomas, Jr.: b 6-8-1760 d 4-8-1835 m Olive Griswold SgtMaj CT
   NY ★

DELANOY,
Abraham: b 9-5-1742 d *p.* 1790 m Rachel Marling Pvt NY

DELANY, (includes DE LANEY, DE LAUNAY, DULANEY, DULANY)
Benjamin: b 11-. .-1755 d 8-18-1839 m Judith Barnes Pvt VA ★
Daniel: b *c.* 1756 d *p.* 1790 m Priscilla White Sol SC
James Anthony: b *c.* 1760 d *p.* 3-20-1831 m Emelie LeBourdais
   Sol GA
John: b 6-6-1718 d 8-17-1803 m Frances Stanton PS VA
Joseph, Jr.: b 5-6-1744 d 7-20-1814 m Frances Hume Pvt VA
Sharpe: b 1729 d 5-13-1799 m Margaret — Col PA
Wm.: b 1752 d 10-20-1805 m Lydia West Sgt Dr PA
Wm.: b 1732 d *c.* 1802 m Elizabeth Butler PS VA
Wm.: b 2-27-1755 d 8-20-1831 m Nancy Rhodes OrdlSgt TN

DELAP,
James: b 5-13-1736 d 10-9-1801 m Susanna Frost Sgt CT
James: b 9-15-1755 d 7- -1841 m — Sidney Pvt NJ ★

DELAPLANE, (includes DE LAPLAINE)
John: b 1741 d 1804 m Sophia Schuler Miller PS MD
Joseph: b 1744 d 1818 m Catherine Miller Ens PA

DE LA PORTE,
Jean (Count): b 1741 d — m Elizabeth Bourdoine Vol NY

DELAPT,
Richard: b 1734 d 6-3-1781 m Mrs Jean Frazer Capt PA

DE LA RONDE,
Pierre Denis: b 4-20-1762 d 12-1-1824 m Elizabeth Eulalie Guerbois
   PS LA

DELATUSH,
Henry: b 1740 d 5-13-1813 m Dena Van Vickle Lt NJ

DELAVAN, (includes DELEVAN)
Nathan: b 5-9-1755 d 11- -1835 m Hannah Vail Pvt NY
Nathaniel: b 9-14-1746 d 8-9-1798 m (1)Mary Underhill (2)Mary
   Thompson Maj NY
Samuel: b 3-23-1752 d 10-27-1785 m Agnes Tyler Capt NY
Timothy: b 5-27-1738 d 1-19-1813 m Sarah Close Lt NY
Timothy: b 7-29-1713 d 2-1-1803 m Hannah Bouton PS NY

DELAVAU,
John: b 1752 d 8-1-1815 m Barbara Kreutzer Sgt PA

DE LA VERGNE,
Benjamin: b 1742 d 1-25-1830 m Anna Baldwin PS Maj NY
Louis: b 1743 d 2-14-1814 m Marianne La Case PS LA
Louis: b 1738 d 6-15-1805 m Rachel Greene PS Lt NY

DELBRIDGE,
Thomas: b 1759 d *a.* 2- -1845 m (1)Nancy Gwaltney (2)Sally Woolsey
   (3)Nancy — Pvt VA

DELERY,
Francois: b 1741 d *p.* 2-25-1814 m Marie Marthe Bienvenue PS LA

DELESDERNIER,
Lewis Frederick: b 1752 d 2-2-1837 m (1)Sarah Brown (2)Sophia
   Clark Lt MA ★

DELESPINE,
Joseph: b 5-20-1743 d *p.* 1789 m Mrs Sarah (Russell) Irvin Dr SC

DELEZENNE,
Christopher: b 3-8-1750 d 6-19-1828 m Mary Dusenberry Capt CL ★

DE LINE, (includes DELINE)
Isaac: b 9-13-1761 d *p.* 1810 m Elizabeth Shallop Pvt NY
Wm.: b *c.* 1740 d *p.* 1790 m Arianntje Wemple Pvt NY

DE LINO DE CHALMETTE,
Ignace: b 8-23-1755 d 2-10-1815 m Victoire De Vaugine PS FrA

DE LISLE,
Charles: b *c.* 1723 d 1803 m Elizabeth Lelande Sol IL
Charles Noel Romand: b *c.* 1755 d 1778 m Letitia Ingraham Maj
   FrA

DELIVAN,
Abraham: b 9-8-1739 d 10-13-1795 m Hannah — Pvt NY

DE LIVAUDAIS,
Francois Enoul: b 1736 d *p.* 9-19-1797 m Pelagie de Vaugine PS LA

Joseph Enoul Dugue: b *c.* 1753 d 5-14-1833 m Jeanne Marie Fleuriau
   PS LA
Juan Enoul Bautista Beaumont: b 1749 d 2-5-1793 m Agata Dufessat
   PS LA

DELK,
Moreland: b 8-1-1749 d 3-28-1823 m Unity Holleman Ens VA

DELLIBER,
Samuel: b 6-20-1759 d 2-22-1816 m Martha Roberts Pvt CT

DELLINGER,
Frederick: b *a.* 1750 d 1815 m Mary Ann Wolf Pvt PA W ★
Jacob: b 7-6-1751 d 4-6-1824 m Christian Shafer Sol PA
Magdalene: b — d *p.* 1782 m Christian Dellinger PS VA

DE LOACH,
David: b 1765 d 1849 m (1)Perifenalla Dixon (2)Hannah Bostick
   (Freeland) (3) — Waltzer (?) Pvt SC
Francis: b 6-19-1751 d 3-6-1814 m Elizabeth Sykes PS NC
Hardy, Sr.: b *c.* 1735 d *p.* 1820 m —, Pvt SC
Hardy, Jr.: b 1758 d 11-18-1828 m Mary Elizabeth Ross Pvt SC
Samuel: b 1762 d 1845 m — Burton Pvt SC
Wm.: b *c.* 1740 d *p.* 5-16-1810 m Purity Ruffin PS NC

DE LONG, (includes DELAUGH)
Elias: b — d — m Isabel Dickinson Lt NY
Francis: b 1739 d *p.* 1816 m Elizabeth Wells NY ★
Francis: b 6-8-1759 d 2-8-1862 m Mary Doody Pvt NC or SC
Henry: b 1733 d 1810 m Susan Margargle PS PA
Henry: b *c.* 1722 d 1785 m Rebecca — PS VA
John: b 1745 d 2-15-1835 m Rachel — Sgt PA ★
John: b 3-27-1723 d 11-22-1813 m Mary Catharine Dussinger PS PA
Joseph: b 1763 d 1821 m Nancy M White Pvt NY
Michael: b 12-26-1739 d 1-26-1819 m Maria Barbara Bollebach
   PS PA
Solomon: b 1750 d *p.* 1796 m Nancy Le Masters Sol VA

DELPH,
Henry: b *c.* 1755 d 1791 m Ann Powell PS VA

DELVA,
Peter: b 1744 d 1807 m Lucy Town Pvt MA

DE MARANVILLE, (includes DEMORANVILLE)
Charles: b *c.* 1744 d *c.* 1834 m Deborah Lombard Pvt MA
Louis, Jr.: b *c.* 1738 d *p.* 1779 m Rebecca Russell Pvt MA
Simeon: b 6-10-1762 d 12-11-1847 m Jane Spooner Pvt MA ★
Stephen: b 8-15-1750 d 9-24-1828 m Deliverance Borden Pvt MM MA

DE MARCILLAC,
Jean Raymond Daney: b 7-9-1753 d *p.* 1808 m Marie Elisabeth Boisson
   Lt FrA

DEMAREST, (includes DES MAREST, DEMARIS)
Adam: b *c.* 1760 d *p.* 1787 m Mary Farmer Cpl NJ
Benjamin: b 3-31-1749 d 3-30-1817 m Catherine Van Orden Pvt NJ
Cornelius: bpt 7-19-1747 d 3-31-1823 m (1)Margaret Demarest (2)
   Elizabeth Wortendyke Sol NY
Daniel: b 9-11-1738 d 7-25-1820 m Effie Westervelt Pvt NJ
David: b 1733 d 3-7-1807 m Magdalena Van Etten Lt NJ
David: b 3-3-1723 d 1796 m Catherine Seckor PS NJ
David, Sr.: b 11-6-1731 d 1808 m (1)Gertrude Lydecker (2)Helena
   Van Vorhees Pvt PA
David A: b 4-26-1742 d 1-2-1816 m Helen Van Wagoner Sol NJ
David P: bpt 4- -1738 d 1820 m Hester Brower Pvt NJ
David S: b 3-7-1736 d 11-24-1810 m Janetje Davids Campbell
   Capt NJ
Gilliam: bpt 9-26-1762 d 12-23-1811 m Breggie Brower Pvt NJ
Jacobus: b 1-23-1732 d 1-29-1808 m Tryntje Lozier Pvt NY
James: b 4-21-1735 d 10-21-1807 m Maria Smith Pvt NJ
James J: b 8-20-1749 d 10-9-1841 m Rachel Smith Pvt NY
Jan: b 5-18-1761 d 10-9-1819 m Annatie Hopper Pvt NJ W ★
John: b 8-2-1720 d 2-1-1783 m Rachel Zabriski Pvt NY
John: b 12-26-1732 d 5-14-1809 m Willemptie Bogert Pvt NJ
Nicholas: b 9-3-1730 d *c.* 1780 m Saurine Ackerman Sgt PA
Nickolas: b 2-26-1762 d 6-10-1845 m Maria Banta (Bouton) Pvt NY
Peter D.: b 6-8-1765 d 1844 m Cathalina Benson Sol NJ ★
Petrus: b 1-13-1759 d 10-1-1820 m Sara DeVoe Pvt NJ W ★
Philip: b 5-26-1761 d 3- -1844 m Maria Oblinus Pvt NJ
Roelof S: b 8-23-1756 d 9-4-1814 m Maria (Demarest) Pvt NJ
Samuel: b 5-29-1754 d 1819 m Grietje Martin Pvt NY
Samuel Peter: b 6-5-1724 d 3-14-1808 m Margaret Brinkerhoff PS NJ
Wm.: b 8-26-1762 d 3-13-1828 m Lavina Hopper Pvt Drm NJ

DEMARY, (includes DEMAREE)
David: b 4-1-1752 d 6-21-1830 m Elizabeth Slagle Pvt PA
John: b 1728 d 11- -1807 m Rebecca Corneille Sgt NH
Petrus: bpt 11-20-1737 d *p.* 1818 m Mary Allen Sol VA
Samuel: b *c.* 10-12-1746 d 12-20-1810 m Susanna Brower Capt NJ

DEMENT,
George: b c. 1741 d 1798 m (1)Sarah Gordon (2)Jocasta Wealaxton Pvt VA

DE MERIT, (includes DEMERITT, DE MERITT, DEMERRITT)
Daniel: b 4-23-1760 d 4-3-1822 m Sarah Hayes Pvt NH
John 2nd: b 5-29-1728 d 1-7-1826 m (1)Elizabeth Cate (2)Mrs Elizabeth Davis Maj NH
Joseph: b 6-17-1741 d 9- -1822 m Susan Runnals PS NH
Samuel: b 6-17-1756 d 11-1-1801 m Sallie Tibbetts Pvt NH

DE MILLE,
Garrett: bpt 8-12-1743 d c. 1826 m Magdalena Eighmay Pvt NY

DEMING,
Aaron: b 3-29-1744 d 3-12-1837 m Lydia Stoddard Pvt CT
Andrew: b 1-14-1761 d 11-25-1828 m Hannah Granger Matr MA
Benjamin: b 9-15-1754 d 1841 m Lovisa Hopkins MM MA ★
Daniel: b 12-31-1753 d 9-10-1828 m Judith (Deming) Sol CT
Daniel: b 3-28-1761 d 10-28-1848 m Sallie Johnson Pvt MA NY
David: bpt 10-20-1751 d 10- -1795 m Anne — Lt CT
David: b 8-16-1729 d 9-8-1789 m Elizabeth Robbins Pvt MA
Davis: b 6-4-1762 d 10-11-1839 m Elizabeth Ann Curtis Pvt CT
Edmund: b 1754 d — m Bethiah Clay Nichols Pvt CT ★
Eleazur: b 1718 d 9-24-1802 m Hannah Woodhouse Sol MA
Elias: b 4-11-1752 d 5-13-1814 m Martha Welles Pvt CT
Elijah: b 5-9-1735 d 10-10-1821 m Lucy Sage Capt MA
Elisha Harris: b 7-20-1759 d 6- -1821 m Mary Bailey Pvt CT
Ephraim: b 1-25-1746 d 7-16-1783 m Martha Deming Pvt CT
Gideon, Sr.: b 2-29-1700 d 5-29-1779 m Elizabeth Case PS CT
Gideon, Jr.: b 9-11-1730 d 3-6-1805 m Prudence Merril Pvt CT
Gideon, 3rd: b 5-30-1756 d 2-11-1846 m Deborah Kellogg Pvt CT
Jabez: b 1742 d 10-16-1799 m Lucy Stoddard Capt CT
John: b 1-8-1738 d 1-17-1815 m Mary Bryant Pvt CT
John: b 10-19-1728 d 1- -1790 m Sibyl — Cpl MA
John: b 3-14-1743 d 4-28-1812 m Purdence Treat Pvt MA
John: b 4-19-1743 d 1-5-1829 m Sarah Robbins Pvt MA
John: b 1761 d 5-22-1837 m Anna Halliday Pvt NY ★
Johnathan: b 11-21-1756 d 4-16-1836 m (1)Sarah Richmond (2)Jane Kelsey Sgt CT ★
Josiah: b 6-7-1758 d 9-6-1805 m Susannah Seymour Pvt CT
Juluis: b 4-16-1755 d 1-23-1838 m Dorothy Champion Capt CT
Lemuel: b 10-16-1735 d 4-25-1790 m Hannah Standish NCapt CT
Lemuel: b c. 1730-35 d 12-19-1801 m Hannah Risley Pvt CT
Moses: b 9-8-1720 d 1-16-1795 m Sarah Chloe Norton PS CT
Peter: b 12-22-1733 d 9-27-1813 m (1)Jerusha Welles (2)Mehitable Stillman PS CT
Phineas: b 1-26-1750 d p. 1778 m Mary Gaylord Pvt CT
Prosper: b 1760 d 3- -1852 m Alice Graves Pvt MA ★
Richard: b 4-11-1750 d 3-4-1805 m Millicent Merrill Vol CT
Samuel: b 1724 d 2-24-1796 m Anna Hart Pvt CT
Samuel: b 11-20-1755 d 12-11-1803 m Huldah Dewey Pvt NY
Selah: b 11-15-1762 d 5-26-1805 m Lovina Curtiss Pvt CT
Seth: b 1749 d 3-11-1827 m Hannah Gilbert Capt CT
Simeon: b 9-28-1751 d 12-9-1830 m Honor Woodford Cpl CT
Simeon: b 9-16-1751 d 8-21-1818 m Mary Curtis Pvt CT
Simeon: b 1763 d 7-30-1850 m Lucy Wolcott Pvt MA
Solomon: b 12-31-1736 d 1-11-1832 m (1)Eunice Harmon (2)Margaret Burt Lt MA
Solomon: b 7-8-1722 d c. 1820 m Sarah Kirkham Sct PS NY
Theron: b 3-13-1761 d 10-17-1839 m (1)Electa Ensign (2)Eleanor Faxon Pvt CT
Titus: b 2-29-1760 d 8-11-1833 m Sibyl Jeffords Pvt CT
Wait: b 5-9-1758 d 7-5-1787 m Ruth Ingraham Pvt CT
Wm.: b 1758 d 4-8-1835 m Bulah — Pvt MA ★

DE MINT,
Jarret: b 1759 d 1850 m Martha Price Nuttall Pvt Spy PA ★

DE MIRABEAU,
Boniface (Vicomte): b 1754 d 1792 m Mademoiselle de Robier FrCdr

DEMMON,
Levi: b 1749 d 3-24-1797 m Dorcas Wakefietd Pvt VT

DE MONBREUN,
Jacques Timothe Boucher, Sieur: b 3-23-1747 d 10- -1826 m Marguerite (Theresa) Archange Gibault PS CtyLt IL VA

DEMONS,
John: b 1-28-1727 d 2-7-1809 m Anna Knowles Pvt CT

DE MOSS,
Abraham Lewis: b 10- -1753 d 9-16-1820 m Hannah — Capt NC
Andrew: b 7-3-1753 d p. 8-15-1837 m Elizabeth — Pvt QM VA
John: b 1732 d 1820 m Sarah Alien Pvt VA
Peter: b 11-11-1752 d 2-27-1841 m Catherine Housman Pvt VA
Peter: b c. 1750 d p. 1830 m Mary — PS VA

DE MOTT,
Abraham: b 3-8-1751 d 1-9-1834 m (1)Christianah Van Allen (2)Hannah Van Horn Pvt NJ
Johannes: b 10-9-1749 d 1832 m Francyntie Roelofse PS NJ

Johannes: b 4-1-1716 d p. 8-21-1780 m (1)Elizabeth Davis (2)Altje — CS NJ
Lawrence: bpt 10-25-1719 d a. 5-14-1800 m Dorothy Vander Beek Pvt NJ
Peter: b 1758 d 10-15-1833 m Mary Terhune Pvt NJ ★
Richard: b 8-18-1759 d 8-13-1850 m Rebecca — Pvt NY

DEMPSEY,
Cornelius: b a. 1758 d 10- -1786 m Ann Iddings Pvt PA

DE MUN,
Wm.: b 1762 d 6-21-1839 m Martha Finley Pvt NJ

DEMUTH, (includes DEMOTH, DE MUTH)
Christian: b 8-22-1755 d 1-27-1822 m (1)Susanna Maria Klein (2)Elizabeth (Schwartz) Ginther Pvt PA
Christopher: b 9-19-1738 d 9-7-1818 m Ann Elizabeth Hartaffel Pvt PA
Gottlieb, Jr.: b 11-18-1750 d 1-25-1825 m Anna Maria Alleman Pvt PA
John Mark: b 1743 d 1785 m Catherine (Demoth) Capt NY

DEMY,
Christian: b c. 1740 d 2- -1813 m — Pvt PS PA

DENBY,
Jonathan: b a. 1761 d a. 4-16-1805 m (2)Mrs Elizabeth Heeley Drm Sol VA

DENCH,
Gilbert: b 1-17-1741 d 1807 m Anne Gibbs Capt MA

DENDY,
Wm.: b c. 1738 d p. 8-14-1800 m — Clary PS SC

DENELSBECK,
Frederick: b 1728 d 4-10-1800 m Barbary Elwell Pvt NJ

DE NEUS, (includes NICE)
John: b 1-26-1739 d 7-5-1806 m Sarah Engle Capt PA

DE NEUVILLE,
Noirmont: b 9- -1736 d 1800 m Marie Bellmare PS France

DENHAM,
Charles: b 12-5-1756 d p. 3-29-1805 m Ann — Sol GA

DENIG,
Ludwig: b 9-17-1755 d 9-17-1830 m (1)Barbara Guntaker (2)Cathrine Rogers Pvt PA

DENIKE,
Davis: b 6-26-1760 d — m Elizabeth Suter Pvt NJ ★

DENIO,
Aaron, Jr.: b 12-11-1755 d 4-21-1846 m Deborah Wood Pvt MA VT ★
Eli: b 10-5-1760 d — m Margaret Burghardt Pvt MA
Israel: b 3-20-1763 d 3-17-1846 m Esther Robbins Pvt MA
Joseph: b 1-8-1734 d 12-23-1820 m (1)Anna Severance (2)Mary Waite CS MA
Seth: b 8-5-1736 d 9-11-1826 m Rebecca Nims Allen Pvt MA
Solomon: b 8-19-1753 d a. 1810 m Esther Pennell Cpl MA

DENISE, (includes DENYSE, DE NYSE)
Daniel: b 4-8-1748 d 5-2-1823 m (1)Jane Schauck (2)Mary Stilwell Pvt NJ
Denise:b 12-22-1745 d 2-9-1796 m (1)Margaret Francis (2)Catherine Schenck 1Maj NJ
Denyse: b 4-5-1726 d 9-21-1806 m (1)Teuntje Van Brun (2)Elizabeth Bennett PS Maj NY
Isaac: b 10-18-1728 d 8-27-1799 m (1)Cornelia Hubbard (2)Seytie Voohees PS NY
Jacques: b 3-5-1744 d 12-24-1791 m Ann Schenck CaptLt PS NJ

DENMAN,
Andrew: b 11-2-1756 d 12-28-1826 m (1)Susanna March (2)Mary Camp Pvt Tms NJ
Christopher: b 3-5-1741 d 10-21-1808 m Abigail Hendricks Pvt NJ
Isaac: b 12-9-1751 d 1835 m Rachel — Pvt NY ★
Joseph: b 1735 d 10-21-1819 m (1)Catherine Townley (2)Sarah Woodruff (3)— (4)Sarah Woolley Tms NJ
Mathias: b 1758 d 9-3-1836 m Rhoda Elston Pvt NJ
Matthias: b 2-19-1751 d 1-24-1841 m (1)Phebe Baldwin (2)Abigail Woodruff Pvt NJ ★
Philip: b 1749 d 1-8-1825 m (2)Abigail Woodruff MM NJ
Stephen: b 1759 d 10-9-1824 m Sarah Whitehead Pvt NJ
Thomas, Jr.: b c. 1749 d 1-24-1823 m Joanna Chandler Sol NJ
Thomas, Sr.: b 1706 d 1793 m Peggy Mulford PS NJ

DENNARD,
Jacob: b 1750 d 1810 m Harriet — Lt SC

DENNETT,
David: b 3-15-1727 d 8-20-1777 m Dolly Downing Pvt MA
Ebenezer: b 8-31-1756/57 d 4-2-1834 m Anna Roberts Pvt MA
Ephriam: b 7-22-1718 d *p.* 1790 m Lydia (Waterhouse) Colby PS NH
Jeremiah: b 12-25-1752 d *p.* 1790 m Susannah Peverly PS NH
John: b 10-15-1716 d 1787 m Phebe Bartlett PS NH
Joseph: b 5-30-1755 d 6-23-1839 m Sally Wakefield Pvt MA ★
Samuel: b 2-6-1755 d 7-21-1836 m (1)Sarah Woodward (2)Abigail Carlyle (3)Hannah Trickey Pvt MA

DENNING,
Samuel: b 11-12-1732 d 1798 m Keziah Bray Smn MA
Wm.: b 4- -1740 d 10-30-1819 m (1)Sarah Hawxhurst (2)Ann (Hawxhurst) McIntosh PS 2Lt NY
Wm.: b 1744 d 12-19-1830 m Mary — Pvt Arfr PA ★

DENNIS, (includes DENNESS)
Adonijah: b 7-12-1759 d 9-15-1842 m Eunice Silbey Pvt MA
Arthur: b 12-25-1745 d 4-24-1825 m Mary Goohue Sgt MA
Benjamin: bpt 7-8-1739 d 10-10-1821 m Sarah Ingalls Pvt MA
Benjamin: bpt 7-27-1740 d 7- -1779 m Hannah Little Capt NJ
David: b 1751 d 1835 m Mary Ann Frambes Pvt NJ
Francis Bowden: bpt 3-9-1745 d 9-2-1812 m Elizabeth — NCdr MA
Henry: b c. 1750 d 1849 m (1)Narcissa Ellen Pitts (2)Mrs Elizabeth (Purnell)Smack Pvt MD
Isaac: b c. 1750 d *p.* 1829 m Sarah Issac Sol GA
Isaac: b 8- -1743 d 5;3;1796 m Tamer Beundige PS NY
Isaac: b 2-12-1742 d 4-4-1813 m Sarah Jarvis 2Lt NY
Jacob: b 2-27-1727 d 1797 m (1)Margaret Price (2)Belphane Capt NJ
James: b 8-27-1761 d *p.* 6-13-1838 m — Pvt Grd PA
John, Sr.: b c. 1725 d *p.* 1797 m Mary — Sol PS GA
John: b 10-30-1760 d 6-8-1850 m (2)Sarah Higbee Pvt NJ ★
John: b 2-26-1726 d 12-21-1806 m Mary Jacques PS NJ
John: b 5-11-1764 d 1-16-1811 m Eve Amigh Pvt NY
John: b 1759 d 11-14-1850 m Mary Dale Pvt SC
John Charles Frederick: b 1750 d 4-4-1835 m Abigail Fox Pvt MA ★
Jonathan: b c. 1745 d 10-12-1817 m Mary — Maj PS NY
Matthew: b 1720 d 1818 m Lavizor Pvt NJ
Moses: b 5-27-1752 d 12-18-1845 m Sarah Frye Pvt MA ★
Robert: b 9-12-1727 d 4-12-1811 m Hannah Coggeshall CS RI
Samuel: b 5-4-1756 d 8-30-1822 m Eunice Gallup Mar NS CT
Samuel: b 1757 d 1820 m Mary Yocum PS CS VA
Thomas: b 1757 d 8-13-1838 m Lydia Crandel Pvt RI
Wm.: b c. 1745 d *p.* 5-29-1800 m Mary Nash Capt NC
Wm.: b 1750 d 9-9-1826 m Amy Nichols NCapt RI

DENNISON, (includes DENISON, DENNISTON)
Amos: b 3-18-1759 d 1835 m Hannah Williams Ens CT
Andrew, Jr.: b 1750/51 d 1822 m (1)Ann Barclay (2)Agnes — Pvt CT
Beebe: b 1-1-1744 d 2-10-1823 m Prudence Holmes Pvt CT
Charles: b 2-25-1736 d 7-2-1820 m Catrien Barheyt Pvt NY
Chauncey: b 1-22-1762 d 7-18-1838 m Sarah Grannis Pvt CT ★
Christopher: b 10- -1743 d 1839 m Cecelia Dudley Sgt NY ★
Daniel, Jr.: b 12-9-1745 d 10-15-1802 m Elizabeth Andross Sgt CT
Daniel, 2nd: b 9-1-1742 d 1-17-1808 m Dorothy Denison Pvt CT
Daniel: b 1758 d 2-3-1824 m Elizabeth Kierstadt Lt NY ★
Daniel, Jr.: b 12-16-1730 d 12-16-1793 m Katherine Avery Sgt NY
David: b 8-16-1734 d 3-5-1799 m Jane Haraden Slr MA
David: b 8-15-1760 d 10-4-1843 m (1)Mehitable Soule (2)Susannah Haraden Griffin Pvt MA
David: b 1-29-1736 d 1-24-1808 m Keziah Smith CS VT
Eleazer: b 12-24-1744 d 1784 m Susanna Elderkin Ens CT
Elisha: b 11-3-1734 d 5-6-1809 m Keturah Minor Cnt CT
George: b 9-16-1753 d 1-25-1835 m Mrs Abigail Gardner Palmer Cpl CT ★
George: b 5- -1746 d 6-3-1833 m Bethiah Crandall Pvt CT
George: b 10-8-1751 d 1-19-1829 m (1)Theody Brown (2)Submit Lyman Sgt CT
Gilbert: b 9-18-1762 d *p.* 9-16-1834 m (1)Huldah Palmer (2)Abigail Stone Pvt CT ★
Henry: b 11-26-1753 d 9-20-1835 m Mary Gallup Lt CT ★
Isaac: b 1-2-1761 d 6-21-1841 m Sarah Rowe Sgt MA ★
Jabez: b 5-4-1759 d 10-8-1809 m Mary Briggs Pvt MA
James: b 4-18-1748 d 1778 m Esther Brown Capt NY
James: b 2-22-1733 d 3-15-1806 m Jane Crawford Pvt NY
James: b 8-25-1745 d 4-26-1813 m Eunice Stanton Grd VT
James: b 12-3-1761 d 9-21-1850 m Taphenah Kirtland Pvt CT ★
Jedediah: b 12-23-1759 d 11-30-1833 m Abigail — Pvt CT ★
John: b c. 1724 d 3-18-1814 m Sarah Hough Sgt CT
John: b 1751 d 1796 m Lucy Wells Pvt NH
John: b 3-26-1749 d 1832 m Phoebe Reynolds Pvt NY
John: b 12-15-1756 d 1-7-1836 m Anna Moffat Pvt NY
John: b 10-29-1748 d 10-29-1821 m Mary McCullough Pvt PA
John: b 1757 d 9-16-1805 m Nancy Cooper Pvt PA
Jonathan: b 5-17-1761 d 9-19-1833 m Sarah Greene Sol NY
Joseph: b 3-20-1750 d 3-12-1833 m Mary Smith Ens CT ★
Joseph: b 10-13-1744 d 1830 m Anna Lay Pvt CT
Joseph: b 9-21-1707 d 2-15-1795 m Bridget (Noyes) Wheeler CS CT
Joseph: b 1-26-1723 d *p.* 1790 m Lucy Chesebrough PS CT
Nathan, Sr.: b 2-20-1716 d 1803 m (1)Ann Cary (2)Hannah Fuller Pvt CT

Nathan, Jr.: b 1-25-1740 d 1-25-1809 m Elizabeth Sill Col PA
Nathaniel: b 1748 d 1795 m Desire Wilcox Sgt CT
Peleg: b 7-6-1755 d 5-21-1800 m Mary Gray Pvt CT
Robert: b 9-26-1749 d 2-9-1820 m (1)Alice Swann (2)Deborah Dewey 3Sgt CT
Samuel: b 1-8-1741 d 1836 m Mary Champlin Sgt CT
Wm.: b 4-8-1756 d 7-21-1820 m Anna Slack Cpl CT
Wm.: b 1741 d 1825 m Hannah Little Capt NY
Wm.: b 1750 d 3-11-1842 m Elizabeth Wilson Pvt NJ PA ★
Wm.: b 1761 d 8-11-1840 m Rachel John Pvt PA

DENNY, (includes DENNEY, DENNIE)
Alexander: b 1747 d 2-5-1827 m (1)Mary Allison (2)Mrs Annie Clinton Adams PS NC
Alexander: b 1744 d 1784 m Frances — Pvt VA
Charles: b 12-25-1759 d 8-6-1839 m Lucinda Allen Pvt NY ★
David: b 1744/45 d *p.* 1820 m Margaret (Denny)Sol PA
David: b 1740 d 11-4-1820 m Martha McClure Capt PA
Ebenezer: b 3-11-1761 d 7-21-1822 m Nancy Wilkins Maj PA
Elijah: b 1755 d 4-23-1863 m — Sgt NC ★
Elijah: b 1737 d 1856 m Rebecca — Pvt SC VA
George: b 1710-14 d c. 1788 m — PS NC
Gideon: b 1750 d 2- -1825 m Mary Rando Pvt PS NJ
Henry: b 1758 d 9-15-1839 m (1)Mary Yonge (2)Ann Bayley Sgt NJ ★
James: b 1715 d *p.* 12-10-1790 m Agnes — PS NC
James: b 1752 d 1835 m Sarah Miller Pvt PA ★
John: b 1725 d 10-15-1782 m (1)Margery B (2)Sarah Smiley Pvt PA
Nicholas: bpt 11-13-1754 d 6-1-1845 m Anna Margaret Stoller Sol NY
Richard: b 7- -1745 d 7-28-1825 m Aseneth Booth Sol NY
Robert: b 5-14-1753 d 4-17-1826 m Rachel Thomas Lt VA
Samuel: b 5-20-1731 d 9-20-1817 m Elizabeth Bass Henshaw Col PS MA
Samuel: b 4-10-1739 d 5-18-1822 m Jane Sterling Pvt PA
Thomas: b 3-19-1725 d 10-23-1774 m (2)Mary Chaplain Storrs Col MA
Walter: b 3-17-1751 d 3-30-1841 m Elizabeth McConnell Capt PA
Walter, Sr.: b 1728 d 5-1-1778 m Margery — Capt PA
Wm.: b 1737 d 1800 m Agnes Parker Cmsry PA
Wm.: b 9-27-1748 d 4-5-1832 m Mary Shields 1Lt VA

DE NOYELLES,
John: b 1734 d 1-11-1775 m Rachel Shatvort Pvt NY

DENSLOW,
Benjamin: b 5-10-1760 d 4-13-1851 m Ruth Spencer Pvt CT
Charles: b 1739 d *p.* 1788 m Martha Alcott Sol MA
Eli: b 2-22-1759/60 d 4-9-1833 m Polly Andrews Pvt CT ★
Elijah, Sr.: b 5-9-1738 d 8-28-1795 m Lydia Fuller Sgt CT
Elijah, Jr.: b 1-6-1764 d 10-1-1849 m Susannah Brown Pvt CT ★
Joseph: b 12-9-1740 d 2-24-1826 m (1)Mary Holliday (2)Abigail Simmons Sol MA
Martin: b 4-25-1745 d 10-24-1817 m Lois Wiard Lt CT

DENSON,
Wm.: b 12-20-1732 d 9-1-1779 m Rebecca Eley Pvt NC

DENT,
Benjamin: b 6-21-1750 d 2-6-1835 m (2)Ann Hancock Pvt MD
George: b 1756 d 12-2-1813 m Anna Magruder Trueman Capt MD
George: b 1756 d 1812 m Mrs Susanna Marbury Cromwell 1Lt MD
George: b 12-21-1756 d 10-15-1842 m Elizabeth Temperance Mills Pvt MD ★
Gideon: b a. 1755 d a. 2-15-1814 m Mary — Pvt MD
Hatch: b 5-20-1751 d 12-30-1799 m Judith Posten Capt MD
Hatch: b c. 1750 d *p.* 1-19-1816 m (1)Susanna Edwards (2)Elizabeth — Pvt MD
Hezekiah: b 8-2-1747 d 9-8-1782 m (1)Catharine Poston (2)Martha Burch Capt MD
John: b 11-7-1732 d 1809 m Sarah Marshall BGen MD
John: b 12-2-1729 d 1778 m Margaret Dyson CS MD
John: b 1735 d 1830 m Violetta Winnett PS MD
John: b 1753 d 3- -1828 m Verlinda Beall PS MD
John: b 1-20-1755 d 9-20-1840 m Margaret Evans Lt VA ★
John: b 1753 d 1835 m Eleanor McGillicuddy Sol VA
John Brewer: b 5-9-1759 d 4-24-1838 m Priscilla Elizabeth Dent Pvt MD
Joseph Manning: b c. 1750 d *p.* 1790 m Mary Manning Ens MD
Michael: b a. 1717 d 1795 m — Manning PS MD
Peter: b 1-10-1728 d 1785 m (1)Mary Eleanor (2)Anne — PS Pvt MD
Thomas: b 1735 d 1788 m Elizabeth Edelen PS MD
Walter: b 1744 d — m Elizabeth Montgomery Pvt MD
Wm.: b 1756 d 1816 m Margaretta Smoot Pvt MD
Wm.: b 1735 d *p.* 1794 m Virlinda Beall PS NC
Zachariah: b c. 1755-60 d 12-18-1828 m Elizabeth — Sgt MD

DENTON,
Benjamin: b 1721 d 5-12-1789 m Rebecca Ketcham Pvt NY
Benjamin, Sr.: b c. 1715 d c. 1780 m Ruth Hopkins PS NY
Daniel: b 8-9-1757 d 3-30-1826 m Martha Bidlack Cpl CT ★
David: b 12-25-1755 d 5-18-1838 m Rachel — Pvt VA
Isaac: b 5-7-1737 d 10-27-1822 m Susanna Pearsall PS NY

James, Sr.: b 1716 d 1799 m (1)Mary Burton (2)Margaret Barton PS NY
John: b — d 1808 m Abigail Walker 1Lt MA
John: b 1750 d 8-4-1819 m Tabitha Mann Sol VA
Jonas: b 1743 d 1786 m Eleanor Jackson Pvt NY
Joseph: b 3-27-1759 d 8-8-1832 m Hannah Yelverton Ens NY
Preston: b 7-1-1755 d 11-13-1826 m Esther Deyoe Pvt NY
Samuel: bpt 1-23-1737 d *p.* 8-21-1813 m Mrs Hannah Weeks PS Pvt NY
Samuel: b *c.* 1745 d *p.* 4-12-1786 m Elizabeth — Pvt NC
Solomon: b 8-4-1754 d 2-11-1828 m Clarissa Fowler Sol CT
Thomas: b 12-27-1742 d — m Elizabeth Griggs PS NY

DENUNE,
John: b 1761 d 11-28-1838 m Sarah Burrell Mus MD

DE PAUW,
Charles: b 3-11-1753 d 8-31-1814 m Rachel Young Pvt CL

DE PEYSTER,
Wm., Jr.: b 2-10-1735 d 3-3-1803 m Elizabeth Brasier Capt NY

DE PLASSE',
Joseph Duguay: b — d 1781 m Catherine Barrois Capt PS VA

DEPP,
Peter: b *c.* 1735 d *p.* 3-13-1807 m Susannah Harris PS VA
Wm.: b 3-25-1761 d 10-9-1834 m Elizabeth Walker Pvt VA ★

DEPPEN,
Christian: b 12-20-1705 d 1782 m Veronica Ruchty PS PA
John: b *c.* 1745 d 10-14-1827 m Anna Barbara — Pvt PA
Joseph: b 1752 d 10-13-1826 m Elizabeth Weigley Pvt PA
Peter: b 6-28-1749 d 10-31-1823 m Barbara Kobel Pvt PA

DE PRIEST,
Robert: b 11-1-1763 d 8-6-1839 m Martha Taylor Pvt VA ★
Wm.: b 1760 d 1844 m Esther Davies Pvt VA NC SC ★

DEPUE, (includes DEPEW, DEPOY, DEPUY, & DE PUY)
Aaron, Jr.: b 1760 d 1845 m Elizabeth La Bar Pvt PA ★
Abraham: b 10-10-1762 d 12-26-1838 m (1)Mary Crab (2)Catherine Crankheit Pvt NY
Abram: b *c.* 1755 d 1816 m Magdalena — Pvt PA
Barnt: b 1717 d 5-1-1777 m Elsie Poillon PS NY
Benjamin: b 12-14-1757 d 6-1-1840 m Osee Stivers Pvt NY
Benjamin: b 1728 d 1806 m Lisabeth Swartwout PS NY
Benjamin: b 6- -1729 d 9-26-1811 m Catherina Van Campen PS CS PA
Daniel: bpt 12-25-1723 d 1793 m Elizabeth Decker 1Lt NY
David: b 10- -1750 d 7-4-1843 m Polly McLeane Sgt NY
Elias: b *c.* 1728 d *a.* 4-18-1779 m Rachel Robinson Pvt NY
Ephraim, Sr.: b 2-8-1730 d *p.* 1790 m Antje Schoonmaker Lt PS NY
Ephraim, Jr.: bpt 1-10-1755 d 1807 m Cornelia Snyder Pvt PS NY
Isaac: b 1760 d 4-15-1839 m Catherine Ketterman Pvt NY ★
Isaac: b 12-15-1728 d *p.* 3-5-1809 m Jane Rose 2Lt PA
Isaac: b 9-16-1758 d 12- -1854 m (1)Jane Jones (2) — Graham Pvt VA
James: b 5-5-1758 d 7-3-1823 m Mary Purnell Capt VA
James: b *c.* 1725 d 12-9-1811 m Prudence Wills Sol VA
John: b 2-20-1756 d 10-1-1832 m Mary Watkins Capt VA ★
John: b 1728 d 4-21-1811 m Catherine Shepherd Pvt VA
Joseph: b 1-14-1750 d 1831 m Maria (DePuy) PS Pvt NY
Moses: b 1-28-1754 d 1-23-1828 m Hellena Hardenbergh Lt NY W★
Moses: b 1-21-1718 d 9-2-1802 m Elizabeth Clearwater PS NY
Moses: b 2-16-1761 d — m Margaret Van Gorden Ens NY
Nicholas: b 8-19-1728 d 4-23-1808 m Eleanor Shoemaker PS CS PA
Peter: b 7-1-1760 d 8-29-1826 m Margaret Martin Lt VA
Peter: b 2-12-1728/29 d *p.* 1788 m Elizabeth Malone Sol VA
Samuel: bpt 10-29-1749 d 1821 m Anna Swartwout Ens NY
Wm.: b 3-19-1752 d 5-29-1818 m Hannah Lacy Pvt NY

DE PUTRON,
Wm.: b 1750 d 2-15-1837 m Prudence — Pvt RI ★

DERAMUS,
John: b *c.* 1759/60 d *c.* 1800 m Ann — Pvt SC

DE RANKE,
Cornelius: bpt 5-21-1745 d *a.* 7-15-1814 m Annatje Terwilliger Sgt NY

DERICKSON,
Jacob: b 1741 d 9-14-1809 m Elenor Stidham Pvt DE
Samuel: b 2-28-1754 d 6-7-1817 m Elizabeth — Lt DE

DERMOND,
John: b 1738 d 7- -1809 m Esther Flenniken Sol NC

DE ROCHE,
Abraham: b *c.* 1740-50 d 1799 m (1)Elizabeth Graff (2)Isabella — Pvt PA

DE ROGUEFEUIL,
Charles Balthasard: b 9-29-1752 d 8-1-1795 m Marie-Jeanne de Roguefeuil Lt FrA

DE RONDE,
John: b 8-2-1760 d 10-9-1851 m Martha Goldtrap Pvt NY ★

DE ROULHAC,
John Gregoire: b 11-23-1738 d 11-4-1810 m (1)Jamina Maule (2)Frances Lee Gray PS FrN
Psalmet: b 10-30-1752 d 10-8-1808 m (1)Anne Hare Maule (2)Elizabeth (Barrow) (Adams) Archbell PS NC

DERR, (includes DARR, DORR)
Abraham: b 1737 d 1-27-1798 m Magdalena Bullinger Pvt PA
George: b 1762 d 2-5-1829 m Fannie Yentzer Pvt PA
George: b *c.* 1750-52 d 1803 m Christina Heger Pvt PA
Jacob: b 2-11-1751 d 8-22-1829 m — Miller Pvt PA
John: b 8-5-1753 d 11-27-1846 m Anna Mary Margaret Roschong Pvt PA
John: b 3-30-1755 d 10-4-1831 m Catharine Brown Pvt PA
Ludwig: b — d *c.* 1785 m Catherine Lorah Derr Pvt PA
Matthias: b 2-15-1744 d 4-17-1836 m Elisabeth Strickler Pvt PA ★
Michael: b 1760 d *c.* 1838 m Elizabeth Miller Ens PA

DERRICK,
Ephraim: b 4-21-1756 d 9-27-1832 m (1)Anna Dodge (2)Elizabeth Gustin Sgt CT
George: b *c.* 1760 d *p.* 1794 m Ann — Pvt PA
Zachariah: b 1756 d 1821 m Hannah — Sol PA

DERRY,
Peter: b 6-6-1755 d 9-4-1824 m Rachel Blending Pvt MA ★

DERUMPLE,
Wm.: b *c.* 1721 d 5-9-1782 m Elizabeth Blood Sgt MA

DE RUSSY,
Thomas: b *c.* 1761 d 2-21-1821 m Marie Madeleine Bessieres Lt FrN W★

DE SAINT AULAIRE,
Marc-Antoine de Beaupoil: b 4-20-1763 d 8-6-1795 m Marie Harpendane de Belleville Lt FrN

DE SAINT EXUPERY,
Georges Alexander Cesaree: b 5-17-1757 d 5-8-1825 m Suzanne Victoire Green de St Marsault 2Lt FrA

DESHA,
Joseph: b 1760 d 10-13-1842 m Margaret Bledsoe Pvt KY
Robert: b *c.* 1738 d *p.* 5-6-1816 m Eleanor Wheeler Pvt VA

DE SHAZO,
Wm.: b 1759 d 4-24-1839 m Jane King Pvt VA ★

DESHLER,
Adam, Sr.: b 1713 d 9-20-1781 m Appolonia — PS PA
Adam, Jr.: b 10-1-1745 d 2-24-1790 m Maria Catherine Balliet Pvt PA
David: b 1733 d 12-4-1796 m Susannah Elizabeth Muhlenburg PS PA
Peter: b 3-18-1743 d 9-28-1800 m Magdalena Mickley Pvt PA

DESHON, (includes DISHON)
Daniel: b 8-9-1754 d 10- -1826 m Mary Ann Packwood NCapt CT
John: b 12-25-1727 d 6-25-1792 m Sarah Starr Capt PS CT
Lewis: b 1763 d 5-21-1843 m Elizabeth Rhody Pvt Mar Pvtr NC ★

DESILLETS,
Antoine Chauvin Deleri: b *c.* 1720 d *a.* 2-16-1789 m Charlotte Dumanoir PS FrA LA

DE SURRENCY,
Samuel: b 7-12-1753 d 1824 m Elizabeth Stafford Pvt SC

DE TOUSARD,
Anne Louis: b 7- -1751 d 5-3-1817 m Marie Francois Reine Joubert Col ADC to Lafayette FrA ★

DE TRAY,
John Peter Anthony: b *c.* 1756 d 1824 m Olive Carpenter Sol FrA

DETTER, (includes DEETER, DIETER)
Adam: b 1-27-1751 d 10-24-1829 m Susanna Lamper Drm PA
Hans Wm.: b *c.* 1730 d *c.* 1790 m Elizabeth — Pvt PA
John: b 12-15-1751 d 4-8-1824 m Maria Magdalena Kohl Capt PA
Matthias: b 1726 d 4-30-1802 m Mary Magdalene Streber Pvt PA

DE TURK,
Abraham: b 3-3-1752 d 4-19-1829 m Anna Weiser Pvt PA
Daniel: b 9-8-1742 d 6-27-1791 m Catharine Levan Capt PA

DE TURK, contd.
John, Sr.: b 9-23-1713 d c. 1781 m Debora High PS Pvt PA
John, Jr.: b 1-20-1747 d 4- -1809 m Elizabeth Bertolet Pvt PA
Philip: b 4-30-1757 d 11-10-1815 m (1)Esther Shenkel (2)Maria
　　　Hock Pvt PA
Samuel: b 5-25-1750 d 11-8-1815 m Catherine Kerst Pvt PA

DETWILER, (includes DETTWEILLER, DETWEILLER)
Christian: b c. 1760 d 1826 m Barbara Fisher Pvt PA
Jacob: b 1735 d 1799 m Sarah — Pvt PA
Jacob: b 1733 d 3- -1804 m (1)Anna — (2)Mary — PS PA
Jacob, Jr.: b 1755-60 d 12- -1831 m Frena (Veronica) — Pvt PA
John: b 1-8-1747 d 7-1-1826 m (1)Catherine Funk (2)Mrs Elizabeth
　　　Horning Pvt PA
John: b c. 1730 d 1788 m Anna Mary — Pvt PA

DEUEL,
Benjamin: b 1726 d 1811 m Mercy Bennett Pvt NY
Wilber: b a. 1750 d 1823 m Phebe (Thorne?) Pvt NY

DE VANE,
John, Sr.: b 1734 d p. 9-14-1783 m Mary Robinson 2Maj PS CS NC
John, Jr.: b 12-25-1755 d 6-15-1802 m Mrs Ann Julian (Davis)
　　　Evans Capt NC W ★

DE VAULT, (includes DE WALD, THERWALD)
George: b 1743 d 4- -1825 m — PS PA
Henry: b 4-10-1733 d 4-16-1817 m Catherine Maria Grover Lt PA
John: b 4-22-1746 d 4-12-1816 m Catherine Dewald Pvt PA
Michael: b 8- -1716 d 12-31-1798 m Maria Barbara Schmidt PS PA

DEVENY, (includes DEVINEY, DEVINNEY)
Aaron: b 4-16-1747 d 3-16-1842 m Sarah — Capt NC ★
Andrew: b c. 1751 d 1816 m Rachel (Lawerence?) Maj PA
John: b 1756 d 2-15-1825 m Ann A. Flemming Pvt PA ★

DEVEREAUX, (includes DEVEREUX)
Benjamin: bpt 9- -1754 d 11-16-1831 m Elizabeth Gatchel Pvt MA
Charles: b 1740 d p. 1-1-1785 m Nancy Woods PS CS VA
John: b 7-13-1748 d 1-3-1788 m Mary Broughton Capt MA
Jonathan: b c. 1750 d 1802 m Lydia Williams Pvt NY
Theodorus: b 7-19-1763 d 4-29-1823 m (1)Hannah Moffitt (2)Betsy
　　　Wood Pvt NY

DE VERGES,
Francois: b 1750 d p. 1780 m Madeleine Josephine de Lino
　　　Chalmette PS LA

DEVIER,
Hugh: b 1752 d 1787 m Margaret Ann Smith Pvt MD

DE VILLENEUVE,
August Clement: b 8-19-1750 d 12-30-1781 m Marie Louise Le
　　　Brett Capt FrA

DE VILLIERS,
Louis: b 1746 d 5-17-1818 m Marie Genevieve Fontenette Ens LA

DEVIN,
Wm.: b c. 1725 d 1802 m Sarah — CS VA

DEVINE,
Asher: b 3-10-1740 d 10-18-1804 m — Pvt NY
John: b 1765 d p. 1806 m Natchen Carle Pvt PA

DEVLIN,
James: b 7-10-1750 d 12-20-1825 m Margaret Ann Grey Pvt SC

DEVOE, (includes DEVEAU, DE VEAUX, DE VOU)
Abel: b 1755 d 4-9-1831 m Jemima Seacor Pvt NY
Abraham: b 1735 d 1826 m Elizabeth Parcells Pvt NY
Anthony: b 3-11-1762 d 1-12-1844 m Helen Vanderberg Pvt NY
Daniel: b 1748 d 1804 m Mary Avery Sol NY
Elizabeth Parcells: b.c 1738 d 1818 m Abraham De Voe PS NJ
Isaac: b 7-9-1750 d 11-24-1824 m Sarah Laird Pvt DE
Jacob: b 1727 d 1824 m Elizabeth Williams Pvt NY
Jacobus: bpt 4-15-1727 d p. 1785 m Catrina Storm Pvt NY
Jeremiah: b 6-15-1757 d p. 3-10-1826 m Lena Danielson Wgn
　　　Pvt NY ★
John, Jr.: b 1744 d p. 1778 m (1)Sarah Frazier (2)Widow Sheever
　　　Lt NY
John: b 1756 d 9-8-1824 m Rebecca (De Voe) Pvt NY
John: b 2-16-1763 d 3-10-1837 m Helen Godwin Pvt NY
John: b — d 8-16-1777 m — Pvt RI
Peter: b 10-10-1752 d 10-6-1826 m (1)Martha Box (2)Mary Eleanor
　　　Box PS Maj GA

DEVORE, (includes DEVOUR)
John: b c. 1752 d 1803 m Esther — Pvt PA
Nicholas: b 2-22-1732 d 3-30-1815 m Sarah Decker Pvt PA
Samuel: b 1751 d 1826 m Charity Johnson Ens PA

DEW,
Arthur: b c. 1728 d 1791-1800 m Mary — Sol NC
John: b 1-4-1764 d 10- -1823 m (1)Rocky Cannon (2)Nancy (Tarver)
　　　Wright Sgt NC W ★
Thomas R.: b 5-28-1764 4-23-1849 m Lucy Gatewood Pvt VA

DEWEES, (includes DEWEESE, DE WEESE)
Cornelius: b 3-22-1731 d p. 1780 m Elizabeth Jones Sol PA
Cornelius: b 1747/48 d p. 10-26-1779 m Elizabeth Draper Sol DE
Henry: b 1716 d 1801 m Rachel — PS PA
Hezekiah: b 3-28-1760 d 7-25-1839 m Annis — Pvt NC ★
John: b 1757 d p. 1785 m Anna Maria Faust Drm PA
Joshua: b 5-3-1742 d p. 12-4-1791 m (1)Elizabeth Bowman
　　　(2)Hannah Birch (3)Elizabeth New Pvt DE
Owen: b c. 1760 d p. 1800 m Mary Lee Pvt PA
Samuel: b c. 1738 d 12- -1777 m Elizabeth — Sgt PA
Thomas: b c. 1738 d 1781 m Hannah Potts PS PA
Wm.: b c. 1740 d 1809 m (1)Sarah Potts (2)Sarah Waters Col PA

DEWEY,
Aaron, Sr.: b 8-25-1734 d p. 1790 m Mary Porter Cpl MA
Aaron, 2nd: b 1-15-1751 d p. Sibyl Calwell Pvt MA
Aaron, Jr.: b 12-13-1759 d 1847 m (1)Eunice Colby (2)Anna
　　　Lawrence Pvt MA
Abner: b 1751 d 1802 m (2)Mrs Rhoda (Stoddard) Jones Pvt MA
Alpheus: b 1760 d 3-25-1813 m Lydia Frink Pvt CT ★
Asaph: b 2-2-1758 d 1-17-1833 m Penelope Sacket Sol MA
Barzilla: b 10-13-1761 d 1841 m — McKee Sol MA
Benjamin: b 4-15-1743 d 10-7-1812 m Rhoda Loomis Sgt MA
Daniel: b 6-31-1731 d 3-9-1816 m Temperance Bailey Capt CT
Daniel: b 3-10-1729 d 4-1-1776 m (1)Ruth Taylor (2)Abigail(Saxton)
　　　Huggins Capt MA
Darius: b 8-22-1757 d 12-13-1849 m Rachel Brigham Pvt CT
David: b 3-9-1741 d p. 1790 m Zibiah Danks Pvt MA
David: b 3-2-1746 d 5-1-1839 m Sarah Witter Pvt MM RI
David: b 4-18-1752 d 1-6-1835 m Seviah Knowlton Cpl MA
Ebenezer, Sr.: b 1-24-1712 d 11-24-1791 m (1)Martha Wilcox
　　　(2)Christina Phelps (3)— Young PS NH
Ebenezer, Jr.: b 3-7-1740 d 2-28-1820 m Temperance Holdridge
　　　Pvt PS CS NH
Eleazer: b 8-1761 d 2-12-1824 m Freelove Booen Tms Pvt CT
Elias: b 1763 d p. 9-16-1833 m Anna Foote Pvt MA
Elijah: b 1-26-1744 d 10-16-1818 m Eunice Brush Capt VT
Eliphalet: b — d — m Rachel Ann Hyde Pvt CT
Enoch: b 10-15-1745 d 2-16-1778 m Martha Foote Pvt MA
Gideon: b 7-7-1758 d 6-11-1830 m (1)Joanna Allen (2)Mrs Eunice
　　　Hawley Weller Pvt MA
Herman: b 10-18-1761 d p. 1805 m Sarah Noble Pvt MA
Hugo: b 12-4-1753 d 4-17-1833 m Hannah Sprague Pvt MA
Israel: b 1-27-1719 d 6-24-1806 m Joanna Noble Sol MA
Jedediah: b 4-11-1714 d 12-21-1778 m (1)Mindwell Hayden
　　　(2)Betty Buck PS VT
Jeremiah: b 3-13-1763 d 1- -1848 m Cynthia Claghorn Fif VT
John: b 12-12-1735 d 6-11-1830 m Rhoda Gillett Pvt CT
John: b 6-27-1743 d 1-17-1807 m Mary Phelps Pvt CT
John: b 1-20-1754 d 12-31-1821 m Achsah Clapp Sol MA
John Woodward: b 12-31-1742 d 11-15-1839 m (1)Abigail Rudd
　　　(2)Mrs Emma Tupper Pvt CT W ★
Joseph: b 5-10-1733 d 2-24-1778 m Deborah Buell Pvt CT
Josiah: b 5-5-1727 d 3-5-1808 m Huldah Frost Ens PS CT
Josiah: b 2-27-1758 d 1-14-1838 m Lydia Davis Pvt CT
Josiah: b 1756 d 5-5-1805 m Fichia Burghard MM Sgt NH MA
Justin: b 1-5-1752 d 8-31-1832 m Lucy Mears Cpl MA
Levi: b 1-28-1764 d 4-30-1827 m Mary Scott Pvt MA
Martin: b 11-1-1756 d 3-15-1849 m (1)Hannah Waterman (2)Olive
　　　Smith Pvt CT ★
Medad: b 12-20-1760 d 4-15-1849 m Tryphena Roberts Pvt MA
Moses: b 3-21-1739 d 10-11-1820 m Hannah Noble Sgt MA
Nathaniel: b 10-27-1750 d 1807 m Margaret Wise Pvt CT
Oliver: b 8-12-1763 d 1-20-1845 m Huldah Morley Pvt MA
Paul: b 3-6-1739 d 8-8-1827 m Susan Reed Sgt MA
Peletiah: b 9-2-1754 d 2- -1822 m Sarah Norton Pvt CT
Russell: b 8-7-1754 d 2-18-1827 m Sophia Chapin QMSgt MA ★
Samuel Rowley: b 12-25-1757 d 1829 m Hannah Gilbert Pvt CT MA
Samuel: b 3- -1763 d 2-7-1854 m (1)Susan — (2)— (3)Sally
　　　Ingraham Tms Pvt VT NY ★
Silas: b 1-9-1761 d p. 6-1-1840 m Elizabeth Spencer Pvt CT ★
Simeon, 2nd: b 2-22-1745 d 9-2-1830 m (1)Hannah Bliss (2)Mrs
　　　Elizabeth (Bridgman) Turner Ens NH
Solomon: b 3-21-1750 d 1-27-1813 m Christina Cone Ens CS CT
Solomon: b 3-1-1743 d 12-11-1818 m Olive Otis Sgt MA
Stephen, Sr.: b 3-13-1719 d 7-25-1796 m (1)Joanna Taylor
　　　(2)Prudence — PS MA
Stephen, Jr.: b 9-8-1760 d 1-3-1826 m Elizabeth Owen Pvt MA ★
Thaddeus: b 7-5-1752 d 4-7-1833 m (1)Ann Noble (2)Mary Salisbury
　　　Pvt MA
Thomas: b 8-20-1747 d p. 8- -1805 m Abigail Davenport PS CT
Thomas: b 11- -1721 d 8-2-1787 m Sarah Martindale PS MA
Timothy, Sr.: b 3-27-1755 d 12-28-1852 m Jemima Griswold Pvt MA
Wm.: b 1-11-1746 d 6-10-1813 m Rebecca Carrier Cpl NH CT
Zebediah: b 10-8-1727 d 10-28-1804 m (1)Mrs Soloman Jackson
　　　(2)Beulah Stearns Maj VT
Zenas: b c. 1750 d p. 1802 m Joanna Root Cpl MA

DEWING,
Hezekiah: b 9-9-1740 d 3-18-1798 m Eunice Draper Bugbee Cpl CT
Jabez: b c. 1763 d p. 1810 m Sally Clark Pvt MA
Jeremiah: b 1762 d 1822 m Prudence Dodge Pvt MA
John: b c. 1756 d p. 1832 m Patience Sumner PS MA RI
Nathan: b 2-8-1758 d 12-17-1831 m (1)Ada Fisher Mills (2)Elizabeth Broad Pvt MA

DE WITT,
Andries: b 1728 d 6-26;1813 m Blandina Elmendorf Ten Eyck PS NY
Barnet: b 1756 d 4-27-1843 m Barbara Geasser Sol NJ
Charles: b 1727 d 8-27-1787 m Blandina Du Bois Col PS NY
Cornelius: b 1759/60 d 2-28-1845 m Margaret Cantine Pvt NY
Garrit: b 11-21-1761 d 11-25-1846 m Elizabeth Baldwin Pvt CT ★
Harris: b 1756 d 1829 m Elizabeth Brockington Cpl SC
Henry, Jr.: b 1-29-1761 d 5-16-1850 m (1)Margaret Schoonmaker (2)Elizabeth — Pvt NY
Jacob: b 8-22-1736 d a. 6-22-1802 m (1)Leah Cortright (2)Sarah — PS NJ
Jacob: b 2-1-1736 d 5-13-1817 m Jane Van Sicklen Capt PA
Jacob Rutsen: bpt 4 -13-1729 d p 1-6-1792 m Jenneke De Puy Capt NY
John: b 1720 d 7-14-1781 m Anne Harris Lt NY
John: b 2-24-1752 d 1808 m Catherine Van Vliet 2Lt NY
John A.: b 11-15-1753 d 10-4-1818 m (1)Rachal Bevier (2)Magdalena Bevier (3)Maria Vernooy Ens NY
John A: b 3-20-1750 d 3-16-1836 m Elizabeth Krums QM NJ
John L: b 5-14-1736 d 5-18-1803 m Anna Maria (DeWitt)Winne Capt NY
Lucas: bpt 8-20-1738 d 1820 m Deborah Perseus Capt NY
Moses: b 7-31-1759 d 9-15-1850 m Lavina — Pvt MA
Moses: b 10-23-1761 d 12-8-1842 m Margaret Wilson Pvt NJ
Paul: b 1763 d 4-21-1839 m Elizabeth Sly Pvt PA ★
Peter: b 9-26-1737 d p. 1800 m Mary Roos Lt PA
Peter: b 7-8-1753 d 4-3-1834 m — Pvt MD VA ★
Reuben: b 10-6-1745 d 7-17-1800 m Elizabeth DePuy Lt NY
Thomas: b 5-3-1741 d 9-7-1809 m Elsie Hasbrouck Maj NY
Wm.: b 1731 d p 1796 m Susanna Chambers Pvt NY
Wm.: b 1750 d p. 7-14-1813 m Mary Devonald Capt SC

DE WOLF, (includes DE WOLFE, DE WOLPH, DOLPH)
Abda: b 10-25-1743 d 10-25-1833 m Mary Coleman Pvt NY
Benjamin: b 3-18-1759 d 5-29-1845 m Jerusha Carter Pvt Smn CT ★
Charles: b 2-25-1745 d 8-20-1820 m (1)Mary Taylor (2)Elizabeth Hogerson (3)Abigail Green PS RI
Daniel: b 10-14-1762 d 2-7-1834 m Polly Fowler Pvt CT ★
Daniel: b 8-9-1763 d 2-21-1834 m (1)Mary Andrews (2)Hannah Ferritt Pvt CT ★
Elisha: b 2-16-1748 d 3-7-1838 m Lydia More Pvt CT ★
James: b 3-18-1764 d 12-21-1827 m Nancy Bradford,Pvt RI
John: b 3-17-1760 d 10-10-1841 m Susan Reynolds Pvt RI
Joseph: b 8-25-1761 d 8-15-1846 m Sarah Gibbons Cpl CT ★
Levi: b 5-9-1764 d 1-23-1849 m Huldah Cushing Pvt RI
Mark Anthony: b 11-8-1726 d 11-9-1793 m Abigail Potter PS RI
Mathew: b 1744 d 5-3-1834 m Esther Higley PS MA ★
Moses: b 1756 d 1826 m Anna MacArthur Sol NY
Peter: b 12-26-1754 d 12-17-1844 m Elizabeth Clemens Pvt CT
Samuel: b 1-4-1752 d 5-8-1834 m Susannah Keeney Pvt CT ★
Seth: b 11-22-1765 d 7-28-1847 m (2)Hannah Austin Pvt CT ★
Stephen: b 1753 d 12-15-1824/25 m (1)Sarah Greenfield (2)Theody Anderson (3)Abigail Beckwith Pvt NS CT ★

DEXTER,
Aaron: b 11-11-1750 d 2-28-1829 m Rebecca Amory Ship Dr MA
Benjamin: b 9-25-1734 d 7-18-1804 m Priscilla Benson Sgt MA
Caleb: b 9-1-1761 d 11-16-1836 m Lucy Dailey Pvt VT ★
Caleb: b 4-13-1751 d 10-3-1831 m Hannah Hatch Pvt MA
David: b 6-17-1760 d 9-14-1854 m Mary Butler Pvt MA
Elisha: bpt 8-8-1731 d p. 1794 m Lydia Smith Pvt CT
Elisha: b 4- -1765 d 1- -1834 m Eunice Bowles Pvt MA ★
Ephraim: b 12-31-1741 d 4-5-1823 m Keziah Tobey Pvt MA
Ichabod: b 6-24-1737 d 2-13-1797 m Abigail Smith Capt CS MA
Isaac: b 6-13-1744 d 12-15-1804 m Keziah Wing Sgt MA
Jeremiah: b 6-20-1745 d p. 1794 m Margaret Naason Pvt MA
Jeremiah: b 1739 d 1782-90 m Lydia — Pvt RI
Job: b 3-8-1741 d 7-10-1827 m (1)Mercy Hinckley (2)Mary Walker Lt MA
John: b 10-28-1753 d 12-10-1840 m (1)Sarah Parker (2)Mrs Sarah Howard Sgt CT ★
John: b 8-12-1735 d 2-7-1800 m Mary Howe Pvt MA
John: b 1701 d 5-4-1790 m Mary Brown PS RI
John: b c. 1717 d c, 1800 m Sabra Whipple PS RI
John Singer: b 6-8-1754 d 6-20-1844 m Mary Pearce Maj RI
Jonathan: b 9-7-1762 d 11;9-1841 m (1)Hannah Church (2)Dolly White Pvt MA
Joseph: b 7-3-1759 d 1-8-1847 m Mary Luce Pvt MA
Luen: b 8-21-1751 d 9-16-1838 m Vashti Sturtevant Cpl MA
Nathan: b 1759 d 7-9-1819 m (2)Irene French Pvt CT
Nathan: b 7-22-1759 d 7-20-1846 m Elsey Warner Pvt RI
Nathaniel Balch: b 7-16-1759 d 4-22-1832 m Lucy Willard Pvt MA
Richard: b 3-2-1756 d 11-3-1842 m Martha Hatch Pvt MA
Samuel: b 10-13-1734 d 5-3-1824 m (1)Thankful Freeman (2)Sibella Therston Capt MA

DEWING, *(column 2)*
Samuel: b 3-16-1725 d 6-10-1810 m Hannah Sigourney PS MA
Samuel: b 2-11-1758 d 1831 m Candace Windsor Ens RI
Seth: b 10-3-1718 d 4-6-1793 m Elizabeth — PS MA
Stephen: b 12-1-1755 d 3-24-1843 m Mrs Prudence (Sumner) Hubbard Slr Fif RI ★
Wm.: b 11-9-1742 d 12-14-1811 m (1)Phoebe Knight (2)Elizabeth Paine Pvt MA
Wm.: b 1728 d 1802 m Phebe Warner Pvt RI

DEY,
Ezekiel: b 7-1-1750 d 7-1-1830 m (1)Elizabeth Cox (2)Sarah M (Egbert) Paul Pvt NJ
James: b 9-15-1728 d 1802 m Margaret Perrine Pvt NJ
John: b 12-28-1741 d 4-26-1829 m Mary Baird Capt NJ W ★
John: b c. 1751 d 1828 m Janette Doremus Pvt NJ
Lewis: b 3-21-1758 d 10-25-1816 m (1)Agnes Bates (2)Fanny (Henley) Williamson Pvt NJ
Peter: b 3-7-1760 d 6-4-1833 m Eleanor Board Pvt NJ
Richard: b 11-19-1752 d 10-7-1811 m Hannah Pierson Maj NJ
Theunis: b 10-29-1726 d 6-10-1787 m Hester Schuyler Col NJ
Wm.: b 10-31-1754 d 12-19-1823 m Margaret Perrine Pvt NJ

DE YAMPERT,
John: b 1755 d 1807 m Mrs Mary Ardis Bradley Dr PA

DEYERLE,
Peter: b c. 1734 d a. 1- -1813 m Regina Ann Bowman CS VA

DEYO, (includes DEYOR)
Abraham, Sr.: b 10-16-1710 d 5-7-1777 m Elizabeth Du Bois PS NY
Abrahan, Jr.: b 2-27-1739 d 9-12-1808 m (2) Mrs Maria Lefever Lt NY
Benjamin: bpt 5-5-1725 d 8-29-1798 m Jeneke Van Vliet PS NY
Christian, Jr.: b 1732 d p. 1777 m Elida Terwilliger PS NY
Christopher: b 2-4-1728 d 1792 m Debora Van Vliet PS NY
Daniel: b 8-27-1740 d 2-27-1823 m Margaret Le Fevre Tms NY
Hendricus, Sr.: b 1731 d 12-17-1805 m Elizabeth Bum PS NY
Hendricus, Jr.: bpt 1754 d p. 1790 m Phebe Woolsey Pvt NY
James: bpt 11-25-1732 d 11-29-1822 m (1)Annatje Cool (2)Margaret Trip Pvt NY
John: b 1750 d 1819 m Rachel — Pvt PA
Jonathan: b 11-14-1745 d 3-8-1833 m Mary Le Fever Sgt PS NY
Peter: b 1738 d 4-6-1812 m Gertrude — Pvt NY
Peter, Sr.: b 11-9-1718 d 12-2-1791 m Elizabeth Helm PS NY
Peter, Jr.: b 4-22-1750 d 10-18-1796 m Elizabeth Freer Pvt NY
Philip: b 9-18-1752 d 12-12-1831 m Gertrude Le Fevre PS NY
Richard: b 1761 d a. 3-17-1829 m (1)Rachel Tator (2)Margaret — Pvt NY
Simon: b 2-13-1743 d p. 1800 m Antje Low Pvt PS NY
Solomon: b 6-13-1759 d — m Bregie Freer Pvt NY

DIAL,
Jeremiah: b 1758 d 9-22-1834 m Nancy Anna McDanel Pvt SC ★
Jeremiah: b a. 1760 d p. 1-1-1805 m Margaret — PS SC
John: b c. 1760 d a. 10-17-1791 m Mary Montgomery Sgt SC
John: b 7-22-1753 d 1813 m Mary Todd Sol SC
Joseph: b c. 1760 d p. 4-13-1827 m Margaret Hinkle Pvt PA
Martin: b 12-30-1744 d 12-26-1844 m (1)Christy Abercrombie (2)Mrs Hannah Abercrombie Pvt SC

DIBBLE, (includes DIBOL)
Benjamin, Jr.: b 9-13-1746 d 7-4-1833 m Elizabeth — Pvt CT ★
Daniel: b 5-18-1754 d 11-5-1842 m Sarah Patterson Lt MA
Ezra: b 1740 d 12-6-1809 m Lydia Benedict Capt CT
Henry, Sr.: b 1726 d 5-21-1808 m Abigail Bulmore Pvt NY
Henry, Jr.: b 11-18-1749 d 2-28-1810 m Lucinda Cleveland Pvt NY
Israel: b 12-7-1742 d 10-9-1824 m Elizabeth Millard Pvt CT
John: b 1735 d 4-14-1815 m Mary Terrill Lt CT
John: b 12-23-1759 d 4- -1852 m Elizabeth Carter Pvt CT ★
John: b 3-18-1754 d 9-5-1826 m (1)Olive Henry (2)Mrs Charity Curtis Dellm Lt MA
John Pierce: b 3-18-1754 d 5-31-1831 m Lucy Champion Pvt CT
Jonathan: b 1748 d 6-27-1827 m Rachel Slosson Pvt CT
Moses, Sr.: b 2-14-1735/36 d 1815 m (1)Mercy Holcombe (2)Elizabeth Holcombe Lt CT
Moses, Jr.: b 10-5-1757 d 11-6-1832 m Elizabeth Hoskins Pvt CT W★
Solomon: b 1755 d 8- -1842 m Charlotte Schermerhorn Pvt NY
Thomas: b c. 1764 d p. 1817 m Rhoda Cleveland Pvt NY

DIBRELL,
Anthony, Sr.: b 5-15-1728 d 1799 m (1)Elizabeth Lee (2)Madaline Burton PS Fif VA
Anthony, Jr.: b 5-24-1763 d 6-22-1816 m Wilmeth Watson Pvt VA ★
Charles: b 10-24-1757 d 7-16-1840 m (1)Martha Burton (2) — Patterson Ens VA ★

DICK,
Archibald: b c. 1724 d 3-9-1782 m Mrs Mary (Barnard) Hewes PS PA
Archibald: b c. 1735 d p. 1787 m Susannah Brock PS VA
Henry: b 10-10-1759 d 11-17-1845 m Lenah Zipperle Pvt NY ★
Jacob: b 1753 d 11-28-1804 m Mary Heirely Pvt PA W ★
Jacob: b 1-18-1754 d 11-10-1834 m Margaretta Zimmerman Pvt PA

DICK, contd.
John: b 1747 d 11-19-1832 m Margaret Wiley Sgt SC W ★
Peter: b c. 1748-50 d 9- -1790 m Barbra — Pvt VA
Samuel: b 11-14-1740 d — m Sarah Sinnickson PS Dr Col NJ
Wm.: b c. 1758 d 1829-35 m (1)Penelope (—) Johnson Lt SC
Wm.: b 11-4-1761 d c. 1831 m Margaret Dubose Lt SC

DICKEN,
Benjamin: b a. 1750 d 1794 m Katherine Stonestreet Johnson Pvt NC
John: b 4-16-1759 d 6-13-1841 m (1)Margaret — (2)Mary (Cook) McCubbin Lt VA ★

DICKENS, (includes DICKINS)
Amos: b 1731 d 12-25-1811 m Mrs Margaret (Dodge) Burdick Sol RI
James: b 1751 d 10-15-1820 m Isabella — Pvt NC
Robert: b 1748 d 1808 m Mary Brown Col PS NC
Thomas: b 1762-65 d 5-23-1852 m Mollie Stevens Pvt NC ★
Thomas: b 4-26-1742 d p. 4-3-1812 m (1)Sarah Franklin (2)Susannah (Mitchell) Rose PS RI
Tristram: b 3-9-1761 d 9-18-1832 m Martha Wilcox Pvt RI

DICKERMAN, (includes DICKMAN)
Chauncey: b 9-28-1750 d 4-29-1820 m (1)Rebecca Bradley (2)Hannah Gill Ens CT
Ebenezer: b 1-1-1748 d 6-9-1811 m (1)Mercy Stone (2)Parnah (Randall) Bonney Pvt MA
Enos: b 11-2-1743 d — m Lois Alling Pvt NY
Enoch: b 4-19-1758 d p. 1786 m Sarah Wales Pvt MA
Hezekiah: b 11-6-1754 d 5-2-1814 m Hannah Rice Cpl CT
Isaac: b 9-16-1740 d 4-3-1801 m Sybil Sperry 2Lt CT
Isaac: bpt 11-28-1731 d 3-26-1784 m Mercy Lasenby PS MA
James: b 5- -1763 d 12-2-1807 m Joanna Crossman Pvt MA
John: b 3-8-1740 d 11-6-1848 m Thankful Smith Pvt VT ★
Jonathan, Sr.: b 1719 d 7-28-1795 m (1)Rebecca Bassett (2)Mrs Hannah (Leavenworth) Moss (3)Deborah Todd PS CT
Jonathan, Jr.: b 1-13-1747 d 5-27-1821 m Miriam Bradley Wgn CT
Manasseh: bpt 5-12-1751 d 2-19-1818 m (1)Ruth Randall (2)Thirza Bryant Pvt MA
Peter: b 10-20-1749 d 8-23-1821 m Mrs Rebecca Tilden Smith Pvt MA
Samuel: b 4-20-1745 d 10-7-1789 m Lowly Pardee Sgt CT

DICKEY, (includes DICKIE)
Adam: b 1722 d p. 1781 m Jane Strahn Sgt NH
Adam: b 4-4-1751 d 10-24-1840 m Jennet Nasmith Pvt NH ★
Adam: b 4-17-1740 d 6-17-1817 m Jane Nahor PS NH
David: b 10-18-1747 d 1834 m Mary — SgtMaj NC ★
David: b 1747 d 4-7-1835 m Mrs Mary Heslip McFadden PS NC
David: b 12-23-1753 d 12-24-1791 m Margaret — Pvt PA
David: b 10-18-1747 d 7-11-1823 m (1)Margaret Robeson (2)Margaret Stephenson Sgt SC
Ebenezer: b 11- -1761 d 6-5-1840 m Mary Graham Pvt NC ★
Eleazer: b 1760 d 6-8-1853 m Mary — Pvt MA
Elias: b 8-11-1751 d 11-29-1836 m Jennet McPherson Pvt NH ★
George: b 6-29-1747 d 5-20-1800 m Ann McKee 1Lt PA
George: b 4-15-1742 d 8-4-1817 m Mary Scott Sgt SC
James: b 8-14-1747 d 12-3-1825 m Mary Davidson Pvt NH
James: b 1753 d 3-18-1849 m Lydia Florence Pvt NH ★
James: b c. 1745 d 1776 m Mary Brown Ens NY
James: b 1754 d 3-13-1813 m Rebecca R — Pvt PA
James: b 10-21-1764 d 12-4-1798 m Leonora Lenoir Pvt PS SC
John: b 1724 d 3-20-1808 m (1)Mary Looney (2)Elizabeth Leasey PS Capt NC W ★
John: b c. 1755 d 9-8-1819 m Mary Logue PS SC
John: b c. 1720 d 6- -1785 m Ailsey (Dickie) PS VA
Matthew: b 11- -1728 d 10-2-1802 m Janet Wallace Sgt NH
Moses: b 1765 d 1835 m Jane Shaw Pvt PA
Robert: b c. 1740-45 d c. 1782 m Agnes Richey Capt PA
Robert: b 11-25-1745 d 5-24-1817 m (1)Margaret Hilhouse (2)Mary Henry Mil SC
Samuel: b 1753 d 12-1-1812 m Catherine Saxton Sgt NC
Samuel: b 1730 d 8-16-1794 m Mary Jackson Pvt PA
Wm.: b c. 1748 d 1823 m (1)Elizabeth Matthews (2)Ann Ranger Sgt NH ★
Wm.: b c. 1736 d p. 12-26-1802 m (1)Rebecca — Pvt PA
Wm.: b 9-22-1756 d 3-10-1848 m Sarah McClellan Pvt PA
Wm.: b 5-6-1764 d 6-26-1832 m Mary Stephenson Gnr VA

DICKINSON, (includes DICKASON, DICKERSON)
Abijah: b 1745 d 2-9-1815 m Hannah Sevey PS ME MA
Abner: b 1-5-1724 d 9-28-1799 m Sarah Smith Pvt MA
Alexander: b 1752 d 11-4-1837 m Elizabeth Valentine Pvt MA
Asahel: b 1-9-1760 d 7-26-1836 m Lucy Russell Sgt CT ★
Benoni: b 12-12-1747 d 7-17-1839 m Phoebe Marsh Pvt MA
Brainard: b 6-28-1752 d 9-12-1819 m Sarah Baldwin Pvt NJ
Charles: b 1695 d 1779 m Sophia Richardson PS CS MD
Charles: b c. 1722 d p. 1809 m Belitze Bogart Capt NY
Cotton: b 1754 d 1826 m Olive Field Pvt MA ★
Daniel: b 10-10-1756 d 5-13-1826 m Sybil Dickinson Pvt MA
Daniel: b c. 1740 d 3-13-1826 m Phoebe Genung Pvt NJ
Daniel: b 9-14-1739 d 11-17-1812 m Mary Palmer Maj NY
David: b 4-18-1757 d 9-9-1822 m Lois Clark Pvt CT

David: b 12- -1705 d 10-17-1790 m Mary Perrin PS CT
David: b — d 1816 m Mercy — Pvt NJ
David: b 3-17-1755 d — m Margaret Redfield Pvt NY
David: b 5-29-1756 d 1812 m (1)Ann Coleman (2)Mary West PS VA
Ebenezer: b 2-21-1734 d 12-4-1824 m Mabel — Sgt CT
Ebenezer, Sr.: b 9-17-1696 d 1780 m (1)Sarah Kellogg (2)Mrs Hamilton PS MA
Ebenezer, Jr.: b c. 1727 d 9-12-1798 m Chloe Holton Pvt MA
Ebenezer: b 1-3-1741 d p. 1781 m Ruth Eastman Pvt MA
Ebenezer: b 1752 d 8-18-1846 m Elizabeth — Pvt MA ★
Eli: b 11-10-1749 d 2-7-1826 m (1)Lois Horton (2)Rachel Eastman Pvt MA
Elihu: b 10-21-1753 d 6-5-1811 m Susanna Lewis Cpl MA
Elijah: b 1760 d 2-1-1820 m Jerusha Smith Col MA
Elisha: b 1737 d p. 1790 m (1)Martha Dean (2)Elizabeth Barns PS CT
Elisha: bpt 3-22-1747 d 3-12-1819 m Martha — Cpl MA
Elisha: b 7-27-1752 d 9-25-1811 m Hannah Billings Pvt MA
Enos: b 3-28-1746 d 12-31-1821 m Lois (Dickinson) Pvt MA
Francis: b 1762 d 1-11-1843 m Olive Ellsworth Pvt MA ★
George: b 3-4-1744 d p. 1790 m Eunice Bunnell Pvt CT
Gideon: b 12-1-1745 d — m (1)Abigail Field (2)Lydia — Pvt MA
Gideon: b 12-1-1720 d p. 1776 m Hannah Edwards PS MA
Griffith: b 8-8-1756 d 10-16-1843 m Susanna Shelton Cpl GA VA ★
Henry: b c. 1730 d 1789 m (1)Elizabeth Walker (2)Deborah Perry LCol PS MD
Henry: b c. 1760 d 7-27-1825 m Ann — Ens PA
Henry: b 10-28-1747 d 7-5-1825 m Mary Powell Lt VA
Israel: b 2-21-1736 d 11-18-1777 m Mercy Partridge Capt PS MA
James: b 1742 d 9- -1828 m Mrs Mary (Cole) Barclay Pvt VA
Jehu: b 1758 d 1814 m Eleanor Pomeroy Pvt MA
Jesse: b 1755 d 3-17-1840 m Rachel — Fif Pvt CT ★
Joel: b 1750 d 1-18-1813 m Hulda Strong Capt MA
Joel: b 5-29-1751 d 2-25-1837 m Eunice Holton Pvt MA
John: b 12-21-1737 d 1830 m Dorothy Scoville Drm CT
John: b c. 1754 d 7-9-1833 m Mrs Catherine Ann (Round) Olendorf Pvt DE ★
John, Sr.: b 4-2-1707 m 2-21-1799 m Mary Coleman LCol MA
John, Jr.: b 10-24-1744 d 10-13-1816 m Lois Bigelow Lt MA
John: b 10-27-1757 d 1-4-1850 m (1)Lydia Eastman (2)Mrs Susanna Wilder Pvt MA
John: b 10-30-1748 d 12-30-1830 m Abigail Alexander Pvt MA
John: b 10-11-1758 d 9-16-1834 m Mary Powers SgnMte NJ
John: b 6-18-1742 d 10-1-1778 m Grace Lindsey Pvt NY
John: b c. 1730 d c. 1783 m Mary Barnes Capt NC
John: b 1731 d 1799 m Martha Usher Capt VA
John: b c. 1735 d p. 4-2-1816 m (2)Judith Douglass Pvt VA
John: b c. 1760 d 1830 m Nancy Clarkson Pvt VA
Joseph: b 11-23-1736 d 12-19-1806 m Lydia Brooks Ens CT
Joseph: b c. 1750 d p. 1791 m Violetta Morse Sgt MA
Joseph: b 1748 d p. 1797 m (2)Rebecca Warren Sgt NH
Joseph: b 4-13-1745 d — m Elizabeth — Pvt NY
Joseph: b 1745 d 4-10-1810 m (1)Anna Hull (2)Sallie — PS NC
Joseph: b 4-11-1742 d 9-18-1818 m Elizabeth Woolridge PS VA
Josiah, Jr.: b 1750 d 1-17-1812 m Sybil Partridge Pvt MA
Lemuel: b 10-22-1752 d 5-14-1835 m Molly Little Sgt MA
Levi: b 1-22-1755 d 1-28-1843 m Bethiah Fuller Pvt CT
Moses: b 4-13-1738 d 11-18-1812 m (1)Lydia Cole (2)Susannah (Langdon) Hooker Grd Pvt CT
Moses: b 1744 d 12-3-1814 m Eunice Wood Pvt MA
Moses: b 1719 d 4-9-1803 m Thankful Smith PS CS MA
Moses: b 1753 d p. 5-29-1832 m Jemima Sullivan Pvt VA
Nathan, Sr.: b 5-30-1712 d 8-7-1795 m (1)Thankful Warner (2)Joanna Leonard (3)Judith Hosmen PS MA
Nathan, Jr.: b 10-19-1735 d 8-3-1825 m (1)Esther Fowler (2)Mrs Jerusha (Dickinson) Blodgett Pvt MA
Nathaniel: b 10-6-1760 d 3-30-1837 m Lucy Gelbert Pvt CT ★
Nathaniel: b 1735 d 9-28-1820 m (1)Deborah Skinner (2)Mehitable Buck (3)Hannah Bancroft Pvt MA
Nathaniel, Sr.: b 9-3-1721 d 7-10-1806 m Thankful — Pvt MA
Nathaniel, Jr.: b 9-1-1750 d 11-10-1802 m Sarah Marsh Pvt PS CS MA
Nathaniel: b 8-10-1745 d 3-25-1814 m Caroline Cummings Pvt NH
Nathaniel: b 1744 d 3-28-1795 m Patience Baldwin Pvt NJ
Nathaniel: b 1747 d 5-30-1797 m Tabitha — Pvt NJ
Nathaniel: b 8-31-1751 d 4-4-1795 m Rebecca Terry Sgt VA
Nathaniel: b 2-5-1742 d 1-9-1782 m Elizabeth Mansfield Sgt VA
Noah: b 3-14-1741 d p. 1808 m Hannah — Lt CT
Noah: b 1719 d 5-28-1815 m (1)Mary Dickinson (2)Susan Ward Lt MA
Obadiah: b 1-7-1754 d 9-2-1824 m Susannah Knowles Pvt CT
Peter: b 1725 d 5-10-1780 m (1)Ruth Coe (2)Sarah (Armstrong) O'Hara Capt PS NJ
Philemon: b 4-5-1739 d 2-4-1809 m Mary Cadwallader MGen NJ
Reuben: b 1729 d 11-12-1803 m Sarah Clark Capt MA
Richard: b 3-4-1731 d 4-18-1820 m Mary Tully Capt PS CT
Richard: b c. 1734 d 7-21-1816 m Rebecca — Sgt MA
Richard: b 10-14-1750 d 1804 m Ann Quarels Sol VA
Robert: b c. 1742 d p. 8-9-1819 m — Cosby Pvt VA
Samuel: b 8-22-1754 d 11-29-1841 m Lois Willard Sgt MA ★
Samuel: b 3-9-1749 d 7-24-1803 m Mary Dickinson Cpl MA
Seth: b 10-6-1759 d 5-9-1839 m Naomi — Pvt MA

Simeon: b 12-25-1757 d 4-17-1837 m Deborah Ackley Sgt CT
Simeon: b a. 1760 d p. 1787 m Sarah McClellan Pvt MA
Simeon: b c. 1726 d 5-23-1806 m Martha Graves CS MA
Stoughton: b 2-17-1755 d p. 1798 m Abigail Nash Pvt MA
Sylvanus: b 1756 d 7-23-1832 m Mary Miles Lt CT ★
Thomas: b 3-17-1737 d 10-5-1811 m Mary Stevens Pvt CT
Thomas: b 4-6-1718 d 4-8-1814 m Prudence Smith Capt MA
Thomas: b 3-5-1756 d 9-18-1845 m Mary Nobles Sgt Mus MA ★
Thomas: b c. 1744 d p. 1-19-1800 m Eleanor — Capt NJ
Thomas: b c. 1756 d c. 1836 m Margaret Davis Pvt PA ★
Thomas: b 5-19-1764 d 12-24-1852 m Mary Curry Pvt PA
Thomas: b 1732 d p. 1785 m Elizabeth Page Pvt VA
Thomas Wells: b 6-14-1751 d 3-16-1835 m Thankful Field 1Lt PS MA
Versel: b 1734/35 d 8-2-1822 m Katherine — Sgt PS NY ★
Waite: b 11-10-1751 d 4-1-1835 m Abigail Russell Pvt CT
Waitstill: b 7-2-1783 d 3- -1843 m Catharine McGot Sgt CT ★
Walter: b 6-17-1763 d 10-8-1855 m (1)Penelope Heaton (2)Sarah Garthwait Pvt NJ ★
Wm.: b 1760 d 9-18-1823 m Ann Hoomes Sol VA
Zebulon: b 1761 d 1835 m Mrs Elizabeth Brush Pvt Fif NY

DICKOVER,
Henry: b 1758 d p. 1799 m Barbara Ventz Pvt PA

DICKS,
James: b — d p. 1788 m Rachel Beals PS NC
Joshua: b 11-21-1758 d p. 1820 m Elizabeth Baldwin PS NC

DIDIER,
Benjamin: b 11-7-1753 d 9-11-1822 m Margaret Fraser Matr PS SC

DIEFENBAUGH, (includes DEFENBAUGH, DIFFENBACH, DEEFENBACH, TEVEBAUGH)
George: b c. 1740 d 1792 m Ava Maria Magdalene Kapp 2Lt PA
Jacob: b c. 1734 d 4- -1790 m — Capt VA
John: b c.1753/54 d 1811 m Maria Buckwalter Pvt PA
Peter: b 1755 d 1838 m (1)Anna Catharine Lebengut Pvt PA

DIEFENDORF, (includes DIEFENDORFF, DIEFENDORF, DIEVENDORF)
Henry: b 1740 d 8-5-1777 m Honestein Moyer Capt NY
Jacob: b 5-1-1740 d 11-17-1818 m Christena Windecker Capt NY
Jacob: b 6-6-1767 d 7- -1847 m (1)Eliza Brookman (2)Elizabeth Baum Fif NY ★
Jacob: b 9-23-1769 d 10-8-1854 m Margaret Bellinger PS NY
Johannes: b 5-10-1742 d 7-26-1834 m Catharine Hess Pvt NY ★
John Jacob: b 5-12-1747 d 3-27-1839 m Catherine Windecker OrdlSgt NY ★

DIEFENDORFER, (includes DEFFENDERFFER, DIEFENDERFER, DIEFFENDORFER, DIEFFENDERFER, DIEFENDERFFER)
David: b 2-9-1752 d 5-10-1846 m Margaret Stein Ens PA
Godfrey: b 2-19-1730 d 4-16-1806 m Anna Margaret Mattern Pvt PA
Jacob: b 6-26-1759 d 1831 m Anna Maria Flick Pvt PA
Jacob: b 2- -1760 d 7-14-1855 m (2)Barbara Baker Pvt PA ★
John: b 2-4-1754 d 1808-18 m Margaret — Pvt PA
John: b 1-25-1754 d 3-27-1815 m Charlotte Elizabeth Shankweiler Pvt PA

DIEFFENBACHER,
Conrad: b 3- -1743 d 8-6-1813 m (1)Catherine Betts (2)Catherine Haas Pvt PA

DIEHL, (includes DEAL & DIEL)
Adam: b 4-14-1762 d 8-28-1825 m Barbara Mary — Drm PA
Charles, Jr.: b 10-14-1750 d 8- -1817 m Christina Stebele Pvt PA
Conrad: b a. 1763 d p. 1784 m Maria Korrin Sgt PA
Frederick: b c. 1708 d a. 10-9-1790 m Ann Maria PS PA
Frederick: b 1-5-1743 d 5-13-1816 m Mary Hawley Pvt PA
Frederick: b 1744 d 12-10-1811 m Susanna — Pvt PA
George: b c. 1750 d 2-11-1822 m Rosina Hoffman Cpl PA
John: b 1730 d p. 1817 m Christina Bosseman Capt PA
Nicholas: b 1741 d 12-5-1818 m Anna Maria Meyerlin Capt NY
Nicholas: b 6-8-1725 d 2-1-1800 m Maria Eva — PS Capt PA
Simon Jacob: b 5-15-1738 d 4-10-1819 m Anna Elizabeth Wagner Pvt PA
Wm.: b c. 1730 d 1807 m Anna Deal Sol PS NC
Wm.: b 1719 d 7-20-1813 m Catherine Schmidt Pvt PA

DIEM, (includes DEAM & DEEM)
Christopher: b 8-13-1744 d 9-7-1828 m Otella Margaretta Sittely Pvt PA
Henry: b — d p. 1802 m Elizabeth Ache Ens PA

DIENER,
Peter: b 4-28-1753 d 11-10-1798 m Anna M Maier Pvt PA

DIETRICH, (includes DEADRICK, DEDERICK, DEDRICK, DEITERICH, DEITRICK, DETRICK, DIETRICK)
Adam: b 10-28-1740 d 3-1-1817 m Maria Barbara Steinbruck Sgt PA
Christian: b 10-12-1752 d 7-11-1822 m Catherine Teal Pvt NY
David, Jr.: b 10-10-1754 d 10-20-1823 m (1)Nancy Knight (2)Margaretta Anderson Adj CS VA ★

Dewald: b 6-16-1762 d — m Margaret Teygert MM NY
Elias: b 1738 d 1795 m Magdalena Hart Pvt PA
George: b 11-12-1742 d 1826 m Catherine Vauman Pvt PA
Jacob: b 1753 d 12- -1801 m Gertrude Wynard Pvt PA
Johan Balser: b 12-23-1754 d 3-18-1838 m Sarah — Pvt PA ★
John: b c. 1740 d 1809 m Anna Margaretha Long Cpl PA
John: b 11-22-1760 d 1795 m Magdalena Snyder Pvt PA
Jurry Wilhelm: b 12-5-1711 d 12-13-1786 m Catharine E Young Pvt PS NY
Ludwick: b 1742 d 1819 m Julia Anne Gushard Pvt PA
Matthew: b 2-14-1736/37 d 12-19-1808 m (1)Maria Emmerick (2)Gertrude Van Luven Capt NY
Peter: b 1741 d 2- -1780 m Elizabeth — PS Pvt PA
Wilhelmus: bpt 2-11-1736 d 1800 m Christina Baer PS NY
Wm.: b 11-8-1730 d c. 1794 m Catherine Brandow Sol NY

DIETZ, (includes DATES, DEATS, DEETS)
Adam: b 10-7-1746 d 9-6-1826 m Annatia Bellinger Ens NY
Dorothea Werner: b 10-6-1723 d 2-7-1871 m Wm. Dietz PS NY
Engeltie Weiner: b c. 1705 d 1782 m Johannes Peter Deitz PS NY
George: b 4-14-1762 d 8-18-1822 m Elizabeth Yeagle Pvt PA
George: b c. 1729 d 2- -1778 m Catherine Mombauer PS PA
Jacobus: b 9-14-1759 d p. 1795 m Elizabeth Eckert Pvt NY
Johannes: b 1701 d 2-7-1782 m Engeltie Weiner PS NY
John: b 4-6-1759 d 10-12-1836 m Elizabeth — Pvt NJ ★
John: b 12-30-1759 d a. 4-23-1812 m Elizabeth Lossing Pvt NY
Peter: b c. 1732-36 d 6-23-1802 m (1)Catherine Lent (2)Mrs Adrianna Dubois Sol NY
Wm.: b 12-7-1749 d 2-16-1794 m Anna Margaretha Bergh Pvt NY
Wm.: b 1720 d 1782 m Dorthy Warner Capt NY

DIGGINS, (includes DIGGENS)
Martin: b 5-5-1760 d 2-23-1846 m (1)Abigail — (2)Lydia P Taft Pvt CT ★
Oliver: b 1735-40 d 1-25-1819 m Mehitable Porter Pvt CT

DIGGS, (includes DIGGE, & DIGGES)
Cole: b 1754 d 4- -1817 m Mary Purdie Maj VA
Dudley, Sr.: b 1729 d 6-3-1790 m (1)Martha Armistead (2)Elizabeth Wormley PS VA
Dudley, Jr.: b 1-15-1760 d 7-16-1842 m Mary Digges Lt VA ★
Edward: b 1-22-1746 d 10-29-1818 m Elizabeth Anne Gaskins Maj VA
George: b 1743 d 1792 m Catherine Brent PS MD
John: b 1735 d 1803 m Elizabeth Harris Capt PS VA
Joseph, Jr.: b c. 1750 d p. 6-12-1816 m (1)Sarah Beverly (2)Jane Tompkins Dr PS MD
Mary: b c. 1730 d'p. 1790 m Augustine Degges PS VA
Robert: b 7-8-1742 d p. 11-17-1786 m Elizabeth Lawson PS NC
Wm.: b 1734 d 1785 m Judy Haley Pvt NC
Wm.: b 1727 d 1797 m (1)Jane Corrie (2)Mary Fox Col VA

DIKE, (includes DYKE)
Anthony: b 1-18-1751 d 3-14-1810 m Molley Pool Cpl MA
Benjamin: b 1747 d 10-17-1777 m Dorothy Stearns Sgt NH
Daniel, Sr.: bpt 5-28-1738 d 8-3-1786 m Mary Pratt Pvt MA
Daniel, Jr.: b 1-17-1760 d 11-28-1838 m (1)Abigail French (2)Mrs Hannah Clarke Pvt MA ★
Ebenezer: b c. 1721 d p. 1805 m (1)Abigail Call (2)Ann — Pvt VT
Gideon: b 10-18-1728 d 8-10-1801 m Mary — Sgt CT
James: b 10-18-1718 d 6-18-1792 m Mary Nariamore CS CT
Jonathan: b 11-26-1751 d 2- -1826 m Abigail Brown Sgt MA W ★
Nicholas: b 2-2-1722 d 7-29-1817 m Mary Hastings Col MA
Samuel: b 4-16-1723 d 10-22-1800 m Mary Perkins Pvt MA
Thomas: b 7-28-1744 d 3-3-1808 m Dorothy Davidson Sgt CT
Wm.: b 4-17-1740 d 1787 m Eunice Woodbury Gallop Cpl MA

DILDINE,
John: b c. 1760 d c. 1820 m Mary Rosencrants Pvt NJ
Jonathan: b c. 1763 d p. 4-4-1742 m (2) Nancy Meelkey Pvt SC ★

DILENO,
Jabez: b 5-7-1760 d 8-24-1848 m Grace Daly Pvt MA

DILGARD,
Jacob: bpt 1-11-1759 d 10-11-1843 m Maria Margaretha — Pvt PA

DILL,
Daniel: b 2-4-1761 d 3-16-1806 m Mary Chubbuck Pvt MA ★
George: b 7-16-1728 d c. 1812 m Dorothy — Sol NY
James: b 1720 d 1796 m Jean Armstrong PS PA
John: b c. 1746 d a. 2-8-1792 m Letitia Carpenter PS CS DE
John: b 1759 d 1862 m Mary Ellen Fonderon Pvt MD
John: b c. 1740 d c. 1790 m Sarah Coffin Pvt MA
Lemuel: bpt 7-12-1761 d 11-1-1836 m Mrs Milcah (Stodder) Bryant Beal Pvt Fif Drm MA ★
Matthew: b 1726 d 4-10-1812 m (1)Martha Jane Bracken (2)Mrs Susanna Waugh Col PA
Solomon: b 1730-35 d c. 8- -1820 m Sarah (Bainard) Lt DE
Thomas: b 1748 d 1797/98 m Priscilla Wierman Pvt PA
Thomas: b 1750 d 7-7-1833 m Mary Boyd Pvt PA ★

DILLARD,
George: b *c.* 1735 d *p.* 3-2-1790 m Priscilla Major Sol PS VA
James: b 1760 d 4-4-1839 m Sarah — Pvt NC
James: b 12-4-1755 d 12-4-1836 m (1)Mary Ramage (2)Mary Puckett Capt SC
James: b 1744 d 10-16-1823 m Sukey — Capt PS VA
James: b 10-29-1755 d 4-4-1832 m Jane Starke Capt VA W ★
James: b 1749 d 6-16-1777 m Martha Motley Pvt VA
James: b 1758 d 1849 m Nancy English Pvt VA
John: b 1751 d 1822 m Sallie Stovall Capt PS VA
John: b 8-12-1760 d 6-5-1842 m Ruth Jane Terry Lt VA ★
Mary Ramage: b *c.* 1757 d *p.* 1787 m James Dillard PS SC
Nicholas Philip: b *c.* 1755 d *c.* 1832 m Elizabeth Adams Sgt SC
Sampson: b 9-2-1753 d 3-12-1830 m Sara Phoebe Neal Sol NC
Thomas: b 1720 d *a.* 9-23-1784 m Martha — PS CS VA

DILLAWAY,
Thomas: b 1754 d *p.* 1806 m Mary Vaux Pvt MA
Thomas: b 8-19-1753 d 4-6-1807 m (1)Mary Pipson (2)Mary Carpenter (3)Hannah (Morrison) Domac NS MA

DILLEHEY,
Charles: b *c.* 1717 d *p.* 8-26-1784 m Eliza — PS VA

DILLENBACK, (includes DILLENBACH)
Andrew: b 12-29-1736 d 8-6-1777 m Catharine Fink Capt NY
John: b 1-31-1747 d 1823 m Maria Eva Spraker Pvt NY
John Balthasar: b *c.* 1733 d — m (1)Anna Maria Metzgar (2)Elizabeth Pvt NY
John Dedrick: b *c.* 1730 d *p.* 1808 m Maria Mynard Pvt NY
Martinus: b *c.* 1729 d 1790-1808 m Catherine Rosner Pvt NY

DILLER,
Adam, Sr.: b 3-8-1723 d 9-8-1777 m Marie Magdalena Ellmaker Pvt PA
Adam, Jr.: b 5-6-1746 d 4-3-1823 m Saloma Yundt Pvt PA
Adam: b 1-31-1751 d 12-27-1792 m (1) — Fessler (2)Elizabeth Brown Pvt PA
Isaac: b 1763 d 1835 m (1)Susanna Roland (2)Maria Graybill Pvt PA
John: b 11-21-1748 d *p.* 1792 m Magdalena — Pvt PA
Leonard Ellmaher: b 2-8-1759 d 12-29-1798 m Mary Magdaline Hinkle Pvt PA

DILLEY, (includes DILLA & DILLE)
Caleb: b 1758/59 d 5- -1839 m Rebecca Martin Pvt PA
David: b 1753 d 10-7-1833 m (1)Nancy Viers (2)Mary Sailor Lt VA
Ephriam: b 11-6-1755 d 7-26-1844 m Lucy Ayers Pvt NJ
Price: b 1754 d 5-22-1826 m (1)Sarah — (2)Roseann — Pvt PA
Revidel: b 3-1-1754 d *p.* 10-26-1828 m (1)Desire — (2)Lovice Simmons Pvt CT

DILLINER,
Augustine: b *c.* 1732 d *p.* 10-19-1824 m Margaret Leonard Pvt PA

DILLINGHAM,
Benjamin: b 2-3-1739 d *p.* 1823 m Ann Hathaway Capt MA
Edward: b 5-6-1743 d 6-3-1828 m Mercy — Pvt MA
Jeremiah: b 1729 d 4-16-1823 m (1)Abigail Chamberlain (2)Mrs Elizabeth Thompson Pettingill Pvt MA
John, Jr.: b 1-9-1735/36 d 10-27-1825 m Sarah Blackmer Lt MA
John: b 8-22-1764 d 8-4-1847 m Susan Crane Pvt MA
John: b 5-29-1737 d 4-15-1815 m Ruth Gifford Pvt MA
John: b 9-25-1762 d 6-24-1853 m (1)Sarah Gilbert (2) Anna (Merrill) Nason (3)Mrs Lydia Milliken Pvt MA ★
Nathan: b 4-30-1759 d 1-21-1836 m Rebecca Fessenden Mus MA ★
Paul: b 10-10-1759 d 7-14-1848 m Hannah Smith Pvt MA ★
Vachel: b 1736 d 1802/3 m (1)Ann — (2)Hester — Pvt VA
Wm.: b 3-1-1760 d 9-8-1832 m Hannah West Pvt MA

DILLMAN,
Andrew, Sr.: b 1705 d 1813 m — Pvt PA
Andrew, Jr.: b 12-3-1753 d 5-21-1823 m Barbara Roush Pvt PA ★

DILLON, (includes DILLEN)
Benjamin: b 1750 d *c.* 1806 m (2)Charlotte Hunning Lt NC
Henry: b 1762 d *p.* 1838 m — 2Sgt VA ★
Jesse: b 1748 d 2- -1779 m Permelia Johnson Cpl VA
Jesse: b 10-13-1753 d 10-3-1823 m Hannah Ruckman Cpl VA
Richard: b 10-7-1745 d 10-7-1833 m Anne Morris Pvt NC
Wm.: b 9-10-1750 d 1830 m Margaret — Pvt PA
Wm.: b 1725 d 1798 m Mary Robinson Pvt Fif VA
Wm.: b 3-3-1764 d 1-9-1847 m Elizabeth Beard Pvt VA

DILLWORTH,
Jacob: b *c.* 1723 d 1809 m Elizabeth Nanna Pvt PA

DILTS,
Jacob: b 4-9-1760 d 9-4-1831 m Sarah Heath Pvt NJ
Wm.: b 1754 d 10-20-1848 m Sarah Ann Jolly Pvt NJ ★

DIMM,
Christopher: b 12-31-1754 d 9-1-1831 m Margaretta Sidtler Lt PA

DIMMICK, (includes DIMICK, DIMMOCK, DIMOCK)
Abel: b 5-8-1748 d 7-11-1829 m (1)Theoda Burbank (2)Sylvania — Capt VT
Amasa: b 11-17-1761 d 9-24-1834 m Matilda Ellis Pvt CT ★
Benjamin: b 9-30-1756/7 d 8-21-1850 m (1)Betsey Lewis (2)Thankful — Lt CT ★
Daniel: b 5-28-1738 d 1790 m Thankful Merriman PS CT
David: b 7-2-1746 d 2-14-1832 m Sarah Green Lt CT ★
Edward: b 6-15-1748 d 9-19-1836 m (1)Peninah Hinkley (2)Esther Tilden Sgt CT ★
Eliphalet: b 3-12-1753 d 1841 m Anna Freeman Sgt CT
Jeduthan: b 1760 d 1831 m Mercy Chamberlain Pvt CT ★
John: b 3-24-1726 d 1800 m Hannah Smith Pvt CT
Joseph: b 2-27-1746 d 2-26-1820 m Prudence — Pvt CT
Joseph: b 3-16-1767 d 12-24-1845 m Fanny Mathews Pvt CT ★
Joseph: b 1734 d 9-21-1822 m Mary Meggs Maj MA
Samuel: b 9-3-1762 d 3-31-1838 m Rachel Nelson Pvt CT ★
Schubel: b 1-31-1731 d 12-8-1840 m Lydia Polk Pvt MA
Shubael: b 10-4-1757 d 3-8-1828 m Elizabeth Wright Sgt CT
Shubel: b 10-1-1752 d 10-29-1839 m Thankful Burbank Sgt NY ★
Solomon: b 4-29-1745 d *p.* 1793 m (1)Elizabeth Beebe (2)Electa Hull Ens CT
Sylvanus: b 9- -1753 d 3-16-1837 m Thankful Dimmick Pvtr MA ★
Timothy: b *a.* 1749 d *c.* 1827 m Hulda Snow Sgt CT
Timothy: b 4-6-1726 d 2- -1795 m Desire Dimmock Pvt CT
Timothy: b *c.* 1748 d *p.* 4-21-1807 m Sarah Beals Ens NH

DIMMITT,
James: b *c.* 1725 d 5-25-1827 m Rachel Sinkler PS MD

DIMON, (includes DIMAN)
Abraham: b 1735 d 1819 m Hannah Foster PS NY
Daniel: b 3-20-1747 d 9-6-1808 m Lois Bradley Ens CT
David: b 1742 d 9-18-1777 m Ann Allen Col CT
Gold: b 6-5-1756 d 3-14-1842 m Abigail Burr Sol CT
James: b 10-19-1735 d 5-30-1809 m Anna Le Favor Pvt RI
John: b 7-5-1730 d *a.* 5-21-1778 m Abagail Fanton PS CT
Joseph: b 1748 d 10-19-1821 m Margaret De Wolf Sgt RI ★
Wm.: b 11-1-1759 d 12-18-1844 m Nancy Munro Pvt RI

DIMOND, (includes DIAMOND, DIAMENT, DYMOND)
Ezekiel: b *c.* 1725 d 2-22-1800 m Miriam Fowler PS NH
Jacob: b 6-3-1760 d 3-16-1826 m Abigail Lawrence Pvt MA
James: b 5-2-1725 d 3- -1776 m — Pvt NJ
John: b 1728-30 d — m Eunice Evans Sailing Master MA
John: b 1- -1764 d 1-14-1830 m Sarah Emerson Pvt NH
Matthew: b 1740 d 1839 m Ann Mosure Pvt NY
Reuben: b 4-8-1755 d 11-17-1825 m Mollie Currier Pvt NH
Wm.: b 7-21-1755 d 7-29-1828 m Rebecca Symonds Drm MA

DINGEE,
Obediah: b 1740 d 1813 m Jane — Pvt DE
Samuel: b 8-14-1748 d 12-27-1822 m Rebecca Merritt Pvt NY

DINGESS,
Peter: b *c.* 1740 d 1800 m Polly Smith Pvt VA

DINGLEY,
Abner: b 1-21-1732 d 6- -1807 m Ruth Bryant Pvt MA
Jacob: b 2-25-1727 d *p.* 1799 m (1)Desire Phillips (2)Susannah Fuller (3)Alethea Fullerton Ford Pvt MA
John: b 1760 d 1816 m Nancy — Dragoon GA
Joseph: b 11-28-1727 d 11-25-1806 m Mary Jackson Capt MA
Levi: b 10-18-1756 d 6-20-1845 m Hannah Peterson Pvt MM MA ★

DINGMAN,
Andrew, Sr.: b 2-11-1711 d 1796 m Cornelia Kermer Pvt PA
Andrew, Jr.: b 9-19-1753 d 2-3-1839 m Jane Westbrook Pvt Cmsry QM NJ ★
Gerardus: b 1762 d 8- -1842 m — Pvt NY ★
Henry: b 1751 d — m Lucretia Van Evra Bohm Pvt NY

DINGS,
Adam: b 1742 d *p.* 8-18-1795 m Marika Knickerbocker Pvt NY
Jacob: b 5-12-1749 d 11-8-1817 m Elizabeth Knickerbocker Pvt NY

DINKEY,
Jacob: b 4-12-1753 d 4-14-1832 m Susannah Leinberger Pvt PA

DINKINS,
John: b *a.* 1731 d 1809 m Fannie Henderson Pvt NC
Samuel Paul: b 1762 d 1814 m Sarah Scott PS SC
Wm.: b *c.* 1746 d *p.* 1800 m (1)Sarah Wright (2)Nancy Smart Pvt PS SC

DINSMORE, (includes DENSMORE, DUNSMORE)
Abel: b 9-27-1736 d 9-27-1803 m Esther Sanderson Capt MA
Abraham: b 2-22-1729/30 d *p.* 1779 m Lydia — PS NH
Elijah: b 1734 d 9-10-1823 m Sarah Willey Capt NH ★
Eliphalet: b 12-23-1734 d 11-11-1811 m Hannah Treadwell Capt MA
James: b 8-15-1760 d 9-23-1837 m Jane McDonald Pvt NC ★
James: b 4-26-1742 d 4-20-1817 m (1) — (2)Mary Walker (3)Elizabeth Carr Lt PA
John: b 3-11-1742 d 3-4-1808 m Elizabeth Amos Lt MA

John: b 1758 d 1815 m Phoebe Robbins Cpl MA
John: b 9-17-1742 d 8-4-1811 m Sarah Winn Pvt MA
John: b 1720 d 11-22-1794 m Ruth Fisher Dr MA
John, Sr.: b 2-22-1721 d 7-23-1793 m Martha McKeen PS NH
John, Jr.: b 1-26-1759 d 4-14-1814 m (1)Susanna Bell (2)Mary Rogers Pvt NH
Robert: b 11-14-1751 d 11-12-1831 m Sarah Dickey Sgt NH
Robert: b 3-24-1752 d 1-10-1824 m Hannah Long Pvt NH
Robert: b 10-7-1757 d 3-16-1836 m (1)Mary Park (2)Mary(David-son) Anderson Fif NH
Samuel: b 1756 d 1846 m Dortohy Glines Pvt MA ★
Samuel: b 7-30-1759 d 11-18-1836 m Gedida Crowell Pvt MA
Samuel: b a. 1754 d 4-15-1776 m Margaret Thompson Pvt MA
Samuel: b 8-10-1757 d 10-31-1822 m Mary Parke Pvt NH
Thomas: b 1748 d 1-7-1837 m Anna True Pvt MA
Wm.: b 5-9-1731 d 11- -1801 m Elizabeth Cochran PS LCol CS NH

DINTURFF,
Philip: b 10-8-1752 d 10-10-1840 m Elizabeth Keischler Pvt PA ★

DINWIDDIE,
David: b 1724 d p. 12-17-1802 m (1)Jean McClure (2)Elizabeth Kerr PS PA
Hugh: b 8-22-1722 d 1-12-1777 m Jean Crawford Maj PA
James: b 5-19-1755 d 10-14-1842 m Sarah Helm Lt VA

DISBROW,
Asael: b 3-23-1746 d 5-2-1813 m Abigail (Disbrow) Pvt CT
Asael: b 4-7-1753 d — m Charity Platt Pvt CT
Elijah: b c. 1750 d 1820 m Phebe Letts Pvt NJ
Henry: b 4-19-1757 d 5-15-1838 m (1)Rebecca Barnum (2)Hannah Merriam Pvt CT
John D: b 1757 d 1835 m Susanna Morgan Pvt NJ
Joseph: b 2-28-1744/5 d 1821 m Phebe Hendricks Cpl CT
Joshua: b 9-29-1750 d p. 1785 m Deborah Squire Sgt CT
Justus: b 6-24-1751 d 1-16-1840 m Elizabeth Sherwood Pvt CT ★

DISHAROON,
Joshua: b 1-2-1749/50 d 1819 m Ebby — Pvt MD

DISHMAN,
David: b a. 1726 d 1794 m — PS VA
Samuel: b 1723 d 1796 m Polly — PS VA
Wm.: b 9-26-1754 d 12-4-1833 m Sallie Salmons Mar VA
Wm.: b — d p. 5-23-1810 m (1)Anne Monroe (2)Elizabeth Monroe PS VA

DISLER,
Jacob: b c. 1744 d 1-20-1830 m Elizabeth — Pvt PA

DISMUKES, (includes DISMUKE)
Elisha: b — d 3-24-1817 m (1) — (2)Ann Thompson PS VA
George: b 1754/5 d 8-12-1827 m — PS NC
James: b c. 1750 d p. 2-8-1810 m (1)Achaeh Fottrell (2)Jenny — Pvt VA
James: b 8-28-1721 d 9- -1787 m Ruth Rowe Pvt VA
Paul: b 5-1-1762 d 2-22-1838 m Sarah Richardson Pvt VA

DISSINGER,
George: b 1747 d 1816 m (1)Judith Louser (2)Catherine Schweitzer Ens PA

DISSOSWAY,
Cornelius: b 1734 d 12-19-1785 m (1)Catharine Corsen (2)Mary (Fitz Randolph) Baldwin PS NY
Mary (Fitz Randolph): b 1748 d 9-10-1808 m (1)Jones Baldwin (2)Cornelius Dissosway PS NY

DITMARS,
John, Sr.: b 1-11-1739 d 4-24-1804 m Sophia Spader Pvt NJ
Lena Van Liew: b 10-15-1724 d 7-6-1778 m Rem Ditmars PS NJ

DITTEMORE,
John: b 1735 d 4-26-1782 m — Pvt MA

DITTO,
Francis: b 1758 d 6-25-1841 m Eleanor Gift Pvt PS PA W ★
John: b 9-25-1758 d 11-13-1816 m Margaret Hinkle Pvt PA

DITZLER,
Peter: b 1756 d 7- -1837 m — Young Pvt PA ★

DIUGUID, (includes DINGUID)
George: b 10- -1762 d p. 9-10-1832 m Nancy Sampson Pvt VA ★

DIVELLY,
Jeremiah: b 5-21-1755 d c. 1800 m Elizabeth — Sgt RI

DIVEN,
John: b 1752 d 1838 m (1) — Baskins (2)Eleanor Means Pvt PA

DIX,
Charles: b 7-11-1730 d 6-13-1811 m (1)Martha Baxter (2)Lydia — (3)Sarah Hooker Lt CT

Elijah: b 3-5-1744 d 4-27-1826 m Margaret Clark Pvt MA
James: b 10-13-1716 d 4-19-1801 m (1)Sarah Bond (2)Mrs Submit Fairbanks Pvt MA
James: b c. 1740 d p. 1-27-1790 m — PS VA
Joel: b 2-16-1755 d 1837 m Martha Wellington Pvt MA
John: b 7-22-1734 d 8-23-1806 m Mary — Capt MA
John: b c. 1728 d 1784 m Kerenhappuck — PS Capt CS VA
Jonas: b 5-21-1721 d 1783 m Lydia Bemis CS PS MA
Jonathan: b 3-23-1745/6 d p. 1818 m (1)Sarah Viles (2)Mary Bullard Pvt MA
Joseph: b 6-25-1748 d 7-13-1827 m Edith Adams Sgt NH
Joseph: b 7-7-1753 d 9-16-1822 m Sarah Fisher Sgt MA
Ozias: b 12-6-1750 d 12-29-1835 m Lucy Hatch Pvt CT
Thomas: b 1- -1755 d 7-17-1824 m Sarah Edmondson CaptLt VA ★
Timothy: b 12-7-1743 d 1824 m (1)Rachel Burbank (2)Mrs Brown (3)Eliza Cunningham Lt NH
Wm.: b 9-25-1755 d 1829 m Martha Hendrick Capt VA

DIXON, (includes DICKSON, DIXSON)
Agnes Carson: b 1747 d 2-23-1826 m Matthew Dickson PS SC
Amos: b 1-6-1765 d c. 1866 m (1)Betsy — (2)Prudence June Pvt CT ★
Andrew: b 1760 d c. 1840 m Mary Ramsey Pvt PA
Andrew: b 1750 d 6-9-1804 m Rachel — Pvt VA
Benjamin: b 12-20-1753 d 3-4-1839 m Esther Morris Lt NY ★
Benjamin: b 1767 d 1849 m Mary Anderson PS SC
Christopher: b 1750 d p. 1794 m Phebe Lewis Bayless Tms NJ
Curtis: b 1752 d 1835 m Lydia Dixon Sgt MA ★
David: b 7-23-1750 d 5-23-1830 m (1)Mrs Sally Aubrey (2)Martha (Ottorson) Cureton (3)Anne Allen Smith Capt SC PA
Edward: b 1-3-1753 d 10- -1834 m Catharine Warren Cpl VA
George: b 1732 d 2-25-1798 m Hannah Gray Pvt PS PA
George: b 12-7-1735 d 12-8-1817 m Rachel McKee Pvt Fif PA
George: b 2-17-1754 d 2-27-1840 m Verona VanBibber Pvt Spy VA ★
George: b 1739 d 1819 m Rachel Beard Sol VA
Henry: b a. 1747 d 7-17-1782 m Martha Wynn LCol NC
Henry: b 1730 d 6-20-1779 m Elizabeth Abernathy Maj NC
Isaac: b c. 1730 d 7-15-1788 m (1)Sarah Lane (2)Betty — Pvt MD
Jacob: b 1758 d 5-18-1833 m Nancy Foote Pvt PA ★
James: b 11-1-1815 m Margaret Gaston Pvt CT
James: b 2-3-1756 d 6-3-1842 m (1)Mary Morris (2)Mrs Rachel Lawrence Capt NY ★
James: b 2-5-1728 d 8-2-1794 m Agnes Burns Capt PA
James: b 12-6-1744 d 9- -1802 m Rebecca Haines Pvt PA
Jared: b 1740 d 1839 m Mercy Ormsby Pvt CT ★
Jeremiah: b 1764 d 7-26-1835 m Elizabeth Goff Pvt NC ★
John: b 1758 d 1835 m Elizabeth Poythrees Pvt NC
John: b 12-25-1756 d 6-30-1840 m (1) — (2)Mary — Pvt NC ★
John: b c. 1737 d 1821 m Margaret Hazelet Pvt PA
John: b 1741 d a. 2-5-1794 m Hannah Marshall Matr PA
John: b 1754 d 1779 m Hannah — Pvt PA
John: b 6-19-1756 d p. 1790 m Mary Nichols Pvt PA
John: b 2-23-1763 d 5-24-1846 m Elizabeth Garrison Cav PA W★
John: b c. 1730-8 d 11-9-1807 m Mary Arthur PS VA
Jonas: bpt 9-21-1755 d 10-23-1821 m Elizabeth Gill Pvt MA
Joseph: b 9-30-1754 d 5-18-1839 m Mercy Raymond QMSgt PS CT ★
Joseph: b 4- -1745 d 4-14-1825 m Margaret McEwen Capt PS NC
Joseph: b c. 1743 d 1803 m Jane Molton CS NC
Joseph: b a. 1760 d p. 1811 m Elizabeth Hurst Pvt PA
Joshua: b 8-1-1750 d 1831 m (1)Phoebe Heald (2)Dinah Battin Pvt PA
Josiah: b 1750 d 8-27-1834 m Isabel Reid Pvt VA ★
Marshall: b c. 1759 d 6-7-1834 m Phoebe Oakley Pvt NY ★
Matthew: b 1731 d 4-10-1830 m Agnes Carson Sol SC
Michael: b 1743 d 12-3-1803 m Mrs Lucy Crawford Atwood Capt GA
Michael: b 1733 d c. 1816 m Sarah Neely Maj SC
Ralph: b c. 1750 d 1788 m Elizabeth — Capt VA
Robert: b 7-22-1736 d 2-6-1799 m Sarusana Dorrance Capt PS CT
Robert: b 12-3-1753 d 12-9-1840 m Sarah Wylie Pvt Slr CT ★
Robert: b c. 1750 d a. 9-10-1783 m Susannah Jones 1Lt GA
Robert: b 1757 d 1836 m Juleyette Armstrong Pvt NY
Robert: b c. 1740-5 d 1790 m (1)Ann Pearsall (2)Barbary (Williams) Sheffield Maj PS NC
Robert: b 1738 d p. 10-26-1792 m Ann Bacon Capt CS VA
Sankey: b 1759 d 11-11-1814 m Anne Cochran Lt PA
Simon: b 1728 d 4- -1781 m Elizabeth Allen Sol PS NC
Thomas: b 3-14-1732 d 3-13-1802 m Lydia A Parks Sgt CT
Thomas: b 7-24-1752 d 3-13-1823 m (1)Abigail Hatch (2)Lydia Griffith Pvt CT ★
Thomas: b 12-9-1754 d 10-9-1819 m Susanna Pollitt 2Lt MD
Thomas: b 4-2-1759 d 1850 m Amy Knapp Matr NY ★
Thomas: b 8- -1761 d 4-9-1826 m Ann Turner Pvt NC W ★
Thomas: b c. 1750 d 12-28-1812 m Martha Adams Pvt VA
Thomas: b c. 1750 d c. 11-5-1827 m Elizabeth — Pvt VA
Thomas, Sr.: b 6-6-1764 d 1848 m Martha Arthur Pvt VA ★
Tilman: b 11-25-1750 d 4-2-1816 m Polly Don Carlos Capt NC
Wm.: b 4-5-1748 d 10-23-1807 m Priscilla Dension Capt CT
Wm.: b 1762 d 7-18-1812 m Hannah Hughé Sgt GA
Wm.: b 1762 d 6-26-1852 m Sarah Smith Cpl NC ★
Wm.: b 1-10-1739 d — m Mary Williams CS PS NC
Wm.: b 10-15-1744 d 1812 m Agnes Dunlop Pvt PA

DIXON, contd.
Wm.: b 1763 d 6-10-1838 m Grizzy Ann Bell Pvt VA ★
Wynn: b 1764 d 1832 m (1)Keturah Payne Lt NC

DOAK,
Benjamin: b 11-28-1760 d 3-4-1836 m Sarah Goodwin Smn MA ★
David, Sr.: b —d 10-2-1787 m Mary — PS VA
James: b — d p. 12-8-1805 m Mary Paisley PS NC
Robert: b 1753 d 10-4-1838 m Sarah McKibben Pvt PA ★
Robert: b c. 1750 d 3-12-1832 m Elizabeth Mitchell Sol VA
Samuel: b 8-1-1749 d 12-12-1830 m (1)Esther H Montogomery
    (2)Margaret Houston McEwen PS VA

DOANE, (includes DOAN)
Amos: b 1758 d 6-22-1842 m (1)Mary Myrick (2)Abigail Libby Pvt
    MA
Edward: b c. 1741 d 1817 m (1)Anna Westcott (2)Sarah McDugle
    Pvt MA
Elisha: b 11-24-1724 d 7-13-1810 m (1)Mary — (2)Mrs Martha Allen
    Capt MA
Elisha: b 6-23-1725 d 1-25-1783 m Hope Rich Pvt MA
Elisha: b 9-9-1744 d 12-26-1805 m Mehitabel Nickerson Pvt MA
Elkanah: b 1738 d 4-15-1802 m Hannah Farnham Pvt CT
Ephraim: b 1741 d 1819 m Lucy — Pvt MA
Hezekiah: b — d 3- -1808 m Elizabeth Crowell Sgt MA
Isaiah: b c. 1742 d 3-12-1830 m Rebecca Smith Pvt MA
Isaiah: b 10-16-1753 d 4-22-1805 m Hannah Bartlett Pvtr MA
Joel: b 1-9-1763 d 11-23-1852 m (1)Lydia Stannard (2)Jemima
    l'Hommedieu Pvt CT ★
John: b c. 1738 d 4-19-1800 m Betsey Snow Pvt MA
Joseph: b 1720 d 1778 m Dorcas Eldridge Col MA
Levi: b 1748 d 4-15-1828 m Anna Rising Pvt VT
Nehemiah: b 3-17-1737 d 1785 m Mrs Lydia (Higgins) Dill Matr Sgt
    MA
Noah: b 7-4-1732 d 4-1-1820 m Bethia — Pvt MA
Oliver: b 1754 d 10-11-1841 m Sarah Doane Pvt MA
Prince: b 1760 d c. 1806 m Jane Smith Sgt CT
Richard: b 7-14-1763-6 d 8-27-1823-6 m Anna Post Pvt CT ★
Seth: b 6-9-1733 d 10-18-1802 m Mercy Parker NCdr PS CT
Thomas: b 4-1-1760 d 7-17-1829 m Mary Plumley Matr PA
Wm.: b 4-11-1759 d 2-13-1812 m Diana Noble Sol CT

DOBBINS, (includes DOBBIN, DOBYNS)
Edward: b 12-30-1743 d 10-5-1789 m Mrs Amory Forrester PS VA
Edward: b 12-7-1747 d 4-3-1794 m Frances Keye Pvt VA
James: b c. 1730 d p. 2-5-1788 m Anna — Sgt NC
James: b 1750 d p. 3- -1813 m Elizabeth Stephenson Pvt SC
James: b 3-7-1753 d 8-24-1853 m Catherine Titman Pvt SC ★
Lodwick: b 1739 d 1- -1781 m Betsy Woodruff Pvt Dep QM NJ
Thomas: b c. 1757 d 1841 m (1) — (2)Nancy Nicholson Pvt NC
Wm.: b 2-17-1740 d 9-23-1814 m Susannah — PS SC

DOBBS,
Chesley: b 1749 d 1-25-1834 m Hannah — Pvt VA NC W ★
Daniel: b 9-9-1765 d 1-15-1830 d (2)Mary Humphrey Pvt NY
Fortune b 1727 d c. 1792 m Mary Adams Guide Cav SC
Lodwick: b 1759 d 6-3-1814 m Sarah Adams (Dobbs) Sol SC
Nathan: b 1760 d 1- -1856 m Fanny Yancey Pvt VA ★
Thomas: b 1750 d 1832 m Janet Mahaffy Pvt PA
Wm., Sr.: b 1718 d 9-6-1781 m Catharine Vansise Capt NY

DOBEY,
John: b 1755 d 1836 m Sarah White Pvt NC ★

DOBKINS,
Jacob: b 1751 d 1835 m — Pvt VA ★

DOBSON,
John: b c. 1752 d 6-20-1780 m — Capt NC
Richard: b 3-16-1763 d 1839 m Sarah — Pvt VA ★
Wm.: b c. 1760 d p. 1803 m Martha Neely PS NC

DOBY,
John: b 1736 d 9-8-1781 m Elizabeth Massey PS SC

DOCK,
Philip: b 8-2-1757 d 7-15-1830 m Elizabeth Killian 1Sgt PA ★

DOCKERY, (includes DOCKARY)
Thomas, Sr.: b 1719 d 1799 m Hannah — PS NC
Thomas, Jr.: b 1745 d 1-30-1805 m (1)Ann — (2)Rebecca Crosnoe
    PS NC

DOCKHAM,
Thomas: b 1750 d a. 5-10-1808 m Dorothy Batchelder Pvt NH

DOCKSTADER, (includes DOXTATOR)
Frederick H: b 1751 d 9-25-1823 m Mary Ecker Pvt NY
George: b c. 1743 d 9-8-1808 m Barbara Schultzin Pvt NY W ★
Henry H: b 3- -1740 d 8-10-1783 m Elizabeth Eckerin Pvt NY
John: b 8-13-1760 d p. 10-11-1832 m Catherine Bellinger Cpl NY
John F: b 5-8-1752 d 8-15-1839 m Barbery Eaker Pvt NY
John H: b c. 1756 d p. 1785 m Maria Serviss Pvt NY

Marks: b 10- -1738 d 10-27-1821 m Elizabetha Schultz Pvt NY
Nicholas, Jr.: b c. 1750 d p. 8- -1811 m Catrina VanDeWerken Lt
    NY
Peter: b 12-25-1751 d 12-1-1842 m (1)Elizabeth Cunningham
    (2)Susanna — (?) Innocent Hurlburt Pvt NY ★

DODD, (includes DOD)
Abijah: b 11-9-1757 d 8-21-1837 m Mary (Dodd)Pvt NJ ★
Amos: b 9-15-1737 d 10-7-1811 m Hannah Condit Capt NJ
Bartholomew: bpt 5-18-1746 d 1808 m Maria Doremus PS NJ
Bishop: b 1755 d 2-9-1826 m Rebecca Hull Sol CT
Caleb: b 5-26-1740 d 1780 m Mary Harrison Maj NJ
Daniel: b 1745 d 10-11-1824 m Charity Freeman Pvt PA
David: b 10-11-1733 d 3-31-1817 m Sarah Harrison Pvt NJ
David: b 1754 d p. 8-17-1813 m Elizabeth — Capt NC
Isaac: b 7-8-1728 d 8-19-1804 m Jemima Williams Capt NJ
Jesse: b c. 1750 d p. 1800 m Mary Bobo 1Lt SC
John: b 3-28-1764 d 9-11-1840 m Betsey Scales Pvt SC
John: b 1759 d 1815 m Elizabeth Bingen Sol VA
Joseph: b 9-12-1731 d 6-4-1789 m (1)Mary Lindsley (2)Sarah
    Williams Pvt NJ
Lebbeus: b 2-15-1739 d 3-31-1816 m Mary Baldwin Capt NJ
Matthias: b 4-29-1753 d 7-23-1801 m Sarah Munn Pvt NJ
Moses: b 12-9-1755 d 12-6-1839 m Lois Crane MM NJ
Permenus: b 1748 d 4-28-1811 m Patience Wright Pvt NJ
Thomas: b 1-7-1723 d p. 9-8-1815 m (1)Sarah Newcombe
    (2)Mrs Phebe Perkins Pvt NJ
Timothy: b — d — m Susannah Gross Pvt CT
Uzal: b 3-9-1759 d 4-9-1827 m Phoebe Freeman Pvt NJ
Wm.: b 1750 d p. 7-11-1793 m (1)Elizabeth Jacobs (2)Sarah
    Heart Pvt DE
Wm.: b 1747 d 10-28-1832 m Anna Childs SgtMaj MA
Wm.: b c. 1758 d 1807 m Rebecca — Pvt VA

DODDRIDGE,
John: b 3-30-1745 d 4-20-1791 m (1)Mary Wells (2)Elizabeth Reeves
    Pvt PA
Joseph: b c. 1710 d 2-14-1779 m Mary Biggs CS PA

DODDS,
Joseph, Jr.: b 10-9-1756 d 4-9-1833 m Catherine Miller Lt PA
Wm.: b 2-15-1753 d 7-16-1831 m Isabella McGrew Capt PA

DODGE,
Abimael: b c. 1760 d 1810 m — Pvt MA
Abner: b 3-30-1755 d 1839 m (1)Eleanor Dodge (2)Elizabeth Sears
    Sgt MA
Abraham: b 3-18-1729/30 d 9-6-1810 m Mrs Elizabeth Warren Pvt
    MA
Abraham: b 7-15-1761 d 10-12-1848 m Amelia Noyes Pvt Fif MA
Abram: b 8-17-1740 d 6-16-1686 m Bethia (Patch) Staniford Capt MA
Ammi: b 1751 d 12-16-1826 m Lucy Dodge MM MA
Amos: b 7-1-1754 d 5-9-1792 m (1)Mrs Hepsibah Dodge
    (2)Lydic Batchelder Pvt MA
Andrew: b 2-14-1739/40 d 12-8-1808 m Mary Rindge Pvt MA
Andrew: b 4-20-1745 d 1828 m Jane Carriel Pvt NY
Asa: b — d c. 1828 m Lydia Buxton Pvt MA
Benjamin: b 1744 d 6-24-1829 m Tabitha Dodge Pvt CT ★
Benjamin: b 4-13-1758 d 1-13-1831 m (1)Eunice Boutwell (2)Mrs
    Sarah Mudgette Pvt MA
Brewer: b 12-4-1749 d 12-29-1826 m (1) — Thompson (2)Anna
    Brainard (3)Anna Sellingham Pvt NH W ★
Caleb: b 12-11-1714 d 3-6-1798 m Hannah Woodbury Capt MA
Caleb: b 12-14-1726 d p. 2-4-1812 m Mariam Gilbert Pvt MA
Charles: b 1-27-1741 d 8-3-1823 m Abigail Dodge Porter Pvt MA
Cornelius: b 1743 d 4-27-1837 m Lydia Poland Pvt MA
Daniel: b 6-6 10-14-1781 m Irena Rowley Cpl CT W ★
Daniel: b 7-19-1757 d 9-14-1807 m Lucy Latimer Pvt CT
Daniel: b 5-23-1743 d 1805 m Sarah Danforth Pvt MA
Daniel, Jr.: b 12-14-1760 d 8-21-1827 m Elizabeth Parson Pvt MA
Daniel: b 2-28-1728 d 2-25-1821 m Mary Brown Pvt NY
Ebenezer: b 1-20-1756 d 5-11-1828 m Eunice Hill Cpl MA W ★
Edward: b 1740-42 d 1783 m Lois Morgan Pvt CT
Edward: bpt 6-9-1754 d 12-11-1833 m Mary Endicott Sgt MA ★
Elijah: b 4-28-1709 d 2-3-1777 m (1)Elizabeth Moulton (2)Dorcas
    Brown PS NH
Elisha, Sr.: b 5-17-1723 d 1786-90 m (1)Eleanor Dodge (2)Sarah
    Foster (3)Mrs Deborah Lovett PS Pvt NH
Elisha, Jr.: b 10-19-1748 d p. 1800 m Ginger Raymond Pvt PS NH
George, Jr.: b 1749 d 5-12-1827 m (1)Mary Cleaves (2)Sally Brown
    Pvt MA
Gideon: b 11-25-1760 d 4-18-1821 m Charity Cole Pvt NH
Henry: b 4-12-1756 d 12-19-1820 m Sarah Rosecranz Capt NY
Isaac: b 2-25-1740 d 10-20-1806 m Sarah Utley Sgt CT
Isaac: b 2-26-1732 d 6-29-1785 m Elizabeth — LCol MA
Isaac: b 6-7-1708 d 6-2-1790 m (1)Mehitabel Tyler (2)Abigail Tyler Sgt MA
Israel: b 9-3-1760 d 1806 m (1)Nancy Hunter (2)Theodosia Lewis
    (3)Mrs Catherine Guion Lt CT
Israel: b 2-21-1739 d 10-3-1822 m Lucia Pickering PS MA
Israel Andrew: bpt 12-10-1749 d 3-18-1823 m Mary Brown Pvt MA
Jacob: b 4-2-1718 d 3-11-1801 m Abigail Edwards Pvt MA
Jacob, Sr.: b 2-19-1715/16 d 12-13-1792 m (1)Sarah Hubbard
    (2)Mrs Martha Dodge (3)Mrs Elizabeth Crowell Pvt MA

Jacob: b 2-9-1752 d 10-25-1810 m Anna Batchelder Pvt NH
Jeremiah: b 5-23-1742 d 10-9-1825 m Elizabeth Chapman Pvt CT
Jeremiah, Jr.: b 7-19-1744 d 1824 m Judith Spofford Pvt MA
Jesse: b 12-1-1748 d 1780 m Bethiah Thorndike Pvt MA
John: bpt 3-10-1723 d 1-22-1794 m (1)Lydia Rogers (2)Elizabeth
    Willis (3)Mrs Martha Shaw Pvt CT
John: b 1-7-1738 d 1800 m Mary Marston MM MA
John: b 10-10-1754 d 8-14-1814 m Abigail Ross Pvt MA
John 3rd: b 5-19-1747 d 5-1-1825 m Mehitable Batchelder Pvt MA
John, Jr.: b 5-28-1748 d 1806 m (1)Susanna Morgan (2)Mrs Katy
    Galer Pvt MA
John Perkins: b 7-27-1760 d 2-4-1830 m Jane Wood Pvt NH ★
John Thomas: b 4-2-1764 d 2-26-1851 m Elizabeth (Dodge) Pvt
    MA ★
Jonah: b 11-19-1738 d p. 1790 m Lydia Herrick Pvt MA
Jonathan: b 8-3-1721 d 1-19-1794 m Marcy Williams Pvt MA
Jonathan: b 1743 d 2-9-1822 m Mary Brown Pvt MA
Joshua: b 12-26-1716 d p. 1790 m (1)Mary Dodge (2)Mrs Anna
    Thorndike (3)Mary Whittridge Pvt MA
Joshua: b 1723-27 d 2-24-1796 m Thankful Morse Pvt MA
Josiah: b 9-8-1740 d p. 1799 m Hannah Connant Pvt MA
Josiah Rogers: b 9-28-1762 d p. 1794 m Zervia Willis Pvt CT
Mark: b 4-6-1743 d 9-18-1824 m Susanna Brown Sgt MA
Moses: b 6-27-1762 d 2-21-1826 m Tryphena McIntyre Pvt MA
Nathan: b 10-20-1758 d 10-7-1797 m Pamelia Pomeroy Pvt NH
Nathaniel: bpt 3-28-1762 d 1850 m Polly Hover Pvt MA ★
Nathaniel: b 7-5-1763 d 5-1-1838 m Rebecca Walton Pvt NH
Nathaniel Brown: b 3-20-1740 d 8-20-1823 m (1)Lydia Barber
    (2)Hannah Robbins (3)Tabitha (Brown) Newhall Pvt MA ★
Nathaniel Hubbard: b 1-21-1738/9 d 4- -1830 m (1)Sarah Hubbard
    (2)Ann Hilliard PS NH
Nicholas: b 11-19-1752 d 12-10-1827 m (1)Hannah Cole (2)Elizabeth
    Myrick Pvt NH ★
Noah: b 11-4-1761 d 5-19-1829 m (1)Hannah Johnson (2)Elizabeth
    (Venning) Comstock Sol MA
Oliver: b 9-2-1745 d 1-1-1802 m (1)Sarah Williams (2)Abigail
    Harris Pvt CT
Paul: b 1745 d 12-20-1820 m Sarah Dodge Lt MA
Phineas: b 9-9-1745 d 3-4-1824 m Lucy Nelson Pvt MA
Richard: b 12-9-1738 d 5- -1802 m Mrs Lydia Dodge Capt MA
Richard: b 12-21-1762 d 9-3-1832 m Ann Sarah Irving Sol Fif NY
Robert: b 9-20-1743 d 6-15-1823 m Mary Bordman Capt MA
Samuel: b 5-24-1756 d p. 1824 m (1)Lydia Sands (2)Mrs Esther
    Conant Pvt MA ★
Samuel: b 1743 d 9-29-1785 m Susannah Washer PS NH
Samuel: b 1740 d 1800 m Deborah North Sol NY
Samuel: b 3-29-1730 d 10-4-1807 m Helena Amerman PS NY
Seth: b 7-24-1765 d 2-27-1825 m Deborah Lawrence Pvt CT
Shadrach: b 8-15-1762 d 7-29-1849 m (1)Lucy Rockwell (2)Susan
    Campbell Pvt NH ★
Simeon: b 1-14-1749 d 6-25-1815 m Abigail Dodge Pvt MA
Simeon: b 3-26-1755 d 12-25-1827 m Mary Balch Pvt MA
Simon: b 8-26-1751 d 12-8-1839 m Abigail Cook Pvt MA
Solomon: b 8-13-1747 d 5-4-1799 m Sarah — Lt MA
Solomon: b 11-8-1759 d 8-8-1831 m Mary Taggart Sgt NH
Stephen: b 3-21-1747 d 1812 m Elizabeth Gardner Lt CT
Thaddeus: b 6-18-1761 d 2-18-1837 m (1)Susan Holloway (2)Esther
    Tyler Pvt MA ★
Thomas: b 1743 d 1816 m Ruth Giddings Capt MA
Thomas: b 1759 d 8-11-1827 m Abigail Putney Pvt MA
Thomas: b 3-13-1763 d 9-29-1842 m Mary Felton Pvt MA ★
Wm.: b 9-5-1758 d 5-11-1828 m Lydia Nichols Pvt CT
Wm.: b 16-1753 d 8-30-1797 m Sarah Williams SgtMaj MA
Wm.: b 3-28-1731 d 11-3-1803 m Mrs Mercy Smith Pvt MA
Wm.: b 10-27-1737 d 10-16-1820 m Elizabeth Thoits PS NH
Winthrop: b 4-26-1759 d 3-2-1818 m Mary Perkins Pvt MA
Zachariah: b 2-14-1732/3 d 10-24-1788 m (1)Martha Cleaves
    (2)Sallie Somes Pvt MA

DODRIDGE,
Philip: b 1737 d 5-6-1822 m Mary Bickerstaff Pvt PA

DORRILL,
James: b c. 1750 d 1806 m — Cpl NC

DODSON, (includes DOTSON)
Caleb: b 1752 d 1837 m Elizabeth Petty Pvt VA
Charles: b 2-2-1747 d 5-2-1831 m Lucy Morgan Pvt NC
Elisha: b 2-22-1727 d 4-27-1791 m — Averett Ens VA
Elisha: b 1758-60 d 8- -1828 m Rachel Henry PS VA
John: b 12-25-1752 d 5-16-1825 m Eleanor Howard PS MD
John: b c. 1740-50 d 1816 m — Pvt MD
John: b 4-10-1720 d 3-10-1818 m Mary Eleanor Evans Pvt PA
Joshua: b 1757 d 1850 m (1)Anne Chilton (2)Sara Brummer Pvt VA
Richard: b 6-26-1731 d 1785 m Susannah Rhodes Capt PA
Richard: b 10-23-1752 d 1847 m (1)Mary — (2)Amelia Pvt Spy VA ★
Samuel: b 1738 d 1-7-1796 m Elizabeth Rhodes Pvt PA
Thomas: b c. 1728 d 1780 m Esther — PS MD
Thomas: b 9-15-1755 d 4-29-1818 m Mehetabel Bixby Pvt PA
Wm.: b 3-29-1758 d 3-11-1840 m Mary Dodson Pvt VA ★

DOE,
Dudley: b 5-25-1747 d 2-16-1833 m Anna Dyer Pvt CS PS ME

Joseph: b 1737 d 1817 m Martha Weeks PS NH
Nathaniel, Jr.: b 1748 d p. 1798 m Molly Fairfield Pvt MA
Reuben: b c. 1736 d p. 1790 m Mary Elliott Pvt NH
Sampson: b 1745 d 1829 m Sarah — Cpl MA
Wm.: b 11-11-1760 d 1-21-1828 m Joanna Hall Pvt Fif NH
Wm.: b c. 1760 d c. 1831/2 m — Sol VA

DOEBLER,
Abram: b 3-17-1765 d 8-17-1849 m Mary Kerlin Drm PA ★
Anthony: b 1-17-1738 d 3-17-1814 m Magdelena Weidman Pvt
    PS PA

DOHERTY,
George: b a. 1755 d 4-23-1792 m Mrs Mary (Freeman) Burke Maj NC
George: b 1-18-1749 d 5-27-1833/4 m (1)Priscilla Goforth (2)Sally
    Randols Capt VA NC ★

DOLAND,
Peter: b 1762 d 1821 m Elizabeth Riche Pvt NJ

DOLBIER, (includes DOLBEARE, DOLBEER)
Benjamin: b 12-25-1760 d 1-26-1837 m Ruth Eddes Pvt MA ★
Edmond: b 3-5-1757 d 4- -1796 m Christina Franks Pvt MA
John: b 9-29-1745 d 4-9-1806 m Sarah Raymond Pvt CT
Nicholas: b 5-8-1749 d 2-24-1796 m Mary Randall Sol NH

DOLE,
Amos, Sr.: b 1-11-1733 d 2-11-1781 m Molly Page Pvt MA
Amos, Jr.: b 9-19-1759 d 7-20-1832 m Matilda Hewes Pvt MA
Enoch: b 10-18-1743 d 3-9-1776 m Eunice Richardson Dr MA
Enoch: b 3-21-1756 d 5-29-1827 m Molly Plummer Cpl MA
John: b 2-5-1760 d 11-11-1814 m Molly Pingree Pvt MA
John: b 9-8-1748 d 6-28-1824 m Eunice Sanderson Pvt MA
Jonathan: b 3-23-1751 d 10-6-1819 m Sarah Clarkson Pvt MA
Parker, Sr.: b 9-14-1740 d 5-19-1813 m Abigail Lawrence PS MA
Richard: b 3-16-1742/3 d — m — Pvt MA
Samuel: b c. 1760 d a. 5-28-1820 m Hannah Merrill Pvt MA
Silas: b 9-10-1755 d 8-7-1831 m Judith Rolfe Pvt MA
Stephen: b 1-17-1752 d 1-22-1804 m Abigail Illsley Pvt MA

DOLES,
Jesse: b 1748-50 d 1831 m Elizabeth — Sol NC

DOLL,
John: b 5-21-1760 d 2-26-1843 m Eva Biery Pvt PA ★
Joseph: b c. 1747/8 d a. 8-3-1819 m Charlotte — PS MD

DOLLAR,
Reuben: b 1745 d 1858 m — Wolbanks Pvt SC
Wm.: b — d 9-6-1838 m Ruth Beezley Pvt VA ★

DOLLINGER,
John: b 9-14-1758 d 11-21-1843 ı.. Veronika — Pvt PA ★

DOLLINS,
John: b 1761 d 1787 m Elizabeth — PS VA

DOLLIVER,
Joseph, Jr.: b 1757 d 9-19-1837 m Abigail Targee Ens RI
Wm.: b 2-3-1759 d 10-10-1841 m Elizabeth Foster Pvt MA
Wm.: b 2-26-1726 d 1793 m Sarah Hinds PS CS MA

DOLLOFF,
Josiah: b c. 1754 d 2-18-1830 m Jane Knox PS NH
Richard: b 1-2-1755 d 10-24-1845 m Tamesin Knowlton Pvt NH
Thomas: b 6-17-1759 d 7-11-1841 m Elice Leavitt Pvt NH ★

DOLSBURY,
Lyles: b 5-11-1760 d 8-23-1850 m Arsula Davis Pvt VA ★

DOLSON,
Isaac: b — d 1795 m Polly Huzzy Drm NY
Jacob: b 11-2-1736 d 5-20-1779 m Mary Cook Pvt NY
John: b 5-15-1737 d 10-28-1794 m (1)Susan Cosman (2)Sarah —
    Pvt PS NY
John: b 6-17-1752 d 4-8-1836 m (1)Magdalena Christie (3)Elizabeth
    Carr Pvt NY ★
Teunis: b 10-6-1735 d p. 8-29-1795 m (1)Rachael Cuyper (2)Mary
    Cross (3)Elizabeth Holland Pvt NY

DOMINICK,
George: b 3-8-1739 d 3-30-1832 m Elizabeth Blanchard Capt NY
Henry: b 1757 d 1-1-1835 m (1)Margaret Fellers (2)Agnes Fellers
    Pvt SC ★
John: b 1740 d 10-6-1824 m Sophia Rickard Sternberg 2Lt NY

DOMINY, (includes DOMINI)
Andrew: b — d 5-2-1817 m Margaret — Pvt SC W ★
Henry: b 12-15-1746 d 1-23-1817 m Elizabeth Dayton Sgt NY
Nathaniel: b 12-14-1714 d 3-30-1778 m Elizabeth Eyres PS NY

DONAGHHO, (or DONAHOO)
John: b 1740 d 1812 m Ann Elizabeth (Meyer)Castle Pvt PA

DONAGHY,
John: b 1732 d 7-5-1817 m Perseverance Stephens Pvt NY

DONALD,
James: b c. 1738 d 1803 m Elizabeth — Pvt SC

DONALDSON, (includes DONELSON)
Altamont: b 11-12-1763 d 1-26-1847 m Anna W Richards Pvt MA
Alexander: b 1-2-1742 d 1783 m Jane Kennedy Pvt PA
Andrew: b c. 1750 d p. 6-23-1817 m Isabella — Pvt PA
Arthur: b 1734 d 1797 m Elizabeth Kaighn Engineer PS PA
Calvin: b 6-4-1755 d 10-24-1845 m Caty McMaster Cpl MA ★
David: b c. 1748 d 1804/5 m Sarah Sloan Pvt DE
Hugh George: b 6-21-1757 d 6-20-1812 m (1)Chloe Demick
  (2)Susannah Snow (3)Hannah Deane Hatch Sgt Dr MA
Isaac: b c. 1747 d 4-1-1781 m Martha Reynolds Pvt PA
John: b 12-8-1727/8 d 2-10-1815 m Ruth Blodget Pvt MA
John: b 1-1-1753 d 9-2-1824 m Abigail Owens Sgt NY ★
John: b c. 1735 d 1782 m — Pvt PA
John, Sr.: b 1718 d 1785 m Rachel Stockley PS CtyLt VA
John, Jr.: b 4-7-1755 d 4-22-1830 m Mary Purnell Capt VA
John: b 7-15-1736 d 8-1-1821 m Jane Wigginton Sgt VA
Moses: b 1745 d p. 2-10-1798 m (1)Mary — (2)Susannah — CS PA
Mrs Moses, (prob Mary): b c. 1745 d 6-12-1778 m Moses
  Donaldson PS PA
Patrick: b c. 1744 d 3-1-1781 m Lucy Pettit PS KY
Robert: b c. 1760 d p. 1798 m Elizabeth (Donelson) Sol NC
Wm.: b 4-17-1743 d 11-8-1825 m Susanna Lane Pvt NJ
Wm.: b c. 1749 d 1789 m Sarah Griscomb Capt Pvtr PA
Wm.: b 1758 d 1800 m Janet Ramsey Capt PA
Wm.: b 9- -1762 d 6-24-1826 m Margaret Barclay Pvt PA
Wm.: b 4-25-1738 d 3-19-1819 m Mary Sweeney Pvt VA

DONAT,
Christian: b 7-16-1740 d 4-5-1815 m Anne Rubican Pvt PA

DONDEL,
Michael: b 11-29-1732 d 2-18-1803 m Sarah Ebert Capt PA

DONIPHAN,
Joseph: b 1757 d 1814 m Ann Smith QM VA

DONNALLY, (includes DONALLY, DONNELLY)
Andrew: b c. 1745 d 1824 m Jane McCreary CS Col VA
Edward O.: b a. 1755 d 10-21-1820 m Nancy — Pvt PA
Jane McCreary: b c. 1750 d p. 1784 m Andrew Donnally PS VA
Peter: b 8-29-1720 d 11-29-1782 m Eleanor McGraw PS MM NY
Thomas: b 5-29-1764 d 2-4-1835 m Ruth Pettinger PS NY ★

DONNELL,
Abraham: b 6- -1749 d 5-4-1831 m Mary Cromwell Pvt MA
Andrew: b 4-17-1757 d 12-24-1835 m (1)Nancy — (2)Mary
  Creswell Pvt NC ★
Benjamin, Sr.: b c. 1720 d c. 1789 m Sarah Kinsbury Capt ME
Benjamin, Jr.: b 12-11-1743 d p. 4-12-1780 m Elizabeth Todd Pvt ME
Daniel: b 1755 d 1835 m Mary Erwin Pvt NC ★
James: b 1739 d 9- -1784 m Catharine Gibson Pvt PA
John: b 1-25-1746 d 4-14-1822 m Sarah Philbrook Slr MA
John: b 1-1743 d 5-7-1822 m (1)Hannah Meeks (2)Elizabeth Denny
  Maj NC ★
Samuel: b 1-9-1745 d 10-9-1827 m Abigail Toppan Pvt MA
Thomas: b 6-11-1765 d 12- -1833 m Nancy Barr PS PA
William: b 1747 d 1798 m Mary Bell Pvt NC
Wm.: b 4-26-1760 d p. 8-28-1833 m (1)Jane — (2)Elizabeth — Pvt
  Wgn NC ★
Zechariah: b c. 1747 d p. 1794/5 m Sarah Hardy Sol MA

DONOHO, (includes DUNAHUGH)
John: b 1718 d 12-29-1822 m Catherine Croompeckler Cpl VA
Thomas: b 1750 d 4-2-1825 m Kesiah Saunders Maj NC

DONOVAN,
Richard: b 11-17-1731 d 8-16-1780 m Sarah Ann Delafield Lt MD

DOOLEY,
James: b 1746 d 6-7-1824 m Margaret McKinney Pvt VA
Moses: b c. 1740 d 1-12-1822 m Mary Boyd Sol VA
Rebecca: b c. 1740 d p. 1-19-1793 m Thomas Dooley PS VA
Thomas: b c. 1735 d c. 1778 m Rebecca Sharp Lt Capt VA

DOOLITTLE,
Abraham: b 8-29-1728 d 1776 m Sarah — Lt CT
Ambrose: b 11-23-1719 d 9-25-1793 m Martha Munson Pvt CT
Amzi: b 11-15-1737 d 4-9-1830 m (1)Jerusha Smith (2)Hannah —
  Lt VT
Benjamin: b 3-5-1738 d 8-3-1802 m Lydia Ives Pvt CT
Benjamin: b 7-15-1753 d 3-29-1831 m Sarah French Pvt Slr CT
Benjamin: b 1-12-1764 d 1854 m Editha Field Pvt MA
Charles: b — d — m — Pvt CT ★
Daniel: b 11-10-1741 d 12-17-1808 m (1)Rebecca Johnson (2)Abigail
  Johnson Ens CT
Daniel: b 2-3-1706 d 9- -1791 m (1)Elizabeth Dayton (2)Martha
  Merriman PS CT

David: b 10-4-1736 d p. 1790 m Tapatha Doolittle Pvt CT
Ebenezer: b 10-12-1736 d 10-1-1807 m Lucy Hall Pvt Sol PS CT
Ephraim: b 9-30-1756 d p. 1788 m Lydia Gridley Pvt CT
Ephraim: b 10-29-1725 d 1807 m Sarah Moreton Col PS MA
Ezra: b 1-3-1752 d 4-5-1829 m Sarah Moss Sgt CT
George: b 6-13-1759 d 2-21-1825 m Grace Wetmore Sgt NY
Hopkins: b 2-22-1764 d 1-28-1827 m (1)Elizabeth — (2)Mary —
  Sol NY
Ichabod: b 8-21-1731 d 12-7-1806 m Deborah Birchard Capt CT
Isaac: b 1721 d 1800 m Sarah Todd Pvt CT
Isaac: b 7-25-1755 d 1793 m Phebe Cook Pvt CT
Joel: b 3-2-1765 d 10-28-1814 m Amelia Wetmore Pvt CT
Joel: b — d 1812 m Rose Lucas Pvt CT
John: b 1-31-1750 d 8-17-1825 m Hannah Guernsey Pvt CT
Joseph: b 9-28-1755 d 3-12-1819 m — Chilson Arfr CT ★
Joseph, Jr.: b 1-13-1757 d 2-25-1814 m Sarah Hart Pvt CT
Joseph: b 1-21-1738 d p. 1790 m Abigail Rockwell Lt NY
Luther: b 1-14-1764 d 8-25-1821 m Mary Hazelton Pvt VT
Obed: b 3-3-1764 d 10-7-1853 m Lozette Blakesley Pvt CT ★
Reuben: b 4-19-1761 d 8-30-1830 m Mary Keeler Cpl NY
Samuel: b 4-11-1749 d 10-5-1810 m Sarah Jones Pvt CT
Solomon: b 2-24-1746 d p. 1797 m Eunice Hall Lt CT
Thomas: b 5-5-1736 d 1807 m Sarah Gitteau Vol CT
Uri: b 9-13-1762 d 9-10-1848 m Jedidah Saxton Pvt CT ★

DORAN, (includes DORN)
Abraham: b 3-16-1756 d 4-24-1838 m Polly Sulivan Sol NY ★
Alexander: b 1-28-1760 d 9-21-1841 m Sarah Reed Pvt Tms NJ ★
Alexander: b 6-2-1760 d 1814 m Elizabeth Lowry Ens VA
George: b c. 1740 d a. 1781 m Elizabeth — PS SC
Jeremiah: b 7-3-1760 d 9-17-1846 m (1)Catharine Veighte
  (2)Elizabeth Karnkrose Pvt NY
John: b 7-3-1740 d 12-2-1815 m Mary Sullivan Pvt NY
Stacy: b c. 1760 d 1850 m (1)Mary Shreve (2)Mary Maginniss Pvt NJ

DORCHESTER,
Alexander: b 1758-60 d 1-23-1843 m Anne Cowle Pvt CT

DOREMUS,
David: bpt 3-24-1750 d 2-2-1799 m Jane Harty Lt NJ
George: b 8-28-1754 d p. 5-31-1828 m Anna Berdan Pvt NJ
Johannes: b 9-1-1720 d 7-22-1784 m Mareytje Lutkins PS NJ
Thomas: b 4-25-1750 d 9-9-1813 m Hester Smith Pvt NJ
Thomas: b 5-9-1725 d 10-7-1801 m Sarah Sanford MM NJ
Thomas: b 8-4-1741 d 5-9-1810 m Rachel Spier PS NJ

DORGAN,
Timothy: b c. 1740 d p. 1781 m — PS PA

DORHMAN,
Arnold Henry: b 1749 d 2-14-1813 m (2)Rachel Banks PS Portugal

DORLAND, (includes DORLAN)
Garrat: b c. 1755 d 3-6-1820 m — 2Lt PA
George: b 1752 d 10-9-1829 m Elizabeth Nesbit Pvt PA
John: b 2-9-1686 d 3-31-1780 m Mary Bedell PS NY
John: b 1754/5 d 8-9-1813 m Ann Robinson Pvt PA
Luke: b 5-23-1749 d 1787 m Eleanor Aulche Pvt NJ
Peter: b 12-27-1758 d 2-11-1833 m Margaret Auble Fif NJ ★
Samuel, Sr.: b 2-24-1721 d 11-7-1809 m Anne Esmond CS NY
Samuel, Jr.: b 7-6-1757 d 5-2-1828 m (1)Rebecca Somes (2)Sarah
  Conkling Pvt NY

DORLON,
John: b 8-13-1751 d 5-22-1824 m Judith (Baker) Bridges Capt NY

DORMAN,
Amos: b 12-20-1735 d 9-11-1811 m Keziah Brown Cpl CT
Daniel: b 9-20-1761 d 4-24-1813 m Esther Hunt Pvt CT
Daniel: b 3-3-1761 d 6-4-1826 m Phoebe Warner Pvt CT
Jabez: b 1744 d p. 1793 m Mary Godfrey Sgt MA
Jesse: b 1718 d 1802 m Eunice Averill Capt MA
Joseph: b 5-25-1723 d 7-5-1779 m Phebe Dorman Pvt CT
Ludwig: b 1755 d p. 4-17-1820 m Mary — Pvt PA ★
Stephen: b 4-3-1749 d p. 1790 m Roxana — Sgt CT
Timothy: b 10-24-1757 d 12-23-1835 m Deborah Perley Pvt MA

DORMEYER,
Jacob: b 1734 d p. 1790 m Hannaricha Christiana Margaret—Pvt PA

DORNBLASER,
Paul: b 10-15-1760 d 6-3-1804 m Elizabeth Pfeifer Pvt PA

DORNEY,
Daniel: b 1725 d p. 1-15-1779 m Elizabeth Jarrett PS PA

DORR, (includes DARE, DOOR)
Benaiah: b 3-15-1764 d 2-21-1854 m (1)Experience Andrews
  (2)Mary Pray Allen Pvt NH MA ★
Ebenezer: b 2-12-1712 d 8-8-1782 m Amy Plympton PS MA
Edward: b 5-28-1752 d 5-24-1839 m Judith Champion Pvt CT
John: b c. 1755 d p. 1-4-1832 m Lucy Whitehouse Pvt MA
Matthew, Sr.: b 6-14-1725 d 9-18-1801 m (1)Elizabeth Palmer
  (2)Lydia (Wood) McClean Capt CT

Matthew, Jr.: b 5-29-1756 d 5-26-1843 m Dinah Mudge Pvt NY
Nathan: b 3-27-1745 d 2-18-1787 m Margaret Odin Pvt MA
Philip, Jr.: b 1746 d *p.* 1782 m Mary (Foss) Locke Pvt MA
William: b 7-13-1757 d 8-13-1840 m Jane Partridge Fif Pvt MA ★

DORRANCE,
David: b 1751 d 1-22-1822 m Anna Brewster Holbert Capt CT ★
George: b 3-4-1736 d 7-3-1778 m (1)Mary Wilson (2)Elizabeth —
    LCol PA
James: b 7-30-1743 d 4-1-1825 m Elizabeth Gordon Cpl QM CT
Lemuel: b 11-28-1746 d 4-28-1812 m (1)Mary Gordon (2)Priscilla
    Bradford Pvt CT
Samuel: b 6-23-1745 d 8-31-1792 m Anne Tully CS RI

DORRIS,
William: b *c.* 1761 d 11-22-1842 m Eleanor Brown Pvt NJ

DORSETT, (includes DOSSET)
Francis: b *c.* 1718 d *p.* 1785 m (1)Jane Prather (2)Rebecca
    MacSwain Sol NC
James: b 11-18-1761 d *p.* 1796 m Eleanor Bennett Pvt NJ
John: b 1-10-1752 d 1834 m Martha Cortelyou Pvt NJ
Samuel: b 1-27-1747 d *c.* 1823 m Elizabeth Stillwell Pvt NJ

DORSEY, (includes DOSSEY)
Basil: b 5-21-1759 d 1806 m Mary Roberson Sol MD
Basil, Jr.: b *c.* 1745 d 8- -1799 m (1)Hannah Crockett (2)Tabitha
    Richardson Capt MD
Bazil John: b *c.* 1762 d 5-9-1803 m Dorothy Dorsey Pvt MD
Caleb: b *a.* 1743 d *p.* 1790 m (1)Sophia—(2)Rebecca Hammond
    PS MD
Charles: b 4-6-1760 d 7-14-1811 m Elizabeth Anchors Cpl MD
Charles: b 11-11-1736 d 1809 m Lydia — PS MD
Daniel: b 3-6-1757 d 5-16-1823 m Eleanor — Capt MD
Edward: b 1759 d *c.* 1851 m Ruth Warfield Pvt MD
Edward: b *c.* 1730 d 1782 m Deborah Maccubin PS MD
Elisha: b 1750 d 11- -1806 m Mary Slade 1Lt MD
Ely: b 1744 d 3-14-1803 m Ruth Dorsey Capt PS MD
Ely: b *c.* 1720 d *p.* 3-9-1793 m (1)Mary Crockett (2)Deborah Dorsey
    PS MD
Francis, Jr.: b 1765 d *p.* 1820 m Rebecca Talbert Pvt MD
John: b 3-31-1751 d 1796 m Margaret Boone Capt MD
John: b 7-3-1734 d *a.* 3-9-1779 m Anne Dorsey LCol MD
John: b 1735 d 1-1-1810 m Mary Hammond PS Col MD
John: b *a.* 1761 d *p.* 8-15-1812 m Mary Cummings PS MD
John Hammond, Jr.: b 2-14-1754 d 3- -1826 m Ann Maxwell Sgt MD
John W.: b 10-8-1751 d 5-13-1823 m Comfort Worthington 2Lt MD
Joshua: b *a.* 1763 d 1791 m Margaret Watkins Pvt MD
Larkin: b 8-17-1744 d 2-22-1822 m Elizabeth Ingram Ens MD
Levin: b 1735 d 10- -1781 m Elizabeth Keene Home Grd MD
Michael: b 10-29-1745 d 1812 m Honor Elder PS MD
Nicholas: b 1712 d 1780 m Sarah Griffith CS MD
Nicholas, Jr.: b 1-1-1759 d 10-16-1821 m Rachel Warfield Lt MD W★
Nicholas: b *c.* 1750 d 1788 m Lucy Belt Sprigg PS MD
Philip: b 8-11-1759 d 4-24-1818 m Barbara Broome PS MD
Richard: b 1754 d 1799 m Rebecca (Hawkins) Pierrepont Capt MD
Richard: b 12-6-1756 d 5-11-1826 m Anne Wayman Lt MD
Samuel: b 12-7-1741 d 9-11-1777 m Margaret Sprigg PS MD
Stephen: b 3-7-1758 d 10-13-1825 m Rachel Ewing Cadet MD
Thomas: b 3-15-1737 d *p.* 1790 m (1)Elizabeth Ridgely
    (2)Elizabeth Ridgely Col MD
Vachel: b 1-27-1756 d 5-14-1814 m Clementine Ireland Pvt MD
Vachel: b 10-20-1726 d — m Ruth — PS MD
William: b 1757 d 1813 m Catey — Ens MD

DORSHEIMER,
Manuel: b 1755 d 8-5-1798 m Christina Shupp Pvt PA

DORTON,
Moses: b *c.* 1762/63 d *p.* 12-18-1811 m Loadicea — Sol VA

DORWART,
Martin: b 1735 d 6-21-1797 m (1)Elizabeth Grim (2)Mary Ann
    Spitzfaden Pvt PS PA

DORWIN,
Russel: b 4-9-1764 d — m — Cassel Pvt MA

DOSS,
John: b 1758 d 12-2-1841 m Mary Jane — Pvt VA ★

DOSTER,
James: b 8-14-1735 d 1818 m (1)Lidia Springer (2)Sarah Winchester
    PS NC
Jonathan: b 1740 d 1827 m Margaret — Sol GA

DOSWELL,
James: b 1755 d 6-23-1825 m Jane Thilman Capt VA
Thomas: b 1714 d *a.* 1783 m Rebecca Drummond Capt VA

DOTTER,
Samuel Solomon: b 5-3-1759 d 1834 m Catherine Elizabeth — Pvt
    PA ★

DOTTERER, (includes DUDDER, DUDDERAR, DUTROW)
Conrad: b 5-26-1738 d 5-1-1831 m Margaret Pennebecker Capt MD
Jacob: b *c.* 1748 d *a.* 1813 m Helena Dildine Pvt NJ
John: b *c.* 1758 d 11-9-1835 m Catherine Summers Pvt Mus MD
Michael: b 10-31-1735 d 3-12-1811 m (1)Anna Reiff (2)Catharine
    Reiff Capt PA
Philip: b 1729 d 1790 m Johanna Guisbert Capt PS PA

DOTY, (includes DOTEN, DOUGHTON, DOUGHTY, DOUTY)
Abner: b 10- -1754 d 7-4-1820 m Leah Risley Holmes Pvt NJ
Absalom: b 1-29-1764 d 10-21-1843 m Hannah Cordery Pvt NJ
Amaziah: b 5-17-1756 d 1-24-1833 m Bethiah Hamlin Pvt MA
Asa: b 11-6-1746 d 1788 m Sarah Barnum Ens NY
Azariah: b 2-18-1745 d 6-7-1851 m Sarah Tucker Pvt NC ★
Barnabas: b 9- -1738 d 1-25-1807 m Catherine Freeman Capt MA
Benajah: b *c.* 1723 d 1780 m (1) — (2)Elizabeth Chatwin Maj PS
    NC
Benjamin: b 1735 d 1802 m Mary — Pvt NJ
Benjamin: b 5-17-1721 d *a.* 1790 m — PS NC
Benjamin: b 7-28-1742 d 3-12-1826 m Phebe Kirtland Pvt CT ★
Christopher, Jr.: b 10-16-1753 d 8-8-1848 m Margaret Morris Pvt
    NJ ★
Cornelius, 1st: b 1736 d 2- -1799 m Ann Harmon Capt NY
Danforth: b 3-24-1767 d 3-24-1842 m Sarah Adams Pvt CT ★
Daniel: b 1762 d 11-23-1823 m Elizabeth Budd Tms NJ
Daniel: b — d *p.* 5-2-1794 m Fif Pvt VA
David: b 1762 d 11-3-1823 m Elizabeth Budd Tms NJ
David: b 5-12-1741 d 2-9-1817 m Hannah Southard Lt NY
Elias: b 1732 d 3-16-1806 m (1)Amy Dean (2)Mrs Hannah Palmer
    Aiken CS NY
Ephraim: b 3-3-1759 d 4-13-1829 m Susannah Morse Pvt MA ★
Ezra: b 9-28-1760 d 6-24-1840 m (1)Anna Mellen (2)Eunice Bishop
    1Sgt MA ★
Henry: b *c.* 1748 d *p.* 1-6-1791 m Elizabeth Cooper Pvt PA
Isaac: b 2-13-1760 d 10-3-1818 m Abigail Le Barion Pvt MA
Isaac, Jr.: b 3-21-1739 d *a.* 1814 m (2)Anna Parks Pvt NY
Jacob: b 1759 d 8-13-1855 m Alchey Huff Pvt NJ ★
James: b — d *p.* 3-24-1836 m — Cpl MA
James: b 1-22-1736 d 8-30-1817 m Elizabeth Kempton Cpl MA
James: b 8-17-1752 d 5-20-1826 m Elizabeth Gilbert Pvt MA
James: b 1765 d 1846 m Mrs Anna Small Leavitt Pvt MA ★
James: b 1-8-1757 d 12-14-1847 m Nancy Locey MM NJ
John: b 10-26-1761 d 11-26-1840 m Eunice Adams Cpl CT ★
John: b *c.* 1743 d 1790 m Martha Mallett Pvt MA
John: b 8-9-1750 d *p.* 1786 m Zebiah — Pvt MA W★
John, Sr.: b 1712 d 1778 m Sarah — Pvt NJ
John, Jr.: b 1756 d *p.* 4-23-1819 m Esther Hunt Pvt NJ
John: b *c.* 1725 d *p.* 1799 m Sarah Clark Sol NJ
John: b *c.* 1760 d 1827 m (1)Elizabeth Ross (2)Dorcas Coombs
    or Mitchell Capt NY
John: b 1-19-1731 d 5-5-1782 m Lucy Smith Pvt NY
John: b 1-16-1740 d 5-4-1827 m Rebecca Jamison Sol VA
John: b 10-13-1738 d *p.* 1793 m (1)Ann Adams (2)Grace Cole PS VA
Jonathan: b 1756 d 9-16-1854 m (1)Abigail McPherson (2)Nancy
    Simpson Dixon Pvt NJ ★
Joseph: b 9-24-1749 d 7-21-1825 m Susanna Smith Cpl MA
Joseph: b 1735 d *a.* 1818 m Grace Colyer Pvt NJ
Joseph: b 1-14-1752 d 12-8-1844 m Martha Allen Pvt NJ ★
Joseph: b 4-7-1759 d 10-11-1844 m Sophia Horton Pvt NY
Joshua: b 1744 d 12-27-1822 m Sarah Boyle Pvt NJ
Levi: b 1752 d 10-1-1839 m Mary Van Deventer Pvt NJ
Nathaniel: b 10-19-1758 d 3-24-1848 m Jane Bockoven Pvt NJ
Peter: b 5-5-1757 d 3-18-1848 m Susanna M. Boyle Pvt NJ ★
Peter: b 1758 d *p.* 1-25-1817 m (1)Catherine Powelson (2)Martha
    — Pvt NJ
Peter: b 1750 d 1811 m Catherine Overrocker Pvt NY
Philip: b *c.* 1742/43 d *p.* 1791 m Jane Churchill Sgt NY
Reuben: b 2-8-1745 d *c.* 1820 m Hannah Delano Ens PS NY
Samuel: b 1816 m Mercy Doty Ens CT
Samuel, Jr.: b 7-15-1758 d 11-2-1847 m Eunice Robbins Smn MA
Samuel: b 6-4-1756 d 8- -1843 m Ann Shepherd Pvt NY
Samuel: b 12-17-1743 d 10-9-1823 m Catherine Baldwin CaptLt PA
Shadrach: b 9-18-1763 d *p.* 1805 m (1)— (2) — Pvt NY
Silas: b 3-31-1749 d 3-11-1824 m Sarah Holmes Pvt MA
Skillman: b 10-17-1755 d 1840 m Hannah Hayden Pvt NJ
Theodorus: b 12-25-1736/7 d *c.* 1783 m Jane Densmore Pvt NY
Timothy: b 7-3-1730 d 1820 m Mercy Meigs FifMaj MA
William: b 7-23-1754 d 8-22-1839 m Ruth Holmes QMSgt CT
Zebulon: b 3-14-1755 d 4-25-1842 m (1)Sarah Rickey (2)Rachel
    Colyer (3)Jane (Eckles) McQuiston Pvt NJ ★
Zebulon: b *a.* 5-18-1813 m (1)Esther Henderson (2)Hepsibeth
    — Pvt NY

DOUBLEDAY,
Ammi: b 4-17-1759 d 1-31-1839 m Lois Tilden Sgt CT
Elisha, Jr.: b 4-15-1740 d 8-6-1796 m Keziah Phelps Cpl CT

DOUCET,
Pierre: b 1752 d 2-6-1807 m Madeleine Como PS LA

DOUDEL,
Jacob, Sr.: b *c.* 1731 d *p.* 1791 m Mary Spengler Pvt PA
Jacob, Jr.: b 6-28-1760 d 9-21-1837 m Catherine Dinkel Drm PA

DOUGLAS, (includes DOUGLASS)
Aaron: b 3-3-1753 d 11-23-1819 m Phebe Lewis Sol NJ
Alexander: b 1753 d 9-30-1827 m (1)Jane Elliott (2)Mary Stapleton Pvt NH
Andrew: b c. 1736 d 8- -1811 m Sarah Houston–McClellan PS PA
Archibald: b — d p. 1794 m — PS VA
Asa, Sr.: b 12-11-1715 d 11-12-1792 m Rebecca Wheeler Capt NY
Asa, Jr.: b 12-24-1739 d 4-17-1812 m (1)Sarah Robbins (2) — Wynkoop Maj PS NY
Barnard: b 2-17-1763 d 9-21-1849 m (1)Hannah Pierce (2)Betsy Cummings Pvt MA
Benjamin: b 12-16-1743 d 8- -1827 m Ann Ward Middleton PS MD
Benjamin: b c. 1755 d p. 1783 m Anne Semmes PS MD
Charles: b 4-29-1732 d p. 7-30-1815 m Anne Adams PS VA
David: b 5-2-1758 d 7-7-1851 m (1)Mrs Elizabeth Chappell Bishop (2)Eunice Swoddle Pvt CT
David: b 1755 d 8- -1839 m (1)Jean Buchanan (2)Elizabeth Reay Ens PA
Domina: b 5-2-1732 d 4-4-1807 m Mary Warner Pvt CT
Ebenezer: bpt 3-4-1747 d 9-3-1798 m Abigail Bailey Lt CT
Edward: b 10-13-1713 d 2-2-1795 m Sarah George Lt NC
Edward, Jr.: b a. 1756 d p. 1781 m Elizabeth Howard Pvt NC
George: b 7-16-1739 d 12-10-1807 m Elizabeth Lucas CS CT
George: b 2-25-1726 d 3-10-1799 m Mary Piersol Capt PS PA
George: b c. 1735 d 1801 m Martha Watson Pvt PA
George: b c. 1745-50 d 1812 m Mary Tucker Sgt VA
Hezekiah: b 1-19-1748/9 d 8-l0-1781 m Esther Witter Ens CT
Israel: b 12-9-1742 d 3-28-1818 m Abigail Hull Pvt CT
James: b 1746 d 8-28-1790 m Rhoda Burnham Pvt CT ★
James: b 3-12-1761 d 1813 m Elizabeth Murdock Pvt CT
James: b 3-15-1762 d 3-29-1851 m Catherine Collier Sgt NC
James: b 1744 d 4-26-1811 m Elizabeth Duffield Capt PA
James: b 8-27-1740 d p. 1796 m Hannah Huston PS VA
James: b 12-5-1750 d 4-10-1832 m Mary Wells Cmsry VA
John: b 4-12-1734 d 9-22-1809 m (1)Susannah Smith (2)Susannah Freyers BGen CT
John: b 6-9-1741 d p. 1790 m Sarah Branch Pvt CT
John: b 4-18-1724 d 12-13-1777 m Ester Leach CS CT
John: b c. 1730 d p. 1801 m — Pvt DE
John: b 10-4-1764 d 11-9-1839 m Nancy — Pvt GA
John: b 8-2-1758 d 10-16-1808 m Hannah Brown Pvt MA
John, Jr.: b 3-11-1752 d 7-30-1828 m Lydia Southworth Pvt MA
John: b 1723 d 1796 m Catherine Marion Pvt NC
John: b c. 1730 d p. 11-9-1805 m Hannah DeBow Pvt NC
John: b 7-8-1750 d 7-9-1840 m Ann Jones Capt PA
John: b a. 1729 d 7- -1799 m Mary — Lt SC
John, Sr.: b 1760 d 1813 m Sara Dunn Sol SC
John Hunter: b 1750 d 12- -1777 m Rebecca James Sol VA
Jonathan: b 4-25-1751 d 11-9-1840 m (1)Mary Young (2)Elizabeth Doyle Sol VA
Joseph: b c. 1755 d 1-1-1810 m Rebecca Lee Capt MD
Joseph: b 1-20-1746 d 10-16-1817 m Sarah — Sol NJ
Joseph: b 5-11-1760 d p. 2-20-1822 m Elizabeth Garten Pvt VA
Lemuel: b 11-18-1743 d 9-11-1801 m Mary Johnson PS NY
Levi: b 1750 d 1787 m Nancy Ann — Mil VA
Nathan, Sr.: b 4-15-1721 d 3-4-1786 m Anne Dennis PS CT
Richard: b 8-19-1746 d 1-9-1828 m Mrs Ann Champlin Jennings Capt CT
Richard: b 10-28-1750 d 3-1-1816 m (1)Abigail Starr (2)Lucy (Way) Palmes Capt CT
Robert: b 1749 d 10- -1834 m Sarah — Lt MD
Robert, Sr.: b 1720 d 11-15-1794 m Elinor Fales Pvt MA
Robert, Jr.: b 3-26-1759 d 2-3-1833 m (1)Martha Johnson (2)Mary Perry Pvt MA
Robert: b 3-10-1758 d 7-10-1837 m Elizabeth Robertson Pvt VA ★
Samuel: b 2-26-1744/5 d 4-20-1821 m Rebecca Avery Pvt CT
Samuel: b 12-26-1723 d 1816 m (1)Molly Conant (2)Tabitha Fletcher Capt NH
Sperry: b 11- -1744 d 4-27-1816 m Rebecca Chapman Sgt CT
Thomas: b 1750 d p. 1783 m Eleanor Seeley Vol MA
Thomas: b c. 1735 d p. 1805 m — PS NC
Thomas: b c. 1730 d 1792 m Margaret McConnell CS PA
Thomas: b 9-2-1740 d c. 1830 m Margaret — PS VA
Thomas James: b 7-12-1748 d 2-2-1829 m Temperance Palmer Pvt MA
William: b 1-27-1742 d 5-28-1777 m Hannah Mansfield Col CT
William: b 2-7-1731 d 10-1-1805 m Mary Lucas PS CT
William: b c. 1745 d 12-15-1791 m Martha — Pvt GA
William: b c. 1720 d 1786 m Rachel — PS MD
William: b 8-22-1743 d 12-24-1811 m (1)Hannah Cole (2)Thankful — Capt MA
William: b 1764 d 12-23-1852 m Mary Scott Sol PA
William: b 1739 d 12-10-1831 m Nancy Laird Pvt PA
William: b c. 1725 d p. 6-3-1780 m (1)Elizabeth (Offutt) Lewis (2)Sarah (Orrick) Chilton CS PS VA

DOUTHET, (includes DOUTHIT)
John, Sr.: b 5-9-1709 d 2-22-1784 m Mary Scott PS NC

DOUTHETT,
Hezekiah: b 4-20-1766 d 8-10-1847 m Mary Brant Pvt PA

DOUVILLE,
Pierre: b 9-9-1745 d 9-2-1794 m Cynthia Aborn Lt RI

DOUW,
Corneluis: bpt 11-16-1746 d p. 1787 m Catharine VanSchaick Pvt NY
John De Peyster: b 1-20-1756 d 2-22-1835 m Catherine Douw Gansevoort Pvt NY
Volckert Peter: b 3-23-1720 d 3-20-1801 m (1)Anna De Peyster (2)Marytje Cadweea PS NY

DOVE,
John: b 1756 d p. 1789 m Dianah Wilmot Sgt QM MD

DOVER,
John: b 1755 d 3-18-1821 m (1)Mary Nice (2)Letitia Steward Lt PA ★

DOW,
Abner: b 8-28-1751 d 1794 m Martha Sawyer Hinckley Capt MA
Asa: b 4-5-1743 d 1825 m Mary Wheeler Sgt NH
Benjamin: b 11-6-1735 d 9-1-1794 m (1)Mary Hutchinson (2)Mercy Killam Sgt CT
Daniel: b 6-27-1723/4 d 6- -1790 m Rachel Brown PS NH
Daniel: b 10-9-1738 d 9-18-1816 m (1)Miss Lyford (2)Mary Grant PS NH
David: b 12-25-1714 d p. 1785 m (1)Abigail Kelly (2)Mary Brown Pvt MA
Ebenezer: b 1737 d 11-19-1817 m Elizabeth (Wilson) Danforth Sgt MA
Ebenezer: b 11-9-1739 d 3-11-1814 m (1)Sarah French (2)Mary Sanborn Sgt NH ★
Jabez: b 8-25-1747 d 9-19-1808 m Ann Jewell Pvt PS NH
Jeremiah: b 6-27-1751 d p. 1807 m Mrs Lydia Andrus Badcock Pvt MA
Jeremiah: b 5-14-1737 d 9-10-1826 m Lydia Kimball Capt NH
Jeremiah: b 5-23-1749 d 1-22-1837 m Rachel Chase PS NH
John: bpt 11-10-1754 d 11- -1835 m Betty Saunders Cpl MA
John: b 1-27-1763 d 1833 m Betsey Strout Sol NH
John: b 8-19-1707 d 1-20-1786 m Mehitable Haynes PS NH
Jonathan: b 3-10-1734 d 1-6-1816 m Comfort Brown Pvt NH
Joseph: b 5-11-1741 d 4-2-1814 m (1)Elizabeth Cummings (2)Sarah Pepper Cpl MA
Joshua: b 10-28-1744 d 5-4-1802 m Achsah Herriman Pvt NH
Lemuel: b 6-3-1737 d 1-23-1818 m Ann Millington Pvt NH
Levi: b 1734 d 1790 m Phebe Taylor Pvt CT
Moses: b 1758/9 d 6-22-1848 m Fanny Molyneaux Pvt MA ★
Moses: b 2-17-1747 d 3-14-1814 m Phebe Emerson PS NH
Nathan: b 3-20-1761 d 1-28-1842 m Nancy Gordon Pvt CT ★
Oliver: b 7-28-1736 d 12-18-1824 m Hannah Pattee Lt NH
Percy: b 9-2-1754 d 1824 m Deborah Barker Fif PS NH
Reuben: b 1729/30 d 2-9-1811 m Lydia Jones Capt NH
Richard: b 2-15-1706 d 11-17-1786 m Phebe Heath Capt NH
Richard: b 10-1-1739 d 1798 m Mary Saunders Capt NH
Samuel: b 3-12-1727 d p. 1790 m Mary Davis Pvt NH
Simeon, Sr.: b 3-20-1733 d 8-15-1827 m Phebe Sanders Pvt MA
Simeon, Jr.: b 6-4-1761 d 2-12-1860 m Phebe Stevens Pvt MA ★
Thomas: b 4-13-1743 d 3-18-1822 m Mary Barker Cpl MA
William: b 5-28-1760 d a. 4-12-1802 m Hannah Hilton Pvt NH
Winthrop: b 1754 d 12-26-1819 m Sarah Cass Pvt NH
Zebulon: b 1755 d 12-20-1843 m Alice Burley Pvt NH ★

DOWD, (includes DOUD)
Benjamin: b 5-10-1761 d 1-6-1852 m Mary Savage Pvt CT ★
Conner: b 10-18-1757 d 3-31-1839 m Hannah Graves Pvt NC
Cornelius: b 1720 d p. 1776 m (1)Mehitable Bailey (2)Eleanor Ludington Pvt MA
Ebenezer, 2d: b 1744 d 1805 m Tamar Wilcox Pvt CT
Elihu: b 4-1-1757 d 9-4-1836 m (1)Sarah Hall (2)Susannah Barnes Pvt MA
Giles: b 7-17-1735 d 1776 m Esther Bacon Capt NY
Isaac: b 1754 d 9-29-1824 m Ellen Osborne Pvt MA
Jesse: b 1754 d 8-25-1831 m (1)Bethany Green (2)Rebecca Grannis Shepherd Pvt VT ★
John: b 1739 d 9-10-1824 m Elizabeth Norton Ens PS CT
Moses: b 1744 d 2-3-1825 m (1)Lydia Foster (2)Ann Nettleton (3)Lydia Wilcox Pvt CT
Owen: b 1728 d 1799 m Judith — PS NC
Reuben: b 1745 d 1805 m Polly Griffin Pvt CT
Richard, Sr.: b 2-9-1724 d 1783 m Phoebe Foster Pvt PS CT
Richard, Jr.: b 7-25-1757 d 3-4-1823 m Rebecca Savage Farrier CT ★
Samuel Miles: b 9-9-1763 d 11-19-1845 m Hulda Roys Pvt VT ★
Stephen: b 1758 d 1823 m Rachel Broughton Pvt CT

DOWDELL, (includes DOWDLE)
James: b 1758 d 1802 m Elizabeth Cropp Pvt VA
Robert: b 1742 d p. 1820 m Mary — PS SC

DOWDEN, (includes DOWTIN)
Clementius: b 1-11-1762 d a. 9- -1836 m Martha Wells Sgt MD ★
John: b 1760 d 1846 m — Pvt NC ★

DOWDY,
Richard: b c. 1744 d 1830 m Peggy — Pvt NC
Thomas: b c. 1745 d p. 1-27-1805 m Rebecca — Sol PS NC
Wm.: b 1759 d 4- -1783 m Elizabeth Seabrook Bartlett PS NC

DOWELL, (includes DEWELL)
Alexander: b 1740 d 7-26-1836 m Lydia Gorman Pvt PA

DOWERS,
George: b 1759 d 2-3-1851 m Nancy Ann — Pvt NC ★
John: b c. 1743 d 1803 m Charity Brooks PS MD
Wm.: b 1755 d 1795 m Judah — Sgt VA

DOWERS,
Conrad: b 8- -1764 d 2-27-1844 m Mary Shields Pvt PA ★

DOWLER,
George: b 1752/3 d 1-6-1830 m Mary Hasbrouck Sgt NY ★
Thomas: b c. 1739 d p. 5-3-1821 m (1)— (2)Mrs Elizabeth Johnson Sol PA

DOWLING,
Daniel: b c. 1740 d 1820 m Rachael Thompson Pvt PA
David: b 1755 d 10-16-1822 m Elizabeth Crawford Capt PA
John: b 1759 d 1826 m Nancy Boutwell Pvt SC
Robert: b 1730 d p. 2-23-1808 m (1)— (2)Sarah Guinn Pvt NC
Wm.: b c. 1750 d 1800 m Ann — Pvt MD
Wm.: b c. 1750 d 1783 m Rebecca Walker Pvt SC

DOWNARD,
Wm.: b 1755-60 d p. 4-18-1814 m Mary McCarty 2Lt PA

DOWNE,
Joseph: b 12-17-1742 d 2-20-1828 m Martha Wood Sgt MA
Nathaniel Holmes: b 1763 d 1-28-1838 m Polly Holmes Symes Mar ME ★

DOWNER, (includes DONER)
Abraham, Sr.: b c. 1732 d a. 11-17-1786 m Magdalena — Pvt PA
Andrew: b 1-30-1726 d 12-17-1819 m Mary Brown Pvt CT
Cushman: b 3-17-1762 d 4-26-1841 m Hannah Garvey Pvt VT ★
Cyprian: b 3-8-1741 d 2-14-1819 m (1)Hannah Willoughby (2)Lydia (Cole) Willoughby Capt VT
Eliphalet: b 4-4-1744 d 4-4-1806 m Mary Gardner SurGen MA
Elisha: b 1-13-1761/2 d p. 1792 m— Sgt CT
Ezra: b 5-27-1730 d 1803 m Hannah Allen Lt NY
James: b 10-23-1761 d 3-8-1849 m (1)Deborah Downer (2)Hannah Little Pvt CT ★
Jason: b 12-21-1756 d 9-15-1841 m Esther West Pvt CT
John: b 10-25-1744 d 12-10-1815 m Lydia Dunham Pvt VT
Joseph: b 2-9-1732 d 7-21-1821 m (1)Alcessa Cushman (2)Asenath — Sgt VT
Joshua: b 8-6-1735 d 7-11-1795 m (1)Margaret Avery (2)Huldah Crary Dr PS CT
Margaret Caruthers: b 1742 d 1829 m Richard Downer PS CT
Samuel, Sr.: b 2-28-1723 d 10-22-1824 m Hannah Potter Pvt NJ
Samuel, Jr.: b 5-24-1760 d 5-29-1846 m Sarah Robinson Pvt NJ
Stephen: b c. 1765 d 1840 m Jane Spinks Pvt VT
Uriah: b 1762 d 11-11-1825 m Desire Hough Pvt CT
Wm., Sr.: b 4-22-1730 d 12-27-1784 m— Pvt PS NH
Wm., Jr.: b 1750 d p. 1790 m (2)Anna Wilson Pvt PS NH
Zaccheus: b 6-7-1737 d 5-16-1811 m Mrs Talitha Packard Cpl NH
Zacheus: b 11-13-1755 d 7-27-1850 m Bethiah Brigham Pvt CT

DOWNEY,
James: b 6-6-1753 d 12-15-1838 m Rosanna Dinwiddle Pvt PA
John: b 8-20-1753 d 9-26-1825 m (1)Rahanna Stockdale (2)Mary Douglas (3)Betsey Owings Pvt PA
Joseph: b — d p. 1820 m— Sol SC

DOWNING,
Benjamin: b 7-22-1722 d 10-17-1805 m (1)Phebe Willis (2)Martha Hopkins Pvt PS NY
Butler Marlow: b 1755 d p. 1821 m Elizabeth Webster Pvt MD ★
Daniel: b 1762 d p. 8-9-1832 m Elizabeth — Pvt CT ★
Daniel: b 5-26-1739 d 6- -1813 m Hannah Adams Ens PA
David: b 1738 d 1798 m Susanna Beecham Sol MA
Francis: b c. 1754 d 4-20-1777 m— Pvt VA
George: b c. 1759 d 10-6-1839 m (1)Eliza Burtis (2)Mary Downing Pvt NY
James: b 1760 d 1832 m Asenath Walters Pvt MD
James: b — d — m Mary — Pvt MA
James: b c. 1729 d p. 1788 m Susannah — Pvt PA
James: b 1750 d 9-22-1822 m Sarah Laughlin Capt Spy IL
John: b 2-1-1766 d 9-12-1852 m Ruth Emery Pvt MA
John: b 5-10-1749 d 1-17-1826 m Susannah Ellis Pvt PA
John: b c. 1762 d 12-18-1838 m Hannah Frakes Pvt PA
Jonathan: b 11-2-1746 d 12-21-1824 m Alice Nutter SgtMaj NH ★
Joseph: b 1708 d 1798 m Martha Howell Muster Master of MM MA
Joseph: b 4-30-1734 d 10-7-1804 m Mary Trimble PS PA
Joshua: b — d 7-30-1825 m Hopestill Smith Pvt MA
Michael: b 12-18-1760 d 1852 m Mary Ann Wells Sol VA
Perigo: b 1-9-1726 d p. 10-2-1782 m Lydia Adams Pvt CT
Richard: b 1716 d 10-29-1793 m Temperance Derby Pvt MA
Richard, Jr.: b 5-14-1750 d 1-15-1820 m Elizabeth Reece PS PA
Roswell: b 5-22-1738 d p. 7-8-1817 m Bethia Sheldon Capt MA
Samuel: b c. 1755 d 1834 m Priscilla Webb Pvt MD
Samuel: b 3-12-1757 d p. 1843 m (1)Susanna Brown (2)Eunice Bridge Pvt MA
Samuel: b 11-30-1761 d 2-18-1867 m Eunice George Pvt NH ★
Stephen: b 2-12-1762 d 7-12-1843 m Susannah Helm Pvt CT ★

Thomas: b 5-23-1744 d 11-14-1799 m (1)Miss Dameron (2)Sarah Anne Rogers (3)Ann Blackwell Capt VA
Wm.: b c. 1755 d 3-5-1835 m (1)Rebecca Cromwell (2)Margaret Shrock Pvt MD
Wm.: b c. 1743 d p. 8-10-1824 m Anne Watt Capt VA

DOWNMAN,
Rawleigh: b 1720 d 3-18-1781 m Frances Ball LCol PS VA

DOWNS, (includes DOWNES)
Benjamin: b 3-23-1734/5 d 4-2-1793 m Temperance Platt Pvt CT
Benjamin: b 12-25-1748 d 1-23-1826 m Comfort Hinman Pvt CT
Chauncey: b 1-9-1743 d 8-16-1814 m Bettee Smith Sgt CT
David: b 4-28-1736 d 12-13-1813 m Sarah Day Capt CT
David: b 1760 d 12-17-1838 m Mary Chatterton Pvt CT
Ebenezer: b 3-28-1707 d 10-1-1790 m Dinah Bristol PS CT
Edward: b 2-26-1742 d 3-14-1800 m (1)Miriam Jordan (2)Rhoda Billings 2Lt MM MA
Henry: b 5-15-1747 d 12- -1816 m (1)Margaret Bayard (2)Margaret Green Maj MD
Henry: b 3-4-1757 d 9-24-1831 m Rebecca Morton 1Lt MD
Henry: b 5-5-1728 d 10-8-1798 m Frances Chew PS NC
Jesse: b 1764 d 10-12-1826 m Naomi Taunt Pvt MA ★
John, Jr.: b 6-5-1745 d 2-10-1819 m Hannah Stone Sgt CT
John: b c. 1745 d 6-2-1805 m Catherine — Pvt VA
Jonathan: b 1738 d 10-18-1818 m Sarah Gary Maj SC W★
Moses: b 9-14-1734 d 2-27-1823 m Anna Hinman Ens CT
Nathaniel: bpt 9-12-1714 d 10-21-1779 m Sarah Chauncey CG CT
Nathaniel, Sr.: b 10-28-1731 d 11- -1801 m Mary Hodge Pvt CT
Nathaniel, Jr.: b 11-11-1767 d 2-8-1836 m Ann Cook Pvt CT ★
Noah: b 1-10-1736 d 6-9-1806 m Julia Prescott Cpl MA
Samuel: b 6-4-1720 d 2-7-1810 m Sarah Humphreyville Pvt CT
Wm., III: b 1742 d 8-23-1781 m Sarah Wells PS NY
Wm.: b 1728 d 1-10-1802 m Jane Douglas Adj SC
Zachariah: b a. 1748 d p. 3-24-1826 m Elizabeth Ann Mason Pvt MD

DOWSE, (includes DOUSE & DOWS)
Benjamin: b 2-6-1716 d 2-6-1793 m Hannah Frost Mears Cpl MA
Ebenezer: b 12-29-1719 d p. 1790 m Elizabeth Corey Pvt MA
Ebenezer, Sr.: b 9-4-1693 d 9- -1777 m Mary Hunt PS MA
Eleazer, Sr.: b 3-2-1728 d 6-25-1807 m (1)Eunice Dana (2)Mehitable (Brentnall) Barker PS MA
Eleazer, Jr.: b 9-1-1750 d 1-12-1826 m Mary Ware Pvt Matr MA
Eleazer, Jr.: b 7-6-1764 d 12-19-1844 m Lucinda Wright Pvt MA ★
Joseph: b 1-1-1760 d 3-29-1839 m Deborah Perry Pvt MA
Joseph: b 2-5-1760 d 11-4-1847 m (1)Sarah Sprague (2)Mary Sprague Pvt MA

DOXEY,
Jeremiah: b 1752 d 4-22-1842 m Rhoda Haney Mrnr VA ★

DOXSEE or DOXSIE,
Samuel: b c. 1758 d p. 1783 m — Johnston Pvt NY

DOYING,
Daniel: b 3-30-1763 d 1843 m Sarah Richards Pvt NH

DOYLE,
Barnabas: b 1754 d 1797 m Mary McElhenny Pvt PA
Daniel: b 12-15-1739 d — m Sarah Stockbridge Pvt MA
James: b a. 1760 d 1815 m Jane Alexander Pvt PA
John: b 1748 d 6-3-1837 m Evaline — Pvt MD ★
John: b 5-10-1758 d 5-12-1850 m Anna Marie Walsh Capt PA
Samuel: b 1752 d 1817 m Mary Arbor Pvt PA

D'OLEY,
Daniel: b 3-19-1763 d 1820 m Anne Rebecca Webb Lt SC

DOYNE,
Jesse: b c. 1735 d 1786 m Anne King PS MD

DRAGOO,
Wm.: b 1747 d 1824 m Temperance Dickerson Sol VA

DRAKE,
Aaron: b 8-30-1735 d 7-27-1825 m Chloe Gillet Pvt MA
Abiel: b 10-27-1734 d 11-13-1824 m (1)Bathsheba Hewitt (2)Susannah Keith (3)Charity Hewit Pvt MA
Abraham, Sr.: b 12-4-1715 d 8-1-1781 m (1)Abigail Weare (2)Abigail Dearborn LCol NH
Abraham, Jr.: b 2-3-1745 d 5-11-1819 m Mary Jenness Lt PS NH
Abraham, Sr.: b 3-1-1726 d 1805 m Martha Eaton PS NH
Abraham, Jr.: b 6-7-1758 d 3-4-1832 m (1)Ann Burnham (2)Mrs Anna Smith Pvt NH W★
Adam: b 2-1-1761 d 7-23-1841 m Susanna Kingman Pvt MA ★
Albritain: b 1760 d 11-4-1847 m Ruth Collins Lt NC ★
Amasa: b 12-8-1750 d 2-10-1838 m Lydia Webb Pvt CT
Andrew: b 8-15-1746 d 10-14-1827 m Eunice Martin Pvt NJ
Archippus: bpt 6-24-1753 d 6-19-1826 m Mary Holmes Pvt MA
Ariel: b 1756 d 10-9-1827 m Phyllis Jillson Pvt NH
Asahel: b 10-10-1745 d 7-26-1825 m (1)Mary Woodruff (2)Naomi Culver Pvt NY

DRAKE, contd.

Benjamin: b 5-10-1746 d 3-26-1810 m Sarah Wood Pvt NJ
Benjamin: b 4-18-1766 d 12-22-1844 m Deborah Ferris Pvt NY ★
Benjamin: b *a.* 1740 d 6-12-1812 m Martha Seaman PS NY
Benjamin: b 1729 d 1-1-1827 m Sarah Buchanan Sol VA
Benjamin: b 6-10-1742 d 3-15-1822 m Rachel Davids Sol VA
Cornelius: b 1756 d 1810 m Polly Masters Pvt NY
Daniel: b 12-21-1743 d 3-27-1810 m Lois Reed Capt MA
Daniel: b 11-14-1732 d 2-8-1818 m (1)Hannah Anderson
    (2)Phebe Reader (3)Thisbie Anderson Britton CS NJ
David: b 1-28-1732 d 1-14-1780 m Hannah Clark Pvt MA
David Grosset: b 12-22-1759 d 6-3-1850 m Mary Smith Pvt NY ★
Ebenezer: b 10-30-1754 d 12-14-1829 m (2)Martha Gurney Pvt MA
Edward: b 7-9-1763 d 2-28-1830 m Hannah White Sol MA
Elias: b 11-25-1754 d 8-7-1804 m Mary Harlow Cpl MA
Elijah: b 7-4-1760 d 4-8-1848 m Abigail Stoddard Pvt PA
Elisha: b 1716 d 10-19-1793 m Christiana — Capt NJ
Enoch: b 2-15-1761 d 10-19-1823 m Catharine Stout Pvt NJ
Ephraim: b *c.* 1760 d *p.* 12-13-1816 m Ann Buchanan Sol VA
Garrardus: b 1685 d 5-20-1797 m Martha Russell PS NY
George: b 9-21-1735 d 1825 m Susannah Collier Pvt NJ
Gilbert: b 1720 d 1-8-1809 m (1)Elizabeth Underhill (2)Ruth Tompkins
    Col NY
Hartwell (Hodges), Mrs.: b *c.* 1729 d *p.* 7-6-1791 m (1)Thomas Davis
    (2)James Drake PS NC
Hezekiah: b 7-19-1736 d 2-24-1799 m Elizabeth Packard Pvt MA
Isaac: b 5-31-1753 d 5-10-1800 m Jane Crossman Pvt MA
Isaac: b 1756 d 1832 m Elizabeth Shotwell Pvt NJ
Isaac: b 2- -1764 d 6-29-1837 m Frances — Pvt NJ PA
Isaac: b *c.* 1756 d 5-13-1815 m June Todd PS NC
Jacob: b 4-21-1732 d 9-18-1823 m (1)Charity Young (2)Esther
    Dickerson Col NJ
Jacob: b 1-13-1746 d 5-23-1827 m Elizabeth Neely 1Lt PA
James: b 11-14-1755 d 2-26-1834 m Hannah Ward Pvt NH ★
James: b 1746-8 d 3-16-1816 m Rachel — Pvt NJ
James: b 5-8-1725 d *p.* 7-6-1791 m (1)Sophia Valentine (2)Hartwell
    (Hodges) Davis PS NC
James: b *c.* 1740 d *a.* 2-1-1806 m Molly — 2Lt VA
Jeremiah, Sr.: b 1726 d 5-6-1784 m (1)Frances Purdy (2)Martha
    Deason Capt PS NY
Jeremiah, Jr.: b 5- -1763 d 6-23-1845 m Phebe Reynolds Pvt NY ★
John: b 8-13-1757 d 2-18-1834 m Molly Cole Pvt MA
John: b 1754 d 1-20-1835 m Phebe Hunt Pvt PS NJ
John: b 1733 d 8-28-1784 m Sarah Perry Sol PS NJ
John: b 9-5-1748 d 3-3-1839 m Jane Neally CS VA
Jonathan: b 1-15-1758 d 3-21-1848 m Sarah Ward Pvt NH
Jonathan: b *c.* 1740 d *c.* 1815 m — Capt NC
Joseph: b 1752-6 d *p.* 9-17-1788 m (1)Elizabeth Barber (2)Olive —
    (3)Abigail — Pvt CT
Joseph, Sr.: b 4-1-1706 d 6-8-1791 m Bethiah Brett Pvt CS MA
Joseph, Jr.: b 10-25-1737 d 2-8-1810 m Ruth Keith Pvt MA
Joseph: b *a.* 1746 d *p.* 1788 m Elizabeth Crow Mil NJ
Joseph: b 1719 d 1-20-1785 m Charity Fowler Col NY
Joshua: b 10-14-1759 d 2-28-1818 m Ann Nelson Capt NY
Lemuel: b 9-7-1754 d 1-17-1837 m Esther Burnham Pvt CT
Lorry: b 5-9-1759 d 3-29-1805 m (1)Amelia Mills (2)Sally Clark Pvt
    CT
Matthew: b 1752 d 1807-10 m Ann Arrington CS NC
Melzar: b 10-30-1761 d 1-19-1812 m Chloe Morse Pvt MA
Nathan, Sr.: b 1-15-1732/3 d 11-15-1815 m (1)Jemima Gay (2)Mrs
    Sarah Smith Pvt MA
Nathan, Jr.: b 11-30-1760 d 4-26-1846 m Jane Tolman Pvt MA
Nathan: b 10-6-1746 d 11-26-1816 m (1)Tamar Jones (2)Mrs Jerusha
    Larrison Pvt NJ
Nathan: b — d 1804 m (1)— (2)Elizabeth Stout (3)Elizabeth Yates
    CS NJ
Noah: b 9-10-1758 d 3-3-1849 m Anna Parsons Pvt CT
Oliver: b 5-15-1758 d 3-3-1828 m Phebe Codding Pvt Mar MA ★
Oliver: b 1754 d 4-6-1838 m Ruth Keith Pvt MA
Paul: b 1-17-1761 d 9- -1828 m (1)Mary Luce (2)Lydia Hays Tms NJ
Perez: b 1-3-1759 d — m Alice Manning Sgt NY
Richard: b 2-7-1745 d 1777 m Mary Young Matr Pvt MA
Richard: b 6-13-1759 d 2-2-1836 m Mary Wood Pvt NY ★
Robert, Sr.: b 11- -1723 d 2-2-1797 m (1)Mary Fobes (2)Susannah
    Chubbuck Thorne Cpl MA
Robert, Jr.: b 4-27-1752 d 8-22-1802 m Rebecca Wade Cpl MA
Samuel: b 9-12-1725 d 1796 m Martha Pratt Pvt CT
Samuel: b 4-30-1730 d 5-14-1794 m (1)Rebeckah — (2)Mary Haight
    (3)Patience — Col NY
Samuel: b 12-15-1714 d 1-3-1786 m Esther Hobbs Pvt NH
Samuel: b — d 1789 m Sarah Handy Capt PA
Samuel: b 1747 d 8-11-1826 m Nancy Hamilton Pvt PA
Simon: b — d 5-30-1826 m Tamson Clark Pvt NH W★
Simon: b 10-4-1730 d 3-6-1801 m Judith Perkins PS NH
Thomas: b 2-12-1739 d 2-9-1798 m Mary Manley Sgt VA
Thomas: b 9-18-1751 d 12-2-1803 m Hannah Hewitt Pvt MA
Thomas: b 3-11-1742 d *p.* 1775 m (1)Patience Towle (2)Lydia Norris
    (3)Molly Burnham Pvt PA NH
Thomas: b 1724 d 3-10-1792 m Dorothy Van Kirk Lt NJ
Thomas: b 7-13-1728 d 7-25-1811 m Eurah Humphreys PS VA
Thomas: b 1760/1 d 3-24-1835 m Catherine Vaughan Pvt VA ★
Timothy: b 5-2-1764 d *p.* 1804 m Polly Dunbar Pvt MA

William, Sr.: b 1729 d *p.* 1787 m (1)Phebe Leonard (2)Olive Crossman
    Pvt MA
William, Jr.: b 9-2-1756 d 1812 m Eunice Hamlin Sol MA
William: b 6-29-1755 d 1-4-1833 m Susannah Harlow Pvt MA
William: b 1762 d 12-14-1848 m Abigail Shaw Pvt MA
William: b 1-3-1757 d 8- -1822 m Anna Turrell Pvt NJ
William: b 1722 d 4-29-1802 m Ruth Elliott Pvt NY
Zachariah: b 7-6-1748 d 1-14-1818 m Mary Smith Pvt MA

DRAKEFORD,
John: b *a.* 1719 d *a.* 1789 m Sarah — Capt SC
Richard: b *c.* 1750 d *p.* 7-15-1826 m Sarah Scott Sol SC

DRANE,
James, Jr.: b 1755 d 10- -1828 m Priscilla Lamar 2Lt MD

DRAPER,
Aaron: b 3-15-1734/5 d *p.* 1790 m Mrs Mary Richards Fisher Pvt MA
Abijah: b 5-10-1737 d 5-1-1780 m (1)Elizabeth (2)Mrs Desire
    Metcalf Maj MA
Daniel: b 11-3-1707 d 4- -1791 m Rachel Pond Capt MA
Jacob: b *c.* 1750 d 1817 m Elizabeth Ladd Pvt NH
James: b 7-24-1747 d 8-29-1825 m Mary Prouty Drm MA
James: b 9-22-1720 d 3-2-1781 m Mehetable Whiting PS MA
James: b *c.* 1748-50 d 1781 m Sussannah— Pvt PA
James: b 1751 d 1835 m (4) Maria Jones Pvt SC
John: b 11-16-1745 d 11-20-1822 m Rebekah Muzzy Sgt MA
John: b 8-8-1725 d 2-3-1805 m Abigail Cheney Pvt MA
John: b 1730 d 1824 m (1)Elizabeth Robertson (2)Mrs Jane Crockett
    Lt VA
Jonathan: b 12-18-1750 d 1848 m — Pvt NH ★
Jonathan: b 7-19-1749 d 5-2-1822 m Edith Gardner Pvt PA
Joseph: b 3-2-1740 d 11-28-1825 m Mary Robbins Sgt MA
Joseph: b 6-9-1731 d 1776 m Lydia Bacon Pvt MA
Joshua, Sr.: b 12-25-1724 d 10-27-1792 m (1)Abigail Fairbanks
    (2)Sarah Wright PS MA
Joshua, Jr.: b 5-25-1749 d 5-12-1839 m Mary Pratt Pvt MA ★
Josiah: b 9-12-1727 d *p.* 1777 m Sarah Ellis Pvt MA
Josiah, Jr.: b 10-14-1756 d 5-17-1819 m Mary Mann Drm MA
Mary (Aldis) Allen: b 4-4-1719 d 11-20-1810 m (1)Abel Allen
    (2)Moses Draper PS MA
Nathaniel: b *c.* 1755 d *p.* 1801 m Anna Jones Pvt MA
Simeon: b 3-28-1764 d 12-28-1848 m Mary Bemis Pvt MA
Stephen: b 2-23-1742 d 3-15-1825 m Elizabeth Fisher Sgt MA
William: b 2-23-1734 d 11-17-1776 m Elizabeth Ellis Capt MA

DRAUGHON,
James: b *c.* 1740 d *p.* 1790 m Elizabeth Wells PS NC

DRAYTON,
William: b 1733 d 5-18-1790 m Mary Motte CS PS SC
Wm. Henry: b 9- -1742 d 9-3-1779 m Dorothy Golightly PS PA

DREHER,
George: b 1-12-1761 d 5-3-1837 m Lydia Heller Pvt PA ★
Godfrey: b — d 11-5-1777 m — PS SC
Peter: b 1752 d 7-2-1822 m Maria Barbara Benzinger Pvt PA

DREIBELBIS, (includes DRIEBLBIS, TRIBLEPIECE)
Jacob: b 5-9-1754 d 4-19-1831 m Maria Magdalene Merkle Capt PA
Martin: b 50-5-1751 d 9-10-1799 m Catherine Merkle Pvt PA

DREISBACH, (includes DRIESBACH)
Adam: b 11-8-1723 d 1-10-1803 m Susanna Koeber Pvt PA
Adam: b 10-15-1762 d 5-6-1849 m Mary Margaret — Pvt PA
Henry: b *c.* 1760 d *p.* 1804 m Margaret Rimmell Pvt PA
Jacob, Sr.: b 7-27-1759 d 1-14-1817 m Anna Margretta Beaver
    Ens PA
Jacob: b — d 1804 m Magdalena Buchs PS PA
John George: b 2-1-1735 d 8-27-1796 m Anna Elizabeth Schmielin
    Pvt PA
Jost, Sr.: b 11-21-1721 d 10-17-1794 m Elizabeth Rachenberger Col
    PA
Martin, Sr.: b 1717 d 2-18-1799 m Anna Eve Hoffman PS PA
Peter: b 11-3-1757 d 8-16-1810 m Susanna Beisel Pvt PA
Simon, Jr.: b 2-18-1730 d 12-17-1806 m (1)Dorothy Dies (2)Anna
    Maria Kuder PS PA

DRENNAN, (includes DRENNING, DRENNON)
Hugh: b *c.* 1762 d 12-26-1842 m Margaret Hughes Pvt PA
Wm.: b 3-8-1739 d 1-24-1810 m (1)Sarah Barnes (2) — Sol PA
William: b — d *p.* 1790 m — Friend Pvt PA

DRESHER,
George: b 10-13-1746 d 10-17-1822 m Maria Yeakel Pvt PA

DRESOR,
John: b 8-18-1735 d 6-24-1814 m Sarah Dresser Cpl PS CT

DRESSER,
Aaron: b 4-12-1758 d 2-25-1845 m Alice Row Pvt MA
Isaac: b 2-22-1759 d 12-4-1835 m Susan Taft Pvt MA

John: b 12-8-1716 d 1-24-1789 m (1)Sarah Scott (2)Mrs Patience Holbrook Cpl CT
John: b 5-10-1748 d 6-28-1778 m Elizabeth Nelson Sgt MA
John: b 8-17-1735 d 6-24-1814 m Sarah Dresser Cpl CT
Jonathan: b 9-14-1757 d 4-3-1814 m Elizabeth Walker Pvt MA
Joseph: b 3-10-1749 d 10-22-1844 m Mary Lane Pvt MA ★
Moses: b 4-17-1753 d 11-29-1813 m (1)Abigail Blood (2)Dolly Makepeace Pvt MA
Oliver: b 9- -1737 d 1809 m Olive Osgood Pvt MA
Richard: b — d 1826 m — Pvt MA ★
Richard: b 9-22-1714 d 8-27-1797 m (1)Dorothy Marcy (2)Susanna Alden PS MA
Samuel: b 9-17-1745 d 6-4-1814 m Lucretia Brown Pvt CT
Stephen: b 10-25-1754 d 9-28-1829 m Abigail Abbott Pvt NH

DRESSLER,
Andrew: b 5-28-1746 d 10-21-1828 m (1)Mary Loy (2)Catherine Hammon Pvt PA

DREW,
Andrew: b 3-25-1758 d 1859 m Joanna Hodgdon Pvt NH ★
Anthony: b 1726 d 2- -1786 m Sarah — PS MD
David: b 2-17-1752 d — m Elizabeth Atwood Pvt MA
Ezra: b c. 1750 d p. 1795 m Elizabeth Holmes Pvt MA VT
Francis: b 1760 d 1831 m Sarah — Pvt NH
Gilbert: b 4-11-1732 d 3-26-1812 m (1)Sarah Hunt (2)Catherine (Muckleworth) Lawrence Sgt NY
Isaac: b 6- -1748 d 11-3-1835 m Welthea Bradford Pvt NS MA W★
Job: b 2-3-1744 d 3-16-1833 m Thankful Delano Prince Sgt MA ★
John: b 5-20-1724 d 3-9-1819 m (1)Mary Northrop (2)Ann Thorp (3)Joanna Lacey Capt PS CT
Joshua: b 3-26-1760 d 2-20-1842 m (1)Mercy Fry (2)Elizabeth Sampson Pvt MA
Michael: b c. 1755-60 d p. 1791 m — Pvt PA
Samuel: b 12-3-1749 d 11-8-1823 m Elizabeth Pierce MM Pvt MA
Samuel: b 1761 d p. 1826 m Elizabeth (Webber) Webster Pvt NY MA NH ★
Samuel: b 3-7-1760 d 10-16-1853 m Mary Toundsend Pvt NY
Seth: b 6-13-1747 d 5-18-1824 m Hannah Brewster Maj MA
Silvanus: b 12-26-1735 d 8-14-1829 m Mercy Clarke NCapt MA
Stephen: b 1754 d 1-12-1825 m Jerusha Bryant Pvt MA W★
Thomas: b 1740 d 4-30-1824 m Lucy Thompson Sgt MA
Thomas Collens: b 8-27-1762 d 4-12-1843 m Betsey Quinton Pvt NH
Thomas Haynes: b 1760 d 1854 m Ann Randolph Harrison 1Lt VA
Wm.: b 9-29-1760 d 12- -1781 m Eunice Howard Drm MA
William: b 1731 d 5-10-1795 m Dorothy Bartlett PS MA
William: b c. 1735 d 1800 m — PS NC
Zebulon: b 11-9-1721 d 1800 m Sarah Chandler 2Lt NH

DRIGGS,
Bartholomew: b 5-9-1745 d 1828 m Elizabeth Spencer Pvt CT
Elisha: b 2-1-1760 d 1-26-1813 m (1)— (2)Charity Dakin Pvt CT
John: b 6-30-1743 d 3-10-1817 m — Pvt CT

DRINKARD,
John: b c. 1730 d p. 6-17-1784 m Ann — PS VA

DRINKER,
Henry: b 2-2-1734 d p. 1807 m (1)Ann Swent (2)Elizabeth Sandwith Pvt PA

DRINKWATER,
Daniel: b 1754 d 9-18-1821 m Rebekah Fisher Pvt MA
David: bpt 11-3-1751 d 11-2-1781 m Rachel Farrer Mstr MA
John, Sr.: b 4-24-1738 d 12-27-1827 m Susanna Brown Pvt MA
John, Jr.: b 3-13-1764 d p. 1790 m Pamela Gray Pvt MA
Joseph, 1st: b c. 1710 m 4-17-1784 m Janet Latham Pvt MA
Joseph, 2d: b 28-1736 d 12-7-1824 m Mary Leach NLt MA
Perez: b 8-28-1761 d 12-25-1847 m Kezia Gray Slr MA

DRISCOLL,
Asa: b 1750 d 1840 m Martha Geer NGnr CT ★
Daniel: b 1753 d 4-3-1812 m Ann O'Leary Cpl MA

DRISKO,
Samuel Gatchell: b 8-13-1749 d p. 1790 m Mercy Chandler Pvt MA

DRIVER,
Matthew: b 8-30-1740 d 7-23-1798 m (1)Margaret Casson (2)Esther Casson LCol PS MD
Robert: b c. 1750 d 1800 m Ann Norsworthy PS VA
Solomon: b 3-20-1744 d 6-16-1831 m Meriam Hooper Pvt MA

DROMGOOLE,
Edward: b 1751 d 1835 m Rebecca Walton PS VA

DRONE,
William: b 1762 d 2-24-1824 m Susannah Scheckells Pvt VA ★

DROWN, (includes DROWNE)
Benjamin, Jr.: b 11-25-1747 d 6-12-1826 m Rachel Scott Sgt RI
Caleb: b 3-4-1753 d 12-11-1819 m Mehitable Tripp Pvt RI ★
Frederick: b 1-31-1742 d 9-6-1804 m Martha Wheeler 1Lt MA

John: b 1757 d 1812 m Abigail Turner Pvt MA
John: b 1766 d 5-8-1847 m Sally Ayres Pvt NH
Jonathan: b 5-5-1745 d 1808 m Sarah Wheeler Capt MA
Jonathan J.: b 8-30-1760 d 6-6-1842 m Hannah Barnes Pvt RI ★
Nathaniel: b 9-21-1740 d 12-27-1817 m Susanna Whitaker Pvt MA
Samuel: b 7-1-1704 d 1795 m — PS NH
Samuel: b 11-5-1749 d 8-7-1815 m Mary Pickering Pvt PS NH
Solomon: b 3-11-1753 d 2-5-1834 m Elizabeth Russell Dr RI

DRULLINGER,
Frederick: b 6-20-1752 d 6-30-1841 m Hannah Summers Pvt NJ ★

DRUM,
George: b 6-12-1762 d 2-27-1831 m (1)Anna Margaret Woodring (2)Mrs Rosina Woodring Pvt PA
Philip, Sr.: b 9-27-1721 d 11-14-1788 m Jonathan — PS PA
Philip, Jr.: b 1752 d 1845 m (1)Margaretta Erb (2)Christina —Pvt PA ★

DRUMGOLD, (or DROOMGOOLE)
James: b — d p. 4-14-1818 m (1)'Frankey' Alston (2)Mrs Jane Mackeye Sgt VA

DRUMHELLER,
Nicholas: b 1750 d 3-27-1823 m Catharine — PS PA

DRUMMOND,
James, Jr.: b 1764 d 7-19-1843 m Nancy Griffith Pvt PA
William: b 1750 d 8- -1797 m Ann Robinson Smith Sgt VA

DRURY, (includes DREWRY)
Asa: b 6-29-1748 d 6-26-1816 m Dolly Gleason Capt MA
Ebenezer: b 10-14-1732 d 4-5-1815 m Mary Bartlett Lt MA
Ebenezer: b 1-17-1734 d 8-19-1818 m (1)Hannah Keyes (2)Thankful — (3)Mary Jackson MM Pvt VT MA
Ebenezer: b 8-4-1743 d 1- -1808 m Miriam Goodale Pvt NH
John: bpt 6-30-1736 d 5-25-1808 m Martha Rice Capt MA
John: b 1755 d 1805 m Sarah Slaughter Capt VA
Jonathan: b 3-23-1744/5 d 11-5-1820 m Mary Pratt PS NH
Joseph: b — d p. 1796 m Sibba Wigington Pvt MD
Luke: b 3-11-1737 d 4-1-1811 m (1)Lydia Sherman (2)Mary Howland LCol VA
Luther: b 11-25-1762 d 11-22-1843 m Rhoda Hopkins Sgt NY
Matthew: b 12-4-1746 d 5-6-1805 m Frances— Sgt VA
Moses: b 8-4-1742 d 9-6-1836 m Cata Adams Capt NH
Nathan: b 9-27-1746 d 4-1-1782 m Abigail Rice Capt MA
Samuel: b 1758 d 1848 m Ann Ijams PS MD
Samuel: b c. 1730 d 2-4-1789 m Elizabeth — Sol VA
Thomas: b 3-9-1734/5 d 4-18-1790 m Martha Emes Capt PS MA
Thomas: b 12-21-1747 d 7-6-1836 m Experience Butler 2Lt MA
Wm.: b 1-11-1758 d 1-20-1850 m (1)Lois — (2)Hannah How Pvt MA W★
Zedekiah: b 4-30-1716 d 1777 m (1)Hannah Axtell (2)Hannah Woolley Pvt NH

DRY,
Jacob: b c. 1762-64 d p. 8-11-1852 m Elizabeth — Pvt NC ★

DRYDEN, (includes DREADEN)
Artemas: b 2-4-1757 d 8-17-1840 m Susanna Perry Pvt MA ★
James: b c. 1730-35 d 1810 m — Pvt VA
Nathaniel: b c. 1745 d 10-7-1780 m Mary — Ens VA
Samuel: b — d p. 4-15-1816 m Martha — Pvt PA
Thomas: b c. 1735 d p. 1775 m Lydia Ward Pvt MA
William: b 1739 d 1832 m Lydia Jester Pvt DE
William: b a. 1755 d 1820 m Rachel Morgan Pvt MD

DRYER,
Allen: b 9-27-1745 d p. 1790 m Molly Wheeler Pvt MA
John, Sr.: b 8-12-1725 d 1785/6 m Mary Read Lt MA
John, Jr.: b 1-23-1754 d 9-29-1826 m Kesiah French Cpl MA
Samuel: b 2-18-1765 d 1837 m Philena Robbins Pvt MA
William: b 10-29-1749 d 9-1-1819 m Deliverance Briggs Sgt MA

DUANE,
James: b 2-6-1733 d 2-1-1797 m Mary Livingston PS NY

DUBÁ,
John: b 1758 d 5-10-1826 m Elizabeth Storm Pvt NY ★

DUBBS,
Daniel: b 10-5-1748 d 9-22-1828 m Elizabeth Schwenk Pvt PA
Frederick: b c. 1760 d 7-2-1850 m Catherine Snyder Pvt PA
Leonard: b 2-23-1840 m Margaret Van Gundy Drm PA
Oswald: b 6-28-1758 d 1-6-1843 m Margareta Thoman Pvt PA

DU BOIS,
Abraham: b 1-19-1728 d 11-7-1792 m Marie LaSiliete Capt NJ
Benjamin: b 3-30-1739 d 8-21-1827 m Phebe Denise CS NJ
Benjamin: b 1-7-1755 d 1796 m Mary Robinson Pvt NJ
Benjamin: b 12-26-1752 d p. 1802 m Catherine Salisbury Capt NY
Benjamin: b 8-18-1716 d 5-18-1787 m Maria Bevier PS NY
Christian, Jr.: b 6-13-1746 d 12-17-1807 m Helena Van Voorhees Lt NY

DU BOIS, contd.
Conraedt: b 1735 d *p.* 1784 m Maria Delamater Pvt PS NY
Cornelius: b 2-14-1727 d 6-5-1803 m Catharine Vanderpoel LCol NY
Cornelius: b 1-24-1743 d 6-24-1829 m Gertrude VanVliet Lt NY
Cornelius, Sr.: b 11-9-1707 d 11-6-1780 m Anna Margaret Houghteling PS NY
Cornelius, Jr.: bpt 7-8-1750 d 1816 m Gertrude Bruyn QM NY
Cornelius: b 7-20-1743 d 4-12-1831 m Charity Griffin Pvt NY
David: b 11-28-1724 d 10-12-1801 m Elizabeth Newkirk Pvt NJ
Elias: b 10-4-1713 d 1786 m Mary Van Voorheis Pvt PS NY
Henry, Sr.: b 3-31-1710 d 6-5-1780 m Janetje Houghtaling PS NY
Henry, Jr.: b 5-1-1743 d 1784 m Rebecca Van Wagner PS NY
Isaac: b 11-2-1752 d 7-14-1820 m Rebecca Deyo Pvt NY
Jacob: b 2-9-1719 d 9-22-1794 m Janitje Van Neinkirk Capt NJ
Jacob: b 1-14-1733 d 2- -1791 m Rebecca Van Wagenen Pvt PS NY
Jeremiah: b 11-22-1760 d 12-29-1844 m (1)Sarah Shute (2)Mrs Rachel Van Meter Pvt NJ
Jeremiah: bpt 1-17-1748 d 2-3-1828 m Catharine Masten Sol NY
Johannes: b 1706 d a. 10-18-1787 m Rebecca Tappen PS NY
Johannes J.: bpt 10-12-1746 d *p.* 1788 m Elizabeth Jansen Pvt NY
John: b 3-25-1760 d 7-31-1841 m (1)Jennette Dies (2)Catharine Bronk (3)Gitty Du Bois (4)Treintje DuBois PS NY
Joshua: b 9-21-1745 d — m Margaret Masten Pvt NY
Koert: b 1-25-1763 d 5-25-1831 m Elizabeth Burroughts Pvt NY
Lewis: b 9-14-1728 d 11-29-1803 m Rachel Jansen Col NY
Louis J.: b 5-20-1733 d 12-29-1795 m Katherine Brodhead Capt NY
Martin: b 10-21-1764 d 7-1-1850 m Margaret Avery Pvt NY ★
Mathusalim: b 9-25-1751 d p. 1790 m (1)Gertruy Bruyn (2)Catherine Bevier Ens NY
Matthew: b 11-17-1724 d 12-29-1799 m Sarah Humphreys PS NY
Matthias: b 2-2-1747 d 12-8-1820 m (1)Mary — (2)Margaret Marshall Pvt NY
Mina: b 3-5-1756 d 3-14-1824 m Marie Pittenger Sgt NJ
Peter: b 4-10-1734 d 8-21-1795 m Amey Greenman Capt NJ
Peter: b 10-19-1739 d 8-14-1814 m Hannah Cheesman Pvt NY
Samuel: b 1- -1741 d 1-8-1811 m Uphan Thompson Pvt NJ
Tobias: b 3-12-1751 d — m (1)Marietje Smith (2)Caty Basten 2Lt NY
Zachariah: b 10-31-1734 d 4-10-1783 m Ruth Ddoge Maj NY

DU BOSE,
Andrew: b a. 1751 d a. 1806 m Elizabeth Mims Capt SC
Andrew: b c. 1749 d 1800 m Rebecca Du Bose Capt PS SC
Daniel: b 10-19-1737 d c. 1797 m (1)Mrs Frances (Villapontout) (2)Mary Nettles 1Lt PS SC
Elias: b 10-19-1737 d 3-16-1789 m Lydia Cassels Capt PS SC
Isaac: b c. 1755 d *p.* 6-30-1824 m Miss James CS GA
Isaac: b 11-5-1742 d 1809 m Elizabeth Norwood Sol SC
Isaac: b 1741 d *p.* 4-18-1816 m Sarah DuBose Lt SC
Isaac: b 5-14-1754 d 5-22-1816 m (1)Catharine DuTarque (2)Catherine — Capt SC
John: b 1715 d *p.* 1785 m Mary Frances DeWitt Pvt SC
Peter: b 3-15-1755 d 7-26-1846 m Lancy Worthington Capt SC
Samuel: b 8-8-1758 d 4-11-1811 m Martha Walter Adj SC

DU BRUTZ,
Gabriel: b 12-25-1761 d 2- -1824 m Deborah Montgomery FrN VA

DUCKETT,
Jacob: b 9-20-1751 d — m Mary Meeks (Claggett) McElderry PS MD
John: b 1726 d 1784 m Sarah Waring CS MD
Joseph: b 11-14-1752 d 3-10-1812 m Mary Turner Pvt SC
Richard, Sr.: b 2-21-1704/5 d 1788 m (1)Mary Nuthall (2)Elizabeth Williams PS MD
Richard, Jr.: b 4-12-1732 d *p.* 1795 m (1)Martha Waring (2)Sophia Buchanan PS MD
Samuel: b 1751 d *p.* 1800 m Ann — Pvt PS MD

DUCKWORTH,
Jacob: b 3-21-1755 d 2-11-1842 m Annie Welborne Capt NC
John: b 1759 d 11-6-1843 m Mary Robertson Pvt NC ★

DUCLOS,
Francis: b 12-8-1754 d 5-7-1844 m (1)Anna Custis (2)Mrs Wheeler (3)Polly Westover NCapt PA

DUDLEY,
Ambrose: b 4-1-1757 d 1-10-1826 m Elizabeth Russell Pvt CT
Ambrose: b 1759 d 11-26-1844 m Betsy Baker Pvt NC
Ambrose: b 1750 d 1-27-1825 m Ann Parker Capt VA
Amos: b 11-3-1747 d 9-8-1823 m (1)Mary Evarts (2)Mrs Deborah Lee Pvt CT
Asa: b 3-12-1754 d 1826 m Lois Baldwin Pvt CT
Banks: b c. 1740 d a. 1805 m — Lt VA
Benajah: b 5-27-1763 d 6-20-1850 m Elizabeth Redfield Pvt CT ★
Benjamin: b 1730 d 12-2-1814 m Mary Walker Pvt MA
Bishop: b c. 1739 d *p.* 11-23-1787 m Rebecca Ward PS NC
Christopher: b 1753 d 1828 m Margaret Ward Capt NC
Daniel: b 1744 d 6-20-1811 m Susy Dinsmore Cpl MA
Daniel, Jr.: b 3-27-1758 d 4-23-1808 m Lucy Vose Pvt MA W★
Davidson: b c. 1708 d 1787 m Anna Ladd PS NH
George: b a. 1735 d *p.* 1790 m Dorothy Tabb 3Lt VA
Gilman: b 5-3-1727 d 6-12-1802 m Sarah Connor Pvt NH

Gwinn: b c. 1750 d 1827 m (1)Mary E. Hale (2)Mary Pasley PS VA
Isaac: b 4-8-1761 d 9-9-1843 m Anna Woodhouse Pvt NY ★
James: b 1745 d *p.* 1817 m — Gliddon PS NH
Jeremiah: b 8-27-1753 d 11-10-1838 m Elizabeth Turner Pvt MA ★
John: b 1730 d 1828 m Lois Brockett Ens CT
John: b a. 1762 d 3-8-1820 m Elizabeth (Jones ?) Pvt GA
John: b 3-24-1758 d 3-21-1833 m Clarissa Collins Pvt MA
John: b 2-25-1758 d 1-2-1846 m Lydia S Booth Pvt NH ★
John: b 2-4-1713 d 11-5-1786 m Elizabeth Hilton PS NH
John: b 4-9-1725 d 5-21-1805 m Elizabeth Gilman PS NH
John: b 9-15-1748 d 10-2-1837 m Olive Kimball PM PS NH
John: b 1748 d 1841 m Mirany Peyton Capt VA
Jonathan: b 3-22-1738 d 8-7-1795 m (1)Mary Garfield (2)Jemima Sterns Sgt MA
Joseph: b 12-20-1738 d 12- -1805 m (1)Prudence Field (2)Diadema Norton CS CT
Joseph: b 1728 d *p.* 1776 m Hannah Leavitt Pvt PS NH
Josiah: b 5-20-1749 d 1826 m Mary Chase PS NH
Medad: b 2-23-1724 d 2-10-1804 m Mary Fowler Pvt CT
Moses: b 5-20-1745 d 11-14-1776 m Anna Stow Lt CT
Nathan: b — d — m Rebecca Stone Pvt CT
Nathan: b 6-17-1755 d 7-17-1835 m Sarah Munroe Lt MA
Nathaniel: b 10-1-1745 d 2-21-1826 m Mary Hart Pvt CT
Paul: b 7-29-1757 d 2-22-1847 m Martha Foster Pvt MA
Paul: b 8-21-1758 d 2-9-1837 m Dorothy Reed Pvt MA
Peter: b 1748 d 1810 m Anna — Ens VA
Phinehas: b 11-28-1752 d 8-20-1793 m Ruth Dowd Pvt CT
Richard: b c. 1750 d 10- -1801 m Mary Manship PS Pvt MD
Robert: b 1740 d 1790 m Ellen Moultrie Lt VA
Samuel: b 2-22-1763 d 7-28-1850 m Margaret McDougal Pvt CT ★
Samuel: b 3-18-1720 d 8-30-1797 m (1)Mary Ladd (2)Mrs Sleeper (3)Mrs Clark CS NH
Samuel: b 8-26-1718 d 12-15-1787 m Deborah Gilman PS NH
Samuel Paul: b 1721 d 1-9-1789 m Jane Hubbard PS NH
Stephen: b 7-2-1735 d 1784 m Lydia Harwood Pvt MA
Stephen: b 10-14-1724 d 8-22-1811 m Hannah Sanborn PS NH
Thomas: b 10-27-1755 d 3-7-1790 m Abigail Weld Lt MA
Timothy: b a. 1750 d 6- -1778 m Mary Leavitt Pvt NH
Trueworthy: b 1727 d c. 1778 m Polly Gilman Pvt NH
Trueworthy: b 9-23-1753 d 11-10-1846 m (1)Hannah Knox (2)Sarah Harvey Rowell Pvt NH
Trueworthy: b 1-5-1757 d 1812 m Sara Stevens Pvt NH
William: b 5-28-1726 d *p.* 1777 m Ann Shepherd PS MA
William: b c. 1740 d — m Judith Curtis Pvt MA
William: b 1750 d *p.* 11-7-1794 m Ann Pinchback Lt VA
William: b 2-10-1756 d 6-22-1819 m Elizabeth Hite Taylor Pvt VA
Winthrop: b 12-17-1749 d 2-11-1820 m Hannah Stevens 2Lt NH
Zebulon: b 7-26-1744 d *p.* 1790 m Abigail Jones Sol CT

DUER,
Wm.: b 3-18-1747 d 5-7-1799 m Catherine Alexander PS NY

DUESLER,
Jacob: b c. 1735 d 1797-1800 m Elizabeth — Pvt NY
Marcus: b 6-3-1763 d 3-6-1846 m Elizabeth Hower Pvt NY ★

DUFF,
Cornelius: b — d c. 1813 m Mary Duff Pvt PA
David: b 9-18-1746 d 10-7-1780 m Mary — Pvt SC
James: b 4-15-1761 d 1843 m Elizabeth Strother PS VA
John: b 1739 d 1802 m Sarah Nash Sol VA
John: b 9-10-1761 d 1840 m — Pvt VA ★
Samuel: b c. 1745-50 d a. 1-19-1825 m Mary Knox Pvt VA
Wm.: b c. 1740 d 1808 m Elizabeth McDowell Pvt SC

DUFFEL,
Edward: b 4-9-1754 d 1-18-1835 m Elizabeth Leonard Pvt NJ
James: b 1761 d 10-21-1835 m Rebecca Leonard Cpl VA

DUFFIELD,
Anthony: b c. 1752 d *p.* 7-28-1785 m Jane — SgtMaj NC
Benjamin: b 11- -1753 d 1799 m Rebecca Potts Dr PA
Edward: b 4-30-1730 d 7-12-1805 m Catherine (Smyth) Parry PS PA
George: b 10-7-1732 d 2-2-1790 m Margaret Armstrong Chp PA
Jacob: b 7-23-1744 d 1-22-1815 m Mary Addis Pvt PA
John: b 1755 d 11-30-1798 m Margarette De Be Voisse Dr PA W★
Patrick: b 1748 d 3-13-1831 m Susan Hardy Sol PA
Thomas: b 12-5-1751 d 2-21-1829 m Rachel Northrop Cpl PA
Wm.: b 1743 d 4-7-1827 m Elizabeth Hassan Pvt PA
Wm.: b 11-24-1731 d 1-7-1799 m Susannah — PS PA

DUFFORD,
Mathias: b 1738 d 5-27-1816 m Judith Trimmer PS NJ

DUFFY, (includes DUFFLE, DUFFEY)
Duncan: b 4-19-1733 d *p.* 1783 m Mary Thompson Cmsry NY
John: b 1752 d 1843 m Margaret Pharr Sol MD

DU FOSSAT, (or DU FUSAT)
Guido: b 9-17-1727 d 1-22-1794 m Claudine Francoise de Dreux PS LA

DUGAN, (includes DOUGAN, DUGGAN)
Daniel: b 1750 d 5-24-1836 m (1)— Kinney (2)Mrs Mary (Daws) Egbert (3)Mrs Catherine Spring Pvt NJ ★

James: b — d 1828 m — Pvt NC
John: b 1-9-1763 d 1-25-1842 m Martha Collier PS NC ★
John: b 1756 d 1825 m — Pvt SC
John: b 1744 d 5-26-1826 m (2)Catherine Robinson Pvt VA
Thomas: b c. 1738 d 1822 m (1)Margaret — (2)Mary — Maj SC
Wm.: b 1744 d 1800 m Chloe Ann Hyman Pvt NC

DUGAS, (or DUGAT)
Pierre: b 1736 d 7-11-1826 m (1)Anne Thibaudot (2)Marie Sondier PS LA

DUGGER, (includes DUGAR)
John: b 1749 d 3-23-1834 m Frances — Pvt VA ★
Julius: b 9-9-1760 d 7- -1838 m Mary Hall Pvt NC
Robert: b 1756 d p. 1819 m Polly — Pvt VA ★
Wm.: b 3-4-1750 d c. 6-16-1839 m (1)Nancy Millard (2)Mrs Nancy A. Brown Pierce PS NC

DUGGINS,
Wm.: b 10-31-1751 d 6-23-1827 m Elizabeth Perkins Pvt VA

DUHAMEL,
James: b c. 1734 d 1803 m (1)Araminta Offley (2)Mrs Ann Morgan PS MD

DUKE, (includes DUKES)
Andrew: b 1730 d 1798 m Keziah Anderson Lt NC
Britain: b c. 1750 d p. 5-8-1800 m Anna Bennett PS NC
Burnley: b 1759/60 d 12-30-1831 m Huldah Brown Sol PS VA
Cliverius: b c. 1760 d 1818 m Ann Overton Pettus Pvt VA
Francis: b 2-11-1751 d 9-1-1777 m Sarah Shepard Cmsry VA
Green: b 1735 d 1811 m Elizabeth Parham PS NC
Hardin: b 7-1-1780 d a. 10-12-1846 m Elizabeth Swift Sgt VA ★
Henry: b c. 1736 d 1780/1 m — Capt GA
Isaac: b 1761/62 d 4-17-1835 m Elizabeth King Pvt MD
John: b c. 1755 d p. 4-3-1803 m (1)— (2)Patsey — Pvt NC
John: b 6-25-1756 d 4-9-1841 m Sally McNeal Sgt PA ★
John, Sr.: b c. 1720 d a. 6-16-1789 m Margaret — PS VA
Joseph: b 1728 d 1800 m Margaret Hazlewood (2) Barbara — Mil SC
Mathew: b 1758 d 2-7-1835 m Martha — Pvt VA
Matthew: b c. 1750 d p. 1-23-1819 m (1)— (2)Mrs Frances Clanton Lanier PS NC
Samuel: b c. 1722 d p. 2-28-1790 m — PS NC
Thomas: b — d p. 12-11-1792 m Sarah — Sol MD
Thomas: b 9-4-1750 d 1846 m Sarah Syphreet Pvt SC
Thomas: b 1742 d 1826 m Jane Thilman PS VA
Wm.: b 11-10-1756 d p. 3-4-1845 m Mary Green Pvt VA ★

DULA,
Wm.: b 3-17-1756 d 1-16-1835 m Mrs Laodocia Beasley Pvt VA

DULIN,
John: b 1753 d 1-15-1830 m Frances — Pvt VA ★

DULL,
Casper: b 6-11-1748 d 7-23-1829 m Hannah Mathieu Capt PA
Christian: b 8-12-1742 d 9-27-1820 m Elizabeth Detor Capt PA
John: b 5-20-1753 d 11-20-1835 m Elizabeth Putnam Pvt PA

DUMAS,
Benjamin: b c. 1756 d p. 8-9-1787 m Susanna — Pvt NC
David, Sr.: b c. 1730 d c. 1803 m Sarah — PS NC
Pierre: b 11-25-1756 d 8-13-1825 m Mary Huntley Sol NY

DUMBAULD,
Abraham: b c. 1753 d 3-28-1825 m Catharine Boyer Pvt PA

DUMBLETON,
John: b 1744 d 6-26-1812 m Ruth Lawrence OrdlSgt NY

DUMM,
Peter: b 9-27-1754 d 4-20-1837 m Catherine Drum Pvt PA ★

DUMMER,
Jeremiah: b 8-27-1763 d 8-18-1834 m Mehitable Moody Pvt MA
Nathan: b 1730 d 9-21-1813 m (1)Tryphena Austin (2)Esther (Tuttle) Dorman Pvt CT
Richard: b 1721 d 1806 m Judith Greenleaf Pvt MA

DU MONT, (includes DU MOND, DUMOND, & DUMONT)
Cornelis: b 10-21-1733 d 1806 m Catharine Suilants Pvt NY
Egenas: bpt 9-23-1753 d p. 1790 m Ariaantje Winne Pvt NY
Elbert: b 5-31-1761 d p. 1800 m Cornelia Hoagland Cpl NJ
Harmanus: b 1740 d 8-26-1778 m Jennie Brink PS NY
Johannes: b 1730 d 1811 m Gertrude Ten Broeck Pvt PS NY
Johannas Philip: bpt 1-22-1744 d 10-13-1805 m Sarah Elmendorph Lt PS NY
John Baptist: b 9-3-1727 d — m Elizabeth Schmidt Pvt NY
Peter: b 11-3-1734 d 1799 m Arrietta Soothoof Pvt NJ
Peter: b 10-1-1744 d 1821 m Mary Lowe Capt NJ
Peter A: b 7-11-1734 d 6-7-1818 m (1)Abigail Tunnison (2)Sarah Hegeman CS NJ

Peter J. B.: b c. 10-15-1759 d 5-19-1846 m (1)Susan Van Middeswart (2)Hannah — Pvt NJ
Peter: b 1730 d — m Maria Van Wagenan Sgt NY

DUNAWAY,
Wm.: b 1751 d 1830 m (1)Eleanor Burton (2)Nancy — Sol VA

DUNBAR,
Aaron: b 1-13-1748 d 1-26-1820 m Mary Potter Pvt CT
Abner: b 4-9-1753 d 6-27-1835 m Lydia Warren Cpl MA
Amos: b 1764 d 8-4-1855 m — Pvt NY ★
Benjamin: b 10-22-1729 d 6-1-1815 m Hannah Garnet Pvt MA
Benjamin: b 1747 d 5-17-1830 m Wealthy Washburn Sol MA
Daniel: b 8-13-1747 d 9-30-1824 m Abigail Kingman Sgt MA
Daniel: b 1752 d 9-15-1825 m Phillipe Damon Pvt MA
David: b 1731 d 12-29-1824 m Margaret Bennett Pvt MA
David: b 11-20-1756 d 3-6-1840 m (1)Elizabeth Ellmes (2)Elizabeth Ornor Horn Pvt MA ★
Ebenezer: b 1-13-1757 d 5-27-1826 m Rebecca Copeland Cpl MA
Edward: b 5-9-1722 d 1-21-1790 m Hannah Curtis Cpl CT
Elijah: b 8-22-1740 d 10-25-1814 m Sarah Hunt PS MA
Hamilton: b 1730 d a. 1784 m Elizabeth — Sgt CT
Jacob: b 10-28-1741 d 9-30-1840 m Abi Gardner Pvt MA
James: b 1721 d 6-30-1778 m (1)Hannah Benson (2)Martha (Packard) Conant Sgt MA
Jesse: b 6-6-1744 d 1806 m Mary Stone Cpl MA
Jesse: b 1742 d 4-9-1816 m Azubah Conant Pvt MA
Joel: b 1752 d 12-31-1827 m Rebecca Curtis Drm CT ★
John: b 9-18-1724 d 10-4-1786 m Temperance Hall PS Pvt CT
John: b 1752 d 6-12-1827 m Eunice Gallup Pvt CT
John: b 1766 d 10-3-1858 m Rebecca Bliss Pvt CT ★ .
John: b 1737 d 6-2-1810 m (1)Mary Mitchell (2)Jane Parker Pvt PA
John: b — d p. 4-17-1794 m Sarah — Pvt VA
Jonathan: b 4-15-1762 d 9-12-1835 m Iscah — Pvt VA ★
Joseph: b c. 1755 d 2-2-1813 m Martha Bassett Sutliffe Cpl CT ★
Joseph: b 1718 d a. 2-27-1801 m Henrietta Carpenter NS MD
Josiah, Sr.: b 4-3-1725 d 6-25-1800 m (1)Mary — (2)Silence (Edson) Packard (3)Abia Goodspeed (4)Mrs Abigail Shurtliff Pvt MA
Josiah, Jr.: b c. 1761 d 1-31-1841 m Martha Russell Pvt MA ★
Melzar: b 1754 d 9-13-1829 m Nabby Loring Pvt MA
Miles: b c. 1758 d 11-12-1837 m Tryphosa Butler FifMaj CT ★
Nehemiah: b 1-14-1765 d 3-11-1833 m Catharine Willard Pvt MA ★
Obed: b 9-16-1744 d 1838 m Abagail Humphrey Pvt MA ★
Peter: b 10-8-1741 d 5-7-1817 m Relief Curtis 2Lt MA
Peter: b 5-29-1750 d 9- -1836 m Alice Alger Pvt MA
Robert: b c. 1760 d p. 1813 m Hannah Maxwell Pvt PA
Robert: b 12- -1744 d 5-7-1821 m Eunice Barker Lt RI
Samuel: b 10-2-1704 d 6-15-1783 m (1)Hannah Danforth (2)Experience Woodward (3)Mary Pierce Chp MA
Silas: b 9-18-1743 d 1827 m Amy Reynolds Sgt MA
Solomon: b 4-18-1709 d 1795 m Rachel Damon Pvt MA
Thaxter: b 1758 d — m Pheba Alger Cpl MA
Thomas: b 8-1-1750 d 4-15-1796 m Lucretia Smith Sgt MA
Wm.: b 2-23-1752 d 1798 m (1)Elizabeth Robison (2)Mrs Sarah (Platt) Myddelton PS SC
William: b 10-31-1760 d 4-18-1852 m Polly Shelton Pvt VA ★

DUNCAN, (includes DUNKAN, DUNKIN)
Andrew: b 3-12-1750 d 1-18-1828 m (1)Ann Smith (2)Elizabeth Andrews Pvt PA
Benjamin: b c. 1735 d 11- -1796 m (1)Sarah Baughman (2)Elizabeth — Pvt VA
Charles: b c. 1742 d 1802 m Sarah Browning Pvt VA
Charles: b 12-12-1751 d 7-17-1818 m (1)Elizabeth Dillard (2)Francis Franklin (3)Ann Grawn Pvt VA
Charles: b 1-19-1761 d 10-24-1838 m Margaret Kirk Pvt VA ★
Daniel: bpt 7-27-1746 d p. 1799 m (1)Sarah Doolittle (2)Elizabeth Williams LT CT
Daniel: b 2-13-1711/12 d 12-9-1792 m Sarah Rice Pvt MA .
Daniel: b 5-11-1729 d 1-1-1791 m (1)— (2)Diana Jacobs Pvt PA
David: b 6-27-1759 d 5-1-1799 m Mary Palmer Pvt NY
David: b 1730-35 d 4- -1792 m Margaret Pomeroy PS PA
George: b 1724 d 5-29-1810 m Mary Bell PS NH
George: b 1730 d 1783 m Ann Hall Capt VA
George: b 3-8-1758 d 11-2-1838 m Elizabeth Phillips Pvt VA ★
Jacob: b c. 1750 d 1814-15 m — PS VA
James: b 1755 d 6-24-1844 m Susan Lear Capt PA
James: b 1758 d 10-14-1843 m (1)Elizabeth Wilson (2)Jane (Dundas) Cook (3)Mrs Peden (4)Sophia (Lashell) Maxwell (5)Martha (Cook) McClelland Pvt PA
James: b 10-14-1747 d 12-9-1843 m Elizabeth Fincher Pvt SC
James: b 2-20-1750 d 10-16-1817 m Elizabeth Strode PS VA
James: b 7-18-1763 d 11-7-1791 m Mary Crockett Sol VA
Jason: b 1-10-1750 d 12-15-1839 m Sarah Gates Capt CS VT
John: b 1780 m— Sol GA
John: b 3-3-1734 d 2-14-1823 m Polly Duncan Capt NH
John: b 3-29-1752 d 6-14-1834 m (1)Margaret Dickey (2)Betsey Prouty Sgt NH
John: b 1727 d 5-21-1794 m (1)Violet Newell (2)Ann Dey Pvt NJ
John: b 9-23-1748 d c. 1806 m Mary Kelley Capt PA
John: b 1743 d 1792 m Jean —— Pvt PA
John: b 5-15-1707 d c. 1783 m Sarah —— PS SC

DUNCAN, contd.
John, Sr.: b c. 1735 d 10-27-1817 m Elinor Sharp Capt VA
John, Jr.: b 2-25-1765 d 4-8-1832 m Mary Laughlin Pvt VA
John, Sr.: b — d p. 7- -1788 m (1)— (2)Wilkey — PS VA
John, Jr.: b c. 1726 d — m Dinah Bradford Sol VA
John: b 　 1730 d 7-26-1806 m Sarah Esther Camden Pvt VA
John: b c. 1750 d p. 1825 m Betty Ann —— Pvt VA
John b 1760 d 4-29-1840 m Margaret Alexander Pvt VA ★
Joseph: b c. 1720 d p. 12-13-1792 m Lyddia —— PS VA
Joseph: b 　 1732 d 　 1802 m Mary Browning Sgt VA
Joseph: b 1730 d p. 2-12-1818 m Nancy Stevens Pvt VA
Joseph: b 5-16-1769 d 5-16-1847 m Ann Laughlin Pvt VA
Rawley: b 11-25-1723/4 d 1786 m— CS VA
Robert: b 　 1718 d 　 1800 m Catherine McCloud PM NC
Robert: b 6-14-1762 d 7-2-1845 m Hannah Carr Pvt NC
Robert: b 12-10-1745 d 12-9-1828 m Esther Reed Pvt PA
Robert: b c. 1751/2 d p. 1799 m — Pvt PA
Roger: b c. 1745 d p. 1830 m Judith Ann Webb Pvt VA
Samuel: b 1745 d 6-30-1784 m Hannah Donnell Dr ME
Samuel: b 1-9-1747 d 7-28-1820 m (1)Betsey Stearns (2)Patience Choate Sgt MA
Samuel: b 　 1760 d p. 1840 m Sarah-- Pvt VA ★
Samuel: b 　 d c. 3-12-1825 m Nancy Withers Sol VA
Simeon: b 5-27-1725 d 6-19-1781 m Bridget Richardson Pvt MA
Stephen: b 1729 d 3-30-1794 m Ann - - Pvt CS PA
Thomas: b 1743 d 12-15-1825 m (1)Sarah Rider (2)Hannah — Pvt NY
Thomas: b 11-20-1760 d 11-16-1827 m Martha Callender Pvt PA
William: b 1716 d 1798 m Naomi Bell PS NH
William: b c. 1755 d p. 1806 m Anne Sivil Kornegay Pvt NC
William: b 1735-1740 d 1794 m Mary Jane Albert 1Lt PA
William: b 1726 d p. 5-17-1790 m Rosanna Norman Pvt VA
William: b 　 d 1781 m Ruth —— PS VA

DUNCANSON,
James: b 3-10-1755 d 3-3-1791 m Mary Macauley Col VA

DUNCKLEE, (includes DUNKLEE, DUNKLEY)
David, Sr.: b 8-16-1746 d 8-13-1826 m Phebe Odell PS NH
Hezekiah: b 6-29-1758 d 1827 m Mehitable White Pvt NH
John: b 3-4-1740 d 8-4-1792 m Elizabeth Chapman PS NH
Joseph: b 9-15-1753 d p. 1802 m (1)Hannah Cook (2)Sabra Whitmore (Adams) Lt MA
Moses: b 12-3-1758 d 2-10-1839 m Sarah Prindel Pvt VA ★

DUNCOMBE,
Edward: b 1760 d 11-12-1837 m Anna Hall Pvt CT

DUNDAS,
James: b 1734 d 1-16-1788 m Elizabeth Moore PS PA

DUNDORE,
John: b 3-20-1751 d 10-14-1823 m Catharine Geiss Pvt PA

DUNGAN,
Benjamin: b 4-27-1743 d 6-23-1816 m (1)Esther Cottman (2)Mary Morgan Capt PA
Elias: b c. 1742 d 1-29-1804 m Diana Carrell Pvt PA
Elisha: b 1735 d p. 12-1-1808 m Hannah —— PS VA
Jeremiah: b c. 1758 d 2-26-1814 m Susannah Walker Pvt PA
Jesse: b 2-22-1756 d 7-12-1823 m (1)Esther Johnson (2)Esther Van Buskirk Pvt PA
John: b 1753 d 3-22-1798 m Mary Hyle 2Lt PA
John, Jr.: b 1-12-1748 d 1798 m Phebe Corbit Pvt PA
Jonathan: b 1752 d p. 1801 m Mary Holmes Lt PA
Joseph: b a. 1725 d 9-15-1785 m Mary Ohl Pvt PA
Joseph: b 4-13-1736 d c. 1816 m Elizabeth Carrell Pvt PA
Levi: b c. 1740 d 1825 m Mary Davis Pvt PA

DUNHAM,
Abial, Sr.: b 1740 d 5-7-1820 m Ruth Cobb Sgt MA
Abial, Jr.: b 2-5-1762 d 1824 m Polly Bishop Drm MA
Amma: b 1764 d 9-15-1845 m (1)Bethia Hallowell (2)Theodate Sawyer Pvt MA ★
Asa: b 1759 d 10-13-1813 m Lydia Cobb Pvt MA
Azariah: b 2-9-1718 d 1-22-1790 m (1)Mary Tuxton (2)Mary (Ford) Stone LCol PS NJ
Bangs: b 2-16-1751/2 d p. 1794 m Submit Phelps Pvt CT
Calvin: b 3-28-1754 d c. 1840 m Ruth Noble Pvt MA ★
Cornelius: b 1740 d 2-23-1819 m Jemima Andrews Pvt CT
Cornelius: b 5-10-1748 d 5-28-1816 m (1)Sarah Butler (2)Lucinda Mayhew Cpl MA
Cornelius: b 9-17-1748 d 7-15-1835 m Lydia Atwood Pvt MA
Daniel: b 2-2-1744 d 5-21-1822 m Anna Moseley 2Lt CT
Daniel: b 1762 d 1862 m Margaret Tritterfield Pvt CT
Daniel: b 1725-7 d 1804 m Elizabeth Martin PS NJ
Daniel, Sr.: b 8-2-1712 d 1- -1796 m (1)Abigail Hart (2)Amy Murphy CS RI
Daniel, Jr.: b 1737 d 4-26-1815 m Elizabeth Dunham NS RI
David: b 2-1-1740/1 d 6-1-1831 m Tabitha Cooley Sol MA
David: b 3-14-1723 d 10-6-1806 m Rebecca Dunn Capt NJ
Ebenezer: b c. 1750 d 1837 m Sarah — Matr MA ★
Ebenezer: bpt 9-3-1759 d 　 1856 m Anna Denne Pvt NY ★
Edward: b 7-24-1753 d 1-25-1844 m Mary Daniels Pvt NY

Elijah: b 1-5-1734 d 1-13-1821 m Sarah Vincent Pvt MA
Elijah: b 5-22-1753 d 8-11-1827 m Eunice Thomas Pvt MA
Ephraim: b 1-23-1751 d 6-11-1832 m Hannah Butler Pvt NY
George: b 1750 d 12-19-1819 m (1)Ann Dunham (2)Mrs Patience Churchill Capt MA
George: b 1753 d 12-6-1800 m Phebe Lucas Pvt MA
Gideon, Jr.: b 10-10-1762 d 5-8-1841 m Anna Merrel Pvtr Pvt CT ★
Hezekiah: b 8-17-1745 d 4-27-1810 m Mary Davis Capt NY
Holtham: b 6-14-1749 d 6-15-1824 m Hannah Cole Lt NY ★
Isaac: b 10- -1743 d 1833 m Sarah Spooner Pvt MA
Israel: b 1741 d 5- -1828 m Hannah Whitney Pvt MA
Jacob: b 4-9-1727 d 4-11-1779 m Elizabeth Pettet Sol NY
James: b 2-9-1754 d- - m Mary Ransom Carver Pvt MA
Jehu: b 9-24-1761 d 4-6-1842 m Elnorah VanTine Pvt NJ ★
Jesse: b 4-21-1757 d 4-4-1845 m Lois Hatch Pvt MA
Jethro: b c. 1754 d 1820 m Lydia —— Pvt MA
John: b 7-12-1726 d 4-13-1814 m Mary Thomas Pvt MA
John: b 1729 d 8-24-1784 m Jane Butler Pvt MA
John: b 8-2-1762 d 3-13-1816 m Anne Round Pvt MA
John: b 8-12-1740 d 9-16-1823 m Mary Gilman Pvt NJ
John: b 1756 d 10-29-1825 m (1)Sarah High (2)Patty Smalley Pvt NJ
John: b 10-7-1762 d 11-26-1840 m Phoebe Williams Pvt NJ ★
Jonathan: b 11-24-1745 d 1821 m Mehitabel Knowlton Lt NY
Jonathan: b 4-6-1758 d 1-4-1840 m Betty Babcock Pvt CT
Jonathan: b 1751 d 1-6-1797 m (1)Sarah Lennox (2)Susanna Halsey Pvt NJ
Jonathan, Sr.: b 8-16-1694 d 3-10-1777 m Jean Piatt PS NJ
Jonathan, Jr.: b 5-23-1721 d p. 11-16-1782 m Keziah Fitz Randolph Pvt NJ
Jonathan, 3d: b 10-30-1752 d 3-19-1833 m Eunice Dunn Pvt NJ
Joseph: b 3-21-1745 d a. 4-7-1778 m Abigail (Hovey) Jennings Pvt CT
Joseph: b 1-12-1739 d 4-20-1823 m Sarah Davis Pvt MA
Joseph: b 4-21-1749 d 1-24-1826 m (1)Sarah Johnson (2)Mercy Twing Pvt MA
Joseph: b 2-6-1741 d 3-11-1796 m Patience Hathaway PS MA
Joseph, Jr.: b 1745-1752 d p. 1789 m Mary Parks Pvt NY
Joseph: b 1735 d 1790 m Hannah Conyer Pvt NJ
Lewis Ford: b 3-31-1754 d 8-26-1821 m Jane Tuthill Dr NJ
Matthew: b c. 1758 d p. 1812 m Ruth Strong Pvt MA
Nathaniel: b 1733 d p. 1800 m (1)Mary Sutton (2)Kesiah Crosley Pvt NJ
Nehemiah: b 11-1-1721 d p. 1783 m (1)Ann Dunn (2)Mary Clarkson (3)Ann McKinney (4)Mrs Bethany (Berdin) Adams PS NJ
Obadiah, Sr.: b 3-13-1730 d 2-17-1813 m Lucy Gillet PS Pvt VT
Obadiah, Jr.: b 11-17-1760 d 10-12-1833 m Lois Hendryx Pvt VT ★
Robert: b 1744 d p. 1791 m Ruth Hatch Sgt MA
Salathiel: b 3-15-1757 d 3-10-1841 m Lucy Stewart Cpl CT ★
Samuel: bpt 2-3-1723 d 10-28-1789 m Elizabeth —— Capt CT
Samuel: b 10-10-1753 d 1804 m Mary Johnson NS CT
Samuel: b 9-22-1754 d 10-13-1854 m (1)Eunice Jennings (2)Asenath Gurley Pvt CT W★
Samuel: b 7-15-1763 d 2-26-1823 m Dorothy Watson Pvt CT ★
Samuel: b 10-9-1758 d 9-25-1827 m Elizabeth Morton Pvt MA ★
Samuel: b 4-13-1750 d 7-4-1822 m Sally Ann Wright Pvt NY ★
Seth: b 7-4-1741 d 5- -1808 m Eunice Hovey Lt CT
Silas: b 3-28-1749 d 7-23/4-1815 m Mary Tilson Pvt MA
Simeon: b 1-25-1739 d 1-11-1817 m (1)Mrs Abijah Phelps (Tallcott) (2)Anna Strong Ens CT
Solomon, Jr.: b a. 8-20-1760 d 7-1-1843 m Sallie Blanding Pvt NH ★
Stephen: b 4-30-1761 d 1-11-1855 m Elizabeth Topliff Pvt CT
Sylvanus: b 1714 d 1796 m Rebecca Crocker Pvt MA
Sylvanus: b 1754 d 9-14-1821 m Mrs Ursula (Wright) Gilbert Cpl NY
Thomas: b 1-22-1738 d 10-5-1804 m Sarah —— PS Sol MA
William: b 2-5-1753 d 2-19-1834 m Experience Pratt Sgt MA ★
William: b c. 1756 d p. 5-2-1786 m Susanna Williams Pvt MA

DUNKEL, (includes DUNCKEL, DUNCKLE, DUNKLE)
John George Garrit: b 7-1-1756 d 5-21-1844 m Elizabeth Countryman Pvt NY
Keleain: b c. 1735 d p. 1790 m Mary Magdalena —— PS PA
Melchoir: b c. 1750 d p. 10-22-1823 m — PS PA
Michael: b c. 1738 d a. 10-1-1800 m Elizabeth —— PS PA
Nicholas: b 5-14-1758 d 2-14-1841 m Anna Shanman Cpl NY ★
Peter, Sr.: b 2-2-1720 d 3-3-1809 m Anna Maria —— Pvt NY
Peter, Jr.: b 2-2-1750 d 3-7-1830 m Anna — Sgt NY
Peter: b 7-11-1742 d 12-22-1827 m Elizabeth Wolf Pvt PA
Peter: b c. 1740 d p. 1790 m — Sol PA

DUNKELBERGER,
Abram: b 1738 d 8-19-1813 m Christina —— Pvt PA

DUNKLIN,
Jean Wathen: b 1740-2 d 1786 m Joseph Dunklin PS SC
Joseph: b c. 1734 d p. 5-7-1776 m Jean Wathen CS SC
Mary: b 2-17-1770 d 6-12-1850 m Hewlett Sullivan PS SC

DUNLAP (includes DUNLOP)
Adam: b 1750 d 1823 m Elizabeth Adams Pvt NH
Alexander: b 10-19-1743 d 3-16-1828 m Agnes Guy Pvt PA
Ebenezer: b 1759 d 6- -1839 m Christina Potter Pvt MA
George: b 1736 d 1796-1807 m Nancy (Craighead) Richardson Capt SC

James: b 1727 d 12-15-1821 m Jane Boggs CtyLt PA
James: b 8-1-1740 d 6-24-1844 m Francois E Wiles Pvt PA ★
James: b c. 1752 d 4-4-1819 m Julianna Cumming PS PA
John: b 5-4-1746 d p. 1790 m Martha Gilmore PS NH
John: b 8-21-1754 d 12-27-1816 m Elizabeth Hammil 2Lt NY
John: b 8-14-1718 d 1813 m Sarah Gillespie Pvt PA
John: b a. 1757 d 10- -1777 m Rabina — Pvt PA ★
John: b c. 1761 d 9-5-1796 m Rachel —— Pvt PA
John: b a. 1748 d 2-5-1804 m Ann Clark Pvt VA
Joseph: b 2-20-1757 d 10-15-1823 m Martha Pain Sgt PA
Joseph: b 1754 d 4-26-1831 m Margaret Flanagan Pvt PA
Nancy Craighead: d 3-17-1740 d 11-9-1790 m (1)Rev William
  Richardson (2)Col George Dunlap PS SC
Robert: b 7-28-1752 d 7-25-1834 m (1)Nancy Giles (2)Mary Letts
  (3)Annie Williams Pvt NJ ★
Robert: b 1737 d 1801 m Julia Alexander Pvt PA
Robert: b 1760 d 1817 m Mary Elizabeth —— Pvt PA
Robert: b 1751 d 7-14-1831 m Mary Dunlap Pvt SC
Robert: b 1741 d 3-15-1781 m Mary Elizabeth Gay Sol VA
Robert: b 8-12-1743 d 4-5-1813 m Eleanor Ruth Wallace PS VA
Samuel: b 1759 d 2-4-1825 m (1)Lucy Howard (2)Elizabeth Temple
  Pvt MA ★
Samuel: b 1751 d 8-2-1830 m Nancy Cochran Pvt NH
Samuel: b 1744 d 1-14-1813 m Mary Ann Howey Pvt PA
William, Sr.: b 1750 d 1778 m Jane Campbell Pvt NY
William: b c. 1753 d 6-11-1835 m Margaret —— Sgt PA ★
William: b 7-25-1765 d 12-20-1838 m Margaret Hunter Pvt SC
William: b 10-19-1743 d 3-5-1816 m Rebecca Robertson Maj VA

DUNLEVY,
Anthony: b 1763 d 2-14-1804 m Mary Crawford Pvt PA
Anthony: b c. 1745 d p. 1792 m Hannah White Pvt VA
Francis: b 1762 d 11-6-1839 m Mary Craig Sgt VA ★
George: b c. 1745 d p. 6-25-1806 m Mary Wake CS VA

DUNN, (includes DUN)
Abner Martin: b 1755 d 7-18-1795 m Priscilla Tyler Lt PA
Alexander: b 12-18-1762 d 12-22-1846 m Christine O'Neal Pvt NC
Bartholomew: b c. 1728 d 1786 m Ruth — Pvt NC
Christopher: b 1760 d p. 1811 m (1)Susanna Lombard (2)Betty
  Fogg Fif MA ★
David: b c. 1726 d 1800 m Frances —— Pvt VA
Duncan: b 1751/52 d 8-29-1839 m — Sgt MA ★
Elinor Brewster: b 1-25-1754 d 11-3-1841 m Samuel Dunn PS VA
George: b c. 1720 d 1776-7 m Rachel Harper Pvt MA
George: b 1749/50 d 7-17-1827 m Margaret Yeomans Pvt NY
George: b 1743 d 5-21-1805 m Mary Curry Lt PA
Gershom: b 10-9-1759 d 10-5-1805 m Catherine — Pvt NJ
Henry: b 1-3-1750 d 6-28-1836 m Elizabeth McDowal Pvt NY
Hugh: b 1740 d 4-4-1826 m Abigail Carman Capt NJ
Hugh Smith: b c. 1760 d 1813 m— PS MD
Isaac: b 12-6-1760 d 1-11-1850 m Jerusha Blackwell Pvt NJ
Isaac: b 1754 d 1836 m Mary Sheffield Pvt NC
Jacob: b c. 1740 d p. 1787 m Mary Taylor Pvt PA
James: b 5-9-1751 d 1788 m Elizabeth Loraine — Capt DE
James: b 1745 d 9-16-1820 m Priscilla Langstaff Lt NJ W ★
James: b 1746 d 2-25-1818 m (1)Rebekah Moore (2)Agnes
  Sterret Capt PA
James: b 1761 d 10-23-1838 m Elizabeth Alexander Pvt PA ★
James: b 1727 d a. 1-12-1805 m Agnes — Sol SC
James: b 4-30-1753 d 1809-15 m Sarah Reed PS VA
James: b 12-10-1759 d 6-15-1846 m Sarah Harvey Pvt VA
James: b 1724-6 d 1806-8 m Martha Long Sol PS VA
Jeremiah: b 1712 d 1794 m (1)Sarah Hull (2)Margaret Carman Pvt
  NJ
Joel: b 10-22-1747 d 7-27-1845 m Rachel Runyon Pvt NJ ★
John, Sr.: b 1710-23 d 1783 m Jane Bothwell Pvt PA
John: b 5-7-1761 d 7-29-1832 m (1)Polly — (2)Mary Puffer Sgt MA ★
John: b 10-10-1719 d 1792 m Ann Martin Pvt VA
John: b 8-21-1758 d p. 1834 m Nancy Harvey Pvt Grd VA
Joshua: b 1760 d 6-7-1848 m Mary Davis Pvt MA ★
Josiah: b 1735 d a. 7-1-1783 m Sarah — Col GA
Josiah: b c. 1732 d 1825 m Sarah Randall PS ME
Justus: b 2-15-1741 d 4-6-1813 m Experience Stelle Pvt PS NJ
Mary Sheffield: b 1758/9 d 5-11-1862 m Isaac Dunn PS NC
Micajah: b 9-12-1714 d 9-11-1779 m Elizabeth Dunham LCol NJ
Nahum: b 4-9-1748 d 1-5-1812 m Elizabeth Dunham Sgt NJ
Nathaniel: b — d p. 1812 m Mercy Dyer Pvt MA
Reuben: b 1-21-1748 d 4-2-1824 m Sarah Fitz Randolph Pvt NJ
Robert: b 1761 d 6-14-1832 m Isabella Vanderbilt Capt PS NY
Samuel: b c. 1735 d 1784 m Sarah Skillings Capt MA
Samuel: b 1753 d 10-6-1836 m Hannah — Pvt NJ PA
Samuel: b 1754 d 11-2-1847 m Anna Stagg Pvt PA
Samuel: b 1761 d 12-19-1843 m (1)Jemima McIntire (2)Hannah
  Morton Pvt PA
Samuel, Jr.: b 1-3-1743 d 12-15-1785 m Lucy Pierce Capt Pvtr RI
Samuel: b 1750 d 8-17-1802 m Eleanor Brewster Pvt VA
Sylvester: b — d p. 9-10-1799 m Janet (Montgomery) Barr PS Mil
  SC

Thomas: b- -p. 1800 m Susannah Sweezy Pvt NJ
Thomas: b 1745 d 1800 m Mary Caldwell Pvt PA
Thomas: b 1740-43 d 1818 m — Sgt VA

Timothy: b 1755 d 6-2-1843 m Mehitable Sweet Pvt NY
William: b c. 1740 d 4- -1806 m (1)Sallie McKinstry (2)Margaret
  (McClelland) Harrison PS Pvt PA
William: b c. 1735 d 1785 m — Pvt VA
William: b 5-7-1751 d 12-19-1837 m Katharine — Pvt VA W ★
William: b 10-17-1752 d 1823 m Hannah Walhouser Pvt VA

DUNNEGAN,
John: b 3-15-1755 d 1813 m Susan — Pvt NC

DUNNING,
Abel: b 7- -1763-4 d 8-16-1841 m Maria Smith Pvt VT ★
Abram: b 3-28-1765 d 8-23-1842 m Tryphena Jewett Pvt VT ★
Andrew: b 7-11-1727 d 3-27-1808 m Hannah Shepard PS ME
Benjamin: b 1-17-1736/7 d 1-8-1808 m Elizabeth Ewing Lt PS MA
David: b 7-9-1753 d 6-7-1835 m (1)Mary Sterling (2)Hannah Hyatt
  Pvt CT
David: b 4-17-1738-40 d 7- -1806 m Elizabeth (Collins) Sperry Pvt
  CT
David: b 12-16-1749 d 4-10-1823 m Elizabeth Hunt Pvt MA
Ebenezer: b a. 1760 d 12-17-1802 m Martha Danes Pvt NY ★
Edmond: b 11-3-1764 d 5-24-1856 m Hannah Hawley Pvt CT
Elias: b 1738 d 8- -1783 m Sarah — PS Capt CT
Isaac: b c. 1740 d p. 1803 m Rachel — Pvt CT
Jacob: b 1746 d 7-27-1781 m Keturah Conkling Lt NY
James: b 7-31-1738 d 3-30-1792 m Jane Woodside Pvt MA
Jesse: b 1745-50 d p. 1790 m Anna (Hill) Davis Sgt NY
John: b 1742 d 1-1795 m Polly Seely Lt NY
John: b 3-8-1753 d 7-11-1839 m Rebecca Spear Sgt MA
Josiah: b 10-1-1755 d 2-27-1842 m Hannah Seeley Sgt NY VT ★
Michael: b 6-3-1726 d 11-29-1813 m Hannah Green Capt NY
Michael: b 8-20-1750 d 9-28-1837 m Hannah Gregory Lt NY ★
Michael: b 7-20-1730 d 2-28-1810 m Abiah Kimberly Lt VT
Richard: b 4-23-1747 d 5-9-1810 m Miriam — Lt VT
Robert: b 1748 d 1789 m Marjorie — Pvt PA
Robert: b 1-10-1731 d 10-7-1804 m Sarah Spear 2Lt PS MA
Silas: b 5-6-1755 d 9-25-1830 m Jerusha Bristol Pvt CT

DUNNINGTON,
Francis: b 1746 d 11-14-1820 m Margaret E. Perry Pvt MD
Hezekiah: b 9-29-1757 d 2- -1822 m Ann McGregor Pvt MD
William: b 4-13-1740 d 1802 m — Beck Pvt MD

DUNSCOMB,
Andrew: b 1745-50 d 1804 m Philadelphia Du Val Sol NY
Daniel: b 6-3-1726 d 3-3-1803 m (1) — Hojer (2)Gertrude Thurman
  PS NY

DUNSTER,
Jason: b 3-27-1763 d 3-21-1828 m Polly Meriam Pvt MA

DUNTON,
Isaac: b 9-8-1765 d 9-8-1791 m Beulah Morse Pvt MA
John: b 1738 d 1808 m Abigail Walker Lt MA
Joseph: b 1736 d 1809 m Abigail — Pvt MA
Richard: b c. 1746 d 10- -1821 m (1)Sophia Harmanson (2)Rosanna
  Clegg (3)Sinah Benthall (4)Lucy Carpenter Maj VA
Samuel: b 11-10-1748 d 5-1-1813 m (1)Lois Pearl (2)Lavina Marcy
  Sgt CT
Thomas: b 3-24-1752 d 5-26-1832 m Joanna (Howard) Blair Pvt MA
Thomas: b 1759 d 8-28-1802 m Sarah Baldwin Pvt VT
Wm.: b 1750 d 1809 m Mary — Pvt NC
Wm.: b c. 1760 d p. 1801 m Sarah George GnrsMte VA

DUNWELL,
Stephen: b 2-11-1762 d 11-21-1840 m Deborah Witter Pvt CT ★

DUNWOODY,
James: b 1741 d 1807 m Esther Dean Splatt PS GA
James: b 1745 d 4-16-1815 m Rachel Burns Pvt PA
John: b 1707 d 9-17-1776 m Susannah Creswell Pvt PA
John: b 1745 d 5-19-1824 m Jane — Sol PA
Robert: b 1744 d 1794 m Mary Creswell Pvt PA
Samuel: b 1755 d p. 8-15-1827 m Martha McClain 2Lt PA

DU PALAIS,
Pierre Alexander De Guemar: b 3-1-1741 d p. 12-1-1831 m Marie
  Mignot Capt FrA

DUPAR,
John: b 1745 d 1788 m Sarah Mulett Pvt MA

DUPEE,
Charles, Sr.: b 10-18-1734/35 d 8-5-1802 m Hannah Smith Fif MA
Charles, Jr.: b 12-30-1759 d 2-19-1803 m Rachel White Pvt MA

DU PLANTIER,
Armand Allard: b 1753 d 9-30-1827 m Augustine Girard Capt FrA

DUPREE, (includes DIPPERY, DU PRE)
Daniel: b 3-26-1768 d 11-22-1848 m Sarah Ellington Pvt NC
Jacob: b c. 1725 d 11- -1803 m — PS PA

DUPREE, contd.
Jeremiah: b 11-16-1754 d *p.* 1838 m Eleanor Huff Ens VA
John: b *c.* 1730 d 10- -1788 m Luvania Lewis Ens PS VA
Joseph: b 11-22-1734 d 4-10-1815 m Nannie Sullivan PS VA
Lewis: b 1727 d 1- -1787 m Elizabeth Warren PS VA
Louis: b 1744 d 8-9-1791 m Lucy Ballou Maj PS NC
Samuel: b 11-24-1761 d 12-13-1799 m Mary Stead Allston Sol SC
William: b 7-7-1759 d 6-16-1854 m Amy Pettis Pvt VA

DURAND,
Alexander: b 2-25-1767 d 2-1-1836 m Elizabeth Whaley Pvt CT ★
Andrew, 2d: b 12-15-1734 d *p.* 1801 m Eunice Hotchkiss PS CT
Ebenezer: b *c.* 1760 d 1-31-1826 m Polly (Stow) Williams Pvt CT ★
Eleazer: b 1754 d — m Mary Canfield Cpl CT
Fisk: b 6-26-1766 d 4-8-1841 m Polly Esther Platt Drm CT ★
Francis Joseph: b 1740 d 6- -1817/18 m Patience Weed Pvt NY
Jeremiah: b 1758 d 6-9-1830 m (1)Hannah Trowbridge (2)Sarah Andrus Vol CT
John: b 1758 d 6-9-1830 m Elizabeth Pond Mar CT ★
John: b 1764 d 4-22-1828 m Philena Beardsley Drm CT
John: b 10-16-1745 d 6-25-1813 m Rachel (Meyer) Post Pvt NJ
Joseph F.: b 1764 d 4-10-1843 m Elizabeth Arnold Pvt CT ★
Lemuel: b 2-25-1762 d 3-3-1847 m Catherine Smith Pvt CT ★
Samuel: b 12-3-1758 d 1-24-1831 m Susanna Hitchcock Pvt CT W★
William: b 4-27-1760 d 4-29-1841 m Mary Baldwin Pvt Smn CT ★

DURANT,
Amos: b 1753 d 1-29-1820 m Sarah Ballard Pvt MA
Benjamin: b 2-13-1760 d 1804 m Miriam Hamilton Pvt MA
Edward, Sr.: b 1715 d 4-10-1782 m (1)Ann Jackson (2)Mrs Mary Allen PS MA
Edward, Jr.: b 3-31-1738 d 1778 m Mary Park Dr MA
Henry: b — d — m Susanna Preston Pvt CL
Henry: b *a.* 1755 d *p.* 1-8-1805 m Sarah Perkins Sct SC
Isaac Preston: b 9-16-1757 d 1-9-1848 m Helena Wendell Pvt MA
John: b 12-19-1749 d 3- -1814 m Sarah Dennie Pvt MA
Jonathan: b 8-20-1739 d *c.* 1780 m Anna Wilkins Pvt NH
Joshua: b 1759 d *p.* 1807 m (2)Mary Hodgman Ens NH
Levi: bpt 8-22-1756 d *p.* 1795 m Mary Wright Sgt NH
Samuel: bpt 9-15-1749 d *a.* 1819 m Merab Coburn Pvt NH
Thomas: b 3-18-1746 d 8-2-1831 m Elizabeth Clark Pvt PS MA W★

DURBIN,
Daniel: b 1729 d 1827 m Molly Johns PS MD
William: b 1-15-1749 d 8-28-1820 m Margaret Bruce Cpl MD

DURBORAW,
Isaac: b *c.* 1740 d 1817 m Martha Holmes PS PA

DURFEE, (includes DURFEY)
Benjamin: b 1-22-1734 d *p.* 1780 m (1)Elizabeth Downing (2)Anna — Pvt CT
Benjamin: b 5-8-1754 d 6-4-1840 m Sarah Bordon Pvt MA ★
Benjamin, Jr.: b *c.* 1742 d — m (1)Sarah Cook (2)Rhoda Brightman Capt RI
Cory, Sr.: b 5-6-1738 d 1-19-1786 m Deobrah Conklin Pvt MA
Earle: b 10-27-1757 d 5-24-1839 m (1)Patience Lake (2)Phebe Hunt Pvt RI
Ebenezer: b 12-24-1761 d 4-18-1840 m (1)Sarah — (2)Abigail Gould Pvt CT ★
Gideon, Sr.: b 2-17-1738 d 9-12-1814 m Anne Bowen Pvt RI
James: b 1-11-1742 d 3-27-1817 m Ruth Slocum Pvt RI
James: b 7-14-1749 d 1805 m Mary Burrington Pvt RI
Job: b 8-19-1733 d *p.* 1790 m Sarah Easton CS RI
John: b 1762 d 1843 m Mary Peck Pvt Pvtr CT ★
John Jenckes: b 1743 d 1830 m Anna Bennett Sgt RI
Joseph: b 12-5-1755 d 10-28-1803 m Allice — Pvt CT
Joseph: b 4-27-1750 d 12-10-1841 m (1)Elizabeth Turner (2)Elizabeth Nichols LCol MA ★
Joseph: b 8-31-1739 d 6- -1775 m Abigail Borden Vol MA
Lemuel: b 4-18-1759 d 8-9-1829 m Prudence Hathaway Pvt RI
Oliver: b 2-27-1754 d 9-11-1798 m Mrs Elizabeth (Lowden) Langley Capt PS CS RI
Richard: b 9-8-1758 d 1-22-1845 m Patience Borden Capt RI ★
Samuel: b 3-1-1702 d 11-8-1788 m Mercy Durfee PS RI
Thomas: b 11-5-1721 d 7-19-1796 m Patience Borden Capt PS MA
Thomas: b 11-4-1759 d 1-17-1829 m Mary Lowden Ens RI ★
Walter: b 8-6-1752 d 1843 m Anna Ashley Pvt VT RI ★

DURGEY,
John: b 1755 d 1835 m Hannah Congo Pvt CT

DURGIN,
Gershom: b *c.* 1750 d 5-8-1827 m (1)Elizabeth Clark (2)Miriam Rowe Pvt NH
John: b 8-13-1756 d 10-16-1848 m Lydia Morrison Pvt NH
Josiah: bpt 6-2-1751 d 7-14-1833 m Hannah Stevens Pvt NH
Wm.: b *c.* 1744 d 2-25-1832 m Rebecca Stuart CS MA
Wm., Sr.: b 1717 d 1789 m Hannah Elliot CS NH
Wm., Jr.: b 9-5-1750 d 5-11-1822 m (1)Elizabeth Morrison (2)Hannah (Hill) Clement PS NH

DURHAM, (includes DURWIN)
Asa: b 1760 d 5-29-1834 m Asenath — Sgt MA ★
Charnel: b 7-1-1754 d 4-13-1836 m Nancy Eckles Capt SC ★
James: b 1- -1753 d 1831 m Margaret McClintock Pvt PA
John: b 2-22-1738 d 9- -1801 m Elizabeth Smithson PS MD
John: b 4-13-1760 d 6-13-1852 m Mary Ann Payne Pvt Mus NC ★
John: b 1732 d 1802 m Molly Hawkins Pvt NC
John: b 10-20-1742 d 5-22-1817 m Martha Bugg Pvt VA
Matthew: b 6-16-1760 d 1-3-1834 m Fannie Spencer Capt NC ★
Matthew, Sr.: b *c.* 1730 d *p.* 12-9-1795 m Susanna Lindsey PS NC
Michael: b 7-5-1761 d 2-14-1832 m (1)Sara Champion (2)Anna Loker Pvt NY
Samuel: b 1740 d 1794 m Mary — PS NC
Samuel: b 5-6-1752 d *a.* 3-19-1838 m Sarah — Pvt VA
Samuel Davis: b *c.* 1755 d 12-27-1801 m Isabel Lindsey Sgt VA W★
Tolford: b 1744 d 11-14-1836 m Jane Brown 2Lt MA
Wm.: b 1760 d 1818 m Ann Tolby Pvt MD W★
Wm.: b 11-21-1754 d *a.* 11- -1839 m Nancy (Cates) Basket Pvt NC

DURKEE,
Andrew: b 11-25-1737 d 11-17-1814 m Mary Benjamin Ens CT
Bartholomew: b 1-14-1739 d 1807 m Ruth Keyes Capt VT
Benjamin: b 10-18-1744 d 4-25-1829 m (1)Abagail — (2)Joanna Parkhurst Capt CT ★
Benjamin: b 8-18-1745 d 1-7-1812 m Susan Clark Pvt CT
Heman: b 6-17-1759 d 10-5-1797 m Susannah Rix Cpl VT
Jeremiah: b 1-21-1727 d 11-29-1775/6 m Abigail Adams Pvt CT
John: b 12-11-1728 d 5-29-1782 m Martha Wood Col CT
John: b 7-4-1762 d 5-2-1838 m (1)Sarah Holt (2)Polly Webber (3)Jemima Strong Pvt CT
John: b *c.* 1761 d *p.* 8-24-1832 m Elizabeth Freeman Pvt NH ★
Joseph: b 3-3-1733 d 7-29-1812 m Elizabeth Fish Capt CT
Nathan: b 9- -1754 d 2-3-1807 m Phebe Bliss Pvt NH W ★
Nathaniel: b 9-3-1757 d 8-5-1823 m (1)Lucy Bostwick (2)Catherine McRea (3)Mrs Melinda Bartlett Qm CT ★
Sabin: b 3-12-1733 d 1-24-1809 m Ruth H. Crocker MM CT
Solomon: b 1761 d 12-29-1833 m Phebe White Pvt CT ★
Timothy: b 5- -1737 d 3-22-1797 m Lucy Ann Smalley Pvt CS VT
Wm.: b 1710 d 1-15-1795 m Abigail — Pvt CT

DURLAND,
Charles: b 3-19-1731 d 12-17-1796 m Jane Swartout PS NY
Joseph: b 3-3-1762 d 8-28-1828 m (1)Martha Board (2)Sarah Satterly Sct NY

DURRELL, (includes DURELL)
Benjamin: b 1715-20 d 10- -1784 m Judith Perkins PS ME
Benjamin: b *c.* 1728 d 1-4-1820 m Mary Sillea Pvt MA ★
David: b 1747 d 5-9-1833 m (1)Mary Lord (2)Mary Lord (3)Judith (Knight) Wentworth Sgt MA
Eliphalet: b 1748 d 11-22-1825 m (1)Dorothy Bennett (2)Mrs Hannah (Batchelder) Teton 2Lt NH
John: b 3-7-1760 d 6-15-1820 m Mary Winchester Pvt MA
Peter: b 1719 d 1810 m Ruth Greenwood Fuller Pvt MA

DURRETT,
Francis: b *c.* 1750 d 1- -1823 m Elizabeth Tunis Pvt VA
James: b *c.* 1760 d 1822 m Nancy Diggs Pvt VA IL
Joel: b *c.* 1749 d *p.* 8-5-1813 m Sarah Chewning PS VA
Richard: b 1735 d 11-30-1820 m Elizabeth Davis Vol VA
William: b 7-28-1745 d 8-11-1813 m Elizabeth Hines Capt VA

DURST, (includes DUST)
John: b 3-12-1740 d 1-7-1807 m (1)Catherine — (2)Elizabeth Pritchard PS VA
Peter: b *c.* 1730 d 1802 m Magdalena Stardin Pvt PA

DURTHICK,
John Ephraim: b 9-9-1752 d 10-10-1832 m Mary Harris Pvt CT

DURYEA, (includes DURYEE)
Abraham: b 5-8-1743 d 3-24-1814 m (1)Eleanor Nagle (2)Sarah Van Pelt PS NY
Charles: b 1746 d 1804 m Hannah Nostrand MM PS NY
Frederick: b 4-18-1755/6 d 9-15-1832 m Charity Sutphen Pvt NJ
Gabriel: bpt 6-23-1750 d *p.* 2-20-1782 m Phebe Hoogland Ens NY
Garrett: b 1-22-1750 d 11-25-1825 m Kezia Tooker Ens NY
George: b 8-6-1747 d 12-19-1832 m Hannah Hudson Pvt PS NY
John: b 8-1-1752 d 10-2-1836 m Mary Lee Brinkerhoff Pvt NJ ★

DUSENBURY, (includes DUSENBERY)
Charles: b 5-18-1730 d 2-9-1809 m Sarah Conklin Pvt NY
Charles: b 3-29-1732 d 8-29-1837 m Margaret Odell Pvt NY
Henry: b 9-3-1760 d 4-12-1825 m Lydia Swayse Pvt NJ
Richard: b 8-30-1758 d 10-30-1830 m Fannie Dusenbury Pvt NY
Wm.: b 4-6-1757 d 3-23-1846 m (1)Elizabeth Compton (2)Catherine Van Bukirk Sgt PS NJ ★
William, Sr.: b 6-30-1739 d 7-2-1784 m Margaret Coe Pvt NY
William, Jr.: b 6-16-1762 d 7-27-1823 m Rebecca Snedeker Sgt NY
William: b 7-10-1760 d 6-18-1853 m Hetty — Pvt NY ★

DUSKIN,
Michael: b 10-27-1752 d 1-15-1816 m Mary Hendon Sol PS NC

DUSTIN, (includes DUSTON)
David: b 9-20-1762 d 4-7-1841 m Abiah Dustin Pvt MA
David: b *a.* 1740 d 8-15-1803 m (1)Lovey Homans (2)Lydia Kenniston Pvt NH
Eliphalet: b 4-9-1750 d 8-30-1833 m Jennet McCollum Cpl NH
Jesse: b 1747 d *p.* 1800 m Elizabeth Swan PS ME
John: b 3-31-1724 d 7-8-1797 m (1)Mary Webster (2)Abigail Kimball (3)Ruth Haseltine Pvt MA
John, Jr.: b 6-10-1754 d 4-29-1837 m Sarah Webster Pvt MA ★
John: b *c.* 1740 d *p.* 1-11-1791 m Mary Peaslee Pvt NH
Jonathan: b 7-4-1719 d 7-4-1812 m (1)Susanna Farnum (2)Ruth Perry MM MA
Jonathan, Jr.: b 1-5-1758 d 10-15-1844 m Aphia Vanalstine Pvt MA
Moody: b 1742 d 8-11-1810 m Alice Kingsbury Capt NH
Moses: b 11-21-1744 d 1-10-1795 m Mary Buck Capt NH
Nathaniel: b 12-25-1751 d 6-21-1803 m Sarah Wellman Pvt NH
Nathaniel: b 9-8-1756 d 3-3-1815 m Judith Knight Pvt NH
Paul: b 9-24-1721 d 1818 m (1)Betty Channon (2)Lydia Bradly Pvt NH
Peter: b 6-7-1746 d 7-23-1825 m Betsy Sawyer Ens NH
Timothy: bpt 4-14-1745 d 3-15-1813 m Eunice Nutting Pvt PS NH
William: b 1740 d 6-4-1818 m Rhoda Petee Lt NH

DUTCH,
John: bpt 11-15-1747 d 9-10-1812 m Mary Calef Capt MA
John: bpt 12-27-1747 d 8-27-1836 m Frances Jones 2Mte MA

DUTCHER,
Christopher: b 9-29-1746 d 7-13-1832 m Mary Belden Pvt NY
David: b 9-14-1740 d 3-2-1802 m Margaret Van Tine Pvt NY
Jacob: b 11-6-1726 d 10-11-1806 m Elizabeth Esselsteyn Pvt NY
John: b 1-5-1759 d 12-2-1848 m Sylvia Beardsley Pvt NY
Roelof, Jr.: b *c.* 1738 d 11-15-1803 m Jane (Ashley) Bull Capt CT
Solomon: b 6-30-1759 d 1847 m Tabitha Roraback Pvt NY MA ★
William, Sr.: b 1741 d 10-13-1794 m Catherine Conkling Capt NY

DUTTON,
Adam: b *c.* 1762 d *a.* 11-26-1833 m Catherine — Pvt VA
Amasa: b 1-28-1754 d 10-25-1842 m (1)Mary Rogers (2)Elizabeth (Bucknell) Wetmore Capt CT ★
Amos: b 10-13-1743 d 10-25-1788 m (1)Thankful Humiston (2)Sarah Turner Sgt CT
Asa: b 10-30-1755 d 9-21-1825 m Clarissa Fitch Sgt CT ★
Asa: b 3-18-1759 d 2-11-1836 m Polly Tarble Pvt MA VT ★
Benjamin: b 5-13-1754 d 10-19-1814 m Patte Cumings Pvt MA
David: b 4-17-1729 d *p.* 1790 m Hannah Whittaker Pvt MA
David: b 6-18-1749 d 3-10-1825 m Mary Higgins Pvt VT
Ephraim: b 8-30-1753 d 7-19-1840 m (1)Susanna Bixby (2)Esther Dutton Pvt MA ★
Francis: b *c.* 1745 d *c.* 1840 m (1)Hannah Talbot (2)Lydia Booth Pvt PA
George: b 6- -1755 d 1813 m Fidelia — PS MA
Isaac: b *c.* 1750 d 3-31-1795 m Elizabeth Lampley Pvt PA
Jacob: b 8-8-1751 d 11-8-1803 m Rhoda Dix Fif NH
James: b 1743 d 3-1-1839 m Lydia Kimbler Pvt PA
Jeremiah: b *.c* 1730 d 11-26-1795 m (1)Damaris Beebe (2)Mrs Mary Russell CT
John: b 11-11-1738 d 5-1-1818 m Susanna Ball Pvt NH
John: b 1-23-1730 d 8-27-1819 m Abigail Webster Pvt CT
Joseph: b 10-26-1760 d 2-6-1836 m (1)Hannah Webster (2)Mary Winchell Pvt CT ★
Kinsman: b 1762 d *p.* 1786 m Mary — Pvt PA
Moses: b 3-20-1763 d 1857 m Hannah Hitchcock Pvt CT
Notley: b *a.* 1734 d 1801 m — Pvt MD
Oliver: b 1-15-1759 d 3-8-1826 m Ruth Lankton Sgt CT ★
Oliver: b 3-11-1760 d 9-10-1843 m (1)Judith Hubbard (2)Mrs Phebe Powers Pvt MA CT ★
Philip: b *c.* 1750 d *a.* 9-30-1826 m Katherine — Pvt VA
Samuel: b 10-26-1746 d 1807 m Ruth Edwards Pvt MA
Samuel: b 3-14-1751 d 12-12-1826 m Mrs Rhoda Bacon Pvt MA
Samuel, Jr.: b 7-11-1743 d 11-21-1829 m Rebecca French Pvt VT
Samuel: b 2-3-1737 d 2-22-1813 m (1)Joanna Root (2)Rachel Benedict Pvt VT
Stephen: b 1759 d 6-25-1800 m Sally Tarble Pvt MA
Thomas, 2d.: b 1-31-1735 d 1-29-1806 m Anna Rice Roys 2Lt CT
Thomas, 3d.: b 3-21-1760 d 9-18-1835 m Thankful Penderson Cnt CT
Thomas: b 1-8-1748 d 12-31-1838 m (1)Sarah Bigelow (2)Betsey Smith Cpl NH ★
Thomas: b 8-28-1713 d 1794 m (1)Mary Hill (2)Sara Fitch PS VT
Timothy: b 2-7-1761 d 11-15-1837 m Lucy Langdon Pvt CT
Titus: b 1747 d 3-8-1832 m Elizabeth Scott Lt CT ★
Wm.: b 1759 d 1807 m Susanna Read Sgt MA

DUTY,
Mark: b *a.* 1750 d 1783/4 m Abigail Woodbury Pvt NH
Moses, Sr.: b *c.* 1710 d *a.* 1790 m Mary Palmer PS NH

DUVAL, (includes DE VALL, DEVOL, DEVOLL, DUELL, DU VAL, DU VALL, DUVALL)
Alexander: b 4-1-1755 d 6-7-1840 m Elizabeth Patterson CS MD
Benjamin: b 1760 d 1-17-1831 m — Sgt MD ★
Benjamin: b 1750 d 1820 m (1)Jemima Taylor (2)Mrs Sally Triplett PS MD

Benjamin: b 10-5-1752 d 1829 m Christiania — Lt RI
Charles: b 7-20-1729 d 1814 m (1)Rebecca Beckett (2)Cassia Brashear CS MD
Cornelius: b 2-23-1735 d 1806-10 m Keziah Duvall CS MD
Daniel: b 1-9-1747 d 1793 m Elizabeth Jennings Lt RI
Daniel: b 7-7-1756 d *p.* 1790 m Avis Jennings NCapt RI
Daniel: b *c.* 1750 d *p.* 8-30-1819 m Mary Polly Herring Capt VA
Daniel: b *c.* 1755 d 1795 m Maria Brooke LCol ADC VA W ★
David: b 10-17-1750 d 6- -1823 m Sarah Bowditch Pvt MA
Frederick Prussia Lewis: b *c.* 1755 d 1830 m Mary Ann Hyatt PS MD
Gilbert: b 11-17-1739 d 6-5-1824 m (1)Ruth Brown Holland (2)Anne Prentice Champlin Hatch CS RI
Jacob: b 1748/9 d — m — Taylor Ens MD
Jeremiah: b 8-24-1745 d 2-12-1832 m Sarah Penn PS MD
Jesse: b 4-4-1748 d 2-18-1814 m (1)— (2)Elizabeth Craycroft PS MD
John: b 2-20-1712 d *p.* 2-20-1790 m Anne Fowler Capt PS MD
John Pierce: b *c.* 1735 d 1803 m — PS VA
Jonathan: b 8-11-1711 d 1782 m (1)Priscilla Allen (2)Mary Sherman CS RI
Lewis: b 12-21-1721 d *p.* 8-6-1789 m Mrs Alice Brown Hardesty PS MD
Lewis: b 10-18-1745 d 1817 m Ann Welch Pvt MD
Mareen: b 1726 d 9-30-1807 m Mrs Sarah Miles PS MD
Marsh Mareen, 3d: b 4-17-1741 d *p.* 1794 m (1)Sarah Hall (2)Mrs Susannah Ijams Capt PS MD
Michael: b *c.* 1751 d *p.* 3-10-1809 m (1)Catharine — (2)Mrs Harriet Parsons Brown Sol SC
Samuel: b 12-24-1748 d 1-7-1821 m Priscilla Ann Dawson QM PS MD
Samuel: b 7- -1740 d 8- -1804 m Mary Higgins Pvt MD
Samuel: b 11-16-1752 d 7-22-1811 m Agnes — Pvt PS PA
Samuel: b 1-22-1714 d 2- -1784 m Lucy Claiborne PS VA
Samuel Sheperd: b *c.* 1750 d 1825 m (1)Margaret Binns (2)Anne Everard Bolling Maj VA
Stephen: b 7-25-1745 d 10-23-1803 m Rose Cook PS RI
Thomas: b 1739 d 8-5-1826 m Ann Ennis Pvt NJ
Wm.: b *c.* 1721 d 4-15-1777 m Priscilla Pruett Lt MD
Wm.: b 3-4-1728 d *p.* 1783 m Mehitable Tripp CS MA
Wm.: b 9-4-1748 d 1-3-1842 m (1)Ann Pope (2)Susan Brown Christian Lt PS VA ★
Wm.: b 1750 d 1807 m Sarah — Lt VA
Zachariah: b 2-10-1743/4 d *p.* 1790 m Zemima Selby Sol MD CL

DUYCKINCK,
Christopher: b 1740 d *p.* 1798 m Catherine Gautier PS NY
James: b 1-8-1741 d 9-24-1822 m Mary Taylor Pvt NJ

DWELLY, (includes DWELLE, DWELLEY)
Abner: b 1-10-1758 d 6-30-1826 m Miriam Martin Lt MA
Abner: b 3-6-1733 d 1803 m (1)Elizabeth Brown (2)Mrs Deborah House Pvt NY
Allen, Sr.: b 1758 d 4-17-1846 m Charity White Pvt MA ★
Jedediah: b 3-15-1737 d 1778 m Lydia Soule Sgt MA
Joshua: b 7-20-1735 d 3-15-1787 m Avis Ramsdell Lt MA

DWIGGINS,
Robert: b *c.* 1740-45 d *a.* 5- -1789 m Lydia — Of MD

DWIGHT,
Ebenezer: b 8-26-1738 d 5-15-1814 m Bethiah Truesdell CS MA
Elijah: b 1-24-1749 d 9-13-1795 m Diana Hinsdale Capt MA
Henry: b 2-18-1752 d 11-20-1819 m Ruth Rich Lt MA
Henry Williams: b 9-15-1757 d 9-15-1804 m Abigail Wells Pvt MA W★
Joseph, Jr.: b 1-23-1744 d 7- -1826 m Lydia Dewey Pvt MA
Nathaniel: b 6-20-1712 d 3-30-1784 m Hannah Lyman PS MA
Seth: b 5-24-1723 d 1-7-1777 m Joanna Kellogg PS CT
Simeon, Sr.: b 2-18-1719 d 2-21-1778 m Sibyl Dwight PS MA
Simeon, Jr.: b 9-13-1755 d 2-1-1815 m Anna Cutler Pvt MA
Timothy: b 5-14-1752 d 1-11-1817 m Mary Woolsey Chp CT
Wm.: b 9-20-1750 d 10-8-1824 m (1)Sarah Elliott (2)Gratia Barrett Cpl CT

DWINELL, (includes DUNNELLS, DWINNEL, DWINNELL, DWINNELLS,
Amos: b 8-26-1753 d 12-19-1777 m — Pvt MA
Archelaus: b 6-10-1754 d 3-21-1835 m Olive Hall Pvt MA
Bartholomew, Sr.: b 4-5-1728 d 11-21-1801 m Sarah Moulton Pvt MA
Benjamin: b 11-10-1726 d 7-29-1805 m Mary Estes Pvt MA
David: b 1762 d 11-23-1792 m Avis — Pvt MA ★
Ebenezer: b 1754 d 1-14-1834 m Hannah Allen Pvt VT
Henry: b 2-22-1762 d 10-17-1805 m Tamar Gale Pvt MA
Jacob: b 7-18-1746 d 8-20-1831 m Elizabeth Brooks Cpl MA
Jonathan: b 6-14-1751 d 7-29-1834 m Esther Wadsworth Pvt NH ★
Solomon: b 10-1-1757 d 7-26-1830 m Mrs Hannah Singletary Gould Pvt MA
Stephen: b 1745 d 1-10-1801 m Susanna Olim Pvt VT
Thomas: b 1711 d — m Hannah Towne Pvt MA
Thomas: b 1752 d 1838 m Sarah Hammond Pvt PS NH

DYASS, (includes DYESS)
Henry: b 1750-60 d *c.* 1835 m Winnifred Boyett Sol SC

DYCKMAN, (includes DEICHMAN, DIKEMAN)

Benjamin: b 1751 d 8-23-1833 m Martha Lent lLt NY
Frederick: b 8-26-1760 d 5-17-1848 m (1)Mrs Mabel Couch
  (Meeker) (4)Mrs Peters Pvt CT
Hezekiah: b 7-28-1763 d 1-13-1815 m Esther Scribner Pvt CT W ★
Jacobus: b 9-18-1748 d 8-20-1832 m Hannah Brown Pvt NY
John: b 5-3-1757 d p. 1790 m Leah Acker Pvt NY
John: b 8-28-1747 d 4-1-1814 m Elizabeth Simon Capt PA
Joseph: b 1737 d 1822 m (1)— Judd (2)Elizabeth Smith Capt NY
Wm., Jr.: b 12-9-1761 d 9-6-1846 m Maria Smith Pvt NY ★

DYE, (includes DEY)

Andrew: b 1744 d 7-15-1835 m (1)Sarah Miner (2)Mrs Ann Lamb
  Evans Capt PA
Avery: b 1753 d 1830-33 m Mary — Sol NC
Brown: b 1761 d a. 3-19-1825 m (2)Mary Martin Sol GA
Daniel: b 2-10-1744 d 7-10-1799 m Martha Nichols Sol CT
Enoch: b 1753 d 1-6-1830 m Rebecca Leet Pvt PA
John: b 5-17-1754 d 6-15-1822 m Anne Ely Pvt NJ
John: b 1753 d 4-23-1836 m Ruth — Pvt PA ★
John: b 10-23-1733 d p. 1800 m Thankful Potter PS RI
John: b c. 1733/34 d 12-27-1822 m Elizabeth — Pvt VA
Peter: b 1734-7 d 4-21-1811 m — Pvt NY

DYER, (includes DYRE)

Ambrose: b 1-29-1730 d 5-10-1792 m Mercy Paine PS MA
Amherst: b 7-10-1759 d 3-3-1840 m Cynthia Kingsley Pvt RI ★
Anthony: b 1-27-1743 d 2-2-1808 m Sarah Bishop Cpl RI W ★
Asa: b 7-26-1739 d 5-3-1831 m Ruth Whitmarsh Lt MA
Bela: b 11-19-1757 d 8- -1830 m Ruth Hunt Cpl MA
Benjamin, Jr.: b 1747 d 1815 m Anna Northway Pvt CT
Benjamin: b 4-1-1750 d 12-7-1833 m Jemima Blake Pvt MA
Brickford: b 11-13-1752 d 5-5-1828 m Dorothy Blake Pvt MA
Charles: b c. 1737 d p. 1790 m Mary Hazard Cpl RI
Charles: b 7-10-1753 d 10-27-1845 m Susannah Wright Capt RI ★
Charles: b 1755 d 9-3-1831 m Mary Hurst Sol VA
Christopher, Sr.: b 9-6-1731 d 10-31-1777 m Elizabeth Reed Lt MA
Christopher, Jr.: b 12-23-1764 d 5-9-1851 m Deborah Reed Pvt MA
Christopher: b 1730 d 5-15-1800 m Sarah Bassett Pvt MA
Daniel: b 1749 d 1814 m Sarah Northway Sgt CT
Ebenezer: b 8-26-1756 d 8-27-1839 m Mehitable Ensworth Tms CT
Edward: b 1729 d 9-12-1785 m (1)Elizabeth Fish (2)Temperance —
  Lt RI
Eliphalet: b 9-14-1721 d 5-12-1807 m Huldah Bowen BGen PS CT
Elisha: b 5-6-1763 d 7-21-1846 m Melvina Wheeler Pvt VA ★
Elkanah: b 1758 d 7- -1820 m Kathrine Brooks Pvt MA ★
Emanuel: b 8-25-1760 d 7- -1836 m Sophia — Fif Pvt PA ★
Ephraim: b c. 1758 d 7-26-1834 m Hannah Thorndyke Pvt MA ★
George: b 1753 d 1827 m Rachel Dalton Lt MD
George: b 12-26-1736 1-9-1817 m (1)Ann Nicholls (2)Amy Wait PS
  RI
Henry, Sr.: b 2-14-1716 d 4-28-1798 m Sarah Ridley PS MA
Henry, Jr.: b c. 1741 d p. 1800 m Betsy Simonton Capt MA
Henry: b 7-12-1759 d 1-2-1855 m Sarah Coy Pvt RI ★
Ichabod: b 12-15-1745 d p. 1790 m Molly Jones Pvt MA
Isaac H.: b 2- -1760 d 10-31-1843 m Mary Watson Pvt MA ★
James: b 4-23-1756 d 3-3-1835 m Mary Marcy Cpl MA ★
James: b 1-13-1752 d 10-1-1843 m Mercy Smalley Pvt MM MA ★
James: b 1-12-1721 d a. 1787 m Mary Marriner Pvt MA
James: b c. 1740 d 1804 m Ann — PS NC
James: b 1727/8 d a. 1802 m Elizabeth — Cpl PA
James: b 10-17-1730 d 6-12-1779 m Phebe — Pvt PA
James: b 1744 d 1807 m (1)Ann — (2)Jane Ralston (3)Nancy Hall
  CS Pvt PS VA
Jesse: b 9-4-1745 d 3-5-1791 m Relief Damon Pvt MA
John: b 2-27-1742 d 1795 m Sarah Haley 1Lt MA
John: b 5-7-1760 d p. 1836 m Marian Culp FifMaj MA ★
John: b 1733-37 d 1790/1 m Bathsheba Dunn Cpl RI
John: b c. 1740-5 d 9-17-1809 m Lucretia Farrington Pvt SC
Jonas: b 7-27-1755 d 3-14-1830 m Elizabeth Clarke Deake Sgt MA
Joseph: b 1762 d 1819 m Charlotte Pettibone Pvt CT
Joseph: b 3-17-1750 d 11-11-1848 m Eunice Holcomb Pvt MA ★
Joseph: b 1-20-1754 d 2-26-1835 m Christina Forster Lt PA
Judah: b 4-23-1729 d a. 4-10-1778 m Anna Harding Pvt MA
Paul: b 1760 d 4-11-1827 m Sarah Waterhouse Pvt MA ★
Roger: b 8-26-1755 d 6-30-1810 m Susannah Blizzard Capt VA
Samuel: b 1-2-1751 d c. 1818 m Elizabeth Griffith PS Pvt MD
Samuel: b 11-11-1724 d 11-2-1811 m Thankful Delano Pvt ME
Samuel: b 1757 d 4-4-1791 m Waity Eldred Capt RI
Samuel: b 10-8-1756 d 12-24-1837 m Celia Bickley PS VA ★
Stephen: b 1-10-1752 d 2-27-1847 m Sarah Mathewson Sgt RI ★
Thomas: b 11-22-1747 d 5-19-1808 m Elizabeth Ripley Col CT
Thomas: b 1728/29 d 1803 m Azubah Humphreys PS CT
Thomas: b 3-26-1734 d p. 1790 m Sarah Preston Pvt PA
Wm.: b c. 1738/9 d 1-27-1808 m (2)Anna Morrison Pvt PS NH

DYGERT, (includes DECHERT, DECKERT, DEICHERT, DYGART)

Henry: b 1725 d 1778 m Anna Margreta — Pvt NY
Henry: bpt 7-3-1744 d p. 1790 m Mary Cunningham Pvt NY
Jacob: b 1757 d 1842 m Mary Vance Pvt VA
Johannes: b — d 8-6-1777 m Dorothea Schumacher Capt PS NY
Nicholas: b 1-22-1760 d 3-31-1806 m Maria (Abeel) Radnour Lt NY

Peter: b 11-24-1759 d 1841 m Maria Snell Pvt NY ★
Peter: b 8-29-1736 d 12-9-1783 m Elizabeth — Maj PA
Peter H.: b 1751 d 1808 m Anna Saert Sgt NY
Peter S.: b c. 1740 d 1801 m (2)Sarah — Maj NY
Severance: b 11-23-1760 d 6- -1849 m Nancy Suits Pvt NY ★
Severinus P.: b c. 1737 d p. 5-8-1791 m Gertrude Ecker Pvt NY
Warner: b 1719 d 1780 m Magdalina Herkimer PS NY
Wm.: b 12-7-1750 d 6-26-1818 m Anna Boom Capt NY
Wm.: b 10-3-1723 d 5-26-1802 m (1)Maria Elizabeth Ecker
  (2)Margaret Cunningham Pvt NY
Wm.: b 7-8-1753 d 8-7-1791 m Agnes Thom Pvt NY

DYSART,

James: b 1727 d 2-1-1781 m Margaret — Sol NC
James: b 1744 d 5-26-1818 m Agnes Beattie Col VA
John: b 12-25-1749 d 9-10-1842 m (1)Martha Patton (2)Martha
  Woods Sgt NC ★

DYSON,

George, Sr.: b c. 1718 d 1- -1791 m X PS MD
John: b 1742 d 6-13-1828 m Elizabeth Davis 2Lt MA
Samuel: b 1743 d c. 1798 m Lydia Murphy PS MD

EADS,

Henry: b 1755 d 8-23-1843 m Sarah Elizabeth Sailors Pvt MD ★
John: b c. 1750 d p. 12-8-1800 m X Sol GA

EADY,

Henry: b 1749 d 1802 m — Barfield Sol SC

EAGER,

Bezaleel: b 12-22-1713 d 10-31-1787 m Persis Ward PS MA
Luke: b 12-8-1748 d 7-16-1807 m Vashti Walker Sgt MA
Micah: b 4-4-1700 d 12-30-1780 m Sarah Brigham Ens MA
Nahum: b 1-19-1739 d 1-15-1805 m Sarah Jennison LCol MA
Oliver: b 5-10-1758 d 11-6-1835 m Seraphina Martyn Pvt MA
Paul: b 4-13-1740 d — m Jane Forbes Sgt MA
Uriah, Sr.: b 4-4-1700 d 12-30-1780 m (1)Sarah Brigham (2)Rebec-
  ca Rice CS MA
Uriah, Jr.: b 2-5-1740 d 9-30-1813 m Triphosa Bush Ens MA
Wm.: b 1728 d 4-15-1813 m (1)Miriam Butler (2)Ann Bull PS NY

EAGON,

James: b c. 1740 d 1821 m Mary — Pvt PA

EAKER,

George: b 1743 d 1-10-1818 m Mary Kennedy Pvt PA

EAKIN,

Samuel: b a. 1760 d p. 1783 m — Wilson Sgt VA

EAMES, (includes EMES)

Alexander: b 4-11-1761 d 1-16-1845 m Beriah Marshall Sol MA
Calvin: b 2-26-1762 d 1812 m Martha Drury Pvt MA
Daniel: b 4-8-1740 d 6-22-1812 m Mary Cutler Capt MA
Ebenezer: b 4-26-1756 d p. 1797 m Elizabeth Coolidge Pvt MA
Ezra: bpt 9-7-1746 d 9-3-1833 m (1)Sarah Jones (2)Hannah
  Twitchell Capt MA
Henry: b 5-6-1751 d 1-21-1829 m Azubah Haven Sol MA
Jacob: b 8-10-1723 d 11-4-1783 m Rachel Wyman Pvt MA
Jacob: b 3-10-1754 d 11-7-1851 m (1)Jenett McKeen (2)Miriam
  Nickerson Parsons (3)Mary E. Hartson Pvt MA
Jacob, Jr.: b 5-26-1762 d 12-3-1839 m Lucy Jones Pvt MA
James: b 5-26-1763 d 9-10-1849 m Ruth Felch Pvt MA
James: b 9-20-1762 d 1-20-1845 m Jerusha Newton Sol MA
Jeremiah, Sr.: b 5-17-1735 d 4-22-1817 m Susanna Peabody Capt
  NH
Jeremiah, Jr.: b 6-30-1762 d 1-5-1828 m Anne Williams Pvt NH
Jesse: b 7-25-1739 d 5-7-1829 m (1)Bette Bent (2)Dorothy (Child)
  Brown (3)Mrs Fanny Parminter Capt MA
John: b 10-30-1743 d 3-13-1832 m (1)Anne Bent (2)Mrs Mercy
  Fuller (3)Sally Kingsbury Lt MA
John: b 12-15-1742 d 4-18-1806 m Ruth Stone Lt MA
John: b 2-19-1727 d 5-24-1804 m (1)Mary Jaquith (2)Hannah
  Cornell Pvt MA
John, Jr.: b 10-25-1746 d 9-7-1819 m Azubah Tidd Pvt MA
Jonathan: b 3-13-1755 d p. 1790 m Olive Young Pvt MA
Jonathan: b 6-11-1761 d 7-2-1840 m X MM Pvt Bbd MA
Joseph: b 9-9-1720 d c. 1795 m Susannah Pike Pvt PS MA
Jotham: bpt 1-25-1756 d 2-21-1841 m Eusebia Goodard Pvt MA
Justus: b 1744 d p. 1818 m (1)Judith Arey (2)Widow Orr Sol PS MA
Nathan: b 11-28-1768 d 9-28-1818 m Susanna Harnden Sol MA
Nathaniel, Sr.: b 4-18-1703 d 3-13-1796 m Rachel Lovell MM MA
Nathaniel, Jr.: b 9-11-1747 d 9-8-1820 m Katherine Rice Pvt MA
Reuben: b 4-10-1743 d 5-16-1818 m (1)Elizabeth Whipple (2)Jane
  Kendall 1Lt MA
Robert: b 3-4-1749 d 7-2-1828 m (1)Jerusha Willis (2)Sarah Adams
  Sgt MA
Timothy: b 11-23-1732 d 9-3-1797 m Hannah Hill Pvt MA

EAN,
Abraham: b 1741 d 6-7-1806 m Catharine VanWagenen Pvt NY

EANES,
Edward: b 5-1-1761 d 1846-8 m Jane Sublett Pvt VA
Josiah: b 6-13-1733 d 1777 m X Pvt VA PA

EARGOOD,
Jacob: b 1745 d 7- -1814 m Anna Retge Pvt PS PA

EARHART, (includes EARHEART)
Jacob: b 1739 d *p.* 9-7-1829 m Catherine — Pvt PA
Jacob: b 1763 d *p.* 1813 m (2)Annie Orum Pvt PA
John: b *c.* 1732 d *p.* 1790 m Polly — Pvt PA

EARING,
Samuel: b 10-19-1750 d 8-4-1836 m Sara Ostrander Pvt NY

EARLE, (includes EARL, EARLL)
Baylis: b 8-5-1734 d 1-6-1825 m Mary Prince PS Cav SC
Christopher: b 5-8-1750 d *p.* 1790 m Mary (Palmer) Earle Drm MA
Daniel: b *c.* 1730 d 3-29-1817 m Mehitable Watson Pvt MA
David: b 7-15-1748 d 11-11-1841 m Martha Earle Pvt NH
David: b 7-1-1756 d 7-10-1808 m Mary Ogden Pvt NJ
Edward: b 6-19-1760 d 6-21-1817 m Phebe Gardner Pvt NJ
Ezaias: b 1758 d 10-30-1826 m Sarah Brownley Maj VA
Ezra: b 1753 d 1806 m Mary Sabin Pvt NY
George, Sr.: b 3-3-1735 d 7-2-1806 m Mary Rice Baker Capt PS VT
George: b 10-11-1759 d 6-23-1847 m Elizabeth Young Pvt VT
Jacob: b 3-8-1747 d 1791 m Relief Bennett Pvt MA
James: b 4-10-1757 d 1-28-1829 m Deborah Sargent Pvt MA
John: b 5-16-1746 d 5-10-1803 m Rebecca Page Pvt MA
John: b 1-3-1723 d 4-24-1799 m Joanna Howard PS NJ
John: b 10-25-1758 d 10- -1813 m (1)Abigail Smith (2)Abigail Haines Cpl NJ
John: b *c.* 1720 d *a.* 8-31-1786 m Rachel — PS NY
John: b 3-16-1738/9 d 5-20-1816 m Dorcas Barney Mstr RI
John: b 6-5-1737 d 11-24-1815 m (1)Thomasine Prince (2)Rebecca Berry Woods Capt SC
John Baylis: b 10-23-1766 d 2-3-1836 m (1)Sarah Taylor (2)Mrs Ann Douglas Sol SC
Jonathan: b 1753 d *p.* 10-9-1832 m Susannah Sheldon Pvt NY ★
Joseph: b 8- -1758 d 3-2-1850 m Sophia — Sgt NY ★
Marmaduke: b 3-8-1749 d 5-29-1839 m Elizabeth Newton Pvt MA
Morris: bpt 4-10-1757 d 3-22-1833 m Elizabeth Terhune Pvt NJ
Oliver: b 3-21-1745 d 7-31-1819 m Mary (Earle) Pvt MA
Peter: b 1748 d 1819 m (1)Elizabeth Bull (2)Lois Clark PS NY
Ralph, Sr.: b 11-13-1726 d *c.* 1808 m Phoebe Whittemore Capt MA
Ralph, Jr.: b 1751 d 1801 m (1)Sarah Gates (2)Ann Whitesides Pvt MA
Reuben: b 5-8-1747 d 1822 m Mary Harrington Pvt MA
Richard Tilghman: b 2-10-1728 d 3- -1788 m Anne Chamberlain Col PS MD
Robert: b 9-4-1757 d 1833 m Mary Cory Maj MA
Robert: b 1759 d 11-25-1833 m Elizabeth Hodge Pvt MA
Samuel: b 11-28-1760 d 11-24-1833 m Harriet Harrison Capt SC
Samuel: b 1-10-1760 d 9-12-1845 m Tabitha Williams OrdlSgt VA ★
Stephen: b 5-4-1754 d 5-28-1834 m Priscilla Hicks Capt MA
Thaddeus: b 4-29-1754 d 11-26-1779 m Dorothy Shaw Pvt MA
Thomas: b 1762 d 2-15-1844 m Rhoda Busick Mil MD
Thomas: b 8-27-1737 d 3-21-1819 m Hannah Southgate Wait PS MA
William, Jr.: b 1763 d 4-3-1844 m Charity Barrett Pvt NY
William: b 1765-8 d 1819 m Sarah Redman Pvt PA
William: b 1758 d 1809 m Mary Margaret — Sol VA

EARLY, (includes EARLEY)
Absalom: b *c.* 1755 d *p.* 1790 m Rachel Williams Pvt NY
Daniel: b — d *p.* 1784 m — Allison Pvt PA
Jacob: b *c.* 1742 d *p.* 1-16-1793 m Elizabeth Robertson Capt VA
James: b *c.* 1750 d 10-11-1822 m Elizabeth Thompson Ens VA
James M.: b 1762/3 d 1807 m Jane Gatewood Pvt VA
Jeremiah, Sr.: b 12-9-1705 d 1787 m Elizabeth Buford PS VA
Jeremiah, Jr.: b 1730 d 1779 m (1)Sarah Anderson (2)Mary Stith Col VA
Joel: b 1745 d *p.* 1794 m X Lt VA
John: b 7-31-1757 d 3- -1811 m Margaret Deininger Pvt PA
Joseph: b *c.* 1740 d 1783 m Jame Paschal Lt VA
Joshua: b 6-13-1738 d 12-1-1812 m Mary Leftwich PS VA
Samuel: b 1735 d 1778 m Alice Jefferies Cpl CL
William: b *c.* 1750 d 1835 m Eve Thomas Pvt VA

EARNEST, (includes ERNEST, ERNST)
Baltzer: b 1744 d 1807 m X Artl Arfr PA CL
Christopher: b 8-23-1748 d 1- -1818 m Anna Margaretta Sichele Pvt PA
Felix: b 9-20-1762 d 2-16-1842 m (1)Sarah North (2)Sarah Oliphant Ens NC ★
George: b 5-20-1762 d 12-31-1840 m Catherine White Pvt VA
Henry: b 1732 d 3-6-1809 m Mary Stephens CS NC
John: b 1752 d 1810 m Elizabeth Kroll Cpl PA
John: b 1723 d 1796 m Catherine — Sol PA
John Frederick: b 4-16-1748 d 10-24-1805 m Maria Clara Peiser Adj PA

EARNHART, (includes EHRENHARDT)
George: b *c.* 1737 d 1823-26 m X CS NC
Philip: b — d *p.* 2-4-1797 m Elizabeth — PS CS NC

EARP(includes HARP)
Joshua: b *c.* 1760 d *p.* 9-30-1811 Eleanor McKinsey PS MD
Josiah: b 3-10-1761 d 11-25-1844 m X Pvt MD
Philip: b 1755 d *p.* 1787 m X Pvt MD
William: b 1729 d *p.* 1778 m X PS MD

EASLAND,
John: b 3-11-1756 d 8-6-1847 m (1)Rachel Hopkins Brasie (2)Sally Webb Pvt MA ★

EASLEY,
Daniel: b 1754 d *p.* 9-13-1832 m Betsy Stevens Pvt VA ★
Daniel, Sr.: b *c.* 1720 d *a.* 1-19-1786 m (1)Ann David (2)Elizabeth Echols Pvt VA
John: b *c.* 1759 d *c.* 1781/82 m Sallie Mann PS VA
Robert: b 5-12-1754 d 12-5-1814 m (1)Wineyfield Dixon (2)Ann — PS VA
Stephen, Sr.: b *c.* 1725 d 1800 m Mary Ann David Burton PS VA
Thomas: b 11-23-1756 d 11-21-1842 m Ecleo Wade Sol TN
William, Jr.: b *c.* 1727 d *a.* 5-19-1796 m Jane Scruggs PS VA

EASON,
Abner, Jr.: b 1749 d 1819 m Martha Tart Pvt NC
Jacob: b *c.* 1760 d *p.* 1830 m X Pvt NC
John: b *a.* 1759 d 12-31-1799 m Mary — Sgt SC

EAST,
Benjamin: b *c.* 1750 d *p.* 1803 m Nancy Pruit Sol VA
George: b 1746 d 1818 m Elizabeth — Pvt MA
James: b 8-10-1753 d 10-4-1844 m Martha Clarkson Pvt VA
John Christopher: b 7-25-1754 d *p.* 11-12-1820 m (2)Mrs Maryann Wagner Pvt PA
Southey: b 1755 d 1819 m Betsey Anderson Pvt VA
Thomas: b *c.* 1740 d 1797 m Obedience — PS VA

EASTBURN,
Benjamin: b 1743 d 8-17-1784 m Jane Robinson Lt PS MD
Benjamin: b 1751 d 11-20-1794 m Margaret Abraham Capt PS PA
Robert: b 2-7-1710 d 1-22-1778 m Agnes Jones PS PA
Thomas: b 2-11-1739 d 1802 m Jane Smedley Pvt PA
W. Benjamin: b 1751 d 11-20-1794 m Margaret Abraham Capt PA

EASTER,
James: b *c.* 1730 d 1791/2 m Sarah — Sol GA
John: b 1-17-1760 d *p.* 11-26-1832 m Margaret Thomas Pvt MD ★
Michael: b *c.* 1760 d *p.* 4-15-1821 m Barbara Essigs Pvt NC

EASTERLING, (includes ESTERLING)
Henry: b 5-24-1733 d *p.* 1791 m Ellen Bennett PS SC
James: b 1760-2 d *p.* 1839 m Millie — Sol SC
Wm.: b 3-10-1757 d 1835 m Elizabeth Sands Covington Pvt SC

EASTERLY,(includes ESTERLY)
Daniel: b 8-27-1758 d 9-27-1822 m Susanna Heckler Pvt PA
Jacob: b *a.* 1750 d 1791 m Elizabeth — Pvt PA
Jacob: b 12-17-1753 d 10-12-1826 m (1)Catherine Rosanna Ried (2)Mrs Eva Price Pvt PA

EASTHAM,
George: b 2-12-1758 d 10-1-1818 m (1)Susan Woodside (2)Mrs Mary Brown Sol VA
Wm.: b *c.* 1733 d 2-8-1811 m Frances Bryd PS VA

EASTIN,
Philip: b 1755 d 1817 m Sarah Hite Smith 1Lt VA
Stephen: b 1-9-1756 d 9-15-1815 m Susannah Johnson Pvt VA

EASTLAND,
Thomas: b 1739 d 1815 m Lucy Towles PS SC
William: b — d *a.* 1-27-1813 m Elizabeth — 2Lt VA

EASTMAN,
Abiathar: b 4-29-1745 d 1-10-1815 m Phebe Merrill PS NH
Amos, Jr.: b 1743/5 d 7-8-1832 m Ruth Flagg Pvt NH
Azariah: b 8-5-1746 d 5-27-1818 m Sarah Booth MM CT
Benjamin: b 1- -1719 d 4-1-1814 m (1)Mary Hitchcock (2)Ruth — Pvt VT
Clark: b 9-30-1763 d — m Mary Conant Mus CT
Cyprain: b 1749 d 5-23-1798 m Rosamond Nelson Sgt VT ★
Daniel: b 1757 d 1847 m Annie Alley Pvt MA
Daniel: b 4-21-1766 d 1-16-1844 m Sarah Whiting Pvt MA
Deliverance: b 9-12-1761 d *p.* 10-22-1832 m Rebecca Minor Pvt CT ★
Ebenezer: b 5-31-1749 d 11-7-1820 m Mary Dickinson Cpl MA
Ebenezer: b 4-24-1746 d 10-27-1794 m Mary Butler Lt PS NH
Ebenezer: b 2-2-1746 d 9-14-1810 m Abigail Barker Ens NH
Ebenezer: b 6-23-1758 d 5-31-1828 m Susannah Wheeler Sgt NH ★
Edmund: b 1766 d 12-9-1812 m Hannah Carter Sgt NH W★

EASTMAN, contd.

Edward: b 2-25-1732 d 4-12-1814 m Anna Judkins Cpl PS NH
Eli: b 4-29-1749 d 6-4-1837 m Rebecca Sears Pvt OrdlSgt CT VT ★
Eliphalet: b bpt 6-7-1752 d 7-2-1821 m X CS CT
Enoch: b 6-6-1725 d — m Rebecca Abbott Pvt NH
Enoch: b 4-24-1748 d 6-23-1829 m Sarah Rising Capt VT
Ichabod: b 5-22-1749 d 9-3-1825 m Mary Whittle Pvt NH
Isaac: b 10-30-1754 d 7-8-1792 m Hannah George Pvt NH
Jacob: b 1762 d 6-23-1855 m Mary Spalding Drm NH
Jacob: b 7-9-1763 d 6-1-1850 m Abigail Kimball Pvt NH
James: b 9-24-1753 d 1-7-1853 m Mary Searles Pvt NH
Jeremiah: b 4-1-1750 d 5-30-1828 m Edner Poor Pvt MA
Jeremiah: b 11-28-1732 d 1802 m Anna Quimby Pvt PS NH
John: b 5-7-1751 d 5-6-1829 m Hepzibah Keyes Pvt MA
John: b 5-11-1739 d 1777 m Judith — Pvt NH ★
John: b 3-4-1759 d 10-18-1838 m Sybil Chamberlain Pvt NH
Jonathan: b 9-17-1746 d 2-19-1827 m Esther Morgan Cpl NH
Jonathan: b 6-3-1724 d p. 1787 m Elizabeth Pearse Pvt NH
Jonathan: b 1759 d 7-5-1829 m Phebe Leach Pvt NH
Jonathan: b 6-10-1746 d 10-19-1834 m (1)Molly Chandler (2)Esther Johnson Pvt NH
Jonathan: b 1717 d 2-26-1807 m Elizabeth Wood Pvt VT
Jonathan: b 1752 d 12-16-1816 m (1)Ruth Davis (2)Ruth Dean Pvt VT
Joseph, Sr.: b 9- -1724 d 9-2-1802 m Phebe Hendricks Pvt CT
Joseph: b 2-1-1715 d 10-29-1790 m Sarah Ingram Pvt MA
Joseph, Jr.: b 1760 d 3- -1844 m (1)Hannah Martin Warner (2)Elizabeth Paddock Pvt CT ★
Joseph: b 7-17-1700 d p. 1790 m (2)Dorothy Lindsay Quimby PS NH
Joseph: b 10- -1715 d 1803 m Abigail Mellen PS NH
Joseph: b 5-26-1720 d 1815 m (1)Elizabeth Jackman (2)Abigail Eastman PS NH
Moses: b 2-28-1732 d 4-14-1812 m Elizabeth Kimball 2Lt PS NH
Moses: b 3-3-1745 d 1796 m Lucretia Tyler Pvt PS NH
Nathaniel, Sr.: b 3-10-1717 d p. 1782 m Phoebe Chandler Sol NH
Nathaniel, Jr.: b 10-9-1755 d 5-7-1839 m Ruth Bradley Vol NH
Noah: b 3-20-1753 d 8-26-1823 m Hannah Hall PS NH
Obadiah: b 4-27-1747 d 1-10-1812 m Mehitable Merrill Cpl NH
Obadiah: b 1-26-1747 d 11-14-1836 m Elizabeth Searle Pvt NH ★
Oliver: b c. 1760 d p. 1820 m Cynthia Hewett Pvt VT
Peter: b 7-22-1746 d 12-29-1829 m (1)Sarah Pierpont (2)Mary Trumbull (3)Abigail Hill Drm Sgt CT
Peter: b 4-20-1710 d 4-6-1794 m Elizabeth Herrimon CS NH
Richard, Sr.: b 8-9-1712 d 12-27-1807 m (1)Molly Lovejoy (2)Sarah (Abbott) Abbott PS NH
Richard, Jr.: b 5-14-1749 d 12-6-1826 m (1)Abiah Hold (2)Mrs Susannah Durgin Pvt NH
Samuel: b 1756 d 1-5-1829 m Mary Tucker Pvt NH
Samuel: b 10-16-1746 d 3-2-1841 m Sarah Currier Pvt NH
Stephen: b 6-23-1755 d 4-25-1819 m Jerusha Jones Pvt Sgt VT
Stilson: b 1-7-1738 d 1837 m Mehitable Hutchins Pvt NH
Thomas: b 12-27-1756 d 1838 m Lydia Holmes Pvt NH ★
Thomas: b 10-11-1740 d 10-17-1828 m Sara Ann Sargent Pvt PS NH
Tilton: b 1741 d 1805 m (1)Polly Owen (2)Remembrance Rowlee Pvt NY
Timothy: b 4-24-1744 d 5-21-1830 m Susannah Curtis Pvt CT
Timothy: b 1733 d 3-29-1820 m Hannah Richardson PS Pvt NH
William: b 2-12-1758 d p. 1801 m Phebe Elliott Pvt NH
William: b 3-9-1719 d p. 1792 m Abigail Harriman CS NH
Wm.: b 10-3-1715 d p. 1803 m (1)Ruth Chase (2)Rebecca Jewett PS NH
William: b 6-13-1734 d 5-3-1807 m Mary Bean PS NH

EASTON,

Ahimaz, Sr.: b 9-19-1739 d 5-20-1795 m Mary Phelps Pvt Cpl PS MA
Ahimaz, Jr.: b 8-11-1765 d 12-14-1817 m Mariah VanBuren Pvt CT
Ashbel: b 9-15-1757 d 10-9-1836 m (1)Sarah Arnold (2)Deidama — Arfr CL ★
Elijah: b 7-14-1736 d p. 1777 m Abigail Noble Pvt CT
Eliphalet: b — d 7-22-1816 m Mary Easton Fif CT
George: b a. 1764 d p. 1810 m Margaret Hutton Pvt NY
Giles: b 4-22-1763 d 6-28-1829 m Anna Haskins Artl Arfr CL
James: bpt 6-9-1728 d 1796 m (1)Rachel Seymour (2)Eunice Pomeroy Col MA
Job: b 12-23-1738 d 6-6-1819 m Susannah Gerrauld PS RI
Johnston: b c. 1745 d 1783-86 m Mary — Ens VA
Normand: b 6-25-1758 d 5-12-1806 m Merab Perry Pvt CT
Samuel: b 5-1-1761 d 5-22-1800 m Ann Dennison Sgt CT
Silas: b c. 1745 d 3-10-1829 m Susannah Pratt Pvt CT

EASTWICK,

John: b c. 1752 d 2-17-1837 m Sarah Smith Pvt PA ★

EASTWOOD,

John: b 9-10-1761 d 12-27-1837 m (1)Elizabeth Brott (2)Hannah Hayes Pvt NY

EATHFORTH,

Samuel: b 1-25-1756 d 4-10-1843 m Elizabeth Clark Pvt RI

EATON,

Aaron: b 3-18-1737 d 5-25-1815 m (1)Lydia Barber (2) Abigail (Alden) Converse Ens CT
Aaron: b 6-12-1763 d 6-27-1816 m Tryphena — Pvt CT
Abel: b 10-9-1754 d 10-15-1812 m Azuba Hurd Cpl NY
Abijah: b 8-16-1759 d 12-23-1833 m Elizabeth Poore Pvt MA ★
Abram: b 1-6-1755 d 5-20-1842 m Mary Barrett Pvt MA ★
Alexander: b 1762/3 d 12-27-1832 m Edna Preston Pvt NH W★
Amos: b 10-18-1751 d 9-11-1811 m (1)Mary Gage (2)Anne Ordway Pvt MA
Benjamin, Sr.: b 10-9-1723 d p. 1790 m Beulah (Fiske) Stone PS MA
Benjamin, Jr.: b 7-27-1754 d 10-20-1800 m Mary Stacy Pvt MA
Benjamin: b 3-4-1762 d 5-24-1839 m Lydia Ireland Pvt MA ★
Brigham: b 8-1-1753 d 4-8-1828 m Anna Eaton Sgt MA ★
Charles Rust: b c. 1743 d 1822 m Elizabeth Jeffreys LCol PS NC
Cyril: b 12-16-1767 d 1-15-1848 m (1)Ruth Willes (2)Alissa — Pvt CT ★
Daniel: b 2-23-1762 d 1-11-1848 m Nancy Charter Pvt CT ★
David: b 3-27-1738 d 5-16-1804 m Elenor Clement CS MA
David: b 8-4-1738 d p. 1790 m (1)Mary Preston (2)Abigail Curtis Sgt NH
David: b c. 1735 d p. 1793 m (1)Mary (Eaton) (2)Elizabeth Razor (?) Pvt PA
Ebenezer, Sr.: b 2-15-1734 d 1815 m Mary Humphrey Sgt CT
Ebenezer, Jr.: b 12-18-1760 d 12-10-1839 m Polly Berry Pvt CT
Ebenezer: b 3-29-1744 d a. 4-20-1800 m ( )Sarah — ( )Elizabeth (Janna)(Hutchinson) Richardson Pvt MA
Ebenezer: b 5-12-1750 d 3-25-1842 m Rebecca Stone Pvt MA ★
Ebenezer: b 4-10-1735 d 8-27-1805 m Ann Brown Cpl NH
Eliab: b 5-2-1763 d 5-3-1843 m Lucretia Flint Pvt MA
Elijah: b 9-20-1742 d 3-3-1805 m Deliverance Mott Pvt CT NY
Elijah: b 11-7-1741 d 1-20-1831 m Sarah Shaw Pvt MA
Enoch: b 11-6-1745 d p. 1780 m Esther Williams: Pvt NH
Ephraim: b 1745 d 1826 m (2)Sarah Stevens CS NH
Henry: b 4-7-1750 d 1782 m Violet Wallace Pvt PA
Isaiah: b 10-15-1757 d 1-21-1847 m Priscilla West Pvt MA
Israel: b 6-9-1760 d 3-19-1833 m (1)Eunice Richmond (2)Keziah Sears Pvt MA ★
Ithmar: b 3-13-1743 d 11-11-1817 m Mary Ordway Ens NH
Jabez: b 1-29-1731 d p. 11-21-1783 m Elizabeth Williams Pvt MA
Jacob: b 4-8-1741 d 11-18-1791 m Elizabeth Thorn PS ME
Jacob, Sr.: b c. 1735 d p. 1800 m Hester Colby PS CS NH
Jacob, Jr.: bpt 3-11-1757 d c. 1816 m Mary Dudley Pvt NH
Jacob: b 2-14-1728 d p. 1790 m Jane Robinson Sol PS NY
James: b 11-6-1733 d 5-16-1775 m . Lois Damon Sol MA
James: b 1-20-1751/2 d 1806 m Sarah Masury Pvt MA
James: b 5-23-1731 d 3-14-1795 m X Sgt NH
James: b 1753 d 10-16-1849 m (1)Martha McClure (2)Sarah (George) White Sgt NH
James: b 5-23-1738 d 6-29-1809 m Abigail Emerson Pvt PS NH
Jeremiah: b 4-25-1738 d 7-17-1792 m (1)Lydia Flint (2)Hannah Wardell Pvt MA
Jesse: b 10-29-1749 d 12-22-1808 m Sarah Worthen Pvt NH
Joel: b 7-27-1751 d 10-19-1851 m Lucy Leonard Pvt MA
John: b 8-20-1745 d 2-13-1817 m Elizabeth George Pvt NH
John: b 8-12-1737 d 7-22-1795 m Patience Shelby Pvt MA
John: b 7-30-1740 d 5-28-1816 m Olive Conant Pvt MA
John: b 1743 d 11-24-1827 m Mary Larkin Pvt MA
John, Sr.: b 5-13-1724 d 9-19-1788 m Hannah Johnson CS MA
John, Jr.: b 2-14-1761 d 12-11-1835 m Mehitable Richardson Pvt MA & NY ★
John: b 7-14-1765 d 1-19-1844 m Phoebe Brockway Pvt NH ★
John, Sr.: b 1727 d 1786 m Sarah — 1Lt PA
John, Jr.: b 1745 d 1783 m Anne Chattel Pvt PA
John Eliot: b 2-9-1756 d 10-12-1812 m Elizabeth Davis SrgnMte NS
Joseph: b 3-12-1716/7 d 7-9-1785 m Lucy Bacon Capt CT
Joseph: b 2-27-1730 d 2-19-1805 m Sarah Webster Capt MA
Joseph: b 1750 d 2-1-1825 m Mary Girdles PS MA
Joseph, Sr.: b 5-10-1730 d 1805 m (1)Elizabeth — (2)Sarah Smith Pvt MA
Joseph: b 1758 d 1840 m Elizabeth George Pvt NH
Joseph: b 11-18-1746 d c. 1835 m Rachel Greenwood Pvt NC ★
Joseph: b 3-18-1756 d 12-15-1832 m Jeanet Ramsay Pvt PA ★
Lemuel: b 2-26-1758 d 10-11-1843 m Sarah Ware Pvt MA
Levi: b 11-6-1757 d 5-13-1834 m (2)Phoebe Walton Pvt NH ★
Lille, Sr.: b 8-3-1738 d 1-6-1812 m Sarah Emerson Pvt MA
Luther: b 9-15-1762 d 7- -1828 m Rebecca Bennett Pvt CT
Luther: b 4-3-1757/8 d 11-9-1828 m Sarah Rice Pvt CT ★
Luther: b 9-15-1762 d 7-4-1848 m Nellie Drury Fif MA
Nathan: b 8-29-1755 d 6-1-1840 m Phoebe Brooks Pvt CT
Nathan: b 12-25-1748 d 3-12-1817 m Lydia Lynde Lt MA
Nathaniel: b 5-5-1743 d 12-29-1796 m Rebecca Dodge Lt. MA
Nathaniel: b 7- -1761 d 1823 m (1)Mary Kent (2)Susannah Hanchett Pvt MA ★
Noah, Sr.: b 7-22-1708 d 10-8-1791 m Hannah Vinton Sgt MA
Noah, Jr.: b 8-7-1733 d 6-12-1814 m Hannah Hunt Sgt PS MA
Noah: b 3-9-1728 d 4-10-1796 m Deborah Wyman Pvt MA
Obadiah: b 4-22-1747 d 4-22-1800 m Betsey Paige Pvt NH
Origen: b 5-8-1765 d 9-22-1839 m (1)Sophia Reed (2)Mrs Ellsworth MA ★
Paul: b 1740 d 1830 m Hannah Emerson Pvt NY
Pearson: b 8-6-1725 d p. 12-3-1781 m Ann Bryant Pvt MA
Peter: b 3-25-1748 d 7-30-1784 m Abigail Greeley Pvt MA

Reuben: b 11-22-1748 d 11-17-1813 m Abigail Lovell Pvt MA
Samuel: b 11-10-1721 d p. 1790 m Millicent Wheeler Sgt MA
Samuel, Sr.: b 4-20-1737 d 3-8-1811 m Mollie Merrill Cpl MA
Samuel: b 12-30-1756 d 3-7-1826 m Lydia Ladd Pvt NH
Samuel: b 7-5-1759 d 3-20-1843 m Alice Hadley Pvt NH
Samuel Phillips: b 1-19-1753 d 2-25-1829 m Sarah Evans Cpl MA W★
Seth: b 4-6-1739 d 2-20-1823 m Bethia — Pvt MA
Silas, Sr.: b 12-1-1750 d 7-18-1828 m Mary Nichols Pvt MA
Solomon: b 1757 d 9-17-1843 m (1)Elizabeth Delano (2)Phebe Carpenter Sgt CT ★
Stephen: b 5-4-1761 d 10-28-1838 m (1)Fannela Knowlton (2)Harmony Knowlton Pvt CT
Stephen: b 1759/60 d 2-23-1819 m Lucy Chaffee Pvt CT
Sylvanus: b 1756 d 1845 m Abigail Jackman Pvt MA
Sylvanus: b 1758 d 1807 m Sarah Goodrich Pvt NY
Thomas: b 5-25-1739 d 8-25-1788 m Susan Rice Pvt MA
Thomas: b 1748 d p. 1790 m Abigail Bancroft Pvt MA
Thomas: b 12-30-1743 d 12-4-1829 m Joanna Flint CS MA
Thomas: b — d p. 6-30-1807 m X Col PS NC
Timothy, Sr.: b 7-31-1731 d 10-14-1811 m (1)Abagale Massey (2)Mrs Mary Coburn Capt PS MA
Timothy: b 2-12-1734 d 1822 m Mehitable Barknap Pvt MA
Uriah: b 5-17-1755 d 7-13-1835 m Eunice Rebecca Corey Pvt MA ★
William: b 2-23-1764 d 6-1-1811 m Eliza (Sykes) Danielson Pvt CT
William: b 1720 d 1800 m Meribah Ruth Wardwell Maj MA
William: b 12-17-1756 d 11-30-1841 m Abigail Littlefield Sgt MA
William: b 12-31-1738 d p. 1800 m Mary Throp Pvt MA
William: b 3-8-1756 d 9-3-1835 m Betsey Swain Pvt MA NH ★
William, Jr.: b 2-29-1754 d 10-11-1837 m Mrs Betsey Swain Pvt NH
William: b 3-3-1756 d 5-27-1852 m Nancy Farrington Pvt CL
William: b c. 1720 d p. 1-18-1785 m X Col PS NC
William: b a. 1723 d 6-16-1787 m Mary Brown Cmsry VA
William: b 4-8-1764 d 4-12-1852 m Margaret Gossom Pvt VA
Ziba: b 9-14-1750 d — m Ruth Leonard Pvt MA

EAVENSON,
Eli: b 1-12-1760 d 7-29-1829 m Rachel Seal Pvt PA
Joseph: b 6-28-1758 d 9-13-1842 m Ann Yearsley Pvt PA

EAYRES,
John: b 1759 d p. 1790 m Margaret Southard PS Maj MA
John, Sr.: b 3-12-1725 d p. 1780 m Mary Eayres Pvt MA

EBAUGH,
John: b 1750-60 d a. 12-6-1833 m Sarah Flowers Pvt PA

EBBS,
Emanuel: b 1743 d 1840 m Nancy Cannon Pvt MD ★

EBERSOL, (includes EBERSOLE, EVERSOLE, & EVERSOULE)
Abraham: b c. 1755 d c. 1810 m Eve Stouffer Pvt PA
Abraham: b 1763 d 5-31-1836 m Mariah — Pvt PA
Christian: b 1758 d 8-4-1834 m Fronica — Pvt PA
Jacob, Jr.: b c. 1757 d 1828 m Anna Garber Pvt PA
Jacob: b 11-30-1760 d 10-3-1832 m Magdalene Wittmar Pvt PA
Jacob: b 8-18-1765 d 9-20-1848 m Catherine Albaugh Pvt PA

EBERT,
George: b 1752 d 1831 m Magdelena Heinrich Pvt PA
John: b 1747 d 2-10-1798 m Catherine — Pvt PA
Martin: b 11-10-1756 d 3-29-1833 m Anna Maria Smyser Pvt PA

EBINGER, (includes EVINGER)
George: b c. 1750 d c. 1821 m (1)Elizabeth Dill (2)Eva — Pvt PA

EBLIN,
Samuel: b 1755 d p. 3-7-1839 m Sarah Grafton Pvt VA ★

EBRIGHT,
Philip: b 3- -1754 d 3-27-1842 m Barbery — Pvt PA ★

EBY, (includes EBEY, EVEY)
Andrew: b 1-11-1747 d p. 1790 m X Pvt PA
Christian: b 2-22-1734 d 9-14-1807 m Catherine Bricker Pvt PA
Christian: b 1743 d 1835 m Catherine Huber Pvt PA
George, Sr.: b a. 1745 d 7-15-1779 m Betsy — Pvt PA
George: b 12-11-1760 d 10-1800 m Barbara Senseig Pvt PA
George, Jr.: b 8-11-1764 d 7-8-1847 m Mary Elebarger Pvt PA
Henry: b — d a. 12-3-1806 m X Pvt PA
John: b 1723 d 1790 m Margaret Eby Pvt PA
Michael: b 6-24-1764 d — m Elizabeth Oberholtzer Pvt PA

ECK,
John: b 1735 d 1821 m Mary Eva PS PA

ECKEL,
Henry: b 8-28-1744 d 5-29-1839 m Magdelene Moser Lt PA

ECKENRODE,
Henry, Sr.: b c. 1726 d 9-11-1813 m Cristina — Pvt PA

ECKER, (includes EACKER)
George: b 1756 d 6-27-1844 m Magdalena Runions Ens NY

George, Jr.: b 5-29-1751 d 6-21-1831 m Catherine Snell Pvt NY
Henry: b 8-12-1767 d p. 1795 m Catherine Dockstader Pvt NY
Jacob: b 2-2-1749 d 5-21-1823 m Margaret Fink Capt NY W★
Wolfert: b 9-19-1730-32 d 1-17-1799 m (1)Sarah Pugsley Lt PS NY

ECKERSON, (includes ACKERSON)
Cornelius: b 2-3-1755 d 2-5-1845 m Mary Keezely Lt NY ★
David: b 1-25-1738 d 3-12-1811 m Agnes Vanderbeek Cpl NY
Garret: b 2-23-1743 d 2-10-1811 m Dorcas Springsteen Capt NY
Garret C.: b 3-7-1724 d 1-7-1798 m Maria Haring Capt NY
Jacob C.: b 2-10-1742 d 6-7-1838 m Maria Westervelt Pvt NY
John: b 1758 d 1812 m Lanie Becker Pvt NY
Teunis: b 2-9-1740 d 10-4-1813 m Lena Slingerland Sol NY
Thomas: bpt 3-24-1713 d 1780 m Margarita Slingerland PS NY

ECKERT, (includes AKART, ECKARD, ECKART)
Adam: b 1741 d 11-3-1791 m Maria Van Steenberg Pvt NY
Conrat: b 2-10-1745 d 1-16-1835 m Rebecca Dipple Pvt PA
Jacob: b 1740 d 9-27-1826 m Susannah M. Latture Pvt PA
John: b 1760 d 2- -1845 m Christina Hummel Ens PA
Michael: b c. 1760 d c. 1816 m Ruth Keykindal Pvt VA
Peter: b 4-29-1742 d 10-29-1823 m Catherine Carpenter Pvt PA
Philip: b c. 1757 d p. 9- -1805 m X Sol VA
Valentine: b 1733 d 1821 m Elizabeth Gernaut Lt PA

ECKLER, (includes ACKLER)
Henry: b 8-11-1739 d p. 1800 m Christina — Capt NY
Leonard: b 5-22-1760 d 1-01-1838 m Catharine Young Pvt NY ★
Peter: b 7-2-1754 d 11-28-1834 m (1)Christina Kramer (2)Hannah Cronkhite Pvt NY

ECKLES, (includes ECHOLS)
Arthur: b 1742 d 1831 m Mrs Abigail Matthews Pvt PA ★
Daniel: b 1755 d 1811 m Mary Crow Pvt PA
James: b c. 1739/40 d a. 4-9-1823 m Elizabeth Palmer PS VA
John: b c. 1737 d p. 11-5-1816 m Lucy Moore Sol VA
John: b 1759 d 1825 m Mary Johnston Drm NJ
John: b c. 1750 d 1817 m Francis Formby Mil VA
Joseph: b 1735 d 1789 m Elizabeth Street PS VA
Nathaniel: b 10-2-1744 d 9-16-1830 m (1)Jean — (2)Mrs Isabel Clendenning Sol PA
William: b 1740 d 1822 m (2)Mrs Mary Armstrong (3)Jane — Pvt PA

ECKLEY,
Joseph: b c. 1752 d p. 7-12-1779 m Susan Ricketts Lt PA
Peter: b 4-12-1753 d 12-4-1833 m Esther Ralph Pvt PA

ECKLIN,
Joshua: b c. 1750 d 1824 m Sarah Hill Pvt NC

ECKMAN,
Henry: b — d p. 1789 m Maria Seegar Pvt PA
Hieronymus: b 3-14-1718 d 4-24-1784 m Barbara Slaymaker PS PA
Jacob: b 1739 d 5-20-1778 m Anna Maria Schneider Pvt PA
Jacob, Jr.: b 3-28-1763 d a. 5-3-1831 m (1)Christina Musser (2)Catherine — Pvt PA
John: b 6-10-1746 d 9-16-1804 m Catharine Foutz Lt PA

EDDINS, (includes EDDINGS)
Benjamin: b c. 1735 d 1818 m Judith Norris PS Sol SC
Samuel: b c. 1754 d 1822 m Kat Wilder Capt VA
William: b 4-21-1758 d p. 3-3-1841 m Mary E. Johnson Lt NC VA ★

EDDY, (includes EDIE)
Abiel: b 11-3-1737 d p. 1798 m Constant Torrey 2Lt CS PS NH
Abner: b 2-20-1747/8 d a. 2-20-1824 m (1)Elizabeth Colton (2)Dorcas Gross Sgt MA
Appollos: b 1752 d 1840 m Martha Woodward Pvt MA ★
Asa: b a. 1739 d p. 1790 m (1)Elizabeth Gore (2)Sarah — Pvt CT
Barnard, Sr.: b 10-11-1729 d 5- -1777 m Patience Eddy PS NY
Barnard, Jr.: b 7-12-1762 d 7-3-1847 m (1)Betsey Walker (2)Julia Granville Westcott Capt RI ★
Benjamin: b 10-21-1739 d 6-11-1832 m (1)Sarah Holland (2)Mrs Tabitha Bixby Sgt MA
Caleb: b 5- -1754 d 4-21-1818 m Nancy Jones Pvt NJ
Caleb: b 5-2-1751 d 1-23-1820 m Prudence Hopkins Pvt RI ★
Charles: b 8-22-1748 d p. 7-8-1813 m (1)Hannah Kelsey (2)Mary Dobson Pvt CT
David: b 10-23-1747 d p. 1784 m Naomi Arnold Capt RI
Devotion: b 3-18-1734 d 6-9-1813 m Mary Sherman Pvt CL
Ebenezer: b 5-3-1743 d 7-18-1830 m (1)Deborah Palmer (2)Elizabeth White Sgt MA ★
Eliakim: b 1740 d 1831 m Eunice Ferrand Pvt MA
Elkanah: b 9-28-1756 d 4-15-1814 m Mary Hopkins Pvt RI W★
Esek: b 12-14-1731 d 8-23-1820 m Mary Perry Capt RI
Gilbert: b 1761 d 5-27-1848 m Prudence Chapman Pvt CT
Ibrook: b 1-9-1754 d 1-6-1833/4 m (1)Lona Pratt (2)Celia (Wilde) Coggeshall Sgt MA
James: b 12-30-1755 d 5- -1833 m Dorothy Wilbur Pvt MA
James: b 12-8-1749 d 6-2-1831 m Miriam Wilkerson Pvt NJ
James: b 1737 d 12-9-1819 m Jane Miller Pvt NY
James: b 5-26-1758 d 8- -1835 m Lydia Ross Pvt VT

EDDY, contd.
James: b 7-8-1764 d 6-29-1849 m Mary Salisbury Pvt VT ★
Joel: b 8-27-1717 d 10-3-1776 m Rachel Vose Pvt CT
John: b 3-22-1754 d 1-27-1817 m (1)Amy (Sage) Cornwall (2)Anna Taber Pvt CT
John: b c. 1739 d p. 1-10-1823 m Huldah — Lt PS PA
John: b 10-3-1748 d 1-21-1821 m Deborah Winsor Capt RI
John: b 1754 d 9- -1823 m Sarah Hill Pvt RI
Jonas: b 11-10-1747 d 12-10-1825 m Lucy Oak Sgt MA
Jonathan: b 8-12-1744 d p. 5-8-1794 m Mercy Cady Pvt CT
Jonathan: b 1726 d 5-4-1804 m Mary Ware Col MA
Jonathan: b 11-26-1733 d 1803 m (1)Ruth Hayford (2)Mrs Joanna Haskins Pvt MA
Jonathan: b 4-15-1757 d 4-21-1823 m Temperance Lewis Pvt VT
Joshua: b 5-5-1748 d 5-1-1833 m Lydia Paddock Capt MA
Josiah: b 2-25-1748 d a. 4-6-1824 m Sarah Dennis Cpl MA
Levi: b 4-25-1745 d 5-6-1821 m (1)Sarah Smith (2)Molly Pratt Pvt MA
Lippitt: b 2-17-1755 d 4-10-1838 m Esther Curtis Pvt RI
Nathan: b 9-8-1733 d 2-28-1804 m Eunice Sampson Pvt MA
Obediah: b 3-21-1742 d 1811 m (1)Lois Palmer (2)Rose Chase Lt MA
Obediah: b 3-10-1751 d 5-4-1826 m Phebe Prouty Pvt MA
Oded: b 2-28-1760 d 7-31-1825 m Wealthy Pratt Pvt MA
Oliver: b 1730 d 1799 m Abigail Harvey Pvt MA
Olney: b 11-16-1750 d c. 1835 m Sarah — Pvt MM RI
Parley: b 8-14-1763 d 12-13-1831 m (1)Amity Parker (2)Hannah Nichols Pvt MA
Paul: b 1747 d 5-27-1843 m Hannah Macomber Cpl MA
Peleg: b 1759 d 2-4-1798 m (1)Anne S. — (2)Charlotte — Drm VT
Peter: b 8-4-1727 d 11-9-1799 m Mary Round Pvt VT
Reuben: b 5-20-1751 d 10-3-1813 m (1)Sibyl Moore (2)Mary Merriam Pvt RI
Samuel: b 11-8-1732 d 8-23-1811 m Rachel Smith Lt MA
Samuel: b 1-23-1742 d 11-29-1821 m Anna Morton SgtMaj MA
Samuel: b 4-29-1760 d 9-25-1813 m Sally Paddock Pvt MA
Samuel: b 1731 d 2-8-1809 m Agnes Cochran CS PA
Seth: b 5-30-1754 d 8-17-1837 m Jerusha Barden Pvt MA ★
Thomas: b 2-28-1756 d 9-21-1842 m Betsey Putnam Sgt MA
Willard: b 1-21-1760 d 4-13-1854 m Dorcas Mathewson Sol Slr RI ★
William: b 4-25-1746 d 6-18-1777 m Elizabeth Smith Sgt MA
William: b 2-5-1725 d 3-16-1805 m Sarah Bellows Sol MA
William: b 7-26-1751 d 2-4-1835 m Huldah Ide Pvt RI MA ★
William R.: b 1760/1 d 12-21-1841 m (1)Zama Severance (2)Martha Hall (3)Philema Cunnabel Pvt MA ★
Zachariah: b 3-17-1712 d 12-6-1777 m Mercy Morton PS MA

EDELEN, (includes EDELIN, EDELINE)
Benedict Joseph: b c. 1754 d 1800 m X PS MD
Richard: b 8-4-1715 d a. 2- -1791 m Sarah Stonestreet PS MD
Edward: b 1752 d 1826 m — Boarman Pvt MD
Edward Thomas: b 11-12-1728 d 8-6-1786 m Elizabeth Marbury PS MD
Louis Victor: b 12-23-1730 d 4-21-1791 m Marie Josepte Thomas 2Capt CS IN

EDELMAN, (includes EDDLEMAN, EDLEMAN)
George: b c. 1732 d p. 4-24-1802 m (1)Anna (Dage) Gaegen (2)Ann Miller, Pvt PA
John: b c. 1740 d 1800 m Maria Barbara — Pvt PS PA
John: b — d p. 1780 m Barbara — Pvt PA
Peter: b 8-15-1762 d 2-13-1857 m Rachel Elrod Pvt NC ★

EDEN,
James: b 1752 d 1814 m Lavinia Anne Davis Maj MD

EDENFIELD,
David: b 1-19-1761 d 4-5-1856 m Elizabeth Apstan Pvt SC ★

EDERS,
Andreas: b 2-1-1741 d 12-16-1808 m Margretta Noll PS PA

EDES,
Benjamin: b 10-14-1732 d 12-11-1803 m Martha Starr Lt PS MA
Isaiah: b 12-11-1730 d 11-17-1803 m (1)Agnes Screech (2)Sarah Parker (3)Mary Kemp PS MA
Peter: b 9-15-1705 d 1-25-1787 m (1)Esther Hall (2)Anna Haskel PS MA
Samuel: b 10-15-1753 d 7-10-1845 m Elizabeth Baker Sol NH
Thomas: b 11-8-1745 d 1784 m Mary Day QMSgt MA

EDGAR,
James: b 1735 d 1784 m Sarah Rowland Pvt NJ
James: b 11-15-1743 d 6-8-1814 m (1)Martha Smiley (2)Mary (McGowan) Stevenson PS PA
John: b 1759 d 9-25-1823 m Mary Peebles Pvt PA
Thomas: b 11-30-1746 d 7-31-1812 m Elizabeth Knapp PS NJ NY
Thomas: b 9-27-1750 d 7-15-1822 m Ann Mathews Wgn VA

EDGE,
John: b 10-10-1744 d 9-14-1816 m Anne — Pvt PA
Nehemiah: b 1754 d p. 1812 m (1)Sarah — (2)Elizabeth James Doster Sol NC

EDGECOMB, (includes EDGCOMB)
Gibbins: b 5-9-1743 d 2-17-1811 m Rhoda Elwell Pvt MA
Gilbert: b 3-3-1762 d 5-18-1843 m Lucy Allen Pvt CT ★
Jabez: b 10-6-1763 d 5-18-1843 m Esther Morgan Pvt CT ★
James: b 7-25-1757 d 5-19-1835 m Anna Burnham Pvt MA W★
Samuel, Jr.: b 2-28-1760 d 2-25-1843 m (1)Katharine Williams (2)Rachael Denison Copp MM CT

EDGELL,
John: b 1729 d — m Rebecca Winship Cpl MA

EDGERLY,
Benjamin: b 1737 d 1- -1817 m Mary Hoyt CS PS NH
David: b 9-15-1741 d 11-9-1785 m Dorothy Hoit PS NH
Edward: b c. 1735 d 9-9-1781 m X Capt MD
James: b 4-13-1737 d 1815 m (1)Jane Phillips (2)Mrs Rachel Carlisle Kent Pvt NH
James: b 3-10-1761 d 1-4-1830 m Hannah Chadwick Pvt NH ★
Jonathan: b 1731 d 9-26-1800 m Betsey Steel Pvt PS NH
Richard: b 1759 d 11-23-1844 m Abigail Bickford Pvt NH ★
Thomas: b 1-6-1745 d 1815 m Agnes Phillips Sgt NH

EDGERTON, (includes EDGARTON, EGERTON)
Ariel: b 10-8-1757 d 10-11-1838 m (1)Edna Huntington (2)Widow Stratton Pvt Pvtr CT ★
Asa: b 3-28-1736 d 5-1-1792 m (1)Hannah Griswold (2)Eunice Storrs PS CT
Daniel: b 3-1-1737 d 2-24-1783 m Mary Douglass Sol VT
Eleazer: b 8-8-1748 d 10-23-1820 m Sarah Hyde Sol Sct VT
Elisha: b 2-28-1728 d 8-22-1782 m Elizabeth Lord Capt CT
Elisha: b 11-20-1753 d 6-9-1832 m Eunice Peck Cpl CT
Hezekiah, Sr.: b 4- -1706 d 7-18-1776 m (1)Ann Abell (2)Freelove Hillard Capt CT
Hezekiah, Jr.: b 4-13-1743 d 6-4-1816 m Bethia Peck Capt CT
Jacob: b 10-29-1760 d 1-22-1845 m (1)Esther Reed (2)Hannah Sheldon Pvt VT
James: b 11-24-1760/1 d 11-27-1842 m Catherine Hinman Pvt CT ★
Jedediah: b 8-28-1759 d 2-12-1848 m (1)Lucy Curtis (2)Widow of Enos Clark Pvt CT VT ★
John: b 12-26-1750 d 11-11-1828 m Abigail Parker Vol MA
Nathan, Jr.: b 3-25-1763 d 1820 m Sally Belshaw Pvt CT
Roger: b 12-12-1761 d 5-24-1844 m Betsey Cole Sol CT
Samuel: b 5-9-1742 d p. 1797 m Elizabeth Paine Pvt CT
Simeon: b 3-9-1732 d 8-27-1809 m Abiah Hough Capt CT
Sims: b 2-14-1739/40 d p. 1781 m Lucretia Horsford Sgt CT
Stephen: b 5-11-1760 d 12-11-1823 m Temperance Bailey Pvt CT
Zebulon: b 3-4-1754 d 4-25-1822 m Abigail Palmer Pvt CT

EDGINGTON,
Jesse: b 12- -1759 d 7-6-1821 m Margaret Paramore Sol VA
Joseph: b c. 1750 d c. 1814 m Eleanor — Pvt PA
Thomas: b 1744 d 1814 m Martha — Pvt PA

EDICK, (includes ITTIG)
Conrad: b 9-15-1763 d 8-22-1845 m (1)Margaret Whitaker (2)Elizabeth Sneeden Cpt NY ★
Conrath: b 1-20-1762 d 9-12-1846 m Nancy Hannah Fikes Pvt NY
Jacob, 2d: b 1764 d 10-3-1807 m Margaret York Pvt NY
Jacob C.: b 6-30-1764 d 10-12-1844 m (1)Miss Cronk (2)Susan Woolaber (3)Catherine Christman Pvt NY ★
Jacob: b 7-21-1755 d 2-23-1821 m Elizabeth Weaver Pvt NY
Michael: b 6-14-1734 d 3-9-1806 m Catherine Orendorf Capt NY

EDINGER, (includes ETTINGER)
Melchoir: b 8-18-1741 d 5-20-1812 m (1)Regina Brandon (2)Maria Barbara Cpl PA

EDINGS,
Benjamin: b 10-24-1742 d 1780 m Mary Baily Pvt SC

EDINGTON,
John: b 3-9-1729 d 7-17-1793 m Rachel Taylor Pvt PA
Jonathan: b 1750 d — m X Pvt CMman PA
Phillip: b 1-20-1750 d 10-16-1815 m Eleanor Hunt Pvt NY

EDLEY,
John: b c. 1750 d a. 1815 m Mary Attaway Sol MD

EDLOE,
Henry: b c. 1760 d p. 3- -1796 m (1)Elizabeth Edmondson (2)Sally Lamb Lt VA

EDMAN,
Samuel: b 8-16-1758 d 10-10-1847 m Dolly Paul Pvt MM NJ ★

EDMANDS, (includes EDMONDS)
Andrew: b 10-4-1740 d 6-28-1814 m (1)Prudence Campbell (2)Esther Campbell Capt CT
Andrew: b 6-17-1760 d 1-1-1813 m Huldah King Pvt PS VT
Benjamin: b 1-9-1752 d 7-17-1828 m Eunice — Pvt Arfr MA ★
David: b 1-11-1741 d 12-9-1823 m (1)Sarah Manning (2)Anna Ford Bbd Cpl MA

Downs: b 1724 d *p.* 5-5-1782 m (1)Experience Hand (2)Mary (Parsons) Hand PS NJ
Ebenezer: b 11-14-1753 d 10-31-1833 m Mary Gale Sol MA
Elias: b 1756 d 1800 m Frances Edmonds LCol VA
Elias: b *c.* 1740 d *p.* 1783 m (1)Frances Garner (2)Frances Denny Lt VA
Eliphalet: b 4-13-1764 d 9-11-1841 m Betsey Robinson Pvt Fif RI VT
Jacob: b 1752 d *p.* 1787 m Elizabeth Mushon Pvt NJ ★
James, Sr.: b 1731 d 1799 m (1) — Alaison (2)Abigail Jenks PS VT
James, Jr.: b 2-25-1762 d 1858 m — Gifford Pvt VT
James, Jr.: b 4-6-1762 d 5-19-1846 m (1)Phebe Williams (2)Olive Robinson (3)Freelove Olin Pvt VT ★
James: b 4-3-1743 d 1-26-1826 m (1)Sarah Lavendar (2)Mary Wooddy PS VA
John: b 1757 d *c.* 5-15-1846 m Sarah Williams Cpl MA ★
John: b 12-20-1757 d 3-29-1851 m Experience Pratt Pvt NY ★
John: b — d *p.* 12-30-1782 m Mary — PS VA
Jonathan: b 4-20-1728 d 1-8-1816 m (1)Prudence — (2)Huldah Hide (3)Hannah Ward Pvt MA
Joseph: b 1756 d 6-20-1828 m Rosamond Barton QM MA
Joseph: b 2-3-1724/5 d 1800 m Mary Fry Pvt MA
Obadiah: b 1759 d 1809 m Sarah Williams Pvt VT
Peter: b 8-1-1760 d 8-4-1854 m (1)Pheby Davis (2)Elizabeth Warner (3)Mrs Martha A. Bechtel Pvt PA
Robert: b 1730 d 1823 m Mary Marks Pvt PS CT
Robert: b *c.* 1743 d 3-28-1818 m Hannah Arnold Mstr Ens RI
Samuel: b 8-27-1760 d 3-14-1826 m (1)Ruth Worth (2)Lydia Worth Cmsry NY
Samuel: b *c.* 1740 d *a.* 1812 m (2)Alcey (Ball) Wright PS VA
Thomas: b *c.* 1746 d 11- -1825 m Sarah Eldridge LCol CS VA
Thomas: b — d 1794 m Martha Short Capt VA
William: b 9-28-1755 d 8-1-1838 m Elizabeth J. Chandler Pvt CT
William: b 10-24-1708 d 9-15-1786 m (1)Rebecca de Beauvoise (2)Margaret Anthony PS PA
William: b 11-14-1734 d 2-19-1816 m Elizabeth Blackwell Col VA

EDMONDSON, (includes EDMISTON, EDMONSON, EDMONSTON & EDMUNDSON)
Andrew: b *c.* 1740 d 10-7-1780 m Ann (Edmiston) Ens CS VA
Archibald, 2d: b *a.* 1734 d 4-14-1787 m Blanchannah — Pvt MD
Benjamin: b 6-5-1752 d *p.* 1801 m Elizabeth Waddy Lt VA
David: b 1750 d 1821 m Sarah Paxton Pvt VA
Edmund: b *c.* 1740 d 1816 m Jane — Cpl VA
Isaac: b 1760-2 d *p.* 5-13-1809 m Nancy Cox PS SC
James: b 1760 d 1845 m Gertrude Harris Sgt NY
James: b *a.* 1751 d 1798 m Penelope — 2Lt VA
James: b 10-7-1746 d 10-7-1817 m Jane Smith Pvt VA
James: b 1750 d *p.* 1780 m Ann McCarthy PS VA
John: b 1764 d 1847 m Elizabeth Robinson Pvt VA
John Montgomery: b 1757 d 1-22-1813 m (1)Anna Montgomery (2)Margaret Robinson Pvt VA
Joseph: b *c.* 1756 d *p.* 3-19-1822 m X Pvt PA
Ninian: b 1735 d 2-4-1816 m Dorothy Brooke Edmonston Pvt PS MD
Peter: b 9-9-1759 d 1799 m Eunice Osbourn PS MD
Richard: b *c.* 1740 d *c.* 1810 m Elizabeth Brown Sgt VA
Robert, Jr.: b 3-17-1753 d 2-16-1816 m Isabella Buchanan Lt VA
Samuel: b 5-3-1738 d 4-4-1808 m Elizabeth Edmondson Pvt VA
Thomas: b 1740 d 3- -1805 m Mary Beall Lt MD
Thomas: b *c.* 1739 d *p.* 1809 m Mary Penrose CS PA
William: b 1730 d 8-11-1803 m Jane Sutherland Ens NY
William: b 1734 d 7-30-1822 m (1)Margaret Montgomery (2)Elizabeth Kennedy Col VA
William: b 1734 d 10-7-1780 m Elizabeth — Capt VA
William: b 1759 d 1820 m Martha Green Sgt VA
William: b 10-17-1750 d 1826 m Mary Cook Sol VA
William: b *c.* 1730 d *p.* 1785 m Martha Campbell CS VA

EDRINGTON, (includes EDERINGTON)
Francis: b 1764 d 6- -1824 m Frances Crosswhite Pvt QM SC
James: b 1742 d 6-4-1847 m (2)Catherine — (3)Mary Forbes Pvt SC

EDSALL, (includes EDSOLL)
Jacobus: bpt 1-5-1725 d *p.* 12-3-1801 m Charlotte Barton Capt NJ
James: b 5-3-1755 d 2-3-1840 m Mary Simpson Pvt NJ ★
Joseph: b 1763 d 5-26-1844 m (1)Sophia —(2)Anna — Pvt NJ
Richard, 3d: b 12-17-1750 d 5-10-1823 m Jemima Seeley Capt NJ ★

EDSON
Abiel: b 1753 d 1823 m Hannah Morton Pvt MA
Abiezer: b 6-10-1715 d 7-24-1791 m (1)Sarah Lathrop (2)Jael Bennett (3)Mary Packard (4)Mrs Earl CS MA
Amasa: b 4-13-1763 d 2-9-1853 m Hannah Morton Pvt MA
Benjamin: b 1-26-1758 d 7-1-1843 m (1)Dinah Washburn (2)Anna Johnson Pvt CT ★
David: b 4-28-1722 d 1795 m (1)Susannah Gannett (2)Sarah Southworth Edson Pvt MA
Ebenezer, Jr.: b 9-5-1755 d *p.* 1791 m Martha Fobes Sgt MA
Jacob: b 4-16-1722 d *p.* 1787 m Betty Packard MM Drm CS MA
James: b 1760 d 1808 m (1)Esther Allen (2)Mrs Elizabeth Washburn Pvt PS MA
James: b 8-19-1759 d *p.* 1786 m Lovina Hancock Pvt Arfr MA
Joel: b 1763 d 1830 m Hannah Packard Pvt MA

John: b 5-20-1748 d 1814 m Judith Shaw Pvt MA
Jonathan, Sr.: bpt 3-27-1727/8 d 2-13-1805 m Mehitable Lilly Pvt MA
Jonathan, Jr.: b *c.* 1749 d 4-18-1816 m Rebecca Graves Pvt MA
Josiah: b 1758 d 10-27-1819 m Sarah Pinney Sgt CT ★
Josiah: b 5-31-1753 d 1-5-1820 m Reliance Fuller Pvt MA
Nathan: b 3-14-1739 d 8-16-1825 m Mary Hall Sgt MA
Samuel: b 7-18-1742 d *p.* 1790 m Anna Hall Pvt MA
Seth: b 1-12-1761 d 10-25-1849 m Desire Comstock Pvt CT ★
Seth: b 6-6-1761 d 9-27-1848 m Thedora Howard Pvt Wgn MA ★
Thomas: b 6-3-1753 d 1836 m Mary Jarvis Sgt MA ★
William: b 2-4-1723/4 d 2-13-1800 m Martha Haward PS MA

EDWARDS, (includes EDWARD)
Aaron: b 7-28-1756 d 9-15-1804 m Desire Minor Pvt NJ
Abel: b 1755 d *a.* 11-9-1846 m (1)Mary Potts (2)Elizabeth Hampton Pvt NY
Abel: b 3-15-1752 d 4-5-1826 m (1)Lucy Hawley (2)Sarah Mann Cpl CT W★
Adonijah: b 9-27-1741 d 9-9-1831 m Polly — Pvt VT
Alexander: b 1765 d 9-15-1816 m (1)Rebecca Noblett (2)Milly Moore Sol NC
Ambrose: b 1750 d 1823 m Jemima — Sol GA
Ambrose: b 2-17-1747 d 1812 m Olive Martin Pvt VA
Andrew: b 1752 d 1820 m Phoebe Meadows Pvt VA
Benjamin: b 8-12-1752 d 11-13-1826 m Margaret Beall Lt MD
Daniel: bpt 2-11-1744 d 7-29-1800 m Jemima Hubbard Sol PS CT
Daniel: b 1742 d 5-5-1820 m Mary Sells Pvt NY
Daniel: b 7-13-1757 d 2-8-1845 m (1)Anna Stillman (2)Lois Stillman Pvt RI ★
David: b 1749 d 2-19-1814 m Deborah Clark Pvt MA
David: b 1743 d 1789 m Deborah Thompson Capt NJ
David: b 1745 d *a.* 12-6-1782 m Elizabeth Morris CS NC
David: b 1750 d 1821 m Mary Elizabeth — 2Lt PA
Ebenezer: b 3-23-1757 d 3-21-1826 m (1)Lucy Wheeler (2)Mary Flint MM MA
Edward: b 6-7-1711 d *p.* 1778 m (1)Jemima Welsh (2)Elizabeth Chilton PS MD
Elisha: b 10-23-1758 d 11- -1832 m Anna Bates Pvt MA ★
Evan: bpt 12-11-1752 d 2-19-1798 m Catharine Jones Maj PA
George: b 12-24-1754 d 3-30-1835 m Elizabeth Monroe Smn VA
Gershom: b *c.* 1740 d *c.* 1805 m Abigail Hallock Sgt NY
Gray: b *c.* 1750 d 1803 m Mrs Elizabeth Lanier Tucker Ingram PS VA
Henry: b 1757 d *p.* 1790 m Ann — Pvt NY
Henry: b 1761 d 11-15-1837 m Sarah Ann Jacobs Pvt NC ★
Hezekiah: b 1-4-1761 d 3-5-1854 m Martha Summers Pvt CT
Isaac: b 1-29-1764 d 2-18-1848 m Esther Foote Pvt CT ★
Jacob: b *c.* 1720 d *c.* 1795 m Affa Speer Pvt NJ
Jacob: b 8-20-1763 d 10-6-1848 m Abigail Tunis Pvt NJ ★
Jacob: b 1760 d 10-4-1837 m Betsy Belote Pvt VA ★
James: b *c.* 1720 d 1810 m Elizabeth Heady Pvt NJ
James: b 6-20-1761 d 10-24-1844 m Phillis Jester Sol NC
James: b *c.* 1730 d 1804 m Sarah Everett Pvt VA
James: b 1750 d *p.* 2- -1823 m Rosa Wren PS VA
Jared: b 1746 d 1-31-1832 m (1)Susan Porter (2)Rebecca Bell Pvt MD
Jasper: b 2-29-1748 d 4-2-1832 m (1) — Cook (2)Elizabeth Quick MM Pvt NJ PA
Jesse: b 3-4-1756 d 11-2-1856 m Catherine Skillman Pvt PA VA ★
John: b 1-13-1753 d 1-22-1837 m Sabra Curtis Cpl MA ★
John: b 6-8-1746 d 1-12-1826 m Hannah Meeker Pvt NJ
John: b 1749 d 1829 m Mercy VanScoy Pvt PS NY
John: b 11-12-1738 d 8-20-1826 m Sarah — Pvt NY
John: b *c.* 1740 d *p.* 12-1-1817- m Lucy H. Curtis Pvt NC
John: b 8-12-1752 d 1834 m Susannah Collins Pvt NC
John, Sr.: b *c.* 1720 d *p.* 4-2-1796 m Mary — CS NC
John: b 1741 d 9-18-1826 m Margaret Brown Maj PA
John: b 1749 d 6-20-1804 m Catharine Buiford Pvt PA
John: b 1-7-1731 d 8-19-1781 m (2)Margaret Peronneau PS PA
John: b 1708 d 8-11-1790 m Sarah Davies PS PA
John: b 12-12-1757 d 7- -1829 m Lydia Roberts Pvt PA
John: b 9-16-1752 d 1-1-1830 m Nancy McGee Pvt VA
John: b 1748 d 1837 m Susannah Wroe PS VA
John: b 10-22-1758 d 5-3-1827 m Sarah Scoggins Pvt VA
John: b 1759 d 3-22-1833 m Martha Elizabeth Rainey Pvt VA ★
John: b *a.* 6-26-1756 d *p.* 1788 m X PS VA
John: b *c.* 1760 d *p.* 1795 m Temperance Parker PS VA
Joseph: b 3-1-1743 d 7-7-1788 m Lucy Jearom Sgt CT
Joseph: b 11-26-1732 d 4-22-1800 m Sarah Newman Pvt MA
Joseph: b 1730 d 7- -1782 m (1)Elizabeth Ingersoll (2)Susanna Ingersoll Pvtr NJ
Joseph: b 3-9-1757 d 3-14-1845 m Sarah Willitts Cpl NJ ★
Joseph: b 1751 d 1827 m Margaretta Kent Pvt NJ
Joseph: b 6-7-1736 d 10-1-1828 m (1)Rachel Reese (2)Elizabeth Vance (3)Lydia Roberts (4)Ann Silver Pvt VA
Joshua: b 1750 d 1834 m Mary Stevens Sgt MA
Justin: b 1752 d 10-6-1795 m Mary Bartlett Cpl MA
LeRoy: b 2-9-1754 d 4-2-1800 m Mary Glasscock Capt VA
Medad: b 1725 d 8-22-1806 m Lois Shattuck Pvt MA
Moses: b 7-28-1756 d 5-4-1827 m (1)Desire Meeker (2)Catherine Ogden Pvt NJ
Nathaniel: b 1739 d 3-2-1825 m Abiah Strickland Lt CT ★
Nathaniel: b 6-21-1752 d 6-14-1828 m Sarah Hunt Sgt MA

EDWARDS, contd.
Nathaniel: b 8-31-1761 d 1-13-1811 m Abigail Bedford Pvt NJ
Nicholas, Jr.: b c. 1747 d 6-29-1812 m Marcy — Pvt RI W ★
Noah, Sr.: b 6-6-1722 d 9-3-1805 m Jerusha Alvord PS MA
Noah, Jr.: b 4- -1750 d 12-3-1788 m Jerusha Rust Sgt MA
Oliver: b 8-29-1755 d 4-4-1829 m Rachel Parsons Pvt MA
Pierrepont: b 4-8-1750 d 4-5-1826 m Frances Ogden Sol PS CT
Richard: b 1754 d 1837 m Elizabeth Owens Sol VA
Robert: b 1759 d 1801 m Mehitable Clemence Pvt RI
Robert: b 2-13-1759 d 11-17-1831 m Nancy F. Quishenbury OrdlSgt NC ★
Robert: b 3-31-1733 d c. 1830 m Elizabeth Crawford Cpl SC
Robert, Jr.: b 2-11-1760 d 5-9-1796 m Hannah Keene 2Lt VA
Robert: b c. 1750 d a. 12-13-1802 m Anne Haynie PS Grd VA
Samuel: b c. 1748 d 1776 m Betty Curtis Pvt CT
Samuel: b 1753 d 8-10-1842 d Silence Judd Cpl MA
Samuel: b 2-16-1750 d 5-13-1839 m (1)Mary — (2)Lucy McDonald (3)Phoebe Pert Pvt MA ★
Samuel: b 10-20-1756 d 8-5-1833 m Jane Shelton Pvt NY
Simeon: b 1754 d 7-16-1830 m Lydia Edwards Cpl MA ★
Solomon: b 9-4-1756 d 1-27-1844 m Sarah Matthews Pvt VA ★
Talmadge: b 1747 d 6-4-1821 m Mary Sherman Pvt NY
Thomas: b 1746 d 1792 m Sarissa Nichols Pvt CT
Thomas: b 8-1-1753 d 8-4-1806 m (1)Sarah Goldthwaite (2)Mary Jewett Adj MA
Thomas: b 3-16-1758 d 4-20-1793 m Deliverance Hicks Smn MA RI
Thomas: b 4- -1735 d 9-5-1816 m Elizabeth Vaughn 2Lt NJ
Thomas: b 1741 d 8- -1832 m Mary Ann McLanahan Pvt SC
Thomas: b 2-17-1757 d 4-12-1837 m Matilda Chandler Sol VT
Thomas: b 1750 d 1791 m Lucy Edwards Pvt VA
Thomas: b 1-28-1752 d 4-20-1798 m Elizabeth Lee CS & Pvt VA
Thomas: b 1764 d 10-8-1846 m Elizabeth Edwards Pvt VA
Timothy: b 7-25-1738 d 10-27-1813 m Rhoda Ogden CS PS MA
William: b 1743 d 8-19-1796 m Sarah Norris Pvt MA
William: b 4-25-1755 d 12-15-1845 m Lydia Baker Pvt MA
William: b c. 1755 d p. 1808 m Christina Smith Pvt NY
William: b 1750 d 9-4-1821 m Mary Irwin Pvt NC
William: b 1757 d 4-23-1837 m Rebecca Ann Brewer Pvt MM NC
William: b 5-13-1746 d 4-9-1818 m Meribah Gaskill PS PA
William: b c. 1741/2 d 1833 m Chloe Stokes Pvt SC
William: b 3-24-1752 d 4-23-1837 m Anne Walton Pvt VA ★
William: b 6- -1754 d 2-16-1827 m Susanah Ayres Pvt VA

EELLS,
Daniel: b 12-5-1757 d 7-17-1851 m Martha Hamlin Pvt MM CT
Edward: b 8-11-1741 d 12-8-1787 m (1)Sarah Edwards (2)Abigail Brandigee Capt CT
Jeremiah Beard: b 12-1-1732 d 11-12-1815 m (1)Lois Benedict (2)Hannah Comstock Lt CT
John: b 1701 d 10-15-1785 m (1)Anna Baird (2)Abigail Comstock Sol CT
John: b 11-16-1755 d 1832 m Anna Mead Cpl CT
John: b 6-21-1760 d 7-14-1839 m Polly Clark Pvt MA VT★
Moses Comstock: b 12-16-1744 d 11-23-1807 m Abigail Reed Pvt CT
Nathaniel, Sr.: b 2-4-1711 d 6-16-1786 m (1)Mercy Cushing (2)Mary Darral Sol Chp CT
Nathaniel: b 9-18-1748 d 1-7-1815 m Hulda White Sol PS CT
Robert Lenthal: b 2-7-1732 d 1-19-1800 m Ruth Copeland Capt MA
Samuel: b 1753 d 9-1-1835 m Ephally Mallory Pvt CT ★
Waterman: b 1731 d 8-16-1777 m Sarah Tubbs Capt MA

EFFORD,
Zachariah: b 2-13-1733 d p. 1792 m (1)Patience — (2)Winneford — PS VA

EFNER, (includes EFFENAAR)
Henderick: b c. 1750/1 d p. 1790 m Maragieta Teator Pvt NY

EGBERT,
Abraham: b 4-12-1736 d — m Elizabeth VanClief Pvt NJ
Abraham: b 12-12-1747 d 2-12-1822 m Ann Ridgeway Pvt NY
Benjamin: b 8-23-1749 d 2-5-1818 m Mary VonArison Capt NY
James: b 5-20-1759 d — m Sarah Smith 2Lt NJ
John: b 1-13-1752 d 10-6-1821 m (1)Elizabeth Bowman (2)Sarah Brandenbaugh Pvt NJ
John: b 6-20-1722 d p. 1794 m Martha — Wgn NJ
Lawrence: b 5-20-1746 d 4-19-1821 m Sarah Norman Pvt PA
Wm.: b c. 1756 d c. 1838 m Rebecca Job Sol NJ

EGBERTS,
Anthony: b 1753 d 1833 m Eve Van Der Zee Ens NY

EGE,
Michael, 2nd: b 2-12-1753 d 6-26-1815 m Ann Dorothea Wolff LCol PA
Samuel: b 6-24-1750 d 8-22-1829 m Anna Titus Pvt NJ
Samuel: b 1-22-1742 d 2-11-1801 m Elizabeth Walker Cmsry VA

EGENBRODE, (includes EIGABROADT, EIGENBRADE)
George: b 1750 d 1838 m Katie Smith Pvt NY
Johannes: b 1746 d 9-28-1828 m Elizabeth Felter Pvt NY
Peter: b 1738 d 1805/6 m Elizabeth Helmar Pvt NY

EGERT,
George: b 1746 d 5- -1814 m Margaret — Capt PA

EGERY,
Daniel: bpt 9-27-1741 d 10-23-1801 m (1)Deborah — (2)Mary Perry (3)Martha Cobb Capt MA

EGGENAAR,
Petrus: b 2-19-1745 d 11-15-1795 m Neltje VanBumble 2Lt NY

EGGLESTON, (includes ECCLESTON, EGGLESON, & EGLESTON)
Abner: b 7-3-1754 d 10- -1788 m Jerusha Whedon Pvt MA
Asa, Jr.: b 2-19-1763 d 8-8-1840 m Content Hadsell Pvt RI ★
Azariah: b 2-23-1757 d 1-22-1822 m Hannah Patterson Maj MA NY
Benedict, Sr.: b 1739 d 8-29-1834 m Agibail Woodard Pvt CT
Benedict, Jr.: b 6-18-1763 d 12-16-1859 m (1)Content Brown (2)Sally Skinner Pvt CT ★
Benjamin: b 1747 d 6-1-1832 m Mary Gordon Pvt MA
Daniel Loomis: b 10-29-1737 d 1810 m Sarah Manley Cpl CT
Daniel: b 6-10-1755 d 8-20-1843 m Katherine FannIng Pvt CT
Eber: b 6-13-1751 d 12-25-1815 m Submit Judd Pvt MA
Edward: b 1-12-1761 d 11-8-1836 m (1)Judith Booker (2)Matilda H. Maury Sol VA
Eliab: b 3-23-1762 d 3-2-1838 m (2)Lucy Ingraham Pvt NY ★
Elisha: b 9-25-1720 d 1804 m Elizabeth Merrill Pvt NY
Gershom: b 7-29-1762 d 5-30-1849 m Avis Lamphere Pvt CT
Ichabod, Jr.: b 10-10-1737 d 11-10-1816 m Abigail Woodward PS CS CT
Jesse: b 1760 d 1812 m Lucinda Curtiss Pvt NY
John, 2d: b 1790 d a. 3-11-1798 m Rebecca Hodson LCol MD
John: b 2-15-1722 d 3-6-1792 m Margaret — CS MD
John: b 1730 d p. 1800 m Elizabeth Cary Sol VA
John G.: b 10-29-1763 d p. 3-28-1797 m Mary Wager Pvt CT
Jonathan: b 5- -1738 d 1791 m Mindwell Hoskins Pvt CT
Joseph: b 8-10-1744 d 1794 m Susanna Mason Pvt CT
Joseph, Jr.: b 2-15-1750 d 1830 m Elizabeth Robbins Pvt CT
Joseph: b 10-28-1736 d 9-6-1799 m Mary — Pvt NY
Joseph: b 11-24-1754 d 2-11-1811 m (1)Sally Meade (2)Judith Cary Eggleston PM Maj VA
Matthew Jacqueline: b 1763 d 9-27-1839 m Anne Cary Cav VA
Richard: b c. 1719 d 3-9-1781 m Rebekah Clough PS VA
Samuel: b 1737 d 2-14-1817 m Dorcas Loomis Pvt CT
Thomas: b c. 1740/41 d 12-25-1822 m (1)Rebecca Drake Ann Clark Pvt CT

EGLE, (includes EAGLE, EAGLES)
Alexander: b 1745 d 11-27-1821 m (1)Electa — (2)Esther Crane (3)Sarah — PS NJ
Casper: b 10-16-1725 d 9-3-1804 m Elizabeth Mentges Pvt PA
Dominick: b 7-18-1760 d 5-18-1829 m Anna Borhman Pvt PA
Thomas: b 1709 d 8-8-1783 m (1)Rachel Nuteman (2)Lois — (3)Jerusha — (4)Mrs Martha Sayre Pvt NJ
Thomas: b 4-3-1743 d 1- -1810 m Magdalene Bussy 1Lt NY
Valentine: b 12-27-1756 d 11-23-1820 m Elizabeth Thomas Lt PA
Wm.: b 1761 d 4-5-1848 m Mary Ann Day Jeffries Pvt VA ★

EHART, (includes AHART)
Michael: b c. 1735 d p. 5-11-1788 m Katherine — PS VA

EHLE,
Harmanus: b 11-12-1762 d 4-12-1844 m Betsey Cornue Pvt NY
Michael: b 10- -1746 d 4-16-1823 m Jannetje Van Der Werken Pvt NY
Peter: b 1729 d 1808 m Mary Magdalen Douw Sol NY
Peter: b 12-23-1746 d 1-25-1829 m Catherin Nellis Cpl NY W ★

EHLER,
Daniel: b 3-10-1757 d 7-22-1832 m Margaret Fundersmith Pvt PA

EHRET,
John: b c. 1756 d 1838 m X Sol PA

EHRENFRIED,
Johan George: b c. 1748 d p. 1810 m Chatarina Barbara — Pvt PA

EIB,
Henry: b — d p. 1782 m Barbara — Sgt PA

EICHELBERGER,
Adam: b 5-9-1739 d 12-9-1787 m Magdilena Bectol Capt PA
George: b 6-23-1739 d 8-30-1780 m Lydia Worley PS Dep QMGen PA
Jacob: b 9-26-1746 d 8-14-1811 m Anna Maria Reinacker PS PA
John: b 1750 d 4-22-1822 m Mary Leonard Pvt MD PA ★
John Frederick: b 2-18-1722 d 1783 m Anna Maria Kintz CS PA
Martin: b 11-16-1716 d 1781 m Anna Maria — CS PA

EICHER,
Peter: b c. 1718 d a. 3-29-1815 m Nancy Smith Pvt PA

EICHOLTZ,
Jacob: b 1742 d 1776 m Mary Shaffner Pvt PA
Leonard: b 9-4-1750 d 4-25-1817 m Katherine Myers SgtMaj PA

EIDSON,
Henry: b c. 1750 d a. 2-8-1819 m Jane Arthur Ens VA
James: b 1760-4 d 1- -1846 m Polly Humphreys Pvt SC ★
Shelton: b 1753 d 8-1-1834 m X Pvt VA ★
Thomas: b c. 1735 d a. 1828 m Sally — Pvt GA

EIGHTS,
Abraham: b 5-10-1745 d 1-10-1820 m Catherine Brooks 2Lt NY

EIGNER,
Henry: b 1-8-1739 d 11-2-1824 m Susanna Romig Capt PA

EILAND,
Absalom: b c. 1750-5 d 7- -1814 m Anne — Sol GA

EILERT,
Christopher:b 6-16-1760 d 8-7-1824 m Maria Magdalena
  Fenstemacher Pvt PA

EISAMAN,(includes ISAMAN)
Michael: b 2-15-1758 d 11-15-1840 m Barbara Baughman Pvt PA ★
Peter: b 1-21-1754 d 1817 m (1)Justina Altman (2)Anna Elizabeth
  — Pvt PA

EISENBEISS,
Andrew: b 8-25-1766 d 4-20-1809 m Mary Wagner Pvt PA

EISENHARD,
Andrew: b c. 1762 d 4- -1817 m Johanna — Pvt PA

EISENHOWER, (includes EISENHAUER & ISENHAUER)
Frederick: b — d 10-4-1777 m Hannah — Pvt PA
John: b 6-24-1727 d 2-23-1789 m (1)Veronica Meyer (2)Barbara
  Steckbeck CMman PA
Martin: b c. 1754 d p. 1820 m Sarah — Pvt PA
Phillip: b 12-19-1754 d 1828 m (1)Elva Klinefelter (2)Elizabeth
  Bixler Pvt PA ★

EISENHUTH,
Bernet: b 5-16-1755 d 6-22-1866 m Catharine Saylor Pvt PA

EISENLORD,
John: b 8-6-1737 d 8-6-1777 m Ann E. Gramps Maj NY

ELAM,
Godfrey: b 1763 d 1835 m Sarah — Pvt VA ★
James: b 1735 d p. 2-6-1796 m Lucy — Capt VA
Joel: b c. 1736 d 9-6-1798 m Mary Ann — PS VA
Josiah: b 1753 d p. 12-29-1819 m Sarah A. Porter Sol VA
Wm.: b 1759 d p. 1810 m Catharine Green Sol VA

ELBERT,
John L.: b 4-12-1760 d 7-10-1835 m Elizabeth Sudler SrgMte MD
Samuel: b 1740 d 11-1-1788 m Elizabeth Rae MGen GA

ELDEN,
Gibeon: b 6-2-1761 d 10-7-1841 m Susanna Whitney Pvt MA ★
John, Sr.: b 2-14-1731 d 5- -1793 m Ruth Sands Capt MA
John, Jr.: b 4-10-1754 d 5-30-1797 m Dorcas Foss Cpl MA

ELDER,
Abram: b 7-27-1754 d 7-27-1827 m Susan Ardry Pvt PA
Andrew: b c. 1745 d 1807 m Margaret — Pvt VA
Charles: b 1731 d 1804 m Julia Ward PS MD
David: b a. 1739 d — m Margery Stewart Pvt PA
David: b 7-8-1752 d 1823 m Jane Boggs Pvt PA
David: b 8-17-1760 d 8-4-1853 m (1)Mollie Reed (2)Pollie Phillips
  (3)Elizabeth Allen Pvt VA
Ephraim: b c. 1735 d 1800 m Martha Patsy Matthews Pvt VA ★
Ephraim: b 10-19-1737 d 10-16-1794 m Mary Mathews Pvt VA
George: b 1740 d p. 9-2-1799 m Sarah Vogan Pvt PA
Isaac: b 1-15-1739 d 7-15-1796 m Mary Hunnewell Sgt MA
James: b 1763 d 4-13-1813 m Martha Robinson Sol PA
James: b 1712 d 9-13-1818 m 2)Elizabeth Maips PS PA
John, Sr.: b 1-26-1706 d 7-17-1792 m (1)Mary Baker (2)Mary
  Simpson PS PA
John, Jr.: b 8-3-1757 d 4-27-1811 m Elizabeth Awl Ens PA
John: b 1762 d 1-19-1835 m Mary Dougherty Pvt PA ★
Joseph: b c. 1756 d 3-19-1829 m Margaret Thompson Sgt NY W★
Robert: b 1730 d 1807 m Mary — Pvt PA
Robert: b 1732 d 1818 m Elizabeth Tomson Pvt PA
Robert: b 6-11-1742 d 9-29-1818 m Mary Thompson Col PA
Robert: b c. 1734 d 1790 m (1)— Cole (2)Mary Taylor Pvt PA
Robert, Jr.: b 1751 d 10- -1837 m Mary Whiteside Pvt PA
Robert: b 1760 d 10-28-1839 m Rebecca — Pvt VA ★
Samuel: b 8-29-1748 d 5-10-1819 m Hannah Freeman Pvt MA
Samuel: b c. 1755 d p. 1810 m Cythia Mackelvain Pvt SC
Wm., Sr.: b 1707 d a. 5- -1776 m (1)Anne Wheeler (2)Jacobi
  Clementina Livers PS MD
Wm.: b 2-19-1754 d 11-21-1786 m Kezia Hanson Pvt MA
Wm.: b 1725 d 11-9-1799 m Mary Akers CS MA
Wm.: b c. 7-20-1757 d 1800 m Sarah Abraham Ens PA
Wm.: b c. 1759 d p. 1790 m — Sol NC

ELDERKIN,
Bela: b 12-10-1751 d p. 1793 m Philena Fitch 1Lt CT
James: b 10-9-1739 d p. 1785 m Martha Bliss PS CT
Jedediah: b 1717/18 d 3-3-1793 m Anne Wood BG CT
John: b c. 2-3-1718 d 11- -1783 m Rebecca Allen Lt QM CT
Joshua: b 10-30-1720 d 2- -1801 m Rachel Wetmore PS CT
Vine: b 9-11-1745 d 8-15-1800 m Lydia White Capt CT

ELDERT,
Henderick: b 7-16-1749 d 9-27-1793 m (1)Catharine Cornell
  (2)Cornelia — PS NY

ELDON,
John: b 1752 d 7-4-1828 m Elizabeth Curtiss Pvt CT

ELDREDGE, (includes ELDRED & ELDRIDGE)
Aaron: b 2-2-1735 d 7-2-1785 m Elizabeth Stilwell PS NJ
Amos: b c. 1761 d p. 1796 m Hannah Littlefield Smn MA
Barnabas: b 5-19-1738 d 7-13-1797 m Patience Crowell Capt MA
Caleb: b — d p. 1825 m Harriet Huntington Pvt MA
Charles, Jr.: b 8-28-1743 d 11-20-1798 m (1)Rachel Avery
  (2)Gloriana Havens Ens PS CT
Christopher, Sr.: b 1-22-1722 d 3- -1811 m Mary Hempstead Vol CT
Christopher, Jr.: b 5-29-1756 d 12-2-1785 m Sally Satterlee Pvtr CT
Daniel: b 2-25-1745 d 1814 m Prudence Warner Lt CT
Daniel: b 12-24-1758 d 12-11-1781 m Lucy Stanton Pvt CT
Daniel: b 9-1-1748 d 5-20-1820 m (1)Amy Vaughn (2)Mrs Margaret
  Carpenter Pvt VT
Edward: b 9-9-1737 d 3-28-1821 m Adna Hammond Sgt MA
Eli: b 2-8-1739 d 4-3-1791 m Priscilla Leaming Maj PS NJ
Elisha: b 1756 d 12-1-1841 m Mary Wheadon Pvt MA
Henry: b 1758 d 3-21-1825 m Elizabeth Tanner Pvt RI CT ★
Hezekiah: b 12-29-1744 d 6-29-1806 m Abigail Whiton Sol CT
James: b 5-18-1745 d 3-29-1811 m (1)Lucy Gallup (2)Mrs Chloe
  Hubbard Capt CT
James: b 11-16-1753 d 8-2-1841 m Sarah Newton Sgt CT ★
James: b 5-12-1749 d 1814 m Phoebe Hunt Pvt NY
James: b 8-29-1740 d p. 1787 m Lucy Reynolds Lt RI
Jehosaphat: b 1716 d 1801 m Betty Swift PS CT
Jeremiah: b 12-18-1738 d 3- -1811 m (1)Audrey Harrington (2)Anna
  Barber Pvt RI
Jesse, Sr.: b 8-9-1715 d 12-17-1794 m Abigail Smith PS CT
Jesse, Jr.: b 4-25-1742 d 5-9-1788 m Mary Pierce Sol CT
John: b 2-7-1756 d p. 1818 m Hannah Buell Sgt CT ★
John: b 5-23-1759 d 2-27-1814 m Rebecca Edwards Pvt NJ W ★
John: b 2-22-1763 d 12-19-1822 m Huldah Austin Pvt RI ★
Jonathan: b 11-19-1752 d 9-10-1840 m Mary Champlin Sgt CT ★
Joseph: b 12-20-1751 d p. 6-15-1820 m Barbara — Pvt MA ★
Joshua: b 7-25-1743 d 1-20-1826 m Jane — Pvt MA
Levi: b 9-27-1753 d 5-30-1830 m Thankful Howes Pvt MA
Levi: b — d a. 7-26-1790 m Esther Edwards PS NJ
Micah: b 3-17-1758 d p. 1795 m Ann Hanks Pvt CT
Nathan: b 5-25-1761 d 1-19-1840 m Lydia Noble Pvt MA
Phineas: b 11-29-1755 d 4-7-1826 m Jane Ham Capt PA
Rolfe: b 12-29-1745 d p. 1790 m Susanna Everard Walker CS VA
Samuel: b c. 1750 d 1-20-1782 m Hannah Fuller Pvt CT
Samuel: b 7-4-1744/5 d 12-18-1825 m Mary Barlow Lt MA ★
Samuel: b 1720 d 1785 m Susanna Casey Pvt RI ★
Simeon: b 1758 d 6-11-1851 m Mary Brittain Pvt NC ★
Thomas, Sr.: b 1733 d 1803 m Helen Brown Pvt CT
Thomas: b 5-15-1742 d 5-4-1810 m Sarah Gage 1Lt MA
Thomas: b 1734 d 3-8-1812 m (1)Isabel Niles (2)Mary Niles Pvt MA
Wm.: b 7-28-1758 d 4-17-1836 m Elizabeth Daggett Smn MA ★
Wm.: b 12-1-1759 d 2-21-1808 m Judith Corson Pilot NJ
Zoeth: b 1751 d 3-18-1828 m (1)Elizabeth Pearl (2)Bethia Hinckley
  Pvt MM CT

ELGIN,
Gustavus: b 9-17-1754 d 1-24-1834 m Nancy — Capt ★
Hesekiah: b 1762 d p. 1796 m Sinai Elgin Mil MD
Samuel: b 7-5-1758 d 1842 m Agnes McClanahan Pvt MD ★
Walter: b 4-12-1756 d p. 3-27-1836 m Mary Fulton Pvt OrdlSgt VA
Wm., Sr.: b 1732 d 9- -1794 m Elizabeth Harrison PS MD

ELIAS,
Henry: b 1751/2 d 8-10-1832 m Ann Snare Pvt PA

ELIASON,
Cornelius: b c. 1750 d p. 1778 m Hester Rothwell Pvt DE

ELKINS,
Archibald: b c. 1756 d p. 8-18-1791 m Margaret — Pvt VA
Henry: b 3-9-1729 d p. 1782 m Mary Moore Capt NH
James: b 4-16-1755 d 6-6-1836 m Martha Jackson PS Spy VA ★
Jonathan: b 8-3-1734 d 12-4-1808 m Elizabeth Rowell Pvt NH
Jonathan: b 10-23-1761 d 5-15-1852 m (1)Judith Foster (2)Eunice
  Stoddard Sct CT Pvt NH
Moses: b 12-16-1743 d p. 1783 m Dorothy Moulton Cpl NH
Peter: b 4-8-1746 d 2-24-1798 m Huldah Buswell Pvt NH
Robert: b 1745 d 3- -1822 m Sarah Reardon PS VA
Thomas: b 6-29-1743 d 10-25-1818 m Mary Hailes Cdr MA
Thomas: b 10-11-1711 d p. 3-31-1785 m Anna Brown PS NH

ELLENBERGER, (includes EILENBERGER)
Christian: b 4-6-1731 d 10-22-1804 m Sara Keres Pvt PA
Jacob: b c. 1735 d 10- -1810 m (1)Anna Huntzaker (2)Veronica —
  Pvt PA

ELLENWOOD, (includes ELLINGWOOD, ELLINWOOD)
Benjamin: b 11-20-1748 d 1826 m Abigail Lamson Pvt NH ★
Hannaniah: b 1-7-1757 d 1-13-1833 m Ester Marsh Pvt MA
John: b 10-2-1756 d 5-23-1836 m (1)Mrs Hannah Glover (2)Esther
  Woodberry Pvt MA
Thomas: b 8-1-1728 d 5-31-1804 m (1)Abigail King (2)Mary Babcock
  Pvt PA CS MA

ELLERBE,
Thomas: b 1749 d 9-16-1808 m Obedience Gillespie Capt SC
Wm.: b 1742 d 12-4-1820 m Hannah Farr Pvt SC

ELLERSON,
David: b 7-4-1750 d 8-24-1838 m Sara Beacraft Pvt VA PA ★

ELLERY,
Benjamin: b 7-28-1744 d 2-15-1825 m Sarah Gouch PS MA
Christopher: b 4-22-1736 d 2-24-1789 m (1)Mary Vernon (2)Rachel
  King PS CS RI
Eppes: b c. 1734 d p. 1782 m Alice Foster Gnr MA
Nathaniel: b 2-13-1753 d 2-22-1833 m Sarah Cunningham Sgt MA
Nathaniel: b 10-20-1726 d 1778 m (1)Rachel Stevens (2)Mary
  Parsons GnrMte MA
Wm.: b 12-22-1727 d 2-15-1820 m (1)Ann Remington (2)Abigail
  Carey SDI RI

ELLICOTT,
Andrew: b 1-24-1754 d 8-28-1820 m Sarah Brown Maj MD
Jonathan: b 11-9-1756 d 1826 m Sarah Harvey Capt MD

ELLINGSWORTH,
Nehemiah Covington: b 12-28-1762 d 8-1-1819 m (1)Sarah
  Workman (2)Patty Workman (3)Lovey — Pvt MD

ELLINGTON,
David: b 9-7-1741 d p. 1791 m Jerusha Fowlkes PS VA
Hezekiah: b c. 1793/4 m Ridley — Pvt VA
Jeremiah: b c. 1737 d p. 11-9-1801 Frances Jones PS VA

ELLIOTT, (includes ELLET, ELIOT, ELLIOTT, ELLIOT)
Aaron: b 3-15-1718 d 12-30-1785 m Mary Worthington PS CS CT
Aaron: b 7-22-1747 d 2- -1829 m Lydia Taylor PS MA
Alexander: b 1763 d 8-23-1852 m (1)Nancy Campbell (2)Polly Stotls
  Mid VA ★
Amos: b 1755 d 4-7-1807 m Martha Stewart Hartshorn Cpl NH
Andrew, Jr.: b 1-11-1743 d 9-26-1805 m Mary Pynchon PS CT
Andrew: b 9-11-1756 d Hannah Dakin Pvt MA
Andrew: b 12-25-1718 d 9-13-1778 m Elizabeth Langdon PS MA
Andrew: b 12-8-1751 d 3-26-1813 m Jane Ayres Pvt NY
Barnard: b 7-16-1751 d 1-15-1828 m Elizabeth Carter Pvt NH
Benjamin: b 1741 d 12-26-1815 m Susanna Cloud Pvt DE
Benjamin: b c. 1750 d c. 1825 m Abigail Webster Pvt NH
Benjamin: b 1752 d 3-13-1835 m (1)Mary Carpenter (2)Sarah
  Ashman (3)Susan Haines PS Pvt PA
Daniel: b c. 1753 d a. 8-2-1785 m Elizabeth Ferguson PS SC
David: b 6-18-1752 d 1-4-1793 m (1)Hannah Adams (2)Mrs Lucy
  Campbell Ens NH
David: b 3-3-1716 d 5-11-1798 m Mehetabel Aldrich PS NY
Ebenezer: b 6-27-1720 d 1794 m Susanna Soden Pvt MA
Edmond: b 1-28-1716 d 10-8-1789 m Mehitable Worthen PS NH
Edmund: b 6-3-1744 d 12-25-1800 m Judith Bartlett Capt NH
Elias, Jr.: b c. 1707 d 2-23-1785 m Ruth Lawrence CS NH
Elias, Jr.: b 6-25-1750 d 11-17-1838 m Sarah Pierce PS NH
Ephraim: b 12-8-1764 d 1-1-1837 m Mary Robie Pvt NH
Ephraim: b c. 1758 d 4-6-1833 m (1)Margaret Heart (2)Sarah Hall
  PS NC
Ezekiel: b 8-11-1746 d 4-12-1834 m Sarah Brown 2Lt NH
George: b 1758 d 11-7-1838 m Eleanor Bears Sgt MA W★
George: b c. 1750 d 1824 m Mary Cloud Pvt PA
George: b 1728 d 1814 m (1)Charity Addidle (2)Florence Bell
  (3)Ann Marshall Capt VA
George: b 6-22-1749 d p. 1780 m Mary Morrett Col VA
Henry: b 1712 d 12-21-1809 m Mary Kegwin Pvt PA
Jacob: b 1-26-1730 d 5-10-1817 m Dorothy Jones Pvt ME
Jacob: b 4-3-1764 d 10-15-1849 m Ann Baker Pvt MA ★
Jacob: b 11-5-1755 d 12-6-1841 m Martha Sleeper Lt NH
Jacob: b 3-5-1758 d 6-8-1834 m (1)Priscilla Ayers Pvt NY
James: b c. 1730 d p. 1790 m Pvt MD
James: b c. 1740 d p. 8-3-1816 m Margaret — Pvt PS NC
James: b c. 1730 d 1803 m — Sol NC
James, Sr.: b c. 1750 d p. 5-5-1799 m Mary Johnston Capt PA
James: b c. 1747 d 1799 m Martha Risk Capt VA
Jedediah: b 1760 d 1844 m Hannah — Pvt NH
John: b 12-2-1732 d 3-9-1797 m Experience Hempsted CS CT
John: b 1753 d p. 1789 m Kezia Todd Pvt MD
John, Jr.: b 1-26-1756 d p. m Mary Huntington Pvt MA ★
John: b 2-8-1761 d p. 1809 m Bathsheba Fields SgtMaj NH
John: b 1724 d 1819 m Hannah Jones Pvt NH ★

John: b 7-7-1745 d 3-4-1827 m Rachel Nutting Pvt NH ★
John: b 1744 d 2-18-1827 m (1)Temperance Durril (2)Mrs Susannah
  Welch Pvt SC NH
John, Sr.: b c. 1720 d p. 1778 m Ruth Flanders PS NH
John: b 1755 d p. 9-29-1837 m Mary — Pvt NC ★
John: b 11-26-1742 d 8-8-1820 m Catherine — Lt PA ★
John: b 1753/4 d 5-23-1835 m (1)Margaret Patterson (2)Mrs. Leech
  Pvt PA MD ★
John: b — d 12-5-1829 m Sarah — Pvt RI
John: b —d 1797 m Peggy — Pvt VA
Johnston: b c. 1748 d 12- -1802 m Rebecca Mayes Pvt PA
Jonathan: b 9-30-1730 d 10-31-1813 m Hannah Wheeler MM MA
Jonathan: b 2-28-1750 d 10-31-1813 m Sarah Chase Pvt MA
Jonathan: b 12-8-1748 d 4-30-1819 m Mary Connor Pvt NH
Jonathan: b c. 1745 d p. 1798 m Mary Drain Sol VA
Joseph: b 2-2-1729 d 8-12-1775 m Jerusha Berry Capt CT
Joseph: b 11-17-1731 d 4-19-1820 m (1)Susanna — (2)Anna Dwight
  Capt MA
Joseph: b 6-25-1749 d 12-15-1777 m Joanna Morse Cpl MA
Joseph: b c. 1727 d 10-31-1796 m — Capt NY
Joseph: b 10-10-1755 d 3-29-1849 m (1)Patience Lewis (2)Deborah
  Lewis Pvt PA NY ★
Joseph: b — d 1819 m Sarah — PS NC
Laban: b 1-4-1757 d 4-27-1830 m Mehitable Harrington Pvt PS NY
Martin: b c. 1750 d 3-14-1832 m (1)Anne Finch (2)Elizabeth
  McCombs Pvt VA
Nathan: b 4-13-1725 d 3-20-1798 m Clarina Griswold PS CS CT
Nathaniel: b c. 1760 d c. 1830 m Hannah — Pvt MA
Oliver: b 4-24-1734 d 3-5-1837 m Mary Fisk Sgt NH ★
Reuben: b 1764 d 1841 m — Renshaw Pvt VA
Richard: b 1762 d 5- -1849 m Polly McIntre Pvt MA
Richard: b c. 1736 d 1799 m — Stewart Col VA
Richard: b c. 1739 d p. 7- -1796 m (1)Martha Merritt (2)Mrs Anne
  Jameson Maj GS VA
Robert: b 1761/2 d 1845/6 m Jane — Pvt PA
Robert: b — d 1794 m (1)Miss Hughes (2)Ann Duncan Adj PA
Robert: b 1747 d 1828 m (2)Margaret Boyd Sol PA
Robert: b 1738 d 1-3-1838 m Elizabeth Childress 2Lt VA ★
Robert: b 1745 d 1806 m Elizabeth — Pvt VA
Robert: b c. 1720 d p. 9-2-1799 m Tabitha Cheatham PS VA
Samuel: b 1757 d 1841 m Keziah Webb Pvt MD ★
Samuel: b 8-26-1748 d 12-1-1795 m Mary Richardson Pvt MD
Samuel: b 3-9-1756 d p. m Susannah Hughes Lt PA
Samuel: b 1751 d 5-24-1831 m Mary — Capt PA
Samuel: b 1745 d 1/2- -1822 m (1)Mary Oldham (2)Nancy Lynn Pvt
  VA
Samuel: b 1754 d 7-16-1821 m (1)Rachel Warner (2)Winnifred Lee
  Pvt VA ★
Teackle: b 1755 d 1803 m Margaret Warrington Pvt VA
Thomas: b 12-25-1725 d 1800 m Martha — PS MD
Thomas: b 1740 d 1797 m Sarah — Capt MD
Thomas: b 9-23-1752 d 3-26-1818 m Sarah Swett Pvt MA
Thomas: b c. 1730 d 6-30-1815 m (1)Catherine Thomas (2)Jane
  Holiday Pvt PA
Thomas: b c. 1740 d a. 1-17-1784 m Winnifred Saunders Sol VA
Wm.: b — d p. 5- -1783 m — PS DE
Wm.: b 1758 d p. 1808 m Rachel Bosely Pvt MD
Wm.: b 1763 d 6-20-1821 m Elizabeth Atkinson PS MD
Wm.: b 9-23-1718 d 4-10-1798 m Emme Trask Pvt MA
Wm.: b 12-1-1748 d 6-4-1830 m (1)Dorothy Merrill (2)Rebecca
  Hildreth CS PS NH
Wm.: b 8-2-1752 d 3-31-1847 m (1)Lucretia Lowre (2)Maria Scutt
  (3)Mrs Hepzibah Mastin Pvt NY
Wm.: b c. 1750 d c. 1792 m Peninah — Pvt NC
Wm.: b 1747 d 12-7-1805 m Mary Barnett PS NC
Wm.: b 2-11-1764 d 4-5-1811 m Deborah White Pvt PS NC
Wm.: b 5-12-1752 d 8-20-1838 m — Ens PA
Wm.: b 1751 d 3-19-1805 m Ruth Crawford Pvt PA
Wm.: b 8-16-1759 d 9- -1796 m Jane Gaston Pvt SC
Wm.: b 1740 d 1788 m Eleanor Burgess Ens VA
Wm.: b 10-20-1754 d 9-23-1836 m Anzele Andros Bradford Pvt VA ★

ELLIS,
Abraham: b 9-27-1753 d 9-26-1837 m Katharine Joel Lt PA VA ★
Amos: b 3-2-1743/4 d 5-30-1817 m Hannah Hill Capt MA
Asa: b 6-6-1744 d 12-25-1840 m Phoebe Smith Pvt MA ★
Augustus: b 4-2-1758 d 8-19-1836 m Desire Slocum Pvt RI ★
Barnabas: b 1745 d 6-26-1838 m Elizabeth Spencer PS Lt NH
Benjamin: b 1751/2 d 10-28-1824 m Roxana Thayer Dr CT
Benjamin: b 3-29-1734 d 8-27-1828 m (1)Comfort Baker (2)Hannah
  Chubb PS CT
Benjamin: b 1750/51 d 1835 m (1)Ruth Pike (2)Lois Mann (3)Zilpha
  Mills Pvt MA ★
Caleb: b 8-16-1754 d 3- -1813 m Mary Crouch Pvt NH MA
Charles: b 6-19-1726 d p. 1800 m Bathsheba Fuller Cpl MA
Charles: b 1-28-1749 d 1828 m (1)Elizabeth Waters (2)Sarah Tucker
  Sol VA
Daniel: b 2-5-1727 d 9-1-1794 m Bathsheba How Pvt NJ
Daniel: b c. 1755 d p. 1778 m Sarah Robinson Pvt NY
David: b 1-30-1763 d 1843 m Sarah Washburn Pvt MA ★
Dudley Brown: b 11- -1760 d 11- -1837 m Elizabeth Watts Pvt VA ★
Ebenezer: b 1-15-1752 d 11-28-1820 m Hannah Wood Pvt MA
Edwin: b 5-16-1749 d p. 10-15-1806 m Hannah Peters PS VA

Eliphalet: b 11-5-1733 d 10-12-1798 m Mary Lewis Lt MA
Enos: b — d *p.* 1794 m Elizabeth — PS VA
Ephraim: b 6-15-1765 d *p.* 1840 m Sarah Fellows Pvt MA ★
Evan: b 2-8-1726 d 12-22-1796 m Sarah — PS NC
Ezekiel: b 1760 d 1839 m Lydia Lawrence Pvt MA
Francis: b *c.* 1740 d 9-14-1817 m Rebecca Ireson Cpl MA
Freeman: b 7-7-1745 d 3-15-1802 m Sarah Bradford Sgt MA
Freeman: b 1747 d *p.* 3-27-1803 m Ann Shackleford CS NC
Garret: b 1756 d 1827 m Mary Tappan PS NY
George: b 5-10-1747 d *p.* 1787 m Phebe Stephens Pvt MA
Gideon: b 1714 d 8-16-1800 m Elizabeth — PS NJ
Gideon, Sr.: b 10- -1724 d 9-30-1793 m (1)Jemima Austin (2)Lydia Reynolds (3)Elizabeth Manchester Pvt CS RI
Henry: b 1748 d 8-3-1838 m Melitiah Thayer Pvt NH
Isaac: b 12-8-1744 d 10-10-1832 m Tabitha Philips Cpl MA
Isaac: b *c.* 1725 d *p.* 2-28-1784 m Mary Shivers CS NJ
Isaac: b 1760 d *p.* 1830 Elizabeth Spencer Pvt VA
Isaac Newton: b 10-29-1752 d 4-10-1833 m Nancy Downing Capt PA ★
Jabez, Jr.: b 12-12-1761/2 d 1-1-1852 m (1)Hannah Mack (2)Prudence Mack Pvt CT
Jabez: b 6-1-1733 d 11-14-1808 m Abigail Morse Capt MA
Jacob: b *c.* 1724/5 d 2-27-1809 m Elizabeth Moore Fif Pvt PA
James: b *c.* 1727 d *p.* 1790 m Mary Veatch Cpl MD
James: b 1734 d 1804 m Elsie Edwards Pvt NY
James: b 5-8-1758 d 1818 m Sarah Riggs Pvt NY
James: b *c.* 1755 d 1827 m Mary — PS VA
Jeremiah: b 1-21-1754 d 1851 m Nellie Harris ‖ Sgt PA
Joel: b 11-14-1724 d 1785 m Elizabeth Clap Pvt MA
Joel, Jr.: b 5-22-1745 d 9-29-1834 m (1)Ruth Green (2)Tabitha White Pvt MA
Joel: b 12-23-1759 d 7-19-1852 m Sarah Walcott Pvt MA ★
John: b 9- -1735 d *p.* 1790 m Elizabeth Sawyer Sgt CT
John: b 3-2-1727 d 10-20-1805 m Bethiah Palmer Chp CT
John, Jr.: b 11-29-1754 d 11-25-1826 m Rhoda Patridge Capt MA
John: b 1-23-1742 d 8-17-1827 m Molly Dimick Lt MA
John: b 3-3-1746 d 5-25-1821 m Hannah Ellis Pvt MA
John: b 1763 d 7-6-1820 m Submit Olds Pvt MA
John: b 10-28-1723 d 3-2-1816 m Mary Baker CS PS MA
John, Sr.: b *c.* 1718 d *p.* 1790 m (1)Eunice Millard (2)Mary — (3)Mary Horton PS NH
John, Jr.: b 4-27-1754 d 3-13-1827 m Rachel Marsh Cpl NH
John: b 10-3-1759 d 9-15-1858 m (1)Sarah Blackmer (2)Anna Wright Converse Cpl MA VT ★
John: b 1-29-1749 d 1797 m Sarah Parrish Sgt VA
Jonathan: b 2-27-1731 d 1790 m Rhoda Keith Pvt CT
Joseph: b 1732 d 3-25-1808 m Jemina Eldridge Pvt MA
Joseph: b 7-28-1736 d *p.* 1790 m Sarah Clark Pvt MA
Joseph: b 11-25-1759 d 11-22-1815 m Elizabeth Child Pvt MA
Joseph: b *c.* 1720 d 1781 m Lydia — PS NH
Levin: b *c.* 1750 d *p.* 2-19-1831 m Isabel — Pvt VA
Luke: b 1755 d *p.* 1784 m (1)Naomi Briggs (2)Elizabeth Macomber Pvt MA
Nathan: b 11-10-1749 d *c.* 1819 m Mary Walker Capt VA PA
Philip: b 10-16-1750 d 4-17-1831 m Rebecca Perry Sgt MA
Philip: b 1725 d 1778 m Mary Staples Pvt MA
Richard: b 8-16-1704 d 10-7-1797 m Jane Phillips PS MA
Richard: b 12-20-1760 d 1841 m (1)Eunice Chilson (2)Chloe Chilson Pvt MA
Richard: b — d 10-20-1804 m (1)Sarah Hogg (2)Elizabeth Greene Sol Asst Cmnsry SC
Robert: b 1712 d 1779 m — LCol NC
Robert: b 1753 d 12-25-1849 m Eliza Robertson Pvt NC
Robert: b *c.* 1755 d 8-20-1818 m Diana — Pvt NC
Samuel: b 8-14-1739 d 10-7-1826 m Sala (Kinsbury) Pvt MA
Samuel, Sr.: b *c.* 1730 d *p.* 7-19-1804 m Mary — PS NC
Samuel: b 5-8-1753 d 1- -1834 m Mary Nye Cpl MA
Samuel, Jr.: b 4-9-1762 d 3-10-1847 m Martha Howard Pvt NC★
Samuel: b 10-22-1754 d 3- -1848 m Mary Frye Sgt PA ★
Sawyer: b 2-13-1757 d 9-4-1830 m Abigail Hutchinson Pvt CT
Simeon: b 1749 d 1-23-1799 m Lydia Comstock Pvt NH
Simeon: b *c.* 1738 d *p.* 10-6-1776 m Priscilla Bates Sol NJ
Simeon: b *c.* 1750 d 9- -1787 m Elizabeth (Millet) QM SC
Stephen: b 10- -1748 d 3-5-1824 m Susanna Thompson Sgt MA
Stephen: b 11-7-1763 d 11-16-1847 m Rebecca Huntington Sgt PA ★
Stephen: b *c.* 1740 d *a.* 3- -1819 m Susan Smith 2Lt VA
Stephen: b 1745 d *a.* 1850 m Diana Lowry Sol VA
Thomas: b 1-1-1728 d 4-4-1797 m Ruth Thomas Pvt MA
Thomas: b 9-26-1744 d 1800 m Jerusha Clark Pvt MA
Thomas: b 12-6-1752 d 12-3-1812 m Eunice Reed Pvt MA
Timothy, Sr.: b 9-14-1724 d 7-13-1817 m Elizabeth—Col PS CS NH
Timothy, Jr.: b 1-5-1746 d 1813 m Anna Page Sgt NH
Timothy: b 1749 d 3-30-1814 m Beulah Pond PS NH
Turner: b 12-23-1733 d 12- -1817 m Mary White Sgt MA
Wm.: b 1758 d 3-1-1837 m Anne Edgerton Sgt CT
Wm.: b 1743 d 9-25-1793 m Agnes Brooks Carr Sol VA
Wm.: b 1730 d 1785 m (1)Amy Matlack (2)Elizabeth Potts Maj NJ
Wm.: b 1755 d *p.* 1812 m Elizabeth Staunton Pvt NC
Wm.: b 1760 d *p.* 1812 m Sarah Ransom Pvt VT
Wm.: b — d 1832 m Frances — Sol VA
Wm.: b 8-12-1755 d 6-19-1823 m (1)Elizabeth Weller (2)Polly (Clark) Leonard Pvt VA
Wm.: b 1760 d 1800 m Elizabeth Shipp Pvt VA

ELLISON,
Alderson: b 1743 d 3- -1808 m Lucretia Smaw PS CS NC
James: b 2-28-1757 d 1838 m Ann Calloway Spy Sol VA ★
John: b 12-7-1761 d 1845 m Ann Paul Spy VA
Joseph: b 1-11-1758 d 5-17-1830 m Mary Kavanaugh Sct VA
Robert: b 1742 d 3-8-1806 m (1)Elizabeth Potts (2)Jennie Seawright Capt SC
Robert: b 1720 d *a.* 1-5-1791 m (1)Elizabeth Scott (2)Frances Avant 1Lt SC
Samuel: b *c.* 1764 d 2-15-1789 m Elizabeth Curtis Pvt NJ

ELLITHORP,
Azariah: b 2- -1760 d 3-17-1835 m Elizabeth — Pvt CT ★

ELLMAKER,
Jacob: b 2-16-1749 d 8-24-1824 m (1)Elizabeth Hoffman (2)Margaret Seeberne Pvt PA
Leonard, Jr.: b 4-12-1741 d 1-14-1829 m Elizabeth Baker Pvt PA
Nathaniel: b 12-1-1751 d 4-24-1837 m Elizabeth Fallenbaun PS Pvt PA

ELLMES, (includes ELLMS)
Joseph: b 5-15-1732 d 3-28-1823 m Mary Lincoln Pvt MA

ELLSBERRY, (includes ELSBREE, ELSBURY)
Frederick: b 9-4-1761 d 5-12-1813 m Jean Culbertson Pvt PA
John: b *c.* 1733/4 d 5-3-1803 m — Pvt VA
Michael: b 1751 d 9-10-1787 m Ann Greenleaf Lt NC
Wm.: b 1-1-1745 d *p.* 1786 m Susannah Woodle Sgt MA

ELLSWORTH, (includes ELSWORTH)
Aaron: b 9-29-1753 d 1-5-1831 m Sarah Chapman Sol NH
Benjamin: b 7-9-1763 d 8-27-1828 m Ann Stiles Pvt CT
Charles: b 12-12-1721 d *p.* 1779 m Betsey Bell PS CS CT
Charles, Jr.: b 2-25-1763 d 11-10-1813 m Sarah Hill Pvt CT
Charles, Jr.: b 1730 d 1-4-1776 m Rachel — Capt CS CT
Daniel: b 1727 d 7-27-1803 m Mary McKinstrey PS CT
David: b 3-28-1741 d 1-4-1821 m Phebe Lyman Cpl CT
Eliphalet: b 5- -1762 d 7-24-1834 m (2)Jemima Ford Pvt CT ★
George: b — d 3-24-1840 m Sarah Reynolds Pvt NY
Gurdon: b 1737 d 6-26-1803 m Lydia Makepeace Sgt CT
Henry: b 1742 d 1816 m Hannah Curtis Pvt NY
Hezekiah: b 1755 d 1815 m (1)Lauranna Loomis (2)Sibyl Harmon Pvt CT
Jacob: b *c.* 1752 d 1854 m Hannah — Pvt VA
John: b 12-7-1762 d 3-6-1848 m (1)Anna Birge (2)Ruth Alling Pvt CT★
John: b 8-24-1735 d 2-14-1779 m (1)Sarah Clark (2)Martha Hall PS CT
John: b 4-17-1757 d 12-9-1840 m Lucy Dean Pvt NH RI CT★
John, Jr.: b 11-30-1756 d 7-14-1844 m Margaret King Pvt NY ★
Jonathan: b 5-29-1742 d 10-6-1806 m Jerusha Ellsworth Cpl CT
Moses: b *c.* 1730 d *p.* 1- -1802 m Mary Hinckle PS VA
Oliver: b 4-29-1745 d 11-27-1807 m Abigail Wolcott PS CS CT
Samuel: b 9-23-1752 d 7-18-1819 m (1)Irene Parsons (2)Elizabeth Bundy Sgt VT
Samuel: b 10-1-1718 d *c.* 1803 m Mrs Amy Matson CS PS VT
Solomon: b 4-30-1737 d 10-19-1822 m Mary Moseley Lt CT
Thomas: b 2-23-1750 d 3-6-1814 m Lucy Lowell Pvt MA
Wm.: b 11-13-1752 d 2-21-1812 m Mary Potter Pvt MA

ELMENDORF, (includes ELMENDORFF, ELMENDORPH)
Abraham: bpt 9-28-1735 d *p.* 9-11-1784 m Arriantje Crispel Pvt NY
Benjamin: b 2-24-1740 d *p.* 1790 m Blandina Van Buren 3Lt NY
Coenraad: b 11-10-1710 d 1789 m Sara DuBois PS NY
Conradt Wilhelmus: b 1755 d 6-16-1826 m Anna Van Steenburgh Sol NY
Gerrit, Jr.: b 3-14-1736 d 1-8-1788 m Henrica Elmendorf Pvt NY
Jacob: bpt 6-19-1737 d *p.* 1790 m Lea Bloemdal Pvt NY
Jacobus, Jr.: bpt 7-18-1736 d *p.* 1794 m Elizabeth Sammons Sol PS NY
John: b 4-27-1725 d 3-18-1812 m Margaret Delamater Capt NY
Jonathan: b 12-26-1723 d *p.* 1797 m (1)Helena or Magdalena Smedes (2)Catharine Bruyn LCol NY
Jonathan: b 7-21-1751 d *p.* 1807 m Margrietje Felten PS NY

ELMER,
Ebenezer: b 8-23-1752 d 10-18-1843 m Hannah Seeley 2Lt Dr NJ
Gad: b 8-31-1760 d 11-13-1819 m Anna Phillips Pvt MA
Hezekiah: b 9-24-1724 d 11-22-1810 m Sarah Wright PS Maj NH
Joseph: b 5-16-1760 d 12-18-1837 m Phebe Stoughton Pvt CT ★
Nathaniel: b 2-14-1733 d 12-17-1797 m Anne Thompson Capt Dr NY
Phineas: b 1762 d 1841 m Ketura Hudson Pvt CT
Samuel, Jr.: b 11-18-1753 d 6-8-1834 m Sarah Loomis Pvt CT ★
Timothy: b 4-4-1748 d 5-16-1780 m Mary Dayton Capt NJ
Wm.: b 1-19-1758 d 5-24-1816 m Mary Allison Pvt Dr NY

ELMORE,
Elijah: b 1743 d 7-30-1804 m Annie Gibbs Pvt CT
Elijah: b 1753 d 5-5-1804 m Mary Mercy Goodale Pvt MA
George: b *c.* 1760 d *p.* 1810 m Elizabeth — Sgt VA
George: b *c.* 1753 d *p.* 1806 m — Pvt VA
John: b *c.* 1740 d *p.* 1815 m Elizabeth Tugwell Sgt NC
John Archer : b 8-21-1762 d 4-24-1834 m (1)Mary Ann Sara Saxon (2)Nancy Martin Pvt VA

ELMORE, contd.
Matthias: b 1755 d *p.* 1835 m Rebecca Kelly Tms SC
Samuel: b 6-19-1720 d 8-23-1805 m (1)Mary Pardee (2)Sylvia Gibbs Col CT
Thomas: b 3-5-1758 d 7-1-1827 m Letitia Williams Matr VA

ELMS, (includes ELMES)
Charles: b 1-6-1756 d 1-6-1835 m Rebecca Withers Pvt SC
Eliphalet: b 12-14-1753 d 8-4-1830 m Chloe Leonard Pvt MA

ELRICK,
George: b 1755 d 1826 m Elizabeth Householder Pvt PA

ELROD,
Christopher, Jr.: b 8-15-1757 d 12-4-1827 m Sarah Douthet PS NC

ELSER,
Peter: b 9-22-1733 d 11-22-1787/8 m Anna Margaretta Stoever Pvt PA

ELSON,
Richard: b 1738 d 12-28-1804 m Mary Turner Pvt PA

ELSTON, (includes ELSTONE)
Abraham S.: b 1750 d 1823 m Mary Jewell Pvt NJ
Benjamin: b 12-25-1759 d 1- -1845 m Elizabeth Long Pvt NJ ★
David: b *c.* 1736 d *c.* 1811 m Fernita Line Sgt NJ
Eli: b 8-6-1764 d 4-15-1814 m Mary Paine Pvt NJ
Josiah: b *c.* 1759/60 d *c.* 1830 m Rebecca Lewis Pvt NJ

ELTINGE, (includes ELTING)
Abraham: b 8-21-1757 d *p.* 1791 m Amaantje Van Deusen Pvt NY
Abraham: bpt 4-13-1735 d 1797 m (1)Dina DuBois (2)Dorothy Bessimer PS Sol NY
Cornelius: b 1744 d 1820 m Blandina Elmendorf Pvt NY
Jacobus: b 12-15-1717 d 1-30-1777 m Elizabeth Hall PS NY.
James: b 2-15-1736 d *p.* 1790 m Marytje Van Steenberg 2Lt NY
John: b 10-17-1756 d — m Rachel Salisbury Sgt NY
Noah: b 12-3-1721 d 9-27-1778 m Jacomintje — Pvt NY
Thomas: b 8-6-1752 d 7-15-1821 m Rosina Rauch Sgt NS NY W★
Wm.: b 2-17-1745 d *p.* 1804 m Jannetje DuBois PS NY

ELTON,
Bradley: b 1741 d 1-3-1830 m Grace Wilcox Pvt PS CT W★

ELWELL,
Abraham, Sr.: b — d *a.* 12-26-1815 m — Lt NJ
Benjamin: b 11-10-1732/3 d 7-4-1801 m Abigail Ingraham Pvt MA
Jabez: b 1747 d 4-17-1813 m Thankful Clark Cpl MA ★
Jabez: b 1728 d 4-22-1809 m Tabitha Jones Pvt NY
Jesse: b 10-30-1761 d 12-3-1812 m Elizabeth McClanathan Pvt MA
John: b 10-8-1758 d 1800 m Judith Train Pvt MA
John: b 1717 d 1787 m (1)Abigail Sawtel (2)—(3)— Butler Sgt NJ
John: b 1744 d 1-8-1835 m Anne — PS NC
Mark: b 9-17-1730 d 11-18-1799 m (1)Mary Hibbard (2)Mrs Dorothy White Lt CT
Samuel: b 1742 d 1806 m Annie Hays Bradstreet Sgt MA
Samuel: b 9-10-1747 d 7-10-1824 m Amelia Morgan Sgt NJ
Thomas, Sr.: b 8-18-1718 d 1-27-1798 m (1)Lucy Pierce (2)Elizabeth Stratton CS MA
Thomas, Jr.: b 1752 d 1-6-1803 m Mary French Pvt MA

ELWOOD, (includes ELLWOOD)
Benjamin: b 2-16-1752 d 6-5-1831 m Elizabeth Coin Pvt NY
Isaac: b 11- -1754 d 2-27-1813 m Magdalene Snyder Cpl NY
Nathan: b 5-9-1762 d 6-19-1829 m Abigail Smith Pvt CT ★
Peter: b 3-5-1754 d 12-30-1831 m Peggy Nellis Pvt NY
Richard: b 3-17-1750 d 9-24-1825 m Catharine Pell Ens NY
Stephen: b 2-14-1762 d 4-14-1812 m Betty Baterson CG CT W★
Thomas: b 7-13-1754 d 11-14-1820 m Susanna Barlow Lt CT
Wm.: b *c.* 1758 d *a.* 2-22-1832 m Jean Stoops Pvt PA

ELY, (includes ELA, EALEY, EALY, & ELEY)
Abner: b 1749 d 1-2-1805 m Mrs. Bridget Brockway Capt CT W★
Adriel: b 4-22-1744 d 5-13-1829 m Sarah Stow 2Lt CT
Benjamin: b 12-25-1730 d 12-25-1802 m Esther Edwards Backus Maj MA
Benjamin: b *c.* 1750 d *p.* 1796 m Mary Scott Pvt VA
Christopher: b 1743 d 1817 m (1)Eve Marvin (2)Esther Hunt (3)Mary Elliot Capt CT
Cullick: b 1733 d 8-29-1821 m Sarah Foot Ens CT
Daniel: b 7-31-1751 d 8-22-1832 m Mary Chapman Pvt Grd CT★
Darius: b 9-29-1761 d 9-23-1844 m Margaret Ashley Pvt MA
David: b 1-24-1759 d 2-19-1822 m Nancy (Fisher) Cunningham Pvt NH★
Elihu: b 11-15-1737 d 6-25-1815 m Anne (Ely) Lt CT NY
Elisha: b 1748 d 1801 m Susanna Bloomer Capt CT
Gabriel: b 1756 d 9-27-1842 m Eunice Merriman Cpl CT
George: b 4- -1745 d 7-21-1820 m Susanna Farley Col NJ
George: b 11-8-1733 d 1-11-1815 m Sarah Magill Pvt PA
Gurdon: b 4-30-1760 d *p.* 8-1-1832 m (1)Parnal Phelps (2)Caroline Willy (3)Sally Russell Pvt CT ★
Jabez: b 1754 d 1841 m Polly Bennett Pvt CT ★
Jacob: b 1-18-1748 d 9-28-1836 m Lois Beebe Sgt MA

Jacob: b 10-3-1743 d 11-28-1815 m Elizabeth Ayer Pvt MA
James: b 10-12-1744 d 1-14-1809 m Catherine Hayes PS CT
Joel: b 11-13-1728 d 7- -1815 m Thankful Leonard Pvt VT
John (Pierce): b 9-24-1737 d 10-3-1800 m Sarah Worthington Col Dr CT
John: b 2-28-1758 d 8- -1847 m Elizabeth Bennett Pvt CT NS
John: b 4-6-1735 d 8-25-1815 m (1)Dorcas Ely (2)Abigail (Montague) Chapin Pvt MA
John: b 1-6-1740/1 d 8-27-1787 m (1)Ruth (Greeley) Whittier (2)Mrs Ruth Sanders PS MA
John: b 10-10-1707 d 3-11-1795 m (1)Phoebe Allison (2)Sarah Warford (3)Deborah Hammel PS NJ
John: b 1755 d *p.* 1832 m Barbara Jane Fry Sgt VA
Jonathan: b 8-2-1762 d 8-26-1836 m Cynthia Morton Pvt PA
Joseph: b 10-19-1756 d 6-19-1850 m Martha Smith Sol MA
Josiah: b 7-20-1739 d 4-26-1825. m Phoebe Denison Sgt CT
Levi: b 11-26-1732 d 10-19-1780 m Abigail Sargent Capt MA
Lewis: b 12-9-1756 d 9-5-1826 m Anna Granger MM MA
Martin: b 7-15-1751 d 4-12-1822 m Elizabeth Roberts PS MA
Micheal: b *c.* 1745 d *p.* 1789 m Mary Regina Pvt PA
Moses: b 11-18-1756 d 7-14-1838 m Rebecca Cook Pvt Tms NJ★
Nathan: b 1-9-1739 d 10-31-1798 m Silence Morgan 2Lt MA
Nathaniel: b 3-20-1737 d 1-14-1823 m Esther Leonard 2Lt MA
Robert: b 6-26-1741 d 12-5-1828 m Jerusha Lay 1Lt CT
Robert: b *c.* 1758 d *a.* 1-7-1811 m Jemima Johnson Pvt VA
Samuel: b 1713 d 2-11-1784 m Hannah Marsh PS CT
Samuel: b 2-27-1724/5 d 1784 m Mary Holman Cpl PS MA
Simeon: b 1-15-1762 d 6-19-1840 m Margaret Smith Pvt MA ★
Simeon: b 1-25-1734 d 6-15-1817 m Ruth Elizabeth Hatch Pvt MA
Thomas: b *c.* 1728 d 1782 m Jane Smith Sol VA
Wm.: b 1752 d 4-6-1838 m Hannah Barker Pvt CT ★
Wm.,3rd: b 10-14-1739 d 1-28-1807 m Lucy Perkins Sol MM NJ
Worthington: b 1760 d 4- -1805 m Prudence Bushnell Fif CT
Zebulon: b 2-6-1759 d 11-18-1824 m Sarah Apama Mills PS CT

ELZEVIEP, (includes ELSEFFER)
Ludovick: b 7-3-1734 d 1-15-1809 m Susanna Reichert Pvt NY

EMANUEL,
David: b 1744 d 1808 m Ann Lewis Sol Capt GA

EMBICH,
Christopher: b 5-6-1725 d *p.* 1783 m Maria Elizabeth Kriter Pvt PA
Jacob: b 10-12-1754 d 10-19-1819 m (1)Magdalene Roland (2)Maria Catherine (Gatz) Frank Ens PA

EMBRY, (includes EMBREE)
Effingham: b 9-24-1759 d 12-3-1817 m Mary Lawrence Pvt CS NY
Jesse: b 1750 d 1800 m Nancy — Sol GA
John, Jr.: b *c.* 1744 d *p.* 6-23-1818 m Fanny Burris PS VA
Wm.: b 1759 d *p.* 7-24-1829 m Frances — PS SC

EMEIGH,
Jeremiah: b 1754 d *a.* 1-8-1812 m Elizabeth Lossing Pvt NY

EMERICK, (includes EMERICH, EMRICH)
Adam: b *c.* 1749 d 1830 m Catherine — Pvt NY
Adam: b *c.* 1735 d *p.* 1-25-1806 m Christina — CMman PS PA
Andrew: b 1747 d 1838 m Christina Heller Pvt PA
Jacob: b 6-17-1728 d 3-12-1797 m Ann Elizabeth Beck PS PA
John: b 9-23-1766 d 1830 m — Pvt PA
Ludwig: b 7-4-1754 d 2-13-1822 m Susanna Emminger 2Sgt PA
Michael: b 2-10-1756 d 10-14-1820 m Christina Kantner Pvt PA
Sebastian: b 7-16-1719 d 8-23-1789 m Maria — LCol PA

EMERSON, (includes EMMERSON)
Abraham: b 1-2-1743 d 8-29-1821 m Hannah Eaton Sgt MA
Amos: b 12-3-1738 d 10-14-1823 m Susan Morse Capt PS NH ★
Arthur, Jr.: b 8-31-1743 d *p.* 1801 m Ann (Tazewell) Nivison PS Chp VA
Asa: b 10-16-1746 d 6-2-1817 m Miriam Corburn Pvt NH
Asa: b 8-19-1749 d 2-10-1822 m Eunice Foster Sgt CS VT
Benjamin: b 1716 d 1794 m Hannah Watts PS NH
Caleb: b 9-3-1741 d 4-15-1811 m Abigail French Pvt NH
Charles: b 3-23-1748 d 4-23-1831 m Remembrance Powers Pvt MA ★
Daniel: b 4-19-1760 d 1-26-1806 m Lucy Pratt Pvt MA
Daniel: b 12-15-1746 d 10-4-1820 m (1)Ama Fletcher (2)Mrs Hannah Mosier Capt NH
Day: b 1-2-1737 d 1776 m Joanna Pattee Pvt MA
Edward: b 7-13-1739 d 3-17-1794 m Elizabeth Shillaber Maj ME
Elias: b 9-9-1759 d 6-16-1835 m Phebe Howard Pvt MA ★
Enoch: b 2-26-1755 d 6-15-1835 m Eunice Dana OrdlSgt VT NH★
Ephraim: b *p.* 6-14-1763 d — m Anna Peck Pvt MA
Henry: b 1763 d 9-5-1842 m Mary — Pvt NC ★
Henry: b 1720 d 1791 m Mary Elizabeth Pvt MA
James: b 1-10-1740 d 10-8-1814 m Lydia Hoyt PS NH
James: b 1746 d 1845 m Beulah Marsh Pvt VT
Jesse: b 3-6-1749 d 8-20-1820 m Lucy Warner Sgt MA
John: b 9-6-1722 d *p.* 1790 m Mary Wood Capt MA
John: b 2-4-1731/2 d 2-19-1803 m Hannah Nichols Ens MA
John: b 4-5-1739 d 11-14-1809 m Katherine Eaton Pvt MA
John: bpt 6-3-1764 d 5-9-1839 m (1)Abigail Chapman (2)Sabra Willson Pvt MA

John: b 11-20-1745 d 6-26-1826 m (1)Sabra Cobb (2)Mrs Betsy Dunbar PS MA
John: b 3-13-1743 d 3-15-1817 m Molly Hyde Sol NH W★
John: b 1761 d 1840 m Kezia Brooks Pvt MA NH ★
John: b 8-13-1757 d 4-3-1844 m Elizabeth French Pvt NH
John: b 1750 d 2-17-1836 m Cathrine Johnson Capt VA ★
Jonathan: b 1744 d 10-19-1785 m Mary Cummings Lt NH
Jonathan: b 6-9-1754 d 9-14-1823 m (1)Sybil — (2)Rhoda Baily Pvt NH ★
Jonathan: b 1749 d 1-26-1825 m Sarah Rollins PS CS Sol NH
Jonathan: b 3-18-1739 d 2-15-1815 m Lydia — PS NH
Joseph: b 3-14-1759 d 5-1-1844 m Mary Bragg Pvt CT
Joseph, Sr.: b 7-27-1723 d 2-2-1785 m Mehitable Hasseltine MM PS MA
Joseph: b 4-7-1754 d 6-23-1850 m Lydia Foster Pvt MA
Joseph: b 5-20-1748 d 10-1-1830 m Pheobe Thayer Pvt MA
Joseph: b 1721 d 5-9-1803 m Pheobe Upton Vol MA
Joseph: b 9-4-1750 d 3-28-1822 m Lydia Durrell Pvt MA
Joseph Sewell: b 6-25-1764/5 d 3-11-1809 m (1)Mary Jones (2)Phoebe Wright Pvt MA
Kendal: b 10-31-1745 d 7-5-1805 m (1)Mehitable Parker (2)Elizabeth Pratt Sgt MA
Mark: b 5-18-1725 d p. 9-27-1788 m Abiah Ingalls MM Fif MA
Moses: b 12-22-1717/8 d 1778 m (1)Rebecca Taylor (2)Abigail Burnham (3)Lydia Burnham Pvt Cmsry MA NH
Moses: b 11-15-1755 d 6-3-1839 m (1)Lydia Sargent (2)Lydia Fitts Pvt NH
Moses: b a. 1760 d p. 1797 m Sarah Drew Pvt NH
Nathaniel: b 5-2-1741 d 4-30-1824 m Sarah Tilton LCol NH
Nathaniel: b 1747 d 9-20-1828 m Dolly Dearborn Pvt NH
Nehemiah: b 1-20-1749 d 12-11-1832 m Mary (Greeley) Whittier Capt NH
Oliver: b 4-7-1737 d 7-18-1778 m (1)Frances — (2)Anna Law Sgt MA
Oliver: b 12-30-1749 d 12-2-1839 m Sarah Eaton Pvt MA
Parker: b 1745 d c. 1805 m — Pollard Sgt MA
Peter: b 7-17-1723 d 10-27-1811 m (1)Miriam Marble (2)Mary Stanton Pvt MA
Peter: b 12-25-1758 d 2-16-1843 m Esther Harvell Pvt NH
Peter: b 11-9-1749 d 2-21-1827 m (1)Rebecca Hobart (2)Mary Muzzey Dr NH
Ralph: b 3-4-1761 d 10-4-1790 m Alice Ames Pvt NH
Samuel: b c. 1754 d 11-25-1812 m (2)Ann Anderson (3)Mary Butler PS MD
Samuel: b 5-9-1736 d 1819 m Mary Little CS PS NH
Samuel: b 1-8-1707 d 9-26-1793 m (1)Sarah Ayer (2)Mrs Dorothy (Sanborn) Dearborn CS PS NH
Smith: b 12-26-1745 d 7-23-1814 m Hannah R. Thompson Capt NH W★
Stephen: b 10-18-1754 d 12-4-1842 m Sarah — Pvt CT ★
Theodore: b 12-5-1757 d 1835 m Lydia Carlton Pvt MA
Thomas: b 1755 d 5-11-1826 m Mary Downey PS MD
Thomas: b 1757 d 2-17-1837 m Ruth Bancroft Capt MA
Thomas: b 7-12-1724 d 1-15-1810 m (1)Elizabeth Bruce (2)Mary Dresseer Sol MA
Thomas: b 4-1-1741 d 1816 m Judith — Pvt NH
Thomas: b 1747 d 5-11-1826 m Mary Downey Capt Pvtr PA MD
Timothy: b 1-29-1740/1 d a. 10-5-1819 m (1)Maria Cole (2)Patty Emerson Pvt MA
Timothy: b 5-24-1746 d 5-19-1788 m (1)Mary Felch (2)Mrs Rachel Walker (3)Frances Prescott (4)Sarah Weston Pvt MA
Timothy: b 5-29-1743 d 1-30-1827 m (1)Abigail Thompson (2)Mary (Jewett-Smith) Woodman Capt CS NH
Timothy, Jr.: b 5-9-1748 d a. 6- -1833 m (1)Molly Ober (2)Mary Harris Eastman PS NH
Wm.: b 6-4-1748 d 1827 m Elizabeth Myrick Sgt MA
Wm.: b 1760 d 7-23-1848 m (1)Sarah Cowdery (2)Mary Vinton (3)Lydia Green Pvt MA ★
Wm.: b 5-21-1743 d 10-20-1776 m Phebe Bliss Chp MA

EMERTON,
Thomas: b 7-1-1744 d c. 1832 m Lydia Burnham Pvtr Sgt MA ★

EMERY, (includes EMORY)
Ambrose: b 2-25-1738/9 d 1824 m (1)Mrs Catherine Foster (2)Rebecca Yocum Pvt PA
Amos: b 1750 d p. 1804 m Anna Foote Pvt PS NH
Amos: b 10-29-1744 d 11-2-1827 m Lucretia Morse Pvt NH
Anthony: b 9-5-1713 d 8-19-1781 m Abigail Leavitt PS NH
Arthur: b 9-12-1740 d 8-13-1801 m Ann Wells LCol MD
Benjamin: b 8-11-1740 d 1-28-1817 m Mary Rawlins Pvt MA ME
Benjamin: b 12-10-1738 d 1821 m (1)Sarah Bailey (2)Sarah — Capt PS NH
Caleb: b 4-6-1741 d 3-4-1825 m (1)Elizabeth Gowen (2)Elizabeth Emery (3)Mrs Hannah Hovey Gould Pvt CS PS ME MA
Caleb: b 5-13-1736 d 1826 m Susannah Worthly Pvt NH
Daniel: b 11-19-1723 d p. 1790 m Anne Emery Pvt MA
Daniel, Jr.: b 12-12-1756 d 3-5-1826 m (1)Elizabeth Farnsworth (2)Hannah Bates Lt MA
Daniel: b 8-18-1731 d 3-11-1825 m Sarah Shackley Pvt MA
Daniel, Sr.: b 5-5-1730 d 8-22-1819 m (1)Jane — (2)Mrs Esther Jaquith PS Pvt NH
David: b 9-24-1754 d 11-18-1830 m Abigail Goodwin Pvt MA ★

Humphrey: b 5-18-1746 d 1-19-1829 m Pattie Reed PS NH
Isaac: b 4-22-1756 d 6-14-1836 m Eunice Perkins Pvt MA
Jabez: bpt 7-13-1718 d 5-19-1790 m Elizabeth Butland Pvt MA
Jacob: b 10-11-1759 d 4-21-1824 m Elizabeth — Pvt PA
James: b 11-22-1738 d p. 1787 m (1)Mary Scammon (2)Sarah Jenkins PS ME
James: b 11-1-1730 d 1814 m Mehitable Emery Pvt MA
Jesse: b 4-13-1753 d 3-9-1812 m Ruth Dwinnell Pvt MA W★
Job: b 1751 d 7-31-1832 m Keziah Webber Pvt MA ★
Joel: b 4-28-1753 d 1837 m Love Ladd Pvt NH
John: b 1758 d 1810 m Mary Betton Sol MD
John: b 5-15-1734 d 4-10-1810 m (1)Adah Emery (2)Mrs Mary Bragdon Dunning 1Lt MA
John: b 3-28-1747 d 10-27-1806 m Mercy Crowell 2Lt MA
John: b 1-2-1725 d 12-10-1802 m Mary Munroe Pvt MA
John: b 7-14-1738 d 1803 m Rachel Sawyer Cobb Pvt Matr MA
John: b 1-28-1753 d 1-28-1828 m Abiah Page Pvt MA
John: b 11-20-1755 d 2-26-1848 m Deborah Colburn Sol MA
John: b 1-22-1758 d 12-27-1831 m Susannah Bartlett Pvt MA
John: b 11-23-1721 d 1807 m Mary Noyes Pvt MA
John: b 9-23-1765 d 3- -1828 m Ruth Sanders Pvt MA
John: b 9-9-1750 d 3-26-1839 m Elizabeth Perkins Pvt PS NH
John: b 4-8-1763 d 5-4-1854 m Mary Smith Drm PA
Jonathan, Jr.: b 8-12-1737 d 11-27-1806 m Elizabeth Tarbox Pvt ME
Joseph: b 6-3-1739 d 11-4-1821 m Hannah Stickney Capt NH
Joshua: b 3-14-1757 d 1-6-1832 m Ruth Nott Pvt MA
Joshua: b 1755 d 4-6-1827 m Tirzah Bean Pvt MA
Joshua, Sr.: b 3-21-1709 d 1796 m (1)Sarah Smith (2)Sarah Short PS MA
Joshua, Jr.: b 2-1-1738/9 d p. 1786 m (1)Hannah Currier (2)Rachel Currier PS NH
Josiah: b 1-31-1745 d 10-20-1816 m (1)Rebecca Woodman (2)Mrs Elizabeth Morrison Pvt MA
Levi: b 11-3-1763 d 1856/7 m Mindwell Ireland Pvt MA RI
Moses: b 10-12-1715 d 4-11-1789 m Lydia (Emery) Pvt MA
Richardson: b 3-10-1753 d p. 1790 m (1)Jane Swan (2)Mrs Winchester Pvt MM NH
Samuel: b 2-9-1755 d 10-2-1836 m (1)Rebecca Wheeler (2)Hannah Boston Sgt MA ★
Shem: b 11-6-1760 d 1-16-1824 m Martha Tibbetts Pvt MA
Thomas: b 9-10-1752 d 10-31-1827 m Hannah Harmon Pvt MA
Thomas: b 4-23-1748 d 12-20-1840 m Mary Sawin Pvt NH ★
Thomas Lane: b 1751 d 1828 m — Hopewell Lt MA
Wm.: b 4-16-1742 d 5-31-1825 m Joanna Elkins Lt NH
Wm.: b 1751 d 1779 m Ruth Thompson Pvt VA
Wm. Wilson: b — d c. 1795 m Elizabeth — Pvt MD
Zachariah, Sr.: b 8-26-1716 d 5-3-1804 m Esther Stevens PS MA
Zachariah, Jr.: b 7-31-1742 d — m Mary Lemon Pvt PS NH

EMIG,
Charles: b c. 9-17-1760 d c. 7-18-1826 m Anna Mary — Pvt PA
John: b c. 1720 d 1786 m Ann — Pvt PA
Philip: b c. 1722 d c. 1819 m Maria Anna — Pvt PA
Valentine: b 11-14-1748 d 4-15-1833 m Barbara Gauvin Pvt PA

EMISON,
Ash: b c. 1753 d p. 7-15-1822 m Mary Mitchell Pvt PA
Hugh: b 9-20-1744 d 1-25-1825 m (1)Mary Baird (2)Elizabeth Marshall 1Lt PA

EMMERT,
George: b c. 1716 d 1796 m Eva Maria Graff PS PA
George: b 1754 d 1846 m Mrs Mary Crowley Pvt VA ★
Leonard: b 1744 d 1804 m Catherine Gunckle Pvt PA

EMMES,
Nathaniel: b 3-23-1760 d 2-2-1847 m Rebecca Ridgeway Cpl MA ★

EMMETT,
John: b 10-2-1759 d 1847 m (1)Margery — (2)Margaret B — Pvt MD ★

EMMINGER,
Andrew: b 1-20-1755 d 9-28-1839 m (1)Elizabeth — (2)Christina — Pvt PA

EMMONS, (includes EMANS, EMMINS, EMMONDS)
Abraham: b c. 1747 d a. 10-7-1795 m Hannah Lane Pvt NJ
Benjamin: b 2-29-1743 d 12-30-1835 m Elizabeth Fellows Ens NH
Benjamin: b 1737 d 1812 m Elizabeth Smith Lt VT
Daniel Spencer: b 10-9-1757 d 9-21-1841 m Luna Beebe Sgt CT ★
Ebenezer: b 9-18-1725 d 1809 m Susannah Spencer Capt CT
Isaac: bpt 3-6-1739 d p. 1778 m Jenny Kilpatrick Pvt PS NJ
James: b 10-2-1761 d 4-5-1839 m (1)Sarah Peterson (2)Sarah Kirk Pvt VA W ★
Jeremiah: b 1749 d 3-8-1790 m Lydia Ackley PS CT
Job: b 6-6-1751 d 1-10-1817 m Hannah Bonham Pvt NJ
John: b 1727 d 1789 m Elizabeth Deering Pvt ME
John: b 1764 d a. 8-24-1833 m Ann — Pvt NJ
John: b 2-19-1755 d 1-2-1821 m Johanna Hampton Sgt NJ
John: b 7-2-1757 d 3-12-1845 m Catherine — Pvt NJ ★
Jonathan: b 12-31-1761 d 12-9-1835 m (1)Mary Brainard (2)Nancy Avery Pvt CT

EMMONS, contd.
Joseph: b 5- -1738 d 4-21-1810 m Lois Gilbert PS CT
Noadiah: b 3-17-1755 d 3-26-1808 m Elizabeth Brainard Pvt MM CT
Noah: b c. 1731 d c. 1799 m Mary Farr Cpl PS NH
Oliver: b 12-15-1759 d 1826 m (1)Anna Brainard (2)Milo Frost Pvt CT
Phineas: b 10-1-1756 d 6-13-1825 m Keziah Palmer Pvt CT
Samuel: b 11-4-1761 d 7-2-1850 m Sarah Lord Pvt CT
Solomon: b 7-19-1754 d 9-5-1835 m Sabra Canfield Sgt CT ★
Thomas: b 8-13-1728 d 12- -1783 m Mrs Frances Gardner Sgt MA

EMPIE, (includes EMPHIE)
Frederick: b c. 1820 m Maria Elizabeth Shultz Pvt NY
John: b 1-20-1753 d 10-25-1854 m Catherine Cool Pvt NY ★
Philip: bpt 10-10-1749 d 1812 m Elizabeth Enslin Cpl NY
Wm.: b 1740 d 1811 m Mariah Bellinger Ens NY

ENCHES,
Jesse: b 5-25-1757 d 11-29-1836 m Sally Pepper Pvt RI ★

ENDERS,
Jacob: b 8-9-1741 d 2- -1807 m Catherine Sternberg Sol NY
Johannes: b 6-20-1754 d 10-7-1825 m Anna Merikle Pvt NY
John: b — d 4-4-1825 m — Ens NY
Peter: b 5-11-1751 d 11-7-1830 m Elizabeth Berg Pvt NY
Wm.: b 10-12-1718 d 9-16-1792 m Elizabeth Margaret Kniskern Pvt NY

ENDICOTT, (includes ENDECOTT, INDICOTT)
Benjamin: b 1741 d 5-31-1792 m Susan Doughty Pvt NJ
James: b 8-17-1738 d 4-4-1799 m Abigail Puffer Capt MA
John: b 6- -1749 d 1-10-1826 m Elizabeth Church Dr Sol CT
Moses: b 10-31-1759 d 5-8-1832 m (1)Martha Hill (2)Mrs Welmet Endicott Pvt NC ★
Samuel: b 12-14-1754 d 4-6-1840 m (2)Damaris Osborn SrgnMte MA

ENDY,
Jacob: b c. 1736 d 1- -1788 m Anna Maria — CMman PA

ENFIELD,
George: b 7-5-1760 d 4-2-1827 m Sarah Augustine Pvt PA

ENGLAND,
Benjamin: b 1765 d 7-17-1814 m Jane Godneer Pvt NY
Daniel: b c. 1752 d a. 1820 m Margaret Gwynn Sol PS NC
David: b c. 1754 d a. 12-8-1801 m Lucy Hodges Sol VA
John: b c. 1730 d 1795 m Ann Grant Pvt NC
John: b 1740-5 d 1816 m Anna Maria — Pvt VA
John: b 9-29-1755 d 9-1-1851 m Ann Musselman Pvt PS VA
Nun: b c. 1760 d 1835 m Margaret England Pvt PA
Stephen: b 7-29-1758 d 5-1-1810 m Sarah Nichols Sgt MA
Wm.: b 1720 d p. 1790 m (1)Elizabeth Wilcox (2)Mary Watson PS NC

ENGLE, (includes ENGEL, INGLE)
Andrew: b 12-5-1755 d 6-2-1810 m Janet Strachan Lt PA
Frederick: b c. 1730 d p. 1784 m Abigail Vernon Pvt CS PA
Henry: b 3-24-1764 d 10-1-1822 m Mary Pechin Pvt PA
James: b 1757 d 1-5-1821 m Margaret (Adams)Marshall Lt PA
John: b 10-16-1745 d 4-20-1826 m Elizabeth Shock Pvt PA
John: b 7-12-1763 d 8-12-1847 m Catherine Sargent Pvt PA
Philip: b 10-8-1743 d 11-21-1830 m (1)Mary Darke (2)Isabella Pollock Sol PS VA
Pitter: b 9-17-1749 d p. 1787 m Sara Werner Pvt NY

ENGLEHAUPT,
John: b 10- -1756 d 12-25-1833 m Barbara Stump Pvt PA W★

ENGLEMAN,
Peter: b 6-7-1754 d 1-1-1812 m Catherine — Pvt PA
Philip: b 1750 d 1826 m Nancy Sillings Sol VA

ENGLER,
Jacob: b c. 1735 d 11-16-1776 m Anna Maria Bayer Pvt PA

ENGLEY,
Timothy: b 6-11-1757 d 3-9-1837 m Levinia Darling Sgt MA

ENGLIS,
Andrew: b 2-15-1752 d 5-26-1832 m Rachel Moore Capt MA ★

ENGLISH,
Benjamin: b 10-8-1705 d 7-5-1779 m Sarah Dayton PS CT
David, Sr.: b c. 1730 d p. 4-22-1790 m Elinor — CS PA
David, Jr.: b c. 1755 d 2- -1806 m Ann — Pvt PA
James: b 4- -1745 d 8-15-1800 m Jerusha Fairfield Ens NH
James: b 7-14-1757 d 12-30-1816 m Hannah Perrine Dr NJ W ★
James: b 1744 d 6-15-1832 m Jane Boatman Pvt PA W ★
James Robinson: b 5-1-1763 d 5-14-1815 m Alice Conover Pvt NJ
John: b 3-3-1755 d 5-22-1832 m Phebe Kent Lt NY ★
John: b 1750 d 1825 m Rebecca Rush Pvt PA
John: b 1750 d 1846 m Fanny Boatman Pvt PA
John: b c. 1725 d a. 1782 m Prudence Thornton Pvt VA
Joshua: b 1745 d 7-19-1795 m Sarah Adamson PS SC

Mizeal: b 1755 d 11- -1839 m Elizabeth — Pvt NJ
Parmenus: b c. 1760 d 5-23-1826 m (1)Sarah Hudson (2)Nancy Starkey Sol GA
Richard: b 10-12-1741 d 2-25-1777 m Freedom Strong PS CT
Samuel: b c. 1762 d p. 1785 m Eunice — Pvt PA
Thomas: b 10-13-1754 d 1836 m Jane Wicker PS GA
Wm.: b c. 1758 d p. 9-10-1815 m Mary Patterson Pvt NY
Wm.: b c. 1755 d 12- -1787 m Catherine — Sol NC
Wm.: b 1758 d 5-2-1827 m Nancy — Pvt VA ★
Wm.: b c. 1760 d 7-4-1815 m Adria Dudley Pvt VA W ★

ENLOW, (includes ENLOE)
Abraham: b 1729 d 1808 m Jemima Elliott PS CS PA
Enoch: b c. 1730 d 1796 m (1) — Spruceband (2)Jane McCord Pvt SC
Isaac: b 2-13-1745 d 6-10-1819 m Violet Porter MM SC
John: b c. 1759 d 1829 m Ann Thompson Pvt SC ★
Luke: b c. 1755 d a. 3-27-1822 m Susannah — Lt PA
Potter: b 1765 d 1833 m Nancy Chumner Pvt SC ★

ENNALLS,
Bartholomew: b 1746 d 1810 m (1)Sally Hooper (2)Nancy Erwin Capt MD

ENNIS, (includes ENNES)
Benjamin: b 4-23-1743 d 4-20-1780 m Magdalena Van Etten Lt PA
Cornelius: b 11-5-1761 d 3-27-1836 m (1)Eleanor Decker (2)Deborah Cole Pvt NJ
Daniel: bpt 12-8-1745 d 12-25-1838 m Magdalena Hornbeck Ens NJ
Henry: b 1752 d 1835 m Nellie Smith Pvt NY
Richard: bpt 1-2-1732 d 1777 m Sarah Beekman PS NJ
Wm.: b 1-10-1711 d 3- -1804 m Elizabeth Quick Pvt NY

ENOCH, (includes ENOCHS)
Enoch: b 9-29-1750 d 1835 m Rebecca Morris Capt PA VA
Gabriel: b 6-19-1741 d 8-22-1821 m Mary — Capt NC
Henry, Sr.: b 5-12-1732 d 7-14-1797 m Sarah — LCol PA VA
Henry: b c. 1725 d p. 1782 m Elizabeth — PS VA

ENOS, (includes ENO)
Abijah: b 1747 d 2-17-1813 m Hannah Griswold Pvt CT
David: b 1760 d 6-16-1843 m Mary — Pvt CT ★
James: b 6-17-1743 d 12-17-1812 m Silence Sessions Cpl CT
Jonathan: b 3-20-1739 d 12-4-1813 m Mary Hart PS Cpl CT
Joseph: b 1-20-1721 d p. 1783 m (1)Rachel Ward (2)Elizabeth White (3)Abigail Keyes Pvt CT
Joseph: b 1753 d 1794 m Ann Morton Lt DE
Joseph: b 8-2-1758 d 6-12-1835 m Thankful Coon Sgt Ens RI W ★
Matthias: b 6-30-1759 d 10-26-1835 m Anna Burdick Pvt Smn PS RI ★

ENSIGN,
Datus, Sr.: b 2-22-1729 d p. 1783 m Lucretia Seymour CS MA
Datus, Jr.: b 5-21-1752 d 1832 m Abigail Woolworth Pvt MA
Eliphalet: b 4-26-1718 d 7-21-1792 m Dorcas Webster MM CT
Eliphalet: b 8-27-1748 d 2-28-1838 m Esther Dickinson Pvt CT
Elisha: b 12-20-1729 d 5-16-1808 m Elizabeth Sedgwick Lt MA
Jacob, Sr.: b 2-2-1723/4 d p. 1790 m (1)Sarah Graves (2)Mrs Rhoda Ford PS MA
Jacob, Jr.: b — d 10-10-1797 m Mary Herrick Pvt MA
John: b 2-2-1723 d 11-16-1810 m Mary Sedgwick Capt PS CT
Otis: b 2-18-1762 d 10-4-1855 m (1)Mary Patrick (2)Mary Briggs (3)Hannah Dickinson Pvt CT ★
Samuel: b 9-15-1745 d 1816/7 m Mary Ives Pvt CT
Solomon: b 5-21-1738 d 9-27-1817 m Irene Allis Pvt CT
Wm.: b 1-20-1748 d 2- -1833 m Mary Wadhams Pvt MA

ENSLEY, (includes ENDSLEY & ENSLOW)
Benjamin: b 1757 d 3- -1823 m Prudence — Wgn NJ
George, Sr.: b c. 1737 d a. 1806 m Elizabeth — Pvt PA
George, Jr.: b 1761 d 2-21-1821 m Elizabeth Martin Capt PA W ★
James: b c. 1743 d 7-9-1806 m Mary — Pvt PA

ENSMINGER, (includes ENTSMINGER)
Conrad: b 1745 d 7-13-1783 m Maria Quickel Pvt PA
George: b c. 1740 d p. 1781 m Mary — Lt PA
Henry: b 1754 d p. 8-11-1820 m Eve Maria Wilson Pvt NJ ★
John: b 9-1-1757 d 10-10-1830 m Jane Reese Pvt VA ★
Peter: b 2-4-1755 d 12-9-1814 m Catherine Gloninger 1Lt PA

ENSWORTH,
Gideon: b 6-24-1744 d p. 1786 m Nancy Bucklin Pvt CT
Jesse: b 9-29-1753 d 12-16-1832 m Lotilla Dyar Pvt CT ★
John: b a. 1758 d 5-20-1823 m Mary Field Pvt CT ★

ENT,
Peter: b 1-11-1749 d 1-28-1829 m Sarah Kent Capt NJ
Theobald: b 8-30-1737 d 2-11-1794 m (1)Elizabeth Roser (2)Mary Hass Pvt PA

ENTLER, (includes ENDIER)
Michael: b 1740 d 1802 m Abigail — Cav VA
Philip: b 1740 d 1793 m Catharine Welsh Pvt PA

ENTREKIN, (includes ENTRIKEN)
James: b c. 1732 d p. 1800 m Elizabeth Hall Pvt PA
Wm.: b 2-28-1762 d 11-2-1844 m (1)Rachel Bryant (2)Sarah Hunnicutt Pvt SC

ENTROTT,
Henry: b 8-10-1755 d 5-15-1837 m (2)Hannah Serrine Pvt MA ★

ENTRUM,
Ebenezer: b 4-24-1746 d 10-27-1794 m Mary Butler Lt NH

ENTWISHILL,
Edmund: b 2-18-1746 d 4-22-1821 m (1)Erinas Harrington (2)Sarah Gale (3)Mindwell Bathrick (4)Mrs Abigail Curney 2Cpl MA

ENZOR,
Summers: b 7-10-1756 d 12-12-1820 m Mary Stevens Sol NC

EOFF,
Abraham: b 10- -1730 d 1788 m Catherine — Pvt PA
Cornelius: bpt 12-18-1743 d p. 1787 m — Pvt NJ
Jacob: b 1700 d 1778-1780 m (1)Mary Magdalene — (2)Mary — PS NJ

EORDAN,
Martin: b 10-31-1761 d 3-22-1812 m Elizabeth Maria Huffnagle Pvt PA

EPES, (includes EPPES, EPPS)
Francis: b 10-19-1740 d 12- -1802 m Mary Frost QM NH
Francis: b c. 1730 d 1789 m Mary Williams CS VA
John: b 3-18-1746 d 9-24-1824 m Elizabeth Baugh PS VA
Joseph: b 1-1-1755 d 8-10-1831 m Betsey Jacobs Pvt MA
Peter: b 3-9-1759 d p. 1-24-1850 m — Capt VA ★
Peter: b 1759 d 12-9-1828 m Lucy Ballard Sol VA
Peter: b c. 1730 d 11-19-1807 m Mary Poythress PS VA
Samuel: b 3-7-1746 d 12-23-1803 m Mary Frost Maj MA

EPLER, (includes EPPLER)
John: b c. 1743 d 1782 m (1)Mary Pfeild (2) — Easley 2Lt PA
John: b 11-30-1745 d p. 1832 m Mary Muller Sol PA
Peter: b 3-13-1740 d 9-1-1805 m — Pvt PA

EPTING,
Adam: b c. 1712 d a. 4-13-1786 m Anna Christina Fenwick Sol SC
Adam Fenwick: b c. 1746 d c. 1780 m Mary Vardiman Pvt SC

ERB,
Jacob: b 4-11-1724 d 12-20-1810 m Magdelena Schautz PS PA
John: b 1714 d 1778 m Barbara Johns PS PA
Lawrence: b 1756 d 4-21-1808 m Anna Maria Dreisbach Lt PA
Peter: b 10-27-1759 d 3-2-1832 m Anna Schaeffer Pvt PA

ERFORD,
John: b 3-31-1754 d 1816 m — Mil PA

ERISMAN,
Christian: b c. 1761/2 d 5-17-1798 m Elizabeth — Pvt PA
George: b 1755 d 11- -1844 m Susanna Hausman Ens PA
Jacob, Sr.: b c. 1728 d 1792 m (1)Adah Hershey (2)Elizabeth (Kendig) Forrer Pvt PA
Jacob, Jr.: b 1759 d 4-19-1794 m Mary — Pvt PA
Jacob: b — d p. 4-18-1812 m Maria Kauffman Pvt PA

ERKENBRACK,
Philip: b 8-15-1752 d 8-12-1834 m Sarah Young Pvt NY

ERMEL,
Wm.: b 6-23-1711 d 1-19-1803 m Mary Laup PS PA

ERNMAN, (includes EHREMAN)
Frederick: b c. 1745 d c. 1824 m Mary Evans Vol FrA

ERRICKSON, (includes EARICKSON)
Charles: b c. 1760 d 1805 m Mary Barnes Ens MD
John: bpt 12-3-1752 d p. 12-4-1806 m Lois Wainwright Ens NJ
Michael: b 5-1-1755 d 11-2-1815 m Ann — Sgt NJ
Thomas: b 1732 d 5-16-1811 m Margaret Abrahams Pvt NJ

ERSKINE, (includes ASKEY, ASKIE & ASKINS)
Alexander: b 1749 d 2-20-1825 m (1)Elizabeth Borland (2)Mary (Poland) Bryant Pvt MA ★
Christopher: b 1758 d 1-1-1819 m Freelove Greene Smn MA
David: b 1759 d p. 8-12-1832 m Catherine Jones Pvt Mrnr MA ★
James: b c. 1747 d 1782 m Elenora Pogue Sgt PA
John: b 3-30-1752 d 2-6-1844 m Phoebe Robinson Pvt NH ★
Robert: b 1-12-1753 d 10-16-1823 m Miriam Colson Pvt MA
Thomas: b 1727 d 1807 m Elizabeth Baker Capt PA
Wm.: b 10-11-1747 d 12-3-1789 m Mary — Cpl VA

ERTZBERGER,
Daniel: b 8-10-1720 d p. 1798 m Regina Leonard Pvt NY

ESHER,
George: b 9-12-1766 d 2-26-1855 m Sarah Shuster Drm PA

ESHLEMAN, (includes ESHELMAN, ESHLMAN, ESLEMAN)
Abraham: b c. 1758 d 1815 m Catherine — Pvt PA
Benedict: b c. 1729/30 d a. 4-20-1795 m Elizabeth Stayman Pvt PA
Henry: b c. 1755 d 1826 m Anna Longnecker Pvt PA
Martin: b c. 1748 d p. 6-6-1808 m Elizabeth Groff Pvt PA

ESKRIDGE,
George: b 2- -1757 d p. 1821 m Nelly Harvey MM Lt VA ★
George: b 7-24-1763 d 8-18-1827 m (1)Frances Kenner (2)Elizabeth Robinson Lt VA W ★
John: b 1743 d p. 8-3-1803 m (1)Rachel Davies (2)Elizabeth Moxley Sol VA
Wm.: b 3-10-1754 d p. 1798 m Ann Edwards Capt VA
Wm.: b 1756 d 10-9-1830 m Elizabeth Scott Lt VA ★

ESLER,
Adam: b 5-16-1756 d 11- -1806 m Anna Maria Schlosser Capt PA
Henry: b 1-24-1749 d 8-28-1798 m Hannah Van Buskirk Lt NY

ESLICK,
Isaac: b 2-8-1744/5 d p. 1791 m (1)Martha Salisbury (2)Ruth Read NC RI

ESLING,
Paul: b c. 1725 d p. 9-21-1798 m Anna Christina Bittenbender Pvt PA

ESMAY,
Thomas: b 9-15-1747 d 1820 m Elizabeth Palmatier Lt NY

ESPY, (includes ESPEY)
David: b c. 1730 d 6-13-1795 m Jane Woods Col PA
George: b 1749 d 4- -1814 m Mary Stewart 2Lt PA
George: b 1732 d 1787 m Elizabeth Crain Pvt PA
George: b 1759 d 1835 m Polly Patterson Pvt PA
James: b 12-7-1759 d 1834 m Sarah Baker Pvt GA
James: b 8-10-1741 d 7-5-1813 m Martha McKnight Lt PA
John: b 12-7-1759 d 1846 m Elizabeth Park Pvt NC ★
Josiah: b 3-10-1742 d 7-22-1813 m Anne Kirkpatrick Pvt PA
Josiah: b 1727 d 1801 m Elizabeth Patterson PS PA
Samuel: b 5-8-1758 d 12-29-1838 m (1)Elizabeth Sloan (2)Mary Renick Capt NC ★
Samuel: b 1753 d — m Martha Chambers Pvt PA
Thomas: b 1739 d 1808 m Anna Hamilton Pvt PA
Wm.: b 1740 d 12-4-1813 m Margaret Hemphill Bbd PA

ESSARY,
John: b 7-5-1744 d 11-17-1828 m Sarah Hester Clark Pvt VA

ESSELSTYNE, (includes ESSELSTYN)
Coenradt: b c. 1739 d p. 1790 m Maria — Pvt NY
Jacob, Sr.: b 1707 d 1795 m Magdalen Brroadhead Pvt NY
Jacob: b 4-27-1762 d 3-31-1850 m (1)Caroline Spoor (2)Maria Van Drusen Pvt NY
Richard: b 5-10-1731 d 6-18-1783 m (1)Moicke Bloom (2)Marie Van Alystyne Maj NY

ESSEX,
Benajah: b 2-27-1762 d 7-22-1843 m Penelope Fones Pvt RI
Corpe: b 7-23-1752 d 12-8-1821 m Mary Matteson Pvt RI

ESSIG,
Adam: b a. 1758 d 1-2-1824 m Mrs Sophia Fickes Pvt PA
Simon: b 12-27-1754 d 3-18-1852 m Julian Schnarin Pvt PA

EST,
Charlotte: b 1761 d p. 1801 George Wenzell PS PA

ESTABROOK, (includes EASTERBROOK(s), ESTABROOKS, ESTERBROOK(s)
Aaron: b 7-15-1750 d 12-26-1841 m Leah Liscomb Pvt RI
Abial: b 8-14-1753 d 3-7-1823 m Ruth Miller Drm RI
Abraham: b 3-12-1744 d p. 1790 m (1)Ruth Lock (2)Olive Adams Pvt PS NH
Benjamin: b 5-21-1744 d 5-24-1830 m Abigail Gates Pvt MA
Benjamin: b 12-20-1729 d 3-8-1803 m Hannah Hubbard Pvt PS CS MA
Daniel: b 1741 d 9-11-1816 m Persis Newton Sgt MA
Joel: b 3-3-1748/9 d 4-14-1834 m Abigail Underwood Pvt MA
John: b 10-20-1729 d 1804 m Anna Bemis Capt MA
John: b 6-15-1725 d p. 1790 m Abigail Abell Matr RI
Joseph: b 3-4-1759 d 4-30-1830 m Lucy Cushing Pvt MA
Joseph: b 4-1-1726 d p. 1790 m Lydia Wheat Capt NH
Nehemiah, Jr.: b 8-27-1749 d 1826 m Elizabeth Slapp Pvt CT ★
Nehemiah: b 3-2-1735 d 10-16-1812 m Elizabeth Winship Drm Sgt MA
Robert: b 11-28-1715 d 12-26-1812 m (1)Olive Townsend (2)Susanna (Tewkesbury) Flagg Pvt MA
Samuel: b 1-24-1738/9 d 1-2-1823 m (1)Rebekah Aspenwall (2)Phebe Palmer Ens NH
Samuel: b 11-27-1738 d 2-25-1784 m Sarah Robinson Pvt MA

ESTABROOK, contd.
Samuel: b 5-4-1752 d 1820 m (1)Esther Rounds (2)Mrs Lucy Hildreth Pvt MA
Thaddeus: b 3-2-1747/8 d 5-13-1818 m (1)Sarah Wyman (2)Deliverance Hunt Sgt MA
Warren: b 8-23-1748 d 6-29-1838 m Rosamond Haile Pvt RI ★

ESTE,
Moses: b 1-18-1752 d 2-4-1836 m (1)Elizabeth Fearels (2)Anne Kirkpatrick Capt NJ

ESTES,
Benjamin: b c. 1753 d a. 7-22-1816 m Cecelia Rebecca Thorpe PS VA
Elisha: b 1749 d 1821 m Catherine Tompkins Pvt VA
Joel: b 1752 d p. 1795 m Anna Harris PS Sol VA
John: b c. 1750 d 1809 m Susannah Montague Pvt VA
Nathaniel: bpt 3-19-1741 d p. 7-16-1794 m Elizabeth Knight Pvt MA
Reuben: b 1754 d 1811 m (1)Rhody — (2)Delphi — Sol NC
Richard: b 1739 d 1800 m Mary Yancey Pvt VA
Samuel: b a. 1746 d p. 1790 m Elizabeth Inman Pvt RI
Ursula: b — d p. 11-23-1803 m John Estes PS VA
William: b c. 1735 d p. 8-11-1807 m Elizabeth — PS Ens VA
William: b c. 1745 d c. 1827 m Frances — PS VA

ESTILL, (includes ESTELL)
James: b 11-9-1750 d 3-18-1782 m Rachael Wright Capt VA
John: b 1720 d 1780 m Ruhama Conover MM NJ
Joseph: b 3- -1745 d 5-29-1793 m Elizabeth Risley Capt NJ
Samuel: b 9-10-1755 d 2-9-1837 m Jane Tees PS VA
Wallace: b 1707 d 1792 m (2)Marcia Boude (3)Mary Ann Campbell Capt VA
Wallis: b 3-8-1758 d 1-22-1835 m (1)Jennie Wright (2)Polly — Lt VA ★
William: b 1756 d 9-7-1804 m Mary Lewis MM NJ
William: b 3-11-1762 d p. 1820 m Martha Jennings Pvt NY ★

ESTY, (includes EASTY & ESTEY)
Benjamin: b 9-21-1743 d 6-17-1775 m Mary — Pvt MA
Elijah: b 8- -1738 d 9-14-1826 m Lydia Gay Pvt MA
Isaac: b 9-30-1731 d 11-15-1807 m Hannah Smith Sol PS NH
John: b 12-14-1733 d 11-28-1811 m Abigail Gould Pvt MA
John: b 5-17-1762 d 3-21-1833 m Irene Sumner Pvt MA
Reuben: b 9-1-1763 d 7-16-1797 m Grace Morse Pvt MA
William: b 8-2-1748 d 11-14-1819 m Phebe Dwinnel Pvt MA

ETCHBERGER,
William: b 1743 d 2-13-1823 m Mary Magdaline Schifler Pvt PA ★
Wolfgang: b c. 1758 d p. 11-3-1827 m Marie — Pvt MD ★

ETHERIDGE, (includes ETHEREDGE)
Henry: b 1757 d 1840 m (2)Jimima Whaley Sgt SC
Stephen: b 1761 d 8-23-1834 m Jane McGaffey Pvt NH ★

ETHERINGTON, (includes EATHERTON & EDENTON)
John: b c. 1752 d 12-31-1830 m Susan E. (Suckley) Pvt VA W★

ETTELIN, (includes ETLEY)
David Gottlieb: b c. 1730 d 1781 m Mary Margaret — PS PA
John Philip: b 4-22-1755 d 8-30-1820 m Mary Gonsell Pvt PA

ETTER,
Abraham: b 10-28-1744 d 5-2-1814 m Susanna Margaretha Haller Pvt PA
George: b c. 1758 d 7-20-1819 m Mary Landers Pvt PA
Peter: b c. 1750 d 1811 m Elizabeth Dout Sol VA
Philip T.: b 8- -1725 d 5-21-1784 m Catharine Friederin Pvt PA

ETTWEIN,
John: b 6-29-1721 d 1-2-1802 m Maria Johanetta Kymbel PS PA

ETZLER,
John George: b 2-15-1734 d 10-22-1813 m Francina — Pvt PA

EUBANK,
Achilles: b 7-31-1758 d 8-16-1844 m (1)Mary — (2)Nancy Ware Pvt VA ★
James: b c. 1725 d 12-3-1799 m Peggy Lewis PS VA
John: b 1755 d p. 9-8-1812 m Katherine — Pvt VA
Richard: b 1758 d 10- -1855 m Susan Gary Sgt VA

EURE,
Stephen: b c. 1736 d p. 12-3-1816 m — Ens NC

EURITT,
John: b c. 1760 d p. 1800 m Emily Tingley Pvt VA

EUSTIS, (includes EUSTACE)
Chamberlain: b 1-9-1743 d 4-24-1801 m Sarah Buckminster Cpl MA
Thomas: b 8-8-1735 d 11-28-1807 m Katherine Wheat Capt MA
Wm.: b 8-19-1756 d 2-11-1834 m (1)Tamsen Wheelright (2)Hannah Coggswell Arfr Smn MA
Wm.: b 1729 d 12-7-1800 m Ann Gaskins Capt VA

EVANS, (includes EAVES, EUANS, EVANCE, EVES, EVINS)
Aaron: b 5-1-1739 d 1-11-1786 m Ruth McPherson PS NC
Abiather: b 1742 d 7-10-1831 m Mary Johnson Sgt CT
Abner: b c. 1717 d p. 1786 m Sarah Thomas Pvt PA
Alexander: b 5-29-1761 d 5-31-1815 m Elizabeth Patton Sol SC
Amos: b c. 1740 d 3- -1796 m Christiana — Pvt PA
Amos: b 1-16-1746/7 d 2-28-1833 m Margaret Evans Pvt PA
Andrew, Sr.: b 1-26-1709 d 12-18-1778 m Mary Richardson Pvt MA
Andrew, Jr.: b 11-20-1734 d 1-28-1799 m Sarah Center Pvt MA
Andrew: b 9-28-1759 d 12-5-1840 m Elizabeth Fain Pvt NC VA ★
Andrew: b 4-1-1763 d 4-9-1839 m Jane — Pvt VA ★
Ann (Meshow) Smith: b a. 1734 d 1-1-1799 m (1)Thomas Rigdon Smith (2)George Evans PS SC
Barnabas: b 1-26-1755 d 9-12-1824 m Elizabeth Phillips Pvt Mus RI ★
Batte: b 10- -1758 d 5- -1828 m Tempie Ellis Pvt VA ★
Benjamin: b 1-9-1749 d 3-30-1826 m Thankful Winslow Lt MA
Benjamin: b 10-12-1760 d 7-10-1830 m Hannah Smith Sol SC
Benjamin: b 1760 d a. 2-18-1806 m Mary Ellis Pvt VA
Charles: b c. 1723 d p. 6- -1799 m Ann Stalcop Pvt PS DE
Daniel: b 1750 d a. 1822 m Mary Jones Pvt GA
Daniel: b c. 1715 d 1775 m (1)Eleanor Bamford (2)Mrs Elizabeth Weymouth Pvt PS NH
Daniel: b 3-22-1750 d 1-1-1829 m Jane Lewis Ens PA
Daniel: b 1735 d 11-21-1793 m Martha James Pvt PA
Daniel: b 9-27-1743 d 10-1-1820 m Esther Benner Pvt PA
David: b 2-15-1747 d 7-23-1834 m Lydia — Pvt CT ★
David: b 12-23-1753 d 10-2-1812 m Mary Carver PS 2Lt NC
David: b 4-12-1754 d 3-21-1824 m Rosanna Millroy Pvt PA
David: b 1738 d 1824 m Susanna Barton Pvt CS PA
David: b 5-11-1761 d 7-19-1839 m Reba Aldrich Pvt RI W★
Edward: b 1736 d 5-26-1818 m Sally Flagg Adj NH
Edward: b 4-27-1760 d 11-3-1843 m Jemima Applegate Pvt PA
Edward: b 6- -1758 d 4- -1836 m Elizabeth Howard Pvt VA ★
Edward: b a. 1749 d p. 1797 m Sarah Wood Vol VA
Eldad: b 4-20-1749 d 6-3-1835 m Betsey Barrett Sgt NH ★
Eleazer: b 12-17-1758 d 8-6-1820 m Christianna Baird Pvt PA
Elijah: b 1746 d 1801 m Mary West Maurice Capt MD VA
Elijah: b 1752 d 1806 m Catherine Schaeffer Lt MD
Elisha: b 7-11-1765 d 1-13-1853 m Mary McDonald Pvt RI
Enoch: b c. 1750 d a. 2-29-1808 m Ann James Kolb 1Lt SC
Evan: b 1753 d 9-18-1817 m (1)Sarah Middleton (2)Patience — Dr NJ
Evan: b 1732 d 1794 m Margaret Nevins Col PA
Evan: b c. 1730 d 3- -1790 m Jennet — Sol PA
Evan: b 12-25-1758 d 6-5-1845 m Susannah Reamey Cpl PA ★
Evan: b — d 1-11-1803 m Catherine Morris Pvt PA
Ezekiel: b 1737 d 1807 m Jane Robinson Pvt SC
George: b c. 1756 d 6-27-1832 m Mary Peyton Dr VA
George: b 1743 d p. 1781 m Ann Hines Maj PS NC
George, Sr.: b a. 1746 d 1788 m Mary — PS VA
George, Jr.: b c. 1760 d 1- -1828 m Sarah — PS VA
Griffith: b 1760 d 10-19-1818 m Mary Burgess Lt MD
Guilford: b 5-4-1754 d 11-30-1829 m (1)Rebecca Reed (2)Elizabeth Howland Lt RI W★
Henry: b 1755 d 1815 m Dolly — Pvt MD
Henry: b a. 1747 d 7-1-1827 m (2)Sarah Fry Pvt MA W★
Henry: b 1734 d 1792 m Abigail — 2Maj NY
Hugh: b 10-7-1730 d 3-27-1808 m (1)Sarah Hardin (2)Lavinia Simpson Pvt PA
Isaac: b 1756 d 5-21-1823 m Hannah Bales Pvt PA
James: b c. 1750 d p. 12-6-1801 m Elizabeth — Pvt NC
James: b 2-8-1724 d 10- -1801 m Elizabeth Thomas Sgt PA
James: b 8-6-1748 d 1-16-1823 m Mary Brooke Pvt PA
James: b 1761 d p. 1802 m Rose Kyle Pvt SC
James: b 1756 d 1833 m Lucy Savage Pvt VA
Jeremiah: b 1749 d 5-14-1826 m Mary — Pvt PA
Jesse: b 12-16-1756 d 7-14-1843 m Lydia Valentine Pvt PA
Jesse: b 7-17-1751 d 1-29-1811 m Sarah Kemp Fif Drm VA
Jesse: b 1740 d 1- -1843 m Elizabeth Breckenridge Capt VA
John: b 1754 d 1801 m Catherine Evans Pvt DE
John: b c. 1716 d a. 10-13-1795 m (2)Catherine Wharton PS DE
John: b 1721 d 12-4-1781 m Elizabeth — PS DE
John: b 1755 d 2-12-1839 m Eleanor Jones SgtMaj MD ★
John: b 12-1-1737 d 5-18-1802 m Hannah Griffith Pvt PS MD
John: b 1760 d 1841 m Elizabeth Marshall Pvt MD
John: b 9-13-1731 d 5-17-1807 m Elizabeth Stickney Capt MA
John: b 8- -1738 d 12-6-1817 m Ann Birney Pvt NJ
John: b c. 1739 d a. 1806 m Ann Culpeper Pvt NC
John: b 1765 d 1821 m Elizabeth McMurray Pvt NC
John: b — d p. 7-24-1801 m — Sol NC
John: b 10-25-1747 d 6-28-1828 m Susan Gabriel Pvt PA
John: b 8- -1749 d 5-9-1826 m Mary Bradley Pvt PA ★
John, Sr.: b 1721 d 1-26-1798 m Sarah Denny Pvt PA
John: b c. 1756 d 6-27-1832 m (1)Sarah Williams (2)Elizabeth Raver Pvt PA
John Jr.: b 11-2-1762 d 7-4-1797 m Jean Grubb Pvt PA
John Sr.: b c. 1733 d 4- -1798 m Sarah — Pvt PA
John: b 1761 d 1831 m (2)Rhoda Evans (3)Judith Bunker Pvt SC
John: b 1760 d 9- -1818 m Eleanor Tarleton Pvt SC
John: b 12-7-1738 d 5-18-1834 m Ann Martin Col PS VA ★
John: b 1743 d p. 1785 m Frances Archer Pvt VA
Jonathan: b c. 1745 d p. 1799 m Hannah Robertson Pvt DE
Jonathan: b 8-5-1739 d 8-5-1806 m Elizabeth True Capt MA

Jonathan: b 1722 d 1797 m Eunice Green Pvt MA
Jonathan: b c. 1740 d 1817 m Sarah Kirk Pvt PA
Joseph: b 10-8-1761 d p. 3-12-1827 m Elizabeth Willard Pvt NC
Joseph: b 4-24-1757 d 7-18-1829 m (2)Ruth Sayer Watson Pvt PA
Joseph: b c. 1729 d 5-17-1805 m Ann — Sgt VA
Joseph: b c. 1720 d a. 5-20-1782 m Susannah Lacy PS VA
Joseph: b c. 1755 d 1830 m Ann Creswell CS VA
Joshua: b 1733 d 3- -1778 m Mary Thomas CMMan PA
Josiah: b 1763 d p. 1-30-1823 m Betsy Fitch Pvt CT ★
Moses: b 1750 d 12-24-1827 m Rebecca Stokesberry Sol NJ
Nathan: b 1742 d 1820 m Mary Thomas Sgt NY
Nathan: b 2-17-1756 d 10-27-1810 m (1)Mary James (2)Mary Mathews Capt PA
Nathan: b 4- -1760 d 5- -1810 m (1)Edith Godbold (2)Zilpha Fore (3)Elizabeth Ann Rogers Pvt SC
Nathaniel: b 1756 d 1826 m Mary Reynolds CS VA
Nehemiah: b 1-8-1744 d 5-20-1797 m Susannah Dumal Ens PA
Obadiah: b 7-23-1749 d 8-23-1821 m Sarah Coleman Pvt NJ
Oliver: b 9-13-1755 d 4-15-1819 m (1)Sarah Tomlinson (2)Hetty Ward Sgt PS DE
Peter: b 10-25-1758 d 2-12-1814 m Ann Newman Capt VA W★
Phillip: b 6-17-1759 d 6-19-1849 m (1)Rebecca — (2)Nancy — (3)Mary — (4)Grace Holland Pvt NC ★
Rees: b 12-4-1758 d p. 1803 m Esther Stretcher Ens PA
Reuben: b 12-28-1741 d 7-18-1785 m Hannah Osgood Lt MA
Richard: b 1751 d 1820 m Katherine McCarter Cmsry Wgm Pvt SC
Richard, Sr.: b 5- -1743 d 9-9-1814 m Mary Gasser PS SC
Richard: b c. 1750 d 2-27-1798 m Mary Mabery Sol VA
Robert: b 4-9-1755 d 12-22-1821 m Mrs Isabella Creigh Alexander 2Lt MD
Robert: b 1744 d 1848 m Sarah — Pvt VA
Rowland: b 1749 d 9- -1781 m — Day Sol SC
Sampson: b 9-15-1752 d 8-15-1842 m Mary Lewis Sgt VA ★
Samuel: b 1725 d p. 1790 m Anne Marshall Capt MD
Samuel: b 7-4-1758 d 4-21-1805 m Frances Lowrey Capt PA
Sherebiah: b 1754 d 8-8-1820 m Elizabeth Dudley Pvt MA
Stephen: b 11-13-1724 d 1808 m (1)Elizabeth Roberts (2)Sarah Nowell (3)Lydia Chesley Col PS CS NH
Stephen: b c. 1743 d a. 11-7-1814 m Obedience Ellington PS Cpl VA
Theophilus: b 11-10-1746 d 1822 m Susan Carver PS NC
Thomas: b 6-19-1749 d 1814 m Rebekah Smith Pvt MA
Thomas: b 5-23-1761 d 3-7-1836 m Prudence Stickney Pvt Smn MA ★
Thomas: b 9-15-1724 d p. 3-11-1789 m Lydia French Cilley Pvt NH
Thomas: b 1739 d 1825 m Sarah — Pvt PA
Thomas: b c. 1760 d p. 1810 m Polly Bullock Sol SC GA
Thomas: b c. 1730 d 12-18-1777 m Margaret Smith PS PM SC
Thomas: b 1743 d 1800 m Elizabeth Hodge Pvt SC
Uriel: bpt 9-23-1753 d 8-21-1825 m Lucinda Evans Sol NH
William: b 9-26-1746 d a. 1807 m Susannah Clement Lt GA
William: b 1752 d 4- -1840 m — Pvt NC GA ★
William: b — d 12- -1794 m Elizabeth — Pvt PA
William: b 7-10-1755 d 10-24-1838 m Meribah Dillingham Cpl MA
William: b 1755 d 1805 m Frances Chesley Sgt & Fif NH
William: b c. 1754 d 1830-40 m — Pvt NC
William: b 1712 d 1783 m Sarah Smith Rogers Col PA
William: b c. 1750 d p. 1794 m Margaret Davis Pvt PA
William: b c. 1749 d 1811 m Rachel Bonner Pvt PA
William: b 1750 d 1795 m Elizabeth Vining Pvt SC
William: b 11-25-1751 d 1827 m Ellie Graves Cooper Lt VA
William: b 4-8-1756 d 9-19-1839 m (1)Martha Hendricks (2)Mary Hendricks 1Lt VA ★
William: b 10-13-1745 d 4-24-1833 m Anna Brown Pvt VA ★
Zachariah: b 1755 d 1841 m Charity Jones Pvt MD ★

EVARTS, (includes EVERTS, EVITTS)
Ambrose: b 11-13-1740 d 7-3-1815 m Hannah Dudley Lt CT
Ambrose: b 9-14-1742 d 3-4-1802 m Achsah Bingham Pvt NY
Daniel: b 1-23-1749 d 12-18-1833 m (1)Charity Van Deusen (2)Molly Redfield Sgt NY CT
Eber: b 9-7-1753 d 9-30-1838 m Hannah Turner Pvt VT ★
Ezra: b 9-12-1755 d 1-13-1837 m Lorain Norton Pvt CT ★
John: b 9-21-1708 d 9-25-1786 m Submit Stone PS CT
Luther: b 5-16-1744 d 1820 m Deborah Newcomb Pvt CT
Matthias: b 8-20-1748 d 1825/26 m (1)Ichy Plass (2)Sara White Pvt NY
Nathaniel Jr.: b 6-17-1748 d 5-17-1835 m Mary Moore Capt CT
Reuben: b 1-7-1763 d a. 1840 m Sarah Allen Pvt CT ★
Samuel: b 1-29-1746 d 12-3-1834 m Sarah Fuller CG CT
Seth H.: b c. 1750 d 2-2-1811 m (1)Neomi — (2)Rebecca Wilson Ens MD
Stephen: b 4-15-1759 d 1835 m Nancy Graves Pvt CT ★
Stephen: b 3-20-1760 d 1-12-1830 m Elizabeth Bignal Pvt CT

EVAUL,
Jacob: b 1746 d 11- -1838 m (1)Abigail Highly (2)Hannah — Pvt NJ

EVELAND,
Peter: b 1752 d 3-4-1836 m X OrdlSgt NJ ★

EVELETH,
Isaac: b 9-13-1738 d 1805 m Emma Buckling Pvt MA

John: b 12-14-1760 d 9-9-1826 m Patience Bartlett Cpl MA
John: b 5-13-1729 d 1-6-1794 m Abigail Knowles Pvt MA
Joseph: b 2-22-1732/3 d 10-11-1790 m Ruth Wetherbe Pvt MA
Joseph: b 7-30-1726 d p. 1785 m Patience Hunt PS MA
Nathaniel: b 8-23-1736 d 11-23-1824 m (1)Sarah Mason (2)Mary Glass (3)Sarah Bartlett Arnold Lt CS MA

EVEREST,
Benjamin: b 1-12-1752 d 3-3-1843 m Martha Fuller Lt VT
Daniel: b 4-16-1752 d 7-2-1825 m Eunice Patterson Pvt CT
Jared, Sr.: b 1729 d 12-7-1792 m Mary Marvin Pvt CT
Joseph: b 8-8-1754 d 9-13-1825 m Sarah Eells PS Cpl VT
Zadock: b 3-5-1744 d 4-30-1825 m Sarah Meacham Capt VT

EVERETT, (includes EVERET, EVERITT)
Abel: b 2-18-1756 d 4-2-1813 m (1)Mary Smith (2)Abigail Guild Pvt MA
Abel: b 5-12-1758 d 11-5-1835 m Brigget McMurtry Pvt NJ
Abner: b 5-12-1761 d 11-25-1852 m Jedidah Bronson Pvt CT
Andrew: b 1755 d 1833 m Abigal North Pvt CT
Andrew: b 6-3-1741 d 2-11-1813 m Mary Smith SgtMaj MA
Asa: b c. 1750 d p. 8-19-1794 m Margaret — Pvt PA
Daniel: b 1-26-1714 d 12-21-1792 m Elizabeth Steele PS CT
Ebenezer, Sr.: b 1722 d 7-4-1810 m Lucy Moulton Pvt CT
Ebenezer, Jr.: b 6-17-1754 d 1-5-1840 m Mabel Elmore Pvt CT
Edward: b 12-9-1739 d 1815 m Ruth Field Capt MA
Eleazur: b 4-25-1761 d 12-22-1828 m Lucy Battelle Sol NH
Eliphalet: b 1756 d 3-27-1815 m Rhoda Peck Pvt CT
Ephraim: b 1742 d 1834 m Beulah Moore Pvt NY
Francis: b 1759 d 12-10-1828 m Mary Moores Sol NJ
George: b 10-26-1763 d — m — Raymond Drm MA NH
Israel: b 12-3-1719 d 4-21-1803 m Sarah Metcalf MM MA
Jacob: b 1735 d 1802 m Hannah Longafelt Dr NJ
Jacob: b c. 1730 d p. 1791 m Anna Margaretha — Pvt PA
Jacob: b 1758 d a. 6-8-1807 m Catherine — Pvt PA
James: b c. 1760 d c. 1820 m Ann Jane Meade PS MD
Jeremiah: b 2-6-1737 d p. 1789 m Lydia — Lt CT
Jeremiah, Sr.: b 11-12-1713 d 3-27-1798 m (1)Rebecca Blackington (2)Mindwell Woodward Pvt MA
Jeremiah, Jr.: b 11-25-1740 d 8-11-1831 m Elizabeth Warren Dr MA
John: b 1-26-1729 d 12-11-1814 m Sarah Gay Pvt CT
John: b 1-30-1745/6 d 7-16-1808 m Elizabeth Gill Pvt NH
John: b c. 1743 d 11-17-1821 m Sarah Fagan Sol NC
John: b 2-28-1753 d 2-13-1845 m(1)Sarah Woodson (2)Sarah Deadman Pvt VA ★
Jonathan: b 8-3-1717 d 12-15-1796 m Jemima Mann MM Cpl MA
Joseph: b 11-1-1757 d p. 1820 m Sarah Elizabeth Davis Ens PA
Joshua: b 9-21-1741 d 2-4-1825 m Molly Titus 1Lt MA
Josiah: b 2-27-1749 d 2-5-1829 m (1)Esther Hinman (2)Nelley Pease (3)Mrs Hannah Butler Stanley Lt PS CT
Josiah, Sr.: b 10-17-1733 d 12-4-1814 m (1)Jane Alexander (2)Mrs Sarah Billings Pvt MA
Josiah, Jr.: b 3-18-1760 d 3-16-1848 m Rebecca Farrington Pvt MA ★
Nathaniel: b 12-1-1745 d 2-14-1791 m Rebecca Connelly MM MA
Nathaniel: b 7-19-1747 d 10-14-1802 m Rhoda Smith Pvt MA
Nathaniel: b 3- -1763 d 5-22-1836 m Elizabeth — Pvt NC ★
Noble: b 3-3-1747 d 12-30-1819 m Abigail Lord Chp CT
Oliver: b 4-24-1764 d 11-3-1845 m Mary Fuller Fif CT
Oliver: b 4-11-1750 d 7-28-1827 m Susannah Capen Pvt MA
Pelatiah: b 3-12-1750 d 10-19-1821 m (1)Mary Cutting (2)Dorcas Fessenden Lt MA ★
Penuel: b 9-3-1758 d 2-5-1813 m Hannah Slack Cpl MA
Peter: b 4-5-1747 d 11-25-1804 m Lucy Whiting Pvt MA
Richard C.: b 3-28-1762 d 3-22-1815 m Persis Wilder Pvt MA
Samuel: b 1739 d 3-11-1821 m Mindwell Strong Pvt CT
Samuel: b 1756 d 1816 m Susanna Walcott 2Lt MA
Samuel: b c. 1745 d 1808 m Mary Barbara Mosser LCol PA
Simeon: b 1755 d 1823 m Elizabeth Nelms Sol VA
Thomas: b c. 1742 d 2-6-1837 m Elizabeth Covington Pvt NC ★
Thomas: b 6-12-1750 d p. 12-4-1777 m Patience Ann Porter 1Lt VA
William: b 5-5-1757 d 5-4-1802 m Sally Blackman Sgt MA
William: b 10-10-1749 d 1-1-1815 m (1)Margaret Buckman (2)Catharine Clark Pvt MA

EVERHART, (includes EBERHARD, EBERHART)
Adolphus: b 1-4-1760 d 1828 m Sophia Speelman Pvt NJ
George: b 8-11-1745 d 4-13-1835 m Eve Elizabeth Zacharias 2Lt MD
George: b 1755 d 11-24-1835 m Barbara Brendel Pvt Wgn Smn PA ★
Jacob: b 6- -1756 d p. 3-2-1848 m — Pvt NC
Lawrence: b 1755 d 8-2-1840 m Mary Beckinbaugh Sgt MD ★
Michael: b 3-31-1732 d 4-15-1783 m Mary — Pvt PA
Paul: b 10-1-1727 d 8-3-1797 m Emma Statler Pvt PA

EVERINGHAM,
John: b 4-15-1764 d 2-15-1852 m Nancy — Pvt NJ

EVERLY, (includes EBERLEY, EVERLEY)
Adam: b 1739 d 1809 m Christiana von Dieu Cpl MD
Casper: b c. 1740 d c. 1800 m — Sol VA
John: b c. 1743 d a. 12-14-1802 m Margaret Boone Pouder PS MD

EVERLY, contd.
Leonard: b 2-7-1760 d 7-7-1830 m Elizabeth Platter Pvt MD PA
Michael: b 1761 d 9-14-1794 m Catherine Walter Lt PA ★
Michael: b 1754 d 1804 m Mary Stuart Capt PA
Simeon: b 10-15-1763 d 3-17-1843 m Prudence Howard Spy VA

EVERMAN,
Michael: b *a.* 1746 d *p.* 10-8-1828 m Jane — Ens PS VA

EVERS,
Andrew: b 3-8-1748 d 7-29-1836 m Amy Carpenter Pvt PS PA ★

EVERSFIELD,
Charles: b 4-15-1750 d *c.* 1851 m Elizabeth Gantt CS MD

EVERSLEY,
John: b — d — m Abigal Hyatt Pvt CT

EVERSON,
Adam: b 8-28-1753 d *a.* 7-9-1821 m Dorothy Dockstader Pvt NY W★
Jacob: b 1-3-1734 d 5-1-1807 m Margaret Bloom PS NY
John: b 9-11-1759 d 1818 m Mrs Jane Barenton Pvt NY W★
Joseph: b 8-3-1759 d 9-22-1836 m Rebecca Cook Pvt MA ★
Samuel: b 9-22-1751 d 3-25-1787 m Sarah Bearce Pvt Fif MA

EVERTON,
Thomas: b 2-16-1762 d *p.* 1840 m Relief Howe Pvt MA ★
Zephaniah: b 1764 d 7-26-1841 m Margaret Watson Drm MA ★

EVERTSEN,
Bernardus: b 11-1-1747 d — m Martina Hoghsen Pvt NY

EVICK,
George: b — d 1800 m Eve — PS VA

EWALT,
Henry: b 1-27-1754 d 9- -1829 m Elizabeth Kellar Ens PA
John, Jr.: b 1760 d 8-19-1828 m Elizabeth Bonnet Pvt PA

EWART,
Robert: b *c.* 1725 d *c.* 1800 m Margaret Adams PS Sol NC

EWELL,
Charles: b 9-29-1760 d 4-1-1830 m (1)Nancy Seldon (2)Mrs Maria
    D. Tucker Craik Capt VA ★
James: b 12- -1757 d 10-19-1827 m Sarah Holbrook Pvt MA
James: b 1745 d 1809 m (1)Mary Ewell (2)Sarah Ewell PS Maj VA
James: b 7-4-1754 d 4-13-1797 m Sarah Ann Conway Lt VA
Jesse: b 9-4-1743 d 9-30-1805 m Charlotte Ewell Col PS VA
John: b 3-4-1734 d 10- -1826 m Deborah Bates Pvt MA
Peleg: b 10-19-1739 d 11-30-1823 m Hannah Johnson Slr NH
Stephen: b *c.* 1760 d 12- -1795 m Mary Diggins Pvt NC

EWER, (includes EWERS)
Barnabas: b 1-13-1756 d 3-8-1835 m Alice Weeks Pvt MA
Henry: b 3-17-1753 d 3-9-1833 m Typhena Scott Cpl MA
John: b 12-27-1735 d 5-9-1815 m Sarah Glading Pvt PA
Lazarus: b 7-9-1746 d 5-2-1835 m Mary Fuller Pvt MA
Paul: b 9-9-1752 d 7-17-1835 m Mercy Crocker Slr NY
Seth: b 3-14-1729 d 4-15-1801 m (1)Elizabeth Rich (2)Mrs Lydia B.
    Holmes (3)Mary Baxter CS MA
Thomas: b 12-25-1743 d *p.* 1810 m Elizabeth — 2Lt VA

EWING,
Alexander: b 6-27-1750 d 12-24-1831 m Jane Wilson Ens PA
Alexander: b 1763 d 1-27-1822 m Charlotte Griffith Pvt PA
Alexander: b *c.* 1754 d 1844 m Margaret McConnell Pvt PA
Alexander: b 3-10-1752 d 4-9-1822 m Sallie Smith Capt ADC VA
    W★
Alexander: b *c.* 1733/34 d *c.* 1829/30 m Rachel — PS VA
Andrew: b 3-15-1740 d 4-30-1813 m Susannah Shannon PS TN
Baker: b 1750 d *p.* 1803 m Letitia Warren Pvt VA
Calvin: b *c.* 1760 d 4-7-1813 m Desire Holbrook Pvt VT
Charles: b 1760 d 1844 m Barbara Boyd Fif Pvt VA
George: b 3-18-1754 d 1-15-1824 m Rachel Harris Lt NJ
George: b 9-1-1737/8 d 1785 m Mary Porter Cmsry PA
George: b 2-3-1760 d 7-4-1840 m Margaret Caldwell Pvt VA ★
Henry: b 1736 d 1796 m Jane Rogers Cmsry CS VA
James, Sr.: b 1725 d 1782 m Elinor Auld Pvt PA
James: b 1733 d 2-20-1825 m Mary McKown Pvt PA
James: b *c.* 1720 d *c.* 1800 m Margaret Sargent Capt VA
John: b 6-22-1755 d 2-14-1799 m Elizabeth Keen Capt PA
John, Sr.: b 1743 d 1813 m Catherine Shell Pvt PA
John: b *c.* 1760 d 1803 m Margaret Townsley Pvt PA
John: b 6-20-1761 d *p.* 5- -1833 m Mary Baker Ewing Pvt Grd PS
    VA ★
John: b *c.* 1760 d 4-25-1832 m (1)Ailse Caswell (2)Mrs Mary
    Dawson McCann Mar VA
John: b *c.* 1730 d 1788 m — PS VA
John: b *c.* 1760 d *p.* 12- -1803 m Martha — PS VA
Joseph: b *c.* 1716 d 10-4-1790 m Elizabeth — PS ME
Joshua: b 11-18-1736 d 1785 m Hannah Harris Capt VA
Nathaniel: b 3-25-1725 d 6-20-1780 m Rachel Porter Capt MD
Nathaniel: b 1747 d 8-23-1822 m Rebecca Osborn Pvt NC

Patrick: b 2-1-1737 d 4-11-1819 m (1)Jane Porter (2)Elizabeth
    Porter CS PS MD
Patrick: b 1720 d 1-1-1786 m Elizabeth Nesbit PS CS PA
Robert, Sr.: b 1718 d 6- -1787 m Mary Baker CS Pvt VA
Robert, Jr.: b 1760 d 7-14-1832 m Jane McLean Sol VA
Samuel: b 1737 d 1793 m Rachel — CS PA
Thomas: b 1730 d *p.* 1790 m Margaret — Col MD
Thomas: b 1743 d 1823 m Mary Ann Leefer Pvt PA
Thomas: b 1740 d 10- -1800 m Sarah — PS SC
William: b 1741 d 1781 m Anna Shannon Pvt PA
William: b 1764 d 1852 m (1)Elizabeth Saunders (2)Mrs Sara Hix
    Wynn Ens VA
William: b 12-24-1756 d 10-22-1822 m Mary McNeill 1Lt VA

EXUM,
Arthur: b *c.* 1750 d *p.* 11-15-1821 m (1)Mary Simmons (2)Eliza-
    beth — (3)Sarah Davidson PS NC VA
Benjamin: b 1725 d *c.* 1789 m Martha — Col PS NC
Etheldred: b *c.* 1735 d 7- -1779 m Rachel — PS NC

EYANSON,
John: b 1-23-1750 d 5-31-1831 m Anna Eddy Pvt NJ

EYCLESHYMER,
Peter: bpt 10-21-1753 d 12-5-1822 m Christina Schmeider Pvt NY

EYE,
Christopher: b — d *p.* 2-21-1797 m Catherine — Pvt VA

EYEMAN,
Henry: b 1-26-1758 d 4-26-1850 m Mary Sager Pvt PA ★

EYLER, (includes EYLAR)
Jonas: b 11-22-1754 d 4-19-1825 m Anna Regina Harbaugh Pvt PA
Joseph: b 9-22-1759 d 7-29-1839 m Mary Ann Rosemiller Pvt PA

EYRE, (includes EYRES)
Benjamin: b 6-1-1747 d 7-1-1789 m (1)Hester Boyd (2)Mary
    Cheeseman LCol NJ
Jehu: b 1-10-1738 d 7-23-1781 m Lydia Wright Col PA
Manuel: b 11-10-1736 d 11-1-1805 m Mary Wright Capt PA
Nathaniel Morgan: b 1-1-1744 d 7-6-1811 m Mrs Catherine Thomas
    Pvt PA

EYSTER, (includes OYSTER)
Christian: b 1710 d 3-3-1792 m Margaret Smyser Pvt PA
Daniel: b 1744 d 9-14-1798 m Elizabeth Reif Capt PA
Elias: b 8-6-1734 d *a.* 4-7-1829 m Anna Maria Law Pvt PA
George: b 1741 d 1810 m Anna Christine Altland Pvt PA
George, Sr.: b *c.* 1710 d 8- -1789 m — PS PA
George, Jr.: b 1736 d 1795 m Hannah Moyer Pvt PS PA
George: b 2-4-1757 d 6-9-1836 m Mary M. Slagle Pvt PA

EZELL,
Balaam: b 10-7-1756 d 1844 m (1)Liddy — (2)Elizabeth Mayo
    (3)Jane Stow Pvt PA ★
Hartwell: b 12-28-1764 d 11-13-1836 m Sealey Lowry Sol GA

FABER, (includes FAUBER)
John: b *c.* 1748 d *p.* 9-24-1832 m Elizabeth Witsel Fif PA
Peter: b 10- -1756 d 1838 m — Sgt PA ★

FABYAN,
Joshua: b 3- -1742 d 6-20-1799 m Sarah Brackett PS ME

FACKENTHAL,
Michael: b 5-23-1756 d 1-21-1846 m Christina Derr 2Lt PA ★

FAGAN, (includes FAEGAN, FAEGANS, FEGAN)
Daniel: b 1743 d 7- -1815 m Violet Coombs Capt VA
James: b 1748 d 1790-94 m Honore Timmons Pvt PA
James: b 1746 d 1794 m Elizabeth Grigsby Pvt VA
John: b *a.* 1760 d 1819 m Martha Lanier Sol NC
John: b *c.* 1750 d 1804 m Sarah Cundiff Pvt VA
Richardson: b 1758 d 1816 m Martha Dowd CS NC

FAGER,
Jacob: b 6-1-1738 d 12-10-1815 m Rosanna Lutz Matr PA

FAGG,
John: b 1737 d 1829 m Lucy Gray Pvt VA

FAHNESTOCK,
Diedrich: b 12-5-1732 d 12-20-1816 m Esther Bowman Pvt PA
John: b *c.* 1735 d 5-22-1812 m (1)Rebecca Groff (2)Catherine
    Studebaker Pvt PA
Peter: b 3-3-1730 d 9-15-1805 m Elizabeth Bolthouser Pvt PA

FAHS,
John Jacob: b 5-3-1741 d 2-27-1813 m Anna Catharine Koehler
    Grd PA

FAILING, (includes FEHLING)
Andreas: b 1753 d 1-27-1830 m Susan Roof Pvt NY
Heinrich: b 1- -1718 d 4- -1790 m Elizabeth Zimmerman Pvt NY
Henry, J.: b 2-1-1748 d 10-4-1825 m Catherine Dygert Sgt NY
Henry Nicholas: b 1750 d 12-22-1831 m Ann Margaret Timmerman Pvt NY
Jacob: b a. 1762 d 1-21-1788 m Mary — Pvt NY
Johan: b 1718 d p. 1790 m Maria Magdalena Wagner Pvt NY
Nicholas: b 1720 d 1-7-1787 m Lisabeth Schnell Pvt NY
Philip: b 2-14-1765 d 5-17-1842 m Margaret Timmerman Pvt NY

FAILOR,
Nicholas: b c. 1750 d p. 10-13-1797 m Barbara — Pvt PA

FAIN,
Charles: b 8- -1742 d 1834 m Juda Spurlock Pvt PS NC ★
Ebenezer: b 8-27-1762 d 12-29-1842 m Mary Mercer Pvt GA NC VA ★
John: b 1755 d 8-8-1788 m Nancy Agnes McMahon Pvt TN
Nicholas: b 1730 d p. 1789 m Elizabeth Taylor Sol NC
Samuel: b 1-20-1753 d 1794 m Rosannah McMahan Sol VA
Thomas: b c. 1760 d 1832 m Mary Parramore Pvt NC
William: b 1757-1760 d p. 7- -1840 m Judy Greathouse 2Lt NC
William: b 7-26-1757 d 1839 m Sallie McMahon Pvt NC

FAIR,
Barnabas: b c. 1730 d 1787 m Elizabeth — PS NC
Jacob: b 5-15-1741 d 5-11-1813 m Christina Beischlein Pvt PA
John: b 1742 d 1827 m Barbara Fair Pvt MD
John: b 1753/4 d 2-24-1839 m Eve Rosana Bowman Pvt Tms PA
Peter: b 6-6-1759 d 9- -1826 m (1)Susannah Bone (2)Rachel Lovisa Chandler Pvt GA

FAIRBANKS, (includes FAIRBANK)
Abel: b 5-12-1754 d 3-27-1842 m Hannah Hobbs Cpl MA ★
Abijah: b 1-27-1745 d 8-13-1830 m Mary Clark Cpl MA
Abner: b 10-21-1758 d 8-23-1803 m Becca Felch Pvt MA
Adam: b 12-3-1763 d 10-23-1831 m (1)Sally Walker (2)Marina Fuller (3)Mary Haven Frail Pvt MA
Amos: b 4-21-1737 d 1-4-1809 m (1)Lucy Gates (2)Rhoda Sawyer Capt PS MA
Asa, Sr.: b 5-30-1731 d 10-28-1809 m Sarah Pond Capt MA
Asa, Jr.: b 6-3-1758 d 8-29-1803 m Julitta Metcalf Bbd Cpl MA W★
Asa: b 3-4-1762 d 7-26-1819 m Hepzibah Adams Pvt MA
Benjamin: b 3-30-1745 d 11-16-1834 m Mary Draper Sgt MA
Benjamin: b 11-20-1746 d 5-28-1828 m (1)Keturah Luce (2)Lydia White (3)Sallie Blue Sgt PS MA
Benjamin: b 9-10-1726 d — m Dorcas Corbin Pvt MA
Benjamin: b 8-7-1759 d 11-19-1838 m Hannah Stratton Pvt MA
Calvin: b 2-11-1753 d 11-1-1836 m (1)Jenny Ayres (2)Elizabeth Holton Pvt MA
Cyrus: b 5-2-1737 d 2-28-1801 m (1)Lucy Wilder (2)Elizabeth Wynn (3)Abigail Wyman Lt MA
Cyrus: b 5-17-1752 d 6-18-1852 m Mercy Hale DrmMaj Cpl MA ★
David: b 1-22-1755 d 9-7-1801 m Lydia Fales Pvt MA
David: b 12-4-1731 d 4-19-1776 m Anna Wight Capt MA
Drury: b 5-1-1733 d 6-19-1786 m Deborah Leland MM MA
Ebenezer, Jr.: b — d — m Mary Hammond Pvt MA
Ebenezer: b 6-1-1734 d 6-6-1812 m Elizabeth Dearth Lt MA
Elisa: b 8-7-1760 d 4-17-1818 m Elizabeth Billings Pvt MA
Elijah: b 9-16-1756 d 5-1-1836 m Elizabeth Hopkins Pvt MA ★
Ephraim: b 1724 d 11-18-1799 m Achsah Goeth Cpl MA
Ephraim, Jr.: b 6-28-1753 d c. 1831 m Prudence Wilder Sgt MA
Isaiah: b 1745 d 1832 m (1)Mary Jones (2)Ruth Eagan (3)Molly Goodale (4)Sarah Nourse Pvt MA
Israel, Sr.: b 3-28-1723 d 2-25-1809 m Elizabeth Whiting Cpl MA
Israel, Jr.: b 1-10-1755 d 9-16-1818 m (1)Anna Bucknam (2)Sarah Holmes Pvt MA
Jabez: b 10-4-1713 d p. 1809 m Susanna Corning 1Lt MA
Jabez: b 3-2-1738 d 10-18-1822 m Meriam Davis Lt PS MA
James: b 3-7-1756 d 12-16-1836 m Betsey Blake Sgt MA ★
Joel: b 1-25-1747 d p. 1782 m Mary Gale Pvt MA
John, Sr.: b 5-4-1731 d 2-9-1817 m (1)Relief Houghton (2)Mrs Tabitha White Pvt MA
John, Jr.: b 5-6-1755 d 10-20-1830 m Fanny Kelton Pvt MA
John: b 5-18-1760 d 1805 m Eunice Payson Pvt MA
Jonas: bpt 10-25-1747 d 5-5-1825 m (1)Mary Carter (2)Freelove Stanley Pvt MA NH
Jonathan: b 3-29-1755 d 2-28-1840 m (1)Hannah Morse (2)Bridget Parmenter Pvt MA
Jonathan: b 11-12-1732 d p. 1782 m Ruth Houghton Pvt MA
Joseph, Sr.: b 11-4-1722 d 1802 m (1)Mary Willard (2)Abigail Tarbell (3)Mrs Mary Willard Capt PS MA
Joseph, Jr.: b 5-25-1743 d 5-12-1784 m Asenath Osgood Pvt MA
Joseph: b 10-27-1741 d 8-29-1813 m Ann Dole Pvt MA
Joshua: b 4-5-1727 d 7-5-1783 m Lydia Ellis 1Lt MA
Joshua: b 9-28-1746 d p. 1783 m Rebecca Richardson Sgt MA
Josiah: b 5-22-1734 d 5-9-1798 m Abigail Carter Pvt MA
Jotham: b 6-4-1757 d 5-24-1834 m Beulah Daniels Pvt MA
Luther: b 7-15-1755 d 12-8-1836 m (1)Thankful Wheelock (2)Anna — Sgt Wgm MA ★
Moses: b 4-13-1740 d p. 1790 m Sarah Smith Lt MA

Nahum: b 8-14-1753 d 12-23-1839 m Lucinda Houghton Sol MA
Nathaniel: b 7-15-1754 d 3-22-1838 m (1)Susannah Metcalf (2)Lydia Chipman Pvt MA
Oliver: b 9-22-1751 d 4-24-1829 m Susanna Gates Cpl MA
Oliver: b 10-8-1752 d 7- -1839 m Elizabeth Norcross Clark Cpl MA ★
Phineas: b 4-8-1719 d 8-22-1800 m Sarah Stone PS MA
Rufus: b 10-20-1759 d 7-7-1842 m Ann Prescott Pvt MA
Samuel: b 1731/2 d 5-25-1794 m Mehitable Hine Sol CT
Samuel, Sr.: b 9-14-1728 d 3-28-1812 m Mary Draper Pvt MA
Samuel, Jr.: b 2-21-1753 d 4-1-1825 m Rachel Lovett Sgt MA
Samuel: b 7-31-1720 d 4-14-1790 m (1)Hannah Corbin (2)Lucy Smith PS NH
Seth: b 12-7-1755 d 12-31-1833 m Relief Sawyer Pvt MA
Silas: b 9-29-1753 d p. 1823 m Mary Day Pvt MA
Thomas: b 1708 d 2-10-1791 m Dorothy Carter PS MA
Timothy Metcalf: b 2-18-1760 d 10- -1844 m Lucy Kendall Pvt MA
William: b 1744 d 7-13-1828 m Priscilla Remington Pvt RI
Zacheus: b 3-22-1759 d 1-6-1845 m (1)Mary Brinley (2)Martha Gates Pvt MA
Zenas: b 11-23-1752 d 6-15-1829 m Mehitable Wood Pvt NH

FAIRBROTHER,
Richard: b 6-29-1755 d 5-26-1838 m Anna Bliss Sgt MA ★
Thomas: b 8-17-1749 d 1-28-1805 m Mary Brown Pvt RI

FAIRCHILD,
Aaron: b 1759 d 10-18-1838 m Elizabeth Smith Pvt MA ★
Abel, Sr.: b 11-4-1761-3 d p. 1806 m Nancy Blackman Pvt CT
Abiel: b 1739 d 5-29-1816 m Zerviah Johnson PS CT
Abijah: b 1756 d — m Damaris Botsford Pvt CT
Abijah: b 9-2-1758 d 1-26-1851 m Sarah Howell Pvt NJ
Abiud: b 1762 d p. 3-30-1850 m Rebecca Jackson Pvt NC ★
Abner: b 1752 d 11-7-1815 m Theodosia Cowger Capt NJ
Abraham: b 11-2-1753 d 7-4-1843 m Phebe Russell Adj NJ★
Anson: b 8-23-1759 d 5-13-1815 m Orpha Spellman Pvt CT
Asher: b 8-16-1734 d 8- -1794/5 m Thankful Hubbard Mstr CT
Caleb: b 10-30-1743 d c. 1807 m Phebe Gard Pvt NJ
Clement: b 5-2-1764 d 1849 m Sarah Platt Pvt CT
Daniel: b 2-18-1719 d 6-9-1807 m Hepzibah Lewis Cmsry CT
Elisha: b 5-16-1736 d 1-25-1777 m Abigail Crowell PS PA
Ephraim: b 3-16-1760 d 5-26-1838 m Mary Plett Pvt CT ★
Gilbert: b 10-21-1759 d 10-31-1835 m Hannah Bennett Sgt CT
Jesse: b 4-19-1754 d 4-28-1813 m Zerniah Doty Pvt NY
John: b 3-4-1765 d 4-27-1814 m Martha Pope Pvt CT
John Curtis: b 2-6-1745 d 2-22-1825 m Elizabeth Burch Sol CT
Jonathan: b 11-3-1751 d 8-5-1813 m Sarah Howell Pvt Matr NJ
Joseph: b 1758 d 1842 m Hannah Wheeler Pvt CT ★
Lewis: b 5-6-1730 d 8-19-1790 m (1)Sarah Watrous (2)Mrs Mehitable Parmelee PS CT
Lewis: b 3-14-1746 d 5-10-1817 m Mary Uffort PS CT
Matthew: b 1720 d 6-5-1790 m (1)Sarah — (3)Rebecca Lyon Pvt NJ
Moses: b 12-1-1756 d 7-7-1825 m Lucinda Hamlin Pvt MA
Nathaniel: b 1-8-1752 d 1- -1838 m Elizabeth Munson Sgt NY ★
Oliver: b 6- -1724 d 1778 m Sarah Turner Pvt NY
Peter: b 3-12-1756 d 9-20-1833 m (1)Eunice Buckley (2)Mrs Rachel Smith Curtis Pvt CT ★
Peter: b 3-22-1715 d 9-21-1834 m Savia Squire MM Pvt NJ ★
Stephen: b 2-3-1725 d 7-31-1802 m Lavinia Beardsley Pvt VT
Zachariah: b 1755/6 d a. 8- -1814 m Hannah Pope Sgt MA

FAIRFIELD,
Benjamin: b 10-6-1708 d 1-12-1788 m Lydia Lamson PS MA
Daniel: b 5-16-1725 d 1797-99 m Mary Moore Pvt MA
John: b 1-8-1757 d 10-17-1828 m (1)Lucy Howland (2)Elizabeth Howland Pvt MA
John: b 1-3-1759 d 6-10-1834 m Hannah Burnham Pvt MA W★
Matthew: b 5-18-1745 d 2-11-1813 m Mrs Abigail Ayers Capt MA
Nathaniel: b 1730 d 7-18-1817 m Judith Perse Pvt MA
Reuben: b 11-7-1747 d p. 12-22-1814 m Abigail Tozer Sgt MA
Samuel: b 1733 d 1816 m Susan Northway Capt MA
Samuel: b 8-19-1753 d 12-15-1828 m Martha Gallup Pvt Drm Fif NH
William: b 12-26-1754 d 3-16-1827 m (1)Sarah Bradbury (2)Mary King Pvt MA

FAIRLAMB,
Frederick: b 2-10-1745 d 12-5-1826 m Mary Pennell Pvt PA
Nicholas: b 8-28-1743 d 11-23-1815 m Hannah Preston LCol PA

FAIRMAN,
Ichabod: b 6-30-1746 d 2-25-1821 m Rebecca Glover Lt PS CT
Jacob: b — d 1821 m — Lt. VT
John: b 8-21-1752 d 1-14-1827 m Elizabeth Pelton Pvt MA
Roswell: b 8- -1762-5 d 12-11-1844 m (1)Sarah — (2)Anna Sanders Pvt CT ★

FAIRSERVICE,
Thomas: b 7-23-1761 d 11-14-1849 m Sarah Tuckerman Pvt MA

FAISON,
Elias: b 10-15-1742 d 4- -1788 m Mrs Frances Gregg Sol NC
James: b 10-23-1753 d 11-28-1812 m Mary Hollingsworth Pvt NC

FAKES,,
George: b c. 1720 d 10-31-1821 m Maria Elizabeth Loanes Pvt NY

FALES,
Aaron Clark: b 7-6-1756 d 9-25-1826 m Hephzibah Everett Fif MA
Abiather: b 6-22-1754 d 4-3-1815 m Sarah Guild DrmMaj Cpl MA
David: b 6-9-1733 d 4-4-1822 m (1)Hannah Thorpe (2)Zibiah
  Partridge CS PS MA
Ebenezer: b c. 1730 d 11-30-1797 m (1)Ruth Bingham (2)Esther
  Bingham PS MA
Eliphalet: b 1743 d 1825 m Melitiah Everett Sgt MA
James: b c. 1724 d 5-20-1793 m Sarah — Pvt MA
John: b 12-26-1742 d 4-9-1803 m Molly Allen Pvt MA
Jonathan: b 10-5-1751 d 6-22-1842 m Elizabeth Wardwell Pvt RI ★
Joseph: b 6-24-1752 d 2-9-1818 m Sarah Kingsbury Pvt MA
Joshua: b 5-6-1755 d 5-30-1837 m Sara Pond Whiting MM Pvt MA
Lemuel: b 8-19-1747 d 2-12-1826 m Elizabeth Hannah White Cpl MA
Moses: b 1- -1730 d 1810 m Rebecca Fisher Pvt MA
Nathaniel: b 1-2-1727 d 4-13-1797 m Sarah Badger Capt MA
Nathaniel: b 1-20-1760 d p. 1805 m Mary Everett Pvt MA
Nathaniel, Sr.: b 7-4-1720 d 12-13-1801 m Sarah Little CS RI
Nathaniel, Jr.: b 5-11-1749 d 2-12-1834 m Elizabeth Bradford Pvt RI
Samuel: b 1756 d 9-29-1841 m Mary McLean Pvt ME MA
Thomas: b 10-22-1752 d 11-14-1830 m Sarah Bowen Pvt RI

FALKENBURY,
Levi: b 2-13-1761 d 11-16-1852 m Hannah Hatch Pvt NY

FALKENSTEIN,
Ludwig: b — d 1778 m Maria Hermannin PS PA

FALL,
Christian: b c. 1740 d p. 1800 m (1) Juliana Finn (2)Magdalena —
  (3)Katherine — PS NC
George: b 1754 d 12-5-1835 m (1)Abra Kenny (2)Tamson
  Wentworth (3)Dorcas Kenney Sgt NH W★
Henry Hatevil: b 1-14-1750 d 7-19-1845 m Sarah Durham Sgt MA ★
Tristram, Jr.: b 5-8-1740 d 2-7-1792 m Martha Pray 1Lt MA

FALLASS,
William, Sr.: b 6-26-1726 d 1801 m Charity Harris PS CS MA

FALLEY,
Richard: b 1-31-1740 d 9-3-1808 m Margaret Hitchcock Lt Armr
  MA

FALLIN,
Daniel: b c. 1735 d 1800 m Elizabeth — Maj & PS MD

FALLIS,
Isaac: b 1762 d 11-26-1851 m Elizabeth Campbell Pvt PA ★

FALLOON,
John: b c. 1750 d 1825 m (1) — (2)Mrs Hannah Shays Pvt PA

FALLS,
Gilbraith: b 1730 d 6-20-1780 m Isabella Kerr Capt NC
Henry: b 4- -1760 d 8-4-1847 m Susannah Kenedey Pvt PA

FAMBROUGH,
Thomas: b 1720 d p. 7-24-1784 m Mary — Pvt VA

FANCHER,
Abraham: b 12-10-1754 d 2-6-1838 m Sarah Newman 2Lt NY
Daniel: bpt 8-10-1755 d a. 9- -1781 m Esther Seymour Pvt NY
David: b 2-11-1747 d p. 1790 m Martha Holmes Pvt CT
David: b c. 1743 d 1781 m Martha Bellamy Lt NY
Isaac: b 12-27-1760 d 3-4-1837 m Hannah McCollum Pvt VA ★
John: b 7-15-1737 d 1-20-1808 m Hannah Weed Pvt NY
John: b 9-4-1756 d 2-17-1838 m Susannah Monroe Pvt NY ★
Richard: b 1756 d 5-21-1829 m Sarah Journegin Pvt VA
Sylvanus: b c. 1732 d p. 1790 m (1)Priscilla Smith (2)Hannah Gray
  Ens CT
Thomas: b 1745 d p. 8-22-1815 m Olive Dunbar Lt CT
William: b 11-13-1739 d 8- -1820 m Sarah Smith Capt CS NY
William: b 7-6-1764 d 2-3-1829 m Lucy Stark Pvt NY W★

FANNING,
Asa: b 7-20-1766 d 11-26-1838 m Jerusha Brown Pvt CT
Asher: b 1745 d 3-10-1816 m Priscilla Kinne Cpl MA
Charles: b 12-16-1749 d 3-22-1837 m (1)Anna Brewster
  (2)Hepsibah Bull Lt PM CT
David: b 3-2-1727 d 1-8-1817 m (1)Abigail Fish (2)Mary Searle Pvt
  CT
Elisha: b 9-16-1756 d 1-29-1818 m Mary Button SgtMaj CT ★
Gilbert: b 1733 d 12-18-1801 m Huldah Palmer Cmsry CT
James: b 1737 d p. 1790 m Sarah Gillett Pvt CT
John: b 1717/18 d 1781 m Abigail Miner PS NJ
John: b 12-21-1758 d 8-22-1830 m Abigail Tracy SrgnMte CT ★
Jonathan: b 3-2-1754 d 5-31-1844 m Eunice Fish Smn CT ★
Joshua: b 9-1-1748 d 3-7-1778 m Ann Read Lt NJ
Laughlin: b c. 1750 d p. 1806 m Winifred — Of PS VA
Nathaniel: b 3-22-1755 d 10-11-1826 m Anna Wells Pvt NY
Nathaniel: b 5-31-1755 d 9-30-1805 m Elizabeth Smith Mid CT
Phineas: b 8-2-1724 d 6-2-1796 m (1)Mehitable Wells (2)Mrs Mary
  Hubbard PS NY

Roger: b c. 1749 d a. 5-3-1779 m Prudence Stanton Mstr CT
Thomas: b 7-18-1750 d 5-24-1812 m (1)Lydia Tracy (2)Lydia Coit
  (3)Lucy Ledyard Dep QMGen CT
Thomas, Sr.: b 1719 d 12-15-1787 m Elizabeth Capron PS CS CT
Thomas, Jr.: b 5-22-1755 d 4-15-1828 m Susannah Faulkner Cpl CT
Thomas Edmund: b 5-17-1765 d 10-1-1821 m Elizabeth Jordan Slr
  CT
Walter: b 5-20-1747 d 4-19-1820 m Grace Benjamin Pvt CT
William: b a.1761 d 1787 m Sarah Cody Cpl MA

FANSLER, (includes FARNSLER)
Henry: b 1761 d 10-10-1843 m Sarah Elizabeth Stone Pvt PA

FANT,
George: b 6-5-1745 d p. 1835 m Elizabeth Sewell Pvt VA ★

FARBER,
Daniel: b 3-4-1765 d 2-21-1847 m Nancy — Pvt NJ

FARDING,
Aaron: b 1761 d 2-21-1834 m Mary Lones Sol MD

FARGO,
Aaron: b 2-5-1729 d — m Elizabeth Reed Pvt CT
Moses: b 1730 d p. 1810 m Mary Turner Sgt CT
Samuel: b 5-11-1761 d 2-27-1846 m Hannah Caulkins Pvt CT ★
Thomas: b 11-9-1699 d — m Mary Nobles Pvt CT
William: b 1757 d 10-14-1801 m Mary Congdell Sgt CT

FARIS, (includes FAIRIS, FARISH, FARRIS)
Alexander: b c. 1740 d a. 8-19-1785 m Jannet James Pvt DE
Alexander: b 1758 d 4-17-1841 m Elizabeth Strain Pvt SC ★
Alexander: b 1740 or 50 d p. 2-16-1824 m Jennie T. (Faires) PS SC
Edward: b c. 1740 d p. 1793 m Agnes — Sgt VA
Elijah: b 1761 d 6-23-1851 m Martha Colter Pvt Spy VA ★
James: b 1755 d 4-7-1823 m Elizabeth Dunn Pvt MA
John: b 6-6-1765 d 8-29-1856 m Jane Hagerman Pvt PA
Martin: b 1762 d 8-15-1857 m Rebecca Amos Cpl VA ★
Richard: b c. 1735 d p. 1785 m X Sol VA
Robert: b 1755 d p. 1828 m Mary Maulsey Capt SC
Robert: b 1735 d 1783 m Anne Dudley Pvt VA
William: b 1750 d 1835 m Mary — Pvt GA
William: b 8-16-1728 d 8-5-1804 m Priscilla Woodward PS MD
William: b 1748 d 7-16-1798 m Ann Biddle 2Lt Matr PA
William: b 1734 d 8-1-1818 m Dorratha Johnston Pvt VA

FARLEY, (includes FAIRLEIGH, FAIRLIE, FARLEE)
Andrew: b 1745-50 d 3-14-1814 m (1)Barbara Combs (2)Hannah
  Templeton Capt PA
Andrew: b c. 1761 d 3-1-1829 m Letitia Rawlings Hart Pvt PA
Benjamin: b 10-17-1759 d 4-25-1824 m Mary Tenny Pvt MA
Benjamin: b 8-28-1708 d 12-23-1789 m Joanna Page Lt NH
Caleb: b 10-19-1730 d 4-5-1833 m (1)Elizabeth Farley (2)Lucy
  Shipley Lt NH
Daniel: b 12-20-1762 d 1-20-1843 m Marietta Pryor Pvt VA
Ebenezer: b 9-19-1747 d 1-28-1827 m Betty Wheeler Pvt NH & MA
Francis, Sr.: b 1726 d 1829 m Nancy Blankenship Pvt & PS VA
Francis, Jr.: b c. 1745 d 1805 m Anne — PS VA
Jabez: b 1755 d 4-5-1836 m Susan Swasey Lt MA ★
James: b 1757 d 10-11-1830 m Maria Yates Maj NY
James: b — d p. 4-15-1808 m Sarah — Arfr PS VA
John: b 10-1-1746 d 10-20-1812 m Sarah Dennis Maj MA
John: b 4-10-1750 d 5-19-1832 m Anne Gray 2Lt NJ
John: b 1715 d 7-4-1799 m Margaret Stuart PS NC
John: b 8-21-1754 d 11-5-1827 m Elizabeth Diemer Pvt PA
John: b 10-14-1751 d 1-9-1816 m Judith Moore Farmer Sol VA
Matthew: b 10-29-1759 d p. 2-27-1837 m Mrs Esther McMullen
  Sct Capt VA
Meindert: b 9-17-1720 d 1790 m Barbara Van Dieren PS NJ
Michael: b 1719 d 6-20-1789 m Elisabeth Choate MGen CS MA
Samuel: b 3-14-1747 d p. 1795 m Polly Merrill Sgt NH
Stephen: b 1-28-1754 d 1-13-1837 m Mary Shattuck Sol NH
Thomas, Sr.: b c. 1725 d 1796 m Judith Clay Pvt VA
Thomas, Jr.: b 1760 d 6-12-1839 m Patty Lester Pvt VA ★
William: b 1752 d 1848 m Martha (Farley) Pvt VA

FARLOW,
William: b 1754 d 5-31-1817 m Drucilla Allred Sol NC

FARMER,
Benjamin: b 9-9-1749 d 11-28-1845 m Sarah Lippenwell Sgt MA ★
Benjamin: b 1735 d p. 3-16-1825 m Elizabeth Dew Pvt NC
David: b c. 1755 d 9- -1834 m Susan Harvey Pvt NH ★
Edward: b 2-24-1734 d 8-4-1804 m Sarah Brown Maj MA
Henry Willard: b 2-7-1753 d 2-16-1813 m Sybil Knight Pvt MA
Isham: b 1751 d 1849 m Elizabeth Johnson Sol PS VA
John: b 7-16-1749 d 7-20-1803 m Catherine Jacobes Stoudtenberg
  PS NY
John: b 1753 d 1810-20 m — Twig Pvt PA
Jonas: b 8-26-1741 d 5-15-1824 m Mary Whitney Pvt MA
Joseph: b 1- -1750 d 11-12-1794 m Zilphia Barnes CS NC
Lodowick, Sr.: b 1722-5 d a. 5- -1780 m — PS VA
Lodowick, Jr.: b 1757 d 9-15-1816 m Elizabeth Knight Capt VA W★

Nathan: b 1755 d 1830 m Mary Elizabeth Garner Sol VA
Nathaniel: b 1753 d 12-11-1838 m Hannah Woodard Pvt MD ★
Nathaniel: b 1-20-1725/6 d *p.* 1775 m Hannah Fessenden MM MA
Oliver: b 10-2-1765 d 4-6-1844 m Catherine Pierce Pvt NH ★
Samuel: b 1758 d 9-8-1838 m Tamar Baily Pvt MA ★
Samuel: b *c.* 1730 d — m Cassandra — PS NC
Shadrach: b 7-9-1755 d 7-23-1836 m Susan — Pvt SC ★
Simon: b 8-18-1757 d 10-7-1809 m Releif Stearns Pvt MA
Thomas: b *c.* 1763 d 4- -1818 m Fanny Tollar CS NC
Thomas: b — d *p.* 7-27-1810 m (1)— (2)Jane Baber PS VA
William: b 4- -1751 d 8-4-1840 m Rebecca Hurst Pvt NC

FARNANDIS,
James: b *a.* 1755 d *c.* 1790 m Ann Elizabeth Wallace Capt MD
Peter: b 1735-40 d — m Elizabeth Grant Lt MD

FARNSWORTH,
Abel: b 5-19-1734 d *p.* 1782 m Elizabeth McFailing Pvt MA
Amos: b 4-28-1754 d 10-29-1847 m Elizabeth Rockwood Ens MA
Asa: b 5-12-1754 d 6-22-1830 m (1)Damaris Gates (2)Mrs Sarah
    Gates Pvt MA
David: b 4-4-1711 d — m Hannah Hastings MM Drm Lt MA
Ebenezer: b 3-22-1725/6 d 11-6-1794 m Sarah Walker Pvt NH
Gershom: b 5-2-1743 d 10-23-1784 m Esther Gilmore Cpl MA
Harbor: b 6-10-1757 d 3-5-1826 m Lucy Haild Pvt MA
Isaac: b 11-30-1723 d 10- -1812 m (1)Anna Green (2)Lydia
    Nutting Moors PS MA
James: b 12-2-1727 d *p.* 5-3-1781 m (1)Susanna — (2)Sarah —
    PS Lt NH
John: b 4-11-1753 d 5-23-1834 m Hannah White Pvt MA
Jonas: b 8-18-1748 d 7-16-1805 m Jean Delap Lt MA
Jonathan: b 9-6-1758 d 8-23-1840 m Anna Willard Pvt MA ★
Joseph: b 7-12-1744 d *p.* 5-27-1794 m Elizabeth Caruthers
    Cmsry Gen CT
Joseph, Sr.: b 1-31-1731/2 d *p.* 1790 m Hannah Flint Pvt CS MA
Joseph, Jr.: b 4-27-1760 d 11-3-1850 m Hannah Danforth Pvt MA
Joseph: b 1760 d 1826 m Chloe Merrills Cpl NY
Josiah: b 1-4-1721 d 9-3-1807 m Hannah Butterick Sgt VT
Lemuel: b 8-6-1740 d *p.* 1778 m Hannah Daby Pvt MA
Manassah: b 4-3-1760 d 5-6-1837 m Charity Spooner Rounsevel
    Pvt MA ★
Matthias: b 9-20-1709 d 1796 m (1)Abigail Shedd Pvt MA
Moses: b 1-17-1756 d 10-23-1837 m (1)Annie Crocker
    (2)Ruhamah Beckwith Pvt NH ★
Oliver: b 12-31-1758 d *p.* 1840 m Hannah Lynde MM NH ★
Oliver: b 11-9-1727 d 4-30-1803 m Sarah Tarbell Pvt MA
Oliver: b 1-16-1732 d 4-12-1810 m (2)Jemima Balch Pvt NH
Oliver: b 12-18-1742 d 1786 m Elizabeth Wheeler CS PS VT
Phineas: b 7-15-1733 d *p.* 1796 m (1)Lydia Whitcomb (2)Hannah
    Gipson Lt MA
Reuben: b 6-4-1751 d 1813 m (1)Keziah Kellogg (2)Anna Kellogg
    Pvt VT
Samuel: b 1750 d 1831 m Anna Wasson Drm Pvt NH
Solomon: b 1762 d 8-14-1850 m Cynthia Whitcomb Pvt NY
Thomas: b 10-23-1752 d 8-10-1839 m Anna Estabrook Pvt MA ★
Thomas: b 4-1-1731 d *p.* 1790 m Elizabeth Tuttle Sol NH
Thomas: b 12- -1762 d 1-30-1814 m Clara Boalch Pvt NH
William: b 1726 d 2- -1806 m Elizabeth Rutherford Col MA
William: b 12-27-1737 d 1837 m (1)Hepzibah Chandler (2)Sarah
    Green Sgt MA ★

FARNUM, (includes FARNAM & FARNHAM)
Abiel: b 1756 /7 d 2-13-1818 m Chloe Simons Sgt CT
Asa: b 11-11-1731 d 1807 m Lydia Bidlake Pvt CT
Benjamin: b 12-16-1746 d 12-4-1838 m Dolly Holt Capt MA ★
Benoni: b *c.* 1738 d *p.* 1790 m Sabra Combs Pvt MA
Bezaleel: b 6-19-1723 d 1-26-1777 m Phebe Kirtland Pvt CT
Caleb: b 11-9-1753 d 1-3-1829 m (1)Lois Taft (2)Azubah Farnham
    Cpl MA
David: b 1749 d 9-6-1814 m (1)Anna Wingate (2)Abigail Smith
    Pvt MA W★
Ebenezer: b 12-17-1750 d 1780/81 m Joanna Benjamin Pvt CT
Ebenezer: b 11- -1755 d — m Olive Woodis Pvt PS NH
Eliab: b 7-24-1731 d 6-9-1806 m Abigail Killum Capt CT
Eliphalet: b 3-21-1725 m *p.* 1790 m Mary Rogers Pvt CT
Elisha: b 9-2-1756 d 8-16-1835 m Thankful Day Pvt MA
Henry, Jr.: b 10-8-1742 d 12-9-1823 m Abigail Rudd Pvt CT
Hiel: b 4-21-1745 d 12-9-1821 m Mary Elderkin Pvt CT
Jared: b 3-13-1760 d 9-10-1828 m Betsey Joselin Pvt MA
John: b 5-30-1760 d 5-21-1834 m Mary Everitt Cpl CT ★
John: b 5-26-1735 d 5-7-1778 m Hannah Card Pvt MA
John: b 4- -1756 d 1-18-1811 m Sarah Dunk Pvt MA
John: b 4-11-1711 d 10-21-1786 m Sarah Frye PS MA
John: b 9-9-1763 d 4-3-1822 m Menda Atkins Cpl NH
Jonathan: b 8-29-1757 d 3-17-1837 m Lydia Chapman Sol MA
Jonathan, Jr.: b 12-7-1753 d 5-29-1823/22 m Dorcas Barnes Sgt
    Maj MA ★
Joseph: b 6-18-1745 d 5-10-1824 m (1)Mary Lyon (2)Tabitha
    Baldwin (3)Edith Smith Lt NH
Joshua: b 4-20-1760 d 7-1-1837 m (1)Polly Boidwell (2)Mrs Abigail
    Kendall Pvt Mus MA ★
Joshua: b 7-20-1730 d 3-4-1816 m Margaret Legg Pvt MA
Joshua: b 11- -1728 d 1-15-1803 m Mary Grow CS ME

Josiah: b 2-6-1726 d 6-1-1807 m Elnor Carew Pvt CT
Levi: b 8-13-1748 d 12-25-1776 m Dorcas Moulton Taylor Cpl CT
Manassah: b 2-15-1717 d 1808 m Keziah Ford Sol CT
Peter: b 2-7-1756 d 2-8-1811 m Sylvia Fletcher MM Sol CT
Peter: b 5-8-1752 d 2-27-1828 m Chloe Wilson Sgt MA
Ralph: b 7-7-1756 d 12-26-1860 m Mehitable Bean Pvt MA ★
Reuben: b 5-20-1749 d 8-26-1826 m Lydia Moulton Sgt CT ★
Reuben: b 5- -1754 d *p.* 1818 m Kesiah Wait Sgt CT
Samuel: b 2-10-1743 d 1-25-1813 m Sarah Abbott Pvt NH
Seth: b 9-28-1733 d 4-18-1820 m Diana Gibbs Pvt PS CT
Simeon: b 10-9-1756 d *p.* 1804 m Elizabeth Johnson Pvt MA
Thomas: b 11-15-1754 d 3-23-1840 m Abigail Durkee Sgt CT ★
Timothy: b 1760 d 1811 m Susannah Berry Sol MA
Zebediah: b 6-18-1721 d 8-8-1814 m Mary Fuller Lt CT

FARQUHAR,
George: b 6-9-1742 d 1796 m Elizabeth Logue Pvt PA
Robert: b 10-23-1743 d 2- -1784 m Elizabeth Fagan PS GA

FARR, (includes PHARR)
Aaron: b 11-6-1743 d *p.* 1790 m Hannah Wheeler Pvt PS NH
Daniel: b 2-1-1744/5 d 4-27-1798 m Lucretia Walton Sgt NH
Ebenezer: b 8-18-1750 d 2-15-1833 m Mary Titus Pvt NH
Edward: b *c.* 1720 d *p.* 8-23-1793 m (1)Rachel Beard (2)Elizabeth —
    Pvt NC
Isaac: b *a.* 1752 d *p.* 1806 m (1)Lydia Stone (2)Mary — Pvt PS NH
John: b *c.* 1760 d 1850 m Polly Waldener Pvt GA
Jonathan: b d 1800 m (1)Mercy — (2) — (3) — Pvt CS NH
Salmon: b 1757 d 1-13-1834 m Mary Swinnerton Cpl VT
Samuel: b 7- -1716 d *p.* 1790 m Rebecca — PS NH
Samuel: b 10-30-1757 d 5-7-1804 m Elizabeth Bailey Lt Wgn NC ★
Silas: b 9-10-1742 d 3- -1813 m Mary Whitney Pvt MA
Thomas: b 1732 d *p.* 1790 m Elizabeth Bray PS MA
Thomas, Jr.: b 10-18-1754 d 11-29-1827 m Elizabeth Waring
    CmsryGen PM SC
Walter: b 1741 d 12-22-1799 m Sarah O'Bryan Pvt NC
Wm.: b 1729 d 3-2-1794 m (1)Mrs Jeter (2)Elizabeth Taliaferro
    Stribling LCol SC

FARRAND,
Bethuel: b 10-4-1741 d 5-27-1794 m Rhoda Smith Lt NJ W★
Daniel: b 1-19-1764 d — m Phebe Plum Pvt NJ
Jared: b 11-18-1764 d 6-28-1862 m (1)Hannah Evans (2)Mrs Emma
    Gallup Pvt MM VT ★
Jonathan: b 8- -1724 d 9-19-1812 m (1)Abigail Wooster
    (2)Rebecca Powell Capt CT
Phineas: b 11-7-1759 d 10-6-1822 m Jemima Kitchell Lt CT W★
Rhoda Smith: b 1747 d 6-30-1839 m Bethuel Farrand PS VT
William: b 11-18-1759 d 3-18-1854 m Jael Manchester Pvt VT

FARRAR, (includes FARRER, FARROR & FARROW)
Amos: b 8-23-1756 d 4-4-1825 m Margaret Ann Whitman PS Pvt
    PA
Benjamin: b 1730 d 3-2-1807 m Deborah — Capt MA
Benjamin: b 3-9-1760 d 7-30-1848 m Lucy Perry Pvt MA
Charles: b 7-24-1758 d 11-28-1835 m Mary Edwards Pvt MA
Daniel: b 3-25-1755 d 11-13-1837 m Lucy Bruce Pvt MA
Ephraim: b 1725 d 4-18-1800 m Mary Dakin Ens MA
Humphrey: b 2-23-1741 d 1820 m Lucy Farrar Pvt MA
Isaac: b 8-10-1719 d 1808 m (1)Sarah Brooks (2)Mrs Mary Nix CS
    MA
Isaac: b — d — m Mary French Pvt NH
Isaac: b *c.* 1750 d 1804 m Ann — PS VA
Israel: b 1738 d 3-13-1819 m Sarah Gilman PS NH
Jacob, Jr.: b 2- -1749 d 1820 m Elizabeth Heywood Sgt Grd MA
James: b *c.* 1732 d *p.* 1786 m Cynthia Miller PS NJ
Jeduthan: b 1740 d 8-10-1812 m — Pvt NH
John: b 4-11-1756 d 3-27-1847 m Hannah — Pvt Smn MA ★
John: b 1759 d 1853 m — Pvt MA
John: b 7-19-1718 d 1-7-1777 m (1)Martha Swift (2)Deborah Winch
    PS CS NH
John: b 1750 d 1808 m (1)Judith Williams (2)Rebecca— Capt NC
John: b 1730 d 1808 m Rebecca Puryear Capt VA
John: b 1741 d 1802 m Polly Minter 2Lt VA
Jonathan: b 7-27-1731 d *c.* 1822 m Hannah Fletcher Lt MA
Joseph: b *c.* 1719 d 4-20-1797 m Deborah Richardson Pvt MA
Joseph: b 9-26-1746 d 9-3-1812 m Lydia Stone Pvt MA
Joseph: *c.* 1742 d 1784 m Elizabeth Masterson Tms PS VA
Josiah: b 9-27-1722 d 11-24-1808 m Hannah Taylor Lt MA
Leonard: b 4-4-1764 d 4-30-1836 m Margaret Hamilton Pvt NC
    VA ★
Matthew: b 10-29-1760 d 1844 m Martha Murrell Pvt VA
Nathaniel: b 12-11-1758 d 8-5-1840 m Sarah Ozier Pvt NC
Oliver: b 3-10-1727 d 1-16-1807 m Mary Cole Pvt MA
Rosannah Waters: b 6-1-1734 d *p.* 1782 m John Farrow PS SC
Samuel, Sr.: b 3-28-1708 d 4-17-1783 m Lydia Barrett PS MA
Samuel, Jr.: b 2-14-1737 d 9-19-1829 m Mercy Hoar Capt MA
Stephen: b 9-8-1738 d 1809 m Eunice Brown Pvt PS NH
Stephen: b 2- -1762 d 8-22-1838 m Elizabeth Rice Pvt VA ★
Thomas: b 4-13-1752 d 11-18-1837 m Rebecca Stoddard Cpl MA
Thomas: b 4-10-1721 d *a.* 12-1-1806 m Jemima Damon Pvt MA
Thomas: b 1726 d 1810 m Elizabeth Howard Maj SC
Thomas: b 10-1-1754 d 8-24-1833 m Margaret Prince Lt SC

FARRAR, contd.
Thomas: b 2-5-1755 d 12-31-1843 m (1)Rebecca Wood (2)Annie Harrison (3)Patience Mountgay (or Mountjoy) Lt NC SC ★
Wm.: b c. 1745 d 1788 m (1)Mary Lovett (2)Lucy Medley Pvt NC
Wm.: b 3-19-1751 d 1800-5 m Amy Oliver Pvt NC W★
Wm.: b c. 1728 d 1788 m Lucy — PS NC
Wm.: b c. 1735 d 1812 m Elizabeth Bibb PS VA

FARREE,
Jacob: b 7-30-1757 d 8-28-1834 m Mary Lias Pvt PA

FARRIN,
John: b c. 1756 d 12-4-1840 m Mary Hall Pvt MA

FARRINGTON,
Abner: b 9-19-1756 d 12-9-1840 m Joanna Kilborn Pvt MA
Daniel: b 8-25-1733 d 9-21-1807 m Azubah Boyden Pvt MA
Daniel: bpt 6-4-1732 d 1819 m Hannah Farnum CS ME
Ebenezer, Sr.: b 7-15-1726 d 8-26-1787 m Mercy Cleveland Pvt MA
Ebenezer, Jr.: b 12-16-1757 d p. 1840 m Mary Cudworth Pvt MA ★
Ebenezer: b 5-13-1734 d 10-23-1810 m Hannah Smith Pvt MA
Elijah: b 6-17-1750 d 7-6-1834 m Elizabeth Sawing Pvt MA W★
Elisha: b 10-12-1734 d 7-2-1814 m Elizabeth George Pvt MA
Frederick: b 1767 d — m Judy — Pvt MA ★
George Lyon: b 4-14-1764 d 11-30-1823 m (1)Rachel Pope (2)Rhoda Baker Pvt MA
Ithamar: b 3-23-1756 d 7-3-1843 m Elizabeth Talbot Sgt MA ★
John: b 12-17-1743 d p. 1809 m Mary Stephens Pvt ME
John: b 4-11-1754 d 10-8-1802 m Phebe Poor Pvt MA
John: b 10-20-1756 d 9-30-1843 m Cynthia Hawes Pvt Gnr MA
Jonas: b 5-26-1754 d 9-29-1822 m Euphemia Lawrence Pvt NY
Jonathan: b 3-2-1757 d p. 8-27-1832 m Freelove Tilden Pvt MA ★
Joseph: b 3-27-1740 d 1-29-1833 m Martha Hodskins Pvt NY
Josiah: b 1756/7 d 2-28-1806 m Thankful Boyden Sol MA
Lewis: b 6-4-1758 d 4-30-1837 m Sarah Morse Pvt Matr MA ★
March: b 10-10-1762 d 4-1-1849 m Elizabeth Colton Drm MA
Samuel: 2-27-1754 d — m Betsey Mann Pvt Fif MA
Samuel: b 1749 d 5-7-1833 m Miriam Eastman Pvt NH
Thomas, Jr.: b 10-1-1760 d 1815 m Elizabeth Holden Pvt MA
William: b 7-15-1734 d 11-1-1808 m Sarah Stocker Capt MA

FARVER,
Christian: b c. 1745 d c. 1814 m Susanna Martain Emrich Sol VA

FARWELL, (includes FAREWELL)
Abel: b c. 1744 d p. 12-10-1817 m Hannah Russell Pvt MA
Abraham: b 8-18-1743 d 8-29-1829 m Priscilla Thurston Cpl MA
Absalom: b 9-4-1741 d 5-18-1819 m (2)Elizabeth Beals Pvt MA
Benjamin: b 7-2-1756 d 10-3-1823 m Lucy Collier Pvt MA
David: b 5-12-1754 d 5-7-1839 m (1)Hannah Taylor (2)Nancy Leason Pvt MA
Edmund: b 7-13-1750 d 3- -1843 m Mary Russell Pvt NH
Eleazer: b 8-18-1759 d 7-31-1848 m (1)Esther Woods (2)Mrs Sarah Brown Pvt MA
Elisha: b 7-1-1754 d c. 1826 m Sarah Parker Pvt NH
Ephraim: b 10-31-1760 d 8-15-1825 m Anna Bartlett Pvt MA
Isaac: b 12-8-1746 d 12-31-1791 m Abigail Willard Capt NH
Isaac: b 3-28-1744 d 5- -1786 m Lucy Page Pvt NH
John: b 1-27-1745 d 4-28-1806 m Sarah Hovey Cpl MA
John: b 1740 d 11-21-1820 m Sarah Pickett PS Cpl NH
John: b 6-23-1742 d 8-24-1823 m Esther Dimmick Pvt VT
Joseph: b 8-26-1759 d 9-17-1834 m Molly Haskell Pvt MA
Josiah: b 8-17-1728 d 1795 m Lydia Farnsworth Cpl NH
Levi: b 1754 d 2-20-1813 m Judith Bingham Pvt NH
Oliver: b 6-28-1741 d 1822 m Abigail Danforth Pvt MA
Oliver: b 1-13-1722 d 3-11-1810 m Rejoice Preston PS NH
Richard: b 9-25-1743 d 1817 m Susanna Pickett Pvt NH
Thomas: b 7-30-1733 d 2-20-1825 m Sarah David Sgt MA
William: b 12-28-1712 d 12-11-1801 m Bethiah Eldridge Sgt NH
Zaccheus: b 6-27-1753 d 6-11-1815 m Lydia Gilson Pvt MA

FASSETT, (includes FASSITT)
Adonijah: b 4-3-1753 d p. 1794 m Anna Allen PS NH
Benjamin: b 3-21-1757 d 2-11-1816 m Hetty Schenck Cmsry Pvt VT
David: b 5-10-1744 d 3-14-1810 m Sabra Safford MM Sgt VA
James: b 5-15-1741 d 1825 m (2)Catherine — 1 Lt MD
John: b 12-7-1739 d 1-12-1834 m Isabel Bogle PS NH
John, Jr.: b 6-3-1743 d 4-2-1803 m Hannah Safford Capt CS PS VT
Jonathan, Sr.: b 3-15-1742 d 5-24-1834 m Sarah Davis Lt MA ★
Jonathan: b 5-7-1745 d 5-21-1825 m Mary Montague Capt VT
Samuel: b 11-8-1741 d p. 1790 m Rebekel Fish PS NH

FAST,
Christian: b 6-22-1762 d 6-25-1841 m Anne Barbary Mason Pvt VA PS ★
Francis: b 10-4-1760 d 11-26-1831 m Elizabeth Yeager Pvt VA
Jacob: b 3-27-1758 d 1827 m Catherine Rudicell PS VA

FATZINGER,
Valentine: b 1740 d 5-12-1807 m Barbara Laury Pvt PA

FAUCETT, (includes FAUCETTE)
Charles: b 1754 d 3- -1797 m Margaret Flowers Pvt PA

James: b c. 1750 d p. 7-18-1801 m Susannah Woods Sol NC
John: b 6-11-1749 d 9-18-1820 m Isabella Snodgrass Sgt PA
John: b 8-10-1752 d 4-23-1838 m Eve Fry Pvt PA ★

FAULCON,
Nocholas: b 1735 d 1795 m Lucy Whitmell Pvt VA

FAULK,
Thomas: b 1749 d 1807 m Mary Hinnant Pvt NC

FAULKNER, (includes FALCONER, FALKNER)
Abiel: b 9-4-1755 d 11-26-1818 m (1)Hannah Abbott (2)Lydia Osgood (3)Clarissa Dillaway Pvt MA
Ammi: b 1756 d 9-12-1845 m (1)Anna Towne (2)Mrs Elizabeth Brewer Cpl MA
Daniel: b 1732 d 10-2-1805 m Sarah Shumway Pvt MA
Benjamin: b 12-17-1714 d a. 7-15-1784 m Frances — PS VA
Caleb, Sr.: b 1740 d p. 1790 m Esther Morse Sgt CT
Caleb, Jr.: b 3-28-1763 d p. 1824 m Martha Chadle Pvt CT
Charles: b 5-11-1731 d 10-18-1803 m (1)Hannah Morse (2)Mary Bly Pvt CT
Francis: b 9-19-1728 d 8-5-1805 m (1)Elizabeth Mussey (2)Rebecca Keys Col PS MA
James: b c. 1730 d 6-26-1796 m Ruth Heald Pvt MA
John: b 11-18-1747 d 6-24-1831 m (1)Elizabeth Purdy (2)Peninah Sands Ens NY
John, Sr.: b 7-6-1726 d 12-24-1804 m Ann Perrine Pvt NY
John: b 1739 d — m — Pvt PA
John: b c. 1754 d a. 8-28-1826 m Margaret Morrison Sol VA
Jonas: b 1764 d 6-24-1837 m Eunice Stone Pvt MA ★
Joseph: b 11-5-1757 d 6-26-1833 m Frances Nelson Pvt Spy VA ★
Joseph, Jr.: b 7-15-1732 d 7-15-1797 m Hannah Hovey Pvt MA
Nathaniel: b 1735 d 7-4-1821 m Catherine Eveleth Lt MA
Nicholas: b c. 1720 d p. 4-3-1789 m Martha Greenhill PS VA
Robert: b 1758 d p. 1720 m — Lt Cmsry PA ★
Wm.: b 8-27-1746 d 12-31-1831 m Jane Rogers Capt NY
Wm.: b c. 1755 d 1834 m Mary — Ens PA ★

FAUNCE,
Ansel: b 1755 d 7-5-1837 m Hope Bessie Pvt MA
Jacob: b 174(8) d 1819 m Catharine Klein Capt PA
Thomas: b 10-22-1745 d 4-28-1832 m Mary Curtis Pvt MA

FAUNTLEROY,
Griffin: b c. 1738 d 1786 m (1)Betty Harding (2)Rebecca Keene -LCol MD
Griffin Murdock: b 6-1-1747 d 1794 m Anne Belfield Lt VA
John: b 1742 d 1787 m Mrs Mary Watkins Stevens Capt CS MD
Joseph: b 5-30-1754 d 1815 m Elizabeth Fauntleroy Pvt VA
Moore: b 1716 d 1-20-1791 m (1)Ann Heale (2)Elizabeth Mitchell PS VA
Samuel Griffin: b 5-7-1759 d 12-8-1826 m (1)Elizabeth Payne Todd (2) Sarah Lowry Capt PS VA
Thomas: b 1760-65 d 2-10-1820 m Isabella Lorimer PS VA
Wm.: b 1713 d 1793 m (1)Elizabeth — (2)Peggy Murdock PS VA

FAUROT,
Henry: b 6-14-1730 d 3-31-1810 m Eleanor Enyard Sol NY
James: b 10-19-1763 d 12-3-1852 m Elisabeth Shay Pvt Wgn NY ★

FAUST, (includes FOUST)
Anthony: b 11-25-1757 d 11-23-1856 m.(1)Christiann Foust Pvt PA
Burrell: b 1-11-1756 d p. 1782 m — Kelly Pvt SC
George: b 6-28-1755 d 2-9-1836 m Mary Barbara Kivett PS NC
Jacob: b c. 1750 d 1796 m Charity — Pvt NC
Jacob: b 12- -1757 d 4-22-1841 m Christenia Alspach Pvt PA ★
Jacob: b 12-25-1757 d 7-27-1834 m Elizabeth Kiefer Pvt PA
John: b 9-9-1719 d p. 12-12-1786 m Anna Barbarah Albright Pvt NC
Peter: b c. 1745 d p. 1795 m Sally Snotherly Pvt PA
Philip: b 10-1-1790 d 7-9-1832 m Barbara — Fif PA
Phillip, Sr.: b 2- -1713 d 4-19-1786 m Magdalene Albrecht PS PA

FAUVER,
Frederick: b c. 1762 d 12-5-1852 m Phoebe Edwards Pvt NJ ★
George: b 1752 d 3-31-1836 m Elizabeth Penton Pvt NJ ★

FAVER, (includes FAVOR, FAVOURS)
Cutting: b 3-11-1737 d 3-8-1822 m Judith Bagley Lt NH
John: b c. 1748 d 1818/19 m (1)prob. Mary Bolton (2)Mary Arnold Pvt GA
John: b 12-27-1740 d p. 1805 m Lydia Hoyt Pvt MA
John, Sr.: b 1712 d p. 7-19-1779 m Isabella Randolph PS VA
John, Jr.: b 1744 d 1789 m Ann Covington Pvt VA
John: b 1763 d 1846 m (1)Henrietta Faver (2)Mahala Lee Pvt VA

FAVILL,
John: b 1749 d 1817 m Nancy Fox Capt NY

FAVROT,
Pedro Josef de: b 7-16-1749 d 6-26-1824 m Marie Francoise Gerard PS LA

FAWN,
Wm.: b c. 1755 d 6-5-1809 m Mrs Elizabeth Stanback Capt NC

FAXON,
Allen: b 9-1-1761 d 2-20-1836 m Margaret Smith Pvt MA
Asaph: b 8-7-1753 d 2-27-1821 m Rachel Wild Fif Arfr MA ★
Azariah: b 3-23-1731 d 7-2-1802 m Dorcas Penniman PS MA
Christopher: b 11-29-1727 d 12- -1815 m Hannah Moses Pvt NH
Ebenezer: b 12-12-1749 d 1-11-1811 m Eleanor Whitman Pvt CT
Elisha: b 11-10-1727 d 1776 m Sarah Allen Pvt MA
Francis: b 7-3-1759 d 2-5-1843 m Dorcas Wild Fif MA ★
Isaiah: b 8-2-1734 d 2-12-1810 m Catherine Fitzgerald Pvt MA
Jacob Allen: b 9-25-1757 d 5-5-1828 m Lydia Stiles Pvt MA
James, Jr.: b 10-6-1744 d 10-5-1829 m Mary Field Pvt MA
Richard: b 11-10-1746 d 7-24-1821 m Susanna Spear Capt PS MA
Thomas: b 2-19-1724 d 6- -1792 m Joanna Allen Pvt MA
Thomas, Sr.: b 10-29-1710 d 1801 m (1)Elizabeth Hobart (2)Anna Clark (3)Phebe Hayden MM MA

FAY,
Aaron: b 8-1-1759 d 10-16-1815 m (1)Molly Hatch (2)Rebecca Winslow Pvt MA
Aaron: b 4-18-1719 d 1- -1798 m (1)Thankful Newton (2)Mrs Eunice Farr CS MA
Adam: b 3-20-1738 d 10-25-1810 m Lydia Babcock Pvt MA
Asa: b 9-19-1761 d 4-17-1837 m Grace Mahan Pvt MA
Barnabus: b 10-30-1758 d 3-27-1830 m Chloe Packard Pvt MA
Benjamin, Jr.: b 11-11-1744 d 3-23-1834 m Beulah Stow Pvt MA
Benjamin: b 3-22-1750 d 1786 m Sarah Robinson Pvt VT
Daniel, Sr.: b 10-21-1728 d 2-28-1815 m (1)Elizabeth Spooner (2)Mary Crosby Lt MA
Daniel, Jr.: b 12-14-1752 d 6-21-1810 m Mary Paige Cpl MA
David: b 1740 d 9-13-1817 m Abigail Ripley Pvt MA
David: b 12-9-1756 d 12-23-1827 m Patience Harvey Pvt MA
David: b 3-5-1755 d 5-4-1806 m Jane Ward Pvt MA
David: b 2-6-1762 d 10-27-1826 m Mercy Perin Pvt MA
Edward: b 5-16-1717 d 1806 m Sarah Joslin Cpl CT
Elijah: b 3-5-1748 d 7-4-1835 m Deborah Lawrence Pvt VT
Francis: b 10-13-1760 d 11-27-1830 m Vira Ball Fif Sgt MA
Gershom: b 3-30-1729 d p. 1778 m Dinah Newton Pvt PS CT
Hezekiah: b 9-15-1737 d 2-5-1800 m Esther Gibbs 2Lt MA
Hezekiah, Jr.: b 10-7-1759 d 1-12-1832 m Martha Brigham Sgt MA
Isaac: b 6-23-1742 d 1-29-1816 m Keziah Doane 1Lt MA
Israel: b 2-24-1744 d 8-17-1797 m Mary Torrey PS CT
James: b 1732 d 3-26-1782 m Mary Winslow Pvt MA
Jedediah, Sr.: b 1727 d 12-16-1799 m Elizabeth — PS CT
Jedediah: b 4-21-1760 d 4-9-1796 m Martha — Pvt CT
Jeduthan: b 10-6-1749 d 1803 m Persis Temple Pvt MA
John, Sr.: b 12-16-1710 d 5-22-1789 m Thankful Taylor CS MA
John, Jr.: b 3-23-1756 d 6-14-1839 m Levinia Brigham Pvt MA
John: b 12- 23-1734 d 8-16-1777 m Mary Fisk Sgt VT
Jonas: b 1-17-1737 d 3-6-1818 m (1)Sarah Fassett (2)Lydia Safford Dr PS VT
Joseph, Sr.: b 9-27-1738 d 11-2-1777 m Lucy Warren Ens NH
Joseph, Jr.: b 12-28-1762 d 4-25-1847 m Sarah Graves Pvt NH
Joseph: b 12-22-1741 d 1-20-1825 m Abigail Twichell Pvt MA
Josiah: b 2-14-1731 d 8-8-1776 m Mary Brent Maj MA
Levi: b 1757 d 5-15-1833 m Nabby Fay Pvt MA
Moses: b 6-30-1763 d 11-3-1839 m Sarah Hedge Pvt MA
Nathan: b 2-6-1747 d 2- -1831 m Lucy Bemis Cpl MA
Nathan: b 1757 d 3-3-1824 m Mollie Perrin 1Lt VT
Peter: b 5-1-1760 d 2-28-1833 m Eunice Matthews Pvt MA
Sherebiah: b 1758 d 3- -1839 m Eleanor Stanley Sgt MA ★
Silas: b 11-14-1747 d 1828 m Anna Gleason MM MA
Stephen: b 5-5-1715 d 5-17-1781 m Ruth Child PS VT
Thaddeus: b 5-12-1731 d 6-22-1822 m (1)Thankful Rice (2)Mary Prescott CS MA
Thomas: b 11-13-1755 d 1837 m Mime Garfield Pvt MA
Thomas: b 10-2-1751 d p. 1798 m Esther Chappelle Pvt MA
Timothy: b 5-2-1754 d 8-24-1799 m Sarah Hager Pvt MA
Wm.: b 1789 d p. 1818 m (1)Bethia Bassett (2)Mrs Wright (3)Dinah — Pvt CT ★

FAYERWEATHER,
John: bpt 10-13-1736 d 9- -1776 m Abigal Curtis Lt CT
Nathaniel: b d 12- -1778 m Charity Summers Pvt CT
Samuel: b 3-1-1761 d 4-29-1848 m Charity Burton Cpl CT

FAYSSOUX,
Pierre: b 1735 d 1795 m Anne Johnson Dr SC

FEAMSTER, (includes FEEMSTER, FEMISTER)
Joseph: b c. 1742 d 10-27-1804 m Elizabeth Berry Capt SC
Thomas: b 1715 d 1797 m Elizabeth — PS VA
Wm.: b 2-20-1759 d 8-28-842 m (1)Mary Sharp (2)Jerusha King Pvt NC ★
Wm.: b c. 1740 d 11-8-1801 m (1)Margaret Black (2)Susan Bratton (3)Mary Fulton Sol VA

FEARALL,
John: b 1722 d 9-24-1782 m Sarah — PS MD

FEARING,
Hawkes, Sr.: b 7-13-1715 d 6-16-1785 m Margaret Lincoln Wgn MA

Hawkes, Jr.: b 11-26-1750 d 6-26-1826 m Leah C. Lincoln Pvt MA
Israel: b 1-9-1758 d 11-27-1825 m Elizabeth Thacher Pvt MA
Israel: b 1747 d 3-20-1826 m Lucy Bourne Maj MA
Noah: b 2-11-1732 d 1809 m Mary Nye Capt CS MA
Shubal: b 5-13-1744 d 1-26-1816 m Mercy Bates Sgt MA
Thomas: b 12-25-1749 d 3-16-1820 m Lydia Ripley Capt MA

FEARIS,
Jacob: b 6-25-1744 d 9-1-1818 m Kezia Sharp Capt DE

FEARN,
John: b 1- -1720 d 1784 m (2)Leanna Lee Capt VA
Thomas: b 10-24-1745 d 10-4-1805 m (1)Sallie Taylor (2)Lucy Coleman (3)Mary Burton PS VA

FEARS,
Thomas: b 1749 d 1790 m Mary — Pvt VA
Wm.: b 2-16-1746 d 3-10-1820 m Ann Bulger Pvt VA

FEARSON,
Attovix: b 1720 d 1792 m Pricilla Newman PS MD
Jesse: b 3-25-1756 d 1-18-1838 m (1)Elizabeth Wellman (2)Mrs Hannah Wells Cdr MD
Joseph: b 1758 d 9-7-1832 m Elizabeth Shaw Pvt MD

FEASTER, (includes FISTER, & PFISTER)
Andrew: b 1735 d 7-15-1821 m (1)—(2)Margaret Fry Cooper Sol PS SC
Durst: b a. 1738 d p. 3-12-1801 m Eve — PS PA
George Adam: b 1754 d 10-25-1839 m Anna Margareth Fisher Lt PA
Henry: b — d p. 7-13-1822 m (1)Ann — (2)Drusilla Johnson Capt MD
Henry: b 1731 d 8-21-1822 m — Pvt PA

FEATHER,
Isaac: b 8-8-1753 d 1-26-1836 m Catharine Schumacher QM PA ★
Jacob: b 9-10-1759 d 5-22-1832 m Mary Connoly Pvt PA W★
Peter, Sr.: b 2-21-1725 d 9-27-1801 m Maria Appolonia Levan CMman PA
Peter, Jr.: b 3-18-1760 d 6-7-1804 m (1)Maria — (2)Margaret Van Kenna Pvt PA

FEATHERLY,
John: b 1760 d c. 1843 m Mary Claus Pvt NY ★

FEATHERSTONE, (includes FEATHERSTON)
Charles: b 1756 d 1840 m Elizabeth Thornton Sol VA
Henry: b c. 1755 d p. 12-1-1827 m Elizabeth Marshall PS VA

FEBIGER,
Christian: b 1746 d 1798 m Elizabeth Carson Col VA

FEDDER,
Conrad: b c. 1748 d 1811 m Sarah Pitcher Pvt PA
Jacob: b 1750 d 11-6-1807 m Barbara Forney Pvt PA

FEE,
John: b 1759 d 8-26-1845 m (1)Patience Kelly (2)Jane Jackson Pvt PA
Michael: b 1760 d 11-26-1847 m Rebecca Matthews Pvt PA W★
Thomas: b c. 1734 d p. 1795 m (1)— Thrasher (2)Sarah Leith Pvt PA

FEECK,
Peter: b 3-19-1742 d 12-14-1814 m Janette Vrooman Pvt NY

FEETER, (includes VEETER)
Wm.: b 1-6-1756 d 5-18-1844 m Elizabeth Bellinger Pvt NY

FEEZEL,
Lawrence: b 1760 d 8-2-1832 m Mary — Pvt PA

FEGLEY, (includes FEGELY, FEIGLEY, FIGLEY, VOEGELI)
Bernhard: b 3-26-1757 d 3-8-1845 m Maria Beiteman Pvt PA
Henry: b 1745-50 d 1829 m Barbara Mertz 1Lt PA
John: b 1-6-1752 d 11-30-1834 m Anna Maria — Lt PA
John George: b 1-25-1726 d 9-7-1784 m Phillipina Crebill Pvt PA
Peter: b 1758 d 1-16-1845 m Catherine Flowd Pvt MD ★
Simon: b a. 1760 d p. 1801 m Agnes — Sct Pvt PA
Zechariah: b — 1761 d 5-10-1853 m — Pvt PS PA

FEHNEL,
Frederick: b c. 1740 d a. 1802 m Elizabeth — Pvt PA

FEITNER,
Henry: b 1753 d 1823 m Christina Barbara Lukens Pvt PA

FELCH,
Abijah: b 9-30-1744 d 9-9-1814 m Lydia Clark Pvt MA
John: b 10-5-1739 d 1821 m (1)Sarah Adams (2)Relief Adams Cmsry CS CT
John: b 4- -1729/30 d 10-28-1776 m Mary Bacon Capt MA
Nathan: b 4-25-1757 d 9-3-1839 m (1)Mary Cheever (2)Sarah Wilkins Pvt MA

FELCH, contd.
Nicholas: b 6-12-1755 d 4-13-1841 m Sarah Gove Pvt NH ★
Samuel, Jr.: bpt 2-21-1747/8 d 8-20-1839 m (1)Mary Richardson (2)Mary Farnsworth Pvt MA

FELDER,
Henry, Sr.: b 1725 d 2-12-1780 m (1)Mary Elizabeth Shaumloffel (2)Catharine Snell CS PS Capt SC
Henry, Jr.: b 9-8-1748 d p. 1799 m Margaret Stoudenmire Capt SC
Peter: b 4-2-1759 d p. 1815 m — Lowe Pvt SC
Samuel: b 6-5-1755 d p. 1790 m (1)Mary Myers (2)Ann Horger Pvt SC

FELDTHOUSEN,
Christopher: b 1725 d 1799 m Sarah Hoogteling Pvt NY

FELIX,
Stephen: b 1741 d 10-21-1821 m Mary Magdalene Eckenroth Pvt PA

FELL,
Amos: b 11-1-1762 d 9- -1825 m Elizabeth Jackson Pvt PA
Benjamin: b 4-11-1739 d 4-4-1811 m Rebecca Casner PS PA
Jesse: b 4-16-1751 d 8-11-1830 m Hannah Welding Pvt PA
John: b 4-24-1721 d 5-15-1798 m Susan McIntosh CS PS NY NJ
John: b 1763 d 1845 m Elizabeth Mason Pvt PA
John: b 4-1-1730 d p. 11-5-1781 m Elizabeth Hartley PS Pvt PA
Joseph: b 8-4-1752 d 2-12-1801 m (1)Margaret Gourley (2)Hannah Fell Pvt PA
Nathan: b 6-4-1760 d 12-10-1835 m Ann Smith Pvt PA
Peter Renaudet: b 1754 d 10-6-1791 m Margaret Colden LCol NJ NY
Thomas: b c. 1738 d 1781 m (1)Mary Toy (2)Anne — Mstr 1Lt PA
Thomas: b 1-11-1746 d p. 2-13-1818 m Grace Parry Pvt PA
Thomas: b 5-14-1759 d 3-2-1849 m Elizabeth Kinsey PS PA
Wm.: b 4-2-1756 d 7-16-1841 m Agnes Anderson Cnt PA

FELLENCER,
John: b 11-19-1722 m 8-3-1809 m Elizabeth — PS PA

FELLER, (includes FOELLER, FOLLER)
Andreas: b c. 1751 d 1818 m Eva Catherine Roth Pvt PA
John, Jr.: b 10-30-1758 d 7-31-1824 m Anna Erkenbergh Pvt NY
Philip: b c. 1720 d 1800 m Susannah E. Schaeffer PS NY

FELLOWS,
Abiel: b 10-1-1764 d 8-18-1833 m (1)Anna Andrus (2)Catharine Mann (3)Dorcas Hopkins Pvt CT
Abner: b 12-5-1720 d c. 1786 m Elizabeth Rowe PS NH MA
Amos: b 1729 d 2-16-1777 m Abigail Lathrop Capt CT
Benjamin: b 10-7-1760 d p. 1792 m Mary Blaisdell Pvt NH
Daniel: b 1-14-1753 d 5-24-1832 m Sarah Osborn Pvt MA
David: b 11-23-1738 d 12-10-1779 m Lois Stevens Sgt CT
Ephraim: b 1760 d 1-16-1803 m Thankful Butler Pvt CT
Ephraim: b 1-20-1754 d 2-5-1810 m Eunice Appleton Pvt MA
Ezekiel: b 8-25-1754 d 10-10-1843 m Ann Blake Sgt NH ★
Isaac: b 1719 d 3-22-1806 m Mary Want Lt CT
Isaac: b 1758 d 2-22-1846 m Anna Grant Sgt CT ★
Isaac: b 8-29-1732 d 2-18-1814 m Mary Merrill Cpl PS NH
John, Sr.: b 1734 d 8-1-1808 m Mary Ashley BGen MA
John: bpt 9-1-1751 d 3-30-1824 m Martha Shatswell Pvt MA
John, Sr.: b 4-27-1720 d 1812 m (1)Elizabeth Blaisdell (2)Mary Kenniston PS Pvt NH
John, Jr.: b 2-7-1764 d 3- -1837 m Prudence Stevens Pvt NH ★
John: b 5-15-1749 d 1823 m Eunice Andrews Pvt NY
Jonathan: b 10-18-1764 d 1842 m Eleanor Weeks Pvt NH ★
Joseph, Sr.: b 1-10-1729 d 3-14-1811 m (1)Margaret Webster (2)Deborah Parvier Cpl NH
Joseph, Jr.: b 8-20-1756 d 10-29-1821 m Mary Huntoon Pvt NH ★
Joseph: b 7-7-1762 d 1847 m Sarah Quimby Pvt NH ★
Josiah: b 11-3-1757 d 3-20-1825 m Jemima Quimby Pvt NH
Moses: b 8-9-1755 d 1-30-1846 m Sarah Stephens Sgt NH
Nathaniel: b 2-4-1738 d — m — Cpl CT
Nathaniel: b 1758 d 7-12-1838 m Mercy Flanders Pvt NH ★
Obel: b 12-22-1742 d 3-15-1809 m Lois — Pvt CT
Parker: b 10-3-1762 d 5-9-1820 m Dorcas Meacham Pvt MA ★
Samuel, Sr.: b 6-15-1712 d 10-27-1781 m Eunice Heald PS MA
Samuel, Jr.: b 1738 d 12-15-1823 m Mary Blodgett Pvt MA
Samuel: b 8-14-1738 d 9-15-1778 m Mary Ring Pvt NH
Willis: b 10-5-1758 d 1-18-1840 m Sarah Hart Pvt MA ★

FELT,
Aaron: b 9-1-1742 d 7- -1801 m (1)Tabitha Upton (2)Azubah Weston PS NH MA
Benjamin: b 10-12-1752 d 9-4-1822 m (1)Waitstill Capen (2)Jerusha Hunt Pvt MA
John: b a. 1730 d 8- -1785 m (1)Deborah Skerry (2)Mrs Catherine Turner Pvt MA
Johnathan: b 4-8-1753 d 2-17-1807 m Martha — Pvt MA
Jonathan: b 4-25-1748 d 11-5-1800 m Eunice Brastow Capt MA
Joseph: b 9-15-1758 d 9-14-1849 m Sarah Hills Pvt MA
Joseph: b 1-12-1757 d 8- -1842 m Elizabeth Spafford Pvt NH ★
Joshua: b 6-21-1751 d 1822 m Hannah Stocker Pvt MA
Oliver: b 12-3-1758 d 12-19-1829 m Mary Dunlap Pvt MA

Peter: b 11-3-1745 d 1-2-1817 m (1)Lucy Andrews (2)Mrs Polly Gilmore Sgt NH
Samuel: b 4-13-1735 d 7-31-1803 m (1)Mehitabel Buell (2)Mercy — Capt CT
Samuel: b 3-17-1755 d 6-26-1826 m Naomi Woods Pvt MA W★

FELTER,
Mathias: b 4-26-1737 d p. 1789 m (1)Catherine Weller (2)Lena Helene Velde Capt NY
Peter: bpt 2-3-1752 d 1824-30 m Elizabeth Brede Pvt NY
Wm.: b c. 1715 d p. 1790 m Elizabeth Parleman PS NY

FELTON,
Benjamin: b 3-12-1739 d 2-20-1819 m (1)Jennie Dorrity (2)Ruth Hamilton Ens MA
Elisha: b 12-30-1733 d 9-3-1805 m Rachel Holt PS NH
Francis: b 8-15-1726 d 1794 m (1)Mehitable Kimball (2)Hannah Turner Capt MA
George Webber: b 4-20-1761 d 7-5-1817 m Hannah Oliver Pvt MA
James: bpt 3-3-1754 d 6-27-1836 m (1)— Ramsdell (2)Olive Alden Standish Sampson Pvt MA
James: bpt 10-8-1738 d a. 1804 m Sarah Houlton 1Lt MA
Joel: b 5-14-1762 d 1-2-1829 m Susanna Hunt Pvt MA
John: b 11-9-1741 d 1820 m Persis Rogers Cpl NH
Matthias: b 3-28-1756 d 12-28-1842 m (2)Relief Kendall Lt MA
Nathaniel: b 5-7-1714 d 2-14-1807 m Anna Jacobs PS MA
Robert: b 12-27-1763 d 7-8-1830 m Sylvia Darling Pvt MA
Skelton: b 12-21-1750 d 7-9-1822 m Silence Hale Pvt MA
Stephen: b 9-14-1752 d 11-3-1827 m Lovinah Stowe Pvt MA
Thomas, Sr.: b 6-20-1732 d 12-20-1805 m Hannah Halfpenny Pvt MA
Thomas, Jr.: b 4-13-1759 d 8-12-1795 m Martha Conway Pvt MA
Timothy: bpt 12-19-1742 d 10-12-1811 m Hannah Proctor Pvt MA
Wm.: b 3-18-1745 d 1820 m Eunice Williams Pvt MA

FELTS,
Cary: b 11-3-1756 d 6-14-1840 m Sallie Foster Pvt NC

FELTY,
George: b 2-14-1742 d 2-14-1800 m Catharine Burkhardt Pvt PS PA
Henry: b 8-10-1758 d 4-25-1836 m Anna Maria Hubert Ens PA ★

FENDERSON,
John: b 7-15-1756 d 6-24-1852 m (1)Sarah Kenney (2)Mary Milliken Sgt MA ★
Wm.: b 7-15-1754 d 6-24-1834 m Annie McKenney Pvt MA

FENIMORE,
Jonathan: b 3-10-1756 d 1-3-1829 m Sarah Watson Arfr Matr PA ★
Thomas: b 1728 d 1812 m Mary Harker Maj NJ

FENLESSON,
Wallis: b c. 1750 d 5-27-1827 m Susannah — Pvt Drm MA

FENN,
Aaron: b 11-25-1746 d 6-13-1821 m Mary Bradley PS Pvt CT
Benjamin, Sr.: b 4-17-1720 d 2-20-1778 m Mary Peck LCol CT
Benjamin, Jr.: b 7-30-1742 d 10-27-1780 m Sarah Treat Lt CT
Isaac: b c. 1749 d 3-18-1825 m Mehitable Humiston PS CT
Jacob: b 8-26-1755 d 3-22-1826 m Sarah Matthews Pvt CT
James: b 9-6-1739 d 1832 m Sarah Baldwin PS CT
Jason: b 11-19-1751 d 3-28-1819 m Martha Potter Sgt CT
Samuel: b 9- -1746 d — m Elizabeth Baldwin Maj CT
Samuel: b 12-27-1737 d 3-7-1823 m Sarah Scott Sgt CT
Theophilus: b 1744 d 10-27-1830 m Martha Rood Capt CT
Thomas: b 12-1-1735 d 8-1-1818 m Aby Welton Capt CT

FENNELL,
Christopher: b 1760 d 1851 m (1)Elizabeth Shaffer (2)Mrs Mary Prugh Pvt PA
Nicholas: b 2-15-1762 d 1-6-1828 m Margaret Robinson Pvt NC W★
Stith: b c. 1749 d 1797 m Mary — PS SC

FENNER,
Arthur: b 1740 d 8-23-1827 m Rachel Westcott Capt RI
Barnet: b c. 1757 d 1-1-1804 m Maria Magdalena — Pvt PA
Felix: b 11-1-1725 d 8-19-1793 m Mary Eve — Pvt PA
Felix: b 9-21-1753 d 3-8-1829 m Martha Eschenbach Pvt PA
Jeremiah: b 1730 d 2-12-1789 m Ann Warner PS RI
John: b 1760 d p. 1795 m Elizabeth Long Pvt PA ★
John: b 1736 d 1828 m Lydia Carpenter Pvt RI
Richard: b 1755 d 4- -1828 m Ann McKinney Geddy Lt NC W★
Richard: b 1718 d 2-17-1799 m Elizabeth Arnold LCol RI
Richard, Jr.: b 8-21-1753 d 9-30-1842 m Sarah Manchester LCol RI ★
Robert: b 1745 d 1816 m Mary Houson Capt NC
Stephen: b —d 10-22-1823 m Mary Fenner Pvt RI
Wm.: b 1764 d c. 1835 m Mercy — Pvt NC

FENNO
Benjamin: b 9-8-1749 d 3-6-1817 m Abigail Bowker Cpl MA
Elijah: b 8-30-1757 d 1819 m Abigail Smith Pvt MA

Enoch: b 3-23-1755 d 9-19-1796 m Mary Holden Pvt MA
John: b 5-4-1732 d 12-5-1812 m Katherine Hodges Pvt Smn MA
Joseph: b 1762 d 4-17-1822 m Helen Derby Pvt MA
Joseph: b 1-1-1758 d 12-29-1822 m Margaret Gibbons Pvt MA

FENSTERMACHER, (includes FENSTERMAKER)
Frederick: b c. 1750 d p. 1820 m Ann Margaret Sgt PA
Jacob: b 11-19-1751 d 7-19-1835 m Elisabeth Basters PS PA
John: b —d 1815 m Anna Maria Wuchter Pvt PA
Michael: b 6-2-1749 d 12-1-1831 m Phillippiana Kerschner Sgt PA
Philip: b 12-10-1746 d 12-20-1807 m Maria Eva Knerr Pvt PA
Wm.: b 10-11-1740 d 11-27-1811 m Margaret Elizabeth Sol PA

FENTON, (includes FINTON)
Asa: b 1-10-1747 d 2-18-1840 m (1)Jerusha — (2)Sarah Johnson Cpl CT
David: b 12-19-1763 d c. 1828 m Margaret Henderson Drm CT
Ebenezer, Jr.: b 4-15-1743 d p. 1783 m (1)Sarah Dunham (2)Rebeckah Johnson Pvt CT
Elijah: b 2-6-1735 d 10-10-1776 m Lois Hovey Maj CT
Elijah: b 8-8-1754 d 4-17-1790 m Rubie Anderson Pvt CT
Gamaliel: b 1-31-1763 d 8-19-1847 m Elizabeth Weber Sol CT
Jacob: b 11-5-1765 d 1-25-1822 m Lois Hurd Pvt CT
John: b 2-12-1760 d 9-7-1826 m (1)Marcia Moulton (2)Anna Guthrie Pvt MA
John: b 5-8-1752 d 2-14-1839 m (1)Phoebe Wells (2)Elizabeth Roberts Arfr Drm Sgt NJ
Jonathan: b 5-17-1741 d p. 1790 m Mary Cary Cpl CT
Joseph: b 1761 d 10-23-1851 m Margaret Swegals Pvt PA ★
Matthew: b 1753 d 1-24-1813 m (1)Lavinia Bigelow (2)Hannah Woods Pvt MA
Nathaniel: b 4-29-1763 d 1-25-1846 m Rachel Fletcher Pvt CT ★
Roswell: b 6-9-1755 d 9-16-1806 m Deborah Freeman Pvt CT
Samuel: b 1756 d 7-3-1842 m Elizabeth Dix Capt PA
Solomon: b 6-23-1750 d 12-25-1831 m Sybbl Snow Lt CT ★
Solomon: b 11-6-1758 d 8-27-1843 m Molly Parker Pvt CT ★
Thomas: b 1745 d 1-17-1778 m Charity Dennis Sgt MA
Thomas: b 1751 d 7-5-1844 m Elizabeth — Sol PA

FENTRESS,
John, Sr.: b c. 1725 d 1803 m Keziah Land PS VA

FENWICK,
Ignatius, Jr.: b 1736 d a. 4-6-1784 m Sarah Taney Col PS MD
John: b c. 1720 d c. 1781 m (1)Elizabeth Guyther (2)Monica Ford CS MD
Richard: b 1760 d 3-26-1829 m Ann Welch Pvt MD
Robert: b. 1741 d c. 1807 m (1)Ann Elizabeth Manning (2)Belinda Miles Pvt MD
Wm.: b 1757 d 6-18-1833 m Catherine — Pvt Smn MD

FERDON,
Abraham.: b 1-25-1755 d 3-19-1831 m Magdalen Powleson Pvt NJ W★
Wilhelmus: b 2-28-1743 d 9-20-1810 m Tieje Verveelan Sol NJ

FEREBEE, (includes FARRABEE)
Caleb: b c. 1738 d 5-4-1792 m Sarah — Capt PS DE
Joseph: b 5-31-1754 d 12-20-1820 m (1)Mary Dauge (2)Nancy Herbert (3)Mary Creekmore Capt CS PS NC
Peter: b c. 1736 d p. 4-15-1786 m Jean Brunt PS NC
Samuel: b 6-20-1761 d 11-7-1845 m (1)Sarah Dauge (2)Margaret Dauge (3)Mrs Jane Brocket Ens NC ★
Wm.: b 4-13-1722 d 7-9-1783 m Elizabeth Cowper CS NC

FERGUS, (includes FARGUS)
Francis: b c. 1758 d a. 3-29-1813 m Catherine — Pvt PA
Francis: b 9-8-1752 d 9-28-1841 m Mary McCormick Wgn Tms PA
Hugh: b c. 1725 d 1804 m (1) — (2)Sarah Gibson Pvt PS PA
John: b c. 1717 d p. 1790 m — Grd PA

FERGUSON, (includes FERGUESON, FERGUSSON, FURGUSON)
Alexander: b 1747 d 12-19-1817 m Mary Parker Pvt VA
Bryant: b c. 1750 d 5-15-1823 m Ann — Pvt VA
Charles: b 1758 d 8-19-1782 m Barbara Ann Blocker Pvt KY
Daniel: b c. 1750 d p. 5-26-1811 m (1)Ruth Riley (2)Mary Riley MM MD
David: b — d 3-18-1780 m — Broadbelt Capt SC
David: b 1758 d 1819 m Lucinda Jackson QM Sgt VA
Gabriel: b a. 1760 d p. 1790 m Hannah Smith Pvt NY
George: b 1759 d 1787 m Catherine Sterrett Pvt MA
Henry: b 1755 d 11- -1826 m Elnor Palmer Pvt PA
James: b 1752 d p. 1783 m Ruth Hallsall Sol MD
James: b 4-5-1759 d 6- -1842 m Sarah Barnett Pvt NC ★
James, Jr.: b 1748 d 9-11-1806 m Margery Denny Pvt PA
John: b 1723 d 12-31-1812/3 m (1)Elener Rezin (2)Catherine Thomas Pvt CS MD W★
John: b c. 1725 d 1796 m Basheba — Pvt MD
John: b 6-15-1756 d 1830 m Lucy Pendleton Pvt MD
John: b 11- -1740 d 1-29-1792 m Dorothy Hamilton Capt MA
John: b 7-12-1756 d 1817 m Sarah Knox Pvt MA
John: b 1757 d 4- -1842 m Mary Woods Pvt NH ★

John: b 8-11-1757 d 11-23-1846 m Ann Gage Pvt NH ★
John: b c. 1734 d 12-18-1824 m Jennet Cowan Pvt NY
John: b 12-25-1758 d 4-5-1841 m (1)Barbara — (2)Mary Campbell Pvt NY ★
John: b 1-15-1755 d 2-14-1842 m (1)— (2)Bethena Deacons Pvt NC VA ★
John: b 3-18-1763 d 1-24-1843 m Any Manning Pvt NY
John: b 1757/8 d 2-20-1838 m Janet Wier Pvt PA
John: b 1756 d 10-19-1846 m Sarah Hanna Pvt PA
John: b 1763 d 1818 m Elizabeth Ferguson Pvt VA
John, Sr.: b c. 1730 d a. 2- -1790 m Elizabeth — PS VA
Matthew: b 10- -1749 d 11-2-1848 m Ann Chestnut Pvt VA
Moses: b 1736 d 1801 m Sarah — Pvt PA
Moses: b 2- -1762 d p. 3-15-1845 m Elizabeth Cox Pvt SC ★
Rezin: b 1762 d 8-6-1808 m Elizabeth Wetzell Pvt MD
Robert: b 1746 d 4-15-1827 m Jean Young Pvt MA
Robert: b 1761 d 4-28-1850 m Bershebia Newbill Pvt VA ★
Robert: b c. 1764 d 1845 m Elizabeth — Pvt VA
Samuel: b 1760 d 1838 m Phoebe Thompson OrdlSgt CT ★
Samuel: b 6-9-1758 d 2-20-1814 m (2)Elizabeth Crooks Blue Pvt PA
Samuel: b c. 1723 d 1785 m Mary McMillin PS PA
Samuel: b 1755 d 6-8-1817 m Isabella Barber Sol PS SC
Samuel: b 3-3-1744 d p. 11-8-1824 m Mary Jameson Ens VA
Stephen: b 4-10-1746 d 12-11-1800 m Shuah Bartlett 1Lt MA
Thomas: b 11- -1753/54 d p. 1832 m — Pvt NY
Thomas: b 1762/3 d 6-19-1843 m Edia Foster Sgt NC
Thomas: b 11-25-1766 d 6-19-1836 m Nancy Young Pvt PS VA
Wm.: b a. 1724 d p. 1776 m Janet Ferguson Pvt MA
Wm.: b 2-9-1754 d 3-21-1817 m (2)Sarah Tod PS NC
Wm.: b 1762 d 2-10-1826 m Patience Franklin FifMaj PA
Wm.: b 1746 d 5-21-1833 m Sarah Liggett Pvt PA
Wm., Abraham: b 5-3-1761 d 7-2-1840 m Nancy Smith Pvt VA ★

FERNALD,
Benjamin: b 4-12-1744 d 11-12-1812 m Sarah Beaver Pvt MA
Benjamin: b 6-27-1721 d 3-4-1798 m Sarah Fernald PS MA
Dennis: b 1730 d 8-2-1785 m Sarah Frost PS ME
Dennis: b 9-29-1757 d 1-1-1837 m Elizabeth Stacey Pvt MA ★
Diamond: b 4-2-1750 d 12-28-1806 m Margaret — PS ME
Ebenezer, Jr.: b 3-27-1729 d 6-9-1807 m Sara Lewis PS Sol NH
Hercules Archelaus: b 12-4-1749 d 7-22-1836 m Miriam Pursley Pvt MA ★
James: b 2-16-1749 d 9- -1823 m Mary Stacy Pvt MA
Joel: b 2-13-1745 d 4-26-1823 m Elizabeth Peters 2Lt ME
John: b 7-10-1737 d 5-16-1825 m Sarah Wentworth Pvt MA
Joseph Weeks: b 6-14-1756 d 11-22-1822 m Catherine Chandler Pvt MA
Joshua: b 8-7-1743 d 12-6-1815 m Elizabeth White Pvt Smn MA
Tobias: b 4-13-1754 d c. 1827 m Elizabeth Mitchell Pvt MA
Wm.: b 2-22-1732 d 1803 m (1)Abigail Tobey (2)Mary Staples Lt MA
Wm.: b 7-9-1759 d 1816 m Mary Colby Pvt NH

FERRIER, (includes FARRIOR)
Andrew Sr.: b 11-17-1732 d 1792 m Jean Marlin Capt PA
John: b c. 1755 d 1812 m Martha McGhee Lt NC
John: b bpt 11-17-1760 d 1803 m Ann Thompson Sol PA
Wm.: b 6-10-1759 d p. 1790 m Isabella Scott Pvt PA

FERRILL, (includes FARRELL, FERELL, FERREL, FERRELL)
Benjamin: b c. 1743 d c. 1796 m (1)Mary Burton (2)Sarah Collier (3)Ann Dortch Capt PS VA
James: b c. 1758 d 1848 m Elizabeth Stone Sol NJ
James: b c. 1759/60 d p. 1807 m Mary Wells Pvt VA
John: b 1740 d 1790 m Margaret Elizabeth Baughman Pvt MD
John: b 1760 d p. 1814 m Barbara Eafland Cav NC
John: b c. 1763 d c. 1824 m Christina — Drm VA
Thomas: b 1757 d 1817 m Sarah Graham Pvt VA
Thomas: b 6-2-1758 d 1-19-1836 m Susannah Burner Pvt VA
Wm.: b — d c. 1826 m (1)Frances Martin (2)Dolly — Pvt VA

FERRIN, (includes FARRAN FERREN)
Barnabas: b 4-6-1739 d 12-13-1820 m Mary Stuart Pvt PA
Ebenezer: b 7-20-1754 d 1790 m Jane — Sgt NH
Enos: b 3-3-1749 d 3-3-1811 m (1)Mary Currier (2)Mrs Judith Corliss Cross Pvt PS NH
Johnathan: b 2-4-1756 d 5- -1829 m Nancy Sawyer Sgt MA
Jonathan: b 6-9-1753 d 6-26-1827 m Hannah Ela Pvt MA NH ★
Moses 2nd: b 1756 d 1-15-1843 m (1)Mary Dellan (2)Aseneah Robinson (2)Jane Blazo Pvt NH ★
Philip: b 10-21-1739 d 1-12-1804 m Ann Currier Lt NH
Zebulon: b 9-18-1727 d 12-6-1805 m (1)Alice Tucker (2)Desire Heminway Pvt CT

FERRIS, (includes FERRISS)
Benjamin: b 1729 d 11-25-1797 m Sarah Palmer Pvt NY
Benjamin: b 10-1-1708 d p. 1779 m Phebe Beecher PS NY
Caleb: b 1737 d 1790 m Susannah Lord Pvt NY
Charity Thomas: b 7-3-1734 d 7- -1809 m James Ferris PS NY
Ebenezer: b — d p. 8-19-1800 m Giddy Edmunds Capt CT

FERRIS, contd.
Ezra: b 9-1-1760 d 11-8-1833 m Charity — Pvt Wgn NY W★
Gilbert: b 9-28-1746 d 12-1-1834 m X Pvt NY
Isaac: b 1735 d 7-11-1819 m Mary Sherwood PS CT
Israel: b 10-25-1751 d 1-2-1844 m Ruth Mead Pvt CT
James: b c. 1732 d 5- -1810 m Mary — Sol PS CT
James: b 7-2-1761 d 3- -1844 m Mary Calkins Pvt NY
James: b 7-30-1734 d 2-25-1780 m Charity Thomas PS NY
Jeduthan: b 2-22-1737 d 6-23-1809 m Phebe Peck Pvt CT
John: b 4-20-1760 d 9-22-1841 m Jerusha Lockwood Pvt NY
John A.: b 1758-1762 d 3-3-1853 m (1)Mary DeWitt (2)Freelove S.
    Addison 4Sgt NY ★
Jonah: b 1744 d 12-26-1815 m Anne Smith Pvt CT W★
Jonathan 1st: b 2-15-1732 d 8-26-1798 m (1)Rachel Dean
    (2)Elizabeth Miller Sgt NY
Joseph: b 9-7-1703 d — m Hannah Welch Pvt CT
Joshua: b — d — m Eliza Hathaway Pvt NY
Nathaniel: b 3-27-1746 d 8-30-1823 m Mary (Johnson) Peck Pvt CT
Oliver: b 11-22-1753 d 8-17-1825 m Abigail Lockwood Lt NCdr CT
    W★
Peter: b 1722 d 1815 m (2) X PS VT
Ransford Avery: b 1752 d 1-2-1824 m Elizabeth June Pvt CT ★
Reed: b 8-16-1730 d 4-3-1804 m Ann Tripp Pvt NY
Reuben: b a. 1750 d p. 1788 m Sarah Strong LCol NY
Richard: b 5-11-1762 d 10-19-1846 m Catherine Lent Pvt NY ★
Samuel Sr.: b 2-18-1733 d 9-17-1798 m Susan Peck Sgt CT
Samuel Jr.: b 8-11-1754 d 12-24-1842 m Phoebe Sherman Pvt
    NY★
Seth: b 6-11-1756 d 8- -1789 m Dolly Mosher Cpl NY
Squire: b 1763 d 1849 m Diadame Callender Slr Sct VT
Stephen: b 12-27-1740 d 2-12-1824 m Sarah Lockwood Pvt NY
Sylvanus: b 8-10-1737 d 6-12-1824 m Mary Meade PS CT
Warren: b 2-19-1763 d 3-26-1813 m (1)Ruth Taber (2)Keziah
    Hawley Sol NY

FERRY, (includes FERRE, FERREE, FIREE, FORE, FOREE,
FOREY, FORRAY, FORRER, FORREY)
Aaron: b 12-24-1724 d 7-19-1783 m Eunice Chapin MM Sgt MA
Charles: b 1-7-1739 d 10-10-1804 m Mary — 2Lt MA
Charles: b 5-12-1761 d p. 1797 m Eunice Chapin Pvt MA
Eliphalet: b 1- -1753 d 2-12-1827 m Mercy Taylor Sgt CT W ★
Elisha Jr.: b 1-7-1738 d p. 1790 m Hannah Jones Pvt MA
Frederick: b 1744 d 1789 m Mary Stuart Interpreter PA
Isaac: b 1752 d 1820 m Mary (Ferree) Pvt PA
Jacob: b c. 1730 d 1782 m (1)Barbara Carpenter (2)Mary — Pvt PA
Jacob : b 6-9-1755 d 9-23-1848 m Susannah Strickler Pvt PA ★
Jacob: b 7-30-1757 d 8-28-1834 m Mary Lias Pvt PA
Jacob: b 8-8-1750 d 9-5-1807 m (1)Rachel Ferree (2)Alice Powel
    PS Pvt PA
Joel: b 2-19-1731 d 6-19-1801 m (1)Mary Copeland (2)Jane Johnson
    (3)Susan (Green) Ferree (4)Mrs Sallie Davis PS PA
John: b 7-9-1754 d 7-16-1832 m Susannah Munn Pvt NY
John: b 2-3-1703 d 1797 m Catherine de Bois Col PA
John: b c. 1740 d a. 7-29-1811 m Elisabeth Meylin Pvt PA
John: b — d 1782 m Margaret Berry Pvt PA
John: b a. 1754 d 1790 m Elizabeth — Pvt PA
John: b 5-17-1761 d 8-17-1839 m Rebecca Marsh Pvt PA
Joseph: b 1742 d p. 1-6-1832 m Anne — Pvt VA
Judah: b 1750 d 4-8-1824 m Hannah Cooley Pvt MA
Moses: b 1757 d 3-9-1832 m Jerusha Easton Pvt CT ★
Noah Jr.: b 10-18-1748 d 10-30-1819 m Hannah Montague Pvt MA
Peter: b 9-25-1745 d 3-20-1844 m Sally Prior Pvt NC ★
Peter: b 1733 d 1795 m Mary — Pvt PA
Philip: b 1730 d 1796 m Anna Copeland Pvt PA
Solomon: b 1744 d 2-7-1810 m Hannah French Cpl MA
Solomon: b 9-26-1752 d 2-8-1835 m Rhoda Sanderson Pvt MA ★
Thaddeus: b 1-3-1761 d 1-13-1847 m Abigail Burgess Fif MA

FERTIG,
John: b 2-24-1736 d 1-13-1831 m Elizabeth Dihm Pvt PA

FERWELL,
Zaccheus: b 6-27-1753 d 6-11-1811 m Lydia Gilson Pvt PA

FESLER,
John: b c. 1745 d 1841 m Eve Moyer Pvt PA

FESMIRE, (includes FISHMIRE)
Christian: b 1733 d 5- -1797 m Martha Nesmith Pvt PA

FESSENDEN,
Benjamin: b 1734 d 5-1-1801 m Barbara Calder Wgn MA
Benjamin: b 1758 d 8-17-1827 m Anne Bucknam Sgt MA
Ebenezer: b 10-1-1756 d 12-30-1834 m Sarah Hutchins Pvt MA
John: b 4-27-1729 d 4-14-1793 m Elizabeth Wyman Cpl MA
Nathan: b 4-10-1749 d 4-24-1797 m Sarah Winship Pvt MA
Nathaniel: b 6-7-1746 d — m (1)Lydia Bemis (2)Elizabeth Webb Pvt MA
Thomas: b 7-10-1741 d 2-25-1804 m (1)Elizabeth Apthorp (2)Lucy
    Lee CS 2Lt MA

FETTER, (includes FEATHERER)
Jacob: b 1756 d 8-31-1836 m Elenore Longaker Pvt NJ

Jacob: b 2-10-1751 d 7-30-1807 m Susanna Catherine Fainot Pvt
    PS PA
Michael: b 1725 d a. 1790 m Catrina — Pvt PA

FETTERMAN,
Johann Phillip: b 5-8-1761 d 10-27-1821 m Mary Sarah Danahower
    Pvt PA

FETTEROLF, (includes FEDDERHAFF, FETERHOFFER,
FETHEROLF)
Jacob: b 2-16-1742 d 4-6-1823 m Catharine Brobst Pvt PA
Jacob: b 7-2-1757 d 2-20-1840 m Ann Gunty Pvt PA
Mathias: b 11-22-1758 d 5-26-1849 m Mary — Pvt PA
Peter: b 3-20-1699 d 8-15-1784 m Anna Maria Rothermel PS PA

FETTERS,
Wm.: b — d 1821 m Ann Madeira Pvt PA

FETZER,
Joachim: b 7- -1752 d 2-10-1827 m Mary — Pvt VA ★

FEW,
Benjamin: b 12-2-1753 d 5-4-1815 m Quen — Pvt PA
Ignatious: b 8-20-1750 d 1810 m (1)Mary Candler (2)Lavinia — Maj
    GA
James: b c. 1745 d 2-22-1794 m Agnes — Pvt PA
Wm., Sr.: b 5-15-1714 d 7-21-1794 m (1)Mary Wheeler (2)Mrs Ann
    Hunt Pvt GA
Wm.' Jr.: b 6-8-1748 d 7-16-1828 m Catherine Nicholson Col GA

FEWELL,
Nathan: b 1757 d 3-9-1830 m Anna Stoyr Sol VA

FICHTHORN,
Andrew: b 1-10-1756 d 3-22-1829 m Susanna Horner Arfr PS PA

FICKETT, (includes FICKET,)
John Sr.: b 8-31-1722 d 2-9-1823 m Mrs Isabel Dyer Roberts Pvt MA
John Jr.: b 3-27-1752 d 8-19-1828 m Lucy Stanford Pvt MA ★
Zebulon: b 1762 d 4- -1858 m Sally — Pvt MA ★

FICKLE,
Daniel: b 1732 d 8-17-1819 m Hester Westenhaver Pvt PA

FICKLIN, (includes FICKLEN, FICKLING)
Benjamin: b 6-1-1740 d 10-7-1805 m — Burwell Lt MD
John: b 1755 d 6-6-1819 m Polly — Pvt VA ★
Joseph: b c. 1752 d p. 1781 m Ester Nuby Capt SC
Mary Herndon: b 1745 d 1816 m Thomas Ficklin PS KY
Philadelphia: b 12-15-1768 d 9-13-1823 m Thomas Bradley PS VA
Thomas: b 1738 d 1812 m Mary Herndon Sol KY
Wm.: b c. 1718 d p. 1789 m Molly Marye Sol VA

FIDLER,
Andrew: b 11-6-1742 d 10- -1808 m Charlotte — Pvt PA
Henry 2d: b 3-21-1752 d 6-6-1831 m Eve Lehnig Pvt PA

FIELD,
Aaron: b 1721 d 1800 m Eunice Frary PS MA
Abizer: b 1762 d p. 1783 m X Pvt MA
Abner: b 7-5-1754 d 12-10-1792 m (1)Chloe Whipple (2)Rebecca
    Payne Maj RI
Abner: b 6-20-1752 d 1831 m Jane Pope Sol VA
Abraham: b c. 1700 d a. 9- -1775 m Eleanor Byrd Sol VA
Asa: b 11-9-1757 d 12-6-1831 m Anna Diggins Pvt MA
Barzillia: b 12-6-1760 d 3- 1839 m Patty (Martha) Packard Pvt MA ★
Benjamin: b 11-11-1755 d 1-3-1842 m Mildred Slaughter Capt VA ★
Bennett: b 4-12-1752 d 1-31-1835 m Elizabeth Pierce Pvt CT
Daniel: b 11-11-1742 d — m Bathsheba Isbell Pvt CT
Daniel: b 8-21-1739 d 1-22-1778 m Lucy Ingersoll 2Sgt MA
Daniel: b 2-17-1709 d 1-22-1778 m Sarah Haynes Pvt ME
Daniel: b 8-30-1743 d 7-6-1824 m Hannah Whitman Drm RI
David: b 1-4-1712 d 4-19-1792 m Thankful (Taylor) Doolittle Col
    PS CS MA
David: b 7-31-1728 d 11-25-1778 m Anna Stone Pvt CT
Dennis: b 5-12-1761 d 4-21-1848 m (1)Mary Boice (2)Cynthia French
    Pvt NJ ★
Ebenezer: b 4-18-1736 d 1777 m Rachel Scranton Pvt CT
Ebenezer: b 11-12-1722 d 1- -1799 m (1)Hannah Wilson (2)Dorothy
    Coit (3)Mary Alcott Sgt MA
Ebenezer: b 10-11-1744 d 3-27-1811 m Eunice Wright Pvt MA
Elihu: b 10-16-1753 d 8-23-1814 m Hepzibah Dickinson Pvt MA
Elijah: b 2-2-1754 d 2-4-1822 m Tryphena Cooley Pvt MA
Elijah: b 4-30-1756 d 10- -1828 m Tamson Crane Sol Drm VT
Elisha Sr.: b 7-1-1717 d 1-18-1791 m Betty Pratt Grd VT
Elisha Jr.: b 3-3-1763 d 2-18-1852 m Ruth Kirkham Pvt Grd VT
Elnathan: b c. 1740 d 1812 m Mary Willet Pvt NJ
Ephraim: b 10-19-1755 d p. 1795 m Ruby Brett Pvt RI
Ezekiel H.: b 1750 d 8- -1783 m Elizabeth (Field) Pvt VA
Francis: b 11-29-1757 d 12-18-1812 m Naomi Wakelee Pvt CT
George: b 1758 d 1842 m (1)Electa Woodard (2)Eunice — Pvt CT ★
George: b 12-22-1742 d 1-22-1803 m Martha Smith Sgt MA

George: b 12-5-1745 d 5-2-1826 m Prudence Whipple Pvt MA
Hendrick: b 9-4-1751 d 9-5-1844 m Hannah Lane Pvt NJ
Henry: b 9-2-1759 d 1-4-1814 m Rhoda Stratton Pvt MA
Henry Sr.: b 1735 d 10- -1787 m Mary — PS VA
Henry Jr.: b 2-3-1755 d 5-27-1823 m (1) — Cardwell (2)Sukey
  Waller Withers Pvt VA W★
Henry: b — d 3- -1778 m Ann Lightfoot Lt VA
Ichabod: b 7-26-1763 d 7-1-1838 m Anna French Pvt CT
Isaac: b 11-18-1743 d 6-8-1780 m Martha Hartshorn Capt RI
Israel: b 3-27-1741 d p. 1785 m Martha — PS VT
James: b 1765 d 6-30-1823 m Anna Spencer Fif CT ★
James: b a. 1745 d p. 1779 m Mary Woodcock PS NH
Jemima: b — d 1793/4 m Thomas Field PS VA
Jeremiah: b 11-7-1753 d 6-20-1832 m Jane Ten Eyck MM Sgt NJ ★
Jeremiah: b 1-27-1713/4 d 1778 m Phebe Van Middleswaert PS NJ
Jeremiah: b 7-4-1746 d 1-8-1842 m Lydia Colwell PS RI
John: b 1756 d 1-1-1829 m Lucy Marsh Ens MA ★
John: b 1740/1 d 4-4-1824 m Hannah Blackman Cpl MA
John Jr.: b 4-16-1752 d 1-8-1826 m Ruth Thayer Pvt MA
John: b 7-10-1758 d 8-9-1842 m (1)Anna McConnell (2)Rahab
  Cooper Pvt NC
John: b 1738 d 9-13-1808 m Abigail Carey Capt Lt RI
John: b 3-22-1748 d 12-11-1811 m Marcy Searle Pvt RI
John: b 1727 d 1794 m Lydia Warren PS RI
John Jr.: b 1748 d p. 8-12-1810 m Diana Field Pvt VA
John: b c. 1745 d 5-4-1827 m Margaret Pearle Cpl VA
John Sr.: b 1720 d 10-10-1774 m Anna Rogers Clark Col VA
John: b 1752 d 1839 m Lavina Shortridge Pvt VA ★
John: b c. 1713 d 1789 m X PS VA
John B.: b 4-2-1756 d 7-6-1836 m (1)Phoebe Brokaw (2)Mrs Ann
  Terhune Pvt NJ ★
John Van Wyck: b 11-13-1729 d 9-8-1794 m Charity Coles Col NY
Joiarib: b 4-12-1742 d 12-11-1836 m (1)Hannah Crampton (2)Anna
  — Sol CT
Jonathan: b 7-30-1737 d 5-21-1814 m Elizabeth Cooley Pvt MA
Joseph: b 1749 d 3-27-1815 m Eunice Hill Lt MA
Joseph: b 11-29-1749 d 6-10-1836 m (1)Mehitable Ludden (2)Relief
  Baxter Cpl MA
Joseph: b 12-22-1714 d 1777 m Abigail Newcomb PS MA
Joseph: b 1763 d 1-14-1847 m Anna Miller Pvt NY
Joshua: b 2-20-1750 d 1-24-1783 m Submit (Field) Collins Pvt CT
Joshua: b 6-5-1746 d 3-26-1837 m Thankful Robbins Pvt NH ★
Levi: b 4-25-1755 d 10-28-1813 m Rhoda Kidder Sgt MA
Lewis: b 7-4-1763 d 1845 m Hannah Lewis Pvt VA ★
Luke: b 2-4-1753 d 3-5-1826 m Patience Griswold Pvt CT
Luther: b 10-18-1761 d p. 2-9-1801 m Hannah Williams Pvt VT
Moses: b 2-16-1722 d 3-7-1815 m (1)Rebecca Cooley (2)Lydia
  Champion Capt MA
Moses: b 1719 d 1787 m (1)Ann Dickinson (2)Martha Root Ens MA
Moses: b 9-17-1754 d 6-30-1832 m Mary Spelman Pvt MA
Moses Dickenson: b 2-10-1742 d 9-8-1828 m Patience Smith Lt NH
Nathaniel: b 1-3-1751 d 6-8-1820 m Sarah Hoar Leonard Cpl MA
Nathaniel: b 1727/8 d 1803 m (1)Mary Goodrich (2)Experience —
  Pvt CT
Nehemiah: b 5-15-1757 d 5-15-1815 m Sarah Whitman Ens RI
Noah: b 11-29-1750 d 7-8-1797 m Mary Brown Sgt MA
Oliver: b 11-15-1752 d 1-15-1801 m Ann Cooley Pvt MA
Pardon: b 9-27-1767 d 1-5-1832 m Rachel Kent Pvt CT ★
Pardon: b 4-13-1761 d 10-28-1842 m Elizabeth Williams Fif NS RI
Phineas: b 1760 d 1833 m Diadama Morgan Cpl MA
Reuben: b 11-11-1757 d 4- -1815 m Fanny Jones Capt VA W★
Richard: b 1734 d 1796 m Rachel Clapp Pvt MA
Richard: b 7-22-1751 d 12-18-1804 m Rebecca Harris Sgt MA
Robert: b c. 1745 d 1824 m (1) X (2)Sarah Green Ens VA
Samuel: b 1704 d 1783 m Bethiah Johnson Pvt CT
Samuel: b 1-20-1754 d 4-7-1829 m Miriam Nash Cpl MA
Samuel Sr.: b 7-6-1719 d 6-6-1789 m Abigail Field Cpl MA
Samuel Jr.: b 3-3-1755 d 5-30-1837 m Elizabeth Mettoon Pvt
  MA ★
Samuel, Jr.: b 10-10-1725 d 9-25-1793 m (2)Hannah — PS Dr CT
Seth: b 9-28-1712 d 5-3-1792 m Susan Doolittle PS MA
Solomon: b 6-28-1746 d 4-20-1828 m Mary Wright CS MA
Spencer: b 9-26-1754 d 11-31-1801 m Betsey Frink Srgmte MA
Stephen: b c. 1730 d p. 3-13-1799 m (1)Jerusha Field (2)Marcy—
  Tms NY
Thomas: b 4-7-1741 d 6-27-1833 m (2)Deliverance Hammon Lt RI
Thomas: b 5-18-1754 d 1- -1804 m Hannah Moses Pvt VA
Timothy: b 3-12-1744 d 1-1-1818 m Anna Dudley Lt CT
Wm.: b 8-27-1745 d 1-24-1824 m (1)Dorothy Kellogg (2)Edith Frary
  Pvt MA
Wm.: b a. 1736 d 1786 m X PS NY
Wm.: b 4-30-1728 d 4-18-1816 m Waite Westcott Capt RI
Zebulon Sr.: b c. 1736 d 1805 m (1)Charity Lincoln (2)Hannah Hall
  Lt MA
Zebulon Jr.: b 1-22-1760 d 9-20-1839 m Olive White Drm Pvt MA
Zenas: b 8-10-1753 d 7-3-1819 m (1)Sarah Burroughs (2)Lydia
  Cathcart Pvt MA

FIELDER,
Dennis: b 4-21-1756 d 5-3-1834 m X Pvt VA ★
James: b 1750 d 1813 m Sally Benge Sol VA
John: b 1742 d 6-27-1807 m Sarah Harris Pvt MA
John: b 1752 d 1842 m Nancy Hawkins Sgt VA

FIELDING,
Eppa: b 1755 d 3-3-1829 m Mary Basye Pvt VA

FIELDS,
John: b 7-5-1759 d 1-31-1843 m (1)Sarah Woodruff (2)Sarah Clarke
  Pvt CT ★
John: b 4-3-1752 d 9-1-1835 m Mary Gibson Sgt NC ★
John: b c. 1745 d p. 1790 m X Pvt PA
Joseph: b 1756 d 1-1-1846 m X Pvt MD ★
Joseph: b 1743 d 1784 m Nancy Noland PS MD
Wm.: b 4-15-1756 d 1825 m Jane — Pvt PA
Wm.: b 5-6-1746 d 3-5-1835 m Mary (Miller) Wright Pvt VA ★

FIEMANN,
Adam: b c. 1760 d p. 1790 m Susanna — Pvt PA

FIERO,
Abraham: b 3- -1764 d 11-4-1826 m Sarah Reightmyer Pvt NY W★
Christian, Sr.: bpt 6-28-1724 d p. 6-25-1793 m (1)Christiana Snyder
  (2)Hilitie — Lt PS NY
Johann Christian: b a. 1720 d 1786/7 m X PS NY
Johannes: b c. 1716 d 7-9-1780 m Anna Margaret Eligh Pvt NY
John: bpt 3-26-1744 d 2-24-1799 m Lena Smith Pvt NY
John Christian: b 12-7-1758 d 1-28-1826 m Mareitje Meirs Sol NY
Peter: bpt 7-3-1762 d 1802 m Mary Mast Post Pvt NY
Stephanus: b 6-25-1750 d 9-16-1831 m Catharina Meyer Ens Sgt NY

FIESTER,
Godfrey: b 6-26-1746 d 6-9-1813 m Mary Magdalene Kepner Pvt
  PA

FIFE, (includes FYFE, FYFFE)
James Sr.: b 1713 d a. 11-22-1791 m Sarah Watson PS MD
John: b — d 1-1-1813 m Elizabeth Strong Pvt MA
John: b c. 1710 d p. 1782 m Jane Garvin PS NH
John Sr.: b 1721 d 11-19-1800 m Margaret Wright Pvt PA
John Jr.: b 1756 d 7-30-1814 m Isabel Thompson Pvt PA
John: b 1747 d 1817 m Elizabeth Fife Pvt VA
Jonathan: b 1755 d p. 1820 m Sarah Harrison PS MD
Silas: b 10-4-1743 d 5-23-1836 m Abigail Houghton PS NH
Wm.: b 5-16-1746 d 1-10-1816 m Phebe White PS NH
Wm., Sr.: b 1720 d 1794 m Jane — Capt PA
Wm., Jr.: b 3-17-1757 d 5- -1838 m Margaret Fife Pvt PA
Wm.: b 1721 d 1799 m Margaret Wright Pvt PA
Wm.: b 1751 d 7-25-1808 m Margaret Boyd Pvt VA W★

FIFIELD,
Abraham: b 8-21-1752 d 6-9-1840 m Abigail Silloway Sgt NH ★
David: b 3-27-1749 d 1-5-1806 m Abigail Larey PS NH
Edward: b 11-29-1755 d 6-21-1812 m Elizabeth Rowe Pvt Fif NH
Edward: b 1751 d 8-19-1834 m Dorothy Sleeper Pvt NH
Jonathan: b 3-19-1746 d 1-15-1828 m Dorcas Pearson Pvt NH
Joseph: b 1740 d 9-29-1813 m — Badger Cpl NH
Moses: b 2-29-1760 d 7-3-1832 m Lucy Levistone Pvt NH W★
Nathaniel: b c. 1740 d 4-2-1813 m Janet Cilley Capt PS NH
Samuel: b 6-14-1735 d 9-3-1812 m Ruth Brown Pvt NH
Winthrop: b — d 1-10-1834 m Mehitable Pettingell MCapt NH

FIGGINS,
James: b 7-23-1763 d 9-23-1844 m Mary Self Pvt Grd VA ★

FIGHT,
Jacob: b 1760 d 1849 m Jane Cummings Pvt PA

FILBERT, (includes PHILBERT, PHILIBERT)
Arnaudt: b 1-22-1755 d 1812 m Marie Doussom PS LA
Peter: b 8-22-1746 d c. 1822 m Anna Catherine Klotz PS Pvt PA
Samuel: b 1-8-1710 d 9-25-1786 m Maria Susanna PS PA

FILER,
Jonathan: b 3-7-1747 d 7-17-1822 m Tryphena Leek PS NY
Roger: b 5-3-1743 d 1-18-1778 m Tryphena (Wolcott) Allyn Pvt CT
Samuel: b 11-6-1730 d 1798 m Mary White PS CT
Thomas: b 2-10-1739 d 10-31-1777 m Esther Osborn Pvt NY

FILES, (includes FILE)
Ebenezer: b 2-24-1758 d 9-30-1833 m Mary (Thomas) Elder Pvt
  MA
John: b c. 1736/7 d c. 10-30-1821 m (1)Elizabeth Richart
  (2)Catarina Hayner Pvt NY
John, Sr.: b c. 1738 d p. 1-17-1781 m Catherine Manley Capt SC
John, Jr.: b 3-31-1760 d 1838 m Mary Foils Pvt SC ★
Samuel: b 8-4-1759 d 4-7-1835 m Esther Thomas Cpl MA

FILHIOL,
Don Juan: b 9-2-1740 d 9-28-1821 m Francoise Poiret Capt LA

FILKINS, (includes FILKIN)
Bernardus: b c. 1724 d 2-25-1800 m X Pvt NY
Francis: b 10-24-1730/4 d 1781 m Catherine Lewis PS NY
Isaac: b 6-1-1755 d 2-5-1834 m — Langdon Pvt NY

FILLEBROWN,
Asa: b c. 1760 d 10-26-1804 m Margaret Shepardson Pvt MA

FILLEBROWN, contd.
Edward: b 6-8-1744 d 7-9-1798 m Lydia Prentice Pvt MA
James: b 11-23-1751 d 8-22-1816 m (1)Elizabeth Prentice (2)Mrs Phebe Barnard Sgt MA
James: b 2-10-1757 d 4-4-1838 m Matilda Williams Cpl MA
Thomas: b 6-16-1734 d p. 1790 m (1)Hannah Phillips (2)Hannah Brown (3)Rebecca Adams Sgt MA
Thomas: b 10-8-1763 d 6-14-1844 m (1)Elizabeth Cheever (2)Sally Cushing Pvt MA ★

FILLER,
Frederick: b 1759/60 d 11-27-1797 m Catherine Border Pvt MD W★

FILLMORE,
Comfort: b 1-25-1742 d 1-24-1814 m Zeruah Bosworth PS CT
Cyrus: b 1758 d c. 1843 m Jemima Kneeland Pvt NY ★
Luther: b 1-14-1749 d 2-9-1809 m Eunice — Sol VT
Nathaniel: b 3-20-1740 d 9-1-1813 m Hepzibah Wood Lt VT

FILSON,
Samuel: b 1757 d 9-15-1831 m (1) — Herron (2)Mary Cooper Sgt MD

FINCH,
Adam: b c. 1724 d 1798 m Mary — Capt VA
Amos: b 1751 d 1845 m Martha Parks Pvt NY
Amos: b 9-22-1754 d 1-22-1849 m Martha Flych Pvt NY ★
Ebenezer: b 1749 d 9-4-1825 m Ruth Foote PS CT
Ezekiel Jr.: b 11-2-1742 d 2-13-1836 m Phebe Sutherland Pvt CT
Foster: b 1761 d 5-23-1843 m Naomi Merrick Pvt NY
Henry: b c. 1745 d p. 5-7-1793 m Anne — Sol VA
Isaac: b c. 1761 d 8-21-1846 m Hannah Rundel Fif CT
Isaac: b c. 1720 d c. 1785 m Ann — PS NY
James Sr.: b 1745 d 1798 m Catherine Gale MM Pvt PS NY
James: b 2- -1755 d 9- -1835 m Mary Finny Pvt NY ★
James: b c. 1753 d 1836 m Judith Hutcherson Pvt VA
Jeremiah: b 1744 d 7-2-1798 m Abigail — Sgt NY
John: b c. 1731 d a. 2-11-1805 m Sarah — Lt NY
John: b 8-20-1757 d 3-3-1841 m Marthy Newman Pvt NY ★
John: b 1717 d 1794 m Mary — Pvt NY
John: b c. 1735 d 7-3-1778 m Christian Carpenter Pvt PA
John: b c. 1760-62 d a. 8-24-1808 m Lavina Fitzgerald Pvt PA
Jonathan: b 11-30-1750 d 4-25-1836 m Deborah Lockwood (2)Rhoda Potts Pvt CT
Jonathan, Jr.: b 3-4-1750 d 7-6-1816 m Hulda Ogden Pvt CT
Jonathan: b 3-31-1759 d 12-13-1831 m Jemima Ferriss Sgt NY ★
Joshua: b 11-3-1748 d 3-9-1807 m Loruhama Brewer Cpl MA
Nathaniel: b c. 1737 d 7-22-1779 m Keziah Allison Lt NY
Peter Sr.: b 4-23-1743 d 1-30-1801 m Phoebe McEwen Pvt CT
Reuben: b 3-3-1759 d 4-8-1847 m Anna Townsend Pvt NY
Silvanius: b 1762 d 10-28-1844 m Betsy Medberry Pvt NY ★
Stephen: b 3-6-1754 d 4-8-1839 m Mindwell Moore Pvt Tms CT ★
Wm.: b 1754 d 5-3-1836 m Mary Huxley Pvt CT ★
Wm.: b 7-25-1741 d 1806 m — Norton 2Lt NJ
Wm.: b 7-15-1762 d 11-22-1842 m Mary Moss Pvt VA ★

FINCHER,
Benjamin: b 3-12-1756 d 1-18-1835 m (1)Mary Miller (2)Hannah Brooks Pvt PA

FINE,
Peter: b 5-5-1753 d 8-11-1826 m (1)Rebecca Holliday (2)Anne Murrell Pvt MD
Phillip: b 1751 d 1824/5 m (1)Mary (Newby) Gaignon (2)Celeste Beaulieu Sol VA

FINEFROCK,
Andrew: b 10-25-1755 d 6-30-1836 m Barbara Neitig Pvt Grd PA ★

FINEL,
Edward: b 10-27-1748 d 6-19-1821 m Anna Morgan Sgt NY

FINK, (includes FINCK)
Andrew, Sr.: b 9-2-1721 d 8-22-1786 m Catherine Elizabeth Loucks Pvt PS NY
Andrew, Jr.: b 2-1-1751 d 2-3-1820 m Mary Markell Maj NY
Christian: b 2-4-1759 d 6-26-1841 m Elizabeth Suts Cpl NY ★
Jacob: b a. 1765 d p. 1790 m X Pvt PA
John: b 1-19-1753 d 7-8-1833 m Dorothy Fox Sgt NY ★
John: b 11-27-1757 d 12-13-1833 m Mary Shorb Pvt PA

FINKEL, (includes FINCKEL)
John: b c. 1740 d p. 1790 m Anna Maria Weger Sol NY
Philip: b c. 1760 d — m Elizabeth Winder Dr PA

FINKS,
Mark: b 7-1-1744 d 5-7-1834 m Eve Fiescher Capt VA

FINLEY, (includes FINDLAY, FINDLEY, FINDLY, FINLAY)
Alexander: b c. 1759 d 9-2-1832 m Nancy Carson Sgt PA
Andrew: b 8-10-1750 d 7-5-1829 m Jane Jack Lt PA

Archibald: b c. 1749 d 1809 m Mary (Poe) Peden PS PA
Charles: b 1743/4 d p. 1820 m Polly Jones Pvt NY ★
Charles: b 11-30-1736 d 3-15-1816 m (1)Hester Hodge (2)Sarah Nancy McDowell PS NC
David: b 3-9-1761 d 9-3-1838 m (1)Martha — (2)Jane Ritchie Pvt PA ★
David: b 1762 d 8-24-1849 m Jane Mitchell Pvt PA
George: b 1756 d 9-7-1814 m Elizabeth Gailbreath Pvt PA
George: b 1749 d 5- -1803 m Margaret Gould Cpl MD
George: b 12-15-1757 d 1-28-1833 m (1)Margaret — (2)Mary Bishop Ross Capt MD
George: b 1-30-1743 d 1828 m (1)Ann Newland (2)Mary Gains Lt VA
George: b 1-4-1748 d p. 1835 m Jean Lyle Lt VA
James: b 1760-2 d a. 3-2-1821 m Isabella — Sol GA
James: b 1743 d 1805 m Jane Craig Pvt NJ
James: b 1739 d 1790 m Jane McQuiston Pvt PA
James: b 2-1-1725 d 1-6-1795 m Hannah Evans PS CS PA
James: b 1755 d p. 10-15-1800 m Mary Henderson Capt VA
James: b 5-8-1747 d 12-14-1830 m Kesiah Martin Sol PS VA
James Edward Burr: b 5-15-1758 d 6-13-1819 m Mary Peronneau . . . . Dr SC
John: b 6-2-1759 d 3-25-1846 m Margaret Roland Pvt MD
John: b 10-20-1741 d 3-21-1778 m Hannah Edwards PS NJ
John: b 5-10-1752 d p. 1790 m Elizabeth Bradley Pvt NC
John: b 7-7-1748 d 4-10-1837 m Hannah Duncan Maj PA
John: b 1726 d 8-5-1783 m Mary Young Maj PA
John: b 10-9-1737 d p. 1804 m Mary Boyd Pvt PA
John Jr.: b 9-28-1760 d 3-11-1846 m Priscilla Hays Pvt PA
John: b c. 1750 d 1790-1800 m Ann — Capt SC
John: b 12-28-1724 d a. 9-20-1791 m Mary Caldwell PS VA
John: b 1-11-1742 d 11-11-1812 m Ann Miller Pvt Cmsry VA
John: b c. 1747 d 1807 m Sarah — Pvt VA
John Sr.: b c. 1724 d p. 1777 m Elizabeth Harris Sct VA
Joseph: b 1730 d 1797 m (1)Jane Taylor (2)Mrs Elizabeth Logan Capt NH
Joseph Lewis: b 2-10-1753 d 5-23-1839 m Jane Blair Maj PA ★
Mathew: b 1758 d 1818 m Jane McCord Pvt GA
Patrick: b 1760 d 1790 m Sarah Anne Black Pvt VA
Paul: b 1- -1762 d 7-12-1843 m Mary Martin Pvt GA SC ★
Robert W.: b 6-9-1756 d 12-8-1840 m Rebecca Bradley Sol SC GA
Samuel: b 1748 d 1834 m Nancy Moore Dr NJ CL
Samuel: b 1-17-1734 d 8-31-1804 m Jane Smith QM PA
Samuel: b 1745 d a. 6-20-1803 m Mary Sutton 1Lt PA
Samuel: b 1742 d 7-26-1816 m Mary Graham Pvt PA
Samuel: b 4-15-1752 d 4-2-1829 m Mary Brown Maj VA
Wm.: b 1-11-1741 d 4-4-1821 m (1)Margot Russel (2)Mary Cochran (3)Mrs Mary Caruthers Capt PA
Wm.: b a. 1714 d 1809 m (1)Martha Dreamer Pvt PA
Wm.: b 6-14-1746 d 1814 m Susanna Skinner Pvt PA

FINN,
Anthony: b 9-7-1748 d 3-27-1797 m Catherine Burt Lt NY
James: b c. 1746 d p. 8-30-1797 m Hannah — PS PA

FINNELL,
Charles: b 1762 d 1842 m Lucy — Pvt VA ★
Reuben: b 1750 d 10-15-1823 m (1)Henrietta — (2)Sarah (Ashford) Mitchell Pvt VA

FINNERTY,
Joseph: b 1760 d p. 1790 m Olive Castle Pvt NJ

FINSON,
Thomas: b 8-21-1757 d 1-30-1807 m Sarah Goss Cpl MA

FINSTER,
John: b 4- -1760 d 11-9-1855 m Mary Fredericka Sneck Pvt NY

FIRESTONE,
Matthias: b 4-5-1744 d 1829 m Mary Beaver Pvt PA
Nicholas: b 4-17-1735 d 1807 m Eva C. Schwab Pvt PA

FIRMIN,
John: b 1713 d 1-21-1802 m Tabitha Green Ammidown PS MA

FIROR,
Leonard: b 1-12-1759 d 3-14-1843 m Elizabeth Pauss PS MD

FIRTH,
James: b 1740 d 1809 m Phoebe Thompson Pvt DE

FISH,
Aaron: b 10-23-1758 d 4-27-1846 m Anna Babcock Pvt NS NY
Abner: b 1761 d 4-14-1849 m Mrs Mary (Ransberry) Brodhead Pvt NY ★
Artemus: b 6-28-1754 d 2-8-1834 m Anne Shrieve Pvt RI ★
Benjamin: b 8-10-1740 d 7-2-1808 m Abigail Howell Tms NJ
Cyrus: b 1761 d 1817 m Bridget Jones Drm CT
Daniel: b 7-13-1737 d 9-13-1809 m Barbara Bowen Pvt MA
David: b 3-14-1734 d — m Lydia Dennis PS RI
Ebenezer: b 1757 d 9-4-1827 m Lydia Fish Vol CT
Elisha: b 2-6-1718 d 8-6-1795 m Hannah Forbush Chp MA

Ephraim: b 3-16-1760 d 10-7-1838 m Mary Potter Lt NY ★
Jabez: b 7-25-1741 d 4-16-1814 m (1)Sarah Avery (2)Susanna Dana Sgt PA
Jacob: b 1751 d p. 8-13-1832 m Sarah Keene Pvt MA ★
John: b c. 1712 d 10-4-1795 m (1)Lucretia Packer (2)Sarah Latham Pvt CT
John: b 2- -1750 d 4- -1813 m Sarah Tupper Pvt MA
John: b 8-14-1749 d p. 1801 m Elizabeth Cook Pvt RI
Jonathan: b 1723 d 12-26-1796 m (1)Abigail Fish (2)Phoebe (Denison) Avery Capt PS CT
Jonathan: b 9-12-1757 d 6-29-1841 m Lillas Mason Pvt MA RI ★
Joseph: b 1-7-1757 d 4-26-1844 m Penelope Fish PS NJ
Joshua: b 1-13-1743 d 2-14-1817 m Phebe Wright Pvt NY
Josiah: b 2-11-1755 d 5-10-1811 m (1)Elizabeth Hazelton (2)Jenniah Phelps Holcomb Capt VT
Moses: b 3-29-1749 d 8-8-1836 m Jerusha Phillips Pvt CT
Moses: b 11-9-1759 d 10-6-1836 m Mary (Avery) Bowers Pvt CT
Nathan: b a. 1737 d c. 1812 m Olive Ensworth Pvt CT
Nathan: b 10-1-1729 d 1-30-1776 m Mary — Pvt MA
Nathan: b 1736 d 12-10-1813 m Catharine Berrien PS NY
Nathaniel, Jr.: b 2-6-1744 d p. 1786 m Mary Bacon Pvt CT
Nathaniel Jr.: b 1763 d P. 1833 m Miriam Hamilton Pvt MA ★
Nathaniel: b 1734d 8-16-1801 m (1)Sarah Reeder (2)Mrs Nancy Campbell Pvt PA
Nicholas: b 8-28-1758 d 6-20-1833 m Elizabeth Stuyvesant Maj NY
Pardon: b 1751 d 1835 m Deborah Mosier Pvt NY ★
Samuel: b 3-31-1751 d 11-26-1837 m Susan Lamb Pvt CT
Samuel: b 1734 d 1816 m Sarah Dimmick Capt MA
Seberry: b 6- -1762 d 1-7-1844 m (1)Elizabeth Allen (2)Mrs Esther Ladd Pvt NY
Simeon: b 5-17-1747 d 3-9-1825 m Tabitha Taft Cpl MA
Stephen: b 1745 d 1- -1782 m Ruth Coggeshall PS MA
Thomas, Sr.: b c. 1720 d p. 1-12-1782 m Jemima Morgan Smn CT
Thomas: b 3-30-1759 d 10-5-1828 m Ursula Crooker Pvt MA
Thomas: b 12-28-1762 d 9-24-1845 m Susanna Crowell Fif Sgt MA W★
Thomas: b 1760 d 4-22-1840 m Mary Young MM Pvt NJ W★
Wm.: b p. 1750 d p. 1840 m Mehitable Tupper Pvt MA
Wm.: b 1751 d 1836 m Juda Asher Pvt CL

FISHBACK,
Harmon: b 11-26-1741 d p. 1-20-1804 m Christine Huffman Sol VA
Jacob: b 4-14-1749 d 9-15-1821 m Phoebe Morgan Pvt Wgn VA
John: b 1757 d c. 1-22-1810 m Patty Pickett Pvt SC W★
John Frederick: b c. 1716 d 9-20-1782 m (1)Ann Elizabeth Holtzclaw (2)Eva Martin PS VA
Phillip: b 1728 d 5- -1819 m (1)— Neville (2)Jane Reed (3)Winifred Nutt PS VA

FISHBURN,(includes FISHBORN, FISHBOURN, FISHBURNE)
Detrich: b 1-29-1760 d 10- -1822 m Catharine Burckardt Pvt PA
Peter: b 4-6-1758 d 2-16-1825 m Maria Myers Pvt PA
Philip Sr.: b 5-7-1722 d 2-22-1795 m Catherine E. Bretz PS PA
Philip Jr.: b 11-15-1754 d 9-7-1851 m (1)Barbara Greiner (2)Ann Maria (Hack) Hadin Pvt PA ★
Wm.: b 9-12-1760 d 11-3-1819 m (1)Sarah Snipes (2)Mary Clay Snipes Capt SC

FISHEL,
Adam: b c. 1759 d 1800 m Elizabeth Zeigler Pvt PA

FISHER, (includes FISCHER, VISSCHER)
Aaron: b 3-3-1756 d 11-22-1839 m Elizabeth Ware Pvt MA
Aaron: b 1-16-1758 d 10-10-1843 m Rebecca Moore Pvt MA ★
Abiel: b 9-22-1755 d 12-23-1829 m Lydia Allyn Pvt MA
Adam: b 5-21-1749 d 1848 m Rebecca Bush Pvt NY
Adam Sr.: b 4-3-1732 d 2-8-1821 m Margaret Hankey Lt PA
Adam: b 1-29-1750 d 5-7-1829 m Susannah Jones Adj PA
Adam: b 11-20-1763 d p. 1844 m Susannah Schlenker Pvt PA
Adam: b 7-24-1740 d 7-5-1812 m Elizabeth Gaar Pvt VA
Adam, Sr.: b c. 1726 d a. 3-11-1783 m Christine — PS VA
Adam, Jr.: b c. 1755 d 1816 m Jemima Mace Sol VA
Asa: b 9-17-1732 d 12-14-1792 m Esther Metcalf Matr MA
Asa: b 4-30-1745 d 4-2-1823 m (1)Elizabeth Draper (2)Hannah Hartshorn (3)Hannah Cole Sgt MA
Asahel: b 12-16-1759 d 11-30-1813 m Anna Borden Sol CT
Barzillai: b 1-16-1730 d 1-21-1813 m Lydia Dexter Pvt CT
Benjamin: b 5- -1721 d 1-18-1777 m Sarah Everett Pvt MA
Christian: b c. 1725 d p. 3-1-1789 m Catherine — Pvt NY
Conrad: b 1757 d 1-5-1793 m Catherine Leger Pvt PA
Daniel: b 3-29-1744 d 8-14-1824 m Sybil Draper Capt MA
Daniel: b 10-16-1713 d 11-23-1799 m Elizabeth Weeks MM MA
David, Sr.: b 5-5-1721 d a. 9-1-1811 m Abigail Lewis Lt MA
David, Jr.: b 6-26-1759 d 11-8-1829 m Mehitable Hewins Pvt MA W★
David: b 9-1-1735 d 2-3-1812 m Jerusha — Pvt MA
David: b 1763 d 10-5-1850 m Sophia Thayer Pvt MA
Ebenezer: b 5-5-1721 d 3-13-1798 m (1)Sarah Chubb (2)Mrs Azuba (Clark) Sanders Sgt MA
Elias: b 1745 d c. 1841 m Hannah Carver Pvt MA
Elias: b 2- -1760 d 3-23-1845 m (1)Nellie Jemima Butler (2)Sarah Cosby Sgt VA ★
Eliezer: b 1-30-1730 d 10-14-1806 m Mary Davis Matr MA

Elijah: b 6-17-1758 d 1- -1842 m Jerusha Keene Pvt MA ★
Elijah: b 4- -1746 d 12-18-1815 m Hester Davids Miller Pvt NY
Ephraim: b 1-27-1751 d 8-6-1834 m Betsey Grinnal Pvt VT
Ezekiel, Jr.: b 8-5-1748 d 8-22-1802 m (1)Sarah May (2)Anna Horton Sgt MA
Frederick: b 1735 d 1797 m Ann McBride MilOf NC
Frederick: b 5-5-1750 d 10-17-1828 m Gertrude Faust Pvt PA
Frederick: b 1762 d 4-24-1846 m Mary — Pvt VA ★
George: b c. 1725 d 1797 m Anna Maria Lehr Ens MD
George: b 6-12-1739 d 12-11-1791 m Anna Barbara Eberhard Pvt PA
George: b 1758 d 1820 m Mary Lewis Pvt PA
George: b c. 1759 d 9- -1814 m Susan Joynes Pvt VA
Hendrick: b 1697 d 5-10-1779 m Elizabeth Bries PS NJ
Henry: b 3-22-1735 d p. 1790 m Margaret W. Shields PS DE
Henry: b 10-14-1756 d 1-22-1820 m Sarah Babcock Sgt NY
Henry: b 1754 d p. 1820 m X Pvt PA ★
Henry: b 12-9-1758 d a. 4-11-1822 m Susanna Ruth Pvt PA
Henry: b 1760 d 5-15-1826 m Mary Keister Pvt PA W ★
Ichabod: b 9-22-1747 d 11- -1818 m Sybil Fisher Pvt MA
Isaac, Sr.: b 8-26-1732 d 7-18-1808 m Hepzibah Adams Pvt MA
Isaac, Jr.: b 6-18-1757 d 8-14-1816 m (1)Abigail Thayer (2)Sarah Barrett Matr MA
Isaac, Jr.: b 1760 d 1842 m Sarah Bruen Pvt NJ
Isaac: b a. 1746 d p. 1787 m Sarah — Pvt VA
J. Jacob: b c. 1721 d 1803 m Mary Elizabeth Frederick PS PA
Jabez: b 11-19-1717 d 10-15-1806 m Mary Adams CS MA
Jabez Pond: b 10-7-1763 d 12-13-1836 m Fannie Auld Pvt MA ★
Jacob: b c. 1737 d 1- -1821 m (1)Sarah Hoppock(2)Anna — Pvt NJ
Jacob: b 10-29-1758 d 1- -1839 m Susan Burns Pvt VA ★
James: b 1766 d 9-5-1830 m Elizabeth Phipher Pvt MD
James: b — d — m Agnes Robinson Capt PA
James: b 1744 d 8-30-1828 m Jane Atkinson Pvt PA
James: b c. 1725 d 1784 m Martha — Pvt VA
Jeremiah: b 5-23-1765 d 10-11-1846 m Sabra Tubbs Pvt Wgn CT ★
Jeremiah: b 2-2-1727 d 5-24-1809 m Esther — Pvt MA
Joel: b 7-4-1743 d p. 1792 m (1)Elizabeth Cummings (2)Elizabeth Atherton Pvt MA
John: b 12-29-1755 d 6-9-1843 m Elizabeth Marcy Lt CT ★
John: b 5-1-1752 d 1829 m Deborah Wilt Cpl MA
John: b 5- -1751 d 10-13-1826 m Eunice — MM Pvt MA
John: b 7-18-1760 d 8-16-1823 m Chloe Smith Pvt MA
John: b 2-17-1734 d 5-18-1814 m Margaret McCrea Pvt NJ
John: b c. 1750 d p. 1783 m Mary Hoagland Pvt PA
John: b c. 1726 d 8- -1805 m Mary — Pvt NY
John: b 2-19-1752 d 5-19-1811 m Elesbeth Enders Sol NY
John: b 1757 d p. 12-27-1819 m Catherine — Pvt NC
John: b 9-11-1756 d 4-11-1837 m (1) X (2)Elizabeth — (3)Lucinda Tramel Pvt SC ★
John: b 12-24-1756 d 3-13-1809 m Susanna B. Bratton Pvt VA
John: b c. 1750 d 1845 m Ann Miller Pvt VA
John Adam: b 10-7-1744 d 11-21-1825 m Margaretta Elizabeth Reid Pvt PA
Jonathan: b 11-25-1743 d 3-10-1777 m Catherine Avery Lt MA
Jonathan: b — d 5-9-1837 m Eunice Holley Pvt MA
Joseph: b 8-5-1735 d 4-23-1827 m Elizabeth Farrington Sgt MA
Joseph: b 10-31-1753 d 11-21-1829 m (1)Elizabeth Pond (2)Submit Lewis Pvt MA
Joseph: b 4- -1734 d 12-29-1819 m Catharine Minegar Pvt NJ
Laurence: b 9-24-1733 d a. 1786 m Catarina Boner Pvt PA
Lemuel: b 12-10-1737 d 1-21-1820 m Mary White Pvt MA
Leonard: b 10-27-1753 d 9-20-1835 m Susana Reigler Lt NY
Lewis: b 1-9-1763 d 4-23-1832 m Rebecca Williams Pvt MA
Martin: b c. 1720 d 11-15-1814 m —Shackelford PS MD
Mary Crosure: b — d — m Samuel Fisher Pvt PA
Matthias: b 2-12-1758 d 2- -1833 m Martha Thompson Pvt PA
Michael: b 5-19-1704 d 9-18-1784 m Charity Chew CS NJ
Michael: b 5-20-1766 d 12-18-1833 m Christiana Barnhart Pvt PA
Michael: b 8-21-1725 d p. 1790 m — Acker PS PA
Micheal: b 1757 d 3-25-1799 m Elizabeth Conrad SIr MD
Moses: b 1-27-1755 d 1-23-1847 m (1)Louisa Thorp (2)Lucy Manning Pvt MA
Nathan: b 9-14-1750 d 9-26-1828 m Mehitable Forbes Capt MA
Nathan: b 3-30-1746 d 10-17-1776 m Rachel — Pvt MA
Nathan: b 2-8-1745 d 10-11-1824 m Esther French Sgt NH
Nathaniel;: b 12-13-1730 d 9-9-1784 m Jemima Richardson Lt MA
Nathaniel: b 10-25-1756 d p. 1- -1799 m (1)Hannah Reed (2)Nancy Simmons Sgt MA
Nathaniel: b 9-29-1740 d 12-6-1796 m Hannah Baker Cpl PS MA
Nicholas: b 1739 d 2-13-1814 m (1)Phebe (Brown?) (2)Susannah Tompkins Lt PS NY
Nicholas: b 1730 d 4-22-1794 m Elizabeth — PS NC
Oliver: b 5-23-1747 d 5-8-1817 m (1)Sarah Morse (2)Sarah Billings Sol MA
Onesiphorus: b 12- -1752 d 3-11-I829 m Ruth Prince Cpl MA
Paul: b 1758-63 d p. 2-15-1827 m Kathrine Kishter Pvt PA
Peter: b a. 1760 d 7-8-1845 m Mary Van Houten Pvt NJ
Peter, Sr.: b 9-8-1735 d 11-23-1787 m Appolonia Heckert Pvt PA
Peter: b — d 4-11-1782 m Anna Elizabeth Heylmann Pvt PA
Philip: b c. 1748/49 d 2-8-1839 m Margaret Albrecht Pvt MD ★
Samuel, 2nd: b 9-14-1732 d 4-4-1816 m (1)Sybil Farrington (2)Jemima (Whiting) Fisher Capt MA
Samuel: b 11-12-1722 d 9-2-1786 m Hannah Blanchard Capt MA

FISHER, contd.

Samuel: b 5-14-1755 d 12-1-1830 m (1)Rena Deane (2)Mrs Jemima Miller Cpl MA
Samuel: b 1-11-1757 d 4-18-1822 m Abigail Mason Cpl MA
Samuel, Jr.: b 2-23-1750 d p. 1-10-1784 m (1)Mrs Lydia Haskell (2)Lydia Hill Pvt MA
Samuel: b c. 1730 d 6-1-1807 m Mary — Pvt MA
Samuel: b 1722 d 4-10-1806 m (1)Sarah Taylor (2)Janet Wilson (3)Sarah Barber Pvt PS CS NH
Samuel: b a. 1757 d 12-3-1813 m (1)Mary Crosure (2)Nancy Layney Capt PA
Samuel: b 1726 d 1801 m Mary Scott Pvt PA
Seth: b 1759 d 1-10-1811 m Hannah Hewins Pvt MA
Stephen: b 1736 d 1817 m Mary M. Gaar Sol VA
Thomas: b 6-14-1761/63 d 12-2-1835 m (1)Elizabeth Evans (2)Sarah Polk (3)Nancy Ricards Pvt DE
Thomas: b 1725 d 10-12-1793 m (2)Catharine Little Capt PA
Thomas: b 2-11-1760 d 12-1-1841 m (4)— Jones Pvt VA ★
Timothy: b 12-28-1760 d 1-10-1833 m (1)Sarah Barton (2)Mrs Freelove (Nash) Jackson Cpl MA ★
Timothy: b 7-1-1746 d 1832 m Mrs Lovica Morse Wood Sgt RI
Timothy, Sr.: b 12-8-1732 d 6-12-1789 m Keturah Pond Pvt MA
Wm.: b c. 1760 d 7-7-1834 m Drusilla Willett Pvt MD
Wm.: b 1742 d 12-4-1804 m (1)Sarah — (2)Abisha — Pvt NY
Wm.: b 1741 d 9-3-1822 m Charity Paguinert Pvt NC
Wm.: b 1-22-1754 d p. 1-18-1816 m (1)Hannah Packer (2)Sarah Moore Pvt PA

FISK, (includes FISKE)

Aaron: b 3-20-1748/49 d 3-3-1839 m Tabatha Metcalf Pvt NH
Abel: b 3-28-1752 d 4-26-1802 m Anna Spaulding Chp MA
Abijah: b 11-1-1755 d 3-14-1833 m Alice Adams Pvt MA
Abner: b 1751 d 1841 m Mary Grout Pvt MA ★
Abraham: b 1762 d 1828 m Betsey Arnold Pvt NY
Amos: b 5-10-1739 d 1802 m Mary Whitney Pvt MA
Asa: b 5-28-1733 m 2-9-1812 m Elizabeth Knight Lt MA
Asa: b 9-3-1746 d 8-26-1830 m (1)Mercy Jones (2)Mary (prob. Godard) Pvt MA
Benjamin: b 5-1-1749 d 11- -1820 m (1)Jemima Holbrook (2)Margery Wood Cpl MA
Daniel: b 5-12-1748 d 7-1-1839 m Elizabeth Morse Pvt MA
Daniel: b 5-18-1742 d p. 1786 m Elizabeth Varnum Pvt MA
Daniel: b 1-26-1758 d 1-22-1841 m (1)Hannah Rockwood (2)Beulah Hayward Pvt MA ★
Daniel: b 8-19-1709 d 3-15-1778 m (1)Deliverance Brown (2)Jemima Shaw CS MA
Daniel: b 4-28-1753 d 5-5-1810 m Celia Freelove Knight Lt RI
David: b 12-17-1726 d 7-4-1775 m Sarah Farnam Pvt CT
David: b 10-8-1731 d 4-11-1800 m (2)Rebecca Garfield Sgt MA
David: b 4-16-1732 d 12-23-1817 m Sarah Bullard Pvt MA
David: b 3-25-1756 d p. 1780 m Mary — Pvt MA
David: b 12-1-1759 d 8-19-1817 m Eleanor Jones Pvt MA
David: b 11-23-1760 d 8-17-1820 m (1)Sarah Hadley (2)Mrs Ruth Trask Pvt Fif MA
David: b 11-23-1760 d 11-20-1803 m Abigail Harrington Pvt MA
David: b 1760 d 10-13-1838 m Prudence Woods Drm MA
David: b 6-25-1757 d 6-23-1843 m Edith Tay Pvt NH ★
Ebenezer: b 7-2-1716 d 1804 m Dorcas Tyler PS MA
Ebenezer: b 1730 d 3- -1784 m Elizabeth Richardson Pvt NH
Ebenezer: b 1748 d 10-7-1816 m Betsey — PS Dr NH
Eleazer, Sr.: b 11-3-1731 d 6-21-1803 m Esther Stewart Pvt MA
Eleazer, Jr.: b 8-24-1760 d p. 8-28-1832 m Elizabeth Foster Pvt NH ★
Ephraim, Sr.: b c. 1732 d 1825 m Mehitable Frost PS Pvt NH
Ephraim, Jr.: b 8-27-1758 d 1849 m Mattha Sawyer Pvt NH ★
Experience: b 11-19-1751 d 3-31-1823-5 m Mary Earll Lt MA VT
Henry: b 8-10-1745 d 12-10-1815 m Sarah (Fiske) Fisk MA
Hezekiah: b 6-2-1756 d 6-14-1819 m Eleanor Cooley Pvt CT
Isaac: b 8-24-1714 d 12-22-1799 m Hannah Haven PS MA
Isaac: b 6-15-1757 d 6-17-1824 m Mercy Fenner Pvt RI
James: b 10-4-1763 d 11-17-1844 m Priscilla West Pvt MA
John: b 4-10-1744 d 9-28-1797 m Lydia Phippen Capt MA
John: b 7-23-1748 d 1781 m Anna Blood Cpl MA
John: b 8-9-1741 d 12-17-1819 m Abigail Howe Pvt MA
John: b 8-16-1749 d 7-4-1802 m Irena Buck Cmsry NY
John: b 2-20-1729 d 2-12-1789 m Mary Bartlett Maj RI
John: b 10-24-1760 d 3-26-1837 m Abigail Ballou Pvt RI
Jonathan: b 8-15-1755 d 1836 m Mehitabel Smith Pvt CT
Jonathan: b 12-15-1739 d 3-12-1814 m Abigail P. — Capt MA
Jonathan: b 5-1-1751 d 1825 m Mrs Mary Bragg Cpl MA
Jonathan: b 8-13-1739 d 12-22-1816 m Hannah — Pvt RI
Joseph: b 1741 d p. 1790 m (1)Eleanor Abbott (2)Margaret Hobbs Lt MA
Joseph, Sr.: b 1727 d 1-8-1808 m Hepzibah Raymond Dr MA
Joseph, Jr.: b 12-25-1752 d 9-25-1837 m Elizabeth Stone Dr MA
Joseph: b 7-16-1754 d 12-26-1843 m Lois Knight Pvt NY
Joseph: b 1737 d 6-10-1793 m Mary — Cpl RI
Joshua: b 1748 d 3-27-1796 m Martha Smith Capt MA
Josiah: b 9-3-1755 d 5-29-1832 m Mary Caldwell Fif NH
Moses: b 7-12-1755 d 3-1-1828 m Betsey Bullard Cpl MA
Moses: b 1746 d 10-2-1810 m (1)Rebecca Clark (2)Mrs Sarah Stone Pvt MA
Moses: b c. 1746 d 11-22-1816 m Hulda W. — Pvt RI

Nathan: b 9-7-1760 d 1-4-1813 m Mary Stearns Pvt MA
Nathan;: b 3-7-1761 d 11-2-1829 m Abigail Lyon Pvt MA
Nathaniel: b 3- -1741 d 4-9-1815 m Lydia Gould Pvt MA
Oliver: b 1-27-1746 d a. 1782 m Olive Wix Smn RI
Peleg: b 1-24-1740 d 5-30-1808 m Lydia Sheldon CS Capt RI
Peter: b 3-16-1743 d 6-17-1775 m Rachel Kemp Pvt MA
Richard: b 2-25-1750 d 3-9-1824 m Zebiah Pond Capt MA
Robert: b 1758 d 4-19-1824 m (2)Elizabeth Jones Sgt MA ★
Rufus: b 3-28-1752 d 12-2-1813 m Dorcas Fleason Cpl CT
Samuel: b 7-9-1742 d 3-13-1813 m (1)Mary Parkhurst (2)Abigail Murdock Sgt MA
Samuel, Jr.: b 4-14-1759 d 5-14-1828 m Rebecca (Fiske) Pvt MA
Simoen: b 7-15-1762 d 1838 m Dinah Whitcomb Pvt MA
Solomon: b 12-26-1757 d p. 1802 m Mary Harris Capt CT
Squire: b 1-10-1756 d a. 11-30-1807 m Amy Lapham Lt RI
Stephen: b 4-7-1759 d 11-13-1847 m Esther Clark Sgt VT ★
Thomas: b 3-12-1746 d 3-15-1818 m Sarah Shipley Sgt MA
Wm.: b 4-14-1733 d 3-9-1818 m Jemima Adams Lt MA
Wm.: b 12-28-1753 d 8-13-1803 m Ruth Smith PS MA
Wm.: b 11-30-1726 d 6- -1777 m Susannah Batchelder PS NH
Wm.: b 4-26-1732 d p. 1800 m — Pvt NY
Zedekiah: b 7-23-1763 d 8-5-1844 m Lucy Sweetser Cpl MA ★

FISKES,

Charles: b a. 1762 d a. 9-25-1804 m Seruriah — PS PA
Garet: b — d a. 11-4-1797 m Mary Magdalena — PS PA

FISLER, (includes FISLAR)

Jacob, Jr.: b 3-8-1754 d 3-4-1841 m (1)H. Jain Sparks (2)Abigail (Ledden) Iszard Pvt NJ ★
Jacob: b 2-29-1720 d 2-18-1803 m Sophia Klein PS NJ
John: b 4-25-1762 d 6-28-1833 m (1)Sarah Plascut (2)Sophia Neddgit Pvt NJ ★
John Ulrich: b 10-15-1757 d 6-23-1814 m Magdeline Barbara Frantz Pvt PA
Leonard: b 3-30-1756 d 4-15-1846 m Nancy Marshall Cpl NJ ★

FITCH,

Abner, Jr.: b 11-18-1749 d 3-23-1797 m Elizabeth Root Pvt CT
Abraham: b 1-22-1737 d 4-1-1821 m Elizabeth Bissell Capt CT
Amos: b 8-2-1760 d p. 9-20-1807 m (1)Lydia — (2)Judah — Pvt MA
Andrew: b 3-22-1747 d 8-22-1811 m Abigail Mason Capt CT
Asa: b 11-10-1765 d 8-24-1843 m Abigail Martin Dr Sgt NY CL
Augustus: b 12-20-1733 d 5-20-1815 m Editha Field Lt CT
Cyprian: b c. 1755 d p. 1784 m Ruth Rand Cpl CT
Daniel: b 1-6-1762 d 11-3-1855 m (1)Mehitable Bushnell (2)Zipporah Allen Cpl CT
Daniel: b 5-28-1744 d 1801 m Lucy — Cpl CT
David: b 5-22-1743 d 7-27-1813 m Mary Fowle Pvt MA
Ebenezer: b 9-9-1755 d 5-14-1817 m Sarah Hobby Pvt CT
Ebenezer: b 8-5-1751 d 1-26-1826 m Persis Bush Lt MA
Ebenezer: b 12-16-1745 d 1-16-1835 m Abigail Taylor Pvt MA
Elisha: b 4-29-1756 d 1826 m Elizabeth Ann (Terry) Tyler Pvt NY
Elisha: b 5-6-1749 d c. 1832 m Rachel Kellum Sgt VT
Ephraim: b 3-22-1730 d 2-2-1832 m Lydia Root Capt PS MA
Haynes: b 1-22-1735 d 8-11-1815 m Anne Cooke Pvt CT
Hezekiah: b 1736 d 12-24-1797 m Jerusha Burr Pvt CS CT
Hezekiah: b 1746 d 9-30-1830 m Prudence Read Pvt NH
Jabez, Jr.: b 3-2-1748 d 6-23-1789 m Olive Ripley Capt CT
Jabez, Sr.: b 1703 d 1-31-1784 m Lydia Gale CS CT
Jabez, Jr.: b 5-23-1728/29 d 12-19-1806 m Lydia Huntington Sol PS CT
Jabez: b 12-2-1737 d 1816 m Mary Huntington Pvt CT
Jabez: b 2-15-1736/37 d 1812 m Hannah Perkins Lt PS CT
James: b 4-9-1739 d 11-8-1815 m Anne Hulbert Pvt CT
James, 3rd: b 4-11-1758 d 7-31-1828 m Esther Camp Pvt CT ★
Jeremiah, Jr.: b 9-25-1742 d 12-29-1808 m Lydia Smith Sgt MA
John: b 7-2-1749 d 8-8-1840 m Irene Warner Sgt CT ★
John: b 12-25-1754 d 8-20-1850 m Ann Buel Pvt Tms VT ★
John: b 4-3-1758 d 7-8-1814 m (1)Rebecca Race (2)Hannah Hollenbeck Cpl MA
John: b 1-21-1743 d 1798 m Lucy Roberts 1Lt NJ
Johnathan: b 4-12-1727 d 9-22-1793 m (1)Sarah Saltonstall (2)Elizabeth Mary Mix Col CT
Joseph: b 1731 d 3-6-1807 m Prudence Drake Ens CT
Joseph: b c. 1709 d 3-29-1789 m (1)Sarah Shaler (2)Abigail Church PS CT
Joseph: b 8-16-1742 d 2-13-1842 m Mary Makepeace Cpl MA
Matthew: b 6-7-1744 d 6-14-1790 m Sarah Reed Cpl CT
Moses: b 3-3-1755 d 10-12-1825 m Rachel Stearns Pvt MA
Nathaniel: b 1763 d 1-2-1837 m Katrine Grout Pvt CT ★
Nathaniel: b 5-5-1748 d c 1800 m Amy Avery Pvt CT
Nathaniel: b 8-9-1745 d 10-29-1798 m Mary Thompson Sol CT
Paul: b 1-4-1744 d 5-2-1818 m (1)Mary Jaquith (2)Joanna (Rice) Walker Pvt NH
Peletiah: b 5-6-1722 d 4-6-1803 m Elizabeth Burrows Dr Pvt NY
Roswell: b 12-7-1765 d 1842 m Sarah Sheffield Pvt NY
Samuel: b 1727 d 11-11-1811 m Elizabeth Platt Sgt CT
Seymour: bpt 1-27-1741 d 4-24-1799 m (1)Elizabeth Hoyt (2)Hannah Raymond (3)Martha St. John Pvt CT
Stephen: b 8-16-1734 d 3-17-1810 m — Pvt PS CS MA
Thomas: b 2-4-1761 d 4-9-1850 m Elizabeth Ellis Pvt CT
Thomas: b c. 1755 d p. 1832 m — PS NC

Timothy: b 1735 d 9-18-1802 m Esther Platt PS CT
Wm.: b 6-23-1764 d 3-10-1843 m Mary Cuyer Pvt CT
Wm.: b 9-18-1734 d 4-30-1785 m Artie Wheeler Capt VT
Zachariah: b 4-1-1734 d 9-2-1820 m (1)Rebecca Davis (2)Lydia
    Tuck (3)Sybil Lakin (4)Elizabeth Tuttle Capt MA
Zoroaster: b 2- 23-1759 d 4-23-1835 m Elizabeth Mayo Pvt VT

FITCHETT,
John: b 1760 d *p.* 1800 m Molly Luke Pvt VA

FITCHJARRELL,
Jarrell: b 1725 d 1798 m Elizabeth — Pvt NC

FITE, (includes FIGHT)
Andrew: b — d *p.* 5-27-1804 m Susanna Essig Pvt PA
John: b 4-1-1758 d 2-18-1852 m Martha Haslet Pvt NJ ★
Leonard: b 2-1-1760 d 3-22-1842 m Margrette Crosse Pvt NJ
Peter: b 1740 d *p.* 1782 m Jennie Barker Pvt PA
Peter: b 1750 d *p.* 1800 m Barbara Hedinger Pvt PA

FITHIAN,
David: b 1728 d 9- -1805 m Esther Conklin Capt NY
George: b 3-27-1761 d 9-6-1831 m Sarah Mulford Pvt NJ
Joel: b 9-29-1748 d 11-9-1821 m (1)Rachael Holmes (2)Mrs Elizabeth
    (Beatty)Fithian Capt CS NJ
Jonathan: b 1740 d 1-7-1815 m Rhoda — Ens NJ
Samuel: b 10-12-1715 d 11-2-1777 m Phebe Seeley PS NJ
Wm.: b 11-22-1757 d 11-13-1808 m (1)Mary Tomlinson (2)Mary
    Clark Pvt NJ

FITTS, (includes FITZ)
Aaron: bpt 2- -1742 d *c.* 12-5-1805 m Mrs Abigail Newman Sgt MA
Abraham: b 10-24-1736 d 8-6-1808 m'Dorothy Hall Lt NH
Andrew: b 4-1-1744 d 1-12-1788 m Phebe Lakeman Pvt MA
Daniel: b 5-2-1725 d 9-7-1775 m Christianna Smith Pvt CT
Daniel: b 4-14-1753 d 2-13-1837 m Chloe White Pvt MA
Ephriam: b 5-10-1745 d 4-13-1800 m Rhoda Worthen Cpl NH
Israel: b 1760 d 11-1-1815 m Sarah Cook Pvt CT
John: b 1747 d *p.* 1802 m (1)Rebecca Stockwell (2)Rebecca Dresser
    Pvt MA
John: b 1730 d 8-28-1802 m (2)Betsy Ferguson Capt SC
Jonathan: bpt 4-24-1720 d 1792 m Mary Hutchinson PS MA
Moses: b 5-18-1755 d 5-18-1815 m Dorothy Belden Pvt CT
Nathan: b 12-13-1739 d 1-29-1781 m Abagail French Pvt NH
Richard: b 8-8-1756 d 12-9-1826 m Dorothea Kimball Pvt NH
Richard: b 1-20-1705 d 2-23-1791 m (1)Sarah Brown (2)Dorothy
    Evans PS NH
Robert, Jr.: b 3-27-1757 d 12-29-1831 m Phebe Patch Pvt MA
Robert Walker: b 1755 d *p.* 9- -1840 m Susannah Pass Pvt VA ★
Samuel: b 12-12-1743 d 4-7-1807 m Martha Sterns Pvt MA

FITZGERALD,
Daniel: b 1765 d 4-30-1822 m Nancy Clark Pvt NH
Edmond: b 5-15-1745 d 6-6-1848 m Mildred Payne 1Lt PS VA
Edward, Sr.: b *c.* 1718 d 1808 m Mehitable Uran Sol PS NH
Edward, Jr.: b 10-24-1751 d 11-21-1817 m Abanezar Corser Lt NH
Garrett: b *c.* 1755 d *p.* 5- -1798 m — Bullard Sol NC
George: b 1734-40 d *p.* 1835 m Betty — Pvt VA
Henry: b 3-2-1755 d *p.* 5-4-1796 m Lydia Wyer PS MA
John: b 7-6-1755 d 3-2-1837 m Sophia Ball Pvt MD
John: b 1752 d 1838 m Sophia Schenck Pvt MA
Wm.: b 1-24-1747 d 10-7-1834 m Ruth Leach Sgt Smn MA ★
Wm.: b 1729 d 1813 m Hannah Driscoll 2Lt NY
Wm.: b 6-7-1750 d 1818 m (1)Sarah Epes (2)Katherine (Crawley)
    Ward Jones Capt VA

FITZHUGH,
Anne Frisby: b.9-5-1727 d 3-26-1793 m (1)John Rousby (2)Wm.
    Fitzhugh PS MD
Henry: b 9-10-1723 d 2-17-1783 m Sarah Battaile PS VA
John: b 6-30-1727 d 5-11-1809 m Alice Thornton PS VA
Peregrine: b 5-10-1759 d 11-28-1811 m Elizabeth Crowley Chew
    Capt CL
Robert: b 8- -1762 d 9- -1818 m Mary Edgar Lt VA
Thomas: b 7-16-1725 d 1-12-1788 m (1)Elizabeth Thornton
    (2)Sarah Stuart PS VA
Wm.: b 1-16-1722 d 7-11-1798 m (1)Martha (Lee)Turberville
    (2)Mrs Ann (Frisby) Rousby PS MD
Wm. Frisby: b 10-6-1761 d 12-29-1839 m Anne Hughes Lt VA
Wm.: b 4-23-1754 d 1817 m (1)Elizabeth Dedman (2)Sarah Digges
    PS VA

FITZPATRICK,
Benjamin: b 12-25-1746 d 11-21-1821 m (1)Mary Perkins (2)Sarah
    Jones Pvt VA
Booth: b *c.* 1762 d *p.* 12-22-1801 m Elizabeth Brown Sol PS VA
James: b 6-20-1760 d 8-23-1841 m Mary Ewen Pvt VA ★
John: b 1- -1758 d 1828 m Mrs Sally Denny Davis Pvt CT
John: b *c.* 1740 d *p.* 12-23-1795 m Behetherland Brent PS CS VA
Rene: b *c.* 1760 d 1839 m Mollie Hardwick Sol GA
Wm.: b 1744 d 1823 m Susan Boswood Lt SC
Wm.: b *c.* 1746 d 1809 m Celia Anne Phillips, Pvt GA
Wm.: b 1742 d 1796 m Elizabeth Carroll Pvt MA

FITZ RANDOLPH,
Asher: b 1755 d 4-16-1817 m Catherine Brown Capt NJ
Edward: b 2-12-1749 d 1-3-1831 m Mary Webster PS NJ
Ephraim: b 1-19-1723/24 d 11-3-1793 m Rachel Stelle MM NJ
Ezekiel: b 12-1-1718 d 1813 m Mary Robinson Pvt NJ
Jacob: b 1754 d 12-23-1839 m Anna Webster PS NJ
James: b 10-1-1730 d *p.* 4-7-1778 m Deliverance Coward Pvt NJ
James: b 8-16-1735 d 6-1-1828 m (1)Hannah Skinner (2)Elizabeth
    Laing PS NJ
John: b 8-21-1752 d 5-6-1826 m Phoebe Stelle Tms NJ
Lewis: b 1756 d 10-7-1822 m Rachel Snowden Ens NJ
Robert: b 10-14-1741 d 7-16-1830 m Sarah Taylor Pvt NJ
Zedekiah: b 11-29-1748 d 4-6-1835 m Sarah Coryell Sol CS NJ ★

FITZSIMMONS,
John: b 3-15-1761 d 7-4-1851 m Mary Fredericks Pvt PA ★
Thomas: b 3- -1761 d 3-12-1840 m Polly — Pvt VA ★

FITZWATER,
Matthew: b 3-25-1745 d 1-24-1803 m Sarah Bewley Pvt PA
Wm.: b 1735-39 d 1807-17 m (1)Ann McCaslen (2)Catherine — PS
    VA

FIVEASH,
Peter: b 1762 d 7-15-1799 m Charlotte Parke Mstr NS

FIX, (includes FICKES)
Isaac: b 1746 d 3-13-1827 m Rachel — Pvt PA
Lawrence, Sr.: b — d 1778 m Catharine Stull PS PA
Lawrence, Jr.: b 10-10-1759 d 1822 m Magdalena Schreffler Pvt PA
Valentine, Sr.: b 1709 d *p.* 3-23-1782 m Elizabeth — Sol PA

FLACK,
James: b 5- -1761 d 12-24-1836 m Martha Harsha Pvt NY
James: b 6-19-1761 d 9-24-1840 m Nancy Ross Pvt NC
James: b 1- -1753 d 3-3-1741 m Anne Nelson Pvt PA ★
Jane McCuiston: b 3-11-1735 d *p.* 1-15-1802 m Thomas Flack PS
    NC
John: b — d 7-21-1810 m Polly Bardoom Pvt PA
John Mathias: b 4-8-1752 d 1-20-1834 m Mary Arnold Pvt PA ★
Wm.: b 8-6-1748 d 1823/24 m Susannah Collison Capt PA

FLADGER,
Charles: b *a.* 1760 d 1785 m Elizabeth Keen Pvt SC
Henry: b 1736 d 1775-83 m Elizabeth Keene Pvt SC

FLAGG,
Abijah: b 5-5-1755 d 11-22-1842 m (1)Thankful Seymour
    (2)Thankful Woodhouse Pvt CT
Benjamin: b 6-26-1751 d 12-22-1831 m Elizabeth Kent Sgt MA
Benjamin J. H.: b 8-23-1723 d 11-8-1818 m Abigail Chadwick LCol
    MA
Bezeleel: b 5-19-1732 d 8-19-1806 m (1)Mary Headley (2)Mary
    Bond Pvt MA
Dimon: b 7-16-1761 d 6-22-1797 m Sarah Carrington Pvt CT
Ebenezer: b 4-7-1756 d 2-17-1828 m Elizabeth Cutting Sgt MA★
Ebenezer: b 10-16-1704 d 11-14-1796 m (1)Lucretia Keyes (2)Mary
    — PS NH
Elijah: b 4-3-1743 d 1843/44 m Elizabeth Cummings Sgt MA ★
Elisha: b 5-12-1728 d 4-1-1804 m Molly Mann 1Lt MA
George: b 9-18-1741 d 2-11-1824 m Mary Henderson PS SC
Gershom: b 4-11-1758 d 1792 m Edith Hitchcock Matr MA
Henry Collins: b 1745 d — m Rachel More Allston Dr RI SC
Hiram: b 11-16-1762 d *p.* 1811 m (1)Sarah Dean (2)Martha Jones
    Pvt MA ★
James: b 5-3-1723 d 4-18-1807 m Anna Morse Pvt MA
John: b 3-21-1730 d 1-7-1809 m Patience Whittemore Pvt MA
John: b 10-6-1758 d 6-23-1820 m (2)Lucy Stebbins (3)Anna Cook
    Pvt MA
John: b 8-29-1746 d 5-24-1825 m (1)Hannah Tidd (2)Abigail
    Thompson Pvt MA
Jonas: b 5-10-1731 d 4-27-1819 m Martha Knight Pvt NH
Jonathan: b 11-15-1751 d 7-2-1842 m (1)Sarah Whitney
    (2)Patience Crane Pvt MA
Josiah: b 6-9-1722 d 1797 m (1)Elizabeth — (2)Hannah (Pierce)
    Wetherbee Sgt MA
Josiah: b 4-8-1748 d 4-25-1799 m Anna Webster Pvt NH
Josiah: b 2-22-1754 d 10-11-1835 m Susanna Freeman Pvt MA ★
Josiah: b 3-28-1737 d 1794 m Elizabeth Hawke LCol RI
Josiah: b *c.* 1761 d 5-9-1849 m Margaret Shively Sgt VA
Solomon: b 1758 d 9-9-1793 m Olive Hart Pvt CT
Solomon: b 12-26-1732 d 5-4-1806 m Lydia Ware Sgt MA
Timothy: b *c.* 3-10-1740 d *p.* 1790 m Elizabeth Peirce Pvt MA
Wm.: b 7-12-1739 d 10-7-1812 m Lydia Child Cpl MA

FLAHARTY,
Amassa: b 12-25-1755 d 7-4-1841 m Mary Ridgely Pvt PA MD ★
Stephen: b 10-28-1743 d 4-21-1799 m Sarah Morgan Sgt MD

FLAKE,
Wm.: b *c.* 1759 d *p.* 11-14-1807 m — PS NC

FLANAGAN, (includes FLENNIKEN)
David: b 1748 d 9-26-1826 m — Lt NC SC ★

FLANAGAN, contd.
Dennis: b 12-21-1731 d 2-26-1800 m Margaret O'Brian Pvt MD
Elias: b 10-22-1745 d 1830 m Mary Dunlap Pvt PA
James: b 8-20-1747 d 8-25-1823 m Jane — Sol PS PA
John: b 5-28-1761 d 12-18-1820 m Mary Hogan Pvt MD
John: b 1745 d 12-4-1810 m (1) — Ranken (2)Hannah McClelland Sol PS NC
Patrick: b 10-4-1739 d 1817 m Sarah Chew Pvt PA
Stephen: b 1762 d 10-15-1832 m (1)Phebe Vance (2)Elizabeth Swart Pvt Smn PA

FLANARY,
Daniel: b c. 1750 d 2- -1820 m Patsy Cofield Sol VA
Silas: b 1750-55 d 1795-1802 m Violet — Sol VA
Thomas: b c. 1730 d a. 1814 m — Sol VA

FLANDER,
Tenus: b 10-10-1759 d 3-19-1848 m Laney Fox Pvt NY

FLANDERS,
David: b 1-19-1758 d 1843 m Hannah Kimball Pvt NH
Elijah: b 3-4-1743 d p. 1790 m Deborah Martin Pvt MA
Enoch: b 10-23-1739 d 6-6-1810 m Anna Crocker Pvt MA
Enos: b 2-8-1745 d p. 1790 m Sarah Langley Pvt PS NH
Ezekiel: b 1759 d 1838 m Betty Rowel Sgt NH ★
Ezekiel: b 9-24-1732 d p. 1786 m Ann Flanders Cpl NH
Ezekiel: b 5-10-1743 d 6-1-1825 m Jerusha Goodwin Pvt NH
Hophni: b 11-7-1746 d a. 5-31-1808 m (1)Mehitable Fitts (2)Betsey Silver Pvt MA
Jacob: b 1-1-1762 d 4-7-1816 m Catherine Fox Pvt NY W ★
Jesse: b c. 1728 d p. 1790 m Ruth Webster PS NH
John: b 1-10-1724 d p. 3-1-1791 Eunice Jackman Sol PS NH
John: b 10-13-1752 d 4-1-1827 m Mrs Elizabeth Jackman Stevens Pvt NH
Jonathan: b c. 1748 d p. 2-1-1796 m Betty Boyd Sol NH
Josiah: b 4-3-1758 d 4-8-1836 m Deborah George Pvt NH
Josiah: b 7-28-1700 d 2-16-1781 m Mehitable Osgood PS NH
Levi: b 2-26-1754-58 d 5-6-1836 m Mary Sargent Pvt MA ★
Moses: b 6-29-1737 d 1803 m Elizabeth Batchelder PS NH
Onesiphorous: b 9-2-1749 d 1827 m Elizabeth Danforth PS NH
Richard: b 4-6-1725 d p. 1776 m Mary Fowler PS NH
Stephen: b 1757 d 11-8-1835 m Sarah Ring Sgt MA CT ★
Thomas: b 5-19-1749 d 4-25-1828 m Eunice Eastman Pvt NH
Thomas: b 12-10-1721 d p. 4-23-1796 m Margaret Lawrence PS NH

FLANSBURGH, (includes FLENSBURGH)
Anthony: b 1-4-1759 d c. 1839 m Susanna Van Alen Pvt NY
David: b 5-3-1761 d p. 1790 m Maria Smith Pvt NY
John: b bpt 6-26-1763 d p. 1807 m Catharine Becker Cpl NY
Mathew: b 3-12-1763 d 9-24-1858 m Maria Clute Pvt NY
Matthew: b bpt 5-23-1742 d p. 1783 m Christina Schneider Lt NY
Wm.: b 9-15-1743 d 3- -1821 m Christianna Bockus 2Lt NY

FLATHERS,
Edward: b 1755 d 5-7-1847 m Clara Legg Pvt VA ★

FLATT,
Andrew: b 11-27-1755 d 3- -1844 m Elizabeth Salmon 2Sgt PS PA ★

FLAUGHER,
Adam: b 1756 d 1781-90 m — Hidler Sgt PA

FLECK,
Adam: b 1739 d 4-27-1820 m (2)Maria Margaret (Gable) Week Pvt PA
George: b 1748 d 6-10-1836 m (1)Mollie Weeks (2)Catherine Ramey Pvt PA

FLEESON,
Plunket: b 1712 d 1791 m (1)Catherine — (2)Martha Linton Pvt PA

FLEET,
John: b 8-12-1724 d c. 1785 m Mary Edwards PS VA
Wm.: b 12-18-1757 d 4-11-1833 m Sarah (Browne) Tomlin Lt VA

FLEETWOOD,
John: b c. 1727 d 5-19-1794 m Mary Palmer Pvt DE

FLEMING, (includes FLEMMING)
Alexander: b 5-24-1734 d 9-12-1821 m Hannah — Capt PA
Andrew: b 1740-45 d 10-19-1785 m Rebecca Paterson PS NJ
Archibald: b a. 1748 d p. 1782 m Jane Speer 1Lt PA
Bailey: b c. 1750 d p. 1802 m Lucy — Capt SC
Benaiah: b 1-10-1762 d 10-12-1845 m Elizabeth Turner Sgt DE ★
Benjamin: b 1747 d 1820 m Phoebe Howell Pvt PA
Benoni: b 1764 d 9-4-1838 m Louisa Squires Pvt CT ★
Boaz: b 1-3-1758 d 3-20-1830 m (1)Elizabeth Hutchinson (2)Eliza Laidley Pvt DE
Charles: b 8-9-1745 d 1779 m Lucy Lewis Capt VA
James: b 1744 d 5-14-1833 m (1)Ann — (2)Mary Whitehair Lt MD
James: b 1762 d 4-13-1835 m (1)Elizabeth Mitchell Pvt NC ★

James: b 1758 d 2-12-1823 m (1)Frances Randolph (2)Margaret Clark 2Lt PA
James: b 1733 d 1778 m Jane Corwin Pvt PA
James: b 1759 d 1822 m Annie Morton Pvt PA
James: b c. 1760 d 2-1-1830 m Jane Glen Pvt PS PA
John: b 12-22-1761 d c. 1841 m Mary Hamilton Pvt DE
John, Sr.: b 1714 d 12-25-1796 m Ann White PS MD
John, Jr.: b 1744 d 7-7-1829 m Nancy Ann Hopkins Pvt PS MD
John: b 1740 d 10-12-1794 m Jane Horde QMSgt NC
John: b c. 1750 d 1800 m — Greene Pvt NC
John, Sr.: b 1731 d 9-2-1814 m Abigail Cowan Capt PS PA
John, Jr.: b 1760 d 12- -1832 m Mary Slaymaker PS PA
John: b 1734 d 5-21-1820 m Mary Hayes Lt PA
John: b — d c. 1780 m Sarah — Pvt PA
John: b 1752 d 12-15-1800 m Mary Jackson Pvt PA
John, Sr.: b 1725 d p. 5-1-1777 m Mary — PS PA
John, Sr.: b c. 1726 d 1788 m Sarah MacMoultrie Pvt SC
Peter: b 1759 d 9-24-1824 m Margaret Heslip Pvt PA
Robert: b 1754 d 1796 m Jane (Fleming) Ens PA
Robert: b 1706 d 4-3-1802 m Jane Jackson PS PA
Robert: b c. 1735 d 1777 m Ann Kyle PS PA
Robert, Sr.: b c. 1733 d 1790 m Pharabe PS SC
Robert, Jr.: b 1759 d 11-5-1840 m Martha Mackie Pvt SC
Samuel: b 10-30-1761 d 8-3-1851 m Sarah Becket Pvt PA
Stephen: b 2-21-1750 d 12- -1821 m (1)Ann G — (2)Ann Morris Capt NJ
Tarleton: b a. 1722 d 1778 m Mary Randolph PS VA
Thomas: b 10-24-1753 d 3-4-1829 m Mary Hayes Pvt NJ
Wm.: b 6-5-1717 d 5-5-1784 m (1)Jean Frame (2)Ann Hudson Pvt DE
Wm.: b 5-8-1761 d 10-14-1852 m Mary Sadler Pvt NC ★
Wm.: b 1736 d 2- -1802 m Mary Parker Sgt PA
Wm.: b 2-18-1729 d 8-1-1795 m Annie Christian CS Col VA
Wm.: b 2-1-1758 d 11- -1809 m Mildred Dalby Pvt VA
Wm.: b 7-6-1736 d 2-15-1824 m Elizabeth Champe PS VA

FLEMISTER,
Lewis: b 1746 d 10-1-1807/08 m Ellender Chessam Pvt CL VA W★

FLENNER,
John, Sr.: b c. 1720 d 12- -1785 m Chreisan — PS MD
John, Jr.: b c. 1742 d p. 1790 m (1)Catherine — (2)Elizabeth — PS MD
Rudolph: b c. 1740 d 1810 m (1)Magdalene Kershner (2)Elizabeth Baum PS MD

FLERL,
John: b a. 1734 d 1777 m (1)Hannah Elizabeth Brander (2)Dorothea Keiffer PS Capt GA

FLESHER, (includes FLEISHER)
Henry: b 1744 d 1802 m Elizabeth — Sgt VA
Henry: b 1734 d 1822 m Susan Catharine Pennegar 2Lt VA

FLETCHER,
Abraham: b 12-17-1755 d p. 1792 m Margaret Twinam Lt PA
Asa: b c. 1735 d 12-12-1822 m Thankful Staples Sgt MA
Asaph: b 6-28-1746 d 1-5-1839 m Sarah Green Dr MA
Benjamin: b 9-18-1746 d 8-25-1823 m Anna Spaulding Capt MA
Briant: b 1713 d 4-11-1791 m Anna Young Pvt MA
Charles: b 1-2-1749 d 4-23-1818 m Sarah — MM Sgt MA
Daniel: b 10-18-1718 d 12-15-1776 m Sarah Hartwell Maj MA
Daniel: b 3-13-1763 d 6-21-1844 m Susan Stone Pvt MA
Ebenezer: b 1-8-1734 d 6-20-1804 m Olive Lawrence Capt CT
Ebenezer: b 1725/26 d 3-17-1799 m Joanna Stearns Pvt MA
Ebenezer: b 2-5-1761 d 5-8-1831 m (1)Mary Cummings (2)Mrs Mary Foster Fif NH
Elijah: b 1735 d 9-21-1798 m Mercy Butterfield Pvt 2Lt MA
Ephraim: b 2-5-1740 d 1-1-1836 m (1)Sarah Davenport (2)Mrs Joanna Stratton Pvt MA
Ezekiel: b 4-3-1741 d 7-7-1806 m Bridget Parker 2Lt MA
Francis: b 10-22-1733 d 8-27-1797 m Sarah Parker Pvt Adj NH
Gershom: b 9-30-1737 d 11-25-1814 m Sarah Robinson Sgt MA
Henry: b 8-17-1751 d 4-17-1829 m Deborah Parker Pvt MA
Henry: b 10-15-1717 d 4-29-1799 m Leah Corbin CS VA
Isaac: b 10-26-1763 d 2- -1838 m Ruth Pierce Pvt MA ★
James: b 9-3-1743 d 9-27-1806 m Rebecca Prescott Sgt MA
James: b 2-28-1757 d 7-10-1834 m Catharine Russell Sgt MA ★
James: b 1- -1747 d 12-23-1834 m Margaret Wood Lt MA
James: b 4-29-1758 d 9-27-1845 m (1)Edy Bywater (2)Mary Smoot Pvt VA ★
Jeremiah: b 4-9-1756 d 10-14-1839 m Elizabeth Perham Cpl MA
Jesse: b 11-9-1762 d 2-14-1831 m (1)Lucy Keyes (2)Sarah Hill Pvt MA
Joel: b 6-23-1743 d 4-16-1825 m (1)Ruth Church (2)Mrs Mary Nichols Capt MA
John: b 5-12-1762 d 8-8-1847 m Silence — Pvt MA ★
John: b 11-14-1751 d 1-4-1810 m Elizabeth Petty Pvt MA
John, Sr.: b 1-14-1765 d 5-23-1860 m Susannah Mizell Pvt SC
John: b c. 1750-60 d a. 11-7-1796 m Grace — Sol SC
Jonathan: b 1-21-1757 d 1-16-1807 m Lucretia Emerson Capt MA
Jonathan: b 3-30-1741 d 3-28-1813 m Lucy Taylor Capt MA
Jonathan: b 8-29-1753 d 2-2-1854 m Abigail Goodnow Pvt NH

Joseph: b — d 7-17-1784 m Elizabeth Underwood Sol MA
Joshua: b 12-26-1724 d 11-13-1814 m Mary Allen Sgt PS MA
Joshua, Jr.: b 2-22-1760 d 4-14-1843 m Lucy Jones Pvt MA ★
Joshua: b c. 1732 d 1785 m Sallie — Sol NC
Joshua: b 3-20-1750 d 4-22-1811 m Agnes Hutchins Pvt VA
Josiah: b 10-19-1749 d 2-27-1825 m Margaret — Adj MA
Josiah: b 1757 d 1831 m Lucy Nource Pvt MA
Josiah: b 3-20-1759 d 2-20-1850 m Zilpah Proctor Pvt MA
Josiah: b 1758 d 8-2-1831 m (1)Grace Wheeler (2)Rachel
    Walton Pvt NH
Luke: b 1760 d 1- -1850 m Bethiah — Pvt NY
Nicholas: b a. 1745 d p. 1790 m (1)Margaret Cozine (2)Mrs Alleta
    Murphy CS NY
Oliver: b 1-25-1751 d 12-20-1831 m Mary Wilson Pvt MA
Paul: b 3-11-1740 d a. 1790 m (1)Anna Willard (2)Abigal Willard
    (3)Thankful Beman Pvt MA
Peletiah: b 5-3-1727 d 2-23-1807 m (1)Dorothy Hildreth (2)Betty
    (Hartwell) Keyes Capt MA
Peter: b 1-1-1745/46 d 4-29-1806 m Martha Farrar Cpl MA
Peter: b 10-31-1733 d 5-11-1812 m Martha Dix Pvt MA
Peter: b 9-5-1762 d 10-12-1843 m Sarah Piper Pvt MA
Peter, Sr.: b 1-22-1736 d 4-11-1811 m Ruth Adams Sol NH
Phineas: b 5-29-1753 d 3-1-1825 m Mary Campbell Pvt MA
Richard: b 4-13-1736 d 6-23-1812 m Lois — MM CT
Richard: b 1738 d 1835 m Sarah Gould PS TN
Richard: b 10-26-1762 d 1834 m Nancy Fletcher Pvt VA ★
Robert: b 7-14-1744 d 2-25-1838 m Sarah Foster Sol NH
Robert: b c. 1738 d p. 8-16-1797 m Christian — Pvt VA
Sampson: b 8-24-1758 d 9-2-1828 m Dorothy Fletcher Pvt MA
Samuel: b c. 1720 d p. 1790 m Mary Carr Pvt MA
Samuel: b 10-13-1745 d 2-5-1822 m Olive Wright Pvt MA
Samuel: b 8-12-1747 d 3-23-1795 m Sybil Caldwell Pvt MA
Samuel: b 9-30-1744 d 9-16-1814 m Mehitable Hazeltine BGen VT
Silas: b 7-20-1762 d 5-25-1837 m Mrs Abis (Franklin)Phelps Cpl VT
Simeon, Jr.: b 1758/59 d 1842 m Mary Colby Pvt NH
Stephen: b 1740 d 1815 m Sarah Shepherd Pvt MA
Thomas: b 9-11-1738 d 12-22-1802 m Rachel Cummines Sgt MA
Thomas: b 5-20-1766 d 9-11-1834 m Mary V. Hadley Thornton Sol
    NC
Thomas: b c. 1753/54 d 7- -1799 m Ann (West) Sorrency Lt PA
Timothy: b 9-20-1750 d 3-17-1823 m Hannah Fosdick Sgt MA
Timothy: b 9-30-1707 d 5-8-1780 m Mary Prescott PS MA
Willard: b 8-21-1749 d 11-30-1825 m Abigal Hadley Cpl MA
Wm.: b a. 1748 d p. 1801 m Lydia — Capt MA
Wm.: b 1742 d 12-8-1806 m (1)Sarah Fisk (2)Sarah (Parrot) Kemp
    PS MA
Wm.: b c. 1750 d 1794 m Sarah — Sgt NJ
Wm.: b 10- -1729 d 1836 m (1)Elizabeth — (2)Elizabeth McIntosh
    (3)Louisa Hendricks Sol SC

FLEWELLEN, (includes FLEWELLYN)
Abner: b 1760 d 8-15-1815 m Ann Lane Pvt NC
Alexander: b 5-12-1762 d 10-10-1821 m Katie Peoples Pvt NC
Wm.: b 1725/26 d 1786 m Betsey Holloway PS NC

FLICK,
Gerlach Paul: b 3-7-1728 d 1-20-1826 m Anna Catherine Fabian
    Capt PS PA
John Casper: b 6-22-1758 d 1840 m Betsy Foulk Pvt PA
Wm.: b c. 1720 d 1790 m — PS MD

FLICKINGER,
John: b 1758 d 3- -1833 m Anna Henshie Pvt PA
John, Jr.: b 12-10-1763 d 4-23-1821 m Elizabeth Ober Pvt PA
Joseph, Sr.: c 1740 d c. 1812 m Ehster — Pvt PA
Peter: b 1730 d 1807 m Mary Dehr Pvt PA

FLICKWIR,
David: b 4- -1744 d 10-9-1793 m Anna Sophia Van Som Pvt PA

FLINCHBAUGH,
Adam: b 1740 d 1801 m Christina Stabley Pvt PA

FLINSCHBACK,
Frederick: b 2-24-1764 d 12-8-1837 m Christina Fister Pvt PA

FLINT,
Aaron: b 1-6-1759 d 2- -1849 m Mary Kimball Pvt CT ★
Adam: b 10-10-1732 d 1831 m Susanna Hand Ens NY
Alexander: bpt 11-6-1737 d 1810 m "Knelia" — Pvt NY
Amos: b 4-17-1718 d a. 11-4-1797 m (1)Mary Graves (2)Mrs
    Elizabeth Trevitt PS NH
Amos: b 4-1-1754 d 3-9-1818 m Elizabeth Ball Pvt MA
Archelaus: b 1-22-1736 d 2-1-1797 m Chloe Elmer PS CT
Austin: b 1-4-1760 d 8-29-1850 m Elizabeth Henshaw Sgt MA
Benjamin: b 3-23-1746 d 5-17-1837 m Olive Richardson Sgt MA
Cornelius: bpt 10-14-1741 d 1- -1817 m (1)Anna Bauman (2)Maria
    Clement Pvt NY
Davis: b 3-10-1749 d 6-11-1836 m (1)Esther Cooper (2)Lucy
    Holmes Lt CT W ★
Ebenezer: b 6-17-1742 d 4-29-1829 m (1)Assenath Holt (2)Mary
    Damon Taylor Pvt MA
Edward: b 3-28-1733 d 11-13-1818 m Mrs Mary How Dr MA

Edward: b 8-14-1749 d 3-18-1812 m Hepzibah Flethcher Pvt MA
Elijah: b 11-15-1747 d 1825 m Sarah Eames Pvt MA
Ephraim: b 5-13-1745 d 9-1-1824 m Catharine Fox Pvt MA
George: b 11-16-1728 d 8-31-1808 m Hannah Phelps Sgt MA
Henry: b 4-19-1752 d 7-18-1830 m Beulah Wheeler Pvt MA ★
Hezekiah: b 4-6-1758 d 1-2-1811 m (1)Esther Coose (2)Mrs Anna
    Annis Pvt MA
Jabez: b 5-2-1756 d 3-28-1844 m Elizabeth Paine Pvt CT ★
James: b 10-5-1751 d 10-4-1843 m Jerusha Lillie Sgt CT
James: b 7-30-1722 d c. 1783 m Jemima Gennings PS CT
James Lazel: b c. 1760 d 10-16-1812 m Jerusha Paddock Warren
    Sgt CT W ★
Jesse: b 1-13-1746 d 11-25-1825 m Mary Hiscock Pvt MA
John: b — d 6-17-1809 m Mary Phelps Pvt CT W ★
John: b 9-8-1749 d 9-2-1810 m Sarah Tilden Pvt CT
John: b 8-9-1752 d 4-6-1824 m Rhoda Keith Pvtr CT
John: b 7-6-1756 d 8-13-1841 m Betty Johnson Pvt MD
John: b 1720 d 2-15-1802 m (1)Joanna Farnum (2)Tamar Kimball
    (or Hunt) Capt MA
John: b 5-16-1745 d 7-31-1830 m Molly Worcester Lt MA
John: b 5-5-1736 d 1-12-1795 m Susanna Bowman Pvt NY
Jonathan: b 11-17-1754 d 12-3-1846 m Mary Amidon Sgt CT ★
Jonathan: b 8-11-1730 d p. 6-24-1749 m (1)Lydia Proctor (2)Sarah
    Smith Cpl MA
Joseph: b 7-22-1745 d 4-13-1807 m Molly M. Harriman Pvt MA
Joseph: b 6-23-1737 d 5-8-1815 m (1)Hannah Herrick (2)Mary
    Hartwell Lt MA
Joseph, Jr.: b 4-21-1759 d 7-19-1787 m Elizabeth Whitridge Pvt MA
Joshua: b 1756 d 4-21-1827 m Sarah Stevens Pvt CT ★
Levi: b 3-4-1756 d 1-5-1845 m Susanna Wheeler Sgt MA ★
Luke: b 12-20-1752 d p. 1837 m Mary Slate Pvt CT ★
Miles: b 1739 d 1831 m Susannah Pilsbury 1Lt MA
Nathan: b 9-6-1734 d 7-6-1816 m (1)Mercy Holton (2)Mrs Sarah
    Goodnow Pvt CT
Nathaniel: b 9-5-1720 d 1- -1795 m (1)Sarah Bidlock (2)Mary Hovey
    MM CT
Nathaniel: b 5-29-1750 d 9-8-1828 m Abigail Allen Sgt MA
Nehemiah: b 4-15-1742 d 1-6-1824 m Sarah Whiting Pvt MA
Robert: b 3-10-1759 d 2- -1837 m Margaret Horning Sgt NY ★
Robert: b 3-12-1742 d 1802 m (2)Deborah Buys Sol NY
Royal: b 1-12-1754 d 1790 m Lora Elderkin CS CT
Samuel: b 4-9-1733 d 10-7-1777 m Ede Upton Capt MA
Samuel: b 10-25-1746 d 7-9-1827 m Lucy Martin Sgt CT
Thomas: b 1731 d p. 1789 m Sarah — PS MD
Thomas, Sr.: b 4-19-1722 d 5-6-1802 m Eunice How Cpl MA
Thomas, Jr.: b 11-2-1748 d 2-19-1827 m Anne Lilley Sgt Matr MA
Thomas: b 10-8-1733 d 1800 m (1)Lydia Pope (2)Martha (Knowlton)
    Kinsman Dr MA
Tilly: b 3-1-1759 d 2-23-1842 m Ruth Fosdick Sgt MA ★
Wm.: b 7-7-1737 d 6-13-1825 m Martha Kimball Pvt MA
Wm.: b 1-12-1758 d 2-6-1843 m Mehitable Peabody Pvt MA ★
Wm.: b 4-14-1714 d 12-7-1790 m Susannah (Flint) CS MA

FLIPPEN,
Robert: b 1749 d 7-22-1830 m (1)Mary Rice (2)Elizabeth De
    Jarnett (3)Sarah R. Bradshaw Pvt VA ★
Robert: b c. 1755 d a. 5- -1821 m (1) — Rice (2)Mary De Jornette
    (3)Lucy Frances Marshall Sol VA
Thomas: b 1745 d p. 1820 m Roda McAdoo PS VA

FLITNER,
Zacharius: b a. 1723 d 1804 m Lucy Colburn Dr MA

FLOCK,
John: b 12- -1734 d 12-12-1818 m Jane Hammell Pvt NJ
John: b 1748 d 12- -1779 m Amy Osborn Sgt NY

FLOOD,
Amos: b 1758 d 8-17-1834 m (1)Hannah Kimball (2)Polly (Whillier)
    Wallace Cpl NH ★
Daniel: b — d p. 1790 m Rachel Annis Capt NH
James, Sr.: b c. 1730 d p. 2-26-1777 m Abigail Thomas Pvt PS MA
John: b 1758 d 8-16-1826 m Mary Fuqua Sol VA
Thomas: b 1732 d 1807 m (1)Elizabeth Gale (2)Judith Strother Pvt
    VA
Thomas: b 1762 d 1815 m Mary Elizabeth Strother Pvt VA

FLORENCE, (includes FLEURY)
Charles: bpt 4-18-1762 d 5-24-1833 m Sarah Humphries Slr MA
Thomas: b c. 1752 d 11-27-1834 m (2)Frances — Pvt NC
Wm.: b 1-7-1736 d 10-23-1822 m (1)Mary Nash (2)Sarah
    Hutchinson Pvt VA W★

FLORY, (includes FLORA)
Abraham: b 1735 d 1827 m Catherine — Pvt PA
Cristopher: b 1-17-1765 d 4-21-1843 m Rachel — Pvt PA
John: b 10-12-1761 d 3-19-1827 m Elizabeth Illick Pvt PA
Joseph, Sr.: b c. 1720 d 9- -1785 m Catharine — PS PA

FLOUNDERS,
Edward: b 1-11-1761 d 7-19-1819 m Judith — Pvt PA

FLOURNOY,
Gibson: b c. 1735 d 1811-21 m Mary Farmer PS VA
Jacob: b 10- -1760 d 4-17-1846 m Edith Farmer Pvt VA ★
James: b 2-23-1763 d 3-18-1858 m Peggy Cundiff Pvt VA
Matthew: b 6-21-1732 d p. 1784 m Elizabeth (Pryor) Smith Pvt VA
Robert: b 5-13-1763 d 7-5-1825 m Mary Willis Cobb Capt GA
Samuel: b 10-4-1724 d 12-21-1780 m Elizabeth Harris Sgt VA
Thomas: b 11-28-1738 d a. 2-16-1801 m Anne Martin Col PS VA

FLOWER, (includes FLOWERS)
Abraham: b 1755 d p.1833 m Obedience Flower Pvt VA
Bildad: b c. 1750 d 1779 m Dorcas — Pvt MA
Christopher: b 2-4-1756 d p. 1790 m Mary Mathlana Pvt PA
George: b 4-26-1760 d 1-3-1827 m Roxaline Crowe Pvt CT
George: b c. 1753 d 1819 m Hannah — Pvt PA
Henry, Sr.: b c. 1729 d p. 1798 m Patsy Savage PS SC
Henry, Jr.: b c. 1761 d 1800 m Rachel Stewart Sol SC
Ignatius: b c. 1740 d p. 10-25-1793 m — Gray PS NC
Isaac: b 8-16-1755 d 1813 m (1)Freelove Hopkins (2)Mrs Barshebe Burr Foote Pvt CT
Ithuriel: b 6-18-1758 d 12-20-1828 m Mehitabel Broughton Sgt CT
James: b a. 1753 d 4-8-1806 m (1)Rebecca Gauslin (2)Rachel Van Blunk Pvt PA
John: b 1718 d 1-19-1803 m Susanna Hooker Pvt MA
John: b c. 1738 d 1786 m Patsy Parks Sgt VA
Joseph: b 3-15-1730 d 9-29-1793 m Hannah Pierce Pvt CT
Lamrock, Sr.: bpt 7-27-1719 d 1-8-1815 m Mehitable Goodwin Pvt MA
Lamrock, Jr.: bpt 3-22-1761 d p. 1797 m Lucy Perkins Pvt MA
Nathaniel: b 7-31-1721 d c. 1800 m Huldah Bradford Steele Capt CT
Ozias: b 12-22-1731 d 1801 m (2)Abigail Leonard Pvt MA
Richard, Jr.: b 8- -1759 d 7-24-1843 m Henrietta Graham PS Pvt PA
Samuel: b 1-17-1742 d 10-28-1815 m Sarah McIntire Capt MA
Thomas: b 4-16-1740 d 10-12-1794 m — Mil NC
Thomas, Sr.: b 1736 d 1784 m Sarah — PS VA
Timothy: b 10-12-1743 d 10- -1832 m (1)Anna Smith (2)Hannah Spencer (3)Martha Jones Cpl MA
Valentine: b 7-19-1765 d 1820-22 m — Flippen Sol VA
Ziphon: b 11-30-1765 d 4-16-1855 m Mary Patrick Pvt CT ★

FLOWEREE,
Daniel: b c. 1736 d 1814 m Susannah French Capt VA

FLOYD,
Abraham: b 5-10-1755 d 12- -1844 m Eve Julen Pvt SC
Benjamin: b 2-22-1738 d 4-22-1812 m Lydia Bond Pvt NH
Benjamin: b 3-3-1746 d 7-17-1817 m Rebecca Greenleaf Pvt MA
Charles: b 3-4-1747 d 9-9-1820 m Mary Fenden Capt SC
Charles: b 1752 d 1797 m Martha Davis PS VA
Francis: b 1756 d 10-22-1804 m Isabella Johnson PS SC
Gallant: b 1754 d 1858 m Nancy Abercrombie Pvt GA
Henry, Sr.: b 1719 d 1- -1816 m Nancy Ann Helm Lt VA
Henry F.: b 1-17-1750 d 12-16-1829 m (1)Eva Troutman (2)Elizabeth Johnson Pvt VA ★
Henry Helm: b 9-21-1761 d 9-6-1850 m Frances Crosby Pvt VA ★
Hugh: b 2-2-1732/33 d 8-6-1800 m Rachael — Pvt MA
Isham: b c. 1748 d 1790 m Lydia Hardin Sgt VA
James: b 10-30-1729 d 10-31-1822 m Hannah Bill Pvt MA
John: b 10-28-1758 d 1-15-1836 m Nancy Andrews Lt NC VA SC ★
John: b 1751 d 4-13-1783 m (1)Mary Burford (2)Jane Buchanan PS CS Col VA
John Helm: b 5-31-1765 d 7-11-1852 m (1)Elizabeth Jeffries (2)Henrietta Hargrave Pvt VA
Joseph: b 9-26-1753 d 9-19-1847 m (1)Abigail Rogers (2)Martha Goodridge Sol MA
Josiah: b c. 1759 d 11-29-1828 m Mary Tillman Pvt VA W ★
Matthew: b 3-7-1763 d 8-29-1844 m (1)Lucy Wilkins (2)Sarah Robbins Pvt VA ★
Samuel, Jr.: b 6-12-1733 d 1-10-1805 m Susannah Sargent Sgt MA
Uriah: b c. 1760 d p. 4-14-1790 m Elizabeth — Pvt NC
Wm.: b 12-17-1734 d 8-4-1821 m (1)Hannah Jones (2)Joanna Strong SDI NY
Wm.: b 1743 d a. 8- -1834 m Elizabeth — Sol NC
Zachariah: b 1755 d p. 1790 m Ann Jones PS VA

FLUCK,
Casper: b 12-25-1759 d 8-20-1848 m Catherine Hoover Pvt PA
John: b 5-8-1750 d 8-23-1840 m Dorothy Ott Pvt PA
John: b 8-30-1750 d 12-9-1841 m Magdalene Leydi Pvt PA

FLUE, (includes FLEU)
Wm.: b c. 1754 d 2-11-1838 m Christina Gorgas Ens PA

FLUEGEL,
John: b 11-27-1762 d 9-3-1845 m Margaret Hahn FifMaj MD

FLUKER,
George: b 4-19-1759 d p. 9-21-1834 m Elizabeth Matthews Sgt NC ★
Owen: b 1756 d 1815 m Nancy Baldwin Pvt GA

FLYE,
Wm.: b 11-21-1750 d p. 1832 m Sarah Rust Pvt MA

FLYNN, (includes FLINN)
Daniel: b 9-30-1742 d 11-17-1824 m Mary Howard Pvt VA ★
Jacob: b 9-1-1757 d 10-28-1827 m Mary Pearson Pvt MA
James: b 3-9-1743 d 9-7-1802 m Mary Kinsella Pvt CS MA
John: b 1750 d 4-5-1803 m Mary Payson Trm Pvt CT
John: b 11-8-1725 d p. 7-10-1783 m Elizabeth Brown Pvt MA
John: b c. 1757 d p. 1790 m Mary Bradshaw Pvt NY
Michael: b 3-9-1754 d 5-14-1827 m Fanny Child OrdlSgt CS CT VT W ★
Wm.: b 10-30-1760 d 12-10-1841 m (1)Sara Adams (2)Nancy West Pvt VA

FOCKEL,
Gottlieb: b 7-12-1724 d 12-17-1778 m Maria Leibert PS NC

FOCKLER, (includes FACKLER)
George: b 1732 d 11-29-1809 m Sussanna Pvt PA
Gotleep: b — d p. 10-15-1816 m Maria Barbara Holzapple Pvt PA
Michael: b 1740 d p. 1790 m Helfina — Capt PS MD

FOERING,
Christian Frederick: b 1736 d 3-29-1779 m Margaret Miller PS NJ

FOGELSANGER,
David: b 1763 d 12-13-1834 m Gertraut Minich Pvt PA

FOGELSONG
Christian: b c. 1749 d p. 3-9-1791 m Barbara — PS MD

FOGG,
Abner: b 12-18-1704 d 8-27-1788 m Bethia Robie Sgt NH
Daniel: bpt 4-6-1759 d 4-23-1830 m Susanna Thayer SgtMaj NH W ★
James: b 2-25-1739 d 1815 m Apphia Collins Pvt NH
Jeremiah, Sr.: b 5-24-1712 d 12-1-1789 m Elizabeth Parsons PS NH
Jeremiah, Jr.: b 10-22-1749 d 5-26-1808 m Lydia Hill PS NH
Jeremiah: b 4-9-1760 d 1-19-1847 m Hannah Eastman Pvt NH ★
Joseph: b 4-22-1753 d 4-17-1822 m Mary Sherburne QM NH
Joseph: b c. 1718-21 d 1786 m Mary — PS VA
Josiah: b 4-15-1728 d 10-6-1790 m (1)Mary — (3) Abigail Eastman LCol VA
Moses: b 7-2-1762 d 1-14-1828 m Hannah Libby Cpl Matr MA W ★
Phineas: b 7-5-1738 d 4-27-1820 m Lydia — Pvt NH
Reuben: b 6-1-1722 d 10-25-1797 m Margaret Elder Col MA
Samuel: b 8-31-1756 d 3-24-1843 m Ruth Lane Drm Pvt NH ★
Samuel: b 2-13-1700 d 12-23-1786 m Mary Denborn PS NH
Seth: b 3-15-1752 d 3- -1832 m (2)Elizabeth Marshall Pvt NH
Seth: b p. 3-29-1730 d 11-20-1806 m (1)Elinor Philbrick (2)Mrs Smith CS PS NH
Stephen: b 8-12-1760 d 12-26-1842 m (1)Sarah Marsh (2)Mary Felch Pvt NH

FOGHT, (includes FOUGHT)
George: b 1749 d 2-17-1829 m Hannah Lesher Capt PA
George: b 3- -1755 d 1834 m Susanna Beaver Pvt Tms PA ★
John George: b 1-14-1758 d 10-26-1841 m Susanna Loy PS PA
John Morris: b 8-31-1749 d 4-2-1836 m (1)Sarah (Vandel) Rynders (2)Rachel (Gilmore) Inglis Capt NY ★
Michael: b 1755 d 2- -1832 m Elizabeth Shivley Pvt PA

FOGLE, (includes FOGEL)
Andreas: b 10-2-1734 d 1-29-1802 m Christina Line Gradwell Pvt PA
Henry: b c. 1764 d 1819 m Susanna Margaret Dick Pvt MD
John: b c. 1720 d 1782 m Mrs Margaret (Conrad)Vogel PS PA
John: b 3-9-1753 d 4-25-1816 m Rosina Schaed PS PA

FÖHL, (includes FEHL)
Andreas: b 4-1-1730 d 3-12-1795 m Barbara Meier CS PS PA
George: b 1-23-1760 d 12-18-1815 m Elizabeth Stautebergerin Pvt PA

FOIL (or FOYL)
John: b c. 1750 d p. 1-15-1815 m Mary — 1Lt GA

FOLEY,
James: b 1737 d 1-8-1808 m Mary Langfitt Capt VA
Richard: b 9-28-1745 d a. 1- -1795 m Margaret — PS VA
Thomas: b c. 1745 d 5- -1828 m Mary Barbee PS VA

FOLGER,
Barzillai, Sr.: b 11-4-1710 d 1790 m Phoebe Coleman PS MA
Benjamin: b 10-8-1731 d 3-21-1819 m Judith Barnard PS MA
Frederick: b 2-17-1724/25 d 7-27-1790 m Mary Trott CS MA
Henry: b 8-5-1762 d 12-24-1811 m Elizabeth Baker Smn MA
Jonathan: b 4-10-1696 d 5-6-1777 m (1)Margaret Gardner PS MA
Latham: b 12-17-1749 d 11-9-1833 m Matilda Worth PS MA
Reuben: b 8-10-1722 d 8-28-1808 m (1)Dinah Hussey (2)Mary Pinkham Smn MA
Seth: b 8-8-1726 d 11-17-1807 m Phebe Coleman Smn MA
Walter: b 1-29-1735 d 9-30-1826 m Elizabeth Starbuck PS MA

FOLLENSBY, (includes FOLANSBEE, FOLMSBEY)
Jeroen: b c. 1750 d 1816 m Elizabeth Witbeck Pvt NY
John: b 2-19-1736 d 10-19-1808 m Susanna Moers Pvt MA
Wm.: b 8-22-1760 d 9-7-1834 m Eleanor Cochran Pvt NH

FOLLETT,
Eliphalet: b 1-16-1741 d 7-3-1778 m Elizabeth Dewey Pvt CT
Frederick: b 3-10-1761 d 5- -1804 m Giffe Babcock Pvt CT
John, Jr.: b 3-5-1752 d 2-20-1829 m (1)Christina Belding (2)Sibyl
    Willard (3)Hannah (Oak) Alexander Pvt NH
Jonathan: b 6-10-1739 d 12-7-1819 m Mary Brown Pvt MA
Martin Dewey: b 7-24-1765 d 2-4-1831 m Persis Fasset Pvt VT
Thomas: bpt 4-16-1758 d 8-31-1823 m Mary Blaney Pvt Smn MA
    W ★

FOLLEY,
Richard: b 1-31-1740 d 9-3-1808 m Margaret Hitchcock Lt MA

FOLLIN,
John: b 9-5-1761 d 5-19-1841 m (1)Catherine Sanford (2)Mary
    Barker Slr VA

FOLSOM, (includes FULSOM)
Abraham: b 4-29-1744 d 1811 m Hannah — PS CS NH
Benjamin: b c. 1730 d c. 1815 m Mercy Taylor Capt NH
Benjamin: b c. 1751 d 2-21-1790 m Mary Baker Pvt NH
Daniel, Jr.: b 8-27-1739 d 3-2-1817 m Mary Moody PS NH
David: b 8- -1732 d a. 6-13-1791 m Sarah Gilman PS NH
David: b 5-20-1750 d 1788 m Dorothy Johnson CS NH
James: b 7-22-1756 d 8-17-1835 m Mary Folsom Pvt NH ★
Jeremiah: b 7-23-1719 d 1802 m Mary Hersey Lt NH
John: b 7-7-1723 d 4-17-1787 m (1)Sarah Veasy (2)Martha Wiggin
    Capt NH
John, Sr.: b c. 1713 d p. 1790 m (1)Elizabeth Hilton (2)Abigail Smith
    PS NH
John, Jr.: b c. 1740 d p. 1785 m — Cpl PS NH
John: b c. 1718 d 1790 m Abiah Carr Pvt NH
John: b 1759 d 1816 m Annie Weymouth Pvt NH
John: b 5-17-1766 d 8-4-1839 m Elizabeth File Pvt NY
Jonathan: b 1724 d 1800 m (1) — Gilman (2)Deborah Hall PS NH
Jonathan: b 1750 d 1813 m Patience — Cpl VT
Josiah: b 7-24-1725 d 7-27-1820 m (1)Elizabeth Bradley
    (2)Abigail Farnom Pvt MA
Josiah: b 11-5-1735 d 2-12-1816 m Elizabeth Gilman Pvt NH
Josiah: b 9-25-1725 d 1820 m Martha (Eastman) Gould PS NH
Levi: b 7-12-1753 d 6-21-1844 m Joanna Weeks Pvt PS NH
Nathaniel: b 1726 d 5-26-1790 m (1)Dorothy Smith (2)Mary
    (Sprague) Fisher MGen NH
Nathaniel: b 1748 d 1830 m Susanna — Pvt NH
Peter: b 1718 d 8-5-1815 m Hannah Morrison PS NH
Peter: b 12-13-1747 d c. 1799/1800 m Sally Dam PS NH
Samuel: b 2-22-1732 d 5-22-1790 m (1)Anna Thing (2)Elizabeth
    Emery PS NH
Samuel: b 5-9-1742 d p. 2-26-1796 m Mrs Persis Montague Clark
    PS NH
Theophilus: bpt 8-27-1756 d 1818 m Sarah Fogg Grd NH
Thomas: b 3-21-1754 d 1840 m Sally Watson Pvt NH
Wm.: b c. 1745 d c. 1785 m Sarah Armstrong Lt GA

FOLTS, (includes FOLTZ, FOLS)
Conrad: b 12-10-1747 d 6-7-1793 m Anna Deichert Pvt PS NY
Conrad: bpt 8-17-1760 d 6-21-1828 m Catharine Lintz Pvt NY ★
Conrad: b. 1735 d 1776-82 m — Sol PA
Frederick: b c. 1757 d 12- -1822 m Mary Eve — Pvt PA
Jacob: b 11-21-1711 d 1-30-1808 m Catrina Petrie Lt NY
Melchert: b 5-5-1746 d 5-2-1829 m (2)Mary Getman Sgt NY
Peter: b 9-15-1750 d 11-16-1827 m Barbara Rasbach Pvt NY

FOLWELL,
Joseph: b 9-14-1748 d 4-3-1824 m Anna Boileau Capt PA
Thomas: b 10-17-1737 d 9-13-1813 m Elizabeth Watts Pvt PA

FONDA,
Abraham: b 1-18-1744 d 1834 m Margaret Grimes Capt NY
Abraham Dow: b 3-25-1733 d 10-10-1799 m Hendricke Lansing
    Maj NY W ★
Adam: b 12-26-1736 d 11-20-1808 m Eleanor Breeze LCol NY
Cornelius: bpt 11-28-1754 d p. 1798 m Elizabeth Miller Pvt NY
Douw: b 9-1-1700 d 5-22-1780 m (1)Marytje Vrooman (2)Deborah
    (Veeder) Wemple PS NY
Isaac, Sr.: b 6-30-1723 d p. 1789 m Cornelia De Foreest Ens NY
Isaac, Jr.: b 5-6-1753 d 9-15-1826 m Antje Van Santvoord Pvt NY
Isaac H.: b 1-13-1751 d p. 1785 m Susanna Vanden Bergh Pvt NY
Jacob: b 2-11-1722 d 1813 m Maria Van Patten Pvt NY
Jacob: b 3-16-1761 d 9-19-1832 m Hannah Becker Pvt NY ★
Jacob D.: bpt 3-29-1741 d a. 9-13-1796 m Dirkje Visscher Pvt NY
Jacob Glenn: b 8-29-1761 d 12-8-1859 m Aletta Willett Pvt NY
Jellis: b 3-24-1727 d 6-23-1791 m Jannette Vrooman Maj NY
Johannes Hendrick: b 2-19-1760 d p. 7-30-1798 m Aaltje Leverse
    Cpl NY
John: b 3-8-1740 d 2-14-1814 m Angelica Hansen Pvt NY ★
John Abraham: b c. 1752 d p. 1810 m Cathalyntje Du Bois Capt PS
    NY

John Douw: bpt 1-10-1731 d 10-10-1804 m (1)Elizabeth
    Ouderkerk (2)Maria Veeder Pvt NY
John Peter: b 10-12-1735 d p. 1790 m Dirckie Winne Lt NY

FONES,
Wm.: b 9-18-1764 d 4-22-1839 m Dorcas Sherman Pvt RI ★

FONTAINE, (includes FOUNTAIN)
Aaron: b 11-30-1753 d 4- -1823 m (1)Barbara Overton Terrill
    (2)Mrs Elizabeth Thurston Ens VA
Andrew: b 5-22-1740 d p. 12-28-1802 m (1)Susannah Horney Capt
    MD
James Maury: b a. 3-19-1749 d 3-11-1795 m (1)Alice Burwell
    (2)Betty Carter Churchill PS VA
Jemima Johnson: b c. 1755 d p. 1803 m (1)Francis Fontaine
    (2)Benjamin Brewton PS SC
John: b 1756 d 1792 m Martha Henry Capt VA
Wm.: b 1-22-1754 d 10-6-1810 m Ann Morris LCol VA

FONVILLE,
Francis: b 1738/39 d 1798/99 m Sarah — Pvt NC
Wm. Brice: b 1736 d 1828 m Ann — Pvt NC

FOOKS, (includes FOWKES)
Daniel: b 5-29-1737 d 1-25-1793 m Violetta Tyndall Pvt MD
Jesse: b c. 1730 d 1807 m Mary — Sol MD

FOOSE, (includes FOOS)
Conrad: b 4-18-1746 d 3-28-1820 m (1)Sarah Rees (2)Catherine —
    (3)Catherina (Shoemaker) Christ (4)Catherine Gottshall PS CS
    PA
John: b c. 1736 d 1803 m (1)Ilse Margarthe Elizabeth Patz
    (2)Hannah Griffith (3)Jane McCandless Pvt PA
Valentine: b 1744 d 10-30-1815 m Rosina Heinrich Pvt PA

FOOTE, (includes FOOT)
Aaron: b 7-5-1738 d — m Mary Bronson 2Lt CT
Abel: b 1754-61 d 9-9-1826 m (1)Anna Daw (2)Jane — Pvt CT
Abraham: b 6-16-1725 d 12-6-1823 m (1)Abigail Rogers (2)Mary
    Ponsonby Capt CT
Asa: b 5-4-1726 d 5-11-1799 m Jerusha Carter PS CT
Asahel: b 4-22-1763 d 3-8-1841 m Anna Abbot Pvt MA
Caleb: b 7-6-1750 d 5-19-1787 m Mary Dedman Sol Slr MA
Charles, Sr.: b 11-10-1723 d 8-25-1795 m Jerusha Chamberlain Pvt
    CT
Charles, Jr.: b 6-22-1753 d 3-11-1833 m Sarah Day Pvt CT
Daniel: b 1717 d 1801 m Margaret Parsons CS CT
Daniel: b 8-16-1755 d 2-6-1820 m Isabella Henry Dr NS
Daniel: b 4-27-1724 d 1801 m Martha Stillman Pvt VT
Daniel: b 4-3-1760 d 8-24-1848 m (1)Sarah Johnson (2)Ellen Scott
    Pvt VT
David: b 1737 d 6-14-1806 m Esther Averill Lt CT
David: b 11-11-1730 d 7-8-1779 m Hannah Bronson Pvt CT
David: b 7-24-1753 d 9-27-1821 m Mary Scovel Pvt CT
David: b 9-4-1760 d 1-31-1851 m Betsey Hamlin Pvt MA
Ebenezer: b 4-12-1756 d 12-28-1829 m Jerusha Purdy Sgt Cmsry
    MA
Ebenezer: b 5-21-1740 d 6- -1778 m Rebecca Barker Pvt CT
Eli: b 10-30-1747 d 9-8-1792 m Roxana Ward Pvt CT
Elihu: b 8-15-1757 d 11-27-1849 m Lucy Williams Pvt Smn CT ★
Elijah: b 3-14-1755 d 1828 m Mary Latimer Pvt CT
Elijah: b 1740 d 10-15-1813 m Unis Peck Sol CT
Ephraim: b 8-11-1725 d 3-24-1791 m Lucy Baker Pvt CS CT
Fenner: b 10-5-1754 d 4-27-1847 m Sarah Wilcox Pvt MA NH VT
Freeman: b 9-22-1759 d 9-30-1842 m (1)Silence Clark
    (2)Bathsheba (Morton) Morton Pvt VT MA ★
George:.b 10-30-1749 d 5-12-1830 m Weltha Ann Woodward Pvt
    CT
George: b 10-11-1749 d 6-27-1820 m Charity Stillson Sol CT
Heli: b 5-3-1755 d 10-30-1827 m (1)Silence (Frisbie) Harrison
    (2)Ruth Polley Sgt Mar CT W★
Ichabod: b 2-24-1746 d 2-26-1835 m Jemima Smith PS CT
Isaac: b 1-4-1746 d 2-27-1842 m Mary Kellogg Sol CS CT
Isaac: b 12-4-1747 d 3-14-1818 m (1)Lydia Tyler (2)Phoebe Benton
    CS PS CT
Isaac: b 1762 d 7-8-1855 m Hannah Blanchard Pvt NH ★
Isaac: b 3-4-1750 d 6-28-1823 m Anne — Gnr Cpl NY ★
Jacob: b 3-20-1732 d 4-25-1818 m Lucy Bunnell Lt CT
James: b 6-20-1747 d 2-28-1831 m Adah Stillson PS CT
Jared: b 8-28-1728 d 1-28-1806 m (1)Hannah Buell (2)Hebzibah
    Phelps (3)Mrs Joanna Jennings PS CT
Jared: b 7-17-1735 d 10-11-1820 m (1)Submit Bishop (2)Sarah
    Stillman (3)Jemima Holcomb (4)Hannah Kimberly Pvt CT
Jehiel: b 4-23-1760 d 1-12-1843 m Lucretia Archer Pvt MA★
Jesse: b 12-25-1756 d 2-17-1822 m Mary Skinner Pvt CT
Jesse: b 1-22-1758 d 1842 (1)Rachel Benedict (2)Elizabeth Taylor
    Pvt CT ★
John: b 1729 d 9-15-1812 m (1)Rosannah Humphrey Sgt CT
John: b 8-21-1742 d 7-5-1809 m (1)Esther Mattoon (2)Mary Peck
    Ens CT
John: b 1757 d 12-13-1833 m Elizabeth Babcock Pvt NY
John: b 1758 d 1817 m Catharine Miller Pvt NY

FOOTE, contd.

John: b 7-14-1754 d 6-16-1826 m Ruth Searl Pvt VT
Jonathan: b 1-28-1737 d 1-11-1801 m Lydia Baldwin CS CT
Jonathan, Sr.: b 3-23-1715 d 11-11-1803 m Sarah Fenner CS MA
Jonathan, Jr.: b 3-20-1752 d 5-26-1837 m Deliverence Gibbs Pvt MA
Joseph: b 2-17-1727 d 9-16-1779 m Azubah Griswold Pvt CT
Joseph Sr.: b 1730 d 1795 m (1)Roselle Chapin (2)Thankful Parcy (3)Mrs Sawyer Pvt MA
Joseph Jr.: b 10-24-1760 d 2-20-1861 m (1)Abigail Dudley (2)Dorcas (Nicholson) Reynolds Drm Pvt MA
Joseph: b 10-26-1758 d 5-27-1789 m Beersheba Burr Pvt NY
Martin: b 10-22-1761 d 1854 m (1)Hannah Dean (2)Mrs Anna Branch Pvt VT
Moses: b 8-4-1734 d 2-9-1819 m (1)Thankful Bronson (2)Amy Richards Capt CT
Nathan: b 1-25-1738 d 7-25-1808 m Merrian Selkrigg Dr VT
Nathaniel: b 2-7-1742 d 1-22-1829 m (1)Jerusha Cadwell (2)Patience Skinner (3)Abigail (Foote) Pvt CT
Stephen: b 1755 d 9-11-1798 m Esther Clark Pvt CT
Timothy: b 10-9-1752 d 8-6-1832 m (1)Abigail Barnes (2)Lucy Throop Pvt CT
Wm.: b 1754 d 3-24-1824 m Ruth Smith Pvt MA
Wm.: b c. 1760 d p. 3-22-1833 m Sarah Alexander PS VA

FORBES, (includes FOBES, FORBIS)

Absolom: b 1751 d 9-   -1778 m Martha Hall Pvt MA
Alexander: b 1763 d 2-22-1838 m Judith Ammonett Pvt VA ★
Alexander Sr.: b 3-3-1760 d 2-2-1846 m Catherine Clifton Pvt VA
Alpheus: b 6-30-1756 d 4-12-1839 m (2)Lucy Backus Pvt MA
Arthur: b 1746 d 1781 m Elizabeth Wiley Col NC
Charles: b c. 1753 d p. 9-2-1819 m Susan Lee Pvt MA
Daniel: b 2-12-1742 d 1814 m Hannah Standish Pvt MA
Daniel Sr.: b 10-23-1710 d 1-5-1780 m (1)Abigail Severns (2)Mary Parker PS MA
Daniel, Jr.: b 9-   -1736 d 3-9-1808 m (1)Persis Crosby (2)Sarah Henshaw (3)Achsah Gilkey PS MA
David: b 1752 d 1-8-1789 m Margaret Sterling Dr VA
Edward: b 3-14-1737/8 d 12-13-1825 m Orpha Leach Pvt MA ★
Edward: b 10-25-1755 d 5-2-1835 m Eunice Amsden Pvt MA
Elisha: b 3-20-1745 d 1-9-1808 m Hannah Flagg PS MA
Ezra: b 1-21-1751 d 8-15-1823 m Mary Shaw Pvt MA
James: b 1731 d 3-25-1780 m Jane Smith PS MD
James: b c. 1762 d 1797 m Elenor Brown Pvt MA
James: b 1755 d 10-24-1839 m Sallie Hubbard Pvt VA
Jason: b 3-17-1745 d 7-12-1809 m Leah Washburn Pvt MA
Jehiel: b 1733 d 4-18-1793 m Mabel Morris PS CT
John: b 1-1-1760 d 10-20-1835 m Ruth Merrill Pvt CT ★
John: b 3-12-1758 d p. 1797 m Rosinda Alden Sgt MA
John: b 1760 d 2-10-1813 m Elizabeth Hayward Pvt MA
John: b 11-4-1761 d 1-22-1842 m (1)Nabby Bailey (2)Mrs Electa Harris Pvt MA ★
John: b c. 1743 d 7-14-1839 m (2)Abiah Ward OrdlSgt NY ★
John: b 1750 d 1788 m Anna House Pvt NY
John: b a. 1749 d 1806 m Mary — PS NC
John: b 3-16-1745 d 9-8-1823 m Jane Forbes Pvt PA
John: b 1739 d 10-24-1829 m Rebecca Barron Lt SC
Joseph: b 3-9-1818 d 1-27-1827 m Susanna Ames Pvt MA
Josiah Sr.: b 9-6-1716 d 9-14-1794 m Freelove Edson PS MA
Josiah Jr.: b 12-21-1740 d 11-4-1776 m Sarah Pryor Pvt MA
Jotham: b 1758 d 8-4-1851 m Lydia Batchelder Fif MA
Lemuel: b 1754 d 1-31-1835 m Anna Bills Pvt MA ★
Levi: b 1739 d 11-29-1795 m Sarah Tuttle Pvt CT W ★
Moses: b 9-28-1733 d 4-17-1822 m (1)Mary Cowles (2)Mrs Mercy Wright Capt CT
Nathan: b 7-24-1758 d 11-23-1833 m Rebecca Parsons Pvt CT ★
Robert: b c. 1735 d c. 1813 m Mary — PS NC
Simon: b 4-5-1756 d 1-30-1840 m Elizabeth Jones Lt CT ★
Steven: b 2-7-1731 d 1-25-1793 m (1)Mary Morise (2)Rebecca — Pvt MA
Timothy: b 6-14-1743 d 9-14-1800 m Mary Roberts PS Sol CT
Wm.: b 1747 d p. 1787 m Mary Miles Pvt MA
Wm.: b 3-27-1763 d 4-   -1846 m Lucy Griffin Pvt MA
Wm. Gilbert: b 12-15-1751 d 1-6-1740 m Catherine Maria Van Gelder Pvt NY

FORCE, (includes VORCE)

David Z.: b 1743 d — m — Pvt NY
Henry: b 2-8-1765 d 2-3-1829 m Lois Quimby Pvt NJ ★
James: b 1758 d — m Mary Steuben Pvt NJ
Joseph: b 1758 d 6-16-1836 m (1)Prudence Phillips (2)Mary — (3)Sarah — Pvt NJ ★
Samuel: b 1757 d 4-4-1826 m Sarah Bird Pvt NJ
Thomas Palmer: b c. 1733 d a. 5-11-1813 m Agnes Elston Pvt NJ
Thomas S.: b 12-21-1758 d 3-30-1827 m Hannah Smith Cpl NJ
Timothy: b 1746 d 8-   -1830 m (1)Elizabeth Simpson (2)Mercy Frazier Sgt NY
Wm.: b 7-29-1752 d 4-3-1826 m Sarah Fergurson MM NJ

FORCEE,

Thomas: b 12-26-1766 d 2-22-1865 m Elizabeth Arnold Drm NJ

FORD, (includes FOARD, FFORD)

Abel: b 1754 d 11-23-1835 m Rachel Littlefield Pvt MA RI ★
Abel: b 8-7-1745 d 5-24-1835 m Abigail Skinner Sgt NY ★
Abijah: b 12-23-1756 d 2-19-1813 m Rebecca Salisbury Pvt CT
Abijah: b 10-22-1744 d 2-22-1809 m Anna Donnison Pvt RI
Abner: b 11-8-1724 d 1796 m Bethiah Sampson Pvt MA
Abraham: b 10-   -1748 d 6-2-1823 m Elizabeth — Sol DE
Absalom: b 12-8-1761 d 2-11-1845 m Zerviah Ford Pvt MA
Alexander: b 1754 d 11-2-1838 m Elizabeth — OrdlSgt MD ★
Amos: b 1761 d 9-7-1835 m Eunice Treat Pvt CT
Andrew: b 11-8-1752 d 10-29-1837 m Sarah Beals Pvt MA ★
Benjamin: b 11-16-1755 d 1782/83 m Mary Anderson Pvt MD
Benjamin: b 4-25-1750 d 8-12-1818 m Sarah Brett Pvt MA
Benjamin: b 5-18-1748 d 10-20-1824 m Mary Lee Ens NY
Chandler: b c. 1755 d 1799 m Elizabeth — Sgt MD
Culverine: b a. 1729 d 1797 m (2)Elizabeth — PS VA
Daniel: b 11-16-1754 d 9-17-1838 m Phebe Camp Pvt CT
Daniel, Sr.: b 4-21-1751 d p. 1778 m Lydia Goodwin Pvt VT
David: b 1754 d 7-14-1836 m (1)Esther — (2)Eleanor — Pvt DE NJ
David: b 4-19-1761 d 11-6-1835 m Anastacia Cook Pvt NJ
Elijah: b 12-8-1759 d 8-1-1832 m Amy Cook Pvt MA
Elisha:b 11-24-1757 d 9-29-1833 m Sara (O'Neal ?) Pvt SC W ★
Gardner: b — d 1805 m Magdalene — Sol PS SC
George: b c. 1761/2 d 2-7-1838 m Charity Calvert Pvt VA
George: b — d — m Martha Hawkins Pvt VA
Hannah Baldwin: b 11-17-1701 d 7-30-1777 m Jacob Fford, Sr. PS NJ
Henry: b c. 1741 d 1782 m Rachel Gillin PS MD
Hezekiah: b 12-29-1759 d 12-19-1848 m Huldah Cobb Pvt MA
Isaac: b 1722 d 1800 m (1)Katherine Mack (2)Dorothy Ingraham Pvt CT
Isaac: b 6-2-1732 d 1-   -1800 m Martha Benham Pvt CT
Isaac: b 7-19-1738 d p. 1790 m Lucy Josselyn Sol MA
Isaac: b 6-25-1752 d 5-29-1813 m (1)Martha Earl (2)Abigail Merry Pvt MA
Jacob, Sr.: b 1711 d 6-9-1794 m Sarah Pool Pvt MA
Jacob, Jr.: b 1738 d 2-21-1818 m Rachel Azur Pvt MA
Jacob, Sr.: b 4-13-1704 d 1-19-1777 m Hannah Baldwin PS NJ
Jacob, Jr.: b 2-19-1738 d 1-11-177/79 m Theodosia Johnes Col NJ
Jacob, Jr.: b 4-22-1744 d 7-24-1837 m (1)Abigail Curtis (2)Ruth Fitch LCol NY
Jacob: b 1759 d 1845 m Lucretia Maxey Pvt Spy PS VA
James: b 5-3-1758 d 4-15-1838 m Lydia Bradford Pvt MA
James: b 3-8-1724 d 3-13-1783 m Deborah Bedlam Pvt MA
James: b 3-20-1731 d 9-24-1799 m Sarah Swan Capt NH ★
James: b IO-1-1756 d c. 1819 m Hannah Davenport Fif NY
James: b 8-9-1715 d 1804 m (1)Ann — (2)Ann Townsend Capt SC
James: b 5-11-1757 d 6-21-1845 m Lucy Shipp Sgt VA ★
James, Sr.: b 1708 d 1810 m Ann Bondurant PS VA
Jesse: b 1737 d 3-5-1812 m Eunice Peck Capt CT
John: b 2-5-1721 d 9-19-1781 m Lucy Mack Pvt CT
John: b 10-29-1739 d — m Sarah Wood Pvt CT
John: b 10-19-1763 d 8-6-1842 m Esther Cook Pvt CT
John: b 1758 d 1803/04 m Mary — Sol GA
John: b 6-   -1752 d 10-   -1824 m (1)Millicent Hyland (2)Catherine Hedrick (3)Mary Wilson Capt MD
John: b a. 1744 d 1793 m (1)Ann Joy (2)Elizabeth Joy PS MD
John: b 1729 d 1-22-1813 m Mary Baker Capt MA
John: b 8-3-1740 d 11-6-1822 m Sarah Barker Capt MA
John: b 1744 d 3-18-1792 m Lydia Auger Lt MA
John: b 9-15-1752 d 8-6-1845 m Hannah Munson Cpl MA
John, Sr.: b c. 1728 d p. 1803 m (1)Rachel Spencer (2)Mrs Catherine Garace (3)Ellenor — Maj SC
John: b c. 1727 d p. 4-25-1798 m Catherine Robinet Pvt PS NC
John, Jr.: b 1750 d — m Rachel — Sol SC
John: b 6-17-1755 d 5-   -1825 m (1) — Myrtle (2)Rosannah Newman Pvt VA
John: b 11-13-1762 d 8-5-1844 m Elizabeth England Pvt VA ★
Jonathan: b 7-3-1736 d 8-11-1831 m Ruth Hamlin Lt NY
Joseph: b c. 1750 d 1812 m — Spinks Capt MD
Joseph: b 1757 d p. 2-   -1834 m — Lt NC ★
Joshua: b 1756 d 1844 m Nancy Cox Pvt CS GA ★
Joshua: b 1-7-1761 d 11-29-1837 m (1)Cele Bisbee (2)Sarah man Pvt MA★
Luke: b 8-18-1742 d p. 1783 m Hannah Reed Pvt MA
Mahlon: b 7-26-1756 d 6-14-1820 m Sophia B. Spencer Lt NJ W ★
Matthew: b 1-17-1761 d 1810 m Mary McKee Pvt CT
Mordecai, Sr.: b 12-19-1727 d 12-   -1795 m Ruth Barney PS MD
Moses: b 11-13-1741 d 6-11-1822 m Eunice Potter Lt CT
Nathaniel: b 1759 d p. 1781 m Abigail Ford Cpl MA
Nathaniel: b 12-25-1734 d p. 1779 m Kiziah Francisco Lt NY
Noah: b 3-19-1762 d 11-15-1817 m Abigail Whitman Pvt MA
Peter: b a. 1760 d p. 1780 m Rebecca Shipe Capt PA
Peter: b c. 1740 d p. 1786 m Agnes — Sol PA
Philip: b c. 1750 d 1806 m Mary Eleanor Thompson PS MD
Richard: b 8-28-1712 d p. 1-4-1784 m Mary Boulden PS MD
Richard: b 1754 d 9-20-1839 m Sarah Kimball Pvt RI
Richard: b c. 1757 d 1809/10 m Mary Gills Sol VA
Richard Boulden: b — d p. 7-9-1806 m Ann — PS MD
Robert: b c. 1750 d 1830 m Elizabeth Patterson Pvt MD
Samuel: b 8-21-1740 d 10-   -1807 m Martha Davis Ens CT
Sanburn: b 4-22-1757 d 10-20-1846 m Ada Shaw Pvt CS CT ★

Seth: b 3-7-1757 d — m Mary Andross Pvt PS NH
Standish: b 4-8-1759 d 4-28-1806 m Sarah Britton Pvt PA
Stephen: b 5-11-1749 d 11-19-1843 m Elizabeth — Pvt CT ★
Stephen: b 10-13-1738 d p. 1791 m Lydia Borden Pvt NJ
Theodosia Johnes: b 9-13-1741 d 8-21-1824 m Jacob Ford, Jr. PS NJ
Thomas: b 2-20-1744 d p. 1782 m Elizabeth Fortt Pvt MD
Thomas: b 3- -1758 d p. 6-22-1831 m Hopeful Buckalue Pvt NJ ★
Warner: b c. 1758 d p. 1835 m Cytha Mellen Pvt VA
Wm.: b 1745 d 10-2-1823-5 m (1)Catherine — (2)Elizabeth Beebe Ens CT
Wm.: b 1742 d 1800 m (2)Elizabeth Townson Pvt PS MD
Wm.: b 1-6-1745 d 1809 m Sarah Hayden Pvt MA
Zadock: b 12-28-1745 d 4-23-1835 m Eunice Bridges Pvt CT

FORDHAM,
Benjamin: b 11-27-1743 d p. 1791 m — Lt NC
Daniel: b 12-6-1740 d — m Phebe Jessup Ens PS NY
Ephraim: b 3-12-1737 d 5- -1832 m Hannah Howell Mstr PS NY

FORDYCE,
Benjamin: b 1759 d 3-1-1819 m Rebecca Horton Pvt NJ
Samuel: b 1734 d 1824 m (1)Elizabeth Hudgins Pvt NJ

FORE,
Peter: b 1719 d 6-1-1780 m Marie — Pvt VA

FOREACRES,
James: b 1754 d 7-2-1849 m (2)Rosanna Saveley Sol VA

FOREHAND,
John: b 3-29-1755 d 2-27-1838 m Rebecca Campbell Pvt VA ★

FOREPAUGH,
George: b 10-19-1743 d p. 9-29-1817 m Margaret — Capt PA

FORGEY, (includes FURJOE, FOGIE)
Hugh: b 1761 d 10-6-1830 m Sarah E. — Pvt PA
James: b 1752 d 5-23-1828 m Rebecca Clements Hawes Pvt NC

FORMAN , (includes FOREMAN)
Caleb: b 12-23-1751 d 2-18-1790 m Elizabeth Bonner Lt NC
Catherine (Parker): b c. 1735 d p. 8-12-1783 m Wm. Forman PS VA
Charles: b c. 1750 d 1- -1806 m Sarah Early Cnt Pvt PA
David: b 10-1-1733 d 3-30-1812 m (1)Anna Denise (2)Elenor Van Brunt CS NJ
David: b c. 1755 d 1795 m Catharine Vogelsong PS VA
Denise: bpt 6-5-1759 d 1-27-1819 m Elizabeth Laird Pvt NJ
Gilbert: b 8-20-1753 d 5-9-1821 m Elizabeth Fowler Sgt NY
John: b 9-16-1739 d 4- -1792 m Rebecca Chamberlin Pvt NH
John: b 1731 d 10-6-1811 m (1)Eleanor Denise (2)Sarah (Vandon) Antonides Capt NJ
John: b 9-14-1716 d 10- -1798/99 m Rebecca Taylor PS NJ
John: b 1725 d 9-20-1811 m Jerusha Sands 2Lt PS NY
John: b 9-25-1762 d 1819 m Elizabeth — Pvt PA
John: b 1725 d 1809 m Mary Hogan PS VA
Jonathan: b 10-16-1755 d 5-25-1809 m (   )Margaret Wyckoff (   )Mary Ledyard LCol NJ
Jonathan: b 5-17-1755 d a. 5-25-1818 m (1)Margaret Harbert (2)Martha Preston Pvt NJ
Joseph: b 7-17-1752 d 1-15-1824 m Hannah Ward Lt NY
Miles: b 9-25-1762 d 2-25-1839 m Anna Platt Pvt NY
Peter: b 1-1-1755 d 1-14-1843 m Esther Tilden Pvt PA ★
Peter: b 3-28-1718 d 12-8-1785 m Eleanor Williamson PS NJ
Robert: b 7-7-1736 d 4-2-1812 m Mary Naylor PM VA
Samuel: b 11-13-1714 d 1-18-1792 m Helena Denise Col NJ
Samuel: b 7-30-1763 d 4-29-1816 m Mary R. Conover Pvt NJ
Samuel Peter: b 12-11-1757 d 1850 m — Lt NJ
Thomas: b 12-18-1740 d 1825 m Jane Throckmorton PS NJ
Tunis: b 7-5-1761/2 d 6-13-1837 m Eleanor Remsen Sgt NJ ★
Wm.: b 8-26-1751 d 1-31-1823 m Franzewsky Hendrickson Sgt NJ
Wm.: b 3-17-1739 d 7-4-1816 m — Dr PS NY
Wm.: b 1726 d 9-27-1777 m (1)Hannah Du Bois (2)Catherine Parker Capt VA
Wm.: b c. 1738 d 5-16-1796 m (2)Lydia — PS VA

FORMBY,
Nathan: b 8-22-1760 d 8-18-1833 m Tabitha Echols Pvt VA ★

FORNEY,
Abraham, Sr.: b c. 1720 d 12- -1784 m Elizabeth Spurgeon Pvt PA
Abraham, Jr.: b 8-15-1758 d 1-18-1821 m Anna Maria Weidman Pvt PA
Abram: b 10-15-1758 d 7-22-1849 m Rachel Gabriel Capt NC ★
Adam: b 2-15-1757 d p. 9-24-1833 m Maria Christina Hoffman PS PA
Henry: b 10-22-1747 d 8-21-1831 m Mary Magdalena — 2Lt PA
Jacob: b 1721 d 1806 m Mariah Bergner PS NC
John: b 11-30-1760 d 10-6-1823 m Elizabeth Lehman Pvt PA
Maria Bergner: b 1724 d 1808 m Jacob Forney PS NC
Peter: b 4-25-1756 d 2-1-1834 m Nancy Abernathy Capt NC
Peter: b 1735 d 1- -1809 m Catherine Forney Pvt PA

Peter: b 1739 d c. 1829 m — Pvt PA

FORREST,
Andrew: b 1754 d p. 1814 m Jane Graydon Dr Capt PA
David: b 6-24-1754 d 7-2-1835 m Abigail Morse Pvt MA ★
David: b 1755 d 1796 m Abigail Forest Pvt MA
Ebenezer: b 11-14-1753 d 9-7-1837 m Hannah Sumner Pvt MA ★
James: b 1-24-1751 d p. 4-11-1838 m — Pvt NC ★
Robert: b 1759 d 12-3-1843 m Elizabeth Robertson Pvt NH ★
Samuel: b 1755 d 10-6-1838 m Charlotte Ware Pvt MA
Thomas: b 1742 d 3-20-1825 m Ann Whitpaine LCol PA
Uriah: b 1756 d 7-6-1805 m Rebecca Plater LCol MD W ★
Wm.: b c. 1753 d 3-5-1840 m (1)Mary Allison (2)Sally Simonds Pvt PS NH ★
Wm.: b 4-5-1756 d 1-7-1817 m Dorothy Worthen Pvt NH W ★
Wm.: b 10-31-1761 d p. 8-13-1833 m — Pvt NC ★
Zachariah: b 11-6-1742 d 1-19-1817 m (1)Nancy Edwards (2)Rebecca Goldsmith Capt PS MD

FORRESTER,
Arthur: b 4-19-1757 d p. 1784 m Jemima Keeler Pvt CT
Robert: b 8-24-1816 d — m Bridget — PS VA
Simon: b 5-10-1748 d 1817 m Rachel Hawthorne Capt Pvtr MA

FORRISTALL,
Joseph: b 3-23-1758 d 4-12-1848 m Hannah Millen Pvt MA W ★

FORSHAY, (includes FOSHER, FOSHAY)
Daniel: b 5-12-1763 d 8-4-1749 m Mavillis Echols Pvt VA
John: b 1-5-1733 d 8-20-1810 m Magdalena Banta Pvt NY
John: b 4-23-1744 d 9-3-1809 m Anna Van Wart Pvt NY

FORSIE, (includes FORSEE)
Charles: b 3-4-1754 d 6-14-1836 m (2)Nancy (Purdie) Robertson (3)Rbecca H. Branch Pvt VA ★
Wm.: b 6-24-1758 d 10-1-1839 m (1)Mary Ann Smith (2)Judy Bledsoe Sgt VA ★

FORSMAN, (includes FORESMAN)
Alexander: b 12-25-1753 d 12-25-1831 m Sarah Keith Capt PA ★
Hugh: b 12-25-1748 d 12-17-1811 m Judith Slocum Lt PA
Robert, Sr.: b 1725 d 6-2-1803 m Jane All Pvt PA
Samuel: b 9-21-1755 d c. 1830 m (1)Jerusha Everett (2)Mary Anderson Pvt PA

FORSYTH, (includes FORSYTHE, FORSAITH)
Andrew: b 7-8-1751 d 11-26-1810 m Agnes Longhead Pvt PA
James, Sr.: b 1720 d 10-11-1804 m Margaret (Means) Vail Pvt VA
James, Jr.: b 1-1-1756 d 4-6-1850 m Susanna Kuykendall Pvt PA
James: b c. 1747 d a. 10-31-1777 m Elizabeth Jones Pvt VA
John: b c. 1760 d c. 1816 m Ann Speer Sgt PS PA
John: b 2-12-1751 d 8-11-1838 m Susanah McConnell Pvt PA ★
Jonathan: b c. 1740 d c. 1795 m Esther Johnson Pvt NY
Joshua: b 1750 d 1782 m Phebe Shreve PS NJ
Josiah: b 1747 d 3-18-1833 m Catherine Richardson Pvt NH
Latham: b 1761 d 10-3-1835 m (1)Eleanor Fox (2)Abigail Lee Pvt CT ★
Matthew: b 1740 d 9-6-1791 m Esther Graham PS NH
Robert: b 6-27-1746 d 5-8-1810 m (1)Mary Tilford (2)Margaret Graham Ens NH
Wm.: b 1759 d 10-29-1830 m (1)Martha Giles (2)Catherine—Pvt MA
Wm.: b 1742 d 1809 m Jane Wilson PS NH

FORT, (includes FEURT)
Abraham: b 8-17-1750 d 8-9-1822 m Jane Monfort Capt NY
Albert: b 4-1-1758 d 1841 m Margaret Norwood Pvt NC
Arthur, Jr.: b 1-15-1750 d 11-16-1833 m Susannah (Tomlinson) Whitehead Lt PS GA
Benjamin: b 11-15-1753 d 9- -1838 m — Pvt NJ
Elias: b 7-2-1730 d 1-14-1819 m Sarah Sugg Col PS NC
Francis: b 1741 d p. 10-27-1827 m (1)Mary — Pvt NJ
Frederick: b c. 1744 d a. 8- -1819 m Mary Knight PS VA
Isaac Danielse: bpt 6-28-1742 d c. 1785 m Sarah Viele Pvt NY
John: b 9-15-1745 d 3-21-1811 m Margaret Heisler Mil NJ
John: b 8-13-1756 d 3-23-1841 m Elizabeth Almy Pvt NY
John: b c. 1740 d 11- -1825 m Franky Broadwell PS NC
Joseph: b 3-13-1751 d 8-1-1806 m Mary Davison Pvt NJ
Lewis: bpt 5-6-1759 d 1792 m Cathaline — Pvt NY
Micaiah, Sr.: b c. 1735 d a. 9-17-1792 m — Sol NC
Simon: b 4-24-1734 d 9-26-1789 m Annetie Van Vranken QM NY
Susannah Tomlinson: b 6-9-1755 d 12-13-1820 m (1)— Whitehead (2)Arthur Fort PS GA
Thomas: b 8-10-1757 d 5-9-1837 m Catriena Sol NJ ★
Turner: b 3- -1763 d 3-29-1850 m Elizabeth Hapgood Pvt NC

FORTIER,
Michel, Jr.: b 7-15-1750 d 9-19-1819 m Marie Rose Durel PS LA

FORTNER,
Benjamin: b 6-26-1768 d 7-10-1838 m (1)Mary — (2)Margaret — Pvt NJ★
Peter: b 1761 d p. 1823 m Nancy Groves Fif PA

FORTNEY, (includes FORTNEUX)
Henry, Sr.: b 1724 d p. 1781 m Maria — Pvt PA
Jacob: b 12-29-1748 d 6-7-1819 m Margaret Fordney Pvt PA

FORTSON,
Thomas, Jr.: b 5-1-1742 d 2-15-1824 m Rachel Wynn Lt VA

FORTUNE,
Zachariah: b c. 1761 d p. 10-9-1833 m Elizabeth Burnett Pvt VA

FORWARD,
Joseph, Sr.: b 12-16-1733 d 1810 m Ruth Morton Capt CT
Joseph, Jr.: b 2-11-1759 d 12-11-1840 m Mary Owen Pvt CT

FOSCUE,
Frederick: b 1766 d 1834 m Dove Simmons Slr Pvt NC ★
Simon: b 1734 d 1814 m (1)Sarah Brockett (2)Nancy Mitchell (3) Mrs Elizabeth Stevenson PS NC

FOSDICK,
James: b 11-20-1716 d — m Elizabeth Darling PS MA
Nicoll: b 4-18-1750 d 1-1-1821 m Abigail Eldredge Slr Sol CT
Samuel: b 3-11-1710 d 1792 m (1)Deborah Shadbolt (2)Mary (Moore) Wright Pvt NY
Thomas, Sr.: b 4-30-1725 d 4- -1776 m Anna Havens Dr CT
Thomas: b 12-28-1756 d 8-30-1801 m Mehitable Hawkins BgdMaj MA
Thomas Updike: b 3-5-1754 d 8-14-1811 m Sarah Howe Ens CT
Wm., Jr.: b 4-27-1762 d 2-6-1851 m Rena Carrington Fif CT

FOSKETT,
Ephraim: b 6-23-1755 d 4-17-1835 m (1)Sabra Tuttle (2)Louisa Munn (3)Sarah — Pvt MA ★
John: b c. 1733 d 3-31-1796 m Abigail Jones PS CS MA
Jonathan: b 10-8-1724 d p. 1802 m (1)Phebe Crouch (2)Mary Glazier Cpl CT

FOSMER,
Hendrick: b c. 1740 d p. 3-23-1782 m Catherine Backus Pvt NY

FOSS,
Benjamin: bpt 1-31-1742 d p. 1810 m (1)Sara Getchell (2)Hannah Miller Pvt MA
David: b 10-12-1744 d 12-8-1786 m Anne Richardson PS NH
Ebenezer: b 5-15-1759 d 3-14-1840 m Sarah Hoyt Vol NH
George, Sr.: b 5-10-1724 d 5-29-1807 m Mary Marden Pvt NH
Isaiah: b 3-20-1755 d 4-18-1850 m Mary Dow Pvt NH ★
James: bpt 8-16-1730 d 7-21-1804 m Abigail Hill PS ME
Jeremiah: b 8-8-1751 d 1-11-1835 m Abiah Hayes Pvt NH ★
Job: b — d p. 1790 m Sarah Land PS NH
John: b c. 1747 d 4-21-1835 m Rachel Milliken Cpl MA
John: b 7- -1757 d 1-1-1819 m Sarah Tucker Cpl NH
John: b 5-6-1757 d p. 9-30-1809 m Sarah Blake Pvt NH
Joshua: b 12-26-1709 d 4-17-1809 m Lydia Rand CS NH
Levi: b a. 1740 d 1-1-1778 m — Cpl MA
Moses: b 2-18-1752 d 1830 m Martha — Pvt NH
Samuel: b 11-9-1750 d 10-24-1825 m Sarah Abbigal Horn Pvt NH
Thomas: b 1733 d p. 1781 m Meribah Rand Pvt NH
Zachariah: b 1760 d 1840 m Olive Carl Pvt MA ★

FOSSBINNER,
Jacob: b 1723 d 10-26-1802 m Sabylla — Pvt PA

FOSSETT,
John: b c. 1750 d p. 1786 m Susanna Ellis Pvt MD

FOSTAIN,
Jacques b — d a. 2-13-1793 m Francoise Trahan PS LA

FOSTER, (includes FORSTER)
Aaron: b 1723 d 12-25-1811 m Ruth Lowe CS MA
Abel: b 7-9-1752 d 2-21-1836 m Mary Wood Cpl MA
Abiel: b 8-8-1735 d 2-6-1806 m (1)Hanna Badger (2)Mary Rogers CS PS NH
Abner: b 4-23-1733 d 1803 m Lydia Nelson Pvt MA
Abraham: b 1702 d 4-2-1784 m Elizabeth Moore PS CT
Abraham: b c. 1760 d 1-27-1813 m Sebra Scott Pvt NY
Alexander: b 9-7-1738 d 12-7-1808 m Esther Pratt Capt MA
Alexander: b 2-10-1759 d 6-27-1843 m (2)Sarah Campbell Pvt PA ★
Alexander: b c. 1755 d p. 1789 m Hannah St. Clair Pvt SC
Amos, Sr.: b 11-30-1727 d 2-19-1798 m (1)Hannah Merrill (2)Sarah French Capt MA
Amos, Jr.: b 5-23-1753 d 10-4-1835 m (1)Beulah Horseley (2)Elizabeth Kittredge Pvt MA
Andrew: b 6-15-1751 d 11-15-1817 m Eleanor Graham Pvt PA
Anthony, Jr.: b 3-13-1741 d 11-3-1816 m Rose Coleman Pvt VA
Arthur: b 1732 d 1814 m Martha Collier Lt VA
Arthur: b 1-15-1757 d 7-25-1840 m (1)Elizabeth Glenn (2)Hannah Johnson Sol GA
Asa: b 10-25-1758 d 12-15-1827 m Sarah Trowbridge Pvt NY CT ★
Asa, 1st: b 6-16-1710 d 7-17-1787 m (1)Elizabeth Abbott (2)Lucy (Rogers) Wise PS MA

Asa, Sr.: b 9-11-1733 d 7-17-1841 m (1)Hannah Symonds (2)Hannah Peters PS NH
Asa, Jr.: b 6-3-1765 d 8-21-1861 m Sarah Morrell Pvt NH
Asa: b 4-15-1721 d p. 1790 m (1)Mary Carr (2)Lydia — PS NH
Asa: b 9-25-1750 d p. 1832 m Mary Foster Sct VT
Benjamin: b 6-17-1726 d 7-4-1818 m (1)Abigail Milliken (2)Elizabeth Scott Col MA
Benjamin, Jr.: b 3-5-1754 d 10-22-1848 m Hannah — Sgt VT ★
Charles: b 1-15-1753 d 1849 m (1)Nancy Turner (2)Mary Penn Capt VA
Chauncey: b 1-15-1759 d 4-22-1824 m Charlotte Hill Pvt CT W ★
Christopher: b c. 1720 d p. 1783 m Hannah Turner Pvt CT
Constantine: b 2-18-1742 d 5-25-1824 m (1)Bathia Eldredge (2)Lydia Edwards PS NJ
Daniel: b — d — m Mary Sawyer Lt CT
Daniel: b 3-12-1762 d 8-29-1833 m Dorothy Pingree Sgt MA
Daniel: b 1750 d 1795 m Elizabeth Read Chp MA
Daniel: b a. 1763 d p. 1783 m Peggy Hodgkins Pvt NH
David: b 1750 d 12-26-1831 m Margaret Greer Pvt PA
David: b 10-21-1755 d 12-16-1844 m Catharien Rogers Pvt CT ★
David: b 3-24-1742 d 4-12-1825 m Phebe Freeman Lt MA
David: b 8-17-1704 d 6-22-1779 m Mrs Hannah Sissons PS NH
David: b 1758 d 1-3-1821 m Susannah — Pvt NY
David: b 5-26-1753 d 1-3-1820 m Melicent How Pvt MA RI ★
Ebenezer: b 1732 d 3-19-1811 m Hannah Parlin Lt MA
Ebenezer: b 7-23-1744 d 10-7-1777 m Hannah (Foster) Pvt MA
Edward: b 5-14-1749 d 3-1-1818 m Rachel Newell Sgt MA
Edward, Jr.: b — d p. 1783 m Margaret Pidge Pvt MA
Elias: b 4-11-1726 d p. 1790 m Abigail Wheeler Pvt MA
Elijah: b 11-11-1727 d p. 1790 m Elizabeth Knight Pvt MA
Elisha: b 4-28-1745 d 7-29-1827 m Grace Barstow Lt MA
Ephraim: b 8-30-1731 d 11-12-1803 m Hannah Moore Ens CS PS NH
Ephraim: b 1750 d 9-15-1828 m (1)Hannah Priest (2)Sarah Harris Pvt NH ★
Ephraim: b 8-27-1738 d 2-2-1794 m Hannah Whiteker Lt NJ
Ephraim: b 1752 d 1824 m Chloe Burnham Cpl MA W ★
Ephraim: b c. 1755 d 1-1-1792 m Rachel Stockham Arfr Lt PA NJ W★
Ezekiel, Sr.: b 1727 d 4-17-1805 m Margaret Henry Lt MA
Ezekiel, Jr.: b 1752 d 1824 m Chloe Burnham Cpl MA W ★
Ezekiel, Sr.: b 9-20-1729 d 4-7-1788 m Martha Austin 2Maj NJ
Ezekiel, Jr.: b 4-9-1759 d 10-8-1821 m Hannah Preston PS NJ
Ezra: b 1762 d 2-22-1856 m Abigail Garland Pvt MA
Fletcher: b 8-16-1751 d p. 1792 m Lois Smith Pvt MA
Frederick: b 8-23-1760 d 1-12-1834 m Mary Eastman Pvt NH
George: b c. 1756 d 1- -1810 m (1)Judith Price (2)Elizabeth Ann Hamblin 2Lt VA
George: b 1758 d p. 1-29-1846 m Judy Purcell Pvt VA
Gideon: b 1748 d 11-1-1845 m Hannah Perry Capt MA
Giles: b 12-10-1756 d 12-30-1843 m Fannie Cook Pvt CT ★
Hachaliah: b 7-4-1740 d—m—Sgt CT
Hachaliah: b 1-29-1740 d 1816 m—Sgt MA
Hatherly: b 4-21-1737 d 1792 m Martha — 2Lt MA
Henry: b 3-31-1737 d 7-25-1791 m Abigail Alexander PS NH
Henry: b 1730 d 1797 m Ann Dunlap Cpl SC
Henry: b 5-31-1762 d 1-25-1849 m (1)Mildred Shultz (2)Esther Whittington Pvt VA ★
Hezekiah: b 8-28-1728 d p. 1776 m (1)Hannah Eastman (2)—Bean (3) Mrs Abigail (Tyler) Pearson Pvt PS NH
Isaac: b 3-8-1745/46 d 5-6-1813 m Lydia Bacon Sgt MA
Isaac,Dr.: b 8-28-1740 d 2-27-1781 m Martha Mason CS MA
Isaac, Sr.: b 1725 d 3-19-1796 m Irena Allen Pvt MA
Issac, Jr.: b 1761 d 1800 m Rebecca Hunt Pvt MA
Issac: b 8-21-1720 d 3-12-1783 m Sarah Brown PS MA
Isaac: b c. 1750 d 1804/05 m Elizabeth Hodges Lt VA
Isaac: b 1760 d p. 1786 m Susan Leach Pvt VA
Jabez: b 1754 d 6-28-1818 m (1)Esther Bliss (2)Cynthia Arms Cpl CT
Jacob: b 3-10-1732 d 12-3-1798 m Hepzibah Prentice Chp MA
Jacob: b 7-15-1746 d 11-8-1791 m Sarah Wheeler Pvt MA
James: b 4-30-1742 d 3-26-1823 m Elizabeth Flint Pvt MA
James: b 7-3-1743 d 1812/13 m Elizabeth Bancroft Pvt MA
James: b 1744 d 3-16-1811 m Mehitable Atwood Pvt MA
James: b 9-29-1743 d 1790 m Hannah Jewett Pvt PS NH
James: b 5-24-1764 d 12-16-1829 m Hannah Stetson Pvt NH ★
James: b 1728 d 5- -1800 m Elizabeth Moore Pvt MA
James, Jr.: b 1753 d 9-19-1837 m Jane Morrow Pvt SC
James, Sr.: b c. 1730 d 1783-85 m Mary — Pvt SC
James: b 8-2-1752 d 11-14-1835 m (1) Mrs Charlotte Foster Brown (2) Mrs Elizabeth Smith Brassfield Pvt SC
James: b 6- -1750 d 9-10-1800 m Elizabeth Grigsby Cpl VA
James: b 4-6-1738 d 4-7-1814 m (1)Ann Barclay (2)Mrs Phoebe Baldwin Dodd Sol VA
Jedediah: b 10-10-1726 d 10-17-1779 m Dorothy Dwight PS CS MA
Jedediah: b 4-20-1749 d 5-7-1819 m Rachael Hollister Pvt MA
Jedediah: b 5-12-1738 d 1832 m Elizabeth Howell Pvt NY
Jeremiah: b 4-21-1750 d 11-21-1820 m Anna Lovett Cpl MA
Jeremiah, Jr.: bpt 1-6-1740 d 12-17-1815 m Sarah Fellows CS MA
Jesse: b 1745 d 1810 m Ann E Toppan QMSgt Arfr CT ★
Job: b 5-3-1756 d 3-10-1842 m Nancy Craycraft Pvt VA ★
Joel: b 8-15-1762 d 8-12-1851 m (2)Mrs Elizabeth Hinton (3)Mary Staples Pvt VA ★
John: b 9-19-1742 d 6-4-1826 m Irene Cross Pvt CT
John: b 1735 d 1-1-1800 m Elizabeth Lewis Pvt MD

John: b 9-3-1757 d 8-17-1848 m Experience Gray Sgt MA ★
John: b 7-31-1752 d p. 1793 m Sally Tweed Lt MA
John: b c. 1752 d 2-13-1829 m (1)Sara Hari (2)Phebe Doan Cpl MA
John: bpt 1758 d 1837 m Susannah Robinson Pvt MA
John: b 3-4-1706 d p. 1778 m Hannah Lovett Pvt MA
John: b 10-24-1760 d 4-27-1835 m Dorcas Towne Pvt MA
John: b a. 7-29-1741 d 7-10-1810 m (1)Sarah Taylor (2)Lydia Foster Ens CS NH
John: b 1734 d 10-16-1811 m Mary McComb Pvt NY
John: b c. 1738 d c. 1824 m Martha Connell Pvt NC
John: b 5-9-1732 d 5-25-1786 m Jane Johnston Capt PA
John: b 1738 d 1782 m Margaretta — Sgt PA
John: b — d 1818 m Elizabeth Ferree Pvt PA
John: b 1725 d 9- -1789 m Catherine Dickey Pvt PA
John, Sr.: b 1752 d 11-17-1812 m Mary Atkins Capt SC
John: b 1755 d 1794 m Elizabeth Boggs Sol SC
John: b 1735 d 1781 m Anne Blacknall Capt VA
John: b 1739 d p. 10-9-1787 m Eleanor Collins Lt VA
John, Jr.: b c. 1752 d c. 1814 m Elizabeth — Lt VA
John: b 4-7-1728 d p. 1784 m Rose — Lt VA
John: b c. 1758 d 5-11-1837 m Sydney — Sgt VA W ★
John: b 1-18-1761 d 3-6-1821 m Elizabeth Savage Sgt VA
John: b 1761 d 7-26-1821 m Frances Borum PS VA
John Harden: b 1755 d 5-18-1801 m Martha Wingfield Lt VA ★
John Lewis: b c. 1742 d c. 1843 m Elizabeth Davis Ens PA
Jonah: b 2-7-1721 d 5-11-1804 m Abigail Jackson Capt CT
Jonah: b 11-14-1751 d 12-17-1815 m Hannah Benedict Pvt CT
Jonathan: b 10-11-1727 d 7-28-1813 m Rebecca Dorman Capt MA
Jonathan: b 5-24-1742 d p. 1794 m (1)Bethia Hill (2)Patience Cady (3)Elizabeth Bosworth Sgt MA
Jonathan: b 6-6-1719 d 3-31-1821 m (1)Mrs Bathsheba Crosby (2)Bettie Hazen (3)Thankful Harrington (4)Mercy Town Pvt MA ★
Jonathan: b 1738 d 1814 m Sarah Townsend Pvt MA
Jonathan: b 8-18-1740 d 11-24-1805 m Hannah Thayer Pvt MA
Jonathan: b a. 1758 d — m Dolly Jenkins Pvt MA
Jonathan: b a. 1760 d 5-17-1813 m Rachel Kitredge Pvt MA W ★
Jonathan: b 7-28-1747 d 1815 m Lucy Rogers Sgt NH
Jonathan: b 11-9-1766 d 9-20-1824 m Elizabeth Greenwood Fif PA W ★
Jonathan: b 6-8-1715 d 11-8-1781 m Anna Jencks Pvt RI
Joseph: b 7-17-1730 d 12-9-1804 m Lydia Giddings Col MA
Joseph: b 6-3-1730 d 5-10-1807 m Susannah Roberts Capt MA
Joseph, Sr.: b 1700 d 1780 m Sarah Brown MM MA
Joseph, Jr.: b 3-21-1750 d p. 1784 m Sarah Baldwin Pvt MA
Joseph: b 4-29-1762 d 11-27-1845 m Chloe White Fif Pvt MA ★
Joseph: b 12-25-1739 d 12-15-1802 m Elizabeth Hilton Pvt MA
Joseph: b 1742 d 7-29-1816 m Jane Reed PS ME MA
Joseph: b 3-24-1733 d 1804 m (1)Sarah Jones (2)Rebecca (Walker) Phelps Pvt MA
Joshua, Jr.: b 7-5-1757 d 10-22-1823 m Lucy Tenny Pvt NH
Joshua: b 6-4-1754 d p. 1- -1829 m Mary Foster Sgt VA W★
Joshua: b — d 1809 m Sarah — Pvt VA
Josiah: b 5-20-1743 d 1-15-1820 m Rachel Burr PS NJ
Jude: b c. 1760 d 3-28-1789 m Lydia M — Cpl MA ★
Lemuel: b 4-30-1764 d 8-25-1824 m Dolly Davis Pvt MA W ★
Luna: b 3-25-1764 d 5-10-1847 m (1)Sally Skinner (2)Lydia White Pvt MA W★
Mary: bpt 3-4-1748/9 d 1-14-1786 m (1)Isaac — (2)John Hurd PS MA
Micah: b 9-27-1742 d 6-27-1827 m (1)Hezediah Crocker (2)Susanna Collamore (3)Mrs Mehitable Stevens Cpl MA
Moses: bpt 11-9-1760 d 10-20-1812 m Mary Story Pvt MA W ★
Moses: b 4-3-1755 d 9-3-1800 m Mary Fuller Sgt MA
Moses: b a. 1765 d 5-9-1842 m Hannah Kennedy Pvt MD
Nathan: b c. 1730 d a. 4-19-1806 m Mirian — Pvt MA
Nathan: b 1-26-1743 d 3-26-1812 m Hannah Haskell Pvt VT
Nathaniel: b c. 1740 d 1792 m (1)Bridgett — (2)Dorothy Chadburne Pvt MA
Nathaniel, Jr.: b 1748 d 1795 m Anna Baker Pvt MA
Nathaniel: b 10-12-1804 m (2)Mary Kendall Pvt MA
Nathaniel: b 4-17-1711 d 10- -1793 m (1)Mercy Thacher (2)Abigail Billings Fif MA
Nathaniel: b 9-28-1751 d 1-21-1823 m Lydia Barnaby Pvt MA
Nathaniel: b 2-7-1760 d 6-11-1841 m (1)Polly Watson (2) Esther Smith Pvt NJ ★
Nathaniel: b 4-17-1725 d 4-15-1787 m (1)Phebe Wing (2)Charity Knowlton PS NY
Nathaniel, Sr.: b 1740 d 1826 m Lydia Frisbee Pvt VT
Nathaniel: b 6-23-1761 d 9-14-1837 m Nancy Mauzy Pvt VA ★
Obediah: b 5-25-1741 d 7-25-1780 m Hannah Ballard Pvt MA
Parla: b 3-1-1759 d 1-27-1852 m Phebe Wells Pvt MA
Paul: b 7-14-1750 d 1814 m Martha Trask Pvt MA
Peletiah: b 11-30-1732 d 7-29-1826 m Phebe Pomeroy CS CT
Peregrine: b 12-27-1759 d 8-17-1804 m Polly Brandshaw Sgt MA
Peter: b 5-31-1764 d 8-31-1842 m Sarah Herridan Pvt VT
Peter: b 3-22-1756 d 12-31-1819/20 m Ann Hall Pvt VA
Philemon: b 6-11-1737 d 5-10-1818 m Ruth Pearley Pvt MA
Richard: b 11-24-1744 d p. 5-7-1814 m Lydia Titus Cpl MA
Richard: b 7-16-1762 d 10-1-1833 m (1)Sarah Greeley (2)Esther Jewell Pvt MA ★
Richard: b c.1750 d 1819 m (1)Judith Walker (2)Obedience Green CS VA

Robert: b 7-12-1738 d 5-30-1782 m Mary Emery CS MA
Robert: b 1760 d 1826 m Sallie Bailey Pvt NC
Robert: b 8-28-1758 d 1-29-1834 m Esther Renick Pvt PA ★
Rufus: b 3-6-1762 d 3-23-1836 m Susanna Hubbard Pvt MA ★
Salathiel: b 1725 d 1792 m Marcy — Capt NJ
Samuel: b c. 1730-40 d p. 4-16-1789 m Margaret — PS MD
Samuel: b 3-4-1745/6 d 8-30-1794 m Mary Ober NCapt MA
Samuel: b 5- -1751 d 5-6-1778 m Margaret Brown Capt MA
Samuel: b 6-14-1743 d 4-7-1825 m Leah Avery Lt MA ★
Samuel: b 2-10-1740 d 11-2-1794 m Bethiah Bennett Sgt MA
Samuel: b 3-31-1758 d 1826 m Mary Colcord SgtMaj MA
Samuel: b 7-14-1746 d 8-13-1808 m Judith Foster Pvt MA
Samuel: bpt 1-8-1741/42 d 4-15-1793 m Susanna Wood PS NY
Samuel: b c. 1742 d 1780 m Tabitha Hodgkins Sol NH
Samuel: b 4-3-1755 d 1-4-1829 m (1)Esther Meeker (2)Elizabeth Taylor Wood Cpl NJ
Samuel: b 8-4-1746 d 1-16-1816 m Waity Wells Sgt RI W ★
Samuel: b 2-1-1763 d 2-19-1844 m Mary M Veath Pvt VA & PA
Silas: b 2-18-1747 d 6-23-1800 m (1)Elizabeth Piper (2)Tamasa Towne Sgt MA
Silas: b 11-12-1756 d 1-4-1826 m Mary Cook Mrnr PA
Stewart: b 4-8-1757 d 8-21-1839 m Jerusha Wadsworth Pvt MA
Theodore: b 4-29-1752 d 1-13-1828 m Ester Bowen Millard PS CS RI
Theophilus: b 3-16-1754 d 10-8-1833 m (1)Susanna Packard (2)Hannah Crosby Sol MA
Thomas: b 7-25-1737 d 6-11-1826 m Martha Elmer Ens CT
Thomas: b 10-14-1736 d 10-9-1806 m Elizabeth Berry Pvt CT
Thomas: b 8-11-1724 d a. 12-8-1789 m Mehitable Peabody Capt MA
Thomas: b — d — m Elizabeth Lathrop Capt MA
Thomas: b 1759 d — m Lucy — Lt MA
Thomas: b 4-9-1762 d 11-11-1809 m Susanna Story Cpl MA
Thomas: b 3-15-1711 d c. 1790 m Mary Hopkins Pvt NY
Thomas: b 1-10-1750 d 7-9-1832 m Hannah Bliss Sgt NY ★
Thomas: b 1746 d 7-5-1804 m Jane Young Maj PA
Thomas: b 1-10-1757 d 10-16-1831 m Esther Wells Pvt RI W ★
Thomas: b 1750 d 1811 m Frances Jones Pvt VA
Timothy: b 4-17-1728 d 1814 m Elizabeth Berry Pvt CT
Timothy: b 6-23-1764 d 4-10-1840 m Susanna Adams Pvt CT
Timothy: b 5-14-1720 d 4-3-1785 m Sebulah Freeman Capt MA
Timothy, Sr.: b 1715 d 5-5-1795 m (1)Mollie May (2)Keziah Lyon (3)Mary Payson PS MA
Timothy, Jr.: b 6-20-1741 d 1-26-1822 m Rachel Robinson Lt MA W★
Timothy, Jr.: b 3-21-1745/46 d 8-1-1825 m Abigail Allen Pvt MA
Wakeman: b 4-20-1738 d 12-20-1829 m (1)Martha Sawyer (2)Phoebe Cleves Pvt NY
Wm.: b 4-29-1734 d 5-16-1825 m Hannah Durkee Sgt CT
Wm.: b 1755 d 10-6-1829 m Susannah Morris Sol GA
Wm.: b 1746 d 1853 m Mary Powell Sol GA
Wm.: b 5-25-1746 d 7-24-1809 m Abigail Chapin Sgt MA
Wm.: b 7-26-1760 d 1792 m Mary Brown Cpl MA
Wm.: b 8-2-1750 d 8-29-1825 m Esther Dodge Pvt MA
Wm.: b 1743 d 6-30-1827 m (1)Jemima Foster (2)Sarah Emes (3)Rebecca Kimball Pvt MA
Wm.: b 2-9-1753 d 11-1-1828 m (1)Margaret Foster (2)Mary Draper Sol MA
Wm.: b 11-11-1716 d 3-14-1786 m Hannah Coburn PS MA
Wm.: b 12-24-1763 d 7-10-1825 m Betsey Morrill Pvt NH
Wm.: b 4-8-1762 d 4-10-1841 m Susanna Wright Pvt NY
Wm.: b 5-5-1750 d p. 1833 m (1)Sarah Grover (2)Mrs Mary (Cross) Gamage (3)Ann Grover Sgt MA ★
Wm.: b 1751 d 1851 m — Sol PA
Wm.: b 6- -1740 d 9-30-1780 m Johanna Blair PS PA
Wm.: b c. 1735 d 1820 m Agnes Allen Pvt SC
Wm.: b 1753 d 3-9-1818 m Mrs Mary Ann (Jones)James Maj VA
Wm.: b 1740 d 7- -1803 m Mary Gilmore Pvt VA
Wm.: b 1747 d 2-7-1824 m (1)Sallie Slade (2)Sarah Hart Pvt Matr VA ★
Wm.: b 3-31-1748 d 4-2-1830 m Elizabeth Heth Pvt VA
Woodin: b 1730 d 2-2-1810 m Frances Scott Pvt MA

FOULKROD,
Jacob: b 4-20-1760 d 9-29-1852 m Mary Bauderman Pvt PA★

FOULKS, (includes FOLCK, FOLKES, FOLKS, FOULKE, FOWLKES, VALCK)
Daniel: b 1760 d 1836 m Elizabeth — Pvt PA ★
James: b 1750 d 9-14-1782 m Jenny Bradford Pvt NC
Johannis: b 1-27-1740 d 11-2-1822 m Marietje Mayerstock Pvt NY
John: b 12-21-1722 d 5-25-1787 m Mary Roberts PS PA
John: b c. 1755 d 1808 m Nancy Newby Adj VA
Joseph: b c. 1728 d p. 4-30-1789 m Mary Jane Jennings PS VA
Samuel: b 2-4-1718 d 1-21-1797 m Ann Greasly PS PA
Stephen: b 10-15-1732 b 11-20-1800 m (1)Margaret Carson (2)Catherine Themburgh Pvt PA
Theophilus: b 12-21-1726 d 11-4-1785 m Margaret Thomas PS PA
Thomas: b 1-14-1724 d 3-31-1786 m Jane Roberts PS PA
Wm.: b c. 1728 d 4-11-1796 m Priscilla Lester Pvt PA
Wm.: b 1743 d 4-25-1805 m Katherine Knibb PS VA

FOURNIER,
Francis: b 1730 d 1-23-1807 m Ester Clark Sol PS NY

FOUSHEE,
Thornton: b *c.* 1753 d *c.* 1801 m Rosa Hobbs Sol VA
Wm: b 10-26-1749 d 8-21-1824 m Elizabeth Harmondson Dr CS VA

FOUTZ, (includes PFOUTZ)
Conrad: b 4- -1734 d 1798 m Elizabeth — Pvt PA
John: b 11-15-1742 d 6-10-1813 m Mary Ann Crane Pvt PA

FOWLE,
Benjamin: b 10-1-1746 d 11-9-1815 m Mary Wyman Pvt MA
Henry: b 1740 d 1810 m Mary Patten PS MA
John: b 2-1-1756 d 12-31-1823 m Mary Cooke Capt MA
John: b 11-10-1755 d 12-9-1834 m Lois Richardson Arfr Pvt MA ★
Joseph: b 3-9-1758 d *p.* 1795 m Caryloine Wyman Ens MA
Josiah: b 7-14-1731 d 2-28-1805 m Margery Carter Pvt MA
Nathaniel: b 7-19-1749 d 1817 m Rhoda Clap Pvt MA
Samuel: b 8-31-1753 d 6-11-1825 m Rachel Lawrence Sgt MA
Wm: b 4-25-1763 d 6-18-1850 m Mary Richardson Pvt MA

FOWLER,
Abel: b 12-17-1745 d 11-29-1833 m Molly Brownell Lt RI
Abner: b 3-17-1753 d 4-30-1833 m Mary Mason Pvt NH ★
Abraham: b 1725 d 9-30-1779 m Elizabeth Bartlett Ens CS PS CT
Adam: b 1749 d 12- -1825 m Elizabeth Haines Pvt PA
Adijah, Sr.: b 6-10-1717 d 12-14-1804 m Abigail Bigelow PS CT
Amos: b 3-17-1758 d 11-30-1837 m Rebecca Dewey Cpl CT W ★
Ashbel: b 5-2-1764 d 7-17-1832 m Lucretia Kellogg Pvt NY
Benjamin: b 2-7-1767 d 12-25-1847 m Sarah Kelsey Smn MA
Bildad: b 8-10-1740 d 11-19-1814 m (1)Mercy Sykes (2)Rachel Hopkins Lt MA
Blachleach: b 1-4-1754 d 9-6-1839 m Miriam Smith Pvt MA
Caleb: b 12-31-1755 d 10-12-1822 m (1)Mollie Chittenden (2)Olive Meigs Pvt CT ★
Daniel: b 9-9-1761 d 4-18-1847 m Rachael Loomis Pvt CT ★
Daniel: b 1714 d 1793 m Mary Jane Rollins Sol NC
Daniel: b *c.* 1715 d *p.* 7-28-1783 m — PS VA
David: b 5-16-1726 d 9-12-1800 m Lucretia Fosdick CG CT
David: b 4-24-1752 d 2-16-1823 m (1)Polly Rising (2)Elizabeth Campbell Pvt CS MA
Ebenezer, Sr.: b 1-11-1719 d 2-9-1800 m Desire Bristol Pvt CT
Ebenezer, Jr.: b 4-17-1747 d 1-1-1833 m (1)Lois Rossiter (2)Mercy Towner Lt CT
Ebenezer, Sr.: b 9-28-1729 d 8-16-1777 m Catherine Root Pvt MA
Edward: b 1753 d 1819 m (1)Ann Roberts (2)Eleanor Roberts Pvt MD
Eliphalet: b 10-11-1743 d *p.* 1790 m Mary Thankful Pixley Pvt MA
Elisha: b 1754 d 1816 m Olive Woodward Pvt MA
Elisha Adams: b 9-29-1755 d 2-20-1839 m Mary Burr Sgt CT ★
Gilbert: b 10-10-1749 d 5-27-1814 m Bridget Tallman Pvt NY
Godfrey: b 1745 d *p.* 10- -1794 m Rahab Cooper PS NC
Issac, Jr.: b 4-3-1746 d 4-10-1821 m (2)Gloriana (Purdy) Merritt Lt NY
Isaac: b 6- -1757 d 4-16-1856 m (2)Susannah Baker Pvt NY
Jacob: b 1730 d 1-23-1785 m Elizabeth Merrill Pvt VT
Jacob: b 4-27-1750 d 5-8-1806 m Phebe Vail Pvt NY
James: b 5-9-1758 d 1-31-1848 m Mary Ozborne Pvt MD
James: b 1758 d 8- -1839 m Mehitable Pvt MA
James: b 1748 d 1803 m Susanna Purdy Cpl NY
Jeremiah: b 7-27-1737 d 1802 m Mary Woodward Cpl NH
Jesse: b — d — m Patience Marton Pvt MA
Job: b *c.* 1748/49 d 2- -1779 m Ruth Gardiner Sgt RI
John, Sr.: b 2-7-1717 d 5-14-1781 m Mary Newton Capt CT
John, Jr.: b 8-21-1748 d 8-17-1787 m Mary Ann Harpin 1Lt CT
John, Sr.: b 6-4-1714 d 7-13-1796 m Abigail Hilliand Hall CS CT
John, Jr.: b 10-5-1745 d 1829 m Ruth Whelpley Pvt CT
John: b 10-10-1750 d 11-17-1824 m Sarah Abbott MM Sgt MA
John: b 3-7-1714 d 9-9-1803 m Mercy Howe Pvt MA
John: b 8-16-1753 d 4-15-1806 m Lucretia Ingersoll Sol MA
John: b *c.* 1758 d 10-11-1845 m Elizabeth Steenberg Pvt MA
John: b 1740 d 1785 m Ann Eliza Keith Pvt NY
John: b *c.* 1725 d 12-18-1799 m Abigail Reeves PS NY
John: b 1739 d 1844 m Elizabeth Fowler Pvt NC ★
John: b 1737 d *p.* 1785 m — Sol SC
Jonathan: b 1757 d 1849 m Elizabeth Lang Pvt NY ★
Joseph: b 1-9-1746/47 d 8-20-1827 m Lydia Ross MM MA
Joseph: b 11-27-1753 d 5-22-1797 m Sarah Whitney Pvt NY
Joshua Cheever: b 1-16-1757 d 1-23-1813 m Lydia Stearns Pvt MA
Josiah: b 3-21-1724 d 5-17-1802 m Ruth Hall Capt CT
Lemuel: b 9-4-1736 d 1828 m Mary Bolter Pvt MA
Mark: b 5-9-1756 d 4-27-1813 m Miriam (Sterling) Warner Pvt CT
Mary Brundage: b *a.* 1735 d 1815 m Moses Fowler PS NY
Matthew: b 1761 d 4-27-1842 m Sarah Burton Pvt MA ★
Moses: b 1755-60 d 1790 m Adah Crane Pvt NY
Moses: b 10-7-1758 d 1810-15 m Hannah Field Pvt NY
Nathan, Sr.: b 7-27-1741 d 9-21-1818 m (1)Susan Miles (2)Mehitable Platt CS CT
Nathan, Jr.: b 2-24-1762 d 10-2-1843 m Sarah Platt Pvt CT
Nathan: b *c.* 1745 d *p.* 9-14-1815 m Nannie Fowler Sol GA
Nathaniel: b 7-14-1758 d 2-24-1841 m Ruth Evarts Pvt CT ★
Noah: b 1730 d 11-15-1815 m Deborah Pendleton LCol CT
Noah: b 9-24-1750 d 1824 m Rhoda Tuttle Pvt CT

Philip: b 1740 d 6-17-1775 m Esther Wood Cpl MA
Richard: b 12-1-1754 d *p.* 1782 m Mary Raynor Pvt NY
Robert: b 1-21-1760 d 6-1-1824 m (1)Mrs Molly Lowell (2)Betsey Morrill Pvt MA
Robert: b *c.* 1749 d 1844 m Ann — Pvt PA
Samuel: b 5-31-1737 d 10-7-1777 m Anna — Pvt MA
Samuel: b 1-9-1748/49 d 4-20-1813 m Sarah Putman Pvt MA
Samuel: b 10-12-1720 d 10-13-1789 m Charlotte Purdy Sol NY
Sherwood: b 1-1-1759 d 5-5-1839 m Mary Wingo Sgt VA ★
Silas: b 5-23-1735 d *c.* 1813 m (1)Kezia Noble (2)Tryphena Pease Capt MA
Stephen: b 1-21-1744 d 12-26-1814 m Temperance Stevens Sol CT
Stephen: b 12-21-1719 d 11-8-1784 m (1)Rhoda Bancroft (2)Mary Wells Pvt MA
Stephen: b 7-25-1747 d 3-14-1824 m Rhoda Weller Pvt MA
Symonds: b 8-20-1734 d 4-6-1821 m Hannah Weeks Pvt PS NH
Theodosius: b 1752 d 10-12-1841 m Mary Steele Capt NY
Thomas: b 7-21-1752 d 12-2-1776 m Beulah Bishop Pvt CT
Titus: b 11-29-1738 d 2-27-1827 m Hannah Burritt Sgt MA
Wm.: b 12-20-1748 d 5-15-1815 m Olive Coan Sgt CT
Wm.: b *c.* 1757 d *p.* 1821 m — Pvt MD
Wm.: b *c.* 1760 d *p.* 1800 m Rebecca — PS MD
Wm. Harrison: b *c.* 1755 d *p.* 1800 m Eleanor Ataway PS SC

FOWLKES, (includes FOWKE)
Chandler: b 5-3-1732 d 2-18-1810 m Mary Harrison Adj VA
Jennings: b 1744 d 1817 m — Clarke Pvt VA
Thompson: b 5-3-1751 d *p.* 1791 m Elizabeth Robinson Pvt VA

FOX,
Abraham: b 11-21-1748 d 2-4-1777 m Martha Couch Pvt CT
Abraham: b 11-21-1748 d *p.* 1736 m Lydia Kneeland Pvt CT
Allen: b 7-1-1755 d 9-17-1831 m Chloe Crittenden Pvt CT ★
Amos: b 3-8-1758 d 3-14-1832 m Mary Stratton Pvt CT ★
Amos: b 7-9-1739 d 1806 m Anna Combs PS VA
Arthur: b 2-27-1761 d 4-11-1794 m Mary Young Pvt VA
Ashbel: b *c.* 1748 d *p.* 12-3-1804 m Jemima Osborn Sol NY
Christopher B: b 2-24-1744 d 12-16-1820 m Elizabeth Hess Maj PS NY
Christopher W: b 8-3-1757 d 1-24-1835 m Margaret Nellis Pvt NY ★
Conrad: b 1700 d 1779 m — PS PA
Consider: b 1759 d 1839 m Susan Green Pvt NY ★
Daniel: b 5- -1752 d 9-28-1824 m Susanna Thompson Cpl NH
David: b 7-14-1720 d 3- -1804 m Mary Chapman Pvt CT
David: b 1756 d 1836 m — Drm CT ★
David: b 2-23-1766 d 4-23-1831 m Mary Elizabeth Roland Trm PA ★
Edward: b 8-27-1755 d 5-7-1839 m Ann Creighton Pvt NH ★
Elijah: b 11-7-1758 d 12-4-1838 m (1)Polly — (2)Sarah Brockway (3)Sabra Nettleton Pvt CT
Elisha: b 10-15-1743 d 4-19-1800 m Anna Fitch Capt CT
Ezekiel: b 4-19-1756 d 4-6-1844 m Susanna Childs Pvt CT ★
Frederick: b 5-10-1751 d 2-27-1837 m Catherine Booker Drm PA
George: b *c.* 1760 d *p.* 1790 m Sara Gosline Pvt PA
Henry: b 3-31-1745 d 6-24-1824 m (1)Anna Sander (2)Maria Ruth Pvt PA
Hubbard: b 5-22-1753 d 1805 m Luna Percy Pvt CT
Issac: b 1712/13 d — m Abigail Prescott Pvt MA
Israel: b 1753 d 2-7-1828 m Elizabeth Porter Slr
Israel: b 10-5-1753 d *p.* 1832 m (1)Sarah Strickland (2)Abigail Hodge Pvt CT ★
Jabez: b 5-6-1745 d 5-20-1780 m Mary Strobridge PS CT
Jacob: b *c.* 1760 d — Lydia Hout Pvt NJ
Jacob: b *c.* 1755 d *p.* 1819 m — Pvt PS PA
Jacob: b 3-12-1764 d 8-16-1849 m Mary Eve Bunzey Pvt CL ★
Jacob: b *p.* 3-22-1807 m Elizabeth Lark PS VA
Jacob MacCoy: b 1744 d 8-10-1827 m Sarah — Lt CT ★
James: b 1756 d 1794 m Rebecca Halloway Pvt MD
James: b 1760 d 1803 m Rebecca Kilgore Pvt VA
Jedediah, Jr.: b 12-19-1759 d 4-12-1858 m Penlope Fox Pvt CT
Jehiel: b 8-21-1762 d 7-25-1823 m Jerusah Baldwin Pvt NY
Joel: b 8-14-1754 d 8-21-1837 m Mercy Gilbert Pvt CT ★
Joel: b 5-6-1757 d 2-8-1849 m Hannah Cheever Pvt MA ★
John: b 8-7-1758 d 12-1-1843 m Priscilla Lyon Sgt CT
John: b *c.* 1755 d 3-29-1841 m Sarah Worcester Pvt MA ★
John: b 5-26-1760 d 4-15-1834 m (1)Deborah Gilman (2)Susan Mills Pvt NH ★
John: b 2-19-1764 d 9-1-1840 m (1)Elizabeth Loving (2)Virlintia Pvt NC ★
John: b 1751 d 4-25-1816 m Ann Margaret Rupert Pvt PA
John: b 1756 d 1864 m (1) — Wennett (2)Mrs Donley Pvt VA ★
John: b *c.* 1765 d *p.* 2-19-1826 m Ann Barber Sol VA
John: b 6-29-1760 d 12-29-1814 m (1)Judith Turner (2)Frances Wyatt Woolfold PS VA
John Nicholas: b *c.* 1740 d 1823 m Elizabeth Barbara Schilp Pvt PS PA
Johnathan: b 1739 d 8-19-1809 m Margaret Cole Pvt CT
Jonathan: b 1738 d *a.* 3-31-1791 m Sarah — PS GA
Jonathan: b 3-26-1716 d 4-17-1790 m Ruth Carter Col MA
Joseph: b 11-22-1749 d 7-9-1827 m Sophia Marcy Capt CS MA ★

Joseph: b 1758 d 12-13-1847 m (1)Jane Wilson (2)Elsey — Pvt PA ★
Josiah: b 2-26-1745 d 1830 m Eunice Clement Pvt MA
Nathaniel: b c. 1750 d 1820 m (1)Mary King (2)Susan Prosser Capt VA
Peter: b c. 1754 d 1820 m Anna Margaret Pvt PA
Peter: b 9-21-1762 d 1-5-1837 m (1)Elizabeth Hudson (2)Amy Williams Pvt NJ ★
Peter: b 10-1-1760 d 5-10-1847 m Mariah Righter Pvt NY
Reuben: b c. 1749 d 1820 m — Williams Pvt CT
Roswell: b 9-9-1751 d 6-6-1825 m Phebe Hough Pvt CT
Rudolph: b 3-29-1739 d 3-4-1806 m Catherine Elizabeth Miller Ens PA
Samuel: b 1725 d 12-15-1810 m Prudence Turner Cpl CT
Samuel: b 10-8-1756 d 10-10-1844 m Mabel Webster Cpl CT
Silas: b 1756 d 4-8-1832 m Mary Cheney Pvt NH ★
Stephen: b c. 1755 d p. 1793 m Sarah Andrews Pvt PS CT
Stephen: b 1760 d 2-25-1842 m Mary Bates Pvt CT ★
Stephen: b a. 1765 d 5-5-1854 m (1) — Collyer (3)Polly Duncan Pvt CT
Thomas: b 9-7-1732 d 5-22-1800 m (2)Patience Kannon Cpl MA
Thomas: b 9-30-1762 d 1849 m Lois Seymour Pvt CT ★
Thomas: b 1765 d 2-6-1834 m Cloe — Pvt CT ★
Thomas: b 1735 d 10-25-1792 m Philadelphia Claiborne 1Lt VA
Thomas: b 1725 d 11-16-1822 m Elizabeth Hancock Sol SC
Timothy: b 4-20-1741 d 1827 m Mrs Abigail Dudley Pvt NH
Veniah: b 1763 d 2-2-1851 m Sarah Cadwell Sgt CT ★
Wm.: b c. 1722 d 6-22-1792 m Mercy (Freeman) Payne Pvt PS CT
Wm.: b c. 1725 d p. 1-21-1783 m (2)Elizabeth — PS GA
Wm.: b 1722 d 5-5-1787 m Mary Langstaff CS NJ
Wm.: b c. 1750 d 12-24-1804 m Margareth Wormuth Pvt NY
Wm.: b c. 1732 d — m Catharine Zimmerman Capt PS NY
Wm.: b 6-28-1760 d 2-17-1822 m Philena White Pvt VT
Wm.: b 4-6-1752 d 3-2-1814 m Mrs Margaret Walden Sol SC
Wm.: b — d p. 4-13-1808 m — Sol PS SC
Wm.: b c. 1763 d. 7-27-1793 m Mary Brown Conrad Pvt VA
Wm.: b 1739 d 4-8-1798 m Patsy Avent Sgt VA

FOXWORTH,
James: b 1742 d 1786 m (2)Mary Alston PS SC

FOXWORTHY,
Wm.: b 4-3-1753 d 6-17-1837 m Clarissa Calvert Pvt VA ★

FOY, (includes FOYE)
James: b c. 1737 d 11-11-1822 m (1)Elizabeth Ward (2)Elizabeth — Capt NC
John: b c. 1720 d p. 1790 m Ruth Huckings PS NH
Moses: b 12-22-1761 d p. 8-15-1832 m Mollie Tibbets Pvt MA W ★
Peter: b 1745 d 1782 m Hamital Moore Pvt SC

FRAILEY, (includes FRALEY & FRALEIGH)
Frederick: b 8-2-1742 d 8-29-1823 m Catharine Frieble Pvt PA
Henry: b 3-27-1744 d 8-20-1821 m Susanna Margaretta Rice Lt PA
John: b 1769 d 1816 m Elizabeth — Cpl NC
John: b 3-6-1761 d 12-16-1848 m Mascy Ann Thomas Pvt PA
Rudolph: b 6-9-1757 d 11-5-1814 m Elizabeth Hergurheimer OrdlSgt PA
Stephanus: b 7-28-1742 d 4-12-1820 m Maria VanBenschoten Pvt NY

FRAMBRIS, (includes FRAMBES)
Andrew: b 10-17-1759 d 1790 m Sarah English Pvt NJ
Nicholas: b 6-1-1758 d 6-25-1835 m Sarah Rape MM NJ

FRAME, (includes FRAIM)
David: b c. 1745 d p. 1797 m Elizabeth — Pvt VA
Jeremiah: b 7-16-1752 d 12-9-1828 m Elizabeth McGill Pvt VA
John: b 1751 d a. 1837 m Elizabeth — Pvt VA
Wm.: b 1745 d — 1827 m Elizabeth Johnston Pvt PA

FRAMPTON,
Arthur: b 1755 d p. 1790 m Martha Lauremore Pvt PS PA
John: b 1714 d 1784 m Elizabeth Critchfield Pvt PS PA
Nathaniel: b 1748 d 6-3-1832 m Martha Coursen Pvt PA
Samuel: b 1746 d — m Nancy Elizabeth Kelly Pvt PA
Wm.: b 11-15-1742 d 10-15-1829 m Sarah Stealey Pvt PA

FRANCIS, (includes FRANCISS)
Amos: b 11-23-1757 d 11-25-1806 m Sarah Curtis Pvt CT
Arnold: b 1738 d 6-10-1802 m Elizabeth Hampstead Capt PA
Asa: b 11-8-1757 d 7-21-1836 m Prudence May Warner Pvt CT
Daniel: b 5-1-1737 d p. 1790 m — Wicks Pvt CT
David: b 1762 d 1-27-1839 m Anna Spencer Pvt CT
Ebenezer: b 12-22-1743 d 7-7-1777 m Judith Wood Col MA
Elijah: b 2-25-1732 d 8-18-1812 m Hannah Buck Lt CT
George: b 11-3-1747 d 2-3-1820 m Ann Elizabeth Shank Sgt PA ★
Henry: b c. 1725 d a. 10- -1780 m Leah — Capt VA
James: b 12-4-1755 d 4-7-1831 m Sarah Coe Cpl CT ★
James: b 10-24-1757 d 4-13-1839 m (1)Sylvia Stanley (2)Mrs Sarah Clark Pvt CT
James: b 2-2-1752 d 6-1-1833 m (2)Hannah Collins Pvt PA ★

John: b 6-20-1744 d 5-30-1824 m Rhoda Wright Capt CT
John: b c. 1764 d 12-29-1856 m Isabelle Erskine Pvt MD
John: b 1723 d 4-22-1776 m Deborah Carter Pvt MA
John: b 1763 d 9-2-1851 m (2)Margaret Kilpatrick Tms NJ
John: b 1747 d p. 1813 m Mary VanOrden Pvt NY
Joseph: b 1- -1765 d 1838 m Judia — Pvt SC
Josiah: b 9-18-1722 d 11-10-1798 m Millicent Stoddard PS CT
Justus: b 1-28-1762 d 2-14-1819 m Abi Stanley Pvt Arfr CT W ★
Justus: b 12-8-1750 d 1-8-1827 m (1)Keturah Andrus (2)Mary Belden (3)Lois Andrus (4)Ruth Barber Pvt CT
Richard: b 1-2-1735/36 d a. 6- -1795 m Hannah Winship Pvt MA
Robert: b 4-26-1762 d 2-13-1855 m (1)Anne Frances (2)Lydia Deming Pvt CT ★
Robert: b. 4-15-1755 d 3-8-1848 m Sarah Hubbard Pvt MA
Roswell: b 1750 d 1816 m Ann Hull Drm CT
Samuel: b 10-21-1752 d 1-31-1840 m Dorcas Sexton Pvt MA
Stephen: b 7-25-1757 d 9-26-1821 m Nancy Green Pvt MA
Thomas: b 3-24-1759 d 8-31-1845 m Mary Huey OrdlSgt PA ★
Thomas: b c. 1757 d a. 4-6-1801 m Susanna Bottom Sol VA
Thomas Davis: b 11-23-1764 d 5-9-1836 m Eunice Millett Smn MA
Titus: b 8-12-1760 d 12-21-1837 m Chloe — Pvt CT ★
Wm.: b 1-21-1754 d 5-28-1831 m Agnes Loomis Pvt CT ★
Wm.: b 3-21-1730 d 3-13-1818 m Phoebe Woodhouse Capt MA
Wm.: b 5-7-1737 d 11-22-1808 m Esther Knapp Pvt MA
Wm.: b 1738 d p. 1820 m (1)Mrs Elizabeth Stiles (2)Sarah Allen Pvt VA ★
Wm.: b 4-28-1763 d 1847 m Mary Romine Sol VA

FRANCISCO,
Cornelius: b 12-4-1759 d 1-12-1837 m Anna Demorest Pvt NY ★
George: b 1739 d 1809 m Mary Murray CS Sol VA
Henry: b 6-11-1686 d 10-25-1820 m (2)Ruth Fuller Pvt NY ★
Levi: b 3-3-1757 d 1-7-1844 m Sarah VanDerKock Pvt NY ★
Michael: b 1-12-1762 d 10-23-1848 m Hannah Wager Pvt NY
Peter: b 1760 d 12-16-1831 m (1)Susannah Anderson (2)Catherine Fauntleroy Brook (3)Mary B (Grymes) West Pvt VA ★
Richard: b c. 1748 d p. 1790 m Elizabeth Oller Pvt NY

FRANK, (includes FRANCK)
Adam: b 3-15-1744 d 6-23-1834 m Catherine Moyer Pvt NY
Adam: b 6-10-1722 d 12-6-1819 m (3)Juliana Omet Dr NY
Baltzer: b c. 1761 d 3- -1796 m Mary Hillibish Pvt PA
Conrad: b 5-14-1755 d 9-10-1800 m Sarah Bowers Pvt PA
David: b 1745 d 1822 m Margarita Carol Sgt NY
Edward: b 9-1-1753 d p. 1813 m Elizabeth Averett CS NC
Frederick: b 1718 d 1798 m Eva — Lt NY
Hendrick: b 1758 d p. 1816 m Mary Myers Pvt NY
Henry, Sr.: b c. 1745 d 1-19-1840 m — Pvt NY
James: b 12-15-1752 d 11-9-1839 m Roxana White Pvt MA ★
John: b 3-23-1756 d 4-19-1840 m Abigail Weeber OrdlSgt PS NY ★
John: b 1760 d 1793 m Sarah Williams Sol NC
John: b 4- -1759 d 10-29-1854 m (1)Polly — (2)Jane Walker McLean Pvt PA
John Michael: b 10-15-1753 d 4-9-1830 m Catharine Oak Pvt NY ★
Lawrence: b 1750 — 1749 d 4-6-1813 m Mary Myers Pvt NY
Robert: b c. 1736 d p. 5-3-1792 m Elizabeth — PS VA
Timothy: b c 1744 d c. 1822 m Ann Elizabeth Bellinger Lt NY
Valentine: b 5-12-1754 d 12-23-1799 m Catharine Kinser Pvt PA
Wm.: b 4-15-1731 d 11-15-1804 m Barbara Walk CS Sol NC

FRANKENBURGER, (includes FRANKENBERGER)
Lewis: b 1750-54 d 1821/22 m Mary Catherine — Pvt PA
Philip: b 2-28-1752 d 9-4-1821 m Hannah Paup Pvt PA

FRANKENFIELD, (includes FRANKENFELT)
Adam: b 1746 d 2-15-1833 m — Pvt PA
Philip Peter: b 11-18-1735 d 3-3-1815 m Maafa Mill Pvt PA

FRANKFORD,
John: b 8-11-1754 d 11-18-1808 m Jane Rutherford Lt PA

FRANKLIN,
Aaron, Jr.: b 3-24-1761 d 1854 m Mary Stowel Pvt VT
Absolom: b 8-4-1764 d 9-3-1835 m Margaret — Pvt VA
Arnold: b c. 1734/35 d p. 1778 m Abigail Foster Pvt PA
Asa: b 1-28-1739/40 d 1-26-1801 m Sarah Paine Lt RI
Benjamin: b 1742 d a. 1791 m — Wilcocks Cpl PA
Benjamin: b 1-17-1706 d 4-17-1790 m Deborah Reed SDI PA
Benjamin: b c. 1760 d 1815 m — Carter Pvt SC
Charles: b c. 1760 d p. 1790 m — Pvt SC
Daniel: b 7-8-1728 d 2-3-1818 m Beriah Titus Pvt MA
David: b 1734 d 1782 m Mary Hubbard Pvt CT
Deborah Morris: b 9-15-1736 d 9-23-1787 m John Franklin PS NY
Ezra: b 8-15-1752 d 1- -1846 m Mary Waters Pvt CT ★
George: b 1744 d 1816 m Vashti Mercer PS Pvt GA
Henry: b c. 1728 d p. 4-1-1792 m Margaret — Sol VA
Henry Johnson: b c. 1741 d 8-3-1800 m Mary Williams Sgt MA
Ichabod, Sr.: b 7-1-1713 d p. 1790 m Easter Porter PS NH
Ichabod, Jr.: b 4-28-1739 d p. 1800 m (1)Molly Whitman (2)Hannah — (3)Loisa McDowell Pvt PS NH
Jabez: b 1759 d 2-25-1828 m Sarah Starr Cpl VT
James: b c. 1750 d a. 3-10-1813 m Anne Crews Capt VA
James: b 1750 d 1828 m Mary Lauderdale Cpl VA

FRANKLIN, contd.
Jerusha Hicock: b 8-17-1740 d 4-15-1781 m Roswell Franklin PS PA
Jesse: b 3-24-1760 d 8-31-1824 m Meeky Perkins Maj NC
Joel: b 9-23-1757 d 9-23-1807 m Susan Lewis Pvt VA
John: b 9-23-1749 d 3-1-1831 m Lydia E. Doolittle Capt CT PA
John: b 4-27-1732 d 8-29-1801 m Deborah Morris PS NY PA
John: b 1753 d 1790 m Susan Wells Lt VA
John: b c. 1760 d 5-29-1820 m Agnes Walker Sol VA ★
Jonathan: b c. 1715 d 7-3-1778 m — Pvt PA
Jonathan: b 3-15-1753 d p. 1832 m (1)Bethiah Grant (2)Mrs Betsey
    Wallace Sgt MA ★
Joseph: b c. 1750 d 11-27-1781 m Elizabeth Ebright 2Lt PA
Joshua: b 7-9-1759 d 2-9-1834 m Laurana Allen Pvt RI ★
Lewis: b 1758 d 4-11-1842 m Polly Ann Lewis Pvt Wgn VA ★
Moses: b 10-24-1763 d 2-4-1854 m Hannah Baringer Pvt VT ★
Nathan: b 12-26-1762 d 6-21-1859 m Sarah Franklin Pvt NY
Owen: b c. 1750 d a. 2-12-1795 m Betesey Steele Capt PS VA
Philip, Sr.: b 2-25-1707 d 2-5-1797 m Rachel Horton Pvt VT
Philip, Jr.: b 1747 d 12-8-1813 m Bethana Rounds Pvt VT
Record: b 1728-30 d — m Rachel Hodges PS MA
Robert: b 1741 d p. 4-1-1825 m Jane Lewis Sol VA
Roswell, Sr.: b 1740 d 1791/92 m (1)Jerusha Hicock (2)Mrs Lester
    Lt CT
Samuel: b 12-29-1762 d 5- -1836 m Rachel Powell Pvt VA ★
Squire: b 6-5-1756 d 2-22-1837 m Anna Westcott Pvt RI ★
Thomas: b 3-22-1734 d — m Mary Rhoads PS PA
Thomas: b 1740 d 1789 m Priscilla — Pvt PS SC
Thomas: b 9- -1758/9 d 3-23-1841 m Letitia Evans Pvt VA ★
Wm., Sr.: b 1733 d 2-13-1797 m Mary — Pvt GA
Wm.: b c. 1754 d 1-20-1806 m (1)Isabella Franklin (2)Charity
    Collison Pvt MD
Wilson: b 4-10-1752 d p. 1810 m Elizabeth Perry Cpl Wgn MA

FRANKS,
Anthony: b c. 1751 d 1820 m Martha Cooke Pvt NC
Henry: b 1751 d p. 1833 m Margaret VanBuskirk Pvt PA ★
Henry: b 6-29-1763 d 5-5-1836 m Christina Mason Pvt PA ★
Jacob: b a. 1728 d 1790 m Mary Ann Ashley Pvt NC
Michael: b c. 1733 d 1814 m Elizabeth Livengood Pvt PA
Nehemiah: b c. 1730 d 11-6-1799 m Mary Peake PS SC
Samuel: b 5-4-1763 d 11-30-1845 m Polly Garner Pvt SC W ★

FRANTZ, (includes FRANCE)
Abraham: b c. 1739 d 1782 m Catharine Dorfi Pvt PA
Adam: b 9-6-1755 d c. 1836 m Sallie Shirk Sgt PA ★
George: b 1750 d 2- -1835 m Mary Frantz Pvt PA
Jacob: b 7-17-1760 d 1841 m Mary Bouck Pvt NY ★
Jacob: b 1745 d 11-4-1819 m Susannah Conrad Pvt PA
John: b 1725 d 1819 m — Pvt PA
John: b c. 1758-62 d 12-26-1842 m Catherine Fones Pvt VA ★
Ludwig: b 11-8-1747 d 1805 m Margaretha — Pvt PA
Mary: b c. 1730 d 5- -1815 m John France, Sr. PS VA
Peter: b 1751 d 4-26-1836 m (2)Elizabeth Snyder Pvt MD ★
Sebastian: b 1732 d 1805 m Magdalena Fritz Pvt PA
Wilhelmus: b 9-16-1754 d 7-13-1848 m Hannah Brink Pvt NY ★

FRARY,
Elisha: b 8-18-1729 d 7-8-1801 m Miriam Warner Pvt MA
Nathan: b 1719 d 5-20-1794 m (1)Elizabeth Barnard (2)Mrs
    Eleanor (Warriner) (Cooley) Barnard Capt MA
Obadiah: b 5-20-1717 d 8-20-1804 m (1)Eunice — (2)Dinah Corse
    PS MA
Phineas: b 4-20-1755 d 5-27-1816 m Rhoda Morton Drm MA
Seth, 5th: b 9-2-1758 d 2-24-1847 m Esther Scott Sgt MA

FRATTS,
Nicholas: b 1760 d 2-20-1809 m Elizabeth Johnson Pvt NY

FRAUNCES,
Samuel: b — d — m Elizabeth — PS NY

FRAVELL,
Henry: b c. 1730 d p. 1-18-1819 m Anna Keller PS VA

FRAZEE,
Benjamin: b c. 1755 d p. 1800 m (1)Susannah — (2)Mrs Phoebe
    Littell Pvt NJ
Benoni: b 1-31-1757 d p. 1798 m Sarah Oliver Pvt NJ
Henry: b c. 1747 d 1-1-1795 m Sarah Maxwell Pvt NJ
Jonas: b 8-4-1759 d 10-7-1858 m (1)Nancy Corwin (2)Sarah Ackley
    Sol NJ ★
Moses: b 1-18-1762 d 3-28-1840 m Priscilla Morris Pvt NJ
Samuel: b 11-5-1753 d 11-12-1849 m Rebecca Jacobs Pvt VA
Wm.: b 4-20-1760 d p. 1817 m Mary Day Pvt NJ

FRAZIER, (includes FRASER, FRAYSER, FRAZER, FRAZOR)
Aaron: b 11-15-1745 d p. 4-12-1780 m Jane Condry PS PA
Alexander: b 1722 d 5-6-1791 m Mary Grimke CS SC
Anthony: b 3-22-1754 d 3-4-1804 m Hannah Herndon 2Lt VA
Daniel: b 1-22-1742 d a. 10-30-1803 m Abigail Haladay Pvt CT
Daniel: b 11-21-1757 d 2-26-1853 m Polly Dix Pvt Sct MA
George: b 10-31-1756 d p. 11-10-1813 m Rebekah Smith Pvt MD

Jackson: b 1761 d 1821 m Mildred Hobson PS VA
James: b c. 1755 d 11-6-1818 m Deborah Emory Lt DE
James: b 1760 d p. 1840 m Elizabeth Hubbard Pvt MD
James: b 12-23-1758 d 12-20-1798 m (1)M. — Thomas (2)Sarah
    Ann Herndon (3)Lucy Smith Sgt VA
James: b a. 1745 d p. 1804 m Jane Anderson Pvt VA
James Carr: b c. 1758 d 9-3-1822 m Margaret Walker Pvt VA
Jeremiah: b 1-20-1763 d 8-16-1847 m — Day Pvt NY ★
Jesse: b 2-5-1764 d 3-28-1827 m Neriah Hobson Sol VA
John: b 1756 d 3-26-1825 m Lenah Bodine Lt GA ★
John: b 7-7-1725 d 9-10-1802 m — Pvt NY
John: b c. 1737 d 1799 m Abigail Millican PS NC
John: b 1733 d 1790 m Mehitable Parsons Pvt PA
John: b — d p. 9-14-1799 m Lydia — Sol SC
John: b — d 1779 m Martha Milligan PS SC
John: b c. 1760 d 1- -1796 m Elizabeth Fox Lt VA
John: b c. 1732 d 8-5-1816 m — Pvt VA
John: b 1760 d 4-24-1810 m Susannah Rebecca Story Pvt VA
Leven: b 5-10-1764 d 7-5-1842 m Elizabeth Eccleston 1Lt PS MD ★
Michajah: b c. 1735 d 1792 m Mary Watson CS NC
Micajah: b 12-25-1753 d 11-9-1843 m Susan Hamilton Pvt VA ★
Persifor: b c. 8-10-1736 d 4-24-1792 m Mary Worrall Taylor BGen
    PS PA
Samuel: b 4- -1749 d 4- -1839 m Rebecca Julien Sol SC
Thomas: b 1760 d 4-2-1844 m Elizabeth Fowler Pvt Mar NC ★
Wm.: b 1752 d 9-24-1817 m Mary Clark Capt DE
Wm.: b 1759 d 2-1-1844 m Jean Lafferty Grd Sct Spy PA
Wm.: b 1730 d a. 12- -1796 m Philadelphia — CaptLt VA
Wm.: b c. 1760 d a. 1795 m Mary Evans Richeson PS VA

FREDERICK, (includes FREDERICKS, FREDRICK, FRIDERICK)
Andrew: b 1734 d p. 1778 m Margaret — CS SC
Felix: b 1748 d 7-13-1832 m Catherine Norris Pvt Cmsry NC ★
Jacob: bpt 6-5-1743 d p. 1-13-1815 m Margaret Young Sol NY
Joseph: b 1742 d 6-8-1822 m Jerusha Pease NS MA
Peter: b 1-10-1750 d 9-25-1814 m Margaretha — Pvt PA
Thomas C.: b 2- -1751 d 5-3-1808 m Ann Margaret Tibbens Pvt PS
    PA

FREEBORN,
Henry: b 6-18-1755 d 10-12-1835 m Mary Simpson Ens RI

FREEDLEY,
Henry: b 1756 d 10-3-1823 m Catherine Isette Sol PA

FREELAND,
Frisby: b 1747 d 4-12-1819 m Sarah Rolle PS Capt MD
Jacob: b c. 1723 d a. 1782 m Dianne Dair PS MD
James: b 12-12-1743 d 10-5-1796 m Mehitabel Mellen Dr MA
James: b c. 1730 d a. 7-24-1805 m Elizabeth — CS NC
John: b c. 1736 d p. 1790 m X Pvt NC
John: b 1759 d 1-13-1851 m Mary — Pvt PA
Robert: b 1762 d 1841 m X Pvt NJ NY ★

FREELOVE,
Thomas: b 1755 d 4-2-1830 m Nancy Read Pvt MA

FREEMAN, (includes FREMAN, FREMOND)
Aaron: b 1-30-1758 d 11-26-1821 m Judith Fleetwood Sgt NC ★
Abiel: b 3-27-1762 d 5-7-1840 m Abigail Stanley Pvt MA ★
Abraham: b 10-10-1743 d 12-29-1828 m Abigail Clarkson Capt NJ
Alden: b 1760 d 5-6-1842 m (2)Precilla Washburn Pvt MA
Alexander: b 3-13-1762 d 1840/1 m Margaret Brown Pvt NJ ★
Alexander: b 6-4-1763 d 1814 m Phebe (Clarkson) Wilson Pvt NJ
Amos: b 10-31-1748 d 4-15-1833 m Mary Crane Pvt NJ
Ashbell: b 11-20-1755 d 6-9-1823 m (1)Anna Crane (2)Zeviah Free-
    Freeman Pvt NJ
Barnabas: b 2-23-1736/7 d 1-17-1781 m Bethia Knowles Pvt PS MA
Benjamin: b 9-9-1725 d 1-5-1784 m Sarah Nye Pvt MA
Benjamin: b 1745 d 6-26-1834 m Hannah Bradfrod Sgt MA ★
Benjamin: b 1-10-1717/8 d 12-10-1786 m (1)Sarah Dillingham
    (2)Mrs Susanna Bangs PS MA
Benjamin, Sr.: b 6-3-1713 d 1-17-1789 m (1)Rachel — (2)Mrs
    Esther (Marsh) Cutler Wgn NJ
Brewster: b 3-27-1765 d 12-9-1823 m Prudence Allen Pvt MA
Chandler: b c. 1756 d 12- -1841 m Elizabeth Millett Pvt MA
Charles: b 7-7-1764 d 5-27-1842 m Rhoda Sutton Drm RI ★
Christopher: b 1-3-1719 d 1798 m Anne E. Claiborne Sol VA
Comfort: b 8-23-1750 d 12-1-1806 m Lucy Walker Sgt MA
Cyrus: b 3-27-1761 d 11-22-1839 m Eunice Williams Pvt NJ ★
Daniel: b — d 1836 m Matilda Freeman Pvt CT ★
Daniel: b 3-23-1733 d 5-5-1806 m Mercy Gates Lt PS CT
Edmund: b 9-30-1711 d 2-11-1800 m Martha Otis PS CT
Edmund: b 3-2-1759 d 4-3-1831 m Ruth Wiley Pvt MA
Edmund, Jr.: b 4-29-1737 d 1813 m (1)Sarah Porter (2)Theoda
    (Porter) Estabrook Capt NH
Edmund: b 8-29-1764 d 9-26-1854 m Zilpha Poole Pvt VT ★
Elijah: b 2-17-1754 d 12-10-1836 m (2)Pernel Follett Sgt NY ★
Elisha: b 11-21-1741 d 1-20-1823 m Elizabeth Percival Lt MA
Elkanah: bpt 1760 d 10-2-1834 m Polly Myrick Cpl MA ★
Enoch: b 5-19-1706 d 9-2-1788 m Mary Wright PS Col MA
Enoch: b 4-11-1754 d 11-12-1844 m Elizabeth Eldridge Pvt NH ★

Frederick: b 10-8-1755 d 6-19-1818 m (1)Abigail Thompson
(2)Abigail Dimmick MM CT
Gideon: b 9-16-1749 d p. 1792 m Eunice Ford Sgt NY
Henry: b 2-2-1760 d 3-27-1838 m Susannah Bloodgood Fif Smn
NJ ★
Henry: b 6-30-1761 d 1-20-1835 m Rachel Freeman Pvt NJ
Henry, Sr.: b 3-23-1717 d 7-16-1784 m Mary Read PS NJ
Holman, Sr.: b c. 1728-30 d a. 1784 m Sally Cox CS GA
Howell: b 1760 d 5-4-1836 m (1)Elizabeth — (2)Hannah Doty Pvt
NC ★
Isaac: b 8-28-1759 d 1-12-1823 m Jane Clark Sgt MA
Isaac: b 1733 d 8-8-1807 m Thankful Higgins Smn MA
Isaac: b 9-14-1747 d 5-18-1824 m Elizabeth Elston Pvt NJ
Isaac: b 12-1755 d 1-1-1841 m Marion Gallop Pvt NY
Isaac: b c. 2-3-1744 d 1821 m Elizabeth — Pvt PA
Israel: b 4-23-1744 d p. 4-   -1833 m Louise Miller Pvt MM NJ
Jacob: b c. 1742 d p. 1810 m (1)Mary Stiles (2)Sarah Heyer Pvt NJ
James, Jr.: b 12-5-1742 d 1820 m Lydia Ford Pvt NY
John: b 3-15-1747 d p. 1799 m Hannah Bicknell Cpl CT
John: b 1756 d 5-29-1806 m Catherine — Lt CS GA
John: b 5-23-1760 d 10-22-1847 m Prudence Follett Pvt MA ★
John: b c. 1750 d c. 1830 m (1)Elizabeth Marshall (2)Mrs Mary
Bishop Pvt NJ
John, Sr.: b c. 1740 d p. 9-17-1797 m Martha Lynn PS NC
John: b 9-18-1756 d 3-27-1844 m Phebe Osten Pvt VA ★
John, Jr.: b 3-15-1764 d 2-5-1841 m Rebecca Read Pvt VA ★
Jonathan: b 5-18-1739 d 6-11-1816 m Sarah Parker Pvt MA
Jonathan: b 3-21-1745 d 8-20-1808 m Sarah Huntington Lt NH
Jonathan: b 8-10-1764 d 11-10-1843 m (1)Margaret Bloodgood
(2)Phebe Barron Pvt NJ ★
Joseph: b 1727 d 3-12-1792 m Caroline Chandler Sgt MA
Joshua: b c. 1745 d 9-   -1832 m (1)Lucy King (2)Margaret — PS NC
Joshua: b 4-10-1764 d 7-4-1828 m Joanna Jones Pvt VT
Matthew: b 5-22-1734 d 5-10-1824 m Margaret Cotheal Capt NJ
Melancthon: b 1746 d 11-   -1806 m Sarah Haines Dr NJ
Michael: b 3-1-1764 d 2-9-1842 m X Pvt NC ★
Moody: b 4-25-1753 d 7-16-1828 m Kezia Freeman Cpl NH
Nathan: b 5-30-1762 d 9-10-1849 m Polly Rice Pvt MA
Nathaniel, Sr.: b 3-9-1712 d 9-6-1791 m Martha — CS CT
Nathaniel: b 3-28-1741 d 9-20-1827 m (1)Tryphosa Colton
(2)Elizabeth (Handy) Gifford BG CS MA
Nathaniel: b 9-29-1740 d 7-22-1793 m Bethia Hodges Pvt MA
Peter: b c. 1760 d p. 1790 m Mary Gammet Sol FrA
Philip: b 1751 d p. 9-12-1837 m Nancy — Pvt NJ ★
Philip: b 1743 d 7-5-1829 m Mary Barbara Bonjour Pvt VA
Phineas: b 1-7-1748 d 11-2-1797 m Martha Morrison Sgt CT
Prince: b 1738 d 1782 m Martha Freeman Pvt MA
Ralph: b 2-17-1740 d p. 1780 m Mrs Phebe Thompson Pvt MA
Reuben: b 7-21-1740 d p. 1790 m Catherine — Pvt MA
Richard: b 1750 d 6-16-1841 m Hannah Lighthall PS Pvt NY ★
Robert, Sr.: b 12-31-1727 d 9-29-1798 m Anna — Maj PS NY
Robert, Jr.: b 7-16-1757 d 5-28-1813 m Elizabeth Williams SolPS NY
Robert: b 1751 d 1810 m Martha Garrett PM VA
Rufus: b 1762 d 7-15-1847 m (1)Phebe Mason (2)Ruth — Pvt MM
NH ★
Russell: b 7-17-1750 d 12-18-1805 m Abia Durkee Pvt NH
Samuel: b 2-1-1753 d 10-11-1837 m Jemima Bigelow Cpl CT ★
Samuel: b 6-15-1743 d 6-15-1831 m (1)Mary Fowle (2)Elizabeth
Ilsley Jones PS MA
Samuel: b c. 1715 d 5-   -1796 m Elizabeth Alexander PS CS NC
Seth: b 2-22-1732 d 7-19-1812 m Experience Hatch PS MA
Silas: b 3-4-1735 d p. 1810 m Mary Brewster Pvt MA
Silas: b 10-11-1746 d 9-8-1837 m Elizabeth Kasson Pvt MA
Skeff: b 9-22-1755 d 1-3-1847 m Mary Aspenwall Pvt CT
Stephen: b 1-24-1759 d 1837 m Ann Baker Pvt NJ ★
Sylvanus: b 4-16-1740 d p. 1790 m Leah Brainerd Pvt CT
Thomas: b 5-1-1743 d p. 1777 m Sarah Southworth Pvt CT
Thomas: b 1748/9 d 12-18-1803 m Sarah Moore Wgn NJ
Thomas: b —— d p. 7-   -1784 m Sallie Mitchell Pvt PA
Thomas: b 3-29-1731 d 5-29-1812 m Phoebe Hall Pvt VT
Thomas: b 4-1-1762 d 2-2-1848 m Rebecca Swift Pvt VT ★
Thomas: b 1749 d 1792 m Susan Latham Pvt VA
Timothy: b 5-4-1747 d 1825 m Zerviah Nickerson Pvt MA
Timothy: b 1758 d 8-21-1839 m Mary Ann Wickwire Pvt MA RI ★
Walter: b 8-20-1759 d 4-8-1810 m Pamelia Child Pvt Arfr MA
Wm.: b 1745 d 1815 m Mary Shotwell Pvt NJ
Wm.: b 10-14-1751 d — m X Pvt NJ
Wm.: b c. 1744 d p. 3-25-1802 m Sarah — PS NC
Wm.: b 1715-20 d 1782 m Tabitha Wilson Sol NC
Wm.: b 10-26-1759 d 1-28-1838 m Mary Bryan Pvt NC ★
Wm.: b 10-14-1751 d 1-   -1822 m — Hanks Capt SC
Wm.: b 7-22-1757 d 1813 m X Sct VT
Wm.: b 1754 d 8-2-1829 m Hannah Epperson Pvt Bbd VA ★
Zenas: b 10-9-1757 d 9-5-1800 m Hannah — Pvt NJ

FREEMIRE,
Johannes, Sr.: b 9-9-1726 d 12-   -1800 m Anna Mattice Pvt PS NY
Johannes, Jr.: b 11-13-1748 d 4-19-1835 m Dorothy Bouck Pvt NY
John: b 1711 d 1778 m X PS NY

FREER, (includes FREAR)
Abraham: b 5-19-1740 d 11-26-1823 m Sarah (Patterson) Mitchell
Pvt NY

Anthony: b 11-3-1734 d p. 1781 m Jannetje Louw Lt NY
Elisa: bpt 8-5-1739 d p. 1788 m Martha Everett Pvt NY
Garret, Jr.: bpt 4-30-1727 d p. 7-20-1804 m Maria — Pvt PS NY
Hugo: b 10-14-1691 d p. 1790 m Bregjen Terpenning PS NY
Hugo: b c. 1754 d 1818 m Maria — Pvt NY
Isaac: b 12-10-1734 d 8-30-1801 m Esther Jansen Pvt NY
Jacob: bpt 5-17-1719 d 1795 m Annitje Van Aken PS NY
Jeremiah: bpt 11-11-1756 d a. 6-2-1822 m Sara VanWagenen Pvt
PS NY
John: b 9-3-1730 d 7-11-1809 m (1)Maria Van Kleeck (2)Hannah
Platt Col NY
John J.: bpt 7-23-1758 d 1828 m Margrietje Bennett Pvt NY
Jonas: b 6-12-1737 d p. 1776 m Magdalena Bevier PS Pvt NY
Paulus: b 11-2-1747 d 8-23-1802 m Elizabeth VanWagner PS NY
Samuel: b 8-6-1762 d p. 1791 m Polly Schoonmaker Pvt NY
Simeon: b 3-10-1753 d 12-17-1818 m (1)Sarah VanKleck (2)Maria
Lemmington Cpl NY
Simon: bpt 2-12-1721 d 1797 m Catherine VanBenschoten Pvt NY
Simon: b 8-9-1741 d p. 1790 m Annetje Blanshan PS Pvt NY
Thomas: b 5-27-1741 d p. 1790 m Sara Vanderberg Pvt NY

FREESE, (includes FREAZ, FREEZE, FRIES)
Abraham: b 1749 d 1800 m Hannah Whittemore Cpl MA
Andrew: b 10-1-1747 d 10-19-1814 m Shuah Thurston PS NH
Isaac: b 1793 d 1840 m X Pvt MA
Jacob: b 10-10-1716 d 4-20-1780 m Susannah Gordon PS NH
John: b c. 1750 d 1818 m Margaret Brunner Capt PA
John: b 1759 d 1823 m Katherine Kearney Pvt PA
Martin: b 1759 d 7-7-1843 m Elizabeth Herzel Pvt PA ★
Michael: b c. 1738 d a. 7-24-1815 m Catharine Nied PS MD
Peter: b 1745 d 1835 m Catharine — Pvt PA

FREETHY,
Joseph: b 1721 d 1835 m Elizabeth Black Cpl MA

FRELIGH,
Peter: bpt 9-7-1729 d p. 10-30-1779 m Maria Wood PS NY
Samuel: b 1-1-1755 d 9-29-1838 m Elizabeth Shoemaker Pvt NY
Solomon: b 5-29-1750 d 10-8-1827 m Rachel Vanderbeck Chp NY

FRELINGHUYSEN
Frederick: b 4-13-1753 d 4-13-1804 m (1)Gertrude Schenck (2)Ann
Yard MM Col CS PS NJ

FRENCH,
Aaron: b 9-8-1739 d 8-31-1805 m (1)Mary Clark (2)Mrs Elizabeth
Fordyce PS NJ
Abel: b 2-21-1725/6 d 8-16-1800 m Elizabeth Jones PS NH
Abraham: b 8-12-1763 d 1812 m Phebe Shute Pvt MA
Adonijah: b 10-3-1758 d 1821 m Elizabeth Linfield Pvt MA
Alexander: b 5-8-1758 d 12-10-1833 m Elizabeth Morrison Pvt PA
Amos: b 3-28-1755 d 1-14-1814 m Judith Swett Pvt MA
Andrew, Sr.: b 1-22-1735 d 11-12-1779 m Ann Williams Ens NH
Asa: b 10-17-1742 d 12-3-1833 m (1)Susannah Smith (2)Thankful
(Bangs) Thrasher (3)Abigail Stone Lt MA
Asa: b 7-7-1760 d 1-30-1841 m Mary Lovejoy Pvt MA ★
Asa: b 1757 d 2-18-1842 m Sarah White Pvt MA ★
Bartholomew: b 10-18-1752 d 7-14-1830 m Susannah Gale Pvt MA
Barzilla: b 9-6-1735 d p. 1790 m Margaret Samborn PS NH
Benjamin: b 2-18-1744 d 2-20-1806 m Bathsheba Hill Sgt MA
Benjamin: b 6-2-1763 d 3-19-1811 m Mary Hartford Pvt MA
Benjamin: b 7-6-1726 d 12-15-1799 m (1)Mary Lovewell (2)Mrs
Mary Cummings PS NH
Christopher: b 3-29-1752 d 12-2-1845 m (1)Margaret Perry (2)Lydia
Perry Cpl MA
Daniel: b 8-21-1708 d 9-1-1785 m Sarah Gould PS NH
David: b 3-30-1742 d 8-29-1821 m Hannah Lines Pvt CT
David: b 7-23-1757 d 3-4-1828 m Elizabeth — Sgt MA
David: b 1755 d 2-19-1836 m (2)Hannah White Pvt NH
David: b 9-15-1754 d 6-13-1790 m Lydia Parker Pvt NH
David: b 2-6-1747 d 10-8-1838 m Sarah Wilcox Pvt NJ
David: b 1-23-1753 d 11-6-1836 m (1)Susannah Blair (2)Elizabeth
Foster Pvt NY
Dependence: b 12-25-1714 d 11-16-1803 m Mary Linfield Pvt MA
Ebenezer: b 1-29-1756 d 9-25-1826 m Rachel Hinman Pvt CT
Ebenezer: b 9-   -1738 d 5-17-1817 m Mehitable Gay Lt MA
Ebenezer: b 5-31-1731 d 4-14-1808 m (2)Susannah Hamblett Sgt MA
Ebenezer: b 4-6-1757 d 11-17-1844 m (1)Lucy Bostwock (2)Rachel
Patrick Pvt MA ★
Ebenezer: b 10-11-1760 d 9-13-1848 m Lucy Beals Pvt CT MA NY
Ebenezer, Sr.: b 8-5-1707 d 2-31-1791 m Elizabeth Hill PS MA
Ebenezer, Jr.: b 5-2-1735 d 1802 m Rebecca Kidder Drm MA
Ebenezer: b 3-24-1755 d 11-22-1839 m Mary Bachelder Pvt NH
Elijah, Jr.: b 2-10-1785 d 3-7-1798 m Susanna White Ens MA W ★
Elijah: b 11-23-1726 d 1-15-1800 m Mary Clark Sgt MA
Elijah: b 6-15-1742 d 2-3-1829 m Elizabeth Phillips Pvt MA
Elisha: b 1-12-1733 d 10-19-1818 m Mary Ludden Pvt MA
Elkanah, Sr.: b 11-9-1727 d 10-16-1808 m Sarah Willmarth 2Lt MA
Elkanah, Jr.: b 6-5-1757 d p. 1795 m Hannah Walker Pvt MA
Ephraim: b 11-25-1708 d p. 1780 m Rebecca Pomeroy PS CT
Ephraim: b 4-25-1734 d 1780 m Elizabeth Presbry Pvt MA
Ephraim: b 11-10-1751 d 9-27-1834 m Hannah Melendy Sgt NH
Ezekiel: b 10-31-1754 d 7-8-1826 m Phoebe Weed Pvt NH

FRENCH, contd.
Ezra: b 5-7-1763 d 3-13-1806 m Jane Titus Pvt MA
Gamaliel: b 4-14-1756 d 1-28-1828 m Susannah Brinsmade Pvt CT
Gould: b 9-17-1741 d 5-12-1823 m Dorothy Whittier Pvt NH
Haynes: b 5-15-1761 d 11-2-1814 m (1)Irene Larned (2)Sarah Hughes Pvt NH
Henry: b 10-7-1743 d 2-22-1810 m Miriam Jewell PS NH
Israel: b 10-8-1709 d 9-27-1788 m Sarah Loveland Pvt CT
Jabez: b 1721 d 10-9-1806 m Hannah Hills PS NH
Jacob: b 9-19-1739 d p. 12-25-1792 m Olive — Pvt MA
James: b 1758 d 7- -1807 m Mary Brinsmade Smn CT
James: b 8-2-1746 d 2-22-1828 m Tabitha Crane Pvt MA
James: b 9-22-1736 d p. 1790 m Mary Collins PS NH
James, Sr.: b c. 1738 d 9-20-1817 m Sarah Brooks Pvt NH
James, Jr.: b 6-6-1761 d 9-1-1822 m (1)Hannah Russell (2)Olive Sawyer Sol NH
James, Sr.: b 1746/7 d — m Catherine Gall Pvt NY
James: b 11-5-1756 d 1835 m Kizzie Calloway Sol KY
Jeremiah: b 6-12-1762 d 7-22-1834 m Hannah Williams Pvt NJ
Jeremiah: b 1762 d 1843 m Margaret VanGorder Pvt NJ ★
John: b 1721 d 8-31-1796 m Elizabeth Edwards Pvt CT
John: b 1733 d p. 1785 m Mary Judd Sgt MA
John: b 1-26-1749 d 7-24-1806 m Damaris Howard Sgt MA
John: b 8-11-1735 d 9-11-1823 m (1)Hayden Shaw (2)Patty Fitch Pvt MA
John: b 9-8-1755 d 4-22-1831 m Nancy Cronhite Sgt NH ★
John: b 1742 d 8-7-1783 m Jane Rutter Sol PA
John: b 3-14-1728 d 4-18-1781 m Olive Hains Pvt VT
John: b 1759 d p. 1810 m Obediance Clay Pvt VA
Jonas: b 8-17-1757 d 6-5-1840 m Betty Marshall Pvt MA
Jonathan: b 3-13-1748 d 1-29-1821 m Desire Titus Pvt MA ★
Jonathan: b 1760 d 12-18-1837 m (1)Huldah Dwinell (2)Mrs Elizabeth Cole Pvt MA ★
Jonathan: b 1763 d p. 1808 m Thankful Barker Pvt MA
Jonathan: b 1-19-1739 d 7-28-1809 m Abigail Richards PS MA
Jonathan: b 1755 d 6-28-1837 m Sarah Place Cpl NH
Jonathan: b 4-29-1760 d 7-18-1841 m (1)Rhoda Currier (2)Mary (Mills) Crawford Pvt NH ★
Jonathan: b 9-22-1751 d 5-17-1838 m Jean Blair Capt NY ★
Joseph: b 9-2-1743 d 10-15-1812 m Elizabeth Deming Sgt MA
Joseph: b 11-1-1762 d 5-20-1802 m Lydia Scarlet Fif MA
Joseph: b 2-27-1702 d 5-3-1794 m Hannah Gould PS NH
Joshua: b 3-9-1734 d 9-11-1791 m Esther Wales Pvt MA
Joshua: b 1752 d 7-28-1783 m Elizabeth Collins Cpl MA
Josiah: b 6-17-1743 d 11-2-1833 m Hannah Coburn 1Lt CS MA
Lafford: b 1753 d 9-11-1834 m (2)Elizabeth Gregory Pvt SC W ★
Martin: b 6-5-1735 d 1786 m Priscilla Anderson Pvt MD
Mason: b c. 1759/60 d p. 7-13-1817 m Ann Lewis 2Lt VA
Matthew: b 2-2-1737 d 1814 m Sarah Payne Pvt VA
Moses: b 9-16-1731 d 1-19-1807 m Elizabeth Hobart Capt MA
Moses: b 12-20-1736 d p. 1790 m Mary Dearborn PS NH
Nathan: b 2-3-1760 d 8-30-1837 m (1)Persis Sheldon (2)Mary Thorp Pvt MA ★
Nathaniel: b 2- -1755 d 12-18-1818 m Bethiah — Pvt MA
Nathaniel: b 4-11-1760 d 11-29-1834 m Susannah Brown Pvt MA
Nathaniel: b 1757 d 1799 m Martha Jewell Pvt NH
Nathaniel: b 4-1-1709 d 4-22-1791 m Abigel Easman PS NH
Nathaniel, Sr.: b 2-2-1721 d 6- -1801 m (1)Elizabeth Frost (2)Joanna Kingsley PS VT
Nathaniel, Jr.: b 1747 d 6-10-1811 m Betty (Nourse) Duncan Pvt VT
Nehemiah: b 3-29-1746 d 11- -1826 m Submit Seeman Pvt NH W ★
Nicholas: b 11-28-1747 d 1-7-1826 m Anne Pike PS NH
Noah: b 1754 d 11-14-1843 m (1)Mary Rolph (2)Joanna Ralph Campbell PS Pvt NJ
Offin: b 7- -1761 d p. 1811 m Susannah Pressey Pvt NH
Ozias: b 5-4-1761 d 1-26-1809 m Elizabeth Dayton Pvt MA
Reuben: b 5-15-1741 d 11-26-1808 m Anna Frost Pvt MA
Robert, Sr.: b 4-9- d 3-15-1813 m Mary Willis PS NJ
Robert, Jr.: b 1754 d 1-28-1830 m Rachel (Drew) Osborn Pvt NJ
Roger: b 9-18-1760 d 8-23-1850 m Achsah Tobey Pvt MA ★
Samuel: b 1-17-1753 d 9-3-1833 m Rebecca Sherman Sgt CT ★
Samuel: b — d 11-24-1814 m (1)Sarah Hall (2)Mary Beardsley PS CT
Samuel: b 7-23-1704 d 2-2-1783 m Martha Chapman PS CT
Samuel: b 9-4-1751 d 3-26-1830 m Lucy Pierce Sgt MA
Samuel: b 5-12-1753 d 6-17-1832 m Lydia Warner Cpl MA
Samuel: b 9-17-1748 d 7-8-1814 m Sarah Heulings Pvt NJ
Silas: b 1752 d 7-2-1837 m Sarah — Pvt NH ★
Sylvanus: b 6-6-1763 d 10-20-1840 m (1)Hannah Thayer (2)Azubah Penniman Pvt MA ★
Thomas: b 4-16-1722 d 9-16-1793 m Keziah Perry Pvt MA
Thomas: b 10-2-1742 d 4-22-1819 m Salome Babcock Pvt MA
Thomas: b 3-28-1751 d 9- -1822 m Hannah Wild Pvt MA
Thomas: b 5-10-1738 d p. 1790 m Mary Glidden 2Lt NH
Truman: b 1750 d 1820 m Deborah Beers Fif CT ★
Wm.: b 5-24-1744 d p. 1793 m Susannah Morgan Pvt PS MD
Wm.: b 3-8-1763 d 1818-22 m Annie Gibson Mus MD
Wm.: b 1-25-1744 d 8-15-1838 m Elizabeth Avery Sgt MA ★
Wm.: b 11-2-1751 d 6-13-1821 m Mary Perkins Cpl MA
Wm.: c. 1740 d 1829 m Hannah Harvey Pvt MA
Wm.: b 1-25-1712/13 d 1793 m Tabitha Pierce Pvt NH
Wm.: b 3-14-1735 d 1803 m Susan Robie CS NH

Wm.: b 8-15-1741 d 4-21-1834 m Nancy MacGenot Pvt PA ★
Zenas: b 4-15-1760 d 12-22-1838 m (1)Relief Thayer (2)Ruth White Pvt Drm MA

FRENEAU,
Philip: b 1-2-1752 d 12-18-1832 m Eleanor Forman PS NJ

FRESHCORN,
Leonard: b c. 1740 d 9-8-1809 m Mrs Margaret Benner Pvt PA

FRESHOUR,
John: b 5-13-1756 d 10-13-1841 m (1)— Dawson (2)Margaret Funkhauser Pvt VA ★
Wendle: b c. 1722 d p. 8-20-1793 m Mary — PS VA

FRETWELL,
Richard: b 12-24-1752 d 1842 m (1)Frances Harris (2)Mary Whitherspoon Pvt VA ★

FRETZ,
Christian: b 1734 d 5-1-1803 m Barbara Oberholtzer Pvt PA
Christian, Jr.: b c. 1750 d p. 1800 m Judith Kulp Pvt PA
Jacob: b 1732 d p. 1790 m Catherine Magdalene Nash Pvt PS PA
John: b 5-24-1758 d 12-20-1804 m Anna Kratz Pvt PA
Marck: b 12- -1750 d 2-24-1840 m Elizabeth Rosenberger Pvt PA

FREW,
Alexander: b 1737 d 9-8-1819 m Ann — Pvt PA

FREYMAN,
George: b 1706 d 1790-1800 m Sabina Lerch PS PA

FRICK,
Abraham: b 6-20-1759 d 2-5-1842 m Christiana Long (Royer) Zug Pvt PA
Christian: b 9-2-1745 d p. 5- -1812 m (1)Anna Witmer (2)Elizabeth Herr Pvt PA
Jacob: b 1751/2 d 1839 m Elizabeth Earnhart Pvt NC ★
Jacob: b 3-23-1717 d 3-23-1799 m (1)Elizabeth Urner (2)Catherine — PS PA
John: b 4-8-1757 d 3-24-1822 m (1)Catharine Grumbacher (2)Mrs Susanna Bartlett Pvt PA
John: b 2-5-1760 d 3-11-1811 m Elizabeth Young Sgt PA

FRICKER,
Andrew: b c. 1733 d c. 1785 m Maria Magdalena — 1Lt PA

FRIDIG,
Gabriel: b 1752 d 6-12-1830 m — Geiger Capt SC

FRIEBELE,
Urban: b c. 1732 d 2- -1793 m X Pvt PA

FRIED,
Henry: b 8-16-1754 d 9-20-1820 m Veronica Schleiffer Pvt PS PA

FRIEDLINE,
Ludwick: b c. 1736 d 6-23-1784 m Marget — Pvt PA

FRIEND,
Edward: b 5-1-1728 d 1-13-1806 m Phebe Osborne CtyLt VA
Gabriel: b 6-17-1761 d p. 12-12-1849 m (1)Elizabeth Bonnell (2)Clara Ann Peck PS Spy 1Lt MD
Jacob: b 1705 d 1789 m Elizabeth Skidmore PS VA
James: b 4-11-1741 d 3-4-1831 m (1Mrs Ann Pratt (2)Mrs Susanna Trow Cpl MA
John: b c. 1732 d p. 1808 m Kerrenhappuch Hyatt Pvt MD
Joseph: b c. 1741 d 1806 m Rachel Rose Pvt PA
Joseph: b c. 1746 d p. 2-14-1822 m Elizabeth Bass Capt VA
Joseph, Sr.: b c. 1735 d 11-15-1827 m Elizabeth Skidmore Capt VA
Nathaniel: b 12-16-1764 d 2-20-1848 m Polly Butman Pvt MA
Tobias: b 9-4-1752 d 7-8-1829 m Anne Margaret Hearsh Pvt PS PA
Wm.: b 4-27-1738 d 1-29-1781 m Elizabeth Hodge Capt MA

FRIERSON,
John: b 1727 d 1797 m Margaret Smith Lt SC
Robert: b 3-6-1743 d 6-9-1808 m Elizabeth McAuley Pvt SC
Thomas: b p. 1730 d p. 1780 m Mary Wilson Pvt SC
Wm.: b c. 1730-2 d p. 1790 m Margarit Gordon Capt SC

FRIETSCH,
Johannes: b 7-14-1744 d 9-13-1823 m Maria Pfaltzgraff PS PA

FRINK,
Andrew: b 12-31-1730 d 9-25-1806 m Sarah Kimball 2Lt CT
Henry: b 2-19-1749 d 8-31-1810 m (1)Desire Palmer (2)Hannah — Pvt NY
Isaac, Jr.: b 7-20-1741 d p. 10- -1782 m Margaret Stanton Pvt CT
Isaac: b 2-4-1761 d 9-13-1834 m Elizabeth Wainwright Sol NY
Israel: b 8-25-1752 d 12-7-1814 m Esther Philips Pvt MA
John: b 5-6-1743 d 1-27-1789 m Mary Tiffany 1Lt CT
John, Sr.: b 10-2-1732 d 1-29-1821 m Anna Wilcox Pendleton Pvt MA

John, Jr.: b 9-12-1750 d 11-3-1823 m Chloe Wright Pvt MA
John: b 9-7-1731 d 9-27-1805 m Elizabeth Davis Pvt MA
Nathan: b 9-10-1765 d 7-17-1843 m Clarissa Tupper Pvt CT ★
Nathan: b 4-8-1759 d p. 1806 m Olive Berry Pvt CT
Samuel: b 3-4-1763 d 3-30-1846 m Esther Nichols Ens MA
Seth: b 3-17-1758 d p. 1793 m Prudence White Pvt CT
Thomas: b 1762/3 d 6- -1852 m Sylvia Pendleton Cpl Fif MA ★
Thomas: b 6-17-1738 d 5-24-1786 m Abigail Willard Dr NH

FRIPP,
John: b c. 1750 d p. 1788 m Martha Scott Pvt SC

FRISBIE, (includes FRISBEE & FRISBY)
Amos: b 2-17-1728/9 d 11-16-1811 m Mary Frisbie Ens CT
Benjamin: b 4-28-1736 d p. 1777 m Margaret Holley Pvt NY
Caleb: b 9-7-1750 d 1791 m Ester Barker Pvt CT
Ebenezer: b 5-29-1757 d 6-22-1830 m Eunice Moseley Pvt CT
Elisha, Sr.: b 8-20-1716 d 1784 m Rachel Levi AM CT
Elisha, Jr.: b 6-22-1754/5 d 10-12-1809 m (1)Martha Harrison (2)Sibbell Dudley Cnt CT
Hezekiah: b 7-11-1738 d 2-28-1817 m Susannah Marvin Capt CT
Ichabod Culpepper: b 8-1-1760 d 11-22-1845 m Thankful Moss Pvt CT
Israel, Jr.: b 6-22-1754 d 2-8-1825 m (1)Active Foot (2)Esther Tyler Sgt CT
Jabez: b 11-30-1730 d 1799 m Jerusha — Pvt CT
Jacob: b 1726 d 9-16-1798 m Ruth Porter MM CT
John: b 12-1-1731 d 2-18-1817 m Freelove Rogers Pvt CT
Jonah: b 12-14-1734 d 1806 m Elizabeth Hickox Lt MA
Jonah: b 8-12-1766 d 8-27-1820 m Amy — Drm Pvt MA ★
Joseph: b 1-3-1741 d p. 1797 m Sarah Kelsey Sgt PS CT
Joseph: b 8-17-1745 d 1826 m Sarah Rogers Pvt CT
Josiah: b 2-12-1752 d 1-5-1842 m Sarah Rogers Pvt Mar CT ★
Judah: b 12-9-1744 d 1-27-1817 m Hannah Baldwin Pvt CT
Levi: b 1-31-1758 d 10-5-1842 m Phoebe Gaylord Pvt CT
Luther: b 7-21-1760 d 11-19-1842 m (1)Mercy Tracy (2)Sally Talcott Arfr CT ★
Noah: b 1732 d 5-7-1815 m Margary Post Pvt CT
Philemon: b 11-29-1759-61 d p. 1795 m Rhoda Butler Pvt CT
Philip: b 1740 d 3-12-1813 m (1)Phoebe Hendricks (2)Sarah Beebe Maj NY
Reuben: b 8-8-1746 d 9-12-1824 m (1)Hannah Wakelee (2)Ruth Seward Pvt CT ★
Wm.: b c. 1722 d 1779 m (1)Mary Young (2)Elizabeth — Capt MD
Wm.: b 2-14-1737 d 1813 m Sarah Campbell Pvt NY

FRISSELL, (includes FRISSELLE, FRIZEL, FRIZELL, FRIZZELL)
Benjamin: b c. 1735 d 1796 m Mary Silvester NS MA
John: b 2-18-1739 d p. 1798 m Abigail Allen Pvt MA
Nathan: b 8-7-1759 d 12-17-1843 m Ruhama — Pvt SC ★
Reuben: b 1742 d 10-31-1822 m (1)Rachel Orvis (2)Mrs Anna (Chamberlain) (3)Esther Lyman CS MA
Wm.: b 7-9-1737 d 12-25-1824 m Judith Mason Capt CT

FRITCHER,
Conradt: b 9-1-1754 d 7-25-1825 m Polly Shely Cpl NY
Henry: b 1755 d 1781 m Barbara Fritcher Pvt NY

FRITTS, (includes FRITZ)
Christian Wm.: b 1744 d 6-8-1797 m Eva Margaret Dorwortan Pvt PA
Frederick: b 11-11-1732 d 5-10-1816 m Cornelia Jewell Pvt NJ
George: b 1753 d 3- -1845 m Mary Wilson Pvt NC ★
Martin: b 1750 d 8-17-1844 m Catherine Wildt Pvt PA
Phillip: b 1755/65 d 6-23-1825 m Charlotte Deborgur Pvt PA
Wm.: b 5-7-1750 d 3-22-1813 m Catherine Mayer Pvt NY
Wooldrich: b c. 1730 d 11-2-1781 m X Pvt NC

FRITZINGER,
Ernst: b c. 1747 d p. 1800 m Mary Elizabeth — Sgt PA

FROELICH, (includes FROELIG)
Martin: b c. 1730 d p. 6-26-1810 m (2)Anna Margretta Niess Cpl PA

FROGG, (includes FROGGE)
John: b 5-26-1745 d 10-10-1774 m Agatha Lewis Capt VA
John, Sr.: b c. 1717 d 1794 m Elizabeth Strother PS VA
Wm.: b 1747 d p. 1804 m Mary — Pvt VA

FROHOCK,
Thomas: b 9-1-1749 d 10-3-1805 m Catherine Kelley Pvt NH

FROMAN, (includes FROWMAN)
Jacob: b 4-9-1749 d 1835 m Barbarry — Pvt VA
Paul, Sr.: b 1708 d 5- -1783 m Elizabeth Hite Capt VA
Paul, Jr.: b 10-16-1734 d p. 1820 m Mary Cartmell PS CS VA

FRONEFIELD,
John: b c. 1739/40 d p. 1790 m Mary Umstead Pvt PA

FROST,
Aaron: b 9-16-1747 d 8-3-1817 m (1)Parnal Wood (2)Margaret Hammond CS CT

Amasa, Jr.: b 5-15-1765 d 8-14-1829 m Rebecca Nash Pvt MA
David: b 9-15-1743 d 12-15-1812 m Mary Beach Pvt CT
David: b c. 1744 d 3-12-1826 m Mary Johnson Cmsry MA
David: b 2-1-1750 d 1-22-1832 m Esther Bixby Pvt MA
David: b 6-3-1743 d 5-5-1826 m Sarah Hyatt Pvt NY
Ebenezer: b 11-23-1746 d 1-7-1824 m (1)Sara Fairchild (2)Elizabeth Wilson PS NC
Eliot: b 12-25-1760 d 1-15-1849 m Jan Clark Pvt MA
Elisha: b 9-21-1758 d 5-10-1836 m Melicent Winch Sgt MA ★
Enoch: b c. 1750 d 6- -1813 m Alice Davis Lt PS MA
Ephraim: b 9-29-1742 d 4-4-1833 m (1)Lydia Perry (2)Martha Boylston Pvt MA
Ephraim: b 7-10-1715 d 3-5-1797 m Mary Cutter CS MA
Frederick: b 1754 d 11-19-1839 m Martha Lewis Cpl MA ★
George: b 4-26-1720 d 1796 m (1)Mrs. Richards (2)Margaret (Weeks) Smith PS NH
George: b 11-24-1750 d 4-18-1808 m Abigail Bell PS NH
George Pepperell: b 1-1-1758 d 1-14-1833 m (1)Elizabeth Goslin (2)Agnes Green Capt NH ★
Henry: b 6-6-1755 d 1817 m Rachel Heustis Pvt NY
Ichabod: bpt 7-14-1755 d 1829 m (1)Susanna Dennison (2)Mary E. — Ens. MA
Jacob: b 7-9-1753 d 6-28-1839 m (1)Lydia Shed (2)Rebecca (Cobb) Stevens Pvt MA
Jesse: b 10-18-1762 d 10-12-1827 m Abigail Culver Pvt Tms CT
Joel: b 9-15-1741 d 3-6-1825 m Mary Gibbs Pvt VT
John: b 5-5-1738 d 1-10-1810 m Mary Nowell BGen MA
John: b 9-18-1743 d 1813 m Elizabeth Mitchell Sgt MA
John: b 12-22-1759 d 10-16-1853 m (1)Amy Tennant (2)Mrs Mary Hunt Cpl MA ★
John: b 8-26-1725 d 1790 m Mindwell Bigelow Pvt MA
John: b 6-23-1734 d 11-1-1818 m Betty Bemis Pvt MA
John: b 9-9-1760 d 5-15-1812 m (1)Susanna Hill (2)Rebecca Hastings Pvt MA
John: b 1762 d 2-26-1800 m Eleanor Ferguson Sol MA
John: b 6-27-1739 d 3-27-1831 m Huldah Munson Pvt NY
Jonathan: b 1751 d 2-22-1782 m Patience Frost Pvt MA
Jonathan: b 10-27-1750 d p. 1781 m Susanna Merrill Cpl MA
Joseph: b 5-22-1754 d 5-24-1844 m Lucy Couch Pvt CT ★
Joseph: b 2-20-1738 d p. 1790 m Anstis Downing Pvt MA
Joshua: b c. 1756 d p. 1790 m X Sol VA
Josiah, Jr.: b c. 1756 d 3-20-1830 d p. 11- -1779 m X Pvt CT
Mark: b 10- -1749 d 10-5-1835 m Hannah Herson Pvt MA ★
Moses: b 1761 d 1-17-1838 m Lucy Getchell Pvt MA ★
Nathaniel: b 1748 d 5-10-1838 m (1)Polly Berry (2)Sally Brown (3)Mrs Rebecca Higgins Lt MA
Noah: b 4-8-1755 d 5-9-1841 m (1)Polly Chapin (2)Erene Edson Cpl MA
Richard: b 8-12-1770 d 12-27-1849 m Rachel Thompson Drm MA ★
Samuel: b 2-15-1736/7 d p. 1782 m Sary Cooper Pvt CT
Samuel: b 7-13-1752 d 11-1-1817 m Mary Hurd Capt MA
Samuel: b 9-16-1733 d p. 1779 m Martha Mace Pvt MA
Samuel: b 12-13-1715 d 3-12-1799 m Rebeckah How MM MA
Samuel: b 12-18-1716 d 10-1-1798 m Abigail Cutter MM MA
Seth: b 3-20-1760 d 1-24-1814 m Sarah Hill Pvt MA
Simon: b 8-7-1757 d 10-1-1803 m Jane Emery Sgt ME
Simon: b 6-21-1745 d 1816 m (1)Eunice Furbush Pvt MA
Solomon: b 5-14-1742 d 9-8-1838 m Thankful Edwards Pvt CT
Stephen: b 5-17-1759 d 11-16-1821 m Mary Cogswell Pvt CT
Stephen: b 6-18-1747 d 11-1-1810 m Susanna Brown Capt MA
Thomas, Jr.: b 3-13-1750 d 7-28-1820 m (1)Deborah Stephens (2)Lydia Pinney Pvt NY
Wm.: b 4-7-1757 d 12-16-1831 m (1)Elizabeth Davis (2)Mary Shipley (3)— Shipley PS MD
Wm.: b 5-26-1747 d 6-2-1827 m Elizabeth Randall Lt MA
Wm. Henry: b 6-6-1755 d 1817 m Rachel Heustis MM NY
Winthrop: b 1753 d 8-4-1810 m Sarah Tuttle Lt NH
Zephaniah: b 1761 d 7-8-1843 m Ruth French Pvt MA ★
Zopher: b c. 1746 d 1828 m Hannah Thorn Pvt NY

FROTHINGHAM,
Benjamin: b 4-6-1734 d 8-19-1809 m Mary Deland Capt MA
Ebenezer: bpt 6-9-1717 d 10-30-1798 m Deborah Paine PS CT
Nathaniel: b 4-6-1746 d 1-22-1825 m (1)Rebecca Austin (2)Mary Townsend (3)Lydia Kettell PS Lt MA
Richard: b 3-15-1748 d 4-1-1819 m Mary Kettell Sgt Cmsry MA
Samuel: b 3-16-1759 d 7-4-1847 m Abigail Kelley Pvt CT ★
Thomas: b 4-7-1743 d 12-2-1790 m Sarah Pecker Sgt MA
Thomas: b 1-27-1755 d 6-25-1827 m Elizabeth Frost Cmsry PS MA

FRUIT,
Robert: b 1732 d 2-4-1820 m Catherine McClure Pvt PS PA

FRUM,
Wm.: b 1755 d 1842 m Anne — Pvt MD

FRUTCHEY,
Frederick: b 1730 d 1- -1779 m (1)Anna Margaret — (2)Catherine Gatterd (3)Anna Maria Gatterd Sgt PA

FRY, (includes FREY & FRYE)
Abraham: b c. 1731 d c. 1806 m Agnes Ann — Pvt PA

FRY, contd.
Adam: b 8-14-1760 d 6-28-1846 m Anna Maria Mielhof Pvt PA
Benjamin: b *c.* 1754 d 9-8-1823 m Mary Ann Jameson Sgt VA ★
Benjamin: b 1730 d 1826 m Catherine — Pvt VA
Benjamin: b 1754 d 4-8-1823 m Magdalena Secrist Pvt VA
Bernard: b *c.* 1750 d 9-10-1802 m Hester Zilpha Swigert Cpl MD
Christopher: b 1764 d 1846 m Elizabeth Allen Pvt NY
Conrad: b *a.* 1733 d 3- -1811 m Barbara Emsminger Pvt PA
Ebenezer: b 9-17-1745 d 3-10-1828 m Hannah Baker Capt NH ★
George: b 8-13-1751 d 1796 m Mary Magdalena Ziegle Pvt PA
George: b 8-15-1756 d 12-7-1810 m — Mowrey Cpl VA
George: b 1735 d 3- -1793 m Anne — Pvt VA
Gottfried: b 8-4-1721 d 5-14-1782 m Maria Margaretha Linn Pvt Grd CS PA
Henry: b *c.* 1762 d 7-15-1829 m Sarah Davis Pvt MA ★
Henry: b 8- -1724 d 4-13-1792 m Fanny — PS VA
Henry: b 10-30-1738 d 7- -1823 m Susan Walker PS CS VA
Isaac: b 2-6-1743 d 11-3-1791 m Elizabeth Holt QM Maj NH
Jacob: b 3-23-1742 d 12-16-1819 m Elizabeth Snell Sgt NY
Jacob: b 11-25-1744 d 5-8-1829 m Catharine Brenler PS Pvt PA
James, Sr.: b 1-24-1710 d 1-8-1776 m (1)Elizabeth Osgood (2)Mrs Sarah Cheever Robie Col MA
James, Jr.: b 1-9-1741 d 1-28-1826 m (1)Mehitable Robinson (2)Phebe Campbell Pvt MA
John: b 12-23-1759 d 1-11-1832 m Betsey Noyes Lt MA
John: b 4-7-1719 d 3-19-1814 m Elizabeth Woodbury PS MA
John: b 4-27-1740 d 4-19-1833 m Anna Gertrude Shoemaker BgdMaj NY
John: b 1748 d 1821 m Phillipina Bauze PS PA
John: b *c.* 1754 d 8-19-1782 m Catherine Spears Pvt VA
Jonathan: b 12-4-1742 d 7-28-1793 m Sarah Peabody Lt MA
Joseph, Sr.: b 3- -1711/2 d 7-25-1794 m Mehitabel Poor MGen MA
Joseph, Jr.: b 7-10-1743 d 1-13-1828 m Mary Robinson Capt MA
Joseph: b *c.* 1735 d 1781 m Ann — CS VA
Joshua, Jr.: b *c.* 1760 d *c.* 1839 m Peachy Walker Pvt VA ★
Leonard: b *c.* 1750-5 d 1815 m Catharine Schneck Pvt PA
Lodowick: b 1730-40 d 1804 m Abigail — PS VA
Martin: b 10-24-1748 d 8-23-1834 m (1)Mary Magdalene Sherer (2)Rebecca — Pvt PA
Martin, Jr.: b 2-12-1751 d 12-21-1830 m Catherine Capp Pvt PA
Michael: b 8-1-1745 d 3-28-1815 m Dorothea — Sol NC
Michael: b 1758 d 1856 m Frances Nancy Howard Pvt PA
Nicholas: b 1748 d 3-23-1840 m (1)Catherine — (2)Margaret Ansell Pvt MD
Peleg: b 1758 d 9-3-1823 m Barbara Sheldon Pvt RI
Philip: b 1735 d 1820 m Susan Ikard Pvt NC
Reuben: b 4-9-1764 d 1-1-1854 m Susan Emerson Pvt MA
Samuel: b 12-22-1729 d 1-10-1819 m Elizabeth Frye Pvt MA
Samuel: b 3-22-1729 d 12-5-1792 m (1)Lucianna Coggeshall (2)Deborah Greene Mar RI
Samuel: b 1729 d 8-15-1814 m Christina Speers Pvt VA
Simon: b 9-29-1737 d 10-1-1822 m Hannah Johnson PS CS ME
Theophilus: b 1750 d 1853/3 d 4-2-1830 m Lucy Lovejoy Sgt MA
Timothy: b 5-8-1735 d 11-6-1811 m Hannah Carleton Pvt MA
Valentine, Sr.: b 5-9-1721 d 9-13-1798 m (2)Anna Maria Barbara (Brinkele) Meyer PS NC
Valentine, Jr.: b 3-8-1748/9 d *p.* 4-14-1814 m Cathrina Petree PS NC
Wm.: b — d — m Deborah Colburn Pvt MA
Wm.: b 7-20-1749 d 10-11-1831 m Tamson Southwick CS MA
Wm.: b 1724 d 1811 m Elizabeth Gor Pvt PA
Wm. A.: b 10-17-1761 d *p.* 1834 m — Spears Pvt VA

FRYBACK,
George: b 1759 d 12-1-1833 m Susanna Steed Pvt PA

FRYBURG,
John: b 1749 d 5-15-1812 m Susanna Becker Pvt PA

FRYER, (includes FRAYER & FRIER)
David: b 1758 d *p.* 1840 m Fytie Hornbeck Pvt NY ★
George: b 1742 d *p.* 1785 m Margery Green Pvt PA
Isaac: b 1-12-1734 d 6-13-1802 m Elizabeth Hilton Pvt NY
John: b 11-20-1759 d 2-14-1818 m Winifred Fenn Pvt GA
John, Sr.: b *c.* 1738 d *p.* 1785 m Elizabeth VanWoert Pvt NY
John, Jr.: b 10-4-1759 d 1-15-1825 m Maria Volwieder Pvt NY
Robert: b *c.* 1745 d *a.* 2- -1818 m Jane — CS VA
Wm.: b *c.* 1730-5 d 1794 m Margaret Love Pvt NC

FUDGE,
Jacob: b 1723 d 1790 m Margaret Gregory Pvt SC

FUGARD,
Samuel: b 1730 d 3-24-1791 m Abigail Fugard Pvt NH

FUGATE,
Jonathan: b 1-25-1738 d 2-21-1859 m X Pvt VA
Randal F.: b 1-26-1762 d 11-30-1836 m Elleanor N. Bond Pvt VA ★
Townsend: b *c.* 1758 d *a.* 7-3-1843 m Malinda Cooper Sol VA

FULBRIGHT,
John: b 1750 d 1825 m Elizabeth Coulter Sol NC

FULCHER,
James: b 1755 d 3-23-1839 m Elizabeth Huff Sol GA

Phillip: b 9-29-1742 d *p.* 1796 m Jane Anderson Sol VA
Richard: b 3-9-1756 d 1834 m Elizabeth Younger Cpl VA ★
Wm.: b — d *a.* 12-27-1797 m X Pvt NC

FULFORD,
John: b 8-14-1737 d 10-20-1781 m (1)Hannah Vickery (2)Eleanor Bodkin Maj MD

FULHAM, (includes FULLAM)
Elisha, Sr.: b 6-26-1727 d 9-22-1801 m (1)Sarah Hagar (2)Elizabeth Knight 1Lt MA
Elisha, Jr.: b 2-25-1752 d 5-20-1824 m (1)Mary Willard (2)Mrs Abigail Nichols Pvt MA
Francis, Sr.: b 3-21-1717 d 2-8-1807 m Susanna Hammond Pvt MA
Francis, Jr.: b 10-26-1744 d 2-12-1832 m Mrs Sarah (Fisher)Perry Pvt PS NH
Jacob: b 1-24-1749 d 10-20-1832 m Elizabeth (Whitcomb) Houghton Pvt MA
Timothy: b 12-14-1741 d 9-10-1829 m Elizabeth Thompson Sgt MA

FULKERSON,
Abraham: b — d *a.* 4-27-1822 m X Pvt CS VA
Caleb: b 1-17-1762 d 3-4-1848 m Deborah Tunison Fif NJ ★
James: b 6-22-1737 d 9-6-1799 m Mary VanHook Capt VA
Joseph: b 3-7-1755 d 7-11-1820 m Betsy Oliphant Sgt NJ ★

FULKINSON,
John: b 1758 d *p.* 1-1-1833 m Alkey Smith Pvt NJ ★

FULLENWIDER,
Henry: b *c.* 1760 d *a.* 2-4-1801 m Ellenor Leonard Ens NC
John: b 1756/7 d 9-4-1826 m Elizabeth Ellis Sol PS NC
Peter: b 1732 d 1799 m Barbara — PS VA

FULLER,
Aaron: b 1-26-1734 d 2-27-1809 m Sarah Holt Capt CT
Aaron: b *c.* 1739 d *p.* 12-5-1780 m Sarah Blodgett Pvt MA
Aaron: b 5-6-1742 d *p.* 1790 m Mary Hall Pvt MA
Aaron: b 2-26-1757 d 10-18-1841 m Hannah Pond Pvt MA
Abiel: b 5-1-1712 d 9-18-1783 m Beulah Daggett Pvt NY
Abijah: b 8-13-1753 d 5-5-1835 m Abigail Meacham Sgt CT ★
Abner: b 12-10-1724 d 1776 m Mary Hilyard Crowfoot Pvt CT
Abner: b *c.* 1756/7 d 1835 m Polly Terrill Pvt NY
Abraham: b 10- -1735 d 9-20-1807 m Lydia Gillett Capt CT
Abraham, Jr.: b 8-19-1760 d 12-22-1838 m Rachel Colton Pvt Fif MA ★
Amasa: b 3-18-1758 d 3-10-1844 m (1)Mary Mason (2)Lois Barr (3)— Bates Sgt MA ★
Amos: b 1731 d 1813 m Mary — Pvt CT
Amos: b 5-10-1744 d *p.* 1782 m Rachel Fuller Pvt CT
Amos (1st): b 2-12-1720 d 12-31-1790 m Abigail Harlow Pvt MA
Andrew: b 5-18-1761 d 1-31-1820 m Hannah Richards Pvt MA ★
Andrew: b 4-21-1743 d 1831 m (1)Mary Putnam (2)Hannah Smith Pvt NH
Archelaus: b 5-4-1727 d 8-25-1776 m (1)Hannah Richardson (2)Mrs Betty Dale Putnam LCol PS MA
Arthur: b *c.* 1725 d *p.* 1779 m Sarah — PS VA
Asa: b 6- -1758 d 7-19-1836 m Abigail Burch Pvt CT
Asa: b 9-20-1752 d 8-11-1836 m Melatiah Metcalf Pvt MA
Asa: b 8-25-1758 d 3-25-1813 m Mary Robinson Pvt MA
Ashbel: b 10-16-1766 d 1850 m Lorain Millard Fif CT
Azariah: b 5-28-1764 d 3-12-1846 m Mercy Bemis Pvt MA
Barnabas: b 9-25-1723 d 3-24-1814 m Rebecca Cushman Pvt MA
Beekman: b 10-13-1750 d 4-8-1832 m Naomi Barnes Pvt NY
Benajah: b 6-4-1756 d 4-4-1836 m Catherine Thompson Pvt CT W ★
Benjamin: b 4-2-1734 d *p.* 1790 m Parthena Hubbard MM CT
Benjamin: b 6-16-1758 d 3-26-1840 m (1)Joanna Trowbridge (2)Clarisa Utley Pvt NS CT ★
Benjamin: b 7-14-1748 d — m Susie Peck Pvt MA
Benjamin: b 1754 d 1832 m Abigale Fuller Pvt MA ★
Benjamin: b 4-26-1746 d 10-20-1834 m Phebe Dow Nichols Pvt NH ★
Benjamin: b 4-11-1750 d 9-23-1808 m Mary Sisson Pvt NY W ★
Benjamin: b 2-11-1741 d 9-6-1824 m (1)Anna Blood (2)Rebecca Wilder Pvt VT
Britian: b 1757 d 1818 m Nancy Jackson PS VA
Brittain, Sr.: b *c.* 1730 d *p.* 3-28-1805 m Elizabeth — PS NC
Daniel: b 3-12-1732 d *p.* 1790 m Lois Nye Sgt CT
Daniel: b 1-17-1724/5 d 5-9-1806 m Katherine Pindar Pvt MA
Daniel: b 4-24-1760 d 4-19-1845 m Charlotte (Fuller) — Pvt MA ★
Daniel: b 9-1-1740 d 5-23-1829 m Hannah Bowers Chp PS MA
Daniel: b 11-6-1760 d 7-21-1847 m Abigail Eaton Drm NH
Darius: b 5-24-1757 d 8-8-1845 m Sarah Sampson Pvt Drm CT ★
David: b 4-18-1751 d *p.* 1781 m Sarah Williams Cpl MA
David: b 12-6-1731 d 4-28-1805 m Elizabeth Dean MM PS MA
David: b 10-20-1744 d 5-28-1809 m Lydia Emerson Pvt MA
David: b 1-27-1760 d 4-17-1845 m (1)Elsea Gleason (2)Jerusha Adams (3)Orinda Bingham Pvt NH ★
David: b 2-11-1764 d 2-7-1845 m (1)Olive Graham (2)Sarah Goodhue Pvt NY ★
Ebenezer: b 7-3-1760 d 9-16-1840 m Juan Fernandes Elderkin Pvt CT ★
Ebenezer: b 5-4-1741 d 11-11-1836 m Abagail Peck Pvt MA

Edward: b 12-31-1735 d 12-10-1810 m Ruth Jackson Capt MA
Edward: b 12-28-1746 d 7-9-1831 m Mary Jones Pvt MA
Edward: b 6-11-1758 d 9-13-1834 m (1)Sarah Colburn (2)Anne Thurston (3)Sarah Goodrich Pvt MA
Eleazer: b 5-3-1746 d 3-8-1828 m Mary Richards Sgt CS PS MA
Eleazer: b 3-17-1752 d 9-5-1819 m Rachel Bartlett Pvt MA
Elijah: b 9-24-1724 d 4-8-1799 m Mary Millington Pvt VT
Elisha, Sr.: b 3-4-1727 d 11-3-1811 m Esther Hungerford Pvt CT
Elisha, Jr.: b 1749 d 8-7-1778 m Sarah Sparrow Sol CT
Elisha: b 10-11-1725 d 1794 m Esther Richardson Pvt MA
Elisha: b 4-8-1754 d 5-15-1850 m (1)Rebecca Waterman (2)Sarah Cleveland Fif MA
Elisha: b 10-8-1761 d 11-3-1822 m Eliner Tyler Mar MA ★
Enoch: b 10-4-1754 d 1-29-184- m Lydia Webb Pvt MA ★
Enoch: b a. 1760 d a. 1814 m Sarah Putnam Pvt PS NH
Ephraim: b 5-23-1762 d 7-31-1842 m Abigail Higgins Pvt MA
Ephraim: b 3-7-1722 d 2-20-1792 m Mary Putnam CS MA
Ezekiel: b 10-23-1758 d 10-16-1838 m Mary Bartlett Sgt MA ★
Gershom: b 1-20-1749/50 d 6-20-1836/7 m Mary — Pvt NY ★
Henry: b — d p. 11- -1800 m Judith Spivey PS NC
Hezekiah: b c. 1730 d a. 1799 m Margaret — Pvt CT
Hosea: b 1748 d 1830 m Mary — Pvt VT
Ignatius: b 10-29-1763 d 12-15-1856 m Anna Reed Pvt MA
Isaac: b 2- -1756 d 12- -1834 m (1)Judith Buel (2)Mrs Elizabeth Chamberlain Pvt CT MA ★
Isaac: b 1754 d 1816 m Mary Jones Pvt GA
Isaac: b 12-15-1738 d 8-22-1803 m Mary Alden Lt MA
Isaac: b 2-8-1751 d 4-27-1833 m Lydia Ellis Sgt MA ★
Isaac: b 1753 d 1832 m (1)Eldridge — (2)— Burch Pvt NY
Isaiah: b 7-7-1744 d 3-10-1809 m Mary Keyzer 1Lt MA
Issachar: b 7-8-1725 d 10-31-1822 m (1)Elizabeth Doten (2)Lucy Tinkham Pvt MA
Jacob: b 9-7-1737 d p. 1795 m Abigail Webb Pvt CT
Jacob: b 1739 d 3-6-1816 m Elizabeth Paine Pvt CT
Jacob: b 11-6-1734 d 5- -1800 m Deborah Tower QM Capt MA
James: b 10-19-1737 d p. 1785 m Abiah Botsford Pvt CT
James: b 9-1-1760 d p. 1807 m Mollie May Pvt MA ★
Jason: b 11-19-1757 d 3-3-1840 m Catherine Farrington Pvt MA ★
Jeduthan, Sr.: b 1714 d 11-15-1779 m Sarah Daggett Pvt MA
Jehiel: b 3-25-1735 d 12-16-1796 m Sarah Day Lt CT
Jeptha: b 1747 d 1794 m Molly Godfrey Pvt NY
Jesse: b 2-14-1752 d 1-17-1832 m Lydia Miller Sgt MA
Job: b 11-25-1751 d a. 10-8-1794 m Susannah Russell Drm CT
John: b 6-28-1757 d 6-21-1813 m Wealthy Kazar Pvt CT W ★
John: b 7-10-1764 d p. 3-2-1833 m Mercy Lucinda — Sgt CT ★
John: b 5-7-1732 d 1-2-1800 m Hannah Kimball Pvt CT
John: b 7-2-1753 d 8-22-1845 m Azubah Vinton Pvt CT ★
John: b 1760 d 5-21-1854 m Mary Williams Pvt CT ★
John: b c. 1764 d 1844 m (1)Ann Maple (2)Wid. Banks Pvt MD
John: b 9-15-1731 d 1801 m Prudence Gibson Capt MA
John: b 9-29-1741 d 10-20-1828 m Rebecca Robbins Sgt MA
John: b 3-18-1753 d 4-15-1809 m Betty Smith Pvt MA
John: b c. 1753 d p. 1782 m Experience Mitchell Pvt MA
John: b 6-23-1744 d 11-2-1829 m Anna Toby CS ME
John: b 7-15-1756 d 2-15-1835 m Betsy Clough Pvt NH ★
John: b 1749 d p. 1810 m Mary Shields Pvt SC
John: b 12-26-1760 d 2-4-1842 m Elizabeth — Pvt VT
Jonathan: b 5-24-1725 d 5-22-1817 m Sibyl Meacham Lt CT
Jonathan: b 7-15-1756 d 11-28-1808 m Hannah Jewell Pvt MA
Jones: b — d p. 5-8-1812 m X PS NC
Joseph: b 1730 d 7-13-1795 m Zerviah Hill Capt CT
Joseph: b 11-28-1738 d 1-29-1805 m Mary Holt Pvt CT
Joseph: b 8-15-1727 d 1807 m (1)Mindwell Stone (2)Mehitable Craft Capt MA
Joseph: b 5-27-1758 d 9-26-1846 m (1)Rachael Miller (2)Alethea — Sgt MA ★
Joseph: b 5-9-1758 d 8-23-1846 m (1)Tabitha Jones (2)Phebe Hoxie Pvt MA ★
Joshua: b 4-21-1725 d 5-20-1808 m Margaret Richardson CS CT
Joshua: b 7-11-1753 d 5-16-1815 m Sybil Champion Pvt CT
Joshua: b 3-2-1747 d 11-8-1817 m Catherine E Jackson Sgt MA
Joshua: b 4-12-1703 d 8-23-1777 m Anna Stearns Pvt MA
Joshua, Sr.: b 10-3-1727 d 3-19-1816 m Joanna Taylor Pvt NH
Josiah: b 10-30-1762 d 12-4-1835 m (1)Deliverance — (2)Dorcas Holt (3)Olivia Moore Pvt CT
Josiah: b 5-15-1722 d 9-3-1805 m Lydia Cushman Capt MA
Josiah: b 1-25-1764 d 6-19-1842 m Eleanor Warren Pvt MA
Josiah: b 12-2-1710 d 5-10-1793 m Abigail Williams CS MA
Levi: b 7-11-1762 d 3-12-1822 m Mary Benton Pvt NH
Lot: b 9-18-1733 d 7-12-1811 m Rachel — Pvt MA
Lot: b 5-6-1760 d p. 1840 m Submit Jones Pvt MA ★
Mathew: b 3-6-1745 d 4-26-1841 m Martha Arnold Pvt VT
Matthew: b c. 1750 d c. 1808 m Adah — Pvt NY
Meshac: b 1755-7 d 5-5-1829 m (2)Bethany Lucas Pvt GA ★
Michael: b 6-28-1741 d 1-22-1822 m Mary Ann Sessions Pvt NY
Moses: b 4-29-1750 d 2-13-1823 m Elizabeth Newell Sgt MA
Nathan: b 6-10-1759 d 11-23-1840 m Hannah Welch Pvt CT ★
Nathan: b 9-3-1763 d 4-25-1852 m Susannah Luce Pvt CT ★
Nathan: b 9-1-1739 d 6-25-1811 m Phebe Harris Pvt NY
Nathan: b 10-12-1750 d 12-13-1800 m Mary Paquinett PS NC
Nathaniel: b 11-18-1710 d 7-12-1780 m Mary — PS CT
Nathaniel, Sr.: b 12-25-1726 d 1778 m (1)Sarah Leatherland (2)Mary Holland Cdr Pvtr MA

Nathaniel, Jr.: b 9-4-1760 d 12-29-1842 m Hannah Hovey Pvt MA ★
Nathaniel: b 3-15-1748 d p. 1784 m (?)Hepzabeth Brown Cpl MA
Nathaniel: b 12-12-1747 d 6-17-1739 m Lydia olmes Sgt MA
Nehemiah, Sr.: b 1-26-1733 d p. 6-6-1806 m (1)Mary Conant (2)Hannah — Pvt MA
Nehemiah, Jr.: b 1-23-1762 d p. 1790 m Hannah Wiswell Pvt MA
Noah: b 9-26-1761 d 2-19-1846 m Lucy Wilson Sol CT
Noah: b 3-26-1758 d 11-9-1843 m Sarah Smith Pvt MA ★
Noah, Sr.: b 1712 d 8-10-1786 m Mary Cushman PS MA
Obidiah: b 10-6-1747 d p. 1785 m Dorothy Dill Pvt CT
Oliver: b 9-30-1742 d 3-9-1817 m (1)Alice Ransom (2)Lois Gillett PS CT
Peter: b a. 1740 d 8-6-1811 m Submit Mighells Pvt MA
Roger: b 7-21-1747 d 9-21-1819 m (1)Martha Phelps (2)Violetta Taylor (3)Lois Taylor PS CT
Samuel: b 10-10-1751 d 4-4-1826 m (1)Mary Dimmock (2)Mary Gildersleeve Pvt CT W ★
Samuel: b 3-22-1736 d 9-26-1812 m Zillah Merrill PS CT
Samuel: b 12-25-1752 d 3-25-1841 m Esther Flagg Pvt CT NH ★
Samuel, Jr.: b 8-11-1765 d 1-13-1844 m (?)Sarah — (3)Polly Beach Pvt NH ★
Samuel: b 10-16-1733 d p. 1781 m Lois Andrews Pvt NH
Samuel: b a. 1744 d 4-17-1849 m Sarah Freeman Pvt VT
Seth: b 10-8-1752 d 9-15-1825 m Rebecca Morse Pvt MA
Simeon: b 10-21-1762 d 12-7-1852 m (1)Mary Cook (2)Wealthy Woodward Horton Pvt MA ★
Simeon: b 1731 d 9-20-1805 m (1)Lois Hyward (2)Eunice Parkes PS PS CT
Solomon: b 10-22-1756 d 1809 m Ziporah Perkins Pvt MA
Solomon: b 10-23-1748 d 4-11-1806 m Mary Colburn Pvt MA
Solomon: b 1756 d 1854 m Martha Moody Pvt MA
Solomon: b 3-12-1757 d 5-21-1847 m (1)Elizabeth Lucas (2)Persis Bennet Sgt VT
Solomon Lathrop: b 12-4-1756 d 3-14-1829 m (1)Martha P. Moody (2)Tamar Smith Pvt MA
Stephen, Jr.: b 11-3-1730 d 5-24-1813 m Mary Abbott Capt CT
Stephen: b 5-4-1734 d 1-28-1807 m Polly Brigham Pvt MA
Stephen: b 5-18-1742 d 3-23-1832 m (1)Jemima White (2)Mrs Abigail Whiting Pvt Drm MA
Stephen: b 12-18-1754 d 2-9-1839 m Hannah Felch Pvt MA
Stephen: b 4-25-1752 d 11-6-1827 m Lydia Putnam Pvt MA
Stephen: b 8-19-1757 d 7-29-1834 m Anna Leppenwell Pvt MA
Thaddeus: b 10-14-1758 d 1-11-1834 m Susannah Oliver Pvt MA ★
Thomas: b 6-10-1732 d 11-14-1813 m Sarah Griffin Lt CT
Thomas: b 4-5-1717 d 11-12-1802 m (1)Martha Rowley (2)Mary (Green)Hosmer PS CT
Thomas: b c. 1744 d 9-9-1803 m (1)Comfort — (2)Hopestill Lethbridge Pvt MA
Thomas: bpt 8-25-1727 d 1789 m (1)Lydia Yonge (2)Mrs Elizabeth Mellechamp Miles (3)Mrs Catherine Mellechamp Foley PS SC
Timothy: bpt 9-21-1707 d 9-14-1796 m Sarah Smith PS MA
Timothy: b c. 1742 d p. 1790 m Mary Gifford Pvt NY
Wm.: b c. 1756 d 10-2-1829 m Ester Fosket Pvt CT
Wm.: b 11-23-1760 d 12-7-1823 m Susannah Knowlton NS CT
Wm.: b 3-22-1761 d 9-2-1842 m Lucy Hodgkins Sgt MA .
Wm.: b 3-10-1743 d 1-17-1802 m Sarah Hunting Lt MA
Wm.: b 12- -1734 d 11-29-1809 m Sarah — Pvt MA
Zadoch: b 9-19-1744 d 9-17-1818 m Alice Porter Pvt MA

FULLERTON, (includes FULLINGTON)
Alexander: b a. 1746 d 1778/9 m Mary Sharp Pvt PA
Araunah: b 1761 d 1800 m Lillis Stetson Pvt MA
Ebenezer: b 1750 d 7-7-1819 m Eunice Beath Pvt MA
Humphrey: b c. 1748 d 1795 m Martha Mitchell Pvt CS PA
Humphrey: b 1724/5 d 9-4-1777 m Ann Dawson Dr VA
James: b 7-12-1756 d 1-30-1833 m Lydia Tibbetts Pvt NH ★
John: b 2-24-1730 d 2-15-1817 m Mary Noyes Lt MA
John: b 9- -1733 d 2-20-1779 m Elizabeth Toomer Capt SC
Thomas: b 1751 d 12-23-1834 m Hannah Kennedy Pvt PA

FULLMAN,
Francis: b 10-25-1744 d — m Sarah (Fisher) Perry Pvt NH

FULLWOOD,
Robert: b c. 1763 d 1822 m Jane Ware Hunter Sol SC
Thomas: b c. 1750 d 1824 m Loana — Sol NC

FULMER, (includes FOLLMER)
Adam: b 1760 d 1-2-1832 m Christina Bone Pvt PA
Casper: b — d 5- -1814 m Mary Roberts Pvt PA
Christian: b 9-25-1762 d 6-6-1813 m Marcellis — Pvt NY
Conrad: b c. 1740 d p. 1786 m Elizabeth Hiltz Pvt NY
George: b 8-16-1751 d 11-9-1830 m Eve Barbara Moyer Pvt PA
Jacob: b 12-14-1738 d 8-24-1804 m Anna Catherine Walters Ens PS PA
Jacob: b 4-28-1757 d 1827 m Anna Sybilla Yost PS PA
Jacob: b 1762 d 1-23-1839 m (2)Elizabeth Able Pvt SC ★
John: b 1-16-1750 d 4-7-1840 m Mary E. Gartner Capt PA
John, Jr.: b 4-4-1760-3 d 8-22-1824 m Mary Krauskopt Pvt PA
Jost: b c. 1730 d 12-5-1802 m Mary Magdalena Pvt PA

FULS,
John Phillip: b 8-15-1754 d a. 10-20-1825 m Elizabeth — Pvt VA

FULTON,
David: b *c.* 1755 d *a.* 8-16-1826 m (1)Mary — (2)Ann McIsaac Pvt PA
David: b — d *p.* 3-7-1822 m Nancy — PS VA
Hugh: b 1759 d 1816 m (1)Sarah (Hall) Tate (2)Jane Rogers Maj VA
James: b 2-2-1751 d 2-15-1833 m Margaret Miller Capt VA ★
James: b 1749 d *a.* 11-10-1833 m — Smith 1Lt VA
James: b 4-15-1751 d 7-15-1839 m (1)Jane Matthews (2)— Fowler Sol VA
James B.: b 1-21-1765 d 4-26-1848 m Anastasia Tuel Mil MD ★
John: b 8-19-1746 d 8-27-1805 m (1)Susanne Steward (2)Anne (Goodrich)Austin Sgt MA
John: b 1736 d 11-9-1790 m Sarah Bradlee PS MA
John: b 1751 d *p.* 3-17-1807 m Martha Hall Cpl NH
John: b 9-1-1740 d 1-20-1832 m Elizabeth Teator Pvt NY
John: b 1713 d 3-20-1796 m Elinor — PS PA
Moses: b 175– d 12-1-1844 m (1)Lydia Clark (2)Martha Lee (3)Rebecca Lee Pvt MA
Richard: b 2-20-1750 d 1806 m Mary Willson Pvt PA
Robert: b *c.* 1749 d *p.* 1783 m (1)Elizabeth Ingraham (2)Polly Ovall Sgt MA
Robert: b 3-27-1745 d 1-13-1777 m Sarah Patten PS MA
Robert: b 1752 d 3-10-1820 m Nancy Sloan Pvt PA
Samuel: b *c.* 1745 d *p.* 4-22-1820 m X PS NC
Samuel, Sr.: b *c.* 1717 d *p.* 1784 m X Pvt SC
Sarah Bradley: b 12-24-1740 d 11-9-1835 m John Fulton PS MA
Wm.: b *c.* 1740 d *p.* 10-21-1806 Jean — 1Lt MD
Wm.: b 9-3-1740 d *p.* 1790 m Elizabeth — Cpl MA
Wm.: b 12-6-1752 d 5-10-1803 m Sara Elizabeth Stuart Cpl MA

FULTZ,
George: b 1756 d 4-14-1826 m Elizabeth — Pvt PA

FUNK, (includes FUNCK)
Abraham: b 11-21-1734 d 4-16-1788 m Mary Landis Pvt PA
Christian: b 2-2-1747 d 2-2-1835 m (1)Anna Shank (2)Magdalin — Pvt PA
Christian: b 1731 d 5-31-1811 m Barbara Cassel PS PA
Henry, Jr.: b 9-23-1750 d 9-9-1799 m Anna Ronk PS MD
Henry: b *c.* 1739 d *p.* 1786 m Barbara Showalter Pvt PS PA
Henry: b — d *p.* 3-22-1800 m (1)Martha — d (2)Magdalene — Pvt PA
Henry: b *c.* 1753 d 11-1-1815 m Elizabeth Miller Pvt VA Heirs ★
Johannes: b *c.* 1730 d 1807 m — Wismer Pvt PA
John: b 10-8-1738 d 1-7-1820 m Elizabeth Lewis Pvt PA
John: b 9-27-1759 d 11-16-1823 m Prudentia Miller Pvt PA
John: b 1741 d *a.* 5-25-1784 m Catherine Stover Capt VA
Martin: b 1-30-1732 d 12-19-1796 m Judie Wenger Pvt PA
Martin: b 2— -1762 d 10-16-1838 m Elizabeth Studebaker Pvt PA ★
Michael: b 2-2-1762 d 6-7-1821 m Elizabeth Gigeley Pvt PA
Rudolph: b 1753 d 12-29-1804 m Catharine Krebile Pvt PA

FUNKHOUSER,
Christian: b 1754 d 1818 m (1)Mary Layman ( )Catherine Boehm Sol VA
Jacob: b 1750 d 11-27-1801 m Dorothy Huddle Pvt VA

FUNSTON,
John: b 2-5-1750 d 12-6-1844 m Mary Aten Pvt PA

FUQUA,
Joseph, Jr.: b *c.* 1754 d 1813 m Catherine Palmer Capt VA
Joseph: b 1762 d 5-4-1829 m Celia Bondurant Pvt VA W ★
Joseph: b 3-18-1764 d 11-26-1832 m Mary Burge Sol VA
Moses: b 1760 d 1844 m Delphia Hoard 2Lt VA
Moses: b *c.* 1738 d 1814 m Judith Woodson PS VA
Thomas: b *c.* 1736 d 12— -1806 m Judith — PS VA

FURBECK,
John: b 4-26-1760 d 1-5-1840 m Susanna Roon Tms NY ★

FURBEE,
Caleb: b 11-22-1752 d 4-16-1837 m (1)Sarah — (2)Mary LeMaster Lt DE
Waitman: b 1750 d 4-20-1835 m Margaret Craig Pvt CS DE

FURBER,
Benjamin: b 1-16-1752 d 4-8-1822 m Deborah Tibbetts Pvt PS NH
Joshua: b 5-24-1744 d 4-27-1827 m Betsey Page Sgt NH
Levi: b 5-16-1751 d 1-19-1829 m Rosamond Fabyan Sgt NH
Richard, Sr.: b 8-6-1725 d 3-8-1807 m Elizabeth Dowing PS NH
Richard, Jr.: b 8-20-1753 d 3-14-1848 m (1)Alice Colman (2)Mrs Mary Wingate Powers Sgt NH ★

FURBUSH, (includes FORBUSH)
Aaron: b 10-31-1722 d 8-10-1811 m Sarah Lamson Pvt MA
Aaron, Jr.: b 5-29-1753 d *p.* 1796 m Catherine Rice Pvt MA
Asa: b 7-7-1760 d 8-31-1818 m Mehitable Fay Pvt MA
Bartholomew: b 1749 d 1808 m Catherine Furrey Pvt NY
Charles: b 5-10-1736 d 2-11-1795 m Sarah Cory Capt MA
David: b 1-5-1718 d 5-19-1803 m Ruth Wood OrdlSgt MA
David: b 12-24-1739 d 4-11-1819 m Sarah Heyward 2Lt MA
David: b 10-20-1721 d 9-25-1787 m Annah Whitney Pvt MA

Ebenezer: b 5-7-1763 d 6-1-1853 m Eunice Warren Pvt MA
Ephraim: b 10-18-1756 d 2-17-1828 m Mary Butterick Pvt MA
Rufus: b 5-6-1757 d 11-27-1818 m Mary Brown Cpl MA
Samuel: b 6-29-1750 d 10-31-1829 m Beulah Whitney Cpl MA
Samuel: b 10-30-1719 d *p.* 1790 m Margaret Parker Pvt MA
Thomas: b 1-18-1749 d 1813 m (1)Submit Ball (2)Elizabeth Flagg Pvt MA

FURD,
Benjamin: b 5-18-1748 d 10-20-1824 m Mary Lee Ens NY

FURLONG,
Lawrence: b *c.* 1735 d 5-21-1806 m Ruth Whitmore Capt MA

FURLOW,
Robert: b 1739 d 12-4-1814 m Katherine Maguire Pvt PA
Wm.: b *c.* 1743 d *p.* 1810 m Elizabeth Nidy Pvt PA

FURMAN,
Moore: b 5-1-1728 d 3-16-1808 m Sarah White DepQMGen PA
Richard: b 10-9-1755 d 8-25-1825 m (1)Elizabeth Haynesworth (2)Dorothea Maria Burn PS SC
Samuel: b 3-2-1753 d 1829 m Elizabeth Gazley Pvt NY
Wm.: b 1751 d 9-1-1826 m Rachel Wolverton Pvt NJ
Wm.: b 1758 d 1818 m Abby Hallock Ens NY
Wood: b 12-4-1712 d 1-2-1783 m Rachel Brodhead PS SC

FURNESS,
Benjamin: b *c.* 1719 d *p.* 1790 m Mary Milliken DepQM MA
Wm.: b 1745 d 1804 m Lettis Douglas PS SC

FURR, (includes FURRER)
Enoch: b 1752 d 4-3-1845 m Sarah Clawson Sol VA
Henry: b 4-6-1762 d 12-22-1851 m (2)Catharine Goodman Sgt NC W ★

FUSSELMAN,
Philip: b *c.* 1745 d 1820 m (1)Mary Hunsicker (2)Catharine — Pvt PA

FUSSELL,
Wm.: b 12-4-1756 d 9— -1836 m Mary — Pvt GA ★
Wm.: b 1729 d 1804 m Sarah Longstreth Sol PA

FUSON,
Wm.: b 4-16-1762 d 1835 m Hannah Bates Pvt VA ★

FUTCH,
Onesimus: b 1750 d *c.* 1809 m Anne Dukes Pvt SC

FUTCHER,
John: b 5-7-1744 d *p.* 1794 m Sarah — PS DE

FUTHEY,
John: b 1762 d 1789 m Jane (Futhey) Capt SC
Samuel, Sr.: b 1725 d 1790 m Ruth Steel PS PA
Samuel, Jr.: b 9-1-1753 d 2-22-1812 m Martha Smith Adj PS PA

FYOCK,
Jacob: b *c.* 1750 d 1810-18 m Barbara B. — Pvt PA

GAAR,
Andrew: b 1750 d 3-4-1811 m Christena Wilhoit PS VA
John: b 1744 d *a.* 3-23-1809 m Margaret Wilhoit Sol VA
John Adam: b 11-24-1711 d *p.* 1-11-1790 m Elizabeth — Pvt VA
Lewis: b *p.* 1734 d 1818 m Catherine Weaver Pvt PS VA
Michael: b *c.* 1740 d *a.* 1803 m Elizabeth Wilhoit Lt PS VA

GABEAU,
Anthony: b 1756 d 2-10-1829 m Elizabeth Brinkley Henley Sgt SC ★

GABEL, (includes GABLE)
Henry: b 5-16-1734 d 3-9-1828 m Elizabeth Brownback Pvt PA

GABEY,
George: b 1747 d 8-23-1828 m Esther Turchell Pvt MA

GABRIEL,
Abraham: b 10-18-1746 d 4-10-1845 m Nancy J. Bartlett Pvt PA

GACKLEY, (includes GOCKLEY)
David Coquelin: b 1765 d 1840 m Elizabeth Saeger Pvt PA
John: b — d *p.* 8-3-1792 m Magdalena Muck Pvt PA

GADD,
Wm.: b 6-30-1759 d 2-14-1835 m Nancy Drake Pvt PA ★

GADDIS,
Alexander: b — d 1786 m Ann — PS VA
John: b 10-7-1741 d 4-12-1827 m Sarah Jenkins Pvt VA
Thomas: b 12-28-1742 d 6-10-1834 m Hannah Rice Col VA ★

GADDY,
Bartholomew: b c. 1760 d 9-20-1822 m Martha Crews Pvt VA W ★
Thomas: b 1753 d p. 2-14-1814 m (1)Jane — (2)Million — Cpl NC

GADSDEN,
Christopher: b 2-16-1724 d a. 9-18-1805 m (1)Jane Godfrey (2)Mary Hassell (3)Mrs Ann S. Wragg BGen CS PS SC

GAFF,
Hugh: b c. 1750 d a. 11-21-1825 m Mary — Pvt PA

GAGE,
Aaron, Sr.: b 2-24-1717/8 d 1790 m (1)Hannah Stevens (2)Sarah Hall Sgt NH
Abel: b 11-18-1755 d 9-3-1846 m Abigail Runnels Pvt NH ★
Abner: b 6-22-1753 d 1814 m (1)Susan Ober (2)Nancy Rogers Pvt NH
Amos: b 7-28-1718 d 9-8-1792 m Mehitable Kimbell 2Maj CS NH
Anthony: b 1763 d 10-22-1831 m (1)Jerusha Ann Sears (2)Sally Bassett Sol MA
Asa: b 7-22-1766 d 1-26-1837 m Mary Bolton Pvt MA
Benjamin: b 1-31-1728/9 d 7-27-1796 m Presila Poor Maj MA
Benjamin: b 8-10-1740 d 12-15-1820 m Sarah Richardson Pvt NH
Daniel: b 6-1-1734 d 4-10-1810 m Priscilla Jones Pvt MA
David: b 12-26-1758 d 8-24-1844 m Rachel Newton Pvt MA ★
David: b 8-9-1750 d 4-26-1827 m Elizabeth Atwood Sgt NH
Ebenezer: b 8-9-1734 d 4-25-1803 m Grissel Elwell 2Lt NY
Elisha: b 1754 d 5-31-1833 m Olive Underwood Pvt CT
George: b 7-9-1740 d 5-4-1806 m Sarah Adams Sol VT
George: b 9-14-1756 d 1846 m — Tupper Pvt VT
Isaac: b 2-10-1761 d 9-27-1813 m Olive Abbott Pvt NH
James: b 12-15-1717 d p. 3-14-1783 m (1)Sarah Baker (2)Mercy (Mary) Baker PS MA
James: b 8-21-1736 d 4-30-1815 m Sarah Lamson Capt NH
John: b 2-10-1754 d 6-29-1812 m Mary Sawyer Sgt MA W ★
John: b 5-26-1757 d 8-27-1846 m (1)Hannah Duston (2)Charlotte Swan Pvt Artf MA ★
John: b 3- -1729 d 10-19-1799 m Judith Twombly CS NH
Jonathan: b 4-24-1747 d 8-27-1824 m (2)Dorcas Swan Cpl NH
Joshua: b 2-24-1747/8 d 12-21-1811 m Jane Anderson Cpl PS NH
Josiah: b 5-3-1738 d p. 1790 m Martha Wilson Pvt NH
Justus: b 1763 d 12-8-1830 m Mary Benjamin Sol NY
Moses: b 4-9-1732 d 1812 m Sarah Buckbee Pvt NY
Nathaniel: b 12-5-1730 d 4-5-1797 m Dorothy Kimball Capt MA
Peter: b 2-12-1751 d 10-14-1831 m Molly Webster PS MA
Phineas: b 5-17-1758 d p. 1784 m Lydia — Pvt NH
Pierce: b 3-29-1741 d 7-14-1821 m (1)Mary Bodwell (2)Eunice Eaton (3)Susannah Noyes Pvt NH
Prince: b 1750 d 12-24-1821 m (1)Priscilla — (2)Thankful — Pvt MA
Reuben: b 5-15-1749 d p. 1790 m Elizabeth Hamlin Pvt MA
Reuben: b 8- -1766 d 2-2-1849 m Mercy Ryder Pvt MA ★
Samuel: b 12-8-1749 d 1820 m Lydia Fish Pvt Cpl MA
Stephen: b 1762 d 1-27-1813 m Jane (Elkridge) Rackel Pvt MA
Thaddeus: b 4-17-1754 d 5-11-1845 m Abigail Merrill Pvt MA ★
Timothy: b 1-30-1749 d p. 1790 m Hannah Thurston Pvt MA
Wm.: b 10-10-1725 d 1803-7 m Mercy Huddlestone Capt VT
Zebulon: b 12-15-1724 d 1-7-1806 m Hannah Clark Sgt MA

GAGEBY,
James: b 1750 d 5-23-1834 m Janet Scroggs Pvt PA

GAILEY,
Andrew: b c. 1755 d 10-13-1845 m Margaret Dawson Pvt PA

GAILLARD,
Charles: b c. 1747 d p. 3-12-1807 m Anne DuPre Pvt SC
John: b 1735 d a. 6-26-1800 m Judith Peyre CS PS SC
Peter: b 1- -1757 d 1833 m Elizabeth Porcher Capt SC
Theodore, Jr.: b 9-3-1737 d 5-26-1805 m Ellen Cordes PS CS

GAINER,
Joseph, Sr.: b c. 1725 d p. 1793 m Susannah — PS NC
Wm.: b 1758 d p. 1799 m Martha Williams Pvt VA

GAINES,
Ambrose: b 7-6-1763 d 1-11-1840 m Mary Moore Pvt VA W ★
Benjamin: b c. 1732 d p. 8-18-1818 m Elizabeth — Sol VA
Daniel: b c. 1740 d 1798/1810 m (1) X (2)Mary Gilbert Col VA
Francis: b — d p. 10-12-1825 m Judy — Sol VA
George: b 1736 d 4-23-1809 m X Maj PS NH
Heirome: b 1758 d p. 3-15-1815 m Ann Thompson Adams SDI VA
James: b 1742 d 1830 m (1) — White (2)Elizabeth Strother Capt NC
James: b 10-14-1760 d 12-4-1854 m (2)Rebecca Lowe (3)Mary Elizabeth Montgomery (4)Cary Kidd Pvt VA ★
James, Sr.: b 1-18-1719 d 3-10-1786 m Mary Pendleton Pvt VA
James, Jr.: b c. 1733 d 11-25-1788 m Mildred Pollard CMman VA
Jonadab: b 1763 d 7-5-1828 m Jennie Johnson Pvt VA
Jude: b 1742-5 d 11-25-1829 m Anna Prindle Pvt CT ★
Moses: b 1735 d 1-12-1821 m Lucy Barbour Sgt VA
Richard, Sr.: b c. 1726 d 1801 m Mildred Hollinger Sgt VA
Richard, Jr.: b 5-19-1750 d 3-20-1835 m (1)Margaret Cunningham (2)Eleanor Miller Capt VA

Richard: b 1729 d 1805 m (1)Ann Cornelius (2)Gemina Pendleton Pvt VA
Richard: b 1752 d 11-9-1837 m (1) — Woods (2)Frances Jolly Pvt PA
Robert: b c. 1740 d p. 1796 m Mildred Bohannon Sol PS VA
Robert: b 1765 d 12-12-1833 m Anne Jenkins Pvt VA
Rowland: b 1758 d 9-4-1805 m Elizabeth Betsy — Cpl QM VA
Thomas: b 1738 d 1-30-1811 m Susan Dabney Strothers Cpl VA
Wm.: b c. 1740 d 4- -1827 m Ann Strother Pvt VA
Wm.: b 3-13-1754 d 1819 m Jeane Botts Pvt PS VA
Wm.: b c. 1757 d p. 10-25-1846 m Milley Banks Pvt VA ★
Wm., Henry: b 1705 d 1796 m (1)Isabella Pendleton (2)Maria Woods PS VA

GAINEY, (includes GANEY)
Bartholmew: b a. 1755 d p. 1820 m — Reddick PS NC
Matthew: b 12-10-1751 d 5-12-1832 m Elizabeth New Pvt NC
Meredith: b c. 1756 d 5-28-1782 m Ann Shotwell Pvt NC W ★

GAITHER,
Basil: b 1751 d 1802 m Margaret Watkins Capt MD
Benjamin: b c. 1728 d 1788 m Rachel — PS NC
Burgess: b 7-16-1757 d 1819 m Milly Martin Ens MD
Greenberry: b 1754 d p. 1781 m Catherine Anderson 1Lt MD
Henry: b 5-15-1724 d 1783 m Martha Ridgely PS CS MD
John: b c. 1741 d p. 9-18-1809 m X Capt MD
Johnsey: b c. 1760 d 1797 m Mary — Pvt MD
Rezin: b c. 1730 d 1807 m Sarah Yieldhall PS MD
Zachariah: b 6-28-1747 d 12-14-1802 m Sarah (Riggs) Warfield Ens MD

GALATIAN,
James, Sr.: b 11-11-1724 d 6-27-1804 m Hannah Little Pvt NY
James, Jr.: b 7-24-1758 d 3-29-1807 m Philandera Bogart Pvt NY

GALBRAITH, (includes GALBREATH, GILREATH)
Alexander: b 11-15-1755 d 1838 m Elizabeth Souther Pvt Sgt NC ★
Andrew: b 1750 d 3-7-1806 m X Maj PA
Arthur: b 1728 d 1818 m Mary Sharp CS VA
Bertram: b 9-24-1738 d 3-9-1804 m (1)Ann Scott (2)Henrietta Huling Col PA
George: b 1750 d 9-13-1822 m (1)Nancy Junkins (2)Hannah Harris Sol PS PA
James: b 1703 d 6-11-1786 m Elizabeth Bertram Lt Col PA
James: b c. 1741 d 1802 m Martha McClellan Col PA
James: b c. 1725 d p. 1792 m Ann Rea PS SC
John: b c. 1750-6 d 12- -1802 m Johanne — Sol NC
John: b 1739 d 12-3-1802 m Mary McColly Pvt PA
John: b 1748 d 1816 m Margaret Hulings Pvt PA
John: b c. 1752 d 1814 m Mary Martin PS VA
Neil: b c. 1740 d p. 1800 m (2)Catherine — Sol NC
Robert: b c. 1748 d 1795 m Mary — Pvt PA
Samuel: b 5-5-1767 d 7-20-1841 m Ann Morrison Pvt PA
Thomas: b 1751 d 2-5-1829 m Elizabeth Hays Pvt PA ★
Wm., Jr.: b 4-28-1753 d p. 1833 m Sally Jones Capt NC ★
Wm.: b 7-24-1736 d 5-3-1789 m Jean Webster Pvt PA
Wm.: b 10- -1757 d 5-3-1839 m Phebe Forman Pvt Sgt VA ★

GALE, (includes GAYLE)
Abraham: b 7-29-1745 d p. 1779 m (1)Abigail Rice (2)Phebe Allison Sgt 2Lt MA
Alpheus: b 9-7-1761 d 1823 m (1)Lydia Hammond (2)Betsey Hayward Pvt MA
Amos: b 3-3-1747/8 d p. 1782 m Hannah Maynard Pvt MA
Amos, Dr.: b 4-20-1744 d 6-8-1813 m Hannah Gilman PS NH
Asa: b 3-16-1751 d 6-11-1838 m (1)Esther — (2)Lydia Longley Pvt NH
Benjamin: b 12-14-1715 d 5-6-1790 m Hannah Elliott Capt CT
Benjamin: b 9-8-1732 d 3- -1786 m Eleanor — Pvt NY
Daniel, Jr.: b 18-1753 d 7-12-1834 m Esther Rice Pvt MA
Daniel: b 6-17-1721 d 12-31-1796 m Sarah Lamson PS MA
Daniel: b 9-2-1739 d 11- -1801 m Patience Eastman Pvt NH
Daniel: b 6-6-1747 d 10-16-1825 m Rhoda Burleigh Pvt NH
Eli: b 2-23-1743 d 1810 m Dorothy Blaisdell Capt MA
Elisha: b 11-26-1743 d 1-17-1827 m Mary Singletary Pvt 2Lt MA
Ephraim: b 4-1-1760 d 7-4-1824 m Molly Rice Pvt VT
Henry: b 3-22-1752 d 8-13-1836 m Elizabeth Drury Pvt MA
Isaac, Jr.: b 9- -1732 d 5-14-1779 m Mehetable Dwinel Sgt MA
Jacob: b 6-20-1736 d 1-22-1784 m Abigail Tappan Col NH
John: b 1-27-1759 d 7-30-1820 m Martha Marble Pvt MA
John: b c. 1730 d p. 1790 m Marie Billups Ens VA
John: b 5-19-1749 d 3-24-1825 m Johanna Walden PS VA
John Collins: b 11-26-1750 d 8-20-1812 m Rebecca Webster Pvt PS NH
Jonathan: b 7-12-1744 d p. 1833 m (1)Violetty Kenney (2)Lucy Temple Pvt MA
Jonathan: b 12-3-1748 d 1-29-1808 m Mary Bancroft Pvt MA
Joseph: b 3-1-1736 d 1799 m Sarah Huntington Capt CT
Joseph: b 1752 d 1834 m (1)Mercy Allen (2)Hannah Mott Pvt NJ ★
Josiah: b 4-8-1722 d 12-7-1794 m Elizabeth — Sgt MA
Josiah: b 6-5-1742 d 11-22-1798 m Rachel Mead 1Lt NY
Josiah: b 1730 d p. 12-17-1794 m X PS SC
Mathias: b c. 1755 d 1794 m Joyce Hall Pvt VA W ★
Matthew: b 8-12-1754 d 9-30-1820 m Mary Reese Cav SC

GALE, contd.
Nehemiah: b 2-12-1736 d 12-17-1820 m Ruth Marsh Lt MA
Noah: b 7-20-1757 d p. 1794 m Rebecca Chase Pvt MA
Peter: b 12-4-1756 d 11- -1818 m Prudence French Pvt MA
Rasin: b — d 11-11-1797 m (1)Martha Moore (2)Rebbeca — Pvt MD
Richard, Jr.: b 10-12-1760 d 6-2-1847 m (1)Lucretia Jones (2)Lucy Cummings Pvt MA
Robert: b c. 1743 d 1779-83 m Sarah — Capt VA
Samuel: b 3-8-1743 d 1-9-1799 m Elizabeth — LCol CT
Samuel: b 5-6-1726 d 5-6-1793 m Anna Fiske MM Pvt MA
Stephen: b 1739 d 9-10-1813 m Susanna Flanders Sol NH
Stephen: b 6-8-1736 d 7-9-1815 m (1)Mehitable Plummer (2)Mrs Phebe Page PS CS NH
Thomas: b 4-17-1750 d 5-24-1824 m (1)Mary Culley (2)Mrs Susannah Brown Lt VA

GALL, (includes GOLL)
Baltzer: b 1726 d 4-7-1799 m (1)Maria Elizabeth — (2)Catherine — PS MD
George, Sr.: b c. 1730 d 2-28-1778 m Marie Stults Cpl VA
George, Jr.: b 6-28-1766 d 7-1-1853 m (1)Susannah Nichols (2)Catherine Roads Pvt VA ★
Henry: b 1-28-1734 d 3-2-1820 m Catherine Kendig Pvt PA

GALLAGHER, (includes GALLAHER)
Bernard: b a. 1765 d p. 1810 m Margaret Strother Sol VA
Ebenezer: b 1-21-1754 d 2-20-1838 m Mary Jones Pvt NJ CL ★
James: b 4-12-1730 d 2-2-1792 m Tobitha Williams Pvt PA
Thomas: b 1751/2 d 1810 m Lucretia Jones Pvt PA

GALLAHUE,
Jeremiah: b c. 1750 d p. 1825 m Nancy Barnes Sol VA

GALLAND,
James: b — d — m Hannah Garland Pvt CT

GALLATINE,
Jacob: b c. 1757 d 1832 m Elizabeth Ritenour Pvt PA ★

GALLEMORE,
Wm.: b 2-14-1750 d 4-10-1794 m Mary Sanders Sol NC

GALLEY,
Peter: b a. 1753 d 1785 m Sophia Sterne Pvt PA

GALLISON,
John, Sr.: b 2-3-1730/1 d 3-26-1786 m (1)Abigail Lee (2)Eunice Bourne PS MA
John: b 8-6-1754 d 1846 m Abigail Winslow Pvt MA NY

GALLOW,
Christopher: b 1750 d — m Deborah Weeks Pvt NY
John: b — d — m (1)Mary Reynolds (2)Mrs Katherine Bell Pettingill Pvt NY

GALLOWAY, (includes GALLAWAY)
Alexander: b 1746 d 7-8-1832 m (1) — Winnon (2)Mary Millen Sol SC
Alexander: bpt 5-4-1747 d a. 1799 m Mary — 2Lt NY
Charles: b 11-19-1758 d 10-25-1846 m Bridget Clifford Sol PS NC
George: b c. 1723 d c. 1786 m Rebecca Junkin PS PA
James: b 4-14-1742 d 11-1-1810 m (1)Ann Smith (2)Rebecca Galloway 2Lt PS NY
James: b 5-1-1750 d 8-6-1838 m Rebecca Junkin Pvt PA VA ★
James: b 9-11-1758 d 8-26-1840 m Jane Bailey Pvt PA ★
John: b a. 1750 d a. 2-26-1780 m Mary Harrison Lt PA
John: b 8-8-1746 d p. 1782 m Mary Cummings Sol PA
Joseph: b c. 1750 d p. 1790 m Mary Galloway 2Maj MD
Joseph: b 1-8-1757 d 8-19-1838 m (1)Isabelle Orr (2)Agnes Cross Pvt PA
Marshall: b 1760 d 12-17-1827 m Hannah Watlin Pvt MD ★
Matthew: b 12-15-1759 d 2-14-1824 m (1) — Beavers (2)Mary East Sol GA
Moses: b 9- -1726 d 7-10-1798 m (1)Mary Nicholson (2)Pamelia Owings PS MD
Peter: b 1757 d 1838 m Phebe Smith Pvt SC
Robert: b — d p. 1790 m McKegg Pvt PA
Samuel: b 1747 d p. 1814 m X Pvt PA
Wm., Jr.: b 11-21-1738 d 8-14-1801 m Ann Waller Ens MD
Wm.: b 6-8-1743 d 9-28-1795 m (1)Catherine Thompson (2)Rebecca Mitchell Pvt PA

GALLUP, (includes GALLOP)
Amos: b 8-1-1755 d 12-1-1843 m Welthean Dean Lt CT ★
Andrew: b 1-26-1761 d 3-16-1853 m Nancy Weldon Sol CT
Benadam, Sr.: b 10-26-1716 d 5-29-1800 m Hannah Avery Maj CT
Benadam, Jr.: b 6-29-1741 d 4-12-1818 m Bridget Palmer Pvt CT
Benadam: b 11-17-1761 d 3-30-1850 m (1)Elizabeth Dorrence (2)Mary Wilson Pvt CT ★
Benjamin: b 7-26-1736 d 7-4-1824 m Amy Kinne Pvt CT
Benjamin Franklin: b 8-23-1739 d 11-4-1841 m (1)Sarah Lawrence (2)Mrs Abiah Everett Cpl MA

Elisha: b 4-21-1727 d 8-24-1800 m Mercy Dennison Pvt VT
Enos: b 10-1-1761 d 12-7-1834 m Ruth Kennedy Pvt MA
Ezra: b 3-13-1763 d 4-5-1846 m Rebecca Hinckley Pvt CT ★
George: b 3-20-1756 d 5-13-1781 m Freelove Packer Ens CT W ★
Henry, Jr.: b 10-17-1758 d 11-22-1831 m Deziah Stanton Pvt CT
Isaac: b 2-24-1712 d 8-3-1799 m Margaret — Capt PS CT
Isaac: b 12-22-1742 d 8-3-1814 m Anna Smith Capt CT ★
Jesse: b 2-2-1751 d p. 1784 m Cathrine Fish Cpl CT
John, Sr.: b 1-29-1720 d 11-1-1801 m Bridget Palmer Cpl CT
John, Jr.: b 1750 d 12-5-1835 m Lydia Clark Sgt CT ★
John: b 12-29-1749 d 3-2-1793 m Hannah Douglas Pvt CT
John: b 2-2-1758 d 12-8-1825 m Hannah Denison Pvt CT
Joseph: b 2-26-1725 d 2-21-1778 m Mary Gardiner Capt CT
Joseph: b 10-18-1760 d 2-18-1849 m Miriam Brigham Sol VT
Levi: b 3-26-1760 d 2-18-1850 m Abigail Packer Pvt CT
Nathan: b 3-13-1727 d 1-29-1799 m Sarah Giddings Col CT
Nathaniel: b 4-29-1718 d 1-11-1786 m Hannah Burrows Grd CS CT
Nathaniel: b 9-22-1760 d 10-19-1843 m Anna York Pvt VT RI
Nehemiah: b 6-19-1751 d 12-27-1843 m Elizabeth Brown Sgt CT
Thomas: b 8-20-1727 d 1-24-1778 m Hannah Dean Sgt NH
Wm.: b 10-9-1722 d 9-29-1803 m (1)Hephzibah Smith (2)Jemima Towne Pvt MA
Wm.: b 7-3-1723 d 4-4-1803 m Judith Reed Sol PA
Wm.: b c. 1739 d p. 1788 m Hannah — Pvt RI VT
Wm.: b 1-16-1735 d 8-13-1803 m Lucy Dennison Pvt VT

GALPIN,
Abel: b 1757 d 2-24-1841 m Mary Wright Pvt MA ★
Amos: b 1-21-1755 d 12-7-1843 m Sybill Tallmadge Ens CT
George: b 1709 d 12-2-1780 m X PS SC
Joseph: b 1754 d 12-26-1840 m (1)Katherine Parsons (2)Rhoda Gurnsey Pvt CT
Samuel: b 1758 d 1840 m Abigail Savage Pvt CT ★
Stephen: bpt 10-27-1734 d 7-19-1806 m Lydia Stone Pvt CT
Thomas: b 2-6-1757 d 11-17-1802 m Ruth Goodrich Pvt CT

GALUSHA,
Amos: b 4-1-1755 d 10-16-1839 m Mary Clark Pvt VT
David: b 1765 d 10-21-1854 m Ruth Osborn Cpl VT
David: b 1748 d 8-26-1804 m (1)Charity Lathrop (2)Rhoda — 1Lt VT
Jacob: b 1725 d 2-13-1792 m (1)Lydia Huntington (2)Thankful King (3)Desire Metcalf (4)Abigail Foster Pvt VT
Jonas: b 2-11-1753 d 9-25-1834 m (1)Mary Chittenden (3)Abigail Ward Capt VT
Jonas: b c. 1730 d p. 1790 m Anne — Pvt VT
Thomas: b 8-2-1756 d 7-24-1844 m Ruth — Pvt CT VT & MA ★

GAMAGE,
Joshua: bpt 1-3-1741 d p. 1785 m Elinor Foster Pvt MA
Samuel: b 8-25-1751 d 8-2-1832 m Marth Swift Lt MA ★

GAMBLE, (includes GAMBRILL, GAMBILL, GEMMILL)
Archibald: b c. 1740 d p. 1790 m Mary Lisle Engineer PA
Archibald: b 6-8-1762 d 7-28-1844 m (2)Elizabeth Patten Pvt NH
Augustine: b c. 1732 d 1790 m Sarah Sappington PS MD
James: b 1759 d 6- -1841 m (1)Sarah — (2)Hannah — (3)Mary — Cpl NY ★
James: b 1744 d 1840 m (2)Martha Miller QM 2Lt PA
John: b 10-16-1762 d 7-24-1844 m Sarah Rogers Pvt MA ★
John: b c. 1760 d 5-5-1817 m (1)Margaret Lawson (2)Rachel Lowery Sol GA
John: b 1745 d 1798 m (1)Agnes Wallace (2)Elizabeth — Pvt PA
John: b c. 1750 d a. 1797 m X Maj SC
John: b 12-11-1757 d 1-14-1831 m Rebecca McPheeters Pvt VA
Joseph: b 1745-50 d 6- -1796 m Mary Flower Pilot PA
Martin: b c. 1760 d 2-20-1812 m Nancy Nall 1Lt Capt NC W ★
Robert: b 9-3-1754 d 4-12-1810 m Catherine Grattan Capt VA
Samuel: b 1748 d 1780 m Mary Miller Pvt SC
Wm.: b 1730 d 1791 m Mary — Pvt MD
Wm.: b 1704 d 12-28-1785 m Anna Stark Aid-de-camp NH
Wm.: b c. 1760 d a. 11-29-1837 m Sarah — Sol SC
Wm.: b 1-15-1735 d 10-29-1784 m Fanny Gregg Pvt VA

GAMBLING,
James: b 8- -1752 d 5-13-1843 m Mary Stalcup Cpl NC ★

GAMMELL,
John: b 5-18-1752 d 2-10-1828 m Margaret Urann PS Pvt MA

GAMMON, (includes GAYMON)
Daniel: b 5-18-1752 d 2-10-1828 m Margaret Urann PS Pvt MA
David: b 1754 d 1836 m Mary Doane Pvt MA ★
Harris: b 9-27-1757 d 2- -1844 m Elizabeth Brawner Pvt VA ★
Isaac: b 6-11-1757 d 11-11-1819 m Elizabeth — Pvt PA
Joseph: b c. 1734 d c. 1810 m Elizabeth — PS MA
Richard: b 8-24-1750 d 1-4-1833 m Sarah Gamble Pvt NC
Smith: b c. 1755 d a. 2-10-1816 m Elizabeth Monk PS NC

GAMMONS,
John: b 4-8-1745 d 3-13-1822 m (1)Hannah Cole (2)Jane Ingraham Pvt MA ★

GAMWELL,
James: b 1758 d 4-3-1830 m (2)Polly Kingston OrdlSgt MA ★

GANCE,
Benjamin: b 6- -1762 d 8-10-1834 m Mary Metcalf Pvt PA

GANDY,
David: b 1758 d 9- -1820 m Sarah Somers Pvt NJ
John: b 7-14-1746 d 2-18-1800 m Lydia Williams Pvt NJ

GANGWER, (includes GANGEWER, GANGEWERE)
Andrew: b 9-15-1757 d 7-10-1844 m Mary Montaigne Lt PA ★
George: b 7-20-1756 d 3-2-1852 m (1)Christine Clader (2)Catherina
    — Pvt PA ★
Jacob: b 2-20-1754 d 8-21-1825 m Margaret Hertz Pvt PA

GANN,
Nathan: b 1759 d 7-18-1839 m Sarah Delaney Lt NC

GANNAWAY
Gregory: b 5-8-1753 d 8-25-1804 m Rhoda Robertson Pvt VA

GANNETT,
Benjamin: b 12-11-1728 d 1813 m (1)Mary Copeland (2)Anna
    Everson Lt MA
Deborah Sampson: b 12-17-1760 d 4-29-1827 m Benjamin Gannett
    Pvt MA
Joseph: b 9-26-1759 d 4- -1842 m (1)Abigail Cobb (2)Sarah Eaton
    White Pvt MA ★
Matthew: b 1725 d — m Submit Joy Pvt MA
Matthew: b 5-8-1755 d 1845 m (1)Alice Latham (2)Priscilla Hayford
    Pvt MA

GANNON,
Wm.: b 2-1-1758 d p. 1832 m Betty Tramble Pvt NC

GANO,
Daniel: b 11-11-1758 d 4-18-1849 m (1)Martha Bryan (2)Jemima
    Robertson Capt NY ★
George: b c. 1758 d 1-24-1813 m Elizabeth Cock Sol NJ
Jacob: b 1735 d 8-7-1812 m Elizabeth Armitage Capt PA
John: b 7-22-1727 d 8-10-1804 m (1)Sarah Stites (2)Mrs. Thomas
    Bryant Chp NY
Stephen: b 12-25-1762 d 8-28-1828 m Cornelia Varasour Dr. NJ

GANSEVOORT,
Conrad: b 3-28-1761 d 8-9-1829 m Elizabeth Roseboom 2Lt NY
Leonard: b 7-14-1751 d 8-26-1810 m Hester Cuyler PS PM NY
Leonard, Jr.: b 1754 d 1834 m Maria Van Rensselaer PS NY

GANSON,
John: b 1750 d 1813 m X Capt MA
Nathan: b 1755 d 5-2-1827 m Rebecca Childs Sgt MA ★

GANTT,
Thomas, Sr.: b 1710 d 1781 m (1)Rachel Smith (2)Mrs Hilleary PS
    MD
Thomas, Jr.: b 1736 d p. 1800 m (1)Susanna Mackall (2)Sarah
    Eleanor Potts PS MD

GANTZ,
George: b 1744 d p. 12-2-1807 m Susannah Arnold Pvt PA
George: b a. 1764 d 1833 m Elizabeth Dorcas Jalim Capt PA

GAPEN,
Stephen: b 5-29-1761 d 12-26-1839 m (1)Sarah Scott (2)Rebecca
    Snider Pvt Spy PA ★
Zacariah: b 8-10-1733 d p. 1800 m Ruth Tindall PS VA

GARBER, (includes GERBER)
Benedict: b 10-13-1732 d 6-12-1817 m Dorothea Loreht Pvt PA
John: b 7-4-1753 d 1-23-1818 m X Pvt PA
Joseph: b c. 1725 d 1791 m X PS PA

GARD, (includes GUARD)
Alexander: b 12-20-1761 d 1-18-1811 m Hannah Keen Pvt NJ
Daniel: b 1737 d 11-1787 m Charity Grey Lt NJ
Daniel: b 12-6-1755 d 6- -1824 m Hannah Merick Pvt PS NJ ★
Gershom: b 1738 d a. 4-7-1807 m Phebe Huntington Pvt NJ
Jeremiah: b 1755 d p. 1813 m Experience — Pvt PA
Jeremiah: b 1717 d 7-19-1783 m Elizabeth Johnson Pvt NJ
John: b 8-11-1742 d 12-28-1824 m Elizabeth Dudley Pvt Wgn NJ

GARDEN,
Alexander: b 12-4-1757 d 2-24-1829 m Mary Anna Gibbes Julia
    Martha Pinckney Maj SC

GARDENHIRE,
Jacob: b 4- -1730 d 1825 m X Sol VA

**GARDNER, (includes GARDENIER, GARDINER, GARDINIER,
    GARTNER)**
Aaron: b 4-1-1741 d 1815 m Azubah Partridge Capt Maj MA

Abel: b 1763 d 4-29-1840 m (1)Lucina — (2)Mrs Mary Mansfield
    Pvt MA ★
Abel: b 1763 d 1834 m Bethiah Pitman Slr MA
Abel: b 9-2-1747 d p. 1780 m Dorothy Sweet Pvt RI
Abraham: b 2-19-1721 d 8-21-1782 m Phoebe Smith Col NY
Amos: b 1756 d 9-28-1827 m Abigail Knowles Pvt PS RI
Amos: b c. 1760 d 1803 m (1)Mary Hammond (2)Mrs Sally
    Champlin Pvt RI
Andrew: b 1749 d 8-26-1840 m Abigail — Pvt MA ★
Andrew: b c. 1754 d p. 1820 m Eleanor — Drm Maj Ens PA
Andries: b 6-9-1723 d 12-22-1801 m (1)Marguereta Goeway
    (2)Sarah Hanson Pvt NY
Asa: b 1760 d 1-22-1835 m Dorothy Jenks Pvt MA
Benjamin: bpt 10-9-1757 d 9-25-1813 m Mary Smith Capt MA
Benjamin: b 8-25-1759 d 8-28-1829 m Mary Thompson Fif NJ
Benjamin: b 9- -1760 d 3-1-1840 m (2)Lucy Hanks Sgt NY ★
Benjamin: b 1731 d 2-2-1809 m Elizabeth Olin Pvt NY
Benjamin: b 11-9-1746 d p. 9-5-1832 m Tabitha Brown Ens RI ★
Benjamin: b 1-4-1750 d 4-3-1819 m (1)Elizabeth Wicks (2)Amey
    Ann Coggshall (3)Mary Howland PS RI
Benoni: b 5-25-1752 d p. 1797 m Silence Grant ArtlMatr NY
Bernard: b 1733 d 3-27-1807 m Barbara Weidman Capt PA
Caleb: b 1727 d 10-23-1801 m Eleanor Phillips — LCol PA
Caleb: b 1-24-1739 d 12-24-1806 m Sarah Ann Robinson PS RI
Christopher: b 1753 d 7- -1849 m Ruth Sherburn Pvt NH ★
Christopher: b c. 1753 d a. 6-27-1805 m Elizabeth — Pvt NJ
Christopher: b 12-2-1726 d 1812 m (1)Mary Easton (2)Elizabeth
    Fones Capt RI
Christopher, Jr.: b 1737 d 6-16-1795 m (1)Mary Wheeler (2)Elizabeth
    Brownell Capt RI W★
Clement: b 1748 d 12-1-1817 m Henrietta Boone Pvt PS MD
Coas: bpt 7-24-1743 d 7-21-1807 m (1)Sarah Perkins (2)Lucy
    Proctor 1Lt MA
Daniel, Jr.: b 5-10-1764 d 7-25-1789 m Anna Crocker Pvt CT
David, Sr.: b 6-26-1720 d 10-1-1796 m Jemima Gustin PS CT
David: b 4-20-1753 d 1-20-1823 m (1)Dennis Holmes (2)Mary
    Lathrop (3)Olive Metcalf Pvt CT
David: b 3-27-1734 d 2-16-1814 m (1)Lydia Loring (2)Ruth Dunbar
    Pvt MA
David, Jr.: b 6-9-1750 d p. 1797 m Zuriah Huntley Seaman MA
Ebenezer: b 9-4-1737 d 11-21-1832 m Damaris Merrill Pvt MA
Elijah: b 3-27-1731 d 1809 m Leah Smith Pvt MA
Elijah: b 9-21-1756 d 1849 m Hannah Reed Pvt MA ★
Elijah: b 1-4-1757 d 6- -1807 m Sarah Force Cpl NJ
Elizabeth Mumford: b 2-26-1743 d 8-24-1834 m John Gardiner PS
    PA
Ezekiel: b 7-1-1753 d 4-18-1828 m Betsey Chubbock Sgt MA
Ezekiel, Sr.: b 9-29-1712 d 8-12-1780 m Dorcas Watson PS RI
Ezekiel, Jr.: b 8-25-1738 d 8-9-1814 m Susannah Congdon RO RI
Francis: b — d 1783 m — Wallace 2Lt PA
George: b 6-8-1741 d 1799 m Barbara Frye Pvt PA
George Adam: b c. 1740 d 7- -1809 m Christine — Pvt PA
Heath: b 1-16-1761 d 8- -1829 m Susannah Weldon PS VA
Henry H.: b 4-23-1727 d 11-21-1805 m (2)Susanna Mayers Capt NY
Isaac: b 5-1-1726 d 4-19-1775 m Mary Sparhawk MM MA
Isaac: b 3-14-1762 d 9-5-1830 m Sarah Thorn Pvt MA
Isaac: b 11-16-1755 d 11-7-1801 m Sarah Lincoln Pvt MA
Isaac: b 1735 d p. 1790 m Hulda — Pvt NC
Jacob: b 2-7-1727 d 5-9-1808 m Dirkje Van der Werken Capt NY
James: b 10-26-1759 d 10-11-1809 m Margaret Skerry Smn MA
James: b 3-8-1763 d 12-26-1831 m (1)Susannah Flagg (2)Content
    Phillips (3)Mary Phillips Pvt MA
James: b 4-26-1755 d 4-21-1849 m (1)Rachel Wilson (2)Tabitha
    Martin Pvt NJ
James: b 12-25-1758 d 6-5-1838 m Elizabeth Froome Pvt Tms NJ ★
James: b c. 1752 d p. 9-12-1790 m Mary — PS NC
James: b 10-26-1750 d 2-4-1795 m (1)Sarah Babcock (2)Patience
    Hall Capt RI
James: b 1755 d 1820 m Sidney Ann Flaherty Drm Maj VA
Jeremiah: b 2-5-1727/8 d 1-29-1815 m (1)Mary Parsons (2)Jemima
    Stratton Ens PS NY
Jesse: b 2-3-1761 d 1-8-1815 m Martha Carpenter Pvt NY W★
Job: b 1730 d 3-9-1806 m Hannah Britton Pvt NY
Job: b 7-23-1723 d p. 1787 m Ann Fry PS RI
John: b — d p. 1-22-1799 m X PS MD
John: b c. 1758 d p. 1783 m Anna Hutchinson Pvt MA
John: b 9-4-1751 d 6-17-1810 m Mary Scott Wgn Capt NJ
John: b 5-19-1747 d 5-29-1813 m (1)Johanna Conkling (2)Rachel
    Mulford (3)Hannah Havens PS NY
John: b 1722 d 1780 m Elizabeth Dayton PS NY
John: b 1750 d 1807 m Mary Douglas Col PA
John: b 1750 d 1808 m Sarah Ann — Pvt PA
John: b 1757 d 9-10-1821 m Elizabeth Clark Pvt PA
John: b 5-9-1737 d 7- -1778 m Elizabeth Mumford PS PA
John: b 1745 d 11- -1808 m Sarah — Capt RI
John: b 6-17-1745 d 9- -1815 m Bathsheba Watson Ens RI
John: b 4-7-1753 d 3-17-1837 m (1)Mary Gardiner (2)Frances Hall
    Sgt RI ★
John: b 1745 d p. 11-5-1796 m Margaret — 1Lt VA
John: b c. 1760 d a. 1832 m Elizabeth Francis Sgt VA
John: b c. 1750 d p. 1780 m Violet Gardner Pvt VA
Jonathan, Jr.: b 12-2-1758 d 5-6-1847 m Jerusha Hyde Stark Pvt
    CT ★

GARDNER, contd.
Jonathan: b 8-15-1745 d 10- -1780 m Abigail Knower Cpl MA
Jonathan: b 1745 d 7-18-1826 m Elizabeth Biddels Pvt MA ★
Jonathan: b 6-29-1760 d 3-31-1836 m Sara — Pvt MA ★
Joseph: b a. 1740 d p. 1782 m Eleanor Collier Pvt MA
Joseph: b 1752 d 1794 m Isabella Cochran PS Dr PA
Joseph: b a. 2-19-1747/48 d c. 1813 m Mary Burts Sol PS NY
Joshua: b 2-5-1734/35 d p. 1790 m Mary Totman Pvt MA
Josiah: b 10-25-1755 d 1-29-1843 m Katherine Fenton Pvt MA ★
Latham: b 10-1-1759 d 9-18-1830 m Priscilla Gardner Smn MA
Lewis: b 1740-44 d a. 8-16-1799 m (1)Hannah — (2)Verlinda — Sol CS GA
Martin: b 1745 d 3-10-1818 m Margareta — Pvt PA
Matthew: b 1750 d p. 1797 m Mary — PS VA
Nathan: b 1754 d 1803 m Martha Thompson Pvt MA
Nathaniel: b 4-10-1744 d 7-14-1801 m Martha Brown Pvt MA
Nathaniel: b 1751 d 2- -1813 m Marcia Spencer Capt RI
Nathaniel: b 6-16-1714 d 1796 m Sarah Pierce CS RI
Nathaniel B.: b 10-11-1765 d 11-16-1851 m Hannah Briggs Pvt NY ★
Nicholas: b 1744/45 d p. 1792 m Catharina Scremling Pvt NY
Nicholas, Sr.: b 12-10-1710 d 1801 m Martha Havens PS RI
Nicholas Easton: b 7-23-1755 d 3-2-1808 m Eunice Bright Pvt Mid & 2Mate RI
Paris: b 7-28-1743 d p. 1790 m Elizabeth Smith Capt RI
Paul: b 1-29-1730 d 3-17-1813 m Rachel Starbuck CS MA
Perez: b 3-26-1762 d 1-31-1841 m Silence — Pvt MA W ★
Prior: b 1-19-1758 d p. 2-1-1827 m Drucilla Rose Rifleman NC
Richard: b 2-8-1767 d 7-4-1858/9 m Lydia Chapman PS PA
Richard: b 2-3-1745 d p. 1790 m (1)Mary Hammond (2)Mercy Hammond CS RI
Robert: b 8-31-1706 d 12-5-1788 m Sarah Dunbar Pvt MA
Robert: b c. 1750 d a. 12-31-1827 m Nancy Milliken Pvt PA
Rufus: b 3-9-1747 d 1809 m Lydia Harris Smn CT
Samuel: b 12-29-1761 d 12-31-1823 m Elizabeth Ford Pvt NJ
Samuel: b 3-18-1733 d 12-30-1806 m Maria Van Everen Lt NY
Samuel: b c. 1740 d p. 1790 m Christina Groat Pvt NY
Samuel: b 1751 d 7-3-1836 m Hannah Owens Pvt PA
Samuel: b 8-29-1742 d 1782 m Catherine Greene CS RI
SarahWayne: b a. 1757 d 1821 m Thomas McCalla PS SC
Seth, Jr.: b 1755 d 10-26-1826 m Eunice Patch Pvt MA ★
Simeon: b 10-22-1754 d a. 9-16-1817 m Abigail — Pvt NY
Simon Stacey: b 7-24-1743 d a. 2- -1787 m Rebecca Knapp Pvt MA
Stephen, Jr.: b 3-27-1735 d 9-29-1811 m (1)Frances Brown (2)Mrs Alice Abbott Pvt CT
Stephen: b 10-27-1727 d p. 1790 m Huldah Chubbuck Pvt MA
Sterling: b c. 1753 d 1843 m — Neal Sol GA
Thomas: b c. 1723 d 7-3-1775 m Joanna Sparhawk Col MA
Thomas: b 2-13-1731/2 d 1788 m Mary Buffington 1Lt MA
Thomas, Sr.: b 3-2-1724 d 10-1-1795 m (1)Phoebe Headley (2)Mrs Abigail Allen Wgm NJ
Thomas, Jr.: b 6-25-1752 d 3-22-1804 m Abigail Allen Cpl NJ
Thomas: b a. 1735 d 1811 m (1)Harriet — (2)Mary Duvall Pvt NY
Thomas: b c. 1750 d 11- -1815 m Eliza Kanard Pvt SC
Thomas: b 9-6-1759 d p. 1833 m Sarah Wadkins Sgt VA ★
Wm.: b 9-5-1741 d 3-31-1800 m Esther Denison Pvt CT
Wm.: b 11-13-1749 d 11-16-1823 m Hannah Blodgett Pvt CT ★
Wm., Sr.: b 1724 d 11-3-1812 m Catherine — CS NJ
Wm.: b 1761 d 1833 m Rebecca Raymond Pvt NY
Wm.: b c. 1750 d p. 1790 m Belinda Teal Pvt SC
Wm.: b 2-12-1758 d 7-19-1840 m Esther Nichols Lt RI ★
Wm.: b a. 1754 d p. 1790 m Miss Draper Matr SC

GARFIELD,
Benjamin, Jr.: b 1740 d 1824 m Lucy Chase Sgt MA
Edward: bpt 8-20-1732 d p. 1787 m Martha Nevers Pvt MA
Eliakim: b 1730 d 12- -1813 m Sarah — Pvt MA
Enoch: b 11-22-1743 d 7-24-1824 m Abigail Slater Sgt MA
Isaac: b 2-19-1716/7 d 1-21-1792 m Mary Brewer PS CS MA
Isaac: b 1743 d 1792 m Margaret Orton CS MA
John: b 10-11-1751 d 6- -1803 m Lucy Smith Pvt MA
John: b 1-23-1764 d 9-20-1837 m Hulda Bird Pvt MA ★
Joshua: b 1726 d 9-28-1795 m Ruth Hammond Pvt MA
Nathaniel: b 10-29-1760 d 2-9-1839 m Eunice Woodward Pvt MA ★
Samuel: b 4-11-1720 d 6-12-1792 m (1)Hannah — (2)Abigail Pierce Pvt MA
Solomon: b 3-5-1753 d 6-12-1821 m Ruth Bird Sgt Lt MA

GARIS, (includes GARRISS)
Henry: b 12-2-1756 d p. 1835 m —Wade Pvt NC ★
John: b 1750 d 1832 m Elizabeth Stout Pvt PS PA

GARLAND, (includes GALLAND)
Amos: b 8-15-1760 d 2- -1832 m (1)Mary James (2)Polly M. Fullerton Pvt NH
Benjamin: b 10-29-1734 d 5-2-1805 m Sarah Jenness MM NH
Christopher: b 5-24-1753 d 1-20-1812 m (1)Sarah — (2)Mary W. Jarvis Sgt VA ★
Dodivah: b 12-26-1722 d 4-19-1798 m Mary — Ens PS NH
Ebenezar: b 1730 d p. 1787 m Sarah Seavey PS NH
Edward: b 1751 d 1817 m Sarah Olds Cpl VA W★
Jacob: b 1738 d 9-30-1797 m Betsey Pettengill Pvt NH
James: bpt 10-1-1752 d 8-17-1841 m (3)Hitty (Kennison) Webster Pvt NH W★

James, Sr.: b 1722 d 1812 m Mary Rice CS PS VA
James, Jr.: b 1753 d 1781 m Anne Wingfield Capt VA
John: b c. 1740 d p. 12-18-1810 m Mrs Joanna Hancock Cpl MA
John: b 1758 d 1815 m (1)Sally Blaisdell (2)Sarah Kimball Pvt NH
John: b 10-4-1758 d 3-24-1844 m Abigail Perkins MM NH
John: b 5-18-1719 d p. 1790 m Molly Rand PS NH
John: b 1743 d 9-17-1840 m Susannah Nichols Pvt NC
Jonathan: b 7-3-1746 d 4-13-1825 m Abigail Fogg Lt NH
Joseph: bpt 6-11-1732 d p. 1790 m Sarah — PS NH
Matthew: b 1750 d a. 1810 m Hannah Fenno Sol VA
Nathaniel: b 1750 d 1793 m Jane Rodes Lt VA
Richard: b 5-28-1763 d 3-5-1855 m Sarah Watson Pvt NH
Vincent: b c. 1745 d 1805 m Elizabeth — PS VA
Wm.: b 1755-60 d 1827 m Lydia Cooley Pvt SC

GARLATIER, DE MAS
Paul Francois Ignace: b 7-31-1733 d p. 1783 m Marie Perrier De la Garde PS FrN

GARLINGHOUSE,
Benjamin: b 1761 d 1850 m Anne Morehouse Pvt NJ
John: b 4- -1759 d 8-12-1810 m Jean Leonard Pvt NJ

GARLINGTON,
Christopher: b 12-17-1756/7 d 4-10-1843 m X Pvt SC VA ★
Christopher: b 12-4-1729 d 1801 m Sarah Young PS SC

GARLOCK, (includes GARLOUGH)
Adam: b 1754 d 1840 m Hannah Grey Pvt NY
Charles: b c. 1735 d 8-6-1777 m X Sgt NY
George Peter: b 7-14-1750 d 3-13-1836 m Margaret Hulshover Pvt NY
Jacob: b 10-16-1761 d 7-19-1848 m Catharine Young Pvt NY ★
John: b 1-16-1763 d 6-9-1823 m (1)— Ettnire (2)Margaretta Ann Eichelbarger Pvt MD

GARMAN,
Adam: b c. 1732 d 1806 m Barbara — Pvt PA
Leonard: b 1-2-1762 d 2-5-1849 m (2)Mary Elizabeth Troop Pvt PA
Michael: b 1747 d 1800 m Susanna Sheetz Pvt PA

GARNER,
Benjamin: b c. 1746 d a. 4-26-1790 m Diana — PS VA
James: b c. 1752 d p. 6-11-1823 m Susanna Britton Pvt MD
J. Michael: b 1728 d 1805-10 m Catherine Seiss Pvt MD
John,: b c. 1740 d 1825 m (1)Alcy Eaton (2)Mrs Margaret Seigler Sol NC
John: b c. 1751 d 1817 m Christina Waugh Pvt PA
John: b 4-18-1761 d p. 1795 m (2)Ann Keen Pvt SC
John Fouche: b 12-25-1749 d 11-25-1839 m (1)Nancy Whittle (2)Betsy Donaldson (3)Gracie Conrad Pvt NC ★
Sturdy: b 4-9-1762 d 3-4-1845 m Sara Smith Pvt NC VA ★
Vincent: b c. 1725 d a. 6-27-1796 m Jemimah — PS VA
Wm.: b — d a. 1820 m Katherine Fairfax Pvt VA
Wm.: b c. 1760 d a. 1815 m Sallie Martin Sol VA

GARNETT, (includes GARNET)
Anthony: b c. 1709 d p. 1800 m Elizabeth Bowles Pvt VA
Augustine: b a. 2-10-1747 d a. 10-16-1786 m Elizabeth — Capt VA
Henry: b 1756 d 6-7-1815 m Elizabeth Aylett Buckner Capt VA
John: b 3-17-1750 d p. 2-13-1830 m Betsy Rogers Pvt VA ★
Reuben: b 10-10-1749 d 1820 m Mary Jameson Ens VA
Thomas: b 1733-6 d 1793 m Rachel Wilson 1Lt GA
Thomas: b c. 1754 d c. 1796 m Susanna Andrews PS VA

GAROUTTE,
Michael: b 4-12-1750 d 4-29-1829 m Sophia Smith Pvtr NJ

GARRARD, (includes GERARD, GERRARD)
Anthony: bpt 2-12-1756 d 1807 m Elizabeth Greene Pvt NC
Elias: b c. 1735 d 12-31-1797 m X Pvt VA
Jacob: b 9-4-1763 d 1814 m Mary Elizabeth Barron Sol GA
James: b 1-14-1749 d 1-19-1822 m Elizabeth Mountjoy Col VA
John: b c. 1730 d 3- -1807 m (1)Mary Bolt (2)Elizabeth — Pvt GA
John: b 3-31-1763 d 6-26-1837 m Leah Hays Pvt VA ★
John: b c. 1720 d p. 8- -1787 m (1)Mehatable — (2)Mary — PS VA
Wm.: b 1735-7 d p. 3-16-1801 m Charity — Pvt PS NY
Wm.: b c. 1715 d p. 9-7-1786 m (1)Mary Lewis (2)Elizabeth Moss Col VA

GARRELL,
John Stephen: b 1758 d 1819 m Abigail Hendricks Pvt PA

GARRETT, (includes GARRIOTT)
Ambrose: b c. 1760 d a. 7-24-1834 m Mary Turpen Sol VA
Andrew: b 2-2-1756 d 1-6-1805 m Olive Blish Pvt MA
Edward: b 8-31-1733 d 8-25-1794 m Anne West Owsley PS SC
Francis, Sr.: b c. 1710 d 4-1729 d c. 1783 m Ruth Case Pvt CT
Francis, Jr.: b 4-12-1759 d p. 1790 m Hannah Robe Pvt CT
Henry: b 1745 d 1815 m Mary Johnson Capt CS VA
Jacob: b c. 1730 d p. 12-3-1796 m X PS VA
James: b 1746 d 6- -1778 m Nancy — Pvt NC
John: b 8-4-1738 d 1-28-1825 m Hannah Barker Pvt CT

John: b 1756 d 2-16-1853 m (2)Widow Carrington Pvt Tms CT ★
John, Jr.: b 1751 d 10-18-1811 m (1)Esther Spencer (2)Mary Case Pvt CT
John: b 2-19-1737 d 3-28-1806 m Elizabeth Yeatman Capt DE
John, Sr.: b 8-15-1727 d 7-3-1778 m Mary Woodford Capt PA
John: b 1727 d 1822 m Martha — Sgt SC
John: b 1-7-1762 d 4-14-1844 m Sarah Baldwin Pvt SC
John: b c. 1750 d 1805/6 m Hannah Harris Adj SC
John: b 5-7-1755 d 3-29-1831 m Hannah Greenwood Sol VA
John: b 1756 d 1836 m (1)Mary Hardin (2)Elizabeth Cunard Sol VA
John Catlett: b 1762 d c. 7-9-1833 m Elizabeth Ware Pvt SC
Robert: b 1-3-1748 d 11-5-1815 m Ann Johnson Pvt PS NY
Robert: b 10- -1750 d 2- -1849 m Malinda Cox Pvt VA ★
Thomas: b 12-17-1721 d 1811 m Margaret Foote Pvt VA
Thomas: b 10-17-1758 d 4-23-1827 m Ann Curry Sol VA
Wm.: b 4- -1847 m Jane Knox Pvt NC SC ★
Wm.: b 1710-5 d a. 5-8-1780 m Elizabeth Ashton PS VA
Wm.: b 12-24-1752 d 7-11-1825 m (1)Elizabeth Taylor (2)Clara Favor Pvt VA

GARRIGUS, (includes GARRIGUES)
David: b 3-12-1748 d 10-8-1815 m Abigail Locy Pvt NJ
Jacob, Sr.: b 1716 d 5-13-1798 m Sarah — Pvt NJ
Jacob, Jr.: b 11-21-1752 d 5-1-1830 m Mary Calvey Pvt NJ
John: b 6-30-1760 d 8-13-1850 m Eliza Shipman Pvt NJ ★
Wm.: b 7-23-1746 d 12-21-1831 m (2)Hannah Briggs PS PA

GARRISON, (includes GARRETSON)
Aaron: b 12-25-1756 d 8-16-1844 m Mary Wanamaker Pvt NJ
Abraham: b c. 1735 d 1824 m (2)Marytie Brower Lt PS NY
Abraham H.: b 8-28-1758 d 1-21-1845 m Ellen — Pvt NJ
Adonijah: b c. 1755-60 d. 5-13-1827 m Judith Pickett Sol NC
David: b c. 1750 d 1838 m Elizabeth Barksdale PS NC
Ephraim: b 1738 d p. 178 0 m Elizabeth Watts MilOf PA
Harmonus: b 4- -1732 d 7-3-1813 m Autty Simonson QM NY
Hendric: b 1724 d 11- -1818 m X CS NY
Isaac: b 1738 d 1816 m Elizabeth Covert Lt NY
Isaac: b 1760 d 8-26-1826 m Martha Denton Pvt NY
Jacob: b 10-6-1755 d 4-16-1836 m Millicent Tomlin Pvt Smn NJ ★
Jacob: b 1734 d 1-16-1812 m Margaret Demerset Pvt NY
James: b 7-13-1760 d 2-3-1858 m Susannah — Pvt NC ★
Jedediah: b 1760-2 d p. 1827 m Jane Williams Sol GA
Joel: b 2-9-1760 d 3-4-1835 m (1)Sarah White (2)Christeny — Pvt Drm NJ ★
Joel: bpt 1-30-1742/3 d 1798 m Catherine DuBois 1Sgt NJ
John: b 2-23-1741 d 12-15-1810 m Mary Griest Pvt DE
John: b 3-26-1763 d 8-1-1842 m Phoebe Schenck Pvt NJ
John: b 1758 d 1842 m X Pvt SC ★
Joseph: b 7-6-1711 d 1794 m (1)Magdalena Van Dyke (2)Alida Ostrander Lt NY
Leonard: b 5-5-1760 d 3-10-1836 m Rebecca — Pvt MM Spy PA ★
Matthias: b c. 1740 d p. 5-1-1784 m Elizabeth Fortner Pvt NJ
Peter: b — d 8-28-1776 m Maria Cook Pvt NY
Richard: b 4-15-1727 d 1803 m Jane Gerow QM NY
Samuel: b 8-24-1763 d 3-27-1833 m Esther Alexander Pvt NC ★
Samuel: b 1745 d 1799 m Margaret Alexander Sol VA

GARROW,
Francis: b 1749 d p. 1780 m Mary Bacon Cpl MA

GARST,
De Walt: b c. 1725 d c. 1789 m Marie Statthalter Pvt PA
Frederick: b 1752 d 1842 m Magadalena Rauch Pvt PA

GARTH,
John: b 8-15-1762 d 11-9-1835 m (1)Anne Rhodes (2)Sarah Griffith Pvt VA
Thomas: b a. 1740 d 1812 m Judith Bocock PS VA

GARTHRIGHT,
Ephraim, Sr.: b a. 1730 d 1789 m X PS VA

GARTHWAITE, (includes GATHEWAITE)
Jeremiah Crane: b 9-10-1765 d 7-29-1822 m Vashti Britton Drm NJ
John: b 12- -1752 d 1834 m Abigail Townley Pvt NJ
Wm., 2nd: b 1731 d 9-3-1807 m Prudence Price Capt NJ

GARTON,
David: b c. 1733 d 12- -1785 m Abigail — Pvt NJ

GARVER,
Christian: b c. 1720 d 1- -1798 m Elizabeth — Pvt PA

GARVEY,
Job: b 1760 d 1-20-1827 m Elizabeth — Pvt VA ★

GARVIN,
Henry: b c. 1750 d p. 1798 m Sarah McKee Cpl PA
Isaac: b c. 1761 d 3-1-1833 m Jane Huston Pvt VA ★
James: b — d 1795 m Sarah Hobbs PS NH
John: b 1748 d p. 1779 m Margaret Laughlin Pvt VA
John: b 1746 d 1820 m X Capt SC

Thomas: b 1745 d c. 1810 m Elizabeth McCullough Pvt PA
Thomas: b 1764 d 11-23-1834 m Elizabeth Young Tms VA

GARWOOD,
Obed; b c. 1729/30 d p. 7-23-1798 m Mary King Pvt PA

GARY, (includes GAREY, GEARY, GERRY, GERY)
Charles: b 1733 d 7- -1808 m Elizabeth — PS SC
Elbridge: b 7-17-1744 d 11-25-1814 m Ann Thompson SDI MA
Enos: b 9-23-1757 d 8-17-1844 m Esther Buckingham Pvt CT ★
Gilbert: b 12-11-1760 d 4-1-1838 m Anna Danna Pvt CT ★
Jacob: b 2-11-1754 d 9-28-1828 m (1)Elizabeth Laurer (2)Anna Treichler (3)Elizabeth Treichler Pvt PA
James: b 1737 d 3-22-1824 m Olive Low Pvt PS CS MA
James: b 11-6-1762 d 1813 m Abigail Littlefield Pvt MA
John: b 1741 d 1805 m X PS MA
John: b 6-3-1759 d p. 1797 m Susanna Wiegner Pvt PA
John: b c. 1750 d p. 1790 m Rachel Davis PS SC
John: b 8-12-1759 d 3-11-1824 m Mary Bush Sgt VA
Jonas: b 1761 d 9-25-1840 m Polly Putnam Pvt MA ★
Jonathan: b 1750 d 1-30-1831 m (1)Mary Mayhew (2)Hepsibah Braybrook Pvt Sgt MA ★
Joseph: b 6-27-1754 d 2-11-1843 m Ruth Nichols Drm MA
Joshua: b 12-2-1762 d 11-29-1831 m Martha Newhall Pvt MA ★
Killyon: b 11-9-1757 d 8-31-1833 m (1)Barbara Miller (2)Miss Shewalter (3)Beckie Walters (4)Catherine Neff Pvt PA
Peter: b c. 1752 d p. 1820 m Phillipinia — Pvt PA
Reuben: b 12-7-1749 d 1-27-1817 m Lucy Brooks Sgt MA
Reuben: b 11-17-1760 d 6-12-1786 m Joanna Oaks Pvt MA
Seth: b 5-19-1761 d 12-12-1842 m Zilpha Pierce Pvt MA ★
Thomas: b 3-15-1732 d 4-5-1819 m (1)Jane Wilder (2)Priscilla Jewett Lt MA
Thomas: b a. 1760 d 1819 m Rebecca Jones Pvt SC
Thomas, Sr.: b c. 1730 d p. 6-5-1796 m Rebecca Newman PS SC
William: b 1755 d 12-4-1829 m (1)Lucy Ann Weaver (2)Rebecca Judkins Sol VA
Zephaniah: b 7-18-1749 d 12-9-1823 m Mary White Pvt MA

GASHA,
Henry: b 7-15-1752 d p. 2-28-1835 m Barbara Schenck Pvt PA

GASHWILER, (includes GARSHWILER)
Joseph: b — d a. 1804 m Barbara — Pvt VA

GASKILL,
Jonathan: b 5-22-1739 d 9-18-1790 m Hannah Estes PS CS NH
Restore: b 1759 d 2-27-1825 m Catharine Stanger Mil NJ
Samuel: b 1-2-1750 d 1820 m (1)Lucretia Hays (2)Catharine Rea Lt NJ
Silas: b c. 1743 d 4-25-1818 m Sarah Jillson PS CS NH

GASKINS,
David: b 1745 d 5-5-1806 m Sarah Oxley CS NC
Ezekiel E.: b c. 1747 d a. 3-10-1812 m (2)Tolitha — PS SC
Thomas: b — d 2-10-1813 m — McClennehan Ens Capt PA
Thomas, Sr.: b c. 1720 d p. 1785 m (1)Sarah Eustace (2)Ann Kerr (3)Sarah Lee CS Col VA
Thomas, Jr.: b c. 1745 d 1805 m Hannah Hull Col VA

GASS
David: b c. 1735 d 1806 m Sarah — Capt VA

GASSAWAY, (includes GASAWAY)
Brice John: b 1745/6 d 1806 m Dinah Warfield Lt MD
Charles: b c. 1751 d 1816 m Ruth Beall 1Lt MD
Thomas: b 1754 d 2-15-1835 m Jane Keller Pvt NC & VA

GASSETT, (includes GASCHET)
Henry: b 1732 d 2-16-1814 m Persia How Pvt CS PS MA
Levi: b 1747 d 1785 m Vashti Brigham Sgt MA

GAST,
Christian: b 12-11-1762 d 9-25-1843 m Margreth Boras Pvt PA
Nicholas: b 2-21-1760 d 12-2-1810 m Anna Catharine Knipe Pvt PA

GASTINEAU,
Job: b 1760 d 1856 m Elizabeth Mercer Brown Pvt VA

GASTON,
Alexander: b 10-28-1754 d 7-12-1823 m Huldah Norton Pvt MA
Esther Waugh: b c. 1715 d 1789 m John Gaston PS SC
Hugh b 3-12-1751 d 6-13-1836 m Martha McClure Sol QM SC ★
James: b 1749 d 1824 m Elizabeth Lyle Pvt SC
James: b 4-15-1747 d 3-6-1840 m Catherine Creighton Pvt SC
John: b 11-16-1730 d 10-3-1776 m (1)Elizabeth Ker (2)Sarah Ogden PS NJ
John: b 5- -1738 d 9-10-1823 m Charity Cheeseman Maj PA
John: b 6-24-1745 d 1- -1808 m Janette Knox Pvt SC W★
John: b 4-4-1703 d 1782 m Esther Waugh PS SC
Joseph: b 5-29-1763 d 10-16-1796 m Ida Vank Arsdalen PM NJ
Joseph: b — d 9-22-1775 m Isabell Simonton PS PA
Joseph: b 2-22-1763 d 10-10-1836 m Jane Brown Pvt SC
Martha: b 11-6-1741 d 4-3-1826 m Joseph Gaston PS SC
Robert: b 1-28-1732 d 9-2-1793 m Rozanna Cooper LCol PS NJ

GASTON, contd.
Robert: b 1749 d 10-9-1779 m (2)Ann Davis Lt SC
Robert: b 1703/4 d a. 1790 m Margeret — PS SC
Thomas: b 3-16-1759 d 1823 m Sarah Chatman Cpl MA
Thomas: b 7-18-1759 d 4-23-1832 m Sarah Nichols Sol SC
Wm.: b 6-5-1743 d p. 1-17-1814 m (1)Jenet Love (2)Ann Porter Capt SC
Wm.: b 1735 d 1790 m Jane Harbison Pvt SC
Wm.: b 7-10-1757 d 1-12-1838 m Mary McClure Pvt SC ★

GATCH,
Benjamin: b 1758 d 1814 m Ruth Taylor PS MD
Conduce: b c. 1712 d p. 1790 m Proseliah Burgin PS MD
Philip: b 3-2-1751 d 12-28-1834 m Elizabeth Smith PS VA

GATES,
Aaron: b 1754/53 d 1-12-1821 m Elizabeth Johnson MM CT
Abraham, Sr.: b 8-7-1741 d 3-7-1806 m (1)Susanna Whittimore (2)Lucy Rumrill Sgt MA
Amos: b 4-15-1735 d 1804 m Mrs Elizabeth Laws Pvt MA
Amos: b 1711 d 1800 m Mary Trowbridge PS MA
Asa: b 1-29-1756 d 11-21-1835 m Fanny Field Sol MA
Benajmin: b 11-27-1737 d 2-11-1797 m (1)Experience Mason (2)Experience Allen Capt MA
Bezaleel: b 10-14-1726 d 3-8-1802 m Mary Brainard PS CT
Bezaleel, Jr.: b 10-2-1751 d 1-24-1789 m (2)Helen Wilder Pvt CT
Caleb: b 8-22-1735 d 4-22-1816 m Elizabeth Branch MM Cpl CT
Charles, Sr.: b 6-15-1738 d 10-9-1805 m Elizabeth — PS VA
Charles, Jr.: b 1-14-1761 d 5-10-1846 m Ann Shackelford Sol VA
Cyrus: b 1753 d 4-2-1836 m Ruth Rockwell Cpl CT
Cyrus: b 4-11-1732 d 7-8-1813 m Ruth Bruce Pvt MA
Cyrus: b 1-20-1756 d 6-5-1838 m (1)Mercy Herrick Pvt CT RI ★
Daniel: b 10-27-1745 d 5-15-1832 m (2)Milcah Ludden Brown Lt MA
Daniel: b c. 1750 d p. 1775 m Susan Alexander Sgt CT
Daniel: b 3-2-1751 d 11-6-1807 m Sarah Moore Lt VT
David: b 1723 d 8-19-1808 m Anna Hale Pvt CT
Ebenezer: b 6-13-1764 d 12-14-1841 m (1)Lydia Chapman (2)Candance Davison Pvt CT
Edmund: Trowbridge: b 7-23-1761 d 10-1-1822 m Elizabeth Tufts Sol MA
Elisha: b — d 12-12-1820 m Lucy Chase PS MA
Ezra: b 1749 d 10-6-1841 m Mercy Gates Pvt CT NY ★
Freeman: b 10-13-1765 d 3-6-1845 m (1)Elizabeth Hyde (2)Sarah — Pvt CT ★
George: b 1760/1 d 2-27-1826 m (1)Phebe Peters (2)Sarah Marshall Pvt CT
Henry: b 3-22-1757 d 2-7-1838 m Anne Eames Pvt MA
Henry: b c. 1763 d p. 2-23-1831 m Maria Catherine Bucher Pvt PA
Hezekiah: b c. 1705 d 6-27-1777 m (1)Mary Sawyer (2)Anna—PS MA
Isaac: b 10-22-1746 d 2-17-1831 m Mary Wheelock Pvt NH
Israel: b 1726/27 d 8-31-1807 m Elizabeth — Pvt Ens MA
Jehiel: b 6-4-1739 d 1837 m Matilda Gross Pvt CT
Jesse: b 4-5-1734 d 2-21-1808 m Elizabeth Lord Pvt CT
John: b 12-24-1745 d 11-10-1826 m Sarah Meach Pvt CT
John: b 10-31-1749 d p. 1796 m Catherine Coolidge 2Lt MA
John: b 1764 d 1839 m Abigail Ball Pvt MA
John: b 2-14-1756 d 7-11-1845 m Margaret Merrin Pvt PA
John Shepard: b 3-11-1744/45 d 2-28-1827 m (1)Hannah Moore (2)Lucy Witt Lt VT
Jonas: b 9-27-1756 d 7-24-1839 m Mary Carter Pvt MA
Jonas: b 7-5-1764 d 1-14-1864 m Anna Robinson Drm MA
Jonathan: b 1744 d p. 1794 m (1)Kate Morse (2)Mary — Pvt MA
Jonathan: b 6-19-1746 d 9-30-1808 m Hepzibah Stone Pvt MA
Jonathan: b 1763 d p. 1832 m Zurviah Gates Pvt MA
Joseph: bpt 2-14-1748 d 1839 m (1)Jane Brockway (2)Mehitabel Warner Pvt CT
Joseph: b 12-7-1759 d 9-4-1830 m Sarah Galera Roper Pvt MA
Joshua: b 11-3-1730 d 12-27-1798 m Anna Branch Pvt CT
Joshua: b 3-4-1760 d 8-17-1830 m Rhoda Clark Pvt NY
Josiah: b 1-15-1723 d 9-20-1807 m Lydia Marvin Pvt CT
Lemuel: b 4-29-1758 d 9-30-1806 m Lydia Whittemore Fif Sgt MA
Luther: b 6-1-1761 d 9-1-1826 m Ann Brown Drm CT
Makepeace: b 5-12-1735 d 9-9-1817 m Katherine Smith PS CS MS
Nathan: b 1754 d 8-8-1838 m Tamerson Kimball Pvt CT
Nathaniel: b 2-18-1738 d c. 1815 m Deborah Deans Sgt PA CT
Nathaniel: b 3-4-1756 d 11-7-1793 m Lucy Gallup Pvt CT
Noah: b 9-12-1747 d 3-31-1798 m Mary Conant Capt MA
Oldham: b 7-27-1759 d 10-12-1843 m Deborah Winch Cpl MA ★
Oliver: b 9-18-1757 d 4-4-1834 m Jemima Freeman Pvt CT
Paul: b 12-12-1754 d 6-25-1826 m Zerviah Spooner Pvt MA
Paul: b 6-20-1758 d 1-15-1843 m (1)Phebe Mahan (2)Sarah Pearce Pvt MA ★
Peter Waldron: b 8-23-1747 d 3-9-1826 m Anna M. Helms Pvt NY
Phineas: b c. 1708 d p. 11-12-1782 m Sarah Hapgood Sol MA
Reuben, Sr.: b 1716 d a. 1783 m Mercy Taylor Pvt CS MA
Richard: b c. 1750 d 1815 m Mary Elizabeth — Pvt VA
Robert: b c. 1750 d 5-6-1790 m Rosamond Cady Sgt CT
Samuel, Sr.: b 9-27-1711 d 4-23-1788 m Margaret — Cpl MA
Samuel, Jr.: b 8-29-1756 d 11-11-1834 m (1)Mary Rand (2)Sarah Lawrence Pvt MA
Samuel: b 11-18-1757 d 1- -1813 m Sarah Benjamin Sol NH
Samuel: b 8-21-1725 d 2-19-1803 m Abigail Blodgett Pvt MA
Samuel: b 3-11-1753 d 1814 m Mary Rowland Pvt VA

Silas: b 1728 d 1781 m Mary White Pvt CT
Silas: b 2-3-1727 d 8-25-1793 m Elizabeth Bragg Capt MA
Silas: b 7-10-1718 d 8-3-1779 m (1)Mary Whitcomb (2)Mary Wheeler (3)Anna Hammond (4)Mary Brown Ens MA
Silas: b 12-1-1756 d 8-21-1828 m (1)Mary Laughton (2)Hannah — Cpl MA
Simon: b 1-6-1756 d 2-2-1849 m Sarah Edgerton Pvt MA
Stephen: b 6-30-1723 d 2-27-1784 m Esther Fuller Ens CT
Stephen: b c. 1744 d p. 1790 m Mary Merrick Sgt MA
Stephen: b 11-15-1750 d 7-21-1837 m Eve Young Pvt Sct NY
Sylvanus: b 6-6-1748 d 5- -1836 m Elizabeth Graham Matr Pvt MA
Thomas: b 8-16-1720 d 12-25-1797 m Elizabeth Mitchell Cpl CT
Thomas: b 7-3-1724 d 1793 m Ruth Randall Sol CT
Thomas Asa: b 3-10-1751 d 2-26-1820 m Margaret Dwight Sgt MA
Timothy: b 4-29-1730 d 10-2-1819 m Hannah Percival Sgt CT
Timothy: b 5-2-1747 d 10-19-1822 m Susannah Marsters Sgt MA
Wm.: b a. 1750 d p. 1790 m Sara Green Pvt MD
Wm.: b 3-14-1729 d 10-28-1808 m Jane Rice Sgt MA
Wm.: b 1734 d 3-9-1816 m (2)Polly Elam (3)Lydia Granger Pvt VA W★

GATEWOOD,
Andrew: b 1740 d p. 1-25-1794 m Margaret Kay PS CS VA
Dudley: b 12- -1747 d 7-7-1836 m (1)Elizabeth Dix (2) Temperance Worsham (3)Mrs Rebecca Wynn Lt NC ★
James: b 1764 d 1852 m Lucy Stewart Pvt VA
John: b 7-10-1761 d 10-6-1835 m Nancy —, Pvt VA ★
Phillip: b 1750 d 1793 m Susannah Wright PS VA
Richard: b 1750 d p. 12-10-1789 m Betty Holliday Sol VA
Wm.: b c. 1749 d 12- -1825 m Jane — Capt VA
Wm.: b 1764 d 9-26-1853 m Clara Dickerson Pvt VA ★

GATHWRIGHT,
Samuel: b 1740 d 6-7-1777 m Sarah Jane Pvt VA

GATLIFF,
Charles: b 5-28-1745 d 6-30-1838 m (1)Christiana McGuire (2)Rachel Cummins Indian Spy Pvt Capt VA ★

GATLIN, (includes GATLING)
Edward: b 1764/65 d 9- -1835 m Elizabeth Smith Pvt NC
James: b c. 1760 d c. 1822 m (1)Mary Cowper (2)Mary Riddick PS NC

GATTIS,
Alexander: b 1761 d 12-2-1842 m (1)Rebecca Ann King (2)Rosannah Wilson Pvt NC

GATTON,
Wm.: b c. 1756/57 d 1816 m Sarah Murphy PS MD

GAUDET,
Joseph: b 1732 d 10-29-1802 m Ann Gertrude Le Blanc Pvt MA

GAUGER,
Johann Wilhelm: b 7-12-1756 d 11-10-1816 m Anna Margaretha Follmer PS PA
Nicholas: b 1718 d p. 1785 m Anna Margeretha Feg PS PA

GAUGLER,
Nicholas: b 8-1-1757 d 2-14-1809 m Anna Mary Wolfart Pvt PA

GAUL,
Jacob: b a. 1750 d p. 6-12-1804 m (1)Catherine — (2)Catherine Lord Pvt NY
John Frederick: b 1757 d 2-4-1844 m (1)Margaret Metsinger (2)Dorothea Kreider Pvt PA ★

GAULDEN, (includes GAULDING)
John: b c. 1742 d - - m Susan — Sol SC
Wm.: b 1752 d 9- -1841 m Malissa Burnett Pvt VA ★

GAULT, (includes GALT, GAUT)
Adam: b 1749 d p. 1790 m Eve Shaffer Pvt PA
Andrew: b 1714 d 1797 m Molly Ayer PS NH
James: b 1742 d 1800 m (1)Mary English (2)Mary Taylor Lt VA
James: b 1737 d 1803 m Elizabeth — Pvt PA
John Minson: b 1744 d 6-12-1808 m Judith Craig Surgeon VA
Matthew: b 3-24-1756 d 10-17-1824 m (1)Elizabeth Bunton (2)Mary McC Emery Drm Sol NH
Matthew: b 10-21-1758 d 5-23-1823 m Mary Bird Pvt MA
Samuel: b 1701 d 1784 m Elsie Carlton PS NH
Samuel: b 12-25-1753 d 6-30-1823 m Anna Gile Pvt NH
Wm.: b 1735 d 1803 m Rebecca Coffey Pvt NC
Wm. Sr.: b - - d 1778 m — PS NY

GAUMER,
Jacob: b c. 1758 d 1820 m Maria Catherine Showash Pvt PA
John Frederick: b 3-12-1750 d 9-2-1815 m Catherine Eisenhard Pvt PA

GAUNT, (includes GAUNNT)
Israel: b 1730-40 d a. 5- -1800 m Hannah Coats PS SC
James: b 1756 d 1817 m Nancy Jane — Sol VA

GAVIT, (includes GAFFIT, GAVITT)
Edward: b 1750 d 6-12-1832 m Mary Champlain Pvt RI
George: b 11-21-1745 d *p.* 1787 m Abigail Hiscox Pvt RI
John: b *c.* 1762 d 8-26-1837 m (1)Rachel Bloomer (2)Mrs Catherine Brook Baker Fif NH ★
John: b 7-13-1743 d 10-23-1815 m Desire Wilcox Maj RI
Sylvestor: b 1755 d 5-2-1829 m (1)Sarah Babcock (2)Keturah Pendleton Pvt RI
Wm.: b 4-2-1766 d 1-6-1854 m (1)Sarah Babcock (2)Mrs Anna Devereaux Pvtr CT

GAY, (includes GUY)
Aaron: b 12-24-1735 d 5-22-1813 m Obedience Fisher Pvt MA
Allen: b 1765 d 6-18-1847 m (1)Celia Rae Elbert (2)Abigail Castleberry (3)Mrs Ann Benton Pvt NC ★
Amasa: b 12-20-1761 d 2-20-1824 m Mary Moore Pvt MA
Asahel: b 6-4-1755 d 3-24-1843 m Temperance Cushman Pvt Mus CT ★
Calvin: b 5-10-1746 d — m Naomi Frizzell Cpl CT
Calvin: b 4-4-1755 d 10-17-1816 m Joanna Kingsbury Pvt MA
Daniel: b 1749 d 6-20-1812 m Sarah — Pvt NY
Ebenezer: b 12-26-1725 d 7-16-1787 m (1)Ann Coles (2)Elizabeth Fairbanks Maj CT
Ebenezer: b 4-12-1749 d — m Elizabeth Leavens Pvt CT
Edward: b 2-3-1763 d 5-15-1846 m Mary White Pvt CT ★
Fisher: b 10-19-1733 d 8-22-1776 m Phebe Lewis Col CT
Jabez: b 12-16-1721 d 10-4-1801 m Hannah Bradford CS SgtMaj MA
James: b 3-20-1744 d 2- -1819 m Margaret Mitchell Pvt Sgt NC
James, Jr.: b 8-24-1758 d 6-22-1840 m (1)Sarah Patton (2)Elizabeth Dunlap (3)Mary Barnes Pvt Spy VA ★
John: b 2-2-1736 d 1795 m Hannah Gay Lt MA
John: b *c.* 1760 d 1817 m Amila Castleberry Sol NC
John, Sr.: b 1-1-1721 d 9-19-1823 m Barbara — Pvt PA
John: b *c.* 1762 d 2-8-1827 m Nancy McKee Ens VA
John: b 1-1-1740 d 10-19-1826 m Sarah Lockridge Pvt VA
Jonah: b 5-2-1721 d 2-26-1778 m Sarah Wellington PS MA
Joshua: b 1764 d *p.* 1830 m Mary Byrd Pvt NC
Lemuel: b 2-4-1745 d 8-10-1809 m Abigail Davenport Lt MA
Lewis: b 3-10-1747 d *p.* 1805 m Mary March Pvt MA
Lusher: b 12-15-1716/17 d 2-19-1803 m (1)Mary Colburn (2)Hannah Cady PS CT
Peter: b 6-27-1743 d 8- -1815 m (1)Hannah Smith (2)Mary Payson (3)Mrs Abigail Pease Smith Sgt MA
Richard: b 12-20-1750 d 8-1-1836 m Lucina Granger Pvt CT
Richard: b *c.* 1756 d *p.* 1790 m Sabrina — Pvt NC
Samuel: b *c* 1740 d 1812 m Catherine — Srgnmte Dr. VA
Solomon: b 3-24-1740/41 d 6-8-1823 m Mrs Abigail Gould Pvt MA
Thaddeus: b 1763 d 8-12-1837 m Charlotte Colburn Pvt MA
Thomas: b a. 1740 d 1784 m Patience — PS NC
Timothy 2d: b 6-28-1744 d 10-29-1822 m Elizabeth Pettee Sgt MA
Wm . Jr.: b 12-3-1730 d 8-20-1795 m (1)Sarah Wight (2)Margaret Lewis Pvt MA
Wm.: bpt 8-12-1746 d 8-20-1789 m Prudence Woods Pvt SC W★

GAYDEN,
George: b 1-4-1739 d *p.* 5-29-1819 m (2)Lois Collins ()Nanny—PS NC
John: b 4-19-1753 d *p.* 1790 m Catherine Collins 1Lt SC

GAYLORD,
Aaron: b 1745 d 7-3-1778 m Katherine Cole Lt CT
Ambrose: b 11-17-1756 d 6-12-1844 m Eleanor Comstock Pvt CT ★
Benjamin, Jr.: b 2-25-1753 d 3-26-1825 m Phebe Ives Pvt CT
Benjamin: b 4-12-1721 d 4-6-1792 m (1)Tyrall Morehouse (2)Ruth Sherman PS CT
Charles: b 9-22-1739 d 7-5-1777 m Hannah Andrus Pvt CT
Chauncey: b 2-14-1757 d 3-31-1844 m Ruth Bunnel Pvt CT ★
Deodate: b 7-20-1760 d 12-20-1840 m Betsey Whitney Pvt CT
Ebenezer: b 6-12-1746 d 8-14-1816 m Catherine Chittenden MM CT
Eleazer: b 3-23-1725 d 12-16-1806 m Eunice Gilbert Pvt CT
Eleazer: b 5-14-1753 d 9-17-1817 m Sylvia Clark Pvt CT
Elijah: b 1736 d 9-25-1796 m Annah Hull Pvt CT
Elijah: b 3-1-1763 d 11-7-1857 m Mary Cotton Pvt CT
Jedediah: b 3-12-1762 d 7-12-1846 m (-)Mercy Kellogg (2)Mrs Lydia NewComb Pvt CT ★
Jesse: b 9-10-1735 d 9-22-1807 m Rachael Hungerford PS CT
Joel: b 5-8-1755 d 7-24-1828 m Lois Cook QM Sgt CT ★
John: b 6-26-1743 d 6-22-1826 m Mary Webster Pvt CT
John: b 12-21-1753 d 3-17-1826 m Phebe Brooks Pvt CT
John: b 1-17-1713 d 1790 m Elizabeth Lathrop Stoughton PS CT
John: b 9-27-1713 d *c.* 1799 m Dolly Taylor PS CS MA
Jonathan: b 10-29-1747 d 1819 m Elizabeth Goodwin Sgt CT
Joseph: b 1722 d 10-20-1791 m Ruth Mathews Sol CT
Joseph: b 2-15-1752 d 11-20-1821 m Ruth Bissell Pvt CT
Jotham: b 1-26-1748/49 d 2-5-1807 m Esther Hotchkiss Cpl CT
Justus, Sr.: b 3-12-1732 d 1820 m Elizabeth — Sol PS PA
Justus. Jr.: b 1757 d 5-28-1830 m (1)Elizabeth Gardner (2)Lucretia Buck Pvt CT
Katherine Cole: b 11-28-1745 d 1840 m Aaron Gaylord PS CT
Lemuel: b 2-14-1765 d 11-7-1854 m Sylvia Murray Tms CT
Levi, Sr.: b 10-1730 d 8-17-1795 m Lois Barnes Capt CT
Levi, Jr.: b 3-30-1760 d 6-6-1846 m Lydia Smith Pvt CT
Nehemiah: b 6-15-1722 d 12-1-1801 m Lucy Loomis Pvt CT
Nehemiah: b *c.* 1740 d 1817/18 m (1)Rebecca Nash (2) Mary — Pvt MA

Oliver: b 10-13-1751 d — - m Betty Hastings Cpl MA
Phebe: b 11-19-1767 d 10-5-1852 m Levi Frisbie PS PA
Samuel: b 9-20-1754 d 9-7-1813 m Azubah Atkins Pvt CT
Samuel: b 10-20-1742 d 6-10-1816 m Penelope Williams Sgt MA
Samuel: b 5-5-1711 d 9-3-1785 m (1)Mrs Margaret Partridge (2)Elizabeth Worthington CS MA
Timothy: b 8-5-1735 d 1825 m Lydia Thompson Capt MA

GAYMAN,
Daniel: b 1757 d 11-20-1849 m (1)Olivia Kees (2)Miss Picksler (3)Olivia Baughman Pvt PA

GAZLEY, (includes GAZLAY)
James: b 1-23-1758 d 8-6-1823 m Huldah Carter Ens NY
John, Sr.: b 7-9-1722 d 8- -1811 m Anna Ward Pvt NY
Jonathan: b 8-17-1760 d 1837 m Karinda Carter Pvt NY ★

GAZZAM,
Wm.: b — d 1811 m Martha Hart PS PA

GEARAN, (or GEREN)
Solomon: b 12-23-1761 d 1-3-1841 m Elender Owens Pvt NC ★

GEARHART, (includes GERHARD, GERHART, GERNHARDT)
Frederick: b 3-20-1715 d 3-30-1779 m (1)Elizabeth Fisher (2)Barbara Rieger PS PA
Heinrich: b *c.* 1740 d 4- -1820 m Rosine Fetterman Pvt PA
Jacob: b 1735 d 1-14-1813 m Catharine Kline Capt NJ
Jacob: bpt 11-26-1751 d *p.* 9-11-1806 m Anna Magdalena—Pvt PA
John: b 2-12-1747 d 4- -1810 m Susanna — Pvt PA
John: b 1754 d 1840 m Catharine Gray Ens PA
John: b 3-26-1754 d 8-27-1829 m Mary Magdalena Hartzell Pvt Ens PA
Peter: b 9-1-1744 d 1-22-1813 m Salome Lauer Pvt PA
Peter: b 12-10-1753 d 8-24-1837 m (1)Susan Gerhart (2)Marcilious Buck Pvt PA ★
Peter: b 1762 d 1854 m Elizabeth — Pvt PA
Wm.: b *a.* 1754 d *p.* 1790 m Eleanor DeKnight Ens NJ

GEARON, (or GERAN)
Thomas: b 3-1-1760 d 4-1-1842 m (1)Elizabeth Amy (2)Barbara OrdlSgt Slr NJ ★

GEBHART, (includes GABBART, GABBERT, GEBBERT, GEPHARD, KEPHART)
Adam: b 3-9-1760 d 1-24-1833 m Eva Rosina Deibert PS PA
George: b 1743 d 5-15-1815 m Anna Margaret Lebo Pvt PA
George: b *c.* 1750 d 1821 m Anne Reed Pvt VA
Henry: 1-8-1745 d *p.* 9-27-1815 m Mary Magdalena — Pvt PA
Jacob: b *c.* 1733 d. 1810 m Barbara Olinger Pvt VA
John: b 8-15-1760 d 9-23-1845 m Phebe Vansickle Drm MD ★
John: b 2-13-1751 d 8-31-1822 m Elizabeth Fretz Pvt PA
Michael: b 1765/66 d *c.* 1840 m Elizabeth Brown Pvt VA
Nicholas: b 1733 d 1829 m Mary Frey Pvt PA
Nicholas: b 5-30-1751 d 7-15-1829 m Anna Appolonia Kornmann Pvt PA
Peter: b *c.* 1720 d *a.* 5-28-1778 m Catarina Meyer PS PA

GEDDES,
Paul: b 1732 d 5-25-1814 m Margaret McGraw McCool PS Pvt PA

GEDDY,
John: b 1748 d 3-4-1800 m Patience McKenny Maj LCol NC

GEDNEY,
Daniel: b 12-15-1739 d 12-15-1790 m Charlotte Fowler Pvt NY
Eleazor: b 9-3-1758 d 4-9-1830 m Mary Belknap Ens NY

GEE,
Charles: b *c.* 1718 d *c.* 1784 m Mary Chappell PS VA
Charles: b *c.* 1755 d *p.* 1800 m Sally Wilson PS VA
Drewry: b 1730 d 1786 m Mary Tiller LCol PS NC
Ebenezer: b *c.* 1755 d *c.* 1830-5 m Olive King Pvt MA
Henry: b *c.* 1733 d *a.* 1815 m (1)Elizabeth Darden (2) — Green Col PS VA
James: b 11-12-1741 d 6-6-1804 m Mary Walker Capt NC
John: b 1-13-1763 d 4-28-1857 m Mary Hutchins Pvt NY ★
Thomas: b 1754 d 8-23-1796 m Mary — QMSgt NY
Wm.: b 4-5-1739 d 9-16-1817 m Abigail Mack Lt CT

GEER, (includes GEAR, GEERS, GEHR, GERE, GHEER)
Aaron: b 5-7-1722 d 12-13-1813 m (1)Mercy Fisher (2)Hannah Utley (3)Miriam Spofford Capt CT
Amos: b 4-14-1736 d 5-19-1821 m Mary Wight PS CT
Asa: b 1737 d *p.* 1832 m — Ens CT
Asa: b 1759 d 7- -1835 m (1)Olive Harris (2)Mary Stead Pvt CT ★
Benajah: b 12-3-1754 d 5-8-1839 m Mary Fairchild Pvt CT ★
Charles: b 1762 d 10-30-1842 m Elizabeth Coon Pvt NH
Ebenezer Stowell: b 6-16-1767 d 1845 m (1)Lucy Hibbard (2)Catherine Johnson Pvt CT ★
Elihu: b 5-3-1750 d 5-11-1801 m Eleanor McClester Sgt CT W★
George: b 1-1-1752 d *p.* 3-4-1836 m — Pvt CT ★

GEER, contd.
Hezekiah: b 4-26-1761 d 8-4-1822 m Sarah Gilbert Pvt CT
Isaac: b 1740-1 d p. 1782 m (1)Mary Leeds (2)Esther Gallup Capt NY
Israel: b 7-29-1757 d 9- -1799 m Mary Newton Pvt MA
Jacob: b 1732 d 1-27-1813 m Ann Patten Pvt CT
John: b 8-6-1729 d 1811 m Jerusha Park Sol CT
John: b 4-2-1759 d 12-25-1840 m Onora Abbe Pvt CT
Joseph: b 6-8-1737 d 12-25-1797 m Anna Maria Clipps Capt PA
Lebbeus: b 12-30-1757 d 8-17-1830 m Rachel Morgan Pvt CT
Philip: b 1741 d 1816 m Catharine LeVan Pvt PS PA
Rezin: b 8-3-1737 d 7-3-1778 m Mary Vanderburgh Capt PA
Robert: b 2-5-1707 d 1-1-1801 m Abigail Greenman CS CT
Robert: b 2-18-1743 d 8-30-1834 m Lucy Fitch Cpl MA
Roger: b 5-18-1753 d 10-21-1845 m Keziah Tucker Pvt CT ★
Walter: b 1759 d 3-22-1808 m Lucy Allen Pvt NH

GEIB,
John: b a. 1747 d p. 3-11-1811 m Veronica — Pvt VA

GEIGER, (includes GEIGHER, GIGHER, GYGER)
Bernard: b 1747 d 7-16-1811 m Mary Smith Capt PA
Charles: b 1754 d 5- -1828 m (1)Anna Mary Dilbon (2)Mrs Margaret Speck Lt PA
George: b 10-10-1742 d 7-31-1803 m Margaret Pechin Lt PA
George Wendel: b 1750 d 1831 m Annie Marie Weimer Pvt PA
Jacob: b c. 1740 d 10-4-1792 m Elizabeth Mohn PS MD
Jacob: b 2-23-1760 d 1823 m Rudy Murph Lt SC
Jacob: b 11- -1763 d 12-25-1804 m (1)Ann Kaigler (2)Mrs Dorothy — Fif Lt SC W★
Jesley: b c. 1720 d 3-28-1790 m Mary Dannenhauer Sgt PA
John: b 1-8-1748 d 9- -1817 m Mrs Anne Ruff Sol PS SC
John L.: b 3-1-1763 d 1838 m Mary Seip Pvt Drm PA
Paul: b 11-15-1723 d 8-2-1798 m Maria Eva Kistler PS PA
Valentine: b 5-14-1755 d 10-30-1821 m Elizabeth — Pvt PA
Wm.: b c. 1752 d 11-14-1824 m Elizabeth — Pvt PA

GEISELMAN,
George: b 3-7-1743 d 7-20-1798 m Hannah Christ Jettin Capt PA
Michael: b 1759 d 1807 m Betty Hershey PS PA

GEISSINGER, (or GEISINGER)
Jacob: b 1729 d 1815 m — Boehman Pvt PA
John, Jr.: b 1760 d 1844 m Hannah Sellers Pvt PA

GEIST,
Andrew: b 1-26-1755 d 12-19-1849 m (1)— Donmayer (2)Maria Christena Snyder Tms PA
Conrad: b 1745 d 1840 m — Capt PA
Thomas: b 1754 d 1846 m (1)Susanna Pickle (2)Mary Palmer Pvt VA
Valentine: b 10-3-1762 d 12-28-1849 m Catherine Dornmeier Pvt PA

GELAT, (or GELETT)
John: b 11-30-1761 d 7-11-1843 m Keziah Mosher Pvt RI MA

GELBACH, (includes GELBAUGH)
Frederick, Sr.: b 8-10-1731 d 2-10-1797 m Anne — Sgt PA
Frederick, Jr.: b 7-9-1763 d 9-9-1815 m (1)Elizabeth Steman (2)Anna Sherer Pvt PA

GELDMACHER, (includes KELTMACHER)
Henry: b c. 1759 d 1839 m Elizabeth Forry PS PA

GELLER,
George: b c. 1754 d p. 9- -1833 m Elizabeth Wiemer Pvt PA ★

GELSTON,
Maltby: b 3-20-1723 d 9-22-1783 m Mary Parsons PS NY
Thomas:b 4-7-1752 d 1-14-1835 m Mary Corwith PS NY
Wm.: b 9-3-1756 d 6-24-1840 m Senah Sears Pvt Pvtr CT

GELWICKS, (includes GELWIX)
Frederick Heinrich: b 2-14-1712 d 4-8-1783 m Mary Dorothea Morgenstern PS PA
George Carl: b 9-16-1741 d p. 1783 m Mary Eva Forney 2Lt PA
Johann Frederick, Sr.: b 10-18-1734 d 11-18-1813 m Susanna Catherine Grove Pvt PS PA

GEMBERLING,
Jacob: b 1736 d 5- -1824 m Catherine Wolfensberger Pvt PA

GENDRON,
Jean Baptiste: b c. 1735 d c. 1-25-1805 m Maria Louise Lachapelle Sol IL

GENSELL,
Adam: b 1757/58 d 3-14-1848 m Philippina Classmeier Pvt PA

GENSEMER,
George: b 1744 d p. 1785 m Margret — Ens PA

GENT,
Wm.: b 1760 d c. 1818 m Mary Anne Gorsuch Pvt MA

GENTLEE.
Thomas: b 1741 d 1788 m Mary Downing Matr Gnr MA

GENTRY,
David: b c. 1724 d 1812 m (2)Mary Estes PS VA
David: b 1754 d 7-16-1846/47 m (1)Eliza J. Smith (2)Mrs Sarah Roberts Johnson Pvt VA ★
Gaddis: b c. 1762 d 7-29-1827 m Patsy Thatcher Pvt VA W ★
George: b 1765 d 10-28-1855 m X Pvt VA
James: b 1754 d 1831 m — Thurmon Capt VA
James: b 1757 d 6-22-1851 m Mary Hicks Pvt Cpl VA
Joseph: b c. 1728 d 5- -1813 m Agnes — PS NC
Martin: b 9-11-1747 d 4-22-1827 m Mary Timberlake Grd VA
Meshack: b c. 1748 d 7-4-1846 m X Capt NC
Nicholas: b c. 1740 d 1782 m Elizabeth — PS NC
Nicholas: b 1726-28 d 1787 m (2)Sarah Dickens Sol VA
Richard: b 12-27-1755 d 2-13-1836 m Justina Hedgepeth Pvt SC ★
Richard: b 9-26-1763 d 2-12-1843 m (1)Jane Harris (2)Nancy Guthrie Pvt VA ★
Samuel: b c. 1760 d p. 2-16-1816 m X PS NC
Simon: b 1735 d 1792 m Susanna Brown PS VA
Wm.: b 1735 d 1789 m Sallie Craiggy Matross VA

GENTZEL,
Adam: b — d 3- -1848 m Phoebe Anne Glossmoyer Cpl PA

GENUNG, (includes GANONG, GANOUNG, GANUNG)
Ananias: b a. 1755 d 12-11-1817 m Abigail Burnett Pvt NJ
Benjamin: b 5-10-1758 d 3-9-1832 m Hannah Whitehead Wgn NJ
Cornelius: b 12-16-1746 d 5-19-1828 m Jemima Hedges Pvt NJ W★
Isaac: b c. 1724 d p. 1790 m Rachel Moseman Pvt NY
Jacob: b 1748 d 12-22-1834 m Hannah Wilson Pvt NY
Jeremiah: b 1743 d 10-13-1823 m Abigail Parrott Pvt NJ
John, Jr.: b c. 1737 d 1807 m X Pvt NY
Reuben: b 9-6-1757 d 12-29-1836 m Elizabeth Craft Pvt NY
Stephen: b 2-4-1760 d 9-8-1828 m (1)Phoebe Magie (2)Mrs Mary Young Howell Pvt NJ
Thomas: b 10-7-1726 d 3-23-1785 m Phebe Ward Tms NJ

GEOGHEGAN,
Anthony: b 6-6-1764 d 5-24-1837 m Anne Lilly Pvt MD W★
John: b 3-23-1755 d 2-20-1826 m (1)Diana Harris (2)Mary Ann — Ens MD ★

GEORGE,
Alexander: b 1748 d 3-3-1814 m (1)Mary Ringland (2)Elizabeth Hosacks Pvt PA
Amos: b 5-31-1754 d 12-23-1827 m (1)Sarah Green (2)Sarah Nichols Cpl MA
Austin: b c. 1760 d — m Sally Bradbury Pvt MA
Austin: b 3-19-1760 d 1-8-1817 m Lydia — Pvt NH
Austin: b 4-11-1756 d p. 1804 m Patty Walker Pvt NH
Benjamin: b 1755 d 9-24-1838 m Abigail Newman Pvt NH ★
Benjamin: b c. 1740 d 3-31-1811 m Hannah — Pvt VA
Francis: b 1761 d 2-28-1852 m (1)Charity Chubbock (2)Tabitha Bessee Pvt MA ★
George: b 5- -1747 d 2-3-1793 m Catharine — Pvt PA
George: b c. 1730 d p. 1790 m Catherine — CS PA
Gideon: b 1714 d 2-11-1787 m Elizabeth Jewett PS MA
Gideon: b 9-12-1740 d 9-17-1822 m Deborah Stevens Cpl NH
Gotleib: b 1760 d 1838 m Anna Burkett Sol SC
Henry: b — d 1815 m Betsey Don Pvt NH
Jacob: b 10-10-1750 d 8-19-1815 m Eve — Pvt PA
James: b 1767 d 1-15-1855 m Mary Mc Clure Pvt PA
Jesse: b c. 1760 d p. 1827 m X Pvt SC
Jesse: b a. 1749 d 1792 m Sarah Simmons Lt VA
Jesse: b 1-18-1758 d 11-4-1845 m Mary Craig Pvt VA ★
John: b 11-30-1753 d p. 1810 m (1)Elizabeth — (2) Frances Clark (3)Elizabeth Johnson PS MD
John: b 1751 d 1-22-1820 m Margaret Mayne Capt MA
John: b 1750 d 1-29-1831 m Ruth Wells Pvt NH ★
John: b 3-15-1748 d 2-4-1822 m Hannah — PS NH
John: b c. 1750 d 1803 m Sarah Scerry Sgt NJ
John: b 1743 d 1813 m Jennie Ford Sgt PS SC
John Conrad: b 4- -1738 d 8-13-1798 m Susanna Knauer Beyer Pvt PS PA
Joseph: b c. 1741 d 4-11-1807 m X PS NH
Joseph: b a. 1745 d p. 7-6-1814 m Lydia Shumate Sol VA
Margaret Whitson: b c. 1724 d p. 1782 m Nicholas George PS VA
Peter: b 1756 d 10-18-1792 m Rebecca Richardson Pvt PA
Reuben: b 11-25-1749 d 1-16-1832 m (1)Mildred George (2)Ailcy — Pvt VA
Richard: b 1746 d a. 2-7-1786 m Sarah — Pvt MD
Richard: b c. 1761 d 1826/27 m Priscilla Breed Sol PS SC
Robert: b 1744 d 8-15-1819 m Christiana Plance Pvt PA
Samuel: b 12-31-1733 d 7-11-1775 m Mrs Rebecca Page MM MA
Sidney: b 10-12-1755 d 11-21-1806 m (1)Ann Harroll (2) Mary Loutitt CS MD
Thomas: b 12-12-1742 d 11-22-1812 m Hannah Brastow Lt MA
Thomas: b 7-6-1754 d 2-3-1839 m Joanna Hayes Pvt NH ★
Thomas: b 10-17-1759 d 11-23-1843 m Betty Wrenn Pvt VA ★
Timothy: b 2-12-1728/29 d 12-20-1808 m Hannah Hoyt PS NH

Wm.: b 11-18-1737 d 1-12-1820 m (1)Ruth Hastings (2)Mrs Abigail Currier PS NH
Wm.: b 10-18-1760 d 9-11-1827 m Nancy Garthright Capt VA
Wm.: b c. 1758-60 d 10-27-1824 m Miss Bylor Capt VA
Wm.: b 1-28-1735 d p. 1815 m Elizabeth — Capt VA
Wm.: b c. 1755 d p. 1804 m (1)Ann Batchelder (2)Elizabeth Greenwood / 2Lt VA

GERBERICH, (includes GARUERICH, GARVERICH)
Andreas: b 7-17-1734 d 1795 m Barbara Babb Pvt PA
John: b 7-18-1740 d 5- -1805 m (1)Mrs Elizabeth Reith (2)Catherine — Pvt PA
John: b 2-7-1759 d 9-18-1843 m (1)Catherine Latschaa (2)Magdalena Bender Pvt PA
Michael: b 1755 d p. 1796 m Margaret — Sol PA
Peter: b 8-12-1730 d 8-13-1805 m Anna Margaretha Rudolph Pvt PA

GERMAN, (includes GARMAN, GERMAIN, GERMAINE, GERMOND)
Adam: b 12-13-1750 d 1-20-1824 m (1)Elizabeth Peter (2)Dorothy Neff Pvt PA
Barnard: b 10-6-1762 d p. 1809 m (1)Mary — (2) — O'Dorothy Fellows Pvt NY
Charles: b a. 1760 d 10-23-1821 m Elizabeth Davis Ens CT ★
Henry: b 12-11-1763 d 10-28-1835 m (1)Elizabeth — (2)Magdalene — Pvt PA
James: b 1728 d 1-24-1788 m Sarah — Pvt NY
James P.: b 1752 d 7-17-1817 m Freelove Bedell Sol NY
John: b c. 1725 d a. 4-6-1791 m Elizabeth Filkin Pvt NY
John: b 11-27-1755 d 9-8-1829 m Sarah Dorsey PS PA
Silas: b 1733 d 8-1-1824 m Sarah Sutherland 2Lt NY

GERNANT, (includes GERNAND)
Christian: b 10-7-1746 d 2-5-1824 m Magdalena Yost Pvt PA
George: b 6-10-1714 d 1-17-1793 m Catharine — PS PA
George: b 6-10-1729 d 8-3-1789 m Barbara Hain PS PA
John: b 4-23-1749 d 3-5-1821 m Anna Maria Bollman 2Lt PA

GEROULD, (includes GERALD, JERAULD)
Dutee: b 1-7-1747/48 d 1786 m Almy Niles Capt RI
Gorton: b 2-22-1752 d 7-5-1822 m (1)Elizabeth Slafford (2)Pheobe Rice Dr PS RI
Jabez: b 11-1-1748 d 6-12-1802 m Demaris Bennett Pvt Drm MA
James: b 2-2-1746 d 4-21-1827 m Mary Rice Lt RI
Joshua: b 2-1-1748 d 11-17-1776 m Prudence Scott Pvt MA
Samuel: b 7-28-1755 d 1-15-1824 m Azubah Thompson Cpl MA

GEROW,
Daniel: b 3-26-1725 d 2- -1791 m Elizabeth Coutant Sgt NY

GERRISH,
Charles: b 1716 d 1805 m Mary Frost 1Maj PS ME
Enoch: b 1-16-1750 d 5-1-1821 m (1)Mary Pearson (2)Hannah Kilburn 2Lt NH
George: b 6-16-1753 d 5-23-1814 m Mary Mitchell Sol MA
Henry: b 5-3-1742 d 5 -16-1806 m Martha Clough LCol NH
John: b 8-29-1756 d 11-14-1831 m (1)Mary Hardison (2)Mary Remick Pvt MA
Joseph: b 9-17-1753 d 11-21-1817 m Mary Bartlett Pvt NH
Paul: b 1754 d 1817 m Ruth Chesley Pvt NH
Samuel: b 4-20-1748 d 11-16-1825 m Lucy Noyes CS NH
Stephen: b 1-22-1711 d 1788 m Joanna Hale PS NH
Wm.: b 6-27-1744 d 6-6-1812 m Esther Parker Lt MA
Wm.: b 7-16-1710 d 8-8-1794 m (1)Mary Preble (2)Mary Morrell Pvt NH

GERRITSON,
Samuel: b 8-7-1750 d 11-7-1822 m Altea Ryder PS Lt NY

GERVAIS,
John Louis: b 1741 d 8-18-1798 m Mary Sinclair PS SC

GESNER,
John Hendrick: b 9-27-1749 d 1833 m Anna Onderdonk PS NY

GESS,
John: b — d 4-18-1799 m Sarah Lucas Pvt VA

GESSELL,
Wm.: b c. 1750 d p. 9-16-1801 m Dorothea — Pvt PA

GETCHELL, (includes GATCHELL, GITCHELL)
Benjamin: b 7-2-1751 d p. 7-23-1802 m (1) X (2)Mehitable Meserve Pvt MA
David: b 3-25-1758 d 3-13-1858 m Sarah Churchman Pvt PA
David: b — d 1803 m Margaret Gallup Cpl NH
Dennis: b 1723/24 d a. 1-6-1792 m (1)Nancy — (2)Margaret — Capt MA
Elihu: b 1742 d 9-6-1806 m X CS MA
Jeremiah: b 11-15-1744 d 2-27-1814 m Eunice Diamond Matr MA
Jeremiah: b 6-29-1756 d 2-27-1814 m Elizabeth Giffords Slr MA W★
John: b 4-25-1719 d p. 1790 m Mary Barbour Pvt MA
Joseph, Sr.: b 1720 d 1815 m Mary Mitchell Brown Pvt MA

Joseph Jr.: b 4-26-1757 d 3-13-1837 m Sally Berry Pvt Matr MA ★
Nathaniel: b 5-14-1759 d p. 1803 m Miriam Blethen Pvt MA
Nehemiah: b 1744 d 6-19-1818 m (1)Annie Bragg (2)Hannah Williams (3)Mrs Anne Dudley Sct CS MA
Samuel: b 1755 d 9- -1819 m Ann Gallison Lt MA
Samuel: b 8-15-1745 d 1822 m Sarah Simmons Sgt MA
Seth: b 11-29-1753 d 7-20-1844 m Mrs Sarah Grant Pvt MA ★
Wm.: b 1757 d 9-21-1842 m Elizabeth Bishop Pvt MA ★
Wm.: b 9-6-1740 d — m Leinah — Lt MA

GETMAN, (includes GETTMAN)
Christian: b 3-6-1734 d a. 7-10-1821 m Anna Eve Timmerman Markell Capt NY
Frederick, Sr.: b 1736 d 1791 m Maria Katharine Frank Capt NY
Frederick: b 1751 d 3-9-1812 m Anna Eva Frank Pvt NY
George Sr.: b 5-1-1723 d 9- -1789 m Delia Shoemaker Pvt NY
George Jr.: b 7-14-1757 d 11-14-1828 m Elizabeth House Ens NY
John: b 7-2-1754 d 1806 m Margaret Loucks Cpl NY
Peter: b 1-5-1764 d 5-22-1845 m Elizabeth Richter Pvt NY ★
Thomas: b 11-17-1752 d 12-25-1820 m Elizabeth Helmer Pvt NY W ★

GETTIG,
Christopher: b c. 1740 d 7-2-1790 m Anna Dorothy — 1Lt PA

GETTY,
Robert: b 1-10-1755 d c. 9-3-1829 m Agnes Lytle Cpl NY
Wm.: b c. 1754 d 1795 m X Pvt PA

GETZ, (includes GATES)
Baltzer: b 8-2-1720 d 6-6-1795 m Maria Catherine Long PS PA
George: b 1759 d 11-28-1842 m Maria Sybilla Stiehl PS PA
Michael: b 6-11-1730 d 9-25-1812 m Barbara — Pvt PA

GETZENDANNER, (includes GEISSENDANNER)
Baltis: b 10-11-1736 d 9-5-1795 m (1)Anna Maria Steiner (2)Phillipona Stull 1Lt MD
Henry: b 7-3-1742 d p. 1826 m (1)Elizabeth Rumph (2)Mary Larey PS SC
John: b 1764 d 4-6-1841 m Catharine Tabler Pvt MD

GEYER, (includes GOWER, GOYER, GUYER)
Andrew: b 11- -1748 d 2-27-1812 m Barbara Boshart Capt PS PA
George Sr.: b c. 1730 d a. 11-9-1799 m Ann Margareth — Pvt PA
George: b 5-2-1752 d 7-31-1846 m (1)Maria Salome Franc (2)Sussanna Keiser Pvt Ranger PA ★
Henry: b 2-12-1756 d 2-24-1807 m Catharine Kurtz Pvt PA
John: b 7-4-1750 d 4-21-1834 m Margaret Garner Capt PA
John, Jr.: b 1760-4 d 5-24-1854 m Elizabeth — Drm PA ★
Joshua: b 1748 d 1826 m Elizabeth Witham Pvt PA
Mary: b 1735 d p. 1820 m Peter Geyer PS PA
Peter: b 1735 d 1820 m Mary — Pvt PA
Robert: b 10-9-1722/23 d 8-29-1806 m (1)Margaret Alexander (2)Mary Henry PS ME
Stephen: b — d p. 1790 m Rebecca Burr Pvt CT

GHISELIN,
John: b 3-7-1754 d 5-7-1809 m Elizabeth Thorogood Capt MD

GHOST,
Philip: b c. 1750 d 1815 m Barbara Keltz Pvt PA

GIBBLE, (or GIBBEL)
Jacob: b c. 1748 d 1833 m Elizabeth — Pvt PA

GIBBON,
James: b 1759 d 7-1-1835 m Elizabeth Phyle Capt PA ★
James: b a. 1765 d — m Agnes Smart Pvt PA
John: b 9-2-1737 d 6-20-1777 m Esther Seeley Sol PS NY

GIBBONEY, (includes GIBONEY)
Alexander: b 1750-5 d c. 1803 m Rebecca Ramsey PS VA
John: b 1749 d 2-22-1831 m Elizabeth Ferree Cpl PA

GIBBONS, (includes GIBBENS)
Bildad: b 2-2-1759 d 8-21-1838 m Hannah Kent Pvt MA ★
Fitch: b 1730-40 d 1804 m (1)Naome Caldwell (2)Margaret Howard Pvt MA
Isaac: b 3-13-1749 d 12-28-1826 m Mary Gangwer Pvt PA ★
John: b 8-19-1763 d 3-7-1821 m Elizabeth Miller Sol MA
Joseph: b — d 1775 m Hannah Martin PS GA
Joseph, Jr.: b 8-30-1738 d 1795 m Margery Hannam PS PA
Peter: b 4-11-1730 d 12-6-1822 m Sarah Green Pvt MA
Thomas: b 9-14-1734 d p. 6-13-1809 m Anne Epps Sol NC
Wm.: b 11-4-1737 d 10-30-1803 m Susanna Ashbridge Col PA

GIBBS, (includes GIBBES)
Benjamin, Jr.: b 12-12-1747 d 1783 m Thankful Landon Cpl CT
Benjamin: b 1759 d 1836 m Deborah Herbert PS NJ
Benjamin Erastus: b 1752 d 1823 m Amanda Zipporah Purnell Col VA
Caleb: b 11-13-1729 d 1801 or 1807 m Marjorie Stuart PS CT
Caleb: b a. 1762 d 11-6-1818 m Catherine Hall Maj MA
Churchill: b 1754 d 5-30-1846 m Judith Richardson Lt VA ★
Cornelius: b 1764 d — m Hopie Pierce Pvt MA ★

GIBBS, contd.

Darius: b 2-9-1759 d 1-9-1811 m Sibbel — Pvt CT
Edward: b c. 1734 d a. 1811 m Hannah Matlack Pvt NJ
Eliakim: b c. 1743 d 1778 m — Pvt NY
Elijah: b 1760 d 1840 m Frances Morton Pvt MA
Elisha: b 10-1-1753 d 4-23-1836 m Silence Harington Pvt MA NH ★
Gershom Sr.: b 7-28-1721 d 12-29-1776 m Tabitha Moore Pvt CT
Gershom Jr.: b 7-18-1750 d 9-22-1843 m Miltie — Pvt CT ★
Herod: b 1750 d p. 1786 m Lucy Anderson 2Lt VA
Isaac: b 4-26-1752 d 10-12-1796 m Lucy Elwell Pvt CT
Isaac: b 1-28-1728/9 d p. 1780 m Lois Townsend Pvt MA
Isaac: b 3-7-1756 d p. 1832 m (1)Jane Stevens (2)Hannah La Grange Sgt MA NH ★
Isaac: b 1744 d 12- -1823 m Anis Culver Pvt MA
Israel: b 1738 d 2-17-1818 m Agnes Wilson Pvt Fif MA
James: b 1752 d 2-6-1825 m Abigail Stimpson Sgt NH MA ★
James: b 5-28-1726 d 8-5-1797 m Martha Newton Pvt MA
John: b 6-30-1747 d 12-8-1836 m Elizabeth Weed Pvt CT
John: b 1741 d 9-17-1836 m Nancy Swayze Pvt NJ
John: b 3-3-1755 d 3-15-1845 m Hannah Muchmore Pvt NC ★
John: b 1756 d 10-18-1848 m Hannah — Pvt VA ★
Jonas Sr.: b 10- -1738 d 4- -1822 m Sarah Townsend Sol MA
Jonathan: b 11-9-1746 d 1834 m Hannah Clark Sgt MA
Jonathan: b 2-2-1753 d 8-26-1848 m Lucy Lumbard Pvt MA
Jonathan: b 1748 d 1- -1827 m Rachel Stoddard Pvtr RI
Joseph: b 1727 d 11-11-1805 m (1)Elizabeth Palmer (2)Mrs Rebecca Albee Pvt MM MA
Joseph: b 10-12-1756 d 6-19-1829 m Elizabeth Laws Pvt MA
Joseph: b 1755 d 1833 m Ann Abigail Bonnel MM NJ
Josiah: b 12-24-1762 d 12-29-1840 m Lucy W. Alvord Pvt MA★
Julius: b 3-27-1753 d 7-26-1834 m Aggy Davis Pvt VA ★
Lemuel: b 3-16-1737 d 1-3-1827 m Esther Johnson Lt CT
Luman: b 3- -1765 d 9-4-1841 m — Rickard Pvt VT ★
Martin: b 1-4-1732 d 1-1-1826 m Phebe Gibson Pvt NJ
Nathaniel: b a. 1747 d p. 1788 m Sarah Holton Cpl MA
Nicholas: b 9-29-1735 d 1817 m Mary Eveland — Sol PS NC
Parnell: b 1720 d 1826 m Mary Wallace Lt PA
Pelatiah: bpt 8-7-1757 d 5-26-1846 m Hannah Littlefield Pvt MA ★
Phinehas: b 10-30-1757 d 11-11-1846 m Olive Walker Pvt MA
Reuben: b 7-30-1753 d 9-29-1827 m Mary Blackwell Pvt MA
Rich: b 1730 d 1796 m Polly — Sol GA
Samuel: b 1-11-1758 d 7-14-1829 m (1)Lucy Brockway (2)Charlotte Tourgee (3)Catherine Johnson Pvt CT ★
Samuel: b 1760 d 8-18-1820 m Lucy Cutler Pvt CT ★
Samuel: b 1754 d 12-22-1836 m Abiah Swift Pvt MA
Simeon: b 9-3-1759 d 3-23-1822 m Esther Orton Pvt NY ★
Solomon: b 9-22-1762 d 9-5-1832 m Sarah Hines Pvt VT ★
Spencer: b 1-26-1762 d 1826 m Olive Cleveland Pvt Sgt CT ★
Sylvanus: b 2-16-1754 d 6-19-1834 m Betsey Elmer Ens CT ★
Sylvanus: b 1750 d a. 12-6-1835 m Hannah Foster Bourne Lt MA
Trueman: b c. 1750 d c. 1830 m Amar Barnes Trumpeter Pvt CT
Warham: b 5-4-1734 d p. 1793 m Eunice Spencer Capt CT
Wm.: b 1-8-1722 d 2-20-1789 m (1)Mary Benison (2)Elizabeth Hasell (3)Mary Cook PS SC
Wm. Jr.: b 1757 d p. 1788 m Margaret Linay Cpl VA
Wm.: b c. 1760 d 7- -1830 m Jane — Pvt VA ★
Wm. Hasell: b 3-16-1754 d 2-13-1834 m (1)Elizabeth Allston (2)Mary Philip Wilson Capt SC
Zadock Sr: b 4-9-1723 d 12-12-1789 m Lydia Townsend Pvt CT
Zebulon: b 8-10-1711 d 1-8-1803 m Eunice Wooduff Pvt CT

GIBERSON,

James: b 1747 d 1836 m Rebecca Reed Pvt NJ
John: b 1754 d 1846 m Hannah Tice Pvt NJ

GIBERT,

Pierre: b 1740-48 d 6-8-1815 m Elizabeth Bienaime Lt SC

GIBSON, (includes GIPSON)

Abraham: b 6-25-1735 d 9-9-1813 m Esther Fox Pvt MA
Abraham: b 8-15-1752 d 4-10-1829 m Mary Brown Pvt MA
Andrew: b 1750 d 1823 m Jane Freeland Sol NC
Andrew: b c. 1724 d 3- -1783 m Elizabeth Carnes Pvt PA
Arrington: b 2-4-1756 d 6-21-1815 m Rachel Longley Pvt Cpl MA
Charles b c. 1750 d p. 1803 m Esther Graham Pvt PA
David: b 1-22-1757 d 1815 m Anna Barton Cpl MA
David: b c. 1743 d 9-23-1833 m X Ens VA
Erasmus: b 1760 d p. 1840 m (1)Dianna Lewis (2)Isabelle Hutts Gibson Pvt VA★
George: b 10-10-1747 d 11-6-1791 m Ann West Capt LCol Col VA
George: b 1732 d 1819 m Elizabeth Smith Maj VA
Gideon: b 3-2-1764 d 2-10-1843 m Mrs Abigail Coulter Crawford Pvt PA
Guyon: b 1-7-1747 d 1795 m Eleanor Kennedy Sol SC
Henry: b c. 1758 d a. 9- -1808 m Dicea — PS VA
Henry B.: b 1760 d 1829 m Sarah — Sol GA
Isaac: b 4-27-1721 d 6-1-1797 m (1)Keziah Johnson (2)Abigail Bennett Pvt MA
Jacob: b a. 1757 d 1794 m Polly Demig Mrnr CT
Jacob: b 1740 d 1815 m Annie Whiteford Maj PA
Jacob: b 1754 d 1778 m Margaret Mc Elhaney 2Lt PA
James: b 9-25-1747 d 3-3-1825 m (1)Anna Forest (2)Betsy Heath Ens NH

James: b 7-12-1741 d 8-2-1831 m Hannah Watts Pvt NH
James: b 1746 d a. 1830 m Jane — Pvt NC
James: b 1745 d 1810 m Margaret — Capt PA
James: b 1745 d 2- -1816 m Annabella Dickson Capt PA
James: b 1755 d 11-24-1836 m Mary Lackey Pvt PA
James: b c. 1760 d 1830/31 m X Pvt VA
John: b 1754 d 5-13-1830 m Martha Parks Pvt PA
John, Sr.: b c. 1715 d 1782 m (1)Sarah — (2)Mary Campbell Alexander PS CT
John, Jr.: b 1759 d 1839 m (1)Frances Flewellyn (2)Elizabeth Dozier (3)Mrs Clara Butts Sol GA
John: b c. 1756 d a. 1833 m Priscilla — Pvt PS MD
John: b 1758 d p. 1818 m X Pvt MD ★
John: b 11-20-1759 d 2-9-1859 m (1)Nancy Gibson (2)Elizabeth Harvey (3)Mrs Elizabeth Smith Sol MD
John: b c. 1745 d 11-27-1797 m Alice — Pvt MA
John: b 1745 d 7-11-1835 m Elizabeth Barnes Sol MA
John: b 2-12-1736 d 1803 m Esther Kasson Pvt NY
John: b 1755 d 9-25-1836 m Margaret Shelp Pvt NY W★
John: b 1744 d 1788 m Tamar Ellis Pvt NC
John: b 9-16-1760 d 5- -1844 m Margaret Joyce Pvt NC ★
John: b 1734 d 12-29-1814 m Mary — Pvt PA
John: b c. 1738 d 1778 m X Pvt PA
John: b c. 1750 d 1816 m Jane Lowry Pvt PS PA
John: b 8-12-1734 d 5-11-1806 m Joanna Crowfoot Pvt CT
John: b 8-26-1765 d 8-2-1843 m Nancy Mills Sol PA ★
John: b — d — m Sarah Mc Dowell Pvt PA
Jonathan: b 12-22-1754 d 12-24-1807 m Bathsheba Bennett Pvt MA
Jonathan: b c. 1725 d p. 1799 m Mary — PS VA
Joseph: b 1749 d 8-31-1846 m Hannah Mary McCree Pvt NC ★
Nathan: b 7-16-1752 d 5-22-1822 m (1)Sarah Howell (2)Mary Bartram 1Lt PA
Nathaniel: b 2-22-1753 d a. 1824 m (1)Hannah Brown (2)Keziah Hayward Pvt MA
Nelson: b 1745 d 5- -1823 m Sarah Williams Pvt NC
Reuben, Sr.: b 2-14-1725 d 7-27-1800 m Lois Smith Sgt PS CS MA
Reuben, Jr.: b 9-21-1748 d 4-20-1836 m Betty Gibson Pvt MA
Robert: b c. 1734 d 1788 m (1) X (2)Elizabeth — Capt PA
Robert: b 1753 d 1801 m Ann O 'Reilly Sgt PA
Robert: b c. 1754 d 8-19-1782 m Mary Britton Cpl VA
Samuel: b 1738 d 5-5-1817 m Mary Kimberly Sgt PS CT
Samuel: b 10-15-1761 d 2-19-1835 m Elizabeth Baird Pvt Spy VA ★
Silas: b 9-1-1747 d 4-25-1834 m Damaris Bennett Pvt MA
Stephen: b6-16-1719 d 10-23-1806 m Sarah Goss Pvt MA
Stephen: b 3-29-1745 d 2-3-1812 m Rebecca Puffer 1Lt MA
Sylvanus: b 1750 d 8-27-1805 m Elinor Taylor PS NC
Thaddeus: b 6- -1760 d 2-23-1834 m Elizabeth Sumner Sgt MA ★
Thomas: b 11-19-1753 d 6-12-1841 m Relief Hartwell Pvt MA
Thomas: b 6-23-1755 d 2-3-1813 m Jemima Shepard Pvt PS NH
Thomas: b c. 1735 d 1804 m Agnes Williams 1Lt NC
Thomas: b 1754 d 1851 m — Buchanan Pvt PA
Thomas, Jr.: b 1740 d 1782 m Pamela Carson Pvt SC
Thomas: b 1750 d 1800 m Martha Riddle 1Lt VA
Timothy: b 2-25-1753 d 9-14-1832 m Sarah Foster Pvt MA
Timothy, Sr.: b 1702 d 1-18-1782 m Persis Rice PS NH
Timothy, Jr.: b 12-17-1738 d 1-16-1814 m Margaret Whitman PS NH
Wm.: b 6-2-1759 d 11-11-1839 m Abigail Sanger Sgt MA ★
Wm.: b 12-25-1753 d 4-9-1835 m Nancy Roarch Sgt NC ★
Wm.: b c. 1740 d 1812 m (1)Nancy — (2)Esther Ma Goffin Pvt PA
Wm.: b — d p. 11-18-1811 m Sally Kirk Capt VA

GIDDINGS, (includes GIDDENS)

Benjamin: b 1753 d 1830 m Afiah Holcomb Sgt CT
Daniel: b 5-9-1734 d 8-18-1816 m Sarah Lord Capt MA
David: b 7-18-1747 d 8-10-1792 m Lois Borden Pvt CT
Francis: b 10-1-1753 d 5-11-1830 m Mary White PS VA
Isaac, Sr.: b — m Elizabeth Goldsmith Pvt MA
Isaac, Jr.: b 6-17-1756 d 1-3-1843 m Elizabeth Knight Pvt MA
John: b 8-4-1748 d 11-1-1835 m Abigail Webber Drm MA ★
Jonathan: b 4-18-1741 d 4-8-1817 m Mary Baldwin Pvt PS CT
Joseph: b 4-9-1759 d 6-27-1832 m Mary Button Pvt CT ★
Joshua, Sr.: b 10-10-1719 d 2-4-1807 m Jane Reed CS CT
Joshua, Jr.: b 5- -1755 d 10-21-1833 m (1)Submit Jones (2)Elizabeth Pease Pvt CT ★
Joshua: b 4-26-1745 d 4-14-1835 m Bethiah Appleton Sgt MA
Solomon: b 1714 d 3-1-1788 m Sarah Burnum Pvt MA
Stephen: b 11-3-1744 d 2-5-1814 m (1)Mary Mighill (2)Polly Pierce Pvt MA
Thomas, Sr.: b 1723 d 5-24-1790 m Mary Coult Capt CT
Thomas, Jr.: b 8-29-1753 d 8-13/14-1845 m (1)Affia Hayes (2)Anna Bishop Pvt CT
Wm.: b 1737 d 2-19-1810 m Lydia Noble Capt CT

GIDEON,

Jacob: b 1754 d 3-3-1841 m Rebecca Sales Trm CL ★
Peter: b 3-22-1752 d 2-5-1844 m Catherine — MM MD ★
Francis: b 17-31-1753 d 1830 m Elizabeth Hopkins Capt GA

GIESEMAN,

George: b 3-3-1754 d 3-18-1810 m Catherine Wagner Pvt PA

GIFFIN, (includes GIFFEN)

Andrew: b 11-11-1751 d 12-10-1812 m Janet Harvey Pvt PA

Edward: b 12-30-1762 d 10-12-1830 m Abigail Holmes Pvt VT
James: b 1760 d 1826 m Elizabeth Ann — Pvt PA
John: b 3-17-1743 d 11-12-1809 m Eleanor Heron Pvt CMman PA
Robert: b c. 1742 d p. 8-15-1777 m Agnes Taggart PS NH
Robert: b 1743 d 8-17-1829 m Mary Bane Pvt PA
Simon, Jr.: b 7-5-1740 d 11-6-1820 m (1)Abigail Higgins (2)Lydia
   Crane QMSgt CT ★
Stephen: b 7-19-1753 d 11-6-1839 m Mary Donegen Pvt PA ★

GIFFORD,
Absalom: b 2-21-1768 d 2- -1849 m Mary Williams Pvt CT
Benjamin: b 3-13-1758 d 2-12-1821 m Esther Crandall Pvt NY
Benjamin: b 5-3-1752 d 2-3-1840 m Hannah Wilkinson Pvt NY
David: b 6-22-1741 d 6-5-1814 m Temperance Dimmick Pvt MA
David: b 11-15-1746 d 6-21-1790 m Abigail Durfee Capt RI
Elihu: b 10-9-1747 d 4-7-1831 m Abigail Chase Capt MA
Elihu: b 7-8-1761 d 9-10-1846 m Deborah Allen PS NY
Elisha: b 1749 d 6-3-1837 m Polly Washburn Pvt NY
Enos: b 3-22-1740 d 11-20-1820 m (1)Mary Wilbor (2)Susannah
   Wilbor CS RI
Gideon: b 5-5-1760 d 1-10-1810 m (1)Ruth Butts (2)Betsey Willey
   Pvt RI W ★
Jesse: b 5-12-1752 d 3-2-1841 m Ruth Perry Pvt MA
Jesse: b 1750 d p. 1804 m Mehitable Thomas Sgt MA
John: b 8-28-1754 d 9-12-1835 m Ruth Luther Pvt MA
John: b c. 1751 d 6-28-1821 m Hannah Crane Pvt NJ
John: b 1747 d 1851 m Isabel Milk Sgt RI
Joseph: b a. 1747 d 11-7-1828 m Sarah Fuller Ens NY
Lewis: b 4-21-1757 d 12-14-1843 m (1)Jedidah Taber (2)Susan
   Ashley Pvt MA ★
Lot: b 6-13-1747 d 2-2-1852 m Olive Weeks Cpl MA
Rowland: b 5-6-1748 d 2-3-1817 m Judith Sutherland Ens NY
Samuel: b 2-10-1720/21 d c. 1796/98 m Maria Handy Cpl MA
Wm.: b 6-29-1722 d p. 1790 m Patience Russel Pvt MA
Wm.: b 1758 d 8-15-1846 m Elizabeth — Pvt NY ★
Wm.: b 12-25-1751 d 2-7-1814 m Annetta Van Voorhis Capt NJ

GIFT,
Adam: b a. 1750 d p. 1793 m Anna Catherine — Pvt PA

GIGLY, (includes GIGELY)
Wm.: b 1741 d p. 1790 m Barbara — Pvt PA

GIGNILLIAT,
James: b 7-30-1746 d 3-12-1794 m Charlotte White Pepper CS SC

GIHON,
James: b a. 1752 d 1795 m Rosanna Ringland Pvt PA

GILBERT,
Abner: b 4-11-1763 d 12-11-1852 m Lydia Stoddard Pvt CT
Adam: b c. 1760 d 2- -1820 m (1) X (2)Barbara Arney Cpl PA
Allen: b 4-23-1756 d 12-13-1840 m Mary Hall Pvt CT
Amos: b 1-15-1753 d 1805 m Elizabeth Ann Alling Pvt CT
Amos: b 1764/65 d 7-26-1832 m Margaret McChesney Pvt MA ★
Asa: b 11-5-1755 d 9-23-1836 m Mary Goodwin MM Pvt CT ★
Asahel: b 12-15-1760 d 11-23-1852 m Anna Goodrich Trm CT
Barnabas, Sr: b 9-5-1724 d 11-30-1802 m Catherine Bender CS PA
Benjamin: b 7-29-1760 d 5-11-1846 m Mary Hamlin Pvt CT
Benjamin: b 5-31-1755 d 6-22-1824 m Mary Starr Cornwall Lt MA
Benjamin, Sr.: b 1724 d 1-14-1792 m Elizabeth Hudson Sol GA
Benjamin, Jr.: B b 1755 d 12-12-1832 m (1)Hannah Butler (2)Emily
   Mc Kenzie Pvt VA
Bernhard: b 5-25-1729 d 2-4-1798 m Maria Elizabeth Meyer Pvt PA
Butler: b 10-22-1747 d 5-3-1827 m Abigail Woodhouse Sgt CT
Caleb: b c. 1748 d a. 3-3-1806 m Ann Buzzardt PS SC
Christian: b 11-9-1743 d 1812 m Anna Margaretta Hartman Capt PA
Conrad: b 4-29-1734 d 1-26-1812 m Anna Elizabeth Stoltz Pvt PA
Daniel: b 2-15-1729 d 4-2-1824 m Lucy Barnes Capt MA
David: b 4-26-1755 d 7-5-1835 m Mary Wakeman Sgt CT NY
Ebenezer: b 7-1-1712 d 4-1-1798 m Rebecca Dayton Sgt CT
Ebenezer: b 4-9-1732 d 3-14-1801 m Anne Phelps Fif CT
Ebenezer: b 6-9-1754 d 4-7-1798 m Ruth Hurlbutt Pvt CT
Ebenezer, Jr.: b 4-24-1760 d 11-29-1829 m Johanna Howard Pvt MA
Elam: b 11-19-1764 d 8-24-1847 m Luna Ray Pvt MA
Eleazer: b 3-25-1744 d 5-14-1804 m Sarah Weeks PS CT
Elias: b 10-27-1748 d 8- -1828 m Lydia Bowen Cpl MA
Elijah: b 1750 d 8-6-1829 m Mary Dunbar Pvt MA
Elisha, Jr.: b 3-27-1747 d 1-12-1823 m Sarah Wheeler Capt NY
Elisha: b 5-25-1736 d 1-6-1778 m Submit Glassier Sgt CT
Felix: b c. 1735 d p. 3-15-1798 m Ann Grant PS VA
Gardner: b 4-15-1758 d p. 1778 m Anna Lathrop Sgt CT
George: b 1753 d 1838 m Susanna — Ens PA
George: b 5- -1754 d 4-20-1803 m Elizabeth Ritter Knouse Pvt PA
Gershom: b 1750 d 1- -1832 m Eunice Whitlock QM Sgt CT ★
Heber: b 10-18-1758 d 6-1-1832 m Lucinda Pennock Pvt CT
Henry: b c. 1748 d p. 1790 m Susan — Smn MD
Hezekiah: b 10-16-1735 d 1790 m — Tameson Pvt CT
Hooker: b 6-5-1754 d 12-6-1840 m (1)Candace Sage (2)Sarah
   Hooker Pvt CT ★
Isaac: b 11-15-1756 d 8-12-1835 m (1)Anna Mix (2)Esther Alling
   Pvt CT ★

Isaiah: b 3-29-1733 d 2-15-1825 m (1)Esther Bull (2)Experience —
   Cpl QM CT
Jacob: b 6-20-1756 d 2-9-1831 m (2)Anna Margaret Fox Sol PA
Jesse: b 3-13-1761 d 10-2-1839 m Sarah Hallenbeck Pvt NY ★
Joel: bpt 7-14-1734 d 11-3-1786 m Elizabeth Bradley Pvt CT
John: b 11-9-1731 d 7-5-1779 m Lydia Ives Capt CT
John, Jr.: b 2-26-1749 d 1817 m (1)Mellicent Goodrich (2)Amelia —
   CS Capt CT
John: b 2-10-1760 d 3-31-1816 m Elizabeth Lyon Sgt CT ★
John: b 12-2-1742 d c. 1795 m Theodosia Marsh QM Capt CT
John: b c. 1790/d a. 7-3-1815 m (2)Mary Strickland Sol GA
John: b 7-28-1723 d 1-15-1806 m Sarah Abbot Sgt MA
John Webster: b 12-27-1738 d 1809 m (1)Sallie Rebecca (2)Mary
   Craig Capt VA
Jonas: b 4-20-1762 d 4-20-1834 m Violaty Luce Pvt MA
Jonathan, Sr.: b 3-28-1713 d 5-9-1800 m Abigail Rogers PS MA
Jonathan: b 8-5-1725 d 8-31-1781 m Hannah Abbott Pvt MA
Joseph: b 1748 d 11-11-1812 m Miriam Webster Hopkins Sgt CT W★
Joseph: b 9-25-1735 d 9-3-1806 m (1)Elizabeth Breck (2)Sarah —
   Pvt CT
Joseph: b c. 1751 d 3- -1777 m Sarah Robbins Capt MA
Joseph: b 11-5-1755 d 2-4-1844 m Jemima Davenport Cpl MA W★
Joseph: b 2-15-1750 d 1844 m X Pvt Arfr VA ★
Josiah: b 12-7-1740 d 1814 m Rachel Bobbit Sgt MA
Josiah: b 10-20-1750 d 7-29-1805 m Lois Brooks Pvt MA
Josiah: b 3-24-1699 d 10-20-1781 m (1)Sarah — (2)Elizabeth —
   PS CS NY
Lemuel: b 11-9-1754 d 12-1-1833 mAmaryllis Mallory Pvt CT
Lemuel: b 2-18-1747 d 4-14-1841 m Ruth — Pvt MA
Lewis: b 4-4-1754 d 1-1-1835 m Naomi Adams Pvt MA
Michael: b 4-17-1754 d c. 1796 m Elizabeth Presbury 2Lt MD
Michael: b 1752 d 1842 m Rose Keyser Capt PA
Michael: b 4-19-1741 d p. 10-16-1829 m Wilmouth Davis PS VA
Moses: b 9-9-1743 d 11-23-1818 m Chloe Cooper Capt CT
Moses: b 5-13-1757 d 4-16-1823 m (1)Mrs White (2)Sarah (Noble)
   Evans Sgt CT
Nathan: b 1750 d 1786 m Elizabeth Scout Sol VA
Nathaniel: b 12-4-1723 d 3-22-1787 m Mary Butler Capt CT
Preston: b c. 1748 d 12-15-1805 m Jemiah Cock Lt VA
Reuben: b 8-18-1756 d 7-20-1840 m Sarah Waite Pvt MA ★
Reuben: b 6-22-1744 d 12-28-1820 m (1)Persis Denny (2) Dorothy
   Moore MM MA
Samuel: b 3- -1742 d 10-12-1813 m Mary Dodge Pvt MA
Samuel: b 3-12-1760 d 10-9-1849 m X Pvt CT ★
Samuel: b 6-3-1734 d 4-24-1818 m (1)Lydia Post (2)Deborah
   Champion CS CT
Samuel: b 2-10-1752 d 12-18-1820 m (1)Rhoda — (2)Susannah
   Elam Lt VA
Samuel: b 1762 d 1845 m Mary — Pvt VA ★
Simeon: b 8-29-1761 d 1-11-1835 m Sarah Nye Pvt MA ★
Solomon: b 2-10-1723 d 8-9-1798/99 m Sarah Alcock Pvt CT
Sylvester: b 10-20-1755 d 1-2-1846 m Patience Barber PS CS CT
Thaddeus: b 1756 d 1833 m Martha Turney Pvt CT
Theodore, Sr.: b 1729 d 4-22-1821 m Mary Waters Pvt CT
Theodore, Jr.: b 10-5-1751 d 8-19-1826 m Hannah Chapin Pvt CT
Thomas: b 12-10-1755 d 1-26-1847 m Mary Loring Cpl CT
Thomas: b 3-1-1723 d 2-19-1788 m Sarah Gilbert Pvt MA
Thomas: b 6- -1760 d 4-28-1848 m Hannah Covell Pvt Fif MA ★
Thomas: b 9-15-1743 d p. 1790 m Lydia Lathrop LCol NH
Truman: b 1756 d 6-15-1841 m Eunice Phippane Pvt CT ★
Wm.: b 6-24-1758 d 7-11-1836 m Hope Burr Pvt CT ★
Wm.: b c. 1758 d c. 1830 m Tamar Strickland Pvt GA
Wm.: b c. 1756 d 5-25-1816 m Betsey Bailey Sgt MA
Wm.: b a. 1744 d 1790 m Sarah Mc Candlass PS NC

GILCHRIST, (includes GILCREAS, GILCREAST)
Adam: b 6-10-1760 d 10-2-1798 m Hester Budd Lt PA
Alexander: b 10-28-1733 d 4-22-1820 m Martha Shirley Sgt NH ★
James: b 11-15-1757 d 6- -1817 m Elizabeth Snyder Lt PA W ★
James: b a. 1723 d a. 1782 m Sarah — Ens PA
John, Sr.: b 2- -1720 d 11- -1801 m Mary Nevins Pvt MA
John, Jr.: b 5- -1756 d 8- -1827 m Abigail Downing Pvt MA
John: b 1745 d 12-25-1809 m (1)Margaret Gillis (2)Jane Cowan
   (3)Abigail Miller Sgt NY
John: b 1740 d p. 5-12-1802 m (1)Effie McMillan (2)Mrs Flora
   McKay Currie Sol NC
John: b 1731 d 9-3-1795 m Mrgaret Cowden Maj PA
John, Jr.: b 1752 d 12-27-1805 m Eleanor Berryhill 1Lt PA
John: b c. 1758 d 1829 m Mary — Sol SC
Matthew: b 1756 d 8-7-1825 m (1)Elizabeth Crouch (2)Eliza Bryson
   Lt PA
Richard: b 2-22-1753 d 6-19-1833 m Mary Swan Pvt MA
Samuel: b 1754 d 5-24-1834 m Hannah Robinson Pvt MA
Sameul: b 1758 d p. 1801 m Betsy Allen Pvt MA
Wm.: b c. 1709 d 8-5-1795 m Elizabeth Glen Miller PS NH
Wm.: b 1752 d 4-9-1819 m Mary Fraser Pvt NY

GILDER, (includes GUILDER)
Isaac: b 1762 d c. 1840 m Elizabeth — Drm Fif NC
Jacob: b — d c. 1786 m Frances Sheppard Pvt SC
Reuben: b 7-9-1755 d 3-17-1794 m Mary Ashbury Alkin Dr DE

GILDERSLEEVE, (includes GILDERSLEVE)
Asa: b 1-28-1755 d p. 1817 m Mary Coffram Pvt CL

GILDERSLEEVE, contd.
Daniel: b 174-- d 3-15-1778 m Esther Wood Sgt PS NY
Finch: bpt 2-17-1751 d 1812 m Mary Seymour Lt NY
James: b 1755 d p. 1820 m Mary — Pvt NY
John: b 12-21-1755 d a. 1799 m Keziah Ketchum PS NY
Nathaniel: b 1753 d 10-30-1840 m Jerusha Powell Pvt NY
Philip: b 7-2-1757 d 10-26-1822 m Temperance Gibbs Cpl NY
Richard bpt 3-22-1730 d a. 2-4-1807 m Elizabeth — PS NY
Silas: b 6-12-1748 d 1826 m Sarah Woodruff Pvt NJ
Stephen: b 1725 d 1783 m Elizabeth Whitehead PS NY

GILE, (includes GUILE)
Asa: b 4-12-1759 d 2-20-1837 m Nancy Monroe Sgt MA
Benjamin: b 11-12-1749 d 5-24-1813 m Ruth Davis Lt NY
Ezekiel: b 3-12-1743 d 3-23-1827 m (1)Gertrude Davis (2)Hannah
    Pecker Capt NH
John: b 1-4-1739/40 d 3-13-1800/1 m Mary Nealley 1Lt CS PS NH
Jonathan: b 1740 d 1815-17 m Sarah Sherburne Sol NH
Joseph: b 1735 d 8-5-1785 m (1)Elethan Harris (2)Mary Franklin
    Vol RI
Moses: b 2-15-1719/20 d 2-14-1786 m (1)Eunice Johnson (2)Mary
    Heath PS VT
Nathan: b 4-11-1758 d 5-5-1814 m Eunice Ladd Pvt CT
Nathan: b 1751 d p. 1793 m Lydia Earl Pvt VT
Noah: b c. 1743 d p. 1786 m Elizabeth Howe Pvt NH
Samuel: b 7-17-1736 d — m Lydia Geer Pvt CT

GILES,
Aquila: b 1758 d 4-8-1822 m Elizabeth Shipton Maj ADC MD ★
Benjamin: b 1717 d 1787 m (1)Martha Geer (2)Ruth Tracy PS NH
Ebenezer: b 1759 d 1838 m (1)Betsey Melvin (2)Abigail Clark
    (3)Lydia Camp Pvt MA
Eleazer: b 10- -1744 d 1809 m Sarah Ellenwood NCdr MA
George: b c. 1762 d 1838 m Martha — Pvt VA ★
Gilbert: b — d — m Elizabeth Neilson Sol NY
Hugh: b 1-13-1750 d 1802 m Sarah Ball Col SC
James: b 8-23-1750 d 5-16-1803 m Martha Gould Pvt MA
James: b 8-24-1760 d 8-9-1832 m Elizabeth Clark Pvt MA
James: b 1759 d a. 7-30-1825 m Hannah Bloomfield 2Lt NY
James H.: b c. 1742 d 8-19-1826 m Susannah Patterson Capt SC
John: b 1744 d 2-12-1823 m Elizabeth — Sol GA
John: b 1736/7 d 3- -1806 m Mary Sias Pvt NH
John: b — d 8-21-1836 m Joanna Young Pvt NY
Jonathan: b 1735 d 1805 m Elizabeth Twiss Pvt MA
Samuel: b 4-1-1765 d p. 1820 m Laura Merriman Pvt MA
Thomas: b c. 1745 d c. 1800 m Rhoda Lowell Slr MA
Thomas: b 10-6-1754 d 11-18-1795 m Mary Soper Marshall Pvt MA
Wm.: b — d p. 2-28-1793 m Anne Branch Col VA
Wm.: b c. 1754 d p. 1797 m Margaret — Pvt VA

GILFILLAN, (includes GILFILLIAN, GILLFILLAN)
Alexander: b 1746 d p. 1802 m Martha Boyd Pvt PA
James: b 4-3-1742 d 12- -1804 m Nancy Watts Pvt PA
Thomas: b 1751 d 3-28-1816 m Agnes High Pvt PA

GILFORD, (includes GUILFORD)
Benjamin: b 1730 d 6-30-1796 m Lydia Goodale Sgt MA
Simeon: b 11-10-1751 d 3-25-1844 m Ruhamah Hayden Sgt MA
Timothy: b 9-10-1749 d p. 1801 m Sarah Hayden Pvt Fif MA

GILKESON,
John: b c. 1752 d 6-19-1793 m Sarah Vance Maj VA

GILKEY,
Charles: b 10-19-1748 d 8-27-1815 m Lucy Avery Cpl CT
James: b c. 1710 d 1790 m (1)Martha Morton (2)Mrs Margaret
    Elder Watts CS PS ME
John: b c. 1744/5 d 9-4-1818 m Sylvania Thomas PS MA
Robert: b c. 1743 d 1810 m Mrs Jean McQuistan Finley Capt NC
Samuel: b c. 1755 d 1- -1818 m Elizabeth L. — Pvt SC
Wm.: b 3-3-1758 d p. 7-22-1838 m Hannah Smith Pvt Drm MA ★

GILL, (includes GILLIS)
Archibald: b 1-16-1757 d 10-12-1803 m Agnes Denton Sol SC
Benjamin: b 6-2-1730 d 4-23-1807 m Bethiah Wentworth Col MA
Charles: b a. 1760 d 1838 m Rebecca — PS MD
Daniel: b 9-25-1734 d 12-7-1793 m Mercy Whitford PS VT
Edward: b 1-2-1744 d 10-7-1818 m (1)Leah Parrish (2)Mary
    McClain PS MD
Elijah: b 10- 1752 d 1826 m Abagail Fisher Pvt MA
Erasmus: b 7-15-1752 d 3-16-1807 m Sarah Newsum Capt VA
James: b 1755 d 8-25-1809 m Mary Louisa Gaston Capt SC ★
James: b 4-14-1760 d 4-14-1842 m Mary Ann Fox Capt SC ★
John: b 5-28-1748 d 11-8-1804 m Hannah — Capt MA
John: b 4-19-1747 d 3-2-1827 m Deborah Lincoln Sgt MA
John: b 5-17-1732 m Ann Kneeland PS MA
John, Sr.: b 12-7-1721 d 1796 m Amy Davis PS NJ
John, Jr.: b 7-16-1758 d 10-13-1838 m Anne Lovett Smith Sol NJ
John: b 1752 d p. 1783 m Agnes Dick Pvt NC
John: b 1748 d 1-9-1822 m Jean Shaw Pvt PA
John: b c. 1727 d 1783 m —X— (2)Elizabeth — Pvt PA
John: b a. 1747 d 1797 m Sarah — Lt PS SC
John, Jr.: b 1754 d 1825 m (3)Elizabeth Faust Pvt SC

John: b — d 9-26-1788 m Margaret Pitman Sol VA
Jonathan: b 1757 d 1797 m Anne Fairfax Matr MD
Joseph: b 1727 d p. 1810 m Ann Wallace Pvt MD
Nathaniel: b 1-3-1742 d 8-22-1818 m Sarah Beal Pvt MA
Obadiah: b 1759 d 5-25-1838 m Anna Martin Pvt MA
Robert, Sr.: b c. 1725 d 1778 m Lydia Musgrave PS MD
Samuel: b 2-22-1758 d 1851 m Bede Bradley Pvt CT
Samuel: b 5- -1740 d p. 1784 m Sara Hatch Sgt MA
Samuel: b 1750 d 11-2-1822 m Ruth VanMeter Capt VA ★
Thomas: b 8-27-1755 d 8-30-1838 m Hannah Griswell Capt SC ★
Wm.: b 1722 d 12-19-1806 m Martha Flynn Pvt MA
Wm.: b c. 1747 d 6-12-1802 m Mary — Pvt PA
Wm.: b 1750 d 4-17-1833 m Elizabeth Leonard Pvt PA ★
Wm.: b 1750 d 9-4-1797 m Susan Younge Maj VA
Wm.: b 7-18-1761 d 2-4-1816 m Mary Wright Pvt VA W ★
Young: b 1765 d 1854 d Ann — Pvt NC

GILLAM, (includes GILHAM, GILLHAM, & GILLIAM)
Devereaux: b c. 1740 d p. 5-2-1809 m Edith Ellis Sol NC
Ezekiel: b c. 1732 d p. 1785 m Sarah Clemens Pvt SC
Isaac: b a. 1760 d p. 1781 m Mary Hand Capt NJ
Isaac: b 11-10-1757 d 9-16-1845 m Jane Kirkpatrick Pvt SC
Jacob: b c. 1753 d p. 1802 m — Garrow Sol VA
James: b — d 6-15-1821 m Frances Hopkins Ens VA
James: b 5-13-1733 p. 10-13-1792 m Martha — Sol VA
John: b — d 3- -1832 m Sarah Clark Cpl SC
John: b c. 1762 d a. 6-20-1825 m X Sol VA
John: b 1747 d a. 1791 m Mary Briggs Harrison Lt VA
John: b 3-6-1761 d 2-23-1823 m Hannah Sampson Pvt Drm VA
John: b 175- d 1821 m Mary Tooley Drm PS VA W ★
Jonathan: b 1753 d 3-24-1835 m (2)Mary Carwile Pvt PA ★
Robert, Sr.: b 10-15-1720 d 12-15-1796 m (1)Phoebe — (2)Mary —
    Maj SC
Robert, Jr.: b 1-11-1760 d 11-7-1813 m Elizabeth Caldwell Capt
    SC W ★
Thomas: b 8-13-1733 d p. 1778 m Mary Burke Pvt PS MD
Thomas: b c. 1710 d p. 1790 m (2)Margaret Campbell PS SC
Wm.: b c. 1750 d 10-27-1825 m Jane McDaw Sgt SC
Wm.: b 1747 d 1804 m Betsy Howard Pvt NC

GILLEN,
John: b a. 1760 d 9-6-1833 m Jane Young Pvt NC ★

GILLESPIE, (includes GALESPIE, GILLASPIE, GILLASPY,
GILLESPY)
Daniel: b 10-31-1743 d 1-17-1829 m Margaret Hall Capt PS NC
David: b 1755 d 7-26-1831 m (1)Abigail Mapes (2)Mrs Nancy
    VanAlstine Pvt NY
David, Jr.: b 1756 d 1835 m Jennie Brown Pvt VA
George: b 1722 d 1796 m Hannah Johnson PS DE
George: b 1735 d a. 2- -1794 m (1)Elizabeth Young (2)Elizabeth
    Allen (3)Martha — PS NC
George: b c. 1745 d 10-11-1822 m Jane Allen Pvt PA
Isaac: b 1755-65 d p. 6-1-1827 m Mary Ann McGuire Pvt NC
James: b c. 1746 d 1-10-1805 m Dorcas Munford Capt PS NC
James: b 1730 d 1800 m Ellen Findley Sol NC
James: b 3-6-1763 d 1-14-1840 m Mary Johnson Pvt PA
James: b 12-2-1754 d 5-18-1828 m Sarah Wild Sgt SC
James: b c. 1735 d p. 8-20-1787 m Elizabeth — Pvt VA
John: b c. 1753 d 1822 m (1)Elizabeth Barnoten (2)Jane—Pvt PA ★
John: b 8-22-1741 d 1-5-1810 m Magdalene Smedes Maj NY
John: b 1725 d 1823 m Mary Graham Capt NY
John: b 1741 d 6-23-1806 m Elizabeth Armstrong Col NC
John: b 1738 d 2-12-1812 m Susan Weir Sol SC
John: b 1750 d 10- -1811 m Mary — Sol VA
Robert: b c. 1760 d p. 9-22-1843 m Martha Edmondson Sgt NC
Samuel: b 9-25-1742 d 9-18-1815 m Esther Raney Lt NY
Thomas: b 7-12-1754 d 9-19-1828 m Agnes Orr Capt TN NC
Thomas: b c. 1760 d 1842 m Margaret Bowen Sol NC
Thomas, Sr.: b 1719 d 12-15-1796 m Naomi — Pvt NC
Wm.: b c. 1741 d 1834 m Polly McSwain Pvt PA
Wm.: b 1756 d c. 1859 m (1)— Rankin (2)Mrs — Dow Pvt PA
Wm.: b 1759 d 8-25-1844 m X Pvt SC ★
Wm.: b 1737 d p. 1831 m Mrs Isabella Houston Henderson Pvt VA

GILLETT, (includes GILLET & GILLETTE)
Aaron: b 5-23-1732 d 6-14-1786 m Anna Pratt Sol CT
Aaron: b c. 1730 d p. 10-17-1786 m Jerusha — Dr PS SC
Amos: b 10-16-1743 d 4-4-1829 m Susannah Webster Pvt CT
Asa: b 6-11-1764 d c. 1839 m Naomi Hosford Pvt CT
Benjamin: b 1-26-1738 d p. 1800 m Abagail Austin Pvt CT
Benjamin: b 1758 d 6-8-1840/1 m Ann Strong Pvt CT
Benoni: b 7-23-1760 d 6-4-1844 m Phebe Dean Pvt CT ★
Benoni: b 8-1-1762 d 4-12-1844 m (1)Penelope Hubbard (2)Mrs
    Polly Seward Pvt CT ★
Charles: b 10-22-1728 d 5-18-1776 m Jerusha Jewett Pvt CT
Daniel: b 11-22-1748 d 8-13-1837 m (1)Amy Palmer (2)Alethina
    Gracia Rowland Capt Vol CT
Ezekiel: b 4-3-1743 d 4-4-1819 m Dorcas Hawkins Pvt CT
Isaac: b 5-16-1720 d 1784 m Hannorah Stevens PS CS CT
Isaac: b 3-5-1745 d — m Susanna Root Pvt CT
Israel: b 9-17-1738 d 7- -1829 m (1)Martha Throop (2)Susanna
    Durkee Pvt PS VT

Jabez: b 7-30-1738 d 4-29-1818 m (1)Anna Loomis (2)Laurana Roberts Capt CT
Jabez: b 1762 d 5-25-1839 m Hannah Holcomb Pvt Drm NY ★
Jacob: b 1756 d 1-23-1777 m Deborah Monroe Pvt CT
Joab: b 11-6-1747 d 3-20-1824 m (1)Sarah Adams (2)Susanna — Pvt CT
Joel: b 1746 d 2-11-1823 m Mrs Rachel (Judd) Hinsdale Capt CT ★
John: b 9-15-1755 d 9-22-1843 m (1)Sybil Anna Platt (2)Mary Johnson Sgt CT ★
John: b 9- -1754 d 11-11-1810 m Mercy Benedict QM CT
John: b 2-9-1733/4 d p. 10- -1779 m Abigail Hough 1Lt NY
John: b 1744 d 1829 m Jemima Smalley Cpl VT
John William: b 1758 d 10-22-1786 m Katherine Beardsley Pvt CT
Jonah, Sr.: b 10-18-1708 d 5-21-1782 m (1)Elizabeth Hoskins (2)Esther Filley CS CT
Jonah, Jr.: b 1729 d 3-14-1792 m Sarah Goodrich Drm Maj CT
Jonathan: b 3-22-1720 d 8-6-1786 m (1)Phebe Marvin (2)Mehetable — Lt CL
Jonathan, Sr.: b 2-4-1738 d 12-9-1779 m Elizabeth Bradford Steele Lt CL
Jonathan, Jr.: b 2-10-1762 d 3-14-1850 m Esther Baker Cpl CT ★
Joseph: b 6-15-1750 d 5-7-1836 m Parcys Sanders Pvt CT
Joseph: b 1755 d 2-15-1842 m X Pvt CT ★
Matthew: b 2-12-1724-1789 m Anne Loomis PS CT
Matthew, Jr.: b 4-10-1741 d 6- -1809 m Lois Douglas Sgt CT
Samuel: b 1759 d 5-8-1845 m Katherine — Pvt Tms Grd CT
Thomas: b 9-14-1748 d 4-27-1821 m Mary Jones Cpl MA
Wm.: b 2-1-1768 d 3-2-1838 m Abigail Bishop Pvt CT ★
Zacheus: b 12-18-1724 d 1-7-1793 m (1)Ruth Phelps (2)Mrs Sarah Dean Capt CT
Zaccheus, Jr.: b 11-11-1745 d p. 1789 m Elizabeth Holcomb Drm Maj CL

GILLIKIN,
George: b c. 1753 d p. 1830 m Martha Sharp PS NC

GILLILAND, (includes GILLILAN)
Alexander: b 11-18-1727 d 10-6-1798 m Rebecca — PS NC
Daniel: b 1765 d 10-5-1838 m Mary Pardun Sgt NJ
David: b 1747 d 1784 m Elizabeth — Lt NJ
David: b c. 1735 d 1831 m X Pvt PA
James: b 1739 d 5-10-1795 m Hannah Adams 2Lt PA
James: b 3-16-1749 d 2-14-1844 m (1)Lydia Armstrong (2)Jane Smith Edmiston Ens VA
James: b 1748 d 1810 m Susanna Young Pvt VA
John: b — d c. 1824 m Leah — 2Lt NJ
John: b c. 1725 d p. 3-24-1795 m Elizabeth — CS Sol NC
John: b c. 1763 d p. 2-4-1826 m Jane Briggs Pvt PA
John: b c. 1706 d c. 1790 m Hester Romar PS PA
Matthew: b c. 1760 d 9- -1843 m X Pvt PA
Thomas: b c. 1735 d c. 1800 m X Pvt GA
Wm.: b 11-25-1761 d 11-25-1840 m Susan Grantham Pvt SC ★
Wm.: b 1734 d 2-2-1796 m Elizabeth Phagan Capt NY

GILLINGHAM,
John: b 2-6-1766 d 5-1-1849 m Ann Preston Pvt PA

GILLIS, (includes GILLES & GILLISS)
Archibald: b 1755 d 12-6-1818 m Catherine McNeil Pvt NY
John: b c. 1756 d 9-3-1813 m Lyde — Pvt PA
John Perry: b 7-1-1757 d 8-6-1835 m Anne — Pvt NY ★
Joseph: b 1738-40 d 1791 m (1)Annie Handy (2)Elizabeth Irving 2Lt MD
Joseph: b 4-27-1732 d c. 1793 m Grace — Pvt MD
Levin: b c. 1761 d a. 7-24-1815 m Elinor Morris Pvt MD
Robert: b 1732 d 1807 m Elizabeth Sharp Pvt PA

GILLISON,
Archibald: b 1728 d 3- -1792 m Jean — Pvt SC

GILLOCK,
John: b c. 1750 d a. 4-7-1783 m Hannah Wolfinburger Pvt VA

GILLON,
John: b 1752 d 9-6-1833 m Jane Young Pvt NC ★

GILLOT,
Francois: b 1761 d c. 1830 m X Pvt NY

GILLPATRICK,
John, Jr.: b 1728 d 6-6-1802 m Elizabeth Clark 2Lt MA

GILMAN,
Antipas: b 7-15-1730 d 2-28-1801 m (1)Joanna — (2)Mrs Mary Gilman Col PS NH
Benjamin: b 4-2-1759 d 8-24-1837 m Sally Clough Pvt NH ★
Bradbury: b 11-5-1755 d 5-10-1842 m Hannah (Gilman) Drm NH
Bradstreet: b 7-29-1745 d 1820 m Mary Marshall Pvt NH
Caleb: b 7-15-1745 d p. 3-15-1833 m Polly Wilson Pvt NH ★
Calvin: b 4-10-1757 d 1-14-1835 m Hannah Bissell Pvt Drm CT ★
Daniel: b 8-17-1705 d 3-13-1797 m Hannah Colcord Pvt NH
David: b 6-9-1735 d 5-9-1827 m (1)Betsey — (2)Sarah (Smith) Hilton (3)Mrs Betsey Ayer Col NH

David: b 1717 d 11-22-1810 m Susannah Folsom PS NH
David: b 6-17-1749 d 3-25-1810 m Lydia C— Wgn NJ
Dudley: b 2-19-1758 d 1-5-1819 m Mary Harriman Sgt NH
Edward: b — d — m Elizabeth — Pvt NH
Eliphalet: b 4-11-1745 d p. 1811 m (1)Joanna Louge (2)Mrs Sally Odlin Fowle PS NH
Epaphras: b 1-6-1751 d 9-28-1811 m Hannah Clark Pvt CT
Israel: b 1730 d 2-20-1777 m Hannah Smith LCol NH
Jeremiah, Sr.: b 6-3-1719 d 1791 m Sarah Kimball Capt PS NH
Jeremiah: b 12-14-1740 d 3-24-1823 m Abigail Johnson LCol NH MA ★
John Taylor: b 12-19-1753 d 9-1-1828 m Deborah Folsom Sgt NH
John Ward: b 5-9-1741 d 6-16-1823 m Hannah Emery Lt NH ★
Jonathan, Jr.: b 4-9-1754 d 11-9-1828 m Joanna Bean Cpl PS NH
Jonathan: b 8-10-1713 d p. 1776 m Elizabeth Sanborn PS NH
Joseph: b 5-5-1738 d 5-14-1806 m (1)Jane Taylor (2)Rebecca Hale Ives PS CS NH
Joseph: b 1748 d 4-17-1818 m Hannah Mazoon Sol PS NH
Joshua: b 6-3-1755 d 10-26-1842 m Tabothy Brown Pvt NH ★
Joshua, Sr.: b 2-2-1716 d 1-7-1792 m Esther Sanborn PS NH
Joshua, Jr.: b 3-21-1745 d 4-21-1825 m Mary Shaw PS NH
Josiah: b 2-25-1710 d 1-1-1793 m Abigail Coffin PS NH
Moses: b 1-5-1756 d 10-22-1813 m Sarah Bean Cpl NH
Nathaniel: b 5-10-1753 d 8-13-1843 m Sally Branscomb 1Lt NH ★
Nicholas: b 10-21-1731 d 4-7-1783 m (1)Ann Taylor (2)Elizabeth Rogers Col PS CS NH
Nicholas: bpt 10-31-1736 d 4-30-1786 m Elizabeth — Pvt NH
Peter: b 1754 d 10-3-1834 m Martha Clough Pvt NH ★
Peter: b 1-5-1739 d 5-30-1797 m Elizabeth Bryant Ens PS NH
Philipp: b 2- -1755 d 5-28-1817 m Maria Clarinda Heasler Pvt PA
Samuel: b 4- -1732 d 11-11-1799 m (1)Deborah Fowler (2)Deborah Thing Capt CS PS NH
Samuel: b 4-20-1725 d 1778 m (1)Tabitha (Gilman) (2)Mrs Lydia (Robinson) Giddings Pvt NH
Samuel: b 3-8-1732 d 5-7-1776 m Hannah Tilton PS NH
Samuel Thing: b 3-13-1759 d 9-12-1841 m Sarah Hurd Pvt NH
Simon: b 1745 d 11-20-1802 m Sarah McDaniels Pvt NH
Simon: b 2-23-1756 d 11-19-1815 m Tabitha Morrill Pvt NH ★
Solomon, Jr.: b 1720 d 1792 m Mary Forbes MM CT
Somersby: b 1734 d 1814 m Sarah Sibley PS NH
Stephen: b 1757 d 3-17-1830 m (2)Dorothy Clough Pvt NH W ★
Thomas: b 8-7-1738 d 9-7-1828 m Priscilla Smith 1Lt PS NH
Zebulon: b 1735 d 10-13-1792 m Elizabeth Colcord Capt PS NH

GILMER,
George, Jr.: b 1-19-1742 d 11-29-1795 m Lucy Walker Lt PS VA
James: b c. 1745-50 d a. 9-27-1813 m Jane Hill Capt VA
John Blair: b 4-26-1748 d 8-11-1793 m Mildred Thornton Meriwether Lt VA
Peachey: b 3-6-1737 d p. 1789 m Mary Meriwether Capt VA
Robert: b — d 1849 m Nancy — QM MD
Thomas Meriwether: b 1763 d 7-17-1817 m Elizabeth Lewis Pvt VA

GILMORE, (includes GILLMOR, GILLMORE, GILMON, & GILMOR)
Adam: b 3-12-1763 d p. 5-27-1833 m Elizabeth Ketcham Pvt MA ★
Alexander: b 6- -1764 d 10-8-1843 m Rebeccah Smith Pvt VA ★
Andrew, Sr.: b 4-10-1726/7 d 8-10-1806 m (1)Abigail — (2)Esther Fales PS MA
Andrew, Jr.: b 7-23-1764 d p. 1809 m Hannah Makepiece Pvt MA
David, Sr.: b 3-27-1732 d 10-21-1831 m Joanna Miller Pvt MA
David, Jr.: b 5-3-1765 d 1-28-1849 m (1)Mary Robbins (2)Mrs Mary Snow Pvt MA ★
Elizabeth: b 1757 d 8-21-1824 m John Berry PS PA
Ephraim: b 1745 d 1823 m Arabella Curry Pvt PA
George: b 1743 d 1-16-1804 m Nancy — Capt NY
Isaac: b 2-2-1744 d 4-14-1822 m Magdalene Ashbach Pvt PA
James: b 11-14-1752 d 1-30-1829 m Nancy — Pvt MA
James: b 8-10-1728 d a. 1804 m Mary Crow Pvt MA
James: b 1734 d 1-18-1809 m (1)Anna — (2)Agnes — (3)Mary Clyde Parker (4)Jeanette — 2Maj NH
James: b 1739 d 1825 m Molly — Ens NH
James: b 11-13-1755 d 1-3-1835 m Mary Hughs Sgt NC ★
James: b 1754 d 12-10-1799 m Mary Scott Pvt NC
James: b a. 1720 d 1782 m Martha Beatle Capt VA
James: b 1-17-1745 d 11-18-1834 m X Sgt Spy VA ★
James: b 1750-55 d 9- -1822 m Martha McElwee Sol VA
John: b 11-8-1759 d p. 3-29-1841 m X Pvt NC
John: b c. 1750 d a. 1790 m Sophia King Pvt NC
Jonathan: b 3-11-1728 d 3-30-1799 m Elizabeth Hunter Pvt NH
Patrick, Sr.: b c. 1750 d a. 2-2-1824 m Martha — Sol NC
Robert: b 7-9-1749 d 11-15-1816 m Elizabeth Andrews Pvt PS NH
Robert: b 1745-1750 d p. 2-15-1814 m X Pvt VA
Roger: b a. 1749 d 11-5-1807 m Ann Hunter Capt NH
Samuel: b 8-11-1765 d 2-27-1845 m Reuhma Hathorn Pvt MA ★
Samuel: b 3-25-1760 d 1-1-1848 m Eleanor Bailey Pvt VA ★
Thomas: b 3-31-1759 d 3-16-1823 m Rachel Young Pvt NH ★
Thomas: b 1757 d 3-27-1808 m Elizabeth Young Pvt PA
Tyrril: b c. 1744 d 5- -1775 m (1)Hannah Cook (2)Rachel—Pvt MA
Whitefield: b 11-12-1745 d 5-12-1786 m Margaret Gilmore 1Lt NH
Wm.: b 11-26-1728 d 8-17-1806 m (2)Elizabeth Fullerton PS MA
Wm.: b 1747 d 9-11-1816 m (2)Sarah Hanna Pvt PA

GILPATRICK, (includes GILLPATRICK, GILPATRIC)
Christopher: b 12-15-1755 d — m Martha Smith Pvt MA

GILPATRICK, contd.
Christopher: b 4-21-1751 d 2-17-1832 m Sarah Wildes Pvt MA
John, Jr.: bpt 10-20-1728 d 6-6-1803 m Elizabeth Clark 2Lt MA
John: b 5-1-1754 d p. 1791 m Eunice Tarbox 2Lt MA
Joseph: b 1760 d 4-13-1854 m Mary Jeffards Pvt ME ★
Nathaniel: bpt 7-12-1752 d 5-30-1834 m (1)Abigail Higgins
    (2)Lidia Higgins Pvt MA ★
Robert: b 10-1-1761 d p. 1810 m Polly Berry Pvt MA

GILPIN,
George: b 3-4-1740 d 12-27-1813 m (1)Catherine Peters (2)Jane
    Peters Maj VA
Gideon: b 12-4-1738 d 8-20-1825 m (1)Sarah Gregg (2)Mrs
    Susanna Hoopes Pvt PA
Israel: b 8-1-1740 d 7-4-1834 m Elizabeth Hannum Col DE ★
Joseph: b 1747/8 d 1836 m — (Giles) Malcolm Capt NLt DE ★
Joseph: b 8-1-1725 d 3-30-1790 m Sarah Elizabeth Reed PS MD
Vincent: b 12-8-1732 d 8-5-1810 m Abigail Woodward Pvt DE

GILSON, (includes GILLISON & GILSTON)
Daniel, Sr.: b 3-28-1736 d 1-13-1778 m Abigal Kent Sgt MA
Daniel, Jr.: b 9-9-1761 d 8-11-1845 m (1)Olive Erwin (2)Rachel
    White Pvt MA ★
David: b c. 1760 d p. 1-18-1836 m Eliza — Pvt VT
Ebenezer: b 6-24-1745 d 1-3-1811 m Elizabeth Lawrence Pvt NH
Eleazer: b 2-19-1720 d 6-10-1777 m Sybil Lakin Pvt MA
John, Sr.: b 5-12-1726 d 1787 m (1)Hannah Green (2)Prudence
    Lawrence Pvt NH
John: b 3-7-1762 d 1-4-1847 m (1)Lucy Derby (2)Mrs Abigail Handy
    Pvt MA ★
Nathaniel: b 9-17-1759 d 11-17-1839 m Lucy Tarbell Cpl MA
Peter: b — 1764 d 5-3-1849 m Esther Spaulding Pvt MA ★
Richard: b c. 1750-55 d p. 4-23-1801 m Rachel Rankin Pvt PA
Samuel: b 1-7-1729 d 9- —1779 m Elizabeth Shedd Sgt MA
Simon: b 12-22-1730 d 5-6-1808 m Sarah Fisk Pvt MA
Wm.: b 1730 d 1806 m (1)Elizabeth Craighead (2)Mrs Sarah Trindle
    (3)Mrs Elizabeth Crawford Pvt PA
Wm.: b 1737 d 3-5-1807 m Alice Shirley Pvt PA

GILSTRAP,
Peter: b c. 1735 d 1795 m Mary — Sol NC

GILTNER,
Bernhard: b 3-1-1749 d p. 1818 m Katherine Lichtenwalter Pvt PA
Francis, Sr.: b 1716 d a. 9-8-1775 m Catharine Weaber Pvt PA
Frantz: b 3-3-1761 d p. 1847 m Otelia Yentzer Fif Pvt PS PA

GINDRAT,
Henry: b 1739 d 1801 m (1)Mary May (2)Dorcas (Stafford) Williams
    Lt CS PS SC

GINGER,
Henry: b 4-4-1758 d 2-8-1842 m Chauncy Luster Pvt PA ★

GINGLE,
George: b c. 1750 d c. 1810 m X Pvt MD

GINN,
James: b 10-4-1745 d 4-17-1818 m Ann Riggs 2Lt MA

GINTHER,
Peter: b 1-12-1740 d 1-11-1814 m (1)Maria Catherine Williams
    (2)Elizabeth Swartz Pvt PA

GIPPLE,
Christopher: b c. 1745 d 1819 m Catherina — Pvt PA

GIRARDEAU,
John: b 3-1-1756 d 4-14-1837 m (1)Mary Westcoat (2)Elinor
    Dashwood Williams Pvt GA
Wm.: b 1752 d 1-21-1822 m Patience — Pvt GA

GIRAULT,
John: b 2-24-1755 d 5-28-1813 m Mary Spain Capt IL

GIRDLER,
James: b c. 1751 d 1-15-1842 m (1)Lenney Miles (2)Nancy (Mincher)
    Soloman Pvt PA
Lewis: b 10-19-1767 d 9-14-1844 m Sarah Brooks Slr MA
Nicholas: b 10-16-1748 d p. 1783 m Elizabeth Palmer Pvt MA

GISH,
Abraham: b c. 1740 d 12-30-1789 m Susanna Kuhns Pvt PA
John: b c. 1740 d 4-21-1783 m Elizabeth Kapp Pvt PA

GIST,
Benjamin: b c. 1730 d c. 1810 m Mary — Capt CS NC
David: b 4-29-1753 d 8-3-1820 m Rebecca Hammond 2Lt MD
Joseph: b 9-30-1738 d 1-22-1803 m Elizabeth Elder QM Maj MD
Joseph: b 8-27-1751 d 7-30-1844 m (1)Hannah Breedon (2)Betsy
    Springer Pvt Spy NC ★
Mordecai: b 2-22-1742 d 8-2-1792 m (1)Cecil Carnan (2)Mary
    Sterrett (3)Mary (McCall) Cattell BGen MD

Nathaniel: b 10-15-1733 d 1796 m Judith Cary Bell Col VA
Nathaniel: b — d 10-7-1780 m Mary Howard Ens NC
Thomas: b 3-30-1741 d 11-22-1813 m Mary Noland Col MD
Thomas: b 10-10-1764 d 1837 m Elizabeth — Pvt NC ★
Wm.: b 1711 d 11-19-1794 m Violetta Howard PS MD

GITHINS, (includes GITHENS)
Joseph: b c. 1752 d 9-30-1776 m Sarah Story Pvt NJ
Joshua: b 1-26-1754 d 5-5-1822 m Margaret Kughler Pvt NJ

GITTINGER,
John: b 1740 d 1793 m Catherine — Pvt PA

GITTINGS,
Benjamin: b 1750 d 11-30-1805 m Jemima Landham Pvt MD
Benjamin: b c. 1740 d p. 5-20-1781 m Ann — PS MD
Henry: b 1730 d p. 1800 m X PS MD

GIVEN,
David: b 1758 d p. 1791 m Elizabeth McDaniel Cpl MA
John: b 1753 d 11-10-1819 m Mary Winchel Sgt MA
Robert: b 1732 d 1-15-1796 m Jane Nickels PS ME

GIVENS, (includes GIVEN)
Daniel: b c. 1745 d p. 10-15-1822 m Martha — Sol VA
George: b 1740 d 1-17-1825 m Rachael Balck Capt VA
James: b 4-8-1764 d 1846 m X Pvt NC ★
James, Jr.: b 1-8-1764 d 7-11-1832 m Jane Givens Sol VA
John: b 1719 d p. 1-14-1790 m Margaret Sitlington Capt VA
Robert: b 5-22-1759 d 10-26-1833 m Martha — Pvt VA ★
Robert: b 1759 d 9- -1825 m Margaret Elliott MM Spy VA
Samuel: b 1763 d 1847 m Jane King Pvt NY
Samuel: b 3-25-1738 d 1-18-1845 m Lucy Pardue Of NC
Samuel Alexander: b 3-26-1753 d 9-4-1784 m Belle Nye Pvt NY
Wm.: b 1740 d 1793 m Agnes Bratton Pvt VA
Wm.: b 5-18-1762 d 1847 m Rebecca Kenney Pvt Tms VA ★

GIVHAN,
Philip: b c. 1750 d a. 12- -1817 m (1)Mary Geiger (2)Frances Molet
    PS SC

GLADDEN,
Wm. W.: b 1761 d 11-11-1848 m Mary Ann Woods Pvt PA

GLADDING, (includes GLADING)
James: b 4-19-1731 d 6-28-1778 m Johanna Wheeler Cpl MA
Jedediah: b 1756 d 11-10-1832 m Elizabeth Page Pvt CT ★
Joseph: b 1753-56 d 5-30-1823 m Susan Fordham Pvt CT

GLADMAN,
Michael, Sr.: b c. 1716 d 9-17-1789 m Rachel — PS MD
Michael, Jr.: b 7-3-1736 d 7-25-1818 m Barbara — Pvt PS MD

GLADNEY,
Richard: b 1741 d 8-10-1793 m Jennet Strong Pvt SC
Samuel: b 1737 d 10-24-1799 m Agnus McCreight Sol SC

GLANCY,
Jesse: b 1756 d 9-16-1831 m Rachel Copeland Pvt PA

GLASBURN,
David: b c. 1730 d c. 1830 m Elizabeth Carpenter Pvt VA

GLASCOCK, (includes GLASSCOCK)
George: b 12-20-1743 d 8- -1787 m Martha Howard PS Dr NC
George: b 1741 d p. 2-10-1815 m Hannah Rector PS CS VA
John, Sr.: b c. 1699 d p. 12-9-1780 m Margaret — PS VA
Spencer: b 1761-3 d 1821-3 m Polly Enochs PS VA
Thomas: b 11-3-1736 d 1793 m (1)Katie Rector (2)Agatha Rector
    Lt VA
Thomas: b 1756 d 1810 m Mary Bacon Lt GA
Wm.: b 5-28-1730 d 1793 m Ann Sellard PS GA
Wm.: b 2-20-1729 d 1785 m Elizabeth Chichester PS VA

GLASGOW,
Arthur: b 1750 d 1822 m Rebecca (McNutt) McCorkle Sol VA
James: b 1761 d 10-11-1840 m Jane McClintock Pvt PA ★
James: b c. 1740 d p. 1790 m Phereby — Maj NC
Robert: b 1762 d 1-17-1835 m Elizabeth Knard Pvt SC
Robert: b 1749 d 1834 m Rosanna Uster Pvt VA

GLASS,
Alexander, Sr.: b 5-1-1746 d 1-2-1834 m Jemima Gustin Sgt CT ★
Consider: b 11-15-1759 d 2-18-1843 m (1)Hannah Parson (2)Tempa
    Beal (3)Mrs Betsy Rowe (4)Mrs Martha Chenery Pvt MA ★
George: b 1740 d 3- -1802 m Eva Albright Sgt PA
John: b 3-21-1737/8 d 1-14-1828 m Bernice Delano Pvt MA
John: b 1763 d 3-16-1839 m Nancy Elizabeth Quint Pvt MA ★
John: b 3-15-1752 d 1836 m Mary Chandler Pvt VA
Joseph: b 1722 d 6-12-1794 m Eliza Wilson PS VA
Levi: b 1766 d p. 1850 m X Pvt NC
Michael: b 8-19-1736 d 4-19-1808 m Christina Hubler Pvt PA

Seraiah: b 1745 d 2-23-1837 m Hannah Oldham Pvt MA ★
Vincent: b 1746 d c. 1834 m (1)Mary Jones (2)Susanna Dean Pvt VA

GLASSFORD,
Alexander: b a. 1759 d 5- -1826 m Margaret — Pvt PA

GLATFELDER, (includes GLATFELTER, GLODFELTER, KLOTFELTER)
Casper, Jr.: b a. 1750 d p. 1796 m Mary — Pvt PA
Felix: b c. 1760 d 1815 m Mary Elizabeth Rennoll Pvt PA
George: b 1757 d p. 10-5-1837 m (1)Elizabeth Leonard (2)Mrs Catherine Sowers Pvt NC ★
Henry: b 8-13-1753 d 4-19-1833 m Margaret Heilman Pvt PA
John: b 10-8-1742 d 1811 m Catharine Simmons Sgt PA

GLATZ,
Jacob: b — d 1798 m Barbara Brenner Capt PA

GLAZE, (includes KLASE & KLOES)
George: b c. 1760-64 d p. 6-7-1823 m Catherine Hetzel Pvt PA
George: b 1-10-1748 d 1826 m Elizabeth Williams Pvt VA
Gideon: b c. 1760 d p. 1790 m Sarah — Sol SC
John: b c. 1758 d p. 1820 m Elizabeth Smith Pvt NC
Joseph: b 1712 d p. 1778 m Ruth — PS MD
Reuben: b c. 1760 d p. 1826 m Elizabeth — Sol GA
Thomas: b c. 1759/60 d 2-13-1805 m Milly Frazer Pvt NC W ★
Valentine: b 4-15-1759 d 4-28-1812 m Eva Smitten Ens VA
Wm.: b 1753 d p. 1806 m Mary O. — PS MD

GLAZEBROOK,
James: b 1738/9 d 12-8-1807 m Mary Bowles Pvt VA
Julius: b 4-15-1752 d 9-14-1847 m (1)Mary Garton (2)Mary Kevil Pvt VA ★
Richard: b 4-10-1753 d 1827 m Catherine Winn Snead Pvt VA

GLAZIER,
Aaron: b 8-4-1756 d 5-5-1833 m Orphie Belnap Pvt MA
Calvin: b 3-18-1759 d p. 1784 m Lydia Pierce Pvt MA
David: b 3-1-1741/2 d 11-17-1824 m Sarah Pratt PS NH
Jacob: b 1759 d 1828 m Annie Rood Pvt CT
John: b 1746/47 d 8-20-1820 m Freelove Sherman Capt RI
John: b 12-4-1755 d 12-4-1831 m Elizabeth Edwards Pvt SC
Jonathan: b 5-16-1751 d 2-24-1836 m Azurah Nye Pvt MA
Oliver: b 5-23-1763 d 2-25-1862 m Rachel Hastings Pvt MA ★
Silas: b 2-12-1748 d 4-8-1816 m Suzee Johnson Pvt CT

GLEASON,
Aaron Jr.: b 4-26-1745 d 1-27-1816 m Dilla — Pvt MA
Abner: b 12-6-1745 d 6- -1816 m (1)Abigal Rich (2)Deborah Baker Pvt MA
Asa: b a. 1763 d p. 1820 m X Pvt MA
Benjamin: b 4-18-1734 d 10-15-1818 m Dorothy Allen MM PS MA
Benjamin: b 12-25-1748 d p. 1802 m Deborah Beard MM Pvt MA W ★
Benjamin: b 5-7-1749 d p. 1803 m Mary Cole PS NH
Benoni: b 1761 d 8-29-1819 m Lucy Hubbard Sol MA
Bezaleel: b 6-9-1749 d p. 1779 m (1)Phoebe Newberry (2)Sarah King Pvt MA
Elijah: b 7-30-1750 d 2-20-1819 m Lucy Scott PS CS NH
Ephraim: b 6-4-1733 d 9-14-1819 m Hannah Kent Pvt MA
Fortunatus: bpt 6-9-1752 d 9-1-1810 m Ester Beamon PS NH
George: b 1748 d 1844 m Betty Sanderson Pvt MA
Henry: b 2-26-1750/49 d p. 7-11-1795 m Hannah — Pvt MA
Isaac: b 9-25-1747 d — m Azubah Pease Pvt CT
Isaac: b 10-24-1733 d 3-18-1791 m Sarah Harrington Capt MA
Isaac: b 8-6-1724 d 1-7-1776 m Eunice Smith Pvt MA
Jacob: b 3-10-1734 d 4- -1805 m (1)Hannah Pease (2)Ruth—Sol MA
James: b 1759 d 10-4-1834 m Lavina Drake Pvt CT
James: b 12-26-1759 d 7-3-1841 m Anna Phelps Pvt MA
John: b 7-22-1744 d 9-20-1827 m Anna Eames 2Maj MA
John: b 10-14-1758 d 8-25-1822 m (1)Sarah—(2)Hannah—Pvt MA
John: b 2-13-1763 d 8-20-1839 m Azubah Duncan Pvt MA
Jonas: b 7-15-1748 d 4-6-1815 m Lucy Harwood Cpl MA
Jonathan: b 11-30-1745 d 6-21-1827 m (1)Lucretia Moore (2)May Fiske Pvt MA
Joseph: b 8-13-1721 d 1809 m Hannah Colton PS CT
Joseph: b 11-16-1752 d 3-4-1808 m Patience Belknap Pvt CT
Joseph: b 3-4-1752 d — m Elizabeth Fox Drm CT
Joseph: b 4-13-1752 d 7-1-1819 m Sarah Bell Pvt MA
Micajah: b 10-17-1740 d 10-28-1776 m Hannah Drury Capt MA
Moses: b 7-12-1762 d p. 10-15-1832 m — Pvt Tms MA
Phineas: b 1732 d 9-10-1808 m (2)Persis Newton Gregory Pvt MA
Phineas: b 8-16-1732 d 3-4-1799 m Lois Robbins Pvt MA
Phineas: b 2-21-1753 d 12-26-1809 m Margaret Kelso Pvt MA
Phinehas: b 7-31-1751 d 12-10-1840 m Hannah Rowell Cpl MA ★
Samuel: b 6- -1756 d 1791 m Submit — Pvt CT
Samuel: b 10-9-1747 d 1823 m Elizabeth Brown Lt MA
Samuel: b 12-13-1715 d 1796 m (1)Elizabeth Howe (2)Dorothy Faux (3)Abigail Livermore Pvt MA
Samuel: b c. 1755 d 6-21-1832 n Hannah Brigham Pvt MA
Simon: b 7-26-1713 d 3-3-1793 m Charity Bellows Pvt MA
Timothy: b 3-22-1748 d 2-7-1827 m Eleanor Lovering Ens NS MA ★
Wm.: b 1730 d 2-3-1818 m(1)Mary Seger (2)Mrs Mary Goss Pvt MA

Winsor: b 5-19-1761/2 d 8-8-1816 m (1)Sally (Gleason) — (2)Patty Follett Pvt NH W ★

GLEAVES,
John: b c. 1739 d 1780 m Hannah — Pvt MD
Wm.: b a. 1750 d 1820 m Elizabeth Turk 1Lt PS CS VA

GLEIM,
George Christian: b 4-7-1736 d 7-21-1817 m Anna Maria Mathias Pvt PA

GLENN, (includes GLEAN, GLEN)
Andrew: b 1754 d 7-25-1842 m Nancy Ferguson Pvt Spy PA ★
Archibald: b 1753 d 6-29-1826 m Sarah Ferguson Pvt PA
David: b 1745 d 6- -1784 m X LCol SC
Gabriel: b 1739 d 1793 m Jane Mills Pvt PA
George: b c. 1720 d p. 12-22-1801 m — Young Pvt VA
Gideon: b c. 1730 d 11-17-1808 m Sally — Sol NC
James: b 2-10-1718 d 8-15-1793 m Angel Boeckout Pvt NY
James: b 7-22-1759 d 7-24-1843 m Martha Craig Boyd Pvt NC ★
James: b 1743 d 2-20-1817 m Elizabeth Nelson Pvt PA
James: b c. 1743 d p. 1-17-1823 m X Pvt PA
James: b 1750 d 3-25-1813 m Jean — Pvt PA
James: b c. 1745 d a. 1-2-1805 m Elizabeth Bowles 2Lt VA
James: b c. 1757 d c. 1832 m (2)Ruth Burns Sct VA
James: b 1763 d 1836 m Elizabeth Calahan Sol VA
John: b 7-2-1735 d 9-28-1828 m Catherine Vedder QM NY
John: b 1726 d 9-24-1828 m (1)Elizabeth Spratt (2)Jane McLean (3)Mary Grissom PS NC
John: b 1741 d 1820 m (1)Ann — (2)Mary Diver Pvt PA
John, Sr.: b c. 1750 d p. 1790 m X Pvt PA
John: b 1752 d c. 1799 m Sarah Bacon Col CS PS VA
Peyton: b c. 1755 d 2-5-1813 m Sara Venable Ens VA
Robert: b 1722 d 11- -1799 m Isabella Clendenin Maj MD
Robert, Jr.: b 1737 d 11- -1807 m Elizabeth — Pvt PA
Wm.: b 12-11-1759 d 9-14-1839 m Rebecca Headington Pvt PA
Wm., Jr.: b 3-14-1741 d a. 1790 m Martha Miller Lt SC
Wm.: b c. 1749 d 1777 m Alice Evans Pvt VA
Wm. Coleman: b 5-16-1761 d 4-13-1827 m Elizabeth Wright Pvt VA

GLENNY, (includes GLENNE & GLENNEY)
Isaac: b 7-7-1761 d 12-30-1835 m Sarah Nutting Sgt MA
John: b 1728 d c. 1800 m Thankful Adams Pvt MA
Wm.: b 1760 d 11-26-1801 m Mary Green Lt CT W ★

GLENTWORTH,
George P.: b 7-22-1735 d 11-4-1792 m Margaret Linton Dr PA

GLENTZER, (includes GANTZERT)
John: b 1-15-1757 d 2-8-1838 m Anna Margaret Hummerlin Pvt PA ★

GLESSNER,
Jacob: b 9-21-1732 d 3-21-1794 m Catherine Elizabeth Miller 2Lt PA

GLICK,
George: b 12-24-1749 d p. 1790 m (1)— Herr (2)Margaret Herr Pvt PA
George: b 4-5-1759 d 4-9-1820 m Hettie Lansing Pvt PA

GLIDDEN,
Andrew: b c. 1737 d p. 1-3-1805 m Maria — PS NH
Arnold: b 1754 d 2-24-1841 m (1)Anna Saward (2)Hannah Davis Pvt MA ★
Benjamin: b 9-6-1746 d p. 1801 m Eunice Averill Pvt MA
Charles: b 5-29-1744 d 8-11-1811 m Alice Mills 2Lt NH
John: b 1738 d 2-15-1816 m Ruth — 2Lt NH
John: b 1754 d 1818 m Abigail Murdock Sgt NH
Joseph, Jr.: b 12-29-1757 d 1-25-1817 m Mary Waters Pvt MA
Robert: b c. 1740 d a. 2-15 -1779 m Phebie Hickson PS NH
Simeon: b c. 1740 d 1833 m Rebecca Smith Ens NH
Tobias: b c. 1720 d 6- -1818 m Miriam Chapman Pvt MA

GLIDEWELL,
Nash: b 1721 d 1795 m Martha — Pvt VA
Robert: b 10-15-1762 d 8-18-1839 m Joanna Lovesy Pvt VA

GLINES,
Benjamin: b 3-13-1764 d 1813 m Love Leavitt Pvt NH
Israel: b 1753 d 10-4-1838 m Mary Virgin Pvt NH ★
James: b — d c. 5-1-1807 m X PS NH
John: b 2-2-1756 d 1835 m Elizabeth Moore Pvt NH
Nathaniel: b 12-1-1744 d 11-7-1825 m Elizabeth Moore Pvt NH W ★
Wm.: b 1736 d 3-28-1830 m Elizabeth Blanchard Pvt NH
Wm.: b 1757 d 9-16-1855 m Elizabeth Williams Pvt NH ★

GLISSON, (or GLISAN)
Daniel: b 7-12-1759 d 2- -1830 m (1)Anne Herring (2)Sarah Kornegay Vol NC
Thomas: b 7- -1735 d 3-29-1809 m Margurete — Matr MD

GLONINGER,
John: b 4-17-1750 d 1-22-1836 m Catharine Orth LCol PA

GLONINGER, contd.
Philip: b 2-12-1719 d 12-11-1796 m Anna Barbara Swope Sub-Lt PA

GLOOS,
John: b 5-3-1709 d *p.* 1779 m Catharine Dexter PS PA

GLOVER,
Alexander: b 2-1-1741 d 7-13-1813 m Hannah Pope Cpl MA
Alexander: b 3-20-1756 d 1-27-1826 m Sarah Salisbury Pvt MA
Alexander: b 11-11-1761 d 8-14-1821 m Nancy Spring Pvt MA ★
Amose: b 4-3-1762 d *p.* 1843 m (1)Anna Katherine — (2)Mrs Nancy (Smith) Holmes Drm DE
Benjamin: b 6-17-1753 d 2-20-1840 m X Pvt NC VA ★
Chesley: b 2-2-1761 d 2-17-1829 m Mary Guerrant Pvt VA
Daniel: b 1-19-1734 d *a.* 1810 m Hannah Jillings Pvt MA
Edmund: b *c.* 1750 d *p.* 1790 m X Sol VA
Edward: b 5-21-1743 d 9-13-1804 m Hannah Fiefield Lt MA
Elisha: b 1-9-1729 d 10-18-1811 m (1)Elizabeth (Glover) — (2)Jerusha Billings Pvt MA
Enoch: b 5-14-1734 d 11-21-1801 m Susannah Bird Pvt MA
Frederick: b *c.* 1740 d 1797 m (1)Elizabeth Cato (2)Sarah — Pvt SC
Henry: b 10-8-1703 d 2-12-1784 m Prudence Stoddard PS CT
Henry: b 8-22-1732 d 8-21-1800 m Hannah Lewis Pvt MA
James: b 6-5-1734 d 4-27-1806 m Lois Bent Capt MA
James: b 9-22-1748 d 2-6-1819 m Rachel Bonney Pvt MA
James: b 7-9-1754 d 10-23-1844 m Margaret Minis Bell Cpl PA ★
John, Jr.: b 2-11-1732/3 d 7-2-1802 m Elizabeth Curtis Capt CT
John: b 12-30-1701 d *a.* 3-30-1784 m Elizabeth Bennett Cav CT
John: b 11-5-1732 d 1-30-1797 m (1)Hannah Gale (2)Mrs Frances Fosdick Col BGen MA
John: b 5-3-1753 d 7-21-1830 m Mercy Colton Lt MA
John: b 1756 d 8-31-1833 m Martha Ann Cheney Ens NC ★
John: b 2-25-1744 d 1825 m Sophia Duncan Pvt VA
John: b 8-18-1747 d 1822 m (1)Judith — (2)Sarah — Pvt KY
Jonathan: b 6-13-1731 d 1804 m (1)Abigail Burnham (2)Mary Breeley Col PS MA
Jones: b *c.* 1750 d 1828 m Judith Love Sol NC
Joseph: b *c.* 1725 d 1786 m Phoebe — PS NC
Joseph: b 6-8-1720 d 8-3-1783 m (1)Margaret Kelly (2)Mrs Anne Wilson Doughty Col SC
Joshua: b 2-3-1736-7 d 9-17-1788 m Elizabeth Swift Drm Pvt MA
Robert, Jr.: b 3-27-1763 d 2-21-1820 m Kezia Barrows Pvt MA
Robert: b 1758 d 1822 m (1)Frances Atwood (2)Rebecca Jeter Mil NC
Robert: b *c.* 1728 d *c.* 1794 m Amey — PS VA
Samuel: b *c.* 1752 d *a.* 11-5-1788 m Elizabeth Dove Pvt MA
Samuel: b 4-24-1756 d 1-17-1808 m Miriam Clarke Pvt MA
Samuel: b 6-2-1750 d 6-7-1820 m Mary Tindale Pvt VA
Samuel Kingsley: b 6-28-1753 d 7-31-1839 m Eunice Babcock Srgn Mte MA ★
Thomas: b 9-1-1723 d 1-11-1811 m Rebeckah Pope Lt MA
Thomas: b 12-2-1745 d 6- -1817 m Zebiah Vose Cpl MA
Wm.: b 1760 d 4-28-1835 m (1)Anna — (2)Elizabeth Pulliam Pvt NC W★
Wm.: b 1741 d 8-6-1806 m X Capt PA
Wm.: b 3-9-1745 d 6-25-1830 m Rebecca Elizabeth Brown Pvt PA
Wm.: b *c.* 1745 d *p.* 4-14-1817 m Mary Mackinson Pvt PA
Wm.: b *a.* 1758 d *p.* 1778 m — Harrelson Pvt VA
Wilson: b 3-28-1758 d *p.* 1790 m Mrs Margaret Heyward Lt SC

GLOYD,
Daniel, Sr.: b *c.* 1736 d *p.* 1790 m Joanna — Pvt MD
Daniel, Jr.: b 1761 d *p.* 1835 m Charity Shaw Pvt MD
Joseph: b 11-10-1763 d 7-15-1842 m Abigail Garnett Pvt MA ★
Thomas: b 11-16-1757 d 1-30-1798 m Chloe — Pvt Fif MA

GOBER,
George: b 1740 d 1786 m Martha Wisdom PS NC
Wm.: b 1744 d 4- -1826 m (1)Lucy — (2)Lucy Appling Sol GA

GOBIN, (includes GOBEN)
Charles: b 1753 d 3-17-1797 m Ann Philips Capt PA
Wm.: b 1758 d 2-26-1842 m (1)Rebecca Braudy (2)Unis Dunham Pvt PA ★

GOBLE, (includes GOBBLE, GOBEL)
Abraham: b *c.* 1760 d 1836 m Lucy Greene Pvt NJ
Benjamin: b 1746-50 d *p.* 1824 m (3)Amelia Howell (4)Catherine Strange Pvt PA
Christian: b 1755 d 5-7-1834 m Sarah Gise Pvt MD ★
Daniel: b *c.* 1759 d *p.* 1790 m Ellen Gooden Pvt NJ
Ezekiel: b *c.* 1746 d 1811 m Phebe Peck Sgt NJ
George: b *c.* 1758 d *c.* 3-13-1806 m Elizabeth Linder Capt MD
George: b 5-26-1750 d 8-22-1831 m Julian Wisner Pvt NJ ★
Jonas: b 1707 d 6-26-1791 m Melatiah — Wgn NJ
Robert: b 7-12-1700 d 3-29-1783 m Mary — CS NJ
Simeon: b 1720 d 8-8-1777 m Abigail Conger Ens NJ
Stephen: b 3- -1759 d *p.* 1840 m X Pvt PA ★

GODBEY,
Wm.: b 9-29-1750 d *a.* 1- -1833 m Zannah — Sol VA

GODBOLD,
John William Ware: b 7-10-1760 d 9-2-1842 m Sarah Ann Cruft Capt CS MA Heirs ★

Stephen: b 1767 d 3-9-1845 m (1)Rebecca Grice (2)— Fore (3)Rebecca Woods Pvt SC
Zachariah: b 4-3-1763 d 7-13-1832 m Rachael — Lt SC

GODDARD, (includes GODARD)
Benjamin: b 11-4-1736 d 3-11-1806 m Mary Flagg Sgt MA
Daniel: b 2-17-1734 d 9-30-1807 m Mary Willard Lt MA
David: b 1730 d 10-7-1777 m Margaret Stone Cpl MA
Edward: b 3-12-1745 d 10-13-1811 m Lois Howe PS NH
Gardiner: b 4-15-1763 d *p.* 1790 m Sophia Rice Pvt MA
Isaac: b 3-12-1752 d 4-16-1840 m Rosanna Holcomb Pvt CT
James: b 4-24-1740 d 2-22-1809 m Betty Goddard Lt MA
James: b 1-6-1731 d 1-13-1815 m Hannah Rice Pvt MA
John, Sr.: b 6-28-1730 d 4-13-1816 m (1)Sarah Brewer (2)Hannah Seaver PS MA
John, Jr.: b 11-12-1756 d 12-18-1829 m (1)Susannah Heath (2)Jane Boyd (3)Mary Langdon (4)Ann White Dr NH
John: b 12-10-1725 d *p.* 1790 m Sarah Sargent Pvt MA
John: b 1-20-1723/4 d 7- -1785 m Hannah Townsend PS RI
Joseph: b 9-27-1761 d 6-28-1844 m Frances Glasscock Cpl VA ★
Levi: b 1758 d 8-13-1803 m Mary Goddard Pvt CT ★
Moses: b 3-26-1746 d 4-11-1832 m Keziah Hayes Pvt CT
Nathaniel: b 3-17-1738 d 10-31-1815 m (1)Mary Cooper (2)Sarah C. Winchester Lt MA
Robert: b 8-13-1728 d 6-9-1807 m (1)Hannah Stone (2)Elizabeth Goddard CS MA
Samuel: b 12-27-1742 d 8-16-1806 m (1)Elizabeth Green King (2)Mrs Catherine Parker Parks PS MA
Wm.: b 4-21-1740 d 6-16-1788 m Rhoda Goddard Pvt MA
Wm.: b 6-14-1731 d 1-28-1820 m Elizabeth White Pvt NH

GODDIN, (includes GODDEN)
David: b *c.* 1724 d 2-7-1790 m (1)Hopeful Wood (2)Elizabeth Stanborough Pvt NJ
John: b 1738 d 1830 m (1)Miranda Isham (2)Priscilla Hamner (3)Lucy Webb (4)Ann Corbett Timberlake Lt VA

GODFREY,
Ard: b *a.* 1758 d 1777/8 m Tamerson Austin Pvt MA
Benjamin: b 1717 d 1781-4 m Elizabeth — Capt PS SC
David, Sr.: b *c.* 1709 d *p.* 1790 m Priscilla Baker Pvt NY
David, Jr.: b 8-18-1732 d 6-21-1813 m (2)Elizabeth Harris Pvt NY
Ezekiel: b 12-22-1751 d 6-5-1817 m Anna Robinson Sol NH
George, Sr.: b 3-19-1720 d 6-30-1793 m (1)Lydia Hodges (2)Bethia Hodges (3)Abigail Dean BGen PS MA
George Jr.: b 9-17-1758 d 2-17-1830 m Abigail King ADC Pvt MA
Isaac: b 11-27-1747 d 2-12-1834 m (1)Abigail Couch (2)Hannah — Pvt CT ★
James: b 2-15-1752 d 3-30-1835 m Abigail Weaver Pvt NJ
John: b 2-26-1754 d 8-1-1829 m Jerusha Hughes Lt MA
Jonathan: b 10-18-1747 d *p.* 1803 m Mary Lane Pvt NH
Joshua, Jr.: b 6-8-1751 d 7-12-1827 m Naomi Kelly Pvt MA
Knowles: b 9-13-1762 d 1794 m Mary Rider Pvt MA
Mathew: b 1739 d *p.* 1782 m Sarah Valentine Cty Lt VA
Nathan, Sr.: b 9-25-1719 d 10-28-1775 m (1)Martha Couch (2)Sarah (Andrews) Nash Pvt CL
Richard: b *c.* 1735 d *p.* 1790 m Lydia Doane Lt MA
Richard: b 3-23-1711 d 1792 m Theodora Deane PS MA
Richard: b 12-8-1760 d 10-16-1817 m Rachel Davis Pvt SC
Samuel: b 7-7-1746 d 3-12-1801 m (1)Elizabeth Hodges (2)Mary Hodges Pvt MA
Seth: b 9-22-1751 d 9-17-1835 m Esther Atwood OrdlSgt MA★
Silliman: b 5-5-1750 d 3-1-1829 m (1)Mary Goodsell (2)Mindwell Osborn PS CT
Thomas: b 1736 d *p.* 1790 m Nancy Hicks Sol SC
Tristram: b 3-11-1763 d 4-5-1808 m Molly Hobbs Sol NH
Wm.: b 5-25-1746 d 7-12-1832 m Anne Dearborn Sol NH
Wm.: b 3-4-1754 d 1-4-1787 m Sarah Britton Pvt SC
Wm.: b *c.* 1760 d 1826 m Helen Ramsay PS VA

GODHARD,
John: b *c.* 1727 d 6- -1797 m Sophia — Pvt PA

GODMAN,
Samuel: b 1740 d 1796 m Anne Henderson Capt MD
Wm.: b 1754 d 7-10-1825 m Allena Gartel CaptLt MD VA

GODOWN,
John: b 4-1-1749 d 12-8-1814 m Mary D. Roundsville Pvt NJ

GODWIN,
Abraham, Sr.: b 11-23-1724 d 2-7-1777 m Phoebe Cole Capt PS NY
Abraham, Jr.: b 7-16-1763 d 10-5-1835 m Mary Munson Fif NY ★
Anthony: b 9-14-1749-52 d 1-1-1779 m Amedora Godwin PS VA
Benjamin: b 1735 d 1799 m Miss Pitt PS VA
David: b 3- -1766 d 1-31-1852 m Catherine Waldron Mus NY ★
Henry: b 2-25-1751 d *p.* 1782 m Catrina Bandt Capt NY
Thomas: b 2-8-1709 d 5- -1779 m Mary Pitt PS VA
Wm.: b 1756 d 1803 m Mary Bowman Pvt NY

GOE,
Wm.: b 8-4-1729 d 3-24-1824 m Dorcas Turner PS PA

GOERTNER,
Peter: b 3-28-1736 d 3-18-1813 m Mary Catharine Bargy Pvt NY

GOETCHIUS, (or GOETSCHIUS)
Abraham: b 9-12-1754 d 3-14-1829 m (1)Genet Campbell (2)Rachel Feister Sol NY
John: b 1745 d 1826-8 m Hannah Dater Maj NJ
John Mauritius: b c. 1753 d p. 4-25-1791 m Tryntie Kip Maj NJ
Stephen: b 10-25-1752 d 1-16-1837 m Elizabeth DuBois PS NY

GOEWEY,
Barent: b 1742 d 11-10-1803 m Rachel Ostrander Pvt NY

GOFF, (includes GOFFE & GOUGH)
Aaron: b 2-16-1754 d p. 1788 m Bethia Briggs Pvt MA
Andrew: b 1754 d 10- -1831 m Grace Gordon Williams Ens TN
Charles: b 10-3-1758 d 10-13-1832 m (1)Deborah Hill (2)Anna (Strong) Brainard Pvt CT
David: b 1761 d c. 1820 m (1)Roxy Fowler Pvt MA
Ezra: b 1760 d c. 1827 m Mehitabel Bliss Fif MA
Hezekiah: b 6-26-1755 d 2-27-1848 m (1)Anna Ward (2)Rebecca Smith Woodard Pvt Mar MA
Jacob: b 3-11-1740 d 10-19-1780 m Mehitable — Pvt MA
Jacob: b c. 1750 d 9- -1779 m Olive Sweet Pvt RI W★
James: b 3-17-1760 d 12-11-1857 m Anna Stubbs Sgt MA ★
James: b 8-25-1759 d 1834 m Jemima Salisbury Pvt RI
Job: b 11-22-1760 d 12-8-1845 m Zerviah Waldo Pvt RI ★
John, Sr.: b 3-15-1701 d 10-20-1781 m Hannah Griggs PS CS NH
John, Jr.: b 2-16-1727 d 2-3-1813 m Jemima Holden Pvt CS PS NH
John: b a. 1730 d p. 2-20-1809 m (2)Elizabeth Hennessey Pvt NC
John: b c. 1752 d 1810 m Elizabeth — Pvt NC
John: b c. 1740 d 1796 m Sarah Wood Pvt VA
Jonathan: b 3-4-1757 d p. 1813 m Lydia Harding Cpl CL
Josiah: b c. 1760 d p. 1804 m Anna Rowley Sgt CT
Nathan: b 1723 d 3-23-1810 m Mary Potter CS MM RI
Richard: b 9-9-1763 d 4-14-1842 m Polly Winchester Slr Sol CT ★
Richard: b 2-21-1749 d 9-1-1836 m Mehitable Bullock Pvt MA
Richard: b 5-16-1729 d 2-2-1796 m Elizabeth Barnwell Capt SC
Roswell: b 10-15-1762 d 10-27-1825 m Mary — Sol NY
Salathiel: b c. 1748 d 6-27-1791 m Elizabeth L. Gray Capt VA
Samuel: b 12-5-1750 d 12-2-1842 m Mercy Vickery Sol NH
Squire: b c. 1763 d c. 1825 m (1)Experience Brainard (2)Mrs Eunice Brainard Pvt CT
Thomas: b 1761 d 5-2-1824 m Margaret Parsons Pvt VA
Wm.: b — d 10-4-1777 m Ann Morse Cpl MA
Wm.: b 1761 d p. 11-29-1837 m Sabra Mathis PS Lt NC
Wm.: b 1753 d 1839 m Margaret Golden Sol VA

GOFORTH,
Preston: b 6-3-1739 d 10-7-1780 m Nancy Elizabeth Potts Pvt NC
Wm.: b 4-1-1731 d 11-2-1807 m Jemima Catherine Meeks CS LCol NY
Wm.: b 9-30-1753 d 12-29-1802 m Elizabeth Wood Auditor PA

GOGGANS,
Daniel: b c. 1730 d c. 1778 m X PS SC

GOGGIN,
Steven, Jr.: b a. 1750 d 1789 m Rachel Moorman Lt VA

GOHEEN,
John: b 7-10-1749 d 4-15-1815 m Mary Jacobs Pvt PA
Richard: b — d p. 1786 m Catherine Bessonett Pvt PA

GOING, (or GOINS)
Drury: b 1749 d 2-22-1796 m Sarah Baxter Pvt SC
Jonathan: b 9-25-1762 d c. 1834 m Sarah Kindall Pvt MA

GOLDEN,
Jacob: b 1730 d 8-31-1811 m Mary — Pvt NJ
Thomas: b 1730 d — m Phoebe — Sol NY
Wm.: b 10-7-1743 d 2-10-1816 m (1)Ruth Drake (2)Christiana Hortman Pvt NJ
Wm.: b 4- -1760 d p. 3-14-1835 m Peggy — Pvt VA ★

GOLDER,
Archibald: b 3-27-1760 d 1807 m Sarah Ashmead Capt PM QM MD W★
Wm.: b 3-1-1759 d 3-18-1846 m Dorcas (Coffin) Dill Pvt PS NY

GOLDMAN,
Christian: b a. 1764 d p. 1818 m Anna Maria Pvt PA

GOLDSBOROUGH, (or GOLDSBURY)
Greenbury: b 4-23-1742 d 2-19-1829 m X Capt MD
Howes: b 9-4-1774 d 1-30-1797 m Rebecca (Goldsborough) CS MD
John, Sr.: b 10-12-1711 d 6-18-1778 m Ann Turbutt CS PS MD
John, Jr.: b 3-26-1740 d 11-18-1803 m Caroline Goldsborough CS PS MD
John: b 1739 d 11-5-1828 m Rebecca Hastings Pvt VT
Robert: b 12-3-1733 d 12- -1788 m Sarah Yerbury PS MD
Wm.: b 12-25-1762 d 3-12-1815 m Bathsheba Walker Pvt VT

GOLDSMITH,
Benoni: b 1-9-1756 d 3-30-1822 m Angelina — Pvt VA

Caleb: b 1755 d 6-23-1818 m (1)Rhoda Finch (2)Elizabeth McWilliams PS Sgt NY
James: b 1760 d 2-20-1837 m X Sgt CT ★
Jeremiah: b 1760 d 7-15-1842 m Sarah Converse Pvt MA
Jeremiah: b 1742 d 11-7-1827 m X Pvt Arfr NY ★
John: b 2-23-1736/7 d — m Martha Lamson Sol NH MA
John T: b 1761 d p. 9-4-1841 m Lovie Caswell Pvt SC ★
Josiah: b 9-9-1744 d 4-26-1816 m Sarah Fox Pvt NH
Wm.: b 1725 d 2-21-1812 m (1)Margaret Cogswell (2)Hannah Burnham Pvt MA
Wm.: b 1762 d 1841 m Elizabeth Rountree Pvt VA
Wilmot: b c. 1730 d p. 1780 m Elizabeth Hobart Capt CT
Zaccheus: b 4-7-1701 d 1776 m (1)Tabitha Dodge (2)Mehitabel Kimball Pvt MA

GOLDSTON,
Wm.: b a. 1753 d p. 3-21-1808 m Sarah — Capt NC

GOLDTHWAITE, (or GOLDTHWAIT)
Jacob: b 1734 d 4-7-1817 m Elizabeth Nightingale Lt MA
John: bpt 5- -1731 d c. 1800 m Hannah — Pvt RI
Joseph: b 1735 d 12-29-1812 m Mary Goldthwait Pvt MA
Philip: b 1757 d 11-25-1832 m Martha Hanscom Pvt Matr MA
Samuel: b 4-14-1760 d 1853 m X Pvt MA
Stephen: b 3-26-1762 d 8-30-1832 m Chloe Aldrich Pvt MA
Thomas: b 1738 d c. 1789 m (1)Lucy Flint (2)Lois Stebbins Sol MA
Timothy: b 5-5-1762 d 6-16-1858 m Polly Briggs Pvt Matr MA
Wm.: b 1743 d 3-29-1808 m Abigail King Pvt MA

GOLDWIRE,
James: b 4-15-1747 d a. 3-16-1781 m Sarah Stuart Capt GA

GOLIGHTY,
David: b 6-30-1757 d 6-27-1842 m Tabitha Mitchell Pvt SC ★
Wm.: b 1730 d 1788 m Any Shand Sol SC

GOLLADAY,
Jacob: b 8-4-1754 d 1795 m Sarah Anne — Pvt PA

GOLSON, (or GHOLSON)
Anthony: b c. 1733 d a. 1-20-1817 m Elizabeth — Pvt VA
John: b 1718 d p. 1782 m Ester Cooke PS VA
John Casper: b 2-11-1756 d p. 1791 m Sarah Miller 2Lt SC
Lewis: b c 1730 d a. 1800 m Elizabeth Stehely Maj PS CS SC
Mary Sandidge: b 1720-22 d p. 1783 m Anthony Gholson PS VA
Wm.: b 1752 d 1-2-1837 m Mary Jarrell Sgt VA ★

GOLTRA,
Oliver: b 1-7-1757 d p. 8-12-1821 m Anna VanTuyle Pvt NJ

GONSOLVE,
John: b 12-29-1752 d 9-15-1834 m Charity Hawkins Smn Sgt RI ★

GONTERMAN,
Henry: b c. 1745 d p. 1815 m X Capt NJ

GONTES,
Peter: b 2-16-1751 d 10-6-1818 m Susanna Elizabeth Hazen Pvt PA

GONZALEZ,
Joseph: b a. 1735 d 4- -1782 m Margaret Dutcher PS NY

GOOCH,
Daniel: b 8-26-1756 d 11- -1837 m Nancy Sneed Sol PS NC
James: b c. 1759 d 9-23-1808 m Mary Davenport Cpl MA
Jedediah: b 4- -1740 d 8- -1832 m Mary Emery Pvt MA
Joseph: b 1732 d p. 1790 m Jane Dudley Sol NC
Pumphrey: b c. 1760 d p. 12- -1794 m Mary Wagstaff Sol VA
Rowland: b c. 1725 d 1794 m Unity — PS VA
Samuel: bpt 4-8-1744 d 2-17-1826 m Sarah Patten Lt MA
Stephen: b c. 1756 d c. 1816 m Mary — PS VA
Thomas: b c. 1750 d c. 1815 m Lucy Grubbs Sol VA
Thomas: b 1743 d 1796 m Sara Wood PS VA
Wm.: b — d 12-22-1802 m Frances Rice Pvt NC

GOODALE, (includes GOODALL, GOODEL, GOODELL)
Aaron: b 1-6-1743 d 8-17-1817 m Eunice Marshall Cpl MA
Abner: b 8-22-1755 d 5-16-1823 m Mary Howe Pvt MA
Amasa: b 7-10-1745 d 2-2-1824 m (1)Lucy Coy (2)Lydia Wheeler CS MA
Asa: b 3-5-1754 d p. 1798 m Mary Rice Cpl MA
Asa: b 2-22-1747 d 8-8-1837 m Alice Corbin Pvt CT ★
Chester: b 9-5-1762 d 1-31-1835 m Aseneth Cook Pvt CT ★
Daniel, Sr.: b 1744 d 4-16-1805 m Frances Craft Pvt CT
David: b 10-5-1738 d p. 1779 m Hannah Abbott Pvt CT
David: b 8-14-1749 d 3-4-1830 m Elizabeth Brigham Pvt MA
Ebenezer: b c. 1734 d p. 1792 m Grace Phelps Capt MA
Ebenezer: b — d — m Hodge Pvt MA
Edward: b 4-20-1715 d 8-30-1784 m Lydia (Eaton) Chandler Cpl PS CT
Enos: b 3-28-1746 d 1836 m Hannah Densmore Pvt PS NH
Ezekiel: b 9-8-1743 d 8- -1824 m Elenor Gill Pvt MA
Isaac: b 11-16-1755 d 11-23-1834 m Jemima Warner Pvt MA ★

GOODALE, contd.
Joel: b 8-12-1760 d 9-20-1830 m Molley Swain Pvt MA
John: b c. 1730 d 1792 m X Sgt VA
Jonathan: b 1741 d 5-9-1826 m Mary McClave Pvt NH
Joseph, Jr.: b c. 1745 d p. 1820 m Ruth Fox Pvt CT
Joseph: b 6-18-1735 d 3-17-1829 m (1)Ann Hopkins (2)Mrs Sarah
  Woodcock PS Pvt MA
Joseph: b 1744 d 1790 m Phebe Brown Cpl PS NY
Josiah: bpt 4-13-1755 d 3-25-1842 m Persis Babcock Sgt MA
Nathan: b 11-11-1743/4 d 3- -1793 m Elizabeth Gates Phelps Capt
  MA
Nathaniel: b 6-22-1753 d 10-3-1818 m Hannah Marble Pvt MA
Parke: b 4-7-1754 d 7-5-1821 m Mary — Ens CS VA
Paul: b 3-9-1747 d 12-4-1828 m Eunice Lovell Pvt MA
Pleasant: b 1757 d p. 1796 m Mary — Pvt GA
Richard: b 4-21-1750 d 6-11-1826 m Mercy Parkhurst Cpl CT
Silas: b 2-13-1747 d 3- -1820 m Sarah Marshall Lt CT
Simeon: b 2-13-1746 d p. 1790 m Martha Williams Ens CT
Thomas: b 5-3-1745 d 3-4-1814 m Judeth Libby Pvt MA
Wm.: b 7-9-1757 d 7-4-1843 m Phebe Newton Pvt MA
Zecheriah: b 7-30-1737 d 1-14-1799 m Hannah Cheney Lt CT

GOODBREAD,
Joseph: b 5-3-1750 d 6-15-1844 m Tomasanne Johnson Sol NC

GOODE, (includes GOOD, GUTH)
Adam: b 1754 d 5-5-1826 m Dorothea Strickler Pvt PA
Bennett: b c. 1744 d 1785 m Isabella Lewis Col PS VA
Daniel: b c. 1715-20 d 1781 m — Campbell Sol VA
Edmund: b 1730 d 10-15-1812 m Sarah Branch Pvt VA
Edward: b 1749 d 1808-10 m Polly Turpin Sol VA
Edward: b c. 1721 d c. 2-1-1796 m Judith Morton PS CS VA
Francis: b 12-20-1744 d 4-23-1795 m Alice Harris Capt VA
Jacob: b c. 1722 d 1797 m Barbara — PS MD
John: b 1761 d p. 1800 m (1)— Johnson (2)Mrs Hester (Gooding)
  Swearingen Sgt MD
John: b 3-12-1738 d 6- -1790 m Sarah Brown Sol VA
John: b 1743 d 1835 m Martha (Embry) Simmons Pvt PS VA
John: b 1750 d 3-11-1840 m (1)Judith Fuqua (2)Mary Oulsey Pvt
  VA ★
John: b a. 1741 d a. 1-10-1803 m (2)Martha Moore (3)Rebecca J.
  Pulley PS VA
Lorentz: b 1-21-1743 d 11-2-1814 m (1)Salome Dorney (2)Ann
  Maria Dorney Pvt PA
Mackerness: b c. 1740 d 1815 m Mary Moseley Cmsry VA
Martha Jefferson: b c. 1719 d 1797 m Bennett Goode PS VA
Peter: b 2-7-1746 d 2- -1823 m (1)Eva Catherine Lehr
  (2)Magdalena — 1Lt PA
Richard: b 1730-40 d 1802 m (2)Rebecca Young Maj NC W★
Robert: b 2-8-1743 d 4-20-1809 m Sallie Bland PS VA
Robert: b 1-22-1765/66 d a. 8-9-1824 m (1)Ann Cheatham (2)Mary
  Watkins Pvt VA
Roswell: b c. 1752 d a. 12-13-1808 m Elizabeth — PS MD
Samuel: b 1763 d 1821 m Susan A. — Pvt PA
Samuel: b c. 1700 d 1797 m Susannah — PS VA
Samuel: b 3-21-1756 d — m Mary Armistead Burwell PS VA
Thomas: b c. 1759 d 12-20-1846 m Sarah Hawkins Pvt VA ★
Thomas: b c. 1760 d p. 2-20-1804 m Elizabeth — PS VA
Wm.: b 10-25-1761 d 9-27-1845 m Phoebe Bass Pvt VA ★
Wm.: b 1765 d 1837 m Sarah James Sol VA
Wm.: b c. 1740 d p. 8-18-1818 m Mlle Marie Morrisette PS VA

GOODFELLOW,
Moses: b c. 1755 d p. 1790 m Louvisa Smith Pvt NY

GOODHART,
Frederick: b c. 1730 d 1791 m Maria Catharina — Pvt PS PA
Henry: b 1751 d 1800 m Elizabeth Caylor Cpl PA

GOODHUE,
Aaron: b 11-12-1761 d 9-20-1847 m Mary Kimball Sol MA
Daniel: b 12-15-1758 d 11-16-1803 m Hannah Shatswell Pvt MA
Francis: b 6-2-1710 d 9-8-1799 m (1)Sarah Fowler (2)Mrs Elizabeth
  Lord Capt MA
George: b 1746 d p. 1791 m (1)Susanna Mitchell (2)Rhoda Calkins
  Pvt MA
Jacob: b 11- -1723 d 9-6-1793 m (1)Joanna Story (2)Rachel (Story)
  Goodhue (3)Mrs Eunice Lord (4)Mrs Sarah Rowe Sgt MA
Jeremiah: b 4-19-1762 d 8-14-1807 m Elisabeth Treadwell Pvt MA
John: bpt 5-20-1722 d p. 1790 m Elizabeth Lamson Pvt MA
John: b 4-23-1745 d 5-4-1817 m (1)Mercey Lampson (2)Mary
  Potter Pvt MA
John: b 4-4-1763 d 1-7-1818 m Rebecca Parham Pvt NH
Joseph: b 10-17-1744 d 1826 m Abigail Choate Pvt MA
Josiah: b 7-7-1728 d 11-14-1797 m Elizabeth Fletcher Pvt MA
Nathaniel: b 1724 d p. 1790 m Lydia Hill PS NH
Samuel, Jr.: b 1719 d 4- -1808 m Deborah Wadleigh PS NH
Zachariah: b 1725 d 1795 m Mary Tool-hacker Pvt MA

GOODIN,
Samuel: b 1733 d 1807 m (2)Elizabeth (Klein) VanMeter PS VA

GOODING, (or GODING)
John: b a. 1752 d c. 1799 m — White PS NC

Jonathan Coolidge: b 1-31-1739 d c. 1825 m Hannah Larned Pvt MA
Joseph: b 7-1-1729 d 12-23-1815 m Rebecca Macomber PS Pvt MA
Matthew: b 4-19-1734 d p. 1781 m Mercy Crane Lt MA
Spencer: b 1749 d 1819 m Margaret — Pvt MA
Wm., Sr.: b 8-23-1736 d 4-2-1778 m Barshabah Walker Pvt MA
Wm., 2nd: b 2-18-1761/2 d 1-30-1803 m Lydia Andrews Sgt MA
Wm.: b 10-13-1736 d p.1835 m Sarah Stearns Pvt MA
Wm. Abraham: b c. 1730 d p. 1789 m Elizabeth Randle Pvt MA

GOODKNIGHT,
Michael: — d 9-1-1781 m (2)Mary Landreth PS CS VA NC
Samuel: b c. 1761 d p. 1800 m X Pvt PA

GOODLETT,
David: b 11-10-1751 d 3-19-1816 m Rachel — Pvt SC
Wm.: b 8-20-1760 d 6- -1836 m Nancy Hooper Lt SC

GOODLOE,
Henry: b 1730 d 1799 m Frances Diana Kemp Sgt VA
Robert: b 4-17-1741 d 1-25-1797 m Sarah Short Capt NC

GOODMAN,
Benjamin: b c. 1730 d 10-7-1781 m Maria Williams Sol SC
Charles: b c. 1741 d 1827 m Elizabeth Horsely PS VA
Eleazer: b 1750 d 12-15-1829 m Rebecca White Capt VT
Joel: b c. 1734 d 1-31-1786 m Annas — PS NC
John: b 1756 d 1829 m Esther Hess Pvt NC
John: b 1750 d 5- -1797 m Elizabeth Whiteman Pvt PA
John: b 6-15-1748 d 6-6-1824 m Anna Maria Miller Pvt PA
John: b 5-28-1762 d 7-5-1830 m Charlotte Shuck Pvt PA
John Reinhard: b 6-5-1753 d 6-6-1822 m Elizabeth Dorothy Hera
  Pvt PA
Moses: b 6-20-1750 d 8-17-1831 m Amy Seymour Lt CT
Noah: b 2-9-1734 d 1797 m Abiel Smith Maj CS MA
Peter: b 1754 d 1-31-1829 m Christina Krauss PS PA
Richard: b 2-10-1761 d 7-20-1845 m Elizabeth Hunt QM CT ★
Richard: b 4-10-1748 d 5- -1834 m Nancy Seymour Sol CT
Roland Horsley: b 1756 d 1827 m Elizabeth Rodes PS VA
Thomas, Sr.: b 1763 d p. 9-3-1851 m Elizabeth — Matr VA ★

GOODNER,
Conrad: b 11-29-1756 d 8-27-1837 m Elizabeth Scherer Pvt NC ★

GOODNOW, (includes GOODENOUG, GOODENOW)
Abraham: b 4-16-1749 d 9-15-1804 m Silence (Tower) Ingersol Pvt
  MA
Adino: b 7-15-1755 d 6-26-1843 m Rebekah Woodard SgtMaj NH ★
Benjamin: b 1747 d 1825 m Mary McBride Cpl NH
Calvin: b 2-15-1762 d 7-29-1853 m Betsy Parker Pvt NH
Daniel: b 6-16-1741 d p. 1781 m Catherine Moore Pvt MA
Daniel: b 7-4-1761 d 3-14-1844 m Hannah Goodnow Pvt MA ★
Daniel: b 1-1-1726 d 12-12-1818 m Martha Banister Pvt PS NH
David: b 8-31-1735 d 10-9-1814 m Abigail Rice QM NH W★
Eber: b 3-15-1765 d 8-8-1843 m Susannan Atwood Sol MA
Edward: b 10-30-1742 d 7-17-1798 m Lois Rice Cpl MA
Eliab: b 2-20-1757 d 8-23-1823 m Jemima Bayley Pvt MA W★
Elijah: b 1753 d p. 1788 m Abigail Dudley Pvt MA
Isaac, Jr.: b — d c. 1812 m Susannah Ockinton Sgt MA
Jesse: b 3-4-1754 d 1-19-1801 m Polly Bond Pvt MA
John: b 12-1-1751 d c. 1843 m Rebecca Tyler OrdlSgt MA ★
John: b 1-30-1762 d 10-13-1863 m Persis Howe Pvt MA
Thomas: b 2-26-1738 d 8-11-1821 m Abigail Willson Pvt MA
Timothy: b 1736 d 6-6-1788 m Sarah Willis Sol MA
Wm.: b 7-18-1751 d 3-22-1809 m Mary Brown Pvt MA

GOODRICH,
Abner: b 2-1-1735 d 11-4-1825 m Ruth Delano Pvt CT ★
Allen: b 10- -1760 d p. 1802 m Lucy Hollister Pvt CT
Benjamin: b 7-7-1740 d 6-30-1834 m (1)Lydia Wilder (2)Abigail
  Witherbee Pvt MA
Benjamin: b c. 1740 d p. 1-15-1803 m Lucy Butler Capt VA
Briggs: b c. 1738 d p. 3-21-1788 m Mary Camp PS CS VA
Caleb: b 9-1-1731 d 7-27-1777 m Huldah Butler Lt MA
Charles: b 8-7-1720 d 11-16-1816 m (1)Lucy Ward (2)Hannah Ward
  Sgt VA
Daniel: b 3-25-1752 d 6-2-1826 m Bertha Shepherd Pvt CT
David: b 10-9-1753 d 1776 m Penlope Holcomb Sgt CT
David: b 12-14-1757 d — m Huldah Booth Pvt CT
David, Sr.: b1705/6 d 1-7-1779 m Sarah Edwards PS CT
David, Jr.: b 5-22-1732 d 10-15-1808 m Prudence Benton Pvt CT
David: b 2-10-1730 d p. 1781 m Hannah Boardman Pvt CT
David: b 7-16-1749 d 10-12-1781 m Anna Strong Pvt CT
Edward: b 1758 d 1818 m Frankie Pierce Pvt VA
Elijah: b 6-3-1755 d 12- -1814 m Betsey Orvis Pvt CT
Elijah, Sr.: b 7-3-1724 d 10-3-1791 m Margaret Gillett PS CT
Elijah, Jr.: b 1-3-1754 d 12-5-1847 m (1)Zilpah Stone (2)Mrs Nancy
  Smalley Pvt MA
Elisha: b 5-27-1734 d 10-2-1789 m Lucy Goodrich Ens CT
Elisha: b 9-2-1712 d p. 6-4-1796 m Rebecca Seymour Pvt CT
Elisha: b 1-3-1748 d 1825 m Deborah Allen Pvt CT ★
Elizur: b 10-8-1730 d 3-16-1785 m Abigail Deming Sgt CT
Elizur: b 3-24-1761 d 11-1-1849 m Anne Willard Allen MM CT
Elizur: b 8-8-1745 d 10-12-1798 m Sarah Kimberly PS CT

Elnathan: b 12-6-1718 d 11-23-1785 m Elizabeth Showers CS PS CT
Ethan: b 11-1-1755 d 10-24-1812 m Abigail Hedden Pvt CT
George: b 8-24-1751 d 8-16-1843 m Lucinda Wells Sgt CT
Gilbert: b a. 1763 d 4-21-1832 m Sarah Taylor Pvt MA W★
Hezekiah: b 5-10-1757 d 6-25-1848 m Rachel Smith Pvt VT ★
Isaac: b 5-2-1743 d 6-28-1814 m Hannah Strickland Lt CT
Isaac: b 5-19-1753 d 4-16-1834 m Sarah Merchant Sgt CT ★
Isaac: b 1752 d 9-27-1813 m Elizabeth Raymond Pvt CT
Jacob: b 9-21-1753 d 12- -1840 m Bethiah — Pvt PS CT ★
Jared: b 1-27-1745 d 1-15-1831 m Zillah Betts Mus CT
Jedediah: b 7- -1717 d 10-3-1803 m Mercy Hooker Sol PS CT
Jesse: bpt 10-18-1759 d 9-21-1852 m Dinah Bishop Pvt MA
Jesse: b 2-9-1764 d 5-1-1816 m Naomi Hubbard Pvt MA
John: b 3-26-1734 d 4-27-1816 m Hannah Dewey Pvt CT
John: b 8-21-1754 d 8- -1814 m Abigail Price Pvt CT
John: b c. 1740 d p. 9-30-1803 m Mary — Pvt VA
Micah: b 12-13-1749 d 1840 m Elizabeth Hills Pvt CT ★
Michael: b 3-23-1747 d 8-17-1820 m (1)Ann — (2)Martha Hollister Pvt CT
Nathan: b 4-13-1765 d 10-8-1836 m Susan Whetzel Pvt CT
Nathaniel: b 7-15-1717 d 5-7-1797 m Martha Deming PS CT
Nathaniel: b 12-20-1744 d p. 1785 m Lucy Hamner Ens CT
Noah: b 1756 d — m Martha Foster Pvt MA
Rosewell: b 1756 d 1-23-1847 m Jane Wilson Arfr CT ★
Samuel: b 4-23-1720 d 5-30-1789 m Martha Langdon Pvt CT
Samuel: b 5-18-1751 d 2-1-1835 m Lurana Trobridge Pvt MA ★
Simeon: b 12-7-1762 d 8- -1847 m Hannah Welles Pvt CT
Simeon: b 9-11-1759 d 2-7-1852 m Sally Howard Sgt CT MA
Stephen: b 1731 d 9-23-1823 m Dorothy — Capt CT ★
Stephen: b 3-29-1757 d 8-18-1825 m Lydia Terry Sol CT
Wait: b 8-28-1735 d 1811 m Hannah Smith PS CT
Waitstill: b 6-9-1729 d 1799 m Mary Hooker PS CT
Wm.: b 4-14-1751 d 3-25-1821 m Phoebe Johns Cpl CT W★
Zebulon: b 6-11-1744 d 1792 m Honor Waples Pvt MA
Zenas: b 8-10-1762 d 3-26-1841 m Mary Lawrence Pvt MA W★

GOODRIDGE, (includes GUTRIDGE)

Abiel: b 5-23-1750 d 2-25-1824 m Rachel Follansbee Pvt MA
Abijah: b 2-21-1754 d 4-12-1842 m Eunice Martin Sol MA
Allen: b 1758 d 10-20-1805 m Sarah Crosby Pvt NH
Benjamin: b 3-15-1720 d 4-29-1805 m Mary Redington CS MA
Benjamin: b 7-9-1746 d 9-8-1805 m (1)Hannah Pingrey (2)Polly Cooper Pvt NH
Daniel: b 8-11-1738 d 4-12-1821 m Hannah Lord Sgt MA
David: b 11-24-1716 d 1-19-1786 m Elizabeth Martin PS MA
Eliphalet: b 3-27-1733 d 3-27-1806 m Rebecca Snow Pvt MA
Ezekiel: b 9-13-1744 d 10-7-1777 m Molly Morss Lt MA
John: b 10-18-1739 d p. 1798 m Lydia Morrison Pvt MA
John: b 4-19-1732 d 12-27-1822 m Martha Holmes PS MA
Joseph: b 12-7-1739 d p. 1790 m Mary Bailey Pvt MA
Joseph: b 9-17-1755 d p. 1788 m Elizabeth — Pvt MA
Joshus, Sr.: b 2-7-1708 d 10-29-1782 m Lydia Stearns CS MA
Joshua, Jr.: b 8-10-1746 d 12-20-1815 m Elizabeth Phelps Pvt MA
Josiah: b 10-10-1734 d p. 1777 m (1)Sarah Tenney (2)Mrs Trifene Edwards 3Sgt MA
Philip, Sr.: b 7-6-1714 d 12-18-1797 m Jane Boynton CS MA
Philip, Jr.: b 10-4-1750 d 3-15-1796 m Sybil Ritter Sgt MA
Robert: b 6-18-1746 d p. 1780 m Hannah Groves Pvt MA
Samuel: b 4-19-1719 d a. 2-24-1776 m (1)Lydia Cue (2)Mrs Sarah (Perley) Putman PS MA
Sewall: b 7-7-1743 d 3-14-1809 m Phebe Putman PS NH
Wm.: b 9-13-1730 d 12-13-1793 m Mrs Molly (Smith) Fletcher Sol MA

GOODRUM,

Thomas: b 1752 d 4-7-1836 m X Sol SC

GOODSELL,

Daniel: b 6-16-1724 d 5-10-1792 m Abigail Moulthrop Pvt CT
David: b 1752 d 1805 m Anna Beers Pvt CT
Edward: b 5-8-1749 d 12-26-1781 m Lidia Luddington Pvt CT
Epaphras: b 5-23-1742 d 1-4-1801 m Jane Bradley Burr Sgt CT
Isaac: b 8-28-1763 d 2-28-1845 m Eunice Elliott Pvt CT
John: b 4-14-1730 d 7-7-1779 m (1)Sarah Bradley (2)Grace C. — Pvt CT
John: b 1749/50 d 1-29-1816 m Abigail Chedsey Pvt CT
Lewis: b 10-23-1744 d 8-22-1829 m (1)Eunice Wakeman (2)Mrs Sarah Sherwood (3)Annie Squire (4)Damaris Thorpe Capt CT
Samuel: b 1746 d 4- -1813 m Abigail Goodrich Pvt CT
Thomas: b 12-4-1732 d a. 6-30-1805 m Miriam Bradley Pvt CT

GOODSON,

James: b c. 1740 d 1833-1835 m Jane — Pvt SC
Thomas: b 1762 d 1840 m X Pvt SC ★
Thomas W.: b 8-18-1755 d 9-3-1837 m Elizabeth Poage Lt VA ★
Wm.: b 12- -1759 d 9-20-1845 m Margaret (Reed) Goodson Ens VA

GOODSPEED,

Abner: bpt 7-7-1754 d — m Patience Bodfish Pvt MA
Anthony: b 4-18-1746 d c. 1825 m Abigail Lothrop Sgt MA
Benjamin: b 2-8-1740 d 1788 m Susanna Smith Sgt MA
Ebenezer: b 2-7-1716 d p. 1812 m Elizabeth Bodfish Pvt MA
Edward: b 6-5-1741 d 1812 m Judith Winslow Pvt MA
Jabez: b 7-31-1737 d 1824 m Margaret Sassett CS MA
Joseph: b 9-13-1736 d 1811 m Sarah Adams Pvt MA
Luther: b 11-1-1762 d 9-19-1832 m (1)Margaret Murdock (2)Elizabeth Rugg Pvt MA
Nathaniel: b 6-17-1749 d 12-25-1834 m Abigal (Cleveland) Perkins Pvt MA ★
Nathaniel: b c. 1740 d 1796 m (1)Mary Yarrington (2)Lois Whitney 2Lt NY
Rufus: b 1-15-1749 d p. 1784 m Abigail Fish Pvt MA
Shearjashub: b 1744 d 11-23-1818 m Elizabeth Ruggles Pvt MA
Simpson: b 11-29-1764 d 3-14-1851 m Mary Hinckley Pvt RI ★
Stephen: b 7-25-1738 d 1818 m Anna Weatherhead Pvt RI
Timothy: b 4-22-1749 d 5-18-1833 m (1)Anna Crocker (2)Sarah Chase Pvt MA
Wm.: b c. 1742 d 1824 m Mary Meigs Pvt MA

GOODWIN, (or GOODWYN)

Abraham: b 1750 d 7-18-1822 m Catherine King Pvt PA ★
Amaziah: b 4-22-1739 d 1798 m (1)Mary Bracy (2)Sarah Butler Sgt MA
Amaziah: b 2-16-1763 d 6- -1863 m Mary Bunker Pvt NH ★
Andrew: b 1-1-1750 d 12-27-1821 m (1)Hannah Stackpole (2)Martha Estey Cpl MA
Benjamin: b 2-21-1732 d 11-30-1792 m Hannah LeBaron Pvt MA
Benjamin: bpt 11-3-1754 d 5-18-1842 m (1)Mary Shackley (2)Elizabeth Linscott (3)Mrs Sallie Newell Bedell Pvt MA ★
Charles: b 5-5-1731 d 11-17-1787 m Thankful Russell 1Lt CT
Daniel: b 11-19-1749 d 12-11-1811 m Sarah Hobbs PS ME
Daniel: b 1757 d 1847-50 m Sarah Story Pvt Sct Grd VT
David: bpt 3-29-1747 d 6-20-1822 m Mehitable Jackson Cpl MA
David: b 1744 d 1825 m Abigail Jenner Pvt MA
David: b 1763 d 11-23-1838 m (2)Nancy Carter Pvt SC ★
Domincus: b 24-24-1741 d 11-20-1827 m (1)Hannah Hill (2)Elizabeth Littlefield Perkins Sol ME
Ebenezer: bpt 5-29-1743 d 5-18-1810 m Anne Webster Lt CT
Ebenezer: bpt 8-9-1747 d 10-20-1803 m Abigail Hubbard Pvt MA
Edward: b 8- -1717 d 5- -1826 m Mary Goodwin Sol VA
Francis LeBaron: b 9-29-1762 d 2-19-1816 m Jenny Prince Robbins SrgMte MA
George: b 1-7-1757 d 5-13-1844 m Mary Edward PS CT
George: b 4-12-1762 d 7-6-1855 m (1)Mary Davis (2)— Jones Pvt MA ★
George: b 1735 d 10-7-1817 m Elizabeth Pearson Capt PA
Hezekiah: b 3-28-1761 d 5-15-1833 m Ellen Burr Cpl CT
Ichabod, Sr.: b 6-17-1700 d 10-27-1777 m Elizabeth Scammon CS ME
Ichabod, Jr.: b 1743 d 1807 m Mary Wallingford Col MA
James: b 12-15-1754 d 6-24-1822 m Hannah Mather Sgt CT
James: b 1737 d 9-21-1808 m Sarah Griffith Lt MA
James: b 4-18-1741 d 9-8-1831 m Bathsheba Robbins Pvt MA
James: b 1754 d p. 1790 m — Copp Ens NH
Jedediah: bpt 5-18-1746 d 7-1-1818 m Hannah Emery Capt MA
Jesse, Sr.: b 9-3-1737 d a. 10- -1805 m Rachel Brace Cpl CT
Jesse: b 1760 d 6- -1848 m Susannah Howard Sol SC
John: bpt 2-3-1745 d p. 1779 m Mary Proctor Lt MA
John: b c. 1763 d 1801 m Mary Plaisted Lt MA
John: b 1719 d 1787 m Martha Nason Pvt MA
John: b 2-11-1739 d 1-5-1809 m Ann Foster Pvt MA
John: b 1740 d 1815 m (1)Noami Potter (2)Annie Heddie Pvt PA
John: b c. 1748 d 1809/10 m Ruth — Pvt SC
John: b a. 1739 d p. 1781 m Abigail Wells Pvt VT
John: b 9-28-1762 d 11-20-1842 m Elizabeth Webb Pvt VA ★
John: b 11-17-1735 d 5-15-1783 m Elizabeth Dozwell PS VA
Jonathan, Sr.: b 3-8-1720 d 1-12-1786 m Sarah Case Pvt CT
Jonathan: b 1740 d 10-28-1811 m Elizabeth — Pvt VT
Joseph: b 12-28-1736 m 4-15-1813 m Rosanna Gillette Sgt CT
Joseph: b 8-11-1747 d 4-15-1822 m Mary Rice Cpl VT
Lemuel: b 1752 d — m Fanny Amis Sgt NC
Levi: b 1-1-1758 d 4-24-1836 m Jerusha Drake Pvt CT ★
Lewis: b 1-9-1749 d 2-27-1795 m (1)Rebecca Zanes Jr. (2)Rachel Nicholson CS NJ
Lyde: b 2-4-1754 d 8-19-1801 m Abby Levy Dr MD
Morgan: b 2-4-1728 d 2-4-1792 m Mary Hawley Pvt PS CT
Moses: b 3-5-1759 d 1-12-1839 m Mary Ann Burnham Mus CT ★
Nathan: b 5-3-1746 d p. 1790 m Sarah Warren Pvt MA
Nathaniel: b 10-21-1727 d 6-18-1777 m Elizabeth Marsh Capt MA
Nathaniel: b 2-8-1760 d 4- -1841 m Rhoda Orton Sgt CT
Nathaniel: b 1748 d 3-8-1819 m (1)Molly Jackson (2)Ruth Shaw Maj MA
Nathaniel: b 1- -1746 d 11-26-1820 m Catherine Lunt Pvt MA
Ozias: b 11-27-1735 d 3-1-1788 m Hannah Vail Ens CT
Paul: bpt 11-23-1746 d 8-12-1834 m Susanna Jacobs Pvt MA ★
Peterson: b 1745 d 2-21-1818 m Elizabeth Peterson Col VA
Reuben: b 4-15-1764 d 2-14-1827 m Ruth Lord Pvt MA W ★
Reuben: b c. 1760 d c. 1810 m (1)Sally Day (2)Mrs Sallie Bradford Grantland Sol VA
Richard: b 1746 d 1821 m Elizabeth Heath Pvt NH
Robert: b 1741 d a. 4-16-1785 m Mary Tucker Col PS SC
Robert: b 1739 d 5-12-1789 m Jane Tulloch Pvt VA
Robertson: b 2-5-1766 d 6-26-1843 m Eve Forney Pvt NC ★
Seth: b 8-4-1763 d 3-26-1850 m Deborah Allen Pvt CT

GOODWIN, contd.
Samuel, Sr.: b 1-27-1716 d 11-9-1802 m Elizabeth Willard PS MA
Samuel, Jr.: b 2-16-1739/40 d 7-3-1798 m Ann Frances Gand CS ME
Samuel: b 1739 d 10-1-1813 m Sarah Thompson Pvt MA
Shadrack: b 1750 d 1828-31 m X Sol GA
Simeon: b 5-24-1746 d 5-20-1816 m Dorcas Evans Ens MA
Simeon: bpt 11-14-1742 d 8-17-1823 m Susanna Heath Adj PS NH
Stephen: b 9-16-1734 d 7-30-1788 m Abigail Gillett Capt CT
Stephen: b 8-6-1733 d a. 12-10-1805 m Olive — Pvt MA
Theodore: b 4-18-1764 d 3-21-1845 m (1)Lucy Adams (2)Harriet Prior Drm CT
Theophilus: b 9-21-1753 d 1799 m Abigail Adams Fif & Cpl NH
Thomas: b 12-9-1756 d 1-11-1838 m Lucy French Pvt MA ★
Thomas: b 5-25-1765 d 4- -1838 m Temperance Harris Pvt VA ★
Timothy: bpt 4-16-1746 d p. 1778 m Mehitable Goodwin 2Lt ME
Uriah: b 5-11-1735 d p. 1782 m Mabel Francis Sgt PS MA
Uriah: b 12-18-1758 d 11-13-1832 m (1)Mary Cummings (2)Mrs Esther Dean Pvt MA ★
Wm.: b 11-10-1733 d 5-26-1805 m Margaret Cook Cpl CT
Wm.: b 1740 d 9-28-1807 m (1)Mary Waters (2)Abigail Johnson Pvt MA
Wm.: b 8-25-1723 d 9-25-1801 m Mary Morris PS NJ
Wm.: b 1739 d 1837 m Winifred Thoroughalkill Pvt NC
Wm.: b c. 1760 d 11-21-1793 m Grace — Capt SC
Wm.: b 1735 d p. 1783 m Mary Hart Lt SC
Wm.: b 5- -1758 d 7-29-1826 m Mrs Mary Wallace Eakin Pvt VA
Willoughby: b — d 1775 m Lydia Knox Cpl NH

GOODYEAR,
George: b 10-11-1751 d 5-29-1837 m Catharine Rummel Pvt PA ★
Jesse: b 6-18-1735 d 5-24-1817 m Hannah Bradley Capt CT
Ludwick: b c. 1758 d 12- -1815 m Regina Gruber Pvt PA
Stephen: b 6-15-1729 d 11-1-1803 m (1)Esther Barnes (2)Mary Peck Capt CT
Theophilus: b 5-25-1735 d 5-28-1793 m Sarah Munson Cpl CT

GOOGINS, (includes GOOKIN, GOOKINS)
Daniel: b 3-2-1756 d 9-18-1831 m Abigail Dearborn Lt PM NH ★
John: b — d 7-7-1777 m Ruth — Cpl ME
Joseph: b 10-9-1745 d 12-28-1831 m Susanna Wescott Pvt MA
Nathaniel: b 2-22-1742 d 11-18-1825 m Mary Clark PS NH
Samuel: b 9-19-1762 d 12-4-1842 m Polly Andrus Pvt CT ★
Thomas: b 4-18-1743 d 6-4-1807 m Jane Welch Pvt MA
Wm.: b 6-6-1765 d 4-5-1814 m Rhoda Munger Pvt VT

GOORLEY, (or GOURLEY)
John: b 1755 d 2-14-1831 m Hannah McDonald Pvt PA
John: b c. 1750 d p. 1790 m Jane Ralston Lt PS PA
Thomas: b 1752 d 1796 m Martha McNeely Capt PA

GOOSHORN, (or GAUGIEN)
Johan Georg: b 3-19-1725 d p. 1-26-1806 m X Ens PA
Nicholas: b 5-14-1753 d 8-8-1835 m Sarah Vaughn 1Lt PA
Simeon: b 1761 d 1813 m Laurenee Udel Sol FrA

GORBY,
Thomas: b c. 1730 d p. 3-24-1814 m Elizabeth Allman Pvt PA

GORDON, (or GORDEN)
Alexander: b 1743/4 d 2-17-1834 m Lydia Linsley Cpl CT
Alexander: b 1-29-1716 d 1-7-1793 m (1)Susannah Pettee (2)Hannah Stanley PS NH
Alexander: b c. 1745 d 1816 m Susannah — Capt NC
Ambrose: b 6-28-1751 d 6-28-1804 m Elizabeth Mead Col NC
Amos: bpt 8-7-1743 d p. 1790 m Mary Smith PS ME
Amos: b 10-5-1755 d 4-5-1830 m Anna George Sol NH
Archibald: b c. 1745 d p. 3-5-1829 m Sara Hart Pvt PA ★
Archibald: b 1-2-1748 d 9-26-1826 m Sychie VanWicklen Lt NJ W★
Chapman: b 1757 d 6-12-1813 m Charity King Pvt NC W★
Charles: b 1750 d — m — Chapman Sol NC
Charles, Sr.: b 1730 d 1811 m Mrs Mary Herndon PS NC
Charles, Jr.: b 1762 d 3-24-1799 m Mary Lenoir Maj VA
Churchill: b 2-10-1761 d 1802 m Ann Sparks Mid VA
Daniel: b 3-15-1743 d p. 1790 m Mehitable Clark Ens PS NH
David: bpt 5-27-1750 d 1819 m Jean Abrahams Capt NJ
David: b 10-23-1759 d 7-23-1852 m Nancy Southard Pvt NJ
David: b 1756 d 1845 m Martha Brower Pvt Drm NJ ★
David: b 3-31-1717 d 1783 m (1)Hannah Lloyd (2)Rebecca Anderson (3)Easter Parent PS NJ
David: b c. 1755 d c. 1836 m Susanna Tiddeback Pvt NJ ★
David: b 1750 d 1810 m Esther McKnight Pvt SC
Enoch: b 12-4-1745 d p. 1-30-1801 m (1)Polly Carter (2)Abigail Ladd (3)Mary Eastman Pvt NH
George: b 6-26-1744 d 9-23-1800 m Sarah Herndon Sol NC
George: b 7-9-1755 d 11-24-1826 m Mary McLean Cpl PA
George: b 5-2-1752 d a. 1-12-1835 m Elizabeth — Sol SC
Henry: b 6-8-1734 d 1809 m Sarah Johnston Pvt PA
Hugh: b c. d a. 9-27-1834 m X PS VA
Isaac: b 1754 d 4-23-1838 m Rebecca — Pvt NC ★
Ithiel: b c. 1735 d 1828 m Mary Glidden CS PS NH
Ithiel, Jr.: b 8-14-1759 d 3-30-1814 m (1)Sarah McCarslin (2)Polly Hunter Pvt NH
James, Jr.: b 3- -1752 d 12-9-1844 m Jerusha Tarbell Pvt NH ★

James: b 10-31-1739 d 1-17-1810 m Mary Ball LCol NY
James, Sr.: b c. 1725 d 1784 m Mary — Pvt NC
James: b c. 1753 d 1819 m Ellenor Dunbar Pvt VA
James: b 1755 d 1814 m Mary Dunlap Pvt PA
James: b 8-7-1750 d 9-29-1796 m Ann Payne PS Col VA
John: b 7-28-1754 d 1-7-1793 m Phoebe Willard Sol MA
John: b 11-27-1749 d 2-13-1810 m Betty Johnson PS NH
John: b 1729 d 1793 m Mary — Pvt NC
John: b 2-12-1745 d 2-27-1815 m Ann Haynes Pvt NC
John: b 1725 d 8-19-1782 m Margaret Tennant Capt VA
John: b 1761 d 8-4-1837 m Penelope Pope Pvt VA
John: b 9-26-1763 d 2-5-1839 m Mary Roundtree Pvt VA ★
Jonathan: b 12-5-1744 d 9-9-1812 m Esther Sanders Cpl PS NH
Kenneth: b 1756 d 5-25-1837 m Nancy — Pvt VA ★
Lawrence: b 5-15-1762 d 3-25-1839 m Nancy — Pvt VA ★
Nathaniel Charles: b c. 1755 d a. 9-23-1809 m Nancy Gordon Lt NC
Peter: b 10-5-1746 d 2-8-1835 m Susannah Hunt Maj NJ
Rachel St. John: b a. 1746 d a. 6-11-1818 m John Gordon PS VA
Roger: b a. 1750 d 6- -1781 m Rectina J. Pressley Lt SC
Samuel: b 1711 d 6-29-1795 m Elizabeth Ker Pvt CT
Samuel: b 10-14-1761 d 7-7-1840 m Elizabeth Brannan Pvt SC ★
Thomas: b 2-19-1751 d 5-1-1808 m Sarah Susanna (Dixon) Pvt CT ★
Thomas: b 11-28-1741 d 7-28-1819 m (1)Dorothy Gilman (2)Mary — Ens NH
Thomas: b 12-4-1749 d 1-24-1834 m Mary Gordon Pvt PA
Thomas: b 9-10-1743 d 11-16-1833 m Mary Caldwell Maj PS SC
Thomas: b 12-21-1758 d 1-23-1826 m Mary Buffington Pvt SC
Thomas, Jr.: b 1752 d 4-2-1814 m Catherine Davis 2Lt VA
Thomas: b c. 1740 d 5-7-1803 m Sarah — Pvt VA
Thomas: b 1718 d 1788 m Sarah Poage PS VA
Thomas: a. 1743 d 1785 m Margaret Murray Pvt VA
Timothy, Sr.: b 3-22-1716 d a. 5-2-1796 m Maria Stockbridge PS NH
Timothy, Jr.: b 12-30-1757 d 1-16-1836 m Lydia Whitmore Pvt MA ★
Wm.: b 10-5-1754 d 6-26-1835 m (2)Nabby Pope Lt MA ★
Wm.: b 3-13-1753 d 10-14-1818 m Hannah Ladd Sgt NH
Wm.: b 1736/7 d 4-15-1777 m Deborah Kinney Canfield Capt NJ
Wm.: b 4- -1748 d 1- -1799 m Lydia Parent MM NJ
Wm.: b c. 1742 d p. 4-19-1781 m Elizabeth — Capt SC
Wm.: b 1750 d p. 1784 m Margaret (Gregg) Scott Capt SC
Wm.: b c. 1738 d p. 1790 m Elizabeth Bacon Pvt VA
Wm.: b 1752 d p. 1811 m Mary Gaitrol Pvt VA
Wm.: b 12-3-1735 d 5-10-1790 m Susan Moore 1Lt VA

GORE,
Asa: b 2-28-1750 d 7- -1778 m Elizabeth Avery Ens CT
Daniel: b 3-13-1746 d 9-3-1809 m (1)Mary Parks (2)Hannah Flinn Lt CT
Ebenezer: b 1743 d 8-23-1796 m Hannah — Capt MA
Ebenezer: b 6-25-1747 d 8-16-1791 m Hannah Seaver Capt MA
Eleazer: b 1752 d 2-14-1830 m Elizabeth Murray Pvt SC ★
James Sr.: b c. 1705 d 1784 m Elizabeth — PS SC
Joseph: b 5-13-1753 d 2-3-1824 m Meriba Thayer Sgt MA ★
Joshua: b c. 1745 d 11- -1820 m (1)Jane McCalpin (2)Frances Osborne Pvt SC
Michael Sr.: b 1727 d c. 3-30-1793 m Sibbel Christian PS MD
Notley: b 6-10-1753 d 1834 m Mary Flint Sgt NC GA W★
Obadiah Sr.: b 7-26-1714 d 1-10-1779 m Hannah Parkes PS PA
Obadiah Jr.: b 4-7-1744 d 3-22-1821 m Anne Avery Lt CT
Rachel Neighbors: b c. 1735 d p. 1784 m Thomas Gore PS SC
Samuel: b 5-24-1761 d 5-2-1834 m Sarah Brokaw Sgt PA ★
Silas: b 12-23-1747 d 7-3-1778 m Keziah Yarrington Ens CT
Thomas Sr.: b c. 1730 d a. 1780 m Rachel Neighbors Pvt SC

GORESLINEUS,
John: b 1752 d 1850 m (2)Hannah Cole Pvt NY

GORGAS,
Jacob: b 8-8-1728 d 3-21-1797 m Christina Mack Sgt PA

GORHAM,
Daniel: b 9-10-1750 d 1- -1838 m Mary Lyon Pvt CT ★
Ephraim: b 3-31-1753 d 8-23-1830 m Sarah Staples Pvt CT
George: b 9-4-1744 d a. 4-5-1838 m Sarah Stevens Arfr CT
George: b 7-20-1759 d 11-17-1848 m Mary Welles Pvt MA
Hezekiah: b 12-25-1725 d 5-11-1790 m Abigail Dickerman Matr CT
Isaac: b 11-14-1730 d 7-4-1798 m Anne Wakeman PS CT
Isaac Jr.: b 11-15-1761 d 5-4-1813 m Sarah Morgan Pvt CT
James: b 8-4-1745 d p. 12-24-1804 m (1)Mary Baker (2)Mrs Sarah Davis McClure Col PS NC
John: b 7-4-1732 d 1805 m Abigail Wakeman Pvt CT
John: b 7-28-1754 d 5-10-1794 m Desire Howland Pvt MA
Jonathan: b 2-4-1753 d — m Mary Davis Pvt MA
Joseph: b 11-20-1741 d 7-8-1779 m Mary Gray Pvt CG CT
Joseph: bpt 4-23-1758 d 1814 m Elizabeth Alley Matr CT W★
Lewis: b 11-11-1753 d 1-16-1821 m Sarah Phinney Pvt MA
Matthias Jr.: b 12-17-1749 d 3-20-1820 m Dorcas Crowell Pvt MA
Nathaniel: b 5-27-1738 d 6-11-1796 m Rebecca Call PS MA
Phineas: b 1758 d 2-2-1842 m Rachel Whitlock Pvt CT
Prince: b 3-14-1730/1 d 12-4-1804 m (1)Abigail Gorham (2)Desire Clap Pvt PS MA
Samuel: b 1753 d 12-12-1805 m Sarah Lines Sol CT
Seth: b 1-18-1763 d 8-28-1852 m (1)Amelia Dunks (2)Louisa Everson Pvt CT ★

Stephen: b 7-29-1735 d 1-28-1806 m Sarah Freeman Lt MA
Sturgis: b 1-28-1742 d 4-26-1895 m (1)Phebe Taylor (2)Desire Taylor PS MA
Thomas: b c. 1740 d 1814 m Margaret Taylor PS VA
Wm.: b c. 1754 d 5-17-1823 m Mary Cannon Pvt CT

GORIN,
Henry: b 4-26-1768 d 6-14-1830 m Sarah Pell Pvt VA
John: b 1760 d 8-5-1837 m (1)Elizabeth Franklin (2)Elizabeth Duval Sgt VA ★

GORMELY, (or GHORMLEY)
Abraham: b 12-26-1758 d 5-13-1848 m Elizabeth McAllister Pvt PA
Hugh: b 3-2-1733 d 11- -1813 m Catherine Covington Pvt PA

GORRELL,
John: b 1764 d 1838 m (1)Hannah Davis (2)Anna Green Pvt PA ★
Ralph: b 1735 d 4-16-1816 m Mary Kerr PS NC

GORSUCH,
Charles Sr.: b 10-12-1729 d 7-3-1792 m Sarah — PS MD
Charles: b c. 1720 d 1806 m (1)Susannah — (2)Margaret — PS MD
John: b c. 1712-14 d p. 9-6-1788 m Mary Price PS MD
Lovelace: b c. 1715 d 1783 m Sarah — PS MD
Thomas: b 4-11-1752 d 1814/15 m Helen Chapman Drm MD

GORTNER, (or GIRDNER)
David: b — d p. 10-3-1809 m Rachel — 2Lt PA
Michael: b 1755 d 1814/15 m Hulda Beech Pvt PA

GORTON,
Benjamin: b 5-28-1758 d 8-14-1836 m (1)Polly Foster (2)Nancy Martin Arfr PS CT
Benjamin: b 7-2-1725 d p. 1786 m Avis Hulett Capt RI
Benjamin: b 4-1-1754 d 11-18-1833 m Thankful Whitford Pvt RI ★
George: b 9- -1748 d 4-30-1829 m Lydia Aylesworth PS RI
Hezekiah: b 3-7-1751 d 4- -1842 m Patience Wood Pvt RI
Israel Sr.: b — d 4-10-1807 m Freelove Burlingame Capt RI
Joseph: b 8-22-1715 d c. 1834 m Susannah Hubbard Lawrence Sgt CT ★
Joseph: b 1741/2 d 8-31-1821 m Mrs Mary Barton Pvt RI
Joseph: b 5-29-1760 d 12- -1814 m Rosannah Remington Pvt RI
Othniel: b 10-1-1718 d 6- -1794 m Theodosia Hopkins CS RI
Peleg: b 1-11-1750 d 1- -1802 m Dorcas Wood Pvt NY
Samuel Jr.: b 8-8-1745 d 3-20-1834 m Eunice Austin Capt RI
Samuel: b 3-7-1717 d 7- -1777 m (1)Ruth Slade (2)Frances (Rice) Graves Cpl RI
Wm. Jr.: b 5-20-1732 d 4-24-1807 m Submit Briggs Lt RI
Wm.: b 7-28-1750 d 11-8-1826 m Wealthy Tillinghast Pvt RI

GOSLEY,
Henry: b 1760 d 10-31-1818 m (1)Sarah Kimbal (2)Mehetible Granis Cpl CT
John: b c. 1750 d 1795 m Hannah Tull Pvt MD

GOSLINE, (or GOSSELIN)
Clement: b 6-12-1747 d 3-9-1816 m (1)Marie Dionne (2)Charlotte Ouimet (3)Catherine Monty Capt NY Heir ★
Louis: b c. 1735 d 8-7-1823 m Anastasia Bourgeois Lt NY ★
Richard: b 1754 d 8- -1817 m Margaret Green Pvt PA

GOSLING,
Samuel: b 1750 d 1835 m Mary — MM NJ

GOSNELL,
Benjamin: b 3-15-1761 d 8-28-1846 m (3)Polly Barlow (4)Dorcas Farnest Porter Pvt VA ★

GOSS, (includes GAUSE, GOSE)
Abraham: b c. 1764 d 4-14-1849 m (1)Elizabeth Erminheiser (2) Mary Shively Mus PA ★
Benjamin: b 5-14-1765 d 1855 m Sarah Codding Pvt NY ★
Charles: b c. 1730 d p. 8-27-1807 m (2)Eleanor (Miller) Leonard Sol NC
Daniel: b 9-14-1741 d 12-10-1809 m Eunice Wilder Capt MA
Ebenezer: b 9-8-1760 d 8-15-1832 m Beda Blakeslee Arfr PA ★
Elizabeth: b 1735/6 d 1810 m George Goss PS PA
Ephraim: b 1732 d p. 1781 m Prudence — Pvt MA
Ephraim: b 4-6-1767 d 11-18-1840 m Anna Bathrick Mus NH
Ephraim: b 1756 d 8-2-1838 m Ruth Campbell Pvt NH
Frederick: b 1744 d p. 1-31-1804 m Isabell — Sol NC
George: b 1729/30 d c. 1780 m Elizabeth — Pvt Fif PA
John: b 2-13-1739 d 9-26-1821 m Catherine Conant Capt NH
John: b 2-5-1748/9 d 7-5-1820 m Hannah Scott PS NH
John: b c. 1740 d p. 6-12-1783 m Susanna Frink Sol NC
Joshua: b 2-21-1748 d 5-29-1814 m Rebekah Necks Cpl MA
Nathaniel: b 1-26-1748/9 d 9-27-1812 m Hannah — Ens CT
Nathaniel: b 1751 d 6-25-1724 m Rachel Gould Pvt PS NH
Needham: b 1755 d p. 9-23-1794 m Hannah — Sol NC
Peter: b 6-17-1737 d p. 1790 m Mary Abbott Cpl NH
Philip Sr.: b 1720 d 4-17-1804 m Hannah Ball Pvt PS NH

Philip Jr.: b 10-17-1757 d 6-23-1840 m Esther Gale Pvt NH ★
Philip: b 11-17-1724 d 11-9-1778 m MaryKendall PS PA
Samuel: b 10-16-1754 d p. 1796 m Lucretia Howe Pvt MA
Solomon: b 6-16-1754 d 7-1-1825 m Olive Scott Pvt PA
Stephen: b c. 1762 d p. 2-12-1842 m Catherine Ketron Sol VA
Thomas: b 5-19-1731 d 1833 m Patience Harraden Slr MA
Wm.: b c. 1740 d p. 3-3-1800 m (1)Mary — (2)Elizabeth (Bacot) Smith CS NC
Wm.: b 3-10-1755 d 1835 m Mary Jackson Beverly Pvt MA
Zebulon: b 1737 d 5-11-1821 m Mary Wood Pvt MA

GOSSARD, (or GASSER)
Jacob Sr.: b c. 1725 d 3- -1779 m Margaret — PS PA
Philip: b c. 1750 d 1812 m Anna Maria Kinny Pvt PA
Tilley: b c. 1744 d c. 1840 m Ada Holcomb Drm CT

GOSSERT,
John: b c. 1750 d 1832-1834 m Mary Keeffer 2Lt PA

GOSSETT,
John: b c. 1760 d p. 12-22-1823 m Honour — Pvt PA
Matthias: b a. 1741 d p. 9-7-1811 m Mary — PS VA

GOSSLER,
Henry: b 7-25-1724 d 1-18-1784 m Dorothea Hedwig Dein PS PA

GOTSHALL, (or GOTSCHALL)
Gotshall: b 4-8-1753 d 3-5-1824 m Elizabeth Ziegler Pvt PA
Michael: b 6-13-1758 d 1817/8 m Catherine Motter Pvt PA

GOTT,
Daniel Jr.: b 12-23-1739 d 6-7-1814 m Hannah Norwood Pvt MA
John Jr.: b 12-8-1754 d 2-3-1812 m Esther Robins Cpl PA
John: b 4-13-1730 d p. 1790 m Ann Trotter Sol NY
Joshua: b 7-30-1754 d 3-22-1846 m Deborah Pool Pvt MA
Nathaniel: b 3-17-1755 d 9-14-1828 m Mrs Sarah Brigham Pvt MA
Story: b 11-30-1764/5 d 6-5-1841 m Mary Wilcox Pvt NY ★

GOTTIER,
Francis: b 1747 d 12-11-1826 m Margaret Ferguson PS MD

GOTWALS,
Henry: b 1749 d 7-25-1832 m Elizabeth Funk Pvt PA

GOUCHER,
Thomas: b c. 1750 d 1795 m Hannah Biddle Pvt PA

GOUDELOCK, (or GOUDYLOCK)
Adam: b — d 1796 m Hannah Stockton PS SC
Davis: b 12-25-1764 d 9-17-1838 m Millie Wilkins Pvt SC ★

GOULD, (includes GOLD, GOOLD)
Abel: b 9-14-1727 d 11-11-1789 m (1)Ellen Burr (2)Amelia (Silliman) Burr PS CT
Abraham: b 4-27-1733 d 4-27-1777 m Elizabeth Burr LCol CT
Abraham: b 5-13-1755 d p. 5-8-1829 m Susannah Foster Pvt MA ★
Alexander: b 8- -1751 d 4-19-1844 m (1)Margaret Emery (2)Betsey Shovey Pvt Mar ME
Amos: b 12-12-1761 d 12-28-1853 m Rebecca Perley Pvt MA
Asa: b 8-26-1752 d 9-11-1849 m (1)Jerusha Derth (2)Lois Owen Sgt MA ★
Benjamin: b 5-15-1752 d 5-30-1841 m Griselda Apthrop Flagg Capt MA
Benjamin: b c. 1744 d 1-10-1818 m Silence Atherton 1Sgt MA
Benjamin: b 1752 d 1818 m Mary Thomson Pvt MA
Benjamin: b 8-29-1742 d 1-5-1804 m Sarah Harvel PS NH
Bezaleel: b 7-4-1756 d 3-18-1818 m (1)Bethsheba Robinson (2)Dinah (Robinson) Hill Cpl MA
Daniel: b c. 1740 d p. 1790 m Martha Nichols Sgt Mus MA
Daniel: b 1-18-1756 d 4-9-1826 m Sarah Bradstreet Cpl MA
Daniel: b 2-5-1746/7 d 9-16-1829 m Mary Porter PS CS MA
Daniel: b c. 1737 d p. 1820 m Widow D. — Pvt PS NH
Daniel: b 4-21-1760 d 9-10-1833 m Anna Philips Pvt NJ ★
Daniel Sr.: b c. 1748 d 1828 m Jamia Gould PS NC
David: b 11-16-1745 d 4-19-1824 m Mary Brewster Lt CT
David: b 1750 d 8-22-1817 m Lovisa Downing Pvt MA
David: b 10-18-1750 d 4-21-1817 m Catherine Seyfried Pvt PA
Ebenezer Sr.: b 2-21-1726 d 4-6-1816 m Olive Parker Pvt MA
Ebenezer Jr.: b 2-27-1755 d p. 1790 m Anna Lane Pvt MA
Ebenezer: b 1760 d 1809 m Anna Cook Pvt MA
Ebenezer: b 8-9-1755 d 6-14-1809 m Rhoda Robbins Sgt NY
Ebenezer Brewster: b — d 3-10-1815 m Beulah Stevens 1Lt MA W★
Eleazer: b 9-23-1740 d 1805 m Sarah Bigelow CS MA
Eli: b 5-5-1766 d 6-24-1848 m Bernice Johnson Pvt MA
Elias: b 1-23-1736/7 d 11-16-1816 m Gertrude Davis Pvt NH
George: b 1-22-1732 d 1-6-1805 m Rachel Dwight Maj MA
George: b 4-23-1722 d 8-29-1792 m Anna Maria Roth Pvt PA
Gideon: b 1741 d 3-1-1821 m Hannah Heath Pvt PS MA
Henry: b 10-5-1757 d 5-13-1820 m Mary Stearns Cpl MA
Isaac: b c. 1750 d — m (1)Sarah Hoar (2)Esther Jones Pvt MA
Isaac: b 4-14-1758 d 1844 m Olive Thayer Pvt MA ★

GOULD, contd.
Isaac: b *c.* 1742 d 1802 m Anna Stevens Tms NJ
Jacob: b 12-27-1752 d 3-7-1816 m Lydia Thayer Capt MA
Jacob: b 2-26-1728/9 d 1809 m Elizabeth Towne Capt MA
Jacob: b 1-16-1703 d 1787 m Dorothy (Goodridge) Woodman PS MA
Jacob: b 10-14-1726 d 6-14-1801 m Elizabeth Holden MM MA
James: b *a.* 1750 d 3-28-1810 m Mary Sill Pvt CT
James: b 1-21-1721 d 1-27-1803 m Elizabeth Chappel PS CT
James: b 6-5-1730 d 1810 m (1)Elizabeth Nason (2)Hannah Hovey Pvt ME
James: b 1-28-1743 d 10-11-1822 m Mary Lovejoy Lt NH ★
James: b 12-23-1755 d 11-14-1793 m Katie Smith Pvt PA
Jedediah: b 8-17-1749 d 1808 m Elizabeth Sanderson Pvt MA
Jeremiah: bpt 7-1-1750 d 12-19-1821 m Mary Putnam Pvt MA
Jesse: b *c.* 1752 d *c.* 1804 m Sarah (Gold) — Pvt CT
John Jr.: b 10-1-1749 d 1-11-1820 m Ruth Perkins Pvt MA
John: b 3-5-1746 d 6-26-1816 m Jane Palmer Pvt MA
John: b *c.* 1750 d *a.* 9- -1816 m Desire Snow Pvt MA
John: b 1-29-1709 d 6-21-1778 m Esther Giles Bixby PS MA
John: b 10-3-1735 d 8-25-1807 m (1)Ann Cobb (2)Dorcas Baldwin Pvt AJ
John: b *c.* 1748 d 9-23-1828 m Mary Stedman Pvt RI
John: b 8-29-1736 d 9-2-1811 m Sarah Coggeshall CS RI
John Jr.: b 3-25-1760/1 d 5-22-1850 m Nancy Graves Pvt VT ★
John A.: b 6-1-1758 d 1837 m (2)Catherine Coughlin MM NJ ★
Jonas: b 1-13-1752 d 6-19-1819 m Elizabeth Waite Pvt MA ★
Joseph: b 11-4-1726 d 6-9-1803 m Elizabeth Emerson 2Maj MA
Joseph: b 1747 d 5-18-1823 m Patience Goodenough Sgt MA
Joseph: b 1752 d 1839 m Lydia Lowell Pvt MA
Joseph: b 7-16-1737 d 12- -1810 m Rebecca Paxton Pvt NJ
Josiah: b 5-22-1761 d 5-25-1845 m Elizabeth Collier Pvt NJ
Morlan: b 6-4-1754 d 9- -1825 m Lucy Gould Pvt MA
Moses: b 7-4-1732 d *p.* 1784 m Submit Holden MM VT
Nathan: b 1-8-1733/4 d 1816 m Martha Gilbert Pvt MA
Nathan: b 5- -1756 d *c.* 1794 m Patience Patchen Smn CT
Nathaniel: b 7-16-1753 d 7-3-1842 m (1)Hannah Killam (2)Betty Andrews Pvt MA
Nicholas: b *c.* 1752 d 2-13-1830 m (1)Bethana — (2)Amy (Bull) Allen Pvt RI
Noah: b 3-4-1763 d 12-27-1828 m Polly Masters Pvt MA ★
Oliver: b 10-3-1733 d 12-19-1792 m Mary Stockwell Pvt PS NH
Samuel: b 3-20-1727 d 1791 m Sarah Gilbert Lt MA
Samuel: bpt 6-26-1743 d 1799 m Eunice Winter Sgt MA
Samuel: b 8-8-1728 d 4-10-1806 m Mary L. Gouch CS PS ME
Samuel: b 1-8-1754 d 3-7-1822 m Ludia Barron Pvt MA
Samuel: b 3-6-1759 d 4-12-1837 m (1)Abigail Lamson (2)Ruth Towne Cpl MA
Sarah (Anthony): b 8-1-1697 d 2-20-1797 m Thomas Gould PS RI
Silas: b 3-11-1760 d 7-5-1842 m Thankful Ditson Cpl CT MA
Simeon: b 8-17-1733 d 1-15-1827 m Elizabeth Pike Sgt Maj NH
Simeon: b 1-13-1759 d 10-3-1828 m Irena Adkins Pvt NH ★
Solomon: b 7-22-1738 d — m Mehitable Perkins Pvt MA
Stephen: b 9-18-1748 d 3- -1806 m Esther Wilder Sgt MA
Stephen: b 2-6-1754 d 1825 m Lydia Fuller Pvt MA
Theophilus: b 10-1-1733 d 1797 m Lydia Hoyt Lt MA
Thomas: b 5-22-1732 d 1778 m Anne Perkins Pvt MA
Thomas: b 11-23-1755 d 1829 m Hannah William Pvt MA
Thomas: b 1698 d 6-13-1786 m Sarah Anthony PS RI
Thomas: b 1698 d 6-13-1786 m Sarah Anthony PS RI
Timothy: b 12-9-1751 d 2-19-1841 m (2)Jemima (Collyer) Lawrence Sgt NJ
Tobias: b 1756 d 2-28-1815 m Rhoda Hammond Pvt MA
Tolcutt: b 6-17-1759 d 9-30-1836 m Anny Barlow Mar CT ★
Wm.: b 1724 d 9-6-1778 m (1)Lydia Smith (2)Hepzibah Smith Pvt MA
Wm.: b 9-11-1760 d 9-11-1833 m Mehitabel Magoon Pvt NH ★
Wm.: b 9-29-1757 d 2-12-1847 m Mehitable Crane Pvt NJ
Zaccheus: b 2-5-1743/4 d 2-13-1823 m Anne Brown Pvt MA

GOULDING, (or GOLDING)
Amos: b 10-14-1756 d 2-20-1843 m Elizabeth Leonard Pvt NY W★
Anthony: b 1756 d *p.* 12-27-1800 m (1)Mary McGill (2)Isabel Reid PS SC
Daniel H.: b 4-20-1735 d 8-14-1817 m Catharine Elizabeth Geltbach Pvt PS PA
Eleazer: b 4-30-1757 d 8-13-1826 m Jemima Bacon Cpl MA
Jesse: b 1755 d 1822 m Elizabeth Barnett Pvt VA
John: b 10-3-1726 d 11-22-1791 m Lucy Brooks Col MA
John: b 10-30-1752 d 7-2-1818 m Elizabeth Twitchell Sgt MA
John: b 2-8-1733 d 4-13-1802 m Phoebe Garretson Pvt Smn PS NJ
Joseph: b 7-13-1747 d 1819 m Kezia Parker Sgt MA

GOULDMAN,
Thomas: b — d 6- -1797 m Sally Wiles PS VA

GOUTY,
John: b *c.* 1740 d 1818 m X PS MD

GOUVENEUR,
Nicholas: bpt 4-19-1713 d 10-20-1785 m Mary — CS NY

GOVE,
Ebenezer: b 4-8-1755 d 1840 m (1)Mary Paige (2)Mary Davis Pvt NH ★
Eleazer: b 4-13-1732 d 1777 m Mary Holt Pvt NH
Elijah: b 5-20-1752 d 10-23-1816 m Sarah Mills Pvt NH
Jacob: b 1764 d 4-9-1823 m Martha Cochran Pvt MA
John: b 1757 d 7-24-1818 m Lois Bradeen Mus MA W★
Jonathan: b 7-18-1742 d 5-29-1832 m (1)Sarah Sweatt (2)Ruth Philbrick PS CS NH
Jonathan: b 8-22-1746 d 3-24-1818 m Mary Hubbard Dr PS NH
Nathan: b 2-8-1758 d 9- -1822 m Rhoda Prescott Pvt NH
Nathaniel: b 4-21-1739 d 9-9-1813 m Esther Tyler Lt CT
Nathaniel: b 4-30-1749 d 3-11-1811 m Mrs Elizabeth Adams Pvt MA
Winthrop: b 11-3-1732 d 6-3-1808 m (1)Elizabeth Ring (2)Elizabeth Griffith Capt CS PS NH

GOVER,
Samuel: b 1750 d 5-17-1860 m Tabitha — Sol NC

GOVERT,
Samuel: b 4-4-1760 d 1-27-1805 m Hannah Atwater Sol CT

GOWARD,
Francis: b 1738 d 7-17-1797 m Mary Presbry Pvt MA

GOWDY, (includes GOUDY & GOWDEY)
Alexander Jr.: b 2-3-1760 d 9-2-1838 m Hannah McGregory Pvt CT ★
Amos: b 10-8-1744 d 6-22-1824 m Sarah Clark 2Lt PS MA
Hill: b 2-13-1763 d 12-14-1837 m Roxana McGregory Pvt CT ★
James: b 1753 d 1842 m Deborah Luther Mar Smn CT
James: b 5-10-1740 d 12-20-1800 m Elizabeth Porter Pvt MA
James: b 9-16-1758 d 1-13-1849 m Catherine Pogue Pvt PA
John: b 5-10-1759 d 1855 m (1)Susanna Ward (2)Mrs — (Coffin) Graves Pvt CT ★
John: b 11-5-1742 d 11-7-1814 m Abigail Ryan Pvt PA
Samuel Sr.: b 8-12-1737 d 11-17-1811 m Abiah Pease Pvt CT
Samuel Jr.: b 6-10-1760 d 4-19-1840 m Alice Gleason Pvt CT ★
Wm.: b *c.* 1745 d 1798 m (2)Jean (Paisley) White PS NC
Wm.: b 1752 d *a.* 8-11-1828 m Isabella Fleming Pvt PA

GOWEN,
John: bpt 9-11-1763 d 6-25-1810 m Mary Storer Pvt MA W★
John: b *a.* 1740 d 1810 m Lettice Winn Bearden Capt Cmsry SC
Stephen: b 6-17-1753 d 3-14-1846 m Mary Powers Pvt MA

GOWENS,
Charles: b 1763 d 1865 m Elizabeth — Pvt VA ★

GOWING,
Daniel: b 10-28-1729 d 5-6-1809 m Sarah Burnap Sgt MA
Jabez: b 3-9-1757 d 9-25-1830 m Sarah Jacques Pvt MA
John: b 4-17-1732 d 9-25-1804 m Lydia Rich Pvt MA

GRABS,
Wm.: b 1-13-1756 d 2-19-1825 m Anna Barbara Pfaff Sol NC

GRACE,
Aaron: b *c.* 1734 d *p.* 3-3-1788 m Ann Boyer Sol PS MD
Benjamin Walker: b 1760 d 11-15-1851 m Rachel Patten Pvt MA
James: b 7-19-1748 d 1826 m Elizabeth — Pvt MA
John: b 1742 d 4-10-1835 m Judith — Pvt Sct NJ ★
Joseph: b 4-8-1756 d 9-7-1823 m Mara Sargent Sol MA
Wm.: b 1759 d 6-1-1824 m Lydia Clows Pvt MD ★
Wm.: b *c.* 1764 d 9- -1814 m Elizabeth Moore Pvt MD

GRACEY, (or GRACY)
John: b 6-30-1759 d 10-8-1839 m (1)Jane Lorance (2)Rachel Ramsay Pvt NC ★
Patrick: b 1-30-1700 d 1-9-1810 m Rebecca Barnett PS NC
Robert: b 12-17-1763 d 10-27-1849 m Prudence Archibald Pvt NC

GRADWOHL,
DeWalt: b 5-11-1753 d 2-26-1827 m Anna Maria Schartz Sol PA
John: b *c.* 1730 d 1811 m Marie Salome Pvt PA

GRADY,
Alexander: b 1744 d 2-26-1821 m Nancy Thomas Mil NC
Elisha: b 1743 d 1794 m Anne Potts Ens PA
Frederick: b 3-5-1753 d 3-19-1818 m Elizabeth (Durham) Bailey Pvt NC
Jonathan: b 1760 d *a.* 10-13-1836 m (1)Harriet Sammons (2)Mary Washburn Pvt VA
Robert Sr.: b *c.* 1725 d *c.* 1800 m X Sol NC
Wm.: b 1734/5 d *p.* 1790 m Ann Barfield Sol NC

GRAFFAM, (or GRAFHAM)
Caleb: b 1711 d 11-11-1784 m Lois Bennett PS CT
Enoch: b 4-3-1753 d 8-28-1827 m Charity Mayberry Sol MA
Peter: b 4-3-1742 d 5-3-1783 m Mary Wilson 2Lt MA

GRAFTON,
Joshua: b — d — m Lydia Masury NCdr MA

GRAGG,
Reuben: b 1745 d 5-231796 m Betty Carleton Pvt MA
Wm.: b *c.* 1736 d 1789 m Elizabeth Martin PS VA
Wm.: b 4-15-1758 d 10-20-1847 m (1)Elizabeth Pulliam (2)Nancy Dunkle (3)Nancy Coffee Pvt VA

GRAHAM,
Alexander: b 1739 d 9-15-1794 m Mary McCormick PS NC
Andrew: b 1-28-1729 d 6-15-1785 m Martha Curtiss Pvt Dr CT
Andrew: b *c.* 1734 d 1821 m (1)Margaret Coalton (2)Margaret Mary Chestnut PS NC
Archibald: b 1-12-1759 d 7-28-1823 m Hannah Johnson Pvt PA
Arthur: b *a.* 1760 d 1805 m Elizabeth Beatty Pvt NC
Arthur: b 8-15-1739 d 7- -1824 m Mary Forgus Pvt VA
Augustine: b *c.* 1750 d 12-26-1815 m Mary Willet 1Lt NY
Charles: b 3-22-1721 d 4-17-1779 m Aseneth Hutton CS MD
Chauncey: b 11-23-1754 d 1-20-1811 m Sarah Merwin Dr NY
Christopher: b 7-9-1755 d 12-14-1841 m Jane Carlile Lt VA
Daniel, Sr.: b 1736 d 1827 m (1)Zerviah Moses (2)Lois Phelps (3)Ann Roberts Pvt CT
Daniel. Jr.: b 1759 d 1808 m X Pvt CT
Daniel: b 1763 d 11-8-1851 m Nancy Anna Calhoun Pvt NC
David: b 1713 d *c.* 1780 m Margaret Patterson Sol PA
Edward: b *c.* 1750/60 d *p.* 2-16-1821 m Sarah Quigley Sol PA
Elisha: b 1734 d 1805 m Anna Humphrey Pvt CT
Francis: b *c.* 1745 d 12-10-1809 m (1)Elizabeth Robinson (?)Nancy Partlow Pvt VA
George: b 1756 d 2-6-1840 m (1)Charity Kimball (2)Sarah (Miller) Shearwin (3)Mary (Patterson) Mason Pvt PA ★
George: b 12-5-1757 d 3-29-1826 m Fannie Cathey Lt NC
Gershom: b 1741 d 6- -1811 m Esther Dunham Patterson Pvt MA W★
Henry: b 6-6-1757 d 5-4-1836 m Elizabeth Furgeson Ens PA
Henry Hale: b 1731 d 1790 m Abigail Pennell Sol PA
Hugh: b *c.* 1755 d *p.* 10-9-1784 m Sarah —Pvt NC
Hugh: b *c.* 1745 d 1792 m Margaret Kennedy Pvt PA
Isaac Gilbert: b 9-4-1760 d 9-13-1849 m Anley (Banker) Garrison Dr MA ★
Jacob: b *a.* 1740 d *p.* 4-14-1812 m X PS VA
James: b 1749 d 9-5-1837 m Mary Van de Mark Cpl CT PA ★
James: b 1-29-1758 d 2-9-1834 m Margaret Porter Pvt NC ★
James: b 10-4-1756 d 9-2-1834 m (1)Elizabeth Ripley (2)Elizabeth (Lasley) Black Pvt PA ★
James: b 1-3-1741 d 1-15-1813 m Florence (Graham) Capt PS VA
James: b 10-10-1743 d 8-14-1803 m Florence — Ens VA
James: b 1735 d 1810 m — Fowler Pvt VA
James: b 1754 d 1799 m Mary Worthington Pvt VA
James G.: b 3-12-1749 d 5-18-1815 m Jemima Forbes Pvt NY
Jesse: b 1761 d — m — Drm CT
John: b 1720 d 3-17-1776 m Jane — Pvt Matr MA
John: b 8-22-1722 d 4-20-1796 m (1)Mary Sheldon (2)Mrs Ruth King Smith Chp CT
John: b 1756 d 5-7-1832 m Julia Ogden Maj NY ★
John: b 1748 d 1801 m Nancy Davidson Pvt NY
John: b *c.* 1740 d 2- -1826 m Margarett — Lt NC
John: b 3- -1761 d 1799 m Jane Donaldson Pvt NC
John: b 12-6-1745 1-1-1797 m Rachel Ferguson Sgt PA
John: b *c.* 1735 d *c.* 12- -1804 m Agnes Walton Brown Pvt PS PA
John: b 12-28-1751 d 11-15-1798 m Rebekah Dixon Pvt VA
John: b 1-1-1763 d 4-20-1835 m Rebecca Witten Pvt VA
John: b — d — 1827 m — Aide to Gen. Washington CL
Joseph: bpt 11-20-1737 d 9-29-1807 m Elizabeth Ingham Pvt CT
Joseph: b 10-13-1759 d 9-11-12-1836 m Isabella Davidson Maj NC ★
Joseph: b 1738 d 1823 m Hannah — Pvt PA
Mathew: b — d 9-29-1786 m X Pvt PA
Michael: b 4-6-1758 d 5-18-1834 m Elizabeth Lyle Pvt VA ★
Patrick: b 1754 d 1844 m Elizabeth McKee Pvt PA
Richard: b 1750 d 1806 m Nancy — Pvt PA
Richard: b 1730 d 1796 m Jane Brent PS VA
Robert: b *c.* 1751 d 1814 m Margaret — Pvt DE
Robert: b 6-19-1747 d *p.* 1794 m Eunice Wood, Cpl MA
Robert: b 1750 d 11- -1811 m (1)Mary Craig (2)Mary Cowan CaptLt VA
Robert: b 7-3-1751 d 1820 m Martha Peyton Gwynn CS VA
Roswell: b 11-19-1761/2 d 12-24-1855 m Nancy Charlotte Grubb Pvt NY
Samuel: b 3-1-1732 8-7-1781 m Bethula (Bethsheba) Graves PS MA
Thomas: b 1758 d 1834/5 m Jane Loyd Sgt VA
Thomas, Sr.: b *c.* 1725 d 6- -1798 m Mary (Graham) Sol VA
Walter: b 3-18-1759 d 2-21-1829 m Sallie Richards CaptLt VA
Wm.: b *c.* 1763 d 5-31-1793 m Elizabeth — Sol DE
Wm.: b 1756 d 1-19-1824 m Mary Cheney Cpl MA NH ★
Wm.: b 8-15-1744 d 9-15-1795 m Margaret Bagley Lt NY
Wm.: b 1750 d 3-17-1829 m Mary Moffat 2Lt NY
Wm.: b 3-17-1750 d 1823 m Mary McBurney Pvt NY
Wm.: b 5-3-1742 d 3-26-1835 m Susan (Belahr) Twitty Col NC
Wm.: b — d *p.* 12-12-1787 m Jean — Sgt NC
Wm.: b 5-1-1758 d 8-3-1858 m Phoebe Frazie Lt PA
Wm.: b 1740 d 7-17-1818 m Margaret Graham Sol PS NC
Wm.: b 1753 d 4-4-1813 m Frances Lyon Ens PA
Wm.: b 1737 d 1-20-1800 m Jane White Pvt PA

Wm.: b 1740 d 9-7-1779 m (1)Mary Ellis (2)Janet Cooper QMSgt SC
Wm.: b 1758 d 1853 m Seelah — Cpl SC
Wm.: b 10-4-1750 d 3-5-1794 m Judith Swan Colston Capt VA
Wm. Montrose: b 4-1-1757 d 9-28-1821 m (1)Mary Campbell (2)Ann (Hartley) Gwynn AsstSgn VA

GRAM,
Conrad: b *c.* 1730 d 1807 m Agnes — Pvt PA

GRAMLICH, (includes GRAMLEY, GRAMLIN(G), GRUMBLING, GRUMLEY)
Adam: b *c.* 1740 d *p.* 1790 m Chloanna Gassaway PS SC
Francis: b 1756 d 1833 m Margaret Spangler Pvt PA
George: b 1-6-1757 d 4-12-1832 m (1)Catherine Wallace (2)Mary Wallace Sol PA
Paul: b 10-28-1754 d 12-6-1829 m Anna Maria Schafer Pvt PA
Philip: b 2-11-1756 d 1828 m Elizabeth Bastian Sgt PA
Valentine: b *c.* 1730 d 1809 m Catherine — PS PA
Wm.: b — d *p.* 9-30-1792 m (1)Hannah — (2)Sarah — PS VA

GRAMMER (includes GRAMER)
Jacob: b 3-15-1749 d 3-13-1815 m Catherine Schaeffer 1Lt PS MD
John: b 1750 d 1793 m Polly — Sgt PA
Johᴿ: b 8-24-1754 d 10-9-1835 m (1)Mary Timberlake (2)Priscilla Winters CS VA
Joseph: b 4-3-1754 d 11-21-1832 m Elizabeth Weber Smn PA

GRAMPS,
Henry: b 1722 d *p.* 1790 m Christina Enge Sol NY
John: b 4-17-1762 d 10-20-1857 m Susan House Sgt PA
John P.: b 1758 d 8-3-1818 m Nancy Bellinger Pvt NY W★
Peter, Sr.: b *c.* 1717 d *p.* 6-30-1801 m Elizabeth Empie Ens NY

GRANADE,
John: b *c.* 1715 d 1791 m (2)Ann — PS NC

GRANBERRY (includes GRANBERY)
George: b *c.* 1750 d *a.* 4-1-1805 m (2)Sarah Jackson Capt NC
John: b 10-17-1759 d 8- -1815 m Susannah B. Stone Mstr VA
Josiah: b *c.* 1740 d *p.* 1790 m Ann Gregory CS PS NC
Moses: b *c.* 1750 d *p.* 2-24-1808 m (1)Susanna Dykes (2)Mrs Elizabeth Powell Sol NC

GRANDIN,
John Forman: b 8-23-1760 d 7-21-1811 m Mary Newell Dr NJ

GRANDY,
Davis: b *c.* 1739 d *c.* 1787 m Mrs Margaret Swan Elligood Ens NC
Edmond: b 11-5-1746 d 8-25-1826 m Mary Hinsdale Pvt CT ★
Reuben: b 6-3-1752 d 4-30-1819 m Sarah Newman Pvt MA
Samuel: b 3-9-1763 d 8-6-1838 m Azuba Bishop Pvt VT

GRANGER, (includes GRAININGER,
Aaron: b 8-25-1736 d 1782 m Mary Ward Pvt MA
Abner: b 2-8-1735/6 d 10-15-1816 m Experience King Capt CT
Abraham, Sr.: b 1-5-1719/20 d 1-19-1810 m Elizabeth Old Pvt PS CT
Abraham, Jr.: b 11-10-1752 d 10-24-1830 m Belinda Loomis Ens CT
Amos: b 10-16-1748 d 11-1-1811 m Ann Phelps Dr CT
Caleb: b *c.* 1725 d 1788 m Mary — Maj NC
Eli: b 3-21-1746 d 4-26-1787 m Margaret Noble PS MA
Elijah: b 8-25-1744 d 12-14-1814 m Mary King PS CT
Elisha: b 7-3-1743 d 4-12-1821 m (1)Sarah Pierce (2)Hannah Harmon (3)Mrs Lydia Green Ens CT
George: b 9- -1740 d 1-12-1812 m Lucy Campbell Lt MA
Gideon: b 1-15-1734/5 d 10-30-1800 m Tryphosa Kent MM MA
Ithamar: b 9- -1740 d 10-23-1831 m Jemima Billington Pvt CT W★
John: b 5-23-1734 d 1-21-1783 m (1)Hannah Messer (2)Rebecca Haskell Capt MA
John Martin: b 1761 d *p.* 1810 m Sarah Griffin Pvt MA
John: b 12-12-1764 d 8- -1812 m Sarah Morse Pvt NY
Jonathan: b 10-19-1743 d *p.* 1782 m Abiah Haliday Pvt PS VT
Luther: b 2-11-1753 d 6-1-1826 m Miriam Wait Pvt MA
Moses: b 10-10-1747 d 2-14-1833 m Lucy Adams Pvt CT W★
Oliver: b 6-20-1747 d 10-23-1827 m Beulah Hanchett Lt CT
Phineas: b 8-9-1738 d 7-20-1781 m Elizabeth Hall Pvt CT
Robert: b 1747 d 8-30-1804 m Elizabeth Kendall Pvt CT
Samuel, Sr.: b 8-13-1702 d 3-6-1790 m Mary Kent MM CT
Samuel. Jr.: b 2-1-1727/8 d 1-16-1795 m Michal King Capt CT
Seba: b 4- -1763 d 3-4-1848 m Mary Molly Clark Pvt MA ★
Simeon: b 12-28-1728 d 5- -1815 m Abigail Dudley Pvt MA
Thaddeus: b 10-9-1765 d 9-4-1825 m (1)Anna Terrill (2)Julia E. Manly Pvt MA ★
Thomas: b 9-11-1765 d 1848 m Jemima Kingsbury Pvt Mus MA ★
Zadock: b 7-20-1736 d 7-17-1799 m Martha Cooley Pvt CT

GRANNIS, (includes GRANNISS)
David: b 4-9-1755 d 1-7-1834 m Clarissa Martin Pvt CT
Edward: b 11-14-1752 d 4-10-1798 m (1)Hannah Wells (2)Elizabeth Bellamy Pvt NH

GRANNIS, contd.
Enos: b 3-15-1754 d 8-2-1824 m(1)Elizabeth Royce (2)Margaret —
  Lt CT ★
Jared: b 8- -1756 d 7-8-1845 m (1)Martha Luddington (2)Eunice
  Munson Pvt Mar CT ★
Robert: b 1-10-1762 d p. 1834 m (1)Elizabeth Andrews (2)Molly
  (Marsh) Tyler Pvt CT
Simeon: b c. 1756 d p. 1795 m Priscilla Brackett Pvt CT

GRANT,
Aaron, Sr.: b 12-12-1724 d 1-31-1804 m (1)Mabel Easton
  (2)Theodosia (Bull) Pitkin PS Mus CT
Aaron, Jr.: b 8-14-1755 d 2-28-1827 m Lucy Sadd Pvt CT
Alexander: b 12-12-1735 d 4-4-1801 m Thankful Lyman Pvt MA
Ambrose: b 9-14-1747 d 12-7-1816 m Hannah Mason CS Sol CT
Andrew: b 1730 d 10-12-1809 m Elizabeth — Capt MA
Benjamin: b 5-7-1750 d 1-20-1839 m Esther Brown Pvt RI
Benjamin: b 1745 d 1776 m Sarah Sloan Lt NH
Boone: b 9-14-1764 d 1-10-1833 m (1)Susan Hand (2)Mary
  (Johnson) Drum (3)Mrs Mary A. Hickman Pvt VA
Christopher: b 2-4-1743 d 4-1-1818 m Sarah Watson Lt MA
Daniel: b 1724 d 1793-6 m Elizabeth Tait PS NC
Daniel: b 1-2-1759 d 2-21-1831 m Jane Smith PS Pvt VA
David: b 12-16-1756 d 10-5-1833 m Mary Skinner Pvt CT ★
Ebenezer: b 10-20-1706 d 3-19-1797 m Anne Ellsworth Capt PS CT
Edward Chapman: b 1-13-1725/6 d 10-30-1811 m Hannah Foster
  PS CT
Eleazer: b 6-24-1748 d 3-13-1806 m (1)Mary Lathrop (2)Esther Rose
  2Lt QM NY
Elijah: bpt 7-15-1722 d p. 3-9-1791 m (1)Sarah — (2)Hannah
  Williams Capt MA
Elisha: b 3-14-1752 d 9-3-1824 m Mary West Pvt CT MA
Elizabeth Boone: b 2-5-1732 d 2-25-1825 m William Grant PS KY
Ephraim, Jr.: b 4-27-1726 d 3-13-1800 m Mary West Capt CT
Ephraim: bpt 4-25-1731 d p. 1799 m Abigail Thurrell Pvt PS MA
George: b c. 1740 d c. 1820 m Mary Worth Capt NJ
Gustavus: b 1759 d 3-11-1841 m Phebe Goodale Pvt CT
Hamilton: b 1759 d 8-22-1822 m Lucy Williams Drm CT
Hezekiah: b 7-13-1763 d 1-15-1844 m Abigail Gilbert Pvt CT ★
Isaac: b 4-4-1760 d 11-9-1841 m Hannah Tracy Sgt Dr CT
Isaac: b 1759 d 1837 m Elizabeth East Pvt VA ★
Jabez: b 9-20-1756 d p. 1792 m Dorcas Blanding Pvt RI
James: b 9-18-1750 d — m X Pvt MD
James,Jr.: b 6-17-1765 d 8-31-1851 m Martha Shackley Sgt MA ★
James: bpt 12- -1726 d p. 1790 m Mrs Sarah Pike Pvt ME
James: b 1723 d — m Ann — PS NC
James: b c. 1755 d c. 11-4-1820 m Dorcus — Pvt SC
Jesse: b 12-10-1742 d c. 1794 m Ann Lewis Capt CT
Joel: b 2-21-1756 d 3-16-1796 m Zilpah Cowles Pvt CT
John: b 7-7-1754 d 8-23-1824 m Thankful Lewis Pvt CT
John: b 1746 d 6-15-1820 m (1)Agnes Reed (2)Sarah Boltwood Sol
  ME
John: b 1753 d 6-22-1820 m Margaret Beasson 2Lt MA ★
John: b 9-1-1746 d 11-3-1825 m Sarah Wise QM MA ★
John: b 1755 d 7-14-1822 m Dorothy Foss Pvt NH ★
John: b c. 1740 d p. 1-13-1802 m Sarah Cotrell Pvt NY
John: b a. 1755 d 4-10-1818 m Eunice Stark Arfr NH ★
John: b 6-30-1754 d 1826 m Mary Moseby Pvt VA
John: b c. 1755 d p. 6-10-1826 m X Pvt VA
Jonathan: b 1755 d p. 1820 m Sarah — Pvt VA
Joseph, Jr.: b 1742 d 1815 m Hannah Drowne Pvt RI
Joshua, Jr.: b 4-2-1756 d 5-16-1825 m Lucy Green Pvt CT
Joshua: b 1744 d 6-5-1825 m Abigail (Grant) QM Sgt MA ★
Josiah: b 1754 d p. 1782 m Mary Letts Pvt NJ
Josiah: b 4-27-1751 d 4-27-1808 m (1)Ruth Woodruff (2)Lysena
  Woodruff Buell Lt VT
Justus: b 8-17-1751 d 10-10-1826 m Anna Kellogg Pvt CT
Matthew: b 6-27-1723 d 6-28-1800 m Hannah Birge Capt CT
Moses: b 3-13-1743 d 12-22-1817 m (1)Elizabeth Brown (2)Sarah
  Pierce PS MA
Moses, Jr.: b 10-11-1747 d 4-14-1816 m Pearly Thare Pvt MA
Noah: b 6-20-1748 d 2-14-1819 m (1)Anna (Buell) Richardson
  (2)Rachel (Miller) Kelly Capt CT
Oliver, Sr.: b 7-18-1729 d 5-22-1798 m Anna Borodel Billings Capt
  CT
Ozias: b 1733 d 5-22-1823 m Lorana Strong Pvt CT
Peter: b 1723 d 10-22-1793 m Eles Guptil Pvt MA
Peter: b c. 1720 d p. 1795 m (2)Jane (Strother) Lewis PS VA
Peters: b 7-7-1746 d 4- -1813 m Anna Bridgman CS Sgt CT
Reuben: b 8-21-1763 d 9-1-1834 m Anna Loomis Pvt CT
Reuben: b 1754 d 1839/40 m (1)— Franklin (2)Martha Skinner Pvt
  NH ★
Reuben: b c. 1756 d a. 1793 m Elizabeth — Capt NC
Reuben: b 1750 d 3-27-1809 m Temperance Freeman Lt. NC
Robert: b 1761 d 7-20-1838 m(1)Mary Wood (2)Susannah Melton
  Pvt VA ★
Roswell: b 3-9-1746 d 12-31-1834 m Fluvia Wolcott Capt CT
Roswell: b 8-18-1762 d 7-7-1837 m Anna Coy Pvt CT
Samuel: b 4-17-1744 d 8-13-1805 m (1)Abby Jones (2)Mrs Elizabeth
  Seward Capt MA
Samuel: b 1-16-1754 d 7-20-1815 m Experience Fisher Pvt RI
Silas: b 1754 d 1842 m Mary Chadbourne Pvt MA ★

Thomas: bpt 10-3-1731 d a. 1815 m Margaret Bubier Capt MA
Thomas: bpt 6-14-1752 d 3-5-1827 m Elizabeth Babcock Sgt MA ★
Thomas: b 8-3-1729 d 9-9-1777 m Hannah Carrol PS MA
Thomas: b 5-21-1757 d 11-27-1828 m (1)Frances Owen (2)Martha
  H. Waddy Ens NC
Thomas: b 11-20-1758 d 6-16-1815 m Deborah Martin AsstQMGen
  PA
Vincent: b 2-20-1761 d 1835-40 m Rebecca Coleman Pvt NY
Wm.: b 6-7-1706 d 11-10-1786 m Sarah Moore Sgt CT
Wm.: b 6-10-1717 d 1802 m Elizabeth Marshall Pvt MA
Wm.: b 11-18-1741 d 2-18-1825 m (1)Lois Foster (2)Polly Yarrington
  Pvt Mar MA W★
Wm., Sr.: b 2-22-1726 d 6-22-1804 m Elizabeth Boone Sol NC KY
Wm.: b 1759 d 11- -1830 m Polly Newet Sol NC
Wm.: b 8-3-1761 d 8-28-1851 m (1)Polly Partman (2)Mary
  Burchfield Lt SC ★

GRANTHAM,
Richard: b 3-16-1754 d 6-22-1846 m Francis Amis Cpl SC ★

GRANTIER
Jacob: b 1756 d 1805 m (1) — Tabor (2)Elizabeth Boes Pvt NY
John: b 10-16-1749 d 4-6-1804 m Elesabeth Kniskern Pvt NY

GRANTS,
Mark: b 1762 d 5- -1841 m (1)Catharine W. Dygert (2)Cathren House
  Pvt NY W★

GRANVILLE,
Joseph: b 1756 d — m Molly Sanborn Pvt MA

GRASTY,
John: b 9-6-1760 d 11-17-1833 m (1)Frances — (2)Lucy Fitzpatrick
  Pvt SC

GRATIOT,
Charles: b 1753 d 4-20-1817 m Victoire Chouteau PS MO

GRATTAN,
John: b c. 1730 d p. 11-3-1791 m Elizabeth Brown CS PS VA

GRATTON,
Thomas: b 12-29-1757 d 5-9-1842 m Mary Dodge Pvt MA ★

GRATZ,
Michael: b 1740 d 9-8-1811 m Miriam Symons PS PA

GRAUTS,
Mark: b 6- -1761 d 5- -1849 m Catherine Dygert Pvt NY

GRAVELY,
Joseph: b 1744 d 10-3-1844 m Eleanor Cox Pvt PS VA

GRAVES,
Aaron, Sr.: b 1749 d 11-18-1834 m Sarah Morton Capt MA
Aaron, Jr.: b 1722 d 8-8-1814 m Phoebe Meigs Pvt NH
Abner: b 1748 d 3-26-1830 m Alice Richardson Lt MA
Allen: b 5-1-1738 d 5-6-1826 m Mary — Pvt MA ★
Amasa: b 6-26-1743 d 11-20-1820 m Phebe Cary Sgt MA
Amos: b 12-10-1753 d 1825 m Hannah Wentworth Canaday Pvt MA
Ann: b c. 1696 d c. 1782 m Thomas Graves PS VA
Ansel: b 2-18-1767 d 1-3-1810 m Caroline Otis Pvt MA
Asa: b 11-4-1755 d 10- -6-1823 m Roxanna Graves Ens MA
Bela: b 5-7-1750 d 1-15-1852 m Sarah Griswold Pvt CT ★
Benjamin: bpt 8-25-1734 d 9-6-1781 m Mary Ransome Pvt CT
Benjamin: b 2-29-1734 d 8-17-1777 m Thankful Field Pvt MA
Benjamin: b 11-22-1760 d 3-22-1843 m (2)Lucretia Marsh (3)Mrs
  Sallie Burroughs Pvt MA CT ★
Boston: b 10-1-1747 d 4-1-1840 m Sarah Ephland Pvt NC ★
Chauncey: b 1762 d p. 8-7-1832 m Olive Graves Pvt VT
Cotton: b 7-31-1762 d 11-1-1847 m (1)Huldah Hubbard (2)Lydia
  Newcomb (3)Ruth Brigham Pvt MA
Daniel: b c. 9-20-1757 d 12-19-1828 m Mary Buxton Cpl MA W★
Daniel: b 3-4-1761 d 1-30-1836 m (1)Rhoda Fay (2)Tirzah Newton
  (3)Beulah Grover Pvt MA ★
Darius: b 1762 d 1-31-1814 m Zeruah — Pvt NH
David: b 10-4-1757 d 1-26-1819 m Sarah Clapp Pvt MA
David: b 10-5-1728 d 1-24-1777 m (1)Hannah Wetmore
  (3)Temperance Dudley Sol MA
David, Jr.: b 6-7-1733 d 12-20-1815 m Mary Smith MM MA
David: b 10-20-1751 d 2- -1837 m Sara Farrington Pvt NY ★
Ebenezer: b 11-24-1730 d 1-14-1814 m Mary Willard Sgt CT
Ebenezer, Sr.: b 3-5-1726 d 4-26-1814 m Prudence Hastings CS PS
  MA
Ebenezer, Jr.: b 3-19-1753 d p. 1800 m Anna Chapin Pvt MA
Edmund: b 1762 d a. 7- -1834 m Nancy — Pvt MA ★
Elias: b 12-21-1760 d 7-14-1830 m Hepzibah Belden Pvt MA
Elihu: b 5-16-1750 d 5-20-1810 m Mercy Carey PS MA
Elijah: b 4-7-1760 d 10-22-1823 m Elizabeth Warner Pvt Drm CT ★
Elijah, Jr.: b 9-2-1755 d 9-17-1835 m Lucy McAllister Pvt NH
Eliphalet: b 1746 d 1836 m Anna Jones Sgt MA ★
Francis: b 1746 d 1845 m X Lt QM NC

Gideon: b 8-25-1758 d 3-8-1834 m (1)Maria Rogers (2)Hannah Dake Sgt MA
Gilbert: b 9-21-1758 d 7-22-1841 m Elizabeth Kelsey Pvt CT
Henry: b c. 1715 d 1797 m Rachel — PS NC
Increase: b — d — m Susan Stetson Bascom Sgt NY
Isaac: b 9-2-1741 d a. 1-23-1818 m (1)Mildred McWilliams (2)Elizabeth Cowherd (3)Jemima Holliday PS VA
Issachar: b 6-8-1755 d p. 1790 m Jemima — Cpl CT
James: b 1730 d 1796 m Mary Copeland Pvt GA
James, Sr.: b — d p. 1787 m — Haskins Pvt MA
James, Jr.: b 5-1-1764 d 7-8-1845 m (1)Wealthy Jones (2)Jemima Acom Pvt MA ★
Jedediah: b 1755 d 8-20-1839 m Polly Crippen Sgt NY
Jeremiah: b 6-2-1754 d 9-4-1839 m Lucinda Hubbard Pvt MA
Jesse: b 1755 d 10-12-1820 m Ruth Remington Pvt VT
Job: b 12-26-1756 d 1-22-1845 m Abigail Wells Pvt MA
Joel: b 8-16-1760 d 2-20-1849 m Lucy Martin Pvt MA
John: b 1759 d 1851 m Rebecca Harris Pvt GA
John: b 6-3-1746 d 1791 m Lois Parker Pvt MA
John: b 2-6-1752 d 1-21-1839 m (1)Mary Hendly (2)Rebecca Thompson Pvt MA
John, Sr.: b 1711 d 6-20-1796 m Lydia Clark CS NH
John, Jr.: b c. 1735-40 d p. 1790 m X Lt PS NH
John: b 1748 d 6-24-1824 m Catherine West Maj VA
John: b 1760 d 1828 m Elizabeth Eddins Maj VA
John: b 12-19-1737/9 d 12-18-1825 m Ann Rice Capt VA
John: b 12-18-1757 d 10-31-1843 m Lydia — Pvt VA ★
John Herndon: b 9- -1749 d 10- -1829 m (1)Nancy Slade (2)Elizabeth Coleman Capt NC
Johnson: b 8-19-1732 d 1-8-1824 m Sarah Staples Pvt MA
Jonah: b 6-20-1728 d 1825 m (1)Ruth — (2)Sallie Graves Capt NY
Jonathan: b c. 1740 d c. 1826 m Bettie Lisk Pvt CT
Jonathan: b 1-31-1750 d p. 1790 m Jemima Scott Pvt MA
Jonathan: b 7-29-1812 m Anne Taylor Pvt MA
Joseph, Rev.: b 5-30-1738 d p. 1790 m Lois Higbee QM PS CT
Joseph: b 9- -1735 d 4-17-1796 m Eunice Dwight Lt MA
Joseph: b c. 1725 d 1785/6 m (1)Sarah — (2)Frances Coleman PS VA
Joshua: b c. 1725 d 3-28-1777 m Lydia Woodcock Pvt NH
Josiah: b 1760 d 4-15-1825 m Mary Dewey Pvt NY
Julius: b 8-18-1762 d 1-25-1844 m Roxie Farnham Pvt MA
Lemuel: b 11-17-1757 d 1802 m (1)Deborah Battle (2)Keziah Harding Pvt MA
Lewis: b 11-7-1755 d 5- -1816 Elizabeth Steele Sgt NY W★
Lewis: b 7-17-1760 d 1839 m Ruth — Sol SC
Lucius: b 12-19-1746 d 5-27-1810 m (1)Irene Dickinson (2)Clarissa Hickox Mus MA
Luman: b 1-1-1760 d p. 1819 m Abigail Todd Pvt CT
Luther: b 4-20-1749 d 1790 m Phoebe Jewett Lt MA
Martin: b 5-25-1744 d 10-20-1822 m Mehitable Edson Sgt MA
Martin: b 2-23-1766 d 1837 m Hannah Jefferson Pvt MA
Matthew: b 9-4-1735 d 10-9-1824 m Hannah Morton Pvt MA
Nathan: b 3-20-1716 d 4-2-1786 m Lydia Leonard Scott MM Pvt MA
Oliver: b 2-9-1761 d 8-11-1854 m Abigail Graves Sol MA
Perez, Sr.: b 4-26-1730 d 12-17-1809 m (1)Martha Gillet (2)Zeruiah (Cole) Perry Capt PS MA
Perez, Jr.: b 1-2-1761 d 11-28-1848 m (1)Eunice Bryant (2)Experience Parsons Cpl MA
Peter: b 11-25-1745 d p. 1798 m (1)Susannah Hager (3)Hannah McIntire (4)Easter Lawrence Pvt MA
Phineas: b 4-30-1726 d 4-20-1806 m Rhoda Smith PS MA
Randall,: b 5-31-1760 d 12-20-1831 m Lydia Coolidge Sol MA
Reuben: b 9-23-1753 d 5-10-1786 m Hannah Kendall Pvt MA NH
Richard Croshaw: b c. 1735 d c. 1798 m Elizabeth Valentine Capt VA
Roswell: b 1740 d 1766/7 m Elizabeth Driggs Sgt CT
Roswell: b 1754 d 12-29-1850 m Hannah — Pvt MA
Rufus: b 9-27-1758 d 2-12-1845 m Experience Graves Sol MA
Russell: b 4-17-1751 d — m Anna Millington Pvt MA
Samuel: b 6-11-1746 d 7-7-1822 m Ann Hern Pvt CT
Samuel: b c. 1718 d 8-22-1794 m Phebe — Sgt MA
Selah: b 5-24-1755 d 8-31-1827 m Mary Strong Sol MA
Selah: b 3-1-1768 d 4-5-1822 m Mary Brush Pvt MA
Seth: b 1760 d 3-8-1838 m Elizabeth Graves Pvt CT
Simeon: b 12-27-1755 d 12-1-1790 m (2)Huldah Hubbard Pvt MA
Simon: b 1-24-1752 d p. 1803 m Persis — Cpl MA
Stephen: b 2-7-1742 d 4-21-1820 m Patience Hatch 2Lt NY
Sylvanus: b 7-17-1729 d 2-4-1801 m Lydia (Hull) Griswold LCol CT
Thomas: b 10- -1763 d 5- -1847 m (2)Marley P. Watchell Pvt MA
Thomas: b c. 1721 d 11-18-1801 m Arabella Bartlett Sol PS VA
Timothy: b 1759 d 1849 m Mabel Munger Cpl NY
Timothy: b 1-1-1754 d 6-20-1848 m Hannah Comstock Sgt CT NY ★
Whitney: b 11-22-1751 d 1838 m Esther Youngs Pvt CT ★
Wm.: b 1755 d 1835 m (1)Mary Kirk Sol GA
Wm.: b 3-24-1757 d 12-10-1841 m Lucy Wheeler Pvt MA ★
Wm.: b 1750 d 1798 m Hannah Ward Sol SC
Wm.: b 7-9-1755 d 2-24-1836 m Sarah Smith Wgm VA
Wm.: b 1-30-1768 d 12-14-1852 m Lydia Williams Pvt VA
Wm. A.: b 1750 d 1799 m Euphan Armistead Cnt VA
Zebediah: b 6-15-1741 d 6-26-1823 m (1)Rhoda — (2)Lydia (Graves) (3)Esther Parker Pvt MA
Zenas: b 1-28-1752 d p. 1800 m Hannah — Mus Pvt MA

GRAVITT, (includes GRAVAT)
John: b 1757 d 1836 m — Pvt VA ★
Wm.: b 5-23-1739 d 7-18-1826 m Jane Fenton Sol NJ

GRAWBARGER,
Daniel: b 1752 d 11-30-1830 m (1)Gertrude Quackenbush Pvt NY

GRAY, (includes GREY)
Aaron, Jr.: b 1748 d 2-25-1812 m Huldah — Pvt NH
Adam: b — d — m Magdalane Loucks Sgt NY
Amos: b 1761 d 1850 m Betsey Read Tyler 3Sgt MA VT ★
Andrew: b 2-23-1759 d 12-17-1823 m Catharine Snell Sgt NY
Andrew: b 1-1-1757-9 d 8-15-1839 m Mary Stewart Pvt PA ★
Arthur: b c. 1743 d 9-27-1779 m Martha Craig Lt SC
Benjamin: b 1740 d 12- -1813 m Temperance Baxter Pvt CT
Benjamin: b c. 1759 d c. 1840 m Nancy Cox Pvt MD
Benoni: b 1742 d 1-12-1809 m Mary Rockwell Pvt NY
Daniel: b 5-12-1728 d 12-14-1803 m (1) — Lamond (2)Mary Dick Pvt MA
Daniel: b 11-29-1760 d 7-18-1833 m Tabitha Allen Pvt MA
Daniel: b 3-20-1749 d 2-19-1843 m ( )Phoebe Butler ( )Susannah — Pvt NJ
Daniel: b 6-4-1756 d 5-23-1830 m (1)Sarah D. Harris (2)Jemima Rix Lt NY
David: b 6-22-1756 d 5-19-1827 m Sarah Smith Pvt NY
David: b c. 1749/50 d p. 4- -1792 m Mary — Pvt PA
David: b 1752 d 12-27-1844 m Nancy Blackburn Pvt PA ★
David: b 1746 d — m Margaret B. Woods Sgt VA
Dominicus: b 1761 d 10-21-1832 m Sarah Plummer Pvt MA W★
Ebenezer: b 7-26-1743 d 6-18-1795 m Sarah Staniford LCol CT
Ebenezer: b 7-1-1743 d 1-18-1834 m (1)Sarah Johnston (2)Agness Berry Sgt MA
Edward: b 9-25-1730 d 1803 m Mary Paddock Capt MA
Elias: b 4-4-1746 d 11-22-1826 m Eunice Allen QM CT
Elijah: b 3-12-1764 d 8- -1847 m Sarai Raymond Pvt CT
Eliot: b 4-28-1736 d p. 1802 m Hannah Barber CS Pvt MA
Elliot: b 9-17-1755 d 3- -1841 m Hannah Crawford Pvt MA ★
Frazer: b 7-26-1761 d 10-11-1849 m (1)Mary Hevelow (2)Elizabeth Lockwood Pvt DE
Frederick: b 1759 d 5-26-1837 m (1)Chloretta Dawkins (2)Mary Geddins Capt SC ★
Gabriel: b 11-29-1762 d 6-1-1844 m Rebecca Wilson Sgt VA ★
George: b 10-26-1725 d 1-22-1800 m Martha Ibison PS PA
George: b c. 1760 d — m Martha — Pvt PA
George: b 5-13-1745 d 12-2-1823 m Mildred Thompson Capt VA
Gideon: b 4-23-1732 d 4-4-1819 m Molly — Pvt PA
Hezekiah: b c. 1760 d p. 1790 m Ann Fair Pvt MD
Isaac: b 3-19-1730 d 9- -1786 m Mary McLain Capt MA
Isaiah: b 1739 d 2-17-1790 m Mary Athearn PS MA
Jabesh: b 4-4-1760 d 1-29-1836 m Ruth Norton Pvt NY
Jacob: b 1752 d 12-24-1842 m Elizabeth Burroughs Pvt NJ ★
Jacob: b c. 1744 d 1792 m X Sol SC
James: b 8-3-1759 d 3-1-1846 m Parthena White Sgt CT NY ★
James: b 5-1-1758 d 11-20-1834 m Mary — Sol GA CL
James: b 1733 d 8-25-1783 m Sarah Spring Col QM MA
James: bpt 2-20-1757 d 9-25-1810 m Priscilla Cressey Pvt MA
James: b 10-8-1749 d 1-10-1822 m (1)Jane Wallace (2)Susannah Parsons Capt NH
James: b c. 1739 d 1829 m Jane Gass Pvt PA
James: b c. 1725 d 5-9-1801 m X PS SC
James: b 1756 d 5-20-1833 m Lucy Webb Pvt VA
Jedediah: b — d p. 8-7-1795 m Eleanor — Sol MD
Jeduthan: b 1756 d 3-2-1830 m Anna Warren Sgt NY
John: b 1721 d 1-15-1817 m Mary — PS MD
John: b 11-29-1732 d 12-27-1796 m Sarah Mitchell Capt MA
John: b 1752 d 12-25-1825 m Mehitabel Brown Pvt MA
John: b c. 1734 d c. 1787 m Martha Savage Pvt NY
John: b 2-14-1762 d 5-14-1801 m Mary Snell Pvt NY W★
John: b 1720 d — 1781 m X Col NC
John: b 1-1-1749 d 11-4-1792 m Jane Greer Capt NC
John: b 1755 d 8-16-1836 m (2)Mary R. — Pvt NC ★
John: b 2-18-1761 d 8-19-1834 m Bythinia Bane Pvt PA ★
John: b 1735 d 1806 m (1)Ailsie Hiatt (2)Elizabeth Hiatt Pvt PS SC
John: b c. 1750 d 1824 m Sarah Marsh Cav SC
John: b 5-19-1750 d 5-22-1814 m Susannah Rider Capt VT
John: b 12-11-1759 d 4-5-1836 m Nancy Pritchard Pvt VA
John: b 1760 d 1856 m — Peyton Drm VA
John: b 1-6-1764 d 3-29-1868 m (1)Nancy McDowell (2)Nancy Ragan (2)Catherine — Pvt VA ★
John: b c. 1735 d 7- -1788 m Jane Guirrant Sol VA
Jonas L.: b 1762 d 8-16-1832 m (1)Lucy Spicer (2)Mrs Mary Vorse Gardner Pvt CT
Jonathan: b 1-3-1754 d 6- -1817 m Mary Needham Pvt MA
Jonathan: b — d 1-11-1801 m (1)Margaret Hardin (2)Elizabeth Willey CS MA
Joseph: b 7-7-1753 d 10-7-1833 m Lydia Keeler Pvt CT MA ★
Joseph: b c. 1750 d 8-8-1820 m Benedictor — Pvt PS MD
Joseph: b 11-18-1732 d 2-23-1821 m Sarah — Pvt MA

GRAY, contd.
Joseph: b 3-19-1761 d 8-26-1846 m Chloe Abbott Pvt NH
Joseph: b 6-12-1732 d 3-29-1796 m X PS NY
Joseph: b 1758 d p. 1790 m Sarah Spain Sol NC
Joseph: b 1734 d 10-13-1794 m Elizabeth Foster Pvt PA
Joseph: b 5-27-1762 d 4-6-1842 m Avis Anthony Sol RI
Joseph: b 6-4-1751 d 1812 m Lucy Bancroft Dr RI
Joseph: b 1763/4 d 1833 m Martha Ann — Pvt VA ★
Joshua: b 1-22-1743 d 3-31-1791 m Mary Hedge Capt MA
Joshua, Sr.: b 11-28-1737 d 12-6-1822 m Susanna Hatch Cpl ME
Kelso: b 1738 d 10-28-1824 m Phebe Gray CS NH
Lot, Sr.: b 2-24-1722/3 d 10-16-1790 m Miriam Smith Pvt MA
Martha Ibbetson: b 1-28-1734 d 6-27-1781 m George Gray N PA
Matthew, Sr.: b c. 1747 d p. 2-23-1836 m Nancy — Pvt PA
Moses: b 8-11-1743 d 10-15-1811 m Sarah Disbrow Pvt CT
Moses: b c. 1745 d 9-11-1775 m Mary Clark Pvt MA
Moses Wiley: b 12-31-1745 d 5-8-1803 m (1)Sally Miller (2)Anna
　　Buckingham MM MA
Nathaniel: b 7-20-1741 d 6-27-1777 m Hannah Bouton Lt CT
Nathaniel: b 3-17-1736 d 6-24-1810 m Deborah Lathrop Ens CT
Nathaniel: b 1745 d 12-20-1777 m Sarah Blair Pvt MA
Nathaniel: b - 1760 d 6-23-1853 m Margaret Harkness Pvt NY
Pardon: b 4-20-1737 d 10-25-1814 m Mary Brown LCol CS RI
Peter: b 1750 d 1814 m — Wilson Capt SC
Philip: b 6-22-1750 d 8-12-1801 m Deborah Bailey Pvt RI
Presley: b 12-23-1764 d 2-19-1838 m (1)Barbara Cotton (2)Agnes
　　Singleton Pvt VA SC
Richard: b 1-4-1755 d 12-25-1833 m Catharine — Pvt Wgn VA
Robert: b 12-23-1734 d 10-6-1799 m Margaret Watts CS PS MA
Robert: b 1747 d 12-21-1843 m Agnes Atkins Pvt CT
Robert: b 7-14-1757 d 12-10-1837 m Kezia Foster Pvt MA ★
Robert: b 10-30-1751 d p. 1813 m Elizabeth Howe Sgt NH MA
Samuel: b 6-21-1751 d 1836 m Charlotte Elderkin DepCmsry Gen CT
Samuel: b 10-28-1736 d 1818 m Eunice Delano 1Lt MA
Samuel: b 1756 d 1812 m Rebecca — Pvt MA
Samuel: b 1-23-1751 d 3-19-1832 m Catherine Suits Lt NY
Samuel: b 5-12-1726 d 4-22-1813 m Deborah Peck Lt RI
Silas: b 5-19-1751 d 1-19-1820 m — Capt NY ★
Solomon: b 4-21-1760 d 3-7-1824 m Mary Locke Pvt NH ★
Thomas: b 5-22-1749 d 2- -1792 m Abigail Wales Dr CT
Thomas: b c. 1709 d 2-5-1796 m (1)ElizabethHutchinson (2)Lydia
　　Graves Pvt MA
Thomas: b c. 1755 d a. 4-29-1823 m — Pvt PA
Thomas: b 1-27-1729 d 11-8-1803 m Abigail Brown LtCol RI
Timothy: b 2-14-1749 d 7-18-1807 m (1)Hannah Blanchard
　　(2)Ruth Burnham Pvt PS NH
Wm.: b 1718 d 1801 m Hannah Laughinghoe Sgt DE
Wm.: b 6-27-1750 d 11-8-1825 m Elizabeth Chipman 2Lt MA
Wm.: b 3-26-1761 d 7- -1812 m Mary Diamond Pvt MA
Wm.: b 3- -1727 d 1780 m Hannah Foss Cpl PS NH
Wm.: b c. 1730 d p. 9-3-1782 m Jean — Pvt NY
Wm.: b 1741 d 1- -1841 m Mary Mourning Lowe Capt NC ★
Wm.: b 9-17-1755 d 3-8-1849 m Ann Thornberry Capt NC SC
Wm.: b 1757 d p. 10-23-1832 m — McNabb 2Lt NC VA ★
Wm.: b c. 1760 d 1791 m Sarah Parker Sol NC
Wm.: b c. 1745 d p. 1792 m Fenella Key Pvt NC
Wm.: b 1745 d 10-7-1780 m Lydia — Pvt NC
Wm.: b c. 1732 d 8- -1794 m — PS NC
Wm.: b 1-17-1731 d 6-23-1801 m Frances Lee Pvt NC
Wm.: b 1738 d 1815 m Agnes Rutherford Capt PA
Wm.: b 1750 d 7-18-1804 m Mary Brady Capt PA W★
Wm.: b —d 1-11-1841 m (1)Mary Allison (2)Jane Taylor Pvt PA
Wm.: b 1750 d 8-14-1816 m Rosannah Giffin Pvt SC
Wm.: b c. 1759 d 1-17-1828 m Katherine Davis Sol SC
Wm.: b c. 1708 d 5-30-1782 m (1)Elizabeth Littlepage (2)Ann
　　Goodrich Capt VA
Wm.: b 1755 d 8-13-1834 m Eleanor (Wardrobe) Blackburn
　　(2)Lucy (Phillips) Neal Ens VA
Wm.: b 1759 d 1837 m Ann Austin Lt QM VA
Wm.: b 10-28-1760 d p. 4-11-1807 m Lucy Wilson Sol VA
Winthrop: b c. 1740 d 6-3-1782 m (1)Mary Gray (2)Rebecca Stone
　　Capt MA

GRAYBILL, (includes GRABILL, GRABLE, GRAYBEEL, GREBIL, GREBLE)
Abraham: b 1756 d p. 1800 m Mary Murdock Pvt PA
Andrew: b c. 1730-35 d c. 1810 m Regina Rosina Shaaf Lt PA
Henry: b 1741 d 10-7-1822 m Mary DuBose Rutherford PS GA
Jacob: b 1730 d 1810 m Catherine — Pvt PA
Jacob: b 1758 d 10-13-1809 m Mary Watson Brown Pvt PA
John: b 1754 d 1785 m Salome Hickman Pvt PA
John: b 4- -1734 d 9-19-1797 m Sarah Carpenter Pvt PA
John: b 8-17-1735 d 2-18-1806 m Barbara Daradinger Pvt PA
Michael: b 4-25-1748 d 1823 m Anna Brubaker Pvt PA

GRAYDON,
Rachel Marks: b 8-22-1723 d 1-23-1807 m Alexander Graydon PS PA

GRAYSBURY, (or GRAISBURY)
James: b 1760 d 1816 m Beulah Warrick Pvt NJ

GRAYSON,
John: b 1733 d 1780-1785 m Sarah Wigg 1Lt SC
Richard: b c. 1760 d p. 1790 m — Bryan 1Lt MD
Spence: b 1732 d 12- -1798 m Mary Elizabeth Wagoner PS Chp SC
Wm.: b 1736 d 3-12-1790 m Eleanor Smallwood Col ADC PS VA
Wm.: b 1732 d 1829 m Ann Smith Capt VA
Wm.: b a. 1750 d 1801 m Rachel Cooley Pvt VA

GREASON,
Wm.: b a. 1755 d 1803 m Agnes Waugh Pvt PA

GREATHOUSE,
Harman, Jr.: b 6-30-1762 d 7-5-1849 m Mercy Buche Pvt PA
Wm.: b c. 1730 d p. 3-25-1792 m Barbara — Pvt PA

GREATON,
John, Sr.: bpt 3-25-1712/13 d 1776 m Catharine (Sharrard) Linton
　　Grd MA
John, Jr.: b 3-10-1741 d 12-16-1783 m Sarah Humphreys BGen VA

GREELEY,
Aaron: b 3-30-1745 d 9-12-1813 m Susanna Burnham PS NH
Benjamin: b 9-26-1708 d 1792 m Ruth Eastman PS NH
Benjamin: b 12-3-1748 d 12-13-1827 m Lydia True PS NH
Enoch: b 8-1-1754 d 2-28-1815 m Dorothy Batchelder Pvt MA
Ezekiel: b 10-21-1725 d 1-21-1793 m Esther Lovell PS NH
Jacob: b 1739 d 1820 m Mary Laiten PS MA
John: b 4-26-1759 d 1844 m Susan Marshall Pvt NH ★
John, Jr.: b 1728 d 3- -1807 m (2)Elizabeth Holmes CS Cpl NH
Jonathan: b 2-26-1731/32 d 7-6-1817 m (1)Ruth — (2)Mrs Phebe
　　Parke Pvt PS NH
Joseph, Sr.: b 2-18-1730 d 11-26-1814 m Prudence Clement Sgt MA
Joseph: b 9-9-1756 d 5-13-1840 m Sarah G— Pvt NH
Mathew: b 9-3-1759 d 6-24-1842 m Abigail Stevens Pvt NH
Nathaniel: b 10-28-1744 d 12-16-1819 m Lydia Cram Pvt PS NH
Noah: b 7-29-1757-60 d 8-2-1836 m Hannah Morrill Pvt NH
Phillip: b 8-6-1750 d 10-22-1832 m Dolly Tilton Pvt NH
Reuben: b 6-26-1742 d 4-1-1778 m Rachel Meloon Pvt NH
Richard: b 9-1-1743 d 9-1-1815 m Edith Page PS NH
Samuel, Sr.: b 5-10-1721 d 3-19-1802 m Abigail Blodgett Capt PS
　　CS NH
Samuel, Jr.: b 9-29-1752 d 9-25-1798 m Olive Read PS NH
Samuel: b 7-7-1759 d 11-25-1803 m Ruth Blaisdell PS NH
Samuel: b 9-16-1746 d 6-14-1824 m Mary Levet PS NH
Shubal: bpt 1-10-1730 d 10-22-1814 m Hannah Pettingill PS Sol NH

GREEN, (includes GREENE)
Aaron: b 1756 d 7-28-1830 m Lydia Needham Pvt MA
Abel, Jr.: b 10- 10-1759 d 1-31-1829 m Prudence Sidwell Pvt PA
Abel: b 10-14-1741 d 1828 m Nancy Ann King Lt RI
Abraham: b 10-10-1740 d p. 1790 m (1)Patience Arnold (2)Mary
　　Reynolds Pvt RI
Abraham: b c. 1750-55 d p. 6-18-1810 m (1)Elizabeth Browne
　　(2)Martha Armistead Capt VA
Allen: b 4-4-1755 d 8-8-1833 m (1)Elizabeth Clarke (2)Elizabeth
　　Greene Pvt Drm RI
Ambrose: b 4-9-1746 d 8-29-1837 m Gulielma Pennington Penn
　　(Lester) Pvt NY
Amos: b 1755 d 11-22-1839 m Lavinia Ross Pvt CT
Amos: b 3-25-1741 d 12-19-1822 m (1)Dorcas Hall (2)Alice
　　Underwood Capt RI W★
Andrew: b 1761 d 12-7-1837 m Jane Daumer Pvt VA ★
Armistead: b — d p. 1783 m Frances Pendleton Sol VA
Asa: b 7-27-1761 d 9-16-1842 m (1)Achsa Sanderson (2)Phoebe
　　Headley Pvt MA ★
Asahel: b 5-15-1751 d 7-5-1844 m Molly Dwinel PS NH
Ashbel: b 7-6-1762 d 5-19-1848 m (1)Elizabeth Stockton (2) —
　　Anderson (3)— McCulloch Sol NJ
Benjamin: b 4-7-1752 d 8-14-1839 m Abigail Dodge Pvt CT
Benjamin: b a. 1763 d 1804 m Eleanor — Pvt GA
Benjamin: b 1730 d 4-16-1808 m Elizabeth Thomas Vol MD
Benjamin: b c. 1756 d 9-1-1837 m Hannah — Pvt MA
Benjamin: b 8-11-1734 d 8-16-1797 m Marcy Taft PS MA
Benjamin: b 5-28-1740 d p. 1790 m Mercy Lawrence PS NH
Benjamin, Sr.: b 2-21-1722/23 d 7-29-1796 m Mary Douglas Sol NJ
Benjamin: b 8-6-1756 d 10-6-1812 m Margaret — Pvt NY
Benjamin: b 9-2-1760 d 1-17-1825 m Lydia Bacon Sgt RI
Benjamin: b 1719 d 1806 m (1)Mercy Rogers (2)Anna Greene Sweet
　　CS RI
Benjamin: b — d — m Anna Low Capt RI
Benjamin: b 8-28-1734 d — m Mary Greene Pvt RI
Benjamin: b 4-26-1755 d 9-28-1835 m (1)Katherine Beam (2)Mrs
　　Martha Lewis Pvt VA ★
Benjamite: b 2-23-1741 d 4- -1777 m Dinah (Greene) Capt RI
Berryman: b 1-26-1754 d 9-13-1825 m (1)Anne Pritchard (2)Nancy
　　Terry Capt PM VA
Bowen: b 8-3-1758 d p. 1811 m Sally Cole Pvt NY
Burwell: b 1750 d p. 1830 m (2)Nancy (Mitchell) King Ens VA
Caleb: b 1- -1753 d 3-29-1817 m Elizabeth Moon Pvt NY
Caleb: b 5-2-1744 d p. 6-20-1790 m Welthian Ellis Lt RI
Caleb: b 1-3-1746 d 2-7-1796 m Mary Lippitt Capt RI
Chafey: b 6-7-1760 d 9-21-1848 m Diana Helms Pvt RI MA ★

Charles: b 6-10-1749 d 1-1-1810 m (1)Waite Bailey (2)Mrs Burdick Lt RI
Christopher: b 5-12-1737 d 5-13-1781 m Ann Lippitt Col RI
Christopher: b 7-3-1748 d 12-22-1830 m (1)Catherine Ward (2)Deborah Ward PS Col RI
Daniel, Sr.: b 7-8-1733 d 4-28-1818 m (1)Ruth Oakes (2)Joanna Oakes Gerry Pvt MA
Daniel, Jr.: b 9-20-1761 d 1-5-1842 m 1)Sarah Evans (2)Mary Evans (3)Elizabeth Evans Ash Pvt MA
Daniel: b 4-2-1760 d 8-4-1833 m Mary Gillson Pvt NY W★
Daniel: b 10-10-1746 d 11-3-1815 m Rebecca Barton 2Lt RI
David, Sr.: b 1714 d 7-17-1781 m Ruth Upham Col MA
David, Jr.: b 2-20-1740 d 5-31-1778 m Elizabeth Woolson Pvt PS NH
David: 1750 d 1814/15 m Isabel Warner Pvt RI
David: b 11-4-1760 d 9-1-1834 m Sarah Allen Pvt RI
Dorastus: b 10-6-1762 d 5-16-1835 m Hannah Porter Pvt CT
Duty: b 1761 d 7-2-1842 m Polly Smith Pvt MA
Ebenezer: b 8-6-1746 d 1786 m Dorcas Grant Capt NH
Ebenezer: b 2-2-1742/43 d 2-25-1826 m Mary Currier CS NH
Ebenezer: b 8-3-1753 d 1823 m Phoebe Ann Allen Pvt RI
Ebenezer: b 6-19-1763 d 12-10-1841 m Priscilla Salisbury Pvt NY ★
Edward: b c. 1740 d 3- -1792 m Sarah McLemore Sol NC
Edward: b 3-20-1760 d 2-24-1845 m Huldah Sweet Pvt RI & NY ★
Edward: b 3-7-1757 d 4-22-1824 m (1)Prudence Davis (2)Sally Rhodes Pvt RI
Edward: b c. 1740 d 1819 m X CS VA
Edward, Jr.: b 3-10-1757/58 d 3-28-1836 m Susannah Crandall Pvt RI
Eleazer: b 1757 d 4-12-1833 m Lucy Brace Pvt CT
Elias: b 1-25-1756 d 3-21-1841 m (2)Mary Willoughby (Young) Sgt MA ★
Elijah: b 1752 d 1842 m X Sol NC
Elisha: b 7-7-1726 d 1802 m (1)Isabel Budlong (2)Sara Johnson PS RI
Elisha: b 1753 d 1845 m Emily — Pvt SC
Ezra: b 1-30-1754 d 9-25-1824 m Amy Church Pvt CT W★
Frederick: b c. 1730 d p. 4-23-1785 m Francis Crittenden PS VA
George: b 9-2-1738 d 8- -1777 m Anna Smith Capt NJ
George: 1755-60 d 7-25-1834 m Lucy Jones Pvt RI
George: b 1-5-1763 d p. 1833 m Jane Livingston Pvt VA ★
Gideon: b a. 1755 d a. 4-15-1799 m Elizabeth Anderson PS NC
Griffin: b 2-16-1749 d 6- -1804 m Sarah (Greene) PM & Maj RI
Henry: b 7-28-1754 d 9-9-1834 m Mercy Corey Sgt CT
Henry: b 6-28-1757 d 5-31-1848 m Sarah Sherwood Pvt MA
Henry: b 8-8-1763 d 2-19-1849 m Submit Clark Pvt MA ★
Henry: b 7-17-1761 d 1-20-1849 m Abigail Moon Pvt VT
Hezekiah: b 11- -1733 d 5-16-1826 m Alice Leavens Capt MA
Isaac: b c. 1729 d a. 8-3-1800 m X Pvt MA
Isaac: b 1742 d 1821 m Elizabeth Ricketts Pvt MD
Isaac: b 1741 d 11-9-1812 m Rachel Howe Dr MA
Isaac: b c. 1747 d p. 1780 m (1)Lois Sprague (2)Mary — Pvt MA
Isaac: b 5-11-1755 d 7-25-1822 m Abigail Chamberlain Pvt MA ★
Isaac: b 3-11-1759 d 4-16-1842 m Ann Barrett Pvt MA
Isaac: b 3-21-1757 d 10-16-1814 m Elizabeth Tillson Pvt MA
Isaac: b 3-28-1764 d 4-19-1833 m Deborah — Pvt NY ★
Isaac: b 11-6-1724 d 1807 m Mary Weaver Cpl RI
Isaac: 1731 d 1799 m Elizabeth Garland Sol SC
Isaac: b 1762 d 2-6-1831 m Phoebe West Sol SC
Israel: b 4-22-1755 d 7-29-1817 m Ruth Goodhue Pvt MA
Israel: b c. 1740 d 1791 m Sarah — Sol NY
Jabez: b 9-8-1718 d 9-22-1806 m Mary — CS PS MA
Jabez: b 6-13-1743 d 10-8-1811 m (1)Lucy Kent (2)Hannah Willis Pvt MA
Jabez: b 12-19-1762 d 9-19-1804 m Abigail Wilcox Pvt NY RI
Jacob: b 3-7-1739 d 11-12-1808 m Margaret (Greene) PS NJ
Jacob: b 1-22-1721/22 d 5-24-1790 m (1)Anna Strong (2)Elizabeth Pierson PS NJ
Jacob: b 1767 d 1820 m Frances Acre Sol SC
James: b 9-17-1728 d 3-11-1809 m Ruth Winslow Marshall Capt CT
James: b 1738 d 1-23-1828 m (1)Martha Brundage (2)Susannah (Marvin) Lyon Capt CT
James, Jr.: b 9-5-1742 d 2-23-1815 m Priscilla Hartwell Pvt MA
James: b 1-15-1751 d 9-13-1837 m Margaret Crowley Pvt NH
James: b 11-15-1740 d 6-3-1812 m Sarah Abbott Ens NY
James: b 1759 d 1847 m Miss Gerow Sgt NY
James: b 7-29-1743 d 1817 m Abigal Hall Pvt NY
James: b c. 1758-60 d 1821 m Sarah Hix Pvt NC
James: b 1764 d p. 1815 m (1)Elizabeth White (2)Elizabeth Lamborn Fisher Pvt MA
James: b 2-14-1757 d 5-2-1857 m Joanna Terry Pvt RI ★
James: b 10-28-1757 d 6-28-1847 m Phebe Warner Pvt RI ★
James: b 1764 d 8-20-1839 m Eunice Case Pvt RI
James: b 10-26-1754 d 10-14-1825 m (1)Rebecca Pitman (2)Mercy Waterman Pvt PS RI
James: b 4- -1760 d 11-5-1823 m Jane Futhey Pvt SC
James: b 1-22-1748 d p. 1794 m Susannah Dunton Pvt MA
James: b 1734 d p. 12-3-1807 m Elizabeth Jones Maj VA
James W.: b 1751 d 1-5-1806 m Elizabeth Bass Pvt GA
Jarvis: b 1750 d 8-19-1782 m Sarah Griggs Pvt KY
Jeremiah: b 6-1-1762 d 5-20-1840 m Martha Green Pvt MA ★
Jeremiah: b 2-15-1755 d p. 1832 m Polly Wiseman Pvt NC ★
Jesse: b 10-25-1752 d 1-13-1823 m Grace Hall Pvt MA
Jesse: b 1-31-1743 d 9-14-1838 m Sarah — Pvt NC

Jesse: b 1755 d 1830 m Elizabeth Cox Cpl VA
Job: b 8-8-1717 d 3-29-1798 m Mercy (Greene) 1Lt RI
Job: b 11-19-1759 d 8-23-1808 m Abigail Rhodes Lt RI
Job: b 3-2-1735 d 1-25-1792 m Maribah Carr Pvt VT
Joel: b 9-9-1738 d p. 1790 m Chloe Tucker Capt MA
John: b 5-16-1736 d 4-19-1803 m Abilene Guild Capt CT
John: b 1756 d 1779 m Sarah Johnson Cpl CT
John: b — d — m Tabitha — Cpl CT
John: b 5-6-1761 d a. 9-4-1846 m Mary Hill Pvt CT ★
John: b 1726 d 1781 m Ann Hardesty PS MD
John: b 4-2-1718 d 2-24-1815 m Rachel Roberds Pvt MA
John: b 1725 d 10-25-1809 m (1)Elizabeth Sharp (2)Elizabeth Rand Pvt MA
John: b 8-14-1736 d 10-29-1799 m (2)Mary Ruggles PS MA
John: b c. 1752 d 5-18-1830 m Agnes Switzer Pvt NY
John: b 11-3-1757 d 11-21-1826 m Hannah Hunt Pvt NC
John: b c. 1760 d 3-5-1823 m (1)Rachel Williams (2)Rebecca Snider Pvt NC
John, Sr.: b 3-31-1736 d 9-24-1796 m Alcie Kollock Capt PA
John: b 1754 d 8-18-1839 m (1)Susan — (2)Elizabeth — Pvt PA
John: b 1757 d 3-8-1813 m Ruth Matteson Pvt RI W★
John: b 1744 d 3- -1830 m (1)Abigail Moon (2)Prudence Saunders Capt RI
John: b 11-10-1743 d 5-27-1813 m Mary (Greene) Ens RI
John: b 6-10-1756 d 7-31-1838 m (1)Catherine Godfrey Nichols (2)Amelia Gavitt OrdlSgt RI NY ★
John: b 8-8-1734 d 6-19-1801 m Mary Allen Pvt RI
John: b 4-23-1711 d 1-2-1800 m Elizabeth Foster Dep RI
John: b 1742 d 5-6-1796 m Elizabeth Nichols PS RI
John: b 4-4-1755 d 3-21-1824 m Esther Holmes Pvt VT
John: b 1730 d 1793 m Susanna Blackwell Col VA
John: b 1752 d p. 9-4-1849 m Nancy Obenchain Pvt VA ★
John Thompson: bpt 7-15-1753 d 8-2-1828 m Jane Davis Capt SC
Jonas: b 3-15-1731 d 6-30-1814 m (1)Jemima Holden (2)Abigail Nevers Pvt MA
Jonathan: b 4-30-1749 d 6-30-1807 m (1)Margaret Budlong (2)Penelope — Capt RI
Joseph: b 2-2-1756 d 6-28-1826 m Lydia Graves Pvt CT
Joseph: b 1-5-1760 d 1-4-1826 m Sarah Clements Cpl MD
Joseph: b 1754 d 6-12-1835 m Mehitable Beall Pvt MA
Joseph, Sr.: b 1735 d 4-6-1801 m Martha Sprague Cpl MA
Joseph: b 12-30-1754 d 10-25-1815 m Lucy Bent Pvt MA
Joseph: b 1739 d 5-28-1822 m Mary Wolcott Mid NH ★
Joseph: b 1-21-1757 d 12-3-1843 m Ann Frazier Pvt NJ
Joseph: b 1-23-1744 d 9-26-1803 m (1)Sarah Whitfield (2)Hannah Gray Haywood (3)Asa Wallace Capt PS NC
Joseph: b 1720 d 1802 m (1)Margaret Abbott (2)Mary Irwin Capt PS PA
Joseph: b 2-26-1767 d 4-16-1852 m (1)Rebecca — (2)Lucy Miller Pvt PA ★
Joseph: b 1758/59 d 1827 m Deborah Clark Pvt RI
Joseph: b 3-20-1745 d 3-25-1825 m Patience Sheffield Sgt RI ★
Joseph: b 2-19-1728 d 1824 m (1)Phoebe Langford (2)Mrs Moon PS Grd RI
Joseph: b 4-27-1740 d p. 1790 m Sarah — Pvt VT
Joseph: b 1754 d 11-24-1832 m Sally — Pvt VA
Joshua: b 4-17-1744 d p. 1796 m Esther Cutler Pvt MA
Joshua: b p. 1750 d c. 1825 m Mary — Pvt PA
Josiah: b 3-5-1735 d 7-30-1814 m (1)Elizabeth Green (2)Sarah Skinner Capt MA
Josiah: 1750 d p. 1791 m Mary Jones Pvt NC
Lemuel: b 9-18-1749 d 1-21-1818 m Sarah May — Pvt MA
Leven: b 1749 d 9-16-1830 m Mary Ellis Mil VA PA
Levi: b 6-6-1758 d 6-24-1851 m Asenath Robinson Pvt PS MA NY
Lewis: b 5-5-1751 d 1835 m Esther Kilgore Pvt VA ★
Lodowick: b 11-15-1759 d p. 1840 m Judith (Judah) Hall Pvt RI ★
Luke: b 9-18-1751 d 1801 m Lois Greene Sgt RI
Mansir: b 10-1-1753 d — m Zilpa Nichols Pvt RI
Mark Wentworth: b 1762 d 9-18-1857 m (1)Polly Hill (2)Nancey Harvey Pvt MA ★
McKeen: b 10-11-1761 d 4-8-1838 m (1)Ellen McCall (2)Frances Dubose Pvt GA NC SC ★
Morris: b 5-26-1751 d 4-21-1801 m Elizabeth Mather Pvt NY
Moses: b 2- -1758 d 1825 m Elizabeth Pede Pvt VA
Nathan: b 1745 d 6-16-1822 m Abigail Williams Sgt MA
Nathaniel: b 1758 d 4-15-1823 m (1)Elizabeth Hall (2)Sarah Rogers Sgt NY
Nathaniel: b 5-27-1742 d 6-19-1786 m Katherine Littlefield MGen RI
Nathaniel: b 6-4-1718 d 9-2-1809 m (1)Alice Lee (2)Mary — Sgt PS CS RI
Nehemiah: b 1753 d 1833 m Pheobe Kirk Pvt PA
Noah: b 8-20-1761 d 12-31-1833 m (1)Becky Converse (2)Sally Davis (3)Betsey Harwood Pvt MA ★
Obadiah: b 5-14-1760 d 1830 m Jerusha Perry Cpl NY
Obadiah: b 9-24-1754 d 7-29-1836 m Submit — Pvt CT ★
Oliver: b 9-10-1740 d 1-22-1778 m Penelope Wells Sgt RI
Oliver: b 2-8-1757 d 10-12-1812 m Judith Giles Pvt RI
Paul: b 2-25-1736 d 12-2-1817 m Sarah Hall Pvt RI
Peleg: b 7-24-1747 d 11-12-1835 m Lucy Green Pvt RI
Perry: b 2-20-1762 d 4-12-1832 m Sarah Nichols Pvt NY
Peter: b 10-1-1745 d 3-31-1828 m (1)Martha Clark (2)Ruth Ayer Dr NH
Peter: b 1736 d 8-3-1803 m Susanna King Pvt NY

GREEN, contd.

Peter: b 1748 d 8-11-1801 m Hannah King Pvt NY
Peter: b 1-18-1752 d 4-3-1834 m Sarah Davis Sgt RI ★
Peter: b 10- -1725 d 10-20-1807 m Judith Love Pvt VA
Philip: b 9-9-1737 d 1813 m (1)Polly Hicks (2)Desire Potter Pvt NY
Philip: b 3-15-1705 d 4-10-1791 m Elizabeth Wickes CS RI
Pliny: b 5-17-1761 d 5-20-1813 m Mercy Upham Pvt MA
Ralph: b — d 1779 Sarah Leigh Slr MD
Richard: b 4-23-1733 d p. 1790 m Sarah Scottow Pvt MA
Richard: b — d 1805 m Eva Gates Pvt NY
Richard: b 10- -1725 d 6-19-1779 m Sarah Fry PS RI
Richard: b 1755 d 1819 m Sarah Virginia — Pvt VA
Robert: b c. 1724 d a. 3-25-1800 m Sarah Rogers Pvt MA
Robert: b c. 1750 d 1782 m Jane Buchanan Pvt PA
Robert: b c. 1754 d 1825 m — Stackhouse Pvt PA
Robert: b c. 1722 d p. 1777 m Mary Ball PS VA
Roswell: b 4-2-1761 d 5-30-1862 m Zebrah Abbey Pvt CT ★
Russel: b 12-27-1760 d 10-6-1833 m Patience Moon Pvt MA
Samuel: b 1-24-1753 d p. 1790 m Anna Clark Pvt CT
Samuel: b 1-14-1762 d 11-30-1843 m Mary Jones Pvt CT ★
Samuel, Jr.: b 12-4-1744 d 2-13-1799 m Abigail Buel PS CT
Samuel: b 1727 d 2-20-1811 m Zerviah Dana Lt MA
Samuel: b 3-21-1760 d 8-18-1841 m Abigail Slate Pvt MA
Samuel: b 6-23-1761 d p. 1791 m Hannah — Pvt MA
Samuel: b 3-1-1723 d 8-21-1807 m Jane White Pvt MA
Samuel Harris: b 3-24-1745 d a. 1826 m Elizabeth Roads QM NS MA
Silas: b 1763 d 10-1-1855 m Deborah Brown Pvt RI
Simeon: b 9-15-1729 d 9-16-1813 m Mary Shattuck Pvt MA
Stephen: b 5-29-1758 d p. 3-4-1842 m X Pvt NY ★
Stephen: b 3-13-1733 d 10-1-1819 m Mary Rhodes Ens RI
Stephen: b 1-9-1757 d 9-15-1829 m Sarah Chase Sol RI
Stephen: b 1742 d p. 7-2-1801 m Jemima Scott Pvt VA
Sylvester: b 11-3-1737 d p. 1786 m Phebe (Greene) Ens RI
Thomas: b 1740 d 1816 m Sarah Helen Wright Smn MD
Thomas: b 5-9-1731 d 1810 m Lydia Swain Ens MA
Thomas: b 1743 d 6-8-1826 m Lydia Kilbourne Cpl MA
Thomas: b 6-17-1748 d 1-13-1826 m Mary Briggs Pvt MA
Thomas: b 4-23-1759 d 1828 m Mollie Peckham Pvt MA
Thomas: b 1753 d 4-29-1813 m Lydia Foster Pvt NH
Thomas: b 5-11-1753 d 11-6-1836 m Elizabeth Whitney Pvt NY ★
Thomas: b 1760 d 1822 m Elizabeth Mathews Capt RI NC
Thomas: b 1757 d 1845 m Mildred Green Pvt NC
Thomas: b 10-11-1729 d 11-14-1813 m (1)Mary Low (2)Sarah Wickes CS RI
Thomas: b 3-21-1733 d 1-20-1816 m Amy Whipple CS RI
Thomas: b 1757 d 1825 m Jane Carol Sol SC
Thomas: b 11-19-1723 d 1805 m Martha Wills Col VA
Timothy: b 9-22-1764 d 1-11-1850 m Elizabeth Richards Pvt CT
Timothy: b 2-18-1763 d 9-1-1842 m Jane Kennedy Pvt CT ★
Timothy: b 4-2-1737 d 3-10-1796 m Rebecca Spooner PS Sol CT
Timothy, Jr.: b 1-4-1748 d 9-7-1821 m (1)Eunice Clark (2)Sybil Hastings Peck Cpl MA
Timothy, Sr.: b 8-9-1723 d 11-1-1796 m Eunice Ellsworth PS MA
Timothy: b 1733 d 2-27-1812 m (1)Effey Finney Robinson (2)Jean Edmundston (3)Mary Innes Col PA
Timothy: b 1725 d — m Silence Burlingame PS RI
Vincent: b c. 1750 d p. 3-11-1800 m Elizabeth Eagleston PS 1Lt MD
Wm.: b 5-12-1755 d 4-14-1817 m Mercy Spaulding Capt CT
Wm., b 1734 d 7- -1806 m Sarah Anne Alston Pvt GA
Wm., Jr.: b 8-3-1764 d 12-13-1819 m Ruth Hunter Pvt NC GA
Wm.: b 10-21-1735 d 4-5-1803 m Joanna Hadley Lt MA
Wm.: b 12-25-1727 d 11- -1810 m (1)Ruth Colburn (2)Hannah Wood Adj MA
Wm.: b 1753 d 3-17-1829 m Phebe Fish Pvt MA
Wm.: b 1-17-1755 d 5-1-1843 m Abigail Ames Pvt MA W★
Wm., Sr.: b 7-6-1716 d 1799 m Rebeckah Tucker Pvt MA
Wm., Jr.: b 2-25-1742 d 3-21-1800 m Lydia Watson Sgt MA
Wm.: b — d 1834 m — Sol NH
Wm.: b 1730 d 8-15-1777 m Sarah Lewis PS NJ
Wm.: b 1743 d 10-30-1815 m Phebe Moore Pvt NJ
Wm.: b 11-26-1739 d 1799 m (1)Mary Christmas (2)Ann Hunt (Macon) Alston (3)Mrs Mary VanDyke Capt NC
Wm.: b 12-19-1757 d 3-23-1803 m Mary Bradley Lt NC
Wm.: b 2-6-1762 d 3-3-1837 m Kezziah — Pvt NC ★
Wm.: b 1754 d p. 7-10-1786 m Patience Speight Sol NC
Wm.: b 1737 d 1817 m — PS NC
Wm.: b 1732 d c. 1790 m (1)Judith Rathbone (2)Sarah Cheesebrough Lt RI
Wm.: b 10-12-1746 d 1-3-1809 m Welthian Lippitt PS RI
Wm.: b 10-8-1757 d 10-6-1818 m Mary Tibbits PS RI
Wm.: b 8-16-1731 d 11-29-1809 m Catherine Ray PS RI
Wm.: b 1740 d c. 12- -1814 m Pheriby — Cav SC
Wm.: b 1756 d 1820 m Ann McClesky Pvt SC
Wm.: b 9- -1754 d 4-8-1835 m Lucy Blackwell Capt VA W★
Wm.: b 1755 d 6-2-1839 m (2)Elizabeth Drinnen Pvt VA ★
Wm.: b 1762 d 1835 m Anne Marshall Vol Mus VA
Wm. B.: b 7-29-1762 d 1-13-1837 m Rebecca (Green) Pvt NJ
Wm. Wills: b c. 1742 d p. 5-2-1811 m Martha Rowlett Col VA
Willis: b 1752 d 1813 m Sarah Reed 2Lt VA KY
Zachariah: b 1-11-1760 d 6-21-1858 m (1)Sarah Fleet (2)Abigail Howard Vol CT
Zacheus: b 3-6-1731/32 d 1-1-1802 m (1)Elizabeth Kidder (2)Mrs Elizabeth Warner Lt MA

Zebediah: b 9-11-1754 d 7-1-1822 m Sarah Cowee MM MA

GREENAWALT, (includes GREENWALD, KREENAWALT)

Abraham: b 1724 d 4-8-1815 m (1)Elizabeth Knight (2)Susan Weyland Pvt PA
Henry: b 1732 d 1-10-1811 m Efa Michael Pvt PA
Jacob, Sr.: b 9- -1720 d 12-8-1810 m Elizabeth Filhower Capt PA
Jacob, Jr.: b 2-18-1751 d 11-18-1839 m Anna Maria Stambach Capt PA ★
Johannes: b 12-18-1755 d 2-20-1826 m Anna Maria Reinhart Pvt Drm PA
John: b 10-11-1760 d 11- -1823 m Regina — Pvt PA
John Philip: b 6-17-1756 d 7-18-1834 m Catharine Schaffner Lt PA
Philip Lorentz: b 6-10-1725 d 2-28-1802 m (1)Mrs Uhland (2)Maria Margaret Foeser PS Col PA

GREENFIELD,

Enos: b 1749 d 11-23-1824 m Mary Curtis Pvt CT ★
James: b 12-25-1753 d 1-23-1812 m Margaret Sweet Pvt NY

GREENING,

James: b 3-22-1752 d 5-5-1830 m Sarah Crostwaite Pvt VA W★
John: b 8-20-1760 d 10-7-1817 m Mary Whitehead Pvt VA
Mason: b c. 1740 d p. 1775 m Margaret Haynsworth PS SC

GREENLEAF,

Benjamin: b 9-8-1759 d 11-2-1843 m Rachel Arnold Pvt MA ★
Calvin: b 3-31-1740 d 8-12-1812 m Rebecca Whitcomb Pvt MA
Daniel: b 11-7-1702 d 7-18-1795 m (1)Silence (Nichols) Marsh (2)Mrs Dorothy Richardson Grd MA
Daniel: b 9-20-1753 d 1839 m Mary Bridges Pvt MA ★
David: b 7-13-1737 d 12-11-1800 m Mary Johnson Pvt MA
David: b 3-9-1763 d 10-13-1819 m (1)Phebe Jones (2)Parmela Grove PS MA
David: b 4-28-1753 d 3-28-1835 m (4)Ruth Stockwell Hutchins Pvt NH ★
Ebenezer: b 1753 d 8-15-1817 m Elizabeth Chapman Pvt MA
Enoch: b 1751 d 12-1-1836 m Sarah Quont Pvt MA ★
Israel: b 3-29-1734 d 3-4-1824 m (1)Prudence Whitcomb (2)Ursula Woods Pvt MA
John: b 11-6-1755 d 6-5-1846 m Anna Pierce Roberts Pvt MA ★
Jonathan: b 6-9-1754 d 8-13-1801 m Joanna Manning Cpl MA
Jonathan: b 7- -1723 d 5-24-1807 m Mary Presbury PS MA
Joseph: b 11-10-1720 d 10-28-1810 m Abigail Paine PS MA
Joseph: b 1751 d 2-24-1814 m Margaret Nason Sgt MA
Moses: b 5-19-1755 d 12-18-1812 m Lydia Parsons Capt MA
Nathan: b 10-16-1761 d 6-13-1831 m Mary Clifford Pvt NH ★
Samuel: b 6-12-1718 d 1792 m Hephzibah Preble Pvt MA
Stephen: b 4-14-1749 d p. 1787 m Ann Worthington PS CT
Stephen: b 10-15-1735 d 6-8-1802 m Eunice Fairbanks PS.CS VT
Stephen, Jr.: b 1-31-1759 d 3-5-1850 m (1)Anna Stager (2)Cynthia Ryan Mus VT
Wm.: b 8-23-1738 d 1-3-1793 m Sarah Quincy LCol MA
Wm.: b 11-28-1725 d 1- -1800 m Ruth Pierson Lt MA
Wm.: b — d 1833 m Mary Soley Lt MA
Wm.: b 10-1725 d 7-21-1803 m Mary Brown CS MA

GREENLEE,

James: b 10-19-1740 d 11-8-1813 m (1)Mary Mitchell (2)Ruth Howard Sol NC
John: b 10-4-1738 d p. 11-12-1802 m Hannah McClanahan PS VA
Robert: b 1756 d p. 1782 m Elizabeth Dunlap Pvt PA
Wm.: b d 5- -1780 m Mary Thomson Pvt PA

GREENMAN,

Benjamin: b 3-9-1757 d 9-19-1841 m Lydia Brown Pvt NY
Jeremiah: b 5-7-1758 d 11-15-1828 m Mary Eddy Lt RI W★
Job: b 12-13-1742 d 11-1-1811 m Lucy Brayman Pvt RI
John: b 7-17-1762 d p. 9-4-1840 m Rachel Grover Pvt MA ★
John: b c. 1765 d 5-7-1821 m Anna Allen Lt RI
Preserved: b 1754 d 2-24-1848 m Ruth Sheldon Pvt NY
Silas: b 6-11-1724 d p. 1800 m Sarah Perkham Ens RI
Wm.: b 1738 d 2-21-1809 m (1)Susannah Gardner (2)Elizabeth Bliss Pvt NY

GREENOUGH,

Daniel: b — d — m Lydia Price Pvt VT
Ebenezer: b 2-18-1753 d 12-15-1827 m Mary Flagg Pvt MA
Joseph: b 5-3-1733 d 7-11-1809 m Sarah Feyeryear NS
Thomas: b 5-6-1710 d 8-10-1785 m (1)Martha Clark (2)Sarah Stodd PS MA
Wm.: b 12-9-1751 d 6-6-1836 m Hannah Wells Drm NH ★

GREENSLIT,

Benjamin: b 1763 d 6-22-1828 m (1)Olive Hebard (2)Martha Cary Pvt CT ★
Elijah: b 8-3-1742/43 d 1809 m Mary Burnham Pvt CT
Joel: b 9-30-1745 d 2-26-1840 m Hannah Kingsbury Sgt CT
John: b —1767 d 4-1-1856 m Saloma Pitts Pvt CT ★

GREENTREE,

Benjamin: b 5-16-1760 d 3-29-1839 m Mary Cash Pvt PA ★

GREENUP,
Christopher: b 1750 d 4-27-1818 m Catherine Pope 1Lt VA
John: b — d p. 9-10-1826 m (2)Elizabeth Witten PS VA

GREENWAY,
William: b 1756 d 4-3-1839 m — Humphreys Pvt PS VA ★

GREENWELL,
Ignatius: b 12-23-1754 d 9-6-1847 m (2)Monica Roack Pvt MD ★

GREENWOOD,
Abel: b 12-25-1755 d 11-29-1837 m Sally Homer PS Drm MA W★
Ajijah: b 1749 d 1-9-1814 m (1)Rhoda Pond (2)Elizabeth Marean Cpl MA
Asa: b 1-12-1762 d 8-16-1823 m Betsy Davis Pvt MA
Bartlee: b 7-18-1764 d 9-28-1837 m Nancy Sublet Pvt VA CL ★
Bela: b 4-4-1760 d 5-9-1838 m Mary Babcock Mus MA
Daniel, Sr.: b 11-27-1704 d 9-25-1775 m Sarah Adams CS MA
Daniel, Jr.: b 6-15-1732 d 6-12-1812 m Jerusha Eaton PS CS MA
Isaac: b 8-13-1759 d 1-19-1832 m Abigail Jackson Pvt MA
James: b 10-2-1730 d 1-18-1809 m Lydia King Capt MA
John: b 5-17-1760 d 11-16-1819 m Elizabeth Weaver Pvt Mus MA
John: b 1-6-1739 d p. 1780 m (1)Rebeccah Hunt (2)Ann Peck Pvt MA
John: b 9-2-1750 d 4-6-1807 m Lucy Whittemore Pvt MA
Jonathan: b 11-12-1755 d 12-20-1821 m Sibbel Holbrook Cpl MA
Joseph: b 1-9-1723 d 12-27-1825 m Sarah Greenwood CS NH
Joshua: b 7-26-1757 d 10-23-1839 m Abigail Bird Pvt MA
Joshua: b c. 1758 d 1830 m Hannah Twitchell Pvt NH
Moses: b 1752 d 3-8-1827 m Betsey Dunlap Pvt MA
Nevinson: b 10-22-1751 d 6- -1805 m Elizabeth Kendrick Pvt MA
Philip: b 11-28-1755 d 9-5-1842 m Sarah — Pvt MD ★
Samuel: b c. 1740-60 d a. 11-25-1809 m (2)Sebel Street Sol PS VA
Thomas: b 1757 d p. 1802 m Mary Goodrich Cpl MA
Thomas: b 12-7-1750 d 3-23-1826 m Deborah Barbour Pvt MA
Thomas: b c. 1730-35 d c. 1811 m Jane — PS VA
Wm.: b 11-4-1721 d 6-28-1782 m Abigail Death Pvt NH

GREEVER,
Philip: b 11-2-1745 d 3-26-1830 m Margaret Bosang Sol VA

GREGG,
Alexander: b 2-9-1755 d 4-1-1830 m Sarah Adams Ens NH
Andrew: b 5- -1763 d 4-25-1846 m Nancy Santee Pvt PA
David: b 1727 d 1797 m Annie Clyde Vol NH
Henry: b 5-4-1763 d 3-31-1848 m Elizabeth Jones Lt SC
Hugh: b 9-5-1754 d 4- -1814 m Lucy Gary Pvt NH
Hugh: b 1730 d p. 1776 m Sarah Leslie PS NH
James: b 12-22-1725 d 3-16-1819 m Mary McCurdy Pvt PS NH
James: b 1728 d a. 1790 m Agnes Smith PS PA
James: b 1752 d p. 1790 m Mary Wilson Capt SC
John: b 1702 d 2-28-1789 m (1)Agnes Rankin (2)Rosanna PS NH
John: b 1749 d 5- -1803 m Jenett Waugh Pvt NH
John: b 12-10-1758 d 2-14-1835 m Mary Taylor Capt NY
John: b 7-12-1755 d 3-29-1808 m Orpha Stubbs Lt PA
John, Sr.: b a. 1732 d p. 1775 m Eleanor — PS SC
John, Jr.: b c. 1754 d p. 1790 m Eleanor McKnight Lt SC
John: b 10-15-1747 d a. 1803 m Sarah — Pvt VA
John: b c. 1755 d 1813 m Hannah Steer Pvt VA
Joseph: b 1740 d 3-6-1804 m Susanna Aiken Lt NH
Joseph: b 1763 d 1840 m Sally Reynolds PS NH
Joseph: b 1740 d 1822 m — Atkins PS SC
Matthew: b 7- -1745 d 3-30-1832 m Nancy Gipson Pvt VA
Reuben: b 1754 d 8-2-1840 m (2)Mary Houston Pvt NH
Richard: b 3-5-1752 d 11-15-1812 m Ann Gregg Pvt PA
Robert: b c. 1732 d 1796 m — Harrison Pvt VA
Samuel: b — d 1-11-1830 m Dinah Chandler Pvt DE
Samuel: b 4- -1739 d 12-10-1808 m Agnes Smiley Maj NH
Samuel: b 1740 d 1809 m Margaret Wallace Pvt PS NH
Samuel: b c. 1705 d 10-1-1778 m Mary Moor PS NH
Samuel: b 12-29-1757 d p. 1838 m Jane — Sol VA
Wm.: b 10-23-1730 d 9-16-1815 m Barbara Aiken Col NH
Wm.: b 7-3-1744 d 10-18-1817 m Isabel Dunlap CS NH

GREGORY,
Abijah: b 12-14-1747 d 1788 m Molly Thorpe Pvt CT
Abraham: b 10-15-1752 d 6-19-1790 m Dorothy Lockwood Capt CT
Asahel: b 1759 d 1842 m Sevia Parks Mus & Sgt MA ★
Bry: b c. 1761 d 1- -1846 m X Pvt NC ★
Daniel: b 7-22-1754 d 7-16-1843 m Phebe Burton Cpl CT ★
Daniel: b 5-29-1734 d p. 1800 m Hannah Smith Pvt NY
Daniel: b 11-13-1752 d 11-13-1817 m Elizabeth (Gregory) Sol NY
Elias: b 10-13-1750 d 6-24-1842 m Elizabeth Raymond Pvt CT ★
Elijah: b 1750 d 1777 m — Corruth Pvt CT
Hezekiah: b 5-13-1752 d 11- -1834 m Abigail Benedict Pvt CT
Jabez: b 2- -1741 d 10-24-1824 m Mercy St John Capt CT
James: b 3-10-1752 d 9-17-1790 m Mary Wynne CS NC
James b c. 1732 d p. 1790 m Agnes Trindle SubLt PA
James: b 5- -1752 d 11-30-1838 m Eleanor Dyche Pvt VA
Jehiel: b 1755 d 4-12-1818 m Elizabeth Andrews Pvt NY
Jeremiah: b a. 1765 d p. 11-28-1828 m Ann — Cav SC

Jesse: b a. 1745 d p. 7-2-1792 m Marcy — Pvt NC
John: b 1729 d 8-10-1812 m Phebe Hawley Pvt CT
John: b 12-25-1755 d 5-4-1808 m (1)Sarah Fairchild (2)Nancy Dickinson (3)Betsey Betts Pvt CT
John: b c. 1705 d 1786 m Mary Smith PS CT
John: b 8-22-1761 d 10-29-1852 m Sarah Robbins Pvt NJ
John: b 1752 d 1825 m Mary Elizabeth Hamilton QM NY
John: b 9-16-1751 d 12-24-1835 m Maria Elizabeth — Capt PA ★
John: b 1752 d 1-18-1841 m Elizabeth Way Sgt PA ★
John, Jr.: b 10-2-1747 d 9-11-1777 m Martha Terrill Lt VA
John, Sr.: b — d — m — Cary Capt VA
John: b 1758 d 5-24-1844 m Barbary Ann Hooper Pvt VA ★
Joseph: b 1737 d 11-10-1800 m (1)Mary Morehouse (2)Anna (Bartlett) Jewett Ens NY
Joshua: b 9-9-1752 d 1840 m Lucy Vail Pvt NY ★
Mark: b 1745 d p. 1778 m Margaret Harvey Pvt PA
Matthew: b 8-13-1759 d 6-4-1848 m Mary DeForest Lt CT
Moses: b 9-13-1762 d 5-23-1837 m Abigail — Pvt CT ★
Nathan: b 1732/3 d p. 1790 m Sarah St. John Pvt CT
Nathaniel: b 10-13-1760 d 4-12-1851 m Betty Porter Pvt CT
Phineas: b 1743 d 12-2-1821 m Elizabeth Hobbs Pvt MA
Richard: b 1-12-1758 d 12-20-1844 m (1)Mary (Ward) Brodnax (2)Elizabeth Wilkinson PS VA
Roger: b 5-1-1729 d 10-2-1803 m (1)Mary Cole Claiborne (2)Fanny (Garland) Loury CS VA
Samuel: b c. 1723 d 9-4-1783 m (1)Eunice Starr (2)Mrs Rachel Starr PS CT
Samuel, Jr.: b 5-18-1712 d 7-6-1836 m Charity Edwards Pvt CT W★
Samuel: b 1750 d 1828 m Martha Gregory Pvt NY
Samuel: b 1761 d 1842 m Sarah Davis Pvt VA
Silas: b 4-7-1762 d 4-18-1809 m (2)Sarah Olmstead Pvt CT W★
Stephen: b 12- -1751 d 12-2-1817 m Rhoda Hall 3Lt CT
Stephen: b 4-7-1738 d 1802 m Mary Benedict Pvt CT
Stephen: b 2-10-1754 d p. 5-13-1833 m Elizabeth Carter Pvt CT ★
Thomas: b 1759 d p. 5-16-1843 m (1)Director Hall (2)Bettie Toller Pvt Wgn NC ★
Thomas: b 1748 d p. 1828 m Patience Nolly Pvt NC ★
Thomas: b 8-2-1750 d 3-25-1843 m (1)Elizabeth LaPrade (2)Elizabeth Baker Pvt Arfr VA ★
Uriah: b 3-21-1754 d 10-2-1844 m Tamor Rowland OrdlSgt CT NY ★
Wm.: b 7-8-1764 d 10-4-1835 m Mary Sherwood Pvt CT ★
Wm.: b 1731 d 3- -1824 m Experience Robbins Pvt Slr MA
Wm.: b 8-11-1757 d 7-10-1836 m Margaret Price Pvt NC ★
Wm.: b 5- -1764 d 9-30-1852 m Martha Bledsoe Pvt NC

GREIDER, (includes GRIDER)
Henry: b 5-9-1755 d 2-5-1843 m Elizabeth Smith Spy Lt VA W★
John: b 7-11-1755 d 10-3-1838 m Isobel Blair Pvt Spy NC
John: b 2-17-1761 d 3-15-1830 m Magdalena Hertzler Pvt PA
Martin: b 1740 d a. 11-26-1785 m Elizabeth — PS PA

GREIM,
John: b 1717 d 1790 m Barbara Webber Pvt PA

GREINER,
Adam: b 6-17-1731 d 5-22-1803 m Catherine — Pvt PA
George: b 1764 d 1828 m Katherine Whitsel Pvt PA
Martine: b 9-10-1758 d 4-5-1841 m Margaretta — Pvt PA
Philip: b 3-12-1749 d 12-2-1822 m Barbara Fishburn Pvt PA
Valentine: b c. 1727 d 8-12-1794 m Barbara — Pvt PA

GRESHAM, (includes GRISSOM)
Ambrose: b 1757 d 1815 m Ann — Sgt VA
John: b 1-24-1759 d 9-19-1818 m Martha W Scott Pvt VA
John: b 3-14-1761 d 6-22-1835 m Martha Halbert Pvt VA ★
Oliver: b c. 1757 d p. 8-13-1830 m Diannah — PS NC
Thomas: b 1761 d 1816 m Mary Thornton Pvt VA
Thomas: b c. 1750 d c. 1803 m Dorcas Lane CS VA

GRESS,
Valentine: b c. 1758 d 1796 m Mrs Elizabeth Butt Pvt PA

GRESSETT,
Wm.: b a. 1758 d c. 1783 m Elizabeth Funchess Col SC

GREVES,
Thomas: b 1746 d 10-1-1802 m Deborah Powell Pvt NY

GRICE, (includes GRISE)
Francis: b 9-22-1726 d 10-9-1798 m Mary Brockenborough 1Lt PA
John: b c. 1745 d c. 1779 m Margaret — Pvt PA
Joseph: b 12-23-1759 d p. 1784 m Mary Smith Gnr PA
Wm.: b 5-10-1764 d c. 9-4-1839 m Patsey Hall Pvt NC ★

GRIDLEY,
Abel: b 9-28-1729 d 2-24-1808 m Hannah Clark Pvt CT
Asahel: b 10-13-1757 d 11-16-1833 m Chloe Hungerford FifMaj CT W★
Asahel: b 3-10-1763-65 d 5-15-1814 m Elizabeth Percival Pvt CT
Elijah: b 3-18-1760 d 5-9-1845 m (1)Sarah Goodman (2)Abigail Eliza — Pvt CT ★
Elisha: b 3-24-1759 d 12-30-1842 m Lois Hopkins Pvt CT ★
Elnathan: b 1726 d 8-9-1781 m Sarah Pratt Lt CT

GRIDLEY, contd.

Hezekiah, Sr.: b c. 7-27-1701 d 7-21-1776 m Sarah Newell PS CT
Hezekiah, Jr.: b 1-3-1732 d 2-18-1816 m Abigail Peck Capt CT
Hosea: b c. 1761 d 12-24-1839 m Sabra E Gridley Pvt Mus CT ★
Isaiah: b 1761 d 3- -1813 m Lucy Lindsley Pvt PA
Judah: b 1-14-1751 d p. 1792 m Katharine VanGelder Sol CT
Noadiah: b 5-27-1750 d 1816 m Rhoda (Woodruff) Brace Pvt CT
Rezin: b 1734 d 2-1-1809 m Sarah Hopkins Capt CT
Samuel: b 1-5-1696/97 d 3-4-1776 m (1)Abigail Sharp (2)Mary George (3)Abigail Baker CS MA
Silas: b 11-7-1757 d 2-28-1839 m Elizabeth Benton Pvt CT
Theodore: b 1759 d 2-26-1826 m (1)Ruth Lewis (3)Amy Lewis Pvt CT
Thomas: b 4-19-1761 d 8-17-1846 m Sallie Barnes Pvt CT ★
Wm., Sr.: b 11-10-1731 d 12-10-1786 m Lydia Blaney Grd MA

GRIEGAR,

George: b 3-12-1727 d 10-4-1818 m Catherine — PS PA

GRIER, (includes GREER, GREIR)

Aaron: b c. 1757 d 1824 m Jean Gibson Pvt GA
Andrew: b c. 1730 d 2- -1810 m (1)Ruth Kincade (2)Mary Vance PS CS TN
Aquila: b 1719 d p. 4-8-1790 m Elizabeth — PS VA
Benjamin: b 2-9-1746 d 10-23-1816 m (1)Nancy Wilcocksen (2)— Cutbirth Pvt NC
George: b c. 1750-55 d c. 1786 m Catherine (Ingham) Pvt PA
Gilbert: b 1760 d a. 4-23-1800 m Frances M — Pvt GA
Henry: b c 1750-5 d 8- -1813 m Charity Ann Mansfield 1Lt PA
Isaac: b 1763 d 8-23-1814 m Elizabeth Cooper Pvt PA
James: b 2-3-1751 d 11-30-1823 m (1)Jane Kinkaid (2)Elizabeth Little Pvt PA
James: b 1-15-1742 d p. 6-13-1825 m Anne (Haynes) Lowe Lt VA
John: b 1743/44 d 6-11-1814 m Jane Stewart Sol PA
John: b 1762 d 7-24-1812 m Sarah — Pvt PA
John: b 1714 d 12-31-1784 m Agnes Caldwell PS PA
John: b c. 1762 d 1836 m Jane McCreary Pvt SC
John: b 1753 d 10-3-1846 m Jane Callaghan Sol VA
Joseph: b 1756 d 1829 m Jane Buchanan Pvt NJ
Joseph: b 8-8-1754 d 2-23-1831 m Mary Ann Harmon Pvt NC
Joseph: b 2- -1750 d 11-10-1830 m Ann Walker Lt PA
Matthew: b 1714 d 9-7-1792 m Jane Caldwell Capt CS PA
Moses: b 1759 d 8-11-1837 m X Pvt NC GA ★
Moses: b 6-2-1744 d 5-10-1834 m Nancy Bailey Capt VA ★
Robert: b 1-20-1755 d 8-6-1822 m Margaret Livingston Lt NC
Robert: b 10-27-1762 d 9-2-1827 m Elizabeth H — Sol SC
Samuel: b 4- -1750 d 5-26-1833 m Mary McCracken Pvt PA ★
Samuel: b c. 1758 d p. 4-26-1820 m Rebecca Howard Pvt PA
Thomas: b 11-2-1763 d 10-6-1823 m Letitia Grier Sol GA
Thomas: b 6-24-1744 d 1-27-1828 m (1)Hannah — (2)Susannah Spratt PS NC ★
Thomas: b 1756 d 10-20-1839 m Johanna Hamilton Pvt NC PA ★
Thomas, Sr.: b c. 1730-40 d p. 11-10-1810 m Sarah — PS SC
Wm., Sr.: b 9-9-1754 d 8-27-1821 m Sarah Corry Sol GA
Wm.: b — d a. 12-6-1786 m Mary — Cav PS SC
Wm.: b 1741 d c. 1788 m Mary McCurdy Pvt SC

GRIESEMER, (includes GREISEMER, GRISEMORE)

Abraham: b 1759 d 7-26-1821 m Catherine Fogel 1Sgt PA
Casper: b c. 1720 d 1794 m Rebecca Ashman PS PA
Jacob: b c. 1755 d 12- -1825 m Christina Rhoads Capt PA
Jacob: b 1738 d 1815 m Elizabeth — 2Lt PA
John: b 1717 d 10-10-1789 m Anna Maria Brunner PS PA
Peter: b 11-28-1751 d 10-2-1811 m Esther Hoch Pvt PS PA

GRIESS, (or GRIES)

Johann Dietrich: b 11-10-1754 d 11-26-1833 m Maria Magdalena Graff Pvt PA

GRIFFEE,

Jonathan: b c. 1745 d p. 1- -1800 m Agnes — Pvt FrA

GRIFFIN, (includes GRIFFEN, GRIFFING, GRIFFITH)

Anthony: b 1745 d 1807 m Mary Ann Pinckney Cook PS SC
Benjamin: b a. 1755 d 1811 m Abigail — Sol NC
Benoni: b 1714-16 d 2-13-1801 m Mrs Mary DeLacy Griffin PS CT
Charles: b 12-1-1734 d 8-1-1832 m Ann Hyatt Pvt PA
Charles: b 6-23-1763 d 8-9-1820 m Mary King Pvt SC
Corbin: b c. 1730 d 1816 m Mary Berkeley PS VA
Cyrus: b 1748 d 12-10-1810 m Christina Stuart PS VA
Daniel: b 1736 d 6-2-1822 m Martha Case Capt NY ★
Daniel: b 1755/56 d p. 1830 m (2)Mary Mitchell Pvt NC
Eliphalet: b 6-8-1760 d 2-4-1798 m Sarah Beckett Pvt MA
George: b 1734 d 8-6-1814 m Eve Dorr Pvt CT
Hugh: b c. 1755 d a. 1812 m Mary Parker PS NC
Isaac: b 2-27-1751 d 10-12-1827 m Mary Morris Capt DE
Jacob: b 1731 d 1800 m Ruth Woolsey LtCol NY
James: b 10-14-1739 d 12-10-1824 m Deziah Terry Pvt NY
James: b 1753 d 12-19-1836 m Sarah Lodge Cpl NC ★
James: b a. 1755 d p. 1800 m Hannah — Pvt PA
James: b 1765/66 d p. 9-17-1850 m Delphia Adams Pvt VA
Jasper: b 3-29-1748 d 11-30-1807 m Jemimah Vaill PS NY CT
Jesse: b 1749 d 1799 m Ann Clary Pvt NC

John: b 1725 d 1819 m Dinah Smith Lt CT
John: b 11-8-1726 d 7-16-1801 m Mary Rogers Mar CT
John: b c. 1745 d 8-16-1780 m Elizabeth Ray Pvt GA
John: b 9-3-1740 d p. 5-25-1815 m Mary Ann Andrews Sol GA
John: b 7-25-1740 d 7-22-1787 m Hannah Gerrish 1Lt NH
John: b 1743 d 1840 m Mary — Pvt SC
John: b 1753 d 9-15-1838 m Cynthia Calvert Pvt VA ★
John: b 6- -1710 d 10-18-1777 m (1)Sarah Paine (2)Anna Swezey PS NY
Joseph: b 5-2-1736 d 12-4-1831 m (1)Rebecca Sawyer (2)Abigail Currier Sgt MA
Joseph: b 11-20-1727 d 12-31-1788 m Sarah Brown Pvt NY
Joseph: b 1761 d 6- -1853 m Rhaunea Peck Pvt NY
Joseph: b 8-9-1763 d 10-3-1850 m (1)Emily Burns (2)Jane Smith (3)Nancy Black Pvt SC ★
Joshua: b 11-8-1755 d 3-16-1841 m Jane Losee Pvt NY
Joshua: b 3-8-1758 d 6-11-1840 m Ann — Pvt NY ★
Lemuel, Jr.: b 1738 d 7-9-1810 m Lydia Willey PS CT
Mark: b c. 1760 d p. 1788 m Polly Simmons Pvt MD
Martin: b 1755 d 12-19-1830 m Anna Brown Pvt CT ★
Micah: b 1737 d 8-6-1815 m Theodosha Phelps Lt CT
Michael: b c. 1758 d c. 1804 m Ann Weldon Pvt GA
Moses: b 9-6-1745 d 7-7-1802 m Sarah Stillwell Mil NCapt PS PA NJ
Nathan: b 1759 d 6-18-1837 m Sarah Sterait Pvt MD ★
Nathaniel: b 9-11-1732 d p. 1790 m Marble Noble Pvt CT
Nathaniel: b 2-4-1752 d 6-2-1790 m Sarah Reynolds Pvt MA
Nathaniel: b 4-9-1743 d 1802 m Frances Babson Matr MA
Oliver: b 9-9-1739 d 6-21-1815 m Mary Wise Sgt MA
Peter: b 9-2-1742 d 1781 m Patience Tabor Capt CT
Ralph: b 1-5-1754 d 1838 m Catherine — Pvt SC ★
Richard: b 3-27-1753 d 10-31-1833 m Sarah Batchelder Pvt PS NH
Richard: b c. 1722 d a. 12-29-1795 m Catherine Vanderhoff PS NY
Richard: b 1734 d 10-25-1805 m Nancy Ann Clark PS SC
Robert: b 1720 d 12-6-1796 m Rhoda Parmelee NCapt LI
Samuel: b a. 1740 d 1805 m (1)Mary Bartlett (2)Mehitable Turner Mus CT
Samuel: b 9-25-1710 d 1789 m (1)Elizabeth Landon (2)Martha Vaill PS CT
Samuel: b 4-18-1736 d 3-19-1812 m Rachel Clark Sgt MA
Samuel: b 1739 d 11-3-1810 m Elizabeth Braxton ADC PS VA
Sarah Stillwell: b 11-13-1753 d 5-13-1804 m Moses Griffing PS NJ
Seth: b 1747 d 3-26-1817 m Mary Brown Pvt CT
Sherrod: b 11-29-1759 d 3-17-1845 m Mary Ann Page Sgt VA ★
Stephen: b — d 1803 m Hannah — Capt CT
Stephen: b 1-22-1754 d 3-1-1841 m Elizabeth Uhl Ens NY CT ★
Theophilus: b 10-25-1754 d 9-23-1814 m Sara Martin Pvt CS PS NH
Thomas: b 10-12-1766 d 7-19-1844 m Polly Brown Pvt CT
Thomas: b 8-20-1749 d 6-26-1819 m Anna Beck Pvt MA NH ★
Thomas: b 3-9-1764 d p. 1833 m Bettie Mullis Pvt NC ★
Thomas: b c. 1745 d p. 12-16-1806 m Mary Elizabeth Mullis Pvt VA
Uriah: b 8-9-1744 d 7-20-1823 m Mary Hazeltine Sgt MA
Wm.: b c. 1740 d 10- -1800 m (1)Sarah Kirksey (2)Elizabeth Strand Pvt NC
Wm., Sr.: b 1725 d 1791 m Rachel — PS SC
Wm., Jr.: b 1754 d p. 9-7-1840 m Nancy — Pvt SC ★

GRIFFIS, (includes GRIFFIN)

Abner: b 3-7-1754 d 5-10-1841 m Martha Cunningham Cpl NY ★
Benjamin: b c. 1739 d p. 3-16-1809 m (2)Polly Robinson (3)Mary — Pvt VT
Charles: b 1755 d 8-10-1844 m Mrs Charity Rich Sol SC
Williams, Sr.: b 2-7-1763 d 1845 m Content Harris Pvt NY ★
Zachariah P.: b 7-5-1750 d 1832 m X Pvt VA ★

GRIFFITH, (includes GRIFFETHS, GRIFFITHS)

Abraham: b 1-10-1745 d 6-21-1841 m Elizabeth Oug Pvt PA
Benjamin: b a. 1760 d 1840 m Rachel Morrell Pvt MD
Benjamin: b 11-22-1732 d p. 1781 m Mary Riggs PS MD
Benjamin: b 12-29-1747 d p. 1811 m Elizabeth Ellis Pvt NJ
Charles Greenberry: b 5-17-1744 d 1792 m Sarah Ridgeley Col MD
Daniel: b 7-8-1726 d c. 1790 m (1)Mary Edwards (2)Mary Eldredge 3Sgt PS CS MA
Dennis: b 3-19-1759 d 1805 m Elizabeth Ridgely Ens MD
Eli: b 3-9-1750 d p. 1833 m Amy — Pvt CT NY
George: b c. 1748 d p. 1790 m Mary — PS MD
Greenberry: b 12-31-1727 d 3-1-1809 m Ruth Riggs PS MD
Henry, Sr.: b 2-14-1720 d 9-28-1794 m (1)Elizabeth Dorsey (2)Ruth Hammond PS CS MD
Henry, Jr.: b 3-16-1744/45 d 4-14-1809 m (1)Sarah Warfield (2)Sara Davis PS 1Lt MD
Hezekiah: b 11-25-1752 d 1825 m Catherine Warfield 1Lt MD
Howard: b 6-18-1757 d 1-4-1834 m Jemima Jacobs Ens MD
Howell: b c. 1735 d p. 1790 m (1)Alice Lunn (2)Elizabeth Pugh Pvt PA
Isaac: b 7-17-1764 d 1834 m Ann Elliott Pvt PA
James: b 6-2-1758 d p. 1791 m Sarah Totten Pvt NY
Jeremiah: b 7-28-1758 d 6-11-1842 m Mary Cropsy Pvt NY CT ★
John: b 1752 d 1799 m X Lt MD
John: b c. 1730 d c. 1812 m Nancy Moore Ens MD
John: b a. 1738 d 1- -1792 m Ruth — MM MD

John: b *c.* 1744 d *c.* 1809 m Anne Mucklerath Pvt NC
John: b *c.* 1740 d *c.* 1815 m Abigail Camp Sol NJ
John: b 8-24-1737 d 1-22-1833 m (1)Mary Faulkner (2)Mary Ellis Pvt PA
John: b *c.* 1740 d 1-16-1792 m X Pvt PA
John: b 1747 d 1842 m (1)Alice Folkner (2)Lydia Wilson Pvt PA
John: b 1756 d 1851 m Anne Francis Pvt VA
Joseph: b 10-31-1745 d *p.* 1786 m Mary Thornton 2Lt PA
Joseph: b 12-1-1743 d 1839/40 m Mary Patterson Pvt PA
Joseph: b 3-8-1757 d 12-23-1810 m Mary Ann Boulware Capt SC
Joseph: b 11-17-1759 d 12-12-1800 m (2)Polly Webb Pvt VA ★
Joshua: b 1763 d 8-22-1819 m Charity Schofield Pvt NY
Moses: b *c.* 1730 d *a.* 4- -1800 m Eleanor Ellegood CS VA
Nathan: b 3-4-1759 d *p.* 1836 m Elizabeth Ensor MM Pvt MD ★
Nathan: b 1759/60 d 8-13-1852 m Mary — Pvt MA ★
Paul: b 5-29-1762 d 1-2-1857 m Margaret Burden Pvt RI CT ★
Philemon: b 8-29-1756 d 4-29-1838 m Elinor Jacobs Maj MD ★
Roger: b *c.* 1740 d 1796 m Faithy Wall Maj NC
Salathial: b 9-11-1738 d *p.* 7-18-1792 m (1)Nancy Owens (2)Martha Braton PS MD
Samuel: b 4-7-1781 d 1-8-1803 m (1)Frenettah Garretson (2)Mrs Presbury Capt PS MD
Samuel: b 5-7-1752 d 5-12-1833 m (1)Rachal Warfield (2)Ruth Berry QM Capt MD ★
Samuel: b *c.* 1787 m (1)Amy George (2)Mary Littler Pvt PA
Samuel: b 1737 d *p.* 1828 m Mary Drake Bevan Pvt PA
Samuel J.: b 6-13-1755 d 12-25-1838 m — Green OrdlSgt NY ★
Southward: b 3-1-1760 d 7-11-1837 m (1)Hannah Tyler (2)Abigail Baker Pvt RI ★
Thomas: b *c.* 1750 d *p.* 1804 m Mary — PS MD
Thomas: b 7-29-1763 d 5-1-1847 m Dorcas Warren Pvt NY VT ★
Thomas: b 4-2-1757 d 4-26-1835 m Mary March Pvt PA VA NJ ★
Wm.: b 1745 d 1821/22 m Hannah (Griffith) Pvt MD
Wm., Jr.: b 1760 d 10-9-1838 m Mary Childs Pvt NY ★
Wm.: b *a.* 1752 d *a.* 4-16-1805 m Freelove Eckle Sol NY
Wm.: b 11-13-1742 d 6-5-1832 m Sarah Hammond Sol PA
Wm.: b 1760 d 1800 m Sarah Baker Sol VA
Zadock: b 7-24-1755 d 3-6-1844 m Susanna Hunter Pvt MD ★

GRIGGS, (includes GRIGG)
Abner: b 1720 d 1795 m Mary Stokes Pvt VA
Benjamin: b *a.* 1750 d 1801 m Jerusha Johnson Pvt MA
Burwell: b 1755 d 1837 m Sabra Elam Lt VA
Burwell: b 4-28-1741 d 1808 m Mary Carroll Ens VA
Frederick: b *c.* 1740 d *p.* 1-1-1805 m Martha — 2Lt PS VA
Henry: b 12-30-1758 d 9-3-1844 m Elizabeth Bush Pvt CS CT ★
Ichabod, Sr.: b 3-8-1718 d 5-9-1790 m Sarah Hatch CS PS CT
Ichabod, Jr.: b 6-7-1744 d 9-30-1776 m Mercy Hatch Sgt CT
Jesse: b 1732 d 1784 m Nancy Webb PS VA
John: b 1757 d 1825 m Fannie Rushing Pvt NC
Joseph: b 10-12-1748 d *p.* 1792 m Rebekah Chaffee Cpl CT
Joseph: b 3-12-1750 d 12-4-1840 m (1)Penelope Goodell (2)Mrs Hannah Hammond OrdlSgt CT ★
Joshua: b 1-8-1743 d 9-9-1813 m Joanna Chapman Adj CS CT
Matthew: b 1746 d 3-30-1832 m Ann Gibson Pvt VA
Moses: b 5- -1755 d 12-14-1830 m Margaret Conley Pvt MA
Samuel: b 12-23-1753 d 1-16-1814 m Beulah Hammond Sgt MA
Solomon: b 1843 d — m Elizabeth Gridley Pvt CT
Stephen: b 6-21-1742 d 10-15-1786 m Sarah Chandler Ens CT
Thomas, Sr.: b 2-25-1715 d 7-17-1782 m Margaret Williams Cpl MA
Thomas, Jr.: b 4-20-1750 d 1800 m Mary Goddard Sgt MA
Thomas: b 11-23-1756 d 2-25-1828 m Catherine Perrine Pvt NJ
Wm.: b *c.* 1740 d 1790 m Mary — QM VA
Wm.: b 1- -1740 d 1779 m Miss Gardiner Pvt VA
Wm.: b 12-3-1746 d *p.* 1802 m Charlotte Williamson Pvt VA

GRIGSBY,
Enoch: b 1715 d 12- -1794 m Mary Butler Lt SC
James: b 11-10-1748 d 2- -1835 m (1)Frances Porter (2)Mrs Rebecca Wallace (3)Mary Ann Madden PS VA
John: b 1720 d 4-7-1794 m (1)Rosanna Etchison (2)Elizabeth Porter PS VA
Moses: b 1763 d 6-16-1838 m Abigail Fritter Pvt VA ★
Mott: b *c.* 1735 d *c.* 1795 m Gracy — PS VA
Nathaniel: b 1716 d *p.* 9-9-1801 m (1)Elizabeth Butler (2)Mrs Susanna Linton Smith PS VA
Taliaferro: b *c.* 1754 d *a.* 1826 m Elizabeth Keith Pvt VA

GRILLS,
John, Jr.: b *c.* 1760 d *a.* 3- -1818 m (1)Margaret Robinson (2)Mary English Pvt VA

GRIMARD,
Pierre: b *c.* 1745 d 1795-1809 m Genevieve Colon PS VA

GRIMBALL,
John: b *c.* 1747 d *c.* 1785 m Elizabeth Robert Lt SC

GRIMES, (includes GRAHAM, GRYMES)
Benjamin: b 2-19-1725 d 1777-79 m (1)Elizabeth Fitzhugh (2)Priscilla Rootes PS VA
Benjamin: b 1-2-1756 d 1803 m Ann Nicholas 1Lt CL
Benjamin, Jr.: b 1744 d 1805 m Molly — Capt VA

Dempsie: b — d 1778 m Penelope Coffield PS NC
George: b 1756 d 10-19-1832 m (1)Elizabeth Turnley (2)Mrs Catherine Hawkins Sgt VA
George: b 1700 d *c.* 1787 m (2)Alice Bellamy PS VA
James: b 1760 d *p.* 1792 m Abigail Johnson Pvt VT
John: b 1758 d *a.* 1803 m (1)Elizabeth Wingfield (2)Sarah Wharry Sol VA
John Charles: b 1-24-1761 d 1-2-1830 m Barbara Frank PS NC
Leonard: b 1759 d *p.* 1-6-1826 m X Pvt PA
Ludwell: b 4-26-1733 d *p.* 1785 m Mary Dawson PS VA
Nicholas: b 1719 d 1798 m Jane — CS VA
Philip: b *c.* 1734 d *p.* 2-20-1805 m Mary Dowdall PS VA
Sampson: b 10-1749 d *p.* 1790 m Bethsheba Winder PS NC
Wm.: b 5-12-1747 d *p.* 1795 m Mary Willard Sgt NH
Wm.: b — d 1-14-1781 m Mary — Pvt NH
Wm.: b 1745 d 5-8-1797 m Chloe — PS NC
Wm.: b 1- -1750 d *a.* 11-2-1785 m Sarah Nicholas Maj VA
Wm.: b 1730 d 8-1-1777 m — Sterling Capt VA

GRIMKE,
John Fancherand: b 12-16-1752 d 8-9-1819 m Mary (Polly) Smith ADC Col SC

GRIMLEY,
Solomon: b 10-4-1730 d 3-18-1806 m Elizabeth Reiner Pvt PA

GRINAGE,
Joshua: b *c.* 1755 d *p.* 7-1-1821 m (1)Sarah Gill (2)Mary (Grinage) Pvt PS VA

GRINDLE, (includes GRINDAL)
Daniel: b 1-7-1754 d *p.* 3-15-1804 m Sarah Gray Pvt MA
Reuben: bpt 12-22-1760 d 9-15-1830 m (1)Hannah Lowell (2)Polly Winslow Pvt MA
Wm.: b 1749 d 1-31-1820 m Eunice Howard Pvt CL ★

GRING,
David: b 2-9-1760 d 2-1-1848 m (1)Anna Maria Waldschmidt (2)Gertrude Stamm Pvt PA ★

GRINNAN,
Daniel: b 1739 d 1800 m Mary Cotten Sol VA
John: b 1761 d 1824 m Frances Stuart Sol VA

GRINNELL, (includes GRENELL, GRINEL)
Amasa: b 1-14-1754 d *p.* 1820 m Ann Isaiah Pvt CT ★
Bailey: b 7-17-1759 d 6-13-1835 m Reliance Spooner Sgt RI ★
Benjamin: b 9-21-1757 d — m (1)Abigail Cudworth (2)Betsy (Evans) Dunham Pvt MA
Billings: b 4-27-1749 d *p.* 1794 m Comfort Wood Cpl RI
Cornelius: b 2-11-1758 d 4-19-1850 m Sylvia Howland Pvt MA
Daniel: b 4-29-1729 d 12-21-1801 m (2)Ann Chapman Pvt CT
Malacia: b 2-1-1737 d 8- -1780 m Lydia Coe Pvt RI
Michael: b 3-20-1752 d 4-13-1858 m Susanna Balcom Pvt CT ★
Richard: b 3-8-1717 d 3-15-1789 m (1)Alice Church (2)Comfort (Billings) Bailey Pvt MA
Royal: b 6-1-1755 d 11-1-1837 m Hannah Briggs Pvt RI
Wm.: b 10-14-1752 d 7-9-1837 m (1)Lucy Clark (2)Lucy Keeney Lt MA ★
Wm.: b 1745 d *a.* 12-9-1783 m Lydia Tillinghast 1Lt RI

GRINSTEAD,
John: b 1755 d 8- -1840 m Mildred Walton Pvt VA ★
Richard: b *c.* 1744 d *a.* 6-9-1806 m Wine — PS VA
Wm.: b 1761 d 8-13-1843 m Lucy Guy Hooker Pvt VA

GRINTER,
John: b 6- -1755 d 5-27-1831 m Elizabeth Hill Pvt VA ★

GRIPPEN,
Jabez: b 5-17-1741 d 8-4-1805 m Abigail Gilbert Sct CT

GRISELL, (or GRISEL)
Edward: b *c.* 1740 d 8-6-1815 m Hannah Taylor Pvt PA
Thomas: b 3-9-1763 d 6-9-1827 m Martha Dingee Pvt PA

GRISS,
Ernst: b 4-12-1746 d 3-19-1816 m Mary M Weiningen Sgt PA

GRISWOLD,
Abiel: b 6-14-1755 d 12-26-1813 m Huldah Pinney Pvt CT
Adonijah: b 6-11-1758 d 9-1-1841 m Mary Barton PS VT
Alexander: b 1745 d 6-2-1813 m Abigail Barnard Sgt CT
Alexander, Sr.: b 10-17-1760 d 4-26-1850 m Lucy Humphrey Pvt CT
Amaziah: b 9-7-1731 d *p.* 1777 m Bertha Parks Pvt CT
Andrew: b 8-12-1745 d 7-4-1813 m Eunice Prince Ens CT W★
Asa: b 5-5-1758 d 5-5-1823 m Desire Potter Pvt CT
Benajah: b 1755 d 1811/12 m Hannah Killiam Pvt CT
Daniel: b 12-28-1746 d 6-26-1786 m Jerusha Gibbs PS CT
Daniel: b 5-25-1762 d 8-4-1836 m (1)Annah Lenthal Ames (2)Mrs Abigail (Davis) Woodberry Tms Pvt CT NY
David: b 1761 d 3-29-1847 m (2)Jane Durham Stull Pvt NY ★
David: b 6-29-1761 d 8-9-1820 m Submit Evarts PS VT

GRISWOLD, contd.

Ebenezer: b 7-29-1725 d 9-30-1810 m Hannah Merrill Pvt VT
Ebenezer: bpt 11-20-1757 d 6-21-1826 m (1)Patty Franklin (2)Martha (Prindle) Stanclift Pvt VT ★
Edward: b 2-11-1758 d 3-21-1843 m Asenath Hurd Pvt CT ★
Elihu: b 8-17-1756 d 1-12-1812 m Mary Wolcott Dr CT
Elijah: b 5-20-1719 d p. 1818 m Abigail Thomas Pvt NY
Elijah: b 8-20-1762 d 1842 m Lydia Adams Pvt CT ★
Elisha: b 10-25-1731 d 3-13-1803 m Eunice Viets Pvt CT
Ezekial: b 2-21-1736 d 5-27-1829 m Anna — Pvt MA
George, Sr.: b 2-1-1823 m Mary Hayden Lt CT
George, Jr.: b 6-8-1762/63 d 1-15-1832 m Eunice Ingersoll Pvt CT
George: b 1-4-1730 d 4-26-1813 m (1)Sarah Jones (2)Susannah Cone Ens CT
George: b 11-5-1752 d 3-6-1834 m Artemesia Stevens Sgt CT
Giles: b 10-28-1748 d 9-24-1818 m Eunice Hough Pvt CT
Isaac: b 4-3-1735 d 2-22-1817 m Abigail Latham Pvt CT
Isaac: b 8-8-1749 d 9-21-1839 m Christiana Holcomb Sol CT
Isaac: b 9-24-1753 d p. 2-22-1800 m (1)Clara Cobb (2)Mrs Lucy Osgood Miller Sgt CS PS NH
Jabez: b 1758 d 1839 m Polly — Pvt NY ★
Jabez, Jr.: b 5-12-1764 d 11-4-1827 m Anna Spencer Pvt NY
Jannah: b 8-15-1758 d 1-31-1835 m Lucy Clark Pvt Tms CT ★
Jedediah, Sr.: b 12-13-1730 d 11-10-1808 m Patience Bates Cpl CT
Jeremiah: b 2-14-1746 d 5-15-1813 m (1)Phebe Case (2)Ester Woodford Ens CT
Jeremiah: b 9-10-1742 d 9-6-1795 m Rebecca Estabrook Pvt NH
Joab: b 9-11-1740 d p. 1790 m Elizabeth Collins PS CT
Joel: b 5-21-1757 d 4-12-1834 m Sarah Kelsey Sgt CT
John: b 6-29-1758 d 12-22-1847 m Rhoda Wetmore MM Pvt CT
John, Sr.: b 3-6-1725/26 d p. 8-27-1776 m Mary Ward Pvt CT
John, Jr.: b 8-4-1749 d p. 1793 m (1)Sarah Brock (2)Abagail Williams Pvt VT
John: b 10-15-1758 d 10-16-1843 m Elizabeth Crittenden Pvt MA ★
John: b 11-6-1733 d 6-25-1810 m (1)Ruth Hewett (2)Elizabeth Porter Maj PS CS NH
John: b 11-3-1747 d 1825 m Eunice Calkins Pvt NY
Jonathan: b — d 1821 m Elizabeth Weeks Pvt CT
Josiah: b 11-19-1731 d 8-15-1800 m Lucy Kelsey Pvt CT
Josiah: b 6-17-1752 d 1-1-1821 m (1)Jemima Parmalee (2)Susanna Simonds Cpl NH
Matthew: b 3-25-1714 d 4-28-1799 m Ursula Wolcott PS CS CT
Midian: b 3-8-1764 d 11-31-1829 m Annie Watkins Pvt CT
Miles: b 11-3-1739 d 5-24-1804 m Abigail Blinn Sgt NY
Moses: b 12-23-1741 d 1813 m Anna Holcomb Sgt CT
Moses: b 11-19-1743 d 5-17-1828 m Lucretia Kelsey Pvt CT
Nathan: b 4-28-1719 d 6-15-1791 m Sarah Hull Capt CT
Nathaniel: b 7-27-1742 d p. 10-19-1795 m Abigail Pinney Sgt PS CT
Noah, Sr.: b 9-11-1722/23 d 9-24-1789 m (1)Abigail — (2)Mindwell (Phelps) Griswold PS CT
Noah, Jr.: b 8-10-1746 d 10-27-1784 m Azubah Strong Sgt CT
Ozias: b 1-16-1735/36 d 12-4-1815 m Anne Stanley PS MA
Phineas: b 8-13-1750 d 2-8-1789 m Vashti Bates Pvt CT
Rebekah: b — d — m Noadiah Hooker PS CT
Samuel: b 1736 d 3-5-1816 m Mary Marvin Sgt CT
Samuel: b 3-29-1759 d 10-16-1851 m Lucretia Abell Pvt CT
Samuel: b 1-15-1760 d 2-12-1844 m Hannah Landon Pvt CT
Selah: b 3-23-1754 d 1-6-1835 m Mary Starkey Pvt CT ★
Seth: b 4-30-1732 d 1816 m (1)Susannah Shurtleff (2)Ann Loper (3)Huldah (Priest) Loomis Pvt CT
Seth: b — d — m Ann Munson Pvt CT
Shubael: b 12-18-1730 d 2-23-1807 m (1)Abigail Stanley (2)Widow Catlin Capt CT
Shubael: b 3-15-1734 d 12-26-1812 m Dorcas — Pvt CT
Solomon: b 1754 d 5-16-1834 m Abiah Allen AsstDepQMGen CT ★
Solomon: b 2-11-1737 d p. 1780 m Sarah Gleason Pvt CT
Solomon: b 8-27-1751 d 8-17-1777 m Sarah Deming PS CT
Stephen: b 11-21-1732 d p. 1805 m (1)Hannah Colmons (2)Mrs Elizabeth Davis Lt CS NJ
Sylvanus: b 1733 d 1-16-1811 m (1)Mary Collins (2)Mrs Hannah Webb (3) — Starr 1Lt CT
Theophilus: b 5-1-1761 d 12- -1821 m Elisabeth Talcott Pvt CT
Thomas: b 9-1-1737 d 1-7-1821 m Hannah Cruttenden MM Cnt CT
White: b 10-26-1727 d 12-2-1777 m Elizabeth Cheney Sol CT
Wm.: b 1734 d 9-7-1806 m Martha Topley Pvt CT
Zenas: b 5-10-1759 d p. 1803 m (1)Mary Lane (2)Mrs Mary Angus Pettibone Pvt CT

GRITTON,

John: b 1755 d 8-7-1839 m Elizabeth — Pvt Spy PA ★

GRIZZEL,

Joel: b 1759 d 1849 m Sarah — Sgt VA

GROAT, (includes GROOT, GROTE)

Abraham: b 1741 d 7- -1818 m (1)Katrina Kittle (2)Elsie McKinney Pvt NY
Cornelius: b c. 1708 d p. 11-8-1781 m Elizabeth Pootman PS NY
Dirk C: bpt 12-31-1758 d 6-26-1847 m Jacomyntje Tymessen Pvt NY
Hendrick: b c. 1710 d p. 5-16-1780 m Maria Catharine Dederick Pvt NY
John: bpt 4-9-1738 d p. 1781 m Angeltie VanPetten Capt NY
Peter: b 12- -1753 d 1835 m Maria Cornicker Pvt NY ★
Simon C: b 11-7-1745 d 2-10-1832 m Annatie (Nancy) Truax Sgt NY

GROENKYKE, (includes GROENENDYKE, GROWENDIKE)

John: b 6-5-1756 d 5-1-1824 m Lucretia Rappleye Pvt NJ
Samuel: b 1740 d 1802 m Polly Devoe Maj NJ

GROESBECK, (includes GROESBEECK)

Johannes W: b 2-14-1742 d 2-23-1820 m Anvatie Davenport 1Maj NY
John D: b 7-12-1741 d a. 1-3-1816 m (1)Aeltje Van Arnhem (2)Catalyna VanSchaick Sol NY
Nicholas W: bpt 5-6-1750 d — m Sara Becker Pvt NY
Walter N: bpt 8-29-1714 d p. 1790 m (1)Maria Bogardus (2)Alida Quackenbos Capt NY

GROFF, (includes GRAEFF, GRAFF, GRAFT, GRAVE, GROVE)

Abraham: b c. 1733 d 1790 m Catherine Ehrwinin Pvt PA
Andrew: b 9-15-1740 d 1-15-1816 m Catherine Graffert Capt PS PA
Christian: b c. 1735 d p. 6-9-1786 m (1)Anna Rhodes (2)Esther Musselman Pvt PA
Daniel: b 10-1-1749 d 9-18-1808 m Margaretha Ruth — Capt PA
Francis: b c. 1760 d p. 1793 m X Sol PA
Frederick: b 12-30-1762 d 3-9-1818 m Margaretta Machemar Pvt PA
George: b 10-11-1747 d 2-2-1835 m Barbara Kohler Capt PA
George Michael: b c. 1757 d 4-12-1825 m Susanna Augustine Sgt PA
Henry: b c. 1745 d p. 1783 m Susanna — Ens PA
Isaac: b c. 1758 d 1778 m Sarah (Pickering?) Sgt MA NH
Jacob, Sr.: b 6-4-1737 d 8-13-1819 m Catharine Staley PS MD
Jacob, Jr.: b 10-1-1759 d 9-3-1834 m Christiana Storm PS MD
Jacob: b 1751 d p. 1-22-1840 m Nancy Kneisley Pvt PA
Jacob: b 1-17-1753 d 12-8-1836 m Elizabeth Hepburn Pvt PA
Jacob: b c. 1757/58 d 1819 m Mary — Pvt PA
Jacob: b 4-20-1751 d 1-15-1824 m Elizabeth Heebner Pvt PA
John: b 1700 d 1780 m Elizabeth Carpenter PS MD
John: b c. 1730 d 1785 m Barbara — Capt PA
John: b 11-5-1757 d 4-4-1828 m Elizabeth Hollinger Pvt PA
John: b 7-23-1750 d 12-11-1819 m (1)Susan Fox (2)Margaret Ann Newkirk Sol Wgn PA W★
John: b — d p. 1810 m Mary Brown Pvt VA
John Peter: b c. 1730 d 1-1-1800 m Anna Maria Yost Pvt PA
Marcus: b c. 1742 d p. 6-11-1804 m (1)Susanna Rhodes (2)Mary Grove PS Pvt VA
Michael: b 1750 d 9- -1827 m X Pvt PA
Peter: b 3-29-1755 d 6-1802/03 m Sarah Whitmore Lt PA W★
Peter: b c. 1743 d 1821 m Anna Maria — Pvt PA
Philip: b 1757 d 2-26-1842 m Elizabeth — Pvt PA ★
Samuel: b 11-10-1745 d 5-20-1790 m Alcha Gulick Ens NJ W★
Sebastian: b 1-31-1747 d 2-19-1822 m Maria Gertraut PS Mil PA
Sebastian: b — d — m Ann Catharine Young PS PA
Wendell: b 1755 d 12-22-1849 m (1)Betsey — (2)Jane Coon Pvt PA W★
Windle: b 1730 d p. 1796 m Mary Wilson Sol VA

GROO,

Samuel, Sr.: b 2-21-1758 d 12-30-1825 m Susanne Brooks Pvt MA

GROOM,

Edward: b c. 1743 d p. 1795 m Elizabeth Souser Pvt PS NY
James: b 7-24-1754 d 4-26-1825 m Margaret Moon Sgt NY
Joseph: b 1753 d 1810 m (1)Rebecca — (2)Rachel — Sgt NY
Major: b 1762 d a. 2- -1846 m Christiana Melinda Bibb Pvt VA ★
Wm.: b a. 1720 d p. 1790 m Sara Cottington PS NY

GROOMS,

Jonathan: b 2-5-1756 d p. 1-28-1833 m Elizabeth Moon Pvt VA ★

GROOVER, (includes GRUBER, GRUVER)

Adam: b 10-19-1735 d 3-6-1807 m (1)Elizabeth — (2)Sarah — Pvt PA
John George: b 2-16-1743 d 8- -1792 m Elizabeth Emrich Pvt PA
Peter: b 1762 d 7-11-1841 m X Sgt NC ★
Philip: b 11-13-1753 d 8-16-1842 m Maria Margaretha Long Pvt PA

GROSCOST,

Daniel: b 11- -1758 d 9- -1841 m Susanah Patterson Pvt PA

GROSH,

Adam: b — d 10-4-1777 m Christine Roemer Lt MD
Conrad: b 1717 d 8- -1794 m Maria Sophis Guttenberg PS CS MD
Michael: b 1750 d p. 3-24-1824 m Christine Roemer Pvt PS MD ★

GROSS, (includes GRASS, GROCE, GROS)

Andrew: b 2-19-1750 d 9- -1803 m Maria Catharina — Lt PA
Andrew: b 1750 d 9-10-1829 m Anna Maria Meyers Pvt PA
Benjamin: b 8-15-1759 d 2-11-1844 m Mercy Hamlin Pvt MA
David: b 4-16-1766 d 1-3-1837 m Sally Newell Pvt NH ★
Elisha: b 3-16-1749 d 9- -1829 m Deborah Sylvester Sgt MA ★
George: b 1759 d 2-24-1828 m Jane Alexander Pvt MA ★
George Daniel: b 1757 d 3-16-1803 m Catherine (Brown ?) Ens PA
Henry: b 1769 d 1875 m Eva Catherine Slotts Sol PA
Isaac: b 1737 d 2-16-1789 m Silence Tower Pvt MA
Israel: b 4-28-1718 d 10-19-1788 m Elizabeth Rich PS MA
John: b 11-17-1749 d 1-2-1823 m Rachel Sahler Capt PA
Jonah: b — d — m Sarah Ladd Pvt CT

Joseph: b 12-20-1739 d 1- -1817 m Tabitha Goodell Pvt MA
Lawrence: b 2-10-1745 d 8-10-1814 m Maria Failing Capt NY
Martin: b 8-17-1736 d 4-4-1827 m (1)Catarine Schuetz (2)Christine
   Beringer Pvt PA
Micah: b 5-8-1750 d 12- -1822 m Elizabeth Dyer Pvt MA
Michael: b 1747 d 7- -1807 m Mary Magdalena Boal Pvt PA
Paul: b c. 1735/36 d c. 1782/83 m Maria Catherine Guth Sgt PA
Peter: b 1-1-1761 d 5-28-1846 m Barbara Troxell Sgt PA
Philip: b c. 1760 d 6-18-1827 m Sarah Kocker Pvt PA
Samuel: b 5-2-1751 d 2-17-1825 m Hannah Owen Pvt CT ★
Samuel: b 1749 d 11-16-1817 m Elizabeth Torrey Cpl MA
Simon: b 5-3-1709 d 2-23-1798 m (1)Betsy Treat (2)Phebe Collings
   NLt CT
Thomas: b 11-12-1758 d 3-18-1843 m (1)Judith Carter (2)Mrs Rhoda
   (Marsh) Pitkin (3)Rebecca Pitkin (4)Phebe Dow (5)Cynthia Porter
   Pvt CT

GROSSCLOSE,
Peter: b 2-23-1730 d p. 11-26-1802 m Mary Magdalene Ott Pvt
   PS PA

GROSSCUP,
Paul: b c. 1752 d 3-14-1812 m Sybilla Rothermel Capt PA

GROSSMAN,
Michael: b 1-22-1748 d 10-7-1810 m Maria Hageman Pvt PS PA

GROSVENOR,
Asa: b 4-6-1745 d 9-28-1834 m Hannah Hall PS Capt CT ★
Caleb: b 8-15-1751 d 1807 m Olive Griffin Pvt CT
Daniel: b 4-20-1750 d 7-22-1834 m Deborah Hall PS MM MA
Ezra: b 6-23-1755 d 1827 m Sarah Carpenter Pvt CT
John: b 5-12-1711 d 2-3-1804 m Hannah Dresser PS CS CT
Leicester: b 10-14-1726 d 6-8-1808 m Esther Weld Pvt PS MA
Lemuel: b 8-11-1752 d 1-19-1833 m Sarah Perkins Lt CT
Moses: b 8-15-1741 d 3-16-1811 m Dorcas Sharp Sgt NY
Oliver: b 5-19-1743 d 5-13-1824 m Zerviah Payson Cmsry CT
Richard: b 10-5-1761 d 1814 m Margaret Graham Drm PA
Seth: b 7-9-1747 d p. 1791 m Abigail Keyes Cpl CT
Theophilus: b 7-29-1755 d 10-8-1797 m Bathsheba Thornton Drm MA
Thomas: b 9-20-1744 d 7-11-1825 m Ann Mumford LCol CT
Thomas: b 3-1-1757 d 12-15-1842 m Theoda Perrin Pvt CT

GROTECLAUS,
Gilbert: b 1763 d p. 4-18-1835 m Mary Gillies Cpl NJ ★

GROUARD,
James: b — d — m — PS NH

GROUT,
Abel: b 2-19-1758 d 1-1-1841 m Dorcas Chase Pvt MA ★
Amasa: b 3-26-1759 d 3- -1837 m Lucinda Heywood Pvt NH VT
Asa: b 2-3-1753 d 8-24-1833 m Sarah Spafford Cpl VT
Daniel: b 3-30-1736 d 7-15-1809 m Elizabeth Adams Capt MA
Elias: b 2-28-1757 d 3-12-1835 m (3)Eleanor Dadmun Cpl MA
Elijah: b 10-29-1732 d 3- -1807 m (1)Mary Willard (2)Widow (Read)
   Hutchins PS CS NH
Hilkiah, Sr.: b 7-23-1728 d 12-19-1795 m Submit Hawkes 1Maj VT
Hilkiah, Jr.: b 10-30-1761 d 4-13-1853 m Abigail Parker Pvt NY ★
Isaac: b 5-24-1758 d 6-24-1835 m (1)Sally Stearns (2)Rebecca
   Brigham Pvt MA
Joel: b 3-6-1734 d 1797 m Sarah Hudson Pvt PS MA
John: b 3-14-1765 d 11-11-1843 m Elizabeth Upham Pvt MA
Jonathan: b 1710 d — m Sarah — PS MA
Jonathan: b 6-27-1744 d 10-17-1828 m Annah Harrington Lt PS MA
Jonathan: b 4-24-1760 d 9-20-1854 m Parthena Page Pvt NH
Silas: b 3-31-1755 d 4-26-1820 m Susanna Clapp Pvt MA
Solomon: b 6-27-1751 d p. 1787 m Ruth Putnam Pvt NH
Wm.: b 4-18-1758 d 1-9-1836 m (1)Rebecca Woodbury (2)Amy
   Campbell Pvt MA

GROVENSTEIN, (or GRUBENSTEIN)
John Justus: b c. 1740 d p. 1789 m Catherine Biddenbach PS GA

GROVER,
Abial: b c. 1743 d 12-17-1821 m (1)Lydia Bate (2)Mrs Mary Skinner
   (3)Mrs Betty Johnson Pvt MA
Amasa: b 3-12-1741 d 1-2-1837 m Elizabeth Jefford Sol CT
Benjamin: b c. 1745 d 1817 m Lucy Bolkom Pvt MA
Benjamin: b 3-30-1760 d 6-6-1833 m (1)Lydia Lancaster (2)Joanna
   Trott Pvt MA ★
David: b 10-15-1755 d 2-23-1844 m Martha Burr Pvt MA ★
Ebenezer: b 3-13-1754 d 3-27-1841 m Mary Palmer Pvt CT ★
Ebenezer: b 1747 d 11-22-1803 m Elizabeth Stowe Pvt MA
Eleazer: b 1758 d p. 1821 m Filena Carpenter Pvt VT ★
Ephraim, Sr.: bpt 12-12-1714 d 12-24-1796 m Jemima Newland PS MA
Ephraim, Jr.: b 4-1-1738 d 3-30-1793 m Marcy Tiffany 1Lt MA
John: b c. 1757 d 1813 m Jerusha Wiley Pvt MA
John: b 8-11-1744 d 7-22-1803 m Margaret Pusley Pvt MA
John: b 10-29-1748 d 5-21-1800 m Elizabeth Shute MM Pvt MA
Jonathan Mason: b 1759 d 5-26-1844 m Sarah Musgrove Cpl MD
Luther: b 8-12-1764 d 12-21-1836 m Anner Bartlett Sol CT
Nehemiah: b 6-30-1730 d p. 1801 m Betty Gamage Pvt MA

Phineas: b 10-16-1747 d c. 1782 m Ruth Nicholas CaptLt CT
Stephen: b 4-3-1747 d 5-29-1831 m (1)Zipporah — (2)Miriam — Pvt CT
Stephen: b c. 1745 d p. 1790 m Zipporah Wheeler Pvt MA
Wm.: b 4-13-1755 d 1816 m Abigail Parsons Sol Smn MA

GROVES,
Abraham: b 3-1-1762 d 12-31-1847 m Rosanna Wetzel Pvt VA
Jesse: b 10-7-1754 d 1-17-1819 m Martha Parley Sgt MA
Jonathan, Sr.: b 1738 d c. 2-23-1789 m Alsa Millikan Sol DE
Peter: b 8-18-1739 d 7-1-1807 m Lydia Lumbard Pvt MA
Robert: b 1763 d 8-25-1855 m Martha Miller Mus DE
Samuel: b 6-5-1758 d 9-5-1829 m Hannah Fiske Pvt MA
Stephen: b 1-6-1740 d 3- -1839 m Isabella Weakly Sol PA ★
Thomas: b a. 1754 d 1814 m Eady — PS NC
Thomas: b c. 1765 d 1822 m Mildred Williams Pvt VA ★
Wm.: b 1760 d a. 1820 m Rebecca Veazey Pvt DE

GROW,
Ambrose: b 7-27-1756 d 7-12-1845 m (1)Jemima Eldridge (2)Mrs
   Anne Parsons Thomas Pvt CT VT ★
Edward: b 10-22-1722 d 5-5-1785 m Olive Farnham Col NOf MA
John: b 5-9-1750 d 1834 m Deborah Davidson Pvt CT
Joseph, Sr.: b 10-16-1717 d 5-3-1782 m Abigail Dana PS VT
Joseph, Jr.: b 3-13-1748 d 3-19-1813 m Tirzah Sanger Cpl VT
Nathaniel: b 5-25-1753 d 7-9-1838 m Susannah Dow Pvt CT
Peter: b 4-30-1763 d 3-13-1837 m (1)Diana Tracy (2)Deborah Tracy
   (3)Mrs Eddy (4)Experience Brown Pvt MA ★
Thomas: b 4-4-1743 d 6-5-1824 m (1)Experience Goodell (2)Mrs
   Sarah Hyde (3)Experience Abbott PS CT

GRUBB,
Amor: b 10-14-1749 d 9-26-1817 m Ann Buckley Sol PS DE
Conrad: b 12-6-1759 d 3-25-1820 m Elizabeth Baugh Pvt PA
Henry: b — d p. 6-8-1804 m Mary Eva Adoretha Dedregh PS Sol VA
Jesse: b 1745 d 1822 m Polly Younger Capt VA
Peter: b 9-8-1740 d 1-17-1786 m Mary Shippen Burd Col PA
Richard: b 1757 d p. 1820 m Rebecca — Pvt DE
Wm.: b 8-20-1759 d 5-31-1841 m Nancy Harris Pvt MA

GRUBBS,
Enoch: b 1755 d 1832 m X Pvt SC
Higgason: b c. 1740 d 6-30-1830 m Lucy Harris Pvt VA
John: b 4-26-1751 d p. 7-8-1818 m Sarah Hopkins Sol VA
Nathan: b 1757 d 1842 m Elizabeth — Pvt VA
Thomas: b — d 1779 m X PS VA

GRUENDIKE,
Samuel: b c. 1730 d 1817 m Mary — Pvt NJ

GRUMBACHER,
Peter: b 1741 d 4-1-1778 m Catthrin — PS PA

GRUMBINE, (includes GRUMBEIN)
Leonard: b c. 1733 d p. 1782 m Catharina — Pvt PA
Peter: b 4-18-1761 d 12-22-1851 m Catharine Cuthbert Pvt PA ★

GRUMMON,
Ichabod, Jr.: b 1755 d 10-29-1794 m Hannah Bruen PS NJ
Joseph: b 1742 d p. 1795 m Hannah Drake Pvt NY

GRUND,
Adam: b c. 1740 d p. 6-24-1822 m Catharine Hoffman PS MD

GRUNDY,
George: b a. 1740 d p. 1780 m Elizabeth Beckham CS VA

GRUNEWALD,
Jacob: b c. 1723 d 1788 m Elizabeth Filhower PS PA
Johannes: b 12-18-1755 d 2-20-1826 m Anna Maria Reinhardt
   Pvt Drm Fif PS PA

GRUWELL,
Peter: b c. 1750 d 1776 m Sarah — Sol DE

GUDTNER,
John: b 1745 d 5-1-1837 m Catherine Dreher Pvt PA

GUE,
Joseph: b 1760 d 1790 m Patience Horton Pvt NY

GUERIN,
Joseph: b 8-3-1748 d 2-6-1828 m Martha Ferguson Wgn NJ
Joshua: b 1737 d 4-4-1808 m Susanna — Ens NJ

GUERNSEY, (includes GARNSEY)
Amos: b 3-31-1743 d 2-12-1813 m Merian Pike Pvt PS NH
Daniel: b 7-18-1760 d 4-28-1840 m Huldah Seymour Sol NY
David: b 3-4-1757 d 9-28-1854 m Hannah Judd Pvt CT ★
David: b 5-30-1764 d 1841 m Esther Fassett Pvt NH ★
Ezra: b 3-29-1750 d 8- -1821 m Sarah Seekins Cpl MA CT
James: b 10- -1758 d 8-24-1810 m Sarah Roe Pvt MA
John: b 1751 d — m X Pvt MA
John: b c. 1720 d — m Lydia Healey Pvt NH

GUERNSEY, contd.
John, Jr.: b 10-28-1734 d 2-27-1799 m Azuba Buel Pvt NY
John, Sr.: b 1709 d 4-3-1783 m Ann Peck PS NY
Jonathan: b 2-28-1729 d 4-28-1804 m Desire Bronson Pvt CT
Joseph: b 1730 d 11-1-1817 m Mary Brown Capt CT
Noah: b 8-18-1746 d 9-18-1820 m (1)Hannah Hollister (2)Thankful — CS CT
Oliver: b 7-16-1744 d *p.* 1778 m (1)Rachel Ware (2)Sarah Perry Pvt NH
Philo: b 9-13-1762 d 12-30-1814 m Irena Murray Pvt CT
Samuel: b 1745 d *p.* 1790 m Mary Brown Weed Skelding Lt CT
Southmayd: b 4-10-1763 d 4-4-1850 m Sabia Scott Pvt CT
Wm.: b 1-11-1749 d *p.* 1794 m Chloe Thurber PS NH

GUERRANT,
Daniel: b 4-23-1747 d 1823 m Mary Porter Lt VA
John, Sr.: b 7-17-1733 d 12-25-1818 m Elizabeth Porter Maj VA
John, Jr.: b 3-23-1760 d 12-7-1813 m Mary Heath Povall Lt PM VA
Peter: b 10-17-1737 d 1819 m Marie Perreau Capt PS VA

GUERRY,
John: b 1751 d 5-22-1822 m Charlotte Jane Michau Sol SC

GUEST,
Moses: b 1- -1750 d 10-1-1837 m (1)Mary Blair (2)Eleandor York Capt NC ★
Wm.: b 12-30-1762 d 7-8-1841 m Anna Allen Lt NC ★

GUFFEY,
Alexander: b 1-1-1764 d 8-27-1844 m Ann Pontiny Pvt PA ★
James: b 1736 d 3-9-1806 m (1)Margaret Campbell (2)Mary Findley Pvt PA
John: b 8-6-1764 d 1845 m (1)Agnes Lowery (2)Rebecca Stewart PS PA

GUFFIN,
Andrew: b 5-29-1756 d 4-26-1842 m Hannah Ostrom Pvt NY ★

GUGEL, (or GUGLE)
David: b 1-21-1764 d 4-24-1842 m Margaret Waldhauer Pvt GA

GUICE,
Nicholas: b *c.* 1755 d *p.* 1820 m X Sol MD VA

GUILD,
Aaron: b 4-5-1728 d 2-3-1818 m (1)Sarah Cony (2)Annah Cony (3)Sarah May Capt MA
Daniel: b 8-18-1738 d 1795 m (1)Sarah Pond (2)Lydia Adams (3)Sarah Fletcher Sgt NH
Ebenezer, Sr.: b 8-22-1722 d 2-25-1803 m Phoebe Day Pvt MA
Ebenezer, Jr.: b 3-1-1759 d *p.* 1796 m Mary Lane Pvt MA
Elias: b 5-4-1758 d 2-5-1840 m Mary White Pvt MA ★
Elisha: b 12-9-1745 d — m Abigail Rea Pvt CT
Heman: bpt 7-28-1751 d 10-28-1792 m Sarah Taunt Sol MA
Jacob: b 4-23-1760 d 4-6-1839 m Chloe May Guild Pvt MA
Jesse: b 4-11-1765 d 6-5-1848 m Zilpah Smith Pvt MA
Joel: b 2-1-1764 d 9-9-1854 m Olive Balch Pvt MA
John: b 2-24-1720/21 d 11-7-1791 m Thankful Harrington Pvt MA
John: b 8-23-1760 d 8-19-1850 m Olive Stuart Pvt MA ★
John: b 7-28-1763 d 9-20-1850 m (1)Margaret Daggett (2)Martha Cook Pvt MA
John, Sr.: b 1712 d 7-10-1787 m Charity Hunt PS NJ
John, Jr.: b 4-23-1749 d 3-23-1825 m Abigail Howell Pvt NJ
Joseph: b 5-11-1735 d 12-23-1794 m Miriam Draper Capt PS MA
Joseph: b 6-22-1716 d 9-18-1792 m (1)Hannah White (2)Elizabeth Thayer Sgt MA
Joseph: b 9-14-1748 d 1794 m Rebecca Pierce Pvt MA
Napthalie: b 1-26-1752 d 1842 m Susanna Bates Fif RI ★
Nathaniel, Sr.: b 3-20-1712 d 9-10-1796 m Mary Boyden PS MA
Nathaniel, Jr.: b 5-29-1739 d 4-4-1793 m Rebecca Hart Pvt MA
Otis: b 7-28-1763 d 2-21-1839 m Lois Robinson Pvt MA
Richard: b 10-17-1762 d 10-20-1819 m Zillah Turner Pvt MA
Samuel: b 10-23-1746 d 5-11-1816 m (1)Elizabeth (Starrett) Fergerson (2)Katherine Leonard Dr MA
Samuel: b 4-21-1734 d 7-18-1816 m Ruth Nimms Sol PS CS MA
Samuel: b 10-23-1727 d *p.* 1790 m (1)Experience Adams (2)Mehitable Clapp Pvt PS MA
Samuel: b 6-16-1739 d *p.* 1784 m Sarah Smith Pvt MA
Samuel: b 12-13-1762 d 12-25-1840 m Ruth Morse Pvt MA ★
Timothy: b 1-15-1732/3 d 4-1-1789 m Jenne Gorden 2Lt MA

GUILFORD,
John: b 2- -1753 d 3-20-1828 m Sarah Flagg Pvt MA
Joseph: b 5-15-1761 d 3-10-1840 m Elizabeth Wallace Pvt NC ★
Paul: b 3-11-1740 d 6-20-1811 m (1)Mary Burt (2)Deborah Bundy Pvt MA
Samuel: b 1756 d 8-26-1832 m Elizabeth Cranson Cpl MA ★

GUILLEBEAU,
Andre: b 1739 d 1814 m Mary Jane Roquemore Pvt SC

GUION,
David: b 4-17-1729/30 d 9-16-1812 m Esther Parcot 2Lt NY

David: b 1737 d 4-20-1821 m Elizabeth — Lt NY
Isaac: b 4-6-1755 d 9-17-1823 m Sarah Lewis CaptLt PM NY

GUITTEAU, (includes GUITEAU)
Ephraim: b 6-22-1737 d 4-21-1816 m Phoebe Humphrey Capt Dr MA
Judson: b 7-6-1751 d 8-31-1823 m Patience Gaylord PS CT

GULDNER,
John George: b 11-20-1752 d 4-23-1803 m Maria Gertrude Herter Cpl PA

GULICK, (includes GULLICK)
Ferdinand: b 11-15-1756 d 6-4-1836 m Hannah Lee Pvt VA NJ ★
Hendrick: b 10-16-1734 d 4- -1798 m Mary Williamson Capt NJ
James: b 7-7-1758 d 11-2-1811 m Elizabeth Snedecker Pvt NJ
Joakim, Jr.: b 9-20-1764 d 2-4-1840 m Jane Wyckoff Sgt NJ
John: b 5-1-1757 d 9-11-1828 m Margaret VanDyke Sgt Trns NJ
John: b 5-28-1753 d 2-8-1810 m Elizabeth Demot Pvt NJ
John, Jr.: b *c.* 1743 d *p.* 1815 m Rebecca Davidson PS NC
Nicholas: b 5-26-1758 d 4-23-1846 m Elizabeth Gano Pvt NJ

GULIKER,
John: b 1738 d 2-3-1789 m Jane Brown NCdr MA

GULLIFORD,
Allen: b — d *p.* 8-24-1812 m Anna — Pvt VA

GULLION,
Jeremiah: b 11-28-1758 d 4- -1815 m Isabella Patty Sol PA

GULLIVER, (includes GULLIFER)
Gershom: b 9-20-1756 d 1-9-1840 m Phebe Harvey Cpl MA
Peleg: b 2-13-1751 d 9-30-1827 m (1)Ruby Sampson (2)Olive — Cpl MA
Reuben: b 2-19-1762 d 11-30-1860 m Ruth Snyder Pvt MA ★

GULLY, (includes GULLEY)
George: b 1750 d 1814 m Frances Franklin Pvt VA
John: b *c.* 1755 d 4-15-1833 m Ann Brown Sgt NC W★
Wm.: b 2-10-1737 d *p.* 1800 m X Sol NC

GUM,
Abraham: b *c.* 1755 d 1806 m (1)Priscilla Callahan (2)Priscilla Wade Cpl VA
Isaac: b *a.* 1753 d *p.* 1796 m Jane McBride Pvt VA
Jacob: b 1763 d 4-15-1847 m Rhoda Bell Pvt VA
Michael: b 1745 d 10- -1815 m Catherine — Pvt PA

GUMAER,
Elias: b 1-22-1748 d 11-7-1820 m Margaret Depuy Pvt NY
Ezekiel: b 8-29-1742 d 5-17-1823 m Naomi Louw Pvt NY
Jacob Dewitt: b 12-12-1739 d 1831 m Alida Decker Pvt NY
Peter, Sr.: b 11-15-1708 d 1779 m Charity DeWitt PS NY
Peter, Jr.: b 2-19-1731 d *c.* 1816 m Hannah (Annatje Elizabeth) Van Inwegan Pvt NY

GUMMEY,
John: b 1743 d 11-16-1811 m Catharine Margaret Muller Pvt PA

GUMP,
Frederick: b 1740 d 11- -1841 m X Pvt PA ★

GUNDY, (includes VAN GUNDY)
Christian: b *c.* 1742 d 1812 m Ann — Sgt PA
Jacob: b 10-13-1765 d 9-23-1845 m Katherine Maury Pvt PA ★
Joseph: b *c.* 1760-2 d 1822 m Frances Coffman Pvt PA
Joseph: b 1740-2 d 1795 m Margaretta Haldeman Lt PA
Joseph: b 1732 d *c.* 1800 m Martha — PS PA

GUNN,
Aaron: b 9-20-1753 d 2-8-1833 m Betsey Stewart Pvt MA CT W★
Abel: b 8-25-1754 d 2-9-1842 m Lucy Wakelee Sol NY CL
Asahel, Sr.: b ★1-16-1730 d 7-11-1796 m Thankful Marsh Capt MA
Asahel, Jr.: b 2-5-1757 d 12-20-1834 m (1)Lucy Root (2)Submit Bardwell Pvt MA ★
Daniel: b 1734 d 2-25-1812 m Submit — Pvt NH
Daniel: b 3-14-1763 d 9-25-1825 m Susan Street Lt NC W★
Elisha: b 8-13-1764 d 5-14-1821 m (1)Lydia Phelps (2)Ann Hathaway Pvt MA
Elisha: b 1759 d 1839 m (1)Retter Weeks (2) — Cox Pvt VA
Gideon: b 1734 d 6-26-1827 m Dorothy Deming Pvt MA
Israel: b 5- -1742 d 12-18-1824 m Mary Root Sgt MA
John: b 3-12-1707 d 10-8-1793 m Hannah Root PS MA
Moses: b 10-12-1728 d 1-3-1794 m Elenor Ingram PS MA
Moses: b 5-3-1754 d 2-6-1844 m (1)Olive Carver (2)Eunice Preston (3)Experience Stebbins (4)Mary Hastings QMSgt MA
Nathaniel, Sr.: b 1-26-1726 d 4-22-1804 m Dorothy Marsh Lt MA
Nathaniel, Jr.: b 1-15-1752 d 3-6-1832 m Hannah Montague Pvt MA
Reuben: b 1752 d 1822 m (1)Mary Goforth (Hudson) (2)Nancy Jones Sol NC ★
Richard: b 6-26-1761 d 6-30-1840 m Elizabeth Radford Sol VA
Salmon: b 1760 d 1850 m — Cpl MA
Starling: b 5-9-1764 d 8-13-1852 m Mary Elizabeth Hooper Pvt VA ★
Thomas: b 1738 d *p.* 11-13-1800 m (1)Susanna Burnett (2)Sarah Davenport (3)Ann Worsham (4)Eleanor — PS VA

GUNNELL,
Henry: b c. 1720 d p. 1-21-1792 m Catherine Daniels PS VA
John, Sr.: b c. 1730 d p. 10-13-1803 m Sarah — PS VA
John, Jr.: b c. 1763 d 1836 m Lucy Fleming Pvt VA
Jonathan: b 1756 d 4-21-1847 m Amelia — Pvt CL ★

GUNNELS,
Daniel: b c. 1762 d p. 1800 m Miss Akins Pvt GA

GUNNISON,
Josiah: b 6-22-1755 d 2- -1835 m Mary Tucker Pvt NH ★
Samuel, Sr.: b 1-27-1720 d 5-14-1806 m (1)Jane Fernald (2)Alice
    Fernald Capt NH
Samuel, Jr.: b 1757 d 1823 m Dorcus Cutts Cpl NH

GUNSALUS, (includes GUNSALIS & GUNSAULUS)
John: b 1717 d 1777 m Marget B— Mil NY
John: bpt 5-16-1742 d a. 4-28-1785 m Machtelt Heemstrast Pvt NY
Manuel: b 11-15-1751 d 1-12-1826 m Sarah Bevier Pvt NY
Richard: b 2-2-1756 d c. 1838 m Statia Ann Lucas 2Lt PA ★

GUNTACKER, (or GUNDAKER)
Johann George: b 9-26-1758 d p. 9- -1800 m Elizabeth Neff Pvt PA

GUNTER,
Isham, Sr.: b c. 1750 d a. 8- -1834 m Hester — Sol NC

GUPPEY,
James: b 9- -1732 d 3- -1826 m (1)Jane Loud (2)Ann Loud FrN NH

GUPTILL,
Benjamin: b 1742 d 5-19-1819 m Mary — Pvt MA

GUPTON,
Abner: b 1756 d 8-20-1859 m (1)Judith Hunt (2)Martha Arthur
    (Ward) Sol NC

GURLEY,
Isham: b 1-13-1759 d p. 1835 m Nancy (Gurley) Pvt NC
Jacob: b 7-28-1742 d 2-20-1804 m Hannah Brigham MM MA
Jeremiah: b 12-29-1759 d 10-28-1843 m Frances — Pvt NC ★
Jonathan: b 4-2-1715 d 11-1-1778 m Hannah Baker PS CT
Phineas: b 3-30-1751 d p. 1795 m Susannah Swift Pvt CT

GURNEY, (includes GURNEA & GURNEE)
Asa: b 10-24-1758 d 12-10-1837 m Molly Reed Pvt MA
Asa: b 1758 d 3-25-1843 m Mary Hersey Fif Pvt MA
Benjamin: b c. 1743 d 7-4/5-1828 m Thankful Ellis Pvt MA
Francis: b 4-2-1735 d 5-12-1822 m Eleanor (Parcelle)Mace Pvt NY
Francis: b 4-9-1758 d 1850 m Susana Knapp Pvt NY ★
Francis: b 1735 d 5-25-1815 m Mary Porterfield LCol PA
Jacob: b 1763 d 2-11-1849 m Lydia Luell Pvt MA
John: b 4-17-1755 d 12-11-1796 m Mehitable Southworth Pvt MA
John: b 12-12-1729 d p. 3-10-1810 m Abigail Coe Pvt NY
Jonathan: b 4-4-1757 d 6-25-1818 m Susannah Byram Pvt MA ★
Joseph, Sr.: b 2-4-1735 d 5-13-1814 m Sarah Shaw Pvt MA
Joseph, Jr.: b 1760 d 5-28-1851 m Sally Reed Drm Pvt MA
Lemuel: b 8-5-1763 d 1-29-1853 m (1)Huldah Blanchard (2)Susan
    Smith Pvt MA ★
Noah: b 5-4-1735 d 7-14-1821 m Ruth Pool Pvt MA
Stephen, Sr.: b 12-22-1733 d p. 1790 m Sarah Halstead Pvt PS NY
Zachariah, Sr.: b 1729 d 1813 m Mary Ames Lt MA
Zachariah, Jr.: b 7-11-1762 d 1-12-1846 m Matilda Packard Pvt MA

GUSEMAN,
Abraham: b 3-19-1753 d 11-27-1821 m (1)Susannah Henlock
    (2)Catharine Bernard (3)Maria Elizabeth Ralph Snider Pvt VA

GUSHEE,
Elijah: b 2-16-1753 d 10-25-1834 m (1)Sally King (2)Jemimah
    Williams (3)Phebe Newcomber Pvt Grd MA ★
Samuel: b 3-14-1760 d 6-4-1840 m Hannah Gilmore Pvt MA

GUSTIN, (includes GUSTINE)
Amos: b 9-7-1753 d 8-9-1823 m (1)— Rogers (2)Susan Jones Pvt
    PA ★
Benajah: b 1-9-1766 d 6-18-1835 m Eleanor Bunton Pvt NJ ★
Ebenezer: b 1734 d 3-1-1794 m Lucy Ayers Pvt MA
Edward: b 4-13-1758 d p. 8-10-1832 m Waltna Martin Sgt CT ★
Elisha: b 1747 d 3-18-1834 m Mary Fletcher Pvt NH ★
Joel Trumbull: b 10-12-1757 d 6-11-1839 m Ann Taylor Green Sgt
    CT ★
John: b 2-12-1743 d 1815 m Lydia Mack Sgt NH
John: b 6-8-1760 d 4-30-1830 m (1)Esther Price (2)Sally Allen Pvt NJ
Lemuel: b 1749 d 10-17-1807 m (1)Susan Smith (2)Rebecca Parker
    Dr PA
Thomas: b 7-19-1725 d p. 1790 m Hannah Griswold Pvt CS
    PS NH
Wm.: b 1752 d 1790 m Priscilla Bunker Pvt PA

GUTEKUNST, (includes GOODYKOONTZ)
Frederick: b a. 1766 d 1785-90 m Margaret — Pvt PA
George: b 2-6-1732 d 1782 m Anna Margaretha — Pvt PA

GUTHRIDGE, (or GUTRIDGE)
John: b c. 1745 d 1824 m Elizabeth Turner Lt VA

GUTHRIE, (includes GUTTRY)
Archibald: b a. 1753 d 8-5-1779 m Rebecca Phillips Pvt PA
Daniel: b 2-14-1737 d 9-17-1806 m Jane — Sol PA
George: b 1755 d 10- -1813 m Margaret Campbell Pvt PA
Henry: b 12-10-1754 d 1-4-1837 m Nancy Ann Shackelford Pvt NC
    W★
James: b 4- -1732 d 4-22-1804 m Abigail Beets CS MA
James: b 2-25-1750 d 3-24-1841 m (1)Polly Welsh (2)Mrs Eunice
    (Cooper) Paul 2Lt PA VA W★
James: b 12-29-1753 d 4-5-1812 m (2)Melinda Teague (3)Rachel
    Pigg Ens VA
John: b 1-11-1749 d 8-12-1832 m Sarah Ann Davis Lt PA
John: b 4-14-1744 d 6-1-1823 m Lydia Baldwin Pvt PA ★
John: b c. 1746 d p. 9- -1795 m Margaret — Pvt PA
John: b c. 1728 d c. 1797 m Mary Jane Reed CS PA
Joseph: b 6- -1733 d 5-30-1808 m (1)Elizabeth (Carpenter) Carey
    (2)Rachel (Hand)Kirby (3) — (Woodward) Cogshell PS CT
Nathaniel: b 12-23-1763 d 1-12-1846 m Nancy John (Johns) Pvt
    VA ★
Robert: b 10-24-1756 d 4-13-1838 m Mary Taylor Pvt SC
Samuel: b 5-23-1756 d 8-23-1808 m (1)Sarah — (2)Anna — Pvt
    PS MA
Wm.: b 1722 d 1798 m Elenor Abbott Pvt NC
Wm.: b 1763 d 1-30-1835 m (1)Mary Batten (2)Hannah Batten Pvt
    PA
Wm.: b 1736 d 3-10-1823 m (1)Esther McClelland (2)Franky Young
    Pvt PA ★
Wm.: b 7-16-1744 d 4-8-1807 m Mary Welch Pvt PA
Wm.: b 7-9-1751 d 3-10-1828 m Mrs Elizabeth G. Brownlee Lt PA

GUY,
Andre: b 1736 d 11-4-1803 m Madelene Setteau Sol FrA
George: b c. 1725 d 11- -1803 m Ann Terry Capt PS VA
James: b a. 12-31-1742 d 4-6-1813 m Isabella Wasson Pvt NC
John: b 5-12-1756 d 3-19-1848 m Ester — Sgt NY ★
Robert: b c. 1753 d p. 2-19-1817 m Olive — PS PA
Timothy: b 1744 d 1784 m Anna White Cpl NY
Wm., Jr.: b 12-21-1754 d 9-15-1841 m Phebe Galencia Cpl Sgt NY
    RI ★
Wm.: b 1752 d 1824 m Nancy Mathias Pvt VA

GUYANT,
Luke: b 3-5-1750 d 9-30-1837 m (1)Abigail Tommas (2)Rachel
    Stark Tms Pvt CT ★

GUYSELL,
Christian: b 1762 d 1810 m Magdalena Earnest Cpl PA

GUYTHER,
George: b c. 1740 d 1797 m Sarah — 1Lt PS MD

GUYTON,
Aaron: b 10-27-1761 d 6-30-1841 m Margaret McCurdy Pvt SC
Joseph: b 1741 d 1818 m Hannah Whittaker PS SC
Moses: b 1750 d 5-27-1807 m Tabitha Saxon Lt SC

GWATHMEY,
Owen: b 11-25-1752 d 12-1-1830 m Ann Clark CS VA
Temple: b 1751 d 3-21-1831 m Ann Baylor PS VA

GWATKIN,
Charles: b 4-3-1741 d 1806 m Mary Calloway Capt CS VA

GWINN, (includes GUINN, GWIN, GWYN, GWYNN, GWYNNE)
Andrew: b 1752 d 1832 m Mary Dudley Pvt VA
Benjamin: b c. 1754 d p. 1820 m Sarah Griffith PS VA
Daniel: b 3-21-1751 d 5-2-1833 m Zipporah Rice Pvt NC
David: b 1745 d 1825 m (1)Jane Carlyle (2)Violet Crawford Capt VA
George: b 1728 d 2-6-1815 m Catharine Brabson Pvt PA
George Holmes: b — d p. 10- -1794 m (1)Nancy Arrington
    (2)Elizabeth — PS VA
Humphry: b 12-8-1727 d 11-30-1794 m Frances Peyton Pvt VA
James: b 1768 d 8-3-1841 m Mary Adair McAdams Pvt PS NC
John: b 1746 d 9-16-1800 m Julia Stull Sgt MD W★
John: b c. 1750 d 1823 m X PS MD
John: b 12-15-1764 d p. 9-11-1839 m Sarah Donnell Pvt NC ★
John: b 1763 d 4-7-1844 m Mary Ammon Drm VA ★
Joseph: b 2-3-1745 d 4-5-1831 m Hester Layton Pvt PA
Nicholas: b 2-24-1745 d p. 1785 m (1)Mary Giroud (2)Mary Elizabeth
    Bland Pvt SC
Richard: b 1738 d 1777 m Sarah Ransome PS NC
Samuel: b 1752 d 3-25-1839 m Elizabeth (Lockridge) Graham Sct
    Spy VA
Wm.: b 1753 d 1828 m Eleanor Pryor Pvt VA

GWINNUP,
George: b 1754 d 8-16-1840 m Margaret Simpson Sgt NJ ★

HAAS, (includes HOSS & HORSE)
Jacob: b *c.* 1734 d *p.* 2-20-1816 m Mary Boone Sol PS NC
John: b 10-29-1757 d 1-28-1838 m Lydia Rue Pvt NJ ★
John: b 3-11-1737 d 10-5-1802 m Elizabeth Hellwig Pvt PA
John, Sr.: b *c.* 1730 d 5- -1784 m Catherine — 2Lt PA
John, Jr.: b *c.* 1757 d *p.* 1784 m Ann Catherine Heller Sol PA
John: b 1756 d 2- -1827 m Elisabeth Wilkin Grd PS VA
Peter: b 12-25-1748 d 6-9-1834 m Maria Christina Trexler Pvt PA
Peter: b *c.* 1750-60 d 3-13-1835 m Eva Hummell Pvt PA
Peter: b 11-4-1758 d 8-1-1808 m Susannah Keil Pvt PA
Simon: b *c.* 1725 d 1779 m Susanna Elizabeth Whittenburg Pvt NC

HABECKER, (includes HAWBECKER)
John: b *c.* 1765 d *p.* 1813 m (1) X Fif PA
Joseph: b 1-24-1754 d 10-26-1800 m Mary Witmore Pvt PA

HABER (or HOOVER)
Johannes: bpt 10-11-1748 d 3-21-1787 m Gertrude Stahl Pvt NY

HABERSHAM,
James, Jr.: b *p.* 1740 d *p.* 1786 m Esther Wylly PS GA
John: b 12-23-1744 d 12-17-1799 m Ann Sarah Camber Maj GA
Joseph: b 7-28-1751 d 11-15-1815 m Isabella Rae Col GA

HACHENBERG,
Johann Peter: b 1741 d 3-4-1820 m Annie Elizabeth Seyfoot Ens PS PA

HACK,
Nathan: b 1733 d 8-27-1809 m (1)Kate Lincoln (2)Rebecca Haskins Lt MA

HACKER,
Hoysted: b — d 7- -1814 m Mary Elizabeth — NCapt RI
John: b 1-1-1743 d 4-20-1824 m Marguerette Sleeth Pvt VA

HACKETT,
Daniel: b 5-25-1753 d 7-11-1841 m Hannah Colby Pvt NH
Ebenezer: b 9-23-1730 d *p.* 1-28-1801 m Abigail Emery Pvt NH
Edward: b 6-5-1748 d 1836 m Sarah (Hedge ?) Sgt MA ★
Elijah: b 4-26-1753 d *p.* 1800 m Wealthy — Pvt MA
Ezekiel: b 5-12-1762 d 3-29-1840 m Susan Graffam Pvt MA ★
Ezra: b — d — m Hannah Plaisted Pvt NH
James: b 10-15-1739 d 10-17-1802 m Joanna Gilman Lt NH
Jeremiah: bpt 1740 d 1797 m Mary Robinson Ens PS NH
John: b 4-28-1743 d *p.* 5-7-1783 m Sarah Walters Pvt NH
John: b *c.* 1740 d *p.* 1-28-1809 m X Mil PA
Josiah: b *c.* 1752 d *p.* 1790 m Abigail Hackett Pvt PS NH
Josiah: b 6-15-1758 d 7-4-1845 m Mary Booth Sgt MA RI ★
Martin: b *c.* 1755 d *p.* 1803 m Faney Garrett PS VA
Moses: b 1755/6 d 4-20-1807 m Keziah Ladd Pvt NH
Peter: b *c.* 1766 d *p.* 1820 m — Adkins Pvt VA
Robert: b *c.* 1740 d 1789/1790 m (1)Margaret Sloan (2)Anna Terrell Willis Pvt SC
Samuel: b *c.* 1751 d *p.* 2-4-1784 m (1)Mary Randall (2)Mrs Meriah Cole Cobb Pvt MA
Thomas: b *c.* 1725/6 d *a.* 1830 m X Pvt VA
Thomas: b 1753 d *a.* 1817 m Mary Johnston Pvt VA
Wm.: b 5-1-1739 d 11-20-1808 m Anna Osgood Pvt MA

HACKLEMAN,
Jacob: b 7-16-1752 d 1-16-1829 m Mary Osborne Pvt NC

HACKLEY,
Francis: b 5-16-1740 d 7-17-1817 m Fanny Lightfoot Sol VA
James: b *c.* 1750 d *p.* 9-17-1804 m Elizabeth — PS VA
Simeon: b 6-1-1748 d 5-19-1825 m Lydia Cogswell Pvt MA

HACKMAN,
Jacob: b 9-12-1747 d 7-19-1804 m Fannie Shiffer Pvt PA
John: b 6-14-1754 d 6-15-1831 m Eve Shrager Pvt PA

HACKNEY,
John: b 1760 d 1-10-1843 m Jane V. — FifMaj DE ★
Joseph: b 7-8-1763 d 5-20-1832 m Margaret Mercer McGrady Pvt NY W★
Joseph: b 1752 d 2-18-1839 m Nancy Hackney Capt NC ★
Wm.: b *c.* 1752 d 1822 m (2)Mrs Peggy Marsh PS NC

HACKWORTH,
George: b 2-28-1752 d *p.* 1810 m Ann — Pvt VA
Thomas: b 4-11-1763 d *p.* 4-23-1855 m Elizabeth Johnson Pvt VA
Wm.: b 1752 d 5-23-1831 m Dorothy Newman Pvt VA W★

HADCOCK,
Daniel: b 1755 d *p.* 5-19-1834 m Betsy Clock Cpl NY

HADDAWAY,
Wm. Webb, Sr.: b 1711 d *a.* 10-16-1786 m Frances Harrison PS MD
Wm. Webb, Jr.: b 1736 d 11-11-1810 m Sarah Lambdin LCol MD

HADDEN, (includes HADDON, HADEN & HEADEN)
Anthony: b 3-26-1746 d 4-28-1828 m (1)Drucilla Roundtree (2)Anna Dabney Capt VA
Anthony: b 1752 d 1835 m Susan Crenshaw Pvt VA
Anthony D.: b *c.* 1763 d 5-23-1829 m (1)Martha Vaughan (2)Rebecca — Pvt VA ★
David: b *c.* 1735 d *p.* 5-13-1791 m — PS VA
Douglas: b *c.* 1750 d *p.* 1800 m Elizabeth — Capt PS NC
John, Jr.: b *c.* 1750 d 1- -1810 m (1)Freedom Polly (2)Delight Litchfield Pvt MA
John: b 1760 d 6-19-1819 m Isabella Elliott Sct VA
Joseph: b 1740 d 1830 m Mary Tully Capt VA
Thomas, Sr.: b 1736 d 9- -1778 m Annabel Crowell LCol NJ
Thomas, Jr.: b 6-24-1760/1 d 7-30-1803 m Mary Baker Pvt NJ
Wm.: b *c.* 1725 d 1789 m Unity — PS NC
Wm.: b *c.* 1760 d *p.* 1823 m Elizabeth Robinson DeFoe Pvt SC
Wm.: b *c.* 1730 d 1781-86 m Mary (Lochard) More PS SC
Wm.: b 1760 d 1827 m Mary Eustace Ens VA
Wm.: b *c.* 1752 d 8-20-1815 m (1)Nancy Johnson (2)Mary Lee Mart Pvt VA

HADDOCK,
Charles: b 1731-3 d 5-6-1796 m (1)Sarah Whitney (2)Susannah Brickett Sol PS MA

HADGER,
Robert: b 6-7-1749 d 5-2-1836 m Sarah Haight Sgt NY ★

HADLEY,
Abraham: b 9-26-1759 d 12-9-1814 m Eunice Evelett Pvt MA
Ambrose: b 10-24-1758 d 11-18-1839 m (1)Anne Bustin (2)Elizabeth Parham (3)Louisa McLeod PS NC
Daniel: b 1-15-1744 d *c.* 1830/31 m (2)Hannah Ordway Pvt PS NH
Ebenezer: b 5-5-1751 d 6-15-1810 m Phebe Winship Sgt MA
Ebenezer: b 11-8-1727 d 4-27-1815 m Abigail Spalding CS VT
Eliphalet: b 5-22-1746 d *a.* 10-18-1796 m Ruth Hadley Sol PS NH
Enos: b 10-24-1755 d *c.* 1839 m Betsey Farmer Pvt MA ★
Frederick: b 1757 d 9-25-1820 m Catherine Purdy Pvt NJ NY
George: b 8-8-1742 d 11-3-1823 m (1)Lydia Wells (2)Mehitable Toy Capt CS PS NH
George: b 8- -1760 d 2-6-1835 m Margaret Parker Pvt NY
Isaac: b 10-19-1752 d 1-14-1836 m Ann Sunacher Sgt NY ★
Jacob: b 3-8-1752 d 10-4-1840 m Elizabeth Putnam Pvt NH ★
James: b *c.* 1763 d 9-5-1832 m Rhoda Jones Sgt PA ★
Jane Fiske: b 5-2-1733 d 1-17-1819 m Josiah Hadley PS MA
Jeremiah: b 1-7-1741 d *p.* 1784 m Mary Dickey PS NC
Jonas: b 5-26-1756 d 1-9-1807 m Azubah Prescott Pvt MA
Joseph: b *a.* 1750 d 1793 m Lydia — Capt NC
Joshua: b 7-13-1753 d 2-8-1830 m Hannah Holmes Capt NC
Joshua: b 5-23-1743 d 8-4-1815 m (1)Ruth Lindley (2)Lydia Hyatt (3)Jane Henshaw PS NC
Josiah: b 5-5-1731 d *p.* 1790 m Jane Fiske Pvt MA
Moses: b 7-20-1756 d 1-8-1826 m Mary Pierce Pvt MA
Moses: b 11-14-1750 d 9-9-1829 m Rebecca Page Pvt PS NH
Samuel, Sr.: b — d *p.* 1790 m Abigail Richardson PS MA
Simon: b 7-26-1761 d — m Olive Porter Pvt MA
Simon: b 1760 d 1835 m Jane Wilkinson Capt NC
Thomas: b 8-11-1712 d 7-15-1788 m Ruth Lawrance MM MA
Thomas: b 1728 d 9- -1781 m Mary Thompson Capt PS MA
Wm.: b 2-1-1732 d 11-22-1801 m Elizabeth Werner PS NY
Wm.: b 4-20-1749 d 1-12-1842 m Sarah — Pvt RI ★

HADLOCK,
Jonathan: b 7-14-1742 d 1801-25 m Betty Pettee Pvt PS NH

HADSELL, (includes HASSELL)
Benjamin: b — d 5- -1792 m Ann Snell PS NC
Elijah: b 4-10-1759 d 6-24-1848 m Anna Michael Pvt RI
James: b 2-4-1726 d 6-30-1778 m Content Worden PS PA
Samuel: b 1753 d 1821 m Betsey — Sol PA

HAFF, (includes HOFF)
Abraham: b *c.* 1725 d 5-19-1812 m Jane Beatty Maj MD
Adam: b 12-12-1758 d 2-13-1834 m Anna Maria Eschinfelt Pvt PA
George: b 10-22-1733 d 8-18-1816 m Justina Margaretta Schneitzel Pvt PA
Henry: b 8-6-1760 d 2-2-1838 m Maria Utz Pvt PA ★
John: b 4- -1734 d 4-3-1818 m Helena Stout Pvt NJ
John: b 1748 d 1823 m Rebecca Storm Pvt NY
Laurens: b *c.* 1746 d *p.* 1784 m Cathrina Shurrie Ens NY

HAFFA,
Henry: b 12-13-1737 d 1-1-1801 m Maria Salome CMman CS PA

HAFLICH, (includes HAFFLICH)
Jacob: b *c.* 1755 d 1816 m Margaret — Pvt PA
Jacob: b 1-3-1755 d 11-12-1813 m Caroline — Pvt PA

HAFT, (includes HALFT)
John, Jr.: b 1757 d 1828 m (1)Elizabeth Thomson (2)Elizabeth Leggett Pvt PA

HAGADORN,
Hendrick: b 9-18-1720 d 10-17-1809 m (1)Angentie Vedder (2)Eva Van Alstyne (3)Santyje Vroman Pvt NY
Jacob: b 1725 d 7-23-1784 m Maretje DeHart 1Lt NY
John: b 11-11-1747 d 11-30-1797 m Hannah Lape Pvt NY
Samuel: b 1-24-1762 d *p.* 1832 m Julia Christenance Pvt NY

HAGAN, (includes HEAGAN)
John: b 1760 d 2-2-1830 m Betsey Stinson Pvt MA
Ralph: b 1753 d 8- -1826 m Rebecca Lavielle Cpl MD

HAGAR, (includes HAGER)
Aaron: b 1759 d 1834 m Rachel Stone Pvt MA ★
Benjamin: b 1-20-1749 d 4-25-1823 m Esther Child Pvt MA
David: b 3-28-1753 d 1-10-1822 m Levina Holden Pvt MA
Ebenezer: b 3-16-1728 d 12-19-1798 m Abigail Stow Pvt MA
Ezekiel: b 3-16-1756 d 3-17-1833 m Esther Hagar Pvt MA
Henry: b 9-1-1702 d 7-13-1796 m Anna Gertrude Petrie PS NY
Isaac: b 9-6-1742 d 1-27-1791 m Anna Bullard Col MA
Jacob: b 8-21-1734 d 8-21-1819 m Cornelia Vrooman Capt NY
John, Sr.: b 9-17-1726 d 7-23-1804 m (1)Hannah Stearns (2)Sarah Child Pvt MA
John, Jr.: b 10-6-1757 d 5-11-1842 m Eunice Whitehead Pvt MA ★
John: b 1-2-1745 d 1-4-1829 m Maria Swart Pvt NY
John: b 1748 d 1810 m Anna Maria Drach Pvt PA
John: b 1749 d 12-6-1813 m Maria Barbara Miller Pvt PA
John: b 12-26-1759 d 1819 m Mary Shrader Pvt PA
Jonathan: b 8-31-1751 d 4-9-1783 m Sarah Mixer Sgt MA
Joseph, Jr.: b 1-1-1736 d 10-1-1776 m Lois Fisk Pvt MA
Joseph: b 1762 d 5-22-1818 m Nancy — Pvt NY ★
Nathan: b 1-26-1744 d 10-3-1802 m Anna Bigelow Pvt MA
Peter: b 3-7-1746 d 10-14-1820 m Mertie Laraway 1Lt NY
Phineas: b 4-6-1755 d 8-24-1817 m Susan Leadbetter Pvt MA
Simeon: b 7-17-1730 d *p.* 1790 m Susanna Priest Sgt MA
Simon: b 1763 d 1-28-1835 m Elizabeth — Pvt NC
Wm.: b 4-19-1749 d 1-23-1820 m Abigail Fullerton Wgn MA

HAGENBUCH,
Andreas: b *c.* 1715 d 1785 m (1)Magdalene — (2)Maria Margaritha PS PA
Christian: b 1747 d 1-25-1812 m Susanna — Pvt PA
Henry: b 1-20-1736 d 4-20-1803 m Susanna Wettsein Capt PA
John: b 9-24-1763 d 3-20-1846 m Maria Madalena Dreisbach Pvt PA
Michael: b 9-17-1746 d 3-23-1809 m Eve Elizabeth Kunz Pvt PA

HAGENS, (includes HAGGINS &HAGINS)
Edmund: b 1732 d 1-1-1777 m Anne Simonton Annie Swanton Dr PS ME
John: b 1753 d 3-1-1825 m (1)Mildred Margaret Johnson (2)Nancy Gibbs Capt VA
Walter: b 10-26-1765 d 9-29-1847 m Mary Libby Pvt MA
Wm.: b 6-25-1766 d 9-8-1833 m Polly — Pvt NC ★

HAGERMAN, (includes HAGAMAN, HAGEMAN)
Adrian: b 8-8-1745 d 6-22-1821 m Jane Lupardus Pvt NJ
Barnett: b 1756-60 d *p.* 1840 m Susan — Pvt PA
Henry: b 1-11-1753 d 1791 m Rebecca Searle PS PA
John: b 1-10-1718 d *c.* 1797 m Jannetje Van Hoorn Pvt NY
Joseph: b 3-27-1740 d 12-18-1817 m Elizabeth Van Wagenen Capt NY
Ruloff: b 3-25-1744 d 11-8-1802 m Catharine Holmes Sgt NJ
Wm. D.: b — d 1835 m Sarah Silvernail Jones Pvt NY

HAGEY, (includes HEAGEY, HEAGIE)
Adam: b 1752 d 1839 m Mary — Sol Grd PA ★
John: b 1-23-1747 d 2-8-1821 m Anna Maria Ens PA
John: b 1748-50 d 7-14-1841 m Catherine Hult Grd FrA
Martin: b 1-18-1761 d 1-1-1812 (1)Margaretha Bauman (2)Maria Elizabetha Beamesderfer Pvt PA
Wm.: b 1-21-1758 d 2-23-1834 m Catherine Katz Sol PA

HAGGARD,
David: b 2-4-1764 d 1843 m Nancy Dawson Pvt VA
James: b 1759 d 8-2-1843 m Elizabeth Gentry Pvt VA ★
John: b *c.* 1753 d 12-29-1792 m X Pvt NC
Nathaniel: b 11-21-1723 d 1805 m Elizabeth Gentry PS VA
Wm.: b 8-7-1753 d 7-23-1852 m Mary Aken Pvt NC VA ★

HAGGERTY, (includes HAGERTY)
John: b 1757 d 1-22-1822 m Mary Taylor Pvt NJ ★
Wm.: b 1750 d 1837 m Nancy Burford Pvt PA

HAGGOTT,
Wm.: b 3-27-1752 d 6-17-1775 m Rebecca Heath Pvt MA

HAUGE,
Wm.: b *c.* 1746 d 12- -1843 m Ruth Mendenhall Pvt PA

HAHN, (includes HANN, HAUN, HAWN)
Bennedick: b *c.* 1747 d 1806-17 m — Houk PS NC
Conrad: b *a.* 1750 d 8-6-1777 m Elizabeth Windecker Pvt NY
Dewalt: b 2-6-1750 d 3-3-1833 m Ann Frany Alleman Sgt PA

Frederick: b 11-16-1747 d 11-25-1815 m Elizabeth Metz Pvt PA
George: b 12-28-1758 d 12-31-1829 m Elizabeth Margaret Sorber Cpl PA
Henry, Sr.: b 3-20-1723 d 10-5-1802 m Catherine Reiffel PS PA
Henry, Jr.: b 6-13-1754 d 10-14-1843 m Catherine Hill PS Pvt PA
John: b 6-12-1712 d 4-21-1793 m Elizabeth Margaretha — PS NC
John: b *c.* 1758 d *p.* 1783 m Mrs. Bear Pvt PA
John: b 10-5-1757 d 4-5-1817 m Catherine Herner Pvt Wgm PA W★
Joseph: b *c.* 1765 d *c.* 1850/1 m Dorcas Fields Pvt PA ★
Peter: b *c.* 1740 d 1810 m Maria Margaret Schmidt Pvt PA
Peter Philip: b 12-15-1715 d 11-12-1800 m (1)Angeline Housman (2)Anna Engle Haussman PS PA
Philip: b 3-31-1736 d 4-16-1821 m Anna Margaretha Hiester Capt PA
Wm.: b 1738 d 2-1-1809 m Anna Maria Sharp Pvt NJ

HAIGHT,
Aaron, Jr.: b 1-11-1750 d 9-3-1816 m Jemmima Waters Pvt NY
Benjamin: b 1737 d 11-19-1805 m Rachel Peck Pvt NY
Cornelius: b 3-17-1758 d 9-17-1841 m Mary Southworth Sol NY
Daniel: b 1732 d 9-4-1812 m Martha Fowler PS NY
Jacob: b 1748 d *p.* 1782 m Phoebe Haviland Lt NY
John: b 8-18-1742/3 d 7-15-1836 m Miriam Swim Capt NY
John: b 1-15-1738 d 3-24-1819 m Abigail Haviland Pvt NY
Jonathan: b 1736-40 d 1779/80 m Elizabeth Rogers Pvt PS NY
Jonathan: b 12-20-1749 d 3-12-1835 m Miriam Hoag Pvt NY
Joseph: b 4-27-1739 d 4-4-1795 m (1)Rebekah Griffith (2)Mrs Hannah Tallman Rogers LCol NJ
Moses: b 1723 d 1805 m — Pvt NY
Samuel: b 4-20-1748 d 1809 m Abigail Simmons Pvt NY
Silas: b *c.* 1750 d *a.* 1805 m Hannah Cudberth Pvt NY
Solomon: b 11-1-1759 d *p.* 1800 m Elizabeth Covert Pvt NY
Stephen: b 5-8-1760 d 12-22-1812 m Abigail Lane Pvt NY
Wm.: b 10-6-1762 d 4- -1837 m Sarah Rogers Mid PS NJ ★

HAIR,
David: b *c.* 1761 d *p.* 3-20-1843 m — Pvt NC
John: b 1754 d *p.* 1840 m Nancy Torbett Pvt PA

HAIRSTON,
George: b 9-20-1750 d 3-5-1827 m Elizabeth Letcher Capt CS VA
Peter: b 2-24-1752 d 12-1-1832 m Alcey Perkins Capt NC
Robert: b *c.* 1717 d *p.* 5-26-1790 m Ruth Stovall Capt CS PS VA

HAISLIP,
Laban: b *c.* 1754 d 12-14-1816 m (1)Ellener Williams (2)Rebecca Welch Cpl PS MD

HAISTEN,
John: b 1762 d 12-15-1835 m Nancy Ellis Pvt VA ★

HAKE, (includes HAAK)
Andrew: b 3-13-1764 d 6-18-1832 m Anna Maria Witmayer Pvt PA
Fredrick: b 7-17-1761 d 4-2-1830 m Kathryn Krome Pvt PA
Johannes Nicholas: b 3-27-1757 d 12- -1811 m Maria Catherine Radebach Pvt PS PA

HAKES,
Caleb: b 7-30-1752 d 3-27-1839 m Sybil Lewis Pvt RI CT
George Solomon, Jr.: b 1-27-1751 d 1826 m Serviah Church Pvt MA
James: b 3-25-1752 d 6-4-1830 m Martha Adams Pvt RI
Jesse: b 1762 d 1813 m Esther Brown Pvt NY W★
John: b 5-20-1755 d 2-9-1841 m Dezier Downing Pvt MA ★
Jonathan, Sr.: b 1724 d 6- -1779 m Hannah F. Brown Sol RI CT
Jonathan, Jr.: b 1757 d 7-11-1835 m Esther Breed Pvt CT RI ★
Richard: b 4-8-1741 d 7-5-1815 m Mary Babcock PS CT
Solomon: b 12-12-1758 d 10-8-1841 m Anna Downing Pvt MA

HALBERT, (includes HOLBERT, HULBERT)
James, Sr.: b 3-7-1734 d 11-16-1777 m Jennette Hunter Lt MA
James, Jr.: b 5-23-1761 d 2-11-1817 m (1)Mary — (2)Ruth Selden Pvt MA
James: b *c.* 1760 d — m Sally Shaddock Sol VA
John: bpt 5-4-1740 d 1784-7 m Eleanor McAllister Lt MA
Wm.: b 10- -1744 d 12-28-1808 m Elizabeth Hill Lt VA

HALDEMAN, (includes HALDERMAN, HOLDEMAN, HOLDERMAN)
Abraham: b 1746 d 1827 m Mary Showalter Pvt PA
Christian: b 1742 d 1832 m Elizabeth Brower Pvt PA
Christopher: b 1730 d *a.* 3-28-1803 m — PS PA
Jacob: b 1752 d 1-1-1799 m Magdalena Halderman Pvt PA
Jacob, Sr.: b 10-7-1722 d 4- -1783 m Maria Miller PS PA
Jacob, Jr.: b 8-14-1747 d 12-18-1790 m Elizabeth Musselman Pvt PA
John: b *a.* 1750 d 12-7-1819 m Maria — Pvt PA
John: b 6-2-1753 d 5-9-1832 m Maria Breneman Pvt PA

HALE, (includes HAILS, HALES & HEALE)
Aaron: b 7-22-1740 d 5-26-1829 m Hannah Daniels Capt NY ★
Abner: b 7-22-1737 d *p.* 8-28-1807 m Abigail Goodridge Pvt MA
Ambrose: b 1740 d 12-27-1811 m Mercy Davy Pvt MA
Amon: b 6-16-1759 d 12-4-1843 m Mary — Pvt MD ★

HALE, contd.

Amos: b 5-25-1752 d 1- -1827 m Sarah Day Cpl MA
Amos: b 1736 d 8-25-1818 m Ruth Esterbrooks Capt RI
Amos: b c. 1745/6 d p. 1796 m Achsah (Haile) Sgt VT
Asa: b 11-6-1759 d 12-2-1843 m Dorcas Mead Pvt CS MA NH VT ★
Benjamin: b 1763 d 8-16-1855 m (1)Susan Whitney (2)Mrs Mercy Rand Pvt MA ★
Benjamin: b c. 1730 d p. 1809 m (1)Kate Ferguson (2)Sally — Capt SC
Benjamin: b 4-30-1735 d 12-4-1781 m Lydia White Pvt NH
Bezaleel: b 10-12-1759 d 10-15-1851 m Abagail Eveleth Pvt MA
Bezaleel: b 10-22-1715 d 12-1-1804 m Abigail Markle MM MA
Daniel: b 1736 d 7-9-1790 m Ruth Hale Pvt CT
Daniel: b 7-30-1758 d 9-5-1830 m Cynthia Buffington Pvt MA
Daniel: b 11-28-1755 d 3-25-1848 m (1)Elizabeth Dow (2)Elizabeth Fellows Cpl MA ★
Daniel: b a. 1754 d 9-2-1821 m Sarah Blake Lt PS NY
David: b 1-11-1727 d 4-7-1796 m Mary Welles Sol CT
David: b 11-24-1749 d p. 1790 m Rachel Foster Pvt MA
David: b 2-17-1756 d 3-2-1822 m Olive Bailey Pvt MA
David: b 3-10-1758 d 10- -1822 m Hannah Emerson Pvt MA
David: b 9-30-1729 d — m Mehitable Eastman Pvt NH
Ebenezer: b 11-11-1758 d 7-26-1805 m Merriam Bunnell Pvt CT
Edward: b 1750 d 1820 m Patsy Pe Due Pvt VA
Eliphalet: b 5-20-1762 d p. 1785 m Rachael Scott Pvt NH
Elisha: b 1729 d 10-6-1809 m Mary Brown Pvt MA
Eiizur: b 1724 d 1790 m Abigail Hollister Capt CT
Enoch: b 10-28-1753 d 1-4-1837 m Octavia Throop Chp CT
Enoch: b 12-10-1757 d 1825 m Mary Woodwell Pvt MA
Enoch: b 11-28-1733 d 4-9-1813 m Abigail Stanley Col NH
Ezekiel: b c. 1764 d 8-9-1791 m Hannah Marshall Pvt MA
Francis: b 3-4-1759 d 1-28-1834 m Olive Harrison Pvt MA
George: b 9-8-1728 d a. 10-27-1806 m Sarah Smith PS VA
Gershom: b 7-10-1756 d 11-28-1832 m (1)Esther Bennett (2)Lois — Pvt CT ★
Henry: b 8-4-1707 d 5-21-1792 m Mary Barlett PS NH
Hezekiah: b 5-4-1737 d p. 1790 m (1)Jerusha Parsons (2)Mrs Rachel Bivins (3)Anna Blake PS CT
Hezekiah: b 8-29-1729 d 5- -1802 m Abigail Hanmer Lt MA
Isaac: b 1757 d 12-7-1832 m Ester — Pvt CT
Isaac: b 3-21-1763 d 11-1-1839 m Elizabeth Lewis Pvt VT
Isaiah: b 3-13-1764 d 1852 m Winnie Olive Pvt NC
Israel: b 6-12-1759 d 5-16-1841 m Esther Taylor Pvt MA
Israel: b c. 1760 d 1-1-1796 m Abigail Willson Pvt VT
Jacob: b 12-8-1744 d 5-3-1832 m Ruth Towne Pvt MA
Jacob: b 1-20-1722 d 7-9-1782 m Elizabeth Holman Pvt MA
James: b 10-30-1745 d 5-4-1808 m Hannah Hicks Sgt VT
John: b 1746 d 1810 m Mehitable Knowlton Ens CT
John: b 6-16-1722 d 1787 m Elinor Knight PS MA
John: b 2-10-1752 d 11-24-1843 m Abagail Hale Pvt MA
John: b 10-24-1731 d 10-22-1791 m Elizabeth Hall Col Dr NH
John: b 9- -1742 d 3-3-1792 m Olive Blake Capt NH
John: b 3-29-1731 d 9- -1803 m Mrs Sarah Severance CS PS NH
John: b 1740 d 1820 m — Lt NC
John: b c. 1715 d c. 1798 m Ann Kellam PS CS Sol NC
Jonathan: b 1718 d 3-7-1776 m Elizabeth Welles Capt CT
Jonathan: b 1753 d 10-29-1807 m Mary Clark Fif Maj CT W★
Joseph: b 3-12-1750 d 4-30-1784 m Rebecca Harris Lt CT
Joseph: b 10-1-1735 d p. 3-27-1790 m Hannah Lovewell Pvt NH
Joshua: b 8-24-1764 d 7-22-1825 m Sally Cutter Pvt NH
Josiah: b 1-27-1747 d 7-8-1808 m Anne Welles PS CS CT
Josiah: b 8-21-1756 d p. 1799 m Abigail Joslyn Pvt MA
Josiah: b 1757 d 7-1-1811 m Abigal Williams Pvt VT
Lewis: b 11- -1742 d 7-2-1802 m Mary Burwell Sol VA
Moses: b 6-5-1742 d 5-31-1828 m Ruth Foster Capt CS PS MA
Moses: b 7-5-1745 d 1814 m Abigail Smith Sol MA
Moses, Sr.: b 2-28-1731/2 d 3-2-1799 m Abigail Emerson PS Sol NH
Moses, Jr.: b 8-7-1760 d 10-25-1829 m (1)Sibyl Adams (2)Mrs Sybil Sawtell Pvt NH
Moses: b 12-8-1754 d 1-16-1827 m Abigail Page Pvt PS NH
Moses: b 6-29-1729 d 11-21-1819 m Mary Edwards Pvt VT
Nathan: b 9-23-1743 d 9-23-1780 m Abigail Grout Col NH
Nicholas: b c. 1723 d p. 4-9-1807 m Ruth — Ens PS MD
Philip: b 4-18-1753 d 10-20-1819 m Catherine Douglas PS VA
Reuben, Sr.: b c. 1732 d p. 1788 m Diantha Ward Pvt CT
Reuben, Jr.: b 4-24-1760 d 4-9-1828 m (1)Esther Mallory (2)Martha Higbee Pvt CT ★
Richard: b 2-28-1717 d 1-1-1802 m (1)Elizabeth Strong (2)Mrs Abigail Adams PS CT
Richard: b 1757 d 1830 m Olive Wheden Pvt RI
Robert: b 10- -1754 d 3- -1816 m (1)— McNichol (2)Susanna Richardson (3) — Marshall (4)Sarah McGinney Capt SC
Samuel: b 4-29-1752 d 1- -1831 m Mindwell Pease Pvt Cpl CT
Samuel: b 10-26-1741 d c. 1809 m Abigail Austin Ens CT
Samuel: b 4-2-1719 d 7-5-1805 m Eleanor Smith Drm MA
Samuel: b 8-24-1718 d 7-10-1807 m Mary Wright CS NH
Samuel: b 1745 d 4-19-1820 m Mindwell Tillotson Pvt NH
Shadrack: b 1731 d c. 1809 m Mary — Sol NC
Silas: b 2-28-1760 d 3-15-1835 m (1)Sarah Parsons (2)Huldah — Pvt MA
Simeon: b 1-18-1739 d 1796 m (2)Sarah Hunt Pvt MA

Stephen: b c. 1745 d p. 1806 m Nancy Hale PS VA
Thomas, Jr.: b 1-22-1743 d 1-2-1834 m Ruth Hardy Lt MA
Thomas: b 1-8-1714/5 d 9-18-1796 m Mary Kimball Lt MA
Thomas: b 10-9-1759 d 4-3-1808 m Elizabeth Wilder Drm MA
Thomas: b 1758 d 1842 m Rachel — Pvt NC SC ★
Thomas: b 10-19-1742 d 1812 m Jane — Capt VA
Thomas: b c. 1750 d a. 12-27-1829 m Elizabeth — Pvt VA
Tilly: b c. 1745-55 d p. 3-26-1811 m Hannah (Bailey) PS MD
Timothy, Sr.: b 1692 d 8-9-1784 m Sarah Frary PS CT
Timothy, Jr.: b 8-3-1727 d 6-25-1801 m Hannah Hale Capt CT
Wm.: b 5-5-1724 d 8-31-1807 m Hannah Brewer Pvt MA
Wm.: b 1761 d p. 1820 m — Williamson Pvt VA ★
Zebulon: b c. 1748 d 3-22-1821 m Rachel Bishop Pvt CT

HALEY, (includes HAILEY & HALLEY)

Anthony: b 1759 d 8-6-1842 m Mary Dennison Pvt VA ★
Benjamin: b — d 1801 m (1)Agatha Hawkins (2)Elizabeth — PS VA
David: b c. 1755 d 1839 m (1)Letitia Cloud (2)Betsy Fleenor Pvt PA
David: b 10-5-1760 d 9-20-1839 m (1)Elizabeth — (2)Mrs. M. C. Griffin Pvt SC
Henry Simpson: b 5-10-1762 d 11-28-1838 m Elizabeth Hampton Pvt VA ★
James: b 5-4-1732 d 8-25-1827 m Frances — Sgt VA
James: b 1743 d 1794 m Mary Jane — Sgt VA
John: b 3-8-1720 d 10-16-1800 m Deborah Fanning Pvt CT
John: b 6-20-1737 d 6-26-1816 m Mary Malcomb Sgt MA
Joseph, Jr.: bpt 9-9-1759 d 11-5-1845 m Jemima Tarbox Sgt MA
Joseph, Jr.: b c. 1753 d 9-29-1832 m Esther Towne Cpl MA
Joshua: b c. 1740 d 2-18-1812 m (1)Elizabeth Wingate (2)Priscilla Emery 2Lt MA
Lewis: b 1748 d p. 1833 m Nancy Loveless Sgt VA ★
Pelatiah: b 10-8-1740 d 10-29-1819 m Elizabeth Lewis Cpl MA
Richard: b 1750 d 1816 m Lydia — Sol VA
Samuel: b 6-10-1759 d 6-12-1837 m Martha Nealley Pvt NH
Thomas: b 12-19-1722 d 1815 m Mary Lamson Pvt NH
Wm.: b 7-27-1748 d 11-24-1830 m Mary Turman Pvt GA
Wm.: b 1737 d p. 1818 m Harriet Forester Pvt MD
Wm.: bpt 3-13-1743 d 5-4-1802 m (1)Miriam Fernald (2)Miriam Johnson 1Lt MA
Wm.: b 1757 d p. 1778 m (1)Dorcas Hilton (2)Sarah Adams Pvt MA
Wm., Sr.: b 1720 d 1796 m Mary — Pvt VA
Wm., Jr.: b 1- -1750 d 1818 m Bathshiba Dulin Pvt VA

HALFERTY,

Edward: b c. 1748 d 3-23-1825 m Margaret Flack Pvt PA

HALL,

Aaron: b 11-11-1760 d 9-29-1839 m (1)Elizabeth Cook (2)Mrs Sarah Hall (3)Anna Brooks Pvt CT ★
Aaron: b 5-23-1751 d 9-4-1835 m (1)Aphia Parkinson (2)Sarah Richardson Pvt CT
Abel: b 10-5-1743 d 12-1-1816 m Caroline Brockway Capt CT
Abel: b 1715 d p. 1790 m Ruth Johnson PS CT
Abijah: b 6-7-1754 d 8-19-1812 m (1)Sarah Read (2)Mary Read Cpl NH
Abner: b 4-28-1764 d 10-5-1844 m (2)Hannah Booth PS Pvt CT ★
Abraham, Sr.: b 9-17-1730 d p. 1797 m Jerusha Bowen Pvt CT
Abraham, Jr.: b 5-29-1755 d 8- -1818 m (1)Mabel Cowan (2)Ruby Marshal Lt VT
Alpheus: b 10-1-1757 d 4-19-1841 m Mercy Blinn Sgt VT ★
Amos: b 11-21-1761 d 12-28-1827 m Phoebe Coe Sgt CT W★
Amos: b 10-1-1760 d 10-19-1854 m (1)Martha Straw (2)Mrs. Wilson QM Sgt PS CT
Amos: b 12-8-1732 d 10-14-1796 m Jemima Carter PS NH
Anan: b 7-6-1757 d 11-29-1840 m Comfort Hodge Pvt CT ★
Andrew: b 9-15-1750 d 8-28-1831 m Jane Merrill Pvt MA
Aquila: b 1-10-1727 d 1779 m Sophia White PS MD
Aquila, Jr.: b 1750 d 2-22-1815 m Ann Tolley PS MD
Asa: b c. 1760 d 1814 m Elizabeth — Pvt CT
Asa: b 7-14-1758 d 6-29-1843 m Lucy Leach Pvt MA
Asa: b 3-24-1761 d 3-12-1833 m Mrs Elenor Wood Pvt MA ★
Asa: b- 1758 d 2-13-1841 m (1)Sarah Adams (2)Mary Vanover Pvt NY ★
Asahel, Sr.: b 1-19-1717 d 11-11-1795 m (1)Sarah Parmelee (2)Mrs Sarah Goldsmith Pvt CT
Asahel, Jr.: b 1-14-1759 d 1-9-1845 m Ruth Johnson Pvt CT
Asaph: b 6-11-1735 d 3-29-1800 m Esther MacNeil Capt PS CT
Baxter: b 10-10-1757 d 7-4-1842 m Lydia Marsh Sgt MA ★
Benajah: b 1762 d p. 8- -1827 m Ruth Francis Fif CT
Benajah: b — d 11-4-1840 m — Fif NY ★
Benjamin, Jr.: b 7-8-1755 d p. 1820 m Sarah Scott Pvt CT
Benjamin: b 7-2-1756 d 11-11-1815 m Lydia Cook Pvt CT
Benjamin: b 11-3-1726 d 7-8-1808 m (1)Mary Ives (2)Phebe (Hall) PS CS CT
Benjamin: b 1719 d 3- -1803 m Eleanor Murdock PS MD
Benjamin: b 2-27-1746 d 8-20-1833 m Elizabeth Mosely Pvt MA
Benjamin: b 4-27-1712 d 10-27-1795 m (1)Rebecca Farnham (2)Mrs Mary Hugget PS MA
Benjamin: b 9-4-1756 d 5-23-1806 m Nabby Emerson Pvt NH
Benjamin: b 12-16-1740 d 4- -1815 m (1)Elizabeth Skidmore (2)Tacy Force Pvt PS NY
Benjamin: b 9-8-1745 d a. 4-19-1824 m Catharine Hicks Pvt NY
Benjamin Holt: b 10-6-1754 d 7-6-1811 m Elizabeth Hall Pvt CT

Bolling: b 1-25-1767 d 2-25-1836 m Jane Abercrombie Pvt VA
Braddock: b 4-7-1767 d p. 1812 m Susannah Wilcox Pvt RI
Brenton: b 4-2-1738 d 11-25-1820 m (1)Lament Collins (2)Abigail
  Guy Ens CT
Caleb: b 8-29-1731 d 9-21-1783 m Prudence Holt Capt CS CT
Caleb: b 4-10-1748 d 2-8-1814 m Hannah Snow Drm MA
Caleb: b 11-1-1738 d 2-15-1835 m Mary Bradley Pvt NH
Caleb: b 7-15-1738 d 10-13-1801 m Meribah Havens Sol RI
Calvin: b 11-4-1758 d p. 1808 m (1)Tabitha Jellison (2)Rhoda
  Austin Sgt VA
Calvin: b 1760 d 11-17-1833 m Mercy Barnes Sol MA
Charles: b 8-21-1742 d 5-22-1783 m Marie Salome LeRoy PS Lt PA
Christopher: b — d 4-6-1829 m Sarah Peck Pvt NY W★
Curtiss: b 1746 d 1799 m Rachel Beecher Pvt CT
Daniel: b 3-1-1758 d 5-26-1837 m Sarah Beers Sgt CT ★
Daniel: b 11-9-1758 d 4-1-1849 m Jernima Turney Ens CT
Daniel: b 6-1-1727 d 10-26-1805 m (1)Patience Baldwin (2)Zervia
  Whitmore (3)Abigail Doolittle Pvt CT
Daniel: b 3-24-1735 d 12-8-1788 m Lorana Winslow Pvt MA
Daniel: c. 1750 d 1-30-1778 m Patience Winslow Pvt MA
Daniel: b a. 1760 d 1793 m Sarah Little 2Mate NS
Daniel: b 7-28-1744 d 11-4-1815 m Jean Barr PS NH
Daniel: b 1-13-1755 d 2-18-1835 m (1)Deborah Davis (2)Elizabeth
  — PS NH
Daniel Johnson: b 7-14-1761 d 12-19-1802 m Abia Humiston Pvt
  CT
David: b c. 1735 d 12-11-1776 m Mehitable Ticknor Cpl CT
David: b c. 1740 d p. 1783 m Lucia Fowler Cpl CT
David: b 11-2-1732 d 3-21-1795 m Ruth Francis Pvt CT
David: b 1-4-1752 d 9-18-1817 m Catherine Tingley Col DE
David: b 3-6-1724 d a. 8-27-1821 m (1)Tamson Sears (2)Ruth Atkins
  (3)Rebecca Crosby Pvt MA
David: b 8-6-1704 d 5-8-1789 m Elizabeth Prescott PS Chp MA
David: b c. 1745 d p. 1790 m — Heath Sol NH
David: b 1750-56 d 4-8/9-1805 m Lydia Graves Pvt NH W★
David: b 9-16-1744 d 9-6-1816 m Mary — CS NH
David: b 8-9-1759 d 11-29-1843 m Hannah Warne Pvt NJ
David: b 6-24-1746 d 12-21-1800 m Naomi — Sgt NC
David: b 3-25-1760 d p. 1832 m Obedience Brazel Pvt Spy NC ★
Dixon: b 1755 d 1820 m (1)Anna Hunt (2)Milly De Jarnett (3)Milly
  Hutchinson (4)Priscilla Baugh Sol VA
Durham: b c. 1745 d c. 3-1-1798 m Frances Hicks PS NC
Ebenezer, Sr.: b 11-9-1730 d a. 1-2-1817 m (1)Anna Pease
  (2)Elizabeth McGregor (3)Rhoda Skinner Sgt MA
Ebenezer, Jr.: b 1755 d 6-28-1818 m Mary Chapin Sgt MA W★
Ebenezer: b 12-7-1741 d p. 1790 m Deborah Cross Sol PS NH
Ebenezer: b 9-19-1721 d 4-24-1801 m (1)Hepzibah — (2)Dorcas
  Abbott PS NH
Edward: b 1706 d 1-15-1794 m (1)Mary Miller Pvt MA
Edward: b 4-19-1717 d 2-8-1797 m Patience Gage PS MA
Edward: b 1740 d p. 1813 m (1) — Willis (2)Temperance Stretch
  (3)Ann Zarrah Maj NJ
Edward: b 1723 d 1796 m Eleanor Stuart Cpl VA
Edward, H.: b 6-28-1760 d 6-28-1838 m Rachel Barnes Sol NC ★
Eliakim, Sr.: b 8-9-1711 d 4-19-1794 m (1)Ruth Dickerman
  (2)Elizabeth Stow CT
Eliakim, Jr.: b 2-13-1740 d 9-6-1806 m (1)Eunice Morse (2)Sarah
  Rogers PS CT
Elihu, Sr.: b 6-16-1723 d 1- -1790/1 m Catherine Orrick LCol MD
Elihu, Jr.: b 8-9-1758 d 3- -1794 m Gertrude VanCowenhaven 2Lt
  MD
Elijah: b 12-9-1746 d 6-22-1830 m Elizabeth Stoodley NLt NH
Elijah: b 8-3-1757 d 12-13-1833 m Lois Tasker Pvt NH ★
Elisha: b 9-15-1730 d 1-19-1800 m Thankful Atwater Capt CT
Elisha: b 1760 d 4-8-1855 m Rosannah Grant Pvt CT
Elisha: b 11-23-1751 d 5-6-1842 m Hannah — Pvt MA
Elisha: b 2-1-1754 d 5-17-1818 m Asenath Sampson Sgt MA
Elkanah: b 1-17-1761 d 6-16-1807 m Mehitable Newcomb Pvt MA
Emerson: b 4-21-1758 d — m Tabitha Fletcher Pvt MA
Enoch: b 7-10-1753 d 4-28-1838 m Berthiah Crocker Pvt MA
Enoch: b 1758 d 8-5-1833 m Keziah Sears Pvt MA
Enoch: b 11-10-1763 d 12-10-1835 m Mitian Furbish Pvt MA ★
Enoch: b c. 1754 d p. 7-10-1812 m Nancy Jackson Sol NC
Enoch: b 1736 d 1806 m Sarah Merrill Lt VT
Ephraim: b 4-25-1723 d 2- -1796/7 m (1)Eunice — (2)Chloe Moss
  Pvt CT
Ephraim: b 2-10-1717 d 2-6-1793 m Eunice Livingston Pvt MA
Ephraim, Jr.: b 1740 d 1821 m Lydia Russell Pvt MA
Evan: b 12-2-1762 d 1841 m Charity — Pvt PA
Ezekiel: b 1741 d 1813 m Mary Leanard Pvt NH
Farnham: b 6-17-1752 d 5-14-1834 m Sally Bailey Pvt MA ★
George: b 3-30-1746 d 6-17-1822 m (1)Ruth Nichols (2)Rachel
  Briggs Sgt NY
George: b c. 1755 d 1792 m Margaret McCoy Pvt PA
George: b 9- -1759 d 2-2-1839 m Mercy Green Pvt RI ★
George Abbott: b 8-25-1742 d 8-1-1791 m Lois Matthews PS SC
Gersham: b 1-20-1744 d 1837 m (2)Keziah Gibbs Pvt MA
Gershom: b 2-28-1735 d p. 9-19-1797 m Mary Hanks Pvt CT
Gershom: b 1760 d 2-26-1844 m (1)Lucy Snow (2)Berthia Collins
  (3)Jerusha Clark Pvt MA
Gideon: b 11-9-1742 d 3-13-1808 m Rachel Clements Lt NY
Giles: b 2-18-1733 d 3-11-1789 m (1)Martha Robinson (2)Thankful
  Merriman NCapt CT

Henry: b 12-1-1761 d 7-25-1850 m Data Hall Pvt MA ★
Henry: b 5-30-1740 d 1829 m Betsey Bradley Lt NH
Henry: b 10-26-1758 d 3-21-1841 m Abigail Keyes Pvt NH
Henry: b 11-23-1712 d 6- -1785 m Joanna Sargent PS NH
Herman: b 1750 d 1795 m Elizabeth Curtis Ens CT
Hezekiah: b 1757 d 8-3-1834 m (1)Relefa—(2)Margaret—Sgt CT ★
Hezekiah: b 7-13-1743 d 9-7-1815 m Elizabeth Merriman Pvt CT
Hezekiah: b 8-9-1730 d c. 1815 m Deborah Daniels Pvt MA
Hezekiah: b c. 1740 d p. 3-9-1811 m Kiziah — PS VA
Hiland: b 5-3-1754 d 7-10-1789 m Hannah Parker OrdlSgt PS CT
Hugh: b 1742 d 1817 m Margaret King Capt NC
Hugh: b 2-8-1764 d 1830-40 m Mary Reid Lt NC
Hugh: b c. 1732 d 9-13-1798 m Sarah Lusk 2Lt PA
Isaac: b 11-4-1737 d 2-7-1798 m Esther Mosely Capt CT
Isaac, Jr.: b 3-7-1745 d p. 1784 m Phoebe Ives Capt CT
Isaac: b 1-12-1714/5 d 7-26-1778 m Sarah Forbes Gates PS CT
Isaac: b 1-24-1739 d 11-24-1789 m Abigail Hasey Capt CT
Isaac: b 1-31-1724 d 1-15-1815 m Joanna Coombes 1Lt MA
Isaac: b 6-29-1757 d 11-25-1844 m (1)Elizabeth Hasey (2)Sarah
  Saywood Keller Cpl MA
Isaac: b 6-22-1764 d 9-22-1830 m (1)Vashti Johnson (2)Sarah
  Taylor Sheldon (3)Martha Taylor Smith Pvt MA ★
Isaac: b 12-6-1760 d 6-30-1836 m Polly Leonard Pvt MA
Isaiah: b 11- -1759 d p. 8-9-1832 m Sarah — Sol RI
Jabez: b 1724 d 1776 m Hannah Lyon PS Capt MA
Jabez: b 12-30-1766 d 11-20-1839 m Tryphena Wilbur Pvt MA
Jacob: b 11-21-1747 d 5-7-1812 m Mary Wilmot Dr NH
Jacob: b 2-2-1749 d 12-22-1840 m Esther Richardson Sol VT
Jacob: b a. 1750 d c. 1820 m — Capt VT
James: b 10-15-1716 d 1807 m (1)Mary Lamb (2)Submit Bosworth
  CS CT
James: b 12-30-1752 d 1-16-1780 m Honor McKean PS CT
James: b 1755 d 12- -1840 m Nancy Cain 2Lt GA
James: b c. 1750 d 1822 m Sarah Burk Pvt MD
James: b 2-22-1750 d 4-3-1819 m Persis Lincoln Capt Lt MA
James: b 9-29-1753 d 8-26-1822 m Thankful-Hildreth Pvt MA ★
James: b 6-5-1751 d 11-9-1826 m Elizabeth Barker Pvt NH
James: b 4-15/19-1757 d 7-29-1835 m Huldah Cooper Mil NH
James: b 4-20-1744 d 8-9-1813 m Phoebe Gardner Pvt NY
James: b 1753 d 1835 m Elizabeth Johnson Pvt NC
James: b 6-10-1756 d 9-20-1826 m Mary McCurdy Pvt NC
James: b 1737 d 1807 m Elizabeth Hill Pvt PA
James: b c. 1752 d p. 1790 m Sarah Winn Pvt PA
James: b c. 1730 d 1794/5 m Martha — Capt VA
James: b a. 1752 d 10- -1816 m — Sol VA
James, Sr.: b a. 1728 d 4-3-1798 m Mary Robe Capt VA
Jehiel: b 5-6-1735 d 9-7-1807 m Catherine Hall Lt CT
Jeremiah: b 6-11-1722 d 10-1-1807 m Elizabeth Bailey LCol MA
Jesse: b 3-22-1760 d p. 8-8-1848 m Phoebe Wilber Pvt NY ★
Jesse: b 1755 d 1833 m Hannnah Kelly Pvt SC ★
Joash: bpt 6-15-1740 d p. 1790 m Sarah — Pvt CT
Joel: b 5-21-1741 d p. 1790 m Hannah Parmelee Pvt CT
Joel: b 2-4-1746/7 d 3-7-1843 m Elizabeth Bush Sol CT
John: b 2-26-1754 d 4-4-1848 m Damaris Evertt Pvt CT
John, Sr.: b 1717 d p. 1790 m Mary Willis PS CT
John, Jr.: b 1-22-1753 d 6-11-1830 m Hannah Nichols PS CT
John, Jr.: b 7-3-1747 d 1842 m Mary Stevens OrdlSgt VT
John: b 8-3-1758 d 7-17-1830 m Hannah Armont Pvt DE
John: b 6-8-1719 d 7-30-1779 m Berthia Stansbury PS MD
John: b 7-17-1739 d 10-27-1822 m Elizabeth Brackett Capt MA
John: b 6-19-1744 d 6-18-1804 m Grace Sprague Capt MA
John: b 10-21-1735 d 4-10-1812 m (1)Esther Slocum (2)Sarah
  Brigs 1Lt MA
John: b 1-14-1753 d 1839 m Phebe Benedict 2Lt MA ★
John: b 5-17-1754 d 4-18-1836 m Hannah Foster SrgnMte MA ★
John: b 4-26-1752 d 2-14-1806 m Dolly Ward Sgt MA
John: b 1-26-1729 d 10-22-1809 m (1)Elizabeth White (2)Mrs Molly
  Leonard Pvt MA
John: b 4-28-1757 d 8-25-1832 m Alice Currier Pvt Smn MA ★
John: b 1744 d 9-12-1827 m Lydia Knowlton Pvt MA
John: b 9-23-1738 d p. 1780 m Hannah Turner Pvt MA
John: b 1-8-1750 d 1827 m Hannah Bickford Lt NH
John: b 1-18-1749 d 12-2-1824 m Deborah Hall Lt NH
John: b 9-22-1758 d p. 1799 m Jane Patten Pvt NH
John: b 9-27-1710 d 5-31-1789 m Sarah Kimball CS PS NH
John: b c. 1747 d 1818 m — Lt NJ
John: b c. 1760 d 3-28-1810 m Chloe — Pvt NJ
John: b 5-9-1753 d p. 1840 m — Fif Maj MM PS NY ★
John: b c. 1750 d 1815 m Tamar Kniffen Pvt NY
John: b 6-12-1746 d 10-12-1821 m Mary Haire Pvt NC
John: b 1735 d p. 12-20-1785 m Jean Deal Sol NC
John: b 12-6-1750 d 12-4-1821 m Sarah Austin Ens PA
John: b 2-2-1749 d 9-25-1809 m Grizelle Coffey Pvt PA
John: b 4-29-1759 d 9- -1822 m Elizabeth Ward Pvt PA
John: b 8-10-1732 d 1820 m Hannah Matteson CS RI
John: b 9-12-1758 d 5-10-1836 m Elizabeth Mar Pvt Wgn ★
John, Sr.: b 5-27-1723 d 8-6-1777 m (1)Olive Spaulding (2)Jemima
  Kinney Reed Capt VT
John: b c. 1735 d p. 1799 m Molly — Capt VA
John: b a. 1760 d 9-27-1817 m Elizabeth Antwell Sgt VA ★
John: b 1750 d 1808 m Ursley Griggs Pvt VA
John: b 1748 d p. 1833 m Mildred Sandige Pvt VA ★
John: b 1762 d 1831 m Nancy — Pvt VA

HALL, contd.

Jonathan: b 7-19-1745 d 3-28-1811 m (1)Ruth Mildrum (2)Mary — Pvt CT
Jonathan: b 6-27-1752 d 12-25-1800 m Alice Gary Pvt CT
Jonathan, Jr.: b 11-11-1754 d 5-11-1805 m (1)Abigail Hall (2)Jerusha Gaylord (3)Ruth Atwater Sol PS CS CT
Jonathan: b 12-11-1757 d 6-3-1812 m Martha Collins Pvt CT
Jonathan: b 10-21-1757 d 9-24-1845 m Mercy Cady Pvt MA
Jonathan: b 2-29-1756 d 4-16-1827 m Abigail Bisbee Pvt MA ★
Jonathan: b 6-19-1759 d 8-21-1825 m Mary Kimball Pvt MA
Jonathan: b 1711 d 8-26-1802 m Mary Smith PS NH
Jonathan, Sr.: b 8-15-1716 d 7-2-1809 m Mehitable Kimball PS NH
Jonathan, Jr.: b 12-19-1745 d 7-5-1831 m Desiah Butterfield Pvt NH
Joseph: b a. 1750 d 7- -1824 m Elizabeth — Pvt MD
Joseph: b 2-25-1748 d 11-22-1822 m Mary Trowbridge Lt NH
Joseph, Sr.: b 1-7-1725 d 2-5-1787 m Abagail Clark PS MA
Joseph, Jr.: b 5-15-1757 d 12-24-1831 m Lucy Sears Cpl MA
Joseph: bpt 11-5-1738 d p. 1785 m Mary Cox Pvt MA
Joseph: b 12-11-1741/2 d 1826 m Mary Foss Pvt PS NH
Joseph: b 1761/2 d p. 1796 m Sarah Allen Cpl NJ
Joseph: b c. 1729 d 9-6-1780 m Tamsen Wilcox Pvt RI
Joseph: b 1762 d p. 1820 m — Hurlbert Pvt RI
Joshua: b 9- -1703 d 10- -1789 m Sarah Burgess Capt PS CT
Joshua: b c. 1708 d p. 4-10-1782 m (1)Diana Spicer (2)Ann Spicer PS MD
Josiah: b 5-16-1743 d p. 1781 m Amiable Hall Lt ME
Josiah: b 1753/4 d 7-2-1809 m Susannah Andrews Cpl MA
Josiah: b 8-26-1723 d 8-23-1786 m Abigail Hall PS MA
Josiah: b 1-15-1754 d 7-5-1855 m Calla Borden Pvt MA
Josiah: b 10-7-1747 d 9-10-1825 m Ruth French Sol NH
Josiah: b — d 8-11-1810 m Abigail Johnson Capt NJ W★
Laban: b 9-9-1755 d 9-7-1843 m (1)Olive Colton (2)Lucy Eddy (3)Marcy Daggit Pvt NH
Lawrence: b 1745 d 6-22-1823 m (1)Henrietta Sylvester (2)Lydia Arthur Ens MD
Lemuel: b 3-7-1761 d 1813 m Mary Root Pvt NY
Levi: b 10-14-1757 d 8-15-1811 m Parthenia Stretch Tms NJ
Levi: b 11-8-1750 d p. 1832 m Martha Silver Putney Pvt RI
Levi: b 1758 d p. 1840 m Jane Jones Pvt MA
Lewis: b — d p. 1786 m Mabel Brush Pvt CT
Lewis: b 6-25-1753 d 4-22-1821 m (2)Nancy Colley Lt NC
Lot: b 4-2-1757 d 5-17-1809 m Mary Homer NLt Pvtr
Luke: b 7-4-1744 d 9-19-1826 m (1)Elizabeth Cooley (2)Martha Davis Lt CT
Luther: b 1750 d 1818 m Zilpha Randall 4Cpl MA
Lyman: b 8-30-1761 d 11-4-1842 m (2)Phebe Palmer Sol Smn RI
Matthew: b 1744 d 1786 m Cornelia — Pvt SC
Miles: b 10-23-1740 d 10-26-1801 m Sarah Bishop Ens CT
Moses, Sr.: b 1732 d 1812 m Sarah Johnson 1Lt CT
Moses: b 7-4-1755 d 5-11-1827 m Lucy Hart Cpl CT
Moses: b 11-28-1750 d 8-3-1826 m Martha Sprague Sgt MA
Moses: b 5-29-1760 d 4-10-1846 m Nancy Snoddy Pvt NC
Moses: b 5-7-1764 d p. 1-16-1838 m Lucy Fowler Pvt VT
Moses R.: b 11-3-1766 d c. 1852 m (2)Asenath Andrus Pvt CT
Nathan: b 5-26-1750 d p. 1783 m (1)Deborah Swift (2)Martha Lyman Pvt CT
Nathan: b 1746 d 1835 m Jane — Pvt VA
Nathan: b 12-25-1715 d 5-7-1807 m Mary Chapman PS NH
Nathan: b 7-30-1738 d 2- -1815 m Anne Hall PS VA
Nathaniel: b 2-8-1724 d 7-27-1816 m Martha Storrs Capt CT
Nathaniel, Jr.: b 12-9-1762 d 2-24-1842 m (1)Experience Brown (2)Elizabeth Saunders Drm CT
Nathaniel: b 4-8-1732 d 1-16-1803 m Margery Doolittle Pvt CT
Nathaniel: b 1731 d 1823 m Mary Williams Pvt MA
Nathaniel: bpt 5-27-1744 d a. 1800 m Jane Downs PS MA
Nathaniel, Jr.: b 8-13-1746 d 2-2-1826 m Mehitable Storrs Lt NH
Nathaniel: b 11-16-1753 d 7-18-1809 m Prudence Chase Pvt NH
Nathaniel: b 12-8-1768 d 8-13-1851 m Belinda Holcomb Pvt VT ★
Nathaniel: b c. 1750 d p. 10-16-1833 m Elizabeth — Ens VA
Nehemiah: b 12-7-1764 d 12-29-1842 m Hannah White Pvt MA
Nicholas: b 5-2-1762 d 9-6-1831 m Mary Sanborn Pvt Drm NH
Percival: b 3-15-1741 d 9-24-1825 m Margaret Ware Dr MA
Percival: b 4-24-1764 d 3-19-1843 m Elizabeth White Pvt MA
Peter: b 8-1-1755 d 10-25-1835 m Mandana Clark Cpl CT VT
Peter: b 6-7-1748 d 9-25-1832 m Lydia Brown Pvt CT
Philemon: b 9-23-1733 d 9-21-1800 m Sarah Page Lt CT
Phineas, Jr.: b 11-11-1751 d 12-27-1819 m Mrs Agnes Collins Sol CT
Ralph: b 12-31-1738 d 6-13-1813 m Hannah Davis Sgt NH
Randolph: b 1751 d 1821 m Sally — PS VA
Rapha: b 2-21-1717 d p. 1790 m Abigail Kimball PS NH
Reuben: b 4-10-1753 d 1828 m Mary — Pvt CT
Reuben: b 4-16-1747 d c. 1821 m Sarah Howes Pvt MA
Reuben: b 1-30-1756 d 2-21-1826 m Betsey Hook Pvt NH
Reuben: b 1755 d 7-11-1834 m Sarah Jones Arfr PA ★
Richard: b 1741 d 9- -1840 m Elizabeth Cole Pvt MD ★
Richard: b 1748 d 9-12-1823 m Sarah Putman Capt MA
Richard: b c. 1755 d 12-20-1821 m (1)— Edwards (2)Phoebe Beggle Pvt Spy PA
Robert: b 10-5-1761 d 11-29-1810 m — Pvt DE
Robert: b 2-23-1755 d 1-14-1797 m Wills Nobbs Dr NC
Robert: b c. 1749/50 d p. 9-1-1797 m Mrs Mary Wawson Sol NC

Robert: b 1761 d c. 9-5-1836 m Nancy Isham Pvt VA ★
Rowland: b 4- -1744 d 11-9-1820 m Martha Brown Pvt NY
Samuel: b 9-25-1742 d 3-10-1828 m Mary Pratt Ens CS CT
Samuel: b 7-16-1739 d 3-29-1791 m Eunice Lee Sgt CT
Samuel: b 10-5-1759 d 5-12-1846 m Lucy Parmelee Pvt CT ★
Samuel: b 8-15-1724 d 4-2-1811 m Elizabeth Wilcox Pvt CT
Samuel: b 8-20-1759 d 4-11-1836 m Esther Strickland Pvt CT ★
Samuel: b 10-4-1695 d 2-26-1776 m Anne Law PS CT
Samuel: b 5-5-1731 d 2-10-1810 m Mamie Ives Pvt MA
Samuel: b 3-3-1757 d — m Sarah Cheney Pvt MA
Samuel: b 1732 d 5-17-1790 m Susannah Chamberlain Pvt NH
Samuel: b 3-19-1747 d 4-19-1831 m Hannah Leighton Pvt NH
Samuel: b 1736 d 1806 m Ruhamah Everett Pvt PA
Samuel: b c. 1760 d p. 1810 m Hannah — Pvt PA
Samuel Read: b 1-27-1755 d 1814 m Elizabeth Taft Hall Pvt NH VT
Seth: b 5-9-1749 d 9-30-1838 m Lois Hall Smn CT ★
Seth: b 10-4-1740 d 2-12-1824 m Diademia Leach Sgt MA
Seth: b 4-10-1751 d 12-24-1807 m Phebe Sears Pvt MA
Seth: b 6-6-1758 d a. 6-19-1816 m Rebekah Rider Pvt MA
Silvanus: bpt 9-5-1759 d p. 2-14-1828 m Hannah Bent Pvt MA
Solomon: b c. 1742 d 10-13-1834 m Hepsibah Allen Pvt MA
Spence, Sr.: b 6-20-1716 d 1-3-1792 m Director — CS NC
Stephen: b 9-5-1739 d 4-25-1783 m Abigail Saxton Capt CT
Stephen, Jr.: b 7-6-1749 d 2-6-1814 m (1)Olive Fuller (2)Fannie Herrick Pvt CT
Stephen: b 1-3-1745 d 9-7-1817 m Mary Hill 1Lt MA
Stephen: b 1764 d 8-30-1856 m Anna Lougee Cpl NH ★
Stephen: b 5-13-1759 d 11-23-1808 m Patience Flanders Pvt NH
Stephen: b 6-22-1760 d 4-5-1833 m Elizabeth Benjamin Pvt NY ★
Street: b 11-12-1721 d 1809 m Hannah Fowler LCol PS CT
Theophilus: b 8-26-1741 d 5-17-1804 m Elizabeth Couch Pvt CT
Thomas, Sr.: b 2-11-1726 d 12-23-1802 m Phoebe Blachley Pvt CT
Thomas, Jr.: b 7-3-1760 d 6-13-1801 m Prudence Northrup Pvt CT
Thomas: b 1749 d 5-14-1825 m (1)Barbara Elizabeth Dickinson (2)Elizabeth Talbot Pvt DE
Thomas: b 6-10-1748 d 9-30-1814 m Hannah — Pvt MA
Thomas: b 6-18-1754 d 12-18-1834 m Priscilla — Pvt MA
Thomas: b 1739 d 12-18-1804 m Elizabeth Sloan 2Lt NC
Thomas: b 3-1-1758 d 9-25-1833 m Nancy Hays Pvt NC ★
Thomas: b 1759 d 1836 m Nancy Chinn Pvt VA
Timothy: b 6-4-1758 d 8-6-1844 m (1)Eunice Hills (2)Mary Goodwin Pvt PS MA ★
Timothy: b 2-18-1752 d p. 1800 m Sarah Keyes PS NH
Titus: b 8-16-1746 d — m Olive Barnes Lt CT
Willard: b 6-12-1730 d a. 5-8-1777 m Ruth Fletcher Pvt MA
Wm.: b 1739 d 1830 m Anna Williams Lt CT
Wm.: b 11-4-1741 d 1824 m Sarah Peck Sol PS CT
Wm.: b 1-21-1753 d 4-3-1835 m Elizabeth Stephenson Ens DE ★
Wm.: b — d p. 12-8-1794 m (1)Sarah Wood (2)Martha — Pvt MD
Wm.: b 1755 d 10-6-1828 m Martha Duckett Sol MD
Wm.: b c. 1735/6 d a. 1-4-1792 m Ann Duckett PS MD
Wm.: b c. 1-1753 d 9-28-1828 m Abigail Pease Sol MA
Wm.: b c. 1740 d 8-3-1787 m Thankful Doak Maj PS NC
Wm.: b 1762 d 5-13-1846 m — Holland Sgt NC
Wm.: b 1761 d c. 1845 m Elizabeth Hicks Pvt VA NC ★
Wm.: b 1760 d 3-11-1815 m Elizabeth Wilson Sol NC
Wm.: b 1741 d 12-26-1825 m (1)Patience Moulton (2)Margaret Pearsall (3)Elizabeth Moulton Pvt NC
Wm.: b c. 1740 d p. 1778 m Elizabeth — Pvt PA
Wm.: b c. 1755 d 4-5-1844 m Sarah — Pvt PA ★
Wm Jr.: b 1756 d 6-15-1840 m Rachael Saunders Pvt RI ★
Wm.: b 4-6-1759 d 5-1-1814 m Ann Wilson NCapt SC
Wm.: b a. 1760 d p. 1788 m Barbara Hawkins Pvt SC
Wm.: b 1760 d p. 1-20-1809 m Ann Tarbert Pvt SC
Wm.: b 1763 d 1812 m Elizabeth Burnett Pvt SC
Wm.: b 3-29-1763 d 3-3-1858 m Mary Cammack Pvt SC
Wm.: b 1756 d 1811 m Urcilla Woodward SgtMaj VA W★
Wm.: b 1760 d 1800 m — Jones Pvt VA
Wm.: b 3-9-1761 d 1838 m Miriam Tullis Pvt VA
Wm.: b c. 1750 d 1832 m — Sol VA
Wm.: b 4-22-1721 d c. 1783 m Ann Bott PS VA
Wm. Jordan: b a. 1737 d a. 5-15-1817 m (1)Sophia Woodcraft (2)Sarah Hill PS DE
Willis, Sr.: b 3-7-1718/9 d 4-1-1800 m (1)Martha Gibbs (2)Anna Coye Sgt PS MA
Zachariah: b 1-11-1735 d 10-30-1795 m Mehitable Patton Pvt MA

HALLADAY,

Eli: b 5-25-1763 d 5-31-1849 m Catherine S. — Pvt CT ★
Jonah: b 3-15-1751 d 5-16-1838 m (1)Mary Rowley (2)Patience Doolittle Pvt MA ★

HALLAM, (includes HALLUM)

Amos: b 2-26-1738 d 1-3-1816 m Desire Stanton Capt CT
John: b 8-23-1750 d c. 1815 m Anna Owens Pvt PS CS SC
Thomas: b 3-10-1748 d 7-31-1829 m (1)Mary Bershire (2)Sally Vorhees Pvt PA

HALLEBURTON,

David: b 10-11-1753 d 1-13-1843 m Lucy Renolds Sol NC VA
Thomas: b 1763 d p. 3-6-1842 m Martha Louiza Humphries Pvt NC

HALLETT, (includes HALLET)
Benjamin: b 1-18-1760 d 12-31-1849 m Abigail Lovell Smn Pvt MA ★
Edward: b 4-6-1762 d 3-6-1848 m (2)Eliza Robbins Pvt MA
Elisha: b 7-23-1758 d 10-2-1847 m Elizabeth Hawes Pvt Smn MA
Enoch: b 1737 d 3-8-1788 m Thankful Hawes LCol CS MA
Isaac: b 8- -1742 d 10-5-1814 m Elizabeth Edridge Pvt MA
James: b 9-11-1752 d 11-18-1824 m Susannah Taylor Pvt MA
John: b 5-4-1756 d p. 1803 m Hannah (Hallett) — Pvt MA
Jonah: b 10-31-1754 d 10-2-1811 m Margaret Lawrence Lt NY
Joseph: b 1-26-1731 d 8-9-1799 m Elizabeth Hazard PS NY
Joseph: b 9-21-1736 d 3-29-1809 m Thankful Baxter Cpl MA
Nathan: b 6-3-1750 d 1820 m Olive Van Tassel Pvt NY
Solomon: b 11-23-1754 d 8-13-1840 m (1)Deborah Chapman (2) Priscilla Crosby Pvt Mrnr CS MA ★
Solomon: b c. 1759 d 6-4-1841 m (2)Eleanor Burgess Pvt NY ★
Thomas: b 7-7-1729 d p. 1790 m Sarah Hamblin Sol MA

HALLOCK,
Caleb: b c. 1748 d 1830 m Kaziah Reeve PS NY
Daniel: b 1732 d 1830 m Phoebe Hunt Pvt PS NY
Daniel: b 1755 d 1844 m Mary Wells Pvt NY ★
Henry: b 11-11-1755 d 8-6-1824 m Mary Jane — PS NY
James: b 1731 d 9-27-1775 m Mary Post PS NY
Jeremiah: b 3-13-1758 d 6-23-1826 m Mercy Humphrey Pvt NY
John: b 5-16-1751 d 8-26-1842 m Mehitable Aldrich Pvt NY
John: b c. 1730 d p. 1782 m — PS NY
Jonathan: b 1738 d 1824 m Mary Dickerson Pvt NY
Josiah: b 1732 d 2-20-1815 m (1)Bertha Young (3)Sarah Reeve PS NY
Moses: b 2-16-1760 d 7-17-1837 m Margaret Allen Pvt PS MA
Noah, Sr.: b 1728 d 11-2-1818 m (1)Nancy Hendrickson (2)Ann — Sgt PS NY
Noah, Jr.: b 5-7-1758 d 10-23-1818 m (1)Sarah Thorne (2)Mehetable Miner PS NY
Peter: b 1724/5 d p. 1776 m Anne Green PS NY
Peter: b 11-15-1728 d 5-13-1791 m Joanna Mapes Pvt NY
Richard: b 1754 d 1828 m Mary — Pvt MM NY
Richard: b 5-13-1724 d 2-12-1821 m Sarah Ludlum PS NY
Samuel: b 2-11-1747 d p. 1785 m Deborah — PS NY
Stephen: b 10-31-1736 d 10-31-1802 m Elizabeth Chamberlain Pvt MA
Wm.: b 1730 d 10-21-1815 m Alice Homan Pvt MA
Wm., Sr.: b 1722 d 1782 m Sarah Saxton PS CS NY
Wm.: b 1764 d 4-11-1818 m Ruth Hawkins Pvt CT
Wm.: b c. 1753 d 1821 m Clarinda Benton PS NY
Wm.: b 1741 d 11-18-1794 m Miriam — Pvt NY
Wm.: b 1750 d 9- -1824 m (1)Deborah Hildreth (2)Deborah Hedges Pvt NY
Zachariah: b 1749 d 1820 m Hannah — 2Sgt PS NY
Zerubabel: b 1722 d 3-31-1800 m Elizabeth Swezey PS NY

HALSEY,
Abigail Howell: b — d 3-26-1777 m Silas Halsey PS NJ
Abraham: b 2-19-1764 d 5-7-1822 m (1)Nancy Beach (2)Lucretia Green Pvt NJ
Benjamin: b 12-10-1721 d 2-19-1788 m (1)Sarah Prudden (2)Mrs Bethia Youngs (3)Mrs Sarah Linsley CS NJ
Cornelius: b 6-15-1721 d 4-12-1782 m Millicent Rogers PS NY
Daniel: b 1739 d 11-16-1801 m (1)Abigail Williams (2)Mary — Capt NJ
Daniel: b 5-25-1757 d 1-14-1827 m Jerusha Topping Pvt NY
David Fithian: b c. 1737 d p. 2-27-1786 m — Haines Pvt PS NY
Ethan: b 1755 d 4-18-1827 m Jane — PS Pvt NY
Isaac: b 5-15-1757 d 4-26-1820 m Sarah Smith Pvt NJ
Isaac: b 1741 d 11-24-1788 m Rebecca Garthwait QM Gen CS PS NJ
Jabez: b c. 1750 d 1804 m Sarah Beach Pvt NJ
Jabez: b 2-13-1762 d 1820 m Euphenia Brouer Cpl NY
Jeremiah: b 6-10-1744 d 8-25-1829 m Esther Parke MM LCol CT
Jeremiah: b 11-29-1737 d 9-8-1782 m Mrs Elizabeth Haines PS CT
Jesse: b 5-18-1739 d 1818 m Charity White Capt NY
Joel: b 1736 d 1817 m Anne — Pvt NJ
John: b 10-17-1756 d 5-19-1827 m Nancy Sayre Pvt NJ
John, Sr.: b 1759 d 11-28-1847 m Rebekah Cook Pvt NJ
Jonathan: b 5-1-1727 d 1-2-1797 m Jane Cooper PS NY
Joseph, Sr.: b 1730 d 7-9-1813 m (1)Mary Armstrong (2)Anna Van Arsdale (3)Elizabeth Ryerson Pvt NJ
Joseph, Jr.: b 1751 d 1796 m (1)Mary Brookfield (2)Sukey Frazee Sgt NJ
Lemuel: b 3-22-1740 d 12-13-1797 m Abigail White PS NY
Luther: b 5-10-1758 d 2-28-1830 m (1)Sarah Foster (2)Demaris Foster (3)Abigail Foster Adj NJ
Matthew, Sr.: b 2-24-1725 d 1802 m Sarah Haines Pvt PS NY
Matthew, Jr.: b 7-25-1753 d 1-28-1841 m (1)Miss Rose (2)Ruth Leonard Pvt NY ★
Paul: b 12- -1741 d 4-1-1830 m Anna Hudson PS NY
Philip: b 1760 d 1846 m Esther Moore Fif NY
Silas: b 1704 d 2-4-1777 m Abigail Howell PS NJ
Silas, Sr.: b 1-17-1718 d 1-3-1786 m Susannah Howell PS NY
Silas, Jr.: b 10-17-1743 d 11-19-1832 m (1)Sarah Radley (2)Hannah (Jones) Howell (3)Abigail Howell Dr NY
Silvanus: b 11-18-1722 d 2-14-1815 m (1)Esther Halsey (2)Mrs. Chard Pvt NY

HALSTED, (includes HALSTEAD)
Ann: b 1761 d 1824 m Joseph Camp PS NJ
Benjamin: b 1740 d 5-25-1801 m X Lt NY
Caleb, Sr.: b 7-8-1721 d 6-4-1784 m Rebecca Ogden PS NJ
Caleb, Jr.: b 5-15-1752 d 8-18-1827 m Abigail Lyon Dr NJ
Edward: b 5-15-1750 d 2-16-1837 m Martha Ferguson Pvt NY
Ezekiel, Sr.: b 11-29-1738 d 2-20-1805 m Abigail Theall 2Lt NY
Gershom: b 10-25-1750 d 6-7-1822 m Mary Smith Pvt NY
Jacob: b 7-26-1757 d 9-15-1821 m (1)Anna Jersey (2)Charity Van Aken Pvt NY
Jacob: b 5-10-1730 d c. 11- -1786 m Rachel Smith Pvt NY
James: b 6-2-1756 d 8-20-1815 m Susannah Miller Pvt NY
John: b 7-12-1754 d 3-17-1840 m Phebe Wade Pvt NJ
John: b 9-9-1755 d 6-27-1827 m Sarah Meyer Pvt NY
John: b 1756 d p. 6-21-1817 m Elizabeth — Sol NY
John: b 1757 d 1-8-1824 m Rachel Knap Pvt PA
Joseph: b 12-28-1759 d 2-13-1845 m Miriam Preston Pvt CT ★
Josiah: b 1735 d p. 5-31-1833 m Elizabeth Young Cpl NY
Richard, Jr.: b 1762 d 1827 m Sibyl Read Pvt CT ★
Robert: b 9-13-1746 d 9- -1825 m (1)Mary Wiley (2)Mary Mills Dr PS NY
Samuel: b 8-7-1763 d 9-30-1844 m Samiah Smith Pvt NY
Thomas: b 1724 d 10-31-1808 m Phoebe Bogardus Pvt NY

HALTIWANGER,
John: b a. 1760 d p. 1799 m Catherine Schmidt Pvt SC

HAM, (includes HAMM & HAMME)
Balthaser: b 4-16-1754 d 5-1-1826 m Catherine Kreber Pvt PA
Casper: b 9-16-1762 d 9-3-1834 m Elizabeth Woolley Pvt NY
Christian: b 8-21-1756 d 5-29-1837 m Anna Maria Hetzer Pvt PA W★
Conradt: b 9-29-1759 d p. 3-10-1806 m Christina — Pvt NY
Daniel: b 3-2-1750 d 1811 m Elizabeth Smith Cpl NH
Daniel: b 1728 d 12-14-1794 m Barbara — Ens PA
David: bpt 1756 d 11- -1811 m Hannah Runnells Sol NH
Ephraim, Sr.: b 8- -1731 d 1806 m Lydia Ham Pvt NH
Ephraim: b 1729 d 11-14-1798 m (1)Mary — (2)Ann — PS NH
George: b 9-29-1764 d 3-8-1846 m Dorothy — Pvt NH
George: b 10-30-1748 d 3-15-1828 m Rachel Garvin Pvt NH
Israel: b 2-14-1759 d 6-25-1801 m Mehitable Hayes Pvt NH
John: b 4-30-1759 d 9-22-1839 m Happy Ryon Pvt VA ★
Moses: b 7-19-1733 d 5-11-1817 m Anna Grafton Lt NH
Peter: b 5-17-1755 d p. 1792 m Catherine Kohl Pvt NY
Samuel: b 10-3-1738 d 1830 m Elizabeth Sherburn Pvt PS NH
Stephen: b c. 1740 d 1811/12 m Mildred Rucker Fif Sol VA
Timothy: b — d p. 1-14-1778 m Mary — PS NH
Tobias: b 7-2-1751 d 5-22-1812 m Elizabeth Herrick Pvt MA
Wm.: b 2-16-1762 d 1825 m (1)Mary — (2)Susan Cooper NLt VA

HAMANT,
Asa: b 3-15-1763 d 12-29-1843 m Mary Draper Pvt RI

HAMBLIN, (includes HAMBLEN)
Amasa: b 7-21-1737 d c. 1800 m Lydia — Pvt CT
Cornelius: b 1752 d 5-30-1811 m Ruth Mudge PS MA
Daniel: b 10-15-1752 d 9-14-1802 m (1)Sarah Davidson (2)Rosamond Kenner CS VA
David: b 1743 d 5-28-1806 m (1)Hannah Townsend (2)Mary Church Bishop 2Lt PS NY
Henry: b 3-25-1740 d 8- -1815 m (1)Polly Dickinson PS VA
Isaac: b 3-14-1735 d 1-28-1805 m Kezia Sears Pvt MA
James: b 5-7-1763 d 5-8-1846 m Charlotte Hartwell Pvt CT ★
Job: b 1736 d 10-20-1815 m Abigail Gifford Pvt MA
Job: b 7-14-1762 d 9-21-1833 m Eleanor Mullings Pvt VA ★
Joshua: b 1721 d 1-2-1797 m Mary Lewis PS NY
Lemuel: b 4-4-1746 d 1819 m Dorothy Fish Pvt MA
Pierce Dant: b 3-24-1756 d p. 1833 m — Pvt VA
Samuel: b 3-30-1760 d 7-8-1830 m Hannah Isbell Pvt MA ★
Simeon: bpt 6-17-1744 d p. 1790 m Martha Hatch Pvt MA

HAMBRIGHT, (includes HAMBRECHT)
Frederick: b 1- -1727 d 3-9-1817 m (1)Sarah Hardin (2)Mary Dover Col PS NC
Johann Adam: b 4-30-1711 d 2-14-1793 m Elizabeth Barbara —PS PA
John, Jr.: b 5-12-1749 d 7-31-1806 m Susanna Gross Lt NLt PS PA

HAMES,
John: b 4-28-1752 d 10-9-1860 m Charity Jasper Pvt SC ★

HAMILL, (includes HAMMELL & HAMMILL)
Hugh: b 1756 d 4-21-1836 m Jane — Pvt PA ★
John: b 10-26-1756 d 7-15-1847 m Elizabeth Kelly Lt NJ
John: b 1758 d 9-28-1845 m Jemima Brower Pvt NY
Nathaniel: b 9-7-1747 d 1-6-1799 m Martha Becket Pvt PA
Robert: b 11-25-1759 d 4-9-1841 m (1)Jeannett Becket (2)Jane
    McKelvey Pvt PA ★
Robert: b c. 1745 d 1-26-1813 m Elizabeth — Pvt PA

HAMILTON, (includes HAMBLETON & HAMMILTON)
Abner: b 1752-62 d 7- -1837 m Mary Clendening Pvt VA ★
Alexander: b 1-11-1757 d 7-12-1804 m Elizabeth Schuyler LCol PS
    NY
Alexander: b 6-5-1725 d 9- -1781 m Ann Reed Capt PS PA
Alexander: b a. 1750 d c. 1788-1800 m Margaret (Whitney)—Pvt PA
Alexander: b c. 1760 d 1825 m Mary Wolf Pvt PA
Alexander: b 9- -1759 d 1843 m Mary — Pvt VA ★
Ambrose: b 7-21-1735 d 1795 m Deborah Soule Pvt MA
Andrew: b 7- -1741 d 1-19-1835 m Jane Magill Maj SC
Andrew, Sr.: b c. 1697 d 9-21-1790 m Martha — PS VA
Andrew: b a. 1760 d 1820 m Isabella Kinkead Ens VA
Archibald: b a. 1750 d 1793 m Martha Means PS NC
Asa: b 5-1-1768 d 4-16-1801 m Rebecca — Dr MA
Audley: b 1738 d 1809 m Eleanor Shanklin Pvt VA
Benjamin: b 1750 d p. 1790 m Judith Ricker Sgt MA
Charles: b 12-7-1760 d 3-25-1845 m Martha Castle Sol VT
Charles: b c. 1758-9/d 10-2-1826 m Margaret Dunlap Capt VA
Daniel: b 1740 d 1784 m Hannah Sparrow Pvt MA
David, Jr.: b 12-18-1756 d 3-14-1840 m (1)Millicent Marks (2)Rachel
    Churchill Sgt CT
David: b 7-11-1742 d 3-23-1817 m Mary Knox Lt MA
David: b 3-10-1750 d 1840 m Margaret Gardner Pvt PA
David: b 5-14-1749 d 11-25-1794 m Elizabeth Norris Reynolds Sol
    PS SC
David: b 2-16-1748 d 8-4-1822 m Elizabeth Harrington Pvt SC
Eden: b 1763 d 6-19-1850 m Zillah Lindley Drm CT
Edward: b 6-4-1762 d 5-27-1824 m (1)Mary Ann Boardman
    (2)Eleanor Hawkins Lt MD
Elisha: b 11-10-1739 d 11-10-1820 m Mary Smith Sgt VT
Erastus: b 9-25-1741 d — m Mary Adams Pvt MA
Francis: b c. 1759 d 2-12-1823 m Mrs Mary McDowell Pvt PA
George, Sr.: b 1722 d 1798 m Elizabeth Schuyler Capt MD
George, Jr.: b 8-2-1754 d 1826 m Agnes Cooper Capt MD
George: b 3-17-1759 d 8-3-1830 m Mercy Haynes Cochran Pvt NY
George: b c. 1750 d 1814 m Ruth — Pvt PA
George: b c. 1750 d 1814 m Ruth — Pvt PA
Hance: b 9- -1763 d 3-31-1816 m Mary McNairy Sol NC
Hosea: b 1752 d 9-8-1796 m (2)Anna Hubbard Capt NY
Hugh: b c. 1761 d 4- -1813 m Martha Moorhead Pvt PA
Ignatius: b 1760 d a. 1808 m Ann Catherine Bush Pvt MD
James: b c. 1720 d 1785 m Mary Ann Coombs Capt MD
James: b 1747 d 3-30-1835 m Caty Bailey Pvt MD
James: b 4-5-1731 d — m Charity Key Pvt MA
James: b 6- -1729 d 1814 m Maria Schoonmaker QM NY
James: b 9-29-1761 d 10-21-1842 m Martha Wallace Pvt NC W★
James: b 9-16-1750 d 11-26-1833 m Elizabeth Lynch Maj PA
James: b 1733 d 1808 m Margaret Loughry Capt PA
James: b 1722 d 11-3-1807 m Mary — Pvt PA
James: b 3-24-1743 d 4-14-1815 m (1)Catherine Carrigan
    (2)Margaret Boyd Lt PA
James: b 1741 d 10-26-1831 m Catherine — PS SC
James: b 5-1-1757 d 4-27-1831 m Jane Gwin Pvt NC ★
James: b c. 1746 d 1837 m Anne Fox Napier 1Lt VA
James: b 9-2-1748 d 1-19-1812 m Jane Gilbreath Pvt VA
James: b 1-15-1757 d 1837 m Robert Kerman Pvt VA
James: b 12-24-1758 d 9-9-1835 m Celia Colyer Pvt VA ★
Jane: b 1764 d 1-10-1831 m Robert McCann Pvt SC
Jeremiah: b 12-19-1756 d 2-6-1814 m Ann Hampton Pvt Wgm PS
    SC
Jesse: b 7-19-1754 d 12-30-1814 m Sarah Stevens Pvt MA
Jesse: b c. 1745 d 5- -1820 m Margaret — Pvt VA
John, Sr.: b 1-25-1732 d 7-11-1809 m Mercy Cornish Pvt CT NY
John, Jr.: b 4-24-1758 d 7-11-1809 m Dolly Campbell Pvt CT
John: b 1720 d p. 1790 m Sydney Brown PM Lt MD
John: b 1753 d 9-4-1843 m Susan Todd Sgt MD ★
John: b c. 1760 d 1824 m Sabra Duckwald Sgt MD
John: b c. 1736 d p. 1790 m Rebecca Canfield Capt MA
John: b 1728 d 6-6-1806 m Joanna Wolcott Pvt MA
John: b 2-8-1757 d 6-22-1816 m Catherine Quigley Pvt MA
John: b 1-20-1760 d 9-20-1859 m Judith Goodwin Pvt MA NH ★
John: b 6-17-1749 d 8-8-1793 m Margaret Alexander Capt PA
John: b 11-1-1765 d 7-11-1849 m Deborah Perkins Pvt PA ★
John: b 11-22-1766 d 9-25-1863 m Rachel Cook PS PA
John: b 1713 d 8-2-1798 m Florence Morrow PS PA
John: b 4-5-1768 d 6-30-1824 m (2)Eleanor Turner Lt Adj SC
John: b c. 1750 d a. 1804 m Martha — Capt VA
John: b 1754 d 9-22-1822 m — Lt VA ★
John: b 1740 d p. 5-4-1811 m Tabitha Thweatt Pvt VA
John: b 1747 d 9-5-1818 m Rebecca Lafferty QM VA
Jonathan: b 5-25-1745/6 d p. 1790 m Mollie Weymouth Pvt PA
Jonathan: b 5-30-1761 d 1-24-1852 m (1)Susan Dilts (2)Martha
    Fowls Pvt PA

Joseph, Jr.: b 9-7-1760 d 1818 m Persis Hill Pvt MA
Joshua: b 1759 d 11- -1851 m Elizabeth Acuff Pvt Spy NC VA ★
Marmaduke: b 1749 d a. 2- -1801 m Mary — Pvt MD
Nathan: b 1739 (?) d p. 1789 m (1)Mary Bemiss (2)Abagail Omsted
    Capt MA
Nathan: b c. 1713 d 1795 m Ruth Wheeler Pvt MA
Patrick: b 1717 d 1790 m Ann — PS MD
Patrick: b c. 1742 d 4-2-1810 m (1)Nelly Coburn (2)Isabel Faris Sol
    SC
Patrick: b 2-16-1748 d 8-15-1821 m Rebekah Fletcher Pvt MA
Paul: b 11-19-1752 d 5-31-1830 m Anna Stevens Sgt CT
Paul: b 10-16-1762 d 6-30-1816 m Mary Wilkinson Pvt SC
Richard: b 10-15-1759 d 6-7-1834 m Mary — Pvt NH
Robert: b 3-31-1742 d 11-13-1820 m Margret Conkey Lt MA ★
Robert: b 5-16-1760 d 2-24-1841 m (1)Susanna Kean (2)Ann Hays
    Cpl PA ★
Robert: b 1753 d 7-2-1834 m Eva Catherine Shindel Pvt PA
Robert: b 9-12-1763 d 6-9-1845 m Anna Jackson Sol PA ★
Robert: b 1720 d 8- -1786 m Margaret McKee Pvt VA
Robert: b 1732 d 4-10-1777 m Jane Hamilton Sgt VA
Rufus: b 4-29-1757 d 11-7-1817 m Polly Kingsbury Vol MA
Samuel: b 11-3-1764 d 3-16-1851 m Wealthy BeBee Pvt CT ★
Samuel: b 5-24-1732 d p. 1777 m Lillis Campbell Lt MD
Samuel: b 2-11-1759 d 12-15-1826 m Betsey Kinston Pvt MA
Silas: b 3-18-1762 d 2-6-1847 m Acksah Barns Pvt MA
Silas: b c. 1726/7 d 11- -1790 m Elizabeth Knapp PS CT
Silas: b 2-21-1736 d 8-7-1816 m Hannah Hoyt PS VT
Solomon: bpt 8-19-1733 d c. 1794 m (1)Sarah Keay (2)Elizabeth
    Pearce Pvt ME
Stewart: b c. 1760 d 1831 m Clarissa Stringer Pvt NC
Thomas: b 1714 d a. 3-6-1784 m (1) — Scott (2)Ann — PS CS MD
Thomas: b 1745 d 6-11-1807 m Ann Hodgkin PS MD
Thomas: b c. 1753 d 3-16-1825 m Jannett McColloch Lt MA
Thomas, Sr.: b c. 1725 d p. 1800 m Jane McCracken Sol PS NC
Thomas, Jr.: b c. 1750 d 1825 m Elizabeth Gwin Sol NC
Thomas: b 12-24-1762 d 2-14-1841 m — Pvt Spy NC ★
Thomas: b 1-18-1752 d 11-29-1829 m (1)Sarah Westfall (2)Mrs
    Lydia Colborn Brailey Pvt PA
Thomas: b 4-9-1758 d 3- -1844 m Temperance Arnold Pvt VA SC
Thomas: b 7-2-1760 d 5-2-1853 m Anne Kennedy Pvt SC
Thomas: b 3-14-1744 d 1-29-1791 m Rebecca Dixon PS SC
Thomas: b 1738 d 1786 m Margaret Gawin Smith Capt VA
Wm.: b 7-30-1748 d 1-8-1806 m (1)Elizabeth Griffin (2)Nancy
    Needles Capt MD
Wm.: b 1750-56 d 1820-26 m Susan Heywood Pvt NJ
Wm.: b 1743 d — m Ann Sophia Dupuy Pvt NY
Wm.: b 1760 d 1815 m — Pvt NC
Wm.: b c. 1740 d 9-22-1822 m Magdalene Bittinger 1Lt PA ★
Wm.: b 8-19-1756 d 7-8-1839 m Jane Allison Pvt PA ★
Wm.: b c. 1740 d p. 1781 m Mary Bitener Pvt PA
Wm.: b 1742 d 1780 m Mary Margaret — Pvt SC
Wm.: b 1750 d 9-24-1827 m Mrs Mary (Wooley) Baughman Capt
    VA
Wm.: b c. 1738 d 12-9-1825 m Isabelle Clemons Capt VA
Wm.: b c. 1740-5 d 10-17-1814 m Anastasia Combs Cpl VA
Wm.: b 1740 d 4-8-1834 m Ruth Wilson Pvt PS VA W★
Wm.: b 1752-4 d 12- -1846 m (1)Mary McClung (2)— Sol VA
Wm.: bpt 8- -1748 d 1795 m Patience Craig Pvt VA

HAMLETT, (includes HAMBLETT)
James: b 2-4-1751 d 10-20-1819 m Mary Bedford Sol VA
Joshua: b 1-27-1725 d 7-17-1803 m Lydia Clement CS MA

HAMLIN, (includes HAMBLIN & HAMLEN)
Africa: b — d 1-28-1808 m Susanna Stone Lt MA
Amasa: b 7-27-1737 d p. 1800 m Lydia — Pvt CT
America: b 10-20-1761 d 10-7-1837 m (1)Sarah Atherton (Parkhurst)
    (2)Elizabeth Brown (3)Mary Giddings Pvt MA
Amos: b 8-8-1766 d 4-17-1843 m (1)Hulda Mudge (2)Elizabeth
    Van Camp Pvt NY
Asa: b 9-22-1761 d 12-3-1831 m Hannah Nobles Sgt NY
Benjamin: b 12-28-1762 d 11-29-1852 m Eunice Burritt Pvt CT
Caleb: b 2-8-1724 d 4-17-1794 m Content Fish Pvt MA
Charles: b 1734 d 1786 m Agnes Cocke PS CS VA
Charles: b c. 1757 d 1797 m Martha Nunnally PS VA
Cornelius: b 6-25-1705 d 2-21-1784 m Marcy Mudge PS CT
Daniel: b 7-23-1755 d 1809 m Ruth Ward Sgt CT
David: b 5-23-1752 d 1839 m Rebecca Beals Pvt MA ★
Edward: b 1735 d 3-4-1783 m Patience Eaton Cnt CT
Eleazer: b 7-18-1732 d 12-1-1807 m (1)Lydia Bonney (2)Mrs Sarah
    Bryant (3)Hannah Fletcher Capt MA
Elisha: b 12-9-1754 d 4-27-1848 m Rachel Bradshaw MM CT ★
Europe: b 11-20-1759 d 6-7-1820 m Dorcas Stowe Pvt MA
Ichabod: b 6-28-1749 d 1834 m Jerusha Isbell Pvt MA
Isaac: b 11-14-1748 d 7-27-1826 m Polly Beals Pvt MA
Isaac: b 1-10-1742 d 8-10-1810 m Damaris Grummon Pvt NY
Jabez: b 7-17-1735 d 9-8-1826 m Dorcas Barnes Lt CT
Jabez: b 7-28-1709 d 4-25-1791 m Mary Christopher CS Col CT
John: b 11-26-1736 d 11-26-1821 m (1)Eleanor Orvice (2)Abiah,
    Phinney (3)Hannah Page Lt CT
John: b 3-12-1761 d 10-31-1825 m Lucy Barton Pvt CT
John: b 10-22-1762 d 4-15-1852 m (1)Sarah Town (2)Mrs Dorothy
    Gove Pvt MA

John: b 7-2-1759 d 3-4-1839 m Rosannah Lard Pvt Tms CS NJ ★
Joshua: b 7-2-1752 d 5-17-1838 m Elizabeth Bearse Pvt MA
Lemuel: b 8-4-1740 d — m Dorothy Fish Pvt MA
Levi: b c. 1763 d 9-27-1814 m Mary Foster Cpl CT ★
Mark: b 2-25-1765 d 5-28-1840 m Roxanna Moses Pvt CT ★
Micah: b 11-11-1741 d 8-8-1797 m Abigail Parker Maj MA
Nathaniel: b 6-7-1739 d 12-27-1818 m (1)Lucy Foster (2)Deborah
    St. John Capt CT
Nathaniel: b 5-29-1732 d 1778 m (1)Lucretia Ranney (2)Abigail
    Moore Capt CT
Nathaniel: b 11-20-1741 d 1-19-1834 m Sarah Baker Pvt MA
Perez: b 2-3-1748 d 1826 m Rhoda Hunt Sol NY MA
Perez: b 9-26-1755 d 7-20-1835 m Sarah Cobb Pvt MA
Samuel: b 9-9-1746 d 4-1-1801 m Thankful Ely Lt RI
Seth: b 9-9-1740 d 1795 m Mary Pitcher Capt MA
Seth L.: b 1-1-1765 d 11-10-1834 m Jerusha Sawyer Drm MA
Simeon: b 3-17-1739 d 9-27-1783 m — Pvt CT
Wm.: b 2-11-1726 d 4-25-1821 m (1)Hannah Allen (2)Mrs Elizabeth
    Wetmore Capt CT

HAMMER, (includes HAMER & HEIMER)
Balsor: b c. 1760 d 1837 m Elizabeth Simmons Pvt VA
Daniel: b c. 1750 d 1784 m Catherine Donnecker Pvt PA
Jonas: b c. 1749 d 1824 m Catherine — Pvt PA
Peter: b 8-19-1757 d 4-18-1838 m (1)Elizabeth White Bonser
    (2)Sarah Pearce Pvt VA ★
Thomas: b c. 1731-1730 d p. 1791 m Elenor Lyons Pvt PA
Tobias: b 1753 d 5-13-1815 m Katherine Otto Pvt MD

HAMMERSLY (includes HAMERSLEY)
John: b 1761 d 3-30-1836 m (1)Sarah Cochran (2)Sally McMullen
    Pvt Cpl PA ★
Wm.: b c. 1757 d 1820 m Sarah Sankey PS VA

HAMMETT, (includes HAMET &HAMMIT)
Benjamin: b c. 1750 d p. 4-6-1790 m Ruth VanMeter Pvt PS VA
Caleb: b 1747 d 1842 m Keziah Potter Pvt RI ★
Malachi: b c. 1741 d p. 1818 m (1)Maplet Hawkins (2)Mrs Hannah
    Low Wicks Capt RI
Richard: b 1-12-1754 d p. 1797 m Nancy Briscoe Pvt MD
Thomas: b 1755 d p. 1782 m Susan Locke Sol PA
Thomas: b 1-15-1750 d 1-18-1786 m Charlotte Bennett PS SC
Wm.: b 11-16-1749 d 8-23-1832 m Martha — Sol GA

HAMMOCK,
John: b c. 1758 d p. 12-29-1829 m (1)Phebe Paschall (2)Mrs Sarah
    Thornton Pvt GA

HAMMOND, (includes HAMMAN, HAMMONDS &
    HAMMONS)
Aaron: b 8-16-1758 d 6-29-1843 m Sarah Bartlett Pvt MA
Abner: b 1-25-1762 d 7-9-1829 m (1)Anne Jones (2)Sarah Dudley
    Lt SC ★
Abraham: b 1753/4 d 3-2-1844 m Charity Hammock Cpl VA ★
Amarian: b 4-18-1719 d 7-3-1778 m Mary Dudley Sol PA
Barzillai: b 3-9-1706 d 6-25-1779 m (1)Mary Barlow (2)Anna Tobey
    (3)Sarah Doty Cpl MA
Bela: b 1-29-1756 d p. 1790 m Jenna Staples Pvt MA
Benjamin: b 6-7-1724 d 9- -1809 m Sarah Brown LCol MA
Benjamin: b 1-8-1735 d 1777 m Sarah Craigie Capt ME
Benjamin: b 6-30-1753 d 3-27-1813 m Sarah Fiske Sol NH
Benjamin: b 1749 d c. 1833 m Deborah Force Pvt NY
Charles: b c. 1740 d 11-29-1795 m Rachel — Capt PS MD
Charles, Sr.: b 6-4-1729 d 1777 m Rebecca Wright PS MD
Charles: b 1765 d 1837 m Polly Garrett Lt SC
Charles: b 11-19-1716 d 8-15-1794 m Elizabeth Steele PS VA SC
Daniel: b 10-18-1727 d 1777 m Lucy Jones Pvt MA
Daniel: b 3-1-1750 d 3-10-1834 m Joanna Baylis Sol PS NY
David: b 1753 d 2-10-1786 m Elizabeth — Pvt MA
David, Jr.: b 8-17-1720 d 1-3-1797 m Susanna Harris Pvt MA
David: b 11-13-1757 d 12-21-1840 m (1)Patience Harris (2)Hannah
    Eastman Pvt NH ★
David: b 9- -1747 d 4-27-1801 m Jane Hanna 1Lt PA
Dudley: b 1757/8 d 1802 m Sybil Huntington Pvt CT
Ebenezer: b 1754/3 d 1815 m Deborah Terry Pvt MA
Edmond: b 3-21-1751 d 1-7-1836 m Mary Wilson Pvt MA ★
Edward: b 5-8-1738 d 5-11-1802 m Mary Lombard Capt MA
Eleazer: bpt 6-10-1733 d p. 1791 m Mehitable Button Pvt CT
Elijah: b 10-7-1711 d 5-3-1800 m (1)Mary Kingsbury (2)Abigail
    Terry PS CT
Elijah: b 3-4-1757 d 4-20-1815 m (1)Mrs Sarah Harrington
    (2)Eunice Davis Sgt MA
Elisha: b 2-4-1752 d 2-22-1839 m (1)Catherine Gardiner
    (2)Margaret Haines Lt MA ★
Enoch: b 10-29-1734 d 7-29-1823 m Lucy Fiske Pvt MA
Experience: b 12-17-1757 d 8-6-1825 m (1)Lettice Wilder (2)Elsie
    Coleman Cpl MA
Faunce: b 5-20-1737 d 2-8-1813 m Mary Holmes Pvt MA
George: b 6-24-1734 d 1-14-1782 m (1)Lucy Sturtevant (2)Betsey
    Thomas Capt MA
George: b 2-25-1750 d 1840 m (1)Sarah Dickerson (2)Unity Smith
    Pvt NC
Gideon: b 11-20-1758 d 5-27-1837 m (1)Rachel Horton (2)Sarah
    Chase Pvt RI

Hezekiah: b 11-4-1733 d 12-9-1813 m Lucy Griffin Cpl CT
Isaac: b 1748 d 6-24-1795 m Mehitable Prime Pvt NH
Isaac: b 4-4-1763 d 2-21-1847 m Margaret Paus Pvt VA ★
Jacob: b 1-16-1752 d 10-9-1804 m Louise Kuchle Pvt PA
Jacob: b 1750 d 2-3-1824 m Anna Hottel PS VA
James: b 6-20-1727 d 7-26-1810 m Nancy Ann Wiley Col NY
James 2d: b 10- -1758 d 2-20-1831 m Mary Brown Sol PA
Jason: b 2-1-1762 d 9-21-1830 m Rachael Hale Pvt CT
Jason: b 5-8-1767 d 2-26-1834 m Mary Vangorder Matr CT ★
Jeduthan: b 4-14-1740 d 5-31-1790 m Mary Jenney Cpl MA
Job: b 1741 d 3-4-1834 m Martha Palmer Pvt SC ★
John: b 10-13-1729 d p. 1781 m (1)Abigail Fuller (2)Abigail Moulton
    Sgt CT
John: b 1742-7 d c. 1785 m Hannah Tubbs Pvt PS CT
John, Sr.: b 1728 d 1780 m Ann Gaither PS MD
John, Jr.: b 4-21-1754 d 9-12-1811 m (1)Tomsey Simpson (2)Rachel
    Roberts Capt MD
John: b 3-24-1741 d p. 1790 m Susan Preble Pvt MA
John: b 8-22-1749 d p. 1805 m Lucy Powers Pvt MA
John, Jr.: bpt 8-21-1746 d 1817 m Freena Romer Pvt NY
John: b — d 1787 m Deborah — Pvt NY
John: b 6-20-1741 d 8-20-1820 m Anna Fisk Ens RI
John: b 2-5-1722 d p. 1820 m Ann Coleman Capt SC
John: b 8-26-1755 d 6-13-1843 m (1)Susanna Hefferling (2)Sarah
    — Pvt VA ★
John, Jr.: b c. 1760 d c. 1825 m Barbara Ann — Pvt VA
John Basil: b c. 1758 d 1819 m Vashti — Sgt NC
Jonathan: bpt 2-3-1747 d p. 1780 m — Pvt NY
Joseph: b 1750 d p. 1804 m Mary Fernald Pvt MA
Joseph: b 2-3-1723 d 1804 m (1)Mrs Esther Gould (2)Abigail —
    (3)Mrs Mary Fiske Col CS NH
Joshua: b 3-10-1720 d 12-31-1792 m Elizabeth Prentice Pvt MA
Joshua: b 6-14-1759 d 3-17-1804 m Olive Adams Pvt MA
Joshua: b 1-1-1757 d 3-22-1853 m Sarah R. Hammond Lt SC ★
Joshua: b 8-6-1749 d 10-3-1803 m Charity Baxter Sol SC
Josiah, Sr.: b 3-12-1700 d 10-5-1793 m (1)Mary Davis (2)Mrs Sybel
    Bishop Pvt MA
Josiah, Jr.: b 1-31-1723 d 8-31-1802 m Abigail Durkee Capt CT
Lebbeus: b 1754 d 7-12-1826 m Lucy Tubbs Pvt MA
Leroy, Sr.: b 1726 d 5-13-1790 m Mary Ann Tyler Cpl SC
Leroy, Jr.: b 5-3-1762 d 1816 m Sarah Quarles Hall Sol SC
Luthan: b 4-3-1758 d 10-22-1806 m Mary Rood Sol NY
Martin: b c. 1760 d 1797 m Susannah Turner Pvt SC
Mathew: b 1759 d a. 1817 m Hannah Hoisington Cpl VT
Nathaniel: b 9-10-1733 d 12-10-1817 m (1)Dorothy Tucker (2)Mrs
    Eleanor Olmstead Burr PS CT
Obadiah: b 12-5-1756 d a. 1750 m Elizabeth — Pvt NC ★
Paine: b 1748 d p. 6-20-1791 m Phoebe Almy PS RI
Paul: b 4-20-1740 d 3-5-1823 m Anna Davis, Jr. Pvt MA
Paul: b 12-27-1757 d 8-8-1838 m Polly Fuller Pvt NY ★
Philip: b 5-23-1744 d 4-21-1799 m Barbara Arianna Raitt PS MD
Philip: b 1753 d 8-3-1832 m Christena Cook Pvt VA ★
Raleigh: b 5-11-1756 d 8-24-1839 m (1)Mary G. — (2)Margaret
    Johnston Pvt Wgm NC W★
Rezin: b 12-25-1706 d — m Ann Catherine Sellman PS MD
Robert: b c. 1762 d 1842 m Mary Ferris Pvt CT
Samuel: b 2-2-1748 d 4-1-1842 m Mary Rogers Pvt PS MA
Samuel: b 9-21-1757 d 9-11-1842 m (1)Mrs Rebecca Rae (2)Eliza
    Amelia O'Keefe Col VA SC ★
Samuel, Sr.: b 3-9-1722 d 10- -1806 m Mary Jenkins Capt VA
Staats: b 11-14-1744 d 7-26-1820 m Elizabeth Martling Sgt NY
Stephen: b 2-7-1764 d 11-16-1847 m (1)Amy Hunt (2)Lorancy
    Edgerton Sol MM Mar RI★
Thomas: b 2-20-1762 d 3-4-1847 m Hannah Cross Cpl MA
Thomas: b 11-12-1744 d 10-28-1824 m Sarah Winchester Cpl MA
Thomas: b 6-11-1747 d 6-8-1827 m Esther Dole Pvt MA
Thomas: b 10-31-1719 d 1782 m Martha Olmstead PS NH
Vachel: b 3- -1751 d 12-18-1821 m Mary Hammond PS MD
Wm.: b 9-19-1735 d 10-18-1793 m Sarah Hutchins Pvt CT
Wm.: b c. 1737 d 9-3-1813 m Eleanor Williams Pvt MD
Wm.: b 7-14-1740 d 5-30-1814 m (1)Mary Livermore (2)Relief
    Baldwin Sgt CS MA
Wm.: b 1739 d 6-16-1816 m Kezia Hawes Cpl MA
Wm.: b 1755-60 d c. 1829 m Mary Wier PS PA
Wm.: b 2-19-1733 d 1-23-1809 m Chloe Wilbur CS RI
Wm.: b 1742 d 1817 m Sarah — Pvt VA
Zedakiah: b c. 1759 d 10- -1787 m Sarah — Pvt MD

HAMNER,
John: b 1-2-1761 d 10-28-1836 m Mary Whobery Pvt VA ★
Nicholas: b 1703 d p. 1779 m X PS VA
Wm.: b 1730 d p. 12-25-1787 m Mary Elizabeth Henly Ens PS VA

HAMPTON,
Andrew: b 1716-20 d 10-8-1805 m Catherine Hyder Col CS NC
Anthony: b 2-3-1715 d 7- -1776 m Elizabeth Preston PS SC
Cary Henry: b 11-16-1750 d 7- -1834 m Elizabeth Plunkett SrgnMte
    VA
David: b 6-1-1764 d 1-26-1842 m (1)Mary Bryan (2)Mrs Mary
    Johnson Pvt VA
Edward: b a. 1740 d 1781 m (2)Sarah Earle Capt SC
Elizabeth Preston: b 1710 d 7- -1776 m Anthony Hampton PS SC
George: b 1725 d 1778 m Mary Colson Pvt VA

HAMPTON, contd.

Joel: b 1753 d 1832 m Hannah Mitchel Pvt NC
John: b 1745 d 8-30-1822 m Mary I. — Capt NJ
John: b 1745 d 12-29-1830 m Anne Williamson Maj SC
John: b 3-15-1735 d 12-1-1805 m Sarah Anne — Pvt PA
John: b 6-22-1761 d 6-19-1837 m Joyce Malone Pvt SC ★
John: b — d 7-12-1803 m — Pvt PS VA
John Thomas: b 1752 d 9-29-1794 m Mercy Harnard Harris Dr NJ
Mary Colston: b 1731 d 1778 m George Hampton PS VA
Moses: b 11-25-1762 d 11-26-1825 m Hannah Van Natta Pvt NJ
Preston: b c. 1752 d 7-10-1832 m Elizabeth — Capt VA
Samuel: b a. 1760 d 12-19-1802 m Bethunia Bostick Capt NC
Thomas: b 4-11-1759 d 6-25-1836 m Elizabeth Hollinger Pvt PA
Thomas: b 10-17-1728 d 1796 m Mrs Sarah Patterson Sgt VA
Thomas: b 1760 d 7-13-1840 m — Pvt VA ★
Wade: b 1752 d 2-4-1835 m (1)Mrs. Epps-Howell (2)Harriet Flud (3) Polly Cantey Col CS SC W★
Zachariah: b c. 1745 d 9-8-1781 m Mary — Pvt NC

HAMRICK,

Benjamin: b 1755 d 1842 m Nancy McMillian MM Cpl VA ★
David: b 1760 d 7-12-1839 m Lettice Wyatt Pvt VA
Wm.: b 1756 d 1830 m Sarah Payne Pvt VA

HAMSHER, (includes HAMSCHER)

Adam: b 1730 d 8- -1809 m Margaret — Lt PA
Adam: b 10-7-1753 d 1-3-1848 m Catherine Weber 2Lt PA
Barnet, Jr.: b 11-18-1761 d 4-20-1815 m Catharine Clippinger Pvt PA
Daniel: b a. 1764 d p. 1790 m Anna Barbara Sparrin Pvt PA

HAMSTREET, (includes HEMSTREET)

Dirk: b 12-14-1740 d p. 1790 m Eve Paford Lt NY
Philip: b c. 10- -1749 d 4-29-1843 m Diana VanVliet Lt NY ★
Wm.: bpt 1-16-1768 d p. 9-6-1787 m Martha Oliver Pvt NY

HAMTRAMCK,

John Francis: b 8-14-1754 d 4-11-1803 m Rebecca McKenzie Capt NY

HANA,

Daniel: b 8-12-1744 d 1841 m Elizabeth Miller Pvt MA

HANAFORD,

Peter: b 1751 d 1-19-1834 m Nancy Pierson Pvt PS NH

HANAWALT,

George: b 1760 d 9-23-1826 m Susannah Rothrock Pvt PA
Henry: b 1730-2 d p. 2-26-1794 m Catherine — Pvt PA

HANBY,

Jonathan: b 12-9-1741 d 3-26-1817 m Sarah Dalton Capt PS VA

HANCE,

Adam, Jr.: b 1750 d 1823 m Hannah Stoebuck Pvt CS VA
Samuel: b 6-1-1730 d 12-10-1798 m Ann Deavor PS MD

HANCHETT, (includes HANCHETTE)

David: b 6-19-1743 d 9-4-1819 m Deborah Sheldon Pvt CT
Ebenezer, Jr.: b 2-7-1747/8 d 5/6- -1795 m Phoebe Holley Pvt PS CT
Jonah: b 1-30-1758 d 5-6-1845 m Sarah Squares OrdlSgt CT ★
Luke: b 2-3-1738 d 9-23-1821 m Sarah Harmon Cpl CT
Oliver: b 8-7-1741 d 5-26-1816 m Rachel Gillet Capt CT
Simeon: b 2-4-1753 d p. 1782 m Mary Raimenton Pvt CT

HANCOCK (includes HANCOX)

Abraham: b c. 1754 d 1813 m Ann — Pvt MD
Austin: b 10-5-1760 d 1849 m Anne Nuckolls Sgt VA ★
Belcher: b 1745-8 d 5-14-1813 m Ann Hancock Capt MA
Benjamin: b c. 1756 d 1817 m Anna Corn Ens VA
Bill: b 6-29-1742 d 1792 m Persis Wood Sgt MA
Ebenezer: b 11-22-1741 d 3-12-1819 m Eliza Lowell CS MA
Edward: b 11-16-1744 d 2-27-1837 m Sarah Sheffield Pvt CT ★
Edward: b 11-15-1754 d 3-9-1836 m Jane Nicholis Sgt VA ★
George: b 1749 d 1799 m Sarah Williams Pvt NH
George: b 6-13-1754 d 7-18-1820 m (1)Margaret Strother (2)Mrs Robinson Col PS VA
Henry: b a. 1750 d 1812 m — Summerell Cpl VA
Jabez: b 7-29-1728 d 1-25-1816 m Rachel Wright Pvt MA
Jacob: b c. 1720 d p. 1-28-1778 m Elizabeth Kezar Pvt NH
James: b 8-25-1745 d 1833 m Elizabeth Hardy Sol PS NC
John: b 7-10-1760 d 1852 m (1) — Hearn (2) — Bell Pvt NC
John: b c. 1735 d p. 1809 m Ann Oliver Lt SC
John: b 3- -1753 d 1827 m Ann Graves Capt VA
John: b c. 1733 d p. 11- -1802 m Elizabeth Maddox Pvt VA
John Lane: b 1757 d 9-6-1835 m Hannah Prescott Pvt MA
Joseph: b 9-10-1740 d p. 1783 m Jerusha Whiting Lt MA
Joseph: b 1759 d 3-2-1831 m (1)Polly Heath (2)Susanna Page Pvt NH
Joseph, Jr.: b 7-21-1758 d 1834 m (1)Katherine Baltimore (2)Dianah Reeder Pvt PA ★
Moses: b 12-20-1758 d 9-22-1828 m Wealthy Bishop Pvt MA
Nathan: b 12-16-1762 d 9- -1823 m Sarah Craig Pvt MA

Richard: b 10-10-1750 d p. 1810 m Eve Burrell Pvt PA
Samuel: b 2-28-1760 d 4-14-1837 m Ann Moon SgtMaj VA ★
Stephen: b 3-25-1747 d 1809 m Margaret Cromwell Pvt MD
Stephen: b c. 1744 d p. 1789 m Catherine Merchant Pvt PS VA
Torrey: bpt 4-6-1746 d 7-17-1778 m Sarah Wyeth Cpl MA
Wm.: b 2-3-1751 d 11-19-1826 m Elizabeth — Pvt MA
Wm.: b 2-3-1761 d 11-19-1836 m Elizabeth Leavitt Pvt MA
Wm. 3d: b c. 1712 d 3-21-1778 m (1)Mabel Chambless (2)Sarah Thompson PS NJ
Wm.: b 2- -1740 d p. 1796 m Sarah — Ens NC
Wm.: b 10-20-1749 d 1837 m (1)Anne Hill (2)Mrs Mary Eliza Fisher Emerson 2Sgt VA
Wm.: b c. 1751 d p. 1790 m Jemimah Brock Sol VA

HAND,

Aaron: b 2-23-1764 d 7-27-1842 m Phebe Smith Pvt NJ ★
Abraham: b 10-17-1751 d 1817 m Ruth Southworth Lt CT
Abraham: b 9-22-1764 d 11-4-1840 m Mary West Pvt MA ★
Christopher: b 1758 d 1834 m Margaret — OrdSgt VA
Daniel: b 1732 d 10-22-1816 m (1)Siba Smith (2)Lizzie Lynde (3)Chloe Boardman Capt CT
Daniel: b 8-12-1744 d 1841 m Elizabeth Miller Pvt MA
Daniel: b 1730 d 4-27-1787 m (1)Hannah — (2)Mary Teel NCapt NJ
Darius: b 1759 d 7-8-1835 m Elizabeth Catlin Pvt MA
David: b 1748 d 4-6-1804 m Martha Yeats Ens NJ
David: b 1730 d 1802 m Zerviah Stuart PS NY
Edward: b 12-31-1744 d 9-3-1802 m Catherine Ewing BGen PA
Elias: b 10-10-1747 d p. 1787 m Sarah Martin Pvt CT
Elijah: b 1-20-1730 d 1790 m Rachel (Hand) Maj Col NJ
Ezekiel: bpt 1711 d 2-13-1781 m Joanna Miller PS NY
Henry: b 1753 d 9-6-1835 m Elizabeth Harrison Pvt GA
Henry: b 1750 d 12-27-1830 m Sarah Bonafield Pvt VA
Hezekiah: b c. 1730 d 4- -1800 m (2)Nancy — (3)Anna Ferrago Pvt NJ
Ichabod: b 6-27-1749 d 1-28-1840 m Mary Graves Pvt CT
Ira: b 6-19-1751 d 10-17-1801 m Mehitabel Bosworth Sgt NH W★
Jeremiah: b 1763 d 9-12-1815 m Deborah (Hand) Pvt NJ
Jesse: b 1-15-1738 d 1-29-1791 m Sarah Laming PS CS NJ
John: b c. 1754 d p. 1795 m Sarah Newton Maj NJ
Jonathan: b 1750 d p. 1793 m Sarah Reeve Ens NJ
Jonathan: b 7-5-1728 d 12-22-1789 m Rebecca Yates PS NJ
Marcus: b 1745 d 12-21-1829 m Mary Nortman Pvt NY
Nathan: b a. 1722 d 1782 m Hannah Eldridge Pvt NJ
Nathaniel: b 4- -1739 d 9-24-1824 m Esther Mulford Lt PS NY
Recompence: b 1764 d p. 1835 m Acsah — Smn NJ
Silas: b 3-5-1728 d 9-5-1818 m Sarah Burnet Wgn NJ
Thomas: b 3-4-1752 d p. 5-3-1783 m (1)Hannah Stites (2)Jerusha Johnson Pvt NJ
Thomas: b c. 1756 d a. 5-10-1796 m Elizabeth Hand PS NJ
Timothy: b 1745 d 1801 m Rhoda Bradley Pvt CT

HANDERSON, (includes HENDERSON)

Gideon: b 10-9-1753 d 7-10-1825 m Abigail Church Pvt MA
Timothy: b 1-18-1756 d 10-14-1833 m Anna Wales Cpl MA ★

HANDLEY, (includes HANDLY)

Archibald: b c. 1730 d 1796 m Jean — CS VA
Handy: b 1755 d p. 9-19-1840 m (1)Mary — (2)Nici Hooper Pvt MD ★
John: b 1746 d 1-13-1811 m Mary Harrison Lt VA
Samuel: b 1752 d 11-24-1840 m Susan Cowan Capt Spy VA NC

HANDWERK,

Peter: b 9-18-1744 d 2-27-1826 m (1)Anna Margaret Weber (2)Maria Eva Stettler Pvt PA

HANDY,

Charles, Jr.: b 7-10-1758 d 6-28-1791 m Rebecca Clarke Capt RI
Ebenezer: b 10-19-1743 d 9-1-1838 m (1)Jemima Teft (2)Sally Wright Sgt RI ★
Edward: b 3-30-1757 d 2-25-1836 m Mary Wing Cpl MA
George: b 11-23-1756 d 7-19-1820 m Elizabeth Wilson Capt MD
George: b 10-13-1727 d 11-6-1782 m Nellie Gillis PS MD
Hannah Hunter: b c. 1745 d p. 1818 m Robert Handy PS VT
Henry: b 1747 d 1787 m Jane Winder Ens MD
Isaac: b 6-17-1746 d 1826 m Amelia Curtis Capt MD
Job: b 7-2-1750 d 1792 m Elizabeth Gifford Slr Pvt MA
John: b 9-3-1757 d 3-15-1840 m Polly Baker Ens PA ★
John: b 10-5-1756 d 11-2-1828 m Desire Potter QM RI
Jonathan: b 9-21-1750 d 6-19-1831 m Tabitha Wing Pvt MA
Levin: b 8-20-1754 d 6-5-1799 m E. Nancy Wilson Capt MD W★
Robert: b c. 1745 d p. 1781 m Hannah Hunter Pvt VT
Samuel: b 6-8-1756 d 12-1-1838 m Sarah Hall QMSgt CT
Samuel: b 1741 d 1828 m Mary Gore Col MD
Wm.: b 3-31-1760 d 12-22-1823 m (1)Caroline Seward (2)Martha Parker Pvt CT
Wm.: b 7-11-1762 d 1852 m Love Swain Sol MA
Zaccheus: b — d p. 1790 m Susanna Freeman Pvt MA

HANER (or HAINER)

Wilhelmus: b 12-23-1760 d p. 1832 m (1)Elizabeth Miller (2)Margaret Fox Sgt NY

HANEY, (includes HEANEY)
James: b 1750 d c. 1825 m Lydia King Pvt VA
Michael: b 5-23-1756 d 11-23-1830 m Hellenah Schaefer Pvt PA

HANFORD,
Daniel: b 6-15-1744 d 4-12-1797 m Susanna Platt Pvt CT
Ebenezer: b 10-1-1757 d 1834 m Lucretia Hanford Sgt CT
Hezekiah: b 1721/22 d 5-2-1812 m Deborah Hoyt Pvt CT
Jesse: b 11- -1746 d 1777 m Mary Whitney Pvt CT
John: b 2-13-1739 d 9-1-1825 m Mehitable Comstock Pvt CT
Levi: b 9- -1759 d 10-19-1854 m Mary Mead Pvt CT ★
Phineas, Sr.: b 1713 d 8-17-1787 m Hannah Comstock PS CT
Phineas: b 1750 d 9-18-1793 m Betty Adams Cpl CT
Stephen: b 1747 d 11-20-1838 m Phebe Fitch Sgt CT

HANGEN,
Jacob: b 9-17-1738 d 12-26-1816 m Barbara Leidy — Pvt PA

HANGER,
Frederick, Sr.: b. 1730 d 1799 m Eve — Sol VA
Frederick, Jr.: b 8-12-1755 d 1812 m Mary Hull Ens VA
Peter, Sr.: b 1729 d 1802 m Hannah Gobbert Pvt VA
Peter, Jr.: b 1-29-1761 d 12-23-1828 m Catherine Link Pvt VA

HANGLEITER,
John, Sr.: b — d p. 6-7-1786 m (1)Ursula — (2)Mary Magdalene —
CS PS GA

HANKERSON,
Wm.: b 6-25-1755 d 3-18-1830 m Martha Thomas Pvt RI ★

HANKINS,
Daniel: b c. 1720 d 1796 m — PS Capt CS VA
Jonathan: b 1-12-1749 d p. 1790 m Almira Hankins MM MA
Wm.: b c. 1750 d 1824 m Elizabeth — 2Lt PS VA
Zachariah: b 1754 d 1849/50 m Phoebe Herbert Pvt NJ

HANKINSON,
Aaron: b 2-7-1735 d 10-9-1806 m Mary Synder Col CS NJ
James: b a. 1760 d 1823 m Joanna — Pvt NJ
Joseph: b 4-15-1745 d 11-30-1825 m Hannah Atkinson Capt NJ
Kenneth: b 1-24-1731 d 10-6-1807 m Eleanor Covenhoven Capt NJ
Wm.: b 10-2-1737 d 4-26-1796 m Susannah Dewitt Pvt NJ

HANKS,
Abner: b 1763 d p. 9-5-1846 m (1)Elizabeth Dale (2)Mary —
(3)Frances Melton (4)Sarah Goodman (5)Nancy Boniface Shouse
Pvt VA ★
Benjamin: b 10-29-1755 d 12-15-1824 m Alice Hovey Drm Pvt CT
Consider: b 4-29-1764 d 2-18-1818 m Sarah Baldwin Pvt CT
Elijah: b 8-30-1761 d 2-11-1839 m Mary Walker Pvt PS CT ★
John, Sr.: b 10-5-1730 d 2-23-1815 m Tabitha Hall Sgt CT
John: b 5-4-1728 d p. 1791 m Susannah — Pvt VA
Levi: b 5-28-1761 d 12-19-1835 m Mercy Waterman Pvt MA
Uriah: b 5-3-1734 d 7-4-1809 m Irene Case PS CT
Wm.: b 10-23-1728 d 1807 m Hannah Sargent Pvt MA
Wm.: b c. 1718 d 12-29-1776 m — Pvt VA

HANLEY,
Patrick: b 1746 d 10-31-1826 m Catherine Keiser Pvt PA

HANLON,
James: b 1754 d 2-2-1829 m Elizabeth — Pvt VA NJ ★

HANMER, (includes HANMORE)
David: b 1756 d 1831 m Eleanor Murphy Pvt NY ★
Francis: b 1709/8 d 12-19-1790 m Elizabeth Curtis PS CT
Francis: b 1739 d 5-4-1816 m Rhoda Bordman Pvt CT
James: b 1747 d 12-9-1789 m Elizabeth Ayrault PS MA
Samuel: b 8-16-1741 d 10-3-1813 m Sarah Wills Pvt PS CT
Turner: b 12-27-1752 d 2-15-1845 m Ann Moore Sol PS VA

HANNA, (includes HANNAH, HANNAY & HANNEY)
Andrew: b 1733 d 1808 m Elizabeth Ricord Towsick PS NY
Andrew: b 8-30-1760 d 4-1-1843 m Jane — Pvt NC ★
Andrew: b 1754 d 3- -1793 m Anne Cunningham Ens VA
David: b — d p. 3-17-1803 m Elizabeth — Pvt PA
Edward: b 1756 d 5-27-1832 m Margaret Daughtery PS PA
Hugh: b c. 1759 d 9-7-1842 m — (3)Elizabeth Barr Sol SC
Isaac: b 1743 d 1816 m Martha Bell 1Lt PA
James: b 3-2-1752 d 10-31-1827 m (1)Hannah Bayless Pvt MD
James: b 1-20-1725 d 12-10-1798 m Elizabeth Glenn Pvt VA
John: b c. 1745 d p. 1810 m Martha — Pvt VA
John: b c. 1760 d 5/6- -1822 m Mary McKnight Pvt NY
John: b 10-26-1748 d 5-4-1838 m Ann MacDill Pvt PA
John: b 1751 d 4-27-1845 m Margaret MacCullum Pvt PA ★
John: b 1752 d 6-9-1832 m Elizabeth Miller Pvt PA
John: b 1756 d p. 4-11-1845 m Jane Graham Sgt VA ★
Joseph: b c. 1720 d a. 7-28-1789 m Anna — PS VA
Robert: b 1755 d p. 1833 m Mary Thomas Pvt MD
Robert: b 1736 d 4- -1786 m Elizabeth Kelly Lt PA
Robert: b 12-10-1744 d 1-24-1821 m Mary Parks Pvt PS SC
Robert: b 1752 d 11-16-1844 m Janet Hancock Pvt PA ★
Robert: b 2-17-1742 d 10-19-1803 m Mary — Lt SC

Robert: b 1755 d 1825 m Mary Moore Pvt SC
Robert: b 1750 d 1825 m Mary Kilpatrick Pvt VA
Robert: b 3-2-1753 d 7-16-1837 m Catherine Jones Sol VA
Robert Cunningham: b 4-1-1761 d 3-25-1841 m Mary Moore Lt SC
Samuel: b 1737 d p. 7-27-1808 m Agnes Sterrett Pvt PA
Thomas: b c. 1750-55 d 1817/18 m Ann — Sol GA
Thomas: b 1760 d 4-9-1839 m Jane Cowden Pvt PA
Wm.: b c. 1740 d 3-18-1818 m (1)Elizabeth — (2)Mrs Foster PS
Pvt PA

HANNAFORD,
Benjamin: b 5-14-1735 d 5-7-1811 m Ruth Page PS NH

HANNAN,
Esom: b 1752 d 3-20-1843 m Mary Greenlee Pvt VA ★
Thomas: b 12-25-1757 d 4-18-1835 m Elizabeth Henry Sol VA

HANNIS,
Henry: b 5-12-1757 d 9-23-1835 m (1)Hannah — (2)Gilly — Pvt
NY ★
John: b 1735 d 8-13-1783 m Mary Glove Pvt PA

HANNUM,
Asahel: b 2-21-1753 d 3-10-1816 m Mary Pomeroy Pvt MA
Joel: b 12-6-1745 d 1-2-1814 m Esther Coleman Pvt MA
John: b 1740 d 2-7-1799 m Alice Park Col PA
Moses, Sr.: b 3-26-1718 d 12-11-1802 m Lydia Warner Pvt MA
Moses, Jr.: b 7-2-1757 d 7-7-1834 m Jerusha Parker Pvt MA
Timothy: b 1751 d 1806 m Selina Clark Cpl MA
Wm.: b 1755 d 8-20-1827 m Mercy Dodge Pvt MA ★

HANSARD,
Wm.: b 6-17-1744 d 3- -1798 m Jennet — Pvt NC
Wm.: b 1763 d 1846 m Martha Christian Pvt VA

HANSBOROUGH, (includes HANSBROUGH)
James: b a. 1724 d 10- -1784 m Lettice Sumner QMSgt VA
John: b c. 1760 d p. 1801 m Sarah Scoggan Pvt VA
Morias: b c. 1740 d p. 7-28-1800 m (1)Jane — (2)Mary Underwood
PS VA
Peter: b 10-16-1758 d p. 1812 m Elizabeth Brown Pvt VA
Wm., Sr.: b c. 1733 d — m Keziah Loving Pvt VA
Wm.: Jr.: b 1755 d 1- -1816 m Sarah Vaughan Pvt VA ★

HANSCOM, (includes HANSCOMB, HANSCOME)
Aaron: bpt 1-7-1739 d 11-4-1826 m (1)Sarah Sevey (2)Lydia Willey
Pvt MA W★
John: b 5- -1751 d 1827 m Anna — Pvt MA ★
Moses: b 12-4-1759 d 8-27-1835 m Mollie McGray Pvt MA
Moses: b 3-12-1717 d 2-26-1793 m (1)Mary Field (2)Martha
Shapleigh PS MA
Stephen: b 1761/2 d 4-2-1802 m Mrs Hannah Remick Tobey Pvt MA
Uriah: b 1757 d 7-19-1825 m (2)Hannah Barnes Pvt NH

HANSELL,
Barnet: b 1759 d 10-11-1809 m (1)Sarah Turner Sutton (2)Sarah
Musgrove Pvt PA
George: b 1756 d p. 1790 m Rosanna Slough Cpl PA
Wm.: b c. 1757 d 7-16-1800 m Sarah Morris Sgt PA

HANSFORD,
Charles: b 12-22-1759 d c. 1850 m — Pvt Slr VA ★

HANSLEY,
John: b 1739 d p. 10-28-1807 m Lilian — Sol NC

HANSON, (includes HANSEN)
Abraham: b 7-15-1759 d 1802 m Susanna Odiorn Pvt NH
Aurt: b 1762 d 6-23-1854 m Meriam — Pvt NY
Charles: b 2-25-1759 d 1830 m Dorcas Mills Pvt NH
Dirk: b 4-18-1743 d 6- -1799 m Helen Low Capt NY W★
Ebenezer: b 6-5-1726 d 1782 m Anna Hodgdon Cpl NH
Elijah: b 2- -1755 d 1802 m Susanna Scruven Sol NC
George Adolphus: b 9-15-1762 d 10-16-1823 m Rebecca Baird Lt
MD
Henry: b 2-18-1721 d 5-20-1780 m Catherine Putnam Lt NY
Hoskins: b c. 1740-5 d p. 9- -1776 m Catherine Queen Thompson
2Lt MD
Ichabod: b 9-22-1741 d 7-5-1818 m Abigail Hayes Lt MA
Isaac: b 1737 d 1807 m Amey Clark Pvt MA
Isaac: b 4-15-1761 d 9-27-1833 m Sarah Church Pvt NH
Isaac: b 1761 d 1820 m Pattie Scammon Pvt MA
John: b 1715 d 11-22-1783 m Jane Contee PS MD
John: b c. 1725 d a. 11-5-1793 m Elizabeth Massey PS MD
John: b c. 1739 d p. 4-22-1819 m Mary Elizabeth Clark Pvt MA
John: b 1760 d 10- -1818 m Mary Magdalena Wall Pvt VA
Nathaniel, Jr.: b 11-1-1761 d 9-27-1836 m Sarah Hodgdon
Lougee Sgt NH
Nicholas: b 9-21-1753 d 3-23-1821 m Deborah Wemple Ens NY
Peter, Sr.: b 1746 d 12- -1776 m Mary — Lt MD
Peter N.: bpt 2-11-1733 d 1817 m Rachel Fonda PS NY
Robert: b c. 1758 d 12-4-1809 m Priscilla Boucher Franklin Sgt MD
Samuel: b c. 1758 d c. 1821 m Peggy Sims Sol GA

HANSON, contd.
Samuel, Sr.: b c. 1716 d 10-21-1794 m Ann Hawkins LCol MD
Samuel: b 10-20-1713 d 11-22-1785 m Eleanor Bailey PS MD
Stephen: b 12-27-1758 d 7-16-1851 m Rachel — Pvt NY
Walter: b 3-11-1711 d 1794 m (1)Jane — (2)Elizabeth Hoskins CS
    MD
Walter: b 10- -1760 d 1792 m Sarah Hatch Maddox Capt MD

HANTZ,
Andreas: b 12-31-1731 d 12-24-1786 m Maria Catharine Altland
    CS PS PA

HANWAY,
Jesse: b 1760 d 5-23-1804 m Rachel Ridgeway Pvt PA

HAPGOOD,
Abraham: b 10-9-1752 d 4-6-1819 m (1)Lucy Davis (2)Mrs Mary
    Wright (3)Mary Foster Lt MA
Asa, Sr.: b 12-6-1728 d 12-23-1791 m Anna Bowker PS MA
Asa, Jr.: b 11-25-1759 d 10-15-1823 m Jeanie Bowker Pvt MA
Daniel: b 11-16-1747 d 5-16-1833 m Esther Gardner Sgt MA
Ephraim, Sr.: b 4-21-1725 d 10-31-1780 m Rebecca Gibson PS MA
Ephraim, Jr.: b 5-3-1755 d 3-28-1828 m (1)Polly Tuttle (2)Molly
    Hunt Pvt MA
Hezekiah: b 12-23-1757 d 10- -1818 m Dorcas Whitcomb Pvt MA
Shadrach: b 11-6-1706 d 10-8-1782 m Elizabeth Wetherbee Pvt MA
Thomas: b 11-13-1747 d 9-13-1822 m Lucy Woods Pvt MA

HAPPES,
Michael: b 1-12-1753 d 7-30-1833 m Catharine Harr Pvt PA ★

HAPTONSTALL,
Abraham: b 4-6-1761 d 10-22-1847 m Rachel Price Pvt NY ★

HARADEN, (includes HARADON, HARRADEN)
Andrew: b 1-14-1733 d 1-27-1786 m Lydia Griffin Pvt MA
David: b 12-18-1744 d 10-7-1821 m Hannah Whipple Pvt MA
Isaac: bpt 5-30-1762 d — m Anna Stone Pvt MA
Joseph: b 8-15-1755 d 5-1-1811 m Lydia (Haraden) Pvt MA
Joseph: b 11-5-1759 d — m Abigail Whitney Pvt MA ★

HARAH,
Charles: b 2-8-1744 d 11-29-1809 m Margaret Gilchrist Pvt PA

HARALSON,
Herndon: b 10-25-1757 d 5-27-1847 m Mary Murphy Capt NC ★
Jonathan: b c. 1758 d 9- -1833 m (1)Jane Huston (2)Mrs Clara B.
    Culberson Pvt NC
Paul: b c. 1730 d p. 2-9-1803 m Nancy Lea Sol NC

HARBAUGH, (includes HARBACH & HERBACH)
Conrad: b c. 1745 d 6-5-1782 m Susanna Downer Sol PA
John: b 5-6-1735 d 2-15-1803 m (1)Christina Elizabeth Mehl (2)Mrs
    Magdalena Neff PS PA
Thomas: b 7-4-1741 d 7-22-1821 m Catharine Bemis Pvt MA
Yost: b 10-22-1741 d 8-16-1831 m (1)Eva Bahn (2)Marie Elizabeth
    Eshelman Capt PA

HARBISON,
Benjamin: b 1728 d 9-24-1809 m (1)Eliphill Harper (2)Margaret
    Combe (3)Catherine — Capt PS PA
David: b 1742 d 1835 m Esther McWilliams Sol VA
Francis: b 1758 d 1823 m Catharine Hart Pvt PA
James: b 8-15-1762 d 11-2-1835 m (1)Margaret McCrory (2)Jane
    Jamison Pvt SC ★
James: b 1763 d 10-16-1841 m (1)Ann Hemphill (2)Rachel Hembree
    Pvt VA ★
John: b c. 1755 d 5-1-1829 m (1)Catharine English (2)Patsey
    Ransdall (3)Nancy Morgan Sol KY
Robert: b 1758 d 1837 m Sallie James Pvt PA ★

HARBORD,
Wm.: b c. 1750 d p. 1788 m — Sol VA

HARBOUR,
Esias: b 1747 d 7-15-1833 m Catherine — PS VA
Noah: b 10-23-1757 d p. 1832 m Judith Strange Pvt VA ★

HARBUCK,
Nicholas: b 1750-60 d p. 10-5-1822 m Barbara — Sol GA

HARBUT,
Samuel: b 1760 d 2- -1847 m Abigail Loofborrow Spy PS VA ★

HARCOURT,
Richard: b c. 1735 d p. 1800 m — Wgn NJ

HARCUM,
Elisha: b c. 1725-30 d p. 2-18-1800 m (1)Margaret — (2)Sarah
    Fasset Capt PS VA

HARD,
Philo: b 8-17-1750 d 3-25-1813 m Currence Hawley 2Lt VT

HARDAWAY (includes HARDEWAY)
Daniel: b c. 1750 d 1807 m Anne Eggleston Sol VA
John: b 1736 d 1824 m (1)Marianna Smith (2)Elizabeth Maclin
    (3)Kate Mason Lt PS VA
Robert: b 3-4-1758 d 11-9-1807 m Sarah Hicks Capt VA
Thomas: b 9-20-1734 d 7- -1781 m (2)Mary Trotter Pvt VA
Thomas: b — d p. 1782 m Agnes Thweatt PS VA

HARDCASTLE,
James: b c. 1756 d p. 11-14-1828 m Rachael — Sol NC
Thomas: b 1736 d 9-29-1808 m Henrietta Downes QM PS CS MD

HARDEMAN, (includes HARDMAN)
Charles: b c. 1757 d p. 1821 m Rhoda — (2)Betsy Willingham PS
    VA
John: b c. 1758 d c. 1804 m Anne Collier Ens VA
John: b c. 1725 d 1796 m Elizabeth — PS VA
Joseph, 2d: b 1745 d 1792 m Elizabeth — PS MD
Thomas: b 1-8-1750 d 6-14-1833 m (1)Mary Perkins (2)Mrs Susan
    Marr Sol TN
Uriah: b 4-12-1752 d p. 4-14-1800 m Fanny Chandler PS VA
Wm.: b 1754 d p. 4- -1824 m Zilphia — Sol GA
Wm.: b 1756 d 4-28-1825 m Ann Willingham PS VA

HARDENBERGH,
Gerardus: b 1744 d 11-23-1808 m Nancy Ryerson Capt NY
Isaac: b 1-25-1756 d 1828 m Rachel Graham Lt NY
Jacob Rutsen: bpt 2-22-1738 d 10-30-1790 m Dinah Frelinghuysen
    PS NJ
Johannes, Sr.: bpt 6-28-1706 d 8-20-1786 m Maria DuBois Col PS
    NY
Johannes, Jr.: b 9-14-1729 d p. 5-15-1799 m Maria LeFevre Col NY
Johannes A.: bpt 4-10-1743 d 1795 m Rachel DuBois Capt PS NY
Johannis Gerardus: b 6-19-1731 d 4-10-1812 m Cornelia DuBois
    Pvt NY
John C.: b 2-22-1756 d p. 8-6-1787 m Jane DeWitte Pvt NY

HARDENBROOK,
Lodwick: b 4-16-1755 d 2-14-1845 m Elizabeth Waldron Pvt NJ ★

HARDESTY,
Francis: b a. 1750 d 1794-1815 m Susanna — Pvt PA
Henry, Sr.: b 1-16-1765 d 2-21-1857 m Sally Dikes Pvt Sct KY
Hezekiah: b 9-2-1763 d c. 1846 m Sarah Griffin Pvt PA ★
Obed: b 1758 d 7-26-1830 m Mary Paris Pvt PA ★
Richard: b 1751 d 1848 m Mary Lamb Pvt PA ★

HARDGRAVE,
Francis: b 3-5-1745 d 8-8-1828 m Sara Skelton Capt NC

HARDICK,
John: b 1752 d 4-17-1843 m Mary Hopper Pvt OrdlSgt NY ★
Jonathan: b 2-20-1740 d 12-26-1816 m Mahalah — Pvt NY

HARDING, (includes HARDIN)
Abiel: b 8-1-1760 d 1849 m Olive Smith SgtMaj CT ★
Abijah: b 8-1-1760 d 3-3-1844 m (1)Lydia Dickinson (2)Elizabeth
    Smith Scott Pvt MA
Abraham: b 12-7-1730 d 3-3-1819 m Abigail Adams Lt MA
Abraham: b 5-12-1746 d 1836/7 m Anna Dolson Capt NY
Abraham, Sr.: b 1720 d 1806 m Anna Dolson PS NY
Abraham: b c. 1750 d p. 1790 m Nancy Griffith Pvt NC
Abraham, Jr.: b 4-14-1744 d 10-22-1815 m Huldah Tryon PS PA
Amaziah: b 4-7-1759 d 5-17-1829 m Hannah — Pvt Smn MA
Amos: b 3-19-1764 d 7-10-1839 m Phoebe Tripp PS PA
Amy Gardner: b 2-17-1725 d 1795 m Stephen Harding PS PA
Benjamin, Sr.: b c. 1735 d p. 1790 m Margaret — Capt NC
Benjamin, Jr.: b 3-15-1764 d 1850 m Elizabeth Scott Pvt NC
Benjamin: b 1739 d 1820 m X Pvt NC
Benjamin: b 1753 d p. 9-25-1832 m (1)Nancy Routt (2)Rebecca
    Jackson Pvt VA ★
Benjamin: b 1739 d 1820 m Sarah Hardin Sol VA
David: b 1-1-1732 d 3-1-1828 m Sarah Brown Pvt MA
Ede: b 1758 d 1-14-1846 m Dorcas — Pvt PA ★
Edward: b 8-17-1757 d 7-11-1802 m Jane Reed Maj SC
Elias: b 1727 d 1799 m Elizabeth Beall Capt MD
Elisha: b 8-17-1763 d 8-9-1839 m Martha Rider PS CT
Enos: b 1742 d 1816 m Mary — Pvt VA
Ephraim: b 5-9-1752 d 3-18-1835 m Susan Wheeler Pvt CT
George: b 10-4-1756 d 1854 m (2)Sallie Gentry Pvt VA ★
Henry: b 1760 d 1830 m Sarah Harris Sol GA
Henry: b 4-12-1761 d 5-8-1845 m Sarah Cook Lt NC
Henry Sr.: b c. 1710 d 1796/7 m Judith Lynch Sol VA
Henry Jr.: b 1752 d p. 1835 m Delilah Allensworth Pvt VA ★
Isaac: b 1736 d 1820 m Elizabeth Brown PS VA
Israel: b 1756 d 1835 m Lydia Reed Pvt CT
James: b 5-10-1757 d 6-26-1837 m Eleanor Davis Pvt PA
Jeremiah: b 12-22-1759 d 7-7-1839 m (1)Lydia Chapman Sgt CT
Job: b 1-4-1762 d 1802 m Dorcas Reed Pvt MA
John: b — d p. 2-21-1818 m Mary (Harding) — Sct PS KY

John: b 1753 d 4-22-1802 m Sarah Peirson Pvt MA
John: b — d 8-18-1812 m Eunice Benson Cpl MA
John Jr.: b — d 8-23-1822 m Lydia — Pvt MA
John: b c. 1750 d 5- -1806 m Lydia — Pvt NJ
John: b 1760 d 1820 m Sarah Katz Pvt NJ ★
John: b 10-12-1749 d 5-22-1813 m Rhoda King Sol PS NY
John: b 12-9-1756 d 7-14-1808 m Sarah Holt Capt NC
John: b — d p. 4-28-1802 m Elizabeth — Pvt NC
John: b 1756 d 1792 m Mary Karr Pvt NC
John Jr.: b 6-2-1733 d a. 6-13-1803 m Isabella Strawbridge Capt PA
John: b 1753 d 10- -1823 m Catharine Snodgrass Pvt PA
John: b 8-14-1767 d 4-3-1850 m Elizabeth Paine PS PA
John: b 11-15-1758 d 4-13-1838 m Magdalena Nier PS PA
John: b 12-1-1763 d 2-28-1816 m Hannah Boyd Pvt PS SC
John Sr.: b c. 1710 d p. 6-4-1788 m Catherine Marr PS Maj VA
John: b 10-1-1753 d 5- -1792 m Jane Davis Lt VA
Joseph: b 4-18-1734 d 7-4-1801 m (1)Jane Gibson (2)Fanny Douglass Maj PS CS NC
Joseph: b — d p. 12-17-1808 m Mary — PS VA
Joshua Sr.: b 3-5-1726 d 2-10-1797 m (1)Sarah Clark (2)Jemima Corbin Pvt MA
Joshua, Jr.: b 1755 d 4-19-1836 m Jemima Fiske Pvt CT ★
Lot: bpt 7-15-1722 d 10-30-1802 m Tamsen Cobb CS MA
Mark: b 5-1-1755 d 9-5-1835 m Sussana Stull Capt PA ★
Mark: b c. 1735 d p. 3-31-1790 m Ann — Sol PA
Mark: b 1730 d p. 4-13-1812 m (1)Mary Hester Hunter (2)Martha Frances Newsom Pvt VA
Martin: b 1720 d 1780 m Lydia Waters Pvt PA
Nathaniel: b 12-19-1746 d 1823 m Thankful Clarke Pvt MA
Nathaniel: b 4- -1756 d 10-6-1834 m Hannah Newcomb Mar Pvt MA
Oliver: b 1753 d 4-8-1838 m Chloe Jones Pvt Matr NY PA ★
Perry: b c. 1748 d p. 12-1-1824 m (1)Elizabeth Bonney (2)Molly Swan Keen Pvt MA
Richard: b 1731 d 8-15-1786 m (1)Anne Brown (2)Abigail Bullock Sgt RI
Samuel Jr.: b 9-25-1766 d 4-16-1850 m Love Mayhew Pvt MA ★
Stephen Sr.: b 3-11-1723 d 10-11-1789 m Amy Gardner Capt CS CT
Stephen Jr.: b 1749 d 1816 m Carrie Jain Pvt PA
Stephen: b 10-21-1754 d 2-4-1807 m Martha Marsh Pvt MA
Thomas: b 5-16-1727 d 7-7-1839 m Mary Richards Sol CT
Thomas: b 1755/6 d 11-20-1845 m Mary Ann McGee Sgt DE ★
Thomas Jr.: b 10-1-1760 d 7-14-1853 m Keziah Bullen Pvt MA
Thomas: b 10- -1737 d 4-24-1798 m Catharine Murphy Sgt NJ
Thomas: b 1751 d 1813 m (1)— Rogers (2)Hannah Stark Pvt PA
Thomas: b 1-8-1758 d 6-20-1840 m Sarah Payne Pvt Spy VA ★
Vachel: b 1762 d 5-11-1837 m (1)Elizabeth Miles (2)Mary Parker Sgt MD ★
Walter: b c. 1752 d c. 5-3-1782 m Mary Elizabeth — Ens MD
Wm.: b 4-25-1741 d 3-4-1810 m Sarah Bledsoe Capt NC
Wm.: b 12-11-1750 d 1797 m Obedience Hutchins Capt NC
Wm.: b c. 1753 d p. 1800 m X Pvt NC
Wm.: b 1747 d 9- -1821 m (1)Winfred Ann Holtzclaw (2)Susannah McGee Pvt VA
Wm.: b 11-8-1743 d 11-28-1785 m Mrs Sarah Perkins Col SC
Wilmoth: b 1720 d p. 12-14-1794 m Henry Harding Sr. PS VA

HARDISON,
Benjamin: b 1753-59 d 1823 m Jane Warren Pvt MA
Benjamin: b 1749 d c. 3-25-1785 m Elizabeth Duggan Sol NC
James: b 1759 d 7-23-1842 m (1)Mary Roberson (2)Mary — Pvt NC ★
John: b a. 1712 d c. 11-20-1778 m Olive — PS NC

HARDWICK, (includes HORTWICK)
Barnet: bpt 12-11-1763 d 12-17-1812 m Dorotha Fisher Pvt Fif NJ W★
Wm.: b c. 1730 d p. 3-23-1802 m Cynthia Parker Sgt SC
Wm. Jr.: b 3-17-1760 d 3-1-1828 m Nancy Shipp Pvt GA
Wm.: b c. 1750 d p. 1811 m Judith Parker Sol VA

HARDY, (includes HARDEE & HARDIE)
Aaron: b 8-30-1742 d 12-26-1775 m Abigail Dutton Sol NH
Abel: b 10-9-1743 d p. 1790 m Sarah Chase Pvt MA
Abner: b 3-13-1735 d 6-22-1777 m Rebecca Hardy Pvt MA
Benjamin: b 1732 d 1790 m Nancy Howell PS NC
David: b 12-12-1750 d 184? m Rebecca Manning Sol MA
Dudley: b 1751 d 2-11-1821 m (1)Sarah Felton (2)Mrs Charity Sanderson Pvt MA
Elijah: b 8-26-1734 d 3-5-1811 m Martha How Pvt MA
Eliphalet Sr.: b 1-27-1719/20 d 3-25-1799 m Hannah Plats PS MA
Eliphalet Jr.: b 3-1-1740 d 7-30-1812 m Mehitable Hardee Capt MA
Ephraim: b 9-16-1745 d 3-16-1793 m Susanna Cheney Sgt MA
George: b 1750 d p. 4-24-1805 m Priscilla Jenkins Pvt MD
Jesse: b 3-16-1757 d 3-5-1846 m Abigail Smith Pvt MA ★
John: b 11-4-1742 d 4-3-1803 m Caroline T. Aldrich NCapt GA
John Sr.: b 11-28-1716 d 4-29-1801 m Abigail Kidder Pvt MA
John: b 1756 d 3-25-1818 m Sarah Sutton Pvt NC
John: b 4-13-1707 d 12-12-1784 m Susannah Tyson PS NC
John: b 1740 d c. 1810-12 m Ann Williams Pvt VA

John: b 1761 d p. 5-18-1839 m Lucinda Sears Pvt VA ★
John Michael Joseph: b 1761 d 6-2-1839 m (2)Lucy Sears Pvt VA
Jonas, Jr.: b 1750 d 5-13-1833 m (1)Molly (Hardy) (2)Mehitable (Hardy) Pvt MA
Joseph: b 2-22-1751 d 5-22-1830 m Margaret Mackenzie Pvt VA
Joshua: b 1753 d 3-22-1812 m Lucy Staples Drm Maj Pvt MA
Moody: b 8-22-1751 d p. 1835 m Hannah Wicom MM Pvt MA ★
Nathaniel: b 8-8-1758-60 d 8-23-1821 m Eleanor Squire Pvt MA CT ★
Nehemiah: b 1751 d 2-4-1837 m (2)Mrs Abigail Hardy Pvt NH
Noah: b 9-17-1758 d 12-21-1835 m Sarah Spofford Pvt NH ★
Paul: b 5-13-1753 d 1794 m Lois Flanders Sgt MA
Peter: b 8-22-1744 d 12-7-1831 m Elizabeth Haskell Pvt MA
Phineas: b 7-11-1726 d 3-7-1813 m Abigail Gage Sol NH
Phineas, Sr.: b c. 1702 d 1776 m Prudence Warren CS MA
Phineas, Jr.: b 6-4-1753 d 4-28-1831 m Sarah Wyman Sgt MA
Robert: b 2-18-1727 d 12-18-1798 m Martha Cogill NCapt PA
Robert: b 9-13-1743 d 1-19-1831 m Abigail Folsom Pvt VT
Samson: b 12-30-1753 d 11-29-1831 m Mary Spalding Pvt MA
Samuel: b 4-26-1744 d p. 1780 m Abigail — Pvt MA
Stephen Jr.: b 10-10-1743 d 11-7-1808 m Hannah Thurston Pvt MA
Theophilus: b 1748 d a. 1812 m Mary Sullivan Vol NH
Thomas: b 6-11-1756 d 7-25-1816 m Lucy Colburn Sgt NH
Thomas: b c. 1730 d 1795 m X Pvt PA
Thomas: b 4-3-1732 d a. 10-24-1814 m Phoebe (Hardy) Pvt VA
Thomas: b c. 1748 d p. 8-10-1811 m Mary — Pvt VA
Thomas: b 2-22-1766 d c. 8-22-1847 m Martha — Pvt VA ★
Wm.: b 2-12-1758 d 11-19-1852 m Mary Hyde Pvt MA
Wm.: b — d m Hannah Parker Pvt MA
Wm.: b — d p. 12-6-1783 m Sarah — CS NC
Wm.: b c. 1720 d 1790/91 m Mary — PS VA

HARE,
Joseph: b 1749 d 9- -1853 m (1)Nannie Clay (2)Phoebe Perdue Sol VA NC
Michael: b 6-10-1727 d 3-3-1843 m Elizabeth — Sol PA ★
Moses: b — d p. 4-12-1793 m Honore — PS NC
Robert: b 1-28-1752 d 3-8-1812 m Margaret Willing Sol PA
Wm.: b 8-28-1736 d 1796 m Sarah Shackelford PS VA

HARFF,
John: b 1733 d 1822 m Mary Hess Pvt PA

HARGIS, (includes HARGETT)
Abraham: b 4-4-1753 d 3-3-1824 m Mary Pentrem 1Lt PA
Abraham: b 1731 d 1811 m Catherine Roe Lt PA
Peter: b c. 1744 d p. 11- -1797 m Ann Isler Sol NC
Shadrach: b 1-4-1740 d 1-25-1816 m Nancy L. — Capt NC
Thomas: b 4-26-1752 d 4-7-1838 m Biddie VanHook Capt NC ★
Wm.: b 7-16-1760 d 3-11-1836 m Elizabeth Jay Ens NC ★
Wm.: b c. 1740 d 9-6-1819 m Miss — Dopson Sol VA

HARGOUS,
Jean I.: b — d — m Marie A. deBrisson NCapt

HARGRAVE, (includes HARGROVE & HARTGRAVE)
George: b c. 1748 d 1802 m X PS MD
Hezekiah: b c. 1762 d 7-24-1838 m Susan McMurtrie Pvt NC
Hezekiah: b 2-21-1748 d 7-16-1833 m Mrs Susannah Murphy Fif VA ★
John: b c. 11-23-1755 d 9- -1834 m Kathryn McNeal Pvt SC ★
Wm.: b 1735 d 6-30-1809 m Mary — PS VA

HARING,
Abraham Jr.: b 4-14-1742 d 2-25-1807 m Sarah Naugle Capt NJ
Cornelius: b 7-14-1744 d 1-9-1824 m Annyte Aryejause Nagle Capt CS NJ
David: b 2-19-1737 d 10-11-1798 m Elizabeth Ferdon Pvt NJ
John: b 9-28-1739 d 4-1-1809 m Mary (Haring) Maj PS NY
John A.: b 4-9-1760 d 9- -1853 m Marie Devereux Pvt NJ

HARKER,
Joseph: b 9-28-1743 d 9- -1815 m Mary Walling Capt NJ

HARKNESS,
James: b 6-15-1759 d 8-18-1836 m Elizabeth Edson Pvt MA
James: b 1722 d 1779 m Nancy Gray Cpl PS CT
John: b 6-15-1760 d 11-14-1843 m Rachel McNall Pvt MA ★
John: b 1760 d 6-4-1821 m Keziah Edson Pvt MA
Nathan: b 9-4-1745 d 9- -1822 m (1)Hannah Buffum (2)Susanna Ballou PS NH
Robert: b c. 1745 d p. 4-12-1791 m — Sol NC
Thomas Jr.: b c. 1748 d 6-3-1819 m Elizabeth Putnam Lt MA
Wm.: b 4-17-1762 d 7-4-1825 m Esther Bridge Pvt MA
Wm.: b 10-1-1739 d 5-4-1822 m Priscilla Lytle Ens PA

HARLAN, (includes HARLAND)
Aaron Sr.: b 1724 d 1798 m Sarah Hollingsworth PS NC SC
Aaron Jr.: b c. 1752 d 8-8-1806 m Elizabeth Stewart PS NC
George: b 1737 d 5-6-1821 m Margery Baker Sol NC
George: b 1756 d 11-26-1813 m Anna Breede Sol SC
George: b c. 1750 d 1815 m Mary Wright Fif VA

HARLAN, contd.

George: b 1761 d 1-24-1837 m Catherine Pope Pvt VA
James: b 1-2-1750 d 8-13-1819 m Elizabeth Swayne Pvt PA
James: b 9-8-1755 d 8-7-1816 m Sarah Caldwell Lt VA
Jesse: b c. 1743 d p. 1810 m Sarah Harlan Pvt PA
John Sr.: b 6-2-1716 d p. 1790 m Martha Ashby PS MD
Jonathan: b 6- -1755 d 6-28-1841 m (1)Mrs Abigail McCall (2)Elizabeth Fawcett Pvt PA ★
Joshua: b 4-17-1726 d 11-9-1804 m Abigail Green Pvt VA
Stephen: b c. 1735 d 8- -1810 m Mrs Deborah Strode Pvt PA
Stephen: b 1750-60 d 1836 m Catherine Wright Pvt PA
Wm.: b 1747 d p. 1785 m Elizabeth Rankin Pvt PA

HARLESS,

Henry: b c. 1747 d p. 3-25-1815 m (1)Charity — (2)Elizabeth — Pvt VA
Philip: b c. 1748 d 1822 m Hannah Boscher Pvt VA
Philip: b 1760 d p. 3-22-1834 m Molly Standley Pvt Spy VA

HARLEY, (includes HARLEE & HARLLEE)

Henry: b 7-4-1754 d 8-18-1840 m Elizabeth Groff Pvt PA
John: b 8-16-1741 d 12-3-1814 m Margaret Rebecca Landis Pvt PA
John: b c. 1750 d — m — Cleland Sol VA
Joseph: b 1720 d 8-17-1807 m (1)Mrs Jane Jackson (2)Elizabeth Jackson Lt SC
Peter: b 1699 d 1783 m Anne Jane Leake PS VA
Thomas: b 1765-7 d 4-6-1827 m (1)Elizabeth Stuart (2)Mrs Anna Bethee PS VA
Thomas: b 2- -1746 d 10- -1814 m Mary Payne Pvt NY CT W★

HARLOW,

Amaziah Sr.: b 12-18-1721 d c. 1782 m Lois Doten Lt MA
Ansel: b 4-25-1743 d 7-28-1832 m (1)Hannah Barnes (2)Thankful Bartlett Pvt MA ★
Benjamin: b 9-12-1723 d 1800 m Abigail Hobbs Pvt MA
Benjamin: b 6-1-1741 d 9-10-1824 m Hannah Horton Pvt NY
Elijah: b 1743 d 8-1-1778 m Patience Drew Pvt MA
Gideon: b 10-28-1743 d 4-19-1811 m Patience Eames Pvt MA
Isaac: b 7-26-1757 d 1-11-1829 m Mehitable Lothrop 1Lt VT NY
James, Sr.: b 4-12-1730 d 9-23-1802 m (1)Mercy Cushman (2)Sarah Bryant Capt MA
James Jr.: b 11-19-1757 d p. 1810 m Phebe Doten Pvt MA
John: b 4-14-1762 d 2-17-1836 m Mrs Eliza Allway Pvt MA
Jonathan: b 1746 d 10-10-1832 m Betsey Blackmar Cpl MA
Josiah: b 1-2-1756 d 8-29-1825 m Olive Hunt Pvt Smn MA
Lazarus: b 8-11-1755 d 6-28-1825 m (1)Sarah Darling (2)Lucy Bradford Pvt MA
Lemuel: b 10-7-1742 d 2-12-1812 m Mary — Pvt MA
Levi: b 1747 d 1-30-1832 m Silence Cobb Pvt MA
Matthew Hobbs: b 4-3-1752 d 10-22-1809 m Lydia — Sgt MA
Stephen: b 2- -1738/9 d 12-27-1797 m Elizabeth Curtis 2Lt NY
Sylvanus: b 6-9-1738 d 8-11-1799 m Desire Sampson Capt MA
Sylvanus: b 1761 d 1854 m Katherine — Pvt MA ★
Zephaniah: b 5-25-1748 d 3-22-1827 m Patience Johnson Pvt MA

HARMCN, (includes HARMAN)

Abner: b 5-15-1756 d 1-30-1839 m (1)Anne Potter (2)Deborah Cary (3)Sarah Waterman Murray Maj MA
Abraham: b 1720 d p. 1778 m Nancy Bateman Pvt PA
Alpheus: b 3-29-1755 d 3-21-1834 m (2)Susannah Smith Pvt NY VT
Amos: b 4-3-1744 d 2- -1824 m Mary Trumbull Pvt VT
Anan: b 10-3-1738 d 5-14-1802 m Sarah Rawson Pvt MA
Andrew Sr.: b c. 1740 d 1777 m — PS PA
Andrew Jr.: b 1764 d 1838 m Irma Catherine Sandles PS PA
Asa: b 12-8-1726 d 8-3-1798 m Miriam King Pvt MA
Benjamin Jr.: b 10-16-1741 d 3-4-1793 m Caroline Austin 1Lt CT
Benjamin: b 5-17-1711 d 12-3-1795 m Hannah Jaques Sgt CT
Benjamin: b 7-28-1744 d 7-18-1806 m Sara Hill 2Lt MA
Christian: b c. 1728 d 1779 m Christina Lenhart Pvt PA
Conrad: b 1748 d 6-9-1823 m Christina Patridge Pvt PA ★
Daniel: b 4-13-1747 d 8-22-1806 m Sarah York Cpl MA
Daniel: b 1-26-1747 d 6-26-1805 m Lucretia Dewey Sgt VT
Daniel: b 1729 d a. 1-25-1820 m Anna Bughsen Sct Pvt VA
David: b 1-27-1741/2 d 9-16-1817 m (1)Jerusha Wilcox (2)Rebecca Sheldon Pvt MA
Edward: b 3-12-1740 d 8- -1797 m (1)Mercy Willard (2)Mary Plaisted Capt MA
Eli: b 10-5-1731 d 5-3-1813 m Anna Southwell 1Lt MA
Elias: b 1-26-1740/1 d 1-27-1793 m Eunice Hanchett Pvt CT
Elias: b 4- -1761 d 5-25-1837 m Olive McKenny Pvt MA
Elijah: b 18-1747 d 11-13-1776 m Mary Brown Pvt CT
Elijah: b 10-31-1751 d 5-9-1830 m Rebecca Clark Cpl MA
Emanuel: b 5-1-1745 d 5-25-1796 m Anna C. Leitner Capt PA
Ezekiel: b 1-24-1750 d 9-9-1816 m Grace Dewey Pvt VT
Ezekiel: b 4-7-1752 d 12-12-1831 m (1)Lydia (Harmon) (2)Ruth Sheldon Sgt VT
Gaius: b 5-7-1754 d 1807 m Mary Parsons Pvt VT
Henry Sr.: b 1726 d p. 2-18-1804 m Nancy Wilburn PS CS NC
Isaac: b 5-9-1751 d 12-11-1839 m (1)Elizabeth Harmon (2)Sylvia Hocum Pvt MA

Israel Sr.: b 10-29-1753 d 12-14-1831 m Elizabeth Kent Pomeroy Pvt CT
Jacob: b c. 1759 d p. 1803 m Elizabeth — Pvt PA
Jacob: b 1755 d 5-12-1823 m Elizabeth Leisenring Pvt PA W★
Jaques: b 9-1-1754 d 6-13-1807 m Ruth Lancton Sgt CT
Jehial: b 10-5-1762 d 3-3-1845 m Elizabeth West Pvt CT ★
Joel: b 2-17-1747 d 3-19-1814 m (1)Chloe Sheldon (2)Ruth Rowe Ens VT
John: b 8-29-1708 d 4-25-1786 m Mary Austin Capt CT
John: bpt 12-11-1743 d 2-2-1813 m Mary Carl Pvt MA
John: b c. 1750 d p. 1810 m Elizabeth — Pvt NC
John: b 3-18-1728 d 1- -1810 m Mary Stanger Sgt PA
John: b 1764 d 10-2-1842 m Nancy Ann Burton Pvt VA ★
Jonathan: b 7- -1744 d 8-7-1828 m Lucretia Bosworth Pvt MA
Jonathan: b 8-6-1743 d c. 1832 m Dorcas (Harmon) — Pvt MA
Joseph: b 1-14-1754 d 4- -1838 m Eleanor King Pvt CT
Josiah: b 11-5-1759 d p. 1838 m Anna Moulton Sgt MA
Mathias: b c. 1736 d a. 3-2-1812 m Elizabeth — Pvt PA
Mathias: b c. 1736 d 1832 m Lydia Scraggs Sol PA
Michael: b p. 7-31-1807 m Margaret Trump Cpl PA
Moses: b 5-25-1757 d 5-22-1841 m Sally Mckinney Pvt MA ★
Naphtali: b 11-18-1722 d p. 1783 m (1)Anne Greenleaf (2)Anna Gray PS MA
Nicholas: b — d 7- -1805 m X Pvt VA
Oliver: b 10-27-1756 d 1-9-1843 m Mary Plumb Sgt VT ★
Peletiah: bpt 10-3-1756 d 6-29-1841 m (1)Olive Fogg (2)Sarah Crockett Pvt MA ★
Philip: b c. 1740 d 1778 m Barbara — PS PA
Rawson: b 2-17-1764 d 6-14-1850 m Lydia Murdock Pvt MA
Reuben, Sr.: b 2-18-1714 d 9-6-1794 m Eunice Parsons PS VT
Samuel: b 5-9-1736 d 5-21-1812 m Abial Sheldon Lt CT
Samuel: bpt 8-28-1743 d p. 1793 m Mary Smith 2Lt MA
Samuel: b 4-5-1740 d 1-31-1830 m (1)Kezia King (2)Deborah Griswold Pvt MA
Seth: b 1-28-1752 d 6-8-1838 m (1)Elizabeth Sheldon (2)Anna Foster Sgt VT ★
Thomas: b 1762 d 1-15-1834 m Lydia Elden Pvt MA
Thomas: b c. 1750 d 1824 m Nancy Walker Sol VA

HARMONSON,

John: b — d p. 4-17-1784 m (1)Lydia Hall (2)Sarah — CS DE

HARMONY,

Nicholas: b 9-13-1758 d 11-4-1830 m Anne Sutton Pvt PA

HARNDEN,

Benjamin: b 12-29-1744 d 10-18-1836 m Hannah Kidder Lt MA
John: b 9-6-1738 d p. 1790 m Ruth Pierce Capt MA
Jonathan: b 5-13-1733 d 7-30-1813 m X PS Sgt NY
Joseph: b 5-2-1736 d 12-24-1775 m Esther Pierce Pvt MA
Joshua: b 10-14-1740 d 9-9-1807 m Sarah Cornell Lt MA

HARNESS, (includes HARNEST)

George: b 1739 d 3-7-1823 m Elizabeth Youcum PS VA
John: b 1725 d 4-28-1810 m Eunice Petty Capt VA
John: b 1759 d 6-11-1835 m Margaret Lair Pvt VA ★
Michael: b 1700 d a. 3- -1785 m Elizabeth Jephobe PS VA

HARNET, (includes HARNED)

Enos: b 10-22-1752 d 1830 m Deborah Comstock Pvt VA
Jonathan: b 5-11-1755 d 1832 m Catharine Arvacost Lt VA PA

HARNEY,

Jonathan: b a. 1745 d 1784 m Isabelle Mills Lt DE
Selby: b c. 1749 d 1799 m Luranah Paderick Col NC

HARNISH,

Christian: b 1764 d 6-23-1846 m Elizabeth Thompson Pvt PA
Jacob: b 1750 d 11-11-1842 m (1)Esther Burkholder (2) Susanna — Pvt PA
John: b 2-15-1754 d 1805 m Anna Eva Burkholder Pvt PA

HARNSBERGER, (includes HARNESBERGER)

Adam: b 10-1751 d 3- -1816 m Cathrine Null Pvt VA
Conrad: b 11-15-1756 d 1814 m Anna Barbara Miller Pvt VA
Robert: b 1761 d 2-7-1840 m Christina Miller Pvt VA
Stephen: b 8-7-1754 d 1819 m Mary Zellars Sol VA

HARP,

Frederick: b 9-17-1756 d 11-21-1835 m (1)Christina — (2)Catherine Eklof Pvt PA ★
Henry: b 1735 d 2-29-1788 m (1)Lydia Wood (2)Eva Klaarwater Sgt NY

HARPAREE,

John: b 1763 d p. 1793 m Jane Rankins Pvt NJ

HARPEL,

Philip, Jr.: b 12-12-1759 d 3-12-1843 m Mary M. Rothrock Pvt PA

HARPENDING,

Andrew Menton: bpt 6-14-1761 d a. 1831 m Sarah Compton Pvt NJ

HARPER,
Abraham: b 1- -1762 d 12-16-1826 m Ann Harper Pvt PA
Adam: b 11-22-1722 d p. 1781 m Catherine Bosler CS PA
Alexander: b 2-22-1744 d 9-10-1798 m Elizabeth Bartholomew
   Capt NY
Ansel: b 1-26-1750 d 11- -1822 m Nancy Parke Pvt GA
Benjamin: b 1758 d 8-22-1798 m Rachel Conrad Pvt PA
Daniel: b 1765 d 8-3-1839 m Mary McAllaster Pvt NH ★
Daniel: b 6-17-1753 d 5-16-1831 m Elizabeth Miller Bosn Gnr PA ★
Francis, Sr.: b c. 1737 d p. 1790 m Elizabeth Bright Lt NC
Francis, Jr.: b — d p. 1790 m Theresa Hopton Pvt NC
George: b 9-11-1763 d 11-27-1839 m Lydia Jane Sexton Pvt GA
Godfrey: b c. 1750 d p. 1777 m Alida Stall Pvt NY
Isaac: b — d a. 4-16-1800 m — PS NC
Jacob: b c. 1743/4 d 1828 m Margaret Simmons PS VA
Jeduthan: b 11-15-1734 d 11- -1819 m Gazeal Parke LCol NC
Jesse: b 1734 d 1811 m Maria Jones Pvt VA
John: b 1769 d 1817 m Ann Thomas Pvt MD
John: b 4-28-1744 d 1819 m (1)Mary Bothwell (2)Martha — Pvt MA
John: b 1762 d 1834 m Anna Wiggs Sol NC
John: b 1745 d 3- -1825 m Elizabeth Proctor Lt NH
John, Jr.: b 5-31-1734 d 11-20-1811 m (1)Miriam Thompson
   (2)Isabelle McKnight Col NY
John, Sr.: b 8-10-1705 d 4-20-1786 m (1)Abigail Montgomery
   (2)Rebeccah — PS NY
John: b 1736 d 9-3-1803 m Phoebe Vernon BgdMaj RegQM PA
John: b 2- -1756 d 9-14-1834 m — Pvt PA
John: b 1-8-1760 d 2-19-1827 m Barbara Backenstoss Pvt PA
John: b c. 1745 d 1840 m Mary Ann — Pvt Sct PS VA
John: b 1758 d p. 1780 m Elizabeth Warren Pvt VA
John: b c. 1740 d 1794 m Frances PS VA
John: b 10-3-1728 d 5-7-1804 m (1)Sarah Wells (2)Mrs Mary
   Reynolds Cunningham PS VA
Joseph Jr.: b 1-14-1727 d 1-11-1783 m Isabel McKnight Pvt CT
Joseph: b 1756 d 6-9-1824 m (1)Patience Allen (2)Hetty West Sgt
   DE MD W★
Nathan: b a. 1760 d 11-10-1843 m Ann Roberts Drm MD
Nathaniel: b c. 1730 d 1794 m — Pvt VA
Nicholas: b 1-25-1706 d 9-15-1803 m Elizabeth Behrn CS VA
Nicholas: b 1738 d 1818 m Elizabeth Peninger Pvt VA
Philip: b — d p. 1810 m — PS VA
Robert: b c. 1760 d 1826 m Lucy Groce Lt GA
Robert: b 8-12-1748 d 7-31-1814 m Sarah McFarland Pvt MA
Samuel: b 1744 d 1834 m Sarah Godfrey Pvt NH
Samuel: b 5-22-1722 d 8-25-1790 m Elizabeth Scribner PS NH
Samuel Sr.: b c. 1730 d p. 1783 m Jane Strang Pvt PA
Samuel: b 1754 d 6-10-1839 m (1)Hannah — (2)Jane McMillan
   Pvt PA
Samuel: b 10-18-1761 d 1812 m (2)Sarah Grimes Pvt PA
Samuel: b 8-23-1757 d 1-27-1837 m Ruth Whipley Chaney Pvt VA
Wm.: b c. 1758 d p. 9-3-1827 m Ann Phelida Hudson Sol CS GA
Wm.: b 1745 d 1828 m Kevan — Pvt MD
Wm.: b 1730 d 1817 m Lady Mortimer PS NY
Wm.: b 1759 d 7-10-1845 m (2)Nancy Ferris Pvt PA
Wm.: b 1-23-1759 d 1850 m Abigail Estabrooks Pvt SC
Wm.: b 1749/50 d p. 1781 m Rebecca Kenton Pvt PA
Wm.: b 1746 d 9-19-1813m Ann Young Sol PS SC
Wm.: b c. 1750 d 1823 m Mary Ingram Pvt VA
Wm.: b 3-14-1761 d 4-18-1829 m Mary Scholl Sol VA

HARPSTER,
Jacob: b 1756 d 1832 m Mary — Sol PA

HARR,
Simon: b 1725 d 3- -1797 m (2)Eve Brouzler (3)Margaret Baer Sol
   VA

HARRELL, (includes HARRALL)
Abraham: b 1747 d 5-1-1810 m Mary Davis Pvt NC
Asa: b 4-21-1762 d c. 1842 m Rachel Beeman Sol NC SC
Benjamin: b c. 1754 d 9-26-1796 m Winnifred Pittman Sol NC
George Edward: b 1744 d 1798 m Barbara Ann — Pvt SC
Housen: b 1731 d 1820 m Frances Delphia Street Pvt VA
Jacob: b 9- -1760 d 2- -1837 m Polly Whiddon Pvt NC
James: b c. 1747 d 1817/18 m — Cotton Pvt VA
Joel: b 1748 d 6-30-1846 m (1)Polly Foster (2)Betsey Shoulders
   (3)Arcadia Smith Pvt NC VA
John: b c. 1746 d 1799 m Unity Fox Pvt NC
John: b 1738 d c. 1827 m Mary Burgess Pvt NC
John: b 1735 d p. 1797 m Sarah — Ens VA
John: b 8-12-1761 d 9-4-1838 m Margaret Montgomery Pvt VA ★
Josiah: b c. 1740 d a. 11- -1783 m — CS NC
Levi: b 1750 d p. 1790 m (1)Mrs — Cole (2)— White Pvt SC
Lewis: b 1741 d 1829 m Sarah Perkins PS NC
Samuel: b a. 1740 d p. 2-13-1811 m (1)Elvey Riddick (2)Sally Bond
   2Maj NC
Wm.: b 1757 d p. 1791 m Priscilla Calvert Houghton Pvt SC

HARRIMAN,
Asa: b 3-5-1736 d 11-29-1823 m Elizabeth Todd Lt MA
Asa: b 5-24-1742 d 7-1-1819 m Joanna Beal Pvt MA
David: b c. 1756 d p. 9-10-1845 m — Pvt MD ★
Ebenezer: b 2-22-1734 d 12-25-1826 m Elizabeth — Ens NH

Enoch: b 10-5-1736 d 9-16-1823 m Martha Palmer CS MA
Ezekiel: b 12-23-1757 d 4-26-1809 m Mary Craige Cpl MA
Jasiel: b 3-11-1726/7 d 8-17-1802 m Mary Davis PS NH
Joab: b 7- -1760 d 5- -1834 m Hannah Beede Pvt MA ★
Jonathan: b 1753 d 6-16-1839 m X Pvt MA ★
Joseph: b 4-18-1726 d 1820 m Abigail Dow Pvt MA
Joshua: b 5-20-1768 d 3-2-1823 m Betsey Keys Pvt MA
Leonard: b 3-12-1739 d 8- -1813 m Rosemond — PS MA
Leonard: b 8-11-1718 d 1800 m Ann Stevens Sol PS NH
Moses: b 4-10-1737 d 8-24-1784 m Jane Hale Lt MA
Moses: bpt 9-22-1734 d 1776 m Eunice Emerson Pvt MA
Nathaniel: b 6-14-1744 d 1830 m Elizabeth Leighton PS NH
Peter: b 4- -1727 d 10-6-1815 m Lydia Jackman Pvt NH
Samuel: b 1-18-1752 d 8-21-1824 m Susanna — Capt NJ
Simon: 10-11-1761 d 7-29-1837 m Elizabeth Gilman Pvt MA ★
Stephen Sr.: b 3-9-1728 d 2-1-1804 m Sarah Mascraft CS PS NH
Stephen, Jr.: b 3-10-1757 d 2-25-1828 m (1)Lucy Story (2)Bridget
   Abbot Ames Pvt NH
Thomas: b 1-19-1744 d p. 1812 m Martha Pool PS NH

HARRINGTON,
Abraham: b 1750 d 2-14-1811 m Anna Russell Cpl MA
Abraham: b 12-11-1756 d 9-9-1824 m Phoebe Allen Pvt RI MA
Abraham: b 9-4-1758 d 10-28-1847 m Electa Galusha Pvt RI
Anthony: b 1762 d 1836 m — Pvt MD ★
Antipas: b 9-30-1753 d 1-27-1803 m Levina Brigham Pvt VT
Daniel: b — m Dorcas Cutler Pvt CT
Daniel: b 9-3-1761 d 2-2-1823 m Relief Smith Pvt MA
Daniel: b 5-3-1707 d 8-31-1795 m Mary — Sol PS MA
Daniel: b 5-25-1739 d 9-27-1818 m Anna Munroe Pvt MA
David: b c. 1745 d 6-12-1811 m Waity Tripp Capt RI
Drury: b-6-22-1752 d 12-22-1839 m Rachel Petty Lt NC SC ★
Ebenezer: b 9-9-1749 d 11-2-1803 m Lucretia Hill Lt CS MA W★
Ebenezer: b 3-16-1743 d 4-2-1824 m Martha Witt Pvt MA W★
Ebenezer: b 1720/1 d 1796 m (1)Rebecca Spencer (2) Mary or Ann
   Morley CS RI
Edward: b 6-17-1702 d 12-6-1792 m Anna Bullard Sol MA
Edward Jr.: b 5-22-1735 d 9-23-1776 m Anne Lawrence Capt MA
Elijah: b 1-27-1745 d 3-8-1818 m Mary Warren Pvt MA
Ephraim: b 4-16-1742 d 7-3-1793 m Sarah Bartlett Pvt MA
Ephraim: b c. 1750 d 7-6-1821 m Sarah Harrindeen Cpl RI W★
Henry, Sr.: b 1-8-1712 d 12-25-1791 m (1)Sarah Laughton (2)Mrs
   Abigail (Marble) Blodgett PS MA
Henry Jr.: b 8-27-1737 d 7-6-1801 m Ruth Blodgett Pvt PS MA
Henry: b 9-27-1738 d 2-3-1824 m Freelove (Harrington) PS RI
Henry William: b 5-12-1747 d 3-31-1809 m Rosanna Auld BGen
   NC
Hezekiah: b 1750 d p. 1832 m Bathsheba Ballard Pvt RI
Isaac: b c. 1735 d 7-8-1805 m Hannah Whipple Capt PS MA
Isaac, Jr.: b 7-11-1754 d p. 1809 m Mrs Mary Parmenter Mil MA
Israel: b 6-12-1754 d 4-6-1812 m Rhoda Mann Sgt RI W★
Israel: b 3-7-1739/40 d 8-10-1825 m Hetabel Shippee Pvt VT
James: b 3-1760 d 12-11-1839 m (1)Margaret Braley (2)Hannah
   Freeman Pvt RI W★
Jeremiah: b 4-19-1742 d 12-11-1818 m Sarah Locke MM MA
John: b 11-25-1743 d 3-13-1824 m Mary — Pvt MA
John: b 3-1-1739 d p. 1783 m Mary Wootten Pvt MA
John: b 1764 d 3- -1847 m Asenath Marvin Pvt MA ★
John: b 9-2-1752 d 10-6-1802 m Deborah Wakefield Sol NH
John: b 1757 d 12- -1818 m Mary Kurtz Pvt PA
John: b 1-1-1759 d 5-18-1862 m Hannah Marshall Pvt PA
John: b c. 1750 d 1792 m Frances Burt PS SC
Jonathan: b 1-12-1741/2 d 1791 (?) m (1)Grace Hagar (2)Catherine
   Wyman Lt MA
Jonathan, Sr.: b 5-21-1723 d 9-14-1809 m (1)Abigail Dunster
   (2)Lydia Stone Milliken Pvt PS CS MA
Jonathan, Jr.: b 7-8-1758 d 3-25-1854 m Sarah Banks MM MA
Jonathan: b 5-17-1759 d 4-6-1842 m (1)Sarah Pratt (2)Susanna
   Penniman Pvt MA
Jonathan: b 3-21-1722 d 4-19-1755 m (2)Ruth Fisk Pvt MA
Jonathan: b c. 1717 d 1785 m Sarah Foster Sol RI
Joshua, Sr.: b 6-12-1709 d 1791 m (1)Elizabeth Truesdale (2)Mary
   Truesdale Pvt MA
Joshua, Jr.: b 1751 d 10- -1817 m Sarah Bigelow Cpl MA W★
Joshua: b 9-13-1755 d 9-20-1834 m Elizabeth Brigham Sgt NH
Loammi: b 9-10-1760 d 9-14-1826 m Sarah Nutting Pvt MA
Moses: b 10-22-1733 d 9-8-1784 m Mary Pierce Capt MA
Nathan: b 10-7-1729 d 2-21-1817 m Elizabeth Flagg Capt MA
Nathaniel: b 1742 d 2-28-1831 m Ruth Stone Lt MA
Nathaniel: b 1-31-1757 d 9- -1836 m Abigail Ailsworth Pvt RI
Peter: b 5-14-1752 d 7-29-1813 m Anne Hammond Pvt MA
Philemon: b a. 1757 d 1803 m Frances — PS NC
Richard: b 4-22-1756 d 6-8-1831 m Roba Perkins Pvt VT
Robert: b 4-26-1719 d 5-30-1793 m Abigail Mason PS CS MA
Sampson: b 1758 d 1853 m Mary Ballou Pvt VT
Silas: bpt 5-21-1752 d 6-15-1831 m Mindwell Willington Pvt MA
Simeon: b 4-22-1743 d 12-31-1811 m Zilpha Bennett Capt RI
Sion: b 1752 d 1828 m Elizabeth Watts Sol NC
Thaddeus: b 9-9-1735 d p. 1790 m Thankful Dodge Sol MA
Thaddeus: b c. 1740 d p. 1790 m Lydia Porter Pvt MA
Theophilus: b 3-27-1762 d 11-11-1813 m Elizabeth Buck Pvt VT RI
Thomas: b 5-12-1748 d c. 1790 m Lucy Perry Pvt MA
Uriah: b 4-11-1760 d 9-11-1839 m Patty Adams Pvt MA ★

HARRINGTON, contd.
Wm.: b 7-5-1767 d 5-13-1829 m Elizabeth Hawley Pvt CT W★
Wm.: b 1-9-1746 d *p.* 9-23-1792 m Esther Bemis Cpl MA
Wm.: b 10-16-1738 d *a.* 1800 m Bethia Peters Pvt MA
Wm.: b *c.* 1744 d 3-14-1820 m Comfort Combs Pvt MA ★
Wm.: b 5-23-1764 d 11-2-1830 m Susan Keith Pvt VT

HARRIOT, (includes HARRIOTT)
George: b 3-13-1720 d 3-24-1802 m Mary — Capt NJ
Israel: b 1748 d 6-22-1836 m (1)Catherine Wool (2)Ann — OrdlSgt NY ★
Samuel: b 6-17-1756 d 5-30-1838 m Abigail Carman Pvt MM NJ

HARRIS,
Abiel: b 12-20-1754 d 1793 m Susanna Snell Capt MA
Absalom: b 5-27-1755 d 11-19-1824 m (1)Elizabeth Tarver (2)Clara Jeter 2Lt VA
Ann Epps: b *c.* 1720 d 1787 m Benjamin Harris PS VA
Arthur: b 6- -1732 d 1800 m Elizabeth Green Lt MD
Arthur: b 10-18-1752 d 3-18-1814 m Celia Mitchell Pvt MA
Asa: b 5-21-1737 d *p.* 1799 m Faith McCall Sgt MA
Asa: b 1-26-1763 d 3-17-1835 m Rachel Farr Pvt NY W★
Asa: b 5-11-1764 d *p.* 1836 m Lucy — Pvt VT
Barton: b *c.* 1760 d *a.* 8-30-1825 m (1)Mary Griffith (2)Elizabeth Dugan (3)Elizabeth Joy PS MD
Benjamin: b 1744 d 1826 m Rebecca Hickman PS MD
Benjamin: b 9-30-1731 d 1-13-1803 m Sarah Snow Lt MA
Benjamin: b 1-29-1761 d 1-1-1840 m Betheny Odam Sgt NC ★
Benjamin: b *a.* 1755 d *p.* 5-14-1816 m — Pvt NC
Benjamin: b 1-1-1740 d 5-23-1802 m Sophia Williams Pvt SC
Benjamin: b 1-30-1754 d 3-25-1834 m Mary Woods Capt VA ★
Benjamin: b 12-22-1742 d 9-26-1820 m Jane Crampton Sol VA
Benjamin: b 11-28-1764 d *a.* 1797 m (1)Frances Jones (2)Nancy Burgin Sol VA
Benjamin: b 1762 d 5-21-1834 m Ruth Byers Pvt VA
Buckner: b 1761 d 1821 m Nancy Matilda Early Pvt GA
Caleb: b 8-9-1740 d 1-17-1812 m Margaret Westcott CS RI
Champlin: b *c.* 1745 d *p.* 1783 m — Pvt CT
Charles: b 6-3-1760 d 7-1-1832 m Meletiah Hawes Pvt MA ★
Charles: b 1739 d 1811 m Sarah Allen Pvt NC
Charles: b 11-23-1762 d 9-21-1825 m (1)Sarah Harris (2)Lydia Bevard Houston Pvt Dr NC
Christopher: b 1732 d *p.* 1780 m Elizabeth Fairbrother Pvt RI
Christopher, Sr.: b 2-5-1725 d 2/3- -1794 m (1)Mary Dabney (2)Agnes McChord PS VA
Claiborn: b *c.* 1740 d *a.* 1800 m Judith — Pvt NC
Daniel: b 5-25-1726 d 9-7-1819 m Prudence Rodgers Pvt CT
Daniel Sr.: b 6- -1743 d 1790 m Dorothy Rude Pvt CT
Daniel: b 7-24-1759 d 4-14-1842 m Lucy Fox Pvt CT ★
Daniel: b 7-26-1752 d 12-16-1820 m Judith Goodale Sgt CS MA
Daniel: b 1758 d 10-22-1838 m Abigail Reed Sgt MA ★
Daniel: b 1758 d 5-26-1846 m Mary Vickers Worthington Pvt NJ
Daniel: b *c.* 1750 d 1827 m Sarah — Pvt PA
David: b *c.* 1750 d *p.* 1787 m Rachel St. John Lt CT
David: b 1743 d 12- -1807 m Mary — Capt GA
David: b 4-14-1752 d 5-10-1830 m Rebecca Woods CS PS Pvt NH
David: b 3-7-1764 d 3/4- -1835 m Sarah Hutchison PS NY
Ebenezer: b 11-21-1738 d 3-13-1823 m Abigail Burnham 2Lt CT
Edward, Sr.: b 9-20-1739 d 4-6-1825 m (1)Lydia Currier (2)Abigail Atkins PS MA
Edward: b *c.* 1750 d 1795 m Jerusha Davis Drm Maj VA
Elijah: b *c.* 1735 d 1822 m (1)Hannah — (2)Mary — Pvt PA
Elisha: b 1759 d 10- -1811 m Elizabeth — Sol VA
Ephraim: b 6-14-1732 d 11-2-1794 m (1)Jane Person (2)Regine Anderson PS CS NJ
Erastus: b 4-8-1731 d 12-25-1806 m Rebeckah Adams Sgt MA
Ezekiel, Jr.: b 9-20-1756 d 6-26-1837 m (1)Mary Bassett (2)Elizabeth Hamilton Pvt NY
Ezekiel: b *c.* 1760 d *c.* 1831 m Mary Davis Pvt GA
Francis: b 10-3-1721 d 1792 m Susanna Benjamin PS MA
Francis Eppes: b 1748 d 1828 m Ann — Ens VA
Frederick: b *c.* 1740 d 6- -1801 m Eliza Terrell PS 1Lt VA
Garrett: b 9-18-1748 d 6-11-1822 m Elizabeth — Sgt NJ
George: b 11-23-1741 d 2-3-1822 m Hannah Tunis Sgt NJ
George: b *a.* 1757 d *c.* 1800 m Frances — Pvt VA
George: b 1753 d 1820 m Keziah Earl Pvt NC
George: b *c.* 1756 d 10-10-1811 m Elizabeth Coxen Pvt PA
Giles: b 11-1-1724 d 4-26-1797 m Mary March Pvt MA
Graves: b *a.* 1761 d *p.* 12-5-1820 m Elizabeth Baldwin Pvt PS VA
Hannah Stewart: b 1741 d 8-13-1805 m John Harris PS PA
Harrison: b *c.* 1725 d *a.* 1795 m Martha — PS VA
Henry: b *c.* 1731 d *p.* 1782 m (2)Abigail — Pvt NY
Henry: b 6-16-1742 d 3-1-1833 m Annie Byrd Pvt VA
Hugh: b 1-7-1755 d 8-11-1825 m Martha Robison Cpl NC
Isaac: b 1741 d 4-24-1808 m (1)Margaret Pierson (2)Sarah Moore Dr NJ
Isham, Sr.: b *c.* 1730 d *p.* 7-3-1815 m Martha — Capt NC
Israel: b 2-27-1747 d 11-28-1834 m Sarah Morse Capt VT MA
Jacob: b 1751 d 2-13-1798 m Rachel Bacon Dr NJ
James: b 12-12-1743 d *p.* 1790 m Mary Drm MD
James, Jr.: b 1760 d 1838 m Henrietta Guy Pvt MD

James: b *c.* 1750 d *p.* 12-3-1810 m Hannah Stapleton Pvt NC
James: b *c.* 1758 d 1817 m Mary Smilley Sol NC
James: b — d 1793 m Nancy Blake Sol NC
James: b 2-26-1756 d 12-2-1826 m Ann Dunlop Pvt PA
James: b 4-27-1754 d 6-13-1843 m Martha Parks Sgt RI ★
James: b 4-6-1763 d 9-23-1804 m Priscilla Gilliam Pvt SC
James: b 1740 d 1796 m Ann McKinney Capt VA
James: b 1745 d 1805 m Ursula Flournoy Capt VA
James: b *c.* 1755 d 1795 m Mary — Sol VA
James: b 1722 d 1792 m Mary — CS VA
Jesse: b *c.* 1755 d *p.* 1810 m Frances Ward Capt NC
Jesse 2nd: b 1760 d 1872 m Cynthia — Pvt NC
Jessie: b — d — m Charity Napp Capt NC
John: b 6-8-1743 d 10-1-1820 m (1)Hannah Rogers (2)Louisa Leech Pvt CT
John: b 4-22-1765 d 12-1-1853 m Susana Smith Pvt CT ★
John: b *c.* 1760 d 1817 m Bethany Lowe Sol GA
John: b *c.* 1736 d *a.* 11-13-1793 m — Pvt MD
John: b 10-7-1730 d 3-8-1812 m Sarah — Pvt MA
John: b 9-13-1733 d 11-26-1814 m Ruth Parlin Pvt MA
John 3d: b 10-19-1746 d 3-8-1812 m Mary Lord Pvt MA
John: b 7-4-1749 d 8-4-1826 m Eleanor Girdler Pvt MA
John: b 7-1-1750 d 1816 m (1)Sarah Burris (2)Mary Hamilton (3)Mary Hampson Pvt NJ
John: b 2-14-1753 d 1-19-1830 m Elizabeth Bacon Pvt NJ
John: b 4- -1744 d 11-27-1814 m Mary Gamble Pvt NY
John: b *c.* 1755 d 1811 m Jane Moore Capt NC W★
John: b 1763 d 9-24-1824 m Martha Hunter Pvt NC
John: b 1754 d 12-25-1838 m Mary Bowen Capt PA
John: b 9-10-1753 d 3-29-1814 m Lydia Smith Bbd PA
John: b 2-1-1724 d 2-28-1794 m (1)Jane Poer (2) Jane Harris SubLt PS PA
John 2d: b 8-22-1727 d 7-30-1791 m (1)Elizabeth McClure (2)Mary Reed PS PA
John: b 1754 d 12-30-1808 m Mary Goodwin Lt VA
John: b 12-6-1762 d 4-24-1845 m Mary Pickens Pvt SC VA ★
John, Sr.: b 1732 d 11- -1800 m Anne Obedience Turpin PS VA
John, Jr.: b 10-13-1758 d 12-4-1815 m Rebecca Brittain Lt VA
John: b 1738 d 6- -1821 m (1)Mary Walker (2)Mrs Milly Price Pvt VA
John: b 3-14-1760 d 6-14-1810 m Margaret Maupin Pvt VA
Jonathan: b 11-17-1757 d 11-4-1822 m Ann Tappan Pvt MA ★
Jonathan: b 5-13-1760 d 1-24-1830 m Huldah Town Pvt MA
Jonathan: b 6-6-1739 d 8-14-1820 m Lodema Tozer Pvt NY
Jonathan: b 1751 d 6-28-1834 m Margaret — Pvt NC ★
Jordan: b 5-20-1763 d 10-7-1826 m (1)Elizabeth Mosby Cannon (2)Ann Jude Lt VA
Joseph: b 4-3-1752 d 2-25-1823 m Hepsibah Bunker Ens RI
Joseph: b *c.* 1735 d 1784 m Sarah — Pvt RI
Joseph: b 1750 d 1831 m Elizabeth Sly Lt NY
Joseph: b 1737 d 9-17-1792 m Mary Clough Pvt NY
Joseph: b 10-1749 d 6-10-1839 m (2)Elizabeth Cribb Pvt NC
Joshua: b 1754 d 8-10-1835 m Miriam Johnson Pvt NH
Joshua, Sr.: b 9-3-1729 d *p.* 1787 m Ruth Simmons Pvt NY
Joshua, Jr.: b 4-9-1761 d 1809 m Hannah Bragg Pvt NY ★
Joshua: b 1759 d 11-6-1841 m Martha Harrell Pvt VA ★
Josiah: b 2-13-1749 d 4-4-1813 m Mehitabel Belcher Pvt MA
Justus: b 1-22-1746 d 10-5-1817 m Jemima Miller Sgt NY
Lawrence Jackson: b 1-9-1713 d 11-10-1784 m — Beassell Capt MA
Lee: b 1725 d 4-16-1792 m Winnie Phillips Capt VA
Luther: b 1-29-1756 d 9-5-1842 m Mary Bennitt PS RI
Matthew: b 1755 d 5-12-1845 m Hannah Ross Pvt GA ★
Matthew: b 1-12-1735 d 12-9-1819 m Sutia Stewart PS PA
Matthew: b 9-9-1737 d 5-19-1805 m Elizabeth Tate PS VA
Micajah: b *c.* 1760 d 1819 m Sarah Shepherd Lt SC
Michael: b 6-12-1748 d 1-28-1816 m Mary Dana Pvt MA
Moses, Sr.: b 5-20-1717 d *p.* 1807 m Dorothy West Pvt PS NY
Moses, Jr.: b 11-8-1746 d 11-13-1836 m (1)Grace (Stevens) (2)Isabella — MM OrdlSgt Spy CS CT ★
Nathan: b 1716 d *p.* 4-30-1793 m Catherine Walton PS VA
Nathaniel: b 4-2-1742 d 3-12-1812 m Mary Tozer Capt CT
Nathaniel: b 4-4-1752 d 6-21-1831 m Abigail Harris Pvt MA
Nathaniel: b 8-26-1759 d *p.* 3-24-1849 m Mary Howard Pvt VA ★
Nathaniel: b *c.* 1762/3 d 4-25-1854 m Martha Byars Pvt VA
Nelson: b *c.* 1760 d *p.* 1806 m (1)Sarah — (2)Lavia (Harris) Sol VA
Nelson: b 2-22-1758 d 1837 m Mary Pryor Pvt VA
Nicholas: b 10-19-1724 d *p.* 1790 m (1)Sarah Adams (2)Lydia (Covell ?) Pvt PS MA
Nicholas: b 8-26-1749 d 4-22-1819 m Phebe Tibbetts Pvt NY
Noah: b 4-26-1755 d 3-26-1821 m Sarah Carroll Pvt NJ
Oliver: b 1759 d 12-20-1841 m (1)Lydia Jencks (2)Mary Ann Gray Pvt RI W★
Overton: b 1730 d 1789 m Ann Nelson PS VA
Pearly: b 5-8-1760 d 4-11-1828 m Aby Snow Pvt CT
Peter: b 9-9-1740 d 2-27-1786 m Sarah Merriel MM MA
Peter: b *c.* 1750 d *p.* 1835 m (1) — Reynolds Ens NY
Reuben: b 1741 d 12-27-1829 m Lucy — Pvt CT
Reuben: b 1760 d 5-6-1842 m (1)Margaret McAlexander (2)Elizabeth Gray Pvt VA
Richard: b 4-14-1740 d 1794 m Hannah — Pvt DE
Richard: b 1719 d *p.* 1780 m Margaret Giles Sol MD
Richard: b 11-13-1705 d 12-20-1776 m Martha **Foster** PS MA

Richard: b 1730 d 1790 m Jemima Young PS NC
Richard: b 11-20-1758 d 1-23-1853 m Judith Simms QM VA ★
Richmond: b 5-23-1762 d 10-4-1853 m (2)Polly Hogan Pvt NC ★
Robert: b 12-12-1766 d 7-22-1826 m Lucretia Kennedy Pvt CT W★
Robert: bpt 9-18-1743 d 12-12-1794 m Sarah Bennet Lt MA
Robert: b 1737 d 3-22-1803 m (1)Mary Wilson (2)Mrs. Davidson Col NC
Robert, Jr.: b 10-4-1733 d 2- -1794 m Margaret Harper Pvt NC
Robert: b c. 1755 d 6-9-1806 m Lucy Stubblefield Pvt NC W★
Robert: b 1756-8 d 9-28-1841 m Jane McCaule Sol NC
Robert: b 1714 d 1798 m (1)Fanny Cunningham (2)Mrs Ann Harris CS NC
Robert, Sr.: b 10-26-1702 d 12-26-1788 m (1)Ann Rodgers (2)Margaret McElmond CS NC
Robert: b 3-8-1741 d 11- -1809 m Lucretia Brown Capt VA
Robert: b 8-24-1749 d 11-18-1833 m Nancy Grubbs Sol KY
Robert: b 5-7-1747 d 1-3-1841 m Lucy Fulham Cpl MA
Robert: b a. 1755 d 1816 m (1) — Jackson (2)Mary Bailey Pvt VA
Roland, Sr.: b c. 1730 d 3- -1797 m (1)Rebecca — (2)Elizabeth — Pvt PA
Roland, Jr.: b 2-28-1762 d 1828 m Mary Ramsay Pvt PA
Sampson: b 4-11-1763 d p. 1798 m Susanne Terrel Willis Lt GA
Samuel: b 1754 d 1829 m (1)Julia Peterson (2)Nancy Evans Pvt MD
Samuel: b 5-7-1747 d 1-3-1841 m Lucy Fulham Cpl MA
Samuel: b 9-14-1725 d 8-28-1798 m Margaret Robbins CS MA
Samuel: b 12-4-1731 d 5-25-1789 m Sarah Moore Pvt MA
Samuel: b 2-16-1751 d 1820 m Hannah Barbara Hoffnagle Ens NY
Samuel: b c. 1742 d 1794 m Fanny — Pvt NC
Samuel: b — d p. 7-30-1800 m Anne Fuller Pvt NC
Samuel, Sr.: b 1715 d p. 3-10-1789 m Martha Laird Sol NC
Samuel, Jr.: b 1742 d 5-30-1825 m Margaret (Harris) CS NC
Samuel: b 1735 d 10-5-1796 m (1)Rebecca Morrison (2)Mary Wilson PS NC
Samuel: b 5-4-1740 d 8-19-1825 m Elizabeth Bonner Capt PA
Samuel: b 1762 d 2-20-1852 m Elizabeth Witt Pvt VA ★
Samuel: b 1-19-1724 d 1799 m Lucy — PS VA
Seth: b 1726 d 7-10-1797 m (1)Abigah Alden (2)Mary Phillips Cpl MA
Sherwood, Sr.: b 1733 d 10- -1805 m (1)Elizabeth Tillman (2)Elizabeth Williams CS NC
Sherwood, Jr.: b 1760 d p. 1820 m Henrietta Searcy Sgt NC
Simeon: b 1761 d 2-21-1847 m (1)Christina Westfall (2)Hannah Smith Pvt VA ★
Simon: b 1766 d 5-11-1831 m Rebeckah Davis Sol VA
Squire: b 4-28-1762 d 7-4-1825 m Mary Davis Pvt NY ★
Stephen: b 7-25-1742 d 10-19-1798 m Sarah Sherrard 2Lt MA
Stephen: b 1-29-1732/3 d — m Sarah Brown Pvt MA
Stephen: b 1725 d 1819 m Mary Angier Sol NH
Sylvanus: b 1744 d 2-26-1827 m Mary Harris Pvt MA
Thomas: b 8-16-1759 d 5-9-1802 m Elizabeth Minor Sgt CT
Thomas: b 1-5-1724 d 2-24-1778 m (2)Sarah Dyar PS CT
Thomas: b 8-1-1741 d 1815 m Ann Gwinn LCol MD
Thomas: b 9-9-1759 d 3-3-1825 m Elizabeth Lawrence Pvt NJ
Thomas: b 1-5-1743 d 1822 m Phoebe Harrison Pvt NJ
Thomas: b 11- -1710 d 4-27-1783 m (1)Sarah Dayton (2)Mrs Susanna Westcott PS NJ
Thomas: b 1736 d 1791 m Mary Patterson Maj NC
Thomas: b 1760 d 1800 m Martha Garrett Pvt NC SC
Thomas: b 5-10-1726 d 4-10-1795 m Elizabeth Charlton PS NC
Thomas: b c. 1760 d 2-6-1825 m Sarah — 2Lt VA
Thomas: b 11-1-1755 d 1830 m (2)Martha Carter Pvt VA
Tucker: b 9-6-1747 d 7-6-1821 m Christiana Boston Dr SC
Tyree, Sr.: b 4-8-1728 d a. 1- -1787 m (1)Elizabeth Chapman (2)Mary Ann Simpson PS NC
Walter: b 6-8-1761 d 12-25-1843 m (1)Jemima Fisher (2)Elizabeth Cleavland (3)Jane Aiken Fif CT ★
Walton: b 2-6-1739 d p. 5-29-1809 m Rebecca Lanier Pvt GA
Walton, Sr.: b 3-2-1739 d 5-23-1815 m Sarah Butler Sol GA
West, Sr.: b 8-13-1715 d 5-14-1795 m Mary Turner PS NC
West, Jr.: b 1757 d 7-19-1826 m Edith Ledbetter Lt NC
Wm.: b 5-23-1734 d p. 3-12-1784 m Ann — Pvt MD
Wm.: b c. 1735 d 1788 m Temperance — Pvt MD
Wm.: b 11-7-1731 d 4-10-1824 m Mary Bradbury Capt MA
Wm.: b 1724 d 11-22-1826 m Elizabeth Herring Sgt MA
Wm.: b 7-2-1744 d 10-30-1778 m Rebeckah Mason Capt MA
Wm.: b 1747 d 10-10-1800 m Elizabeth Longford Pvt MA
Wm.: bpt 1-12-1756 d 12-28-1838 m Elizabeth Smethurst Pvt MA ★
Wm.: b 11-3-1746 d 12-3-1797 m Sarah Runyon Pvt NJ
Wm.: b 1763 d 4-15-1833 m Sarah Rich Pvt NJ
Wm.: b 1726 d p. 6-19-1782 m (2)Hannah — CS NJ
Wm.: b c. 1755-7 d 9-24-1840 m Rachel Rundle Pvt NY ★
Wm.: b 1752 d 8-30-1828 m Cynthia Stewart Sol NY
Wm.: b 1760 d p. 1802 m Margaret Sloane Capt NC
Wm.: b 1-1-1755 d 2-15-1828 m (1)Elizabeth Corzine (2)Ann Headley Sol NC
Wm.: b 10-7-1757 d 9-4-1812 m Mary Campbell Capt PA
Wm.: d 1737/8 d p. 12-13-1813 m (1)Mary Hudson (2)Elizabeth — Capt VA
Wm.: b 1750 d p. 10-24-1834 m (1)Bersheba Barbee (2)Jemima Withers Pvt VA
Wm.: b 6-14-1757 d 1-23-1806 m Doshea Thorpe Ens VA
Wm.: b 1763 d 1850 m (1)Anna Oldham (2)Mary Dunbar Pvt VA
Wm.: b 8-25-1755 d p. 1833 m Lou Rita Harris Pvt VA ★
Wm.: b 12-18-1762 d 10-18-1825 m Keziah Sneed Pvt VA W★

Wm.: b 10-2-1755 d 1840 m Martha Smith Pvt VA
Wm.: b c. 1713/14 d 1788 m Mary Netherland PS VA
Wm. Overton: b 1-13-1753 d 1-26-1802 m Diana Chisman Goodwin Pvt VA W★
Wooten: b 3- -1759 d 2-11-1840 m Francis Adams Pvt VA

HARRISON,
Aaron: b 5-3-1726 d 9-5-1819 m Jerusha Warner PS CT
Abijah: b 2-14-1751 d 2-26-1846 m Sarah Ogden Pvt NJ
Almond: b 6-2-1761 d 4- -1826 m Jerusha Bacon Pvt MA
Amos: b 1-12-1712 d 3-3-1785 m Hannah Johnson Lt NJ
Andrew, Sr.: b c. 1735 d c. 1798 m Jane Dillard Sol PS NC
Benjamin: b c. 1739/40 d 11-19-1809 m Esther Hunt Sol MD
Benjamin: b 10-25-1755 d 8-14-1811 m (1)Celia Lawhorn (2)Charity Williams Capt NC W★
Benjamin: b 1741 d 1819 m Mary McClure Col VA
Benjamin, Sr.: b 1726 d 4-24-1791 m Elizabeth Bassett PS SDI VA
Benjamin, Jr.: b 1755 d p. 11-15-1787 m (1)Ann Mercer (2)Susan Randolph Col CS VA
Benjamin: b c. 1745 d 1808 m (2)Mary Newell Capt VA
Benjamin: b 2-15-1743 d 8-7-1807 m Evelyn Taylor Byrd PS VA
Benjamin, Sr.: b c. 1720 d 1789/90 m — PS VA
Benjamin, Jr.: b 1742 d 1799 m — PS VA
Burr: b 6-16-1734 d p. 2-5-1790 m Mary Anne Barnes Col VA
Burr: b 9-20-1738 d 8-18-1822 m Elizabeth Dargan 1Lt VA
Butler: b 2-16-1757 d 4-10-1832 m Mercy Linsley Smn CT
Carter Henry: b 1732 d 1796 m Susanna Randolph PS VA
Charles: b 9-30-1742 d 1796 m Mary Herbert Claiborne BGen VA
Christopher: b c. 1750 d a. 6-2-1796 m Mary Shelton Sol VA
Cuthbert: b c. 1718 d 1783 m Frances Osborne Barnes PS Capt VA
Cuthbert: b c. 1758 d 7- -1815 m Elizabeth — Capt VA
Daniel: b 7-5-1753 d 1829 m (1) — Munn (2)Mary Parrott Cpl NJ
Daniel: b 9-2-1760 d 3-16-1823 m Ann Patton Pvt VA
David: b 4-5-1756 d 1820 m (1)Hepzibah Roberts (2)Lydia Hotchkiss Pvt CT
Edward: b 6-19-1753 d 1-28-1833 m Sarah Dudley Pvt CT
Edward: b c. 1760 d 7- -1833 m (1)Matilda — (2)Fannie Michem (3)Susan Gideon Pvt GA
Elihu: b 2-23-1740 d 5-3-1806 m Theda Woodruff Sgt CT
Ezekiel: b 10-6-1752 d 4-17-1836 m Sarah Bryan Pvt VA
Gabriel: b c. 1747 d c. 1790 m Martha Kenan Pvt VA
George: b 1756 d 1849 m Dorcas Wood Pvt NC
Gideon: b 1762 d 9-8-1838 m — Pvt VA ★
Gideon: b 1760 d 1797 m Mary Brian PS VA
Isaac: b 6-20-1757 d 3-8-1823 m Mary Kingsland Pvt NJ ★
Isaac: b c. 1739 d 1786 m Martha Smith Pvt NJ
Isaac: b 1744 d 1-31-1806 m Sarah Stevens Pvt PA
Isham: b 1760 d 9-14-1835 m Amy Gillam Lt NC ★
Ithiel: b 7-27-1759 d 1-1-1818 m Amy Linsley Fif CT
James: b 1740 d 1804 m Jane Carlyle Pvt PA
James: b 7-20-1748 d 1-18-1815 m Elizabeth Hampton Pvt PS SC
Job: b 5-30-1764 d 2-19-1833 m Lydia Lewis Pvt NJ
John: b 9-25-1749 d 2-11-1814 m Mary Ashford Pvt MD
John: b 1760 d 1821 m Delilah Youngblood Fif NC
John: b c. 1750 d p. 8-25-1825 m (1)Eleanor Kelly (2)Sarah Lloyd Pvt VA
John: b 1730 d 1789 m Mary Malone Capt SC
John: b 1751 d 1819 m Sally Speed Lt VA
John: b 1730 d 12- -1827 m (1)Bettie Headly (2)Nancy Miller Pvt VA
John: b 1750 d 1797 m Sarah Ellis Pvt VA
John: b 1760 d 1846 m Miss Cambell Pvt VA ★
John: b 1754 d 7-23-1821 m Mary Ann Johnston Lt VA
John Peyton: b c. 1752 d 7-24-1807 m (1)Frances Peyton (2)Elizabeth Peyton Capt VA
Jonathan: b c. 1732 d p. 1-12-1796 m (1)Temperance Shipman (2)Susan — Pvt VA
Joseph 3d: b 12-19-1747 d 3-1-1837 m (1)Rhoda Freeman (2)Phebe Thompkins (3)Mary Kirk Ens NJ ★
Joseph: b 1750 d 2-21-1803 m Sarah Giles Capt NY
Joseph: b 8-8-1735 d 8-27-1811 m Margrete Hill Pvt NC
Joseph: b c. 1763 d 8-22-1813 m Mary Gayle Lt VA W★
Joseph: b 10-23-1752 d p. 2-26-1828 m Elizabeth — Capt CL
Lawrence: b 1737- d 11-12-1813 m Mary Allison Lt VA ★
Moses: b 1758 d 1850 m Sarah Vincent MM NJ
Nathan: b 3-25-1762 d 11-7-1839 m (1)Thankful — (2)Lois Barker Pvt CS CT ★
Nathaniel: b 9-30-1742 d 12-24-1782 m (1)Mary Ruffin (2)Anne Gilliam CS VA
Nathaniel: b 1703 d 10-1-1781 m Mary Cole Digges PS VA
Noah: b 11-19-1737 d 3-7-1823 m (1)Hannah Rogers (2)Anne Carter Pvt CT
Noah B.: b 7-12-1759 d 9-25-1789 m Huldah Bacon Drm MA
Peter: b 11-11-1739 d 10-22-1829 m Mercy Frisbie PS CT
Reuben: b 4-28-1762 d 1-2-1833 m Nancy Baldwin Cpl MA
Reuben: b 1731 d 1807 m (1)Lydia Harrison (2)Mary McDonald Capt PS CS VA
Reuben: b 1754 d 8-15-1840 m Mary Matthews Pvt CS VA ★

HARRISON, contd.
Reuben Henry: b *a.* 1760 d *p.* 3-13-1835 m (1)Sarah Burgess (2)Nancy — Pvt SC
Richard: b 1754 d *p.* 1800 m Mary Johns Pvt MD
Richard: b 3-18-1752 d 10-22-1791 m (2)Ann Patillo Maj Dr NC
Richard: b 12-10-1757 d 2-7-1848 m Mary Clarkson Pvt NC
Robert: b 11-5-1740 d 5-16-1802 m Milcah Gale Col CS PS MD
Robert: b 3-23-1745 d 3-23-1820 m Sarah — PS MD
Robert: b 1759 d 2-10-1844 m Elizabeth Rhodes Pvt RI ★
Robert: b 2-11-1755 d 7-8-1797 m Henrietta Maria Hardyman Pvt VA
Robert H.: b *c.* 1735 d 11-13-1826 m Mrs Mary Williams Wgn GA
Robert Hanson: b 10- -1745 d 4-2-1790 m (1)Sarah Anne Johnstone (2)Grace Dent LCol ADC VA
Samuel: b 4-26-1756 d 4-6-1813 m Rebekah Keeler Lt VT
Silas: b 5-1-1755 d *p.* 1832 m Sarah Brown Pvt CT ★
Stephen: b 1734 d 1812 m Lydia Williams Pvt NJ
Stephen: b 1742 d 12-22-1793 m Abigail Mulford MM NJ
Theodore: b 1756 d 5-20-1836 m Clotilda Wright Pvt CT ★
Thomas: b 1743 d 1808 m Eleanor Hargrove Sgt MD
Thomas: b 1734 d 1801 m Mary Porter PS CS MD
Thomas: b 1747 d *a.* 1- -1799 m (1)— Pendleton (2)Mary Kennon 2Maj NC
Thomas: b 1760 d 11-6-1839 m Nancy Pack Pvt NC ★
Thomas: b *c.* 1740 d *p.* 4-4-1809 m Caty — Pvt SC
Thomas: b 1750 d 1815 m (2)Hannah Dennis Sol VA
Thomas, Jr.: b 1756 d *p.* 6-4-1799 m (1)Sarah Briggs (2)Sarah Oliver Sol VA
Thomas: b 1704 d 1785 m (1)Jane Delahage (2)Sarah — PS VA
Valentine: b *c.* 1750 d — m Nancy Peyton Capt VA
Wm.: b 9-2-1745 d 1813 m Ruth Skinner Sol MD
Wm.: b 10-24-1747 d 7-21-1789 m (1)Rebecca Dent (2)Ann Jordan PS CS Col MD
Wm., Jr.: b 1720 d 4- -1787 m (2)Martha Bowlby Capt NJ W★
Wm.: b 1733 d 1797 m Elizabeth Simmons Lt NC
Wm.: b 11-29-1739 d 2- -1811 m Anne Payne PS CS VA
Wm.: b 1730 d 1812 m (2)Worlanda Davis PS VA
Wm. Butler: b — d 7-28-1835 m Penelope Russell Cnt VA
Zebulon: b 1718 d 1792 m Margaret Cravens PS VA

HARROD,
James: b *c.* 1756 d *p.* 1820 m Elizabeth Stewart Pvt VA
John: b 1736 d 12-28-1781 m Rachel Sheperd Brig Maj PA
Levi: b 1-22-1750 d 10-2-1825 m Rachel Mills Lt PA
Noah: b 5-8-1764 d 4-8-1820 m Eusebia Kendall Pvt MA
Thomas: b 1-13-1761 d 5-30-1803 m (1)Jane Bowen (2)Ester Templin Ens PA
Wm.: b 12-9-1737 d 10-9-1801 m Amelia Stephens Capt VA

HARROLD, (includes HERROLD)
Christopher, Sr.: b *c.* 1722 d *c.* 4-1-1787 m Catherina or Mary — PS PA
Jeremiah: b 10-30-1756 d 5-6-1834 m Sarah Osborne Pvt SC ★
John: b 1745 d 2-28-1828 m Barbara Altman PS PA
John: b 1750 d 1825 m Deliah — Pvt PA
John George: b 8-18-1725 d 10- -1803 m Anna Maria Benesch PS PA
Simon: b *c.* 1754 d 3- -1827 m Elizabeth — Ens PA

HARROUN,
David: b 1736 d 5-7-1789 m Elizabeth Anderson Capt MA
John: b 1737 d 10-18-1819 m Martha Henry Pvt MA

HARRY,
Amos: b 1751 d 1829 m Sarah Davis Pvt PA
Charles: b 1811-1760 d 4- -1843 m Barbara Bowman Pvt PS PA ★
John: b 10-14-1736 d 6-13-1800 m Alice Meredith Pvt PA
Martin, Sr.: b 5-27-1720 d 8- -1788 m (1)Anna Maria — (2)Elizabeth — Pvt PS MD
Thomas: b 1730 d 5-23-1827 m Betsy Evans Pvt PA

HARSH, (includes HERSH)
George: b 1759 d 8-16-1833 m (2)Catherine Strieker Pvt PA
Henry: b 1733 d 2-21-1819 m Maria Margaretha Scholl Pvt PA
Henry: bpt 11-4-1759 d *a.* 2-25-1839 m (1)Maria Magdalena — (2)Margaret — Pvt PA
Henry: b 1758 d 6-5-1828 m Catherine Lider Pvt PA

HARSHA,
Hugh: b *a.* 1758 d *p.* 1798 m Mary McWhorter Pvt NY
John: b 1747 d 5-8-1831 m Mary McCraig Pvt NY

HARSHBARGER, (includes HERSHBERGER, HIRSCHBERGER)
Bernard: b *c.* 1735 d 1798 m Elizabeth — PS MD
Christian: b 9-20-1755 d 6-29-1827 m (1)Barbary Ammen (2)Mrs Susanna Beckner Garman Pvt PA
Christian: b *a.* 1756 d *p.* 2-28-1805 m prob. Caroline — PS VA
Henry: b *c.* 1750 d *a.* 3-12-1828 m Magdalena Schenk Pvt PA
Jacob: b 1757 d 1850 m Margaret Keller Pvt PA
John: b 1759 d 1847 m Christiana E. Fehler Pvt PA
Samuel: b 9-19-1759 d 1849 m Elizabeth Gish Pvt PA

HARSHFIELD,
Henry: b 1758 d 11-19-1836 m Elizabeth Rumbaugh Pvt PA ★

HARSHMAN,
Peter: b 1745 d 1827 m (2)Elizabeth Burres Sol VA

HART, (includes HARTE, HARTT, HEARTT)
Abel: b 2-22-1741 d 8-15-1802 m Mary Galpin 2Lt MA
Abner: b 1-31-1762 d 1-7-1825 m Jane Creinyonce VanCleve Pvt NJ
Adam: b 3-17-1757 d 1-27-1847 m — Pvt Wgn NC
Amasa: b 6-19-1754 d *p.* 1794 m Phebe Roberts Pvt CT
Amos: b 2-20-1722 d 4-10-1798 m (1)Ann Gridley (2)Mary Dunham (3)Lois Clark Pvt CT
Anthony: b 1743 d *a.* 4-25-1795 m Mrs Susannah Martin Capt NC
Anthony: b 1756 d 11- -1845 m Nancy Hart Pvt VA
Ard: b 5-17-1761 d 3-5-1851 m (1)Millicent Roberts (2)Mrs Lucy Hotchkiss Pvt CT ★
Benjamin: b 3-5-1752 d 1-30-1831 m Hannah Curtis Pvt CT ★
Benjamin: b 3-25-1761 d 4-17-1829 m Mehitable Jerome Pvt CT
Benjamin: b 10- -1732 d 1-2-1802 m Nancy Morgan Sol GA
Benjamin: b *c.* 1735 d *p.* 1786 m Mary Ann Lee Cnt QM NC
Benjamin: b 1720 d 1806 m Hannah Cook Pvt NJ
Bliss: b 3-10-1761 d 3-6-1831 m Sylvia Upson Pvt Fif CT ★
Daniel: b 8-13-1762 d 1848 m Margaret Bund Sol NJ
Daniel: b 12-17-1749 d 12-7-1832 m (1)Hannah Potter (2)Prudence Potter Pvt NJ ★
Daniel: b 1-22-1747/48 d 5-9-1812 m Bethiah Mackintire Pvt MA
David: b 1725 d *p.* 1790 m Susanna Nunn CS NC
Ebenezer: b 1762 d 3-26-1840 m Polly Smith Cpl CT ★
Edward: b 12-20-1755 d 10-6-1812 m Nancy Deborah Stout Pvt NJ ★
Elias: b 5-11-1759 d 2-22-1834 m Philomela Burnham Pvt MA CT ★
Elijah 3d: b 5-7-1759 d 8-4-1827 m Anna Andrews Sgt CT
Elijah: b 9-10-1749 d 2-2-1829 m Rebekah Mershon PS NJ
Elnathan: b 9-10-1735 d 8-26-1831 m Ruth Judd PS CT
George, Sr.: b 1730 d 4-14-1807 m Phebe Brewster PS NH
George, Jr.: b 2- -1755 d 7-14-1792 m Martha Sumner Sol NH
George: b *c.* 1758 d 2-28-1833 m Magdelena Schappert Pvt PA ★
Gilbert: b 4-19-1762 d 1847 m Sarah Linsley Sol CT
Hawkins: b 2- -1736 d 5-26-1824 m Abigail Hall Lt CT
Hawkins, Jr.: b 1-3-1736/7 d *p.* 1-26-1800 m (1)Huldah Woodruff (2)Ruth Chubs 1Lt CT
Henry: b 3-13-1744 d 3-27-1806 m Alice Downing PS NH
Henry: b 9-10-1759 d 2-1-1835 m Anna Efan Van Kiltz Pvt NY ★
Henry: b 1724 d 1785 m Priscilla Sessoms Col NC
Israel: b *c.* 1763 d *p.* 11-12-1838 m Elizabeth Price Pvt MA
Jabez: b 1756 d 12-20-1832 m Jemima Brace Pvt MA
Jacob: b 1746 d 5-9-1822 m Leah Nathan PS MD
Jacob, Jr.: b 4-16-1761 d 11-4-1833 m Jerusha King Cpl MA ★
Jacob: b *c.* 1755 d 11- -1800 m Elizabeth Smith Pvt PA
James: b *c.* 1747 d 5-4-1825 m Martha Kenniston Maj MA
James: b 4-17-1729 d *p.* 1780 m (1)Hannah Crane (2)Hannah Valentine Pvt MA
James: b 3-21-1756 d 10-21-1839 m Nancy Strayhorne Pvt NC
James: b 3-17-1759 d 4-22-1826 m Ann Hankinson Pvt PA
James: b *c.* 1760 d *p.* 1-21-1822 m Elizabeth — Sgt SC
James: b 6- -1738 d *c.* 7- -1822 m Elizabeth Hopkins Pvt VA
James: b 1757 d 1823 m Margaret Muse Pvt VA
Jeremiah: b 4-5-1745 d 7-4-1822 m Abigail Pearsall Sol NY
Jesse: b 11-19-1742 d *p.* 5-1-1789 m Martha Mathison PM RO NJ
John, Jr.: b 1733 d 4-4-1811 m Lydia Curtis Sgt MA
John: b 1762 d 1821 m Patience Lane Pvt GA
John: b 1754 d 9-9-1843 m Jane Thompson Smn MA
John: b 10-23-1751 d 4-27-1836 m Mary Gould Dr LCol MA
John: b 10-4-1740 d 2-20-1784 m Anne Ottilie Schwartzbagen Pvt PA
John: bpt 2-21-1713 d 5-11-1779 m Deborah Scudder SDI PS NJ
John: b 5-5-1753 d 4-15-1849 m Sarah Vernon Sgt PA
John: b 11-29-1743 d 6-5-1786 m Rebecca Reese 2Lt PA
John: b 3-6-1758 d 3-17-1814 m Mary Esther Screven Capt SC W★
John R.: b 9-25-1752 d 1-23-1845 m Mary Dean Pvt NJ ★
John R.: b 1753 d 3-18-1817 m Martha Thompson Pvt PA
Jonathan: b 1744 d 10-18-1785 m Elizabeth Bloomer Pvt NY
Joseph: b 1700 d 3-10-1777 m Mary Bird CS CT
Joseph: b 8-17-1739 d 12-15-1806 m Eunice Burrell Sgt CS MA
Joseph: b *c.* 1760 d 1793 m Anna Sugg Pvt NC
Joseph, Sr.: b 9-1-1715 d 2-25-1788 m Elizabeth Collet Col PS PA
Joseph, Jr.: b 12-7-1758 d 4-15-1811 m Ann Folwell Ens PA
Joseph, Jr.: b 6-16-1761 d 6-20-1841 m (1)Nancy Shanklin (2)Mary Means Pvt VA
Joshua: b 9-17-1738 d 10-3-1827 m Abagail Howell PS NY
Josiah: b 5-20-1764 d 4-6-1845 m Judith Tanner PS VA
Josiah: b 4-28-1742 d 8- -1812 m (1)Abigail Sluman (2)Abigail Robbins Dr CT
Josiah: b *c.* 1750 d *p.* 1812 m (1)Mehitable — (2)Mrs Susanna Putnam Pvt NH
Josiah: b 7-17-1749 d 12-25-1800 m Anne Watts Col PA
Judah: b 9-10-1750 d 4-28-1795 m Sarah North PS CT
Lemuel: b 8-24-1759 d 5-2-1822 m (1)Rosanna Winstone (2)Mary Dunham Pvt CT
Lent: b — d — m Olive Hickox Pvt CT
Leonard: b 1753 d 1843 m (1)Sallie Goodman (3)Phoebe Proffit Pvt TN

Leonard: b c. 1744 d p. 1802 m (1)Mary — (2)Catherine — Sol VA
Levi: b 1751 d p. 1806 m Mary Hunt Pvt NJ
Lewis: 3-26-1757 d 7-15-1817 m Anne Elliott Trm Maj CT
Luke: b 1-8-1738 d — m Deborah Barnes Pvt CT
Martin: b 12- -1758 d 8-7-1842 m Levinah Bidwell Pvt CT
Matthew: b 1-23-1737 d 1811 m Elizabeth Hopkins Cpl CT
Michael: b 1738 d 3-23-1813 m Leah — Cpl PA
Nancy: b 3-17-1747 d 1840 m Benjamin Hart PS Spy GA
Nathaniel: b 9-5-1729 d 1810 m (1)Alice Hall (2)Mrs Phebe Johnson PS CT
Nathaniel: b 7-16-1746 d 8-19-1830 m Abigail Scudder Pvt NJ
Nathaniel: b 10-29-1747 d 1825 m Elizabeth Stout PS NJ
Nathaniel: b c. 1748/9 d 1816 m Lydia Redman PS NJ
Nathaniel: b 5-8-1734 d 8-11-1782 m Sarah Simpson PS Capt NC
Nehemiah, Sr.: b 4-19-1717 d 11-20-1796 m Mercy Lewis Pvt PS NY
Nehemiah, Jr.: b 10-27-1745 d 8-27-1808 m (1)Martha Titus (2)Mary Brewster Pvt NY
Nicholas: b 1738 d 7-10-1821 m Rachel Geyer Pvt PA
Nicholas: b c. 1760 d c. 1831 m (1)Catherine Honey (2)Ann New PS VA
Oliver: b 7-5-1723 d 12-31-1795 m (1)Sarah Bress (2)Anna Maria Grimball PS SC
Philip: b 1755 d 1831 m Hannah Palmer Pvt NJ
Philip: b 1-12-1749 d 8-31-1837 m Susanna Akins Pvt PS NY
Reuben: b 9-5-1729 d 12-6-1788 m Rhoda Peck Lt CT
Robert: b c. 1760 d p. 5-5-1838 m (1)Sarah Pattison (2)Elizabeth — Pvt GA
Robert: b 1756 d 4-7-1811 m Hannah Holliday Cpl NC
Robert: b 1739 d 10-18-1811 m Mary Dick DrmMaj VA
Samuel, Sr.: b 1-21-1738 d 8-21-1813 m (1)Rebecca Norton (2)Lydia Hinsdale Capt CT
Samuel, Jr.: b 5-17-1761 d 3-27-1835 m Mary Wilcox Fif CT
Samuel: b 7-18-1735 d 1-12-1805 m Abridget Fowler Lt CT
Samuel: b 12-2-1721 d 2-2-1801 m Lydia Gridley Sgt CT
Samuel: b 1-8-1741 d 12-15-1813 m Elizabeth Lambert Pvt NH
Samuel: b 8-31-1761 d 6-23-1838 m (1)Rosanna Clark (2)Patience Andrews Pvt NY W★
Samuel: b — d — m Amy Soper MM NY
Samuel: b 1755 d p. 12-3-1807 m Susanna Boring Lt NC
Samuel: b 1756 d 1837 m Elizabeth Hall Pvt NC ★
Simeon: b 12-29-1735 d 1-12-1800 m Sarah Sloper Capt PS CT
Stephen: b 8-2-1712 d 9-16-1788 m Sarah Taber CS RI
Thomas: b 1-12-1738 d 1-7-1830 m Mahitable Bird Pvt CT
Thomas: b 3-3-1757 d 1-14-1847 m Ruth Payne Pvt CT ★
Thomas: b 5-27-1723 d 2-26-1813 m Concurrence Bartlett PS CT
Thomas: b c. 1715 d 6-23-1808 m Susanna Gray PS Cmsry NC
Timothy: b 5-24-1731 d p. 1790 m Phoebe Fenn Pvt CT
Titus: b 7-4-1757 d 7-27-1844 m (1)Lucy Johnson (2)Elizabeth Andrews Pvt CT ★
Titus: b 7-1-1757 d 1797 m (1)Rebecca Scudder (2)Phebe Guild Pvt NJ
Wm.: b 6-24-1746 d 8-29-1817 m Esther Buckingham MajGen CT
Wm.: b 10-11-1743 d 1812 m Abigail Thompson Sgt CT
Wm.: b 1738 d 1826 m Hannah Lanning Cpl NJ
Wm., Jr.: b c. 1750 d p. 1775 m Elizabeth Hart Pvt VA MD

HARTER, (includes HARDER, HERRTHER, HERTER, HORTTER)
Andrew: b 2-8-1733 d 12-2-1814 m Anna Barbary Kareksner Pvt PA
Frederick: b 1726 d 7-28-1812 m Appollonia Bellinger Pvt NY
Henry: b 2-15-1730 d 4-12-1822 m (1)Catherine Piper (2)Abelona Holman Capt NY
Henry: b 1760 d 10-21-1831 m Catharine — Sol VA
Jacob, Sr.: b 3-7-1714 d 2-24-1792 m Maritje VanHoesen Pvt NY
Jacob: b a. 1761 d p. 1785 m Catherine — Pvt NY
Jan: b 10-20-1740 d 9-11-1835 m Magdelena Maul Pvt NY
Johan Martin, Sr.: b 4- -1706/9 d 1800 m (1)Magdalene — (2)Mrs Catharine Maurer PS PA
Lorence: b 12-26-1742 d 5-2-1815 m (1)Larry McCombs (2)Catharine — Pvt NY
Lorentz: b 10-14-1698 d 1792 m Appolonia Schuttin PS NY
Martin: b 1740-45 d 1800 m Christiana Margaretha Maurer Sgt PA
Mathias: b c. 1740 d 1- -1790 m Anna Maria — Pvt PA
Nicholas: b 3-8-1761 d 7-26-1854 m — Damworth Pvt NY ★
Peter: b 3-27-1753 d 8-14-1842 m Eva Land Pvt NY ★
Valentine: b 1739 d 1816 m Magdalena Rice Pvt PA

HARTFORD, (includes HARFOR)
Ephraim: b c. 1756 d 2-18-1825 m Ruth Scofield Cpl PS NY W★
John: b 9-21-1751 d 1825 m Sarah Spencer Pvt NH
John: b 1769 d 8-4-1843 m Rachel Compton Smn VA
Mathew: b — d p. 3-27-1821 m Ann Dyer Pvt PA
Solomon: b 1758 d 1820 m (2)Mary Farnham Sol ME
Solomon: b 10-16-1748 d p. 1790 m Joanna Beale Pvt MA

HARTH,
John: b 1740 d 1836 m Elizabeth Holstien PS NC

HARTLE,
George: b 5-10-1722 d 9-13-1776 m Margaret — PS MD

HARTLESS,
Henry: b c. 1725 d 7-3-1803 m Isabella — PS VA
James: b c. 1752 d 1804 m Elizabeth — Sol VA

HARTLEY,
Anthony: b 1753 d 1803 m (1)Drusilla Dixon (2)Isabella Stewart Pvt PA
Anthony: b 10-3-1730 d 1811 m (1)Elizabeth Smith (2)Sarah Betts Sol PA
Benjamin: b c. 1740 d p. 1790 m Elizabeth Simcock Pvt PA
Daniel: b 1743 d 1850 m — Brown Pvt GA
James: b c. 1760 d 1827 m Mary Smalley Pvt PA
John: b c. 1748 d p. 1790 m Elizabeth — Pvt MD
Laban: b c. 1753 d p. 1835 m Sarah Feagley Pvt NC ★
Thomas: b 9-7-1748 d 12-21-1800 m Catherine Holtzinger Col PA
Thomas: b 1760 d 1806 m Elizabeth Williams PS VA

HARTLINE,
George, Sr.: b 1732 d 2-9-1794 m Christina Boehn Pvt PA

HARTMAN,
Adam: b 9-5-1743 d 4-5-1836 m — Pvt NY ★
Adam: b 5-5-1761 d 3-21-1846 m Elizabeth — Pvt PA ★
Christian: b c. 1740 d 12- -1829 m Barbara Brubaker Pvt PA
Christian: b 11-22-1753 d 10-9-1841 m Mary — Pvt PA
Christopher: b 5-6-1750 d 3-16-1833 m Mary Hutchinson Pvt NJ ★
George: b — d 1831 m Elizabeth Hortline Pvt PA
George: b 1759 d 1810 m Maria Elizabeth Hench Drm PA
Henry: b 1755-60 d a. 8-22-1814 m — Pvt MD
Henry, Jr.: b 10-14-1752 d 10-14-1836 m Sarah Harner Pvt PA
Jacob: b 1751 d c. 1811 m Peggy Cox Pvt PA W★
Jacob: b a. 1750 d 1823 m (1)Sallie Sahler (2)Eva Maria Dankel Pvt PA
John: b 11- -1757 d p. 1840 m — Pvt PA ★
John: b 6-24-1757 d 11-30-1842 m Christina Keller Pvt PA W★
John: b 7-6-1761 d 10-10-1815 m Sarah Hildebrand Pvt PA
John: b c. 1755 d 1799 m (1)Margaret Ritter (2)Magdalina Ritter Sol PA
John: b a. 1725 d 1785 m (1)Margaret Moses (2)— PS PA
John, Sr.: b c. 1728 d p. 5-13-1777 m Eva Mary — PS VA
John, Jr.: b 10-3-1760 d p. 1810 m Barbara — Pvt PA
John: b 12-28-1731 d 10-18-1786 m (1)Eva Catharine — (2)Mrs Anges Bleiler CMman Pvt PA
Mathias: b 5-22-1743 d 12-29-1825 m Catharine Wagner PS PA
Peter: b 4-2-1740 d 9-30-1810 m (1)Catharine Mary Stein (2)Margaret Metzler Maj PA
Peter: b 1750 d 1787 m Susanna Knerr Cpl PA
Philip: b 4-10-1752 d 4-3-1812 m Christina Scharman Pvt PA

HARTNESS,
Robert: b 3-17-1756 d 1799 m (1)Jean Richey (2)Jane Beard Pvt SC

HARTRANFT,
John: b 1763 d 1824 m Betsey Buchard Pvt PA
Leonard: b 11-6-1759 d 7-24-1841 m Christina Moyer Pvt PA

HARTSFIELD,
John: b c. 6-11-1758 d 9-28-1838 m Peggy — Pvt NC
Richard: b 2-17-1748 d c. 1830-5 m Anna — Pvt NC

HARTSHORN, (includes HARTSHORNE & HORTSHORN)
Andrew: b 4-7-1755 d 8-27-1809 m Sarah Abbe Pvt CT
Beriah: b 1-1-1757 d 11-3-1827 m Lydia Hunt Pvt CT
Ebenezer: b 10-2-1742 d 1-1-1825 m Abigail Barstow Pvt CT
Eli: b 1-5-1758 d 5-2-1825 m Elizabeth Sumner Pvt CT
Jacob: b 1761 d 8-26-1835 m Lucy Larcher Pvt RI ★
John: b 2-13-1731/2 d 7-27-1778 m Sarah Ellis Sol CT
John, Sr.: b 2-1-1725/6 d 9-16-1778 m Mary Fisher Pvt MA
John, Jr.: b 3-30-1757 d 7- -1823 m Catherine Allen Sgt MA
John: b 3-7-1756 d 3-26-1805 m Sarah Bachelder Pvt MA
John: bpt 1744 d 5-26-1830 m (1)Naomi Upton (2)Hannah Prince (3)Mrs Lucy Jones (4)Mrs Nancy Durant Sol PS NH
Jonathan: b 1748 d 1812 m (1)Hannah Eastman (2)Kezia Start Pvt PS NH
Nathan: b 7-23-1756 d 12-31-1836 m Irene Pember Pvt CT
Nathaniel: b 4-26-1747 d 4-7-1791 m Sarah Jones Sgt MA
Oliver: b 11-1-1761 d 12-18-1810 m Hannah Prentice Pettingill Pvt CT
Richard: b 7-3-1741 d 12- -1820 m Nancy Paine Sgt MA
Rufus: b 9-17-1728 d p. 1785 m (1)Lucy Avery (2)Mrs Jemima Spicer Pvt CT
Samuel: b 2-9-1764 d 11-5-1844 m Sarah Trowbridge Pvt CT
Samuel: b 4-20-1749 d 1830 m Mary Mann Pvt MA
Thomas: b 3-24-1718/9 d 2-7-1809/10 m Abiah — Sgt MA
Wm.: b 3-17-1754 d 10-1-1831 m (1)Elizabeth Fish (2)Betsey — Pvt CT
Wm.: b 6- -1742 d 12-14-1816 m (1)Susanna Saunders (2)Mrs Susannah Shreve PS VA

HARTUNG,
Christopher: b 9-2-1751 d 10-12-1834 m Catherine — Sgt PA ★

HARTUPEE,
Wm.: b 8-21-1756 d 9-1-1844 m Jane Mershon Capt NJ

HARTWELL, (includes HEARTWELL)
Abraham: b 6-2-1743 d 8-24-1820 m (1)Mary Lawrence (2)Patience
— Capt NY
Benjamin: b 7-18-1759 d 3-17-1844 m Meriah Nichols Sgt MA
Daniel: b 10-11-1755 d 4-3-1844 m Mehitabel Copeland Pvt MA
Ebenezer: b 1746 d 4-2-1813 m Hannah Bangs Sgt PS NY
Edward: b 8-23-1689 d 2-17-1785 m Sarah Wilder PS MA
Edward: b 8-22-1747 d 3-30-1844 m Lydia White Sgt MA ★
Ephraim: b 1-8-1745 d 5-30-1816 m Mary Brown Capt MA
Isaac: b 11-27-1752 d 6-2-1831 m Abihal Lothrop Lt RO MA
John 5th: b 8-21-1747 d 11-2-1820 m Hepsibah Brooks Lt MA
John: b 4-2-1758 d 9-8-1832 m (1)Hannah Moore (2)Mercy Cartwright
(3)Mrs Mary Brown Pvt Arfr MA ★
Jonas: b 3-30-1761 d — m Rubanah Fenno Sgt MA
Jonathan: b 4-30-1750 d 1-26-1814 m Mary Boynton Pvt MA
Jonathan: b 10-25-1748 d 5-11-1800 m Nancy Daggett Sgt NH
Joseph: b 1728 d 4-18-1811 m Rebecca Sherman PS CT
Joseph: b 1-17-1722/3 d 7-7-1792 m Jemima Batchelder Pvt PS MA
Joseph: b 5-14-1727 d 1807 m (1)Tabitha Dodge (2)Mrs Phebe
Eaton Hart Pvt MA
Joseph: b 2-2-1742 d 8-9-1812 m Elizabeth Pierce Capt NH
Josiah: b 8-7-1748 d 11-19-1822 m Rebecca Walker Capt MA
Nathan: b 10-11-1765 d 1822 m Sally Ripley Pvt MA ★
Oliver: b 9-7-1761 d 11-1-1854 m (1)Ruth Farnsworth
(2)Hannah Benedict Pvt CT ★
Oliver: b 9-7-1761 d 11-1-1854 m (1)Rachel Shattuck (2)Mrs
Keziah Matthews Chase Pvt MA
Paul: b 1742 d 10- -1804 m Mary — Capt VA
Phineas: b 1-2-1731 d 3-18-1803 m Mary Pierce CS MA
Samuel: b 6-25-1742 d 8-12-1829 m Mary Flint Sgt QM MA ★
Samuel: b 9-8-1755 d 6-10-1826 m Susannah Burr Pvt MA
Samuel: b 4-20-1760 d 6-6-1848 m Mrs Ann Barnum Pvt MA ★
Solomon: b 7-18-1751 d 9-12-1847 m Dorcas Polly Pvt MA ★
Solomon: b 4-20-1739 d p. 1790 m Abigail Davis Pvt MA
Stephen: b 11-24-1746 d p. 1775 m Sally Reed Pvt MA
Wm.: b 1-7-1743 d 8-28-1820 m Mary Lovell MM Sgt MA

HARTZELL,
Christian: b 8-6-1747 d 11-6-1826 m Anna Maria Bruch Pvt PA
Conrad: b 1748 d 1-17-1831 m Catherine — Pvt PA
George, Sr.: b c. 1718 d c. 1812 m Katrina — Pvt PA
George: b 10- -1733 d 12-11-1795 m Mrs Catherine Nyce Pvt PA
George: b c. 1760 d 1829 m Anna Maria Margaret — Fif PA
Heinrich: b 1-11-1717 d 6-21-1784 m Margaret — Sol PA
Jacob: b 9-27-1751 d 3-24-1839 m (1)Mary Catherine Klein
(2)Margaret Smith Pvt PA ★
John Adam: b 4-24-1747 d 1824 m Anna Maria Clara — Pvt PA
Paul: b 1-9-1749 d 8-20-1806 m Catherine Wambold Sol PA

HARTZLER,
John, Sr.: b a. 1737 d 4- -1801 m Ceronica Reichenbach Pvt PA
John, Jr.: b 1-17-1757 d 3-22-1836 m Ulrica Reichenbach Pvt PA

HARVELL,
John: b 1736 d 4-6-1821 m Rebecca Parham Walton CS PS NH

HARVEY, (includes HARVIE, HERVEY & HERVY)
Alexander: b 1747 d 12-14-1809 m Janet Brock PS VT
Amasa: b 1-30-1756 d 4-21-1830 m (1)Eunice Hungerford (2)Annie
Stewart Pvt CT
Andrew: b c. 1735 d 11-10-1801 m Margaret — Pvt PA
Archibald: b 1754/5 d 11-28-1807 m Elizabeth McFadden Pvt PA
Arnold: b 5-14-1727 d 12-14-1834 m Sinthney Wood PS Sol Mrnr SC
Asa: b 1-11-1749 d p. 1789 m — Selden Sgt CT
Asa: b 10-10-1739 d 9-13-1826 m (1)Elizabeth — (2)Esther Cone
PS CT
Benjamin: b 1734 d 3- -1848 m Sarah — Pvt NY ★
Benjamin: b 4-4-1727 d p. 1790 m Juliana Baker PS NC
Benjamin: b 7-28-1722 d 11-27-1795 m (1)Elizabeth Pelton (2)Mrs
Catharine Draper Pvt PA
Charles: b c. 1710 d 3-16-1800 m Frances — CS GA
David: b c. 1750 d p. 1779 m Marcia Chandler Sgt MA
David: b 1735 d 6-19-1814 m Content Byram Drm MA
David: b 4-24-1726 d 6-16-1802 m Judith Chase CS MA
David: b 9-5-1743 d 11-4-1810 m Abigail Dunham Sol NY
Edmund: b 2-25-1757 d 4-29-1807 m Mary Harvey Pvt MA
Edward: b 1752 d 1-6-1823 m Mary — Pvt VA ★
Elisha: b 1-8-1755 d 5-6-1846 m (1)Rachel Wetmore (2)Sarah Prout
SIr PS CT
Elisha: b 10- -1758 d 3-14-1800 m Rosanna Dixon Jameson Pvt PA
Ephraim: b 8-25-1751 d 9-25-1822 m Rhoda Hayward Pvt CT
Evan: b 1753 d p. 10-9-1812 m (1)Charity Powell (2)Ursula Jackson
Sol GA
Ezra: b — d 1805 m (1)Zipporah Blake (2)Esther Hows PS NH
Henderson: b c. 1755 d p. 1801 m Martha McConnell Pvt PA
Henry: b 1755 d 1813 m Sarah Ann McDaniel PS MD
Isaac: b 9-21-1718 d 11-3-1802 m Martha Newlin Sol PA
Ithamar: b 2-11-1743 d 5-31-1813 m Anna Cone Capt CT
James: b 1755 d 1807 m Sarah Clarke Pvt GA
James: b — d — m Elizabeth Eliott Pvt Fif MA

James: b 8-17-1762 d 4-10-1844 m Sarah Judkins Pvt NH
James: b 1751 d 1844 m — Pvt NC
James: b c. 1739 d p. 4-18-1822 m (1)Mary Gibbes (2)Betty Francis
Holcombe (3)Jane Hannah PS SC
Job: b 4-4-1738 d 10-19-1816 m Sarah Dawes Sol PS DE
Job: b 2-9-1738 d 1820 m Hannah Anderson Lt PA
John: b 1752 d p. 1801 m Barbara — Pvt MD
John: b 6-17-1764 d 4-22-1852 m Lintha Lincoln Pvt MA
John: b 3-4-1752 d 2-29-1841 m Sarah Stevens PS NH
John: b 8-4-1745 d 2- -1812 m Sarah Blake Lt QM NH
John: b 10-15-1744 d p. 1792 m Hannah Hilton PS NH
John: b a. 1730 d 1775 m Mary Bonner PS NC
John: b 1757 d 1819 m Jane Beauchamp Pvt PA
John: b c. 1730 d p. 1810 m Margaret — Col VA
John: b c. 1745 d 1813 m Ann — Capt VA
John, Jr.: b 1740 d 2-27-1807 m Margaret Morton Jones PS Col VA
Jonathan: b 1-28-1761 d 9-6-1833 m Fannah Burdick Pvt CT
Jonathan: b 2-27-1761 d 3-29-1832 m Wealthy Pool Gnr OrdlSgt
MA W★
Jonathan: b 1712 d 1797 m Freelove Hicks PS MA
Joseph: b 1730 d 4-9-1778 m Betty Chandler Pvt MA
Joshua: b 1761 d 1849 m Lucy Powell Pvt PA
Josiah: b 10-19-1745 d 6-22-1808 m Elizabeth Bates Dr Capt MA
Kimber: b 4-15-1755 d 2-1-1828 m Polly Hazelton Sgt NH
Levi: b 7-14-1745 d 4-7-1807 m Elizabeth Randlett Sgt NH
Mathew: b 3- -1760 d 9-19-1823 m Madgalen Hawkins Pvt MD
Matthew: b 3-1-1749 d 2-25-1799 m Hannah Sargent CS NH
Miles: b 12-17-1728 d 12-12-1776 m (1)Elizabeth Baker (2)Elizabeth
Jones Col PS NC
Moses: b 7-20-1723 d 1-17-1795 m Esther — Capt MA
Nathan: b 8-14-1757 d 1815 m Mehitabel Harvey Pvt Drm MA
Obed, Sr.: b 3-10-1722 d 1808 m — Capt NY
Paul: b 8-26-1762 d 5-4-1859 m Hannah Nickerson Pvt MA
Richard: b 1747 d 1784 m Mary Catherine — Sol GA
Richard: b 1759 d a. 7-2-1817 m Elizabeth Morel Sol VA
Robert, Sr.: b 12-26-1731 d 12-18-1800 m Rachel Stewart Pvt CT
Robert, Jr.: b 4-25-1760 d 4-1-1840 m Asenath Cone Pvt CT
Robert: b 10- -1756 d 5-9-1831 m (1)Mrs Martha Hawkins (2)Nancy
Moore Pvt VA
Rufus: b 10-7-1758 d 9-9-1807 m Sarah Jones Sgt MA
Samuel: b 8-20-1762 d 7- -1843 m Mehitable Burnham Pvt NH
Samuel: b 7-1-1742 d 5-1-1778 m Martha Martin Pvt PA
Samuel: b 1751 d 11-4-1807 m Mary Saunders Pvt PA ★
Simeon: b 6-20-1743 d 8-28-1815 m Mary Arms PS MA
Thomas: b 1740 d 3-26-1826 m Grace Willey Capt NH
Thomas: b c. 1740 d p. 2-12-1806 m (1)Bettie Pritchett (2)Sarah
Anne Col NC
Thomas: b 10-14-1742 d p. 1783 m Jane Angus Manning Pvt PA
Thomas: b 1730 d 1799 m Rachel — Sol GA
Wm.: b 10-26-1754 d 8-26-1826 m Jane Beebe Pvt CT ★
Wm.: b c. 1740 d p. 1791 m — Lt MD
Wm.: b 1749 d 1836 m Lenah Gentry Pvt NC ★
Wm.: b 1740 d 1818 m Sarah Hudson Pvt PA
Wm.: b c. 1748 d c. 1840 m (1)Mary — (2)Sarah — Pvt PA
Wm.: b — d 10-4-1777 m Mary Struper Pvt PA
Wm.: b 1744 d p. 1818 m Jane Robinson Pvt VA
Wm.: b a. 1769 d p. 1802 m Judith Cosby Pvt VA
Zephaniah: b 1760 d 1832 m Nancy Smith Pvt SC

HARVIN,
John: b 1740 d 1805 m — Lt SC
Richard: b 8-13-1746 d 12-15-1807 m Frances Ragan Pvt SC

HARVOUT,
Wm.: b 1752/3 d 1784 m Rebecca John Pvt PA

HARWELL,
Loudon: b 8- -1764 d 7- -1838 m Mary Hodge Pvt SC
Samuel, Sr.: b — d p. 10-30-1793 m Abigail — PS VA

HARWICK,
Jacob: b 1752 d 11-22-1833 m Catherine — Pvt NC ★

HARWOOD,
Andrew: b 9-20-1743 d 2-23-1823 m Rachel D Higgins Pvt MA
Archibald: b 1762 d 1837 m Susannah House Pvt NH
Christopher: b c. 1760 d 1793 m Margaret Roane Pvt VA
Daniel: b 1736 d 2-28-1823 m Lydia Gould Pvt MA
David: b 1-3-1733 d 9-28-1808 m Rebecca Twiss Pvt MA
Edward: b 3-4-1757 d 12-6-1812 m Mary Hill Lt VA
Francis: b 8-14-1763 d 5-20-1835 m Lucinda Foward Pvt MA
James: b 10-4-1730 d 6-21-1803 m Martha Barnes Pvt MA
James: b c. 1736 d 12-1-1777 m Mary Clogson Pvt NH
James: b c. 1735 d 1- -1805 m Eunice Brooks Sgt VT
John: b 11-28-1744 d 1810 m Mary Hall Pvt PS MD
John: b 4-28-1730 d 1796 m Huldah Bannister Capt MA
John: b 6-5-1736 d p. 1784 m Mary Pulsipher Pvt VT
John: b 1753 d 1823 m (1)Mary Murray (2)Rebecca Champion Ens
VA
John: b 1737 d 3- -1778 m Mary Curtis Pvt VA
Jonathan: b c. 1751 d 10-24-1822 m Eunice Briggs Pvt MA ★
Marville: b 1756 d 2-28-1838 m Polly Southworth Pvt MA

Nathan: b 2-22-1736 d 2-3-1790 m Huldah Bannister Capt MA
Oliver: b 12-16-1763 d 7-10-1822 m Fear Ripley Pvt MA
Peter, Sr.: b 7-10-1740 d 1-14-1805 m Phebe Prouty Maj MA
Peter, Jr.: b 9-16-1765 d 4-13-1836 m Elizabeth Airmet Pvt MA
Peter: b 10-26-1727 d 1815 m Mary Webb MM MA
Peter: b 7-14-1735 d 6-12-1815 m Margaret Clark Pvt VT
Richard: b 12-11-1738 d 2-21-1826 m Margaret Hall LCol CS MD
Samuel: b 1740 d *p.* 1787 m Joyce Mayjor Maj VA
Stephen: b 1741 d 1804 m Abigail Streeter Pvt MA
Thomas: b 12-8-1726 d 5-15-1791 m Rachel Sprigg Capt MD
Wm., Sr.: b *c.* 1710 d *a.* 1782 m Mary — PS VA
Wm., Jr.: b 1737 d 10-1-1795 m (1)Frances Langley (2)Martha —Col VA
Zachariah: b 3-11-1742 d 6-6-1821 m (1)Lovina Rice (2)Antice Alma Pvt VT

HASBROUCK,
Abraham: b 8-21-1707 d 11-10-1791 m Catherine Bruyn PS Col NY
Benjamin: b 1767 d 1841 m Rachel Storm Pvt NY
David: b 6-8-1740 d 3-12-1806 m Maria Hoogland PS Sol NY
Elias: b 5-8-1743 d 10-8-1791 m Elizabeth Sleight Capt NY
Isaiah: bpt 4-13-1746 d *p.* 1796 m Mary Bevier Pvt NY
Isaac: b 3-11-1722 d 6-15-1789 m Maria Bruyn Pvt PS NY
Jacob, Jr.: b 4-5-1728 d 6-6-1806 m Janetje Dubois Maj PS NY
Jacob I.: b 9-29-1746 d 6-21-1818 m Sara DuBois PS NY
Jacobus Bruyn: b 12-1-1753 d *p.* 11-6-1824 m Annatje Abeel Pvt PS NY
Jonas: b 5-5-1736 d 8-11-1824 m Kathryn Rine DeBois PS NY
Jonathan: b 4-23-1722 d 7-31-1780 m Tryntje Debois Col NY
Joseph: b 3-3-1744 d 2-26-1808 m (1)Elizabeth Bevier (2)Mary DeWitt LCol NY
Joseph, Jr.: b 9-8-1754 d *p.* 1828 m Margaret Hoornbeck Lt NY
Josiah: b 1755 d 1821 m Sara Decker 2Lt NY
Petrus: b 8-20-1738 d *p.* 1789 m Sarah Bevier Lt NY
Solomon: b 4-1-1750 d 12-27-1834 m Annatje Van Steenberghen Sgt NY ★

HASELWOOD,
Thomas: b *c.* 1740 d 1799 m — Sol SC

HASH,
Wm.: b *c.* 1750 d *c.* 1818 m — Osborne Pvt VA

HASKELL, (includes HASCALL & HASKEL)
Abijah Wheeler: b 3-19-1754 d 2-27-1832 m Sarah Cole Pvt MA
Abner: b 1-1-1735 d 4-4-1809 m Martha Ward Pvt MA
Abner: b 12-5-1721 d 1-14-1799 m Grace Slack Sgt RI
Andrew: b 3-8-1710/11 d — m (1)Jane Clark (2)Susanna Paine Pvt MA
Andrew: b 7-22-1748 d 11-3-1781 m Lois Bullen Sgt MA
Benjamin: b 1746 d 10-8-1804 m Sarah Foster Ens CT
Caleb: b 7-1-1754 d 1-12-1829 m Ednah Hale Fif Pvt MA ★
David: b 1755/6 d 1-4-1828 m (1)Elizabeth Putnam (2)Mary More Pvt NH ★
Elias: b 7-31-1752 d *p.* 1791 m (1)Sarah Roberts (2)Mrs Mary Riggs Cpl MA
Elias: b 3-24-1751 d 10-10-1824 m Mercy Tilson Cpl MA
Elisha: b 3-2-1744 d 2-24-1829 m Anna — 1Lt MA
Elnathan, Sr.: b 1725 d 4-16-1783 m Dorothy Peckham Pvt MA
Elnathan, Jr.: b 9-4-1755 d 12-16-1825 m Charlotte Thomson Bgd Maj MA
George: b 4-23-1761 d 5-25-1837 m Comfort Knowlton Pvt MA
Henry: b 5-2-1738 d 6-10-1807 m (1)Rebecca Willard (2)Martha Little (3)Charity Pratt Capt MA
Hubbard: b 5-3-1720 d 4-9-1811 m Anna Millett PS MA
Jabez: b 1746 d 9-4-1816 m Elizabeth Bissell Pvt CT
Jacob: b 10-27-1718 d 1800 m Tabitha Day 1Lt MA
Jeremiah: b 1741 d 3-3-1838 m Hanna Nichols Sgt MA
Jeremiah, Jr.: b *c.* 1759 d 1835 m Letty Benjamin Pvt MA
Job: b 10-27-1751 d *p.* 1788 m Elizabeth Hammond Cpl MA
Job: b 11-22-1744 d 1837 m (1)Isabel Winship (2) — Estabrooke Capt NH MA ★
John: b 2-28-1763 d 10-22-1845 m (1)Amy Chandler (2)Grace Barnard Pvt CT
John: b 7-17-1749 d *p.* 1783 m Deborah Meacham Pvt MA
John: b 11-11-1756 d 9-22-1819 m Mary Paine Pvt MA
Jonathan: b 1755 d 12- -1814 m Phoebe Green Adj MA
Jonathan: b 4-13-1735 d 7-22-1779 m (1)Tamer Moffitt (2)Ann Lothrop Lt PA
Joseph: b 3-29-1746 d 12-22-1827 m Mercy Parker Pvt MA
Joseph: b 4-4-1752 d 2-9-1837 m Hannah Gary Pvt MA
Josiah: b 1761 d 5-5-1844 m (1)Abigail Wallace (2)Abigail Berry Pvt MA W★
Josiah: b 7-5-1737 d 5-19-1819 m Mary Gates Lt MA
Lot: b 10-18-1758 d 3-13-1844 m (1)Desire Vincent (2)Betsey Cotton Pvt MA
Moses: b 12-20-1757 d *p.* 1781 m Priscilla Hinckley Pvt MA
Moses: b 1763 d 1-13-1837 m Hannah Lebaron Pvt MA ★
Nathaniel: b 2-14-1742 d 2-14-1794 m Deborah Bailey Lt ME
Nathaniel, Sr.: b 2-26-1731 d 7-16-1821 m Lydia Foster Pvt MA
Nathaniel, Jr.: b 7-25-1762 d 1842 m Mary Stacy Pvt MA ★
Nehemiah: b 1726 d 5-4-1787 m Mrs Elizabeth Fitts Pvt MA

Philip: b 6-7-1754 d 4-8-1849 m (1)Joanna Brooks (2)Sarah Finch Pvt MA
Prince: b 4-24-1758 d 3-23-1841 m Leah Wilder Drm Pvt MA ★
Roger: b 6-11-1742 d 11-14-1813 m Judith Nelson Cpl MA
Roger: b 4-2-1753 d 4-8-1847 m Mary Webster Pvt MA ★
Samuel: b 2-17-1734 d 11-15-1820 m Elizabeth Macomber PS MA
Samuel, Jr.: b 6-12-1749 d 8-16-1825 m Ruth Safford Sgt MA
Samuel: b 9- -1754 d 9-17-1849 m Mary Jane Turner Pvt RI ★
Simeon: b 4-25-1758 d 9-20-1846 m (1)Sarah Parsons (2)Sally Lord Cpl NY
Solomon: b 2-19-1740 d — m Elizabeth Davis Pvt MA
Squire: b 6-1-1706 d 1787 m Elizabeth — Pvt CT
Stephen: b 4-11-1763 d 2-21-1847 m Rachel Green Larned Pvt CT MA MA
Stephen: b 9-9-1765 d 12-3-1830 m Rebecca Marston Pvt MA ★
Thomas: b 1-2-1753 d *p.* 8-27-1800 m Eunice Morse Pvt MA
Wm.: b 6-15-1728 d 11- -1776 m (2)Anna Merrill Pvt Fif MA
Wm.: b 1759 d 9-15-1827 m Rhoda Bragg Pvt MA ★
Wm.: b 3-20-1761 d 10-16-1843 m Rebecca Haskell Pvt MA
Zebulon: b 8-4-1747 d 10-28-1820 m Abigail Swift Pvt MA
Zebulon: b 2-17-1753 d 1831 m (1)Thankful Dexter (2)Susanna Sherman Sgt MA

HASKET,
Isaac: b — d 1782 m Lydia Elliott PS SC

HASKINS, (includes HASKIN & HOSKINS)
Aaron: b 5-31-1752 d 12-31-1816 m Rhoda Risley Pvt CT
Abraham: b 4-6-1756 d 3-4-1826 m Lois Watts Pvt MA ★
Anthony, Sr.: b 4-12-1731 d 4-13-1819 m Rhpda Goodrich Sgt CT
Anthony: b 1-23-1750 d 9-11-1811 m Rest Crepo Pvt MA
Asa: b 6-11-1762 d 3-18-1847 m Abigail Case Pvt PS CT
Asahel: b 1764 d *p.* 1827 m Jeanette Cochran Pvt MA ★
Benjamin: b 1754 d 1824 m (1)Dille Prior (2)Thankful Francis Pvt VT
Benjamin: b *c.* 1729 d 6-9-1798 m Phoebe Haskins PS VA
Bennet: b — d 1804 m Ruth Boynton Pvt MA
Benoni: b 5-7-1746 d 1830 m Mehitable — Sgt MA
Daniel: b 3-21-1744 d *c.* 1832 m Abigail Roberts Pvt VT
David: b 4-12-1759 d 2-22-1844 m Phebe — Pvt CT ★
Edward: b 1741 d 1805 m Lucy Carter Maj VA
Eli: b 11-21-1759 d 11-12-1846 mRhoda Drake Pvt MA RI ★
Eliphalet: b 2-26-1731 d 3-18-1800 m Faith Cook Pvt MA
Elkanah: b 9-11-1741 d 9- -1805 m Mindwell Barney Pvt Sgt MA
Enoch, Sr.: b 5-5-1740 d 3- -1833 m Mary Williams Pvt MA
Enoch, Jr.: b 7-23-1765 d 1838 m Lydia Ackley Pvt MA ★
George: b *c.* 1755 d 9- -1822 m Alice Pope Capt MA
Henry: b 1-20-1761 d *p.* 1831 m Abigail Townsend Pvt MA ★
Jacob: b 6-20-1736 d 1-4-1819 m Mercy Pitts Capt MA
James: b *c.* 1755 d *p.* 1830 m Mary Sanford Pvt Cpl MA
John: b 1750 d 4-12-1850 m Lavicia Winchel Pvt CT ★
John: b 12-6-1742 d 3-14-1814 m Charity — Pvt MA
John: b 1748 d 1825 m Lydia Cole Pvt MA
John: b 3-25-1751 d 12-19-1813 m Elizabeth Chaney Capt VA
John: b 3-12-1729 d 10-27-1814 m Hannah Upham PS MA
Joseph, Jr.: b 1736 d 12- -1818 m Eunice Coe Trm CT
Joseph: b — d *c.* 1813 m Ann Bulwin Sol VA
Joshua: b 3-26-1755 d 8-31-1849 m Hannah Myrick Pvt MA
Lemuel: b 2-6-1734 d 6- -1840 m — Pvt NY ★
Nathan: b 2-20-1745 d 12-10-1802 m Phebe Linkon Sgt CS MA
Nicholas: b 1762 d 1846 m Susanna Smith Pvt NY
Preserved: b 1761 d 4-2-1854 m Deborah Fisher Pvt MA ★
Richard: b *c.* 1740 d 4- -1796 m Winifred Wiggins PS NC
Robert: b 1732 d 12-2-1804 m Elizabeth Hill Col VA
Samuel: b 9-9-1753 d 6- -1825 m Lydia Presby Pvt MA
Samuel, Jr.: b 2-2-1759 d 2-25-1818 m Persis Johnson Pvt MA
Thomas: b *c.* 1738 d 1804 m Mary Roberts PS CS NC
Thomas: b 4-9-1724 d 12-12-1798 m Anne Owen PS Col VA
Thomas: b 1760 d *p.* 1820 m Betsey Ellington Marshall Pvt VA
Wm.: b 6-17-1745 d 2-28-1833 m Susanna Grover Sgt MA ★
Wm.: b 3-7-1717 d 3- -1812 m Rebekah Lincoln PS MA
Wm.: b 1-4-1736 d 5-30-1786 m Lydia Box CS ActCmsry Gen MA
Wm.: b 4-16-1740 d 7-11-1781 m Joanna Hackett Pvt MA
Wm.: b 5-20-1754 d 4-18-1827 m Sarah Caswell Pvt MA
Wm.: b *c.* 1730 d *p.* 11-18-1780 m Mary — PS VA
Winnifred Wiggins: b — d 1807 m Richard Hoskins PS NC

HASLAM,
George: b 1735 d *p.* 1798 m Polly Westcott Capt MA

HASLETT, (includes HASLET)
John: b *a.* 1738 d 1-3-1777 m Mrs Jemima Molleston Brinckle Col DE
Wm.: b 1738 d 8- -1791 m Jane Wilson Pvt PA

HASLIP, (includes HESLEP)
Thomas: b 1750 d *c.* 1820 m Mary Nettles Pvt NC
Thomas: b — d *p.* 7-17-1817 m Mary — PS PA
Thomas: b 8-5-1740 d 2-28-1826 m Jane Lackland Pvt VA ★

HASSAM,
Samuel: b 5-15-1729 d *c.* 1777/8 m (1)Hannah Simpson (2)Mary Finney Pvt MA
Stephen: b *c.* 1761 d 2-4-1861 m (1)Theodosia Hastings (2)Lucy A Miller Vol MA

HASSINGER,
Herman: b 1751 d 1817 m Elizabeth — Pvt PA

HASSLER, (includes HOSLER)
Abraham: b 1-29-1759 d 5-15-1832 m Catharine Waldschmidt Cpl PA
Christian: b 8-28-1752 d 1813 m Magdalena — Ens PA
Frederick:b 1- -1749 d 3-8-1829 m Catharine Elizabeth Palm PS Pvt PA
Joseph: b 9-8-1750 d p. 3-30-1798 m Anna Mary Roemer Sgt PA
Michael Jr.: b 12-15-1754 d 9-4-1826 m Christina Geiselman CS Sgt PA
Sebastian: b c. 1720-5 d p. 1785 m Barbara Degan PS PA
Stephen: b c. 1753 d p. 1790 m Maria Margaret Katzemayer Pvt PA

HASSON,
Hugh: b 1744 d 1815 m Elizabeth McClair Pvt PA

HASTINGS,
Abijah: b 5-9-1730 d 2-24-1826 m Martha Ingraham Ens MA ★
Amos: b 2-3-1758 d 7-28-1828 m Elizabeth Wiley Pvt MA
Andrew: b a. 1750 d p. 1790 m Sarah — Pvt PS NH
Asa: 12-28-1751 d 1836 m Molly Lowell PS NH
Benjamin: b 12-7-1728 d 1-21-1806 m Mary Porter Lt MA
Benjamin: b 1763 d 11-9-1845 m Experience Ball Pvt MA
Charles: b 11-26-1760 d 11-28-1850 m Anna Woods Capt MA
Daniel: b 7-5-1732 d 9- -1807 m Priscilla Keyes Pvt MA
Daniel: b 8-23-1734 d 1815 m Submit Jordan Pvt VT
Eliphalet: b 10-10-1734 d 11-16-1824 m Susan Fiske Ens MA ★
Enoch: b c. 1728 d 1-6-1812 m Sally Anderson Capt PA
Henry: b 9-3-1758 d 7-2-1803 m Abigail Hawes Pvt MA
Henry Sr.: b c 1727/28 d 5-7-1812 m Elizabeth — Sol NC
Isaac: b 12-26-1755 d 7-2-1831 m Sarah Stearns Pvt MA
James: b 10-6-1745 d p.1785 m Mary Perry Pvt MA
James: b c. 1758-60 d 1822 m Hannah Crabtree Sol NC
John: b 9-24-1743 d 5- -1829 m Mehetabel Berry Capt MA
John: b 3-23-1754 d 2-16-1839 m Lydia Dana Capt MA
John: b 8-27-1738 d 9-28-1802 m Elizabeth Howe 2Lt MA
John: b1-10-1738 d 12-6-1811 m Content Little PS MA
John: b 1-23-1717/8 d 11-24-1794 m (1)Rebecca Bailey (2)Mary Amy PS MA
John: b 10-5-1744 d p. 1781 m Submit Russell Pvt MA
John: b 2- -1741 d 3-1-1823 m Sarah White Pvt PA
John: b 1748 d 1797 m Sarah Hubler Pvt PA
Jonathan: b 7-10-1738 d 12-28-1804 m (1)Esther Smead (2)Abigail Smith 1Sgt MA
Jonathan: b 10-23-1752 d 10-3-1822 m Hannah Shaw Cpl MA
Joseph: b 6-13-1711 d 12-10-1787 m Zerviah Crocker PS CT
Joseph: b 1-25-1753 d 3-7-1825 m Rebecca Amey Pvt NH
Joseph: b 11-25-1757 d 1-30-1816 m Susannah Holloway PS NC
Josiah:b 2-28-1728 d 8-10-1802 m Lydia Ball Pvt MA
Josiah: bpt 8-27-1727 d 12-14-1810 m Mary Hartwell Ens NH
Matthew: b 9-18-1718 d 1790/1 m Mary — CS ME
Nathaniel, Jr.: b 1738 d 1820 m Elizabeth Goodnow Pvt MA
Nathaniel, Jr.: b 5-28-1745 d 9-16-1847 m Jemima Bennett Pvt MA
Nevenson: b 6-5-1756 d 8-13-1835 m (1)Experience Wright (2)Lucretia Worthington Sgt MA
Oliver: b 11-23-1755 d 2-2-1826 m Dorothy Cary Pvt MA
Peter: b 1738 d 1823 m Rachel Sloan Sgt PA
Robert: b 1-20-1738 d 1790 m Patience Colby Pvt MA
Roswell: b 1-8-1756 d 2-25-1825 m Lucy Sumner Pvt CT
Samuel: b 1735 d 9-9-1823 m Anna Bigelow Lt MA
Samuel, Sr.: b 1-30-1721 d 2-8-1820 m Lydia Tidd CS PS MA
Samuel, Jr.: b 7-11-1757 d 1-8-1834 m Lydia Nelson Pvt MA ★
Samuel: b 2-22-1750 d 12-20-1834 m (1)Nancy Lush (2)Frances Lamb PS MA
Seth: b 12-6-1745 d 4-29-1830 m Eunice Parmele Dr CT
Silas: b 1746 d — m Hannah Reed Pvt MA
Simon: b 3-28-1735 d 8-15-1785 m Sarah Coolidge Pvt MA
Sylvanus: b 3-23-1721 d 1-12-1806 m Jemima Willard Pvt NH
Theophilus: b 12-25-1764 d 10-31-1842 m Betsy Prince Ames Pvt MA ★
Thomas: b 1-28-1721 d 1-22-1787 m Mary Belden Lt MA
Timothy: b 1763 d 6-14-1849 m (1)Susan Sawyer (2)Hannah Abels Pvt MA

HASTY,
David: b 1762 d 10-8-1834 m Susannah Jordan Pvt ME ★
John: b 1753 d 4-19-1826 m Rebecca Mordock Pvt PA ★
Joseph: b 1738 d 8- -1805 m Abigail Warren Pvt MA
Nathaniel: bpt 3-23-1746 d p. 1792 m Sally Beeman Pvt MA
Robert: b 1-1-1757 d 12-19-1821 m Margaret Patterson Sgt MA
Samuel: b 1743 d 1-3-1835 m (1)Lucy Warren (2)Anagail Wadline Sgt NH MA ★
Wm.: b — d c. 1809 m Jemima — Sol GA

HASWELL,
Anthony: b 4-6-1756 d 5-26-1816 m (1)Lydia Baldwin (2)Mrs Elizabeth Rice Sol PS MA

HATCH,
Abel: b 3-29-1752 d 5-16-1814 m Fear Weeks Pvt MA
Abraham: bpt 3-18-1744 d p. 1786 m Olive Penny Pvt MA

Alexander: b 11-15-1764 d p. 11-21-1845 m Rhody Snipes Pvt VA ★
Anthony Eames: b 4-18-1753 d 9-11-1842 m Bethia Rogers Sgt MA
Asa: b 1-30-1757 d 12-25-1798 m (1)Rebecca Crockett (2)Jane McIntosh Pvt MA
Asa: b 1760 d 1840 m Sara Wilder Pvt NH
Asa: b 1741 d 1813 m Lucy Warner Pvt VT
Asa: b 8-15-1759 d 4-28-1847 m (1)Roxanna Delano (2)Jane Black (3)Ruhamah Na Smith Pvt CT NH ★
Benjamin: b 4-22-1722 d 1-4-1796 m Jerusha Phillips Sgt MA
Benjamin: b 4-7-1755 d 1-9-1854 m Christina Price Pvt Arfr NY ★
Benjamin: b 12-16-1748 d 10-3-1821 m Ruby Thatcher Pvt VT
Bogardus: b 7-3-1761 d 5-24-1836 m Deborah Gray Pvt MA
Charles: b 1-18-1755 d 10-13-1828 m Joanna Winslow Pvt MA
Charles Ozias: b 4-12-1763 d p. 1790 m Esther Palmer Pvt Fif MA
Dan: b 12-29-1757 d 2-20-1825 m Lucy Jones Sgt CT
David: b 11-10-1725 d 1778 m (1)Mary (Mercy) Tobey (2)Elizabeth Fuller Pvt MA
Ebenezer: b 1740 d 6-26-1826 m (1)Elizabeth Hatch (2)Rebecca — (3)Hannah Strong Pvt CT
Ebenezer: b 7-28-1766 d a. 1852 m Eunice — Pvt NY
Ede: b 9-20-1761 d 12-6-1848 m Eunice Chapman Pvt Drm CT
Edmund: b 1708 d p. 1778 m Lucy Richards PS NC
Eleazer: b 11-19-1744 d 11-26-1809 m (1)Thankful Lathrop (2)Mary Hyde Pvt CT
Elijah: b 4-7-1730 d 1809 m Keziah Barrows Sgt MA
Elisha: b 4-6-1743 d 9-15-1843 m (1)Elizabeth Howland (2)Rebecca (Whitehouse) Hilton (3)Nancy Wellman 1Lt MA
Elnathan: b c. 1745 d 1803 m (1)Silence Hungerford (2)Mrs Anna Prentice Champlain Sgt CT
Gilbert: b 8-14-1764 d 2-22-1835 m (1)Sally Nichols (2)Martha Royse Pvt CT ★
Heman: b 6-14-1760 d 12-26-1843 m (1)Mary Jane Baker (2)Voadicia Tucker Pvt CT ★
Isaac: b 1760 d 1830 m Mary — Pvt NH
Israel: b 9-15-1754 d 5-19-1837 m Lois Holmes Pvt MA
Jabez: b 2-17-1737 d 7-16-1802 m Deborah Hewes Col DepQMGen MA
James: b 2-22-1728/9 d 2-11-1821 m (1)Mary Moore (2)Sarah Cushing Capt MA
Jeremiah: b 9-25-1766 d 5-23-1850/1 m Elizabeth Haight Mus MA ★
Jethro: b 9-17-1722 d 9-29-1817 m Martha Clark Maj CT
Joel: b 8-29-1764 d 3-26-1855 m Ruth Gray Pvt NY
John: b 12-8-1760 d 6-16-1849 m (1)Anna Wadhams (2)Elizabeth Wadhams (3)Polly Straight Pvt CT ★
John: bpt 2-23-1728/9 d p. 6- -1793 m Bathsheba Goodale Pvt MA
John: b 5-4-1761 d 7-26-1839 m Martha Bassett Sol NY
John Jr.: b 6-8-1762 d 1852 m Waitsell Tracy Ensworth Pvt VT
John Sr.: b 6-9-1727 d 4-24-1806 m Sarah Richards Pvt VT
Jonathan: b 5-26-1739 d 11-28-1819 m Lucy Cole Lt MA
Jonathan: b 1741 d 7-28-1796 m Anna Davis Pvt MA
Jonathan: b 12-17-1743 d — m Mary Sears Pvt MA
Jonathan: bpt 6-2-1745 d 1838 m Laruhama Maxwell Pvt MA
Joseph: b 8-15-1718 d 3-6-1802 m Sarah Stearns Sgt & PS NH
Joseph: b 4-13-1750 d 5-7-1823 m Sarah Parks Pvt CT
Joseph: b 3-14-1750 d 6-3-1834 m Mercy Davis Sgt MA
Joseph: b c. 1762 d 1850 m Rose Landers Pvt MA
Joseph: b 5-28-1754 d 1796 m Phebe (Tilden) Lewis Pvt MA
Joseph: b 3-8-1734 d 10-17-1785 m (1)Mehitable Johnson (2)Mary Hamblin PS MA
Joseph: b 12-2-1762 d 1819 m Anne Blackledge Sol NC
Joseph: b 5-13-1738 d 11-12-1811 m (1)Elizabeth Brown (2)Harriet Freeman Capt VT
Joshua: b p. 1735 d 7-7-1777 m Susanna Heath Pvt MA
Josiah: b 7-27-1754 d 10-6-1834 m Elizabeth Conant PS CT ★
Josiah: b 1758 d 1-14-1837 m Mary Cook Sgt NH ★
Lemuel: b 2-29-1735 d 1827 m Temperance (Hatch) Sol NY
Lemuel: b c. 1730 d p. 11-17-1776 m Mary Fonville PS LCol NC
Lewis: b 12-30-1760 d 12-3-1847 m (1)Mary Davis (2)Parnell Poole Cpl MA
Matthew: b 5-14-1735 d 5-2-1804 m Freelove Sherman Pvt MA
Moses: b 3-15-1760 d 12-21-1837 m Abigail Loveland Drm CT
Nailer: bpt 2-21-1731 d 7-14-1804 m (1)Abigail Smalley (2)Martha Atkins Capt MA
Nathan Jr.: b 1740 d 11-9-1828 m Betsy Hungerford Pvt CT
Nathan: b 11-16-1757 d 11-10-1847 m Jerusha Fisher Pvt MA
Nathan: b 1757 d 6-1-1841 m Hannah Marcy Pvt NH ★
Nathaniel: b 7-1-1726 d 8-8-1776 m Achsah Parmelee Pvt MA
Oliver: b 2-2-1755 d 11-20-1839 m (1)Tamar Gillett (2)Rebecca Hatch (3)Phebe Perry Mstr Sgt NY W★
Phillips: b 1757 d 1-4-1848 m Sarah Perkins PS Pvt MA ★
Reuben: b 3-3-1741/2 d 8-4-1811 m Prudence Benton CS CT
Reuben: b 10-7-1743 d 1-15-1818 m Eunice Denison Pvt VT
Robert: bpt 8-14-1757 d 2-6-1814 m Mary Manning Pvt MA
Samuel: b 11-15-1757 d p. 9-4-1840 m Hannah Landers Pvt MA ★
Samuel: b 6-6-1720 d 4-30-1797 m Mrs Hannah Sweet Sol NY
Samuel: b 7-5-1764 d 8-16-1820 m Elizabeth Reed Pvt NY
Seth Sr.: b 1728 d 8-12-1799 m Mary Turner PS MA
Seth Jr.: b 8-25-1755 d 5-14-1836 m Molla Hatch Sgt MA
Simeon: b 1755 d 10-5-1802 m Jemima Pease Pvt MA
Solomon: b 1761 d 1-10-1838 m Huldah Andrews Pvt MA
Stephen: b 3-16-1754 d 7- -1835 m Tabitha Low Pvt MA
Sylvanus: b c. 1745 d p. 7-13-1818 m (1)Sylvina Bodfish (2)Anna Turner Pvt MA

Timothy: b 1757 d 6-10-1838 m (1)Lucretia Rockwell (2)Lucy
    Bassett (3)Lucinda Martyn Danford Sol CT ★
Timothy: b 12-12-1758 d 1847 m Ruth Welles Pvt CT
Timothy: b 6-22-1728 d 1-21-1810 m Eunice Beardsley Pvt CT
Walter: b 6-28-1751 d p. 1787 m Deborah Cushing 2Lt MA
Walter: b 10-15-1758 d 1841 m Eunice Kingman Sgt MA ★
Zaccheus: b 1749 d 4-23-1833 m (1)Mary Glidden (2)Persis Dunbar
    (3)Mary Hawks Lt MA W★
Zephaniah: b c. 1730 d 3-7-1807 m Esther Dickinson PS CT

HATCHER,
Benjamin: b a. 1759 d p. 5-13-1800 m Elizabeth — PS NC
Benjamin: b c. 1740 d 11 or 12-1781 m Lucy — Capt PS SC W★
Frederick: b 1734 d 1783 m Sarah Woodson PS VA
Henry: b 5-7-1756 d 7-19-1836 m Nancy Haskins Pvt VA ★
Jeremiah: b 10-3-1731 d 6-25-1804 m Edith Logwood PS VA
John: b 7-15-1750 d 4-20-1835 m Mary Brady Sol GA
John Sr.: b c. 1760 d 12-12-1825 m Christian Crusoe Pvt SC
John: b 1756 d 7-21-1837 m Nancy Gentry 1Lt VA ★
Josiah: b 1761 d 6-24-1847 m Lavenia Clay Pvt GA
Seth: b 1759 d 1843 m (2)Elizabeth Ligon Pvt VA
Thomas: b a. 1740 d 1797 m (1)Sarah Porter (2)Lucy Curd Capt VA
Wm.: b 1755 d 1833 m Priscilla Scott Pvt GA
Wm.: b c. 1725 d p. 3-13-1788 m Lucy — PS VA

HATCHESON,
Benjamin: b 9-15-1759 d p. 1799 m Martha — Pvt MD

HATCHETT, (includes HATCHITT)
Abraham: b 2-2-1753 d 4-22-1841 m Mary Farley Pvt VA
Thomas: b 1754 d 9-27-1811 m Phoebe Chaffin Wgm VA
Wm.: b c. 1760 d p. 3-28-1826 m Jane Roberts Sol GA

HATCHMAN,
John: b 1763 d 3-22-1831 m Martha Rumney Pvt PA ★

HATFIELD, (includes HETFIELD)
Aaron: b 9-27-1739 d 4- -1797 m Phebe Terrill 1Lt NJ
Abner: b c. 1747 d 8-17-1784 m Mary Boudinot Pvt NJ
Daniel: b 10-13-1752 d 8-17-1830 m Mary Griffen Pvt NY
Elias: b 3-11-1760 d 5-19-1839 m Ann Lindsey Pvt NJ ★
John: b 5-5-1745 d 8-4-1813 m (1)Sarah Patton (2)Nancy Berryhill
    (3)Elizabeth Cochran Pvt PA
John: b 1746 d a. 3-29-1824 m Mary Magdalena George Pvt PA
Joseph: b 6-19-1756 d 12-29-1815 m Anna Rannels Pvt NJ
Joseph: b c. 1735-40 d 8-29-1832 m (2)Rachael Smith Pvt Sct Spy
    VA ★
Joshua: b 8-6-1746 d 8-8-1820 m (1)Sarah Oakley (2)Hannah
    Oakley (3)Martha Loder Capt NY
Morris: b 4-12-1757 d 9- -1820 m Abigail Clark Pvt NJ
Moses: b 1750 d 10-16-1809 m Hannah DeMoney Pvt NJ
Nathan: b 3-17-1752 d 5-9-1821 m Margaret Schrack Pvt PA
Stephen: b 1759 d 5-19-1824 m Elizabeth Freeborn Pvt Drm NJ
Zophar: b 1760 d 8-28-1837 m Mary — Pvt NJ

HATHAWAY, (includes HATHEWAY, HATHWAY)
Abner: b 2-6-1759 d 10-24-1827 m Abigail Stone Pvt MA
Abraham: b 1747 d 5-13-1831 m Sarah Goble Sol PA
Alfred: b 12-18-1755 d 1-14-1829 m Rebecca Alford Pvt VT
Arthur: b 6-11-1756 d 6-17-1823 m Esther Tobey Cpl MA
Arthur: b 1756 d — m Sarah Gurney Pvt MA
Benoni: b 11-6-1743 d 4-18-1823 m Ruth Ludlum LCol NJ ★
Clement: b 5- -1745 d 9- -1801 m Hannah — Pvt NJ
David: b 10-15-1744 d p. 1781 m (1)Priscilla Hiller (2) Deliverance
    Atwood Pvt MA
Ebenezer: b 7-15-1718 d 6-16-1791 m Wealthy Gilbert Pvt MA
Ebenezer: b 2-25-1757 d 1844 m Mehitable Cowdry Sgt NY
Edward: b 1759 d 1829 m Elanor — Pvt MA
Eleazer: b 8-5-1739 d 8-29-1803 m (1)Alce Pope (2)Ann Pope 2Lt
    MA
Ephraim, Sr.: b 1719 d 1816 m (1)Hannah Talbert (2)Mrs Hannah
    Walker (3)Mrs Ruth Talbot Capt MA
Ephraim, Jr.: b 12-12-1752 d 1809 m (1)Elizabeth Simmons (2)Isabel
    Baker (3)Hannah Andrews Pvt MA
Ephraim, Jr.: b 1757 d 2-15-1836 m Jemima Godfrey OrdlSgt MA ★
Erastus: b 8-27-1760 d 9-21-1844 m Anna Warner Pvt VT ★
Isaac: b 7-29-1729 d 12-25-1798 m Phebe Bailey Adj QM MA
Isaac: b 7-23-1749 d p. 1789 m Judith Hoar Pvt MA
Isaac: b 10-28-1755 d 3-1-1823 m (1)Jemima Comstock (2)Elizabeth
    Richmond Pvt MA
Jacob: b 1727 d 10-5-1793 m Hannah Clarke Pvt MA
James: b 10-23-1737 d 4- -1817 m Abagail Pearce 1Lt MA
Jethro: b 7-31-1720 d 6-15-1803 m Hannah West Pvt MA
Job: b 10-28-1737 d 2-11-1796 m Mary Chase Pvt MA
Job: bpt 11-27-1749 d p. 1786 m Lydia Johnston Pvt NJ
Joel Sr.: b 11-2-1721 d 1789 m Joanna Adams PS CT
Joel Jr.: b c. 1750 d 5-7-1803 m Elizabeth Granger Sol CT
Joel: b 7-12-1762 d 11-9-1838 m Sally Trafton Pvt MA
John: b 8-10-1724 d 6-27-1800 m (1)Elizabeth Eldredge (2)Alles
    King Col MA
John: b 11-2-1754 d 1-16-1842 m Edith Robenson Pvt MA
John Jr.: b 2-27-1760 d 5-1-1823 m Rebecca Wilkinson Pvt MA

John: b 5-17-1733 d 4-19-1786 m Sarah Timberlake Maj VA
Jonathan: b 1738 d 8-26-1814 m (1)Lydia Peck (2)Sarah Pruden
    Pvt NJ
Joseph: b 10-9-1742 d 11-3-1812 m Eunice Winslow Pvt MA
Joseph: b 5-5-1751 d 3-12-1842 m Bathsheba Simmons Pvt MA
Joseph: b 4-24-1752 d 9-30-1834 m Sarah Crapo Pvt MA W★
Joshua: b 1-19-1727 d 5-4-1807 m Mary (Reed) Evans Maj MA
Joshua: b 8-18-1761 d 12-10-1836 m Elizabeth Lord Pvt VT
Lawson: b a. 9-20-1819 m Elizabeth King 2Lt VA
Lazarus: b c. 1749 d 1823-28 m Olive Pratt Pvt MA
Lemuel: b 2-16-1737 d 11- -1815 m Prudence Hoskins Sgt MA
Philip Jr.: b 7-19-1740 d 1-24-1816 m Lucy Valentine Lt MA
Philip: b 2-23-1756 d 6-14-1839 m Abiah Ashley Sgt MA ★
Philip: b 1731 d 9-29-1777 m Catura Fairchild PS NJ
Richard: b 9-28-1750 d — m Sarah Hathaway Pvt MA
Salathiel: b 1769 d p. 1802 m Love (Hathaway) Pvt MA
Savory: b 7-26-1739 p. 1787 m Dorothy Clifton Pvt MA
Seth: b 12-21-1760 d 1-19-1838 m Tryphena Crane Pvt MA W★
Shadrach: b 6-9-1752 d c. 1780/1 m Hannah Chase Pvt MA
Silas Sr.: b 9-2-1721 d 9-8-1790 m Deborah Carlisle Sgt MA
Silas: b 5-29-1754 d p. 1798 m Mary Valentine Pvt MA
Silas: b 10-12-1749 d 2-17-1803 m Prudence Baldwin PS NJ
Simeon: b 6-25-1719 d 4-12-1804 m Deborah Austin PS Lt Adj VT
Simon: b 4-20-1752 d 3-20-1799 m Eunice Wing Pvt MA
Stephen: b 9-4-1745 d 4-29-1819 m Hopestill Pierce Pvt MA
Stephen: b c. 1750 d p. 8-7-1780 m Abigail Smith Pvt MA
Timothy: b 3-27-1756 d 8-31-1849 m Rhoda Clark Pvt MA
Wilber: b 11- -1761 d p. 1801 m Lucy Rice Pvt CT
Wm.: b c. 1747 d p. 1790 m Mary Randall Sgt MA

HATLER,
Michael: b 7-15-1750 d 1843 m (2)Myram Bracken Pvt VA ★

HATMAKER,
Adam: b 1730 d p. 1790 m — Pvt NY

HATTER,
John: b 1750 d p. 12-18-1834 m — Pvt PA

HATTON,
Francis: b c. 1760 d p. 1800 m Elizabeth Jolly Pvt SC
Joseph: b 6-3-1731 d 1791/2 m Mary — PS MD
Reuben: b 1762 d 5-16-1841 m Johanna Bellew OrdlSgt VA ★
Samuel: b 1728 d 1839 m Rosena Queen Sol VA
Wm.: b 1764 d 8-27-1842 m — Kiger Pvt VA ★

HAUENSTEIN,
George: b 1761 d p. 1803 m Rosanna Avey Pvt PA

HAUGHEY,
Thomas: b 7-20-1759 d 4-17-1847 m Violet Clanch Sol VA

HAUGHT,
Peter: b 7-1-1755 d 2-12-1853 m (1)Christeny Yeager (2)Sarah
    Jones Spy Pvt PS VA ★

HAUMAN,
Frederick: b 1740 d 1800 m Sarah — Pvt PA

HAUPT,
Henry: b 7-21-1744 d 1-1-1809 m Maria Catherina Jungst Pvt PS
    PA
John, Jr.: b — d a. 12-14-1812 m Catherine — Sgt PA
Jon' Nicholas: b c. 1722 d 1792 m Anna — PS PA
Valentine: b c. 1745 d c. 1814 m Anna Maria — Lt PA

HAUSHALTER,
George Adam: b 1724 d 1794 m Margaretha Balmer PS MD
George Michael: b 2-20-1753 d p. 1822 m Susanna Hager PS MD
Simon: b c. 1745 d p. 1781 m Elizabeth — PS MD

HAUSKNECHT,
Jacob: b 1745 d 4- -1782 m Anne Catherine Pvt PA

HAVEN, (includes HAVENS)
Amariah Jr.: b 11-6-1757 d 1-1-1807 m Elizabeth Frail Sgt MA
Clark: b 8-31-1742 d 4-6-1821 m Mary Flagg Pvt MA
Constant: b 9- -1734 d 9- -1797 m (1)Rhoda Brown (2)Martha —
    (3)Temperance — Cpl NY
Daniel: b 2-5-1750 d 5-25-1780 m Elizabeth Bostwick Pvt NY
David: b 6-14-1734 d 9-5-1805 m Abigail Prentiss Pvt MA
Elias Sr.: b 6-18-1742 d 4-19-1775 m Jemima Whiting Pvt MA
Ezra: b 12-19-1755 d 10-26-1794 m Mary Glover Pvt MA
Gideon: b 3-10-1734 d 1829 m Comfort Pike 2Lt MA
Isaac: b 10-7-1746 d 12-10-1825 m Fanny Havens Pvt NY
James: b 9-18-1731 d 3-12-1782 m Mehitable Bixby Pvt MA
James: b 2-12-1742 d 3-15-1810 m Elizabeth Bowditch PS NY
Jason: b 1733 d 5-17-1803 m Catherine Dexter PS MA
Jedediah Jr.: b 12-6-1743 d 9-17-1811 m Susannah Vaile Pvt MA
Jesse: b 2-20-1745 d 12-28-1813 m Catherine Marsh PS Lt MA
Jesse: b c. 1753 d 1814 m Content Downard Pvt NJ
John: b 1758 d 4-29-1824 m Mary Saunders Pvt CT ★

HAVEN, contd.

John Sr.: b 5-7-1726 d 7-12-1827 m Susannah Drury PS CS MA
John Jr.: b 10-24-1756 d 11-8-1831 m Martha Death Pvt MA
John: b 6-13-1735 d 4- -1813 m Anne Stone Capt NH
Joseph: b 1698 d 2-27-1776 m Mehitable — PS MA
Joseph: b 2-7-1717/18 d 2-22-1801 m (1)Miriam Bayley (2)Mrs
　Rebecca Newell Chickering PS MA
Noah: b 6-17-1749 d 8-27-1817 m Olive Kingsbury Sgt CS MA
Obadiah: b 1747 d 8-22-1786 m Phoebe — 1Lt PS NY
Peleg: b 1761 d p. 8-15-1832 m Hannah Besse Sgt CT ★
Peter: b 4-14-1762 d 7-26-1841 m Sarah Cadman Pvt NY ★
Samuel: b 1-4-1762 d 9-22-1840 m Deziah Clayes Pvt MA
Samuel: b 8-4-1727 d 3-3-1806 m (1)Mrs Mehetabel Appleton
　(2)Margaret Marshall PS NH
Simon: b c. 1737 d p. 1783 m Ruth — Pvt MA
Thomas: b 1748 d 11-10-1820 m Mary Smith Pvt RI
Wm.: b 6-5-1751 d 6-4-1824 m (1)Lucy Winch (2)Miriam Heminway
　(3)Mrs Lucy (Child) Shepard Pvt MA
Wm.: b 5-4-1759 d 1846 m Rebecca Jacob Sol NH

HAVERSTICK, (includes HABERSTICK)

Michael Sr.: b 1718 d 1793 m Salome — Col PS PA
Michael, Jr.: b 1762 d — m Eve Bender; Almonar PA
Wm.: b 1753 d 1823 m Mary Deshler Lt PA

HAVERSTOCK,

Philip: b 6-12-1749 d 12-19-1831 m Barbara Breber Pvt PA

HAVILAND,

Benjamin: b 5-1-1740 d 12-2-1801 m Mary Haight Sol NY
Isaac Jr.: b 8-21-1755 d 10-10-1843 m Polly Ann Aken Pvt NY
Thomas: b 10-9-1744 d 3-31-1827 m Tamar Miller Pvt NY

HAWES, (includes HAWS)

Benjamin: b 6-11-1731 d 3-10-1813 m Olive Cowell Col MA
Benjamin: b 12-5-1745 d 8-7-1817 m (1)Elizabeth Holbrook (2)Mary
　Sumner Cpl Slr MA
Daniel: b 6-4-1733 d 9-29-1815 m Lois Mann Capt MA
Daniel: b 5-22-1757 d 8-8-1811 m Jemima Cheever Sgt MA
David: b 10-16-1752 d 10-2-1812 m Rebekah Parker Pvt MA
David: b 8-4-1758 d 3-24-1842 m Hannah Batchelder Pvt MA W★
Eli: b 8-19-1748 d 6-17-1825 m Susanna (Easton)Bigelow Pvt MA
Elisha: b 2-5-1747/8 d 1-26-1797 m Sarah Wentworth Sgt MA
Elisha: b 6-1-1750 d 5- -1818 m Margaret Hayden Pvt MA
Ichabod: b 9-18-1720 d 12-18-1777 m (1)Elizabeth Fisher (2)Mrs
　Keziah Mann (3)Mrs Ruth Williams Pvt MA
Isaac: b c. 1719 d p. 11-3-1786 m Elizabeth — CS VA
Jacob: b 5-3-1740 d 8-9-1809 m (1)Elizabeth Hewins (2)Mrs Anne
　Carr Pvt MA
James: b 1-21-1761 d 6-18-1826 m Jemima Farrington Pvt MA
Jesse: b 1768 d 1808 m Anne Pierce Pvt MA
Joel: b 4-12-1757 d 10-15-1839 m (1)Judith Clark (2)Philadelphia
　Thayer Sol MA
John: b 12-24-1748 d 3-9-1836 m Lydia Pratt Cpl MA
John: b c. 10-6-1753 d 10-6-1824 m Mercy Hopkins Pvt Smn MA
John: b 7-27-1715 d 1799 m Sarah Niles Pvt MA
John: b c. 1760-63 d a. 1817 m Hannah Anders Sgt NC
John: b c. 1759 d 11-19-1812 m Catherine Boyer Pvt PA
Jonathan: b 12-28-1742 d p. 1785 m Mary Partridge Pvt PS MA
Joseph: b 3-21-1728 d 2-21-1818 m Hannah Fisher Lt MA
Levi: b 3-29-1750 d p. 1796 m (1)Jerusha Wadsworth (2)Phebe
　Henry Pvt MA
Matthias: b 10-6-1754 d 11-4-1828 m Sarah Payson Pvt Gnr MA
Nathan: b 8-29-1760-2 d 11-7-1845 m Phebe Stevans Pvt NH
Peletiah Sr.: b 1713 d 8-27-1791 m Judith Peck Pvt NY
Samuel Sr.: b 2-7-1727 d 4-1-1794 m (2)Anne Walker PS VA
Samuel: b 1739 d 8-14-1786 m Margaret — CS VA
Seth: b a. 1755 d p. 1789 m Catherine — Pvt NY
Shubael: b 7-7-1737 d 1781 m Elnathan Wrightington Capt MA
Stephen: b 12-13-1757 d 8-17-1799 m Mary Gannett Pvt MA
Thomas: b 11-13-1761 d 2-9-1834 m Bathsheba Moore Pvt Mrnr
　MA ★
Wm.: b 5-19-1753 d 4-21-1804 m Esther Smith Pvt MA

HAWKINS,

Abraham: b 3-26-1760 d 5-10-1849 m (1)Lydia Bucklin (2)Elizabeth
　Perry (3)Mrs Bixby Pvt Spy VT ★
Alexander Sr.: b 6-17-1713 d 5-2-1787 m Tabitha Satterly PS NY
Alexander Jr.: b 5-19-1741 d 4-27-1810 m Miriam (Hawkins)Pvt
　NY
Alexander Smith Henly: b c. 1755 d p. 11-1-1807 m — (2)Nancy
　Powell Cpl MD
Amaziah: b 1-30-1758 d 9-8-1847 m (1)Sally Stearns (2)Thankful
　Hinsdale Pvt CT ★
Benjamin: b 8-14-1755 d 3-3-1819 m Ruth Smith PS NY
Benjamin: b 8-14-1754 d 6-6-1816 m Louvrenia Downes Sol PS NC
Benjamin: b 5-8-1759 d 1-10-1836 m Elizabeth Arnold (Colby) Sgt
　RI ★
Benoni: b 10-15-1762 d c. 1843/4 m Elizabeth — Pvt RI ★
Darius: b 5-29-1759 d 5-28-1849 m Esther — Pvt RI
David: b 8-15-1714 d — m Mary Mills Pvt NY
Dexter: b 3-19-1761 d 4-19-1830 m (1)—Arnold (2)Hipzabah
　Gould Pvt RI

Ebenezer: b 10-20-1762 d 11-22-1852 m (1)Mary Gray (2)Hulda
　Cornish Pvt CT ★
Eleaser Sr.: b 4-16-1716 d 4-24-1791 m Ruth Mills PS NY
Eleaser Jr.: b 4-25-1750 d 4-24-1791 m — PS NY
Eli: b 4-21-1729 d 11-27-1797 m (1)Hannah Botsford (2)Hannah
　(Chatfield)Coe (3)Sarah — PS CT
Elijah: b 2-20-1756 d 4-22-1813 m Rhoda — Ens RI
Ezeriah: b 5-15-1730 d 7-10-1798 m Elsie Rosa Howe Arirette Capt
　NC
Gersham: b c. 1742 d p. 9-25-1815 m (1)Hannah Bridgette (2)Mary
　— Pvt NY
Jacob: b c. — 1753 d 6-30-1839 m (1)Charity Longbottom (2)Huldah
　Corwin PS NY
James: b c. 1763 d 3-2-1819 m Jane — Capt VA
Jeriah: b 1742 d 11-28-1840 m Polly Knight Pvt RI
John: b c. 1730 d 3- -1799 m Elizabeth Jones MM MD
John: b c. 1746 d p. 1792 m Phoebe Lambert Pvt NJ
John: b 5-14-1750 d 1799 m Mary Newton MM PS NY
John: b 1744 d p. 1790 m Sallie Macon Col NC
John: b 12-22-1762 d 7-24-1840 m Rebecca Kester Pvt NC ★
John: b 2-14-1733 d 12-19-1786 m Mary Waller Wilby CS NC
John: b c. 1735 d p. 1800 m (2)Sarah Emerson Capt VT
John: b c. 1750 d 1805 m Alice Corbin Thompson Capt VA
John: b 10- -1750 d p. 9-5-1835 m — Pvt Arfr VA ★
John: b c. 1718 d 5- -1778 m Mary Langford Cmsry VA
John: b 1754 d 1821 m Anna Gabriella Jones (?) Pvt VA
John H.: b 4-7-1744 d 12-30-1820 m Lydia Bunker SgtMaj NH
Jonas: b 8-28-1752 d 4-24-1811 m Ruth Mills Pvt NY
Joseph: b 2-6-1730/1 d p. 7-9-1786 m (1)Sarah Southworth
　(2)Zerviah Howard Pvt MM CT̄
Joseph: b 11-3-1759 d 11-17-1848 m (1)Elizabeth Winslow
　(2)Abigail Evarts Pvt CT ★
Joshua: b 1750-4 d 7-25-1832 m Susan Johnson Pvt VA ★
Josias: b c. 1735 d 10-30-1789 m Ann Waring Col MD
Laban: b c. 1760 d 5-18-1820 m Catharine McGehee Pvt VA W★
Matthew: b c. 1753 d 1820 m Betty — Sol VA
Moses: b 8-9-1761 d 9- -1835 m Salonne Hurlburt Pvt CT ★
Moses: b a. 1750 d 10-4-1777 m Susannah Strother Capt VA
Nathaniel: b 1750 d 10-3-1817 m Rebecca Kent LCol RI
Nathaniel: b 1716 d a. 11-4-1794 m Catherine — CS VA
Nicholas: b c. 1755 d 1833 m — Pvt GA
Philemon Sr.: b 9-28-1717 d 9-10-1801 m Delia Martin PS Col NC
Philemon Jr.: b 12-3-1752 d 1-28-1833 m Lucy Davis Col PS NC
　HEIRS ★
Richard: b 1748 d p. 8-9-1811 m (1)Elizabeth Cox (2)Averilla Durbin
　CS PA
Robert: b 1695 d 11-5-1801 m Lydia Cruchet PS MD
Samuel: b 6-9-1760 d 7-7-1840 m Hannah French Capt CT
Samuel: b 6-7-1721 d 3-15-1810 m Mary Green PS NY
Samuel: b 1762 d 1814 m Christena Worthington Pvt VA
Samuel B.: b 5-18-1735 d 5-6-1836 m Pharaba Spears OrdlSgt
　MA ★
Stephen: b 2-21-1754 d 1-19-1844 m Eunice Potter Pvt RI ★
Thomas: b 1741 d 5-15-1826 m Sarah Hargrove Lt MD
Uriah: b 3-8-1757 d 2-19-1840 m Mary Keith SgtMaj RI ★
Uriah: b c. 1731 d p. 1-23-1809 m (1)Deborah — (2)Elizabeth —
　Sol RI
Wm.: b 3-15-1737 d 9-23-1819 m Sarah Belknap Sgt CT
Wm.: b 1766 d 3-13-1854 m Jane Bayne Pvt VA
Wm. Adrian: b 1-18-1742 d 12-16-1817 m Abigail Keyes Capt NH
Zachariah: b 4- -1715 d c. 1800 m Abigail Jayne PS NY
Zechariah: b 2-8-1717 d 6-27-1806 m (1)Sarah Davis (2)Mary
　Tomlinson (3)Mrs Rachel Perry (4)Lydia (Thomas) Taylor PS CT

HAWKS, (includes HAWK & HAWKES)

Adam: b 12-8-1743 d 10-20-1778 m Hannah Newhall MM Smn
　MA
Daniel: b 10-20-1749 d 5-8-1831 m Rhoda Perham Pvt MA
Eleazer: b 8-25-1747 d 1-1-1827 m Rhoda Kingsley Lt VT
George: b 1738 d 1836 m Elizabeth — Pvt PA
Henry: b — d p. 5-3-1800 m (2)Catharine — PS VA
John: b 7-14-1754 d 5-3-1811 m Rachel Bancroft Pvt MA
Moses: b 5-19-1737 d 6-16-1806 m (2)Rhoda Childs Ens MA
Nathan: b 7-1-1745 d 10-17-1824 m Sarah Hitchings Lt MA
Paul: bpt 11-7-1736 d 10-15-1814 m Lois Wait CS MA
Thomas: b 2-5-1742 d 4-12-1808 m Esther Newhall Sgt MA

HAWLEY,

Aaron: b 1739 d 7-21-1803 m (1)Elizabeth Hawley (2)Sarah
　(Comstock) Pickett (3)Rachel Comstock BgdMaj CT
Abel Jr.: b 10-5-1755 d 4-4-1836 m Elizabeth Peck Pvt CT
Abel: b 5-2-1763 d 3-1-1855 m Sarah Nichols Pvt CT
Abner: b 12-15-1739 d p. 1805 m Margaret — Capt NY
Amos: b 2-14-1755 d 8-19-1825 m Achsah Strong Sol CT
Andrew: b 6-22-1732 d 6-24-1801 m Ann Hard Pvt VT
Benjamin: b 11-18-1730 d 10-26-1815 m Mary Johnson Pvt PA
Caleb: b 4-23-1757 d a. 7-5-1809 m Hannah Battin Pvt PA
Chapman: b 12-5-1759 d p. 1839 m Mary Ludlow Pvt NY ★
Clauson: b 1756 d 8-11-1832 m Sarah Waller Pvt CT
Daniel: b 12-11-1725 d — m Anne Salmon Pvt CT
Daniel: b 9-4-1741 d p. 1787 m Hannah Warner Pvt NY

David: b 4-22-1715 d 1796 m (2)Sarah Judson Sol PS CT
Ebenezer Jr.: b 2-11-1747 d 2-22-1827 m Mehitable Rich Pvt CT
Ebenezer: b 1758 d 1821 m Sarah Ives Pvt CT
Ebenezer: b 1764 d 1-25-1822 m Lucy French Pvt CT W★
Elijah: b 12-30-1744 d 8-11-1825 m Mercy Bennett PS CT
Elijah: b 1-15-1762 d 12-2-1846 m Abigail Wilcoxson Pvt CT
Elisha: b 3-26-1744 d 1-4-1819 m (1)Azuba Russell (2)Hannah (Dean)Sayles QM Lt NY VT
Ezekiel: b 1748 d 9-21-1776 m Elinor Olmstead Sgt CT
Ezekiel: b 9-9-1731 d 2-6-1788 m (1)Ruth Lyon (2)— Morehouse Lt NY
Gad: b 9-9-1746 d 4-5-1836 m Lydia Gillett Pvt CT ★
Gideon: b 1744 d 5-18-1840 m Sarah Curtis Pvt CT
Ichabod: b 11-12-1756 d 3-30-1814 m Huldah Root Pvt CT
Israel: b 6-11-1751 d 1-3-1837 m — Pvt CT ★
James: b 5-8-1760 d 4-14-1836 m (1)Bridget Stanton (2)Martha (Stevens) Waterhouse Pvt CT ★
James: b 7-19-1758 d 6-29-1846 m Parnel Picket Pvt NY
Joseph: b 1763-65 d 9-15-1818 m Phebe Smith Pvt CT
Joseph: b 1749 d 1791 m Anna Lewis Pvt CT
Joseph Chrysostom: b 10-10-1757 d 4- -1845 m Amy Bradley Pvt CT
Joseph Ebenezer: b 10-8-1723 d 3-10-1788 m Hannah Ripbon PS MA
Josiah: b 1731 d 10-22-1791 m Hannah Warner Pvt VT
Lemuel: b 1753 d p. 1797 m Rebecca Tilton Pvt VT
Liverus: b — d 7-16-1819 m Anna Blackman Pvt CT
Moses: b 10-19-1748 d 10-14-1830 m Mary Martin Pvt CT
Robert Sr.: b 6-5-1726 d p. 6-2-1797 m Anna Beach PS CT
Robert Jr.: b 1-20-1762 d 1-5/7-1833 m Mary Elizabeth Nichols Grd Pvt CT ★
Thomas: b 1739 d 11-19-1797m Anna Gregory Sgt CT
Thomas: b 7-29-1759 d 8-6-1850 m Mary Beardsley Pvt CT ★
Thomas: b 2-28-1755/6 d 11-19-1840 m Keziah Scribner Pvt CT ★
Wm.: b 1732 d 4-9-1791 m Mary Glover Pvt CT
Zachariah: b 5-13-1753 d 6-1-1824 m Rebecca Edwards Pvt MA

HAWTHORNE,
Adam: b 1739 d 1810 m (1) — (Montgomery) McMeekin (2)Elizabeth Bradford Pvt SC
Alexander: b 3-17-1756 d 10-1-1827 m Nabby Hathorn Slr MA
Collin: b — d — m Sarah Deane Sol NH
Daniel: b 1731 d 4-18-1796 m Rachel Phelps NCdr MA
James: b c. 1755-60 d a. 10-22-1811 m — Pvt PS SC
John: b 1-19-1744 d 4-1-1815 m Tabitha Gowan SB CT MA
John: b 1-9-1749 d 2-19-1825 m Elizabeth Welling Col NY
John: b c. 1754 d 7-4-1796 m (1)Mary Calvery (2)Elizabeth Rhoads Pvt PA
John: b 1- -1748 d p. 3-4-1834 m Margaret Greene Pvt SC ★
Joseph: b 7-10-1756 d 10-30-1849 m (1) — (2)Frances Ellis Pvt SC ★
Seth: b 11-3-1751 d 3-2-1831 m (1)Sarah Thwing (2)Rebecca — Pvt MA

HAXTON,
Benjamin: b 6-15-1741 d p. 5- -1817 m Mary — Sol NY

HAY,
Adam: b 1736 d 5-18-1818 m Mary Elizabeth Wagener Pvt PA
Alexander: b 1- -1755 d 6-3-1849 m Elizabeth Haggart Pvt NY ★
Ann Hawks: b 8-14-1745 d 4-18-1786 m Martha Smith Col NY
David: b 8-8-1752 d 8- -1834 m Margaret Newell Lt NJ
Hardy: b c. 1740 d p. 1784 m — Pvt SC
Isaac: b 6-16-1751 d 1832 m (2)Mary Hix Pvt NC
John: b 12-15-1737 d 4-10-1815 m Sarah Ring Pvt MA ★
John: b 1733 d 4-11-1810 m (2)Juliana Moul LCol PS PA
John: b 11-16-1766 d 11-7-1846 m Mary Best Pvt PA
Melchoir: b 2-2-1726 d 8-15-1794 m Susanna Brotzman PS Capt PA
Samuel: b 11- -1739 d 11-27-1803 m Mrs Elizabeth (Mallum)Neil LCol PA
Thomas Jr.: b 12-29-1759 d 3-2-1839 m Rebecca Poole Pvt NH
Wm.: b 9-18-1744 d p. 1790 m Pheba Brown Pvt MA
Wm.: b c. 1740 d 2-28-1779 m Betsy Williams PS NY
Wm.: b — d 1812 m Sarah Atkinson LCol PA
Wm.: b 1743 d 11-8-1813 m Sarah Galloway Pvt VA

HAYCOCK, (includes HAECOCK)
David: b c. 1740 d p. 1790 m — Bartoff Capt NY
Jeremiah: b 6-8-1747 d 1-1-1797 m Sarah Morgan Pvt PA
Ralph: b 1732 d a. 9-26-1791 m (1)Martha — (2)Elizabeth — Pvt ME

HAYCRAFT,
Samuel: b 11-19-1752 d 10-15-1823 m Margaret VanMetre Pvt VA ★

HAYDEN,
Aaron: b 5-4-1750 d 8-11-1804 m Sarah Rice Cpl MA
Allen: b 4-9-1753 d 3-10-1837 m Annis Moss Peck Pvt CT
Augustine: b 8-24-1740 d 2-24-1823 m Cynthia Fyler Sgt CT
Benjamin: b 1760 d a. 1853 m Hannah McPike Pvt VA ★
Charles: b 2-14-1764 d 6-14-1842 m Mary Howard Pvt MA

David: b 10-8-1738 d 2-3-1813 m Jemima Ellsworth Cpl CT
Enoch: b 3-21-1734 d 11-11-1813 m Amy Thayer Sgt MA
Ezekiel: b 1734 d p. 8-8-1788 m Sarah — PS VA
Ezra: b 2-27-1758 d 7-3-1819 m Olive Witmore Pvt CT
George: b c. 1730 d p. 1790 m Elizabeth Potter PS MA
Isaac: b 3-12-1748 d 2-19-1827 m Lucy Phelps Pvt CT
Jacob: b 1760-2 d 1849 m Mary — Sol CT
James: b 12-25-1766 d 4-13-1840 m Susannah Gore Pvt Spy VA ★
John: b 11-4-1750 d 1814 m Anna Trumbull Pvt CT
John: b 9-1-1740 d 4-17-1824 m (3)Mrs Rhoda (Daniels)Whitney 2Lt MA
John: b 10-26-1749 d 7-24-1836 m (1)Charity Gard (2)Mary Snyder Pvt NJ ★
John: b — d p. 5-27-1801 m (1)Mary — (2)Lucy Morton PS VA
Joseph: b 12-7-1742 d 5-4-1807 m Mary Hayden PS CS CT
Joseph: b 1725 d 1776 m Lettice Hammond Pvt MA
Jonathan: b c. 1760 d p. 1835 m Lydia Young Pvt MA
Josiah: b 5-15-1734 d 9-2-1818 m Silence Howard Maj MA ★
Josiah: b 3-5-1733 d 12-29-1810 m Ruhamah Thayer Cpl MA
Levi: b 5-28-1747 d 8-24-1821 m (1)Margaret Strong (2)Mrs Mary Kent Sol CT
Moses: b 1754 d 11-9-1809 m Bethoir — Pvt MA
Nathaniel: b 12-14-1738 d 5-17-1795 m Rhoda Lyman Capt CT
Nathaniel: b 7-11-1763 d 10-9-1843 m Alice Peakes Pvt MA ★
Noah: b c. 1755 d 2-25-1829 m Jemima Damon Pvt MA
Oliver: b 1-29-1753 d 3-29-1802 m Keziah Ellsworth Bissell Pvt CT
Peleg: b 1760 d 1829 m Rhoda Jenkins Pvt MA
Richard: b 11-7-1741 d 1829 m Mary Jordan Sgt MA
Robert: b 1-7-1735 d 1822 m Elizabeth French Lt MA
Samuel: b 7-1-1748 d 1-26-1834 m Katherine Palmer Capt MA
Silas: b 2-24-1760 d p. 1793 m Rebecca Morris Pvt MA
Thomas: b 6-14-1745 d 11-28-1817 m Abigail Parsons Lt CT
Uriah: b 10-1-1746 d — m Lydia Eaton Pvt MA
Wm.: b 1743 d 3-24-1817 m Susana Buckman Sol MD
Wm. Sr.: b c. 1722 d 1801 m Anna Stetson Pvt MA
Wm. Jr.: b 11-9-1744 d 6-7-1810 m Mrs Sarah Wade Pvt MA
Wm.: b 1736 d 9-13-1807 m (1)Ann Spear (2)Deborah Noyes Pvt MA W★
Wm.: b 10-5-1727 d 7- -1823 m Lydia Kierstede Sgt VA
Wm.: b a. 1740 d p. 1792 m Ann Ballard PS KY
Zebah: b 1748 d 1784 m Sarah Allen Sgt MA

HAYES, (includes HAYS)
Aaron: b 2-2-1762 d 1-30-1851 m Phoebe Wood Pvt NH ★
Aaron: b 3-3-1727/8 d 1-3-1793 m (1)Abigail Huckings (2)Susannah Keating PS CS NH
Abraham: b 8-9-1758 d 10-18-1851 m Elizabeth Ruscoe Pvt NY ★
Adam: b c. 1745/6 d 3- -1789 m — Pvt PA
Andrew: b 5-29-1737 d 9- -1807 m Mehetable Fox Pvt CT
Andrew: b c. 1726 d 1786 m Margaret Walker Ens VA
Benjamin: b 4-13-1747 d 6-12-1810 m (1)Rosanna Hayes (2)Mrs Martha Hecock Bishop (3)Hannah Fuller Sgt CT
Benjamin: b 7-28-1758 d 11-14-1841 m Alathea — Pvt CT ★
Benjamin: b 3-1-1723 d 4-14-1797 m Abigail Young PS CS NH
Charles: b 1714 d 1780 m Rachel Turner PS MD
Charles: b 8-24-1752 d 2-6-1810 m Mary Campbell Walker Ens VA
Christopher: b 1738 d 1808 m Eve May Apple Col PA
Daniel: b 8-26-1723 d 2-26-1807 m Sarah Plummer PS NH
Daniel: b c. 1760 d a. 8-11-1849 m Priscilla Lewis Pvt NJ
David: b 1732 d 1-28-1811 m Mary Crane Pvt NJ
David: b 2-15-1753 d 1838 m Hannah VanWys Pvt NY
David: b 3- -1732 d 10-17-1812 m Esther Etting PS NY
Dudley: b c. 1760 d 1-13-1844 m (1)Mercy Messenger (2)Beda Dewey Pvt CT ★
Elijah: b 1-15-1740/41 d 11-10-1805 m Elizabeth Chadbourne CS ME
Enoch: b 6-14-1763 d p. 1791 m — Pvt CT
Enoch: b 8-27-1757 d 3-6-1837 m Susanna Knowles Pvt NH ★
Enoch: b 1759 d 1802 m Elizabeth P. Stevens Pvt PA
Ezekiel: b 1748 d 7-21-1834 m Mary Cossit Pvt CT
Ezekiel: b 11-21-1724 d 10-17-1807 m (1)Rebecca Russell (2)Abigail (Hitchcock)Brown PS CT
George: b 11-23-1760 d 3-20-1834 m Ann Hawkins Sol NH ★
George: b 11-23-1760/1 d p. 9-15-1832 m Margaret Gerrish Pvt NH ★
George: b 1760 d 1839 m — Pvt NC ★
George: b 10-1-1753 d 4-26-1835 m Sarah McCannis Ens PA ★
Henry: b 1-27-1756 d 6-27-1832 m Catherine Bellinger Pvt NY
Henry: b — d 7-7-1806 m (1)Elizabeth Scott (2)Jane Todd Sol PA
Hezekiah: b 2-2-1719 d 2-4'1791 m Margaret Cate PS NH
Hugh: b 2-25-1739 d 6-6-1786 m Elizabeth Diggs Lt VA
Ichabod: b 12-13-1718 d 10-15-1794 m Elizabeth Hayes PS NH
Ichabod: b 1-17-1744 d 2-21-1817 m (1)Tamsen (Hayes) (2)Mrs Mehitable (Libby) Pray PS NH
Isaac: b 9-20-1733 d 9-26-1805 m Anne Thatcher Pvt CT
Isaac: b 11-13-1736 d 4-29-1815 m Deborah Hays Sol PA
Jacob: b 8-5-1757 d 12-21-1848 m Jane Grey Pvt MA
James: b 1752 d 6-6-1819 m Sarah Long 2Lt VA
James: b 1748 d 5- -1823 m Elizabeth Ham Pvt PS NH
James: b 2-18-1740 d 2-7-1823 m (1)Elizabeth Smith (2)Hannah Minewell Pvt NY
James: b 2-29-1740 d 2-14-1817 m Sarah Brown Lt PA
James: b 2-3-1764 d 8-5-1841 m Lititia Rankin Sol PA

HAYES, contd.
James: b 1760 d 1832 m Polly Miles Pvt SC
James: b c. 1763 d 12-11-1812 m Mary Bustard Pvt VA
Jeremiah Sr.: b c. 1720 d 1783 m Sarah — PS MD
Joel: b 10-2-1728 d 5-27-1800 m Rebecca Post Lt CT
John: b 1759 d 1820 m Susanna Howard Ens MD
John: b 2-26-1740 d 1-7-1821 m Hannah Waldron PS NH
John: b 2-7-1766 d 12-18-1830 m Olive Hine Pvt NY★
John: b 1728 d 11-3-1796 m (1)Barbara King (2)Jane Walker Capt PS PA
John: b 1726 d 12-26-1801 m (2)Jean — Lt PA
John: b 1764 d p. 1812 m Anne Nancy Berry Pvt SC
John: b 11-2-1751 d 6-17-1839 m Mary — Pvt PS VA ★
John: b 3-20-1760 d p. 1819 m Mary Regan Pvt VA
Jonathan Jr.: b 1744 d 3-8-1791 m Anna Noble Pvt MA
Joseph: b 6-29-1756 d 9-29-1843 m (1)Sarah Bradley (2)Grissel Burr Pvt Smn CT ★
Joseph: b 10-18-1760 d 6- -1851 m (1)Deborah Wimmer (2)Martha Thomas Pvt MD
Joseph: b 12-16-1732 d 1812 m Johanna Passmore Capt PA
Joseph: b — d 1793 m Sarah Hays Pvt VA
Joshua: b 12-9-1765 d 2-22-1826 m (1)Deborah Brown (2)Eleanor — Pvt NH
Judah: b 1-3-1730/1 d — m Honora Lamson Pvt CT
Levi: b 10-1-1752 d p. 7-16-1825 m Eleanor Harris Sol MD
Michael: b 1-17-1741 d 2-3-1829 m Nancy — Pvt PA
Moses: b 3-9-1750 d — m (2)Mrs Lucy (Brooker)Noble Pvt MA
Moses: b 1760 d 2-24-1837 m Jemima Paterson Pvt Grd Tms PS NJ
Moses: b 1748 d 11-18-1824 m Rachel Elizabeth — Pvt PA
Moses: bpt 1750 d p. 1794 m (1)Mary — (2)Mrs McCarty Pvt PA
Nathaniel: b 4-1-1744 d 5-28-1810 m Rachel Webb Capt DE
Nathaniel: b 11-17-1757 d 1-7-1832 m Elizabeth Bickford Pvt NH
Obadiah: b 6-14-1754 d 3-23-1817 m Ohinoam Holcomb Pvt CT W★
Oliver: b 3-4-1756 d 9-11-1847 m Miriam Yokum Pvt CT ★
Patrick Jr.: b 4- -1734 d 4-16-1813 m Nancy McAllister Capt PA
Pliny: b c. 1757 d 3-8-1841 m (2)Ann Clinger Pvt MA
Richard: b 5-12-1753 d 10-6-1826 m Lydia Watson Pvt NH
Richard: b c. 1710-20 d p. 1801 m Mary Venable PS VA
Rpbert: b 2-2-1733 d 6-30-1809 m Margaret Wray 1Lt PA
Robert: b 1760 d 4-12-1823 m Nancy Plumer Pvt PA
Robert: b — d c. 9-9-1794 m — Pvt PA
Robert: b a. 1760 d p. 1788 m Jane Donelson Lt NC
Robert: b 1742 d 7- -1819 m Allison Lt PA
Rutherford: b 7-29-1756 d 9-25-1836 m Chloe Smith Ens CT
Samuel: b 3-26-1730 d 12-25-1801 m Rosanna Holcombe Capt CT
Samuel: b 3-12-1729/30 d 4-22-1776 m Sarah Cate Capt PS NH
Samuel: b 1728 d 6-2-1811 m Sarah Bruen Maj NJ
Samuel: b c. 1735 d p. 1785 m Elizabeth Job Pvt PA
Seth: b 6-2-1753 d 1-3-1839 m Mehetabel Topping Sgt CT
Solomon: b 1755 d 1816 m Mary Craig 2Lt PA
Solomon: b 5-27-1755 d 1- -1807 m Lois Keating Pvt NH
Thomas: b 7-12-1762 d 2-18-1831 m — Cpl CT
Thomas: b 5-10-1762 d 8-25-1847 m Rebecca Padgett Pvt MD ★
Thomas: b 5- -1734 d 3-12-1777 m Sarah Ayres Lt NJ
Thomas: b c. 1735 d 1789 m Chloe — 2Lt VA
Titus: b 2-5-1746 d 6-20-1811 m Deborah Beckwith Pvt CT
Wentworth: b 1-27-1727/8 d 1-14-1802 m (1)Mary Main (2)Susannah (Burnham) Roberts PS NH
Wm.3d.: b 1750 d 1800 m Eleanor Boughton Cpl CT
Wm.: bc. 1730 d 1777 m Mary Plumer Pvt NH
Wm.: b 1715 d 1794 m Elizabeth Hawkins Pvt PA
Wm.: b 1742 d 8-26-1804 m Jean Taylor Pvt PA
Wm.: b 1754 d 12-13-1804 m Susanna Boone Capt KY
Wm.: b c. 1758 d 3-9-1838 m Nancy — Pvt VA ★
Zebedee: b 1757 d 11-9-1832 m (1)Chloe Fisher (2)Mehitable Knowlton Pvt Gnr MA ★

HAYFORD,
Ebenezer: b 6-18-1751 d 9-22-1839 m (1)Priscilla Booth (2)Abigail Caswell Cpl MA
Ira: b 11-10-1762 d 2-2-1833 m Lydia Munson FifMaj NY ★
John: b 4-17-1743 d 9-5-1821 m Elizabeth Riley Pvt CT
John: b 3-2-1730 d p. 1790 m Sarah Conant Pvt MA
Nathaniel: b 9-11-1755 d 4-25-1851 m Philena Gannett Pvt NH ★
Samuel: b 8-8-1744 d 5-3-1783 m (1)Rebecca Freeman Waterman (2)Diadama Bishop (3)Bathsheba Tinkham Pvt MA
Wm., Sr.: b 5-16-1740 d 10-12-1801 m Betsey Bonney Pvt MA
Wm.: b 4-18-1763 d 9-23-1844 m Philena French Pvt MA

HAYGOOD,
Benjamin: b 6-30-1758 d 6-4-1841 m Mary Stewart Pvt NC

HAYHURST,
John: b 1728/29 d 3-5-1811 m Mary Wiggins PS PA

HAYMAKER,
Adam: b 1717 d p. 8-29-1783 m Ann Anna — Pvt PA
David: b c. 1752 d p. 1810 m (1)Ann Herr (2)Margaret Stout Pvt PA

HAYMOND,
Calder: b 1733 d 3-7-1815 m (1)Eleanor Owen (2)Catharine — Pvt VA
Edward: b 6-6-1755 d 6-14-1820 m Sarah Woodfin Pvt PA VA ★

Henry: b 1758 d 1835 m Mary Goodall 1Lt GA
Jabez: b 6-9-1741 d 5-2-1807 m Priscilla Delano Pvt MA
Wm.: b 2-22-1740 d 9-21-1823 m Ann Wayne NCapt PA
Wm.: b 1-4-1740 d 11-12-1821 m (1)Cassandra Clelland (2)Mary Pettyjohn Powers Maj VA

HAYNES, (includes HAIN, HAINES, & HAINS)
Aaron, Sr.: b 12-25-1727 d 1-23-1783 m (1)Rebecca Willis (2)Ruth Woods Capt MA
Aaron: b 12-6-1745 d 3-25-1827 m Mary Armstrong Sgt VT
Aaron, Jr.: b 4-19-1759 d 2-16-1842 m (1)Mary Johnson (2)Desire Homer Sgt MA
Abel: b c. 1758 d 11-10-1828 m Abigail Robinson Pvt MA W★
Asa: b 1739 d p. 1794 m Deborah Hunt 2Lt NY
Benjamin: b 3-4-1733 d 1780 m Martha Morgan Pvt MA
Benjamin: b 3-18-1725 d p. 9- -1800 m (1)Elizabeth Roberts (2)Margaret Balanger (3)Sarah Butcher Matr NJ
Benjamin: b 1741 d 7-22-1822 m Sophia Smith Pvt NY ★
Caleb: b 10-22-1736 d 7-26-1823 m Sophia (Billings)Stoddard 1Lt NY
Charles: b 9-7-1736 d 10-22-1806 m Elizabeth Winn Pvt MA
Christopher: b 6-8-1760 d 9-9-1846 m Tallitha — Pvt VA★
Cotton: b 10-28-1745 d 4-25-1823 m Martha Nudd PS NH
Daniel: b 12-30-1759 d 3-3-1846 m Hannah Webber Pvt MA
Daniel: b 5-19-1757 d 10-23-1824 m (1)Mary — (2)Hannah Marion Davies Pvt VA
David: b 9-29-1756 d 10-24-1837 m Eunice King Grd NY
David: b 4-13-1762 d 4-2-1844 m Margaret Ewart Pvt PA ★
Ebenezer: b c. 1751 d p. 1780 m Mary Gammage Pvt MA
Elisha: b 1762 d 1834 m (1)Betsy Bartlett (2)Mary Johnson Pvt NH
Ezekiel: b 3-25-1721 d 1781 m Abigail Kemble PS VA
Frederic: b 1-18-1756 d 11-23-1812 m Catharine Hawk PS PA
Frederick: b c. 1730 d p. 1-27-1807 m (1)Catrina Decker (2)Temperance Decker Pvt NY
Frederick: b 9-17-1750 d p. 8-5-1834 m Anna Maria Eckert Ens PS PA
George: b 5-14-1746 d 12-31-1803 m (1)Magdalena Ruth (2)Magdalena Ruth Pvt PA
George: b 12-1-1757 d p. 1829 m Margaret McInturff Pvt VA ★
Henry: b 12-8-1759 d 2-1-1842 m Elizabeth Ort Pvt PA
Henry: b c. 1727 d 2-5-1795 m Anna Christina — PS PA
Henry: b 3-12-1763 d 12-2-1784 m Mary Smith PS VA
Isaac: b — d p. 1790 m Catherine Diffenbaugh Pvt PA
Isaac: b 9-23-1745 d 8-4-1781 m Elizabeth Hutson Col SC
Israel: b 12-11-1728 d 8-24-1808 m Sarah Darby Pvt MA
Jacob: b 7-27-1758 d 3-28-1837 m Ruth Haines Pvt NH
Jacob: b 3-4-1749 d 3-4-1832 m Nancy Reddick Lt NY
James: b 10-12-1767 d 1867 m Jemima Callaway Pvt DE
James: b 5-25-1721 d p. 1777 m Eleanor Lee Pvt MA
James: b 7-8-1757 d p. 1797 m Mary Brown Pvt MA
James: b 1723 d 6-7-1789 m Ann Huggins PS NC
Jason: b c. 1741 d 8-12-1816 m Lydia Conant Cpl MA
Job: b 8-10-1756 d 5-28-1807 m ( )Margaret Smith ( )Margaret W. Thomas Pvt NJ
Johan Jacob: b 10-6-1724 d 9-16-1804 m Anna Rickert Pvt NY
John: b 9-15-1742 d 2-2-1783 m — Pvt MD
John, Jr.: b 10-6-1738 d 1810 m Mary Dudley PS NH
John, Jr.: b c. 1735 d p. 1803 m Mary Shreve Pvt NJ
John: b — d — m Rachel Austin Pvt NJ
John: b — d 10- -1819 m (1)— (2)Hannah Haight Pvt NY
John: b 1730 d 1805 m Anna Eliza Snyder Pvt NY
John: b 1758 d p. 1850 m Mary Stice Pvt NC
John: b 11-24-1759 d 10-25-1838 m Margaret Andrews Pvt NC ★
John: b 8-12-1740 d 9-18-1815 m Esther Guschwa Ens PA
John: b 7-12-1735 d 1-3-1815 m Anna Regina Schuster Pvt PA
John: b 1-21-1747 d 5-21-1800 m Anna Margaret Guschwa Pvt PA
John: b 1755 d 1786 m Sarah Simmons Cpl VA
John: b 1751 d 1827 m Sarah — Pvt VA
John: b 10-15-1756 d p. 1810 m Nancy Shields Pvt VA
John, Sr.: b 1731 d 1807 m — PS VA
John George: b 1-15-1757 d 5-21-1832 m Catharine Miller Pvt PA
Jonas: b 4-26-1759 d 12-21-1835 m Hannah Cutler Sgt MA
Jonas: b 1731 d 1-11-1814 m Mary (Haynes)Pvt MA
Jonathan: b 4-23-1759 d 2-26-1833 m Polly Corliss Pvt MA
Jonathan, Sr.: b ? -25-1712 d 4-28-1786 m (1)Elizabeth Kingsbury (2)Ruth Page Pvt VT
Jonathan, Jr.: b 7-16-1753 d 5-13-1813 m Lydia Haskins Pvt VT
Joseph: b 5-30-1742 d — m Hannah Stratton Pvt MA
Joseph, Sr.: b 2-15-1715 d 12-26-1801 m Elizabeth Clement PS MA
Joseph: b 10-17-1745 d 1- -1828 m Betsey Hoitt Cpl NH
Joseph, Jr.: b 3-25-1743 d 1810 m Anna Heath 1Lt NH
Joseph: b 10-15-1749 d 6-3-1845 m — Pvt NC ★
Joseph: b 8-3-1742 d 8-3-1815 m (1)— (2)Jeanette Young Capt VA
Joshua: b 12-31-1731 d 12-29-1814 m Susannah Puffer Lt MA
Joshua: b 2-26-1756 d 7-21-1813 m Hannah Rich Pvt PA
Josiah: b 1696 d 4-19-1775 m Persis Knight Pvt MA
Josiah: b 8-13-1748 d p. 1806 m Rebecca Austin PS NJ
Josiah: b c. 1739 d p. 11-24-1789 m (1)Abigail Ridgway (2)Mary — CS NJ
Josiah: b 1733 d 2-6-1822 m (1)Mary Cook (2)Jane — (3)Ann — Pvt PA
Marcus: b 9-17-1719-23 d 9-19-1797 m Anna Elizabeth Kerber PS NC

Matthias: b 8-5-1750 d 1796 m Molly Cammet 2Cpl MA
Matthias: b 10-11-1744 d 8-22-1818 m Sarah Hall Pvt NH
Matthias: b 1-3-1750 d 3-20-1838 m Mary Edgerly PS NH
Moses: b *c.* 1743 d 1829 m Sarah — Sol GA
Moses: b 2-5-1741/42 d *p.* 1784 m Dorcas Jones Pvt MA
Nathan: b 1- -1731 d 7-14-1790 m (1)Rebecca Ballinger (2)Mrs.
   Dorcas Davis PS NJ
Nathan: b 7-14-1754 d 8-29-1824 m Mary McPherson PS VA
Nathaniel: b 8-4-1748 d *p.* 1797 m Comfort — PS NH
Nicholas: b 1735 d 1797 m Elizabeth — PS VA
Parmenas: b 7-1-1742 d 3-1-1813 m (1)Elizabeth Baber (2)Delia
   Greer Capt VA
Perley: b 4-7-1756 d 10-21-1833 m Jane Hopkins Drm MA
Peter: b 9-2-1743 d 1801 m Anna Russell Pvt MA
Peter: b 5-28-1760 d 3-5-1832 m Martha Lewis Pvt NJ
Peter: b 1754 d 1843/44 m Margaret Willis Pvt VA ★
Richard: b 9-19-1763 d 2-2-1850 m Margaret Majors Pvt VA ★
Robert: b 10-17-1741 d 7-11-1821 m Rachael Venicomb PS NJ
Samuel: b 2-25-1737 d 12-29-1821 m Hannah Seavey Sol MA
Samuel: b 11-29-1738 d 5-6-1825 m Polly Hammond Pvt MA
Samuel: b 8-26-1747 d 10-29-1838 m Hannah Johnson Sgt MA
Samuel: b 3-1-1763 d 12-19-1800 m Rachael Stanton Pvt VT
Simeon: b 5-9-1752 d 5-8-1828 m Eunice Gilman Pvt NH
Simeon: b 2-22-1759 d 10-12-1846 m Welthea Spencer Pvt NH ★
Stephen: b 2-11-1733 d 7-1-1810 m Joanna Sale Pvt NJ
Stephen: b 5-23-1759 d 2-3-1807 m Hannah Carter Pvt NH
Thomas: b 7-3-1754 d 4-18-1817 m Anne Moorers Pvt MA
Thomas: b 1735 d 1781 m Lucretia Pettit Pvt NJ
Thomas: b 3-19-1748 d 10-14-1823 m Frances Stith PS NC
Thomas: b *c.* 1750 d *p.* 7-22-1799 m Mary — Sol PA
Thomas: b 7- -1735 d 11-26-1789 m Miriam Marsh Pvt VT
Valentine: b 3-16-1719 d 9-4-1793 m (1)Margaret Beidler
   (2)Margaret Schuetz PS PA
Walter Weeks: b 1754 d 5-16-1808 m Rachel Knowles Pvt NH
Wm.: b 1753 d 10-15-1834 m Sarah Porter Pvt CT
Wm.: b 2-12-1746 d 1806 m Judith Rowe Pvt NH
Wm.: b 10-20-1759 d 1814 m Agnes Lippincott Pvt NJ
Wm.: b 7-9-1747 d *a.* 3-13-1817 m Lydia Austin PS NJ
Wm.: b 1754 d *p.* 1790 m Sarah Bennett Pvt NC
Wm., Sr.: b 1730 d 1804 m Anna Barbara Wink Pvt PA
Wm.: b 8-4-1740 d 8-3-1827 m (1)Hannah Ellis (2)Sarah (Seeley)
   New Pvt VA
Wm.: b 1762 d 1846 m Sarah Hill Matr VA
Wm.: b *c.* 1710 d *p.* 4-8-1780 m Elizabeth — PS VA
Wm. Baker: b 10- -1760 d 8-12-1830 m Mary Jones Pvt VA

HAYNESWORTH,
Henry: b 11-27-1746 d 1823 m Sarah Furman PS SC

HAYNIE,
Bridgar: b *c.* 1745 d *p.* 11-7-1783 m Sarah Shearman 2Lt VA
Ezekiel: b 9-29-1760 d 9-6-1799 m Betsy Bayly Dr MD
Spencer: b 3-7-1758 d *a.* 1- -1825 m Katherine (King) Sol VA
Wm.: b 11-12-1739 d 12-7-1816 m Sarah Halley Sgt VA
Wm.: b *c.* 1753 d 8-25-1825 m Ann Bradley Lt NC W★

HAYTER,
Israel: b 10-2-1754 d 2-11-1829 m Anne Crawford Sol VA

HAYWARD, (includes HAYWOOD, HEYWARD, HEYWOOD & HOWARD)
Abner, Jr.: b 5-17-1746 d 6-1-1805 m Abigail Howard Capt MA
Amos: b 3-27-1730 d 1816 m Mary Ripley Lt MA
Amos: b 10-3-1719 d 2-7-1792 m Mary Buttrick Pvt MA
Barzillai: b 1753 d *p.* 1795 m Rebecca — Pvt MA
Benjamin: b 12-1-1752 d 10- -1838 m Lucy Hunt Pvt MA
Benjamin: b 4-3-1767 d 11-26-1795 m Hannah Way Fif Pvt MA
Benjamin, Sr.: b 8-23-1713 d 1784 m Mary Wheaton MM CS VT
Benjamin: b 9-10-1740 d 10-29-1783 m Elizabeth Thayer Pvt
   MA
Benjamin: b 10-22-1753 d 2-1-1829 m Sally Flagg Pvt MA
Caleb: b 1746 d 1811 m — Clark Cpl MA
Charles: b 12-24-1723 d *a.* 1825 m Abigail Hubbard Pvt MA
Daniel, Sr.: b 1723 d 5- -1798 m Martha (Hayward) MM MA
Daniel, Jr.: b 2-21-1750 d *p.* 1790 m Elinor Davis Pvt MA
Daniel: b 2-1-1752 d 1-8-1842 m Bethiah Howard Sgt MA
Daniel: b 10-13-1754 d 8-12-1837 m Mary Hobart Denton Pvt MA
David: b 4-28-1743 d 9-20-1822 m Priscilla Knowlton Pvt CT
David: b 5-4-1755 d 11-2-1826 m Abigal Bixby Pvt MA
Edmund: b 5-12-1720 d 2-12-1781 m Anna Snell Pvt MA
Egbert: b *a.* 1740 d 1801 m Sarah Ware 2Maj PS NC
Eleazer: b 1752 d 1789 m Keziah Shedd Pvt MA
Elijah: b 11-3-1732 d 2-24-1808 m Mary Pulcipher Pvt MA
Ephraim: b 4-27-1760 d 9-29-1849 m (1)Phoebe Dickinson
   (2)Deborah George Pvt Drm NY ★
Ezekiel: b 8-22-1741 d 11-5-1821 m Hannah Johnson Pvt MA
Isaiah: b 10-1-1755 d *p.* 1778 m Sarah Bartlett Pvt MA
Jabez, Jr.: b 3-24-1754 d 11-24-1835 m Nabby Graves Pvt MA
Jacob: b 1745 d *p.* 1784 m Betsey (Hayward) Pvt MA
Jacob: b 3-27-1749 d 2-15-1822 m (1)Elizabeth Gibbs (2)Elizabeth
   Albee (3)Mrs. Elizabeth (Thayer) Heath Pvt MA
James: b 4-14-1763 d 1834 m Elizabeth Chase Pvt MA ★
James: b *c.* 1740 d 1793 m Keziah Butler Pvt NH

John: b 1743 d 1825 m Marian Forbush Capt MA
John, Sr.: b 12-11-1718 d 6-20-1794 m Margaret Albee Pvt MA
John, Jr.: b 5-6-1760 d *p.* 1803 m Mary Pease Pvt MA
John: b 1745 d *p.* 1784 m Betsey (Hayward) Pvt MA
John: b 10-9-1750 d 2-17-1830 m Mary Penniman Pvt MA
John: b 2-20-1760 d 4-25-1825 m Hannah Poore Pvt VT W★
Jonas: b 8-21-1721 d 7-28-1808 m Ann Prescott Capt MA
Jonathan: b 5-18-1749 d 1815 m Lydia Wood Sgt MA
Jonathan: b 5-6-1755 d *p.* 1795 m Lydia Davison Pvt CT
Joseph, Sr.: b 4-16-1715 d 2-4-1802 m (1)Abigail Hosmer (2)Anna
   Saunderson MM PS MA
Joseph, Jr.: b 1-16-1745 d 5-9-1835 m Rebecca Prescott CS NH
Joseph: b 1746 d 1-16-1836 m Olive Manley Pvt MA
Joseph: b 7-17-1753 d 2-12-1843 m Lydia Barrows Pvt MA
Josiah, Sr.: b 5-29-1707 d 5-6-1783 m Mary Hosmer PS MA
Josiah, Jr.: b 2-15-1737/8 d 10-9-1821 m Lucy Conant Pvt MA
Lemuel: b 3-22-1749 d 3-20-1821 m Sarah Henshaw Dr MA
Levi: b 9-15-1752 d 5-14-1838 m Bethia Chapin Pvt MA ★
Nathan: b 1720 d 1794 m Susanna Latham Pvt MA
Nathan: b 1754 d 8-6-1818 m Sarah Hayward Cpl MA
Nathaniel: b 11-5-1748 d 11-18-1834 m (1)Hannah Curtis (2)Mary
   Chamberlain Lt MA ★
Nathaniel: b 1766 d 4- -1851 m Harriet Manigault Pvt SC
Paul: b 2-25-1751 d 1792 m Bulah Howard Pvt VA
Peter: b 1725 d 8-1-1791 m (1)Ruth Rutter (2)Esther Holmes Pvt PS
   CS NH
Phineas: b 7-18-1707 d 3- -1776 m Elizabeth Moore PS MA
Samuel: b 4-19-1763 d 3-22-1837 m (1)Jerusha Benton (2)Sarah
   Cranston (Young)Bliss Pvt CT ★
Samuel: b 1- -1760 d 5-16-1834 m Bethiah Cobb Cpl MA
Samuel: b *c.* 1735 d 1-15-1797 m Susanna — Pvt MA
Samuel, Sr.: b 4-5-1713 d 3-6-1791 m Mary Stevens PS MA
Samuel: b 3-14-1733 d — m Catherine Field Sgt RI
Seth: b 1738 d 8-24-1826 m Martha Temple Lt MA
Silas: b 2-20-1746 d 11-21-1825 m Hannah Goddard Pvt MA
Simeon: b 9-7-1743 d 9-6-1807 m Hepsibah Curtis Pvt MA
Simeon: b 4-17-1717 d 6-18-1797 m Sarah Hosmer PS MA
Solomon: b 6-27-1754 d 10-24-1832 m Zerviah Washburn Pvt MA
Solomon: b 8-2-1755 d 9-29-1831 m Martha Burr Pvt MA ★
Stephen: b 9-19-1759 d 9-19-1839 m Hannah Tracy Sgt MA ★
Stephen: b 6-2-1747 d 5- -1818 m Ruth Dinsmore Pvt MA W★
Sylvanus: b 5-16-1757 d 10-1-1817 m (1)Olive Metcalf (2)Lucinda
   Lee Champlin (3)Mary Webb Pvt NH
Thomas: b 2-23-1753 d 1820 m Hannah — Pvt MA
Thomas, Sr.: b 1-26-1723 d 10-20-1795 m Anne Miles PS SC
Thomas, Jr.: b 7-28-1746 d 3-6-1809 m (1)Elizabeth Mathews
   (2)Elizabeth Savage SDI PS Capt SC
Timothy: b 2-22-1739/40 d 8-14-1825 m Patience Stebbins Lt CS MA
Waldo: b 3-20-1758 d 11-18-1834 m Lucy Bartlett Sgt MA★
Wm.: b 8-6-1758 d 2-23-1834 m Nancy Greene Sgt MA
Wm.: b 7-28-1728 d 2-4-1803 m (1)Lydia Hastings (2)Joanna
   Wetherbee Maj NH
Wm.: b 1730 d 12- -1779 m Charity Hare PS Col NC
Zimri: b 9- -1731 d 6-14-1798 m Jane Foster Capt MA

HAZEL,
Delia: b 1764 d *p.* 1810 m Thomas Chappell PS SC
Henry: b 1745 d 6-16-1838 m Sarah Johnson Matr VA MD
Henry: b 1740 d 1823 m Mary (Hazel) Pvt SC

HAZELGROVE,
John: b *c.* 1750 d *p.* 1781 m Ann Timberlake Sgt VA

HAZELRIGG,
James: b *c.* 1738 d *a.* 12- -1819 m (1)Margaret — (2)Lucy Flan-
   nin Pvt PA
Joshua: b 12-4-1760 d 12-21-1836 m America Frances Wright Pvt
   PA
Wm., Jr.: b *c.* 1764 d 3-16-1826 m Sarah Knox Pvt PA

HAZELTINE, (includes HASELTINE, HASELTON, HAZELTON, HEASELTINE, HESSELTINE & HESSELTON)
Arnold: b 3-29-1740 d 1815 m — Brainerd Capt CT
Asa: b 11-20-1740 d 4- -1823 m Mary Woodard Lt MA
Benjamin: b 8-7-1763 d 10-12-1826 m Abigail Mayo Pvt Dr MA
Daniel: b 12-20-1761 d 6-26-1828 m Susanna Jones Pvt MA
Daniel: b *c.* 1737 d *p.* 1790 m (1)Abigail — (2)Eleanor Emerson Pvt
   NH
David: b 4-17-1759 d 2-26-1824 m Anna Carter Pvt VT
James: b 10-16-1723 d 10-11-1788 m Hannah — PS CT
James: b 7-20-1729 d 11-1-1803 m (1)Rebecca Milliken (2)Hannah
   Kimball Pvt PS MA
John: b 6-9-1736 d 6-27-1815 m (1)Anna Dearborn (2)Hannah
   Chase Pvt NH
John: b 1-4-1756 d 7-22-1832 m Elizabeth Haynes Pvt NH MA ★
John: b 1702 d 1777 m Jane Wood PS NY
John: b 4-11-1758 d 10-11-1834 m Barbara Slaughter Pvt PA
John: b 5-14-1759 d 7-1-1822 m (1)Lucy Doolittle (2)Tapha Weeks
   Dr VT
John: b *a.* 1736 d 1- -1797 m Sarah Beadle Pvt VT
Jonas: b 1753 d *p.* 1799 m Rachel Wood Pvt MA
Joseph: b *a.* 1750 d 1812 m Elizabeth Marsh Pvt NH
Joseph: b 12-27-1731 d 5-30-1798 m Elizabeth Abbott PS NH

HAZELTINE, contd.
Nathaniel: b 10-23-1747 d 7-4-1825 m Abigail Nastings Cpl MA
Paul: b 11-20-1728 d p. 1790 m Mary Rice Pvt VT
Peter: b 9-14-1725 d p. 1795 m Mrs. Sarah Jones Pvt MA
Philip: b 1-25-1744 d 2-25-1829 m Patience Rowell Sgt MA
Richard: b 4-28-1757 d 8-20-1810 m Jane Campbell Cpl MA W★
Richard: b 9-19-1755 d 4-6-1835 m Susannah Clark Pvt MA ★
Richard: b 10-2-1742 d 1- -1819 m Lucy Cross PS NH
Ruth Ladd b 5-11-1712 d 3-23-1796 m James Haseltine PS MA
Samuel: b 6-28-1740 d 10-22-1808 m Elizabeth (Haseltine)Lt NH
Solomon: b 4-13-1761 d 8-11-1842 m Elizabeth Page Pvt NH ★
Stephen: b 5-11-1765 d 1-30-1811 m Sibyl Moseley Pvt MA
Thaddeus: b 9-13-1760 d p. 1807 m Content — Pvt VT
Thomas: b 9-4-1763 d 9-4-1835 m Ruth Merrill Cpl NH ★
Wm.: b 1753 d 12- -1811 m Mary Rebecca Bradley Sol SC

HAZEN,
Abraham: b 4-8-1761 d 2-8-1838 m Levinah Albertson Pvt NJ ★
Andrew: b 5-22-1764 d 1836 m (1)Betsy Haynes (2)Jane Truman (3)Sally Hamlin Pvt CT
Andrew: b 4-6-1766 d 10-18-1829 m Polly Drake Pvt CT W★
Asa: b 11-16-1749 d 3-12-1819 m Susannah Tracy Lt CS VT
Benjamin: b 12-7-1745 d 1807 m Lydia Woods Pvt MA
Benjamin: b 10-21-1758 d 1814 m Elizabeth Gates Fif NH
Caleb, Sr.: b 4-4-1720 d 3-5-1777 m Sarah Hamblin Pvt NY
Caleb, Jr.: b 11-17-1749 d 3-31-1806 m Ruth Wright Lt NY
Daniel: b 7-17-1761 d 11-22-1814 m Olive Bartholomew Pvt VT
Edward: b 5-2-1738 d 1796 m (1)Sarah Willard (2)Mrs. Jemima Dodge Bathrick Pvt NH
Elijah: b 11-25-1752 d 2-2-1832 m Esther Hollister Capt CT
Frederick: b 9-25-1762 d 5-21-1825 m Sarah Stedman Sol CT
Hezekiah: b 3-15-1756 d 7-25-1829 m Sally Marsh Cpl VT
Jacob: b 6-20-1753 d 5-11-1834 m Abigail Burnham Pvt CT
Jacob, Sr.: b 1739/40 d 1795 m Abagail (Perley)Spofford Sgt MA
Jacob, Jr.: b 1762 d 8-13-1843 m Hannah Wood Pvt MA ★
Joshua: b 10-19-1745 d 4- -1796 m Mercy Hazen Capt PS VT
Moses: b 12-1-1731 d 7-11-1812 m (1)Elizabeth Merrill (2)Mrs Johanna Sampson PS CT
Moses: b 12-9-1743 d p. 6-16-1823 m Rebecca Cheney Pvt MA
Nathan: b 6-24-1756 d 6-6-1812 m Cynthia Ayers Pvt VT
Nathaniel: b 3-17-1745 d 11-3-1835 m Mary Bell Pvt PA
Samuel: b 5-24-1740 d 5-6-1815 m Elizabeth Little Capt MA
Solomon: b 11-24-1759 d 7-26-1849 m Theodora Pease Pvt NH
Thomas: b 9-30-1719 d 8-19-1782 m Ann Tenney Pvt VT
Thomas: b 8-9-1758 d 9-9-1816 m Eleanor Lanning OrdlSgt NJ
Thomas: b 1-16-1733 d 12-27-1802 m Mary Giles Sol NJ
Thomas, Jr.: b 3-13-1758 d 8-9-1835 m Abigail Dutton Pvt VT
Wm.: b 7-10-1760 d 1801-03 m Martha Folsom Pvt CT

HAZZARD, (includes HAZARD)
Carder: b 8-11-1734 d 11-24-1792 m (1)Alice Hull (2)Alice Hazard PS CS RI
Charles: b 1752 d 1838 m Polly — Pvt NJ ★
Cord: b 5-13-1749 d 3-13-1831 m Comfort Conwell Capt DE
David: b 5-13-1749 d 1790 m Elon(McIlvain)Rhoads 2Lt DE
Ebenezer: b 1-15-1745 d 6-13-1817 m Abigail Arthur CS PA
James Carr: b 8-2-1759 d 3-24-1837 m Betsey Greely Cpl NH W★
John: b 4-29-1754 d 12-26-1825 m (1)Mary Houston (2)Hannah Horseman (3)Mrs. Elizabeth Wolfe 2Lt DE
Jonathan J.: b 1731 d 7-29-1812 m (1)Patience Hazzard (2)Hannah Brown (3)Miriam Gage PS RI
Joseph: b 6-9-1728 d 9-27-1794 m Mary (Purnell)CS PS DE
Joshua: b c. 1742 d p. 1790 m — Pvt NY
Stewart: b 5-11-1745 d 6-11-1833 m (1)Rachel Clark (2)Sybil — Pvt NY CT ★
Robert: b 4-11-1755 d 1795 m Hannah Gardner Pvt RI
Thomas: b 9-15-1720 d 8-17-1798 m Elizabeth Robinson PS RI
Tiddeman: b 7-1-1760 d 6-15-1813 m Alberta Fonda Pvt RI
Wm.: b 1753 d 1821 m Amelia Potter Pvt DE
Wm.: b 6-15-1759 d 12-19-1819 m Mary Fuller Lt SC

HEAD,
Benjamin: b 1731 d 8-19-1803 m Martha Sherman Capt PS VA
Benjamin: b 1760 d a. 1- -1809 m Mildred Long Pvt VA
George: b — d 2-18-1818 m Catherine Newport PS NC
James: b 11-16-1727 d 8-31-1777 m Mrs. Sarah Thurston Maj NH
James: b 12- -1767 d 10-28-1851 m — Pvt SC
James: b 9-23-1758 d 10-23-1795 m Elizabeth Janet (Powell)Ens VA
John: b 3-15-1767 d p. 1802 m Elizabeth Bond Drm MD
John, Sr.: b 2-8-1721 d 12-7-1795 m (1)Mehitable — (2)Sarah Kimball PS CS MA
John: b 9-28-1748 d 3-19-1809 m Lydia Merrill Pvt NH
John: b c. 1735-45 d a. 6-25-1807 m Sarah Waters Pvt NC
John: b 10-2-1723 d 2-2-1792 m (1)Mary Hudson (2)Elizabeth Hastings (3)Margaret White PS PA
John Stromatt: b 8-5-1763 d 1852 m Barbara — Pvt SC ★
Jonathan: b 1738/39 d 1778 m Ruth Little Pvt MA
Joseph: b 2-24-1761 d 12-18-1837 m Rebecca Sandford Pvt MA
Moses: b 4-20-1761 d 4-20-1850 m Rebecca Gowell Pvt NH ★
Nathaniel: b 10-9-1742 d 10-14-1823 m Abigail Stickney Capt NH
Nathaniel: b 3-6-1754 d 10-24-1829 m Anne Knox Capt NH
Richard Mace: b 1734 d 5-15-1827 m Charlotte Bird Cnt PA

Robert: b 11-30-1757 d 12-25-1838 m Martha Elder Pvt NC
Wm. Beckwith: b 1747 d 12-28-1833 m Ann Lilly lLt MD

HEADINGTON,
Zebulon: b 1740 d 1839 m Sarah Bosley Sol MD

HEADLEY, (includes HEADLEE, HEADLY)
Cary: b 2-14-1756 d 2-1-1823 m Phebe Stiles Pvt Wgn NJ
Cary: b 1760 d 7-13-1839 m Mary Hathaway Pvt NJ ★
Elisha: b 5-18-1760 d 10-8-1845 m Mary Fairchild Pvt NJ
Ephraim: b 1-21-1758 d 12-6-1822 m Mary Fordyce Sol NJ
Isaac: b 1735 d 5-14-1802 m (1)Mary Frazee (2)Mrs. Catherine Clark Pvt NJ
Jacob: b 2-23-1763 d 12-15-1838 m Hannah Hindes Pvt NJ ★
John Thompson: b 1751 d 2-4-1828 m Catherine Smith Pvt NJ W★
Joseph: b 1758 d 8-27-1842 m Martha Riker Pvt NJ
Joseph: b 2-3-1746 d 2-22-1840 m Abigail (Morris)Pvt NJ
Joshua: b 10-17-1727 d 5-30-1815 m Sarah Bidgood PS CS PA
Samuel: b 1731 d 9-3-1792 m Martha — Pvt NJ
Samuel: b 4-18-1759 d 2-8-1831 m Hannah McAfee Pvt PS NJ

HEADY,
James: b c. 1758 d p. 1804 m Eleanor Jackson Pvt VA
James: b 1758 d 9-20-1818 m Mary Doolen Pvt VA

HEAGLE,
Johannis: b c. 1760 d — m Catrina Plantz Pvt NY
Michael: b 9-17-1753 d 3-12-1814 m Eva — Pvt NY

HEAGY, (includes HEGE)
Balthaser: b 10-31-1714 d 11-10-1785 m Maria Juliana Frey PS NC
Christian: b 1751 d 5-13-1815 m (1)Maria Stouffer (2)Maria Shank Pvt PA
Jacob: b 1762 d 8-24-1842 m Margaret Michael Pvt PA

HEALD,
Amos: b 5-3-1749 d 6- -1836 m Esther — Pvt NH
Asa: b 10-16-1750 d p. 1803 m (1)Rebecca Morrill (2)Jerusha Carter Pvt MA
Benjamin: b 6-25-1764 d 10-12-1841 m Rebekah Spaulding Pvt MA
Daniel: b 7-14-1739 d 9-17-1833 m Abagail Wheeler Pvt MA
Ebenezer: b 6-30-1754 d 4-23-1814 m Sarah White Pvt MA
Ephraim, Sr.: b 2-19-1711 d 4-29-1802 m Eleanor Robbins MM MA
Ephraim, Jr.: b 9-29-1734 d 9-12-1815 m Sarah Conant Sol PS NH
Ephraim: b 11-26-1753 d 11-6-1834 m Sarah Hardy Pvt MA ★
Isaac: b c. 1760 d a. 12-10-1822 m Lydia — Pvt MA
Israel: b 8-16-1736 d 10-28-1815 m Susannah Robbins Capt MA
John: b 2-14-1721 d 11-26-1810 m Elizabeth Barrett Lt MA
John: b 8-3-1760 d 10-26-1825 m (1)Elizabeth Hindkley (2)Lydia Cooper Cpl MA
John, 3d: b 8-8-1693 d 5-16-1775 m Mary Hale MM MA
John: b 4-29-1746 d 10-31-1816 m Mary White MM MA
Jonathan: b 8-28-1757 d 12-28-1816 m Sarah Brown Capt MA
Josiah: b 12-10-1747 d 7- -1822 m Tryphena Corey CS MA
Nathan: b 2-26-1735 d 12-14-1826 m Rebecca McBride Pvt PA
Oliver: b 1734 d 1- -1790 m Lydia Spaulding MM PS NH
Peter: b c. 1722 d c. 1784 m Deborah Chesley Pvt MA
Peter: b 1736 d 9-25-1811 m (1)Sarah — (2)Rebecca Russell Vol NH
Samuel: b 3-27-1744 d 5-11-1829 m Mary Hunt Capt MA
Silas: b 10-26-1760 d 6-21-1811 m Sarah Wetherbee Pvt MA
Stephen: b 7-18-1729 d 10-3-1814 m Hazadiah Howe Sol MA
Thomas: b 5-5-1764 d 2-12-1850 m Lucy Longley Pvt ME ★
Thomas: b 1733 d 8-20-1806 m (1)Sybil Adams (2)Deliverance Blanchard Col NH
Timothy: b 1749 d 5-17-1817 m Abigail Cragin Capt MA
Timothy: b 2-19-1756 d 5-1-1814 m Lois Smith Cpl MA
Timothy: b 10-14-1723 d 8-18-1785 m Elizabeth (Stevens)Brooks PS ME

HEALY, (includes HEALEY)
Benjamin: b 5- -1755 d 6-25-1820 m Rachel Spaulding Pvt MA
Eliphaz: b 2-18-1755 d 10-10-1833 m Lucy Robinson Pvt MA
Hugh: b 1758 d 8-31-1824 m Sophia Hargraves Pvt NJ ★
Jabez: b 9-29-1763 d 12-1-1838 m Grace Bailey Pvt MA
James: b 7- -1756 d 10-4-1820 m Ruth Bristow Sgt VA
John: b 1-13-1756 d 5-27-1835 m Elizabeth Dalrymple Sgt MA ★
John: b 1-6-1733 d 8-19-1810 m Mary Wright Pvt MA
John: b 6-27-1745 d p. 1784 m Martha Powers Pvt MA
Lemuel: b 12-26-1759 d 9-11-1837 m Dolly Corbin Pvt MA
Nathaniel: b 9-3-1736 d 10-5-1817 m Abigail Carter 1 Maj MA
Samuel: b 12-9-1738 d 11-24-1817 m Phebe Curtis Capt MA
Thomas: b 2-12-1746 d 1813 m (1)Ann — (2)Hannah Dillard (3)Mrs. Sarah (Batchelder) Mitchell PS 2Lt VA
Thomas: b 12-9-1740 d p. 1837 m Penelope Mott Pvt RI ★

HEAP, (includes HEAPE)
Archibald: b 9-1-1758 d a. 1-26-1841 m Sarah Bay Pvt MD
John: b 1750 d a. 3-25-1828 m (1)Margaret Kerr (2)Mrs. Sarah Smith, Jr. (3)Mrs. Jane (Mahon) Wilson Pvt PA
Sarah: b c. 1730 d c. 1800 m Benjamin Heape PS SC

HEARD,(includes HURD)
Barnard: b 1739 d p. 1784 m Nancy Germany Maj GA
Benjamin: b 8-2-1715 d 1804 m Anna Downs PS MA

Benjamin: b 1744 d 2-2-1817 m Mary Andrews Pvt MA
Charles: b c. 1734 d p. 8-25-1792 m Margaret Logan Lt SC
David: b 6-2-1758 d 1-22-1813 m (1)Eunice Baldwin (2)Sibyl
   Sherman Pvt MA
George: b c. 1761 d p. 4-29-1816 m (1)Edna Perrin (2)Mrs
   Elizabeth Goode Pvt SC
George: b 1744 d 1791 m (2)Nancy Dean Pvt VA
Jacob: b 1745 d — m Betsey Home Pvt NH
James: b 5-25-1747 d 3- -1833 m Elizabeth Hodgkins Pvt MA
James: b 1749 d p. 1780 m Lizebeth Hopkins Pvt MA
Jessie: b 1740 d a. 3-3-1803 m (1)Judith Wilkinson (2)Elizabeth Early
   Capt VA
Jethro: bpt 5-10-1753 d 11-17-1815 m Sarah Hartford Lt NH
John: b c. 1754 d 2-16-1826 m Mary Sargant Capt NJ
John: b 1744 d 1797 m Susannah Meador Pvt GA
John: b 7-20-1718 d 2-19-1794 m Phebe — PS NH
Joseph: b 5-3-1751 d 5-3-1820 m Sarah Wentworth Pvt NH
Mark: b 6-19-1748 d p. 1800 m (1)Sarah Smith (2)Nancy McCobb
   Pvt MA
Nathaniel, Jr.: b 8-27-1758 d 11-9-1840 m Susanna Spiller Pvt MA ★
Nathaniel: b 1730 d 10-28-1792 m Mary Ford BGen NJ
Phineas;: b c. 1748 d 1812 m (1)Mary Tooker (2)Hetty Board Capt
   NY
Richard: b 4-2-1720 d 5-16-1792 m Sarah Fiske MM PS MA
Samuel: b 11-13-1723 d p. 1790 m — CS NH
Stephen: b 4-13-1741 d 11-15-1815 m (1)— Germany
   (2)Elizabeth Darden PS CS Capt GA
Stephen: b 1748 d 1815 m (2)Margaret — PS VA
Stephen: b 1713 d 1797 m (1)Margaret — (2)Isabella — PS PA
Thomas: b c. 1740 d 1-23-1817 m Mary Wentworth PS ME
Thomas: b 1742 d 1-17-1808 m (1)Elizabeth Fitzpatrick (2)Mary
   Veasey Capt VA
Thomas: b c. 1760-65 d 1- -1813 m Dorcas Morris Sol VA
Wm.: b 1750 d p. 4-12-1825 m (1)Mary Nancy McLendon (2)Rachel
   Pvt GA
Wm.: b 5-28-1755 d 5-15-1829 m (1)Betsey Dix (2)Thirza Williams
   Fif MA
Wm: b 1750 d p. 1798 m Abigail Crockett PS ME
Wm.: b 4-7-1750 d 9-18-1784 m Joanna Crane 2Lt NY
Wm.: b 1747/48 d p. 11-19-1803 m Margaret — PS VA

HEARNE,
Daniel: b c. 1760 d 9- -1818 m Sarah Marsh Sgt VA
Drury: b 1760 d 10-14-1839 m (2)Keren Bledsoe Pvt NC
Ebenezer: b 10-11-1760 d 1-16-1840 m Dovey Walker Pvt NC ★
Elisha: b 1755 d 1- -1812 m Fereby Johnson Slr Pvt GA
Wm.: b 1746 d 9-21-1832 m Tabitha (Hearne) Pvt NC

HEATH, (includes HETH)
Aaron: b 1754 d 1-29-1843 m Rhoda Edson Pvt MA CT ★
Andrew: b c. 1725 d 6- -1777 m Magdalena — Pvt NJ
Andrew: b 1756 d p. 11-8-1817 m Hannah Smalley Lt VA
Bartholomew: b 1724 d 8-1-1813 m Hannah Kelly Pvt PS NH
Bartholomew: b c. 1735 d p. 1788 m Ann Millard Adj NY
Benjamin: b 11- -1752 d 11-27-1839 m Dolly Willey Pvt NH W★
Daniel: b 2-25-1733 d 1788/89 m Elizabeth Call Pvt Drm MA NH
Daniel: b 1-22-1764 d 4-15-1849 m (1)Joanna Ingalls (2)Tryphena
   (Ladd)Goodwin Pvt NH ★
Daniel, Sr.: b 5-6-1740 d 12- -1805 m Anna — Lt NY
Daniel, Jr.: b 3-26-1760 d 10-1-1841 m (1)Hannah Gates (2)Azuba
   Reynolds Sgt NY ★
David: b c. 1724 d 1820 m Mary Worthington Pvt NJ
Dearborn: b 4-15-1758 d 8-22-1831 m (1)Mrs. Marsh (2)Mary Hays
   Pvt NH W★
Eleazer: b 1754 d 1-1-1850 m Abigail Robins Pvt CT
Henry: b 1718 d 6-12-1793 m Agnes McMahon Capt VA
Henry: b 1753 d 4-3-1797 m Susanna Williams Capt VA
Henry: b c. 1758 d c. 1787 m — Gilbert Lt VA
Jacob: b 1740 d 1816 m (2)Mary Smith Pvt MA
James: b 1739 d 1814 m Sarah Shepard Pvt NH
Jesse: b 4- -1759 d 4-27-1839 m Phoebe Straw Pvt NH ★
Job (1): b c. 1750 d p. 1785 m Susanna Stevens PS NH
John: b 9-12-1732 d 4-11-1804 m Susannah Craft Pvt MA
John: b 1726 d 1783 m Judith —Lt VA
Jonathan: b 1764 d 12-1-1831 m Rebecca Stoddard Pvt RI W★
Jordan: b 4-12-1758 d 2-13-1840 m Christian Wimberly Pvt GA
Joseph: b 3-19-1758 d 10-9-1836 m Patience Markham Fif Arfr
   MA ★
Joseph, Jr.: b 4-7-1754 d 6-21-1830 m (1)Mabel Rising (2)Mrs.
   Bethiah Hatch Pvt NY
Joshua: b 1-12-1730 d 1776 m Hannah Dearborn Sgt NH
Josiah: b 12-16-1747 d 9-4-1838 m (1)Hannah — (2)Mary — Pvt
   NY ★
Levi: b c. 1740 d p. 1792 m (2)Abigail Doud Pvt MA
Nathaniel: b 7-4-1732 d 5-8-1812 m Mary Adams Maj MA
Nathaniel: b a. 1745 d 8-6-1777 m Katrine Walrad Lt NY
Nathaniel: b 1-29-1745 d 5-19-1829 m Rebecca Brown Lt RI
Peleg: b 3-23-1747 d 7-4-1786 m Anna Kent Maj PS RI
Reuben: b 9-9-1754 d 6-15-1818 m Mary Farwell Pvt NH
Richard: bpt 4-9-1738 d 6-28-1778 m Mehitable Copp Pvt NH
Robert: b 11-5-1762 d p. 1810 m Sebra — Pvt MA
Samuel: b 9-7-1754 d 6-13-1833 m Sarah Webster Pvt MA ★
Samuel: b c. 1738 d 3-22-1815 m Elizabeth — Lt PA

Samuel Corbin: b 3-18-1759 d 5-29-1836 m Leah Tracy Pvt CT ★
Simeon: b 5-6-1749 d p. 1785 m Sarah Carleton PS NH
Solomon: b 3-31-1741 d 12-6-1776 m Chloe Johnson Sgt MA
Starling: b 1759 d 10-28-1828 m Elizabeth Ladd Pvt NH
Stephen: b 5-2-1750 d 5-19-1810 m Sarah Osborn Pvt CT
Stephen: b 1758 d 11-12-1832 m Anna Milliman Cpl MA
Sylvanus: b — d 2-26-1787 m Azubah Sawer Sgt Sct Grd VT
Thomas: b 1755 d 9-27-1842 m Polly Calkins Pvt CT ★
Thomas: b c. 1750 d 1821 m Martha Gilbert 1Lt VA
Wm.: b c. 1750 d 3- -1794 m Mary Collver Pvt CT W★
Wm.: b 3-2-1737 d 1-24-1814 m Sarah Lernard MGen MA
Wm.: b c. 1721 d p. 1730 m Mary Bannister PS MD
Wm.: b 9-28-1758 d 6-29-1850 m Katherine Robbins Pvt CT ★
Wm.: b 3-24-1756 d 6-6-1789 m Abigail Davis Capt MA
Wm.: b 9- -1764 d 9-6-1840 m Hannah Allen Pvt NH ★
Wm.: b 1764 d 1827/8 m (1)Polly Taylor (2)Sally Hardwick Sol
   NC ★
Wm.: b 7-19-1750 d 4-8-1807 m Eliza Briggs Col VA
Wm.: b 1759 d 1849 m Sallie Bell Watson Pvt VA
Wilson: b 1733/34 d 4- -1785 m Rachel (Heath)Gibbons Pvt MD

HEATHERINGTON,
John: b c. 1750-55 d p. 1792 m Ruth Smith Pvt PA

HEATHLY,
Wm., Jr.: b 8-8-1741 d 11-23-1800 m Mary McCleland PS SC

HEATON,
Amos: b c. 1740 d 1794/95 m Elizabeth — Lt VA
Calvin: b 8-14-1755 d 3-26-1820 m Esther Humiston Pvt CT
David: b 12-15-1742 d 9-11-1839 m Phebe Johnson Pvt NJ
Ebenezer: b 6-18-1750 d 1-12-1837 m Joana Sutton PS PA & VA
Isaac: b 1744 d 2-7-1800 m Thankful Baker Sgt MA
Isaac: b 5-10-1731 d 4-1-1814 m (1)Mary Booth (2)Hannah Bowen
   Sgt PA
James: b 5-30-1752 d 4-1-1811 m Susanna Grimes Ens NH
John: b 12- -1760 d 1820 m Sarah Morgan Pvt PA
John: b 1756 d 4-30-1778 m Ann Stowe Pvt Cpl VA
Jonathan: b 12-10-1750 d 7-13-1837 m Thankful (Sawyer) Clark
   Pvt NH
Moses: b 12-2-1747 d 9- -1815 m Deborah — Dr MA
Samuel: b 7-23-1759 d 4-1-1830 m Sally Boynton Cpl NH
Seth: b 2-3-1710 d 6-3-1797 m Thankful Field PS NH
Thomas: b 1761 d 9-19-1858 m Susan Taylor Pvt VA
Wm.: b 6-5-1732 d 3-15-1814 m Irena King Capt VT

HEAVENOR, (includes HEAVNER)
Charles: b 1760 d 4- -1854 m Margaret Burns Pvt MA
Jacob: b 1746/7 d c. 1810 m Mary Mallow Ens VA

HEBB,
Joseph: b c. 1745 d 1782 m Mary Cole Pvt MD
Vernon: b 1742 d — m Anna Hopewell LCol MD
Wm.: b c. 1757 d 1831 m Mrs Jemima Washington Jenkins Pvt
   VA ★

HEBRON,
John: b 5-10-1760 d 12-15-1811 m Abigail Banks Pvt PA

HECHLER,
John: b 8- -1732 d 8-25-1782 m Hannah — PS PA

HECK,
Frederick: b c. 1760 d p. 1830 m — Pvt PA
Jacob, Sr.: b c. 1727 d 1795 m Mary — Pvt PA
Johann Yost: b 5-10-1754 d 8-20-1825 m Susanna Exline Pvt PA

HECKENDORN,
Christian: b 10-19-1753 d 2-11-1830 m Veronica Frances Deppen
   Pvt PS PA

HECKERT,
John: b 1733 d a. 2-7-1800 m Elizabeth Gertrude Fisher PS CS PA
Philip: b 10-15-1744 d 9-18-1804 m Anna Maria Hain Pvt PA

HECKEWELDER,
John: b 3-12-1743 d 1-21-1823 m Sarah Ohneberg PS PA

HEDDEN,
Aaron: b 12-5-1752 d 5-7-1825 m Martha Lamson PS NJ
Caleb: b 1761 d 6-16-1846 m Rhoda Peck Pvt NJ
David: b 6-30-1750 d 1835 m Esther Baldwin Pvt MM NJ
Elisha: b c. 1760 d c. 1840 m — Sol NC
Job: b 12-25-1753 d 5-25-1843 m Phoebe Ogden Pvt NJ ★
Jonathan: b 1733 d 12-25-1795 m Phoebe Canfield Pvt NJ
Joseph, Jr.: b 1728 d 9-27-1780 m Sarah Canfield PS CS NJ
Joseph: b 1742 d 1833 m Martha Oliver Pvt NJ
Zadock: b 1- -1757 d 4-29-1840 m Rachel Baldwin Pvt Wgn NJ

HEDGER,
Thomas: b 3-25-1747 d 12- -1845 m — Pvt VA★
Wm.: b 8-20-1757 d 9-6-1837 m Mary Campbell Pvt NY ★

HEDGES, (includes HEDGE)
Andrews: b c. 1719 d 12-3-1782 m Mercy Taylor Pvt MA
Charles, Sr.: b 1712 d 1795 m Mary Stille PS MD
Charles, Jr.: b 3-4-1749 d 12-21-1831 m Rebecca Hedges CS VA
Daniel: b 5-11-1734 d 11-26-1797 m (1)Sarah Baker (2)Susannah
    Pierson MM Capt PS NY
David: b 1735 d 1829 m Hannah Shaw Pvt CT
David: b 6-15-1744 d 11-8-1817 m Charity Howell PS NY
Eleazer: b 4-7-1757 d 8-20-1839 m Amanda Dennison Pvt NY ★
Elisha, Jr.: b c. 1729 d 12- -1777 m Deliverance Stearns Pvt MA
Ezekiel: b 1719 d 11-17-1789 m Elizabeth — PS NY
John: b — d 1804 m Elizabeth Eppes PS VA
Jonathan: b 1724/5 d 6-3-1804 m Phoebe — LCol NY
Joseph: b 1750 d 1805 m Sarah Biggs Ens PS MD
Joseph: b 1730 d 4-30-1777 m Mary — CS Sgt MD
Joseph: b 1738 d c. 1828 m Elizabeth Rawlings Capt VA
Joseph: b c. 1740 d 9-30-1821 m Margaret VanMetre Sol VA
Joshua, Sr.: b 4-14-1714 d a. 2-16-1790 m Elizabeth Chapline PS VA
Matthew: bpt 6-15-1735 d 5-27-1817 m (1)Hannah Hudson
    (2)Naomi Wells Pvt PS NY
Silas: b 12-3-1736 d 5-17-1811 m (1)— Mummy (2)Margaret
    Hoaglin Pvt VA
Sylvanus: b 10-23-1737 d p. 1815 m Mary Ann Wheeler Pvt NJ
Thomas: bpt 1744 d 9-6-1785 m Elizabeth Barnes PS NY
Wm.: b c. 1742 d p. 4-19-1777 m Elizabeth — Lt MD
Wm., Sr.: b 1706 d p. 1775 m Temperance — PS NY
Wm., Jr.: b 12- -1737 d 2-16-1815 m Mary Chatfield PS Ens NY

HEDGLIN,
Wm.: b 2-25-1752 d 3- -1833 m Sarah Gomo Pvt NJ ★

HEDGPETH,
John: b 9-11-1757 d 10-15-1818 m Sarah Nicholson Pvt NC

HEDRICK, (includes HADRICK, HEDERICK, HEDRICH,
HETRICK, HETTRICK)
Charles: b c. 1741 d c. 1802 m Barbara Conrad PS VA
Christin: b c. 1750 d c. 10-6-1781 m Agnes — Pvt PA
Jacob: b 10-26-1761 d 12-4-1834 m Lydia Shaffer 1Lt PA
Jacob: b 1736 d 1826 m Barbara — Pvt PA
Jacob: b 7-25-1763 d 9-4-1834 m Margaret Hines Pvt PA ★
John: b 7-4-1763 d 2-8-1845 m Susan Feeman Pvt PA ★
John: b 1725 d p. 1810 m Susan Maria Horn Pvt VA
John Nicholas: b — b p. 5-3-1806 m (1)Anna Catherine Brosius
    (2)Anna Mary — Ens PA
Peter: b 12-17-1733 d 1-24-1798 m Margaret Herrick Capt NC
Peter: b a. 1738 d p. 1787 m — LCol PA
Philip: b 1755 d 1833 m (1)— (2)Louvicey or Louvisa — Capt PA
Varner: b 7-7-1744 d a. 11-12-1805 m Garttrout Flick PS MD

HEEBNER, (includes HEUBNER)
Christopher: b 4-19-1731 d 6-27-1817 m Susanna Wiegner Pvt PA
George: b 1756-58 d 182- m — Haines Reed Pvt PA
Hans George: b 1720 d 1792 m Anne Veronica DoHerer CS PA

HEERMANCE,
Jacob: b 9-2-1707-17 d 3-12-1788 m Catherine Vosburgh Capt NY
Jacob: b a. 1738 d p. 1790 m Morretje Whittaker Pvt NY
Peter: b 9-16-1724 d 5-21-1804 m (1)Elizabeth Knickerbocker
    (2)Maria Schepmoes VanWagenen Pvt NY

HEFFERNAN,
Stephen: b 8-25-1758 d 9-27-1836 m Abigail Dyer Pvt RI ★

HEFFLEFINGER,
Philip: b c. 1757 d 12-13-1839 m Catharine Eichholtz Fif PA

HEFFLEY, (or HAFFLE)
Charles: b 9-29-1737 d 1827 m Margaret Hausmann PS PA

HEFFNER,
George: b 6-10-1757 d 4-29-1818 m Maria Hummel Pvt PA
Jacob: b 9-23-1752 d 11-23-1848 m (1)Elizabeth Miller (2)Mrs.
    Elizabeth Priest Pvt MD ★
Jacob: b 11-11-1736 d 5-31-1829 m (1)Elizabeth Lyass (2)Maria
    Barbara — CMman PA
Valentine: b 1758/9 d 1848 m (1)Barbara Miller (2)Mary — Pvt PA

HEGEMAN,
Adrian: b 7-19-1736 d 10-2-1809 m (1)Katherine Pollock (2)Jane
    Johnson 1Lt NY
Adrian: b 9-9-1722 d 3- -1788 m Cynthia Stryker PS NY
Elbert: b 6-2-1742 d 10-18-1816 m Mary Smith PS NY
Peter: b a. 1760 d p. 1783 m Lettie Fletcher Pvt NY

HEILIG, (includes HELICK)
George Michael: b 2-27-1761 d 1828 m Catharine Roseman Pvt PA
Philip: b c. 1750 d p. 12-27-1791 m Eva Elizabeth Muller Pvt PA

HEILMAN, (includes HILEMAN)
Ansten: b 3-3-1742 d 3-15-1815 m Regina Barbara Maurer Pvt PA
Jacob: b 7-10-1762 d 8-25-1828 m (1)Eva Rumbold (2)Christina
    Diehl Pvt PA

John: b 12-17-1744 d 2-10-1812 m Anna Maria — Pvt PA
John Adam: b 8-2-1745 d 10-4-1827 m Catherine Schmidt Lt PA
Michael: b 9-30-1756 d 10-6-1849 m (1)Mary Young (2)Margaret
    Hooper Pvt PA
Peter: b 5-16-1743 d 4-16-1810 m Barbara Umburger Pvt PA
Peter: b 1750 d 6-1-1833 m Elizabeth Harter Pvt PA

HEIM, (includes HEIMS)
John: b 1756 d 1824 m (2)Sophia Kohl Pvt PA
Wm.: b 12-11-1760 d 3-3-1856 m Elizabeth — Pvt PA

HEIMBACH,
David: b 4-10-1760 d 8-23-1837 m Fannie McKay Pvt PA

HEIMBAUGH, (includes HEIMBAUCH)
Jacob: b 1760-64 d 1816 m Dorothea — Pvt PA
Michael: b 8-18-1762 d p. 1787 m Katharina Werthmann Pvt PA

HEINER, (includes HENER)
Frederick: b c. 1752 d p. 1783 m Magdalena — 1Lt PA
Johannes: b c. 1725 d p. 1803 m Eva VanEtten Pvt NY
Johannes: b c. 1745 d p. 1801 m Catherina Theter Pvt NY
John: b 1745 d 1798 m Rachel — Pvt PA
Lewis: b c. 1766 d 1830 m Nancy Myers Pvt NC

HEINEY,
Jacob: b c. 1730 d p. 1781 m — Diffenbaugh Pvt PA

HEINLEIN,
George: b 1742 d 10-2-1805 m Sarah Bucher Capt PA

HEINLY,
David: b 10-17-1728 d 10-3-1784 m (1)Eva Kuser (2)Sabina Kuder
    PS PA
George: b 6-15-1758 d 8-17-1840 m Eva Dunkel Pvt PA
John: bpt 10-26-1730 d 12- -1818 m Elizabeth Kickline Pvt PS PA

HEINTZ,
Philip: b c. 1752 d p. 1814 m — Moyers Pvt MD

HEISER, (includes HEIZER, HEYSER)
John: b 8-12-1739 d 6-14-1798 m Mary — Pvt PA
John: b 3-17-1747 d 6-26-1837 m Elizabeth Mowry Pvt VA
Samuel: b 9-25-1749 d a. 1-26-1815 m Elizabeth — Pvt VA
Wm.: b c. 1745 d p. 12-23-1789 m Anna — Capt MD

HEISKELL, (includes HISKILL, HYSKELL)
Adam: b 1754 d 7-28-1822 m Margaret Upp Capt VA
Benjamin: b 3- -1729 d 3-20-1811 m Margaret Secord PS MD
Frederick: b 1752 d 1815 m Catherine Steidinger PS MD
Peter: b 1760 d 1840 m Susanna Wetzell Ens VA

HEISLER,
Frederick: b 10-17-1759 d 3-12-1843 m Mary Gardner Pvt PA

HEISLEY,
Michael: b 10-10-1755 d 1815 m Mary Heisley Pvt PA

HEISS,
Frederick: b 1750 d p. 1- -1817 m Anna Catherine — Pvt PA

HEITLER,
Christian: b 4-3-1758 d 6-2-1835 m (1)Maria Kauffman (2)Elizabeth
    Wickel Pvt PA

HELFFERICH, (includes HELFRICH)
George, Sr.: b 12-27-1734 d 1-11-1814 m Mary Magdalena
    Bobbinmyer Pvt PA
George, Jr.: b 5-13-1761 d 12-22-1836 m Elizabeth Christina
    Schaffer Pvt PA
Michael: b 4-27-1760 d 10-19-1841 m Catharine Hill Pvt PA

HELLEN,
Wm.: b c. 1750 d 1780 m Dorcas Johnson PS MD
Wm.: bpt 7-9-1749 d 11-23-1811 m Susannah Hallenbeck Pvt NY

HELLER, (includes HALLER, HOLLER)
Berndt: b a. 1753 d 10- -1809 m Oshel Jedelin Pvt PA
Christopher: b 4-5-1731 d a. 6-20-1804 m (1)Mary Keiper
    (2)Elizabeth — Pvt PA
Frederick: b 7-19-1763 d 8-1-1837 m Catharine Brecht Cpl PA
Henry: b 1720 d 9- -1793 m Chrishamer — Col Wgn PA
Henry: b 12-4-1753 d 5- -1838 m Jane McClimans Pvt PA
Jacob: b 3-6-1750 d 10-8-1822 m Susanna Weyland Capt PA
John: b 10-29-1756 d 1834 m Susan Hammond Pvt PA
John: b 1757 d p. 3-4-1826 m (1)Christina — (2)Susan Hauser Pvt
    PA
John: b 9-21-1758 d 1833 m Mary Jones Pvt PA ★
John: b 1752 d 1830 m Susanna — Pvt PA
John: b c. 1755 d p. 5-9-1814 m — Fogwell Pvt PA
John: b 11-24-1739 d 8-4-1822 m Anna — Pvt PA
John: b 1748 d 9-12-1824 m Mary Magdalena — Pvt PA
Joseph: b 3-19-1756 d 3-26-1838 m Margaret Butz Pvt PA

Michael: b 2-12-1724 d 1803 m Magdalena Catherine Keiper Pvt PS PA
Peter: b 9-18-1762 d 5-12-1852 m Katherine — Pvt PA
Simon: b 6-18-1721 d 5-20-1785 m (1)Louisa Deitz (2)Margretha Sgt PS PA

HELLMAN, (includes HELMAN)
Christian: b 1735 d 4- -1815 m Rosanna Hubler Pvt PA
George, Jr.: b c. 1752 d 1- -1832 m Elizabeth — Pvt PA

HELM, (includes HELME, HELMS)
Daniel: b 10-29-1758 d 7-9-1838 m Sara — Sol NY
George: b 8-22-1747 d 7-9-1821 m Frances Coppage Pvt VA
James, Jr.: b 3-12-1749 d p. 1795 m Sarah Clarke PS RI
Job: b 7-10-1762 d 6-18-1846 m Mary Moore Pvt PA
John: b 8-14-1741 d 4-20-1825 m Mary Carson Lt VA
John: b 1761 d 5-31-1838 m Anna Ockerman Pvt NC VA ★
John Daniel: b 9-1-1741 d 9-27-1819 m (1)Sophia Moore (2)Mrs. — Jones Pvt VA
Leonard: b 1758 d 12-23-1824 m Elizabeth Jackson Pvt VA ★
Lynaugh: b c. 1715 d 1789 m Hester — PS VA
Meredith: b 1724 d 1804 m (1)— Calmes (2)Frances Sanford Fowler CS VA
Robert: b 1754 d 11-10-1792 m Sara Linn Capt NJ
Samuel: b 10-11-1760 d 4- -1846 m Hannah Westfall Pvt Spy NJ ★
Samuel: b 1-6-1762 d 10-11-1837 m Catherine — Pvt NJ ★
Thomas: b 9-14-1731 d 4-27-1816 m Jane Pope Lt VA
Thomas: b 7-22-1748 d 3-15-1781 m Nancy Ann Gilbert 1Lt VA
Thomas: b 1727 d 1-6-1778 m Margaret Neill CS VA
Wm.: b 5-22-1758 d 7-14-1826 m Elinor Dobbin Pvt VA ★
Wm.: b 1766 d 8-28-1809 m Deborah Cranston Pvt RI
Wm.: b 1745 d 1826 m (1)Matilda Taliaferro (2)— Pickett Maj VA
Wm.: b 4-10-1760 d p. 3-27-1806 m (1)Margaret Rankin (2)Agnes Pickett Capt VA

HELMER,
Adam F.: b 1754 d 4- -1830 m Anna Bellinger Lt NY W★
Frederick: b — d 8-6-1777 m (1)Sabina — (2)Elizabeth Dygert Capt PS NY
Frederick A.: b 8-16-1725 d 3-5-1804 m Barbara Elizabeth Homan Pvt NY
George: b 8-8-1740 d 3-23-1823 m Margaret Myer Lt NY
Henry A.: b 1747 d 5-15-1815 m Maria Elizabeth — Sgt NY
John F.: b 9-3-1765 d 11-26-1829 m Margaret Munterbach Pvt NY ★
Joseph: b 2-18-1762 d — m Susanna Flint Pvt NY
Philip: b 6-11-1757 d p. 1820 m — Pvt NY ★
Philip F.: b 8-7-1740 d 6-8-1830 m Anna Mayer Sgt NY

HELMERSHAUSEN,
Henry Frederick: b 3-27-1751 d 7-2-1831 m Anna Marsh Pvt MA

HELMICK,
Peter: b 9-12-1750 d 4-17-1824 m (1)Mary M. Storms Pvt VA

HELPHENSTINE,
Peter: b 6-17-1724 d p. 8- -1776 m Catherine Berger Maj VA
Philip: b 1754 d 10-12-1830 m Rebecca Wolf Pvt VA ★

HELSLEY,
Jacob: b 8-10-1756 d 4-15-1833 m Rosana Foltz Pvt PA ★

HELTON,
Peter: b c. 1731/2 d 1803 m Susanna — PS NC

HELTZINGER, (or HILTSINGER)
Peter: b 3-20-1755 d p. 1790 m Elizabeth Finck Pvt NY

HELWIG,
Andrew: b 1756 d 1827 m (1)Catherine Bader (2)Catherine Truckenmiller PS PA

HELZEL, (includes HELTZEL, HOLTZEL)
John T.: b 1-3-1760 d 6-16-1843 m Hetty Imler Pvt PA
Nicholas: b 7-17-1763 d 11-29-1841 m Catharine Hershinger Pvt PA
Philip: b 4-14-1761 d 3-26-1838 m Mary Willis Pvt PA
Tobias, Sr.: b c. 1732 d 1792 m (1)Anna Elizabeth Moore (2)Mrs. Anna Mary Brenner Pvt PA

HEMBREE, (or HEMBRY)
Joel: b 1755 d p. 1806 m Hannah — PS SC

HEMINGER,
John: b 5- -1758 d 4-5-1842 m Mary — Pvt PA ★

HEMINGWAY, (includes HEMENWAY)
Abijah: b 10-19-1755 d 7-30-1824 m Lydia Smith Pvt MA
Abraham, Jr.: b 4-10-1751 d 7-22-1813 m (1)Anna Smith (2)Mary — (3)Margaret — Pvt CT
Abraham: b 4-1-1727 d 8-25-1796 m Mercy Tuttle Pvt CT
Abram: b 12-3-1699 d — m — Capt CT
Asa: b 9-19-1750 d 4-18-1810 m (1)Rebecca Rice (2)Sara Nicholson Pvt MA

Daniel, Sr.: b 2-2-1719 d 11-15-1794 m (1)Ruth Bigelow (2)Elizabeth Johnson (3)Abigail Wheelock PS MA
Daniel, Jr.: b 6-6-1745 d p. 1790 m Mary Carroll Pvt MA
Daniel: b 1732 d 12-1-1815 m (1)Margaret Bellows (2)Thankful Joslin (3)Desire Cloyes Pvt PS MA
Ebenezer, Sr.: b 10-24-1712 d 1781 m Mary Eve PS MA
Ebenezer, Jr.: b 5-6-1740 d 12-11-1831 m Bathshebah Stone Lt MA
Ebenezer: b 5-26-1760 d 10-21-1839 m Ruth Gates Sol MA
Elias: b 12-22-1757 d 10-1-1835 m Molly Patterson Cpl MA
Enos: b 9-17-1755 d 3-4-1845 m Sarah Hemingway Sgt CT ★
Isaac, Sr.: b 7-17-1730 d 1-31-1778 m Elizabeth Haven Pvt MA
Isaac, Jr.: b 10-24-1762 d 2-21-1833 m Patty Maynard Pvt MA
Jacob: b 1-1-1765 d 8-28-1838 m Abigail Linsley Pvt CT ★
Jacob: b 5-21-1747 d 12-19-1822 m Nabby Eaton Pvt MA
Jacob: b 3-17-1753 d 1820 m (2)Sarah Saddler Pvt MA
John: b 9-3-1762 d 1-21-1816 m Deborah Adams Sgt MA
Jonas: b 12-13-1758 d 3-12-1827 m Sarah Whitney Pvt MA
Jonathon: b c. 1742 d 2- -1818 m Martha Resign Wilder Pvt MA
Joshua: b 4-28-1755 d 3-18-1817 m Miliscent — Cpl MA
Josiah: b 10-5-1733 d 1808 m (1)Zerviah Mellens (2)Mary — Lt MA
Phineas: b 1762 d 11- -1835 m Mary Ann Conn Pvt NH ★
Phineas: b 2-19-1744 d 4-18-1815 m Elizabeth Sarah Taylor Pvt VT
Rufus: b 3-30-1764 d 12-22-1839 m (1)Lydia Brown (2)Polly Curtis Pvt Fif Maj MA ★
Samuel: b 3-12-1713 d 10-25-1777 m Mehitabel Dennison CS CT
Samuel: b 8-3-1724 d 6-18-1806 m Hannah Rice Sgt MA
Samuel: b 4-17-1748 d 3-15-1818 m Sarah Fitch Sgt MA
Samuel: b 2-26-1755 d 1-26-1813 m Martha Salmon Pvt MA
Silas: b 4-6-1744 d 8-12-1830 m Mary Smith 2Lt MA
Thomas: b 1753/4 d 2-6-1847 m Elizabeth — Pvt MA

HEMINOVER,
Anthony: b — d p. 2-4-1824 m Else — Pvt NJ

HEMPERLY, (includes HEMBERLY)
Anthony, Sr.: b— d 1788 m Mrs. Julina Gessele Bauman Pvt PA
Lodwick: b c. 1732 d 1790 m Mary — Pvt PS PA

HEMPHILL,
Andrew: b c. 1750 d 5-24-1804 m McKown PS SC
James: b 11-14-1761 d 4-15-1816 m Ruth Harthorn Pvt NH W★
Jonathan: b 1760 d 1825 m Esther Walker Pvt SC
Joseph: b 1732 d 1793 m Ann Mills Pvt PA
Moses: b 11-11-1746 d 2-16-1822 m Agnes Sharpe Pvt PA
Robert: b — d 3- -1813 m Nancy Carney PS PA
Thomas: b c. 1750 d 5-4-1826 m Mary — Capt NC

HEMPINSTALL,
Abraham: b 1740 d p. 1783 m Mary Wilson Ens VA

HEMPLEMAN,
George: b 6-24-1732 d p. 4-7-1852 m Margarett Duffy Pvt PA

HEMPSTEAD,
Benjamin: b 5-8-1753 d 9-2-1798 m Elizabeth Copp Cpl CT
Hallam: b 6-1-1763 d 7-25-1833 m Polly Barron Pvt CT
John: b 12-26-1709 d 6-2-1779 m Hannah Salmon CS CT
Joshua, Sr.: b 6-4-1724 d 9-6-1806 m Lydia Burch Sol CT
Joshua, Jr.: b 6- -1744 d 8-16-1782 m Anna Hempstead Cdr CT
John: b 7-2-1733 d 1-17-1821 m (1)Keziah Havens (2)Ann Buck Pvt CT
Joshua Havens: b 9-30-1756 d p. 1811 m Mrs. Ursula (Phelps) Clark Pvt CT
Nathaniel, Sr.: b 2-5-1727 d 11-21-1792 m Hannah Booth Sol CT
Nathaniel, Jr.: b 10-30-1747 d 1846/7 m Esther Greene Lt NY
Robert: b 2-27-1747 d 5-17-1834 m Annie Avery Sgt CT
Robert: b 11-12-1702 d 3-5-1779 m (1)Mary Youngs (2)Mahitable (Tuttle) Reese PS NY
Samuel Booth: b 1755 d 6-5-1795 m Lucretia Goddard Pvt CT
Stephen: b 6-12-1752 d 10-3-1832 m Mary Lewis Sgt CT
Wm.: bpt 1-22-1749 d 1821 m Lydia Hempstead Sol CT

HEMSLEY,
Wm.: b 1-23-1737 d 6-5-1812 m (1)Henrietta Maria Earle (2)Sarah Williamson (3)Anna Maria Tilghman Col CS PS MD

HENCH,
Christina Schneider: b a. 1720 d a. 1790 m John Hench PS PA
George: b 1756 d c. 1814 m Catharine — Pvt PA
John, Sr.: b 1712 d p. 1800 m Christina Schneider PS PA
John, Jr.: b 1750 d 11- -1800 m Margaret Rice 2Lt PA

HENCHMAN,
Nathaniel: b 5-4-1762 d 5-27-1800 m Anna Crosby Pvt MA

HENDEE,
Caleb, Sr.: b 11-29-1730 d 5-13-1814 m Hannah Holmes Capt CT
Caleb: b 8- -1745 d 10-2-1823 m Caroline Ellsworth Pvt VT
Eliphalet: b 4-28-1743 d 2-28-1827 m Mary Loomis Sgt CT
Joshua: b 7-14-1748 d 11-19-1819 m Lydia Woodward Capt NH

HENDER,
Thomas: b 1751 d 6-4-1796 m Sally Farnsworth Ens CT

HENDERSHOT,
Jacob: b 7-6-1747 d 2-14-1828 m Effie Paugh Pvt NJ
Michael: b 1762 d 1848 m (2)Mary Space Pvt NJ
Michael: b 10-7-1745 d p. 12-13-1809 m Sarah VonSchall Pvt PA

HENDERSON,
Alexander: b 3-2-1737 d 1815 m Sarah Moore PS VA
Andrew: b 1747 d 1837 m Mehitable Saunders Sgt NH
Andrew: b — d p. 5-7-1803 m — Pvt PA
Archibald: b 6-7-1743 d 11-8-1827 m Hannah Cookson Pvt PA
Benjamin: b 12-3-1761 d 6-28-1836 m Mary Bray Pvt Slr MA
Bennett: b c. 1750 d 1793 m Elizabeth Lewis Pvt CS VA
David: b 7-21-1756 d 5-8-1831 m Lydia Fitch Pvt VT ★
David: b 1754 d p. 1832 m Elsey Anderson Sgt VA ★
Edward: b 1761/2 d 1800 m Sarah Lufkin Pvt MA
Edward: b 1811 m Mary Mathias Lt VT
Gideon: b 8-25-1713 d 12-6-1791 m Sarah Baker PS CS MA
James: b 9-22-1737 d p. 1791 m Rachel McFarlan Cpl MA
James: b c. 1715 d a. 4-1-1776 m (1)Sarah Harper (2)Elizabeth Roley Sol MA
James: b 7-23-1753 d a. 9-4-1836 m Mahetable Shepherd Pvt NY VT ★
James: b — d p. 9-9-1793 m Violet Lawson PS NC
James: b 1758 d 12-5-1795 m Sarah Park Pvt PA
James: b 1758 d 10-17-1834 m Margaret Wiggins Pvt PA
James: b c. 1741 d 1793 m Sarah Estill LCol CS VA
James: b c. 1734 d 1801 m Isabella — Pvt VA
John: b 1751 d 1786 m Elizabeth Hays Capt PA
John: b 1747 d 6-5-1814 m Martha Long Ens PA
John: b 1739 d 12- -1807 m Margaret McMahan Capt PA
John: b c. 1762 d 1795 m Hannah — Pvt PA
John: b 10-7-1753 d 8-20-1815 m Martha Pickens Pvt QM SC W★
John: b c. 1740 d 1813 m Mary — Capt CS VA
John: b c. 1756 d p. 1800 m — Capt VA
John: b c. 1750 d 1-1-1816 m Elizabeth Lyles Capt VA
John: b 1748 d 1822 m Sara — Pvt VA
John: b 1760 d 1830 m Margaret Hammond Pvt VA
John, Sr.: b c. 1718 d 1786 m Anne Bennett PS VA
John, Jr.: b 1752 d 1790 m Frances Moore Pvt VA
John: b 1-17-1740 d 3-24-1787 m Anne Givens Capt VA
John G.: b 3-30-1754 d 5-17-1839 m (2)Margaret Collins Sol GA
Joseph: b 1737 d 1812 m Delphia Lee PS NC
Joseph: b 1742 d 1778 m Nancy Osborne Pvt VA
Joseph: b c. 1745 d a. 1- -1792 m Sarah Miller Pvt VA
Kearns: b 4-25-1724 d 4-25-1793 m Elizabeth Robinson PS CS NC
Matthew: b 1745 d 4-8-1796 m Margaret Kearsley Capt PA
Matthew: b 1735 d 10-2-1795 m Mary Ferris PS PA
Michel: b 1752 d p. 1788 m Jane Green Capt VA
Nathaniel, Jr.: b 1750 d 1821 m Jemima Branson Pvt SC
Nathaniel: b 12-1-1736 d 2-28-1794 m (1)Mrs. — Jones (2)Mrs. — Morgan PS VA NC
Pleasant: b 1-9-1756 d 12-10-1842 m Sarah Martin Maj NC ★
Richard: b 2-5-1736 d 7- -1802 m Sarah Brice PS MD
Richard: b 4-20-1735 d 1-30-1785 m Elizabeth Keeling PS Col NC
Richard: b 3-17-1767 d 1-31-1850 m Anna Wagener PS PA
Robert: b 1758 d 1819 m Martha (Henderson) Sgt NC
Robert: b c. 1750-55 d a. 10-5-1788 m Isabell — PS NC
Robert: b c. 1736-8 d p. 1790 m — PS PA
Robert: b 5-18-1751 d 2-22-1839 m Mary Carroll Pvt VA
Robert: b a. 1758 d 1815-1826 m Frankey Savage Sol VA
Robert: b 2-1-1745 d 11-11-1824 m (1)Nancy Stewart (2)Elizabeth Hatfield PS VA
Samuel: b 1740 d 1820 m Priscilla Miles Capt NC
Samuel: b 11-29-1759 d 12-5-1828 m Lucy Ryckman Pvt NC
Samuel: b 2-6-1746 d 1826 m Elizabeth Callaway Maj PS NC
Samuel: b c. 1742 d a. 3-6-1799 m Mary — Pvt PA
Samuel: b 1753 d 2-5-1822 m Elizabeth — Pvt VA
Samuel: b 1737 d 1821 m Mary Ann Waldrup Lt SC
Samuel, Sr.: b 1713 d p. 5-20-1782 m Jane — Pvt VA
Samuel 3d: b 1759 d c. 1804 m Amanda Fraime Pvt Matr VA
Thomas: b 8-14-1743 d 12-15-1824 m Rachel Burrowes LCol NJ
Thomas: b 3-19-1753 d 11-11-1821 m Jane Martin Pvt NC
Thomas: b 1762 d 11-23-1846 m Mary Patterson Pvt PA
Thomas: b c. 1762 d 5-20-1841 m Elizabeth Ratchford Lt SC ★
Thomas: b 1734 d 11-27-1801 m Jennet Breckenridge Sol VT
Thomas: b 8-28-1744 d 5-3-1827 m Sara Wharton Pvt VA
Wm.: b 1753 d 1829 m Nancy Milbern Pvt MD
Wm.: b 1732 d 11-25-1825 m Elizabeth (Henderson) Pvt MA ★
Wm.: b 1756 d 9-9-1811 m (1)Margaret Wilkins (2)Mercy Little Capt PA
Wm.: b 3-5-1748 d 1-29-1788 m Mrs. Leticia (Davis) Nelson PS BGen SC
Wm.: b c. 1723 d p. 9-9-1786 m Susannah — Capt VA
Wm.: b 1757 d 1807 m Rebecca Hudson Capt VA
Wm.: b 8- -1752 d p. 4- -1803 m Lockey Trigg Capt VA
Wm.: b 1760 d 1834 m (1)Margaret Broadwater (2)Dorcas Towers Pvt VA ★
Wm.: b 10-16-1756 d 1807 m Hannah Johnson Sol VA
Wilson: b 10- -1758 d 1847 m Sarah Frost Pvt SC

HENDLEY,
John: b 10-10-1753 d 10-8-1819 m Lucy Lewis Pvt MA
Wm.: b 1747 d 2- -1830 m — Cpl MA ★

HENDON,
Isham: b 1725 d 1804 m Kesiah Johnson PS Pvt NC

HENDREN,
Downey, Jr.: b 1759 d 1810 m (1)— Schuyler (2)Mary Rutter Cpl QMSgt VA
Downer: b a. 1753 d p. 1779 m — Oldham Sgt VA
Wm., Sr.: b 1712 d 1783 m Amara Howell Pvt VA
Wm., Jr.: b 5-30-1744 d 1792 m Priscilla Oldham Sgt VA

HENDRICKS, (includes HENDRAKE, HENDRICH, HENDRICK, HENDRIX, HENDRYX, HINDRICKS)
Abijah: b 8-9-1761 d 11-26-1840 m Hepzibah Sweetland Pvt MA
Abram: b 11-5-1749 d 1-2-1819 m Ann Jameson 2Lt PA
Albert: b 5-2-1759 d 9-14-1843 m Margaret Barnett Sgt NC ★
Andrew: b 1752 d 10-15-1819 m Elizabeth Davenport Pvt CT ★
Benjamin: b 4-9-1761 d 8-18-1831 m Esther Clemens Pvt PA
Benjamin: b c. 1760 d p. 1789 m Ann — Pvt VA
Bernard: b c. 1749 d p. 1781 m Prudence — PS VA
Coe: b 8-26-1752 d 2-26-1839 m Nancy Smith Smn Pvt CT ★
Daniel: b 2-20-1745 d a. 6-22-1787 m Jean Buckles Sgt VA
David: b — d 3-27-1828 m Anne Westcott Pvt CT
David: b 1734 d 2-12-1788 m Margaret Elizabeth Pillsbury Pvt NC
Eleazer: b c. 1760 d 3-31-1798 m Martha Stone Drm Mus CT
Elijah: b 6-23-1758 d 9-11-1830 m Nancy Harrison Sgt VA ★
Ezekiel: b c. 1750 d 1817 m Mary Wood Pvt VA
Isaac: b 1740 d a. 9-22-1811 m Sarah Crane Pvt NJ
Isaac: b 1718 d 2-10-1788 m Lydia Craig PS NJ
Israel: b 1-18-1724 d c. 3-2-1797 m Rachel Boutwell Pvt MA
Jabez: b 12-19-1720 d 1-18-1808 m Lois Marcy PS MA
Jacob: b — d 1843 m Kate Thompson Pvt NY
James: b 9-12-1745 d 3- -1816 m Lois Beamen Capt MA
James: b 2-6-1758 d 6-3-1828 m Huldah Parsons Pvt MA
James: b 1-3-1759 d 3-17-1817 m Sarah Anderson Pvt VA
James: b 1722 d 1795 m Priscilla Pabbit PS VA
John: b 1730 d 2-6-1807 m Eunice Bradley Pvt CT
John, Sr.: b 1758 d 1820 m (1)Lucy Ellington (2)Mrs. — Abernathy Drm Pvt NC GA
John: b 12- -1753 d 7-6-1810 m Mary Woodruff Pvt NJ
John: b 1739 d 1803 m Margaret — Pvt PA
John: b 8-7-1756 d p. 1845 m Hannah Kelley Pvt VA
John: b c. 1736 d p. 1784 m — PS VA
Moses: b 11-19-1756 d 9-4-1844 m Elizabeth — Pvt MA ★
Moses: b c. 1757 d p. 1781 m Susan — Pvt MA
Moses: b 1-25-1765 d 1-22-1849 m Nellie Overby Pvt VA ★
Thomas: b c. 1737 d 10- -1778 m Elizabeth Turner Pvt NC
Wm.: b 1750 d p. 1786 m Sarah — Capt SC
Wm.: b 12-1709 d 3-14-1795 m (1)Elizabeth Mekie (2)Eunice Thorpe Pvt VT

HENDRICKSON, (includes HENDRICKSEN)
Benjamin: b 8-21-1743 d 1-24-1832 m (1)Marcia Jones (2)Joanna Temple (3)Phebe Dean Sgt NJ
Cornelius: b c. 1737/38 d p. 2-28-1812 m (1)Rhoda — (2)Anna — Pvt NJ
Cornelius: b 8-28-1747 d 10-1-1802 m Lydia Vanderbilt Pvt NJ
Daniel: bpt 12-25-1736 d p. 4-4-1797 m Catharine VanBrunt Col PS NJ
Daniel: b 2-14-1737 d 9-19-1812 m Ann Steward Pvt NJ
David: b 1745 d p. 8-5-1782 m Leah Lawrence Col NJ
Garrettson: b 2-11-1734 d 12-21-1801 m (1)Catherine Denise (2)Helena VanLieu (3)Nelly VanDoorn Smock Lt NJ
Hendrick: b 5-2-1758 d 12-1-1840 m Fransinkie Covenhoven Pvt NJ
Hendrick: b 2-25-1742 d 6-23-1812 m Johanna Hubbard 2Sgt NY
Henry: bpt 5-22-1726 d p. 1790 m Annatje Merkle CS NY
Isaac: b c. 1753 d a. 2- -1840 m — Pvt NC ★
Jacob: b 4- -1744 d 8-15-1810 m Elizabeth Mount PS NJ
John: b 1735 d 3-5-1820/1 m Anne Coxe Artl Matr NJ
John: b 11-5-1733 d 9-12-1815 m Nancy Burtis Pvt NY
Okey: b c. 1734 d 1830 m Mary Ann Steepe Pvt NJ
Tobias: b 6-23-1740 d 5-25-1811 m Rebecca Coward Lt NJ
Wm.: b 2-23-1757 d p. 5-8-1840 m Charlotte — Cpl MD ★

HENDRY,
David: b 1-19-1754 d 2-10-1827 m Selina Hotchkiss Pvt NY
Robert: b 3-17-1752 d 3-31-1830 m Ann Lee Sol NC
Samuel: b 1754 d 10-15-1823 m (1)Phebe Chandler (2)Elizabeth Anderson (3)Mrs. Mary Hughes Capt NJ ★
Thomas: b c. 1722 d a. 4-7-1780 m Anne Miller PS NY

HENEKER,
Emanuel: b 1757 d 5-14-1832 m (2)Rachel — Pvt NY

HENFIELD,
Edmund: b 4-9-1720 d 2-24-1790 m Lydia Hardy Pvt CS MA
Joseph: b 8-25-1743 d 3-16-1809 m Mrs. Anna Mansfield PS MA

HENLEY, (includes HENLY)
David: b 2-5-1749 d 1-1-1823 m Sarah Hazelrigge Col MA
James: b 1743 d 1805 m Frances — Capt PS VA
John: b c. 1742 d 3-16-1815 m (1)Mary Albertson (2)Elizabeth Wilson Sol NC
Leonard: b 1748/9 d 11-19-1798 m Mrs Elizabeth (Dandridge) Aylett QMSgt VA

Leonard: b 10-25-1755 d 12-5-1835 m Elizabeth Oglesby Pvt VA
Richardson: b c. 1754 d 1814 m (1)Elizabeth Brown (2)Judith Tisdale Sol PS VA
Samuel: b 1718 d 8-28-1795 m (1)Elizabeth Cheever (2)Katherine Russell Capt MA
Wm.: b 9-28-1728 d a. 7-20-1800 m Mary Ann Osborne Pvt VA

HENNEN,
Mathew: b 11-21-1752 d p. 1-15-1834 m Elizabeth — Pvt VA ★

HENNIG,
Adam: b 7-18-1757 d 7-4-1839 m (1)Anna Wierbaugh (2)Catherine Rickel (3)Barbara Vonedia Drm Pvt PA

HENNIGAN, (or HANAGIN)
Joseph: b 2-6-1759 d 4-6-1833 m Rhoda Harris Pvt NY W★

HENNING, (includes HANNING)
Conrad: b 11-8-1751 d 10-29-1833 m Mary Magdalene Baer PS Gnr PA
Daniel: b 1-10-1755 d 12-10-1831 m Margaretta Wolfersberger Sgt PA
Jacob: b 10-19-1744 d 2-29-1824 m Margaretta — 1Lt PA

HENNION,
Cornelius: b c. 1727 d 1800 m Maria Blauvelt Capt NJ ★
John: b 3-6-1753 d c. 1815 m Sara — Pvt NJ
Joseph: b 11- -1761 d 6-28-1841 m Margaret Morrow Pvt PA
Theunis: b c. 1722 d 5-19-1801 m Annetje Doremus Tms NJ

HENRITZ,
Balser: b 1745 d p. 1777 m Dartha — Arfr PA

HENRY,
Aaron: b 1740 d c. 1824 m Rebecca — Pvt VA
Adam: b 4-27-1741 d 6-16-1838 m Elizabeth Mary Wilson Capt MA ★
Andrew: b 10-26-1762 d 10-8-1838 m Jael Elder Cpl PS MA
Andrew: b 1-31-1751 d 9-28-1837 m Thankful Norris Pvt MA
Benjamin: b 12-25-1760 d 10-17-1824 m Ruth Steer Mrmr Pvt RI ★
Benjamin: b 5-12-1742 d 5-10-1816 m Martha Ayer 1Lt VT
David: b 4-12-1734 d 12-22-1809 m Hannah Watson PS CS MA
Edward: b 1750 d 1855 m Mrs. Christina Trout Pvt VA
Francis: b 1753 d 12-23-1824 m (1)Agnes Carson (2)Eleanor — Pvt PA★
George: b 1737/8 d p. 1815 m Margaret Young Pvt PA
George: b c. 1745 d a. 1810 m Lydia Wheatley Pvt VA
Hugh: b 1756 d 1838 m (1)Mary Long (2)Mary Upton Sol NC
Hugh: b 1745 d 2-7-1825 m Phoebe Ann Morris PS Pvt PA
Hugh: b 4-1-1750 d 6- -1814 m Elizabeth Martin Pvt MA
James: b 8-3-1762 d 4-27-1831 m Mrs. Abigail Woodruff McCrea Pvt NJ
James: b c. 1740 d 1812 m Agnes Mitchell Pvt SC
James: b 5-7-1765 d 5-1-1845 m Anna (Henry) Pvt SC
James: b 1750 d 11-25-1816 m Mary Murphy PS SC
James: b 1750 d 1792 m Jean McNabb Pvt VA
James, Sr.: b c. 1729 d 10- -1806 m Mary — PS VA
James, Jr.: b c. 1760 d p. 1809 m Mary Berry Sol VA
James: b 1731 d 12-9-1804 m Sarah Maria Scarborough PS VA
John: b 12-4-1753 d p. 1793 m Nancy Waterman Capt CT
John: b 1-8-1742/43 d 1-9-1819 m Mary Gager Pvt CT
John: b a. 10-1-1715 d p. 4-21-1781 m Dorothy Rider PS MD
John: b 11- -1750 d 1798 m Margaret Campbell PS MD
John: b 3-3-1744 d 5-5-1817 m Leah Brevoort Cmsry Gen NY
John: b 2-25-1750 d 1780 m Jane Mills Pvt NY
John: b 1737 d 7-24-1823 m Margaret Polk Pvt PA
John: b 1750 d 4-23-1838 m Margaret McMillan Pvt PA
John: b a. 1750 d 10-3-1825 m — Pvt VA
John: b 4-15-1757 d 12-29-1833 m Nancy Newman Capt SC ★
John: b 2-14-1752 d 7-22-1833 m Jane E. Dale Pvt SC ★
John: b 10-30-1745 d 1-18-1810 m Catherine Houston Pvt PS SC
John: b 1758 d 1823 m Sarah — Pvt VA
Joseph: b c. 1765 d 9-22-1816 m Mary McCaslin Pvt NC W★
Malcolm: b c. 1739 d 10-10-1816 m Dorothy Blair Capt PS MA
Malcolm: b 12-21-1755 d 4-24-1840 m (1)Nettie Gordan (2)Elizabeth Geiger Capt NC★
Moses: b c. 1757 d 7- -1781 m Margaret Baldrich Pvt NC
Patrick: b 5-29-1736 d 5-6-1799 m (1)Sarah Shelton (2)Dorothea Spottswood Dandridge PS VA
Robert: b 1732 d p. 1794 m Susannah Young Sgt MA
Robert: b 1750 d 1829 m Jane Kennedy Pvt MA
Robert M.: b 1-10-1765 d 1-6-1863 m Dorcas Bell Love Pvt NC
Samuel: b 5-25-1734 d 6-30-1790 m Lurana Cady Pvt MA
Samuel: b 8-3-1740 d 9-29-1819 m Jeney Crook Pvt MA
Samuel: b 1762 d 7-13-1824 m Mary — Sgt VA
Samuel: b — d p. 10-21-1821 m Sarah Thompson CS VA
Silas: b 1754 d 8-5-1832 m Relief Knight Pvt MA
Wells: b 8-6-1753 d 8-5-1805 m Elizabeth Rowley Pvt NY
Wm., Sr.: b 5-29-1729 d 12-15-1786 m Anne Wood PS CS PA
Wm., Jr.: b 3-12-1757 d 4-21-1821 m Sabina Schropp PS PA
Wm., Sr.: b 1715 d 10-22-1819 m Margaret Isabella McKeown Sol SC
Wm., Jr.: b 1753 d 9-12-1807 m Rosannah Moore Capt SC
Wm., Sr.: b 3-1-1734 d 5-30-1811 m Isabelle Gilmore Lt VT

Wm., Jr.: b 10-5-1760 d 5-11-1845 m Ann Brownson Sol VT
Wm.: b 1734 d p. 1784 m (1)Lucy Taylor (2)Peggy McNair Capt VA
Wm.: b 4-12-1761 d 11-23-1824 m (1)Elizabeth Julia Flournoy (2)Hester L. Clarke Pvt VA

HENSEL, (includes HENSELL)
Lawrence: b 1747 d 11-30-1808 m Esther — Pvt VA
Michael: b 11-9-1753 d 7-15-1836 m Barbara Harsh Pvt VA ★
Wm.: b 12-8-1755 d 9-14-1842 m Maria Eve East Pvt PA ★

HENSELMAN, (or HEINTZELMAN)
Andrew: b 8-8-1748 d 5-23-1848 m Anna M. — Pvt PA

HENSHAW, (includes HINCHER, HINSHAW)
Benjamin: b 1-12-1729 d 8-2-1793 m (1)Elizabeth Lord (2)Mrs. Huldah (Stillman) Sumner Lt CT
Daniel: b 12-3-1701 d 11-18-1781 m (1)Elizabeth Allen Bass (2)Elizabeth DeJersey PS MA
David: b 8-19-1744 d 5-22-1808 m Mary Sargent Capt MA
John: b c. 1734 d a. 5-6-1794 m Sarah — Pvt VA
John: b 1728 d 1790 m Mary (Rachel) — Capt PS VA
Josiah: b c. 1751/52 d 1829 m Sarah Phipps Cpl MA
Wm.: b a. 1736 d 1798-1800 m Elizabeth Gilbert Lt PM CT
Wm.: b 9-20-1735 d 2-21-1820 m (1)Ruth Sargent (2)Phebe Swan AdjGen MA
Wm., Sr.: b 12-21-1715 d 9-10-1801 m (1)Priscilla Read (2)Ruth Wilcutt Pvt MA
Wm., Jr.: b 5-9-1742 d 6-21-1807 m Mehitable Moffit Sgt MA
Wm.: b c. 1729 d 1818 m (1)Sarah — (2)Mary (Hinshaw) PS NC
Wm.: b 3-6-1736 d 7-8-1799 m Agnes Anderson Capt VA

HENSHY,
Henry, Sr.: b c. 1736 d c. 10-9-1795 m Barbara — Pvt PA

HENSLEY,
Richardson: b c. 1746-48 d 1823 m Winnifred — Sol VA
Wm.: b c. 1755 d c. 1815 m Elizabeth Appleberry Pvt VA

HENSON, (includes HYNSON)
Charles, Jr.: b 10-9-1741 d 11-15-1794 m Sarah Waltham Pvt MD
Daniel: b 8-17-1764 d 1-1-1843 m Fariba Pool Pvt VA ★
John Carville: b 12-11-1743 d 2- -1816 m Rebecca — Pvt MD

HENSZEY,
Joseph: b 1733 d 10-21-1796 m Deborah Marshall Pvt PA

HENTON,
Evan: b c. 1754-56 d a. 1803 m — Pvt VA
George: b 4-8-1758 d 9-22-1837 m Mary Rigney 1Lt VA
Thomas, Sr.: b c. 1720 d 1796 m Ann Yarnall CS VA
Thomas, Jr.: b c. 1756 d p. 9-18-1829 m Christina Branner Sol VA

HEPBURN,
John: b c. 1740 d 1796 m (1)Deborah (Montgomerie) (2)Rachel — Sol NJ
Peter, Sr.: b 4-28-1732 d c. 1815-17 m (1)Susan (Fenn) Baldwin (2)Mary Cobb Pvt LT CT
Stacey: b c. 1758 d p. 1790 m Sarah Duffield Pvt PA
Thomas, Jr.: b c. 1750 d p. 5-3-1815 m Margaret Dwyer Pvt MD
Wm.: b 1753 d 6-25-1821 m (1)Crecy Covenhoven (2)Elizabeth Huston Capt PA

HEPENSTALL,
Francis: b 4-28-1745 d 1778 m Ann Spenny Pvt MA

HEPLER, (includes HOPLER, HOPPLER)
Casper: b 5-20-1751 d 12-27-1816 m Anna Maria Schmitt Pvt PA
Christopher: b c. 1745/6 d 1816 m Catharine — Pvt PA
Conrad: b c. 1730 d 5-26-1815 m Elizabeth — Pvt NJ
Jacob: b 1745 d p. 1809 m Elisabethe Pvt PA

HEPNER,
John: b 1753 d p. 1820 m Mary Hitchner Pvt NJ ★

HEPPICH,
Christian: b 1754 d 1803 m Elizabeth Catherine Ettele Pvt PA

HERBERT,
Francis: b c. 1730 d 9-4-1802 m (2)Catherine Mount PS NJ
James: b 12-20-1744 d 11-7-1814 m Elizabeth Conover Pvt NJ
James: b 3-14-1746 d 1834 m Mary VanDeventer Pvt NJ
John: b 11-19-1759 d 6-22-1846 m Fanny Poinset Pvt NJ
Josiah: b 8-22-1755 d p. 1833 m Sarah — Drm VA
Obediah: b 9-9-1731 d 10-12-1777 m Elizabeth Warne Pvt NJ
Reuben: b 10-18-1743 d 6-23-1803 m Betty Sparrow CS MA
Richard: b 12-31-1729 d 7-17-1823 m Hannah Hall Lt NH
Thomas: b 1753 d 1833 m Alice Hill Pvt NJ ★
Thomas: b 10-3-1754 d 10-25-1844 m Zilpha Murphy Pvt NJ
Wm.: b 3-9-1733 d 1776 m Sarah — Capt VA
Wm. II: b 6- -1761 d 1831 m Mary Christian Pvt VA

HERBST,
Andrew: b 6-16-1760 d 1847 m Barbara Barrett Pvt PA
Peter: b 7-19-1763 d 3-8-1847 m Tacy — Pvt PA ★

HERDMAN,
John: b 9-29-1739 d 1-26-1791 m Eleanor Hamilton Sgt PS DE

HEREFORD,
John: b 1725 d 1794 m (2)Margaret Ammon PS VA
John: b 2-3-1758 d 5-13-1846 m (1)Betsy Patterson (2)Sarah Mauzey Adj PS VA ★

HERGESHEIMER,
Christopher: b 3-3-1737 d 1806-08 m Sarah Elizabeth — Pvt PA

HERITAGE, (includes HERRITAGE)
Benjamin: b 2-14-1740 d 3-27-1815 m Priscilla Clark PS NJ
Wm. Martin: b c. 1755 d p. 3-28-1807 m Mary Green LCol NC

HERKELRODE,
Christian: b 1754 d 1826 m (2)Christina Bartruff Lt PA
Henry: b 10-21-1749 d 2-19-1836 m Elizabeth Emmert Pvt VA

HERKIMER,
George: b 1744 d 8-24-1788 m Alida Schuyler Col NY
Hanyost, Sr.: b 1695 d 8-26-1775 m Catherine — PS NY
Hendrick: b 1730 d 8-1-1779 m Catherine Tygert Capt NY
Joseph: b 10- -1751 d 4- -1825 m Catherine Elizabeth Schuyler Capt NY

HERMAN, (includes HEERMAN)
Christian: b 10-20-1761 d 10-23-1829 m Elizabeth Bowers Pvt PA
Conrod: b 1747 d 6-9-1822 m Christena — Pvt PA
Frederick: b c. 1745-50 d p. 1818 m — Reiger Sgt PA
Frederick: b 4-7-1765 d 9-16-1843 m Catharine Lutz PS PA
Frederick Wm.: b 1752 d p. 1832 m Sallie Priest SgtMaj MA ★
George: b 12-20-1763 d 10-16-1850 m Elizabeth Eslinger Sol NC
Ludwig: b 1720 d 11- -1790 m Eberhardina Regina Frederica Fritz Pvt PS PA
Martin: b 1732 d 1804 m Anna Dorothea Borst Pvt PA

HERMANY,
John: b 3-7-1743 d 11-23-1831 m Elizabeth Lowe Pvt PA

HERNDON,
Benjamin: b 12-10-1749 d 12-30-1819 m (1)Sarah Pines (2)Patience Terry LCol NC VA
Benjamin: b c. 1760 d 1814 m Nancy Newton Pvt VA
David: b 1712 d p. 9-8-1794 m Mary — PS VA
Edward: b 7-16-1738 d 5-11-1831 m Mary Gaines PS VA
Edward: b 1-15-1761 d 1837 m Margaret Whitelaw PS VA W★
Edward, Sr.: b 3-5-1730 d 12- -1799 m Mary Duerson PS VA
Edward, Jr.: b 11-19-1762 d 5-19-1808 m Mary Elizabeth Sharpe Pvt VA
George: b 1731-34 d 1796 m Sarah — Capt NC
George: b 6-14-1762 d 4-29-1848 m Frances Rogers Pvt NC ★
James: bpt 1737 d 1815 m Isabella Thompson Capt NC
James: b c. 1743 d 1810 m Nancy Rice CS PS VA
John: b 1746 d 1821 m Mary Ann Clarkson 1Lt VA
John: b 1-16-1756 d 2-13-1812 m Judith Hampton QM VA W★
John: b c. 1741 d 1805 m Mrs Sarah (Chapman) Mountjoy PS CS VA
John: b c. 1722 d 1782/3 m Mary Lewis PS VA
Joseph: b 1756 d 8-30-1853 m — Stewart Pvt NC
Joseph: b 5-1-1737 d 10-28-1810 m (1)Philadelphia Foster (2)Mary Minor PS VA
Lewis: b 1738 d 1796 m Frances Thompson PS VA
Pomfrett: b c. 1746 d p. 10-28-1820 m Martha Bryant PS NC
Reuben: b 1765 d p. 1809 m Frances Canada Pvt VA
Thomas: b 1760 d p. 1800 m Sarah Woodson Pvt VA
Wm.: b 2-29-1764 d 1846 m Mary Rucker Pvt VA ★
Zachariah: b 1738 d p. 3-23-1796 m Mary Scott Capt VA

HERNLY,
Isaac: b 4- -1742 d 3-30-1824 m Maria — Pvt PA

HEROY,
Clarkson: b 11-27-1760 d c. 1805/6 m Bethenia Golden Pvt NY

HERR, (includes HARE)
Christian: b 9-19-1732 d 11-26-1815 m Maria Bowman Pvt PA
Christian: b 12-30-1746 d 1822 m (1)Frances Martin (2)Barbara (Dombach) Funk Pvt PA
Christian: b 1744 d 1819 m Fannie Eshleman Pvt PA
Emanuel: b 1745 d p. 1826 m Catherine — Pvt PA
Henry: b c. 1725 d 7-26-1780 m Esther Hershey Pvt PA
John: b 6-26-1726 d 4-9-1796 m Mary Myers PS PA
John: b c. 1729 d 1806 m Ann Shirk Pvt PA
John: b 8-30-1748 d 10-29-1813 m Sarah Randall Pvt PA
Rudolph: b 8-30-1752 d 3-6-1822 m Anna Charles Pvt PA

HERRENDEN,
Nehemiah: b c. 1720 d a. 5- -1791 m Hannah — PS MA

HERRICK,
Amos: b 12-5-1744 d 12- -1825 m (1)Deborah Fillmore (2)Eunice Searless Pvt VT
Andrew, Jr.: b 4-7-1752 d c. 1827 m Priscilla Gady Pvt CT
Andrew: b 8-13-1742/3 d 1812 m (1)Sarah Goodwin (2)Abigail — (3)Judith — (4)Elizabeth — (5)Mercy Closson Pvt MA
Asa: b 7-11-1742 d 4-27-1821 m Elizabeth Stacey Pvt MA
Benjamin: b 2-9-1752 d p. 1796 m (1)Elizabeth Dodge (2)Rebecca Chase Pvt MA
Daniel: b 12-5-1755 d 4-28-1792 m Olive Fiske Pvt CT
Daniel: b 10- -1751 d — m Ruth Avery Pvt MA
Daniel: b 5-18-1742 d p. 1785 m (1)Zillah Marvin (2)Mary Guile Capt NY
Ebenezer: b 12-10-1766 d 6-3-1842 m (1)Polly Lamb (2)Phoebe Alger Steele PS CT
Ebenezer: b 1764 d 1846 m Mary Washburn Pvt MA ★
Ebenezer: b 6-24-1739 d 6-17-1775 m Phoebe Carlton Sol MA
Ebenezer: b 3-2-1759 d 1-7-1842 m (1)Lydia Eaton (2)Abigail Nims Pvt NH
Edward: b 10-9-1754 d 2-25-1811 m Mary Holt Sgt MA
Elijah: b 1758 d 1808 m Hannah Russell Pvt MA W★
Elijah, Sr.: b 1-25-1736/7 d 1-18-1806 m Anna Kinnie Capt PS NY
Elijah, Jr.: b 7-22-1760 d 9-26-1847 m Rhoda Cissen Pvt NY ★
Ezekiel: b 6-15-1729 d 10-28-1810 m Abigail Wilson Capt MA
George: b 1734 d 1786 m Mary Rogers 2Maj NY
Henry: b 10-5-1716 d 12-9-1780 m Anna Batchelder Col MA
Henry: b 9-11-1741/2 d 7-25-1820 m Mary Foster Sgt MA
Henry: b 1738 d 12-20-1827 m Sally Yemmons Sgt VT
Isaac: b 12-16-1719 d 1819 m Elizabeth (Herrick) Cpl CT
Isaac: b 2-8-1748 d 9-30-1809 m (1)Olive Worthington (2)Prudence (Avery)Starkweather Pvt MA
Israel, Jr.: b 7-3-1750 d 10-6-1837 m Ruth Tracey Pvt CT ★
Israel: b 12-3-1721 d 9-14-1782 m (1)Mary Bragg (2)Abagail Kilham Pvt MA
Jacob: b 6-12-1754 d 12-18-1832 m Sarah Webster Pvt Adj MA Heirs ★
Jason: b 1763 d 1819 m Damaris Baxter Pvt MA
John: b 7-4-1731 d 1-14-1806 m Anna Brown Pvt CS MA
John: b 1753 d 1-30-1789 m Avice Newton Cpl CT W★
Jonathan: b 8-10-1710 d p. 1790 m Mary Dodge Sgt MA
Jonathan: b 10-18-1760 d 1847 m Patience Palmer Pvt NY ★
Joseph: b 9-14-1752 d 1820 m Mercie Scales Preston Pvt MA
Joshua: b 11-2-1751 d 4-4-1830 m Rachel Adams Pvt MA ★
Josiah, Jr.: b 11-10-1733 d 4- -1799 m Mary Lowe Pvt MA
Nathan: b 11-24-1743 d 1-15-1826 m Mary Kidder 1Lt NY
Nathaniel: b 10-31-1736 d 1807 m Susannah Messer Lt MA
Nehemiah: b 4-9-1737 d p. 1794 m (2)Miriam Upton Capt MA
Rufus: b 3-13-1734 d 1-30-1811 m (1)Sarah Gibbs (2)Lydia Leonard LCol NY
Samuel, Sr.: b 1713 d 1792 m Elizabeth Jones Pvt MA
Samuel, Jr.: b 2-14-1745 d 2-9-1807 m Elizabeth Flint Pvt MA
Samuel: b 2-23-1757 d 5-24-1824 m Margaret Per Lee Capt Adj NY
Samuel: b 4-2-1732 d a. 1798 m (1)Silence Kingsley Col VT
Stephen: b 3- -1760 d 11-3-1841 m Rebecca McCrary Pvt Tms CT ★
Stephen, Sr.: b 1727 d p. 1776 m (1)Anna Fargo Pvt NY
Wm., Sr.: b 12-25-1709 m 4-10-1783 m Mary Tuck Cdr Pvtr MA
Zacharia: b c. 1740 d 11-20-1812 m Anna Pool Pvt MA

HERRING, (includes HERRIN)
Arthur: b c. 1740 d p. 12-29-1811 m Elizabeth — Pvt NC
Benjamin, Jr.: b 9-3-1761 d 2-3-1845 m Esther Robinson Pvt MA
Benjamin: b 10-21-1738 d 4-16-1795 m Miriam Dean Pvt MA
Benjamin: b 9-1-1727 d 1781 m Experience Annis Pvtr MA
Daniel: b 1726 d p. 1787 m (1)Sarah Whitfield (2)Charity (Whitfield) O'Daniel Sol NC
Henry: b 1759 d 11-4-1791 m Catherine Peckempaugh Pvt MD
Henry: b 10-2-1753 d 12-1-1840 m — Sol PA
Isaac: b 3-2-1761 d 10-23-1833 m Nancy Ann Shotwell Gainey Pvt SC ★
Jacob: b 10-28-1758 d 2-10-1812 m Magdalene Gettleman Pvt PA
Joel: b — d p. 4-9-1828 m Mrs Sophia King Gilmore Lt NC
Jonathan: b 1738 d 1808 m Elizabeth Harrison Pvt VA
Joshua: b 11-23-1723 d 4- -1801 m Elizabeth Matchett CS NC
Matchett: b 1755 d 1825 m Elizabeth Whitfield Lt NC
Pelatian: b 9-6-1721 d p. 1775 m Hepsibah Lyon Pvt MA
Richard: b 2-23-1726 d 4-4-1803 m Sarah Anders PS CS NC
Stephen: b c. 1738 d p. 9-21-1797 m Sarah — Sol NC
Thomas: b 4-12-1755 d 10-2-1832 m (1)Mary Finley (2)Agnes Johnson Pvt PA
Wm.: b 2-19-1762 d 12-15-1823 m Penelope — PS NC
Wm.: b c. 1760 d p. 10-8-1812 m (1)Susannah Parham (2)Betsy T. Pvt VA

HERRINGTON,
Benjamin: b 1740 d 1785 m Abigail — Cpl CT
Daniel: b 1-4-1756 d 8-13-1836 m Mary McCrea Pvt PA ★
Ephraim: b 1750-60 d p. 7-25-1839 m — Sol GA
Jonathan: b 1-2-1764 d 5-4-1847 m Patience Stevens Pvt RI ★
Richard: b 3-6-1756 d 11-2-1839 m (1)Elizabeth — (2)Martha — (3)Martha Striggles Pvt GA

Richard: b 4-16-1724 d 1784 m Sarah Bates Pvt RI
Silas: b 6-24-1740 d 12-8-1819 m Freelove Fiske PS RI

HERRIOTT, (includes HERIOT)
Andrew: b *a.* 1743 d *p.* 1791 m Hester Walker Pvt MD
Ephraim: b 5-8-1763 d 12-11-1817 m Mary Kerr Pvt PA
Robert: b 7-28-1739 d 7-22-1792 m Mary Ouldfield Col CS SC

HERRON,
Allen: b *c.* 1758 d *p.* 1833 m — Pvt NC ★
David: b 1730 d *p.* 1833 m — Sol VA ★
Hercules: b — d — m Elizabeth (Mildenburgh)Bingham Pvt NY
James: b 1754 d 4-24-1829 m Margaret Davidson Sol PA
James Gordon: b 1- -1749 d 12-30-1809 m Eleanor Evans Capt NJ
John: b 1-12-1740 d *p.* 8-24-1814 m Mary Stratson Pvt MD
John: b 1750 d — m Nancy Cook Sgt PA
Thomas: b *a.* 1760 d 11-8-1814 m Jean Brown Pvt PA
Wm.: b 1742 d 1-8-1819 m Mary Jennings PS Spy CT

HERSEY, (includes HEARSAY)
David: b 11-3-1746 d 11-17-1827 m Elizabeth Jenkins Lt MA
Isaiah, Sr.: b 1-29-1720/1 d 3-20-1803 m Margaret Sprague MM MA
Isaiah, Jr.: b 10-13-1745 d 2-16-1831 m Rebecca Sprague Sgt MA
James: b 12-12-1758 d 3-27-1846 m Althea Poole Sgt MA
Jeremiah, Jr.: b 10-18-1741 d 10-7-1796 m Mary Hersey Pvt MA
John, Sr.: b 8-18-1732 d 3-11-1777 m (1)Elizabeth Humphrey (2)Sarah Lincoln Pvt MA
John, Jr.: b 9-24-1761 d 12- -1849 m Anna Cushing Pvt MA
John: b 1753 d 5-14-1815 m Experience Thomas Pvt MA
Jonathan: b 10-28-1742 d 1822 m (1)Margaret Tower (2)Mary Berry Sgt & DrmMaj MA ★
Jonathan: b 1746 d 10-16-1837 m Mary Wiggin Drm NH
Joseph: b 6-23-1726 d 9-30-1801 m Mary Reed Pvt MA
Joshua: b 12- -1704 d 11-1-1784 m Mary Lincoln Pvt MA
Nathaniel: b 6-29-1742 d 10-24-1817 m Lucy White PS ME
Noah: b 10-6-1746 d 3-12-1826 m Lydia Waterman Lt MA
Obadiah: b 12-1-1755 d — m Naome Reed Pvt MA
Peter: b 12-5-1757 d 5-16-1844 m Rachel Stowell DrmMaj MA
Thomas: b 9-22-1734 d 1-12-1810 m (1)Rebecca Magoon (2)Abigail Cushing Capt MA
Zadock: b 1-16-1752 d 1-13-1850 m Abigail Lewis Pvt MA ★

HERSHER, (or HERSTER)
Andrew: b *c.* 1731 d 12-25-1776 m Anna Maria Marsteller Sgt PA

HERSHEY,
Andrew, Jr.: b 1734 d 7-16-1806 m (1)Magdalena Backmen (2)Maria Acker Pvt PA
Christian: b 2-12-1765 d 10- -1824 m Elizabeth Shelley Pvt PA
Christian: b 12-13-1757 d 10-12-1854 m Elizabeth Hoke Pvt PA
John: b 1741 d 1811 m Magdalena Hoover PS PA

HERSHNER, (or HERSCHNER)
Lawrence: b *c.* 1740 d *a.* d *a.* 3-18-1807 m Anna Maria — Pvt PA

HERTZ
David: b 7-12-1752 d 4- -1816 m Christina — Pvt PA
Ludwig: b 4-15-1759 d 3-28-1821 m Rosanna Rhein Pvt PA
Peter: b 1742 d 12-31-1824 m Catharine Barbara Clader Pvt PA

HERTZLER,
Jacob: b 1733 d 4- -1795 m Barbara Yoder Sol PA
John: b *c.* 1740 d 2- -1795 m Barbara Newcomer Pvt PA

HERTZOG, (includes HARTZOG)
Catherine: bpt 4-14-1747 d 1786-89 m George Hartzog PS SC
Philip: b *c.* 1721 d *c.* 1785 m Anna Margretha Dorster Lt PA

HESLEY,
Lenard: b *c.* 1750 d 10- -1815 m Rosina — Pvt PA

HESS,
Augustines, Sr.: b 12-21-1718 d 7-15-1782 m Catherine Kasson PS NY
Christian: b 3-10-1765 d 10-22-1826 m Catherine Brua Pvt PA
Conrad: b *c.* 1726 d 1797 m Maria — Pvt PA
Conrad: b 3- -1762 d 5-19-1839 m Margaret Frank Pvt NY
Conrad: b 1-27-1746 d 3-16-1832 m Anna Dorothy Frankenfield PS PA
Daniel: b 11-3-1757 d 11-2-1842 m (1)Katy Fox (2)Mariaugh — Pvt NY ★
Frederick: b 5-10-1751 d 1806 m Catherine Nellis Pvt NY
George: b 4-18-1760 d 4-9-1848 m Elizabeth Knepley Pvt PA
George Baltzer: b 3-25-1747 d 12-27-1806 m Mary Eve Hansel Sgt PA
Han Jost: b 11-3-1758 d 8- -1844 m Mrs Elizabeth Edic Piper Pvt NY ★
Henry: b 2-2-1730 d 2-25-1810 m Maria Elizabeth Garlock Pvt NY
Henry: b 9-23-1757 d 4-23-1831 m Magdalena — CMman PA
Jacob: b 1740 d 7-1-1815 m Margaret Orndorf Pvt MD
Jeremiah: b 11-19-1751 d 10-24-1819 m (1)Elizabeth — (2)Susannah — Lt PA

Johannes: b 3-4-1743 d 8-13-1802 m Eva Copperwall Pvt NY
John: b 12-22-1747 d 5-22-1805 m Margaret Fulmer Pvt NY ★
John: b *c.* 1760 d *p.* 1809 m Dorothea Cronmiller Pvt NY
Michael: b 1752 d 1838 m Margaret Showers Pvt NY
Michael: b — d *p.* 5- -1789 m Gertrude VanCortlandt Pvt PA
Nichoas: b 1723 d 1- -1800 m Catherine Funk PS PA
Peter: b 9-8-1757 d 8-8-1825 m Susannah Pvt PA
Philip: b 5-1-1750 d 1828 m Mary Moyer Pvt PA
Wm.: b 1741 d 1827 m Ann Catherine Godhard Ens PA

HESSER,
Frederick: b 7-6-1763 d 1851 m Mary Elizabeth Reed Boyer DrmMaj PA ★
George Nicholas: b 5-7-1747 d 11-14-1804 m Catherine Boyer Ens PA
John: b 8-10-1761 d *c.* 1825 m Elizabeth Frey Pvt Fif PA
John: b — d 1779 m Madalina — Pvt PA
Leonard: b 1733 d 9-10-1792 m Magdalen Meyer Pvt PA

HESTER,
Abraham: b 1750 d *a.* 1- -1847 m Elizabeth Norman Pvt NC ★
Barbara: b *c.* 1720 d *p.* 1782 m Robert Hester PS VA
Conrad: b 1755 d 1781/2 m Eleanor Cathrine Kunkle Pvt PA
John: b *c.* 1754 d *a.* 2-18-1820 m — Mus NC
Joseph: b *c.* 1751 d *p.* 1784 m Winnefred (Champion ?) Pvt VA

HESTON,
Edward: b 3-16-1745 d 2-14-1824 m (1)Mary Griffith (2)Sarah Hall LCol PA
Isaiah: b 8-20-1744 d 9-7-1785 m Anne Leonard Pvt PA
Thomas: b 4-4-1753 d 10-13-1802 m Hannah Clayton 1Lt PA W★

HETER, (includes HEETER & HIETOR)
Adam: b *c.* 1730-35 d *p.* 12-28-1805 m Elizabeth — 2Lt CS PA
George: b 1751 d *a.* 6- -1843 m Charlotte Speere Pvt MD ★
Sebastian: b 2-28-1760 d 6-5-1846 m Elizabeth Rarick Pvt PA

HETZEL,
John: b 1-21-1760 d *p.* 1818 m Mary Pool Pvt PA

HEUGH,
Andrew: b 1727 d 2- -1789 m Sarah Needham PS MD

HEVERLY,
Adam: b *c.* 1730 d 1803 m Maria — PS PA

HEWELL,
Wyatt: b 10-15-1756 d 1842 m (1)Sarah Worthy (2)Frances Davenport Sgt VA ★

HEWENDEEN,
Hezekiah: b 1761 d 9-16-1842 m Peggy — Pvt CT

HEWINS,
Benjamin, Jr.: b 6-18-1747 d 11-18-1826 m Anna Rhodes Pvt MA
Ebenezer: b 11-9-1731 d 5-8-1806 m Mercy Guild Lt MA
Enoch: b 5-16-1741 d 8-10-1821 m Sarah (Hewins) 2Lt MA
Increase: b 4-16-1739 d *a.* 1-4-1791 m Jerusha Bryan Capt MA
Jacob, Sr.: b 1-13-1728 d — m Damaris Bird Lt MA
Jacob, Jr.: b — d — m Hannah Alger Fif MA
Wm.: b 12-16-1735 d 3-4-1802 m Ruth Cummings Cpl MA

HEWITT,((includes HUERD, HUYETT, HUIET)
Acres: b *c.* 1748 d 8- -1830 m Elizabeth Parmenter Pvt MA
Andrew: b 4-2-1761 d 8-11-1852 m (1)Rachel — (2)Phebe — Pvt CT ★
Daniel: b — d 1-8-1826 m (1)Desire Williams (2)Sarah Tyler Sgt CT ★
Dethic: b *c.* 1747 d 7-3-1778 m Elizabeth Searle Capt CT
Elisha, Jr.: b 2-18-1758 d 11-8-1846 m Mary Malry Pvt Artr CT ★
Gershom: b 5-16-1743 d 9-11-1834 m (1)Elizabeth Stevens (2)Elizabeth — Capt CT ★
Gideon: b 3-12-1748 d *p.* 9-4-1835 m (1)Susan Dunbar (2)Jane Smith Pvt NY
Henry: b 7-7-1730 d 1821 m (2)Phebe Prentice Pvt CT
Henry: b 1763 d 11-8-1851 m Phebe Morgan Pvt CT ★
Increase: b 11-2-1742 d 8-30-1829 m Elizabeth Tyler Cpl CT
Israel: b 10-10-1760 d 7-19-1834 m Sarah Williams Pvt CT ★
Jacob: b 3-8-1766 d 1-19-1831 m (1)Rosina Bechtel (2)Catherine Bechtel Pvt PA
Jacob: b 4-23-1732 d 4-2-1802 m Anna Maria Gegin PS PA
John: b 1-25-1761 d 6-6-1848 m Elizabeth Ratliff Sgt NC ★
John: b 10-30-1763 d 11-27-1825 m (1)Susanna Bechtel (2)Mary — Pvt PA
John: b 11-14-1763 d 12-19-1844 m Margaret Hewitt Pvt VA ★
Joseph: b 5-2-1731 d *p.* 11-18-1784 m Sarah Babcock Cpl CT
Lewis: b 11-14-1757 d 3-15-1837 m Charlotte Dean Ens CT
Ludwig: b 1739 d 4-17-1828 m Margaret Potter Pvt PA
Nathaniel: b 2- -1763 d 1831 m Sarah Avery Pvt CT
Nicholas: b 1751 d 5-30-1835 m Elizabeth Gerhart Pvt PA
Philip: b 3-8-1754 d 5-14-1846 m Elizabeth Lutz Pvt NC
Philip: b *c.* 1750 d *p.* 2-14-1815 m Patience — Sol NC
Randall: b 6-28-1760 d 5- -1850 m Experience (Hewitt)Pvt CT ★
Reuben: b 1738 d 6-28-1808 m Hannah Hakes 2Lt RI

HEWITT, contd.
Richard: b 1737 d 9- -1825 m Experience Leeds Capt CT ★
Richard: b 5-27-1766 d 1845 m Abigail — Pvt CT ★
Robert: b 6-5-1760 d 11-5-1829 m Abigail Meach Pvt CT
Simeon: b 6-21-1766 d 7-10-1843 m Mahala Hewitt Pvt CT ★
Sterry: b 4-7-1756 d 7-29-1845 m Hannah Barnaby Pvt CT ★
Thomas: b 3-20-1757 d 1828 m Electa Chittenden Pvt CT
Thomas: b 1725 d p. 6-23-1790 m Rebecca Dugan CS PA
Wm.: b 6-3-1749 d — m Sarah Coye CS CT
Wm.: b 1750 d 4-11-1826 m Sarah King Cpl NH

HEWSON,
Daniel: b 1-5-1762 d 12-27-1821 m Elizabeth Geyer Pvt NY
John: b 8- -1744 d 10-11-1821 m (1)Mary — (2)Zibiah Smallwood
   Capt PA

HEXT,
Philip: b 6-15-1749 d p. 10-25-1784 m Susannah Glaze Ford
   Webster Lt SC

HEYBERGER,
John Christian: b 12-17-1757 d — m Eva Wieder Sgt PA

HEYDRICK,
Abraham: b 11-5-1742 d 8-30-1826 m Susanna Yeakel Pvt PA

HEYL, (includes HEIL)
George: b — d 1-25-1815 m Sarah Steward Pvt PA
Jacob, Sr.: b 4- -1712 d 9-5-1783 m Anna Catherine Ruehl PS PA
John: b c. 1758 d a. 9-6-1788 m Susanna Albert Sol PA
Philip: b 9-15-1739 d 12-29-1811 m Maria Jacobina Zieglerine
   Ens PA

HEYSHAM,
Wm.: b 1720 d 9-26-1797 m Mary — CS PS PA

HIBBARD, (includes HEBARD, HEBERD, HEBBARD,
   HIBBART)
Aaron: b 1-17-1761 d 2-12-1835 m Sarah Merrill Pvt Fif CT
Ahimaaz: b 5-31-1759 d 1-16-1802 m Asenath Millard PS VT
Andrew: b 10-30-1754 d 8- -1803 m (1)Elizabeth Frost (2)Ruth
   Loomis Capt CT
Asa: b 10-3-1755 d 5-17-1829 m Abigail Armstrong Sgt CT ★
Augustine: b 3-27-1748 d 12-4-1831 m (1)Eunice Ashley (2)Sophia
   Stone Chp NH
David, Jr.: b 12-2-1755 d 2-18-1845 m Eunice Talcott DrmMaj CT
David: b 4-23-1748 d 9-29-1817 m Leah Kronkite Pvt NY
Ebenezer: b 1740 d p. 1790 m — Pvt CT
Ebenezer: b 9-15-1761 d p. 1832 m Susanna Carver Pvt CT ★
Elihu: b 1-14-1759 d 3-1-1812 m Mary Haley Pvt CT
Elisha: b 7-18-1749 d 3-31-1829 m Thankful Wood Pvt VT
Ithamar: b 6-18-1745 d 3-2-1802 m (1)Esther Haskins (2)Hannah
   Wood Chp PS VT
Jacob: b 1753 d 2-24-1823 m (1)Eliza Colby (2)Elizabeth Salter
   Toby Pvt MA ★
James: b c. 1750 d 5-31-1777 m Mary — Sgt NY
John: b 12-9-1727 d p. 1786 m Elizabeth Pearl Pvt CT
John: b 10-8-1743 d 1-29-1829 m Sarah Parker Pvt MA ★
John: b 9-17-1744 d 3- -1831 m (1)Dolly Walker (2)Tabatha Briggs
   Pvt MA
Joseph: b 12-22-1723 d 1801 m Lois Ingersoll NCapt MA
Joseph: b 1754 d 5-11-1824 m Dorothy Eastman Pvt MA ★
Moses: b 6-20-1745 d 3-21-1823 m (1)Elizabeth Whitaker (2)Hanna
   Alden Pvt NH
Nathan: b 1-16-1739 d 1825 m (1)Mehitable Crosby (2)Phoebe
   Fitch CS CT
Nathaniel: b 1-18-1741 d 5-30-1803 m Mary Abbe Pvt CT
Ozias: b 12-1-1763 d 5-9-1851 m Mary Flower Pvt CT ★
Perez: b 2-21-1752 d 5-17-1820 m Martha Burnett Pvt CT
Robert: b 9- -1737 d 5- -1798 m Lydia — Ens NY
Rufus: b 1758 d 4-17-1848 m Lydia Bradford Pvt CT ★
Southwick: b 1723 d 2-11-1806 m Abagail Collier Pvt MA
Thomas: b a. 1758 d 7-1-1800 m Lucy Sylvester Sgt VT
Timothy: b 1758 d 7-24-1804 m Mrs Abigail Frances Pvt CT
Timothy: b 2-20-1757 d 1-4-1829 m Sarah Chamberlain Pvt CT ★
Uriah: b 11-10-1749 d 5- -1819 m Hannah Scoville Pvt CT ★
Wm.: b 10-30-1730 d 3-17-1811 m Dorthy Burnham Capt CT
Wm.: b 12-12-1750 d 6-4-1834 m Bathsheba Strong Ens CT ★

HIBBEN,
Thomas: b 1760 d 5-12-1833 m Mary Entriken Pvt PA

HIBBETS,
James: b 8-10-1751 d 8-18-1832 m (3)Margaret Hill Pvt PA

HIBBLER,
Jacob: b 10-5-1762 d 6-11-1835 m Jinsey Belcher Pvt NJ

HIBBS,
Jonathan: b c. 1750 d 1800 m Mary Wazey Pvt PA

HIBSCHMAN,
Heinrich: b 8-5-1748 d 6-2-1818 m (2)Catharine B Leisey Pvt PS PA
Wendel: b 1-2-1740 d 9-3-1819 m Hannah Heffley Maj PA

HICHBORN,
Robert: b 11-20-1740 d 10-18-1800 m Susannah Ellingwood 1Lt MA
Thomas, 3d: b 6-30-1708 d 1776 m (1)Isannah Fadree (2)Elizabeth
   Green PS MA

HICKENLOOPER,
Andrew: b 2-10-1757 d 3-12-1830 m Rachel Long Lt PA

HICKERNELL,
David: b c. 1745 d p. 1790 m Anna Maria — Cpl PA

HICKERSON,
Joseph: b 1747 d 11-8-1777 m — Whiting Pvt VA

HICKLE, (includes HICKEL)
Lewis: b — d c. 1- -1808 m — Sol VA
Samuel: b 4-5-1760 d 5-13-1832 m Elizabeth Huber Pvt VA ★

HICKLIN, (includes HICKLING)
Arthur: b 3-7-1758 d 11-19-1799 m Elizabeth Williams Mil SC
Thomas: b 9-21-1747 d 12-19-1834 m Mary Barbot Sol SC
Thomas: b 1730 d p. 1795 m — Capt VA
Wm., Jr.: b 5-21-1742 d 6-2-1790 m Elizabeth Hudson PM Adj MA
Wm.: b 1734 d 10-10-1819 m Sarah Isbell Pvt SC

HICKMAN, (includes HECKMAN)
Adam: b 1753/54 d 8-12-1824 m Mary Stillwell Pvt PA
Adam: b 1730 d 7-2-1818 m Elizabeth Kreider Fif PA
Andrew: b 8-27-1743 d 1825 m (2)Elizabeth — Pvt PA
Benjamin: b 9-13-1762 d 5-5-1838 m Judith — Pvt NC ★
Charles: b 1725 d 6- -1790 m Morila Grable Pvt Dr PA
Ezekiel: b c. 1725 d 1793 m Elizabeth Trammel Lt PA
George: b 1- -1748 d 3-22-1835 m Maria Magdalena — Pvt PA
George: b 10-16-1766 d 4-17-1856 m Margaret McWherter Pvt PA
Isaac: b 6-4-1757 d 8-15-1845 m (1)Susannah Gwin (2)Susannah
   Lunnon Lt NJ
James, Sr.: b 3-3-1724 d 4-16-1824 m Hannah Lewis Pvt VA
James: b 10- -1761 d 4-7-1843 m Elizabeth — Pvt VA ★
James Lewis: b 12-18-1759 d 8-10-1828 m Elizabeth Bryan Capt VA
Joel: b 8-10-1761 d 7-16-1852 m Frances Geretta Wilson Pvt VA ★
John: b c. 1750 d 1802 m Elizabeth Bright Matr SC
Lewis: b c. 1755 d 1780 m Elizabeth Mason Pvt PA
Peter: b 1758 d 9-25-1825 m Abigail Faucett Pvt PA
Richard: b 1757 d 1732 m Lydia Irvine Calloway Sol VA
Sotha: b 6-10-1748 d 4-2-1834 m Elizabeth Davis Pvt VA ★
Wm.: b c. 1730 d 1787 m (1)Mildred Smith (2)Lucretia Strickland
   Lt PS NC
Wm.: b 12-25-1756 d 1835 m Ann — Pvt NC ★
Wm.: b 3-14-1732 d 4-17-1816 m (1)Mary McFerson (2)Lettice
   Cole PS SC
Wm.: b c. 1730 d p. 8-9-1788 m Jane Talbot PS VA
Wm.: b 2-4-1747 d 1-24-1834 m (1)Elizabeth Shackleford (2)Mrs
   Elizabeth Abbot Pvt VA

HICKOK, (includes HECOX & HICKOX)
Amos: b 5-19-1715 d 3-1-1805 m Mary (Prichard)Richards Cpl CT ★
Amos: bpt 4-2-1738 d p. 1793 m Phoebe Curtis PS CT
Asa: b 6-4-1754 d 3-29-1836 m Hester Hinman Pvt CT ★
Asa: b 1-23-1755 d 1829 m Mary Porter Sgt NY
Benjamin: b 1750 d 1-13-1816 m Rachel Barnum Maj CT
Benjamin: b 4-20-1744 d 7-2-1829 m Mary Pierce Capt CT
Benjamin: b 10-30-1743 d 3-21-1825 m Rebecca Gregory Capt VT
Daniel: b 1748 d 12-29-1835 m Lucy Starr Capt CT ★
Durlin: b 3-22-1759 d 7-30-1837 m Betsey Fletcher Sgt MA ★
Ebenezer: b 5-29-1755 d 1844 m Abigail Smith Pvt CT
Elihu: b 9-4-1759 d 1810 m Sabra Comstock Pvt MA
Gideon: b 9-6-1705 d 4-18-1798 m Sarah Upson PS CT
Giles: bpt 2-28-1765 d 4-2-1836 m Caroline Matilda Case Pvt NY
   MA ★
James: b 8-5-1755 d 10-16-1825 m Eunice Collins Sgt CT
Joel: b 11-5-1752 d 3-18-1840 m Anna Trowbridge Pvt CT
John: b 4-17-1734 d 4-5-1810 m Lydia Kellogg Ens CT
Joseph: b 4-6-1729 d 10-28-1776 m Martha Wilcox Capt CT
Levi: b 4-25-1751 d 1-7-1811 m Sybil Moore Pvt MA
Nathaniel: b 3-3-1758 d 2-20-1844 m Esther — Pvt CT ★
Samuel: b 4-16-1752 d 5-2-1835 m Lucena — OrdlSgt CT ★
Samuel: b 9-11-1739 d 4-29-1830 m (1)Ellinor Warner (2)Charity
   (Johnson)Dixon Pvt CT
Silas: b 3-9-1721 d p. 1790 m Sarah Stiles CS CT
Simeon: b a. 1760 d p. 1791 m Annie Parmley Ens CT
Stephen: b 6-30-1749 d 9-9-1836 m ( )Rebecca Robinson Capt
   MA ★
Thomas, Jr.: b 4-4-1737 d p. 1781 m (1)Lois Richards (2)Thankful
   Seymour PS CS CT
Truman: b 4- -1765 d 8-29-1837 m Sarah — Pvt CT ★

HICKS, (includes HIX)
Barney: b 6-9-1754 d 1-5-1832 m Sally Cook Pvt Slr MA
Benjamin: b 1755 d 3-25-1843 m Alice — Pvt NH ★
Benjamin: b — d 5-23-1836 m Deborah Doty Capt NY
Conrad: b 7-13-1740 d 12-21-1814 m Anna Maria Heyer PS PA
Daniel: b — d 1853 m Katharine VanName Pvt NY ★
Daniel: b c. 1762 d p. 4-14-1855 m Fanney Delony Pvt SC ★

David: b 3-1-1745 d 7-5-1816 m Jane Hellen 1Lt RI
David: b c. 1725 d 1790 m Mary Gildersleeves Pvt VT
David: b 5-9-1739 d 8-16-1812 m Mary Johnson Sgt VA
David: b c. 1756 d c. 1840 m Nancy Thomas Pvt VA
Durfee: b 3-12-1757 d 2-12-1844 m (1)Lucy Potter (2)Eunice Potter (3)Susannah Potter (4)Mrs. Chase Sol & Mar RI ★
George: b 5-2-1763 d 8-3-1833 m Nancy Hemmondway Pvt NY
George: b c. 1730 d 1-23-1793 m (1)Naomi — (2)Sarah (James) Gardner Col PS CS SC
Hezekiah: b 1719 d 1788 m Desire Carpenter Sgt MA
Isaac: b 1755 d 6-20-1817 m Nancy Cryer Capt GA
Isaac: b 1758 d p. 1824 m Elizabeth Hines Pvt NC ★
Israel: b 9-19-1743 d 2-12-1813 m Elizabeth Bowen Capt MA
Jabez: b 1-23-1763 d 4-9-1827 m Anna Francis — Pvt MA
Jacob Giles: b c. 1759 d 1841 m Elsie Lamborn Capt-Lt PA
James: b c. 1750 d 1819 m (1)Mary Harris (2)Elizabeth Harris Cpl VA
James: b 5-5-1754 d 10-4-1840 m Ann Frost Cpl VA
John: b 4-1-1761 d 7-29-1842 m Eunice Fish Preston Pvt CT ★
John: b 5-23-1725 d 4-19-1775 m Elizabeth Nutting PS MA
John: b 12-12-1746 d 9-25-1826 m Dorthy West Pvt MA
John: b c. 1763/4 d 10-6-1845 m Elizabeth Butts Pvt VT
Joseph: b 8-12-1714 d 4-3-1803 m (1)Margaret Lester (2)Catharine Filkins (3)Elizabeth — Pvt NY
Joseph: b 3-23-1725 d 6-14-1797 m Hannah Schellinger PS NY
Jotham: b 5-26-1752 d 4-19-1829 m Chloe Wheeler Pvt MA
Lawton: b 5-8-1764 d p. 1802 m Priscilla Borden Pvt MA
Meshack: b c. 1740 d 1826 m (1)Ann Dawson (2)Elizabeth Moreland PS VA
Nathan: b 4-20-1762 d 10-10-1845 m Prudence Round Pvt Cpl MA
Nathaniel: b 11-23-1751 d 1-31-1836 m Rebecca Sheldon Pvt RI
Nathaniel: b c. 1745-50 d p. 8-4-1801 m Jena Chrisman PS VA
Pewid: b c. 1715 d a. 1-21-1793 m (2)Mrs Temperance — PS VA
Robert, Jr.: b 1759 d 1829 m (1)Mary Dudley (2)Sally Raven Pvt NC
Robert: b c. 1720 d p. 1-22-1780 m — PS VA
Samuel: b 1757 d 7-23-1840 m Lydia Hastings Pvt CT ★
Samuel: b 1-5-1755 d 8-20-1834 m Ann Doughty Cpl MA
Samuel: b 5-30-1735 d p. 1790 m Keziah Salisbury Pvt MA
Samuel: b 12-9-1759 d 11-12-1835 m Catherine Johnson Pvt NJ
Samuel: b 11-10-1742 d 8-29-1825 m Patience Burrington 1Lt RI
Simeon: b 8-22-1755 d 1-24-1855 m Barbara Barney Pvt MA NH VT ★
Stephen: b 1-25-1755 d 2-19-1833 m Hanna Goff Pvt RI MA ★
Thomas: b 1722 d c. 1785 m Mrs Rosanna Brown Lt MD
Thomas: b 1745 d 3-21-1834 m Anna Doughty 2Lt NY
Thomas: b c. 1745 d p. 1790 m Catherine Filkins Pvt NY
Thomas: b 3-13-1725 d 4-1-1797 m Elizabeth Williams PS NC
Wm.: b a. 1758 d 1812 m Mary Elizabeth Harris Pvt VA
Zachariah: b 11-1-1749 d 10-6-1833 m Rebecca Sherrill Pvt NY

HIDDEN,
Jeremiah: b c. 1749 d p. 1797 m (1)Elizabeth Watts (2)Mrs Rebecca Hazeltine Sol NH
Samuel: b 2-22-1760 d 2-13-1837 m Elizabeth Story Price Pvt Smn MA ★

HIDER, (includes HYDER)
Benjamin: b c. 1750 d 1826/7 m Catharine — PS NC
John: b c. 1756 d 7-11-1815 m Julianna — Pvt PA
Michael, Sr.: b a. 1740 d 6-25-1790 m Elizabeth Woods Sol PS NC

HIDLAY,
George: b a. 1735 d 1794 m Sophia — Pvt PA

HIERS,
Jacob: b c. 1730 d a. 1790 m — Sol SC

HIESTAND, (includes HEASTON, HEISTAND)
Abraham: b 8-11-1762 d 2-13-1848 m Magdalena Strickler Pvt PA
Jacob: b 1750 d 9-12-1824 m Mary Eby Sol PA
Jacob: b c. 1730 d 1798 m Elizabeth Brumbaugh Pvt VA
John: b 1741 d 4- -1821/2 m (3)Mary Osmer Pvt PA
Peter: b c. 1740-3 d a. 3-24-1818 m — Pvt VA

HIESTER,
Daniel: b 11-5-1761 d 4-16-1827 m (1)Magdalena Albright (2)Barbara Kauffman (3)Susan Auman CS PA
Gabriel: b 6-17-1749 d 9-1-1824 m Elizabeth Bausman Maj PA
John: b 4-9-1746 d 10-15-1821 m Hannah Pauling Col PA
John Christian: b 4-25-1757 d 1827 m Susan Rieser Pvt PS PA
Joseph: b 11-18-1752 d 6-10-1832 m Elizabeth Witman LCol PS PA
Wm.: b 1-10-1757 d 7-13-1822 m Anna Maria Myer Pvt PA

HIGBEE, (includes HIGBIE & HIGBY)
Aaron: b 10-19-1749 d 5-25-1827 m Marcy Heartt PS NY
Absalom: b c. 1761 d 1833 m Rachel Scull Pvt NJ
Charles: b 1-21-1754 d 7-28-1828 m Abigail — Pvt NH
Daniel Elton: b 5-17-1739 d p. 1796 m Martha Ives Pvt CT
Edward: b 4-5-1714 d 9- -1793 m (1)Jemima Risley (2)Sarah Leeds Pvt NJ
Elihu: b 8-6-1749 d 12-30-1777 m Martha Green Ens CT
Elijah: b 2-23-1750 d 9-13-1821 m Lucretia Barnes Pvt MA
Elisha: b c. 1735 d p. 1785 m — Sol NJ

Elnathan: b 3-6-1754 d 9-2-1839 m Abigail Chapman Sgt MA NY ★
Hendrick: b 10- -1759 d p. 1820 m Elizabeth — Pvt NJ ★
Isaac: b 6-17-1761 d 4-12-1839 m Sophia Somers Pvt NJ
James: b 1745 d 1808 m Mary Jackson Pvt NY
John, Sr.: b 12-17-1732 d 10-16-1821 m (1)Mindwell Lewis (2)Thankful — (3)Lois — Pvt PS NY
John, Jr.: b 6-5-1757 d 2-18-1817 m Sarah Clinton Pvt NY
Jonas: b 1730 d 11-10-1789 m Sarah Davis Pvt NY
Lemuel: b 12-26-1762 d 10-24-1806 m Abigail (Higby)Pvt CT
Noah: b 3-14-1735 d p. 1790 m Mary Cooper Pvt CT
Obadiah: b 11-13-1732 d 1808 m Anna May Brower Sol NJ
Peter: b 1760 d 1845 m — Pvt NJ
Richard: b a. 1750 d p. 3-3-1822 m Abigail Steelman Capt NJ
Samuel: b 8-14-1758 d 4-23-1843 m Hannah Galpin Pvt CT ★
Wm.: b c. 1730 d 1788 m (3)Abigail Dean Pvt NY
Wm.: b 1742 d 1792 m Betsey Bartram Pvt NY

HIGDON,
John: b 1758 d 9-16-1816 m Mary — GnrMte VA
Joseph: b 7-18-1759 d 2-6-1836 m Margaret Holbrook Cpl MD W★
Leonard: b 1754 d 9-11-1837 m Susannah Harris Pvt NC

HIGGINBOTHAM,
Aaron, Sr.: b c. 1720 d 1785 m Clara Graves PS VA
Aaron, Jr.: b c. 1753 d 1794 m Nancy Croxton Sol VA
Jacob: b 9- -1752 d 1- -1836 m Annie — Capt VA
James: b 12-25-1729 d 3- -1813 m Rachel Campbell Col VA
John: b 1726 d 7-25-1814 m Rachel Banks Capt VA
Joseph: b 1730 d 1805 m Hannah — Pvt VA
Joseph: b — d p. 1788 m (2)Jean — Sol GA
Samuel: b c. 1745 d 1803 m Jane Satterwhite Capt CS VA
Wm.: b 1761/62 d 1-12-1832 m Mary Shannon Pvt VA

HIGGINS,
Abisha: b 6-12-1753 d 1-17-1812 m (1)Mary Snow (2)Hannah Harding Cpl MA
Cornelius, Sr.: b 7-21-1722 d 10-14-1803 m (1)Sarah Hawes (2)Mrs Mary Smith Capt CT
Cornelius, Jr.: b 7-22-1744 d 1834 m (1)Eleanor Hazelton (2)Esther Kelsey Lt CT ★
Daniel: b 8-25-1759 d 1848 m Mary Pegg Pvt PS VA ★
Daniel: b 1763 d 10-30-1851 m Mary Ann — Pvt VA ★
David: b 8-6-1761 d 6-19-1842 m Eunice Gilbert Pvt CT
Ebenezer: b 2-12-1757 d 4-25-1742 m Mary Knowles Pvt CT★
Ebenezer: b 6-21-1721 d 4-21-1779 m (1)Martha Burgess (2)Mrs Hannah Yates 1Lt MA
Edward: b c. 1714 d p. 1783 m Ann — Pvt PA
Eleazer: b 9-15-1759 d 11-17-1831 m Lurania Gross Sol MA
Elisha: b 11-1-1727 d p. 3-23-1801 m Thankful — Cpl MA
Elisha: b 1750 d p. 1790 m Mary Butler Pvt MA
Elisha, Sr.: b 1-13-1701/2 d 1-22-1777 m (1)Sarah Lewis (2)Hannah Doane Atwood PS VT
Elkanah: b 12-1-1729 d 11-4-1815 m Sarah Knowles Pvt MA
Hawes: b 4-10-1752 d 5-6-1834 m Lucinda Bushnell Sgt CT
Isaiah: b 4-5-1727 d p. 1790 m Joanna Mayo Capt MA
Israel: b 10-3-1728 d a. 4-1-1793 m (1)Hannah Arnold (2)Elizabeth Aiken Pvt CT
Israel: b c. 1742 d 11-11-1818 m Mary Snow Pvt MA
James: b 1732 d 1-18-1816 m Luraner Becraft Pvt PS MD
James: b 5-22-1767 d 10-12-1826 m Rebecca Jeffers Pvt NJ W★
Jedediah: b 9-12-1733 d 5-29-1817 m (1)Phoebe Paine (2)Azubah Paine Pvt MA
Joel: b 1748 d 1807 m Drucilla Winn Ens VA
John: b c. 1753 d p. 1790 m (1)Sarah Sparrow (2)Sarah (Mayo) Sparrow Pvt MA
John: b 1-16-1747 d 1829 m Nancy Woodruff Pvt VA
Joseph: b 12-31-1761 d 7-18-1797 m Nancy Williams Dr CT
Joseph: b 3-1-1737 d 3-27-1781 m Hannah Pepper Pvt MA
Josiah: b c. 1762 d 6-21-1834 m Persis Eggleston Pvt MA
Judah: b 10-14-1751 d 5-20-1824 m (1)Mary Hill (2)Rachel McPherson Tms Wgm NJ
Levi: b 6-27-1743 d 6-22-1825 m (1)Bathsheba Young (2)Mary (Higgins) Hopkins 2Lt MA
Michael: b 12-5-1739 d 6-20-1818 m (1)Mary — (2)Ruth Brush MM NJ
Moses: b 3-1-1746 d 10-7-1832 m Elizabeth Holmes Pvt NY ★
Nathaniel: b c. 1738 d a. 2-2-1806 m (1)Mary — (2)Elizabeth Haviland Pvt MA
Paine: b 12-15-1758 d 6-4-1812 m Elizabeth Harding Matr MA
Peter: b c. 1741 d p. 1810 m (1)Susannah Craig (2)— Leigh Lt VA
Philip: b 1-28-1757/8 d a. 5-27-1796 m Mary Wiley CS PS MA
Reubin: b 5-18-1739 d 9-2-1823 m Mercy Dyer Capt MA
Richard: b 4-5-1762 d p. 1806 m Lydia Cole Pvt MA
Robert: b 1738 d 1834 m Maria Armstrong Pvt NY
Robert H.: b 12-8-1746 d 5-30-1825 m (1)Miss Wright (2)Mary Joliffe BrevMaj VA
Samuel: b c. 1752 d 4- -1785 m Eleanor — Pvt PS MD
Samuel: b 3-5-1756 d 6-5-1829 m Rebecca Frazee Pvt NJ
Samuel: b 1743 d 6-30-1811 m Temperance Kelsey Pvt VT
Simeon: b 1746 d 3-23-1824 m Martha Knowles Pvt MA
Solomon: b 12- -1738 d p. 1780 m (1)Bethia Chase (2)Esther Dean Capt MA

HIGGENS, contd.
Sylvanus: b 6-8-1735 d 10-2-1785 m Lucy Stocking Ens CT
Sylvanus: b 10-2-1736 d 1802 m (1)Abigail Knowles (2)Hannah Higgins Pvt CS MA
Timothy: b 1754 d 7-12-1829 m Hannah Alling Pvt CT
Wm.: b 1744 d 1794 m Susannah Duvall Pvt PS MD
Wm.: b 11-11-1745 d 2-11-1842 m Margaret Mooney Pvt VA ★
Zaccheus, Sr.: b 10-8-1728 d 1817 m (1)Mercy Crosby (2)Hannah Knowles Sparrow Pvt MA

HIGGINSON,
Robert: b c. 1730 d 1800 m Mary Cary PS VA
Stephen: b 11-28-1743 d 11-22-1828 m (1)Susan Cleveland (2)Elizabeth Perkins (3)Sarah Perkins PS MA

HIGGS,
John: b 1738 d 11- -1781 m Judath Harrell Pvt NC
Leonard: b 1755 d 1851 m Sallie Kitrell Pvt NC
Zachariah: b 1735 d 1816 m Elizabeth Kenelm PS NC SC VA

HIGH, (includes HOCH)
Alsabrook: b 1-5-1758 d 11-22-1822 m Agnes Martin Capt NC
Daniel: b 1-18-1731 d 8-27-1789 m Mary Bertolet PS Pvt PA
Frederick: b 1-18-1751 d 3-22-1843 m Christine (Kale) Pvt VA
George: b c. 1750 d p. 3-14-1811 m Elizabeth Schmid Pvt PA
Isaac: b 3-7-1753 d 5-18-1795 m Sarah Hottenstein Pvt PA
John, Jr.: b 3-15-1759 d 9-10-1836 m Rachel Squire Pvt NJ
John: b 1750 d a. 5-5-1792 m Martha Madison Pvt NC
Nathan: b 1724 d 1807 m Mary (Post) Jolly Pvt NJ
Philip: b 3-9-1755 d 9-4-1828 m Anna Bechtel Pvt PA
Robert: b 1746 d p. 1810 m Sarah Winston PS NC
Samuel: b 7-7-1750 d p. 9-12-1812 m (1)Clara Jackson (2)Media Garett Sol NC
Samuel: b 5- -1723 d 7-19-1795 m Esther Herbein PS PA

HIGHNOTE,
Philip: b 3-15-1753 d 4-18-1839 m Agnes Scott Pvt Spy GA ★

HIGHSMITH,
Moses: b 3-4-1760 d 12-27-1846 m Esther — Pvt SC ★

HIGHT,
George: b 7-3-1755 d 8-21-1837 m Lovia Lunsford Pvt VA ★
Hanson: b 1760 d 1810 m Sarah Lord Pvt MA
James: b — d — m Dorcas Mills Pvt NH
John: b 1731 d p. 1779 m Hannah Richards Pvt NJ
John: b 1757 d 1824 m Elizabeth Stone Sol NC
John N.: b 1-9-1756 d p. 1832 m Hannah Savage OrdlSgt NJ ★
Thomas: b 9-21-1757 d p. 1844 m Priscilla May Lt VA
Wm.: b 10-20-1753 d 10-10-1831 m Catherine Barcley Pvt NJ

HIGHTOWER,
Thomas: b c. 1755 d p. 1830 m Martha — Pvt SC
Thomas: b 1751 d p. 9-9-1803 m Milly Arnold Pvt VA
Wm.: b c. 1760 d p. 1830 m Miss Fann Pvt GA

HIGLEY,
Asa: b 1-31-1745 d 2- -1805 m Eunice Cotton Cpl CT
Brewster 2d: b 12-12-1709 d 3-21-1794 m (1)Esther Holcombe (2)Mrs Mindwell Bull Lt PS CT
Brewster 3d: b 3-14-1735 d 4-11-1805 m Esther Owen Ens VT CT
Brewster 4th: b 3-14-1759 d 6-20-1847 m Naomi Higley Pvt CT VT ★
Daniel: b 1738 d 3-15-1812 m (1)Ruth — (2)Basha Lincoln Lt CT
Joel: b 1-1-1739 d p. 1810 m Eunice Haskins 2Lt CT
John, Sr.: b 2-17-1722 d 5- -1802 m (1)Apphia Humphrey (2) — Clark Pvt CT
Joseph, Jr.: b 5-22-1741 d 12-17-1823 m Azubah Gillette Pvt MA
Josiah 2d: b 11-6-1725 d 11- -1778 m Hepzibah Cotton Pvt CT
Obed: b 10-25-1757 d 1-24-1841 m Rebecca Mills Pvt CT
Ozias: b 3-20-1748 d 6-22-1827 m Martha Gillette Sol CT
Roswell: b 12-19-1756 d 11-10-1834 m Sarah Garnsey Pvt NY ★
Seth: b 10-29-1746 d 2-28-1794 m Mindwell Higley Cpl CT
Seth: b 9-27-1757 d 1829 m (1)Lucy Holcomb (2)Lucy Heron Pvt NY

HIGNETT, (or HIGGNUTT)
Daniel: b c. 1750 d 1808 m Sarah H. — Pvt MD

HIKES,
George: b 3-8-1725 m 1-3-1800 m Maria M. Muller Pvt PA

HILBERT,
Wm.: b 8-12-1752 d 5-24-1841 m Betsy Dickinson Pvt MA

HILBORN,
Robert: b 1740 d 1-8-1834 m Lucy (Riggs)Chadbourne Pvt MA ★

HILDEBRAND,
Conrad: b 5-28-1741 d 7-9-1824 m Elizabeth Mull Sol PS NC
Felix: b 11-14-1749 d 3-26-1820 m Maria Elizabeth Simon Pvt PA
George: b 1753 d 7-2-1827 m Mary Elizabeth Kinsley Pvt PA

Johannes: b 1715 d 4-2-1783 m Barbara Glattfelter Pvt PA
John George Nicholas: b 8-12-1733 d 12-19-1804 m Anna Maria Hill PS PA
Michael: b 11-17-1766 d 10-8-1850 m Elizabeth Schlenger Pvt PA
Stephen: b 1744 d 1790 m Hannah Bailes Pvt PA

HILDRETH,
Abel: b 3-18-1756/7 d 9-4-1836 m Huldah Edwards Pvt MA ★
Elijah: b 5-23-1728 d 5-14-1814 m (1)Hannah Colburn (2)Susannah Barker (3)Mrs Hannah Coburn Pvt MA
Elijah: b 2-21-1751 d 11-17-1798 m Mary Reed Drm MA
Ephraim: b 2-21-1718 d 7-15-1797 m Elizabeth French PS MA
Ephraim: b 1754 d 10- -1853 d Nance Rodah Pvt NH
Ephraim: b 1760 d 10-27-1852 m Rhoda Barnes Pvt NH
Ephraim: b 1736 d p. 1787 m (1)Elizabeth Ellenwood (2)Elizabeth Williams PS NH
Hosea: b 11-21-1744 d 12-20-1776 m Experience Keep Cpl MA
Isaac: b 1750-55 d 1804 m Sarah Wheeler Pvt PS NH
Isaac: b 1756 d 4-1-1822 m Abigail Halsey PS NY
Israel: b 10-11-1755 d 9-6-1839 m Susannah Hale Pvt MA
James: b c. 1721/2 d 1778/9 m Phebe Howell PS NY
Jeremiah: b 2-22-1761 d p. 1808 m Abigail Parker Pvt MA
John: b 11-5-1738 d 8-13-1802 m (1)Abigail Parker (2)Ellzabeth Gates Pvt MA
John: b 5-8-1729 d p. 1796 m (1)Anna Squires (2)Christiana Topping Ens NY
Jonathan: b 8-30-1727 d p. 1805 m (1)Mary — (2)Phebe Farr (3)Dinah Davis CS NY
Jonathan: b 1753 d 5-14-1825 m Lucy Brigham Pvt NH
Jonathan, Jr.: b 2-1-1760 d 1850 m (1)Hannah Britton (2)Christiany — (3)Amanda — Pvt NJ ★
Joseph, Sr.: b 4-4-1724 d 7-4-1796 m Lydia Fletcher PS VT
Joseph, Jr.: b 1-31-1747/8 d 5-22-1812 m Submit — Sgt VT
Josiah, Jr.: b 1-17-1746 d 10-17-1812 m Hannah Varnum MM MA
Oliver: b 7-11-1723 d 2-1-1793 m Ann Blaisdell Pvt MA
Reuben: b 5-4-1755 d 4-1-1846 m Susanna Sanderson Pvt NH
Samuel: b 1750 d 8-6-1823 m Abigail Bodwell Dr MA
Simeon: b 10-7-1736 d 1776 m Hannah Spalding Pvt NH
Stephen: b 2-1-1742 d p. 10-23-1800 m Esther Manning Cpl NH
Wm.: b 11-6-1757 d 9-5-1813 m Mary Hildreth Pvt MA
Zachariah: b 12-28-1728 d 4-18-1784 m Elizabeth Prescott PS MA
Zachariah: b 1754 d 3-17-1829 m Elizabeth Keyes 2Lt MA

HILEY,
Jacob: b c. 1755-60 d c. 1820 m Mary Magdalene Theus Pvt SC
John: b 1759 d 1824 m Polly — Sol PA

HILL,
Aaron: b 1750 d 1809 m Abigail Bell SrgnMte MA
Aaron: b 12-12-1755 d 9-18-1827 m Hannah Fisk Pvt NY
Aaron: b a. 1750/51 d p. 1800 m (2)Rachel Perry Capt NC
Abel: b c. 1730 d a. 3-14-1803 m Elizabeth — CS NC
Abraham: b 5-26-1763 d 9-30-1840 m Lydia Murray Pvt CT ★
Abraham, Sr.: b 1734 d 12-16-1812 m Susanna Wellington Sol MA
Abraham, Jr.: b 1759 d 2-18-1838 m Ruth Blodgett Pvt MA
Abraham, Sr.: b 4-23-1732 d 2-4-1792 m Christian Walton CS NC
Abraham, Jr.: b 1-14-1759 d 4-24-1818 m Elizabeth McGehee Pvt SC
Abraham: b 1-29-1758 d 11- -1840 m Prudence Hall Pvt SC ★
Abram: b c. 1760 d 8- -1843 m — Pvt NC ★
Adam: b c. 1760 d 1817 m Rosanna Jordan Pvt PA
Ambrose: b 3-21-1744 d 2-26-1816 m Lucy Beach Capt MA W★
Andrew: b 1732 d 1810 m Catherine Horton Maj NY
Asa: b 1-12-1760 d 3-10-1828 m Sarah Bancroft Pvt MA ★
Asa: b 1760 d p. 1829 m Lucy Johnson Fif MA
Bellias: b 1735 d 10-17-1807 m Lydia Birge Pvt MA
Benjamin: b 10-21-1754 d 12-25-1818 m Ruth Haskins PS MA
Benjamin: bpt 9-7-1727 d 9-17-1796 m Elizabeth Dudley Sgt NH
Benjamin: b c. 1762 d a. 9-13-1841 m Mary Wooten Pvt NC
Bernard: b 11-17-1761 d 11-24-1832 m (1)Sarah Wheetin (2)Cloe Munger Pvt MA ★
Caleb: b 5-23-1716 d 3-25-1788 m Hannah — Capt PS MA
Caleb: b 12-24-1756 d 6-9-1842 m Rebecca — Pvt NY ★
Caleb: b 8-17-1736 d p. 1778 m Hannah (Fisk)Fairbanks Pvt MA
Caleb: b 1731 d 5-6-1804 m Mercy Stafford Lt RI
Charles: b 2-21-1756 d 4-29-1804 m Mary Wait Cpl MA
Charles: b 8-15-1734 d 1819 m Sarah Prentiss Sct NH
Charles: b 9-10-1744 d p. 1805 m (1)Amy Hyde (2)Lydia Metcalf Lt NH
Clement, Sr.: b 1-4-1707 m 2-12-1782 m Mary Digges PS MD
Clement, Jr.: b 11-6-1743 d 2-6-1807 m PS 2Lt MD
Comfort: b 8-25-1756 d p. 1796 m Mary Mason Cpl MA
Cyrus: b 1757 d 1-1-1849 m Relief Howard Pvt MA ★
Daniel: b 7-6-1756 d 3-10-1835 m (1)Sarah Leavitt (2)Phebe Paine Ens MA
Daniel: b 5-1-1752 d 1-22-1834 m (1)Jane Whitney (2)Alice De Gross Sgt MA W★
Daniel: b 8-9-1744 d 2-6-1837 m Mary Clark Pvt MA
Daniel: b 9-29-1755 d 5-28-1814 m Mercy Hayward Pvt MA
Daniel: b 7-16-1761 d 10-28-1826 m Elizabeth Burleigh Pvt NH
Daniel: b 9-4-1757 d 11-1-1846 m Ellen — Pvt NC ★
Daniel: b 10- -1756 d 5-28-1826 m Martha Hickman Sol NC
David: b 3-15-1761 d 5-30-1850 m Elisabeth Rouse Pvt MA

David: b 3-29-1762 d 11-4-1813 m Mercy Holbrook Pvt MA
David: b 1752 d 1-1-1813 m Abigail Stanborough Pvt MA
Ebenezer: b 2-26-1742 d 3-27-1798 m Mabel Sherwood Capt CT
Ebenezer: b 3-17-1768 d 3-30-1833 m Mary Bronson Pvt CT ★
Ebenezer: b 1-30-1758 d 3-20-1853 m Sarah Bryant Pvt NH ★
Ebenezer: b 7-8-1744 d 10-1-1834 m Esther Pratt PS NH
Ebenezer: b c. 1762 d 1840 m Margaret Montgomery Cpl NY
Edward: b — d 7- -1800 m Mary Willey Sgt NH
Eliphalet: b 1727 d 7-18-1821 m Isabel Bun Pvt CT
Frederick: b c. 1732 d 7- -1794 m Maria (LeVan)Huttenstein Pvt PA
Frederick: b 4-13-1750 d 5-2-1838 m Elizabeth Defenbaugh Pvt PA ★
Frederick: b 1755 d 10-13-1840 m Mary Klinglesmith Pvt PA
Frederick: b 9-8-1758 d 5-7-1833 m (1)Betsy Myers (2)Mary Elizabeth Dockerty Pvt PA
George: b c. 1736 d 11-20-1786 m (1)Ruth Virden (2)Polly — Pvt DE
George: b 1725 d 1812 m Ann — Pvt PA
Green: b 11-3-1741 d 9-11-1826 m (1)Nancy Thomas (2)Mary Seawell Maj PS NC
Henry, Jr.: b — d a. 1822 m Hester Brooke Capt PS MD
Henry: b 1762 d 1828 m Eleanor Patterson Drm NY
Henry: b 1730 d 1804 m Sarah Cotton Pvt NC
Henry: b 1725 d 1800 m Ann — PS NC
Henry, Jr.: b 1750 d 1804 m Sarah Walton Pvt NC
Henry: b 10-17-1743 d 9-12-1815 m Ann Powell Capt VA
Hiram: b c. 1760 d 1851 m Millie Shelton Pvt SC
Hugh: b 8-1-1740 d 2-17-1829 m Jane Brown NCapt MA
Ira: b 7-17-1755 d 10-13-1841 m Esther Post Pvt VT
Isaac: b 4-16-1740 d p. 1832 m Eunice Mallory Pvt CT ★
Isaac: b 1748 d 1825 m (1)Lucy Wallace (2)Mrs Lydia Hill Drm MD
Isaac: b 2-10-1761 d 8-15-1833 m Nancy Crain Pvt NC ★
Isreal: b 8-17-1719 d 8-25-1777 m Beriah Latham Pvt MA
Jabez: b 6-17-1744 d 10-9-1779 m Sarah Read Maj CT
Jacob, Jr.: b 10-29-1756 d 3-22-1827 m Anne Tribon Pvt MA
Jacob: b 5-9-1750 d 1-9-1824 m Christena Gortner Capt PA
Jacob, Sr.: b 1726 d 12-8-1815 m Magdalena — Ens PS PA
Jacob: b 5-21-1750 d 2-9-1809 m Christina Schad Pvt PA
Jacob: b 1755 d c. 8-21-1783 m Eva Schmidt Pvt PA
James: b 11-30-1749 d 11-26-1802 m Eleanor Hull Pvt CT
James: b 12-31-1734 d 8-22-1811 m (1)Sarah Coffin (2)Sarah Burleigh (3)Martha Wiggins Brackett Folsom LCol NH
James: b 4-2-1754 d 12-29-1811 m (1)Eunice Gruard (2)Sally M. Briard Capt & PS NH
James: b c. 1747 d p. 1790 m Elizabeth Tompkins Pvt NY
James: b 1730 d p. 1787 m Betsey Chittenden Lt VT
James: b 1- -1750 d 1781 m Sarah Williams Capt VA
James: b 12-3-1745 d 4-9-1854 m Mary — 2Lt VA
James: b 6- -1758 d 6-18-1831 m Anne — Sgt VA
James Plaisted: b 12-4-1739 d 7-28-1788 m Abigail Furber Capt PS MA
Jared: b 8-10-1736 d 4-20-1815 m Eunice Tuttle Lt CT
Jedediah: b 3-29-1761 d 4-28-1841 m Abigail Kilby Pvt CT ★
Jeremiah, Sr.: b 1-22-1724 d 8-12-1779 m (1)Mary Smith (2)Mary Langdon Storer AdjGen MA
Jeremiah, Jr.: b 4-30-1747 d 6-11-1826 m Mary Emery Capt MA ★
Job: b 7-21-1748 d 3-18-1779 m Abigail Cook Cpl MA
Job: b 4-9-1720 d p. 1777 m (1)Hannah Morse (2)Eunice — Pvt MA
Joel: b 1734 d 1834 m Priscilla Bell Sol VA
John: b c. 1760 d p. 1806 m Elizabeth Champion Pvt GA
John: b 2-26-1739 d 9-20-1829 m Kesia Ball Sol MD
John: b 3-4-1742 d 11-24-1793 m Mary Rouel Lt MA
John: b 1749 d 1811 m Keturah Smith Sgt MA
John: b 11-11738 d 6-26-1798 m Dorcas Bowes Pvt MA
John: b 10-3-1750 d 1834 m Rachel Rice Pvt MA
John: b 7-19-1751 d — m Rody Holt Sol MA
John: b c. 1750 d p. 6-24-1802 m Jane Kenan Lt NC
John: b 6-12-1761 d p. 1804 m Elizabeth (Jones)Neal Lt NC
John: b 4-19-1736 d 2-10-1814 m Mary Gibbons Pvt PA
John: b 1755 d 1815 m Mary Leet PS PA
John: b 1750 d a. 1- -1823 m Agnes Stuart Pvt PA
John: b c. 1723 d 1785/6 m Hannah Martha Kuhn PS PA
John: b 3-13-1750 d 9-12-1834 m Priscilla Wilbur Pvt RI ★
John: b c. 1740 d p. 12-4-1812 m Mary — PS VA
John Stephen: b 1-14-1758 d 1830 m (1)Nancy Miller (2)Jenny Wynns (3)Martha Douglas Sol MD
Jonathan: b 1-30-1734 d 2-10-1793 m Elizabeth Perry Pvt CT
Jonathan: b 4-8-1755 d 3-17-1835 m Mary Coddy Pvt CT
Jonathan: b 6-12-1741/2 d 10-16-1826 m (1)Lois Reed (2)Betsey (Wheeler) Cole Lt MA
Jonathan: b 1751 d 11-26-1830 m Rosella Combs Pvt MA W★
Jonathan: b 1753 d 1840 m Annie Wild Pvt MA
Jonathan: b 12-29-1759 d 10-31-1820 m Sarah Wiggin Drm NH
Joseph: b 10-18-1741 d 9-2-1825 m Phebe Thayer Pvt MA
Joseph: b 1750 d 12-6-1831 m Susanna Stowell Pvt MA ★
Joseph: b 2-13-1745 d 10-3-1819 m Esther Smith Pvt MA
Joseph: b 6-24-1748 d 10-24-1828 m (1)Margaret Ackley (2)Margaret Joy Pvt PA
Joseph, Sr.: b c. 1716 d 1797 m (2)Elizabeth — PS PA
Joseph: b c. 1754 d 1819 m — Ellender Sgt SC
Joshua: b 1757 d 11- -1833 m Sophia Purser MM Pvt NC ★
Joshua: b 5-26-1763 d 6-20-1855 m Nancy Ann Wyatt Collier Sol VA

Levin: b c. 1743 d p. 12-18-1800 m — Ens MD
Lodowick: b 4- -1765 d 7-27-1822 m Susan Grigsby Sgt SC
Martin: b 1750 d 8-13-1777 m Rachel — Slr Pvt VA
Moses: b 8-24-1754 d 5-19-1836 m Lucy Adams MM Pvt MA ★
Moses: b 8-17-1757 d 9-1-1800 m Dinah Robinson Drm MA
Moses: b 1728 d 7-16-1799 m Hannah Currier Pvt NH
Moses: b 1750 d 1820 m Sevilla Rhoden Pvt SC
Nathaniel: b 12-4-1748 d 7-4-1801 m Martha Crockett Pvt MA
Nathaniel: b 5-7-1746 d 1-28-1854 m (1)Elizabeth Goodrich Sgt MA
Nathaniel: b c. 1740 d c. 1807 m Nanny Parrish Sol VA
Nicholas: b 12-22-1766 d 6-14-1856 m (1)Anna Newkirk (2)Catherine Row (3)Sarah Mosher (4)Sarah Hegeman Sgt NY ★
Nicholas Dudley: b 3-1-1759 d 12-15-1838 m Mary Crockett Pvt NH ★
Noah: b 2-22-1751 d 4-29-1826 m Caroline Parmelee Sgt CT
Paul: b 7-9-1742 d 8-11-1784 m Dorcas Wilson Pvt MA
Peter: b 3-9-1747/48 d 2-21-1823 m (1)Mrs Elizabeth Bacon (2)Mrs Lucy (Fitch) Hill Pvt 1Lt MA
Peter: b 1726 d 3-21-1814 m Sarah Woodbury Fif MA
Peter: b a. 1758 d 3-17-1829 m Susanna Bryant Fif MA
Peter: b 3-10-1755 d 10-14-1795 m Isabella Trimble Capt NY
Peter: b 1-1-1746 d 10-5-1813 m Catharine Fairlamb PS PA
Reuben: b 3-7-1746 d 9-23-1835 m Hannah Scranton Pvt CT
Reuben: b — d 1794 m Abigail Piper PS NH
Reuben: b 1-19-1765 d 1-31-1858 m Patience — Pvt NY ★
Reuben: b 1764/5 d 7-25-1858 m — Pvt NC ★
Richard, Sr.: b 4-15-1728 d 12-13-1793 m Permelia Pullen 1Lt CL
Richard: b 7- -1763 d 1849 m Nancy McNeel Sol VA
Robert: b 10-7-1756 d 6-20-1798 m Sarah Collins Smn MA
Robert: b 2-17-1752 d 8-2-1835 m Martha Halbert Capt NC ★
Robert: b 1735 d 6-12-1800 m (1)Margaret Stephenson (2)Mary Logan Pvt NC
Robert: b 2-15-1761 d 6-20-1845 m Rosamond Welsh Pvt PA
Robert: b 1745 d 1795 m Margaret Allison Pvt SC
Robert: b 3-10-1750 d 7-28-1833 m Margaret Vawter OrdlSgt VA ★
Robert: b 1745 d 1783 m Mrs Priscilla Bowen Gaddes Pvt VA
Robert: b 1755-60 d a. 11-16-1818 m (2)Rebecca Bailey (3)Miss Phinney Pvt VA
Robert: b 2-5-1758 d 1-15-1822 m Rebecca Caldwell Pvt VA
Sampson: b 4-15-1742/3 d 2-18-1825 m Prudence Rugg Pvt MA
Samuel: b 1732 d 9-6-1781 m Esther Killum Pvt CT
Samuel: b 4-27-1751 d 10-28-1818 m Martha Comstock Sol CT
Samuel: b 1751 d 2-10-1836 m — Sgt MA NH ★
Samuel: b 1-25-1734 d 9-21-1797 m Sarah Knight Capt PS MA
Samuel: b 1732 d 6-21-1797 m Sarah Cutler Pvt MA
Samuel: b 10-6-1721 d p. 1783 m Abigail Huckins PS NH
Samuel: b 3-5-1725 d 3-5-1788 m Bathsheba Sexton Pvt NJ
Samuel: b 11-5-1755 d 8-22-1795 m Constance Bimley Pvt MA
Samuel: b c. 1760 d 1817 m Mary — Pvt SC
Smith: b 2-16-1751 d 1-9-1822 m Elizabeth Nutt QM NJ
Solomon: b 1760 d 3-29-1839 m Amy Stone Pvt CT
Spencer: b 2-26-1762 d 10-8-1852 m (1)Mary Denny (2)Mary Rutherford Pvt VA
Squire: b 8-14-1747 d 11-17-1826 m Dorothy Walker Capt CT
Stukely: b 12-23-1755 d 2-16-1843 m Sarah Kenyon MM RI ★
Thomas: b 1762 d 1-1-1853 m Mary Williams Pvt CT
Thomas: b 1759 d 1821 m Sarah Howard Pvt MD
Thomas: b 4-23-1746 d 11-1-1821 m Rebecca Train Pvt MA
Thomas: b 5-31-1747 d 8-14-1814 m Charity Jerolmon Capt NJ
Thomas: b c. 1725 d p. 11-27-1787 m Sarah (Hill)Pvt NC
Thomas: b 12-22-1759 d 4-5-1849 m Cathrine Shropshire Pvt NC ★
Thomas: b 1762 d 1824 m Elizabeth Hannah Pvt PA
Thomas: b 1752 d p. 1800 m Sally Mayson Maj VA
Thomas: b 1750 d p. 1-15-1827 m Alianna — Ens VA
Thomas: b 3-17-1763 d 5-22-1848 m Mary Stone Sol VA
Uriah: b a. 1760 d 2-24-1834 m Rowena Marvin Pvt CT
Uriah: b 1758 d 1841 m (1)Mary Swartout (2)Catherine (Davis) Crispell (3)Mabel (Barlow) Taylor Pvt NY ★
Valentine: b c. 1730 d 2-18-1825 m Sarah Burley PS NH
Violett: b c. 1725 d 8-12-1803 m Robert Hill PS VA
Whitmel: b 2-12-1743 d 9-26-1797 m Winifred Blount Col PS NC
Whitney: b 5-13-1748 d 7-26-1800 m Rachel Daniels Sgt MA
Wm.: b 11-7-1760 d 6-30-1850 m Pheobe Flournoy Pvt GA
Wm.: b 10-16-1743 d 6-13-1815 m Mercy Perry Pvt MA
Wm.: b c. 1759 d 9-20-1806 m Lucy Leighton Sgt NH
Wm.: b 12-4-1760 d 11-29-1851 m Nancy Pinkney Pvt NY
Wm.: b 4-20-1764 d 10-10-1844 m Abigail Jane Knapp Pvt NY ★
Wm.: b 4-15-1737 d 8-22-1783 m Margaret Moore Capt NC
Wm., Sr.: b 1710-15 d 1787 m Susannah Smithers PS NC
Wm., Jr.: b 1737 d 1792 m Hanniniah Elizabeth Halbert PS Chp NC
Wm.: b 12-22-1758 d 5-13-1830 m (1)Rhoda Stephenson (2)Sarah Twiggs Pvt VA
Wm.: b 1740 d 12-1-1816 m Jane McCall Col SC
Wm.: b a. d p. 1-1-1799 m Elizabeth — Pvt SC
Wm.: b 1746 d 6-25-1828 m (2)Lydia Woodward PS CS VT
Wm.: b 1740 d 4- -1812 m Mary Jane Wood Pvt VA
Wm.: b 1740 d 1812 m Ann Davis Pvt VA
Wm.: b 4-12-1759 d 3-14-1841 m Sarah Cowins Pvt VA ★
Willy: b 1760 d 1847 m Miriam Lamos Fif NH ★
Zechariah: bpt 3-27-1737 d 3-11-1812 m (1)Rebecca Wellington (2)Ruth Robbins Pvt MA

HILL, contd.
Zenas: b 1-4-1730 d *p.* 1780 m Kezia — Pvt MA
Zimri: b 1762 d 11- -1844 m (1) — Hurlbut (2)Melinda Palmer Pvt VT

HILLAN,
James: b 1758 d 4-19-1846 m Kissiah Bailey Pvt NC ★

HILLEGAS, (includes HILLEGASS)
Frederick: b 10-12-1746 d *p.* 1803 m Anna Hunt Pvt NY
George: b *c.* 1747 d 12-31-1806 m Elizabeth Young Pvt PA
Michael: b 4-22-1729 d 9-29-1804 m Henrietta (Cox) Bonde PS CS PA
Peter: b 2-2-1735 d 9-24-1810 m Anna Barbara Hornecker Pvt PA

HILLER, (includes HELLER)
Edward: b 1736 d — m Mary Boyles Cpl MA
Jacob: b *c.* 1740 d *p.* 1785 m Elizabeth — Ens NY
Jacob: b 1760 d *p.* 1783 m Amanda Harmon Pvt SC
Joseph: b 1748 d 1814 m Margaret Cleveland 1Maj MA

HILLERY, (includes HILLEARY)
George: b *a.* 1760 d *p.* 1806 m Sarah Smith Pvt MD
Henry: b 2-15-1726 d 5- -1783 m Cassandra Magruder 1Lt MD
John: b 1741 d 12-27-1782 m Mary — Pvt MD
John: b 1751 d 5-30-1813 m Margaret Boise Pvt NH ★
Ralph Crabb: b 12-27-1740 d 10-2-1823 m Mary Beall Capt MD

HILLHOUSE,
James: b 10-21-1754 d 12-29-1832 m (1)Sarah Lloyd (2)Rebecca Woolsey Capt CT
John: b 5-11-1744 d 1801/2 m Margaret Chambers Sol SC
Wm.: b 8-25-1728 d 1-12-1816 m Sarah Griswold Maj CT

HILLIARD, (includes HILLYARD & HILGIRT)
Benjamin: b 1-29-1753 d 5-5-1801 m Sabra Smith Sgt CT
Daniel: b 1-31-1759 d 11-20-1834 m Rebecca Washburn Pvt CT ★
David: b 9-21-1726 d 7-27-1816 m Ann Mercy Irish LCol RI
Francis: b 2-1-1722 d 8-19-1797 m Christina — PS PA
Isaac: b 7-28-1738 d 6-25-1790 m Leah Crafford Sol NC
Jacob: b — d *p.* 1802 m — Sol PA
John: b 10-4-1756 d 3-1-1826 m Betsey Worthington Mather Cpl CT
John: b 1729 d 1793 m Elizabeth Smith PS CT
Jonathan: b 1748 d 1803 m Mary — Pvt CT
Joseph: b 1-15-1737 d 2-3-1820 m Sarah Burr Lt CT
Joshua: b 1-7-1757 d 8-27-1849 m (2)Elizabeth (Moore) Stickle Pvt Mrnr CT ★
Levi: b 12-11-1744 d 10-15-1776 m Experience Edgerton Pvt CT
Miner: b 4-29-1764 d 2-26-1847 m (1)Abigail Hill (2)Mrs Silence Story Pvt CT ★
Peter: b 12-7-1754 d 4-24-1834 m Elizabeth —Pvt PA ★
Samuel: b 11-16-1747 d 11-16-1831 m (1)Phoebe Yerrington (2)Caroline Lathrop Drm NH
Stephen: b 4-12-1752 d 7-29-1777 m Joanna Darling Cpl MA
Wm.: b *c.* 1750 d *p.* 12-1-1786 m — CS VA

HILLIKER, (includes HILLAKER)
Herman: bpt 4-23-1737 d 11-24-1822 m (1)Christine Storm (2)Jean Soulice Pvt NY
John: bpt 11-15-1746 d 11-25-1824 m (1)Elizabeth Storm (2)Eva Yerks Pvt NY

HILLIS, (includes HILES)
Abraham: b 1740 d 1826 m Ann Edwing Pvt PA
Jacob: b — d *a.* 1-24-1807 m — PS NJ
John: b *c.* 1760 d 7-20-1836 m — Pvt VA ★
Matthew: b *a.* 1742 d 12-8-1803 m Elizabeth — Vol PA
Wm.: b 1737 d 1818 m Jane Curruthers Pvt PA

HILLMAN, (includes HILMAN)
Benjamin: b 1725 d 1784 m (1)Love Cathcart (3)Abigail Manter Pvt MA
Daniel: b *c.* 1760 d 1800 m Martha Ellis Pvt NJ
Daniel: b *c.* 1755 d 4-1-1820 m Heathy Craig Pvt PA
John: b 1740 d 3-29-1822 m Elizabeth De Pue Van Campen Pvt PA
John: b 10-12-1751 d 12-22-1848 m Susan Lucas Pvt PA
Joseph: b — d *p.* 5-25-1814 m Esther Witherspoon Sol VA
Lot: b 1758 d 11-14-1805 m Lore Luce Pvt MA
Samuel: b *c.* 1730 d 1-27-1801 m Phebe Cathcart PS MA
Samuel: b 7-7-1759 d 6-6-1812 m Mary A. Arnold Pvt NJ W★

HILLS,
Abner: b 1-19-1733 d 8-13-1822 m (1)Mary Comstock (2)Elizabeth — Pvt CT
Amos: b 1- -1745 d 4-9-1813 m Rachel Lewis Pvt CT
Asahel: b *c.* 1759 d *c.* 1853 m (1)Hannah Burroughs (2)Mary Gilligan (3)Sarah Brown Pvt CT ★
Benoni: b 1701 d 6-24-1793 m Hannah Strong PS CT
Daniel: b 12-14-1761 d 1845 m Ruth Dickenson Pvt CT ★
Daniel: b 1730 d *p.* 1-16-1810 m Hannah Emery Capt MA
Ebenezer, Jr.: b 2-7-1756 d 4-14-1826 m Ruth Damon Pvt CT
Elijah: b 1- -1758 d 5-2-1819 m Lucy Marsh Pvt CT

Elijah: b 3-15-1738 d 1-3-1828 m (1)Lois Kidder (2)Miriam Kidder Lt NH
Eliphalet: b 2- -1761 d 10-27-1803 m (1)Jerusha Judson (2)Jerusha Smith Pvt CT
Elisha: b 1741 d *c.* 1820 m Rebecca Loveland Pvt CT
Elisha: b 4-17-1753 d 8-19-1804 m Elizabeth Porter MM CT
Erastus: b 2-26-1758 d 5-27-1840 m Sally Kellogg Pvt CT
Ezekiel: b 4-11-1718 d 5-14-1790 m Hannah Varnum PS NH
Israel: b 1757 d 9-18-1827 m Ruth Hollister Pvt CT
Jacob: b 1741 d 8-8-1817 m Love Pease Pvt CT
James: b 7-25-1732 d *p.* 1782 m Abigail Allbee Pvt MA
James: b 1763 d 1846 m Thankful Coburn Ens NH
Jeremiah: b 3-1-1727 d 4-4-1810 m Hannah Dow PS NH
John, Sr.: b 9-20-1735 d 1-21-1782 m Mindwell Wright Pvt CT
John: b 12-13-1732 d 3-15-1808 m Jerusha Lewis Capt PS CT
John: b 1731 d 1777 m Anna Loomis Pvt CT
Jonathan: b 1729 d 10-13-1776 m Mabel Stanley Pvt CT
Medad: b 4-27-1729 d 4-9-1808 m Sarah Smith LCol CT
Nathan: b — d 12-31-1781 m — Cpl CT
Obadiah: b 8-23-1751 d 6-17-1825 m (1)Sarah Merrill (2)Mrs Lois Foss Pvt MA
Reuben: b 9- -1752 d 9-28-1828 m Sarah Currier Pvt NH
Samuel: b 8-24-1761 d 1839 m Felinda — Pvt CT ★
Samuel: b 1-25-1701 d 2-14-1792 m Hannah Turner PS CT
Samuel: b *c.* 1730 d 1800 m Sarah Graves Pvt PS NH
Samuel: b 3-4-1754 d 5-28-1832 m (1)Aseneth Scott (2)Mrs Hannah Healey Pvt NH
Samuel: b 10-25-1759 d 6-12-1840 m (1)Elizabeth Cobb (2)Anna — Pvt NY
Samuel: b 2-14-1740 d 3-14-1833 m Rhoda Phillips Capt RI
Seth: b 9-13-1736 d 6-3-1826 m Abigail Soper Wgm CT ★
Stephen: b 1746 d 2-8-1831 m Anna — Pvt NH
Thomas: b 3-30-1751 d 5-21-1833 m Ruthe Whittemore Pvt NH
Zimri: b 11-16-1762 d 7-16-1835 m Milla Catlin Pvt CT ★

HILLSGROVE,
John b 1752 d *p.* 1776 m Mary Harcourt Pvt MA

HILLSMAN,
John: b 11-17-1764 d 12-8-1850 m (1)Kitty Chenault (2)Rebecca Thrasher Pvt VA

HILLYER, (includes HILYER)
Andrew: b 6-4-1743 d 2-2-1828 m Lucy Tudor Capt CT
Asa: b 8-21-1738 d 12-11-1820 m Rhoda Smith Pvt Dr CT ★
James, Jr.: b 10-6-1746 d 4-22-1826 m (1)Ruth Holcomb (2)Hannah (Wadsworth) Bigelow Tilley (3)Dorcas Eldridge (4)Penelope (Holcomb) Goodrich Hubbard Capt CT
Lawrence: b 2-24-1734 d 7-20-1809 m Ann Lockman 1Lt NY
Seth: b 8-16-1756 d 6-22-1841 m Sibil Case Pvt CT
Simon: b 2-24-1762 d 12-24-1822 m Elner Vactor Pvt NJ
Theodore: b 1741 d 1836 m Lodumy Humphrey Mus CT ★

HILT,
Peter: b 1748 d 1785 m Mary Klaus Cpl MA

HILTEBEITEL,
Adam: b 10-30-1742 d 7-25-1823 m Salome — Pvt PA

HILTON,
Abraham, Jr.: b 6-12-1760 d 10-24-1815 m Mary Libby Pvt MA
Charles: b 9-28-1754 d 4-5-1812 m Mary Wadleigh Pvt NH
David: b 4-27-1755 d 10-9-1822 m Mary Anna Hammond Pvt MA
Ebenezer: b 10-23-1753 d 1-28-1839 m Abigail Arnold Pvt MA ★
Edward: b 1764/5 d 4-26-1833 m Mary Moody Pvt MA ★
Edward: b 8-30-1730 d 8-31-1794 m Elizabeth Folsom Capt NH
James: b 6-27-1737 d 1799 m Sarah Tasy Capt MA
James: b *c.* 1764 d 1845 m Patty Brewer Sol SC
Jeremiah: b *c.* 1735 d *a.* 3-29-1800 m (1)Sarah Becket (2)Abigail Hunking PS NH
John: b 5-11-1756 d 12-31-1835 m Rachel Gray Lt MA
Joseph: b 1753 d 1833 m Miriam Getchell Pvt MA ★
Joseph: b 8-29-1747 d 11-26-1826 m (1)Sarah Thurston (2)Anna Mills Lt NH ★
Josiah: b 11-6-1724 d *p.* 1789 m Sarah Marston Ames PS NH
Moral: b 9-6-1755 d 2-3-1840 m Lydia Gould Grant Sgt MA
Moses: b 1728 d 6-16-1820 m (1)Rachel Thompson (2)Mrs Dorcas Gray Greenlief (3)Mrs Ruth Young Lt MA
Peter: bpt 11-19-1728 d *p.* 1790 m (1)Machtel Wyngaat (2)Anna Broecks Capt NY
Richard: b 6-30-1753 d 8-14-1842 m Anna — Lt NY
Robert: bpt 11-5-1749 d 6-9-1829 m Elizabeth Burgess Pvt NY
Samuel: b 10-7-1741 d 8-29-1809 m Judith Carter Pvt MA
Thomas: b 6-14-1752 d *p.* 1799 m Sarah Stratton Pvt MA
Wm., Sr.: b *c.* 1730 d *p.* 1790 m Hepzibah Boynton Pvt MA
Wm., Jr.: b 8-15-1759 d 7-14-1846 m Catherine Mc Kenney Pvt MA

HILTZ,
Nicholas: b 4-15-1733 d 12-15-1809 m Elizabeth Fox Pvt NY

HIMMELRIGHT, (includes HIMMELREICH)
John: b 10-1-1751 d 3-31-1821 m Margaret — Pvt PA
John: b *c.* 1760 d 7-15-1815 m Catharine Brill Pvt PA W★

HIMROD,
Aaron: b 8-18-1757 d 12-4-1820 m Isabella Kirk Pvt PA
Simon: bpt 12-16-1731 d *p.* 1783 m Marie Cathrine Moelich Lt PS PA

HINCHMAN,
James: b *c.* 1726 d *c.* 6-1-1785 m Sarah Bickham PS NJ
John S.: b *c.* 1740 d *c.* 1811 m Abigan Bartum Dr NJ
Robert: b 3-14-1734 d 1-29-1784 m Joanna Ludlum PS NY

HINCKLEY, (includes HINKLEY)
Aaron: b 9-13-1715 d 1793 m Mary Larrabee CS ME
Abel: b 4-10-1743 d 3-20-1818 m Sarah Hobart Sgt PS CT
Adino: b 12-12-1735 d 2-5-1793 m Marcy Otis Pvt CS MA
Benjamin: b 2-20-1750 d 5-18-1782 m Pannah Nye Pvt CT Heirs★
Benjamin: b 1743 d 5-24-1824 m Dinah Swett Lt MA
Ebenezer: b 9-23-1754 d 9-5-1822 m Esther May Pvt MA
Ebenezer: b 2-10-1733 d 3-31-1776 m Susan Brown Lt MA
Edmond: b 6-29-1745 d 8-18-1807 m Mary Pettingell Pvt MA
Elkanah: b 7-18-1759 d *p.* 1792 m Bathsheba Paddock Cpl NY
Enoch: b 3- -1751 d 11-29-1842 m Mercy Crocker Pvt MA
Gershom, Sr.: b 9-4-1730 d 1-15-1809 m Catherine Wightman Pvt NY
Gideon: b 1730 d *p.* 9-25-1779 m Mary Russell Pvt MA
Heman: b 1-27-1754 d *p.* 1793 m Lydia Lovewell Pvt MA
Ichabod: b 10-13-1735 d 2-23-1807 m (1)Mary — (2)Hannah Kingsbury Capt CT
Ira: b 3-16-1756 d 8-21-1825 m Elizabeth Hyde Pvt CT
Jabez: b 10-24-1741 d 2-19-1817 m Deborah Wing Pvt MA
Jared, Sr.: b 10-8-1731 d 2-5-1820 m (1)Anne Hyde (2)Mary Newman PS CT
Jared, Jr.: b 11-8-1759 d 4-12-1828 m Hopestill Brewster Pvt CT★
John: b 9-2-1761 d 10-22-1846 m Anna Whipple Pvt CT★
John: b 9-26-1733 d 7-28-1779 m Hannah Oliver Capt MA
John: b 9-13-1748 d 12-19-1835 m (1)Elizabeth Hinckley (2)Lydia Cobb Cpl MA
Josiah: b 2-18-1742 d 7-1-1811 m Kazia Hutchins Lt MA
Josiah: b 1760 d 9-28-1851 m Elizabeth Ellis Lambert Pvt NY ★
Levi: b 5-17-1764 d 1-31-1830 m Sarah Crocker Pvt MA
Nathan: b 2-23-1748 d 1814 m Mary Babcock PS CT
Nehemiah: b 10-13-1762 d 10-22-1837 m Edith Wood Pvt MA
Nymphas: b 9-13-1753 d 12-12-1832 m Chloe Jenkins Pvt MA W★
Phillip: b 12-16-1747 d 6-18-1843 m (1)Polly Covil (2)Rebecca Covil Cpl MA★
Prince: b 12-27-1758 d 11-30-1844 m Eunice Goodspeed Pvt MA
Samuel: b 12- -1757 d — m Dorothy Strong Pvt MA NY
Seth, Jr.: b 6- -1759 d 4-30-1851 m Lydia Berry Pvt MA ★
Sylvanus: b 8-25-1756 d 8-1-1841 m (1)Mary Hawes (2)Bethiah Hinckley Pvt MA★
Thomas: b 4-28-1751 d 1-18-1831 m Phalla Slack Cpl CT
Thomas: b 12-7-1736 d 12-11-1821 m Elizabeth Mitchell Sgt MA
Thomas: b 7-22-1731 d 3-7-1807 m (2)Susannah Chase Pvt MA
Wyatt: b 1-18-1739 d 1810 m Eunice Breed Pvt CT

HINDMAN,
David: b *c.* 1745 d *p.* 1782 m Agnes Linville Pvt PA
John: b 1-24-1754 d 1827 m Mary Ann Latcha Dr MD

HINDS, (includes HINE, HINES)
Abel: b *c.* 1736 d 2-2-1810 m Silent (Syley) Shears Pvt MA
Ambrose: bpt 6-26-1726 d *p.* 4-27-1794 m (1)Sarah Terril (2)Betsy Ford Capt PS CS CT
Andrew: b 6-12-1752 d 12-21-1843 m Keziah Thorpe Pvt CT
Bartlett: b 4-4-1755 d 10-11-1822 m (1)Ruth Pickens (2)Agnes Rugg Post Capt MA ★
Benjamin: b 7-7-1725 d 10-29-1794 m (1)Elizabeth Temple (2)Tabitha Holland PS Pvt MA
Corlis: b 4-28-1724 d 1821 m (1)Janet McMasters (2)Mrs McCutter PA MA
Corlis: b 4-10-1748 d 1832 m (1)Adah (Hill) Brownell (2)Susannah Henry PS MA
Daniel: b 2-18-1748/9 d 1-14-1835 m Lydia Beecher CS CT
David: b *c.* 1725 d 1793 m Nancy — Pvt NC
Ebenezer: b 9-21-1746 d *p.* 1799 m Esther Potter Pvt CT
Ebenezer: b 1-25-1753 d 4-26-1831 m Charity Canedy Sgt MA
Ebenezer: b 7-29-1719 d 4-19-1812 m (2)Lydia Bartlett PS MA
Elijah: b 1-5-1730-34 d 3-2-1818 m Molly Coe Cpl CT
Henry: b 1732 d 10- -1810 m (1)Dorcas Kelley (2)Elizabeth Harvey Pvt VA
Hezekiah, Sr.: b 1733 d 9-13-1807 m (1)Lois Bristol (2)Eunice Bristol Ens CT
Howard: b 3-6-1755 d 1850 m Anna Paine Pvt MA
Jacobus: b 10-28-1752 d 1844 m Priscilla Evans Pvt MD ★
James: b 1767 d 11- -1851 m Mason Potter Sol GA
James: b *c.* 1750 d *p.* 4-28-1799 m Drusilla Lewis Pvt NC
James: b 5-10-1760 d 3-20-1851 m Zipporah Morgan Scott Pvt PA
Jesse: b 7-10-1759 d 5-26-1842 m Martha Wing Sol MA
Joel: bpt 9-26-1736 d 7-19-1819 m Martha Rogers Pvt CT
Joel: b 1-30-1752 d 6-20-1826 m (1)Mary Perkins (2)Sally Sperry Pvt CT
John, Jr.: b 9-8-1750 d 5-13-1837 m (1)Comfort Baldwin (2)Susannah Johnson Cav CT

John: b 1744 d 10-6-1816 m Gertrude Deitch Mil MD
John: b 9-19-1759 d 10-4-1830 m Olive Valentine Pvt MA
John, Sr.: b 1732 d 3-10-1806 m Hannah Sutton Pvt NJ
John, Jr.: b 1760 d 1818 m Elizabeth Prudden Pvt NJ
John: b 9-17-1749 d 3-25-1806 m Juliana Schneider Pvt NC
John: b 1760 d 5-18-1807 m Sally Greswitt Pvt VA
Jonathan: b 9-17-1722 d 8-30-1809 m (1)Sarah Baldwin (2)Abigail Parker Pvt CT
Joseph: b 1-17-1743 d 1799 m (1)Susannah Powers (2)Elizabeth Scott Sgt MA
Joseph: b *c.* 1735 d *c.* 1812 m — Grider PS NC
Leonard: b 8-19-1761 d *p.* 1797 m Mary Rounseville Drm MA
Nathan: b 4-22-1732 d 7-26-1818 m (1)Elizabeth Welch (2)Mary Terrill Capt CT
Nimrod: b 1-12-1758 d 2-12-1835 m Betsey Pishon Pvt MA
Noble: b 8-12-1745 d 10-15-1795 m Patience Hubbell Capt CT
Richard: b *a.* 1755 d 7-26-1834 m Abiah Jenkins Sgt MA
Samuel: b 11-15-1742 d 7-1-1833 m Mary Harlequin Pvt CT ★
Samuel: b 1745-48 d *p.* 6- -1803 m Elizabeth Wright Capt PA
Simon: b 1750 d 12-14-1838 m (1)Eva B. Miller (2)Anna Margaret Braugh Pvt PA
Stephen: b 1-13-1754 d 2-27-1833 m Naomi Peck Pvt CT
Thaddeus: b 8-18-1739 d 11- -1816 m Mary Humphries Pvt CT
Thomas: b 3-4-1741 d 5-5-1796 m Abigal Rose 1Lt MD
Thomas: b 7-16-1734 d 9-28-1828 m Mary Todd Hubbard Dr VA
Timothy: b 12-3-1741 d 6-4-1844 m Mary — Pvt MA
Titus: b 2-9-1744 d 4-18-1822 m Mary Merchant Pvt CT ★
Wm.: bpt 1-9-1703/4 d *a.* 9-5-1781 m (1)Elizabeth Hollingsworth (2)Hannah (Howell) Sherman PS CT
Wm.: b 1-25-1736 d 1-7-1816 m Martha Blow Pvt VA

HINESMAN, (or HINZMAN)
Henry:b — d 12-24-1827 m Charity Coon Pvt PA

HINKLE, (includes HENCKEL, HENKEL, HINCKLE)
Abraham: b 3-20-1749 d 1815 m Mary Catherine Teeter PS VA
Anthony: b 1737 d *c.* 1811 m Maria Magdalena Zwicker Pvt NC
Anthony: b 11-30-1754 d 2-18-1838 m Salome Lechner Ens PA
Baltis: b 12-25-1737 d 2-4-1804 m Elizabeth Grove PS MD
Charles: b *c.* 1741 d *a.* 1790 m Elizabeth Johnson Capt PS NC
George: b 1727 d 3-13-1778 m Barbara Roland Pvt PA
Hans Leonard: b *c.* 1730 d 1810 m Marcellas — Pvt PS PA
Isaac: b *c.* 1760 d 1824 m Mary Cunningham Capt VA
John, Jr.: b 9-30-1755 d 7-15-1828 m Catherine Kaufman Pvt PA
John: b 4-30-1733 d 10-8-1816 m (1)Elizabeth Lovering (2)Rachel — PS CS PA
Joseph: b 10-29-1758 d 2- -1828 m Catharine Dollin Cpl PA
Joseph: b *c.* 1761 d 3-17-1793 m Lydia Cook Mil PA
Justus, Sr.: b 12-30-1706 d *a.* 8-24-1778 m Mary Margareta Eshmann PS VA
Justus, Jr.: b 1-14-1752 d 4- -1794 m Christina Nagley Ens VA
Michel: b 1750 d 1810 m Sarah — Sol PA
Nathan: b 3-31-1759 d 12-25-1848 m Rebecca Ledford Pvt PA ★
Paul: b 12-15-1754 d 11-27-1825 m Elizabeth Nagley Pvt PS VA
Philip: b 1739 d 1814 m Mary Johnson Pvt PA
Wendel: b 3-17-1757 d 7-11-1838 m Elizabeth Fox Pvt PA

HINKSON,
John, Jr.: b *c.* 1765 d 2-17-1819 m Abigail Engle Pvt PA
John: b 1740 d 1810-15 m Margaret Mc Cracken Maj VA
Samuel: b 1-17-1747 d *p.* 1785 m (1)Apphia Farnum (2)Abigail Allen Pvt PS NH

HINMAN,
Abijah: b 3-12-1733 d 3-23-1807 m Rebecca Minor Pvt MA
Adoniram: b 12-6-1757 d 12-23-1830 m Martha Barber Pvt MA
Asahel: b 3-23-1742 d 9-5-1825 m Mary Harris Hinman Capt NJ
Asher: b 3-13-1742 d 3-8-1809 m Mary Harris Sgt CT
Azur: b 1-14-1759 d *c.* 1810 m Esther Munn Pvt CT
Benjamin: b 4-1-1720 d 3-22-1810 m (1)Molly Stiles (2)Mrs Sarah Hickok Col CT
Benjamin: b 1757 d 4-7-1821 m Anna Keyser Capt CT ★
Bethuel: b 6-27-1742 d *p.* 1790 m Hannah Hicock Lt CT
Daniel: b 10-15-1752 d 11-24-1807 m Annis — Pvt CT
Eleazer: b 1704/5 d — m Hannah Scovill CS CT
Elijah: b 4-1-1733 d 1823 m Hester Curtis Capt CT
Elisha: b 3-9-1732 d 8-29-1805 m Abigail Dolbear Capt CT
Ephraim: b 4-5-1753 d 12-11-1829 m Sylvania French Asst Cmsry Gen CT
Gideon: bpt 11- -1725 d — m Hannah Curtis Capt MA
Joel: b 3-3-1748 d 3-9-1813 m Sarah Curtis Col CT
John: b 8-1-1732 d 10-17-1801 m (1)Abigail Graham (2)Mary (Way) Wentworth Capt CT
Jonas: b 2- -1730 d *c.* 1790 m Sarah Downs Lt CT
Jonas: b 3-30-1752 d 1833 m Caty Fairchild Pvt CT
Josiah: b 12-16-1747 d 9-10-1818 m Phebe Summers Pvt CT
Lewis: b *c.* 1759 d 4-17-1807 m (1)Margaret Bissell (2)Lucy Adams Sgt NY W★
Moses: b 1755 d 1836 m Mary Shaw Pvt MA
Phineas: b 3-31-1740 d 3-8-1829 m (1)Rhoda Hubbell (2)Ruth Colt Pvt CT
Reuben: bpt 9-7-1735 d — m Mary Downes Pvt MA
Samuel: b 7-26-1736 d 1840 m Anna Colt Pvt CT

HINMAN, contd.
Samuel: b 1705 d 1784 m — PS CT
Samuel: b 10-21-1739 d 10-16-1794 m Lois Crane Capt NJ
Timothy: b 7-21-1762 d 4-29-1850 m Phebe Stoddard Pvt CT ★
Titus: b 10- -1733 d 7-3-1778 m Joanna Hurd Ens CT
Wait: b 1748 d 6-2-1826 m Mary Howe Sol CT

HINNANT,
Wm.: b 1728/9 d 1801 m Mary — CS NC

HINSDALE,
Ariel: b 9-11-1750 d 3-10-1828 m Thankful Severance Cpl MA
Barnabas: b 2-23-1738 d 4-29-1890 m Magdalen Seymour Lt CT
David: b 6-30-1754 d 11-8-1822 m Frazina Bemis.Pvt MA
Elisha: b 2-28-1761 d 6-22-1827 m (1)Asenath Barnes (2)Elizabeth
　　Holcomb Pvt CT
Ezra: b 1-5-1741 d 1804 m Sarah Hopkins Sgt CT
Jacob: b 9- -1734 d 11-22-1815 m (1)Mary Brace (2)Mrs Rachel
　　Goodwin Capt CT
Jacob: b 4-18-1759 d 10-26-1839 m Sarah Barber Pvt MA
Joseph: b 9-14-1747 d 8-18-1800 m Hannah Bingham Ens VT
Joseph: b 8-9-1720 d 12-30-1800 m Elizabeth Kellogg Sol VT
Samuel, Sr.: b 4-24-1708 d 11-23-1786 m (1)Rebecca Leonard
　　(2)Mrs Eunice McDowell (3)Sarah — PS MA
Samuel, Jr.: b 8-22-1741 d 5-10-1825 m Mary Stebbins Pvt MA

HINSEY,
John: b c. 1734 d p. 11-11-1787 m Elizabeth Post Pvt DE

HINTON,
Benjamin: b a. 1761 d p. 4-16-1804 m Sarah Hopkins Sol VA
David: b 1750 d 1779 m Mary Van Meter PS VA
Dempsey: b c. 1750 d 1779 m Mary Ann Benefield PS GA
James: b c. 1750 d 6- -1794 m Delilah Hunter Col PS NC
John, Sr.: b c. 1720 d 1784 m Grizelle Kimbrough PS Col NC
John, Jr.: b 3-14-1748 d 1818 m Pheriba Smith Maj NC
John, Jr.: b — d 1845 m Elizabeth Norman PS NC
John: b c. 1732 d p. 1-1-1781 m Esther — PS VA
Malachi: b a. 6-20-1730 d a. 2- -1808 m Sarah Wimberly PS NC
Wm.: b 1750 d 12-7-1783 m Phebe Smith Drm NY
Wm.: b 1748/9 d 1839 m Martha Chamberlin Pvt PA

HIPKINS,
Lewis: b 5-20-1753 d p. 7-26-1794 m Susanna Adams PS VA

HIPP,
Valentine: b 5- -1760 d 11-9-1838 m Margaret Allison Pvt NC

HIPPLE,
Conrad: b 1762 d 6-17-1838 m Elizabeth Schrack Drm PA ★
John: b 10-8-1755 d 12- -1851 m Elisabeth — Pvt PA ★
Laurentz: b 1-28-1729 d 10-1-1795 m (1)Mary — (2)Rosina — Pvt
　　PA

HIRES, (includes HIERS)
Conrad: b 6-12-1744 d 5-30-1782 m Christina Hitchner Pvt NJ
John: b 1751 d 6-20-1832 m Eleanor — Pvt NJ

HIRONS,
Simon: b c. 1725 d 9-25-1778 m Grace Raiford PS SC

HISCOCK, (includes HISCOX)
Clarke: b 10-14-1760 d 2-8-1842 m Sarah Saunders Cpl RI
David: b 1751 d 3-3-1839 m Anstus Bugbee Lt CT
John: b c. 1761 d — m Mary Flint Pvt MA
Richard: b 9-15-1758 d 6-17-1840 m Sarah Cody Pvt MA W★
Thomas: b 10-25-1753 d 5- -1826 m Anna Knowlton Pvt MA

HISE,
Jacob: b 1752 d 1830 m Phebe — Pvt NJ
John: b 1758 d 2-5-1819 m Barbara Mesh Kreitzer Pvt PA

HISERODT,
Hindrick: b 1759/60 d 10-18-1823 m Catherine Holzapple Pvt NY

HISEY,
Christian: b c. 1759 d 1827 m Christiana Hultz Pvt PA

HISLE,
Samuel: b 1764 d — m Ludia Ann — Pvt VA ★

HISSOM,
Thomas: b 1750 d 1815 m Mary Parker Pvt PA

HISTED,
Thaddeus: b 12-20-1763 d 11-26-1854 m Esther Sayles Pvt NY ★

HITCH,
Christopher: b c. 1736 d 1805 m Susannah or Rebecca — PS MD
Ezekiel: b 1748 d 9-3-1828 m Betsy Piper Pvt MD
Louther: b 1743 d 1831 m (1)Mary Nicholson (2)Elizabeth Douglas
　　Pvt MD
Samuel: b 1741 d 3-12-1825 m Lydia Allen Cpl MA

HITCHCOCK,
Aaron: b 12-6-1759 d 1-9-1835 m Ruth Tuttle Sol CT
Aaron: b c. 9-1-1756 d 11-29-1836 m Desire Maxwell Pvt MA
Abner, Sr.: b 11-17-1721 d 1903 m (1)Margaret Burt (2)Sarah
　　Knowlton Pvt MA
Abner, Jr.: b 4-20-1750 d 1-6-1805 m Lucy — Pvt MA
Abraham: b 4-6-1765 d 7-26-1846 m (1)Rachel Schlippe (2)Elizabeth
　　Smith Pvt NY ★
Amasa: b 10-3-1739 d 2-27-1827 m Sarah Bradley 2Lt CT
Amos: b 1738 d 7-17-1801 m Azubah Benham Cpl CT
Amos: b 6-12-1724 d 11-20-1791 m Dorcas Foote PS CT
Asael, Sr.: b 4-26-1719 d 1790 m Sarah Norris PS MD
Bela, Sr.: b 10-27-1719 d 10-12-1796 m (1)Sarah Atwater
　　(2)Hannah Atwater Pvt CT
Benjamin, Sr.: b 2-23-1724 d 10-4-1792 m Rhoda Cook Pvt CT
Benjamin: b 10-11-1760 d 11-19-1816 m Mary Johnson Pvt CT
Dan, Jr.: b 10-19-1752 d 1817 m (1)Anna Perkins (2)Catherine
　　Douglas PS CT
Daniel: b 1763 d 4-2-1810 m Chloras Mills Pvt CT
David: b 11-10-1751 d 11-27-1829 m Lois Cook Capt CT
David: b 6-29-1742 d 7-27-1814 m Hannah Doolittle Pvt MM CT
David: b 5-11-1745 d c. 1784-90 m Lydia Parmlee Pvt CT
David: b 1733 d 3-8-1825 m Rachel Knappl Pvt NY
David: b 5-1-1742 d c. 1820 m Miriam Merrick Lt VT
Eldad: b 1-20-1757 d 1826 m Esther Hoar Sol MA
Elijah: b 8-9-1741 d 8-5-1813 m Sarah Townsley Pvt MA
Gad, Sr.: b 12-2-1719 d 8-8-1803 m Dorothy Angier PS MA
Gad, Jr.: b 1-2-1749 d 11-29-1835 m Sarah Sage Bailey Dr MA ★
Gaius: b 4-30-1764 d 8-5-1843 m Sarah Wells Pvt MA
Heli: b 3-8-1756 d 5-26-1818 m Tryphena Goodell Pvt MA
Ichabod: b 12-18-1756 d 5-26-1820 m Lydia Cook Pvt CT
Ira: b 6-16-1765 d 3-12-1824 m Hannah Hotchkiss Tms RI W★
Jacob: b 7-4-1739 d 1810 m Phoebe Ives Sgt CT
Jacob: b 2-24-1748 d — m Bathsheba Holbrook MM MA
Jarid: b 6-14-1759 d 11-17-1836 m Irene Bartholomew Cpl CT
Jason: b 1760 d 3-30-1804 m Patience Langdon Cpl CT
Joel: b 1739 d 2- -1813 m Lois Scott Pvt CT
John: b 5-17-1753 d 8-20-1827 m Rachel Littlehale Pvt CT
John: b 5-13-1760 d 5-10-1836 m Lucy Ripley Pvt CT ★
John: b 4-21-1722 d 10-11-1807 m Thankful Burt Lt MA
John, Jr.: b 1-23-1746/7 d 10-29-1822 m (1)Martha Hitchcock
　　(2)Lucy Colton Pvt MA
Johnathan: b 1-12-1724 d 1-11-1808 m Abigail Beecher Pvt CT
Jonathan: b 10-16-1727 d p. 1777 m Christian Warner Sgt CT
Jonathan: b 9-21-1757 d 12-3-1832 m Mollie Wood Pvt MA
Joseph: bpt 7-14-1728 d 2-18-1790 m Hannah Ball Pvt CT
Joseph: b 4-28-1742 d 12-6-1811 m Hannah Livermore Sgt MA
Joseph: b 8-25-1719 d 5-7-1788 m (1)Abigail King (2)Patience
　　Stebbins (3)Mary Burt Pvt MA
Josiah: b 11-29-1726 d 1-6-1819 m Martha (Hitchcock) Pvt MA
Justin: b 5-27-1752 d 2-10-1822 m Mercy Hoyt Fif Sol MA
Lemuel: b 12-20-1749 d 6-27-1827 m (1)Mamre Hotchkiss
　　(2)Patience Dice Lt CT ★
Luke: b 12-27-1744 d 2-21-1782 m Sarah Cornish Capt CT
Luke: b 2-22-1723/4 d 8-9-1777 m Lucy Merrick PS MA
Luther: b 6-13-1754 d 11-1-1836 m Beulah Chapin Cpl MA ★
Lyman: b 3-15-1746 d 2-15-1819 m Sophia Cabot BgdMaj MD ★
Medad: b 11-24-1757 d 1820 m Martha Stebbins Sgt MA
Mirick: b 4-15-1754 d 8-25-1820 m Abigail Strickland Fif MA
Moses: b 10-25-1743 d 1800 m Hannah Williston CS MA
Nathaniel: b 5-13-1732 d p. 1790 m Sarah Severance Pvt MA
Noah: b 1-14-1715 d 3-12-1799 m Mary Burt Pvt MA
Oliver, Jr.: b 2-24-1755 d 3-19-1838 m Mercy Parker Pvt CT
Oliver: b 2-18-1760 d 10-28-1836 m Elizabeth Hitchcock Pvt MA
Phineas, Sr.: b 1-1-1734/5 d 1- -1786 m (1)Elizabeth Stebbins
　　(2)Mrs Elizabeth Montague Phillips Pvt MA
Phineas, Jr.: b 1761 d 1828 m (1)Mabel Mott (2)Prudence — Pvt MA
Samuel, Sr.: b 4-1-1730 d 5-8-1798 m Tamar — Sol CT
Samuel, Jr.: b 2-27-1757 d 10-20-1841 m Mary Munson Pvt CT
Samuel: b 12-16-1744 d 9-13-1819 m Thankful Hawks 1Lt MA
Samuel: b 2-28-1731 d 1801 m Betsey — Pvt MA
Samuel: b 8-14-1755 d 10-4-1829 m Jemima Barlow Pvt NY ★
Seth: b 2-19-1732 d 1790 m Mary Bates Pvt MA
Silas: b 10-6-1739 d p. 1775 m (1)Martha Bliss (2)Mary Taylor Pvt MA
Thomas: b 8-30-1757 d 12-29-1813 m (1)Clemence Reynolds
　　(2)Mary Tinpenny (3)Hannah Betts Pvt CT
Timothy: b 11-8-1748 d 8-6-1820 m Abigail Clark Sol PS CT
Zachariah: b 1742 d 12-20-1819 m Mercy Byington Pvt CT
Zina: b 11-6-1755 d 5-2-1832 m Mabel Lockwood PS NY

HITCHINGS,
John: b 4-4-1747 d p. 1780 m Lois Hawkes Pvt MA
Thomas: b 11-15-1762 d 2-14-1839 m Ruth Burchsted Pvt MA

HITCHMAN,
Saulsbury Alexander: b 10-10-1752 d p. 8-17-1784 m Hannah
　　Cubbach Cpl MA

HITE,
Abraham, Sr.: b 5-10-1729 d 1-17-1790 m Rebecca VanMeter PS
　　VA
Abraham, Jr.: b 10-25-1755 d 7-12-1832 m Elizabeth Erickson Capt
　　VA

Andrew: b 1758 d 2-24-1819 m (1)Anna — (2)Magdalene Gaylor Pvt VA

Conrad: b 1-1-1763 d 1835 m Maria A. — Pvt PA ★

George: b 10-28-1761 d 12-16-1816 m Deborah Rutherford Lt VA W★

Isaac, Sr.: b 5-12-1723 d 9-18-1795 m Eleanor Eltinge CS VA

Isaac, Jr.: b 2-7-1758 d 11-24-1836 m (1)Eleanor C. Madison (2)Ann Tunstall Maury Lt VA

Jacob: b 3-14-1719 d 1778 m (1)Catherine O'Bannon (2)Frances (Madison) Beale PS CS

Jacob: b 2-14-1761 d 10-27-1839 m Catherine Sheiner Pvt VA ★

John, Jr.: b 1741 d 1786 m — Pvt PA

John, Sr.: b 1710 d 1792 m Sara Eltinge CS VA

Joseph: b 1753 d p. 1815 m Mary — Lt VA

Julius: b 10-10-1756 d 12-2-1851 m Agnes Land Cpl VA ★

Matthias: b c. 1740-2 d 1-9-1823 m Sarah Daugherty Lt VA

Thomas: b 1751 d 8- -1779 m Frances Madison Beale Lt VA

Wm.: b 1756 d 1828 m Elizabeth Henning Cadet VA

HITES,
John: b 6-3-1762 d 1833 m Catherine — Pvt CL

HITT,
Herman: b — d p. 1783 m Mary Weaver PS VA
John: b 10-24-1746 d p. 1790 m Sarah (Pace) Day Sol SC
Peter: b — d 8-31-1802 m Hannah — Pvt VA ★

HITTEL, (includes HITTLE)
Adam: bpt 7-21-1748 d 8-19-1834 m Elizabeth Fisher Pvt PA
Adam: b c. 1747/48 d 1789 m Barbara — Pvt PA
Nicholas: b 1747 d 1825 m Susanna Wescoe Pvt PA

HIXON, (includes HIXSON)
Abner: b 12-11-1753 d 5-15-1820 m Mary Hogg Pvt NJ
Isaac: b 10-18-1762 d 3-18-1852 m Elizabeth Harding Pvt MA
James: b 6-10-1763 d 9-5-1833 m (1)Isabella Lee (2)Sarah Gibson (3)Mary Hampton Pvt VA ★
John: b c. 1755 d p. 6-15-1813 m — Sol SC
Jonathan: b c. 1750-52 d p. 1820 m Hannah Rockafellow Pvt NJ ★
Samuel: b '12-9-1734 d p. 1778 m (1)Hannah Harlow (2)Mary White Pvt MA
Seth: b 1734 d 7-13-1821 m Bethia Partridge Pvt Fif MA
Timothy: b 1730-40 d 1811/12 m (1)Rachel — (2)Margaret (Hixon) Capt VA

HOADLEY,
Culpepper: b 9-10-1764 d 5-21-1857 m Mollie Lewis Drm CT ★
Daniel: b 10-21-1736 d 1806 m Mary Barker Pvt CT
James: b 2-25-1738 d 2-18-1815 m Mrs Lydia (Buell) Hoadley CS CT
Jared: b 3-18-1753 d 1833 m Ann Kellogg Cpl MA
Jonathan, Jr.: b 5-5-1755 d c. 10-21-1822 m Rachel Leete Pvt CT
Nathaniel: b 5-4-1755 d 3-15-1822 m Eunice Tyler Pvt CT
Philemon: b 6-11-1755 d 1-18-1811 m Mary Rogers Pvt MA
Rufus: b 2-26-1740/1 d 1-22-1811 m (1)Ruth Peck (2)Mrs Obedience (Stevens) Ives PS CT
Silas: b 3-14-1757 d 10-28-1835 m Rachel Hoadley Pvt CT ★
Thomas: b 1737 d 6-20-1829 m Mary Stone Pvt MA ★
Wm.: b 1734 d 12-21-1820 m Esther Porter Pvt CT

HOAGLAND, (includes HOAGLIN, HOGELAND)
Abraham: b 4-29-1759 d p. 1840 m Anna Bennett Pvt NJ ★
Albert: b c. 1745 d p. 1-18-1810 m Johanna (Annatye) Stoothoff Pvt NJ
Amos: b 8-21-1741 d 1807 m Mary Titus Pvt NJ
Cornelius: b 4-12-1750 d 7- -1806 m Mary Tuttle Capt NJ
Daniel: b 4-14-1738 d 11-19-1813 m Elsie Kroesen Capt PA
Derrick: bpt 12-26-1762 d 2-8-1837 m Judith VanFleet Pvt NJ
Derrick: b 12-10-1743 d 11-12-1827 m Elizabeth Chamberlin Pvt NJ
Derrick: b 8-7-1743 d p. 1788 m Molly Montross Pvt NY
Derrick: b 5-26-1740 d 2-6-1811 m Ida Bennett Pvt PA
Harmanus: b 10-27-1750 d p. 1798 m Jane Vroom Pvt NJ
Jacob: b c. 1735 d c. 1808 m Mary Dubois Pvt NJ
James: b 5-9-1760 d 3-11-1849 m Margaret Clausen Pvt NJ ★
James: b 1750 d 1833 m Marcy Hooey Lt VA
John: b 11-25-1759 d 12- -1831 m Phoeba Baird Pvt NJ ★
John: b 1755 d 1784 m Francina Opdyke Pvt NJ
John: b 11-21-1761 d 10-5-1835 m Sarah Bergen Sol NJ
Joseph: b 12-11-1737 d 3-16-1815 m (1)Jessie Jane Jewell (2)Alice Slack Pvt NJ
Lucas: b 4-24-1753 d 5-22-1821 m Mary Bunn Pvt NJ
Martin: b 5-17-1739 d p. 1783 m Rebecca Opdyke Capt NJ
Martin: b 10-27-1716 d 3-24-1804 m Annatje — Pvt NJ
Peter: b c. 1754 d a. 3-4-1816 m Maria VanClief Pvt NJ
Richard: b 1730 d p. 1784 m Martha — Pvt NJ
Tunis: b c. 1754 d 7-13-1837 m Aaltje VanDoren Pvt NJ ★
Wm.: bpt 10-9-1720 d p. 11-25-1799 m Rachel — Pvt NJ

HOAR, (includes HORR)
Braddock: b c. 1754 d 4-13-1831 m (1)Sarah Valentine (2)Charity Snow Pvt MA
Daniel: b 1713 d — m Rebecca Brooks Pvt MA
Elijah: b 3- -1741 d 3-1-1808 m Anna Paddock Cpl VT

John: b 1-6-1707 d 5-16-1786 m (1)Esther Pierce (2)Elizabeth Coolidge PS MA
John: b 1756 d 1831 m Abigail Pierce Pvt RI
John: b 7-21-1765 d 2-3-1827 m Theodosia Durkee Pvt VT
Jonathan: b 1-9-1747 d 2-19-1813 m (1)Sarah Heard (2)Lucy Glezin Lt MA
Jonathan: b 4-12-1739 d 9-6-1805 m Anna Smith Pvt MA
Joseph, Sr.: b 12-5-1707 d 9-7-1797 m Deobrah Colton PS MA
Joseph, Jr.: b 6-22-1740 d 2-5-1816 m Mary Hitchcock Capt MA
Josiah: b 1-2-1717 d 1779 m Mary Walker Capt MA
Leonard: b 1-29-1758 d 12-12-1842 m Eunice Wheeler Pvt MA
Nathan, Sr.: b 1720 d 1801 m Miriam Colton Pvt MA
Peter: b c. 1757 d 1840 m (1)Mary Pierce (2)Mrs Eusebia (Warren) Richardson Lt MA
Philip: b c. 1732 d 11-14-1822 m Hannah Harraden Pvt MA
Robert: b 6- -1748 d 1818 m Sarah Reed Sgt MA
Samuel: b 10-17-1743 d 2-26-1807 m Elizabeth Waite Lt MA
Shadrach: b 9-18-1743 d p. 1802 m — Cpl MA
Stephen: b 1-15-1758 d 10-28-1810 m Hannah Wood Cpl MA
Timothy: b 3-15-1759 d 1-10-1832 m Lydia Hunt Matr MA
Wm., Jr.: b 7-28-1743 d p. 1790 m Mrs Phebe Carey Pvt RI
Wm.: b 2-18-1745/46 d 1810 m (2)Miriam Riggs (3)Ruth Pitcher Ens VT

HOBART,
Aaron: b 6-18-1729 d 3-11-1808 m (1)Elizabeth Pillsbury (2)Thankful Adams PS MA
Adam: b 6-9-1743 d 5-18-1824 m (2)Avis Thayer Sgt MA
Caleb: b 8-16-1744 d 12-15-1837 m (1)Anna Hopkins (2)Hannah Wright Pvt MA
Caleb: b 12-13-1754 d 8-12-1846 m Lydia Marsh Pvt MA
Caleb: b 8-18-1725 d 6-5-1795 m Elizabeth French CS MA
Daniel: b 2-24-1748 d 10-23-1776 m Kezia Weston Cpl MA
Edmund: b 3-14-1747 d 5-22-1808 m Mehitabel Peck Sol CT
Edmund: b 8-14-1755 d 4-3-1847 m (1)Elizabeth Cushing (2)Persis Cushing Cpl MA
Elijah: b 8-31-1763 d 9- -1847 m Mary Orcutt Pvt MA
Gershom: b 3-25-1740 d p. 1792 m Phebe — Pvt NH
Israel: b 7-2-1722 d 8-31-1796 m Anna Lawrence PS MA
James: b 1-27-1739 d 2-3-1834 m Hannah Cummings Pvt NH
Japhet: b 10-28-1727 d 1-17-1822 m Hannah Humphreys Sgt MA
John: b 10-5-1731 d 7-22-1791 m Miriam Lincoln Pvt MA
John: b 4-26-1755 d 2-18-1834 m Deborah White CS MA
Jonas: b 11-15-1744 d c. 11-15-1833 m Betty Kemp Pvt NH ★
Joshua: b 8-1-1747 d 12-28-1813 m Sarah Thayer Pvt MA
Justin: b 1-27-1731 d 4-7-1809 m Hannah Penfield PS CT
Nehemiah: b 3-13-1717 d 1-1-1789 m Rachel Shattuck CS MA
Peter, Sr.: b 10-19-1727 d 10-8-1798 m Lucretia Gill PS MA
Peter, Jr.: b 7-31-1750 d 1793 m Mary Cushing Dr MA
Samuel: b 4-25-1752 d 4-18-1801 m (1)Abigail Leavitt (2)Mrs Jane (Sherow) Stowell Sgt MA
Shubael: b 12-15-1746 d 11-8-1813 m Susannah Bradford Cpl MA
Solomon: b 7-21-1760 d 4-6-1849 m (1)Abigail Brooks (2)Mrs Nancy Merchant Pvt NH ★
Wm.: bpt 6-15-1740 d 5-19-1812 m (1)Abigail Curtis (2)Mercy Burrill Lt MA
Wm.: b 5-23-1751 d 1-1-1801 m (1)Patience Flagg (2)Dolly Smith Chp MA
Wm.: b 1-26-1743 d 7-23-1821 m (1)Heziah Brown (2)Sarah Taylor Pvt NH

HOBBS,
Amos: b 1752 d 6-3-1839 m Lucy Robinson Pvt MA
Benjamin: b 4-18/29-1728 d 4-22/23-1804 m Elizabeth Fogg PS NH
Benjamin: b 9-29-1751 d 1825 m Frances — Sol VA
Daniel: b 5-30-1744 d 3-30-1805 m Elizabeth L. Chubb Cpl MA
Elisha: b 2-8-1742/3 d 9-22-1807 m Lois Hastings CS MA
Frederick: b 12-25-1756 d 10-21-1833 m Sarah Moss Pvt VA
George: b 4-7-1764 d 9-1-1853 m (2)Jane Pearson Pvt MA ★
James: b — d 1-26-1808 m Sarah Gage Cpl NH
James: b a. 1735 d a. 6-27-1785 m — Pvt VA
John: b c. 1760 d 1808 m Charlotte — PS MD
Jonathan: bpt 3-31-1754 d 2-13-1833 m Rachel Foster Pvt MA
Joseph: b c. 1740 d p. 10-25-1809 m Ann Maynard Lt MD
Joseph, Sr.: b c. 1715 d p. 3-19-1791 m — PS MD
Joseph: b 8-23-1747 d c. 1825 m Elizabeth Peabody Pvt NH ★
Josiah: b 10-27-1762 d 10-29-1849 m Mary Patrick Sgt MA ★
Josiah: b 1721 d 1802 m Mary Harrington Pvt MA
Mattias: b 1734 d 1798 m Mary Rencher Cpl MD
Morrell: b 11-23-1753 d 10-20-1826 m Miriam Bracket Sgt MA
Morris: b 6-27-1730 d 6-20-1810 m Theodate Page PS NH
Moses: b c. 1756 d p. 1820 m Emily Walton Pvt NC
Nathaniel: b 1742 d 2-4-1830 m Anna Leavitt Capt NH
Nicholas: b 2-22-1747 d 10-7-1793 m Elizabeth Cumming PS Lt MD
Robert: b 5-30-1754 d 6-7-1845 m Mary Marion Corwell Pvt SC ★
Samuel: b c. 1748 d p. 8-7-1806 m Priscilla Busey PS MD
Sheldon: b 3-26-1760 d p. 1831 m (1)Ruth Stillings (2)Patience Neal Pvt MA
Thomas: b 1741 d 12-29-1818 m Nancy Baker Pvt MD
Thomas: b 4-26-1765 d 9-21-1808 m Abigail Patton Pvt MA
Thomas: b 3-25-1728 d p. 1790 m Mary Abbott CS ME
Thomas: b c. 1760 d 4-27-1844 m Sarah — Pvt NC ★
Vincent: b c. 1720 d p. 1804 m Mary Shelby Pvt VA
Wm. Hubbard: b 1755 d 11-9-1817 m Martha Meridith Pvt VA

HOBBY,
Benjamin: b 1721 d 1796 m Amy Knapp Pvt CT
David: b 12-18-1743 d 2-27-1812 m Sarah Knapp Maj NY
John: b 11-4-1739 d 2-6-1812 m Clarissa Holmes Capt PS CT
Jonathan: b 5-4-1739 8-24-1795 m Hannah Mead Pvt NY MA
Joseph: b 7-10-1741 d p. 1787 m Eunice Knapp Capt CT
Mills: b a. 1760 d 6-22-1802 m Ruth Holmes Pvt CT
Thomas, Sr.: b 1-6-1723 d 7-30-1798 m (2)Rebecca Merritt LCol CT
Thomas, Jr.: b 6-15-1745 d 10-20-1801 m (1)Hannah Holmes (2)Clemence Hobby Ens CT

HOBDAY,
Edmund: b 1760 d 1848 m Ann Harrell Pvt VA
Richard: b 1759 d 1830 m (1)Mary — (2)Jane — Sgt VA

HOBLITZELL,
Adrian: b 2-6-1745 d 1802 m (1)Martha Barton (2)Christena — PS MD

HOBSON,
Benjamin: b c. 1754 d a. 10-28-1817 m Elizabeth Moore Pvt VA
Charles: b 5-14-1744 d 10-24-1829 m Sarah Beck Mil NC
Joana Lawson: b 3-17-1721 d p. 1790 m Adcock Hobson PS VA
John: b 1751 d 1824 m Susannah Hatcher Pvt VA
Matthew: b c. 1755 d 1801 m Ann Lipscomb PS VA
Nicholas: b 1745/6 d 1809 m Sarah deGraffenreid Capt VA
Samuel: b c. 1739 d p. 10-30-1805 m Sarah Povall PS VA
Wm.: b 3-25-1730 d 9- -1827 m (1)Hannah Johnson (2)Lydia Parsons (3)Margaret — Pvt MA
Wm.: b c. 1753 d 2-9-1816 m Janette McLaurine Capt VA
Wm.: b 1745 d p. 1794 m Sarah Benbow Ens VA
Wm.: b 9-7-1748 d c. 1836 m Nancy Brackett Sgt VA
Wm.: b 1730 d 1805 m Lucy Harris Sol VA

HOCHLAENDER,
George: b 1-20-1764 d 4-20-1844 m (2)Ann Catharine Geiger PS PA
Michael: b c. 1742 d 12-7-1794 m Catharine — PS PA

HOCKADAY,
James: b c. 1732 d p. 1786 m Mary — PS VA
John: b c. 1750 d a. 7-11-1799 m Hannah Clarke Capt VA
Wm.: b 10-28-1762 d 1822/3 m Elizabeth Brademham Sol VA

HOCKENBERRY,
Casper: b c. 1720 d — m Miss Greenwood Pvt PA
James: b c. 1752 d 1844/5 m Eva Meyer Pvt PA

HOCKENMILLER,
Jacob: b 12-24-1757 d 1814 m Maria Mullen Pvt PA

HOCKENSMITH,
George: b c. 1740 d p. 12-8-1798 m — Lt MD

HOCKER,
Adam: b 12-19-1763 d 2-4-1847 m Ann Dillet Pvt PA
George: b 4-14-1734 d 10-14-1821 m Margaret — Pvt PA
John: b 9-26-1761 d 9-26-1798 m Elizabeth Mason Pvt PA
Nicholas: b 3-5-1752 d 2-14-1813 m Sarah Barnes Ens PS MD
Philip: b 1729 d 1780 m Margaret Snowden PS MD
Philip: b 1750 d p. 6-25-1820 m Dorcas — Sol PS MD
Wm.: b 1752 d 1823 m Margaret Chrisman PS MD

HOCKSTRASSER,
Paul I.: b 9-12-1761 d 11-11-1843 m Dorothy Fisher OrdlSgt NY★

HODGDON,
Benjamin: b a. 1757 d p. 1798 m Betsey Tyler Pvt MA
Benjamin: b 5-20-1750 d 3- -1823 m Rosamond Coleman Pvt NH
Caleb: b 1-27-1732/3 d 5- -1814 m (1)Priscilla Austin (2)Elizabeth Twombly Maj NH
Hanson: b 1-4-1758 d 10-8-1840 m Mary Caldwell Pvt NH ★
Peter: b 10-18-1742 d 4-19-1827 m (1)Mary Brodey (2)Patience Chase PS NH
Phinehas: b 2-10-1759 d 2-21-1845 m)Kesiah Nutter Pvt NH
Samuel: b 1755 d 8-31-1825 m Ann Libby Pvt NH
Samuel: b 9-3-1745 d 6-9-1824 m (1)Mary Ranger (2)Mary Hodge CmsryGen PA
Shadrach: b 1709 d 11-15-1791 m Mary Ham PS NH
Thomas: bpt 7-5-1730 d p. 1793 m (1)Sarah Seaver (2)Rebecca Emerson Capt MA

HODGE,
Abel: b 3-8-1731 d 4-25-1802 m Rebecca Trowbridge Pvt CT
Abel: b 12-2-1757 d 6-2-1850 m (1)Tabitha Elwell (2)Keturah Jones Pvt CT
Alexander: b 1762 d 8-17-1836 m Ruth Hodges Sol SC
Benjamin: b 2-1-1753 d 2-23-1837 m Sarah Churchill Sol CT
Charles: b 8-20-1716 d 4-27-1779 m Elizabeth Titcomb PS MA
David: b 1754 d 1832 m Amy Webster Pvt CT
Elijah: b 11-11-1752 d 11-6-1821 m Elizabeth Ellis Pvt CT
Hugh: b 8-20-1755 d 7-14-1798 m Mary Blanchard Dr PA
Isaac: b 5-9-1757 d p. 4-25-1837 m (2)Tryphena — Pvt CT ★
James: b 1730 d 6-9-1809 m Susannah Averill Pvt MA

James: b 11-30-1744 d 11-11-1827 m Sarah Runyan Pvt NJ
James: b 1760 d p. 1783 m — Lifely Pvt NY
John: b c. 1725 d 9-1-1799 m (1)Sarah Taylor (2)Abigail Dodge PS CT
John: b 1732 d 4-6-1798 m Margaret McDowell NCapt
John, Jr.: b 5-19-1742 d 4-22-1831 m Amy Rouse Sol NY
John: b 1741 d 1797 m Jane Hamilton Pvt VA
Joseph: b 1755 d 1822 m Euphemia Agnew Pvt NC
Philo: b 2- -1756 d 1-31-1842 m (1)Keturah Armstrong (2)Lucy Weston Pvt CT ★
Thomas: b 9-8-1758 d 8-10-1840 m Lucy Webber Pvt CT
Thomas: b c. 1742 d p. 1790 m — Pvt SC

HODGEN,
Robert: b 8-7-1742 d 2-5-1810 m (1) — Atkins (2)Sarah LaRue Sol VA

HODGES,
Abednego: b 1759 d a. 12-9-1842 m Sally A. — Pvt VA
Abiel: b 1739 d p. 1805 m (1)Experience Williams (2)Abigail Williams (3)Thankful Ameden Pvt MA
Abijah: b 1728 d 1807 m Jerusha Leonard Lt MA
Abijah, Jr.: b 1755-8 d 6-8-1812 m (1)Wealthy Godfrey (2)Freelove Luther Sgt MA
Andrew: b 1729/30 d 1777 m (1)Mehitable Leonard (2)Abigail Hoskins PS MA
Benjamin: b 1-6-1745 d 5-8-1814 m (1)Esther Allen (2)Miriam Pratt Pvt MA
Benjamin: b 1757 d 6-6-1818 m (2)Jane Ann Phelps Sol GA
David: b 2-15-1752 d 1806 m Lydia (Hodges) Pvt MA
Edmund: b 8-17-1744 d p. 1788 m (1)Rachel Godfrey (2)Ruth (Fletcher) Paddock Capt MA VT
Elijah, Sr.: b 1724 d 7-28-1809 m Elizabeth Reed Pvt MA
Elijah, Jr.: b 4-5-1751 d 4-14-1837 m (1)Sarah Morey (2)Mrs Betsey Burt MM Pvt MA
Eliphalet: b c. 1761 d p. 1832 m — Pvt MA ★
Ezekiel: b 11-14-1751 d 3-22-1850 m Mercy Foster Pvt NY
Ezra: b 5-23-1762 d 9-29-1851 m (1)Mehitabel Pollard (2) Elizabeth Kersey Pvt RI ★
Francis: b c. 1745 d 1798 m Martha Sproat Pvt NC
George: b 6-4-1759 d 12-21-1828 m Phebe Arnold Pvt MA
George: b 7-18-1765 d 7-28-1827 m (1)Lydia Gale (2)Hannah Phippen Slr MA
George: b c. 1760 d 1826 m Sarah Cherry Sol SC
Henry: b 1718 d 6-29-1778 m Mercy Eddy Capt PS MA
Hercules: b 1743 d 6-20-1821 m Lydia (Phinney)Hinckley Pvt MA
Isaac, Sr.: b 2-4-1728/9 d 3- -1807 m Mary Pratt LCol MA
Isaac, Jr.: b 8-25-1757 d 7-25-1840 m Chloe Bishop Sgt MA RI ★
James, Sr.: b 2-22-1732 d p. 9-17-1816 m Sarah Granger Sol MD
James: b 4-22-1737 d 1818 m Mary Briggs 2Lt MA
James: b 11-1-1757 d 4-29-1838 m Abigail Cable Sgt NY
Jesse: b 10-3-1755 d 12-15-1819 m Olive White Cpl MA
Jesse: b 1760 d p. 1832 m Mrs. George Pvt VA ★
Job, Sr.: b 1721 d 8-5-1808 m Ruth Andrews Pvt PS MA
Job, Jr.: b 1744 d 8-15-1822 m Margaret White Pvt MA
John: b 3-20-1749 d 8-11-1816 m Margaret Lacy Capt NC
John: b 1747 d p. 1797 m Anna Magee Pvt SC
John: b 1765 d 12-24-1834 m (1)Margaret Long (2)Frances Anderson Pvt SC ★
Jonathan: b 1747 d 1823 m Abigail Carpenter Sgt MA
Joseph, Jr.: b 11-15-1752 d 4-10-1810 m Lurana Williams Lt MA
Joseph: b 1- -1763 d 1828 m Sarah Carr Pvt NC
Joshua: b 10-13-1736 d 3-13-1809 m Ann Raiford Sol NC
Leonard: b 3-25-1759 d 3-25-1841 m Sarah Spafford Pvt CT ★
Nathaniel: b 1759 d 1843 m Mercy Delano Pvt MA
Nathaniel: b 5-21-1750 d 1828 m (1)Hannah Skinner (2)Martha Dean Pvt MA
Philemon: b 1760 d 1848 m Winefred Kittrell Pvt NC ★
Seth, Sr.: b 3-10-1722 d 4-1-1809 m (1)Anna Hoar (2)Elizabeth Tyler PS Capt VT
Seth, Jr.: b 2-19-1753 d 7-26-1847 m Margaret Hodges Pvt VT ★
Silas: b 12-1-1741 d 1-9-1804 m (1)Mary Bacon (2)Rachel Freeman (3)Mary Gould Dr NH
Simeon: b 6-4-1740 d 11-2-1815 m (1)Susannah Cobb (2)Sarah Fisher Pvt MA
Thomas: b 1747/8 d 9-8-1822 m Sarah Cooper Pvt MA
Timothy: b 10-11-1718 d 4-9-1791 m Lydia Cox PS Pvt MA
Wm.: b 1711 d p. 5-1-1776 m Lydia Andrews PS MA
Willis: b 4-25-1745 d 11-9-1804 m Arabella Davenport Pvt NC
Zebulon: b 1755/6 d 5-12-1839 m (1)Amy Pierce (2)Elizabeth Howe Pvt MA ★

HODGKINS,
David: b 8-22-1737 d 4-14-1824 m Patience Winslow Cpl MA
Hezekiah: b 9-3-1757 d 10-3-1821 m Lydia Cummings Sgt MA W★
James: b d 7-27-1821 m Mary Herrick Pvt MA
John: b 9-30-1756 d 3-5-1835 m Abigail Lord Pvt MA
John: b 12-25-1763 d 6-11-1850 m Hannah Spooner Pvt NY ★
Jonas: b 7-20-1761 d 8-29-1844 m (1)Lucy Fulham (2)Anna Grover Pvt NH VT W★
Nathaniel: b 1-3-1761 d 2-15-1839 m Jerusha Spencer Pvt CT ★
Samuel: b 5-16-1753 d 9-15-1818 m Jemima Allen Pvt MA
Samuel: b 6-6-1757 d 10-13-1845 m (2)Lydia Wright Pvt MD

Thomas: b 6-17-1756 d 7-25-1835 m Tryphena Durkee CS Lt CT ★
Thomas: bpt 2-25-1746 d 6-11-1797 m Abigail Ross 1Lt MA
Wm.: b 8-29-1758 d 1-25-1842 m Ruth Brown Pvt NH ★

HODGKINSON,
Bethaniah: b 1-17-1746 d 10-26-1831 m (1)Catharine Zimmerman (2)Mary (Bunting) Wright Pvt PA

HODGMAN, (includes HODGEMAN)
Amos: b 1-26-1756 d 5-18-1822 m Jemima Stone Pvt MA
Benjamin, Sr.: b 12-18-1722 d 1-26-1802 m Lydia — PS NH
Benjamin, Jr.: bpt 5-25-1746 d 12-4-1823 m Elizabeth Merriam Cpl MA
Job: b 7-13-1758 d 2-4-1834 m Anna Hosmer Pvt NH
Jonathan: b 1-26-1725 d 2-17-1801 m (1)Marcy Buttrick (2)Sarah Conant Pvt VT
Joseph, Jr.: bpt 11-18-1753 d 4-8-1841 m Sarah Lawrence Pvt NH ★
Lot: b 5-27-1756 d 3-30-1831 m Azubah Lull Pvt VT

HODGSKIN,
Aaron: b 1741 d 4-17-1813 m Eunice — Cpl NH

HODGSON,
Abel: b 1745/6 d 1817 m Margaret Frier Pvt PA

HODNETT,
Benjamin: b 1761 d 1820 m Elizabeth Wyatt Collier Pvt VA
John: b c. 1710 d 1799 m — PS VA

HODSDON,
Moses, Jr.: b 7-26-1740 d 12-20-1810 m Dorcas Lord Pvt ME
Thomas, Jr.: bpt 6-10-1739 d p. 4-16-1816 m Margaret Goodwin Capt MA
Wm.: b 3-20-1746/7 d — m Amy Nason Pvt MA
Wm.: b c. 1725 d a. 1797 m Sarah Bridget Capt VA

HOES,
John D.: b 5-25-1753 d 1-25-1789 m Maria Quackenboss PS NY

HOEY,
Samuel: b c. 1745 d 1814 m Mary MacNeil Pvt PA

HOFFECKER, (includes HUFFAKER)
George: b 8-7-1757 d 11-8-1850 m (1)Agatha Lee (2)Mary Creswell Pvt VA
Philip: b 1746 d 10-9-1795 m Elizabeth Benner Pvt PA

HOFFER,
Matthiah: b 8-24-1718 d 5-19-1803 m (1)Maria Wohlweider (2)Ann Groh Pvt PA
Rudolph: b 6-7-1747 d 10-6-1826 m Mary Catherine — Pvt PA

HOFFERT,
Christian: b c. 1710 d a. 10-8-1788 m Anna Margaretha — PS MD
Henry: bpt 5-13-1759 d p. 6-1-1816 m Susanna — Pvt PA

HOFFMAN, (includes HUFFMAN)
Adam: b 4-15-1739 d 1-7-1809 m Elizabeth VanWagenen Sol PS NY
Ambrose: b 11-22-1753 d 6-24-1849 m Mary Railsback Pvt VA ★
Anthony: b 3-4-1711 d 2-25-1790 m Catherine VanGaasbeck PS NY
Charles: b 1727 d 4-14-1808 m Elizabeth Sypher Ens NY
Christian: b 1752 d 9- -1845 m Susannah Deibler Pvt PA
Christian: b 1730 d p. 1790 m Barbara — Pvt PA
Christian: b 1756 d 12-13-1822 m Margaret Cole Pvt PA ★
Conrad: b 1734 d p. 1790 m — VonOntz Pvt PA
Cornelius: b 9-9-1741 d 1-3-1832 m Elizabeth Alspach Pvt PA ★
Daniel: b 1750 d c. 1812 m Elizabeth Patton Pvt NC
Daniel: b 8-21-1748 d 1-17-1833 m Eva Mary Emmert 2Lt PA
Daniel: b 1755-60 d p. 1788 m Rebecca — 1Lt PA
Dietrich: b 6-23-1751 d 3-10-1826 m Sussana Alter PS PA
Frederick: b 1749 d 6-5-1816 m Anne Margarete Schreiner Pvt PA
George: b 2-26-1735 d 9-24-1789 m Anna Maria Hornberger Pvt PA
George: b 1762 d 1855 m Barbara Butt Pvt VA
Hanrick: b 1719 d 2-4-1789 m Sybil Magdalene Yunkhaus Pvt NY
Henry: b 1-6-1761 d 1840 m Catherine Vetterly Pvt NY
Henry: b 3-18-1749 d 6-19-1835 m Eleanor Connor OrdlSgt RI ★
Herman: b 6-3-1745 d 9-1-1829 m (1)Catherine Douw (2)Cornelia Vredenburgh (3)Catherine Verplanck Capt NY
Jacob: b 6-5-1757 d — m Sarah Whitlock Pvt NY
Jacob: b 4-18-1765 d 12-11-1828 m Catherine Slough Pvt PA
Jacob: b 1752 d 1786 m Rachel Butts Pvt SC
Jacob: b 1746 d 1816 m Elizabeth Shetley Pvt NC
Jacob: b c. 1741 d a. 1816 m Barbara — Sol VA
John: b 8-19-1755 d 3-19-1831 m (1)Catherine Gibbs (2)Elizabeth Steiner Pvt MD
John: b 7-12-1746 d 4-22-1828 m Elizabeth Ann Young Pvt NJ
John: b 8-14-1746 d 12-28-1838 m Margaret Moyer Pvt PA
John: b 1-1-1756 d 1823 m (1)Margaret Upp (2)Nancy Sprinkle Pvt PA
John: b 10-23-1741 d p. 1790 m Margaret — PS PA
John: b 1760 d 1827 m (1)Mary Blake (2)Sally Newcomer Pvt VA
John: b 1728 d 1802 m Katharine — Pvt VA

John: b 1760 d 9-24-1832 m Margaret Hovie Pvt VA
John Nicholas: b 1-10-1749 d 1829 m Margaret Harman Pvt PA
Lewis: b 7-25-1755 d 11-2-1833 m Catherine — Pvt PA ★
Michael: b 5-27-1752 d p. 1798 m Dorothea Reidenauer Pvt PA
Nicholas: b 12-18-1717 d 11-21-1784 m Mary — PS PA
Peter: b c. 1760 d p. 4-19-1810 m Anna — Sol VA
Philip: b 11-20-1736 d 9-27-1823 m Mercy — Cpl PA
Valentine: b c. 1750 d p. 1781 m Susanna Henson Capt PA
Wilhelm: b 1-14-1749 d 3-16-1824 m Elizabeth Gerber Pvt PA
Wm.: b 1742 d 1-26-1826 m Mary — Pvt NJ
Wm.: b — d 12-11-1822 m Susanna — Pvt PA

HOFFNER,
John George: b 4-20-1735 d 1799 m Mary Zumwalt Lt PA

HOGAN,
Edmund: b 6-17-1762 d 2-13-1838 m Patsey Wilburn Pvt NC ★
James: b c. 1721 d 1-4-1781 m Ruth Norfleet PS BGen NC
James: b 1752 d 1811 m Elizabeth — Pvt VA
John: b c. 1740 d c. 1810 m Mary Lloyd Col NC
John: b c. 1750 d 1830 m Sally Hudgens Pvt NC
Jurian: bpt 8-25-1745 d a. 1-13-1813 m Annatje White Capt NY
Pat: b 1747 d 3- -1830 m Catharina Cool Pvt NY ★
Wm.: b 9-9-1760 d 4-21-1836 m Jemima — Lt SC ★

HOGATE,
Philip: b 7-15-1762 d 11-22-1854 m Priscilla Carter Pvt NJ

HOGEBOOM,
Bartholomew: b a. 1751 d p. 1787 m Polly VanValkenburg Pvt NY
Cornelius: b 7-2-1739 d 10-22-1791 m Sarah Vosburgh Capt NY
James: b 1- -1750 d 1848 m Catherine VanAllen Lt NY ★
Jeremiah: b 4-5-1712 d 1783/4 m Jannye VanAlen Pvt NY
Johannes, Sr.: b 7-4-1708 d 1784-6 m Albertia VanAlen PS NY
Johannes, Jr.: b 9-3-1735 d a. 2-16-1814 m Gertruuy Muller Pvt NY
Lawrence: b 8-3-1737 d 3-14-1805 m Hester Leggett Pvt NY
Stephen: b 8-16-1744 d 4-2-1814 m Helletje Muller LCol NY

HOGENKAMP,
John: b 10-18-1747 d p. 11- -1781 m Aeltje Haring Pvt NJ
John M.: b 7-11-1742 d 5-13-1813 m Elizabeth VanHouten Capt NY
Martines: b 10-20-1749 d 3-22-1833 m Sophia Christie Pvt NJ ★

HOGG, (includes HOAGG, HOGE, & HOGUE)
Abner: b 2-15-1759 d 10-16-1856 m Rosannah Ferson Sgt NH ★
Andrew: b 5-20-1753 d 1805 m Rebecca Lewiston Pvt MA
George: b 2-6-1733 d 1805 m Elizabeth Blackledge Pvt VA
Hussey: b 1740 d 11-15-1824 m Abigail Stickney Pvt NH
James: b 1730 d 11- -1804 m McDonald Alves PS NC
James: b 11-30-1741 d p. 1819 m Margaret Parkes Pvt PA
James, Sr.: b 1760 d 6-2-1795 m (1)Agnes Crawford (2)Nancy Griffith PS VA
James, Jr.: b 6-12-1832 d 4-5-1812 m Elizabeth Howe Sol VA
James: b 1754 d 10-31-1827 m Margaret Irvin Pvt PA
John: b 9-12-1751 d 5-10-1834 m Martha R. Quale Lt PA ★
John: b 1738 d 1814 m Lucy — Pvt VA
John: b c. 1733 d p. 1788 m Mrs Margaret Jones Burton Pvt SC
John: b 9-15-1763 d p. 3- -1844 m — Pvt VA
Jonathan: b c. 1761/2 d p. 1800 m — Pvt PA
Lewis: b 1750 d 1820 m Clara Smith Pvt SC
Moses: b 2-15-1752 d 7- -1820 m (1)Elizabeth Poage (2)Susan (Watkins) Hunt Vol VA
Peter: b 1703 d 4-20-1782 m Elizabeth Taylor CS VA
Richard, Sr.: b c. 1717 d a. 1786 m Mary Austin PS VA
Robert: b 2-25-1732 d 1-23-1795 m Margaret Gregg PS NH
Robert: b 1743 d 1824 m Mary Jackson Pvt VA
Thomas: b 1765 d 4- -1849 m Martha Chandler Pvt SC
Wm.: b 1760 d 8-7-1850 m — Pvt NH
Wm.: b 1755 d p. 1832 m Eliza Green Pvt VA
Wm.: b c. 1688-1706 d 1789 m (1)Anne — (2)Mrs Mary Pancoast PS VA
Wm.: b 1-4-1726 d p. 10-6-1804 m Esther Ewing PS VA

HOGGATT,
Anthony: b 9-28-1749 d 9-27-1818 m Sallie — Sol VA
John: b 1738 d 6-5-1816 m Ruth Beals Pvt NC

HOGLE,
John: bpt 12-11-1757 d 1-12-1818 m Polly Lampman Cpl NY

HOGMIRE,
Conrad: b 5-25-1725 d 12-20-1797 m Mary Magdalena — Capt PS MD

HOGSHEAD,
David: b c. 1760 d p. 1-7-1814 m Catherine Graham CS VA
James: bpt 4-6-1746 d a. 4-26-1802 m Sarah Gordon Sol VA

HOHNE,
Christopher: b 1758 d 3-29-1833 m Mary Holland Pvt MD

HOISINGTON,
Bliss: b c. 1750 d 2-6-1810 m Phoebe Hawkins Pvt VT W★
Ebenezer: b 1729 d 7-25-1804 m Elizabeth Miller PS VT

HOISINGTON, contd.
Elias: b 12-12-1759 d 1-15-1810 m Mary Stowell Sgt VT
Elisha: bpt 8-11-1754 d 1-14-1827 m Mindwell Wells Pvt CT
Joab: b 9-19-1736 d 2-1-1777 m Mary Boardman Col VT
Vespasian: b 6-8-1762 d 5-21-1841 m Hannah Wood Pvt VT

HOKE,
Adam: b 1760 d 8-7-1832 m Catherine Hoffheins Pvt PA
Andrew: b 1734 d 1-3-1800 m Barbara — Pvt PA
Andrew: b 1758 d 1813 m Catharine Light Pvt PA
Frederick: b 1760 d 1825 m (1)— Hafer (2)Elizabeth Lorance
(3)— Stirewalt Pvt PA
John: b 1740 d p. 10-22-1781 m Sabina Swope Pvt PA
Peter: b 1739 d 12- -1804 m Maria Dorothea Smyser Sgt PA

HOLABIRD,
Timothy: b 1716 d 1810 m Abagail Charles CS CT

HOLBEN,
Lorentz: b 1-29-1750 d 6-23-1842 m Catherine Kramlich Pvt PA ★

HOLBERTON,
Wm.: b 8-15-1740 d 12-11-1797 m Eunice Burr Pvt CT W★

HOLBROOK,
Aaron: b 8-31-1730 d 4-4-1818 m (1)Hannah Partridge (2)Elizabeth
Daniels Sgt MA
Abel: b 12-4-1762 d 7-15-1842 m Hannah Clark Sgt CT ★
Abel: b 10-9-1761 d — m Betsey Caperman Pvt MA
Abner: b 6-21-1762 d 11-25-1827 m Martha Simpson Pvt MA
Abner: b 3-9-1741 d 5-29-1788 m Jerusha Vining Pvt MM MA
Amariah: b 12-21-1750/1 d 7-5-1799 m Hannah Henshaw Cpl MA
Amariah: b 6-6-1756 d 9-7-1797 m Molly Wright Pvt MA
Amos: b 1-23-1754 d 6-17-1842 m Jerusha Robinson Dr MA
Amos: b 3-4-1764 d 4-5-1813 m (1)Mary Badger (2)Lydia Owen
Pvt MA
Asa: b 3-21-1737 d p. 1813 m Abigail (Nabby)Stacey Pvt VT
Asahel: b 1710 d 1-3-1801 m (1)Anna Puffer (2)Mrs Marcy Holbrook
Pvt MA
Daniel: b 9-21-1747 d 4-24-1813 m Anne Hitchcock Capt CT
Daniel: b 2-14-1757 d 4-17-1839 m Mary Edwards Pvt MA
Daniel: b c. 1760 d p. 1807 m Joanna Benson Pvt MA
David: b 7-28-1760 d 11-29-1832 m Mehitabel Wells SgtMaj MA
David: b 6-26-1717 d 3-11-1782 m Mary Hayden Pvt MA
David: b 6-10-1726 d 5-26-1793 m (1)Lydia Bragg (2)Abigail
Black Pvt MA
David: b 5-1-1758 d 7-21-1828 m Judith Bullard Pvt MA
David: b 1-21-1764 d 12-12-1850 m Hepsibah Smith Pvt MM
NH ★
Ebenezer: b 1-24-1724 d 9-19-1808 m (1)Sarah Griffin (2)Mary
Osgood Capt PS CT
Ebenezer: b 4-24-1756 d 5-21-1838 m Diadana Durkee Pvt CT ★
Eli: b 2-11-1746 d 11-9-1828 m Sibyl Thompson Pvt MA
Elias: bpt 6-8-1740 d 5-8-1815 m Elizabeth Benton Sol PS CT
Elias: bpt 4-7-1757 d p. 1790 m Abigail Shumway Sgt VT
Elijah: b 1755 d 5-19-1808 m Abigail Wilson QM MA
Elisha: b 11-4-1752 d 11-9-1805 m Sarah Burrill Cpl MA
Henry: b 8-27-1756 d 10-1-1833 m Elizabeth Cook Pvt MA ★
Henry: b 5-2-1757 d 7-8-1821 m Martha Perry Pvt MA
Ichabod, Jr.: b 5-26-1748 d 3-31-1822 m Elizabeth Niles 2Lt MA ★
James: b 9-25-1753 d — m Rhoda Vinton Pvt MA
James: b 7-24-1754 d 11-30-1843 m (1)Hannah Fisher (2)Mary
Morse Cpl MA ★
Jesse: b 7-21-1729 d 4-18-1815 m Abigail Thayer Capt MA
Jesse: b 1764 d 5-25-1844 m Susannah Meanley Pvt VA★
John: b 11-1-1738 d 3-18-1832 m Susanna Cabot Lt CT
John: b 1735 d 1803/4 m Sarah — Ens CT
John: b 8-12-1726 d 1-28-1801 m Jean Esther Nichols PS CT
John: b 6-7-1730 d 1-5-1815 m Sybil Lane Lt MA
John: b 6-2-1748 d 7-27-1817 m Rhoda Thayer Pvt MA
John: b 6-20-1745 d p. 1792 m Anna Wild Lt MA
John: b c. 11-1-1751 d 1-31-1839 m Lucretia Babbitt Pvt MA
John: b 3-12-1758 d 12-12-1835 m Sarah Griggs Pvt MA
John: b 6-14-1762 d 8-6-1838 m Sarah Higgins Pvt MA ★
Jonathan: b 6-30-1743 d 11-2-1776 m (1)Mary Ware (2)Sarah
Bedlow Cpl MA
Jonathan: b 6-29-1760 d 1796 m Abigail Benson Pvt MA
Joseph: b 10-15-1748 d 4-18-1817 m Meletiah Fisher Sgt MA
Joshua: b 10-31-1743 d 1818 m Experience Dana Pvt MA
Josiah: b 9-27-1727 d 11-25-1805 m Sarah Porter Pvt MA
Josiah, Jr.: b 4-4-1755 d 11-16-1831 m Rachel Wright Pvt CS MA
Luke: b 3-20-1724 d 11-3-1775 m Mercy Pond Lt MA
Micah: b 3-11-1744 d c. 1807 m (1)Rhoda Thayer (2)Mary
Thompson Pvt MA
Nathan: b 2-14-1743 d 9-7-1820 m Susannah Wadhams Capt MA
Nathaniel: b 10-1-1758 d 5-28-1828 m Allis Davis Pvt CT ★
Nehemiah: b 5-6-1745 d p. 1779 m Elizabeth Hobart CS Sgt MA
Peletiah: b 8-25-1743 d 1798 m Mary Clark Sgt CT
Peter: b 7-22-1742 d 7-13-1792 m Huldah Wood Pvt MA
Peter: b 1753 d 1844 m Martha Greenleaf Pvt MA ★
Peter: b 11-23-1762 d 12-3-1839 m Mary Bates Pvt MA W★
Peter: b 7-12-1765 d 5-12-1823 m (1)Mary Taft (2)Anna
(Davenport) Torrey Pvt MA

Peter: b 1740 d 7-12-1807 m Lydia Darling Pvt NH
Samuel: b 9-27-1730 d a. 1790 m Lydia Staples Capt MA
Samuel: bpt 5-18-1729 d 7-24-1784 m Elizabeth Williams PS MA
Samuel: b 1757 d 9-4-1836 m Martha Clark Slr NH
Seth: b 11-24-1751 d 11-13-1839 m Dinah Holbrook Sgt MA ★
Silas: b 3-18-1757 d 3-22-1835 m Tirzah Taylor Pvt MA
Stephen: b 4-30-1737 d 6-11-1812 m Rachel Cook Cpl MA
Thomas: b 1-30-1739 d 5-3-1808 m Hannah Harding Pvt MA
Wm.: bpt 5-12-1745 d p. 1780 m (1)Lucy Fernald (2)Elizabeth
(Fernald) Underwood Capt MA
Wm.: b 4-2-1747 d 4-26-1808 m Melatiah Swan Sgt MA
Ziba: b 8-8-1752 d 7-7-1829 m Rebecca Kimball Pvt MA

HOLBURTON,
Wm.: b 12- -1740 d — m Eunice Burr Pvt CT

HOLCOMB, (includes HOLCOMBE)
Abner: b 9-16-1752 d 10-14-1839 m Mindwell Bull Pvt CT ★
Adonijah: b 9-27-1757 d p. 1820 m Charity Gillett Pvt CT
Amos: b 6-1-1732 d 5- -1814 m Mary Dibble Pvt CT
Asahel: b 1720/1 d 2-21-1817 m Thankful Kent Pvt CT
Asahel, 2d: b 11-12-1742 d 1816 m Sarah Eno Capt CT
Asahel, 3d: b 1764 d 1832 m Martha Flagg Pvt CT ★
Asahel: b 10-15-1752 d 10-2-1832 m Abigail Hoskins Pvt CT ★
Azariah: b 1735 d 1781 m Hannah Loomis Pvt MA
Azariah: b 1758 d 9-1-1835 m Christiana Shephard Tms Pvt MA ★
Benajah: b 9-17-1737 d 1-2-1828 m Lydia Forward Capt CT
Benajah: b 11-12-1741 d p. 1790 m Huldah Post Cpl NY
Benjamin: b 3-3-1745 d 9-15-1807 m Mercy Kimball Lt CT
Beriah: b 8-16-1746 d 3-15-1824 m Lucretia Pease Sgt NY
Ebenezer: b 5-14-1761 d 3-15-1826 m Chloe Bacon Pvt CT ★
Eldad: b 1-9-1734 d 1789 m Michel Church Sgt MA
Eli: b 2-2-1741 d 5-10-1823 m Hannah Crofut Cpl MA
Elijah: b 1759 d 10-4-1841 m (1)Lucy Holcomb (2)Betsey Post
(3)Betsey Ives Pvt CT ★
Elijah: b 9-29-1750 d 9-10-1845 m Nancy Briton Pvt NJ ★
Elisha: b c. 1760 d a. 4- -1805 m Mary — Pvt SC
Enoch, Sr.: b 9-4-1717 d 3-11-1808 m Anna Fowler PS CS MA
Ezra: b 1735 d 4-23-1813 m Phebe Gillet Pvt CT
George: b 4-9-1747 d 5-12-1811 m Achsah Knowles 2Maj NJ
Grimes: b 1725 d p. 8-14-1786 m (1)Elizabeth Busbee (2)— Graham
Pvt SC
Henry: b 9-22-1762 d 5-22-1824 m Frances Tanner Capt VA SC
Henry: b c. 1740-2 d p. 1796 m Mary — Pvt SC
Hezekiah, Sr.: b 1-27-1726 d 7-17-1794 m Susanna Alderman Capt
CT
Hezekiah, Jr.: b 9-2-1750 d 11-8-1820 m (1)Chloe Pinney
(2)Dorothy Bates Pvt CT
Increase: b 1-31-1761 d 12-4-1836 m Mary Reed Pvt CT
Jacob: b 10-27-1764 d 10-15-1856 d m (1)Theodocia Bacon
(2)Susannah Rowe (3)Hanna Holcomb Sol CT
Jacob: b 12-7-1741 d 1-11-1820 m Rachel Hyde Lt NJ
James: b 6-8-1764 d p. 1836 m Irene Williams Pvt MA
Jedediah: b 1740 d 11-27-1779 m Mary Hitchcock Cpl CT
Jesse: b c. 1764 d 9- -1837 m (1)Nancy Porter (2)Nancy—Sol SC
Joel: b 1760 d 6-1-1847 m Sarah Warner Pvt CT W★
Joel, Jr.: b 1744 d 1839 m Sarah Whitney Pvt MA
John: b 1760 d a. 8-17-1786 m Eleanor — Pvt SC
John: b c. 1750 d 1817/18 m Martha Venable Capt VA ★
Jonathan: b c. 1758 d p. 1816 m — Pvt SC
Jonathan: b 1712 d — m Mary Gillett Pvt CT
Jonathan: b 6-19-1762 d 10-1-1847 m Hannah Everest Pvt MA ★
Jordan: b 11-19-1762 d 7-3-1846 m — Pvt SC ★
Joseph: b c. 1763 d 1851 m Susannah Russell Pvt SC
Joshua: b 2-2-1724 d 1784 m Martha Griffin Pvt CT
Josiah: b 9-19-1743 d 6-15-1827 m Dorcas Smith Sol MA
Judah, Sr.: b 1705 d 1-5-1802 m Hannah Buttolph CS PS CT
Judah: b 9-27-1745/46 d 11-2-1826 m Anna Hubbard Pvt CT
Martin: b 11-21-1725 d 11-8-1798 m Christian Winchell Lt CT
Michael: b 7-11-1733 d 1-20-1817 m Mary Hillyer Lt MA
Nathaniel: b 11-10-1740 d p. 1786 m (1)Hannah Holcomb
(2)Jemime Smith Pvt MA
Nevil G.: b 1760 d 1832 m Laodicea Bobo Pvt PS SC
Obed: b 1-8-1736 d 11-27-1789 m Mercy — Lt CT
Peter: b 4-15-1715 d 4-20-1800 m (1)Margaret Case (2)Tryphena
Corse Pvt CT ★
Philemon, Sr.: b 1720 d c. 1798 m Ann Walthall CS VA
Philemon, Jr.: b 12-21-1762 d 1833 m Lucy Maria Anderson Maj
VA ★
Philip: b c. 1756 d 3-20-1820 m Sarah Farmer Pvt SC
Phineas: b 3-17-1759 d 2-7-1831 m Elizabeth Moore Pvt CT ★
Phineas: b 2-4-1726/27 d 9- -1781 m Sarah Tuller PS VT
Return: b 1742 d 6-2-1832 m Hannah Niles Pvt CT
Richard: b 12-3-1752 d 1-26-1835 m Hannah Emley Pvt NJ
Roger: b 10-18-1742 d 10-22-1824 m Mercy Gillet Cpl CT
Samuel: b 3-18-1745 d 2-6-1817 m (1)Mrs Mary (Stillwell)
Stevenson (2)Sarah Emley Sct NJ
Seth: b 1-3-1755 d 7-28-1810 m Polly Gillet Pvt CT
Sherwood: b 1763 d p. 12-10-1844 m Jane Keith Pvt SC ★
Silas: b 11-27-1734 d 10-6-1806 m Mary Post Lt CT
Thomas: b 11-19-1754 d 6-9-1822 m (1)Leah Deremer (2)Mary F.
Holcomb Pvt NJ
Timothy: b 7-19-1740 d 12-3-1776 m Abigail Robbins Lt CT

Zephaniah: b 8-19-1750 d 3-16-1822 m (1)Tryphena Niles (2)Mehetable Wetmore Pvt NY

HOLDAWAY,
Henry: b 9-15-1753 d 5-17-1835 m Eleanor Anderson Pvt VA

HOLDCROFT,
Edward: b c. 1755 d 1818 m Frances Bullifant Pvt VA

HOLDEN,
Aaron: b 1-26-1731/32 d 9-30-1802 m Anna Clark Capt MA
Abel: b 9-26-1728 d 1797 m (1)Emma Blood (2)Elizabeth Henry Pvt MA
Abel: b 10-2-1752 d 8-3-1818 m Thankful Catling Capt MA
Abner: b 11-2-1722 d 10-22-1805 m Elizabeth Darby PS MA
Amos, Sr.: b 6-16-1726 d 3-28-1803 m (1)Prudence (Holden) (2)Sarah Blood Pvt MA
Amos, Jr.: b 9-21-1752 d 4-16-1806 m Lydia Sloan Pvt MA
Asa: b 12-5-1758 d 1-24-1850 m Dorcas Sawtelle Pvt NH ★
Benjamin: b 3-10-1729 d 11-24-1820 m Katherine Richards LCol MA
Benjamin: b 1- -1749 d 9-20-1783 m Abigail Bacon Pvt MA ★
Benjamin: b 8-29-1752 d 4-20-1822 m Mary Elizabeth Ballard Pvt MA
Charles: b 7-17-1747 d a. 4-4-1822 m (2)Deborah Crawford Sol MA
Daniel: b 5-22-1732 d 1-21-1803 m Milescent Hosmer Pvt MA
Daniel: b 10-15-1763 d 7-23-1849 m (1)Elizabeth Hill (2)Polly Hill (3)Statira Whiteman Pvt MA ★
Daniel: b 1745 d 1-12-1811 m (1)Jemima Tucker (2)Dorothy Johnson Pvt MA W★
Ebenezer Mitchel: b 1-7-1764 d 7-13-1845 m Hepsabeth Goodrich Pvt MA ★
Francis: b 5-6-1743 d p. 1799 m Abagil Closson Pvt VT
Isaac: b 1743 d 6-29-1827 m Nancy — Lt MA ★
Jabez: b 5-12-1735 d 8-11-1787 m Rachel Farnsworth Capt MA
James: b 2-15-1756 d 6-20-1839 m Eunice Hinman Sgt VT MA
Jeduthan: b 3-4-1739 d p. 1790 m Hannah Hayward Pvt MA
John: b 1730/31 d 10- -1785 m Susanna Ellsworth Pvt CT
John: b 3-4-1737 d 2-9-1818 m Marjorie Amidon Capt MA
John: b 7-26-1753 d 3-13-1828 m Zipporah Hall Lt MA ★
John: b 10-24-1738 d 2-28-1807 m Mary Knight Lt MA W★
John: b 5-21-1765 d 1847 m (1)Sarah Sanderson (2)Patience Sanderson (3)Sarah Boynton Fif MA ★
John: b 5-18-1724 d — m Dorothy Rice Lt RI
Jonas: b 9-8-1751 d 4-19-1835 m Sarah Reed Lt MA W★
Jonas, Sr.: b 1721 d 1800 m Abigail Kendall Pvt MA
Jonas: b 1756 d 1820 m Molly Thompson Pvt MA
Jonathan: b 1-19-1703 d 1782 m Joanna Wyman Pvt MA
Jonathan: b 12-21-1745 d 1790 m Mary Ann Baker Pvt MA
Joshua: b 2-8-1729 d 12-1-1817 m Huldah Simpson Pvt MA
Josiah: b 7-24-1721 d 1-2-1777 m Abigail Bond Capt MA
Josiah: b 9-30-1751 d 6-29-1829 m Polly Forbes Pvt MA
Lemuel: b 6-27-1751 d p. 1790 m Lucy Bartlett Pvt MA
Levi: b 1-12-1754 d 4-19-1823 m Hannah Plympton Capt MA ★
Nathaniel: b 5-7-1739 d 1-21-1817 m Mary Richardson MM Capt MA
Nathaniel: b 8-15-1753 d 7-21-1841 m (1)Lettice Grout (2)Hannah Parker Pvt NH ★
Nehemiah: b 1763 d 12- -1849 m (2)Abbie Bassett Pvt MA ★
Nehemiah: b 3-12-1731 d 1809 m Elizabeth — Sol MA
Philemon: b 2-28-1725 d 7-19-1810 m Lucy Walker Fif MA
Phineas: b 1-31-1744 d 1819 m Thankful Baker Dr MA
Richard: b 8-25-1734 d 1777 m Dorothy Adams Sgt NH
Robert: b 3-5-1743 d 6-22-1826 m (1)Sarah Tuttle (2)Joanna Bruce Whitcomb Pvt MA ★
Samuel: b 1737/38 d 4-27-1808 m Hannah Kelton Capt MA
Sawtell: b 5-13-1752 d 4- -1850 m Hannah Cook Pvt MA ★
Simon: b 1731 d 12-5-1816 m Sarah Brown Lt MA
Stephen, Jr.: b 5-16-1755 d 11-15-1803 m Elizabeth Miller Pvt MA
Stephen: b 6-11-1720 d 2-22-1791 m Sarah Wheelock CS MA
Thomas: b 6-17-1741 d 2-22-1823 m (1)Freelove Barton (2)Mercy Wightman BGen RI
Thomas: b c. 1753 d c. 1807 m Margaret Spurgeon Sol SC
Timothy: b 7-12-1760 d 8-9-1833 m (1)Hannah Glidden (2)Mary Page (3)Katherine Humphrey Pvt NH
Wm.: b 2-19-1723 d 11-28-1807 m Annis Nutting Capt MA

HOLDER,
John: b c. 1720 d 2- -1792 m Suffiah — Pvt MD
John: b 1744 d p. 1797 m Frances Calloway Capt VA
Michael Henry: b 8-25-1734 d 11-4-1781 m Maria Catherine — Pvt PA
Nathaniel: bpt 10-1-1732 d a. 9-1-1777 m Susanna Harsham Matr MA

HOLDERBAUM,
Michael: b c. 1740 d 2- -1802 m Juliana Ulrich Capt PA

HOLDERBY,
Wm.: b 1753 d 10-10-1812 m (1)Priscilla Pendleton (2)Fannie Lewis Pvt VA

HOLDRIDGE,
John: b 1746 d 12-10-1834 m Charlotte Watterman Lt MA ★

Thomas: b 1-1-1744 d p. 1805 m Anna — Pvt NY
Wm.: b c. 1755 d 1803 m Mary Pollard Pvt SC

HOLE, (includes HOLL)
Daniel: b 4-6-1757 d p. 4-25-1829 m Mary Bedell Pvt VA ★
Jacob: b 2-27-1758 d 2-1-1842 m Mary Thomas Mus PA
John: b 4-30-1755 d 1-6-1813 m (1)Hannah Clark (2)Mercy Ludlow Dr PA
Peter: b 1-5-1744 d 5-16-1819 m Elizabeth — Pvt PA

HOLGATE,
Cornelius: b 1-27-1758 d 4-14-1829 m Mary Levering Sgt PA
Wm.: b 7-15-1762 d 5-12-1843 m Mary Ann Davis Lt PA ★

HOLLAND,
Abraham: b — d a. 9-12-1800 m Asenath Spiers PS MD
Abraham: b 1751 d 2-18-1847 m Abigail Baldwin Pvt NH
Charles: b 4-2-1758 d a. 3-16-1846 m — Pvt SC ★
Drury: b 1760 d 7-31-1826 m Sally Turner Pvt VA
Edward: b c. 1737 d 3-4-1810 m Sally — Artl MD
Ephriam: b 6-21-1714 d 8-20-1786 m Thankful Howe Pvt MA
George: b c. 1720 d p. 1-7-1788 m (1)Sarah Ford (2)Mary Coleman PS VA
Henry: b 3-1-1757 d 6-26-1852 m — Pvt NC ★
Isaac: b 5-12-1745 d 9-10-1810 m Mrs Hannah Leggett Pvt NC
Ivory: b 12-27-1739 d 7-3-1820 m Martha Rogers Lt QMReg MA
Jacob: b 3- -1764 d 9-17-1838 m (2)Mary Smith Cpl MD ★
Jacob: b 1763 d 10-1-1852 m Sarah Miller Pvt SC ★
Jacob: b c. 1750 d 10-17-1815 m Mary Harrison Pvt GA
James: b 1728 d p. 1790 m (1)Patience Watkins (2)Jerutha White PS NC
James: b 1733 d 9-20-1820 m Mary Bell Pvt MA
James: b 1754 d 5-19-1823 m Sarah Gilbert 2Lt CS NC
Joab: b 1-9-1758 d 1-6-1832 m Abbie Rice Pvt MA ★
John: b 1749 d 1-9-1826 m (1)Lydia Crowford (2)Elizabeth Stevens Ens DE
John, Sr.: b 9-11-1726 d 9-25-1804 m Elizabeth Fallas Arfr MA
John, Jr.: b 1-26-1758 d 1-18-1824 m Sarah May NCarp MA
John: b 1766 d 8-3-1842 m (1)Christina Robinson (2)Mrs Jane Marshall Pvt SC
John: b a. 1748 d p. 10-17-1807 m Margaret Wilkins PS VA
Joseph: b 4-24-1733 d a. 1790 m Mary — PS CT
Joseph: b 2-12-1746 d 11-15-1777 m Mrs Sarah Wells Pvt MA
Joseph: b 2-22-1768 d 3-27-1827 m Polly Howe Pvt MA ★
Luther: b 6-7-1750 d 6-5-1820 m Elizabeth Spooner 2Lt MA ★
Michael: b 1748 d 5- -1828 m Susanna Ingersoll Pvt MA
Moses: b 11-17-1758 d 9-8-1829 m (1)Mary E. Barton (2)Grace King Pvt VA
Nathan: b — d 1801 m Sarah Waters PS MD
Park: b 11-19-1752 d 5-21-1844 m Lucy Spooner Lt MA ★
Reason: b c. 1760 d 8-14-1802 m — Pvt NC
Richard: b c. 1750 d 1798 m Mary Edwards Sol NC
Richard: b 1755 d 4- -1818 m Mrs Martha Walker Capt VA
Thomas: b 1758 d 1799 m Ledy Meadow Pvt VA
Thomas: b 2-12-1762 d 10-3-1815 m Jane Adair Pvt SC
Thomas: b c. 1750-60 d p. 12-1-1820 m Elizabeth — Sol GA
Wm.: b 9-21-1763 d 2-19-1839 m Lavina Lewis Pvt MD ★
Wm.: b 1760/62 d a. 1-23-1838 m Sophia Pitts Pvt MD
Wm.: b 1747 d 9-19-1837 m Margaret Hall Capt NC ★

HOLLENBECK, (includes HALENBECK, HALLENBACK, HALLENBECK, HOLLENBACK, HOLLENBAUGH, HOLLENBECK)
Abraham: b 5-19-1760 d 5-22-1841 m Margaret Storms Pvt MA
Anthony: b 12-20-1738 d — m Cornelia Cooper Pvt NY
Bernardus: bpt 4-15-1744 d 10-21-1792 m Neeltje Clark Sol PS NY
Conrad: b c. 1750 d 9- -1832 m Anna Catherine — Pvt PA
George: b 1748 d 6-28-1824 m Hannah Bartor Pvt PA
Jacob: b 1746 d 7-3-1813 m Hannah — Lt NY
Jacob: b 11-14-1740 d 9-11-1811 m Elizabeth Vischer Pvt NY
Jan: b 5-16-1731 d p. 1800 m Callyntje Spoor Capt NY
John: b 1747 d 1820 m Esther Stanton Lt CT ★
Matthias: b 1752 d 1802 m Maria Muller Pvt NY
Matthias: b 2-15-1752 d 2-18-1829 m Mrs Sarah Hibbard Ens PA
Robert: b c. 1732 d 1806 m Lena — Pvt NY
Samuel: b a. 1753 d p. 1790 m Supenra Woodruff Pvt NY
Wm.: b 12-4-1739 d p. 1790 m Amy Clark Pvt NY

HOLLEY, (includes HALLEY, HOLLY)
David: b 1-17-1751 d 5-14-1834 m Sarah Southard Sgt MA ★
James, Sr.: b 6-14-1707 d 7-6-1792 m Elizabeth Simpson PS VA
John: b 12-28-1760 d 1-11-1848 m Fanny Thompson Pvt CT
John, Jr.: b 2-16-1746 d 7-17-1817 m Hephzibah Marchant Pvt MA
John: b 1750 d 7-4-1812 m Rebecca Lewis Sgt NY
John: b 4-16-1747 d 7-14-1825 m Hannah Rose Pvt RI ★
John: b 11-17-1760 d 1846 m (1)Anne Gaddy (2)Nancy Douglas Pvt VA ★
Joseph: b — d 2-3-1828 m Jane Russell Pvt MA
Joseph: b 1733 d p. 1784 m Mary Drake PS NY
Justus: b 2-5-1763 d 4-29-1849 m Elizabeth Field Fif VT MA
Nathan: b 2-26-1729 d 10-10-1811 m Hannah Jager PS CT
Robert: b 2-14-1759 d 4-18-1836 m Hannah Hewitt Sgt RI

HOLLEY, contd.
Silas: b 1756 d 12-20-1833 m Esther — Sgt NY W★
Stephen, Jr.: b 1-12-1763 d 3-23-1833 m Deborah Ferris Pvt CT ★

HOLLIDAY, (includes HOLLADAY, HOLLYDAY)
Adam: b 1728 d 1799 m Sarah Campbell PS PA
Amos: b 1-6-1747 d 4-9-1853 m Azubah Brewer Pvt CT ★
Benjamin: b c. 1720 d 3-21-1785 m (1)Susannah — (2)Mrs Mary Scott CS VA
Daniel: b 1752 d 2-14-1837 m Martha Knighton Sgt SC ★
Henry: b c. 1725 d 9-9-1800 m Mary Fayle PS NC
James: b 11-1-1758 d 1-7-1807 m Susanna Tilghman PS MD
James: b 7-20-1754 d 9-9-1834 m Agnes Gamble Pvt PA
James: b 6-15-1753 d 1823 m (1)Mary Ann Lewis (2)Sophia Sandridge Ens VA
John: b 1747 d 8-19-1823 m Dorcas Roddy Capt PA
John: b c. 1746 d p. 9-12-1812 m Susannah — Sol SC
Joseph: b c. 1753 d 1798 m Patience Godwin Capt VA
Joseph: b 1726 d 9-23-1795 m Elizabeth Lewis PS CS VA
Lewis: b 8-22-1751 d 10- -1820 m Elizabeth Littlepage Lt VA
Samuel: b 1742 d 9-10-1806 m Sarah Campbell Capt PA
Samuel: b 1730-2 d c. 2- -1805 m (2)Susanna Korlin Pvt PA
Samuel: b 11-26-1755 d 11-10-1841 m Jeannette Campbell Pvt PA
Stephen: b 9-8-1760 d 3- -1837 m Anne Hickman Pvt VA
Thomas: b 1750 d 7-30-1798 m Martha Dickerson Sol GA
Wm.: b c. 1760 d 11- -1826 m Jane Cooper Pvt GA
Wm.: b 12-26-1750 d 2-20-1855 m Catherine Pamphlyia Hitt Pvt NY ★
Wm., Sr.: b a. 1727 d 1796 m Mary McClellen Of PA
Wm., Jr.: b 9-1-1749 d 10-29-1821 m Susanna Johnston Lt PA
Zacharias: b 1761 d 1846/47 m Kitty Anderson Drm VA

HOLLINGER, (includes HULLINGER)
Christophel: b 10-20-1753 d 4-20-1814 m Catharine Lauber Pvt PA
Daniel: b 3-12-1757 d 7-22-1839 m Ann Shockey Lt PA ★
Daniel: b 4-9-1734 d 9-23-1800 m Catharine — Drm PA
Philip: b 5-20-1758 d 9-5-1821 m (1)Elizabeth Hess (2)Mary Hess Pvt PA

HOLLINGSHEAD, (includes HOLLINSHEAD)
Benjamin: b 1762 d 1840 m — Pvt NC ★
James: b 7- -1755 d 2-22-1845 m — Pvt PA ★
John: b 6-28-1748 d 6- -1798 m Hepsata Thomas Maj NJ

HOLLINGSWORTH,
Henry: b 9-17-1737 d 9-29-1803 m Sarah Husband Col MD
Henry: b 8-18-1757 d 11-16-1840 m Elizabeth Griggs Pvt NC ★
James: b c. 1742 d p. 1784 m Betsy Merritt Sol NC
Jeptha: b 8-30-1745 d 1816 m (1)Miss Ray (2)Nancy Gordon Sol SC
Jesse: b 3-12-1732 d 9-30-1810 m (1)Sanai Ricketts (2)Rachel L. Perkins PS MD
John W.: b 1755 d 4-20-1843 m (2)Susan Ritter Pvt PA
Joseph: b 9-22-1765 d 4-8-1844 m Rosannah Nichols PS SC
Levi: b 11-29-1739 d 3-24-1824 m Hannah Paschall QM Sgt PA
Robert: b 1744 d 1799 m Susanna Rose PS PA
Samuel: b 1-17-1757 d 5-9-1830 m Sarah Adams Sol DE
Samuel: b c. 1740-2 d 1814 m (2)Sarah Murphy PS NC
Thomas: b 12-12-1729 d 3-1-1799 m Jane Smith Pvt DE
Valentine: b 1748 d p. 1790 m Deborah Harlan Pvt PA
Zebulon: b 6-17-1735 d 3-21-1812 m Mary Evans PS MD
Zebulon: b 11-6-1761 d 4-22-1836 m Elizabeth Chestnutt Pvt NC ★

HOLLIS,
Hezekiah: b 1740 d 1776-82 m Sarah Jackson Pvt MA
John: b 1746 d 5-25-1845 m — Pvt PS NC
John: b 12-5-1751 d 11-4-1836 m Nancy — Capt SC ★
Samuel: b 7-9-1738 d 2- -1812 m Abigail Drew Pvt MA
Samuel: b c. 1766 d a. 3- -1815 m Nancy Strother PS NC
Thomas, Jr.: bpt 12-13-1741 d 9-1-1820 m Lydia Holbrook Capt MA

HOLLISTER,
Abel: b a. 1746 d 1- -1821 m Abigail Chamber Pvt CT
Abner: b 10-28-1754 d 9-12-1813 m (1)Sarah McKee (2)Mrs Elizabeth Granger Sol MA
Amos: b 5-5-1726 d 11-6-1786 m Bathsheba Hollister PS CT
Appleton: b 11-2-1761 d 12-16-1831 m (1)Sarah Carver (2)Lucina Carver (3)Anna Carver Pvt CT
Asa: b 12-9-1758 d 4-16-1839 m (1)Anna Allen (2)Mary Wilson Pvt NY ★
Asahel: b 1763 d p. 1832 m Elizabeth Ware Pvt CT
Ashbel: b 3-4-1759 d 5-4-1840 m Mary Pepper Pvt CT ★
Benjamin: b 8-16-1760 d 12-6-1825 m Sarah Hall Pvt NY
David: b 10-9-1758 d 7-20-1836 m Hope Clark Drm CT ★
David: b 8- -1761 d c. 1850 m (1)Prudence Miller (2)Mrs Prudence Baird Pvt CT
Elijah: b 4-24-1754 d 1838 m Mary Tryon Sgt CT ★
Elijah: b 5- -1729 d 1-10-1785 m Mehitable Judd PS CT
Elijah Strong: b 1763 d 1-12-1813 m Lucy Clark Sgt MA
Elisha: b 1722 d 11-12-1800 m (1)Experience Robbins (2)Mrs Penelope Graves Dwight Capt CT
Gideon: bpt 9-21-1725 d 12-30-1813 m (1)Esther Preston (2)Patience Hurd Pvt CT
Innett: b 3-16-1761 d 2-8-1844 m Mary Kendall Pvt CT VT ★

Israel: b 1741 d 2-28-1818 m Sarah Skinner Sgt CT
John: b 2-2-1756 d 2-27-1835 m Mary Wells Pvt CT
Joseph: b 8-26-1752 d 8-21-1848 m Patience Hollister Sgt CT ★
Josiah: b 3-19-1754 d 7-4-1832 m (1)Mehitable Andrews (2)Naomi Tredwell Pvt CT
Josiah: b 2-22-1754-6 d 9-8-1849 m (1)Mary House (2)Asenath Sweetland Sol CT
Lazarus: b 3-22-1745 d 9-22-1798 m Sarah — Cpl MA
Nathan: b 11-21-1759 d 12-10-1843 m Abigail Goodrich Pvt CT ★
Nathaniel: b 5- -1731 d 1810 m Mehitable Mattison Pvt CT
Nehemiah: b 6-8-1748 d c. 1820 m (1)Abigail House (2)Elizabeth Fox (3)Mehitable Chapman Cpl CT
Salmon: b 1746 d 11-26-1826 m Millicent Goodrich Pvt CT
Solomon: b 5-9-1747 d 7-22-1822 m Mary Davis PS MA
Thomas, Sr.: b 1-13-1707 d 9-17-1784 m Abigail Talcott Ens PS CT
Thomas: b 9-10-1762 d p. 1803 m Sarah Hurlbut Pvt CT
Thomas C., Jr.: b 9-23-1738 d 1-27-1813 m Jemima Goodrich Lt CT

HOLLMAN,
Anthony: b 1735 d 11- -1826 m Mary Streeper Pvt PA

HOLLOWAY,
Benjamin: b 1759 d 9-16-1846 m Elizabeth Evolt Pvt NJ
Daniel: b 1755 d 11-29-1837 m Maria Bates Pvt MA
Elijah: b 3-11-1754 d p. 1820 m — Pvt MD
Elizabeth Cammack: b — d p. 2-3-1783 m George Holloway PS VA
George: b c. 1760 d p. 1810 m Frances Tiller Pvt VA
George: b 10-23-1740 d c. 1800 m (1)Mary Emley (2)Elizabeth Laurie Pvt VA
Isaac: b 1751 d 1808 m Elizabeth — DrmMaj PA
James: b 1759 d 9-10-1829 m Martha Owen Spencer Capt VA
John: b c. 1745 d p. 6-3-1789 m Ann — PS NC
John: b 1757 d c. 1820 m Elizabeth Allen Pvt SC
John: b 1761 d 2-29-1825 m Anne Starling Pvt VA
Joshua: b 174- d 3-1-1813 m — Gordy Pvt MD
Lewis: b c. 1753 d 9- -1815 m Mrs Rachel Williams Sgt GA
Peter: b 3-19-1751 d 3-11-1832 m Abagail Gooding Pvt MA
Reuben: b 1753 d 10- -1806 m Peinniah — Pvt SC
Thomas: b c. 1752 d 1- -1815 m Catherine Windle Pvt PA
Wm.: b 6-18-1747 d 5-10-1831 m Molly Trask Sgt MA
Wm.: b 1754 d 4-30-1831 m — Pvt VA ★
Wm.: b 1740-45 d p. 1790 m Miss Carter Sol VA

HOLLOWELL, (includes HALLOWELL)
Abner: b c. 1734 d 7-20-1811 m Tabitha Rice Pvt MA
John: b c. 1715 d — m Christian — CS NC
John: b 9-11-1757 d 5-7-1826 m Lydia Trump Pvt PA
Miles: b 2-4-1761 d 2-6-1843 m Ann Smithwick Pvt NC ★
Silas: b 1754 d 1789 m Mary Riddick Pvt NC
Theophilus: b 9-21-1750 d 9-28-1833 m (1)Bridget Newhall (2)Susanna Bread Pvt MA
Wm.: b 9-1-1754 d c. 1807 m Grace Trump Pvt PA

HOLMAN, (includes HALLMAN, HOLEMAN & HOLLIMAN)
Abraham: b c. 1730 d 1782 m (1)Abigail — (2)Prudence Mills Pvt MA
Anthony: b — d p. 1783 m Mary Strieper Pvt PA
Conrad: b a. 1732 d p. 1790 m Mary Ann — PS SC
Daniel: b 9-1-1743 d 11-16-1812 m Elizabeth Pitts Cpl MA
David: b 1757 d 1815 m Mary — Sol GA
David: b 2-19-1737 d 6-15-1813 m (1)Lucy Thurston (2)Hannah Waters Lt MA
Edward: b 9-11-1766 d 2-28-1837 m Martha Hemenway Pvt CS MA ★
Edward: b 10-13-1730 d p. 1790 m (1)Rebecca Gale (2)Sarah Kinney Pvt MA
Eli: b 1755 d 1825 m (1)Nancy Agnes McGrady (2)Betsey Perkins Pvt PA
Eliphalet: b 1761 d 5-30-1838 m Tamar Dagget Pvt MA
Elisha: b 5-13-1739 d 7-20-1812 m Jerusha Snow Sgt MA
George, Jr.: b 2-11-1762 d 5-24-1859 m Elizabeth Fisher Pvt PS VA ★
Henry: b c. 1758 d p. 1816 m Catherine Shepler Pvt PA
Henry: b 1735 d 8-17-1789 m (1)Mary Rennick (2)Rebecca — (3)Jane Gordon Sol VA
Isaac: b 3-20-1757 d 4-5-1843 m (1)Catherine Wilcox (2)Lillis Mitchell Pvt NC ★
Isaac, Sr.: b c. 1725 d p. 8-15-1807 m Mary — PS NC
Isaac: b 2-15-1752 d 8-25-1834 m Elizabeth Johnson Pvt SC ★
Johannes: b c. 1750 d p. 1790 m Mary Hoffmals Pvt PA
John: b 12-25-1736 d c. 8- -1833 m Elizabeth Burton Pvt VA ★
John: b 4-21-1757 d 1-13-1852 m Nannie Wright Pvt VA ★
Jonathan: b 8-13-1732 d 2-25-1814 m (1)Hannah Sibley (2)Susanna Trask Col MA
Jonathan: b 3-18-1741 d 1790 m Olive Farr Capt MA
Nathaniel: b 8-30-1733 d 1-14-1805 m Abagail Atherton Pvt MA
Nathaniel: b c. 1734 d. 2-7-1804 m Ann Winn 1Lt VA
Solomon: b 10-25-1723 d p. 1781 m Sara Waite Cpl MA
Stephen: b 10-20-1763 d 2-19-1850 m Rhoda Russell Pvt MA ★
Stephen: b 4- -1744 d 10-4-1821 m Mary Hipple Pvt PA
Thomas: b 1-13-1743 d p. 1789 m Lydia Bates Pvt MA
Thomas: b c. 1715-8 d 1798 m Susannah — PS NC

Thomas: b 9-8-1755 d 6-27-1850 m (1)Huldah — (2)Mary Vaughn Draper Pvt CT ★
Wm., Jr.: b 1737 d p. 5-5-1819 m (1)Elizabeth Johnson (2)Sarah Johnson Sol NC
Wm.: b 1739 d 1794 m Martha Benton Ens VA
Wm., Jr.: b 5-14-1749 d 1806 m Sophronia Carter Ens VA
Yancy: b 3- -1760 d 2-23-1854 m Nancy Beecher Pvt VA ★

HOLME,
Benjamin: b 2-28-1728 d 7-14-1792 m Esther Seeley Gibbon Col NJ
Thomas: b 1-16-1749 d 5-26-1826 m (1)Rebecca — (2)Hester — Capt PA

HOLMES, (includes HOMES)
Abijah: b 4-3-1741 d 3-6-1785 m Rachel Seeley LCol NJ
Abner: b 1753 d 1-30-1814 m Sarah Kent Pvt MA
Abraham: b 6-9-1754 d 9-7-1839 m Bethiah Blackwell Nye Sgt MA
Alexander: b — d c. 8-27-1776 m Sarah — Pvt PA
Andrew: b 10-26-1730 d 2-10-1810 m Jean Graham Pvt PA
Asa: b 3-22-1754 d — m (1)Tabitha Fuller (2)Elizabeth Carver Pvt MA
Asher: b 2-16-1740 d 6-20-1808 m Sarah Watson Col NJ
Barnabas: b a. 1764 d p. 1786 m Mercy Bates Pvt MA
Bartlett: b 1744 d p. 1790 m Lucy (Bartlett) 2Lt MA
Benjamin: b a. 1760 d a. 1825 m Mary Cleveland Pvt CT
Christopher: b 7-15-1762 d 2-1-1812 m Esther Beckwith Pvt CT
David: b 10-27-1760 d 9-15-1820 m Chloe Strong Pvt CT ★
David: b 8-11-1721 d 3-19-1779 m (1)Mehitable Mayo (2)Temperance Bishop Dr CT
Ebenezer: b 11-1-1748 d 1-29-1810 m Marsala Colburn Sgt CT
Ebenezer: b 9-28-1718 d 7-17-1797 m Lucy Nichols Drm CT
Ebenezer: b 2-27-1761 d 2-3-1848 m Hannah Paul Pvt MA
Ebenezer: b 5-12-1733 d 6-24-1801 m Jemima Lyon PS MA
Edward: b 9-20-1762 d 4-17-1837 m Abigail Brooks Pvt CT MA ★
Edward: b c. 1744 d c. 1814 m Sarah Ann Starke Pvt VA
Eliphalet:b 5-23-1748 d 5-2-1826 m Amy Hatch Sgt MA W★
Elisha: b 10-27-1758 d 9-21-1845 m Sarah Harris Pvt CT ★
Elisha: b 9-4-1732 d a. 4-16-1816 m Sarah Ewer Pvt MA
Elkanah: b 12-22-1744 d 1-17-1832 m Eleanor Miller Chp Pvt NJ
Ezra: b 7-8-1756 d 10-13-1845 m Reliance Hows Pvt CT ★
Francis: b 1739 d 8-6-1825 m Jane — Pvt PA
Gabriel, Sr.: b c. 1724 d c. 1792 m Mary Caison Pvt NC
George: b 10-9-1761 d 9-1-1843 m Rachel Allen Pvt MA
George: b c. 1740 d p. 1786 m Anna Hill Pvt VA
Gershom: b 1739 d p. 1789 m (1)Deborah Delano (2)Mercy King Pvt MA
Ichabod: b 8-4-1741 d p. 1780 m Dimias Worden 2Lt NY
Isaac: b 1746 d 12-17-1843 m (1)Susanna Griffiths (2)Mrs Anne Brewster Pvt MA W★
Isaac: b 3-9-1758 d 9-12-1793 m Elizabeth Thacker Brookin Lt VA
Jacob: b 12-26-1735 d 1-18-1803 m (1)Elizabeth Gates (2)Anna Harrington Pvt MA
James: b 1-1-1732 d 2-21-1812 m (1)Sarah Jewell (2)Sarah Roberts Stoddard Lt CT
James: b 1731 d p. 1790 m Surviah Mason Pvt CT
James: b 8-8-1759 d 4-13-1827 m Jerusha Rawson Pvt Smn MA ME
James: b 6-12-1754/5 d 6-27-1853 m Mercy Hunt Pvt OrdlSgt NJ
James: b 2-13-1748 d 2-2-1826 m Nancy Ann Whittaker 3Lt PA
James: b 9-18-1743 d 6-7-1833 m Margaret Lewis 1Lt VA
Jedediah: b 3-18-1763 d 5-1-1840 m (2)Hannah Brown Pvt NY ★
Jeremiah: b 11-12-1751 d 3-8-1790/1 m Mary Denison Sgt CT
Jeremiah: b 1745 d 11-15-1832 m Betsey Louis PS NH
Jezaniah: b 1-20-1763 d 4-17-1840 m Olive Goodell Pvt CT
John, Sr.: b 8-10-1702 d 1783 m (1)Abigail Frink (2)Mary Smith (3)Hannah Halsey PS CT
John, Jr.: b 9-3-1749 d 7-12-1809 m Martha Stanton Capt CT
John: b c. 1730 d 8-27-1776 m Lois Tiffany 1Lt CT
John: b 1756 d 7-12-1823 m Anna Rathbone Cpl CT
John: b c. 1735 d p. 9-4-1802 m Chloe Bentley Chp GA
John, Sr.: b a. 1734 d 1777/8 m Isabella — CS MD
John, Jr.: b a. 1754 d 1797 m Mary Turner CS MD
John: b c. 1720 d 9-22-1805 m Hannah Jones Capt MA
John: b 11-27-1759 d p. 1798 m Experience Samson Sol MA
John, Sr.: b c. 1762 d p. 1783 m Rachel Fellows Capt MA
John, Jr.: b 12-31-1760 d 5-12-1849 m (1)Ruth Fowler (2)Esther Wilcox Ensworth Pvt MA ★
John: b 2-1-1764 d 4-13-1840 m (1)Mary Carroll (2)Sally Snow (3)Polly Berry Pvt NH ★
John: b 1709 d 2-10-1777 m Grizel Given PS NH
John: b 1729 d 1780 m Catherine Brown Pvt NJ
John: b 12-31-1752 d 12-25-1839 m Catherine Slawson Pvt CS NY ★
John: b 1736 d 4-22-1814 m Ruth — PS NY
John, Sr.: b 1710 d 1790 m Elizabeth Jacques CS PA
John, Sr.: b c. 1730 d p. 9-6-1794 m Sarah — Sol SC
John, Jr.: b 1738 d 1809 m Margaret — Pvt PA
John Bee: b 4-23-1760 d 9-5-1827 m Elizabeth Edwards Sol SC
John Garrison: b 9-3-1758 d 2- -1840 m Mary Knott Pvt NJ
Jonathan: b 3-19-1749 d 3-8-1814 m Eunice Richards Pvt CT
Jonathan: b 4-27-1736 d 10-18-1806 m Rebecca Holmes Pvt MA
Jonathan: b 1-3-1755 d p. 1814 m Mercy Churchill Pvt MA
Jonathan: b 12-2-1738 d 8-4-1777 m Lydia Throckmorton Sol PS NJ

Joseph: b 1758 d 9-1-1826 m Lydia Curtis MM Pvt CT
Joseph: b 10-29-1755 d 10-21-1819 m Nellie Schenck Matr NJ
Joseph: b 1699 d 7-25-1777 m Elizabeth Ashton PS NJ
Joseph: b 8-22-1746 d 1806 m Rebecca Hunter Col VA
Joshua: b 12-28-1726 d 11-21-1799 m Prudence Wheeler Pvt CT
Josiah: b c. 1700 d c. 1778/9 m Hannah Dennis PS NJ
Lazarus: b 1755 d 12-1-1841 m Polly Hight Pvt NH W★
Levi: b 11-28-1747 d 5- -1795 m Lydia Bradford Pvt MA
Lothrop: b 1-26-1740 d 12-17-1808 m Mary Bartlett Ens MA
Mather: b 10-21-1756 d 7-29-1834 m Silence Fisher Pvt MA
Moses: b c. 1760-5 d 4-22-1837 m Sarah Goodson Sol NC
Nathaniel: b 10-1-1728 d 1783 m Hannah Smith PS MA
Nathaniel: b 4-14-1751 d — m Mary Rickard Pvt MA
Nathaniel: b 9-5-1759 d 9-10-1832 m Katherine Allison Sol NH
Nathaniel: b 3-17-1757 d 1-28-1834 m Hannah Hand Pvt Mar NJ
Obadiah: b 9-8-1760 d 6- -1834 m Jane Richardson Ens PA
Oliver: b 5-4-1740 d 9-26-1806 m Bethiah Morse Lt PS NH
Orsamus: b 10-11-1757 d 8-26-1835 m Ruth Webb Pvt VT & NY
Peter: b c. 1730 d 6- -1799 m Mary Holmes Pvt NY
Philip: b 4-22-1731 d 3-2-1795 m Mary Waters Fif MA
Reuben: b 1731 d 4- -1808 m (1)Mary — (2)Ruth Wood Pvt CT
Richard: b c. 1755-60 d a. 12- -1818 m Elizabeth McGaughey Pvt NC
Robert: b 9-28-1742 d 7-19-1827 m Mary Wier Pvt NH
Robert: b 1-5-1748 d 2-24-1838 m Margery — Lt PS NC PA
Roswell: b 1764 d 2-20-1854 m Polly Earle Pvt NY
Samuel: b 9-4-1726 d 5-26-1786 m Sarah Trask Pvt MA
Samuel: b 6-10-1733 d 2-5-1803 m (1)Susannah Commings (2)Abigail Tilden Pvt MA
Samuel: b 11-28-1755 d 4-12-1826 m Rachel Fisher Pvt MA
Samuel: b 3-25-1760 d 3-19-1813 m Salina Scott Pvt VT & NY
Samuel: b 1742/3 d 1800 m Mary Morrison Pvt PA
Samuel (2): b 11-17-1754 d 12-14-1825 m Mercy Winsor Lt RI
Seth W.: b 2-2-1738 d 12-12-1821 m (1)Sarah Rodgers (2)Mary Bradford Capt CT
Simeon: b 8-24-1755 d 3- -1835 m Emma Baldwin Sgt CT ★
Simeon: b 2-27-1740/1 d 10-30-1812 m Mercy Weston Pvt MA
Solomon: b 4-17-1759 d 1812-5 m Nancy Clayton Ens VA
Stephen: b 7- -1759 d 2-2-1835/6 m (1)Mercy — (2)Mrs Lydia Merrill Sgt VT ★
Stetson: bpt 3-25-1753 d 8-20-1824 m Anna Shurtleff Pvt PS NH
Thomas: b c. 1746 d c. 1786-90 m Tamar Harris Pvt CT
Thomas: b 12-9-1746 d 4-9-1822 m Margaret Patterson Pvt NH
Thomas: b c. 1740 d 1817 m Sarah — Pvt PA
Walter: b 6-27-1761 d 6-18-1831 m Abigail Bradford Pvt MA
Wm.: b 11-23-1755 d 10-4-1831 m Judith Goss Walker Sgt MA
Wm.: b 1754 d 8-8-1801 m Sibbel Smith Pvt MA
Wm.: b 10-10-1716 d 7- -1785 m Rebecca Dawes PS MA
Wm.: b c. 1707 d p. 1780 m Mary Taylor PS NH
Wm.: b 1756 d 6-20-1821 m Mary Kirby Pvt NJ
Wm.: b 9-22-1755 d 1852 m Phebe Cromwell Pvt NY
Wm.: b 1- -1751 d 8-21-1836 m Elizabeth Ann Love Pvt PA
Zebulon: b 4-28-1736 d p. 1780 m Abigail Savell Pvt MA

HOLSAPPLE,
Johannes:b c. 1710 d 1800 m Anna Maria Scholder Pvt NY

HOLSART,
John: b 5-9-1759 d 12-6-1846 m Mary Polhemus: Pvt NJ ★

HOLSENBAKE,
Derrick: b 1764 d 6-7-1826 m Mary Mosley Pvt SC

HOLSHUE,
George W.: b 3-24-1760 d 1815 m Elizabeth — Pvt VA

HOLSINGER,
George: b 3-2-1762 d 4-3-1813 m (1)Rosanna Friedley (2)Elizabeth Reichard Pvt PA
Jacob: b 6-24-1731 d 2-9-1817 m Susanna Yeakle Pvt PA

HOLSTEIN, (includes HOLSTON)
George: b 10-11-1733 d 3-11-1805 m Elizabeth Lower Pvt PA
John: b c. 1739 d p. 3-11-1795 m Martha Sill Pvt PA
Peter: b 5-25-1759 d p. 1807 m Catherine Blake Capt PA
Stephen: b 1729 d p. 1776 m Lucy Jane Looney Pvt VA

HOLT, (Includes HOULT)
Abel: b 6-14-1740 d 2- -1815 m Eunice Keyes Pvt MA
Abiel: b 4-3-1746 d 11-17-1824 m Lydia Lovejoy Pvt MA
Abiel: b 7-18-1748 d 1- -1811 m Sarah Abbott Pvt NH
Asa: b 5-3-1742 d 2- -1793 m (1)Dinah Holt (2)Mrs Lydia Stevens Patten Pvt MA
Benjamin: b 9-8-1748 d 6-22-1809 m Esther Webb Col CT
Benjamin: b 7-23-1709 d 1784 m Sarah Frye PS CS NH
Benjamin: b 3-5-1753 d 2-16 1830 m Edith Easton Pvt RI W★
Caleb: b 3-6-1729 d 8-18-1810 m (1)Mary Merrick (2)Chloe Hatch Sgt CT
Dan: b 10-18-1744 d 1-24-1829 m Anne Hitchcock Lt CT
Dane: b 4-7-1740 d 12-18-1818 m Lydia Ballard Pvt MA
Daniel: b 5-3-1738 d 6-11-1811 m Mary Pierpont Lt CT
Daniel: b 1744 d 1813 m Abigail Lovejoy Sol NH
Darius: b 3-6-1765 d 8- -1854 m Chloe Holt Pvt MA ★

HOLT, contd.
Ebenezer, Jr.: b 8-15-1760 d 6-30-1835 m Elizabeth Christopher Pvt CT
Eleazer: b 8- -1752 d 1835 m Elizabeth Stone Pvt CT
Ephraim: b 12-3-1762 d 6-3-1844 m Jerusha Kinney Pvt MA ★
Evan: b 12-2-1762 d 1841 m Charity — Pvt PA
George: b 4-6-1757 d 11-19-1839 m (1)Hannah — (2)Sarah — (3)Lovisa Cpl CT
Humphrey: b c. 1-1-1751 d p. 4-21-1794 m Edith — Sgt MA
Isaac: b 10-14-1720 d 11- -1806 m Mercy Morris PS CT
Jacob: b 5-19-1760 d 5-11-1826 m (1)Hannah Jeffords (2)Eleanor Hammond (3)Mrs Penelope Green Fif CT
Jacob: b 3-29-1739 d p. 1788 m Rhoda Abbott Pvt MA
James: b 8-27-1746 d 9-30-1818 m (1)Esther Orven (2)Lucy Sawin Matr CT
James: b 5-2-1762 d 7-22-1837 m Olive Dean Pvt MA ★
Jedediah: b 2-13-1744 d 2-12-1790 m Phebe Barker Sgt MA
Jeremiah: b 3-31-1734 d 1816 m Hannah Abbott Pyt NH
Joel: b 1764 d 6-16-1848 m Mary Coburn Cpl NH
John, Sr.: b 1-11-1719 d 5-15-1786 m Sarah Strickland Cmsry Sgt CT
John, Jr.: b 12-6-1746 d 9-6-1781 m Martha Coit PS CT
John: b 5-12-1764 d 7-16-1830 m Lydia Russell Pvt MA
John: b 2-1-1758 d 8- -1831 m Sarah Milliken Ens PA
Jonathan: b 1-3-1758 d 8-11-1833 m Ann Faulkner Pvt CT
Jonathan: b 5-16-1756 d 12-12-1832 m Molly Bailey Sgt MA ★
Joseph: b 8-14-1739 d 3-28-1785 m Elizabeth Crocker Cpl CT
Joseph: b 8-20-1740 d 12-15-1801 m Ruth Johnson Sgt MA
Joseph: b 1754 d 12-10-1817 m Mary Carter Pvt MA
Joseph: b 1730 d 1794 m Elizabeth — 1Lt VA
Joshua: b 6-30-1730 d 7-24-1810 m Phebe Farnum Capt MA
Jotham: b 1-10-1765 d 3-3-1839 m Lydia Fairbanks Pvt MA ★
Mastin: b 8-17-1747 d p. 1785 m Abigal Wheeler Pvt MA
Michael: b 5-6-1723 d 1799 m (1)Miss O. Neill (2)Jean Lockhart PS NC
Nathan: b 1739 d 3-3-1818 m Sarah Chamberlain Pvt NH
Nathaniel: b — d 4-8-1814 m Abigail Stanton Pvt CT
Nehemiah: b 11-28-1756 d 6-5-1824 m (1)Mary Lamphear (2)Sarah Dunlap (3)Eunice Fuller Sgt CT
Nicholas: b 10-4-1755 d 4-16-1832 m (1)Ketura Pratt (2)Sarah Bingham (3)Mrs Lydia Phelps Pvt CT
Nicholas: b 2-29-1715/6 d 3-16-1798 m (1)Hannah Osgood (2)Lois Phelps LCol PS MA
Nicholas: bapt 1751 d 1833 m Phoebe Bachelor Sol MA
Obadiah: b 3-23-1758 d 6-9-1815 m Susannah Jones Pvt NH
Paul: b 1-4-1743 d 10-27-1827 m (1)Sarah Welch (2)Phoebe Welch Cady (3)Dinah Stowell Pvt CT
Peter: b 9-3-1752 d 1-9-1830 m Hepzibah Stevens Pvt MA
Reuben: b 6-27-1744 d 3-2-1836 m Lydia Small PS NH
Samuel: b 5-1-1749 d 12-5-1799 m Lydia Adams Pvt NH
Stuart: b c. 1750 d 1792 m Ann Johnson PS VA
Thomas: b 1743 d 7-12-1799 m Martha Morgan Sgt CT
Thomas: b 3- -1712 d 11-21-1776 m (1)Hannah Kimball (2)Dorcas Holt Pvt MA
Thomas: b a. 1730 d p. 1782 m Mary — PS VA
Thomas D.: b a. 1735 d 1788 m Elizabeth Hunter Capt VA
Timothy: b 12-2-1739 d 2-7-1847 m Rebecca Fenton 2Lt NY
Timothy: b — d a. 3-15-1822 m Elizabeth Chambers PS VA
Uriah: b 1722 d 1812 m (1)Anise Willard (2)Sarah Goodridge Pvt MA
Valentine: b 12-25-1763 d p. 1840 m (1)Nancy Goodrich (2)Hannah Day Sol NH
Wm.: b 9-7-1763 d 12-23-1810 m Elizabeth J. — Pvt MA
Wm.: b 3-6-1763 d 9-29-1827 m Nancy Young Pvt MD
Wm.: b 1765 d — m Lucy Hutchings Pvt MA
Wm.: b 1744 d 2-28-1784 m Sarah Tew CS RI
Wm.: b 2-12-1757 d 9-10-1826 m Lucy Saunders Pvt VA
Zebediah: b 9-13-1734 d 12-15-1811 m Jemima Simonds Pvt PS CT

HOLTER,
George: b c. 1750 d p. 1798 m Margaret Arnold Pvt PA

HOLTINGER,
Jacob: b 1750 d 1825 m Barbara Leixin Lt PA W★

HOLTON, (includes HOLTEN)
Arad: b 11- -1752 d 10-8-1841 m (1)Anna Haven (2)Rebecca Houghton (3)Eunice Spaulding Pvt VT ★
Benjamin: b 1740 d 1797 m Abigail Adkinson Pvt NJ
Elisha: b 11-12-1756 d 9-17-1827 m Lois Benjamin Pvt MA
John: b 10-22-1747 d 3-22-1825 m Hannah Sheldon Sgt MA
John: b 12-2-1747 d 10-2-1822 m Priscilla Beath Cpl MA
Jonathan: b 1743 d 11-19-1821 m (1)Hannah Olcott (2)Nancy Walker Lt NH
Lemuel: b 6-17-1749 d 10-1-1786 m Lydia Shattuck PS CS MA
Robert: b 1759 d 1804 m Catherine Fenwick Pvt MD
Samuel: b 6-9-1738 d 1-2-1816 m Mary Warner PS Maj MA
Solomon: b 4-8-1755 d 10-9-1824 m Mary Lyman Pvt MA
Thomas: b 1717 d 12-22-1800 m Sarah — PS CS VT
Wm.: b c. 1739 d 12-21-1831 m Abigail Gorman PS VA

HOLTZ,
Jacob: b 11-30-1753 d p. 1795 m Anna Barbara Morgenstern Pvt MD

HOLTZCLAW
Benjamin: b 1755 d 4- -1826 m Catherine M. Russell PS VA
Catherine James: b c. 1745 d 1810 m Joseph Holtzclaw PS VA
Jacob: b 2-17-1738 d 10-21-1812 m Susannah — Sol VA
John: b 1762 d 1827 m Catherine Hicks PS NC

HOLTZMAN,
Jacob: b c. 1758 d 1814 m Christina Winter Pvt PA

HOLYOKE,
Elizur: b 9-25-1739 d 9-4-1794 m Sarah Gates Sgt MA
John: b 8-27-1743 d 4-21-1807 m Elizabeth Treat PS MA

HOLZENDORF,
Wm.: b c. 1714 d 1798 m Elizabeth Stafford PS GA

HOMAN,
Ebenezer: b c. 1752 d p. 1775 m — Woodruff PS Pvt NY
Eber: b 9-9-1764 d 3-25-1840 m (3)Anna Marshell Pvt PA ★
Joseph: b 12-14-1765 d 2-2-1830 m Sarah Walton Pvt NH ★
Joseph: b 10-10-1757 d 9-23-1841 m Temperance Corey Pvt NY
Mordecai: b 1750 d 5-15-1805 m Mary Leek PS NY
Mordacai, Jr.: b 1757 d 4-6-1829 m Charity — PS NY
Samuel: b 2-17-1755 d 2-15-1824 m (1)Juliana Rapp (2)Christiana Reitmyer Pvt PA
Thomas: b 12-24-1758 d 1-20-1832 m Tabitha Glover Pvt Smn MA

HOMANS,
Joshua: b 5-10-1758 d 3-22-1814 m (2)Nancy Wherry Cpl NY
Wm.: b 12-15-1749 d 8-15-1839 m Relief Brown Matr MA

HOMER,
Robert: b 1730 d 10-24-1822 m Rebecca Richardson Pvt MA
Stephen: b 4-15-1734 d p. 1790 m Elizabeth Chapman Pvt MA

HOMMEL,
Abraham: bpt 2-23-1757 d p. 1-19-1793 m Rachel Snyder Pvt NY
Peter: b 10-31-1750 d 2-1-1828 m Rachel Hommel Cpl PS NY

HONAKER,
Henry: b 2-10-1756 d 9-16-1830 m (1)Ann Baker (2)Edith Smith Pvt VA

HONEYMAN, (includes HONYMAN)
John: b 1729/30 d 8-18-1822 m (1)Mary Henry (2)Elizabeth Burrows Spy NJ
Robert: b 12-21-1747 d 4-21-1824 m Mildred Brown Dr VA
Wm.: b 6-3-1759 d 6-25-1788 m Jane Davison 2Lt PA

HONIE,
Elias: b 1763 d 1804 m Frances Paul Matr SC

HOOD,
Amos: b 8-12-1757 d 11-13-1792 m Phebe Perkins Pvt MA W★
Andrew: b c. 1745-55 d p. 1803 m Massa Sudduth Pvt VA
Benjamin Landon: b 5-20-1750 d 3-8-1839 m Deziah Liscome Pvt MA
George: b 1-10-1763 d 6-23-1846 m Elizabeth Goist Pvt PA
George: b 12-15-1761 d 3-16-1835 m Catherine Mullen Pvt VA ★
George: b 1749/50 d 7-18-1823 m Anna Christina Schmidt Ens PA
James: b 1755 d 1819 m Kitty Franklin QMSgt MD W★
James: b 1729 d 8-20-1805 m Catharine — Pvt PA
John, Jr.: d 1740 d 1795 m (1)Hannah Barnes (2)Rachel Ridgely Howard (3)Elizabeth Gaither PS MD
John, Jr.: b 2-26-1760 d 7-19-1836 m (1)Anne Kimball (2)Ruth Gould Sgt MA ★
John: b 1747 d 1-24-1806 m Amey Hood Pvt NC
John: b 2- -1751 d 1-14-1831 m Ann Stewart Pvt PA
John: b 1755 d 1832 m Mary — Pvt PA
John: b c. 1750 d p. 1799 m Mary — Lt SC MD
John: b 1750 d p. 1834 m — Pvt SC ★
John: b 5-1-1759 d 2-12-1827 m Rebecca Reeves Pvt VA
Joseph: b 2-10-1746 d 10-27-1795 m Mrs Dorcas Hovey Sgt MA W★
Joseph M.: bpt 2-16-1746 d 6-10-1826 m Mary — Pvt CT
Mathew: b 1756 d 1821 m Mary Smith Sol NC
Nathaniel: b 1758 d 1838 m Elizabeth Bullard Pvt SC
Philip: b 10- -1728 d 1-30-1798 m Eve Elizabeth Weiss Lt PA
Reuben: b 10-4-1762 d 5-13-1845 m Jane Irwin Pvt Wgn NC ★
Richard: b 3-1-1751 d 11-19-1835 m Lydia Tarbox Pvt MA
Robert: b c. 1740 d 5-14-1811 m Mary Newbold Sgt CS DE
Robert: b 1-18-1741 d 1813 m Mary Rowley Pvt MA
Samuel: b c. 1752/3 d 1805 m Mary — Pvt PA
Tunis: b c. 1750 d 1801 m — Pvt NC
Wm.: b 1762 d 8-8-1858 m (3)Sally McLean Pvt NY
Wm.: b 12-29-1739 d 8-26-1809 m Christiana — Pvt NC
Wm.: b c. 1752 d 2-22-1822 m Rebecca Lee Pvt PA
Wm.: b 1750 d 1843 m Martha Blair Ens VA

HOOE,
John: b 2-23-1729 d p. 1782 m Anne Fowke Maj PS VA
Robert Howson: b 11-22-1748 d p. 10-13-1833 m Mary Waugh Lt VA
Charles: b 2-20-1768 d 10-18-1843 m (1)Bertie Williams (2)Kitty Dickson (3)Mary Ann Hunter Pvt NC

HOOK, (includes HOOKE & HOOKS)

Francis: b 2-10-1742/3 d *p.* 1782 m Mary Rand Pvt MA
George: b 10-1-1750/1 d 3-7-1835 m Jean Bleakly Sgt NC VA ★
Humphrey: b 7-27-1722 d 1-8-1801 m (1)Hannah Philbrick (2)Sarah Reddington PS NH
Jacob: b 1752 d 1815-25 m Susannah Cockley Boone PS MD
Jacob: b 1724 d 12-14-1804 m Mary Bachelder PS NH
James: b *c.* 1716 d *p.* 6-10-1798 m — PS MD
James: b 1749 d 1-23-1824 m Mary — Capt VA ★
James: b 1726 d 9- -1783 m Betsey —Lt VA
James: b *c.* 1752 d *p.* 1784 m Letitia McCulloch Ens VA
Josiah: b 5-29-1744 d 9-20-1829 m Sarah Pike 2Lt VA
Martin: b *c.* 1755 d 1820 m (1)Sarah Senn (2)Katie Lever Sgt SC
Mathias: b 1747 d 4-27-1836 m Sarah — Pvt PA
Robert, Sr.: b *c.* 1712 d *p.* 10-16-1802 m Jean — PS VA
Wm.: b 1759 d 1-30-1837 m Mary McKee OrdlSgt VA ★
Wm., Sr.: b *c.* 1738 d *p.* 9-25-1817 m Sarah Campbell Pvt VA

HOOKER,

Asahel: b 12-13-1736 d 11-10-1810 m Anne Parmelee Capt CT
Brainard: b 3-4-1747 d 10- -1808 m Mary Deming Tms CT W★
Daniel: b 1730 d 9-12-1802 m Mary Sedgwick Dr CT
Daniel: b 6-25-1750 d 2-15-1817 m Mary Gates Pvt MA
Elijah: b 4-12-1746 d 9-27-1823 m Mrs Susannah Seymour PS CT
Gilbert: b 5-14-1758 d 1-9-1849 m Rebecca Andrews Pvt MA
Hezekiah: b 10-30-1717 d 1796 m Elizabeth Stone Pvt CT
Ira: b 3-12-1760 d 11-30-1838 m Amy Barnes Pvt CT
James, Sr.: b 1-30-1720 d 6-18-1798 m Dorothy Parmalee Sol CT
James, Jr.: b 12-25-1760 d 8-9-1844 m Lucina Christy Cpl CT ★
James: b 8-15-1742 d 12-10-1805 m Mary Chaffee PS CT
James G.: b 6-16-1764 d 1855 m Mary Powell Pvt VA ★
Jesse: b 4-23-1752 d 1791 m Sabrina Smith Pvt MA
John: bpt 10-15-1758 d *p.* 1800 m Hannah Field Pvt MA
Joseph: b 1704 d 1784 m Ruth Powers Capt MA
Martin: b 9-25-1759 d 1843 m Mary Judd Pvt CT ★
Noadiah: b 8-29-1737 d 6-3-1823 m Rebecca Griswold Col CT
Philip: b 1749 d 3-20-1832 Hannah Chapman Pvt MA
Riverius: b 2-12-1749 d *p.* 1776 m M. Mehitable Baker Pvt MA
Samuel: b 8-3-1762 d 6-2-1835 m Elizabeth Martin Pvt CT
Samuel: b 5-6-1745 d 1-13-1822 m Mary Pierce Pvt MA
Sarah Whitman: b 2-27-1747 d 6-5-1837 m (1)Thomas Hart Hooker (2)Seth Collins PS CT
Seth: b 10-26-1759 d 5-31-1844 m Abigail Gay Pvt MA
Simeon: b 4-14-1739/40 d 2-21-1841 m Lydia — OrdlSgt MA ★
Thomas: b 12-24-1754 d 8-31-1838 m (1)Ruth Parmalee (2)Ruth Hickok (3)Mary Coleman Pvt CT
Thomas Hart: b 9-3-1745 d 11-26-1775 m Sarah Whitman Pvt MA
Wm.: b 7-1-1729 d 10-30-1815 m (1)Rachel Waller (2)Mary Moseley Pvt CT
Wm.: b 9-15-1756 d 2-4-1826 m Hannah Jones Sgt CT
Zibeon: b 2-12-1752 d 12-2-1840 m Sarah Barber 1Lt MA

HOOKEY,

George: b 5-6-1759 d 9-29-1793 m Mary Gilbert Pvt PA
Nicholas: b 3-26-1718 d 8-3-1785 m (1)Catherine Kleyss (2)Catherine Demuth Pvt PA

HOOMES,

Benjamin: b 1755 d — m Mary Pendleton Col VA

HOON, (includes HONE)

Anthony: b *c.* 1735 d 1792 m Elizabeth Carter Pvt PA
Henry: b *c.* 1735 d *a.* 3-7-1785 m Ruth — Pvt PA
Henry: b 1760 d 12- -1836 m (2)Frances Sargeant Pvt PA

HOOPER,

Absalom: b *c.* 1740 d 1813 m — Pvt SC
Absalom: b 1765 d 12-9-1845 m Sarah Salers Pvt SC GA W★
Aeneas: b *c.* 1760 d 1800 m (2)Anne Young Pvt NC
Benjamin: b 1720 d 1802 m Lydia Ladd Smith Capt PS MA
David: b 6-9-1745 d 2-19-1835 m Rachel Story Pvt MA ★
Elisha: b 10-11-1736 d 11-23-1814 m Hannah Stevens Pvt MA
Enoch: b *c.* 1755 d 1815 m Lettitia Birding Pvt Spy SC
Henry: b *c.* 1718/20 d *p.* 1790 m Anne Enalls BGen PS MD
Henry: b 1759 d 7-10-1820 m (2)Margaret Creighton PS MD
Hezekiah: b 1832 d *p.* 1800 m (1)Elizabeth Leonard (2)Hannah Conant Lt MA
Isaac: b *a.* 1758 d *c.* 1820-30 m Jane Crage PS MD
Jacob: b *c.* 1760 d *p.* 1836 m Mary Cord Pvt MD
James: b 10-3-1703 d 11-3-1789 m Mary Woolford PS MD
James: b 5- -1746 d 10-31-1828 m Susanna Washburn Cpl MA
James: b 1760 d 1835 m (1)Lucy Hall Flora (2)Mary Ann Childress Pvt VA W★
John: bpt 8-9-1752 d 9-10-1810 m Mary Roundy N1Lt MA
Levi: bpt 5-16-1742 d 10-22-1806 m (1)Susannah Leach (2)Sarah Hall Capt NH
Luther: b 2-21-1745/6 d 5-11-1831 m Phebe Washburn Pvt MA
Noah: b 3- -1745 d 5-15-1814 m Sarah Gilpatrick Fif MA
Obadiah: b 12-15-1755 d 5-31-1839 m (1)Elizabeth Carter (2)Sarah Sanders Pvt VA
Richard B.: b 5- -1756-8 d *p.* 7- -1836 m (2)Elizabeth Adams Ward (3)Adenia Miller Sgt PS VA ★

Robert: bpt 4-6-1755 d 1779 m Patience Pool Sol MA
Robert: bpt 7-12-1741 d 1-20-1814 m Mary Ingalls Pvt MA
Robert Lettice: b 1709 d 4-25-1785 m Christina Ebrington QM NJ
Thomas: b 7-31-1737 d 1777 m Deborah Cushman Cpl MA
Wm., Sr.: b 4-29-1719 d 7-26-1809 m Elizabeth Emery CS MA
Wm., Jr.: b 3-31-1746 d 1- -1827 m Mary Lord Pvt MA
Wm.: b 1-25-1735/6 d 1798 m Mary Salkins Capt MA
Wm.: b 10-22-1742 d 8-18-1823 m Abigail Gilbert 2Cpl MA
Wm.: b 10-12-1763 d 3-27-1825 m Mary Tilson Pvt MA
Wm.: b 6-7-1742 d 10-14-1790 m Anne Clarke SDI NC

HOOPES,

Ezra: b 7-31-1751 d 10-13-1811 m Ann Hickman Pvt PS PA
Francis: b 4-3-1752 d *p.* 11-6-1784 m Mary Pratt Sol PA
Thomas: b *c.* 1740 d 1-10-1791 m Sarah Bane Pvt PA

HOOTMAN,

Christian: b 1757 d 8-31-1845 m Miss Revenaugh Sol VA

HOOTON, (Includes HOOTEN)

Charles: b *c.* 1755 d 1832 m Nancy — Pvt NC
Francis: b *c.* 1750 d *p.* 1800 m Mary Hodson Pvt MA
John: b 9-4-1754 d 9-16-1844 m Catherine Thompson Sgt MA ★
Wm.: b *c.* 1730 d *p.* 1-24-1794 m — Lt NC

HOOVEN,

Henry: b *a.* 1755 d *p.* 1789 m Elizabeth Boulton Pvt PA

HOOVER, (includes HOVER & HUBER)

Adam: b 8-23-1761 d 4-19-1826 m Hannah Katherine Bolter Matr PA
Andrew, Sr.: b 12-1-1722 d 1794 m Margaret Fouts PS NC
Andrew, Jr.: b 9-21-1752 d 12-29-1834 m Elizabeth Waymire PS NC
Anthony: b 1745 d 5-14-1813 m Mary Staley Sgt PA
Christian: b 1765 d *p.* 1806 m (1)— Hooker (3)Elizabeth Zeigler Pvt PA
Conrad: b *a.* 1740 d 1806 m Anna Maria Lentz Pvt PA
Emanuel: b 3-5-1748 d 8-9-1824 m Mary Schoonover Capt NJ
Henry: b 4-4-1740 d *p.* 1803 m (1)Cornelia Cortright (2)Mary Van Ness Capt NJ
Henry: b 1749 d 11-13-1822 m Catherine — Pvt PA ★
Henry: b 12-1-1751 d 4-9-1809 m Margaret — PS PA
Jacob: b 4-17-1760 d 1-22-1847 m Margaret Auyerbroat Pvt NY
Jacob, Sr.: b *c.* 1720 d 1782 m Harriet Magdalena Breckbill Sgt PA
Jacob: b *c.* 1730 d *p.* 12-10-1800 m Anna — Pvt PA
Jacob: b 1748 d *p.* 1790 m Maria — Sol PA
John: b 1739 d 10- -1840 m Gertrude Crim Capt NY
John: b 3-1-1744 d 2-26-1804 m Letitia — Pvt PA
John: b 2-19-1755 d 1840 m Margaret Smith Pvt PA ★
Lodewyk: b *c.* 1748 d *p.* 1814 m Hester VanGarden Cpl PA
Martin: b 9-5-1762 d 1841 m Catherine — Pvt PA
Peter: b *c.* 1730 d 1807 m Mary — PS VA
Thomas: b 4-5-1750 d 4-10-1833 m Maria Barbara Warlick PS NC

HOPE, (Includes SCHOPF)

Adam: b 6-13-1741 d 9-26-1821 m Sarah Dunham Capt NJ
Adam: b 11-1-1761 d 12-26-1841 m Rachel — PS CS VA
Francis: b 1752 d 4-15-1814 m Elizabeth Musselman Pvt PA
George: b 3-28-1749 d 1812-14 m Rebecca Ballard Sol PS VA
James: b 1-22-1758 d 9-8-1828 m Jane McPherson Pvt PA
James, Sr.: b 12-28-1732 d *a.* 1790 m Ellen Demorse Pvt SC
James: b 1754 d 10-15-1811 m Margaret Dryden Pvt VA
John: b *c.* 1700 d 1790 m — PS SC
Robert: b 11-2-1750 d 7-14-1808 m Catherine Allison PS NC
Thomas: b 6-10-1742 d 3-20-1815 m Hannah Nelson Capt MD

HOPEWELL,

Hugh: b — d 7-22-1777 m Elizabeth Biscoe PS MD
John: b 1751 d 8-6-1826 m Sarah Edwards Pvt VA ★

HOPKINS,

Abijah: b 1716 d 1797/8 m Elizabeth King Capt NJ
Alexander: b *c.* 1755 d *c.* 1840 m Rosanna Laird Ens PA
Alexander: b *c.* 1730-35 d *p.* 1790 m Mary Phillips Capt RI
Allen: b *c.* 1718 d 1794 m Sarah — Sgt PS MA NH
Archibald: b 1760 d 1-25-1848 m (2)Margaret Shanklin Pvt VA ★
Archibald: b *a.* 1737 d 5-8-1799 m Jannet Love PS VA
Benjamin: b *c.* 1720 d *p.* 1775 m Phebe Ives Pvt CT
Benjamin, Jr.: b 2-10-1727 d 11-7-1820 m Anna Powers PS NH
Benjamin: b 1745 d 9-6-1780 m Zaresh Rudd Lt VT ★
Benjamin, Sr.: b 5-23/25-1701 d 6-11-1787 m Hannah Wilson PS NH
Caleb: b 1759 d 7-19-1824 m Ruth Hull Lt NJ
Caleb: b 7-6-1743 d 12-8-1836 m Thankful Paine Sgt MA ★
Christopher: b *c.* 1730 d *p.* 1792 m (1)Mary — (2)Abigail Newbit Pvt MA
Consider: b 6-10-1723 d 8-22-1795 m Lydia Gilbert Pvt CT
Constant: b 5-16-1747 d 3-28-1817 m Elizabeth Paine Sgt MA
Daniel: b 10-16-1734 d 12-14-1814 m Susanna Saunders PS MA
Daniel: b 6-16-1758 d 7-13-1844 m Hannah Tanner Pvt RI ★
Daniel: bpt 10-1-1751 d *p.* 1810 m Olive Kinne Sgt VT
David: b 12-2-1753 d 3-7-1824 m (1)Mrs Mary Howard (2)Polly Dorsey (3)Isabella Ford (4)Mrs Hannah Greenleaf Maj MD

HOPKINS, contd.

David, Sr.: b 2- -1713 d 6-6-1783 m Sarah Polk Pvt NY
David, Jr.: b 11- -1748 d 1-26-1813 m Hannah Parrish Ens NY
David: b 1739 d a. 2-8-1816 m Mary Bowles LCol SC
David: b 8-8-1754 d 2-14-1800 m Susanna Drake 2Lt VA
Dennis: b 7-13-1760 d 6-26-1850 m — Pvt NC
Ebenezer: b c. 1750 d a. 4-14-1827 m Abigail Davis Sol RI
Ebenezer: b 6-1-1761 d 7-16-1838 m Rachel Mead Pvt VT W★
Ebenezer: b 6-24-1699 d 1784 m Susannah Messenger PS VT
Edward: b c. 1750 d a. 12-31-1806 m Rebecca Marlin Pvt NJ
Ehud: b 2-1-1741/2 d 11-17-1809 m (1)Chloe King (2)Mrs Hannah Benjamin Sgt PS MA
Elias: b 3-2-1741 d c. 1793 m Polly — Sgt CT
Elijah: b 6-28-1741 d 4-23-1813 m (2)Lois Fuller (3)Joanna Parish (4)Jane Husted Pvt CT
Elisha: b 1762 d 1840 m Rebecca Mereen Pvtr MA
Elisha: b c. 1742 d 11-14-1798 m Mary — Sgt RI
Elkanah: b 5-18-1758 d 9- -1828 m Temperance Snow Pvt MA
Esek: b 4-26-1718 d 2-26-1802 m Desire Burroughs BGen NCommo PS RI
Ezekiel: b 1732 d 1834 m Sarah Hazzard Sgt PA
Garner: b 7-16-1750 d 6-4-1832 m Mary Chambers Pvt NY ★
George: b 1-11-1750 d 1-24-1829 m Nancy Davis Pvt CT RI
George: b 2-19-1758 d 7-18-1842 m Rachel Russell Pvt VT
Gerad, Sr.: b 1-7-1709 d 7-3-1777 m Mary Hall PS MD
Harris: b 3-1-1744 d 12-16-1820 m Margaret Peck Pvt PS CT
Hezekiah: b 1758 d 5-18-1834 m Eunice Hubbell Pvt CT
Ichabod: bpt 12-9-1744 d 10-20-1819 m (1)Mary Nash (2)Mrs Sarah Ransom Pvt PS MA
Isaiah: b 2-29-1742 d 1-4-1823 m Mollie — Sgt NY
James: b c. 1748 d 10-22-1831 m Mary Ann McGregor Lt NH
James: b a. 1730 d 1777/8 m — PS NH
James: b 7-11-1746 d 8-20-1818 m Mary Presby PS NH
James: b 6-17-1765 d 1849 m (2)Elizabeth Billingsly Pvt NC
James: b 1748 d 1830 m Miriam Kent Holcombe Capt VT
James: b 2-17-1739 d c. 1797 m Ruth Hopkins Ens VT
Jeptha: b 1750 d 1820 m Annie Bucklin Pvt RI
Jeremiah: b 8-16-1762 d 10-17-1829 m Thankful Stone Pvt NY
Jesse: b c. 1730-5 d p. 9-17-1799 m — Sol SC
John: b 4- -1741 d a. 3-3-1789 m (1)Hessie Stevenson (2)Mary Vint (3)Sophia McIlvaine Pvt DE
John: b c. 1727 d 1796 m Eleanor Wallace Pvt MD
John: b a. 1748 d 1-25-1814 m (2)Catherine Collier Pvt MD
John: b c. 1707 d p. 2-5-1779 m Elizabeth Dinsmore PS NH
John: b 7-6-1737 d 3-2-1806 m Sara Mickle Pvt NJ
John: b 1750 d 11-29-1820 m Mary Richardson Pvt PA
John: b 1-12-1765 d 10-13-1832 m Amy Goodwyn Pvt SC
John: b 1752 d 5-5-1833 m Charity Bromley Pvt VT
John: b c. 1763 d 1832 m Hannah Mead Pvt VT
John: b c. 1726 d 1807 m Mary Martin Col PS VA
John: b 1732 d 6-1-1791 m Jean Gordon Capt VA
Jonah: b 1724 d 11-18-1805 m Abigail Whitman MM RI
Jonathan, Jr.: b 5- -1757 d 1835 m Jane Townsend Pvt NY
Jonathan, Sr.: b 12-17-1719/20 d a. 1790 m Rebecca Freeman Pvt NY
Jonathan: b 1748 d 1797 m Elizabeth Lambert Cpl NC
Joseph, Sr.: b 6-6-1730 d 3-27-1801 m Hepzibah Clark PS CS CT
Joseph, Jr.: b 1-9-1760 d 2-20-1829 m Ruth Gilbert Pvt CT
Joseph: b 1-27-1760 d 1837 m Lois Wills Pvt MA
Joseph: b 11-5-1761 d 9-19-1853 m (1)Patience Hale (2)Martha Crooker Pvt MA ★
Joseph: b 4-6-1750 d 1-31-1833 m Elizabeth Townsend Pvt NY
Joseph: b 3-16-1736 d 3-9-1793 m Mary Austin Capt RI
Joshua: b 9-28-1754 d 3-19-1842 m Ruth Linnell Pvt MA
Josiah: b 7-28-1754 d 10-26-1824 m Anna Peirce Pvt CT
Levi: b 3-31-1753 d 9-1-1835 m (1)Abigail Stevens (2)Elizabeth Looper Pvt MA ★
Moses: b c. 1760 d 1-6-1810 m Susannah — Pvt PS MD
Nathan: b — d 1784 m Hannah Drial Sgt NJ
Nehemiah, Sr.: b 4-14-1730 d c. 1814 m Tryphena Smith Pvt VT
Nehemiah, Jr.: b 1763 d 1844 m Lucy Millard Pvt VT
Noah: b 1-26-1730/1 d 5-6-1805 m Mary Paine 1Lt NY
Oliver: b 1-18-1756 d 4-7-1839 m Susanna Bennett Pvt RI ★
Peleg: b 4-29-1755 d 4-7-1846 m Elizabeth Place Pvt RI
Peter: b c. 1740 d — m Silence King Pvt MA
Reuben: b 6-1-1748 d 8-12-1822 m Hannah Eliot 1Lt NY
Richard: b c. 1760 d c. 1826 m Hannah Hammond PS MD
Robert: b c. 1715 d 1788 m (1)Martha — (2)Elenor Wilson PS NH
Robert: b 3-15-1756 d 8-11-1838 m Catharine Harper Pvt NY
Robert: b 1752 d 12-29-1827 m Grace Hopkins Pvt VT
Roderick: b 1756 d 11-3-1841 m Mary M. — Cpl CT ★
Roswell: b 5-18-1733 d 1817 m Mary Cook Col NY
Samuel: b 10-21-1748 d 3-18-1818 m Mary Miles Vol CT
Samuel: b 1750 d 1828 m Elizabeth (Houston) Campbell Pvt NY
Samuel: b 10-31-1729 d 3-8-1811 m Mrs Sarah Porter Williams Chp MA
Samuel: b 5-6-1759 d 2-23-1813 m Louisa Sibley Pvt MA
Samuel: b 4-4-1744 d 9-8-1807 m Elizabeth Woodhull Pvt PS NY
Samuel: b 8-2-1753 d 2-6-1820 m Mary Smith Pvt MA
Samuel, Sr.: b 1-6-1704 d 4-4-1790 m Honor Brown RO NY
Samuel, Jr.: b 10-15-1734 d 1813 m (1)— Waite (2)Phebe Case Capt RI

Samuel: b c. 1724 d p. 1816 m Pheobe Arnold Pvt RI
Samuel: b 4-9-1753 d 9-16-1819 m Elizabeth Bugg Col VA
Seth: b 7-1-1753 d 4-26-1841 m Mercy Rogers Pvt MA ★
Silas: b 8-9-1741 d 9-5-1815 m Mary Swazey Pvt PA
Simeon: b 2-7-1731 d 1821 m Betty Cobb PS ME
Solomon: b 3-28-1757 d 1840 m Hannah — QM Mar MA ★
Solomon: b 3-12-1757 d 12-2-1812 m Esther Plummer Pvt MA
Solomon: b 5-31-1739 d 9-22-1792 m Elizabeth Crosby Lt NY
Stephen: b 5-10-1762 d 2-24-1813 m Mary Taylor Pvt MA
Stephen: b 11-12-1707 d 7-13-1785 m (1)Sarah Scott (2)Ann Smith SDI RI
Stephen: b 1757 d 1819 m Leah Crocket Lt RI
Stephen: b 2-22-1744 d 3-28-1813 m Rhoda Dewey Pvt VT
Thatcher: b 1754 d 7-7-1830 m (1)Eleanor Regan (2)Mrs Mary Green Pvt NY
Theophilus: b 3-13-1757 d 12-20-1837 m (1)Betsey Higgens (2)Thankful Freeman (3)Betsey Stevens (4)Martha Spencer Pvt MA ★
Thomas: b c. 1759 d c. 1829 m Catherine Hurd Pvt MD
Thomas: b 8-12-1761 d 2-2-1833-5 m Hannah — Pvt MA
Thomas: b 3-24-1742 d 4-12-1808 m Hannah Baker Pvt RI
Timothy, Jr.: b 11-25-1750 d 10-10-1803 m (1)Sarah Ransom (2)Phebe Marvin Pvt CT
Timothy, Sr.: b 7-25-1725 d 3-18-1812 m (1)Penelope — (2)Lillis Hinds CS PS RI
Timothy, Jr.: b 8-1-1751 d 1-29-1816 m Sarah Carver Adj RI W★
Uriah: b 12-26-1738 d 4-3-1825 m Lucy Lanksford Pvt RI
Wait: b 10-9-1738 d 7-15-1779 m Mindwell Dewey Maj VT
Wm.: b 1743 d 3-5-1813 m Elizabeth Anderson Pvt NH
Wm.: b 1725/6 d 7-17-1793 m (2)Eunice Howell Arfr NJ
Wm.: b 1740 d a. 12-18-1820 m Maky — PS VA

HOPKINSON,

Caleb: b 7- -1747 d 2-18-1841 m Sarah Clay Scafford Pvt MA ★
Caleb: b 4-14-1759 d p. 1786 m Peggy Williams Pvt NH
David: b 8-21-1751 d 5-14-1830 m Sarah Kennedy Pvt NH
Ebenezer: b 5-26-1752 d 5-22-1810 m Mary Pillsbury Pvt MA
Francis: b 2-21-1737 d 5-9-1791 m Ann Borden PS SDI NJ
John, Jr.: b 7-27-1740 d 1-24-1817 m Rebekah Tenney Pvt NH
Jonathan: b 2-10-1717 d p. 1786 m Margaret Burbank Pvt NH
Jonathan: bpt 10-23-1748 d 1786 m Lydia Smith Pvt NH

HOPPER,

Albert: b 5-5-1717 d a. 7-27-1795 m Rachel Alje PS NJ
Cornelius: b 2- -1756 d 2-22-1814 m Hannah Rockwell Pvt NY
Garret A.: b 1-28-1755 d 12-18-1830 m Catherine — Pvt Grd NJ
Henry: b p. 1746 d 1821 m (1)Aeltje Hopper (2)Hettie — Pvt NJ
Jacob G.: b c. 1727 d 1814 m (1)Catherine Kejoyne (2)Cornelia Ackerman PS NJ
John: b 1750 d 3-11/12-1852 m (1)Anna Wilson (2)Catherine Piles Pvt NC ★
John: b c. 1750 d 1817 m Barbara — Gnr VA
Peter A.: b 10-13-1749 d 2-16-1816 m Elizabeth VanHorn Pvt NJ

HOPPING, (includes HOPPIN)

Benjamin: b c. 1732 d 1798-1811 m — PS NY
Benjamin: b 5-12-1747 d 11-13-1809 m (1)Anna Rawson (2)Mrs Mary Whitney Capt RI
John: b 1762 d 1839 m Elizabeth Hoppin Pvt MA
John: b 1750 d 7-16-1823 m Betsey Looker Pvt NJ
Nicholas, Sr.: b 12-29-1725 d 5-3-1804 m (1)Susanna Hancock (2)Hannah Lamson Cpl MA
Samuel: b 1743 d 2-13-1824 m (1)Sarah Miller (2)Sarah Frost Pvt NJ
Samuel R.: b 8-21-1757 d 2-6-1800 m Elizabeth Curtis Pvt MA
Silas: b c. 1740 d p. 1781 m — Pvt NJ
Thomas, Jr.: bpt 7-18-1762 d 12-21-1831 m Dorcas Clewly Pvt MA

HOPSON,

Henry: b 1725 d 1810 m Martha Neville Capt VA
John: b c. 1750 d c. 181? m Polly Hopson Ens NC
John: b 4-20-1720 d 9-20-1804 m Anna Margaretha Fey Young PS PA
John: b 1742 d 3-26-1796 m Abiah Hazen Lt VT
Joseph: b 3-10-1752 d 12-20-1815 m Sarah Boyd Lt VA
Linus: b 1736 d p. 1790 m Martha Shattuck Lt CT
Rew: b 8-12-1745 d 6-28-1824 m Sarah Tibbals OrldSgt CT
Samuel, Jr.: b 7-29-1738 d 4-29-1826 m Mamra Hall Ens CT
Simeon: b 10-14-1747 d p. 7-4-1837 m Naomi Moss Sol PS CT

HOPWOOD,

John: b 1745 d a. 6-2-1802 m Hannah Humphreys Aide VA

HORD, (includes HOARD)

David: b 5-13-1757 d 12-1-1807 m (1)Naomi Knapp (2)Polly Briggs Sgt MA
Isaac: b 5-14-1754 d 6-20-1841 m Sarah Shaw Sgt NY
James: b — d 1-3-1815 m Nancy Curd Ens Capt VA
James: b 4-18-1744 d 8-2-1815 m Mary Dismukes Lt VA
Jesse: b 10-31-1749 d 1814 m Antoinette — Capt VA
John: b c. 1744 d c. 1780 m Mary Snyder Capt VA
John: b 1739 d 1808 m (1)Annie Minnie Peyton (2)Margaret Hawkins Capt VA

Mordecai Miller: b — d *a.* 6-29-1789 m Sarah Carr PS VA
Peter: b *c.* 1749 d 1817 m (1)Honora Whitney (2)Rebecca Wilkinson Pvt VA
Samuel: b 2-25-1758 d 6-16-1848 m (1)Lucy Gates (2)Susanna Herrington Pvt NY
Wm.: b 1747 d 8- -1781 m Mary Thorpe Sol VA

HORGER,
Jacob: b 1725 d 1800 m Lovisia Shaumloffel Pvt SC
John: b 11-28-1758 d *p.* 1810 m Rachel — Pvt SC

HORLACHER,
George: b 10-6-1738 d 11-22-1813 m Eva Hillegas Capt PA

HORLBECK,
John: b 2-11-1729 d 4-1-1812 m Elizabeth Geiger Pvt GA

HORMELL,
Henry: b 1-1-1747 d 2-16-1834 m Ellinor Lee Ens PA
Jacob: b 1737 d 1821 m Jane Miller Pvt PA

HORN, (includes HORNE)
Abishai: b *c.* 1750 d 1795 m (1)Mary — (2)Ann Ricks PS NC
Abraham: b 12-31-1757 d 5-22-1826 m Susanna Hay Lt PA ★
Andrew, Jr.: b 1755 d 10-12-1821 m (1)Mary Wentworth (2)Dorcas Nock Pvt NH ★
Benjamin: b 1753 d 5-7-1834 m Ruth Hanson Pvt NH ★
Christopher: b 7-28-1745 d 12-14-1809 m Catherine Watson Pvt PA
Christopher: b 12-8-1752 d 3-9-1837 m Elizabeth — Pvt VA ★
Ephraim: b 1734 d 10-15-1826 m Elizabeth Williamson PS SC
Frederick: b 3-26-1756 d 3-25-1838 m (1)Susanna — (2)Catharine Sinn Pvt PA ★
George: b *a.* 1757 d 7-29-1813 m Sarah — Pvt PA
George: b 10-15-1766 d 3-22-1835 m Elizabeth Todd Pvt PA
George: b 8-6-1756 d 3-14-1827 m Margaret Milhoff PS VA
Hardman: b 6-6-1747 d 10- -1811 m Elizabeth Hough Pvt CS PA
Henry: b 10-15-1758 d 5-8-1845 m Elizabeth Pretzman Pvt PA ★
Henry: b 10-8-1755 d 11-17-1839 m Elizabeth Trone Pvt PA
Henry, Sr.: b 11-24-1716 d 4- -1798 m (1)Ann ⤴ (2)Patience — *Purcell* PS NC
Henry, Jr.: b 1750 d 1839 m Charlotte Gulley 2Maj NC
Henry, Jr.: b 10-6-1744 d *p.* 1783 m Sarah Hilliard Mus NC
Ichabod: b 1757 d *p.* 1818 m (1)Betsey — (2)Eliza — Pvt NH ★
Joab: b 12-30-1753 d 7-28-1840 m Nancy Ricks Pvt NC ★
John: b 1765 d 2-21-1840 m Elizabeth Reed Pvt GA
John: b 9-5-1711 d 1790 m Jemima Hopper Pvt NY
John: b 1751 d 9-26-1826 m Catherine — Pvt PA
Joseph: b 10-29-1748 d 7-17-1829 m (1)Barbara Harrell (2)Winne Bruce PS NC
Nathan: b 5-27-1762 d *p.* 1834 m (1)Nancy Jennings (3)—Dishmun Sgt NC
Peter: b 1735 d 1795 m Mercy Wentworth PS NH
Samuel: b 2-26-1753 d 7-15-1789 m (1)Elizabeth Harrington (2)Mittia Angier Pvt MA
Sebastian: b 6-18-1726 d 6-30-1812 m (1)Anna Rosina (2)Barbara Ahl Pvt PA
Wm.: b 1746 d 9-3-1799 m Martha Lyon Lt PA

HORNBECK, (includes HOORNBECK)
Abraham: b 1758 d 11-14-1834 m Hannah Cleaver Pvt VA ★
Abraham: b 10-21-1761 d 1-25-1833 m (1)Eliza Trumbo (2)Mrs Betsy Mappin Bracken Sol VA
Benjamin: b 5-29-1739 d *p.* 1792 m Rebecca Wells Pvt NY
Benjamin: b 1754 d 4-6-1827 m (1) — VanScoy (2)Lydia Currence Sgt VA
Elisha: bpt 2-2-1735 d *p.* 1790 m Catrina Hardenburg PS CS NY
Isaac: b 1-27-1751 d 1805 m Ariantje Low Pvt NY
Jacob: b 4-2-1753 d 6-19-1796 m Sara VanWaggenen Capt NY
Johannes: b 8-26-1739 d 7-21-1811 m Maria Vernoy Pvt NY
Michael: b *c.* 1745 d *p.* 1787 m — Pvt VA
Philip: b 10-9-1747 d 3-22-1817 m Maria Schoonmaker 1Lt NY

HORNBERGER,
Conrad: b *a.* 1730 d 1796 m Catherine Huffert Pvt PA

HORNBLOWER,
Josiah: b 2-23-1729 d 1-21-1809 m Elizabeth Kingsland PS NJ

HORNEY,
John: b 3-1-1749 d 7-22-1821 m Mary Chipman Pvt MD
Wm.: b *c.* 1750/1 d 1829 m Hannah Chipman Pvt MD

HORNING,
Adam: b *c.* 1760 d *p.* 2-22-1789 m Dorothy VanAlstine Pvt NY
Dederick: b *c.* 1730 d *a.* 4-19-1827 m Maria Margaretta Kraus Lt NY
George: b 10-18-1765 d 4- -1843 m Maria Mareness Pvt NY

HORNOR, (includes HARNAR, HERNER, HORNER)
Abraham: b — d *a.* 7-8-1830 m Elizabeth — Pvt PA
Andrew: b 4-19-1743 d 10-10-1821 m (1) — Klick (2)M. Barbara Klick Pvt PA
Christian: b *c.* 1729 d 1795 m Barbara Krebs Pvt PA
David: b 1739 d *p.* 1785 m Mary Love 1Lt PA

Gustavus Brown: b 2-28-1761 d 1-24-1815 m Frances Harrison Scott SrgnMte VA
Hugh: b 10-20-1743 d 4-15-1806 m Elizabeth Wilson Sol PA
Jacob: b 4-2-1755 d 11-8-1837 m Elizabeth Baum Pvt PA
James: b 1-24-1759 d 5-25-1824 m Jean Walker PS PA
John: b 10-27-1750 d 3-19-1819 m Patty Richards PS NJ
John: b *c.* 1740 d *p.* 3-29-1814 m Susanna — Pvt PA
John: b 10-1-1747 d 9-15-1806 m Mary Darrah Pvt PA
Nathan: b 3-25-1729 d 10- -1799 m Mrs Jane Wigfield PS MD
Nicholas: b 3-26-1732 d 1-15-1814 m Barbara — Sol PA
Samuel: b *c.* 1750 d *c.* 1810 m Margaret — Pvt NJ
Solomon: b 11-10-1757 d 9-4-1839 m (1)Elizabeth — (2)Elizabeth Johanna John Cpl PA
Thomas: b 1749 d 1825 m Jane Patterson Ens PA
Timothy: b *c.* 1744 d 1808 m Hannah — Pvt NJ
Wm.: b 10-30-1746 d *p.* 4-15-1823 m Elizabeth Aldridge PS NC

HORRELL, (includes HORRALL)
James: b *c.* 1757 d 10- -1829 m Elsie — Capt PA
John: b 5-20-1762 d 10-13-1805 m Sarah Likens Capt PA
Wm.: b 1757 d 1851 m (1)Priscilla Calvert Houghton (2)Elinor Wallace Pvt VA ★

HORSEWELL,
Philip: b 11-28-1754 d 7-22-1838 m Mercy West Pvt RI ★

HORSEY,
John: b 1750 d *a.* 12-13-1810 m Amelia Leatherbury Lt MD
Thomas: b 1743 d 6-19-1789 m Eunice Hawkins Capt CT

HORSLEY,
Valentine: b 1-18-1758 d 9-18-1843 m Sarah Kendrick Sol GA
Wm.: b 1745 d 1791 m Martha Megginson Lt VA

HORSOM, (includes HERSOM)
Jacob: b 2-5-1736 d 8-8-1823 m (1)Lydia Door (2)Hannah — Pvt NH ★
John: b 1749 d 5-6-1833 m Margaret Frost CS MA

HORT,
Wm.: b 1-14-1749 d 1-18-1826 m (1)Alice Gibbes (2)Catherine Simons Sol SC

HORTER,
Jacob: b *c.* 1735 d 8-16-1806 m Maria Magdalena Rausch Pvt PA

HORTH,
Francis: b 1-23-1757 d 8-6-1844 m (1)Lucy Dickson (2)Anna Albro Sgt MA VT ★

HORTON, (includes HAUGHTON)
Aaron: b 11-12-1758 d 10-25-1832 m Sarah Harris Pvt MA
Abel: b 7-14-1756 d 1842 m Seviah Hopkins Sgt RI ★
Abraham: b 5-9-1759 d 12-11-1842 m Dithy — Pvt NC ★
Adonijah: b 12-19-1755 d 2-24-1852 m (1)Susanna Horton (2)Olive Rugg Pvt MA
Barnabas: b 1742 d 10-16-1819 m Abigail Dickerson PS NY
Barnet: b 5-6-1744 d *p.* 1834 m Mehitabel Cole Pvt MA
Benjamin: b 4-2-1755 d *p.* 2-18-1830 m (1)Mehitabel Osborn (2)Harmony Reeves Pvt NY
Caleb Paulding: b 9-21-1739 d 4-18-1831 m Jane Martine 2Lt NY
Comfort: b 3-29-1743 d 6-14-1805 m Joanna Wood Sgt MA
Cushing: b 5-10-1757 d 3-17-1811 m Abigail Snow Smn MA
Daniel: b 7-30-1749/50 d *p.* 1790 m Mary Goff Sgt MA
Daniel: b 9-13-1744 d 12-9-1807 m Anna French Ens NY
Daniel: b 4-23-1692 d 12-10-1777 m Esther Lane PS NY
David: b 9-2-1750 d 3-10-1843 m Olive Skellinger 1Sgt NJ ★
David, Jr.: b 12-18-1744 d 5-4-1813 m (1)Theodocia Allen (2)Temperance Owens Pvt NY
David: b 1751 d 1808 m Mary Case 2Lt NY
David: b *c.* 1724 d 1784 m Ann — PS NC
Edward: b *c.* 1757 d 1818 m (1)Deborah Gregory (2)Abigail Walton PS NC
Elijah: b 6-19-1724 d 10-7-1799 m Lydia Sweazy CS NJ
Elijah: b 8-7-1739 d 8-14-1821 m Jemima Curris Pvt PA
Elisha: b 1-2-1745 d 6-2-1826 m Ruth Bishop Case Pvt CT
George: b 3-23-1741 d 10-28-1835 m Else Shoemaker Pvt NY
Gilbert: b 4-20-1758 d 8-26-1833 m Sarah — Pvt NY
Henry: b 12- -1766 d 12-8-1845 m Lavina Cook Pvt CT ★
Hezekiah, Jr.: b *c.* 1740 d *p.* 1800 m — Sol VT
Isaac: b 4- -1759 d 1840 m Lovisa Brown Pvt MA
Israel, Jr.: b 9-23-1756 d 7-22-1813 m Anna VanDeVort Pvt NY
James: b 7-10-1741 d 8-10-1833 m Freelove Pierce Lt MA ★
Jason: b 12-18-1758 d 12-28-1837 m Mary Terry Pvt NY ★
Jeremiah: b 1730 d *a.* 9-20-1796 m Mary Sylvia — PS NC
Jesse: b 1757 d 6-24-1838 m (1)Nancy Potter (2)Caroline M. Wheeler Pvt MA
John: b 9-28-1735/6 d 5-14-1799 m Mary Beecher Pvt CT
John: b 2-26-1752 d 4-20-1810 m Mary DeLaMontaigne Lt NJ
John: b 7-30-1763 d 4-28-1848 m Deborah Terry Pvt NY
Jonathan: b 4-3-1737 d 8-11-1827 m (1)Gertrude Purdy (2)Ann Secor Maj NY
Jonathan: b *c.* 1741 d 1817 m (1)Deborah Pratt (2)Deborah Norcom PS NC

HORTON, contd.

Jonathan Paulding: b 1-6-1711 d 3-31-1795 m Margaret — Capt NY

Joseph: b 6-12-1749 d 5-13-1841 m (1)Hannah Ross (2)Mary Dean Pvt MA

Joseph: b 8-24-1759 d 6- -1813 m Mary Beedle Ens NY

Joseph: b 1759 d 6-11-1833 m (1)Susannah — (2)Mary Jenkins Pvt VA ★

Joseph Lee: b 4-27-1765 d 7-10-1831 m Hannah Todd Pvt NY

Joshua: b 11-27-1742 d 3-11-1814 m Anna Dyer PS ME

Joshua: b 9-22-1751 d 11-11-1811 m (1)Phebe Swartout (2)Sarah Colgrove Pvt NY

Jotham, Jr.: b 7-30-1753 d p. 2-24-1830 m Grizzell Bowen Pvt MA

Jotham: bpt 7-16-1749 d 1795 m Sarah Francis Capt RI

Lemuel: b 1761 d 10- -1851 m Hannah Holt Sgt MA

Michael: b 5-5-1736 d p. 1790 m Elizabeth Esselstyn Capt NY

Nathan: b 2-25-1757 d 7-22-1824 m Elizabeth Eagles Capt NJ W★

Nathaniel: b 2-28-1740 d 8-13-1824 m Susanna Robinson Capt NJ

Nehemiah: b 1759 d 1819 m Experience Vail PS VT

Prosser: b 1756 d 3- -1823 m Sarah — Pvt GA

Samuel: b 4-11-1757 d 11-22-1822 m Hannah Morris Cpl CT

Samuel: b 8-21-1716 d 1-10-1800 m Elizabeth — Pvt CT

Silas: b 12-25-1730 d 3-10-1820 m Margaret Bull Pvt NY

Silas, Sr.: b 1730 d p. 1790 m Experience Vail PS NY

Silas, Jr.: b 8-24-1756 d 12-25-1816 m Mary Danes PS NY

Simeon: b c. 1730 d p. 1790 m Mary Martin Pvt MA

Solomon: b 1-15-1742/3 d 6-27-1804 m Hannah Talbot Sgt MA

Stephen: b 5-24-1753 d 7-12-1825 m Submit Henshaw Sgt MA

Stephen: b 4-30-1731 d 12-7-1814 m (1)Sarah Owens (2)Elizabeth Frost Pvt NY

Thomas: b 1728 d 1-30-1778 m Susanna Conklin Capt PS NY

Thomas: b 6-6-1745 d 4-6-1825 m (1)Hannah Hix (2)Esther Haskell Sgt NY

Thomas, Sr.: b c. 1724 d p. 5-19-1821 m Mary Knapp Pvt NY

Thomas, Jr.: b 10-10-1763 d 2-17-1841 m Hepzibah Taylor Pvt NY ★

Thomas: b c. 1752 d 7-26-1841 m (2)Orander Bush Sgt Maj VA SC ★

Valentine: b 1750 d 7-1-1811 m Anna Hix Pvt MA

Wm.: b 4-21-1745 d p. 1797 m Content Brayton Pvt MA

Wm.: b 7-16-1762 d 4-4-1842 m Mary Wright Sgt NY VT ★

Wm.: b 1-10-1743 d 1-28-1831 m Elizabeth Covert Pvt NY

Wm.: b 12-25-1757 d p. 1809 m (1)Hannah Crossman (2)Elizabeth Masters Pvt NY

Wm.: b c. 1740 d 2- -1820 m Amy — Sol NC

Wm.: b a. 1750 d a. 7-18-1834 m Elizabeth — PS SC

Wm.: b 5-8-1730 d 1-5-1817 m Maggie Craven Pvt VA

Zephaniah: b 11-13-1760 d 4-5-1844 m Jane McCurry Pvt NJ ★

HOSACK, (includes HOSICK)

David: b c. 1750 d p. 12- -1814 m Janet Morrison Capt PA

Wm.: b 1753 d 5-3-1819 m Elizabeth Hall Pvt VA ★

HOSBROOK,

John: b a. 1760 d 1798 m Lydia Kitchel Sgt NJ

HOSCH,

Jacob: b — d p. 9-5-1818 m Rachel — Pvt PA

HOSE,

Jacob: b 1736 d 1801 m Mary Boone Sgt PA

HOSFORD, (includes HORSFORD)

Aaron: b 12-25-1748 d 7-19-1818 m Lucy Strong Pvt VT

Daniel: b 11-8-1723 d 1788 m Martha Dibble Adj MA

Elihu: b 6-2-1750 d p. 1790 m Abigail Chamberlain Sgt VT

Jeremiah, Sr.: b 9-14-1736 d 5-18-1820 m Lucy Burnham Pvt PS CT

Jeremiah, Jr.: b 9-12-1760 d 2-9-1832 m Hannah Dean Pvt CT

John: b 9-16-1740 d 2-8-1812 m Naomi Loomis Pvt CT

Joseph, Jr.: b 12-7-1761 d 1-5-1847 m Mary Williams Pvt NY ★

Obadiah: b 1-26-1724 d 7-11-1783 m Mary Buell LCol CT

Samuel: b 10-29-1762 d 2-3-1808 m Anna Densmore Pvt CT

Wm., Sr.: b 7-21-1731 d p. 1791 m Esther Smedley Pvt MA

HOSHAL,

Jesse: b a. 1759 d 7-15-1830 m Mary Hurst Pvt MD ★

Michael: b 1739 d p. 7-3-1790 m (1)Ruhamah — (2)Ruth — (3)Rachel Peck PS NJ

HOSIER,

Samuel: b c. 1755 d a. 5-2-1834 m — Sol VA

HOSKINSON,

Basil: b 3-29-1752 d 9-9-1834 m Eleanor Downs Pvt VA ★

Isaiah: b 12-27-1749 d 8-26-1836 m (1)Rachel DeMoss (2)Hannah Winchel Pvt VA ★

Josiah: b 1756 d 2-12-1836 m Margaret Summers Sgt Maj MD ★

Josiah: b 1759 d 1- -1836 m (2)Alcy Cutsinger Sgt PS MD

HOSLEY,

David: b 1743 d 7-5-1802 m Lucile Hosley Sgt MA

James: b 1-19-1734 d 4-19-1809 m Sarah Shedd Capt MA

Jonathan Jewett: b 3-27-1759 d p. 1810 m Abagail Gibbs Pvt MA

Joshua: b 12-8-1753 d 2-17-1830 m Sarah Gilson Pvt MA

HOSMER,

Aaron: b 7-26-1729 8-3-1803 m Susanna Chamberlin Pvt NH

Abel: b 3-27-1747 d 11-3-1832 m Lucy Lee Pvt MA

Amos: b 6-28-1734 d 11-2-1810 m Lucy Merriam Lt MA

Amos: b 11-9-1759 d 1-18-1831 m Sybil Parker Pvt MA

Ashbel: b 4-30-1758 d 4-1-1812 m Mary Belden Cpl CT ★

Daniel: b 1749 d 4-28-1800 m Mary Belding MM CT

Daniel: b 1-28-1746 d p. 8-10-1832 m Hannah Baker Cpl MA ★

Elijah: b 3-22-1749 d 5-31-1828 m Sarah Gardner MM MA

Ephraim: b 11-22-1722 d 3-17-1811 m Sarah Jones Pvt MA

Graves: b 2-25-1756 d 1-17-1838 m Amy Congdon Cpl Mid CT ★

James: b 12- -1761 d 8- -1835 m Rhoda Eastman Pvt MA

John: b 6-17-1752 d 2-16-1836 m Mary Vassal Prescott Pvt MA

John: b 5-10-1758 d 9-17-1839 m Anna Fosgate Pvt MA ★

Jonas: b 10-24-1758 d 2-1-1840 m (1)Elizabeth Willard (2)Mrs Abigail Sparhawk Pvt MA

Jonathan: b 8-28-1734 d 7-10-1822 m Submit Hunt Sgt MA

Joseph: b 10-24-1749 d 5-21-1823 m (1)Jerusha Prior (2)Betsey Prior (3)Miriam Newberry Ord CT

Joseph: b 12-25-1735 d 1-14-1821 m Lucy Barnes Maj MA

Joseph: b 12-27-1735 d 1805 m Rhoda Eastman Lt MA

Samuel: b 5-12-1734 d 1-22-1796 m Ann Parlin 2Lt MA

Samuel: b 9-11-1761 d 1-27-1848 m Sarah Hosmer Pvt MA

Simeon: b 5-27-1754 d 1831 m Lucretia Steele Sgt CT

Stephen: b 2-1-1739/40 d 3-28-1807 m Sarah Davies Cpl MA

Stephen: b 11-13-1709 d 2-4-1782 m Millicent Wood Capt MA

Thomas: b 2-7-1703 d 1-7-1787 m Prudence (Hosmer) PS MA

Timothy: b 9- -1745 d 11-29-1815 m Elizabeth Smith Dr CT

Titus: b 1736 d 8-4-1780 m Lydia Lord PS CT

Wm.: b 12-15-1745 d 7-18-1839 m Elizabeth Barker PS CT

Wm.: b 10-19-1729 d 3-26-1802 m Anna Heald Pvt MA

HOSTERMAN,

Jacob, Jr.: b 10-14-1749 d 2-5-1812 m Christina — Pvt PA

Peter: b 9-27-1746 d 1-27-1805 m Elizabeth — Col PA

HOSTETLER,

Joseph: b c. 8- -1742 d a. 8-24-1812 m (1)Anna Blank (2)Barbara Kauffman Pvt PA

Nicholas: b 1725 d 12-19-1795 m Anna Hostetler Pvt PA

HOSTETTER, (includes HOCHSTEDLER, HOFSTALER, HOOFSTATTER, HOOFSTITLER, HOSTETER, HUFFSTUTTER)

George: b 1763 d p. 9-4-1843 m Anna — Pvt NC

Henry: b 8-23-1760 d p. 1820 m Anna Maria Sherman 1Lt PA

Henry: b 11-27-1756 d 6-8-1822 m Margaret — Pvt PA

Jacob: b 9- -1745 d — 1826 m Mary Metzler Pvt PA

John: b 1733 d 3- -1805 m (1)Catherine Hertzler (2)Anna Schrock Pvt PA

Ulrich: b c. 1748 d 1839 m Catherine — Ens PA

Ulrich: b 1749 d 2-26-1840 m — Ens PA

Ulrich: b c. 1752 d p. 9-28-1801 m (1)Catherine — (2)Mary Baxter Pvt PA

HOTCHKIN,

Beriah: b 3-27-1752 d 2-17-1829 m Thankful Dickinson Pvt CT

HOTCHKISS,

Ambrose: b 2-16-1762 d 4-10-1841 m Sallie Barnard Pvt CT ★

Amos: b 11-24-1751 d 5-13-1820 m Abigail Scott Lt Capt CT

Amos: b 1-2-1739 d p. 1801 m Desire Dowd Pvt CT

Asahel: b 1760 d 1841 m (1)Sarah Williams (2)Phebe Merriman Pvt CT

Caleb: b 6-6-1712 d 7-5-1779 m Phebe Atwater Pvt CT

Daniel: b c. 1750 d p. 1790 m Lucia Beecher Pvt CT

Eben: b 12-13-1757 d 7-26-1853 m Mary Sanford Pvt CT ★

Eli: b 9- -1759 d 5-13-1831 m Eunice Atwater Sol CT

Eliphalet: b 11-1-1727 d 7-5-1803 m Comfort Harger CS CT

Elisha: b 4-4-1762 d — m Lydia Lee Pvt CT

Enos: b 5-13-1731 d p. 1781 m Elizabeth Shepard Pvt CT

Ezekiel: b 3-14-1726 d 7-5-1779 m Hannah Alling Pvt CT

Gideon: b 12-5-1716 d 9-3-1807 m (1)Anna Brockett (2)Mabel Stiles PS CT

Harris: b 5-24-1763 d 11-21-1854 m Lucy Carey Smn Pvt CT ★

Henry, Sr.: b 4-1-1715 d 6-9-1799 m (1)Sarah Benham (2)Mrs Lydia Ives PS CS CT

Henry, Jr.: b 9-2-1737 d 3-10-1821 m Esther Smith PS CT

Ira: b 5-6-1758 d 3- -1826 m (1)Mary Rose (2)Abigail Frisbie Pvt CT

Isaac: b 1756 d 8-24-1835 m Ann Spinning Pvt CT

Isaac: b 1758 d 5-11-1828 m Elizabeth Clark Pvt CT

Israel: b 5-30-1767 d 2-21-1840 m Martha Royce Pvt CT

Jared: b 2-27-1761 d 8-21-1838 m Elizabeth Knight Pvt CT

Jason: b 5-13-1759 d 11-19-1816 m Ursula Hull Pvt CT

Jesse: b 1738 d 9-29-1776 m Charity Mallory Pvt CT

John: b 11-12-1731 d 7-5-1779 m Susannah Jones Pvt CT

Jonah: b 6-12-1749 d 11-11-1811 m Elizabeth Atwater Pvt CT

Joseph: b 2-10-1736 d 1-21-1823 m Hannah Atwater Sol CT

Joseph: b 7-31-1756 d 5-2-1825 m Temperance Andrews Pvt CT

Josiah, Jr.: b 12-26-1742 d 7-4-1812 m Sarah Perkins Pvt CT

Ladwick, Sr.: b 1-18-1723 d 3-7-1803 m (1)Molly North (2)Mercy Hills (3)Lydia Hart Capt CT

Ladwick, Jr.: b 5-25-1752 d 12-1-1823 m Martha Lee Pvt CT

Lemuel: b 11-8-1741 d 2-18-1802 m Penelope Mather Capt CT
Lent, Jr.: b 8-10-1737 d 1802 m Parthenia Murray 2Lt CT
Lent, Jr.: b 9-2-1753 d 12-2-1805 m Sarah Ball Ens CT
Leverett: b 10-6-1762 d 10-3-1826 m Sarah Burritt Sol CT
Levi: b 5-2-1754 d 9-11-1831 m (1)Phebe Hitchcock (2)Betsy — (3)Sarah — (4)Susannah — Lt CT ★
Robert: b 4-4-1754 d 5-21-1829 m (1)Hannah Hotchkiss (2)Mrs Lucy Matthews (3)Mrs Sarah Francis Pvt CT
Roswell: b 7-24-1762 d 12-28-1845 m Margaret Harper Sgt CT ★
Samuel: b 10-22-1755 d 3-19-1843 m Rachel Upson Pvt CT
Stephen: b 12-1-1718 d 5-16-1807 m (1)Thankful Cook (2)Ann Johnson (3)Thankful Brooks PS CT
Stephen, Jr.: b 7-15-1754 d 2-13-180? m Mary Upson Lt CT
Stephen: b 10-31-1761 d 11-4-1847 m Hannah Brown Pvt CT
Titus: b 6-27-1755 d 1-29-1835 m Rachel Gurnsey 2Lt CT ★
Truman: b 6-18-1760 d 5-30-1833 m Ruth Frost Pvt CT ★
Wait: b 11-13-1733 d 1799 m Deborah Alcott Pvt CT

HOTT, (includes LE HOTTE)
Louis: b 4-16-1762 d 1823 m Rebecca Ann Sledd Smn VA

HOTTEL, (includes HUDDLE)
George: b 1728 d 1787 m — PS Pvt VA
Jacob: b 6-20-1752 d 8- -1820 m Mary Dorothea Rinker Pvt MD
Joseph: b c. 1761 d 1814 m Barbara Dull Pvt VA

HOTTENSTEIN, (includes HORTENSTINE)
David: b 2-8-1734 d 5-6-1802 m (1)Sarah Herbein (2)Catherine — Lt PA
Jacob: b c. 1735 d p. 6-7-1803 m Catherine Widener Sol PA
Wm.: bpt 8-15-1730 d 1784 m (1)Susanna — (2)Sarah Hoch CMman PA

HOTZENPELLER,
Peter: b c. 1745 d 1782 m Anna — Pvt VA

HOUCHINGS, (includes HOUCHINS)
Bernard: b 1755 d p. 1819 m Elizabeth Randolph Pvt VA ★
Edward: b 2-28-1760 d 4-14-1846 m Nancy Clements Pvt VA ★
Edward: b c. 1756 d p. 1799 m — Pvt VA
Francis, Jr.: b 2-17-1764 d p. 3-30-1843 m Mary Jones Sol VA
John: b c. 1725 d p. 1784 m Martha Orford CS VA
John: b — d p. 7-23-1810 m Sarah Quarles Sol VA
John: b 1748 d p. 12-19-1837 m Patsey — Pvt VA

HOUCK, (includes HAUK, HOUK, HOUKS)
Barnet: b 1747 d 1835 m Barbara Wolfe Cpl PA
George Michael: b 1757/8 d 1-12-1845 m Margaret Funck Pvt MD
Henrick: b 5-9-1762 d 9-14-1822 m Catherine Kniskern Pvt NY
Jacob: b 1750 d 1823 m Magdalene — Sgt PA
John: b a. 1753 d 1819 m Catherine Kemp PS MD
John: b 1750 d a. 11-25-1819 m Christina Storg Pvt PA
Mathias: b 1759 d 1831 m Susan Morgenstein Pvt MD
Peter: b 10-1-1737 d 11-7-1808 m Christina Enders Pvt NY
Philip: b 1740 d 1805 m Barbara Fessler Pvt PA
Wm.: b 1763 d 1853 m Ellen McClanskey Pvt PA

HOUGENDOBLER, (includes HOGENTOGLER)
Isaac: b 8-18-1754 d 1822 m Elizabeth Peters Pvt PA
John: b 1745 d 1820 m Catharine Boyer Pvt PA
Joseph: b 12-20-1756 d 9-4-1830 m Eve Straub Pvt PA
Nicholas: b c. 1748 d p. 1790 m Elizabeth Stoneking Pvt PA

HOUGH, (includes HUFF)
Azel: b 7-5-1761 d 3-11-1849 m (1)Mary Edgerton (2)Lusena Fann Pvt CT
Bernard: b 1763 d p. 1790 m — Pvt VA ★
Caleb: b 2-13-1757 d 1828 m Rebecca Andrews Pvt CT
Daniel: b 1-12-1752 d 9-11-1820 m Lydia Edgerton Pvt NH
Daniel: b a. 1747 d p. 10-23-1795 m Southy — PS VA
David: b 1-27-1724 d 7-8-1798 m (1)Desire Clark (2)Jemima Baldwin Capt CT
David: b 3-13-1753 d 1828 m Abigail Huntington PS NH
Ebenezer: b c. 12-22-1726 d 10-27-1782 m (1)Lydia Buell (2)Mrs Abigail Bacon Plumb PS CT
Elijah: b 1-29-1748 d 1-28-1828 m Mary Ives Pvt MA ★
Elisha: b c. 1760 d 1810 m Rachel Iams Pvt VA
Hezekiah: b 1737 d 1807 m Mary Ingram PS CS NC
Isaac: b 11-15-1726 d 4-13-1786 m Edith Hart Pvt PA
Jabez, Jr.: b 5-26-1760 d 2-20-1831 m Eunice Clement Pvt CT W★
Jacob: b 1751 d 7-15-1831 m Chatherine Smeltzer Pvt PA
Jacob: b c. 1747 d p. 3-28-1803 m Charlotte Smith Pvt PA
James: b 7-31-1743 d 9-14-1799 m Deborah Meriam Rice Lt CT
James: b a. 1757 d p. 1-21-1825 m (1)Mary — (2)Tabitha — PS VA
Joel: b 1-4-1757 d 9-9-1843 m (1)Sarah Rice (2)Thankful Rice (3)Mrs Munson Pvt CT ★
John: b 3-2-1761 d 3-20-1847 m Elizabeth Newton Pvt Sgt NC ★
John: b 1750 d 1816 m Sarah — PS NC
John: b 1-19-1758 d 3-14-1843 m Mary Corder Pvt VA
John: b 1763 d 5-10-1840 m (1) — DeWeiss (2) — Ferguson (3)Elizabeth Guilliams Pvt VA ★
John: b 1-30-1720/1 d p. 2-21-1797 m Sarah Janney Sgt VA
Joseph: b 1758 d 1818 m Elizabeth Trask Pvt MA

Joseph: b c. 1751 d p. 1806 m (1) — McLendon (2)Sara Bivens PS SC
Justice: b 7-10-1762 d 4-27-1829 m Sarah Whitney Pvt MA
Nicholas: b 1750 d p. 1832 m Elizabeth — Pvt NJ ★
Peter: b 3-10-1756 d 184? m Abigail Bucaw MM NY
Philip: b — d p. 7-25-1822 m Rachel — PS VA
Richard: b 5-13-1757 d 7-30-1843 m Elizabeth — Pvt NJ ★
Richard: b 1760 d 2-25-1835 m Pamelia Walton Pvt PA
Samuel: b 4-26-1754 d p. 1818 m Thankful Hough Pvt CT ★
Samuel: b c. 1750 d p. 1822 m — Pvt VA
Thomas: b 2-22-1732 d 1839 m Elizabeth Isham Pvt VA
Thomas: b 10-1-1749 d 12-4-1815 m Rebecca Ives PS MA
Walter: b 12-15-1753 d 3-15-1818 m Martha Lockwood Dr CT
Wm.: b a. 1750 d 4-16-1801 m Prudence Atwell Pvt CT
Wm.: b — d p. 12-13-1792 m Mary — PS NC
Wm.: b 7-23-1754 d 1838 m Rachel Bean OrdlSgt VA
Wm.: b 11-24-1744 d 2-18-1815 m Eleanor Hite Pvt VA

HOUGHHAM,
Moses: b c. 1747 d c. 1845 m Catherine Pitts PS MD

HOUGHTALING, (includes HOGHTAILING, HOGHTELING, HOOTELING)
Abraham: b 10-4-1756 d 1-15-1821 m Jennie Counover Pvt NY
Abraham: b 1753 d p. 1798 m Catherine Brewer Pvt NY
David: b c. 1738 d p. 1790 m Hilletze VanDerZee 1Lt NY
Garret: bpt 5-26-1751 d p. 11-27-1816 m Annajte Osterhout Pvt NY
Jeremiah: b 4-28-1740 d 10-15-1825 m Margaret DeLa Martre Pvt NY
Johannes: b 4-16-1721 d 2-18-1802 m Geertruy Ploeg Pvt PS NY
John: b 11-16-1753 d 10-8-1793 m Anna Margritta Roosa Pvt NY
John: b 1755 d 1814 m Hannah — Pvt NY
John: b 3-18-1757 d 3-31-1816 m (2)Jane Burhans Pvt NY
Storm VanDerZee: b 1758 d 1-14-1843 m Miss Terwilliger Pvt NY
Teunis: bpt 6-30-1723 d 1788 m Elizabeth Beekman PS NY
Thomas: b 11-14-1731 d 2-21-1824 m Elizabeth Whitbeck Capt NY
Thomas: b 10-1-1749 d 4-20-1817 m Elizabeth Van Steenburgh Sgt NY

HOUGHTON,
Aaron: b 4-15-1761 d 10-8-1835 m Elizabeth Sexton Pvt NJ ★
Abel: b 1756 d 4-19-1823 m Rebecca Willard Pvt MA
Abiathar: b 1-21-1725 d 1777 m Melliasant Carter Pvt MA
Abijah: b: 9-23-1723 d 1-23-1802 m Alice Joslin Pvt MA
Abijah, Jr.: b 1747 d 12-15-1831 m Mary Sawyer Pvt MA ★
Abram: b 11-27-1725 d 3-7-1813 m Sarah Divol Pvt VT MA
Asa: b 1-28-1727 d 3-14-1808 m Elizabeth Rand PS MA
Benjamin: b 9-5-1739 d 7-31-1802 m Zervia Moore Capt MA
Darius: b 4-4-1754 d 8- 23-1830 m Sybel Eastman Sgt NH ★
Edward: b c. 1735 d 9-29-1820 m Sarah Smith Cpl NH
Edward: b 12-25-1730 d 7-30-1782 m Lucretia Richardson Pvt NY
Elijah: b 6-18-1728 d 7-7-1810 m (1)Katherine Sparhawk (2)Mary Allen Pvt MA
Elijah: b 1729 d 2-17-1822 m Mary Andrews Pvt MA
Elijah: b 6-2-1739 d 7-20-1819 m Mercy Whitney Pvt MA
Elisha: b 7-20-1746 d 7-7-1810 m — MM MA
Israel: b 12-13-1723 d 4-21-1801 m Alice Campbell Pvt NH
Jacob: b 1-1-1748 d 3-20-1790 m Phebe Golden Capt NJ
James: b 9-4-1728 d p. 1777 m Phebe Holt Pvt CT
James: b 1755 d 12-1-1842 m Hannah Russell Pvt NH
James: b c. 1729 d 1797 m Sallie Burke Pvt NC
James: b 11-18-1764 d 2-27-1843 m Lois Farr Cpl VT
Joab: b 7-10-1725 d 10-17-1798 m Catherine Runyon LCol NJ
Joab, Jr.: b 1756 d 1-17-1844 m (1)Phoebe — (2)Abigail Wood Fif NJ
John: b 6-14-1738 d 8-8-1819 m Esther Tarbell Sgt 1Lt MA
John: b 9-14-1739 d 1807 m Keziah Ross Pvt MA
Jonas: b 1728 d 11-21-1801 m (1)Rebecca Nichols (2)Lucy Johnson Pvt MA
Jonathan, Sr.: b 11-7-1737 d 12- -1829 m Susannah Moore Capt MA
Jonathan: b 2-3-1761 d 1-11-1840 m (1)Rachael Hale (2)Mary Bryant Pvt MA
Jonathan: b 3-8-1752 d 8-30-1831 m Joanna Burgh Pvt VT
Josiah: b 1723 d 1808 m (1)Bethesda Brabrook (2)Grace Whitney (3)Abigail Godfrey Pvt MA
Nathaniel: b 2-8-1753 d 4-26-1821 m Annah Stone Pvt MA ★
Nehemiah: b 3-23-1738 d 11-23-1789 m Eunice Curtiss Capt PS NH
Ralph: b 2-20-1729 d 1-16-1809 m Ruth Wadsworth 1Lt MA
Rufus: b 1764 d 7-25-1814 m Mary Gleason Pvt MA
Samuel: b 9- -1759 d 8-24-1819 m Sarah Cooke Pvt MA W★
Seth: b 3-13-1757 d 5-4-1815 m Sarah Wheeler Pvt MA
Silas: b 10-7-1742 d 6-9-1797 m Sarah Gregory 2Lt MA
Simon: b 5-16-1737 d 3-25-1814 m Martha Stearns Pvt MA
Wm.: b 9-25-1757 d 6-28-1835 m Margaret Saxton Pvt NJ ★
Zarah: b 7-26-1751 d 10-6-1829 m Eleanor Derby Pvt MA

HOUNSHELL,
John: b 11-5-1756 d 8-11-1827 m Susanna — Pvt VA

HOUSE, (HAUSE)
Andrew: b 12-1-1747/8 d 8-15-1843 m Hannah Snapp Pvt Spy PA
Benjamin: b 8-27-1757 d 9-5-1846 m (1)Martha Woodbridge (2)Submit West Pvt CT ★

HOUSE, contd.

Caleb: b 1-18-1738 d *a.* 1790 m Elizabeth Randall Pvt MA
Christian: b *c.* 1748 d 10-11-1809 m Christina Rechtmagerin Capt NY
Dudley: b — d *p.* 8-23-1816 m Sarah — Pvt NC
Eleazar: b 8-25-1760 d 10-27-1833 m Sibbyl Wright Pvt CT
Eleazar: b — d *p.* 8-27-1776 m — Capt CT
Elias: b 6-3-1708 d 5-14-1791 m Maria Louchs Pvt NY
George: b 1754 d 9-8-1826 m Mary Talcott Cpl CT ★
George: b 1750 d *a.* 2-22-1821 m Elizabeth — Pvt PA ★
Henry: b 4-7-1765 d 6-5-1834 m Nancy House Pvt NY ★
Jacob: bpt 3-11-1716 d *p.* 1782 m Maria Pruyn Pvt NY
Job: bpt 4-8-1753 d *p.* 1784 m Sarah Norton Pvt MA
Joel: b 8-8-1761/2 d 10-29-1835 m Lois Risley Pvt CT ★
John: b 1757 d 11-14-1798 m Esther Hooker Sol CT W ★
John: b 5-2-1741 d 7-4-1831 m Jane — Lt MA
John: b 1744 d 2-17-1825 m Susannah Peters Capt NH
John: b *a.* 1760 d *p.* 1822 m (1)Lena VanSlyke (2)Rhoda — Pvt NY
John: b 12-27-1733 d 12-9-1808 m Mary G. — 2Lt PA
John: b 6-23-1760 d 3-10-1838 m Joanna Pridden Pvt PA
John Michael: b 1751 d 1793 m Anna Maria Ommuth Pvt PA
John Valentine: b 1738 d 1825/6 m — Harbison 2Lt MD
Jonathan: b 1748 d 10-7-1804 m Mary Smith Pvt NY
Lazarus: b 4-14-1748 d *p.* 1817 m Rebecca Ripley Pvt CT
Nathaniel: bpt 4-2-1758 d *p.* 1823 m Lillis Palmer Pvt MA ★
Nathaniel: b 1743 d 8-1-1824 m Heletia Hasbrouck Capt NY
Nicholas: b 1757 d 7-1-1829 m Catherine Spoon Pvt PS NY W★
Peter: b *c.* 1740 d 10-19-1780 m Maria — Sgt NY
Peter: b *c.* 1750 d *p.* 7-19-1819 m (1)Mary Boyer (2)Hannah — Cpl PA
Reuben: b 1760 d — Mary Chandler Lt SC
Rynard, Jr.: b 1-2-1756 d 9-27-1822 m Fanny Smith Pvt NY
Samuel: b *c.* 1760 d *a.* 6-21-1828 m Cassandra Eagon Pvt PA
Wm.: b 1743 d 12-17-1801 m Elizabeth Risley Pvt CT
Wm.: b — d *a.* 8-13-1816 m Ann — Pvt MD

HOUSEAL,

Wm.: b 1730 d 2-9-1807 m (1)Mary Elizabeth Stromer (2)Anna Margaret Geiselhart Capt CS SC

HOUSER, (includes HAUSE & HOWSER)

Andrew: b 4-2-1755 d 10-31-1842 m (1)Margaret R. — (2)Elizabeth Huffman Pvt SC ★
George: b 8-28-1755 d 11-3-1818 m Mary Magdalena Shore Lt NC
George, Sr.: b 2-8-1730 d 2-28-1801 m (1)Anna Margaretha Elrod (2)Barbara Stolz Mil CS PS NC
George H.: b 8-20-1754 d 1-10-1823 m Elizabeth Hunnick Pvt PA
Henry: b 5-19-1748 d 8-14-1810 m Margretha Heller Pvt PA
Jacob: b 10-16-1733 d *p.* 9-1-1804 m Eleanor Margaretha Fiscus Pvt NC
Jacob: b 1760 d 2-14-1832 m Barbara Shirk Pvt PA
Jacob: b *c.* 1730 d 8- -1793 m — Pvt PA
Jacob: b 4-2-1752 d 12-26-1812 m Eva Ehro Pvt PA
John Philip: b *c.* 1758 d *p.* 1811 m — Pvt PA
Martin: b *a.* 1757 d *p.* 1799 m Mrs Mary Offutt Pvt PS MD
Martin: b 10-16-1733 d 11-9-1794 m Susanna Maria Keissler CS NC
Martin, Sr.: b 6-22-1731 d 4-22-1800 m Elizabeth Hess Pvt PA
Martin, Jr.: b *c.* 1753 d *c.* 1830 m Anna Katherine Cary Pvt PA
Martin: b 1756 d 1840 m Anna — PS PA
Michael, Sr.: b 9-29-1731 d 4-24-1789 m Anna Cunigunda Fiscus PS CS NC
Peter: b *a.* 1760 d 1840 m Eva Katherine Dome Pvt PA
Ulrich: b 1-16-1741 d 6-5-1824 m Barbara Germanton Pvt PA

HOUSHILL,

Frederick: b *a.* 1756 d 1800 m Margaretha — Pvt PA

HOUSMAN, (includes HAUSMAN & HOUSEMAN)

Christopher: b 1732 d 1809 m Sarah — Pvt PA
Jacob: b 1731 d *p.* 10-15-1792 m Christina — Pvt PA
Jacob: b 1755 d 5-10-1814 m (1)Sarah Johnston (2)Elizabeth Hill Pvt PA
John: b 1751 d 10- -1826 m Augusta Perry Capt NJ
Paul: b 1730 d 1789 m Barbara Krug Pvt CS PA
Wm.: b *c.* 1747 d 3-29-1813 m Elizabeth Barnett Ens NY

HOUSTON, (includes HOUSTOUN, HUSTON & WHOSTON)

Alexander: b 11-29-1739 d 1-11-1826 m Agnes Wallace Sol PS NH
Archibald: b 10-26-1751 d 3-18-1836 m Rosannah Cunningham Pvt NC ★
Caleb: b 6-1-1740 d 11-5-1776 m Priscilla Coffeen Sol PS NH
Christopher: b 2-18-1744 d 5-17-1837 m (1)Sarah Mitchell (2)Elizabeth Simpson Capt NC
Christopher: b — d 12- -1784 m Susanna Wilson PS PA
Daniel: b 1754 d 1839 m Hannah Johnston 2Lt PA
George: b 1744 d 1795 m Ann Moodie PS GA
George: b 1763 d 12- -1826 m (1)Jane Hunter (2)Julia (Thompson) Gale Grd NY
George: b *a.* 1730 d *p.* 1783 m Margaret Ware PS NC
George: b 1750 d *p.* 1824 m Susanna Snapp Capt VA
Henry: b *c.* 1746 d 1820 m Sarah Elizabeth Miller Lt NC
Isaac: b — d — m Mary Purnell CS MD

Isaac: b 7-3-1760 d 3-25-1833 m (1)Molly Abbott (2)Ruth Gale Pvt NH MA ★
James: b *c.* 1755 d *p.* 7-2-1837 m Mary Hughey Sol GA
James: b 1746 d 1818 m Nancy Todd Pvt MD
James: b 1726 d 2-28-1797 m (1)Anne Kerr (2)Abigail — Capt NY
James: b 6-22-1747 d 8-2-1819 m Asenath Brevard Capt NC
James: b 1- -1751 d 1-18-1839 m Elizabeth — Pvt NC ★
James: b 1729 d 1-4-1802 m Grace — PS NC
James: b 1-29-1721 d 12-3-1789 m (1)Jane Eliot (2)Abigail Brown Pvt PA
James: b 4-16-1758 d 9-16-1841 m Mary Reed Pvt PA
James: b 1758 d 5-5-1801 m Catharine Ewing Pvt PA
James: b 11-12-1757 d 1839 m (1)Esther Houston (2)Polly Gillespie Pvt Ens VA ★
James: b 1726 d 1818 m Nancy McCreary Sct VA
James: b 1760 d 8-15-1836 m Anna Braddock Pvt VA ★
John: b 7-24-1748 d 4-27-1826 m Ann Starbird 2Lt MA
John: b *c.* 1745 d 8-25-1785 m Mahitable Ayers Pvt MA
John: b 1757 d 1850 m Sarah Estus Pvt MA
John: b 4-21-1739 d *p.* 1776 m Priscilla Coffin Pvt NH
John: b 1762 d 1835/6 m Rachel Balch Pvt VA NC ★
John: b 4-26-1737 d 6-19-1812 m Pheobe Spear Lt PA
John: b 4-16-1732 d 6-17-1836 m Catherine Anderson Lt PA
John: b 1-19-1751 d 10-16-1820 m Elizabeth Ottinger Lt PA
John: b *c.* 1709 d *p.* 1790 m — PS PA
John: b 1738 d — m Mary Watson Pvt PA
John: b 6-10-1732 d 11-20-1799 m Margaret Hathaway Sol PA
John: b 1744 d 12- -1828 m Margaret — Pvt PA
John: b 7-26-1758 d *p.* 9-15-1824 m Elizabeth Brown Pvt PA
John: b 1743 d 6-9-1809 m Susannah Wright Dr PA
John, Sr.: b 1735 d 12- -1802 m Jean — PS SC
John, Jr.: b 4-10-1760 d 5-24-1835 m Mary Wilson Pvt SC ★
John: b 1732 b 1793 m Elsa — Pvt SC
John: b 1744 d 1832 m Lydia Armstrong Pvt SC
John: b 1726 d 1795 m Sarah Todd Pvt CS VA
Joseph: b *c.* 1746 d 4- -1821 m Mary Nottingham Sgt MD
Joseph: b 1722 d 1778/9 m Margery Cunningham Capt CS PA
Levi: b 8-20-1750 d 2-11-1824 m Dolly Schoolfield Pvt PS MD
Margaret Weir: b *c.* 1740 d *p.* 1800 m (1)George Houston (2)George Gibson PS VA
Mathew: b 1730 d *p.* 1790 m Martha Lysle Sol VA
Purnell: b 2-1-1755 d 3-9-1835 m Mary Carey Pvt Smn PA DE ★
Robert: b *c.* 1730 d 1788 m (1)Mary Purnell (2)Priscilla Laws PS DE
Robert: b 3-6-1758 d *p.* 1810 m Katherine Taylor Smn MA
Robert: b 3-8-1756 d 7-20-1838 m Deborah Smith Robertson Pvt NJ
Samuel: b 1734 d 4-15-1815 m Elizabeth — PS DE
Samuel, Sr.: b 1726 d 2-8-1819 m (1)Isabel Dickey (2)Esther Rogers Capt PS MA ME
Samuel, Jr.: b 1754 d 1-9-1835 m Sarah Boyce Pvt NH
Samuel: b 2-29-1745 d 5-23-1824 m (1)Rachel — (2)Mary Colby Lt NH
Samuel: b 2-6-1728 d *c.* 1827 m Sarah Henderson Sol NC
Samuel: b 1710 d 1784 m Isabella Sharon 2Lt PA
Samuel: b 1760 d 1840 m Anne Hamilton Pvt SC
Samuel: b *c.* 1745 d 1807 m Elizabeth Paxton Maj VA
Samuel: b *a.* 1760 d *a.* 3-1-1824 m Grazella P. Huston Pvt SC
Samuel: b 1760 d 11-29-1820 m Nancy Agnes Lecky Pvt PA
Samuel: b 1735 d *p.* 1822 m Elizabeth Hubbard PS NC
Samuel: b 1-1-1758 d 1-20-1839 m (1) — Hall (2)Margaret Walker Pvt VA SC
Thomas: b 1739 d 5-11-1824 m Janet Walker 1Lt Capt PA
Wm.: b 12-28-1756 d 11-11-1849 m Elizabeth Campbell Pvt CT ★
Wm.: b 3-8-1746 d 1831 m (2)Mary Smith QM PS MD
Wm.: b 1755 d 1830 m (1)Betsy Miller (2)Isabel Campbell Pvt NH
Wm.: b 1742 d 1-25-1822 m Margaret Williams Capt NC
Wm.: b 2-8-1760 d 1820 m Susan Allen Pvt NC
Wm.: b 1755 d 10-28-1823 m Margaret Nelson Capt PA
Wm.: b *a.* 1760 d 1799-90 m Susanna Woodruff Lt PA
Wm.: b *c.* 1750 d 1822 m — 1Lt PA
Wm.: b 1729 d 1- -1803 m Hannah — Pvt PA
Wm.: b 1750 d 12-15-1781 m Elizabeth Taylor Pvt PA
Wm.: b 10-12-1754 d 9-6-1827 m Mary Morrison Pvt PA
Wm.: b 11-9-1755 d 12-31-1813 m Elizabeth Fleming Pvt PA
Wm.: b 5- -1757 d 10-28-1834 m Jane Watson Pvt PS PA
Wm.: b *c.* 1762 d *a.* 4-3-1843 m Hannah Sherrill Pvt VA ★
Wm. Churchill: b 1746 d 8-12-1788 m Jane Smith Capt NJ

HOUTZ, (includes HOUT & HOUTS)

Christopher: b 11-24-1758 d 10-23-1820 m Mary Johnson Pvt PA
Henry: b *c.* 1745 d 1796 m Barbara — Pvt PA
Jacob: b 1755 d 3-9-1820 m Barbara — Pvt VA ★
John George: b 1725 d 9-20-1786 m Catherine — Pvt PS PA VA
Peter: b 2-18-1762 d 6-11-1813 m Rosanna Miller Pvt PA

HOVEY,

Abijah: b 12-9-1719 d *a.* 2-3-1795 m (1)Lydia Graves (2)Lydia Ingalls (3)Mrs Mary Ann Faulkner PS CS MA
Amos: b 1753 d *p.* 1790 m Emilia Calkins Pvt CT
Azel: b 11-5-1763 d 9-14-1838 m Lucy Rockwell Pvt CT ★
Benjamin: b 3-12-1758 d 1806 m Lydia Haven Pvt MA
Daniel: b 12-20-1741 d 1776 m Content Ramsdell Lt MA
Daniel: b 7-24-1764 d 3-2-1850 m Beulah Pingree Pvt VT ★

David: b 8-5-1757 d 1-6-1814 m Anna Robinson Pvt CT
Dominicus: b 4-5-1740 d *p*. 1811 m (1)Ruth Hammond (2)Mehitabel 1Lt MA
Ebenezer: b 7-24-1744 d 1777 m Reliance Pratt Pvt MA
Ivory: b 12-29-1748 d 10-17-1818 m (1)Mrs Mary Lord (2)Frances Hight Dr NH MA
Ivory: b 7-14-1750 d 9- -1832 m Lucy Peabody Lt MA
Jacob: b 5-16-1760 d 8-24-1830 m Olive Grow Pvt CT
James: b 1740 d 6-15-1829 m Hannah Tomlinson Capt CT
Jonathan: b 12-2-1734 d 5-31-1811 m (2)Eunice Woodward Pvt MA CT
Joseph: b 12-17-1762 d 10-9-1825 m (1)Sally Burnham (2)Ruth — Pvt MA
Josiah: b 8-24-1743 d 4-24-1820 m Theodora Downer Pvt NH
Moses: b 5-11-1753 d 11-12-1805 m Love Prentice Sgt MA
Moses: b 10-28-1748 d 10-29-1813 m Phebe Tenny Cpl MA
Nathan: b 12-22-1740 d *p*. 1790 m Jemima Phelps Pvt CT
Nathaniel: b 6-22-1719 d 1799 m Abigail Hatch CS PS NH
Phineas: b 1-18-1746 d 10-2-1786 m Hannah Preston Pvt MA
Richard: b 2-4-1761 d 5-10-1842 m Asenath Hall Pvt MA
Roger: b 2-20-1759 d 4-6-1841 m Martha Otis Freeman Pvt CT
Samuel: b 12-12-1718 d 2-9-1796 m Elizabeth Colson Pvt MA
Samuel: b 2-24-1742/3 d 5-12-1833 m Abigail Cleveland Sgt CT ★
Solomon: b 3-27-1751 d 3-25-1804 m Lucy Barlow Pvt MA
Thomas: b 8-14-1740 d 5-12-1807 m Elizabeth Brown Capt MA
Wm.: b 7-6-1749 d 10-20-1834 m Lucinda Downer Sgt CT ★

HOVIS,
Frederick: b *c*. 1752 d 9-20-1825 m (1)Maria Magdalena Cramer (2)Catherine — Pvt PA
John: b *a*. 1765 d *p*. 1810 m Sarah Katherine Rhyne Pvt NC

HOWARD, (includes HOWERD)
Aaron: b 1711 d 1789 m Mary Bass Pvt MA
Abijah: b 1750 d 1818 m Priscilla Cushman Vol VT
Adam: b 1754 d 3-30-1838 m Polly Mann Pvt CL ★
Adam: b 1764 d 4-6-1848 m Catherine Bungardner Pvt VA ★
Allen: b 2-16-1763 d 6-7-1835 m Phebe Marshall Pvt NC ★
Amos: b 4-24-1739 d 12-9-1826 m Hannah Lynde Sgt MA
Andrew: b 8-21-1765 d 9-14-1849 m Clarissa Clark Pvt MA ★
Barnabas: b 6-19-1730 d 11-8-1813 m Mehitable Packard Pvt MA
Benjamin: b 2-17-1742 d 6-4-1828 m Prudence Sater Pvt MD
Benjamin: b *c*. 1740 d 11-24-1787 m Elizabeth Burd Sgt MA
Benjamin: b 8-15-1759 d 2-21-1849 m Sarah Worcester Pvt MA ★
Benjamin: b 5-11-1762 d 3-3-1842 m Rhoda Burge Pvt NY
Benjamin: b 9-6-1755 d 4-15-1835 m Rebecca Turner 2Lt NC ★
Beriah: b 12-16-1757 d 7-27-1840 m Roxy Chapin Pvt MA ★
Caleb: b 12-15-1760 d 1-4-1831 m (1)Sylvia Alger (2)Abigail Snell Pvt MA
Cary: b 6-15-1759 d 9-1-1820 m Mary Thompson SgtMaj MA
Charles: b 3-6-1750 d *a*. 1813 m Polly Lewis Pvt VA
Daniel: b 1-15-1744 d 4-14-1806 m Amy Beckwith Ens CT
Daniel: b 6-8-1746 d 3-23-1782 m Mary Hayward 1Lt MA
Daniel: b 3- -1760 d 8-15-1813 m Esther Spencer Pvt CT
Daniel: b 16-1750 d 4-20-1821 m Vesta — Sol CS MA
Daniel: b 1724 d 6-16-1777 m Rachel Latimer PS Pvt NJ
Daniel: b 7-20-1752 d 9-14-1824 m Dorothy Clarke Sgt RI W ★
Ebenezer: b 7-30-1751 d 10-14-1830 m (1)Bathsheba Alton (2)Prob Mrs Mercy Day Pvt CT
Ebenezer: b 8-31-1752 d 4-22-1818 m Silence Snell Pvt MA
Edmond: b 1760 d 1840 m Edith Murphy Pvt NC
Edward, Jr.: b 1-24-1756 d 1-18-1842 m Milly Howard Pvt MA ★
Edward: b 12-22-1724 d 10-1-1801 m Phebe Hart Pvt NY
Eleazer: b 5- -1739 d *p*. 1783 m Anna Badger Sgt MA
Eliakim: b 5-8-1739 d 1-31-1827 m Mary Howard Capt MA
Elihu: b 1764 d *c*. 1825 m Elizabeth McCaslin Pvt NJ
Elijah: b 9-6-1744 d 7-10-1831 m Kaziah Hayward Ens PS MA
Elijah: b 1-1754 d 10-17-1838 m Patty Williams Pvt NY
Enos: b 7-5-1760 d 5-15-1845 m Martha Soule Pvt NY ★
Ephraim: b *c*. 1760 d *p*. 1796 m Eleanor Ridgely 1Lt PS MD
Ephraim: b 1-25-1731 d *p*. 1790 m Hannah Brett Pvt MA
Ezekiel: b 4-29-1759 d 4-19-1824 m Rebecca Anderson Pvt VA
Ezra: b 1-12-1744 d 4-27-1808 m Sarah Lynde Pvt MA
Francis: b *c*. 1740 d 1-6-1785 m (1)Ann Allen (2)Sarah Johnston PS NC
Frederick: b *c*. 1750 d *p*. 8-7-1805 m Catherine — Pvt PA
Gamaliel: b 7-17-1751 d 7-18-1831 m Olive Babbit Sgt MA
George, Sr.: b 1-31-1722 d 4-3-1815 m Abigail Copeland Pvt MA
George, Jr.: b 9-8-1753 d 9-22-1812 m Parnel Ames Cpl MA
George: b 6-8-1749 d 6-8-1806 m Ann — Pvt NC
Gordon: b 12-2-1752 d 10-3-1843 m Sarah — Pvt PA VA ★
Groves: b 11-5-1733 d 1806 m (1)Mrs Hawkins (2)Hannah Allen PS Sol NC
Henry: b 12-14-1735 d 1-4-1789 m (1)Mary Kingman (2)Silence Bryant Pvt MA
Henry: b 1727 d 1790 m Hannah — Sol VA
Isaac: b 4-14-1753 d 9-28-1794 m (1)Patience Smith (2)Mary Mott Fif MA
James: b *c*. 1752 d 12-9-1817 m Margaret Wilson Pvt PS MD
James: b 1753 d 3-10-1804 m Abigal Snell Sgt MA
James: b 1702 d 5-14-1787 m (1)Mary McCurdy (2)Susanna — CS PS MA
James: b 1751 d 1839 m Rebecca — Pvt MA

James: b 1755 d 1835 m (1)Mary Bryan (2)Rhoda Deboard Pvt NY ★
James: b *c*. 1735 d *p*. 1- -1790 m (1)Cassandra Brice (2)Elizabeth Partridge 2Maj CS PS NC
James: b 1760 d 1820 m Sarah Ashburn Pvt NC
James: b 1-16-1759 d 4-14-1846 m Jane Simmons Pvt RI ★
James: b 1755 d *p*. 1798 m Mary — Pvt VA
Jeremiah: b 2-8-1756 d 4-25-1837 m Sarah Humphrey Sgt CT ★
Jeremiah: b 8-28-1749 d 11-11-1817 m Zilpha Lumbard Sgt MA
Jesse: b 7-20-1740 d 1-3-1828 m Melatiah Dunbar Lt MA
Job: b 5-19-1758 d 10-1-1844 m Hannah Capen Pvt MA
John: bpt 7-20-1735 d 5-4-1816 m Mary Adams Sgt CT
John: b 7-24-1742 d 6-18-1775 m Zerviah Hewitt Sgt CT
John: b 8-23-1756 d 1830 m Margaret Fudge Pvt GA
John: b 1740 d 9- -1814 m Huldah Sibley Capt MA
John: b 12-20-1726 d 1792 m Abigail Hudson 2Lt MA
John: b 1-2-1755 d 8-9-1849 m Jemmia Young Sgt MA ★
John: b 2-9-1753 d 1825 m Silence Burr Pvt MA
John: b 3-26-1748 d 1788 m Eleanor Cobb Slr MA
John: b 1730 d *a*. 4-5-1785 m Mary Ashburn Sol NC
John: b 2-22-1733 d 1836 m Mary Preston Vol NC
John: b 10-4-1761 d 4-12-1822 m Jane Vivian Pvt SC
John: b *c*. 1756 d 1831 m — Tubb Sgt SC
John Beale: b — d 7-15-1799 m Blanch Carvil Hall Lt MD
John Beale: b 11-30-1748 d 4-1-1788 m Rebecca Boone Pvt MD
John Eager: b 6-4-1752 d 10-12-1827 m Margaretta Chew LCol MD
Jonathan: b 1729 d 1809 m Phebe Ames Pvt MA
Jonathan: b 3-14-1748 d 10-13-1805 m Martha Willis Pvt MA
Jonathan: b 1-6-1754 d 10-9-1828 m Mary Gardener Sgt NY
Joseph: b 11-17-1753 d 11- -1805 m Dorcas Howard Pvt MD
Joseph: b *c*. 1760 d *a*. 11-12-1788 m Mary Duyer Pvt MD
Joseph: b 9-28-1758 d 1-17-1838 m Eunice Carrier Pvt MA ★
Joseph: b 3-31-1762 d 1834/5 m (1)Amelia Howard (2)Rhoda — Pvt NC
Joseph: b 1760 d 1843 m Sophia Smith Sol SC
Joseph: b 1750 d 1817 m Sally — Sgt VA
Joshua: b 11-13-1743/4 d *p*. 1797 m Elizabeth — 2Lt MA ME
Joshua: b 1742 d 1-8-1839 m Nancy Rice Capt CS MD
Josiah: b 1-3-1758 d 2-6-1833 m Mary Stanley Pvt MA W ★
Nathan: b 10-22-1733 d 4-5-1820 m Lydia Lynde Ens MA
Nathan: b *a*. 1745 d *p*. 1782 m Sybel — Sgt MA
Nathan: b 12-27-1746 d 1833 m Susanna Bryant Pvt MA
Nehemiah: b 1730 d *p*. 1- -1798 m Edith Smith PS Sol SC
Nehemiah: b 4-13-1740 d 1825 m Hannah Dean Pvt MA
Obediah: b 1741 d 10-4-1804 m Priscilla Breed Pvt SC
Oliver: b 6-19-1758 d 1-24-1845 m Susanna Reynolds Pvt MA
Peter: b 4-4-1762 d 5-9-1827 m (2)Sarah Strickland Pvt VA ★
Richard Seabury: b — d 6-28-1778 m Rachel Pack Sol NY
Robert: b 1-29-1735 d 2-10-1808 m Abigail Snell Pvt MA
Robert: b *c*. 1725 d *p*. 3-11-1799 m Ann — PS SC
Robert: b 1743 d 8- -1793 m Anne — PS SC
Robert: b — d — m — Col SC
Samuel: b 11-3-1752 d 4-22-1819 m Rachel Talcott Pvt CT
Samuel: b 1701 d 4-22-1785 m Margaret Lithgow PS ME
Samuel: b 5-2-1747 d 6-1-1840 m Mary Haley Pvt MA ★
Samuel: b 10-5-1739 d 2-11-1815 m Elizabeth Barrett Lt NH
Samuel: b 1761 d 1842 m Nancy Clark Pvt PA ★
Samuel: b 1762 d 12-5-1840 m Cloe Osborne Pvt VA ★
Samuel Harvey: b 8-23-1750 d *p*. 1804 m (1)Susannah — (2)Mary Higginbotham Capt MD
Seth: b 11-21-1762 d 1843 m Desire Bailey Pvt MA
Seth: bpt 4-7-1745 d 8-25-1825 m Mercy Whitman Pvt MA
Seth: b 3-3-1746 d 6-20-1810 m Narcissa Collins Sol SC
Solomon: b 2-12-1762 d 10-7-1834 m Anna Cary Pvt CT ★
Solomon: b 12-6-1756 d 6-23-1840 m Cynthia Stoodley Pvt MA ★
Solomon: b 8-27-1756 d 1-7-1834 m Moanen Barron Sgt NC ★
Stephen: b 7-28-1747 d *p*. 1796 m (2)Esther Lyman Pvt CT
Thadeus: b 2-28-1756 d 1813 m (1)Keziah Ames (2)Seabury Keith Pvt MA
Theophilus: b 5-5-1758 d 5-23-1838 m Bathsheba Keith Cpl Gnr MA ★
Thomas: b 9-5-1742 d 10-18-1805 m Priscilla Grow Pvt CT
Thomas: b 7-24-1737 d 11- -1811 (1)Martha Barker (2)Martha Hoar Pvt MA
Thomas: b 1742 d 1-24-1837 m (1)Sarah Westcott (2)Leah Hopkins (3)Dilys Clemens Ross (4)Anne Myers Pvt MA ★
Thomas: b *c*. 1757 d 10-22-1830 m Rhoda Wren Pvt PA ★
Thomas: b 11-15-1758 d 5-25-1825 m Elizabeth Armstrong Pvt PA
Thomas: b 1759 d 12-14-1836 m (1)Martha Vincient (2)Lydia Eaton Pvt RI ★
Thomas: b 2-25-1760 d 2-24-1838 m Mary — Sol SC
Thomas Cornelius: b *c*. 1745 d 1- -1801 m Eleanor — Ens MD
Thomas Gassaway: b 1735 d 1803 m Frances Holland PS MD
Uriah: b 1763 d 7-9-1845 m Lydia Rice Sgt NH VT ★
Wm.: b 1-7-1749 d 7-13-1822 m (1)Phebe Fuller (2)Lucy Greer Capt CT
Wm.: b 8-30-1744 d 10-28-1776 m Zilpha Bugbee Pvt MA
Wm.: b 1740 d 4-7-1810 m Martha Howard LCol ME
Wm.: b 8-14-1730 d 5-28-1792 m Mary Coe Pvt PS NY
Wm.: b 1728 d 1800 m Elizabeth — Pvt NC
Wm.: b 1747 d 1820 m Mary — Pvt NC
Wm.: b 2- -1747 d 6-22-1813 m (1)Deborah Shelton (2)Hope Cooke Capt RI W★
Wm.: b *c*. 1750 d 1781 m Mary Thorpe Pvt VA

HOWARD, contd.
Wm.: b 1732 d 1815 m Hannah Psalter PS VA NY
Wilson: b 1753 d 11-4-1840 m Mary Mayo Pvt NC ★

HOWD,
Joel: b 1735 d 1820 m Abigail Pond Pvt CT

HOWE, (includes HOW)
Aaron: b 1-22-1761 d 7-1-1833 m Betsy Hale Pvt MA ★
Abel: b 8-16-1757 d 5-12-1842 m Hannah Needham Pvt MA
Abner: b 6-28-1736 d 12-20-1776 m Sarah Lane Capt MA
Abner: b 10-20-1731 d 7-13-1781 m Mehitabel Holton PS NH
Abner: b 11-17-1747 d 1781 m — Pvt VT
Abraham, Sr.: b 1-2-1724/5 d 11-5-1797 m Mrs Lucy Appleton Capt MA
Abraham, Jr.: b 9-18-1754 d 1-8-1795 m Eleanor Spofford Cpl MA
Abraham: b 4-21-1746 d 3-24-1811 m Patience Blake Sgt MA
Adonijah: b 9-7-1737 d 9-10-1800 m Lydia Church Lt MA
Alvin: b 11-4-1753 d 5-17-1820 m Mary Wellington Cpl MA
Amasa: b 7-28-1765 d 1-16-1853 m Sarah Harrington Pvt MA ★
Antipas: b 8-19-1746 d 3- -1833 m Joanna Lawrence Pvt NH ★
Artemas: b 3-23-1734 d p. 1790 m Abigail — Capt MA VT
Artemas: b 1-15-1742/3 d 11-17-1813 m Mary Bigelow Pvt MA
Asa: b 3-30-1760 d 7-6-1844 m (1)Eunice Buck (2)Priscilla Gray Pvt CT ★
Asa, Sr.: b 1-1-1728 d 1814 m Mary Stow Capt MA
Asa, Jr.: b 10-18-1762 d 9-7-1843 m Esther Bowker Pvt MA
Azar: b 2-12-1764 d 11-6-1841 m (1)Lydia Pratt (2)Ruth Cheesman Pvt MA ★
Bezaleel, Jr.: b 12-9-1750 d 9-3-1825 m (1)Hannah Merritt (2)Catherine Moffat Capt NH
Cyprian: b 3-29-1726 d p. 1790 m (1)Dorothy — (2)Mary Williams Col CS MA
Daniel: b 3-1-1764 d 4-16-1843 m (1)Hannah Day (2)Mrs Boyd Pvt MD ★
Daniel: b 10-4-1741 d 10-21-1819 m Demaris Dutton Pvt MA ★
Daniel: b 3-20-1729/30 d 5-12-1810 m (2)Esther Pierce Pvt NH
Daniel: b 9-20-1758 d 1-2-1838 m Nancy Haven Lt VA
Darius: b 6-16-1746 d 2-23-1833 m Lovisa Church Lt MA
David: b 1757 d 1-27-1814 m Phebe Cole Pvt CT
David, Sr.: b 6-3-1717 d 11-14-1802 m Abigal Hubbard Pvt MA
David, Jr.: b 1-7-1756 d 10-13-1803 m Sibbel Rockwood Pvt MA
David: b 12-10-1759 d 2-9-1842 m (1)Persis Whittier (2)Betsey Reddington (3)Sally White Pvt MA
David: b 6-10-1764 d 10-10-1840 m Hannah Marden Pvt MA
David: b 9-27-1761 d 4-15-1847 m Unice Crapo Pvt NY ★
David: b 3-8-1747 d 10-29-1833 m (1)— Dunlap (2) — Woods Sol SC ★
Ebenezer: b 9-8-1762 d 4-15-1829 m Hannah Mallon Cpl MA
Edith: b 10-11-1744 d 1822 m Timothy Bradford PS NH
Edward: b 1743 d 1823 m Anne Lyne Capt VA
Edward C.: b 1742 d 9- -1821 m — PS MA
Eli: b 2-25-1757 d 9-21-1836 m Polly Oakes Pvt MA ★
Eliakim: b 1-17-1723 d p. 1801 m Rebecca Bush PS NH
Elijah: b 12-7-1731 d 2-24-1808 m Deborah Smith Pvt MA
Ephraim: b 12-19-1750 d 10-10-1826 m Abigail Hubbard PS CT
Ephraim: b 11-23-1733 d 1795 m Sarah Gilbert Pvt MA
Ephraim: b 1736 d 3-24-1806 m Damaris Seward Pvt MA
Estes: b 6--24-1747 d 3-3-1826 m Susannah Dwight Dr MA
Ezekiel: b 4-5-1720 d 10-14-1796 m (1)Bathsheba Stone (2)Rebecca Ruggles Col MA
Ezra: b 3-22-1719 d 4-4-1789 m Phebe Bush Sol MA
Fisk: b 6-23-1741 d 1-26-1807 m (1)Lydia Bigelow (2)Rachel Davis Pvt MA
Fortunatus: b 3-26-1760 d 12-12-1831 m Sarah Bruce Pvt MA ★
Francis: b 6-26-1750 d 2-28-1833 m Mary Hapgood CS MA
Gardner: b 11-20-1759 d 7-4-1854 m Abagail Sherman Pvt MA ★
Gideon: b 3-15-1732 d 2-8-1815 m Damaras Hapgood Pvt MA
Ichabod: b 1-9-1731/2 d 1-16-1810 m Sarah — PS ME
Isaac: b 12-16-1743 d 8-21-1825 m Mary Cande Sol CT
Isaac, Sr.: b 1-9-1710/11 d 10-8-1779 m (1)Abigail Webb (2)Kezia Mead PS CT
Isaac, Jr.: b 2-11-1749 d 12-29-1823 m Lucy Mead Capt CT
Isaac: b 6-26-1755 d 9-2-1830 m Sarah Wiswell Sgt MA
Isaac: b 2-28-1753 d 12-9-1831 m (1)Hannah Fay (2)Mrs Louisa Morse Pvt MA
Isaac: bpt 2-18-1759 d 3-10-1843 m Lois Dadmun Pvt MA
Isaac: b 1-27-1735 d 10-16-1800 m Sibyl Proctor Adj NH
Isaac: b 2-27-1741 d p. 1800 m Damaris Burch Pvt CT
Israel: b 9-8-1759 d 4-16-1845 m Hannah Washburn Pvt CT
Jaazaniah: b 1762 d 3-19-1838 m Lois Stevens Pvt MA ★
Jacob: b 4-9-1758 d 9-1-1799 m Hannah Johnson Pvt MA
Jacob, Jr.: b 7-9-1760 d 1-31-1830 m Betsey Foster Pvt MA
James: b 11-29-1746 d 1-12-1798 m Susannah Richardson Pvt PS MA
James: b 3-23-1755 d 10-13-1807 m Lucy Fisher SrgnMte NH
James: b c. 1745 d p. 1-19-1808 m Sarah — Pvt PA
James: b 2-5-1763 d 3-19-1838 m (1)Rebecca — (2)Margaret Dean Pvt VA ★
Jane Dunlap: b 3-16-1743 d 7-11-1804 m John Howe PS SC
Jeremiah: b 2-17-1734 d 11-20-1783 m Elizabeth Gaylord Sgt CT
Jesse: b 1758 d 6-20-1827 m Mary Wood Cpl NY W ★
Jesse: b 7-30-1754 d p. 1790 m Elizabeth Spurbeck Sol NY

Joel: b 1760 d 1-9-1854 m (1)Elizabeth Bemis (2)Esther Bemis Pvt MA ★
Joel: b 11-2-1748 d p. 1794 m Mary Gates PS Pvt MA
John: b 6-15-1725 d 5-13-1807 m Sarah Ayer CS MA
John: b 5-2-1763 d — m Courrance Parker Pvt Sct MA ★
John, Sr.: b 6-4-1718 d 3-10-1778 m — PS NY
John, Jr.: b 3-11-1750 d p. 1-31-1820 m Catherine K. — Pvt NY
John: b 8-26-1740 d 12-17-1817 m Jane Dunlap PS SC
John: b 6-24-1754 d 5-16-1830 m Rachel Pindell Sgt VA ★
John W.: b 1752 d 4-30-1835 m Mary Ann — Sol Spy VA
Jonah: b 1-2-1749 d 7-2-1826 m (1)Prudence Bowcker (2)Candace Allen Lt MA
Jonah: b 7-2-1746 d 11-10-1832 m Sarah Newton Cpl MA
Jonathan: b 1746 d 10-7-1787 m Lucy Read Pvt MA
Jonathan: b 2-26-1761 d 10-27-1847 m (1)Parna Howe (2)Susanna Kuhn Pvt MA
Jonathan: b 8-13-1753 d 4- -1840 m Hannah Webster Pvt MA ★
Jonathan: b 8-2-1761 d 9-20-1841 m Betsy Stickney Pvt NH
Joseph: b 2-1-1728/9 d 9-26-1800 m Grace Rice Sgt MA
Joseph, Sr.: b 3-6-1724 d 8-17-1794 m Sarah Stone MM MA
Joseph, Jr.: b 4- -1754 d p. 1787 m Hulda Stacy Sgt MA
Joseph: b 12-1-1760 d 1-27-1808 m Hepzibah Belknap Pvt MA
Joseph: b 2-18-1748/9 d 7-16-1799 m Isabella — Capt PS CS SC
Joseph: b c. 1729 d a. 3-4-1794 m Ellen Dunbar CS VA
Joshua: b 1730 d 1-25-1800 m Miriam Blakeslee Pvt CT
Jotham: b 6-17-1754 d 1821 m Dorothy Smith Pvt MA
Jotham: b 7-23-1733 d 4-5-1812 m Mary Kimball Lt NH
Lebbeus: b 7-2-1756 d 11-17-1834 m Anna Austin Pvt NY
Lemuel: b c. 1758 d p. 1790 m Sarah Goodwin Pvt MA
Luther: b 4-10-1747 d 9-24-1811 m Elizabeth Watson PS CS MA
Mark: b 12-31-1736 d 5- -1818 m Mary Payson Dr NH
Matthias: b 5-27-1742 d 3-18-1829 m Azubah Davis Pvt MA
Micah: b 9-22-1759 d 7-22-1842 m (1)Louisa Amsden (2)Persis Welch Pvt MA
Moses: b 7-3-1754 d 11-28-1838 m Love Gallup Pvt MA
Moses: b 1749 d 12-18-1817 m Submit Scott Lt VT
Nathan: b 6-17-1730 d 3-21-1781 m (1)Hepzibah Taylor (2)Zillah Taylor Capt MA
Nehemiah: b 1-13-1721 d 4- -1777 m Beulah Wheeler PS CS VT
Oliver: b 2-18-1748/9 d 9-23-1783 m Sibyl Fuller Sgt MA
Oliver: b 10-5-1759 d 3-5-1823 m Sarah Schultz Pvt MA
Otis: b 10-3-1748 d — m Lucy Goodale Pvt NH
Perley: b 2-3-1742/3 d 1795 m (1)Tamar Davis (2)Abigail DeWolf Capt CT
Perley: b 6-17-1755 d 11-7-1839 m Sarah Dunning Sol MA ★
Perley: bpt 9-24-1749 d 4-6-1825 m Anna Hill Pvt MA
Peter: b 11-17-1753 d 11-3-1831 m Mary Noyes Pvt NH
Peter, Jr.: b 12-23-1730 d p. 1777 m Mary Smith Lt MA
Peter: b 8-1-1756 d 12-12-1842 m Orrinda Fuller Pvt VT ★
Phineas: b 10-22-1735 d 9-19-1807 m Susanna Goddard PS MA
Reuben: b 5-9-1755 d 7-18-1836 m (1)Lucy Wood (2)Judith Tenney (3)Elizabeth Bailey Pvt MA ★
Robert: b 1732 d 11-12-1785 m Sarah Grange MajGen NC
Samson: b 7-26-1751 d 9-7-1824 m Huldah Davis Pvt CT
Samuel: b 9-23-1719 d 6-28-1784 m Hannah Smith PS Col MA
Samuel: b 10-2-1756 d 4-7-1842 m Mercy Rosebrook Pvt MA ★
Samuel: b 6-15-1727 d 4-9-1806 m Abigail Dudley Pvt MA
Samuel: b 5-18-1759 d 8-6-1836 m Judith Clough Pvt NH ★
Samuel: b 1742 d 1-22-1814 m Elizabeth Deamer Pvt PA
Samuel: b 1749 d 1-24-1822 m Sarah Rose Pvt NY
Silas: b 4-15-1747 d 12-13-1810 m Susannah Franklin Sgt VT
Simeon: b 3-6-1755 d 5-28-1819 m Hannah Foster Cpl VT
Simon: bpt 9-21-1740 d 1836 m Sally Rice Sgt MA
Simon: b 10-20-1722 d 8-26-1806 m Lydier Baker MM MA
Squire: b 1751/2 d 11-20-1807 m Martha Field Capt VT
Sylvanus: b 1727 d 1802 m Mary Rice Sol MA
Thomas: b 8-24-1735 d 3-23-1816 m Hannah Leeds Pvt MA
Timothy: b 12-1764 d 5-21-1829 m Keziah Powers Pvt MA ★
Timothy, Jr.: b 6-27-1765 d 3-25-1839 m (1)Elcy — (2)Phoebe Babcock Pvt NY ★
Timothy: b 10-6-1742 d 1826 m Elizabeth Andrus 1Lt PA
Titus: b 6-27-1765 d 1837 m Rhoda Ferris Pvt NY ★
Uriah: b 10-27-1745 d 1813 m Martha Graves Pvt NH
Wm.: b 10-18-1735 d 9- -1814 m Susanna Shoop Pvt PA
Wm.: b 1740 d c. 10- -1820 m (1)Margaret Jackman (2)Elizabeth — Sol PA

HOWELL, (includes HOWEL)
Abraham: b c. 1740 d p. 1787 m Rebecca — PS NY
Amos: b 5-22-1754 d 2-16-1819 m Martha Jones Pvt NJ
Arthur: b 12- -1756 d 10-18-1820 m (1)Euphamia Hensilwood (2)Leah Swaim CS Asst Cmsry NJ W ★
Asher: b 10-19-1758 d 1-2-1809 m Phebe — Pvt NJ
Benjamin: b 10-10-1725 d 12-26-1798 m Abigail Cook CS NJ
Caleb: b c. 1745 d a. 1792 m — Col GA
Caleb: b 3-8-1752 d 1-12-1805 m Rebecca Stiles PS NJ
Charles: b 1741 d 1-9-1797 m Abigail Diament Ens NJ
Daniel: b a. 1757 d p. 10-5-1809 m Civility — Maj GA
Daniel: b 1759 d 3-5-1836 m (2)Frances Bartlett Pvt VA ★
David: b 11-26-1739 d 6-23-1827 m Phebe McCord Coulter Pvt NJ
David: b 1736 d 4-3-1778 m Mary Douglas Capt NY
David: b 1751 d 12-29-1839 m Mehetable Halsey Capt PS NY

David: b 1-1-1747 d 7-31-1824 m Mary Brown PS RI
David: b 6- -1724 d 2-13-1803 m Elizabeth Havens PS NY
Ebenezer: b 1727 d 1790/1 m Sarah Bond PS CS NJ
Edward: b 8- -1745 d 8-29-1809 m Clement Albertson Pvt NY
Edward, Jr.: b 4-28-1750 d 8-10-1817 m Ann Phillips Sol NC
Ellett: b 12-6-1756 d 4-23-1821 m Catharine Flick Lt NJ
Ezekiel: b 1755 d 1831 m Charity Lott Pvt NJ
Ezekiel: b 3-27-1758 d 6-16-1831 m Susannah Hill Pvt NJ
George: b a. 1756 d 4-2-1829 m Eunice Horton Pvt NY
Gideon: b 1-16-1728 d 1-20-1803 m Sarah Gordon Pvt NJ
Hezekiah, Sr.: b 5-6-1709 d 6-27-1784 m Susanna Sayer PS NY
Hezekiah, Jr.: b c. 9-13-1741 d 4-2-1815 m Julianna Woodhull Maj NY
Isaac: b 12-27-1735 d 9-17-1825 m Abigail Freeman PS NY
Israel, Sr.: b 3-14-1715/6 d p. 1790 m Anna White PS NY
Israel, Jr.: b 1- -1742 d 11-24-1805 m Tabatha Hulse Pvt NJ
Jacob S.: b 3-14-1749 d 9-20-1793 m Mary Cannalt PS PA
James: b 10-15-1734 d 12-12-1808 m Lucretia Havens Pvt NY
James: b 1744 d 1844 m Martha Denny Pvt VA
Jedediah: b 6-28-1713 d 1795 m Elesabeth Gold CS NY
Jeremiah: b 1748 d 2-17-1846 m Mary — Pvt NJ
John: b 9-23-1756 d 9-18-1830 m Eleanor Seely Capt NJ W ★
John, Sr.: b 6-14-1727 d 9-15-1779 m Naomi Hart Pvt NJ
John, Jr.: b 2-5-1765 d 5-8-1848 m Mary Geassarrh Pvt NJ
John: b 1745 d 12-25-1790 m Sarah Dougherty Pvt NY
John: b 1759 d 3-11-1837 m Hannah Corwin MM NY
John: b 7-11-1710/11 d 6-16-1791 m Desire White PS NY
John: b c. 1732 d p. 1780 m — Pvt NC
John: b 8-3-1758 d 8-8-1828 m Hannah Johnson Pvt NC
John: b 8-8-1721 d 7-27-1808 m Elizabeth Yerkes CS PA
John Ladd: b 3-15-1738 d 7-30-1785 m Frances Paschall PS Capt PA
Jonah: b c. 1700 d p. 1776 m Elizabeth Foster PS NY
Jonathan: b 1720 d 3-26-1804 m Elizabeth Sherry MM NY
Jonathan: b 6-20-1760 d 1843 m Elizabeth — Pvt PA ★
Joseph: b 1735 d 1789 m Ruth — PS NY
Joseph: b c. 1745 d 10-11-1819 m — Sol SC
Joseph: b 6-30-1750 d 8-8-1798 m Rebecca Betterton Capt PA
Joseph: b 1733 d 1835 m Margaret Elenor Gormon Pvt NC
Josiah: b 1-12-1738 d 8-17-1808 m (1)Mary Howell (2)Phebe Pierson Capt NJ
Lewis: b 1755 d 4-27-1833 m (1)Mary Ann Kirk (2)Mrs Leona Sisk Pvt VA ★
Luther: b 4-2-1747 d 4-8-1792 m Mary Young Pvt NJ
Matthew: b 2-12-1726 d 3-5-1786 m (2)Margaret Carr Pvt NY
Nathan: b 1729 d 3-29-1803 m Sarah — Pvt NJ
Nathaniel, Jr.: b 10-3-1742 d 2-14-1809 m Ruth Toppin Lt NY
Paul: b 1751 d 9-26-1807 m Susannah Knight Pvt NY
Philip: b c. 1750 d p. 1810 m Margaret Cooper Lt PA
Phillip: b 3-29-1737 d 4-2-1823 m Cleopatra Herrick Lt NY
Reading: b 1743 d 11-26-1827 m Catharine Yerkes QM Maj NJ
Reeves: b 1738 d 9-3-1802 m Bathsheba Clark Pvt NY
Richard: b 10-25-1754 d 4-28-1802 m Keziah Burr Maj NY
Samuel: b 1-14-1754 d 1834 m Elizabeth Tuthill Cpl PS NY
Samuel, Sr.: b 1729 d 1807 m Sarah Stretch PS PA
Samuel, Jr.: b 11-23-1749 d 11-6-1806 m Margaret Emlen Pvt PA
Samuel: b 1750 d 9-7-1824 m Mary Hutson Pvt SC
Seth: b 1739 d 1794 m Sarah Jessup Pvt NY
Silas: b c. 1746 d 4-9-1812 m (1)Hannah White (2)Hannah Vaughn Capt NJ
Silas: b c. 1737 d 12-18-1792 m Mary Benjamin PS NY
Stephen: b 10-23-1744 d 1-18-1828 m Susannah — Capt NY
Theophilus: b 5-2-1760 d 12-6-1829 m (1)Susanna Carpenter (2)Hannah Denton Pvt NY
Thomas: b 4-30-1719 d 5-18-1797 m Mary White Cmsry CT
Thomas: b 1750 d 1791 m Rebeca Lock PS NC
Wm.: b 1755 d 10-7-1823 m Ann Elizabeth — Sol MD
Wm.: b 6-10-1758 d 3-15-1841 m Hannah — Pvt Smn MA ★
Wm.: b 1750 d p. 1780 m Rebecca Cook Pvt NJ
Wm.: b c. 1745-50 d 1817 m Martha Marks Sgt VA
Wm.: b 1725 d 1779 m Letitia Lewis Pvt Wgm VA
Wm.: b 1748 d 3-28-1842 m Elizabeth Gray Goff Pvt VA ★

HOWER,
Frederick: b 12-9-1720 d 7-30-1797 m Kathrine Wenner Pvt PA
Jacob: b c. 1760 d 1- -1826 m — PS MD
Michael: b 4-18-1751 d 10-28-1824 m (1)Anna Elizabeth Margretta (2)Salome — Pvt PS PA
Nicholas: b 2-6-1751 d 2-14-1829 m Elizabeth Dreisbach Lt PA
Sebastian: b — d p. 1790 m Maria Friedrichin Pvt PA

HOWERTON,
John: b 1757 d 1830 m — Faulkner Pvt VA
Wm.: b 1730 d a. 11-19-1781 m Mary Hayes PS VA

HOWES, (includes HOWSE)
Barnabas: b 7-24-1724 d c. 12-25-1778 m (1)Lois Mayo (2)Hannah Sears Pvt Smn MA
Benjamin: b 1757/8 d 2-14-1839 m (1)Rachel Camp (2)Eunice Pomeroy Pvt CT ★
Daniel: b 1762 d 2-4-1824 m Rahamah — Pvt NY
Ebenezer: b 8-9-1737 d 2-20-1811 m Ruth Hallett Pvt MA
Edmund: b 8-21-1743 d 9-10-1828 m Abigail Crosby Pvt MA

Elkanah: b 1-8-1751 d 3- -1823 m Desire Eldredge Pvt MA
James: b 11-5-1764 d 9-11-1846 m Priscilla Sears Pvt MA
Jeremiah: b 12-26-1743 d 1824 m Priscilla Hall 1Lt MA
John: b c. 1740 d p. 11-8-1808 m Mary — PS MD
Joseph: b 11-25-1752 d 2-4-1831 m Martha Howard Cpl CT
Joshua: b 9-17-1746 d — m (1)Mary Sears (2)Mary Paddock Pvt MA
Josiah: b 5-13-1739 d 6-12-1801 m Lydia — Pvt MA
Kimball: b 2-5-1750/1 d 1-20-1820 m Elizabeth Howes Pvt MA
Moody: b 7-18-1724 d 4-9-1806 m (1)Hannah Snow (2)Sarah — Pvt NY
Sylvanus: b 7-4-1763 d 3-12-1857 m Sarah Lincoln Pvt MA W ★
Thomas: b 4-15-1727 d 7-16-1793 m Bathsheba Sears Pvt MA
Thomas: b 2-27-1745 d 6-10-1796 m Jerusha — Pvt MA
Zachariah: b 3-23-1753 d 12-1-1832 m (1)Lavinia Sears (2)Mrs Sarah Cranston Pvt MA ★
Zenas: b 5-20-1756 d 12-21-1831 m Eunice Hunt 2Sgt CT ★

HOWEY,
John: b 1725 d 1782 m Nancy Houston Pvt PA
Thomas: b 6-11-1763 d 5-27-1835 m Lodema Harris Pvt PA

HOWISON,
Stephen: b 1-31-1736 d 2-1-1815 m Mary Brooke PS VA

HOWLAND,
Abraham: b 9-22-1756 d 12-3-1829 m Elizabeth Hathaway Pvt MA
Abraham: b 9-6-1762 d 2-6-1853 m Anna Staples Pvt MA
Ansel: b 12-3-1728 d 2-23-1802 m Elizabeth Bodfish Lt MA
Caleb: b 5-4-1758 d p. 9-5-1838 m Mary Simonds Pvt VT RI
Charles: b 6-4-1764 d 1-1-1830 m Amy Allen Fif MA
Consider: b 8-17-1752 d 9-1-1834 m Elizabeth Hall Sgt MA
Daniel: b 3-7-1759 d 1-11-1821 m Sarah Wood Pvt MA
Elijah: b 4-5-1763 d 7-18-1855 m Mary — Smn MA
George: b 4-25-1743 d 5-16-1815 m (1)Marcey Baker (2)Doratha Baker Pvt MA
Gershom: b 3-3-1734 d 1823 m Elizabeth Parker Pvt MA
Israel: b 6-13-1713 d 1787 m Drusilla Wood Pvt NY
Jabez: b 1-29-1762 d 1806 m Sarah Chapin Pvt MA
James: b 7-18-1760 d 10-10-1850 m Sarah Mason Pvt MA ★
Job: b 6-18-1726 d 1794 m Hannah Jenkins Matr MA
John: b 1742 d 1-13-1810 m (1)Lydia Pierce (2)Beulah Bemis (3)Mrs Rachel Perkins Ens MA
John: b 2-16-1755 d p. 1799 m Mary Kerby Pvt MA
John: b 1-14-1743 d 5-13-1835 m Lois Eddy Sol RI
John: b 5-19-1734 d 12-6-1792 m Mary Coggeshall PS RI
John, Sr.: b 9-27-1713 d 8-21-1786 m Martha Wardwell PS RI
John, Jr.: b 3-9-1738 d 1792 m (1)Elizabeth LeFavour (2)Elizabeth DeWolfe PS RI
John: b 10-31-1757 d 11-5-1854 m Mary Carlisle Pvt RI ★
Joseph: b 5-2-1763 d 7-15-1848 m Avis Chase Pvt MA ★
Lemuel: b 11-28-1742 d 1- -1802 m Abigail Hamlin Pvt MA
Nathan: b 2-27-1742 d 6-21-1831 m Priscilla Drew Lt VT
Nathaniel: b 10-9-1736 d 11-28-1804 m Martha Fearing Thatcher Pvt MA
Prince: b 1745 d 1-17-1834 m Abigail Wadsworth Cpl MA
Robert: b 9- -1742 d 4- -1821 m Ruth Crooker Sgt MA
Samuel: b 1744 d 2-18-1798 m Lydia Robinson Cpl MA
Thomas: b 12-1-1718 d 10-28-1798 m Ruth Wing Pvt MA
Thomas: b 2-26-1742/3 d 1815 m (1)Mary Kimball (2)Mary — Pvt RI
Wm.: b 7-1-1747 d 1835 m Mary Richmond Pvt RI ★
Wing: b 5-28-1750 d 8-16-1805 m Elizabeth Huttlestone Pvt MA
Zebulon: bpt 8-12-1739 d 2-19-1824 m (1)Lydia Cushing (2)Margaret — 1Lt MA

HOWLE,
Epaphroditus: b 3-5-1729/30 d c. 1804 m Mary — PS VA
Wm.: b 8-7-1755 d 1844 m — Pvt GA SC ★

HOWSON,
Samuel: b 1726 d — m Lydia Clark Pvt MA

HOXIE, (includes HOXSIE)
Gideon: b 12-12-1729 d 6-13-1805 m Dorcas Congdon LCol RI
John: b 5-21-1737 d p. 2-9-1815 m Hannah Bill CaptLt RI
Peleg: b 9-15-1756 d p. 1818 m Lucy Babcock Lt RI
Stephen: b 9-28-1713 d 10-24-1793 m Elizabeth Kenyon PS RI

HOXWORTH,
Edward: b 9-22-1760 d 1-11-1847 m Mary Hoxworth DrmMaj PA ★

HOY, (includes HOYE)
Albert: b c. 1737/8 d p. 1801 m Susanna Sneavely PS PA
Paul: b 3-26-1736 d 10-13-1816 m Mariam Waller Lt MD
Thomas: b 1760 d p. 1793 m Agnes Scott Pvt MD
Thomas: b 6-13-1763 d 9-15-1846 m Sussanna Bush Pvt VA ★
Wm., Sr.: b 1727 d 9-9-1806 m Agnes Guthrie Pvt NY
Wm.: b 1743 d 1790 m Sarah Callaway Maj VA

HOYER,
George: b 1757 d 5-25-1841 m Catharine Schultz Lt PA

HOYER, contd.
George Frederick: b 1752 d 5-25-1815 m Mary Elizabeth Staring Pvt NY
Jacob: b 1-1-1752 d p. 1834 m Catherine Crow OrdlSgt PA ★

HOYLE, (includes HOYL)
John: b 6-1-1740 d 9-4-1809 m Margaret Castner CS PS NC
Joseph: b 1741 d 4- -1800 m (1)Sarah Field (2)Mrs Patience Manchester CS RI
Michael: b 1-12-1732 d 3-12-1792 m Margaret Dellinger PS NC

HOYSRADT,
Adam: b 7-5-1737 d 1793 m (1)Mary Knickerbocker (2)Eve Gertrude Dennis Capt NY

HOYT, (includes HAIT, HAYT, HOIT & HOITT)
Abner: b 1-25-1731 d 10-22-1807 m Hannah Eastman Pvt NH
Abner: b 4-15-1759 d 12-28-1852 m (1)Elizabeth Blanchard (2)Mrs Martha Livingston Phillips Pvt NH
Agur: b 6-30-1761 d 11-30-1836 m (1)Lois Boughton (2)Mrs Sarah Grubb Pvt CT
Asa: b 10-13-1763 d 5-31-1844 m (2)Olive Barnum Pvt CT
Asa: b 8-23-1744 d 4-14-1806 m Ruth Kellogg PS CT
Barnard: b 4-6-1730 d 1-8-1810 m Annie Stuart Maj MA
Benjamin, Sr.: b 12-20-1727 d 1802/3 m (1)Eunice Ray (2)Mary Stearns (3)Elizabeth Barry Pvt MA
Benjamin, Jr.: b 12-11-1761 d 10-29-1843 m Lydia Joslyn Cpl MA
Benjamin: b 1-25-1757 d 2-3-1815 m (1)Mary Jewett (2)Jane French 2Lt NH
Benjamin: b 4-2-1742 d 1798/9 m Sarah Downing Cpl NH
Benjamin: b 8-10-1763 d 1839 m Betty Johnson Pvt NH
Benjamin: b 9-17-1739 d 10-25-1807 m Sarah Cooper CS NH
Comfort, Sr.: b 2-20-1723/4 d 5-19-1812 m Anna Beach Capt CT
Comfort, Jr.: b c. 5-15-1751 d 3-11-1836 m Eunice Mallery Sol CT
Daniel: b 5-2-1756 d 8-31-1824 m Anne Gunn Pvt CT
Daniel: b 2-27-1759 d 7-5-1843 m Mary Fancher Fif CT ★
Daniel: b 1-13-1741 d p. 1787 m (1)Thankful Weeks (2)Mary Bartlett Ens PS NH
David: b 10-3-1728 d a. 8-7-1810 m Hannah Crissey Capt CT
David: b 2-21-1730/1 d 6-23-1800 m (1)Sarah Lockwood (2)Mrs Hannah Hoyt Pvt CT
David: b 11-17-1757 d 9-18-1803 m Elizabeth Bull Cpl MA
David: b 3-20-1743 d 3-27-1822 m (1)Rachel Judd (2)Lucy Dudley (3)Sarah Fowler Lt VT CT
Dennis: b 5-1-1744 d 4-22-1818 m Elizabeth Fabyan PS NH
Drake: b 1717 d 4- -1805 m Hannah Knapp Pvt CT
Ebenezer: b 3-9-1758 d 10-1-1834 m (1)Mary Saint John (2)Ruhamah Williams (3)Sarah Brown Pvt CT ★
Ebenezer: b 6-15-1754 d 12-19-1836 m Sarah Nichols Pvt MA W ★
Ebenezer: b 1-27-1756 d 11-19-1816 m (1)Nancy Merrill (2)Mrs Abigail Clement Pvt NH
Elijah: b 3-6-1753 d 11-14-1815 m Elizabeth Weeks Sgt CT
Elijah: b 5-1-1734 d 10-8-1804 m Mary Raymond Sol CT
Elijah: b 1-13-1762 d 4-15-1837 m Polly Canfield Pvt CT ★
Eliphalet: b 6-2-1723 d a. 1795 m Mary Peaslee PS NH
Elisha: b 1750 d 3-4-1827 m Hannah Blood Pvt MA
Ephraim: b 1-20-1758 d 9-15-1841 m Sarah Stevens Pvt NH ★
Ezekiel: b 12-25-1758 d 8-19-1833 m Mary Weed Pvt CT
Frederick: b 11-16-1757 d 9-25-1814 m (1)Sarah Hait (2)Phoebe — Pvt CT
George: b 6-7-1748 d 1841/2 m Rhoda Blaisdell PS NH
Gideon: bpt 3-20-1736/7 d 7-26-1801 m Elizabeth Weed Pvt NY
Gilbert: b 1-27-1751 d a. 8-20-1832 m Hannah Bishop Pvt NY ★
Goold: b 1-9-1732 d 6-2-1803 m Elizabeth Dimon PS CT
Israel: b 11-18-1733 d 1809 m Joanna Holmes Pvt NY
Jabez: b 11-8-1734 d 8-7-1817 m Abigail Hasseltine PS CS NH
Jacob: b 4-8-1762 d 3-10-1832 m (1)Sarah Kellogg (2)Nancy M Twitchell Sol CT
Jared: b 5-20-1762 d 4-17-1826 m Mary June Pvt CT
Jedediah: b 11-23-1758 d 1840 m (1)Hannah Elliot (2)Mrs Sarah Farnum Pvt NH
Jesse: b 1-23-1743 d 12-17-1831 m Bethiah Sherwood Cpl NY
Jesse: b 4-24-1743 d 6-6-1831 m Lydia Ferris Sol NY
John, Sr.: b 12-20-1720 d 4-18-1807 m (1)Miriam Currier (2)Mrs Mary Moulton Capt MA
John, Jr.: b 12-18-1752 d 10-17-1832 m (1)Hannah Rogers (2)Abigail Clark Cpl MA ★
John: b 9-23-1752 d 9-2-1827 m Hannah Prescott Pvt NH
John: b 9-10-1732 d 2- -1804/5 m Abigail Carter PS NH
John: b 10-9-1762 d 9- -1806 m Elizabeth Colby Pvt NH
John, Jr.: b 5-8-1755 d 2-9-1839 m Ruth Gregory Pvt CT ★
John: b 11-15-1740 d 3-1-1825 m (1)Abigail — (2)Rebecca Jeffery PS CT
John Millet: b 4-17-1745 d 2-5-1829 m Nabby Teal Pvt MA
Jonathan: b 4-20-1750 d 3-9-1835 m Hannah Abbot Pvt CT
Jonathan: b 5-31-1745 d 5-20-1825 m Mary Brackett PS NH
Jonathan: b 5-4-1754 d 7-17-1821 m Lois Bradley Pvt PS VT
Joseph: b 8-2-1725 d 6-11-1820 m (1)Jane King (2)Mrs Anna Nichols LCol CT ★
Joseph: b 12-12-1739 d 12-24-1799 m Sarah Weed Sgt CT
Joseph: b 1727-34 d 1776-78 m Deborah Bell Pvt CT
Joseph: b 1727 d 12-14-1807 m (1)Sarah Collins (2)Ruth Brown Capt NH

Joseph: b 6-3-1739 d 1815 m Abigail Flanders Pvt NH
Joseph: b 7-19-1761 d 4-17-1839 m Polly Elliot Pvt NH
Joseph: b 10-22-1717 d 7- -1789 m (1)Sarah Jewett (2)Mrs Deborah Light PS NH
Joseph: b 9-20-1717 d 1788 m Susanna French PS NH
Joseph: b 11-3-1751 d p. 1778 m Betsy Folsom PS NH
Joseph Brown: b 4-15-1762 d 10-16-1846 m Anna Sawyer Pvt NH ★
Josiah: b 5-17-1736 d 5-23-1811 m Elizabeth Tuttle PS CT
Justus: b 1742 d 1823 m Elizabeth Fitch Ens CT
Levi: b 12-15-1746 d p. 1790 m Ann Curier Pvt MA
Levi: b 9-5-1759 d 5-7-1788 m Mrs Hannah Aldrich Pvt NH
Matthew: b 5-6-1741 d 4-14-1821 m (1)Mary Lockwood (2)Mrs Mercy Hayes Pvt CT
Micah: b 7-23-1738 d 6-9-1807 m Miriam Currier Lt NH
Moses: b 7-22-1763 d 3-9-1840 m Amaryllis Dibble Pvt CT
Moses, Sr.: b 3-1-1708 d c. 1784 m Mary Carr PS NH
Moses, Jr.: b 3-22-1737/8 d 3- -1820 m Lydia Gould PS NH
Nathan, Jr.: b 2-6-1728 d 3-12-1810 m Sarah Jeffrey Sgt CT
Nathan: b 4-29-1718 d 10-21-1799 m (1)Elizabeth Lockwood (2)Sarah — PS CT
Nathan: b c. 1745 d 1-9-1820 m Mary Page Lt CS NH
Nathan: b 5-12-1765 d 5-20-1847 m Merribah Fogg Perkins Pvt NH
Nathaniel, Jr.: b 12-27-1751 d 2-12-1840 m (1)Anna White (2)Lucretia Braman Ens CT ★
Neazer: b 11-8-1751 d 2-15-1811 m Prudence Weed Pvt CT
Nehemiah: b 5-14-1752 d 1809 m Widow Moulton Pvt VT
Noah: b 11-3-1753 d 12-23-1827 m (1)Jerusha Abbott (2)Mary Seely Pvt CT
Noah, Sr.: b 3-26-1741 d 10-31-1810 m (1)Abigail Curtiss (2)Sarah Comstock (3)Elen Purdy PS CT
Oliver: b 11- -1748 d 9-11-1826 m Rebecca Gerald PS NH
Peaslee: b 10-23-1749 d 11-27-1827 m Margaret Hubbard PS NH
Peter: b 10-24-1764 d 6-26-1843 m Obedience Haynes PS NY
Rice: b 10-21-1740 d 4-26-1830 m Theodosia Dibble Pvt NY
Richard: b 11-25-1759 d — m Mrs Mercy Leighton Pvt NH MA ★
Robert: b 5-6-1753 d 10-17-1843 m Jane Hall Pvt MA ★
Samuel, Sr.: b 6-30-1720 d 3- -1799 m (1)Dinah Hanford (2)Hannah — PS CT
Samuel, Jr.: b 10-21-1752 d 12-30-1832 m Anna Seymour 2Lt CT
Samuel: b 4-3-1744 d 10-5-1826 m (1)Clotilde Wilcox (2)Mrs Mary Stone Pvt CT
Samuel: b 10-19-1764 d 9-18-1819 m Elizabeth Olmstead Pvt CT
Samuel: b 1-24-1739/40 d 11-22-1821 m (1)Joanna Brown (2)Anna Sibley Stevens (3)Mehitable Kilborn Pvt PS NH
Seth: b 1759 d 6-6-1831 m Catharine Ruble Pvt MA ★
Silas: b 3-2-1738/9 d 1-9-1825 m Sarah Lockwood Pvt CT
Simeon: b 3-17-1757 d 4-9-1824 m Miriam Morrill Pvt NH ★
Stephen: b 1760 d 1834 m Hannah Delavan Pvt CT
Stephen: b 9-23-1746 d 5-17-1824 m Sarah Straw Lt NH
Stephen: b 1744 d p. 1809 m (1)Lydia Buzzell (2)Mrs Rachel Piper (3)Mrs Hannah Clapham Pvt PS NH
Sylvanus: b — d 7-12-1825 m Anna Smith Pvt NY W ★
Thaddeus: b 11-21-1763 d 3-17-1842 m Jemina Benedict Pvt CT
Thaddeus: b 1-26-1742 d 10-3-1826 m Hannah Holmes Pvt CT
Thomas: b 5-17-1731 d 9-1-1778 m Miriam Kimball Pvt NH
Thomas: b 12-24-1752 d 5-24-1831 m Mary Hoyt Sgt CT
Thomas: b 7-17-1743 d p. 1790 m Eunice (Hoyt) CS PS Pvt NH
Timothy: b 5-28/9-1739 d 1-9-1815 m Sarah Benedict Pvt CT
Timothy: b c. 1745 d p. 1796 m Sally Judge Pvt CT
Uriah: b 2-5-1749 d 1830 m Elizabeth Lockwood Pvt NY
Walter: b 2-7-1753 d 11-25-1828 m Grace Hoyt Pvt CT
Wm.: b 12-16-1737 d 2- -1820 m (1)Elizabeth Challis (2)Apphia Worthen Pvt MA
Wm.: b 7-24-1755 d 7-7-1818 m Susanna Balch Sol VT

HUBBARD, (includes HUBBART, HUBBURD, HUBERT)
Aaron: b 6-10-1753 d 3-1-1814 m Martha Nason Sgt MA
Abel: b 7-24-1760 d p. 1840 m Luey Taynter Cpl MA
Abigail Smith: b 10-16-1726 d 9-28-1813 m Israel Hubbard PS MA
Abijah: b 8-28-1755 d 1825 m Sarah Tryon Sgt CT
Abner: b 3-10-1750 d 3-13-1834 m Esther Hamlin SgtMaj CT
Abner: b 1759 d 9-7-1820 m Catharine Webster Pvt MA
Amos: b 9-30-1745 d 6-8-1792 m Leah Farr PS NH
Benjamin: b c. 1720 d 1793 m Mrs Mary Williams Pvt NC
Benjamin: b 1712 d 1784 m Elizabeth Todd PS VA
Caleb: b 1748 d p. 8-3-1776 m Prudence Chapman Pvt CT
Caleb, Jr.: b 3-11-1748/9 d 7-4-1802 m Elizabeth Johnson PS CT
Caleb: b 4-23-1754 d 4-7-1850 m (1)Tryphena Montague (2)Lucretia Ashley Sgt MA
Charles: b — d 4-20-1794 m Lucy George Smn VA W ★
Daniel: b 3-1-1729 d 1825 m Eunice Clark Pvt CT
Daniel: b 4-27-1753 d 2-27-1834 m Mary Sargent OrdlSgt MA
Daniel, Jr.: b 1714 d 12-19-1777 m Naomi Root Pvt MA
Daniel, Jr.: b 12-27-1737 d 9-11-1798 m Rachel Falley PS MA
David: b 9-2-1758 d 3-11-1806 m Jemima Chamberlin Pvt CT
David: b 1756 d 11-14-1814 m Abigail Labarre Drm MA
Ebenezer: b 3-1-1725 d 10-1-1807 m Hannah Estabrook MM PS MA
Eleazer: b 1730 d 7-15-1812 m Abigail Hollister Capt CT
Eli: b 5-23-1745 d 1-10-1814 m — Pvt MA
Elijah: b 1745 d 1808 m Hannah Kent Cmsry CT
Eliphalet: b 9-10-1748 d p. 1790 m Abigail Johnson Pvt CT

Elisha: b 10-1-1754 d 1-28-1837 m Martha Roberts Sgt CT
Elisha: b 12-20-1744 d 7-17-1814 m Mercy Hubbard Lt MA
Elisha: b 1750 d 12-28-1834 m Tamer Moore Cpl VT
Elizur: b 8-25-1736 d 9-14-1818 m (1)Lois Wright (2)Huldah — Capt CT
Ephraim: b c. 1695 d 4-14-1780 m Mary — PS CT
Ephraim: b 11-8-1710 d p. 1790 m (1)Ruth — (2)Sarah Billings Pvt MA
Ephraim: b 11-30-1742 d 2-24-1828 m Lucy Willard Sgt CS NH
Francis: b 12-17-1761 d 3-22-1838 m Mehitable Judkins Pvt MA
George: b 2-6-1731 d 1-7-1809 m Mary Stocking Capt CT
George, Sr.: b 11-30-1739 d 4-16-1818 m Thankful Hatch Lt CT
George, Jr.: b 2-12-1765 d 1839 m Mehetable Tyler Drm CT
Giles: b 9-7-1742 d 7-21-1824 m Editha Field PS MA
Henry: b 1- -1751 d 7-11-1825 m (1)Lydia Dickinson (2)Hannah Smith Pvt CT
Hezekiah: b 3-29-1742 d 11-30-1804 m Esther Foster Lt CT
Hezekiah: b 1737 d 5-1-1775 m Mabel Hubbard Capt MA
Isaac: b 9-24-1749/50 d 3-10-1848 m Ruth Coleman PS Sgt CT
Isaac: b 1-6-1730 d 1810 m Submit Graves Sgt CS MA
Israel: b 1-18-1725 d 4-21-1817 m Abigail Smith Capt MA
Jacob: b 1-8-1759 d p. 1790 m (1)Sarah Hobby (2)Sarah Hall Sol CT
Jacobus: b 5-23-1744 d 8-18-1807 m Rebecca Swart Dr NJ
James: b 12-23-1732 d 7-15-1808 m Hepsibah Smith Pvt CT
James: b 2-29-1728 d a. 1776 m Mary Bean Capt MA
James: b 4-15-1744 d 8-13-1813 m Martha Livermore LCol MA
James: b 1707 d 11- -1812 m Elizabeth Maddox Pvt NC
James: b 1740 d 1782 m Elizabeth Filmer Capt MA
Jeremiah: b 10-27-1732 d 3-7-1814 m Betty Meigs Lt CT
Jeremiah: b 1-29-1746 d 8-23-1808 m Flora Hazelton Ens PS CT
Jeremiah: b 3-9-1758 d 10-21-1825 m Hannah Hobbs Pvt MA
Job: b 1739 d 5-2-1822 m Thankful Clark Pvt CT
Joel, Sr.: b 1728 d 3-25-1802 m Anne Clark Pvt CT
Joel: b 12-10-1758 d 1-9-1853 m Lucy Bartlett Pvt MA
John: b 12-28-1748 d 9-11-1830 m Susannah Mills Sgt CT
John: b 1-14-1751 d 1837 m (1)Anna Atwater (2)Martha Bradley (3)Sally Thompson Pvt CT
John: b 1-27-1727 d 11-18-1786 m Rebecca Dickerman Chp CT
John, Sr.: b c. 1731 d a. 2-15-1800 m Sally — Pvt GA
John, Jr.: b 1763 d 5- -1831 m Elizabeth Flint Sol GA
John: b 3-14-1761 d 1-5-1850 m (1)Patty Tyler (2)Eunice Moore (3)Agnes — (4)Patience Wheeler Pvt SrgnMte MA ★
John: b 10-29-1758 d 6-10-1837 m Susannah Mitchell Cpl MA ★
John: b 4-4-1740 d 10-7-1780 m Elizabeth Braswell Pvt NC
John: b 7-16-1756 d 9-2-1832 m Mildred Brassil Pvt NC W ★
John: b 4-22-1759 d 12-27-1819 m Lydia Snow Lt RI
John: b 10-24-1738 d 7-31-1793 m Keziah Pigg PS VA
Jonas: b 5-21-1739 d 12-31-1775 m Mary Stevens Capt MA
Jonathan: b 10-25-1742 d 3-20-1813 m Katherine Roberts 2Lt CT
Jonathan: b 11-20-1720 d 3-11-1806 m (1)Nancy Lester (2)Sarah Forbes (3)Jemima Dickenson PS CT
Jonathan: b 9-17-1734 d 5-13-1806 m Mary Keep Pvt MA
Jonathan: b 1744 d 1-1-1825 m Christie (Annie)Deane Sgt MA
Jonathan: bpt 6-27-1762 d p. 1833 m Frances Parsons Pvt MA ★
Jonathan: b 1- -1748 d 3-29-1828 m Eunice Wheeler Pvt NH
Joseph, Jr.: b 2-14-1748/9 d 2-19-1830 m Honour Roberts Cpl MA
Joseph: b 8-1-1741 d 11-25-1819 m (1)Anna Gowen (2)Alice Wheelwright PS MA ME
Joseph: b c. 1750 d p. 1777 m Thankful Rowley PS NH
Joseph: b c. 1717 d p. 6-13-1799 m — PS VA
Josiah: b 3-6-1732 d 1796 m (1)Abigail Wetmore (2)Susanna Marks Pvt CT
Josiah: b 9-13-1758 d 7-13-1833 m Mary Hovey Pvt CT ★
Lazarus: b 1748 d — m (1)— Dinsmore (2)Abigail Gilmore Sol MA
Lemuel: b 1755 d p. 1800 m Mrs Sarah Fuller Ens PS NH
Leverett: b 7-21-1725 d 10-1-1794 m Sarah Whitehead Dr CT
Levi: b 2-24-1764 d 4-13-1834 m Abigail Jones Pvt MA
Lucy Stearns: b 10-6-1727 d — m Elisha Hubbard PS MA
Manoah: b 8-14-1739 d 9-7-1801 m Hannah Woodward Pvt CT
Matthew: b 2-22-1757 d 11-29-1812 m Martha Wallace Pvt VA
Moses: b 1-5-1746 d 3-27-1830 m (1)Mrs Abigail Sheldon (2)Lucy Williams Lt MA
Moses: b 1762 d 8-20-1837 m (1)Mary Frong (2)Mrs Ann Carson Pvt MA ★
Nehemiah: b 4-10-1752 d 2-6-1837 m (1)Cornelia Wyllis (2)Lucy Starr (3)Hannah Latimer DepQMGen CT
Noadiah: b 3-14-1735/6 d 5-4-1816 m (1)Mrs Phoebe Crowell (2)Mrs Sarah Seward (3)Phebe Thayers Lt CT
Noah: b 2-15-1754 d 8-4-1844 m (1)Prudence Kellogg (2)Mary Bosworth Pvt MA
Paul: b 1754 d 1817 m Mary Elizabeth — Pvt CL
Peter, Jr.: b 11-21-1742 d 5-19-1809 m Susannah Clark Ens MA
Peter: b 3-17-1754 d 8-26-1826 m Phebe Brigham Pvt MA
Peter: b 7-31-1756 d p. 1832 m Mary — Lt SC ★
Philip: b 1718 d 8-8-1792 m Hannah Plummer Capt MA
Philip: bpt 9-14-1755 d 9-11-1808 m Mehitable Underwood Pvt MA W ★
Richard Steers, Sr.: b 1723/4 d 12-14-1796 m Esther Hallock PS NY
Richard Steers, Jr.: b 1753 d 1821 m Mary Tuthill Sgt PS NY
Russell: b 6-28-1732 d 1785 m Mary Gray PS CT
Russell: b 1769 d 1814 m Olive Rood Pvt MA

Samuel, Sr.: b 7-21-1731 d 6-20-1813 m Sarah Smith Pvt CT
Samuel, Jr.: b 8-10-1750 d p. 6-5-1821 m Mary Barrett Sgt MA
Samuel, Sr.: b 5-24-1714 d 12-3-1783 m (1)Eunice Woodward (2)Abigail — (3)Mrs Elizabeth Drury PS MA
Samuel, Jr.: b 8-6-1741 d 6-24-1823 m Lucy Davis Capt MA
Samuel: b 3-8-1761 d 7-14-1843 m (1)Lucy Wheeler (2)Mrs Sarah Bell Pvt MA
Samuel: b 4-25-1742 d 2-10-1835 m (1)Catherine VanBrunt (2)Ann Emmens Lt NY
Samuel: b 1757 d 1820 m (1)Miss Stone (2)Mary McHovey Pvt VA
Seth: b 1-11-1751 d 12-13-1834 m (1)Ruth — (2)Belsora — Pvt MA ★
Solomon: b 7-8-1744 d 12-21-1822 m Rachel Tryon PS Pvt CT
Stephen: b 7-27-1756 d 12- -1828 m Lucy Boltwood Pvt MA
Thomas: b 1760 d 4-22-1821 m Silence Bartlett Pvt CT
Thomas: b 6-8-1730 d 10-12-1810 m Abigail Brown Capt MA
Thomas: b 12-28-1745 d 5-25-1807 m (1)Eliza Conant (2)Lois White Pvt MA
Thomas: b 11-26-1754 d 7-31-1841 m Molly Blaikley Swann Bgd Maj VA ★
Timothy: b 1734 d 5-15-1809 m Sarah Bailey Pvt MA
Titus: b 12-27-1762 d 3-22-1845 m Rachel Miller Pvt CT ★
Watts, Jr.: b 10-10-1753 d 1-24-1826 m Lois Corey Pvt VT
Wm.: b — d 8-12-1813 m — Pvt CT
Wm.: b 1762 d 1858 m Jane Reeder Pvt NC ★
Wm.: b 12-19-1744 d c. 1805 m Frances Thruston Maj VA
Wm.: b 10-13-1758 d 6-11-1847 m (1)Nancy Jones (2)Elizabeth Guthrie (3)Letitia Francis Sgt VA ★
Zadoc: b 1749 d 1827 m (1)Lois Pomeroy (2)Sally Sprague Pvt MA

HUBBELL,
Aaron: b 10-10-1762 d 10-13-1848 m Sarah Silliman Pvt CT W ★
Aaron: b 9-14-1757 d 12-26-1844 m (1)Sarah Dewey (2)Lucinda Moody Lt CT
Abijah: b 4-27-1763 d 7-18-1841 m (1)Hannah White (2)Betsey Case Pvt NY ★
Amos: b 1747 d 8-13-1817 m Lucy Holmes Capt CT W ★
Comfort: b 11-10-1729 d 7-5-1797 m (2)Susannah Baxter PS Capt CT
David: b 1752 d 4-5-1820 m Abiah Leavenworth Pvt CT W ★
David: b 1755 d 10-9-1845 m Elizabeth Williams Pvt MA
Ebenezer: b 1726 d 1812 m Mary Brooks Pvt CT
Elnathan: b 9-22-1717 d 7-21-1788 m Mehitable Sherwood Pvt VT
Enoch: b 8-10-1735 d 10- -1827m Sarah Wooding Pvt CT
Ephraim: b 12-21-1712 d 12-17-1795 m (1)Johannah Gaylord (2)Alice Hatch CS CT
Ezbon: b 1759 d 9-4-1821 m Molly — Sgt CT
Gershom: b 1724 d c. 1790 m Mehitable Hall Pvt CT
Gershom: b 7-29-1729 d 4-14-1802 m (1)Mary Bradley (2)Sarah Wakeman (3)Sarah St. John Lt CT
Gideon: b 1755 d 4-11-1838 m — Capt CT
Henry: b 5-31-1754 d 6-7-1827 m Mary Bunn Pvt PA
Hezekiah Bloomfield: b 1755 d 10-12-1855 m Nancy Drummond Sol NJ
Isaac: b c. 1747 d 5-22-1787 m Frances — CaptLt CT
Jedediah: b 8-22-1720 d 8-14-1819 m (1)Abigail Northrup (2)Susanah Hickok (3)Mary Hulbert (4)Eunice Johnson (5)Mrs Cleo Bemen Pvt MA
John, Sr.: b 2-20-1709/10 d 5-7-1782 m Hannah Wheeler Lt CT
John, Jr.: b 1751 d 9-22-1822 m Sarah Curtis Pvt CT
John: b 8-10-1734 d 3-10-1810 m (1)Eleanor Burr (2)Elizabeth Bradley Sgt CT
John: b 1754 d 4-17-1834 m Mary Robinson OrdlSgt NJ ★
John: b 6-10-1746 d p. 1788 m Phebe Davis Pvt NY
Justus: b c. 1732 d p. 1793 m Waitstill Bishop Pvt PS NY
Lemuel: b 1755 d 4-11-1845 m Rebecca Clark OrdlSgt VT ★
Matthew: b 9-4-1723 d — m Abiah Hawley Pvt MA
Nathan: b c. 1763 d p. 1808 m (1)Phebe Lake (2)Hannah Edwards Sgt CT
Nathaniel: b a. 1734 d 3-5-1802 m Ruth Jacques Maj PA ★
Parrach: b 1730 d 1819 m Lydia Beardsley Ens CT
Peter: b 4-10-1743 d 1826 m Sarah Stewart Pvt CT
Richard: b 10-20-1696 d 6-26-1787 m Penelope Fayerweather PS CT
Samuel: b 6-10-1754 d 6-23-1813 m Mary Beardslee Pvt CT ★
Seth: b 9-7-1759 d 12-7-1832 m (1)Elizabeth Guise (2)Salome Bennett Pvt CT
Seth: bpt 5-30-1736 d p. 1790 m (1)Jane Rockwell (2)Prudence Phelps PS NY
Shadrach: b 1739 d 9-18-1816 m (1)Phebe Dunning (2)Esther — 1st Lt CT
Shadrach: b 7-22-1740/1 d p. 1787 m Hannah Mosher Pvt CT
Silas: b 1752 d 11-30-1812 m Elizabeth Lampson Ens CT
Silas: b 2-24-1738 d 8-27-1805 m (1)Elizabeth Edmond (2)Mrs Hannah Wheeler Pvt CT
Silliman: b 1764 d 7-27-1847 m Hannah Taylor Pvt CT
Thaddeus: b 3-12-1725 d 4-8-1806 m (1)Ruth Betts (2)Mrs Phebe Squire CS CT
Wm. Gaylord: b 1736 d p. 7- -1779 m X Capt CT
Wolcott: b 1752-4 d 1839 m Mary Curtis MM MA
Zadock: b 1756 d 2-1-1813 m Mary Hubbell Pvt CT

HUBBS,
Alexander: b 1742 d 3-4-1834 m Mercy Cabel Lt NY ★

HUBBS, contd.
Charles: b c. 1752 d p. 1795 m Miriam Coffin Pvt NY
Jacob: b 10-30-1762 d 2-15-1843 m Asenath Williams Sol MD VA ★
James: b 1741 d 4-17-1809 m Mary Blatchly Cpl NY
John: b c.   12-25-1763 d 9-12-1844 m (2)Rebecca Woolsey (3)Mrs Mary Hill Pvt SC ★
Samuel: b 1765 d 2- -1845 m Mary McKinster Pvt NY ★
Wm.: b 1-10-1755 d 1811 m — Pvt NY W ★

HUBER,
Andrew: b 5-17-1762 d p. 1802 m — Kline Pvt PA ★
Conrad: b 1757 d 8-11-1842 m Mary Bender Pvt PA
George: b 8-6-1735 d 10-6-1815 m (1) — Shearer (2)Catharine Miller Sol PA
Henry, Sr.: b 1719 d 11-4-1798 m Ann Huber Capt PA
Henry, Jr.: b 6-8-1756 d 5-18-1850 m Mary Magdalene Shull Pvt PA
Henry: b 11-14-1753 d 12-24-1845 m Anna Maria — Pvt PA
John: b 1-10-1751 d 9-21-1821 m Christine Brinkle Col PA
John: b 3-25-1750 d 1811 m Esther Senseny SubLt PA
John: b 1723 d 4- -1791 m Margaret — Capt PA
Michael: b 6-23-1743 d 10-29-1822 m Anna Schwartz Capt PA
Michael: b 9-22-1737 d 6-26-1816 m Anna Mary Binkley Pvt PA
Michael: b 1-14-1750 d p. 1797 m Christine Germaine Sol PA
Rudolph: b 5-1-1722 d 3-29-1779 m Anna — Pvt PA

HUBLER,
Jacob: b 1711 d 5- -1789 m Barbara — PS PA

HUBLEY,
Bernard, Sr.: b 10-19-1719 d 1-27-1803 m (1)Magdalena Belzner (2)Anna Maria Hubley PS PA
Bernard, Jr.: b 1754 d 3-17-1810 m Elizabeth McCalla Capt PA W ★
Frederick: b 11-16-1751 d 12-23-1822 m Anna Maria Deering Maj PA ★

HUCKINS,
Israel: b 9-15-1760 d 5-20-1823 m Ruth Dame Pvt NH ★
James: b 10-14-1746 d 3-2-1837 m (1)Dorcus Bickford (2)Ruth — (3)Mrs Huldah Garland Pvt NH
John: b c. 1704 d 7-30-1789 m Abigail Edgerly PS NH
John: b 1759 d 8-13-1811 m Mary Pearl Pvt NH
Joseph: b 6-30-1736 d 4-3-1819 m (1)Mary Kelly (2)Sarah Merrill PS NH
Thomas, Jr.: b 3-28-1736 d 1786 m Sarah — Pvt NH

HUCKLEBERRY,
George: b a. 1743 d a. 1-9-1813 m (1)Rosanna Wise (2)Barbara Peckintaw Pvt PA

HUCKSTEP,
Charles: b 2- -1763 d 12-29-1854 m (1)Mazy — (2)Martha Gillum Pvt VA ★
Samuel: b c. 1750 d 1815 m (1)Elizabeth Anne — (2)Anna Miles PS VA

HUDDLESTON, (includes HEDDLESTON & HUDELSON)
Daniel: b c. 1720 d a. 1790 m Mary Ball Capt VA
David: b 1741 d 1790 m Sarah Easley Pvt VA
James: b c. 1736 d 1815 m Jane Montgomery Pvt VA
John: b 1715 d 1785 m Sarah Brown Pvt VA
John: b 1754 d 1818 m Margaret — Sol VA
Nathaniel: b 1730 d 1794 m Esther — Pvt PA
Seth: b 4-30-1746 d 9-7-1794 m Lydia Gifford Pvt MA
Wm.: b 11- -1756 d 9- -1845 m (2)Elizabeth Brockman Pvt Spy PA ★
Wm.: b — d p. 7-10-1803 m Jane — PS SC

HUDDY,
Joshua: b 11-8-1735 d 4-12-1782 m Mary — Capt NJ

HUDGINS, (includes HUDGENS)
Ambrose: b 1762 d 1-30-1844 m Elizabeth Henderson Sgt SC ★
Anthony: b 1759 d 9-4-1834 m Sarah Hundley Pvt VA ★
John: b c. 1758 d c. 1803 m (1)Amelia Foster (2)Ann Soper (3) — Soper PS VA
Robert: b 1-15-1759 d 11-10-1820 m Ann Burton Pvt VA
Wm.: b a. 1760 d 1781 m — Lt VA

HUDNALL,
John: b 1734 d 1814/5 m Jemima Jennings Pvt VA
John: b 6-22-1763 d 10- -1844 m (1)Patty Newman (2)Frances Miles McGee Pvt VA ★
Joseph: b c. 1739 d 1779 m Mary Taylor CS VA
Thomas: b c. 1742 d 11-24-1824 m Lucy — CS VA
Wm.: b 1736 d p. 1-31-1813 m Frances Smith Lt VA

HUDNUT,
Richard: b 8-4-1760 d 12-19-1818 m Grace Anderson FifMaj NJ

HUDSON,
Abraham: b 1750 d 1-15-1829 m (1)Abigail Howard (2)Sarah O'Hara Sgt NJ ★
Asa: b 1-14-1749 d 2-15-1840 m Mary Scott Sgt NY

Benoney: b 4-4-1761 d 1-28-1827 m Mercy McAlister Cpl RI ★
Chamberlain: b c. 1760 d 1843/4 m — Pvt NC
Cuthbird: b 1733 d p. 9-30-1799 m Elizabeth H — Capt NC
Daniel: b 4-27-1738 d 8- -1821 m (1)Mary Coe (2)Dorothy Hubbard (3)Abigail Watson Pvt NY
Darius: b c. 1750 d p. 1782 m Elvira — Pvt MA
David, Sr.: bpt 10-29-1721 d 1798 m Rebecca Fowler PS CT
David: b 1754 d p. 1-22-1823 m Elizabeth — Cpl VA
David: b 12-6-1762 d p. 1838 m Mary Cobb Booker Pvt SC VA ★
Dennis: b c. 1738 d p. 8-20-1810 m (1)Sarah Selby (2)Polly Melvin Pvt MD
Eli: b 1751 d 12-11-1828 m Sarah Perkins Sgt MA ★
Elisha: b 9-24-1744 d 4-17-1815 m Susanna Brigham Sgt MA
Enos: b 1-15-1759 d 6-10-1827 m Patty Brown Cpl MA ★
Ephraim: b 1757 d 5-3-1805 m Hannah Claus Lt NY
George: b c. 1749 d p. 1817 m Catherine Hudson Pvt PA
George: b 1745 d 6-15-1820 m (1)Isabella Abernethy (2)Isabella Buchanan Pvt PS PA
Hezekiah: b 6-11-1738 d a. 1782 m (1)Mary Lincoln (2)Mary Woodward (3)Abigail Marble Pvt MA
Irby: b 1752 d 1806 m Phoebe Featherstone Pvt VA
Isaac: b 4-18-1761 d 1834 m — MM DE
Isaac: b 9-19-1763 d 8-7-1848 m Dolly Shepherd Pvt NC
James: b c. 1760 d p. 1816 m Sarah — Sol GA
James: b 10-23-1719 d 11-29-1792 m Mary Rolfe Capt PS MA
James: b 3-14-1759 d 4-16-1849 m Martha McSwain Pvt NC
James: b c. 1755 d a. 4-18-1820 m Sarah — Pvt VA
John: b 9-9-1749 d 2-29-1780 m Hannah — Cpl CT
John, Sr.: b 1713 d 8-6-1799 m (1)Elizabeth McAllister (2)Bethia Wood Pvt MA
John, Jr.: b 11- -1758 d 3-12-1845 m Hannah Nelson Cpl MA ★
John: b 1739 d 1814 m — Allen Pvt NC
John: b c. 1750 d 1801 m Ann Barbour Capt VA
John: b 1760 d 3-4-1842 m (1)Catharine Lanier (2)Ann Williams Drm VA ★
Nathaniel: b c. 1737 d 1800 m Margaret Swesey Ens NY
Richard: b 1760 d 1843 m Elizabeth Reddin Pvt VA
Robert: b c. 1753 d p. 1806 m Mary — Pvt GA
Samuel: b 1738/9 d 3-7-1812 m Elizabeth Terry Pvt MM NY
Stephen: b 6-12-1761 d 3-21-1827 m Louisa Williams Pvt MA
Stukely: b c. 1734 d p. 4-8-1806 m (1)Rose Potter (2)Amey Roberts (3)Jane — Capt RI
Wm.: b 1-26-1755 d 2-5-1817 m Susan Tuthill Sol NY
Wm.: b 1745 d p. 1-23-1821 m (1)Elizabeth Jean Baker (2)Taffeness Moore Pvt VA
Wm.: b c. 1727 d 4- -1800 m Frances — PS VA

HUDSPETH,
Giles: b c. 1730 d p. 9-11-1796 m Elizabeth — CS NC
John: b — d p. 6-2-1780 m (2 ?) Mary Vaughn CS NC
Thomas: b c. 1762 d p. 10-7-1835 m Sarah Glen PS NC

HUFFINGTON,
Jonathan: b c. 1751 d 1802 m Sarah — Pvt MD

HUFFNAGLE, (includes HOOFNAGLE, HUFNAGLE)
Christian: b 3-1-1755 d 1836-8 m Mary Lorah — Pvt PA ★
George: b 1760 d 1818 m Mary — Pvt PA
Michael: b 1755 d 12-31-1819 m Rachel Kaufman Capt PA
Peter: b 1757 d 1816 m Maria Christina — Drm PA
Valentine: b 10-31-1756 d 12-6-1829 m Eve Berger Pvt PA

HUFFSMITH,
Adam: b c. 1758 d 1850 m (1)Julianna — (2)Catharine — (3)Christine — Pvt PA
Peter: b c. 1729/30 d 3- -1794 m Anna Maria — Pvt PA

HUGER,
Benjamin: b 12-30-1746 d 5-11-1779 m (1)Mary Golightly (2)Mary Esther Kinloch Maj SC
John: b 1-5-1744 d 6-22-1804 m (1)Charlotte Motte (2)Ann (Bourn) Cusack PS SC

HUGG,
Joseph: b c. 1741 d 1796 m (1)Sarah Smith (2)Elizabeth Homer PS NJ

HUGGINS,
David: b 1744 d 7-21-1821 m Hannah Ayres Pvt NH
Ebenezer: b 12-17-1748 d 10-15-1825 m Mary Dickerman Pvt CT
James: b 6-17-1750 d 9-14-1793 m Mary Brevard Pvt NC
John: b 1712 d 12-16-1781 m Hannah Ayres CS NH
John: b 1752 d 1826 m Margaret Brevard Pvt NC
John: b 1-12-1748 d 7-13-1825 m (1)Elizabeth Simons (2)Clarissa H — Capt SC
Jonathan: b 1741 d 1-7-1809 m Rhuama Brown Pvt NH
Joseph: b 1761 d 9-20-1849 m (1)Rebekah Burrell (2)Hannah Turner (3)Jerusha Austin Sgt MA
Luke: b a. 1750 d 1784 m Nelly — Pvt NC
Medad: b 1746 d 4-26-1812 m Merial Cutting Pvt MA
Nathan: b c. 1755 d a. 1842 m — Pvt SC
Nathaniel: b 5-10-1754 d 6-1-1828 m Phebe Ayres Sol NH
Samuel: b 1753 d 8-21-1837 m Lydia (Richards) Judd PS NH

Wm.: b 1745 d 2-2-1815 m Tryphena Ranston Cpl NY
Wm.: b c. 1749 d a. 6-18-1792 m Elizabeth — Pvt PA

HUGHART,
Thomas: b c. 1725 d a. 5-23-1810 m Rebecca Estill Col VA

HUGHES, (includes HEWES, HUES & HUSE)
Archelaus: b 9-25-1747 d 1798 m Mary Dalton Col VA
Benjamin: b c. 1763 d c. 1808-12 m Susannah — Pvt VA
Benjamin: b 10-7-1763 d 6-24-1838 m (1)— Tucker (2)Polly White Pvt VA ★
Bodwell: b p. 1723 d p. 1783 m Mercy Collins Pvt CT
Carr: b 6-29-1740 d 4-10-1833 m (1)Sarah Wells (2)Joanna Buswell Sgt CS PS NH
Christopher: b 1724 d 9-16-1777 m Jean Hines Pvt PA
Cornelius: b 1739 d 1814 m Rachel Campbell Sol PA
Daniel: b 1755 d 2-22-1846 m Sarah Cushman Pvt Pvtr MA CT ★
David: b 9-9-1749 d 11-23-1815 m Rachel Hand Pvt NJ
David: b c. 1755 d p. 1790 m Judith Daniel Lt VA
David: b c. 1756 d 1805 m Margaret Frame Pvt VA
Elias: b 1757 d 12-22-1844 m — Pvt Sct VA ★
Elias: b 1743 d 1800 m Jane Sleeth Pvt PA
Ellis: b 1745 d 1817 m (1)Eleanor (Hirst)Whillden (2)Judith Hudyer PS NJ
Felix: b 1723 d 1805 m Cinthia Kaighn PS PA
Gabriel: b 11-7-1762 d 10-20-1836 m Mary Williams Pvt VA ★
George Robert Twelves: b 8-25-1742 d 11-5-1840 m Sarah Sumner PS Pvt Smn MA
Henry: b c. 1756 d 4-27-1814 m Jane Cooper Capt VA
Hugh: b 9- -1738 d 12-11-1790 m Martha Breckenridge PS NJ
Hugh: b c. 1755 d 11-22-1838 m Mary Hutton Cpl PA
Isaac: b 9-16-1757 d 9-6-1833 m Joanna Rowell Pvt MA ★
Isaac: b 12-1-1747 d 4-26-1782 m Hannah Holstein LCol PA
Isaac: b 6-15-1740 d 1803 m Mary Warne Pvt VA
Jacob: b 1756 d 12-22-1854 m Elizabeth Jones Sgt VA
James: b — d 1819 m Mary Ann Stansbury Pvt MD
James: b 9-11-1744 d 5-6-1829 m Abigail Ayer Sgt NH
James: b 1750 d 1807 m Cassandra Dunn Sol PA
James: b 1756 d 1802 m Mary — Sgt VA
Jasper: b 1757 d 8-19-1821 m Ann Tompkins Cnt VA
Jesse: b c. 1751/50 d 1829 m Grace Tanner Sct VA
Jesse: b 12-20-1756 d 3-1-1838 m Jemima Sandus Lt VA ★
John: b 8-9-1759 d — m Margaret Robins Chamberlaine Capt MD
John: b 10-4-1750 d 2-9-1850 m Rebecca Taylor Pvt MD ★
John: bpt 8-3-1740 d 12-15-1805 m (1)Elizabeth Kingsbury (2)Jemima Elwell Maj ME
John: b 8-7-1739 d 9-25-1802 m Anne Webster 1Lt MA
John: b 10-31-1758 d 9-15-1832 m Molly Bean Pvt MA
John: b 1744 d 10-7-1819 m Mehitable Buzwell Lt NH W★
John: b 1729 d 1802 m Martha Moore Sgt NC
John: b 1747 d 9-19-1830 m Esther — OrdlSgt NC
John: b 1750 d 9-15-1818 m Sarah Wiley Capt PA ★
John: b 7-15-1737 d 9-27-1814 m Anna Harriman Pvt VT
John: b 10-28-1758 d 7-26-1826 m Ann Moore Capt VA W★
John: b 8-11-1763 d 12-11-1842 m Anne Meriwether Lt VA ★
John: b c. 1760 d 2-19-1831 m Mildred Bland Pvt VA
John Hall: b 7-10-1742 d 2-7-1802 m Ann Everett Lt MD
Jonathan: b 3-25-1753 d 9- -1849 m (1)Vercetta — (2)Abigail Jackson Ens PS VA ★
Joseph: b 2-11-1733 d 2-21-1811 m (1)Abagail Johnson (2)Sarah Moody LCol MA
Joseph: b 1761 d 9-4-1834 m (1)— Leonard (2)Annie Brown Capt NC SC ★
Joseph: b 9-20-1752 d 2-7-1839 m Sarah Swan Pvt PA
Joseph: b 6-6-1759 d 1837 m Catherine Dear Pvt PA
Memucan: b 4-12-1739 d 1-8-1812 m (1)Martha Hughes (2)Rhoda Allen PMCmsry PS NJ
Moses: b 4-13-1740 d 2-6-1831 m Abigail Fuller PS NH
Nathaniel, Sr.: b 1725 d p. 1790 m Abigail Walker Sol NH
Nathaniel: b 1747 d 12-16-1808 m Sarah Freeman Sgt NH
Owen: b 1740 d 1805 m Elizabeth Jenkins Pvt PA
Powell: b 6-22-1740 d 3-5-1823 m Elizabeth Colman Pvt VA
Ralph: b 1726 d 1804 m (1)Margaret Ferguson (2)Barsheba —Pvt VA
Reuben: b 12-27-1763 d 3-19-1829 m Betsy Gray Pvt VT
Reuben: b 1763 d p. 8-4-1814 m Keziah Taylor Pvt VA
Richard: b 1727 d 1-7-1832 m (2)Elizabeth Scarlett Pvt PA
Richard: b 1765 d 9-24-1822 m Leticia — Sol SC
Rowland: b 1750 d 1800 m Melinda Tuly Pvt VA
Samuel, Jr.: b 3-7-1740 d 2-3-1814 m Elizabeth Asten Sgt MA
Samuel, Jr.: b 9- -1766 d 1825 m Sarah Dole Cross Pvt MA
Samuel: b — d 10-3-1816 m Betsey Foot Cpl NH
Samuel, Sr.: b 2-21-1744 d 10-22-1820 m Sarah Hale Capt MA
Samuel: b 1725 d 4-19-1784 m Elizabeth Rain Pvt PA
Solomon: b 12-4-1734 d 10-15-1806 m (1)Sarah Masters (2)Elizabeth Wendell Hunt (3)Sarah Hunt PS MA
Stephen: b 1738 d p. 1784 m — Pvt VA
Sylvester: b 8- -1747 d c. 1780/1 m Mary Burns Pvt VA
Thomas: b 1752 d 5-16-1826 m Lucy Tandy 2Lt PM VA
Thomas: b c. 1750 d 7- -1791 m Frances Dorcas Forrester LCol MD
Thomas: b 5-5-1749 d 2-4-1823 m Elizabeth Swan Maj PA MD
Thomas: b 5-30-1752 d 12-10-1821 m Welthian Greene Maj RI
Thomas: b 1725 d 1777 m Martha Tucker Jolley Pvt SC
Thomas, Sr.: b 1727 d 1778 m Susanna Baker Pvt VA

Thomas: b c. 1740 d 1793 m — Pvt VA
Timothy: b 1748 d 7-5-1792 m Ann — Capt NY
Wm.: b 9-22-1760 d 1-10-1828 m Martha Swan Pvt MD
Wm.: b 8-22-1760 d 1839 m Rachel Bryer Pvt NH
Wm.: b 3-22-1761 d 6-3-1855 m Abigail Woodcock Pvt NH ★
Wm.: b 1748 d 1835 m Elizabeth Dawson Pvt PA
Wm.: b c. 1760 d 11-30-1843 m Hannah — Sol SC
Wm.: b 1740 d a. 10-14-1805 m Ruth — Capt PS VA
Wm.: b 11-23-1753 d 10-4-1832 m Susan Bowles Ens VA
Wm.: b 1750 d 11-14-1834 m Mary Sampson Capt VA
Wm.: b 1723 d 1824 m Molly Daten Sol VA
Wm.: b 1735 d a. 9-6-1813 m Mary Ball PS VA

HUGHEY, (includes HEWEY, HUEY & HUIE)
Jacob: b c. 1750 d p. 1-9-1792 m Margaret Cook PS NC
James: b 2-17-1744 d 4-3-1828 m Mary Lynn Sol GA
James: b 1742 d p. 1- -1839 m Sarah — Sgt SC ★
James: b 5-8-1759 d 4-5-1836 m (1)Polly Coffee (2)Jane Walker Pvt Sct SC
John: b 1-31-1752 d 5-2-1837 m Elizabeth King Pvt PA ★
John: b c. 1745 d 1794 m Mary — Pvt SC
Lewis: b 4-20-1762 d 1841 m Nancy — Pvt NC ★
Robert: b — d — m Catharine Wootman Pvt NJ
Robert: b c. 1750 d 1832 m Agnes Elliott Pvt PA
Robert: b c. 1741 d a. 1790 m Mary Boyd Pvt SC
Wm.: b c. 1751 d 5-12-1826 m Mary Kelly Berry Pvt NJ

HUGUENIN,
Pieter: b 7-3-1752 d p. 1795 m Rachel Holland Lt NY

HULETT, (includes HEWLETT, HOWLETT, HUGHLETT & HULET)
Charles W.: b 1760 d 5-27-1835 m Catharine Miller DrmMaj NJ Heirs ★
Daniel: b 5-11-1748 d 8-27-1838 m Abigail Paul Pvt CT
David: b 1762 d 10-3-1832 m Martha Wilkins Pvt CT
John, Sr.: b c. 1760 d p. 10-11-1848 m Drusilla Johnson Pvt MD
John: b 3-31-1756 d 8-26-1842 m (1)Sallie Howe (2)Hannah Walker Sgt MA ★
John: b 2-17-1731 d 4-4-1812 m Sarah Townsend PS NY
Joseph: b 11-1-1752 d 10-26-1850 m Hannah Larabee Pvt MA ★
Nehemiah: b 2-24-1764 d 8-5-1848 m Elinor Gray Pvt MA ★
Parley: b 1754 d 7-29-1803 m Bathsheba Parker Sol VT
Sylvanus: b 11-7-1758 d 11-10-1824 m Mary —Pvt MA ★
Thomas: b c. 1739 d p. 3-15-1791 m Sarah — PS VA
Wm.: b c. 1760 d p. 1818 m — Sgt VA
Wm.: b 5-12-1756 d p. 1820 m Nancy Watkins Pvt VA ★
Wm. Thrift: b 11-11-1757 d 1-16-1827 m Mary Tate Capt NC ★

HULICK,
John: b 10-12-1754 d 7-30-1841 m Mary Lott OrdlSgt NJ W★

HULIN,
Walton: b 1745 d 10-5-1823 m Abiah Mosher Pvt NY

HULING,
Andrew: b 1761 d 4-8-1844 m Susan Koontz Pvt VA ★
John, Sr.: b 5-14-1731 d p. 1790 m Susannah Raymond PS NY
John, Jr.: b 4-10-1762 d 1-2-1837 m (1)Theodosia Randall (2)Charity Eighmy Pvt NY ★
John: b 1-1-1743 d 7-9-1802 m Sara Seely Maj PA
Marcus, Sr.: b 2-11-1704 d 1786-8 m Rebekah Godfrey PS PA
Marcus, Jr.: b 10-22-1742 d 1804 m Masser Daugherty Ens PA
Thomas: b 3-3-1755 d 3- -1808 m (1)Elizabeth Watts (2)Rebecca Berryhill Ens PA

HULL, (includes HOHL & HULLS)
Aaron: b 9-11-1736 d 1825 m Abigail Whitlock Pvt CT
Aaron: b 7-17-1745 d p. 1780 m Sarah Merchant Pvt CT
Abel: b 8-24-1745 d a. 1815 m Abigail — Pvt CT
Abijah: b 6-10-1747 d — m Rachel Thompson PS CT
Andrew: b 1748 d 1827 m Elisabeth A. Atwater Pvt CT
Caleb: b 2-4-1695 d 9- -1788 m Mercy Benham Pvt CT
Daniel: b 10-1-1747 d 2-6-1816 m Ruth Barnum Cpl CT
Daniel: b 5-23-1728 d 2- 1790 m Eunice Hill MM CT
Daniel: b c. 1753 d p. 1776 m Mary — Sol MD
Daniel, Sr.: b 8-20-1725 d 8-26-1811 m Mary Betts Lt NY
Daniel, Jr.: b 1766 d 1842 m Phebe Green Pvt NY
David: b — d 12-8-1831 m Mary Davis Lt CT
David: b c. 1746 d 1830 m Margaret — Pvt NJ
Edmond: b c. 1740 d p. 1794 m Jane Graham Sol PS SC
Edward: b 5-1-1741/2 d 9-11-1804 m Mary Weeden PS RI
Eli: b 3-20-1764 d 4-3-1828 m Sally Beckwith Pvt CT ★
Elias: b 4-13-1748 d 1834 m (1)Mary Campbell (2)Cynthia Carpenter Lt RI ★
Eliphalet: b 12-14-1749 d 3-30-1813 m Huldah Patchen Pvt NY
Ezekiel: bpt 3-17-1765 d 1810 m Mary Denton Sol NY
Francis: b c. 1727 d c. 1806-8 m — Pvt VA
George: b 1-5-1757 d p. 1790 m Jamima Willman Pvt CT
George: b 10-15-1757 d p. 1832 m Hannah Keister Pvt Spy VA ★
Henry: b 4-1-1760 d 9-16-1835 m (1)Elizabeth — (2)Elizabeth Hawkins Pvt VA ★
Hezekiah: b 5-29-1754 d 2-3-1818 m Lucy Randall Lt NY
Isaac, Sr.: b 11-17-1731 d p. 1780 m Anne Dunham 1Lt NJ

HULL, contd.
Isaac, Jr.: b 11-17-1753 d *p.* 1800 m Massie Vaughn Pvt NJ
Jacob: b 11-23-1750 d 1804 m Catherine Abel Pvt PA
James Wake: bpt 5-3-1748 d 1-16-1823 m Rebecca Draper Sgt MA
Jedediah: b 7-24-1732 d 2-14-1796 m (1)Mary Chapman (2)Mary Osborne Lt CT
Jehiel: b 2-28-1728 d 2-3-1822 m Ruth Phelps Ens CT
Jeremiah, Sr.: b 1-5-1729 d 8-24-1790 m Mary Merriman PS CT
Jeremiah, Jr.: b 12-17-1763 d 10-10-1843 m (1)Sarah Barker Beadles (2)Phoebe Hart Pvt CT ★
Jesse: b 1-27-1745 d 1781 m Ruth Preston Pvt CT
John: b 1756 d 10-29-1832 m Sarah Baldwin Pvt CT
John: b 3-17-1739 d 6-1-1788 m Sarah Wilcox Drm CT
John: b 5-28-1762 d 11-8-1853 m (1)Ann Bowne Pvt NJ
John: b 1752 d 1807 m Jane Hastings Sgt VA
Joseph: b 4-29-1716 d 7-14-1786 m Syble Coe Pvt CT
Joseph: b 2-18-1728 d 9-24-1775 m Elizabeth Clark Sol CT
Joseph: b 10-27-1750 d 1- -1826 m Sarah Bennett Lt CT
Joseph: b 1757 d 1832 m Sara Miller Sol NC
Josiah: b 4-4-1759 d 3-27-1836 m Mehitable Chalker Pvt CT ★
Nathaniel: b 2-20-1726 d 1787 m Abigail Platt Pvt NY
Oliver: b 3-26-1747 d 1831 m Sara Platt Pvt CT
Oliver: b 3-16-1731 d 8-1-1803 m Penelope Fones PS NY
Peter: b 1738 d 1818 m Esther Parmalee Lt MA
Peter: b 1733 d 1- -1818 m Barbara Ann Keith Capt VA
Peter Thomas: b *c.* 1716 d 2- -1776 m Susanna Margaretha Dieffenbach PS VA
Roswell: b 1-16-1745 d 3-18-1825 m Charity Chatfield Pvt CT
Samuel: b 5-15-1744 d 1806 m Abigail Hitchcock PS CT
Samuel, Sr.: b 3-22-1730 d 4-27-1791 m Eunice Cook Sgt CT
Samuel, Jr.: b 5-27-1759 d 10-27-1828 m Abigail Doolittle Pvt CT
Samuel, Sr.: b 9-1-1707 d 1-17-1789 m Sarah Hall Pvt CT
Samuel: b 1755 d 1840 m Freelove Kelsey Sol CT ★
Samuel: b 7-20-1755 d 1803 m Bathena Norton Pvt NY
Samuel: b 5-5-1756 d 1831/2 m Grace Lytton Sgt NY
Samuel: b 1735 d 1814 m Martha Glover Pvt VA
Seth: b 1755 d 1828 m Sarah Patchen Sgt NY
Stephen, Sr.: b 1715 d 2-21-1798 m Martha Morey Pvt CT
Stephen, Jr.: b 9-17-1743 d 1803 m Comfort Babcock (Welles)Ens CT
Titus: b 8-15-1746 d — m Olive Barnes Lt CT
Titus: b 3-25-1751 d 8-13-1817 m (1)Lucy Parmalee (2)Mrs Olive Lewis Parmalee Dr CT
Trustrum: b 4-6-1720 d *p.* 4-2-1794 m Elizabeth — PS NJ
Warren: b 3-30-1762 d 1838 m Polly Gillett Pvt MA ★
Wm.: b 4-24-1753 d 11-29-1825 m Sarah Fuller LCol MA
Zalmon: b 4-22-1759 d 5-18-1839 m Eunice Belden Pvt CT ★
Zephaniah: b 1763 d 3-22-1841 m Rachel Gilbert Cav CT

HULSE,
Benjamin: b 2-22-1752 d 1810 m Abigal — PS NY
David: b 1755 d *a.* 5-4-1808 m Mary Jones Pvt NY
Gilbert: b 10-1-1735 d 1-9-1811 m Charity — Pvt NY
Jacob: b 10-10-1755 d 5-19-1833 m Rebecca VanTassell Pvt NY ★
John: b *a.* 1756 d 1811 m Abigail Williams Pvt NY
Jonah: b 1731 d 5-18-1809 m Joanna Raynor Pvt PS NY
Matthias: b 11-3-1755/6 d 4-11-1846 m Elizabeth Tyse Pvt NJ ★
Paul: b *c.* 1718 d 2-7-1799 m Esther Mapes PS NY
Silas: b 10-7-1754 d 12-1-1799 m Margaret Brown PS 2Lt NY
Wm.: b 10-14-1753 d 10- -1830 m Elizabeth Brown Sgt VA

HULSEY,
Jennens: b 1765 d 12-16-1850 m Rebecca Pate Pvt NC

HUMBER,
John: b *c.* 1735 d *c.* 1806 m Mary Elizabeth Christian PS VA

HUME, (includes HUMES)
Aaron: b 9-25-1762 d 6-11-1837 m Hannah Hibbard Pvt MA
Archibald: b 1739 d 2-1-1832 m Mary — Sgt PA
Charles: b 10-7-1739 d 4-7-1821 m Hannah James Sol VA
David: b 2-27-1763 d 1-13-1827 m Elizabeth Morris Pvt MA
Francis: b 1730/1 d 1813 m Elizabeth Duncan Capt VA
George: b 1729 d 1802 m Jane Stanton Sgt VA
George: b 10- -1756 d 1821 m (1)Elizabeth Proctor (2)Susan Hutchinson Chp LA
John: b 1732/3 d 1802 m (2)Helinor Manson (3)Jean Glen Pvt ME
John: b 1761 d 1840 m — Crawford Pvt PA ★
John: b 1761 d 9-16-1827 m Mary (Duncan)Chambers Pvt PA
Robert: b 6-18-1731 d *c.* 1782-4 m Merriam Shepard PS CS MA
Robert: b *a.* 1733 d 3- -1790 m Anna— Pvt PA
Stephen: b 3- -1754 d 4-24-1843 m Mary Hovey Pvt MA
Wm.: b *a* 1809 m (1)Susan Elzephan (2)— Granville (3)Mrs Sarah Baker Pvt VA
Wm.: b 1734 d 1795 m Anne — Pvt VA

HUMISTON, (includes HUMMASON & HUMMASTON)
Daniel: b 6-29-1727 d 4-8-1798 m (1)Desire Dorman (2)Abigail Atwater Pvt CT
Ephraim: b 12-5-1730 d 5-3-1806 m Susanna Bassett Lt CT
James, Jr.: b 10-28-1734 d 2-18-1812 m Hannah Hitchcock Pvt CT
Jesse: b 12-4-1749 d 1-21-1837 m Abi Blakeslee Pvt CT
Jesse: b 3-12-1764 d 3-12-1832 m Lois Doolittle Pvt CT
Joel: bpt 12- -1758 d 8-8-1832 m Anna Wheeler Pvt CT

HUMMEL,
Adam: b 1755 d 8-21-1836 m (1)Margaret — (2)Elizabeth — Pvt PA
David: b 1-9-1761 d 10-3-1793 m Mary Toot Pvt PA
Frederick, Sr.: b 4-14-1726 d 6-24-1779 m (1)Rosina Kauffer (2)Barbara Blessing 2Maj PS PA
Frederick, Jr.: b 10-4-1758 d 12-7-1802 m Rachel Reichert Pvt PA
George Adam: b *c.* 1752 d 2- -1808 m Magdalene — PS PA
Jacob: b 2-21-1756 d 2-22-1832 m Anna Elizabeth Heffner PS PA
John: b 8-10-1750 d 10-5-1776 m Christine Catherine Grundel Pvt PA
Mathias: b 2-23-1746 d 11-29-1828 m Catharine Barbara Young Cpl PA
Michael: b 1-12-1723 d 1-24-1805 m Anna Margaret — Pvt PA

HUMPHREVILLE, (includes HUMPHREYVIL)
Lemuel: b 6-25-1737 d 4-25-1798 m Mary Beecher Ens CT
Timothy: b 9-17-1746 d 1-14-1800 m Rebekah Burnet Sgt NJ

HUMPHREY, (includes HUMFREY, HUMPHREYS, HUMPHRIES, HUMPHRIS & HUMPHRY)
Abner: b 10-27-1763 d 12-17-1824 m Mary Purcell Sol VA
Absalom: b 8- -1760 d 12-9-1834 m Barthena Wall Pvt SC ★
Amasa: b 1-12-1756 d 2-19-1799 m (1)Lucy Case (2)Abigail Griswold Pvt CT
Amaziah: b 1-28-1754 d 2-26-1822 m Elizabeth Harris Pvt CT
Arthur: b 3-15-1763 d 1812 m Mary Kingsbury Sgt MA
Asahel: b 7-22-1747 d 10-21-1827 m Prudence Merrill Sgt CT ★
Asher: b 4-16-1759 d 3-12-1826 m Chloe Humphrey Pvt CT
Benjamin: b 5-18-1734 d 5-19-1805 m Bethsheba Beal Sgt ME
Benjamin: b *c.* 1758 d 7-27-1814 m Jane Lawrence Lt NC VA
Benjamin: b *a.* 1752 d *c.* 1822-33 m Chloe Biggs Sol NC
Charles: b 2-13-1743 d 3- -1826 m Naomi Worcester Pvt CT
Charles, 2d: b 3-6-1734 d 1779 m Sara — Pvt CT
Charles: b 8-28-1748 d 2-28-1815 m Sarah Evans 2Lt PA
Cornelius: b 10-10-1735 d 3-10-1812 m Sarah — Col NY
Daniel: b 8-17-1737 d 8-27-1813 m Rachel Phelps PS CT
Daniel: b 1750 d 1805 m Hester Williams Pvt NC
David, Sr.: b 6-5-1726 d 3-23-1814 m Lucy Marshall Pvt CT
David, Jr.: b 2-16-1758 d 7- -1831 m Lucy Marshall Pvt CT
David: b 5-15-1757 d 1-2-1837 m Lydia Shores Cpl MA
David: b *c.* 1740 d *c.* 1790 m Jane Wells Pvt PA
David: b 5-25-1753 d 2-25-1839 m Martha Word Capt NC ★
Ebenezer: b 6-22-1741 d 6-20-1836 m (1)Ruth Shumway (2)Mrs Abigail Marsh Capt MA
Elihu: b 4-14-1738 d 2-25-1777 m Asenath Humphrey Maj CT
Elijah: b 4-27-1746 d 7-2-1785 m Anna Mansfield Maj CT W★
Elijah: b 1750 d 2-10-1817 m Esther Brown Pvt MA
Evans: b 9- -1750 d 1-15-1806 m Elizabeth Lightbody Ens NY
Ezekiel: b 8-28-1719 d 1795 m Elizabeth Pettibone PS CT
Frederick: b 12-9-1753 d 7-13-1821 m Ruth Tuller Capt CT
George: b 11-11-1756 d 7-16-1813 m (1)Elizabeth Pettibone (2)Rachel Humphrey Fif CT
George: b 1764 d 4-10-1840 m (1)Martha Gerard (2)Mary Rose — Pvt VA ★
George: b 12-19-1749 d 3-26-1834 m (1)Jane Wilson (2)Elizabeth Jolly Pvt VA
Henry: b 8-1-1726 d 2-11-1793 m Abigail Clap Sgt MA
Hugh: b 1748 d 10-25-1840 m Deziah Rixley Sgt MA ★
Isaac: b 1755 d 10-15-1817 m Mary Chapman Pvt CT
Isaac: b 11-29-1735 d 1788 m Esther North Sol CT
Jacob: b 1751 d 1-21-1826 m (1)Ann Charlesworth (2)Jane Charlesworth Capt PA W★
James: b 6-5-1753 d 7-13-1845 m Elizabeth Capen Capt MA
James: b 12-5-1754 d 3-12-1819 m Deborah Tirrell Pvt MA W★
James: b 6-22-1711 d 5-2-1798 m (1)Ann Torrey (2)Silence Whitmarsh PS CS MA
James: b 3-20-1722 d 5-8-1796 m Esther Wiswell PS MA
James: b 11- -1752 d 5-26-1828 m Jean Fisher Pvt NH
James: b 12-23-1755 d 9-15-1834 m Phoebe Howell Sgt NY ★
John: b 12-22-1755 d 1-25-1837 m (2)Hannah Mayo Sgt MA
John: bpt 11-11-1753 d 8-18-1801 m (1)Mary Caswell (2)Mercy Eaton Cpl MA
John: b 1741 d *p.* 1779 m (1)Pamelia Eaton (2)Achsah Larison (3)Rachel Stilwill Pvt NJ
John: b 3-27-1754 d *p.* 1790 m Urie Eaton Pvt PA
John: b 4-8-1757 d 5-1-1816 m Elizabeth Bullock Sgt RI W★
John: b 8-9-1727 d — m Martha Walker Pvt RI
John: b 1754 d 1829 m Mary Clary Sgt SC
John: b *c.* 1745 d 1815 m Elizabeth Thomas Sol SC
John: b *c.* 1719 d 12-31-1775 m Eurah — Capt VA
John: b 1741 d *p.* 1796 m Ann North 2Lt VA PA
John: b 11-25-1755 d 4-7-1825 m Margaret Murphrey Pvt VA ★
Jonathan, Sr.: b 6-8-1715 d 9-13-1794 m (1)Desire Owen (2)Lois (Phelps)Viets Col PS CT
Jonathan: b 4-5-1737 d 1796 m — Capt CT
Jonathan: b 7-29-1764 d 8-2-1836 m Rebecca Vinal Pvt MA
Joseph: b 1-24-1743/4 d 9-21-1809 m Annis Pettibone Ens CT
Joseph: b 1745 d *a.* 1-7-1811 m Rebeccah Phelps Pvt PS GA
Joseph: b 1-14-1745 d 5-19-1804 m — Pvt MD
Josiah, Jr.: b 1752 d 1829 m — Sgt RI
Josiah, Sr.: b 1717 d 1778 m Habijah Brown PS RI
Levi: b 5- -1765 d 8-6-1845 m Loraina Eaton Pvt CT ★
Lewis: b *c.* 1753 d 3-4-1805 m Elizabeth — Smn MD

Lot: b 4- -1762 d 2-11-1836 m (1)Chloe Moses (2)Mary McGloughlin Pvt CT
Martin: b c. 1734 d c. 1810 m Susannah (Humphrey)Ens CT
Nathaniel: b 5-20-1735 d 6- -1822 m (1)Maria (Humphrey) (2)Lucy Moses 2Lt CT ★
Nathaniel: b 8-22-1759 d 11-4-1824 m Lucy Darby OrdlSgt RI ★
Noah: b 3-25-1735/6 d 6-13-1803 m Lydia Leavitt Pvt MA
Oliver: b 4-13-1720 d 10-30-1792 m Sarah Mills Garrett PS CS CT
Ralph: b 1735 d 9-20-1789 m Agnes Wilson Col VA
Richard: b c. 1750 d 1810 m (2)Jane Asenath Sol NC
Robert: b 10-9-1751 d 8-19-1834 m Martha Alexander Pvt PA ★
Royal: b 9-22-1761 d 4-30-1848 m Eusebia Humphrey Pvt MA ★
Samuel, Jr.: b 1-14-1755 d 6-15-1850 m Zerviah Wilcox Pvt CT ★
Solomon, Jr.: b 8-2-1752 d 12-24-1834 m (1)Lucy Case (2)Hannah Brown Sgt CT ★
Theophilus: b 1744 d 1826 m (1)Hepzibah Cornish (2)Diana Averitt Pvt CT
Thomas: b 10-27-1737 d 1818 m (1)Elizabeth Hopkins (2)Joanna Flint Pvt NY
Thomas: b 6-2-1742 d 6-6-1824 m Mary Marks Capt VA
Thomas: b 12-18-1756 d 7-25-1827 m Mary Wall Capt VA
Uriah: b — d a. 3-21-1818 m — CS VA
Wm.: b 3-5-1730 d 1818 m (1)Olive Pratt (2)Elizabeth — Capt NH
Wm.: b a. 1711 d 1- -1791 m Elizabeth Wiltse Col NY
Wm.: b 6-4-1760 d 12-23-1820 m Ann Blount Sol NC
Wm.: b c. 1746 d 7-1/3-1832 m Lydia Munro Capt RI
Wm.: b 12-13-1733 d p. 1785 m Susannah Webb Pvt VA
Wm.: b a. 1755 d 1- -1805 m Mary Summers PS VA

HUMRICHOUSE, (includes HUMRICKHOUSE)
Peter: b 10-10-1753 d 2-13-1837 m Mary Hadelman Lt PA ★

HUMSTON,
Edward: b 9-22-1737 d 1-23-1821 m Susannah Quarles PS CS VA

HUNGATE,
Charles: b 1745 d 1820 m (1)Mollie Hale (2)Catharine Odel Pvt VA
John: b 1750 d 1811 m Elizabeth Hale Pvt VA

HUNGERFORD,
Amasa: bpt 5-21-1749 d p. 1790 m Elizabeth Seeleye Sgt VT
Benjamin: b 6- -1741 d 9-1-1775 m Zezia Walker 2Lt CT
David: b a. 1740 d 1-29-1777 m Rosanah Williams Pvt CT
Elijah: b 11-10-1756 d 12-8-1834 m Rhoda Harvey Pvt CT ★
Elisha: b 7-5-1743 d p. 1-20-1811 m Keziah Conger Pvt NY
Ezra: b 2-15-1761 d 9-1-1832 m Caroline Wilcox Pvt CT
Isaiah: b 1-23-1757 d 6-16-1833 m Esther Mead Pvt CT
James: b 9-7-1747 d — m Sarah Steevens Pvt CT
James: b 3-5-1760/1 d 12-6-1832 m — Pvt CT ★
Jehiel: b 6-3-1758 d 1844 m Hannah Spencer Pvt CT ★
Joseph: b 11-10-1761 d 1835 m (1)Sarah Tuttle (2)Eunice — Pvt CT ★
Josiah: b 12-20-1763 d 9-19-1841 m Hannah Bigelow Pvt CT
Nathaniel: b 5-23-1733 d 1807 m Rachel Cone Pvt CT
Reuben: b 9-9-1748 d 11-10-1828 m Olive Gaylord Pvt CT
Robert: b 1-3-1751/2 d 12-29-1834 m Olive Ely Lt CT ★
Samuel: b 5-10-1725 d 9-3-1789 m Mary Graves CS CT
Stephen: b 1743 d 6- -1814 m Alathea Cogswell Pvt CT
Thomas, Jr.: b 7-19-1742 d 1810 m (1)Naomi Moody (2)Elizabeth Matthews Capt CT
Thomas: b c. 1739-41 d 5-3-1803 m Anne Washington Lt VA
Uriel: b 2-12-1755 d 4-18-1834 m Hannah Wilcox Sgt CT ★
Zechariah: b 3-20-1741 d 11-1-1816 m Lydia Bigelow Capt CT

HUNKINS,
Robert: b 10-8-1758 d 3-20-1836 m Abigail Hoyt Pvt MA
Robert: b 1738 d 4-1-1818 m (1)Phebe Emerson (2)Lydia Chamberlain Capt VT

HUNN, (includes HUN)
Derrick: b 12-5-1760 d 3-7-1795 m Annatse Lansing AsstCmsry NY
Enos: b 3-1-1745 d 3-21-1805 m Esther Smith Pvt CT
Gideon: b 3-12-1710 d 1785 m Rebecca Beldin PS CT
John: b 1746 d 4-22-1810 m Mary Silsby Capt DE
Samuel: b 5- -1763 d 1840 m Polly Tillotson Pvt CT ★
Thomas: b 10-8-1735 d 9-15-1796 m Catherine Van Emburg Maj NJ
Wm.: b 8-28-1734 d 5-17-1814 m Sarah deForest Capt NY

HUNNEWELL, (includes HONEYWELL)
Enoch: b 4-9-1725 d 9-11-1813 m Elethea Searles Sol NY
Israel, 3d: b 3-13-1744 d 10-27-1790 m Elizabeth Oatley Capt NY
Rice: b 1- -1760 d 1840 m Ruth Allen Pvt VT MA NY
Richard: bpt 7-18-1736 d 10-16-1798 m Eunice Thompson Pvt MA
Thomas: b 1756 d 4-22-1829 m (1)Molly Dean (2)Elizabeth — Pvt MA ★
Wm.: b 1751 d 8-23-1820 m Rebecah Snell Smn ME ★
Zerubbabel: b 4-15-1714 d 8-23-1803 m (1)Hannah Haskell (2)Hannah (Cobb) Swett PS MA

HUNSICKER,
Henry: b 3-7-1752 d 7-8-1836 m Esther Detweiler Pvt PA
Johannes: b c. 1728/9 d 1800 m Magdalena — PS PA

HUNSIKER,
Casper: b — d p. 1810 m Margaretha — Pvt PA

HUNSPERGER, (includes HUNSBERGER)
Christian: b 4-21-1732 d 1-28-1806 m Catharine — Pvt PA
Christian, Jr.: b 10-15-1757 d 3-20-1829 m Catherine Souder Pvt PA

HUNT,
Aaron: b 11-2-1737 d 4-26-1818 m Levina Howe Sol MA
Abell: b 1736 d 1816 m Betsey Calkins 2Lt NY
Abijah: b 1743 d 12-27-1822 m (1)Prudence Fitch (2)Abigail Bracket 2Lt MA
Abner: b 7-28-1731 d 8-21-1814 m Abigail Miller Pvt MA
Abraham: b 6-2-1748 d p. 1794 m Mary St. Leger Capt MA
Abraham: b 1740 d 10-27-1821 m Theodosia Pearson LCol NJ
Arnold: b 1723 d 11-14-1792 m Phoebe Drake Pvt NY
Asa: b 1744 d 1791 m Rebecca — Pvt MA
Brimsmead: b 10-7-1708 d 5-12-1802 m (1)Patience Henshaw (2)Abigail Matthews Pvt MA
Daniel: b 1754 d 4-14-1826 m Hannah Miller Pvt CT ★
Daniel: b 10-17-1761 d 2-13-1837 m (1)Judith Chaffin (2)Nancy Jones Lt NC ★
David: b 3-3-1756 d 4-1-1815 m Mary Warren Cpl NJ
David: b 9-4-1757 d 11-16-1819 m Phebe Oakley Pvt QM NY
David: b 1745 d 2-14-1826 m Nancy Richardson Capt VA
Ebenezer: b 5-9-1735 d 9-28-1804 m Rachel Kingman Cpl MA
Ebenezer: b 1758 d 5-11-1814 m Elizabeth Tepel Pvt NJ
Ebenezer K.: b 8-26-1755 d 7-26-1831 m Mary Beal Pvt MA
Edward: b 1734 d c. 4-11-1786 m Mary Shuel PS NJ
Eldad: b 10-21-1742 d 1822 m (1)Jerusha West (2)Huldah Benton Cpl CT
Eleazor: b 11-12-1762 d 11-22-1840 m Lydia Worley PS NC
Elijah: b c. 1751 d 4-13-1832 m Mary Knapp Pvt NY
Elijah: b c. 1737 d 1-31-1795 m Sarah Richardson CS PS VA
Eliphaz: b 1-12-1739 d 6-12-1820 m Hannah Stiles Capt CT
Enoch: b 1-1-1760 d 2-17-1824 m Sally Page Pvt NH ★
Ephraim: b 1-4-1729 d 6-3-1812 m Delight Mann 2Lt MA
Ephraim: b 4-8-1734 d 4- -1820 m — 2Lt MA
Ephraim: b 1-4-1744 d 3-28-1832 m Abigail Cates Pvt MA
Ephraim: b 1760 d 1843 m Vashti Thayer Pvt MA ★
Esli: b 1-10-1759 d 5-8-1837 m (1)Nancy Lacey (2)Hallie Agnes Cockran (3)Tamma Mosely Pvt NC ★
Ezekiel: b 4-6-1735 d 1-5-1803 m Eunice White Pvt MA
Fitz Maurice: b 3-21-1756 d 9-9-1822 m Sarah Robeson Pvt GA
Gad: b 1-16-1749 d 5-6-1806 m Elizabeth Woodward Sgt CT
Gideon: b 9-8-1763 d 6-10-1839 m Prudence Crane Pvt MA ★
Humphrey: b 3-4-1762 d 5-29-1828 m Peggy Moore Pvt NH W★
Ichabod: b 1756 d 4-30-1821 m (1)Mary Stone (2)Eunice Stone Pvt MA ★
Isaac, Sr.: b 1729 d 1-12-1812 m Lois Armstrong Pvt CT
Isaac, Jr.: b 3-18-1756 d 9- -1841 m Rebecca Mitchell Pvt CT ★
Israel: b 8-27-1758 d 3-2-1850 m Catherine Nowell Sgt MA ★
Jacob: b 9-18-1754 d 1-18-1842 m Hannah Littlefield Pvt MA ★
James, Jr.: b 6-6-1762 d 3-23-1832 m Jemima Carter Sol GA
James: b c. 1756 d a. 1841 m Una Lovelace Sol MD
James: b 5-19-1739 d 5-12-1832 m Jemima Green Capt NJ
James: b 11-4-1758 d 3-26-1837 m Mary Cochrane Pvt NJ ★
James, Sr.: b 7-24-1732 d a. 2- -1805 m Mary — Sol VA
James: b 1729 d 2-8-1803 m Rhoda Nunnelie OrdlSgt VA W★
James: b 1720 d a. 9-7-1795 m Sarah Whitlock Sol VA
James Booth: b 10-28-1753 d 8-5-1824 m Sarah Ewing PS Pvt NJ
Japheth: b 1711 d 3-7-1808 m Elizabeth Davis Dr MA
Jared: b 11-21-1760 d 9-24-1812 m Asenath Clark Cpl MA
Jeremiah, Jr.: b 4-1-1754 d 1-27-1815 m Nancy Blodgett Pvt MA
Joel: b 1759 d 10-30-1820 m Beda Moulthrop Pvt CT ★
John: b 5-31-1744 d 12-12-1816 m Asenath Jennings Pvt CT
John: b 1-15-1752 d 8-16-1828 m (1)Lydia Bullock (2)Anna Webster Sol CT
John: b 1750 d 1825 m Joanna Holbrook PS MD
John: b 7-9-1737 d 1813 m (1)Rebecca Pain (2)Mary Thayer CS Sgt MA
John: b 1712/3 d 1-9-1785 m Esther Wells Pvt MA
John: b 1716-18 d 12-19-1789 m Mary — Pvt MA
John: b 6-9-1738 d 4-4-1816 m Hannah Dakin Pvt MA
John: b 11-19-1716 d 1-19-1777 m Ruth Fessenden PS CS MA
John: b 2-20-1719 d 1806 m Rachel Carpenter PS MA
John: b c. 1758 d p. 1780 m Anne Brewster PS NJ
John, Sr.: b c. 1719 d p. 2-20-1787 m — Pvt NJ
John: b c. 1760 d a. 1826 m Rhoda Reed Pvt NJ
John: b 8-5-1755 d 10-9-1807 m Mary Jeffreys CS NC
John: b 9-19-1748 d 5-7-1829 m Margaret Wilson Pvt NC
John: b 1750 d 4-30-1834 m Charity — Pvt NJ ★
John: b c. 1750 d p. 1809 m — Pvt NC
John: b 3-12-1752 d 8-10-1818 m Frances Penn PS Pvt NC
Jonas: b 5-24-1757 d 8-9-1831 m Anna Myal Bond Pvt MA
Jonathan: b 8- -1736 d p. 3-4-1782 m Sarah Vining Sol MA
Jonathan: b 12-25-1760 d 1835 m Millisant Brown Pvt MA ★
Jonathan: b c. 1724 d p. 1790 m Miriam Trussel PS NH
Jonathan: b12-1-1741 d 7-25-1825 m Christian — Sgt NJ
Jonathan: b 5-24-1756 d 11-18-1822 m (1)Sarah Stout (2)Mary Salter Pvt NJ
Jonathan: b 1760 d p. 1843 m Rachel Hampton Cpl NC ★

HUNT, contd.

Jonathan: b 10-17-1707 d 9-5-1783 m (2)Isabella Hampton (3)Margaret Lawrence PS NC
Jonathan: b 9-12-1738 d 6-1-1823 m Lavinia Swan LCol CS VT
Joseph: b 12-7-1746 d 12-12-1822 m Eunice Copeland Pvt MA
Joseph: b a. 1755 d 1-24-1835 m Mollie Littlefield Matr MA
Joseph: b 11-22-1757 d 5-16-1831 m Anne Estabrook Matr MA
Joseph: b 12-8-1759 d 1-10-1810 m Betsey Fay Pvt MA
Joseph: b 1733 d 1804 m Nancy Anne — Pvt PA
Joseph: b 3- -1758/9 d 1799 m Sarah Glover Pvt PA
Joshua: b 1759 d 3-3-1814/15 m Elizabeth Whittlesey Pvt NH
Josiah: b 3- -1727 d 3-26-1827 m Abigail Lawrence Pvt MA
Josiah: b 3-18-1760 d 5-21-1841 m (1)Sarah Miller (2)Esther Smith Sgt NJ ★
Jotham: b 2-15-1755 d 4-10-1832 m Elizabeth Prey Pvt NY
Judkins: b 1747 d 1817 m Martha Batts Capt VA
Lemuel: b 10-4-1761 d 1804 m Nancy Curtis Pvt MA
Melzar: b 10-18-1756 d 6-24-1828 m Mercy Cooley Pvt MA
Memucan: b 8-23-1729 d 1808 m Mary Polly Wade CS PS NC
Mesech: b 12-16-1766 d 11-30-1849 m Sahra Roby Sol MD
Moses: b 10-28-1756 d 7-10-1822 m Esther Jenney Pvt MA
Nathan: b — d a. 4-13-1808 m Elizabeth — CS NJ
Nathaniel: b 1738 d 11-6-1783 m Elizabeth Woodwell Pvt MA
Oliver: b 8-15-1756 d 3-27-1841 m Elizabeth Carle Furman MM NJ
Paul: b 7-19-1753 d 11-28-1832 m Elizabeth Shattuck Pvt MA
Pelatiah: b 5-28-1748 d 11-26-1814 m Hannah Benson Pvt NY
Perley: b c. 1763 d 6- -1828 m Persis Gleason Pvt MA
Peter: b 5-2-1720 d 6- -1814 m Mary Kimball Pvt MA
Peter: b 9-23-1757 d 8-25-1836 m Hannah Benson Pvt NY ★
Philip, Sr.: b 10-27-1720 d p. 1790 m Elizabeth Goodwin PS Pvt NH
Ralph: b 1732 d 1821 m Elizabeth Phillips Pvt NJ
Reuben: b 8-6-1744 d 6-30-1816 m (1)Rebecca Barrett (2)Mary Taylor Sgt MA
Richard: b 3-25-1752 d 1-2-1835 m Elizabeth Warren Pvt MA ★
Richard: b 3-23-1720 d 8-27-1819 m Mercy Hull Pvt NJ
Richard: b 6-13-1756 d 7-29-1838 m (1)Hannah Phillips (2)Rhoda Barcroff Pvt NJ ★
Richardson: b 9-2-1762 d 1-6-1818 m Nancy Martin Carter PS VA
Robert: b 1-20-1754 d 8-14-1824 m Jane Turner Sgt MA
Russell: b c. 1733-6 d 10-18-1806 m Lydia Peck 2Lt CT
Russell: b 3-11-1766 d 8-26-1831 m Esther Beebe Sgt CT
Samuel: b 5-9-1735 d c. 12-22-1790 m Abigail Day Sgt MA
Samuel: b 3-9-1730 d 12-7-1804 m Elizabeth Ring Pvt MA
Samuel: b 1744/5 d 3-8-1812 m Submit Graves Pvt MA
Samuel: b 1-18-1764 d 1-5-1840 m Lydia F. Green Pvt MA ★
Samuel, Jr.: b 9-29-1734 d 8-24-1799 m Esther Strong LCol NH ★
Samuel: b 1758 d 12-1-1798 m Sarah Howard PS Sol NC
Samuel: b 9-20-1743 d p. 1817 m Mary Weaver Pvt RI
Samuel: b 9-27-1736 d 8-13-1799 m Sarah Osgood Pvt VT
Seth: b 1732 d 1-8-1828 m Mary Irish Pvt VT
Sherebiah: b 7-23-1758 d 3-6-1826 m (1)Ruth White (2)Mrs Dorothy (Mirick) Garfield Sgt MA
Simeon: b 12-20-1762 d 10-14-1852 m (1)Ruth Coudrey (2)Elizabeth Folsom Pvt CT
Simon: b 4-8-1734 d 4-1-1820 m Lucy Raymond Capt MA
Simon: b 1711 d 8-9-1777 m (1)Submit — (2)Anna Barron Pvt MA
Solomon: b 1743 d 8-10-1814 m Mary Sutton Pvt NY
Stephen: b 10-9-1736 d p. 11-2-1784 m Margaret Wortman Col PS NJ
Thomas: b 1747 d p. 1833 m Elizabeth Parker Pvt MD ★
Thomas: b 9-17-1754 d 8-18-1808 m Eunice Wellington BgdMaj MA
Thomas: b 12-5-1746 d 2-18-1825 m Experience Thayer Pvt MA ⟵
Thomas: b 7-27-1746 d 12-25-1818 m Jerusha Woodworth Capt NY W ★
Thomas: b — d 1826 m Celia Hunt Sol SC
Thomas: b 1760 d c. 1845 m — Morgan Pvt VA
Timothy: b 3-7-1757 d 8-22-1838 m (1)Dolly Worcester (2)Hannah Stickney Pvt MA ★
Timothy: b 9-16-1744 d 9-16-1824 m Rosanna Cynthia Vermilye Sol NY
Turner: b 1756 d 8-8-1847 m (1)Mary — (2)Martha Turner (3)Elizabeth — Sol NC
Willard: b 5-7-1741 d p. 11-24-1795 m Martha Wadkins Pvt MA NH
Wm.: b c. 1764 d 12-8-1809 m Gertrude Russel Sol GA
Wm., Sr.: b 4-13-1726 d 4-4-1802 m Mary Wheeler Pvt MA
Wm., Jr.: b 3-7-1753 d 9-18-1845 m Mary Plympton Pvt MA
Wm.: b 8-10-1737 d 8-20-1801 m Mary Storm Lt NY
Wm.: b 8-16-1763 d 10-20-1846 m Nancy Colborn Pvt PA ★
Wilson: b 1-16-1754 d 1-28-1833 m (3)Margaret Shotwell Pvt NC W★
Zebulon: b 1759 d 1839 m Lucy Whittlesey Pvt NH
Ziba: b 1-4-1746 d 9-10-1820 m Joanna Blount Capt CT

HUNTER,

Abraham: b 1720 d 1-14-1786 m — 2d Lt MA
Andrew: b 1750-2 d 2-24-1823 m (1)Ann Riddle (2)Mary Stockton Chp NJ
Andrew: b c. 1750 d p. 3-2-1823 m (1)Elizabeth Longshore (2)Rachel Flowers Pvt PA
Andrew: b 7- -1757 d 9-18-1837 m Rachel Moore Pvt PA
Andrew: b c. 1737 d 1822 m (1)Matilda Hickman (2)Mary Andrews Sct SC

Arthur: b 4-5-1749 d 2-24-1829 m Sarah Winchell PS ME
Charles: b c. 1755 d 8-16-1782 m Rebecca Dumford Sol KY
Daniel: b 4-8-1742 d 2-3-1783 m Maria Lease Col PA
David: b 7-6-1756 d 10-12-1823 m Lucy Barnes Cpl MA
David: b 2-1-1732 d 1776 m Rebecca Morgan Pvt NY
Edward: b 1716 d 5-9-1797 m (1)Tabitha — (2)Mrs Elizabeth Moore CS MA
Elijah: b 8-4-1749 d 12-22-1815 m Anna Drake Capt PS NY
George: b 12-3-1753 d 2-18-1803 m Mary Andrews Sgt NY
George: b c. 1745 d c. 1825 m Sarah Paxton Pvt PA
George: b 3-14-1755 d 2-23-1823 m Phoebe Bryant SrgnMte PA W ★
Henry: b 1725 d 1-11-1799 m (1)Sarah Wyer (2)Sarah Wyer Capt MA
Henry: b 8-11-1751 d 5-18-1836 m Martha Sloan Pvt NC ★
Henry: b 1734 d 1783 m Fanny Starke CS SC
Humphrey: b 5-14-1755 d 8-21-1827 m Maryland Jane Ross Lt NC
Isaac: b 8-29-1759 d 1816 m (3)Mary Gordon Pvt NC
Jacob: b 1737 d 6-8-1784 m Sarah Hill PS 2Maj NC
Jacob: b c. 1745 d a. 1792 m Sarah Rogers PS NC
Jacob: b 1755 d 1806 m Polly — Sol SC
Jacob: 3-16-1766 d 9- -1836 m Anne Clarke Pvt VA
Jacob: b c. 1740 d 1780 m (2)Elizabeth Boush PS VA
James: b 4-15-1735 d 2- -1809 m Abigail Williams Col MA
James: b 10-4-1744 d 1822 m Frances Galatian 1Lt NY
James, Jr.: b 4-8-1740 d 1-30-1821 m Mary McFarlane Maj CS PS NC
James: b 1738 d 1794 m Christian Trice PS NC
James: b 1743 d 10-3-1824 m Martha (Barclay)McAfee Capt PA
James: b 12-6-1738 d 1809 m Elizabeth McDonald Pvt PA
James: b c. 1752 d p. 1783 m Martha Lewis Pvt PA
James: b 1718 d c. 1795 m Frances (Dott)Fayssoux PS SC
James: b 11-17-1746 d 12-25-1788 m Marianna Spence Pvt VA
John: b 7-6-1754 d 8- -1828 m Jane MacGregor Pvt NH
John: b a. 1750 d p. 1787 m Mary Stratton Pvt NJ
John: b 1755 d 9-23-1805 m Phebe — Ens NY
John: b — d 6/7- -1823 m Barbara Bowman Sol NC
John: b 1747 d 9-3-1821 m Ann Levis Capt PA
John: b 1751 d 7-2-1829 m Margaret Want Pvt PA
John: b c. 1737 d 1796 m (1)Rachel McFarland (2)Mary (Stith)Early Capt PS VA
John: b a. 1746 d 1815 m Jane Broadwater 2Lt CL
John: b c. 1735 d 1800 m Elizabeth Chapman Pvt VA
John Chapman: b c. 1760 d c. 1848 m Sarah Dade Triplett Pvt VA
Jonathan: b 1-24-1754 d 3-21-1834 m Hannah Walkup Pvt MA ★
Joseph: b c. 1745 d p. 1783 m Margaret Barnes Pvt NC
Joseph: b 8-5-1763 d 6-6-1834 m Margaret McGaughey Pvt PA
Joseph, Jr.: b 1757 d 1825 m Catherine Phillip Pvt PA
Nathaniel: b 4-5-1758 d 1-20-1845 m Sarah Strong Pvt CT NY ★
Nathaniel: b 1764 d 1812 m Sarah Ann Tyler Pvt VA
Nicholas: b 9-10-1757 d 8-26-1828 m Hannah Van Reed Maj PA
Patrick: b 6-1-1760 d 5-9-1848 m Nancy Jack Ens PA
Robert: b 1748 d 1-28-1820 m — Pvt MA
Robert: b 6- , 5-1745 d 2-19-1808 m (1)Susanna Thompson (2)Margaret Randall 1Lt CS PS ME
Robert: b c. 1730 d 5-22-1791 m (1)Marey — (2)Catherine Shaw Lt MA
Robert: b 1761 d 1846/7 m Elizabeth Hunter 2Lt NY
Robert: b c. 1740 d — m —Pvt PA
Robert: b 9-16-1750 d 3-11-1830 m Catherine Keyes Pvt SC ★
Samuel: b 1732-6 d 4-10-1784 m Susannah Scott Col PA
Samuel: b c. 1757 d 4-18-1813 m Susan Alexander PS VA
Theophilus: b c. 1725 d 1798 m Jane Lane LCol NC
Thomas: b c. 1720 d — m Mary Whitmel Maj PS NC
Wm.: b 12-2-1723 d 8-1-1790 m Ann — Pvt MD
Wm.: b 10- -1754 d 11-30-1827 m Mary Newell Lt NH ★
Wm.: b c. 1713 d 1800 m Mary — Capt NC
Wm.: b 1737/8 d 12-18-1803 m Jane — Pvt PA
Wm., Sr.: b 1722/3 d 1787/8 m Martha Taliaferro PM VA

HUNTING,

Amos: b 3-15-1763 d 1-23-1846 m Olive Newell Pvt MA
Benjamin: b 11-18-1753 d 8-17-1807 m (1)Anna Rhodes (2)Mehitable Cooper PS NY
Converse: b 5-5-1760 d 7-4-1851 m Mary Parker Sol MA
Ebenezer: b 5-3-1748 d 2-8-1821 m (1)Lois Hunting (2)Hannah Ordway CS NH
Isaac Mulford: b 11-14-1731 d 2-8-1812 m Ruth Stratton 1Lt NY
Israel: b 4-23-1758 d 6-1-1834 m Rhoda Dewing Pvt MA ★
Jonathan: b 1758 d 1837 m (1)Marcy Sawin (2)Chloe Felt Pvt MA ★
Nathaniel: b 4- -1730 d 9- -1801 m Mary Murdock PS NY
Timothy: b 1752 d 10- -1793 m Lucy Savage Pvt MA
Wm.: b 6-3-1738 d 7-6-1816 m Puah Osborn PS NY

HUNTINGTON,

Abner: b 7-21-1752 d 1-8-1819 m Abigail Leavens Pvt CT
Amos: b 9-4-1739 d 7-2-1822 m Peace Clark Capt VT
Andrew: b 5-9-1747 d 7-16-1811 m Ruth Hyde t CT
Andrew: b 6-21-1745 d 4-7-1824 m (1)Lucy Coit (2)Hannah Phelps Cmsry CT
Andrew: b 7-8-1740 d 1830 m Lucy Landphere Pvt CT
Andrew: b 11-11-1761 d 1845 m Lydia Davis Pvt CT ★
Asa: b 4- -1741 d 1825 m Polly Hine Pvt CT

Azariah: b 6-6-1756 d 11-7-1833 m Parnell Champion Cpl CT
Barnabas: b 5-29-1728 d 4-14-1787 m Anne Wright PS CT
Benjamin: b 4-19-1736 d 10-16-1800 m Anne Huntington PS CT
Christopher: b 1719 d 1800 m Sarah Bingham Pvt CT
Christopher: b 11-11-1761 d 11-11-1854 m Eunice Shaddock Pvt CT
Ebenezer: b 12-26-1754 d 6-17-1834 m (1)Sarah Isham (2)Mary Lucretia McLellan LCol CT
Eleazer: b 9-19-1734 d 1808 m Phebe Hartshorn Capt CT
Eliphalet: b 4-24-1737 d 6-15-1799 m Dinah Rudd Pvt CT
Elisha: b 12-17-1754 d 1838 m Esther Ladd Pvt MA
Enoch: b 12-15-1739 d 6-12-1809 m Mary Gray PS CT
Frederick: b 10-26-1750 d 10-3-1830 m Lydia Andrews NCdr CT
Gamaliel: b 11-28-1760 d 2-2-1813 m Keturah Armstrong Cpl CT
Hezekiah: b 10-3-1728 d 9-17-1807 m Submit Murdock Maj CT
Hezekiah: b 12-30-1759 d 5-27-1842 m Susan Kent Sol CT
Hiram: b 8-24-1758 d 5-8-1835 m Lucy Perkins Pvt CT ★
Jabez: b 8-7-1719 d 10-5-1786 m (1)Elizabeth Tracy Backus (2)Hannah Williams MajGen CT
Jabez: b 4-15-1738 d 11-24-1782 m Judith Elderkin PS CS CT
Jacob: b 6-16-1741 d p. 1790 m Elizabeth Goodin Pvt MA
James: b 6-23-1760 d 11- -1811 m Rose McDinsmore Drm CT
James, Sr.: b 2-2-1706 d 9-21-1785 m Elizabeth Darby CS CT
James, Jr.: b 10-1-1743 d 3-22-1808 m Hannah Curtis Sgt CT
Jared: b 1-20-1740/1 d 4-16-1819 m Amy Gorton Sgt CT
Jedediah: b 8-4-1743 d 9-25-1818 m (1)Faith Trumbull (2)Ann Moore BGen CT
Jeremiah: b 2-8-1751 d 1831 m Lois Bates Sgt VT
John: b 10-26-1745 d 9-30-1815 m Abigail C. Abel Sgt CT
John: b 5-11-1749 d 9-18-1834 m Sarah Rebecca Newell 2Sgt CT W★
John: b 8-15-1737 d 3-26-1826 m Hannah Weed Pvt MA
John: b 12-24-1714 d c. 1784 m Abigail Jones PS NH
John S.: b 10-21-1759 d 3-22-1842 m Katurah Davis Pvt CT ★
Jonas: b 8-19-1754 d 11-26-1830 m Rhoda Baldwin MM CT
Joseph: b 6-18-1752 d 11-25-1841 m Suzannah Fuller Pvt CT ★
Joshua: b 8-16-1751 d 1820/1 m Hannah (Huntington)Col CT
Roger: b 12-3-1757 d 11-29-1835 m Susanna Elderkin QM CT ★
Roger: b 4-1-1758 d 12-4-1850 m Polly Dyer Pvt CT ★
Samuel: b 6-3-1759 d 12-7-1823 m Bethia Daggott Sgt CT
Samuel: b 10-16-1723 d 3-20-1797 m (1)Rebecca Fairbanks (2)Dorothy Gates PS CS CT
Simeon: b 4-2-1740 d 8-10-1817 m (1)Freelove Chester (2)Patience Keene 1Lt CT
Simon: b 9-12-1719 d 12-27-1801 m Zipporah Lathrop PS CT
Theophilus: b 11-23-1753 d 7-11-1830 m Phoebe Hall Sgt CT ★
Thomas: b 1-13-1744/5 d 2-22-1835 m Mary Ward Dr CT
Uriah: b 4-11-1760 d 9-11-1839 m Martha Adams Pvt MA ★
Wm.: b 8-20-1732 d 5-31-1816 m Bethia Throop Capt CT
Wm.: b 2-1-1736 d 7-19-1816 m (1)Anne Pride (2)Lois Durkee (3)Elizabeth Waterman Cpl CT
Wm.: b 9-19-1757 d 5-11-1842 m Prescendia Lathrop Fif CT

HUNTLEY, (includes HUNDLEY)
Aaron: b 1752 d 2- -1818 m Rachel — Pvt NH
Amos: b 10-31-1727 d 9-1-1804 m Phebe Mack CS CT
Andrew: b 1-16-1747 d 4-16-1836 m Selinda Bosworth Pvt CT
Charles: b c. 1740-50 d p. 11-19-1796 m Elizabeth A. — PS VA
Elihu: b 10-23-1743 d 9-13-1836 m (1)Mary Chappel (2)Naomi Brockway Pvt CT W★
Elijah: b c. 1723/4 d 11-20-1815 m (1)Anna (Munsell)Downer (2)Zerviah Abbe Pvt CT
Elisha: b 12-15-1760 d 1-17-1835 m Clarry Gustin Pvt NH
Ezekiel: b pt 4-4-1731 d p. 5- -1782 m (1)Mary — (2)Naomi Tiffany Mar CT
Hoel: b 1-10-1750 d 8-17-1842 m ( )Hannah Holmes ( )Sarah Huntley Pvt CT ★
Isaiah: b 11-12-1752 d 12-21-1820 m Elizabeth Church Pvt NH
Jabez, Sr.: b 1718 d c. 1810 m — Sgt MA
Jabez, Jr.: b 1760 d 10-1-1816 m Betty Smith Pvt MA
James: b 4-17-1725 d 2-25-1816 m Lucretia Smith Capt CT
Joel: b c. 1745 d — m Catherine Jennings PS VA
Josiah: b 1756 d 8-11-1827 m (1)Elizabeth Motley (2)Ann Holmes Pvt VA W★
Martin: b 9-27-1750 d 4-16-1834 m (1)Mehitable Sill (2)Phebe Mack Pvt CT
Nathan: b 6-2-1726 d 4-30-1798 m Lucy Smith Sol MA
Reuben: b 9-25-1752 d p. 9- -1837 m (1)Lovice Huntley (2)Azubah Huntley (Widow Huntley Pvt CT ★
Robert S.: b 1762 d 1-11-1854 m Betsy Wilson Sol NC
Rufus: b 1749 d p. 1783 m Esther Moore Cpl NH
Russell: b 8-9-1758 d 3-9-1808 m Ann Miller Pvt NH
Solomon: b 3-29-1754 d 3-4-1847 m (1)Ruth — (2)Abigail Plato Pvt CT ★
Thomas: b 5-15-1745 d 1802 m Zilpha S. Meadows Pvt NC
Wm.: b 2-15-1755 d 2-3-1842 m Hannah — Pvt NY
Zachariah: b c. 1740 d p. 1783 m Sarah — PS VA

HUNTOON, (includes HUNTON)
Aaron: b 6-9-1758 d p. 6-20-1820 m Elizabeth Smith Pvt NH ★
Benjamin: b 9-4-1729 d 12-12-1815 m (1)Judith Clough (2)Abigail Page (3)Mrs Mercy Quimby (4)Mrs Hannah Dearborn Sgt PS NH
Benjamin: b 7-13-1744 d p. 1790 m Deliverance Goss PS NH

Charles: b 3-18-1755 d 11-21-1829 m Susannah Sleeper Pvt MA ★
Charles, Sr.: b 10-12-1725 d 5-27-1818 m Maria Smith PS NH
Daniel: b 7-9-1738 d 10-16-1802 m Martha Fifield PS Sol NH
John: b 1-4-1753 d 1838 m Susanna Chase Capt NH
Jonathan: b 1756 d 10-16-1833 m Hannah Chase Pvt MA
Joseph: b 1731 d 3-13-1813 m Sarah Davis Lt NH ★
Josiah: b 5-1-1758 d p. 2-28-1794 m Hannah Glidden Pvt NH
Nathaniel: b 6-18-1721 d a. 9-10-1793 m (1)Anna Dearborn (2)Martha Judkins Capt NH
Philip: b 6-18-1749 d p. 1790 m Polly Willard Sgt NH
Samuel: b 6-18-1718 d 5- -1796 m (1)Hannah Ladd (2)Margaret Newley Pvt NH
Thomas P.: b 11-2-1753 d 1-2-1831 m Elizabeth Huntoon Pvt NH
Wm.: b c. 1729/30 d p. 5-12-1809 m Judith Kirk Sol VA

HUNTRESS,
Christopher: b c. 1728 d — m — Pvt NH
Darling: bpt 4-19-1730 d p. 1-12-1795 m Love Hearle PS ME
Solomon: b 6-16-1749 d p. 1799 m Lucy Burleigh Pvt NH

HUNTZINGER,
John George: b 3-25-1754 d 10-15-1815 m Anna Mary Deibert Pvt PS PA

HUPP,
Ann Rowe: b 1757 d 6-23-1823 m John Hupp, Sr. PS PA
Everhart: b 1745 d 1824 m Margaret Thomas Lt PA
John: b c. 1750 d 3-26-1782 m Ann Rowe Pvt PA

HURD,
Abner: b 1-7-1744 d p. 1821 m Rebecca Savage Lt VT
Abraham: b 1724 d p. 1790 m Mrs Mary Stevens Wilcox Pvt CT
Adam: b 3-24-1757 d 2-14-1844 m (1)Martha — (2)Hepzibah — Pvt VT CT ★
Asahel: b 10-20-1747 d 9- -1776 m Rebecca Blakesley Lt CT
Benjamin: b 11-19-1759 d 7-24-1844 m Mary Carey Mus CT
Bethel: b 11-27-1750 d 5-17-1817 m Mary Hurd Sgt VT
Crippen: b 1761 d 12-14-1845 m Elizabeth Hurd Pvt CT
Curtis: b 10-27-1751 d 3-11-1831 m Abigail Judson Pvt CT
Daniel: b 2-24-1762 d 3-29-1835 m (1)Phoebe Conger (2)Nancy Conger Pvt NJ
Daniel, Jr.: b 8-22-1758 d 1-1-1826 m Lucinda Hamilton Sgt VT
Ebenezer: b 10-26-1732 d 7-13-1820 m Hannah Allen Sol NY
Ebenezer: b 4-10-1756 d 10-28-1824 m Abigail Kempton Pvt NH
Eleazer: b 8-15-1758 d p. 1810 m Catharine — Sgt VT
Elijah: b 4-10-1755 d 10-7-1835 m (1)Burzinah Leavenworth (2)Polly Hamilton Pvt CT ★
Elnathan, Sr.: b 10-18-1730 d c. 1794 m Abigail Carter Sol CT
Elnathan, Jr.: b 1-10-1755 d 4-27-1846 m Anne Ray Pvt CT ★
Isaac: b 5-11-1759 d 1-5-1852 m (1)Mary Quicksal (2)Mary Moore Pvt CT ★
Jacob, 3d: b 3-28-1762 d 12-16-1861 m Abigail Carey Pvt CT
Jacob: b 1747 d 1828 m Elizabeth Horn Pvt NH
Jedediah: b 12-11-1763 d 11- -1818 m Jerusha — Sgt VT
Jesse: b 10-13-1765 d 7-21-1831 m Drusilla Dart PS CT
John: b 1758 d 1795 m Amanda Farnham Pvt CT
John: b 1-25-1751 d 12-25-1827 m Lois Hurd Pvt CT
John: b 12-9-1727 d 7-19-1809 m (1)Elizabeth Foster (2)Mrs Mary (Russell)Foster Col CS PS NH MA
Joseph: b — d 2-11-1778 m Prudence — Cpl CT
Josiah, Jr.: b 6-7-1734 d 6-29-1807 m Hannah Brown Lt NJ
Justus: b 1721 d 3-31-1804 m Rachael Fuller PS CS NH
Lewis: b 5-26-1759 d 12-18-1847 m Catherine Sanford Sgt CT ★
Lovewel: b 12-22-1760 d 3-25-1809 m Margery Hurd Pvt CT
Moses: b 1746 d 8-6-1832 m Eunice — Sgt VT
Nathan: b 8-4-1727 d — m Eunice Hinman Capt CT
Nathan: b 2-2-1746 d 1810 m Ruth Larabee PS Cpl NH
Nehemiah: b 12-12-1726 d 1797 m Sarah Mead Pvt CT
Philo: b 7-26-1755 d 8-25-1829 m Elizabeth Clark Pvt CT ★
Reuben: b 3-9-1722 d p. 1790 m — Walton Sgt NH
Robert Lane: b 2-29-1765 d 8-27-1856 m Lydia Russell Mus VT ★
Samuel: b 1722 d — m Tainor Levenworth 2Lt CT
Samuel: b 11-1-1734 d 10-14-1810 m Lydia Wilcox Capt PS NH
Simeon, Sr.: b 7-24-1725 d p. 1783 m Ruth Hicock Pvt CT
Simeon, Jr.: b 5-22-1759 d 1- -1832 m Sarah Tallman Capt CT
Solomon: b 12-25-1750 d 9-26-1819 m — Hurlburt Pvt CT
Thaddeus: bpt 12-28-1743 d 2-12-1827 m (2)Elizabeth Wakely Capt CT
Thomas: b 3-12-1754 d p. 1794 m Mary Ray Pvt CT
Thomas: b 10- -1760 d 12-7-1833 m (1)Sarah Hutchins (2)Esther Church Pvt Mar PS MA ★
Wilson: b 2-8-1763 d 3-2-1853 m Abigail Holbrook Pvt CT ★

HURDLE,
Hardy, Jr.: b 1754 d 6- -1828 m Christian Outlaw PS NC

HURLBURT, (includes HOLBERT, HULBERT, HULBURD, HURLBUT & HURLBUTT)
Abiram: b 5-12-1764 d 3-24-1846 m Mary Barrett Pvt CT
Adam: bpt 10-24-1736 d p. 7-19-1809 m Rebecha — Capt CT
Alvin: b c. 1759/60 d 6-12-1798 m Abinoam Phelps Pvt CT
Amos: b 12-3-1752 d 11-1-1835 m Esther Geer Sgt CT ★
Asher: b 1-20-1762 d 11-25-1836 m Anna Wright Pvt CT ★

HURLBURT, contd.
Azor: b 8-17-1746 d *p.* 1781 m Mary Mead Ens PS CT
Benoni: b 1735 d 9-29-1791 m Phoebe — Sgt NY
Betsy: b 6-27-1769 d 7-26-1850 m Noah Hickok PS CT
Caleb: b 1753 d 1824 m Lydia Mitchell Pvt CT
Christopher: b 5-30-1757 d 4-21-1831 m Elizabeth Mann Pvt RI W★
Daniel, Jr.: b 1740 d 2-11-1827 m (1)Naomi Stuart (2)Esther Patrick Lt CT W★
Daniel: b 8-14-1758 d 1-1-1847 m Lucretia Noble Sol CT
Ebenezer: b 9-16-1747 d 7-11-1819 m (1)Mary Sheldon (2)Hannah Parker Hall Pvt VT
Elijah: b 6-15-1753 d 9-25-1831 m (1)Zilpha Foote (2)Ruth Frisbie Pvt CT ★
Elijah: b 12-9-1719 d 2-8-1803 m Elizabeth Belden PS CT
Eliphalet: b 8-31-1752 d 4-17-1834 m Mehitable Deming Pvt CT ★
Elisha: b 1760 d 5-29-1824 m Hannah Landon Pvt MA ★
Gideon: b 6-9-1729 d 7-1-1823 m Deborah Brainerd Cpl CT
Gideon, Jr.: b 4-5-1744 d 8-12-1828 m (1)Elizabeth Judson (2)Martha Warner Pvt CT
James: b 11-3-1756 d 1-1-1815 m (1)Nancy Pearsall (2)Anna Hays Pvt CT
James: b 9-20-1755 d 1-9-1824 m Eleanor Pomeroy Lt MA
Jehiel: b 9-10-1762 d 2- -1813 m Eunice Bacon Pvt CT
John: b 4-10-1751 d 3-7-1832 m Judith Homer Cpl CT ★
John, Jr.: b 3-12-1730 d 3-10-1782 m Abigail Avery Tiffany PS CT
John: b 1-29-1735 d 6-7-1815 m Mercy Hamlin PS MA
John: b 12-14-1741 d 3-4-1829 m Mary Bellis Capt NY
John: b *c.* 1739 d 7-4-1811 m Philippa Emerson Cpl NH
Joseph: b 5-23-1744 d 9-21-1796 m Sarah Roberts Pvt CT
Joseph: b *c.* 1708 d *p.* 1781 m (1)Elizabeth Buttolph (2)Elizabeth Christopher Hinman CS CT
Joshua: b 10-26-1746 m Rosanna Wilcox Pvt CS MA
Matthias: b 6-18-1755 d 4-13-1814 m Clemence Kellogg Pvt CT ★
Rufus: b 1741 d 9-6-1781 m Hannah Lester Sgt CT
Salmon, Jr.: b 10-5-1734 d 9- -1815/6 m Anna Everett Pvt MA
Samuel: b 4-15-1737 d 3-23-1818 m Prudence Hinman Capt CT
Samuel: b 4-21-1748 d 8-12-1816 m Jerusha Higgins Lt CT
Samuel: b 1748 d 3-23-1831 m Rebecca Beach 1Lt CT
Samuel: b 8-28-1750 d 6-11-1815 m (1)Mary Kilbourne (2)Prudence Couch Pvt CT
Seth: bpt 7-24-1763 d 1813 m (1)Priscilla Pomeroy (2)Elizabeth Elliott Pvt MA
Stephen: b 12-12-1760 d 5-1-1807 m Abigail Meeker Pvt CT W★
Thomas: b 1754 d 10-7-1814 m Eunice Grant Sgt CT
Wm.: b 1730 d 1782 m Tabitha Warner Sgt VT

HURLEY,
Cornelius: b 1730 d *a.* 12-9-1788 m Mary — CS MD
James: b 4-1-1761 d *p.* 1818 m Lydia Riddle Pvt PA
John: b 1751 d *a.* 1815 m Amelia Lewis Pvt MD
Thomas: b *a.* 1744 d 1778 m — Buchanan Pvt VA
Wm.: b 1750 d *p.* 1795 m Mary Evans Pvt MD
Wm.: b 10-17-1760 d 3-29-1837 m (1)— Newman (2)Rhoda Remine Pvt NJ ★

HURST, (includes HEARST & HORST)
Eliphaz: b 1-5-1739 d 6-12-1825 m Hannah Stiles Ens CT
Henry: b *c.* 1763 d 11-4-1825 m (1)Judith Hudnall (2)Rosanna — PS VA
Henry: b 10-27-1762 d 11-2-1844 m Elizabeth Kizer Pvt VA ★
John: b — d 1806 m (1)Martha Carson (2)Phoebe — Pvt PS SC
John: b 1732 d 1825 m (1)Lydia Smith (2)Mrs Mary (Duncan)Lindsay Lt VA
John: b *c.* 1720 d 1787-9 m (1)Elizabeth — (2)Sybel — PS VA
John: b *c.* 1735 d 1817 m (1)Nancy Nunn (2)Elizabeth Breedwell Pvt VA
Joseph: b 1760 d 5-21-1814 m Jane Pressley Sol SC
Nathaniel: b 1749 d *p.* 2-12-1807 m Lydia — Pvt PA
Peter: b *c.* 1728 d *p.* 1795 m Anna — Pvt VA
Phillip: b 1738 d 1-24-1823 m Elizabeth Dannehower Sol PA
Samuel: b 1764 d 10-26-1822 m (1)Lavinia Littleton (2)Elizabeth Yardley Pvt MD ★
Wm.: b *c.* 1750 d *p.* 10-19-1800 m Mary — Sol NC

HURT, (includes HURTT)
Benjamin: b 1759 d 7-27-1834 m (1)Frances Richerson (2)Mary Stewart Pvt VA ★
James: b *c.* 1760 d 1819 m Agnes Harrison Pvt VA
James, Jr.: b 1766 d 10-9-1834 m Polly Wommack Pvt VA
John: b 1752 d 1824 m (2)Sallie Franklin BgdChp VA
Moza: b *c.* 1728 d *p.* 12-15-1791 m (2)Phebe Mann PS VA
Philemon: b 10-6-1758 d 7-19-1837 m Elizabeth Mann Cpl VA
Richard: b *c.* 1760 d 1794 m Araminta VanSant Pvt MD
Wm.: b *c.* 1750 d 10-1-1812 m (1)Priscilla Yancey (2)Polly Hunnicutt Sol GA NC
Wm.: b 9-16-1757 d 11-12-1842 m (1)Sarah White Field (2)Elizabeth McMurray Pvt VA ★
Zachariah: b 1763 d 8-11-1841 m Frances Mitchell Pvt VA

HUSBANDS,
Herman: b 10-3-1724 d *p.* 5-12-1795 m (2)Mary Pugh (3)Amy Allen CS PA

HUSH,
Conrad: b *c.* 1757 d *p.* 1801 m Eleanor Putney PS MD

HUSKE,
John: b 1740 d 1794-6 m Elizabeth Hogg PS CS NC

HUSSEY,
Batchelor: b 11-29-1728/9 d 4-12-1805 m Ann Coffin PS MA
Christopher, Sr.: b 6-3-1724 d 6-28-1785 m Mary Coffin PS MA
John: b *c.* 1733 d *p.* 1795 m Jane Rollins Pvt MA
John: b 1737 d 2-7-1781 m Mary Jessup Pvt NC
Mary: b 12-5-1740 d *c.* 1821 m John Hussey PS NC
Samuel: b 10-10-1748 d 4-17-1814 m Mercy Evans Pvt NH
Stephen: b 9-27-1738 d 2-9-1796 m Elizabeth Swain PS MA
Stephen: b 7-10-1739 d 3- -1812 m Martha Chambers PS NC

HUSTED, (includes HUESTED)
Abraham: b 5-29-1739 d 6-9-1819 m Hannah Knapp Sgt CT
Abraham: b *c.* 1760 d 1820 m Sarah Palmer Pvt NY
David: b 2-1-1741 d 1835 m Patience Palmer Lt NY ★
Ebenezer, Sr.: b 1693 d 1790 m (1)Sarah Holmes (2)Sarah Smith PS NY
Ebenezer, Jr.: b 1736 d 1811 m Sarah Germond Maj NY
Hosea: b 6-2-1753 d 5-25-1823 m Mary Montgomery Pvt NJ ★
John: b 11-23-1731 d *c.* 1810 m Ann — Pvt NY
Moses: b 5-15-1745 d *p.* 6- -1835 m (1)Mary Goodwin (2)Margaret Davis Pvt Spy VA ★
Nathaniel: b 3-12-1757 d 1-20-1826 m Ruth Sniffen Sgt CT W★
Nathaniel: b — d — m Hannah Webb Cpl CT
Peter: b 4-25-1762 d 8-13-1808 m Polly Smith Pvt NY
Reuben: b 1755 d 5-14-1827 m Ruth Johnson Pvt NJ
Robert: b 3-7-1755 d 6-26-1838 m Sarah McDonald Sgt Spy PA ★
Silas: b 10-19-1743 d 1-24-1827 m Sarah Hoff Capt NY

HUSTIS, (includes HUESTIS)
Aristides: b 1748 d 2- -1832 m Prudence Baxter PS NH
Joseph: b 10-11-1719 d 6- -1805 m Mary Hunt Pvt NY
Robert: b 6-7-1759 d 2-15-1833 m (1)Jemima Weeks (2)Tamer Budd Pvt NY

HUTCHCRAFT,
Thomas: b *c.* 1762 d *c.* 1822-25 m Nellie Harrison Apperson Pvt MD

HUTCHINS, (includes HUTCHENS & HUTCHINGS)
Amasa: b 9- -1748 d 3-3-1826 m Hannah Leffingwell Pvt CT
Benjamin: b *c.* 1730 d 3-10-1842 m Elenor — LCol CT
Benjamin: b 4-10-1757 d 9-4-1828 m Abigail Tibetts Pvt Mrnr MA
Benjamin: b 7-25-1756 d 9-8-1810 m Nancy — Pvt MA
Benjamin: b 1-11-1727 d 5-27-1813 m (1)Lucy Davis (2)Sarah — Pvt VT
Bulkeley: b 6-19-1765 d 5-16-1850 m Elizabeth Johnson Pvt VT ★
Charles: b 10-10-1742 d 6-3-1834 m (1)Mary Perkins (2)Mrs Nelly Bowles PS ME
Charles: b 1750 d 1783 m Martha Green Sol VA
Christopher: b 1730 d *a.* 5-20-1807 m Elizabeth — PS VA
David: b 7-13-1754 d 2-3-1819 m Joanna Abell Pvt MA
Drury: b 1708 d 1788 m Magdalen Pintard Capt SC
Gabriel: b 1758 d 1831 m Mrs Lydia Hinkle Pvt NJ ★
Gordon: b 1733 d 12-8-1815 m (1)Dorothy Stone (2)Lucy Lund LCol NH
Hezekiah: b 1727 d 6-13-1796 m Anne Sweet Capt NH
Hollis: b 1744 d 8-5-1822 m Elizabeth Boynton Pvt MA ★
Jeremiah: b 1-15-1736 d 11-11-1816 m Mehitable Corliss Pvt NH
John: b 8-18-1748 d 10-23-1787 m Anne Skinner Pvt CT
John: b *c.* 1721 d *p.* 5- -1782 m Lydia Weeks Pvt MA
John: b 6-19-1751 d 12-2-1825 m Phoebe Strong Drm NY
John: b 1733 d 1829 m (2)Jennie Braswell PS VA
John Church: b 10-8-1753 d *c.* 1812 m Irena Chapman Pvt CT
Jonathan: b— bpt 9-22-1728 d *p.* 1790 m Elizabeth Higgins Sgt MA
Joseph: b 6-28-1745 d 11-12-1814 m Martha Corliss Capt NH
Joseph: b 1735 d 1785-90 m Anna — Pvt NH
Joseph: b *c.* 1739 d *p.* 5-3-1776 m Amanda Lawson Col VA
Levi: b 8-17-1761 d 6-13-1855 m Phebe Hannaford Fif RI ★
Moses: b 3- -1754 d 4- -1836 m Lucy Parks Lt VA
Nathan, Sr.: b 4-1-1722 d 9-26-1811 m Mary Whittier Capt CT VT
Nathaniel: b 1742 d 1-10-1832 m Mehitable Ordway Capt NH ★
Noah: b 3-28-1758 d 8-13-1838 m (2)Lydia Joy Sgt MA ★
Phineas: b 1740 d 2-18-1785 m Abigail Reed Capt PS NH
Richard: b 1741 d 7-23-1826 m Zana Phyllis Standiford 2Lt MD
Samuel: b 9-3-1749 d 12-25-1791 m Olive Robbens Pvt MA
Shubael: b 7-22-1759 d 4-14-1841 m Avis Borden Pvt CT ★
Strangeman: b 1707 d 2-10-1792 m Elizabeth Cox PS VA
Thomas: b 1-31-1730 d 10-15-1807 m Anna Briant Pvt MA
Thomas: b 1750 d 1804 m Katherine Donelson Capt VA
Wm.: b 1735 d *p.* 1776 m Jerusha Wiswall Pvt MA
Wm.: b 10-6-1764 d 5-2-1866 m (1)Mercy Wardwell (2)Sarah Staples Pvt MA ★
Wm.: b 3-16-1739 d 6-3-1826 m (1)Abigail Flood (2)Mrs Hannah Belknap (3)Mrs Mary Shepard Lt MA NH ★
Wm.: b 11-7-1750 d 3-18-1822 m Nancy — Pvt PA
Wm., Sr.: b 4-16-1741 d 1825 m Lois Bingham Capt VT
Wm., Jr.: b 6-8-1767 d 2-7-1852 m (1)Lucina Aseneth Allen (2)Mary Cowdry Pvt VT ★
Zadoc: b 3-5-1755 d 2-17-1835 m Elizabeth Spalding Pvt CT ★

HUTCHINSON,
Abijah: b 7-4-1756 d 2-11-1843 m Mariam Farnum Pvt CT
Amasa: b 12-14-1762 d 10-3-1823 m Betsy Mack Pvt CT
Asa: b 11-17-1759 d 6-27-1848 m Eunice Davis Pvt NH ★
Bartholemew: b 6-28-1734 d 1820 m (1)Ruth Haven (2)Rebecca Monroe 1Lt MA
Benjamin: b 6-9-1754 d 9-12-1832 m Susanna Peabody Pvt PS NH
Benjamin: b 2-27-1760 d 3-28-1813 m Irena Clark Pvt NY
Charles: b — d p. 11-12-1807 m Frances Collier 2Lt VA
Cornelius: b 1757 d 10-3-1843 m Eleanor McGuire Pvt PA ★
Ebenezer: b 3-22-1753 d 1828 m Hannah Littlefield Pvt PS NH
Eleazer: b 2-19-1735 d 11-25-1813 m Ruth Long Capt CT
Elisha: b 11-22-1746 d 5-11-1824 m Eunice Hyde Sgt CT
Elisha: b 12-6-1751 d 10-12-1800 m Sarah Buxton Sgt MA
Ezra: b 11-2-1726 d 1807 m Elizabeth Chapman Pvt CT
Israel: b 11-12-1727 d 3-15-1811 m (1)Anne Cue (2)Mehitable Putnam Col MA
Israel: b 3-3-1765 d 6-12-1850 m Jane Doke Pvt PS NH ★
James: b 2-16-1755 d 2-11-1830 m Sarah Tindall Pvt NJ
James: b c. 1725 d p. 9-   -1776 m — Pvt NC
James: b 10-24-1744 d 6-12-1812 m Elizabeth Fulton Pvt PA
James: b 1740 d 7-28-1806 m Margaret Alsop Pvt VA
John: b — d 10-5-1804 m Mary Collins Cpl CT
John: b 1736 d 1830 m Lydia Goodell Pvt MA
John: b c. 1731 d 1-13-1791 m Jerusha — Pvt NJ
John: b 1754 d 2-11-1827 m Mary Henry Pvt PA ★
John: b 3-26-1732 d 5-27-1818 m Phebe Moore Pvt PA
John: b c. 1725 d 1787 m (1)Derector — (2)Sarah — NCapt VA
John: b c. 1739 d 3-   -1780 m Sarah Johnston Pvt VA
John: b 4-27-1755 d 1843 m Sarah Henderson CS Pvt VA ★
John: b c. 1750 d c. 1-21-1799 m — Sol VA
Jonathan: b 2-17-1712 d 9-26-1796 m (1)Anna Carter (2)Hannah Sawyer CS CT
Jonathan: b 1715 d 8-5-1801 m Theodate Morrill PS NH
Joseph: b 1749 d 2-3-1828 m Sybil Mack Pvt CT
Joseph: b 1746 d 1818 m — Marshall NCO VA
Levi: b 2-28-1761 d 2-12-1823 m (1)Ester Melchor (2)Elizabeth Norris Pvt NH
Nathan: b 2-10-1717 d 1-12-1795 m Rachel Stearns PS NH
Nathan, Jr.: b 2-   -1752 d 12-26-1831 m Rebecca Peabody Sgt NH
Nathaniel: b 7-6-1745 d c. 1782 m Rebecca Center Sol MA
Nathaniel: b 1-8-1719 d 1-30-1780 m Catharine Bryant PS MA
Nehemiah: b 1763 d 1836 m Mary Johnson Sgt NH
Paul: b 4-18-1736 d c. 1817 m Susanna Sprague Pvt CT
Richard: b c. 1750 d 1780/1 m Nancy Westcott Pvt MA
Samuel: b 8-10-1748 d 3-11-1838 m Betsey Johnson Pvt MA ★
Samuel: b 1749 d 9-27-1821 m Mary Wilkins Cpl NH
Samuel: b 3-30-1750 d 1-24-1824 m (1)Jane Rutherford (2)Mrs Jane Wallace 1Lt PA
Samuel: b 9-6-1751 d 10-1-1839 m Hannah Burr Sgt VT
Thomas: b 1-31-1756 d 6-20-1797 m Mary — Pvt NJ
Timothy: b 7-24-1758 d 11-22-1830 m Prudence Elliott Pvt MA
Walter: b 1760 d 1-1-1838 m Mary Payne Sol VA
Wm.: b 3-28-1751 d 9-16-1821 m Sarah Blood PS MA
Wm.: b c. 1760 d 1845 m Mary Breese Pvt PA
Wm.: b 1725 d 10-19-1804 m — Pvt SC
Wm.: b 1736 d 1799 m Margaret Henderson Pvt VA
Wm.: b 1748 d 7-12-1835 m Elizabeth Redd Pvt VA ★

HUTCHISON,
James: b 1743 d 12-29-1817 m Jane Kelly Pvt PA
James: b c. 1790 m Ann Semple Ens PA
James: b 1760-5 d 6-   -1835 m Martha Findley Pvt PA
John: b 1740 d 5-   -1806 m Elizabeth — Pvt PA
John: b c. 1730 d a. 4-13-1782 m Elizabeth Chiles PS VA
Joseph: b 10-15-1751 d 3-12-1815 m (1)Frances Curtis (2)Elizabeth Majors Sgt VA
Joseph: b 1723 d 11-23-1804 m Elizabeth Gray Pvt VA
Letitia Wright: b c. 1751 d p. 8-27-1796 m John Hutchison PS SC
Richard: b 1744 d 1-   -1807 m Mary Childs Ens VA ★
Samuel: b 1737 d 1-24-1822 m Jane Ross Pvt PA
Thomas: b c. 1759 d 1813 m Verlinder — Cpl VA
Wm.: b 1750 d 11-23-1833 m Catherine Bradshaw McDonald Capt NC ★

HUTSON, (includes HUSTON)
John: b 1758 d 6-   -1812 m Mrs Mary Elizabeth Davis Sol SC
John: b 1756 d 1821 m Lydia Hutson Pvt VA
Joshua: b c. 1750 d a. 2-   -1804 m Suzanna Hooker PS MD
Skinner: b a. 1759 d p. 1824 m Jane — Pvt PA
Thomas: b 1-9-1750 d 5-4-1789 m Esther Maine Col SC

HUTT,
John: b 9-5-1763 d 8-25-1833 m Elizabeth Crockwell Sgt VA

HUTTO,
Ann: b c. 1727 d c. 1790 m Charles Hutto PS SC
Henry: b 5-26-1753 d 9-24-1817 m Ann — Cpl SC
Henry: b 12-25-1750 d p. 9-14-1833 m — Pvt SC ★

HUTTON,
George: b 2-   -1738 d p. 1782 m Mary Moore Gnr PA
James: b 12-21-1756 d 2-24-1843 m Jane Spottswood Pvt PA

James: b 4-6-1761 d 6-13-1833 m Hannah Woods Ens VA ★
Moses: b 1733 d 1806 m Elizabeth — Col VA
Timothy: b 11-24-1746 d 10-10-1824 m (1)Jane McChesney (2)Elizabeth Deline Lt NY W★
Timothy: b 3-10-1764 d 10-19-1833 m Arrietta Smedes Lt NY ★
Wm.: b 6-7-1736 d a. 9-4-1809 m Rebecca Craig Capt SC
Wm.: b 1755 d c. 1781 m Martha Gilmore Pvt VA

HUTZ,
John Peter: b 7-12-1735 d 1-3-1815 m Hendrietta — Pvt PA

HUXFORD,
Harlock: b 10-25-1752 d p. 7-23-1822 m Judith Jones Pvt SC
Henry: b 1752 d 1-   -1816 m Esther Huxford Cpl CT
John: b 4-22-1755 d 1846 m Mary Huxford Pvt CT
Joseph: b — d 4-8-1843 m Mary Arey Pvt MA
Joseph: b c. 1728 d 1804 m Esther Egin Eagen PS MA

HUXLEY,
Dan: b 5-15-1743 d 7-22-1822 m Ruhamah Holcomb Pvt MA
James: b 7-20-1769 d 4-9-1828 m Ann Mead Drm NY ★

HUY,
Jacob: b 1748 d 1820 m Mary Geruant Pvt PA

HUYCK,
Barnet: b 1747 d a. 6-6-1835 m Barbara — Cpl PA
John A.: bpt 6-27-1730 d p. 1790 m Fitje Derkarr Sgt NY
Wm.: b 2-20-1764 d 2-   -1849 m Margaret Westbrook Pvt PA ★

HUYLER, (or HYLER)
Adam: b 1735 d 9-6-1782 m Ann Nafey Capt NJ

HYAM,
Richard: b c. 1757 d p. 1778 m Abigail Gould Matr MA

HYATT, (includes HIATT & HIETT)
Abraham: b 6-17-1747 d 6-30-1820 m Sarah Ryder Lt NY
Abraham: b 4-14-1760 d 1-28-1834 m Anna Whelpley Pvt Pvtr NY CT ★
Alvan: b 11-19-1751 d 6-26-1835 m Abigail Grumman Cpl CT ★
Eli: b 10-16-1754 d 7-28-1815 m Mary Ann Warfield PS Sol MD
Elisha: b 8-24-1751 d 5-24-1835 m Sarah — Pvt NY
Evan: b 1748 d 1815 m Sarah Smith PS VA
Jesse: b 7-15-1753 d 7-18-1835 m Sabra Chapin Sgt CT
John: b 6-   -1761 d 4-24-1853 m (2)Rachel Wolfe Pvt NY
John: b 1736 d 6-11-1818 m Mary Wynn LCol NY
John Vance: b 1755 d 1806 m Sarah Tatlowe Lt DE
Joshua: b 4-26-1738 d 9-1-1801 m Mary Bashford Pvt NY
Meshack: b c. 1723 d 1807 m (1)Sarah — (2)Susannah Hobbs PS MD
Peter: b 1728 d 1800 m Martha Vance Capt DE
Samuel: b 3-20-1759 d 10-14-1839 m Juda Pope Sgt CT ★
Shadrack: b 8-15-1749 d 3-9-1835 m Elizabeth — Pvt MD ★
Stephen: b 1762 d 5-21-1842 m (1)Elizabeth Whitlock (2)Eunice Hoyt Pvt CT
Wm. Sr.: b 2-18-1717 d p. 9-25-1784 m Elizabeth Walker PS MD
Wm.: b 10-22-1738 d 5-22-1817 m Tabitha Johnston Pvt DE
Wm. 2d Jr.: b 1748 d p. 1790 m Martha Duvall PS MD
Wm.: b 1760 d 8-6-1835 m (2)Catherine — Pvt NY

HYDE, (includes HEYDE, HIDE & HIDY)
Agur: b 2-27-1757 d 12-24-1831 m (1)Elizabeth — (2)Sarah Olds Pvt CT
Andrew: b 1748 d 1835 m Mary Tracy Pvt CT
Andrew, Jr.: b 9-9-1757 d 7-11-1845 m Rebecca Galpin Pvt MA
Asa: b 7-21-1741 d 3-26-1797 m Lucy French Pvt CT
Benjamin: b 1757 d 8-3-1839 m Elizabeth Hyde Cpl CT
Benjamin: b 4-28-1717 d 1781 m (1)Abigail Lee (2)Abigail Chadwick (3)Elizabeth Lord PS CT
Benjamin: b 4-11-1723 d 11-20-1797 m Dorcas Dyer Pvt MA
Caleb: b 7-29-1739 d 12-25-1820 m Elizabeth Sacket LCol PS MA
Charles: b 10-8-1748 d 5-1-1839 m Mary Abel Pvt CT
Comfort: b 8-24-1737 d 5-2-1820 m Deborah Faulkner PS CT
Daniel: b 3-1-1756 d 12-24-1831 m Mary Hyde Drm CT
Ebenezer: b 1-13-1743 d c. 1790 m Lois Thatcher Lt CT
Eli: b 10-12-1736 d 10-6-1815 m Rhoda Lothrop Capt PS CT
Elihu: b 9-24-1752 d 7-29-1838 m Hannah Abel Pvt CT
Elihu: b 8-3-1734 d 10-9-1815 m Sarah Griswold PS NH
Elijah, Sr.: b 6-17-1735 d 12-31-1800 m Mary Clark Maj CT
Elijah Clark: b 6-19-1758 d 1835 m (1)Sarah Taylor (2)Ann Hyde Sgt CT ★
Elijah: b 12-10-1754 d 12-12-1820 m (1)Elizabeth Edgerton (2)Rebecca Stark Sgt VT
Eliphalet: b 5-9-1744 d 3-   -1825 m (1)Naoma Flint (2)Abigail Washburn Cpl CT
Elisha: b 9-6-1730 d 1779 m Mary Knapp Pvt MA
Ephraim: b 1-6-1745/6 d 10-13-1812 m Sarah Lamphear Pvt MA
Ephraim Samuel: b 10-29-1762 d 5-3-1836 m Rebecca Hurlburt Sol VT ★
George Michael: b 1-25-1757 d 11-12-1821 m (2)Elizabeth Herr (3)Elizabeth Platz Pvt PA
Gershom: b 12-2-1755 d 1-21-1836 m Catherine Wilson Pvt MA

HYDE, contd.
Henry: b 1-19-1748 d 1-30-1813 m Therina Ward Pvt VT
Ichabod: b 4-30-1749 d *p.* 1832 m Lucy Abigail Burnham Pvt CT RI ★
Isaac, Jr.: b 4-24-1735 d 4-29-1829 m Sarah Marshall 2Lt CT
Jabez, Sr.: b 9-16-1713 d 3-6-1805 m Lydia Abel PS CT
Jabez, Jr.: b 6-17-1740 d 11-15-1835 m Martha Pettis Pvt CT
Jacob, Sr.: b 1-20-1703 d 1-22-1782 m Hannah Kingsbury CS CT
Jacob, Jr.: b 8-1-1730 d 1815 m Hannah Hazen Pvt VT
Jacob Dana: b 4-9-1761 d 7-18-1827 m Mary Fitch Dr VT
James: b 4-6-1741 d 1-25-1785 m Eunice Backus Seacapt CT
James: b 7-17-1752 d 4-9-1809 m Martha Nevins Lt CT
James: b 3-18-1760 d 10-4-1834 m (1)Betty — (2)Eunice Pennock Pvt CT ★
Jedediah: b 8-24-1738 d 5-20-1822 m (1)Mary Waterman (2)Elizabeth Parker Capt CT ★
Job: b 3-10-1752 d 4-5-1824 m Elizabeth Ward Pvt MA
Joel: b 1764 d 1- -1853 m Mary Belcher Pvt CT
John: b 7-12-1750 d 4-10-1808 m Olive Bascom Pvt MA
John: b 1746 d 1806 m Hannah Rittenhouse Wgn NJ
John: b 1751 d 3-19-1823 m Christina A. Teexler Sgt PA
Joseph: b 1-3-1761 d 12-3-1850 m Arete Jesup Pvt CT
Joseph: b 12-12-1756 d 12-10-1834 m Susanna Moore Pvt MA W ★
Joseph, Sr.: b 11-16-1714 d 9-28-1786 m Susanna Livermore PS MA
Joseph, Jr.: b 2-25-1748/9 d 1787 m Anna Jackson Pvt MA
Joshua, Sr.: b 10-12-1722 d 1794 m Rebecca Hubbard Pvt VT
Joshua, Jr.: b 1753 d 3-28-1813 m Sarah Graham Pvt VT
Matthew: b 4-28-1711 d 3-18-1792 m (1)Elizabeth Huntington (2)Hannah Pember PS CT
Moses: b 9-11-1751 d 1828 m Sarah Dana PS MA
Noah: b 9-26-1717 d 11-9-1786 m Ruth Seger Cpl PS MA
Oliver: b 11-2-1754 d 11-15-1837 m Mary Lee Pvt CT
Othniel: b 7-12-1752 d 8-26-1832 m Mrs Rachel Streeter Rood Pvt MA
Phineas: b 11-15-1849 d 9-5-1820 m Esther Holdridge Dr Mte CT
Robert: b 1761 d 12-11-1835 m Mrs Ann East Arfr VA
Samuel: b 10-24-1725 d 10-2-1776 m Anne Fitch Pvt CT
Samuel: b 8-2-1741 d 1-1-1810 m Hannah McKlem Pvt MA
Thaddeus: b 1-10-1751 d 1-9-1821 m Elizabeth Grimes Sol MA
Thomas: b 5-11-1735 d 10-4-1819 m Edna Burleigh Ens CT
Thomas: b 3- -1725 d 3-15-1795 m Elizabeth Bishop CS MD
Uriah: b 9-17-1741 d 1806 m Mehitable Marvin PS CT
Walter: b 2-17-1735 d 9-18-1776 m (1)Sarah Bissell (2)Sarah Wattles Capt CT
Wm.: b 2-24-1742/3 d 1802 m Lydia Bruce Pvt MA
Zabdial: b 6-3-1763 d 1842 m Mary Lyman Pvt CT

HYDEN,
Henry: b 12-2-1735 d *p.* 1782 m — PS VA
Wm.: b 2-14-1761 d 12-24-1858 m (2)Martha Baldwin Pvt VA ★

HYER, (includes HEYER, HIER & HYRE)
Conrad: b 4-10-1749 d 2-19-1856 m Mary — Pvt ME MA
George: b *c.* 1717 d 4- -1790 m — PS PA
Jacob: b 5-25-1757 d 3-6-1841 m Elizabeth Powers Pvt Spy VA ★
Leonard: b *c.* 1715 d 1786 m — PS VA
Lewis: b 7-20-1730 d *p.* 1782 m Maria Eve — Pvt PA
Walter: b 8-14-1744 d 1795 m Francis Ketcham Pvt PS NY
Wm.: bpt 12-4-1723 d 4-24-1800 m (1)Geertje Brestede (2)Neeltje Stoutenburgh Col NY

HYLAND, (includes HILAND & HYLANDS)
Amasa: b 1761 d 1843 m Prudence Whitcomb Pvt MA ★
Edward: b 1-10-1755 d *p.* 5-3-1799 m Julianna Arrents PS MD
John: b 11-27-1746 d 1806 m Elizabeth Worrall Lt MD
Lambert: b 1751 d 1819 m (1)Eliza Rigby (2)Elizabeth Gale Capt MD
Nathaniel: b 1749 d 1824 m Isabel Marks Pvt PA
Samuel: b 3-22-1758 d 1-24-1828 m Hannah Studley Pvt MA
Stephen: b 2-23-1743 d 3-19-1806 m (1)Rebecca Tilden (2)Araminta Hamm Col MD

HYNDSHAW,
James: b 12-22-1758 d 1810 m Esther Bailey Pvt PA

HYRNE,
Henry: b 10-18-1734 d *p.* 1-4-1784 m Mary Ann Girardeau Capt SC

HYSLOP,
Levin: b 1754 d 4-27-1835 m Susan Davis Pvt VA W ★

HYSON,
Archibald: b *c.* 1744-46 d 1815 m Catherine Ramsey Sol PA

ICE,
Adam: b 6-1-1760 d 7-5-1851 m Phoebe Bayles Sol VA
Andrew: b 10-16-1758 d 3-13-1848 m Mary Bayles Pvt VA ★
Wm.: b *c.* 1730 d 1830 m (1)Mary Scott McMillan (2)Margaret Higginbotham (3)Elizabeth Shreve Pvt VA

ICKES,
John: b 8-23-1742 d 1-19-1829 m (1)Magdalena Stambaugh (2)Elizabeth — Pvt PA
John: b 1740 d *p.* 1785 m Margaret Krauss Pvt PA
Michael: b *c.* 1741 d 5- -1778 m (1)Alice Koplin (2)Catherine Acker PS PA
Nicholas: b 1764 d 3-25-1848 m (1)Mary Magdalene Christman (2)Mrs Susan L. Bernheisel Pvt PA

IDDINGS,
Wm., Jr.: b 11-21-1749 d 1804 m Hannah Sharpless Pvt PA
Wm.: b 1757 d 10- -1833 m Ann Myers Pvt PA ★

IDE,
Amos: b 4-10-1756 d 4- -1816 m Sarah Carpenter Cpl RI
Benjamin: b 10-27-1754 d 4-13-1813 m Hannah — Pvt MA
Ezra: b 2-6-1736/7 d 9-7-1785 m (1)Sarah Allen (2)Sarah Loring Lt MA
Ichabod, Sr.: b 3-31-1717 d 1-23-1785 m Mary Mason Pvt VT
Ichabod, Jr.: b 4-10-1755 d 2-24-1831 m (1)Mary — (2)Phoebe — Pvt VT
Jesse: b 7-22-1760 d 7-2-1848 m (1)Laensca Sheldon (2)Lucy Hicks OrdlSgt VT ★
John, Jr.: b 8-25-1742 d 2-14-1815 m Deborah Pond Lt MA
John: b 10-20-1752 d 10-22-1824 m Anna Short Cpl MA ★
John: b 2-27-1728 d *p.* 12- -1782 m (1)Priscilla Wilmarth (2)Patience Lyon PS CS MA
Joseph: b 5-22-1753 d *p.* 1790 m Lydia — Pvt VT
Josiah: b 10-16-1728 d *a.* 10-1-1793 m (1)Bethiah Blanding (2)Mrs Jemima Freeman Sweet Pvt MA
Nehemiah: b 11-3-1746 d 2-8-1823 m Mary Bennett Sgt MA
Timothy: b 4-10-1745 d *p.* 1810 m Elizabeth Bates MM MA

IDEN,
John: b 11-5-1755 d 6-6-1847 m (2)Hannah Russell Pvt VA ★

IDOL,
Barnett: b *c.* 1735 d *a.* 2- -1786 m Elizabeth Meier PS NC
Jacob: b 11-16-1761 d 1-21-1851 m Chloe Johnson Sgt NC ★

IGLEHEART,
Jeremiah: b — d *c.* 1802 m Mary — PS MD
John: b *c.* 1748 d 1811 m Mary Denune PS MD

IGOU,
Joshua: b 1760 d 4-20-1833 m Mary Roller Pvt PA

IHRIE,
Conrad, Sr.: b 6-27-1731 d 7-18-1813 m Mary Elizabeth Bapp Pvt PA
Conrad, Jr.: b 1758 d 1-19-1807 m Christina Seip Pvt PA

IJAMS, (includes IAMS, IIEMS)
John, Sr.: b 1712 d *p.* 10- -1783 m Rebecca Jones Capt PS MD
John, Jr.: b 1755 d 4- -1823 m Mary Waters 1Lt MD
John: b 1750 d 7-4-1823 m Elizabeth Gill Hampton Pvt MD
John Frederick: b 1765 d 1-24-1839 m Mary Denune Pvt MD
Plummer: b 1716 d 11-26-1792 m Ruth Childs PS MD
Plummer, Jr.: b 10-29-1748 d 2-2-1795 m Jemima Welsh PS MD
Thomas: b 12- -1754 d 6-24-1834 m Catherine Hampton Pvt MD ★
Thomas: b 4-20-1745 d 1806 m Mary Ijams PS MD
Vachell: b *c.* 1759 d 2-20-1833 m Martha Cunningham Sgt MD NC ★

IKERD,
Henry: b *c.* 1756 d *p.* 7-31-1800 m Elizabeth — Sol NC

ILGENFRITZ,
Frederick: b 1753 d 1823 m Ann Elizabeth — Pvt PA

ILIFF,
John: b *c.* 1745 d *p.* 9-11-1805 m Margaret Williams CS PA

ILLICK, (includes ILLIG)
Christopher: b 2-2-1746 d 11-27-1818 m Elizabeth Huber Pvt PA
Leonard: b 1732 d 12-23-1797 m Dorothy Bassler Pvt PA

ILLSLEY, (includes ILSLEY)
Daniel: b 5-30-1740 d 5-10-1813 m Mary Jones Maj PS MA
Enoch: b 12-16-1730 d 11-10-1811 m Mary Parker PS ME
Jewett: b 3-19-1763 d 7-12-1845 m Fannie Peabody Dale Cpl MA
Jonathan: b 1738 d 5- -1819 m Dorcas Ingersoll Pvt MA
Paul: bpt 7-11-1762 d 3-3-1844 m Sarah Hale Pvt MA
Stephen: b 8-3-1734 d 9-7-1816 m Elizabeth Noyes Lt MA

IMBODEN, (includes IMBODY)
John: b 9-20-1761 d *p.* 1795 m Catherine Fernsler Pvt PA
John Sweigert: b 10-23-1733 d 7-29-1819 m Elenora Diller Pvt PA
Nicholas: b 1747 d *p.* 1790 m Margaret Lynn Sol PA

IMLAY,
David: b *c.* 1759 d 2-16-1803 m Abagail Akin Capt NJ
Isaac: b 3-5-1756 d 11-11-1836 m Mary Lawrence Lt NJ ★

John: b c. 1749 d 1814 m Elizabeth DeBow Sol NJ
Peter: b 1730 d 1789 m Susannah — Pvt PS NJ
Wm.: b 11-12-1742 d 8-5-1808 m Mary Nevins Church PS CT
Wm. Eugene: b c. 1725 d p. 4-3-1788 m X Capt NJ

IMMEL, (includes IMLER)
George Michael: b c. 1739 d 1-23-1816 m Catharine Walter Pvt PA
Leonard: b 10-10-1748 d 6-2-1839 m Barbara Kuster Capt PA ★

IMPSON,
Benjamin: b 1740 d 1821 m X Pvt NY

IMUS,
Wm.: b 5- -1739 d 3-20-1835 m (1)Lucy Hurd (2)Anna Rising Pvt VT

INABINET, (includes INABNIT)
Christian: b 3-17-1749 d p. 1790 m Peggy Horger Pvt SC
John: b a. 1722 d 1788 m Margaretta Negely Pvt SC

INGALLS, (includes INGELL & INGLES)
Abijah: b 1739 d 1777 m Elizabeth Hutchinson MM Pvt MA
Benjamin: b c. 1712 d c. 1785 m Mercy Jencks Pvt MA
Caleb: b 2-22-1756 d 1847 m Mary Chatsey Pvt VT NY
Daniel: b 1-13-1758 d 1832 m Mary (Tapley) Tarbell Cpl MA
Ebenezer: b 11-18-1745 d p. 3-19-1834 m Mercy — Pvt NH ★
Ebenezer: b 4-13-1747 d p. 1790 m Mary Longee Pvt NH
Edmund: b 3-18-1739/40 m Esther Sallsbury Pvt MA
George: b 2-20-1746 d 8-15-1827 m Elizabeth Morgan Pvt PA
Henry: b 4- -1719 d 1803 m (1)Sarah Putnam (2)Mrs. Sarah (Putnam) Andrews Sol MA
Henry: b 10-12-1738 d 6-18-1813 m Sybel Carpenter Lt CS PS NH
Isaiah: b 7-13-1756 d 6-2-1831 m (1)Esther Stevens (2)Phebe Curtis Pvt MA
Israel: b 3-30-1760 d p. 1799 m Elizabeth French Sgt NH
Jacob: b 6-27-1764 d 10-17-1841 m Susanna Goff Pvt MA ★
Jacob: b — d c. 1791 m Mary Tucker Pvt MA
James: b 3-12-1749 d 1-13-1815 m Catherine (Boone) DeHart Pvt PA
John, Sr.: b 6-1-1723 d 3-11-1815 m (1)Mary Hazeltine (2)Elizabeth Copp PS NH
John, Jr.: b 4-3-1751 d p. 1793 m Mrs Hannah (Massey) Ordway Pvt MA
Jonathan: b 12-7-1757 d 1845 m Freelove Andrews Pvt MA
Jonathan: b 2-25-1762 d 7-9-1837 m Sarah Berry Pvt MA ★
Jonathan: b 1750 d 1834 m (1)Martha Jane Locke (2)Edna Hastings Pvt NH
Joseph: b 8-22-1723 d 10-18-1790 m Sarah Abbott PS CT
Joseph: b 6-8-1744 d 3-23-1799 m Susanna Babbitt Pvt MA W ★
Joseph: b 6-8-1744 d 3-2-1813 m Roby Horton Pvt MA
Joseph: b 4-22-1752 d 8-15-1834 m Sarah Parker Pvt VT ★
Joshua: b 8-13-1732 d a. 7-5-1785 m Elizabeth Steele Pvt MA
Lemuel: b 12-6-1755 d 11-17-1837 m Dorothy Sumner Pvt MA
Luther: b 8-24-1758 d 7-4-1855 m Lucy Utley Pvt CT ★
Moses: b 6-1-1754 d 10-1-1845 m Susannah Heath Sgt NH ★
Nathaniel: b 1-8-1730 d 8-11-1806 m Mercy Pratt Pvt MA
Phineas: b 11-14-1758 d 1-5-1844 m Elizabeth Stevens Pvt MA ★
Samuel: b 4-20-1723 d 1795 m Ruth Moulton Pvt MA
Simeon: b 5-28-1754 d 5-23-1827 m (1)Olive Grosvenor (2)Eunice Wheeler (3)Rachel Harris Pvt CT
Simeon: b 9-3-1764 d 1799 m Elisabeth Fish Pvt MA
Solomon: b 6-16-1750 d 9-22-1840 m (1)Abigail Carleton (2)Mercy Wilson (3)Hannah Harris Sgt MA ★
Stephen: b 6-30-1755 d c. 1827 m Sarah Miller Pvt MA ★
Thomas: b 1751 d p. 1809 m Eleanor Grills Capt VA
Wm.: b 1729 d 1782 m Mary Draper Col VA
Zadock: b 3-9-1760 d 12-22-1832 m Christain Bell Pvt MA
Zebadiah: b 11-3-1729 d 6-11-1800 m Esther Goodell Capt VA

INGALSBE, (includes INGOLDSBY)
Ebenezer: b 1-30-1730 d 8-17-1802 m Susannah Robins Capt MA
Ebenezer: b 2-25-1752 d 7-12-1828 m Phoebe Estabrook Pvt MA
John: b 5-15-1753 d 8-17-1836 m Lovisa Maynard Pvt MA ★

INGERSOLL, (includes INGERSOL, INGERSON)
Artemedores: b 5-9-1762 d 9-21-1839 m Sarah Newberry — Pvt MA ★
Daniel: b 1739 d p. 1781 m X Sgt PA
David: b 12-1-1759 d 1-26-1839 m Sarah Parsons Pvt MA
Ebenezer: b 9-16-1755 d 6-26-1835 m Margaret Whitcomb 1Sgt Arfr MA ★
Ebenezer: b 1757 d 7-19-1837 m (1)Ann Springer (2)Deborah Springer (3)— Spencer (4)Mary Scull Pvt NJ
Francis: b 2-23-1758 d 6-2-1830 m Rachel Case Pvt MA ★
Jared: b 1-9-1757 d 6-1-1822 m Betsy Noble Pvt MA
John: b 2-26-1731 d 3-1-1792 m Margaret Moseley PS Sol MA
John: b 10-11-1758 d 5-30-1840 m Martha Bull Pvt CT ★
John: b 6- -1756 d 2- -1840 m Hannah Bowditch NCapt MA
John: b 12-20-1733 d p. 1781 m Abigail Dolliver Cpl MA
John: b 3-11-1764 d 8-20-1839 m (1)Mary Beyea (2)Mary Terrell Pvt NY
Jonathan: b 1713 d 10-2-1778 m Dorcas Moss PS CT
Jonathan: b 2-9-1735 d 1-12-1819 m Abigail Clark Pvt NY

Jonathan: b 8-9-1751 d 7-9-1840 m (1)Mary Hodges (2)Polly Poole (3)Mrs Sarah Blyth 2nd Lt MA ★
Jonathan: b 4-10-1747 d 5-20-1817 m Martha Haskell NCdr MA
Josiah, Sr.: b 7-21-1716 d 1-13-1789 m Bethiah Sargent Pvt MM MA
Josiah, Jr.: b 1-10-1743 d p. 1792 m (1)Anna S Elwell (2)Lydia Willett Mrnr MA
Josiah: b 1716 d p. 1790 m (1)Rebecca Rundle (2)Eleanor Moe Mil NY
Moses: b 1765 d 1834 m Lavina Lee Pvt MA
Moses: b 7-14-1748 d 9-9-1813 m (1)Eunice West (2)Prudence Taylor Pvt MA
Nathaniel Low: b 3-23-1754 d 4-20-1834 m Sally Haskell Pvt MA ME ★
Peter: b 5-11-1733 d 1785 m Anna Severell Capt MA
Philip: b 2-14-1744 d 12-26-1835 m Elizabeth Bausman Pvt NY ★
Samuel: b 1-22-1744 d 8-18-1818 m (1)Phebe Wilson (2)Ruth Peck (3)Jerusha Gaylord Pvt CT
Simon: b 1736 d 3-19-1777 m Elizabeth Schofield Lt CT
Thomas: b 1749 d 1812 m Elizabeth Dewey Capt MA
Wm.: b 4-1-1723/4 d 8-10-1815 m Lydia Ingersoll PS MA
Zebulon: b 9- -1757 d 1-1-1826 m Ruth (Moody) Pike Pvt MA

INGHAM,
Alexander: b 2-18-1738 d 8- -1776 m Catherine Noble Pvt CT
Benjamin: b 3-29-1756 d 7-7-1810 m (1)— Ensign (2)Anne Steele Cpl MA
Daniel: b 5-1-1723 d 5-21-1801 m Mehitable Phelps PS CT
Ebenezer: b 6-18-1738 d 6-12-1832 m Sarah Ford Pvt CT
Jonas: b 1746 d 10-28-1820 m Elizabeth Beaumont Capt PA
Jonathan, Sr.: b 1720 d 1799 m Deborah Bye Pvt PA
Jonathan, Jr.: b 7-16-1744 d 10-1-1793 m Ann Welding PS Dr PA
Joseph: b 11-8-1742 d p. 1790 m Mehetabel Brown Pvt MA

INGLE, (includes INGLEE)
Ebenezer: b 3-7-1764 d 10-29-1851 m Elizabeth Otis Smith Pvt MA ★
Jonathan: b 1754 d 12-3-1845 m Freelove Andrews MM Pvt MA

INGRAHAM, (includes INGHRAM, INGRAM)
Alexander: b c. 1729 d a. 4-25-1794 m Ann — PS SC
Arthur: b 1746 d 10-28-1834 m Allive Smith Pvt PA
Benjamin: b c. 1735 d p. 1-28-1794 m Elizabeth Nelms PS VA
Comfort: b 3-7-1744 d 8-21-1821 m Molly Cheeney Cpl MA
Daniel: b 3-25-1737 d 1823-6 m Margaret Hill Pvt CT
Duncan, Jr.: b 1752 d 1804 m Susanna Greenleaf Pvt MA
Edwin: b 4-17-1751 d 5-11-1843 m Nancy Montgomery Ens NC ★
Francis: b 1754 d 1847 m Elizabeth Duffield Pvt MA
Humphrey: b c. 1750 d c. 1835 m Rachel Ryker Sol NY
Jeremiah: b 12-8-1731 d 9-30-1807 m Rebecca Monroe Capt MA
Jeremiah: b 5-20-1733 d 2-22-1814 m Abigail Hartwell Pvt PS MA
Jeremiah: b 3- -1735 d 12-8-1785 m Elizabeth Taylor Pvt VA
Jeremiah: b 1759 d 9- -1844 m Sarah Willis Pvt VA ★
Job: b 9-15-1755 d 11-27-1834 m Lucy Tolman Pvt MA
John: b — d p. 7-15-1820 m Mary — PS NC
John, Jr.: b 1730 d 11-5-1800 m Mrs Rebecca Jerman Owen Pvt PA
John: b 1-10-1759 d 10-6-1810 m Rebecca Williams Pvt PA
John, Jr.: b 1-25-1727 d 8-3-1799 m Mary Gladding Pvt RI
John: b c. 1755 d 9-16-1828 m Ruth White Pvt SC
John: b c. 1710 d p. 9-26-1786 m Patience Berry PS VA
Jonathan: b 4-4-1760 d 4-26-1847 m Mary Haward Pvt CT MA ★
Jonathan: b 1745 d 10-26-1820 m Joanna Kellogg Pvt MA
Joseph: b 6-19-1753 d 6-21-1832 m Betty Taylor Pvt CT
Joseph: b 7-1-1759 d 10-23-1848 m Bradbury Keen Pvt MA
Joseph: b 1745 d 1799 m Ann Montgomery Pvt NC
Joseph: b 1744 d 3-22-1828 m Winifred Nelms Sol NC
Joshua: b 2-12-1705 d 3- -1793 m (1)Martha Lawton (2)Mary Richmond PS RI
Leatham: b 9-30-1735 d 5-28-1786 m Annie Ford Pvt PA
Moses: b c. 1750 d 1784 m Elizabeth Croft PS VA
Nathaniel: b 8-23-1743 d 8-19-1815 m Hannah Warren Pvt MA
Nathaniel: b 6-6-1760 d 2-28-1818 m Louisa Hall NVol MA
Peter: b 1753 d 8-15-1832 m Elizabeth Taylor Pvt PA
Philip: b 8-27-1727 d p. 1790 m Experience (Montague) Pierce Pvt MA
Samuel: b 12-27-1756 d 11-23-1819 m Jerusha Blodgett Pvt MA
Samuel: b c. 1740 d 1799-1801 m Anne — CS Pvt VA
Thomas: b 1755 d 7-27-1820 m Elizabeth Blackmer Pvt MA
Wm.: b 12-16-1738 d 1805 m Jemima Bushnell Pvt CT
Wm.: b 10-7-1764 d 2-23-1810 m Louis Durkee Sgt CT
Wm.: b 9-23-1746 d 1-2-1821 m Esther Carpenter Pvt MA
Wm.: b c. 1750 d c. 1809 m Agnes — Pvt PA

INMAN,
Abednego: b 7-1-1752 d 2-2-1831 m Mary Ritchie Sol PS NC GA
Benjamin: b — d p. 5-17-1813 m Rachael — PS NJ
Daniel: b 1751 d 5-16-1837 m Ava Allen Pvt GA
David: b c. 1755 d 1778 m X Sol PA
Edward: b 11-23-1763 d 10-20-1848 m Jerusha Dilley Pvt PA
Richard: b 8-17-1751 d 7-25-1831 m Hannah Spencer Sol PA
Rufus, Sr.: b 5-4-1765 d 2-25-1848 m (1)Mehitable — (2)Mrs Betsy Mayhew Pvt MA ★
Shadrack: b 1-25-1747 d 10-7-1831 m Mary Jane McPheeters PS NC

INNES, (includes INNIS)
Harry: b 1752 d 9-20-1816 m (1)Elizabeth Calloway (2)Mrs Shields PS CS VA
Hugh: b c. 1740 d 3-22-1797 m Hannah Eggleston Capt VA
James: b 1730 d 1818 m Sabra Ross Pvt NY
James: b a. 1762 d 10-21-1826 m (1)Ann Arbuckle (2)Isabella Oliver Pvt PA ★

INSKEEP,
Abraham: b 10-23-1745 d 9-15-1823 m Susan Hedges Vause PS VA

INSLEE,
Grace Moore: b 1726 d 10-3-1794 m Jonathan Inslee PS NJ
John: b 5- -1746 d 4-23-1791 m (1)Elizabeth Pike (2)Sarah Freeman Pvt NJ
Jonathan: b 1716 d 2-24-1777 m Grace Moore PS NJ

INYARD, (includes ENYART, ENYEART)
Benjamin: b 5-28-1741 d a. 1-7-1818 m (1)Johanna Tombs (2)Mrs Mary Runyan Cpl NJ
John: b 1753 d 1818 m Mary Anne (Wright) Ens PA
Wm.: b 1748 d 9-2-1828 m (1)Catherine Shell (2)Jane Norris 2Lt PA

INZER,
John: b 1760 d 8-30-1831 m (2)Mary Dowdy Mid Pvt MD

IRBY,
Charles: b c. 1730 d p. 1783 m Mehitable Kolb Cmsry PS SC
Joseph, Sr.: b 9- -1728 d 11-19-1781 m Mary Carter Sol SC
Wm.: b 1752 d 12-5-1811 m Elizabeth Williams Sol VA

IREDELL,
James: b 10-5-1751 d 10-20-1799 m Hannah Johnson CS NC

IRELAN,
Japhet: b 11-22-1744 d 2-20-1810 m Mary Townsend Pvt NJ

IRELAND,
Abraham: b 4-8-1713 d 4-29-1799 m Anne Bird Pvt MA
James: b 12-15-1752 d 8-17-1826 m Agnes Fleming Ens NC
James: b 10-2-1759 d 8-12-1815 m Lydia VanEmmons Pvt PA
John: b 1752 d 1833 m (1)Margaret Ager (2)Ann Kerns Montgomery Pvt PA
John: b 1755 d p. 1799 m Catherine Hoose Pvt VA
Joseph: b 1713 d 6-1-1793 m Elizabeth Losee PS Pvt NY
Stephen: b 1751 d 1828 m Mary Cosman Pvt NY
Thomas: b 1745 d 12-10-1811 m Sarah Sieley Pvt NY
Wm.: b c. 1756 d 1806 m Jane Miller PS VA

IRES,
Joel: b 5-19-1749 d 8-14-1825 m Mary Heaton Pvt CT NY

IRESON,
John: b 7-20-1758 d 9-20-1822 m Sarah Sargent Cpl MA

IREY,
John: b 1-29-1757 d 12-20-1837 m Sarah Ann Poole Pvt VA

IRION,
Francis Lewis Charles: b 4-10-1757 d p. 10-20-1808 m Charlotte Holderness PS NC

IRISH,
Abner: b 1748 d 3-25-1825 m Thankful Brown Pvt NY
Benjamin: b 1-11-1753 d p. 1795 m Martha Irish Sgt CT
George: b 1739 d 10-11-1801 m Sarah Babcock Col RI
James, Jr.: b 1-21-1736 d 4-1-1816 m Mary Gorham Phinney Sgt MA
Jesse, Jr.: b 11-11-1739 d 11-10-1803 m Ruth Wing PS VT
John: b 4-13-1724 d p. 1800 m Sarah — Pvt MA
Joseph: b 4-12-1728 d p. 1802 m Hannah Doane Pvt MA
Nathaniel: b 5-8-1737 d 9-11-1816 m (1)Elizabeth Thomas (2)Mary Ann — Capt PA
Thomas: b 1-29-1737 d 8-14-1832 m Deliverance Skillings Sgt MA
Wm.: b — d 3-0-1817 m Sarah Murch Pvt NH MA

IRONMONGER,
Cornelius: b c. 1730 d 1811 m Esther Dunton Lt VA

IRONS,
Garrett: b 2-14-1759 d 6-14-1838 m Hester Applegate Pvt NJ ★
James: b 1-31-1757 d 8-29-1833 m Didamia Cooper Pvt NJ
Jeremiah: b 1748 d 5-5-1840 m Barbery Tucker Lt RI

IRWIN, (includes ERWIN, IRVIN, IRVINE)
Abram: b 5- -1725 d 6-1-1814 m Mary Dean Sol VA
Alexander: b c. 1752 d p. 1799 m Penelope Lawson Capt GA
Alexander: b 12-29-1750 d 6-20-1830 m (1)Sarah Robinson (2)Mrs Cynthia Margaret Crawford Col PS NC
Alexander: b 1729 d 1790 m Margaret Chestnut PS NC
Andrew: b c. 1755 d p. 1791 m Sarah McCollough Pvt PA
Andrew: b 1748 d 4-25-1830 m Elizabeth Mitchell 1Lt VA W★
Andrew: b 1728 d 1790 m Elizabeth Mitchell 1Lt VA

Archibald: b 1728 d 1-23-1798 m Jean McDowell QM PA
Arthur: b 1726 d 6-9-1791 m (1)Mary Scott (2)Mary Kennedy Col PA
Arthur: b 3-1-1738 d 8-21-1821 m Margaret Brandon Sol PS NC
Christopher: b c. 1725 d p. 1-22-1791 m (1)Jane — (2)Mary Lyall CS NC
Christopher: b 9-11-1755 d 10-6-1786 m Lydia Calloway Ens VA
Christopher: b c. 1730 d 1815 m (1)Louisa Tucker (2)Lucinda Echols Pvt VA
David: b 5-18-1758 d 12-9-1831 m Catharine Munson Sol NJ
Edward: b 3-20-1760 d 1820 m Sarah Yates Pvt PS PA
Edward: b c. 1728 d 1798 m Mary — Pvt VA
Ezekiel: b a. 1-2-1761 d 7-28-1843 m (1)Betsie Martin (2)Elizabeth Braden Pvt PA ★
Francis: b 1743 d 12- -1802 m Elizabeth Clements PS VA
Henry: b 1750 d 10-4-1777 m Elizabeth Lackey LCol PS NC
Henry: b 1751/2 d 5- -1844 m Mary Naasin Pvt PA W★
Hugh: b c. 1725 d 1805 m Martha Alexander Sol GA
Hugh: b c. 1753 d p. 7-15-1805 m Mary — Sgt SC
Hugh: b c. 1730 d 9-25-1785 m (1)Mary Ellison (2)Elizabeth James PS SC
Isaac: b 3-15-1741 d 1783 m Margaret Creighton Pvt PA
James: b 1745 d 1814 m Jane Doud Pvt NY
James: b 1747 d 10-28-1820 m Mary McAuley Galloway Pvt NY
James: b 1757 d 12- -1829 m Margaret Cooper Sgt PA
James: b 1740 d 2- -1822 m Mary Carson Pvt PA
James: b 1742 d 1819 m Olivia Bard Pvt PA
James: b 4-14-1758 d 11-9-1843 m Margaret Piper Sol PA
James: b 10-16-1758 d 2-10-1847 m Agnes Irwin Sol PA
James: b 1754 d 1812 m Sarah Daniel Lt SC
James: b 1754 d 1851 m Lettie Irvin Pvt VA ★
Jared: b 1750 d 3-1-1818 m Isabella Erwin Sol GA
Jared: b 1732 d 9-25-1815 m Polly Laverty Pvt PA
Jennet Brewster: b 4-11-1761 d 7-17-1839 m Samuel Irvin PS VA
John: b 1755 d 1834 m Martha Wiley MM NJ
John: b 1762 d c. 1835 m Mary Holt Pvt NC ★
John: b 1753 d 3-5-1808 m Mary Pattison Maj PA
John: b 5-24-1757 d 7-31-1835 m Mary Welsh Pvt PA
John: b 3-25-1754 d 6-10-1820 m (1)Jane Witherspoon (2)Margaret Ervin (3)Mrs Hannah Blackwell Col SC
John: b 1740 d 2-15-1822 m Elizabeth Cunningham Col DepCmsry Gen PA
John: b c. 1751 d a. 7-9-1814 m Mary Ann Tucker Capt VA
John: b a. 1745 d p. 1802 m Ann — CS Pvt VA
John: b c. 1736 d 1- -1826 m Margaret McFarlane Pvt VA
John: b 1749 d 1823 m Eleanor Vance Mil VA
John Lawson: b 8-29-1764 d 1-1-1822 m Rebecca Sessions Pvt GA
Joseph: b 6-7-1762 d 4-14-1829 m Mrs Lavinia Thompson McKamie Sol NC
Joseph: b 8-15-1736 d 8-28-1803 m Violette Porter Lt PA
Matthew: b 1740 d 3-10-1800 m Esther Mifflin Col PA
Moses: b 1722 d 10-14-1805 m Hannah — CS PA
Nathaniel, Sr.: b c. 1712 d 2-18-1794 m (2)Leah Julian PS NC
Nathaniel: b 12-28-1757 d 4-17-1836 m Elizabeth Hunter Sgt PA ★
Peter: b 1752 d 4-30-1846 m Elizabeth Armstrong Pvt NJ CL
Richard: b 1740 d 1812 m Ann Steele 1Lt PA
Robert: b 8-20-1738 d 12-23-1800 m (1)Mary Alexander (2)Mary Barry PS Col NC
Robert: b — d 1808 m Margaret — Pvt PA
Robert: b c. 1740 d a. 3-6-1796 m Agnes Campbell Irwin Pvt SC
Robert: b c. 1750 d 1798/9 m Mary South 1Lt VA
Samuel: b 1-25-1747 d 3-9-1806 m Mary Miller LCol PA
Samuel: b 1745 d 1-26-1826 m Mary Potts PS PA
Samuel: b 2- -1760 d 8-3-1837 m Jane Brewster Pvt SC
Samuel: b 4-4-1749 d 2-24-1811 m Mary Curry Pvt VA
Sarah Anne Robinson: b 11-29-1750 d 4-7-1785 m Alexander Erwin PS NC
Thomas: b 1758 d 4-13-1843 m (1)Mary Montgomery (2)Elizabeth Biggers Pvt NC ★
Thomas Henry: b 1755 d p. 9-5-1836 m — Pvt SC ★
Wm.: b 1759 d p. 1785 m Nancy Whitaker Sol GA
Wm.: b 11-3-1741 d 7-30-1804 m Anne Callender BGen PA
Wm.: b 1738 d c. 1815 m Eleanor Brisbane Pvt PA
Wm.: b 1734 d 5-20-1814 m Sallie Ross Pvt SC
Wm.: b 9-26-1763 d 9-25-1850 m Mary Pigman OrdlSgt Wgn VA ★
Wm.: b 1761 d 1817 m Elizabeth Hockaday Sol KY
Wm.: b 1745 d 1809 m Elizabeth Holt PS VA

ISAACS, (includes ISAACKS)
Jacob: b c. 1718 d 3- -1798 m Rebecca Mears PS RI
John: b 1757 d p. 1834 m Mrs Mary Swan Pvt VA
Samuel: b 1759 d p. 9-5-1844 m Mary Wallace Pvt Spy SC NC ★
Samuel Brown: b 1756 d 11-22-1819 m Hannah Marshall Pvt CT

ISBELL, (includes ISBEL)
Chauncy: b 7- -1752 d 4-27-1777 m Deborah Beach Pvt CT
Eleazer: b 4-7-1740 d 9-17-1777 m Hannah Pamely Pvt CT
Eliab: b 7-31-1759 d 12-31-1825 m Deborah Stevens Fif CT
Elias: b 2-5-1747/8 d 2-6-1834 m Temperance Ward Drm CT
Garner: b 9-2-1762 d 10-27-1835 m Mary Graves Pvt CT ★
Lyttleton: b a. 1762 d a. 3-3-1829 m Anna — Capt SC
Pendleton: b 6-2-1757 d 3- -1829 m (1)Sarah — (2)Margaret Lawhon Pvt PS VA ★

Thomas: b 6-27-1753 d 10-27-1819 m Discretion Howard Pvt VA ★
Wm.: b c. 1722 d a. 10-3-1807 m Ann Dillard PS VA

ISGRIGG,
Michael: b 1751 d 6-15-1831 m Barbary Love Sgt PS MD

ISH,
John: b 1760 d 7-24-1794 m Elizabeth Keppener Pvt PA

ISHAM,
Daniel: b 6-22-1751 d 6-27-1841 m Rhoda Lord Pvt CT ★
Jehiel: b 6-17-1761 d 9-17-1851 m Sarah Mobbs Pvt CT ★
Jirah: b 4-22-1760 d 12-9-1837 m Lois Kellogg Pvt CT ★
John, Jr.: b 5-7-1742 d 5-5-1828 m Eunice Baldwin Capt CT
Joseph: b 1735 d 1810 m Esther Taintor Capt CT
Samuel: b 1752 d 1827 m (1)Mary Adams (2) "a widow" Pvt CT
Wm.: b 10-1-1759 d 5-25-1849 m Tabitha Brainard Pvt CT ★

ISHERWOOD,
Francis: b 10-26-1747/8 d 10-25-1828 m Elizabeth Grimes PS PA

ISHMAEL,
Benjamin: b c. 1736/7 d 7-10-1822 m prob. Jane — Pvt PA ★

ISRAEL,
Basil: b 4-9-1757 d 10-13-1829 m Eleanor Mansel 1Lt MD
Israel: b 11-20-1745 d 3-18-1822 m Hannah Erwin PS PA
John: b 6-13-1749 d 1-30-1822 m Rachel Clary Cadet VA
Joseph: b 11-12-1753 d 12-15-1807 m Susanne Pusey Capt DE
Robert: b c. 1709 d 1795 m Priscilla Baker PS MD

IVENS,
Solomon: b 1-22-1761 d 1-4-1802 m Catherine Scott Pvt CL ★

IVERS,
Thomas: b 1730 d 1805 m Elizabeth Beach PS Capt NY

IVES,
Abel: b 5-6-1711 d 1-31-1791 m Sarah Reed PS CT
Abner: b 8-20-1745 d 10-8-1801 m Anna Ferguson Pvt CT
Abraham: b 11-20-1746 d 4-27-1814 m Eunice Hull PS CS VT
Amasa: b 11-22-1747 d p. 2-22-1833 m (1)Bethia — (2)Mary — Pvt MA ★
Ambrose: b 5-22-1736 d p. 1810 m Deborah — Pvt CT
Amos: b 8-11-1749 d 1841 m Lucy Hall OrdlSgt CT ★
Benjamin: b 1749 d 10-29-1791 m Elizabeth Giles NS
Bezaleel: b 1726 d 11-24-1798 m Hannah Merriman Capt CT
Charles, Sr.: b 9-5-1735 d 6-18-1790 m Sarah Butler PS CT
Charles, Jr.: b 4-14-1760 d 1837 m Mary Francis Pvt CT ★
David: b 1-15-1740 d 12-11-1815 m Dolly Hough Cpl MA
Elam: b 12-26-1761 d 1-24-1846 m Sarah Hitchcock Pvt CT
Elnathan: b 12-21-1748 d 12-14-1841 m Olive Blakeslee Pvt NY CT
Elnathan: b 1706 d 2-16-1777 m Abigail Frisbee PS CT
Enos: b 10-25-1753 d 3-9-1830 m Eunice Merriman Pvt CT
Enos, Sr.: b 5-14-1727 d p. 1783 m Annah Cook Pvt VT
Enos, Jr.: b 4-25-1759 d 11- -1827 m Ruth Bingham Pvt CT
George: b a. 1743 d p. 4-7-1789 m Sarah Old Lt VA
Ichabod: b 8-14-1759 d 2-15-1845 m Mary Clark Sol MA
Joel: b 5-19-1749 d 8-14-1825 m (1)Mary Heaton (2)Sarah Harrison Pvt CT
Joel, Jr.: b 4-16-1760 d 6-3-1808 m Olive Ives Pvt CT
John: b 7-4-1729 d 2- -1816 m (1)Mary Hall (2)Sarah — Pvt CT
John: b 4-3-1749 d 4-16-1814 m Sarah Henderson Pvt CT
John: b 2-5-1757 d 12-10-1847 m Esther Tuttle Sol CT
John P.: b 1754 d 1835 m Elizabeth C. Marchant Pvt NC ★
Joseph: b 1-17-1737 d 11-25-1785 m Elizabeth Grannis Pvt CS PS NH
Josiah: b 3-13-1739 d p. 12-13-1808 m Anna — Lt CT
Jotham: b 8-20-1745 d 4-1-1825 m (1)Anna Foster (2)Lydia Mix Pvt CT
Jotham: b 1753 d 1816 m Lillis Fisk Pvt CT
Lazarus: b 11-2-1734 d 9-17-1812 m Lydia Grimes Lt CT
Lent: b 11-28-1758 d 6-30-1738 m Mary Mighell Pvt CT VT ★
Levi: b 6-4-1750 d 10-17-1826 m (1)Lydia Auger (2)Margaret Bird Sol Dr CT
Levi: b 5-25-1761 d 4-12-1850 m Caroline Pratt Pvt CT ★
Noah: b 12-4-1730 d 1800 m Abigail Pierpont Capt CT
Phineas: b 6-12-1746 d 6-27-1824 m Martha Moss Cpl CT
Reuben: b 3-10-1743 d 1823 m Lydia — PS CT
Samuel: b 3-9-1745/6 d p. 1801 m Lola Parker Pvt CT
Stephen: b 3-26-1741 d 1786 m Sarah Ames Pvt CT
Thomas: b 2-2-1753 d 3-8-1814 m Ruth Foster Maj MA
Titus: b 2-28-1732 d 9-26-1810 m Dorothy Halsey Capt PS CT
Titus: b 2- -1746/7 d 9-2-1776/7 m Martha Gaylord Pvt CT
Wm.: b 1755 d 1829 m Sarah Hotchkiss Smn CT

IVEY,
Adam: b c. 1723 d p. 8-3-1789 m Mary — PS VA
Curtis: b c. 1735 d 1795 m Eunice Willis Capt NC
Elijah: b 1758/9 d 1-15-1840 m (4)Mary Harten Pvt SC ★
Ephraim: b 12-24-1751 d a. 7-6-1840 m — Pvt VA
George: b c. 1740 d p. 7-29-1814 m — PS VA
Robert: b 4-2-1763 d 6-6-1845 m Elizabeth West PS NC

IVINS,
Solomon: b c. 1721 d p. 12-17-1790 m (1)Elizabeth Everingham (2)Mary — Asst QM PS NJ

IVORY,
John, Jr.: b 5-17-1756 d 3-1-1818 m Lucy Russel Pvt MA

IVY,
Henry: b c. 1754 d 7-27-1834 m Jane Howell Pvt NC W★

IZARD, (includes ISARD)
Henry: b 12-28-1765 d 3-9-1845 m Deborah — Pvt NJ
Ralph: b 1-23-1741 d 5-30-1804 m Alice de Lancey PS CS SC

JACK,
Andrew: b 6-30-1756 d 1-23-1846 m Nancy Clemson Pvt PA
James: b 1731 d 12-18-1822 m Margaret Houston Capt NC
James: b 1758 d 10-5-1824 m Nancy McKinney Sgt PA
James: b 1748 d 1847 m Nancy Wiseman Matr VA
Jeremiah: b 11-13-1750 d 6- -1833 m Martha Gillespie Sol NC
John: b 3-11-1726 d 4- -1808 m Eleanor Stevenson Pvt PA
John: b 1747 d 4-1-1815 m Nancy McCoy Pvt PA W★
Matthew: b 2-1-1755 d 11-26-1836 m Nancy Wilson Capt PA
Michael: b 1752 d 9-30-1829 m Susannah Dunlap Pvt PA
Patrick: b 1700 d 10-5-1780 m Lillias McAdoo PS NC
Patrick: b 1-23-1721 m Martha Finley Capt PA
Patrick: b 1745 d 2-17-1817 m (1)Margaret Bryant (2)Mrs Anna Story Watson (3)Mrs Leslie Capt PA
Robert: b c. 1752 d 7-9-1831 m (1)Margaret Reed (2)Susanna — Pvt MA ★
Thomas: b a. 1760 d p. 1794 m Jane Kinkade Sgt PA
Wm.: b 1751 d 2-20-1821 m Margaret Wilson 2Lt PA
Wm.: b c. 1745 d c. 1820 m Lucretia Ann Gear Pvt PA

JACKMAN,
Abel: b 8-2-1762 d 6-24-1820 m Dorothy True Pvt MA
Benjamin: b 5-7-1743 d 11-26-1836 m Jane Woodman Lt NH
Edward: b c. 1735 d p. 10-1-1805 m Barnett Pvt PA
Enoch: b 10-13-1753 d 12-25-1833 m (1)Elizabeth Fells (2)Hannah French Sgt Mar MA
George: b 10-28-1735 d 11- -1829 m (1)Martha Webster (2) — Thompson PS NH
Humphrey: b 7-16-1761 d — m Judith Pettingell Pvt NH
John: b 1745 d 9-15-1825 m Margaret Morton Pvt PA
John: b 8-21-1743 d 3- -1813 m Mary Danforth Pvt VT
Richard: b 1746 d 3-30-1801 m Mary Neavil Pvt VA
Robert: b — -1739 d 8-26-1813 m (1)Sarah Whittaker (2)Ann Dixon Capt PA
Samuel: b 3-17-1749 d 8-20-1844 m (1)Submit Brown (2)Hannah Winslow Pvt NH ★
Samuel: bpt 3-17-1748 /9 d p. 1790 m Anna Fowler PS NH
Timothy: b 7-13-1729 d 7-8-1795 m Mary Thurston Capt MA
Timothy: bpt 10-25-1747 d 1815/16 m Mary Burbank Pvt MA
Wm.: b 11-16-1759 d 8-5-1805 m Elizabeth Morriel Sgt NH

JACKSON,
Aaron: b 1758 d 6-3-1802 m Lucy Dewing Sgt MA
Abraham: b 12-4-1721 d 1-15-1807 m (1)Mary Hide (2)Margaret Hammond Marean (3)Mrs Hannah Woodward Pvt CS MA
Abraham, Sr.: b 1-16-1726 d 9-18-1791 m Eleanor Bump Capt VT
Abraham, Jr.: b 7-10-1751 d 8-9-1833 m (1)Jerusha Steele (2)Mary Button Kinne PS CS VT
Absolem: b a. 1760 d a. 2-5-1795 m Pharabee Webster Pvt GA
Alexander: b 6-12-1728 d 3-14-1818 m Martha Drake Pvt NY
Alexander: b 1722 d 1803 m Deborah Mauduitt PS MD
Andrew: b 8-7-1729 d 12-31-1815 m Jane Sloan Sol VA
Andrew: b 5-30-1754 d 4-30-1837 m Elizabeth Sargent Pvt VA
Asa: b 12-17-1749 d 9-11-1844 m (2)Mrs Polly Adams Pvt NH ★
Barnabas: bpt 4-25-1753 d 1-2-1819 m Lydia Oldham Pvt MA
Benjamin: b c. 1750 d a. 3-3-1798 m — Sol GA
Benjamin: b 3-5-1752 d 6-5-1842 m Abigail Mitchell Sgt NJ ★
Caleb: b 4-16-1760 d 12-15-1815 m Rhoda Pratt Pvt MA
Charles: b 5-15-1760 d c. 1830 m (2)Allie Barlowe 1Lt SC
Charles: b 1745 d p. 1784 m Cloe Ann Calvert Pvt VA
Christopher: b c. 1758-60 d p. 1800 m Magdaline Boggess Pvt VA
Christopher: b 1-8-1768 d 7-22-1831 m Catherine Rhodes Sol VA
Daniel, Jr.: b 1763 d 8-25-1841 m Elizabeth Whitney Pvt VT ★
Daniel: b 12-26-1753 d 4-9-1836 m (1)Jemima Benjamin (2)Sarah Campbell Pvt NJ ★
Daniel: b c. 1754 d p. 1828 m Elizabeth Alden Lt MA ★
Daniel: b 1735 d 1812 m Nancy High Pvt SC
David: b 10-28-1736 d a. 2- -1814 m (1)Anna Sanford (2)Esther Ward Pvt CT
David: b c. 1730 d c. 8- -1811 m Elizabeth Reed Pvt PA
David: b 1745 d 4-23-1818 m Mary Morrison Sol SC
Drury: b a. 1748 d p. 6-21-1792 m Nancy Mayfield Sol GA
Ebenezer: b 1- -1762 d 1-25-1839 m Abigail Keys Pvt VT ★
Edward: b 1730 d p. 5-7-1807 m Martha Miller Pvt PA NJ
Edward: b c. 1740 d 1804 m Margaret McMullin Pvt MD
Edward: b 9-3-1739 d 9-25-1830 m Jemima Trowbridge Pvt MA

JACKSON, contd.

Edward: b 4-26-1755 d 5-25-1826 m (1)Abigail Smith (2)Mrs Judith Bacon (3)Lucy Claflin (4)Mrs Sarah Stevens (5)Mrs Patty Winch Pvt MA

Edward: b 2-14-1755 d 2-22-1845 m (1)Charity Hill (2)Mary Hall Pvt SC ★

Edward: b 3-1-1759 d 12-26-1828 m (1)Mary Hadden (2)Elizabeth Brake Sol VA

Eleazer: b 8-22-1748 d 4-19-1834 m (1)Levina Child (2)Huldah Dresser (3)Mrs Olive Fitch Ens NH

Elias: b 12-31-1753 d p. 1801 m Nancy Alexander Pvt NY

Elisha: b 2-12-1737 d 7-10-1814 m Beulah Taylor Capt MA

Elizabeth Cummins: b 1724 d 1825 m John Jackson PS VA

Ephraim: b 1741 d 10-19-1828 m Martha Hull Pvt CT

Ephraim: b 10-12-1729 d 12-19-1777 m Mary Davis LCol MA

Ephraim: b c. 1745 d 5-29-1814 m (1)Bathsheba Trask (2)Hannah Delano Lt MA

Ephraim: b c. 1754 d 1825 m Lucretia Tucker PS VA

Francis: b 8- -1757 d 1835 m Martha Maddera Pvt VA ★

George: b 10-11-1746 d 5-10-1818 m Elizabeth Walker Ens NJ

George: b 11-5-1737 d 8-3-1805 m Rachel — 2Lt PA

George: b 1-9-1757 d 5-17-1831 m (1)Elizabeth Brake (2)Mrs Nancy Richardson Adams Capt VA

Giles: b 1-27-1733 d 5-4-1810 m (1)Anna Thomas(2)Sarah Atwood Orton LCol MA

Henry: b 1760 d p. 1785 m Sallie Mopp Pvt GA

Henry: b p. 1742 d p. 3- -1810 m Elizabeth — PS Sol VA

Henry: b — d p. 10-8-1789 m (1)Mary — (2)Ann — PS VA

Hugh, Sr.: b 5-20-1709 d 8-25-1782 m Mary — PS MD

Isaac: b 1733 d 3- -1805 m Nancy Mopp LCol GA

Isaac, Jr.: b 5-29-1732 d 5-9-1795 m (1)Jemima Jones (2)Sarah Cheney (3)Mary Hammond Lt MA

Isaac: b c. 1755 d a. 4-30-1821 m (1)Ann Richardson (2)Eliza Howell (3)Elizabeth Durman Pvt SC

Isaac: b 2-6-1758 d 10-1-1845 m (1)Submit Scott (2)Betsey Bessey Pvt MA ★

Isaac: b c. 1718 d 1809 m Elizabeth Claiborne Pvt VA

Jacob: b 1756 d 1832 m Freelove Foote Sgt NY

James: b 9-21-1757 d 3-19-1806 m Mary Charlotte Young LCol GA

James: b 11-10-1721 d 1791 m Mary Scripture PS NH

James: b 4-1-1758 d 3-26-1816 m Sarah Smith Adj NY

James: b 11-18-1746 d 4-17-1814 m Mary Read Sgt VA

Jarvis: b 1728 d 1802 m Mary — PS VA

Jedediah: b 2-4-1753 d 6-11-1818 m Betsey Swift Ens VT

Jehiel: b 12-7-1734-39 d 1804 m Mehitabel Rood Pvt CT

Jeremiah, Sr.: b 8-13-1739 d 1802 m Phebe Murry Ens MA

Jeremiah, Jr.: b 1-27-1761 d 8-22-1837 m Sarah Simpson Lamphere Pvt Wgn MA ★

Jeremiah: b a. 1764 d 1822 m Martha Keys Pvt MA

Jesse: b c. 1750 d 6-10-1834 m Hannah DeCoursey Pvt PA

Job: b 1759 d c. 1829 m Sarough — Sol GA

John: b 10-6-1750 d 11-7-1820 m Delight Foster Pvt CT

John: b 1762 d 8-15-1833 m (2)Ruth Godfrey Pvt MA ★

John: b 1755 d a. 1790 m Anna Gowan Smn MA

John: b 6-16-1743 d 1-11-1816 m Phoebe Everit Capt NY

John: b 1750 d p. 1780 m Jane Newlands Pvt NY

John: b c. 1752 d p. 1789 m Margaret Crawford Pvt NC

John: b 10-16-1712 d 5-31-1791 m Sara Miller Pvt PA

John: b 1731 d 1823 m Elcy Armstrong PS PA

John: b 8-29-1759 d 9-4-1829 m Katherine White Pvt PS VA W★

John: b 1719 d 9-25-1804 m Elizabeth Cummins Pvt VA

John: b 6-10-1762 d 2-10-1833 m Mary Forrest Hancock Pvt VA

Jonas: b 3-12-1723 d p. 1790 m Martha Hyde Pvt MA

Jonathan: b 6-4-1743 d 3-5-1810 m Hannah Tracy PS MA

Jordan: b c. 1750 d p. 1820 m — Wright Pvt GA

Joseph, Jr.: b 3-7-1756 d 1-29-1837 m Mary Edmunds Pvt CT

Joseph: b 1730 d 8-25-1803 m Elizabeth — PM MA

Joseph: b 1753 d 9-3-1788 m Rebecca Green Pvt 2Cpl MA ★

Joseph: b 8-2-1729 d 11-16-1803 m Abigail Brown Pvt MA

Joseph: b 5-11-1752 d 6-19-1831 m Hannah Kennedy Pvt MA

Joseph, Sr.: b 11- -1728 d p. 1790 m Sarah Burr PS NY

Joseph: b 1760 d 10-11-1844 m Margaret Lyster Pvt NC ★

Joseph: b c. 1758 d 9-24-1842 m Sarah Kirkman PS NC

Joshua: b 5-2-1762 d 7-31-1849 m Eleanor Fiske Pvt MA

Josiah: b 4-23-1730-32 d 2-5-1778 m Mary Darby Pvt MA

Josiah: b 3-5-1732 d p. 1791 m Ruth Steer Pvt VA

Josiah: b 12-19-1746 d 8-6-1836 m (1)Dolly Ashurst (2)Sarah (Ray)Strupes Sol VA ★

Lemuel: b 1738 d 1818 m (1)Jemima Sampson (2)Susanna Cole Pvt MA

Lyman: b 2-29-1756 d 3-20-1835 m Deidama Dunham Sgt MA NY ★

Mark: b 11-12-1742 d p. 1832 m Elizabeth Leanna Pvt SC ★

Mathew: b 1-16-1763 d 7-14-1823 m Jane Campbell Fif Pvt MA CT ★

Michael: b c. 1755 d 6-26-1828 m Deborah Jencks Pvt CT ★

Michael: b 12-18-1734 d 4-10-1801 m Ruth Parker BG MA

Michael: b 8-11-1708 d 1-15-1789 m Eleanor McDowell PS NY

Michael: bpt 7-13-1735 d 10-24-1802 m Susanna Willcoxson Pvt VT

Moses: bpt 6-28-1761 d 7-23-1824 m Sarah Maxwell Pvt MA ★

Nehemiah: b 9-11-1744 d 4-18-1825 m Esther Abbot Cpl CT

Obadiah: b c. 1730 d 1799 m Alma Seaman PS NY

Oliver: b 11-22-1757 d 4-13-1816 m Abigail (Beard)Pierce Pvt MA

Peter: b 4-22-1757 d 3-4-1842 m — Sgt PA ★

Phillip: b c. 1750 d p. 1790 m Rosanna Murphy Pvt PA

Phineas: b 11-3-1755 d a. 10- -1815 m Ruth Wood Cpl MA

Reuben: b 6-5-1753 d 9-16-1829 m Hannah Tucker Cpl VA

Richard: b c. 1750 d 1820 m Phoebe Updike Pvt PA

Robert: bpt 3-21-1736 d 1809 m Olive Varnum Pvt MA

Robert: b 4-5-1760 d 4-28-1829 m Albertie Hogeboom Pvt NY

Robert, Sr.: b 3-17-1733 d 9-28-1809 m Mary Hewthorn Pvt PA

Robert: b 1740 d 1799 m Elizabeth Ann — Pvt PA

Robert: b 1758 d 9-26-1828 m Elizabeth McCorkie Pvt PA

Salah: b 1755 d 2-6-1802 m Annie Wheelwright Saxton PS CT

Samuel: b 1758 d 4-1-1843 m Susanna Hawley Cpl CT ★

Samuel: b 9-16-1755 d 5-2-1836 m Elizabeth Catherine Woodrow 1Lt GA ★

Samuel, Sr.: b 4-10-1737 d 7- -1801 m Lois Woodward Sgt MA

Samuel, Jr.: b 2-16-1764 d 5-10-1836 m (1)Comfort Houghton (2)Mercy Macomber Pvt MA ★

Samuel: b 1756 d p. 1800 m Hannah Southworth Pvt MA

Samuel: b 1- -1731 d 3-27-1805 m Experience Atwood CS PS MA

Samuel: b 1752 d 7-20-1822 m Mary Jackson Cpl NH

Samuel: b c. 1750 d p. 4-21-1832 m Margaret Kelch Pvt NJ

Samuel: b 1758 d 6-18-1834 m Hannah Gibson Pvt NC ★

Samuel: b 1747 d 1801 m — Woodward Pvt PA

Samuel: b 1757 d 3-12-1834 m Margaret Cree PS PA

Samuel: b c. 1755 d 1815 m Mary Farrow Pvt VA

Simon: b 11-20-1760 d 10-17-1818 m (2)Sarah Spring 1Lt PM MA

Stephen: b 7-25-1755 d p. 1820 m Hannah Jackson Sgt NH VT ★

Stephen: b 9-8-1744 d 3-28-1812 m (1)Mary Burwell (2)Mary (Minturn)Allen Capt NJ

Stephen, Jr.: b c. 1760 d p. 1807 m Tempie Rushing Pvt SC

Thomas: b 1733 d 11-23-1806 m Mary Knight Pvt CT

Thomas: b 7-2-1751 d 8-7-1833 m Rachel Colburn QMSgt MA

Thomas: b 1754 d 11-10-1840 m (1)Lucy Sampson (2)Sarah LeBaron Pvt MA

Thomas: b — d — m Mary Jackson Pvt MA

Thomas: b 1703 d 7-10-1775 m Hannah Woodworth PS CS MA

Thomas: b 12-24-1754 d 11-29-1842 m Elizabeth Jackson Pvt PS NY

Thomas: b 5-9-1757 d 11-20-1844 m Frances Richardson Pvt SC ★

Thomas: b — d p. 8-8-1792 m Mary Franklin PS VA

Timothy: b 8-3-1756 d 11-22-1814 m Sarah Winchester OrdlSgt MA

Uri: b c. 1750 d p. 1781 m Sarah Burchard Cpl CT

Walter: b c. 1737 d 1816 m Mary Chauncey Clark Sol GA

Wm.: b 1750-54 d 1835/36 m Mary — Pvt GA

Wm.: b c. 1760 d c. 1804 m Elizabeth Borland Pvt GA

Wm.: b 3-4-1756 d 6-27-1828 m Tryphena Mason Ens MD

Wm.: b 8-10-1760 d 8-10-1849 m Barbara Ann Snively Pvt MD

Wm.: b 1726 d 1792 m Mary Ann Cheseman Cmsry NJ

Wm.: b 6-22-1752 d 10-5-1802 m Ruth Woolley Pvt NJ

Wm.: b 9-3-1747 d 1776 m Mary VanVechten Capt NY

Wm.: b c. 1760 d p. 1798 m Abigail Gilham Pvt NC

Wm.: b 1745/6 d 9-11-1777 m Ann Rudolph Pvt PA

Wm.: b 3-9-1759 d 12-17-1828 m Elizabeth Willing ADC PA

JACOBIE,

Bastian: b 1742 d p. 11-17-1791 m Catherine Smith Pvt NY

Bastian: b c. 1719 d 4-4-1785 m Catherine Scholdis Pvt NY

John: b 1-22-1750 d 4- -1834 m Catharine Fritts Pvt NY

JACOBS, (includes JACOB)

Asa, Jr.: b 4-18-1760 d 11-27-1844 m (1)Sarah Emerson (2)Phebe Greenwood Pvt CT RI ★

Benjamin: b c. 1750 d p. 1813 m Eleanor Odell PS MD

Benjamin: b 3-4-1741 d 10- -1814 m Sarah Moulton 1Lt MA

Benjamin: b 1743 d 6-10-1795 m Susanna Beal Sgt MA

Cornelius, Jr.: b 5-19-1754 d 4-18-1811 m Elizabeth Lyon Pvt NY ★

David: b c. 1759 d 5-18-1835 m Elizabeth Rice Pvt PA ★

Elisha: b 8-29-1735 d 12-8-1779 m Lusanna Randall Pvt MA

Elnathan: b 9-9-1750 d 2-13-1813 m (1)Margaret — (2)Rachel — Pvt MA

Enoch: b 12- -1746 d 3-6-1797 m (2)Lois Parker Pvt CT

Ezekiel: b 6-20-1755 d 3-5-1834 m Eleanor Walter Pvt CT ★

James: b 3-6-1742 d 9-12-1827 m Deborah Richmond Cpl MA

Jermiah, Jr.: b 1745 d p. 9-9-1813 m Rebecca Dowden PS MD

John: b 5-25-1725 d 3-3-1820 m Sarah Plank Slr CT

John, Jr.: b 9-12-1751 d 6-8-1837 m Dinah Tourtellotte Pvt CT

John: b 5-23-1735 d 2-7-1817 m Hannah Tolman Col MA

John: b 8-14-1732 d 12-4-1806 m Lydia Beal Pvt MA

John: b 2-18-1757 d 1-9-1820 m Lydia Reed Pvt MA

John: b 1759 d 7-8-1838 m (1)Margaret Bennett (2)Sarah Eton Pvt MA ★

John: b 1748 d 3-15-1831 m Elizabeth Pensil Pvt NJ PA ★

John: b 1752 d 1820 m Elizabeth — Pvt PA

John: b 3-6-1722 d 1782 m Elizabeth Havard PS PA

John: b 1738 d 1811/12 m Sarah Crawford Capt CS VA

John Jeremiah: b 1-17-1757 d 3-23-1839 m (1)Mary (Cresap) Whitehead (2)Susan McDavitt Lt PM MD ★

Joseph: b 11-4-1729 d p. 1790 m Bethiah Hodges Pvt CT

Joseph: b 10-8-1741 d 7-25-1817 m Hannah Aldrich Mus NY

Joseph: b *c.* 1755 d *p.* 1-7-1814 m Elizabeth — PS VA
Joshua: b 6-27-1737 d 8-9-1808 m Elizabeth Richmond Lt MA
Nathaniel: b 7-6-1760 d 4-5-1845 m Elizabeth Starr Pvt CT
Peter: b *a.* 1763 d 10-12-1820 m Elizabeth Rice Pvt PA W★
Richard: b 5-28-1724 d 1-14-1809 m (1)Thankful Kellogg
   (2)Susannah Hosmer CL PS MA
Richard, Sr.: b 1-30-1697/8 d *c.* 6-25-1779 m Hannah Howard PS
   MD
Samuel: b 2-26-1739 d 11-5-1810 m Elizabeth Perkins Pvt PS CT
Samuel: b 11-4-1734 d *p.* 1790 m (1)Bithiah Oley (2)Elizabeth Gray
   1Lt MD
Samuel: b 3-23-1760 d 1-26-1840 m (1)Elizabeth Martin (2)Lydia
   Groves Pvt VA ★
Simeon: b 1757 d 4-7-1833 m (1)Abigail — (2)Sarah Davis Sgt
   Grd MA
Solomon: b 3-24-1740 d *p.* 1800 m Elizabeth H. Gillett Sgt CT
Whitman, Jr.: b 5-1-1759 d 10-2-1825 m Hannah Walker Pvt MA
Wm.: b 6-19-1755 d 6-3-1836 m Sarah Thomas 2Sgt MD ★
Wm.: b *c.* 1757 d *a.* 7-16-1816 m Dorcas Stokes PS VA

JACOBUS,
Cornelius: b *c.* 1755 d 2-8-1835 m Abigail Gould Pvt NJ
Cornelius: bpt 6-21-1746 d 1-8-1832 m Catherine Garrison PS NJ
James: b 1776 d *a.* 8-22-1794 m Maritje Kip PS NJ
Richard: b — d 1806 m Eleanor Spreer Pvt NJ

JACOBY,
Bartholomew: b 1747 d *p.* 1816 m Katherine Mayer PS PA
Francis: b *c.* 1738 d *p.* 5-17-1788 m Frederica Lotspeig PS VA
George: b 1748 d *p.* 1810 m Anna Maria Philip Cpl PA
Henry: b 1733 d 11-12-1809 m Maria Kern Pvt PA
John: b 3-2-1745 d 1-27-1805 m Anna Margaret Eberhard Capt PA
John: b 5-18-1761 d 8- -1825 m (1)Anna Christina Raub (2)Anna
   Maria Laubach Pvt PA
Philip: b 12-4-1755 d 8-31-1827 m Catherine Klinker Sol PA
Phillip: b 1760 d 11-7-1823 m Mary Toole Pvt PA ★

JACOCKS,
Gershom: b 1763 d 7-30-1819 m Mary Elizabeth Fisher Pvt NY ★
Jonathan: b *c.* 1720 d 5-24-1787 m Elizabeth Hill PS NC

JAGGERS, (includes JAGGER)
Jeremiah: b 3-19-1750 d 9-13-1826 m Esther Jewell MM NJ
John: b 1-24-1733/4 d. 9-28-1800 m Mercy Brown Pvt NY
Nathan: b 10-16-1759 d 12-19-1839 m —Pvt SC ★

JAMES,
Abel: b 1738 d 10-11-1814 m (1)Hannah Kenyon (2)Mary — Pvt
   MA
Abel: b *c.* 1717 d 11-9-1790 m Rebecca Chalkley PS VA
Able: b 1749 d 1798 m Elizabeth Barton Lt PA
Allen: b 3-17-1743 d 7- -1821 m (1)Elizabeth Pettis (2)Sarah
   Conklin Ens RI
Amos: b 5-25-1760 d 2-9-1845 m (1)Polly Lee (2)Mrs Phebe
   Chadsey James Adj RI ★
Benjamin: b 1740 d — m Sarah Holmes Smn MA
Benjamin: b 4-22-1763 d 11-15-1825 m Jane Stobo Pvt VA
Daniel: b *c.* 1737 d 3- -1809 m Susan Baylert Bbd PA
David: b 12-28-1756 d 7-18-1834 m Philothea Watson Sgt NJ
David: b 1761 d 1866 m Catherine Park Fif VA
David: b 4-25-1764 d 12-25-1843 m Nancy Atchison Pvt VA ★
Ebenezer: b *c.* 1758 d 6-23-1838 m — Cpl NY
Edward: b 1760 d 1856 m Elizabeth — Pvt VA
Elias: b *c.* 2- -1744 d 1789 m Anne Matson Pvt PA
Evan: b 1750 d 12- -1825 m Rachael Evans Lt PA
Griffith: b *p.* 1739 d 1812 m Mary Gyger PS PA
Henry: b 11-11-1764 d 11-10-1811 m Frances Webb Pvt VA
Jabez: b 3-14-1760 d 6-18-1846 m Joanna Hutchinson Pvt NH ★
James: b — d *p.* 3-14-1790 m Mary Holmes PS NC
John: b 1745 d 5-31-1799 m Esther Dennison Sgt CT
John: b 1741 d 4-3-1799 m Elizabeth Evans PS DE
John: b 1739 d 1794 m Margaret Wood Lt MD
John: b 1752 d *p.* 1795 m Dinah Haynes Pvt MD
John, Jr.: b 1744 d 7-11-1810 m Lois Beals Pvt MA
John: b 1754 d 2-6-1844 m Lydia Door Pvt NH ★
John: b 11-14-1758/9 d 6-20-1834 m Sarah Whatley Pvt QM PS
   NJ ★
John.: b *c.* 1729 d *p.* 1800 m (1)Rosanna Martin (2)Leah — Pvt
   NC
John: b 1732 d 1791 m Alice Hinton Capt NC
John, Jr.: b 1750 d *p.* 10- -1794 m Mary Pierce Capt NC
John, Sr.: b 1720 d 7-1-1784 m (1)Priscilla McGirth (2)Sarah
   Moore PS SC
John, Sr.: b 4-12-1732 d 1-29-1791 m Jean Dobein Maj PS SC
John, Jr.: b 5-26-1757 d 10-12-1825 m (1)Mary Ervin (2)Elizabeth
   Wilson Capt SC
John: b *c.* 1755 d *p.* 9-8-1801 m Elizabeth Wright Lt VA
John: b 1751 d *p.* 4-6-1823 m Clara Nalle Pvt VA
John: b — d *p.* 11-6-1777 m Dinah Allen PS VA
John: b 1760 d 1833 m Jane Woodward Pvt PA
Joseph: b 1-31-1753 d 2-3-1795 m Elizabeth Green Lt RI W★
Joseph: b 1743 d 1804 m Mary — Capt VA

Richard: b *c.* 1744 d *p.* 11-29-1800 m Mary Jefferson Turpin PS VA
Robert: b *c.* 1752 d *a.* 1833 m — LCol VA
Robert Briton: b 1762 d *c.* 1803 m Ann Pinkerton Drm Pvt NJ ★
Samuel: b 1745 d *p.* 1807 m Rachel Haas Pvt PA
Samuel: b *c.* 1730 d 1804 m Anna Keshlen Sol PA
Sherwood: b 1726 d *a.* 10-14-1783 m Martha — PS SC
Sherwood: b *c.* 1764 d *c.* 1818 m Nancy — Pvt VA
Stephen: b 1748 d 1782 m Polly Pickett Cpl VA
Thomas: b 1756 d 9-12-1842 m (1)Elizabeth McFall (2)Mary Egan
   Pvt MD ★
Thomas: b 11-5-1761 d 11-12-1822 m Sarah Riehl Pvt NJ
Thomas: b *c.* 1750 d *p.* 1793 m Elizabeth Hinton (Rand) Capt NC
Thomas: b *c.* 1757 d *p.* 2-2-1821 m Elizabeth Robinson 2Lt VA
Thomas: b 1740 d 12-7-1780 m Mrs Martha Burton Pvt VA
Thomas: b 1746 d *c.* 1815 m Nancy — Pvt VA
Thomas: b 2-20-1755 d 6- -1779 m Mary Jones Pvt VA
Wm.: b 1-22-1764 d 5-15-1855 m Elizabeth Gallagher Pvt NJ
Wm.: b 8-15-1761 d 2-24-1850 m (1)Rachel Thomas (2)Mrs Anna
   Shipton FifMaj PA ★
Wm.: b 1747 d 1796 m Betsey Hicks Cpl VA
Wm.: b 4-14-1759 d 1836/7 m Elizabeth Wells Sol VA
Wm. Dobein: b 12-20-1764 d 6-4-1830 m Sarah Ford Sol SC

JAMESON, (includes JAMISON & JEMSON)
Alexander: b 12-25-1760 d 11-17-1819 m (1)Janet Brown (2)Mrs
   Parks Sgt NH
Alexander: b 1743 d 9-1-1807 m Jenny Moore Pvt NH
Daniel: b 2-25-1762 d 7-9-1814 m Hannah Burnham Pvt NH
Daniel, Sr.: b *c.* 1720 d 3- -1802 m Mary Magdalene Baxter PS PA
David: b 1715 d 1799 m Elizabeth Davis Col PA
David: b 8-19-1752 d 10-2-1839 m Mary Mennis Lt VA ★
David: b 3-10-1757 d 6-23-1833 m Hannah Richards Pvt VA
David: b 10-15-1757 d 1812 m Sally Gray Capt VA
George: b 1732 d *p.* 10-11-1799 m Ellinor — Pvt VA
Hugh, Sr.: b 1710 d *c.* 1790 m (1)Christine Whitehead (2)Jane
   (McHenry) Barr PS CS NH
Jacob: b 10-5-1735 d *p.* 1781 m Rebekah Pangburn Pvt NJ
James: b 7-3-1751 d 7-3-1821 m Elizabeth Ewing Pvt PA
James: b 1736 d 7-27-1812 m Mary Smith PS Pvt VT
James: b *c.* 1741 d *p.* 1810 m Lucy Hackley Lt VA
John: b 6-17-1749 d 7-8-1782 m Abigail Alden 1Lt CT
John: b 1758 d *p.* 1807 m Rhoda — Pvt MA
John: b 3-8-1750 d 2-14-1806 m (1)Sally Mills (2)Mrs Elizabeth
   (Fulton) Ely Pvt NH
John: b 12-3-1755 d 3-23-1836 m Nancy McDuffy Capt PA
John: b 1743 d 1-28-1811 m (1)—Barkley (2)Sarah McFadden
   Gilmore Pvt PA
John: b 1748 d *p.* 1792 m — Caldwell Pvt PA
John: b 1736 d 3-27-1796 m Martha Grier PS PA
John: b 5-5-1742 d 7-7-1790 m Barbara Allen Stewart Sol VA
John: b 1752 d 8- -1837 m Nancy Harter Sol VA ★
John: b 10-22-1763 d 2-3-1841 m Mary Rice Pvt VA ★
John Harvey: b 1738 d 1817 m Lucy Townsend Pvt VA
Joseph: b 1750 d 6-13-1829 m Mary Bean Pvt PA
Paul: b 10-17-1720 d 1795 m Elizabeth Pebbles Pvt MA
Robert: b 11-20-1753 d 1828 m (1)Martha Porterfield (2)Deborah
   Simmons 2Lt MA
Robert: b — d 3-7-1825 m Sarah McKinney Pvt MA
Robert: b 1739 d 9- -1811 m Hannah Baird Ens PA
Robert: b 1755 d 8-24-1825 m Mrs Elizabeth Gaff PS PA
Robert: b 1756-62 d *c.* 1844/5 m Isabelle Mahan Pvt VA ★
Thomas: b 1760 d 6-12-1839 m Mary Steele Pvt NH
Thomas: b *c.* 1738 d *p.* 9-6-1823 m (2)Rachel McCollock Sgt VA
Thomas: b 11-7-1732 d 4-6-1830 m (1)Jane Dickey (2)Hannah
   Taggart Pvt PS VA
Thomas: b 5-3-1743 d 8-14-1827 m Judith Ball Hackley PS Sgt VA
Wm.: b 1746 d 12-2-1804 m Susanna Lockhart Pvt VA
Wm.: b 1-15-1745 d 5-10-1785 m Anne Read PS Capt VA
Wm.: b *c.* 1745 d *p.* 1-30-1797 m Rachel McCreery PS VA

JANES,
Ebenezer: b 7-31-1736 d 1-22-1808 m (1)Sarah Field (2)Mehitable
   Alexander Lt PS MA
Elijah: b 4-17-1744 d 1826 m Anna Hawkins MM MA
Eliphalet: b 2-23-1743 d 1836 m Elfleda Lyons Pvt MA
Elisha: b 3-7-1734 d 2-20-1808 m Sarah Phelps Pvt MA
Israel: b 1-26-1734 d 5-2-1793 m Abigail Fay Pvt MM MA
Israel Champion: b 8-26-1760 d 8-15-1847 m Mary Ann Marsh Pvt
   MA
Jonathan: b 4-1-1726 d 1825 m (1)Esther — (2)Hannah Parsons Pvt
   MA
Jonathan: b 1756 d 6-29-1823 m Martha Plympton Pvt MA
Noah: b 11-19-1753 d 3-23-1808 m Naomi Strong Cpl MA
Obadiah: b 7-9-1760 d 9-2-1832 m (1)Polly Oliver (2)Harmony
   Bingham Pvt MA
Peleg Cheney: b 12-2-1760 d 6-25-1834 m Patty Coy Pvt MA
Samuel: b 9-13-1724 d 1788 m Hannah Brown Sgt MA
Solomon: b 20-1748 d 4-4-1812 m Beulah Fisk Sgt MA

JANEWAY,
George: b 10-9-1741 d 9-2-1826 m Effie (Ten Eyck)Poppellsdorph
   Capt PS NY

JANIS,
Jean Baptiste: b 9-18-1759 d 10-22-1836 m Reine Julia Barbau Ens VA ★

JANSEN,
Abraham: b 4-18-1749 d 12-   -1826 m Catalyntje Sammons PS NY
Cornelius T.: b 2-14-1748 d 8-22-1796 m Christina Moores Capt NY
Henry: b 4-26-1731 d 8-18-1794 m Helena Sleght PS NY
Jacobus: bpt 9-10-1740 d p. 1798 m Lydia Mynderse Pvt NY
Johannes: b 11-15-1696 d a. 9-8-1792 m Anna Schepmoes PS NY
Mathew: b 3-22-1738 d 3-14-1796 m Rachel Hardenbergh Capt NY
Nicholas: b 5-20-1750 d 12-29-1825 m (2)Margaret Ten Broeck Pvt NY
Thomas: b 3-22-1735 d 12-2-1802 m Elsie Osterhoudt LCol NY
Thomas H.: b 3-14-1754 d 10-14-1813 m Janeke DuBois Pvt NY

JANUARY, (includes JANVIER)
Ephraim: b 10-   -1759 d 8-5-1823 m Sarah McConnell Pvt PA
Peter: b c. 1725 d 1789 m Deborah McMahon Ens PA
Philip: b 8-25-1751 d 4-22-1822 m (2)Rebecca Golden Lt DE

JANUS,
George: b 1735 d 1-27-1796 m Margaret (Muller)Foering Dr PA

JAQUA, (includes JACQUA & JACQUAY)
Gamaliel: b 1-29-1764 d 4-20-1835 m Eleanor Campbell Pvt CT ★
Jonathan: b 7-2-1739 d 9-20-1824 m Lucretia Wells Pvt CT
Simon: b 6-11-1754 d 6-25-1825 m Ruth Hanchett Sol VT

JAQUES, (includes JAQUAYS, JAQUESS, JAQUEWAYS, JAQUISH)
George Augustus: b c. 1730 d p. 1790 m (1)Estelle Bowen (2)Margaret — Pvt NY
John: b 5-29-1758 d 6-10-1810 m Hannah Eames Pvt MA
Jonathan: b 4-5-1744 d 4-4-1804 m Mary Lee Pvt NJ
Jonathan, Jr.: b 4-28-1753 d 6-29-1843 m (1)Sally Jaquess (2)Esther E. Koy (3)Rebecca Rankin Pvt NJ
Moses: b 2-1-1742 d 1-17-1816 m (1)Zipporah DeCamp (2)Elizabeth Winans Col NJ
Nathan, Jr.: b 1757 d 6-14-1829 m Sally Northup Pvt RI ★
Parker: b 3-11-1754 d 5-13-1848 m Mary Newman Cpl MA
Samuel: b 7-19-1764 d 3-30-1828 m Rachel Langstaff Pvt NJ
Samuel: b 11-20-1728 d 6-4-1824 m Mary Noyes Pvt MA

JAQUETTE, (includes JACQUET)
Joseph: b c. 1726 d 8-27-1776 m Susanna Jacquett Lt PA
Peter: b 10-12-1760 d 11-4-1816 m Katherine Longhead Capt DE

JAQUINS,
John: b 4-14-1763 d — m (1)Tamsin — (2)Lavina Stevens Pvt MA CT ★

JAQUISH,
John: b 6-17-1755 d 8-3-1845 m Catherine Wheaton Sgt NY ★

JAQUITH,
Abraham: b 6-15-1760 d 11-26-1808 m (1)Elizabeth Stevens (2)Hannah Meader (3)Hannah Curtis Pvt MA
Adford: b 4-15-1710 d 7-16-1791 m (1)Margaret Jaquith (2)Olive Davis Pvt MA
Benjamin: b 6-27-1716 d 2-20-1801 m Hannah Walker PS MA
Benjamin: b 2-28-1737 d 2-11-1810 m Phebe Heacock Marshall Pvt NH
Ebenezer, Sr.: b 12-24-1732 d 12-29-1802 m Esther French Pvt MA
Ebenezer, Jr.: b 11-20-1758 d 6-18-1844 m Sarah Harthorn Pvt MA ★
Ebenezer: b 1742 d 12-12-1811 m Ruth Wright Pvt NH
Jonathan: b 9-13-1749 d a. 1778 m Lydia Johnson Pvt MA
Joseph: b 7-7-1745 d 3-20-1827 m Elizabeth Needham Sol MA
Nathan: b 5-7-1756 d p. 1787 m Anna Crosby Pvt MA
Samuel: b 12-13-1742 d 4-20-1825 m Martha Richardson Pvt MA

JARALOMAN, (includes JARALAMAN)
Henry: b 8-31-1733 d 1807 m Mary VanderPoel Capt NJ
John: b c. 1740 d 1811 m Liedga — Ens NJ ʼ

JARBOE,
Henry: b 1-   -1710 d 4-   -1795 m Elizabeth Stiles PS MD

JARMAN,
John: b 1746 d 11-10-1813 m Ann Hopkins Pvt SC
Wm.: b c. 1748 d 1813 m Sarah Maupin Ens VA

JARRARD, (includes GARRARD)
Joseph: b 1745-55 d 1-   -1803 m — 3Sgt NY
Wm.: b 6-3-1758 d 9-22-1827 m Ane Elizabeth Rolston Capt VA

JARRATT, (includes GARRED, JARED, JARRET, JARRETT)
Abraham: b c. 1735 d a. 3-   -1776 m Martha Bussey Capt MM MD
Archelaus: b 1-5-1725 d 1794 m Elizabeth Mims PS VA
David: b c. 1740 d a. 10-8-1811 m — PS VA

Devereux: b 1730 d 1790 m Elizabeth Williamson PS GA
Devereaux: b c. 1754 d 1818 m (1)Joannah Wade (2)Molly Duiguid (3)Christian Humber PS VA
Henry: b 1725 d 11-   -1801 m Elizabeth Magget Sol PS VA
Isaac: b 1738 d 6-   -1790 m Catherine Wetzell Pvt PA
Jesse: b a.1761 d 8-27-1839 m (1)Alice Anna Bond (2)Elizabeth Bosley Ens MD
John: b 3-   -1715 d p. 1790 m Alice Conrad Pvt PS PA
John: b 6-23-1737 d p. 1803 m (1)Hannah Whitacre (2)Rachel — Grd VA
Jonathan: b 1-31-1735 d 9-8-1824 m Hannah Mather Pvt PA
Joseph: b 1-2-1760 d 1-7-1848 m (1)Martha Agnes Beard (2)Bessie Baker Pvt VA ★
Robert: b c. 1744 d 1785 m Dorothy Lane Lt GA
Wm.: b 1758 d 1821 m Elizabeth Morris Cpl PA

JARVIS,
Austin: b 1737 d 1806 m Jemima Whitehead PS NY
Field: b 4-25-1756 d p. 1-21-1833 m Asenith Adams Pvt VA ★
John: b c. 1735-40 d a. 6-17-1799 m Sarah — CS VA
Joseph: b 5-14-1752 d 10-17-1806 m Abigail Church Pvt SgnMte MA
Joseph: b 1-26-1732 d 1789 m Elizabeth Rogers Pvt NY
Nathaniel: b 9-9-1743 d 5-12-1778 m Phoebe Allen Cpl MM NY
Philip: b 11-13-1762 d 12-3-1831 m Anne Head PS MA
Solomon: b 1753 d 1830-40 m Margaret Haythorne Sgt MD

JASPER,
Nicholas: b 6-7-1752 d 1827 m Elizabeth Wyatt Lt SC

JAUNCEY,
Joseph: b — d 2-11-1779 m Susannah Nicoll NCapt SC

JAY,
James: b 1-1-1744 d 1835 m Mary Voss Pvt NC
John: b 4-5-1750 d 1810 m Eunice Johnson Pvt NY
Joseph: b 1755 d 11-30-1835 m Eleanor Nelson 2Lt NJ ★
Wm.: b 1745 d 1812 m (1)Elizabeth Jay (2)Margaret — PS SC

JAYNE,
David: b 5-14-1751 d 3-9-1837 m Elizabeth DeWitt Pvt Chp PA
Ebenezer: b 2-19-1754 d 5-27-1826 m (1)Elizabeth Riggs (2)Mary DeWitt Pvt NJ
Isaac: b 11-26-1746 d 1-12-1809 m Anna Lauterman Pvt PA
John: b 12-25-1748 d 4-25-1838 m Cornelia Decker Pvt PA
Nathaniel: b 12-8-1719 d 1-5-1818 m Elizabeth Owen PS NY
Timothy: b 4-15-1741 d 3-20-1790 m Sarah Allen Capt NY PA
Wm.: b 1759 d 11-   -1836 m Nancy Bell Kenner PS NY
Wm.: b 4-12-1712 d 1-2-1798 m Tabitha Norton PS PA

JEFFERIS,
Emmor, Sr.: b c. 1732 d 9-10-1802 m Elizabeth Taylor Pvt PA
Emmor, Jr.: b 3-2-1760 d 8-8-1813 m Charity Grubb Pvt PA

JEFFERSON, (includes JEPHERSON)
Aaron: b 7-2-1754 d 3-31-1825 m Deborah Sherman Pvt MA
Jedediah: b 9-19-1758 d 7-23-1845 m (1)Susannah Emerson (2)Jerusha (Cox) Blackman Pvt Mar MA ★
John: b 1759 d 11-23-1844 m Mary Morse Pvt MA
Joseph: b 6-5-1751 d 1813 m Ruth Emerson Cpl MA
Peter Field: b 3-14-1735 d 1794/5 m Elizabeth Allen CS PS VA
Thomas: b 4-13-1743 d 7-4-1826 m Martha Wayles Skelton SDI PS VA
Wm.: b 1717 d 3-29-1802 m Sarah Thayer 2Lt MA

JEFFERY, (includes JEFFERIES, JEFFERS, JEFFRESS, JEFFREY, JEFFRIES & JEFFRY)
Aaron: b c. 1750 d p. 1796 m Sarah Sylvester NCapt VA
Alexander: b 1762 d p. 1841 m — Haltzclaw Pvt VA
Allen: b 1-3-1758 d 11-9-1820 m Cornelia Berkley Pvt SC
Benjamin: b 1749 d 1833 m Annie Swan Pvt PA
Charles 2d: b 1759 d 8-12-1842 m Abigail Jeffery DrmMaj CT
Edward: b 11-14-1738 d 11-16-1826 m Hannah Parker Ens PS CT
Francis: b c. 1762 d 7-21-1830 m Elizabeth Martin Pvt NJ
Henry: b c. 1757 d 1-   -1822 m Mary Chamberlain Sol PA
Humphrey: b 9-   -1756 d 12-   -1835 m Ann Martha Chadwick Pvt NJ CL
James: b 7-23-1728 d — m Mary Colleten Pvt SC
James: b c. 1732 d 1805 m Susanna — Pvt VA
John: b c. 1753 d p. 1794 m Sybil Foster Pvt NH CL
John: b 9-14-1757 d — m Hannah — Pvt NJ ★
John: b 5-1-1754 d p. 3-30-1819 m Mary Ann — Pvt NY ★
John: b 4-14-1757 d 11-2-1832 m Anna Wilson Capt PA
John: b 3-6-1760 d 1-29-1851 m Rachel Barnett Pvt SC ★
John: b 1761 d 10-29-1829 m Mary Jordan Pvt VA
John, Sr.: b 9-5-1707 d 2-8-1792 m Ann Swepson PS VA
Joseph: b 8-20-1760 d 6-28-1845 m Eunice Giddings Pvt MA ★
Joseph: b 1736 d 11-26-1814 m Jane Harper Cpl PA
Joseph: b 1733 d p. 10-24-1783 m Margaret Smith Sol VA
Matthew: b 1-4-1747 d 6-3-1791 m (1)Mary Alexander (2)Isabella — Sol VA
Nathaniel: b 1762 d 1833 m Eunice Fowler Pvt CT
Nathaniel, Sr.: b 1-8-1733 d 9-29-1823 m (1)Prudence Jefferies (2)Mary Chalfant Pvt PA

Nathaniel: b 1733-5 d 1-29-1812 m (2)Sarah Brown Steen Capt SC
Osborne: b *c.* 1715-17 d 12-9-1793 m Patience Spier CS NC
Richard: b 10-19-1726 d 10-4-1794 m Rebekah Wall PS NJ
Richard: b 2-24-1730 d 3-27-1817 m (1)Jane Logue (2)Ann Davis Pvt PA
Samuel: b 1755 d 10-31-1820 m Elizabeth Drew Capt RI
Thomas: b 1-12-1745 d 8-31-1820 m Lucy Parmer Pvt NY
Thomas: b 3-9-1756 d 12-31-1815 m Martha Ferguson Sgt VA
Thomas: b 6-10-1761 d 5-9-1822 m (1) —Motley (2)Mary Hamlett Sol VA
Wm.: b *a.* 1750 d 5-31-1802 m Mary Gray Pvt NC
Wm.: b 9-5-1761 d 5-27-1848 m (1)Ann Woodward (2)Martha Mendenhall Pvt PA
Wm.: b 1764 d 5-30-1850 m Nancy Connell Pvt VA ★

JEFFORDS,
Ann: b *c.* 1754 d *p.* 11-30-1796 m (1)John Jeffords Jr (2)Dr. Thomas Kennedy (3)Duncan Littlejohn PS SC
John: b 1740 d *p.* 3-27-1807 m (1)Hannah Williams (2)Anna — Lt CT
John, Sr.: b 1728 d *p.* 8-1-1779 m (1)Magdalen Miller (2)Hannah — Pvt NC
John, Jr.: b 1-11-1752 d *a.* 8-19-1779 m Ann Townsend Pvt SC
John: b 8-3-1766 d 5-3-1831 m Phebe Sherman Slr MA
Wm.: b 3-4-1765 d 8-8-1832 m (1)Sarah Rublee (2)Jemima — Pvt MA ★

JELKS,
Wm.: b *c.* 1730 d 1782 m Ann — Cpl PS SC

JELLEFF,
James: b 4-8-1760 d 10-24-1840 m Lydia Blackley Pvt CT ★

JELLISON,
Benjamin: b 1715-20 d 1787-93 m Agnes Patten Pvt MA

JENIFER,
Daniel: b 1727 d 1795 m Elizabeth Hanson Dr. MD

JENKINS, (includes JENKINSON)
Aaron: b 1-7-1743 d 11-11-1807 m (1)Rebecca Baldwin (2)Mrs. Charity Garwood Pvt PA
Abiah: b 2-5-1755 d 3-17-1822 m Hannah Luther Pvt MA
Abraham: b *c.* 1729 d 3-29-1814 m Martha Sherman Pvt MA
Benjamin: b 6-30-1707 d 6-1-1787 m Mehitable Blush PS MA
Benjamin, Jr.: b *c.* 1758 d 1826 m Hannah Tripp Ens SC
Benjamin: b *c.* 1735 d *a.* 6-29-1782 m Mary Grimball PS CS SC
Bethia Harris: b 9-14-1752 d 8-12-1842 m John Jenkins PS RI
Calvin: b 1761 d 5-22-1846 m Eunice Jackson Mus Pvt CT ★
Calvin: b 6-22-1758 d 12-1-1845 m Elizabeth Litchfield Pvt MA ★
David: b 7-2-1731 d 6-27-1797 m Martha Armor Col PS PA
Dempsey: b 11-25-1760 d *p.* 1824 m Mary Perry Sol NC
Ebenezer: b 7-6-1736 d *p.* 1790 m Elizabeth Clark Capt PS MA
Eleazer: b 1752 d 4-6-1824 m Rebecca — Pvt PS PA
Enoch: b 8-16-1763 d 1-5-1846 m Hannah Day Pvt NY MA
Gera: b 5-16-1742 d 8-17-1818 m Lillie Coleman Pvt MA
Gideon: b 1753 d 1830 m Mercy Lincoln MM MA
Isaiah: b 1750 d 1-11-1828 m Huldah Gurney Sgt MA
James: b 12-9-1735 d 4-10-1807 m Mercy Price Pvt MA
James: b 9-16-1749 d 12-28-1831 m Ruth Lincoln Sgt MA
James: b 9-26-1758 d 10-29-1801 m Hannah VanGelder Pvt NJ ★
James: b 11-29-1764 d 1-24-1847 m Elizabeth Ann Gwynn Pvt SC ★
Joel: b 9-11-1757 d 6-23-1827 m Elizabeth Garrison Lt MA
John: b 1736 d 10-24-1810 m Ann Hill Ens MA
John: b *c.* 1740 d *p.* 1788 m Rebecca — Wgn NJ
John II: b 1742 d 7-13-1805 m Elizabeth Walker Lukens 2Lt PA
John, Sr.: b 2-6-1727 d 11- -1784 m Lydia Gardener CS PS PA
John, Jr.: b 11-27-1751 d 3-19-1827 m Bethia Harris Lt CT ★
John: b 5-15-1750 d 1813 m Mary Frippe Capt SC
John: b *c.* 1750 d *p.* 1793 m Sarah Smythe Pvt VA
John: b 1-17-1760 d 1-20-1847 m Mary Rutherford Pvt VA ★
John Jacob: b *c.* 1757/58 d *c.* 1837/38 m Mary Winton Pvt NC
Joseph: b 3-17-1725 d 1-8-1808 m Sarah Barron Pvt MA
Joseph: b 1756-58 d 1828 m Elizabeth Evans Lt SC
Joseph: b 3-22-1755 d 2-12-1832 m (1)Rachel Lewis (2)Ann Jenkins (3)Margaret — Sol SC
Joshua: b 7-25-1744 d *p.* 1781 m (2)Ruth Sparrel Pvt MA
Josiah: b 9-20-1750 d 10-21-1831 m Prudence Davis Capt MA ★
Lemuel: b 7-3-1757 d 3-16-1844 m Hannah Luce Pvt Fif MA ★
Lewis, Jr.: b 1760 d *p.* 1840 m Annie Jones Pvt NC ★
Lot: b 3-13-1737 d 7-21-1776 m Mercy Howland Pvt Drm MA
Micah: b 1754 d 1830 m (1)Mary Fickling (2)Margaret Meggett PS SC
Nathaniel, Jr.: b 5-4-1721 d 3-19-1776 m Abigail Baldwin CS MA
Obadiah: bpt 6-18-1718 d *p.* 8- -1777 m Lydia — Pvt MA
Philip: b *c.* 1755 d *p.* 1822 m Elizabeth Hungerford Pvt MD
Reuben: b *c.* 1757 d *p.* 1827 m Betty Oakley Lt SC
Samuel, Jr.: b 9-20-1743 d 1777 m Anna Upton Lt MA
Samuel: b 1754 d 1-3-1798 m Elizabeth Goodwin Pvt MA
Samuel: b 10-20-1727 d *p.* 1783 m Mary Chipman PS MA
Samuel, Jr.: b 7-17-1759 d 7-22-1825 m Margaret Crawford Sol Cmsry SC
Seth: b 11-10-1735 d 8-1-1793 m Dinah Folger CS MA

Southworth: b 12-10-1742 d 12-11-1820 m Huldah Wright Cpl MA
Sterling: b *c.* 1750 d *p.*! 10-2-1819 m (1)Mary — (3)Mrs Catherine (Anderson) Nowland Pvt GA
Thomas: b 1-18-1751 d 11-14-1821 m Mrs Mary (Neale) Corry Smn PS MD
Thomas: b 1761 d *p.* 1-21-1836 m Mildred Atcherson Pvt MD ★
Thomas: b 6-6-1727 d 3-24-1792 m Jemima Smith PS MM MA
Thomas: b *c.* 1760/1 d *p.* 12-5-1817 m Delilah Gadd Pvt PA
Thomas: b 1758 d 1815 m (1)Elizabeth Major (2)Mary Washington SrgnMte MM VA
Thomas: b *c.* 1745 d *p.* 9-5-1791 m Tabitha — PS VA
Thomas Shepard: b 9-28-1735 d *p.* 1799 m Grace Keene Pvt ME
Wm.: b *c.* 1746 d 1806 m Demarius Roberts Pvt GA
Wm.: b — d *p.* 1781 m Susan Guttridge Sgt VA
Wm.: b 3-1-1762 d 5-21-1833 m Susannah Walker Pvt VA

JENKS, (includes JENCKES & JENCKS)
Amos: b 1-6-1746 d 6-6-1825 m Amey Savage Lt RI
Boomer: b 2-19-1761 d 6-8-1847 m Anna King Pvt RI ★
Caleb: b 1-27-1750 d 8-23-1803 m Abigail Brown CS RI
David: b 6-21-1739 d 7-26-1828 m Martha Whipple Capt RI
Dickinson: b 3-10-1754 d 2-20-1836 m Susannah Mattison Pvt NY ★
Edmund: b 1732 d 11-29-1816 m Keziah Olney Pvt MA
Eleazer: b 3-3-1747 d 8-28-1822 m Silence Shaw LCol RI
Esek: b — d *p.* 1783 m Sarah Bucklin Lt RI
George: b 11-26-1757 d 5-25-1825 m Ruth Miller Fif RI ★
Ichabod: b 1-2-1732 d 5-6-1803 m Margaret Bagley Lt RI
Jacob: b 4-16-1761 d 5-20-1842 m Martha Morey Pvt RI ★
James: b — d *p.* 1811 m Phebe Tripp Pvt VT
Jeremiah: b 11-29-1739 d 1-4-1811 m Lucy Whipple Lt NH
Jeremiah: b *c.* 1755 d 9-7-1809 m (1)Anne Tillinghast (2)Priscilla Bacon (3)Nancy Whipple Ens RI
Jesse: b 1-22-1734/5 d 3-19-1827 m (1)Mary Smith (2)Abigail Sayles PS RI
John: b 6-14-1743 d 1775 m Sarah Seymour Pvt MA
John: b 1736 d 1818 m Anna Bishop PS RI
John: b 11-4-1730 d 1-2-1791 m (2)Freelove Crawford PS RI
John: b 2-4-1743 d — m Elizabeth Davis PS RI
John Seymour: b 6- -1768-70 d 10-19-1843 m Penelope Webb Drm CT CL ★
Jonathan: b 1718 d 1-31-1787 m Harriet Pullen Slr RI
Jonathan: b 8-30-1746 d 1-31-1787 m Cynthia Brown CS RI
Joseph: b 1714 d 5-25-1784 m (1)Sarah King (2)Mrs Sarah (Moon) King Capt RI
Lory: b 3- -1756 d 5-1-1839 m (1)Sarah Wilcox (2)Mary Griffith Lt RI
Nicholas: b 1750 d 7- -1819 m Betsey Bryant Sgt RI Heirs ★
Samuel: b 7-17-1745 d 3-20-1813 m Abigail Griffiths Pvt RI W★
Stephen: b 5-3-1726 d 11-16-1800 m Sarah Hawkins PS RI
Stephen: b 3-12-1759 d 8-9-1819 m Anne Sayles Pvt RI
Thomas: b 12- -1699 d 5-4-1797 m Mercy Wildman PS PA
Zachariah: b 12-20-1753 d 2-12-1827 m (1)Ruth Jackson (2)Sarah Tyler Pvt VT

JENNER,
Stephen: b 3-14-1749 d *p.* 1800 m Mary Kirkham Pvt VT

JENNESS,
Francis: b 12-1-1715 d *p.* 1-20-1784 m Sarah Garland PS CS NH
John: b — d — m Temperance Follett Col NH
Richard Sr.: b 6-28-1718 d 1782 m (2)Abigail (Coffin) Sleeper PS NH
Richard, Jr.: b 1747 d 1819 m (1)Betsey Berry (2)Hannah Seavey Pvt NH
Simon: b 1751 d 4-4-1798 m Olive Shapleigh CS NH
Thomas: b 11-24-1748 d 7-18-1826 m Sarah Yeaton PS NH

JENNEY, (includes JENNE & JENNY)
Jethro: b 9-18-1724 d 6-24-1802 m Desire Mitchell Pvt MA
John, Jr.: b 3-16-1755 d 8-23-1814 m Hannah Perry Pvt MA
Nathaniel: b 10-3-1720 d 1-13-1802 m Mercy Mitchell Pvt MA
Prince: b 4-11-1759 d 7- -1837 m Lettice Hayden Pvt MA ★
Seth: b 3-27-1732 d 4-27-1806 m Hannah Rider Pvt MA
Timothy: b 1752 d *p.* 1795 m Lydia Seekins Pvt MA

JENNINGS,
Aaron, Jr.: b 11-11-1762 d 1-29-1839 m Eunice Taylor Pvt CT ★
Abner: b 10-1-1762 d 6-7-1858 m (1)Hannah Landers (2)Mrs Betsey Fordham Pvt MA ★
Abraham: b *c.* 1752 d *p.* 1832 m Cherry Resden Pvt CT
Augustine: b 1708 d 8-24-1778 m Hannah Williams Pvt VA
Baylor: b 1755 d 1805-7 m (1)Susanna Bradford (2)Sally Morehead Ens VA
Benjamin: b 1758 d 5-12-1845 m Rhoda Spencer Pvt PA ★
Beriah: b 1731 d 5-12-1776 m Eunice Stebbins Pvt MA
Burritt: b 12-21-1758 d 2-22-1848 m Ruth Crofoot Smn CT ★
David: b 2-24-1723/4 d 3-28-1797 m Sarah Turner Pvt CT
Elias: b — 1790 m Dorothy Purple PS NY
Eliphalet: b 8-26-1765 d 8-17-1853 m Mary Butterfield Drm Pvt MA
Ephraim, Sr.: b 5-27-1720 d 4-3-1802 m Sybil Rice Lt MA
Ephraim, Jr.: b 9-6-1749 d *a.* 1819 m Marium Smith Lt MA
Ezra: b 1-14-1747 d 4-22-1802 m Martha Bennett Sgt CT
Gershom: bpt 11-12-1738 d 1-9-1809 m (1)Rhoda Sanford (2)Mrs Abigail (Wakeman) Meeker CS CT
Gideon: b 2-17-1753 d 2-11-1814 m Ann — Capt SC

JENNINGS, contd.

Hannah: b c. 1719 d 12- -1809 m Augustine Jennings PS VA
Isaac: b 5-18-1743 d 6-6-1819 m Abigail Gould Sgt CT
Isaac: b c. 1759 d 2-1-1836 m Abigail Cousins Pvt MA
Isaiah: b 1737 d 1792 m Margaret Baird Pvt PA
Israel: b 3-10-1752 d 1-1-1841 m Elizabeth Mount Sol VA
Jacob: b 12-5-1739 d 4-11-1817 m Grace Park CS CT
Jacob, Sr.: b 1711 d 1787 m Anne — Pvt NJ
Jacob, Jr.: b 1744 d 2-17-1813 m (1)Mary Kennedy (2)Mrs Hannah Carnahan Dr Capt NJ
Jacob: b — d c. 1820 m Mrs Phoebe Bonnell Pvt NJ
James: b 2-14-1757 d 12-4-1837 m (2)Hannah Martin Pvt VA NC ★
James: b 1755 d 8-24-1834 m Polly — Pvt SC ★
James: b 12-23-1756 d 4-11-1826 m Nancy Dickerson Pvt VA
James R.: b 1749 d 4-3-1822 m Sarah Corwin PS NY
Jeremiah 2d: b 9-21-1740 d 10-3-1828 m Elizabeth Smith PS CT
Jesse: b 1759 d 1847 m (2)Jane Davis Sgt NY
Joel: b 7-13-1753 d p. 1787 m Grace Perry Pvt CT
Joel: b 5-24-1762 d 10-21-1813 m Zillah Walker Pvt MA
John: b 10-1-1759 d 1825-29 m Mercy Sikes Pvt MA
John, Sr.: b 1710 d 1794 m Lydia Batte CS NC
John, Jr.: b 1761 d 1806 m Elizabeth Lanier Cpl NC
John: bpt 8-25-1748 d 1-22-1807 m Elizabeth — PS SC
John: b 1735 d p. 1-20-1784 m Temperance Thompson PS VA
Jonathan: b c. 1725 d c. 8- -1780 m — PS VA
Jonathan S.: b 9-29-1752 d 10-19-1830 m Mary Hart Pvt NY ★
Joseph: b 9-21-1737 d 2-10-1781 m Hannah Hardy Cpl MA
Joseph: b 1739 d 12-24-1804 m Ann Billups Capt VA
Joshua Sr.: b 1727 d 2-1-1818 m Esther Burr Pvt CT
Justus: b 8-31-1755 d 4-19-1844 m Mary Jenny Pvt NJ ★
Lemuel: b 6-5-1748 d 6-12-1823 m Abia Bierce Sol CT
Lemuel: b 8-29-1763 d 8-10-1824 m Alice Dodge Pvt VA
Levi: b 11- -1735 d p. 1782 m (1)Bethia Tucker (2)Mary Hill Capt MA
Lyman: b 11-16-1753 d 9-4-1806 m Deborah Mitchel Pvt CT
Nehemiah: bpt 8-3-1729 d c. 1811 m (1)Patience Jackson (2)Elizabeth Seely Pvt CT
Oliver: b 7-15-1749 d 8-27-1776 m Joanne Clark Cpl CT
Peter: b 9-9-1764 d 5- -1841 m Sarah Wakeman Pvt Grd CT ★
Philip, Sr.: b c. 1720 d 1795 m Elizabeth Hasfort CS SC
Robert: b c. 1740-5 d 1828 m Catherine Sallee PS NC
Robert: b 1760 d p. 1831 m Elizabeth Arnold Sol VA
Robert: b — d p. 10-1-1794 m Rachel — PS VA
Robert G.: b c. 1740 d p. 2-21-1805 m Mary Ann Clement Capt CS VA
Royal: b 1762 d 2-1-1839 m Catherine Daniels Pvt VA ★
Samuel: b 11-16-1742 d a. 1800 m Keziah Bearse Pvt MA
Samuel: b 11-15-1762 d 3-23-1842 m Olive Tupper Pvt MA
Silvanus: b c. 1742 d p. 1776 m — Pvt NY
Thaddeus: b 8-31-1732 d 1811 m Lavinia Burritt Pvt CT
Wm.: b 1726 d 1793 m Agnes Dickerson PS VA
Wm.: b c. 1745 d 6-14-1796 m Elizabeth — Pvt PA
Wm.: b 1749 d 1789 m Betsy Jennings Pvt NC
Wm.: b — d 9-9-1815 m Mary Billups Ens Lt VA
Wm.: b c. 1745 d p. 1790 m Mary Smith Capt VA
Wm.: b 2-26-1761 d 7-17-1840 m Polly Kidd Pvt VA ★
Zachariah, Jr.: b 3-25-1745 d c. 1816 m Eunice Risdon Pvt CT
Zebulon, Jr.: b 11-12-1737 d 10-16-1776 m Joanna Little Pvt NY

JENNISON, (includes JENISON & JENNERSON)

Abijah: b 11-19-1747 d p. 1793 m Mary Robinson Pvt MA
Daniel: b 9-1-1757 d 2-4-1839 m Molly Putnam Pvt MA
Israel: b 1713 d 9-19-1782 m (1)Mary Heywood (2)Margaret (Oliver) Coolidge PS MA
John: b 6-15-1744 d 10-16-1804 m (1)Keziah Spring (2)Sybil Bishop Capt NH
Joseph Brooks: b 1-5-1756 d 3-5-1839 m Damaris Howe Pvt MA ★
Moses: b 11-17-1755 d 9-24-1842 m Sarah Longley Pvt MA
Peter: b 1-6-1750 d 1821 m Mehitable Singletary Pvt MA
Phineas: b 9-27-1743 d 2-11-1825 m Susan Newton Pvt MA
Robert: b 18-1758 d 2-3-1835 m Hannah Howe Pvt MA
Wm.: b 1-18-1760 d 2-14-1838 m Judith Kenney Pvt MA ★

JEPSON, (includes JIPSON)

David: b 9-5-1762 d 3-29-1849 m Priscilla Bates Pvt MA ★
John: b 2-18-1728 d 1797 m (1)Thankful Cox (2)Ann Gooding CS MA
John: b 4-11-1754 d 7-7-1830 m Elizabeth Leach Pvt MA ★
John: bpt 8-3-1760 d p. 3-16-1812 m Mary Morse Pvt MA
Micah: b 8-2-1716 d 1798 m (1)Elizabeth Southard (2)Mrs Mary Joy Pvt MA

JERNIGAN, (includes JARNAGIN & JERNEGAN)

Jesse: b 1725 d p. 1790 m — Bishop Sol NC
Lewis: b — d p. 9-11-1807 m — PS NC
Thomas: b 1746 d 1802 m Mary Witt Capt NC
Wm.: b 8-1-1728 d 7-26-1817 m Mary Osborn CS MA

JEROLD,

Reuben: b 1734 d 5-8-1800 m Johannah Spaulding Lt NH

JEROME,

Benjamin: b 1743 d 12-31-1824 m Desire Brown Pvt CT

John: b 6-10-1755 d 1-20-1839 m Mary StJohn Pvt MA
Samuel: b 1728 d 4-9-1796 m Lucy Foster SgtMaj MA
Thomas: b 1766 d 2-3-1837 m Ruth Hill Tms CT ★
Timothy: b 1757 d 1799 m Mary Isaacs Pvt MA
Timothy 3d: b 1713 d 1784 m Ann Norton Pvt CT
Wm. 2d: b — 1756 d 8-10-1821 m (1)Phoebe Barnes (2)Mrs Polly (Andrews) Byington Pvt CT
Zerubbabel: b c. 1714 d 1783 m (1)Mary Frisbie (2)Phebe Cook Pvt CT

JERROLDS,

Thomas: b 1750 d a. 1810-14 m Abigail Keeney Sgt CT

JERSEY,

John: b 12-28-1740 d 9-2-1821 m Annetje Blaubelt Pvt NY
Richard: b 1759 d 2-10-1831 m Isabel Palmer Pvt NY

JERVEY,

Thomas: b 1740 d 6-14-1796 m Grace Hall Capt SC

JESS,

Samuel: b c. 1756 d 1812-20 m Hannah Atkinson Pvt NJ CL

JESSE, (or JESSEE)

John: b c. 1750 d a. 11-17-1815 m Frankey Lea Mus NC

JESSEMAN,

George: b 10- -1731 d 1-4-1822 m Jemima Wood Pvt MA

JESSUP, (includes JESSOP, JESUP)

Blackleach: b 12-14-1735 d 3-22-1816 m (1)Sarah Stebbins (2)Mary Kellogg (3)Mrs Mary Sturges PS CT
Ebenezer: b 3-14-1739 d 12-8-1812 m (1)Eleanor Andrews (2)Abigail Squire (3)Anna Wyankoop Ens Dr CT
Jonathan: b 9-12-1734 d 4-22-1805 m Ann Lockwood Pvt CT
Silas: b c. 1732 d c. 1800 m Susannah — Lt PS NY
Thomas: b 1715 d 12-13-1783 m (1)Sarah Small (2)Hannah Bishop (3)Ann (Matthews) Floyd PS NC
Zebulon: b 9-15-1755 d 6-8-1822 m Zerviah Huntting Pvt NY

JESTER,

Daniel: b 3-9-1756 d 1-5-1840 m Elizabeth — Pvt DE ★
John M.: b a. 1765 d 1821 m (2)Mary Turlington Slr VA
Levi: b 1760 d 6-17-1841 m Rozannah Frazier Pvt GA

JETER,

Ambrose: b a. 1735 d 1803 m (1)Jane Stern (2)Mrs Mary Farley Ens VA
Dudley: b 9-20-1754 d p. 9-19-1838 m (1)Sarah Jones (2)Rebecca Wynn Pvt NC ★
Henry: b 1744 d 1821 m Elizabeth Bell 1Lt VA
James: b 1-15-1759 d 3-16-1840 m Mary Crosby Pvt SC
Littleton: b 1754 d 5- -1842 m Jane Alsop Pvt VA ★

JETT,

Francis: b a. 1761 d a. 5-12-1835 m — PS VA
Francis: b — d 10-22-1791 m Barsheba — PS VA
James: b c. 1740 d c. 1803 m Rosey Duncan Pvt VA
Wm. Storke: b 1761 d 4- -1844 m Jane Turner Lt VA CL

JETTON,

Lewis: b 1-24-1749 d 9-21-1826 m Priscilla Sharp Sol NC

JEWELL, (includes JEWEL)

Aaron: b 12-23-1742 d 10-15-1829 m Hannah Curtis Pvt MA
Archibald: b 4-8-1716 d 12-26-1777 m Rebecca Leonard PS MA
Asahel: b 8-2-1744 d 4-30-1790 m Hannah Wright PS NH
Benjamin: b 5-25-1759 d 6-5-1832 m Olive Lamb Pvt MA
Daniel: b 5-25-1744 d 3-29-1831 m Sarah Sanborn Capt NH
David: b c. 1716 d 5-20-1798 m Elizabeth Lowe PS NH
Elisha: b 2-27-1757 d 3-15-1842 m Rhoda Giberson Pvt NJ
Enos: b 1754 d 1831 m (1)Deborah Hall (2)Abigail Chamberlain Pvt MA
Ephraim: b 8-19-1760 d 7-13-1845 m Rebecca Brigham Pvt MA ★
Henry: b 3-5-1753 d 8-20-1827 m Sarah Greely Pvt NH
Hubbard: b c. 1750 d 10-4-1777 m Mary Little Pvt NJ
James: b 6-13-1753 d 9-24-1851 m Sarah — Pvt NH ★
John: b 1-17-1764 d 12-2-1838 m Elizabeth Lawrence Pvt NY
Joseph: b 1759 d 1812 m Anna Daniels Cpl NH
Joseph: b 5-13-1741 d 8-11-1822 m (1)Susan Graves (2)Miriam Currier PS NH
Joseph: b 6-18-1744 d 12-13-1822 m Mary Crane Lt NY
Nathaniel, Jr.: b 9-17-1762 d 7-16-1848 m Elizabeth Crane Pvt MA
Oliver: b 3-14-1738/39 d 4-8-1817 m (1)Phebe Tubbs (2)Amy Stevens (3)Sarah Sears Tms PS CT
Seth: bpt 10-12-1760 d p. 1821 m Mary Temple Pvt NJ ★

JEWETT, (includes JOUETT)

Aaron: bpt 5-27-1744 d 1-6-1824 m (1)Hannah Pearson (2)Elizabeth Bradstreet Pvt MA
Abel, Sr.: b 4-3-1760 d 5-8-1821 m Sarah Dwinnell Pvt NH
Alpheus: b 1-15-1756 d 10-5-1841 m Abigail Sears Cpl NY ★
Andrew: b 10-28-1750 d 2-11-1819 m (1)Mary Piper (2)Lydia Morrison PS NH

Benjamin: b 11-30-1739 d *p.* 9-6-1795 m (1)Hannah Bidlack (2)Abigail Bates Pvt CT
Benjamin: b — d *p.* 1777 m Mary Dearborn PS NH
Caleb: b 6-25-1710 d 1-18-1778 m (1)Rebecca Cook (2)Mrs Faith Brewster Capt PS CT
Caleb: b 1-16-1741 d 2-8-1820 m Hannah Curtis Pvt CT ★
Daniel: b 2-24-1743/44 d 3-30-1829 m Zilpha Hibbard Lt VT
David: b 1738 d *p.* 1800 m Elizabeth Hughes Capt CT
David: b 8-11-1714 d 3-17-1785 m (1)Patience Phillips (2)Mrs Mary Prince Chp CT
David: b 9-30-1742 d *p.* 1783 m (1)Sybil Gilson (2)Abigail Walker Pvt MA
David: b 5-31-1746 d 7-15-1799 m Elizabeth Goodwin Pvt MA
David: b 6-30-1758 d 10-24-1842 m Esther — Pvt Fif MA ★
David: b 1754 d 9-13-1836 m Mary Shepard Pvt NH ★
David Hibberd: b 8-21-1745 d 4-26-1814 m Patience Bulkeley Dr CT
Dummer: b 4-25-1732 d 10-26-1788 m Mary Staniford PS MA
Ebenezer: b 8-28-1747 d 12-7-1834 m Abigail Hammond Pvt CT
Elam: b 3-5-1746 d 5-29-1812 m Eunice Richardson Sgt MA
Eleazer: b 8-31-1731 d 12-17-1817 m Sarah Farnham PS CT
Enoch: b 7-25-1759 d 1-21-1849 m (1)Lydia Pike (2)Mrs Sarah Willoughby Pvt MA ★
Epes: b 6-7-1761 d 12-14-1834 m Betsy Hidden Pvt MA ★
Ezekiel: b 5-28-1736 d 7-25-1818 m (1)Lucy Townsend (2)Anna Williams Pvt NH
Ezekiel, Sr.: b 2-22-1727 d 2-7-1786 m Hannah Platts PS NH
Gibbons: b 11-1-1738 d 8-10-1789 m (1)Hannah Ayres (2)Rhoda Hyde Dr CT
Ichabod: b 2-5-1738 d 5-1-1796 m (1)Mary Carpenter (2)Elizabeth Miner Pvt CT
Jacob, Jr.: b 1744 d 11-2-1813 m Elizabeth Cummings Sgt PS NH
Jacob: b 5-1-1743 d 12-12-1787 m Deborah Light Pvt NH
Jacob: b 10-30-1760 d 3-29-1830 m Ruth — Pvt NH
James: bpt 6-29-1718 d 5-3-1790 m Martha Scott Pvt MA
James: b 9-14-1739 d 12-5-1811 m Alice Cothrin Pvt MA
Jedediah: b 1752 d 1832 m Mary Atkinson Pvt VT
Jedediah, Sr.: b 9-5-1719 d 5-12-1804 m (1)Elizabeth Shattuck (2)Mrs Hannah Baldwin CS MA
Jedediah, Jr.: b 4-22-1754 d 4-2-1840 m Sally Hall Pvt MA
Jedidiah: b 1-3-1749 d 1-22-1823 m Naamah Bridges Pvt Cmsry NH
Jeremiah: b 12-24-1757 d 4-22-1836 m Temperance Dodge Pvt MA
Jeremiah: b 1-10-1745 d 4-22-1808 m Sarah Jackman PS MA
John: b *c.* 1730 d *p.* 1784 m Hannah Jewett Sol NH
John, Sr.: b 1730 d 1802 m Mourning Harris PS VA
John, Jr.: b 12-7-1754 d 3-1-1822 m Sally Robards Capt VA
John Cole: bpt 1-29-1739 d 1-6-1811 m Elizabeth Smith Pvt MA
Jonathan: b 1761 d *p.* 2-15-1785 m Mehitable Kilbourne Pvt MA
Jonathan: b 3-12-1739 d 4-28-1786 m Martha Belsher Pvt NH
Jonathan: b 7-25-1760 d 2-26-1834 m Sarah Stearns Sgt NH ★
Joseph: b 12-13-1732 d 8-31-1776 m Lucretia Rogers Capt CT
Joseph: b 8-15-1742 d 12-16-1820 m Rachel Nichols Lt CT
Joseph: b 6-15-1740 d 8-25-1814 m (1)Rebecca Abbott (2)Hannah (Richmond) Spaulding Pvt MA
Joseph: b 6-29-1743 d 5-4-1792 m Phebe Richardson Pvt NH
Joseph M.: b 2-7-1764 d *p.* 1833 m Phebe Drake Pvt CT ★
Matthew: b *c.* 1735 d *p.* 9-9-1779 m Sarah — PS NC
Maximilliam: b 1-27-1742 d 10-16-1823 m Rebecca Burpee Pvt MA
Moses: b 4- -1722 d 7-31-1796 m Abigail Bradstreet Capt MA
Moses: b 1-29-1737 d *c.* 1827 m (1)Mary Meade (2)Mary Sawyer (3)Mrs Mary (Fry) Varney Pvt NH
Nathan Hibbard: b 1760 d *p.* 1840 m Mary Griffin Pvt CT
Nathaniel: b 10-20-1710 d 10-5-1791 m Susannah Gooden Pvt NH
Nathaniel: b 4-27-1760 d 5-27-1828 m Ruth Powers Pvt NH
Noah: b 2-11-1758 d 1839 m Lydia Boynton Pvt NH ★
Oliver: b 2-24-1747 d 8-22-1829 m (1)Betsey Houghton (2)Keziah Snow (3)Mrs Sarah (Snow) Bride Sgt MA
Purchase, Jr.: b 11-19-1739 d 10-11-1814 m Sarah Gould Pvt MA
Richard Dummer: b 9-24-1756 d 1-15-1825 m Lucy Kinsman QM MA
Samuel: b 1746 d 1815 m Abigail Folsom Cpl MA
Samuel: b 1-1-1756 d 12-17-1839 m Apphia Smith Pvt NH
Sarah: b *c.* 1737 d *p.* 9-9-1779 m Matthew Jouett PS NC
Stephen: b 10-15-1735 d 5-29-1823 m Mehitable Harris Sgt CT
Stephen: b 11-28-1743 d 1822 m Elizabeth Little Sgt MA
Stephen, Sr.: b 12-28-1727 d 5-23-1803 m Hannah (Farwell) Cummings Sol PS NH
Stephen, Jr.: b 10-14-1753 d 2-22-1829 m Elizabeth Pool Sol NH
Thomas: b 4- -1758 d *a.* 1-18-1839 m Prudence Reede Pvt CT ★
Thomas: b 7-19-1736 d 5-29-1812 m Eunice Slafter 1Lt PS VT
Thomas Frederick: b 11-18-1759 d 11-15-1820 m Elsie Green Pvt VT
Timothy: b 3-5-1763 d 8-13-1852 m Elizabeth Phelps Pvt MA
Wm.: b 7-15-1705 d 6-16-1786 m Hannah Pickard CS MA
Wm.: b 1736 d 3-4-1813 m Anna Town Pvt MA

JILLSON,
Amos: b 4-27-1743 d 1- -1794 m (1)Mrs Mehetable Hunn (2)Hannah — Capt Lt RI
David: b 2-1-1761 d 8-27-1850 m (1)Joanna Thompson (2)Sarah Cudworth Pvt NH VT ★

Jonathan: b 1-29-1729 d 6-6-1803 m Cloe Cargill PS NH
Levi: b 6-1-1747 d 1-7-1822 m Elizabeth Hunt Pvt MA
Oliver: b 12-5-1761 d 7-6-1840 m Nancy Potter Slr Pvtr MA ★
Stephen: b 2-16-1741 d 12- -1801 m (1)Hannah Nicholas Peck (2)Susan Cole (3)Chloe Tolman Capt RI
Uriah: b 1713 d 9-16-1781 m Sarah Ballou Sol RI

JINGST,
Henry: b 5-20-1736 d *p.* 1780 m Catharine — Pvt PA

JOB, (includes JOBE)
Andrew: b 1735 d 1796 m Elizabeth Johnson Sol PA CL
Archibald: b 1726 d 1805 m Margaret Rees PS MD
Morris: b 5-26-1753 d 5-1-1803 m Lydia Bond PS MD
Nicholas: b 1760 d 1827 m Minnie Wien Almoner PA
Samuel: b *c.* 1753 d *p.* 8-18-1803 m Rachel — Sol NC
Samuel: b 1735-38 d *p.* 1806 m Rachel — Sol NC

JOBS,
Peter: b 1743 d 9-30-1803 m Ann — Pvt NJ
Wm.: b 6-10-1763 d 6-18-1851 m Alice Kirdy Pvt NJ CL

JOEL,
Thomas: b *c.* 1740 d 11-15-1785 m Hester Dutarque PS SC

JOHNES,
Timothy, Jr.: b 9-27-1748 d 10-13-1818 m (1)Sarah — (2)Abigail Juline Blanchard Dr NJ
Timothy: b 5-24-1717 d 9-17-1794 m (1)Elizabeth Sayre (2)Keziah Oldfield Ludlow PS NJ
Wm.: b 5-19-1755 d 12- -1836 m Charlotte Pierson Capt NJ

JOHNS, (includes JOHN)
George: b 8-25-1754 d 2-23-1841 m Dorothy Wells Sol PA
Griffith: b 8-26-1729 d 8-21-1811 m Sarah Lloyd Pvt PA
Henry: b 4-21-1757 d 3-26-1833 m (1)Charity Nicke (2)Nancy Duncan (3)Ann Lane Pvt NY
Jacob: b 10-1-1762 d 8-22-1845 m Elizabeth Smith Mar DE ★
Jehiel: b 2-19-1756 d 8-12-1840 m Elizabeth Saxton Pvt VT
Jehu: b 12-22-1759 d 1-30-1837 m Elizabeth David Pvt PA
John: b 9-28-1733 d *p.* 1792 m Hannah Davis Sol PA
John: b 2-29-1748 d 5-19-1830 m Elizabeth Miller Pvt PA
John: b *c.* 1740 d *a.* 12-23-1815 m Barbara Evans Sgt VA
Philip: b *c.* 1740 d 9-24-1820 m Jane Townsend Pvt PA
Thomas: b 1-3-1761 d 2-15-1817 m Elizabeth Brown Pouncey Pvt SC
Thomas: b 1758 d 1794 m Gartie Hood Glover Ens VA
Thomas: b 1742 d *p.* 1824 m Mary Mahone Pvt VA ★
Wm.: b 1743 d 10-4-1814 m Mary Davies Lt VA

JOHNSON, (see also JOHNSTON)
Aaron: b 1-26-1747 d 2-6-1826 m Elizabeth Rider Cpl MA
Abel: b 3-26-1748 d 5-21-1815 m Mary — PS CT
Abel: b 1760 d 1830 m Curtis Frazier Pvt NC
Abel: b *c.* 1740 d 1820 m Anna Alexander Pvt PA
Abijah: b 6-13-1745 d 5-10-1809 m Mary Reed Cpl MA
Abner: b 9-6-1759 d 10-26-1826 m Anna Delano Pvt CT
Abner: b 9-10-1737 d 5-12-1777 m Miriam Jones Sol MA
Abner: b 6-9-1759 d 1-15-1832 m (1)Jemima Hampton (2)Jane Kirkpatrick Pvt NJ
Abner: b 11-22-1762 d 9-16-1828 m Abagail Lee Pvt NJ
Abraham: b 10-5-1762 d 9-12-1849 m Aretas Fitz Randolph Pvt NJ ★
Abraham: b 4-16-1749 d 6-12-1828 m Amy Smith OrdlSgt NY ★
Abraham: b 10- -1754 d 1834 m Elizabeth Bogardus Capt VA ★
Abraham, Sr.: b *c.* 1720 d *p.* 7-20-1792 m Rachael — PS VA
Adam: b 1718 d 12-17-1813 m Abigail Carleton Lt NH
Adam: b 1750 d 11-5-1804 m Sarah Laggon Pvt NH VT
Alexander: b — d *a.* 12-8-1807 m Mary Lewis PS VA
Allen: b 7-22-1748 d 9-5-1812 m Anna — Capt RI
Amos: b 1732 d 3-5-1803 m Elizabeth Pierce Capt CT
Amos: b 2-23-1753 d 11-1-1824 m (1)Patience Hickox (2)A. — Curtiss Ens CT
Amos: b 1738 d 12-21-1776 m Jemima Chamberlain Sgt CT
Amos: b 3-4-1726 d *p.* 1785 m Abigail Holt Pvt CT
Amos: b 9-16-1760 d 12-7-1858 m Abia Moss Pvt CT ★
Amos: b *p.* 1756 d *p.* 1790 m — Cpl MA
Andrew: b 2-22-1732 d 1837 m Jane Berger 1Lt NJ
Andrew: b 1-25-1750 d 1-25-1826 m Jane Faulkner PS KY
Archer: b *c.* 1735 d 1813 m — PS VA
Archibald: b 6-18-1763 d 2-18-1822 m Mary Idol PS NC
Artemas: b 4-5-1740 d 8-14-1784 m Mary — Pvt CT
Arthur: b 1747 d 3- -1823 m Elizabeth Harrison Capt VA
Arthur: b 8-7-1757 d 10-16-1839 m Lucy Harmon Pvt VA ★
Asa: b 1738 d 1810 m Hannah Tuttle Pvt CT
Asa: b 2-16-1728 d 8-13-1820 m Tamar Whitcomb Pvt MA
Asahel: b 8-15-1739 d 6-14-1811 m (1)Lois Williams (2)Miriam Fowler Trent Pvt CT
Ashahel: b 9-25-1743 d 6-26-1818 m Eunice Wetmore PS CT
Ashley: b 7-17-1765 d 6-26-1848 m Mildred Johnston Sol VA
Azel, Sr.: b 7-9-1732 d *a.* 1810 m Rebecca Wilson Cpl MA
Azel, Jr.: b 11-27-1762 d 5-4-1838 m Rebecca Brown Pvt MA ★
Bailey: b *a.* 1763 d 9- -1805 m Hannah Moffett Pvt VA

JOHNSON, contd.

Baker: b 9-30-1747 d 6-18-1811 m Catharine Worthington Col PS MD
Barachiah: b 12-8-1746 d 5-11-1826 m Lydia Green Lt MA
Barent: b 8-26-1746 d 2-2-1813 m Elizabeth Terhune Pvt NJ
Barent: b 4-2-1740 d 11-6-1782 m Ann Remsen Maj NY
Benjamin: b 1762 d 9-19-1828 m Susannah Hull Sgt CT ★
Benjamin: b 1716 d *p.* 1790 m Mary Doolittle Sol CT
Benjamin: b 7-6-1727 d 5-17-1785/6 m (1)Mrs Sarah Backus (2)Catherine Bull Col MD
Benjamin: b *c.* 1718 d *c.* 1-10-1795 m Rachel Summers PS MD
Benjamin: b 11-21-1741 d 11-12-1810 m (1)Lydia Richards (2)Lydia Breed (3)Rachel Roberts 1st Lt PS MA
Benjamin: b 6-4-1744 d 10-21-1832 m Elizabeth Boardman Cpl PS NH
Benjamin: b 1763 d 11-11-1849 m (2)Priscilla Robinson Pvt NH ★
Benjamin: b 5-5-1719 d 7-2-1811 m Rachel Garland PS NH
Benjamin: b 1729 d 1805 m Mary James Sol PA
Benjamin: b 1-23-1749 d *p.* 1792 m Mary Weaver 1Lt RI
Benjamin: b 5-8-1751 d 11-14-1801 m Betsey Barbour LCol VA
Benjamin: b *c.* 1740 d 1787 m Elizabeth — 2Lt VA
Benjamin: b 6-18-1756 d 1809 m Mary Henley Sol VA
Benjamin: b *a.* 1758 d *p.* 1779 m Mary — Pvt VA
Benoni: b 5-23-1762 d 5-17-1848 m (1)Olive Wilcox (2)Abigail Wood Pvt CT ★
Burrell: b 1755 d *p.* 1823 m Mary — Spy Sol Arfr SC
Caleb: b 1740 d *p.* 1794 m Martha Davies Pvt PA
Caleb: b *c.* 1740 d *p.* 1794 m Martha Davies Pvt PA
Caleb: b 3-23-1740 d 1819 m Mary Bennett Pvt PA
Calvin: b 12-20-1755 d 10-7-1843 m Sarah Armstrong Pvt CT ★
Cave: b 11-15-1760 d 1-19-1850 m Elizabeth Craig Ens Ky ★
Charles: b 5- -1750 d *a.* 3-4-1821 m — Pvt MD ★
Charles: b 9-2-1757 d 10-21-1821 m Polly Huston Pvt NC
Charles: b *a.* 1755 d *a.* 5- -1820 m Hannah — PS NC
Charles: b 9-27-1753 d 1-17-1819 m Mary Moorman Pvt VA
Christopher: b 1-3-1755 d 1-2-1823 m (1)Mary Austin (2)Mrs Phoebe Waterhouse Sgt CT
Christopher: b *c.* 1752 d 1801 m Catherine — Capt PA
Christopher: b 11-21-1731 d — m Elizabeth Moorman Ens VA
Comfort: b 1755 d 8-19-1840 m Sarah Sumner Sgt MA ★
Daniel: b 3-24-1746 d 9-2-1830 m (1)Rebecca Hitchcock (2)Lucy Dudley 2Lt CT
Daniel: b 2-2-1760 d 9-13-1840 m Mary Norton Pvt CT ★
Daniel: b 11- -1763 d 5-31-1847 m (3)Elizabeth Mosley Pvt MD
Daniel: b 7- -1725 d 1802 m (1)Lucy — (2)Abigail (Spring) Brown Pvt MA
Daniel: b *c.* 1761 d *p.* 1812 m Sarah Jones Cpl NY
Daniel: b 9-26-1726 d 1783 m Ann Anderson Pvt NC
Daniel: b 5-24-1747 d 9-23-1777 m Betsey Lee Chp MA
Daniel: b 1-8-1766 d 9-9-1824 m (1)Sarah Mendenhall (2)Jane Mendenhall Pvt PA
Daniel: b 8-10-1751 d 1-10-1854 m Margaret Mann Pvt SC
David: bpt 9-24-1738 d 8-16-1813 m Susanna (Russell) Smith Lt CT
David: b 9-29-1762 d 12-27-1827 m Eunice Avery Pvt CT
David: b 12-4-1744 d 5-17-1823 m Sarah Standiford PS MD
David: b 1746/7 d 7-29-1812 m (1)Phebe — (2)Mary Brewster 1Lt MA
David: b *a.* 1735 d *p.* 11-5-1787 m Mary Berryman Sol VA
David: b 9-17-1763 d 1849 m Lucinda Carter Pvt VA ★
Dennis: b 1-20-1764 d 1-6-1833 m Mary Carter Pvt ME
Ebenezer: b 2-25-1731 d 12-11-1804 m Anna Willes Ens CT
Ebenezer: b 7-7-1723 d 1795 m Thankful Upson PS CT
Ebenezer: b 8-29-1741 d 8-26-1823 m Elizabeth Rice Pvt MA
Ebenezer: b 2-6-1749/50 d 2-24-1823 m Eleanor Edmonds Pvt MA ★
Ebenezer: b 5-9-1760 d 2-8-1841 m Deborah Lathrop Pvtr VT CT
Ebenezer: b 1752 d *p.* 1850 m Elizabeth — Pvt MM Spy PA
Ebenezer: b 2-19-1736 d 9-4-1840 m Rebecca Tingley Pvt RI ★
Edmond: b *c.* 1750 d 4-12-1803 m Sarah — Pvt VA CL
Edmund: b 5-4-1741 d 12-31-1812 m Sarah Potter Capt PS RI
Edward: b 12-30-1729 d 1776 m Mary Phillips Pvt CT
Edward: b 1737 d 1797 m Ann Arnold PS MD
Edward: b 10-23-1743 d 1779 m Mary Godfrey Pvt NH
Edward: b 11-2-1746 d 7-21-1828 m Releif Johnson Pvt MA
Edward: b 1766 d 2-26-1846 m Deborah St. Clair Sol VA
Eleazer: b 2-27-1719 d 7-3-1791 m Lucy Ball Pvt MA
Eleazer, Sr.: b 1697 d 5-12-1792 m (1)Elizabeth Toppan (2)Sarah Bailey PS MA
Eleazer, Jr.: b 1743 d 7-3-1788 m Hannah Pearson Capt MA
Elias: b 12-3-1758 d 3-28-1837 m Susan Spencer Pvt CT ★
Elihu: b 1735 d *p.* 1790 m Sarah (Webb) Converse Pvt CT
Elihu: b *a.* 1733 d 2-25-1811 m Sarah — Sgt VT
Elijah: b 3-25-1751 d *p.* 1797 m Abigail — Pvt MA
Elijah: b 4-13-1754 d *p.* 10-21-1836 m — Pvt NC ★

Elisha: b 7-1-1753 d 11-28-1832 m (1)Abigail Newton (2)Sarah Perry Pvt MA
Elisha: b 9-22-1759 d 1824 m Mary Reeve Pvt NY CT
Elisha Moses: b 1762 d 6-8-1828 m — Pvt CT NY ★
Ephraim: b 3-31-1742 d 9-4-1834 m Mary Farley Sol MA
Ezekiel: b 1754 d 1-27-1832 m Elizabeth Crossman Pvt MA
Ezra: b 11-4-1751 d 5-18-1804 m Ruth Marston Pvt MA
Francis, Jr.: b 4-2-1746 d 9-18-1805 m Abigail Brooks Pvt★
Francis: b *c.* 1750 d 1780 m Margaret Searight Lt SC W★
Frederick: b 3-29-1759 d 10-10-1810 m Rhoda Reed Pvt MA
George: b *c.* 1738 d 1828 m Elizabeth Blakemore Maj VA
George: b 1762 d 5-23-1837 m Catharine — Fif VA ★
Gideon: b 11-7-1754 d 11-1-1843 m Polly (Baker) deGraffenreid Pvt NC ★
Griffith: b 3-7-1739 d 1805 m Elizabeth Thomas Capt MD
Haynes: b 8-28-1749 d 9-2-1775 m Elizabeth Elliot PS VT
Henry: b 1745 d 4-26-1801 m Polly Cheapton Pvt MA
Henry: b — d *p.* 9-27-1780 m Mary — PS MD
Henry: b 10-5-1737 d 1-5-1826 m Susanna Hover QM Capt NJ
Henry: b 1738 d 1815 m Rachel Holman Pvt NC
Henry: b — d *p.* 1786 m Elizabeth — Pvt PA
Henry Ashton: b *c.* 1760 d *p.* 1-9-1806 m Ann Michie 2Lt VA
Henson: b 2-25-1763 d 1-9-1858 m Jane — Pvt VA ★
Hezekiah: b 11- -1749 d 11-15-1826 m Rebecca Tuttle Cpl CT
Hezekiah: b 3-12-1733 d 2-21-1810 m Ruth Merriman Capt CT
Hezekiah: b 1- -1730 d 10- -1811 m (1)Hepzabah (Beall) Ford (2)Frances Smoot Pvt MD
Horatio: b 1755 d 2- -1811 m Elizabeth Warfield 1Lt MD
Hugh: b 8-12-1750 d 2-4-1835 m Winea Flanegan Sol NC
Isaac: b 3-24-1728 d 11-5-1814 m Jerusha Gager Capt PS CT
Isaac: b 10-6-1735 d 4-10-1813 m Lois Hopkins Pvt PS CT
Isaac: b 1-24-1756 d 5-13-1805 m Anna Farnam Pvt CT
Isaac: b 1733 d 1799 m Elizabeth — Sol MD
Isaac, Sr.: b 8-9-1721 d 5-2-1807 m Mary Willis Maj MA
Isaac, Jr.: b 2-27-1755 d *p.* 1800 m Mary Wright Sgt MA
Isaac: b 3-26-1729 d 1-15-1817 m Elizabeth Coffin Cpl MA
Isaac, Sr.: b 2-28-1735 d 2-16-1801 m Patience Joslyn Sol MA
Isaac, Jr.: b 3-16-1760 d 10-24-1833 m Olive Hixon Pvt MA
Isaac, Jr.: b 7-17-1761 d 8-7-1832 m Dinah Walker Pvt MA W★
Isaac: b 7-17-1724 d *p.* 1786 m (1)Lydia Pierce (2)Elizabeth Dean Pvt NY
Isaac: b 5-10-1760 d 8-14-1838 m Agnes Wright Pvt NJ
Isaac: b 4-14-1761 d *p.* 1835 m (1)Sarah — (2) — (3)Nancy — (4)(4)Lecy Williams Pvt NC ★
Isaac: b 3-30-1753 d 3-29-1821 m Catharine Roberts Lt RI
Isaac: b *c.* 1730 d *p.* 1-21-1815 m (1)Ann Williams (2)Rebecca Bowen 1Lt VA
Isaac: b 1745 d 5- -1814 m Elizabeth Holeman Cpl VA
Isaiah: b 1756 d 7-18-1841 m Sarah Whittlesey Sgt CT ★
Jacob: b 5-19-1727 d — m Sarah Dolliver Pvt MA
Jacob: b 7-21-1742 d 6-10-1816 m Esther Hotchkiss Pvt MA
Jacob: b 10-18-1754 d 4-10-1846 m Sarah Garrison Lt Tms NJ W★
Jacob: b 4-21-1751 d 4-25-1780 m Anna Vail Trooper NJ
Jacob: b 1738 d *p.* 1-16-1781 m Mary W — PS CS PA
Jacob: b 4-7-1713 d 3-15-1797 m Mary Giddings PS PA
Jacob: b 1760 d 1817 m Deliah Cummings Sol VA
Jacob: b 5-15-1752 d *p.* 1814 m Sarah Knowling Pvt PS VA
Jacob Weller: b 3-7-1747 d *c.* 1839 m Christianna Fishbaugh Sol NJ
James: b 3-10-1751 d 3-7-1833 m Hepzibah Hubbard Pvt CT ★
James: b 8-21-1761 d 1-3-1835 m (1)Olive Armstrong (2)Rhody Ransted (3)Phebe Wirt (4)Phebe (Church) Kidder (5)Jemima Broughton Pvt CT★
James: b 8-8-1752 d *c.* 1843 m Eunice — Pvt CT NY ★
James: b 9-30-1736 d 12-3-1809 m Margaret Skinner Col MD
James: b 5-14-1735 d 6-3-1831 m Elizabeth Porterfield Maj MA
James: b 1750 d 1814 m Hannah Hutchinson Sgt MA ★
James, Sr.: b 1712 d 4-1-1788 m Susanna — Pvt MA
James, Jr.: b 5-19-1739 d 10-12-1816 m Hannah Harding Pvt MA
James: b 3-3-1759 d 2-10-1838 m (1)Hannah Bates (2)Mrs Hannah P Fickert Pvt Smn MA ★
James: b 10-20-1739 d 10-24-1816 m Sarah — Pvt MA
James: b *c.* 1755 d *p.* 1820 m Elizabeth Hunt Ens NJ
James: b 1746 d 9-1-1818 m Mary Farril Pvt NJ
James: b 10-31-1757 d 2-9-1837 m Christianna Swing Pvt NJ
James: b — d *p.* 5-21-1830 m (1)Jane McKnight (2)Lydia Elrod Pvt NC
James: b — d 9-8-1826 m Elizabeth Lindsey LCol PA
James: b *c.* 1732 d 1839 m (1)Ann McMillan (2)Catherine DeMos PS PA
James: b *c.* 1725 d *a.* 10-11-1787 m Susannah — Maj VA
James: b 4-27-1747 d 9-15-1845 m Martha Fulgham Capt VA ★
James: b 1745 d 4-7-1817 m Margaret — Sol VA
James: b 1757 d 1839 m Hannah Sanford Pvt VA ★
James: b 1764 d *p.* 1855 m Mary Jane Richardson Pvt VA ★
James: b 1760 d 1850 m Agnes Baker Pvt VA ★
James: b *c.* 1735/6 d 1-26-1820 m (1)Milly Moorman (2)Penelope Anthony PS VA
Jedediah: b 1758 d 7-18-1843 m Elizabeth Torry Pvt VT ★
Jeffery: b — d *p.* 3-23-1788 m Rachael — PS NC
Jemima Suggett: b 6-29-1753 d 2-23-1814 m Robert Johnson PS VA
Jeremiah: b 1739 d 1814 m Cassandra — PS CS MD
Jeremiah: b 1763 d 11-2-1847 m (1)Thomazin Blanchard (2)Sybil Kimball Pvt NH

Jesse: b 11-7-1746 d 4-30-1832 m (1)Mary Stevenson (2)Mrs Abigail Butler Goodwin PS CT
Jesse: b 1734 d 3-17-1822 m Sarah — Pvt MA
Jesse: b 3-16-1755 d 4-3-1839 m Sarah Harrington Pvt MA ★
Jesse: b 7-27-1753 d 1-11-1826 m Mary Lewis Sol NC
John: b 1745 d 5-2-1834 m (1)Hannah Clark (3)Clarissa (Parker) Miner Rock Capt Wgm CT ★
John: b c. 1741 d 1838 m Sarah Lee Capt CT
John: b,1748 d 6-28-1842 m (1)Lois Brainard (2)Mary Bailey Pvt CT ★
John: b 9-14-1757 d 4-17-1850 m Rachel Baker Pvt CT ★
John: b 10-21-1722 d a. 2-16-1803 m Gracie Morris PS CT
John: b 3-23-1730/1 d 3-13-1804 m Phyllys Pellet PS CT
John: b c. 1760 d a. 5-22-1829 m Elizabeth — Capt GA
John: b 3-28-1764 d 1-14-1828 m Ann Ealy Sol GA
John: b — d p. 12-30-1814 m Elizabeth — Sol GA
John: b 1740 d p. 5-23-1791 m Sarah (Upton ?) Pvt GA
John: b 1- -1732 d 3-19-1838 m Anne Almany Pvt MD
John: b 5-14-1737 d 5-28-1833 m Eleanor Lamb Sgt MA
John: b 5-24-1737 d 5-28-1820 m Jane Libby Pvt ME
John: b 2-14-1757 d 11-22-1792 m Achsah Simonds Sol MA
John: b 6-9-1748 d 4-10-1833 m Persis Sherman Pvt MA
John: b 11-16-1758 d 10-3-1833 m Abigail Abbot Pvt MA ★
John: b — d 1777 m Abigail Carlton Pvt NH
John: b 3-16-1740 d 5-24-1825 m (1)Abigail Morrison (2)Mary Smith Pvt PS NH
John: b 6-25-1758 d 6-29-1847 m Sally Cate Pvt NH
John: b 5-2-1758 d 9-3-1833 m Betty Ward Sgt NJ
John: b 10-12-1760 d 1824 m Sarah McDonald Pvt Cav NJ
John: b 1731 d 3-31-1802 m Jane Sauyberry Pvt NJ
John: b a. 1750 d 9- -1820 m Rebecca — Pvt NJ
John: b 1750 d 1829 m Abigail Bach Canfield Pvt NJ
John: b 11-6-1736 d 1821 m Abigail Fowler Capt NY
John: b 5-4-1753 d 12-8-1829 m Anne Maria Styres Lt NJ W★
John: b 1752 d 9-4-1833 m Mary Cooper Pvt NY
John: b 4-18-1756 d 6-26-1838 m Elizabeth Peck Pvt NY ★
John: b 2-9-1756 d 1816 m Priscilla Scovil Capt PA
John: b 5-23-1732 d 1804 m Jean Bell Capt PA
John: b c. 1744 d 9- -1792 m Isabelle Todd Pvt PA
John: b 1735 d 2-18-1808 m Mehitable Sperry Pvt NJ
John: b 8- -1748 d 3-25-1825 m Annie Honeycut Ens VA ★
John: b c. 1738 d 1827/8 m Lydia Watkins Sol VA
John: b 5-14-1762 d 8-7-1860 m — Pvt VA
John:Boswell: b 5-10-1715 d 3-22-1785 m Mary Cornwell Capt VA
Jonathan: bpt 3-12-1736 d 1815 m Mary Whitmore LCol CT
Jonathan: b — d — m — Lt CT MA
Jonathan: b 1741/2 d p. 1778 m Jane Gibbs Pvt CT
Jonathan: b 5-12-1762 d 4-26-1838 m Lydia Todd Sol CT
Jonathan: b 10-4-1754 d 12-17-1832 m (1)Miriam Booker (2)Mehitable Hersey Cpl MA
Jonathan: b 12-12-1754 d 9-16-1820 m Rhoda Abbot Pvt NH W★
Joseph: b 6-17-1750 d 11-17-1808 m Jerusha Foot Cpl CT
Joseph: b a. 1752 d 12-5-1790 m Abagal Wright Pvt CT
Joseph: b 11-9-1717 d c. 1787 m Elizabeth Durand Pvt CT
Joseph: b 5-21-1726 d 2- -1787 m Mary Rogers PS CT
Joseph, Jr.: b 9-6-1751 d 6-25-1818 m Hannah Banks Cav CT
Joseph: b 1756 d 1806 m Catherine Miller Pvt MD
Joseph, Sr.: b c. 1716 d 6-30-1792 m Hannah Hack Pvt MA
Joseph, Jr.: b 1-8-1737 d 9-18-1823 m Mary Whittemore Pvt MA
Joseph: b 3-9-1709 d 2-25-1795 m Elizabeth Shepard PS NH
Joseph: b 4-10-1734 d 10-8-1794 m (1)Anna Lane (2)Dinah — PS NH
Joseph: b 1-21-1745 d 12-29-1831 m Martha Vail Pvt Wgm NJ W★
Joseph: b 5-5-1753 d 11-16-1838 m Nancy Lytle Pvt NC
Joseph: b a. 1753 d 1835 m Martha House Capt PA
Joseph: b c. 1752 d 3-4-1789 m — Sgt PA ★
Joseph Shirley: b 8-4-1758 d 7-23-1842 m Sarah — Pvt VA ★
Josiah: b 1-27-1757 d 2-25-1833 m Anna Hedges Pvt CT ★
Josiah: b 3-7-1746 d 2-21-1827 m Martha Arms Taylor Lt MA
Lawrence: b 1749 d 9-22-1822 m (1)Lydia Comstock (2)Grace Harris Pvt CT W★
Lawrence: b 7-4-1757 d 7-23-1843 m Margaret Mesler Pvt NJ NY ★
Lemuel: b 12-8-1750 d 8-22-1817 m (1)Susanna Peabody (2)Nancy (Morrison) Boyd PS NH
Lemuel: b 1-1-1746 d — m Jerusha Norton Pvt MA
Levi: b 2- -1762 d 12-10-1833 m (1)Huldah Beecher (2)Ruth Judd Pvt CT ★
Levi: b 1744 d 8-7-1809 m Anna Manning Pvt CT MA
Lewis: b 1-4-1738 d 9-11-1778 m Mary May Lt MA
Mathias: b 1720 d 1794 m Elizabeth — Ens NJ
Mathias: b c. 1744 d 1799 m — Smith Pvt NC
Matthew: b c. 1710 d 1780 m Judith — PS NJ
Matthew: b 1734 d 1780 m Jane Gaston Pvt SC
Michael: b 4-15-1756 d 1798 m Susanna Minch Pvt NJ
Miles: b 1741 d 1909 m Ruth Hall Capt CT
Moses: b 7-26-1737 d 1815 m (1)Marcy Fox (2)Ruth Whitman (3)Mollie Tower Pvt MA
Moses: b 7-7-1751 d c. 1790 m Mary Bly Pvt NH
Moses: b 2-23-1741 d 9-3-1835 m (1)Margaret Moore (2)Lydia Wheeler Lt VT
Nathan: b 1732 d 5-26-1805 m Nancy Elizabeth Hutchins Pvt GA
Nathaniel: b 2-11-1732 d p. 1776 m Susannah Smith Capt MA CT
Nathaniel: b 3-6-1732 d 1777 m Anna Child Pvt PS CT
Nathaniel: b 3-25-1749 d 9-30-1845 m Rebecca Pierson Pvt CT W★

Nathaniel: b 8-19-1753 d 2-10-1822 m Sarah Spooner Pvt CT ★
Nathaniel: b 11-13-1749 d 5-17-1826 m (1)Ruth Sanborn (2)Sarah (Batchelder) Marston Pvt NH
Nathaniel: b 1735 d 2-1-1777 m Anna Johns Pvt PA
Nicholas: b 11-28-1752 d 10-30-1825 m Mary Perkins SeaCap MA
Nicholas: b c. 1758 d 1832 m (1)Mary Perkins Cpl VA
Noble: b c. 1758 d 1800 m Sara — Pvt VA
Obadiah: b 2-18-1736 d 10-27-1801 m (1)Mary Howard (2)Lucy (Cady) Spaulding Col CT
Obadiah: b c. 1754 d 1813 m Lois Winchell Pvt MA
Obadiah: b 1723 d 7- -1793 m Sarah Nichols Pvt RI
Oliver: b 1755 d 4- -1816 m Hannah George Pvt NH
Peter: b 1745 d 6-18-1813 m (2)Comfort (Clark ?) Capt CT
Peter: b 6-7-1756 d 8-29-1806 m Isabel Simpson Pvt NH
Peter, Sr.: b 7-11-1714 d p. 1790 m Sarah Dow PS NH
Peter: b c. 1730-32 d a. 5-18-1816 m Rebecca — Pvt NJ
Peter: b 1745 d 1825 m Anna Trissel Pvt PS PA
Peter: b 1753 d 1830 m Eleanor Peters Pvt PA
Philip: b 11-16-1756 d 10-7-1831 m Sarah Noyes Vol MA
Philip: b 5- -1764 d 3-18-1845 m — Susanna Petit Pvt NY ★
Philip: b c. 1728 d 3-15-1788 m Elizabeth Bray PS VA
Phillip: b 1758 d 1835 m Susannah — Pvt VA ★
Phillip: b c. 1760 d 1823 m Phebe Clay Pvt VA
Phillip: bpt 1722 d 1785/6 m (2)Elizabeth Philbrook (3)Mary Brackett Pickering Pvt NH
Phineas: b 1761 d p. 7-5-1820 m Mary Skeels Pvt CT ★
Phineas: b 1747 d 1844 m Hannah Poor MM MA
Reuben: b 1751 d 8-12-1804 m Kezia Baldwin Pvt MA
Reuben: b 1758 d 1-26-1833 m Nancy Greenlee Pvt NC W★
Richard: b 7-22-1734 d 12-2-1811 m Mary Brooks Lt CT
Richard: b — d 1- -1793 m Sarah Poppino Pvt NY
Richard: b 8-17-1743 d c. 1828/9 m (1)Dorcas Dungan (2)Elizabeth Nash Lt PA
Richard: b c. 1750 d p. 1799 m Susan Garrett 2Lt VA
Richard: b c. 1758 d 8-30-1842 m Frances Phelps Cpl VA
Robert: b 1744 d 3-16-1831 m Mary Vannoy Pvt MD
Robert: b 1724 d 10-3-1802 m Mary Millions Capt MA
Robert: b 1-25-1727 d 12-28-1796 m ( )Margaret Morgan ( )Jane Gibbon PS NJ
Robert: b 12-9-1763 d 1-16-1821 m Civil Littleton Ives Sol NC
Robert: b 8-2-1732 d 5- -1808 m Cecelia Elmore Sol NC
Robert: b 7-17-1745 d 10-15-1815 m Jemima Suggett Capt PS VA
Robert: b 4-7-1759 d 6-4-1838 m Mary Sloan Pvt VA ★
Robert: b 2-2-1750 d 8-1-1835 m Mattie Ralston Pvt VA
Roger: b 3-15-1749 d 3-3-1831 m Elizabeth Thomas Maj MD
Roland: b 1758 d p. 5-8-1838 m Milly — Pvt VA ★
Rufus: b 11-8-1753 d 6-9-1837 m (1)Elizabeth Goff (2)Anna Gardner 2Lt VA
Samuel, Jr.: b 2-20-1754 d 3-10-1793 m Lucy Atkins DrmMaj CT
Samuel: b 12-23-1719 d 1788 m Mary (Durand ?) Pvt CT
Samuel: b 1751 d 3-13-1843 m Sarah Pearl Pvt CT ★
Samuel: b 1752 d 9-2-1840 m Chloe Barnes Pvt NY
Samuel: b 3-23-1713 d 11-12-1796 m Elizabeth Gage Col MA
Samuel: b 4-5-1743 d 9-2-1824 m Anna Kimball Capt MA
Samuel: b 5-18-1725 d 4-12-1789 m Elizabeth Kendall Pvt MA
Samuel: b 8-21-1738 d 1789 m Mary Spence Pvt MA
Samuel: b 4-22-1748 d 3-10-1814 m Susanna Searle Pvt MA
Samuel: bpt 9-13-1754 d — m Lydia Phelps Pvt MA
Samuel: b 4-25-1756 d 7-24-1847 m Elizabeth Fisk Pvt NH
Samuel: b 9-12-1739 d 3-30-1822 m (1)Lydia Roberts (2)Elizabeth Brackett CS PS NH
Samuel: b c. 1735 d 5- -1808 m (1)Betty Headley (2)Mrs Sarah Davis Wgm NJ
Samuel: b 4-11-1760 d 11-20-1848 m Anney Brower Pvt NJ ★
Samuel: b 1757 d 9-15-1834 m Mary Hammond Lt NC ★
Samuel: b 1744 d 2-28-1833 m Miss Johnston Pvt VA NC★
Samuel: b 3-21-1726 d c. 1801 m Lydia Ross Pvt PA
Samuel: b 1746 d 7-5-1822 m Barbara Young Pvt PA
Samuel: b 1757 d 1834 m Nancy — Cpl RI
Samuel: b 1758 d 1849 m Susan Erwin Sgt SC
Samuel: b 11-27-1762 d 6-16-1845 m Sarah Sawyer Pvt VT ★
Samuel: b c. 1760-65 d p. 1813 m — Pvt VT
Samuel Wm.: b 10-23-1761 d 10-25-1846 m Susan Edwards PS CT
Sarah Nightingale: b 8-28-1751 d 10-5-1825 m William Johnson PS SC
Seth: b 10-27-1746 d p. 1782 m Jemima Miller Pvt CT
Seth: b 1-10-1748 d 1-9-1833 m Mrs Abigail Hutchins Carleton Pvt CT ★
Shadrach: b 1-17-1762 d 6-26-1823 m Hannah Toocker Pvt CT ★
Silas: b p. 1758 d c. 1819 m Phebe Ward Pvt VA
Simeon: b c. 1760 d 1733 d c. 1823 m (1)Elizabeth Gardner (2)Elizabeth Stone Pvt PS NH
Solomon: b 1735 d p. 1786 m Eleanor Pierce Pvt CT
Solomon: b 5-4-1740 d 4-4-1799 m Mary Barker Sol CT
Stephen: b 1754 d — m Ruth Smith Pvt CT
Stephen, Sr.: b c. 1737 d 1801 m Elizabeth Pelton Pvt CT
Stephen, Jr.: b 3-17-1762 d 7-31-1832 m Phoebe Burr Pvt CT ★
Stephen: b 8-28-1704 d 1797 m (1)Mercy Wilmot (2)Sarah Hull PS CT
Stephen: b 5-17-1724 d 11-8-1786 m (1)Elizabeth Diodati (2)Mary (Gardiner) Blague (3)Abigail Leverett Chp CT
Stephen: b 9-9-1736 d p. 1794 m Hannah Baxter Pvt MA
Stephen: b 5-17-1759 d 4-21-1837 m Elizabeth Jordon Pvt MA
Stephen: b a. 1729 d c. 1808 m Dorothy Whitcomb PS MA

JOHNSON, contd.

Stephen: b — d 1802 m (1)Phebe — (2)Avey — PS VA
Stephen Wm.: b 6-13-1749 d 6-29-1834 m Martha Smith Sol CT
Thomas: b c. 1745 d 1805 m Penelope Sanders Pvt GA
Thomas: b 3-10-1742 d 3-5-1816 m (1)Mary — (2)Agnes Greer Lt GA
Thomas: b 11-24-1732 d 10-24-1819 m Ann Jennings BGen MD
Thomas: b 9-15-1742 d 1819 m Thankful Smith Pvt MA ★
Thomas: b 1-15-1750 d 9-11-1826 m Abigail Berry Sol NH
Thomas: b — d — m Ann Varnum Pvt PA NC
Thomas: b 3-22-1742 d 1-4-1819 m (1)Elizabeth Lowell (2)Abigail (Merrill) Pool (3)Abigail Carleton Col PS NH VT
Thomas: b c. 1752 d 10-28-1776 m Mary Anne — Pvt PA
Thomas: b 11-14-1749/50 d c. 1834 m Ann — Capt VA
Thomas: b 1762 d 1837 m Dolly Dunton Sol VA
Thomas: b c. 1722 d 1799 m (1)Elizabeth Ashton (2)Ursula Row PS VA
Thomas: b 3-6-1735 d 8-12-1803 m Elizabeth Merriwether PS CS VA
Thomas Baker: b 1754 d 1795 m Catharine Rhoda Dimmick PS MD
Timothy: b 6-2-1729 d 9-29-1812 m Mary Phelps Pvt CT
Timothy: b c. 4-17-1737 d p. 1790 m Mary Greeley Capt MA
Timothy: b 9-21-1744 d p. 1798 m Penelope Eaton 2Lt MA
Timothy: b 10-15-1759 d p. 1802 m Sarah — Pvt NH
Tunis: b c. 1729 d p. 8-8-1807 m Jaminah — Pvt NJ
Uzal: b 1731 d 9-10-1804 m (1)Phebe Wick (2)Mary Scudder Hole MM NJ
Wm.: b 2-20-1761 d 12-5-1838 m (2)Hadassah Smith Pvt CT ★
Wm., Jr.: b 8-2-1725 d 9-12-1804 m Dorcas Chamberlin Capt CT
Wm.: b 1744 d 3- -1832 m Sarah — Pvt CT ★
Wm.: b 4-11-1753 d 9-7-1801 m Jemima Hubbard Pvt CT
Wm.: b 4-23-1754 d 8-20-1831 m Mary Nye Pvt CT
Wm.: bpt 5-2-1762 d p. 1843 m Abigail — Pvt CT
Wm.: b 1734 d 1806 m Margaret Scott Capt GA
Wm.: b 1755-60 d 1821 m Nancy Hill Capt GA
Wm.: b — d 1795 m Elizabeth Hayes Sgt MD
Wm.: b 12-7-1745 d 9-13-1821 m Mary Marble 2Lt MA
Wm.: b — d — m Martha Roper Sgt MA
Wm.: b 4-3-1749 d 6-1-1834 m Sarah Cheney Sgt MA
Wm.: b 4- -1710 d 8-3-1793 m Elizabeth Pierce Pvt MA
Wm.: b 6-26-1732 d 4-11-1811 m Abigail Little Pvt MA
Wm.: b 2-25-1733 d p. 1788 m Sarah Kendall Pvt MA
Wm.: b 1742 d 7-22-1828 m Mary (Eddy) Owen Pvt MA
Wm.: b 1-17-1753 d 4- -1818 m Jane Robinson Pvt MA
Wm.: b 4-16-1734 d c. 5-31-1814 m Rachael — Capt NJ
Wm.: b — d 1812 m — Ens NJ
Wm.: b 1751 d 1823 m Hetty Woodruff Sgt NJ
Wm.: b 3-20-1751 d p. 3-9-1809 m Ann Perrine Pvt NJ
Wm.: bpt 7-23-1736 d p. 1-11-1818 m Mary — Pvt NY
Wm.: b 12-27-1749 d 2-8-1830 m Sarah McClaren Pvt NC
Wm.: b c. 1750 d 1816 m — Higgs Pvt NC
Wm.: b 4-16-1751 d 1835 m Mary Parks Pvt NC ★
Wm.: b 9-9-1731 d 6-9-1800 m Catharine Tarter Ens PA
Wm.: b 8-14-1754 d 2-17-1832 m Lanah Zimmerman Pvt PA
Wm.: b c. 1750 d p. 1790 m Sally Murfee Ens CS SC
Wm.: b 10-16-1757 d 4-23-1854 m — Sgt SC ★
Wm.: b 5-21-1741 d 3-21-1818 m Sarah Nightingale Sol SC
Wm.: b c. 1740 d 1816 m Rebecca Kindall PS SC
Wm.: b 10-10-1750 d 5-6-1830 m Rosannah — Cpl VA
Wm.: b 1759 d 1849 m Elizabeth Hunter Cpl Cav VA
Wm.: b 1755 d 12-22-1805 m Amy — Pvt VA
Wm.: b 6-25-1758 d p. 4-15-1826 m (1)Agnes Scott (2)Lucy Dabney Pvt VA
Wm.: b c. 1762 d 5-2-1801 m Mary Cathrine Parker Pvt VA
Wm.: b 1759 d 1820 m Betty Robinson Pvt VA
Wm.: b 6-9-1728 d 1789 m Elizabeth Madox PS VA
Wm.: b 1735 d 2-26-1814 m (1)Martha — (2)Pattie — PS VA
Wm.: b 11-2-1740 d p. 5-29-1823 m Agatha Moorman PS VA
Wm.: b c. 1745 d 1782-92 m — Capt VA
Wm. Pearce: b 1745 d 4-6-1804 m Sarah Greenleaf Capt MA
Wm. Samuel: b 10-7-1727 d 11-14-1819 m Ann Beach PS CT
Willis: b 1744 d — m Jemima Smith Pvt MA
Zachariah: b 1757-61 d 1840 m — Pvt VA NC ★

JOHNSTON, (includes JOHNSTONE)

Abraham: b 4-5-1754 d 7-7-1823 m Jean Labar Capt NJ
Abraham: b c. 1730 d 1789-91 m (2)Susannah — Pvt NC
Alexander: b c. 1752 d 1803 m Catherine — Capt PA
Alexander: b 1755 d 1823 m — Sgt PA
Andrew: b c. 1745 d 1805 m (1)Mary Greg (2)Mrs Else Black Capt VA
Archibald: b 1732 d 2-14-1789 m Sarah Dawson Capt PS NY
Archibald: b c. 1-17-1750-7 d p. 1834 m Jemima O'Bannon Lt VA ★
Charles: b 5-29-1737 d 3-5-1813 m Ruth Marsh LCol NH
Clabourn: b 6-17-1760 d 8-22-1840 m Elizabeth Sims Pvt VA ★
Daniel: b 10-2-1748 d 8-25-1822 m Mary Haille Pvt VA
David: b 7-25-1746 d 1815 m Margaret Nixon Capt NJ
David: b c. 1757 d 2-18-1829 m Elizabeth — Pvt NC ★
David: b c. 1726 d 1786 m Nannie Abbott Pvt VA
Edward: b 1750 d 1832 m Sarah Cunningham Sol NC
George: b 1736 d 1786 m — McNeil Sol NC
George: b 2-20-1762 d 12-4-1830 m Mary Mulhollen Sol NC

Gideon: b 11-10-1717 d p. 10-2-1807 m Ursula Allen PS NC
Gilbert: b c. 1740-44 d 1827 m Jane Smith Pvt NY
Gilbert, Jr.: b c. 1725 d 1793 m Margaret Warburton PS NC
Hepzebath Tyler: b 12-5-1754 d 7-8-1846 m (1)James Bell (2)Col Robert Johnston PS VT NH
Hugo: b 1751 d 5- -1794 m Susannah Barefield Maj NC
Jacob: b 1744 d a. 5-8-1808 m (1)Mary Randall (2)Mrs Barbara Franck Shine PS NC
Jacob: b c. 1738 d 1781 m Mary — PS Pvt PA
James: b 1735 d 1782 m Mary Graham Pvt NY
James: b 8-10-1742 d 7-23-1805 m Jane Ewart Col NC
James: b 9-16-1759 d 4-22-1850 m (1)Rebecca Porter (2)Jane Greer Sol NC
James: b 6-22-1758 d 9-19-1842 m Mary Graham Kelso Ens PA
James: b 1738 d 12-5-1832 m Jane Anderson Pvt PA ★
James: b — d 9- -1783 m — Pvt PA
James: b 1751 d p. 1789 m Mary Houston Pvt PA
James: b 9-25-1754 d 1-4-1820 m Elizabeth Brown Pvt PS PA
James: b a. 1760 d 3-13-1797 m Mary Johnston Capt SC W★
James: b 1750 d 1817 m Mary Elizabeth — Capt VA
James: b 1763 d — m Esther Turk Lt VA
James: b 1757 d 4-30-1841 m Joice Wells OrdlSgt VA
James: b c. 1762 d 1816 m Rachel Copley Pvt VA
James: b 1-16-1761 d 7-2-1852 m Ann Cole Pvt VA ★
John: b 1757 d 9-7-1816 m Ruth Ballard MarSgt NS ★
John: b 1736 d 1816 m Mary Coward Pvt MD
John: b 5-12-1753 d 3-13-1802 m Rosannah Lytle Capt NC
John: b 3-17-1734 d 3-1-1816 m Elizabeth Locke Maj PS CS NC
John: b 1736 d 1797 m Elizabeth Whitmel Williams PS NC
John: b — d a. 5-2-1796 m Margaret Edmundson Maj PA
John: b 5-24-1748 d 10-21-1826 m (1)Rebecca Smith (2)Anabella McDowell Maj PA
John: b 1-10-1737 d 9-18-1803 m Margaret (Robinson ?) Pvt PA
John: b 1747 d 7- -1810 m (1)Mary Reed (2)Martha Miskimans Pvt PA
John: b 1-5-1753 d 10-5-1818 m Martha Allison Sgt SC W★
John: b 5-31-1740 d 3-16-1801 m Jane Lowry Pvt SC
John: b 1757 d 8-25-1832 m — Pvt VA ★
Jonas: b 1740 d 7-29-1779 m Esther Maund Col PS NC
Jonas: b 10-19-1766 d 3-17-1842 m Elizabeth Tuten Pvt SC
Joseph: b 1739 d 1835 m — Sgt PA
Joseph: b 2-28-1745 d 8-15-1825 m Margaret Graham Sgt VA
Lancelot: b 4-17-1748 d 9-19-1832 m Zeruah Rice Dr NC W★
Lancelot: b 1756 d 1822 m — Pvt VA
Larkin: b 5-1-1727 d 3-16-1816 m Mary Rogers Pvt Cav VA
Lyttleton: b 2-18-1761 d 7-7-1842 m (1)Lucy Childs (2)Sarah Dirby Cpl NC
Matthew: b 1731 d 8-26-1806 m Ann — Sol PA
Michael: b 4-19-1764 d 10-12-1842 m Sarah Atkinson Pvt NH ★
Nathan: b 1740 d 1800 m Elizabeth Henry Capt SC
Peter: b 1735 d 9-13-1798 m (1)Jane Mundle (2)Susannah Johnson (3)Mrs. Benedict Pvt NY
Peter: b 10-15-1762 d 4-14-1835 m Anna Drieslein Cpl PA
Peter: b 1-6-1763 d 12-8-1831 m (1)Mary Wood (2)Ann Barnard Lt VA W★
Philip: b 8-27-1741 d 8-1-1776 m Rachel Stewart Col NJ
Philip: b c. 1750 d 1-15-1799 m Elizabeth Ann Taylor Maj VA
Randolph: b 1759 d 1846 m (3)Mary Holcombe Pvt NC
Richard: b 1760 d 10-29-1834 m Elizabeth Mullen Pvt VA ★
Robert: b 1745 d p. 1791 m Ann Haughabout Pvt NJ
Robert: b c. 1738 d p. 1785 m Jane Graham Pvt PA
Robert: b 1730 d 1-26-1803 m Amie Willson Newburn Pvt PA
Robert: b 1750 d 11-25-1808 m Eliza Sproul Dr PA
Robert: b 9-13-1739 d 2-29-1824 m (1)Abigail Hadlock (2)Abigail Way (3)Jane Bell (4)Mrs. Hepzibah (Tyler) Bell Sct LCol VT
Samuel: b 1756 d 1794 m Sarah Sage Adj CT
Samuel: b 1748 d 4- -1803 m Mary Powers CMman PA
Samuel: b 1706 d 1785 m (1)Sarah Oakley (2)Mary Crazier CS PS NC
Samuel: b 12-22-1748 d 5-6-1825 m Elizabeth Miller Dean Pvt NY ★
Samuel: b 1729 d 4-4-1779 m Mary Sproul Sgt PA
Samuel: b c. 1750 d p. 1795 m — Pvt PA
Thomas: b 3-28-1735 d 4-28-1811 m (1)Mary McFarland (2)Anne Sproul Pvt MA
Thomas: b c. 1720 d 1804/5 m Rebecca — 1Maj NC
Thomas: b 1744 d 12- -1819 m Martha Beatty Capt PA
Thomas: b a. 1740 d 10- -1813 m Mary Patton 1Lt PA
Thomas: b 1-20-1751 d 2-5-1829 m Anna Houston Pvt PA
Thomas: b c. 1753 d 1830 m Martha Glenn Pvt PA
Thomas: b 1754 d 1820 m Mary Rankin Pvt PA
Thomas: b c. 1760 d a. 3-7-1825 m Winnifred — Pvt SC
Wm.: b 1756 d 7-1-1819 m Mary Elmsley Matr MA
Wm.: b 8-11-1751 d 2-10-1843 m Deborah Ayres Capt NJ ★
Wm.: b 2-16-1756 d 10-18-1813 m Sarah Providence Davidson Douglass OrdlSgt NJ
Wm.: b 1713 d 1783 m Anne Witter Cummings PS NY
Wm.: b 1735 d 1-20-1798 m Elizabeth Dickey Pvt NC
Wm.: b 1737 d 5-3-1785 m Ann Hobart PS NC
Wm.: b 8-2-1752 d 1-31-1813 m Mary — Capt PA
Wm.: b 3- -1731 d 1-17-1804 m Anna Maria Sibald Sgt PA
Wm.: b 1744 d 1789 m Elizabeth Duncan Pvt NonCom PA
Wm.: b 1745 d 1825 m Mary Clugston Pvt PA

Wm.: b c. 1750 d 1792 m Rachel Davis Pvt PA
Wm.: b c. 1750 d 6-4-1829 m Elizabeth Laughlin Sol PA
Wm.: b 12-10-1749 d 5-22-1809 m Nancy Ford Pvt SC
Wm.: b 1751 d 1815 m Ann Mason Simpson Capt VA
Wm.: b 1753 d 1838 m (2)Millison Hogan Pvt VA ★
Wm.: b 1758 d 12-25-1802 m Rebecca Moseley Ens VA
Wm. Patrick: b 12-1-1748 d p. 1800 m Emily Elliott Ens MD
Windsor: b 1762 d 11-16-1853 m Miss Nichols Pvt NJ ★
Witter: b 9-30-1753 d 10-4-1839 m Jane Campbell Lt NY ★
Zachariah: b 9-26-1742 d 1-7-1800 m Ann Robertson Capt PS VA

JOHONNET,
Prince: b 7-6-1749 d 5-25-1836 m Mehitabel Emerson Pvt MA ★

JOLLEY, (includes JOLLY)
Bourland: b 1766 d 1844 m Hannah Passmore Pvt VA
David: b c. 1739 d c. 1799 m Elizabeth Kelly Pvt PA
Henry: b 12-26-1757 d 7-29-1842 m Rachel Ghriest Pvt VA ★
John: b 1737 d 3- -1781 m Sarah Palmer Lt SC W★
Joseph: b 5-25-1754 d 7-15-1831 m Sophia Crawford Sol SC
Lewis: b c. 1751 d — m — Pvt NJ
Marcus: b c. 1730 d p. 1789 m — Pvt VA
Nelson: b c. 1740 d p. 1790 m — Pvt VA
Thomas: b 5-25-1756 d 5-25-1841 m Betsey Mitchell Pvt VA

JOLLIFF, (includes JOLLIFFE)
John: b 6-18-1751 d 4-5-1777 m Mary Dragoo 1Lt VA
Wm.: b 5-30-1761 d 5-4-1827 m (1)Katherine Collins (2)Charity
   Prickett Pvt PA

JOLLS,
John: b 11-18-1743 d p. 1782 m Mary Cole Pvt RI

JONAS,
John: b —d p. 1806 m Lucy Squires Pvt NJ

JONES,
Aaron: b 12-4-1754 d 6-11-1836 m Abigail Billings Cpl MA
Aaron, Sr.: b 6-10-1723 d 4-19-1820 m (1)Silence Cutting
   (2)Elizabeth Prescott (3)Miriam Brewer Pvt MA
Aaron: b 2- -1751 d a. 10- -1783 m Nancy Clayton Sol NC
Abel: b 1757 d 9-1-1831 m Margaret Lewis Pvt DE ★
Abraham: b 1752 d 5- -1811 m Sarah Bugg Pvt CS GA
Abraham, Jr.: b 3-3-1746 d 12-1-1816 m Olive Bates Pvt MA
Abraham: b 7-19-1853 d p. 1812 m Elizabeth Bolton Pvt NJ
Abraham: b 3-5-1761 d 2-2-1851 m Margaret Garret Pvt VA ★
Abraham Parham: b 11-11-1752 d 6-28-1821 m Ann Cole 2Lt GA ★
Adam: b 1759 d 1830 m Nancy Harrison Pvt VA
Adam Crain, Jr.: b 12-10-1760 d 1-12-1807 m Margaret Swain Sol
   SC
Adonijah: b 8-20-1748 d 12-18-1820 m (1)Sarah Lyman (2)Anna
   MacElwain Sgt MA
Albridgton: b c. 1745-8 d 11- -1809 m Mary Calvert 1Lt VA
Allen: b 12-25-1739 d 11-15-1807 m (1)Mary Haynes (2)Rebecca
   Edwards BGen PS NC
Ambrose: b 8-10-1756 d 6-12-1833 m Martha Craig Cpl VA ★
Ambrose, Sr.: b c. 1740 d p. 10-8-1820 m Winnifred — PS VA
Ambrose: b c. 1745 d p. 4-9-1810 m (2)Mary Waggoner PS VA
Amos: b 7-2-1734 d 7-9-1824 m Mary Cone Capt CT
Amos: b 1-17-1748 d 9-10-1840 m Lydia — Pvt CT ★
Amos: b 7-23-1754 d 9-12-1827 m Anne Lewin Pvt MD
Amos: b 1-21-1755 d 4-24-1836 m Azubah Russell Pvt MA
Amos: b 2-11-1761 d 4-20-1842 m Mary Pattee Pvt MA ★
Anthony, Sr.: b 6-8-1723 d 4-8-1782 m Elizabeth Alden Pvt MA
Aquilla: b 1748 d 4-18-1830 m Prudence Wise Pvt VT
Asa: b 4-7-1755 d 1834 m Lucy Parks Sgt CT
Asa: b 12-12-1758 d 5-17-1846 m Mary Martin Pvt MA
Asa: b 1-9-1739 d 6-15-1810 m Sarah Treadway Lt NH
Asa: b 5-15-1740 d 11-26-1832 m Elizabeth Monell Sgt NY ★
Asaph: b 1758 d 8-31-1837 m (1)Prudence Dixon (2)Hannah —
   Pvt PA ★
Augustus: b 8-11-1752 d p. 9-10-1832 m (1)Mehitable Chapman
   (2)Hetty (Buell) Holmes Pvt CT ★
Batt: b 3-4-1754 d c. 12-18-1821 m Mary Jones 1Lt GA
Batte: b 1755 d 1797 m Margaret Ward Lt VA
Benaiah: b 8-12-1755 d 8-19-1839 m Jemima Skinner Pvt CT
Benjamin: b 1-21-1757 d 10-20-1840 m (1)Lydia Murdoch (2)Sallie
   Miles Sgt QM CT
Benjamin: b 2-5-1757 d 6-22-1821 m Esther Woodruff Pvt CT
Benjamin: b 1748 d p. 1798 m Mercy Wilder Pvt MA
Benjamin: b 2-7-1838 m (1)Tabitha Leavitt (2)Sarah
   Dillingham Pvt MA
Benjamin: b 8-13-1751 d 1-12-1819 m Elizabeth Cleves PS NH
Benjamin: b c. 1740 d — m Hannah Chesley PS NH
Benjamin: b 6-9-1724 d — m Jemima Delavan Pvt NY
Benjamin, Jr.: b 6-9-1763 d 8-10-1835 m Miriam Russ Pvt PA NY ★
Benjamin: b 1750 d 1821 m Elizabeth Foster Pvt NC
Benjamin: b 3-28-1754 d 1833 m — Ens NC VA
Benjamin: b c. 1760 d 1800 m — Sol PA
Benjamin: b 12-26-1741 d 2-7-1802 m Elizabeth — PS PA
Benjamin: b 4-25-1752 d 8-22-1843 m Elizabeth Reamey Pvt VA
Berryman: b c. 1750 d p. 1781 m — Pvt VA
Brereton: b 1-4-1716 d 1795 m Lettice Warner PS VA

Bridger: b 8-11-1759 d a. 11-1-1819 m Rachel Barry Sol NC
Cadwallader: b 1755 d 1796 m Mary Pride Maj VA
Catesby: b — d — m Lettice Corbin Tuberville Capt VA
Catlett: b 10-15-1749 d 9-6-1829 m (1)Mrs Ann Douglas Barksdale
   (2)Sarah Crew Pvt VA
Charles: b 7-1-1738 d 8-11-1807 m Catherine Cling Pvt DE
Charles: b 1705 d 1798 m Elizabeth Coats PS MD
Charles: b 2-2-1758 d 10-14-1811 m Prudence — Sol PS MD
Charles: b c. 1760 d 2-1-1822 m (1)Sara Chandler (2)Nancy Darby
   Pvt SC
Charles: b 1749 d p. 2-13-1841 m Patsy Adcock Capt VA
Charles: b 6- -1754 d p. 1795 m (2)Elizabeth Ellis PM 1Lt VA
Charles: b 1753 d p. 11-22-1838 m Frances Dorcas Thorpe Pvt VA ★
Charles Grigsby: b 6-4-1746 d a. 10-3-1805 m Winifred Rogers PS
   VA
Christopher Paul: b 1763 d 10-26-1848 m Mercy Briggs Pvt MA
Churchill: b 1723 d 1790 m — Minitree Maj VA
Cornelius: b 9-27-1741 d 1792 m Joanna Harrison Pvt NJ
Cornelius: b 9-19-1740 d 11-11-1823 m Martha — Pvt NY
Cornelius, Jr.: b 6-3-1758 d 3-26-1841 m Julianne Armstrong Pvt
   NY ★
Daniel: b a. 1740 d 3-19-1786 m Mindwell — Pvt CT
Daniel: b c. 1750 d p. 1802 m Mary Thomas Pvt DE
Daniel: b 9-25-1750 d 8-25-1819 m Bethiah Root Cpl MA
Daniel: b 7-1-1756 d 4-14-1847 m Bethany Pierce Pvt MA
Daniel: b 1-6-1751 d 9-8-1815 m Mary House Capt NC
Daniel: b 3- -1757 d 9-27-1841 m — Franklin Pvt NC ★
Daniel: b c. 1747/8 d 1795 m (1)Susannah Hardyman (2)Catherine
   (Crawley) Ward Capt VA
Daniel: b 1752 d 12-16-1822 m Mary Morris PS VA
Darling: b 1764 d 10-9-1848 m (1)Nancy J. Nelsons (2)Nancy Huff
   Pvt TN
David: b 10-1-1753 d 1-20-1804 m Kezia Filley Pvt CT
David, Sr.: b 7-27-1716 d 1-24-1795 m (1)Hannah Fox (2)Mary
   (Hall) (Pratt) Godfrey Lt MA
David, Jr.: b 2-12-1740/1 d p. 3-25-1819 m (1)Molly Bailey (2)Mrs
   Judith Lee (3)Hannah (Abbott) Bodwell Pvt MA
David: b 3-26-1749 d 3-27-1822 m Elizabeth Hobart Dr ME
David: b c. 1755 d c. 1830 m Mary — Pvt NJ
David: b 1745 d a. 3-23-1829 m Mary Brooks Lt PA
David: b 5-12-1736 d 2-5-1820 m Anne Stillwell Chp PA
David: b 12-10-1740 d 1-18-1785 m Rebecca Carter Pvt PA
David: b 8- -1709 d 9- -1784 m Elizabeth Davies PS PA
David: b 1-25-1761 d 2-7-1838 m Jane Rebal 2Sgt VA ★
David: b c. 1730-50 d p. 1-8-1817 m Sallie — PS VA
Dearing: b 1746 d 1815 m Mary Clarke MM MA
Deodate Pratt: b 6-16-1762 d 11-19-1852 m Sarah Dickerman Pvt
   CT ★
Dorothy Chamberlayne: b 1710 d 1781 m Peter Jones PS VA
Eaton, Sr.: b 1729 d 1791 m Elizabeth Catlin Lt CT
Eaton, Jr.: b 11-9-1762 d 1-5-1838 m Mary McNeil Pvt CT ★
Ebenezer: b 1752 d p. 4-3-1823 m Susannah Blackmore Cpl MA
Ebenezer: b 1763 d 2-2-1835 m Mary Vining Pvt MA ★
Ebenezer: b 4-8-1718 d p. 1779 m (1)Abigail Long (2)Zerviah Loomis
   PS MA
Ebenezer: bpt 2-3-1740 d p. 5-9-1795 m Rebeckah Stirke Pvt PA
Edmund: b 1749 d 1834 m Rachel Alston Pvt NC
Edward: b 1735 d 1790 m Sarah White PS MD
Edward: b 1741 d 9-1-1823 m Rachel Lewis 2Lt PA
Eli: b 1756 d 5-9-1811 m Anna Brown Sol MA
Elias: b c. 1760 d 3-4-1843 m (1)Jermina Darling (2)Chloe House
   Pvt MA ★
Elijah: b c. 1750 d c. 1817 m Hannah Raymond Pvt CT
Elijah: b 4-20-1756 d 7-18-1808 m Patience Fisher Sol MA
Elijah: b 1742 d 4-6-1782 m Rhoda Stoddard Cmsry MA
Eliphaz: b 5-30-1758 d 12-30-1796 m Lavinia Barber Drm CT
Elisha: b 5-23-1744 d 2-1-1810 m Elizabeth Farrar MM MA
Elisha: b 4-27-1761 d 4-17-1838 m Elizabeth Bates Pvt MA
Elisha: b 1757/8 d 10-27-1848 m — Sol VA
Elisha: b 1757 d 1817 m Sarah — Pvt VA
Elisha: b 1758 d p. 1-19-1844 m Jerusha Watson Pvt VA ★
Enoch: b 1758 d 12-15-1834 m (1)Deborah — (2)Elizabeth — Pvt
   NJ ★
Enoch: b c. 1740 d a. 1798 m Jane Boggs Pvt DE PA
Enos: b 5-31-1734 d 8-15-1803 m (1)Amplias Wadsworth
   (2)Prudence Lincoln Sgt MA
Enos: b 7-4-1742 d 12-30-1825 m Mary Whitmore Pvt MA
Erasmus: b 1743 d 9- -1811 m Frances Daley Sol VA
Etheldred: b 10-8-1749 d 10-2-1835 m Jean Lane Capt NC
Evan: b c. 1730 d 1790-4 m Tamer — PS SC
Ezekiel: b 3-29-1731 d 11-30-1791 m Mindwell Beach Fif CT
Ezekiel: b 7-5-1754 d 10-10-1833 m Hannah Holly Cpl MA ★
Ezekiel: b 4-3-1764 d 11-1-1825 m Rosannah Gill Pvt NC W★
Ezra, Jr.: b 4-13-1752 d 8-11-1841 m (1)Susanna Stone (2)Esther
   Roys (3)Mary Farrar Pvt PS NH
Ezra: b 10-1-1762 d 7-24-1842 m Martha Ingraham Pvt CT
Fielding: b 1756 d 1-29-1832 m Sarah Hardin Sol VA
Frederick: b 1732 d 1797 m Jean Swann PS NC
Frederick: b 1754 d 11- -1808 m Elizabeth Best Pvt NC
Frederick: b c. 1749 d p. 6-8-1807 m Mary — PS VA
Freeman: b 1763 d 8-26-1835 m Christina Parrish Pvt NC ★
Gabriel: b c. 1740 d 1776/7 m (1)Mary Waller (2)Martha Slaughter
   Capt VA

JONES, contd.

Gabriel: b 5-17-1724 d 10-17-1806 m Margaret (Strother) Morton PS VA
George: b 1754 d 2- -1841 m Lucretia Cooke Pvt CT
George: b 1765 d 1835 m (1)Kitty Howe (2)Thankful — (3)Sicha Dawson Pvt PA ★
George: b 1753 d p. 1782 m Mary Churchman Sgt VA
George: b 6-13-1743 d p. 12-3-1828 m Phoebe Foster Pvt VA
George: b 11-17-1762 d 3- -1841 m — Foster Pvt VA ★
Gershom: b 3-10-1752 d 5-1-1809 m Desire Ely Capt RI
Gideon: b 6-6-1754 d 1-3-1824 m Lydia Wolcott Cpl MA
Gray: b 1760 d 6-13-1849 m Elizabeth Winfield Pvt VA ★
Hardy: b 1746/7 d 6-21-1819 m (1)Sarah Phillps (2)Jane Allison (3)Ann Clemmon (4)Mary Ann (Williams) Brown Doby Pvt NC
Harrison: b 10-14-1757 d 1-12-1841 m Ann Ligon Pvt VA ★
Henry: b 1-9-1727/8 d p. 9-26-1802 m Keziah — Col PS GA
Henry: b c. 1734 d 1806 m Hope Wallace Pvt NJ
Henry: bpt 4-4-1747 d 11-19-1811 m Mary Pou PS SC
Henry: b c. 1750 d 1807 m Emily Jane Carlile Pvt VA
Henry: b 12-7-1751 d 2-6-1838 m Rachel — Pvt VA ★
Hezekiah, Jr.: b 6- -1735 d 3-10-1823 m Elizabeth Bagg Pvt MA
Hezekiah: b 1730 d p. 1796 m Mary Ann Sowell Pvt NC
Holmes: b 6-15-1758 d 1810 m Susanna Morse Sgt VA
Horatio: b 11-19-1763 d 8-18-1836 m (1)Sarah Whittlemore (2)Elizabeth Starr Fif Pvt PA
Hugh: b 3-12-1748 d 12-29-1796 m Mary Hunter Cpl PA
Hugh, Jr.: b 7-7-1727 d — m Sarah Fletcher Pvt MA
Income: b 6-16-1757 d 1-19-1845 m Mary Kingsley Pvt RI ★
Isaac: b c. 1755 d 10-3-1814 m Sarah Finch Pvt CT
Isaac: b 5-6-1748 d 1-4-1823 m Mary Pond Pvt CT
Isaac: b 2-7-1756 d 1-14-1801 m Ellen Gaither Pvt MD
Isaac: b 1748 d 5-28-1834 m Anna — Pvt NY ★
Isaac: b 1755 d 1842 m (1)Mary Canada (2)Mary Faust Drm Pvt PA
Isaac: b 10-1-1756 d 8-3-1840 m Sarah Glezen Pvt RI ★
Israel, Sr.: b 3-18-1716 d 12-28-1798 m Jemima Clark Capt CT
Israel, Jr.: b 9-2-1753 d 9-1-1812 m (1)Rhoda Parsons (2)Lois Wadsworth 2Lt CT
Jacob: b 9-23-1737 d 1-20-1814 m Mary Winn Pvt MA
Jacob: b 2-15-1759 d 5-4-1839 m Hannah Jones Pvt NY W★
Jacob: b 1753 d 10-7-1848 m Martha — Pvt NC ★
Jacob: b 1732 d 1828 m Dinah Stanton Sol PA VA
James: b 9-25-1747 d 10-11-1788 m Susanna Loveland PS CT
James, Sr.: b c. 1715/16 d 5-26-1786 m Susanna Williams PS DE
James: b 4-28-1764 d 10-10-1828 m Elizabeth Mills Pvt GA
James: b — d 7-18-1839 m Anna Coolidge Sol NH
James: b 7-22-1754 d 7-26-1803 m Catherine Dennison 2Lt NY W★
James: b 1730 d 1777 m Charity Alston Capt PS NC
James: b 1752 d 1810 m Sarah (Jones) Pvt NC
James: b 1750 d 1805 m Roseanna — Pvt PS NC
James: b 7-4-1760 d 9-22-1851 m Susanna Kinkaid Pvt NC ★
James: b 11-11-1761 d 8-18-1811 m Eleanor Moulton Pvt PA
James, Jr.: b 4-6-1756 d 4-29-1830 m Mary Creighton Dr PA
James: b 3-26-1758 d 12-12-1815 m Sallie Schooler Pvt VA
James: b 4- -1759 d p. 1780 m Catherine Robinson Pvt VA
Jasper: b . 1759 d p. 1780 m Lucy Clark Cpl CT
Jehu: b 12-17-1749 d 1813 m Elizabeth Clark Pvt PS NH
Jeremiah: b 12-27-1759 d 5-31-1848 m Elizabeth Mercer Pvt SC ★
Jesse: b 10-2-1757 d 2-4-1826 m Hannah Kidder Pvt NH
Joel: b 4-16-1733 d 6-17-1792 m Margaret Day LCol CT
Joel: b 7-7-1764 d 8-11-1845 m (1)Sally Southgate (2)Rhoda Swrague Pvt MA W★
John: b 5-7-1738 d 5-7-1816 m (1)Phebe Smith (2)Sarah Burr (3)Rebecca Smith (4)Mary Keeler Lt CT
John: b 1-9-1762 d 10-8-1841 m Esther Bolles Pvt Grd CT
John: b c. 1735 d 1810 m Margaret Walker PS Col GA
John: b 1-20-1748 d 10-9-1779 m Mary Sharpe Maj ADC GA
John: b 1745 d a. 1817 m Susanna Strobhar Pvt GA
John: b 1753 d 1800 m Mary Ogletree Pvt GA
John: b 1720 d 1790 m Mary — Sol GA
John: b c. 1745 d a. 12-10-1788 m Mry Mary Powell (Brown) Sol GA
John: b 9-4-1755 d 2-7-1848 m Cassandra Chew Johns Capt MD
John: b 2-11-1757 d — m Elizabeth Dashiell Ens MD
John, Sr.: b 1711 d 1790 m Hannah Wooley PS MD
John, Jr.: b 4-9-1739 d 10-21-1785 m Ester — Pvt MD
John: b c. 1755 d 1809 m — Sol MD
John: b 12-7-1730 d 12-18-1811 m Phebe Brewer Capt MA
John, Jr.: b 2-4-1744 d 7-4-1776 m Betty Hapgood Capt MA
John: b 3-23-1744 d 1828 m Abigail Cheney Cpl MA
John, Sr.: b 7-15-1709 d 1798 m Elizabeth Gibbs Pvt MA
John, Jr.: b 11-10-1751 d 7-20-1826 m (1)Mary Belknap (2)Margaret Stone Cpl MA
John: b 6-25-1764 d 2-1-1855 m (2)Nancy Mallory Pvt MA ★
John, Sr.: b 1709 d 12-20-1792 m Mehitable — Smn MA
John, Jr.: b 1740 d 12-7-1808 m Mary — Pvt MA
John, Sr.: b 10- -1691 d 2-7-1773 m (1)Elizabeth Simpson (2)Mrs Hannah Alden (3)Mrs Mary Alden PS MA
John, Jr.: b 1-9-1721/22 d 9-5-1797 m Mary Mellen PS MA
John: b 1745 d — m Hannah Woodman QM NH
John: b 8-15-1736 d 3-7-1806 m Abigail Peck Pvt NJ
John, Sr.: b 12-22-1732 d 2-9-1808 m (1)Sarah Curry (2)Rachael — Sgt NY ★
John, Jr.: b 1761 d 12-5-1844 m Sarah Swim OrdlSgt NY ★

John: b c. 1735 d p. 7-28-1812 m Ann Williams Capt NC
John: b a. 1750 d 9-18-1794 m Mary Hubbard PS NC
John: b 1737 d a. 5-7-1816 m (1)Ann Ridgely (2)Hannah (Wood) Mitchell Pvt PA
John: b 6-24-1737 d 12-19-1795 m Jane Godfrey Maj PA
John: b 6-10-1748 d 4-24-1821 m Sydney Wynne Roberts QM Sgt PA
John: b 8-10-1756 d p. 4-15-1833 m Lina — Pvt PA ★
John: b 4-27-1748 d 4-15-1815 m (1)Hope Miller (2)Rebecca Burroughs (3)Mary (Miller) Cornell Pvt RI
John: b c. 1743 d 10-12-1796 m Margaret Benson Pvt SC
John: b 3-19-1756 d p. 3-10-1846 m Sarah Shepard Pvt SC ★
John: b 1-27-1764 d p. 1835 m Patience Hartley Pvt SC
John: b 12-14-1744 d 9- -1829 m Anna Brown Sol SC
John: b 1733 d 6-13-1813 m Hannah Tupper Pvt VT
John: b 1728 d 1793 m Elizabeth Monroe Col VA
John, Sr.: b 2-14-1735 d 6-11-1803 m Elizabeth Binns PS CS VA
John: b 1-26-1740 d 1797 m Frances Barber Jones Capt VA
John: b c. 1743 d p. 1797 m Ann Shackleford Sgt VA
John: b 1746 d 1842 m (1)Annie Norman (2)Judith Lynch Pvt VA
John: b 5-8-1750 d 9-16-1841 m Barshaba — Pvt VA ★
John: b 2-2-1755 d 1-7-1838 m Frances Morris Pvt Spy VA ★
John, Jr.: b 3-30-1764 d 1845 m (1)Lucy Binns Cargill (2)Mrs Esther Moore Pvt VA
John: b 1766 d 1836 m (2)Mrs (Leftridge) Tinder Pvt VA ★
John Gabriel: b 6-6-1752 d 12-25-1776 m Elizabeth — PS Sol VA
John K.: b 6-15-1747 d 12-11-1835 m Deborah — Pvt PA
Jonathan, Jr.: b 1-23-1750 d 9-18-1836 m (1)Mrs Susannah Parker (2)Mrs Bethier Fletcher (3)Abigail Wright Sgt MA
Jonathan: b 3-24-1737 d 3-16-1783 m Sarah Wheeler Pvt MA
Jonathan: b 8-11-1746 d 7-30-1814 m Mary Ball CS MA
Jonathan: b 1738 d 9-26-1782 m Margaret Davis LCol PA
Joseph: b 1750 d 8-16-1832 m Abigail Seward Pvt CT ★
Joseph: b c. 1748 d p. 9-16-1836 m Ann — PS MD
Joseph: b 9-12-1752 d 10-2-1834 m Lucena Barnes Sgt MA ★
Joseph, Jr.: b c. 11-1-1734 d 1-29-1816 m Lurena Cornwall Pvt MA
Joseph: b 9-29-1737 d 8-22-1799 m Ruth Nelson Pvt MA
Joseph: bpt 7-25-1742 d 1787 m Dorothy Haley Pvt CS ME
Joseph: b 2-21-1757 d 3-3-1835 m Anna Harmon Pvt MA
Joseph: b 10-1-1702 d 5- -1782 m Mary Prouse PS NH
Joseph II: b 11-17-1739 d 1816 m Phoebe Harrison Sgt NJ
Joseph: b c. 1750 d 1793 m — PS NC
Joshua: b 1750 d a. 1811 m Mary — Pvt MD
Joshua: b c. 1760 d 1-11-1830 m Sarah Burns Pvt NH W★
Joshua: b 1756 d 1820 m Amaryllis — CS PS Arfr NC
Joshua: b 8- -1760 d p. 6-20-1845 m Mary Sech Pvt PA ★
Joshua: b 10-9-1760 d 10-5-1823 m Eleanor Thomas Pvt PA
Joshua: b c. 1750 d p. 3-20-1808 m Sarah Whitmore Pvt SC
Joshua: b 5-5-1739 d 11-8-1816 m Hannah Todhunter Sol VA ★
Joshua: b 4-25-1761 d 1-6-1844 m Mary — Pvt VA ★
Josiah: b 10-4-1725 d 4-22-1795 m Mabel Woodbridge Sgt MA
Josiah: b 9-5-1735 d p. 1790 m Sarah Annice Pvt MA
Lazarus: b 11-21-1752 d 11- -1836 m Betsy Buzzell Pvt MA
Lemuel: b 5-5-1729 d a. 1783 m Anna Stimson Pvt MA
Levi: b 9-23-1749 d 3-17-1807 m Rhoda Avery Pvt CT
Lewis: b c. 1750 d p. 9-20-1803 m Cherry — Sol NC
Lewis: b c. 1750 d p. 8-29-1799 m (2)Milly Chilton Lt VA W★
Luke: b 12-13-1751 d 12-23-1838 m Eleanor Condon Pvt MA
Matthew: b c. 1748 d 1793 m Elizabeth — Maj PS NC
Matthew: b 3-18-1758 d 7-18-1836 m Mary Crumpler Pvt VA ★
Meredith: b 1722 d 1788 m Elizabeth Fusman Pvt NJ
Michael: b c. 1750-5 d 1794 m (2)Mrs Sabina (Symmes) Thomas Sgt PA
Michael: b 1760 d p. 1800 m Leeana Dibrell Pvt VA
Miles: b 1764 d 4-17-1812 m Mehitable Adams Pvt MA
Morris: b 1757 d 2-13-1847 m (1)Sarah — (2)Deziah — Sgt CT ★
Morton: b 8-10-1747 d 11-8-1841 m Frances Foster Sgt VA ★
Moses: b 12-15-1762 d 11-21-1835 m Mary Scott MM NJ
Moses: b 9- -1762 d c. 1852 m Elizabeth — Pvt NC ★
Moses: b — d 1-1-1830 m Mary Florence Sol VA
Musgrove: b 10-30-1761 d p. 3-26-1850 m Elizabeth — Pvt NC ★
Nathan: b 12-30-1731 d 1822 m Elizabeth Bidwell Sgt CT
Nathan, Jr.: b 2- -1763/4 d 1-12-1847 m Priscilla Brown Pvt CT
Nathan: b 1760 d 1807 m Cartna — Sol GA
Nathan: b 11-3-1760 d 8-20-1856 m Ann Brittania Buxton Pvt MD
Nathan, Sr.: b 4-13-1721 d 9-2-1799 m Elizabeth Coburn PS NH
Nathan, Jr.: b 2-25-1748 d 11-6-1813 m Mrs Mary Bradford PS NH
Nathan: b 6-29-1757 d 11-26-1824 m Temperance Sawyer Pvt NY
Nathaniel: b 12-22-1745 d 178- m Susanna Harris Pvt MA
Nathaniel: b — d 9-1-1779 m Sarah Dodge Dr MA
Nathaniel: b 1745 d 2-8-1815 m Amelia Blanchard PS NC
Nehemiah: b 6-17-1760 d 12-19-1838 m Anna Pomeroy Pvt MA
Noah: b 9-12-1758 d 9-24-1850 m Deborah Holbrook Pvt MA NH
Noble Wimberly: b 1723 d 1-9-1805 m Sarah Davis PS GA
Oliver: b 2-5-1738/9 d 8-11-1820 m Hannah Wooly Sgt MA
Oliver: b 5-6-1762 d 10-4-1816 m Dorothy Clement Pvt MA
Paul: b 10-4-1737 d 9-16-1821 m — Pvt PA
Peter: b 1760 d 7-3-1842 m Mary Branson Pvt MD
Peter: b 1747 d 12-10-1795 m Elizabeth Rose Pvt PA
Peter: b 1758 d 1820 m Cassandra — 1Lt PA
Peter: b 10-10-1749 d 11-24-1809 m Catherine Kirlin Pvt PA
Peter: b 1752 d 1829 m Rebecca Scott Pvt PA
Peter: b 11-17-1720 d 1799 m Sarah Tanner Pvt VA

Peter: b 4-15-1751 d 1-24-1815 m Jane Stokes Sol VA
Peter: b 11-2-1733 d p. 9-24-1796 m Martha Jones Sol VA
Peter: b c. 1748 d p. 1792 m Catharine — Pvt VA
Philip: b 7-16-1759 d 11-6-1789 m Eliza Jones Pvt GA
Phillip: b 7-12-1752 d 10-1-1831 m Elizabeth Dowden Pvt PS MD
Phineas: b 2-17-1762 d 5-13-1850 m Lucy Baldwin Sol MA
Rees: b 7-10-1749 d 12-25-1801 m Charity Britton Pvt PA
Reuben: b 10-5-1766 d 2-1-1836 m Rebecca Golding Sol Wgn SC
Richard: b 2-2-1757 d 4-18-1821 m Susannah Culver Pvt MD W★
Richard: b — d p. 12-17-1792 m Elizabeth Maloon MM PS MA
Richard: b — d 1790 m Sara Hunt Pvt NJ
Richard: b 1755 d 1819 m Hester VanBibber Pvt NY
Richard: b 4-2-1737 d 1781 m Hannah Harper Pvt PA
Richard Lord: b 5-15-1767 d 7-23-1852 m Elizabeth Clarke Fif CT ★
Robert: b 3- -1766 d 11-15-1838 m Susan Grant Allen Pvt GA
Robert: b 1753/4 d 1803/4 m Ann Ward Sgt VA
Robert Strattell: b 7-21-1745 d 3-16-1792 m Ann Shippen PS PA
Roger: b c. 1732 d p. 1783 m Elizabeth — Capt MD
Roger: b 12-3-1756 d 4- -1808 m (1)Hannah Case (2)Acenath
  Dennison Sol NY
Rowland: b 4-19-1738 d p. 1810 m Anne Crawford Sol VA
Russell: b c. 1745 d 1828 m Sarah — Sol GA
Samuel: b 5-15-1752 d 7-9-1836 m Parthenia Patterson Vol Of NY
Samuel: b 12-3-1759 d 6-26-1847 m Talitha Bishop Pvt CT ★
Samuel: b 10-31-1754 d 8-18-1813 m Huldah Pepoon Fif CT
Samuel: b 7-31-1749 d 3-29-1822 m Ruth Ackley Pvt CT
Samuel: b 6-15-1740 d p. 1786 m Hannah Adams Cpl PA
Samuel: b 2-3-1747 d 5-9-1824 m Mary Richards Sol MA
Samuel: b 8-25-1742 d 4- -1835 m (1)Sarah Pratt (2)Mrs Mercy
  Haskell Pvt MA
Samuel: b 11-18-1746 d 1-22-1820 m Anna Gates Pvt MA
Samuel: bpt 3-17-1759 d 2-20-1833 m Rachel Haynes Pvt MA
Samuel, Sr.: b 10-27-1707 d 6-7-1802 m Sarah Hubbard CS MA
Samuel: b 12-19-1746 d p. 1809 m Hannah Hoar Pvt PS NH
Samuel: b 3-6-1759 d 7-16-1831 m Elizabeth Hawkins Sgt NJ
Samuel: b 1726 d — m Abigail — Wgm NJ
Samuel: b — d 7-22-1779 m Hannah Jackson Capt PS NY
Samuel: b 1761 d 10-8-1849 m Elizabeth Thurston Pvt NY ★
Samuel: b 7-26-1734 d 11-21-1819 m (1)Eleanor Turk (2)Cornelia
  Haring PS NY
Samuel: b 10- -1755 d 10- -1831 m Elizabeth Goodloe Capt NC W★
Samuel: b 6-24-1747 d 10-28-1781 m Patience Barden Lt NC
Samuel: b 1-14-1735 d 2-7-1814 m Sylvia Spicer Chp PA
Samuel: b 9-22-1756 d 1-20-1847 m (1)Elizabeth Middleton
  (2)Elizabeth Welsh (3)Elizabeth Hilton Pvt SC
Samuel: b 1750 d 6-6-1816 m Patsey Eans Capt VA
Samuel: b 1742 d 1810 m Leah Thomas Capt VA
Samuel: b — d 4- -1784 m Mary Giles Sol VA
Samuel: b 7- -1762 d 1837 m Elizabeth Reeves Pvt VA ★
Samuel Paine: b 1758 d 5-1-1819 m Pernelia Hayden Pvt MA ★
Seaborn: b 6-15-1759 d 7-24-1815 m (1)Sarah H. Wilkinson (2)Mrs
  Elizabeth Cooper Harris Pvt GA
Seth: b 3-21-1748 d 4-27-1827 m Mary Dagget Pvt MA
Seth: b 9-28-1755 d 9-10-1824 m (1)Sarah Pitts (2)Esther Ford Pvt
  MA NY ★
Silas: b 5-7-1738 d p. 1790 m Beulah Stone Pvt MA
Silas: b 5-26-1760 d 10-14-1832 m Mercy Scriven Pvt RI ★
Simon: b c. 1750 d a. 8-12-1797 m Sarah Winter PS NC
Simpson: b 4-7-1756 d 6-28-1825 m (1)Abigail Hammond (2)Mrs
  Mercy (Holbrook) Hill Cpl MA
Solomon: b 4-20-1742 d 2-18-1806 m Bulah Stratton Sgt MA
Solomon: b 8-19-1758 d p. 1801 m Hannah Gates Pvt MA
Solomon: b 1-26-1759 d 1-27-1842 m Olive Bristol Pvt MA
Solomon: b — d 1793 m Sarah Scarrett (Lewis) Pvt VA
Stephen: b 1-13-1746 d 12-17-1811 m Anna Brooks Sgt MA
Stephen: b 1-8-1762 d 3-1-1846 m (1)Martha Ricker (2)Mehitable
  Moody Pvt Mar PS MA W★
Stephen: b 8-19-1750 d 1836 m — Pvt NC ★
Strother: b 1758 d 4-11-1790 m Frances Thornton Pvt VA
Sylvanus: b 6-10-1755 d 12- -1840 m Ruby Taber Sol MA
Sylvester: b 9-6-1738 d p. 1785 m (1)Deborah Linkhorn (2)Mercy
  Lincoln (3)Marcy Pratt Lt MA
Theophilus: b c. 1735 d p. 9-6-1794 m Grace — Pvt NY
Thomas: b 1749 d 8-19-1828 m Sarah Fling Sgt CT ★
Thomas: b 6-6-1751 d 6-13-1832 m Susannah Adams Pvt CT
Thomas: b 1-9-1750 d 8- -1854 m Rebecca Smith Pvt DE
Thomas: b c. 1750 d 2- -1805 m (2)Sarah — Sol GA
Thomas: b 3-12-1735 d 9-27-1812 m (1)Elizabeth Baxter (2)Mrs
  Elizabeth McClure Maj MD
Thomas: b 1723 d 3-24-1808 m Elizabeth Fells Col MD
Thomas: b 3-24-1747 d 8-7-1830 m Alice Morris Cpl MD
Thomas: b 11-4-1742 d 2-19-1808 m Sarah Lane Sgt MA
Thomas: b 5-29-1730 d 2-7-1802 m Berthia Whitney Pvt MA
Thomas: b 1739 d 2-14-1825 m Sarah Bush Pvt MA
Thomas: b 2-23-1756 d 1830 m Lydia Rockwood Pvt MA ★
Thomas: b 5-21-1732 d 1823 m Hannah Gardner Ens NH ★
Thomas: b 1741 d 2-6-1835 m (1)Sarah Mead (2)Mary — Pvt NH ★
Thomas: b 1750 d 1825 m Martha Dickey Adj NJ
Thomas: b p. 1737 d p. 6-20-1807 m Mary Jones Dep Cmsry NY
Thomas: b 1-13-1737 d 1810 m Sarah Bunch Lt NC
Thomas: b c. 1730 d 12-1-1820 m Sarah Butler PS NC
Thomas: b 2-11-1736 d 10-25-1802 m Mrs Arabella (Hamilton)
  Erwin Pvt PA

Thomas, Jr.: b 1742 d 3- -1800 m Mary Bromfield PS PA
Thomas: b c. 1740 d a. 2-25-1785 m Catherine Littleton Capt SC
Thomas, Jr.: b a. 12-5-1733 d p. 1787 m Mary Burnett Capt VA
Thomas: b 11-6-1754 d 1826 m Elizabeth Johns Ens VA
Thomas, Sr.: b a. 1746 d 1787 m Mary — Lt PS VA
Thomas, Sr.: b 12-25-1726 d 1785/6 m Sallie Skelton CS VA
Thomas, Jr.: b 1760 d 1800 m (2)Frances Carter Lt VA
Thomas: b 1755 d 7-8-1835 m Catherine Clarkson 1Lt VA ★
Thomas: b 1748 d 8-26-1839 m Lavinia Thomas Pvt VA
Thomas: b 1751 d 1832 m Ann Thompson Sol VA
Tignal, Sr.: b 11-25-1720 d — m Penelope Cain LCol CS PS NC
Timothy: b 3-11-1748 d 6-1-1804 m Rebecca Bateman Lt MA
Timothy: b — d 1785 m Judith Gilman Pvt NH
Vinkler: b c. 1759 d 1817 m Elizabeth Armistead PS NC
Vinson: b a. 1755 d p. 1804 m — Sol VA
Walter: b 12-15-1753 d 1815 m Alice Flood Dr VA
Wilie: b 12-24-1740 d 6-18-1801 m Mary E. Montford PS NC
Wm.: bpt 7-15-1759 d 3-17-1850 m (1)Hannah Mead (2)Elizabeth
  White Pvt CT ★
Wm.: b 11- -1744 d 10-4-1801 m Mary Ghiseling Pvt DE
Wm.: b 1762 d 1834 m (1)Elizabeth Eubanks (2) — Grinage (3)Mary
  Grinage Sol GA
Wm.: b — d 1825 m Elizabeth Mastin Pvt GA
Wm.: b c. 1737 d 1796 m Elizabeth Gregg Pvt MD
Wm.: b 1724 d 9-28-1811 m (1)Margaret Huston (2)Mrs Jane
  (Rogers) Young Col MA
Wm.: b 11-8-1760 d 11-29-1833 m Dorothy Blair Pvt MA
Wm.: b 8-23-1724 d p. 1790 m Rebecca Jenkins PS NH
Wm.: b 4-5-1757 d 4-6-1839 m Abigail Moores Pvt NJ ★
Wm.: b 1754 d 10-28-1831 m Jane McCord Pvt PA
Wm.: b — d — m Margaret Fitz Randolph Pvt PA
Wm.: b 10-8-1734 d — m — Capt RI
Wm.: b 10-31-1735 d 1823 m Mary Whittlock Sol SC
Wm.: b 1754 d 1806 m Martha Hughes PS Capt VA
Wm.: b c. 1755 d 5-20-1816 m (2)Mrs Nancy Thorp Mead 1Lt VA
Wm.: b 11-17-1756 d 2-15-1841 m (1)Mary Hancom (2)Emilia
  Patterson Sgt VA ★
Wm.: b 1750 d 1830 m Patsy Brown Pvt VA
Wm.: b 12-13-1759 d 7-24-1834 m Mary Fishback Pvt VA ★
Wm.: b 1745 d 3-15-1781 m Agnes Walker Sol VA
Wm. Clark: b 5-9-1760 d 9-25-1841 m (1)Elizabeth Hayes
  (2)Rebecca Rolland (3)Lorany Brockway Cpl CT ★
Willis: b 1753 d 10-15-1778 m Hannah Sikes Pvt NC
Wood: b c. 1710-20 d a. 10-22-1783 m (2)Amey (Jones) Watson
  Capt VA
Zachariah: b 1761 d 1814 m Mary Rennick Pvt VA
Zebediah: b 3-12-1753 d 8-2-1823 m Mrs Joanna Goodhue Cpl MA
Zebulon, Jr.: b 3-19-1747 d 11-25-1836 m Mary Cooley Pvt VT ★

JOPLIN,
Josiah: b 1747 d 1797 m Elizabeth Ware MM VA
Thomas: b 5- -1708 d 1-17-1789 m Hannah — Capt VA

JORALEMON,
James: bpt 2-9-1752 d 8-24-1834 m Mary Kingsland Lt NJ

**JORDAN, (includes JAUDAN, JAUDON, JORDON, JOURDAN &
JURDEN)**
Abner: b 1760 d 1819 m Hannah Wentworth Pvt MA
Absalom: b c. 1745 d p. 9-23-1824 m Mary Ann — PS VA
Amos: b c. 1762 d 8-5-1843 m Sarah Davis Pvt PA
Arthur: b 1720 d 1793 m Elizabeth Turner Pvt NC
Benjamin: b 1738 d 1814 m Hannah Weiman Lt MA
Benjamin: b c. 1754 d 1786 m Elizabeth — Lt NC
Benjamin: b c. 1745 d 1807-1810 m Isabella Potter Ens PA
Benjamin: b 3-19-1760 d 7-18-1845 m Mary Walker Pvt Fif RI ★
Benjamin Allen: b 1749 d p. 1783 m Sarah Trundy Sol ME
Charles: b 6- -1749 d 8-31-1832 m (1)Anne — (2)Elizabeth Lockett
  (3)Frances — Pvt GA
Clement: b 4-12-1720 d 4-5-1789 m (1)Elizabeth Allen (2)Mrs Sarah
  Gray Dunham (3)Sarah Wentworth Dr CS MA
David: b 4-12-1761 d 5-30-1847 m Temperance Russell Pvt MA ★
David: b 1758 d 3- -1822 m Mary Braun Pvt PA
Dominicus: b 4-5-1740 d 1834 m Susanna Simonton Pvt PS MA
Ebenezer: b 1742 d p. 1788 m (1)Lucy Tarbox (2)Judith Trewargy Cpl
  Matr MA
Edmund: b 1762 d 8-6-1840 m Rebecca — Pvt MA ★
Edmund: b 1761 d 12- -1836 m Polly Ridley Pope Cpl VA
Edward: b c. 1745 d p. 7-21-1820 m Susanna — Capt VA
Eleazer: b a. 1750 d 1820 m Phebe — Pvt NH ★
Elias: b 5-17-1739 d 7-18-1809 m Mary Dixon Sol SC
Ezekiel: b 1749 d 1818 m Mary Simonton 2Lt MA
Fleming: b 2-12-1763 d 8-12-1837 m Martha Gaines Moore Sol GA
Francis: b 8-19-1733 d 11-12-1804 m Catherine Kendall Pvt PA
Frederick: b 9- -1744 d 8-20-1784 m Catherine Eckel Sgt NJ
George: b c. 1731 d a. 6- -1792 m (1)Patience Warren (2)Hannah
  Smith PS NC
George: b 1-26-1754 d 3-1-1842 m Martha Jordan Pvt VA ★
Henry L.: b c. 1755 d c. 1831 m Francis Rives Pvt VA
Hezekiah: b 9-9-1759 d 5-16-1828 m Eunice Davis Pvt MA ★
Hugh: b 10- -1757 d 1840 m Ann Polk Pvt MD ★
Israel: b 1712 d 1782-6 m Susanna Thorndike Pvtr Mstr Mrnr MA
Jacob: b 1764 d 2-22-1849 m Mary Ann Swiver Sol PA

JORDAN, contd.
James: b 1716 d p. 11-10-1778 m Phoebe Mitchell Matr MA
James, Jr.: b 1746 d 3- -1813 m Hannah Roberts Pvt MA W★
James: b 10-17-1757 d 9-20-1835 m Elizabeth McKenney Pvt MA
James: b 8- -1759 d 3-15-1844 m Margaret Armstrong Pvt NJ ★
James: b c. 1759 d a. 9- -1796 m Barbara Cole Sol NC
James: b c. 1725 d 1802 m Mrs Margaret Miller Cmsry SC
James: b 11-15-1755 d 7-9-1835 m Mary McElwayne Pvt SC ★
James: b 1-17-1745 d 12-1-1807 m Eleanor Sara Anderson PS SC
James: b 1743 d 1790 m Margaret Galloway Pvt VA
James, Sr.: b c. 1745 d p. 1813 m Sarah — PS VA
Jeremiah: b 1753 d 1840 m (1)Ruth Chute (2)Mrs Rebecca Rice Pvt MA
John: b 12-8-1752 d 3-19-1813 m Rebecca Dyer Pvt MA
John: b c. 1754 d 1812 m Hannah McNeal Sgt NH
John: b c. 1758 d p. 1845 m Mary — Pvt NJ ★
John: b 1736 d 1798 m Elizabeth Smith PS NC
John: b c. 1755 d 8- -1799 m Sarah — PS NC
John: b c. 1730 d 12-6-1799 m (1)Mary — (2)Mrs Agnes Steel Capt PA
John: b 10-25-1755 d 5-4-1835 m Catharine Beale Capt PA W★
John: b 4-10-1757 d 12-24-1835 m Katherine Scherer Pvt PA ★
John: b — d p. 3-10-1808 m Sarah — Capt VA
John: b 5-8-1756 d 8-20-1828 m Winifred Jordon Sol VA
Joshua: b 1752 d 1800 m Abigail Hatch Pvt MA
Josiah: b 8-1-1760 d 8-9-1840 m (1)Abigail Farrar (2)Esther Caryl (3)Asenath Reid Pvt Matr MA ★
Mark: b 5- -1761 d 5-2-1833 m Eve Ann Bloom Pvt PA
Melatiah: b 12-2-1753 d 12-22-1818 m Elizabeth Jellison Pvt MA
Nathaniel, Sr.: b 12-24-1718 d p. 1779 m Hannah Woodbury LCol MA
Nathaniel, Jr.: b 1757 d p. 1807 m Joanna Sawyer Pvt MA
Reuben: b 1756 d p. 4-23-1812 m (1)Ann Howard (2)Jeannette Harvie PS VA
Rishworth: b 1719 d 4-18-1808 m Abigail Gerrish CS ME
Robert: b 5-17-1748 d 3-2-1835 m (1)Hannah Hill (2)Catherine Redding Pvt NY ★
Samuel: b 1744 d 5-10-1809 m Sarah Jackson Pvt MA
Samuel: b 2-7-1707 d 7-21-1789 m (1)Ruth Meredith (2)Judith (Scott) Ware Col CS PS VA
Solomon: b 4-20-1755 d 1815 m Sarah Staples Sol MA
Samuel: b 1752 d 1800 m Abigail Hatch Pvt MA
Solomon: b 9- -1756 d 3-4-1846 m Lydia Russell Cpl MA ★
Thomas, Sr.: b c. 1720 d p. 2-6-1790 m Ann — PS MD
Thomas: b 4-5-1747 d 4-15-1850 m Rebecca Starbuck Ens PA ★
Thomas: b — d 11-8-1819 m (1)Miss — Hood (2)Ann Steele PM PA
Thomas: b c. 1758 d 1850 m Priscilla Applewhite Pvt VA
Timothy: b 10-19-1764 d 1849 m Esther Mann Pvt MA ★
Tristram: b 1743 d p. 1790 m Hannah Lassell Sgt MA
Tristram: b 1743 d p. 1790 m Hannah Lassell Sgt MA
— (3)Hannah Frost Col MA
Wm.: b 1747 d — m Comfort Palmer Pvt CT MA
Wm.: b 3-31-1744 d 9-23-1826 m Annie Medlock Sol GA
Wm.: b 9-2-1751 d 6-10-1833 m Ruth Ferris Sol NY
Wm.: b 1750 d 1819 m Emily Garrett Pvt NC
Wm.: b 2-15-1709 d 10-29-1787 m Mildred Hill PS NC
Wm.: b c. 1753-6 d p. 2-15-1817 m (1)Elizabeth Woodson (2)Lucy Stith Capt VA
Wm.: b 1765 d 1810-20 m — Sol VA
Wm.: b 10-5-1748 d 7-24-1822 m Sarah Wood Pvt VA

JOSEPH,
Daniel: b c. 1759 d p. 1799 m Eve Hanger Pvt VA
Wm.: b c. 1746 d 6-30-1828 m Sarah Stafford Sol VA

JOSSELYN, (includes JOCELYN, JOSLEN, JOSLIN & JOSLYN)
Abijah: b 1-24-1745 d 9-1-1811 m Kezia Farrar PS CS Capt MA
Abraham, Sr.: b 11-18-1717 d 5-28-1778 m (1)Mary Soule (2)Mary Bolyston Pvt MA
Asa: b 12-13-1749 d 12-25-1832 m Keziah Morse Pvt MA
Benjamin: b 7-31-1728 d 10-7-1801 m Abigail Barrett Pvt CT
Benjamin: b 6-2-1753 d 1-26-1846 m Susanna Robinson Cpl CT
Charles: b 5-7-1739 d 11-21-1812 m Rebecca Keen Pvt MA
Darius: b 8-22-1751 d p. 1790 m Sibyl Herrick Pvt MA
David: b 8-24-1760 d 1- -1844 m Catherine Snell Pvt CT ★
David: b 4-25-1765 d 4-9-1825 m Rebecca Richardson Cpl MA ★
Ebenezer: b 11-2-1732 d 9-11-1806 m Lydia Church Pvt MA
Eleazer: b 9-14-1762 d 1838 m Bethia Bourne Pvt MA
Elias, Sr.: b 4-29-1763 d 12-10-1824 m Prudence Lincoln Pvt MA
Gideon: b 3-1-1724 d 10-18-1795 m Sarah Merrill Pvt MA
Henry: b 4-24-1748 d 3-14-1813 m Mary Tefft Pvt RI
Hezekiah: b 2-18-1757 d 2-13-1836 m Chloe Hall Pvt Smn MA ★
Isaac: b 11-4-1743 d p. 12-2-1814 m Lois Ramsdell Pvt CS MA
Jabez: b 1744 d 1828 m Lydia Seward Pvt MA
James: b 7-31-1747 d 7-12-1824 m Mary Daby Pvt MA
John, Sr.: b 12-10-1710 d 8-1-1788 m Lucy Wilder Capt MA
John, Jr.: b 9-17-1735 d 9-6-1810 m (1)Susannah Carter (2)Martha Wilder (3)Mrs Martha Phelps Capt MA
John: b 3-30-1761 d 9-18-1845 m Lucy Lowden Cpl MA ★
John: b 9-9-1734 d 10-25-1811 m (1)Joanna Andrews (2)Content — PS RI
John: d 1739 d p. 6-29-1793 m Dianah — Cpl VA
Joseph: b 3-18-1753 d 3-7-1819 m Dorothy Osgood MM MA

Joseph, Jr.: b 3-12-1757 d p. 1804 m Debra Hatch Pvt MA
Joseph: b 4-9-1759 d 8-1-1843 m Lydia Bucklin Pvt Tms CT
Lindsey: b 8-12-1749 d 8-12-1826 m (1)Susan Welch (2)Mrs Richards Pvt MA
Nathaniel: b 7-6-1722 d 5-2-1790 m Sarah Low Pvt MA
Nathaniel: b 11-11-1729 d 5-27-1806 m Martha Fairbanks Pvt MA
Peter, Sr.: b 12-13-1730 d 1802 m Elizabeth Greenleaf Pvt MA
Peter, Jr.: b 10-12-1759 d 12-12-1837 m Sarah Kidder Pvt MA ★
Reuben: b 8-9-1755 d 4-10-1834 m Mary Rice Pvt CT
Zebediah: b 1753 d 11-27-1828 m Hannah Hale Sgt MA W★

JOST,
Johan: b 1695 d 8-26-1775 m Catherine — PS NY

JOURNEY, (includes JOURNEAY)
John: b c. 1725 d 1803 m (1)Martha — (2)Patience Cole PS NY
Joseph: b 2-16-1755 d 7-2-1797 m Margaret Magee Pvt NJ

JOUVET,
Wm. Louis: b 7-13-1751 d 8-31-1815 m Mary Downer Arfr FrA RI

JOY,
Abiather: b 3-20-1762 d 7-31-1851 m Elizabeth Burt Pvt VT ★
Amos: b 5-27-1761 d 1837 m Rachel Fletcher Pvt VT
Asa: b 5-21-1754 d 11-14-1820 m Mary Blanchard Pvt MA
Benjamin: b 1-25-1741 d 6-3-1830 m Rebecca Smith Sgt ME
Benjamin, Sr.: b 9-14-1712 d 11-27-1809 m (1)Sarah Sawyer (2)Phoebe Parsons PS MA
Daniel: b c. 1724 d 6-20-1784 m Mary McElroy Capt PS PA
David, Jr.: b 7-5-1754 d 3-7-1813 m Hannah Partridge Pvt CT
David, Jr.: b 3-31-1743 d 3-15-1812 m (1)Phebe Coffin (2)Phebe C. Meader Pvt MA
David: d c. 1738 d 9-12-1820 m (1)Mrs Margaret (Torrey) White (2)Mrs Lydia Blanchard 1Lt MA
David, Sr.: b 12-16-1724 d 1809 m Elizabeth Allen Pvt MA
Edward: b 1750 d 1819 m Mary Macklin Pvt PA
Francis: b 3-2-1739 d 8-31-1822 m Phebe Folger CS MA
Jacob, Sr.: b 1734 d 1812 m Jerusha Ripley Pvt MA
Jacob, Jr.: b 3- -1760 d 6-18-1839 m Susanna Snow Pvt MA
Jared: b 12-19-1749 d 2- -1803 m Olive (Litchfield) Lincoln Pvt MA
Micah: b 1753 d 7-9-1826 m Mercy Tirrell Sgt VT MA
Nathaniel: b 1759 d 7-9-1833 m Sarah Ward Pvt MA
Nehemiah, Sr.: b 8-30-1726 d 9-11-1802 m (1)Miriam Turner (2)Mrs Susannah Joy Sol MA
Nehemiah, Jr.: b 8-21-1757 d 5-5-1830 m Hannah — Sgt MA
Samuel: b 9-21-1742 d 4-4-1829 m Lydia Hamilton Pvt MA W★
Thomas: b 11-28-1762 d 10-21-1820 m Polly Day Pvt MA

JOYAL,
John B.: b 1744 d 12-18-1848 m Mary — Pvt NY ★

JOYCE,
Edward: b 1746 d 1807 m Elizabeth Hopkins Pvt VA
Henry: b 1755/6 d 3-11-1826 m Martha Stafford Pvt SC
John: b c. 1760 d 1833 m — Pvt SC
Seth: b c. 1731 d 7-4-1788 m Abigail Thomas Pvt MA

JOYNER, (includes JOINER)
Edward: b 1742 d 5- -1814 m Mary Munn Pvt MA
Henry: b 1734 d 1790 m (1)Mrs Hannah Bunch (2)Rebecca — Sgt NC
John: b 1746 d p. 1790 m Jerusha Bixby Sgt NH
Lewis: b a. 1732 d 1787 m Martha — PS VA
Nathan: b c. 1719 d p. 1798 m — PS NC
Robert: b 1725/6 d 11-11-1802 m Lucy Loomis Pvt MA
Thomas: b c. 1760 d 7-24-1824 m Mildred Burn Sol NC
Wm.: b a. 1757 d 12-24-1834 m (1)Mrs Elizabeth (Fairchild)Joyner (2)Susan Greene Grayson Pvt SC ★

JOYNES,
Levin: b 1-6-1753 d 10-22-1794 m Anne Smith LCol VA
Reuben: b a. 1756 d 1789 m Margaret Dunton Lt VA

JUCKETT,
Elijah: b 6-8-1760 d 8-5-1839 m Anna Benson Sgt MA ★

JUDD,
Anthony: b 8-24-1752 d 3-12-1843 m Rebecca Belden Pvt CT ★
Arunah: b 12-16-1747 d 7-11-1836 m Sarah Spring Pvt MA ★
Balmarine: b 9-20-1755 d 3-19-1840 m Abigail Thompson Pvt CT ★
Calvin: b 3-21-1754 d 10-27-1817 m Mary Ingham Pvt CT
Chandler: b 4-30-1763 d 12-21-1791 m Abigail Mills Scott Pvt CT
Daniel, Sr.: b 10-10-1724 d 10-23-1807 m (1)Lydia Jones (2)Hannah Hinkley Sol CT
Daniel, Jr.: b 10-13-1751 d 5-29-1805 m Mehetable Clark Pvt MA
Demas: b 5-26-1753 d 1-4-1841 m Maranah Garnsey Pvt CT
Eben Warner: b 4-12-1761 d 9-18-1837 m Lydia Giddings Pvt CT
Elihu: b 7-4-1755 d 2-23-1795 m Lois Dikeman Pvt CT
Freeman: b 8- -1755 d 3-5-1840 m Deborah Boughton Sgt CT
Isaac, Sr.: b 1730 d 1808 m Anna Williams PS CT
James, Jr.: b 1-27-1757 d 11-10-1822 m Esther Allen Pvt CT W★
Jehiel: b 3-7-1763 d 8-24-1826 m Hannah Clarke Cpl CT
Jesse: b 8-3-1739 d p. 1781 m Mary Buell Ens CT
Job: b 10-21-1757 d 7-23-1846 m Mary Andrews Pvt CT ★

John: b 8-4-1733 d 12-23-1793 m Elizabeth Richards Pvt CT
Jonathan: b 10-23-1751 d 12-25-1802 m Mabel Bishop Pvt CT
Levi: b 10-22-1757 d 11-30-1810 m Eunice Hubbard Pvt CT
Nathan: b 1750 d 1809 m Elizabeth Brown Sol CT
Oliver: b 6-10-1761 d 10-27-1844 m Tryphena Heath Pvt MA
Orange: b 8-14-1763 d 5-10-1844 m Abigail Dike Pvt MA
Philip: b 12-31-1715 d 9-15-1776 m Mary Peters Cpl CT
Phineas: b 2-4-1715 d 12-22-1790 m Ruth Seymour Capt CT
Reuben: b 8-9-1750 d 8-12-1799 m Naomi Brown Pvt CT
Reuben: b 1733 d 3-7-1815 m (1)Elizabeth White (2)Elizabeth Smith
  (3)Submit Gallaway Lt MA
Samuel: b 12-26-1734 d 9-11-1825 m Bede Hopkins Capt CT
Samuel: b 1743/4 d — m Lucy Hawley Pvt CT
Stephen: b 8-14-1751 d 7-15-1820 m Sarah Russell Pvt CT
Thomas: b 1723 d 12-21-1802 m (1)Esther Jones (2)Esther Graves
  (3)Thankful Allen (4)Ruth Taylor Pvt MA
Timothy: b 12-28-1713 d 1-23-1796 m Millescent (Gaylord)
  Southmayd PS CT
Timothy: b — d 1819 m Mindwell Cowles Pvt MA
Uriah, Jr.: b 12-20-1745/6 d 10-17-1839 m (1)Lucy Miller
  (2)Elizabeth Brattle Cpl MA
Walter: b 11-11-1758 d 4-2-1833 m Margaret Terrell Sgt CT ★
Wm.: b 7-20-1743 d 11-13-1804 m Elizabeth Mix Maj CS CT
Wm.: b 5-18-1733 d 11-28-1804 m Susanna Gilson Pvt MA

JUDKINS,
Charles: b c. 1748 d a. 1808 m Elizabeth Cryer 2Lt VA
James: b 12-9-1735 d 4-10-1807 m Mercy Price Pvt MA
Jonathan: b 12-20-1759 d p. 6-7-1820 m Mary Sleeper Pvt MA ★
Leonard: b 8-11-1741 d p. 1776 m Sarah Cram Pvt CS NH
Samuel: b 1-8-1736 d 1809 m Sarah Bohonon Mus Maj NH

JUDSON,
Abel: b 11-28-1740 d p. 1820 m Abigail Clark Pvt CT
Abel, Jr.: b 2-21-1746 d 1-3-1799 m Ann Bennett PS CT
Agur, Sr.: b 3-23-1724 d 7-6-1791 m (1)Hannah Curtis (2)Mehitable
  Toucey Maj CT
Agur, Jr.: b 5-3-1750 d 1820 m Ann Mills Sgt CT
Benjamin: b 2-17-1735 d 9-11-1811 m (1)Mehitable — (2)Anna
  Camp (3)Lydia Murray PS CT
Curtis: b 9-27-1756 d 2-16-1804 m Huldah Curtis Pvt CT
Daniel: b 4-26-1728 d 11-4-1813 m (1)Sarah Curtis (2)Mercy (Burton)
  Burritt PS CT
David: b 3-9-1755 d 2-14-1818 m Elizabeth Davies Bgd QM CT W★
Elijah: b 12-15-1716 d 1-10-1798 m Sarah Hollister Pvt CT
Elisha: b 1765 d 10-26-1826 m Lucy Case Pvt CT
Gideon: b 3-8-1748 d 6-25-1821 m Lydia Handy Sgt CT
Isaac: b 7-5-1731 d 12-7-1787 m Mary Stoddard Pvt CT
Isaac, Sr.: b 6-3-1700 d 3-14-1789 m (1)Elizabeth Hawley
  (2)Rebecca Sherman Hollister PS CT
James: b 10-20-1728 d 3-12-1807 m (1)Mary Edwards (2)Deborah
  Judson (3)Ann Nichols Capt CT
John: b 10-6-1746 d 1808 m Martha Camp Ens CT
John B.: b 1759 d 12-21-1829 m Hepkibah Lake Pvt CT
Joseph: b 2- -1715 d a. 11-12-1783 m Jerusha Sherman Pvt CT
Joshua: b 12-14-1732 d 1776 m (1)Ann Walker (2)Deborah
  Levenworth Pvt CT
Lemuel: b 12-9-1759 d 11-16-1839 m Abagail Booth Sgt CT
Nathaniel: b 1753 d 10-17-1838 m Lydia Lewis Adj CT ★
Nathaniel: b 3-2-1754 d 3-15-1815 m Rhoda Hall Adj CT
Phineas: b 8-29-1760 d 1835-40 m Martha Bogue Sgt CT
Seth: bpt 6-15-1755 d 12-12-1790 m Mary Munn Pvt CT
Silas: b 8-31-1754 d 12- -1808 m Mary Whiting Drm CT
Stiles: b 11-18-1752 d 3-10-1834 m Naomi Lewis Capt CT ★
Timothy: b 4-22-1737 d 9-10-1821 m Sarah Hooker Capt CT

JUDY, (includes JUDAH & TSCHUDY)
Jacob: b 1740 d 1807 m Elizabeth Sprater PS PA
John: b 2-2-1759 d 3- -1834 m (1)Appolina — (2)Charity — Pvt PA
John: bpt 3-4-1759 d 4-27-1841 m Phoebe Lamaster Artl PA
Martin: b 12-22-1744 d p. 1835 m Anna Barbara Adams Cpl PA ★
Martin, Jr.: b 11-7-1757 d 9-28-1831 m Elizabeth Judy Pvt PA
Martin, Sr.: bpt 7-31-1735 d p. 1810 m Anni Boni Pvt PA
Matthias: bpt 5-12-1749 d 1811 m (1)Rose — (2)Elizabeth — Pvt PA
Samuel: b 8-19-1728 d 10-19-1781 m Jesse Jones PS NY
Wm.: b 1724 d 1782 m Mary — 2Lt MD

JULIAN, (includes JULIEN)
Isaac: b 1741 d p. 4-26-1839 m Susannah Hedges Pvt PA ★
Isaac: b 1714 d 7-8-1778 m Barbara White Sol NC
Isaac, Jr.: b 1751 d 2-17-1831 m Sarah Long PS NC
John: b 1753 d 8-4-1830 m Elizabeth Butler Pvt MD
John: b c. 1738 d c. 1787 m Margaret Isabella Lounds Dr VA

JUNE,
Joshua: b c. 1756 d c. 1812 m Sarah Cox Pvt MA
Reuben: b 4-17-1759 d 2-26-1839 m Mary Scofield Pvt CT

JUNGHEN, (includes YOUNKIN)
Henry: b 1-31-1717 d a. 3-13-1787 m Catharine Scherer PS PA
Herman: b c. 1720 d a. 3-26-1788 m Magdalana — PS PA
Jacob: b 1756 d 1811 m Hannah Nicols Pvt PA

JUNKIN, (includes JUNKINS)
John: b 7-19-1733 d 5-3-1783 m Eunice Young Pvt MA
Joseph: b 1-22-1750 d 2-21-1831 m Eleanor Cochran Capt PA
Lancelot: b 1753 d 6-10-1833 m Martha Galloway Pvt PA
Wm.: b 1744 d 4-25-1825 m Jane Galloway Pvt PA

JUSTICE,
Benjamin: b 1-3-1750 d 11-15-1799 m Mary Jones Pvt Sct PA
David: b 1750-60 d p. 10-10-1832 m Sarah High Cpl NC
David: b 8-14-1763 d 12-24-1829 m Susannah Pyle Pvt NC
Jacob: b 1751 d 4-23-1829 m Elisabeth — Pvt PA ★
James: b 3-15-1751 d 1843 m Nancy Campbell Pvt PA ★
Jesse: b 1762/3 d 8-6-1826 m Elizabeth — Pvt NJ
John: b 1755 d p. 1805 m Susanna Turner Pvt DE
John: b c. 1725 d 1788 m Elizabeth — Sgt PA
Lawrence: b 12-1-1754 d 10-8-1797 m Elizabeth Smith PS Ens PA
Ralph: b — d p. 12-31-1792 m (1)Siner Simpson (2)Bridget Clemmons
  PS VA

JUSTIN,
George: b 9-12-1761 d 2-15-1828 m Lucy Galusha Pvt CT ★

KAHN,
Henry: b 1725 d a. 4-24-1798 m Anna Barbara Bortner Pvt PA
Michael: b 9-12-1750 d 12-23-1829 m Mary Schenck Capt PA

KAIGLER,
Andrew: b 1730 d p. 1809 m Katy Copplepower CS Lt SC

KAIME,
Joseph: b c. 1740 d p. 1789 m Phebe Gowen Pvt MA

KALBACH,
Adam: b 9-4-1740 d 3-14-1801 m Maria Eva — Sol PA

KALEHOFF,
Frederick: b 1760 d c. 1846 m Margaret Launcern Pvt PA ★

KALLAM,
Luther: b 1-3-1760 d 6-5-1845 m Amy Hewitt Pvt RI CT ★

KANTNER,
George: b c. 1745 d a. 6-15-1816 m Catharine — Pvt PA
Valentine: b c. 1760-2 d p. 1825 m — Pvt PA

KAPLE,
John: b 11-12-1750 d 1834 m Sarah Richardson Pvt CT

KARCH,
Jacob: b 1742 d 8-19-1819 m — Pvt PA

KARMANY, (includes CARMANY)
Anthony: b 3-3-1730 d 8- -1813 m Anna Christiana Hetzler PS PA
John, Sr.: b c. 1739 d c. 1808 m Christina — Pvt PA
John: b 6-15-1760 d 5-19-1840 m Barbara Wunderlich Sol PA
Peter: b 2-3-1741 d c. 1810 m Mary Martin Pvt PA
Philip: b 2-5-1737 d 7-4-1808 m Ann Catherine Miles Pvt PA

KASSON,
Adam: b 11-30-1743 d 9-6-1828 m Dorothy Taft Capt MA
Archibald: b 1742 d 6- -1816 m (1)Sarah Parke (2)Martha Douglas
  MM CT
James, Sr.: b 11-7-1714 d 7-5-1791 m (1)Esther Duncan
  (2)Margaret Dixon PS CT
James, Jr.: b 6-19-1748 d 1-26-1803 m Reliance Hatch Sol CT
Robert: b 1741 d 9-25-1826 m Jennie Gaston Sgt MA

KATHAN,
Charles: b 3-26-1743 d 5-22-1793 m Elizabeth Moor LCol VT
Daniel: b 2-1-1741 d 10-17-1807 m (1)Ruth Barrett (2)Sibyl Tarbel
  McFarland 1Lt VT NY
Daniel: b 10-15-1760 d 9-4-1804 m (1)Olive Lamb (2)Sybil
  McFarland Pvt VT

KATTERMAN, (includes CATHERMAN)
Jacob: b c. 1750 d — m Catherine Mook PS PA
Jacob: b — d 1802 m Mrs Anna Catherine (Reed)Anspach PS PA
John: b 7-17-1751 d 1829 m Margaret Elizabeth Zeller Sol PA

KATTS,
Michael: b 4-21-1758 d 4-6-1833 m Margaret — Pvt PA

KATZEMEYER,
Michael: b 9-24-1759 d p. 1790 m Christina Muller Pvt PA

KAUFMAN, (includes COFFMAN, KAUFFMAN)
Christian: b c. 1740 d 1811 m (1)Barbara — (2)Catherine — Sol
  PS PA
Christian, Sr.: b c. 1730 d 3-1-1799 m Barbata Baer Pvt PA
Christian, Jr.: b 3-1-1755 d 8-31-1823 m (1)Catherine —
  (2)Elizabeth — (3)Elizabeth — Pvt PA
Christian: b c. 1757 d 1822 m Elizabeth — Cpl PA
Frederick: b 1758/9 d p. 1800 m Katie Spohn Pvt PA

KAUFMAN, contd.
George: b 2-20-1751 d 9-9-1817 m Catherine Hofer 2Lt PA
Jacob, Sr.: b c. 1727 d p. 9-8-1800 m Anna Maria — PS PA
Jacob, Sr.: b c. 1737 d p. 9-29-1804 m Hannah Hill PS PA
Jacob, 2d: b 3-10-1757 d 4-27-1843 m Susanna Keim Pvt PA
Jacob: b 1-3-1763 d 4-20-1815 m Elizabeth Stump Pvt PA
Jacob: b 1748 d 4- -1796 m Elizabeth — Pvt VA
John: b 8-8-1750 d 4-21-1812 m (1)Anna Swarr (2)Barbara Reebly Sol PA
Michael: b 1764 d 10-6-1827 m (1) — (2) —Pvt PA
Philip: b 12-21-1757 d 11-11-1843 m Maria Magdalena Seaman Pvt PA
Samuel: b 10-30-1752 d c. 1828 m (1)Elizabeth Reist (2)Anna Hoffman (3)Barbara Brumbach Sol PA

KAULL,
John: b 1750 d 3-31-1839 m Catherine Hargill Pvt NY

KAUP,
Christian: b 1753 d p. 1783 m Sarah — Pvt PA
Peter: b c. 1760 d p. 1832 m Mary Shrater Cpl PA ★

KAY,
John: b 9-12-1723 d 11-4-1793 m Elizabeth Smart Pvt PA
John: b c. 1755 d p. 1-29-1812 m Mary Gatewood Ens VA

KAYS,
John: b 3-9-1739 d 7-13-1829 m Sarah Duer Hull Lt NJ

KEAGY,
Abraham: b 5-2-1726 d 11-5-1784 m Ann Brenneman Pvt PA
Christian: b 8-3-1751 d 8-31-1805 m Mary Resh Pvt PA

KEASIS,
Nathan: b 10-12-1740 d 10-15-1795 m Barbara Low Capt CS NC

KEARNEY,
Anthony: b 2-15-1756 d 5-1-1829 m Sarah Shepherd Thornburg Pvt VA
John: b c. 1745 d 1805 m Susanna Tabb Capt VA
Philip: b 1733 d 1794 m Elizabeth Kinchen Pvt CS NC

KEARSLEY,
Jonathan: b 1718 d 12-26-1782 m Jane — PS PA
Samuel: b 9-15-1750 d 3-22-1830 m Sarah Kirkpatrick Capt PA

KEASBEY, (includes KEASBY)
Edward: b 10-5-1760 d p. 11-18-1805 m Lydia Carll Mil NJ
Edward: b 1726 d 15-1779 m (2)Sarah Quinton PS NJ

KEATING,
Richard: b 1751 d 4-22-1839 m Miriam Bridges Pvt ME
Wm.: b 12-7-1760 d 6-28-1830 m Mary Elizabeth McLane Pvt MA

KEATLEY,
Christopher: b 6-3-1752 d 10-18-1831 m (1)Esther Graham Cpl PA

KEATON,
Keader: b c. 1735 d p. 1794 m Hester — PS SC

KEATOR,
Cornelius: bpt 3-22-1730 d p. 8-29-1801 m Sarah — Sol NY
Cornelius: b 1761 d 8-29-1855 m Elizabeth Krom Pvt NY ★
Jacob N.: b 4- -1760 d 9- -1838 m (1)Susanna Keator (2)Catherine Keator Pvt NY ★
John: bpt 4-24-1737 d 1826 m Maria Keator Pvt NY
John C.: b 7-14-1756 d 10-12-1847 m Rebekah Elmore Sgt NY ★
Matthew: b 1736 d 1781 m Ann Peck PS NY
Nicholas: b 9-22-1728 d 1798 m Mary Nottingham CS NY
Peter: bpt 5-5-1745 d p. 1- -1804 m Gertrude Roosa Pvt NY

KEAZER,
Reuben: b 10-15-1752/3 d 5-25-1836 m Lydia Hancock Pvt NH ★

KECK,
Andrew: b c. 1752 d 5- -1828 m (1)Barbara Bank (2)Susanne — Pvt PA
George: b 1733 d 1808 m — Warren Pvt NY
George: b 1748 d 1816 m Catherine H. Shaub Pvt PA
John: b c. 1735 d 10- -1803 m Anna Margaret — Lt PA
Michael: b 1760 d p. 8-9-1808 m Catherine Kerns Pvt PA

KEEBLE,
Wm.: b 5-21-1755 d 12-30-1834 m Mary Keeble Pvt VA W ★

KEECH,
George: b 1753 d 1-5-1830 m Mary — Pvt NY
James: b 1745 d p. 1790 m Ann Estep Pvt MD
Jeremiah: b c. 1757 d 12-26-1799 m Rachel Coller Pvt RI W ★
Stephen: b 5-18-1721 d 3-6-1794 m Dorcas Paine CS PS RI
Zephania: b 1737 d 1823 m Lydia — Ens RI

KEEFER, (includes KEIFER, KIEFER, KIEFFER)
Abraham: b 11-18-1758 d 8-18-1855 m Catherine Beaver Capt PA
Andrew: b 7-9-1755 d 8-27-1776 m Barbara Eckert Sgt PA

Frederick: b 12-10-1758 d 11-6-1834 m Ann Maria Krause Drm Fif RO PA ★
George: b 1728 d 4-11-1809 m Margaret Schisler PS MD
Jacob: b 9-9-1750 d 1809 m Magdalena Barnett Pvt PA
John: b c. 1750 d p. 1790 m Anna Eva Schuman Pvt PA
Lawrence: bpt 12-24-1749 d p. 1790 m Helena Van Keuren Pvt NY
Theobald De Wald: b c. 1735 d p. 1793 m Hannah Fox Pvt PA

KEELE,
Richard: b 1757 d 1849 m Lydia Richmond Pvt NC ★
Simon: b 8-18-1763 d 5-4-1842 m (1)Permelia — (2)Penelope James Pvt NC ★

KEELER, (includes KEELOR)
Aaron: b 12- -1756 d 10-22-1816 m Gloriana Hubbell Ens CT
Aaron: b 6-17-1761 d 12-31-1811 m Mary Brooks Pvt NY
Benjamin: b 5-23-1742 d 11-7-1830 m Mercy — Pvt MA
David: b 1746 d 1-22-1812 m Amy Ingersoll Pvt NY
Edward: b 11-9-1761 d 11-25-1826 m Elizabeth Grey Pvt NJ ★
Elijah: b 1-12-1756 d 5-27-1835 m Eleanor Squire Sgt MA
Elisha: b 1764 11-12-1814 m Lucina Warner Pvt CT
Henry Haydon: b 1760 d 1825 m Martha — Pvt CT
Hezekiah: b 12-4-1761 d a. 9-12-1846 m Mercy Brooks Pvt CT ★
Isaac: b 7-25-1761 d 1-23-1837 m (1)Sarah St. John (2)Catherine Tuttle Capt CT
Isaac: b 8-8-1739 d 1-14-1807 m (1)Rachel Northrup (2)Sarah Smith Lt NY
Isaiah: b 1-1-1761 d 10-26-1852 m Sarah Mosher Pvt NY ★
Jabez: b 1751 d p. 1800 m Sarah Benedict Pvt CT
Jeremiah: b 5-6-1760 d 2-9-1853 m Huldah Hull Cpl CT
John: b 1722 d 9-7-1795 m Abigal Copely Pvt CT
John: b 1764 d 1848 m (1)Elizabeth Smith (2)Eleanor Wilson Pvt NY ★
Justus: b 5-21-1750 d 10-23-1821 m Charlotte Olmstead Pvt CT
Levi: b 4-4-1758 d 5-5-1812 m Dorcas Smith Capt CT W ★
Matthew: b 3-4-1717 d 4-16-1793 m Sarah — Pvt CT
Nathan: b 11-1-1755 d 11-5-1826 m Rebecca Nichols Pvt NY
Nathan: b 10-25-1757 d 8-1-1818 m Huldah Baldwin Pvt CT
Nathaniel: b 10-10-1757 d 9-30-1853 m (1)Jemima Barnum (2)Ann Stephens Pvt Trm NY ★
Nathaniel: b 11-2-1760 d 1-14-1807 m Rhoda Lawrence Pvt NY
Nehemiah: b 6-13-1753 d 10-28-1838 m Elinor Rockwell Pvt CT ★
Paul, Jr.: b 4-9-1756 d 11-16-1812 m Sarah Burt Cornwell Trm CT
Phineas: b 1-11-1744 d 6-26-1833 m (1)Mary Camp (2)Rebecca Mead Pvt CT
Samuel, Sr.: b 2-9-1716 d 6-17-1781 m Mary Kendrick PS CT
Samuel, Jr.: b 6-23-1737 d 11-29-1811 m Abiah Benedict Capt CT
Stephen: b 3-2-1751 d 9-14-1798 m Margaret Pynchon Pvt NY
Thaddeus: b 4-2-1752 d 3-13-1803 m Ruth Keeler Sgt 1Lt QM CT
Thomas: b c. 1743 d 10-5-1807 m Anna Squires Pvt CT
Thomas: b 2-16-1764 d 5-8-1851 m Elizabeth Woolson Pvt NJ ★
Timothy: b 10-9-1721 d 4-1-1799 m Mary Hoyt PS CT

KEELEY, (includes KEELY, KIEHLEY)
Conrad: b 2-25-1758 d 4-14-1847 m Margaret Laubach Pvt PA
Henry, Sr.: b 2- -1731 d 10- -1793 m Anne Margaretta Held Pvt PA
Henry, Jr.: b 1757 d 8- -1826 m Hannah Lembar Pvt PA
John: b 10-1-1742 d 4-22-1818 m (1)Anna Maria Barbara Smellen (2)Susan Smellen Pvt PA
John: b 12-5-1742 d 1-22-1822 m Mary Hatfield PS PA
Joseph: b 1757-61 d 1-12-1838 m Mary — Pvt PA
Matthias: b 9-15-1722 d 1-28-1808 m Eva — PS PA

KEELING,
Adam: b 1751 d 1805 m Elizabeth Edey Lt VA

KEELS,
John: b 5-4-1750 d 4-10-1789 m Elizabeth Frierson Pvt SC

KEEN, (includes KEAN, KEANE, KEENE)
Andrew: b 8-6-1752 d 8-3-1838 m Margaret Foy Pvt PA ★
Benjamin: b 3-2-1727 d 11-25-1797 m Mary Stevens Capt MD
Conrad: b 1761 d 5-8-1833 m Christiana — Pvt PA
Ebenezer: b 1736 d 7-11-1815 m Hannah Cole Pvt RI
Hezekiah: b 9-8-1746 d 12-8-1809 m Hannah — Pvt MA
Isaac: b 1754 d 1853 m Mercy Main Pvt MA
Isaac: b 5-8-1737 d 3-22-1830 m Bethiah Tobey Pvt MA
Isaiah: b 8-19-1761 d 1-22-1838 m Lydia Bourne Fif MA
Jacob: b 11-21-1731 d 10-10-1788 m Deborah Keen Pvt MA
Jacob: b c. 1738 d 1796 m Hannah Holme Pvt NJ
James: b — d p. 1780 m Elizabeth — Capt PS NJ
James: b 1759 d c. 1835 m (2)Jane Clark Fif Pvt VA
Jesse: b 1758 d 2-12-1833 m Huldah Hall Sgt MA ★
Job: b 1760 d 6-9-1843 m (1)Charity Toby (2)Nancy McMillen Pvt MA
John: b 5-9-1760 d 8-15-1842 m Priscilla Robinson Pvt MA W★
John: b 7-16-1729 d p. 1-17-1831 m (1)Keziah Lincoln (2)Jerusha Blake PS MA
John: b 1750 d p. 12-12-1803 m Elizabeth Curlee Sol NC
John: b 3-29-1747 d 10-29-1832 m Mildred Cooke Pvt PA
John: b 1759 d 1809 m Margaretta Hoffman Pvt VA
Joseph: b 7-14-1762 d 5-12-1821 m Margaret Williams Pvt PA
Joshua: b 12-13-1730 d 12-10-1823 m Abigail Ames 2Lt MA
Meshach: b 8-19-1758 d 1-4-1844 m Kezia — Pvt MA ★
Peter: b 1756 d 1840 m Jemima Gard Pvt PA

Roger: b 2-17-1756 d 11-17-1801 m Jane Stoll Capt PA
Seth: b 1-31-1752 d *p.* 1800 m Lydia Winslow Pvt MA
Snow: b 3-7-1734 d *p.* 1811 m Rebecca Burbank Pvt MA
Thomas: b 3-5-1756 d 10-18-1814 m Ann McAdam Pvt VA
Wm.: b 4-27-1753 d 7-21-1821 m Celanah Wadsworth Pvt MA
Zebulon: b *a.* 1733 d *p.* 2-3-1781 m Mary — PS MD

KEENAN, (includes KENAN)
Felix: b *c.* 1730 d *c.* 7-18-1785 m Mrs Catherine Norris Love CS PS NC
James: b 9-23-1740 d 5-23-1810 m Sarah Love Col PS NC
Michael Johnston: b 8-26-1746 d 1817 m Ann Holmes PS Pvt NC
Owen: b 1743 d 1783 m Nelle Routledge Col NC
Thomas: b *c.* 1725 d *p.* 7-9-1778 m (2)Mary Savery (3)Mary Robinson Pvt NJ

KENNEMORE,
George: b *c.* 1745 d *p.* 12-7-1824 m Elizabeth — Pvt SC

KEENER,
Christian: b 8-12-1752 d 11-21-1817 m Susanna Swope PS MD
George: b 1757 d 1857 m Nancy Stetley Pvt PA
Melchoir: b 9-25-1720 d *a.* 8-29-1798 m Margaret — PS MD
Sebastian: b 9-15-1755 d 4-28-1826 m Margaret — Pvt VA

KEENON,
Peter: b 12-4-1756 d 8-5-1814 m Jane Sloan Pvt NJ

KEEP,
Caleb: b 12-10-1741 d 10-6-1816 m Mercy Merrick Capt MA
Jabez, Sr.: b 12-13-1736 d 1-21-1821 m (1)Phoebe Crosby (2)Mrs Elizabeth Rogers Sgt MA ★
Jabez, Jr.: b 9-8-1759 d 6-22-1822 m Lydia Parkhurst Sgt MA W ★
Jabez: b 3-2-1728 d 9- -1805 m Sarah Chandler PS MA
John: b 9-29-1753 d 10-20-1838 m (1)Elizabeth Smith (2)Abigail Lewis Pvt MA ★
Jonathan: b 8-7-1745 d *p.* 1-19-1816 m (1)Hannah Hildreth (2)Ruth Scott 1Lt MA
Josiah: b 8-30-1743 d 12-9-1799 m Love Kibbe Cpl MA
Matthew: b 3-24-1745 d 2-6-1827 m (1)Mehitabel Chandler (2)Mrs Miriam Colton Cpl MA
Samuel: b 1731 d 1802 m — Capt VT
Samuel: b 5-26-1739 d 10-20-1823 m Sabina Cooley Sgt MA
Simeon: b 2-15-1737 d 7-22-1829 m Esther Hoar Lt NH

KEEPER, (includes KEIPER)
John: b 10-18-1751 d 7-3-1833 m Mary Catherine Schmidt Pvt PA
Peter: b 10-21-1755 d 8-14-1813 m Catherine — Sgt PA
Thomas: b 1753 d 1806 m Tabittha Jones Pvt NJ

KEEPORTS,
Jacob: b 1718 d 3-8-1792 m — CS MD

KEESEE,
Richard: b — d *p.* 3-9-1789 m Ann — PS VA

KEEZER,
David: b 1755 d 1815 m Mary — Pvt NH

KEFAUVER,
Nicholas: b 7-20-1756 d 7-24-1811 m Margaret Beckenbaugh PS MD

KEEFER,
Jacob: b 6-20-1734 d *p.* 1784 m Anna Maria Nass Pvt PA

KEGEREIS,
Michael: b *a.* 1750 d 3- -1804 m (1)Anna Margaretha Hettler (2)Elizabeth — Pvt PA

KEHL,
Jacob: b 9-15-1756 d 4-1-1836 m Catharine Weiser Pvt PA W ★
Michael: b *c.* 1734/5 d 1794 m Mary Catherine Kraft CMman PA

KEIBEARD,
Thomas: b *a.* 1760 d *c.* 7-30-1811 m Margaret S. Beale PS MD

KEIGHER, (includes KYGER)
Christian: b *c.* 1750 d *p.* 1796 m (1)Margaret — (2)Mrs Caty Dundore Lt VA
George: b 1740 d 4-3-1800 m Margaret — Pvt PA

KEIGWIN,
Thomas: b 8-15-1744 d 9-27-1827 m Jerusha Gates Pvt CT

KEIM, (includes KIME)
Conrad: b *c.* 1734 d *p.* 8-15-1776 m Anna Maria — PS PA
David, Sr.: b 1760 d 10-24-1833 m Dorothy Coble Pvt NC
George: b 12-3-1753 d 12-3-1836 m Catherine Schenkel Pvt PA
Henry: b 10-3-1756 d 8-22-1833 m Hannah Rudolph Pvt PA
John: b 7-6-1749 d 2-10-1819 m Susanna de Banneville Capt PA
Nicholas: b 4-2-1719 d 8-2-1802 m Barbara Schneider CS PA

KEISLY,
Paul: b *a.* 1761 d *p.* 1783 m Mary Monohan Pvt NY

KEITER,
George: b 12-25-1756 d 3-26-1850 m Esther Buzzard Sol PA

KEITH,
Alexander: b 6-7-1762 d 12-21-1839 m Abigail Dean Sgt MA
Alexander: b 7-2-1748 d 1824 m (1)Mary Gallihue Thornton (2) — Yancey Lt VA
Alexander: b *a.* 1754 d 3- -1824 m Margaret Harned Pvt VA
Andrew: b *a.* 1745 d *p.* 1800 m — Porter Sgt PA
Asa: b 11-6-1758 d 8-17-1841 m Susannah K. — Pvt MA
Asa: b 6-10-1750 d 12-26-1792 m Susanna Cary CS MA
Benjamin: b 11-18-1763 d 9-9-1814 m Martha Cary Pvt MA
Caleb: b 5-6-1755 d 10-9-1843 m (1)Susanna Mitchell (2)Molly Stowers Lt MA ★
Comfort: b 3-26-1742 d 9-8-1823 m (1)Deborah Nelson (2)Jerusha Aldrich Pvt MA
Cornelius, Jr.: b 1743 d 6-13-1820 m Mary Laffoon Cpl SC ★
Daniel, Sr.: b 5-2-1725 d 4-28-1803 m (1)Elizabeth Conant (2)Lydia Keyser CS PS MA
Daniel, Jr.: m — Melatiah (or Millicent)Hooper Sgt MA
David: b 12-27-1728 d 7-3-1812 m Charity Brett Pvt MA
Ebenezer: b 10-25-1716 d 4-12-1778 m (1)Mary Pierce (2)Mrs Hepsibah Carver PS MA
Ephraim: b 1707 d 2-25-1781 m Sarah Washburn PS MA
Ephraim, Jr.: b 1739 d 1782 m Mary Smith Sgt MA
Henery: b 5-1-1738 d 1825 m (1)Hannah Wheelock (2)Hannah Cummings Pvt MA
Isaac: b 1759 d 11-19-1822 m Betty Keith Sgt MA
Isaiah: b *c.* 1743 d 1796 m (1)Ann Mann (2)Isabella — Pvt PS PA
Isham: b *c.* 1735 d *a.* 9-24-1787 m Charlotte Ashmore Lt VA
Israel: b 6-20-1744 d 12-3-1808 m Abigail Leonard Sgt MA
James: b 4-4-1727 d 6-20-1803 m Sarah Holman Pvt MA
James: b 3-31-1740 d — m Comfort — Pvt MA
Jeremiah: b 1749 d 1822 m Agatha Bryant Pvt MA
John: b 5-23-1761 d 5-21-1846 m Abigail House Sgt PS MA ★
John, Sr.: b 7-23-1756 d 4-8-1833 m Azubah Thayer Pvt MA
John: b 1735 d *a.* 8- -1809 m Mary Elizabeth Doniphan Sol VA
Jonathan: b 11-19-1754 d 6-23-1810 m Hannah Snell Pvt MA
Joseph: b 1732 d 1814 m Chloe Packard Capt MA
Josiah: b 10-11-1732 d 4-9-1803 m (1)Susanna Williams (2)Rebecca (Lathrop)Williams (3)Hannah Wetherill Capt MA
Levi: b 1738 d 1813 m Jemima Perkins Pvt MA
Luke: b *c.* 1748 d *p.* 1790 m Martha Littlefield Cpl MA
Nathan: b 12-16-1714 d 1-9-1786 m Hannah Snell PS MA
Nehemiah: b 10-29-1746 d 3-28-1821 m (2)Mary Eddy Pvt MA
Noah, Sr.: b 6-10-1723 d 10-9/1800 m Deborah Taft CS MA
Noah, Jr.: b *a.* 1750 d 1779-82 m Mary Legg Pvt MA
Robert: b 10-18-1742 d 7-10-1818 m Silence Hartwell Sgt MA
Scotland: b 11-16-1752 d 11-2-1815 m Parnel Howard Pvt MA
Seth: b 6-7-1758 d 8-16-1830 m Hannah (Keith)Cole Sgt MA
Simeon, Jr.: b 5-6-1742 d 1-3-1776 m Rebecca Leland Pvt MA
Simeon: b *c.* 1743 d *p.* 1798 m Thankful Lincoln Pvt MA
Simeon: b 1-19-1749 d 6-28-1828 m Mary Cary Sgt MA
Solomon: b 3-24-1749 d 11-14-1822 m Lois Cary Pvt MA
Thomas: b *a.* 1755 d 1805 m Judith Blackwell Capt Cmsry VA W★
Thomas: b *c.* 1756 d *p.* 1839 m Judith Key PS VA
Wm.: b 1714 d 4-16-1781 m (1)Margaret Stockton (2)Elizabeth Wilson PS PA
Zephaniah: b 3-8-1730 d 1-29-1820 m Mary Hooper Maj MA

KEITHLEY,
John: b 1-1-1755 d 7-28-1835 m Mary Ann Riblin PS NC

KELCHNER,
Jacob: b 1760 d 10-5-1823 m (1)Magdeline Wanner (2)Maria Wanner Pvt PA
Michael: b 1-1-1734 d 4-22-1820 m Elizabeth Roth Cpl PA

KELKER,
Anthony: b 12-30-1735 d 3-12-1812 m Mary Magdalena Meister Lt Wgm PA

KELL,
James: b 3-6-1760 d 2-22-1848 m Lettice Kneal Capt NC
John: b 1736 d 11-2-1819 m Jane Tyler Pvt SC
Samuel: b *a.* 1748 d *p.* 1820 m Elizabeth — Pvt PA
Thomas: b *c.* 1747 d *p.* 1790 Aliceanna Bond Seacap MD

KELLAM,
Houston: b *c.* 1756 d 1-15-1847 m (1)Betty Turlington (2)Elizabeth Ward (3)Elizabeth Rogers Pvt VA ★

KELLER, (includes KELLAR)
Adam: b 4-28-1757 d 10-27-1834 m Mary Ashton 2Lt PA
Christopher: b 10-12-1743 d 6-10-1795 m Christina Possert Capt PA
Christopher: b 12-15-1751 d 7-8-1820 m Margaret Frauch Ens PA
Conrad: b 1750 d 1836 m Catherine Manning Pvt VA
Frederick, Jr.: b 1757 d 1833 m Barbara Baylor Pvt PA
Frederick: b 1757 d 1847 m Elizabeth Peter Pvt PA
George: b *c.* 1753 d 7-13-1796 m Catherine — PS GA
George: b — d 9-7-1735 m Margaretta Pfeifer Pvt FifMaj PA
George: b 3-6-1759 d 3-1-1836 m Maria Eva Laubscher Pvt PA

KELLER, cont.
George: b 1712 d *c.* 1783 m Barbara Ann Hottel PS VA
Henry: b 5-13-1755 d 2-13-1838 m Catharine Seitz Pvt PA
Henry: bpt 6-22-1755 d 10-25-1825 m Anna Christina Waldschmidt Pvt PA
Jacob: b 1-10-1763 d 10-15-1831 m Magdalene Nellis Pvt NY
Jacob: b 2-15-1753 d 3-6-1828 m Eve Elizabeth Doxter Sol PA
Jacob: b 7-23-1759 d 12-28-1848 m Elizabeth Hess Ens PA
John: b 1740 d 1806 m Christina Spease Pvt NY
John: b 1740 d 11-4-1806 m Barbara Windecker Pvt NY
John: b 2-24-1732 d 3-1-1831 m Dorothea Rub Pvt PA
John: b 1-11-1758 d — m Annie Ball Pvt PA
John: b *c.* 1750 d 11- -1815 m Mary — PS VA
Joseph, Jr.: b 1-15-1751 d 4-15-1832 m Maria Magdalene Andre Lt PA
Martin: b 1733 d 1809 m Elizabeth Landis Sol PA
Michael: b 9-25-1731 d 4-1-1828 m Anna Maria Kummer Pvt PA
Michael: b *c.* 1760 d *p.* 1788 *m* Jennie Monroe Pvt VA
Philip: b *c.* 1764 d 4-9-1834 m Lidya — Pvt SC

KELLETT,
Joseph: b *c.* 1735 d *p.* 10-9-1785 m Jane — PS SC

KELLOCH, (includes KALLOCK)
Alexander: b 1740 d 2-14-1826 m Eleanora Gaut Lt ME
Matthew: b 3-29-1737 d 3-22-1824 m Mary Robinson Pvt Slr ME ★

KELLOGG, (includes KILLOUGH)
Aaron: b 1742 d 4-3-1826 m (2)Hannah Robbins PS CT
Aaron: b 7-19-1762 d 5-8-1835 m Susan Huntington Branch Sol MA
Abner: b 11-9-1746 d 7-24-1821 m Lydia Bartlett Lt CT
Abner: b 11-9-1747 d 6-9-1812 m Phebe Westover Lt NY
Amos: b 7-7-1760 d 3-6-1826 m Lucretia Harwood Sgt VT
Asa: b 2-19-1745 d 6-4-1820 m Lucy Powell Sgt MA
Benjamin: b 2-18-1761 d 12-16-1859 m Lauranah Spalding Pvt MA ★
Benjamin: b 10-11-1724 d 12- -1779 m Comfort Thompson PS VT
Benjamin: b 4-22-1744 d 11-3-1824 m Phebe Stark Pvt NY
Bradford: b 3-24-1759 d 1832 m Mary Tompson Pvt CT
Cotton: b 12-22-1759 d *p.* 1804 m Lydia Williams Pvt MA
Daniel: b 1727 d 2-4-1817 m (1)Hannah Fairchild (2)Elizabeth Boalt Pvt CT
Daniel: b 4-5-1758 d 1830 m Abigail Crow Pvt CT
Daniel: b 11-5-1746 d 1- -1776 m Rhoda Callender Ordl ME
Daniel, Jr.: b 7-26-1753 d 3-1-1826 m Mercy Eastman Pvt MA
David: b 1744 d 1776 m Mrs Eunice Brown Sol CT
Ebenezer: b 9-6-1751 d 7-17-1843 m Mollie Bissell Pvt CT
Ebenezer (Rev): b 4-5-1737 d 9-3-1817 m Hannah Wright Pvt CT
Ebenezer, Sr.: b 1722 d 11-22-1776 m (2)Sarah Clapp Pvt MA
Ebenezer, Jr.: b 5-29-1749 d 3-29-1807 m (1)Elizabeth Crocker (2)Tamer Wright Cpl MA
Ebenezer: b 2-29-1748 d 5-10-1827 m Sarah Austin Cpl MA
Eldad: b 12-29-1752 d 10-1-1838 m Elizabeth Waterhouse Pvt CT W★
Eleazer: b 4-10-1749 d 5-13-1813 m Esther Fuller Ens CT
Elijah: b 6-3-1757 d 3-23-1845 m Sarah Jones Pvt CT ★
Elijah: b 2-25-1764 d 12-26-1839 m Mary Karner Pvt CT MA ★
Elijah: b 1761 d 3-9-1842 m Eunice McLellan Mus MA ★
Elijah: b 1751 d 2-14-1819 m Tryphena Westover Pvt VT
Eliphalet: b *c.* 1735-40 d *p.* 1787 m Sarah Brown Pvt NY
Enoch: b 12-2-1761 d 11-30-1842 m Elizabeth Wood Pvt CT
Enos: b 12-24-1742 d 12-13-1803 m Abigail Seymore Pvt MA
Enos: b 7-28-1761 d *p.* 1837 m (1)Lydia Alvord (2)Demise Wells CS MA
Ephraim: b 9-20-1740 d 2-11-1819 m Ruth Hosmer Pvt MA
Ezekiel: b 11-24-1732 d 6-16-1785 m Ann Owen Pvt CT
Ezekiel: b 3-23-1753 d 2-20-1839 m (1)Eunice Foster (2)Juliett (Parker)Cahoon Sgt MA
Ezekiel: b 9-17-1748 d 7-7-1823 m (1)Elishaba Wells (2)Philotha (Clark)Tracy Pvt MA
Gad: b *c.* 1729 d *c.* 1812 m Lucy Sackett Stl Pvt MA
Gardner: b a. 1730 d 10-6-1814 m Thankful Chapin CS MA
George: b 7-7-1737 d 8-24-1803 m Sarah Clark Ens CT
Helmont: b 3-17-1762 d 3-28-1846 m Susanna Moore Sol CT ★
Isaac: b 1-17-1697 d 7-3-1787 m Mary Webster PS CT
Isaac: b 1-14-1745 d 4-5-1829 m (1)Hannah Fitch (2)Sarah (Burgess) Gardner Pvt CT
Jabez: b 2-11-1734 d *c.* 1791 m Abigail Catlin Sgt MA
Jarvis: b 1731 d 3-22-1815 m (1)Elizabeth Smith (2)Hannah Meeker Sol CT
Jason: b 2-11-1754 d 9-5-1821 m (1)Miriam Dewey (2)Martha (Benedict)Sacket (3)Lucretia (Dart)Rockwell Sgt MA
Joel: b 10-12-1733 d 10- -1787 m Susanna Hosmer Pvt MA
John: b 12-20-1743 d 2-22-1826 m Mary Newton Pvt CT
John: b 5-25-1737 d 1821 m Sarah Smith Pvt CT
John: b 7-5-1727 d 12-17-1806 m (1)Lucy Ann Terry (2)Anna Lord (3)Jemima Wood Capt MA
John: b 4-17-1755 d 10-27-1834 m Lydia Church Pvt Fif MA ★
John: bpt 9-4-1726 d 4-23-1780 m Union Stoddard Pvt MA
Jonathan: b 1730-33 d *p.* 1792 m Susannah Chichester Pvt CT
Jonathan: b 10-24-1760 d 2-28-1823 m Mary Holland Pvt MA
Joseph: b 11-14-1742 d 11- -1795 m Lucy Warner Capt CT
Joseph: bpt 9-21-1746 d 3-22-1823 m Mary Niles Cpl MA

Joseph: b 10-5-1748 d *p.* 1820 m Mrs Eleanor Stephenson Hancock Pvt MA ★
Joseph: b 1749 d 10-31-1836 m (1)Susanna Bailey (2)Mrs Elizabeth Bouldrey Stone Pvt NY
Josiah: b 8-7-1770 d 1847/8 m (1)Clarissa Alford (2)Sally Fox Fif CT
Josiah: b 11-21-1760 d 12-21-1835 m Jerusha Taylor Pvt MA
Judah: b 1740 d 1820 m Mary Tomlinson PS CT
Levi: b 10-3-1760 d 1-13-1848 m Cynthia Wright Sol NY ★
Loomis: b 5-9-1758 d 10-6-1848 m Anna Truman Pvt MA W★
Martin, Sr.: b 8-2-1718 d 12-7-1791 m Mary Boardman Capt PS CT
Martin, Jr.: b 1746 d 8-19-1828 m Hannah Robbins Lt CT
Martin: b 10-10-1740 d 9-1-1824 m Mercy Benedict Pvt CT
Martin: bpt 3-29-1741 d 11-28-1789 m Sarah Treadway Pvt CT
Martin: b 11-2-1757 d 3-4-1850 m Lucy Dunham Pvt MA ★
Martin: b 1-8-1744 d 11-7-1827 m Hannah Crocker PS MA
Martin: b 7-16-1758 d 4-14-1840 m Lucy Seymour Pvt NY
Medad: b 2-23-1749 d 10-29-1841 m Anne Brooks Pvt CT ★
Moses: b 11-23-1736 d 2- -1820 m Jerusha Spencer Pvt CT
Moses: b 1733 d 5-28-1815 m Mary Sheldon Capt MA
Moses: b 2-21-1746 d 9-20-1795 m Lydia — Cpl MA
Nathan Fairchild: b 1752 d 1824 m Hannah Wasson Morehouse Pvt CT
Nathaniel: b 7-10-1739 d 8-8-1808 m (1)Hannah Barnard Hastings (2)Mrs Lydia Sargent Watson Lt MA
Nathaniel: b 2-24-1758 d 10-24-1846 m (1)Palm Hawkins (2)Annice Gray Pvt MA NY ★
Nathaniel: b 10-1-1763 d 2-24-1851 m (1)Chloe Drake (2)Betsey (Coles)Moody Pvt MA ★
Nehemiah: b 10-14-1752 d *p.* 1807 m Hannah Marble Pvt MA
Noah, Sr.: b 12-13-1729 d *p.* 1777 m Clemence Merrill Capt CT
Noah, Jr.: b 5-8-1756 d 3-3-1822 m (1)Deborah Knowlton (2)Lucy Crow Pvt CT
Ozias: b 12-17-1760 d *c.* 1789 m Isabella Williams Cpl MA
Phineas: b 6-7-1756 d 12-2-1835 m (1)Olivia Fraser (2)Ruth Bird Pvt CT
Pliny: b 11-12-1752 d 1842 m Mary (Kellogg) Pvt MA ★
Preserved: b 10-25-1742 d 11-6-1833 m Lucy Palmer Pvt VT ★
Russell: b 11-12-1753 d *a.* 1813 m Esther Bridges Pvt CT
Samuel: b 1740 d 1780 m Hannah Strong Cpl CT
Samuel: b 6-29-1749 d 10-12-1829 m Elisabeth Waring Pvt CT
Samuel: b 2-20-1755 d 3-9-1839 m (1)Sarah Rogers (2)Ruth (Rogers) Pierce Sol CT
Samuel: b 6-9-1734 d 9-2-1788 m Chloe Bacon Pvt CS PS MA
Samuel: b 2-1-1739 d 1816 m (1)Lucy Snow (2)Sally (Fisk) Southwick Pvt MA
Samuel: b 10-26-1761 d 3-2-1826 m Elizabeth Lathrop Sol CT
Samuel: b 1756 d 11-6-1834 m Agnes — Pvt PA NC
Seth: b 7-7-1732 d *c.* 1792 m Lois — Pvt CT
Seth: b 2-8-1740 d 6-28-1819 m Eunice Judd Pvt CT
Seth: b 1753 d 11-30-1827 m Jerusha White Pvt MA ★
Silas: b 8-25-1742 d 12-11-1812 m Sarah Cook Pvt NY
Silas, Sr.: b 4-7-1714 d 1-24-1792 m Ruth Root PS MA
Silas, Jr.: b 4-7-1757 d 11 or 12-28-1838 m Rhoda Root Pvt MA ★
Solomon: b 1733 d 4-27-1828 m Vashti Hobbs Drm CT ★
Stephen: b 4-7-1758 d 4-21-1806 m (1)Cynthia (Andrus)Stephens (2)Sarah Kirkham Pvt CT
Stephen: b 8- -1757 d 6-25-1834 m Comfort Fisk Pvt Drm MA ★
Stephen: b 1761 d *p.* 1809 m Thankful Button Pvt MA
Titus: b 1765 d 10-28-1832 m (2)Rachel Southwell (Southworth) Pvt MA ★
Wm.: b 2-1-1739 d 10-7-1826 m Nancy Holton Pvt MA
Wm.: b 10-27-1750 d 3-2-1823 m Ruth Wood Pvt NY
Wm.: b 5-6-1759 d 10-20-1824 m Urania Bishop Pvt PA ★
Wm.: bpt *c.* 1743 d 5-5-1802 m Bathsheba Karley Pvt VT

KELLS,
John: b *c.* 1740 d 1799 m Elizabeth Hagedon Pvt NY

KELLY, (includes KELLEY)
Aaron: b *c.* 1750 d *c.* 1825 m Mary Canady Pvt MA
Alexander: b 1766 d 8-17-1841 m Mary Morrison Pvt PA
Alexander: b *c.* 1755 d *p.* 1838 m Nancy Robinson Capt VA
Craig: b *c.* 1754 d 2-14-1815 m Sibbel Morris OrdlSgt CT W★
Darby: b *c.* 1705 d 1788 m (1)Sarah Huntoon (2)Sarah Dudley PS NH
David: b 2-25-1751 d 6-5-1848 m Susan Jones Pvt NY
Dennis: b 8-25-1758 d 12-11-1834 m Elisabeth Thompson Pvt DE ★
Dudley: b 1763 d 1836 m Ruth Dow Pvt NH
Edmund: b 2-25-1767 d 6-10-1854 m Lavinia Liscom Pvt NY ★
George: b 1738 d 5-9-1801 m Persus — Pvt NJ
Hannah Bartlett: b 11-16-1704 d 4-6-1789 m Richard Kelly PS MA
Henry: b 1742 d 6- -1832 m — Cpl NC
Jacob: b 3-4-1755 d 8- -1835 m (1)Susannah — (2)Jane Hanner Sol GA
Jacob: b *c.* 1756 d *p.* 12-13-1817 m Esther — Sol VA
James: b *c.* 1750 d 1803 m Sarah Meek Pvt PA
James: b 3-12-1737 d 4-8-1802 m Susan Wilson Capt VA
James: b *c.* 1750 d *p.* 1785 m — Sgt VA
James: b 1752 d 8-30-1837 m Catharine Stewart Pvt VA ★
Jared: b 4-17-1764 d 9-3-1822 m Mary Hall Pvt NJ ★
John: b 1757 d 4-14-1825 m Molly Cheever Pvt MA ★
John: b 10-22-1736 d 3-29-1821 m Elizabeth Hoyt PS MA

John, Sr.: b 10-9-1697 d 4-27-1783 m Hannah Somes PS NH
John, Jr.: b 10-15-1724 d 12-18-1807 m Hannah Hale CS NH
John: b 9-5-1747 d 1-19-1798 m Elizabeth Casteau Maj NJ
John: b c. 1740 d p. 12-4-1822 m Jane — Pvt NC
John: b 8-22-1755 d p. 1827 m Polly — Pvt NC ★
John: b 2- -1744 d 2-8-1832 m Sarah Polk Col PA
John: b 1759 d 10- -1803 m Mary Robinson Pvt PA
John: b 3-22-1761 d 3-4-1821 m Nancy Dite Pvt PA
John: b c. 1756 d 6-11-1853 m Elizabeth Brannon Pvt VA ★
John: b 1760 d 1840 m Polly Manning Pvt VA
John: b c. 1755 d p. 9- -1848 m Elizabeth Askins Pvt VA
Jonathan: b 1765 d 10-7-1840 m Jerusha — Pvt NH
Joshua: b 1751 d a. 10-10-1834 m — 2Lt PS MD
Joshua: b 2-13-1742 d 5-1-1822 m Deborah Page Pvt Sct NH
Lawrence: b 1740 d 9-24-1823 m Martha Smith Pvt PA
Lloyd: b c. 1758 d 1834 m Elizabeth Gonder Pvt SC ★
Luke: b 4-3-1757 d 11-25-1821 m Mary Keyser Pvt VA
Matthew: b 8-1-1734 d 12-31-1796 m Jane — Pvt MD
Matthew: b c. 1734 d 3- -1801 m Betty — CS PA
Micajah: b 5-15-1761 d 12-19-1844 m (1)Mary Page Gilman
 (2)Sarah Gale Patten Pvt NH
Moses: b 3-15-1739 d 8-2-1826 m Lydia Sawyer Col NH
Nathan: b 9-30-1760 d 7-6-1845 m (1)Hannah Miller (2)Mary Pierce
 Van Meter Pvt PA
Nathaniel: b 4-1-1763 d 7-4-1843 m Sally Andrews Pvt NH ★
Nathaniel: b 1734 d 1826 m Ann Smiley Pvt PA
Oliver: b 1756 d 9-30-1827 m Jane Morris Pvt PA
Peter: b 1751 d 3-24-1838 m Jane Ewing Pvt SC ★
Richard, Sr.: b 11-2-1727 d 1789 m Esther Palmer PS NH
Richard, Jr.: b 9-20-1758 d 12-1-1816 m Sybil Fletcher Pvt NH
Richard: b 3-26-1763 d p. 1840 m Catherine Howell Pvt VA ★
Robert: b 4-26-1714 d 7-1-1783 m (1)Ruth Wheelock (2)Lydia
 Marrs 2Lt MA
Samuel: b 3-2-1732/3 d p. 1780 m Elizabeth Hall PS Capt NH
Samuel: b 1733 d 6-28-1813 m Elizabeth Bowdoin Lt NH
Samuel: b 11-27-1759 d 12- -1839 m Elizabeth Hemphill Pvt PA ★
Stephen: b 11-15-1740 d 10-7-1784 m Louis Sargent Sgt NH
Stephen: b 1-18-1755 d 8-18-1846 m Hannah Wells Pvt RI ★
Thomas: b c. 1740 d p. 9- -1812 m (1)Abigail Cromet (2)Mrs Emmy
 Steele Cpl MA
Thomas: b 1747 d 1814 m Mary — Pvt PA
Thomas: b 1742 d a. 4-29-1808 m Peggy Biles Pvt VA
Wm., Sr.: b c. 1716 d p. 1-2-1784 m (1)Elizabeth — (2)Eleanor—
 (3)Mary Miller PS MD
Wm.: b c. 1740 d c. 1800 m Sarah Nellie Buncephataly Sol GA
Wm., Jr.: b 4-11-1751 d 2-22-1818 m Martha Lovell Capt MD
Wm.: b 3-17-1739 d 12-13-1826 m Mary Durham'Pvt NC
Wm.: b 1750 d p. 1790 m Susanna Anderson Sub-Lt PA
Wm.: b — d 11-1-1779 m Martha McCourtney Pvt PA
Wm.: b 1747 d 1-27-1829 m Rebekah Martin Cpl RI
Wm.: b c. 1735 d 9-9-1783 m — Smith Maj VA
Wm.: b 1759 d 7-14-1841 m Elizabeth — Pvt VA
Wm.: b 1-10-1760 d 3-18-1846 m — Pvt VA
Wm. P.: b 1762 d 7-21-1832 m Sally Blake Pvt NH W★

KELSEY,
Abner: b 6-29-1755 d 11- -1816 m Ann Eaton Pvt CT
Amos: b 4-16-1733 d 11-13-1804 m Mable Parmelee PS CT
Daniel: b 9-23-1734 d 10-20-1810 m (1)Jemima Bronson
 (2)Susannah — Pvt MA
Elias: b 3-3-1825 m Tamsen Jones Pvt CT
Enoch: b 8-27-1717 d 6-2-1788 m Mary Bidwell PS CT
Ezra: b 3-20-1761 d 3-20-1847 m Phebe Carter Pvt CT
George: b 2-6-1757 d 1827 m Mrs Susan Smith Brooks Pvt CT
Giles: b 1747 d p. 1790 m Elizabeth Buell Pvt PS NH
Heth: b 1755 d 2-5-1850 m Rhoda — Pvt CT ★
Hugh: b c. 1755 d 6-18-1817 m Margaret Mills Sol PS SC
Isaac: b 3-28-1712 d 11-7-1781 m Hannah Bushnell Cpl CT
Israel: b 11-20-1745 d 5-16-1824 m Mary Sanborn PS CT
Job: b 1742 d 7-22-1797 m Sybil Lay 2Lt CT
Joel: b 8-6-1761 d 3-6-1860 m Jemima Buell Pvt CT
John: b 11-30-1746 d 3-4-1832 m Agnes R. — Pvt CT
John: b 6-3-1743 d 11-3-1822 m Molly Park Sgt MA
Jonas: b 1743 d 12-22-1817 m (1)Jane Du Bois Capt NY
Jonas: b 7-21-1756 d 11-12-1837 m Sarah Woolsey Pvt NY
Nathan, Jr.: b 1750 d 1800 m Huldah Ray Pvt CT
Samuel, Jr.: b 1755 d 1828 m Mary Mills Pvt PS SC
Seymour: b 6-30-1751 d 4-26-1817 m Sarah Augur Pvt PS NH
Silas: b 4-16-1733 d 8-28-1802 m Lydia Wellman Capt PS CT
Stephen: b 1-6-1757 d 3-22-1833 m Lois Griffin Pvt CT W★
Stephen, Sr.: b 1-8-1732 d 6-15-1812 m Anna Platt Cpl PS NY
Stephen, Jr.: bpt 4-22-1758 d 5-19-1814 m Elizabeth Conklin Pvt NY
Thomas: b 3-12-1754 d 4-30-1835 m Eunice Thomas Pvt NY
Timothy, Jr.: b 3-21-1735 d 8- -1781 m — Pvt CT
Wm.: b c. 1745 d a. 8- -1806 m Nancy Gowdey 1Lt CT

KELSO,
Alexander: b 3-30-1758 d 9-2-1835 m Margaret Balch Pvt SC NC ★
Hugh: b c. 1760 d p. 6-23-1817 m Elizabeth — Sol NC
John: b 1729 d 7-11-1814 m Sarah Crawford PS MA
John: b 1755 d 4-17-1813 m Mary McCormick Sgt PA
Wm., Sr.: b 1737 d 11-26-1788 m Jean Simpson Pvt PS PA

KELTON, (includes KILTON)
Amos: b 3-11-1760 d 8-25-1841 m (1)Phebe Cornell (2)Alice Chace
 Pvt MA ★
Elihu: b 6-9-1733 d 10-12-1792 m Thankful Davenport Pvt MA
Enoch: b 6-19-1726 d 3-31-1812 m Elthear Hicks Pvt MA
James: b 2-16-1750 d 1-26-1831 m Lois Ingalls Cpl MA
John Jenckes: b 3-1-1749 d 5- -1784 m Sarah Brayton Pvt RI
Jonathan: b 5-27-1730 d 11-20-1804 m Margaret Lucas Pvt MA
Samuel: b a. 1750 d a. 3-21-1812 m Marcy Harris Tms RI
Wm.: b 9-26-1753 d 5-18-1813 m Elizabeth Ramsey Sol NC

KELTY,
John: b 1751 d 5-27-1812 m Catherine Quine Capt MD W★
John: b 1750-2 d 12-5-1833 m Margaret Connor Pvt PA

KELTZ,
George, Sr.: b c. 1734 d 1784 m Mary — Pvt PA
George, Jr.: b 1758 d 6-1-1837 m Sarah Shannon Pvt PA

KEMMER, (or KEIMER)
Nicholas: b 1758 d 10-19-1841 m Sarah Fehler Cpl PA ★

KEMMERER, (includes KAEMMERER, KAMERER)
Frederick: b 5-24-1746 d 12-1-1843 m Magdalena — Pvt PA ★
Henry: b 4-4-1740 d 10-10-1804 m Anna Maria Rischel Ens PA
Jacob: b c. 1760 d a. 12- -1829 m (1)Eve Schleppi (2)Magdalena
 Yetter Pvt PA
John Nicholas: b 3-17-1750 d 8-7-1820 m Elizabeth Kern Pvt PA
Peter, Sr.: b c. 1734 d a. 4-6-1784 m Juliana — Pvt PA
Philip: b 4-10-1759 d 4-13-1827 m Roseann Hyle Pvt PA

KEMP,
Amasa: b 1744 d c. 1780 m Tamorsen Henley Sgt MA
Benjamin: b 1733 d 7-12-1809 m Judith Reed Pvt MA NH
Ebenezer, Jr.: b 1-11-1750 d 1833 m (1)Relief Phillips (2)Lydia Elder
 Cpl MA ★
Frederick: b 2-11-1747 d 2-17-1814 m Dorothy Hensetbergern PS MD
Frederick: b 1725 d 1804 m Regina — PS MD
Garret: b 2-23-1749 d 4-14-1837 m Eve— Pvt PA
George: b 1748 d 9-19-1833 m Susanna Levan Capt PA
Gilbert: b 1717 d 1794 m Margartha Goetzandomern Sol MD
John: b 9-22-1761 d 1822 m Rhoda Edwards Sol GA
John W.: b 2-15-1745 d 11-16-1844 m Mary Miller Pvt MD
Jonathan: b 1742 d 12-9-1814 m (1)Elizabeth Womack (2)Sallie
 Cox Capt NC
Lawrence: b 1734 d 10-2-1805 m Dorothy Stebbins Capt MA
Lewis: b 1738 d 4-3-1805 m (1)Elizabeth — (2)Barbara Norris 2Maj
 MD
Oliver: b 1742 d 1820 m Dolly Middleton Pvt MA
Peter: b 6-28-1749 d 2-26-1811 m Mary Lehman Pvt MD
Reuben: b 1754 d 1834 m (2)Patsy Crofton Pvt VA ★
Samuel, Jr.: b 1745 d 1830 m Elizabeth Keser Pvt MD
Thomas: b 10-4-1741 d p. 12-23-1805 m Rachel Denny PS MD

KEMPER, (includes KAMPFER)
Abraham: b c. 1755 d p. 4-22-1830 m — Pvt PA
Charles: b 6-27-1756 d 12-1-1841 m Susanna Manzee Ens VA
Charles: b 1758 d p. 1787 m — Pvt VA
James: b 11-23-1753 d 8-20-1834 m Judith Hathaway Pvt VA
John: b 9-25-1756 d 8-11-1842 m Elizabeth Ann Hopper Mid Wgm
 NY ★
John: b 11-27-1757 d 1-22-1833 m Judith Burdett Cpl VA
John: b 1749 d p. 8-14-1832 m (1)Sarah James (2)Hannah Carner
 Pvt VA ★
John: b 5- -1722 d p. 1782 m Ann Weaver PS VA
Peter: b c. 1748-50 d 7- -1824 m (1)Mary Whitesides (2)Scytha
 Riley Ens VA
Peter: b 1-25-1743 d 7-23-1829 m (1)Isabella Nicholls (2)Mrs Susan
 Ball Culpepper Capt VA
Tillman: b 4-11-1759 d 12-3-1836 m Dinah Hitt Pvt VA ★

KEMPLIN,
Wm.: b 7- -1752 d 12-9-1836 m Elizabeth Garlick Pvt PA

KEMPTON,
Ephraim: b 12- -1741 d p. 1790 m Hannah Battles Pvt MA
Lemuel: b 1758 d — m Hannah Wilbur Pvt MA
Thomas: b 4-20-1740 d 1-27-1806 m Deborah Price Col MA
Wm.: b 7-22-1732 d p. 1788 m Ruth Damon Pvt MA

KENCH,
Thomas: b 1744/5 d 1-17-1831 m Mary Maker Sgt MA ★

KENDALL, (includes KINDLE)
Asa, Sr.: b 3-16-1735 d 7-26-1816 m (1)Sarah Williams (2)Mary
 Rice Lt MA
Asa, Jr.: b 5-27-1761/2 d 7-9-1844 m Mary Wallace Pvt MA
Benjamin, Jr.: b 1745 d 1841 m Kezia Twitchell 2Lt MA
Benjamin: b 9-12-1731 d 2-28-1805 m Jane Rogers Sol MA
Caleb: b 5-15-1748 d — m Priscilla Savory Sol MA
Cheever: b 8-5-1756 d 3- -1835 m Dolly Parish Sgt MA ★
David: b 11-11-1754 d p. 1805 m Sally Eustice Pvt MA
Ebenezer: b 10-5-1736 d 11-2-1802 m Martha Walton CS NH

KENDALL, contd.
Eleazer: b 10-20-1756 d 1-29-1840 m Content — Sgt MA ★
Ephraim: b 2-16-1756 d p. 1-24-1798 m Elizabeth Knight Drm MA
Ezra: b 1-1-1721 d 5-1-1817 m (1)Mrs Ruth Frost (2)Abigail Chandler Pvt MA
Heman: b 5-20-1740 d 6-9-1800 m Mary Fairbanks PS MA
Henry: b c. 1760 d p. 11-11-1825 m Elizabeth Penny Wright Sol VA
Isaac: b 10-6-1734 d 10-15-1776 m Mary Russell Pvt CT
Jabez: b 1742 d 10-20-1803 m Mary Pool Pvt MA
Jacob: b 8-9-1729 d 2-25-1809 m Elizabeth Cutler Pvt MA
Jacob: b 1758 d 6-3-1823 m Sarah Lamson Pvt NH
James: b c. 1740 d 1798 m Ann — Pvt PA
Jeremiah: b 11-16-1760 d p. 1789 m Susannah Flaker Sol GA
Jeremiah: b 2-6-1758 d 1-28-1843 m Rhoda McIntyre Sgt VA ★
Jesse: b 5-15-1727 d 4-14-1797 m Elizabeth Evans PS MA
John: b 5-5-1723 d 2-13-1809 m Hannah Whitmore Pvt MA
Jonathan: b 1-29-1743 d 7-8-1817 m Anne Oliver CS MA
Joseph: b 10-15-1738 d 9-2-1808 m (1)Mary Dearing (2)Hannah (Bowen)Smith Ens CT
Joseph: b 7-19-1753 d 5-26-1812 m Mary Geiger Cpl PA
Joshua: b 6-20-1746 d 6-29-1837 m Dorothy Warner Pvt MA ★
Josiah: b 9-1-1712 d 7-22-1785 m Tabitha Wyman 1Lt MA
Moses: b a. 1748 d 1799 m Amy — PS VA
Nathan, Jr.: b 7-28-1755 d 8-11-1846 m Sarah Kendrick Fif NH
Nathan, Sr.: b 1726 d 11-10-1791 m Rebecca Coulburn Sol NH
Paul: b 4-30-1744 d 2-15-1832 m Mary Bayley 1Lt MA
Peter: b 2-7-1763 d 3-22-1844 m (1)Mary Hart (2)Hephzibah Green Pvt VT ★
Reuben: b 11-25-1739 d p. 1790 m Molly Hartwell Pvt MA
Robert: b 1752 d 1843 m Nancy Wilson Pvt PA
Silas: b c. 1746 d 7-25-1826 m Eunice Conant Cpl MA
Temple: b 8-10-1730 d 3-6-1822 m Abigail Cummings Lt MA
Thomas: b 4-15-1745 d 12-5-1836 m Ruth Waters Chp MA
Thomas: b a. 1745 d 1804 m Margaret — Pvt PA
Wm.: b 9-11-1759 d 8-11-1827 m Abigail Chase Pvt MA
Wm.: b 4-22-1734 d p. 1794 m (1)Mary Lipinwill (2)Sarah Bradstreet Pvt MA
Wm.: b 9-14-1749 d p. 1784 m Mary Brooks Fif MA
Wm.: b 1755 d 1824 m Jane Linn Pvt PA
Wm.: b 8-30-1749 d p. 6-29-1825 m Becca — Pvt VA
Wm.: b 1759 d p. 1800 m Mary — Pvt VA
Wm.: b 1760 d 2-13-1852 m — Pvt VA ★
Woffendall: b c. 1740 d p. 1-3-1792 m Susannah — Capt PS VA
Zebedee: b 6-6-1755 d 8-12-1839 m Molly Dakin Pvt MA
Zimri: b 9-20-1763 d 1-28-1842 m Lucy Robbins Pvt MA

KENDRICK, (includes KENDIG, KENRICK, KINDIG & KINRICK)
Abraham: b 2-24-1755 d a. 4-19-1833 m Catherine — Pvt PA
Adam: b 1735 d 9-10-1807 m Alice Graft Pvt PS PA
Benjamin: b 1-30-1723/4 d 11-13-1813 m Sarah Harris PS NH
Benjamin: b 1722 d 6-12-1830 m Nancy Corbin Pvt VA
Burwell: b c. 1760 d 5- -1817 m Ruth Harvey Pvt NC
Caleb: b 1-29-1739 d 7-16-1808 m Elizabeth Parker 2Lt MA
Daniel: b 10-4-1735 d 5-20-1789 m (1)Hannah Harris (2)Mary Poole Capt PS CS NH
Daniel: b 1760 d 1853 m Rebecca Eaton Pvt NH
Edom, Sr.: b c. 1730 d c. 1840 m Mary — Sol VA
George: b 11-8-1745 d 11-17-1823 m Elizabeth Eshleman Pvt PA
Henry: b 1735 d 1787 m Anna Graft PS PA
Henry: b 1742 d 1809 m Barbara Herr Capt PA
James: b c. 1733 d p. 1796 m Susannah Roberson CS NC
John, Sr.: b 1732 d 1793 m Ellenor — Lt GA
John: b 1759 d 2-17-1843 m (1)Rebecca Day (2)Mary Atkinson Pvt GA ★
John: b 1759 d 1836 m Sarah Franklin Pvt MD
John: b 1745 d 4-23-1808 m Kezia Baldwin Lt MA
John: b 1740 d 1800 m Hulda Pease Capt of Pvtrs
John: b — d 8-10-1816 m Dolly Kingston Cpl MA
John, Sr.: b 8-8-1722 d 9-8-1805 m Anna Dana Sol MA
John, Jr.: b 11-6-1755 d 3-28-1833 m Mehitable Meriam Pvt MA
John: b — d 12-14-1802 m Martha Montgomery Lt NC ★
John: b 1730 d 1810 m (1)— Hill (2)Ann Witmer Pvt PA
John: b 6-31-1735 d p. 10-16-1807 m Amy Fox Capt VA
Jonathan: b — d 9-17-1823 m Mary Burgess Smn MA
Lemuel: b 2-17-1735 d a. 1790 m Experience Church Pvt MA
Patrick: b c. 1730 d p. 9-10-1803 m Jane — Pvt VA
Samuel: b 3-28-1753 d 3-13-1845 m Anna Smith Sgt NH
Samuel: b 1752 d 3-27-1850 m Margaret Fawby Pvt VA
Wm.: b c. 1758 d 2-26-1838 m (1)Eliza Ann Thompson (2)Margaret Watt PS NC

KENEA,
John Jordan: b 3-21-1763 d 1-14-1840 m Obedience Alcox Pvt CT ★

KENLY, (includes KENLEY)
Richard: bpt 11-3-1761 d 1825 m Avis Ward Sol MD
Samuel: b 8-22-1758 d — m Jean — Pvt PA
Wm.: b 3- -1741 d 11- -1806 m Hannah Jenkins PS PA

KENNAMER,
George: b a. 1755 d 1828 m Elizabeth — Pvt SC

KENNARD, (includes KINARD, KINNEARD)
James: b 1-7-1748 d 1-9-1837 m Ann Parry Slr ME

John, Jr.: b 2-14-1747 d 3-14-1806 m Martha Frisby Pvt MD
Martin, Sr.: b 1730 d a. 10-14-1805 m Mary — Sol SC
Michael: b 11-30-1754 d 5-6-1839 m Katherine Swittenberg Pvt SC
Nathaniel: b 5-4-1755 d 6-24-1823 m Margaret Peverly Pvt Smn ME
Wm.: b 1750 d 7-30-1822 m Sarah McGraw Sol PA

KENNEBREW, (or KINNEBREW)
Jacob: b c. 1745 d p. 3-30-1807 m (1)Edith Kirby (2)Elizabeth Swisher Sol GA

KENNEDY, (includes CANADY, CANEDY, CANNADY, KENNEDAY)
Alexander: b 1762 d 1850 m Elizabeth Cloud Pvt PA
Alexander: b 12-6-1743 d p. 8-10-1824 m Agnes Fears Sol SC
Andrew: b 10-16-1729 d 5-10-1788 m Amy Wentworth Cpl MA
Andrew: b 8-12-1752 d 5-5-1834 m Rachel Penny Pvt NC ★
Andrew: b c. 1751 d 9-23-1811 m Elizabeth Potts Sol PA
Andrew: b 2-3-1764 d 1-31-1825 m Agnes McCreary Pvt VA
Ann: b 1760 d 3-24-1836 m Thomas Hamilton Messenger SC
Benjamin: b 3-19-1754 d 6-25-1821 m Abigail Babcock Pvt MA
Daniel: b 1750 d 9-15-1802 m Margaret Hughes Capt PS CS NC
David: b 7-6-1730 d p. 1-3-1792 m Mary Campbell Pvt CT
David: b 3-17-1741 d 12-26-1802 m (2)Susannah Pugh Cpl DE
David: b 9-21-1767 d 9-21-1850 m Jane Cox Pvt KY ★
David: b — d 1780 m Maria McKesson Col VA
Francis: b c. 1752 d 1796 m Rebecca Williams Pvt PA
George: b 1751 d 5-18-1828 m Mindwell Higby Sgt NY
Henry: b 1750 d 5-22-1828 m Mary Quick Pvt NJ
Hugh: b 1725 d 1814 m (1)Catherine Hughes (2)Elizabeth Scullion Pvt PA
Hugh: b c. 1750 d 1837 m Sarah Canada PS PA
James: b 1745 d 11-20-1813 m Phoebe Alley Pvt MA
James: b 11-30-1751 d 11-21-1822 m Mary Fuller Pvt NY
James: b c. 1753 d 1837/8 m Margaret Clark Pvt PA ★
James: b 1730 d 10-7-1799 m (1)Jane Maxwell (2)Jane Macalla Pvt PA
James: b 1750 d 1811 m Rebecca Spurgeon Pvt PA
James: b 1752 d 1820 m Margaret White Lt QM SC
James: b c. 1760 d p. 1816 m — Sol SC
James: b a. 1755 d 3-28-1828 m Barbara Smith Lt VA
James: b c. 1755 d a. 3-3-1817 m Elizabeth Raikes Pvt VA
John: b 1720 d 1777 m Mary Barron Pvt NH
John: b 5-8-1761 d 4-12-1847 m (2)Barbara Slaugh Pvt NJ
John: b 4-20-1749 d 6-10-1831 m Hannah Olmsted Pvt NY
John: b 1750 d p. 4-3-1813 m (1)Magdalena Vedder (2)Nancy Wasson Pvt NY
John: b c. 1760 d 11-29-1832 m Cherry Rountree Pvt NC ★
John: b 1760 d 1823 m Elizabeth King Sol NC
John: b 1735 d 9-1-1801 m Apsley Hubbard PS NC
John, Sr.: b 9-29-1747 d 1-31-1823 m Sarah Croom PS NC
John: b 4-24-1739 d 8-20-1809 m Marie Van Vliet Pvt PA
John: b 10-14-1741 d 3-17-1815 m Elizabeth Wiley Pvt PA
John: b c. 1740 d 1- -1805 m — Pvt PA
John: b 1751 d 1835 m Margret Burkhart Pvt PA
John: b c. 1755 d a. 1790 m Elizabeth (Blocker)Loftin Sol SC
John, Jr.: b 2-17-1744 d 6-12-1820 m Hannah Barnet Pvt VT
John: b 3-14-1763 d 12-15-1836 m Mary Shearer Pvt VA ★
John, Sr.: b 1720 d p. 1810 m — PS VA
John, Jr.: b a. 1748 d 1780 m Mary Anderson Sol PS
John: b 10-16-1742 d 6-21-1781 m Esther Stilly Pvt VA
Joseph: b 8-28-1760 d 11'30-1844 m (1)Pattie Perrin (2)Elizabeth Morrison Spy Lt VA NC ★
Lemuel: b 3-4-1759 d 1-14-1829 m Rebecca Pope Pvt MA
Margaret White: b 1756 d 1820 m James Kennedy PS SC
Michael: b 1756 d 3-4-1816 m Eleanor McCaffrey Pvt MD
Robert: b 9-18-1748 d c. 1820 m Jane Pratt Sgt NY
Robert: b — d — m Alice — Dr PA
Robert Campbell: b 1761 d c. 1800 m Esther Edminston Pvt VA
Samuel: b 7-30-1743 d 1-28-1822 m Ruth Spencer Lt CT
Samuel, Sr.: b — d c. 1793 m Mary — Pvt MA
Samuel: b 1730 d 6-17-1778 m Sarah Ruston Dr PA
Sherwood: b 10-14-1760 d 4-6-1842 m Rebecca Connor OrdlSgt NC ★
Thomas: b c. 1741 d 8-1-1821 m Dinah (Davis)Piersol Pvt PA
Thomas: b 4-2-1753 d 8-15-1823 m (2)Sarah Gibson Pvt SC ★
Thomas: b 1-22-1744 d p. 1787 m (1)Ann Locker (2)Mrs Daniel (Graham)Cook PS KY
Wm.: b 12-5-1757 d 11-21-1836 m Mary Brown Pvt MA
Wm.: b 1744 d 9-1-1783 m Agnes Grier Maj PA
Wm.: b 1741 d 1777 m Mary Sterling Sgt PA
Wm.: b c. 1730 d p. 1790 m Mary Ann Brandon Pvt SC
Wm.: b 1755 d 1827 m Mary Hamilton Pvt SC
Wm.: b c. 1755 d c. 1825 m Martha Whittier Pvt SC
Wm.: b 1755 d 1817 m Martha — Ens QM VA
Wm.: b 3-15-1733 d p. 1813 m Martha Campbell Sgt CS VA
Wm.: b c. 1755 d c. 1799 m Mary Lindsay Pvt VA
Wm. J.: b — d 1785 m Elizabeth Elliott Col NC

KENNELL,
Peter: b c. 1729 d a. 1800 m Catherine — Pvt PA

KENNELLY,
John: b 12-21-1768 d 8-25-1829 m (1)Sarah — (2)Mindwell — Drm NY ★

KENNEMORE,
George: b c. 1745 d p. 12-7-1824 m Elizabeth — Pvt SC

KENNER,
Francis: b c. 1734 d 1784 m Elizabeth Howard Sol NC
Margaret Eskridge: b 1715 d 10-8-1801 m Howson Kenner PS VA
Rodham: b c. 1740 d 1777 m Elizabeth Plater PS VA

KENNERLY,
Everton: b a. 1761 d a. 6-22-1795 m — Sol MD
James: b 1752 d 1817 m Elizabeth Rahlls PS SC
James: b 8-13-1734 d 1827 m (1)Susannah Long (2)Mary (Bear) Harpine Sol VA
Samuel: b 1754/5 d 2-3-1840 m (1)Mary Talbot (Hancock) Radford (2)Mary (Lockhart) Jones Pvt VA ★

KENNETT,
Charles: b 1760 d 10- -1803 m Susannah — Pvt VA

KENNISON, (includes KENISON, KENNISTON, KINERSON)
Aaron: b c. 1730 d 8-26-1823 m (1)Phebe Kennison (2)Mary Dutch PS Pvt NH
David: b 11-10-1736 d 2-24-1852 m — Pvt PS MA ME ★
David: b 1750 d c. 1800 m Elizabeth Dearborn Pvt NH
Hugh: b— d — m (1)Anna Stacy (2)Meribah Stach Slr ME
Joseph: b 1764 d 2-20-1853 m Hannah Bodge Pvt NH ★
Wm. Sr.: b 1726 d 5-8-1803 m — Cilley Pvt PS NH
Wm. Jr.: b 10-10-1760 d 10-30-1853 m Sarah Morrison Pvt NH

KENNON,
Andrew: b 4-20-1754 d p. 1789 m Peggy Smith Cpl MA
Isaac: b 12-6-1757 d — m Ruth Burnham Pvt MA
John: b 12-20-1721 d 10-12-1812 m Elizabeth Woodson Lt NC
Richard: b 1752 d 1804 m Celia Ragland PS NC
Richard: b 1759 d p. 2-4-1805 m Elizabeth Beverly Munford Capt VA
Robert: b 4-14-1725 d p. 4-13-1781 m Sarah Skipwith PS VA
Wm.: b 3-11-1751 d 10-3-1804 m (1)Elizabeth Bullock (2)Elizabeth Harrison PS NC

KENT,
Abel: b 9-20-1752/3 d 1806 m Thankful — Pvt MA
Abel: b 1769 d p. 1778 m S. Lancaster Pvt MA
Abel: b 8-7-1730 d 10-14-1826 m Hannah Hobart PS MA
Absalom: b 10-16-1752 d 3-4-1839 m Tabitha — Ens PA ★
Alexander: b 7-29-1755 d 4-7-1841 m Mary Carter Pvt VA ★
Amos Jr.: b 5-21-1744 d — m (1)Lydia Bush (2)Abigail Marritt Pvt NY
Bela: b 5-19-1757 d 12-16-1834 m Lucretia Remington Sgt CT
Cephas Sr.: b 4-13-1725 d 12-5-1809 m Hannah Spencer PS CS VT
Cephas Jr.: b 4-2-1754 d 1- -1813 m Lydia Sheldon ADC Cpl VT
Dan: b 4-10-1758 d 7-21-1835 m (1)Abigail Sykes (2)Betsey Griswold Sgt VT ★
Daniel: b 8-3-1745 d 1784 m (1)— Sedwick (2)Anne Wheeler Ens MD
Daniel: b a. 1756 d 1805 m — Pvt MD
David: b 1745 d 1825 m Lydia Daman Pvt RI
Ebenezer: b 5-12-1759 d 3-26-1812 m Lucy Sanger Ens MA
Ebenezer: b 12-8-1745 d 1-8-1806 m Esther Stone Cpl MA
Elihu, Sr.: b 6-1-1733 d 2-12-1814 m (1)Rebecca Kellogg (2)Susannah Lyman (3)Sibyl Dwight Maj CT
Elihu, Jr.: b 12-15-1757 d 5-12-1813 m Elizabeth Fitch Pvt PS CT
Elijah: b 12-30-1727 d 9-22-1815 m Hannah Perren Pvt MA
Elisha: b c. 1710 d p. 1786 m Susanna Ford PS CS MA
Elisha: b 10-30-1734 d 3-19-1811 m Anna — Pvt VT
Ezekiel: b 6-22-1744 d 5-17-1842 m (1)Ruth Gary (2)Lois — Drm MA
Ezra: b 6-28-1734 d 5-10-1799 m Ruth Cushing 1Lt MA
Jacob: b 1-31-1750 d 8-5-1825 m (1)Desire Prouty (2)Mary Tucker (3)Abigail Barnes Pvt MA
Jacob: b 10-1-1757 d 7-23-1840 m (1)Affie Edwards (2)Keziah Dodd Pvt NJ ★
Jacob: b 6-12-1726 d 12-13-1812 m (1)Abigail Bailey (2)Mary White Col NH VT
James: b 1760 d 7-16-1805 m Catherine Parliament Pvt NJ
Job: b 3-31-1743 d 12-26-1837 m E. Alice Little Ens NH
John: b 10-17-1764 d 2-18-1852 m Mary Griswold Pvt CT ★
John: b 8-9-1749 d 5- -1795 m Grace Root Ens MA
John: b 12-7-1755 d 8-17-1835 m Betsey Walker Cpl MA ★
John: b 9-11-1759 d 6-1-1807 m Huldah Bowen Cpl VT
John: b 10-31-1749 d 6-4-1849 m Lucy Sykes Sol VT
John: b 1753 d 8-11-1834 m Mary Whipple Pvt VT
Joshua: b 1746/7 d 8-24-1806 m Anna Low Pvt RI
Josiah: b 4-8-1747 d 1799 m Elizabeth Bullock Pvt MA
Moses: b 4-3-1756 d 9-28-1842 m Abigail Harmon Pvt CT ★
Noah: b 8-27-1737 d 1813 m Loes Warren Pvt MM MA
Peleg: b 9-4-1748 d 9- -1819 m Elizabeth Ford Pvt MA
Phineas: b 9-16-1756 d 5-1-1808 m Sarah Brown Pvt NJ
Remember: b 1-7-1754 d 4-7-1822 m (1)Lucy Ide (2)Martha Ide Sgt MA
Robert: b c. 1710-15 d p. 10-13-1782 m Mary — PS VA
Samuel Jr.: bpt 11-23-1760 d 4-4-1835 m Rhoda Hill Pvt MA
Samuel: b 1-19-1733 d 12-7-1821 m Ruth — Pvt RI
Seth: b 3-16-1738 d 8-4-1800 m Susanna King Pvt MM CT

Simeon: b 1762 d 1-21-1851 m Sarah Jane Lewis Sol NY
Thomas: b 3-1-1748 d 1-8-1835 m Anna Ralston Pvt MD ★
Thomas: b 6-6-1750 d 9- -1823 m Anne Webster Sol NC
Thomas: b 1746 d 9-28/10-6-1846 m — Pvt VA
Wm.: b 10-3-1763 d 3-24-1849 m Sarah Perrin Pvt PA ★
Wm.: b 1756 d c. 1820 m Jane Tyler Sol VA
Zenas: b — d 10-23-1822 m Ann Plum Pvt CT CL

KENTFIELD, (includes KENFIELD)
David: b 9-22-1752 d 2-17-1834 m Mary Smith Pvt MA ★
Napthali: b c. 1764 d p. 1786 m Jemima Kenfield Pvt MA
Salmon: b 1735 d 7- -1787 m Bethia Stearns Pvt MA
Wm.: b 1727 d 1791 m Sarah — Pvt MA

KENTON,
John: b 1757 d 4- -1829 m Catharine Russell Sgt VA
Simon: b 4-3-1755 d 4-20-1836 m (1)Martha Dowden (2)Elizabeth Jarbo Capt KY ★
Wm.: b 9-20-1737 d 5-21-1822 m Mary Clelland Lt VA

KENYON, (includes KINYON, KUNNIAN)
Amos: b a. 1757 d 5-15-1808 m Lydia Nye Pvt RI W★
Benjamin: b 3-24-1720 d 7-31-1814 m Lydia — Pvt NY
Caleb: b 1758 d 10-19-1822 m Martha Allen Pvt RI
Clark: b 7-9-1762 d 3-8-1842 m Mary Card Pvt RI
David: b 6-24-1756 d 2-4-1834 m Mary Rogers Pvt RI ★
Enoch: b 1760 d 3-27-1831 m Sibyl Griswold Pvt NY
Gardiner: b 9-24-1755 d 8-9-1825 m Mercy (Kenyon) Pvt RI
John: b 2-3-1745 d 10-20-1843 m Hannah Ketchum Pvt NY
John Sr.: b 9-29-1730 d 8-31-1823 m (1)Freelove Reynolds (2)Lydia Ennos (3)Welthon Reynolds Pvt RI
John Jr.: b 7-3-1760 d 5-17-1849 m Hannah Crandal Pvt RI ★
Nathaniel Sr.: b c. 1728 d p. 1790 m Eleanor Utter PS RI
Payne: b 7-30-1755 d 7-20-1836 m Theda Radelia Howard SgtMaj CT
Phineas: b 10-3-1744 d 1829 m Elizabeth — Capt CS RI
Robert: b 1-10-1735 d 10-2-1805 m Ruth Barber CS RI
Samuel: b 9-10-1731 d p. 1798 m Martha Seaman Pvt RI
Samuel: b c. 1759 d a. 11-27-1822 m Hannah — PS RI
Thomas Webster: b 3-9-1757 d p. 1833 m Sylva Saunders Pvt Lt RI
Wells: b 1-16-1758 d — m Elizabeth Stillman Cpl RI
Wm.: b 8-22-1755 d 9-26-1841 m (1)Nancy Greene (2)Mercy Johnson OrdSgt CS RI ★
Wm.: b 1-30-1731 d p. 1776 m Hannah Niles PS RI

KEOUS,
Wm.: b 6-20-1741 d 9-1-1814 m Deborah Thing CS NH

KEOWN,
Thomas: b 1740 d 6-8-1808 m (1)Polly Caldwell (2)Elizabeth Young Adj SC

KEPLER,
Barnard: b c. 1732 d 1809 m Eva Catherine Myer Pvt PA
Bernhard: b c. 1740 d 1804 m Rebecca Zieber Pvt PA
John: b 1-1-1743 d 12-12-1845 m Helena DeAvarie Pvt PA
Matthias: b 1726 d 1822 m — Pvt PA

KEPNER,
Benjamin: b 1-17-1765 d 5-30-1818 m Elizabeth Huebache Pvt PA
Bernard: b 8-10-1764 d 2-27-1848 m Cathrine Koenig Pvt PA
Bernard: b 6-8-1720 d 10-21-1792 m Maria Lindenmuth PS PA

KEPPLE, (includes COPPLE)
Daniel: b 1753 d p. 1820 m Catherine — Pvt PA ★
Michael: b 1-14-1759 d 1821 m Dorothy Yeron PS PA
Nicholas: b c. 1735-8 d 1804 m Anna Maria Williams PS PA

KERAN,
Patrick: b c. 1730 d p. 1805 m Rebecca — PS VA

KERBER, (includes KERPER)
Julius: b 1730 d 1801 m Catherine — Pvt PA
Paul: b 1728 d 4-30-1778 m Katrina Bingeman QMSgt PA

KERCHEVAL, (includes KIRCHIVAL)
Benjamin: b a. 1759 d 4-19-1812 m Elizabeth Fulton Sgt VA
John, Jr.: b 9-12-1762 d 10-1-1839 m Jane Berry Pvt VA W★
John, Sr.: b 1736 d 10- -1788 m (2)Winifred Gholson Pvt VA

KERFOOT,
Margaret: b c. 1750 d p. 3-4-1814 m George Kerfoot PS VA
Wm. Jr.: b 5- -1749 d 2-4-1811 m (1)Mary Bryarly (2)Ann Peters Sgt VA

KERLIN,
John Sr.: b 1722 d 3-19-1812 m Elizabeth — CS PA

KERN, (includes CAIRNS, CARNES, CARNS, KAIRNES, KARN, KERNS)
Edward: b 9-8-1730 d 8- -1782 m Joanna Jenner 2Maj MA
George: b a. 1721 d p. 1788 m Catherine Elizabetha — Pvt PA
Godfrey: b 1750 d 7-17-1843 m Mary McDowell Pvt PA ★

KERN, contd.
Jacob: b 1734 d 5-20-1799 m Catharine Funk Pvt PA
Jacob Christopher: b *a*. 1755 d 1793/4 m Catherine Utt 1Lt PA
John: b 7-11-1723 d 10-12-1802 m Mary Lewis Chp MA
John: b 1760 d 1838 m Isabel Burch Pvt PA
John: b 1755 d 8-18-1815 m Polly Nicely Pvt PA
Leonard: b 8-15-1723 da. 4-19-1810 m Charlotta Scharadin PS PA
Michael: b 12-4-1757 d 3- -1834 m (1)— House (2)Mary (Ostrender) Marshall Pvt NY CT ★
Michael: b 5-4-1757 d 2-11-1850 m Mary Boone Pvt PA ★
Michael: b *c*. 1749 d 2- -1807 m (1)Catherine Shaver (2)Elizabeth — Pvt VA
Michael: b *c*. 1740 d p. 6-21-1831 m (1)Mrs Susanna Wetherhold (2)Mrs Riddle Sol PS VA
Nicholas Sr.: b 1727 d *p*. 1798 m Eva (Karns) LCol PA
Nicholas Jr.: b 4-1-1760 d 6-15-1829 m Mary Olwine Lt PA
Thomas Peter: b *c*. 1750 d 5-8-1822 m Elizabeth Bostwick Pvt GA
Peter: b 1748 d 5-28-1821 m Catharine Deshler Pvt PA
Wm.: b 1752 d 1844 m Catherine Hoover Lt PA ★
Wm., Sr.: b 1725 d 8-1-1800 m Maria Salome Pvt PA
Wm.: b *c*. 1740 d 1803 m Margaret — Pvt PA

KERR, (includes CARR, KEHR, KER, KURR)
Andrew: b *c*. 1759 d 1-7-1849 m Elizabeth Phillips Pvt PA
Charles: b 1743 d 1811 m Susan — PS VA
Daniel: b *a*. 1760 d 12-3-1820 m Elizabeth Murphy Pvt NC W★
David: b 2-3-1749 d 11-2-1814 m (1)Hamutel B. (Hammond) Bishop (2)Rachel Leeds (Bozman) Edmondson 1Lt MD
David: b 2-18-1757 d *p*. 4-23-1838 m Dorothy Rodes Pvt VA ★
Edward: b 1721 d 1790 m Margaret Shepperd PS VA
Frederick: b *c*. 1740 d 1808 m Anna — Pvt PS PA
James: b 1740-50 d *p*. 1807 m Mary Moore Slr MD
James: b 1743 d 1-16-1816 m Jean Davidson Capt PS CS NC
James: b 1734 d 1816 m Nancy Mitchell Pvt NC
James: b 2-28-1733 d 2-25-1825 m Elizabeth Porter Pvt PA
James: b 1744 d 3-23-1827 m Jane McKinstry Pvt PA
James: b *c*. 1751 d 6-2-1825 m Agnes Carrick Pvt PA
James: b 1737 d 1-5-1812 m Jane — Pvt VA
John: b *c*. 1745 d 10-2-1807 m Mary Doherty Pvt 2Lt PA
Joseph: b 7-15-1733 d 1-5-1824 m Elsy Hampton Ostler Tms NJ
Joseph: b 8-9-1760 d 7-24-1848 m Jane Chambers Bingham Pvt PA
Matthew: b 1754 d 1828 m Margaret Work Pvt PA
Moses: b 11-15-1747 d 11-5-1813 m Lydia Beard Sgt MA
Nathan: b 9-7-1736 d 12-14-1804 m Anna Livermore Chp NY
Nathaniel: b *c*. 1750 d 2-7-1826 m Margaret (Graham) Barrett Sol NC
Robert: b 1-19-1756 d 11-28-1846 m (1)Mary Benjamin (2)Mary Christina (Pitts) Parcell Sol NY
Robert: b *c*. 1759 d 6-13-1817 m Agnes Elder Pvt PA
Robert: b 1720 d 1-22-1808 m Elizabeth Bailey Pvt PS PA
Samuel: b 10-13-1750 d 10-19-1818 m Margaret McDowell Pvt PA
Samuel: b 1-8-1757 d 12-31-1829 m (1)Rhoda Becherer (2)Isabell — Ens NJ
Thomas: b — d *p*. 5-29-1806 m Martha — Pvt PA
Thomas Sr.: b 1717 d 7- -1791 m Elizabeth — PS PA
Thomas Jr.: b 1754 d 11-28-1832 m Elizabeth Kintzer PS PA
Wm.: b 1730 d *p*. 1783 m Agnes Martin Ens PA
Wm.: b 6-2-1756 d 1-1-1843 m Elizabeth Aiken Pvt NC
Wm. Sr.: b *c*. 1737 d 1803 m Nancy Love Pvt PA
Wm. Jr.: b 1-5-1758 d 1-20-1832 m Margaret Young Pvt PA ★
Wm.: b 1760 d 7-16-1828 m Mary Ann Grove Pvt PA

KERSEY,
James: b 1762-4 d *p*. 1834 m Susanna Bell Pvt NC ★
John: b 3-11-1764 d 12-9-1852 m Lucretia Hutchinson Pvt VA ★

KERSH,
Andrew: b *c*. 1755 d 1800/1810 m Eve Margaret Gislar Pvt SC

KERSHAW,
Joseph: b 3-16-1728/9 d 12-28-1791 m Sarah Mathis Col SC

KERSHNER, (includes KERCHNER)
Conrad, Jr.: b 8-1-1744 d 1801 m Catharine Rieser Pvt PA
Frederick: b 1750 d *a*. 1828 m Barbara Fetterman Pvt PA
John: b — d *a*. 10-2-1822 m Anne Marie Capt PS MD
Martin: b 1743 d 11-19-1817 m Elizabeth Schnebele PS MD
Michael: b 1758 d 4-25-1823 m Mary Motter Pvt MD ★
Peter: b 4-17-1747 d 9-11-1809 m Catharine — Lt PA

KERSTETTER,
Leonard: b *c*. 1747 d 1822 m Anna Christena Lenker Pvt PA

KESLING, (includes KEESLING, KISLING)
Conrad: b 1762-4 d 12- -1818 m Rebecca Ann Kegley Pvt PA
Jacob: b 1-18-1760 d 5-23-1835 m Barbara Lingell Pvt VA ★
John: b 3-2-1758 d 12-31-1839/40 m (1)Eve Miller (2)Barbara Staley Pvt Wgn PA ★
Teter: b 8-16-1754 d 12-23-1841 m (1)Elizabeth Fudge (2)A. Roller Pvt VA ★

KETCHUM,
Azariah: b 2-15-1755 d 12-10-1832 m Elizabeth Thorp Cpl NY W★

Benjamin: b 4- -1716 d 10- -1817 m Elizabeth Sprague Pvt NY
Benjamin: b *c*. 1735 d 5-18-1833 m Mary — Pvt NY
Daniel: b 2-17-1753 d 3-17-1828 m Keziah Lewis PS MD
Epenetus: b 10-3-1736 d 2-26-1829 m Amy — Pvt MA
Jesse: bpt 10-27-1734 d 9-6-1826 m Temperance Brush Sgt NY
John: b 3-17-1722 d 6-28-1786 m Wentiah Cook Pvt NJ
John: b 9-27-1756 d 3-29-1808 m Phoebe Van Velzor Pvt NY ★
John: b 1-24-1716 d 4-21-1794 m Sarah Matthews PS NY
Jonathan: b 1751/2 d *p*. 1790 m Betsy Bristol Pvt NY
Joseph Sr.: b *c*. 1720 d *p*. 5-6-1793 m Elizabeth Hurlbut PS NY
Joseph Jr.: b 10-1-1754 d 9-6-1794 m Phebe Moore QM NY
Joseph: b 1-25-1757 d 10-23-1823 m Charity Austin Cpl NY
Joshua: b *c*. 1717 d *p*. 1-16-1787 m Jerushia Whitman PS NY
Joshua Jr.: bpt 5-7-1738 d 1812-19 m Ruth — Pvt NY
Joshua: b 3-6-1759 d 3-8-1808 m Eleanor Soule Sol NY
Levi: b 9-19-1754 d 8-17-1839 m (1)Elizabeth Allen (2)Hannah Fisher Pvt NJ
Nathaniel: b *c*. 1750 d 12-9-1827 m Polly Drake 1Lt NY W★
Nathaniel: b 1724 d 1816 m Mary Scudder PS NY
Phillip: b 6- -1750 d *p*. 1782 m Deborah Conklin Pvt NY
Philip: b 7-5-1752 d 6-18-1830 m Susanna Brush PS NY
Philip: b 6-17-1746 d 1816 m Elizabeth Youngs Pvt NY
Samuel: b 11-13-1757 d 1843 m Phebe Lyon Pvt NY
Solomon Sr.: b 6-8-1724 d 9-21-1781 m Hannah Conklin CS PS NY
Solmon Jr.: b 9-6-1757 d 2-19-1851 m Rebecca Platt Smn NY
Stephen: b 8-26-1761 d *p*. 6-10-1798 m Nancy Peck Pvt NY
Thomas: b 2-8-1748 d 5-17-1834 m Mary Doughty Pvt NY
Timothy: b 1731 d 3-20-1827 m (2)Rebecca La Due Pvt PS NY
Zebulon: b 10-11-1740 d 2-2-1823 m Hannah Conklin PS NY
Zophar: b 1-20-1746 d *c*. 1815 m Asenath Buckbee Pvt NY
Zophar: b 1746 d 1837 m Jemima Scudder Rusco PS NY

KETTELL, (includes KETTLE, KITTEL, KITTELL, KITTLE)
Abraham Sr.: b 1- -1731 d 9-16-1816 m (1)Christina Westfael (2)Mary Scott Pvt NJ
Andrew: b 6-10-1759 d 9-2-1807 m Eleanor Bennett Sgt MA
Edmund: b 11-4-1758 d 7-5-1833 m Patience Fiske Pvt RI W★
Jacob: b 7-26-1757 d 10-10-1842 m Mary — Pvt PA ★
James: b 12-3-1740 d 2-15-1778 m Mary Gookin Sgt MA
James Sr.: b 9-15-1720 d 1793 m (1)Sarah Call (2)Sarah Hill (3)Elizabeth Wilson Pvt MA
James Jr.: b 1745 d 1829 m (1)Joanna Sweetser (2)Sarah Bradish Pvt MA
John: b 1760 d 1805 m Margaret Duyker Pvt NY
Wm.: b 6-14-1740 d 8-28-1826 m Anneke Toll Sol NY

KETTNER, (or KETNER)
Heinrich Adam: b 10-6-1725 d 10-19-1805 m Catherine — PS PA
Johannes: b 11-10-1763 d 7-28-1848 m Anna Margaret Bruetle Pvt PA

KEY,
George: b 1753 d 1-15-1836 m Susannah Craighead Pvt VA ★
George: b *c*. 1749 d 1799 m (1)Nancy Edward (2)Mary Center (3)Isabel Kennedy PS VA
Henry Jr.: b 4-11-1759 d 8-23-1810 m (1)Elizabeth Garrett (2)Phoebe Tolbert Capt SC
James: b 1740 d 1817 m Judith Keith PS MD
John: b *c*. 1735 d *c*. 1795 m — Capt NC
John: b 1760 d 1827 m Elizabeth Watson Pvt VA
John: b 1731 d *p*. 1789 m Agnes Witt PS VA
John Ross: b 9-19-1754 d 10-13-1821 m Ann Phoebe Penn Dagworthy Charlton 2Lt MD
John Walter: b 5-11-1751 d *p*. 12-2-1827 m Virginia Wade Ens VA
Jonathan: b 1748 d 1829 m Ann Adams Pvt NC
Martin Sr.: b 1715 d *p*. 11-24-1785 m Nancy Bibb PS VA
Martin Jr.: b 1752 d 1814 m — Pollard 2Lt VA
Phillip: b 1750 d 1-4-1840 m (1)Rebecca Rowles (2)Sophia Hall PS MD
Price: b 6-3-1754 d 7-14-1829 m Sarah McQueen Pvt QMSgt Ord-Sgt VA
Tandy: b 10-29-1754 d *a*. 7-23-1838 m Mildred Perkins Lt PA ★
Tandy Clark: b 5-19-1763 d bet 1807-15 m Mary Harvey Pvt PS SC
Thomas: b 1-18-1750 d 7- -1821 m (1)Frances Garrett (2)Elizabeth Scott Capt SC
Wm.: b 4-2-1761 d 1802 m (1)Sarah Gibson (2)Fanny Talbot Pvt SC
Wm.: b 10-14-1761 d 1-19-1834 m Elizabeth Gaines Pvt Mar VA
Wm. Bibb: b 10-2-1759 d 12-7-1836 m Mourning Clarke Pvt VA ★

KEYES, (includes KEES, KEESE, KEYS, KIES)
Abner Sr.: b 1738 d 12-17-1820 m Mary Shedd Sgt NH
Charles: b 1764/5 d 5- -1841 m Hannah Hink Pvt MA ★
Cyprian Jr.: b 1735 d *c*. 1805 m Martha Bush Pvt MA
Danforth: b 7-6-1740 d 9-14-1826 m Sarah Cutler Col MA
Daniel: b 6-4-1741 d 10-31-1797 m Abial — Sgt MA
Daniel: b 11-30-1731 d 4-1-1814 m Abigail Proctor PS Pvt NH
Ebenezer: b 10-24-1760 d 5-31-1838 m Jemima Jackson Pvt MA
Ebenezer: b 11-18-1755 d 1828 m Esther Hildreth Pvt NH
Edward: b 6-4-1750 d 5-1-1827 m Mary Works Pvt CT
Ephraim: b 7-4-1715 d 12-15-1804 m Sarah Wadkins Pvt NH
Ezra: b 1-27-1763 d 12-29-1841 m Hannah Knowlton Pvt MA ★
Israel: b 7-20-1760 d 9-18-1841 m Dollie Temple Pvt MA ★

John: b 1744 d 4-13-1824 m (1)Mary Wales (2)Mercy Scott Maj
  1st Adj Gen CT
John: b 9- -1736 d 1813 m Anna — Pvt NY
John: b 1760 d 2- -1854 m Sarah Clymer Cpl PA
John: b 1755 d 6- -1809 m Rhoda Appleby Asst Dep QMGen PA
John Wade: b 9-25-1752 d 2-13-1839 m Louisa or Luvica Talbott
  Capt VA
Jonathan: b 1-21-1728 d 1786 m Sarah Taylor Sgt MA
Joseph: b a. 1753 d 8-20-1834 m Mary Nichols Pvt NH ★
Joseph Sr.: b c. 1740 d 4-10-1808 m Rebecca Mullen Pvt NC
Matthew: b 2-5-1761 d 1833 m Ruth Calvin Pvt VA ★
Richard: b 1756 d 4-28-1830 m Mary Bailey Lt PA
Salma: b 1761 d p. 1805 m Mary Andrews Pvt MA
Samuel: b 11-16-1746 d 1814 m Thankful Hunt Capt MA
Simon: b 10-17-1742 d 10-29-1802 m Lucy Wheeler Pvt MA
Solomon: b 2-22-1756 d 12-21-1820 m Thankful Lincoln Sgt MA W★
Stephen: b 7-15-1717 d 4-2-1788 m Abigail Peabody Lt CT
Stephen: b 2-8-1738 d 2-17-1812 m (1)Elizabeth Ward (2)Mrs Molly
  Cross Sol MA
Thomas Sr.: b 12-24-1737 d 12-21-1812 m Mary Temple Cpl MA
Thomas: b 7-8-1755 d 11-2-1845 m (2)Eunice Knight Pvt MA
Wm.: b 10- -1740 d 4-21-1813 m Hannah Stowell Scarborough
  Capt NH

KEYSACKER, (or KEESUCKER)
George: b 1749-60 d 8-15-1851 m Catherine — Pvt VA

KEYSER, (includes KEISER, KISER, KYSER, KYSOR)
Andrew: b 12-16-1758 d 11-23-1833 m Sarah Rinehart Pvt VA
Charles Jr.: b c. 1750 d c. 1796 m Elizabeth Baker Pvt VA
Derrick: b 2-4-1737 d 1808 m Rachel Ottinger Pvt PA
George: b — d 1807 m Elizabeth — Pvt SC
Jacob: b c. 1758 d c. 1833 m Catherine Stumbaugh Sgt PA
Johannis: b c. 1750 d p. 1784 m Margaret Bedine Capt NY
John: b 12-8-1758 d 10-8-1837 m Ruth White Pvt NY
John: b 1719 d 1821 m (2)Mary Hamilton (3)Christina Fox Pvt PA
John: b 5-23-1730 d 5-2-1813 m Elizabeth Rinker PS PA
Michael: b 1740 d 1802 m Mary Lingle Pvt PA
Michael: b 8-30-1745 d 8-5-1825 m Catherine Knorr Pvt PA
Michael: bpt 12-25-1746 d p. 1-20-1808 m Catherine Liess PS PA
Michael: b — d 1794 m Catherine — Pvt PA
Peter: b 10-28-1726 d 4-6-1804 m Anna Margaret Biery Pvt PA
Wm.: b a. 1755 d 12-3/4-1837 m Keziah Snead Pvt VA

KEYT,
John: b 10-20-1755 d 1834 m (1)Elizabeth Carter (2)Sarah Carnes
  Pvt MD ★

KEZER, (or KEZAR)
David: b 1761 d 9-4-1839 m Anne Stevens Pvt MA ★
John: b 3-4-1763 d 7-20-1843 m (1)Apphia Lancaster (2)Mrs Lucy
  Barrows Pvt MA

KIBBE, (includes KIBBEY & KIBBIE)
Amariah: b 1747 d 1829 m (1)Hannah Kibbe (2)Maria Grover Capt
  CT
Daniel: b 1720 d12-15-1809 m Mary Pratt Pvt CT
David: b 9-1-1723 d — m Miriam — PS MA
Edward: b 11-7-1750 d 1-3-1827 m Mary Cody Sgt MA W★
Ephraim: b 12-10-1754 d 4-22-1809 m Phoebe Ann — Sgt NJ
Frederick: b 3-29-1762 d 1-25-1841 m Zelinda Pratt Pvt CT ★
Gideon: b 11-3-1734 d 6-6-1818 m Bridget Wood Lt MA
Isaac 3rd: b 2-3-1732/3 d 2-11-1880 m Margaret Terry Ens PS CT
Israel: b 12-28-1759 d 3-28-1836 m Ruth Wood Pvt CT ★
Jacob: b 1754 d 8-25-1818 m (1)— (2)Abilene Collins Pvt MA
Jedediah: b 12-25-1755 d 1-28-1834 m (2)Louisa — Pvt CT ★
John: b 2-28-1755 d 10-17-1839 m Olive Parrish Pvt MA ★
Lemuel: b 1752 d 8-17-1827 m Love Parsons Pvt CT W★
Moses: b 9-6-1752 d 4-26-1819 m Mary Parish Pvt MA
Peter: b 6-15-1731 d 2- 2-15-1808 m (1)Esther Wood (2)Anne
  (Marsh) Pratt Hills (3)Dorcas (Hubbard) Arnold PS CT
Philip W.: b 5-19-1761 d 11-5-1853 m Sara Meigs Pvt NH

KIBLER,
George: b 1-2-1758 d 3-4-1841 m Katherine Siegel Pvt PA ★
John: b 1760 d 6-22-1827 m (1)Mary Munford (2)Mary Riffe Pvt PA

KIBLINGER, (or KIPLINGER)
Adam: b 8-15-1762 d 7-15-1844 m Elizabeth Prince Pvt VA ★
Jacob: b 12-14-1753 d 1839 m Sarah Coolidge Pvt MA W★
John Sr.: b 1722 d 4-4-1777 m Catherine Wolfe CS MA
John Jr.: b 9-3-1755 d c. 1849 m Betty Fisher Pvt MA
Philip: b c. 1750 d p. 1788 m Abby — Sol VA

KICHLEIN, (includes KACHLEIN, KACHLINE, KEICHLINE)
Andrew: b 11-20-1752 d 1-24-1821 m Elizabeth — Pvt PA
Charles: b 1726 d 1788 m Susanna — PS PA
Johann Andreas: b 11-22-1728 d 9-22-1781 m (1)Susanna —
  (2)Mrs Catherine Texter Col PA
Peter: b 11-8-1722 d 11-27-1789 m (1)Margaretta Umbehendin
  (2)Anna Doll (3)Catherine Gwinner Col PA

KICHLEY,
Michael: b 1720 d 3- -1784 m Magdalena — PS PA

KIDD,
Alexander Jr.: b 1746 d 7-22-1822 m Mehetable Haines Lt NY
Benjamin: b 1753 d 6-23-1806 m Magdalena Kelchner Matr PA
John: b 1753 d 1826 m Mary Royston Pvt MD
John: b c. 1742 d p. 1809 m — Jennings Pvt VA
Nathaniel: b 1740 d 6-3-1824 m Hannah Britton Pvt PA
Robert: b — d p. 1791 m Mary McGowan Pvt NY
Webb: b c. 1730 d p. 8-16-1803 m Elizabeth White PS VA
Wm.: b 12-16-1763 d p. 9-6-1844 m Judith Carter Pvt VA ★
Wm.: b 1734 d 1803 m Eliza — Pvt VA

KIDDER,
Benjamin: b 2-8-1735 d 2-17-1822 m Lois Reed PS NH
Elijah: b c. 1762 d 1810 m Mary Sargent Pvt NH
Enoch: b 12-30-1697 d 1-5-1781 m Sarah Hunt PS MA
Francis: b 2-6-1743 d c. 1814 m Mary Chase Pvt MA
Francis: b 1752 d 2-10-1822 m (1)Abigail Russell (2)Lydia Abbot
  (3)Mrs Sally Davis Pvt MA
Isaac: b 3-28-1752 d 3-16-1825 m Sarah Stickney Pvt MA
James: b 5-14-1745 d 6-10-1820 m Deborah Wood Lt MA
John: b 7-5-1749 d 3-15-1825 m Sarah Dodge Pvt MA
John: b 11-8-1761 d 1-9-1852 m Dorothy Joslin Drm MA
John: b 1736 d 9-7-1828 m Jenny Lind Pvt NH
Jonas: b 11-16-1743 d 11-1-1837 m (1)Huldah Putnam (2)Alice
  (Taylor) Barron Capt NH
Josiah: b 4-18-1745 d 8-18-1803 m Mary Jewett Pvt MA
Nehemiah: b 4-9-1749 d 12-7-1811 m Abigail Kittridge Pvt MA
Oliver: b 12-19-1743 d 11-29-1812 m Eunice Burr Lt VT
Samuel: b 2-8-1734 d 1778 m Sara Corbin Ens MA
Samuel: b 1720 d 1777 m (1)Mary Thompson (2)Joanna — PS MA
Samuel: b 10-13-1740 d 10-8-1824 m Mehitable Maynard Lt NH
Thomas: b 9-16-1750 d 3-5-1827 m Ruth Page Sol NH

KIDDOO,
James: b 1762 d 9-30-1823 m (1)Elizabeth — (2)Mary Tidball
  Pvt PA

KIDNEY,
John: b 1-26-1749 d 11-26-1809 m Maria Winner Capt NJ
Jonathan: b 12-11-1759/60 d 3-20-1849 m Hannah Van Zantt Pvt
  Mar NY ★

KIDWELL,
Benjamin: b 5-25-1754 d 12-10-1810 m Elizabeth Mudd Pvt MD
Hezekiah: b c. 1760 d 1810-18 m Susanna — PS MD
Jonathan: b 9-20-1750 d 2-15-1835 m Rebecca — Pvt Arfr NC ★
Joshua: b 7-15-1757 d 3-25-1835 m Mary Britton Pvt NC

KIERSTED,
Christopher: b 8-23-1736 d 3-23-1791 m Leah Dubois Dr PS NY
Jacobus: b 1747 d p. 1803 m Charity Taylor Pvt NY

KIESTER, (includes KEISTER)
Frederick: b 1730 d 1815 m Hannah Dyer Lt VA
Philip: b 2-15-1747 d 11-15-1834 m Ann Elizabeth — Cpl PA

KIFF,
Andrew: b 1760 d 1826 m Mary Mabie Pvt NY

KILBOURN, (includes KILBORN, KILBOURNE, KILBURN)
Abraham: b 11-15-1759 d 12-4-1806 m Elizabeth Moranville Pvt CT
Abraham: b 4-12-1708 d 2-25-1776 m Rebecca Dickinson PS CT
Ashbel: b 4-17-1759 d 6-3-1814 m Laurena Evans Pvt CT
Benjamin, Jr.: b 6- -1761 d 6-3-1828 m Diana Denning Sgt PA ★
Calvin: b 10- -1757 d 1852 m (1)Mary Stratton (2)Mrs Sanderson
  Fif MA
Ebenezer: b 4-19-1744 d 8-3-1810 m (1)Jemima Ford (2)Sarah Bill
  Lt NH
Eliphalet: b 12-11-1752 d 12-12-1844 m Mary Thorla Sgt MA
Elisha: b 6-7-1749 d 1829 m Jemima Chamberlain Pvt MA
George: b 1733/4 d 2-7-1777 m (1)Rebecca Belding (2)Abigail
  Pierpont PS CT MA
Giles: b 1-25-1728 d 9-13-1797 m (1)Mary Pettibone (2)Chloe
  Munger Pvt CT
Hezekiah: b 11-7-1752 d 10-25-1804 m Prudence — Sgt MA NY
Jacob: b — d — m (2)Mary Fletcher Sgt MA
Jacob: b c. 1750 d 12- -1813 m (1)Anna Smith (2)Hannah Alden
  Pvt MA
Jedediah: b 8-15-1725 d 3-30-1803 m Hannah Platts Pvt MA
Jehiel: b c. 1748 d 4-18-1803 m Amy Vail Sol CT
Joel: b c. 1750 d p. 1785 m Sarah Bliss PS CT
John: b 4-12-1735 d 9-5-1820 m Anna Smith Capt MA
John: b 6-28-1750 d 9-8-1842 m Mary Howe Sgt MA ★
John Sr.: b 1704 d 4-8-1789 m (1)Mehitable Bacon (2)Hannah Fox
  PS NH
John Jr.: b 4-1-1736 d 7-20-1819 m Content Carpenter Lt NH
Jonathan Sr.: b 6-8-1707 d 10-12-1785 m Mary Skinner PS CT
Jonathan Jr.: b 4-12-1742 d 1807 m Hannah Chapman Capt CT
Joseph: b 7-2-1719 d — m Mary Sawyer PS MA

KILBOURN, contd.
Josiah: b 5-28-1706 d 1793 m (1)Mary Mack (2)Mrs Abial Day PS NH CT
Josiah: b 8-21-1731 d 3-23-1804 m (1)Deborah Attwood (2)Martha Thwing Pvt MA
Lemuel: b 10-7-1784 d 1820 m (1)Sarah Hastings (2)Anna O'dell Sol CT
Robert: b 5-12-1764 d 12- -1857 m Sarah Hubbard Sol MA
Roswell Sr.: b 6-29-1734 d 2-8-1777 m (1)Irene Bacon (2)Patience Jenkins Pvt CT
Samuel: b 11-7-1750 d 11-14-1834 m Elizabeth Stillman Pvt CT ★
Simeon: b 11-23-1759 d 11-6-1839 m Eunice Kirkham Pvt CT W★
Timothy: b 5-26-1757 d — m Relief Richardson Sgt MA
Wm.: b 1-12-1758 d 6- -1816 m Sarah Sage Pvt CT

KILBURY,
John: b c. 1730 d 1820 m (1)Zerviah — (2)Dorcas — Pvt VT NH

KILBY,
James: b c. 1755 d a. 7-19-1830 m (1)Lucy Sparks (2)Mrs Frances Burbridge Rice PS VA
John: b 11-8-1760 d 1842 m Mary Baxter Pvt CT ★
John: b 9-15-1758 d 2-9-1826 m Elizabeth Thompson Gnr VA

KILGORE,
Benjamin: b c. 1740 d c. 1810 m (1)Anne McCreary (2)— McDavid Capt SC
Charles Sr.: b 1-18-1744 d p. 5-16-1823 m (1)Winnie Clayton ( ) Martha — Pvt VA ★
Charles, Jr.: b 1-4-1764 d 11-28-1844 m Avarilla Simpson Pvt VA ★
David: b 2-28-1745 d 7-11-1814 m Sarah Mickey Capt PA
George: b a. 1745 d 1818 m — Lt VA
James: b 1758-60 d 5-5-1845 m (1)Abigail Lord (2)Mrs Abigail Dresser Pvt MA ★
Jesse: b 1751 d 1794 m Jane (Kilgore) Pvt PA
John Sr.: b c. 1730 d 4-20-1818 m Elizabeth Brackett Smn MA
John Jr.: b 4-14-1766 d 4-10-1843 m (1)Anna York (2)Abigail Shurtleff Cpl MA
Joseph: b c. 1752 d 12- -1815 m Isabella Stephen Pvt PA
Patrick: b c. 1744 d 1- -1808 m Jean — Pvt PA
Robert: b 1760 d p. 1797 m Ann Smith Pvt GA
Thomas: b c. 1715 d 1824 m Lydia — Sol NC
Wm.: b 1759 d 1823 m Margaret — Pvt GA

KILL,
Christopher: b 1747 d 10- -1829 m Polly Nier Pvt Matr NY ★

KILLAM,
Benjamin: b 5-20-1740 d 8-31-1811 m Sarah Foster Sol NH
Eliphalet: b 2-23-1753 d 10-31-1830 m Submit Abbe Cpl CT
Ephraim: b 7-18-1751 d 1836 m Abby Bundy Pvt PA ★
John: b 5-12-1729 d 10-11-1818 m Priscilla Bradstreet Pvt MA
Moses: b 1747 d 5-16-1831 m Polly or Mary — Sol NY
Thomas: b 7-18-1859 d c. 1850 m Hannah Jaquith Pvt MA ★
Thomas: b 1744 d 1782 m Sarah Fuller Pvt MA

KILLEN,
Daniel: b c. 1740 d 1813 m Mary McClatchey Pvt PA
Henry: b 1730 d 1786 m Susannah Griffith PS DE

KILLIAN, (includes KILLION, KILLOM)
Daniel: b c. 1752 d p. 1788 m — Pvt NC
Jacob: b 3-16-1755 d p. 9-5-1838 m Jennie Killion Pvt NC ★
Jacob: b 12-29-1761 d 11-10-1828 m Susanna Beck Pvt PA
John, Sr.: b c. 1725/6 d c. 1800 m Mrs Elizabeth Zimmerman PS NC
Michael: b c. 1750 d c. 1783 m Eva Elizabeth Ziegler Pvt PA

KILLICUT,
Thomas: b 1723 d p. 1784 m Mary — Pvt NH

KILLINGER,
George: b 1759 d 1813 m Elizabeth — Pvt PA
Michael: b 5-15-1731 d 7-11-1815 m Catharine — Pvt PS CS PA

KILLINGSWORTH,
Jacob: b c. 1745 d 1798 m Mary Salisbury Lt PS SC

KILMER, (includes KULMER)
Hendrick: b 2-5-1728 d 1795 m Callin Hollenbeck Pvt NY
John: bpt 8-27-1739 d 1823 m Elizabeth Mickle Pvt NY
Wm.: bpt 1746 d 1792 m Gertrude Pulver Pvt NY

KILPATRICK,
Andrew: b 1746 d 3-27-1814 m (1)Jane Nichols (2)Elizabeth Barr Pvt NC
Robert: b 8-2-1735 d 6-30-1840 m (1)Martha Isabella Dunn (2)Anne MacDonald Sgt SC ★
Roger: b 1740 d 1797 m Jean — Pvt VA
Samuel: b c. 1735 d c.,1812 m Elizabeth Oliphant Pvt NJ
Thomas: b 1753 d p. 1828 m Martha Scott Sol GA

KILTS,
Adams: b 8-27-1730 d p. 1790 m Catherine Franck Pvt NY

Conrad: b 8-8-1761 d 1-11-1839 m Anna Elizabeth Saret Pvt NY ★
Conrad A.: b 9-7-1756 d 5-12-1846 m Catharine Leip Pvt NY
Peter: b — d p. 7-25-1784 m Anna Maria Bellinger Pvt NY

KIMBALL, (includes CIMBAL, KEMBLE, KIMBELL & KIMBLE)
Aaron, Sr.: b 2-15-1729 d 11-20-1807 m Mary Brooks Capt MA
Aaron, Jr.: b 6-29-1760 d 11-13-1843 m Mary Goulding Pvt MA ★
Aaron: b 9-12-1747 d 12-2-1837 m (1)Eunice Lee (2)Abigail — (3)Judith Lendall PS NH
Abel: b 2-10-1731 d 6-4-1790 m (1)Sarah Pearl (2)Mary Haggett PS Lt MA
Abel: b 1755 d 1832 m Sybil Chapman Pvt PA
Abraham: b 1757 d p. 1807 m (1)Sarah Smith (2)Susan Hodgkins Pvt MA
Abraham: b 4-18-1742 d 5- -1828 m Phoebe Runnels Pvt NH
Abraham Tyler: b 8-6-1757 d 5-5-1834 m Sarah Babbitt Cpl CT
Amos: b 9-8-1707 d 1-26-1788 m (1)Margaret Hale (2)Mrs Abigail Sessions Pvt MA
Amos: b 8-31-1750 d 9-20-1820 m Abigail Corliss Pvt NH
Andrew: b 9-27-1750 d 5-11-1826 m Mary — Pvt NH ★
Aquilla: b 9-28-1755 d 3-4-1826 m Ann Tenny Sgt MA
Asa: b 3-27-1737 d 2-3-1797 m Hannah Sweet LCol RI
Benjamin: b 8- -1761 d — m Ann — Sol MA RI CL
Benjamin: b 3-10-1734 d 1779 m Joanna Lee Capt MA
Benjamin: b 1756 d 7-16-1833 m Mary Huldah Gould Pvt ME
Benjamin: b 10-24-1756 d 6-20-1822 m Lois Warner Sgt MA
Benjamin: b 8-5-1741 d 8-23-1779 m Sarah Little Capt PM NH
Benjamin: b 6-30-1761 d p. 1832 m Joanna Fry Pvt Mar MA NH ★
Benjamin: b 5-27-1707 d 10- -1784 m Elizabeth Greeley PS NH
Boyce: b 6-18-1731 d 5-13-1802 m Rebecca Hayward Sol MA
Boyce: b 3-4-1757 d 4-6-1820 m Mary Pike Pvt MA
Buckner: b c. 1812 m Pattie Harriss Capt NC
Caleb: b 10-10-1744 d 1830 m Hannah Noyes Capt MA
Caleb: b 12-10-1753 d 7-30-1807 m Elizabeth Hammon Pvt MA
Caleb: b 9-24-1748 d 12-19-1825 m Sarah Sawyer Pvt NH
Charles: b 1745 d 3- -1825 m Jerusha Walker Pvt CT
Daniel: b 9-15-1752 d 2-4-1836 m Mary Sterry CS CT
Daniel: b 1-4-1736 d 12-29-1801 m Sarah Day PS Lt MA
Daniel: b 6-11-1747 d 8-19-1800 m Elizabeth Tenny Lt MA
Daniel: b 7-5-1751 d 5-24-1813 m Lucy Dutton Lt MA
Daniel: b 10-25-1773 d 5-24-1843 m (1)Elizabeth Osgood (2)Abiah Holt Pvt MA ★
Daniel: b 11-11-1711 d 12-19-1785 m Hepzibah Howe Pvt MA
Daniel, Jr.: b 10-6-1750 d 10-24-1814 m Mary Stevens Pvt MA
Daniel: bpt 6-6-1738 d a. 6- -1791 m Martha Wentworth PS NH
David: b 12-10-1739 d 9-4-1804 m Abigail Burwell Pvt MA
David: b 4-12-1760 d 10-18-1842 m Lydia Simmons Pvt MA ★
David: b 3-11-1765 d 11-30-1839 m Olive — Pvt MA
David: b 6-15-1749 d 1-12-1817 m (1)Ruth Whitmore (2)Mehitable Clement Pvt NH
David: b 4-2-1743 d 3-24-1810 m Rebecca Flint Pvt MA
David: b 8-3-1760 d 8-8-1799 m Priscilla Herrick Pvt NH
David: b — d p. 8-18-1838 m — Sol NC
Ebenezer: b 3-17-1755 d 7-8-1826 m Sarah Baker Pvt MA
Ebenezer: b 12-3-1763 d p. 1801 m Judith Hunt Pvt MA
Edmund: b 5-2-1751 d 2-11-1813 m Rebecca Gage Pvt MA
Edward: b 2-3-1763 d 1814 m Sarah Emerson Pvt NH
Eliphalet, Sr.: b 2-10-1730 d 5-5-1805 m Elizabeth Woodward Sgt NH
Ephraim, Sr.: b 8-16-1722 d 2-14-1782 m Mary Weatherbee PS MA
Ephraim, Jr.: b 2-15-1752 d 5- -1825 m Betty White Pvt MA
Ezra: b 9-11-1744 d p. 1820 m Sally Holmes Sgt MA ★
George: b 2-29-1723/24 d 10-13-1790 m Sarah Mulliken Capt MA
Hasadiah: bpt 9-11-1749 d p. 1818 m (1)Mary Stevens (2)Mrs Mary Lassell Sgt MA
Isaac: b 1-29-1741 d 8-3-1815 m Abigail Raymond Pvt MA
Jacob: b 10-12-1706 d 5-4-1788 m (1)Mary Peake (2)Anne — (3)Martha — PS CT
Jacob: b 12-1-1735 d 5-18-1826 m Esther Phillips CS PA
James: b c. 1740 d p. 1778 m — Pvt MD
James: bpt 7-11-1742 d 1833 m (1)Elizabeth Gilpatrick (2)Eunice Stone PS ME
Jedediah: b 12-21-1749 d 1825 m Eunice Love Pvt CT VA
Jeremiah, Sr.: b 7-25-1735 d 11-6-1808 m (1)Abigail Runnells (2)Sarah Parker Heath 1Lt MA
Jeremiah, Jr.: b 6-26-1762 d p. 1806 m (1)Judith Snow (2)Mary Tucker Pvt MA
Jesse: b 3-19-1760 d 11-18-1857 m (2)Elizabeth Rollifson Pvt CT
Joab: b 4-15-1762 d 11-19-1843 m Elizabeth Reed Pvt MA
John, Sr.: b 8-9-1735 d 10-28-1810 m Jerusha Meacham Capt CT
John, Jr.: b 10-8-1760 d 8-14-1839 m Priscilla Spalding Pvt CT ★
John: b 1740 d p. 1790 m Sarah Burham Pvt ME
John: b 1-10-1736 d 12-1-1814 m Dorothy — Pvt MA
John: b — d 1820 m (1)Elsie Edgerly (2)Sarah Crosby Lt NH
John: b 1-26-1735 d — m Dorothy Dudley Lt NH
John: b 6-9-1737 d p. 1779 m (1)Merriam Hadlock (2)Mary Kimball Sol NH
John, Sr.: b 12-20-1699 d 1- -1785 m (1)Abigail Lyford (2)Sarah Wilson PS NH
John, Jr.: b 11-20-1742 d 1807 m (1)Huldah Bachelder (2)Mrs Mary Weeks PS NH
John: b 2-5-1738/39 d 12-31-1817 m Anna Ayer PS NH
John: b 2-11-1764 d 1844 m Dolly Hoyt Pvt Smn RI ★

Jonathan: b 7-23-1761 d 7-31-1823 m Mary Cheney Pvt MA ★
Jonathan: b 4-19-1759 d 4-2-1814 m (1)Sarah Currier (2)Lois Hoyt Pvt NH
Jonathan: b 10-22-1764 d 9-9-1853 m Betsey Noyes Pvt NH
Joseph: b 8-1-1760 d 3-8-1838 m (1)Sarah Mallory (2)Ede Felch Pvt MA ★
Joseph: b 1-29-1739-41 d 11-6-1814 m (1)Mary Sanborn (2)Sarah Smith Cpl RI
Joseph: b 12-29-1731 d 10-22-1822 m (1)Hannah Morgan (2)Mary Clift (3)Eleanor Dunlop Pvt NH
Joseph: b 9-10-1749 d 10-27-1821 m Eunice Gallup Pvt NH
Joseph: b 9-13-1735 d 4-14-1803 m Elizabeth — Capt RI
Joshua: b a. 1747 d 4-15-1823 m Martha Elden Pvt MA
Joshua: b 2- -1761 d 1807 m Hannah Crowell Sol MA
Lebbeus: b 2-25-1751 d 9-4-1839 m Sarah Crafts Sol NY
Mellen: b 10-16-1760 d 2-7-1834 m Mary Worthen Pvt NH
Michael: b 7-6-1748 d 7- -1803 m (1)Elizabeth Runnells (2)Anna — PS NH
Moses: b 5-6-1741 d 1835 m Mary Satterlee Pvt CT
Moses, Jr.: b 1-9-1752 d 1-7-1829 m Mary Jones Cpl MA
Moses: b 1-18-1736 d 7-26-1822 m Dorothy Robinson Pvt MA
Moses: b 9-14-1747 d 11-9-1828 m Jemima Clement OrdlSgt NH W ★
Nathan: b 1749 d 11-8-1802 m Mary Poore Pvt MA
Nathaniel: bpt 9-9-1705 d 1785 m (1)Abigail Cousens (2)Mehitable Scammon PS CS ME
Nathaniel: b 3-24-1757 d 10-12-1843 m Salley Stickney Sgt MA ★
Nathaniel: b 2-3-1743/44 d p. 1780 m Mary Woodman Cpl MA
Nathaniel: b 7-8-1733 d 6-3-1819 m Elizabeth Low Pvt MA
Nathaniel: b 11-7-1748 d 1800 m Susanna Sawyer QM Sgt NH
Nathaniel: b 1749 d 4-28-1810 m Lydia Livermore Pvt PS NH
Noah Brooks: b 5-19-1756 d 8-21-1856 m (1)Persis Brigham (2)Mary Chase Pvt MA
Oliver, Sr.: b 5-24-1724 d 11-3-1801 m Mary Ober PS NH
Oliver, Jr.: b 12-7-1745 d 4-20-1821 m Mary Allen Cpl NH
Peter: b 10-16-1739 d 12-11-1811 m (1)Elizabeth Thurston (2)Priscilla — Capt PS NH
Peter: b c. 1730 d p. 1730 m Miss Clendennis PS VA
Peter Sanborn: bpt 8-3-1760 d p. 1796 m (1)Abigail Dean (2)Mrs Elizabeth Small Pvt NH
Phineas: b 12-8-1745 d 11-6-1826 m Lucy Pearl Pvt NH
Reuben: b 5-3-1758 d 6-13-1815 m Miriam Collins Capt NH
Reuben: b 4-17-1738 d 5- -1811 m Hannah Annis Cpl NH
Richard: b 8-21-1762 d 11-23-1828 m Susanna Holden Pvt CT
Richard: b 12-20-1722 d 3-2-1803-05 m Sarah Hayden Pvt MA
Richard: b 12-25-1728 d 1809 m Anne Robinson Pvt MA
Richard: bpt 4-12-1747 d — m (1)Susannah Lord (2)Sarah Hidden Sgt MA
Richard: b 10-13-1732 d 1780 m Sarah Harriman PS CS MA
Richard: b 5-21-1746 d 3-8-1815 m Lois Patten Ens NH
Richard, Sr.: b 6-11-1710 d 12-19-1785 m (1)Mercy Kimball (2)Elizabeth Seeton PS NH
Robert: b 1735 d 10-24-1808 m Anna — Sol NH
Samuel: b 6-5-1750 d 11-14-1835 m (1)Phoebe Burrill (2)Mary Jephson Pvt CT
Samuel: b 12-7-1750 d 11-15-1800 m Mary Goodrich 2Lt MA
Samuel: b 5-6-1748 d 1802 m (1)Eunice Apton (2)Mrs Mary (Mugford) Putnam Cpl MA
Samuel: b 4-9-1755 d 1835 m Elizabeth Hoyt Pvt NH MA
Samuel: b 2-26-1736 d 10-23-1814 m Elizabeth Carlton Pvt NH
Samuel, Sr.: b 8-17-1714 d 1789 m Hannah Abbott PS NH
Samuel, Jr.: b 7-5-1745 d 12-6-1802 m Abigail Eastman Pvt NH
Sargent: b 4-27-1761 d 3-10-1851 m (1)Love Ladd (2)Abigail — (4)Mrs Betsy (George) Marsh Pvt NH ★
Stephen: b 9-13-1738 d 9-1-1782 m Mrs Margaret (Barkey) Daugherty Pvt MD
Stephen: b 2-10-1740 d 2-23-1791 m Meriam Stone LCol RI
Thomas, Sr.: b 2-5-1730 d 5-21-1805 m (1)Mary Cross (2)Elizabeth Stratton Capt MA
Thomas, Jr.: b 2-26-1756 d 12-27-1810 m Huldah Porter Pvt MA
Thomas: b 2-12-1730/31 d 1789 m Hannah Kimball Cpl MA
Thomas: b 7-17-1753 d 1825 m Olive Lovejoy PS NH
Timothy: b 8-16-1741 d p. 1790 m Anna Dow Cpl MA
Walter: b 1754 d p. 1810 m Elizabeth Jennings Pvt PA
Wm.: b 9-29-1757 d 9-25-1844 m Abigail Hamlet Pvt MA
Wm.: b 12-16-1757 d 1-29-1813 m (1)Lucy Abbott (2)Bethia Gordon Pvt MA
Wm.: b 12-19-1757 d 7-25-1795 m Ruth Kimball Pvt MA
Wills: b 3-31-1760 d 1-17-1844 m Mercy Roberts Pvt NH ★
Ziba: b 9-1-1754 d 1781 m Rebecca Colbourn Pvt NH

KIMBER,
Richard Preddy: b 1737 d 1822 m Gertrude Griffith Sol PA
Sanuel: b 9-11-1762 d 1835 m Mary — Pvt NY

KIMBERLIN,
Jacob: b 1757 d 7-4-1801 m Sarah Hines Sol VA

KIMBERLY,
Abraham: b 1-6-1739 d 1-31-1808 m Tamar Burrett Lt CT
Ephraim: b c. 1738 d 1796 m Mary Riggs Capt CT

Ezra: b 1-18-1764 d 8-28-1844 m (1)Phebe Bradley (2)Lucy (Ball) Beecher (3)Lucy Ball PS CT
Fitch: b 12-22-1736 d 5-31-1813 m Abigail Woodruff Pvt CT
George: b 1746 d 7-25-1817 m Beulah Morse Pvt CT
Gilead: b 1755 d 2-12-1831 m (1)Mary Brockett (2)Mrs Mary (Merrick) Bradley Sgt CT
Isaac Sherman: b 1-23-1733/4 d c. 1842/3 m Sarah Wheaton Lt CT
Nathaniel: b 5-12-1743 d a. 8-18-1806 m Mabel Thompson Cpl CT
Silas: b 1743 d 1-17-1803 m Sarah Smith Capt PS CT
Thomas: b 1712 d 12-30-1801 m Lois Tuttle Sol CT

KIMBROUGH,
John: b 1745 d 5- -1799 m Ann Legrande Lt GA
Joseph: b c. 1760-2 d c. 1804 m Elizabeth Yancey Sol VA
Samuel: b c. 1735 d 1810 m Sarah (Cary) Thomson PS VA
Wm.: b 1735 d 9-28-1803 m — Pvt GA

KIMMEL, (includes KIMMELL)
Adam: b 9-12-1733 d 1-27-1778 m Barbara Miller PS 1Lt PA
George: b 12-25-1743 d 4-18-1818 m Julia Ann Ruby Pvt PA
Jacob: b 9-7-1757 d 11-14-1824 m Mary Hoffman Pvt PA
Michael: b 3-14-1736 d 5- -1818 m Julianna Asper PM Capt PA

KIMMIS,
John: b 1731 d 6-22-1822 m Mary Darragh Pvt NY

KIMPTON,
Rufus: b 9-2-1762 d 2-17-1822 m Abigail Breck Pvt Drm MA ★

KINCAID, (includes KINKEAD)
Andrew: b c. 1755 d 1826/27 m Martha — Pvt PA
Archibald: b c. 1750-55 d 2-7-1823 m Janette Townley Pvt PA
Charles: b 1737 d 12-29-1782 m Hannah — Pvt PA
David: b 1747 d 1805 m Martha Sproul Pvt DE
George: b c. 1744-46 d — m Margaret Renick Pvt VA
James: b 1754 d 7-22-1836 m Jane Reed Pvt NC ★
James: b 1752 d 10-20-1801 m Mary McMorris Capt SC
James: b 3-10-1763 d 7-8-1841 m Sarah Wilson Lt VA ★
John: b 1762 d 9-15-1840 m Susanna Dracket Pvt Pvtr MA ★
John: b 8-9-1749 d 8-10-1836 m Anna Gregory Capt SC ★
John: b 1734 d 1819 m Margaret — Capt VA
John: b c. 1750 d c. 1810 m Anne Graham Pvt VA
John: b 1-11-1758 d 8-11-1835 m Alice Dean Sol VA ★
John: b 3-10-1760 d p. 4-21-1834 m Elizabeth Galespei Pvt VA ★
John: b c. 1712 d p. 1782 m Elizabeth — CS VA
Joseph: b c. 1750 d 8-18-1782 m Jane — Capt VA
Robert: b 2-28-1764 d 6-26-1736 m Margaret Dunn Pvt NC ★
Samuel: b 11-9-1763 d 12-9-1865 m Merrium Stewart Pvt PA
Samuel, Jr.: b c. 1734 d 1-23-1819 m Margaret Clark CS VA
Thomas: b 12-13-1755 d 7-13-1819 m Mary Patterson Sgt VA
Thomas: b 1749 d c. 1830 m Hannah Tincher Pvt VA
Wm.: b 1-9-1736 d 5-3-1823 m Eleanor Guy Capt VA

KINCANNON,
Andrew: b 10-27-1744 d 11- -1829 m Catherine McDonald Capt VA

KINCHELOE, (includes KINSLOW)
Daniel: b 1-8-1723 d 1785 m (1)Elizabeth Wickliffe (2)Mrs Susan (Davis) Wickliffe PS VA
Peter: b 1734 d p. 1810 m Margaret Walls Pvt VA
Thomas L.: b 10-8-1761 d 11-10-1845 m (1)Hannah Robinson (2)Nancy Edwards RO OrdlSgt VA
Wm.: b 5-26-1736 p. 10-10-1788 m Mary White Capt VA

KINCHEN,
John Dawson: b 1740 d 1793 m Elizabeth Marshall PS NC
Wm.: b c. 1735 d c. 1832/33 m Sarah — Pvt NC

KINDER, (includes GINDER & GUNDER)
Peter: b — d p. 1-23-1827 m Dolly — Pvt PA
Phillip: b 1747 d 2-21-1829 m — Pvt PA ★

KINDRED,
Bartholomew: b 1734 d 1805 m Paradine — Pvt VA
Thomas: b 1760 d 1836 m Nancy Sharp Pvt VA ★
Wm.: b c. 1743/44 d p. 10-15-1829 m — Pvt VA ★

KINDT,
Nicholas: b c. 1730 d a. 10-24-1783 m (1)Christena — (2)Elizabeth — Pvt PS PA

KING,
Aaron: bpt 5-18-1729 d 4-21-1782 m Sarah Kibbe PS MA
Abraham H.: b 2-11-1762 d 11-8-1852 m — Pvt Mus NJ ★
Adonijah: b 2-18-1757 d 7-25-1825 m Elizabeth — Pvt MA
Alexander: b 12-6-1749 d 2-6-1831 m Abigail Olcott Ens CT
Alexander: b 1754 d 8-8-1826 m Nancy Jackson Sgt PA ★
Amos: b 3-12-1758 d 7-13-1839 m Esther Robinson Pvt MA
Apollos: b 6-15-1763 d 12-18-1842 m Mary Rhodes Pvt MA ★
Asaph: b 1- -1747 d 10-10-1832 m Mary Robbins Lt MA
Ashbel: b 1-26-1748 d 5-21-1808 m (1)Jemima Burnham (2)Mrs Jemima Smith Ens CT

KING, contd.

Barzillia, Sr.: b *c.* 1730 d *p.* 1790 m Lydia Hinckley Pvt NY
Baxter: b *c.* 1749 d 3-10-1801 m Eleanor Johnston Capt NC W ★
Benjamin: b *c.* 1747 d 9-20-1810 m Susannah Blake NCapt MD
Benjamin, Sr.: b *c.* 1722 d — m Sarah Taylor Pvt NH
Benjamin, Jr.: b 5-23-1749 d 8-30-1801 m Ruth Bartlett 2Lt MA
Benjamin: b 10-21-1720 d 12-4-1803 m (1)Abiah Leonard (2)Deliverance Eddy PS DE
Caleb: b 11-20-1756 d 5-5-1840 m (1)Lydia Sherwin (2)Lovice (Carter) Ens MA ★
Charles: b *c.* 1730 d — m Charity Pennington PS SC
Clement: b 3-15-1756 d 12-18-1835 m Mary Woodward Pvt RI NY ★
Constant Victor: b 10-11-1752 d 11-14-1800 m Adah Hull Lt NJ W ★
Cornelius: b 11-21-1753 d 8-26-1839 m — Sgt VA ★
Cushing: b 2-18-1764 d 11-29-1843 m (1)Chloe Warrinner (2)Eliza Bates Pvt MA
Dan: b 2-8-1740 d 7-21-1816 m (1)Rebecca Austin (2)Hannah Harmon Pvt CT
Dan: b 10-11-1741 d 9-1-1833 m (1)Thankful Brownson (2)Delight Parks Pvt CT
Daniel: b 9-2-1749 d 3-15-1815 m Hannah Lord Capt MA
David: b 9-19-1756 d *p.* 1789 m Eunice Dart Pvt CT
David: b 8-21-1726 d 3-11-1807 m Elizabeth Gray Sgt MA
Douglass: b 10-30-1729 d 9- -1814 m Hannah Sheldon Pvt MA
Edmund: b 1740-45 d *a.* 7-7-1817 m (1)Miss Beavers (2)Mrs Thomas (3)Elizabeth (Woodson) Thomas Capt PS CS VA
Edward: b 1746 d 1800 m Feely Lewis Pvt NC
Eli: b 11-17-1759 d 12-25-1835 m (1)Lydia Vinson (2)Mrs Brown Cpl MA
Eli: b *c.* 1760 d *p.* 1790 m Hannah Temple Pvt PA
Elijah: b *a.* 1745 d *p.* 1781 m Mary Baker Pvt CT
Elijah: b 2-9-1758 d 9-24-1825 m (1)Mary Benjamin (2)Mrs Isabella (Williams) Pvt Sgt MA
Elijah: b 12-14-1737 d 1794 m Maria Cooke CS MA
Eliphalet: b 2-6-1743 d 8-29-1821 m (1)Mary Remington (2)Silence Rumrill 1Lt CT
Ephraim: b 5-14-1709 d *p.* 1777 m Elizabeth Vail PS NY
Francis: b 11-25-1757 d 10-24-1830 m Mary Jones Cpl MD ★
Francis: b 6-30-1747 d 9-15-1784 m Isabella McCullough Pvt PA
Frederick: b 10-6-1738 d 4-4-1796 m Mary Ayres QM NJ
George: b 1723 d 1-19-1777 m Hannah — Capt MA
George: b 11-27-1744 d 1-16-1827 m Betty Shaw Sgt MA
George, Jr.: b *c.* 1753 d *p.* 1777 m — PS NH
George: b 1744 d 1799 m Maria Phoenix PS NJ
George: b — d 1792 m Catharine — Ens PA
George: b 5-5-1758 d 3-24-1840 m Margaret McDowell Sol PA
George: b *c.* 1740 d *c.* 1787 m Mary Hannah Capt SC
George: b 5-12-1751 d 2-7-1838 m Mary Saunders OrdlSgt VA ★
George: b 1732 d 1819 m Sarah Garrard Sgt MA
George: b 1761 d 12-5-1838 m Mary Bowling Pvt VA ★
George: b 1730 d *p.* 5-6-1806 m Mary Niblett Sol VA
George H.: b 7-25-1762 d 11-24-1848 m Erley Haxstine Pvt MA ★
Gideon: b 3-4-1747 d 8-5-1798 m (1)Mary Kendall (2)Ruth Graham Pvt CT
Gideon: b 8-24-1729 d 12-11-1802 m Charity Tucker PS CS CT
Gideon: b 1754-59 d 1800 m Grasilva Hendricks Pvt MA
Godfrey: b 2-9-1750 d *p.* 1832 m Abagail Macomber Sgt RI ★
Heman, Sr.: b 10-15-1727 d 1-21-1812 m Elizabeth Cartwright Pvt NY
Henry: b 1750 d 1799 m Penina Wimberly Cmsry MD
Henry: b 5-9-1748 d 1-2-1822 m Prudence Dudley Sgt MA
Henry: b 10-28-1763 d 9-6-1822 m Ann Vila Pvt MA
Henry: b *c.* 1708 d 2- -1784 m Abigail Green PS MA
Henry: b 5-28-1721 d 8-16-1818 m Mrs Susannah Cochran PS VA
Hezekiah: b 11-20-1740 d 8-20-1807 m Ruhama Smith Pvt MA
Hezekiah: b 11-20-1755 d 5-6-1823 m Mercy Thornton Pvt MA
Hophni: b — d *p.* 1789 m Joanna Holton Capt MA
Hugh: b *c.* 1736 d *p.* 1-13-1779 m Mary — Lt DE
Hugh: b 12-17-1754 d *p.* 1846 m Mary Montgomery Pvt NC
Hugh: b 1-29-1750 d 5-21-1811 m Abigail Voorhees Capt PA
Ichabod: b 5-14-1756 d 12-18-1834 m Lovisa Adams Pvt CT
Ichabod: b 7-14-1758 d 7-1-1820 m Mary Huston Cpl MA
Isaac: b 9-17-1762 d 11-8-1859 m Sally Putnam Pvt MA
Jabez, Sr.: b 1-10-1729 d 2-15-1813 m Mary Washburn Pvt MM MA
Jabez, Jr.: b 6-1-1763 d 12-5-1846 m Abigail Udall Pvt VT
Jacob: b *a.* 1750 d *p.* 1790 m Abigail Johnston Pvt PA
Jacob: b *a.* 1733 d *a.* 8-3-1781 m Anna Catharine Illick PS PA
James, Jr.: b 4-26-1752 d 12-17-1819 m Nancy Forquehr Pvt DE
James: b 9-20-1742 d 12-20-1811 m Lydia Pierce Sgt MA
James, Sr.: b 1765 d 12-2-1850 m Nancy Young Pvt NH
James: b 1-6-1737 d 1-6-1815 m (1)Sarah Hall (2)Sarah Brevard Sol NC
James: b 1755 d 1836 m (1)Rachael Rhodes (2)— Molsey Pvt NC
James: b 6-15-1757 d *p.* 9-23-1839 m (1)Sarah — (2)Elizabeth — Pvt NC ★
James, Jr.: b 3-28-1765 d 11-13-1844 m (2)Roby Howland Pvt RI
James: b 1752 d 8-17-1825 m Sarah Goodson Sol VA
Jeremiah: b 1737 d 9-28-1786 m Hannah Youngs Pvt NY
Job: b 6-12-1743 d 8-27-1825 m Zipporah Williams Pvt MA
Joel: b *c.* 1760 d *a.* 1827 m Mary — Sol GA
John: b 5-26-1762 d 10-27-1836 m Jane Knight Pvt CT ★

John: b 1733 d 2-25-1832 m Sinia E. Atkins Cpl DE
John: b — d 7-15-1806 m Letitia — Cpl DE
John: b 12-3-1759 d 2-25-1832 m Margaret — Pvt DE ★
John: b 1738 d 1816 m Eleanor — PS MD
John, Sr.: b 8-26-1730 d 3-6-1814 m Katharine Leonard Capt MA
John, Jr.: b 9-9-1752 d 4-29-1827 m (2)Hannah Randall (4)Sally (Leonard) Weed Pvt MA
John, Sr.: b 9-11-1730 d 5-1-1808 m Elizabeth Fenner Capt PS MA
John, Jr.: b 9-4-1753 d 8-8-1841 m Mrs Caroline (Haxton) Gage Pvt MA ★
John: b 4-8-1740 d 9-13-1806 m Rebeckah Phelps Capt MA
John: b 1-19-1737 d 1795 m Elizabeth Town Capt MA
John: b 1730 d 5-14-1806 m (2)Rachel Clapp Pvt MA
John: b 10-21-1740 d 4-2-1812 m Betty McEllwain Pvt MA
John: b 1765 d 11-2-1855 m (1)Sarah Hawkins (2)Sarah Bovie Mus MA ★
John: b — d 1807 m Sarah Wiswall Dr Pvt MA
John: b 9-17-1758 d 9-18-1837 m (1)Mary McKinley (2)Sarah White Pvt PA NC ★
John: b 1731 d 7-4-1809 m Isabel Hunter Capt PA
John: b 1726 d 12-9-1801 m Margret Lois Miller Lt PA
John: b 1759 d *p.* 1818 m Maria Barbara Hildebrand Ens PA
John: b 9-22-1753 d 10-18-1805 m Jean Dickson Ens PA
John: b 1751 d 1811 m (1)Anna Maria Snyder (2)Elizabeth Wagoner Pvt PA
John: b — d 10-19-1777 m Johanna Hamilton PS PA
John, Jr.: b — d — m Betsey — Pvt PA
John: b *c.* 1722 d *p.* 9-3-1798 m Isabella — Pvt VA
John: b 12-1-1740 d *p.* 1795 m Mary Hampton Pvt VA
John: b 1754 d 6-22-1840 m Eleonor Karr Pvt VA ★
John: b 1-12-1758 d 3-25-1842 m Sarah Lemaster Life Grd VA ★
John Edwards: b 12-21-1757 d 5-13-1828 m Sallie Clifton Pvt VA
Jonah: b 3-3-1752 d 3-11-1833 m Susannah Hale Pvt Arfr CT MA ★
Jonas: b 1-27-1754 d 9-20-1832 m Abagail Leonard Cpl MA
Jonathan: b 2-28-1742 d 9-18-1776 m Bethia Austin Pvt CT
Jonathan: b 10-22-1748 d 1-28-1822 m Mary Clark Sgt MA
Jonathan: b 1-17-1736 d 1800 m Abigail (Manning) Dr MA
Jonathan: b 1761 d 1827 m Lucy Blanchard Pvt MA ★
Joseph: b 4-15-1741 d 3-19-1814 m Tryphena (Kendall) Bowker Pvt CT
Joseph: b 1752 d 9-25-1807 m Mary Church Pvt MA
Joseph: b *c.* 1759 d 1821 m Mourning — Pvt VA
Joshua: b 11-24-1758 d 8-13-1839 m Anne Ingersoll Fif RegQM CT MA ★
Joshua: b 6-13-1748 d 1814 m Martha Pearl Pvt RI
Joshua: b *c.* 1757 d *c.* 1802 m Rachel Kennedy Sol VA
Josiah: b 8-5-1731 d 7-24-1815 m Sarah Kellogg MM Capt CT
Josiah: b 10-2-1739 d — m Ruth Basset Capt MA
Lemuel: b 9-20-1765 d 11-17-1827 m Jane Bronson Pvt CT
Mathias: b *a.* 1734 d 1810 m Eva Christena Hurtzel Cpl PA
Micah: b 5-18-1754 d *p.* 1790 m Sarah — Pvt CT
Michael, Sr.: b *c.* 1715 d *p.* 11-27-1783 m Mary — PS NC
Michael: b *c.* 1741 d 5- -1801 m Susanna Passmore Pvt PA
Miles: b 11 2-1747 d 6-19-1814 m (1)Barbara Jones (2)Martha Kirby Capt VA
Miles: b — d 1823 m Mrs Elizabeth (Barr) Potter Dr PS VA
Moses: b 1761 d 8-10-1803 m Mary Pushard Pvt MA
Nathan: b 1744 d 11-1-1780 m Damiras Hathaway Pvt MA
Nathan: b 11-7-1750 d 1839 m Ailse Lee Capt NC ★
Nathaniel: bpt 9-27-1753 d *p.* 1790 m Hannah Doty Pvt MA
Nathaniel: b 1760 d 1840 m Anna Mead Pvt NY
Paul: b 1734 d *p.* 12-31-1808 m Mary Alexander Lt MA
Peter: b 1745 d 8-22-1828 m (2)Mrs Mehitable (Pike) Old Pvt CT
Peter: b 2-11-1757 d 4-19-1855 m Abigail Ingram Pvt MA ★
Philip: b 10-23-1738 d *c.* 1794 m (1)Mary Wales (2)Martha Bowers Capt MA
Philip: b 12-30-1761 d 11-28-1854 m (1)Hannah Warren (2)Mrs Rebecca Dodge Davis Pvt NY MA ★
Philip: b 1748 d 5-13-1818 m Ann — Pvt PA
Phillip: b 5-22-1760 d 8-14-1836 m Nancy Woodson Cpl VA
Philip Jacob, Sr.: b 17?? d 2-25-1792 m (1)Maria Barbara Wilhelm (2)Catherine Ziegler Capt CS PS PA
Philip Jacob, Jr.: b 2-24-1764 d 3-2-1829 m Catharine Ruth Pvt PA
Phineas: b 8-24-1761 d 3-27-1810 m Lowly Smith Pvt MA
Richard: b *a.* 1739 d 1805 m (1)Lucy Butterfield (2)Sarah Wooley Pvt NH
Richard: b 1757 d 1853 m (2)Rachel Dearmon Pvt NC SC
Richard: b *c.* 1720 d *p.* 5-7-1779 m Margaret — Sol NC
Richard: b 1-7-1762 d 2-6-1827 m Sally — Pvt VA
Robert: b 1749 d 1806 m Mary — CS PS NC
Robert: b 1-3-1747 d 12-20-1826 m Elizabeth McCallup Lt PA ★
Robert: b 1753 d 3-29-1848 m Susanna Pierson Lt PA
Robert: b 9-24-1744 d 8-14-1827 m Jennet Smith 1Lt PA
Robert: b 11-9-1750 d 12-13-1826 m Tabitha Dolley Pvt SC
Rogers, Sr.: b 1728 d — m Lydia Woods MM MA
Reuben: b 2-22-1752 d 12-26-1834 m Susanna Millard Pvt CT
Rufus: b 3-24-1755 d 4-29-1827 m (1)Mary Alsop (2)Amelia Laverty Capt ADC MA
Samuel: b 12-14-1751 d 9-13-1785 m Molly Whitney Col CS PS VT
Samuel: b 5-24-1721 d 6-1-1794 m — Lt MA
Samuel: b 9-30-1737 d 2-3-1815 m Sarah Thompson Pvt MA
Samuel: b 1760 d 1813 m Ruth Marble Pvt MA

Samuel: b 9-29-1740 d 4-2-1810 m Mary Young 2Lt NY
Samuel: b 4-5-1737 d 2-1-1804 m (1)Freelove Phillips (2)Dinah Burton Pvt RI
Samuel: b 2- -1745 d 1829 m Deborah Greene Mil RI
Samuel: b 1748 d 1828 m Elizabeth Davenport Pvt VA
Solomon: b 2-17-1748 d 9-11-1775 m Lydia Ely Pvt MA
Solomon: b c. 1720 d 1795 m Abigail Lee PS NC
Stephen: b 1756 d 9-10-1828 m Elizabeth Dakin Pvt NY
Stephen: b 1752 d p. 1832 m Lurana Maupin Pvt VA ★
Thaddeus: b 6-25-1749 d 1-20-1792 m (1)Alice King (2)Lucy Johnson Lt CT
Thaddeus: b 6-9-1757 d 2-25-1814 m Naomi Warner Pvt MA
Theodore: b 12-2-1750 d 9-8-1822 m (1)Anna Mather (2)Sibbel Hanchett Pvt CT
Thomas: b 2-25-1729 d p. 1783 m (1)Abigail Warriner (2)Mercy Vincent 2Lt MA
Thomas: b 1719 d 5-18-1801 m Jemima — PS MA
Thomas: b 11- -1764 d 4- -1864 m Lettie Hall Pvt NY
Thomas: b 3-17-1754 d 6-18-1847 m Susan Sharp Pvt PA NC ★
Thomas: b 7-28-1716 d 1786 m Ann Coppock PS PA
Thomas: b 7-29-1747 d 1-27-1804 m Polly Butler Pvt VT
Thomas: b 1757 d 1832 m Tabitha H. Pulliam Sol GA
Thomas: b c. 1760 d 1820 m Elizabeth Cotton Pvt VA
Valentine: b c. 1750 d p. 1817 m Sophia — Sol VA
Wm.: b 10-10-1721 d 3-8-1791 m (1)Sarah Fuller (2)Lucy Hathaway Ens CT
Wm.: b 8-1-1752 d p. 1840 m Elizabeth Sharp Pvt Spy NC ★
Wm.: b 5-5-1740 d 11-29-1815 m Hannah Lamphear Pvt MA
Wm.: b 12-29-1744 d 5-17-1813 m Sarah Clark Pvt MA
Wm.: b 10-27-1734 d 12-3-1825 m Silence Dwight PS CS MA
Wm.: b 1762 d 12-19-1840 m (1)Lydia Goodell (2)Caty Morse Pvt NH MA ★
Wm., Sr.: b 1717 d 9-21-1797 m Jemima Bliss Lt PS MA
Wm., Jr.: b 1-20-1743 d 2-5-1817 m Thankful Warner PS MA
Wm.: b 1-24-1724 d 10-8-1793 m Elizabeth Cushing Pvt VT
Wm.: b 10-28-1734 d 6-6-1822 m Marytie Cadmus Pvt NJ
Wm.: b 5-9-1756 d 8-2-1818 m Hannah Fenimore Pvt NJ
Wm.: b c. 1750 d p. 8-28-1816 m Margaret DeVane Sol NC
Wm.: b 9-30-1753 d 11-12-1798 m Amelia Slade Pvt NC
Wm.: b 1-29-1745 d 10-2-1802 m (1)Rachel Tharp (2)Martha Reeder Lt PA
Wm.: b 1754 d 2-23-1815 m Ann McIlhenny Pvt Arfr PA W ★
Wm.: b 1756 d 1811 m Mary Ann Miles Pvt PA
Wm.: b 1- -1764 d 9-19-1863 m Nancy Waugh Pvt PA
Wm.: b 6-28-1834 d 10-6-1834 m Lucy — Pvt RI ★
Wm.: b 2-22-1745 d p. 1800 m Letitia Bland Pvt VA
Wm.: b c. 1755 d p. 1840 m Betty Brown Pvt VA ★
Wm.: b 1755 d 1835 m Elizabeth — Pvt VA ★
Wm.: b 3- -1760/63 d p. 1833 m Ann Bunt Pvt VA ★
Zephaniah: b c. 1734 d p. 1778 m Draden Clarke Pvt PS MD

KINGMAN,
Abner: b 6-20-1735 d 2-22-1812 m Susannah Leonard Lt MA
Alexander: b 4-14-1765 d 10-20-1849 m Nancy Robinson Pvt MA ★
David: b 2-26-1733 d 5-11-1805 m Abigail Hall Capt MA
Edward: b 10-8-1744 d 10-1-1777 m Sarah Newcomb Ens MA
Eliab, Jr.: b 6-13-1762 d 2-12-1835 m Ann King Sgt MA W ★
Isaac: b 8-8-1747 d 11-11-1839 m Content Packard Pvt MA ★
James: b a. 1754 d 10-15-1821 m Relief Clark Pvt Fif MA W ★
John: b 1758 d 6-18-1817 m Anna French Pvt MA
John: b 12-23-1747 d 11-15-1807 m Dolla Waterhouse PS NH
Joseph: b 10-17-1763 d 12-18-1839 m Eunice Josleyn Pvt MA
Mathew: b 9-8-1732 d 11-22-1809 m Jane Packard Pvt MA
Mitchell: b 1744 d 10-22-1819 m Keturah Latimer Pvt CT
Molbory: b 1-3-1756 d 6-20-1805 m Sybil Haskell Pvt MA
Seth: b 7-7-1757 d 2-18-1843 m (1)Judith Washburn (2)Jennet Edson (3)Olive Curtis Pvt MA
Wm.: b 1720 d 1776 m Elizabeth Webster Pvt NH

KINGSBURY,
Aaron: b 1743 d 10-18-1794 m Elizabeth Richardson 2Lt MA
Absalom: b 2-13-1730 d 4-5-1805 m Rebecca Rust Pvt NH
Andrew: b 4-24-1759 d 10-6-1837 m Mary Osborn Sol NY
Asa, Sr.: b 4-7-1729 d 9-5-1775 m Sarah Huntington Capt CT
Asa, Jr.: b 3-12-1757 d 3-13-1839 m Laurena Hartshorn Sgt CT ★
Benjamin, Sr.: b 12-27-1715 d 2-20-1787 m Jedidah Cook PS MA
Benjamin, Jr.: b 10-30-1742 d 6-10-1827 m (1)Abigail Sawin (2)Lucretia Lock Pvt MA
Daniel: b 9-20-1749 d p. 1788 m Rose Pease Ens CT
Daniel: b 3-11-1715 d 3-25-1783 m Beriah Mann Pvt MA
Daniel, Jr.: b 10-6-1742 d 8-10-1825 m Mary Thurston Lt PS NH
Ebenezer: b 2-11-1716 d 9-6-1800 m Priscilla (Kingsbury) PS CT
Eleazer: b 2-7-1718 d 10-6-1785 m (1)Freelove Rust (2)Mrs Elizabeth Russell PS CT
Elijah: b 5-3-1747 d c. 1809 m Lois Leonard Cpl MA
Eliphalet, Sr.: b 4-21-1721 d p. 10-22-1794 m Abigail Fuller PS MA
Ephraim: b 3-13-1738 d 3-10-1826 m Phoebe French Ens PS CT
Ephraim: b 9-2-1759 d 2-26-1826 m Hannah Leonard Pvt NH
Jabez: b 3-10-1756 d 3-25-1844 m Anna Hatch Pvt CT
Jacob: b 1756 d 1833 m Milly Smith Cpl MA
Jeduthan: b 1743 d 7-7-1821 m (1)Susannah Woodward (2)Mary Curtis (3)Anna Greenleaf Pvt NH
Jeremiah: b 1735 d 4-23-1816 m Ruth Ballard Capt MA

Jonathan, Sr.: b 1722 d 1812 m — Haxmal Pvt MA
Jonathan, Jr.: b 1744 d 1816 m Jemima Skinner Sgt MA
Joseph: b 4-17-1753 d 4-13-1828 m Lois Richards Porter Lt CT
Joseph: b 11-30-1756 d 8-29-1822 m Roxana (Allyn) Wadsworth Fif Sgt CT
Joseph: b 2-23-1755 d 9-7-1835 m Ruth Benton Cpl CT ★
Joseph: b 3-27-1721 d 6-6-1806 m Mary Loomis PS CT
Joseph: b 12-25-1751 d 6-20-1820 m Mary Eaton MM Cpl MA
Joseph: b 12- -1732 d 1792 m (1)Elizabeth Milberry (2)Sarah Milberry Pvt MA
Joseph: b 9-6-1734 d p. 1790 m Elizabeth Amidown Pvt MA
Joseph: b 12-27-1760 d 8- -1850 m Martha Deming Pvt MA ★
Joseph: b 8-5-1760 d p. 1789 m — Pvt NH
Joshua, Sr.: b 7-30-1723 d p. 3-4-1780 m (1)Martha Fisher (2)Hannah Lewis Pvt MA
Joshua, Jr.: b 10-17-1749 d 5-3-1801 m Rhode Sumner Pvt MA
Josiah: b 6-30-1759 d p. 1-18-1811 m Esther Craig Ens MA
Lemuel: b 9-14-1752 d 9-14-1846 m Alice Terry Cnt CT
Lemuel: b 11-20-1750 d 12-20-1844 m (1)Lucy Crittenden (2)Louisa (Hutchins) Smith Pvt CT MA ★
Moses: b 8-8-1736 d 1801 m Sarah Fuller Pvt MA
Nathan: b 5-4-1752 d 5-5-1837 m Azuba Smith Pvt MA
Nathan: b 3-14-1730 d 1806-15 m (1)Sarah Adams (2)Zerviah Blake PS MA
Nathaniel: b 10-4-1757 d 2-5-1829 m Asenath Daggett Sgt CT
Nathaniel: b 2-18-1739 d 1-26-1803 m (1)Mehitable Johnson (2)Hannah Ware (3)Rebecca Bigelow Pvt NH
Obadiah: b 5-3-1763 d p. 5-11-1803 m (1)Eunice Crane (2)Alice White Pvt NH
Phineas: b 5-9-1731 d 2-4-1799 m Hannah Hutchinson PS CT
Samuel: b 25-1745/46 d 1-6-1794 m Olive Scribner Sol CT
Samuel: b 11-18-1760 d 1-29-1823 m Sophia Moore Cpl MA
Samuel Rust: b 2-27-1754 d 12-21-1839 m Ruth Steele Pvt CT
Sanford: b 4-7-1743 d 11-12-1833 m Elizabeth Fitch Maj CT ★
Seth: b 5-18-1720 d 11-25-1800 m Miriam Holbrook PS MA
Solomon: b 11-24-1745 d 1-2-1822 m (1)Ruth Kingsbury (2)Kesia Meriam Cpl MA
Stephen: b 12-17-1735 d 1799 m Sarah Spalding Pvt CT
Thomas: b 9-1-1754 d 3-7-1839 m Esther Baker Pvt CT ★
Willard: b 8-26-1747 d 1817 m Hannah Lawrence Pvt CT

KINGSLAND,
Edmond: b 4-7-1742 d 10-30-1822 m (2)Anna Low PS NJ
Isaac: b 7-10-1710 d 7-28-1803 m Johanna Schuyler Pvt MM NJ

KINGSLEY, (includes KENSLEY & KINSLEY)
Adam: b 1763 d 10-12-1840 m Sarah — Pvt MA
Amos, Sr.: b 6-3-1731 d 3-23-1796 m Mary Wadsworth Pvt MA
Asahel: b 6-12-1762 d 4-4-1849 m Naomi Hill Pvt Grd CT
Azel: b 7-5-1750 d 3-14-1854 m Patty Howard Pvt Fif MA ★
Benjamin: b 3-27-1738 d 1810 m Innocent Mason Cpl MA
Calvin: b c. 1745 d p. 8-30-1811 m Susannah Lathrop Pvt MA
Daniel: b 4-22-1764 d 9-28-1828 m Lucy Montague Sgt VT W ★
David: b 1-22-1749 d 1804 m Patience Woods Pvt MA VT
Ebenezer: b 1752 d p. 1797 m Thankful Burke Pvt CT
Elijah: b 1740 d 10-30-1839 m Dorothy — Sgt PS MA
Enos: b 9-20-1757 d 10-21-1836 m (1)Rachel S. Crane (2)Sarah Wadsworth Pvt MA
Enos: b 10-16-1740 d 12-1-1822 m Abigail Pomeroy CS MA
Hezekiah: b 12-5-1739 d 5-20-1820 m (1)Mary Luther (2)Mary Cole Pvt MA
Jabez: b 1756 d 6-18-1846 m Dolly Averill Pvt CT
Jacob: b 1755/56 d 8-4-1837 m Catherine Dorothea Rummel Sgt PA
James: b 1-7-1758 d 3-23-1813 m (1)Mary Call (2)Burradell Cheney Pvt ME
James: b 1737 d 3-24-1782 m Elizabeth Welsh Matr NJ
Jedediah: b 11-15-1753 d p. 1811 m Mary Cary Sgt MA
Jeremiah: b 4-3-1736 d 7-4-1833 m Hannah Lillie Sgt MA
John: b 1734 d 2-24-1813 m Mary Burnap Cpl CT
John: b c. 1721 d p. 8-16-1777 m Thankful Washburn Pvt VT
Jonathan: b 2-12-1760 d — m — Sol NH NY
Jonathan, Jr.: b 7-1-1752 d 2-17-1835 m Elizabeth Gray Sct MM VT
Martin: b 6-1-1756 d p. 1840 m Bethena (Allen) Sgt MA ★
Moses: b 1-29-1744 d 4-29-1829 m Abagail Lyman 2Lt MA
Nathan: b 1-23-1743 d 1822 m Roccelana Wareham Lt CT
Nathan: b 6-3-1715 d a. 12-5-1796 m Betty Dunbar CS PS MA
Nathaniel: b 4-23-1727 d p. 1805 m Sarah Walden PS CS MA
Phineas: b 2-21-1750 d 5-25-1825 m Abigail Woods Pvt VT
Rufus: b 4-11-1763 d 5-26-1846 m Lucinda Cutler Drm CT ★
Salmon, Sr.: b 9-27-1728 d 1812 m Lydia Burges MM PS CT
Salmon, Jr.: b 9-17-1755 d 9-23-1827 m (1)Alethea Smith (2)Betsey Chubb Farge Pvt CT
Samuel: b c. 1752 d p. 1803 m Phebe Wakefield Pvt MA
Silas: b 12-8-1735 d 5-15-1775 m Rebecca Littlefield Ens MA
Thaddeus: b 4-10-1759 d p. 6-20-1833 m Ruth Ames Pvt Drm MA ★
Thomas, Jr.: b 5-8-1763 d — m Joanna Short Pvt MA
Uriah: b 1760 d 11-26-1852 m Parnell Lathrop Smn ★
Wareham: b 5-7-1766 d 12-31-1845 m Urania Turrell Pvt CT

KINNAN,
Edward: b 5-29-1763 d 8-25-1833 m Lucy Britton Drm NJ
Peter: b 5- -1749 d 4-18-1836 m Mary Fine QM NY ★

KINNEY, (includes KEENEY, KENNY, KINNE & KINNIE)
Aaron: b 9-24-1744 d 7-14-1824 m Anna Morgan Chp CT
Alexander: b 1738 d 3-27-1819 m Elizabeth — Capt CT
Alexander: b 1758 d 8-1-1798 m Elizabeth Glassford Pvt PA
Amos: b 1748 d 1-11-1807 m Anna Rogers Pvt CT
Amos: b 6-11-1742 d 3-16-1821 m Esther Utley Sgt CT
Amos: b 2-11-1765 d 3-15-1813 m Hannah Rowland Pvt NY W★
Asa, Sr.: b 9-26-1723 d 1-12-1810 m Bethiah Kimball Capt CT
Asa, Jr.: b 9-7-1752 d 4-9-1842 m (1)Thankful Bellows (2)Mary Colton Ens CT ★
Ashbel: b 1754 d 1-23-1823 m Mrs Sarah (Hills) Keeney Pvt CT W ★
Barnett: b 1726 d p. 1786 m (1)— Kramer (2)Mary — Sgt PA
Cyrus: b 8-11-1746 d 8-8-1808 m Comfort Palmer Pvt NY
Daniel: b 1743 d p. 1787 m Mary Hill Pvt MA
Daniel: b 2-27-1751 d 2-7-1813 m Sarah Fletcher Pvt MA
Ebenezer: b 1718 d 1-10-1795 m Betty Davis PS CT
Edward D.: b 1763 d 3- -1846 m Nancy — Pvt PA ★
Elijah: b 8-7-1743 d 2-6-1830 m Jerusha Kinney Cpl NY
Elijah: b 1740 d 1795 m Anna Kinne PS NY
Elisha: b 10-21-1753 d 1807 m Thankful Fitch MM MA
Ezra: b 9-26-1727 d 9-8-1795 m Sarah Dennison Capt CT
James: b — d 1784 m — Ens PA
James: b 11-29-1752 d 3-15-1815 m (1)Mary Frame (2)Margaret Johnston Pvt VA
Jeremiah: b 8-30-1702 d 6-24-1798 m Mary Starkweather CS CT
John: b 1746 d 1811 m Abigail Lester Sea Capt
Jesse: b 9-3-1752 d 4-13-1813 m Hannah Stearns Pvt MA VT
John: b 8-10-1729 d 4-3-1811 m Ann Ayre Pvt CS MA
John: b 3-1-1751 d 7-17-1832 m Phebe Arnold Ens NJ ★
John: b c. 1760 d 1824 m Betsey Sherman Pvt NJ
Joseph: b 2-22-1757 d 6-3-1841 m Sarah Spalding Sgt CT ★
Joseph: b 2-17-1717 d 10-15-1793 m Mrs Jemima Newcomb Lamb Capt NH
Mark: b 5-1-1740 d 10-7-1804 m Abigail B Lee Sol CT
Matthew: b c. 1745 d a. 6- -1821 m Elizabeth Houston CS VA
Michael: b — d p. 1787 m Catherine Lewis Sol VA
Nathan: b 1751 d 10-6-1798 m Deborah Knight Sgt PA
Parley: b 4-7-1753 d 1833 m Sarah Hine OrdlSgt CT ★
Peaboby: b 7-14-1757 d 2-16-1817 m Elizabeth Crary Pvt CT
Peter: b 1755 d p. 8-14-1832 m Margaret Biggs Sgt NJ ★
Reuben: b 1746 d 1829 m Jemimah Webster Pvt CT
Richard: b 7-22-1765 d 12-16-1851 m Margaret Porter Pvt CT ★
Robert: b 1738 d 10-24-1831 m Abagail Brown Pvt CT
Robert: b 7-1-1758 d 12-22-1843 m Caroline Gryder Pvt PA
Robert: b — d p. 1-4-1804 m Phoebe (Huston ?) Capt VA
Roger: b 1740 d 1806 m Huldah Skinner Capt NY
Samuel: b 1741 d c. 1813 m (1)Patience Wing (2)Abigail Chubback Cpl MA
Spencer: b 2-3-1732 d 6-22-1816 m Merribee Brumbly Pvt CT
Stephen: b 1-24-1743 d 11-8-1806 m Mary Bartlett Pvt MA
Stephen: b 3-6-1762 d 7-19-1848 m Rebecca Coates Pvt CT RI ★
Thomas: b 5-10-1751 d 1-10-1840 m Mercy Lamb Pvt CT ★
Thomas: b 1730 d 10-16-1804 m Sarah Jeralds Sol CT
Thomas: b 1729 d 11-19-1815 m Jemima Foster Sgt MA
Thomas: b 5-11-1717 d 1-20-1795 m (1)Hannah Gallup (2)Mrs Eunice Twogood Pvt CS MA
Thomas: b 1761 d 4-11-1825 m Hannah White Pvt MA ★
Thomas: b 4-9-1731 d 4-2-1793 m Elizabeth Kinney Capt NJ
Thomas: b a. 1760 d p. 1782 m — PS VT
Timothy: b 1741 d 1821 m Delight (Kinney) Pvt MA
Wm.: b 7-16-1757 d 4-9-1837 m Betsey Moore Sgt CT ★
Wm., 2d: b 11-4-1755 d 1-12-1819 m Mary Snow Pvt MA
Wm.: b a. 1755 d p. 1821 m Sallie Parks Pvt NC

KINNICUTT, (includes KENNICUT & KINNECUT)
Daniel: b 7-14-1735 d 5-12-1817 m Hannah Kent Lt RI
Edward: b 2-24-1763 d 10-24-1832 m R Allen Sol RI
Hezekiah: b 3-24-1743/4 d 4- -1828 m Lydia Luther Pvt RI W★
Josiah: b 4-2-1765 d 3-25-1838 m Rebecca Townsend PS RI
Shuball: b 3-28-1738 d 5-18-1810 m Elizabeth Burr Ens RI

KINSAUL,
John: b 1759 d 1839 m Mary — Pvt NC ★

KINSEY,
Benjamin: b 10-22-1727 d 7-12-1789 m (1)Susanna Brown (2)Martha White Pvt PA
Henry: b a. 1740 d 1820 m Eva Wampler Pvt PA
Jacob: b — d 1790 m — Pvt PA
James: b 1732 d 1802 m Hannah Decon PS NJ
John: b c. 1750 d 7-19-1823 m Margaret Kitchen Sol PA
Jonathan: b 1728 d 1785 m Jemima Heston Pvt PA
Samuel: b 5- -1734 d c. 3-1-1793 m Sarah Ingham Lt PA
Thomas: b c. 1730 d p. 1785 m Margaret Smith Pvt PA
Wm.: b 1755 d c. 1825 m Catharine DeGuyant Pvt PA

KINSMAN,
Aaron: bpt 8-21-1743 d 1810 m (1)Rose Burnham (2)Mary Hall Capt NH
Daniel, Jr.: bpt 5-13-1744 d 12-12-1818 m Abigail Morse Sgt MA
Ephraim: b 1-9-1761 d 6- -1817/8 m Mary Hall Pvt NH
Jeremiah, Jr.: b 10-6-1748 d 3-11-1828 m (1)Martha Andrews (2)Lydia Campbell Pvt MA

John: b 5-7-1753 d 8-17-1813 m Rebecca Perkins Ens CT
Michael: b 4-6-1746 d 11-25-1795 m Mary Knowlton MM Pvt MA
Wm.: b 8-27-1752 d 9-30-1843 m Anna Brown Pvt MA

KINTER,
John: b 5-15-1755 d 4-29-1836 m Isabella Findley Pvt PA ★

KINTZ, (or KEANS)
Anthony: b 7-10-1749 d 4-29-1824 m Anna Eliza — Pvt PA

KINTZER, (includes KINCER, KINSER & KINZER)
Henry: b c. 1744 d p. 9-10-1821 m — Pvt PA
Jacob: b 7-8-1750 d 8- -1815 m (1)Elizabeth Unruh (2)Barbara Fohrer (3)Catharine Fohrer Pvt PA
Michael: b 10-27-1751 d 2-13-1808 m Magdalena Diller Pvt PA
Nicholas: b 11-15-1715 d 1-20-1794 m Juliana Schneider PS PA

KIPP, (includes KIP)
Abraham: b 3-22-1743 d — m Phoebe Haight Pvt NY
Benjamin: b 3-21-1703 d 5-24-1782 m Dorothy Davenport CS NY
Boudewin: b 1-14-1757 d 6-16-1820 m Catherine Kipp Pvt NY
Cornelius: b 6-18-1762 d 5-3-1840 m Christina Demarest Pvt NJ
Ignas: bpt 10-17-1736 d p. 1788 m Annatie VanVechten Lt NY
Jacob: b 1699 d p. 1775 m Klaartje VanWagensen PS NY
Jacobus: b 8-19-1706 d 10-1-1777 m Catherine Kip PS NY
James: b 1751 d — m Cornelia Ryckman Pvt NY
John: b — d a. 4-2-1810 m Mary Catherine — Lt PA
Peter: b 12-26-1743 d 3-8-1813 m (1)Willemynge VanWinkle (2)Jemima VanWinkle PS NJ
Peter: b 1754 d 11-4-1825 m Margaret Finton Sgt NY ★
Peter: b 5-9-1740 d p. 1780 m Ida Adams Pvt NY

KIPPERS,
John: b 3-4-1762 d 10- -1844 m Rebecca Patterson Pvt VA ★

KIPPS,
Jacob: b 11-11-1760 d 4-20-1849 m Elizabeth Zerkel Pvt VA ★

KIRBY, (includes KERBY)
Abraham: b 7-14-1730 d 4-3-1796 m Eunice Starkweather Pvt MA
David, Sr.: b 1738 d p. 4-6-1811 m Elizabeth — PS VA
Ephraim: b 2-23-1757 d 10-20-1804 m Ruth Marvin Lt CT
Isaac: b 9-23-1756 d 2-1-1834 m (1)Hannah — (2)Phebe Hains Pvt NJ W★
James: b 11-23-1751 d 3-17-1819 m Margaret Brown Pvt SC
Jacob: b 1758 d 1822 m Elizabeth Horner Pvt NJ
Jesse: b 10-23-1757 d 12-17-1852 m Sophia Choice Pvt VA ★
John: b 1726 d 1795 m Sarah — Pvt VA
John: b 12- -1752 d 1798 m — Drm Fif VA
Ruth Marvin: b 12-20-1763 d 10-17-1817 m Ephraim Kirby PS CT
Samuel: b 1733 d 1816 m Helena Hartshorn Pvt NJ
Seth: b 5-31-1751 d 1-2-1825 m Olive Treat Cpl CT
Silas, Sr.: b c. 1720 d 1785 m Elizabeth Russell PS MA
Silas, Jr.: b 11- -1742 d p. 1797 m Susannah Rogers Pvt MA
Stephen: b 2-1-1749 d 3-18-1842 m Mary — Pvt NY
Thomas: b 1742 d 1803 m Sarah Fairfax Pvt VA
Wm.: b 7-16-1736 d 1782 m Margaret Howard Capt VA
Wesson: b 12-14-1731 d 10-9-1798 m Hannah White PS CS MA

KIRK,
Caleb: b 8-3-1759 d 3-8-1836 m Lydia Updegraff Pvt PA
George: b 5-18-1747 d 6-1-1815 m Mary — Mus NY
Henry: b 2-9-1753 d 9-9-1827 m Elizabeth Foset Pvt PA
Isaac: b 10-23-1735 d a. 8-16-1803 m Rachel — Pvt PA
Jacob: b 7-30-1735 d 10-13-1829 m Elizabeth Cleaver Pvt PA
James: b — d — m (1)Susannah Blair (2)Susannah Ogden Pvt NY
James: b 11-4-1759 d 1-21-1857 m (1)Ann Horton (2)Mahala Chamberlain Pvt VA
James: b c. 1720 d p. 5-9-1783 m (1)Agnes Edmiston (2)Jean — PS VA
John: b c. 1745 d p. 1790 m Sarah Steele Pvt NC
John: b 8-14-1755 d 1831 m Rebecca Lukens Ens PA
John: b 10-10-1754 d 12-5-1850 m Elizabeth O'Bryant Pvt VA ★
John: b c. 1751 d 1808 m Mary Ann — Capt CS VA
Lewis: b 1759 d 1800 m Bine — Sol NC
Mary Story: b 1720 d 11-1-1804 m Moses Kirk PS PA
Roger: b 6-5-1751 d 3-20-1809 m Rachel Hughes Capt PA
Thomas, Sr.: b 1726 d p. 8- -1819 m — Ens MD
Thomas: b 9-26-1744 d 1815 m Hannah Cadwalader Pvt PA
Timothy: b 11-17-1717 d 11-15-1784 m Ann Gatchell CS MD PA
Wm.: b 3-1-1751 d 10-2-1825 m (1)Ann White (2)Prudence Stevens Pvt MD ★
Wm.: b 9-9-1764 d 8-27-1841 m Edith Shortledge Capt PA
Wm.: b 1763 d 1843 m Jane Knox PS PA
Wm.: b a. 1727 d 1812 m Mary Bennoit Pvt SC
Wm.: b c. 1759 d c. 1820 m Nancy — 2Lt VA
Wm.: b 1754 d 1837 m Agnes — PS VA

KIRKBRIDE,
Robert: b 11-23-1737 d 9-30-1798 m (1)Hannah Bidgood (2)Hannah Wilson Pvt PA

KIRKHAM, (includes KIRKUM)
Michael: b 8-29-1746 d 1835 m Nancy Campbell Ens VA ★

Philemon: b 12-8-1763 d 7-15-1854 m Elizabeth Mills Sgt CT ★
Robert: b 1754 d *p.* 1800 m Jane Boyd Sol KY

KIRKLAND,
Benjamin: b 1756 d 2- -1811 m Martha Jones Pvt VA
Daniel: b *c.* 1746 d *p.* 1783 m (1)Abigail Knight (2)Theodosia Mixer 1Lt MA
Francis: b *c.* 1745 d *p.* 10-12-1790 m Mary Watts Pvt SC
Jabez: b 1752 d 11-16-1834 m Eunice Burnham Pvt CT ★
John: b 11-15-1735 d 3-7-1820 m Anna Palmer Capt MA
John: b 1753 d *p.* 3-24-1837 m — Porter Pvt Spy VA ★
Reuben: b *a.* 1760 d 1822 m Mary Clark Sol SC
Richard: b *c.* 1750 d 10-23-1813 m Mary — Sol PS SC
Wm.: b 1759 d 6-10-1830 m Margaret Stone Pvt NY
Wm.: b *c.* 1730 d 1806 m (1)Elizabeth McKinnie (2)Lucretia Pearson Capt SC

KIRKPATRICK,
Abraham: b 1749 d 11-17-1817 m Mary Ann Oldham Maj VA
Alexander: b 9-3-1751 d 9-24-1827 m Sarah Carroll (Carle)Lt NJ
Alexander: b 1741 d 8-17-1825 m Jane Stewart Pvt NC
Andrew: b 1721/22 d *p.* 1790 m Margaret Gaston Capt NJ
Andrew: b 1739 d 1-15-1827 m Elizabeth Bowen Pvt VA
Benjamin: b *c.* 1755 d 1826 m Mrs Jane Scott McKean Pvt PA
David: b 2-17-1724 d 3-19-1814 m Mary McEowen PS NJ
Hugh: b 1739 d 1829 m Polly Gordon Pvt NJ
Isaac: b 11-1-1755 d 11-15-1838 m Nancy Graham Pvt PA ★
James: b 1755 d 1839 m Mary Larimer (Larimore) PS PA
James: b *a.* 1730 d *p.* 6-8-1786 m Susannah Gillham Pvt SC ★
John: b 1741 d 2-28-1808 m Margaret — Sol NC
John: b 1741 d 3- -1812 m Jane Wilkins Pvt NC
John: b 1738 d 4-17-1822 m Lydia Lewis Capt NJ
John: b *c.* 1758 d 2-19-1833 m Jeannette Moore Pvt PA
John: b *c.* 1745 d *c.* 1813 m Martha — Lt VA
John Robert: b 7-3-1743 d 8-1-1828 m Agnes Patterson Lt PA
Joseph: b *c.* 1745 d 1823 m Ann — PS Pvt PA
Lydia Lewis: b 1742 d 1832 m John Kirkpatrick PS NJ
Moses: b *c.* 1750 d 4- -1820 m Mary — Pvt PA
Moses: b — d 1786-89 m Mary Johnson Pvt PA
Robert: b 1-19-1754 d 2-24-1835 m — Pvt SC ★
Wm.: b *c.* 1725 d *p.* 1782 m Augusta — Lt VA
Wm.: b 1723 d 1791 m Mary — Mil VA

KIRKSEY,
Christopher: b 1734 d 10-12-1818 m Perthany — PS NC

KIRKWOOD,
Robert H.: b 1756 d 11-4-1791 m Sarah England Capt DE

KIRTLAND,
Abner: b 12-6-1745 d 8-8-1834 m Mercy Doty Pratt 1Lt CT
Daniel: b 10-27-1745 d 7-7-1824 m Louisa Lord Lt CT ★
Gideon: b 1731 d 4-18-1805 m Lydia — Pvt NH
John: b 12-20-1759 d 5-19-1843 m (1)Lucy A. Burbank (2)Mrs Mary Tyler Benham Pvt CL
Martin: b 3-31-1735 d *p.* 1818 m Sarah Meigs Capt CT
Martin, Jr: b 3-29-1759 d 8-9-1833 m (1)Eunice Bushnell (2)Mrs Betsey — Pvt CT ★
Nathan: b 1-14-1763 d 8-5-1844 m Rachel Towner Pvt CT ★
Samuel: b 8-31-1760 d 10-4-1825 m Statira Cone Pvt CT
Samuel: b 1-10-1732 d 9-4-1805 m (1)Thankful Bushnell (2)Mehitable Lord (3)Hepsibah Bushnell CS PS CT
Turhand: b 1755 d 1844 m Mary Potter Btm NY
Zebulon: b 1755 d 1-2-1803 m Elizabeth Cooke Pvt CT

KIRTLEY,
Francis: b 1756 d *p.* 1786 m Elizabeth Walker Sol VA
Wm.: b *c.* 1725 d 1795 m Sarah Early Capt VA

KISCKER, (or KEESECKER)
John: b *c.* 1724 d *p.* 3-26-1794 m Christianna — PS VA

KISE,
Peter: b 1760 d *p.* 1818 m Mary Morgan Pvt NJ ★

KISSAM,
Benjamin: b 1728 d 10-25-1782 m Katharine Rutgers PS NY
Daniel: b 1739 d 6-3-1812 m Mary Betts PS NY

KISSINGER, (includes KESSINGER)
Abraham: b 1750 d 1833 m Maria Agneiez Kieszling PS PA
Charles: b 1731 d 1799 m Gertrude — Pvt PA
Jacob: b 1730 d 10-25-1806 m (1)Anna Maria Ursula (2)Susannah — (3)Maria Elizabeth Koch 2Lt PA
Mathias: b *c.* 1738 d 1799 m Judith — Pvt VA
Michael: b 1717 d 1-4-1791 m Mary Catharine Ruland PS PA

KISTLER, (includes KISNER, KISTNER)
George: b 1744 d *p.* 7-22-1807 m Christina Deitrich Pvt PA
Jacob: b 2-12-1751 d 10-20-1811 m Phoebe — Pvt PA
Michael: b 1749/50 d *p.* 1790 m Barbara Haahl Pvt PA
Philip: b 10-19-1745 d 8-28-1809 m Elizabeth Barbara — Pvt PA

Samuel: b 9-20-1754 d 4-24-1822 m (1)Mary Elizabeth Ladich (2)Catharine Brobst Ens PA
John: b 1744 d *p.* 10-24-1804 m Eva Catherina (Clymer)Pvt PA

KITCHELL, (includes KITCHEL)
Aaron: b 1744 d 6-25-1820 m Phebe Farrand Pvt PS NJ
Abraham: b 8-26-1736 d 1-11-1807 m (1)Charity Ford (2)Rebecca Farrand PS NJ
Asa: b 10-28-1748 d 6- -1811 m Rhoda Baldwin Pvt NJ
Daniel: b 1746 d 1800 m Esther — MM NJ
James: b 11-1-1759 d 10-1-1842 m Hannah Day Pvt NJ ★
Moses: b *c.* 1739 d *p.* 1806 m Phoebe Hedges Lt PS NJ
Obadiah: b 1740 d 10-3-1798 m Sarah Reynolds Capt NJ
Phineas: b 8-13-1763 d 7-29-1853 m Esther Mulford Pvt NJ

KITCHEN,
Benjamin: b 1763 d 1849 m (1)Mason Daniels (2)Levisa Wilson Capt NC ★
Daniel: b 12-21-1757 d 1-25-1838 m Mary Barker Pvt VA ★
James: b *c.* 1750 d 3-23-1832 m Jane Patterson Pvt PS VA ★
Jesse: b 1760 d 1827 m Sarah Jones Hinton Sol NC

KITE, (or KYTE)
Isaac, Jr.: b 12-24-1754 d 9-21-1823 m Sarah Sellers Ens PA
Thomas: b — d *p.* 1800 m Leah Keator QM PS NY
Wm.: b 10-24-1748 d *p.* 1790 m Margaret Kyle Ens PA

KITLEY,
Wm.: b 1758 d *p.* 3-4-1835 m Sarah — Pvt MA ★

KITTREDGE, (includes KITTRIDGE)
Benjamin: b 3-7-1740/41 d 1-18-1822 m (1)Rebecca Ball (2)Mrs — Graham Sol CS PS MA
Francis: b 7-1-1728 d 4-17-1808 m Abigail Richardson Dr NH
Joshua: b 3-15-1761 d 2-18-1834 m Beulah Baker Pvt NH MA ★
Nathaniel: b 5-10-1753 d 1816 m Martha Dows Pvt MA NY
Solomon: b 6-9-1736 d 8-24-1792 m Tabitha Ingalls Sol PS NH
Solomon, Jr.: b 8-3-1755 d 10-22-1845 m (1)Ann (Kittredge) (2)Betsey Holt Sol NH
Thomas: b 7-13-1746 d 10-16-1818 m Susanna Osgood Dr MA
Thomas: b 11-9-1731 d 1-16-1806 m Anne Thorndike Pvt MA
Wm., Sr.: b 2-11-1698/99 d 4-25-1789 m (1)Molly Wright (2)Mary Harden CS MA
Wm., Jr.: b 4-25-1737 d 9-6-1790 m (1)Rebecca Shed (2)Hannah Patton Pvt MA
Zephaniah: b 8-24-1757 d 8-17-1843 m Elisabeth Stickney Sol NY

KITTRELL,
Jonathan, Sr.: b *c.* 1720 d 1812 m Elizabeth — CS NC
Jonathan, Jr.: b 1753 d *p.* 1800 m Tabby Bryant Pvt NC
Moses: b *c.* 1745 d *c.* 1805 m Elizabeth Goodman Capt NC

KITZMILLER,
Jacob, Sr.: b 1731 d 1808 m Elizabeth — 1Lt PA

KIVETT,
Peter: b 1730 d 11- -1794 m Anna Barbara Kivett PS NC

KLAHR, (includes KLAUR)
Philip: b *c.* 1758/60 d *p.* 1790 m — Pvt PA
Simon: b 1756 d *p.* 1780 m Margaret Clay Capt PA

KLEBER, (includes CLEAVER, CLEVER, KLIPPART)
Barnhart: b 1746 d 6-29-1816 m Margaret Bollinger Pvt PA
Ezekiel, Sr.: b 2-4-1724 d 1783-87 m Mary Lewis Pvt PA
Ezekiel, Jr.: b 3-25-1757 d 9-22-1832 m Abigail Richards Pvt PA
Isaac: b — d *p.* 1790 m Jemima Draper Pvt PA
John: b *c.* 1743 d 1832 m Sarah — Sol PA
John: b *c.* 1740 d 1790 m (1)Rebecca — (2)Catharine Kline PS PA
John Jacob Earnest: b 4-30-1754 d 9-24-1842 m Susannah Kline Pvt PA
Martin: b *c.* 1760 d 11- -1825 m Catherine Lutzen Pvt PA
Peter: b 1756 d 1836 m Elizabeth Arenhart Pvt PA
Wm., Sr.: b *c.* 1730 d *p.* 8-28-1805 m Hannah — CS VA
Wm.: b 1761 d 1835 m Charlotte — Pvt VA ★

KLEINPETER,
Adam: b 1748 d 4-12-1832 m Anna Maria Long Ens PA

KLINE, (includes CLINE, KLEIN)
Abraham: b 11-18-1735 d *p.* 9-2-1819 m Charity Ann Kramer Pvt PA
Barnhart: b 12-16-1756 d 8-3-1837 m Margaret — 2Lt PA
Conrad: b 1757 d 1837 m Nancy — Pvt PA
Conrad: b 1743 d 1816 m Betsy Tanquary Capt NY
George: b 1740 d 1795 m Susannah Buck Sgt PA
Godfrey: b 10-30-1726 d *p.* 1785 m Ida Lena Mellick Cpl PA
Henry: b 2-17-1755 d 11-5-1840 m (1)Mary Cole (2)Sarah — Pvt NY ★
Jacob: b 4-14-1749 d 3-14-1828 m Katherine Barkman Pvt MD
Jacob: b 1751 d 10-22-1823 m Phebe Nevius Pvt NJ
Jacob: b 6-20-1756 d *p.* 6-3-1807 m Magdalena — Pvt PA
John: b 4-1-1764 d 5-6-1829 m Deidamia Howard Fif MA

KLINE, contd.
John: b 1-20-1760 d 4-23-1837 m Elizabeth Shipman Drm NJ ★
John: b c. 1758 d 1802 m Barbara Mace Pvt PA
John: b 9-3-1761 d 10-12-1827 m Magdelene Sassaman Pvt PA
Jonas: b 6-21-1760 d 7-20-1840 m Catherine Roos Pvt NY ★
J. Michael: b 8-4-1744 d 8-21-1828 m Ann Maria — Pvt PA
Michael: b 1761 d 1-9-1840 m Fanny Killian Pvt NC W★
Michael: b a. 1725 d a. 1781 m Dorothea — Pvt PA
Nicholas: b 1754 d 8-10-1825 m — Pvt PA
Peter: b —d — m Sophronica Myer Pvt PS NY
Peter: b 4-27-1741 d 12-22-1819 m Margaret Stettler Pvt PA
Peter: b 2-15-1760 d 11-27-1836 m Eva Margaretha Lichtey Pvt PA ★
Philip: b 6-17-1742 d 5-9-1815 m Elizabeth — Pvt PA
Philip: b 2-2-1751 d 3-16-1835 m Mary — Pvt PA
Philip: b 12-9-1763 d 7-22-1834 m Elizabeth Adams Pvt PA
Philip: b 1-1-1760 d 6-21-1842 m Elizabeth Schweitzer Cpl VA CL
Wm.: b 1-23-1747 d 8-23-1853 m (1)Susannah Lance (2)Jane Woten Pvt MD
Wm.: b 1-4-1737 d 4-   -1814 m Maria O'Reagen Pvt NY

KLINEFELTER,
George: b 1758 d 1830 m Katharine — Pvt PA
Michael: b 6-10-1736 d 7-17-1807 m (2)Maria Elizabeth Pvt PA
Peter: b c. 1753 d a. 9-28-1796 m Elizabeth Scheffer Pvt PA

KLINESMITH,
Andrew: b 1749 d 6-9-1836 m Barbara Need Sgt PA

KLING,
Ludwig: b 1753 d 1826 m Anna France Sgt NY

KLINGER,
Henry: b 8-15-1758 d 2-14-1808 m Mary Shearer Pvt PA

KLINGENSMITH,
Andrew: b c. 1755 d 1800 m Agnes — Pvt PS PA
John Philip: b 7-5-1760 d 11-29-1832 m Barbara Broadsword Pvt PA
Phillip: b c. 1730 d 7-2-1781 m Christiana — PS PA

KLINGER, (includes KLINKER)
Johan Ernst: b 1-17-1723 d 6-23-1798 m (1)Catharine Elizabeth — (2)Catharine Hutchinson Pvt PA
John Philip: b 7-11-1723 d 9-30-1811 m (1)Eve Elizabeth — (2)Anna Eva — Pvt PA CL
Philip: b 11-10-1753/54 d 1841 m Barbara Ecos Pvt PA ★

KLINGLER,
Peter: b 6-4-1756 d 3-13-1833 m Mary Elizabeth Hoag Pvt PA

KLOCK, (includes CLOCK)
Adam: b 5-22-1751 d 12-10-1823 m Catherine Staurin Pvt NY
George: b 1790 d 1790 m Catherine — Pvt NY
George G.: b 11-12-1742 d 7-26-1834 m (2)Catherine Bellinger Pvt NY
Hendrick J.: b 8-7-1749 d 6-22-1810 m Margaret M Waggoner Pvt NY
Jacob: b c. 1725 d p. 1798 m Catherine Nellis Col NY
Jacob: b 9-14-1738 d 6-9-1811 m Hannah Forbes Pvt NY
Jacob G.: b 3-9-1738 d 9-8-1814 m (1)Anna Nellis (2)Maritje Beekman PS NY
Jacob I.: b 10-17-1745 d 2-22-1828 m Anna G. Klock Ens NY
Johannes: b 10-30-1711 d 1787 m Anna Margaretha Fox PS NY
John: b 9-1-1730 d 1-15-1815 m Anna Margaret Schumaker Pvt NY
John J.: b 10-13-1740 d 12-28-1810 m (1)Catherine Fultz (2)Catherine (Fox) Nellis 1Lt NY
John Peter: b 1-1-1743 d 12-9-1817 m Margaret Druckenmiller Pvt PA

KLOTZ,
John: b 5-20-1743 d 12-28-1795 m Franconia Krouse Sgt PA

KLUM,
Johannes: b 1736 d 1816 m Maria Pulver Capt NY

KLUMPH,
Jeremiah: b 1763/64 d 10-26-1855 m Amanda Norton PS Tms NY
Thomas: b c. 1729 d 1-   -1818 m Margaret Davis PS NY

KNAB,
Michael: b 4-17-1717 d 6-17-1778 m Eva Magdalena Seltzer PS PA

KNAPP, (includes KNAP)
Aaron: b 1731 d 1777 m (2)Lydia Crozier Pvt NY
Abial: b 9-3-1738 d 5-25-1832 m Keziah Cheney Pvt MA
Abraham: b 12-28-1737 d p. 1780 m Elizabeth Wright Pvt NY
Abraham: b — d 1809 m Martha Comstock Pvt VT
Amos: b 1740 d p. 1784 m — Nelson Drm CT
Charles: b c. 1731 d p. 2-11-1793 m Hannah — Ens NY
Daniel: b 7-2-1763 d 6-25-1842 m Lucy Gray Pvt CT
Daniel: b 9-7-1743 d 11-16-1832 m Mary Field Sgt MA
David: b 1744 d 1810 m Deborah — MM MA

David: b 3-4-1738 d 8-30-1804 m Phebe Horton Pvt NY
Ebenezer: b 6-2-1739 d p. 6-11-1809 m Mary — Pvt NY
Edward: b 9-23-1763 d 3-23-1821 m Esther — Pvt MA ★
Elijah: b 1736 d 10-17-1823 m Irene Ferris Sgt CT ★
Elnathan: b 1735 d 2-20-1818 m Ann Kellogg Pvt CT
Enos: b 1744 d 9-21-1824 m Mary Lockwood Cpl CT
Henry: b 8-25-1763 d c. 1815 m Jemima Fish Pvt NY
Hezekiah: b 10-14-1749 d 12-11-1840 m Mary Peck Pvt CT
Isaac: b 5-14-1750 d 12-3-1834 m Mary Gould Pvt CT
Israel: b 1737 d 11-7-1789 m Mary Henion Capt NY
Jabez: b 1752 d 5-1-1801 m Hannah Holley Lt NY
Jacob: b 7-1-1761 d 12-22-1833 m Mary Smith Cpl CT ★
James: b 1-27-1764 d 2-3-1847 m Hannah Holley Pvt CT
James: b 5-15-1735 d 7-22-1779 m Esther Drake Pvt NY
James: b 1-31-1764 d 12-13-1831 m Lucy Griswold Ball Sol Drm NY ★
Jared: b 7-27-1753 d 10-12-1848 m Catharine Baldwin Sgt CT
Job: b 12-8-1739 d 5-26-1786 m Ruth Reed Capt MA
Joel: b a. 1750 d 2-   -1813 m Mary Davids Pvt NY
John: b 1745 d 9-   -1838 m Esther Haight Lt CT
John: b 3-24-1753 d 1843 m Mary Wilson Pvt CT ★
John: b 12-8-1741 d 11-23-1818 m Jane Foster Ens MA
John: b 5-11-1757 d 2-4-1836 m Eunice Wilcox Pvt Arfr NY ★
John: b 1761/62 d p. 1840 m (1)— Dawson (2)Prudence Hadley Fif VA ★
Jonah: b 1740 d p. 1-24-1811 m Ann Park Sgt CT
Jonathan: b 4-11-1752 d 12-20-1838 m Persis Melvin Pvt MA
Jonathan: b 1756 d 1817 m Abigail Palmer Lt NY
Joseph, Sr.: b 6-9-1740 d 10-16-1811 m Susannah Packard Pvt MA
Joseph, Jr.: b 6-9-1763 d 8-7-1839 m Eunice Carver Pvt MA ★
Joseph: b 12-12-1731 d — m Amy Rundell Pvt NY
Joseph: b 11-28-1762 d 8-10-1833 m Margaret Dickson Pvt PA
Joshua, Sr.: b 2-5-1716 d 8-8-1798 m (1)Hannah Taylor (2)Abigail Bostwick Dibble MM CS PS CT
Joshua, Jr.: b 5-6-1762 d 7-9-1829 m Lodemia Warner Ens CT
Joshua, Jr.: b 1-6-1761 d 2-10-1831 m Charity Mead Pvt CT
Justus: b 1-19-1735 d 3-12-1812 m Sarah Reynolds Ens NY
Lebbeus: b c. 1745 d 3-14-1835 m Rachel Storms Pvt NY
Moses: b 3-12-1743 d 11-7-1809 m Margaret Tiffany Maj MA
Moses: b 9-3-1755 d 12-13-1846/47 m Amy Sprague Pvt NY ★
Nathan: b 1-12-1735 d 1-27-1797 m (1)Rebecca Wardwell (2)Mary Lockwood Cpl CT
Nathaniel, Sr.: bpt 11-29-1726 d 1-2-1804 m (1)Jemima Ward (2)Margaret Rowlins PS NY
Nathaniel, Jr.: b 7-6-1753 d 1787 m Sarah Sutton Pvt PS NY
Nehemiah: b 10-29-1741 d p. 12-21-1807 m (1)Mary Hill (2)Jane — Smn CT
Oliver: b 12-9-1751 d 2-15-1827 m Abigail Gale Pvt MA
Peter: b 7-14-1741 d 2-2-1811 m Sarah Raynolds Cpl CT
Peter: b 2-25-1755 d 4-13-1839 m Dina Guyon Pvt NY
Peter: b 1741 d 12-21-1804 m (1)Huldah — (2)Mrs Jerrusha Owens Mason Pvt MA
Phineas: b 1737 d 4-13-1814 m Mercy Rundel Pvt NY
Samuel: b c. 1726 d 3-12-1816 m (1)Phebe Lockwood (2)Nancy Bouton PS CT
Samuel: b 3-7-1747 d 11-16-1824 m Mercy Holt Pvt CT
Samuel: b 7-5-1747 d 8-5-1827 m Rachel Grover Sgt MA
Samuel: b 1738 d 8-22-1779 m Mehitabel — Lt NY
Samuel: b 11-24-1758 d 7-22-1841 m Hannah Secor Sol NY
Samuel: b 12-   -1759 d 7-16-1847 m Charity Westfall Pvt PA ★
Silas: b 10-15-1758 d 1-8-1826 m Ann Guion Pvt NY
Uzal: b 10-22-1759 d 1-11-1856 m Abigail Hoyt Sgt CT
Wm.: b 10-23-1751 d 6-12-1817 m Mary Holly Cpl NY
Wm.: b 1-4-1758 d 9-23-1842 m Olive Rowley MM NY
Wm.: b 11-29-1764 d 8-6-1846 m Fanny Temple Pvt VT ★
Zephaniah: b 5-6-1736 d 1-21-1816 m Millah Roe Pvt NY

KNAPPEN,
Thomas: b 1741 d 10-16-1815 m Sybelia — Pvt CT

KNAPPENBERGER,
Conrad: b 1747 d 1818 m Barbara Blos Pvt PA
Henry: b 9-19-1744 d 8-   -1818 m Anna Margaret — Pvt PA

KNEDLER,
Peter: b 1764 d 1798 m Maria Magdelena — Pvt PA

KNEELAND,
Aaron: b 11-10-1749 d 10-4-1838 m Hannah Ramsdell Pvt Grd MA
Bartholomew: b 11-11-1725 d 4-19-1792 m Susanna Sewall PS MA
Benjamin: b 11-21-1746 d p. 1779 m Mehitable Lord Pvt CT
David: b 4-23-1752 d 2-24-1834 m Mercy (Kneeland)CS CT
Ebenezer: b 9-8-1753 d 9-20-1786 m Elizabeth (Sedgwick)Taylor Pvt CT
Hezekiah: b 6-26-1722 d 1779 m Mercy Pepoon Pvt CT
Isaac, Sr.: b 8-15-1716 d p. 1784 m (1)Sarah Beach (2)Content Rowley PS CT
Isaac, Jr.: b 10-13-1741 d p. 1784 m Hannah Adams MM CT
Jonathan: b 8-26-1744 d 5-25-1780 m Mary Spencer Pvt CT
Joseph: b 11-22-1752 d 1828 m Ruth Hartwell Pvt NH
Nathaniel: b 5-3-1729 d 2-26-1786 m Sarah Hastings Pvt MA
Timothy: b 2-1-1737 d 4-4-1818 m Maria Stone Pvt MA

KNEISEL,
Stephen: b *a.* 1743 d *a.* 1807 m Catharine — Pvt PA

KNEISLEY, (includes KNEISLY, KNISELY, NEISLEY, NESSLY, NICELY, NISLY)
Adam: b *c.* 1730 d 1826 m Elizabeth Eichert Pvt PA
Christian: b 5-21-1751 d 6-2-1835 m Elizabeth Ohment Sol PA
Christian: b 1759 d 1822 m (1)— Stauffer (2)Catherine Bossler Pvt PA
George: b 8-2-1751 d 2-26-1816 m (1)Mary Meyer (2)Elizabeth Furry Pvt PA
Jacob: b 5-31-1753 d 11-3-1832 m Elizabeth Groff Pvt PA
John: b 9-27-1746 d 8- -1825 m Barbara Hertzler Pvt PA
John: b *c.* 1750 d *a.* 12-28-1812 m Elizabeth — PS PA
John: b 9-21-1752 d 12-15-1834 m Mary Miller Pvt PA
Michael: b *c.* 1750 d *p.* 7-3-1793 m Barbara Baer Pvt PA

KNEPPER,
Abraham: b 1734 d 1823 m Catharine — Pvt PA
David: b 6-5-1759 d 11-18-1824 m Esther Foreman Pvt PA

KNERR,
Abraham, Sr.: b 1716 d 4-21-1793 m Mary Eva — PS PA
Abraham, Jr.: b 1750 d 1778 m Eva Elizabeth — Pvt PA
Andrew: b 6-5-1758 d 12- -1840 m Catherine Elizabeth Schall Pvt Fif PA
Heinrich: b *c.* 1735 d *p.* 1790 m Elizabeth Miller Pvt PA

KNIBB. (or NIBB)
John: b 1732 d *p.* 9- -1791 m — Sgt VA

KNIBLE, (includes KNIPPLE, KNIPPEL)
Christopher: b — d — m — Pvt PA

KNIBLOE,
Ebenezer: b 10-7-1729 d 12-20-1795 m Betty Prindle PS NY

KNICKERBOCKER, (includes KNICKERBACKER, KNIKKABAKKER)
Harmon Jansen: b 1748 d *p.* 1732 m Susanna Bossoon Lt NY
James: b 1734 d 8-12-1810 m Grietje Hardenbroek Pvt NY
John, Sr.: b 3-17-1723 d 8-16-1802 m Rebecca Fonda Col NY
John, Jr.: b 1-29-1751 d 11-10-1827 m Elizabeth Winne Pvt NY
Lawrence: bpt 10-25-1747 d *p.* 1809 m (1)Maria Gertrude Snyder (2)Nancy Race Pvt NY
Petrus: b *c.* 1750 d *p.* 5-20-1780 m Margerie Bain PS NY
Philip: bpt 2-24-1745 d 1819 m (1)Anna Maria Dings (2)Hannah (Gardinier)Herder Ens NY
Rulef: bpt 4-16-1745 d 6-28-1807 m Catherine Dutcher Ens NY

KNIFFEN, (includes KNIFFIN)
Amos: b 3-26-1757 d 2-5-1842 m (1)Sarah — (2)Hannah Angevine Pvt NY ★
Jacob: b 7-19-1760 d 10-10-1859 m Jemima Springsteen Pvt NY
Jonathan: b *p.* 1755 d *p.* 1817 m Elizabeth Patience — Pvt NY
Samuel: b 2-1-1750 d 3-9-1828 m Jane Hughson Pvt NY

KNIGHT, (includes KNECHT, KNIGHTS)
Amaziah: b 8-25-1745 d 1-4-1835 m Lydia Wright Pvt NH
Amos: b 4-7-1737 d *p.* 9-25-1804 m Ann Sawyer Pvt MA
Amos: b 9-27-1758 d — m Betsey — Pvt ME
Amos: b 3-6-1747/48 d *p.* 1788 m (1)Susanna Maynard (2)Lydia Johnson Pvt NH
Artemas: b 2-15-1748 d 2-7-1838 m Tabitha Sanderson 2Lt MA
Asher: b 6-26-1761 d 7-31-1825 m Martha C. Clark Pvt MA
Barzilla: b 1757 d 3-20-1821 m Eleanor Carpenter Pvt RI W★
Benjamin: b *c.* 1735 d *p.* 1778 m Elizabeth — Pvt MA
Benjamin: b 12-25-1751 d 7-5-1827 m Lydia Lake Pvt MA
Benjamin: b 1757 d 8-16-1843 m Sally Coffin Pvt MA
Benjamin: b 4-20-1755 d 7-26-1831 m Sally Jackman Sgt NH
Charles: b 9-20-1760 d 1-4-1833 m Martha Bartlett Pvt VA
Daniel: b 1756 d 10-10-1799 m Betty Bradbury Pvt ME
Daniel: b 1-29-1739 d *p.* 1780 m Mary Goodwin Sgt MA
Daniel: b 12-20-1715 d *p.* 1783 m Jerusha — Pvt MA
Daniel: b 3-18-1744 d 1-8-1798 m Mary Winslow Pvt MA
Daniel: b 1760 d 1-31-1853 m Sally Dolly — Pvt MA ★
Daniel: b 9-12-1759 d 6-29-1838 m (3)Mary Ridgway Drm PA
Edward: b 10-29-1751 d 9-15-1819 m (1)Elizabeth Flagg (2)Sarah Jenkins Pvt MA
Elisha: b 10-3-1723 d 8-8-1798 m Sarah Holden PS MA
Enos: b 12-29-1729 d 1804 m Louisa Gould Pvt MA
Giles: b 11-17-1719 d 12-19-1799 m (1)Elizabeth James (2)Phebe Thomas PS PA
Hans Ulrich: b 2-18-1738 d 2-26-1818 m (1)Maria Catharina Schlouch (2)Eva Lannaschmidt Pvt PA
Jacob: b 1757 d 1-27-1843 m Mary — Pvt MA
James: b 1759 d 8-31-1841 m — Shufelt Pvt NY ★
James: b 8-20-1750 d 2-3-1838 m Margaret Prigmore Pvt Mar PA ★
James: b 1734 d 8- -1786 m Jane Haney Sgt VA
James: b 2-3-1760 d 4-18-1858 m (1)Sarah Patterson (2)Jane Davis Sgt VA
James: b 3-9-1750 d 10-24-1831 m Betsy Williams Sgt VA ★

Job: b 1738 d 1792 m Abigail Bennett 2Lt MA
Joel: b 12-11-1761 d 5-5-1841 m Esther Farr Drm VT
John: b 12-15-1753 d 5-18-1803 m Susanna Allen Pvt MA
John: b 1741 d 6-12-1813 m Mary Coran PM Pvt PA
John: b 1747 d 1848 m Polly Rutledge Pvt SC ★
John: b 2-10-1754 d 4-23-1838 m Abigail Town Pvt VT ★
John: b 1748 d 3-12-1838 m Mary Stephenson Dr VA
Johnathan, Jr.: b 2-18-1760 d 2-15-1842 m Elizabeth Fiske Mar Pvt RI ★
Jonathan: b 1-10-1758 d 3- -1829 m Anna Fitch SrgnMte CT
Jonathan: b 12-11-1737 d 2-10-1828 m Mary Atkins N2Lt MA
Jonathan: b 1720 d 1814 m Mary Perkins Pvt MA
Jonathan: b 1756-59 d 11-19-1837 m Sarah (Weed) Pettingell Pvt MA ★
Jonathan: b 1-21-1761 d 12-15-1836 (1)Obedience Root (2)Elizabeth Dudley Pvt MA
Jonathan: b 1721 d 1809 m Judith Woodson Of NC
Jonathan: b 1-3-1732 d 3-13-1819 m Tamer Keyes Capt CS PS VT
Joseph: b 5-29-1744 d *p.* 1778 m Mehitable Putnam Pvt MA
Joseph: b 10-1-1744 d 12-14-1805 m Sarah Holden Pvt MA
Joseph: b 1749 d 1-24-1829 m Sarah Stuart Pvt MA
Joseph: b 5-1-1740 d 2-27-1825 m Elizabeth (Knight) Maj PS RI
Josiah: b 11-22-1763 d 1840 m Marguerite Nalour Pvt CT ★
Mark: b 7-1-1731 d 12-6-1813 m Margaret Johnson Lt MA
Moses: b *c.* 12-23-1757 d 2-22-1828 m Abiah Page Pvt NH W★
Moses: b 1764 d 5-20-1822 m (1)Sarah Stockwell (2)Rebecca Rexford Ryon Pvt RI
Moses: b 5-27-1763 d 10-1-1836 m Frances — Pvt SC
Nathaniel: b 1752 d 4-27-1826 m Judith Eastman Pvt MA
Nicholas: b 3-19-1755 d 9-12-1828 m Elizabeth Case Pvt NY
Peter: b — d — m Catharine Raub Pvt PA
Peter: b *c.* 1745 d *p.* 1800 m Eva — Cpl PA
Phineas: b 1731 d 5-12-1806 m Abigail — PS CT
Phineas: b 1755 d 2-28-1833 m Hetty Sanford Pvt CT ★
Richard: b 1767 d 11- -1850 m (1)Sarah Boyer (2)Sarah Berry (3)Sarah Rembaugh Drm PA
Robert, Jr.: b 6-12-1750 d 7-31-1823 m Elizabeth Hammond Pvt RI W★
Samuel: b 2-3-1743 d 8-22-1792 m Betty Elderkin Sgt MA
Samuel: bpt 12-7-1729 d 1804 m Prudence Bennett PS NY
Samuel: b *c.* 1742 d 1806 m Hannah — Pvt MA
Samuel: b 2-21-1757 d *p.* 1832 m Sarah Bradley Pvt NH
Samuel: b 1759 d 7-2-1826 m Lucina Mowry Pvt RI
Samuel: b 2-10-1731 d 7-23-1804 m Mary Covill Pvt VT
Silas: b 5-5-1757 d 9-8-1842 m Martha Goodenow Pvt MA ★
Thomas: b 1-26-1748/49 d 1776 m (1)Elizabeth Gould (2)Mrs Ann Thomas Pvt MA
Thomas: b 1760 d 7-2-1848 m Elizabeth Wisner Pvt QMSgt NJ NY
Wm.: b *c.* 1721 d *p.* 4-4-1789 m Sarah — PS MD
Wm.: b 1760 d 8-9-1834 m Rachel Stevens Pvt MA ★
Wm.: bpt 1-2-1731/32 d 3-14-1788 m Hannah Knight 1Maj MA
Wm.: b 5-11-1761 d 5-17-1820 m Lydia Cleverly Pvt MA ★
Wm.: b *c.* 1758 d 4-12-1831 m Phoebe Hays Drm Smn NH
Wm.: b 1751 d 4-30-1820 m Priscilla Corbly Pvt PA
Wm.: b 1728 d 1782 m Polly — Sol VA

KNIGHTON,
Thomas: b 3-23-1753 d 9-3-1835 m Jane Freeman Pvt SC VA ★

KNIPE,
Christian: b 7-4-1753 d 8-7-1813 m Mary Wismer Pvt PA
John: b 8-16-1744 d 10- -1812 m Anna Maria Connors Pvt PA

KNISKERN,
Johannes, Sr.: b 6-14-1721 d 10-11-1781 m Sophia Schaeffer Pvt NY
Johannes, Jr.: b 3-26-1746 d 12-19-1826 m Margaret Enders Pvt NY
Peter: b 10-8-1748 d *p.* 1790 m Lea Windecker Pvt NY

KNOOP, (or KNOPF)
Jacob: b 6-1-1724 d 5-24-1785 m Christine Metz Pvt PA

KNORR,
Christian: b 1749 d 6-11-1836 m Anna Maria — Pvt PA
George: b 12-11-1761 d 8-22-1854 m — Pvt PA
Jacob: b 1-9-1759 d *c.* 1820 m Jemima Warner Pvt PA
John: b 5-21-1731 d 9-28-1807 m Alice Jones Pvt PA
Matthias: b 4-7-1737 d 7-30-1825 m Susanna Bachman Pvt PA

KNOTT, (includes KNOTTS, NOTT)
Abraham: b 7-31-1719 d 1794 m Mercy Dimock Pvt CT
Benjamin: b 1744 d 1812 m — Jones Pvt SC
David: b *c.* 1732 d 1788 m Isabel Little PS NJ
Epaphras: b 1754 d 3-13-1843 m Jemima — Cpl CT ★
Ignatius: b 4-17-1747 d 7-15-1835 m — Pvt MD ★
James: b 1752 d 1805 m Elizabeth — Pvt VA
John: b *c.* 1755 d 1824 m Polly — Sol NC
John: b 1740 d 1798 m Mary — PS NC
John: b 9-24-1731 d 1815 m (1)Ruth (Kilburn) (2)Eunice Powers Sgt CS VT
Nathaniel: b 1750-56 d 1791/92 m Ruth — Pvt NY
Thomas Percy: b 1745 d *p.* 1790 m Jane Hart Ens MD
Wm.: b 1-7-1743 d *p.* 1798 m Elizabeth Goodrich SeaCapt CT

KNOUF, (or CNOUFF)
Peter: b 1749 d 3-3-1833 m Mrs Judy Sullivan PS MD

KNOUSE, (includes KNAUSS, KNOUSS)
Abraham: b 3-1-1754 d 8-3-1836 m Elizabeth Boeckel Pvt PA
Daniel, Sr.: b 7-27-1726 d 2-1-1792 m Salome — Pvt PS PA
Daniel: b c. 1738 d a. 1-7-1779 m Elizabeth Ritter Pvt PA
Daniel, Jr.: b 9-5-1756 d 2-23-1845 m Susanna Meyer Cpl PA
George: b c. 1727 d p. 1782 m Maria Charlotte — QM CMman PA
George Frederick: b 10-12-1748 d 12-11-1817 m (1)Mary Magdalena Roth (2)Mary Magdalina Saeger PS PA
Godfrey: b 1-15-1742 d 2-15-1806 m Anna Maria Griesemer Capt PA
Heinrich: b 11-22-1741 d 5-6-1810 m Anna Maria Ehrenhart Pvt PA
Henry: b 1-8-1746 d 10-30-1816 m (1)— Brant (2)Elizabeth Van Rith (Reed) (3)Eva Boyer Capt PA
John: b 11-6-1748 d 5-23-1822 m Catherine Romig Sgt PA
John Ludwig: b 5-19-1759 d 4-24-1832 m (1)Mary Magdalena Klein (2)Catherine Werner Pvt PA
Leonard: b 1-8-1745 d 5-14-1823 m Joanna Salome Mueller Pvt PA
Ludwig, Sr.: b 2- -1730 d 6-4-1809 m Elizabeth — CS PA
Ludwig, Jr.: b 2-28-1760 d p. 1808 m Elizabeth Schumaker Pvt PS PA
Paul: b 4-13-1747 d 1-19-1808 m Anna C Griesemer Capt PA

KNOWER,
Benjamin: b 11-4-1754 d 11-4-1806 m Elizabeth Weld Pvt MA
Daniel: b 9-5-1725 d c. 10-10-1780 m Abigail Whittemore Smn MA

KNOWLAND, (includes NOWLAND)
James: b c. 1735 d p. 3- -1785 m Mrs Hannah Richardson Carr Pvt MA
John: b c. 1753 d 2-15-1815 m Lydia Welden Pvt MD

KNOWLES,
Amos, Jr.: b 2-9-1752 d 8-26-1810 m Olive Batchelder Pvt PS NH
Amos: b 11-4-1722 d 1804 m Elizabeth Libby PS NH
David, Sr.: b 9-1-1725 d 3- -1806 m Deborah Palmer PS NH
David, Jr.: b 8-23-1751 d p. 1790 m Mary Hobbs Pvt NH
Freeman: b 12-17-1754 d 11-27-1797 m Susan Nash Pvt MA
Henry: b 1763 d 7-15-1847 m Catharine Mountz Cpl MA
James: b 1752 d 6-18-1830 m Martha Smith Pvt CT ★
James: b 8-6-1745 d 6-1-1777 m Prudence Benton NLt MA
James: b 2-26-1720 d 1802 m (1)Mary Libbey(2)Comfort Wallis (3)Experience Chamberlain PS NH
John: b 6-9-1744 d 11-5-1806 m Susannah Walker Pvt MA
John: b 4-25-1759 d 5-16-1832 m Lydia Chaplin Sgt NH ★
John: b 4-8-1760 d 12-22-1845 m (1)Lois Hoit (2)Phoebe Whittier (3)Widow Quimby Pvt NH ★
John: b 1-25-1732 d 3-26-1777 m Lydia Philbrick Pvt NH
John: b 10-12-1714 d 4-26-1798 m Sarah Moulton PS NH
Joseph: b 12-13-1727 d 3-3-1823 m Love Brackett Pvt NH
Joseph: b 6-15-1758 d 2-16-1815 m Sarah Locke Pvt NH
Joshua: b 1730 d 5-7-1779 m Mary — Pvt MA
Joshua: b 1756 d 1822 m Hannah Atkins Pvt MA
Nathan: b 11-14-1748 d 4-30-1837 m Susannah Shackford Sol PS NH
Paul: b 1-24-1758 d 3-2-1816 m Thankful Snow Pvt MA
Robert: b c. 1760 d 1821 m Sallie — Pvt DE
Seth: b 3-7-1760 d 3-20-1829 m (1)Mercy — (2)Dorcas Chapin (3)Mehitable Bills Pvt CT ★
Seth, Sr.: b 1-20-1722 d 3-18-1787 m Ruth Freeman Of MA
Simon: b 6-3-1759 d 3-26-1834 m Lydia Fuller Pvt NH ★
Walker: b 4-1-1762 d 8-30-1837 m (1)Elizabeth Wells (2)Lydia Brainerd Porter Cpl CT ★
Willard: b 11-6-1711 d 3-11-1786 m Bethiah Atwood CS PS MA
Wm.: b c. 1755 d c. 1815 m Mary Ann Wilson Pvt MD

KNOWLTON,
Abraham: b 1731 d 6-9-1812 m (1)Comfort Holman (2)Susanna Jordon Lt MA
Abraham: bpt 10-24-1731 d 10-2-1797 m (1)Sarah Lord (2)Mrs Sarah (Giddings) Fitts 2Lt MA
Abraham: b 11-25-1750 d 9-12-1807 m (1)Lydia Batchelder (2)Lucy Whitney Pvt MA
Abraham: b 9-5-1756 d 2-13-1829 m Anna Taylor Pvt MA ★
Amos: b 7-6-1746 d 6-30-1778 m Mrs Mary Warren Sgt MA
Andrew: b 1750 d 1845 m Ruth Ridlow Sgt MA
Benjamin, Sr.: b 12-10-1728 d 7-21-1809 m Phoebe Wright Lt PS NJ
Charles: b c. 1747 d 8-1-1822 m Eunice Packard Pvt MA
Daniel: bpt 12-31-1738 d 5-31-1825 m (1)Elizabeth Farnham (2)Rebecca Fenton Lt CT
Ebebenezer: b 8-14-1759 d 6-11-1845 m Elizabeth Rowlings Pvt NH
Edmund: b 1747 d 11-24-1827 m Mary Austin Pvt MA
Ephraim: b c. 1758 d 5-15-1831 m Molly Murphy Pvt MA
Ezekiel: b 5-1-1736 d 12-1-1810 m Anna Miles Capt MA
Ezra: b 7-29-1739 d 10-25-1814 m Abigail Dodge Pvt MA
Grant: b 9-17-1753 d p. 1818 m Frances Evans Pvt SC ★
John: b 1- -1764 d 10-18-1798 m Dorcas Shapleigh Pvt MA
John: b 1-24-1745 d 4- -1835 m (1)Martha Jennings(2)Elizabeth Wight Sgt NH
John: b 8-17-1747 d 7-19-1838 m Mary Manning Ens NY ★
John: b 1740 d 1800 m Lydia Ingles Pvt NY
Jonathan: b 7-28-1750 d 11-5-1819 m Mary Blunt Oakes Pvt MA

Jonathan: b 12-19-1755 d 6-30-1837 m Hannah Morgan Pvt MA
Jonathan: b 6- -1739 d 6- -1814 m Ruth Page PS NH
Joseph: b 1739 d 5-1-1834 m (1)Ruth Dodge (2)Reliance Cole Cpl CT
Joseph: b 7-27-1749 d 7-7-1845 m Marta Wheeler Sgt MA ★
Joseph: b 8-11-1742 d c. 1790 m Rachel Patch Pvt MA
Joseph: b 6-27-1760 d 3-28-1836 m Betsey Sprague Pvt MA ★
Luke: b 10-24-1738 d 12-12-1810 m Sarah Holland CS VT
Malachi: b 1-10-1759 d 9-13-1830 m Abigail Patch Fif MA
Nathan: b 5-15-1760 d 5-24-1856 m Olive Pomeroy Cpl MA ★
Nathan: b 8-31-1760 d p. 1840 m (1)Patience Miller (2)— Jennings Pvt MA ★
Nathan: b 6-28-1733 d 12-22-1807 m Sarah Boyde Pvt MA
Nehemiah: b 4-19-1745 d 8-13-1834 m (1)Elizabeth Potter (2)Susanna Fellows (3)Martha Tilton Sgt MA
Reuben: b 7-17-1744 d p. 1790 m Mary Morse Pvt MA
Rice 3d: b 4-27-1740 d p. 2-17-1778 m (1)Sarah Coey (2)Judith Lane Pvt MA
Robert: b 1-28-1757 d 1825 m Betsey Davis Pvt MA
Robert: b 2-10-1759 d 12-10-1851 m Mary Gay Pvt NY
Roswell: b 10-20-1738 d 1806 m (1)Ann Dutton (2)Sophia Goodell Pvt MA
Stephen, Sr.: b 8-26-1730 d 1-29-1814 m (1)Abigail — (2)Rebecca — (3)Mary Purple Sgt CT
Stephen, Jr.: b 7-15-1753 d 5-30-1830 m Diadema Chubb Pvt CT W★
Thomas, Sr.: b 11-22-1740 d 9-16-1776 m Anna Keys LCol CT
Thomas, Jr.: b 7-13-1765 d 5-2-1858 m Martha Marcy Sol CT
Thomas: b 4-27-1750 d 8-27-1829 m Elizabeth Bachelor 1Lt MA
Thomas: b 1-28-1759 d 10-10-1827 m (1)Joanna Martin (2)Mrs Hannah Lincoln Rhoades Pvt MA ★
Thomas: b 10-26-1760 d 2-13-1832 m Abigail Goodhue Pvt MA
Thomas: b 1760 d — m Susannah Hollis Pvt Matr MA
Thomas: b 5-10-1749 d 3-7-1832 m Betsey Giles PS NH
Timothy: b 1745 d 6-20-1815 m Sarah Mansfield Pvt MA
Wm.: b 12-23-1738 d 1-9-1784 m Mehitable Eaton Pvt CT
Wm.: b 4-29-1741 d 9-13-1820 m Hannah Hastings 1Lt MA

KNOX, (includes NOCK)
Absalom: b 1738 d 1808 m Mary Marrison Pvt NC
Andrew: b c. 1733 d a. 1776 m Christian Halsey PS LCol NC
Andrew: b 1727 d 10-17-1807 m Isabell White CS Pvt PA
Archibald: b c. 1750 d 12-17-1815 m (1)Elizabeth Ann McKee (2)Martha McClellan Pvt SC
Benjamin: b 6-5-1760 d 9-2-1842 m Datie Wilson Pvt NC ★
Benjamine: b 4-10-1759 d 2-27-1842 m Rebecca Simmons Pvt NC
David: b 1757 d 5-9-1830 m Mary Wood PS NH
David: b 10-17-1760 d 9-13-1822 m Isabella Caldwell Pvt PA
Elijah: b 8-23-1761 d 6-22-1833 m Ruth Huntley Cpl MA
George: b 9-27-1757 d 3-10-1834 m Ann Bell SgtMaj PA
George: b 1761 d 8-30-1833 m Sarah — Pvt VA
Henry: b 7-25-1750 d 10-25-1806 m Lucy Flucker Col MGen MA
Hugh: b — d 3- -1821 m Jane Nesbit Capt NC ★
Isaac: b a. 1735 d p. 2-26-1819 m Charity — Cav SC
James: b 6-20-1755 d 2-23-1839 m Lydia Stratton Sgt MA ★
James: b 8-12-1755 d 2-18-1825 m Sabra Huntley Sgt MA
James: b 1752 d 1794 m Lydia Gillespie Capt NC
James: b c. 1760 d 10-19-1822 m Nancy Morse Pvt RI ★
James: b 5-18-1760 d 1847 m (1)Janet McElroy (2)Eliza Smith Sol SC
James, Sr.: b 1713 d 1785 m Elizabeth Craig PS SC
James, Jr.: b 1749 d 1781 m Jannet Miller Pvt Cav SC
John: b a. 1748 d 8- -1811 m Jane Robinson Pvt MD
John: b 1745 d p. 1820 m Molly Grant Gerrish Pvt MA
John: b 1-15-1759 d 10-13-1847 m Anna Gunn Pvt MA
John: b c. 1720 d 11-25-1800 m Rachel Freeland PS CS MA
John: b 9-16-1754 d 1-18-1839 m (1)Mary Ann Knox (2)Mrs Lettice (Forest)Mann Pvt NH
John: b 10-26-1751 d 4-10-1820 m Mary Forrest PS NH
John, Jr.: b a. 1740 d 1802 m Hannah Reid Pvt NC
John: b 7-31-1744 d p. 1799 m Pharaby Matthews Pvt NC
John: b 1748/9 d 12-24-1818 m Elizabeth Oaff Lt SC W★
John: b 1743 d 1811 m Nancy Gilbreath Sol VA
Joseph: b c. 1747 d 8-31-1835 m (1)Magdalene Allison (2)Jean Crockett Pvt NC ★
Nathan: b 2-13-1761 d 5-7-1833 m Polly Fuller Pvt MA W ★
Oliver: b 1-23-1752 d p. 1791 m Leddy Moore Pvt MA
Robert: b 4-11-1758 d 10-3-1836 m (1)Elizabeth Gill (2)Milly Bohannan Sgt SC ★
Samuel: b 1-1-1747 d 11-2-1837 m Mary Luckey Lt NC ★
Sarah: b 1751 d 6-2-1835 m John Johnston PS PA
Wm., Sr.: b 1721/2 d 3-19-1802 m Isabel Ferguson PS Capt MA
Wm., Jr.: b 9-15-1750 d 3-12-1815 m (1)Submit Black (2) Mrs Elizabeth Osborn Lt MA
Wm: b 7-11-1742 d 12-19-1824 m Jennette Campbell 2Lt MA
Wm., Sr.: b 1716 d 4-27-1799 m Mary Ann McNeal PS NH
Wm., Jr.: b 1752 d 9-26-1823 m Elinor McDaniel Sol NH
Wm: b 1736 d 7-19-1776 m — Allen Capt NC
Timothy: b 1725 d 4-1-1807 m Abigail Dike Sct Pvt CS VT

KOCH, (includes COGH & KOUGH)
Adam: b 10-20-1752 d 1844 m Barbara Leddermann Pvt PA ★
Adam: b c. 1745 d 1807 m Catharine — Pvt PA

Adam: b 4-13-1764 d 5-22-1827 m (1)Mary Loescher (2)Catherine—
   Pvt PA CL
Casparus: b 10-5-1761 d 11-3-1839 m Margaret Harring Pvt NJ
Henry: b 1758 d 1824 m Catharine Gerhard 2Lt PA
Jacob: b 1758 d p. 1825 m Elizabeth Wright Pvt PA
John: b 1757 d 11-23-1843 m Catherine Myers Pvt PA
Michael: b 1730 d 3-31-1785 m Dorothea — PS PA
Nicholas: b 4-22-1737 d 9-21-1818 m Elizabeth Hertzel Pvt PA
Severivus: b 2-15-1752 d 10-21-1841 m Elizabeth — Pvt NY ★
Soverinus: b 1737 d p. 1790 m Catharina Loucks Capt NY
Wm.: b 4-1-1747 d 5-3-1832 m (1)Phillipina Dreibelbis (2)Maria Mag-
   dalena Neufang Pvt PA

KOCHER,
John Peter: b 3-29-1742 d 4-19-1819 m Maria Messenger Pvt PA

KOCHERSPERGER,
Martin: b — d a. 10-28-1822 m Rosina — Pvt PA

KOERCHER, (includes KARKER)
John Phillip: b — d p. 1787 m (2)Anna Marie Meyer Sct PS NY
Martin: b 3-27-1718 d 8-3-1787 m Anna Elizabeth Kascherm Maj PA

KOGER,
Joseph: b 9-25-1749 d 2-11-1835 m Mary Cook Sol SC

KOINER, (includes COINER, COYNER, KEINER & KOINER)
Casper: b 9-25-1764 d 10-31-1853 m Margaret Berrier Pvt PA
Conrad: b 1755 d 3-11-1816 m Elizabeth Stumbaugh Ens PA
George Adam: b 8-7-1753 d 1820 m Barbara Smith Pvt PA
George Michael: b 6-10-1758 d 6-30-1840 m (1) — Foster
   (2)Susanna Hawpe Pvt PA
Michael: b 1-29-1720 d 11-7-1796 m Margaret Diller PS PA

KOHL,
Jacob: b c. 1752 d 4-1823 m Elizabeth Buck Pvt PA

**KOHLER, (includes KALER, KAYLER, KAYLOR, KOEHLER,
   KOLLER)**
Antony: b 1710 d 1783 m Maria Barbara — Pvt PA
Baltzer: b 1751 d 1790 m Elizabeth — Pvt PA
Charles: b 1-2-1747 d 1832 m Elizabeth — Pvt MA
George: b — d p. 1779 m — Pvt PA
Heinrich: b 9-17-1750 d 2-13-1830 m Margaretha Zimmer Pvt PA
John: b 1726 d 12-27-1799 m Anne Margaret Hassin PS PA
John: b 1750 d 11- -1815 m Elizabeth — Pvt PA
Matthias: b 2-2-1751 d 10-4-1825 m Catharine Sands Ens PA
Michael: b 9-27-1753 d 4-11-1836 m Maria Elizabeth — Pvt PA
Michael: b c. 1745 d a. 5-28-1807 m Elizabeth — Pvt VA
Peter: b 4-2-1735 d 9-27-1793 m Juliana Margaret Guth Ens PS CS
   PA

KOLB, (includes CULP, KULP)
Abel: b c. 1750 d 4- -1781 m Sarah James Col SC
Benjamin: b 1740 d 10-29-1819 m (1)Dorothy Ofhenchine (2)Mary
   Rachel Cline PS SC
Daniel: b — d p. 1791 m Esther — 1Lt VA
Dillman: b c. 1756 d p. 1802 m Barbara Cassel Pvt PA
Jacob: b 3-2-1745 d 8-3-1820 m Annie Yoder Pvt PA
Jehu: b 1758 d 5-2-1844 m (1)Lucretia — (2)Angelina — Pvt SC ★
Jeremiah: b c. 1758 d p. 12-29-1829 m (1)Anna Catherina —
   (2)Elizabeth Rieser Pvt PA
John: b 1763 d 1842 m Mary Polly Alexander PS SC
Martin: b 2-2-1728 d 7-6-1788 m Mary Wilds CS SC
Peter: b 11-25-1762 d 12-8-1835 m Thenny Gates Pvt SC ★
Peter: b a. 1732 d p. 1790 m Ann James PS CS SC
Yelles: b 1-9-1750 d p. 1783 m Catherine Sabel (Savocool) Pvt PA

KOLLOCK,
Philip: b 4-22-1748 d 6-28-1824 m (1)Comfort Wiltbank (2)Penelope
   Rodney Sol PS DE
Royal: b 1726 d 11- -1806 m (1)Susanna Man (2)Mary Randall 1Lt
   MA
Shepard: b 9- -1750 d 7-28-1839 m Susan Arnett Capt PA

KOOKEN,
Henry: b — d p. 2-1-1805 m (1)Mary — (2)Anna Elizabeth — PS PA

KOOKOGEY,
Samuel: b c. 1740 d 1827 m Elizabeth McSwain Mus PA ★

KOON,
John: b 2-16-1755 d a. 3-6-1804 m A Catherina Hausman Pvt PA

KOONCE,
Daniel: b — d p. 9-22-1821 m Wenny— PS NC
Philip: b 1-29-1765 d 2-2-1841 m (1)Nancy Griffis (2)Nancy Dodson
   Megee Pvt NC ★

KOONS, (includes COONTZ, COUNCE, KOONTZ & KOUNS)
Christina: b 1759 d 12-5-1837 m Anna Lamb Sol VA
Daniel: b 3-15-1754 d 11-12-1826 m Agnes Martin Pvt PA
De Walt: b 1736 d 1808 m Susannah Dicks Sgt PA

Jacob: b 1734 d 2-7-1823 m Mary Elizbeth Rohuemus Pvt MD ★
John: b 11-17-1754 d 8-6-1842 m Dorethae Clodfelter Pvt NC ★
Nicholas: b 5-26-1742 d 10-14-1813 m (2)Philetta — MM NY
Peter: b 1759 d 1847 m Margaret Snyder Pvt PA

KOPLIN, (or COBELANCE)
Harman: b 8-16-1735 d 7-31-1806 m Julianna — PS MD

KORNEGAY,
Jacob: b c. 1735 d 1795/6 m (1)Mrs Elizabeth Fontaine (2)Mary
   Ward Capt NC

KORNMAN, (includes CORMAN)
George: b 10-6-1750 d 8-3-1820 m Christina Webber PS Pvt PA
John: b 1748 d 12- -1832 m Elizabeth — Pvt PA
Ludwig: b 1754 d 1835 m Catharine Nunemaker Pvt PA
Valentine: b 1742 d 2-28-1823 m (1)Elizabeth — (2)Margaretha —
   Pvt PA

KOSER,
Jacob: b 7-11-1749 d 2-6-1828 m Anna Margaretha Kindt PS PA

KOTTS, (includes COTZ)
Christoff David: b 10-17-1741 d 12-6-1800 m Anna Catherine — Pvt PA
Conrad: b — d 1810 m Margaret Plaskett Cmsry NJ

KOUGHER,
Daniel: b 7-14-1755 d p. 3-4-1829 m Sara Schleyhofin Pvt PA ★

KOYLE, (or KYLE)
Ephraim: b 1749 d 1839 m Mrs Abigail Reading Kincaid Sgt NH

KRACK, (or KRAKE)
Gottlieb: b 1757 d 10- -1833 m Elizabeth Sitts Pvt NY ★

KRAFT, (includes KRAFFT)
Andereas: b c. 1708 d p. 8-29-1794 m Mary — PS PA
Conrad: b c. 1744 d p. 10-22-1792 m Dorothy Rush Cpl PA
George Michael: b a. 1748 d 12- -1788 m Joanna Maria Kieferen Pvt PA
Wm.: b 1753 d 4-17-1829 m Catherine Nicodemus Pvt MD

**KRAMER, (includes CRAMER, CRAMMER, CRANMER,
   KRAEMER, KREAMER & KREMER)**
Adam: b 1755 d 2-1-1829 m Margaret Jacobs Pvt MD
Christopher: b 11-8-1758 d 1825/6 m Catharine VanWoert Pvt NY
Christopher: b — d 1793 m Ann Catherine Hangleiter 1Lt GA
Conrad: b c. 1748 d 5-29-1837 m Catherine Helphenstine QM Sgt
   PA ★
Daniel: b 12-24-1763 d 5-25-1843 m Anna Margaretha Kern Lt PA
David: b 4-3-1748 d 3-25-1813 m Mary Pratt Tomkins Pvt NJ
Frederick: b 2-28-1751 d 6-30-1834 m Elizabeth Willett Capt NH
George: b c. 1750 d 1812 m Christina Dupps Pvt PA
Jacob: b 1745 d 1826/7 m Mary Wilson Lt PA
Jacob: b — d 6- -1795 m — 1Lt PA
Jacob: b 11-22-1749 d a. 1-15-1811 m Catherine Margaret Minich
   Pvt PA
John: b 1740 d p. 1779 m Catherina Flegelar Sol NY
John: b 1760 d 1815/6 m Christiana — MM NY
John: b 10-29-1753 d 1836 m Susannah Kutz Ens PA ★
John Jacob: b 1758 d 1814 m Clarissa Paul Bassett Lt PA
John Nicklaus: b 1-22-1743 d 10-18-1806 m Elizabeth Tippel Pvt NY
Lawrence: b 1755 d 8-7-1818 m (2)Susan Cressman Pvt PA
Martin Luther: b — d 1799 m Sarah Reynolds PS PA
Matthias: b 1737 d 3-24-1783 m Anna Maria Henn Ens NJ
Peter: b 1740 d 1812 m Margarget — Pvt PS MD
Philip: bpt 7-12-1758 d p. 1790 m Elizabeth Overhuyser Pvt NY
Philip: b 4-5-1743 d 2-25-1812 m Mary Magdalena Imler Lt CS PA
Seymour: b 1730 d p. 1783 m Mary Smith Pvt NJ
Wm.: b 3-6-1763 d 4-5-1828 m (1)Phoebe Orsborn (2)Phoebe
   Johnson Fif NJ ★
Zacherias: b 3-26-1753 d 2-11-1818 m Rebecca Scriver Pvt NY

KRANICH, (or CRONICK)
John Peter: b 6-6-1756 d 5-16-1816 m Rachel Funderburk Pvt SC

KRANTZ,
George: b 9-25-1747 d 2-6-1791 m Elizabeth — Pvt PA

KRATZ,
Abraham: b 1741 d 1817 m Barbara Moyer Pvt PA
Isaac: b 7-15-1749 d 9-15-1823 m Mary Yellis Pvt PA
Philip: b 1739 d 1818 m Susanna Krout Pvt PA

KRATZER,
Frederick: b c. 1732 d p. 9-6-1802 m (1)Anna Maria Dorstlinger
   (2)Elizabeth — PS PA
Philip: b c. 1712 d p. 5- -1780 m (2)Mrs Elizabeth Dauber PS PA
Philip: b 12-12-1763 d 1841 m Catharine Jacoby Pvt PA

KRAUSER,
Baltzer: b 10-12-1764 d 1-26-1845 m Eve Meyerly Pvt PA

KRAUSKOP,
George: b 1728 d *p.* 11-3-1783 m (1)Maria Christina Walterin (2)Susanna Magdalena Baselrin (3)Anna Margaretta Wild Ens PA

KREIDELBACH,
John: b *c.* 1750 d 1820 m Dortha Mundschaner Pvt PA

KREILDER,
Frederick: b *c.* 1738 d 1819 m Barbara — Pvt PA

KREISELER,
Sylvester: b 2-14-1761 d 1820 m Marytje Schram Pvt NY

KOPLIN,
John: b *c.* 1720 d *p.* 1783 m Mary — Pvt Tms PA

KREISHER,
Simon: b 5-4-1754 d 5-4-1806 m Susan Keim Pvt PA

KREPS, (includes KRIBBS)
George: b *c.* 1750 d *p.* 1790 m — Pvt PA
John: b 1-11-1755 d 11-4-1791 m Katharine Harrold Pvt PA
Michael: b 1750 d 1799 m Catherine Schnee Cpl PA

KRESS, (or CRESS)
Charles: b 4-29-1739 d 10-26-1792 m Catharine Margaret Pvt PA

KRESSLER, (or CRESSLER)
Michael: b 1740 d 1792 m Elizabeth — Pvt PA

KRETSINGER,
Jacob: b 4-14-1754 d 4-17-1827 m Gertrude Mareenus Pvt NY

KRETZER, (includes KREITZER)
James: b 1740 d 1800 m Maria Elizabeth Clay Pvt VA
Leonard: b — d 4-12-1828 m Elizabeth Cool Btm Cpl NY W ★
Michael: b 9-11-1750 d 1-12-1816 m Barbara Stroh Pvt PA

KREWSON,
John: b 1750 d 1800 m Dana Phillips Lt PA
Simon: b 3-2-1755 d 11-18-1844 m Rebeckah Jones OrdlSgt PA

KRICHBAUM, (or KREIGHBAUM)
Wilhelm: b 10-10-1754 d 11-20-1815 m Catherine Garman Pvt PA

KRICK,
Frantz: b 11-6-1736 d 4-20-1814 m (1)Maria Spohn (2)Mrs Catherine (Schlegel) Gehrling Pvt PA
Jacob: b 1760 d 12-15-1841 m — Pvt PA
John Peter: b 6-27-1756 d 7-31-1829 m Catherine Rader Pvt PA

KRIEBEL,
Abraham: b 5-26-1760 d 9-2-1814 m Salome Yeakel Sol PA

KROESEN, (includes CRUZER)
Abraham: b 6-1-1733 d 4-12-1819 m Martha Doolhagen Sol NJ
Jacob: b 1754 d *p.* 4-27-1829 m Elsje Vansant Ens PA
Johannes: b 1729 d 6-17-1812 m Janetje Nevins 2Lt PA
John: b 1740 d 10-4-1796 m Jane Coursen Pvt PA

KROHN, (includes CRONE)
Jacob: b *c.* 1754/5 d *a.* 1813 m Margaret Dritt Pvt PA
John P: b *c.* 1740 d *a.* 6-25-1804 m Maria Elizabeth — Pvt PA
Martin, Jr.: b 1750 d 1825 m Magdalena Kutz PS PA

KROM, (includes CRUM)
Cornelius: b 3-26-1754 d 1842 m Barbara Davis Pvt NY ★
John: b 2-13-1748 d *p.* 1784 m Hester Leroy Pvt NY
Jan: bpt 4-28-1717 d 1799 m Rebecca Bogart PS NY
John: b 3-20-1811 d 12- -1776 m Rachel DuBois Pvt NJ
Petrus: b 8-16-1752 d 1-17-1835 m Annatje Teffenbor Pvt PS NY
Simeon: b 9-4-1758 d 4-25-1833 m Anna Roosa Pvt NY W★

KROSGE,
Conrad: b *c.* 1740 d 1805 m Anna Margaret Kohl Pvt PA

KROWS, (includes KROUS, KROUSE & KROSS)
John: b 1-9-1712 d 6-6-1795 m Ann Maria — Pvt PS PA
Leonard: b 3-24-1759 d 3- -1838 m Deborah Ostrander Sgt NY ★

KRUG,
Jacob: b 2-4-1750 d 10-8-1817 m Rebecca Hopson Capt PS PA
Valentine: b *c.* 1754 d 1817 m Eva Graff 2Lt PA

KUDER, (includes KUTER)
Elias: b 1754 d *p.* 1790 m Catherine Skinner Capt PA
Valentine: b 5-25-1759 d 9-18-1852 m Christine Fuchs 1Lt PA ★

KUMLER,
Jacob: b 7-1-1742 d 10-22-1815 m (1)Elizabeth Young (2)Sophie Breitenstein PS PA

KUNKEL, (includes CONKLE, GUNCKEL & KUNCKLE)
Adam: b 7-15-1750 d 11-27-1827 m Margaretta Giltner Lt PA

Baltzer: b *a.* 1762 d 9-8-1812 m Anna Maria Kunckel PS PA
Christian: b 7-10-1757 d 9-8-1823 m (1)Katharine Hoyer (2)Anna Maria Elizabeth Welshaur Ens PA
Christian: b 6-15-1746 d 6-4-1813 m Anna Catherine Haagen Pvt PA
John: b 1722 d *p.* 3-11-1785 m Margaret Leonard Pvt PA
John: b 9- -1730 d 2-15-1829 m Margaret — Sol PS VA

KUNSTMAN, (or KUNSMAN)
Philip: b *c.* 1755 d 10- -1820 m (1)Elizabeth Ernst (2)Margaret Enders (3)Barbara (Wildanner) Staufer Pvt PA

KUNTZ, (includes COENS, COONS, KUEHN, KUHN, KUHNS & KUNS)
Abraham: b 5-3-1752 d 7-17-1841 m Anna Hegeman Pvt NY
Bernard: b 12-3-1723 d 7-14-1807 m (1)Anna Catharine Eberhard (2)Anna Oblinger PS PA
Daniel: b *c.* 1756 d *p.* 1786 m Christina — Pvt PA
George: b 4-1-1751 d 10-2-1817 m Margaret Snyder 1Lt PA
George: b 1762 d 2-4-1842 m Leah Corbin Pvt PA
George: b 11-26-1762 d 1-16-1831 m Susan Hubbert Pvt PA W ★
George Frederick: b 11-22-1759 d *p.* 1820 m Maria Elizabeth Luetzelberger Pvt PA
Henry: b 1749 d 1839 m Catherine — Pvt PA
Jacob: b *c.* 1721 d 11- -1793 m Susanna — Pvt PS PA
Jacob: b 2-28-1759 d 10-31-1841 m Christina Mosser Pvt PA
John: b 3-8-1760 d 12-23-1834 m Caroline Allen Pvt NY ★
John: b 9-18-1746 d 1-23-1811 m Susanna Jones PS Dr PA
John: b 4-27-1761 d 3-28-1823 m Elizabeth Marchand Pvt PA CL
Ludweg: b 8-13-1731 d 9-8-1815 m Sevilla Moselle Pvt PA
Peter: b 9-12-1757 d 12-16-1846 m Barbara Reeg Pvt PA
Philip: b 1747 d 1822 m Emma Margarethea Steinbach Sol PA
Phillip: b 5-8-1745 d *a.* 1800 m Maria Harshberger Pvt PA

KURTZ,
Adam: b 1747 d 1815 m Mary Sperry Pvt VA
Johann Nicholas: b 10- -1720 d 5-12-1794 m Anna Elizabeth Seidel PS PA
Michael: b 3-27-1741 d 8-29-1823 m Fredericka Binder Pvt PA
Peter: b *c.* 1743 d 4-12-1816 m Sarah Young Pvt PA

KUTZ, (includes COOTS)
George: b 1730 d 1788 m Mary Margaret Bieber PS PA
Jacob: b 5-13-1741 d 12-23-1821 m Christina Bozzert Pvt PA
James: b *c.* 1755 d 1820 m Mary — Lt NC
Peter: b 12-6-1754 d 4-6-1817 m Catharine — Pvt PS PA

KUYKENDALL, (includes COYKENDALL, CUYKENDALL, KIRKENDALL)
Abraham: b 10-18-1719 d *p.* 12-17-1778 m — CS PS NC
Benjamin: bpt 9-11-1723 d 10-18-1789 m Sara Ferree CS VA
Harmon: b 9-17-1756 d 7-23-1833 m Catherine Beemer Pvt NJ W★
Jonathan: b *c.* 1754 d *a.* 11-14-1826 m — PS SC
Martin: b 2-18-1764 d 12-14-1843 m Anna Cole Pvt Spy NY ★
Mathew: b 10-24-1758 d 10- -1845 m Margaret Hardin Pvt NC ★
Matthew: b 2-9-1758 d 8-15-1841 m Nancy Johnson Sol NC
Petrus: b 11-15-1732 d 1-1-1822 m Catherine Kittle PS NY
Samuel: b 5-28-1752 d 11-26-1835 m (1)Lydia VanCamp (2)Sara Compton Capt NJ ★
Wm.: bpt 12-13-1744 d *p.* 8-21-1787 m Leah Decker Pvt NJ
Wm.: b 4-1-1762 d 8-15-1848 m Jane Gumaer Pvt NY

KYLE, (includes KILE)
George: b *c.* 1750 d 1794 m Hannah — Pvt PS VA
Hartman: b *c.* 1750 d *a.* 5-3-1843 m Catherine Herschberger Pvt PA
John: b 1756 d 8-31-1845 m Jane Watson Pvt PA
John: b *c.* 1745 d *p.* 4-15-1808 m Anna Crawford Pvt PA
John: b 1742 d 1787 m Hannah — Capt PA
Joseph: b 1749 d 7-2-1821 m Katherine Chambers Pvt PA
Joseph: b 1746 d 12- -1807 m Jane Diuguid Sol VA
Robert: b *c.* 1739 d 10-17-1820 m Leah Brooks Capt TN NC
Robert: b 1751 d 1815 m Sarah Pierce Ens PA
Thomas: b 1757/8 d *p.* 3-20-1837 m Mary — Pvt PS PA ★
Wm.: b *c.* 1730 d 1821 m Sara Ann Stevens Sol PS VA

LAAR,
Jacob: b 1752 d 4-18-1837 m Catherine Cratser Pvt PA

LABAGH,
Isaac: b 6-30-1734 d 1-7-1815 m Judith Ozee Pvt NJ

LABAR, (includes LA BAR, LA BARE, LABARR & LABARREE)
Abraham: b *a.* 1750 d *p.* 1777 m Margaret Gordon Col PA
Daniel, Sr.: b *c.* 1726 d *p.* 1790 m Anna Crowner Sgt PA
Daniel, Jr.: b 8-25-1763 d 2-11-1846 m (1)Elisabeth Chambers (2)Cornelia — Pvt PA
George, Jr.: b *c.* 1763 d *p.* 1802 m Clara Bloom Pvt PA
Henry: b 4-15-1755 d 5-13-1849 m Elizabeth Schutt Pvt PA
Joseph: b 8-14-1761 d 2-22-1831 m Esther Marvin Cmsry FrA
Peter, Sr.: b 1724 d 8-3-1803 m Ruth Putnam PS NH
Peter, Jr.: b *c.* 10-24-1750 d 1805-10 m (1)Sarah Kennedy (2)Sarah Longfellow Sgt CS NH
Wm.: b 5-3-1730 d 10-10-1800 m Elizabeth Long Pvt PA

LABOYTEAUX,
Peter, Sr.: b 1737 d 9-14-1813 m Keziah Sebring PS NJ

LA BRANCHE,
Alexandre: b — d *p.* 1820 m Marie Jeanne Piseros PS LA

LABREE,
Peter: b *c.* 1750 d *c.* 1848 m Mehitable Smith Smn MA ★

LACEY, (includes LACY)
Abraham, Jr.: b 10-6-1755 d 10-16-1827 m Susan Willis Pvt NJ
Archibald: b 4-12-1758 d 10-3-1822 m Sarah Martin Sol VA
Benjamin: b 1755 d 1827 m Judith Christian — PS VA
David: b 1719 d 1801 m Martha Parrot Pvt VA
Ebenezer: b 4-19-1727 d 12-12-1807 m Freelove Canfield Sgt CT
Ebenezer: b 8-30-1749 d 1819 m Mary Hurd Pvt CT
Edward: b 9- -1742 d 3-20-1813 m Jane Harper Col SC
Enoch: b — d — m Eleanor Rowland Pvt CT
Ephraim: b 12-20-1750 d 10-14-1839 m Mehitable Kimball Pvt MA
Isaac: b 4-2-1754 d 11-2-1830 m Lydia Pratt Pvt CT
John: b 12-4-1752 d 2-17-1814 m Anastasia Reynolds BGen PA
John: b *c.* 1723 d 1794 m Jane Chapman CS PA
John: b 1728 d 1803 m Frances Littlepage Maj VA
John: b *c.* 1761 d 6-3-1842 m Sarah Porter Sol VA
Josiah: b 1746 d 10-28-1812 m (2)Ruth Silliman Capt CT
Matthew: b — d 3-7-1823 m Susannah Rutherford Ens VA W★
Philemon: b *c.* 1725 d 1808 m Ann — PS NC
Spencer: b 1742 d 1810 m (1)Brittingham (2)Mary Fletcher Pvt Drm DE
Thaddeus: b *c.* 1726 d 10-3-1776 m (1)Mary — (2)Anna — Capt PS CT
Thomas: b *c.* 1730 d *p.* 10-1-1793 m (2)Keziah Griffith CS PS NC
Wm.: b 12-2-1761 d 5-2-1814 m Lucy Gregory Sol CT
Zachariah: b 11-15-1754 d 10-22-1837 m Betty Rowland Cpl CT

LACKEY, (includes LASKEY, LAKEY)
Adam: b 1759 d 2-13-1836 m Catherine — Pvt VA ★
Adam: b *c.* 1748 d *a.* 5- -1789 m Mary — PS VA
Andrew: b 4-24-1757 d 8-27-1821 m Ann Orne Cpl MA ★
James: bpt 4-1-1733 d 3-30-1806 m Margaret Hawley Lt MA
James: b 7-20-1757 d 3-11-1827 m Charlotte Forbes Cpl MA
Matthew: b 10-21-1742 d 1809 m Dorcas Woodbury Pvt MA
Robert: b 9-26-1737 d 12-22-1811 m Elizabeth Corral Pvt MA
Thomas: b 1756 d 1824 m Janett Lackey Pvt GA
Thomas: b 1747 d 2-2-1845 m Margaret Stephenson Pvt NC ★
Thomas: b 1728 d 9-1-1801 m Agnes Leach Sct VA

LACKLAND,
James: b 1756 d 1835 m Catharine Lynn 2Lt MD

LADD,
Abner: b 5-11-1740 d 2-2-1819 m Abigail Perkins Capt PS CT
Amasa: b 10-18-1762 d *p.* 1791 m Elizabeth Cox Pvt VT
Ashbel: b 1-15-1759 d 10-11-1840 m Irene Babcock Pvt VT
Banajah: b 1751 d 1-20-1823 m Deborah Grant Pvt CT
Benjamin: b 9-25-1753 d 12-12-1830 m (1)Deborah Allen (2)Deborah — Pvt MA NH ★
Bodwell: b 12-12-1760 d 10-15-1829 m Martha Lewis Pvt MA
Constantine: b 1- -1753 d *p.* 10-25-1801 m (1)Elizabeth — (2)Mary McNally PS CS NC
Daniel: b 1-8-1735 d 2- -1823 m (1)Hannah Boynton (2)Rebecca Armstrong (3)Elizabeth Cady Pvt CT
Daniel: b 4-9-1747 d 4-25-1825 m Persis Davis Pvt CT
Daniel: b 4-21-1740 d 10-9-1826 m Dorothy Foote Pvt NH
Daniel: b 1-25-1725 d 4- -1809 m (1)Johanna Dudley (2)Susanna Dow (3)Ruth Bradley CS PS NH
Daniel: b 8-21-1742 d 8-28-1808 m Judith Lyford PS NH
Dudley, Sr.: b *c.* 1725 d 3-6-1811 m Alice Hurley CS MA
Dudley, Jr.: b 7-8-1707 d 12-23-1841 m Berthia Hutchins Pvt MA
Edward: b 6-22-1707 d 7-5-1787 m Catherine Thing PS NH
Eliab: b 4-21-1754 d 12-15-1800 m Suzalla Lathrop Pvt CT
Elias, Jr.: b *c.* 1741 d *p.* 1796 m Nancy Thompson PS NH
Eliphalet: b 2-19-1755 d 4-27-1827 m Alice Boyd Park Sgt NH
Elisha: b 3-17-1753 d 1840-3 m Tabitha Strong Pvt CT
Ephraim: b 5-22-1749 d 5-4-1836 m Lois Chapman Pvt CT
Ezekial: b 8-6-1731 d 7-21-1803 m Ruth Hyde Pvt CT
Ezekiel: b 4-10-1738 d 7-12-1818 m Ruth Hutchins Capt NH
James: b 4-10-1752 d 12-5-1836 m Hannah Lock Lt NH ★
Jesse: b 4-10-1732 d 12-14-1816 m Rachel Taylor Sol CT
John: b 9-19-1737 d 1804 m Prudence Shephard Pvt CT
John, Jr.: b 5-8-1756 d 12- -1820 m (1)Sarah Lewis Barber (2)Hannah Reynolds Cpl MA
John: b 4-17-1746 d *p.* 1798 m Hannah Eastman Ens NH
John: b 12-11-1737 d 3-15-1784 m Mary Moody PS NH
Jonathan: b 12-10-1760 d 3-11-1833 m Sarah Looke Pvt NH
Joseph: b 12-15-1764 d 12-21-1836 m Sarah Ring Pvt NH
Joseph: b 6-2-1760 d 6-12-1834 m (1)Cathrine Bacey Damron (2)Mary Angell Pvt NC
Nathaniel: b 1749 d 1832 m Rachel Tilden Pvt CT
Nathaniel: b 10-4-1751 d 10-31-1837 m Abigail Scripture Pvt CT
Nathaniel: b 6-17-1722 d 1790 m Sarah Clifford Pvt MA
Nathaniel: b 10-22-1755 d 2-16-1837 m Sarah Noyes Pvt MA
Nathaniel: b 5-12-1753 d 6-8-1824 m Sally Marshall MM PS NH

Noble: b *c.* 1731 d *a.* 11- -1782 m Judith Damarel PS NC
Paul: b 3-6-1719 d 2- -1783 m Martha Folsom PS NH
Samuel: b 9-14-1727 d 2-16-1816 m Ann Woodward Pvt CT
Samuel: b 6-7-1742 d 5-18-1814 m Margaret Chapman PS CT
Samuel: b 2-21-1744 d 4-9-1801 m Abigail Flanders 1Lt NH
Simeon: b 1-15-1757 d 1-13-1823 m Lizzie Hines PS NH
Thaddeus: b 1-5-1758 d 1-23-1832 m Hannah Dow Drm Pvt MA
Trueworthy: b 5-21-1726 d 4-26-1778 m Lydia Harriman Pvt NH
Wm.: b 1-24-1738 d *p.* 9-6-1821 m Hannah Ayer Lt PS MA
Wm.: b 9-30-1743 d *p.* 1820 m Elizabeth Vining Pvt MA
Wm.: b 2-8-1760 d 5-9-1834 m Mary Crew Pvt VA ★
Wm.: b 10-30-1736/7 d 12-4-1800 m Sarah Gardiner Capt PS RI

LADEY,
Daniel: b *a.* 1757 d *a.* 6-24-1806 m Anna — Pvt PA

LADNER,
Robert: b 1755 d 2-15-1830 m Elizabeth Martin Pvt NJ W ★

LADSON,
James: b 7-7-1753 d 1-21-1812 m Judith Smith Capt SC

LADUE, (includes LA DOUX, LA DUE, LADU)
Abraham: b *c.* 1725 d 6-21-1797/8 m Anna — Ens NY
John: b 2-28-1765 d 6-2-1832 m Deborah Mott Pvt NY
Oliver: b 8-23-1746 d 10-6-1817 m Sarah Caniff Pvt NY
Peter: b 10-8-1762 d 1812 m Mary Lawerence Tallman Pvt NY

LA FAR,
Joseph: b 5-16-1753 d 1795 m Catherine Boillat Sgt SC W ★

LAFAYETTE,
M. Joseph Paul Y. R. G. du Motier, Marquis: b 9-6-1757 d 5-20-1834 m Marie Adrienne Francoise de Noailles MGen FrA

LAFFERTY,
Edward: b *c.* 1733 d *c.* 1810 m Elizabeth Ramage Pvt PA
James: b 2-14-1759 d 11-23-1834 m Elizabeth Morrison Pvt PA
John: b 1759 d 1815 m Sarah Lindsey Pvt NC
Thomas: b *a.* 1751 d 1824-6 m (1)Eleanor — (3)Catherine — PS Sol VA

LAFFOON,
James: b 1763 d 12-27-1852 m — Burk Pvt GA VA ★

LAFLER,
Coonrod: b *a.* 1765 d *p.* 1800 m Agnes Darch Pvt NJ
John Christopher: b 1753 d 1818 m Jemima Kendell Ens NY

LAFLIN,
Joseph: b *c.* 1720 d 1788 m (1)Phebe Wilson (2)Martha Cumins Sgt MA
Matthew, Sr.: b 6-13-1735 d 3-15-1810 m Lucy Loomis Lt MA
Matthew, Jr.: b 7-1-1765 d 12-2-1822 m Lydia Rising Fif MA

LA FOLLETTE,
Joseph: b *c.* 1745 d 1- -1834 m (1)Lydia Carter (2)Phoebe Goble Pvt NJ

LAFON,
Nicholas: b *c.* 1760 d 1831 m Maria Upshaw Sgt VA
Richard: b 1760-2 d 8- -1824 m Anna Bondurant Maxey VA W ★
Thomas: b 3-18-1764 d 9-15-1815 m Catherine Gale Pvt VA

LA FORGE, (includes LA FARGE)
Benjamin: b *c.* 1750-60 d *p.* 1717 m Catherine Linkletter Pvt NJ
Peter: b 10-28-1756 d 4-27-1837 m Martha Webb Pvt NY

LAGENAUER, (includes LOCKENOUR)
George Friedrich: b 5-1-1756 d 3-30-1834 m (1)Christina Hoshns (2)Catharine Crum Kastner Pvt NC ★
Jacob: b 11-7-1751 d 1-15-1843 m (1)Luliana Rominger (2)Elizabeth Clewell Clouse Pvt NC ★

LA GRONE,
Adam: b 1755 d *p.* 1800 m Mary — Pvt SC

LAIDLEY,
Thomas: b 1-1-1756 d 3-17-1838 m Sarah Osborn NCdr PA ★

LAING,
Abram: b 5-1-1758 d 1811 m Susannah Thorn Pvt NJ
Benjamin: b 1745 d 1-6-1819 m (1)Mary Jenkins (2)Mrs Sophia Manning Capt NJ
John: b 1724 d 3-23-1793 m Nellie Paisley Pvt NY

LAIR,
Andrew: b 1750 d 2-5-1828 m Lady Frances Hubbard Pvt KY
Mathias, Sr.: b 1714 d 1787 m Catherine Margaretha Moyer CS VA
Matthias, Jr.: b 2-16-1752 d 10-16-1795 m Ann Elizabeth Rush Sol KY VA

LAIRD,
David: b 1743 d 1820 m Anne Scott Lamme Capt VA

LAIRD, contd.
David: b 1755 d 1829 m Margaret Craig Pvt VA
Jacob: b *c.* 1755 d 11- -1792 m Jane Johnston Lt PA
James: b 5-11-1761 d 1-15-1846 m Mary Macfarlane Pvt PA
James: b 1735 d 10-8-1780 m Lucy Pickens Ens VA
James: b 1730 d 1803 m Sarah — Pvt VA
John: b *c.* 1750 d 12-13-1797 m Sarah Finley LCol PA
Matthew: b 1737 d 1821 m (1)Margaret — (2) — McClennhen 1Lt PA
Moses: b 5-19-1736 d 1798 m (1)Elizabeth English (2)Catherine H. English PS NJ
Richard: bpt 6-22-1760 d 5-6-1828 m Lucy Compton Sgt NJ ★
Robert: b 1742 d *c.* 3-17-1834 m Elizabeth — Capt SC
Robert: b 4-7-1758 d 9-5-1811 m Elizabeth — Pvt NJ
Samuel: b 1760 d 5-21-1820 m Mary Laird Pvt MA
Samuel: b *c.* 1725-30 d 11-16-1821 m Margaret Gibson Pvt PS SC
Wm.: b 1750 d 6- -1828 m (1)Elizabeth Boss (2)— Boss Pvt NJ
Wm.: b 10-27-1727 d 4-11-1820 m (1)Catherine Spencer (2)Martha Wilson Capt PA
Wm.: b *c.* 1760 d 4- -1809 m Elizabeth — Pvt PA

LAISSARD, (or LAYSSARD)
Etienne Marafret: b *c.* 1724 d *p.* 1786 m Helene Fazande Capt LA

LAKE,
Abraham: b *c.* 1730 d *p.* 4-16-1796 m Elizabeth — CS NJ
Abraham, Sr.: b 1741/2 d 1-6-1828 m (1)Rachel — (2)Henrietta Bard (3)Lydia — Sgt NY
Andrew: b *a.* 1756 d *a.* 2-26-1805 m Mary Ingersol Pvt NJ
Asa: b -1764 d 8-8-1843 m Chloe Abbott Fif VT
Benjamin: b 8-27-1764 d 6-28-1838 m Sarah Hollingshead Pvt NJ
Daniel: b 6-22-1726 d 9-26-1810 m Sarah Bixby Pvt NH
Daniel: b 1740 d 1799 m (1)Elizabeth Lucas (2)Susannah (Ingersoll) Edwards Pvt NJ
Daniel: b 3-8-1763 d 10- -1836 m Hannah Sawdey Pvt RI ★
Eleazer: b 9-12-1724 d 3-29-1796 m Sarah Perkins Pvt MA
Eli: b 6-25-1758 d 10-18-1809 m Elizabeth Read Pvt MA
Enos: b 10-26-1756 d 8-5-1841 m (1)Prudence Page (2)Abigail Hudson (3)Abigail (Sawtell)Platts Cpl NH
Garret: b 3-8-1753 d 11-21-1838 m Charity Lake Pvt NY
George Bixby: b 11-7-1750 d 4-16-1816 m Sarah Lovejoy Pvt VT
Gershom: b 6-21-1739 d 5-7-1797 m Sariah Chatfield Ens VT
Henry: b 1739 d 11-28-1804 m Rhoda Jewett Capt MD
Henry: b 4-11-1761 d 9-24-1851 m Jemima Waldo Pvt NY
Joseph, Jr.: b 10- -1740 d 4-24-1813 m Dinah Beardsley Sol CT
Laban: b 2-16-1751 d 2-22-1832 m Patience Goff Pvt MA
Mary(Bird): b *c.* 1728 d 4-27-1796 m Archibald Lake PS NY
Noah: b 1-20-1745 d *p.* 5-1-1803 m (1)Mrs Wealthy Chase Greenman (2)Sarah — Pvt RI
Pardon: b 8-15-1762 d 5-20-1839 m Ruth Macomber Pvt RI ★
Peter: b 8-1-1762 d 9-30-1846 m Hannah Cummings Pvt NY ★
Phineas: b 5- -1736 d 4-6-1819 m Elizabeth Stilson Pvt CT ★
Richard: b *c.* 1756 d 1800 m Sarah Elizabeth Lanning Pvt NJ
Thomas: b 1734 d 3-6-1815 m Mrs Eunice Seavey Davis PS NH
Thomas: b 1735 d *p.* 8-20-1814 m Elizabeth Reeder Pvt NJ
Wm.: b 1748 d 10-22-1823 m Mary Tysen Pvt NY
Wm.: b 1-7-1750 d 3-21-1783 m Elizabeth Poillon Sgt NY

LAKEMAN,
James Fuller: bpt 1-13-1754 d 8-21-1833 m Mercy Brown Pvt MA
Richard: b 3-10-1719 d 8-6-1805 m Lidia York Sgt MA
Samuel: b 10-11-1721 d 10-10-1810 m Hannah Fuller Cpl MA
Samuel: b 1736 d 2-24-1823 m Margaret Kimball Pvt PS NH

LAKIN,
Abraham: b 10-16-1722 d 1- -1796 m Sarah — PS MD
David: b 10-10-1753 d 3-3-1846 m Rebecca Blanchard Pvt MA
Ebenezer: b 7-19-1707 d *p.* 12-28-1786 m (1)Lydia Lakin (2)Mrs Eunice (Lakin) Lakin CS MA
James: b 6-2-1749 d 6-10-1821 m Elizabeth Shattuck Drm MA
Joel: b 1767 d 1837 m Sally Martin Pvt MA
Nathaniel: b 1728 d 10-2-1817 m Sybil Parker 1Lt MA
Robinson: b 2-17-1720 d 8-16-1796 m Hannah Dodge MM MA
Simeon: b 3-6-1760 d 12-10-1842 m Lois Hartwell Pvt NH
Wm., Sr.: b 5-22-1732 d 1816 m Anna Gregg PS NH
Wm., Jr.: b 10-11-1757 d 2-23-1835 m Elizabeth Wilson Pvt NH
Winslow: b 8-27-1759 d 9-23-1840 m Esther Sawtelle Pvt MA W ★

LA LANDE De FERRIERE,
Nicolas Luis: b 11-5-1765 d *p.* 1801 m Marie Magdalena Jacinta Arnoul PS LA

LAMAR,
Basil: b 1764 d 11-5-1827 m Rebecca Kelly Sol GA
Basil: b 1748 d *a.* 2-10-1801 m (1)Jane Patton (2)Charlotte Pennington Pvt GA
James: b *c.* 1724 d *p.* 1786 m Verlinda Osborn Pvt GA
John: b *c.* 1745 d — m (1)Mary Elizabeth Bugg (2)Priscilla Bugg (3)Lucy Appling Capt GA
John: b 7-17-1763 d 10-18-1842 m Frances Breedlove Pvt GA SC
Robert: b 1731 d 1815 m Sarah (Lamar) PS MD
Thomas, Jr.: b *c.* 1760 d *p.* 1801 m Lydia Murphy Sol SC
Thomas: b 1735 d 1800 m (1)Eleanor — (2)Ann Gresham PS SC

Wm.: b 1755 d 1-8-1838 m Margaret Worthington Capt MD ★
Wm. Bishop: b 8-3-1745 d 8-29-1812 m Elizabeth Smith PS MD

LAMB, (includes LAMM)
Abijah: b 9-14-1739 d 5-21-1824 m Elizabeth Wheelock Capt MA
Amos: b 1744/5 d *p.* 1793 m Mary Hulett Pvt MA
Archibald: b *c.* 1760 d *p.* 1830 m Betsy Austin Pvt VA
Asa: b 7-12-1761 d 4-1-1839 m Silence — Pvt CT ★
Benjamin: b 11-13-1750 d 10-22-1835 m Nabby Rice Pvt MA ★
Daniel, 2d: b 1735 d 1819 m Content Pendleton Pvt MA
David: b 2-24-1755 d 7-16-1838 m Amy Wightman Pvt NS CT ★
David: b 12-14-1739 d 4-26-1814 m (1)Mary Howe (2)Jemima Rice Sgt MA
David: b 10-5-1758 d 3-20-1846 m Judith Fitts Pvt MA ★
Ebenezer, Jr.: b 1736 d 1- -1819 m Mary White Pvt MA
Gad: b 12-20-1744 d 4-5-1824 m (1)Penelope Leonard (2)Jerusha Ripley Sgt MA
Gideon: b 2-20-1740 d 11-8-1781 m (1)Mary Gregory (2)Mary Burgess Col NC
Isaac: b 9-12-1749 d 1825 m — Pearsley Pvt MA
Isaac: b — d *p.* 1790 m Elizabeth Delis PS NY
Israel: b 2-7-1762 d 2-1-1841 m Amanda — Pvt MA ★
Jacob: b 5-4-1764 d 1-6-1845 m Catrinka Conklin Pvt NY
James: b 1732 d *p.* 1778 m Hannah Rich 1Lt MA
James: b 11-16-1746 d 5-31-1824 m Ann — Sgt PA
James: b 7-15-1756 d 9-22-1841 m Hannah Boone Sgt VA
Johannes: b 12-1-1759 d 10-28-1817 m Anna Margretta Brossman Pvt PA
John: b 9-26-1749 d *p.* 1804 m Zilpha Hoggs Cpl CT
John: b 6-3-1756 d 1-9-1825 m Susannah Haven Pvt MA ★
John: b 1-1-1735 d 5-31-1800 m Catherine Jandine BGen NY
John: b 5-22-1757 d 4-9-1811 m Beulah Curtis Pvt NY
John: b 12-27-1748 d 7-14-1813 m Hannah Richey Capt PA
Jonas: b 6-24-1755 d 9-3-1822 m Mehitable Pierce Pvt MA
Joseph: b 5-22-1764 d 3-25-1848 m (1)Dorcas (Massey)Marcy (2)Clara Willard Pvt MA CT ★
Joseph: b 2-9-1755 d 10-9-1837 m (1)Thamor Hunt (2)Martha Thompson Pvt NY
Joshua: b *c.* 1757 d 12-27-1813 m Mercy Brooks PS MA
Lemuel: b 11-5-1738 d 5-28-1812 m Desire Swan Capt CT
Luke: b 7-17-1734 d 5-31-1824 m Ann — PS NC
Matthew: b *c.* 1757 d 8-24-1781 m Jane Coe Sol PA
Nahum: b 7-13-1759 d 5-22-1842 m (1)Lydia Dagget (2)Lucinda Marsh Pvt MA ★
Peter: b 10-12-1747 d 1804 m Catharine Kiplinger Pvt PA
Phinehas: b *c.* 1758 d *p.* 1810 m Anna Garfield Sol PS MA
Reuben: b 9-14-1742 d 11-11-1819 m Rebecca Nichols Pvt PS CS MA
Richard: b — d 1786 m Clarissa Boswell QM CS VA
Samuel: b 7-10-1748 d 7-8-1834 m Tabitha Wightman Pvt PS CT
Samuel: b 7-4-1743 d 7-27-1796 m Elizabeth Davis Capt MA
Samuel: b *c.* 1734 d *p.* 5-27-1778 m Sarah Dana Cpl MA
Samuel: b 4-5-1741 d 10-26-1810 m Rebeckah Cozzens Pvt MA
Thomas: b 12-19-1735 d 1795 m Deborah Brown Matr CT
Thomas: b 11-20-1753 d 1-13-1813 m Roxanna Duncan Lt MA
Wm.: b — d — m Elizabeth Haskell Pvt MA

LAMBDIN, (includes LAMDIN)
Daniel: b 5-16-1759 d 9-7-1809 m Mary Spry Sol PS MD
Wm.: b 7-24-1755 d 6-25-1823 m Dorcas Morsell Pvt MD

LAMBERSON, (includes LAMBERTSON)
Cornelius: b 3-3-1752 d 2-11-1815 m Mary Johnson Pvt NJ
David: b 1-7-1760 d 7-29-1848 m (1)Mary Owens (2)Mrs Sarah Johnson Pvt NJ ★
Nicholas: b — d 1826 m Eleanor Seeburn Drm NY
Samuel: b *a.* 1755 d *a.* 10-14-1806 m Esther Joynes Sol MD

LAMBERT,
Alexandre Etienne: b 12-26-1752 d 12-21-1826 m Marie Francoise Noelle Charlotte Jacqueline Laignel Lt FrN
Christopher: b — d *a.* 10-9-1786 m (1)Salome — (2)Catherine Crider Pvt VA
David: b 12-2-1731 d 11-8-1815 m Martha Northrop Pvt CT
Gideon: b 3-21-1729 d 12-15-1819 m Susannah Luce 2Sgt CS MA
Henry: b *c.* 1742 d 3-14-1826 m Hannah Beal Pvt MA
Jacob: b 11-6-1755 d *a.* 1824 m — Capt VA
James: b *c.* 1745 d *c.* 1804 m — Capt GA
James, Sr.: b 1701 d 6- -1778 m Elizabeth Acken PS NJ
James, Jr.: b 7-14-1755 d 4-2-1842 m Hannah Littell Pvt NJ
Jeremiah: b 1- -1764 d 8-30-1844 m (1)Elizabeth Holcombe (2) — Archer Pvt NJ
John: b 1752 d 1794 m Mary Rea Pvt Seacap MA
Joshua: b *a.* 1746 d *a.* 6-17-1799 m Catharina — Pvt PA
Josiah: b *c.* 1745 d *p.* 1815 m Joannah Woodward Slr NJ
Michael: b 5-17-1744 d 1826 m Rosina Strauss Pvt PA
Nicholas: b 12-27-1759 d 2-17-1828 m Mary Magdalena Hill Drm PA
Peter, Sr.: b 1727 d 7-10-1806 m Elizabeth Lipe Pvt NY
Peter, Jr.: b 8-15-1760 d 10-25-1844 m Nancy Lipe Sgt NY
Samuel: b 12-21-1758 d 4-11-1815 m Mary Chase Pvt MA
Samuel: b 1-9-1758 d 10-10-1850 m Elizabeth Hager Pvt NJ ★
Thomas: b 3-10-1747/8 d 12-11-1793 m Apphia Gage Pvt PS MA
Wm.: b 3-19-1760 d *p.* 1832 m Elizabeth Cypher Sgt NJ

LAMBERTH,
John: b *c.* 1755 d 1826 m (1)Jerusha Morgan (2)Sarah Brazeal Pvt NC

LAMBERTON,
James: b 5-10-1750 d 9-10-1822 m Ursala Wood Pvt PA
James: b 9-25-1761 d 1-12-1841 m (1)Miriam Dinsmore (2)Hannah Chamberlin Pvt MA ★

LAMBETH,
Aaron: b 1735 d 1805 m Flobella Williamson Pvt NC
Meredith: b *c.* 1726-28 d *p.* 1-6-1800 m Frances Bernard PS VA
Moses: b 1757 d 8-18-1843 m Tabitha — Pvt NC ★

LAMBORD,
Luke: b 1730 d 1821 m Rachel Allen Pvt MA

LAMBORN,
Josiah: b 3-19-1738 d 1818 m Sarah Jackson Pvt PA
Thomas: b 3-19-1738 d 12-25-1812 m Dinah Carson Pvt PA

LAMBRIGHT,
Nicholas: b 1741 d 1804 m Martha Coleman Sol VA

LAMME,
James: b 11-26-1745 d 11-26-1815 m Elizabeth Givens Sgt VA
Nathan: b 1755/6 d 1-15-1834 m Nancy Ralston Capt VA ★
Samuel: b *c.* 1754 d 1-1-1826 m Nancy Agnes Steele Pvt VA
Wm.: b *c.* 1715 d 1797 m (1)Anna — (2)Margaret Read PS VA

LAMONT, (includes LAMOND & LEMONT)
Archibald: b 1749 d 12-3-1826 m Mary Blackmer Sgt MA W★
Archibald: b 1724 d 4-24-1795 m Abiah Smith Pvt NY
Benjamin: b 1734 d 1799 m Susanna Hunter Capt ME
David: b 2-25-1759 d 6-6-1835 m Elizabeth Philbrook Pvt MA ★
James: b 11-23-1736 d 9- -1829 m (1)Mary Hunter (2)Mrs Sarah Springer Capt MA
John: b 8- -1740 d 10-23-1827 m Mary (Robinson)Simonton Capt MA
John: b 9-18-1753 d 4-10-1843 m Elizabeth Sullivan Pvt NY MA ★
Thomas: b 2-20-1759 d 9-18-1842 m (1) — Woodside (2)Jane Coffee (3)Mrs Chase (Woodside) (4)Abigail (Winter) Clifford Capt MA ★
Thomas: b 2-14-1748 d 10-11-1777 m Lucy Mitchell Pvt MA W★
Wm.: b 1755 d 11-1-1848 m (1)Phoebe (Goss)Perkins (2)Mary Rodman Pvt NY ★

LAMOREUX, (includes LAMOREE, LAMOUREUX, LAMOUREAUX)
Isaac: b 11-15-1732 d 3-17-1817 m Hannah T. Conklin Pvt PS NY
John: b 12-31-1723 d 1809 m Charity Davenport Pvt NY
Joseph: b 10-11-1753 d 11-11-1840 m Abigail Sneden Pvt PS NY
Peter: b 9-3-1726 d *a.* 3-3-1821 m Phoebe Wood Pvt NY
Thomas: b *c.* 1745 d 1829 m Keturah Tuttle Ens PS NY

LAMPHEAR, (includes LAMPHEER, LAMPHERE, LAMPHIER, LANFAIR & LANPHEAR)
Abner: b 7-12-1753 d *p.* 1790 m Rachel Clarke Pvt CT
Benjamin: b 2-19-1761 d 3-24-1848 m Elisabeth Dye Pvt CT ★
Isaiah: b *c.* 1740 d *p.* 1790 m Thankful Allen Pvt CT
James, Sr.: b 11-22-1710 d *p.* 9- -1791 m Sarah Meyhew PS CT
James, Jr.: b 1747 d 3-6-1820 m Grace Deshon Mid CT ★
Leonard: b *c.* 1746 d 4-7-1835 m (1)Lovina Dodge (2)Mrs Mary Willaims Pvt MA
Nathan, Jr.: b 2-18-1742 d *p.* 1790 m (1)Amy Crandall (2)Catherine Greenman (3)Sarah Saunders Pvt RI
Oliver, Jr.: b 1749 d 5-7-1812 m Phebe Rogers Pvt CT
Samuel: b 12-23-1723 d *p.* 1781 m Mary — Pvt RI
Solomon: b 4-10-1708 d 12-7-1782 m Mary Palmer PS CT

LAMPKIN, (includes LAMKIN)
John: b 1739 d 7-27-1830 m Mary (Story)Lee Pvt VA W★
Newcomb: b 1743 d 3-4-1836 m Armesel Northrup Pvt MA
Peter: b *c.* 1735 d *p.* 1790 m Mary Elizabeth Sharp Pvt VA
Wm.: b 1750 d 12-3-1777 m Jane Moore Pvt VA

LAMPMAN,
Henry: b 1734 d *c.* 11-1-1784 m Elizabeth Empie Pvt NY ★
Peter: b 1730 d *p.* 11-4-1784 m — Pvt NY

LAMPREY,
Daniel: b 3-4-1759 d 12-12-1840 m (1)Sarah Lane (2)Abigail Lane Foule Lt NH
John: b 8-17-1707 d 7-23-1788 m Hannah Johnson PS NH
John: b 12- -1748 d 8-10-1835 m Molly Marston PS NH
Morris: b 12-20-1711 d 10-27-1809 m Rebecca Moulton PS NH

LAMSON, (includes LAMPSON)
Benjamin: b 1756 d 11-12-1832 m Mary Terry Pvt CT W★
Ebenezer: b 5-19-1754 d 3-14-1835 m (2)Martha Holbrook Pvt CT ★
Ebenezer: b 4-13-1741 d 7-4-1834 m Ruth Phillips PS CT
Eleazer: b 4-17-1720 d 3-24-1789 m Jane — PS NJ
James: b 7-30-1754 d 3-18-1795 m Mary — Pvt MA

John: b *c.* 1750 d *p.* 1800 m Mercy Morton Sgt MA
Jonathan: b 2-20-1755 d 12-6-1807 m (1)Sally Morton ( )Anna Cobb Sgt MA
Jonathan, Jr.: b 8-10-1747 d 9-28-1825 m Bethial Whipple Pvt MA
Jonathan: b 9-29-1726 d 12- -1815 m Mehitable Holt Pvt NH
Joseph: b 1728 d 1789 m Susannah Frothingham Pvt MA
Joseph, Sr.: bpt 12-28-1718 d 1802 m (1)Mehitable Batchelder (2)Pernal Giddings CS PS NH
Joseph, Jr.: b *c.* 1745 d *p.* 1790 m Rachel Sanborn Pvt NH
Nathaniel, Sr.: b 1-28-1720 d 1802 m Tabitha Hawley Cpl CT
Nathaniel, Jr.: b 1745 d 8-19-1807 m Abiah — Pvt CT
Samuel: b 9-18-1736 d 7-17-1795 m Elizabeth Sanderson LCol MA
Thomas: b 12-9-1762 d 4-5-1830 m Anna Martin Pvt MA W★
Wm.: bpt 4-3-1757 d *a.* 5-8-1796 m Katherine Weare Matr MA
Wm.: b 3- -1746 d 11- -1800 m Mary Lummas PS NH

LA MUNYON,
Thomas: b 7-1-1763 d 8-3-1849 m Lydia Sawdy Pvt RI ★

LANCASTER,
Daniel: b 11-27-1747 d *a.* 1800 m Mehitable Clifford Pvt MA
Henry: b 1752 d 2-1-1836 m (1)Susan Swanson (2)Persey (Piercy) Houghton 1Sgt SC ★
John, Sr.: b *c.* 1732 d *p.* 8-5-1794 m Mary — CS PS MD
John: b 3-3-1763 d 1-28-1826 m Margaretta D. LeGrand Pvt VA
Joseph: b 2-16-1757 d 6-23-1846 m Martha Preble Cpl MA ★
Moses: b 2-2-1752 d 12-9-1811 m (1)Ann Duncan (2)Sarah Barnet Highlands Pvt NH
Nathaniel: b 11-2-1734 d 1809 m Hope Walker PS VA
Paul: b 5-25-1735 d 7-18-1814 m Mary Gage Lt MA
Richard: b *c.* 1745 d 1815 m Joanah Singleton Pvt VA
Samuel: b 3-13-1757 d 3-13-1846 m Mehitable Lambert Pvt MA
Timothy: b 8-31-1718 d — m Sears Sargent Pvt MA
Wm.: b 1760 d 1840 m Vashti Strickland Pvt GA
Wm.: b 3-2-1733 d *p.* 1786 m (1)Sarah — (2)Ann Outland PS NC
Wm.: b 11-17-1746 d 11-4-1843 m (2)Mrs Sarah Blades Pvt VA ★
Wm. Sanders: b *c.* 1760 d 1814 m Sarah Turman Sol GA

LANCE, (includes LANTZ)
Andrew: b — d 9- -1825 m Margaret — Pvt PA
George: b 9-21-1757 d 7-17-1840 m Anna — Pvt NJ
Henry: b 1747 d 9-14-1802 m Margaretha Sigfriendin Sol PA
Jacob: b *c.* 1721 d 1789 m — PS VA
Joseph: b 1758 d 1818 m Susanna — Pvt VA

LANCEY,
Samuel: b 8-10-1760 d 10-25-1837 m Elizabeth Pierce Pvt MA

LANCISCO,
Henry: b — d *p.* 8-6-1799 m Clara Shobe Pvt VA

LANCK,
Peter: b 12-31-1753 d — m Emily Heiskell VA

LANCRAFT,
George: b — d 9-17-1807 m Sarah Jocelin Vol CT

LAND,
John: b *c.* 1740 d 3- -1781 m Mary — Capt SC
Moses: b 1764 d 1848 m Charity Beshears Pvt VA ★
Robert, Sr.: b *c.* 1720 d *p.* 4-1-1789 m Mary — PS VA
Thomas: b 1760 d 1822 m (2)Sallie Allen Pvt SC

LANDER,
Charles: b 12-29-1754 d 8-15-1833 m (1)Katherine Foreman (2)Elizabeth Jones Sgt VA ★
Henry: b *c.* 1730 d 11- -1809 m Hannah Skinner PS VA
Peter: b 2-26-1764 d 3-4-1847 m Sophia Dills Pvt NJ

LANDERKIN,
Daniel: b 1759 d 2- -1842 m (1)Mehitable Chaple (2)Mrs Lydia Riggs Mar. Pvt MA ★

LANDERNEAU,
Jean Pierre: b *c.* 1746 d 6- -1819 m Suzanne Joffrion PS LA

LANDERS,
Asahel: b 7-7-1766 d 3-27-1842 m Mercy Goodspeed Pvt MA
Ebenezer: b 11-8-1758 d 2-14-1846 m Olive Osborn Sgt MA ★
John: b 9-15-1757 d 10-30-1840 m (¹)Lucy Johnston (2)Morning Mitchell Pvt VA ★
Joseph: b 1722 d 1801 m Anna Landers PS CT
Joseph: b 2-2-1763 d 9-9-1845 m Deborah Rider Pvt MA ★
Seth: b — d — m Susan Landers Pvt CT
Thomas: b 4-27-1727 d 10-24-1811 m (2)Mary Lake Pvt MA

LANDIS, (includes LANDES & LANTES)
Benjamin: b 1759 d 1829 m Barbara Burkholder Pvt PA
Felix: b *c.* 1756 d 1825 m (1)Ann Knupp (2)Elizabeth — Sol PA
Frederick: b 3-4-1739 d *c.* 1802 m (2)Elizabeth Hock Pvt PA
Henry: b 4-10-1744 d 3-4-1825 m Mary Brubaker Cpl PA
Henry: b 12-22-1763 d 12-22-1840 m Susanna — Pvt PA
Henry: b 8-16-1763/4 d 9-8-1844 m Veronica Long Pvt PA

LANDIS, contd.
Jacob: b c. 1738 d p. 1794 m — Pvt PA
Jacob: b 3-20-1749 d 5-27-1834 m Dorothea — Pvt PA
Jacob: b 1750-60 d p. 9-8-1831 m Elizabeth Mellinger Pvt PA
Jacob: b 9- -1751 d 10- -1821 m Catharine — Pvt PA
John, Sr.: b 11-11-1720 d 12-9-1796 m Elizabeth (Bechtel)Eshbach Pvt PA
John: b c. 1745 d a. 10- -1819 m Catherine Miller Pvt PA
John: b 4-3-1761 d 4-4-1827 m (1)Elizabeth Musser (2)Maria Hoover Pvt PA

LANDON, (includes LANDING)
Daniel, Jr.: b 2-23-1737 d 4- -1814 m Chloe Smith Pvt CT
David: b 10-30-1743 d 9- -1796 m Rebecca Ruggles Capt CT
David, Sr.: b 8-5-1718 d 5-4-1804 m (1)Mary Osborn (2)Thankful Dickinson Pvt MM CT
David, Jr.: b 10-13-1741 d 5-30-1817 m Chloe Buell Pvt CT
Ebenezer: b 12-10-1760 d 8-23-1854 m Pamela Clemons Pvt CT
Edward: b 4-30-1762 d 8-24-1834 m Triphena Hewitt Pvt NJ ★
James: b 5-20-1750 d 9-13-1838 m Elizabeth — Pvt NJ ★
Jared: b 1-29-1740 d 2-10-1816 m (1)Martha Hutchinson (2)Deborah Reeve (3)Christian Conkling PS NY
Jonathan: b 10-30-1743 d 1815 m Isabella Graham LCol PS NY
Laban: b 1-13-1759 d 6-28-1828 m Elizabeth Gilles Pvt NJ ★
Luther: b 9-16-1752 d p. 1803 m Mary Way Pvt CT
Nathaniel: b 1-9-1757 d 1851 m Hannah Greene Pvt PS NJ NY PA ★
Reuben: b 3-28-1757 d 11-23-1854 m Mary Way Pvt CT
Rufus: b 2-4-1759 d 4-10-1847 m Sarah Hunt Pvt CT ★
Samuel: b 5-20-1699 d 1-21-1782 m (1)Bethia Tuthill (2)Mary Youngs PS CS NY
Thomas: b 9-19-1752 d 10-9-1847 m Nancy Hopkins Pvt NJ
Wm., Sr.: b c. 1730 d 4- -1792 m Phebe —Sol NC

LANDRUM,
James: b 1762 d 1-15-1840 m Mary Clark Alford Pvt VA ★
Jehu: b c. 1730 d c. 1779 m — Sol SC
Thomas: b 1744 d 1840 m Dorothy Alcock Pvt VA
Thomas: b 1750 d 1832 m Margaret (Herndon)Miller Pvt VA ★
Thomas: b 10-6-1759 d 1832/3 m Nancy Bell Pvt VA ★
Young: b c. 1740 d p. 9-19-1796 m Patsey — Capt VA
Zachariah: b c. 1762 d 7-19-1833 m Letitia — Pvt GA

LANE, (includes LAIN, LAINE & LAYN)
Aaron: b c. 1720 d a. 5- -1805 m Sarah Conover Lt NJ
Aaron: b 1740 d 9-21-1807 m Eleanor Green PS VA
Abial, Sr.: b 1736 d 7-29-1803 m Susannah — Ens MA
Abial, Jr.: b 3-29-1763 d 2-27-1837 m Mary Corss Pvt MA ★
Abraham: b 11-27-1748 d 2-3-1838 m (2)Mary — Lt NJ ★
Abraham: b 1748 d 2-25-1840 m Mary Hoffman 2Lt NJ
Abraham S.: b 1759 d 1849 m Betsy Mills Pvt GA
Alexander: b 10-17-1761 d 12-25-1844 m Abigail Mills Pvt NY
Aquilla: b 5-18-1753 d 11-24-1819 m Agnes Fitzgerald Pvt VA
Asaph: b 1758 d 9-22-1845 m Lydia Osgood Pvt MA ★
Benjamin: b 3-17-1754 d 12-20-1835 m (1)Anna Page (2)Isabel Hill Cpl MA
Caleb, Sr.: b 11-16-1729 d 2-10-1783 m Lydia Riggs Pvt MA
Caleb, Jr.: b 5-23-1759 d 4-5-1850 m Abiah Saville Pvt MA ★
Cornelius: b c. 1722 d c. 1792 m Elenor Compton Capt NJ
Cornelius: b 12-21-1755 d 5-10-1837 m Elizabeth Wolf Sgt NJ ★
Cornelius: b c. 1740 d c. 1823 m Rebecca — PS NJ
Daniel: b 5-11-1740 d 9-11-1811 m Mary Woodman Capt MA
Daniel: b 12-19-1736 d c. 1804 m Mary Griswold Sol CT
Daniel: bpt 1-5-1734/5 d p. 1781 m Mary Green Capt MA
Daniel: b 2-27-1750 d 10-23-1821 m Lydia Joy Cpl MA
Daniel: b 7-8-1735 d 3-28-1825 m (1)Mary Butterfield (2)Abigail Batchelder Pvt NH
David: b 3-11-1759 d 9-10-1842 m Molly Lane Fif MA
Derich: b 3-26-1755 d 5- -1831 m (?)Maria Lansing (?)Engletie Van Rensselaer Lt QM NJ
Doxey: b c. 1760 d p. 7-2-1800 m Mary Matthews Pvt NY
Ebenezer: b 4-17-1713 d 5-12-1790/1 m Bethia Shaw PS MA
Edward: b 12-23-1721 d 1798 m Ann Evans PS PA
Edward: b 1723 d 8-27-1817 m Sarah Richardson PS PA
Edward: b 1750-60 d p. 5-23-1830 m Rhoda Lane Sol MA
Eleazer: b 1-8-1761 d 3-17-1826 m Henrietta Dodge Pvt MA W★
Elisha: b 6-17-1753 d 1-31-1831 m Nancy Dillingham Pvt NY
Elkanah, Sr.: b 4-1-1719 d 12-6-1811 m Hannah Tingley MM Mil NH
Elkanah, Jr.: b 1-14-1745 d 10-21-1811 m (1)Esther Dinsmore (2)Annis Knight Sgt PS NH
Ephraim, Sr.: b 9-10-1717 d 4-9-1800 m Mehitable Stone LCol MA
Ephraim: b 7-9-1739 d 4-9-1826 m Elizabeth Copeland Lt MA
Francis: b 8-31-1760 d 5-1-1823 m (1)Hepzibah Coolidge (2)Sarah (Cushing) Burr Capt MA
Gad: b 8-31-1744 d 11-27-1833 m Olive Tree Pvt CT
Gershom Flagg: b 7-30-1753 d 11-20-1838 m Lydia Thomas Sgt MA
Gilbert: b 4-23-1739 d 4-14-1816 m Martha Williamson Pvt MM NJ
Hendrick: b 7-20-1760 d 9-27-1834 m Catherine Conover Pvt NJ ★
Henry: b 4-12-1762 d p. 3- -1850 m Mary Hazlett Pvt NJ ★
Hermanus: b c. 1740 d 1797 m Elizabeth Dildean CS NJ
Hezekiah: b 1-22-1739 d 11-6-1809 m Abigail Rutty CS CT
Isaac: b 1762 d 11-24-1854 m Abigail Foster Pvt MA ★
Isaac: b 2-14-1760 d 11-9-1851 m Sarah Russell Lt VA NC ★

Isham: b 9- -1757 d 6-20-1852 m Cinda Lamb Sgt VA ★
Jabez: b 9-21-1743 d 4-30-1830 m Sara Woodman Capt ME MA
Jacob: b 5-29-1753 d 10-9-1837 m (1)Alice Chamberlain (2)Mrs Jane Hulshart Lt NJ
Jacob: b 1-15-1757 d 5-6-1798 m Rachel (Lane) PS Pvt NY
Jacob: b c. 11-27-1760 d c. 9-15-1830 m Susan Leigh Pvt NC
James: b 1745 d 7-26-1819 m Eunice Chase Pvt MA
James, Jr.: b 3-8-1725/6 d 1-4-1799 m Mary Wellington PS MA
James: b 1718 d 1790 m Lydia Hardage CS PS VA
James Hardage: b 11-7-1735 d p. 1-2-1787 m Mary Jane Smith Capt PS VA
Jeremiah: b 3-10-1732 d 6-21-1806 m Mary Sanborn PS NH
Jesse: b 12-1-1746 d 8-23-1819 m Hester Wright Ens NH
Jesse: b 7-3-1733 d 10-28-1806 m Winnifred Aycock Pvt NC
Job: b 9-27-1718 d 6-11-1796 m Susanna Fasset Pvt MA
Joel: b 1-4-1740 d 3-29-1795 m (1)Martha Hinton (2)Mary Hinton PS CS NC
Joel: b 10-18-1751 d 8-18-1806 m Elizabeth Atkins Pvt CT
John, Sr.: b 4-14-1733 d 8-26-1796 m Joannah Stevens Pvt CT
John, Jr.: b 3-17-1759 d 1821 m (1)Roxanna Redfield (2)Hannah Platts Pvt CT
John, 3d: b 7-4-1734 d 7-14-1822 m (1)Elisabeth Hancock (2)Hannah (Boynton) Hazelton (3)Hannah Bean Capt MA
John: b 10-2-1720 d 12-7-1789 m (1)Ruth Bowman (2)Sarah (Abbott) Hildreth PS MA
John: b 7-1-1722 d p. 1797 m Martha Flagg Sol MA
John: b 2-14-1726 d 3-21-1811 m Hannah Dow 1Maj NH
John: b 12-22-1739 d a. 1811 m (1)Jane Bruce (2)Mollie Shepard (3)Sarah Laskey Priest Capt PS NH
John, Jr.: b 10-17-1733 d 3-11-1813 m Mary Colby Lt NH
John: b c. 1733 d 1825 m Mary Dodge Cpl NH
John: b 10-12-1709 d 2-13-1784 m (1)Hannah Lamprey (2)Mary Knowles PS NH
John: b 10-24-1750 d 3-12-1823 m Hannah Godrey PS CS NH
John: b 2-22-1758 d 2-9-1833 m Catherine Price Pvt PS PA ★
John, Jr.: b 9-12-1717 d 1798 m Olive Jennings Pvt VT
John: b c. 1727 d 1785 m Elizabeth Cloud PS VA
Jonathan: b 3-4-1747/8 d 8-24-1816 m Sarah — Pvt MA
Jonathan: b 2-16-1761 d 9-6-1819 m (1)Lydia Leavitt (2)Mary Towle Cnt NH
Jonathan: b 12-18-1764 d 7-30-1844 m Anna Wright Pvt VT
Joseph: b 1740 d 1801 m (2)Mary Gilpin Maj SA
Joseph: bpt 9-8-1745 d 11- -1828 m (1)Rachel Rowe (2)Sarah Davis Lt MA
Joseph: b c. 1745 d p. 1785 m Katherine Newton Capt VA
Joshua: b 6-8-1724 d 1-13-1794 m Ruth Batchelder CS NH
Josiah: b 7-6-1736 d 8-13-1813 m Lucy Tower 2Lt MA
Josiah: b 5-19-1738 d 1-16-1821 m Betsey Perkins PS Pvt NH
Lambert: b c. 1740 d 1804 m (1)Nancy Anderson (2)Rebecca (3)Anne — Pvt VA
Larkin: b 5-22-1762 d 8-10-1847 m Sarah Price Pvt VA ★
Leavitt: b 5-26-1761 d 7-15-1840 m Elizabeth Loring Pvt MA ★
Levi: b 11-10-1754 d 6-23-1806 m (1)Elizabeth Gyles (2)Susanna (Newman)Lane Pvt MA
Martin: b 1755 d 7-12-1825 m Courtney Seville Capt NC
Matthias, Sr.: b 1-18-1721 d 1-17-1804 m Elizabeth Sutphen PS NJ
Matthias, Jr.: b 10-7-1746 d 11-7-1819 m Gertrude Sutphen Pvt NJ
Nathaniel: b 6-15-1743 d p. 1775 m Rebecca Cobb Sgt MA
Noah: b 1-30-1756 d — m Mehitable Burnham Pvt NH
Richard: b 1740 d 1811 m Catherine Groom Pvt MD
Richard: b 1759 d 1838 m Hannah Morris Pvt MD
Richard: b c. 1700 d p. 1790 m Sarah — PS MD
Richard: b 2-9-1759 d p. 7-6-1793 m Mary Flint Pvt NC
Robert: b 11-20-1713 d 1794 m Mary Thacher PS CT
Robert: b 7-11-1758 d a. 4-22-1845 m Elizabeth — Pvt VA ★
Roswell: b 3-15-1740 d p. 1806 m Sarah Dudley Pvt CT
Samuel: b 7-1-1737 d p. 1799 m (1)Ruth Davis (2)Hannah French (3)Mrs Frances Blood Pvt MA
Samuel, Jr.: b 10-21-1737 d 6-26-1802 m Elizabeth Fitch Pvt MA
Samuel: b 1757 d 7-7-1831 m Ruth Pettee Pvt MA ★
Samuel: b 10-6-1718 d 12-29-1806 m (1)Mary James (2)Rachel Parsons Colcord PS NH
Samuel: b 1-9-1759 d 1-26-1845 m Eunice Scott Pvt NH ★
Samuel: b 8-16-1754 d 2-16-1814 m Phoebe Coates Pvt PA
Sarah Richardson: b 1732 d 7-8-1818 m Edward Lane PS PA
Simon: b 7-3-1733 d 11-30-1813 m Sarah Robie Pvt NH
Solomon: b 8-7-1756 d 2-1-1837 m Sarah Stearns Pvt MA
Thomas: b 1754 d 1825 m Mary Crafton Pvt VA
Tidence: b 8-31-1724 d 1-30-1806 m Esther Bibber Chp NC
Timothy: b 7-10-1722 d 12-3-1793 m Lydia Lane Davis Sol MA
Timothy: b 1758 d p. 7-22-1829 m Charity Raynor Sol PS NY
Wilkison: b 4-1-1742 d a. 2-7-1814 m Jane — Pvt PA
Wm.: b 2-24-1763 d 2-12-1840 m Sarah Harris Cpl MA
Wm., Sr.: b 6-11-1723 d 12-20-1802 m Rachel Ward CS PS NH
Wm.: b 5-27-1727 d 10-14-1797 m (1)Jannetze Rapellyea (2)Maria Brokaw Pvt NJ
Wm.: b 1740 d 1790 m Rebecca Montanye Pvt NJ
Wm.: b 12-20-1743 d 4-1-1811 m Kezia Mather Pvt NY
Wm.: b 1757 d 10-25-1833 m Jane — Pvt NY
Wm.: b 12-3-1757 d 4-27-1838 m Mary Bean Pvt PA
Wm.: b 8-30-1740 d 3-16-1808 m Sarah (Lane) Pvt VA
Wm., Jr.: b c. 1751-3 d 1822 m Susan Linton Jennings Capt VA
Wm.: b c. 1740-44 d c. 1829 m Nancy Allen Pvt VA

Wm.: b c. 1760 d p. 1807 m — Shannon Pvt VA
Ziba: b 7-5-1756 d 8 - -1807 m Lydia Danforth Pvt MA

LANFORD,
James: b c. 1730 d c. 1822 m Mary Lowrey Sol SC

LANG,
Benjamin, Sr.: b 9-19-1734 d 5-4-1816 m (1)Eleanor Burleigh (2)Deborah Verrill Cpl NH
Bickford: b 1738 d 1804 m Martha Locke PS NH
Edward: b 9-3-1742 d 1-25-1830 m Rachel Ward 2Lt MA
Francis: b c. 1760 d 7-19-1847 m (2) — Kennedy (3)Susannah Hunter Phillip Pvt MD
George, Jr.: b 6-24-1761 d 3-4-1837 m Mary Ann Gregory Pvt PA
Jacob: b 1710 d a. 8-22-1807 m Anna Catherine Berger Pvt PA
James: b 1734 d 5-5-1817 m Margaret Helm Pvt PA
Johannas: b c. 1730 d 1789 m Elizabeth — Pvt NC
John: bpt 5-15-1726 d 2-10-1789 m Catherine Pople PS NH
John: b 5-26-1765 d 8-18-1840 m Elizabeth — Sol NC
John: b 1738 d 12-23-1809 m Margaret Jolly Pvt PA
Killian: b 4-14-1733 d 3-5-1808 m Magdalena Fridruhen PS PA
Lowell: b 9-17-1754 d 10-25-1822 m Susanna Prescott Pvt Fif NH
Mark: b 1741 d 7-26-1808 m Salome Goss PS NH
Robert: b c. 1740 d 8-4-1817 m Sarah — Sgt SC
Samuel: b 1754/5 d 9-8-1829 m Susan Salter Pvt NH
Thomas: b 6-27-1741 d 4-12-1829 m (1)Mary Weeks (2)Mary Holmes (3)Mary Simpson Pvt NH
Thomas: b 1735 d 1790 m Mary Goss Pvt NH
Wm.: b 1-16-1750 d 8-11-1827 m Bridget Derby Vol MA
Wm.: b 7-6-1740 d 12-2-1818 m Semperace Thurman Sol SC

LANGDELL,
Livermore: b 11-5-1751 d 5- -1826 m Abagail Dodge Pvt NH
Wm.: b c. 1726 d 1799 m Mary Witrage PvtrCdr MA

LANGDON, (includes LANGTON & LANKTON)
Amos: b 12-25-1761 d 1-9-1842 m (1)Abigail Rockwood (2)— Underwood Pvt MA
Asahel: b 3-30-1765 d 5-19-1852 m Violetta Hitchcock Pvt CT
Benjamin: b 1763 d 1833 m Tamer Barnes Pvt NY
Daniel, Sr.: b 12-24-1738 d 1-20-1812 m Phoebe Clark Capt PS CT
Daniel, Jr.: b 5-9-1759 d 5-21-1841 m Sally Coles Pvt CT ★
Giles: b 5-24-1763 d 2-11-1847 m Sarah Carter Capt CT
John: b 7-28-1747 d 8- -1793 m Mary Walley Capt MA
John: b 6-21-1728 d 10-10-1822 m (1)Sarah Stebbins (2)Eunice Torrey Sgt MA
John: b 5-28-1707 d 1780 m Mary Hall PS NH
John: b c. 1738 d 1786 m Lucy Morehouse Lt NY
John Wilson: b 3-11-1759 d 2-13-1842 m Elizabeth Lucy Ashley Sol MA
Joseph: b 12-12-1740 d 2-26-1812 m Ruth Hooker Ens CT
Josiah: b 1-12-1765 d 2-5-1855 m Sally Hall Pvt MA
Levi: b 1754 d 1843 m (1)Elizabeth Crane (2)Eunice Fish PS CT
Lewis, jr.: b 6-15-1749 d 1829 m Submit Cooley Sgt MA
Martin: b 4- -1756 d 9-8-1838 m (1)Lydia Chapin (2)Hannah — Pvt Matr MA
Noah: b 8-10-1728 d 9-20-1817 m Rebecca Porter Capt MA
Paul: b 12-16-1728 d 6-23-1804 m Thankful Stebbins Capt MA
Paul: b 6-6-1752 d 11-22-1834 m Mary Kimball Pvt MA
Philip: b 1759 d 8-31-1853 m Dorcas Langdon Pvt MA
Samuel: b 1-12-1723 d 11-29-1797 m Elizabeth Brown Chp PS MA
Seth, Sr.: b 10-6-1759 d 12-20-1851 m (1)Amy Dowd (2)Lois Phelps Pvt MA
Thomas: b 1-6-1714 d 10-12-1783 m Abigail Richards CS CT
Thomas: b c. 1730 d 1781/2 m (1)Elizabeth — (2)Mary — Capt SC
Timothy: b 2-7-1746 d 1808 m Sarah Vans PS MA
Wm.: b 1-25-1750 d 5-18-1820 m Susana Sankey Pvt NCdr PA
Woodbury: b 1739 d 1805 m Sarah Sherburne PS NH

LANGFITT,
Francis: b 12-30-1760 d 12-16-1847 m Embly — QMSgt VA ★
Francis: b 1748 d 1840 m — Sgt VA
Philip: b 1758 d 1825 m Margaret Campbell Pvt VA
Wm.: b 1737 d 8- -1831 m Margaret Campbell Sgt VA

LANGFORD, (includes LANKFORD)
George: b 1755 d 3-16-1827 m Abigail Elliott Sgt MA
John: b 1758 d 1830 m Martha Whitehead Sol NC
John: b 10-10-1705 d 5- -1785 m Barbara Rice PS RI
Stephen: b c. 1735 d p. 11-2-1785 m Sarah Watkins PS VA
Thomas: b 1740 d p. 11-20-1789 m Elizabeth Westry Lt VA
Wm.: b 1744 d 1830 m Nanch Dickinson Pvt NC
Wm.: b 10-11-1764 d 11-18-1838 m Elizabeth Pankey Kelso Pvt VA ★

LANGHAM,
Elias: b 1759 d 4-3-1830 m — Lt VA ★
Wm.: b 1743 d 1800 m — Smith Bbd Wgn VA

LANGHORNE,
John Scarsbrook: b 1760 d c. 1797 m Elizabeth (Langhorne)Lt VA
Maurice: b 1721 d 1791 m (1)Elizabeth Trotter (2)Mary Maulson PS VA
Wm.: b 1720/30 d 1798 m Elizabeth Scarsbrook PS VA

LANGLEY, (includes LANGLY)
Benjamin: b 9- -1757 d 11-15-1836 m Betsey Dow Pvt NH ★
James: b c. 1754 d c. 8- -1796 m Elizabeth Ann Snale PS VA
Peter: b 12-5-1751 d 7-7-1781 m Elizabeth Lowden PS RI
Samuel: b 1-5-1724 d p. 3-13-1777 m Hannah Runnels PS NH
Thomas, Sr.: b c. 1721 d a. 4-22-1778 m (1)Sarah Trickey (2)Hannah Kent (3)Esther Ross PS NH
Thomas, Jr.: b 1743-48 d 1794 m Eleanor Libbey PS NH

LANGSTON,
James: b c. 1750 d p. 1791 m Johanna Davis Sol SC
John: b 1710 d 1790 m Agnes Maugham Sol SC
Laodicea: b 1759 d 1837 m Thomas Springfield PS SC
Solomon: b 1732 d p. 1810 m Sarah Bennett 1Lt SC
Wm.: b 4-15-1762 d 12-7-1853 m Mary — Pvt NC

LANGWORTHY,
James: b 7-2-1752 d 6-15-1800 m Ann De.... .vt VT
Joseph: b 2-6-1749 d 5-6-1824 m Lois Lewis PS RI
Samuel: b 11-27-1745 d 10-1-1818 m Mercy Saunders PS RI

LANHAM,
Edward: b 1750 d 4-7-1791 m Susannah Page Capt MD
George: b c. 1760 d p. 1790 m Ann Jarmain PS MD
Henry: b 5-28-1761 d 11-20-1849 m Eleanor (Millia)Pvt MD
Ralph: b c. 1750 d — m Murphy PS MD
Shadrick: b 1729 d p. 1814 m Sarah — PS MD
Stephen, Sr.: b 5-28-1726 d p. 6-25-1806 m (1)Leah — (2)Susannah — PS MD
Thomas: b 1757 d p. 3-25-1840 m Patience Sappington Pvt MD ★

LANIER,
Benjamin: b 12-14-1732 d 8-2-1817 m (1)Susannah Green (2)Ann Jones CS PS Sol GA
Benjamin: b c. 1720 d p. 9-14-1790 m Elizabeth — PS VA
Burwell: b 1737 d 1812 m Elizabeth Hill PS NC
Clement: b 1764 d 1840 m Sally Newton Sol GA
David: b c. 1750 d p. 1792 m Mary Hicks 2Capt VA
James: b 2-2-1750 d 4-27-1806 m Sarah Chalmers 2Lt NC
James: b 1726 d 1786 m Mary Cooke PS NC
Lewis: b c. 1754 d a. 8-16-1794 m Margaret — Sol NC
Lewis: b c. 1756 d 2-12-1839 m (1)Ann Butler (2)Mrs Esther Thorn Capt VA NC
Robert: b 6-30-1743 d 5-21-1828 m Elizabeth Washington PS NC
Thomas: b c. 1720 d 2- -1801 m Elizabeth Hicks Pvt VA

LANIUS,
Henry: b 8-21-1738 d 9-15-1808 m (1)Anna Margaret Fishel (2)Elizabeth Kunzel Pvt PA
Jacob: b 8-14-1732 d p. 4-23-1786 m (1)Barbara Weiss (2)Barbara Buhler Pvt PA
Johannes: b 3-24-1751 d 9-12-1837 m Catherina Rominger PS NC

LANMAN,
James: b 1752 d 1844 m — OrdlSgt SC ★

LANNING,
John: b 1736 d 1816 m Martha Hunt Pvt NJ
Joseph: b 1745 d p. 3-15-1814 m Anna — Pvt NJ
Ralph: b a. 1757 d 1800 m (1)Elizabeth Smith (2)Mary Hart 2Lt NJ
Robert: b 2-24-1747 d 10-4-1828 m Sarah Coryell Pvt NJ
Stephen, Sr.: b c. 1725 d c. 1780 m Abigail Hart Pvt NJ
Stephen, Jr.: b 1746 d 1798 m Elsie Reed CS NJ

LANSDALE,
Charles: b 1742 d 1795-1800 m Catherine Wheeler PS MD
Isaac: b c. 1760 d 1844 m (3)Sarah (Gentry)McCool Pvt DE ★
Thomas Lancaster: b 8-14-1727 d 1785 m Martha — Maj MD

LANSDOWN,
George: b c. 1750 d a. 5-5-1798 m Elizabeth — PS CS VA

LANSING,
Abraham: b 6-2-1750 d p. 6-3-1809 m Maria Bloodgood Ens NY
Abram Jacobus: b 4-8-1720 d 10-8-1791 m Catherine Leversee PS NY
Christopher: b 1-29-1743 d 10-25-1819 m Sarah Van Schaik QM NY
Cornelius: b 7-6-1756 d 4-23-1842 m Helen VanDerHeyden Pvt NY
Franciscus: bpt 7-18-1708 d p. 1780 m Maritje Lievense PS NY
Gerret I.: b 7-8-1745 d 12-24-1837 m Sarah Sharp Pvt NY ★
Gerrit: bpt 4-26-1752 d 1835 m Maria VanArnhem Pvt NY
Gerrit G.: b 12-11-1760 d 5-27-1831 m Manette Antill Ens NY ★
Gerrit J.: b 3-4-1711 d — m Jane Waters PS NY
Hendrich J.: b 3-14-1747 d 7-6-1792 m Helena Winne Pvt NY
Isaac: b 10-24-1725 d 10-10-1799 m Annalie VanWoert Lt NY
Jacob, Jr.: b 7-12-1714 d 1-18-1791 m Marytje Egberts Col NY
Jacob Franse: bpt 4-30-1738 d a. 7-8-1819 m Jannetje Visscher Lt PS NY
Jacob H.: b 4-4-1742 d p. 1790 m Maria Onderkirk Pvt NY
Jacob J.: b 11-22-1713 d 9-8-1794 m Hybertje Yates Capt NY
Jacob J.: b 11-2-1739 d 5-31-1796 m Willempye Bratt Lt NY
John: b 1-31-1754 d 12-12-1829 m Cornelia Ray MilSec NY
John Evert: b 5-1-1743 d 1821 m Maria Staats QM Adj NY

LANSING, contd.
Levinus: b 8-1-1749 d 10-16-1836 m Catherine Van der Huyden 2Lt PS NY
Obadiah: b 6-29-1740 d — m (1)Cornelia vanBenthuysen (2)Cornelia Cooper 1Lt NY
Philip: b 2-23-1729 d p. 1778 m Elsie Hun PS NY

LANTER,
Jacob: b 8-11-1762 d 7-1-1837 m Mary Webb Pvt VA ★

LANTERMAN,
John: b 1714 d 1794 m Elizabeth Peterson Pvt PA
Peter: b 1-8-1749 d 6-14-1821 m Aletta Applegate Pvt PA

LAPE,
Thomas: b 1752 d 5-2-1813 m — Pvt NY

LAPHAM,
John: bpt 11-14-1731 d 8-18-1801 m Bathsheba Eames Pvt MA
John: b 7-6-1745 d 10-6-1826 m Amy Bucklin Pvt RI
Jonathan: b 5-6-1728 d 1798 m Mary Soper Sol NY
Lemuel: b 4-14-1761 d 12-20-1843 m Lydia Macgoun Pvt MA ★

LAPSLEY,
John: b 12-29-1753 d 10-8-1816 m Mary Armstrong 1Lt VA

LARA,
James: b 7-4-1755 d 1-31-1840 m Mollie Hobbs Cpl MA

LARAWAY,
Jacob: b 3-1-1759 d 1-26-1847 m Elizabeth Murray Pvt NY ★
Peter P.: b 1734 d 1801 m Gertrude Vrooman Pvt NY
Phillip: b 12-20-1757 d 9-5-1844 m Ruth Smalley Pvt MA ★

LARCHAR,
John, Sr.: b 8-28-1726 d 12-6-1804 m Lucy Crowell Sol RI
John, Jr.: b c. 1753 d 1787 m Lillias Gladding Mstr RI

LARCHER,
Timothy: b c. 1750 d p. 12- -1777 m Nancy Brown NLt RI

LARCOM, (includes LARKCOM & LARKUM)
Henry: b 9-17-1751 d 7-7-1780 m Priscilla Woodbury NLt MA
Jonathan: b 4-30-1742 d 1778 m Abigail Ober Pvt MA
Paul: b 2-16-1764 d 1-21-1843 m Comfort Norton Pvt MA
Thomas: b 10-31-1756 d 7-27-1823 m Sarah Hutchinson Smn CT

LAREY,
Michael: b 6-8-1752 d 1794 m Mary Catherine Deramus Pvt SC

LARGE,
John: b 12-15-1759 d 7-21-1850 m Nancy Low Pvt NJ

LARGENT,
James: b c. 1745 d p. 5-14-1810 m Margery — Sol VA

LARIMORE, (includes LARIMER)
James: b 4-16-1759 d 9-16-1842 m (1)Caty Morgan (2)Leanna Southern Sgt NC W★
John: b c. 1742 d 10- -1818 m Elizabeth — Pvt PA
Thomas: b c. 1740 d 1816 m Catherine — Pvt PA

LARKIN, (includes LARKINS)
Abel: b 1749 d 1826 m Sarah Foster Pvt RI
Benjamin: b 1759 d 5-12-1833 m (2)Susannah — Capt NC ★
Ephraim: b 3-28-1753 d 7-8-1846 m Dinah Baker Pvt MA ★
James: b 1749 d 7-13-1828 m Catherine (Keiger) Gerlinger Sgt PA ★
John: b 10-22-1724 d 4-1-1798 m Katharine Frothingham Pvt MA
John: b 5-1-1731 d 5-4-1777 m Amie Enos PS RI
Joseph: b 1739 d 8-13-1826 m Ann Salkeld Pvt PA
Joshua: b 7-7-1752 d 12-10-1834 m Jerusha Blackman Pvt CT
Lorin Nehemiah: b 9-30-1755 d 10-24-1845 m Christiana Cutler Pvt CT ★
Matthias: b 1-5-1724/5 d p. 2-3-1778 m Demaris Sawyer Sgt MA
Peter: b 7-29-1727 d 1815 m Azubah Wheeler Cpl MA
Samuel: b 2-6-1748 d 11-10-1802 m Abiel Rand Sol MA
Timothy: b 10-10-1736 d p. 1793 m (1)Sarah Nye (2)Rachel Langworthy Pvt RI
Wm.: b c. 1730-35 d p. 4-19-1802 m — Capt NC

LA ROCHE,
James: b — d 3- -1783 m Annis Upham Maj SC

LA ROSE,
John Jacob: b 2- -1755 d 11-17-1844 m Mary Barbara Gift Pvt PA ★

LARRABEE, (includes LARRIBEE)
Benjamin: b 5-23-1740 d 4-17-1829 m Hannah H. Skillings Capt MA
Benjamin: b 2-5-1739 d 11-24-1816 m Lydia Bailey Capt PS MA
Eleazer: b 8-31-1756 d c. 1835 m Mary Grant Pvt VT NH ★
Isaac: bpt 1729 d p. 1790 m Deborah — Sgt MA
Isaac: b 1749 d 4-18-1801 m Mary Flinn Pvt MA
Isaac: b 1750 d 1840 m Sarah Freeman Pvt MA ★

John: b 1753 d 2-6-1846 m (1) — Hicks (2)Dorothy Smith Pvt NH ★
John: b 1732 d 6-7-1818 m Mary Spaulding Cpl VT
Jonathan: b — d — m Margaret Wellington Cpl MA
Samuel: b 7-1-1753 d 6-9-1836 m Elizabeth Blake Sol NH
Thomas: b 9-4-1722 d 8-15-1792 m (2)Abiah Stratton Pvt MA
Thomas: b 8-15-1752 d 5-10-1832 m Bathsheba Morse Pvt MA
Timothy: b 10-8-1730 d 1-7-1810 m Abigail Wood PM CT
Timothy: b 7-6-1763 d 8-21-1831 m Elizabeth Grover Pvt VT
Wm.: b a. 1760 d p. 1800 m (1)Ammy Howard (2)Millie Royce Pvt VT
Zebulon: b 3-11-1757 d 1798 m Susan Goodwin Pvt MA

LARRICK, (or LERRICK)
Casper: b c. 1730 d c. 1801 m Elizabeth Sundown PS VA

LARRISON, (includes LARASON)
Peter: b c. 1755 d p. 1817 m — Wgn NJ
Roger: b 1-21-1750 d 5-4-1812 m Lenah — Sgt NJ
Thomas: b 1745 d p. 1817 m Mary — Pvt NJ
Wm.: b c. 1747 d 1777 m Patience — Sgt NJ

LA RUE, (includes LAREW & LARUE)
Henry: b 10-7-1745 d 3-1-1850 m (1)Merretje Mandeviel (2)Betsy Emmons Pvt NY ★
Isaac: b c. 1747 d 1792 m Mary — Pvt PA
Isaac: b 1712 d 3- -1795 m Phebe Carman PS VA
Jacob: b 5-1-1744 d 9-15-1821 m (1)Mary Frost (2)Jane Morgan PS VA
John: b 1-24-1746 d 1-4-1792 m Mary Brooks PS VA
Peter: b 1745 d 12-24-1832 m Catherine McKissic Pvt VA
Peter: b 4-21-1745 d 4-16-1816 m Elizabeth (La Rue) Sol VA
Wm.: b 1744 d 1822 m Nellie Covenhoven Pvt NJ

LARY,
Daniel: b 12-24-1754 d 5-13-1827 m Elizabeth Lary Cpl NH
Dennis: b a. 1753 d 1811 m — Sol VA

LARZELERE,
Nicholas, Sr.: b c. 1721 d 1791-99 m Elizabeth Bessonette Pvt PA
Nicholas, Jr.: b c. 1734 d 1-12-1818 m Hannah Britton Pvt PA

LASCELLES,
Edward: b — d 8-15-1805 m Hannah — Pvt NY

LASH,
Adam: b c. 1738 d p. 1825 m Nancy — Pvt PA
Jacob: b 1752 d 9-21-1836 m Elizabeth Yost Sol PA

LASHBROOKS (includes LASHBROOK)
John: b 1-30-1757 d 2-11-1835 m — Lee Pvt VA
Wm.: b 1756 d 3-30-1839 m Zeruah Mitchell Pvt Fif CT ★
Wm.: b 1745 d 1816 m Effy — PS VA

LA SHELLS,
George: b 4-24-1756 d 5-27-1844 m (1)Margaret Hontz (2)Anne Moore Pvt NJ ★

LASHER, (includes LOESCHER)
Adam: b c. 1750 d p. 5-14-1803 m Catharina Schoonmaker Pvt NY
Conrad B.: bpt 8-2-1749 d 1824 m Catharine Clum Pvt NY
Gerrit: b 12-29-1723 d 1802 m Catherine Dillenback Pvt NY
John: b 3-3-1726 d 2-23-1806 m (1)Helena Piers (2)Eva Ernest Col NY
John: bpt 11-27-1733 d p. 8-3-1795 m Christina Holtzappel Sgt NY
John: b 1758 d 1838 m Catherine Mesick Pvt NY
Wm.: bpt 1-24-1762 d p. 1800 m Susanna Klein Pvt NY

LASSELL, (includes LASSELLE)
Caleb: b 3-19-1761 d 11-23-1846 m Dorcas White Pvt MA
Josiah: b 5-5-1741 d 4-8-1809 m Lydia Bingham Pvt MA

LASSITER, (includes LASSATER, LASSETER)
Jacob: b 1732 d 3-16-1778 m Sarah Harrell Pvt NC
James: b a. 1760 d 4-20-1828 m Elizabeth Butt Pvt GA
Jonas: b c. 1740 d 1814 m Winifred — Pvt NC
Wm.: b 12-22-1756 d 2-11-1845 m Rebecca Gunter Pvt NC ★
Wm.: b 1725 d p. 1-4-1784 m Keziah — PS NC

LASSLEY,
John: b — d p. 1785 m Sarah Tyler Sgt NY

LATANÉ,
Wm.: b c. 1753 d — m Ann Waring Lt VA

LATCH,
Jacob: b 10-31-1758 d 6-29-1845 m Jane Rose Sgt PA ★

LATCHA,
Abram: b 5-29-1741 d 1814 m Mary Ann — Maj PA
Jacob: b 2-24-1763 d 5-9-1835 m Anna Margaret Stine Lt PA

LATHAM, (includes LEATHAM)
Andrew: b — d p. 5-6-1790 m Jean — PS SC
Arthur: b 2-16-1758 d 11-25-1843 m Mary Post MM MA
Benoni: b 12-13-1759 d 6-25-1826 m Sarah Appleby Matr RI

Cary: b 1733 d 9- -1780 m Mary Packer Pvt CT
Eliab: b 5-14-1764 d 3-24-1818 m Lucy Latham Pvt MA
Elizabeth: b c. 1728 d 1782 m (1)John Manley (2)John Latham PS MD
Hubbard: b 1-4-1746 d 6-9-1816 m Ruth Brown Seacap CT
James: b 1748 d p. 1799 m Esther Baker Pvt MA
James, Sr.: b 2-14-1736 d 11-10-1785 m (2)Agnes — PS NC
Jasper: b 1715 d 1-11-1799 m Deborah Avery Pvt CT
Jasper: b 1753 d 3-31-1835 m — Pvt CT ★
Joseph: b c. 1750 d 11-5-1834 m Abigail Fish Pvt CT
Joseph: b 1724 d 4-2-1798 m Mary Pryor Pvt MA
Nehemiah: b 11-1-1733 d 11-21-1807 m (1)Lucy Harris (2)Mrs Hannah Allen Lt MA
Phinehas, Sr.: b c. 1720 d 9- -1781 m (1)Mary — (2)Rebecah — (3)Anne Catherine — CS NC
Stephen: b 1751 d p. 9-16-1815 m — Pvt RI
Wm.: b 1-27-1741 d 1-27-1792 m Eunice Forsythe Capt CT
Wm.: b 1765 d 1-29-1849 m Sabrina Ashbey Pvt CT
Woodward: b 12-24-1729 d 12-13-1802 m Rebecca Dean Cpl MA

LATIMER, (includes LATTEMORE, LATTIMER & LATTIMORE)
Aholiab: b 9-1-1762 d 1-10-1852 m (1)Eleanor Loomis (2)Lois Loomis Pvt CT
Alexander: b 1758 d 4- -1832 m Nancy Wells Pvt PS PA
Benjamin: b 6-14-1743 d 5-5-1785 m Louisa Cazey Pvt MD
Francis: b c. 1754 d p. 4-18-1817 m — Lt SC
George: b 7-29-1749 d 10-8-1837 m Rachel Smith Pvt CT ★
George: b 11-15-1757 d 6-5-1850 m (1)Hannah Loomis (2)Eunice Rowland (3)Louisa Holcomb Moses Wgn CT ★
George: b — d a. 10-19-1793 m Margaret Potter PS PA
Giles, Sr.: b 1745 d 6-29-1829 m Ziba Wilcox Pvt CT
Hezekiah: b 5-5-1736 d 4-29-1818 m (1)Tryphena Gillet (2)Rebecca — (3)Mindwell — Capt CT
Jacob: b a. 1730 d 8- -1784 m (1) — Brandt (2)Judith Swann PS MD
James: b 1761 d 1827 m Mary Ann Walker Ens PA
John: b c. 1745 d 1777/8 m — Pvt NY
John: b 1745 d 3-12-1821 m Jemima (Stockton) Pvt SC
Jonathan: b 5-27-1724 d p. 11-13-1802 m Lucretia Griswold Col CT
Marcus: b 1740 d 1790 m Ann — Sol PS MD
Pickett: b 7-27-1747 d 1825 m Eunice Douglass Capt CT
Robert: b c. 1735 d c. 1800 m Nancy King Pvt PS PA
Stephen: b 1749 d 11-30-1800 m Joannah — Pvt CT
Thomas: b 1750 d 9-23-1826 m Ann Ford PS MD
Wait: b 7-16-1741 d 7-8-1804 m Martha Tuller Pvt CT
Wetherel: b 3-18-1757 d p. 1803 m (1)Abigail Fitch (2)Margaret Anderson Adj CT ★
Wm.: b 1763 d 11-11-1833 m Mary Ralston Pvt PA

LATOUR,
Anthony: b 1751 d p. 1824 m Elizabeth C. Hughes Pvt MA ★

LA TOURETTE,
Peter: b 4-13-1755 d 4-1-1836 m Margaret Stout Pvt NJ

LATTA,
Ephraim: b 1759-60 d p. 11-28-1803 m Mary Thompson Pvt PA
James: b 1748 d 11-13-1816 m Sarah Jackson PS CS NY
James: b c. 1735 d p. 8-16-1804 m — PS NC
James: b 1732 d 1-29-1801 m Mary McCalla Sol Chp PA
John: b 1722 d 1798 m Mary Dougherty Pvt PA
John: b 9-15-1756 d 10-4-1843 m Margaret Potter PS PA
John: b 1727 d 1-9-1795 m Sarah Ramsey (Dunlap)PS SC
Moses: b a. 1760 d p. 1790 m Elizabeth Jearman Pvt NY

LATTIN, (includes LATTING)
Ambrose: b 1-11-1750 d 8-1-1814 m Johanna Morehouse Pvt NY
Luke: bpt 6- -1742 d p. 1800 m Betsy Blackman PS CT
Richard: b 6-11-1755 d 2-7-1841 m Kezia Seeley Pvt VT W★
Jacob: b 1756 d a. 4-27-1824 m Derica Ann Waring Pvt NY

LAUB,
Conrad: b 12-25-1751 d 2-26-1807 m Mary Elizabeth Jost Pvt PA

LAUBACH,
Adam: b 1-20-1763 d 2-8-1847 m Margaret Newhard Pvt PA
Frederick: b 5-10-1744 d 4-7-1797 m Catherine Bitting Ens PA
George: b 11-11-1729 d 10-19-1802 m Elizabeth Janson Sol PA
Peter: b 1734 d 1818 m Catharine Knepley Pvt PA

LAUDENSLAGER,
George: b c. 1730 d p. 1790 m Catherine — Sol PA
Valentine: b c. 1756 d 5- -1806 m Magdalene Kochendoerfer Pvt PA

LAUDERDALE,
John: b 1725 d 1800 m Jane — Pvt VA
Wm.: b 1741/2 d 1838 m Helen — Spy Pvt VA ★

LAUFFER,
Henry: b c. — -1753 d 2- -1821 m Barbara Alliman Pvt PA
John: b 3-8-1760 d 2-8-1851 m (1)Susan Kemerer (2)Barbara Erret Pvt PA
Peter: b 10-18-1752 d 7-21-1830 m Magdalena Althaus Pvt PA

LAUGHINGHOUSE,
John: b 2-4-1757 d 8-29-1831 m (1)Elizabeth Wall (2)Elsie Knox (3)Mary Harrenton Pvt NC

LAUGHNER, (includes DELAUGHTER, LAUGHTER)
Christian: b 1729 d 1799 m Margaret Brisch Pvt PA
George: b 1760 d 11-18-1830 m Charlotte Pace Sol SC
John: b 3-17-1746 d 6-13-1816 m Mary Langford PS NC

LAUMAN, (includes LOWMAN)
Christopher: b 11- -1735 d p. 3-21-1806 m Catherine Elizabeth Meem Capt PA
George: b 8-26-1743 d 6-26-1809 m Esther King Pvt PA
George: b 1765 d 1848 m Susan Herman Pvt PA
Jacob: b 1755 d 1860 m — Pvt PA
John: b c. 1735 d 10- -1819 m Magdalen — Pvt PA
Michael: b c. 1755 d 4-25-1822 m Rosanna — Pvt PA

LAURENS,
Henry: b 2-6-1724 d 12-8-1792 m Eleanor Ball PS SC
John: b c. 1756 d 8-27-1782 m Elizabeth Earpe Col ADC CL

LAUTZENHEISER,
Henry: b 1761 d 4-6-1834 m Judith Marchand Pvt PA

LAVAL,
Jacint: b 1762 d 9-2-1822 m Rebecca Withers Cnt FrA

LAVEILLE,
John: b c. 1750 d 1813 m Ann Frazier PS MD

LAVENDER,
George: b 1755 d 5-14-1778 m Barbara Panther Pvt VA
Hugh: b 11-11-1754 d p. 9-8-1834 m — Pvt SC ★
Wm.: b c. 1760 d 1-17-1835 m Sarah Stratton Pvt VA ★

LAVERGNE,
Lois: b 1743 d a. 2-14-1814 m Marianne LaCaze PS LA

LAVERTY,
Ralph: b c. 1715 d 1792 m (1)Elizabeth Stuart (2)Jane Hicklin PS VA

LAW,
Benedict Arnold: b 12-20-1740 d 11-19-1819 m (1)Sarah Bryan (2)Henrietta Gibbs PS CT
Consider: b 1756 d 8-4-1820 m (1)Martha Allen (2)Sarah Groman Pvt NY
John: b 1743 d 6-9-1811 m Agnes Herrin Pvt NY
Jonathan: b 12-5-1705 d 9-24-1790 m Eunice Andrew PS CT
Joseph: b c. 1733 d 4-18-1803 m (1)Sarah Henley (2)Mary Jones (3)Mary Bradwell (4)Elizabeth Spry Maj CS GA
Matthew: b 1743 d 1798 m Margaret Snodgrass Sol PA
Nathaniel: b c. 1752 d 1823 m Rachel — PS VA
Reuben: b 10-22-1751 d 8-21-1840 m (1)Alice Piper (2)Ruth Piper Pvt MA
Richard, Sr.: b 3-17-1733 d 1-26-1806 m Ann Prentis PS CT
Richard, Jr.: b 3-17-1763 d 12-19-1845 m Lucretia Wolcott Mid CT
Wm.: b 9-2-1751 d 3-14-1824 m Sarah Hotchkiss Lt CT
Wm.: b 12-17-1764 d 10-18-1812 m Mary DuBose Pvt SC

LAWALD, (includes LAVAL & LAWALL)
Michael: b 5-24-1716 d 9-12-1796 m Maria Sibilla PS PA
Henry Wm.: b 1-31-1740 d 12-6-1802 m Elizabeth Neulin Col PA

LAWLER,
James: b — d p. 1-2-1813 m Anna — Sol VA
Mathew: b 1754 d 1830 m Ann Bevan SeaCap PA
Michael: b 12-10-1761 d 2-2-1826 m Mary Mathney Pvt MD ★
Nicholas: b 9-10-1743 d 1837 m Dinah — Pvt VA ★
Patrick: b c. 1764 d p. 5-4-1805 m Margaret Kent Pvt MA

LAWLESS,
Augustine: b 1752 d 10-9-1832 m Sarah Dillon Pvt VA ★
John: b 3-11-1751 d 8-12-1847 m Mary Stoddard Pvt VA ★
Wm.: b c. 1739 d 3-15-1791 m Rebecca Dyer Capt RI

LAWRENCE, (includes LARRANCE & LAURENCE)
Abraham: b 7-9-1752 d 6-14-1837 m Eunice Miner QMSgt NJ
Abraham: b 5-8-1759 d 10-17-1838 m Leanna Jones PS NC
Amos, Jr.: bpt 3-12-1758 d 1-2-1842 m Sabra Eggleston Pvt Tms NY ★
Amos: b 1765 d 10-4-1838 m Desire — Pvt NS RI ★
Amos, Sr.: b 7-24-1738 d p. 1790 m Sarah Webster Sgt CT
Amos: b 8-7-1748 d 6-9-1840 m (1)Sarah Wetherbee (2)—White Pvt PS MA
Amos, Jr.: b 9-9-1750 d 5-1-1798 m Betty Hubbard 1Lt MA
Amos: b 1-15-1755 d 12-15-1841 m Hannah Daniels Pvt MA
Asa: b 1745 d 1812 m Lucy Miller Pvt CT
Asa: b 6-14-1737 d 1-16-1804 m Abigail King Capt MA
Benjamin: b 5-17-1741 d 3-5-1814 m Urith Randall Owings 2Lt PS MD
Benjamin, Sr.: b 11-6-1720 d 7-5-1807 m Rebecca Dodge Lt MA
Benjamin, Jr.: b 9-1-1746 d 6-8-1824 m Rebecca Woods 1Lt MA

LAWRENCE, contd.
Benjamin: b *a*. 1763 d 4-22-1826 m Rachel Weems Lt SC W★
Bigelow: b 5-27-1741 d 1-21-1818 m Asenath Curtis Maj VT
Caleb: b 2-10-1723 d *p*. 4-19-1799 m Sarah Burling Capt NY
Daniel: b 9-29-1747 d 7-13-1832 m Elizabeth Graves Pvt MA
Daniel: b 12-13-1713 d 1788 m Charity Mills Matr NJ
Daniel: b 8-14-1737 d 11-19-1821 m Pheba Seaman Lt NY
Daniel: b 11-26-1739 d 11-7-1807 m Eve VanHorne Capt PS NY
David: b 1-26-1742 d 2-18-1836 m (1)Elisabeth Eastman (2)Sarah
   Clark (3)Hannah Clark Pvt MA
David: b 2-22-1731 d *p*. 1805 m Sarah Chamberlin PS CS NH
David, Jr.: b 2-27-1740 d 10-30-1821 m Lydia Sias PS NH
David: b *a*. 1752 d *c*. 1816 m Elizabeth Poppino Pvt NY
David: b 1-1-1748 d 5-13-1834 m Abigail Birch PS NY
David: b 2-18-1738 d 10-18-1809 m Sybil Sterry Lt RI
Ebenezer, Jr.: b 5-11-1721 d 10-4-1796 m (1)Mary Haws (2)Mary
   Harding CS MA
Edward: b 1755 d 10-4-1825 m Elizabeth Thomas Sgt CT MA ★
Eleazor: b 1707 d 1789 m Lucy Tuttle Pvt MA
Eleazer: b 8-11-1735 d 3- -1818 m Rebecca Haynes Pvt MA
Elijah: b 10-17-1763 d 3-15-1809 m (1)Hannah Clark (2)Lucinda
   Butterfield Grd CL
Elisha: b *c*. 1744 d *p*. 1791 m Elizabeth Drake Col QM NJ
Enoch, Sr.: b 11-15-1710 d 9-28-1778 m Sarah Stevens Pvt NH
Enoch, Jr.: b 7-24-1738 d 12-11-1809 m Esther Woods Pvt NH
George: b 4-20-1750 d *p*. 1805 m Esther (Mercey)Warren Pvt MA
Gideon: b 3-15-1716 d *p*. 1789 m Eunice Parkhurst Pvt NY
Henry: b 11-23-1751 d 10- -1831 m Elizabeth Parrish Pvt VA
Isaac, Sr.: b 2-25-1704/5 d 12-2-1793 m (1)Lydia Hewitt (2)Amy
   Whitney PS CT
Isaac: b 10-19-1756 d 1828 m Anna Hodgman Cpl MA
Isaac: b *c*. 1728-30 d *p*. 3-4-1793 m — Pvt NY
Isaac, Jr.: b 3-5-1737 d *p*. 1793 m Mary Brown PS VT
Jacob: b *c*. 1750 d *c*. 1820 m Elizabeth Kip Lt NY
Jacob: b 1732 d 3-8-1813 m Marah — Pvt NY
Jacob: b 8-7-1759 d 5-24-1855 m Rebecca Beard OrdlSgt NC ★
Jacob: b 2-10-1761 d 10-17-1854 m Barbra Mackey Randolph Pvt
   PA ★
James: b 1758 d 1828 m Lois Teller Pvt CT
James, Jr.: b 4-11-1736 d 4-15-1821 m Elizabeth Fish Lt MA
James: b *c*. 1742 d *c*. 10-28-1805 m Jane (Davis)Symmes PS MA
John: b 10-26-1743 d 4-4-1782 m Martha West PS MD
John: b *c*. 1750-52 d 9-6-1844 m Jane Huddlestone Sgt MA
John: b 11-13-1741 d 12-26-1799 m Sarah — Pvt MA
John: b 10-7-1754 d — m Hannah Davis Pvt MA
John: b 3-25-1745 d 11- -1810 m Catharine Beekman 2Lt NY
John: b 7-5-1758 d 8-29-1817 m (1)Elizabeth Berrien Lawrence
   (2)Patience Riker NS NY
John: b *c*. 1739 d 1801 m Lavinah — Sol NY
John: b 1740 d 11- -1800 m Ann — Sol NC
John: b *c*. 1747 d 10-23-1796 m Mary Duke Sol NC
John: b 9-15-1751 d *c*. 1799 m Elizabeth St. Clair Capt PA
John: b *a*. 1748 d 1-4-1818 m Catherine — Sgt PA
John: b *a*. 1728 d 8-27-1798 m Catharine Heuss Pvt PA
John: b 3-2-1746 d 10-27-1825 m Mary Cleveland Pvt VT
John: b *c*. 1745 d *p*. 11- -1787 m Mary Bridger Col PS VA
John: b 9-4-1760 d 1-29-1841 m Behesland Smith Pvt VA ★
Jonas: b 1728 d 5-22-1793 m Tryphena — PS CT
Jonathan: b 4-15-1736 d 6-5-1816 m Zerviah Ormsby Cpl CT
Jonathan, Jr.: b 2-20-1761 d 2-5-1851 m (1)Lucy Clark (2)Lydia
   Lawrence Pvt CT ★
Jonathan, Sr.: b 10-4-1703 d 12-8-1789 m (1)Tryphena Powers
   (2)Lydia Fletcher Pvt MA
Jonathan: b 9-2-1725 d 4-12-1806 m Esther Shedd Pvt MA
Jonathan: b 12-27-1724 d 8-1-1793 m Rachel Wright CS MA
Jonathan, Sr.: b *c*. 1721 d 7-22-1808 m Elizabeth VanKleck PS NY
Jonathan, Jr.: bpt 9-20-1759 d 4-27-1802 m (1)Janette Neale
   (2)Mary Mann Capt NY
Jonathan: b 10-4-1737 d 9-4-1812 m (1)Judith Fish (2)Ruth Riker
   PS NY
Joseph: b 4-6-1749 d 1-5-1829 m Lydia Shattuck Cpl MA
Joseph: b 1734 d 1779 m Nabby Brown Pvt MA
Joseph: b *a*. 1757 d 6-5-1777 m Silence — Ens NH
Joseph: b 3-21-1723 d 1-28-1793 m Patience Moore PS NY
Joseph: b 1761 d 12-6-1834 m Frances (Jones)Vaughn Pvt NC
Joseph: b *a*. 1749 d 1-1-1797 m Sarah Moffitt PS PA
Joseph: b 1-12-1736/7 d *a*. 1790 m Susannah — Sgt VT
Joshua: b 3-4-1755 d 2-12-1826 m Thankful Snow 2Lt MA ★
Joshua: b 4-18-1753 d 5-20-1827 m Ruth Nims Pvt MA
Josiah, Sr.: b 8-11-1735 d 4-11-1802 m Mrs Mary Branch Sol VT
Josiah, Jr.: b 11-29-1763 d 8-3-1835 m (1)Sally Willoughby
   (2)Mrs Huldah Smith Pvt VT ★
Levi: b 4-14-1759 d 7-24-1831 m (1)Elizabeth Holden (2)Sarah Tripp
   Pvt MA
Levi: b 3-9-1766 d 12-10-1838 m (1)Abigail Burdick Janes (2)Mary
   Miller Pvt VT ★
Levin: b 1750 d 3-31-1805 m Sarah Dorsey Capt MD
Martin: b 5- -1751 d 1823 m Sarah Puffer Pvt MA
Nathaniel: b 7-11-1761 d 7-5-1797 m Elizabeth Berrien Lt NC NY
Nathaniel: b 1735 d 1800 m Louisa — Sol NC
Nathaniel: b 1743 d 8-25-1849 m *Miss* Martin Lt VT
Nehemiah: b 3-18-1730 d 7-2-1800 m (1)Sarah Boardman
   (2)Elizabeth Robbards (3)Abigail Sutton Capt CT

Nehemiah: b — d — m Abigail Burral Capt CT
Nehemiah: b 1-14-1752 d 7-13-1796 m Esther Fitch Sgt MA
Nicholas: b 9-18-1764 d 2-7-1838 m Sarah Cummings Pvt NH
Oliver: b 10- -1759 d 3-23-1848 m Patty Wait Pvt NY ★
Peter: b 10-17-1742 d 10-21-1798 m Persis — Lt MA
Phineas: b 2-19-1749 d *p* 1786 m Elizabeth Stearns Cpl MA
Roseamus: b 1753 d 8-1-1835 m Hannah — Smn CT
Rowland: b 3-25-1763 d 6-17-1812 m (1)Mahala Worcester
   (2)Azubah Parker Pvt MA
Samuel: b 4-22-1752 d 11-8-1827 m Susannah Parker Cpl MA
Samuel, Sr.: b 5-2-1714 d 1789 m Mary Hildreth Pvt MA
Samuel, Jr.: b 1-24-1738 d 7-26-1799 m (1)Rebecca — (2)Susanna
   Jones Pvt MA
Samuel: b 3-9-1739 d 5-27-1796 m Rhoda Benedict Capt NY
Samuel: b 1750 d 11-26-1834 m Abigail Pell Pvt NY ★
Samuel: b *c*. 1755 d *p*. 1815 m (1)Sarah Grayson (2)Elizabeth (Ellis)
   Givens (3)Harriet (de Treville)Gerrard Lt SC
Simon: b 1-11-1739 d 10-15-1795 m Sybil Robbins Pvt MA
Thomas: b 4-3-1758 d 7-28-1822 m Anna Shattuck FifMaj MA
Thomas: b 8-18-1734 d 3-22-1821 m Sarah Bailey Pvt MA
Thomas: b 3-14-1746/7 d 10-2-1815 m Ruth Raymond Pvt MA
Thomas: b 1748 d 7-26 1825 m Abigail Britton Pvt MA
Thomas: b 4-25-1756 d 2-3-1833 m Sarah Parker Pvt MA W★
Thomas: b 7-31-1724 d 11-4-1795 m Mary Willett Lt NJ
Thomas: b 1764 d 6-12-1837 m (1)Sarah — (2)Catherine Kesler Pvt
   NY ★
Thomas: b 11-21-1733 d 12-3-1817 m Elizabeth Fish PS NY
Uriah: b 12-25-1720 d 11-30-1803 m Mary Clark PS NY
Wm.: b 4- -1767 d 9-4-1854 m Elizabeth Friend Pvt MD ★
Wm.: b 4-10-1752 d 12-12-1804 m Eunice Brown Pvt MA
Wm.: b 7-27-1729 d 1-13-1794 m (1)Anna Brinkerhoff (2)Mary
   Palmer Capt NY
Wm.: b 3-8-1754 d 7-7-1833 m Elizabeth Stewart MM Sgt NY ★
Wm.: b 3-27-1761 d 3-27-1851 m Mary Shadbolt Pvt NY
Wm.: b *c*. 1714/5 d 6-18-1802 m Mary Stilwell PS NY
Wm.: b 1766 d 7-12-1822 m Catherine Pvt NC

LAWS,
Bolitha: b *c*. 1720 d *c*. 4-26-1783 m Leah Sturgis PS DE
Elijah: b *c*. 1725 d *p*. 2-6-1794 m Comfort CS MD
Elijah, Jr.: b 1744 d 1- -1814 m Patty Bird Pvt MD
George, Sr.: b *c*. 1710 d *p*. 1-12-1798 m — PS NC
George: b *c*. 1750-55 d *p*. 6-24-1815 m (2)Sarah Carpenter PS
   NC
John: b 1757 d 2-27-1840 m (2)Margaret Ransdale Pvt VA ★
Thomas: b 11-20-1737 d 9-14-1803 m Hannah — Pvt MA
Wm.: b *c*. 1753 d *p*. 1829 m Ann Fooks Pvt MD

LAWSON,
Andrew: b 1-23-1760 d 6-27-1822 m Mary Moore Barry Pvt GA NC
Andrew: b 1736 d 2-16-1785 m Mary Calvert Col PS VA
Ebenezer: b 1-26-1760 d *p*. 1795 m Elizabeth — Pvt CT ★
Hugh: b 6-14-1755 d 2-20-1802 m (2)Sarah Whittaker Capt GA
Isaac: b 8-19-1760 d 2-3-1838 m Deborah Mark Pvt NY
James: b 3-11-1760 d 11-11-1844 m (2)Sophia Johnson (3)Phebe
   — Pvt VA
John: b 6-30-1724 d 6-20-1798 m Mary Brown Pvt CT
John: b *c*. 1755 d *p*. 1820 m — Pvt GA
John: b 11-3-1757 d 4-18-1816 m Alice Moore Sol GA
John: b 1756 d 2-1-1802 m Jane White Pvt NJ
John: b — d *p*. 12-5-1804 m Sarah — PS NC
Joseph: b *c*. 1765 d *p*. 10-24-1814 m Magdalena Baughman Pvt PA
Matthew: b 6-18-1756 d 9-17-1812 m Eleanor Hoffman Pvt NY
Nathan: b 3-15-1755 d *p*. 1840 m (1)Mildred — (2)Christian High
   Pvt VA ★
Robert: b 1-23-1748 d 4- -1805 m Sarah Merriwether Pierce BGen
   VA
Robert: b 1-11-1759 d 4-18-1835 m Anna Horton Sol CT
Roger: b 5- -1730 d 8-6-1803 m (1)Hannah Thompson (2)Margaret
   McGill Sol GA
Thomas: b 12-11-1727 d 1-5-1825 m Esther Paul Capt CT
Thomas: b 1718 d 10-20-1795 m Hannah Farley Cpl PA
Wm.: b 1763 d 1-30-1852 m Nancy Baker Pvt NC
Wm.: b 1740 d 1799 m Mary Graham 1Lt VA

LAWTON, (includes LAUGHTON)
Benjamin: b 11-16-1751 d 1835 m (3)Rhoda Cahoone Pvt Drm RI ★
David: b 10-22-1760 d 1837 m (2)Ruth L. Melvin Pvt VT ★
Elisha: b 7-22-1734 d 7-2-1811 m Jane Luscomb PS RI
George: b — d — m Patience Turner (Lawton) Pvt RI
Israel: b 1-30-1758 d 9-26-1844 m Dolly Billings Sgt MA ★
James: b 11-21-1741 d 6-20-1833 m Lydia Howland Sgt MA ★
John: b 1- -1730 d 3- -1786 m Jane (Derby)Lampson MM MA ★
John: b 10-8-1759 d 1-30-1838 m Mary Hooker Pvt MA ★
Joseph: b 10-18-1753 d 3-5-1815 m Sarah Robert Lt PS SC
Oliver: b 1739 d 1815 m Ann Rathbone Pvt RI
Robert: b 11-17-1718 d *p*. 1783 m Mary Hall Pvt PS RI
Samuel: b 1721 d 1814 m Susanna Melvin Pvt VT
Thomas: b 1730/1 d 11-12-1814 m Rebecca Derby Pvt VT
Thomas: b 1745 d 6-9-1829 m — Bosworth Pvt VT
Wm.: b 4-9-1759 d 1799 m Abigail Farrington SrgnMte MA
Wm.: b 12-26-1755 d 1-22-1846 m Sarah Barker Pvt RI

LAWYER,
Abraham: b 6-19-1759 d 1-20-1825 m Eve Dietz Cpl NY
Abraham L.: b 9-3-1758 d 9-20-1839 m Catharine Reddick Pvt NY
David: b 1- -1760 d 8-13-1835 m Catharine Sternbergh Sgt NY
Jacob F.: b 10-4-1723 d 11-9-1803 m Elizabeth Sternbergh Pvt NY
Jacob S.: b 8-13-1748 d 2-3-1827 m Anna Eva Bergh Ens NY
Johannes: b 7-8-1746 d 6-25-1800 m Anna (Bouck)Lawyer Pvt NY
Johannes L.: b 9-4-1748 d 12-1-1840 m Eva Steenberg Pvt NY
John Adam: b c. 1750-5 d 1799 m Eva Margrette Conrad Lt PA
Lawrence: b 10-16-1758 d 8-23-1848 m Elizabeth Lawyer Sgt NY ★
Lawrence: b 11-26-1727 d 9-9-1810 m Elizabeth Berg Pvt NY
Peter: b 12-15-1761 d 1836 m Elizabeth Heiney Pvt PA

LAY,
Abraham, Sr.: b c. 1700 d 1784 m Sarah Grimes PS VA
Asa: b 1749 d 2-23-1814 m Sarah Wolcott Capt CT
John, Sr.: b 12-29-1737 d 1-8-1813 m Anna Sill Cpl CT
John, Jr.: b 11-23-1764 d 1841 m Rhoda Watrous Pvt CT
John, 2d: b 9-13-1714 d 4-3-1792 m Hannah Lee PS CS CT
Lee: b 1-1-1745 d 2-13-1813 m Louise Griswold Capt RI CT
Peter: b 3-6-1743/4 d 5-12-1802 m Hepzibah Peck CS CT
Reuben: b 9-10-1751 d 1835 m Elizabeth — Pvt NY
Simeon: b 12-10-1748 d 8-10-1806 m Hetty Dennison Capt CT
Thomas: b 1763 d 7-15-1846 m Polly Lawrence Pvt NC ★

LAYFIELD,
Josiah: b 1758 d p. 4-19-1855 m — Cowhorn Pvt GA

LAYMAN, (includes LAMONT, LAMAN & LAMENT)
Cornelius: b 1755 d 6-1-1842 m Zilla Carmer Pvt NY
George: b 1760 d 6- -1854 m Barbara Baumgardner Pvt VA

LAZARUS,
Leonard: b 10-1-1760 d 10-20-1846 m Mary Magdalena Krumerine Pvt PA
Marks: b 2-22-1756 d 11-1-1835 m Rachel Doris SgtMaj SC ★

LAZEAR,
Cornelius: b c. 1762 d 8-5-1826 m Catherine Lobdell Sol NY

LAZELL, (includes LAZELLE)
Calvin: b 1766 d 1831 m Sarah Stocking Pvt MA
Daniel: b 1734 d 1776 m Huldah Leach Pvt MA
Edmund: b 1750 d 1840 m Mary Ford Pvt MA
Isaac: b 12-12-1725 d 1796 m Bethia Alger Pvt MA
Joshua: b 9-21-1760 d 3-21-1851 m Susannah Pratt Sgt MA
Joshua: b 9-6-1753 d 12-3-1832 m Levina Cook Pvt MA W★
Sylvanus: b 5-17-1752 d 1827 m Abigail Robinson Pvt MA
Wm.: b 4-20-1732 d p. 1790 m Eunice Davenport PS VT

LAZENBY,
Elias: b 3-18-1752 d 7-31-1819 m Martha Jones Ens MD
John: b c. 1750 d p. 10-22-1787 m Deborah — PS MD
Joshua: b 1759 d 9-2-1840 m Keziah Belt Pvt MD
Robert: b 1750 d a. 1835 m Margery Ridgway Pvt PS MD
Thomas: b 1755 d 4-5-1840 m Sarah Ridgeway Sol MD

LEA,
Francis Wainwright: b 1741 d 3-1-1815 m Mary Sanders PS Pvt VA
Gabriel: b 3-23-1758 d 7-23-1834 m Elizabeth Ashurn Sol PS NC
George: b 1760 d p. 1786 m Jane Douglas Pvt NC
James, Sr.: b 3-26-1723/4 d 10-2-1798 m Margaret Marshall CS DE
James, Sr.: b 1718 d 6-2-1788 m Annie Tolbert Sol NC
Major: b 1742 d p. 7-25-1837 m (1)Elizabeth Herndon (2)Sally Farley Lt NC ★
Mary Sanders: b 1748 d 9-19-1821 m Francis Wainwright Lea PS VA
Wm.: b c. 1740 d 1794 m Nancy — Pvt GA
Wm.: b 1733 d 1802 m Susannah Pike Pvt NC

LEACH, (includes LEACHE, LEECH & LEITCH)
Abisha: b 1739 d 1-31-1817 m Patience Woods Pvt PS MA
Abner: b 5-4-1750 d 2-9-1846 m Mary Hull Pvt NJ ★
Andrew: b c. 1750 d 10-1-1776 m Margaret Augustina Brice Maj VA
Andrew Silas: b — d 1814 m Mary Pilcher Pvt VA W★
Benjamin: b c. 1744 d p. 1825 m (1)Mary Keith (2)Anne Short Pvt MA
Benjamin 2nd: b 12-16-1750 d 12-20-1838 m (1)Elizabeth Sample (2)Sarah Knowlton (3)Elizabeth Bean Pvt Slr MA
Benjamin, Sr.: b 1735 d 4- -1776 m Mary Rogers Pvt NH
Benjamin, Jr.: b 11-26-1760 d 2- -1840 m Abigail Harriman Pvt NH
Caleb: b 6-12-1748 d 1845 m (1)Experience Strong (2)Sarah Fowler Pvt CT
Caleb: b 1759 d 11-14-1783 m Mary Adams Pvt MA
Daniel: b 12-9-1735 d 4-19-1800 m Bethia Keith Capt MA
David: b 1740 d 6-2-1824 m Prudence Maclehanne Capt SC
Ebenezer: b 1756 d p. 1817 m Lettice Ferguson Drm Cpl CT
Elisha: b 6-22-1754 d 11-12-1784 m Lucy Cady Cpl CT
Ephraim, Jr.: b 3-24-1751 d 9-30-1843 m Phebe Coombs Pvt CT
Ephraim: b 1761 d 2-28-1840 m Chloe Shattuck Pvt MA
George: b 8-1-1756 d 2-20-1838 m Nancy Ann Bigbee Pvt VA ★
Giles: b 12-27-1749 d 1780 m Deborah Jackson Pvt MA

Hezekiah: b 1740 d 1823 m Sarah Bartholomew Pvt CT
Ichabod: b 7-25-1735 d 11-3-1807 m Penelope Standish Cobb Pvt MA
Isaac: b 1737 d p. 1802 m Jerusha Leach PS NH
Isaac: b 3-12-1754 d 6-26-1834 m Sarah Holcombe PS PA
Jabez: b c. 1750 d 1778-90 m Sarah Chilson Pvt CT
James, Sr.: b 4-28-1759 d 8-2-1835 m Sybel Cady Pvt CT
James: b 8-2-1737 d 12-29-1799 m Hazadiah Keith Pvt MA
James: b c. 1745 d 12- -1823 m Jane Reynolds Pvt PA
Jedediah: b 1754 d 4-12-1823 m Phebe Kasson Pvt CT
Jedediah: b c. 1742 d 3-8-1813 m Phoebe Keith Pvt MA
Jeremiah: b 8-29-1749 d 7-17-1812 m Eunice Hughes Cpl CT
John: b 11-8-1760 d 1845 m Mary Simpson Pvt MA
John: b 4-19-1757 d 2- -1847 m Ruth Riggs Pvt MA ★
John: b 10- -1725 d 2-27-1807 m Betty Eddy Pvt MA
John: b 8-10-1735 d 6-27-1811 m (1)Martha Wanzer (2)Hannah Page Pvt NY
John, Sr.: b 1724 d 6-10-1789 m Sarah Coffin PS MA
John, Jr.: b 3-10-1752 d 1805 m Elizabeth Bacon SeaCap Pvtr
John: b c. 1735 d 2-26-1779 m Jean — Pvt PA
Jonathan: b 7-26-1742 d a. 9-2-1794 m Experience Hartwell Sgt MA
Jonathan: b 11-20-1741 d 12-26-1829 m (1)Abigail Leach (2)Anne Williams Pvt MA
Joseph: b 4-15-1743 d 3-30-1819 m (1)Jerusha Dodge (2)Hannah (Driver) Perry SeaCap MA
Joseph: b c. 1747 d 8-5-1820 , Elizabeth Burnham Sgt MA ★
Joseph: b 2-2-1735 d 2-22-1809 m Abigail Stickney Sgt NS NH
Joshua: b 5-10-1756 d 6-6-1845 m Priscilla Wilkinson Sgt MD W ★
Lemuel: b 10-15-1745 d 9-18-1825 m Rebecca Washburn Ens MA
Lewis: b 1763 d 8-30-1821 m — Cpl CT ★
Libeus: b 1762 d 10-19-1816 m Margaret Starr Pvt MA
Mark: b 11-29-1742 d 1-23-1822 m Margaret Jackson Pvt MA ★
Micah: b 3-13-1757 d 1840 m Lucy Pratt Pvt MA
Nathan: b 1746 d 2-1-1826 m Deborah (Leach) Pvt MA
Nathan: b 3-28-1733 d 2-11-1813 m Anne Herrick PS MA
Nathaniel: b 10-25-1741 d 9-29-1776 m Deborah Waite NCdr MA
Oliver: b 1-25-1759 d 10-10-1832 m Sarah Sarle Sgt RI ★
Samuel: b 1720 d 1775 m (1)Lydia Hatch (2)Mary (Marcy) Simpson (3)Rebecca Harris Pvt MA
Samuel: b 12- -1756 d 11-21-1844 m (1)Elizabeth Wright (2)Anna Horn (3)Olive Stevens Pvt MA NH ★
Silas: b 1748 d 1844 m Mrs Alice (Howard) Leach Pvt MA ★
Simeon: b 1734 d 1777 m Elizabeth Curtis Capt MA
Stephen: b 3- -1726 d 9-25-1807 m (1)Lydia Flora — (2)Sara Hooper Lt RI
Thomas, Jr.: b 5-10-1760 d 4-11-1828 m Ann Bradley Drm CT
Thomas: b c. 1747 d p. 1790 m Elizabeth Riggs PS MD
Thomas: b 1764 d 1848 m (2)Sarah Owens Pvt VA ★
Valentine: b 1-7-1755 d 9-20-1821 m Molly Furrow Sgt VA
Wm., Sr.: b 1718 d p. 8-27-1779 m Martha — PS MD
Wm.: b 1750 d 1830 m — Wolfe Pvt PA
Zephaniah: b 12-17-1739 d 6-21-1819 m Sarah Britton PS NH

LEACOCK,
John: b 12-21-1729 d 11-16-1802 m Martha Ogilby PS PA

LEADBETTER, (includes LEDBETTER)
Drury: b c. 1743 d p. 1801 m Winifred Lanier Col CS PS NC
Drury: b 11-24-1734 d 11- -1789 m Susanna — Pvt VA
Henry: b c. 1717 d a. 1-15-1785 m Edie Clark PS NC
Increase, Sr.: b 4-5-1724 d 7-13-1800 m Katherine Babcock PS MA
Increase, Jr.: b 10-29-1749 d 1-25-1842 m Elizabeth McCordy Calderwood Mrnr MA
Increase: b 3-3-1738 d 4-28-1802 m Sarah Harrington Pvt MA
John: b 9-5-1764 d 11-16-1859 m (1)Mercy Brown (2)Lucy Poole PS MA
Rowland: b 1764 d p. 9-2-1839 m Sara Vaughan Pvt NC

LEADENHAM,
Edward: b 1742 d 8-21-1821 m Nancy — Sol MD

LEADER,
Frederick: b 1-31-1760 d 4-29-1844 m Susanna Schreiten Pvt PA ★
George: b 10-2-1753 d 8-11-1845 m Elizabeth Rupert Pvt PA ★

LEAKE, (includes LEAK & LEEK)
Amos: b 1747 d 1822 m Anne White Pvt NJ
Benjamin: bpt 5-11-1707 d 6-25-1798 m Charity Alexander PS NY
David: bpt 5-11-1740 d p. 1779 m Mary Conkling PS NY
Elisha: b c. 1739 d 10-19-1806 m (1)Joyce Thompson (2)Frances Curd Capt PS VA
John: b c. 1739 d 5-18-1790 m Martha Rose Capt RO NJ
Josiah: b 1730 d p. 9-21-1795 m (1)Ann Fenton (2)Ann Minter (3)Anne Foster Capt VA
Mask: b 1735 d 9-1-1813 m Patience Morris PS Capt VA
Nathan: b 1729 d 12-24-1790 m (1) — Brick (2)Hannah Fithian CS NJ
Nicholas: b 9-29-1749 d 1-31-1824 m Mary Farrell Mar Sgt MD
Phillip, Jr.: b 1742 d 4-10-1786 m Eleanor Miller Ens NY
Samuel: b 1756 d 1806 m Anne Bryant Pvt VA
Samuel: b 1733 d 1790 m Miss — Raner Pvt VA
Thomas: b 5-29-1762 d 10-28-1821 m Rhoda Alling PS CT

LEAKE, contd.
Thomas: b 6-10-1756 d 3-1-1811 m Catherine — Pvt VA
Walter: b 11-30-1761 d 7-3-1844 m Hannah Pickett Pvt PS NC ★
Wm.: b 3- -1734 d 1797 m Judith Mosely PA VA
Wm.: b c. 1760 d 1811 m — Sharp PS VA

LEAMING,
Aaron: b 7-6-1715 d 8-28-1780 m Mary Foreman PS NJ
Christopher: b 10-2-1739 d 1-2-1788 m Sarah Spicer PS NJ
David: b 1757 d 9-9-1829 m Deborah Jennings Pvt CT ★
Jonathan: b 7-5-1738 d p. 1778 m (1)Margaret Stites (2)Judith Hand PS NJ
Judah: b 1753 d 6-7-1829 m Thankful Pvt CT
Persons: b 7-23-1756 d 3-29-1807 m Charlotte Eldredge PS NJ
Thomas (3): b 8-20-1748 d 10-29-1797 m Rebecca Fisher OF PA

LEAR, (includes LARE, LEER, LEHR, LEHRE, LOHR)
Adam: b 12-21-1758 d 10-9-1798 m Rebecca Schwartz Pvt PA
Eve: b — d — m George Piper (Peiffer) PS PA
Henry: b 1718-20 d 8-25-1802 m Anna — Pvt PA
Jacob: b c. 1758 d 1827 m Mary Francis Stutsman Pvt PA
Jacob: b 2-3-1726 d 10-30-1806 m Mary Duff PS PA
John, Jr.: b 1734 d 1780 m Jemima Struman Pvt VA
Joseph: b 1750 d 1-29-1819 m (1)Elizabeth Rand (2)Mercy Woodward Sgt PS NH
Philip: b 2-12-1711 d 11-10-1782 m Anna Christian PS PA
Phillip: b 1745 d 2-19-1837 m (1)Elizabeth — (2)Catherine — Pvt PA
Samuel: b 1762 d 11-20-1842 m Sally Salter Pvt NH ★
Ulrich: b 10- -1747 d 10- -1795 m — Drm PS PA

LEARN,
Jacob: b 7-12-1758 d 8-31-1844 m (1)Elizabeth Ramage (Roming) (2)Elizabeth — Pvt PA

LEARNED, (includes LARNARD & LARNED)
Abijah: b 2-2-1760 d 1-10-1844 m Anna Sellingham Pvt MA ★
Abijah: b 4-26-1729 d 1776 m Anna Wales PS NH
Asa: b 2-17-1750 d 7-31-1813 m Mary Child Pvt MA
Benjamin: b 1-23-1741 d 9-5-1818 m (1)Elizabeth Wilson (2)Margaret Swan PS NH
Bezaleel: b 3-5-1720 d p. 1790 m (1)Jerusha Bond (2)Susanna Bowman Pvt PS MA
Daniel: b 11-16-1743 d 12-29-1797 m Rebekah Wilkinson Lt CT
Ebenezer: b 3-11-1723 d 12-6-1779 m Keziah Leavens Pvt CT
Ebenezer: b 4-18-1728 d 4-1-1801 m (1)Jerusha Baker (2)Eliphal Putnam BGen MA
Edward: b 6-18-1749 d 1792 m Sarah Willard Pvt MA
Elijah: b 11-14-1739 d 9-2-1819 m Rachel Kingsbury Sgt MA
Elisha: b 8-12-1737 d p. 3-15-1779 m Sarah Bemis PS MA
Henry: b 4-13-1745 d 10-27-1807 m (1)Rachel Lowe (2)Sally Merrill Sol CT
Hezekiah: b 10-25-1739 d 1- -1821 m Lydia Perham Pvt MA
Isaac: b 1749 d 10-10-1827 m Elizabeth Winship Sgt MA
Isaac: b 2-5-1760 d 6-19-1827 m (1)Rachel Phillips (2)Mary Austin Matr Bbd MA
Jedediah: b 10-17-1736 d p. 1780 m Mary Grant Sol MA
John: b 6-20-1758 d 12-8-1844 m (1)Martha Wakefield (2)Abigail (Marsh) Wakefield Pvt MA ★
Jonas: b 8-30-1748 d 11-13-1821 m Hannah Titterton Cpl MA ★
Moses: b 2-13-1728 d 4- -1799 m Ruth Hill MM MA
Samuel: b 6-7-1756 d 12- -1833 m Hannah Walker Pvt MA
Samuel Smith: b 5-15-1740 d 8-31-1808 m (1)Sarah Gardner (2)Mary Fisk Pvt MA
Simon: b 8-13-1753 d 11-16-1817 m Ruth Buell Capt MA
Sylvanus: b 5-30-1760 d 5-28-1826 m Martha Davis Sgt MA
Thaddeus: b 10-26-1756 d 1-19-1818 m Abigail Russell Pvt CT
Thomas: b 5-22-1731 d 2-12-1812 m Hannah Brooks Pvt MA
Thomas: b 8-3-1734 d 4-7-1784 m Deborah Brown Pvt MA
Thomas: b 1-5-1762 d 6-15-1848 m Hannah Morris Pvt MA
Wm.: b 4-1-1752 d 2-22-1828 m (1)Mrs Angell (2)Sarah Smith QMGen RI
Wm.: b 4-15-1725 d 5-15-1806 m Elizabeth (Davis) Mayo Maj MA

LEARY,
Cornelius: b c. 1756 d p. 7-2-1784 m Catherine Litzinger PS MD
Cornelius: b 1738 d 1782 m Anne Civil Davis Pvt VA
Wm.: b 12-17-1754 d 12-12-1832 m Harriet (Leary) Lt NJ

LEAS,
John: b 9-1-1754 d 5-20-1847 m Sophia — Pvt PA ★
Leonard: b c. 1757 d 1810 m Lovice Forney Pvt PA

LEASURE, (includes LEASER)
Abraham: b 1763 d 4-4-1849 m Jane Marshall Pvt PA ★
Abraham: b 1713 d 3-15-1803 m Margaret — PS PA
Daniel: b 1758 d 12-9-1830 m Elizabeth Ryan Pvt PA
Frederick: b c. 1738 d 1810 m Catharina (Leaser) Pvt PS PA
John: b 5-13-1760 d 1-17-1845 m Sarah Crow PS 1Sgt PA ★
John: b 5-28-1762 d 12-20-1844 m Jane Culbertson Sol PA

LEATH, (includes LEATHE)
Elijah: b 8-12-1755 d 12-13-1835 m Hepsibah Brooks Pvt MA ★

James: b 1751 d 1792 m (1)Elizabeth Freeman (2)Susannah Barker Sol NC
John: b 1750 d p. 1785 m Mary Ann Addison Cpl VA

LEATHERBURY,
John: b 1744 d a. 12-11-1784 m — 2Lt MD

LEATHERMAN,
Jacob: b c. 1737 d 6-11-1805 m Esther Stauffer Pvt PA
Michael: b 1-9-1761 d 9-23-1811 m Catherine Palmer Pvt PA

LEATHERS,
Abednego: bpt 3-28-1725 d 6-3-1802 m (1)Charity Boody (2)Hannah — Pvt NH
John: b — d a. 9-28-1818 m Ann — CS VA
Robert: b 1735 d 4-13-1814 m Deborah Follett Pvt NH

LEAVELL,
John: b 1757 d 5- -1826 m (1)Margaret Jones (2)Frances Williams Sol SC

LEAVENS, (includes LEVENS)
Benjamin: bpt 9-9-1716 d 7-27-1798 m (1)Elizabeth Cady (2)Dorothy Morris Perrin Pvt MA
Benjamin, Jr.: b 7-2-1763 d 5-26-1851 m Sybil Learned Pvt MA
Charles: b 1747 d 8-4-1822 m Lydia Glover Pvt CT
Darius: b 3-28-1738 d 7-12-1785 m Martha Fairbanks Cpl CT
Elijah: b 8-1-1747 d p. 1790 m Rachel Blood Pvt MA
Henry: b 5-26-1744 d p. 1828 m Elizabeth Dodridge Pvt PA ★
Isaac: b 5-18-1735 d 5-29-1810 m Mehitable — Pvt CT
Jacob: b 10-15-1736 d 1-7-1788 m Elizabeth Haskell Pvt CT
Jedediah, Sr.: b 8-19-1755 d 5-1-1833 m Patience Whittaker Pvt MA
John: b 9-23-1734 d 7- -1799 m Esther Williams MM CT
Joseph: b 2-5-1754 d 1845 m Phoebe Atwill Pvt NY

LEAVENWORTH,
Amos: b 8-9-1753 d 9-2-1828 m Esther Warner Pvt CT
David: b 1737 d 3-25-1820 m (1)Olive Hunt (2)Mary Downs Capt CT
Ebenezer: b 12-29-1734 d 3-18-1778 m Elizabeth Hurd Lt CT
Edmond: b 1725 d 7-17-1785 m Abigail Beardsley Capt CT
Eli: b 12-10-1748 d 1-15-1819 m Sarah Elliott Maj CT
Gideon: b 1751 d 4-19-1816 m (1)Sarah Ward (2)Mary Ann Kasson Hull Capt CT
Gideon: b 10-26-1759 d 10-15-1827 m Loisa Hunt Cmsry FrA
Gideon: b c. 1745 d 1810 m — (2)Sarah Eliot Pvt CT
James: b 7-8-1737 d 5-6-1806 m Jehodah Moss Pvt CT
Jesse: b 11-22-1740 d 12-12-1824 m (1)Catherine (Conkling) Frisbie (2)Eunice Sperry Capt CT
John: b 7-18-1739-41 d 6- -1802 m Abigail Peck Capt CT
Lemuel: b 10-9-1743 d 4-30-1825 m Sybil Parker Pvt VT
Mark: b p. 8-11-1711 d 8-20-1797 m (1)Ruth Peck (2)Sarah Hull PS CT
Morse: b 7-1-1764 d 11-12-1822 m Sarah Benedict Pvt CT
Samuel: b 1751 d 4-12-1807 m Sarah Nettleton Sgt CT

LEAVERTON,
John Foster: b 1755 d 3-1-1837 m Hannah Wilson Pvt MD

LEAVITT,
Andrew: b 1752 d 8-29-1846 m Sarah Hastings Pvt NH
Benjamin: b 10-4-1732 d 3-14-1805 m Esther Towle Pvt NH
Caleb: b 11-29-1730 d 9-10-1810 m (1)Mary Hatch (2)Sarah Beal 1Lt MA
Carr: b 7-2-1751 d 9-20-1825 m Huldah Hobbs Ens NH
David: b 1722 d 1818 m Maria Lewis Vol CT
Edward: b 1757 d 7-27-1831 m (1)Hannah Sias (2)Abigail Peavey Sgt NH
Jacob: b 10-6-1740 d 1-7-1826 m Leah Fearing Lt MA
Jacob, Sr.: b 2-4-1732 d 1-27-1814 m Sylvia Bonney Pvt MA
James: b 12-24-1739 d 1-12-1804 m Elizabeth Rowe Pvt NH
James: b 6-22-1760 d 8-23-1839 m Betsey Batchelder Pvt NH
Jeremiah: b 1743 d 3-29-1816 m (1)Lydia Linscott (2)Hannah McIntire PS ME
John: b 7-16-1724 d 4-9-1798 m Abiah Kent MM CS CT
John: b 10-7-1740 d 7-7-1785 m Elizabeth Lamprey PS CS NH
John, Jr.: b 5-29-1755 d 10- -1815 m Silence Fitch Pvt CT
Jonathan: b 9-9-1743 d 3-19-1819 m Marion Mitchell CS ME
Jonathan: b 1756 d 1-27-1810 m Mrs Mary (Perkins)Wood CaptLt NH
Jonathan: b 1760 d p. 1821 m (2)Elizabeth Hutchins Pvt Fif NH ★
Joseph, Jr.: b 1739 d 4-4-1809 m (1)Sarah Bradbury (2)Nancy Ann Bradbury Sgt MA
Joseph: b 1757 d 1839 m (1)Anna Stevens (2)Hannah Chandler (3)Elsea Caswell Pvt MA
Joseph, Sr.: b 3-21-1722 d 10-21-1804 m Abigail — SgtMaj NH
Joseph, Jr.: b 1751 d 5-7-1801 m (1)Sarah Gilman (2)Eunice Pike Pvt PS NH
Joseph: b 3-22-1699 d 1793 m Mary Wadleight PS NH
Joshua: b 2-2-1732 d 5-13-1825 m (1)Deborah Fearing (2)Sarah Gilbert Pvt MA
Joshua: b c. 1735 d p. 1795 m Elizabeth James PS NH
Josiah Gold: b 6-15-1753 d 9-11-1830 m Sarah Sherwood Sgt CT
Levi: b 7-2-1761 d 3-31-1839 m Sarah Burleigh Pvt NH
Moses: b 7-12-1759 d 10-3-1827 m (1)Ruth Leavitt (2)Mrs Abigail Chellis Sanborn Cpl NH

Nathaniel: b c. 1750 d a. 1810 m Mary Brown Pvt MA
Nathaniel: b 1757 d 2-14-1825 m Mary Elkins Lt NH W★
Peter: b 8-18-1741 d 11-9-1815 m Elizabeth Cram Pvt NH
Samuel, Sr.: b 2-2-1762 d 7-22-1831 m Lydia Wheeler Fif CT
Samuel: b 1732 d 1797 m Sarah Phinney Pvt MA
Simon: b 6-4-1753 d 8-20-1842 m (1)Sarah Krake (2)Mrs Abigail L Cotton Drm NH
Thayer: b 1761 d 1838 m Abigail Snell Pvt MA
Thomas: b 10-15-1744 d 3-20-1830 m Mary Fogg QM NH
Thomas: b 1747 d p. 1792 m Abigail Tuck PS NH
Wadleigh: b 12-18-1763 d 12-8-1853 m Elizabeth (Leavitt) Pvt RI ★
Wm.: b 3-21-1752 d 10-22-1837 m Betsey Hardy Pvt NH ★

LEAYCRAFT,
George: b c. 1740 d 4- -1811 m Elizabeth Arden 1Lt NY
Wm.: b 10-26-1757 d 6-7-1827 m Eleanor Bogert Lt NY

LE BALLISTER, (includes BALLISTER)
Charles: bpt 9-7-1746 d 1815 m Hannah Martin SeaCap MA

LE BARON, (includes LE BARRON)
David: b 4-27-1740 d 2-1-1819 m Martha Chatfield Pvt CT
Francis: b 4-20-1762 d 7-3-1856 m Jane Haskell Pvt MA
Issac: b 9-10-1762 d 3-30-1815 m Lydia Ryan Pvt MA
James: b 12-10-1726 d 10-3-1780 m Hannah Turner Cpl MA
James, Jr.: b 11-30-1759 d 6-9-1856 m Elizabeth Washburn Pvt MA
Joshua: b 10-10-1729 d 3-9-1806 m Grace Bush Pvt MA
Lemuel: b 9-1-1747 d 11-26-1836 m Elizabeth Allen Chp MA
Wm.: b 4-20-1757 d 7-4-1827 m Lurany Bennett Lt MA
Zebulon: b 12-6-1752 d a. 1793 m Elizabeth Lucas Sol MA

LE BAS,
Francois Isaac: b 1754 d c. 1840 m Sarah Jennings Sol FrA

LEBEY,
Andrew: b 10-7-1758 d 7-1-1793 m Mary Judith Hines Sol GA

LEBKICHER,
Michael: b 3-19-1759 d 1-27-1848 m Susan — Pvt PA ★

LEBO, (includes LEBOT)
Henry: b 1752 d 7-4-1828 m Sarah Eoff Pvt PA ★
John Adam: b 10-4-1761 d — m Catharine — Mil PA

LE BON, (or LABOON)
Pierre: b 1-6-1745 d 12-12-1799 m Anne Gervais FrN

LE BOSQUET,
John: b 12-20-1737 d 2-8-1803 m Sarah Brooks Pvt MA

LE BRETON D'ORGENOY,
Francois Joseph: bpt 10-10-1750 d 9-21-1814 m Anna Margarite Harang Sol LA

LE BRETT,
Charles: b 1756 d 1835 m Sally — Pvt CT ★

LECHLER,
John: b c. 1752 d p. 8-19-1806 m — Cpl PA

LECHNER,
Nicholas: b 2-22-1759 d p. 8-8-1836 m Maria Elizabeth Mueller Pvt PA

LECKY,
John: b 1744 d 7-18-1821 m Mary Wilson Pvt PA

LE CLERE,
Charles: b 9-10-1767 d a. 5-14-1821 m Jane Metayer Sol FrA

LECOMPTE, (or LE COMPTE)
Charles: b 1749 d 1822 m Elizabeth (Coons) Waite Sol VA
John: b — d — m Mary — 2Lt MD
John, Sr.: b c. 1721 d p. 3-25-1790 m Sarah Peterkin PS MD
John, Jr.: b 1745 d 5-5-1795 m Mary — Ens MD
Moses: b 10- -1748 d 10-22-1800 m (1)Eliz Edmonson (2)Elizabeth Woodward Lt MD
Moses: b c. 1755 d p. 1800 m Elizabeth Wheeler 1Lt MD

LE CONTE,
John Eatton: b 9-2-1739 d 1-11-1822 m Jane Sloane PS GA

LE CRONE,
John Leonard: b 12-17-1726 d 2-18-1810 m Barbara — Pvt PA

LEDERER, (or LATHERS)
Johan: b 9-21-1759 d 6-22-1812 m Marie Vander Werken Cpl NY W★

LEDGERWOOD,
James: b 1753 d p. 12-25-1806 m (1)Elizabeth McCoun (2)Jane — Pvt VA KY

LEDLIE,
James: b 1751 d 1809 m Isabel Cannon Pvt PA
Wm.: b 1746/7 d 1-5-1835 m Mary Lusk Andrews PS Lt PA

LEDYARD,
Benjamin: b 3-5-1753 d 11-9-1803 m ( )Catherine Forman (2)Anne Rhea Maj NY
Ebenezer: b 1736 d 9-29-1811 m Mary Latham Cmsry Col CT NY
Isaac: b 11-5-1754 d 8-28-1803 m Ann MacArthur Dr NY
Mary: b 9-3-1758 d 5-3-1806 m Jonathan Forman PS CT
Robert: b 1755 d 5-6-1835 m Mary Cady Pvt MA ★
Youngs: b 6-24-1751 d 9-6-1781 m Bridget Billings Capt CT

LEE,
Abiather: b 1750 d 11-13-1837 m Elizabeth Mason Pvt MA
Abijah: b 8-19/20-1764 d 7-30-1806 m Anna Fellows Pvt MA
Abner: b 1760 d 10-7-1852 m (1)Franky McFarland (2)Sally Miller Pvt VA
Agnes Dickinson: b 3-21-1745 d 7-2-1830 m Samuel Lee PS CT
Alexander: b — d p. 9-2-1805 m Nancy Anny Ens PA
Amos: b 6-5-1760 d 10-2-1849 m Hannah Bowen Pvt MA
Andrew: b 5-7-1745 d 8-25-1832 m Eunice Hall Chp CT
Andrew: b 1739 d 1821 m Priscilla Espy Stewart Capt PA
Andrew: b 1-25-1758 d 7-16-1846 m Elizabeth Walton Pvt GA SC
Andrew: b c. 1745 d 1- -1796 m Nancy Ann Wilson Pvt PS SC
Ann: b 8-4-1750 d 8-5-1797 m William Lee PS SC
Benjamin, Sr.: b 4-4-1712 d 4- -1777 m Mary Ely CS CT
Benjamin2d: b 2-27-1740 d 7-2-1826 m Mary Door MM CT
Benjamin: b 1-5-1718 d 5-4-1796 m (1)Hannah Morse (2)Esther Baker (3)Mehitable Jenkins Capt CS MA
Benjamin: b 1753 d 3-7-1790 m Maria Lewhart Pvt NY
Cato: b 1757 d 9-26-1832 m Nancy Holland Pvt NC
Charles: b c. 1723 d 3-19-1792 m Joannah Morgan LCol VA
Charles: b 3-4-1744 d 3- -1785 m Sarah Hull Capt PS VA
Charles: b c. 1720 d 1799 m Ann Dabbs PS VA
Daniel: b 1-20-1753 d 7-1-1806 m Sarah Whittaker Sgt CT
Daniel: b 1740 d 4-5-1825 m (2)Patience Calendar Capt MA ★
Daniel, Sr.: b 9-29-1732 d 9-12-1792 m Agnes Campbell Pvt MA
Daniel, Jr.: b 9-20-1762 d 9-15-1841 m (1)Jerusha Page (2)Mrs Hannah (Butts)Carpenter Pvt MA
David: b 1764 d 1840 m Ezubah — Pvt CT ★
David: b 12-16-1763 d 6-4-1842 m Elizabeth Hayes Sol CT
David: b 1-17-1739 d p. 1783 m Tabitha — Pvt MA
David: b c. 1745-50 d — m Martha Blackman Sol NC
David: b 10-12-1753 d 12-13-1821 m (1)Ann McAllister (2)Elizabeth Crafts Sol SC
David: b 1740 d p. 3-17-1809 m Margaret Perrine PS VA
David: b 1-27-1766 d 1-10-1852 m Mary Osborn Pvt VA KY
Drury: b 8-31-1744 d 8-17-1830 m Nancy — Pvt SC
Dudley: b 5-5-1759 d 4-10-1815 m Margaret Fetters Pvt MD
Ebenezer, Sr.: b 10-29-1727 d 5-9-1811 m Abigail Bull Dr CT
Ebenezer, Jr.: b 1-7-1757 d 10-29-1837 m (1)Martha Parsons (2)Anna Hyde Sgt CT
Eber: b 1760 d 5-31-1855 m Huldah Bishop Pvt CT
Eber: b 5-27-1746 d 2-4-1813 m Bertha Jenkins Pvt MA
Elias: b 7-26-1723 d 2-25-1795 m (1)Sarah Royce (2)Kezia — Sgt CT
Elijah: b 1-21-1742 d 5-3-1811 m Silence Washburn Sgt CT
Elijah: b 1751 d 6-23-1829 m (1)Sarah Conklin (2)Mary (Brown) Palmer (3)Letitia Brown (4)Sophia Williamson Cpl NY
Elisha: b 3-3-1740 d 10-15-1815 m Abigail Murdock Capt CT
Elliott: b c. 1760 d p. 4-14-1828 m Lucy — Sol SC
Elon: b 5-16-1724 d 5-10-1806 m Elizabeth Hotchkiss Pvt CT
Ezra: b 1-21-1749 d 10-29-1821 m Deborah Mather BgdQM CT
Ezra: b 5-9-1743 d 3-12-1820 m Sarah Hackley Lt NY
Francis: b 1749 d 5- -1815 m (1)Jane Alexander (3)Margaretta Cloyd (4)Elizabeth Cloyd Pvt VA
Francis: b c. 1735 d c. 1794 m Elizabeth Higginson Asst Cmsry VA
George: b 1760 d 1831 m Mary W Zimmerman Pvt DE
Gershom: b c. 1735 d 1821 m Rebecca Hunt PM CS NJ
Gideon: b 3-11-1811 m Lucy Ward Pvt MA
Greenberry: b c. 1750 d 1784 m Elizabeth Few Col CS PS GA
Henry: b c. 1745 d 1806 m Mary Elizabeth Pipkin Sol NC
Henry: b 4-2-1757 d 10-24-1845 m Mrs Mary (Young) Fox LCol VA
Henry, Sr.: b 1729 d 1787 m Lucy Grimes PS VA
Henry, Jr.: b 1-15-1777 d 3-25-1818 m (1)Matilda Lee (2)Anne Hill Carter MajCmdt VA
Hezekiah: b 1736 d 1-15-1777 m Lydia Thompson Pvt CT
Isaac: b 1-17-1716 d 12-13-1802 m (1)Tabitha Norton (2)Elizabeth Grant (3)Mary (Johnson) Hall Col CT
Issac 3rd: b 9-29-1752 d 4-11-1828 m Abigail Goodrich Sol CT
Isaac: b 1752 d 1-5-1828 m Mary Boone PS PA
Isaac: b 12-12-1738 d 3-14-1806 m Rachel Hooper NCdr MA
James: b 9-30-1742 d 2-14-1823 m Lucy (Boras)Gridley PS CT
James: b 5-9-1743 d p. 1810 m Kezia Fuller Pvt MA
James: b 1760 d 1844 m Celia Rogers Pvt NC ★
James: b c. 1754 d 7- -1827 m Elizabeth — PS NC
James: b 1760 d 1817 m Elizabeth Jane Jones Sgt PA ★
James: b 1748 d 1810 m Mary Lewis Pvt SC
James: b 1750 d p. 1820 m Mary Kenny Pvt VA ★
Jared: b 1712 d 1780 m Rhoda Judd CS CT
Jedediah: b 4-7-1755 d 10-24-1824 m (1)Elizabeth Wood (2)Mary Perry (3)Mary Denison Holmes Pvt CT

LEE, contd.
Jeptha: b 3-1-1764 d 3-11-1855 m Esther Franklin Pvt NY
Jesse: b c. 1740 d 8- -1816 m Miriam Baggett Sol NC
Jesse: b 12-21-1740 d 10-29-1831 m Susannah Johnson Pvt NC
John: b 1749 d 2-22-1813 m Olive Towner Pvt CT
John: b 1763 d 8-30-1803 m Martha Howlett Pvt MD
John: b 2-12-1716 d 8-24-1789 m Joanna Raymond Col PS MA
John, Sr.: b 9-20-1726 d 3-12-1816 m Sarah Perine Pvt NY
John, Jr.: b 10-18-1753 d 9-22-1835 m Esther Horton Pvt NY ★
John: b 8-25-1755 d 10-15-1836 m Morning Altman Pvt NC
John: b c. 1755 d c. 1835 m — Sol NC
John: b 1734 d 10-30-1816 m Margaret Holliday Pvt PA
John: b c. 1757 d 1817 m — Cpl SC
John: b 4-19-1733 d 1789 m Lucy Graves Sgt VT
John: b 1730 d 5-19-1818 m Sally (Lee) Capt VA
John: b c. 1738 d 1803 m Elizabeth Bell Maj VA
John: b 1750 d 2- -1820 m — Capt PS VA
John: b 1763 d 1824 m Catherine Chambers Pvt VA
John: b c. 1745 d 1788 m Elizabeth Thompson Pvt VA
John: b 1738 d p. 4-24-1777 m Susanna Smith PS VA
Jonathan: b 10-26-1745 d 9-1-1814 m Mabel Little Dr CT
Jonathan: b 7-15-1752 d 3-4-1812 m Elizabeth Lee Pvt MA
Jonathan: b 1-26-1759 d 4-17-1833 m (1)Sallie Heywood (2)Sybil Butterfield Pvt MA
Joseph: b 4-22-1762 d 8-24-1837 m Eleanor Davidson Pvt PA NJ ★
Joseph: b 1713 d a. 4-17-1790 m (1)Sarah — (2)Phebe — Pvt PS NY
Joseph: b 3-1-1765 d 3-1-1855 m Esther Franklin Pvt NY
Joseph: b 11-24-1705 d 8-29-1779 m Mary Allen PS NY
Joseph: b 8-12-1730 d 7-4-1800 m Ruth Weatherhead Cpl RI
Joseph: b 11-11-1742 d 11-15-1814 m (1)Mary Hay Thorne (2)Anges Harper PS SC
Joshua: b 1758 d p. 1840 m — Pvt GA ★
Joshua: b 1764 d 1846 m Fanny King Pvt Cav CL
Lemuel: b 5-3-1760 d 7-25-1826 m Sally Sterling Pvt CT
Milo: b 6-27-1760 d 4-29-1829 m Ruth Camp PS CT
Moses: b 5-15-1762 d 12-14-1804 m Electa Guilford Pvt Fif MA
Nancy Ann Wilson: b 1758 d p. 1815 m (1)Andrew Lee (2)Nicholas Vaughan PS SC
Nathaniel: b c. 1737 d p. 1795 m Sarah Hubbell (Hubbard) Pvt MA
Nathaniel, Jr.: b c. 1756 d 1827 m Sarah — Sol VA
Noah: b 10-15-1745 d 5-5-1840 m Dorcas Bird Col VT
Owen: b 1-11-1761 d 6-21-1817 m Betsy Wright Pvt NC
Parker Hall: b 1- -1759 d 5-6-1829 m Elisabeth Dallam Lt MD
Paul: b 9-5-1757 d 4-6-1814 m Eunice Lindsley Pvt NJ W★
Peter: b c. 1759 d 3- -1823 m Rebekah Taylor Pvt VA
Peter Perrine: b 3-10-1756 d 11-10-1848 m Ruth Huntington Gard Pvt NJ
Philip: b 12-20-1759 d 8- -1836 m (1)Eunice Washburn (2)Sally Graham Pvt MA ★
Philip: b 3-21-1761 d 1825 m Susannah Byram Pvt PS NJ
Randolph: b 1757 d 12-26-1822 m Jane Carson Pvt VA ★
Richard: b 5-2-1758 d 2-12-1838 m Sarah Marsh Pvt NJ ★
Richard: b c. 1764 d p. 1830 m Nancy Hogan Pvt NC
Richard: b 1752 d p. 1836 m Frances Harrison Pvt VA
Richard: b c. 1726 d c. 1795 m Sally Poythress PS VA
Richard Evers: b a. 1754 d 6-8-1814 m Letty Kelly PS VA
Richard Henry: b 1-20-1732 d 6-19-1794 m (1)Anne Aylett (2)Mrs Anne (Gaskins) Pinkard SDI VA
Samuel: b 9-27-1749 d 9-3-1829 m Elizabeth Brown Capt CT
Samuel: b 10-1-1742 d 5-31-1819 m Agnes Kickinson Lt PS CT
Samuel: b 1744 d 12-7-1805 m Sarah Marsh Dr CT
Samuel: b 10-2-1757 d 3-31-1803 m Sarah Burnett Pvt CT
Samuel: b 7-25-1737 d 4-11-1811 m Hannah Briggs Pvt MA
Samuel: b 3-8-1767 d 10-17-1839 m (1)Mehitable Jinkins (2)Mary Mixter Pvt MA
Samuel: b 1759 d 1841 m (1)Abigal Smith (2)Mary Ann Peters Pvt NJ
Samuel: b 1753 d p. 1798 m Susannah Bonner Pvt VA
Seth: b 3-31-1736 d 2-17-1803 m (1)Susanna (2)Joanna Johnson Pvt CT
Simon: b 1752 d 4-4-1829 m Mary — Capt NC ★
Solomon: b 3-29-1747 d 9-20-1811 m Anne Brewster Tms CT
Stephen: b 1-21-1750 d 11-7-1807 m Dorothea(Smiser)Alison Lt PS SC
Steven: b 1735 d 7-1-1779 m (1)Matha Pollock (2)Mary Fagan PS NC
Thomas: b 12-17-1717 d 1-11-1806 m Ezbal Sedgwick PS CT
Thomas: bpt 5-17-1728 d 1-7-1805 m Dinah Perrine Pvt NJ
Thomas: b 5-15-1756 d 6-8-1847 m Anne Bishop Pvt NJ ★
Thomas: b 11-15-1739 d 1-22-1814 m Waty Shearman Capt NY
Thomas: b 12-3-1729 d 7-2-1816 m (1)Mary Griffin (2)Mary Bryan Capt NC
Thomas: b 1749 d 1843 m (1)Hannah Murphy (2)Sarag Smith Pvt PS SC
Thomas: b 12-5-1734 d 10-8-1811 m Sarah Vary Col VT
Thomas Ludwell: b 12-31-1730 d 4-13-1778 m Mary Aylett PS VA
Thomas Sim: b 10-29-1745 d 11-9-1819 m Mary Digges PS MD
Timothy: b 11-26-1740 d 10-1-1813 m (1)Lucy Camp (2)Esther Stanley Pvt CT
Timothy: b 1748 d p. 1785 m Mary Walpole Sgt MA
Westbrook: b 12-4-1759 d 3-4-1840 m Seney Gainey Pvt NC
Wm.: b 1741 d 4-29-1795 m Eunice Hotchkiss Pvt CT

Wm.: b 4-27-1710 d 1-6-1791 m Sarah Bates Pvt CT
Wm.: b 1745 d 12-12-1828 m Elizabeth Gilbert Drm CT
Wm., Sr.: b 2-24-1728 d 5- -1794 m Elizabth Chilchase 2Lt MA
Wm.: b c. 1740 d p. 1790 m (1)Sarah Wadsworth (2)Sarah Baldwin Capt CS NH
Wm.: b 1-24-1763 d 12-5-1839 m Abigail Bryam Pvt NJ ★
Wm.: b 15-1764 d 1826 m Elizabeth — Sol NC
Wm.: b c. 1723 d p. 4-18-1801 m Hannah Saunders Maj PA
Wm.: b 1- -1747 d 1-6-1828 m Mary Barbara Shoemaker Sgt Maj PA
Wm.: b 1750 d 3-1-1807 m (1)Eliza Ann Smith (2)Elenor Greenup Cpl PA
Wm.: b 8-15-1745 d 8-15-1803 m (1)Susannah Chaffings (2)Sarah McMullen Capt SC
Wm.: b 6-21-1747 d 11-29-1803 m Ann Theus Capt PS SC
Wm.: b 1751 d p. 1791 m Jane Payne Capt VA
Wm.: b 1-24-1754 d 2-12-1835 m Drusilla Staples Sgt VA
Wm.: b 1734 d 9- -1803 m Ava Noel Pvt VA
Wm.: b c. 1735-40 d a. 6-5-1810 m (2)Sarah — Pvt VA
Wm.: b 1753 d a. 1806 m Nancy McCallister Pvt VA
Wm.: b 8-31-1739 d 6-27-1795 m Hannah Philippa Ludwell PS VA
Wm.: b c. 1730 d c. 1795 m — Cmsry VA
Wm.: b c. 1749 d 1785 m Susannah Dawson PS VA
Wm. H: b 2-10-1761 d 3-31-1829 m Phebe Davis Fif CT W★
Wm. Raymond: b 7-30-1745 d 10-26-1824 m Mary Sweet Lemmon Col MA
Zachariah: b 1765 d 1838-54 m Jane Wright Pvt VA ★
Zebulon: b 5-16-1758 d 8-9-1848 m Margaret Cortwright Pvt CT
Zebulon: b 9-23-1742 d 1-31-1833 m Mary Taylor Pvt VT

LEEDOM,
Richard: b 11-9-1739 d 7-5-1825 m Sarah Twining Cawley Pvt PS PA
Thomas: b 9-23-1754 d 1-18-1840 m (1)Mary Smith ( )Mrs Hannah Humphrey Sgt PA ★

LEEDS,
Daniel: b 12-16-1760 d 4-1-1851 m Ann — Pvt NJ
Felix: b c. 1752 d 1797 m Sarah Doughty Pvt NJ
Jeremiah: b 3-4-1754 d 10- -1838 m (1)Judith Steelman (2)Millicent Steelman Ingersoll Lt NJ
John: b 4-10-1738 d 7-22-1824 m Jersha Packard Pvt MA
Nathen: bpt 3-2-1753 d 7-21-1809 m Elizabeth Tilstone SgtMaj MA W★
Samuel, Sr.: b 11-15-1709 d 3-18-1778 m Thankful Bird Pvt MA
Samuel, Jr.: b 6-9-1735 d 1778 m Ann Atkins Pvt MA
Thomas: b 9-17-1747 d 5-26-1796 m Mary Haley Cpl CT
Wm.: b 5-24-1738 d 2-7-1828 m Mary Osborn PS NJ

LEEDY,
Abraham: b 1753 d 1-5-1835 m Catherine Long Pvt Grd MD
Samuel: b c. 1745 d 1815 m Catherine Weldner Sol PA

LEEF,
John: b — d 1836 m — PS MD

LEEMAN, (includes FLEEMAN)
Daniel: b 6-9-1755 d 5-23-1812 m Martha Gray Cpl MA
Nathaniel: b 1748 d 5-26-1792 m Elizabeth Blackledge Sgt MA
Thomas: b 1749 d 1-14-1835 m — Pvt VA ★

LEEPER,
Allen: b 1720 d 10-29-1788 m Elizabeth Cummings Pvt PA
Charles: b a. 1755 d p. 1800 m Margaret Miller Pvt PS PA
James: b c. 1755 d 4- -1781 m Susannah Drake Capt NC
James: b 1749 d 1799 m Helen Robertson Lt NC
James: b 9- -1761 d 1-7-1842 m Margaret Henry Pvt NC ★
James: b 2-20-1743 d 4-11-1811 m Mary Blair Sol PA
James: b 1748 d 3-13-1814 m Nancy McCleary Pvt PA
Matthew: b — d 10-21-1801 m Amytiah — PS NC
Samuel: b c. 1745-50 d 8- -1805 m Margaret Clark Lt PA
Wm.: b 6-4-1748 d 11-5-1807 m Matilda Graham Pvt PA

LEET, (includes LEETE)
Absalom: b 9-3-1747 d 10-27-1800 m Jane Dudley Pvt CT
Allen: b 10-13-1728 d 1783 m (1)Rachel Morgan (2)Abigail Kelley Sgt CT
Amos: b 4-25-1758 d 4-15-1808 m Hannah Ward Pvt CT
Asa: b 7-21-1726 d 1-9-1799 m Hannah Raynor PS NH
Daniel: b 4-17-1742 d 2-13-1824 m Charity Norton Pvt CT
Daniel: b 11-6-1748 d 6-18-1830 m Wilhelmina (Ballou) Carson BgdMaj QM VA
Elijah: b 12-21-1753 d 4-19-1825 m Leah Hill Pvt CT
Gideon, Jr.: b 5-5-1731 d p. 1790 m Ann Parmelee Ens CT
Isaac, Sr.: b 1726 d 5-5-1800 m Rebecca Vaughan CS PA
Isaac, Jr.: b 3-13-1753 d 12-15-1839 m Nancy Sutton Pvt PA
Pelatiah: b 3-7-1713 d 5-18-1783 m Lydia Crittenden PS CT
Simeon: b 4-14-1753 d 6-19-1781 m Zuriah Norton Pvt CT
Solomon, Sr.: b 9- -1722 d 9-6-1803 m Tripporah Stone Pvt CT
Solomon, Jr.: b 12-3-1746 d 1822 m Hannah Norton Pvt CT
Wm.: b 8-4-1758 d 4-8-1833 m Susan Laycock Capt PA

LE FEVRE, (includes LA FEVER, LE FAVOUR, LE FEVER, LE VIER, LEFAVOUR & LEFEVER)
Adam: b 2-27-1745 d 2-15-1814 m Elizabeth Paules Pvt PA

Amos: b 10-20-1745 d 4-7-1795 m Anna Delleware Sgt MA
Andries: b 3-18-1722 d 5-25-1812 m Rachel Du Bois PS NY
Daniel: b 11-8-1725 d 2-10-1800 m Catherine Cantine PS NY
Daniel: b c. 1750 d 1806-14 m Elizabeth — Pvt PA
George: b 2-18-1739 d 8-20-1820 m Anna Barbara Slaymaker 3Lt PA
Isaac: b 3-24-1753 d 1790 m Marie (Le Fevre) PS NY
Jacob: b 2-24-1753 d 1-8-1827 m (1)Susanna — (2)Catherine Peterman Sol PA
John: bpt 10-7-1753 d p. 1804 m (1)Lydia Orne (2)Lucy Day Sgt MA
John: b 6-21-1730 d 10-18-1810 m Anna Margaret Henning Sol PA
Matthew: b 8-3-1749 d 1-31-1825 m Elizabeth (Le Fevre) 2Lt PS NY
Matthew: b 11-10-1710 d p. 1783 m Margaret Bevier 2Lt PS NY
Minard: b 1744 d 1800 m Mary Vail Pvt NJ
Minard: b 1753 d 1832 m Charity Elinor Teets Pvt NJ ★
Minard: b 1754 d 1805 m Mary Curtis Pvt NJ
Nathaniel: b 2-19-1749 d 6-30-1817 m Maria Deyo Pvt PS NY
Noah: b 10-29-1754 d p. 1799 m Cornelia Bevier Sgt NY
Peter: b 1-5-1733 d 1-12-1799 m Catherine (Le Fever) Pvt PA
Petrus: b 12-25-1720 d 10-25-1806 m Elizabeth Vernooy Sol NY
Philip: b 11-19-1763 d 9-6-1840 m Elsie DuBois Pvt NY
Samuel: b 6-28-1719 d — m Lydia Ferree PS PA
Simon: b 6-17-1744 d p. 12-6-1797 m Janneke Swart Capt PS NY

LEFFEL,
Balzar: b 2-2-1721 d 7-11-1796 m Sybilla — PS PA

LEFFERTS, (includes LEFFERSON)
Jan: b 3-16-1719 d 10-20-1776 m (1)Sarah Martense (2)Lammetie Vanderbilt PS NY
Leffert: b 11-25-1712 d 5-6-1795 m Mary Smith PS NY
Leffert: b 2-20-1723 d 9-24-1800 m Elsie Boerum PS NY
Oukey: b 11-8-1747 d 6-29-1809 m Sarah Schenck PS NJ
Peter: b 12-27-1753 d 10-7-1791 m (1)Jannetie Vanderveer (2)Fennetie Hegeman 1Lt NJ
Peter: b 6-11-1739 d 1-19-1823 m Lemmetje VanArsdalen Pvt PA

LEFFINGWELL,
Benajah: b 1-11-1737/8 d 9-26-1804 m Lucy Backus LCol RI
Christopher: b 6-11-1734 d 10-27-1810 m (1)Elizabeth Harris (2)Elizabeth Colt (3)Mrs Ruth Perit Capt PS CT
Daniel: b 2-7-1752 d 9-15-1778 m Elizabeth Whiting Lt CT
Elisha: b 11-4-1743 d 6-4-1804 m Alice Tracey Ens CT
Jonathan: b 5-22-1731 d p. 9- -1783 m Lycia Camp PS CT
Samuel: b 5-28-1718 d 1799 m Mercy Gorton CS PS CT

LEFFLER,
Jacob, Sr.: b c. 1741 d a. 3-30-1738 m Elizabeth Buett Capt PA
Jacob, Jr.: b 9-8-1765 d 2-3-1844 m Jane Smith PS PA

LEFOY,
Abraham: b c. 1741 d 1806 m Harriet Montanys Pvt NJ

LEFRAGE,
Wm.: b 8-10-1748 d 1-1-1835 m Margaret Barriman Pvt SC

LEFTWICH,
Augustine: b 9-10-1744 d p. 1835 m (1)Mary Turner (2)Mrs Sarah Turner Capt VA ★
Augustine, Sr.: b 1712-15 d 1795 m (2)Elizaeth Stovall PS VA
Joel: b 11-27-1760 d 10-20-1846 m Nancy Turner Ens VA
Thomas: b 1740 d 5-3-1816 m (1)Mary Challis (2)Bethenia Ellis (3)Jane Stratton Capt VA
Wm.: b 10- -1737 d 5-31-1820 m Elizabeth Haynes LCol PS VA

LEGARE,
Samuel: b 2-10-1745 d 1- -1797 m Eleanor Hoylan Lt SC
Thomas, Sr.: b 1732 d 2-9-1801 m Elizabeth Basnett PS SC

LE GENDRE,(or GENDAR)
Francosi: b 1738 d 1799 m Mary L Foos Pvt FrA

LEGG,
Aaron: b 1731 d 9-7-1801 m (?)Experience Fish (?)Hannah Bacon Pvt MA
Benjamin: b 1-1-1748 d p. 1790 m Abigail Holbrook Pvt MA
Caleb: b 11-4-1746 d 8-14-1799 m (1)Sarah Fletcher (2)Susannah — Pvt MA
Cornelius: bpt 10-13-1745 d p. 1790 m Annetje Osterhoudt Pvt NY
David: b 5-11-1756 d 4-25-1844 m (1)Majorie Holbrook (2)Comfort White (3)Thankful Holbrook 3rd Sgt MA ★
David: b 5-11-1755 d 1840 m Hannah Dewing (2)Olive — Pvt MA ★
Edward: b c. 1755 d 1834 m Mary Grover PS VA
James: b 8-8-1754 d 11-2-1822 m Elizabeth Hughes CS VA
Joel: b 5-28-1758 d 2-8-1845 m Sarah Holbrook Pvt MA
John, Jr.: bpt 2-19-1716 d p. 9-10-1788 m (1)Beeletjen Kool (2)Geertrude (Maklein) Davis Sol NY
Reuben: b 5-28-1754 d 5-28-1832 m Elizabeth Fletcher Pvt MA ★
Samuel: b c. 1730 d c. 1790 m Mary Clayland Pvt MD
Thomas: b 6-13-1723 d p. 1790 m Mary White Pvt MA
Wm.: b — d — m Hannah Nelson Pvt MA

LEGGETT,
Abraham: b 1-3-1755 d 1-16-1842 m (1)Rebecca Morgan (2)Catherine Wyley Lt NY
Elijah: b 9-27-1737 d 1784 m Sarah Angevine Pvt NY
Gabriel: b 1715 d — m Mary Wiggins Pvt NY
Gabriel: b 1696 d 1786 m (1)Bridget — (2)Mary Wiggins (3)Sarah Brown PS NY
John, Jr.: b 1730 d 1780 m Mary Haviland Pvt NY
Thomas, Jr.: b 1-17-1755 d 10-10-1843 m (1)Mary Height (2)Mary Underhill PS NY

LE GORE,
John: b 1755 d 7-7-1829 m (1)Margaret Funk (2)Mrs Hester Casey Pvt PA

LE GRANDE, (includes LE GRAND)
Abraham: b c. 1730 d 1801 m Agnes Nicholas PS VA
Alexander: b 12-25-1732 d a. 3-21-1822 m Lucy Walker PS VA
Josiah: b 9-3-1760 d 9-14-1836 m (1)Elizabeth Anderson (2)Sally D Meadows Sol VA

LE GROSS,
Francis: b c. 1760-4 d 9-11-1809 m Dolly Barker Pvt MA

LE GROW, (or LE GRO)
Elias: b 3-1-1741 d 10-24-1815 m Elizabeth Dodd Pvt MA
John: b 1-29-1733 d 8-4-1800 m Sarah — Pvt NH
Thomas: b 8-30-1763 d 1-30-1845 m (1)Eunice Farham (2)Eunice Knox (3)Jane Brock PS ME

LEHMAN, (includes LEMAN)
Anthony: b 1753 d 4-24-1827 m Catharine Arnick Pvt PA
Christian: b 7-29-1744 d 6-22-1819 m Eva Maria Koppenhaffer Sol PS PA
George: b 11-11-1758 d c. 1844 m Lydia Johnson Pvt PA
Jacob: b 1756 d p. 1790 m — Meredith Ens PA
Jacob, Sr.: b a. 1740 d 2- -1785 m Margaret — Pvt PA
Jacob, Jr.: b 1760 d 1821 m Catharine — Pvt PA
John: b 12-25-1743 d 7-25-1824 m Anna — Baer Pvt PA
John Adam: b 11-20-1732 d 8- -1823 m Anna Margaretha Steltz PS MD
Wm.: b c. 1748 d 1838 m Elizabeth Wetzel Pvt PA

LEHMER,
Jacob: b 8-1-1758 d 12-4-1836 m Catherine — Pvt PA

LEI,
Michael: b 1740 d 7-12-1823 m Margaret Lambert PS PA

LEIB,
John: b — d c. 1821 m — Sol PA

LEIBELSPERGER, (includes LEIBERSPERGER)
Jacob: b 8-15-1755 d 11-3-1822 m Eva Elizabeth — Pvt PA
John: b 8-26-1757 d 9-15-1823 m Marie Catherine — Lt PA

LEIBERT,
George: b 12-26-1735 d 6-19-1804 m Elizabeth Ehrenhardt Pvt PA

LEIBY,
Frederick: b 5-7-1735 d 3-28-1817 m Susanna Jergen Pvt PA
Jacob: b 7-22-1746 d 3-24-1797 m Anna Maria — Pvt PA

LEIDY, (includes LATTIG, LAUDIG, LEIDIG, LEYDE, LIDEY, LYDICK)
George Henry: b 10-9-1755 d 9-2-1841 m Elsia Barbara Raudenbush Pvt PA
Jacob, Sr.: b 7-25-1719 d 8-18-1794 m Barbara Nyce Pvt PA
John: b 1732 d 11-10-1810 m Arrantje Rosekrans Pvt PA
John: b 1748 d 8-10-1803 m Mary May — Pvt PA
John: b — d 1784 m Elizabeth — Dr PA
Jacob, Jr.: b 1-22-1759 d 4-23-1834 m Feronica Schell Lt PA
Joseph: b c. 1744 d 1800 m Lydia — Pvt PA
Peter: b 3-2-1742 d 7-31-1824 m Maria Elizabeth Bruch Pvt PA
Peter: b 1-28-1760 d 8-6-1831 m Catherine Lantzer Pvt Tms PA ★
Phillip: b 5-21-1755 d 3-14-1822 m Rosina Bucher Sol PA
Samuel: b 9- -1757 d a. 1-27-1845 m Mary Goughnour Pvt PA VA ★

LEIGH,
Benjamin: b 6-13-1754 d 1-15-1832 m Abigail Pierce Fif MA
Daniel: b 1-21-1762 d 11-5-1823 m Phoebe Waters Pvt NJ
Elijah: b 7-4-1757 d 3-25-1813 m Charity — Sgt NJ
John: b c. 1760 d 1-27-1827 m Catherine Huff Pvt NJ
John: b 1737 d 8-14-1785 m Sarah Greenhill Sgt VA
Samuel: b 7-13-1745 d 3-19-1835 m Amy Blackwell Pvt MM NJ
Zachariah Greenhill: b 11-13-1762 d 1-28-1817 m Priscilla Townes Sol VA

LEIGHTON, (includes LAIGHTON, LAYTON)
David: b 10-5-1733 d 6-17-1810 m Helena VanWicklen Capt NY
Francis: b 7-22-1734 d 4-19-1806 m Lydia Fitch Pvt MA
Gideon: b 2-14-1731 d 1776 m Abigail Titcomb Cpl NH
Hatevil, Jr.: bpt 8-18-1751 d c. 1796 m Martha Denbow Pvt NH

LEIGHTON, contd.
James: b 10-12-1749 d 2-22-1824 m (1)Sarah Thompson (2)Abigail (Mather) Mooney Smn NH ★
Jedediah: b 7-31-1756 d 6-24-1837 m Rebecca Swain Pvt NH ★
Joel: b 9-24-1754 d 12-29-1810 m (1)Betsey Huntress (2)Betsey Smith Pvt NH
Joseph: b 4-3-1754 d *p.* 1832 m Betsey Jordan Pvt NH ★
Louder: b *c.* 1730 d *p.* 10-23-1793 m Tabitha Laws PS DE
Richard: b *c.* 1752 d *p.* 1810 m Rebecca Dodge Cpl MA
Robert: b *c.* 1739 d *p.* 10-9-1786 m Rose — PS DE
Robert: b 1746/7 d 3-8-1838 m Ann Stamps Capt VA ★
Samuel: b 3-16-1740 d 2-27-1802 m Abigail Frost Maj ME
Samuel: b 12-20-1729 d 3-21-1812 m Abigail Goodwin Pvt MA
Thomas: b 9-1-1740 d 9-12-1803 m Lydia Tracy Sgt MA
Thomas: b 11-13-1725 d 3-9-1813 m Margaret Murray Pvt MA
Thomas: b 2-11-1738 d 6-9-1824 m Lydia — Pvt NJ
Tobias, Jr.: b 8-31-1742 d 1818 m Mary Wooster Pvt MA
Tobias: b 5-9-1736 d 1812 m Ann Tuttle Lt NH
Wm.: b 9-17-1723 d 1-11-1793 m (1)Katherine Rogers (2)Mary Bane PS MA
Wm.: bpt 10-6-1701 d *p.* 8-10-1775 m Margaret Kettels PS NY
Wm.: b 2-15-1755 d 1823 m Elizabeth McKinney Pvt PA

LEINBACH, (includes LEIMBACH)
Christian: b 2-2-1739 d — m Rosina Paus Pvt PA
Henry: b 1750 d 1832 m Catherine Keller Pvt PA
John Daniel: b 1-19-1746 d 4-8-1811 m (1)Catharine Graul (2)Catherine Hoffman (3)Maria Magdalena Hartman Capt PA

LEININGER,
George: b 12-23-1742 d 4-16-1791 m Magdalena — Pvt PA
Jacob: b *c.* 1727 d *a.* 4-2-1802 m Elizabeth — Pvt PA
Peter: b 9-21-1755 d 9-11-1835 m Christina Wenrich Pvt PA

LEIPER,
John: b *c.* 1760 d *p.* 1790 m Catherine McCauley Pvt PA W★
Thomas: b 12-15-1745 d 7-7-1825 m Elizabeth Coultes Gray Lt PS PA

LEISENRING,
Conrad: b 11-6-1759 d 2-10-1824 m Catherine Grob Pvt PA

LEIST,
Andrew: b 11-30-1755 d 11-11-1821 m Elizabeth — Sgt PA

LEITHEISER,
Hartman: b *c.* 1750 d 5-11-1830 m Elizabeth Sauerbier Ens PA ★
Jacob: b 12- -1754 d 1-27-1810 m Catherine — Pvt PS PA

LELAND, (includes LEALAND)
Adam: b 4-10-1745 d 3-10-1827 m Prudence (Leland) Pvt MA
Amariah: b 12-11-1710 d 1790 m Ursula Lovett PS MA
Asa: b 1738 d 1822 m Lois Marshall Pvt MA
Asaph: b 2-7-1730 d 8-7-1812 m Beulah Littlefield Pvt MA
Daniel: b 1-8-1742/3 d 12-14-1835 m Sibella Eames Pvt MA
David Warren: b 1758 d — m Mary Rawson Pvt MA
Ebenezer: b 7-7-1749 d 11-1-1837 m Molly Lyon Sgt MA ★
Ebenezer: b 1737 d 1806 m Abigail Cutter Pvt MA
Eleazer: b 12-18-1717 m 1789 m Mary Lovett Pvt MA
Eleazer: b 3- -1755 d 3- -1827 m Elizabeth Sherman Pvt MA
Henry: b 4-11-1729 d 4-24-1797 m Kisiah Bullard Capt MA
Isaac: b 8-29-1730 d 9-3-1777 m Mary Smith Pvt NH
James: b 1720 d 1807 m Lucy Warren Pvt MA
Jeremiah: b 8-22-1752 d 10-5-1808 m (1)Mary Harding (2)Sarah Hawes Matr MA
John: b 5-14-1754 d 1-14-1841 m Sarah Devine PS MA
John, Sr.: b 6-10-1713 d 1-15-1789 m Lydia Leland Pvt MA
John, Jr.: b 1-12-1744 d 1824-6 m Hephzibah Leland Capt MA
Joseph: b 1698 d 1776 m Esther Thurston Pvt MA
Joshua: b 8-8-1741 d 6-22-1810 m (1)Phebe Howard (2)Waitstill Greenwood Capt MA
Levi: b 1-26-1742 d 3-3-1797 m Sarah Woody Pvt MA
Micah: b 8-19-1741 d 6-27-1810 m (1)Betty Mason (2)Ann Pratt Sgt MA
Moses: b 1717 d 3-23-1797 m Abigail Robbins Pvt MA
Moses: b 7-18-1751 d 4-4-1835 m Mercy Twitchell Pvt MA
Oliver: b 8-2-1760 d 6-11-1838 m Abigail Perry Pvt MA
Thomas: b 1760 d 5-23-1830 m Lydia Sherman Pvt MA W★
Phineas: b 1-28-1753 d 1820 m (1)Sarah Winchester (2)Mrs Polly King Rawson Pvt MA
Samuel: b 1755 d 7-6-1833 m Abigail Gale Sgt MA
Solomon: b 5-12-1742 d 7-21-1808 m Lois Haven Lt MA
Thomas: b 3-20-1750 d 10-19-1847 m Anna B. Rawson Pvt MA ★

LEMANT,
James: b 1740 d *c.* 1780 m Martha Smyth Pvt SC
Jeannette Lemon: b 1768 d 10-8-1856 m Wm. Walker PS SC
Martha (Smythe): b *c.* 1741 d *c.* 1808 m (1)James Lemant (2)John Walker Sr. PS SC

LEMASTERS, (includes LE MASTERS & LEMASTER)
Andrew: bpt 1750 d 1818 m Barbara Heck Sol PA

Benjamin: b 6-15-1756 d 2-16-1837 m Rebecca Martin Sgt VA ★
James: b *c.* 1758 d 1831 m Mary — Pvt VA
John: b 1749 d *p.* 10- -1779 m Jemima Floyd Pvt VA

LEMLEY,
George: b 1742 d 6-11-1813 m Katherine Yoho Pvt PA
Solomon: b 1752 d 10-6-1820 m Sally — Pvt NY

LEMMOND,
John: b 1755-60 d *p.* 7-19-1806 m (1)Elizabeth Queary (2)Martha — Sol NC
Wm.: b *c.* 1730 d 1810 m (1)Margaret Buchanan (2)Ann Ghent Sgt CS Dr NC

LEMON, (includes LEAMON, LEMAN, LEMEN & LEMMON)
Alexander: b 12-10-1738 d *p.* 12-13-1790 m Mary Reynolds PS VA
Alexis, Jr.: b 3-12-1746 d 6-21-1826 m Rachel Stansberry Capt MD
Alexis, Sr.: b — d 1786 m Martha — PS MD
Daniel: b *c.* 1745 d *c.* 1841 m Hannah Leslie Ens PA
Frederick: b — d *p.* 1786 m Mary Sea Cpl VA
Jacob: b 5-7-1763 d 11-6-1848 m Jane Gilliland Sgt VA ★
James: b 1-10-1731 d 2-5-1811 m Mary — Pvt MA
James: b 1757 d 1842 m Rachel Fleming Pvt VA
James: b 11-20-1760 d 1-8-1823 m Catharine Ogle Pvt VA
James: b 4- -1765 d 7-4-1857 m (1)Sarah Carr (2)Amy Rawlings Pvt VA
John: b 11-6-1740 d 4- -1811 m Sarah Stansbury Smn PS MD
John: b *c.* 1730 d *p.* 6-28-1794 m Mary — Pvt PA
John: b *c.* 1750 d *c.* 8-15-1812 m Elizabeth Michy Pvt PA
John: b 1761 d 1850 m Catherine Shrowyer Pvt PA ★
John: b *c.* 1740 d *p.* 1809 m Mary Cox Capt VA
John: b 1750 d *p.* 1802 m Millison Foster Pvt VA
Joseph: b *c.* 1762 d *p.* 1806 m — PS PA
Matthias: b 2-18-1762 d 12-15-1841 m (1)Catherine — (2)Mary Stewart Hunnell Pvt PA
Michael: b 1760 d 1856 m Mary Johnson Pvt PA
Robert: b 1730 d *p.* 1800 m Eleanor — Capt CS MD
Robert: b 10-16-1752 d 7-12-1848 m (1)Isabelle Jennings (2)Mary McCowen Sgt PA NC ★
Samuel: b 2-4-1753 d 8-22-1834 m Jane Holmes Pvt MA ★
Wm.: b *c.* 1744 d 1807/8 m Martha — Lt PA
Wm.: b 1-1-1756 d 4-17-1809 m (1)Margaret (Manning)Martin (2)Mersey Thornburg Pvt VA
Wm. Slough: b 1760 d 3-25-1845 m (1)Margaret Fleming (2)Lydia Dunwoody (3)Agnes Ewart Pvt Sct PA ★

LEMOND,
Alexander: b 2-8-1761 d *p.* 1815 m Terissa Neely Pvt NC ★

LEMUNYON,
Philip: b 9-7-1756 d 7-23-1850 m Silva — Pvt RI

LENDALL,
John: b 1729 d 1785 m Eunice Lee Pvt MA
John, Jr.: b 10-17-1759 d 10-17-1814 m Anne Tewksbury Pvt MA W★

LE NEVE,
Samuel Cobbs: b *c.* 1753 d *p.* 1795 m Mildred Booker Sgt VA

LENHERT, (includes LENHART)
George: b *c.* 1738 d *p.* 9-10-1790 m Catherine — Pvt PA
Jacob: b 11-18-1736 d 8-3-1793 m (1)Anna Maria Kuhl (2)Barbara — Pvt PA
Philip: b 1763 d 1-3-1841 m Barbara Hollinger Pvt PA

LENIG,
Peter: b 3-8-1759 d 8-19-1840 m Barbara Stephon ADC PS PA

LENINGTON,
Thomas: b 1747 d 4-2-1827 m Sarah Sickerton Capt QM NJ NY ★

LENNINGTON,
Thomas: b *c.* 1750 d *a.* 7-14-1834 m (1)Phebe Chamberlan (2)Lydia Lash Capt NJ

LENNON,
John: b — d 3-7-1827 m Deborah Newcomb Mil NY

LENOIR, (includes LANOIR)
Thomas: b 8-11-1741 d 1816 m (1)Martha Blanche Atkinson (2)Mary Blanchard (3)Sarah (Ransone) PS SC
Wm.: b 5-20-1751 d 5-6-1839 m Ann Ballard Capt NC ★

LENOX,
James: b 1756 d 1820 m Hannah Smith Pvt MD

LENT,
Abraham, Sr.: b 1723 d 1786 m Anna Brinkerhoff Col NY
Abraham, Jr.: b 12-31-1755 d 8-16-1829 m Margaret Waldron Lt NY
Abraham: b 1727 d *p.* 1778 m (2)Jennetje Coursen PS NY

Hendrick: b 2-9-1761 d 2-9-1824 m Mary Montross Cpl NY
Hendrick: b c. 1750 d c. 1813 m Margaritta Montrass PS NY
Henry: b 1745 d 2-15-1801 m Catherine Croft Pvt NY
Hercules: bpt 10-18-1737 d 10-2-1816 m Lavinia VanTastel Pvt NY
Isaac, Jr.: b 1-4-1764 d 9-5-1849 m Margaret Christian Vought Pvt
    NY
Jacob: bpt 5-11-1740 d p. 1790 m Annetje — Cpl NY
James: b 8-24-1761 d 8-4-1849 m Elizabeth McCaul Pvt NY
John, Jr.: b 3-8-1763 d 11-6-1837 m Barbara Croft Pvt NY ★
John: b 10-1-1723 d 8-10-1808 m Phoebe Winter Pvt NY
Wm.: b 1755 d 8- -1832 m Elizabeth — MM Pvt VA ★

LENTNER,
Conrad: b c. 1740 d p. 6-4-1782 m (1)Barbara Davis (2)Elizabeth
    Graffley Pvt PA

LENTZ, (includes LINTS)
Jacob: b 11-14-1754 d 1841 m (1)Catherina Bender (2)Mary
    Elizabeth Reman Pvt NY ★
Peter: b 1762 d p. 1790 m (2)Margaret Roma Pvt NY

LENUD,
Henry: b c. 1740 d a. 6-7-1795 m Elizabeth (Leger)Capt PS SC

LEONARD, (includes LINNARD)
Abiathar: b a. 1742 d 7-13-1810 Sarah Williams Pvt MA
Abiel: b 1-14-1754 d 8-14-1777 m (1)Mrs Dorothy Huntington
    (2)Mary Greene Chp CT
Adam: b 1732 d p. 1780 m Margaret Neel Pvt MD
Adam: b 1745 d p. 1799 m Susannah — Pvt PA
Amos: b 10-11-1741 d — m Mary Partridge Pvt MA
Amos: b 3-15-1748 d 3-26-1825 m Mercy (Sweatland) Green Pvt MA
Archelaus: b 1742 d 3-6-1813 m Lydia Caswell Pvt MA
Archippus: b 12-4-1758 d 1-13-1833/4 m Asenath Cobb Sgt MA ★
Asa: b 1-30-1759 d 3-24-1836 m Olive Churchill Pvt CT ★
Barney: b 1757 d 4-21-1821 m Phebe Basset Cpl MA
Benjamin: b 12-4-1745 d 9-8-1801 m (2)Hannah Pratt Sgt MA
Benjamin: b 1732 d c. 1800 m (2)Mary Renough Pvt MA
Caleb: b 1750 d 7-17-1845 m Sarah Burt Pvt PA
Daniel: b 12-3-1753 d 1804 m Mary Starkweather Sgt MA
Daniel: b 5-13-1754 d 7-12-1830 m Phoebe Leonard Pvt MA
David: b 1737 d 1777 m Mary Miller Col MA
David: b 7-29-1734 d 11-24-1813 m Mary Hall Lt MA
David: b 1754 d 1834 m Betsey — Pvt NJ
Ebenezer: b 6-2-1753 d 3-6-1813 m Elizabeth Marsh Sgt MA
Edmund: b 1722 d 12-31-1803 m Mary Jones Pvt MA
Elias: b 7-24-1753 d 9-1-1831 m Susannah Selden Pvt MA
Elijah: b 1748 d 1808 m Joanna Tuttle Pvt NJ
Eliphalet: b 1702 d 2-4-1786 m Ruth Fenno PS MA
Ezekiel: b 7-30-1757 d 8-30-1834 m (1)Hudah Sexton (2)Rhoda
    Sexton Pvt MA ★
Ezra: b 9-19-1711 d 6-29-1798 m Olive Smith PS MA
Gamaliel, Sr.: b 4-30-1733 d 3-12-1809 m Bethiah Howard Pvt CS
    MA
Gamaliel, Jr.: b 5-31-1757 d 8-7-1827 m Anna Wiherell Pvt MA
George: b 10-22-1735 d 12-5-1809 m Lucy Palmer Pvt MA
George: b 7-17-1753 d 2-29-1832 m Mary Allen Pvt MA
George: b 10-6-1723 d 1-20-1801 m Charity Nelson PS MA
George: b 9-13-1755 d 5-7-1847 m (1)Elizabeth Yost (2)Catherine
    Evans Pvt PA ★
Gideon: b 9-20-1744 d p. 1790 m (1)Mary Warriner (2)Mrs Phoebe
    Parmelee Capt MA
Jacob: b 4-8-1742 d 8-13-1816 m Rhoda Wheeler Cpl MA
Jacob: b 1747 d 9-11-1790 m Eleanor Miller Capt NC
Jacob: b 11-16-1758 d 1-27-1835 m Elizabeth Shoaf Pvt NC ★
Jacob: b 11-18-1736 d 8-3-1793 m Anna Maria Keck Fif PA
James: b 1723 d 7-14-1793 m Eunice Smith Capt PS MA
James: b 1716 d p. 12-8-1786 m Jemima Hefford Pvt MA
James: b 1751 d 5-6-1817 m — Pvt NY
Job Strong: b c. 1740 d 1821 m Betsy (Robbins)Walker Pvt PS MA
John: b 12-23-1746 d p. 1790 m Ruth Bigelow Pvt MA
John: b c. 1747 d 1808 m Cornelia Rechter Lt NY
John: b 1760 d 8-23-1826 m Ruth Eastman Lt NY
John: b 1755 d 1813 m Nancy — Pvt PA
John: b c. 1738 d 1- -1783 m Elizabeth Lawrence Pvt PA
Jonas: b 9-19-1745 d 5-19-1837 m Sarah Mason Pvt MA
Jonathan: b 4-17-1738 d 9-12-1807 m (1)Eleanor Campbell
    (2)Rebecca Smith Cpl MA
Joshua: b 1-5-1725 d 11-27-1816 m — Capt MA
Josiah: b 5-6-1750 d 11-9-1818 m Elizabeth Hillard CS MA
Justin: b 5-15-1763 d 12-14-1835 m Theodosia — Pvt MA
Laughlin: b 1748 d 11- -1781 m Mary Golden Capt SC
Lot: b 11- -1755 d 11-7-1847 m (1)Elizabeth Hoge (2)Francis
    Willis NJ PA ★
Michael: b c. 1728 d c. 1790 m Elizabeth Catharine — Pvt PA
Moses, Jr.: b 1-17-1737 d 2-3-1818 m (1)Rhoda Smith (2)Anne
    Emerson Pvt MA
Moses: b 11-24-1761 d 6-2-1845 m Sarah (Sally)Pratt Pvt VT
Nathan: b 8-22-1717 d 1783 m Abigail Herrick PS MA
Nathan: b 9-25-1743 d 10-10-1813 m Amittai Cutler MM Capt MA
Nathaniel: b 1729 d 2-10-1795 m Mary Williams LCol MA
Nathaniel: b 12-7-1751 d 7-4-1833 m Hope Bennett Pvt MA
Nathaniel: b c. 1743 d 1804 m Phebe Lee Capt NJ

Nathaniel: b 12-10-1746 d 10-15-1823 m Esther Heath PS Capt
    NJ W★
Nehemiah: b 1751 d 1831 m — Pvt MA
Noadiah: b 9-10-1737 d 4-26-1790 m Jerusha Smith Capt MA
Oliver: b 2-13-1749 d — m Hannah Day Pvt MA
Patrick: b c. 1740 d 8-11-1822 m Margaret Delaney Pvt CT PA ★
Philip: b 1718 d 1785 m Mary Richmond Pvt MA
Philip: b 8-25-1746 d 12-31-1822 m Elizabeth Schappelle Pvt PA
Phineas: b 8-19-1751 d 11-16-1847 m Sybil Leonard Cpl MA
Preserved: b 3-13-1728 d 5-18-1801 m (1)Sarah Keep (2)Mary
    Morley Capt MA
Reuben, Sr.: b 11-25-1716 d c. 8-22-1805 m Miriam Day CS MA
Robert: b c. 1738 d 3-18-1814 m Sarah — Pvt PA
Robert: b a. 1740 d 8-16-1780 m Honor Prichard Pvt MD
Rowland: b 7-5-1755 d 7-6-1806 m Lydia Smith Pvt MA
Samuel: b 11-12-1740 d 4-8-1841 m (1)Silence Ripley (2)Rachael
    Tenney (3)Abigail (Ripley)Robinson Pvt MA
Samuel: b 8-28-1753 d 12-7-1840 m Deborah Mitchell MM MA
Samuel: b 1757 d 3-24-1822 m Abigail Pierson Arfr NJ ★
Seth: b 9-26-1750 d 8-30-1775 m Silence Packard Sgt MA
Silas: b 1754 d 1798 m Polly Hacket Cpl MA
Silas: b 2-15-1757 d 12-15-1845 m (1)Anna Tyler (2)Hannah
    Hawley MM Capt MA
Simeon: b 11-24-1737 m 9-20-1793 m Ann Smith Pvt MA
Solomon: b 5-30-1759 d 7-1-1734 m (1)Lydia Bassett (2)Sarah
    Sears Sgt MA
Timothy: b 7-3-1757 d 7-10-1830 m Susan Presbrey Cpl MA
Valentine: b 10-13-1718 d 11-13-1781 m Elizabeth — Pvt NC
Wm.: b c. 1730 d p. 1798 m Sarah Hoar Pvt MA
Wm.: b 5-27-1751 d 12-28-1819 m (1)Hannah Thayer (2)Dinah
    Burt Pvt MA
Wm.: b 1-8-1734 d 8-5-1805 m Mary Christina — Capt NY
Wm.: b c. 1750 d 9-20-1835 m Mary McMullen Capt PA
Zephaniah: b 1-18-1736 d 4-11-1814 m Abigail Alden LCol MA
Ziba: b 10-13-1756 d 7-7-1845 m Chloe Shaw Pvt MM MA ★

LEPLEY,
Michael: b 1738 d 4-26-1779 m Mary Ann — Pvt PA

LEPPER,
Frederick: b 1750 d 4-17-1820 m Mary — Pvt NY W★
John: b 1765 d 8-17-1840 m (2)Mary Prime Pvt NY ★
Wyant: b 5-26-1746 d 1-10-1839 m (1)Margaret Garlock
    (2)Margaret Snell Pvt NY

LEQUIER,
John: b 3-9-1765 d 2-9-1844 m Martha Ackerson Pvt NJ
Wm.: bpt 8-18-1730 d 10- -1819 m Ariantje Springstien Pvt NJ

LERCH, (includes LARK)
Anthony, Sr.: b 9-20-1720 d 8-28-1793 m Anna Margaret Lauer
    PS PA
Anthony, Jr.: b 3-18-1750 d 4-21-1798 m Anna Welsh — PS PA
Christopher: b 1759 d 1830 m Rachel Buffington Cpl PA
Frederick: b 4-17-1759 d 8-1-1826 m Elisabeth Sweetzer Pvt PA
John: b 11-6-1747 d 3-17-1818 m Sybilla Christina Mory Pvt PA
John: b 8-1-1765 d 10-25-1834 m Anna Catherine Lash Pvt PA
John: b 1723 d c. 1787 m Rachel Blakeley Wgm SC
Peter: b 3-7-1764 d 2-24-1813 m Anna Margaret Riegel Pvt PA

LERMOND,
Alexander: b 1707 d 12- -1790 m Mary Harkness CS ME
John: b 1750 d 2-20-1805 m Elizabeth Lamb PS MA

LE ROY,
Francis: b 1733 d 11-12-1797 m Geertruy (Gertrude) Middagh Pvt
    NY
Francis: b c. 1736 d p. 1785 m Sara Ellis Pvt NY
Francois: b c. 1740 d p. 1804 m (1)Mary Holt (2)Eunice Moulton
    SgtMaj FrA
Henry: b c. 1765 d c. 1833 m Anna Mors Pvt NY
Magnon: b 8-23-1702 d 10- -1795 m Marie LaValley SeaCap RI
Michael: b 1745 d 2- -1815 m Anna Kidney PS NY
Philip: b 10-13-1754 d 2-1-1829 m Elizabeth David Sol SC
Robert: b 1760 d p. 1800 m Blandina Palmatier Pvt NY
Simon: b 1-15-1759 d 3-26-1854 m Polly Wolfen Pvt NY ★
Simon: b 4-13-1712 d 1780 m Blandina (Freer)VanKleek PS NY

LESESNE,
Charles Frederick: b 1759 d 1821 m Binkey McDonald 2Lt SC

LESH, (includes LOESCH)
Baltzer: b 1730 d 9-9-1802 m (1)Anna Marie Moyer (2)Christina
    Loesch Pvt PA
Herman: b 3-15-1726 d 4-28-1791 m (1)Anna Barbara Beroth
    (2)Anna Margaretha (Heinsch) (3)Maria Johannes Beroth Hirte
    Pvt PA
Jacob: b 3-30-1757 d 4-21-1820 m Anna Moyer Pvt PA

LESHER, (includes LOSCHIER & LOUSER)
Abraham: b 5- -1742 d 5- -1839 m Elizabeth Humbert Sgt PA
Conraedt: b — d p. 1794 m Lydia Fiero Pvt NY
Hans George: b c. 1719 d p. 7-28-1789 m Margaretha Barbara
    Karnagel PS PA

LESHER, contd.
Henry: b 8-8-1740 d 11-7-1821 m — Zette Pvt PA
Jacob: b 12-27-1764 d 3-6-1843 m (1)Catherine Livengood (2)Susanna Strunk (3)Catherine (Weand) Moore Pvt PA
John: b 1-5-1711 d 4-5-1794 m (1)Mary Johanna Yoder (2)Marie Maegaret Hess PA PA
John: b 3-17-1759 d 4-20-1839 m Elizabeth Bosler Pvt PA
Johannes: b 1-18-1762 d 6-9-1813 m Christina Miller PS PA
Michael, Sr.: b c. 1732 d 1- -1786 m Catharine — PS PA
Michael, Jr.: b 3-29-1752 d 9- -1823 m Elizabeth — Pvt PS PA

LESLIE, (includes LESLEY)
Alexander: b 1756 d 10-3-1820 m Lucy Warner AsstQM Pvt NH
Patrick: b 1739 d p. 1795 m Mary Dyer PS VA
Robert: b 10-25-1763 d 1822 m Elizabeth Compton Sol VA
Thomas: b c. 1751 d a. 2-26-1800 m — Pvt PS SC
Wm.: b 11-25-1762 d 12-23-1832 m Sarah Wallace Pvt NC ★
Wm.: b 11-10-1754 d 12-30-1821 m Anna Caldwell Sol PS SC
Wm.: b 1757 d p. 1792 m Jane White Pvt PS SC

LESNETT,
Christian: b 1726 d 1804 m Christinana — Pvt PA

LE SOURD,
Jean: b 1757 d 8-20-1822 m Mary Curtiss SeaCap FrN

L'ESPERANCE,
Joseph: b 1760 d 1829 m Tryphena Plumbley FifMaj PA ★

LESSIG,
Christian: b 3-5-1745 d 9-10-1821 m Elizabeth Reifschneider Pvt PA

LESTER,
Alexander: b 8-8-1754 d p. 9-7-1833 m Martha — Sgt VA ★
Amos: b 1730 d 9-10-1789 m Anna (Lester)Ens CT
Benajah: b —d — m Jane Pinker Pvt CT
Bryant, Sr.: b 1730 d p. 5-25-1795 m Sarah Winbush PS VA
Christopher: b 1763 d 1827 m Mary Fish PS CT
Elihu: b 12-25-1759 d 3-22-1836 m Nancy — Pvt CT ★
Elijah: b 5-26-1753 d 8-22-1823 m Darmaris Lord Pvt CT
Guy: b 9-10-1760 d 11-4-1845 m Cynthia Lawrence Pvt NY
James: b 1754 d 6-18-1819 m Henrietta — Sol GA
James, Sr.: b c. 1714 d 1808 m Catherine — PS SC
Jason: b 1750 d 1826 m Irine — Pvt NY
Jeremiah: b 4-15-1762 d 3-4-1837 m Abigail Champlain Pvt CT ★
John: b 10-13-1740 d 9-6-1781 m Dorothy Morgan Ens CT
John: b 11-15-1750 d 12-1-1821 m — Pvt NY ★
John: b 1-31-1738 d 6-14-1801 m Jane Antrim Pvt PS PA
John: b c. 1750 d c. 1795 m Mary — Sgt VA
John: b 1-11-1752 d 1-29-1825 m Catharine Plick Pvt VA
Jonathan: b 1724 d 1797 m Hannah Latham PS CT
Joshua: b 5-7-1763 d 8-29-1846 m Polly Tubbs Pvt CT
Nathan: b 7-25-1742 d 1813 m Susan Gallup Pvt CT
Samuel, Jr.:b 1720 d — m Abigail Mason Pvt CT
Thomas: bpt 9-1-1734 d 1776-8 m Lucretia Beebe Pvt NY
Timothy, Sr.: b 8-27-1718 d 2-2-1795 m (1)Mehitable Belcher (2)Rebecca Aryart PS CT
Timothy, Jr.: b 3-18-1748 d 1796 m (1)Elizabeth Kinney (2)Betsey Dunlop PS CT
Wm.: b 10-3-1761 d 6-3-1842 m (1)Susanna Fields (2)Chloe Faris (3)Elizabeth(Dillon) Echols (4)Nancy Webb Pvt PS Wgn VA

LESUER, (includes LESUEUR & LESURE)
Martel: b 3-6-1758-61 d 8-10-1843 m Elizabeth Bacon Sol Cav VA ★
Samuel: b 11-1-1762 d 12-27-1826 m Hannah Cummings Sgt MA ★

LETCHER,
Wm.: b 1741 d a. 9- -1780 m Elizabeth Perkins Col NC

LETCHWORTH,
Benjamin: b 10- -1757 d 1834 m Eleanor Adams Pvt VA ★

LETSON,
Ephram: b c. 1740 d — m Mercy Maxfield Pvt RI
John: b 10-14-1761 d 1-6-1851 m Christiana — Pvt NJ ★
Thomas: b 5-16-1756 d 12-2-1846 m Lydia Jackson Pvt NJ
Wm. T.: b 10-21-1725 d 3-24-1800 m Elizabeth — Pvt NJ
Wm. Warren: b 9-23-1739 d 9-25-1800 m Esther Stillwell PS NJ

LETTS, (includes LETT)
James: b 1747 d 1828 m Patty Whitfield Pvt NC
Nehemiah: b 10-5-1763 d 9-3-1822 m Rhoda Ann Reed MM NJ

LETZENBERGH, (includes LETZENSBERG, LITZENBERG)
Adam: b 1720 d 2-6-1786 m Catharine Lohrman PS PA
George: b 9-22-1758 d 5-10-1841 m Grace Coates PS Lt PA

LEVAKE,
Augustus: b 4-16-1759 d p. 10-17-1820 m Lucy Clarke Pvt NY ★

LEVAN, (includes LE VAN)
Abraham: b 9-5-1748 d 5-27-1823 m Magdalene Siegfried Adj PA

Abraham: b c. 1733 d 1786 m Margaret — PS PA
Daniel: b 1748 d 2-18-1792 m (1)Justina — (2)Mary — CS CMman PA
Isaac.: b c. 1700 d 8- -1786 m Mary Margaret — PS CMman PA
Isaac, Jr.: b 1732 d 1800 m Anna Marie Ellmaker QM PA
Isaac, 3d: b 1754 d 1826 m Elizabeth — Pvt PA
Jacob: b c. 1736 d c. 1778 m Catherine Wink Lt PA
Jacob: b 1738 d 1-22-1814 m Susanna Ludwig Pvt PA
Sebastian: b 3-17-1727 d 12-22-1790 m Susanna Schneider CS Col PA

LEVERETT,
Thomas: b 5-12-1755 d 6-8-1834 m Mary G. Griffin Pvt GA W★
Wm.: b c. 1760 d 1-5-1812 m Cealey Anne Moseley Pvt GA
Wm.: b 1726/7 d 12-1-1791 m Rachel Watts Lt MA

LEVERICH,
Elnathan: b 1741 d 4-25-1784 m Mary Coe Sol NY

LEVERING,
Aaron: b 12-7-1739 d 10-14-1794 m Hannah Righter LCol MD
Anthony, Sr.: b c. 1725 d a. 1787/8 m Agnes Tunis PS PA
Anthony, Jr.: b 1-11-1759 d 3-24-1826 m Sarah Howell Pvt PA
Anthony: b 7-5-1752 d 8-8-1818 m Mary Sterne Pvt PA
Benjamin: b 9-15-1728 d 2-25-1804 m Catherine Righter Pvt PA
Enoch: b 2-21-1742 d p. 10-29-1795 m Mary Righter Pvt PA
Jacob: b 9-18-1746 d p. 1798 m Mary Brownfield Spy PA
John: b 4-25-1750 d 7-28-1832 m Hannah Howell Capt PA
Joseph: b 4-25-1747 d 9-12-1822 m Abigail Ramsey Sgt PA
Wm.: b 1-8-1734 d 6-1-1806 m Martha Deaves Pvt PA

LEVERS,
Robert: b c. 1728 d 5- -1788 m Mary Church PS Col PA

LE VERT,
Alexandre André: b 9-30-1759 d 3-22-1824 m Julie Philippine D. A. Caffieri Lt FrA
Claudius: b 1750 d 1810 m Ann Lea Metcalf Dr FrN VA

LEVEVER,
John: b 1753 d 8-17-1839 m Nancy Huston Pvt VA W★

LEVICK,
Caleb: b 1755 d 1817 m Rachel Bedinger Sgt VA

LEVINESS,
Thomas: b — d 11-7-1838 m Levina Fisher Pvt NY

LEVIS,
Samuel: b 8-21-1711 d a. 11-25-1794 m Mary Thomson PS PA
Thomas: b 5-8-1740 d 10-8-1817 m Sarah Pancoast CS PA

LEVY, (includes LEAVY & LEVI)
Benjamin: b — d — m Rachel Levy PS PA
Hayman: b 1721 d 8-19-1789 m Sloe Myers PS NY
Isaac: b 1750 d p. 1832 m Mary Dunn Pvt VA ★
Judas: b c. 1760 d 6-24-1829 m Mary McGraw Pvt VA ★
Michael: b 1759 d 5-19-1843 m Bata (Betsy)Hernstreet Pvt NY
Wm.: b 1755 d 9-21-1831 m Sarah Gatewood Pvt PA

LEWERS,
Thomas: b c. 1758-60 d p. 1798 m Mary Gray Sol SC

LEWIN,
John, Sr.: b c. 1720 d p. 1790 m Jemima Luther Lt MA
John, Jr.: b 1743 d a. 1805 m Bethia Eddy Pvt MA
Thomas: b 11-12-1758 d 12-14-1843 m Phebe Slode Pvt MA

LEWIS,
Aaron: b 1-25-1761 d p. 1840 m Mary — Pvt NC ★
Aaron: b a. 1750 dc. 1811 m Mary South Col VA
Abel: b c. 1730 d 9-22-1795 m Thankful Maccoon Sgt NY
Abisha, Sr.: b 8-9-1728 d 1797 m Sarah Stodder Sprague Pvt MA
Abisha, Jr.: b 7-16-1755 d 3-28-1828 m Deborah Wilder Sgt PS MA
Abner: b 1-28-1736/7 d 3-7-1778 m Margaret Cruikshank Pvt PA
Abraham: b 8-10-1752 d 12-14-1838 m Thankful Lewis Capt CT ★
Abraham: b 1734 d p. 1786 m Maria VanWagenen Sgt NY
Addison: b 1758 d 1820 m Susan(Susanna)Fleming Capt VA
Alexander: b 1730 d 12-13-1814 m Mary Smith PS PA
Amos: b 9-26-1746 d 7-23-1812 m Lydia Newhall CS MA
Amos: b 7-25-1730 d 1821 m (2)Rachel Hubbs Pvt PA
Andrew, Sr.: b 4-23-1720 d 9-26-1781 m Elizabeth Given BGen VA
Andrew, Jr.: b 10- -1758 d 9-25-1844 m (1)Elizabeth Madison (2)Margaret Briant Pvt VA ★
Anne Montgomery: b 1726 d 1808 m Col William Lewis PS VA
Anthony: b c. 1750 d a. 5-25-1779 m Jean — Sgt VA
Archelaus: b 2-15-1753 d 1-2-1834 m (1)Rebecca Hubbard (2)Eliza Brown (3)Frances Angier Lt MA
Asa: b 1-2-1765 d 8-17-1843 m (1)Bridget Rix (2)Betsey Millard (3)Mrs Ann Perkins Thompson Pvt CT
Augustus: b 4-30-1753 d 1845 m Esther Lewis Pvt CT ★
Augustus Johnston: b 10-10-1759 d 3-18-1851 m Susannah Perry CG RI

Barnabas: b 8-17-1733 d 7-3-1811 m (3)Rachel Curtis PS CT
Benajah: b a. 1740 d c. 1777 m Sarah Simmons SeaCap RI
Benjamin 3d: b 9-14-1729 d 5-2-1800 m Sarah DeForest Pvt CT
Benjamin: b 1760 d 12-1-1838 m Polly Case Pvt CT ★
Benjamin: bpt 10-16-1743 d 5-4-1829 m (1)Joannah Roboson (2)Desire Bacon Pvt MA
Benjamin: b 12-10-1752 d 9-1-1809 m Mary (Molly) Seavy Pvt MA
Benjamin, lst: b 6-5-1705 d 9-23-1777 m Elizabeth Jaquith PS MA
Benjamin, 2d: b 9-28-1729 d 1-13-1796 m Mary Drown Cpl MA
Benjamin, 3d: b 5-6-1753 d 2-1-1817 m Sarah Blanchard Pvt MA
Benjamin: b 9-12-1733 d p. 3-17-1810 m Priscilla Rich Bbd MA
Benjamin: b 1763/4 d 11- -1821 m Celia Martin Pvt NC
Benjamin: b 9-6-1763 d 1834 m Charlotte Shurg Pvt Tms PA ★
Benjamin: b 7-16-1744 d 7-1-1803 m Martha Bickerton Sgt VA
Benjamin: b — d 1790 m Mary Myrick CS VA
Benjamin: b 1761 d 9-25-1824 m Elizabeth Edmunds Pvt VA
Beriah: b 4-4-1750 d 1826 m Lois Wells Capt RI ★
Charles: b 1730 d a. 5- -1779 m Mary(Lewis)Col VA
Charles: b 1736 d 10-10-1774 m Sarah Murray Col VA
Charles, Sr.: b 10-13-1696 d 1779 m Mary Howell Col PS VA
Charles, Jr.: b 3-14-1721 d 5-14-1782 m Mary Randolph PS VA
Charles Crawford: b 5-26-1761 d 12-13-1833 m Elizabeth Russell Sgt NC ★
Charles Linburn: b p. 1747 d p. 1789 m Lucy Jefferson Lt PS VA
Chauncey: b 1-15-1760 d 4-28-1855 m (1)Lois Woodruff (2)Sibyl Hill Pvt CT ★
Daniel: b 1-8-1763 d 3-23-1806 m (3)Anna Stickles Pvt NJ
Daniel: b 1755 d 6-9-1836 m (1)Margery — (2)Elizabeth Belt Pvt NC ★
Daniel, Sr.: b c. 1730 d 1801 m Hannah Wilcox PS NC
David: b c. 4-15-1756 d p. 1800 m Elizabeth Benham Pvt CT
David: b 4-29-1757 d 3-3-1845 m Rebecca Hotchkiss NS CT
David: b 1732 d 1808 m Lydia Vernon PS DE
David: b 3-6-1765 d 5-2-1839 m Priscilla Guild Pvt MA
David: b 3-21-1747 d 6-23-1822 m (1)Ann Beason (2)Penelope — Pvt NC
David: b c. 1714 d p. 1784 m Jane Lawrence Pvt PA
David: b 1720 d 1787 m (1)Rebecca Stovall (2)Elizabeth Lockhart Pvt SC
David: b 1751 d 1797/8 m Elizabeth — PS VA
David: b c. 1763 d 5-8-1839 m Rachel Salmon Pvt SC
Ebenezer: b 4-14-1715 d 4-16-1776 m Sarah Everett Pvt CT
Ebenezer: b 1751 d 1-13-1776 m Sarah Bennett Pvt MA
Edward: b c. 1760 d 1813 m Mehitable Horton Lt NJ
Edward, Sr.: b 8-8-1722 d 6-22-1792 m Sarah Morris Pvt NJ
Edward, Jr.: b 5-10-1750 d 5-27-1817 m Nancy Crowell Cmsry NJ
Edward: b 2-11-1740 d 11-28-1787 m Mary Bressie Sol VA
Eldad: b 2-7-1755 d 7-15-1825 m (1)Mehitable — (2)Ruth Collins SgnMte MA
Eldad: b 2-13-1711 d 6-29-1784 m (1)Sarah Wiard (2)Mrs Jerusha Cowles (3)Mrs Sarah Root PS MA
Eleaser: b 1-8-1756 d 4-26-1835 m Catharine Vose Pvt CT
Eleazer: b 1-11-1737 d 12-15-1816 m Thankful Lewis Pvt PS CT RI ★
Eli: b 4-15-1743 d 2-11-1831 m Anna Collins Pvt CT
Eli: b 1-31-1750 d 2-2-1807 m Pamela Webster Maj PA
Elias: b 11-25-1746 d p. 1790 m Prudence Hewitt Sol PS RI
Elijah: b 4-1-1751 d 12-30-1834 m Martha Thompson Sgt QM CT ★
Elijah: b 11-14-1740 d 6-2-1823 m Elizabeth Whiton Pvt MA
Elijah: b 3-27-1764 d 9-18-1852 m Lucy Odell Pvt PA ★
Elijah: b 8-10-1741 d — m Prudence Babcock Capt RI
Enoch: b 12-17-1746 d p. 1821 m (1)Sarah — (2)Hannah Lockwood Ens CT
Enoch: b 2-19-1753 d 5-28-1841 m Eunice Smith Pvt Slr RI ★
Ephraim: b 10-4-1735 d 7-18-1808 m Lois Ransom Pvt CT
Evan: b 7-10-1740 d a. 7-20-1830 m Sarah Hunter Pvt PA
Evan: b 4-13-1740 d 3-1-1808 m (1)Esther Massey (2)Jane Meredith Pvt PA
Evan: b 5-25-1760 d 10-3-1823 m Sarah Tennison Pvt VA
Exum: b c. 1732/3 d p. 6-26-1795 m Elizabeth Figures Col CS NC
Ezekiel: b 1755 d 4- -1850 m Martha McCollester Pvt PA ★
Fielding, Sr.: b 7-7-1725 d 12-7-1781 m (1)Katharine Washington (2)Elizabeth Washington BGen PS VA
Fielding, Jr.: b 2-14-1751 d 7-5-1803 m Nancy Ann Alexander Capt VA
Francis: b 3- -1713 d 12-19-1803 m Elizabeth Annesly SDI CS NY
Francis: b c. 1755 d 1783 m Lucy Dudley Matr NC
George: b 3- -1734 d 1815 m Mary Wheeler PS Pvt CT
George: b 1747 d 1826 m Elizabeth Penfield Pvt CT
George: b 4-9-1741 d 7-24-1819 m Mary Davis Maj MA
George: b 3-14-1756/7 d 1821 m Catherine Daingerfield Capt VA
Harbert: b 1759 d 1836 m Charlotte Betty Pvt VA
Henry: b c. 1750 d p. 10-20-1832 m Sarah Clark Ens NY ★
Henry: b 6-1-1752 d 1-18-1832 m Juliana Carll Sgt NY
Henry, Sr.: b c. 1720 d a. 6-7-1808 m Eva Lehr PS NY
Henry: b 1716 d 1-18-1797 m Margaret James Pvt PA
Henry: b c. 1724 d c. 1810 m Ann Buford Pvt VA
Henry: b c. 1707 d 1785 m Martha — PS VA
Hezekiah: b 10-24-1744 d 1798 m Ann Main Pvt CT
Howell: b 9-13-1731 d 11-20-1813 m Mary Isabella Willis CS NC
Ichabod: b c. 1721 d 10- -1776 m Sarah Beardslee Col CT
Ichabod: b 1749 d 2-19-1807 m Martha Gale Pvt NY
Isaac: b 1-21-1746 d 8-27-1840 m Hannah Beale Chp CT

Isaac: b 1764 d p. 3-8-1833 m Lydia Judd Pvt CT ★
Isaac: b c. 1743 d 1784 m Keziah Moss PS CT
Isaac: b 1718 d 10-12-1784 m Keziah Moss PS CT
Isaac: b c. 1743 d 1799 m Catherine Higginson Pvt MD
Isaac: b 5-20-1755 d 8-27-1837 m Lydia Loomis Pvt MA ★
Isaac: b 8-4-1749 d 5-23-1821 m Abigail Bullard Pvt MA
Isaac: b c. 1750 d p. 1790 m Sarah Ransom Pvt NC
Isaac: b 2-25-1725 d 1806 m Mary Phipps Lt PA
Isaac: b 8-1-1751 d 9-21-1821 m Mary (West)Jones Pvt PA
Isaac: b 4-15-1752-62 d 11-17-1825 m Sarah Owen Pvt PA
Isaac: b 1760 d p. 2-22-1839 m Nancy Overfield Sol PA
Isaac: b 1762 d 2-24-1843 m Elizabeth (Lewis) Sol VA
Israel: b 3-28-1750 d 6-7-1850 m Amie Gardner Seacap CT
Jabez: b 1755 d 3-11-1838 m Lucy Rockwell Pvt CT ★
Jacob: b 10-27-1734 d 6-29-1801 m Mary Beabout Pvt Wgm NJ
Jacob: b 5-24-1750 d a. 11-23-1812 m Sarah Aubry Noland Pvt NC
Jacob: b a. 1762 d p. 1804 m Elizabeth — Pvt NC
Jacob: b 4-15-1755 d 6-23-1840 m (1) — Curtis (2)Mary(Parker) Watson Ens VA ★
James: b 1751 d 12- -1811 m Polly — Pvt MD
James: b 5-14-1744 d 12-7-1826 m Hannah Seaver Pvt MA
James: b 12-6-1760 d 10-20-1827 m Mrs Hannah Pierce Sol MA
James: b c. 1730 d c. 1790 m Martha Collins Capt PS NH
James: b 1747 d 1819 m Abigail Douglas Pvt NJ
James: b 1759 d 5-15-1830 m (2)Polly Shelley Pvt NJ
James: b 8-28-1755 d p 1790 m Susanna Anderson Pvt NC
James: b 5-21-1748 d 10-14-1813 m Hanna — Ens PA
James: b c. 1732 d 1815 m Elizabeth Iddings PS PA
James: b 1755 d p. 1793 m Tryphena Barber Lt VT
James: b 1745 d p. 9-10-1819 m Alice Forrester PS VA
James: b 4-6-1756 d 9-21-1849 m (1)Lucy Thomas (2)Mary C. Marks 2Lt Cmsry VA ★
James Hawke: b 12-27-1724 d 4-3-1802 m Lydia Pratt Pvt MA
James Martin: b 1762 d 1830 m Mary Boswell Herndon Lt NC
Jared: b 5-10-1761 d 5-14-1826 m Rhoda Munson Pvt CT
Jehu: b 1723 d 1804/5 m Alice Maris Sgt PA
Jeremiah: b 3-30-1745 d 11-22-1822 m Jane — Sol PS MD
Jesse: b 4-6-1752 d 6-20-1824 m (1)Isabel Burdick (2)Mary Potter Pvt CT
Jesse Pitman: b 5-13-1763 d 3-8-1849 m Nancy Clarkson Sol VA
Joel: b 8-28-1760 d 2-22-1816 m Myrian Eastham Capt VA
John, Sr.: b 4-14-1711 d 2-24-1799 m (1)Mary Munn (2)Amy Smith Capt CT
John, Jr.: b 12-10-1740 d 3-5-1812 m Sarah Gordon Capt CT
John, Jr.: b 8-31-1753 d p. 1-21-1817 m Elizabeth Howell Kennon Pvt GA
John: b 12- -1757 d 3-25-1825 m Elizabeth Harding Capt MA
John: b 5-26-1758 d 8-7-1834 m Rebecca Wheaton Sgt CT MA ★
John: b 1-3-1754 d 2-3-1828 m Mary Phelps Pvt Arfr PA
John: b 8- -1759 d 4- -1833 m Anna Pratt Pvt MA
John: b 7-14-1717 d 3-4-1803 m (1)Mary Howland Mitchell (2)Mrs Lydia Paul Worthley PS MA
John: b 11- -1752 d 2-1-1845 m (2)Abigail Gee Pvt NH ★
John: b c. 1747 d c. 1825 m Sarah Putnam Sgt NY
John: b 7-27-1760 d 1808 m Margaret Hayes ADC NY
John, Sr.: b c. 1720 d 6-10-1802 m Priscilla Brooks Pvt NC
John: b 1758 d 1835 m Nancy Reed Pvt NC
John: b a. 1755 d 1842/3 m Zila — Sol NC
John: b 1733 d 1-3-1818 m (1)Nancy Lavinia Ward (2)Susanna Johnson PS NC
John, Sr.: b 8-31-1725 d 1-21-1788 m Catherine Fauntleroy PS NC
John: b 2-10-1757 d p. 1790 m Rachel Fox Pvt PA
John: b 4-19-1719 d 1808 m Thankful Lewis Sol RI
John: b 8-25-1733 d — m Abigail Austin Pvt RI
John: b 11-10-1747 d 4-13-1833 m Amey Sheldon Pvt RI
John, Sr.: b 11-29-1764 d 4-18-1827 m Anna Cleveland Pvt VT
John: b a. 1765 d 1820 m Polly Smith Pvt VT
John: b c. 1755 d p. 1790 m Rachel Viney Capt VA
John: b 1758 d 6- -1823 m (1)Jane S. Thompson (2)Mary Preston Capt VA
John: b a. 1751 d p. 1819 m Elizabeth — Capt VA
John: b 6-23-1748 d 2-17-1835 m (2)Mary Power Drm Sgt VA ★
John: b c. 1740 d 4- -1787 m Mary — Pvt VA
John: b c. 1753 d 1804 m Lydia Reese Pvt VA
John: b 1757 d 11-4-1840 m Anne Berry Earle Pvt VA ★
John: b c. 1760 d 1804 m Margaret — Pvt VA
John: b c. 1718 d a. 1-6-1800 m — PS VA
John: b 10-18-1729 d 9-12-1790 m Ann Lewis PS VA
John Zachary: b a. 1753 d 3-7-1784 m (1)Elizabeth Woolfolk (2)Elizabeth Brock Ens VA
Jonathan: b 4-10-1731 d 10-10-1779 m Persis Crosby Pvt MA
Jonathan: b 8-15-1752 d 5-9-1815 m Martha Bowdish Pvt RI
Joseph: b 5-4-1756 d 1835 m Mrs Hannah Patterson Pvt CT ★
Joseph: b 1740 d 9-6-1781 m Deborah Warner, Lt CT
Joseph: b 4-7-1750 d 1838 m Mary Stanton Pvt CT
Joseph: b 1750 d 4-1-1838 m Esther Burnham Pvt CT ★
Joseph: b 4-17-1753 d 3-9-1791 m Elizabeth Duncan Lt MD
Joseph: b 12-23-1748 d 7-30-1814 m Anne Johnes QM PM NJ
Joseph: b 1763 d p. 1800 m Sarah Odell Pvt NY
Joseph: b — d — m Mary Jarret Lt PA
Joseph: b 9-30-1763 d 3-24-1845 m Sarah Elizabeth Magee Pvt SC
Joseph: b 11- -1746 d 6-18-1833 m Experience Burr Dr VT
Joseph: b 1757 d 4- -1817 m Rebecca — QM Cmsry VA
Joseph, Sr.: b c. 1706 d p. 1783 m Sarah Cocke PS VA

LEWIS, contd.
Josiah, Jr.: b 1739 d 12-20-1803 m Abigail Jerome QM CT
Josiah: b *c.* 1750 d 11-10-1783 m Susanna — Chp GA
Josiah: b *c.* 1725 d *a.* 3-31-1808 m — Mullington Lt NC
Josiah: b — d 1798 m Molly Cole ADC VT
Lemuel: b 1736 d 9-9-1822 m (1)Sarah Royce (2) — Lindsley Pvt CT
Lemuel: b 9-28-1725 d *c.* 1816 m Temperance Bearce Pvt MA
Levi: b 1743 d 3-9-1810 m Sarah Strange Pvt MA
Martin: b 4- -1761 d 8-23-1854 m Abigail Thayer Pvt CT ★
Matthew: b 2-6-1756 d 6-7-1807 m Hannah Ingraham Cpl MA
Mordecai: b 9-21-1748 d 3-13-1799 m Hannah Saunders Pvt PA
Mordecai: b 1751 d *p.* 1793 m Mary Segler Pvt VA
Morgan: b 7-1-1737 d 11-17-1784 m Sarah Tripp Capt MA
Morgan: b 1730 d 2- 1789 m Lucy ——Pvt NC
Morris: b *c.* 1730 d *p.* 1795 m Phebe Doughty Pvt NY
Nathan: b 1-29-1755 d 10-26-1845 m Jerusha Bertram Pvt CT
Nathan: b 1724 d 1807/8 m — Pvt NC
Nathan: b *c.* 1731 d 1-30-1792 m Mary Adams Pvt RI
Nathaniel: b 12- -1747 d 2-24-1839 m (1)Sarah Gridley (2)Lydia (Alcott)Frisbie Lt CT
Nathaniel: b 2-29-1732 d 3-24-1821 m Elizabeth Hull Sgt CT
Nathaniel: bpt 1-23-1719 d 4-4-1777 m Ruth Beardsley Pvt CT
Nathaniel: b 11-21-1757 d 2-24-1834 m Abigail Wooster Pvt CT
Nathaniel: b 11-14-1751 d 2-25-1818 m (1)Hannah Drew (2)Lucy Shaw Lt MA
Nathaniel: b *c.* 1736 d 7-14-1826 m — Pvt NC
Nathaniel: b 10-22-1740 d *p.* 1781 m Esther Tuttle Pvt VT
Nathaniel Sherman: b 6-3-1730 d 2-14-1812 m Mary Jones Pvt CT
Nehemiah: b 1751 d 1780-84 m Amy Hawkins Sol CT
Nehemiah: b 9-11-1739 d 7-30-1810 m (2)Sarah Peck Pvt CT
Nicholas: b 1-19-1734 d 12-8-1808 m Mary Walker PS Col VA
Noadiah: b 11-21-1736 d 1803 m Irene Clapp Pvt MA
Oliver: b 1-25-1758 d 3-13-1839 m Lucinda North Pvt CT
Ozias: b 1752 d 3-8-1812 m Lucia Bigelow Ens PS CS CT
Paul: b 2-19-1760 d 1-29-1834 m Eunice Worsley Pvt MA
Peter: b 1-7-1756 d 4-10-1793 m Mehitable Hinckley Cpl MA
Peter: b *c.* 1718 d 4- -1811 m Lena Lehr PS NY
Philip, Sr.: b *c.* 1730 d 1840 m (1)Betty Wasson (2)Mrs — (Anderson) McBride Pvt PA
Phineas: b 4-11-1722 d 10-31-1800 m (2)Sarah Norton Sol CT ★
Randall: b *c.* 1740 d *p.* 1790 m Alse Rathbun Pvt RI
Reuben: b 1-31-1748/9 d *p.* 1786 m Esther Hall Pvt CT
Richard: b 1749 d 1809 m Ann Warren Sgt MD
Richard: b 11-1-1747 d 1809 m Caroline Booker Sgt NC
Richard: b 7-22-1759 d 7- -1827 m Lydia Field Pvt NC
Richard: b 1765 d 1831 m Sarah Miller Pvt NC
Richard: b 5- -1759 d 2-8-1839 m Ann Williams Pvt PA
Richard: b *c.* 1763 d 1826 m Mary — Sol SC
Richard: b 11-26-1764 d 1-22-1852 m (1)Isabe (Isabel) — (2 or 3) Isabelle McEndre Pvt VA
Richard Mullington: b 2-20-1763 d 2-29-1844 m Sarah — Sol NC
Robert: b 1739 d *p.* 11-7-1780 m Mary Frances (Lewis)PS NC
Robert: b 5-29-1739 d 1-10-1803 m Jane Woodson Col VA
Samuel: b 6-23-1731 d 2-26-1808 m Eunice Patterson Sol CT
Samuel, Jr.: b 1756 d 1796 m (2)Rebecca Tomlinson Pvt CT
Samuel: b 7-6-1718 d 4-11-1788 m Eunice Beebe PS CT
Samuel: b 1749 d *p.* 1790 m Mary Nichols Pvt MA
Samuel: b 6-6-1752 d 4-23-1806 m Susannah Meacham Sol MA
Samuel: b 6-28-1752 d 8-25-1822 m Sarah VanVoltzenburg Lt NY
Samuel: b *c.* 1750 d *c.* 1816 m Dorcas Fincher Pvt NC
Samuel: b 9-29-1754 d 8-25-1822 m Elizabeth Godfrey Ens PA
Samuel: b 8-5-1726 d 12-13-1798 m Margaret Trotter Pvt PA
Samuel: b 5-20-1744 d 2-9-1818 m Sarah Edwards Pvt RI
Samuel: b 9-17-1766 d 3-9-1851 m Cassandra Le Sueur Pvt VA
Seth: b 6-24-1759 d 3-26-1808 m Rhoda Cole PM CT
Shadrack: b 1730 d 1800 m Sarah Grice Pvt VA
Solomon: b 1750 d 3-6-1843 m Catharine (Moon) Pvt Spy NC ★
Stephen: b 8-4-1749 d 7-16-1839 m Jerusha Curtis Pvt CT ★
Stephen: b *c.* 1744 d 1811 m (1)Mrs Sarah Dickinson (2)Mrs Deborah (Luff) Pleasanton (3)Ann Polk (4)Mrs Leah (Laws) Capt DE
Stephen: b 1751 d *p.* 9-3-1834 m Alice Sheldon Pvt RI ★
Stephen: b 1722 d 1790 m Elizabeth Offutt QM VA
Thomas: b 4-11-1745 d 1810 m Mary Turrell PS CT
Thomas: b 1742 d *c.* 1814 m Mary Ellis PS MD
Thomas: b 3-5-1755 d 9-10-1831 m Olive Spaulding Pvt MA
Thomas: b 1-27-1723 d 4-25-1804 m Dorothy Elie Sgt NY
Thomas: b *c.* 1750 d *p.* 11-21-1791 m Martha — Pvt SC
Thomas: b 1-9-1742 d 8-4-1822 m Judith Ferguson Capt VA
Thomas: b 5-8-1749 d 9- -1809 m Elizabeth Payne 1Lt VA
Thomas: b 4-27-1718 d 1-31-1790 m Jane Strother PS VA
Thomas: b 5-3-1755 d 8-1-1849 m Hannah Hopkins Pvt PS Spy VA ★
Thomas: b 1759 d 3-2-1851 m (1)Sarah Clark (2)Susannah Rayfield (3)Sarah Ann Hart Pvt PA ★
Thomas: b 12-18-1764 d 7-28-1833 m (1)Nancy Rey (2)Sarah Condly Pvt VA ★
Thomas: b *c.* 1752 d 1-12-1836 m Susannah — Pvt NC ★
Thomas: b *c.* 1750-52 d *p.* 1802 m Jane Baxter PS VA
Timothy: b 5-24-1764 d 6-2-1858 m Thankful Bradley Pvt MA
Valentine: b 11-2-1749 d 3-30-1819 m Sally Clarke Pvt CT W★
Waitstill, Sr.: b *c.* 1734 d 5- -1778 m Sarah Bliven Pvt NS MA
Walker: b 7-7-1755 d 7-17-1826 m Sarah Gunn Pvt CT

Waller: b 9-11-1739 d 1- -1808 m Sarah Lewis PS VA
Warner: b 10-10-1720 d *p.* 7-5-1779 m Mrs Eleanor Bowles Gooch PS VA
Wm.: b 12-1-1737 d 4-9-1822 m Elizabeth Scott Ens CT
Wn.: b 7-10-1756 d 11-8-1841 m Experience Rice Pvt CT ★
Wm.: b *c.* 1725 d 12-15-1806 m Naomia Brockway PS CT
Wm.: b 1737 d 10-7-1820 m (1)Hannah Mather (2)Azubia Gridley PS CT
Wm.: b 1755 d 5-20-1827 m Mary Falkler Pvt MD ★
Wm.: b 10-14-1754 d 3-6-1834 m (1)Sarah Pinkham (2)Mary . . . . Lamson (2)Hannah Brooks Pvt MA
Wm.: b 8-13-1754 d 3-3-1829 m Margaret McLean Pvt NY
Wm.: b *c.* 1740/1 d *p.* 1813 m Mourning Herring Pvt NC
Wm.: b 1746 d 1825 m Elizabeth — Sgt PA
Wm.: b *c.* 1756 d 7-11-1810 m (1)Catherine Geiger (2)Elizabeth Jones Pvt PA
Wm.: b 6-24-1760 d 8-8-1835 m Hannah Thompson Pvt Smn RI ★
Wm.: b 3-29-1749 d 11-2-1796 m Mary Abigail (Miller)Child Pvt RI
Wm.: b *c.* 1740 d 1811 m Morning VanPelt Pvt SC
Wm.: b 10-9-1759 d 5-18-1841 m (1)Mrs Sarah (Hirons)Taylor (2)Frances Raines Pvt SC
Wm.: b 11-17-1724 d 1811 m Anne Montgomery Col VA
Wm.: b *c.* 1735 d 11-14-1781 m Lucy Meriwether Lt VA
Wm.: b *c.* 1740 d 1812 m Mary John Maj VA
Wm.: b 1750 d *c.* 1824 m Anne Montgomery Pvt VA
Wm.: b 1762 d 6-17-1838 m Mary Dodson Pvt VA ★
Wm.: b 4-8-1763 d 6-18-1851 m Polly Brown Pvt VA ★
Wm.: b 1767 d 1-17-1825 m Sarah Poe Tms Pvt VA
Wm.: b *c.* 1745 d 1822 m Jane Shelton PS VA
Wm. Terrell, Sr.: b 1718 d 1802 m Sarah Martin PS NC
Wm. Terrell, Jr.: b 1757 d 1813 m Mary Ann Hipkins Sol NC
Zachary: b 5-6-1731 d 7-21-1803 m Ann Overton Terrell CS VA
Zebulon: b 9-3-1734 d *c.* 1828 m (1)Lydia Enos (2)Mary York Pvt RI
Zebulon: b *a.* 1738 d 1799 m Sandal Jackson 1Lt VA
Zephaniah: b 7-16-1734 d 1-18-1777 m Ann Doty Pvt NJ

LEWMAN,
John: b 1735 d *a.* 1800 m Mary — PS MD

L'HOMMEDIEU,
Constant: b 2-5-1730 d 1-25-1810 m Deborah Young Capt PS NY
Ezra: b 8-30-1734 d 9-25-1811 m Mary Catherine Havens PS NY
Grover L.: b 8-3-1741 d *p.* 1807 m (1)Esther Vail (2)Elizabeth Tracy Sgt NY
Henry Mulford: b 1-1-1757 d 1813 m (1)Sarah Cooper (2)Jerusha Schoville MM NY
James: bpt 1752 d *p.* 12-9-1797 m — PS NY
John: b *c.* 1728 d 9-12-1794 m Prudence Goodale MM PS NY
Samuel: b 2-20-1744 d 3-7-1834 m Sarah White Capt NY

LIBBY, (includes LEBBE, LEBBY, LIBBEE & LIBBEY)
Abraham: b 12-29-1739 d 8-3-1799 m (1)Abigail Page (2)Mary Tarlton Sgt PS NH
Allison: b 4-6-1757 d 5-14-1816 m Sarah Dam Pvt MA
Arthur: b 4-5-1728 d 7-7-1798 m Deborah Smith PS NH
Arthur Bennick: b 1-1754 d 9-7-1837 m Elinor Haynes Pvt NH ★
Asa: b 1737 d 11-5-1828 m Abigail Coolborth Sgt MA
Azariah: b 1740 d 5-5-1820 m Elizabeth Paul Pvt ME
Benjamin: b 9- -1762 d 8-2-1831 m (1)Elizabeth Hunnewell (2)Hannah Moody Pvt MA
Benjamin: b 11-4-1756 d *c.* 6-12-1812 m Sarah Hamilton Sgt MA W★
Benjamin: b 1-18-1758 d 5-24-1834 m Polly Hearl Mrnr PS MA W★
Charles: b 12-16-1749 d *c.* 1791 m Sarah Pray Sgt ME
Daniel: b 2-21-1715 d 7-31-1804 m (1)Abigail — (2).Mrs Lois Jones Wentworth PS ME
Dominicus: b 12-27-1751 d 12-18-1822 m Dorothy Small Sgt MA
Edward: b 2-10-1759 d 3-15-1848 m Elizabeth Libby Pvt MA ★
Eliakim: b 4-20-1745 d 12- -1836 m Mehitable Cummings Sgt MA
Eliakim: b 1756 d 9-20-1833 m Rachel Jameson Pvt MA
Elijah: b 12-11-1748 d 2-22-1825 m (1)Mary Dresser (2)Mindwell Dresser Cpl MA
Francis: b 3-17-1761 d 1-24-1847 m Lucy Moulton Pvt ME
George: b 1-21-1760 d 10-19-1838 m Mary Bartlett Pvt MA ★
Ham: b 1735 d 1790 m Ester Drew PS NH
Harvey: b 12-18-1763 d 2-28-1849 m (1)Sarah Small (2)Polly Strout Pvt MA
Hatevil: b 11-28-1736 d 9-24-1820 m Jane Watson Lt ME
Ichabod: b 1742 d 11-18-1828 m Mary Fickett Pvt MA
Isaac: b 2-28-1725 d 8-20-1810 m (1)Ann Symmes (2)Margaret Kalderwood PS NH
Jacob: b 1747 d 1805 m Unity Parker Pvt MA
Jethro: b *c.* 1726 d *c.* 1795 m (1)Mary Libby (2)Mrs Hannah (Woodbury)Moody Pvt MA
John: b 1-29-1760 d 6-20-1812 m Sarah Leathers Pvt NH
John Skillings: b 11-23-1761 d 12-8-1807 m Rhoda Cummings Pvt MA
Jonathan: b 1752 d 3-21-1805 m Abigail (Libby)Capt MA
Joseph: bpt 3-15-1747 d 11-15-1844 m Jane Cole Pvt MA ★
Josiah: b 2-26-1746 d 3-1-1824 m (1)Eunice Libby (2)Elizabeth (Parcher)Foss (3)Mrs Mary Jones 1Lt MA
Josiah: b 9-13-1745 d 1-15-1826 m Sarah Libby Pvt MA
Josiah: b 2-17-1758 d 4-11-1828 m Sarah Holmes Pvt MA

Luke: b 8-22-1756 d 1-8-1844 m (1)Nancy Crocker (2)Widow
  Goodwin Pvt NH ★
Matthew: b 4-25-1729 d c. 1804 m (1)Sarah Hanscom (2)Hannah
  Hasty Pvt MA
Moses: b 5-13-1756 d 5- -1804 m Anna (Libby) Pvt MA
Nathan: bpt 8-19-1759 d p. 1809 m Polly Larrabee Pvt ME
Nathaniel: b 9-5-1735 d 10-18-1798 m Mary Meserve Pvt MA
Nathaniel: b 2-22-1763 d 5-23-1855 m (1)Miriam Gilpatrick
  (2)Eleanor Staples (3)Mrs Catherine Milliken (4)Abigail B.
  Guppey Pvt MA ★
Nathaniel: b 1740 d 1805 m Elizabeth Howard PS SC
Peter: b 3-8-1736 d 11-7-1822 m (1)Ruth — (2)Anna Lazzel 2Lt MA
Rebecca Weston: b 1755-60 d 7- -1819 m Reuben Libby PS ME MA
Reuben: b 8-11-1734 d 1820 m (1)Sarah Goss (2)Sarah Tucker Pvt
  MA
Reuben: b 7- -1745 d 7- -1833 m Rebecca Weston Pvt MA
Reuben: b 3-2-1754 d 3-13-1825 m Mercy Marr Pvt MA
Samuel: b 2-1-1737 d 3- -1825 m (1)Mary Frost (2)Jemima
  Leighton Capt MA
Samuel: b 12-17-1759 d 3-8-1819 m Abigail Graffam Pvt ME
Samuel: b 7- -1757 d 2-27-1843 m Mehitable Seavey Pvt NH
Seth: b 5-4-1755 d 12- -1836 m Lydia Jordan Sgt MA ★
Simeon: b 1-11-1755 d 3-11-1830 m (1)Abigail Smith (2)Mrs Ann
  (Huston)Phinney Cpl MA ★
Solomon: b 8-26-1759 d 3-3-1832 m Sarah Seavey Pvt MA
Stephen: b c. 1741 d 5-8-1793 m (1)Alice Guptill (2)Hannah Young
  PS ME
Thomas: b 3-23-1743 d 4-14-1824 m (1)Hannah Plummer (2)Mrs
  Dorcas (Fogg)Ring Sgt MA
Thomas: b 11-16-1733 d 1-6-1821 m Mary Larrabee PS MA
Wm.: b 1-30-1749 d 1-5-1835 m Elizabeth Clark Pvt MA ★
Zebulon: bpt 4-10-1757 d 12-6-1835 m Lydia Andrews Pvt MA ★

LIBERGER, (includes LYBARGER & LYBERGER)
Henry: b 12-28-1759 d 7-31-1820 m Barbara — Pvt PA
Ludwock, Sr.: b 1735 d p. 2-20-1827 m (1)Barbara — (2)Phebe —
  Pvt PA
Nicholas, Sr.: b 1733 d 1808 m Mary Anne — Pvt PA
Nicholas, Jr.: b 1754 d 2-16-1836 m Christina Ried Sol PA ★

LIBHART,
Valentine: b 10-30-1751 d 1-31-1807 m Appolonia Mate Pvt PA

LICHTENBERGER,
Casper: b 10-4-1762 d 1834 m Magdalena Nieman Pvt PA
George: b 4-1-1764 d 10-30-1820 m Maria Elizabeth Bohn Pvt PA
Killian (John): b 2-3-1753 d 5-13-1833 m Catherine Bohn Pvt PA

LICHTENWALTER, (includes LICHTEWALTER)
Abraham: b 7-12-1753 d 3-13-1814 m Eve Catharine Sarger Pvt PS
  PA
John: b 6-28-1738 d 10-30-1794 m Catherine Stettler Lt PA

LICHTY,
Mark: b 3-16-1753 d 5-5-1817 m Anna Barbara Altendorfer Pvt PA

LICK,
Wm.: b 2-15-1734 d 6-28-1801 m Catherine — Pvt PA

LIDDELL,
Andrew: b 1756 d 4-7-1833 m (1)Jean Johnson (2)Jane Gordon Pvt
  SC
George: b 1754 d 12-28-1789 m Rachel Thomson Capt PS SC
Moses: b 12- -1755 d 8-2-1802 m Elizabeth (Haney)Johnson Col
  SC
Wm.: b 3-10-1762 d 8-23-1836 m Ruth Keith Pvt SC ★

LIDDON,
Benjamin: b 3-30-1754 d 1805 m Mrs Sarah (Rutledge)Ivy Pvt NC

LIDE,
Robert: b 5-17-1734 d 3-12-1802 m (1)Mrs Priscilla Fort (2)Sarah
  Kolb (3)Mrs Mary (Westfield)Holloway Maj SC
Thomas: b 1-9-1722 d 2-10-1787 m (1) — Kimbrough (2)Mary
  Foster (3)Mehitabel Irby Capt SC

LIDEN,
Shadrach: b c. 1750 d p. 2-9-1811 m Rebecca Foxwell Capt MD

LIERLY, (includes LYERLY)
Christopher: b c. 1760 d 9-30-1832 m (1) X (3)Barbara — Pvt NC
Zachariah: b 6-2-1755 d 4- -1847 m — Harkey Pvt NC ★

LIESS,
Peter, Sr.: b 11- -1746 d 12-2-1820 m Anna Margaret Seyler Sgt
  PA

LIEUZADER,
Abraham: b 1757 d 12-14-1825 m Leah Hogue Pvt VA W★

LIEVERSEE,
Peter: b 9-7-1729 d p. 1790 m Maria Fonda Pvt NY

LIGGETT,
John: b 1751 d 1-29-1791 m Mary Shield Pvt PA
Robert: b 10-6-1743 d 6-19-1806 m Isabella Darragh Pvt PA
Wm.: b 1748 d 8-18-1836 m Mary — Pvt VA

LIGHT, (includes LICHT & VON LICHT)
Henry: b 1740 d 1803 m Jemima Barrett Pvt NY
Henry, Sr.: b 3-7-1738 d 1-7-1806 m Barbara Landis PA
Henry, Jr.: b 11-21-1760 d 10-3-1830 m Magdalena Funck Pvt PA
Jacob, Sr.: b 8-7-1730 d 4-24-1788 m Elizabeth Landis Pvt PA
Jacob: b 11-4-1758 d 2-2-1837 m Veronica Ellenberger Pvt PA
Jacob: b 9-11-1763 d 9-5-1840 m Barbara Brandt Pvt PA
John: b 1759 d 1835 m Ellender Light Sol NC
John: b 2-21-1726 d 3-11-1806 m Anna Landis Pvt PS PA
John: b 12-25-1754 d 7-2-1834 m Catherine Britzius Cav FifMaj PA
Lodowick: b 7-23-1752 d 8-26-1830 m Martha Seely Pvt PA
Wolsey: b 7-7-1762 d 4-11-1828 m (2)Judith Horton Pvt NY

LIGHTBURNE,
Richard: b a. 1741 d 11- -1794 m Patsy Jones NLt VA ★

LIGHTCAP,
Solomon, Sr.: b c. 1729 d a. 12-21-1781 m Catherine — PS PA
Solomon, Jr.: b c. 1758 d c. 8- -1825 m Anna Maria Hauswirtin PS
  PA
Solomon: b 1729 d c. 1804/5 m Mary — PS PA
Solomon: b 1764 d 8- -1825 m Anna Maria Alexander Pvt PA

LIGHTFOOT,
John: b c. 1730 d a. 1782 m Mary C. — Capt PS VA
Philip: b 1751 d 1786 m Mary Warner Lewis Lt VA
Wm.: b c. 1720 d 11-5-1805 m Elizabeth — PS VA
Wm.: b 1750 d p. 4-27-1829 m (1)Anne Cocke (2)Ann Clopton
  Ellyson Lt VA
Wm.: b c. 1758 d 1808 m Lucy Armestead Digges 2Lt VA

LIGHTHALL,
Abraham: b 9-14-1740 d 12-31-1831 m Katherine Bellinger CplNY ★
Francis: b 1-17-1765 d 5-20-1836 m Sarah Fye Pvt NY
John: b 2-12-1759 d 8-4-1835 m Nancy VanSlyck Pvt NY
Nicholas: b 3-7-1724 d p. 1781 m Margarit Ittich (Ydich)Pvt NY
Wm.: b 1756 d 10-5-1822 m Sarah Marselis Lt NY ★

LIGHTNER,
Adam: b 9-10-1760 d 1-3-1843 m Susannah Harper PS PA
George Daniel: b 1750 d 1784 m Miss Werner Lt PA
Ignatius: b 8-6-1736 d 5-23-1818 m Margaret Rutter Pvt PS PA
John: b 8-5-1733 d 1812 m Barbara Rutter Pvt PA
Nathaniel: b 1709 d 10-21-1782 m Margaret La Rue PS PA
Wm.: b 1735 d 1813 m Margaret Mackerel Pvt PA
Wm.: b c. 1730 d c. 1812 m Elizabeth Ann — PS PA

LIGON,
Blackman: b 1757 d 5-3-1831 m Elizabeth Townes Pvt VA ★
Joseph, Sr.: b 1725-30 d p. 1-27-1779 m Judith — Capt VA
Joseph, Jr.: b 11-1755 d 9-21-1842 m (1)Mrs Lettice May Sims
  (2)Diana Coleman Clay Ens VA
Samuel: b c. 1720 d p. 11-11-1783 m Agnes — CS VA
Seth: b 4-1-1762 d p. 5-16-1809 m Janett Mayo PS VA
Wm.: b 1756 d 1838 m Sarah Hewing Sgt VA ★
Wm.: b 11-24-1762 d 3-4-1841 m Ann D. Moseley Pvt PS VA ★
Wm.: b a. 1725 d 1796 m Ann Webber PS VA
Wm.: b 1737 d 1788 m Edith Turner PS VA

LIKINS,
Andrew: b c. 1750 d 2-15-1819 m Ann — Sgt NJ PA ★

LILLARD,
Benjamin: b c. 1740 d 1829 m Frances Crow Capt VA
James: b c. 1725 d p. 4-15-1804 m Kesiah Bradey PS VA
John, Sr.: b 11-3-1737 d 5-30-1801 m (1)Susanna Ball (2)Anne
  Moore Thomas Capt VA
John: b 1765 d p. 1832 m Rachael Garrett Pvt VA ★
Thomas: b c. 1726 d 1806-1815 m Anne — Sgt VA

LILLEY, (includes LILLIE & LILLY)
Abner: b 1-3-1761 d 1-14-1782 m Sybil Hale Pvt CT W★
Bethuel: b 3-25-1762 d 10-13-1840 m Hannah Smith Pvt MA ★
David: b 11-6-1736 d 1821 m Azubah Bissell Ens CT
David: b 10-27-1742 d 9-1-1827 m Huldah Blodgett Cpl CT
David: b 4-24-1739 d c. 1801 m Elizabeth Gibbs Pvt MA
Ebenezer: b 5-5-1759 d 9-9-1840 m Jerusha Williams Pvt VT ★
Edmund, Sr.: b 1728 d 1815 m (1) — Lightfoot (2)Elizabeth
  Billingsby CS NC
Elijah: b 1757 d 1844 m Anna (Amy)Smith Capt VT
Jared: b 1759 d 1827 m Susanna Tuckerman Pvt CT
John: b 7-18-1753 d 9-22-1801 m Elizabeth Vince Capt NY
John: b 1725 d 1800 m Elizabeth Dennis Pvt RI MA
John: b 1753 d 1825 m Eleanor Dumas Pvt NC
Jonathan: b 5-1-1739 d 1-10-1828 m Sarah Foster Sgt MA
Joseph: b 7-20-1757 d p. 1789 m Deborah Holman Pvt MA
Nathan: b 5-26-1755 d p. 1790 m Lydia Robinson Sgt CT

LILLEY, contd.
Reuben, Jr.: b 2-14-1745 d 10-15-1804 m Rachel Sherman Lt MA
Thomas: b — d p. 1784 m Lucy Burwell Capt VA
Turner: b 10-8-1755 d p. 1801 m Elinor Churchill Pvt CT

LILLIBRIDGE, (includes LILLABRIDGE)
David: b 9-18-1744 d 1-19-1831 m Marion Moore CS RI
Gardner: b 9-19-1758 d 7-22-1834 m Sarah Dawley Pvt RI ★
Jonathan: b 8-28-1751 d 10-13-1836 m Mary Waite Reynolds Ens RI
Thomas, Sr.: b 12-4-1729 d 1-20-1822 m Mary Hoxsie CS PS RI
Thomas, Jr.: b 3-6-1761 d 4-27-1838 m Alice Sweet Pvt RI ★

LILLINGTON,
John Alexander: b 1725 d 1786 m Sarah Waters BGen NC

LILLISTON,
Wm.: b 1756 d 1-18-1830 m Elizabeth VerNelson Pvt VA ★

LIMBOCKER,
John: b 1754 d 8-29-1829 m Livina Hearn Pvt NY

LINCOLN, (includes LINKON)
Abiel: b 3-5-1719 d 10-9-1808 m Sarah Fisher Pvt MA
Abiel, 2d: b 5-26-1750 d 9-3-1821 m (2)Lois Smith Sgt MA
Abierther: b 6-4-1759 d 10-22-1844 m Mary Babbitt Pvt MA ★
Abraham: b 12-12-1740 d 9-29-1823 m Sarah(Lincoln) Pvt MA
Abraham: b 10-18-1736 d 1-31-1806 m Annie Boone SubLt PS PA
Abraham: b c. 1751 d 10-19-1811 m Elizabeth Shrum Pvt PA
Abraham: b 5-13-1744 d 5- -1786 m Bathsheba Herring Capt VA
Ambrose: b 2-28-1756 d 4-13-1830 m Lois Smith Cpl MA
Amos: b 3-18-1753 d 1-14-1829 m Deborah Revere Capt MA
Barnabas: b 9-5-1751 d 11-18-1822 m Olive Gilbert Pvt MA
Benjamin: b 1-24-1733 d 5-9-1810 m Mary Cushing MajGen MA
Benjamin: b 11-17-1740 d 1-31-1828 m Elizabeth White Sgt MA
Benjamin: b 1754 d 11-29-1822 m Zilpha Lincoln Pvt MA
Benjamin: b 10-29-1756 d 10-6-1821 m Elizabeth Ores Pvt PA
Beza: b 7-17-1756 d 3-1-1835 m Sarah Ward Pvt MA
Caleb: b 11-10-1750 d 6-26-1829 m Elizabeth (Lincoln)Pvt MA
Caleb: b 6-5-1757 d 3-26-1822 m Mercy Thayer Pvt MA
David: b 10-17-1734 d 2-7-1814 m Elizabeth Fearing Pvt MA
Elisha: b c. 1752 d 7-29-1833 m Reuhama Crossman Pvt Mus CT ★
Elisha: b 9-22-1759 d 5-3-1824 m Molly Gurney Pvt MA ★
Elkanah: b 4-30-1747 d 7-29-1816 m Susannah Torrey Sgt MA
Ezekiel: b 4-21-1734 d 1-1-1812 m Elizabeth Whitcomb Pvt Matr MA
Ezekiel: b 1759 d 1-31-1828 m Jane Lincoln Pvt Smn MA ★
Gideon: b 12-2-1760 d — m Martha Perkins Pvt MA
Hananiah: b 1756 d p. 1898 m Sarah Jerrfries Capt PA
Isaac: b 1738 d 1808 m Lydia Drake Pvt MA
Isaac, Jr.: b 7-10-1744 d p. 1785 m Experiance Willis Pvt MA
Isaac: b 8-5-1717 d 3-1-1776 m Ruth Beal PS MA
Jacob: b 11- -1761 d 4-30-1850 m Chloe (Lincoln) Pvt MA
Jacob: b 11-18-1751 d 2-20-1822 m Dorcas Robinson Lt VA ★
James, Sr.: b 7-23-1731 d 5-16-1804 m Susannah Humphrey Capt MA
James, Jr.: b 4-22-1761 d 5-23-1835 m Abigail Mitchell Fif MA
James: b 6-20-1752 d 7-17-1839 m Mrs Hannah Everson Cpl MA
Jeremiah: b 10-28-1733 d 11-26-1803 m Sarah Hersey Pvt MA
Jerome: b 11-13-1752 d 12-11-1832 m Elisabeth Lincoln Sgt MA
John: b 7-28-1726 d 6-7-1810 m (2)Anna Martin Stowell Pvt CT
John: b 8-14-1735 d 6-3-1811 m Lydia Jacob Capt MA
John: b 2-15-1755 d 4-11-1824 m Polly Clark Pvt MA ★
John: b 3-28-1758 d 1839 m Mary Lafferty Pvt PA ★
Jonah: b 1759 d 6-18-1829 m Polly Gooding Sol MA
Jonathan: b 1-1-1750 d 12-15-1821 m Lydia Nichols Sgt MA
Joseph: b 12-28-1753 d 4-13-1816 m Susanna Todd Marsh Mrnr MA
Joshua: b — f p. 1790 m Elizabeth Seekins Cpl MA
Joshua: b 11-14-1737 d 9-3-1810 m Tamar Sprague Pvt MA
Lazarus: b 10-3-1756 d 12-5-1836 m Fanny Kilby Pvt MA
Levi: b 3-5-1738 d 5-12-1819 m Elizabeth Norton Lt MA
Levi: b 11-16-1763 d 1-2-1815 m Cynthia Franklin Cpl MA
Levi, Sr.: b 5-5-1749 d 4-14-1820 m Martha Waldo MM MA
Loring: b 5-6-1746 d 11-23-1786 m Dorothy Moore Capt MA
Lot: b 8-4-1762 d 4-17-1814 m Sarah Hathaway Pvt MA
Macey: b 11-21-1759 d 7-23-1838 m Relief — Pvt MA
Matthew, Jr.: b 6-10-1735 d 12- -1821 m (1)Susanna Gill (2)Rebecca Lincoln Pvt MA
Michael: b 11-9-1761 d 8-11-1849 m Rachel Thompson Pvt PA ★
Mordacai: b 5-9-1730 d 3- -1812 m Mary Webb CS PA
Nathan: b 5-11-1746 d 3-19-1814 m Eunice Cross Pvt CT ★
Nathan: b 8-4-1738 d 12-19-1809 m Martha Fearing Lt MA
Nathaniel: b 2-15-1738 d 9-22-1804 m (1)Lucy Beal (2)Susanna Lincoln Pvt MA
Persis: b 8-1-1759 d 9-29-1828 m (1)Allen Lincoln (2)James Hall PS MA
Royal: b 9-15-1754 d 3-29-1837 m Jerusha Waterman Pvt MA ★
Rufus: b 11-10-1751 d 2-11-1838 m Lydia Sprague Capt MA
Samuel: b 2-14-1714 d 12-10-1783 m Mary Bates Pvt Matr MA
Seth: b 4-27-1751 d 3-6-1839 m (1)Mary Fearing (2)Mrs Chloe (Whiton)Fearing Sgt MA
Seth, Jr.: b 3-23-1754 d 12-1-1826 m Jemima Miller Cpl MA
Silas: b c. 1750 d p. 1804 m Hannah Luce Sgt MA

Simeon: b 1757 d — m Huldah Porter Sgt RI
Solomon: b 10-5-1739 d 1-25-1819 m (2)Deborah Randall Pvt MA
Stephen: b 12-3-1751 d 3-16-1840 m Lydia Foster Pvt MA
Thomas: b 1752 d 1799 m (1)!Phoebe Keyes (2)Lucy Holbrook (3)Mrs — (Swingle)Walls Pvt MA
Thomas: b 9-4-1759 d 8-10-1836 m Esther Newland Pvt MA ★
Thomas: b 11- -1758 d 7- -1819 m Priscilla Dickinson Sol PA
Timothy: b 1754 d 2-24-1793 m Mary Barney Pvt MA
Welcome: b 11-6-1729 d 6-25-1814 m Sarah Gill Pvt MA
Wm.: b 5-23-1738 d a. 5-17-1814 m (1)Prudence Buss (2)Relief (Whitcomb)Sawyer (3)Sarah Meriam Lt MA
Zenas: b 9-8-1757 d 12-19-1820 m Mary Lincoln Pvt MA

LIND,
John: b 5-11-1761 d 10-23-1823 m Susanna Gonter Pvt PA

LINDEMUTH, (includes LINDAMOOD & LINDENMUTH)
Christopher: b 1750 d a. 3-7-1825 m (1)Mary — (2)Elizabeth Miller (3)Francey Hammon PS VA
George: b 6-20-1752 d 11-4-1819 m Christeann Woolf Pvt PA
John Michael, Sr.: b c. 1716 d 10- -1785 m Maria Margaretha Wolf Sol PA
John Michael, Jr.: b 4-25-1737 d p. 3-10-1812 m (1)Maria Eva Noerken (2)Anna Katarina Geschwindin Col CS PA
Martin: b 2-14-1757 d 9-12-1829 m Magdalena Wolff Cpl PA
Peter: b 11-2-1750 d 6-16-1830 m (1)Barbara Wolf (2)Mrs Catharine (Murray)Etter Pvt PA

LINDERBERGER,
John: b 3-6-1754 d 9-30-1817 m Dorcas Sprague 1Lt PA W★

LINDER,
Daniel: b c. 1750 d c. 1840 m Rebecca VanMeter Ens VA
John: b c. 1750 d 1-14-1834 m (1)Mary Mosgroves (2)Jane Wright Pvt NC
John: b c.1755 d 10- -1833 m Martha Apemon Sol NC

LINDERMAN,
Cornelius: b 3-31-1757 d 2-8-1848 m Anna Young Pvt NY ★
Jacob: b 1722 d 10- -1792 m (1)Catherine Maklin (2)Catherine Felton Pvt NY

LINDESMITH,
Joseph: b 3-19-1751 d 6-10-1817 m Nancy Bauman Mus PA

LINDLEY,
Caleb: b 12-25-1756 d 3-24-1837 m (1)Mary White (2)Rachel — (3)Keziah Jennings (4)Elizabeth Conklin Pvt NJ ★
David: b 1760 d 4-21-1845 m Hannah Woods Matr MA ★
Demas: b 6-3-1733 d 1-22-1818 m Joannah Pruden PS Pvt PA
Isaiah: b 1-26-1728/9 d p. 11-8-1796 m Anna Channing Pvt MA
Jonathan: b 6-15-1756 d 4-5-1828 m (1)Deborah Dix (2)Martha Henley PS NC
Philip: b 9-10-1736 d 5-20-1820 m Mary McFarran (Feran)Pvt NJ
Thomas: b c. 1730 d 10- -1809 m (1)— Harrison (2) — Hall (3)Elizabeth Ridgeway Sol GA
Thomas: b 2-25-1706 d 9-14-1781 m Ruth Hadly PS NC

LINDSEY, (includes LINDSAY, LINDSLEY & LINSLEY)
Aaron: b 1748 d 1797/8 m Abigail Halsey Sol NJ
Abiel: b 1730 d 5-7-1800 m Thankful Pond QMSgt CT
Abraham: b 2-17-1744 d p. 4-26-1786 m Elizabeth Barker Pvt CT
Abraham, Sr.: b c. 1740 d c. 1825 m Mary Frost Lt VA
Anthony: b 1736 d 1808 m Rachel Dorsey PS MD
Archibald: b 1744 d — m — Pvt MA
Benjamin: b 5-26-1754 d 6-9-1840 m Mary Dennis Cpl MA
Benjamin: b 2-22-1732 d 11-18-1815 m Sarah Kitchell Lt QM NJ
Benjamin: b 1753 d 1841 m Elizabeth — Pvt SC
Brainard: b 7-14-1761 d 9-13-1837 m Rhoda Ford Pvt CT
Daniel: b 5-15-1764 d 9-24-1827 m Hannah Doolittle Pvt CT ★
Daniel: b 5-14-1753 d 11-7-1827 m Deborah Ingalls Pvt MA
David: b 7- -1744 d 10-17-1837 m Mary Shawgessey Pvt PA ★
David: b c. 1740-50 d a. 2-7-1842 mMary Casey Sol VA
Ebenezer: b 11-7-1711 d 5-2-1787 m Sarah Wilford PS CT
Eleazer: b 12-7-1737 d 6-1-1-1794 m Mary Miller LCol NJ
Elisha: b 1755 d 5-9-1816 m Jane Carr Sol NC
Ephraim: b 3-26-1738 d p. 3-2-1779 m (1)Ann Howland (2)Ann Bonney Sgt MA
Ephraim: b 11-3-1762 d p. 1811 m Mercy Willey Cpl MA
Hezekiah: b 1747 d p. 1820 m — Pvt VA ★
Isaac: b a. 1742 d p. 1783 m Susanna Smith CS TN SC VA
James: b 7-9-1763 d 11-23-1828 m Sarah Maltby Pvt CT
James: b 7-29-1755 d 1-19-1849 m Phebe Pettingill Pvt MA
James: b 8- -1743 d 1804 m Martha Breckenridge Pvt PA
James: b c. 1758 d 7- -1838 m Delilah (Hodgson)Brewer Sgt VA
John: b 9-6-1750 d 6- -1808 m (1)Mary (Sims) Lindsay (2)Clarissa (Bullock) Sims Maj GA
John: b 8-27-1738 d a. 12-16-1800 m Mary Masterson Maj GA
John: b 3-15-1758 d 5-3-1840 m Rachel Dorsey Pvt MD
John: b 1732-5- d p. 1792 m Susanna Robinson Pvt MA
John: b 1728 d 9-10-1784 m (1)Joanna Hudson (2)Sarah Raynor Capt NJ
John: b c. 1748 d p. 10-20-1793 m Mary Robertson PS NC

John: b 1724/5 d 9- -1787 m Alice — Col PS SC
John: b 1740 d 8-11-1795 m Elizabeth Humphreys Pvt VA
John: b 10-5-1760 d 2-28-1837 m Sarah Rea Pvt VA
Joseph: b 6-7-1736 d 10-8-1822 m (1)Anne Lums (2)Mary Gardner
　　Maj NJ ★
Levi: b 4-27-1731 d 2-4-1801 m (1)Polly Stillwell (2)Anna Davison
　　PS NJ
Micajah: b 1759 d 1796 m Jane McNutt Pvt VA
Moses: b 1734 d 5-7-1793 m Irany Raynor Pvt NJ
Nathaniel: b 3-2-1746 d 8-20-1798 m Sarah Lee Capt MA
Obed: b 8-13-1747 d p. 1790 m Lydia Beach CS PS CT
Opie: b 1745 d 1815 m (1)Margaret Lampkin (2)Frankie Jett
　　(3)Sarah Howerton PS VA
Philip: b 9-10-1736 d 6-20-1820 m Mary McFeran Sol Wgn NJ
Philip: b 1758 d 1828 m Henrietta Gilpin Pvt MM VA
Reuben: b 1-15-1747 d 1831 m (1)Sarah Walker (2)Hannah Tidwell
　　Col VA
Robert: b c. 1740 d 1801 m (1)Miss Mabane (2)Ann McGee CS PS NC
Samuel: b 1760 d 6-18-1820 m Phoebe Williams Pvt NJ
Samuel: b 1725 d 4-16-1800 m Nancy Ferguson Capt PA
Silas: b 9-21-1766 d 1-17-1845 m Jane Lindsley Wgn NJ
Solomon: b 7-21-1759 d 8-8-1839 m (1)Katharine — (2)Lucy
　　Fairbanks Sgt CT ★
Stephen: b 3-22-1759 d 8-14-1846 m Sally McNitt Pvt CT ★
Stephen: b 1761 d 3-18-1849 m (1)Elizabeth Tyler (2)Deborah Irwin
　　Pvt CT ★
Thomas: b c. 1750 d 1816 m (2)Hester Clark Pvt PS NC
Walter: b 1746 d 4-4-1801 m Letitia Causey Pvt NC
Wm.: b 6-16-1747 d 3-31-1831 m Hannah Leadbetter Pvt PS MA
Wm.: b 4-15-1760 d 10-8-1836 m (1)Elizabeth Mace (2)Clarissa
　　Prior Pvt Spy Wgn PA ★
Wm.: b 1-5-1735 d 1810 m Margaret Thompson Pvt PA
Wm.: b 3-1-1742 d 3-23-1827 m Katherine Woodbury Pvt RI W★
Wm.: b 1743 d 9-15-1792 m Ann Calvert Maj VA
Wm.: b 1757 d 9-15-1838 m Nancy Ferguson Capt VA
Ziba: b 11-4-1762 d 6-20-1849 m Abigail (Lindsley) Pvt NJ

LINE,
John: b c. 1757 d 1-15-1843 m Mary Baltzell Capt VA ★

LINEBERRY,
Jacob, Jr.: b 1751 d p. 9-29-1821 m Mary Catherine Youngblood PS
　　NC

LINENSHEET,
Charles: b a. 1766 d p. 1790 m Margret — Sol PA

LINES, (includes LINE, LIONS & LYNES)
Abel: b 1758 d 1823 m Army(Anna)Lines Pvt CT
Ashbel: b 4-9-1751 d 5-11-1823 m Eunice Murray Pvt CT
Benjamin: b 8-16-1762 d 10-22-1840 m Sally Brown Pvt CT ★
Conrad: b 1730 d 9-6-1815 m Claracy — Sol CT
David: b 6-20-1764 d 8-29-1856 m Polly Bradley Pvt CT ★
Ebenezer: b 1768 d 11-23-1811 m Mercy Tuttle Matr CT ★
Holly: b 7-15-1751 d 5- -1841 m Martha Pearse Pvt CT
James: b 9-30-1748 d 1816 m Susanna Alling Pvt CT
James: b 1722 d 1- -1792 m Thankful Sperry PS CT
John: b 3-13-1720 d p. 1790 m Deborah Hotchkiss Pvt CT
Major: b 10-14-1747 d 3-2-1814 m Susannah Mansfield Lt CT
Rufus: b 1764 d 7-24-1835 m Tamar Durand Pvt CT ★
Samuel: b 9-20-1733 d 2- -1810 m Mary Carrington Pvt CT
Wm.: b 1716 d 3-10-1779 m Deborough Allen Pvt NJ

LINFIELD,
David, Sr.: b 7-13-1726 d 1-6-1816 m Hannah Vinton Lt MA
David, Jr.: b 10-19-1752 d 7-31-1790 m Esther French Cpl MA
Wm. 2d: b 12-10-1718 d 2-26-1779 m Jemima Clerk Pvt MA
Wm. 3d: b 10-4-1742 d 2-23-1823 m Sarah White Sgt MA

LINGAN,
James McCubbin: b 5-31-1751 d 8-28-1812 m Janet Henderson
　　Capt MD

LINGEL, (includes LENGEL)
John: b 1739 d 5-29-1806 m Anna Margretha Fehler Pvt PA
Stephen: b 1748 d p. 1-3-1824 m Susanna Schmidt Pvt PA
Thomas: b 1742 d 1811 m Mary Feggen Pvt PA

LINGO,
Henry: b 1755/6 d 11-9-1835 m — Pvt PA ★
Wm.: b 1753 d 1836 m Susannah — Pvt DE ★

LINGRELL,
Nehemiah: b 1752 d 7-6-1825 m Rosanna Paul Pvt MD ★

LINING,
Charles: b 10-26-1753 d 8-16-1813 m Mary(Blake)Rose Capt SC

LINK,
Adam: b 10-13-1721 d 4-24-1805 m Maria Elizabeth Miller PS MD
Adam: b 11-14-1760 d 8-15-1864 m Elizabeth Link Pvt PA ★
George: b 5-16-1753 d 5-5-1838 m Elizabeth Schwerer Pvt PA
Jacob: b c. 1739 d 8- -1780 m — Pvt PA

John Adam, Sr.: b 10-13-1721 d 4-24-1805 m Marie Elisah Miller
　　PS MD
John Adam, Jr.: b 12-31-1756 d 9-28-1835 m Jane Ogle Ens MD
Nicholas: b c. 1756 d 6-23-1816 m Rebecca Pence PS Pvt VA MD
Wm.: b 1749 d 3-23-1830 m (1)Zella Maria Plass (2)Janetje Decker
　　Pvt NY
Wm.: b 3-28-1753 d 2-28-1849 m Maria Kilmer Pvt NY

LINKENFELTER,
Mical: b c. 1752 d 1818 m Catrina Ergensinger Pvt NY

LINNELL, (includes LINNEL)
Joseph: b 8-12-1755 d 1827 m Sarah Lombard Cpl MA
Joseph: b 12-3-1754 d 1-21-1834 m Zeruiah Knowles Pvt RI MA ★
Josiah: b 12-19-1755 d 1822 m Alice — Mrnr MA ★
Samuel: b 1-12-1762 d 5-12-1837 m (1)Anna York (2)Susannah
　　Newcomb Pvt MA ★
Thomas: b 8-8-1750 d 8-27-1817 m Priscilla Rogers Slr MA
Uriah: b 2-16-1756 d 1836 m Thankful Crosby Pvt MA ★

LINNEN,
Thomas: b 7-14-1760 d 1-28-1841 m Mary Oliver Sgt ME

LINSCOT, (includes LINSCOTT)
Joseph: b 2-2-1723/4 d p. 1790 m Eliza Peaks PS ME
Samuel: b 5-10-1751 d 11-17-1816 m (2)Dorcas Dunning Cpl ME

LINSENBIGLER,
Daniel: b 1750 d 1824 m Elizabeth — Pvt PA

LINSTER,
Moses: b 11-1-1740 d 7- -1817 m Sarah Wells PS NC

LINTHICUM, (includes LINCECUM)
Archibald: b a. 1757 d 1812 m Nancy (Mary)Leake(Lake)Pvt PS MD
Francis: b 5-18-1734 d p. 1804 m Mary Mayo Pvt MD
Gideon: b 12-17-1746 d 3-10-1779 m Miriam Bowie Sol GA
John: b 1751-5 d p. 1810 m Ann Edwards Ens MD
Richard: b 4-12-1752 d 8-24-1817 m Mary Lee Drm MD
Zachariah: b 1735 d a. 6-4-1808 m (1)Sarah Prather (2)Ann Clegatt
　　Pvt MD

LINTNER, (includes LINDER)
Christian: b c. 1737/8 d a. 4-12-1803 m Elizabeth — CS PA
George: b 8-14-1739 d 1-27-1826 m Elizabeth Hilbert Pvt NY
Peter: b 4-25-1760 d 1-31-1836 m Mary Douglass Pvt PA ★

LINTON,
Elijah: b c. 1760 d 1835 m (2)Eleanor Robertson Pvt VA
John: b 1749 d 8-2-1824 m Mary Moore Capt PA
John: b 1750 d 12-4-1836 m Ann Mason Capt VA
Joseph: b 1-6-1763 d 10-25-1848 m Sara Daggett Pvt NC
Samuel: b 1722 d 7-14-1807 m Elizabeth Brees Pvt PA
Samuel: b 8-17-1755 d 12- -1826 m (1)Ruth Brown (2)Elizabeth
　　Montgomery QM SC

LINVILLE,
David: b 1752 d p. 1-24-1787 m Dorothy Fair PS NC
John: b c. 1755 d 4-30-1801 m Martha McAllister Pvt PA
Peter: b 1750 d 4-19-1834 m Lucretia Laing Sol PA

LIONBERGER,
John: b a. 1756 d a. 9-11-1815 m (1)Barbara Boyer (2)Barbara
　　Stover (3)Barbara Herschberger Sol PS VA

LIPE,
Adam: b c. 1740 d 2-27-1804 m Elizabeth Mathieus Capt NY
Johannes: b c. 1740 d a. 12-19-1814 m Elizabeth — Pvt NY
John Godfrey: b c. 1760 d c. 10- -1849 m Barbara House Pvt PA
Leonard: b 1763 d p. 4-12-1849 m — Pvt NC ★

LIPEHITE,
John: b 8-18-1750 d 4-4-1831 m Polly Duffy Pvt CL ★

LIPES,
John: b 9-2-1758 d 7-24-1832 m Sarah Britton Pvt NJ

LIPFORD,
Henry:b 1753 d 1-12-1841 m — Pvt VA ★

LIPHART,
Henry: b c. 1740 d 8- -1796 m Barbara Smith Lt PA

LIPPERD, (or LIPPARD)
Wm.: b 7-17-1760 d 5-5-1834 m Mary Cress Pvt SC ★

LIPPINCOTT,
Caleb: b 7-2-1732 d p. 1790 m Hannah Wilkins Pvt NJ
John: b c. 1745 d p. 1830 m Abigail Collins Pvt NJ
Samuel: b 8-29-1759 d 2-24-1853 m Amy Maxson Pvt NJ ★

LIPPITT,
Charles: b 3-2-1754 d 8-17-1845 m Penelope Low Lt Asst Cmsry RI

LIPPITT, contd.
Christoper: b 10-28-1744 d 6-18-1824 m Waite Harris BGen RI Heirs ★
Jeremiah: b 1-27-1711 d 10-20-1776 m Welthian Greene PS RI
John: b 2-14-1763 d 7-19-1830 m (1)Ann Maria Bawler (2)Celia (Allen) Carpenter Pvt RI
Moses: b 12-16-1752 d 4-11-1833 m Eliza Lippitt Seacap RI
Moses: b 9-10-1751 d 12-15-1844 m Anstis Holden Pvt RI ★

LIPPS,
John: b c. 1758 d a. 12-14-1824 m Elizabeth Tompkins Sol NC

LIPSCOMB, (includes LIPSCOMBE)
Ambrose: b c. 1745 d 1794 m Elizabeth Claiborne Capt VA
Archibald: b 1763 d 3-22-1837 m Dorothy(Palmer)Lipscomb Pvt VA ★
Bernard: b c. 1755 d a. 1829 m Mary Hill Capt VA
John: b 10-31-1761 d 10-27-1827 m Sarah Smith Pvt VA
Mourning: b 1758 d 1817 m (1)Sarah Norrel (2)Mrs Jane Lipscomb Pvt VA
Reuben: b 1754 d 1808 m Ann Pleasants Capt VA
Thomas: b 3-25-1737 d 6-12-1825 m Mary Smith PS Sol VA
Uriah: b c. 1746 d a. 10-6-1825 m (1)— (2)Mary — (3)Susanna G. — PS VA
Wm. Sr.: b 3-28-1731 d 3-13-1810 m Elizabeth Smith PS VA
Wm., Jr.: b 2-12-1756 d 11-17-1802 m Elizabeth Ragland Hall FifMaj VA
Yancey: b c. 1750 d 5-1-1813 m Elizabeth — Capt VA

LIPSEY,
John: b 1723 d 6- -1835 m Catharine — Pvt VA

LISCOMB,
Darius: b 4-10-1757 d 9-7-1838 m (1)Olive Slader (2)Sarah Paine Pvt Fif CT ★
Nehemiah: b 11-26-1753 d 8-29-1835 m Rebecca Parsons Pvt VT
Samuel: b 5- -1765 d 3-12-1813 m Bethany Perry Pvt NY

LISENBY,
Reuben: b c. 1735 d 12-14-1782 m — Pvt SC

LISPENARD,
Leonard: b 12-14-1715 d 2-20-1790 m Alice Rutgers PS NY

LIST,
Jacob: b 1760 d 11-30-1842 m (1)Mary Quick (2)Mrs — Demaree Pvt Sct Grd PS NY ★

LISWELL,
Thomas: b 11-28-1758 d 11-4-1814 m Hannah Crosby Pvt MA

LITCH,
John: b 4-14-1752 d 4-17-1817 m Martha Steward Cpl MA

LITCHARD,
Joseph: b 1748 d 7- -1833 m Anna Maria Prawl Pvt PA ★

LITCHFIELD,
Amos: bpt 7-22-1753 d 9-15-1830 m (1)Bathsheba Litchfield (2)Assenath Stockbridge Pvt MA
Caleb: b 5-8-1760 d 1-19-1843 m Betsey Dunbar Pvt Mar MA ★
Daniel: b 3-21-1742 d 10-26-1820 m Sarah Whitcomb Pvt MA
Eleazer: b 4-15-1757 d 1840 m Keziah Witter Pvt Matr CT
Eleazar: b 1715 d 1780 m Desire White PS MA
Elisha: b c. 6-8-1733 d 10-20-1813 m Ruth Cole Pvt MA
Elisha, Jr.: b 1754 d 1787 m Delight Beals Pvt MA
Ephraim: b 9-26-1743 d p. 1792 m Penelope Lichfield Sgt MA
Isaac, Sr.: bpt 9-4-1720 d 12-11-1800 m (1)Lydia Cowing (2)Hannah Hersey Pvt MA
Isaac,Jr.: b 6-10-1746 d 12-11-1800 m Mrs Hannah Damon Pvt MA
Israel: bpt 6-2-1728 d p. 1790 m (1)Penelope Burden (2)Phoebe Holt Sol CT
Jacob: b 3-12-1750 d 5-7-1818 m Sarah Litchfield Pvt MA
James: b 11-12-1734 d 4-5-1812 m Hannah Pratt Pvt MA
James: b 2-10-1738 d 10-10-1786 m (1)Anna Gordon (2)Elizabeth (Litchfield) Pvt MA
John: b 1721 d 1-20-1785 m Lucy Cady PS CT
Josiah: b 2-23-1716 d p. 1777 m (2)Abigail Studley PS MA
Lawrence: b 2-19-1749 d 9-4-1814 m Mrs Rachel Clapp Lt MA
Lothrop: b 7-31-1741 d 12-30-1831 m Rhoda Perry Pvt MA
Nathaniel: b 12-8-1727 d p. 1789 m Priscilla Nash Pvt MA
Roland: b 3-19-1759 d 1828 m Lucy Curtis Cpl MA
Samuel: b 4-5-1757 d 9-8-1798 m Sarah Curtis Pvt MA
Thomas: bpt 7-14-1723 d 3-5-1803 m Lydia Cole Pvt MA
Ward: b 5-9-1757 d 5-1-1820 m Betsey Merritt Pvt MA

LITER,
John: b c. 1745 d 11- -1825 m Catherine — Pvt PA

LITS,
Wm.: b — d — m Eva Wust Pvt NY

LITSEY,
Anthony: b c. 1745 d p. 6-28-1791 m Susannah (Ogden)Sol VA

LITTIG,
Peter: b 12-10-1754 d 4-3-1799 m Magdalena — PS MD

LITTLE, (includes LIDDLE, LITTELL & LYTLE)
Abraham: b c. 1715 d 1- -1789 m Amy — PS NC
Absalom: b c. 1752 d 3-17-1825 m Mary Norris Pvt PA
Alexander: b 5-6-1748 d 5-26-1833 m Martha (Gregory) Riley 2Lt PA
Amos:b 12-10-1757 d 9-17-1831 m Hannah Moody Pvt MA
Andrew, Sr.: b 1718 d 5-18-1795 m Mary Stewart Pvt NY
Andrew, Jr.: b 2-8-1750 d p. 1795 m Jane Gregg Pvt NY
Andrew: b 1731 d 8-15-1784 m Jane Skiles 1Lt PA
Andrew: b c. 1760 d p. 1807 m — Knight Fif PA
Archibald: b — d p. 2-18-1777 m Sarah Wood Capt NY
Archibald: b 1730 d 1790 m (1)Margaret Johnson (2)Katherine — Col NC
Barzillai: b 1750 d 12-31-1835 m Betsey Blush Trm CT
Benjamin: b 4-13-1760 d 8-30-1846 m (1)Rhoda Bartlett (2)Persis Herbert Pvt NH
Caleb: b 3-19-1759 d 1-27-1848 m Abigail Rogers Pvt NH
Christy: b 9-11-1761 d 10-17-1850 m Rachel Cook Wgn NJ
Daniel: b 3-19-1750 d 1-13-1841 m Hannah Mores Pvt NH ★
Daniel: b 1731 d 12-10-1775 m Mary — CS NC
Daniel: b c. 1750 d a. 4-15-1807 m Phillippina — Sol NC
David: b 1-1-1751 d 12-28-1812 m Hannah Miller 2Lt NJ
Eliakim: b 1744 d 1805 m (1)Hannah Jewel (2)Mary Gillam SeaCap NJ
Enoch: b 5-21-1728 d 10-21-1816 m (1)Sarah Pettengill (2)Hannah Hovey PS NH
Ephraim, Jr.: b 11-27-1748 d 12- -1822 m Mrs Ann Wright Bulkley Pvt CT
Ezekiel: b 3-6-1721 d 12-28-1799 m Margaret Fitz MM Cpl MA
Forbes, Sr.: b 1710 d 5- -1801 m Sarah — Pvt RI
Forbes, Jr.: b 10-23-1736 d 1795 m Sarah Wilcox Ens RI
Friend: b 1-19-1756 d 11-19-1836 m Mary Couch Pvt NH ★
Gamaliel: b 1742 d 1800 m Sarah Phelps Cnt CT
George: b 11-7-1754 d 2-22-1808 m Rachel Rogers SeaCap MA
George: b 10-21-1749 d 3-7-1806 m Phebe Ensign PS NY
George: b 1730 d 1-28-1800 m Mary Ann Person Col NC
George: b 1735 d p. 2-1-1815 m (1)Mary (Little) (2)Mary (Handley) Douglass Capt PS SC
Henry: b c. 1747 d 4-24-1820 m Mary Ann Clark Pvt NJ
Henry: b 2-14-1758 d 4-4-1839 m — Pvt NY
Isaac: b 3-10-1764 d 2-25-1825 m Hannah Frazee Pvt NJ
James: b 8-16-1758 d 3-24-1843 m (1)Sarah Hodges (2)Rosetta Allen Pvt CT ★
James: b 1737 d 4-5-1807 m Isabella Hamilton Col GA
James: b 7-22-1717 d 4-5-1798 m Sarah Thompson 2Lt NY
James: b 1749 d 1833 m Mary Simpson Cpl NY
James: b a. 1726 d 1783 m Martha McConnell Pvt PA
James: b 1747 d 12-7-1820 m Mary Skyles Pvt PA
James: b — d p. 1808 m Agnes Gray Pvt SC
John: b 9-13-1743 d 2-28-1825 m Ruth Hale Pvt MA
John: b 1757 d 1845 m Betsey Montanye Pvt NJ
John: b 1712 d 1785 m Mary Longstreet PS NJ
John: b 1745 d 9-29-1822 m (1)Leah Crawford (2)Catherine McIntyre Capt NY
John: b 1750 d 7-22-1779 m Experience Horton Capt NY
John: b 1720 d 1793 m Eleanor Laurie Pvt NY
John: b 11-28-1748 d — m Elizabeth Everson Mus NY
John: b c. 1747 d p. 2-26-1819 m (1)Bellany Erwin (2)Jean Hall Pvt NC
John: b 1739 d 4-6-1806 m — Capt PS PA
John: b 2-16-1746 d 1798 m Mary Scofield Sgt PA
John: b 8-1-1760 d 1810 m Caroline Parks Pvt PA
John: b 1755 d 8-3-1822 m Rachel Kenny Pvt PA
Joseph: b 5-30-1761 d 3-26-1843 m Anna Morrill Pvt MA ★
Joseph: b 4-21-1730 d 2-1-1792 m Elizabeth Hazen Pvt MA
Joseph: b 1-19-1741 d 11-20-1819 m Mary Knight PS Lt NH
Joseph: b 6-22-1727 d 1811 m (1)Elizabeth Ingalls (2)Sarah Mills PS NH
Joseph: b c. 1743 d 3-21-1818 m Margaret Little Arfr NJ
Joseph: b 1732 d 5-29-1817 m Susannah — Lt VT
Joshua: b 9-17-1741 d 11-3-1821 m (1)Lydia Brown (2)Ruhamah (Burnham)Blaisdell Lt MA
Joshua: b 7-8-1747 d 6-25-1836 m Eunice Atkinson Pvt MA
Josiah: b 2-16-1747 d 12-26-1830 m Sarah Bailey Topham Pvt MA
Josiah: b 1727 d 1795 m Martha Hudson Lt NC
Luther: b 4-15-1757 d 3-22-1842 m Hannah Lovell Mid NS MA
Micajah: b c. 1761 d 1809 m Mary Brackenbury 2Lt NC
Moses: b 5-8-1724 d 5-27-1798 m Abigail Bailey Col MA
Moses: b 10-19-1747 d 3-21-1829 m Hannah Cole Pvt MA
Moses: b 8-3-1742 d 9-5-1813 m Mary Stevens Lt NH
Moses: b 4-15-1739 d 8-30-1798 m (1)Mary Milk (2)Sarah (Titcomb) Fernald CS NH
Nathaniel: b 11-10-1745 d 3-25-1839 m Mary Toppan 2Lt MA
Nathaniel: b 1759 d 11-20-1808 m Pamela Bradford Ens MA
Nathaniel: b 3-16-1755 d 5-27-1835 m Joanna Mizzy Plumer Pvt MA
Nathaniel: b 11-10-1746 d 8-11-1827 m Mary Carlton Ens NH
Nathaniel: b 1733 d 3-16-1796 m Susan Colie Pvt NJ
Nathaniel: b 1755 d 2-17-1826 m Catherine Corsner Pvt NJ ★
Nathaniel: b 1758 d 1843 m — Hill Matr NC

Paul: b 4-1-1740 d 2-11-1818 m Sarah Louther PS ME
Peter: b 1-27-1724 d 4-7-1783 m Ursual Schriever PS MD
Peter: b 9-13-1752 d 3-14-1822 m Christena Agner Sol NC
Richard: b 6-6-1725 d 2-13-1806 m Jane Noyes Pvt MA
Robert: b 8- -1753 d 7-9-1853 m Isabella Barclay Sgt NJ ★
Robert: b 1741 d 9-7-1822 m Elizabeth — Pvt NY
Robert: b c. 1763 d 2- -1813 m Esther (Lytle) Pvt NY
Robert: b 1730/1 d 1-21-1822 m Margaret Denniston(Denison)Pvt PA
Robert: b — d c. 1781 m Margaret — Pvt PA
Robert: b c. 1760 d 12- -1811 m Ann Mason Pvt PA
Robert: b 6-28-1753 d 6- -1838 m Margaret Sanderson Pvt PA ★
Samuel: b 2-18-1713 d 9-29-1792 m Dorothy Noyes PS NH
Stephen: b 5-19-1719 d 8-30-1793 m Judith Bailey PS MA
Theophilus: b 2-14-1744 d 2-19-1825 m Mary Polhemus Capt NJ
Thomas: b 7-7-1741 d 12-18-1810 m Lydia Drummond Capt NJ
Thomas: b 6-6-1750 d 5-31-1835 m Susanna Perkins Capt NC ★
Thomas: b 1740 d 12-5-1814 m Mary Campbell PS VA
Wallis: b 1751 d 1823 m Jane Shearer Pvt MA
Wm.: b c. 1766 d c. 1799 m Alathea — Drm CT
Wm.: b 1755 d 1835 m Hannah — Sol GA
Wm.: b 1720 d 7-20-1797 m Elizabeth Wallis Pvt MM MA
Wm.: b 10-13-1757 d 10-24-1819 m Phebe Meeker Pvt NJ
Wm.: b 1754 d 7-8-1833 m Meriam Cooly Pvt NY ★
Wm.: b 9-17-1755 d 9-4-1829 m Anne Taylor Capt NC
Wm.: b c. 1740 d p. 5-4-1790 m Elizabeth — PS NC
Wm.: b 10-15-1728 d 8-14-1797 m Mary Steel Pvt PA
Wm.: b 1745 d 7- -1825 m (1)Mary McDole (McDowell)(2)Elizabeth Walker Pvt PA ★
Wm.: b 1749 d 1-3-1823 m Ann — Pvt PA
Wm.: b c. 1749 d 6-21-1803 m Margaret Howe Capt VA
Wm. Adam: b 1- -1737 d 12- -1797 m Susanna Wallace Sol SC

LITTLEFIELD,
Aaron: b 8-2-1759 d 7-8-1840 m Meribah Thayer Pvt MA ★
Asa: b 2-18-1713 d 11-10-1837 m Mary Adams Pvt MA
Caleb: b 4-9-1733 d 8-12-1809 m Mary Dickens PS RI
Daniel: b a. 1760 d 2-25-1779 m Hannah Low Maj MA
Daniel: b 10-23-1737 d 2- -1820 m (1)Rachel — (2)Catherine Cole Sgt MA
Edmund: b 4-3-1724 d p. 1790 m Mary Caswell Pvt MA
Elijah, Jr.: b 6-4-1757 d c. 2-5-1836 m (1)Mary Tukey (2)Hannah Cooper Pvt MA ★
Ephraim: b 5-1-1749 d 1-10-1828 m Sarah Grant Pvt MA
James: b 1748 d 4-23-1801 m Mary Wheelright Capt MA
Jeremiah: b 7-17-1736 d 10-21-1816 m (1)Elizabeth Barbar (2)Elizabeth Everett Pvt MA
John: b 1753 d 3-11-1790 m Mirriam Winn Lt MA
John: b 8-18-1717 d 1796 m Susanna — LCol PS MA
Joseph: b 7-17-1737 d 4-4-1807 m Lydia Stevens Pvt MA
Jotham: b 1747 d 1834 m Mrs Martha Littlefield Pvt MA
Nathaniel: b 9-11-1762 d 1-29-1833 m Rebecca Tucker Pvt MA ★
Noah Moulton: b 1737 d 10-25-1821 m Martha Richardson LCol MA
Peter: b 3-19-1738 d p. 7-16-1808 m Esther Banks Pvt MA
Samuel, Jr.: b 5-28-1726/7 d p. 1783 m Susannah Bellamy PS ME
Seth: b 7-20-1757 d 1-21-1804 m Lucy Bartlett Pvt MA
Simeon: b 1761 d 9-11-1835 m Lydia Andrews Pvt MA
Wm.: b 1753 d 11-1-1822 m Elizabeth Brinley Capt RI

LITTLEHALE,
Abraham: b 1-23-1725 d 1-7-1811 m (1)Mary Stearns (2)Abagail Bailey Pvt MA
James: b 8-4-1731 d 12-17-1803 m Hannah Jaquith Pvt MA

LITTLEJOHN,
Samuel: b c. 1748 d 1813 m Sarah Cofer Lt SC
Wm.: b 12-7-1763 d 2-24-1826 m Deliverance Muxham Pvt MA
Wm.: b 2-22-1740 d 3-4-1817 m Sarah Blount PS CS NC

LITTLEPAGE,
John Carter: b 1753 d p. 1833 m — Puvall Capt VA ★

LITTLER,
John: b 1740 d 1-3-1819 m Rosannah — Sol VA
Thomas: b 10-10-1734 d a. 11-3-1818 m Magdaline — Pvt DE

LITTLETON,
Charles: b c. 1760 d 3-28-1848 m (1)Sarah(Earls)Hampton (2)Elizabeth Henderson SC W★
Wm. (Josiah John): b c. 1740 d a. 11-3-1843 m (1)Sarah — (2)Eleanor Elliott NS VA

LITTON, (includes LETTON & LITTEN)
James: b 1736 d 1798 m Sarah Osborne PS NC
Michael: b 4-4-1740 d 1819 m Mary Willett Pvt PS MD
Solomon: b 12-22-1751 d 2-24-1844 m Martha(Litton) 2Lt VA

LITZ,
Wm.: b c. 1740 d c. 1786 m Mare Catherine Dinninger Pvt VA

LITZINGER,
Henry: b 5-3-1735 d 12-5-1827 m (1)Mary Ann Cyprus (2)Sarah Charlotte Cyprus Pvt MD

LIVELY,
Cottrell: b 5-16-1763 d 12-2-1838 m Sarah Maddy Pvt VA

LIVENGOOD, (includes LEVERGOOD & LIVINGOOD)
Jacob: b c. 1728 d 1788 m Catharine Derr Capt PA
Jacob: b 1723 d 12-6-1783 m Christina — Pvt PA
Peter: b 9-15-1755 d 5-15-1825 m (1)Phoebe Yocum (2)Hanna (Gardner)Litzenberger Pvt PA
Peter: b 3-21-1763 d 4-10-1846 m Hannah Sands Sol PA
Peter: b 1758 d 11-14-1834 m Mary (Povator)Sellers Pvt VA

LIVERMORE,
Abigail Hagar: b 8-11-1725 d 1-17-1824 m Jason Livermore PS MA
Abijah: b 12-12-1737 d 1-18-1817 m (1)Anna Graves (2)Sarah Howe Lt MA
Abraham: b 8-13-1749 d 3-11-1826 m Hephzibeth Williams Pvt MA
Braddyll: b 10-4-1763 d 9-24-1845 m Mary Flint Fif Pvt MA ★
Daniel: b 1-26-1746 d 12-14-1804 m Elizabeth Hitchcock MM Cpl MA
Daniel: b 11-24-1734 d 10-19-1787 m Lucy Stratton CS MA
David: b 1745 d 12-13-1818 m Anna Haywood MM MA
Elijah: b 3-4-1730/1 d 8-5-1808 m (1)Dinah Harrington (2)Hannah (Cutting)Clark Pvt MA
Elisha: b 1-9-1720 d 2-13-1795 m Sarah Bigelow Pvt PS MA
Elisha: b 5-20-1751 d 9- -1836 m Ruth Ward Eddy Pvt MA
Isaac: b 5-11-1720 d p. 1790 m Dorothy Walker Pvt MA
Isaac: b 6-11-1752 d 1838m Hannah — Pvt MA
Jason: b 12-1-1726 d 10-14-1797 m Abigail Hagar Pvt MM MA
Jason, Jr.: b 4-28-1750 d 4-1-1816 m Mary Jackson Pvt Bbd MA
John: b 5-4-1761 d 9-14-1807 m Rachel Morse Pvt MA
Jonas: b 2-28-1763 d 1-31-1825 m Sarah Green Ward Pvt MA
Joseph: b 7-11-1740 d 12-13-1823 m (1)Anna Rice (2)Martha Maynard Capt MA
Josiah: b 5-12-1761 d 1-29-1840 m Rebecca Worcester Pvt MA
Moses: b 3-31-1759 d 4-14-1831 m Lydia Harrington Cpl MA
Moses: b 7-14-1729 d 10-18-1797 m Hannah Allen PS CS MA
Nathaniel: b 4-13-1713 d 10-2-1783 m Martha White PS MA
Oliver: b 7-15-1735 d 6-16-1782 m Catherine Bond Pvt MA
Samuel: b 5-14-1732 d 5- -1803 m Jane Brown PS NH
Silas: b 9-15-1756 d 5- -1833 m Abigail Livermore Sgt MA
Solomon: b 4-4-1762 d 7-12-1849 m Lois Warren Pvt MA ★
Wm.: b 1-12-1752 d 4-23-1806 m Mary Bigelow Pvt MA

LIVERS,
Arnold: b 1763 d 1837 m Mary Brawner PS MD

LIVEZEY, (includes LEVISEY)
Daniel: b 12-14-1752 d 1796 m Margery Croasdale Pvt PA
George: b 1764 d 5-19-1837 m Nancy Anderson Pvt VA
John: b 11-7-1758 d 9-9-1834 m Ann Hampton Pvt PA
Nathan: b 4-11-1739 d 6-8-1823 m Hannah Williams Pvt PA

LIVINGSTON, (includes LEVESTONE & LEVISTON)
Abraham: b 1754 d 7-3-1802 m Maria Peebles Capt NY
Asa: b 6-3-1755 d 5-8-1806 m Olive Peacock Pvt MA
Benjamin: b 4-8-1743 d 4-22-1837 m Margaret Scott Capt MA
David: b 1760 d 7-2-1843 m Annie Mishler Pvt MD ★
Duncan: b — d c. 1782 m Janett Wiley Pvt PA
George: b 10-3-1756 d 4-1-1849 m Susan Ennis Sol MD
Gilbert: b 12-17-1742 d 1806 m Catherine Cannell PS NY
Gilbert James: b 10-14-1758 d 4-7-1833 m Susanna Lewis Capt NY
Henry: b 9-8-1714 d 2-10-1799 m Susan Conklin PS CS NY
Henry: b 8-13-1748 d 2-29-1828 m Jane Patterson Maj NY
Henry: b 1761 d 6-12-1836 m Mary Frazier Pvt SC ★
Henry Brockholst: b 11-26-1757 d 3-18-1823 m Catharine Ketellas LCol NY
Isaac: b 1751 d 1-30-1823 m Anna — Sgt CT ★
Isaac: b 1-13-1755 d p. 1802 m Judith Sanders Pvt NY
Jacob: b 11-9-1746 d p. 1790 m Sarah House Pvt NY
James: b 5-23-1741 d 1812 m Silvia Martindale QM Sgt MA
James: b 3-27-1747 d 11-29-1832 m Elizabeth Simpson Col NY
James: b — d — m Judith Newcomb PS NY
John: b c. 1740 d p. 1789 m — Boyd Pvt NY
John: b 9-1-1739 d p. 7-12-1815 m Anna Sternberg Pvt NY
John, Sr.: b 1729/30 d 12- -1779 m Esther Conger Pvt PS CS PA
John: b 12-18-1764 d 12-11-1823 m Mary Isabella Hipps Pvt SC
Peter: b a. 1755 d 1-10-1835 m Elizabeth Osborne PS VA
Peter Robert: b 4-27-1737 d 11-15-1794 m Margaret (Livingston) PS Col NY
Peter VanBurgh: b 10- -1710 d 12-28-1792 m (1)Mary Alexander (2)Mrs — Ricketts PS NY
Philip: b 1-15-1716 d 6-12-1778 m Christina Ten Broeck SDI PS NY
Richard: b 10-19-1744 d 1786 m Elizabeth Rencour LCol NY
Robert: b 12-27-1708 d 11-27-1790 m (1)Mary Thong (2)Gertrude (VanRensselaer)Schuyler PS NY
Robert Gilbert, Sr.: b 12-24-1712 d 10-27-1789 m Catharine McPhaedres Maj NY
Robert G., Jr.: b c. 1732 d 1789-1792 m Margaret Hude DepAdjGen
Robert H.: b 10-25-1760 d 8-31-1804 m Catharine Tappan Lt NY
Robert R., Sr.: b 8- -1718 d 12-9-1775 m Margaret Beekman PS NY
Robert R., Jr.: b 11-27-1746 d 2-26-1813 m Mary Stevens PS NY

LIVINGSTON, contd.
Samuel: b 1757 d 10-6-1834 m Phoebe — Pvt VA ★
Thomas: b 8-3-1714 d 9-5-1807 m (1)Elizabeth Frost (2)Phoebe Stone CS PS MA
Thomas: b 1756 d *a.* 8-22-1809 m (1)Mary Childs (2)Nancy Childs Pvt VA
Walter: b 11-27-1740 d 5-14-1797 m Cornelia Schuyler PS NY
Wm.: b 2-19-1761 d 3-4-1834 m Elizabeth Saunders Pvt MA
Wm., Sr.: b 11-30-1723 d 7-23-1790 m Susanna French BGen NJ
Wm., Jr.: b 3-21-1754 d 5-17-1817 m Mary Lemington CS Wgn PS NJ
Wm.: b 4-26-1752 d *c.* 1804 m Elizabeth Roberts Capt SC
Wm. Smith: b 8-27-1755 d 6-25-1794 m Catharine Lott LCol CT

LLEWELLYN, (includes LEWALLEN & LEWELLEN)
Doctor: b 8-25-1757 d 2-3-1847 m Catherine — PS VA
John: b *c.* 1716 d 9- -1785 m Elizabeth Jordan PS MD
Philip: b *c.* 1747/8 d 1833 m — Pvt PA
Richard: b 1763 d 5-8-1833 m (1)Gracey Stokely (2)Parazeda Vowell Pvt VA ★
Wm.: b 1748 d 11-26-1825 m Susanna Wilson Pvt PA

LLOYD, (includes LOYD)
Bateman: b 8-28-1756 d 5-5-1814 m Abigail Lefferts Capt NJ
Edward: b 12-15-1744 d 11-19-1796 m Elizabeth Tayloe PS MD
George E., Sr.: b 2-4-1758 d 1-19-1853 m Ann Brown Pvt VA
Henry: b — d *p.* 1816 m — Ens VA
Hugh: b 1-22-1742 d 3-20-1832 m Susannah Pearson Col PA
Jaconias: b 2-25-1761 d *p.* 1804 m Elizabeth McCrief Pvt NJ
James: b *c.* 1742 d *p.* 12-31-1811 m Sarah Martin Capt MD
John: b 6-23-1723 d 10-14-1784 m Catherine Craig Pvt NJ
John: b 1-26-1743 d 2-4-1817 m (1)Sarah Couvenhoven (2)Anna Longstreet (3)Elizabeth Brown Swain Cmsry PS NJ
John: b 1733 d 8-11-1817 m Eunice — Lt NY
John: b 1762 d 1822 m Rachel VanderVeer Pvt PA
John: b *c.* 1738 d 1814 m Elizabeth Brooks Pvt PA
John: b 9-22-1735 d 11-8-1807 m Rebecca Savage PS SC
Joseph: b 1767 d 11-29-1831 m Euphemia Huyler Drm Fif NJ ★
Nicodemus: b 1762 d 1- -1844 m (1)Eleanor Hersh (2)Rebecca Firestone Pvt PA
Samuel: b 5-27-1747 d 4-24-1834 m — Pvt NC ★
Stephen: b *c.* 1759 d *a.* 3-1-1791 m Martha — PS NC
Thomas: b 1736 d 1792 m — PS NC
Thomas: b 12-26-1763 d 4-15-1857 m Martha Jane McCullough Lt NC
Thomas: b — d *a.* 12-20-1783 m Anna Chew Ward PS MD
Thomas: b 10-2-1744 d 12-1-1805 m Patience McCracken Pvt VA
Wm.: b 1734 d 11-2-1815 m Isabella Black Pvt MA
Wm.: b 1747 d *c.* 1820 m Sarah Chowning Pvt VA ★

LOBACH, (includes LOBAUGH)
Abram: b 2- -1746 d 1808 m Mary Burkholder Pvt PA
Andrew: b 11-30-1751 d 7-29-1818 m Eve Knisley Pvt PA
Peter: b 1- -1720 d 1-20-1785 m (1)Helen Pallio (2)Susanna Betz PS PA

LOBB,
Abraham: b 12-28-1733 d 1-27-1784 m (1)Dinah Thomas (2)Naomi — Pvt PA

LOBDELL,
Abraham: bpt 8-25-1765 d 6-5-1823 m Sarah Kennard Pvt MA
Daniel: b *c.* 1740 d *p.* 1783 m Elizabeth Lockwood Pvt NY
Darius: b 10-18-1729 d 11- -1796 m Mary Baldwin Pvt NY
Ebenezer, Jr.: b 7-13-1735 d *p.* 1783 m Eunice Bradley Pvt NY
Isaac: b 3-8-1755 d 3-24-1838 m (1)Mirriam Pomeroy (2)Jerusha Lobdell Pvt MA ★
Isaac: b 12-26-1717 d 1-26-1802 m Ruth Clark Pvt MA
Isaac: b 10-5-1755 d 6-18-1806 m Mary Stetson Pvt MA
Jacob: b 1732 d 4-16-1816 m Ruth Boughton Pvt NY
Jacob: b 1756 d 2-27-1834 m (1)Betty Whitney (2)Rebecca Morehouse Pvt NY
James: bpt 7-13-1757 d 1827 m Mary Venable Pvt MA
John: b 3-10-1743 d 10-15-1812 m Elizabeth Sherwood Pvt NY
Samuel: b 10-7-1728 d 1792 m Elizabeth Blain 2Lt NY
Uriah: b 3-11-1740 d *p.* 1779 m Phoebe Chapman Pvt CT

LOBINGIER,
Christopher: b 10- -1741 d 7-4-1798 m Elizabeth Muller PS PA

LOCKE, (includes LOCK)
Abraham: b 6-3-1752 d 2-28-1820 m Hannah(Locke)Cpl MA
Alexander: b 6-27-1757 d 11-8-1824 m Rachel Clarey Pvt NC
Amos: b 12-24-1742 d 7-27-1828 m Sarah Locke Pvt MA
Ayers: b 1763 d 3-27-1839 m Lydia Blodgett Pvt MA ★
Benjamin: b 8-6-1738 d 12-7-1791 m Mary Pierce Capt MA
Benjamin: b 5-7-1756 d 6-4-1842 m Betsey Wyman Pvt MA
Benjamin: b *c.* 1762 *p.* 1790 m Sara Roots Sol NC
David: b 2-22-1740 d 8-19-1800 m Betsey Kibbe Pvt MA
David: b 8-24-1735 d 6-3-1810 m (1)Annah Lovering (2)Mrs. Olive (Marden) Elkins PS CS NH
Ebenezer: bpt 3- -1735 d 9-12-1816 m Lucy Wood Pvt MA

Ebenezer. Sr.: b 8-5-1737 d 9-24-1812 m Phebe Moore PS NH
Ebenezer, Jr.: b 8-6-1763 d 11-12-1856 m (1)Hannah Gustin (2)Mrs Susan Campbell Pvt VT
Edward: b 5-18-1701 d 6-29-1788 m Hannah Blake PS NH
Elijah, Sr.: b *c.* 1714 d 1782 m Huldah Perkins PS NH
Elijah, Jr.: bpt 12-15-1754 d 8- -1838 m Elizabeth Brown Pvt NH
Elisha: b 5-7-1761 d 1-28-1844 m Mehitable Stickney Cpl NH ★
Francis: b *a.* 1750 d 9-15-1777 m Ann McMurtrie Capt NJ
Francis: b 12-29-1754 d *p.* 1805 m Blanche Rutherford Lt NC
Francis: b 1732 d 1796 m Anna Brandon Col NC
Frederick: b 6-6-1758 d 1-17-1834 m Anna Farwell Pvt MA
George: b — d *p.* 9-22-1823 m Sarah — PS VA
James: b 12-5-1728 d 1-19-1808 m Hannah Farnsworth 2Lt PS MA
James: b 4-7-1752 d 7-6-1831 m Sarah Symmes Pvt MA
James: b 3-11-1759 d *p.* 1790 m Susannah Kimball Pvt MA
James: b 1753 d 12-8-1831 m Martha Seavey Pvt NH
Jeremiah: b 8-4-1728 d 1-28-1795 m Mary Elkins PS NH
Jesse: b *c.* 1755 d 11-9-1815 m Sarah Bruce Sol MD
Jethro: b 6-27-1727 d 10-29-1807 m Hannah Rand PS NH
John: b 7-4-1755 d 10-4-1818 m Salome — Pvt MD
John: b 9-2-1752 d 3-31-1837 m Ruth Faxon Sgt MA
John: b 10-19-1746 d 5-5-1801 m (1)Sarah Jones (2)Thankful Blago (Blaisdell) PS NH
John: b 1755 d 1845 m Lucretia (Hicks) Jordan Sgt NC ★
John: b *c.* 1726 d 2-7-1795 m Nancy — Cpl VA
John: b 1752 d 1834 m Mary Ann Raider Sol VA
Jonas: b 1727 d 3-5-1812 m Mary Dwight Capt MA
Jonas: b 2-22-1757 d 8-23-1833 m (1)Sarah Russell (2)Eunice Winship (3)Deborah (Robbins) Blodgett Pvt MA
Jonathan: b 1-17-1716 d 1-10-1799 m Phoebe Pierce Pvt MA
Jonathan: bpt 4-19-1762 d 5-27-1803 m Alice Pearson Pvt NH W★
Jonathan: b 3-29-1732 d 9-13-1813 m Abigail Towle PS NH
Joseph: b 4-23-1729 d 1777 m Mary Ayres Maj MA
Joseph, Jr.: b 3-28-1734 d 4-27-1791 m Sally Baldwin Pvt MA
Joseph: b 4-14-1750 d 9-13-1823 m Mary Butterfield Pvt MA
Joseph: b 10-23-1753 d 4-22-1790 m Martha Dow PS NH
Josiah: b 2-6-1735 d 4-18-1819 m Persis Matthews Capt MA
Josiah: b 5-21-1757 d 4-12-1841 m Elizabeth Gelpatrick Cpl MA
Josiah: b 2-3-1753/4 d 8-5-1811 m Elizabeth Richardson Pvt MA
Matthew: b 1730 d 12-17-1801 m (1)Mary Elizabeth Brandon (2)Elizabeth Gostler BGen NC
Moses: b 9-2-1754 d 1827 m Hannah — Pvt MA
Moses: b 7-8-1733 d 1797 m Mary Organ Pvt NH
Reuben: b 3-13-1748 d 1-25-1823 m Jerusha Richardson Pvt Slr MA
Richard: b 9-4-1744 d 10-20-1823 m Huldah Hobbs Pvt NH
Richard: bpt 6-7-1750 d 12-26-1827 m Sarah Palmer Pvt PS NH
Richard: b 1-11-1762 d *p.* 1835 m Mary Thackston Pvt VA ★
Samuel: b 12-15-1748 d 9-13-1819 m Margaret Adams Lt MA
Samuel: b 7-28-1740 d 10-22-1818 m (1)Deborah Veazey (2)Esther Dow (3)Hannah Magoon (4)Sally James PS NH
Simeon: b 3-31-1760 d 8-12-1836 m Abigail Blake Pvt NH
Simon: b 9-20-1752 d 9-6-1831 m Lydia Foss Pvt NH
Stephen: b 3-29-1750 d 11-4-1822 m Sally Hopkins Pvt MA
Thomas: b 6 11-1753 d 2-19-1831 m Abigail Gowen Lt MA
Thomas: b 10-14-1751 d 4-16-1816 m Martha Worthen CS NH
Thomas: b *c.* 1735 d *a.* 3-9-1801 m — Slater Sol NC
Timothy: b *c.* 1700 d 1797 m Miriam Brooke Capt RI
Timothy Blake: b 10-30-1735 d 5-12-1822 m (1)Lydia Dow (2)Patience Perkins Sgt NH
Wm.: b 6-16-1758 d 4-9-1828 m Abigail Saunders Pvt NH
Wm.: b 4-12-1748 d 3-20-1829 m Rebecca Barrett CS NH
Wm., Sr.: b *c.* 1704 d *c.* 1784 m (1)Meribah Page (2)Elizabeth Rand PS NH
Wm., Jr.: b 8-9-1745 d *p.* 4-18-1826 m (1)Betsey Babb (2)Mary Hayes PS NH
Wm.: b 7-26-1738 d 11-16-1825 m (1)Christiana Paine (2)Mrs Mary Dustin PS NH
Wm.: b 2-2-1756 d 11-29-1823 m Margaret McCoy Pvt PA ★
Wm.: b 3-1-1744 d 3-11-1843 m Sarah Neal Pvt VA ★
Wm.: b 1730 d 1785 m Agnes Thweatt Hardaway Pvt VA

LOCKER, (includes LOCHER & LOKER)
Henry: b 9-20-1724 d 6-4-1813 m Hannah Barber Sgt MA
Henry: b 1747 d 1839 m Elizabeth Hoffman Pvt PA
Isaac: b 3-5-1739 d 10-4-1824 m Nancy Brintnell Capt CS MA
Jonas: b 12-3-1730 d 6-17-1775 m Abigail Barber Sol MA
Thomas: b 8-17-1751 d 10-27-1803 m Rebecca Mackall PS MD

LOCKERMAN,
Thomas Nyer: b 1738 d — m Catharine Ryal Lt MD

LOCKHART, (includes LOCKART)
Aaron: b 1749 d 12-20-1798 m Sarah Miles Lt PS SC
Jacob: b *c.* 1715 d 1783 m Mary — Pvt VA
James: b *c.* 1740 d *p.* 1791 m Rachel Ann — LCol NC
James: b *c.* 1730 d *p.* 1790 m Elizabeth — Pvt NC
James: b — d 1800 m Hannah Hawkins Smith PS NC
James: b *c.* 1740 d *p.* 1805 m (1)Polly Mitchell (2)Rachel Totten Pvt VA
Joel: b 1757 d 1827 m Charlotte Vincent Pvt NC
Patrick: b *a.* 1750 d *p.* 1781 m Mary McDonald Maj VA
Richard: b — d *a.* 10-25-1800 m Mary — Sol GA
Robert: b 1744 d 5-13-1817 m Margery (Denny) Wilson Sgt PA

Samuel: b *a.* 1745 d *p.* 1783 m Sarah Barrett LCol PS NC
Samuel: b 1727 d *a.* 1786 m Catherine — Capt PS NC
Wm.: b *c.* 1736 d 1795 m Mary Campbell CS VA

LOCKLIN, (includes LOCKLING)
Dennis: b 9-16-1725 d 12-12-1798 m Abigail Houghton PS VT
Jonathan: b 8-28-1754 d 12-27-1841 m (1)Rachel Parker (2)Sally
   Houghton Fif VT

LOCKMAN,
Vincent: b *c.* 1762 d 10-29-1843 m (1)Anne Kirkland (2)Christina
   (Miller) Hagan Pvt NC

LOCKWOOD,
Abraham: b 12-26-1748 d 11-11-1790 m Patience Greene Capt RI
Abraham: b 1-9-1761 d 4-21-1831 m Bethiah Field Pvt VT
Abraham: b 4-19-1751 d 1830 m (1)Lydia Pollard (2) — Sastelle Pvt
   VT
Abram: b *a.* 1760 d *p.* 1801 m Anna Hyatt Pvt CT
Armwell: b 4-28-1738 d 1-30-1806 m Gertrude Muncey Capt DE
Benejah: b 11-20-1757 d *p.* 1800 m Abby Webb Pvt RI
Benoni: b 11-27-1733 d 2-19-1781 m Phebe Waterman Capt RI
Charles: b 5-8-1766 d 9-13-1834 m Elizabeth Waterbury Pvt CT ★
Daniel: b 6-5-1734 d 11-28-1807 m Mary Bellamy Pvt CT
David: b 1737 d 7-6-1789 m Martha Trowbridge Pvt CT
David: b 6-21-1760 d 12-24-1841 m Sarah Closson Pvt NY
David: b 3-16-1762 d 11-27-1840 m Rebecca Thomas Pvt Slr NY
Ebenezer: b 1741 d 1821 m Mary Godfrey Pvt CT
Ebenezer: b 3-31-1737 d 7-29-1821 m (1)Hannah Smith (2)Sarah
   — Maj PS NY
Eliphalet: b 10-17-1741 d 3-19-1814 m Mary Goold Capt Cmsry CT
Ephraim: bpt 4-22-1744 d 12-25-1829 m (1)Sarah Slawson (2)Sarah
   Waring Capt NY
Ezra: b 5-30-1747 d 3-8-1821 m Hannah Clauson Pvt CT
Gershom, Sr.: b 1728 d 1798 m Eunice Close Pvt CT
Gershom, Jr.: b *c.* 1754 d 3-12-1816 m Polly Waring Cpl PS CT
Gilbert: b 1747 d 8-9-1836 m Phoebe Hall Capt CT ★
Henry: b 6-14-1762 d 1-1-1839 m (1)Esther Smith (2)Sarah
   Schofield (3)Clarissa Newton Capt VT
Hezekiah: b 11-15-1755 d *p.* 1785 m Catherine Seymour Pvt CT
Hezekiah: b 1752 d 1795 m Mary Birdsall Pvt NY
Isaac: b 5-21-1741 d 1816 m Rebecca Seeley Capt CT
Isaac, Jr.: b 12-22-1761 d 12-16-1838 m Ruth Aner Nichols Pvt CT ★
Isaac: b 12-12-1749 d 1-19-1830 m Susannah Wygant Pvt NY ★
Jacob: b 10-3-1761 d *p.* 1790 m Mary Pellum Drm CT
Jacob: b 10-15-1756 d 7-27-1819 m Esther Field Pvt VT
James: b 10-25-1746 d 10-30-1833 m (1)Phebe — (2)Abigail
   DeForest (3)Elizabeth Waring Richards Sgt CT
James: b *c.* 1752 d 1799 m Rachel Lockwood Pvt CT
Jared: b 7-7-1758 d 8-2-1823 m Elizabeth Skelking OrdlSgt CT
Jeremiah: b 1733 d 11- -1786 m Abigail Smith Pvt CT
Jesse: b 7-2-1745 d 1-13-1823 m Mary Hawes Pvt NY
John: b 1-10-1738 d *c.* 12- -1776 m Hannah Hoyt Pvt CT
John: b — d — m (1)Ann Kirkley (2)Frances Cummins (3)Priscilla
   Blackiston CS DE
Jonathan: b 1719 d 1-24-1798 m Mercy Finch Pvt CT
Joseph: b 1747 d *p.* 1806 m Cordelia Filly Pvt CT
Joseph, Jr.: b 6-30-1731 d 3-17-1792 m Hannah Close Capt PS NY
Joshua: b 11-5-1729 d 11-5-1809 m Mary Lee PS SC
Lambert: b 1757 d 2-11-1825 m Elizabeth Roe Sgt CT
Moses: b 9-26-1749 d *a.* 2-26-1809 m Sarah Bunce Sgt CT
Nathan: b 4-28-1759 d 9-29-1841 m (2)Mary Mead Pvt CT ★
Nathaniel: b 5-20-1717 d *p.* 1790 m Mary Patchin Pvt CT
Nathaniel: b 1756 d *p.* 1798 m (1)Elizabeth Ellison (2)Rebecca
   Raymond Pvt NY
Nathaniel: b 7-19-1751 d *p.* 1790 m Joanna Benedict Pvt CT
Philip: b 2-28-1750 d 10-29-1831 m Hannah Clason Pvt CT
Reuben: b 4-17-1762 d 5-11-1838 m Elizabeth Raymond Tms CT
Reuben, Sr.: b 12-15-1715 d 1776 m (1)Sarah Cramp (2)Elizabeth
   Stevens Pvt NY
Reuben, Jr.: b *c.* 1751 d 5-30-1831 m Mary Mead Pvt CT W★
Richard: b 11-29-1736 d 3-21-1786 m Margaret Jackson PS CS
   Capt DE
Samuel, Jr.: b 11-25-1737 d 8-26-1807 m Letisicia (Letitia) Davis
   Capt CT
Samuel: b 4-3-1748 d 12-6-1825 m Jemima Northrup Lt CT
Samuel: b 4-18-1756 d 5-22-1821 m Sarah Betts PS CT
Stephen: b 8-16-1754 d 2-13-1830 m Sarah Betts Pvt CT
Timothy: b 10-26-1735 d *c.* 1782 m Abigail Mead Capt CT
Timothy: b 12-21-1749 d 1-13-1818 m Susannah Silkworth Pvt NY
Titus: b 1749 d 12-20-1815 m Hannah Dan Pvt CT
Wm.: b 8-15-1753 d 2-13-1837 m Jemima Lounsbury Pvt Slr CT ★
Wm.: b 1-21-1753 d 1-23-1828 m Sarah Sturges Chp CT
Wm.: b 1730 d 11-27-1801 m Sarah White PS VT

LODER,
John: b 8-24-1765 d 2-10-1844 m Martha Armstrong Pvt NY
Jonathan: b 5-28-1741 d 12-31-1832 m Ann Bouton Capt NY

LODGE,
Benjamin, Jr.: b 3-28-1749 d 5-16-1801 m (1)Elizabeth Carnahan
   (2)Martha Latimer Lt PA
Jonathan: b — d 11- -1783 m Margaret Hammon 1Lt CS PA

Jonathan: b 2-28-1762 d 3-21-1844 m Elizabeth Leslie PS PA
Wm. O: b 1740 d 1814 m Johanna O'Neal PS MD

LOFLAND,
Dorman: b *c.* 1734 d *a.* 11-26-1792 m (1)Comfort Smith (2)Mary
   Hogshead CS PS DE

LOFTIN,
Elkanah: b 1726 d 1792 m Rachel Herring Sol NC
Francis: b 1752 d 1810 m prob Louvisa — PS NC

LOGAN, (includes LOGGAN)
Alexander: b 7- -1758 d 12-15-1836 m Eliza Watts Pvt PA ★
Andrew: b 8-17-1763 d 4-14-1856 m (1)Mary Hyde (2)Nancy
   Merwether Pvt SC
Benjamin: b 1743 d 12-11-1802 m Ann Montgomery Col VA
David: b *c.* 1758 d 1825 m (1)Susannah Cord (2)Margaret — Lt PA
David, Sr.: b 1750 d 11-28-1815 m Margaret Logan Vol PA
David: b *a.* 1756 d 2-14-1826 m Elizabeth Arbour Pvt PA
Francis: b 1734 d 11-6-1826 m Hannah Tremble Capt SC
George: b 1759 d 12- -1816 m Dorcas Logan Pvt PA
Hugh: bpt 3-24-1745 d 12-25-1816 m Sarah Woods Pvt VA
James: b 6-30-1731 d 3-15-1805 m Rachael Weeks Pvt CT
James: b 1738 d 7-1-1808 m Mary Ward Bbd MA
James: b 6-27-1754 d 1-14-1803 m Elizabeth Alcott Sgt NJ
James: b 1733 d 6- -1825 m Hannah Erwin Pvt VA
John: b 1753 d 1821 m Mary (Logan) Pvt PA
John: b 1757 d 9-11-1841 m Christena Barringer Pvt NJ ★
John: b 1729 d 2-21-1788 m Hannah Sawyer Pvt PA
John: b 3-15-1760 d 1- -1818 m (1)Elizabeth Briarley (2)Mary
   Thompson Pvt PA
John: b 5-10-1747 d 7- -1807 m Jane McClure LCol CS KY
John: b 5-2-1742 d *p.* 1791 m Ann McClure Ens VA
John: b 11-30-1761 d 7-8-1820 m Rachel Foster Pvt VA
Matthew: b 12-15-1742 d 6-6-1824 m Sarah Savage Pvt CT
Patrick: b 1752 d 1-17-1828 m Sarah Nancy Harper Pvt VA ★
Robert: b *c.* 1760 d *p.* 4-10-1846 m Elizabeth Dickey Pvt PA
Robert: b 7-12-1739 d 12-26-1812 m Ruth Beckwith Sgt VT
Samuel: b 1760 d 3-3-1845 m Rebecca Walker Pvt PA ★
Samuel: b 1745 d 4-4-1825 m Abigail Clark Maj NY ★
Timothy: b 1759 d 3-21-1848 m (1)Sarah — (2)Sarah Alexander
   (3)Sally Smith Pvt VA ★
Wm.: b 1-2-1735 d 1-16-1803 m Margaret Lewis Capt NJ
Wm.: b 3-18-1736 d 1-8-1814 m Rebecca Gaston Capt NJ
Wm.: b 11-11-1748 d 1-7-1833 m Jane Margaret Black Pvt NC
   SC ★
Wm.: b 8-3-1762 d 9-12-1838 m Eleanor Craig Pvt SC
Wm.: b 1-8-1726 d 6-5-1802 m (1)Mary Baker (2)Margaret Crockett
   PS SC
Wm.: bpt 7-14-1749 d *c.* 1795/6 m Agnes McConn Pvt KY VA
Wm.: b 10-13-1767 d 7-24-1836 m Sarah Haskins Pvt VA
Wm.: b *c.* 1721 d 1791 m Elizabeth — Sol VA

LOGEE,
Caleb: b 7-19-1756 d 9-23-1825 m Rachel Battles Pvt RI

LOGSDON,
John, Sr.: b *c.* 1716 d 10- -1797 m Margaret Wooley PS MD
Ralph: b *c.* 1736 d 1818 m Mary Durbin PS MD

LOGUE,
James: b 9-6-1750 d 10-1-1825 m Anna Logue Ens PA
John: b 1758 d 6-6-1833 m Mary Sproul Pvt PA

LOGWOOD,
Thomas: b 1740 d 9-10-1821 m (1)Ann Aiken (2)Mrs Martha
   Minnis Capt VA

LOHR, (includes LORE)
George: b *c.* 1752 d 1788 m Barbara Nagle Capt PA
Martin: b 1720 d 5-24-1799 m Elizabeth Hays Pvt PA
Michael: b 10-6-1755 d 1835 m Catherine Schriner Pvt MD ★
Peter: b 1750 d 9-21-1841 m Catharine — Pvt MD ★
Valentine: b 1747 d 1826 m Eva Winkler Pvt PA

LOHRA,
Conrad: b — d *a.* 8-20-1791 m Dorothea — PS PA

LOMAX,
Thomas: b 1-25-1746 d 10-17-1811 m Ann Corbin Tayloe PS VA
Wm.: b 2-14-1745 d 7-2-1813 m (2)Sarah Knight Pvt NC

LOMBARD, (includes LUMBARD)
Aaron: b 11-2-1747 d 12-22-1824 m Lucy — Pvt MA
Benjamin: b 3-23-1723 d 1-3-1794 m Elizabeth — Sgt MA
Calvin: b 5-25-1748 d 1808 m (1)Martha Grant (2)Mary Walker PS
   MA
David: b 10-29-1756 d 2-21-1839 m Beulah — Pvt VT ★
Elijah: b 1-20-1750 d *a.* 1779 m Eunice — Sol MA
Jedediah, Sr.: b 4-8-1728 d 1-24-1820 m Susan Dlrsett Slr MA
Jedediah, Jr.: b 1760 d 3-16-1842 m Lydia Rand Pvt MA
John: b 8-11-1764 d 7-31-1853 m Elizabeth Sawyer Pvt MA

LOMBARD, contd.

Joseph, Sr.: b 7-16-1720 d 5-25-1805 m Ruth — (2)Lydia Leach PS MA

Joseph, Jr.: b 3-1-1744 d 10-15-1825 m Mary Faulkner Pvt MA

Nathaniel: b 1757 d 6-29-1837 m Ruth Hamblin Sgt MA W★

Richard: b 2-23-1743 d 10-21-1825 m Lydia Bangs LCol MA

Solomon, Sr.: b 4-5-1702 d 1781 m Sarah Purrington PS CS MA

Solomon, Jr.: b 5-15-1738 d p. 1779 m Lydia Grant Pvt MA

Thomas, Jr.: b 3-26-1751 d — m (1)Mary — (2)Anne Shaw Sgt MA

LOMMASON,

Lawrence: b a. 1751 d a. 12-11-1810 m Bridgett VanNatta 2Lt NJ

LONAS, (includes LONASS & LONES)

Adam: b 1754 d 4-4-1839 m Elizabeth Bront Pvt NY

George: b 1764 d 1852 m (1)Barbara Helsely (2)Katherine Barbe Pvt VA ★

John: b — d 10-2-1782 m Mary Keplinger Pvt MD W★

John: b 6- -1728 d 5- -1833 m Margaret Sporbeck Pvt NY

LONDON,

John: b c. 1728 d 1779 m Elizabeth — Pvt NJ

LONG, (includes LANG)

Abraham: b 1743 d 4-19-1794 m Maria — Pvt PA

Alexander: b c. 1750 d 1-13-1829 m Elizabeth — Pvt PA

Alexander: b 10-3-1756 d 1843 m Sarah Graham Pvt PA ★

Andrew: b 1730 d 11-4-1812 m Mary Carr Capt PA

Andrew, Jr.: b 5-11-1758 d 11-16-1830 m Jemima Santee Pvt PA W★

Armistead: b 4-26-1762 d 3-9-1831 m (1) — Greenough (2)Elizabeth Burgess Ball (3)Mrs. Latham Sol VA

Benjamin: b 7-13-1757/8 d 1828 m Elizabeth — Pvt PA ★

Benjamin: b 1745 d 1816 m Priscilla Turner Maj SC

Brumfield: b c. 1750 d p. 3-17-1823 m Elizabeth Mitchell PS VA

Christopher: b 5- -1746 d 8-14-1829 m Sarah Turner ColorSgt VA

Cookson: b — d 1786 m Rebecca McNight Col PA

David: b 8-10-1761 d 12-22-1852 m Margaret Harkness Pvt MA

David: b 1758 d 1-24-1845 m Mary Howe Pvt NC

David: b 3- -1758 d p. 1821 m Sarah — Pvt PA

Edward: b 10-22-1739 d 10-18-1792 m Sarah Comstock Capt NY

Elias: b 1746 d 1827 m Betsey — Pvt PA

Evans: b c. 1759 d 1819 m Lucy Apperson Sgt VA

Felix: b 1720 d 8-21-1784 m Mary — PS SC

Gabriel: b 2- -1751 d 2-3-1827 m (1)Elizabeth Stubblefield (2)Ann (Slaughter) Stubblefield Capt VA

George: b 1741 d 4-9-1819 m (2)Margaret (McCurdy) — Pvt PA

George: b 1766 d 3-11-1854 m Isabella McCormick Pvt PA ★

George: b 1754 d 2-16-1836 m Catherine Bowers Sol SC

Gideon: b 1756 d 2-16-1834 m Hannah Phillips Pvt PA W★

Henry: b 4-25-1756 d 1824 m Ann Pope Pvt NC

Henry: b 2-6-1764 d 1-18-1842 m Margaret (Zimmerman) Pvt PA

Henry: b 1745 d 1816 m Margaret — Sgt PA

Henry: b a. 1763 d a. 3- -1803 m Rebecca Harris Pvt SC

Herman: b c. 1736 d 1804 m (1)Ann Hershey (2)Anna Kaufman (3)Mrs Elizabeth Gerringer Pvt PA

Herman: b 7-5-1748 d 1820 m — Pvt PA

Hugh: b c. 1740 d 1778 m Mary Corbit 1Lt PA

Jacob: b 10-2-1754 d 4-11-1831 m Elizabeth — Pvt PA

Jacob: b 1754 d 12-22-1842 m Eve Funk Pvt PA VA W★

Jacob: b 1742 d 1799 m Elizabeth Minnick Pvt SC

Jacob: b c. 1760 d a. 8-16-1834 m Katherine — Pvt SC

Jacob: b c. 1745 d p. 7-22-1810 m Mary Ann — Sgt PS VA

James: b c. 1750 d 5-12-1806 m (1)Catherine — (2)Mrs Patience Pratt PS MD

James: b 1758 d 12- -1841 m Elizabeth Douglass Cpl PA

James: b 11-18-1764 d 12-28-1848 m (2)Susannah Knight Pvt PA

James: b c. 1753 d 4-6-1825 m Margery Thomas Pvt SC W★

James: b 12-24-1767 d p. 1820 m Priscilla Laswell Pvt VA

Jeremiah: b 1756 d 7-4-1820 m (1)Mary Ivers (2)Jane — Pvt PA

John: b a. 1763 d p. 1798 m Elizabeth Shafer Pvt MD

John: b 9-3-1747 d 1-24-1805 m Esther Hows Dr PA

John: b 1737 d 1826 m Jane (Young) Henry Pvt TN

John: b 1756 d 1826 m Mrs Ann Graham Beaty Pvt NC

John, Sr.: b 1718 d 1786 m Maria Barbara LaBar Pvt PA

John, Sr.: b 1737 d 5-25-1830 m Betsy — Pvt PA

John, Jr.: b — d p. 1-16-1814 m — Pvt PA

John: b c. 1742 d 4- -1813 m Catherine — Pvt PA

John: b 1755 d 3-15-1826 m Elizabeth Bennet Capt VA

John: b 1753 d 1829 m Maria Whitzel Ens VA

John: b 12-25-1755 d 5-20-1828 m Delilah Eliott Pvt VA ★

John: b 11-18-1749 d 1-18-1832 m Mary Haynes Pvt VA

Joseph: b 1750 d 1854 m Nancy Henard Pvt MD

Joseph: b 10-24-1761 d 7-9-1824 m Elizabeth — Pvt MD

Joseph: b 1747/8 d 2-11-1800 m Sara Dildine Pvt PA

Joseph: b c. 1750 d a. 7- -1829 m Catherine Thompson Capt VA

Lawrence: b 5-10-1756 d 1803 m Priscilla Cogswell QMSgt VA

Levi: b 7-23-1758 d 9-11-1849 m (1)Abigail Baker (2)Martha Kimball Pvt Tms CT ★

Littleton: b 1760 d 1827 m Martha Shelton Pvt NC

Ludwick: b c. 1750 d 4- -1829 m Christina — Pvt PA

Ludwick: b c. 1730 d 12-3-1795 m Elizabeth — PS PA

Mathew: b 9-7-1757 d 12-21-1821 m Betty Hawes Pvt MA

Matthew: b c. 1753 d a. 1790 m Mary Kennedy Of PA

Matthew: b 4-19-1753 d 6-7-1838 m Rebecca Maxwell Pvt Spy PA ★

Michael: b c. 1761-3 d 10- -1802 m Christina Stober Pvt PA

Michael: b 2-14-1756 d 7-13-1822 m Mary Agnes Small Pvt PA

Moses: b 10-16-1760 d 3-3-1848 m Lucy Harriman Pvt MA

Nicholas: b 1728 d 8-22-1819 m (1)Mary Reynolds (2)Mary McKinney Dep QM NC

Nicholas, Sr.: b 1730 d 1796 m Gretchen Wilhelm Pvt PA

Nicholas, Jr.: b 8-2-1754 d 3-7-1832 m Elizabeth Miliron Pvt PA

Nicholas: b 5-15-1754 d 1846 m — Pickett BgdMaj VA ★

Nicholas: b a. 1762 d 1825/6 m Elizabeth Brannin Sgt VA

Nicholas: b 4-12-1764 d 7-27-1839 m Margaret — Pvt VA W★

Peter: b 8-21-1755 d 2-16-1827 m Elizabeth Worman Pvt PA

Philip: b 12-18-1742 d 2-5-1826 m Elizabeth Arey Pvt Matr VA

Reuben: b 1730 d p. 12-29-1791 m Mary Harrison 2Lt PS VA

Richard: b 9-22-1758 d 5-30-1848 m (1)Sarah Hall (2)Nancy — Sgt VA ★

Robert: b 3-9-1763 d 1-20-1840 m Elizabeth (Ralston) Finny Pvt SC ★

Samuel: b 1753 d 7-7-1822 m Ann Williamson Pvt PA

Sarah (Brown): b 1718 d p. 1782 m Brumfill (Bromfield) Long PS VA

Solomon: b 1744 d 1786 m Catherine Julian Cpl SC

Stephen: b 3-15-1754 d 5-23-1816 m Nancy Lawson Sgt MA

Thomas: b c. 1738 d p. 1780 m Elenor Long MM NJ

Thomas: b 1740 d 2-22-1810 m Rachel (Smith) Morgan Maj PS CS PA

Wm.: b 1-2-1756 d 9-13-1856 m Zilpha Holloway Pvt Mar MA ★

Wm.: b 7-16-1759 d 6-10-1859 d Hannah Paine Cpl NC ★

Wm.: b c. 1800 m Hannah Young Capt PA

Wm.: b 1727 d 1793 m Elizabeth Henderson Pvt PS PA

Wm.: b 1739 d 12-12-1806 m Elizabeth Templeton Pvt PA

Wm.: b 1746 d 6-27-1818 m Agnes Culbertson Pvt PA

Wm.: b c. 1756 d p. 5-11-1813 m Rachael Douglas Pvt PA

Wm.: b c. 1755 d 8-26-1814 m — Capt VA ★

Wm.: b 1755 d 1822 m Catherine Surface Capt VA

LONGACRE,

Daniel: b 1740 d 1812 m Elizabeth — Pvt PA

Jacob: b 12-6-1751 d 5-21-1837 m Juleah — Pvt PA

Joseph: b c. 1745 d a. 12-1-1806 m Elizabeth Watson Capt CS VA

LONGBOTTOM,

James: b 9-27-1729 d — m (1)Mary Farnum (2)Sarah Avery Pvt CT

LONGDON,

John: b 1754 d 3-31-1830 m Elizabeth Evans Sol VA

LONGENBERGER,

George: b 4-6-1755 d p. 5-30-1814 m (1)Catharina — (2)Elizabeth — Pvt PA

LONGENDYKE,

Cornelius: b 8-27-1758 d 9-2-1838 m Christina Snyder Pvt NY ★

LONGENECKER,

Abraham: b 7-1-1748 d 7-23-1823 m Barbara Fretz Pvt PA

Jacob: b 8-6-1741 d 2-6-1825 m Cathrina — Pvt PA

Peter: b 1733 d 1803 m Anna Good Pvt PA

LONGFELLOW,

Nathan: b 1746 d 1-8-1828 m Tahphenes Huntley Lt MA

Nathan: b 12-31-1743 d 4-9-1796 m Margaret Bigelow Pvt MA

Samuel: b 1756 d 2-3-1834 m Mary Perkins Pvt NH W★

Stephen: b 11-18-1746 d 1824 m Mary Pritchard Pvt MA

Stephen 2d: b 2-7-1723 d 5-1-1790 m Tabitha Bragdon PS MA

Stephen 3d: b 8-3-1750 d 1825 m Patience Young PS MA

Thomas: b 6-6-1754 d 8-18-1780 m Nancy Reed Pvt MD

Wm.: b 4-9-1755 d 9-5-1843 m Sarah Knowlton Pvt MA

LONGGON,

Samuel: b 9-23-1752 d 8-22-1819 m Abagail Chandler Pvt MA

LONGINO,

Thomas: b 1755 d 1810 m Mary Ransom Sol NC

LONGLEY,

Edmund: b 11-11-1745 d 11-29-1842 m Alice Lawrence Capt MA

Eli: b 12-13-1762 d 9-7-1839 m Mary Whitcomb Pvt MA

Ezekial: b 8-4-1756 d 4-9-1835 m Mary Swan Pvt MA ★

James: b 11-4-1753 d 1-15-1837 m Molly Bartlett Pvt MA

John: b 1-6-1710 d 3-17-1792 m Elizabeth Patterson MM MA

Jonas: b 1-22-1712 d 9-24-1799 m Esther Patterson Pvt MA

Joseph, Jr.: b 8-6-1744 d 5-20-1836 m (1)Elizabeth Thayer (2)Lucy Shattuck Cpl MA ★

Joshua: b 7-23-1751 d 11-7-1814 m Bridget Melvin MM MA

Robert: b 3-11-1733 d 8-10-1802 m Anna Whitcomb LCol MA

Wm.: b 1761 d 11-7-1841 m Mary Ann — Pvt VA ★

Zachariah: b 6-29-1729 d 2- -1814 m Jemima Moore QM MA

Zachariah: b 1758 d 6-28-1825 m Betsey — Pvt MA ★

LONGMIRE,

Wm.: b 1764 d 1843 m Emeline Ann Good Sol SC

LONGSDORF, (includes LANGSTAFF)
John: b 1744 d 11-1-1834 m Charity Stille Pvt NJ
Martin: b 5-12-1749 d 9-17-1804 m Anna Margaret Boor Ens PA

LONGSTREET,
Aaron, Jr.: b 1741 d 5-25-1829 m Ann Wetherill Capt NJ
Garret: b a. 1750 d 1818 m Catharine Smock Capt NJ
Gilbert: b 10-15-1750 d 9- -1787 m Helena Hankinson Lt NJ
John: b 1744 d 6- -1819 m Lucy Tapscott Pvt NJ

LONGSTRETH,
Benjamin: b 9-17-1746 d 8-4-1802 m Sarah Fussell Pvt PA
Daniel: b 4-28-1732 d 11-19-1803 m (1)Grace Michener (2)Martha
   Bye PA PA
Isaac: b 12-16-1742 d 4-12-1817 m Martha Thomas Pvt PA
John: b 4-14-1754 d 5-7-1819 m Esther Kirkbride Capt PA
John: b 1751/2 d p. 8-23-1833 m Margaret Ann George Lt PA ★
Philip: b 1749 d 12-10-1836 m Salome Heaton 2Capt PA★

LONGSWORTH,
Solomon: b c. 1750 d 1830 m Lucretia McElfresh PS MD

LONGWELL,
David: b 2-3-1737/8 d 4-7-1795 m Mary Tyler Pvt NY
James: b 1754 d c. 1820 m Nellie Slack Pvt PA
Stephen: b 4-15-1748 d 11-4-1812 m Jane Sellick Pvt CT W★
Wm.: b 9-5-1751 d 11-6-1829 m Rachel Walker Pvt PA ★

LONGWORTH,
Burgess: b 6-10-1740 d 12-30-1817 m Mary McKinee Smn Gnr VA

LONGYEAR,
Christopher: b 2-14-1758 d 11-22-1848 m Mary Conyes Pvt NY
Jacob, Sr.: b — d p. 11-1-1785 m Maria Cox (Kokin) Pvt NY
Johannes: b 3-24-1754 d 8-31-1824 m Annatje Winne Pvt NY

LOOK,
Cheney: b 6-17-1749 d 1844 m Anna Chapman Pvt Smn MA ★
Daniel: b 6-7-1733 d 4-1-1825 m Anne Butler Pvt MA
Elijah, Sr.: b 11-17-1713 d 1-28-1800 m Joanna Luce PS MA
Elijah, Jr.: b 3-27-1759 d 8-27-1852 m Mary Russell Pvt MA ★
John: b —d 6-13-1823 m Jane Holmes Pvt MA
John: b 11-26-1733 d 1778 m Elizabeth Weaver Sgt NS
Jonathan: b c. 1748 d 6-6-1835 m Drusilla Luce Pvt MA
Noah: b 11-27-1719 d 8-16-1790 m Hannah Holley Pvt MA
Samuel: b 1-14-1744 d 4-28-1725 m Margaret Chase PS MA

LOOKER,
Johnson: b 1762 d 2-13-1840 m Betsey — Pvt NJ
Othniel: b 10-6-1757 d 7-23-1845 m Pamela Clark Pvt NJ ★

LOOMER,
Joseph: b a. 1746 d 10-31-1778 m Lucy House Pvt MA

LOOMIS, (includes LAMMAS)
Abijah: b 3-10-1743 d 1820 m Mary Kellogg Fif CT
Abner: b 11-26-1727 d 1-18-1809 m (1)Sarah Grant (2)Chloe
   Barber PS CT
Amasa: b 2-19-1738 d 7-1-1793 m (1)Hannah Hurlburt (2)Priscilla
   (Hammond) Birge Capt CT
Asa: b 4-2-1750 d 1-30-1805 m Mary Stanton Pvt CT
Benaiah: b 7-15-1752 d 3-8-1838 m (1)Rachel Patterson (2)Mrs
   Prudence Corbin Pvt MM MA
Benjamin: b 11-27-1757 d 9-17-1830 m Chloe Brown Sol CT
Benjamin: b 9-5-1750 d 1814 m Lucy Leonard Pvt MA
Benoni: b 2-27-1758 d 2-20-1820 m Jemima Barber Pvt CT
Caleb: b 1738'd 3-5-1821 m Mary Sessions Pvt MA
Dan: b 1-22-1758 d 8-22-1841 m Sarah (Wells) Field Pvt Cav Tms
   CT ★
Daniel: b 12-31-1739 d 12-13-1807 m Mary Sprague Lt CT
Daniel: b 7-25-1739 d 2-28-1798 m (1)Sarah Crawford (2)Sybil Knox
   Lt CT
Daniel, Sr.: b 6-16-1735 d 9-18-1790 m Alice Chamberlain 2Lt CT
Daniel: b 6-5-1761 d 8-19-1833 m Mary Huston Pvt CT
Daniel: b 10-10-1749 d 2- -1791 m Amy Peck Pvt MM MA
Daniel: b 4-4-1750 d 7-21-1833 m (1)Sarah Webb (2)Elizabeth
   (Karner) Winchell Sgt MA
Dyer: b 2-18-1756 d 8-14-1839 m Esther Johnson Mar MA ★
Elijah: b 10-16-1730 d 10-16-1802 m Rachel Wolcott Pvt CT
Elijah: b 7-17-1761 d 12-29-1848 m Rachel Chapman Pvt CT ★
Enos: b 12-2-1741 d 12-2-1817 m Eunice Noble Cpl MA
Epaphras: b 11-13-1732 d 9-10-1812 m Mary Hills Capt CT
Ephraim, Sr.:b 4-1-1731 d 4-4-1812 m (1)Ruth Hoffurd (2)Jane
   Campbell PS CT
Ephraim, Jr.: b 7-12-1758 d 1824 m (1)Jane Tyler (2)Zerviah Hill Pvt
   CT
Ezra: b 1-8-1752 d 8-22-1842 m Lydia Spoor Pvt MA
Francis: b 6-12-1726 d 1783 m Elizabeth Pinney Sol PS CT
George: b 10-6-1752 d 9-22-1836 m Deborah Stewart Pvt CT ★
Gideon: b 12-30-1735 d 5-7-1802 m Hannah Booth PS CT
Giles: b 11-6-1756 d 7-3-1812 m Esther (Loomis) Pvt CT

Grove: b 1-30-1763 d 1825 m Olive McCoe Pvt CT
Ichabod: b 1-17-1742 d 7-31-1785 m Mindwell Lewis Pvt CT
Isaiah: b 8-3-1758 d 4-11-1841 m (1)Sybil Pryor (2)Mrs Sarah
   Gager Pvt Tms Wgm CT ★
Isaiah: b 6-28-1730 d 1811 m Abigail Barber PS CT
Israel: b 6-4-1744 d c. 1823 m Irene Chamberlain Pvt CT
Israel: b 12-20-1753 d 1800 m Ruth Risley Pvt CT
Israel: b 12-26-1754 d 2-22-1834 m Sarah Adams Pvt CT ★
Israel: b 10-29-1756 d 5-11-1826 m Hannah — Pvt CT ★
Jabez: b 9-8-1741-5 d 1796 m — Sweatland Cpl CT
Jacob: b 1-22-1755 d 6-2-1835 m Lucy Eunice McCall Pvt CT ★
Jacob: b 6-1-1756 d 12-2-1840 m Thankful Hubbard Pvt CT
James, Sr.: b 11-15-1714 d 9-7-1778 m Eunice Stricklen Pvt MA
James, Jr.: b 3-7-1754 d 6-19-1779 m Dorcas — Pvt MA
Jerome: b 8-20-1757 d 4-19-1840 m Elizabeth Tippets Pvt CT
Joel: b 6-21-1722 d 6-19-1788 m (1)Naomi Elmer (2)Sarah
   (Buckland) Spencer Capt CT
Joel: b 5-22-1760 d 1825 m Prudence West Pvt CT
John: b 6-6-1741 d 5-4-1811 m Rachel Harris Ens CT
John: b 3-4-1733/4 d 9-18-1807 m Redexalina Wolcott Pvt PS CT
John: b 11-3-1751 d 5-24-1841 m Elizabeth Tilden Tms CT W★
John: b 3-16-1760 d 4-20-1833 m (1)Salome Scott (2)Elizabeth
   Standish Pvt CT MA ★
Jonah: b 5-5-1743 d 4-22-1813 m (1)Mehitable Cram (2)Martha
   Post Ens VT
Jonathan: b 12-16-1753 d 12-12-1832 m (1)Martha Blackman
   (2)Mrs Patience Pelton Cpl CT
Jonathan: b 8-13-1722 d 7-7-1785 m Margaret — Pvt CT
Jonathan: b 3-25-1757 d 10-3-1814 m Hannah Barber Pvt CT
Jonathan: b 1-23-1719 d 1798 m Hannah Seldon Pvt MA
Joseph: b 4-29-1743 d 4-27-1811 m (1)Lydia Bosworth (2)Ruth
   Bingham Sgt CT
Joseph: b 8-29-1725 d 6-19-1786 m Kezia Loomis Pvt CT
Josiah: b 5-19-1737 d 1800 m Deborah Williams Drm MA
Justus: b 3-7-1754 d 1818 m Mary Bowe Cpl MA
Luther: b 6-24-1754 d 10-20-1812 m Jemima Bronson Pvt CT
Michael: b 9-5-1741 d 1793 m Mary Karner Lt MA
Moses: b 12-24-1734 d p. 7-16-1783 m Eunice Webster Pvt CT
Nathaniel: b 8-28-1747 d 12-16-1825 m (1)Mary Simms (2)Lavinia
   Clark (3)Rachel White Ens CT
Nathaniel: b 7-8-1758 d 12-27-1794 m Bethena Bronson Pvt CT
Nathaniel: b 1731 d p. 1795 m (1)Hannah White (2)Sarah Rockwell
   PS CT
Nathaniel: b 5-28-1734 d 1795 m Tabitha Kingsley Pvt MA
Nehemiah: b 11-8-1739 d 10-12-1808 m Elizabeth Morley Pvt MA
Noah: b 1-13-1745 d 11-6-1817 m (1)Sybil Williams (2)Mrs Dorcas
   Crawford Pvt CT
Noah: b 5-12-1724 d 8-9-1808 m Rhoda Clark Pvt PS MA
Oliver: b 2- -1760 d 3-3-1844 m Sarah Upson Pvt CT ★
Oliver, Jr.: b 9-24-1763 d 1-4-1837 m (1)Judith Adams (2)Mrs
   Deborah Hamlin Pvt CT ★
Reuben: b 3-4-1719 d 10-12-1801 m (1)Anne Moore (2)Rebecca
   Goodrich (3)Mary Hoskins Sol CT
Richard: b 12-25-1758 d 8-9-1826 m Rachel Higgbee Pvt CT
Roger: b 10-1-1732 d 2-11-1817 m Priscilla Baker Pvt CT
Roswell, Sr.: b 4-26-1754 d 5-8-1846 m Abigail Graham Pvt CT
Samuel: b 5-12-1760 d 2-1-1825 m Betsey Dunham Cpl CT
Seth: b 5-22-1737 d 7-15-1809 m (1)Lurane Knapp (2)Mindwell
   Porter Pvt NY
Simeon: b 5-14-1755 d 8-3-1829 m Martha Buckingham Pvt CT ★
Simon: b 8-24-1760 d 12-28-1841 m Sarah Holbrook Cpl CT ★
Simon: b 3-7-1768 d 11-26-1842 m Mary Carpenter Pvt Tms CT ★
Solomon: b 11-4-1732 d 8-5-1805 m (1)Mary Chapman (2)Mary
   Johnson Pvt PS CT
Solomon: b 12-17-1748 d 1-26-1794 m Prudence Robbins Pvt CT
Stephen: b 4-13-1745 d 1795 m Mary Mumford Pvt CT
Thomas: b 4-18-1756 d 9-5-1842 m Mary Williams Capt CT ★
Thomas: b 7-6-1756 d 5-1-1842 m Eunice Mann Sgt CT
Thomas: b 1714 d 2-27-1792 m Susannah Clark PS CT
Timothy: b 6-3-1750 d 2-15-1832 m Anna Roberts Pvt CT
Timothy: b 2-12-1752 d 2-12-1838 m Mary Orton Pvt CT
Uriah: b 6-27-1760 d 3- -1844 m Sarah Sheldon Pvt MA
Zadock: b 2-23-1741 d 6- -1808 m Bathsheba Huggins Cpl MA

LOONEY,
David: b c. 1735/6 d p. 5-1-1801 m Mary McClellan Maj NC
David: b 8-9-1758 d 2-18-1828 m (1)Isabella Kinkead (2)Mrs
   Elizabeth Boyd Sol SC
John: b 1750 d p. 1809 m Esther — Capt VA
Michael: b c. 1755 d p. 11-12-1827 m Temperance Cross Pvt VA
Peter: b 11-24-1755 d 1-1-1830 m Rachel — Pvt VA

LOOP, (includes LUPP)
Christian: b 1754 d 1826 m — Pvt NY
Henry: b c. 1740 d p. 1800 m Nellie Sharp Ens NY
Peter: b 1723 d 10-22-1824 m (2)Miss Bailey (3)Mrs Prudence
   Bushnell Pvt NY

LOOSE, (includes LOOS)
George: b c. 1758 d 3-13-1834 m Elizabeth Snider Ens PA
Jacob: b 12-11-1743 d 12-7-1830 m Magdalena Schneider Pvt PA
Johann George: b c. 1722/3 d a. 3-28-1803 m Anna Margaretta
   — 1Sgt PA

LOPER,
Abraham: b 1754 d 1851 m Rebecca Montgomery Lt NJ
Abraham: b 9- -1748 d 8-25-1821 m — Sgt NJ ★
Abraham: b 1740 d 1815 m Elizabeth Conkling Sgt NY
Samuel: b 1743 d 1799 m Abigail Chittenden Lt CT
Wm.: b *p.* 1735 d 1783 m Bethinia Packer Pvt CS NJ

LORAH, (includes LORA)
Conrad: b — d 8-20-1796 m — Pvt PA
George: b 1745 d 8-1-1823 m Dorothy Elizabeth Rhoades Maj PA
Henry: b 1751 d 1817 m Christine Wicks Pvt PA
John: b *c.* 1747 d *p.* 1809 m Maria Elizabeth Zellers Pvt PA

LORAIN,
John: b 1755 d 9-11-1834 m Mary Parker Ens PA ★

LORD,
Aaron, Sr.: b 5-25-1732 d 3-24-1811 m Hannah Lord Pvt MA
Aaron, Jr.: b 12-10-1758 d 12- -1832 m Elizabeth Powerling Sgt MA
Abner: b 3-20-1733 d 11-21-1790 m Temperance Colt Capt CT
Abraham: b 1722 d 3- -1777 m Phebe Heard PS MA
Adam: b — d 4- -1782 m Olive — Pvt MA
Asa: b 6-29-1760 d 9- -1855 m Sarah Beecher Smith Pvt CT ★
Benjamin 1: b 1-3-1728/9 d 2-6-1805 m Hannah Lay Pvt CT
Benjamin: b 1692 d 1784 m (1)Ann Taylor (2)Elizabeth Tisdale PS CT
Benjamin: b 6-27-1761 d 7-8-1818 m Susannah Sutton Pvt MA
Charles: b 12-20-1753 d 5-1-1825 m Mrs Sarah Goodhue Sgt MA
Daniel: b 1726 d 1785 m Lydia Chapman Ens CT
Daniel: b 1-4-1762 d 9-17-1825 m Anna Choate Pvt CT
David: b 8-4-1756 d 1-25-1804 m Hannah Hanks Pvt VT
Dominicus: b 7-12-1762 d 1849 m Mary Currier Pvt MA ★
Ebenezer: bpt 3-29-1740 d 1-31-1836 m Sarah Perkins Drm MA
Ebenezer, Sr.: bpt 1-19-1721 d 1811/2 m (1)Martha Emery (2)Mrs Jane Plaisted PS ME
Eliphalet: b 1754 d 8-5-1826 m Hannah — Pvt NH
Elisha: b 3-18-1745 d 4-13-1819 m (1)Eunice Bulkeley (2)Sarah Omstead Pvt CS CT
Elisha: b 8- -1764 d 12-11-1818 m (1)Lydia Hayes (2)Lydia Upham Pvt CT
Epaphras: b 12-26-1709 d 11-25-1799 m (1)Hope Phillips (2),Lucy Bulkley CS CT
Ichabod: bpt 4-2-1759 d *p.* 1802 m Lois Shackley Pvt MA
Jabez: b 4-16-1745 d 4-2-1794 m Elizabeth Clark Pvt CT
Jabez: b 6-14-1732 d 1799 m Sarah Nason PS ME
James, 3d: b 3-26-1737 d 2-13-1830 m Mrs Elizabeth Brown Lt MA
Jeremiah: b 1755 d 10-14-1812 m Tryphena Pease Sgt CT
Jeremiah: bpt 2-2-1754 d 1795 m Martha Marshall Pvt MA
Jeremiah: b 5-18-1738 d *p.* 1816 m (1)Elizabeth — (2)Mary Tapley Sgt NH
Joel: b 3-27-1754 d 12-22-1824 m Jerusha Webster Pvt CT MA
John: b 2-22-1757 d 1-4-1837 m Olive Everett Pvt CT ★
John: b 1745 d 1801 m Charity Curtis Lt MA
Jonathan: b 10-3-1726 d 5-8-1805 m Ruth Rogers Pvt VT
Joseph: b 1720 d 10-28-1778 m Esther Chapman CS Ens CT
Joseph, Sr.: b 3-11-1727 d 3-13-1788 m Sarah Wade Pvt CT
Joseph, Jr.: b 11-29-1757 d 8-10-1839 m Caroline Sterling Pvt CT ★
Joseph: b 7-16-1766 d 7-5-1833 m Chloe Booth Pvt CT
Joseph: b 7-26-1728 d 8-21-1800 m Prudence Hodgdon Cpl MA
Levin: b *c.* 1758 d *p.* 1800 m Keziah — Pvt MD
Lynde: b 2-3-1733 d 6-1-1801 m Lois Sheldon CS Capt CT
Martin: b 6-5-1742 d 12-15-1821 m Concurrance Seward Capt CT
Moses: b 4-18-1762 d 1-30-1834 m (1)Lucy Heard (2)Abigail Berry Pvt MA
Nathan: b 11-27-1738 d 10-1-1833 m (1)Abigail Ingraham (2)Mary Nevins Ens CT
Nathan: b 4-14-1758 d 4-3-1807 m (2)Elizabeth Brewster Ens MA
Nathan: b 2-17-1744/5 d 11-24-1827 m Hannah Fields Pvt MA
Nathaniel: b 11-10-1755 d 2-20-1842 m Abigail Barnes MM CT
Nathaniel: b *c.* 1740 d *p.* 1790 m Sarah Pierce Ens VT
Nicholas: b 1747 d 1828 m Elizabeth Chick Cpl MA
Philip, Sr.: b 2-16-1723 d 3-22-1816 m Sarah Brown Pvt MA
Philip, Jr.: b 11-4-1749 d 9-12-1785 m Elizabeth (Boardman)Warner Pvt MA
Richard: b 9-15-1752 d 7-29-1818 m Ann Mitchell Sol CT
Samuel: b 1755 d 1840 m Mary Andrews Sol CT
Samuel: b 9-4-1759 d 2-8-1855 m (1)Abigail Allen (2)Mrs Mary (Roberts) Wentworth Pvt NH ★
Simeon: b 12- -1750 d 10-28-1815 m Polly Frost Capt MA
Solomon: b 1732 d 1820 m Meriam Coleman Pvt CT
Theophilus: b 5-8-1756 d *p.* 1834 m (2)Abigail — Pvt CT ★
Theophilus: b 1757 d 1831 m Olive Hungerford Pvt CT
Thomas: b 1-17-1736 d 12-3-1810 m Leonard Smith Capt MA
Thomas: b 3-5-1767 d 1-5-1843 m Esther Bradbury Pvt NH
Tobias, Sr.: b 8-27-1724 d 1-12-1809 m Jane Smith Capt ME
Tobias, Jr.: b 2-22-1748/9 d 1-16-1808 m Mehitable Scammon (2)Hephzibah Conant Lt MA
Wentworth: b 9-14-1755 d 2-28-1845 m Patience Brackett Sgt MA ★
Wm.: b 1-22-1751 d 2-6-1839 m Ruth Wyman Sgt MA ★
Wm.: b 4-14-1732 d 3-9-1780 m Sarah Espey CS Col NC

LOREE,
Job: b 11-16-1759 d 2-25-1843 m Elizabeth Hull Pvt NJ ★
Samuel, Jr.: b 1759 d 8-17-1803 m Sarah Price Pvt PS NJ

LORING,
Abner: b 1743 d — m Thankful Davis Pvt MA
Bezaleel: b 4-13-1739 d 6-27-1822 m Elizabeth Mason PS ME
Braddock: b 8-21-1760 d 3- -1822 m Mary Mather Pvt MA
Daniel: b 5-28-1752 d 1822/3 m (1)Bathsheba Howe (2)Lucy (Eaton) Moore Rice Adj MA
Daniel: b 1-8-1751 d 7-27-1831 m Mary Thayer Cpl MA
David: b 8-5-1714 d 1781 m Hannah Vickery Pvt MA
Ezekiel: b 7-27-1742 d 3-6-1825 m Hannah Stetson 2Lt MA
Ignatius: b 8-14-1729 d 1-9-1803 m Bathsheba Bass Ens CS MA
Job: b 2-12-1739/40 d 2-11-1825 m Judith Whitton Pvt MA
John: b 1-28-1742 d 8-17-1824 m Elizabeth Howe Cpl MA
Joseph: b 2-17-1752 d 5-13-1799 m Anna True Lt MA
Joseph, Sr.: b 8-21-1713 d 9-13-1787 m Kezia Gove PS MA
Joseph, Jr.: b 12-27-1747 d 10-11-1839 m Betsey Pollard Pvt Slr MA
Joshua: b 11-19-1757 d 6-18-1799 m Hannah Campbell Lt MA
Joshua: b 3- -1756 d 11-8-1810 m Lydia Fearing Pvt MA
Levi: b 12-3-1750 d *p.* 1805 m Joanna Mitchell Lt MA
Matthew: b 9-18-1751 d 11-7-1829 m (1)Nancy Floyd (2)Sarah Blake (3)Mercy Bates PS MA
Nathan: b 11-27-1721 d 4-25-1803 m (1)Kezia Woodward (2)Elizabeth Clapp Sol MA
Nathaniel: b 9-22-1751 d 3-28-1837 m (1)Elizabeth Hayden (2)Mrs Sarah Lloyd Pvt MA
Nathaniel Thomas: b 1749 d 9-28-1817 m Sarah Watson Cpl MA
Perez: b 8-26-1729 d 8-22-1827 m Sarah Freeman PS MA
Samuel: b 5-1-1747 d 10-16-1816 m Prudence Chapman 2Lt MA
Samuel: b 2-3-1720/1 d 9-19-1813 m Jane Goold Pvt MA
Samuel: b 9-7-1760 d 5-27-1840 m Hannah Goff Pvt RI ★
Solomon: b 12-23-1767 d 2-19-1842 m (2)Mary Sawyer (3)Angelina Sawyer ADC MA
Solomon: b 11-18-1728 d 3-31-1798 m Hannah Dunbar Pvt MA
Solomon: b 9-29-1751 d 2-5-1831 m Hannah Davis Pvt MA
Thomas: b 4-25-1718 d 6-28-1795 m Sarah Lobdel Capt MA
Thomas, Jr.: b 10-22-1757 d 10-11-1794 m Lydia Lincoln Pvt MA
Thomas: b 6-7-1747 d 2-4-1781 m Mary Brown PS MA
Wm.: b 1-5-1756 d 2-2-1788 m Zerviah Lord NCapt CT
Wm.: b 10-11-1741 d 10-18-1815 m Alethea Alden Pvt MA
Wm.: b 9-15-1756 d 6-10-1791 m Jane Brown Matr Bbd MA

LORTON,
Israel: b *c.* 1727 d *a.* 1808 m Sarah — Capt VA
Robert: b 2-15-1747 d 5-16-1833 m Tabitha Ganaway Sgt VA ★

LOSEE, (includes LOSEY)
Cornelius, Sr.: b 6-27-1732 d 8-14-1783 m — Pvt NY
John A.: b 4-16-1753 d 8-22-1837 m Sarah — Pvt NY
Simeon: b 1741 d 1784 m (1)Hannah Hoff (2)Miriam Carpenter Pvt NY
Wm.: b 1761 d 1852 m Rosanna Cole Pvt NJ

LOSH,
Andrew: b 10-26-1752 d 4-12-1849 m (1)Magdalena Haines (2)Sarah Such Pvt PA

LOSSING,
Nicholas: b 9-27-1738 d 9-9-1827 m Christiana Woolweaver Pvt NY
Peter: b 1730 d 1791 m Margaret Cook Lt NY
Simeon: b *c.* 1735 d *p.* 7- -1775 m Margaret VanKeuren PS NY

LOTHROP, (includes LATHROP & LOTHROPE)
Andrew: b 4-20-1728 d 7-9-1803 m Abigail Fish Capt CT
Arunah: b 12-1-1735 d 6-22-1817 m (1)Martha — (2)Sarah Wattles Pvt CT
Asa: b 2-2-1756 d 1827 m Allis Fox Pvt CT
Azariah: b 1728 d 2-25-1810 m (2)Abigail Huntington PS CT
Azariah: b 8-21-1754 d 10-1-1808 m Mercy Bennett Pvt CT
Daniel, Sr.: b 5-2-1721 d 3-18-1818 m Rhoda Willis Maj MA
Daniel, Jr.: b 12-10-1745 d 3-18-1837 m (1)Hannah Howard (2)Lydia Willis (3)Mary Turner 2Lt MA
Dixwell: b 1753 d 1841 m (1)Rebecca Rogers (2)Eunice Davis (3)Mahala (Phillips) Bennett Pvt CT ★
Ebenezer: b 2-7-1702/3 d 1-28-1781 m (1)Lydia Tracy Leffingwell (2)Mrs Hannah Lynde Capt CT
Ebenezer, Jr.: b 1743 d 1804 m Deborah Lathrop 2Lt CT
Ebenezer: b 5-15-1743 d 1-27-1815 m Elizabeth Davis Capt MA
Ebenezer: b 7-24-1759 d 8-23-1826 m Ruth Bettys Cpl NY
Elisha: b 12-29-1723 d *p.* 1788 m Abigail Avery PS CT
Elisha: b 3-13-1714 d 7-2-1787 m (1)Margaret Sluman (2)Hannah D. Hough PS NH
George: b 6-13-1765 d 1839 m Polly Thayer Pvt MA ★
Isaac: b 9-6-1758 d 3-11-1835 m (1)Betsey Scudder (2)Mary Crocker Pvt MA
James: b 7-11-1752 d *p.* 1778 m Mary Stark Pvt CT
Jedediah, Sr.: b 1-4-1718 d 6-9-1792 m (1)Abigail Hyde (2)Jemima Birchard Pvt CT
Jedediah, Jr.: b 2-9-1747 d 1811 m Amy Gardner Pvt CT
Jedediah: b 4-17-1748 d 6-19-1817 m Civil Perkins Pvt CT

John: b 1736 d 11- -1814 m Lydia Freeman PS CT
John: b 10-27-1754 d 3-19-1840 m Rebecca Cox Pvt MA
John: b 11-12-1737 d 11-21-1836 m Sarah Cook Cpl MA
Jonathan: b 7-3-1734 d 12-14-1817 m Thede Woodworth Pvt CT
Josiah, Sr.: b 2-14-1726 d 5-15-1808 m Sarah Church Pvt MA
Josiah: b 10-15-1759 d 1848 m Susannah Howard Pvt MA
Mark: b 3-4-1746 d 3-8-1841 m Elizabeth Dickerman Pvt MA
Melatian: Sr.: b 2-20-1714 d 9-5-1787 m Mercy Hatch PS NY
Samuel: b 11-23-1756 d 6-12-1821 m Lois Huntington Pvt CT ★
Septimus: b 1756 d 10-12-1819 m Abigail Adams Pvt CT
Seth: b 8-3-1722 d 3-2-1804 m (1)Lydia Packard (2)Mehitable Daily Pvt MA
Seth: b 7-7-1729 d 7 11-10-1815 m (1)Martha Conant (2)Martha Kinsley (3)Hannah Smith PS MA
Simeon: b 1-15-1722/3 d c. 1804 m Hannah Abel Cpl CT
Simon: b 1-1-1744 d 12-27-1820 m Hannah Davis Ens NY
Solomon: b 2-9-1761 d 10-19-1843 m Mehitable White Pvt MA
Thatcher: b 1-26-1734 d 12-30-1806 m Submit Loomis Ens CT
Thomas: b 11-9-1738 d 9-4-1813 m Ruth Nichols Col PS CS MA
Thomas: b 3-6-1736 d c. 1800 m Sarah Mayhew Smn MA
Uriah: b 4-30-1750 d 12-11-1828 m Lois Hinckley Pvt CT
Zachariah: b 3-25-1742 d 12-26-1817 m Mehetable Cleveland Pvt CT

LOTT,
Bartholomew: b 2-11-1761 d 11-30-1858 m Catherine Fitzgerald Drm Pvt NJ
Cornelius: b 4-16-1738 d 12-15-1816 m Henrietta Brokaw Capt NJ
Hendrick: b 6-26-1716 d a. 1795 m Katherine — Pvt NJ
Henry: b 1707 d 12-21-1784 m (1)Mercy — (2)Catherine Kroeson Jones Capt PA
Janetje Probasko: b 1-24-1722 d 10-28-1802 m Johannes Lott PS NY
Jeremiah: b 1757 d 8-31-1822 m Elizabeth Laycock Pvt Trm PA ★
Johannes E.: b 9-1-1746 d 8-13-1811 m (1)Adriaeztje Voorhees (2)Catrintie Vanderbilt PS NY
John: b 11-27-1758 d 3-21-1853 m Sarah Probasco Pvt NJ ★
John: b c. 1742 d 7- -1810 m Sallie — Sol SC
Peter: b c. 1759 d 1787 m Mary Hyer QM Lt NY
Richard: b 1723 d 1784 m Letitia Phillips LCol NJ
Zephaniah: b 3-14-1742 d 2-26-1829 m Else VanPelt Capt PA

LOTTRIDGE,
Thomas: b — d p. 1790 m Maria Bratt Pvt NY

LOUCHNORE,
Christian: b 1740 d a. 1-14-1799 m Margaret — Cpl PA

LOUCKS, (includes LAUCK & LAUCKS)
Adam: b 12-14-1715 d 2-14-1790 m Catherine Elizabeth Snell Pvt NY
Adam: b 1747 d 1828 m Magdalena — Pvt NY
Andrew: b 10-15-1739 d 4-8-1838 m Catharine Hummell Pvt NY
Andrew: b 1738 d 4-9-1838 m Mariah — Pvt NY
George: b 7-10-1759 d 9-2-1835 m Elizabeth Bellinger Cpl NY
George: b 1743 d 1808 m Anna Catherine Keiser PS PA
Jacob: b 7-7-1763 d 10- -1839 m Elizabeth — Sol PA
Jeremiah: b 11- -1747 d 6-19-1834 m Magdalene Bellinger Pvt NY ★
Jeremiah: b 10-15-1767 d 3-19-1854 m Hannah Borst Pvt NY
John: b 12- -1742 d 1-31-1814 m Cathrine Frey Pvt NY
John: b 12-14-1756 d 5-8-1820 m (1)Anna (Rosenberger) Leatherman (2)Anna (Wisner) Augeney Pvt PA
Peter: b 12-19-1760 d 7-10-1825 m Anna Overholt Pvt PA
Peter: b 3-21-1752 d 10- -1839 m Amelia Heiskell Pvt PA
Simon: b a. 1760 d 2-21-1815 m Katherine Starr Pvt VA
Wm.: b 1750 d 1-12-1837 m Margaret Liter Pvt Wgm PA ★

LOUD,
Caleb: b 4-18-1747 d 5-4-1782 m Susanna Bates Pvt MA
Eliphalet: b 12-30-1755 d 10-4-1832 m Anna Blanchard Pvt MA ★
Ellet: b 7-28-1743 d 3-28-1813 m Sarah Pratt PA
Esau: b 3-17-1750 d 3-24-1798 m Huldah Palmer Pvt MA
Jacob, Sr.: b 5-24-1723 d 11-15-1779 m Mary Smith Pvt MA
Jacob, Jr.: b 3-6-1747 d 1779 m Lydia Joy Pvt MA
Solomon: b 9-4-1740 d 1810 m Sarah Heard Cpl NH
Sylvanus: b 6-1-1760 d 1-1-1844 m Lydia Lovell Pvt MA
Wm.: b 2-1-1739 d 8-6-1810 m Lucy Vining Pvt MA

LOUDERBACK,
John: b 1756 d 1-10-1802 m Amelia Harris Pvt PA

LOUDON, (includes LOUDIN)
John: b c. 1763 d p. 11-11-1822 m Sarah Lindsey Pvt PA
Matthew: b 1729 d 1-10-1801 m (1)Elizabeth McCormick (2)Ann Copenger Lt PA
Wm.: b 8-22-1759 d 11-9-1796 m Eunice Yeomans Drm NY W★

LOUGEE,
John: b c. 1722 d 1811/2 m (1)Molly Leavitt (2)Susan Hull (3)Mrs Judith Beal Pvt NH
John: b 1-2-1752 d 8-8-1836 m Molly Avery Pvt NH
Joseph: b 6-28-1751 d 2- -1845 m (1)Apphia Swazey (2)Mariam Fogg Fif NH

LOUGHBOROUGH, (includes LOOFBOURROW)
David: b 3-2-1755 d 1846 m Amy Gaskill Pvt NJ ★
John Wade: b 4-28-1746 d 1814 m Mary Hoff Pvt PA

LOUGHEAD,
David: b 3- -1755 d 6-29-1824 m Elizabeth Mitchell Sol PA
Wm.: b 1733 d 1799 m Martha Jane Pvt PA

LOUGHRIDGE, (includes LOCKRIDGE)
Andrew: b c. 1740 d p. 1-7-1791 m Jean Graham Maj VA
John: b 10- -1762 d 10-11-1851 m Margaret Henderson Pvt VA ★
Robert: b c. 1750 d — m Susannah Carpenter Sol GA

LOUGHRY, (includes LOCKRY)
Archibald: b 4-15-1733 d 8-24-1781 m Mary Erwin LCol PA
Wm.: b 5-22-1756 d 9-27-1825 m Esther Allison Capt PA

LOUNSBURY, (includes LOUNSBERRY)
Edward: b 1738 d 1809 m (1)Jane VanWagener (2)Elizabeth Kator (3)Jane Du Boise CaptLt NY
Enos: b 5-31-1763 d 1816 m Caty Waterbury Pvt CT
Jacob: b 5-7-1753 d p. 1792 m Bethia Newman Pvt CT
Jairus: b 1751 d 9-4-1832 m Amelia Chapman Pvt CT ★
John: b 3-22-1731 d 12-30-1811 m Sarah — Sol NY
Joshua: b 10-4-1745 d 4-4-1826 m Susannah Smith Pvt NY
Linus: b 1-13-1749 d 7-15-1836 m Prudence Scott Pvt CT
Michael: b 9-12-1744 d p. 1790 m Abigail Hillman Pvt CT
Nathan: b 1722 d 1793 m Elizabeth Seeley Pvt CT
Nathan M.: b 1754 d 4-26-1857 m Lucy Pelton Pvt NY ★
Nehemiah: b 12-23-1717 d 9-26-1790 m Sarah Webb Pvt NY
Stephen: b c. 1730 d p. 1790 m Hannah Sperry Pvt NY
Stephen: b 2-3-1758 d 12-3-1839 m Sarah Raymond Pvt NY ★

LOVE,
Alexander: b 1718 d 3- -1784 m Margaret Moore PS SC
Amos: b c. 1749 d a. 4- -1798 m Mary — Capt NC
Andrew: b 9-12-1747 d 3-26-1821 m Anna Latimore Col SC
Benjamin: b 1723 d 9-25-1795 m Jean — PS SC
Charles: b 1753 d 3- -1824 m Susanna Chiles Pvt VA ★
David: b c. 1740 d 11-30-1798 m Jean Blewitt LCol PS NC
Henry: b 1745 d 12- -1808 m Catherine Bensley Pvt PA
Hezekiah: b 10-10-1752 d 6-11-1833 m (1)Elizabeth Cartmount (2)Nancy Duren Pvt SC W★
Hugh: b c. 1750 d p. 2-4-1819 m Mary Gaston Pvt PA
Isaac: b c. 1754 d p. 1787 m Martha Chappell Lt SC
James: b c. 1740 d 9-23-1820 m Jannett — Pvt SC
James, Jr.: b 1-24-1763 d 12-6-1807 m Janet Lockert Pvt SC
John: b a. 1762 d 4-25-1809 m Louisa Duffle SgnMte GA
John: b 1762 d 1842 m Mary King Pvt NC ★
Joseph, Sr.: b 1728 d 11-10-1804 m Mary Tees Sol PS VA
Joseph, Jr.: b 1752 d p. 2-25-1830 m Mary Marshall Sol VA
Mark: b 1763 d 11-30-1831 m Louise Orr Frazer Pvt SC ★
Robert: b c. 1750 d — m Eleanor Tillman MM MD
Robert: b 2-2-1755 d 2-19-1846 m (1)Mary Cutting (2)Dolly Tompkins Pvt MA ★
Robert: b 12-17-1762 d p. 8-13-1850 m — Pvt NC ★
Robert: b 6-21-1734 d 12-28-1828 m Jennie — Pvt PS PA
Robert: b 1730 d 1809 m (3)Sarah Blanchard Sgt RI
Robert: b 8-23-1760 d 7-17-1845 m Mary Anne Dillard Lt PS VA ★
Samuel: b 1728 d 4-23-1779 m Rozanna Graham Pvt MD
Samuel, Sr.: b 1720 d 4-24-1787 m Mary Haw PS MD
Samuel: b c. 1735 d p. 1790 m Dorcas Bell CS VA
Thomas: b 3-23-1730 d 1-21-1815 m Sarah Burnett Pvt CT
Thomas: b 1-28-1739 d 12-20-1825 m Martha Guthrie Lt PA
Wm., Sr.: b 1728 d 1797 m Mary Elizabeth — Sol PA
Wm.: b 1733 d 1786 m Susanna — CS PS RI
Wm.: b c. 1760 d 2-18-1821 m Rachel McCool Lt SC W★
Wm.: b 1746 d 7-26-1826 m Isabella Swansea Lt SC
Wm.: b 1-27-1764 d 11-12-1828 m Nancy C. Walker Pvt SC
Wm.: b c. 1720 d p. 10-4-1793 m — PS VA

LOVEALL,
Henry: b c. 1755 d a. 3-10-1829 m Mary — PS MD
Wm.: b 10-15-1753 d — m Mary — Ens MD

LOVEJOY,
Abial: b 12-11-1731 d 7-4-1811 m Mary Brown CS MA
Abial: b 3-17-1737 d 3-27-1817 m Anna Stickney PS NH
Benjamin, Sr.: b 5-2-1724 d 8-28-1776 m Mary Meriam PS NH
Caleb, Sr.: b 10-5-1718 d 1781 m Mehitable Chandler PS NH
Chandler: b 12-3-1741 d 11-30-1827 m (1)Miriam Virgin (2)Azuba Graham Pvt NH
Daniel: b 2-23-1746 d 1-29-1829 m Sarah Wyman Pvt NH
Daniel: b 6-2-1762 d 12-17-1842 m Lorenza Havens Pvt NH VT ★
Daniel: b 1738/9 d 7-28-1795 m Prudence Cady Pvt NY
David: b 10-15-1715 d 2-18-1819 m Elizabeth Chandler PS NH
Edward: b c. 1738 d p. 1794 m Jemima Mobley Sol SC
Francis: b 10-30-1734 d 10-11-1818 m Mary Bancroft PS Pvt NH
Henry: b 1716 d 3-15-1788 m Phoebe Chandler Pvt PS NH
Hezekiah: b 10-29-1729 d 4-6-1793 m Hannah Phelps Capt NH
Isaac, Sr.: b 3-29-1724 d 12-3-1799 m Debora Shelden Pvt MA
Isaac, Jr.: b 3-16-1757 d 12-8-1832 m Mary Morse Pvt MA
Jacob: b 2-7-1752 d 6-20-1841 m Elizabeth Baxter Drm NH
Jeremiah: b 1738/9 d 10-1-1806 m Dorothy Ballard Pvt MA

LOVEJOY, contd.
John: b 1- -1740 d 4-20-1808 m Rebecca (Naylor)Ranson PS MD
John: b 9-24-1751 d 1-11-1831 m Martha Odell Pvt NH
John, Sr.: b 1-5-1720 d 1795 m Sarah Pierce PS NH
John, Jr.: b 1749 d 1835 m Mary Galoupe PS NH
Jonathan: b 7-3-1754 d 7-21-1852 m Rebecca Ball Sol NH
Joseph: b c. 1734 d 10-18-1814 m Patience Bradford Pvt NH
Joshua: b 1744 d 1-28-1832 m Sarah Perkins Lt MA
Nathan: b 8-22-1726 d 4-15-1783 m Apphia Hoyt Slr MA
Nathan: b 11-11-1757 d 3-8-1829 m Louise Davis Pvt NY ★
Peter: b 1742 d a. 1790 m Silence Bartlett Pvt MA
Peter: b 1755 d 11-29-1793 m Anna Averill Pvt NH
Samuel: b 9-23-1750 d 10-6-1801 m Lydia Abbott Maj NH
Samuel: b 9-11-1753 d 9-13-1822 m Esther Morse Pvt MA
Samuel: b 8-24-1757 d 11-26-1841 m Elizabeth Elliott Pvt MA ★
Wm.: b 7-6-1759 d 9-30-1830 m (1)Mary O.Dane (2)Polly Barker
    Cpl MA

LOVELACE,
Charles: b — d p. 10-8-1796 m Catherine Beall Pvt MD
Gershom: b 3-28-1757 d 1-19-1844 m Mary Adams Pvt NJ ★
Wm.: b 7-29-1747 d 8- -1815 m Margery Beall CS Sol NC MD

LOVELAND,
Abner: b 4-18-1764 d 9-6-1847 m Lois Hodge Pvt CT ★
Amos: b 9-1-1762 d 12-30-1851 m Jemima Dickson Pvt CT
Amos: b 2-6-1764 d 2-14-1836 m Hannah Haff Pvt CT
Asa: b c. 1748 d 10-24-1775 m Mary — Pvt CT
Charles: b c. 1738 d 1781 m Mary Gleason Lt NJ
Daniel: b 1757 d p. 1797 m Ruth Keeny Pvt CT
Elijah: b 5-31-1745 d 5-27-1826 m Anna Deming Cpl CT
Elijah: b 11-16-1742 d 1-2-1829 m Sara Smith Pvt MA
Eliphaz: b 12-31-1745 d 8-28-1823 m (1)Jemima Porter (2)Mrs
    Rachel Kneeland Pvt CT
Elisha: b 5-4-1738 d p. 1780 m Lucy (Sparks) Stratton Pvt CT
Elizur: b 4-12-1738 d 1818 m Ruth Sparks Pvt CT
Epaphroditus: b 6-16-1758 d 6-26-1808 m Eunice Bascum Pvt CT
George: b 1758 d 11-29-1843 m (1)Hannah Combs (2)Thankful
    Fanny Beebe Pvt MA ★
Isaac: b a. 1764 d 4-28-1832 m Ruth Judith Holden Pvt CT
Joel: b 1729 d 2-28-1776 m — Van Zandt Stoepel Pvt CT
John: b 12-25-1740 d 10-30-1809 m (1)Elizabeth Buck (2)Esther
    (Buck)Seward PS CT
Jonathan: b 6-6-1741 d 1822 m (1)Bethiah — (2)Their Winslow Pvt
    CT
Joseph: b 2-8-1739 d p. 1782 m Lois Chatfield Capt CT
Joseph: b 4-14-1747 d 9-8-1813 m Mercy Bigelow Cpl NH
Levi: b 11-19-1749 d p. 1803 m Esther Hill Pvt CT
Malachi: b 5-7-1736 d 10-13-1799 m Priscilla Norkott Ens CT
Pelatiah: b 1-13-1748 d 4-28-1823 m ( )Mary Ruth Sparks ( )Mary
    Goodale Pvt CT
Samuel: b 12-12-1735 d 10-17-1791 m Rebecca — Sgt NJ
Solomon: b 1729/30 d 10-19-1820 m (1)Experience — (2)Lucy
    M. Morley PS MA
Thomas: b 8-30-1726 d 3-30-1811 m (1)Mary White (2)Hannah
    Norkott Pvt CT

LOVELL,
Alexander: b 1747 d 4-13-1814 m Margaret Westcott Pvt RI
Amos, Sr.: b 1753 d 1815 m — Pvt MA
Asahel: b c. 1760 d 3-17-1835 m Hannah — Pvt NJ
Caleb: b 10-2-1759 d 3-19-1833 m Ruth Fullerton QM Gnr MA
David: b 8-8-1752 d 1-24-1840 m Keziah White Pvt MA
Dyer: b 8-23-1749 d 10-22-1818 m Abigail Chickering Pvt MA
Elijah: b 4-20-1749 d 8-15-1816 m Abigail Goldsbury PS VT
Ezra: b 3-29-1749 d 8-14-1821 m Mary Jennerson lLt MA
Jacob: b 3-29-1724 d 11-27-1805 m Hannah Lumbart Capt MA
Jacob: b 8-25-1737 d a. 10-6-1776 m Mary Tower Pvt MA
James, Sr.: b 10-31-1737 d 7-14-1814 m Mary Middleton PS MA
James, Jr.: b 7-9-1758 d 1850 m Deborah Gorham Adj MA
John: b 1731 d 11-3-1789 m Priscilla West Pvt CT MA
John: b 10-20-1746 d 12-15-1803 m Martha Corey Pvt VT
Joseph: b 1-20-1717 d 2-11-1796 m Patience Barrows Pvt MA
Joseph: b 1741 d 1827 m (1)Jemima Adams (2)Elizabeth (Partridge)
    (Wheeler)Leland Capt MA
Joshua: b 8-6-1761 d 9-20-1843 m (1)Rebekah Thayer (2)Sarah
    Tower (3)Annah Brewster Pvt MA ★
Josiah: b 10-26-1757 d p. 1823 m Lydia Vining Pvt MA
Nathaniel: b 9-23-1748 d 6-29-1824 m Mary Barber Knowlton Pvt
    MA
Obadiah: b 2-17-1729 d 9-27-1810 m Ruth Beal Pvt MA
Oliver: b 5-1-1739 d p. 1785 m (1)Hannah Smith (2)Irena — Maj VT
Robert: b 1719 d 8- -1778 m (1)Sarah Marshall (2)Elizabeth — Lt
    VA
Samuel: b 8-8-1753 d 8-7-1807 m Olive Gould MM Sgt MA W★
Solomon: b 6-1-1732 d 9-4-1801 m Hannah Reed Pittey BGen MA
Wm.: b 4-20-1753 d 12-30-1821 m Dorothy Eldridge Pvt MA
Wm.: b 1758 d 1826 m Janet Irvine Urquhart NS VA

LOVERIDGE,
Wm.: b 1752 d 1805 m Sarah Douglass Pvt PA
Wm.: b 5-28-1761 d 9-18-1836 m (1)Lucy Welch (2)Lucretia
    (Jewett) Frink Pvt CT

LOVERING,
Ebenezer: b 12-9-1720 d 12-14-1806 m Mary Dearborn PS NH
Ebenezer: b 9-24-1734 d 8-23-1808 m Dorothy Brown PS NH
Jesse: b 3-27-1746 d 9-10-1844 m (1)Mercy Jennings (2)Lydia
    Sheffield Marsh Drm Sgt MA ★
John: b 8-21-1715 d 1778 m Anna Sanborn PS NH
Jonathan: b 8-7-1748 d p. 9-5-1823 m Elizabeth Dudley Pvt NH
Joseph: b 1735 d 1802 m Sarah Ellis Pvt MA
Samuel, Sr.: b 12-5-1715 d 8-22-1781 m Mary Hunt Leland Pvt MA
Samuel, Jr.: b 8-13-1741 d 2-22-1819 m Phebe Smith Cpl MA
Simeon: b 1752 d 6-9-1837 m Sarah Sanborn Pvt NH ★
Simeon: bpt 4-3-1743 d 1820 m Anna — Pvt NH
Theophilus: b 1-3-1759 d 4-15-1852 m Susana Dudley Sgt NH

LOVETT,
Aaron: b c. 1738 d a. 3-31-1818 m Charity Rodman Pvt PA
Benjamin, Jr.: b 11-2-1729 d 2- -1805 m Hannah Killiam Pvt PS MA
James: b 1762 d 3- -1832 m Rosamond Gould Pvt MA
Jeremiah: b 6-3-1756 d 2-4-1828 m Elizabeth Butler Pvt MA
John: b 7-1-1743 d 2-25-1792 m Elizabeth Herrick PS MA
John: b 1760 d 8- -1818 m Nancy McClellan Sol NY
Joseph: b 9-9-1747 d 7-23-1829 m Elizabeth Way Ens CT W★
Joseph: b 4-24-1739 d 1-10-1819 m Lucy Rea Pvt MA
Rebecca: b 6-1-1707 d 2-13-1787 m Josiah Lovett PS MA
Reuben: b 1730 d p. 3-20-1802 m Leshea — PS VA
Wm.: b 1-29-1748 d 4-9-1810 m Elizabeth Lufkin Pvt MA

LOVEWELL,
Joseph: b 10-27-1729 d 10- -1801 m (1)Hannah Warren (2)Mrs
    Ruth Walker Pvt MA
Nehemiah: b 1-9-1726 d 3-23-1801 m Raechel Farwell Capt NH
Zaccheus: b 11-8-1758 d 2-23-1847 m (1)Hepsibah Taplin (2)Irene
    Loveland Pvt NH VT ★

LOVING, (includes LOVIN)
Adam: b 11-12-1751 d 1-28-1819 m (1)Patty Arnold (2)Polly
    Gibbons Pvt VA
Christopher: b 12-30-1763 d 9-27-1830 m Judy Sea Pvt SC ★
Christopher: b c. 1750 d p. 6-25-1790 m Mary — Sol SC
Gabriel, Jr.: b c. 1750 d p. 7-25-1808 m Rachel Sisk Lt NC
John: b 10-4-1739 d 5-10-1804 m Naomi Seay Capt VA
Randolph: b c. 1749 d 2- -1810 m — Pvt VA
Richard: b 1760 d 6-24-1834 m Mary Harlow Pvt VA W★
Wm.: b 2-14-1740 d 1-30-1792 m Elizabeth Hargrove PS CS Capt
    VA

LOVINGOOD,
Harmon: b c. 1745 d 7-16-1800 m Ann — Pvt VA

LOVINS,
Arthur: b 1754 d 1815 m — Pvt NC

LOVIS,
Ambrose: bpt 4-17-1743 d c. 1789 m Susannah Dennis Pvt Smn MA

LOVRIEN,
Samuel: b 1753 d 12-12-1829 m Mehitable Rowe Pvt NH

LOW, (includes LOUW & LOWE)
Aaron: b 5-3-1755 d 8-20-1840 m Anna Burnham Pvt MA
Abraham: b 2-11-1755 d 10-23-1834 m Charlotte Hale Sol MA NY
Abraham: bpt 10-13-1719 d p. 1780 m Ida Stoothoff CS NJ
Abraham: bpt 1-23-1743 d a. 11-28-1812 m Rachel Dewitt Pvt NY
Abraham: b — d — m Dinah Cuddeback Pvt NY
Abraham: b 8- -1764 d p. 2-6-1830 m Mary Martin Pvt NC
Abraham: b — m Maria VanVliet Pvt PS NY
Anthony: b 1-12-1725 d 10-8-1802 m (1)Phebe Greene (2)Sarah
    Stafford Sgt RI
Asa: b 3-13-1761 d 10-11-1839 m Sally Brown Pvt MA
Basil: b 1759 d 9-22-1846 m Teresa Wood Cpl MD ★
Benjamin: b 12-13-1728 d 11-12-1796 m Maria Bogardus Lt NY
Caleb: b 7-7-1739 d 5-10-1810 m Sarah Shillaber Maj MA
Cornelius: b 2-12-1758 d a. 4-17-1844 m Jane Allen Wgn PS NJ
Cornelius: b 1730 d 10-13-1812 m Catherine McKenney Pvt NY
Cornelius: b 7-25-1763 d 9-15-1835 m Johanna Hornbeck Pvt
    PA NY ★
Daniel: b — d c. 1822 m Martha Scott Sol GA
David, Sr.: b 5-5-1728 d 7-24-1782 m Abigail Choate Capt MA
David, Jr.: b 1753 d a. 8-7-1797 m Hannah Haskell Sgt MA
Dirck: b 9- -1717 d 1802 m Rebecca Emmons PS NJ
Ebenezer: b 10-4-1741 d p. 1790 m Martha Story 1Lt PA
Ephriam: b c. 1736 d p. 1790 m Maria Rosa Pvt NY
Isaac, Sr.: b c. 1725 d p. 1-4-1790 m (1)Grace — (2)Ann Money Sol
    CS PS GA
Isaac: b 9-19-1759 d 2-25-1850 m Deliah Hitchcock Ens MD
Issac: b 2-1-1730 d p. 1792 m Francisca Everet PS NY
Jacob: b 9-9-1760 d p. 1830 m Nancy Warner Sgt MD
Jacob G.: b 8-13-1755 d 4-9-1845 m Catherine Kortright Sgt NY ★
James: b c. 1760 d c. 1826 m Sarah Jane (Napier) Zeigler Pvt NC
James: b c. 1-5-1755 d 1814 m Rosana Hayback Pvt VA
Jennison: b 9-16-1756 d 12- -1835 m Dinah Haynes Pvt MA
Jesse: b c. 1750 d a. 4-11-1814 m Susanna Sublette Sol VA
Johannis: b 3-17-1706 d p. 4-29-1775 m Rebecca Freer PS NY
John: b 1736 d 1820 m Nancy Butler Pvt GA

John: b 3-5-1757 d 1-1-1816 m Hannah Hewitt Sgt MD
John, Sr.: b 5-17-1728 d 11-3-1796 m Sarah Gee Col CS MA
John, Jr.: b 9-1-1754 d 2-10-1801 m Lucy Rogers Lt MA
John: b 7-3-1760 d 10-30-1845 m Elizabeth Warner Pvtr MA
John: b 3-2-1752 d 3- -1813 m (2)Elizabeth D — Pvt NJ
John: b c. 1750 d 1816 m Jean — Pvt PA
John: b 6-19-1731 d 4-22-1817 m Sarah Wickes LCol VA
John: b 1730 d 1801 m Rebecca — Pvt VA
John Hawkins: b 1732 d 1820 m — Lawson LCol MD
Jonathan: b 1752 d — m Sarah Googe Cpl MA
Jonathan: b 1724 d 4-22-1813 m (1)Magdalene Auchmoodie
  (2)Gertjen VanWagenen Pvt NY
Joseph: b 5-6-1712 d 10-10-1784 m Abigail Low Pvt MA
Michael: b 1741 d p. 1818 m Anne Magruder Capt MD
Michael: b 5-2-1736 d 6-2-1795 m Anna Mary — Pvt PA
Nathan: b 1743 d 7-24-1804 m Lucy Lord Pvt MA
Nathan: b 12- -1762 d p. 1834 m Bitheath — Pvt NC ★
Nicholas: b 1763 d 1819 m Keturah Baker Pvt MD
Nicholas: b 3-7-1733 d a. 1790 m Sarah — Capt NY
Obadiah: b 1760 d 1813 m Sally Hobbs Sol ME
Peter: b 1-4-1750 d 4-10-1820 m Johanna (Ten Eyck) Sutphen Lt
  NJ
Peter: b 1728 d 9-4-1805 m — Pvt PA
Peter: b 3-14-1760 d 11-21-1835 m Elizabeth Coddington Pvt NY
Peter G.: b 1750 d 1847 m Catrina Hess Pvt PS NY
Petrus: bpt 10-24-1708 d 4-17-1776 m (1)Marytjen VanKeuren
  (2)Helena Kiersted PS NY
Philip: b 6-27-1751 d 9-28-1758 m Mary (Sharpe) Jones Ens GA
Ralph: b 1759 d 1845-1854 m — Lt NC
Robert: b 10-30-1759 d 1-10-1858 m Judith Elwell Sol MA
Robert: b c. 1745 d 1797 m Eleanor Polk Bbd PA
Samuel: b 5-27-1739 d 5- -1807 m Alma Stafford Capt MA
Samuel: b 10-29-1762 d 12-16-1812 m Lydia Smith FifMaj MA W★
Samuel: b 10-23-1758 d 9-17-1839 m Abigail Holden Bacon Arfr
  MA
Stephen: b 1704 d 11-29-1788 m (1)Alice Gorton (2)Sarah — PS
  RI
Thomas: b 8-10-1756 d 5- -1780 m Molly Allen Pvt Mid RI W★
Thomas: b 1755 d 10-27-1835 m Mary Holman QMSgt VA ★
Wm.: b 2-13-1748 d 9-13-1812 m Elizabeth Knowak Pvt MA
Wm.: b 1745 d 1818 m Nancy Yarborough Fif NC
Wm.: b 2-17-1756 d 3-19-1835 m Margaret F. — Pvt SC
Wm.: b 1757 d c. 1781 m Elizabeth Davenport Pvt VA

LOWDERMILK,
Jacob: b c. 1756 d 1843 m Mary Meyer 2Lt MD
Jacob: b 1716 d 6-15-1807 m Mary Myers PS NC

LOWDON, (or LOWDEN)
John: b 1730 d 2- -1798 m Sarah Gailbreath Capt PA

LOWELL,
Abner: b 12-28-1740 d 9-20-1828 m Mercy Paine Capt MA
Barnard: b 1-21-1760 d 3-28-1807 m Sarah Merrill Pvt NH
Benjamin: b 3-11-1759 d 3-11-1834 m Lydia Anice Pvt MA
Daniel: b 2-20-1743/4 d 3-14-1828 m Mercy Davis PS NH
David, Sr.: b 1-12-1716 d p. 1784 m Mary Blood Pvt NH
Gideon: b 1730 d 1730-35 m Molly Morrill PS MA
Isaac: b 5-30-1739 d 5-10-1796 m (1)Anna Chase (2)Sarah Pillsbury
  Pvt MA
Jacob: b 6-3-1752 d 8- -1828 m Jane McFadden Cpl MA
Jacob: b 4-7-1762 d 8-2-1819 m Sarah Keyes Pvt NH
James: b 10-12-1725 d 6-15-1830 m Mary Clark Pvt NH
John: b 6-17-1743 d 5-6-1802 m Sarah Higginson CS PS MA
John: b 10-19-1733 d 1-25-1790 m Martha Hasting Sol NH
John: b 1761 d 5-10-1840 m Elizabeth — Pvt CL ★
John: b 8-11-1748 d — m Mary Chapman Pvt VT
John E.: b 11-2-1757 d 11-16-1846 m (1)Nancy Bachelder
  (2)Hannah Rogers Pvt MA ★
Jonathan K.: b 1756 d 1852 m Rachel Morton Pvt MA
Joseph: b 5-8-1720 d p. 1778 m Martha Bradbury Pvt NH
Joshua: b 1744 d 11-22-1839 m Sarah Mayberry Pvt MA
Moses: b 8-17-1726 d 1817 m Sarah Bradbury Pvt PS NH
Paul: b 1758 d 1-14-1835 m Elizabeth Hunt Pvt MA
Peter: b 12-28-1752 d 1840 m Eunice Frink Pvt NH ★
Reuben: b 6-29-1739 d 6-1-1824 m (1)Priscilla Bartlett (2)Sarah
  Williams PS NH
Samuel: b 2-17-1738 d a. 2-23-1784 m (1)Susan Ellen Philbrook (2)
  Charity Berry Pvt MA
Samuel: b 10-11-1754 d 2- -1800 m Olive Wright Mil NH
Simeon: b 10-6-1745 d 8-26-1830 m Annie Wadleigh Pvt MA
Solomon: b 7-28-1749 d p. 1797 m Hannah Smith Pvt MA
Stephen: b 10-6-1728 d 6-15-1801 m Agnes Bolton Pvt MA
Thomas: b 1763 d 8-4-1843 m (1)Sarah Ayer (2)Lucinda Corliss Pvt
  MA ★
Timothy: b 2-21-1754 d 11-8-1834 m (1)Olive Carlton (2)Mary —
  Pvt MA ★
Wm.: b 1734 d 9-27-1809 m Mehitable Gould Pvt NH
Willoughby: b 6- -1749 d 6-17-1823 m Sally Sloan Pvt CT

LOWER, (includes LAUER)
Adam: b 1755 d 4-16-1833 m (1)Elizabeth Keiser (2)Nancy Diggins
  Pvt PA

Christian: b 4-19-1713 d 9-8-1786 m Anna Catharine Sterf PS PA
Christian, Jr.: b 5-11-1751 d 1- -1807 m Eva Christiana Anspach
  Col PS PA
Michael: b c. 1720 d p. 1786 m Maria Barbara Frey PS PA
Philip: b 9-29-1754 d 6-5-1793 m Hannah Parker Sgt PA

LOWES,
James: b 1753 d 12-15-1810 m Jane Andrew Ens PA

LOWING,
Wm.: b 4-11-1758 d 12-29-1802 m Anna Height Cpl RI W★

LOWMILLER,
Henry: b c. 1730 d p. 6-29-1786 m Fronica Snevely Pvt PA

LOWNDES,
Christopher: bpt 6-19-1713 d 1-8-1785 m Elizabeth Tasker CS PS
  MD
Rawlins: b 1- -1722 d 8-24-1800 m (2)Mary Cartwright PS SC

LOWREY, (includes LAURY, LAWREY, LOWERY, LOWRY)
Alexander: b 12- -1733 d 1-31-1805 m (1)Mary Waters (2)Anne
  West (Aldrichs) (3)Mrs Sarah Cochran Col PS PA
Alexander: b 1-30-1767 d 8-20-1846 m Amie Gist Pvt VA
Andrew: b 1752 d 9-13-1796 m Margaret Hood 2Lt PA
Daniel: b 1-27-1749 d 5-14-1819 m Anna Monson Cpl CT
Esther Fleming: b 4-15-1739 d 10-13-1814 m Thomas Lowrey
  PS NJ
Giles: b 12-25-1733 d p. 1833 m Anne — Pvt VA ★
Godfrey: b 11-22-1756 d 6-27-1824 m Susannah Rockel Pvt PA
Isham: b 1725 d 1788 m Mary — Pvt SC
Jacob: b 10-12-1758 d 1841 m Ann Washabaugh Pvt PA MD
James: b c. 1760 d p. 6-3-1841 m Margaret — Pvt PA
James: b 1749 d 1840 m Sarah Preston Pvt SC
John: b 1735 d 1790 m Hannah Phinney Pvt MD
John: b 1749 d 4-17-1849 m Hannah Vance Sol NC
John: b 1744 d 10- -1792 m Dorcas Montgomery Lt VA
John: b 1760 d 1835 m Betty Hill Pvt VA
Levi: b 8-1-1764 d 3-18-1847 m Martha (Wilson) McCuller Pvt SC
  NC GA ★
Michael: b 1-3-1760 d 1833 m Maria Washabuagh Pvt MD ★
Michael: b c. 1717 d 1777 m Barbara Gottchalk Pvt PA
Philip: b 1757 d 3-7-1848 m Margaret Masters Pvt PA
Robert: b 3-13-1730 d 5-10-1800 m Judith (Boggan) May Pvt SC
Robert: b c. 1752 d p. 6-5-1813 m Penelope — PS SC
Robert: b 1743 d 1823 m Elizabeth — CS SC
Stephen: b c. 1760 d p. 3- -1796 m Margaret Lewis Pvt VA
Stephen: b 1747 d 12-29-1821 m Sarah Spencer CmsryGen NJ
Thomas: b 9-3-1737 d 11-10-1806 m Esther Fleming Col NJ
Thomas: b 8-17-1734 d p. 1783 m Phoebe Benedict Pvt NY
Thomas: b c. 1760 d 11-25-1846 m Nancy Dedman Pvt VA ★
Wm.: b 2-11-1759 d 3-13-1802 m Martha Howe QM NJ
Wm.: b 1760 d 5-22-1842 m Sarah Wilson Pvt PA ★
Wm.: b 3-13-1742 d p. 1790 m Rebecca Kerr Pvt PA
Wm.: b 1762 d 1836 m Mary Gray Pvt PA
Wm.: b 6-12-1747 d 9-12-1804 m Agnes Strong Sol SC

LOWTHER, (includes LAUTHER & LOUTHER)
David: b — d 9-18-1845 m Sarah Menoher Sol PA
James: b c. 1758 d 1826 m Margaret Freeman Lt PA
Robert: b 10-1-1765 d 11-16-1832 m Catherine Cain Sct VA
Wm.: b 1742 d 10-28-1814 m Sudna Hughes Col CS VA

LOXLEY,
Benjamin: b 12-20-1720 d 10-15-1801 m (1)Jane Watkins
  (2)Catherine Cox Col PA

LOY,
John: b 1747 d 5-3-1840 m Mary Holt Pvt NC ★

LOYER,
Adrian: b 11-19-1730 d 3- -1780 m Christiana Irwin PS GA

LOZIER,
Abram: b 1755 d 11-14-1839 m Jane Peck Sgt NY
Hillebrant: b 7-1-1757 d 6-2-1836 m Elizabeth Campbell Pvt NJ ★
Jacob: b 1760 d 1831/2 m Christiana Peck Pvt VA ★
Oliver: b 1747 d 1849 m Eleanor Erkells Matr NY ★
Peter: b 12-12-1735 d 1814 m Rebecca Peck Pvt NJ

LUCAS,
Abijah: b 2-5-1759 d 9-11-1838 m Mary Robbins Pvt MA
Barton: b 1729 d 5- -1785 m Priscilla Smoot Capt MD
Basil: b 1757 d 7-6-1841 m Elizabeth — Sgt MD ★
Charles: b c. 1730 d 6- -1783 m Tabitha — Cmsry VA
Daniel: b 2-7-1762 d 11- -1838 m Martha Brown Pvt MA
David: b 8-27-1745 d 10-21-1827 m Sarah Stanley PS CT
Edward: b 12-3-1738 d 3-19-1809 m Elizabeth Edwards 2Lt VA
Elijah: b a. 1759 d 7-8-1806 m Sarah Shaw Pvt MA
Elnathan: b 3-1-1762 d 8-27-1826 m Lydia Cornish Pvt MA
George: b 2-19-1750 d 1-18-1841 m Lilly Ann Dobson OrdlSgt
  PA ★
Hugh A.: b 1744-54 d p. 5-2-1826 m — PS NC
Isaac: b 1-6-1759 d 4-8-1848 m Janet Smith Pvt MA ★

LUCAS, contd.
Israel: b 1-26-1753 d 3-22-1834 m Mabel Bidwell Pvt NY
James: b 1755 d p. 1795 m Mary Free Pvt GA
James: b 1760 d 1820 m Ruth Holmes (Lewis) Sgt MD
James: b 3-9-1753 d 3-2-1835 m Anne S. Whiteman 2Lt PM NH
  W★
James: b c. 1758/9 d 12-8-1814 m Mary (Lucas) Col VA W★
John: b 5-5-1735 d 9-23-1776 m Miss Gardner Pvt CT
John: b a. 1740 d 1785 m Rebecca Mooring ADC GA
John: b 6-26-1750 d 9-22-1823 m (1)Mary Simmons (2)Rachel
  (Belt)Marriott Sgt MD
John: b c. 1755 d p. 1833 m Jemima Lary Pvt NH ★
John: b c. 1756 d p. 1807 m (1)Ann Mikell (2)Clarissa Denmark Sol
  SC
John: b 7-15-1749 d 4-19-1836 m Mary Wilson Capt VA ★
John: b 1-11-1765 d 10-1-1831 m Mary Simons Pvt VA
Joseph: b 1-12-1729 d p. 1790 m Mary Rickard Pvt MA
Joseph: b 10-3-1742 d 10-22-1806 m Ruby Fuller Pvt MA
Moses: b 1749 d 11- -1829 m Eunice Barnes Pvt PS CT
Nathaniel: b a. 1755 d 5-5-1807 m Sarah Rivers Capt VA W★
Richard: b 7-19-1732 d p. 4-1-1791 m (1)Elsie — (2)Rachel (Duval)
  — Sgt PA
Samuel: b 1755 d 5-24-1823 m Margaret Downy Sgt PA
Thomas: b 9-12-1758 d 10-11-1824 m Abigail Gillum Pvt CT
Thomas: b 1732 d 1-11-1819 m — PS MD
Thomas: b — d 11-3-1823 m — Lt PA
Wm.: b 4-11-1760 d 4-16-1836 m Jane Brown Pvt CT
Wm.: b 1757 d 1803 m Hannah — Pvt NH
Wm.: b 7-7-1730 d a. 5-14-1811 m Sarah — Pvt PA
Wm.: b c. 1746 d p. 3-7-1803 m Frances — LCol PS VA
Wm.: b c. 1720 d p. 5-20-1813 m Rebecca Rust Capt VA
Wm.: b 1-18-1742 d 7-2-1814 m Susannah Barnes Lt VA
Wm.: b 7-25-1749 d p. 1834 m Elizabeth Price Pvt PS VA

LUCE, (includes DE LUCE & LUSE)
Abijah: b 10-22-1760 d 10-8-1821 m Mary Lambert Pvt MA
Abner: b 4-16-1762 d 4-18-1819 m Armelia Luce Pvt MA
Benjamin, Sr.: b 1730 d 1814 m Elizabeth Hopkins Pvt NJ
Benjamin, Jr.: b 2-5-1761 d 2-12-1806 m Jane Hines Wgn NJ
Benjamin: b 10-4-1756 d 11-12-1834 m Demaris Allen Pvt MA ★
David: b 1752 d — m Hannah Look Cpl MA
Ebenezer: b 1-27-1727 d 7-30-1794 m Annah Robinson Pvt CT
Eleazer: b 1740 d 1820 m (1)Elizabeth — (2)Jemima Oliver Lt NJ
Eleazer: b 1729 d 5-4-1792 m Prudence Young PS NY
Elijah: b 6-23-1746 d 10-29-1819 m (1)Lydia Cleveland (2)Love
  Cleveland NCdr MA
Francis: b c. 1742 d p. 1790 m (1)Mary Davenport (2)Mary
  Bradley Pvt MA
Hezekiah: b 7-8-1723 d 5-14-1809 m Thankful Look PS MA
Israel: b c. 1746 d a. 1828 m Deborah Swayze Pvt NJ
Israel: b 1761 d 1820 m Apphia Parker Pvt MA
Ivory: b 10-21-1756 d 2-10-1847 m (1)Mary Look (2)Sabra —
  Sgt VT ★
James: b c. 1756 d 5-21-1813 m (1)Hannah Harding (2)Lucy Pease
  Pvt MA
Jesse: b 1-5-1746 d 4-2-1813 m Elizabeth West Sgt MA
Jonathan: b 9-28-1760 d 3-29-1838 m Rachel Lurvey Pvt VT ★
Joseph: b 1734 d 6-20-1814 m Priscilla Loomis Sol CL
Joseph: b 9-25-1726 d 3-22-1808 m Jedidah Claghorn Pvt MA
Josiah L.: b c. 1741 d 7-27-1786 m Elizabeth Walden Pvt MA
Malachi: b 8-27-1755 d 3-20-1838 m Ann Weeks Pvt MA ★
Nathan: b 6-23-1747 d 10-13-18l3 m Damaris Luse Col NJ ★
Roland: b 8-26-1756 d 10-2-1835 m Elisabeth Clark MM MA
Shubael, Jr.: b c. 1754 d p. 1790 m Mary Atsatt Pvt MA
Solomon: b 8-4-1762 d 2-8-1839 m (1)Martha Tilton (2)Anna
  Norton Pvt MA
Stephen: b 9-25-1714 d 5-13-1801 m Content Presbury PS CS MA
Sylvanus: b 11-26-1750 d 11-4-1803 m Elizabeth Ferguson Pvt MA
Thomas: b 1758 d 9-17-1843 m Thankful (Luce) Pvt Smn PS MA ★
Zimri: b 3-12-1759 d 4-13-1843 m Molly Murray Pvt VT MA

LUCK,
Francis: b c. 1723 d a. 7-17-1781 m Sarah — Capt VA
Sarah: b 1730 d a. 3-12-1821 m Francis Luck PS VA

LUCKETT, (includes LOCKETT)
David: b c. 1750 d 10-7-1799 m Susannah (Luckett) Lt MD
David: b 1730 d 1796 m Sally Lucy Winfrey Pvt VA
Jacob: b 1754 d a. 6-4-1820 m Lucy Waddell Sgt VA
Samuel: b 7- -1755 d 1-23-1838 m Susanna — Capt MD
Thomas Hussey: b — d 1787 m Elizabeth Noland Lt VA
Thomas Hussey: b c. 1755 d 1800 m Eleanor Douglas PS MD
Wm.: b 1711 d 1782 m Charity Middleton LCol MD
Wm.: b 1747 d 5- -1820 m Clarissa Nelson PS MD

LUCKEY, (includes LUCKIE)
John: b c. 1735 d 1824 m — Pvt NC
Joseph: b 1750 d 10-30-1823 m Mary J. Bralock Capt PA
Robert: b c. 1753-8 d 1797 m Catherine MacIlvaine Pvt PA

LUCY, (includes LUCEY)
Alexander: b c. 1700 d p. 1790 m Eunice Dame PS Lt NH
Isham: b 1740 d p. 1806 m Sarah Dickerson Pvt NC
Isham: b a. 1745 d p. 1820 m Ann — Sol NC

LUDDEN,
Asa: b 1750 d 4-8-1825 m — Wait Lt MA
Ezra: b 1748 d 11-24-1833 m Hannah Wolcott Pvt MA
James: b 9-5-1743 d p. 1790 m Elizabeth Wales Sol MA
Joseph: b 10-25-1753 d 8-4-1829 m Sarah Brown Sgt MA
Seth: b 2-4-1744 d p. 6-23-1781 m Parnel — Sol MA

LUDINGTON, (includes LUDDINGTON)
Comfort: b 1740 d 9- -1805 m Elizabeth Wickerson Capt NY
Daniel: b 7-30-1751 d 8-21-1824 m Naomi Searl Pvt MA
Henry: b 5-25-1738 d 1-24-1817 m Abigail (Ludington) Col NY
Isaac: b 1742 d 1-10-1782 m Mary Goodsell Pvt CT
Jesse, Jr.: b 2-2-1757 d 1-1-1841 m (1)Thankful Chidsey (2)Sarah
  Moulthrop Pvt CT ★
Lemuel: b 5-8-1747 d 1-16-1839 m Hopestil Trescott Pvt CT ★
Nathaniel: bpt 11-29-1761 d 12-8-1831 m Polly Stewart Sol CT
Samuel: b 4-13-1744 d 3-14-1814 m Ruth Galpin Pvt CT

LUDLAM, (includes LUDLUM)
Christopher: b 3-7-1756 d 9-18-1805 m (1)Amelia Hand (2)Elizabeth
  Morris Homes 2Lt NJ
Daniel: b 12-6-1729 d 3-18-1807 m Joanna Smith Pvt NY
Henry: b 5-13-1752 d 10-20-1837 m Hannah Somers Smith Lt NJ
Jacob: b 1760/1 d 2-7-1838 m Margaret Pool Pvt NJ
Povidence: b 1725 d 7-5-1792 m Hannah Gardner CS NJ
Reuben: b c. 1728 d 1783 m Hannah Spicer PS NJ
Wm.: b 4-3-1757 d 4-24-1850 m Temperance Weeks Pvt NY
Wm.: b 10-5-1746 d 11-22-1816 m Judith — Capt NY

LUDLOW,
Anthony: b 10-21-1748 d 1809 m Elizabeth — PS NY
Cornelius: b 1729 d 4-27-1812 m (1)Catherine Cooper (2)Martha
  Lyon (3)Polly Wall LCol NJ
Henry: b c. 1743 d p. 1820 m Hannah Cooper Pvt NY
Joseph: b 7-10-1757 d 2-28-1833 m Chloe Moore Biddle Pvt NJ
Richard: b 8-17-1745 d a. 11-17-1820 m (1)Jane Van Nostrand (2)
  (2)Elizabeth Van Campen Maj PS NJ
Ziba: b c. 1750 d p. 11-3-1815 m Phoebe Baker Pvt NJ

LUDWIG, (includes LUDWICK)
Conrad: b 1-15-1760 d 6-10-1821 m Mary Lieb Fif PA
Daniel: b 1754 d p. 12-12-1812 m Mary DeHart Ens PA
Daniel: b 6-4-1748 d 6-9-1825 m (1)Appelona Miller (2)Eva
  Grissmer (3)Elizabeth Shupert Pvt PA
Jacob: b 1730 d 1-1-1826 m Marguritte Hilt Capt MA
Jacob: b 1738 d 9-14-1800 m Madalen (Baker) Pvt PA
Jacob: b 2-22-1761 d 1-26-1813 m Ellenora Sadler Pvt PA
John: b 1753 d 1786 m Ann Margaret Elizabeth Misshatt Capt PA
John: b 6-4-1747 d 7-2-1802 m Rachel Morris Capt PS PA
Joseph Henry: b 1790 d 1833 m Elizabeth Kaler Pvt CS PS MA
Leonard: b — d p. 12-24-1803 m — Pvt MD
Mattias: b 1735 d 1-22-1794 m Mrs Anna Elizabeth Walbert Pvt PA
Michael, Sr.: b 8-3-1707 d 12-24-1784 m Eva Rosanna Bechtel PS
  PA
Michael, Jr.: b 2-7-1745 d 4-17-1806 m Susanna Lutz Pvt PS PA
Phillip: b 3-10-1760 d 2-8-1827 m Anna DeHart Pvt PA

LUFF,
Nathaniel: b 4-23-1756 d 1-21-1806 m (1)Elizabeth Fisher (2)Lydia
  Boon Dr PA
Nathaniel: b 1-4-1736 d 1-21-1806 m (2)Ann Archer Clark PS Capt
  DE

LUFKIN,
Benjamin: b 4-8-1763 d 11-9-1844 m (1)Mehitable Abbott
  (2)Sarah E. Bunker Mar Pvt MA ★
Moses: b 6- -1755 d 6-7-1846 m (1)Mary Brown (2)Martha Giddings
  Drm Sol MA
Nathaniel, Jr.: bpt 3-30-1755 d 2-19-1838 m (1)Mary Butler (2)
  Mehitable Haskell Pvt MA
Samuel: b 1762 d 7-30-1838 m Sarah Livingston Pvt MA ★
Stephen: bpt 7-22-1733 d 7-9-1803 m Sarah Choate PS Pvt NH

LUGAR,
Christopher: b 11-9-1753 d 3-4-1810 m Sarah Ashfield Pvt NY

LUKE,
Coenradt: b c. 1731 d p. 1790 m Geertruy VanDeusen Pvt NY
Isaac: b 11-26-1729 d 10-31-1784 m Rachel Dale PS VA
Peter: b 1726 d 1806 m Catherine Elizabeth Keiser QM VA
Philip C.: bpt 6-17-1753 d 1782 m Magdeline VanWie 2Lt NY
Wm.: b 1741 d c. 1835 m Jane Ferris Sol VA

LUKENS,
Charles: b a. 1746 d 1784 m Margaret Sanderson Maj Cmsry PA
David: b 10-10-1753 d 1831 m Sarah Lloyd Pvt PA
John: b 10- -1720 d 10-21-1789 m Sarah — CS PA
John: b 10-17-1729 d 4-16-1813 m Rachel Robinson Pvt PA
Mathias: b 1750 d p. 3-6-1783 m Jane — Pvt PA
Peter: b c. 1752 d 3-16-1811 m Martha Jones PS PA
Seneca: b 2-14-1751 d 12-9-1829 m Sarah Quimby Pvt PA
Wm.: b 8-1-1742 d p. 1790 m Rachel Kenderdine Pvt PA

LULL,
Benjamin, Sr.: b 1724 d 1810 m Elizabeth — PS NY
David: b 11-2-1759 d 6-29-1832 m Mary Cilley Pvt MA ★
John: b c. 1752 d p. 1800 m Deborah Winslow Pvt VT
Nathan: b 5-17-1761 d 9-27-1842 m Ruth Moore Pvt NY
Timothy: b 1730 d 9-   -1811 m Mary — Capt VT
Wm.: b 1761 d 1837 m Charlotte — PS NY

LUM,
Adam: b 11-11-1753 d 1830 m (1)Hannah Bassett (2)Elizabeth Hawkins Sol CT
Andrew: b 2-25-1743 d p. 1790 m Hannah Pvt MA
Israel: b 1756 d 10-4-1837 m (1)Betsey Day (2)Patience Pierson Pvt NJ
Janes: b 6-7-1747 d 5-4-1805 m Elizabeth (Young) Ens NJ
John Clark: b 12-26-1759 d 8-4-1838 m Ruth Baker Pvt NJ ★
Joseph: b 1-14-1715 d 2-24-1796 m Sarah Washburn PS CT
Matthew: b 5-31-1763 d 5-14-1837 m Hannah Ludlow Pvt NJ
Matthias: bpt 11-8-1747 d 3-20-1815 m Hannah Leonard Pvt NJ
Stephen: b 1-26-1754 d a. 3-29-1806 m Abigail Thompson Pvt NJ

LUMPKIN,
Dickerson: b c. 1765 d 1856 m — Sol VA
George: b c. 1723 d p. 1785 m Mary Cody Capt VA
Henry: b 12-1-1741 d 11-4-1803 m Anne Burke Capt VA
John: b 1763 d 1834 m Lucy Hopson Sol VA
Moore: b c. 1756 d 12-6-1841 m (2)Catherine Richardson Pvt VA

LUMSDEN,
Jeremiah: b c. 1760 d 1-18-1837 m Elizabeth Belcher Sol VA
John: b 11-10-1758 d 4-21-1843 m Elizabeth Eastland Ens VA ★
John: b c. 1738 d 1788 m Wilmoth Steele Cpl VA

LUNA,
Peter: b 10-1-1760 d p. 3-25-1848 m Elizabeth — Pvt VA

LUND,
John: b 2-22-1749 d 3-11-1822 m Hannah Phelps Lt NH W★
Thomas: b 3-12-1739 d 2-   -1821 m Sarah Whitney Pvt NH

LUNDY, (includes LUNDIE)
Ebenezer: b 9-19-1751 d p. 12-3-1778 m Hannah Bard PS PA
Samuel: b 12-13-1727 d 2-14-1801 m (1)Anne Schooley (2)Sarah Willets PS CS NJ
Theophilus: b 1760 d p. 1800 m Frances McLinn 2Lt GA
Thomas: b 1741 d 2-   -1798 m Lucy Yates PS VA

LUNGER,
Jacob: b 10-11-1743 d — m Juliana Hulshizer Sol NJ

LUNSFORD,
Anthony: b 1-9-1719 d 1784 m (1)Sarah Carpenter (2)Elizabeth Watts Pvt VA
George: b 6-8-1762 d 12-8-1808 m Mary Ann Judy Pvt VA
Rodham: b a. 1739 d p. 1791 m (2)Lettice (Lynton)Carter Sol PS VA
Rodham: b 1761 d 3-   -1841 m (1)Clementine Ball (2)Sally Cox Pvt VA ★
Swanson: b 1759 d 8-7-1799 m Rebecca Wade Capt SC VA

LUNT,
Abner Coffin: b 10-2-1752 d 5-4-1792 m Elizabeth Hodgdon Sol MA
Daniel: b 11-19-1749 d 11-23-1823 m (1)Molly Starbuck (2)Eunice Conant Capt MA ★
Daniel: b 3-12-1745 d 7-20-1787 m Sarah Knight NCdr MA
Ezra: b 1736 d 1804 m (1)Mary Pike (2)Mrs Annie Lowell Burnham Maj MA
Henry: b 1755 d 1805 m Sarah Orcutt 1Lt MA
Joseph: b 1-20-1730 d 1796 m Sarah Stickney Sol MA
Joseph, Jr.: b 2-19-1753 d 12-26-1811 m Priscilla Crooker Mar MA
Micajah: b 9-2-1763 d 5-22-1828 m Mary Smith Pvt MA ★
Micajah: b 11-9-1764 d 8-30-1840 m (1)Sarah Giddings (2)Sarah B. Swett Smn MA
Moses: b 6-7-1751 d 10-5-1813 m Sarah Noyes Sgt MA
Paul: b 3-30-1747 d 11-26-1824 m (1)Margaret Coffin (2)Hannah Adams Lt MA
Richard: b 4-17-1742 d 10-27-1796 m Elizabeth Chapman Smn MA
Wm.: b c. 1744 d — m Bethana Hoxie Sol RI

LUPHER, (includes LUPFER)
Casper: b 10-10-1760 d 3-5-1846 m Barbara Leyen Pvt PA
Jacob, Sr.: b 10-31-1725 d 9-10-1803 m Anna Kumbert PS PA
Jacob, Jr.: b 8-12-1765 d 4-3-1838 m Mary Magdalena Bernheisel Pvt PA
John: b 1761 d 6-26-1826 m Margaret Reed Pvt PA

LUPTON,
Joseph: b c. 1750 d p. 1780 m Susan (Boyer)Pearce Sgt VA
Josiah: b 11-1-1727 d 4-29-1803 m Sarah Fanning Capt NY
Stephen: b 9-15-1745 d 12-8-1787 m Rhoda (Platts)Garrison Sol VA

LURTY,
John: b — d p. 7-12-1794 m Rosa Bronaugh NCapt VA

LURVEY,
Jacob: b 10-25-1761 d 9-11-1853 m Hannah Boynton Pvt MA
Moses: b 1754 d 12-   -1836 m Elizabeth Potter Sgt MA ★

LUSCOMB,
Richard: b 9-27-1740 d 1829 m Bathsheba Austin Sgt MA
Robert: b 5-22-1709 d 2-14-1801 m (1)Bathsheba Walker (2)Elizabeth White Chandler (3)Margaret Leonard (4)Elizabeth Bucknam PS MA

LUSH,
Richard: b a. 1760 d 5-3-1817 m Lyntje Fonda PS NY

LUSHBAUGH, (or LORSHBACH)
Harmon: b 1761 d 11-   -1800 m Elizabeth — Pvt PA

LUSK,
David, Sr.: b c. 1730 d 7-6-1793 m Prudence Hurlbut Pvt CT
David: b 2-17-1744 d 9-   -1828 m Elizabeth McKinley Pvt PA
Hugh: b 1754 d p. 1834 m Elizabeth McMortrey Pvt VA ★
Jacob: b 1766 d c. 1800 m Elizabeth Phillips Pvt NY ★
James: b 4-17-1746 d 9-23-1831 m Love Graham Capt CT
James: b 8-15-1754 d 9-27-1803 m (1)Letitia Thomas (2)Sarah McElwayne Maj SC
John: b 2-10-1748 d 5-6-1813 m Elizabeth Kellogg Pvt MA
John: b 1754 d 1820 m — McMurtie Pvt VA
Joseph: b 3-15-1753 d 8-15-1839 m — Pvt NC ★
Patrick: b 1750 d 3-17-1816 m Eleanor — Pvt PA ★
Samuel: b 1-29-1752 d 11-4-1828 m (1)Naomi Bryant (2)Anne Hyde Cpl CT
Samuel: b 4-9-1750 d 8-14-1825 m Elizabeth Whiteside Pvt NC ★
Thomas: b c. 1735 d p. 1790 m Elizabeth Goodrich Maj MA
Wm.: b c. 1764 d 3-29-1825 m Hannah — Pvt NY
Wm.: b — d 8-25-1799 m Martha McClure Capt PA
Wm.: b 11-3-1743 d 10-7-1780 m Margaret Vance Sol VA

LUTER, (includes LEWTER)
Giles: b c. 1750 d p. 5-6-1819 m Sally — Sol NC
Hardy: b 1740 d p. 1840 m — Bunn Pvt NC ★

LUTES,
John: b 1755 d 1800 m Elizabeth Ray Pvt NY

LUTHER,
Amos: b 2-24-1759 d 3-28-1840 m Bethany (Luther)Smn PS MA
Benjamin: b 1-31-1754 d 6-6-1837 m Waity Sheldon Sgt RI ★
Caleb: b 1751 d 1-27-1840 m (1)Rebecca Brown (2)Molly Foss Pvt RI W★
Cromwell: b 1761 d 3-   -1839 m Esther Smith Pvt CT ★
Eleazer: b 8-28-1732 d 1781 m Mary Chase Pvt MA
Ellis: b 1755 d 2-15-1837 m (1)Sibyl Post (2)Sarah Merrils Pvt CT
Ezra: b 6-30-1751 d 7-15-1847 m Rebecca (Sheldon)Hart Sol RI
Frederick: b 2-15-1730 d 5-13-1822 m Johanna Luther PS RI
Gideon: b 5-26-1756 d 2-28-1815 m (1)Olive Fowler (2)Mary Jowis Pvt RI
Harler: b 11-19-1737 d 1-24-1827 m Rachel Salisbury Pvt MA
Hezekiah: b 2-16-1763 d 6-10-1850 m Mary Luther Pvt MA
Jabez, Jr.: b 12-18-1759 d 12-23-1818 m Lydia Brown Pvt RI
James: b 2-19-1747 d p. 1833 m Sarah Bowen Pvt RI
Job: b 12-29-1738 d p. 1790 m Lydia Traffen Pvt MA
Josiah: b c. 1760 d 11-   -1801 m Priscilla Hill Pvt RI W★
Martin: b 4-19-1761 d 11-27-1841 m Rachel Cole Pvt RI
Peleg: b 8-18-1756 d 11-7-18I0 m Mary Nichols Sgt MA
Theophilus: b 5-27-1734 d 1802 m (1)Esther Cole (2)Martha Eddy Pvt MA
Theophilus: b 11-7-1760 d 4-24-1848 m Zilpha Sherman Pvt MA RI W★
Wheaton: b 12-3-1757 d 10-28-1833 m Hannah Cranshaw Pvt MA

LUTTERLOH,
Henry Emanuel: b 1743 d 3-6-1785 m Rachel Webber Col VA NY

LUTTRELL,
James: b 2-12-1755 d 11-1-1848 m Elizabeth Witt MM Pvt VA
Richard: b 1735 d c. 1800 m Sarah Churchwell Pvt VA
Richard, Jr.: b — d p. 1819 m Rachel Stallard Ens VA

LUTZ, (includes LOTZ)
Benedict: b 10-12-1735 d 2-5-1818 m Anna Maria Odenwelder Pvt PA
Frederick: b 1742 d 1798 m Maria Elizabeth Eckroth Ens PS PA
Jacob: b 12-21-1761 d 10-12-1839 m Sarah Wolfe Pvt VA ★
Johann Caspar: b c. 1737 d 1791 m Eva Mann Pvt PA
John: b 1-9-1762 d 9-4-1824 m Elizabeth Demuth Pvt PA
Nicholas: b 2-20-1740 d 11-28-1807 m Rosina Meyer Col PA
Peter: b c. 1718 d 1803 m — PS PA
Wolley: b c. 1740 d 1790 m Elizabeth Dice Pvt PA

LUX,
Darby, Jr.: b 1737 d 4-10-1795 m Rachel Ridgely Col MD

LUYSTER,
Peter: b 1760 d 12-2-1826 m Rachel VanOrden Pvt NJ

LYBROOK,
Henry: b 4-2-1755 d 8-22-1837 m Hannah Hankey PS VA

LYDECKER,
Garret G.: b 11-19-1728 d 10-22-1806 m Lydia Demarest Capt NJ

LYDSTON,
Wm.: b 1754 d 1800 m Sarah Gowell Cpl MA

LYE,
Joseph, Sr.: b 1737 d a. 7-12-1792 m Elizabeth Gray Slr MA
Joseph, Jr.: b 2-4-1759 d 10-16-1807 m Anna Hart Pvt MA W★

LYFORD,
Biley: b 3-10-1716 d 2-10-1792 m Judith Wilson Pvt NH
Francis: b 10-20-1760 d 5-25-1821 m Mary Gilman Pvt NH
James Gilman: bpt 8-24-1746 d p. 1802 m Mary Hardy PS NH
John: b 9-13-1766 d 9-3-1859 m Mima Morse Pvt NH
Moses: b c. 1728 d 4-13-1799 m Mehitable Smith PS NH
Nathaniel Lad: b 1-26-1762 d 10-14-1850 m Mary Johnson Ens Mrnr NH
Oliver Smith: b 8-24-1758 d 1788 m Elizabeth Johnson Pvt NH
Stephen: b 8-10-1758 d 12-8-1844 m Sarah (Lamprey)Hilton Pvt NH
Thomas: b 1738 d 4-15-1804 m Mehitable Robinson Lt NH
Thomas: b 5-12-1743 d 7-27-1787 m Ann James PS NH

LYKE,
John: b 8-18-1760 d 10-29-1838 m Catherine Whaling Pvt NY

LYLE, (includes LYELL)
Aaron: b 11-17-1759 d 9-24-1825 m Eleanor Moore Sgt PA
Aromanus: b 1748 d 9-2-1817 m Rebecca Valentine Capt SC
Daniel: b c. 1725 d a. 8-3-1784 m — Paxton PS VA
Ephraim: b 1760 d 1-4-1820 m (1)Susannah Edrington (2)Elizabeth — Sol SC
Hugh: b 1755 d 2-27-1797 m Isabella Creighton PS VA
James: b c. 1751 d p. 2-3-1801 m Sarah Lyle Ens VA
James: b c. 1753 d 3-31-1791 d Hannah Alexander CS VA
John: b 12-2-1752 d 4-17-1826 m Elizabeth Hays Capt PA
John: bpt 2-18-1736 d 1793 m (1)Isabella Paxton (2)Frances Stuart Capt VA
John: b 1728 d 11-1-1815 m Elizabeth Wayne Pvt PA
John: b 7-10-1746 d 9-18-1815 m Flora Reid PS VA
John: b 1758 d 1808 m Sarah Glass Pvt VA
John: b 2-12-1732 d p. 11-14-1787 m Sarah — PS VA
Maher Shallal Hasby: b 3-14-1737 d 1-30-1814 m Elizabeth — Gibson Pvt PS VA
Moses: b 3-30-1756 d — m Catharine Schuyler Sgt NJ
Richard: b 9-29-1757 d p. 1834 m (1)Harriett Magruder (2)ElizabethJones SgnMte MD
Robert: b 10-8-1754 d 11-25-1843 m Sarah Rea Sgt PA
Robert: b c. 1740 d p. 1784 m — Capt SC
Samuel: b 1758 d 8- -1834 m (1)Elizabeth White (2)Marjorie Hadley Pvt VA
Samuel: b 1725 d 9- -1796 m Sarah McClung PS VA
Thomas: b 9-29-1754 d 1840 m Mary Jones Ens MD
Wm.: b 1750 d p. 1795 m (2)Sarah Magruder CS MD
Wm.: b 1752 d 9-10-1837 m (1)Julia Anna Stuart (2)Elizabeth Lyle Capt VA

LYMAN,
Abel: b 1-15-1752 d 1-17-1823 m Hannah Storrs Lt NH
Abner: b 8-16-1746 d 1794 m Lydia — 1Lt MA
Asa: b 1755 d 1817 m Mary Bowen Pvt CT
Azariah: b 12- -1747 d 10-28-1833 m Jemima Kingsley Pvt MA
Benjamin: b 7-27-1759 d 4-3-1823 m Mary Wright Pvt MA
Benjamin: b 3-9-1761 d 6-5-1846 m Polly Temple Pvt VT ★
Dan: b 1-6-1761 d 6-13-1848 m (1)Sarah Benton (2)Hannah Lovejoy Pvt CT
Daniel: b 1-27-1756 d 10-16-1830 m Mary Wanton Col CT
David: b 5-20-1747 d 7-29-1813 m Mary Brown Pvt CT
David: b 12-14-1737 d 1-10-1822 m Sarah Wright Lt MA
David: b 5-20-1763 d 1-26-1849 m Submit Gould Sol MA
Ebenezer: b 3-17-1750 d 3-7-1813 m Ann Young Pvt CT
Eleazer: b 1-30-1767 d 1-11-1844 m Clarissa Hitchcock Pvt VT
Elias: b 5-15-1710 d 4-17-1790 m Hannah Allen PS MA
Elias, Sr.: b 9-30-1715 d 2-18-1803 m Anne Phelps PS CS MA
Elias, Jr.: b 6-27-1752 d 5-26-1804 m Eunice Sheldon Pvt MA
Elijah: bpt 8-8-1736 d 4-7-1783 m Esther Pomeroy 2Lt MA
Elisha, Jr.: b 6-27-1765 d 2-23-1849 m (1)Abigail Bloyd (2)Abigail Dewey Pvt CT ★
Elisha: b 6-22-1734 d 8-13-1798 m Abigail Jones Lt MA
Ezekiel: b 10-23-1733 d 6-27-1802 m Elizabeth Bliss Pvt CT
Ezekiel, Jr.: b 8-18-1762 d 7-4-1845 m Mabel Mitchell Pvt CT ★
Francis: b 1755 d 3-23-1840 m Abigail Coles Pvt CT ★
Gideon: b 1-26-1758 d 5-22-1824 m Dolly Spencer Pvt VT
Ichabod: b 1724 d 4-2-1813 m Honora Casey Pvt CT
Isaac: b 8-18-1759 d 3-1-1827 m (1)Sallie Edgecomb (2)Laura Pierce (3)Patience Mann Spafford Lt QM VT
Isaac: b 5-30-1762 d 10-3-1821 m Sabrina Williams Sgt CT
Israel: b 2-7-1746 d 6-8-1830 m Rachael Beals Sgt MA
Jacob: b 5-6-1746 d 3-25-1819 m Mary Woodward Pvt CT

James: b 1748 d 1801 m Jerusha Woodward Sol CT
James: b 1-9-1747 d 1-25-1804 m (1)Mary Crouch Nash (2)Abigail Wright Lt MA
Jesse: b 6-20-1764 d 10-5-1814 m Mrs Jerusha Hunt Pvt CT
Joel: b 9-20-1758 d 7-6-1840 m Achsah Parson 2Lt MA
John: b 3-4-1760 d 7-27-1840 m Hulda Brinsmade Pvt CT
John, Jr.: b 10-17-1723 d 11-4-1797 m Hannah Strong Lt MA
John: b 10-12-1693 d 1-3-1783 m Abigal Mosely PS MA
Jonathan: b 5-8-1737 d c. 1790 m Sarah Davis Ens CT
Jonathan: b 1748 d 3-28-l788 m Lois Clapp Pvt MA
Joseph: b c. 1734 d 1784 m (1) — Southard (2)Sally Longfellow Cpl CT
Joseph: b 7-6-1744 d 2-20-1820 m Sarah Edwards Pvt CT
Joseph: b 5-4-1731 d 1798 m Mary Sheldon Capt MA
Josiah: b 3-9-1736 d 3-18-1822 m Sarah Worthington Maj MA
Justus: b 12-1-1768 d 12-4-1846 m Nancy Carey Pvt MA
Lemuel: b 8-28-1735 d 7-16-1810 m Lydia Clark Pvt MA
Luke: b 1-8-1753 d 1-12-1825 m Susanna Hunt Pvt MA
Moses: b 3-30-1743 d 9-29-1829 m (1)Ruth Collins (2)Mary (Buell) Judd Col CT
Noah, Jr.: bpt 6-21-1747 d 4-1-1801 m Eleanor Rossiter PS CT
Richard: b 8-13-1755 d 6-8-1802 m Philomela Lommis Sgt CT
Rufus: b 12-13-1751 d 6-5-1807 m Martha Burt Cpl MA
Samuel: b 11-28-1759 d 1861 m Ruhamah Allen Pvt CT
Seth: b 2-1-1736 d 10-14-1817 m Eunice Graves Sgt MA
Simeon, Sr.: b 1725 d 1800 m Abigail Beebe Pvt CT
Simeon, Jr.: b 1-17-1754 d 4-19-1820 m Joannah Palmer Pvt CT
Simeon: b 11-26-1730 d 5-19-1809 m (1)Sarah Field (2)Mrs Molly Smith Stratton Sgt MA
Stephen: b 8-9-1742 d 12-8-1811 m (1)Anna Blair (2)Hannah Clark Pvt MA
Timothy: b 7-25-1745 d 1-23-1818 m Hannah Colson Lt MA
Timothy: b 12-31-1744 d 10-12-1815 m Dorothy Kinney CS PS MA
Wm.: b 8-12-1738 d 4-2-1827 m Mary Barker Pvt CT

LYMASTER,
Wm.: b 6-10-1741 d 6-20-1817 m Elizabeth Wagner Pvt PS PA

LYNAM, (includes LINAM)
George: b c. 1746 d p. 3-9-1815 m Mary Hodges QM Lt SC
John: b 3-3-1747 d 12-16-1830 m (1)Ann Springer (2)Mary Rice Long Pvt DE

LYNCH, (includes LINCH)
Anselm: b 6-8-1760 d 2-18-1826 m Susannah (Miller)Baldwin 1Lt VA
Charles: b 1736 d 10-29-1796 m Anna Terrell Col VA
George: b 1748 d 1816 m Margaret McCorkle Cpl PA
Henry: b 1763 d 7-19-1849 m Sarah Ferris Pvt VA ★
James: b c. 1753 d a. 11-29-1822 m Sarah Willis Pvt MD
James: b 1741 d 1790 m Nancy Raymond Pvt NY
James: b 1760 d 1827 m Nancy — Pvt PA
James: b 1732 d p. 1804 m Francis Elizabeth Maupin Pvt VA
John: b 1735 d 1-27-1797 m Anne — Capt MD
John: b 1750 d p. 1780 m Sarah — Sgt NC
John: b c. 1755 d 1819 m Nancy Pierce Pvt PA
John: b 1740 d 1820 m Mary Bowles Pvt VA
Peter: b 1-29-1751 d 3-8-1823 m Hester Saffron Pvt VA
Thomas: b 1758 d 1831 m Elizabeth Watts Pvt MD ★
Wm.: b c. 1755 d p. 1-1-1833 m — Pvt VA

LYNDE, (includes LINE & LYND, LYNDS & LYNE)
Abraham: b 2-20-1758 d 7-16-1820 m Christina Eby Ens PA
Benjamin: b 1747 d 3-4-1827 m Hannah Phipps 1Lt MA
Benjamin: b 1754 d 1818 m Rebecca Jewell Capt PA
Benjamin;: b 10-2-1758 d 9-26-1829 m Mary Sprague Pvt MA
Conrad: b 2-7-1763 d 1843 m Huldah Locke MM Pvt NJ
Cornelius: b 8-5-1751 d 2-17-1836 m Rebekah Davis Ens VT ★
David: b 5-15-1724 d p. 1790 m Jerusha Pierce PS NH
David: b 6-10-1753 d 8-10-1814 m Anna Bear Ens PA
George: b 1718 d c. 11-12-1788 m Salome (Zimmerman) Carpenter MM PA
Jabez: b 1-10-1744 d 12-28-1816 m (1)Phoebe Paine (2)Phoebe Jenkins Sgt MA
Jacob: b c. 1760 d 1842 m Barbara Schaack Pvt PA
John: b 3-29-1745 d 8-17-1817 m Sarah Warner Ens MA
Johnson: b 7-8-1741 d p. 1796 m (1)Abigail White (2)Mrs Molly Prouty Pvt MA
Jonathan: b 3-24-1756 d 12-25-1829 m Polly Franklin Sol MA ★
Joseph, Sr.: b 7-4-1716 d 7-4-1798 m Mary Sprague Pvt MA
Joseph, Jr.: b 2-10-1745/6 d 1-20-1805 m Mary Porter Pvt MA
Nathan: b 7-13-1732 d 1-12-1819 m Lydia Green Lt MA
Peter: b c. 1760 d a. 12-15-1818 m Annatje Vandervoort Pvt NJ
Samuel: b 10-14-1736 d 11-2-1792 m Phoebe Waterhouse Pvt CT
Samuel: bpt 9-5-1756 d 8-17-1811 m Deborah Marston Pvt MA
Wm.: b 4-12-1749 d 6-12-1822 m Mary Bear MM PA
Wm.: b 1740 d 9-27-1808 m Lucy Foster (Lyne) PS VA

LYNN, (includes LINN)
Adam: b c. 1750 d 6-1-1832 m (1)Sidney Ewing (2)Sarah Burden Pvt VA
Andrew: b 1728 d 1794 m Mary Ashcroft Capt PA
Andrew: b c. 1760 d c. 1836 m Elinor Scott Wgm PA
David, Sr.: b — d — d. 12- -1779 m Elizabeth Lamar CS MD

David, Jr.: b 7-15-1758 d 4-6-1835 m Mary Galloway Ens MD ★
James: b 1750 d 12-29-1820 m Mary Livingston Maj NJ
James: b 10-17-1761 d p. 1822 m Griselda Patterson Sgt PA
James: b 1757-60 d 12-24-1838 m Eleanor Young Pvt PA ★
James: b c. 1740 d 1833 m Hannah Wright Bruntz PS PA
Johann Nicolaus: b 11-29-1727 d 1802 m Mary Catherine — Pvt PA
John: b 8-17-1754 d 4-28-1834 m Rebecca Anderson Pvt MA ★
John: b 1737 d 9-2-1820 m Jenet McCollough Sol PS SC
John: b 12-3-1763 d 1-5-1821 m Martha Hunt Sgt NJ
John Richie: b 9-4-1755 d 9- -1847 m Jane Darrough Pvt PA
Joseph: b 1741 d 2-19-1823 m Molly Gilchrist Pvt PS NH
Joseph: b 1725 d 4-8-1800 m Martha Kirkpatrick Lt NJ
Matthew: b 1746 d 8-1-1822 m (1)Anna Horsford (2)Beulah
    Chittenden Galusha Lt VT
Robert: b a. 1760 d p. 1801 m Margaret Leonard Pvt NC
Samuel: b c. 1750 d 2-17-1835 m — Grd PA
Wm.: b 1749 d 2-11-1813 m Martha Scott 2Lt PA
Wm.: b 1-30-1734 d 12-23-1808 m (1)Agnes — (2)Isabel Gibson
    Pvt PS PA
Wm.: b 2-27-1752 d 1-8-1808 m Rebecca Blair Chp PA
Wm.: b 1734 d p. 7-8-1780 m Letitia — Col VA
Wm.: b 1757 d 1837 m Deborah Morgan Capt VA
Wm': b c. 1750 d a. 7-6-1795 m Elizabeth — PS VA

LYON, (includes LYONS)
Aaron, Sr.: b c. 1730 d p. 1798 m Mary Mason PS MA
Aaron, Jr.: b 1757 d 1802 m Jemima Shepard Pvt MA
Aaron: b 7-28-1758 d 11-9-1819 m Elizabeth Nelson Ens NY
Abel: b 1742 d 10-1-1815 m Susannah Leach Pvt CT
Abiel: b 6-8-1736 d p. 1775 m Mehitable Osgood Pvt CT
Abraham: b 1748 d p. 1820 m Phoebe Bobbet Capt NJ
Alpheus: b 5-25-1760 d 2-13-1825 m Lucy Blake Drm Pvt MA
Alvin: b 12-2-1762 d 9-13-1841 m Mary Ascough Sgt NY
Amos: b 3-7-1732 d 2-26-1812 m Bethiah Dana Pvt CT
Benjamin: b 12-31-1730 d 7-14-1807 m Sarah May Capt CT
Benjamin: b 6-30-1732 d c. 1797 m (1)Thankful Humphrey
    (2)Rachel Stetson (3)Ruth Wentworth Pvt MA
Benjamin: b 5-23-1754 d 1836 m (1)Joanna Wilcox (2)Gertrude
    Muncy Rogers Pvt NJ
Benjamin: b 3-7-1733 d 12- -1822 m Mary Hyatt Pvt NY
Benjamin: b 1752 d 1826 m Mary (Lyon) Capt PA
Bezaleel: b 1739 d 6-24-1796 m Mary Davenport MM MA
Caleb: b 4-15-1709 d 11-14-1792 m Margaret (Lyon) PS CT
Caleb: b 1760 d 9-15-1835 m Mary Dupont PS CT
Caleb, Sr.: b 10-26-1718 d 8-30-1809 m Eunice Mead Pvt NY
Caleb, Jr.: b 12-3-1744 d 8-16-1832 m Rachel Mead Pvt NY
Cyrus: b 2-22-1759 d 2-12-1831 m Mary Abell Pvt MA
Daniel: b 2-22-1734 d 6-20-1820 m Prudence May Capt CT
Daniel: b c. 1740 d p. 1785 m Eunice Fitz Randolph Pvt NJ
Daniel: b 1760 d p. 1800 m Lydia Trask Pvt MA
David: b 7-21-1739 d 10-24-1808 m (1)Jerusha Barton (2)Lydia
    Burbank Sol CS MA
David: b 8-12-1737 d 9-8-1803 m Abigail Draper CS MA
David: b 1745 d 3- -1802 m Charity Woodruff Capt NY
David: b 5-25-1740 d 1787 m Freelove Forman 2Lt NY
Eliab: b 7-2-1735 d 4-2-1814 m Meriah Smith Pvt MA
Ebenezer: b 4-5-1764 d 4-4-1829 m Chloe Jackson Pvt CT
Elias: b a. 11-7-1755 d 1800-10 m Sarah Lyons Pvt NJ
Eliphalet: b 9-7-1727 d 12-28-1812 m (1)Sarah Hinman (3)Easter
    — PS NJ
Enos: b 1-4-1761 d 9-23-1830 m Naomi Jones Pvt NJ ★
Ephraim: b 1737 d 5-25-1798 m Ester Bennett Lt CT
Ephraim: b 1745 d 5-24-1813 m (1)Eunice Leach (2)Hannah Pearl
    Lt CT
Ephraim: b 1736 d 2-24-1820 m Elizabeth Axtell Capt MA
Ethelbert Child: b 4-13-1744 d 7-1-1787 m Mary Fuller MM Pvt MA
George: b 3-10-1723 d 1-3-1807 m Zerviah Marcy Pvt CT
Gershom: b 7-10-1725 d 5-3-1801 m Mary Buckley CS CT
Gideon: b 1751 d 9-20-1838 m Anna Savage Sgt NJ
Gilbert: b 1751 d 9-12-1819 m Mary — Capt NY
Henry: b 4-2-1738 d p. 5-1-1785 m Anna — Pvt CT
Henry: b c. 1750 d c. 1780 m Martha Drake Pvt NY
Isaac: b 11-16-1745 d 4-1-1821 m Rachel Edwards Pvt CT
Isaac: b 1747 d p. 1788 m Rebecca Condit Pvt NY
Isaiah: b 1-29-1743 d 8-25-1813 m Elizabeth Lyon Pvt CT
Israel, Sr.: b 12-20-1734 d 12-28-1816 m Abigail Husted PS
    NY
Israel, Jr.: b 2-12-1755 d 1816 m Hannah Merritt Pvt NY
Jabez: b 1-26-1756 d 3-16-1843 m Mehitable Woodward Pvt MA
Jacob: b 10-12-1754 d 1-3-1829 m Jerusha Tucker Pvt MA
James: b 7-1-1735 d 6-12-1794 m (1)Martha Holden (2)Sarah
    Skillen Chp MA
James: b 8-31-1755 d 9-20-1841 m Elizabeth Williams Arfr NJ
James: b 10-19-1761 d 4-2-1850 m Martha Banks Pvt NY ★
James: b 12-19-1749 d 1795 m Susanna Marvin Pvt NY
James: b — d c. 1800 m Elizabeth Martin Sol PA
James: b 1755 d 12-15-1836 m Mary (Longwill)Lorman Pvt VA ★
James: b 1736 d 12-29-1817 m (1)Christina Harmon (2)Sarah —
    LCol PS VA
Jedediah: b 9-7-1721 d 2-9-1807 m Mary Cushman Cpl MA
Jedediah: b 1758 d 6-10-1824 m Mary Brice Gorman Cpl NJ
John: b 4- -1756 d 2-7-1817 m Sarah Lockwood Cpl MA
John: b 12-22-1730 d 9-26-1778 m Mary Evans Pvt CT

John: b 1-12-1748 d 4-24-1807 m Elizabeth Moore Pvt CT
John: b 4- -1740 d 1813 m Liddie Billeasly Sol PS NC
John: b 6-28-1717 d 2-5-1800 m (2)Esther — MM Pvt NJ
John: b 2-24-1740 d 1-18-1803 m Martha Burlingame Capt MA
John: b 8-26-1753 d p. 1832 m Martha Babbitt Sgt NJ
John: b 1762 d a. 1812 m Jemima Smith Pvt NJ
John: b c. 1760 d 1-1-1801 m Mary McKinney Lt PA
John: b 1744 d 1820 m Mary Harris QM PA
John: b c. 1755 d 1807 m Sarah Davis PS PA VA KY
Jonathan: b 2-20-1760 d 1824 m Olive Poole Pvt MA ★
Jonathan: b c. 1753 d 8-2-1831 m Lucy Read Pvt NH
Joseph: b c. 1712 d 12-23-1776 m (1)Mary Disbrow (2)Anne — Pvt
    CT
Joseph: b 10-1-1733 d 11-27-1817 m Lois Thorp Sol CT
Joseph: b 1755 d p. 1832 m Mary Montgomery Pvt VT
Joseph: b 1755 d 6-27-1836 m Mary Carey Pvt VT ★
Joseph Emanuel: b 2-13-1754 d 1820-40 m Mary Ann Marshbank
    Sol SC
Joshua: b 2-5-1754 d 10-2-1841 m Elizabeth Purdy Pvt CT ★
Josiah: b 1757 d 1-21-1829 m (1)Susana Selby (2)Mercy Andrews
    Pvt CT
Lemuel: b 6-4-1738 d p. 1790 m (1)Hannah Dresser (2)Mary — 1Lt
    MA
Lyman: b 3-10-1753 d 2-3-1824 m Hannah Corbin Pvt CT
Matthew: b 7-14-1750 d 8-1-1822 m (1)Ann Hosford (2)Beulah
    (Chittenden)Galusha Col CS VT ★
Matthias: b 1738 d 11-11-1797 m — Clark Capt NJ
Moses: b 1731 d 3-27-1813 m Mary Harris Pvt NJ
Moses: b 3-22-1752 d 12-11-1834 m Katherine Scadden (Karsmad-
    den) CS NJ★
Moses: b 10-8-1762 d 2-24-1844 m Diadamia Banks Pvt NY ★
Nathan: b 2-24-1756 d p. 1792 m Elizabeth — Cpl MA
Nathaniel: b 7-3-1758 d 9-2-1833 m Mary Wilcox Pvt NJ ★
Nehimiah: b 10-16-1719 d 10-1-1807 m (1)Mehitable Child
    (2)Mrs Elizabeth Squire PS VT
Nehemiah Webb: b 6-8-1759 d 4-19-1860 m Sarah Treadwell Pvt
    CT ★
Noah: b 3-16-1759 d 9-23-1820 m Mary Mead Pvt NY W★
Obadiah: b 8-18-1747 d 9-27-1817 m Lydia Cushman Pvt MA
Peter: b 5-28-1745 d 7-4-1824 m Jerusha Palmer Pvt PS NY
Peter: b — d 8- -1809 m Mary Power CS VA
Philip: b 4-6-1729 d 1-30-1811 m Lydia Green Sgt MA
Roger, Sr.: b 12-15-1715 d 5-13-1797 m Mary Wilson Capt NY
Roger, Jr.: b 1736 d 10- -1824 m Phebe (Lyon) Pvt NY
Samuel: b 6-26-1729 d 2-9-1780 m Phebe — PS NJ
Samuel: b 5-14-1747 d 1-23-1819 m (1)Mary Lounsbury (2)Elizabeth
    Flemming Maj NY
Samuel: b 12-22-1754 d 2-24-1828 m Maplhet Miller Pvt NY
Samuel: b 10-11-1725 d 11- -1805 m Mary Kniffin PS NY
Samuel: b c. 1751 d p. 1780 m Eleanor Blaine Col PS PA
Spencer: b 4-8-1757 d 12-26-1827 m Mary Barney Pvt MA
Stephen: b 7-3-1755 d 9-4-1845 m — Sgt NJ ★
Stephen: b 11-16-1756 d 5-6-1820 m Elly Perkins 1Lt VA
Thomas: b 5-16-1760 d 8-6-1824 m Thankful Fisher Pvt CT
Thomas: b 10-9-1749 d 3-4-1835 m (1)Thankful Russica (2) —
    Green OrdlSgt MA ★
Thomas: b 4-5-1764 d 11-11-1847 m Sarah Pierce Pvt MA
Thomas: b 5-31-1766 d 9-29-1847 m Benjamin Valentine Pvt NY
Thomas: b 10-23-1747 d 9-3-1827 m Jean Bennett Lt VT ★
Wm.: b 4-29-1736 d 3-30-1808 m Mary Tufts Lt CT
Wm.: b 3-6-1742 d 10-12-1830 m Lois Mansfield Sol CT
Wm.: b 3-17-1729 d 2-7-1809 m Ann Fleming Lt PA
Wm.: b 11-15-1755 d p. 1832 m Margaret Gibson Pvt PA ★
Wm.: b 1751 d 8-14-1823 m Mary Radick Pvt PA
Wm.: b 3- -1757 d 3-10-1828 m Anna Dilts Pvt PA
Zebulon: b 1751 d 1823 m Eleanor Porter Skinner Lt VT

MABEN, (includes MABIN)
John: b 1753 d 6-1-1813 m Sally Pierce Pvt NY

MABIE, (includes MABEE, MEBIE)
Abraham: b 1727 d 8-7-1817 m Sarah Gates Pvt NY
Abraham: b 12-21-1731 d p. 1805 m (2)Wynite Quackenboss Pvt NY
Albert: b 4-27-1735 d 1-7-1797 m Engeltia Vrooman Pvt NY
Casparus: b 1-10-1741 d p. 9-23-1782 m Willimpye Eckeson Sgt NY
Cornelius: b 3-18-1741 d 5-10-1789 m Hester Groot 1Lt NY
Cornelius: b 3-17-1754 d 8-6-1843 m Elizabeth Blauveldt Pvt NY
Harmanus: bpt 9-9-1737 d 8-26-1808 m Susanna Wemple Capt NY
Jacob: b c. 1740 d p. 1791 m Christiana Fedley Pvt NY
Johannes: b 1-10-1728 d 11-24-1796 m Alida Toll Cpl NY
John Peter: b 1740 d 1798 m (1)Maria Bell Pvt NY
Peter: b 10-13-1717 d 1787 m Jannetye Hogenkamp Pvt NY

MABILLE,
Thomas: b 6-5-1750 d p. 1800 m Sol Fr A

MABRY,
Braxton: b 5-22-1750 d p. 1838 m — White Pvt 1Lt VA
David: b 1749 d 7-11-1834 m Jean Bledsoe Pvt NC ★
Joel: b 1732 d 6- -1784 m Winifred Smith PS VA

MABRY, contd.
Reps: b 1755 d 1-29-1819 m Martha De Fore Pvt GA
Robert: b 1755 d 1838/9 m Rebecca Adams Lt VA
Seth: b c. 1752 d 10-5-1803 m Elizabeth Seawell PS NC

MAC CLUNG, (includes McCLUNG)
Mathew: b 10-11-1757 d 6-2-1844 m Jane Cummins Pvt PA ★

MACE,
Andrew: bpt 12-25-1757 d 4-6-1845 m Jane Hale Sgt NH
Andrew: b 1709 d 1-23-1790 m Deborah Moulton PS NH
Eliphalet: b 1763 d 1830 m Mary Clark Batchellor Pvt MA
Joseph: b 1-17-1758 d p. 1839 m Margaret Murphy Pvt PA ★
Samuel: b 9-22-1737 d 3- -1825 m Sarah Nay PS NH

MACHEMER,
Wm.: b 1755 d 9-21-1831 m Anna Elizabeth Berlet Pvt PA

MACHIN, (includes MACHEN)
Henry: b 12-9-1745 d 12-10-1821 m Frances Ballinger Sgt SC
Thomas: b 5-10-1741 d 4-5-1816 m Susan Van Nostrum Capt NY
Thomas: b c. 1720 d 5- -1782 m Bettie Wale CS NC

MACHIR,
Alexander: b 10-2-1738 d 5-4-1790 m Magdalena Ann Keller Capt
   CS VA

MACK,
Alexander: b c. 1740 d 1811 m — Pvt PA
Andrew: b 5-10-1751 d 7-7-1839 m Sally Pease Pvt CT ★
Andrew: b 1748 d 1820 m Elizabeth Clark Pvt PS NH
Archibald: b 12-13-1753 d 10-26-1840 m Mary Dayton Pvt NH ★
Benjamin: b 1756 d p. 1781 m Nabby Lord Pvt CT
Bezaleel: b 9-18-1760 d 7-22-1829 m (1)Rachel Hurd (2)Olive
   (Gibbs)Temple (3)Lucy (Hill)Smith Sol CT CT
David: b 12-10-1750 d 3-24-1845 m Mary Talcott Pvt MA
Elisha, Sr.: b 5-25-1728 d 5-24-1783 m Mary Ellis Ens CT
Elisha, Jr.: b 5-13-1759 d 12- -1850 m Sarah Blossom Howes Pvt
   CT
Elisha: b 7-16-1745 d 11-15-1820 m (1)Diademia Rathburn
   (2)Widow Burt Capt NH
Henry: b 10- -1759 d 1843 m Mehitable Hall Pvt CT
Hezekiah: b 7-14-1754 d 6-9-1839 m Ann — Pvt CT ★
Joel: b 11-14-1761 d 11-4-1805 m Susannah Andrews Pvt CT W★
John: b 1758 d 1810 m — Rickenbaker Pvt SC
John: b c. 1750 d p. 1819 m Sarah Sophia Blair Sol VA
Josiah: b 1-25-1741 d 5-8-1805 m Betsey Bennet Pvt CT
Nathan: b c. 1753 d 11-30-1821 m (1)Molly Diggins (2)Hannah
   Foster Pvt NH
Nehemiah: b 5-18-1754 d 1-3-1828 m Caroline Niles Pvt CT
Orlando: b 10-10-1747 d 1815 m (1)Mehitable Chapman (2)Lucy
   Baldwin Lt CT
Ralph: b 6-13-1759 d 6-25-1836 m Lydia Gilbert Pvt CT ★
Richard: b 1765 d 1844 m Betty Harvey Pvt CT
Robert: b 5-9-1739 d 1- -1824 m Elizabeth Ewins Pvt NH
Samuel: b 5-3-1743 d 1836 m Martha Rawson Pvt CT
Silas: b 5-21-1755 d 4-14-1836 m Mary Brown Cpl NH
Solomon: b 9-15-1732 d 8-23-1820 m Lydia Gates Pvt Pvtr NH
Warren: b 6-16-1763 d 7-3-1843 m Polly — Sol MA
Wm.: b 10-31-1749 d 2-12-1813 m Agnew Gantz Pvt PA

MACKALL,
Benjamin: b 4-14-1764 d 9-6-1830 m Rebecca Dawson Pvt MD ★
Benjamin: b 8-14-1745 d 1807 m Mary Taylor PS MD
Benjamin, 2d: b 2-16-1723 d 1795 m Rebecca Covington PS MD
Elijah: b 1720 d 6-18-1790 m Mehitable Arnold Ens RI
James: b 1730 d 1789 m Anne Brooks Ens MD
John: b 1738 d 5-19-1813 m Margaret Cough Capt MD
John: b 5-10-1744 d p. 1791 m Margaret Reynolds PS MD

MACKEY, (includes MACKAY, MACKIE)
Aeneas S.: b c. 1740 d 2-14-1777 m Mary Carter Col PA
Alexander, Sr.: b 1738 d 4-23-1796 m Thankful Tuthill Pvt NY
Alexander, Jr.: b 1-20-1764 d 10-5-1843 m Elizabeth Woolsey Pvt
   Fif NY ★
Alexander: b 1726 d p. 10-23-1793 m Susannah Lewis Sol NC
Andrew: b 7-12-1742 d 4-27-1817 m Charity Fearing Dr PS MA
David: b c. 1736 d 10-30-1820 m Agnes Curry LCol PA
James: b 5-24-1759 d 6-30-1834 m Rebecca Scott Pvt NC ★
James: b 1739 d 11-24-1793 m — Sgt SC
John: b a. 1726 d 9- -1784 m Elizabeth Young Col NJ
John: b 1745 d 5- -1818 m Hannah Ruger Pvt PS NY
John: b c. 1735 d c. 1809 m Jemima Campbell Pvt NC
John: b c. 1725 d 9- -1787 m Jane — PS PA
John: b c. 1726 d 1787 m Ann Alexander PS NC
John: b 1765 d 12-14-1831 m Abigail Mills PS SC
John: b c. 1726 d p. 8-1-1802 m — Pvt VA
Joseph: b 4-12-1741 d 10-19-1798 m (1)Margaret Wilhelm
   (2)Rachel Hendershot Capt NJ
Joseph: b 1736 d 1812 m Elizabeth Brewster Pvt NJ
Samuel: b 1761 d 12-5-1845 m Mary Clark Pvt NC ★
Stephen: b 3-2-1759 d 3-2-1836 m Agnes Gumm Pvt PA
Thomas: b c. 1740 d 1796 m Rosannah — PS NC

Thomas: b 2-12-1762 d 1-8-1842 m (1)Charity Perry (2)Mary Ann
   Crenshaw Pvt SC ★
Thomas: b 1753 d 12-24-1821 m Joanna Cook Sol PA
Wm.: b 1748 d 1821 m Mary — Sgt MD
Wm.: b 1724 d 1801 m Frances Thompson PS MA
Wm.: b 1738 d 11-4-1812 m — Capt PA
Wm.: b c. 1749 d 3-3-1814 m Mary — Sol SC

MACKLIN, (includes MAUGHLIN)
James: b a. 1760 d 2-2-1819 m ElizabethJohnson Pvt PA
Wm.: b 1738 d 2-11-1813 m Martha Reed Pvt PA

MACKNESS,
Perygren: b 1722 d p. 5-8-1800 m (1)Sarah Hamrick (2)Mary —
   PS NC

MACKNET,
Charles: b 4-17-1758 d — m Sarah Pastorius Lt PA ★

MACKRES,
Samuel: b 7-22-1743 d 6-4-1831 m Rebecca Huggin Sgt NH

MACLAY
John: b 5-10-1734 d 10-17-1804 m Jane Dickson PS PA
John, Sr.: b c. 1721 d 4- -1779 m Elizabeth McDonald Pvt PA
John, Jr.: b 1748 d 1800 m Eleanor Maclay Pvt PA
Samuel: b 6-17-1741 d 10-5-1811 m Elizabeth Plunket LCol PA
Wm.: b 7-20-1737 d 4-16-1804 m Mary McClure Harris PS PA

MACLIN, (includes MASLIN)
Frederick: b c. 1720 d a. 12-26-1808 m Lucy Rollins PS Col VA
Henry: b c. 1735 d p. 2-24-1810 m Tabitha — PS VA
James: b 12-8-1734 d 1794 m Elizabeth (Maclin) Pvt VA
Thomas: b c. 1755 d p. 10-11-1807 m Martha Glenn Lt MD
Wm.: b c. 1735 d 1802/3 m Sarah Clack Capt VA

MACOMBER,
Abiel: b 1738 d 11-18-1821 m Phoebe Deane Lt MA
Archer: b 4-4-1751 d 5-29-1832 m (1)Eunice Corne (2)Margaret —
   Pvt NY
Constant: b — d 1826-30 m Mary (East) Hicks Pvt MA
David: b 9-2-1752 d 5-13-1819 m Kathrine Littlefield Pvt MA
Elijah: b 5-4-1740 d p. 1810 m Hannah Gridley Sol MA
Elijah: b 1-25-1750 d p. 1790 m Zilpha (Briggs)Thresher Pvt MA
Ephraim: b 3-5-1749 d 7- -1839 m Patience Fish Pvt RI ★
George: b 7-7-1740 d 7- -1820 m Susannah Paul Pvt MA
George: b 7-2-1751 d 4-5-1813 m Amitta — Sgt MA
Henry: b 1726 d p. 1795 m (1)Hannah — (2)Susanna (Pratt)
   Thrasher Pvt MA
Jacob: b c. 1715 d 4-3-1787 m (1)Eleanor Turner (2)Elizabeth Niles
   PS MA
James: b 1726 d 1-20-1820 m (1)Ruth(Reed)Williams (2)Hannah
   Simmons Capt MA
Job: b 11-3-1737 d c. 1810 m Abigail Pitts Sgt MA
John: b 1-26-1734 d 4-13-1802 m Mary Deuel Pvt MA
John: b 5-18-1760 d 10-11-1841 m Mary Dean Pvt MA
Jonathan: b 1752 d 8-17-1821 m Elizabeth Dagan Pvt MA ★
Joseph: b 3-28-1732 d 1-24-1800 m Thankful Canedy Lt MA
Josiah: b 2-9-1711 d 11-18-1801 m Ruth Paul Pvt MA
Michael: b 1-1-1732/3 d p. 1798 m (1)Mary (Macomber) (2)Sarah
   Manchester Pvt RI
Nathan: b 10-15-1752 d 10-15-1847 m Mary Reed Pvt MA
Nehemiah: b c. 1765 d a. 9-14-1807 m Charlotte Davis Pvt MA
Wm.: b 3-26-1740 d 6-9-1824 m Sarah Brownell Pvt MA
Zenas: b 12-30-1754 d 6- -1831 m (1)Jane Kiser (2)Hannah Huff
   PS CL

MACON,
Gideon Hunt: b c. 1761 d 1809 m (1)Mary Green (2)Mary Hartwell
   PS NC
Harrison: b — d c. 1790 m Hannah Glenn Capt NC
Henry: b 9-1-1727 d 1785 m (1)Rebecca Mayo (2)Frances (Netherland)
   Carlye PS VA
John: b 6-17-1755 d 4-28-1803 m (1)Joanna Tabb (2)Bettie Williams
   Capt VA
John: b c. 1753 d 1808 m Elizabeth Bowden PS NC
Nathaniel: b 12-17-1757 d 6-29-1837 m Hannah Plummer Pvt NC
William: b 1-4-1725 d 11-24-1813 m Lucy Scott PS VA

MACY,
Barachiah: b 2-24-1760 d 1844 m Lucinda Barnard PS NC
Caleb: b 9-28-1719 m 9-20-1798 m Judith Folger Gardner CS MA
Francis: b 6-2-1715 d 5-21-1793 m Judith Coffin CS MA
Paul: b 4-22-1740 d 2-8-1832 m (1)Bethiah Macy (2)Deborah
   Coggeshall PS NC
Tristram: b 4-26-1745 d 1781 m Miriam Barnard Slr MA
Zaccheus: b 12-7-1713 d 10-27-1797 m Hepzabeth Gardner CS PS MA

MADDEN, (includes MADAN, MADEN & MAIDEN)
Champness: b 8- -1763 d 7-17-1839 m Frances Duncan Pvt VA ★
David: b 7-14-1763 d 1842 m Anna Battle Pvt MA ★
Dennis: b c. 1734 d c. 1790 m Anestascia — Sol GA
George: b c. 1759 d 1823 m (1)Edith (Harvey)Reynolds (2)Elizabeth
   Carter Pvt PA

James: b 1750-55 d c. 1797 m Theodosia Lee Pvt VA
John: b 1755 d 3- -1841 m Jane Fling Sgt MA
John: b 6- -1760 d 5-13-1840 m Jane Thompson Pvt PA
Joseph: b 1744 d 1823 m Martha Smith Pvt PA ★
Mabra: b — d p. 5-27-1805 m Jane — PS VA
Michael: b c. 1740 d 4-1-1811 m Mary Bullard Ens MA
Michael: b 1755 d 5-20-1823 m Esther Cody Pvt MA ★
Neal: b c. 1723 d 1808 m Marina Sheila Moran Pvt PA

MADDING, (or MADING)
John, Jr.: b 1745 d 8-31-1800 m Sarah — PS VA
Thomas: b c. 1760 d 1810 m Rachel — Pvt VA

MADDOX, (includes MADDOCK, MADDOCKE, MADDOCKS MADDUX, MATTOCKS, MATTOX)
Ignatius: b c. 1730 d p. 1-19-1777 m Sarah Gray Pvt MD
James: b 1734 d p. 11-26-1798 m — PS MD
John: b 1760 d 1836 m Sarah — Pvt MM GA
John: b 1763 d 7-9-1844 m Eleanor Ashton Pvt VA ★
John: b 1755 d 7-9-1811 m Sarah Fernandis Pvt MD
Joshua: b 4-1-1732 d p. 1790 m Susannah Austin Pvt MA
Matthew: b 1752 d 1-1-1831 m Rachel Bonnifield Pvt VA ★
Michael McKenzie b 1777 d p. 1-18-1815 m Elizabeth — Sol NC
Nathan: b c. 1760 d p. 8-19-1829 m Michel Robey Pvt MD
Notley: b 4-13-1731 d 3-11-1820 m Susannah Burch Sgt PS MD
Notley, Sr.: b1714 d p. 11-1-1779 m — PS MD
Notley: b c. 1754 d 11-8-1813 m Mary Ann Compton Pvt VA
Richard: b 3- -1756 d 1837 m Mary — Pvt PA ★
Robert: b 1727 d 4-2-1788 m Sarah — PS NJ
Samuel: b 12-12-1762 d 1855 m (1)Abigail Day (2)Rebecca Clements Pvt MA ★
Samuel, Sr.: b 4-10-1739 d 1-18-1804 m Sarah Burdell Capt VT
Samuel, Jr.: b 12-23-1765 d 1823 m Lucy Sage Smith Pvt VT
Sherwood: b 12-15-1761 d 3-4-1839 m Elizabeth Ferguson Pvt VA ★
Thomas: b 1720 d p. 10-15-1782 m Margaret Tombly Sol VA
Thomas: b c. 1755 d 1811 m Sarah Harrison Pvt VA
Wm.: b — d 1800 m Isabel Cahoon Capt PA
Wm.: b c. 1750 d 1810 m (1)Peggy Wharton (2)Hannah Mount Sgt VA
Wilson: b 9-30-1757 d 6-30-1834 m Delilah — Pvt VA ★

MADDY,
James: b c. 1739 d 1783 m Anna Morris Sol VA

MADERIA, (includes MADARA, MADERA, MADEIRA, MATHERY)
Christian: b 1759 d 3-15-1822 m Anna Bierly (Bailey) Ens PA ★
Jacob: b 1736 d p. 3-29-1804 m (1)Margaret Pullinger (2)Hannah Shute Pvt NJ
Michael: b 5-17-1756 d 12-13-1833 m Anne Elizabeth Dick Pvt PA
Nicholas: b 12-26-1763 d 9-7-1835 m Susanna Adamson Pvt Drm PA
Nicholas: b c. 1731 d 4-29-1782 m Mary Elizabeth PS PA

MADISON,
Ambrose: b 1-27-1755 d — m Mary Willis Lee Capt VA
Gabriel: b 1755 d 4-14-1804 m Miriam Lewis Capt VA W★
Henry: b c. 1740 d 1811 m Martha White 1Lt PS CS VA
James: b 8-27-1748/9 d 3-6-1812 m Susan Tait Capt VA
James, Sr.: b 3-27-1723 d 2-27-1801 m Nelly Rose Conway Col PS VA
John: b c. 1709 d 12-19-1783 m Agatha Strother CS Pvt VA
John: b c. 1745 d a. 1810 m Mary Cheverseus Pvt VA
Rowland: b 1753 d c. 1798 m Anna Lewis Capt VA
Thomas: b 1751 d c. 1793 m Susanna Henry Capt VA
Wm.: b 5-1-1762 d 7-20-1843 m (1)Frances Throckmorton (2)Nancy Jerald Lt VA ★

MAECK,
Frederick: b 1765 d 6-30-1826 m Abigail Newell Pvt MA

MAGARR,
James: b 1749 d 1-1-1827 m Rachel Patterson Pvt MA

MAGAW, (includes McGAW)
John: b 1757 d 1805 m Sarah Patterson Capt SC
Robert: b 1738 d 1-5-1790 m Marietta Van Brunt Col NY
Samuel: b 1735 d 12-1-1812 m (1)Sarah Ridgely (2)Lucy Bell (3)Martha Doz Flowers PS DE PA
Wm.: b 1800 d 5-1-1829 m — Lt Dr PA
Wm.: b 2-8-1750 d 5-31-1836 m Mary Patterson Capt SC W★

MAGEE, (includes MAGIE)
Charles: b c. 1740 d c. 1800 m Martha Leggit Pvt PA
Daniel: b 1745 d 4-24-1810 m Catherine Kyser Pvt PA
Ezekiel: b 1-26-1759 d 12-3-1824 m Zurviah Woodruff Pvt NJ
James: b 12-6-1762 d 1835 m — Pvt NC ★
James: b 1733 d 11- -1823 m Margaret McCracken SgtMaj DE ★
John: b 9-30-1733 d 9-26-1781 m Phoebe Ogden Pvt NJ
John: b 1756 d 6-24-1804 m Elizabeth Holt 2Lt PA

Michael: b 1-8-1757 d 1-6-1810 m (1)Katherine Haines (2)Mary Meeker Pvt NJ
Ralph: b 9-14-1755 d p. 1840 m Polly Bell Sgt VA ★
Robert: b c. 1758 d a. 5-6-1816 m — Sol NC
Samuel: b 1759 d 12-13-1819 m Nellie Baker Pvt DE
Willis: b a. 1764 d 8- -1827 m Asha — Pvt NC

MAGGARD,
Margaret: b c. 1723 d p. 1785 m David Maggard PS VA

MAGILL,
Charles: b 7-10-1760 d 4-16-1827 m (1)Elizabeth Daingerfield (2)Mary Buckner Thruston Col VA
James: b 1756 d 8-24-1840 m (1)Betsy Evans (2)Mary McMeans Pvt VA
John: b 1759 d p. 6-20-1832 m — Pvt VA
Wm.: b 1741 d 1797 m Joan Fowler QMSgt VA

MAGINNIS, (or McGINNIS)
Daniel: b c. 1762 d c. 1-2-1831 m Mary Eve — Pvt PA ★
James: b 1735 d 1799 m Mary — Ens PA
James: b 1750 d 2- -1836 m Martha — Pvt Sct PA
John: b 1759 d 1813 m Martha — Pvt PA

MAGLATHLIN,
Daniel: b 1744 d 9-12-1830 m Asenath Stetson Pvt MA

MAGOON,
John: b 4-10-25-177- m — Pvt NH

MAGOWN,
Josiah: b — d 1841 m Ann Sleeper Pvt NH

MAGRUDER,
Alexander: b 1716 d 11-10-1779 m Elizabeth Howard PS MD
Archibald: b 11-4-1751 d 1-6-1842 m Cassandra Offutt Pvt MD
Dennis: b 7-1-1759 d 5-21-1836 m Ann Contee Lt MD
Enoch: b — d a. 1736 m — Meeks Sgt MD
George Fraser: b 3- -1733 d p. 12-30-1793 m Eleanor Bowie PS CS MD
Haswell: b 1736 d 1811 m (1)Charity Beall (2)Ann Allen CS MD
Hezekiah: b a. 1743 d a. 11-4-1806 m Susannah Talbot Lt MD
Isaac: b 1755 d 1- -1809 m (1)Sophia Baldwin (2)Ann Hill PS Pvt MD
James: b 1723 d 1795 m Mary Bowie PS MD
Jeffrey: b 4-21-1762 d 10-31-1805 m Susanna Bowie Pvt MD
John Read: b 6-17-1736 d 9-24-1812 m Barbara Contee CS MD
Joseph: b 10-16-1742 d 8- -1793 m (1)Mary Jackson (2)Katherine Fleming Capt MD
Nathan: b c. 1718 d 1786 m Rebecca Beall PS MD
Nathaniel: b a. 1730 d 1785 m Margaret Magruder CS MD
Nathaniel: b 1726 d p. 11-28-1793 m Elizabeth Offutt PS MD
Ninian, 3d: b 1744 d 1800 m Mary Harris PS Sgt MD
Ninian Beal: b 11-22-1735 d 5-7-1810 m Rebecca Young PS MD
Norman Bruce: b 1754 d 2-16-1836 m Nancy Paugh Pvt MD ★
Samuel: b 1723 d 1708 d 6- -1786 m Margaret Jackson PS MD
Samuel Beall: b c. 1759 d 1812 m Martha Ellis Pvt MD
Samuel Brewer: b 10-14-1744 d 1-20-1818 m (1)Rebecca Magruder (2)Eleanor Waring Ens MD
Samuel Wade: b 1728 d 7-20-1792 m Lucy Beall Maj MD
Wm.: b 3-25-1747 d 10-11-1802 m Sarah Greenfield PS MD
Zachariah: b 1711 d p. 3-26-1789 m Sarah — PS MD
Zadock: b 1729 d 4-12-1811 m Rachel (Pottinger)Bowie Col MD
Zadock: b c. 1766 d a. 2-8-1820 m (1)— Talbot (2)Tracy Rearden Pvt MD

MAHAN, (includes MAHON, MEIGHEN)
Cornelius: b 1755 d 5-22-1831 m Mary Shaver Pvt PA
James: b 1755 d 12-17-1839 m Nancy — Spy Capt NC ★
John: b 7-16-1759 d 1789 m Sarah Hemenway Pvt MA
John: b 1760 d p. 1820 m Catharine Britton Wgn NJ
John: b 1750 d 4-7-1820 m Mary Scott Lt VA
Thomas: b 1750 d 1840 m — Johnson Pvt VA

MAHOLLAND,
John: b 4-10-1752 d 8-4-1835 m Lucy Smith Pvt NC ★

MAHONEY, (includes MAHONY & MAHORNEY)
Edward: b 1735 d 1800 m Alice — Pvt MD
James: b 1763 d1821 m Elizabeth Harris Pvt VA ★
Timothy: b 9-13-1743 d 9-30-1817 m Huldah Estes Pvt RI W★

MAINE, (includes MAIN & MANE)
Amos: b 7-2-1735 d 8-17-1815 m Abigail Brown Capt CT
Andrew: b 8-5-1723 d 4-18-1802 m Fear Holmes Pvt CT
David: b 8-26-1752 d 12-27-1843 m (1)Hannah Worden (2)Judith Palmer (3)Mrs Esther Palmer (4)Philena Sawyer Pvt CT ★
Ezekiel: b 7-8-1742 d p. 1790 m (1)Deborah Meacham (2)Mary Crandall Newcomb PS CT
James: b c. 1753 d 9-28-1820 m Eve Leatherman (Castler) Pvt PA
Jonas: b 2-7-1735 d 1-24-1804 m (1)Patience Peckham (2)Content Bromley Ens CT
Josiah: b 12-27-1735 d 11-11-1823 m Molly Palmer CS NH
Nathaniel: b 7-12-1754 d 1823 m Abigail Thurston Cpl CT

MAINE, contd.
Peter, Jr.: b 6-9-1742 d *p.* 1790 m Patience Eggleston Sol CT
Philip: b 10- -1747 d 4-19-1835 m — Rou Pvt VA ★
Rufus: b 11-15-1758 d 2-22-1836 m Sarah York Pvt CT ★
Sabeers: b 3-23-1757 d 11- -1809 m Hannah Cole Spy Pvt NY
Thomas: b 8-8-1747 d 1822 m Lucy Tyler MM CT
Timothy: b 1- -1790 m Elizabeth Brown Sol PS CT
Wm.: b 10-12-1740 d 1-29-1816 m Abigail Horton Matr MA

MAJOR, (includes MEAGHER)
Jerem: b 1747 d 1789 m — Yancey Pvt VA
John, Sr.: b 1740 d 1808 m Elizabeth Redd Pvt VA
John: b 1746 d 6- -1810 m Martha Marable Pvt VA
John: b 1750 d *c.* 1830 m (1)Elizabeth Porter (2)Euphry Sleet Pvt Artl VA
Peacock: b 5-10-1748 d 12-19-1829 m Amy Barton Lt PA
Richard: b *c.* 1750 d *p.* 1792 m Lydia Yates 1Lt MA
Wm.: b 1746 d 5-1-1793 m Elizabeth Jones Pvt PA

MAJORS,
John: b 1759-60 d *c.* 1820 m Rachel Baxter Pvt MD
John: b 1759 d 11-7-1843 m Barbara Myers Pvt VA MD ★
Samuel D.: b 1762 d 6-24-1842 m (1)Elizabeth Green (2)Nancy Perkins Pvt VA ★
Thomas: b 3- -1764 d 4- -1857 m Rebecca — Pvt NC ★

MAKEMSON,
John: b *a.* 1750 d 1- -1814 m Elizabeth Brown Sol PS MD
Thomas: b 1753 d *p.* 7-19-1828 m Jane Lindsey Pvt PA

MAKEPEACE,
Elliot: b 8-13-1751 d 1813 m Lucy Brinton Sgt MA
Gershom, Sr.: b 1708 d 1798 m (1)Jane Elyot (2)Mary Weeks PS MA
Gershom, Jr.: b 2-8-1738 d — m Lydia Knight Pvt MA
Isaac: b 10-1-1760 d 7-23-1839 m Anna Hodges Pvt MA
Peter: b 4-18-1730 d 10-7-1796 m Abigail Morey PS MA
Seth: b 1755 d 9-7-1829 m Lydia Dean Grd Pvt MA W★
Wm., Sr.: b 5-4-1738 d 10-31-1822 m (1)Anna Cobb (2)Deborah Briggs (3)Ruth Hunt Sgt MA
Wm., Jr.: b 7-19-1763 d 3-23-1855 m Mary Whiting Pvt MA
Wm.: b 1735 d 1827 m Sarah Presbery Pvt MA

MALBONE,
James: b *c.* 1750 d *p.* 4-22-1791 m Dorcas — PS VA

MALCOLM, (includes MALCOM)
Henry: b 12-12-1756 d 4-18-1831 m Rebecca Olney Dr PA
James: b 1752 d 2-23-1829 m (1)Nancy Ganaway (2)Sally — Pvt VA
Joseph: b 1743 d 9-29-1816 m Frederica Lang Sgt NH
Wm.: b 11-7-1720 d *p.* 1790 m Elizabeth Smarte Pvt VA
Wm.: b 1-23-1745 d 9-1-1791 m (1)Abigail Tingley (2)Sarah Ayscough AdjGen NY

MALEY,
Lawrence: b 1755 d 1808 m Agnes Margaret Harper Pvt PA

MALICK, (includes MELICK, MELLICK, MOELICH & MOLICH)
Aaron: b 10-17-1725 d 4-7-1809 m Charlotte Miller PS NJ
Andreas: b 12-7-1729 d 6-29-1820 m Catherine — Capt NJ
Henry: b 12-3-1759 d 4-9-1851 m Rebecca Stewart Pvt CS NJ
John: b 12-7-1853 d 5-10-1834 m (2)Eleanor Todd (3)Mary Oyster Wgn Sgt NJ ★
Leonard: b 1760 d 1815 m Mary Glaspey Pvt NJ
Peter, Sr.: b 8-29-1719 d *p.* 4-26-1789 m (1)Maria Sophia Abal (2)Anna Maria Faber PS PA
Peter, Jr.: b 4-18-1752 d 2-11-1830 m Rachel Clingham Pvt PA
Phillip: b 10-9-1736 d 3-5-1797 m Maria King PS NJ
Tunis Anthony: b 3-6-1730 d 11-27-1795 m Eleanor VanHorn CS NJ

MALLARD,
John: b 1763 d 11-8-1844 m Polly Fay Pvt MA ★
Lazarus: b *c.* 1734 d 3-12-1814 m Mrs Mary Boyd Norman Pvt GA
Wm.: b 1757 d 3-30-1833 m (1)Sarah — (2)Miriam Severance Pvt NH

MALLETT, (includes MALLET & MALETTE)
Antoine: b 1759 d *p.* 11-1-1788 m Catherine Bordeleau PS VA
Gideon: b 6-14-1759 d 9-3-1822 m Hannah E. DeRoche Pvt SC
Lewis, Sr.: b 3-19-1734 d 4-1-1804 m Mary Merwin Capt CT
Lewis, Jr.: b 5-31-1756 d 1-14-1825 m Anna Beach Cpl CT W★
Peter: b 11-14-1744 d 2-2-1805 m (1)Eunice Judson Curtis (2)Sarah Mumford Cmsry PS NC
Philip: b 5-20-1750 d 3-7-1819 m Sarah Frost Cpl CT
Philo, 5th: b 5-5-1760 d 4-2-1820 m Eunice Wheeler DrmMaj CT
Wm.: b 1757 d 6-10-1844 m Deborah Collamore Pvt MA

MALLISON, (includes MALLERSON)
Thomas: b 1753 d 11-7-1813 m Ame Newton Sgt CT
Wm.: b *c.* 1740 d *p.* 8-30-1810 m (2)Sarah Reed Pvt PS NC

MALLORY, (includes MALLERY)
Abner: b 7-28-1723 d 12- -1804 m Susanna Walker Capt CT
Amasa: b 2-20-1763 d 11-9-1855 m Calome Smith Pvt CT

Asa: b 1- -1754 d 10-2-1832 m (1)Hannah Chidsey (2)Mercy — Cpl Slr CT ★
Benajah: b 12-22-1765 d 3-2-1837 m Hannah Welch Sol CT
Caleb: b *c.* 1740 d *p.* 1778 m — Pvt CT
Daniel: b 5-29-1725 d 7-18-1805 m Sarah Lee PS CT
David: b 1753 d 6-1-1841 m (1)Ruth Ann Trowbridge (2)Susanna (Baker)Botsford Pvt CT ★
Francis: b 1741 d 3-8-1781 m (3)Mary King Col VA
Gideon: b 6-13-1764 d *c.* 1845 m Anna Labarie Cpl CT ★
Giles: b 7-2-1755 d 9-20-1803 m Hannah Keeler Cpl CT
Isaac: b 1731 d 12-20-1786 m Mabel Luddington Cpl CT
Jacob: b 1766 d 3-4-1834 m (1)Hannah Foote (2)Sarah Leach Pvt CT ★
Jesse: b 1762 d 11-27-1825 m Hannah Howe Pvt CT
John: b 1714 d 1793 m Ann — Pvt CT
John: b 8-20-1752 d 6-5-1831 m Esther Webb Sgt CT
John: b 3-11-1759 d *p.* 10-22-1844 m (1)Lucy Sutherland (3)Elizabeth — (4)Nancy Brown Cpl VA
John: b 1761 d 5-14-1845 m Elizabeth — Pvt VA ★
Lemuel: b 5-22-1763 d 2-16-1851 m Rebecca (Regan)Long Pvt NY ★
Levi: b 5-2-1725 d 1-21-1798 m Mary Hyatt Smn CT
Moses: b 3-10-1724 d 12-7-1794 m Frances Oviatt Pvt CT
Nathaniel: b 11-9-1766 d 11-1-1842 m Sarah Boyd Sgt CT ★
Ogden: b 1720 d 1811 m Sarah Mallory PS VT
Peter: b 1741 d 3-21-1842 m (1)Lucy Baker (2)Amy Dorwin Pvt MA
Philip: b *c.* 1725 d 1811 m Lucinda Pynes Capt VA
Roger: b 5-12-1755 d *p.* 9- -1837 m — Pvt VA ★
Samuel: b 1-27-1744 d 5-5-1822 m Mary Carley Sgt NY
Truman: b 10-20-1759 d 1-3-1830 m Olive Hubbell Ens CT W★
Uriel: b 1- -1738 d 11- -1824 m Hannah Cave Capt VA
Wm.: b 12-3-1742 d *p.* 1810 m Mary Whelan Pvt NY

MALLOW,
George, Sr.: b 1725 d *c.* 1788 m Anna Barbara — PS VA
George, Jr.: b 3-17-1752 d 4-14-1837 m Anna Catherine — Ens VA ★
Henry: b 1759 d *p.* 1833 m Magdaline — Pvt VA ★

MALONE, (includes MALLONEE & MELOAN)
Andrew: b 2-18-1754 d 8-14-1834 m Rachel Zilerfrow CPL MD
Hallory: b 12-13-1758 d 6-17-1854 m Katie Lyon Pvt VA
John: b *c.* 1728 d 8-2-1783 m (1)Edith Cole (2)Rebecca — Pvt MD
John: b 1750 d *a.* 3-10-1802 m (2)Mary Bamer Kennerley Pvt PS SC
John: b 1730 d *a.* 2-6-1794 m Mary Harper Pvt VA
Jonathan: b *c.* 1753 d 1824 m Mary Duncan Pvt SC
Michael: b *c.* 1748 d *a.* 2-1-1798 m(1)Mary — (2)Cecily Pertway (3)Anne — Pvt VA
Nathaniel, Sr.: b *c.* 1715 d *c.* 1785 m Rachel Robinson Pvt PS NH
Richard: b 1735 d *c.* 1801 m (1)Rebecca — (2)Mrs Mary Shirk Pvt PA
Thomas: b 1744 d 11- -1820 m Mary Harper Pvt MD ★
Wm.: b 11- -1755 d *c.* 1842 m — Sgt SC ★

MALOY,
James: b *c.* 1750 d *p.* 10-11-1787 m Rachel — Sol VA

MALTBIE, (includes MALBE, MALTBY, MALTY)
Benjamin: b 5-10-1750 d 1-1-1847 m Abigal Munger Pvt CT ★
Benjamin: b 6-20-1717 d 7-9-1796 m Elizabeth Fowler PS CT
Daniel: b 10-29-1715 d 10-26-1776 m Mary Harrison PS CT
David: b 2-1728 d 10-5-1797 m Sarah Holly Sol CT
Jonathan, 3d: b 12-17-1744 d 2-11-1798 m Elizabeth Allen NLt CT
Noah: b 9-23-1744 d 12-2-1785 m Huldah — Pvt CT
Wm.: b 6-13-1742 d 1812 m (1)Lydia Ritter (2)Catherine Lee Pvt MA
Zacheus: b 6-10-1753 d 6-19-1833 m Jerusha Rose Pvt CT ★

MAMAN,
Joseph Charles: b 6-3-1748 d 5-1-1813 m Oloce Bicknell NCdr RI

MANAHAN,
John: b 1757 d 5- -1818 m Mary Nesmith Pvt NH

MANBECK,
Rudolph: b 1740 d 1794 m Christina — Cpl PA

MANCHESTER,
Abraham: b 8-6-1761 d 4-27-1848 m Anna Cook Pvt RI ★
Elias: b 8-15-1758 d 3-14-1846 m Patience Boyce Pvt NY
Gershom: b 5-10-1761 d *p.* 1800 m — Pvt MA
Isaac: b 11-6-1717 d 1791 m Hannah Cundall PS RI
Isaac: b 6-27-1731 d 7-17-1792 m (1)Abigail Brown (2)Deborah Cook PS RI
John: b 1752 d 1804 m Anna Gould Cpl PA
John: b 7-27-1752 d 5-14-1794 m Mary Whitman Lt RI
John: b 3-28-1761 d 10-28-1833 m Mary Brayton Pvt RI ★
John: b 3-23-1757 d 1-23-1838 m Phebe Stedman Pvt RI ★
John: b 11-7-1749 d 1812 m Sarah Church Bailey Pvt RI
Joseph: b 9-27-1757 d 6-26-1827 m Hannah Cranston Ens RI
Joseph: b 9-15-1755 d 8-12-1839 m Mary Arnold Pvt RI ★
Joseph: b 2-13-1760 d 1-8-1841 m Hannah Tabor Pvt RI ★
Matthew: b 10-1-1720 d 9-14-1801 m Freelove Gorton PS RI

Nathaniel: b 4-2-1744 d 4-8-1833 m Elizabeth Coxe Pvt RI
Stephen: b 5-23-1717 d 6-24-1807 m (1)Grace Farrow (2)Sea Fair
Mayberry (3)Mary Bailey Pvt MA
Thomas: b 1726 d 10-13-1817 m Eunice Norton Pvt MA
Thomas: b 1739 d 1777 m Hannah Bailey Pvt NH
Thomas: b *c.* 1761 d 2-25-1840 m Elizabeth Brewer Pvt Mar RI ★

MANDELL,
Moses: b 12-16-1751 d 6-18-1826 m Abigail Mason Pvt MA
Paul: b 1723 d 9-16-1809 m Susanna Ruggles BgdMaj MA

MANDERFIELD,
John: b 1758 d *p.* 1790 m Catherine — Pvt PA

MANDEVILLE, (includes DE MANDEVILLE)
Anthony: b 4-30-1741 d 10-26-1828 m (1)Willempie VanHouten
(2)Margrit J. Mandeville (3)Charity VanDevort Lt NJ
David: bpt 10-30-1717 d 1782 m Anna — PS NY
Francis: b *a.* 1749 d 1836 m Deboratha Clark 1Lt NY
Hendrick: b 10-21-1729 d 9-17-1793 m (1)Sarah Berthoff
(2)Margaret Jones CS NJ
Henry: b 2-25-1760 d 2-2-1847 m (1)Elizabeth Ryerson (2)Lidia
Jones Pvt Grd Sct NJ
Jacob: bpt 1-10-1711 d 8-27-1784 m Sarah Davenport PS NY
Jacob: b 4-22-1752 d 1-17-1839 m Sarah Clark ADC NY
John: b 10-11-1753 d 4-17-1827 m Sarah Drake Capt NY W★
Michael: b *c.* 1760 d *p.* 1805 m (1)Elizabeth Clark (2)Jane Cross
(3)Mrs Lewis Pvt NY
Wm.: b *c.* 1739 d *c.* 1818 m Elisabeth Jacobus Pvt NJ
Yellis, Sr.: b 1-25-1708 d 8-8-1776 m Leah Bruin CS NJ
Yellis: b 6-6-1746 d 6-27-1812 m Christian — Pvt NJ

MANDIGO,
Jeremiah: b 10-15-1755 d *a.* 1-24-1842 m Sarah Ellsworth MM Pvt
NH ★

MANER,
John: b 4-8-1759 d 8-16-1833 m Keziah — Pvt GA
Wm., Jr.: b 12-1-1747 d 8-4-1819 m (1)Jane Asenatha May
(2)Elizabeth Tison Capt SC

MANGAM,
John: b *c.* 1755 d 1846 m Sarah — PS NC
John: b 1-19-1763 d 3-23-1843 m (1)Betsy Murdock (2)Gurnine
Gouglin (3)Rebecca Knowles Pvt SC ★

MANGOLD,
Frederick: b *c.* 1752-8 d *a.* 9-25-1798 m Barbara Kneil Pvt PA

MANHART,
John: b *c.* 1760 d 6-10-1835 m (1)Mrs Lyons (2)Rebecca Plimett
Pvt NY ★

MANICKE, (or MANIQUET)
Christian: b 2-5-1736 d 1806 m Anna Magdalena vonWeylandt Lt
PA

MANIFOLD,
Benjamin: b *c.* 1748 d 9-23-1820 m Mary Payne Pvt PA
Joseph: b 6-8-1736 d 7-16-1801 m Eleanor Cougle Pvt PA

MANIGUALT,
Gabriel: b 4-21-1704 d 6-5-1781 m Ann Ashby PS SC
Gabriel, Jr.: b 3-17-1758 d 11-4-1809 m Margaret Izard Pvt SC
Joseph: b 10-19-1763 d 6-5-1843 m (1)Henrietta Middleton
(2) Charlotte Drayton Sol SC

MANKER,
Wm.: b 1-7-1765 d 4-29-1839 m (2)Sarah.Powers Sol VA ★

MANLEY, (includes MANLY)
Ancil: b 1763 d 6-22-1853 m Elizabeth Butler Pvt VA ★
Asa: b 2-23-1735 d 1788 m Eunice (Dimmock)Gurley Pvt CT
Basil: b 6-8-1742 d 5-15-1824 m Elizabeth Maultsby Capt NC
Daniel, Sr.: b 1721 d 1-18-1804 m (1)Rebecca Manly (2)Sarah
Monk Pvt MA
Daniel, Jr.: b 1752 d — m Phebe Howard Pvt MA
David, Jr.: b 1754-60 d *p.* 1838 m Desire — Pvt MA
Jacob: b 4-18-1747 d 12-13-1794 m Rebecca Lum PS MD
Jesse: b 5-28-1755 d *p.* 1802 m Eunice Holmes Pvt MA
John: b *a.* 1751 d *p.* 1808 m (1)Bethia — (2)Elizabeth — (3)Tryphena
Elmer Pvt MA
John: b 6-9-1737 d 11-23-1807 m Charity Addis Wgt NJ
John: b 1733 d 2-12-1793 m Martha Hickman NCommo MA
John: b 1750-60 d 10-8-1829 m Mary Hardaway Lt GA
John, Jr.: b 1711 d 11-29-1803 m Mary Arnold PS VT
John, Jr.: b 1737 d 1816 m Jerusha Paddock Pvt VT
John: b 6-5-1759 d 1814 m Susannah Cox Sgt VA
Luther: b 3-26-1757 d 1-9-1824 m Hannah — Fif Pvt MA
Nathan: b 7-15-1750 d 4-5-1833 m Hannah Kent SgtMaj VT
Samuel: b 1742 d 1827 m (2)Anna Howard Sgt MA
Setha, Sr.: b 2-18-1739 d 1-6-1810 m (1)Mercy Keith (2)Elizabeth
Taylor Cpl MA

Thomas, Jr.: b 10-25-1729 d *p.* 12-13-1783 m Temperance Swift
PS MA
Wm.: b 11-25-1761 d 1824 m Lucy Freeman Pvt MD
Wm.: b 2-19-1758 d 2-25-1835 m Betsy Morse Pvt VT

MANLOVE,
Matthew: b 12-17-1736 d 12-20-1777 m Sarah Mott Capt DE

MANN, (includes MAN)
Abijah: b 8-7-1734 d 1809 m Sarah Porter CS CT
Amos: b 1762 d 11-1-1841 m Mary Blagdon Pvt MA
Andrew: b 3-18-1755 d 10-5-1846 m Hannah Phelps Pvt CT ★
Andrew: b 1740 d 1-13-1818 m Rachel Egnor Capt PA
Ariel: b 6-20-1748 d 1-4-1777 m Zilpha Gratrax Sgt MA
Arnold: b *c.* 1759 d *p.* 10-14-1818 m Rebecca Wright Cpl NC
Benjamin: b 10-23-1739 d 12-7-1831 m Martha Deane Capt PS NH
Benjamin: b 1750 d 1826 m Mildred Timberlake Pvt VA ★
Bernard: b 5-9-1740 d 6-6-1817 m Maria Stumb Capt PA
Bezaleel: b 6-15-1725 d 10-3-1796 m Beebe Carpenter PS Dr MA
Charles: b 1-15-1744 d 2-7-1832 m (1)Elethan Ide (2)Elizabeth
McCobb (3)Zeviah (Williams) Parker Pvt PS VT
David: b 1759 d 12-26-1834 m Sarah (Tibbetts)Osgood Pvt MA W★
Denton: b *c.* 1765 d *a.* 1812 m Sarah Wheeless PS NC
Ebenezer: b *a.* 1739 d *p.* 1790 m Anne Berry BgdSrgn CT
Elias: b 7-27-1754 d 5-12-1825 m Asenath Wright Adj MA
Elijah: b 8-9-1751 d 3-15-1836 m (1)Mary Perkins (2)Ruby Baxter
Pvt CT
Ensign: b 7-15-1740 d 12-21-1829 m Alice Whitney PS MA
Ephraim: b 4-3-1752 d 1824 m Comfort Jewett Pvt MA
Ernest: b — d 1813 m Maria Magdalena Summers CS NJ
Frederick: b 3-4-1754 d 7-15-1814 m Maria Young Sgt PA
Frederick: b 6-23-1756 d 8-8-1823 m Anna Post Pvt VT
George: b 1725/6 d 5-24-1821 m Elizabeth Herrmann Pvt PA
Gideon: b 9-1-1735 d 1800 m Rachel — PS NH
Jacob: b 1725 d *p.* 1788 m Barbara Miller PS VA
Jacob, Jr.: b *c.* 1745 d 1815 m Mary Kessinger Pvt Sct VA
James: b *c.* 1720 d 1785 m (1)Abigail Willard (2)Anne Parker Capt MA
James: b *c.* 1745 d 1816 m Judith Pvt SC
James: b — d *p.* 8-7-1810 m — Cav SC
Johannes: b 6-24-1730 d 4-14-1815 m Anna Catherine Meder Pvt
PA
John: b *c.* 1710 d *p.* 1-19-1786 m Anne Vincent PS GA
John: b 12-25-1743 d 5-9-1828 m (1)Lydia Porter (2)Mrs Barber PS
NH
John: b 7-23-1742 d 11-7-1819 m Elizabeth McGlaughlin Capt PA
John: b 1746 d 1826 m Ann Dean Pvt PA
John: b 12-13-1734 d 10-9-1807 m (1)Mary Stafford (2)Anna
Aldrich CS RI
John: b 10-27-1767 d 5- -1841 m Mary Hubbard Pvt SC
Jonathan: b 3-28-1745 d 12-22-1822 m Mary Gilbert Cpl MA
Joshua: b 7-14-1759 d 10-20-1827 m M. Mary Cushing Pvt MA
Josiah, Sr.: b 12-9-1715 d 1802 m Mary Chubbuck Pvt MA
Josiah, Jr.: b 5-12-1745 d 1820 m Sage Clark Pvt MA
Levi: b 9-9-1757 d 1-12-1818 m Anne Cooley Pvt MA
Luke: b 1736 d 1802 m Anne Butler PS Capt GA
Moses: b 7-14-1750 d 5-10-1834 m Rebecca Bullard Pvt MA
Moses Hamilton: b 1761 d *p.* 1810 m (1)Jane Kinkead (2)Sarah
Lewis CS VA
Nathan: b 7-20-1741 d 1796 m Abigail Blood Wight Pvt MA
Nathan: b 4-13-1757 d 12-31-1854 m (1)Betsey — (2)Polly
Adams Pvt MA
Obadiah: b 3-4-1737 /8 d 1824 m Hannah — Lt MA ★
Oliver: b 1- -1756 d 7-4-1832 m Lucy Adams SrgnMte MA
Peter: b 11-29-1759 d 3-13-1842 m Hannah Haney Pvt PA
Robert: b 2-7-1732 d *p.* 7-14-1780 m Phoebe — Pvt VA
Rufus: b 8-26-1755 d 8-26-1837 m Sybil Allen Sgt MA ★
Samuel: b 5-25-1755 d 12-20-1826 m Margaret Keith Pvt PA
Seth, Sr.: b 1724 d 1-28-1815 m (1)Rachel Spear (2)Elizabeth Dyer
(3)Deborah Dyer Pvt MA
Seth, Jr.: b 2-13-1747 d 7-20-1822 m (1)Mary Haywood (2)Deborah
Dyer Lt MA
Theodore: b 3-6-1707/8 d 10-1-1783 m Abigail Day Pvt MA
Thomas: b 11-26-1717 d 6-29-1795 m Deborah Briggs PS MA
Thomas: b *a.* 1722 d *p.* 6-6-1792 m Elizabeth — PS CS NC
Timothy: b 1746 d 1843 m Elizabeth Parker Capt MA
Willard: b 8-24-1758 d 9-29-1835 m Mary Cook Pvt Wgn PS VT
Wm.: b 1764 d 3-25-1841 m Rebecca — Pvt MA
Wm.: b *c.* 1730 d 1787 m Mary — PS NH
Wm.: b 1731 d 3-20-1778 m Jane Hamilton Sol VA
Zadock: b 2-7-1759 d 9-29-1846 m (1)Esther Warner (2)Hannah
Williams Pvt CT

MANNERS,
John: b 1760 d *p.* 1810 m Sallie Couch Pvt PA

MANNING, (includes MANNEN & MANRING)
Abraham: b *c.* 1751 d 11-11-1811 m Esther Hammond CS NJ
Andrew: b 7-8-1755 d 11-29-1849 m Elizabeth Lathrop OrdlSgt
CT ★
Andrew: b 2-1-1739 d 4-19-1818 m Mary Stelle Pvt NJ
Anthony: b *c.* 1760 d *a.* 1800 m Rebecca Griffith Lt MD
Benjamin: b *a.* 1763 d *p.* 8-27-1831 m Charity Gray Sol GA
Benjamin: b 2-23-1763 d 6-2-1839 m Phebe Drake Pvt NJ

MANNING, contd.
Benjamin: b 8-12-1744 d 12-23-1801 m (1)Mary Martin (2)Rachel Cutter PS NJ
Daniel: b 9-29-1753 d 12-29-1836 m Lydia Peters Pvt CT W★
David: b 1-14-1726/7 d 9-29-1807 m (1)Anne Hamilton (2)Miriam Simonson Pvt CT
David: b c. 1759 d 9-14-1816 m (1)Lucy Peck (2)Annis Jackson Pvt MA
Diah: b 8-24-1760 d 8-25-1815 m Anna Gifford Drm CT
Edward: b — d 1778 m Debora Vroome Pvt NY
Eliphalet: b 4-16-1757 d 8-9-1826 m Sarah Goodwin Pvt MM MA
Frederick: b 1758 d 10-21-1810 m Anne Young Sol CT
Hezekiah: b 8-8-1721 d 4-20-1802 m Mary Webb PS CS CT
Hillery: b c. 1758 d 1809 m Sarah Lewis PS NC
Isaac: b 1-20-1755 d 6-27-1825 m Sarah Pike FifMaj MA ★
Isaac, Jr.: b 7-25-1742 d 6-29-1827 m Elsey Merrill 2Lt NJ
Isaac: b 12-31-1758 d 3-31-1843 m Rosannah Runyon Pvt NJ ★
Israel: b 1-29-1756 d 1-3-1821 m Lydia (Richardson)Wright Cpl MA
Jacob: b 11-8-1739 d 7-16-1808 m Sarah Butterfield Pvt MA
Jacob: b 1745 d 10- -1819 m Sarah — Sol NY
Jeremiah: b 5-25-1736 d 6-10-1803 m (1)Ursula Drake (2)Rachel Randolph (3)Mary Ford Capt CS NJ
Jesse: b 8-17-1745 d a. 11-15-1825 m (1)Anne Carleton (2)Elizabeth Abbot (3)Abigail Baldwin Pvt MA
Joel: b 4-1-1756 d 8-13-1805 m Abigail Bundy Pvt CT
John: b 3-30-1753 d 12-20-1828 m (1)Mary Perkins (2)Irena Wood Pvt CT
John: b 1727 d 6-14-1837 m Nancy Woodle Pvt PA DE ★
John, Sr.: b 1738 d 10-24-1824 m Lucy Bolles Dr MA
John: b 6-3-1749 d 8-5-1829 m Lydia Pike Cpl NH
John: b 1742 d 4- -1817 m (1)Sarah Shawhan (2)Elizabeth Harnett Sgt PA
John, Jr.: b 10-19-1761 d 11-5-1841 m Hannah Goodhue Srgn Mte RI
Jordan: b 1760 d 11-15-1837 m Elizabeth Clark Pvt NC ★
Joseph: b 3-24-1728 d 10-3-1776 m Ruth Child Pvt CT
Joseph: b 12-9-1761 d 2- -1849 m Lydia Everett Pvt CT ★
Joseph: b c. 1740 d 7-7-1790 m Deborah Elgin Pvt MD
Joseph: b 1749 d p. 1790 m Elizabeth Dunnington Sol MD
Joseph: b 1-26-1730 d 3-26-1808 m Mary Allen Chp MA
Lawrence: b 1756/7 d 12-20-1804 m Susannah Richardson Lt VA
Levi: b a. 1753 d 1796 m Elizabeth — PS SC
Marcom: b — d p. 10-18-1792 m — Sol NC
Moses, Sr.: b c. 1760 d p. 1-2-1791 m Liddia — PS NC
Moses, Jr.: b c. 1731 d p. 1-14-1810 m Kezziah Lott PS SC
Nathaniel: b 3-16-1760 d 3-9-1814 m Matilda Morgan Pvt CT
Peter: b 11-25-1758 d 12-25-1839 m (1)Rebecca Carter (2)Sarah Stone Pvt MA
Phineas: b 10-7-1756 d 10-22-1832 m Abigail Alden Pvt Fif MA
Robert: b 1748 d a. 3-6-1781 m Abagail Eustas MM Sgt MA
Samuel: b 11-3-1723 d 11-9-1783 m Anne Winship Pvt CT
Samuel: b 10-22-1725 d 4-5-1812 m (1)Abigail Clark (2)Eunice Frink Pvt CT
Samuel: b 8-26-1729 d 4-3-1824 m (1)Mary Woods (2)Sarah Woods Pvt PS
Samuel: b 3-15-1732 d 1-28-1809 m Abigail Avery PS MA
Samuel: b 11-16-1752 d 4-7-1821 m Mehitable (Spaulding)Burt Sgt MA
Thomas: b 6-15-1764 d 12-22-1853 m Anna Todd Pvt CT ★
Thomas: b 11- -1750 d 1-8-1794 m Rebecca Goodwin Pvt MA
Thomas: b 1753 d 10-21-1819 m Mary Stelle Pvt NJ
Wm.: b 11-28-1733 d 9-16-1807 m Mary (Johnson)Payson Capt CT
Wm.: bpt 1-20-1760 d 1-8-1847 m Sarah — Pvt CT ★
Wm., Jr.: b 5-21-1747 d 10-21-1814 m Sarah Heywood 2Lt MA
Wm.: b 10-15-1756 d 3-9-1843 m (1)Hannah White (2)Mary (Simonds) Avery Pvt MA

MANNON,
Patrick: b c. 1755-60 d p. 1790 m — Pvt PA

MANNY, (includes MANE, MANI & MAUNEY)
Adam: b c. 1759 d a. 2-23-1818 m Mary Caterina — Cpl PA
Barnabas: b 1735 d 4-28-1815 m Anne Everitt Pvt PS NY
Christian: b 1741 d 1-13-1815 m Caty — PS NC
Henry: b 3-23-1730 d 11-26-1811 m Alida Vanderburg Pvt NY
Jacob, Jr.: b — d p. 9-7-1813 m Nancy — PS NC
James: b 1761 d 1812 m Eunice Wines Pvt NY
Valentine: b 1737 d 12- -1805 m Katherine — PS NC

MANROSS,
Elijah: b 1761 d 10-28-1832 m Martha Manross FifMaj CT ★
Theodore: b 1-6-1760 d 8- -1825 m Martha White Pvt CT

MANSELL,
John: b 1723 d p. 6-3-1801 m Leah Simons Pvt MA
Samuel: b 12-4-1715 d 1779 m Susanna Gassaway PS MD

MANSFIELD,
Charles: b 12-19-1762 d 1-12-1830 m (1)Molly Howard (2)Elizabeth Howard Fif CT ★
Daniel: b 12-27-1741 d 3-29-1816 m Lydia Norwood Pvt NH
Daniel, Sr.: b 11-24-1717 d 4-2-1797 m (1)Lydia Newhall (2)Mrs Ruth B. Newhall PS MA

Ebenezer: b 7-16-1757 d 10-8-1819 m Mary Lewis Pvt MA ★
Epes: b 3-24-1757 d 5-9-1832 m Sally Smith Pvt MA
Isaac: b 3-27-1750 d 9- -1826 m Mary Clapp Chp MA
James: b 1748 d 11-6-1813 m Rebecca — Pvt MD
John: b 8-18-1748 d 6-1-1823 m (1)Eunice Kirtland (2)Esther Lewis LT CT ★
John: b 2-19-1721/2 d 8-27-1809 m Sarah Cheever PS MA
Jonathan: b 10-14-1753 d 4-18-1833 m Martha Howard Pvt MA CT ★
Joseph: b 4-16-1737 d 6-6-1821 m Hannah Punderson Capt CT
Joseph: b 10-9-1728 d 9-10-1806 m Sarah Waters Pvt MA
Nathan, Sr.: b 3-15-1718 d 3-13-1783 m Deborah Dayton PS CT
Nathan, Jr.: b 11-30-1748 d 11-5-1835 m Anne Tomlinson Pvt CT ★
Richard: b 6-17-1744 d 4-3-1793 m Elizabeth Whittemore Pvt MA
Robert: b 12-19-1762 d 10-1-1833 m Mourning Clark Pvt VA ★
Samuel: b 1740 d 9-16-1819 m Charity Boyles Fif MD ★
Samuel: b 12-22-1750 d 10-5-1828 m Hepzebah Williams Pvt MA
Samuel: b 12-16-1757 d 2-8-1810 m Esther Hall Capt NY
Thomas: b 9-14-1750 d 1-19-1837 m (2)Anna Wilkinson Pvt MD ★
Thomas: b c. 1736 d p. 1790 m Mary Hawks PS MA
Wm., Sr.: b 4-1-1750 d 5-28-1842 m (1)Elizabeth Lyon (2)Lucy Peck Culver Lt CT
Wm.: b 5-20-1749 d 9-28-1809 m Betty Townsend Pvt MA

MANSKER,
George: b c. 1745 d a. 1822 m — Sol NC

MANSON,
David: b 10- -1753 d c. 1835 m Jean Johnston Pvt PA ★
Frederick: b 8-16-1745 d 10-25-1826 m Ann Hemenway QM MA
Nehemiah: b 1761 d 11-19-1832 m (1)Hannah Lincoln (2)Mercy Jenkins Pvt MA
Peter: b 12-24-1733 d c. 1794 m — Capt VA
Wm.: b 3-27-1750 d 11-27-1819 m Rachel — Pvt MA

MANSPERGER,
John: b 1-28-1742 d 1825 m (2)Rachel Long Capt PA
John George: b 10-3-1751 d 1823 m Mary — Pvt PA

MANSUR,
John, Jr.: b 6-21-1734 d 8-5-1776 m Ruth Varnum Sgt MA
Samuel: bpt 7-4-1742 d p. 1790 m Sarah Varnum Sgt MA
Wm.: b 1-1-1737 d 1808 m Isabella Harvey Pvt NH
Wm.: b 12-21-1757 d 8-16-1863 m Gertrude Horton Pvt NH

MANTER, (includes MANTOR)
David: b 11-5-1763 d 6-5-1820 m Keziah Robbins Pvt MA
Jonathan: b 3-3-1730 d 4-11-1820 m Sarah Chase Pvt MA
Robert: b 1724 d 1797 m Elizabeth Milliken Capt MA

MANTLE,
Christopher: b 1752/3 d 1828/9 m Elizabeth Pvt PA

MANTON,
Daniel: b 1742/3 d 11-15-1808 m Patience Eddy Col RI
Jeremiah: b 2-13-1762 d 12-25-1843 m Mary Austis Borden Trm Sgt RI ★

MANTZ,
Nicholas: b 8-11-1750 d 3-1-1828 m Marie Heilman Pvt PA
Peter: b 11-8-1752 d 1-16-1833 m Catherine Haner Maj MD ★

MANUS,
James, Jr.: b 1742 d 1837 m Elizabeth — Sol VA

MANVILLE, (includes MANVEL)
Daniel: b 6-8-1740 d c. 1785 m Hannah Sherman Pvt VT
John: b 9-5-1736 d p. 1780 m Elizabeth Weed Sol CT
Nicholas: b c. 1725 d 7-3-1778 m Mary Murray Pvt PA
Simeon: b 2-9-1760 d 1825 m Electa Benham Pvt CT

MANWARING,
John: b 1736/7 d 2-22-1782 m Lydia Plumb Pvt CT

MAPES, (includes MAPS)
David: b c. 1737/8 d p. 1790 m (1)Hannah Bull (2)Mary Cornwall Pvt PS NY
Frederick: b 1756 d 1-9-1818 m Sibyl Riggs Sgt NJ ★
Henry: b c. 1725 d p. 1783 m Ruth Rumsey Pvt NY
James: b 12-16-1756 d 6-3-1835 m Anna Many Pvt NY ★
Samuel: b 2-14-1735 d 2-6-1820 m Mary Smith Pvt PS NY
Stephen: b 6-23-1765 d 7-9-1820 m Susannah Decker Pvt NY
Thomas: b 1712 d p. 1779 m Hannah Huydelkoop PS NY

MAPLES (includes MAPEL, MAPLE)
Jacob: b c. 1745 d p. 1779 m Elizabeth Stanford Pvt NJ
Josiah: b 5-15-1762 d 7-2-1847 m (1)Deidamia Comstock (2)Esther Hedges Pvt CT ★
Stephen: b 1-14-1749 d 5-3-1829 m (1)Bathsheba — (2)Lydia Vergason Pvt CT
Stephen: b 2-17-1759 d 10-23-1844 m Mary Betsey Slack MM Pvt NJ ★

Thomas: b c. 1740-8 d p. 9-28-1831 m — PS NC
Wm., Sr.: b 6-15-1727 d 4-13-1821 m (1)Prudence Comstock (2)Joanna Stebbins PS CT
Wm., Jr.: b 4-7-1759 d 1834 m Priscilla Leffingwell Lt CT
Wm.: b c. 1738 d a. 8- -1813 m (1)Keziah Larrison (2)Anny More Tms NJ
Wm.: b 6-22-1755 d 1842 m Eleanor — Pvt NJ ★
Wm. D.: b 1766/7 d 10-26-1847 m Nancy Long Sol VA

MAPP,
John: b c. 1733 d a. 2-10-1789 m Betty (Jacob)Haggoman LCol VA

MAPPIN,
James: b 1748 d p. 1797 m Sarah — Pvt PA

MARABLE,
Edward: b c. 1752 d p. 6-9-1805 m — Lt VA
Hartwell: b c. 1750 d 1789 m Elizabeth Mason Capt VA

MARBLE,
Aaron: b 6-6-1763 d 12-9-1825 m Rebecca Putnam Pvt MA W★
Alpheus: b 8-7-1753 d 7-21-1807 m Anne Dudley Sgt MA
Coker: b 9-8-1765 d p. 1815 m Rhoda Judkins Smn MA
Daniel: b 1755 d — m Ruth Woodbury Pvt MA
Ebenezer: b 12-13-1741 d c. 1776 m Hannah Sawyer Pvt MA
Enoch: b 11-25-1726 d 1-12-1815 m Abigail Holland Lt MA
Jabez: b 9-15-1755 d 12-22-1845 m Mary Salter Pvt MA
John: b 5-10-1751 d 5-25-1830 m Lucretia Richardson Pvt MA
Jonathan: b 11-25-1755 d 1-18-1812 m Mary Stevens Cpl MA
Joseph: b 1-28-1753 d 7-26-1805 m Rebecca Harris Pvt MA
Malachi: b 9-25-1736 d 10-7-1810 m (1)Mary Hayden (2)Abigail Keyes CS MA
Nathaniel, Sr.: b c. 1722 d p. 4-12-1794 m Abigail Houghton CS MA
Oliver: b 9-15-1755 d 7-29-1827 m Deborah Bayley Pvt MA
Sampson: b — d c. 1- -1783 m Sarah Shepard Sgt VT ★
Solomon: b 4-14-1758 d 2-18-1834 m Jerusha Greenwood Pvt MA
Stephen: b 4-17-1753 d 12-18-1817 m Betty Putnam Pvt MA
Thaddeus: b 2-24-1758 d 3-19-1827 m Olive Putnam Pvt MA

MARBURGER,
Simon: b 8-18-1732 d 12-20-1802 m Anna Maria — Pvt PA

MARBURY, (includes MARBERRY)
Leonard: b c. 1750 d 9-22-1796 m Anne Sommerville LCol GA
Luke: b 10-5-1767 d 1852/3 m Elizabeth Bullen PS GA
Thomas: b 1756 d 1823 m Charity — Pvt GA

MARCH,
Clement: b 1707 d 1777 m Eleanor Veazey PS NH
Jacob: b 7-17-1747 d 9-29-1814 m Eleanor Moore Pvt MA
James: b 2-9-1769 d 3-29-1823 m Sarah Jose Fif Pvt MA
James: b 1728 d 5-5-1785 m Margery Jones Pvt NH
John: b 8-18-1738 d 6-10-1809 m (1)Sarah Dole (2)Sarah Emery Pvt NH
Paul: b 1736-42 d p. 1780 m Rhoda Clough Sgt MA
Samuel: b c. 1730 d 10-30-1804 m Anna Libby LCol MA
Stephen: b 7-27-1741 d 1813 m Miriam Bean Pvt NH

MARCHEND, (or MARCHIN)
David: b 5-4-1745 d 7-22-1809 m Elizabeth Kaemerer Capt PA

MARCUS,
John: b c. 1755 d a. 4-7-1806 m Hannah — Pvt GA

MARCY,
Asael: b 3-25-1738 d 3-2-1819 m Priscilla Dunham Cpl CT
Ebenezer: b 2-7-1741 d 3-20-1790 m Martha Spencer CS CT
Elijah: b 9-6-1761 d 10- -1806 m Mary Hobbs Pvt MA
Gardner: b 6-12-1762 d 10- -1837 m Elizabeth Danforth Pvt MA
Griffin: b 1745 d p. 1785 m Temperance Kelsey Pvt NY
Jedediah: b 7-26-1757 d 9-16-1811 m Ruth Larned Pvt MA
Jonathan: b 1-20-1742/3 d 4-5-1822 m Hannah Stone Pvt CT
Nathaniel: b 2-25-1733 d 11-29-1798 m Hannah Grosvenor Capt CT
Reuben: b 11-28-1732 d 1-14-1806 m Rachel Watson Capt CT
Samuel, Jr.: b 10-8-1739 d 2- -1820 m Lois Peak Lt CT
Zebediah, Sr.: b 8-27-1732 d 12-1-1806 m Priscilla Morris Pvt CT
Zebulon: b 5-28-1744 d 9-21-1826 m Jerusha Coult PS PA

MARDEN,
Benjamin, Jr.: b 2-4-1751 d p. 1817 m (1)Hannah Rand (2)Deliverance Johnson Pvt NH
David: b a. 1720 d 6-28-1777 m Mehitable Hardy Pvt MA
Edward: b 1751 d 3-16-1835 m Sarah Elmers Pvt NH ★
Israel: b 2-4-1731 d p. 1777 m Prudence Locke PS NH
Joseph: b 3-22-1738 d p. 1786 m Mary (Rand) Hunt Drm NH
Lemuel: b 8-30-1745 d 1-9-1819 m Hannah Greenough Pvt MA
Nathaniel: b 3-22-1746 d 3-30-1823 m Elizabeth Moulton Fif MM NH

MARDERS,
James: b c. 1755 d p. 1830 m Mildred — PS VA

MAREAN,
John: b 2-6-1739 d 2-1-1786 m Abigail Hammond CaptLt MA
Wm.: b c. 1759 d 1811 m Mary Fletcher Pvt MD
Wm.: b 12-12-1742 d 5-10-1826 m Sibyl Parker Capt MA W★

MARGERUM,
Wm.: b c. 1761 d 1810 m Rebecca O. — Pvt PA

MARIM,
John: b 1751 d 2-18-1815 m Hannah Stevens Lt DE

MARINER, (includes MARRINER)
Gilbert: b a. 1748 d 1795 m Elizabeth Kollock Pvt DE
Joseph: b 8-29-171- d 7-20-1811 m Abigail Hanscom CS MA

MARINUS,
David: b 10-17-1751 d 1-16-1778 m Effy Marritje Cadmus Capt NJ W★

MARION,
Bartholomew: b c. 1755 d 7-10-1833 m — Harrison Pvt NC ★
Benjamin: b c. 1720 d 9-20-1778 m (1)Martha Allston (2)Esther (Bonneau)Simmons Maj SC
Isaac: b 1730 d 5-31-1781 m Rebecca Alston Sol PS SC
Joseph: b a. 1752 d 1795 m Elizabeth Robertson Collis Pvt SC
Samuel: b 9-21-1756 d p. 10-26-1843 m Tabitha (Barron)Barnet Pvt VA ★

MARIS,
Caleb: b 8-26-1744 d 10-26-1839 Ann Fawkes Pvt PA
David: b 4-23-1753 d p. 1814 m Sarah Fawkes Pvt PA
George: b 2-28-1744 d 12- -1783 m Eleanor Lindley Pvt PA
John: b 10-12-1736 d 11-6-1817 m Jane Mace Pvt PA

MARKELL, (includes MARKEL, MARKLE & MERKEL)
Abram: b 2-23-1760 d 2-28-1841 m Rachel Blackburn Col PA
Casper: b 9-15-1751 d 7-9-1821 m Blandina Hottenstein Pvt PA
Christian: b 11-26-1761 d 4-4-1846 m Nancy Catherine Boyer Pvt Tms PA ★
Gaspard: b 1732 d 9- -1819 m (1)Elizabeth Grim (2)Maria Rothermel PS PA
George: b c. 1723 d 1779 m Christina Hill Pvt PA
George: b 1761 d 2-3-1850 m Barbary — PS PA
Henry: b 4-23-1727 d 12-29-1809 m Anna Margaretha Eaker 2Maj NY
Michael: b 3-9-1724 d 8-17-1778 m Margarett Schaeffer Pvt NY
Peter: b 3-24-1765 d 5-25-1837 m Elizabeth Koch Pvt NY ★

MARKER,
George: b 12-10-1722 d 5-13-1823 m (1)Anna Maria — (2)Margaretta Stellwagon Pvt PA

MARKEY,
Wm.: b 1753 d 1846 m Margaret Holland Sgt MD

MARKHAM, (includes MARCUM)
Abijah: b c. 1742 d p. 1790 m Abigail Chadwick 2Lt MA
Asa: b 1740 d p. 1798 m Rebecca — Pvt MA
Barzillai: b 11-4-1740 d 6-1-1824 m Annie Whitaker Ens CT
Benjamin: b 4-8-1746 d 5-6-1789 m Mercy Bentli 2Lt PS NY
Bernard: b 1737 d 7-13-1802 m Mary Harris PS VA
Darius: b 1745 d 1800 m Lucy Alden Pvt CT
Ebenezer: b 9-5-1749 d 2-17-1814 m Dorothy Johnson PS CT
Isaac: b 5-26-1754 d 10-15-1840 m Cynthia Terry Cpl CT ★
James: b 1752 d 9-1-1816 m Elizabeth Kenner NCapt VA
Jeremiah: b 1-20-1734 d 11-17-1827 m Amy Deming 2Sgt CT
John, Sr.: b 12-28-1705 d 3-3-1788 m Desire Sears PS CT
John, Jr.: b 4- -1756 d 4-15-1852 m (1)Asenath Smith (2)Anna Estabrook Niles OrdlSgt CT ★
John: b 1764 d 1838 m Sallie Brown Pvt VA ★
Joseph: bpt 8-29-1742 d p. 2-20-1830 m Mehitable Spence Sgt CT ★
Josiah: b 5-2-1759 d c. 1852 m Eada McDonald Pvt VA ★
Nathaniel: b 5-5-1754 d 1-11-1829 m (1)Margaret Hall (2)Polly Strong (3)Hannah Rogers Pvt CT
Richard: b c. 1750 d p. 8-20-1829 m Ann Roberts Pvt NC
Stephen: b 1763 d 6-21-1829 m Dorothy Jocelin Pvt MA
Thomas: b 1-4-1752 d 2-13-1839 m Fanny — Pvt Arfr NC ★
Thomas: b 7-15-1757 d 5-14-1840 m Nelly Wilkerson Pvt VA W★
Wm., Sr.: b c. 1730 d 5-1-1792 m Abigail Cone Willey Sgt PS NH
Wm., Jr.: b 8-29-1762 d 1-3-1826 m Phebe Dexter Pvt NH

MARKLAND,
John: b 8-8-1755 d 2-23-1837 m (1)Christiana Heisz (2)Sophia Bicker Lt PA ★
Matthew: b 8-31-1727 d p. 1793 m Ancibell — Sol NC
Richard: b c. 1759 d a. 7-4-1814 m Alley — Pvt PA

MARKLEY,
Benjamin: b 7-13-1751 d 7-10-1819 m Hanna Wentz Capt PA
George: b 11-24-1755 d 9-19-1816 m — Pvt PA
Henry: b c. 1740 d 1788-90 m Barbara Frick Maj PA
Jacob: b 7-11-1701 d 8-29-1784 m (1)Barbara Dotterer (2)Barbara Kausch Maj PA

MARKLEY, contd.
Jacob: b 8-28-1747 d 9-26-1821 m Maria Koplin Pvt PA
John: b 12-28-1764 d 7-28-1834 m Elizabeth Schwenck Pvt PA
Philip: b 8-27-1725 d 4-5-1800 m Mary Johnson PS PA

MARKOE,
Abram: b 1729 d 8-28-1806 m (2)Elizabeth Baynton Capt PA

MARKS, (includes MARCK, MARK, MARQUES & MARX)
Adam: b 3-20-1757 d 10-20-1814 m Margaritta Miller Lt PA
Conrad: b 1743 d 1823 m Margaret Shaeffer Pvt PS PA
Conrad: b 6-12-1745 d 1-16-1807 m Margaret — Pvt PA
Edward, Sr.: b 1757 d p. 3-4-1837 m Elizabeth — Sol VA
Isaac: b 1732 d p. 1776 m Miriam Simons Sol NY
James: b 8-24-1745 d 4- -1816 m Elizabeth Harvie PS CS VA
Johannes: b 1758 d p. 3- -1823 m (2)Mary — Pvt PA ★
John: b 1759 d 1806 m Rosetta Humphrey Pvt CT
John: b 1746 d 12-29-1832 m Anna McCurdy Pvt PS NH
John: b c. 1745-50 d p. 1796 m Lucy (Meriwether)Lewis Capt VA
Joseph: b 1752 d 1820 m (1)Julia — (2)Catherine Plaugher Pvt PA
Samuel: b 10- -1757 d 9-19-1836 m (2)Abigail Polley Pvt Wgn MA ★
Wm.: b 1760 d p. 1820 m Christeanna Drm PA ★

MARKWARD,
Mordea: b 1762 d 1806 m Hannah VanLear PS PA

MARKWELL,
Wm.: b 1750 d p. 6-30-1816 m Amelia — Pvt MD

MARLER,
James: b 1753 d 10-18-1834 m Lydia — Pvt SC

MARLETT, (includes MARLATT, MARLETTE)
Abraham: b 1761 d 7-23-1828 m Ann Linder Pvt VA ★
Gideon: b 1-14-1747 d 12-13-1822 m Mary Quackenbush Adj NY
John: b 1720 d 1775 m Batie — PS NY

MARLEY,
Adam: b c. 1720 d 1789 m Rosannah — PS NC
Robert: b 8-4-1741 d p. 1800 m Martha — PS NC

MARLIN,
Joshua: b 12-27-1745 d 3-30-1828 m Agnes McCulloch Pvt PA
Nathaniel: b c. 1755 d a. 5-18-1807 m — Pvt NJ

MARLOW,
James: b 1740 d 1779 m Ellen Evans Pvt SC
Robert: b 5-5-1740 d 11-18-1802 m Ann — Pvt SC

MARNEY,
Amos: b 9- -1760 d 8-28-1839 m Sarah Vance Pvt VA ★

MARONEY, (includes MERONEY)
Alexander: b 3-14-1760 d 3-13-1865 m Abigail Barton Drm NY ★
Philip DeLancy: b 1736 d 12-3-1830 m (1)Sarah Nelson (2)Martha Massey Capt MD
Em: b c. 1740 d 1786/7-m Rachel Tomlinson Pvt DE

MARPLE,
Isaiah: b c. 1750 d p. 1-27-1814 m Elizabeth — Sol NJ

MARQUART,
John George: b c. 1733 d p. 8-23-1795 m Barbara Dipple Pvt NY
Peter: b 3-8-1759 d p. 7-16-1798 m Margaretha Escher Pvt NY

MARQUET, (includes MARQUARDT)
Johannes: b c. 1735 d 6-12-1815 m Margaretha Weger Sol NY

MARQUIS,
Thomas: b 1753 d 9-27-1827 m Jean Park Lt PA
Wm.: b 1749 d 1-15-1815 m Elizabeth Vance PS VA

MARR, (includes MAR & MARRS)
David: b 12-20-1740 d p. 1790 m Sarah — Pvt PA
Dennis: b 7-29-1735 d 6-19-1812 m Sarah (Manson) Hutchins Pvt MA
James: b c. 1762 d 11-1-1814 m Anna Shanon Sgt VA
John: b 11-22-1752 d a. 12-10-1821 m Agnes — Sol VA
John: b 5-30-1750 d 1796 m Susannah Perkins Pvt VA
Thomas: b 9-3-1734 d 2-12-1777 m — Pvt VA
Wm.: b 1743 d 8-14-1802 m Isabel Hamilton Pvt MA

MARRETT,
Amos: b 2-4-1738 d 3-24-1805 m Mary Dunster Pvt MA

MARROW,
Daniel, Sr.: b c. 1735 d 4-3-1812 m Elizabeth Harding Pvt PS ME MA
Samuel: b 3-19-1760 d 2-19-1842 m Jennette Nelson Pvt SC ★

MARSDEN,
George: b 1738 d 12-15-1821 m Wilmot Lee Lt MA

James: b 1732 d 9-14-1780 m Mary Calvert PS VA
John: b 2-14-1757 d 9-15-1844 m Elizabeth Murdock Pvt PA ★

MARSELIS, (includes MARSELUS & MERSELIS)
Ahazuerus: b 6-26-1726 d p. 1777 m Maria Vrooman Sol NY
Ahazuerus G.: b 4-12-1740 d 4-9-1799 m Hester Visscher Capt NY
Edo: b 1-27-1729 d 10-12-1799 m Areantje Sip PS NJ
Garrett: b 8-30-1760 d 2-8-1853 m Charlotte Pederrick Pvt NY ★
Henry A.: b 5-25-1753 d 8-12-1821 m Cornelia Putnam Lt NY
Richard: b 1-5-1700 d 12- -1785 m Lysbet VanEps PS NY

MARSH, (includes MERSCH)
Aaron: b 7-26-1751 d 4-29-1807 m Sarah Fuller Pvt MA
Abel: b 1735 d 1822 m Dorothy Udall Capt VT
Abijah: b 2-4-1757 d 5-24-1844 m Barsha Snow Pvt MA
Abner: b 1740 d 5-31-1778 m Hannah — Pvt CT
Abraham: b c. 1760 d 1847 m (1)Elizabeth Dreisback (2)Eliza Catharine Metzgar Pvt PA
Adam, Sr.: b 1727 d 4-20-1796 m Juliana Dieter Cpl PA
Adam, Jr.: b 1755 d p. 1799 m Mary Elizabeth — Pvt PA
Allen: b 3-9-1762 d 10-17-1830 m Mabel Case Cpl CT ★
Amariah: b 2-27-1747 d 11-8-1815 m Lois Fisk Pvt MA
Amos: b 9-25-1736 d — m Abigail Dimick Pvt CT
Benjamin, Sr.: b 4-1-1711 d p. 1795 m (1)Desire Moulton (2)Rebekah Carriel Pvt MA
Benjamin, Jr.: b 11-9-1745 d 3-16-1834 m Maleson Davenport Pvt MA
Benjamin: b 1758 d 1845 m Sarah — Sol NY
Benjamin: b 1744 d 1785 m Margaret Harris Lt PA
Charles: b 12-23-1755 d 3-31-1833 m Abigail Marsh Pvt NJ
Christopher: b 5-7-1743 d 10-6-1810 m Anna Brown Capt NJ
Cutting: b 3-20-1728/9 d 1-14-1818 m Ruth White PS MA
Daniel, Jr.: b 2-6-1732 d 9-28-1818 m (1)Anne Morrison Normand (2)Hannah (Smith) Gleason (3)Mrs Anna (Stanley) Pitkin (4)Margery Spencer Capt CT
Daniel: b 6-3-1765 d 8-9-1857 m Jane Adams Pvt NH ★
Daniel: b 1736 d 4-16-1803 m Esther Skinner QMGen NJ
Daniel: b 1764 d 12-29-1827 m Rhoda Taft Pvt Drm MA ★
David: b 1730 d 4- -1798 m (1)Sophia — (2)Elizabeth Smith Pvt PA
Ebenezer: b 1731 d p. 1781 m Achsah Stearns Lt MA
Ebenezer: b 1750 d p. 1785 m Eunice Sprague MM MA
Ebenezer: b 1721-3 d 5-29-1795 m Sarah Eastman PS CS MA
Elias: b 5-24-1755 d 4-23-1836 m Esther Brown (Berry)Cpl MA
Eliphalet: b 1742 d 1828 m Sarah — Pvt VT
Elisha: b 3-28-1750 d p. 1790 m Hannah Spring Cpl NH
Enos, Jr.: b 3-18-1760 d 2-28-1842 m Mercy Marsh Pvt MA
Ephraim: b 2-24-1736 d 10-12-1796 m Susanna Todd Sgt MA
Ephraim: b 4-2-1738 d 11-6-1825 m Sarah Farnum Pvt NH
Ephraim: b — d 1784 m Phebe Ludlow Pvt NJ
Ezekiel, Sr.: b 5-27-1711 d 1798 m Sarah Buffington Pvt MA
Ezekiel, Jr.: b 1-26-1740 d 9-15-1822 m Abiah Hartshorn Lt MA
Gravenor: b 2-10-1751 d — m Ann Matson Pvt PA
Hartshorn: b 2-14-1748/9 d 1791 m Mehitable Broad Pvt MA
Isaac: b 10-18-1747 d 8-27-1792 m Lucy Smith Capt MA ★
Isaac: b 9-4-1761 d 1-13-1821 m Catharine Terrill Capt NJ
Jasper: b 8-17-1760 d 4-29-1841 m Submit Belden Pvt MA
Jesse: b 12-16-1761 d 4-29-1834 m Charity Stearns Pvt MA
Job: b 5-12-1755 d 4-20-1835 m Salome Beach Pvt CT ★
Joel: b 6-11-1745 d 3-11-1807 m Ann Mason Col VT
John: b 10-20-1712 d 12-27-1780 m Sarah Webster CS CT
John: b 11-10-1718 d 8-19-1802 m Elizabeth Claflin Pvt MA
John: b 5-26-1750 d 7-30-1778 m Frances Foster Pvt MA
John, Jr.: b 7-24-1751 d 7-15-1814 m Sarah Colburn PS Pvt MA
John: b 1738 d p. 1797 m Nancy Searing Pvt NJ
John: b 1750 d 1- -1821 m Susanna Catharine Pvt PA
Jonathan: b 1-1-1714 d 1794 m Elizabeth Sheldon Pvt CT
Jonathan: b 3-4-1759 d 10-1-1830 m Elizabeth Sawyer Pvt NH
Joseph: b 12-26-1731 d p. 1781 m Deborah Staples Sgt MA
Joseph: b 10-26-1754 d 8- -1783 m Mindwell Pomeroy Pvt MA
Joseph: b 12-26-1755 d 2-12-1824 m Elizabeth Matteson Pvt MA
Joseph: b 8-8-1762 d 1-2-1841 m Ruth Rapelje Smith PS NJ
Joseph: b 10-21-1735 d 12-26-1826 m Sarah Beasley LCol PA
Joseph: b 1-12-1726 d 2-9-1811 m Dorothy Mason Col LGov VT
Joseph Clark: b 9-14-1763 d 2-4-1850 m Susannah Sanger Pvt MA ★
Joshua: b 1757 d 11-5-1825 m Temperance Harryman Capt MD
Joshua: b 2-21-1944 d p. 1815 m Lois Gideon Pvt MA
Judah, Sr.: b 7-25-1712 d 5-7-1801 m Hannah Olmstead Pvt MA
Judah, Jr.: b 5-22-1757 d 2-10-1817 m (2)Jerusha Collins Cpl MA
Lot: b 11-28-1757 d 1-12-1843 m (1)Delight Lincoln (2)Lydia French Pvt MA
Moses: b 3-20-1718 d 4-10-1796 m Hannah Cooke PS Capt MA
Moses, Jr.: b 1-6-1743 d p. 1790 m Jerusha Owne Pvt NH
Moses: b 1747 d 5-29-1828 m Chloe Clark Pvt PS MA
Nathaniel: b 1-28-1746 d 3-29-1795 m Delight Wilson Pvt CT
Nathaniel: b 9-6-1745 d 3-26-1827 m (1)Rebecca Wright (2)Grace Prentice (3)Elizabeth Grinman (4)Widow Rhodes Pvt CT
Peter: b 6-24-1760 d 6-10-1818 m Sarah Wright Pvt MA
Reuben: b 8-18-1758 d 3-9-1843 m (1)Tryphena — (2)Lydia Rathbun Pvt MA ★
Richard: b c. 1760 d a. 12-13-1797 m Barbara Lowdenslager 2Lt MD
Rolph: b 1748 d 10-26-1804 m Janett Brown 1Lt NJ

Roswell: b 7-15-1761 d 9-26-1843 m Anna Crow Pvt CT
Samuel: b 10-8-1751 d 5-14-1822 m Miriam Leach Pvt CL
Samuel: b 1738 d 1832 m Rebekah Wilder Pvt MA
Samuel: b 1-18-1733 d 5-15-1820 m Abigail Merrell Pvt NH
Silas: b 5-26-1764 d 2-23-1848 m Mary Hare Tms CT W★
Silas: b 5-24-1747 d 6-3-1836 m Deliverance Fisk Pvt MA
Simeon: b 3-1-1753 d 10-22-1825 m Jane Cole Lt NJ
Stephen: b 12-20-1735 d 6-27-1810 m Nancy Dodge Pvt MA
Thomas: b *c*. 1805 m Polly Peck Pvt CT
Thomas: b *c*. 1740 d *p*. 1800 m — PS MD
Thomas: b 12-21-1753 d 3-3-1821 m Nancy Ann Mackey PS DE
Thomas: b 8-14-1741 d 6-14-1813 m (1)Mary Thomas (2)Lois Thayer Sgt MA
Timothy: b 1736 d 1776 m (1)Sarah Andrews (2)Mary Coe Pvt CT
Wm., Sr.: b 12-12-1734 d 10- -1790 m Sarah Webster PS NJ
Wm., Jr.: b 8-12-1754 d 1802 m Sarah Frazer Pvt NJ
Wm.: b 1-25-1759 d 11-2-1854 m Sarah Stuart Pvt NC ★
Wm.: b 2-2-1747 d 12-6-1823 m Elizabeth Cornwallis Capt PA ★
Wm., Sr.: b 2-22-1732 d 1824 m Rachel Coates Sol VT

MARSHALL, (includes MARCHEL)

Aaron: b 7-7-1758 d 7-18-1839 m Elizabeth Davis Pvt DE ★
Aaron: b 1740 d 1826 m Sarah Snowden PS Pvt PA
Abel: b 9-9-1764 d 1-22-1855 m Polly Flint Pvt MA
Abner: b 2-9-1727 d *p*. 12-25-1801 m (1)Hannah Marshall (2)Lydia — PS CT
Abraham: b 1748 d 4-15-1819 m Ann Waller Chp GA
Abraham: b 2-12-1730 d 11-30-1811 m Susannah Calvert Pvt NY
Abraham: b 9-25-1747 d 3-17-1829 m Alice Pennock Capt PA
Alexander: b *c*. 1747 d *p*. 5-26-1807 m Ann Walthall 2Lt VA
Amon: b 1722 d 6-10-1891 m Jane Smith PS NY
Andrew: b 1745 d 5-19-1811 m Elizabeth Seymour Pvt CT
Archibald: b 1755 d 5-24-1832 m Anne Elder PS PA
Archibald: b 3-29-1762 d 11- -1835 m Margaret Wilson Pvt PA
Benjamin: b 1744 d 1785 m Margaret Harris Lt PA
Benjamin: b 1-22-1759 d 8- -1841 m Sarah Pulliam Sgt VA ★
Benjamin: b 1755 d 3-29-1834 m Elizabeth — Pvt VA W★
Benjamin: b 1-22-1759 d *p*. 1832 m Rebecca Jeffress Sol VA
Caleb: b 5-25-1761 d *p*. 1807 m Mary — Pvt PA
Christopher: b 3-20-1743 d 10-23-1804 m Rachel Harris Capt MA
Christopher Sr.: b 11-16-1709 d 5-4-1797 m Sarah Thompson PS PA
Christopher, Jr.: b 1740 d 1806 m Ann Eddy Pvt PA
Conrad: b 1729/30 d 9-7-1813 m Anne Barbara PS NJ
Daniel: b 8-24-1706 d 11-2-1784 m (1)Hannah Drake (2)Martha Stearns Chp CA
David: b 10-21-1728 d 3-31-1776 m Naomi Griswold Lt CT
David: b 12-13-1750 d 11-20-1828 m Lucy Mason Pvt MA
David: b 10-12-1752 d 9-3-1826 m Margaret Dover Lt PA ★
David: b 2-23-1754 d 4-24-1821 m Sarah Graham Lt PA
David: b 1-21-1749 d 9-4-1833 m Elizabeth Gloninger PS PA
Dempsey: b *c*. 1740 d *a*. 3-26-1792 m Charlotte 2Lt VA
Dietrich: b 5- -1738 d 5-25-1814 m Julianna Hart Pvt PA
Dixon: b 7-1-1754 d 8-22-1824 m Lucy Nichols 2Lt NC ★
Ebenezer: b 9-18-1721 d 11-15-1802 m — PS MA
Edward: b 1710 d 11-7-1789 m (1)Elizabeth Oberfeldt (2)Elizabeth Weiser PS PA
Eliakim: b 10-28-1754 d 12-26-1831 m Anne Palmer Pvt CT
Elihu: b 1-18-1750 d 4-18-1806 m Susanna Brown BgdMaj NY
Elisha: b 9-16-1763 d 1791 m Anna Carter Pvt CT
Francis: b 8-11-1750 d 1-1-1836 m (1)Phebe Hatcher (2)Sarah Jacobs Pvt VA ★
Gideon: b 1751 d 1807 m Abigail Randall Cpl NH
Gilbert: b 1750 d 1795 m Sarah Brown Cpl CT
Gilbert: b *c*. 1715 d 4-1-1801 m Martha Rowan PS VA
Henry: b 1747 d 1798 m Mary Weir Pvt NH
Humphrey: b 1756 d 7-1-1841 m Mary Marshall Capt VA
Ichabod: b 8- -1741 d 11- -1792 m Lydia Stearns Sgt VT
Isaac: b *c*. 1725 d *c*. 1796 m Amy Baremore Cpl CT
Isaac: b 3-1-1737 d 5-14-1813 m Abigail Brown Lt MA
Isaac: b 12-22-1759 d 11-15-1840 m (1)Elizabeth Trull (2)Mehitable Tenney Pvt MA ★
Isaac: b 1746 d 1804 m Lydia Hawley Sgt CT
Jacob: b 1755 d *p*. 1795 m Mary Morse 2Lt MA
James: b 1729 d 1805 m Elizabeth — 1Lt PA
James: b 1-13-1725 d *p*. 1790 m Sarah Waite Pvt PA
James: b 1745 d 2-20-1829 m Lydia Carson Pvt PA
James: b *c*. 1750 d *p*. 8-2-1811 m (2)Charity — Capt SC
James: b 1735 d 4-15-1818 m (1)Anne (Harrison) Williams (2)Amy (Robinson) Robertson Capt VA
James: b — d 1788 m Euphan — Capt VA
James Markham: b 3-12-1764 d 4-26-1846 m (1)Hester Morris (2)Elizabeth Hurst Lt VA ★
Jenifer: b *c*. 1742 d 4-1-1792 m Euphemia — SeaCap VA
Jeremiah: b 1729 d 6-5-1816 m Rebecca Daniels Pvt CT
Joel: b 5-24-1744 d 8-3-1829 m Anne Mooers Pvt MA
John: b 8-30-1764 d 3-20-1863 m Lydia Brown Pvt CT
John: b 1726 d 1802 m — — Maj MD
John: b 1756 d 1-1-1820 m Sarah March Pvt Mar MA ★
John Jr.: b 8-29-1747 d *p*. 1785 m Elizabeth Hayward Pvt MA
John: b 11-6-1716 d 5-30-1776 m Martha Horton PS NH
John: b 1725 d 10-9-1811 m Susannah Cole Pvt NJ

John: b 4-26-1762 d 3-26-1808 m (1)Rebecca Hart (2)Winifred Hoff Pvt NJ
John: b 11-26-1744 d 1807 m Mary Bragg Sol CS NC
John: b *c*. 1752 d 1782 m Tabitha — PS NC
John: b 1746 d 9-27-1821 m Mary Park — Capt PA
John: b *c*. 1755 d *c*. 1797 m Ann Catherine Williams Capt PA
John: b 1749 d *p*. 1818 m Hannah Jane Baldwin Capt PA
John: b 1736 d *a*. 11-16-1818 m — Pvt PA
John: b 1750 d 11-24-1824 m Jane Scott Pvt PA
John: b 1730 d *p*. 12-19-1801 m — PS CS
John: b 9-24-1755 d 7-6-1835 m Mary Willis Ambler Capt PS VA
John: b *c*. 1735 d 1786 m Margaret Carter Capt VA
John: b 1-24-1756 d 8-10-1810 m Mary Herald Capt VA
John: b *c*. 1720 d 1785 m — PS VA
Jonathan: b 12-23-1762 d 5-1-1830 m Phebe Ashley Sgt VT
Joseph: b 1734 d 1-27-1805 m (1)Sarah Frost (2)Susanna Walker Pvt NH
Joseph: b 8-12-1759 d 6-13-1844 m Louisa Edwards Pvt RI ★
Joshua: b 10-6-1756 d 10-21-1827 m Esther Mores Pvt MA
Josiah: b 1751 d 1-9-1814 m Keziah — Pvt MA
Levi: b 11-3-1754 d 5-2-1807 m Sarah Wynne Sol GA
Matthew: b 1748 d 4- -1794 m Rhoda — Lt GA
Michael: b 1755 d 8-2-1841 m Mary Thompson Ens PA
Moses: b 11-30-1760 d 6-1-1830 m Hannah Choate Pvt MA W★
Moses: b 11-20-1758 d 10-1-1813 m Alice Pennock Dr PA
Nathaniel: b 7-17-1755 d 1839 m (1)Hannah Marsh (2)Martha Kemp (3)Rhoda Kemp Pvt MA ★
Nehemiah Jr.: b 1755 d *p*. 1790 m Abigail Thorne Sol NY
Obed: b 1-30-1744 d 8-8-1817 m Susanna — CS MA
Oliver: b 10-31-1756 d 10-27-1783 m Charlotte Woodford Pvt CT
Peter: b 1759 d 7-25-1806 m Rachel Overfield Pvt NJ
Richard: b 175- d 1-18-1816 m Margaret Hardy Pvt PS MD
Richard: b 2-14-1751 d 1-7-1837 m Esther Pierce Pvt PS NH
Richard: b 1730 d 1798 m Mary Boswell Sgt VA
Richard: b 1753 d 1842 m Keziah Sherer Pvt Cav VA ★
Robert: b *c*. 1745 d 5-3-1790 m Jane — Sol SC
Robert: b 1745 d 1828 m Elinor Hayes Pvt PA
Robert: b 1760 d 6-16-1832 m (2)Elizabeth Glass Pvt PA
Samuel Jr.: b 3-27-1744 d 8-13-1800 m Sabra Mills Pvt CT
Samuel: b 10-2-1742 d 6-6-1812 m Sarah French Lt MA
Samuel Sr.: b 5-10-1732 d *p*. 1815 m Esther Frost Pvt PS MA
Samuel: b 1750 d 1816 m Nancy Haylesrigg Pvt PA
Samuel: b 1745 d 1810 m Cassandra Alfriend Capt VA
Samuel: b 1745 d 2-15-1835 m — Pvt VA
Sylvanus: b 5-4-1746 d 9-28-1833 m — Capt CT
Thomas: b 8-24-1738 d 5-5-1810 m Desire Tuttle Pvt CT
Thomas: b 6-29-1759 d 2-8-1829 m (1)— Edgerton (2)Freelove Edgerton Pvt CT ★
Thomas: b 5-17-1744 d 2- -1830 m Rebecca Ackley PS CT
Thomas: b *a*. 1747 d *p*. 1783 m Elizabeth Stradling Pvt PA
Thomas: b 4-2-1730 d 6-22-1802 m Mary Randolph Keith Col VA
Thomas Jr.: b 10-27-1761 d 3-19-1817 m (1)Susanna Adams (2)Frances Maitland Kennan Capt VA
Thomas: b *c*. 1752 d *p*. 1800 m Sallie Johnston Pvt VA
Thomas Hanson: b 4-9-1731 d 3-8-1801 m Rebecca Dent Capt PS MD
Wm.: b 3- -1735 d 1793 m Susan Whitley PS MD
Wm.: b 1739 d 8-3-1813 m (1)Mrs. Mary Snow (2)Elizabeth Dorrell Pvt MA
Wm.: b 5-5-1724 d 8-28-1803 m Rebecca Dixon PS NC
Wm.: b *c*. 1765/6 d 8-29-1830 m Sara Lanier Pvt NC
Wm.: b *c*. 1722 d *p*. 11-19-1792 m Elizabeth Armstrong Pvt PA
Wm.: b *c*. 1740 d *p*. 6-13-1794 m Jean — PS Pvt PA
Wm.: b 9-9-1748 d 8-11-1828 m Mary Fell Pvt PA
Wm.: b *c*. 1740 d *c*. 1818 m Mary Speers Pvt PA
Wm.: b 1750 d 1-10-1822 m Mary Evans PS PA
Wm.: b 12-17-1757 d 11-5-1810 m Lucy Ann Goode Col VA
Wm.: b 1730 d 1800 m Ann McLeod Capt VA
Wm.: b *c*. 1755 d 1819 m Rebecca — PS VA
Wm.: b 2-2-1756 d 7-21-1830 m Eleanor Ralston Sol VA
Wm.: b 1735 d 1809 m Mary Ann Pickett Sol VA
Zaccheus: b 2-5-1746 d 7-7-1830 m (1)Anna Totten (2)Susannah Dean 3)Jane Quimbley Pvt NY
Zaacheus: b *a*. 1760 d *p*. 1812 m Abigail Carpenter 1Lt NY

MARSTELLER, (includes MOSTOLLER)

Frederick: b 2-29-1735 d 12-2-1815 m Catherine Smith Pvt PA
George Sr.: b 5-14-1731 d *p*. 12-29-1785 m Margaret — PS PA
John George: b 5-24-1736 d 1799 m Elizabeth Custer Pvt PA
Philip: b 1-4-1741 d 1803 m Magdalena Rice PS LCol PA
Valentine: b 12-26-1738 d *p*. 8-4-1804 m Magdalena Hennrick Pvt PS PA

MARSTERS,

Andrew: b 3-7-1735 d 12- -1780 m Elizabeth Allen Haskell Capt MA

MARSTON,

Brackett: b 1747 d *a*. 10- -1781 m Mary Gerrish PS MA ME
David: b 9-24-1757 d 1-21-1851 m Mary Wadleigh Pvt MA ★
David Sr.: b 12-31-1716 d 2-23-1799 m Abigail Garland PS CS NH
David Jr.: b 2-5-1756 d 1-30-1835 m Mary Page Pvt NH ★
Ephraim: b 1-5-1727 d 8-26-1810 m Ruth Batchelder PS Pvt NH

MARSTON, contd.

Jeremiah Jr.: b 2-22-1745 d 8-10-1834 m (1)Hannah Towle (2)Lydia Cumings (3)Abigail (Marston) Chase Pvt PS NH
Jeremiah: b 1-2-1753 d *p.* 1798 m Hannah Lamprey Pvt NH
John: b 3-17/27-1756 d 12-13-1846 m Anna Randall Lt MA
John: b 2-26-1720 d 8-26-1786 m (1)Hannah Welland (2)Mrs. Elizabeth Blake (3)Elizabeth Greenwood PS MA
John: b 7-8-1820 d 4-18-1800 m — Pvt MA
John: b 1748 d 11-20-1793 m Mary Hilton Sgt NH
John: b 10-18-1756 d 1824 m Elizabeth Davis Pvt NH
Joseph: b 12-22-1745 d 1831 m (1)Hannah Brown (2)Jemima Jones Pvt NH
Levi: b 7-22-1763 d 1-11-1852 m Olive Lord Pvt MA
Levi: b 3-14-1753 d 11-8-1834 m Abigail Fogg Pvt NH
Nathaniel: b 1760 d 9-2-1823 m Jane Potter Pvt NH ★
Nathaniel: b 1-2-1747 d *p.* 1782 m Ruth Lunt PS NH
Paul Smith: b 10-24-1738 d 12-12-1823 m (1)Catherine Elkins (2)Annie Trow Pvt Cpl NH
Reuben Sr.: b 10-2-1722 d *p.* 1790 m Mary Batchelder PS NH
Samuel: b 12-23-1754 d 11-10-1797 m Rhoda Melcher Ens NH ★
Samuel: b 10-7-1760 d 11-6-1828 m Sarah Hall Pvt NH
Samuel: b 1-2-1741 d *p.* 1781 m Rhoda Edgerly PS NH
Samuel: b 10-19-1743 d 2-9-1825 m Mary Moulton PS NH
Simon: b 2-3-1737 d 12- -1810 m Hannah Wedgewood Capt NH
Theodore: b 28-1755 d 5-25-1830 m Joanna Ladd Pvt NH
Thomas: b 11-10-1756 d 5-17-1847 m Hannah Knowles Pvt PS NH

MARTENIS,
Christopher Sr.: b 2-19-1745 d 4-19-1822 m Ann — Pvt NJ

MARTIN, (includes MARTAIN)

Aaron: b 10-7-1762 d 3-7-1810 m Mercy Horton Pvt MA
Aaron: b 8-14-1763 d 2-18-1842 m Mary Eggleston Pvt NY
Aaron: b 7-30-1742 d 3-12-1819 m Eunice Flint Pvt VT
Abraham: b 1730 d 1805 m Charity — Pvt NC
Adam: b 8-27-1739 d 7-26-1818 m Abigail Cheney Capt MA
Adam: b 9-28-1755 d 4-14-1835 m Mary McMillin Sol VA
Alexander: b 4-24-1762 d 12-8-1843 m (1)Lovice Prescott (2)Mary Darling Slr NJ ★
Alexander: b 3-27-1737 d 9-18-1816 m Catherine Henry Pvt PA
Alexander: b 1760 d 9- -1816 m Jane Black Mil VA
Amasa: b 12-13-1760 d 2-18-1849 m Sarah Dunham Pvt NY CT ★
Amos: b 10-1-1728 d 4-7-1800 m Prudence Tuttle PS CT
Amos: b 1762 d 12-9-1840 m — Pvt NH ★
Andrew: b *c.* 11/10-6-1726 d 5-8-1805 m Eunice Mitchell Capt CT
Anthony: b 4-21-1760 d 2-14-1840 m Susanna Allen Pvt RI
Anthony: b 9-26-1737 d 6-19-1805 m Sarah Holman Pvt VA
Arnold: b 2-26-1738 d *p.* 1789 m Sarah (Griste) Mugford Gnr MA
Ashbel: bpt 11-27-1760 d 12-7-1833 m (2)Lydia Chamberlain (3)Mary Roat Martin Pvt CT ★
Azariah: b *c.* 1748 d 12-6-1822 m Sarah Dunn QM NY
Ben: b 11-30-1757 d 12-26-1852 m (2)Mrs Melissa Highnot Sol NC
Benjamin: b 7-5-1734 d 6-23-1814 m Sarah Kingsley Pvt MA
Benjamin: b — d 1801 m Priscilla Martin MM NJ
Benjamin: b 1720 d *p.* 4-30-1791 m Luce Perry Pvt RI
Benjamin: b 4-8-1746 d 10-31-1821 m Diana Harrison Ens VA
Benjamin: b 7-8-1758 d 9-20-1838 m Nancy Kemper Sgt VA
Charles: b 3-7-1759 d 11-9-1838 m Mary Galer Pvt Pvtr CT W★
Charles: b 8-14-1753 d 10-24-1818 m Catharine — SgtMaj PA
Charles: b — d *p.* 11-4-1798 m (1)Elizabeth Buress (2)Mary Bell Col PS CS VA
Charles: b 1745 d 1808 m Patsy Moon Pvt VA
Christian Jr.: b 1744 d 7- -1806 m Mary Barr Sol PA
Christian: b 1760 d *p.* 1820 m Mrs Barbara Prillaman Snidow Pvt VA
Christian Frederick: b 12-22-1727 d 6-13-1812 m (1)Rosina Barbara Schertlin (2)Maria Miller Dr PA
Comfort: b 1752 d 1826 m Susannah Cummings Pvt MA
Cyrus: b 10-21-1763 d 9-26-1831 m Charlotte Bridgham Pvt MA
Daniel Jr.: b 9-23-1737 d 9-11-1796 m Rebecca Horton Lt MA
Daniel: b *c.* 1751 d10-3-1850 m (1)Elizabeth Wynne (2)Sarah Painter (3)Eve Everly Pvt NJ ★
David: b 1760 d 2-13-1808 m Huldah Freeman Pvt NJ
David: b 3-18-1751 d 1832 m Catherine Becker PS NY
David: b *c.* 1730 d *a.* 8- -1779 m Mary — PS NC
David: b — d 2-24-1812 m Margaret Aiken Pvt SC W★
David: b 3-23-1743 d 4-23-1819 m Susanna Groff Pvt PA
David: b 11-22-1751 d 1784 m Ann Stauffer Pvt PA
David: b 1-13-1737 d 12-31-1777 m Anne Ellison Pvt VA
Ebenezer: b 1741 d 1-10-1800 m Prudence Merritt Pvt Gnr MA
Enenezer: b 4-12-1761 d 11-20-1841 m Bethany Mason Pvt MA
Edmund: b 3-6-1745 d 11-28-1811 m (1)Hannah — (2)Susanna (Fristoe) Dulin Pvt NJ
Edward: b 12-7-1746 d 3-27-1782 m Deborah Brown Lt MA
Edward: b 1-28-1745 d *p.* 1812 m Ruth Rounds Pvt MA
Edward: b 10-15-1759 d 12-11-1831 m Susanna Hammons Sgt NH ★
Edward: b 10-11-1758 d 12-21-1813 m (1)Margaret Olive McClure (2)Mary Jane Aiken Capt SC W★
Eleazer: b 2-10-1748 d 4-5-1828 m Mehitable Peters Cpl NH W★
Elijah: b 1751 d 1819 m Mary Van Der Burg Pvt SC
Elizabeth Marshall: b 3-1-1726 d *p.* 5-2-1797 m (1)John Smith Jr (2)Abraham Martin PS SC

Ephraim: b 2-2-1745 d 8-8-1833 m (1)Mary Burnham (2)Jerusha — Sgt CT
Ephraim: b 5-9-1758 d 10-30-1830 m Rebecca Salisbury Drm MA
Ephraim Sr.: b 12- -1733 d 2-28-1806 m Katherine — Col NJ
Ephraim Jr.: b 1760 d 1840 m Mercy Alward Sgt NJ
George: b 1743 d 3-27-1827 m Dorothy Brown Pvt CT ★
George(3): b 11-16-1753 d 10-20-1830 m Sarah Simmons MM CT
George: b *c.* 1760 d *a.* 1-7-1834 m Elizabeth Nicholls Sol MD
George: b 1748 d 1822 m Mary Robinson PS NH
George: b 6-4-1754 d 1821 m Alice Freeman Capt SC
George: b 1760 d 1821 m Phoebe — Pvt VA
George: b 3-6-1765 d 11-19-1827 m Elizabeth Hoard PS VA
Gideon: b *c.* 1732 d 1837 m (2)Innis Franky (3)Mary Houseright (4)Sophia Stephenson Pvt VA ★
Gotlop: b 1746 d 11-2-1832 m Ann Catharine Shoemaker 1Lt NY
Hendrick: b 1-30-1715 d *p.* 4-29-1786 m Elizabeth Emmerick PS NY
Henry: b 7-1-1760 d *p.* 4-15-1818 m Marie Salome Fetterman PS PA
Hezekiah Jr.: b 3-22-1748 d 11-16-1834 m Mary Pierce Sgt MA
Hudson: b 7-3-1752 d 3-28-1830 m Jane W. Lewis Lt VA W★
Hugh: b 1738 d 1823 m Jane Knox Capt PA
Hugh: b *a.* 1744 d 3-25-1784 m Margaret Grant Pvt PA
Hugh: b *a.* 1748 d *p.* 1823 m Mary Mc Donald Pvt VA
Hugh: b 1760 d 1798 m Mary Stewart Pvt VA
Isaac: b 3-15-1756 d 1-27-1838 m Mehitable Peck Sgt MA ★
Isaac: b 1736 d *c.* 1790 m (2)Phoebe (Webb) Harland Pvt NJ
Isaac: b *c.* 1740 d 1823 m Sebiah Levering Pvt PA
Isaac Sr.: b *c.* 1750 d 3- -1806 m Margart — Pvt PA
Jacob: b 1759-61 d 6-24-1837-9 m Magalena — Pvt MD
Jacob: apt 4-20-1740 d *p.* 1790 m (1)Lucy Shotswell (2)Mary Brewer NCapt MA
Jacob: b 9-13-1742 d 5-1-1830 m Elizabeth Dunham Capt NJ
Jacob: b 2- -1749 d 10-19-1828 m Catherine Wilson Pvt PA
Jacob: b *c.* 1760 d *p.* 2-22-1825 m Mary Bagby Sol VA
James: b 10-14-1749 d *p.* 1788 m Obedience Bugg Col GA
James: b 1750 d 10-26-1838 m Elizabeth — Sol MD
James: b 1-7-1745 d 2-12-1781 m Elizabeth St. Clair Ens NH
James: b 2-15-1750 d 2-13-1829 m Ann Wright Pvt NJ
James: b 3-21-1742 d 10-31-1834 m (1)Ruth Rogers (2)Mrs. Martha (Loftin) Jones Col NC ★
James: b 9-6-1758 d 7-25-1825 m Mary Fitz Randolph Pvt NJ
James: b 1738 d 1- -1788 m Elizabeth — Col NC
James: b *a.* 1740 d 5-12-1809 m Sarah Thomas Capt PA
Janes: b 7-12-1749 d 2-3-1807 m Judith Reed Ens RI
James: b 1749 d 9-22-1797 m (1)Sarah Caldwell (2)Sarah (Brown) Bennoit Dr SC
James: b *c.* 1758 d 7-7-1811 m (1)Nancy McKenzie (2)Martha Nutt Sol SC
James: b 1745 d *p.* 5-30-1811 m — Ens VA
James: b 8- -1758 d 5-11-1848 m Judah Young Pvt VA ★
James: b *c.* 1759 d *c.* 1836 m Nancy Weisiger Pvt VA
Jesse: b 1751 d 11-3-1832 m Naomi Hopkins Pvt MA NH ★
Jirah: b 1762 d 2-17-1843 m Hannah Cross Pvt MA ★
Joel: b 6-23-1745 d *a.* 2-23-1789 m Lucy — Pvt CT
John: b 1760 d *p.* 1798 m Nancy Willis Pvt DE
John: b 1753 d 7- -1808 m Elizabeth Allen Sol GA
John: b 1759 d *p.* 1826 m Drusilla Williams Pvt SC GA ★
John: b 2- -1756 d 2-27-1825 m Barbara Ann Funfrock Pvt MD ★
John: b 10-30-1743-5 d *a.* 1811 m Margaret Richardson MM Pvt MA
John: b 1760 d 2-21-1844 m Rachel Cobb Cpl MA W★
John: b *c.* 1750 d — m Lydia McKenney Drm MA
John: b 1759 d 1846 m Rebecca Adams Pvt NH ★
John: b 1710 d 8-8-1785 m Margery — PS NH
John: b 10-10-1753 d 6-11-1832 m Catherine Munford Pvt NJ
John: b *a.* 1756 d 2-16-1801 m Margaret Roeden Pvt NY
John: b 7-26-1758 d 1823 m Sally Hunt Pvt NY
John: b 1756 d 4-5-1823 m Nancy Shipp Lt NH W★
John: b 8-23-1756 d 6-29-1810 m Elizabeth Green Sol NC
John: b 5-6-1756 d 3-24-1836 m Margaret — Pvt NC
John: b *c.* 1760 d *p.* 1810 m — Lt PA
John: b 1-12-1748 d 5-14-1814 m Sarah Kline Pvt PA
John: b 1737 d 9-20-1777 m Elizabeth Clark Ens PA
John Jr.: b 1-13-1761 d 9-16-1823 m Elizabeth Harrison Pvt PA
John: b 1718 d 12-8-1801 m Mary Reid Capt RI
John: b *c.* 1730 d *p.* 1790 m Isabella — Capt SC
John: b 11-19-1751 d 8-7-1813 m (1)Miss Bugg (2)Elizabeth Terry (3)Mrs. Barksdale Capt SC
John: b 1-20-1766 d 4-13-1827 m Margaret Feris Sol SC
John: b 3-20-1749 d 12-3-1837 m Elizabeth Lewis Maj VA
John: b *c.* 1735 d *p.* 11- -1830 m Rachel Pace 2Lt VA
John: b 7-11-1740 d *a.* 1809 m Ann Barbara Lewis Pvt VA
John Nicholas: b 1720 d 7-27-1795 m Ann Catherine PS SC
Jonathan: b *c.* 1750 d *c.* 1824 m Phebe Varnham PS NH
Joseph: b 5-6-1754 d 8-29-1828 m Abigail Butler Pvt CT ★
Joseph: b 1-14-1764 d 10-10-1845 m Rebecca Girard Pvt PA
Joseph: b 9-18-1740 d 12-18-1808 m (1)Sarah Lucas (2)Susannah Graves LCol VA
Joseph: b 1741 d 9-17-1832 m Mary Sanders Pvt VA
Joseph: b 1755 d 2-14-1832 m Patsy Bailey MM Pvt VA ★
Joseph: b *c.* 1758 d 1835 m Talitha Sol Spy VA
Joshua: b *c.* 1735 d *c.* 1796 m (1)Mary — (2)Martha Battas Capt PS CS NH

Joshua: b 4-18-1760 d 9-7-1797 m Elizabeth Markland Capt VA
Josiah: b 2- -1757 d 9-17-1835 m Mary Mc Clary Lt NC
Kinchen: b 1-6-1762 d 6-14-1841 m Chloe Hough Ens VA ★
Lewis: b 3-27-1762 d 6-23-1852 m Elizabeth Dains 2Sgt PA ★
Louis Daniel: b c. 1745 d 10- -1815 m Sarah Wallace Capt SC
Luther: b 1-20-1752 d 8-10-1799 m Elizabeth Humphreys Ens CT
Luther: b 4-21-1752 d 11-13-1832 m Hannah Brewster Pvt Grd CT ★
Maria Staats: bpt 10-19-1744 d 1833 m Peter Martin PS NY
Marshall: b 2-7-1761 d 9-11-1819 m Mary Isham Key Lt SC
Martin: b c. 1745 d 4-1-1812 m Isabella Graham Pvt SC
Martin: b 1755 d 2-24-1837 m Dicy Hicks Pvt SC
Mathew: b c. 1755 d a. 5-14-1800 m Agnes — Pvt SC
Matt: b 12-26-1763 d 10-16-1846 m Sarah Clay Pvt SC GA VA ★
Matthew: b 1750 d 1835 m — Sol SC
Melatiah: b 3-23-1736 d 9-9-1794 m Phebe Bowen Pvt MA
Merrick: b 3-19-1763 d 4-19-1816 m Rebeckah Jacques Pvt NJ
Moses: b 8-4-1763 d 5-30-1850 m Anna Parker Pvt MA
Moses: b 1746 d 6-14-1792 m Lydia Moore Adj NY
Moses: b 1-12-1755 d 8-29-1837 m Ann Heath Drm NC ★
Mulford: b 1741 d 1-28-1788 m (1)Anna Ludlum (2)Hannah (Trembley) Spinning Pvt NJ
Nathan: b 7-30-1734 d 11-5-1792 m Ellen Bradley Pvt CT
Nathan: b 6-28-1760 d 6-2-1812 m Martha (Holt) Clark Pvt CT
Nathan: b 4-3-1763 d 2-27-1834 m Hannah Boynton Pvt NH W★
Nathaniel: b 8-31-1762 d 6-14-1854 m Phyla Potter Pvt NJ
Nathaniel: b 1- -1723 d 1-15-1806 m Susanna Kent Col PS RI
Nathaniel: b c. 1763 d 1813 m Anna Goodwin Pvt VT W★
Nathaniel Ford: b 11-24-1759 d 9-26-1847 m (1)Jerusha Lincoln (2)Naomi Fitts Drm CT ★
Nicholas: b 1743 d 1808 m Ann G. Oldham Capt MD
Obediah: b c. 1761 d c. 1826 m Winneford Cook Sol NC
Oliver: b 8-23-1762 d 5-8-1829 m (1)Susanna Marsh (2)Ann Richards Pvt NJ
Orson: b c. 1735 d a. 7-24-1786 m Ann Forsee PS VA
Paul: b c. 1750 d 5- -1802 m (2)Rosana Logan Sgt PA
Peter: b 2-22-1759 d 6-23-1820 m Hannah Dean Pvt MA
Peter: b c. 1745 d p. 1790 m — Lt NY
Peter: b c. 1750 d 9-11-1777 m Sarah Campbell 2Lt PA
Peter: b 1739 d a. 11-2-1812 m Cartarina — PS PA
Peter: b 2-8-1741 d 3-4-1807 m Sarah Redding Pvt PS VA
Philip: b 6-11-1756 d 5-6-1821 m Mary Granger BGen MA RI PA
Pleasant: b 12-21-1755 d 10-16-1836 m Rebecca Joplin Lt VA ★
Ralph: b a. 1760 d 2- -1836 m Anna Shoemaker Pvt PA
Reuben: b 6-22-1765 d 2-14-1836 m Sally Minor Sol CT
Reuben: b 1- -1746 d 9-30-1838 m Sallie Williams Pvt NH ★
Reuben: b c. 1748 d c. 1851 m Mary Van Buren Pvt NJ ★
Richard: b 2-15-1766 d 10-17-1824 m Hannah Faxon Pvt NH
Richard: b 1-29-1755 d 12-15-1841 m Frances Turner Pvt NC ★
Richard: b 1760 d 6-16-1836 m Sophie Reece 1Lt PA ★
Robert: b 9-6-1754 d c. 1832 m Eleanor Jones Cpl MD
Robert: b 1- -1755 d 11-30-1836 m Nancy Phebus Pvt MD ★
Robert: b 11-22-1756 d 6-9-1820 m Hannah — Slr PA
Robert: b 1-20-1759 d 12-24-1839 m Abigail McCriss Pvt NH
Robert: b 1759 d 1823 m Betsey — Cpl NC
Robert: b 4-10-1755 d 7-20-1840 m — Thompson Sol NC ★
Robert: b 1747 d c. 1800 m Nancy Lindsey Sgt SC
Robert: b 1729 d 12-29-1811 m (1)Rebecca (2)Mary — Pvt SC
Robert: b 1720 d 1800 m Mary Bloomfield CS PS PA
Roger: b — d p. 9-24-1800 m (2)Mrs. Joanna (Taylor) Pvt NC
Salathiel: b — d 5-6-1827 m Mary Cook Capt NC W★
Samuel: b 1732 d 11-18-1836 m Margaret Mc Curdy Capt NC ★
Samuel: b 12-12-1747 d 8-15-1812 m Mary Dickey Cpl NH
Samuel: b 1722 d 10-5-1795 m Nancy Ankrim Pvt PA
Samuel: b 1725 d 1-20-1804 m (1)— McNeary (2)Jean Allison Pvt PA
Samuel: b 1744 d 9-28-1828 m Margaret — Pvt PA
Samuel: b 1750 d 1825 m (1)Isabella Stockman (2)Jane Guthrie Pvt PA
Samuel: b 9-24-1749 d 6-29-1826 m Susannah Wickliffe Pvt VA
Seth: b 8-12-1745 d 7-15-1817 m Mary Horton Lt NH
Silvanus: b 7-1-1727 d 8-17-1800 m Martha Wheeler CS PS Capt MA
Silvanus Jr.: b 3-19-1748 d 11-25-1818 m Amey Brown Lt CT
Simeon: b 4-18-1755 d 8-2-1816 m Esther Mason Sgt MA
Simeon: b 10-20-1754 d 9-30-1819 m Abigail Durfee Capt MA
Solomon: b 1752 d 7-10-1845 m Lydia — Lt NY ★
Stephen: b 1-26-1761 d 12-19-1834 m Bethia Barrows Pvt CT ★
Thomas: b 11-16-1752 d 8-5-1847 m Hephzibah Willard Pvt CT ★
Thomas: b 11-15-1759 d 6-1-1830 m Hannah Hicks Pvt MA
Thomas: bpt 10-8-1721 d p. 9-18-1780 m Sarah Goodwin Mrnr MA
Thomas: b 11-20-1752 d 1842 m Charita Hurd 2Sgt NY ★
Thomas: b 5-11-1756 d 5-5-1835 m Sabra — Pvt Sct NC ★
Thomas: b c. 1755 d p. 1785 m Susanna — Ens PA
Thomas: b c. 1758 d p. 1795 m — Rainey Pvt PA
Thomas: b 1759 d 11-16-1828/9 m Mary Montgomery Pvt PA W★
Thomas: b c. 1751 d 11-15-1811 m Mary O'Brien Pvt PA
Thomas: b 1752 d 1818 m Susan Washington Ledbetter Capt VA
Thomas: b 1714 d a. 12- -1792 m (1)Ann Moorman (2)Miss Glover (3)Mary Suddarth Capt VA
Thomas: b c. 1750 d c. 1801 m Susannah Walker Pvt VA
Thomas Newbold: b 11-1-1761 d 10-28-1822 m Lydia Gates Pvt Fif MA

Wait: b 1752 d 1808/9 m Lydia Williams Sgt MA
Wheeler: b 2-8-1765 d 4-7-1844 m (1)Hannah Blinn (2)Lucena Wright Pvt CT
Wm.: b 4-13-1751 d 11-27-1816 m Anna Slate Pvt CT
Wm.: b c. 1732 d c. 1791 m Mary Burns 2Lt PS MA
Wm.: b 7-7-1753 d 5-30-1825 m Olive Averell Pvt MA NH ★
Wm.: b 1744 d 1842 m Lois Varbeck 2Lt NH
Wm.: b 12-28-1757 d 8-6-1824 m Margaret Brown Pvt NJ W★
Wm.: b 10-10-1763 d 8-21-1851 m (1)Susan Stout (2)Jane Powers PS NJ
Wm.: b 1745 d p. 1823 m Marybelle Coventry Pvt NY
Wm.: b c. 1749 d p. 1838 m (2)Elinor Doneley Pvt PA
Wm. Sr.: b 3- -1718 d 1-16-1780 m Margaret — Pvt PA
Wm. Jr.: b 12-15-1754 d 4-4-1820 m Hannah Chapman Pvt PA
Wm.: b 9-26-1745 d 9-15-1780 m Grace Waring Capt SC GA
Wm.: b 5-16-1729 d 1-13-1807 m (1)Mary — (2)Jenny Cherry (3)Susanna Boggs PS SC
Wm.: b 1743 d 1822 m Martha Martin Pvt VA
Wm.: b c. 1750 d c. 1792 m Hannah Mitchell Sol VA
Wm.: b 3-8-1762 d 4-13-1836 m Letitia Mc Clanahan Pvt VA ★
Wm.: b 11-26-1765 d 11-4-1846 m Frankie Ferress Pvt VA
Wm.: b 5-24-1735 d 1-19-1824 m Jane Holman Sol VA
Wm.: b c. 1725 d p. 1-17-1793 m Ursley — PS VA
Wm.: b c. 1750 d p. 1815 m Nancy — PS VA
Wm. Peters: b 1742 d 1809 m Rachael Dalton Capt VA

MARTINDALE,

Gershom Sr.: b 1727/8 d 12- -1775 m Bathsheba Nash PS MA
Gershom Jr.: b 6-15-1760 d p. 1797 m Ruth Gray Pvt MA
James: b 1754 d 7-7-1840 m (1)Miss Bishop (2)Margaret Alexander (3)Mary Gilmour Lt SC ★
Samuel: b — d p. 1801 m Mary — Pvt MD
Uriah: b 8-15-1758 d 6-2-1842 m Cloe Hitchcock Pvt MA
Wm. Jr.: b 3-8-1753 d 1-24-1854 m Martha Bishop Pvt SC
Zadock: b 1728 d 12-1-1797 m Sybil Shipman Sol MA

MARTINE,

John: b 1751 d 5-1-1817 m Sarah Allaire Sol NY
Samuel: b 5-15-1753 d 3-1-1814 m Auly Archer Pvt NY

MARTLING,

Abraham: b 1761 d p. 1791 m Fannie Knickerbocker Pvt NY ★
Abraham: b 4-21-1719 d 6-16-1786 m Jennet Ackerman Pvt NY
Daniel: b 8- -1737 d 6-14-1788 m Mary Van Wart Capt NY
Deliverance: b 12-17-1754 d p. 1790 m Katrina Van Wart Pvt NY
Isaac: b 12-13-1741 d 5-27-1779 m Elizabeth — Sgt NY

MARVEL,

Stephen: b 8-4-1737 d 3-4-1806 m Ann Le Moyne Pvt MA

MARVIN,

Barnabas: b 12-25-1739 d 1-19-1810 m (1)Molly Adams (2)Mabel Tuttle Pvt CT
Benjamin: b 11-17-1762 d 5-7-1754 m (1)Hannah Hanford (2)Sarah Hoyt (3)Mrs Urania Parmelia (Miner) Hall Pvt NY CT ★
Benjamin: b 9-30-1737 d 6-26-1822 m Mehitable Marvin Capt NY ★
Brush: b 10-19-1741 d p. 1785 m Abigail Squier Pvt CT
Dan: b 2-12-1731 d 12-30-1776 m Mrs. Mehitable Selden CS Capt CT
Daniel: b c. 1735/6 d 1780 m Abigail Grumman Pvt CT
David: b 12-2-1764 d 6-19-1841 m (1)Sylvia Everett (2)Deborah Baldwin Pvt CT
David: b 4-13-1759 d 1840 m (1)Eunice Hayden (2)Abigail Fitch (3)Mrs Crowley (4)Mrs Jones Pvt PA
Ebenezer: b 4-17-1740 d 11-1820 m Sarah Minerva Adams Capt Dr VT
Elihu: b 12- -1752 d 9-13-1798 m Elizabeth Rogers Adj Bgd Maj CT
Elihu: b 10-10-1719 d 8-24-1803 m Abigail Yelverton LCol PS NY
Elisha: b 3-8-1717/8 d 12-31-1801 m Catharine Mather PS CT
Ephraim: b 12-26-1745 d 7-27-1793 m Abigail — Adj PS NY
Ezra: b 7-15-1744 d 12-26-1811 m Susannah Peck CS MA
Giles: b 12-23-1751 d 11-5-1801 m Lucy Barron Pvt NH
Ichabod: b 12-15-1744 d 1-21-1792 m Martha Kellogg Pvt CT
Isaiah: b c. 1760 d a. 1816 m Sarah Keeler Pvt CT
John: b 1-30-1726 d 12-24-1792 m Sarah Brooker PS CS NH
John: b 4-8-1757 d 6-23-1809 m Fanny Woodhull Pvt NY
John Case: b 3-24-1765 d 4-12-1834 m Clarissa Case Smn CT ★
Joseph: b 2-14-1755 d 11-18-1839 m Phoebe Sterling Pvt CT
Joseph: b c. 1754/5 d 1790 m Anna Anderson SrgnMte CL
Matthew: b 2-2-1742 d 8-22-1806 m Elizabeth Deming Lt CT
Matthew: b 6-7-1754 d 9-22-1846 m Mary Weed Sgt CT
Matthew: b 4-27-1760 d 1829 m (1)Girthrude Carnwright (2)Mary Cole Pvt NY
Moses: b 4-17-1745 d p. 1802 m Zilpah (Pratt) Gillete PS CT
Nathan: b 2-7-1753 d 2-21-1805 m (1)Grace Deming (2)Rebecca — Pvt MA ★
Ozias: b 1-29-1737 d 5- -1807 m Sarah Lockwood Pvt Capt CT
Ruth Welch: b 12-19-1739 d 5-12-1783 m Reynold Marvin PS CT
Sampson: b 3-16-1756 d p. 11-13-1797 m Mrs Ruth Gleason Cpl MA
Samuel: b 4-13-1757 d 12-10-1807 m Ruth Custis Pvt CT
Seth: b 2-15-1745 d 8-25-1815 m Mary Little Capt NY

MARVIN, contd.
Seth: b 12-21-1749 d 7-6-1836 m Hannah Gregory Pvt NY
Seth: b 1761 d 7-21-1865 m (1)Mercy Noble (2)Priscilla — Pvt PA
Stephen: b 4-6-1731 d 1798 m Mercy Hoskins Pvt NY
Thomas: b 1-15-1763 d 8-11-1835 m Anna Norton Sol CT
Uriah: b 2-17-1742/3 d 1824 m (1)Sarah Scott (2)Martha Scott Pvt CT
Uriah: b 1742 d 1799 m Phebe Nesbit Pvt NY
Wm.: b 3-24-1740/1 d 3-4-1810 m Susanna Wright Pvt NY

MARYE,
James: b 1731 d 1780 m (1)Sarah Vausx (2)Elizabeth Osborne Grayson PS VA
Peter: b 2-20-1737 d 10-15-1810 m Eleanor Green PS VA

MASCOLL, (or MASKELL)
Daniel: b 10-15-1728 d p. 9-8-1794 m (1)Mary Vaughn (2)Elizabeth Garrison (3)Sarah Woodruff 2Maj CS NJ
Stephen: b a. 1744 d 1-1-1777 m Hannah Dean Cdr MA

MASCRAFT,
Jacob: b 8-13-1723 d 12-17-1806 m (1)Mary Wilson (2)Hannah Austin (3)Mrs. Hannah (Carrol) Crosby PS CT
John: b 6-22-1756 d 9-28-1815 m Molly Wilson Pvt CT

MASE,
Samuel: b 1758 d 3-6-1843 m Phoebe Elston Pvt NJ

MASK,
John Jr.: b a. 1750 d p. 4-24-1813 m — PS NC
Wm.: b c. 1748 d c. 1811 m Ann Smith 2Lt NC

MASON, (includes MEASON)
Aaron: b 6-1-1748 d 7- -1837 m (1)Lydia Aldrich (2)Chloe Baker Drm MA
Abel: b 4-3-1739 d 4-3-1826 m Ruth Hobbs Capt MA
Abner: b 4-26-1740 d 3-7-1825 m Phoebe Harding Pvt MA
Amos: b 3-22-1749 d 12-2-1806 m Jane Buffum Pvt MA
Benjamin: b 9-4-1739 d p. 1802 m (1)Anne Mason (2)Freelove Barney Cpl MA
Benjamin: b 7-14-1717 d 7-5-1801 m Martha Fairbanks Pvt Fif NH
Benjamin: b c. 1755 d 4-13-1803 m Margaret Lear PS NH
Benjamin: b 1761/2 d 1859 m Sarah Crawford Pvt VA
Brook: b 10-2-1737 d 6-15-1825 m Anna Eddy Pvt MA
Caleb Sr.: b 11-28-1724 d 5- -1808 m Martha Mason Pvt MA
Caleb Jr.: b 2-11-1756 d 7-12-1812 m Mary Ann Gardner Pvt PA
Charles: b 3-24-1760 d 9-30-1810 m Elizabeth Manlove Matr PA
Christopher Jr.: b 10-22-1737 d 7-13-1805 m Anna Chase CS PS MA
Christopher: b c. 1730 d p. 5-26-1773 m Sarah Chappell Sgt VT
Comer: b 3-26-1761 d 4-21-1827 m Elizabeth (Mason) Pvt MA
Daniel: b 3-30-1761 d 9-20-1839 m Ruth St. John Cpl MA ★
Daniel: b 8-15-1757 d 10-9-1817 m Esther Mason Pvt MA
Daniel: b 4-3-1753 d 1-16-1820 m Tabitha Jenkins Drm MA
David: b 3-28-1726 d 9-17-1794 m Hannah Symmes LCol MA
David: b 3-6-1744 d 8-8-1822 m Mary Day 1Lt MA
David: b 1-13-1741 d 5- -1823 m (1)Anna Harvey (2)Rebekah David PS NC
David: b 6-14-1758 d p. 1800 m Sarah Lee Pvt MA
David: b 2-19-1761 d 9-11-1829 m Isabella Teague Sol SC
David: b c. 1733 d 2- -1792 m Mary — Col PS VA
Ebenezer: b 3-27-1749 d 7-25-1824 m Mary Hastings Sgt CT
Ebenezer: b 3-1-1732 d 3-23-1798 m Elizabeth Bright Capt MA
Ebenezer: b 11-12-1732 d 6-3-1816 m (1)Rebecca Winslow (2)Anna Cleaves (3)Mary Collins Pvt MA
Ebenezer: b 6-7-1763 d 1-16-1849 m (1)Susanna Chruchill (2)Mrs. Hannah (Bass) Norris Pvt MA ★
Edward: b 4-25-1757 d 2-12-1840 m Annie Calley SgtMaj NH
Edward: b 6-18-1752 d 12-22-1830 m Sarah Arnold Sgt RI
Edward: b 1748 d p. 1832 m Elizabeth Russell Pvt VA ★
Elias: b a. 1740 d 10-24-1781 m Sarah — Pvt DE
Elijah: b 1-25-1754 d 1841 m (1)Sarah Childs (2)Miss Carat Pvt CT
Elijah Sr.: b 2-12-1743/4 d 5-13-1818 m Susanna Mills Sol CT
Elijah: b 9-26-1756 d 6-27-l833 m (1)Mary Marsh (2)Lucretia Green Pvt VT
Elijah: b 2-27-1760 d 1-27-1808 m Hannah Bond Pvt MA
Elisha: b 4-4-1759 d 6-1-1858 m Lucretia Webster Arfr CT
Gardner: b 8-28-1744 d 3-6-1795 m Mary Munro Sgt RI
George: b c. 1760 d p. 1792 m Charity Johnson Slr MA
George Sr.: b 10-9-1725/6 d 10-7-1792 m (1)Ann Eilbeck (2)Sarah Brent PS VA
George Jr.: b 1753 d 12-5-1796 m Elizabeth Mary Ann Barnes Hooe Capt VA
Henry: b 4-3-1758 d 4-24-1836 m Amey Williams Sgt CT
Hezekiah: b 8-11-1732 d 1-22-1801 m Parnell West Sgt MA
Hezekiah: b 11-18-1754 d 3-9-1825 m (1)Sarah Wood (2)Abigail Sheldon Pvt MA
Hugh: b 12-23-1758 d 8-25-1838 m (1)Elizabeth Clark (2)Lydia Moore Pvt MA ★
Isaac: b 5-24-1743 d 9-11-1826 m (1)Tabitha Martin (2)Abigail Martin (3)Martha Francis Pvt MA
Isaac: b 4-4-1767 d 1-30-1856 m (1)Catherine — (2)Margaret White Pvt NY

Isaac: b c. 1748 d — m Catharine Harrison Pvt PA
James: b 4-7-1759 d 9-10-1820 m Abigail Beaumont Pvt CT ★
James Sr.: b 1-17-1724 d 11-29-1795 m (1)Mary Cornell (2)Mrs. Avis(Anthony) Lee Pvt MA
James Jr.: b 3-2-1752 d 4-17-1790 m Rhoda Wood Pvt MA
James: b 1-11-1743 d 1784 m (1)Elizabeth Harrison (2)Rebecca Thweatt Capt VA
Japhet Jr.: b 8-19-1742 d 3-4-1787 m Patience Hempstead Ens CT
Jenks: b 3-25-1762 d 9-26-1819 m (1)Sibbil Wood (2)Elizabeth Cory Pvt MA
Jeremiah: b 2-22-1730 d 4-16-1813 m Elizabeth Fitch Col CT MA
Jeremiah: b 2-3-1757 d 4-10-1848 m Phebe Luther Pvt MA
Jesse: b 3-21-1737 d 10-17-1823 m Lois (Mason) Pvt MA
Job: b 4-27-1727 d 6-23-1801 m Martha Gardner Pvt MA
John: b 1755 d 1795 m Elizabeth Hix SgtMaj GA
John: b c. 1735 d p. 9-19-1801 m Mary Sabin Pvt MA
John: b 10-4-1716 d 6-27-1801 m Zerviah Ormsby PS MA
John: b 1734 d 4-19-1792 m (1)Catharine Van Wyck (2)Sarah Van Alstyne Chp NY
John: b 2-22-1753 d 8- -1805 m Hannah Frost Maj PA
John: b 9-1-1745 d 4-11-1831 m Ann Shirley Lt VA
John Sr.: b 1716 d 1785 m Elizabeth Chappell CS VA
John Jr.: b 4-17-1741 d 9-12-1802 m (1)Elizabeth Gee (2)Jane (Parham) Thweat Pvt VA
John: b 1724 d 1790 m Mary Nelson Pvt VA
John: b 1752 d p. 1786 m Selah Jeffries Sol VA
Jonas: b 12-25-1748 d 1810 m Susannah (Daggett) Foster Sgt MA
Jonas: b 10-21-1708 d 3-13-1801 m Mary Chandler CS MA
Jonathan: b 3-24-1733 d 1777 m Susannah Rossiter Lt CT
Jonathan: b 1737 d 1814 m Mary Howard 1Lt MA
Jonathan: b 2-21-1758 d 12-14-1833 m Deborah Lyon MM CT ★
Jonathan Sr.: b 4-20-1734 d 8-18-1798 m Patience Mason Pvt RI
Jonathan Jr.: b 1-3-1756 d 3-27-1822 m Mary Kirby Pvt Slr RI ★
Joseph: b 3-6-1751 d 2-18-1834 m Lucy Flint Fif Sgt MA ★
Joseph: b 6-12-1759 d c. 1796 m Lovina Rounds Pvt MA
Joseph: b 12-4-1722 d 11-14-1785 m Mary Manlove Pvt PA
Joseph: bpt 9-11-1748 d 3-11-1806 m Anne Prentiss Pvt MA
Joseph: b 9-22-1757 d p. 1835 m Jane Henderson Sgt VA ★
Joseph: b c. 1750 d p. 3-3-1795 m Elizabeth Watson PS VA
Josiah: b 10-3-1734 d 9-9-1814 m Anna Livermore Pvt MA
Lemuel B.: b 1-14-1759 d 3-3-1851 m Mary Chamberlin Lt NH
Levi: b 10-15-1755 d 8-20-1844 m Amy Gillson Vol MA
Littleberry: b 3-7-1753 d p. 11-10-1806 m Rebecca Blunt PM VA
Luther: b 3-30-1757 d 10-3-1843 m Polly Catlin Sgt CT
Malachi: b 6-9-1764 d 3-6-1838 m (1)Polly Hall (2)Elizabeth Hall Pvt MA
Marmaduke: b 9-14-1732 d 6-28-1798 m (1)Hannah Anthony (2)Mrs Elizabeth O'Kelly Pvt RI
Moses Jr.: b 4-26-1757 d 10-1-1836 m Eunice Ayres Pvt NH
Nathan: b 4-16-1747 d 8-19-1816 m Experience French 2Lt MA
Nathan: b 11-12-1726 d 3-23-1812 m Elizabeth Wood PS MA
Nathan: b 2-21-1741 d 1826 m (1)Mehitabel Carpenter (2)Rhobe (Wood) Mason Pvt MA
Nathan: b 11-15-1756 d 6-16-1847 m Elizabeth Cole Pvt MA ★
Nathaniel: b 1759 d 1827 m Judith Stewart Capt VA
Noble: b 11-23-1747 d 8-13-1827 m Lydia Thurber Pvt MA
Oliver: b 3-3-1740 d 8-15-1822 m Lucy Johnson Pvt MA
Oliver: b 2-21-1738 d 7-1-1798 m (1)Phoebe Martin (2)Mary Thurber PS NH
Pardon: b 8-14-1748 d 5-18-1845 m Anna Hall Pvt MA
Paul: b 2-15-1761 d 4-9-1824 m Elizabeth Priest Pvt MA W★
Pelatiah: b 3-9-1740 d 1-4-1823 m Sarah Allen Pvt MA
Peres: b 4-9-1747 d 3-19-1825 m Martha Barney Pvt NH
Peter: b 8-1-1752 d 12-28-1831 m Elishaba Farnum Ens CT
Peter: b 8-22-1764 d p. 1840 m Mary — Pvt VA ★
Philip: b 1-29-1744 d 7-21-1813 m Mercy Scott Capt MA
Reuben: b 9-4-1757 d 11-2-1806 m Thankful Tobey Pvt MA
Reuben: b 8-14-1749 d 2-22-1790 m (1)Dorcas Olney (2)Hannah Pierce Dr RI
Robert: b 11-12-1755 d 7-21-1837 m (1)Judith Wright (2)Mehitable Ingram (3)Mrs. Betsey Hovey Pvt NH
Sadey: b 11-1-1730 d 9-4-1804 m Sarah Ellis CS MA
Samson: b 2-2-1765 d 7-3-1845 m Hannah Mason Fif MA
Samson: b 4-8-1750 d 10- -1825 m Lucy Sherman Pvt MA
Sampson: b 11-4-1733 d p. 1791 m Abigail Stone Matr MA
Samuel: b c. 1754 d p. 1795 m Elizabeth Rogers Pvt CT
Samuel: b 8-22-1744 d 2-7-1831 m Sarah Beal Pvt MA
Samuel: b 5-7-1749 d 4-7-1839 m Sara Whitney Pvt MA
Samuel: b 11-8-1739 d 7- -1803 m Miss Dorsey Capt VA
Shubael: b 6-15-1759 d 7-2-1830 m Amy Jones Pvt MA
Silas: b 1741 d 10- -1792 m Priscilla Wheelock Pvt MA
Simeon: b 3-14-1735 d p. 1-15-1809 m (1)Hannah Thomas (2)Experience Baker Pvt MA
Simeon: b 1-17-1758 d 2-19-1835 m Abigail Buzzell Pvt NH
Thomas: b 12-16-1760 d 10-4-1846 m Mary Dawson Pvt DE ★
Thomas: b 6-14-1733 d 11-28-1814 m Mary Baxter Lt MA
Thomas: b c. 1730-40 d p. 1830 m Reancy Whatley Pvt VA
Thomas: b 1740 d 1782 m Charlotte — Pvt VA
Thomson Sr.: b 1730 d 2-26-1785 m (1)Mary King Barnes (2)Mrs Elizabeth (Westwood) Wallace PS VA
Tilly: b 1760 d 6-8-1847 m Hannah Wetherby Pvt MA ★
Timothy: b 8-14-1747 d 12-22-1832 m (1)Chloe Brown (2)Mrs. Elizabeth Brown Lt MA

Wm.: b 11-21-1727 d 4-10-1819 m Hannah Child MM MA
Wm.: b *c.* 1758-60 d *p.* 1792 m Mrs. Hannah Goodwin Dobson Pvt MA
Wm.: b *c.* 1760 d *p.* 5-4-1840 m Nancy Acree Pvt NC
Wm.: b 1760 d 1830 m Sarah Murphy Pvt PA
Wm.: b 1764 d 8-2-1826 m (1)Rebecca Sharp (2)Sally Shockley Pvt PA
Wm.: b 1750 d *p.* 1795 m Lucy Benson Capt VA
Wm.: b 1756 d 1818 m Ann Stuart Pvt VA
Wm.: b — d *a.* 2-25-1803 m — PS VA

MASSENGILL,
Henry Sr.: b *c.* 1720 d *c.* 1800 m Mary Cobb PS CS NC
Henry, Jr.: b 10-17-1758 d 9-23-1837 m (1)Penelope Cobb (2)Elizabeth Emmert (3)Mary McCorkle Pvt NC ★
Michael: b 3-1-1756 d 10- -1834 m Susan Stone Pvt NC ★
Solomon: b *c.* 1760 d *p.* 6-12-1830 m Tabitha Cobb Sol NC

MASSEY, (includes MASSIE)
Caleb: *c.* 1750 d 5-6-1827 m (1)— Dickerson (2)Sarah — Pvt VA W★
Charles: b 1727 d 1817 m Mary Davis Sgt VA
Daniel: b 8-5-1714 d 8-30-1787 m (1)Abigail Kimball (2)Mary Ayres (3)Rebecca Kelly PS NH
Daniel Toas: b *c.* 1722 d 1779 m Catharine — Pvt MD
Ezekiel: b 1-15-1766 d 12-19-1844 m Esther Oliver Mar NJ ★
Frederick: b 7-24-1750 d 6-8-1809 m Marilda — Pvt NC
Henry: b 1763 d 1836 m Betsy Cureton Pvt SC ★
John: b 12-3-1762 d *p.* 1790 m Elizabeth Hamblet Pvt MA
John: b 7- -1758 d 5-12-1835 m Lydia Sandlin Pvt NC ★
John: b *c.* 1743 d *p.* 1820 m Rebecca — PS VA
Jonathan: b 7-16-1747 d 3-20-1830 m Betsey Woodbury Sgt NH
Josiah: b 9-4-1757 d *p.* 12-16-1789 m Elizabeth — Pvt MD
Lee: b 9-22-1732 d 9-23-1814 m (1)Mary Johnston (2)— Burwell (3)— Bronaugh PS VA
Mordecai: b *c.* 1745 d *p.* 1812 m Sarah Griffith 2Lt PA
Nathaniel, Sr.: b 8-2-1727 d 4-6-1802 m (1)Elizabeth Watkins (2)Mrs Ann Clarke Venable Capt VA
Nathaniel Jr.: b 12-28-1763 d 11-3-1813 m Susan Everard Mead Pvt VA
Reuben: b *c.* 1740 d *a.* 1820 m Mary Carter Pvt VA
Thomas: b 1740 d 1-9-1817 m Mary Peeples Pvt NC
Thomas: b 8-22-1747 d 2-2-1834 m Sally Cocke Capt VA ★
Thomas: b 12-26-1759 d 8-19-1835 m (1)Fannie Hudson (2)Rebecca Collyer Pvt Spy VA
Wm.: b *c.* 1743 d 3-21-1841 m Elizabeth Rives PS LCol SC
Wm.: b 1755 d *p.* 1-20-1799 m Betty (Parks) Fif Maj VA

MAST,
Jacob: b 1738 d 1808 m Magdalena Holly PS PA
John Sr.: b *c.* 1740 d *p.* 1780 m Barbara Harman Sol NC
John Jr.: b *c.* 1762 d 9-3-1823 m Susanna Hoover Pvt NC

MASTEN, (includes MASTIN)
Abraham A.: b 10-20-1763 d 6-5-1819 m Gertrude Kierstead Pvt NY
Benjamin: b 12-28-1707 d *p.* 12-9-1780 m (1)Tjaatjen VanKeuren (2)Maria de Witt PS NY
Cornelius: b *a.* 1730 d *p.* 1785 m Catharine VanSteenberg Capt NY
Cornelius C.: bpt 11-24-1754 d *p.* 1790 m Rebecca Roosa Pvt NY
Jacob: b 12-20-1760 d 6-4-1852 m Catherine Helm Pvt Spy NY ★
James: b — d 1848 m Elizabeth Rose MM NY
Johannes: b *a.* 1733 d *p.* 1800 m Madlena Swart PS NY
John: b 9-5-1759 d 12-20-1834 m Giertje Traver Pvt NY
Matthias: b 3-9-1765 d 11-9-1856 m Sarah Stanly Sol DE
Peter: b *c.* 1729 d *p.* 1790 m (1)Sarah DuBois (2)Greetje Freer Pvt NY

MASTERMAN,
James: b 4-4-1759 d 5-10-1842 m Hannah Dows Pvt Smn MA ★

MASTERSON,
James: b 4-7-1752 d 12-15-1838 m Margaret Wimer Ens NC ★
James: b 1730 d 1790 m Elizabeth — Pvt Spy VA

MASTICK,
Benjamin: b 6-21-1761 d 6-6-1830 m Cynthia Wood Pvt MA ★

MASURY,
Stephen: b 9-1-1751 d 6-10-1782 m Elizabeth Woodbury Pvt MA

MATCHETT,
Edward: b *c.* 1755 d *a.* 1-21-1797 m — Pvt NC
John: bpt 6-11-1764 d 1844 m Catherine Gordon Pvt NJ

MATHENY, (includes MATHENEY)
Daniel: b *c.* 1735-38 d *p.* 12- -1803 m Judah — Ens VA
Luke: b 1753 d 8-5-1839 m Elender Orr Pvt VA
Nathan: b 1741 d 1846 m Rachel Thompson Sol PA
Wm.: b 1759 d 1838 m Mary Harrison Pvt VA ★

MATHER,
Abner: b 2-13-1751 d 4-1-1838 m (1)Lucy Lord (2)Deborah Carr Pvt CT ★
Asaph: b 8-22-1753 d 1-1-1849 m Mary Austin Cpl NH

Benjamin: b 9-19-1731 d 12-25-1821 m (1)Irene Pearsons (2)Abigail Worthington Sgt CT
Charles: b 3-20-1734 d 6- -1825 m Ruth Kelsey Sgt CT
Charles: b 10-26-1742 d 6-3-1822 m Rhoda Mosley PS CT
Cotton: b 1745 d 11-26-1791 m Martha Stoughton Pvt CT
Cotton: b 1745 d 11-26-1791 m Zilpha Huxley Pvt CT
David: b 10-7-1738 d 8- -1817 m Hannah Dunham Pvt CT
Ebenezer: b 1729 d *p.* 1790 m Margaret Downs Pvt NY
Eleazer, Sr.: b 11-17-1716 d 11-21-1798 m Annie Watrous Dr CT
Eleazer, Jr.: b 6-22-1753 d 9-17-1837 m Irene Starlin Sgt Dr CT
Elijah: b 12-1-1743 d 12-11-1796 m (1)Mary Strong (2)Ruhama Roberts Pvt CT
Elisha: b 4-4-1740 d 3-22-1807 m Eunice Mosely Pvt MA
Erastus: b 10-14-1760 d 9- -1822 m Olive Higley Pvt VT
Increase: b 8-12-1725 d 5-7-1799 m Appbia Norton Pvt CT
Increase: b 1725 d 12-20-1794 m Anna Brown PS NY
Jehoida: b 11-16-1740 d 3-11-1811 m Eunice Miller PS CT
John, Sr.: b 7-31-1721 d 1-1-1804 m (1)Mary Higgins (2)Mrs Ruth Robbins Pvt CT
Joseph: b 7-21-1753 d 2-29-1840 m Sarah Scott Ens CT ★
Joseph, Jr.: b 1749 d 7-10-1833 m (1)Mary Burritt (2)Mrs Hannah Treat Sage Pvt CT ★
Joseph: b 1-27-1756 d 3-21-1848 m Ruth Adams Pvt CT ★
Moses: b 2-23-1719 d 9-21-1806 m (1)Hannah Bell (2)Elizabeth Whiting (3)Rebecca Raymond PS CT
Nathaniel: b 5-30-1759 d 1-30-1852 m Eunice DeWolf Pvt CT ★
Nathaniel: b *c.* 1746 d 1803 m (2)Mrs Lois Cooley PS NY
Oliver: b 3-21-1749 d 8-27-1829 m Jemima Ellsworth Lt CT
Phineas: b 1-15-1751 d 3-30-1838 m Huldah Taylor Sgt VT
Robert: b 1743 d 7-8-1818 m Susannah Watson Pvt PA
Samuel: b 2-10-1742 d 5-17-1834 m Alice Ranson Capt Dr CT ★
Samuel: b 12-19-1765 d 10-22-1842 m Sarah Scofield Pvt CT ★
Samuel: b 2-22-1745 d 3-26-1809 m Lois Griswold PS CT
Samuel: b 10-19-1737 d 1808 m Grace Moseley CS MA
Stephen: b 2-9-1758 d 6-1-1837 m Elizabeth Peck Pvt CT ★
Sylvester: b 9-1-1758 d 1810 m Elizabeth Wait Pvt CT
Timothy, Jr.: b 3-2-1757 d 3-8-1818 m Hannah Church Pvt VT
Zachariah: b 9-22-1743 d *p.* 1816 m Lucy Gaylord CS CT

MATHERS,
James: b 1750 d 8- -1811 m Sarah — Sgt PA
Wm.: b 5- -1760 d 11-30-1844 m Esther Thorn Pvt PA ★
Wm. H.: b 8-2-1761 d 8-25-1835 m (1)Margaret — (2)Sarah — Pvt GA ★

MATHES, (includes MATHEWS)
Abraham: b *c.* 1744 d *p.* 1790 m Mary (Saunders) Thomas Pvt NH
Alexander: b 3-12-1740 d 1806 m Ann Leith Capt VA
James: b 1737 d *c.* 1790 m Sarah Netherington Lt VA
Samuel: bpt 1-27-1722 d *a.* 12-19-1802 m Ruth Lord PS NH
Valentine, Sr.: b 1720 d 2-2-1814 m Hannah Burnham PS NH
Valentine, Jr.: b 1746 d 4-4-1801 m Dolly Rogers CS NH

MATHIEU,
Andre: b 1761 d 11-9-1857 m Hannah Davis Pvt FrA

MATHIOT,
George: b 10-13-1759 d 4-4-1840 m Ruth Davis Sgt Slr PA ★

MATKINS,
John: b 12-24-1762 d 2-8-1845 m Sarah Conley Pvt MD ★

MATLACK, (includes MATLOCK)
George: b 7-16-1753 d 1782 m Sarah Matson Pvt PA
George: b 4-16-1758 d 10-3-1826 m Anne Smedley Pvt PA
Jacob: b 12-19-1762 d 2-2-1857 m Sebilla Ellis Pvt NJ ★
Joseph: b 3-7-1753 d 11-20-1795 m Julia Scott Pvt PA
Nicholas: b 1735 d 1824 m Elizabeth Terrill Sol NC
Timothy: b 4-26-1734 d 4-14-1829 m (1)Ellen Yarnall (2)Elizabeth (Claypole) Copper Col PS PA
White: b 11-17-1743 d *c.* 1820 m Mary Hawkshurst MM NY
Wm.: b 12-7-1762 d 9-18-1829 m Catherine Sevier Sol NC
Wm.: b 5-15-1752 d 10-12-1805 m (1)Mary Matson (2)Letitia Harris Sgt PA

MATSINGER,
Michael: b 1735 d 1834 m — Leech Pvt PA

MATSON,
Aaron: b 1745 d 5-6-1837 m Mary McMinn Pvt PA
Asa: b 1739/40 d 2-9-1825 m Amy — Pvt CT
Israel: b 12-10-1755 d 1803 m Catherine Muff Pvt PA
John: b 1740 d 10-1-1804 m Jane Harrison Capt PA
John: b *c.* 1743 d *p.* 1810 m Sarah — Pvt PA
Joseph: b 3-10-1738 d 2-18-1810 m Elizabeth Porter Pvt CT
Levi: b 11-13-1749 d 12-12-1835 m Sarah Worrall Pvt PA
Nehemiah: b 5-6-1755 d *p.* 11-5-1827 m Rachel Worrel Pvt PA

MATTER,
George: b 1746 d 1790 m Catherine — Pvt PA
Jacob, Sr.: b 1742 d 5-20-1790 m Mary Anna Wendling 2Lt PA
John, Sr.: b *c.* 1737 d 1802 m (1)Anna Catharine (2)Salome Stahlscmidt Pvt PA
John, Jr.: b 8-7-1759 d 6-30-1832 m Elizabeth Bergner Cpl PA

MATTESON, (includes MATTISON)
Aaron: b 1723 d 1801 m Sarah Cook Pvt NJ
Allen: b 1-20-1755 d 7-9-1839 m Jemima Johnson Ens RI ★
Daniel: b 10-17-1748 d 2-7-1824 m Dorcas Chapman Pvt RI W★
David: b 3-1-1742/3 d p. 1810 m Mary Sweet Pvt NY
David: b 10-25-1763 d c. 7-31-1847 m Dorcas Waite Pvt RI
David: b 5-23-1750 d 9-7-1818 m Sarah — Sgt VT W★
Dyer: b 11-4-1762 d 11-3-1844 m (1)Freelove Johnson (2)Lydia Eddy Goodell Pvt RI ★
George: b 3-20-1742 d p. 1780 m — Pvt RI
Jacob: b 11-8-1743 d 3-11-1823 m Catherine Mattison Pvt NJ
James: b 8-20-1762 d 7-3-1849 m Frances Wyatt Sol VA
Job: b 4-12-1758 d 5-4-1809 m Lucy Johnson Pvt RI W★
Joseph: b 11-19-1742 d 3-11-1823 m (1)Catherine Bodine (2)Lena Boss Lt NJ
John: b 12-30-1749 d 4-26-1821 m Sarah Ketchum MM NJ
Jonathan: b 1762 d 9-25-1846 m (2)Katherine Carter Cpl RI ★
Moses: b c. 1732/3 d p. 1790 m Patience Cahoon Pvt RI
Nathan: b 3-15-1735 d 1810/11 m Freelove Bowen Pvt RI
Peleg: b 2-27-1747 d 4-6-1837 m (1)Barbara Bowen (2)Susannah Andrews Capt VT
Peter: b 1753 d 2-13-1825 m Phebe — Pvt VT
Philip: b 1759 d 5-3-1827 m Sarah Curtis Sgt VT ★
Rufus: b 10-24-1752 d 9-6-1834 m Rhoda Andrew Pvt RI ★
Samuel, Sr.: b 1725 d p. 4-19-1794 m Clarissa — Pvt VT
Samuel, Jr.: b 10-16-1762 d 4-9-1848 m Hannah Richardson Pvt PS VT ★
Thomas: b 8-23-1762 d 7-7-1833 m Thankful Sweet Pvt VT
Thomas: b 6-22-1742 d 6-5-1809 m Sarah Doolittle CS VT
Wm.: b 1-20-1762 d 4-6-1858 m Mehitable Matteson Pvt NJ
Wm.: b 10-20-1733 d 3- -1814 m Sarah Lee Pvt RI

MATTHAY,
Jacob: b 1760 d 1796 m Rachel Jones Pvt PA

MATTHEWS, (includes MATHEWS, MATHIAS)
Aaron, Sr.: b 11-19-1721 d 2-24-1806 m Huldah Frisbie Ens CT
Aaron, Jr.: b 3-23-1745 d 1813 m Hannah Tuttle Pvt VT
Aaron: b 1-23-1742/3 d 9-13-1778 m Mary Hubbard Sgt MA
Abel, Jr.: b 2-25-1746/7 d 5-1-1822 m (1)Eunice Pardee (2)Molly Woodard PS CT
Abner: bpt 12-29-1737/8 d p. 1790 m Eunice — Sgt NH
Alexander: b — d 10-30-1788 m Grizelle — PS VA
Amasa: b 2-9-1751 d 5-4-1829 m Rebecca Kortright Pvt NY
Archer: b a. 1744 d 8-13-1786 m Letitia McLanahan PS VA
Barnabas: b 7-15-1749 d 12-2-1821 m Desire Ryder Cpl MA
Benjamin: b 6- -1756 d 1-13-1843 m — Pvt MA
Caleb: b 12-16-1743 d 12-20-1814 m Anna Carrington Lt RI
Daniel: b 9-28-1725 d 12-27-1803 m Huldah Putman PS MA
Daniel: b 7-31-1743 d 4-6-1821 m Ann Canfield Pvt NJ
David: b 5-11-1727 d 7-11-1819 m Sarah Hedge Pvt MA
Ebenezer: b 1758 d 1848 m Mercy Peckham Pvt NY
Edmund: b c. 1719 d 1803 m Mary Price Pvt PS NC
Edward: b 1755 d 1-17-1814 m Eleanor Thomas Pvt PA
Elijah: b 3-12-1749 d 9-12-1779 m Martha Smith Slr NS NJ
Ezekiel: b 1740-50 d p. 9-16-1816 m — PS PA
George: b 1726 d 1795 m Isabella Lee Capt PA
George: b c. 1750 d p. 1-11-1815 m Mary Saltus Pvt SC W★
George: b 8-30-1739 d 9-30-1812 m (1)Anne Paul (2)Margaret Reed (3)Mrs Mary Flowers BG VA
Gideon: b 10-12-1741 d 2-17-1807 m Esther Eggleston Cpl MA
Hardy: b 4-1759 d p. 6-29-1836 m Phebe — Pvt NC
Henry: b c. 1750-55 d p. 1787 m Mary — Lt MD
Henry: b 4-9-1759 d 12-8-1842 m Rosannah Wolverton Pvt NJ
Henry: b 1748 d 1806 m — Capt PA
Isaac: b — d 3-25-1791 m Anne — Sol SC
Jabez: b 1743 d 1827 m Sarah Tufts Maj MA
Jabez: b 1764 d 10-9-1827 m Louisa Owen Pvt MA
Jacob: b 10-23-1704 d 5-7-1782 m Margaret — PS MD
Jacob: b 9-3-1746 d 6-10-1813 m Anna Leibon Lt NY
James: b 3-1-1753 d 12-23-1828 m Desire Crowell Pvt Smm CT W★
James: b 5-6-1737 d 1803 m (1)Charity Coombs (2)Sarah Rhodes (3)Elinor Jones Barbour Lt MA
James: b 1742 d 1816 m Hannah Strong PS NY
James: b 12-10-1750 d 1-25-1802 m Susanna Lathland Pvt NC
James: b 7-11-1764 d 12-28-1850 m (1)Margaret Sloan (2)Mary Ann Newkirk Pvt NC
James: b c. 1760 d 1810 m Nancy Dickenson Sol NC
James: b 1750 d p. 10-22-1784 m Margaret — PS PA
James: b 1760 d 1845 m Prudence Gorden Pvt PA
James: b 10-15-1755 d 6-5-1828 m Rebecca Carlton Pvt SC
James: b 1764 d 1844 m Nancy Gaines Pvt VA
Jeremiah: b a. 1760 d p. 1790 m Sarah Brinkley Pvt NC
Joel: b 9-22-1750 d p. 1786 m Rachel Gilbert Pvt NH
John: b 4-30-1750 d 12-1-1800 m Olive Roys PS CT
John: b 6-25-1749 d 12-1-1800 m Catharine Weller Pvt MD
John: b 6-29-1743 d 1782 m Elizabeth Coombs 1Lt CS MA
John: b 2-18-1765 d 10-31-1828 m Sarah Woodbridge Pvt MA
John: b 1758 d 10- -1800 m Betty Fonger Lt NJ
John: b 11-4-1764 d 1860 m Margaret Green Pvt NJ ★
John: b 1690 d a. 10-23-1779 m Alice Higbee PS NJ
John: b 3-15-1742 d 11-3-1824 m Susannah Thomas Pvt NC
John: b 1762 d 1839 m Agnes Calhoun Sol CS

John: b c. 1746 d p. 1814 m Francis Burgess Smith PS VA
Joseph: b a. 1754 d p. 1790 m Catherine E. Bartholamew Pvt NC
Luke: b 3-15-1739 d 1788 m Lucy Fox PS VA
Moses: b 8-14-1757 d 3-8-1834 m Amy Mallory Pvt CT ★
Moses, Sr.: b 1725 d 1806 m Sarah Findley PS SC
Moses: b c. 1760 d c. 1809 m Martha Matthews PS SC
Musentine: b 1752 d 3-7-1839 m (1)Anne Sloan (2)Jane Knox Brandon Maj NC
Philip: b 1760 d p. 1845 m — Pvt SC
Philip: b 1756 d p. 4-19-1839 m Molly — Lt VA ★
Reuben: b 1734 d 1820 m Elizabeth Jones Pvt SC
Richard: b 1750 d c. 1800 m — Ens PS NJ
Richard: b c. 1740 d 1799 m Eleanor — Ens VA
Robert: b 1750 d 8-31-1818 m (1)Sarah Baxter (2)Elizabeth Gibson Pvt PS NH
Sampson: b 1737 d 1-20-1807 m (1)Mary Lockhart (2)Mrs Catherine — PS Col VA
Solomon: b 2-2-1745 d 4-2-1834 m Agnes Van Reed 1Lt PA
Stephen: b 5-1-1725 d p. 5-24-1796 m Hannah Parker Capt CT
Thomas: b 6-3-1755 d 12-25-1796 m Ann Poston Sgt MD
Thomas: b c. 1756 d 1829/30 m Mary Rutherford Sol SC
Thomas: b 1742 d 4-20-1812 m Mollie Miller LCol VA
Timothy: b 11-17-1764 d 9-4-1857 m Lois Damon Pvt MA ★
Wm.: b 4-10-1763 d 7-18-1855 m Rachel Wakefield Pvt NC
Wm.: b 9- -1755 d 11- -1819 m Mary A. Pvt MD
Wm.: b 5-24-1721 d 3-15-1789 m Abigail Atkins Pvt MA
Wm.: b 1744 d 1784 m Deborah — Pvt NJ
Wm.: b 2-14-1754 d 4-14-1834 m Rachel Gordon Pvt PA
Wm.: b c. 1735 d 1811 m — Sol VA
Wm.: b 1746 d 1788 m Frances Crowe Pvt VA
Wm.: b 1758 d 1825 m Jane Dunbar Hall Pvt VA

MATTHEWSON, (includes MATHEWSON)
Abraham: b 3-22-1737 d 5-4-1801 m Alice Mathewson CS RI
Charles: b 6-29-1757 d 4-15-1848 m Rebecca Wadkins Pvt RI ★
Daniel: b 1-17-1749 d 9-28-1832 m Abigail Shippee Lt RI ★
Elisha: b 9-8-1756 d 4-11-1805 m Elizabeth Satterlee Cpl CT W★
James: b 9-10-1764 d 5-6-1847 m Barberry Lockwood Pvt RI
John: b c. 1740 d 3-10-1815 m Avis Aldrich Capt RI
Joseph: b 3-3-1737/8 d 10-15-1825 m Prudence Bowen Pvt RI
Nicholas: b 10-14-1752 d 10-18-1822 m Abigail Cooke Pvt RI
Noah: b 7-5-1735 d 9-17-1824 m Judith Peirce PS RI
Wm.: b 9-28-1745 d 1-1-1835 m Tabitha Chaffee Pvt RI

MATTICE,
Adam: b 1-10-1741 d 5-22-1820 m Anna Swart Pvt NY
Conrad: b 9-9-1744 d p. 9-2-1821 m Eva Hager Pvt NY
Elias: b 10-1-1763 d 8-20-1817 m Marget Soop Sol NY
Frederick: b 9-7-1719 d 3-6-1794 m Gertrude Zimmer Pvt NY
John, Jr.: bpt 12-25-1750 d p. 6-29-1792 m Dorotha Hager Pvt NY
John H.: b 1-1-1749 d 9-24-1824 m Gertrude Vroman Pvt NY

MATTINGLY, (includes MATTINGLEY)
John: b 1756 d 1831 m Elizabeth — Pvt VA
John: b 2-15-1759 d 2-23-1824 m Dykander Boswell Pvt VA ★
Wm.: b c. 1760 d 1820-30 m (1)Catherine Spalding (2)Elizabeth Clarke Pvt MD

MATTOON,
Amasa: b 1-9-1758 d 5-11-1829 m Elizabeth Dayton Sol CT
Caleb: b 1755 d 3-12-1840 m Sarah Spencer PS CT
Ebenezer, Sr.: b 12-21-1720 d 4-27-1806 m (1)Dorothy Smith (2)Sarah Alvord Pvt CS MA
Ebenezer, Jr.: b 8-19-1755 d 9-11-1843 m Mary Dickenson Lt Adj MA ★
Gershom: b 8-18-1730 d 1790 m Ruth Parker PS CT

MAUCK,
Daniel: b c. 1742 d a. 1-10-1803 m (1)Miss Hansberger (2)Rebecca PS VA

MAULDIN,
Benjamin: b — d 3-3-1804 m Mary Morrey PS MD
James: b c. 1735 d a. 1798 m Caty Tyler CS TN & NC
Rucker: b 1-18-1760 d 1-16-1846 m Nancy Posey Pvt SC

MAULL,
John: b 10-9-1742 d 1-9-1831/2 m Mary Marsh PS DE
Nehemiah: b 10-15-1737 d 1780-86 m Mary Moulder PS PA

MAUPIN,
Cornelius: b 2-3-1758 d 12-9-1840 m (1)Mourning Harris (2)Nancy Tomlinson (3)Mary Paul (4)Mary Ellis (5)Ann Bratton Pvt VA
Daniel, Sr.: b 1728/9 d p. 10-11-1803 m Elizabeth Dabney PS VA
Daniel, Sr.: b c. 1700 d 1788 m Margaret Via PS VA
Daniel, Jr.: b 12-6-1760 d 8-29-1832 m (1)Elizabeth Gentry (2)Margaret McWilliams OrdlSgt VA ★
Daniel: b 9-16-1756 d 1838 m (1)Sara Jarman (2)Patsy Gentry (3)Hannah Harris Pvt VA ★
David: b 1760 d p. 2-10-1820 m Sarah Spencer Sol VA
Gabriel: b 2-12-1737 d 1800 m (1)Esther Page (2)Dorcas Allen Capt VA
Gabriel: b c. 1720 d 1794 m Ann Ballard PS VA

Mosias: b 1756 d 10-29-1816 m Leah Sol VA
Thomas: b 1760 d 8-2-1838 m (1)Judith Cobbs (2)Margaret Maupin Pvt VA
Thomas: b 1764 d 2-25-1855 m (1)Elizabeth Michie (2)Margaret Burnsides Pvt VA
Wm.: b c. 1740 d 6-18-1814 m Mildred White Pvt VA
Wm.: b 11-19-1759 d p. 1816 m Jane Jameson Pvt VA ★

MAURAN,
Joseph Charles: b 6-3-1748 d 5-1-1813 m Olive Bicknell NCapt RI

MAURER,
Adam: b 3-16-1727 d 6- -1814 m Catharine Sgt PA
Baltzer: b 6-8-1743 d 8-20-1822 m (1)Margaretha (2)Christiana Pvt PA
Daniel: b 5-3-1749 d 3-3-1832 m Regina Wagner Pvt PA
John: b 1746 d p. 2-26-1823 m Anna Maria 1Lt PA
John: b 2-12-1763 d 2-24-1833 m Elizabeth Stimmell Pvt PA W★
Peter: b 6-13-1757 d 4-15-1847 m Elizabeth Graffort Pvt PA ★

MAURY,
Abraham: b 4-28-1758 d 3-23-1833 m Mildred Washington Thornton Lt VA ★
Abram: b 3-18-1731 d 1-22-1784 m Susanna Poindexter PS VA
James: b 1746 d 2-23-1840 m (1)Catherine Armistead (2)Margaret Rutson PS VA

MAUS,
George: b 1748 d 8-1-1825 m Ann Mary Kitzmiller Pvt PS PA
Philip: b 1731 d 4-27-1815 m Francis Heap Pvt PA

MAUZY,
Henry: b 1721 d 12-31-1799 m (1)Ann Withers (2)Elizabeth Taylor Morgan PS VA
John: b c. 1745 d p. 3-3-1802 m Lydia Duncan 2Lt VA
Peter: b 5-19-1748 d p. 12-30-1834 m Elizabeth — Sol VA
Peter: b 3- -1751 d 8-15-1841 m Sarah Hughes Pvt VA ★
Wm.: b 12-27-1755 d 4-6-1837 m Ursula Arnold Pvt VA ★

MAVERICK,
Samuel: b 1742 d 7-3-1784 m (1)—Reavis (2)Lydia Turpin PS SC

MAVITY,
Wm.: b 11-8-1747 d 1832 m Mary Jones SgtMaj VA

MAWNEY,
John: b 1750 d 3-9-1830 m (1)Nancy Wilson (2)Elizabeth Clark Dr RI

MAXEY,
Benjamin: b 5-11-1740 d 7-26-1791 m (1)Sarah Fuller (2)Amy Ide 2Lt MA
Edward: b c. 1749 d 2- -1782 m Mary Bondurant PS VA
Jesse: b 1750 d 1808 m (2)Elizabeth Loraine Pvt VA
Joel: b 1762 d 12-27-1844 m (1)Susan Hill (2)Betsey Ann Howard Pvt VA ★
John: b c. 1730 d 1803 m Mary Ann PS VA
John: b 1756 d c. 1846 m Mary Maxey Pvt VA ★
Levi: b 3-28-1741/2 d 1826 m Ruth Newell Pvt MA
Walter: b — d p. 3-5-1791 m Mary — PS VA
Wm.: b 2-11-1759 d 5-27-1833 m Nancy Williams Pvt VA W★

MAXFIELD,
Abraham: b 8-5-1759 d p. 1797 m Elizabeth Hathaway Pvt MA
David: b 1729 d 1820 m Judith Clough Pvt NH
Eliphalet: b 8-8-1744 d p. 1782 m Lida Jones PS NH
John N.: b 3-25-1755 d 5-11-1836 m Rhoda French Pvt MA
Joshua: b 1743 d p. 1787 m Sarah Currier Pvt MA
Nathaniel: b 5-24-1743 d 1797 m Mehitable Rowe Pvt PS NH
Wm.: b 1763 d 8-23-1820 m Abigail Belcher Pvt NH

MAXHAM,
Adonijah: b 12-28-1754 d 11-22-1850 m (1)Zilpha Whitten (2)Catherine Hosford Pvt NY CT ★
Edmund: b 1752 d 2-22-1800 m Rebecca Faunce Pvt MA
Jabez: b 4-27-1743 d 10-19-1831 m Anna Shurtleff Pvt MA
Nathan: b 11-30-1741 d 1805 m Martha Chubbuck Pvt MA
Samuel: b 9-12-1748 d 12-6-1820 m Margaret Lucas Cpl MA

MAXSON, (includes MAXON)
Asa: b 3-6-1752 d 11-18-1842 m (1)Lois Stillman (2)Polly—Lt RI ★
Benjamin: b 2-21-1733 d 4-9-1822 m Eunice Reynolds Pvt RI
David: b 7-24-1729 d c. 1786 m Abigail Greenman PS Sol RI
Ephraim: b 1743 d 1799 m Elizabeth Davis Pvt NJ
George: b 10-10-1756 d 10-10-1796 m Anna Marriott Lt RI
John: b 2-14-1761 d 12-18-1835 m Leah Benjamin Pvt NJ W★
John: b 3-13-1748 d 4-15-1822 m Sarah Shrieve Pvt RI
John: b 8-27-1725 d 8-28-1791 m (1)Sarah Burdick (2)Mrs. Darcis Davis CS RI
Jonathan: b 8-24-1737 d 7-31-1823 m (1)Mary Woodmansee (2)Tabitha Tucker LCol RI
Joseph: b c. 1750 d a. 4- -1794 m Hannah Ogborne Sol NJ
Joseph: b 3-23-1721 d p. 1-15-1790 m Keturah Randall 1Lt PA
Matthew, Sr.: b 4-27-1727 d 2-28-1791 m Martha Potter PS RI

Matthew, Jr.: b 1-6-1754 d 5-20-1826 m Fanny Peckham Pvt RI W★
Nathan: b 1720 d 1786 m Elizabeth — Sgt NJ
Paul: b 1757 d 7-13-1818 m Susannah Stillman Pvt RI
Phineas: b 2-1-1755 d 1851 m Betsy Burdick Capt RI ★
Silas: b 12-29-1750 d p. 1833 m Sarah Clarke Ordl Sgt CT ★
Stephen: b 8-25-1757 d 11-30-1841 m Caty Whitford Pvt RI
Sylvanus: b 5-3-1735 d 1820 m Lydia Lewis Lt RI
Torry: b 1-22-1732/3 d p. 1790 m Martha Lamphere PS RI
Zacheus: b 6-6-1756 d 9-17-1844 m Amelia Crandall Pvt RI ★

MAXWELL,
Adam: b 1752 d 5-1-1837 m Elizabeth Wallace 2Lt PA ★
Alexander: b 12-5-1748 d 1843 m Philadelphia Rankin PS ME
Anthony: b 12-12-1754 d 5-24-1825 m Eva Platner Capt NY
Audley: b c. 1705 d 10-8-1776 m Hannah Powell PS GA
Benjamin: b 3-17-1737 d 2-2-1829 m Anna Winslow 1Lt MA
Bezaleel: b 12-20-1751 d 1-9-1828 m Margaret Anderson Pvt VA
Cornelius: b 1755 d 1809 m Judith Smith Sgt NY
David: b 6-19-1750 d 1-20-1820 m (1)Susanna Maxwell (2)Mary Capt DE
David: b 1742 d p. 7-28-1794 m Elizabeth — Pvt VA
Edward: b 1744 d 9-1-1828 m Jane Montgomery Sol SC
George: b 1751 d p. 11-14-1821 m Sarah — Lt VA
Henry: b c. 1730 d 1791 m Agnes Carson Pvt VA
Hugh: b 10-27-1733 d 10-14-1799 m Bridget Monroe LCol MA
James: b 7-26-1742 d c. 1780 m Hannah Phillips Drm CT
James: b c. 1737 d 3-1-1792 m Ann Way Maj PS GA
James: b 9-2-1764 d 1848 m Chloe Burt Drm MA
James: b a. 3-23-1735 d 3-23-1823 m Phebe — Pvt NH ★
James: b 1757/8 d 7-27-1843 m Ann Grant Capt NJ
James: b 1750 d p. 2-27-1811 m — Pvt NC
James: b 1734 d 10-4-1795 m Helen Calvert NCapt VA
James: b c. 1750 d 1821 m Jane Roberts Capt VA
James: b 1766 d 3-3-1825 m Grizella Berry Pvt VA
John: b 5-9-1763 d 10-5-1840 m Agatha Henry Sol GA
John: b c. 1725 d 11-21-1778 m Elizabeth — CS MD
John: b 11-25-1739 d 2-15-1828 m (2)Mary Ann Clifford Capt NJ
John: b 1755 d 11-30-1828 m Anna Hubbell Pvt NJ
John: b 2- -1740 d 4-30-1833 m Mary Taylor Pvt PA
John: b 1718 d 9-7-1781 m Jane Mitchel PS PA
John: b 1723-5 d p. 1798 m Fannie Garner Capt VA
John: b 1741 d 7-1-1819 m Sarah McClain Mil VA
Joshua: b c. 1720 d p. 1790 m Mary Phipps Pvt PS CT
Nathaniel: b 1741 d 1-6-1834 m Esther Carson Pvt PA
Robert: b 1745 d 9-26-1798 m Eleanor Sloan Lt NJ
Robert: b c. 1730 d 1790 m (2)Elizabeth — Pvt PA
Samuel: b 7-13-1760 d 8-5-1825 m Lydia Brooks Pvt MA
Squire: b 4-29-1756 d 4-12-1813 m Phebe Rice Pvt MA
Thomas: b 1-11-1740 d 3-15-1795 m Chency — Maj GA
Thomas: b 9-7-1742 d 12-12-1837 m Mary Pemberton Sol GA
Thomas: b 1738 d 1785 m Ann Blackmar Ens PA
Thomas: b 1746 d 12- -1795 m Agnes — Pvt VA
Thompson: b 9-11-1742 d 10-24-1832 m (1)Sibyl Wyman (2)Mrs Mary Little (3)Mrs Eleanor Hickox Capt NH ★
Wm.: b 1739 d 12-28-1807 m Constant Butler PS NCapt GA
Wm.: b 6-27-1754 d c. 1790 m Margaret Gleaves Capt MD
Wm.: b 3-8-1758 d 3-13-1856 m (1)Sarah Bragdon (2)Isabel Webster (3)Ruth Moore Pvt MA

MAY,
Alexander: b — d p. 5-19-1801 m Mary — Pvt PA
Benjamin: b 3-17-1736 d 8-8-1808 m Mary Tyson Maj PS NC
Benjamin: b 2-23-1743 d 1835 m Hopestill Dexter Pvt MA
Benjamin: b c. 1750 d 1824 m Mary Harrison Lt SC
Caleb: b 9-13-1719 d 6-11-1777 m (1)Elizabeth Payson (2)Mehitable Holbrooke CS CT
Cassmore: b 1752 d 5-31-1836 m Mary Horne Pvt PA ★
Charles: b c. 1725 d 1793 m — PS CS VA
Chester: b 11-1-1759 d 2-22-1811 m Lycy Wales Pvt MA
Christian: b 1-30-1762 d p. 1819 m (1)Margaret Smith (2)Anna Pvt PA
Daniel: b 2-24-1738 d 9-17-1819 m Sarah — Cpl NY
Eleazar: b 3-11-1733 d 7-9-1803 m Sibyl Huntington PS CT
Eleazer: b 3-1-1757 d 2-21-1853 m Abigail Prince Cpl MA ★
Eliakim: b 7-10-1744 d 3-27-1816 m Martha Lyon Pvt CT
Elisha: b 1728/29 d 11-15-1811 m Ruth Metcalf Lt MA
Ezra: b 12-16-1731 d 1-11-1778 m Margaret — Col MA
Ezra: b 9-10-1761 d 9-10-1811 m Bathsheba Armstrong Pvt MA
George: b 2-6-1756 d 5-26-1822 m Anna Fitzhugh Pvt VA
Hezekiah, Sr.: b 12-14-1696 d 9-3-1783 m Anna Stillman PS CT
Hezekiah: b 11-13-1728 d 12-20-1797 m Mary George Sol CT
James: b c. 1745 d 1792 m Lydia — Pvt GA
John: b 11-24-1748 d 7-16-1810 m Abigail May Col MA
John, Jr.: b 1748 d 1826 m Hannah Warren Pvt MA
John: b 1757 d 2-19-1836 m Mercy Foster Sgt MA ★
John: b 7-18-1753 d 4-18-1826 m Sophia — Pvt PA
John: b 1756 d 1819 m Mary B. — PS SC
John: b 2-27-1757 d 3-20-1844 m Elizabeth Hunter Capt NC ★
John: b 1760 d 1-25-1813 m Sarah Phillips Pvt VA
Jonas W.: b 1756 d 12-19-1821 m Ann — CS NC
Joseph: b 1732 d 1829 m (1) — Baker (2)Jane McLean Pvt SC
Joseph: b c. 1750 d a. 12-27-1807 m Letty — Pvt NC

MAY, contd.

Joseph, Sr.: b c. 1734 d p. 10-24-1824 m Elizabeth Moser Pvt PA
Ludwick: b 1-20-1764 d p. 1833 m — Ephland Pvt NC ★
Nehemiah: b 1-31-1729 d 12-27-1793 m Anna Lyon Capt MA
Samuel: b 2-20-1738 d 11-19-1805 m (1)Abigail Davis (2)Katherine Williams Capt MA
Samuel: b 2-17-1722 d 8-9-1794 m (1)Catherine Mears (2)Abigail Williams PS CS MA
Samuel: b 11-24-1739 d 5-3-1810 m Priscilla Reynolds Maj RI
Stephen: b 3-23-1755 d 1840 m Hannah Murray Pvt CT
Theodore: b 3-27-1747 d 8-19-1820 m Elizabeth Ellis Pvt MA
Thomas: b 2-14-1723 d 8-7-1803 m Lucy Goddard Child Sgt CT
Thomas: b 7-26-1757 d 6-20-1816 m Eunice Brooks Pvt MA W★
Wm.: b c. 1747 d 7- -1832 m Lucy — Sol CL
Wm.: b 10-21-1740 d p. 1800 m Sarah Simpson Pvt MA
Wm.: b c. 1746 d 9-8-1781 m Betty Dyer Pvt VA

MAYBANK,

Joseph: b 12-19-1735 d 1783 m Hester Bonneau Col SC

MAYBERRY,

George: b 10- -1760 d 11-11-1848 m Christiann — Pvt VA ★
Henry: b 1753 d 1832/3 m Magdalene Carnes Sol VA
John: b 10-22-1763 d 4-1-1841 m Rachel Wilson Pvt MA ★
Richard: b 1735 d 11-5-1807 m Martha Bolton Capt MA
Thomas: b 8-22-1738 d 3-4-1819 m Mary St. Clair Maj NJ
Wm.: b 1745 d 1829 m Jane Miller Sgt MA

MAYBIN,

Wm.: b c. 1748/49 d 8-18-1780 m Jane Duncan Pvt NC

MAYFIELD,

John: b 1720 d 1784 m Mary — Lt SC
John: b 1745 d 1816 m Clarinda Pleasant Pvt VA
Stephen: b c. 1758 d c. 1846 m Margaret Cook Pvt NC

MAYHEW, (includes MAYHUGH)

Brian: b 10-10-1756 d 7-4-1833 m (1)Ann Conley (2)Ann Dophey Pvt MD
Eleazar: b 4-8-1756 d 11-17-1828 m (1)Sarah Van Meter (2)Mrs. Norah Lawrence Pvt CS NJ
Freeborn: b 8-25-1758 d 7-4-1824 m Hannah Skiff Cpl MA
James: b 1762 d c. 1840 m Mary Varvil Sol VA
Jeremiah: b 1705 d 6-14-1790 m (1)Deborah Smith (2)Mrs Fear Hillman PS MA
John: b 4-28-1747 d 2-27-1832 m Abigail Cloyes Lt MA
Matthew: b 7-26-1723 d 10-10-1799 m Phebe Manning Capt MA
Richard: b 1754 d 1841 m Rebecca Watt Pvt NJ
Wilmet: b 8-11-1762 d 12-10-1840 m Nancy Tilton Pvt MA

MAYNARD, (includes MINARD)

Abiather: b — d 9-23-1815 m Abby — Pvt CT
Benjamin: b 1760 d 1-18-1834 m Martha Earle Pvt MA
Bezaleel: b 7-23-1731 d 1795 m Elizabeth Keyes Pvt MA
Caleb: b — d — m Elizabeth Moore Pvt NH
Christopher: b 1753 d 3- -1826 m Lucretia Tinker Pvt CT ★
Daniel: b 10-25-1750 d 2-7-1834 m Hannah Harrington Pvt MA
Daniel: b 9-10-1760 d 10-3-1815 m Cyrene Dinsmore Pvt MA
Ephraim: b 8-29-1745 d 8-25-1826 m Eunice Jewell Pvt MA
Foster: b 6-17-1742 d 12- -1818 m Margaret Aldern Pvt PS MD
Gardner: b 2-14-1746 d 12-16-1814 m (1)Anna Ross (2)Patience Perry Sgt MA
Hezekiah: b 6-17-1708 d 10-28-1781 m Tabitha Howe PS MA
Hezekiah, Jr.: b 1-20-1742 d 3-14-1824 m Hannah Brigham Sgt MA
Isaac: b 10-27-1747 d 6-25-1797 m Mrs. Rebecca Haynes Pvt MA
James: b 1750 d 10-13-1852 m Chaney Smith Pvt NC ★
Jesse: b c. 1730 d p. 6-9-1798 m Anna Watrous Pvt CT
John: b 5-14-1753 d 1-21-1823 m Martha Wilder PS Lt MA ★
Joseph: b 10-10-1759 d 5-4-1845 m Abigail Merriam Sgt MA
Joseph: b 5-17-1750 d p. 1808 m Deborah Twitchell Pvt MA
Joseph, Sr.: b 12-31-1750 d 12-30-1785 m Lovina Barnes Pvt MA
Jotham: b 3-14-1741 d p. 1775 m Dinah Powers Sgt MA
Lemuel: b 3-1-1739 d 5-4-1808 m Sarah Craig Cpl MA
Levi: b 1745 d 1822 m Esther Maynard Pvt MA
Malachi: b 11-1-1745 d 2-29-1824 m (1)Elizabeth Hinds (2)Anna Hale PS MA
Michah: b 10-24-1735 d 8-19-1778 m Dorcas Maynard Pvt MA
Moses: b 1697 d 1782 m Lois Stow Pvt MA
Nathan: b 1-2-1722 d 1811 m Lucy Pratt Pvt MA
Nathan, Jr.: b 10-2-1751 d — m Mary Williams Sol MA
Nathaniel: b 5-7-1744 d 1805 m Martha Smith Capt MA
Samuel: b 3-8-1752 d 1776 m Sarah Noyes Sgt MA
Stephen: b 12-26-1762 d 8-24-1822 m (1)Elizabeth Wright (2) Dorcas Cornish Pinney Fif CT
Thomas, Sr.: b c. 1720 d p. 9-13-1792 m Anna — PS MD
Timothy: b 12-31-1763 d 2-21-1863 m Sibyl Wipple Pvt MA
Wm.: b 3-28-1745 d 1788 m Mary Pepper Lt MA
Wm.: b 10-18-1752 d 2-14-1827 m Lucy Balcom Pvt MA
Zachariah: b 1-15-1719/20 d p. 1778 m (1)Sybilla Brigham (2)Mrs Mary Walker Pvt MA
Zebediah: b 1760 d 7-29-1825 m Anne Atwell Pvt CT

MAYO,

Ebenezer: b 3-22-1757 d 4-29-1814 m Sarah Burgess Sgt MA

Isaac: b 11-21-1757 d 10-12-1844 m Hannah Cahoon Pvt MA ★
Issachar: b c. 1754 d 10-19-1819 m Deborah Gould Pvt MA ★
James: b 1741 d 9-5-1828 m Abigail Cole Pvt MA
James: b 6-16-1761 d p. 1806 m (1)Mary Nickerson (2)Deborah Crosby Pvt MA
John: b 2-21-1743 d 3-4-1776 m Mary Allen 1Lt MA
John: b 4-19-1733 d 2-26-1816 m (1)Lydia Cook (2)Priscilla Walker Pvt MA
John, Sr.: b 7-17-1737 d 2-15-1786 m Mary Tabb PS VA
Joseph: b 1747 d 1829 m Ruth Snow Sgt MA
Joseph, Sr.: b 2-28-1720/21 d 2-14-1776 m Esther Kendrick PS MA
Joseph, Jr.: b 7-25-1749 d 4-18-1817 m (2)Lucy Richards 1Lt MA
Joseph: b c. 1750 d p. 1791 m Jeanne Richardson 2Lt VA
Joseph: b 1739 d 1802/3 m Martha Tabb PS VA
Joshua: b 7-25-1735 d 1-11-1820 m Lydia Pepper Pvt MA ★
Nathan: b 9-22-1742 d 3-14-1811 m (1)Julia Williams (2)Mrs. Elizabeth Hyman Lt NC
Nathan: b 4-5-1736 d p. 1790 m Hannah Atwood Pvt MA
Stephen: b 1757 d 3-16-1847 m (1)Ann Isbell (2)Susan Trent (3)Rebecca Dawson Pvt VA ★
Thomas, Sr.: b 9-23-1713 d 11-30-1792 m (1)Elizabeth Farley (2)Mary Heath (3)Catherine Williams PS MA
Thomas, Jr.: b 1741 d 1805 m Anna Davis Capt MA
Thomas: b 10-28-1718 d 6-28-1794 m (1)Hannah Atkins (2)Sarah Higgins Pvt MA
Thomas, Sr.: b 4-1-1725 d 1778 m Elizabeth Wing Pvt MA
Thomas, Jr.: b 10-8-1753 d 8-1-1825 m (1)Hannah Atwood (2)Hannah — Pvt MA
Uriah: b 5-27-1749 d 7-12-1824 m (1)Mercy Sparrow (2)Bethia Knowles (3)Mercy Howes Pvt MA
Wm.: b 1-7-1754 d 10-21-1802 m Catherine Swann Col VA
Wm.: b 9-26-1757 d 8-12-1837 m (1)Elizabeth Poythress (2)Lucy Fitzhugh Capt VA

MAYRANT,

John: b 1762 d 8- -1836 m Isabella Norvill NLt SC ★

MAYS, (includes MAYES, MAYSE, MAZE)

Benjamin: b 9-10-1757 d 5-25-1835 m (1)Susanna Brown (2)Leutitia Pvt VA ★
George: b 1-10-1755 d 3-31-1820 m Elizabeth — Pvt PA
James: b c. 1720 d 1795 m Mary — PS VA
John: b 1760 d 1828 m (2)Alzera Brinalee Sol GA
John: b 3-18-1719 d 11-2-1789 m Margaret Pvt PA
Joseph: b 1722 d p. 7-25-1786 m Rebecca Lewis Lt VA
Joseph, Jr.: b 3-17-1752 d 4-16-1840 m Agnes Hicklin Sol VA
Joseph, Sr.: b c. 1732 d a. 6-18-1798 m Sarah — Pvt VA
Joseph, Jr.: b 4-18-1756 d a. 6-1-1825 m Jane — Pvt VA
Matthew: b 1762 d 1820 m Frances Brown Pvt VA
Nicholas: b 11-24-1741 d 1813 m Sussanah Laubsher Pvt PA
Samuel: b 5-7-1759 d 7-22-1841 m (1)Mary Scott (2)Mary McCottery Frierson Pvt SC
Samuel: b 1-25-1765 d 1816 m Nancy Grigsby Pvt SC
Sherod: b c. 1737 d p. 4-11-1829 m Elizabeth Smith PS VA
Thomas: b c. 1730 d p. 1790 m Jean Rutherford Pvt PA
Thomas: b 1753 d 3-27-1830 m Mary Hamilton Pvt SC
Wm.: b 1750 d p. 1791 m Mary Wadkins Pvt GA

MAYSON,

James: b 1739 d 10- -1799 m (1)Meriam — (2)Anne — (3)Henrietta Hart Col SC
James Robert: b c. 1762 d p. 1805 m Nancy Conway Sol MA

MAZUZAN,

Mark: b c. 1745 d 11-30-1777 m Amy Palmer 1Lt CT

MAZYCK,

Daniel: b 11-24-1747 d 1813 m Elizabeth Deristoe Capt SC

MC ADAMS, (includes MAC ADAMS)

John: b 1760 d c. 1823 m Seby M— Sol NC
John: b 3-30-1763 d 6-16-1839 m Catherine Steward Pvt PA ★
Joseph: b 1755-57 d 9-22-1840 m (1)Jemima Murray (2)Sarah Bradford Pvt NC ★
Joseph: b 5-28-1719 d 1788 m Mrs Sarah Anne (Gaskins)Pinkard SrgnMte PS VA
Wm.: b 1760 d 9-4-1843 m Mary Hendricks Pvt NC ★
Hugh: b c. 1735 d 1-20-1781 m Catrine Scott PS NC

MC ADOO,

John: b c. 1716/7 d 1802 m Martha — CS MD
John, Sr.: b c. 1730 d p. 1783 m Ann — CS NC
John, Jr.: b 2-6-1757 d 12-26-1830 m Martha Frills Sol NC

MC AFEE, (includes MC AFFEE)

Benjamin: b 3-9-1764 d 7-11-1844 m Rachel Potter Pvt NJ ★
George: b 4-13-1740 d 4-14-1803 m Susan Curry Pvt VA
James: b 1762 d 1844 m Margaret Cole Pvt NC
James: b 1745 d 1814 m Jane Durham Pvt PA
James: b 1736 d 6-25-1811 m Agnes Clark Capt PS VA
James, Sr.: b 10-17-1707 d 1785 m Jane McMichael PS VA
Robert: b 7-10-1745 d 5-10-1795 m Ann McCoun Sol PS KY
Samuel: b 10- -1748 d 6-8-1801 m Hannah McCormick Capt VA

MC ALEVY,
Wm.: b 1728 d 8-21-1822 m (1)Margaret Harris (2)Mary Hays (3)Margaret Allen Col PA

MC ALEXANDER,
Wm.: b 1760 d *p.* 12-19-1820 m (2)Tamar Booth PS VA

MC ALILEY,
Wm.: b 5-13-1758 d 11-18-1818 m Mary Wiley Pvt SC

MC ALLISTER, (includes MC ALISTER)
Alexander: b 1715 d *p.* 1790 m (1)Mary McNeill (2)Flora McNeill (3)Jean Colvin Col PS NC
Andrew: b 9-6-1741 d 1816 m Rebecca Robinson Pvt NH
Archibald: b 1735 d *p.* 1790 m Mary Boyce Capt MA
Archibald: b *a.* 1752 d *p.* 1790 m Maria McKeen Pvt PS NH
Archibald: b 4-17-1756 d 1831 m Elizabeth Carson Capt PA
Edward: b 3-4-1758 d 5-30-1833 m — De Hart Pvt VA
Hugh: b 1736 d 9-22-1810 m Sarah Nelson Maj PA
Isaac: b 9-25-1736 d 1-8-1809 m Hannah Goddard Sgt NH
James: b 2-29-1752 d 8-27-1823 m Sally McClary PS NH
James: b 1727 d 1790 m Sally Vance Pvt PA
James: b 1752 d 1843 m Eleanor Anderson Pvt PA
James: b 2-11-1754 d 11-27-1840 m Caty Hughes Pvt PA ★
John: b 1-18-1739 d 1828 m Anna Steel Pvt NH
John: b 2-12-1765 d 12-24-1848 m (1)Lilly McRae (2)Kiziah Dugar (3)Mrs Mary Dumas (4)Mrs Sarah (Digges)Hailey Sgt NC ★
John: b 8-14-1724 d 1802 m Catherine McKnight Pvt PA
John: b 1732 d 2-1-1808 m Elizabeth — Pvt PA
John: b *c.* 1745 d 6- -1821 m Elizabeth McReynolds Ens VA
Joseph: b 1754 d 7-22-1833 m Nancy Gilmore Pvt VA ★
Randal: b 9-21-1744 d 5-23-1819 m Mary Blair Pvt NH
Richard: b 9-25-1760 d 2-11-1848 m (1)Peggy Cunningham (2)Mrs Sarah Thomas Sgt MA NH ★
Richard, 2d: b 10-20-1749 d 2-11-1813 m Susan Dimond Pvt NH
Richard: b *c.* 1715 d *p.* 1776 m Ann Miller PS NH
Richard: b 9-5-1725 d 9-7-1795 m Mary Dill Col PS PA
Wm.: b 2-17-1787 m Jerusha Spofford Ens MA
Wm.: b 1745 d 7-7-1819 m Sarah Thompson Pvt PA

MC ALPINE,
Alexander: b *c.* 1748 d *c.* 1814-16 m Mary — Pvt GA
John: b 6-24-1764 d 9-23-1842 m Caroline Keefer Pvt NY

MC ANULTY,
John: b 3-10-1755 d 9-12-1795 m Mary Holliday Pvt PA
John, Jr.: b *c.* 1756 d 12-10-1839 m Isabella McLane Pvt PA

MC ARTHUR,
Daniel: b 1741 d *p.* 1796 m Jennette McArthur Pvt NC
John: b 1742 d 12-20-1816 m Margaret Aiken Lt NY
Peter: b 1762 d 2-5-1841 m Christana McDougal Pvt CT NY ★
Wm.: b 1-27-1758 d 2-24-1843 m Isabella Carson Capt SC ★

MC BEE,
Israel: b 1756 d 1- -1860 m Nancy Hale Pvt VA
Silas: b 11-24-1765 d 1-6-1845 m (1)Katherine Katz (2)Dicy — Pvt SC ★
Vardry: b 1745 d 1787 m Hannah Echols Capt SC

MC BRAYER,
David: b 1744 d 1813 m (1)Nancy — (2)Agnes — (3)Delilia — Pvt PA
David: b *c.* 1745 d 10-19-1816 m (1)Agnes Dickson (2)Agnes — Pvt PA
Wm.: b 1754 d 1-5-1820 m (1)Jane Philips (2)Jennet Walker Pvt KY

MC BRIDE, (includes MAC BRIDE, MC BRRIDE)
Alexander, Jr.: b 1754 d *a.* 3-26-1805 m (1)Tabitha Patterson (2)Juliann — Pvt PA
Duncan: b 1762 d 12-11-1838 m Mary Jeanette Brown Pvt NC
Henry: b 6-5-1757 d 1814 m Mary Anne Newberry Ofr PA
Hugh: b 12-30-1725 d 6-19-1803 m Helen — PS PA
Hugh: b 1- -1762 d 11-16-1833 m Martha Dale Sol SC
Isaac: b 1757 d 12- -1830 m Mary Jane Carr Pvt VA
James: b 1750 d 1-23-1836 m — Pvt NC ★
James, Sr.: b 1708 d 1812 m Mary — Pvt PA
James, Jr.: b 3-15-1758 d 12-21-1837 m Martha Young Pvt PA ★
James: b 1743 d 10-6-1827 m Sarah Sprouls Pvt PA
James: b 4-2-1748 d 10-16-1819 m Margaret Campbell Pvt PA
James: b 8-17-1756 d 6-11-1808 m Mary — Pvt SC
James: b *c.* 1750 d *p.* 1782 m Mary White Sgt PA
James: b *c.* 1735 d *p.* 5-20-1817 m Mary — PS VA
John, Jr.: b 6-9-1743 d 7-18-1827 m Eliza Gilmore Ens PA
Maggie: b 4-24-1769 d *p.* 1790 m Robert Stewart PS NC
Robert: b 1740 d *a.* 1826 m Anne Yarnell 1Lt PA
Stephen: b 10-2-1759 d 3-8-1827 m (1)Hannah Smith (2)Jane Howel Pvt VA
Thomas: b 2-7-1742 d *c.* 1793 m Sarah Snow Pvt MA
Wm.: b 1750 d *p.* 4-18-1822 m Margaret — CS NC
Wm.: b *c.* 1740 d 1-17-1781 m Martha — Pvt SC
Wm.: b 1-5-1745 d 8-19-1782 m Martha Lapsley Capt CS VA KY

MC BROOM,
Andrew: b 7- -1754 d *p.* 5- -1850 m — Pvt NC ★
Henry: b 1750-60 d 1825 m Nancy Jones Pvt PA

MC BURNEY,
James: b *c.* 1747 d *c.* 1816 m (1)Martha McGoffin (2)Elizabeth Gillespie Sol PA

MC CABE,
James: b 1735 d 1795 m Mary Hughes Lt PA
John: b 1752 d 4-21-1818 m Mary Strayhorn PS NC
John: b *c.* 1735 d 1-20-1800 m Mary — Pvt DE
Michael: b 1743 d 1785 m Elizabeth Spates Pvt VA
Stephen: b 10-26-1755 d *p.* 1802 m Mary Farrar Sol NJ

MC CADDON,
John: b 1-27-1757 d 1846 m Elizabeth Silverthorn Pvt VA

MC CAFFERTY,
Joseph: b 1753 d 12-1-1845 m Deborah Beebe Pvt NJ

MC CAIN,
Barnet: b 1748 d 1829 m Margaret McGowan PS NH
Hugh, Sr.: b 1729 d 8-26-1821 m (1)Mary — (2)Jane (Pickens) Davis Sol PS CS NC
Hugh, Jr.: b 1748 d 3-6-1832 m Isabel Baskin Pvt NC ★
John: b 1733 d *p.* 5-7-1812 m Elizabeth Logan Pvt NJ
John: b 12-10-1753 d 3-9-1835 m Mary Huey Pvt NC ★
Wm.: b 1758 d 4-6-1823 m Eleanor Johnson Pvt SC
Wm.: b — d 9- -1807 m Charlotte Johnson Pvt PS NY

MC CALEB,
Alexander: b 2-21-1761 d 5-16-1845 m Hannah Young Pvt NY
James: b *c.* 1744 d *c.* 1827 m Mary — Pvt NC
Wm.: b 1747 d 4-19-1813 m Anne McKey Sol SC

MC CALL,
Benijah: b 9-12-1743 d 12-18-1824 m (1)Abigail Comstock (2)Mrs Naomi Crampton (3)Lois Brinsmade Pvt NY
Charles: b 1732 d 1814 m (1)Ann (Nancy)Williams (2)Hannah Eberett PS Pvt SC
Francis: b 1710 d 1794 m — Sol NC
George: b 9-10-1760 d 1-9-1837 m (1)Elizabeth Burnett (2)Elizabeth Sanders Pvt SC
James, 1st: b *c.* 1721 d *p.* 1790 m Janet Harris Sol PS NC
James, 2d: b 8-11-1741 d 4-1-1781 m Elizabeth — Col SC GA
John: b 3-21-1720 d 10-9-1812 m Elizabeth Ford Capt CT
John: b *c.* 1730 d *p.* 8-24-1809 m Jane — CS NC
John: b 1726 d 1810 m Jane McCall Pvt PA
John: b 1745 d 1821 m Jenny Robinson Pvt PA
John: b 3-20-1741 d *p.* 1790 m (2)Jane Proctor Lt SC
Josiah: b — d — m (1)Sara M. Smith (2)Sara Robertson Pvt PA
Robert: b 1751/2 d 4-9-1820 m (1)Virginia McFall (2)Elizabeth Aiken Sol SC
Samuel: b 1750 d 1795 m Rebecca Sherry Sgt VA
Thomas: b 3-19-1764 d 4-4-1840 m (1)Henrietta Harriet Fall (2)Elizabeth Ann Smith Sol SC
Thomas Harris: b *c.* 1730 d 7-20-1793 m Jane — PS NC
Wm.: b 1766 d 1-12-1830 m (1)Nancy Fletcher (2)Mary Pierce Pvt SC

MC CALLA,
David: b 1754 d 11-1-1826 m Mrs Mary (Adair) Nixon Pvt SC
Mary (Adair)Nixon: b 1755 d 11-16-1807 m (1)John Nixon (2)David McCalla PS SC
Robert: b *c.* 1739 d *p.* 1782 m Ruth Morrey Pvt PA
Sarah: b *a.* 1755 d *p.* 1781 m Thomas McCalla PS PA
Thomas: b 9-16-1756 d 10-15-1811 m Sarah Wayne Gardiner Pvt SC PA
Wm.: b 1732 d 1-26-1815 m Elizabeth Means Capt PA

MC CALLEY,
Alexander: b 1707 d 10-11-1788 m Mary Pinkerton Pvt NH
James: b 4-1-1745 d 1-24-1812 m Isabel Jameson Pvt NH
John: b 1-10-1742 d 12-22-1834 m Elizabeth Gibson Lt NH

MC CALLOM, (includes MC CALLON)
James: b 5-3-1743 d *p.* 1832 m Love — Pvt SC ★
Robert: b 10-1-1732 d 10-1-1800 m Isabella Lock Capt PA

MC CALMONT,
John: b *c.* 1756 d *c.* 1806/7 m Jane Jamison 1Lt PA
John: b 1746/7 d 1817 m Mary Livingstone Pvt PA
John: b 1-11-1750 d 8-3-1832 m Elizabeth Conrad Pvt PA

MC CAMANT,
James: b 1753 d 11-5-1825 m Abigail Graham Ens PA

MC CAMISH,
James: b 1754 d 11-30-1822 m Agnes Galbreath Sol VA
Thomas: b 1759 d 1-4-1840 m Jinney Wilson Pvt VA ★

MC CAMLY,
David, Jr.: b 9-9-1743 d 6-16-1817 m Phebe Sands Capt NY

MC CAMPBELL,
James: b 10- -1750 d 5-18-1809 m Martha Anderson Ens VA
Samuel: b c. 1743 d 1804 m Martha Cooper Ens CS VA

MC CANDLESS,
Alexander: b 1750 d 1-24-1817 m Jenny Wilson Pvt PA
James: b c. 1748 d p. 1830 m Mary Nott Pvt NC
James, Sr.: b c. 1735/6 d 1788 m Ruthia Capt PA
James, Jr.: b 2- -1760 d 2-17-1846 m Margaret Johnson Lt PA
John: b 6-10-1754 d 1-12-1840 m Susanna Farmer OrdSgt NC ★
John: b 1755 d 2-2-1827 m Jane Mason Pvt VA W★
Wm., Jr.: b c. 1745 d p. 1- -1797 m Agnes Smith Pvt PA

MC CANLEY,
Alexander, Jr.: b 1751 d 6-21-1822 m Esther Gregg Pvt NH

MC CANN,
James: b 1728 d p. 12-16-1797 m Mrs Mary Arnold Dr PS NC
James: b 1759 d 3-4-1839 m Jane Quail Pvt Fif PA ★
John: b 5-1-1740 d 10-4-1777 m Jane Goff Lt NC
John: b 11-11-1747 d 1803 m Flora — Pvt VA
Lawrence: b c. 1736 d 1814-20 m Mary — Sol PA
Patrick: b 1760 d 1853 m Hannah Johnson Pvt MD

MC CANNON,
Christopher: b c. 1754 d c. 1831 m Hannah Haddix Sgt VA
James: b 1761 d 1831 m Ann Worthington Pvt PA

MC CANTS,
Nathaniel: b 1745 d 7-9-1816 m Elizabeth Gautier Pvt SC
Thomas: b 1741 d 4-4-1830 m Ann Reed Pvt SC

MC CARGO,
Radford: b 1762 d p. 6- -1838 m — Harvey Pvt CS VA ★

MC CARROLL,
John: b 3-13-1757 d p. 1833 m Elizabeth Graeme Pvt Wgn PS PA ★

MC CART,
John: b 1-3-1754 d 5-19-1807 m Sarah Humphrey Sgt VA

MC CARTER,
Alexander: b 1755 d p. 1800 m Barbara Poffenbarger Pvt PA
Christopher: b 1760 d 10-19-1823 m Hannah Sol SC
James: b 5-28-1765 d 9-9-1844 m Nancy — Pvt SC ★
John: b 1759 d 1851 m Sarah Gillispie Pvt NY
Moses: b c. 1720 d 1788 m Catren — Sol SC

MC CARTNEY,
Daniel: b c. 1744 d 1818 m — Pvt PA
James: b 4-11-1745 d c. 1835 m Mary Taggart Pvt PA ★
Jeremiah Michael: b 1753 d 12-29-1831 m Rhoda Clark Pvt NC
John: b a. 1750 d p. 1780 m Bridget — SgtMaj PA
Joseph: b 11- -1742 d 1- -1823 m Sarah Galbreath Pvt PA
Robert: b 1-2-1763 d c. 1781 m (1) — Mitchell (2)Mary Mitchell Lt PA
Samuel: b 4- -1753 d 4-14-1817 m Nancy Penelope Young Pvt PA

MC CARTY, (includes MC CARTHY)
Charles: b 8-23-1741 d p. 11-11-1784 m Winifred Tarpley Maj CS VA
Clark: b 5-15-1755 d 12-3-1818 m Mabel Treadway Pvt CT
Daniel: b 2-22-1754 d 1844 m Elizabeth Joy Pvt MA ★
Daniel: b 1753 d 4-9-1829 m Letitia Johnson Pvt PA ★
Daniel: b 1-20-1762 d 1852 m Winifred Anderson Pvt VA ★
Daniel: b 1727 d 1791 m Sinah Ball PS VA
David: b 1737 d 1812 m Charlotte Witbeck PS NY
Edward: b 12-18-1756 d 8-25-1824 m Elizabeth Miller Sgt VA
Henry: b 1760 d 1849 m Margaret McDowell Pvt PA
James: b 1744 d 2-14-1804 m — Sgt PA
James: b c. 5-20-1754 d c. 1820 m Elizabeth Pruett Pvt NC
Michael: b 1755 d 6- -1813 m Elizabeth — Pvt PA
Nicholas: bpt 5-27-1742 d 2-26-1810 m Albertina Kohl Pvt PA
Philip: b 6-23-1754 d p. 1804 m Mary Van de Mark Pvt PA
Thomas: b 1746 d 8-25-1825 m Sarah Gaylord Pvt NY ★
Thomas: b 2-12-1741 d 10-9-1804 m Elizabeth Lancaster Pvt PA
Thomas: b 1756 d 1828 m Elizabeth McCarty Ens Spy VA
Thomas: b c. 1747 d 11-28-1822 m Ann Scott Sgt VA ★
Timothy: b c. 1760 d c. 1808 m (1)Nancy Honeyman (2)Jane Waugh Drm VA

MC CASKEY,
Alexander: b c. 1740 d p. 8- -1778 m Hannah Mifflin PS PA

MC CASKILL,
Finlay: b 1754 d 1811 m Margaret — Pvt SC

MC CAULEY, (includes MC AULEY, MC CAULY)
Alexander, Jr.: b 1-23-1751 d 6-21-1820 m Esther Gregg Pvt NH
Daniel: b 7-1-1756 d 12-24-1840 m Prudence — OrdSgt PA ★
James: b 4-1-1745 d 1-24-1812 m Isabel Jemeson Pvt NH
James: b c. 1755 d 4-28-1794 m Agnes Frierson Capt SC
James: b 1758 d 4-3-1818 m Catherine Chapman Capt SC

John: b 1-1-1733 d 4-1-1839 m Priscilla Howard Pvt PA
Mathew: b c. 1755 d 9-6-1820 m Martha Johnston Capt NC W★
Thomas: b 1757 d 5-23-1853 m — Pvt MD
Wm.: b 6-18-1757 d 4-6-1842 m Margaret Green Pvt NY
Wm.: b c. 1747 d p. 1818 m — Sol NC

MC CAUSLAND, (includes MC CASLAND, MC CASLIN)
Andrew: b c. 1750 d p. 1792 m Keziah Berry Pvt MA
Andrew: b 1758 d 7-8-1830 m Christiana Brown Pvt PA
Henry: b 1759 d 8-28-1829 m Abial Stackpole Pvt MA ★
James: b 1750 d 3-11-1826 m Mary Berry Pvt RI ★
John: b 1731 d 4- -1788 m Esther Stewart Pvt PA
John: b c. 1741/2 d 4- -1809 m (1)Martha — (2)Mary — Pvt PA
Samuel, 1st: b 1742 d 1-21-1816 m (1)Hester Mackey (2)Esther Sides Pvt PA
Wm.: b 1755 d 11-21-1821 m Rebecca Clemson Ens PA
Wm.: b 1760 d 1821 m Nancy Jane Pvt VA

MC CAW,
James: b 1762 d 9-4-1839 m Sarah McWilliams Pvt SC ★

MC CHAIN,
John: b 12-31-1755 d 1-31-1828 m Ann Hoyt Pvt NY

MC CHESNEY,
Benjamin: b 1760 d p. 1840 m Margaret — Pvt VA ★
Hugh: b 1741 d 2-15-1819 m Johanna Plum Pvt NY
John: b c. 1730 d 3- -1775 m (1)Mrs Newell (2)Mary McGuire PS NJ
John: b 1749 d 9-22-1822 m Rebecca — Pvt PA
Samuel: b 6-22-1753 d 4-4-1803 m Susannah — PS VA
Samuel: b c. 1761 d 1834 m Jemima Martin Pvt NJ
Wm.: b 1750 d p. 1790 m Mary McCauley PS MD

MC CLANAHAN, (includes MC CLENAHEN)
Alexander: b 1734 d a. 5-6-1797 m (1)Sallie Shelton (2)Elizabeth Clymer Col VA
Charles: b 8-28-1760 d 2-26-1836 m Elizabeth Bell Pvt PA ★
Elijah: b c. 1718 d p. 5-2-1794 m (1)Ann Ewing (2)Lettice Breckenridge (3)Margaret — PS CS VA
James: b — d 1-23-1802 m Letitia — PS VA
Robert, Jr.: b c. 1748-50 d 10-10-1774 m Catherine Madison Capt VA Heirs ★
Samuel: b 1-4-1730 d 10-17-1807 m Rachel Abbe McClennan BG CT
Thomas: b 1732 d 1806 m Mrs Isabella Hughes Walker 2Lt PA
Thomas: b 1753 d 10-15-1845 m (1)Ann Green (2)Tabitha Williams Pvt VA W★
Thomas, Sr.: b 1734 d 1809 m Margaret Strother Sol VA
Thomas, Jr.: b 1758 d 7-25-1834 m Mrs Elizabeth Field Pvt VA
Wm.: b 5-25-1740 d 9-25-1819 m Sarah Neilly LCol VA
Wm.: b c. 1730 d p. 5-15-1802 m Mary Marshall Capt VA
Wm.: b 7-25-1762 d 2-8-1842 m (1)Miss Johnson (2)Sarah Franklin Pvt VA ★

MC CLANATHAN,
Samuel: b 1740 d 6-14-1825 m Mary Blair Sgt MA
Thomas: b 1743 d 1-6-1818 m Catherine Shaw PS MA

MC CLARRAN,
Alexander: b 1754 d p. 2-15-1816 m Jane PS NC
Mathew: b c. 1760 d 1827 m Mary Kinkaid Pvt PA

MC CLARY, (includes MC CLEARY)
Andrew: b 9-8-1720 d 6-17-1775 m Elizabeth McCrillis Maj NH
Daniel: b 12-2-1740 d 7-26-1797 m Elizabeth Savage Lt NY
David: b 9- -1742 d 6-18-1823 m Elizabeth — Pvt PS NH
John: b 1764 d 5-5-1837 m Sarah Raffield Pvt SC
Michael: b 12-26-1752 d 3-27-1823 m Sarah (Sally)Dearborn Col NH
Robert: b 1749 d 1830 m (2)Mary Logan Robinson Pvt PA
Robert: b 1760 d 12-14-1814 m Anne Crow Pvt PA
Robert: b 1760 d 1827 m Jane — Pvt PA
Robert: b c. 1755 d 1781 m Mary Cameron Pvt SC W★

MC CLATCHEY,
James, Sr.: b — d a. 9-26-1808 m Jane — Pvt PA
James, Jr.: b 5-17-1767 d 4-28-1842 m (1)Margaret—(2)Elizabeth— Pvt PA

MC CLAUGHRY,
Andrew: b 1742 d 1-7-1826 m Elizabeth Jane Harsha Pvt NY
Matthew: b 1736 d 3-5-1789 m Anne Morrison Pvt NY
Richard: b 2- -1739 d 8-20-1819 m Anne Burrhus Pvt NY
Thomas: b 1747 d 9-10-1827 m (1)Agnes Harsha (2)Jennie Smith MM VA

MC CLAVE,
Wm.: b c. 1752/3 d 1803 m Maria Hofman Sgt NY

MC CLAY,
Wm.: b 1743 d 9-22-1829 m (2)Polly Farnsworth Pvt VT

MC CLELLAN, (includes MC CLALLEN, MC CLELLAND, MC LALLEN)

Alexander: b c. 1761/2 d 1824 m Catherine Coursin Lt PA
Cary: b 3-15-1753 d 3-8-1846 m Hannah Myers Pvt PA ★
Daniel: bpt 7-15-1753 d 7-29-1833 m (1)Mary Holmes (2)Margaret Holmes (3)Mrs Mary Gerrard Boyd Capt PA
David: b 1740/41 d 3-3-1790 m Jane Buchanan Ens MD
Hugh: b 4-4-1744 d 8-16-1816 m Sarah Wilson Capt MA
Hugh: b 1749 d 1799 m (1)Hannah Moore (2)— Kronkhite PS NY
Hugh: b 1756 d 1824 m — McFarland Capt PA
Hugh: b 1753 d 9- -1825 m Sarah Armstrong Pvt PA ★
James, Sr.: b 6-22-1727 d 9-11-1794 m Sarah Axtell Lt MA
James, Jr.: b 8-8-1758 d 6-26-1841 m Beulah Bacon Pvt MA
James, Sr.: b 10-19-1735 d 2-15-1816 m (1)Margaret Lamberton (2)Olive White Pvt MA
James: b 4-9-1761 d 3-8-1835 m Lydia Case Pvt NY
James: b 1758 d 1842 m (1) — Hughes (2)Sarah McKinley Pvt PA ★
James: b 11-14-1760 d 1809 m Sarah Hanna Pvt PA
John: b 1755 d 1848 m Sarah Thompson Pvt NY
John: b c. 1740 d 6-5-1782 m Martha Dale LCol PA
John: b 1732/3 d 12-12-1817 m Sydney Smith Roddy Capt PA
John: b 1734 d a. 2-23-1819 m Margaret Kimble Capt PA
John: b c. 1740 d 1-1-1777 m Sarah Lowry CS Pvt VA
Joseph: b 4-28-1747 d 10-13-1834 m Keziah Parke Capt PA
Robert: b 1716 d 8-24-1789 m Nicola Gordon Mil PS NY
Samuel: b 1-4-1730 d 9-17-1807 m (1)Jemima Chandler (2)Rachel Abbe (3)Eunice Folunsbee Col CT
Samuel: b a. 1753 d 3-5-1829 m Elizabeth Oliver 1Lt PA
Samuel: b 1745 d 3-9-1806 m Sarah Morrison Pvt PA
Thomas: b a. 1727 d 4-17-1809 m (1)Elizabeth Mitchell (2)Janet Trimble Pvt PA
Thomas: b 1757 d 11-10-1839 m Agnes Fergus Pvt PA NC ★
Wm.: b 1-11-1765 d 12-25-1828 m Sarah Guyer Fif MA
Wm.: b 1735 d 10- -1796 m (1)Eleanor McMichael (2)Mary Reynolds Capt PA
Wm.: b c. 175 ' d c. 1809 m — Lt PA
Wm.: b 1742 d '1-12-1812 m Martha Miller Ens PA
Wm.: b 1733 d 7-.?-1815 m Esther — Pvt PA
Wm.: b 1761 d 4-8-1817 m Margaret Patterson Pvt PA
Wm.: b 8- -1755 d 2-19-1834 m Janet Thompson Pvt VT
Wm.: b c. 1741 d 1825 m Barbara Walker Capt VA
Wm.: b c. 1745 d 1824 m Sarah — Pvt VA

MC CLENDON,

Isaac: b 1740 d 1825 m Elizabeth Stribling Pvt GA
Isaac: b c. 1753 d 1823 m Mary Fincher Pvt GA
Jacob, Sr.: b c. 1715 d 1793 m Martha — Pvt GA
Jacob, Jr.: b c. 1752 d 1779 m Elender E. — Pvt GA
Joseph: b a. 1756 d 1837 m (2)Olive Blake Pvt GA
Josiah: b 1766 d 1856 m — Granbery Pvt NC
Samuel: b 1741 d 12-11-1838 m Sarah Ware Pvt GA
Shadrack: b 1753 d p. 1846 m — Pvt SC ★
Thomas: b c. 1728 d p. 1824 m Sarah Cooper Sol GA
Thomas, Jr.: b 1758-60 d 1-1-1831 m Elizabeth — Pvt GA
Travis: b 1755 d 1835 m Sallie Edmonds Capt GA

MC CLIMAN,

John: b 4-29-1756 d 8-8-1829 m Mary Creviston PS PA
John: b 1752 d 6-16-1817 m Elizabeth Hannah Pvt PA

MC CLINTOCK,

Alexander: b c. 1741 d p. 1790 m Janet Gambler Pvt PS NH
Alexander: b a. 1748 d 9-18-1777 m Sarah May Lt PA
Alexander: b 1732 d 1803 m Mary Esten Pvt PA
Daniel: b 9-16-1716 d 1-9-1799 m Frances — Pvt PA
Hugh: b c. 1750 d 1807 m Ann Crouthers Pvt PA
James: b c. 1740 d p. 1790 m Mary Williamson Sgt PA
John: b c. 1740 d 1807 m Isabella Starrett PS NC
John: b c. 1730 d a. 9-30-1805 m Mary Ann Sgt PA
Joseph: b c. 1744 d 8-13-1825 m Rebecca Patton Pvt PA
Michael: b c. 1700 d p. 1790 m — PS NH
Samuel: b 5-1-1732 d 4-27-1804 m Mary Montgomery Chp NH
Wm.: b c. 1720 d p. 1780 m Agnes Oglebee PS NH
Wm.: b c. 1734 d 1804 m — McClintock Pvt PA
Wm.: b c. 1743 d p. 1790 m Jean Sharp Pvt PA
Wm.: b 1750 d 3-20-1820 m Elizabeth Torrence Pvt PA
Wm.: b 1759 d 9-13-1786 m Alice Mann Pvt VA
Wm.: b 1717 d 1801 m Nancy Shanklin PS VA

MC CLISTER,

James: b c. 1756 d 1837 m Sarah Roan Pvt PA

MC CLOSKEY, (includes MC CLESKY)

James: b 1-20-1755 d 10-20-1842 m Isabell Rhea Pvt PS SC ★
Joseph: b 1735 d 1805 m Agnes — Pvt PS SC
Joseph: b 1756 d 2-25-1837 m Mary Green Pvt SC ★
Wm.: b 1766 d 9-29-1836 m Mary — Pvt SC ★

MC CLOW,

Cornelius: b c. 1755 d 3-20-1812 m Elizabeth Brewer Pvt NJ

MC CLUNG,

Charles: b c. 1757/8 d p. 1790 m Margaret Young Pvt PA
Charles: b 9-27-1761 d 8-19-1810 m Margaret Martin PS PA
James: b 1720 d 1798 m Ann Gray Pvt PA
James: b 1736 d 8-28-1790 m Nancy Dickenson CS VA
John, Jr.: b 1733 d 1830 m Sarah McCutcheon Lt VA
John: b 1731 d 1817 m Elizabeth Alexander Spy Sol VA
John: b 1706 d 1788 m Rebecca Stuart PS VA
Joseph: b c. 1744 d 2-3-1819 m Margaret Bell PS VA
Matthew: b c. 1730 d a. 1802 m Martha — Pvt PA
Matthew: b 10-11-1757 d 6-2-1844 m Jane Cummins Pvt PA ★
Samuel: b 1744 d 4- -1806 m Rebecca Bourland Pvt VA
Thomas: b 1753 d 5-4-1832 m Nancy Graham Pvt PA
Wm.: b 10-25-1746 d 7-28-1779 m Jean Leach Pvt PA
Wm.: b 1738 d 1-18-1833 m Abigail Carpenter Sol VA
Wm.: b c. 1742 d 1794 m Jean Dun Sol VA
Wm.: b 1761 d 2-14-1837 m Euphemia Cunningham Tms VA
Wm.: b c. 1705 d p. 9-20-1783 m — CS VA

MC CLURE,

Abdiel: b 6-8-1751 d 6-14-1823 m Mary Cummins Lt PA ★
Alexander: b 1730 d 3- -1803 m Martha — Cpl PS PA
Alexander: b c. 1760 d 10-15-1850 m Nancy Shepherd Pvt VA
Alexander: b c. 1762 d p. 3-4-1842 m Nancy Dupuy Pvt VA
Alexander: bpt 1749 d p. 3-14-1789 m Martha — PS VA
Andrew: b 1752-56 d 6-27-1850 m (2)Mary Allen Sgt NJ ★
Andrew: b 1755 d 1793 m Rebecca Allen Lt VA
Andrew, Sr.: b 1720 d 1789 m Eleanor Wright Pvt VA
Arthur: b c. 1753 d 1800 m Martha — PS CS VA
Benjamin: b 9-9-1759 d 8-31-1821 m Agnes Wallace Lt PA
Charles: b 1739 d 2-8-1811 m (1)Mary Blair (2)Amelia Blair (3)Rebecca Parker PS PA
Daniel: b 2-13-1754 d 12-24-1825 m Martha Baird Pvt PA
David: b 1-1-1733 d 5-6-1813 m (1)Janet Moocher (2)Hannah Richardson (3)Lucy Kibbe Lt PS CT W★
David: b 1758 d 5-24-1835 m Martha Wilson Pvt NH★
David: b 1726 d 7-14-1796 m Jane McCormick Pvt VA
Francis: b 10-5-1739 d 4-22-1843 m Margaret McClure Pvt PA
George: b 6-4-1754 d 9-5-1829 m Jane Gilmore Pvt PA
George: b 1755 d 12-1-1819 m Sarah Stewart Pvt PA
Hugh: b 1760 d 3-3-1802 m Jane — Capt SC
James: b 4-17-1753 d 5-17-1840 m Mary Nesmith Lt PS NH ★
James: b 1-11-1746 d 10-2-1821 m Esther — Capt PA
James: b 7-9-1748 d 8-16-1821 m Martha — Capt PA
James: b c. 1740 d p. 7-2-1816 m — Scott Lt PA
James: b a. 1760 d 1813 m Margaret Pollock Lt PA
James: b 1733 d 1778/9 m. Mary Espy PS PA
James: b c. 1740 d p. 1825 m Elizabeth — Bennett Sol SC
James: b c. 1750 d p. 1790 m Jane Martin PS SC
John: b 1739 d 4-11-1817 m Ann McKragan Pvt NC
John: b 1737 d 1813 m Violet McElhaney Sgt PA
John: b c. 1740 d c. 1795 m — Scott Sgt PA
John: b 1722/3 d 7- -1811 m Martha Denny Pvt PA
John: b 7-12-1745 d 6-14-1814 m Mrs Jane McClintoc Pvt PA
John: b 1746 d 1789 m Rebecca Chambers Pvt PA
John: b 12-2-1758 d 3-25-1839 m Martha Loughead Pvt PA
John: b 1730 d 8-18-1780 m Mary Porter Capt SC
John: b c. 1764 d p. 1790 m Ruth Pratt Mil VT
John: b 4-15-1760 d 5-24-1856 m Margaret OrdlSgt VA
John: b c. 1717 d 8-28-1791 m Mary — Pvt VA
John: b 11-11-1750 d 1820 m Nancy Steele McCluer Pvt VA
John Graves: b 1760 d 12-30-1840 m — Pvt SC ★
Jonathan: b 1745 d 12-11-1799 m Sarah Hayes Capt PA
Joseph: b 11-24-1744 d 3-8-1817 m Rebecca Densmore Drm MA
Joseph: b 9-3-1761 d 8-15-1829 m Margaret Carson Pvt NH ★
Josiah: b 1752 d p. 12-31-1826 m Sarah Harris PS VA
Mary Gaston: b 1712 d 1802 m James McClure PS SC
Matthew: b c. 1755 d 2-28-1805 m — PS NC
Richard: b 6-16-1754 d 7-9-1835 m (1)Margaret Laird (2)Mary McClure Sgt PS PA
Robert: b 7-19-1718 d 4- -1818 m Martha Rogers Pvt NH
Robert: b 1753 d 9-11-1830 m Margery Buffington Pvt SC
Samuel: b 1736 d 1790 m Jenet Graham Pvt PA
Samuel: b 10-1-1753 d 4-6-1816 m Phebe Edgerton Pvt VT
Samuel: b 5-16-1748 d 12-18-1845 m Jane Hamilton Pvt VA ★
Thomas: b 9-5-1748 d 1832 m Mary — Ens NC
Thomas: b 1760 d 1832 m Mary Moorehead Pvt NC
Thomas: b c. 1739 d 1778 m Mary Harvey Pvt PS PA
Thomas: b 9-2-1762 d 9-3-1832 m Margaret Beyers Pvt PA
Wm.: b 12-14-1749 d 12-14-1811 m Margaret Mosman CS Capt PA ★
Wm.: b 1740 d 1-14-1814 m Rebecca Harvey Pvt PA
Wm.: b 1750 d 1815 m Mary McAllister Pvt PA
Wm.: b c. 1752 d 11- -1791 m (2)Margaret — Pvt PA
Wm.: b 3-31-1759 d 10-1-1823 m (1)Agnes McKeehan (2)Margaret McKeehan Capt PA
Wm.: b 1738 d 1785 m Margaret Wright Ens PA
Wm.: b 1758 d 10-28-1832 m Rebecca Leggett Pvt Sct VA
Wm.: b 1752-61 d 1814 m Mary Shields Pvt VA

MC CLURG,

James: b 1748 d 1825 m Elizabeth Selden Dr PS VA

MC CLURKIN,
John: b c. 1755 d 1- -1819 m Elizabeth — Pvt SC
Mathew: b 1761 d 5-1-1847 m (1)Jennet — (2)Mary Gaston Elliott Pvt SC ★
Samuel: b c. 1752 d a. 5-2-1795 m — Pvt SC
Thomas: b 1756 d 3-22-1845 m Elizabeth Smith Pvt SC ★

MC COBB,
James: b 1710 d 7-17-1788 m (1)Beatrice Rogers (2)Mrs Hannah Miller PS ME
Samuel: b 11-20-1740 d 7-30-1791 m Rachel Denny Col MA
Samuel: b 1707 d 2-8-1791 m Mary — PS ME

MC COLLISTER,
Hamilton: b 3-25-1742 d 5-13-1825 m Sarah Dick Pvt PS NY

MC COLLUM,
Cornelius: b 1-4-1749 d 2-14-1837 m Rebecca Leeds Ens NJ ★
Daniel: b 1-24-1754 d 4-12-1842 m Sarah Moore Ens PA
Daniel: b 1740 d 2-7-1807 m (2)Isabella Sellers Sol SC
David: b 1752 d 11-22-1830 m Lucy Cook Pvt NJ
James: b 1724 d 1800 m — Fif PA
John: b c. 1745 d p. 5-19-1794 m Elener — Sol VA
Mary: b c. 1743 d 2- -1783 m Daniel McCollum PS NC
Patrick: b 12-27-1749 d 1838/39 m Mary McClain OrdlSgt NY ★
Thomas: b 8-20-1751 d 7-1-1806 m Mary Veneman Pvt PA

MC COMB,
Allan: b 1749 d 8-8-1830 m Hannah Bovard Lt PA
Andrew: b c. 1739 d p. 3-15-1788 m Jane Raeburn PS VA
David: b 1759 d 12-18-1837 m Margaret Scott Pvt PA
George: b 1754 d — m — Pvt PA
James: b 1739 d 10-10-1813 m Mary — Sol PS NC
James: b 1758 d 7-13-1814 m Nancy Jack Pvt PA
John: b 1732 d 12-24-1811 m Mary Davis Pvt Cpl NJ
John: b 2-27-1747 d 2-27-1822 m Elizabeth Marshall Pvt PA
Robert: b 1752 d 1-9-1830 m Jane Stephenson PS PA
Wm.: b c. 1748 d 1807 m Mary — Pvt PA
Wm.: b c. 1750 d p. 1786 m Temperance Cole Pvt PA
Wm.: b 1-10-1757 d 2-10-1835 m Rebecca Kearsley Pvt PA W★

MC CONAUGHY,
David: b 1716 d 12-8-1815 m Margaret Ramsey PS PA
James: b c. 1759 d p. 1800 m Isabella Moore Sol PA
John: b 4-15-1762 d 3- -1846 m Jane Davis Pvt VA ★
Robert: b — d 3- -1800 m Hannah Finley Capt PA

MC CONICK,
John: b 6-10-1756 d 4-21-1838 m Abigail Hartshorn Pvt MA ★

MC CONKEY,
Hugh: b 3-14-1754 d 8-11-1837 m Jane Neeper Pvt PS PA
Wm.: b 1-22-1744 d 9-10-1825 m Hannah Mather Capt PA

MC CONNELL,
Abram: b 10-16-1757 d 8-7-1830 m Rosannah Fryatt Sol VA
Alexander: b 1-5-1761 d 7-18-1822 m Judith Pemberton Lloyd Sgt PA
Alexander: b 7-10-1755 d 4-2-1825 m (1)Esther Reed (2)Elizabeth McCrory Pvt PA
Alexander: b 1-26-1758 d 11-12-1821 m Rebecca Thompson Pvt VA
Andrew: b c. 1730 d 8-19-1782 m — Pvt KY
Francis: b 4- -1754 d 2-21-1833 m Mary Treadway Pvt NJ ★
Hugh: b a. 1752 d 1820 m Jane Ferguson Pvt NJ
Hugh: b 1759 d 9-4-1826 m Rebecca Whiteside Pvt PA
Hugh: b 1758 d 1835 m Elizabeth Jolly — Ens VA
James: b 3-9-1747 d 12-29-1820 m (1)Mary Cunningham (2)Mrs Griffith Capt PA
James: b 2-14-1743 d 1-24-1807 m Rebecca — Capt PA
James: b 1756 d 2-18-1816 m Mary — Pvt SC
James: b 11-1-1758 d 2-22-1832 m Elizabeth Pvt PA
John: b 1752 d 2-9-1822 m — Sol SC GA
John: b 1746 d 8-14-1819 m Mary Dawson Capt PA
John: b 1732 d 1789 m Elizabeth Pvt PA
John: b 5-10-1740 d 6-2-1800 m Margaret Johnsey PS SC
John A.: b 1-20-1745 d 7-10-1825 m Mary Hannah Capt SC
Manual: b 1757 d 9-9-1842 m Martha Armstrong Pvt SC GA ★
Mathew: b 12-2-1739 d 6-21-1817 m (1)Elizabeth (2)Mary Porter Sgt NY
Matthew: b 1748 d 11-11-1816 m Ruth Hall BgdMaj PA
Philip: b c. 1738 d p. 9-10-1778 m Sarah McClelland Pvt NC
Robert: b 1758 d 1-24-1829 m Catharine Weiser Capt PA
Robert: b a. 1750 d p. 1800 m Agnes Willson Sgt PA
Samuel: b 11-26-1739 d 12-26-1817 m Ann Cunningham Maj NH
Thomas: b 6-9-1749 d 1-1-1801 m Mary Blakely Pvt SC
Wm.: b c. 1750 d 4- -1823 m Rosannah Kennedy PS KY
Wm.: b 1734 d 1812 m Hetty — Pvt PA
Wm.: b 2-8-1751 d 9-18-1831 m Sarah January Pvt PA
Wm.: b c. 1750 d p. 2-10-1807 m Mary Cowen Pvt PS VA

MC CONOUGHEY,
David: b 2- -1732 d 9-15-1805 m Anna Carnahan 1Lt MA

MC COOL,
Joseph: b 1750 d 1825 m Mary Thomas Sol PS SC
Samuel: b c. 1743 d p. 7-3-1815 m (2)Mrs Barbara Raynor Pvt PA

MC CORD,
David: b c. 1745 d p. 9-30-1818 m (1)Mary — (2)Elizabeth Cowden CS NC
David: b 3-10-1747 d 6-4-1818 m Anna Shiply PS NC
James: b 1739 d 11-4-1824 m Jane Scruggs PS NC
James: b c. 1750 d p. 7-31-1793 m Jean — Pvt SC
John: b 12-18-1747 d 10-24-1837 m (1)Ida Hoffman (2)Sarah Terwilliger Pvt NY ★
Mark: b 1745 d 1781 m Catharine Miller Cpl PA
Samuel: b 1730 d — m Miriam Applebe Pvt NY
Samuel: b 6-6-1756 d 7- -1835 m Agnes Jamison Sol VA
Wm.: b 1748 d 3-1-1832 m (1)Rachel Gandy (2)Sarah Kingsland Sgt PA ★
Wm.: b 1745 d 9-9-1806 m (1)Agnes McKinney (2)Rachel Scudder (3)Miss Patterson Pvt PA
Wm.: b 1755 d 1798 m Catharine Pressley Sgt VA
Wm.: b 1762 d 3-20-1846 m — Pvt VA ★

MC CORKLE,
Alexander: b a. 1723 d 12-25-1800 m (1)Nancy Agnes Montgomery Sol NC
Andrew: b 1750 d 1-12-1777 m Elizabeth Ruth Pvt VA
Archibald: b 10-27-1754 d 6-6-1844 m — White Pvt SC ★
Francis: b 1742 d 10-19-1802 m (1)Sarah Work (2)Elizabeth Brandon Capt CS PS NC
George: b a. 1754 d 1814 m Catherine Pvt PA
James: b c. 1740 d 1782 m — Pvt PA
James: b 1750 d 1806 m Elizabeth Anderson Pvt PA
James: b — d 2-22-1780 m Mary Todd Pvt PA
James: b c. 1740 d 1-17-1781 m Margaret McCollom Ens VA
John: b c. 1755 d p. 8-24-1810 m (2)Susannah — CS NC
John: b 1745 d 1-1-1781 m Rebecca Anderson McNutt Ens VA
John: b 11-22-1753 d 5-6-1814 m Lydia Tyler Forrest Pvt VA
John: b c. 1738 d — m Elizabeth Ruth Sol VA
Joseph: b 1753 d 7-25-1828 m Margaret Snoddy Sol NC
Robert: b 3-6-1760 d 3-10-1833 m Elizabeth Tyler Forrest Ord Sgt VA ★
Samuel: b 8-23-1746 d 6-21-1811 m Margaret Gillespie PS NC

MC CORMICK, (includes MC CORMACK)
Adam: b 1735 d 7-12-1791 m Elizabeth — Sgt PA
Andrew: b c. 1755 d 12-7-1797 m Catherine Adams Pvt NC
Archibald: b 10-10-1762 d 8-4-1839 m Susan Woodburn Pvt VT ★
Francis: b 4-17-1734 d 1794 m (1)Ann Province (2)Ann Frost Lt VA
Francis: b 6-3-1764 d 7-26-1836 m Rebecca Easton McCormick Pvt VA ★
George: b 1757 d p. 1-15-1802 m Rachel Moore Pvt VA
George: b 4-6-1742 d 1-20-1820 m (1)Mary — (2)Mary Chaplain Capt VA ★
Hugh: b 1725 d 1777 m Sarah Alcorn Wgm PA
Hugh: b 1720 d 1810 m Mary Price PS PA
Hugh: b 1735 d 1799 m Catharine Sanderson Pvt VA
Hugh: b 12-12-1741 d 6-5-1819 m Mattie Johnson Sol SC
James: b 2-22-1762 d 9-10-1834 m Mary — Pvt PA
James: b 2-3-1813 d 4-1-1814 m (1)Mary Ann Fletcher (2)Catharine Oliver Sol PS SC
John: b 3-20-1738 d 2-8-1814 m Barbara McEachern Sol NC
John: b 3-14-1748 d 5-22-1844 m Betsy Fleming Ens PA
John: b c. 1750 d p. 9-12-1828 m Elizabeth McMillen Pvt PS PA
John: b 7-9-1756 d 1-23-1861 m Christinia E. Hillicoss Pvt PA
John: b 8-30-1754 d 4-18-1837 m Catherine Drennen Pvt VA PA ★
John: b — d p. 5-28-1814 m — Capt VA
John: b c. 1750 d 9- -1822 m Ann Hutchins Pvt VA
Joseph: b 1744/45 d 1840 m Peggy Watson Pvt GA ★
Patrick: b c. 1760 d p. 1850 m Margaret — Pvt PA
Robert: b 1738 d 10-12-1818 m Martha Sanderson Sol VA
Thomas: b 1760 d 1842 m Mary Ann Day Pvt GA ★
Thomas: b 1759 d 1827 m Catherine Fisher Fif VA
Wm.: b 1732 d 1810 m Mary Wiggin Pvt PA
Wm.: b 1740 d 1815 m Nancy Craig Pvt PA
Wm.: b c. 1760 d 3-5-1817 m Grissil Porter Pvt PA W★
Wm.: b c. 1760 d p. 1793 m Maria Cary Eggleston Pvt VA

MC COTTRY,
Robert: b 3-2-1748 d 3-4-1805 m Mary White Capt SC

MC COWN, (includes MC CONN)
Alexander: b 11-25-1755 d 9-23-1835 m Susanna Uncel Pvt PA ★
Alexander: b c. 1730 d p. 1798 m Elizabeth — Pvt SC
James, Sr.: b 1717 d 10- -1800 m Margaret Walker Pvt VA
James, Jr.: b 3-11-1745 d 12- -1790 m Anne Tilford Pvt VA
James: b 9-2-1758 d 1-9-1845 m Phebe Casto Pvt VA ★
John: b — d 6-8-1818 m Sarah Cusack Adj SC
John: b 1755 d 1817 m (1)Nancy Kinnear (2)Eleanor McCampbell Sol VA
Justus: b 5-28-1745 d 1810 m Susannah — PS NY
Moses: b — d p. 11-2-1784 m Mary Pvt PS SC
Patrick: b 1739 d 1-24-1779 m Margery Fullerton PS ME
Thomas, Sr.: b c. 11-7-1763 d 3-7-1848 m Isabella Wilson Pvt PA

MC COY, (includes MC CAY)

Alexander: b 7-2-1752 d 9- -1794 m Eleanor Graham Bbd CT W★
Alexander: b 11-16-1744 d 5-27-1832 m Lydia Spaulding Pvt PS NH
Alexander: b 1730 d 1-30-1822 m Jane Watts Capt PA
Alexander: b c. 1741 d p. 11- -1807 m Margaret — Pvt PA
Alexander: b 1752 d 3-7-1829 m Frances Catherine Sutherland
    Pvt PA ★
Alexander: b c. 1753 d p. 1804 m Nancy Campbell PS PA
Daniel: b 1760 d 1809 m Mary — Sol GA
Daniel: b 1755 d 1818 m Christina Sutherland Pvt PA
Daniel: b 1757 d 5-16-1841 m Jane Parish Pvt PA
Daniel: b 1750 d 1814 m Nancy Nelms Pvt VA
Daniel: b 10-15-1761 d 2-23-1836 m Agnes Kemper Pvt VA ★
David: b c. 1742 d 1805 m Nancy Wallace Pvt PA
Gavin: b 1738 d 4-20-1800 m Susanna Kinan Capt NJ
James: b c. 1740 d p. 1776 m Jane McNeely CS NC
James: b c. 1719 d 9-30-1801 m Ann Bruce Pvt PA
John: b 1745 d 6-30-1831 m Elizabeth Arbuckle Pvt MD
John: b 1728 d 3-17-1794 m Frances — PS MD
John, Sr.: b a. 1724 d p. 1776 m Jane — Pvt PS NH
John: d 1-9-1823 m Margaret Boyd Pvt NH
John: b 2-11-1743 d 12-14-1809 m Mary Cook Pvt NY
John: b c. 1758 d a. 9-3-1836 m (1)Sarah — (2)Mary — Pvt NC
John: b — d c. 1787 m Sarah Coffey Pvt PA
John: b c. 1725 d a. 4-19-1794 m — Pvt PA
John: b 1760 d 4-13-1834 m — Pvt SC
John: b 1748 d 1790 m Catharine — Sol SC
John: b 1749/50 d 1856 m Elizabeth Finch Pvt VA
John: b 1750 d p. 1784 m Rebecca Blair Pvt VA
John: b c. 1735 d p. 8-20-1796 m Sarah Oliver Capt VA
John: b 1754 d 1821 m Martha Humphreys Cpl VA
Joseph: b — d 1799 m Mary PS SC
Malachi: b c. 1755 d 1-5-1829 m (1)Ann Lassell (2)Clarkie Maudlin
    Pvt NC
Nathaniel: b c. 1758 d 12-3-1826 m (1) — Haughton (2)Rebecca
    Ferguson Pvt DE
Neal: b 1737 d 3-3-1814 m Rachel Thornton Pvt PA
Perry: b c. 1740 d 1-1-1822 m Mary — 1Lt MD
Redden: b 9-29-1757 d 1-9-1843 m Susan Pringle Sgt SC ★
Richard: b — d p. 10-24-1792 m Susanna Pvt VA
Robert: b 7-14-1753 d 10-7-1823 m Rachel Collett Pvt PA
Robert: b 11-26-1761 d 11-30-1852 m Margaret Drake Pvt VA ★
Thomas: b 1754 d 10-13-1810 m Catherine Park Pvt MD
Thomas: b c. 1750 d 1781 m — Lt PA
Thomas: b c. 1757 d c. 1822 m Hannah — Pvt 2Lt PA
Wm.: b 1746 d p. 1789 m Nancy Smith Pvt NY
Wm.: b 6- -1762 d 1848 m Eunice Carswell Pvt NY ★
Wm.: b 1730 d 1797 m Elizabeth — Sol NC
Wm.: b 1751 d p. 1790 m Racheal — Sgt PA
Wm.: b c. 1730 d 3-14-1791 m Rebecca Smith Pvt PA
Wm.: b 1730 d 1800 m Jean — Pvt PA
Wm.: b 1754 d 8-2-1813 m Elizabeth Rice Pvt PA
Wm.: b 1758 d 1806 m Elizabeth Spear Pvt PA
Wm.: b 1746 d p. 1790 m Sarah Sibley Sol SC
Wm.: b 1758 d 2-10-1842 m (1)Mary Washington (2)Nancy Waple
    (3)Susan Buchanan Sgt VA
Wm.: b 1740 d p. 1795 m Jane Mann Lt VA

MC CRACKEN,

Cyrus: b — d 5- -1794 m Elizabeth Palmer Sol VA
Henry: b — d 5-31-1778 m — PS Pvt PA
James: b 1750 d 1-18-1802 m (1)Jane — (2)Elizabeth Davidson
    Sol NC
James: b c. 1753 d p. 1- -1807 m Rebecca Greenwood Pvt PA
John: b 1755 d 1817 m Esther — Pvt PA
Joseph: b 1737 d 5-5-1825 m Sarah Turner Maj NY ★
Philip: b 1760 d 12-29-1810 m Mary McKeever Pvt NJ
Samuel: b c. 1746/7 d 9-9-1794 m Jerusha McIlhenny Sgt PS PA
Seneca: b 1789 d 9-8-1829 m Rebecca Reynolds Pvt PA
Wm.: b 1764 d 7-6-1830 m (1)Hannah Younglove (2)Mary Thompson
    Fif NY ★
Wm.: b 1754 d 1-16-1803 m Mrs Elizabeth Peebles Lt PA
Wm., Jr.: b c. 1757 d 11-4-1782 m Anne Higgins Capt VA

MC CRAW,

Francis: b 5-9-1760 d 9-28-1834 m Mary Harrison Word Pvt VA ★
Jacob: b c. 1750-60 d 7-10-1815 m Elizabeth Waller PS Tms VA
Wm.: b c. 1745 d 1816 m (1)Susannah Walker (2)Jane Towles
    Medley PS VA

MC CREA, (includes MC CRAY)

John: b — d 1811 m (1)Sarah Beekman (2)Helen McNaughton Col NY
John: b c. 1751 d p. 1790 m Ann Baker Pvt PA
John: b c. 1755 d 1777 m Jane Porter Pvt PA
John: b a. 1765 d p. 1817 m Mary DuBose Sol SC
John: b c. 1740 d a. 1810 m — Pvt SC
Phineas: b 10-21-1762 d 8-29-1838 m Sarah Jane Peters Pvt PA
Samuel: b 9-16-1749 d 6-16-1809 m Margaret Sloan Pvt NY
Samuel: b c. 1724 d p. 1-2-1777 m Elizabeth McClelland Pvt PA
Samuel: b c. 1740 d p. 1791 m Rebecca Douglass Pvt PA
Thomas: b 9-6-1754 d 7-21-1833 m (2)Jeannette Cooper (3)Esther
    DuBose Pvt SC

MC CREADY, (includes MC CREDY)

Robert: b 11-20-1743 d 11-20-1814 m Jane Mulrae Pvt NY
Robert: b 3-28-1752 d 8-10-1846 m Anne Levins Pvt PA

MC CREARY, (includes MC CRAY, MC CREERY, MC CRERY)

Amos: b — d p. 1790 m Hannah Whinery Pvt PA
George: b 1752 d 2-26-1842 m Mary — Sgt PA ★
James: b 1737 d 1820 m Isabella Giffin Capt NC
James: b 2- -1763 d 12-31-1813 m Jean Agnew Sol PA
John: b a. 1741 d 1800 m Rebecca Wallace CS DE
John: b c. 1740 d p. 2-7-1814 m Rebecca — Pvt PA
John: b 1739 d p. 1785 m Susanna Estill Lt VA
Robert: b — d p. 4-16-1814 m Mary Fortune LCol PS SC
Robert: b c. 1740 d 9- -1803 m Mary — Col SC
Robert: b 1740 d p. 1790 m Polly McClanahan Capt VA
Samuel: b 6-22-1739 d 10-6-1784 m Mary Caughey Pvt PA
Thomas, Sr.: b c. 1737 d c. 1793 m Littie Brandon Sol SC
Wm.: b 1762 d 1816 m Deborah — PS PA

MC CREIGHT,

David: b 1749 d 2-7-1817 m Martha Orr Pvt SC
Robert: b 1761 d 12-22-1842 m Margaret — 2Lt SC ★

MC CRILLIS, (includes MC CRELLIS)

David: b 9-2-1754 d 5-31-1825 m (1)Mrs Susanna Moore (2)Mary
    Gerrish Pvt PS NH
Henry: b 1-20-1747 d 8-15-1814 m Margaret McGaffry Ens NH
Robert: b 1740 d 6-9-1819 m Mary Kenney Pvt NH
Wm.: b 1733 d p. 1790 m (1)Eleanor King (2)Mrs Sarah Palmer
    Sol MA
Wm.: b 1750 d 6- -1775 m Lydia Morrell Pvt NH

MC CRORY,

James: b 5-15-1758 d 11-24-1840 m Jean Gilmore Ens NC ★
Thomas: b 1735 d 1788 m Hannah Crawford Capt NC

MC CROSKY, (includes MC CROSKEY)

David: b — d 1778 m Grizelda Poage CS VA
John: b 9-26-1757 d 8-17-1843 m Ann Montgomery Pvt VA ★

MC CRUM,

Wm.: b 1753 d 12- -1833 m Hepzibah Stout Sgt PA

MC CUBBIN, (or MC CUBIN)

James: b 5-15-1755 d 3-16-1824 m Polly Cook Pvt NC
Nicholas: b c. 1724 d a. 3-15-1787 m Mary Clare Carroll Capt MD
Richard: b 1710 d 1779 m Elizabeth Creigh PS MD
Zacharias: b 1756 d p. 1800 m Sarah Lane Capt MD

MC CUE,

John: b 1715-20 d p. 10-27-1798 m Eleanor Mathews CS VA

MC CULLAR,

Alexander, Sr.: b 12-24-1758 d 1848 m Esther — Pvt GA ★

MC CULLERS,

John: b 1740 d 1822 m Mary — Capt NC
Matthew: b 6-14-1759 d 6-28-1825 m Sarah Lane Capt NC W★

MC CULLOCH,

Abram: b 1760 d 5-5-1839 m Alcy Boggs Pvt PS VA ★
Benjamin: b 1737 d 1809 m Sarah Stokes PS NC
James: b 6-4-1756 d 8-15-1843 m Sarah Otis Pvt MA ★
John: b c. 1763 d 1812 m Nancy Butt Pvt GA
John: b 1755 d 1850 m Nancy Murdock Pvt NC
John: b 4-29-1749 d 4-13-1800 m (1)Ann Todd (2)Ann Bringhurst
    Maj PA MA
John: b 1740 d 3-10-1808 m Elizabeth Huston Sol PA
John: b 1752 d 4-6-1821 m Mary Bulkey CS Pvt VA
Joseph: b 1738 d 5-2-1823 m Sara Spring Cpl MA
Robert: b 1790 d 1799 m Sarah McCartney Pvt PA
Roderick: b 11-6-1741 d 11-1-1821 m Elizabeth Horsley Capt CS
    VA
Thomas: b 1735 d 10-12-1780 m Isabella Patrick Lt VA

MC CULLOUGH,

Alexander: b 1745 d 10-20-1831 m — Pvt PA
Benjamin: b 3-27-1734 d 3-27-1789 m Hannah Cook Henry Capt PS NJ
David: b.4-7-1738 d 7-3-1795 m Phebe Boyd NCapt GA
George: b — d p. 8-29-1791 m (1)Mary Crosby (2)Mary Eynon
    (3)Sarah Phillips Sol DE
George: b 1751 d 9- -1784 m Sarah Hoge Pvt PA
George: b 1750-60 d c. 1814 m — Pvt PA
James: b c. 1730 d a. 4-24-1788 m Ann PS PA
James: b 1745 d 1786 m Mrs Morrow Lt PA
John: b 1748 d 1-4-1823 m (1)Mary McKinnie (2)Elizabeth
    Cunningham Pvt PA
John: b 1751 d 1812 m Margaret Peters Pvt PA
John: b 4-3-1766 d 2-1-1842 m Esther Gamble Pvt PA
Joseph: b 7-23-1750 d 10-16-1807 m Sarah Brown Pvt NJ
Patrick: b 1735 d 1-8-1811 m Hannah Smith CS Pvt PA
Robert: b 1750 d 9-15-1824 m (1)Prudence Grubb (2)Mary
    Blakely Pvt PA

MCCULLOUGH, contd.
Robert: b 1754 d 4-19-1811 m Susanna Barbour Pvt PA
Robert: b 1756/7 d 6-17-1823 m Jane — Pvt PA
Samuel: b 1760 d 1823 m Frances Paine Sgt GA
Thomas: b 1762 d 8- -1858 m Rose Ann Addison Pvt PA
Wm.: b 1756 d1824 m Mary — Cpl MD
Wm.: b 12-18-1759 d 2-9-1840 m (1)Keturah Hunt (2)Elizabeth
    Budd (3)Mrs Mary Grandin Capt NJ ★
Wm.: b *c.* 1750 d *p.* 1782 m — Capt PA
Wm.: b 1748 d 3-18-1831 m Isabella Sol PA

MC CULLY,
Andrew: b 6- -1747 d 8-27-1790 m Lois Townsend Lt MA
James: b *c.* 1737 d *p.* 1798 m Elizabeth Greene Pvt PA
John: b *c.* 1744 d 10-17-1821 m Margaret Peters Pvt CT
Thomas: b *c.* 1760 d *p.* 1802 m Anne Cummins Pvt PA
Wm.: b 7-19-1757 d 12-22-1840 m Sarah Mitchell Pvt PA

MC CUMSEY,
Robert: b 1754 d 1831 m — Pvt PA

MC CUNE,
James: b *c.* 1730 d 1808 m Elizabeth Rotherham Pvt PA
James: b *c.* 1750 d 1778 m Abigail Miller Pvt PA
Robert: b 1753 d 8-29-1816 m Mary Brewer 2Lt PA
Thomas: b *c.* 1741 d 5- -1802 m Margaret Kerr Pvt PA
Thomas: b 7-12-1756 d 4-12-1842 m Mary Brady Pvt PS PA ★
Wm.: b *c.* 1748 d *p.* 2-10-1810 m Susannah — Pvt PA
Wm.: b 1729 d 12-28-1807 m Elizabeth Whitney Capt VT
Wm.: b 1751 d 1830 m (1)Elizabeth — (2)Elizabeth Maxwell PS VA

MC CURDY,
Alexander: b 1754 d 1-6-1839 m — Pvt PA ★
Archibald: b 4-16-1752 d 11-10-1843 m (1)Margaret Seller
    (2)Elizabeth Greeley Lt NC ★
Hugh: b — d 4-10-1832 m Grasselia Walker Pvt PA
James: b 1756 d *p.* 2-17-1834 m Nancy McKinney Pvt PA ★
James: b 1751 d 8- -1828 m Mary McCreary Pvt PA
James: b *c.* 1735 d *p.* 2-26-1803 m Elizabeth — PS PA
John: b 1724 d 11-10-1785 m Anne Lord PS CT
John: b 3-4-1760 d *p.* 1812 m Mary Reeves Pvt MA ME
John: b 1746 d 6-4-1824 m Nancy Cochran Pvt NH ★
John: b 1718 d 8-6-1813 m Mary Scoby PS NH
John: b *c.* 1735 d 1820 m Mary Fox 2Lt PA
John, Jr.: b *c.* 1758 d *p.* 1809 m Elizabeth Groves Pvt PA
Robert: b 1736 d 5-16-1810 m Ann Creighton Capt PA
Thomas: b 1741-51 d 9- -1821 m Mary — Pvt PS NC
Wm.: b 1730 d 1822 m Mary — Capt PA

MC CURRY,
Angus: b *c.* 1755 d *p.* 6-16-1836 m (1)Flora — (2)Katherine—
    Pvt GA
Malcolm: b 1- -1742 d *p.* 1-24-1789 m Rachel Freeman PS NJ

MC CUTCHEON,
Frederick: b 1751 d 2-9-1844 m Ann Brown Pvt NH
George: b 9-22-1761 d 10-14-1846 m Nancy Robertson Pvt MA ★
John: b *c.* 3-8-1755 d 1-17-1835 m (1)Ann — (2)Cassandra Gray
    Pvt SC ★
John: b 1739/40 d *c.* 1800 m Elizabeth — Ens VA
John: b 1747 d 1793/4 m Elizabeth Ware Pvt VA
John: b 8-13-1750 d 4-7-1842 m Elizabeth Hodge Pvt VA ★
Samuel: b — d 1824 m Rebekah — Capt VA
Samuel: b 4-13-1759 d 2-19-1816 m Catharine Bell Ens VA
Wm.: b 11-17-1758 d 6-29-1848 m Jean Finley OrdlSgt VA ★
Wm.: b 11-11-1760 d 10-22-1827 m (1)Margaret — (2)Ann Shaw
    Pvt VA

MC DADE,
James: b 2-10-1750 d 7-15-1820 m Elizabeth — Pvt SC
John: b 1748 d 1848 m Margaret Langley Pvt VA ★

MC DANIEL,
Clement: b 12-19-1759 d 9-25-1836 m Elizabeth Coleman Lt VA W★
David: b *c.* 1749 d 7-19-1808 m — Sol MD
Edward: b 3- -1756 d 3-12-1824 m Elizabeth McCaw Pvt SC ★
George: b 5-17-1722 d 1821 m Margaret Gough Pvt VA
Henry: b 11- -1763 d 9-28-1838 m Hannah Bryan Pvt VA ★
James: b 1717 d 4-11-1801 m Sussana Pvt NH
James: b 6-27-1762 d 9-27-1830 m Ann Rodgers Pvt NC
James: b 1764 d 12-29-1853 m Nancy — Pvt VA
James W.: b 12-26-1755/6 d 1847 m Rebecca Lewis OrdlSgt VA
John: b *c.* 1750 d *p.* 1787 m — Pvt PS MD
John: b 9-11-1764 d 9- -1842 m Elizabeth McDaniel Pvt MA
John: b 1751 d 1839 m (1)Margaret Rucker (2)Mrs Lucy Dawson Pvt
    VA
Mathew: b 1766 d 1-10-1840 m Jane Lowry Sol SC
Nehemiah: b 1715 d 4-15-1799 m — PS NH
Randall: b 4-14-1754 d 6-27-1848 m Martha Russell Pvt NH
Robert: b 1757 d 7-4-1826 m Luann McDonnell Pvt PA
Wm.: b 6-24-1754 d 12-24-1836 m Pricilla Ann Winn Sol MD
Wm.: b 11-18-1744 d 10-24-1824 m Mary Bickford Pvt PS NH

Wm., Sr.: b 1732 d 3-10-1817 m Mary Duff Faed Pvt VA
Wm., Jr.: b 1753 d 1844 m Elizabeth — Pvt VA

MC DAVID,
James: b 2-10-1766 d 6-5-1853 m Penelope Rogers Pvt SC
John: b 1735 d 1789 m Rosanna — PS SC

MC DERMOT, (includes MC DERMUT)
James: b 8- -1758 d 6-25-1859 m Agnes Bell OrdlSgt PA ★
John: b 1725 d 1814 m Mary — Matr PA ★

MC DILL,
David: b 3- -1763 d 3-7-1843 m Isabella Mc Quiston Pvt SC ★
James: b 1740 d 9-12-1801 m Jane — Pvt PA
John: b 1748/9 d 3-15-1824 m Jane Bell Sol SC
Thomas H.: b 1725 d 12-4-1794 m Margaret Chestnut PS SC

MC DOEL,
Wm., Sr.: b 1720 d 11-4-1784 m Rosanna Mc Laughlin Pvt NH
Wm., Jr.: b 1762 d 10-2-1840 m Mary Witherspoon Pvt NH

MC DOLE,
Alexander: b 6-5-1761 d 1-17-1814 m Olive Abbott Pvt NH
George: b *c.* 1750 d *p.* 1790 m Catherine Seger Pvt Cpl NY

MC DONALD, (includes MAC DONALD)
Adam: b *c.* 1740 d 2- -1778 m — Flud Col SC
Alexander: b 1750 d 1844 m Christian Mc Leod Sgt Maj SC
Alexander: b *c.* 1736/7 d *p.* 6-19-1811 m Margaret — Pvt VA
Andrew: b 1724 d 3- -1799 m Hester — Pvt VA
Angus: b 1750 d *p.* 1790 m Mary Mc Lain Cpl PA
Angus: b *c.* 1727 d 8-19-1778 m Anna Thompson LCol VA
Archibald: b 10-11-1759 d 9-11-1840 m Margaret McDonald Pvt PA
Archibald: b 1760 d 3-12-1838 m Elizabeth Brownlee Mus PA ★
Archibald: b 1740-45 d *p.* 3-29-1785 m (1)Margaret Neilson
    (2)Martha Richardson Col SC
Benjamin: b 1-27-1754 d 7-29-1824 m Sarah Green Pvt PA
Benjamin: b *a.* 1746 d *p.* 1827 m — Massay Pvt VA
Bryan: b 7-8-1732 d *a.* 2-11-1777 m Susan Ogle Sol VA
Charles: b 10-4-1758 d 9-12-1841 m Sarah — Sgt CT ★
Collen: b — d 8- -1819 m — Pvt PA
Daniel: b 1751 d 1811 m Margaret Mc Cloud Pvt PA
Daniel: b 1723 d 1797 m Rebecca Middleton Pvt SC
Donald: b 7-6-1748 d 1-29-1824 m Helen Mc Gregor PS NY ★
Edward: b 3-10-1761 d 4-19-1855 m Mary Rowland Pvt VA
Edward: b 1761 d 1835 m Keziah Stephens Lt VA
Elizabeth: b 6-8-1726 d 1795 m Joseph Mc Donald PS VA
Henry: b *c.* 1750 d 1816 m Sarah Hodge Pvt VA
Hugh: b *a.* 1757 d 8-24-1828 m Rebecca — OrdSgt SC
James: b 9-19-1759 d 3-1-1837 m (1)Huldah Foote (2)Rachel
    Davies Sgt CT NY ★
James: b *c.* 1730 d *p.* 3-17-1795 m Elizabeth Belden PS NY
John: b 1731 d 1831 m Jane Wilson Capt PA
John: b 4-30-1738 d 1-17-1815 m Martha Noble CS PS PA
John: b 1-15-1746 d 1-30-1812 m (1)Christiana — (2)Eliza Yongue
    Sgt SC
John: b 9- -1758 d 12-12-1845 m Elizabeth English Pvt SC ★
John: b 6-26-1748 d 8-29-1831 m Lydia Sturgeon Maj PA
John: b 1756 d 1807 m (1)— Sawyers (2)Cannaday — Sol VA
Jonathan: b *c.* 1740 d *p.* 1782 m Prudence Daboll PS CT
Joseph: b 9-3-1748 d 1815 m Sarah Towel Cpl MA
Joseph, Sr.: b 4-4-1722 d 2- -1809 m Elizabeth Ogle Sol PS VA
Joseph, Jr.: b 1758 d *c.* 1839 m Nancy Sawyer PS VA
Michel: b 1729 d 1823 m Margret De Bois Pvt NY
Peletiah: b 5-20-1754 d 1840 m (2)Dorcas Stuart Sgt MA
Peter: b 1753 d 3-6-1825 m Katheeine Wise Pvt VA W★
Richard: b 1735 d 1820 m Catherine Castner Maj NJ
Robert: b — d 6-9-1840 m Mary — Pvt PA ★
Susanna Ogle: b — d *a.* 3- -1801 m Bryan Mac Donald PS VA
Wm.: b 1745 d 9-6-1823 m Effie Mc Donald Lt PA
Wm.: b 1720 d *p.* 1782 m Martha Richardson LCol SC
Wm.: b 1766 d *p.* 1840 m Ursula Hough Pvt VA
Wm.: b 11-21-1740 d *p.* 1804 m Charlotte Massey Pvt VA
Willis: b 1-10-1760 d 3-7-1840 m Dorsia Owen Pvt VA

MC DONNAUGH,
John: b 8-8-1737 d 3-19-1809 m (1)Roseabella — (2)Elizabeth
    Wilkins Pvt VA
Thomas: b 1747 d 11-20-1795 m Mary Vance Col DE

MC DOUGALL,
Alexander: b 1754 d 9-15-1847 m (1)Mary Ellsworth (2)Jane Gibson
    Sgt NY ★
Alexander: b 5-1-1742 d 3-3-1845 m Hannah Doan Lt SC ★
Daniel: b *a.* 1756 d *c.* 1786 m Eve Sommer Pvt NY
Dougall: b — d *p.* 1790 m Mary Shaw Pvt NY
Duncal: b 1744 d 8-25-1795 m Nancy Weaver PS NY
John: b 3-11-1731 d 7-1-1778 m Charity Duvall Pvt MD
John: b 4-4-1753 d 4-8-1813 m Elizabeth Beattie Ens NY

MC DOW,
John: b *c.* 1743 d *p.* 1803 m (1)Catherine Caryl (2)Mary — Sol SC

MC DOWELL,
Alexander: b 1763 d 2-19-1816 m Sarah Parker Pvt PA
Alexander: b c. 1739 d 1790-93 m Mary — Pvt PA
Andrew: b 2-3-1757 d 8-25-1834 m (1)Elizabeth Sutphin (2)Jane Merrill Lt NJ ★
Charles: b 10-28-1743 d 3-31-1815 m Mrs Grace Bowman BG CS NC
Daniel: b 4-16-1757 d 1-19-1852 m Martha Halstead Pvt NY ★
Daniel: b 11-23-1763 d 11-28-1806 m Ruth Drake Sgt PA
David: b 1715 d 1807 m Elizabeth — PS SC
Edward: b — d 1810 m — 2Lt PA
James: b 1740 d 9-12-1815 m Elizabeth Langhead Capt PA
James: b 1728 d 2-5-1811 m Jane Smith Lt PA
James: b 1754 d 1829 m Elizabeth Deweese Pvt PA
James: b 4-29-1760 d 12-31-1843 m Mary Paxton Lyle Ens VA ★
James: b 4-9-1747 d 7-6-1809 m Sarah Gorrel Pvt VA
John: b 1751 d 3-24-1822 m Hannah Keller Maj NC
John: b 8-10-1758 d 1-1-1841 m Sarah Thomas Pvt NC
John: b 1748 d 1-1-1825 m Martha Johnston Capt PA
John: b c. 1756 d 1808 m Mary Sutphin Lt PA
John: b 1734 d 5-23-1809 m Elizabeth Reed Pvt PA
John: b 1716 d 6-6-1794 m Agnes Craig Pvt PA
John: b 1748 d 2-21-1814 m Mrs Margaret Lukens Dr PA
John: b 9-23-1736 d 8-12-1809 m Agnes Bradford CS PA
John: b 5-20-1714 d 9-25-1779 m Hannah De pui Ens PA
John: b 1743 d 7-30-1795 m Jane Parks Col SC
John: b c. 1757 d 7-18-1835 m Martha Jane Fairburn Lt VA ★
John: b 1757 d p. 1812 m (1)Sarah (2)Lucy Le Grand 1Lt VA
Joseph, Sr.: b 1715 d 1775 m Margaret O'Neal PS NC
Joseph, Jr.: b 3-8-1756 d 8-11-1801 m Margaretta Moffett Col NC
Joseph: b 2-25-1758 d 4- -1795 m Mary Moffett Capt NC
Margaret O'Neal: b a. 1723 d p. 1780 m Joseph Mc Dowell PS NC
Mary McClung: b 1734 d 1826 m Samuel McDowell PS VA & KY
Matthew: b 1739 d 4-6-1829 m Lucy Turner Pvt PA
Matthew: b c. 1750 d 1799 m Jane Borland Pvt PA
Nathan: b 1759 d 2-1-1830 m Mary Mc Lanahan Pvt PA
Nathaniel: b 1739 d 4-27-1826 m Sarah Gryst Pvt PA
Samuel, Sr.: b 10-27-1735 d 9-25-1817 m Mary Mc Clung Col PS VA
Samuel, Jr.: b 3-8-1764 d 8- -1834 m Anna Irvine Pvt VA
Stephen: b 1753 d p. 11-1-1815 m Sarah — Pvt NC
Thomas: b 1760 d p. 1791 m Ruth Mac Intyre Pvt MD
Thomas: b 11-4-1744 d 12-5-1806 m Elizabeth Hodge Pvt NY
Thomas: b c. 1730 d 11-19-1796 m Janet Clark Pvt PA
Wm.: b c. 1750 d 1-2-1823 m Mary Ann Mc Dade Pvt NC
Wm., Sr.: b 1720 d 9-17-1812 m Mary Maxwell Ens CS PA
Wm., Jr.: b 1750 d 6-19-1835 m Elizabeth Van Lear Lt PA
Wm.: b c. 1745 d — m Catherine Tomlinson PS SC
Wm.: b 1761 d 18-24-1835 m Elizabeth Burgess Pvt VA ★

MC DUFF,
Daniel: b 1757 d 3-26-1831 m Hannah Green Farr Capt SC ★

MC DUFFEE,
Archibald: b 1736 d 2-23-1830 m Sarah Emerson PS NH
Daniel: b 3- -1739 d 12-15-1824 m Margaret Wilson PS NH
James: b 1726 d 1800 m Mercy Young PS NH
Wm.: b a. 1732 d 1801- 4 m Martha Allen Capt NH

MC ELDERRY,
John: b — d — m Anna Sinclair Lt VA

MC ELHANNON,
John: b 9-25-1752 d 5-31-1834 m Eleanor Branham Pvt PA ★

MC ELHERRON,
James: b 1755 d 12-23-1835 m (1)Fannie Mc Cobb (2)Sarah — Sgt MA ★

MC ELNAY,
John: b 7-11-1755 d 11-21-1841 m Hannah Brown Pvt PA ★

MC ELROY,
Adam: b c. 1720 d p. 1794 m Agnes — Pvt PA
Archibald: b c. 1730 d 2-4-1806 m Sarah Mc Cleeland LCol PA
Daniel: b 1755 d 1830 m Rebecca Wishart Pvt PA
Hugh: b 1734 d 1823 m Esther Irvine Pvt PA
James: b c. 1740 d p. 1775 m Elizabeth Robinson PS NH
James: b 1764 d p. 10-4-1850 m — Lt NY
James: b 1738 d 11-20-1820 m (1)Margaret Shields (2)Margarette Mays Pvt PA
James: b 1757 d 4-15-1813 m Ann Mc Elroy Pvt PA
James: b 9-1-1759 d 2-9-1848 m Fanny Langston Pvt SC ★
John: b c. 1740 d p. 1790 m Martha — Lt SC
Micajah: b 9-30-1760 d 10-19-1832 m — Pvt NC ★
Samuel: b 1745 d 1806 m Mary Irvine PS VA
Wm.: b 3-1-1750 d 3-11-1838 m Elizabeth Maxwell Sgt NJ ★

MC ELWAINE,
Andrew: b 1745 d 1820 m (1)Elizabeth Shannon (2)Margaret Bell Sgt PA
Andrew: b c. 1725 d p. 6-18-1789 m (2)Comfort Waples PS DE

Andrew: b 3-18-1737 d 3-1-1811 m Mary Larimer Pvt PA
Andrew: b 1753 d p. 1794 m Margaret Workman Pvt PA
George: b 1742 d 9-16-1807 m Jane Hamilton Lt PA
George: b 1754 d 1844 m Ruth — Pvt PA
James: b c. 1746 d p. 7- -1803 m Jean Pvt SC
John: b 11-20-1742 d 8-25-1833 m Elizabeth Donaldson Capt PA
John Allan: b 3-12-1743 d 2-28-1814 m Hannah Malvin Sgt MA
Joseph: b 1748 d 1787 m — Col PA
Moses: b 1750 d p. 9-12-1805 m Margaret Larimer Pvt PA
Roger: b 8-23-1759 d p. 1800 m Delina Hill Pvt MA
Samuel: b c. 1755 d 2-3-1806 m Elizabeth Purdy Ens PA
Timothy: b 1709 d 9-7-1790 m (1)Ann Spear (2)Susanna Thompson PS MA
Wm.: b 7-18-1750 d 9-16-1806 m Mary Shippen Dr NJ
Wm.: b 1745 d — m Margaret — Sol SC

MC ELWEE,
James: b 1735 d 1800 m Jane Carmichael Pvt SC
James, Jr.: b 9-16-1753 d 6-10-1818 m (1)Nancy Johnson (2)Feriba Cannon Pvt NC
James: b 8-19-1758 d 1-13-1832 m Rhoda Black Pvt SC W ★
Wm.: b c. 1718 m 6- -1807 m Janet Black Sol SC
Wm., Jr.: b 2- -1761 d 11-15-1854 m Rachel Newman Sol SC

MC EWEN,
Alexander: b 7-5-1750 d 8- -1795 m Margaret Houston Pvt NC
Duncan: b 1-1-1755 d 4-11-1808 m Martha Dickerson Sgt NY W ★
Henry: b 1753 d 10-9-1825 m Elizabeth Gregg Pvt PA ★
James: b 1730 d p. 9-18-1781 m — Drm PA
John: b 1730-35 d 1788 m Jane Mc Cullough Sol PA
Margaret Houston: b 3-10-1758 d 9-2-1831 m Alexander Mc Ewen PS NC
Wm.: b 1744 d 2- -1816 m Sarah Kerr Sgt PA

MC FADDEN,
Conley: b 1753 d 1-31-1840 m Jennie Dillaplain Pvt NJ ★
Isaac: b 1753 d p. 2-13-1818 m (1)Elizabeth — (2)Jane (3)Mary — PS SC
Patrick: b c. 1720 d p. 7-16-1788 m Uphanas Riddle Pvt SC
Robert: b 1763 d 6-29-1829 m (1)— Dickey (2)Mrs Lenora Lenoir Dickey Pvt SC
Robert: b c. 1760 d p. 1790 m (1) — Steele (2) — Buford Pvt SC
Thomas: b 10-28-1740 d 11-18-1840 m Hannah Savage Lt MA
Thomas: b 1759 d 1823 m Sarah Witherspoon Sol PA

MC FALL,
Hugh: b 1740 d 2-9-1786 m (2)Ann Sebring Pvt PA
John: b 1745 d 1- -1800 m Hanna Craig McFall Lt PA

MC FARLAND,
Alexander: b a. 1718 d 1775 m Jane Harper Pvt MA
Andrew: b 1751 d 1833 m Elizabeth — OrdSgt NY ★
Andrew: b 1729 d 2- -1777 m Margaret Graham Capt PA
Andrew: b a. 1754 d 11-7-1829 m Margaret Lynn Lewis Lt PA
Benjamin: b 1-12-1750 d 1834 m Margaret Merry Pvt MA
Benjamin: b 4-16-1747 d 5-9-1823 m Mary Blackburn Pvt VA
Daniel: b 2-13-1723 d 1797 m Margaret Dunn Pvt MA
Daniel, Jr.: b 1762 d 2-5-1844 m Avis Reynolds Pvt MA
Daniel: b 9-9-1731 d 12-14-1817 m Sarah Barber Col PA
Ebenezer: b 6-16-1751 d 4-23-1837 m Elizabeth Gibson Sgt MA
Elijah: b 1722 d 11-29-1777 m Laurana Bradford Pvt MA
George: b c. 1763 d p. 1-2-1834 m Margaret — Pvt SC ★
James: b c. 1750 d c. 1820 m — Pvt CS GA
James: b 9-19-1758 d 12-22-1835 m (1)Betsey Moore (2)Elizabeth Cutting Cpl MA ★
James: b 1759 d 1812 m Elizabeth Findley Lt PA
James: b 11-22-1754 d 11-9-1830 m Mary McCormick Louden PS PA
James: b a. 1746 d 6-8-1825 m Margaret Campbell Pvt PA
James: b 1752 d 1829 m Margaret Lewis CS VA
John: b — d p. 1800 m Martha Pratt Sgt MA
John: b 1727 d 9-24-1778 m Martha Glover Pvt MA
John: b 1750 d 5-24-1824 m Nancy Manees Sol NC
John: b 1733 d 1-17-1787 m Mary — 1Lt VA
John: b 10-25-1748 d 10-7-1839 m Susannah Cox Lt PA
John: b 1738 d 5-8-1802 m Sarah Heald Pvt PA
John: b 1708 d 1784 m Mary PS VA
Moses: b 2-19-1738 d 4-7-1802 m Eunice Clark Maj MA
Robert: b 1-12-1740 d 1-22-1823 m Jean Cochran Pvt PA
Robert: b 3-15-1759 d 5-20-1834 m (1)Margaret McNutt (2)Mary Cox Lt VA ★
Robert: b 1710 d 1798 m Esther Huston PS VA
Thomas: b 1750 d 1818 m Hannah Stuart Sgt PA
Wm.: b 6-10-1755 d 6-1-1825 m Rebecca White Pvt PA
Wm.: b 12-17-1756 d 6-2-1823 m Hannah Kelsey PS PA
Wm.: b 1758 d 8-3-1839 m Rebecca Foster Sgt PA
Wm.: b 1751 d 1-25-1840 m (1)Elizabeth Jack (2)Mrs Mary Thompson Capt PA
Wm.: b 1738 d 1795 m Nancy Kilgore Lt VA

MC FEE,
Alexander: b c. 1747/8 d 3-13-1816 m Peggy Clark Sol NY

MC FEELY,
John: b — d *a*. 11-13-1834 m Elizabeth Line Pvt PA
Roger: b 1740 d 1804 m Eleanor McGranathan Pvt PA

MC FERRIN,
Henry: b 1-20-1764 d 4-19-1834 m Susanna Knepper Pvt PA
Samuel: b c. 1756 d 12-17-1790 m Margaret Sniverly Lt PA
Wm, Sr.: b c. 1722 d c. 1802 m Isabell Nelson Pvt PA
Wm, Jr.: b 11-26-1757 d 7-6-1826 m Polly Scott Ens PA
Wm: b 1755 d 1845 m Jane Laughlin Pvt VA

MC GAFFEY,
Andrew: b 1743 d 8-20-1826 m Hannah Wallis Lt NH ★
John: b 1728 d 8- -1810 m (1)Jane McClary (2)Margaret Sanborn
    PS NH
Neal: b 9-30-1756 d 11-29-1785 m Sarah Babb Lt NH
Samuel: b 1-13-1760 d 3-23-1823 m Lydia Sanborn Sgt NH

MC GALLIARD,
James: b 1-27-1755 d 6-7-1831 m — Sgt NJ

MC GANNON,
Darby: b 5-18-1756 d 2-1-1830 m Sallie Cogwell Cpl VA

MC GARRAH,
Joseph: b 1745 d 1809/10 m Mrs Elizabeth Rinich Maj PA
Wm: b 1756/7 d 1845 m (1)Elizabeth Walker (2)Mary McKeag
    Pvt VA

MC GARVEY,
Francis: b 7-6-1754 d 10-19-1834 m Sarah McWillians Pvt PA

MC GARY,
Hugh: b 1744 d 1806 m (1)Mrs Mary Ray (2)Catherine Yocum
    (3)Mary Ann Col VA

MC GAUGHEY,
John: b 1756 d 11-7-1813 m (2)Mary Simpson Pvt PA ★
Samuel: b 7-15-1763 d 1-5-1841 m Jane Laughlin Capt NC ★
Wm.: b 10-26-1741 d 1875 m Ann Kincaid Pvt PA
Wm.: b 1762 d 9- -1829 m Prepare Clark Pvt PA ★
Wm.: b 1740 d p. 1812 m Elizabeth Lackey Pvt VA

MC GAVOCK,
Hugh: b 9-21-1761 d 4-2-1844 m (1) — Campbell (2)Nancy Kent
    Lt VA
James, Sr.: b 1728 d 3-22-1812 m Mary Cloyd PS VA

MC GEE,
David: b 7-25-1762 d 3-25-1857 m Mary Cook Pvt VA
John: b 1761 d 6-16-1836 m Martha Johnston Pvt NC
John: b 3-20-1761 d 11-2-1844 m Martha Ellison Pvt NJ ★
John: b 1730 d 1810 m Mary McCoun Pvt VA
John: b c. 1760 d 1-1-1820 m Esther Clendenning Pvt VA
Jonathan: b 3-1-1752 d 12- -1815 m Jane Thompson Pvt MA
Michael: b 6-26-1759 d 6-21-1834 m Anna Melvina Sims Pvt SC
Patrick: b c. 1740 d a. 10-18-1811 m Jane Hall Pvt PA
Patrick: b 1750 d 1818 m Esther Pilson Pvt PA
Robert: b 3-25-1756 d p. 1796 m Isabella Park Lt PA ★
Thomas: b 1714 d 10-27-1793 m Anne Stewart PS MA
Thomas: b 3-11-1757 d 1849 m Margaret Fairfax Pvt NJ ★
Thomas: b c. 1760 d 1-8-1822 m Amy Williams Lt NC
Wm.: b 1745 d 9-20-1777 m Amy — Ens PA

MC GEHEE,
Daniel: b 1747 d 1801 m Jane Brooke Hodnett PS GA
Jacob: b 1707 d 12-6-1783 m (1)Eleanor De Jarnette (2)Ann —
    PS VA
Micajah: b 1730 d 1811 m Anne Baytop Scott Sol GA
Mumford: b c. 1735 d p. 1790 m — Ofr NC
Samuel: b c. 1759 d 6-9-1821 m Olivia Muse Lt VA
Wm.: b 8-29-1745 d 10-1-1827 m Margaret Jackson Pvt PA
Wm.: b 12-17-1740 d 4-17-1806 m (1)— Forrest (2)Sarah Harris 1Lt
    VA
Wm.: b 1749 d 2-2-1829 m Catherine Clem Sol VA

MC GIBBONS,
Peter: b a. 1761 d p. 1809 m Margaret Smith Sgt NY

MC GIFFIN,
Nathaniel: b 1752 d 11-22-1819 m Margaret Duncan Pvt PA

MC GILL,
Angus: b c. 1758 d 1820 m (1)Anne Fairley (2)Polly Fletcher Pvt NC
Arthur: b 1764 d 6-1-1847 m Elizabeth Arters Pvt PA
Daniel: b 1750 d 1789 m Margaret McNair Pvt NC
James: b 1756 d 9-20-1834 m Sarah Brashears Sgt PA ★
James: b 9-3-1721 d 2- -1788 m Ann — PS PA
Patrick: b 9-27-1760 d 12-13-1813 m Elizabeth Connor Pvt NJ
Roger: b 8-28-1742 d p. 1787 m Elizabeth Westbury PS SC
Samuel: b 9-12-1747 d 1781 m Hannah Plowden Sol SC

MC GINNIS,
James: b 1758 d 1839 m Elizabeth Williams Sol NC
James: b c. 1750 d p. 1790 m Sarah Davis Sol VA
John: b 4-4-1765 d 12-28-1820 m Sarah Clark PS PA
John: b 1748 d p. 1788 m Elizabeth Green Pvt VA
Samuel: b c. 1740 d 1801 m Margaret Kennedy Ens PA
Thomas: b 12-19-1743 d 1848 m Nancy Tenly Pvt PA
Wm.: b 10-26-1736 d 8-3-1814 m Elizabeth Barris Sol NY

MC GINTY,
Robert: b 1746 d a. 2-10-1841 m Deborah — Sol GA

MC GLATHERY,
Isaac: b 1752 d 1834 m Rachel McGlathery Lt PA

MC GLOGAN,
Patrick: b c. 1750 d 1803 m Margaret Taylor Pvt PA

MC GOHAN,
Mark: b c. 1750 d 2-15-1848 m Elizabeth Dunn Pvt PA ★

MC GOODWIN,
Daniel: b 1763 d 10-25-1839 m (1)Elizabeth Kerr (2)Jane Kennedy
    Pvt NC SC ★

MC GOUGH,
John: b 8-21-1761 d 10-17-1847 m Elizabeth Carson Pvt SC

MC GOWEN,
David: b c. 1760 d p. 1820 m Elizabeth Crocket Pvt PA
James: b 4-16-1750 d 10-16-1831 m Margaret Clark Pvt NY
John: b 1742 d 6- -1826 m Margaret Lusk Pvt PA
John: b 3-3-1746 d 11-9-1815 m Elizabeth — Pvt NY
John: b c. 1749 d 1824 m Sarah Gooch PS Nova Scotia
Stephen: b 10-13-1762 d 10-10-1842 m Margaret Wilson Pvt NY
Wm.: b 8- -1756 d p. 1832 m Sarah — QMSgt SC ★

MC GRANAHAN,
John: b c. 1760 d p. 1801 m Nellie Smith Pvt PA

MC GRAUDY,
Gaun: b 1736 d 4-16-1812 m Mary Wilson Sol PS PA

MC GRAW,
Levin: b 1733 d a. 3-27-1792 m Sarah — Cpl MD
Peter: b c. 1745 d p. 1792 m — Pvt SC

MC GREGOR,
David: b 1756 d 7-4-1828 m Elizabeth Holland Capt NH ★
Joel: b 11-23-1760 d 10-31-1861 m Martha Bellows Pvt CT ★
John: b 1743 d 1820 m Betsey Shepard Capt CT

MC GREGORY,
Ebenezer: b 1754 d 7-16-1822 m Susanna Bradley Pvt CT

MC GREW,
Alexander: b 1727 d 1797 m (1)Sarah Hall (2)Martha Kirk Capt PA
Wm., Sr.: b c. 1730 d c. 1800 m (1)Margaret Bracken (2)Mrs Isabella
    Long PS PA
Wm.: b 4-24-1752 d 1-2-1815 m Mary Goodwyn Sol SC

MC GRIFF,
Partick: b c. 1750 d 12- -1810 m Mary Hall Col SC

MC GUFFEY,
Robert: b 1755 d 7-14-1815 m Sarah McClelland Maj PA
Wm.: b 2- -1742 d 2-21-1836 m Anna McKettrick Pvt PA

MC GUFFIN,
Robert: b 10-9-1746 d 1-30-1824 m Elizabeth King Sgt DE

MC GUIRE,
Edward: b 1720 d 1806 m (1)Susannah Wheeler (2)Millicent D'Obee
    Capt PS VA
Hugh: b 1750 d 1807 m Patience Lyons Pvt PA
Hugh: b c. 1749 d p. 1805 m — 1Lt MD
James: b 1747 d 8-28-1838 m Clementine L. — Pvt VA ★
James: b c. 1749 d p. 1780 m — Pvt VA
John: b 1750 d a. 1800 m Mary Tipton Capt VA
Michael: b 1717 d 11-17-1793 m Rachel Brown Pvt MD
Patrick: b c. 1750-55 d p. 2-19-1831 m Catherine Prigmore Pvt PS
    PA
Peter: b 1763 d 1-30-1850 m Charity Shirley Pvt MD
Wm.: b 1765 d 11-24-1820 m Mary Little Lt VA
Wm.: b 3-12-1748 d 1834 m Mary Shirley Lt VA ★
Wm.: b c. 1722 d Rachel — Spy VA

MC GUNNEGLE,
George: b 1736 d 7-21-1821 m Margaret Kennedy Pvt PA

MC HANEY,
John: b 8-6-1752 d 1840 m Mary Mitchell Pvt VA
Terry: b 1757 d 7-2-1838 m Sarah — Pvt GA ★

MC HARD,
Joseph: b 2-14-1750 d 7-2-1829 m Mary Gingles Pvt PA
John: b 1733 d 12-23-1803 m Griselda Kelly Pvt NY

MC HARG, (includes MC HARGUE)
Wm.: b 8-5-1745 d 8-7-1836 m Sarah McBroom Pvt NC ★

MC HATTON,
Alexander: b 1743 d 4-23-1837 m — LCol PA ★
John: b 6-21-1740 d 2-21-1831 m Martha Lytle Capt PA ★

MC HENRY,
Henry: b 7- -1762 d 9-10-1826 m Priscilla McClure Pvt PA
Isaac: b 1734 d 1812 m Jane Smythe Lt PA
John: b c. 1752-6 d 7- -1823 m (2)Rachel Brown Sol NC
John: b 1725 d 1785 m Susanna McNeail Pvt PS PA
John: b — d p. 2-17-1805 m (1)Susannah Viney (2)Hannah Crabtree
    CS VA
Richard: b 1746 d p. 1818 m Dolly — Pvt PA ★
Thomas: b 2-16-1760 d 2-19-1835 m Mary Reed Pvt PA ★
Wm.: b 5-6-1744 d 11-25-1808 m Mary Stewart Capt PA
Wm.: b 1743 d 1809 m — Butterfield Lt PA

MC ILDUFF,
John: b 1744 d 9-22-1816 m Ann Wallace Pvt PA

MC ILHENNY,
Felix: b 1755 d 8-7-1841 m Jane — Pvt PA ★
George: b 1753 d 1815 m Martha Stringer Pvt PA
James: b 1745 d 3- -1813 m — McCracken Pvt PA
James: b 1759 d 1841 m Grizella — Capt SC ★
James: b 9-22-1749 d 9-17-1804 m Margaret Williams Capt VA
John: b 1745 d p. 1783 m Anne Coil Capt SC
Robert: b 1715 d 1786 m Agnes Crawford 1Lt PA
Robert: b 1-31-1761 d 8-9-1832 m Martha King Pvt PA
Thomas: b c. 1744 d 9-1-1828 m — Mil PA
Wm.: b 1749 d 8-24-1833 m Agnes King Pvt PA

MC ILHOES,
Robert: b 1745 d 1788 m Mary — Pvt PA

MC ILRATH,
Andrew: b 9-30-1758 d 2-25-1836 m (1)Abigail Cozad (2)Alice
    Ward Pvt CT ★
Robert: b c. 1750 d 5-19-1797 m Jane Shields PS SC
Samuel: b 12-25-1718 d 8-9-1804 m Isabel Aikman Pvt NJ

MC INTIRE,
Andrew: b 6-20-1760 d 5- -1799 m Rachel Hovey Lt MA
Andrew: b 1746 d 1-18-1835 m Elizabeth Edmondson Pvt PA ★
Charles: b a. 1742 d p. 10- -1779 m Elender — Pvt VA
Daniel: b 1760 d 6- -1826 m Jane — Pvt PA
Ebenezer: b c. 1746 d c. 6- -1814 m Hannah Linscot Ens MA
Eleazer, Jr.: b c. 1739 d p. 3-25-1782 m Elizabeth — CS MA
Ely: b 1-1-1761 d 4-10-1845 m (1)Dianna Robinson (2)Sabra — Pvt
    MA ★
Ezra, Sr.: b 1730 d 8- -1799 m Elizabeth March Pvt MA
Hugh: b c. 1756 d 1794 m Jane — Lt PA
Jacob: b 12- -1749 d 1828 m Phebe Hutchinson Pvt MA
James: b 1750 d p. 1788 m — Sgt NC
James: b 1735 d 5-27-1818 m Lucretia — CS NC
Jesse: b 8-2-1739 d 4-14-1826 m Abigail Flower Lt MA
John: b — d 2-16-1816 m Mary — PS MD
John: b 1-1-1765 d 4-5-1850 m (1)Sallie Stockwell (2)Susanna
    Buckman Pvt MA ★
John: b 1724 d 11-30-1796 m Mrs Lamb PS MA
John: b 1755 d p. 1820 m — Pvt PA
John: b c. 1759 d 1823 m Catharine Harbaugh Pvt PA W ★
Joseph: b c. 1731 d p. 1790 m Rebecca Harwood Pvt MA
Nathan: b 4-21-1736 d 3-4-1823 m Jemima Ames Pvt MA
Phineas: b 1750 d 1830 m Lucy Stover Pvt MA
Phineas: b 6-15-1752 d 3-4-1838 m Lydia Haywood Pvt MA ★
Robert: b — d p. 8-16-1785 m Ann — PS DE
Robert: b 1750 d 1812 m Jean — Sol SC
Robert: b 6-17-1761 d 1837 m Ann Hyatt Pvt VA
Samuel: b 7-23-1743/4 d 1-3-1810 m (1)Dorothy Rogers (2)Mary
    Johnson Capt ME
Wm.: b 1757 d 4-1-1816 m Judith Davis 2Lt MA
Wm.: b 1750 d 12-8-1821 m Ann Campbell Pvt MA
Wm.: b 5-29-1758 d — m Sarah Leonard Pvt MA
Wm.: b 4-27-1747 d 8-3-1786 m Ruth McIntyer NS MA
Wm.: b c. 1755 d p. 1786 m Jane Kennedy Pvt PA
Wm.: b c. 1719 d 1803 m Mary Rippy PS PA
Wm.: b c. 1750 d 4- -1792 m Elizabeth Shepard QM VA
Wm.: b 5-15-1753 d 12-20-1815 m Eliza Tanner Pvt VA PA
Willin: b c. 1747 d 7-11-1807 m — Sol MD

MC INTOSH,
Alexander: b — d 11-18-1780 m Elenor James BG SC
Ebenezer: b 6-20-1737 d 1812 m (1)Elizabeth Maverick (2)Elizabeth
    Chase PS Pvt NH
George: b 4-27-1728 d p. 1777 m Anne Houston PS GA

Jeremiah: b 4-13-1751 d 1-21-1843 m Susannah Blake Sgt MA ★
John: b 1755 d 11-12-1826 m (1)Sarah Sewinton (2)Mrs Hillery
    LCol GA
John: b 10-6-1762 d 6- -1814 m (2)Sarah Hart Sol SC
Laughlin: b 3-5-1727 d 2-20-1806 m Sarah Treadcraft BG GA
Peter: b 10-6-1758 d 11-16-1836 m (2)Susan — Pvt MA
Peter: b 10-6-1758 d 11-23-1846 m Sybil Hayden PS MA ★
Simon: b 1761 d 1-29-1853 m Sally Phelps Bates Pvt NY
Stephen: b 8-19-1754 d p. 1799 m Sarah Griggs Pvt MA
Wm.: b 1-27-1726 d 2-7-1801 m Katherine McKay PS Capt GA
Wm.: b 6-16-1722 d 1-3-1813 m Abigail Whiting Col MA
Wm.: b 1760 d 1800 m Fannie Mikell Capt SC
Wm.: b 4-7-1764 d 6-24-1843 m (1)Miss Gambel (2)Mary Redon
    (3)Elizabeth Harrington Pvt SC ★
Wm.: b 1756 d 10-25-1846 m — Pvt VA ★

MC IVER,
Evander: b 3- -1760 d 11-13-1823 m Sarah Kolb Pvt SC
James: b 1752 d 1-24-1829 m Lois Howard Pvt MA ★

MC JUNKIN,
Joseph: b 6-22-1755 d 5-31-1846 m Anne Jane Thomas Maj SC
Samuel: b 1725 d 1805 m Mary Bogan PS SC

MC KAIG,
Patrick, Jr.: b 1759 d p. 1818 m (1)Margaret King (2)Rachel Starr
    Pvt PA

MC KAMY,
James: b 1-19-1753 d 5-2-1845 m Agnes Telford Pvt VA ★

MC KAUGHAN,
Archibald: b c. 1745 d p. 1810 m Jane Mercer Pvt PA

MC KAY,
Alexander: b 2-2-1752 d 8-29-1820 m Barbara — Pvt NC
Alexander: b c. 1742 d p. 2-23-1793 m — PS NC
Alexander: b 2-22-1732 d p. 1787 m Mary Sackett Sol PA
Daniel: b 9-3-1756 d 1-1-1814 m Catherine Little Pvtr PA
Duncan: b c. 1760 d 9-17-1833 m Elizabeth — Sol NC
James: b 1754 d 8-2-1833 m (1)Margaret Denham Burke
    (2)Elizabeth Brown Pvt MD ★
James, 2nd: b c. 1750 d 1789 m Mary Cheek Pvt VA
Neal: b 1-11-1749 d 1-11-1835 m Nancy Montgomery 2Lt PA ★
Richard: b 1750 d 1823 m (1)Nancy Hebb (2)Mrs Shumate (3)Mary
    Murphy Pvt VA
Robert: b 1755 d 1816 m Sarah — PS MD
Robert: b 2-12-1760 d 9-28-1835 m Lydia Leith Pvt VA ★
Wm.: b 1754 d 8-14-1814 m (2)Mary Mc Culley Pvt MD
Wm.: b 10-25-1759 d 10-6-1836 m Nancy Agnes Pvt NC ★

MC KEAN, (includes MC CAIN, MC KEEN)
Alexander: b 1761 d 2-15-1838 m Mehitable Hutchins Sol NH ★
Alexander: b c. 1730-32 d p. 8-28-1815 m Jane — PS SC
David: b 6-12-1750 d 12-2-1824 m (1)Margaret McPherson (2)Lydia
    Ingalls Pvt VT
Hugh: b 1-14-1755 d 1835 m (1)Joanna Danforth (2)Mary Gragg
    Pvt NH
James: b 1749 d 2-28-1802 m Ann Wilson PS DE
James: b 1745 d 1-4-1797 m Jane Scott Pvt PA
John: b 4-24-1760 d p. 9- -1845 m (1)Mary Gregg (2)Martha Dunn
    Pvt NH ★
John: b 1714 d 10-9-1795 m Mary McKeen PS NH
Robert: b 1749 d 10-27-1810 m Mary McPherson PS NH
Samuel: b 1763 d 8-25-1846 m Ellen Cambell Pvt NY
Thomas: b 3-19-1734 d 6-24-1817 m (1)Mary Borden (2)Sarah
    Armitage SDI PS DE
Thomas: b 1753 d 12-29-1837 m Nancy — Pvt PA ★
Wm.: b 1- -1754 d 12-11-1824 m Nancy Taylor Pvt NH

MC KEAND,
John: b 1742 d 1791/2 m Elizabeth Willis Sol PS VA

MC KECHNIE,
John: b — d 4-14-1782 m Mary North Dr ME

MC KEE,
Alexander: b 1753 d 1834 m Sarah McGuire Pvt PA
Andrew: b 1721 d 4-16-1802 m (1)Margaret Anderson (2)Ann
    Stevenson Capt PA
Andrew: b 1747 d 6-18-1833 m Mary Blandford Pvt PA ★
Daniel: b c. 1748 d a. 11-16-1818 m — Pvt SC
Daniel: b 5-6-1759 d 11-16-1839 m Frances Herndon Lt PS VA ★
David: b c. 1750 d 12- -1801 m Margaret Cunningham Capt PA
Guian: b 5-5-1751 d 12-9-1827 m Abigail Lane Pvt PA ★
Hugh: b 1760 d 1820 m Margaret Leigo Pvt DE
Hugh: b 1759 d 3-22-1821 m Elizabeth Thompson 2Lt PA
James: b 7-7-1760 d 6-14-1843 m Elizabeth Wilson Pvt NY W★
James: b c. 1735 d p. 7-8-1821 m Abigail — Sol NC
James: b c. 1733 d p. 10-18-1790 m Elizabeth — Capt PA
James: b 1750-5 d 1820-30 m Agnes — Pvt VA
James: b c. 1750 d a. 3-2-1803 m — Pvt VA

MC KEE, contd.
James Logan: b 3-14-1752 d 8-14-1832 m (1)Jane Telford (2)Nancy L Scott Ens VA ★
John: b 1-1-1754 d 11-10-1830 m Mary Hoge Pvt PA
John: b 1756 d 10-20-1831 m Mary Seaburn Pvt PA
John: b 1-5-1761 d 2-17-1847 m Martha Hindman Pvt PA
John: b 1755 d 9-12-1780 m Polly McCoy Pvt SC
John: b c. 1740 d 1778-82 m Esther Houston Sol VA
Joseph: b 11-3-1729 d 6-15-1808 m Ruth Webster Sgt CT
Joseph: b 1733 d 3-31-1810 m (1)Elizabeth Witherspoon (2)Ann Witherspoon (3)Elizabeth — PS SC
Nathaniel: b 1728 d 2-16-1815 m Prudence Hollister PS CT
Robert: b 1726 d 1797 m Mabel Hollister Pvt MM CT
Robert: b 2-27-1725 d 6-12-1794 m (1)Anna Klatz (2)Isabella Semple Capt PA
Robert: b c. 1740 d 1782 m Susanna — Capt PA
Robert: b c. 1740 d 10-16-1800 m Elizabeth — Dr VA
Samuel: b 1-3-1744 d 1824 m Rachel Davidson Pvt PA
Samuel: b 7-3-1764 d 6-3-1842 m Elizabeth Lowry Pvt VA ★
Thomas: b 1749 d 1815 m Martha Hogue Pvt PA
Wm.: b c. 1745 d 2-17-1820 m Mary McHenry Pvt NC ★
Wm.: b 1742 d 12-2-1831 m Susannah Greer Pvt PA ★
Wm.: b 1732 d 12-10-1816 m Miriam McKee Capt VA

MC KEEHAN,
Alexander: b 9-2-1731 d p. 1790 m Jane — Pvt PA
Benjamin: b 8-2-1748-51 d 10-23-1814 m Margaret Wilson Pvt PA
Brice: b 1748 d 5-22-1825 m Sarah — Pvt PA
Duncan: b 1750 d 1792 m — Capt PA
John: b 8-15-1736 d 3-7-1813 m Elizabeth — Pvt PA

MC KEEL,
John: b c. 1744 d p. 1779 m Frances Davenport Lt NY

MC KEENRY,
Wm.: b c. 1742 d p. 2-1-1805 m — PS VA

MC KEEVER,
John: b c. 1755 d 1810 m Jemima Edwards Flower Pvt PA

MC KEITH,
Thomas: b 10-14-1756 d 5-17-1823 m Sarah Haseltine Pvt VT

MC KEITHAN,
Duncan: b 3-10-1755 d 7-19-1810 m Molly McColl Sgt NC

MC KELLOP,
Archibald: b 1755 d 5-6-1847 m Mary Young Pvt NY
Samuel: b 9-22-1747 d 7-23-1836 m Mary Terrill Pvt NH ★
Wm.: b c. 1751-2 d p. 1784 m Sarah Lent Sgt NY

MC KELVEY,
Hugh: b 1762 d 3-13-1835 m Sarah Aiken Pvt SC
James: b c. 1730 d p. 1791 m Sarah — Pvt PA
John: b 1759 d 1809 m Martha Hamill Sgt PA
John: b c. 1761 d a. 2-5-1827 m Mary — Pvt SC
Wm.: b 1759/60 d 1839 m Mary Topping Pvt PA
Wm.: b 1744 d 8-11-1834 m Mary Mason Pvt SC ★

MC KENDRY,
Archibald: b 4-14-1756 d 4-7-1806 m Sarah Crane Cpl MA

MC KENNAN,
Wm.: b 1758 d 1-14-1810 m Elizabeth Thompson Capt DE

MC KENNEY, (includes MC KINNEY)
Andrew: b a. 1758 d 9-22-1817 m — Pvt CT
Andrew: b 3- -1753 d 11-12-1825 m Mary Parker Pvt PA ★
Charles: b c. 1753 d 2-27-1834 m Elizabeth — Pvt VA ★
Collin: b 1735 d 1811 m Rebecca — CS VA
Daniel: b 1725 d 8-1-1802 m Margaret Stanhouse Pvt NY
Daniel: b c. 1738 d 3-17-1822 m Mary Connelly Pvt NY
Daniel: b c. 1745 d 5- -1807-9 m Mercy Blatchley Pvt VA
David: b 1746 d 3-19-1819 m Jennet Smith Pvt PA
David: b a. 1741 d 9-13-1784 m Rebecca Lane PS PA
David: b 1755 d 5-7-1822 m (1)Mary Stuart (2)Margaret Wallace Pvt VA
Humphrey: b a. 1748 d p. 1779 m Elizabeth Small Pvt MA
James: b 2-21-1749 d 8-31-1826 m (1)Sarah Mitchell (2)Susan Reeder (3)Ann Fletcher Capt PA
James, Jr.: b 1732 d 3-10-1815 m (1)Mary Paine (2)Deborah Kibbe Cpl CS CT
John, Sr.: b 12-15-1759 d 8-25-1837 m (1)Katy — (2)Mildred Kennedy Lt GA SC
John: b 2-9-1737 d 11-18-1818 m Mary Rand Sol MA
John: b 9-11-1757 d 2-8-1838 m Eleanor Davison Pvt NJ
John: b — d 7- -1804 m (1)Jean — PS CS NC
John: b — d 1793 m Elizabeth Pope PS CS NC
John: b 1742 d p. 5-18-1818 m Jane Laird Pvt PA
John: b c. 1760 d p. 1787 m Mary Llewellyn Pvt PA
John: b c. 1744 d 1805 m — PS PA
John: b a. 1760 d 1843 m Katherine Evans Pvt SC
John, Jr.: b 4-2-1757 d 8-24-1837 m Hannah Evans Capt SC ★
John: b 12-17-1759 d 1833 m Sarah Taliaferro LCol CL

John, Sr.: b 1735 d 1805 m Elizabeth McDowell Lt VA
John: b c. 1754 d 9-27-1825 m Polly Trimble Sol VA
Joseph: b 1748 d 2-10-1844 m Elizabeth Wiswell MA ★
Joseph: b 11-17-1720 d 1785 m Mary MacKensie Capt PA
Joseph: b 6-10-1756 d 10-15-1848 m Susan Frances McVey Pvt VA
Mordecia: b 1727 d 4-4-1782 m Agnes Bodine Lt PS NJ
Moses: b 5-5-1742 d p. 1736 m (1)Eunice Larrabee (2)Lucy Plummer 2Lt MA
Peter: b 1768 d 4-22-1849 m Mary Shorts Fif PA ★
Richard: b 1752 d 1-27-1800 m Sallie Fellows CS NC
Robert: b — d p. 1784 m Easter Ley Pvt PA
Samuel: b 1744 d 1840 m Lydia Rand Pvt MA
Walter: b 1748 d 1806 m Jane Rusk Capt PA
Wm.: b c. 1765 d 4-20-1813 m Jane — Sol GA
Wm., Sr.: b 1728 d p. 1-26-1793 m Miss Grimes PS NC
Wm.: b 1743 d 10-13-1809 m Mary Alesander Pvt PA
Wm., Jr.: b 2-19-1749 d 9-17-1790 m Mary Jernigan Maj NC
Wm.: b c. 1736 d 4-27-1785 m Barbara Culp PS Pvt SC

MC KENZIE,
Alexander: b 1762 d 6- -1852 m (1)Caroline Weathers (2)Sarah Butler (3)Sarah Quarles Sol SC
Alexander: b c. 1755 d 9-17-1821 m Tabitha Hill Sgt VA W★
Andrew: b 1726 d 1827 m — Pvt NC
Daniel: b 1755 d 9-7-1825 m Mary Ann Chapman PS MD
Ebenezer: b 1757 d 2-4-1812 m Elizabeth Brown Sgt MA ★
John: b 11-12-1747 d 4-10-1812 m Margaret Garland Gnr MA
John: b 9-17-1757 d 11-5-1842 m Martha Bonner Capt SC NC ★
John: b c. 1730 d 2-16-1818 m Jane — Sol VA
Joseph: b a. 1755 d p. 1-20-1821 m Rebecca — PS SC
Joshua: b 3-20-1764 d 1835 m Mary Jones Drm MD
Moredock O: b 1738 d 1813 m (1)Jemima Chapman (2)Eunice Allen (3)Sally — Sol VA
Owen: b c. 1760 d 1834/5 m Elizabeth Dyer Cpl MA
Samuel: b c. 1740 d 6- -1781 m Jane Isabelle Warner Dr PA
Thomas: b 1720 d 1789 m (1)Rebecca Johnson (2)Ann Johns Drm MD
Wm.: b 8-28-1758 d 4-13-1835 m Elinor Campbell Sol NC
Wm., Sr.: b c. 1740 d p. 4-2-1782 m Mary — Capt SC

MC KERLIE,
John: b c. 1730 d 12-28-1814 m Mary — Pvt NY

MC KIBBEN,
Jeremiah: b c. 1750 d 1820 m Mary Chambers Cpl PA
John: b c. 1750 d 1814 m Jane — PS PA
John: b 1728 d p. 8-25-1798 m Sarah — PS PA
Joseph: b c. 1748 d 10- -1801 m Mary — Lt PA
Thomas: b 6-16-1755 d 5-7-1822 m Margaret — Pvt PA

MC KIM,
Alexander: b 1748 d 1-18-1832 m Catherine Sarah Davey PS MD

MC KINLEY,
Alexander: b 1764 d 1819 m — Wilson Pvt VA
David: b 5-16-1755 d 8-8-1840 m Sarah Gray Pvt PA ★
John: b 1751 d 7-15-1811 m Sarah Benedict Arfr CT W ★
John: b c. 1720 d 2-18-1779 m Margaret — Pvt PA
John: b 1720 d 1779 m Esther Wilson Sol SC
John: b 10-10-1744 d 6-10-1782 m Mary Connelly Capt VA
Wm., Sr.: b c. 1740 d 8-16-1780 m Pvt MD
Wm.: b 8-10-1744 d 4-22-1798 m Mary Beatty Sol SC

MC KINSTRY,
Amos: b 3-24-1759 d 3-6-1844 m Sarah Pike Pvt MA ★
Ezekiel: b 8-17-1753 d 11-25-1803 m Rosina Chapman Capt CT
James: b 1-3-1752 d 12-8-1819 m Lois Dix Pvt MA
John: b 1745 d 6-9-1822 m Elizabeth Knox LCol NY
Wm.: b 10-8-1732 d 3-21-1776 m Priscilla Leonard SurGen NS

MC KISSACK, (includes MC KISSICK)
Daniel: b c. 1755 d 11-18-1818 m Jane Wilson Capt PS NC ★
Isaac: b 9-19-1752 d 1-20-1830 m Mary Cochran Pvt PA
James: b 6-18-1747 d 1-25-1838 m Mrs Letetia Caldwell Pvt PA
John: b 1740 d 1807 m Margaret — Pvt PA
Thomas: b 12-24-1756 d 4-24-1826 m Mrs Lucy Edwards Pvt NC ★
Wm.: b 1754 d 2- -1831 m — McDonald Capt NJ

MC KITRICK, (includes MC KITTRICH)
Alexander: b c. 1760 d p. 1790 m Susannah Baker Sgt PA
John: b 1745 d 1833 m (1)Mary McCready (2)Mary Ross Pvt PA
John: b 1760 d 2-1-1839 m (1)Jane Hogshead (2)Sally — Capt VA ★

MC KNIGHT,
Benjamin: b 1756 d 1848 m Ann Fullerton Pvt VA ★
Charles, Sr.: b c. 1710 d 1-1-1778 m Elizabeth Stevens PS NY
Charles, Jr.: b 10-10-1750 d 11-16-1791 m Mrs Mary Morin Scott Dr PA
David: b 1752 d 1819 m Jane McKissick Lt PA
David: b 8-29-1764 d 11-16-1839 m Hannah Gill Pvt PA
George: b 1741/2 d 6-18-1808 m Jane Beattie 1Lt NY
James: b — d 1802 m Ann Pine Decatur NLT
James, Jr.: b 1-13-1754 d 12-18-1824 m Mary Taggert Lt MA

James: b 1747 d 1-24-1822 m Eleanor McEwen PS NC
James: b c. 1750 d 6-16-1820 m Elizabeth Gillien Pvt PS PA
John, Jr.: b 1734 d 8-17-1798 m Elizabeth Stewart Pvt PA
Robert: b 1747 d 4-15-1843 m Elizabeth Sears Pvt PA ★
Robert: b 1758 d p. 3-27-1790 m Lydia Lee Sol NC
Wm.: b 1725 d p. 5-28-1793 m Elizabeth McCormick PS PA

MC KUNE,
Joseph: b 1753 d 1851 m (1)Esther Many (2)Annie Gillet (3)Mrs
    Winters Pvt NY

MC LARTY,
Alexander: b c. 1730 d p. 1790 m (2)Mary McMath (3)Barbara
    McNaught PS NC VA SC

MC LAUGHLIN, (includes LAUGHLIN, MCGLOTHIN)
Alexander: b 1748 d 1832 m Ann Sharp CS VA
Charles: b 1750 d p. 10-29-1797 m Elizabeth Asbury Pvt VA
Colin: b 3-24-1746 d 1-14-1831 m (2)Mrs Elizabeth M. Sullivan Sgt
    NJ
Daniel: b 2-10-1755 d 1-15-1830 m Mary Key Pvt VA
Hugh: b 1750 d p. 3-27-1819 m Polly Brading Pvt PA
Hugh: b 1758 d p. 1814 m Jane Wiley Pvt VA
James: b 1743 d 2-22-1829 m Elizabeth Mickey Pvt PA
James: b c. 1745 d p. 10-7-1809 m Margaret Mitchell Pvt PA
James: b a. 1755 d p. 8-20-1795 m Elizabeth — Pvt PS PA
James: b 3- -1758 d 4-7-1823 m Sarah Coleman Ens VA
James, Sr.: b c. 1736 d 3-27-1810 m Jane Dunkin Pvt VA
John: b c. 1753 d 1825-30 m Catherine Thompson Pvt MD
John: b 6-1-1720 d 10-28-1807 m Jannet Taggart PS NH
John: b 1756 d 1830 m Frances Calhoun Pvt PA
John: b c. 1759/60 d 1812 m Sarah Casner Pvt PA
John: b 1-26-1758 d 2-17-1848 m Juda Leathers Pvt NC ★
John: b 5-20-1764 d 3-19-1838 m (1)Lucretia — (2)Anne Wiley Pvt
    VA ★
Randall: b 1740 d p. 1807 m Elizabeth Warnick CMman PA
Robert: b 5- -1739 d 9-26-1825 m Mary Keen Pvt MA
Robert: b 1729 d 7-26-1809 m Mary Patton Pvt PA
Samuel: b 1755 d p. 1792 m Mary Hall PS PA
Thomas, Sr.: b c. 1733 d 1820 m Margaret Ayers Capt NH
Thomas: b 1758 d 3-29-1829 m Jane Moorehead Pvt PA
Thomas: b 5-8-1763 d 5-29-1844 m Elizabeth Duncan Pvt NC VA ★
Thomas: b — d 12-13-1801 m Sarah Madison PS VA
Wm.: b 1762 d 5-12-1829 m Catharine Sweetser Pvt NH W ★
Wm.: b 1740 d 6-6-1828 m Elizabeth Huey Pvt PA

MC LAURINE,
James: b 11-25-1753 d 1848 m Catherine Steger Pvt VA
Wm.: b 9-12-1761 d p. 10-3-1844 m Eizabeth Swann Pvt VA ★

MC LEAN, (includes MC CLEAN, MC LAIN, MC LANE &
    MC LENE)
Alexander: b 5- -1755 d 12-28-1849 m Anne Hais Sol NC
Alexander: b 12-2-1746 d 6-7-1834 m Sarah Holmes Lt CS
    PA ★
Allen: b 8-8-1746 d 5-22-1829 m Rebecca Wells Maj DE
Andrew: b 2-19-1741 d 9-5-1831 m Margaret Bell Pvt PA
Andrew: b 3-9-1755 d 5-17-1840 m Margaret Anderson Sgt PA
Archibald: b 12-20-1728 d 1791 m Elizabeth Rowan PS NC
Archibald: b 10-16-1736 d 7-16-1786 m (1)Ann Trump (2)Mary
    Leech Treat PS PA
Archibald, Jr.: b 6-18-1740 d 5-13-1791 m Anne Charlesworth Dr
    PA
Charles: b 1748 d 1810 m Elizabeth Mac Nair LCol PS CS NC
Charles: b 12-20-1734 d 4-10-1825 m Marie Smith Maj NC
Cornelius: b 1758 d 12-29-1838 m Sarah Wilson Pvt NY
Daniel: b 1749 d 6-6-1821 m Nancy Jordan Pvt PA
Daniel: b 1752 d p. 1803 m Sarah — Pvt SC
Ephraim: b 1730 d 1823 m Elizabeth Davidson PS CS NC
George: b 10-14-1760 d 11-30-1834 m Rebecca Alexander Pvt NC
Henry: b 5-10-1750 d 1841 m Esther Henderson Pvt VA ★
Ichabod: b 1746 d 1836 m — Chadwick Pvt MA ★
James: b 1755 d p. 1845 m Abigail Strickland Pvt CT
James: b c. 1740 d 10-20-1804 m Agnes — Lt PA
James, Sr.: b 10-14-1730 d 3-13-1806 m Christian Brown PS PA
James, Jr.: b 3-22-1763 d 1815 m Barbara Campbell Pvt PA
John: b 8-17-1737 d 4-7-1805 m Deborah Adams PS CT
John: b 5-28-1727 d 3-24-1785 m Margrit Christ Lt NY
John: b 7-3-1756 d 2-28-1821 m Ann Burnett Sol NY
John, Jr.: b c. 1750 d 1795 m Dorcas McComb Capt NC
John: b 1760 d 7-8-1844 m Mary — Capt NC ★
John: b 6-11-1748 d 8-9-1841 m Sarah Armstrong Pvt PA ★
John: b c. 1755 d 7-31-1829 m — Powell Pvt SC
John: b 1730 d 6-26-1796 m Elizabeth — Pvt VA
Joseph: b 9-13-1752 d 12-23-1832 m Margaret Mebane Pvt NC ★
Joseph: b c. 1740 d p. 1783 m Rachel Wood Capt VA
Joseph: b 1760 d 1828 m Lettie Latta PS PA
Laughlin: b 12- -1740 d 1805 m — Durell Pvt VA
Moses: b 1-10-1737 d 8-25-1810 m (1)Sarah Charlesworth (2) Sarah
    Watkins LCol PA
Peter: b 1760 d 10-7-1817 m Lucy Weathersby Pvt NC
Samuel: b 9-30-1744 d 1820 m Margaret Porter Pvt PA
Wm.: b c. 1735 d p. 3-30-1798 m Elizabeth Johnson Pvt CS ME

Wm.: b 4-2-1757 d 10-25-1828 m Mary Davidson Dr NC
Wm.: b 12-26-1735 d 9-12-1807 m Jane Witherow Capt PA

MC LELLAN,
Alexander: b 1- -1742 d 10-4-1779 m Margaret Johnson Capt MA
Arthur: b 1753 d 3-6-1835 m Jane Ross PS ME
Cary: b 5-1-1745 d 5-12-1805 m (1)Eunice Elder (2)Mary Parker Lt
    CS MA
Hugh: b 1710 d 1-2-1787 m Elizabeth — Capt PS ME
Joseph, Sr.: b 1732 d 7-5-1820 m Mary — Capt PS MA
Samuel: b 1747/8 d 1778 m Ann Dyer NCapt MA
Stephen: b 2-26-1766 d 10-25-1823 m Hannah IIsley Pvt MA
Thomas: b 10- -1753 d 1- -1829 m Jane Patterson Pvt MA

MC LEMORE,
Atkins, Sr.: b c. 1724 d c. 1788-91 m Sarah — PS NC
James, Sr.: b c. 1718 d c. 1800 m Nancy Jones PS NC
Joel: b c. 1750 d p. 2- -1794 m Elizabeth Wyche Capt SC
John: b 1762 d 6-30-1844 m Sarah Carner OrdSgt NC ★

MC LEROY,
Andrew: b 1740-50 d p. 5-28-1821 m (1)Johannah Hancock
    (2)Phoebe — Pvt NC

MC LOUTH,
John: b 3-18-1758 d 9-13-1820 m Sarah Peirce Sgt MA RI W★
Lawerence, Sr.: b 1743 d 4- -1803 m Molly Pratt Pvt MA
Lawerence, Jr.: b 4- -1757 d 12- -1810 m (1)Esther Brownell
    (2)Welthea Thayer Sgt RI W★
Lewis: b 9-12-1760 d 2-4-1836 m Elizabeth Fuller Sol MA
Peter: b 6-28-1763 d 10- -1834 m (1)Lavina Wells (2)Lydia Osgood
    Pvt MA
Solomon: b 4-15-1761 d 9- -1841 m Charity Mason Pvt MA

MC MAHON, (includes MC MAHAN)
Archibald: b 1760 d 5-26-1841 m Annie Payne Pvt NC
Benjamin: b 6-10-1754 d 5-17-1829 m — McCleese Pvt PA
Daniel: b 1-1-1751 d 9-21-1838 m Eleanor Farmer Pvt NC
James: b 1744 d 3- -1823 m Mary Murry Capt PA
John: b 1728 d c. 1800 m Isabella Barnes CS NC
John: b 1750 d 12-23-1823 m Mary Oliver Pvt SC
John: b c. 1734 d p. 1-23-1784 m Deborah Stockton Lt VA
Joseph: b 2-28-1753 d 8-15-1825 m Sarah — Pvt MA ★
Joseph: b 5- -1761 d 4- -1838 m Mary — Fif VA ★
Robert: b 1759 d 1823 m (2)Nancy Kester Sol VA
Wm.: b 1725 d 1797 m Susan Margaret Pvt PA
Wm.: b 1-9-1749 d 6-30-1794 m Ann Cox Dr VA

MC MANIGAL,
Neal: b c. 1740 d 10-25-1806 m Margaret Thompson PS Pvt PA

MC MANNERS,
Daniel: b 1763 d 6-1-1851 m Elizabeth Tarr Pvt MA
John: b 3-9-1758 d 5-16-1845 m (1)Hannah Rooms (2)Lucy
    Calkins Pvt CT W★

MC MANUS,
Christopher: b 12-8-1753 d 6-14-1849 m Annice — Sgt NJ ★
Hugh: b — d p. 1790 m — Lt SC
Thomas: b a. 1760 d 1791 m Mary Lynch Pvt MD

MC MASTER,
Edward: b 1751 d 4-22-1833 m (1)Hannah Brown, (2)Rhoda
    Fairchild Pvt NJ W★
Gilbert: b c. 1755 d 5- -1825 m Catherine Kirke Sgt PA
Hugh: b 1714 d 8-28-1803 m Mary Farrand Pvt PA
Hugh: b 12- -1752 d 9-25-1837 m (1)Rebecca Paterson (2)Martha
    Williams Pvt NY W★
Hugh: b 1754 d 7-19-1787 m Margaret Killoch Pvt SC
James: b 3-22-1837 m Kathrine Mae Mitchell Pvt NY
James: b 10-8-1750 d 1818 m Rachel Bogardus Pvt NY
James: b c. 1733 d 1788 m Susanna — Sol NC
James: b 10-18-1750 d 3-13-1837 m (1)Sarah Grosscross (2)Jane
    Clary Speer PA ★
James: b a. 1764 d 1806 m Mary Kerr Pvt PA
James: b a. 1752 d p. 6-5-1819 m Margaret — Lt SC
John: b 1714 d 3-16-1793 m Milicent Ferrel PS MA
John: b 7-14-1743 d 11-30-1829 m (1)Lydia Nutting (2)Mrs Springer
    Pvt NY
Joshua: b 12-5-1758 d 6-8-1822 m Rebecca Thompson MM Pvt
    PS MA W★
Robert: b 6-18-1739 d p. 1790 m Elizabeth Young Pvt NY
Robert: b 1755 d p. 1788 m Hester Palmer Pvt PA
Samuel: b 9-10-1744 d 5-25-1811 m Nancy Gillet PS MD
Wm.: b 1726 d 1815 m Eleanor Laffin Pvt PA
Wm.: b c. 1759 d 3-18-1824 m Rebecca Townes Pvt SC

MC MATH,
Alla: b 1-11-1738 d 10-4-1804 m Mabel Kelsey Pvt PA
Daniel: b c. 1740 d 1819 m — Pvt PA
James: b 1759 d 3-14-1837 m Hannah Keller Pvt DE
James: b c. 1745 d 1794 m Susanna — PS VA
Joseph: b 1750 d 1825 m Elizabeth Wilshire Pvt GA
Samuel: b 1743 d p. 1790 m Ella Baxter Pvt PA

MC MEANS,
Andrew: b c. 1740 d 1780 m Anne Wilson Pvt VA

MC MECHEN,
James: b 12-25-1748 d 7-8-1825 m Hannah Davidson Pvt VA
Joseph: b 1753 d 2-10-1818 m Elizabeth Campbell Pvt PA
Wm.: b 1724 d 11-27-1797 m (1)Rachel Rosanna Nivens Capt VA

MC MELLEN,
John: b 1704 d 8-4-1797 m Rachel Steele Pvt RI

MC MICHAEL,
Alexander: b c. 1742 d p. 11-7-1811 m Martha Johnson Pvt PA
Alexander Van Eps: b 1-22-1758 d 5-12-1817 m Angelica Van
    Patten Pvt NY
Christopher: b — d p. 1800 m — Pvt PA
James: b 1761 d 1845 m Sarah Patterson Pvt MA
James: b c. 1740 d p. 7-16-1788 m Priscilla — Pvt PA
John: b c. 1758 d 1817 m Mary Crawford Pvt PA
John: b 1757 d p. 7- -1841 m Emily Green Sol SC
Wm.: b 1747 d 1817 m Sarah Mackeson 2Lt PA
Wm.: b c. 1753 d p. 1-17-1809 m Elizabeth Harrell PS SC

MC MICKEN,
James: b 12-29-1756 d 3- -1835 m Elizabeth Walker Pvt PA

MC MILLAN, (include MAC MILLAN)
Alexander: b 8-12-1749 d 8-23-1837 m Margaret — Pvt MA VA
Andrew: b 1731 d 1800 m Hannah Hazen Osgood Pvt MM NH
Archibald: b 1748 d a. 2- -1824 m Mary — Sol NC
Daniel: b 1757 d 8- -1838 m Jane Sconce Sgt MD ★
Daniel: b 1752 d 8-14-1838 m Jane Thompson Pvt SC ★
George: b 1745 d 1805 m Mary Crain Capt PA
George: b 1735 d 1786 m Susan Crane Capt PA
Hugh: b 1750 d 1791 m Anne Boone Sgt MD
James: b 5-6-1764 d 8-30-1840 m Jane — Pvt NJ ★
James, Sr.: b c. 1730 d a. 1787 m Jean — Pvt PA
James, Jr.: b 1750-60 d 1790 m Jennet — Pvt PA
James: b 8-20-1735 d 3- -1821 m Eleanor — Pvt PA
James: b 1747 d 1812 m Nancy Morgan Ens VA
James, Sr.: b c. 1720 d p. 1-23-1793 m Margaret White Pvt VA
John: b 1761 d 1-5-1841 m Nancy White Pvt NJ ★
John: b 1736 d 7-17-1812 m Mary Arnott Pvt NY
John: b 3-14-1752 d 10-3-1832 m Mercy Comstock Capt PA
John: b 11-11-1752 d 11-16-1833 m Catharine Brown PS Pvt PA
John: b c. 1750 d 1-2-1807 m Catherine Murphy Pvt SC
John: b 1748 d 10-7-1825 m Mary Arnot Pvt VA
John: b 6-20-1760 d 1840 m Elizabeth Brown Pvt VA ★
John: b 1756 d 1848 m Nancy Dickens Pvt VA
Margaret: b c. 1722 d p. 1787 m James McMillan PS VA
Peter: b 1749/50 d p. 1821 m Sarah — Cpl MA
Robert: b 1758 d 9-4-1835 m Christiana Slater Pvt PA ★
Robert: b 1758 d 10-16-1834 m Mary Harbinson Pvt PA ★
Robert: b — d p. 10-17-1791 m Jean — Sol SC
Rowley: b c. 1743 d c. 1843 m — Wallace Pvt SC
Samuel: b 1750 d 9-26-1832 m Isabella Long Pvt MD
Thomas: b 1759/60 d 11-5-1836 m (1)Mary Cobean (2)Hannah —
    Lt PA ★
Wm.: b c. 1729 d p. 1810 m Mary Leeper Pvt CS VA

MC MINN,
John: b 1750 d 8-15-1799 m Jean Forset Lt PA
Robert: b c. 1731 d p. 6-20-1795 m Sarah Harlan PS MD

MC MORDIE,
Robert: b 1720 d 6-22-1796 m Jennett Boyd PS PA

MC MORRIS,
Wm.: b 9-21-1735 d 9-18-1801 m Lady Jane Donovan Sol SC

MC MULLEN, (includes MC MULLAN & MC MULLIN)
Archibald: b 1759 d p. 1823 m (1)Sarah Robbins (2)Sarah Lufkin
    (3)Abigail Curry Pvt MA ★
Charles: b c. 1750 d p. 1812 m Mary — Pvt NY
Daniel: b 1757 d 8- -1838 m Jane Sconce Sgt MD ★
Duncan: b 1-7-1760 d 10-11-1825 m Catherine McFarland Pvt PA
Edward: b c. 1735 d 1788 m (2)Sarah Robinson CS VA
James: b — d 1- -1818 m — Slr PA
James: b 1758-60 d a. 1853 m Sarah Minton Pvt SC
John: b c. 1756 d 7-10-1822 m Mrs Mary Long Pvt PA
John: b 1740 d 12- -1817 m (1)Theodosia Beazley (2)Elizabeth
    Stowers Pvt VA
Michael: b 1752 d — m Esther — Pvt PA
Neal: b 5-24-1751 d 7-21-1824 m Susannah Mann Pvt PA ★
Patrick: b 1761 d p. 1798 m (1) — Walker (2) — Dobbs Pvt GA
Patrick: b 4-1-1724 d 5-18-1797 m Mary Collister Pvt MA
Wm.: b 3-29-1756 d 8-1-1835 m (1)Hannah Smith (2)Jane
    Lindsey (3)Hannah Thompson Pvt MA
Wm.: b 11-24-1729 d 11-20-1797 m Margaret Gordon Capt PA

MC MURPHY,
Archibauld: b 12-2-1744 d 2-19-1816 m Isabel Auld PS NH

Daniel: b 1737 d 10-27-1819 m Susannah Crossley LCol CS GA
George: b 1746 d 3-28-1834 m Nancy Ayers Pvt NH
Robert: b 1-8-1723 d 1-26-1814 m Mrs Jane Shirley PS NH

MC MURRAY,
James: b c. 1750 d a. 2- -1805 m (1)Elizabeth Brown (2)Elizabeth
    Smith Sol NC
John: b a. 1754 d 3- -1830 m Agnes Blaine Pvt PA
John: b 5-6-1750 d 6-3-1842 m (1)Martha — (2)Margaret Adams
    Lt SC
Robert: b 1744 d 1-23-1814 m Susanna Cowan Pvt NY
Samuel: b c. 1755 d 1821 m Nancy Bogle Sol NC
Wm.: b 7-19-1754 d 3-28-1839 m Ann Long Pvt PA ★
Wm.: b 1743 d 1808 m Martha Suttle Pvt SC
Wm.: b c. 1730 d 11-29-1798 m Mary — Sol VA

MC MURTRY,
John: b 2-15-1749 d 10-22-1890 m (1)Margaret Robinson (2)Mary
    Todd Hutton Capt KY
John: b c. 1760 d 1782 m Nancy Ann Campbell PS NC
John: b 2-15-1752 d 3-16-1841 m Margaret Gomer Ens PA ★
Robert: b 2-2-1749 d 2-9-1822 m Agnes McVicar Pvt NJ
Thomas: b 1725 d 1788 m Mary — Pvt NJ
Wm.: b 1728 d 4-1-1807 m Ann Gordan Pvt PS PA
Wm.: b c. 1759 d a. 1-19-1825 m Alice — Mil VA

MC MYER,
Andrew: b c. 1745 d 10-4-1777 m Mary Henry Capt NJ

MC NABB,
David: b 1757 d 5-3-1826 m Elizabeth Taylor Capt NC
John: b 1757 d 1840 m Sarah Jamison Capt NC
Wm.: b 1760 d 8-12-1835 m Mary Crawford Pvt PA

MC NAIR, (includes MAC NAIR)
Daniel: b c. 1748 d 1811 m (1)Catherine — (2)Elean Martin Sol GA
David: b 1736 d 1776/77 m Anna Maria Dunning Sol PA
Hugh: b 1-1-1765 d 12-27-1844 m (1)Phoebe Torbert (2)Eliza Tate
    Duncan Pvt PA
John: b 1735 d 6-30-1819 m (1)Jennet Smylie (2)Catherine Buie
    PS NC
John: b 1738 d 1818 m Margaret Denny Pvt PS NC
John: b c. 1750 d a. 1795 m Sarah — Pvt PA
Samuel: b 9-25-1739 d 4-20-1816 m Mary Mann Sol PA
Thomas: b 1737 d 7-25-1830 m Ann Wallace Pvt PA
Wm.: b 1727 d 1823 m (1)Margaret Wilson (2)Sarah Horner Pvt PA

MC NALL,
Alexander: b — d 7- -1782/3 m (1)Elizabeth — (2)Mary — (3)Annie
    Moor Sol CT

MC NAMARA,
James: b 6-16-1746 d 10-14-1841 m Margaret White Pvt PA
Levin: b 1740-50 d p. 1830 m Sarah Ross PS MD
John Stewart: b 1754 d 7-8-1823 m Lavina Lake 1Lt MD

MC NAMEE,
Wm.: b — d 11-26-1830 m Abigail Mead Cpl NY

MC NARY, (includes MC NAIRY)
David: b 1757 d 1817 m Esther Cowden Pvt PA
Francis: b 1726 d p. 11-16-1807 m Mary Boyd PS NC
Hugh: b 8-21-1762 d p. 1832 m Elisabeth — Pvt NC ★
James: b c. 1741 d 2-11-1815 m Margaret Paxton Pvt PA
John: b 1738 d 3-16-1802 m Esther Boyle Pvt PA
Martin, Jr.: b 1757 d 8-8-1825 m Kate Snyder Pvt CT ★
Thomas: b 1744 d 1820 m Jennet Robinson Capt PA
Wm.: b — d 2-16-1778 m — Cpl VA

MC NATT,
James: b 9-3-1758 d 1-23-1842 m Ferebe Jones Sgt NC ★
John: b 1750 d 1843 m — Benson Pvt DE ★

MC NEE,
Wm., Sr.: b 1711 d 12-23-1789 m (1)Mary Eckless Brownley (2)Mrs
    Sarah Smith Bell PS NH
Wm., Jr.: b 1740 d 1810 m Betsey Russell PS NH

MC NEELY,
George: b 1756-8 d 2-24-1829 m Abigal Hoops Pvt PA
Michael: b 1752 d 1848 m (1)Susan Pushaw (2)Jane Harriman Pvt
    PA

MC NEES,
Robert: b 1-5-1755 d 12- -1836 m Mary Henderson Lt SC ★
Wm.: b c. 1756 d 1805 m Jane McCormick Pvt PA

MC NEIL, (includes MC NEAL, MC NEILL)
Alexander: b 1725 d 4- -1795 m Deborah Phelps Pvt CT
Archibald, Sr.: b 1708 d 1-8-1789 m Sarah Johnson PS CT
Archibald, Jr.: b 7-17-1738 d 1-31-1813 m Jemima Orton Capt CT
Archibald: b c. 1745 d 3-19-1777 m — Sol KY
Daniel: b 1750 d 1835 m Martha Parker Lt NH

Edward: b 1-17-1739 d 4-21-1796 m Ann Vail Lt NY
George: b c. 1720 d 6-7-1805 m (1)Mary Coats Chp NC
Hector: b 1756 d 7-28-1830 m (1)Jane McNeil (2)Ayles McNeill Lt NC
Hugh: b c. 1733 d a. 1795 m Martha — Pvt VA
Jacob: b 6- -1759 d 2- -1841 m (1)Annie Stevens (2)Peggy Cool Pvt VA ★
James: b 1744 d 1823 m Sarah Webb Cpl PA
John: b a. 1749 d 6-12-1775 m Rachael — Smn ME MA
John: b 1744 d 10- -1819 m Anna Howell Pvt PA
John: b 1740 d 1788 m Anna McVeigh Pvt PA
John: b 5-18-1761 d 11-25-1836 m Abigail Gorham Pvt VT
John: b 1745 d 1825 m Martha Davis Pvt VA
John: b c. 1750 d p. 3-20-1806 m Amy Parsons Pvt VA
Patrick: b — d p. 2-20-1786 m Martha — PS VA
Robert: b a. 1757 d 7- -1823 m Jean — Pvt PA
Samuel: b 8-29-1753 d 5-8-1817 m Mary Palmer Sol Bgd QM PA
Samuel: b 1713 d 1-5-1799 m Sarah Skillen Pvt PA
Thomas: b 1758 d 1837 m Elizabeth Sabin Sgt NH ★
Thomas: b 1747 d 1810 m Mary Iveson Sgt VA
Wm.: b 1748 d 5-23-1824 m Martha Hartford Pvt NH
Wm.: b 1759 d 4-23-1823 m Sarah Bailey Pvt PA

MC NEIR,
Alexander: b 1727 d 10-1-1816 m Margaret — Pvt PA
Thomas: b c. 1747 d p. 1777 m Nancy Burgess Sgt MD

MC NISH,
Alexander: b 1748 d 3-24-1827 m Sarah McCoy Ens Lt NY W★
John: b 3- -1744 d p. 1790 m (1)Ann Black (2)Mary Catherine Rivers PS SC

MC NITT,
Adam: b 9-15-1763 d 6-24-1848 m (1)Margaret Clark (2)Mrs Percy Sparks Pvt MA
Alexander, Sr.: b 1720 d 11-29-1817 m (1)Elizabeth — (2)Jane — Capt NY
Alexander: b — d 1793 m Ann Williamson Pvt PA
Daniel: b 1740 d 11-21-1829 m Mary Gault Sgt PA
John: b 4-25-1749 d 4-13-1835 m Patty Wilson Pvt MA ★
John: b 2-24-1759 d 4-17-1843 m Eleanor — Pvt NY ★
John: b 1730 d 4-16-1826 m Nancy Hazelett Pvt PA
John: b 1739 d 1-20-1822 m Mary Brown Pvt PA

MC NUTT,
Alexander: b 12-10-1754 d 3-29-1812 m Rachel Grigsby Sgt VA
George: b 1750 d 1-5-1823 m (1)Isabella Collison (2)Catherine Kain (3)Ginny Anderson Sol VA
James: b 1738 d 1810 m Margaret McElroy Lt VA
James: b c. 1755 d 9-6-1811 m Margaret — Sol VA

MC PEEK,
Jonathan: b 12-2-1756 d 2-26-1839 m Catherine Youst Pvt NJ ★

MC PEETERS,
David: b 1-14-1756 d 3-27-1846 m Susannah Loyd Pvt NC ★

MC PHATRIDGE,
Malcolm: b c. 1755 d 1820 m Ann — Sgt PA

MC PHEETERS,
Andrew: b 3-22-1761 d 4-30-1850 m (1)Achsah Smith (2)Sarah Ogles Pvt PA NC ★
John: b 1762 d 1839 m Margaret Anderson Pvt VA ★
Wm.: b 1729/30 d 10-28-1807 m Rachel Moore CS VA

MC PHERRAN,
Andrew: b 1759 d 6-16-1829 m Mary Adams Pvt PA ★

MC PHERSON, (includes MAC PHERSON)
Abell: b 6-9-1754 d 2-14-1811 m Nancy McDaniel QM Sgt NC
Alexander: b 1754 d 1-21-1821 m Elizabeth Murray PS NC
Daniel: b 10-22-1755 d 10-17-1844 m Susannah Kinchloe Sol VA
Frederick: b a. 1755 d p. 1810 m Isabella Collins Pvt PA
James: b 1760 d 11-14-1826 m Mary McClintock Starrett Pvt NH
James: b 3-10-1761 d 4-2-1837 m (1)Cathrine Hoffman (2)Dorothy Tullis Pvt PA ★
John: b a. 1760 d p. 1797 m Agnes McLaughlin Pvt NH
John: b 1753 d 8-2-1827 m Elizabeth Slaymaker Mid PA ★
Joseph: b 1725 d 1783 m Ann — Pvt NH
Mark: b 2-14-1754 d 2-8-1847 m Mary Middleton Lt MD ★
Matthew: b 1758 d 8-5-1843 m Elizabeth Wilson Pvt NC
Nathaniel: b a. 1752 d 1789 m Anne — PS NJ
Robert: b 6-10-1730 d 2-19-1789 m Agnes Miller Col PA
Samuel: b 6-11-1739 d 9-4-1808 m (2)Elizabeth Goldsmith Capt MD
Thomas: b 12-16-1729 d 8-22-1793 m Elizabeth Hanson PS MD
Wm.: b 9-23-1740 d 1-18-1809 m Mary Smoot Capt MD
Wm.: b 1752 d 9-28-1828 m Mary Gregg Pvt NH
Wm.: b 1756 d 11-5-1813 m Margaret Stout Maj PA

MC PIKE, (includes MAC PIKE)
James: b 1751 d 5- -1825 m Martha Mountain Sgt PA
Roger: b c. 1740 d 1814 m Sarah Drake Pvt PA

MC QUAIDE,
James: b 1758-61 d 5-23-1828 m (1)Isabell Pearce (2)Mrs Ann Davis Pvt PA
Patrick: b 1743 d 5-24-1820 m Catherine Graham Pvt PA

MC QUEEN,
Alexander: b 1723-8 d p. 1810 m Isabel More PS NY
Alexander: b 1754 d — m Elizabeth Fuller Lt SC
David: b 7-21-1754 d 1-21-1788 m Margaret Tate Capt PA
John: b 8-18-1751 d 1807 m Ann Smith PS Capt SC
Joshua: b 1756 d 1851 m (2)Jemima Cornelison Sgt VA ★
Thomas: b 12- -1761 d 1838 m Sarah Vaughn Pvt VA ★

MC QUIDDY,
John: b 3-22-1760 d 12-24-1841 m (1)Sarah Elizabeth West (2)Susan (Hanks) Smith Pvt VA ★
Wm.: b 1752 d 10-27-1832 m Alice McKee Sol VA

MC QUIE,
Wm.: b 5- -1758 d 1837 m Sarah Brook Pvt VA ★

MC QUIGG,
David: b 6-4-1752 d 7-14-1817 m Mary Harvell Ens NH
John: b a. 1750 d 1804 m (1)Molly Gilmore (2)Sarah Coburn Pvt NH

MC QUILKIN,
James: b c. 1750 d 12-2-1802 m Anna Robinson Pvt CL
John: b 1761 d 1826 m Eliza Jane McClure Pvt PA

MC QUISTON, (includes MC CUISTON, MC QUESTEN, MC QUISTION)
David: b 9-27-1757/8 d 7-29-1824 m Margaret Fisher Pvt NH
James: b 11-23-1758 d 4- -1826 m Jean Nicholson Sol NC
James: b 11-29-1736 d 10-24-1804 m Margaret Trindle PS PA
Jane: b 1706 d 4-11-1783 m James McCuistion PS NC
Thomas: b 10-31-1762 d 2-14-1853 m Mary Nicholson Pvt NC ★
Thomas: b 12-17-1731 d 12-9-1783 m Ann Moody PS NC
Wm.: b 1732 d 10-28-1802 m (1)Margaret Nahor (2)Anna (Osgood) Parker 2Maj NH
Wm.: b c. 1760 d c. 1800 m Jane Chestnut Pvt SC

MC QUOWN,
John: b 4-25-1751 d 3- -1827 m Mary — Pvt VA ★

MC RAE,
Duncan: b 1743 d a. 2-6-1820 m Margaret McQueen Pvt NC

MC REE,
John Griffeth: b 1-1-1723 d 4- -1801-3 m Helen Purdy LCol NC
Samuel: b c. 1754 d p. 5-5-1798 m Mary — Sol NC

MC REYNOLDS,
Hugh: b 1- -1750 d 2-28-1797 m Elizabeth Snoddy Pvt PA
Joseph: b 12-12-1762 d 10-30-1840 m (1)Henrietta Browning (2)Elizabeth J. Simpson Pvt NC ★
Robert: b c. 1738 d p. 1796 m Martha Rich — Ens NC

MC ROBERTS,
Alexander: b c. 1755 d c. 1800-05 m Nancy Highland Sol CS VA
James: b c. 1760 d 7-18-1823 m Nancy Nishart Pvt PA
John: b 1752 d 1813 m Lucy Bradford OrdlSgt NY W ★
John: b 1757 d 4-4-1813 m Lucy Bradford OrdlSgt VT
John: b 11-5-1740 d 6-5-1833 m Margaret Taylor Pvt VA
Wm.: b c. 1740 d p. 2-24-1808 m Hannah — Pvt PS PA

MC SHANE,
Francis: b 12-2-1717 d 1800 m — CS NJ

MC SHERRY,
Patrick: b 1725 d 7-13-1795 m Catherine Gartland PS PA

MC SPADDEN,
John: b c. 1754 d 1798 m Esther Thompson PS NC
Samuel: b 10-19-1756 d 8-4-1844 m (1)Sarah Keyes (2)Nancy Harris Pvt VA ★

MC SWAIN,
Wm.: b 1762 d 12-9-1838 m (1)Judith Moore (2)Elizabeth — Pvt NC W ★

MC TEER, (includes MATEER, MC TEEAR, MC TIER, MC TYER, MC TYERE, MC TYIERE & MC TYRE)
Frizzell: b 2- -1734 d 4-14-1823 m (1)Mary — (2)Mary (Rhodes) Murphy Sgt VA
James, Jr.: b 4-16-1732 d 1790-1800 m — De Nelson Pvt PA
John: b 1746 d 6-10-1821 m (1)Sarah (Carter) Henning (2)Molly Doggett (3)Lucy Shelton (4)Anne McCabe (Barrie) (5)Anne Esther — VA PS
Robert: b 9-15-1741 d 4-8-1811 m (1)Jane Coulter (3)Elizabeth Martin Capt PA
Robert: b 1-25-1740 d 4-6-1824 m Agnes Martin Ens P A
Samuel: b 4-12-1752 d 10- -1800 m Rosannah Quigley Pvt PA
Wm., Sr.: b c. 1778 m Sarah Ann Adair PS NC
Wm., Jr.: b 1760 d 1817 m Elizabeth Whittington Bbd Cpl NC
Wm.: b — d 1800-20 m Margaret Caruthers Pvt Fif PA

MC VANEY,
Christopher: b 1755 d 1852 m Mary Paul Pvt VA ★

MC VAY, (includes MC VEAUGH & MC VEY)
Benjamin: b 1754 d 1818 m Phebe Brinson Pvt NY
James, Jr.: b 7-18-1743 d p. 1790 m Mary McCormack Pvt VA
John: b 1748 d 1805 m Mary Bumpass Sol NC
John: b 1747 d 1824 m Sarah Wakefield Pvt PA
John: b 12-16-1759 d 2-21-1826 m Sarah Rood Pvt PA
John: b 1727 d 1823 m Sarah Snedinger Sgt VA
Jonathan: b 9-1-1743 d 9-16-1824 m Elizabeth Bull Sol PA
Roger: b — d — m Catherine Galiher Pvt PA

MC VEAN,
Daniel: b 1734 d 5-19-1814 m Jennet McNaughton Pvt NY

MC VICKER,
Duncan: b 1739 d 1-19-1818 m Nancy McCollum Capt NJ

MC VITY,
Cromwell: b c. 1737/8 d 1789 m (1)Margarete Hudson
  (2)Margaret Anderson (3)Margaret McCurdy Pvt PA

MC WAIN,
John: b 9-8-1739 d 2-10-1818 m Joanna Burge Pvt VT

MC WATTERS,
John: b 1746 d 8-30-1828 m Celia Lott Sgt SC

MC WETHY,
Isaac: b 10-26-1745 d p. 1784 m — Pvt NY

MC WHINNEY,
Thomas: b 1755 d 1828 m Eleanor — Pvt PA

MC WHORTER, (includes MC WHIRTER)
Alexander: b 7-15-1734 d 7-20-1807 m Mary Cumming Chp NJ
David: b 1740-45-d 1789 m Mary Poston PS NC
George Gray: b 1765 d p. 6-18-1829 m Elizabeth — Sol SC
Henry: b 11-13-1760 d 2-4-1848 m Mary Fields Pvt NY ★
Hugh: b 1737 d 3-6-1812 m Kezia Tyler Sgt NY
John: b 8-10-1729 d 4-23-1804 m (1)Jean Faries (2)Rebecca
  Thomas (3)Mrs Sarah Dushane PS DE
John: b c. 1755 d p. 5-16-1827 m Margaret Potts Sol GA
John: b c. 1762 d a. 6-5-1797 m Margaret Carr Pvt NY
John: b 1739 d 1-6-1813 m Bethia Hall Pvt NY
John: b c. 1763 d 3/4- -1840 m Rhoda — Pvt SC ★
John, Jr.: b 1749 d 6-7-1833 m (1) — Jasker (2)Elizabeth McClure
  Pvt SC ★
Moses: b 1744 d 1-24-1832 m Mrs Jean (Finley)Morrison OrdlSgt PA

MC WILLIAMS,
Hugh: b 5- -1735 d 12-24-1778 m Rebecca Dunwoody Pvt PA
James: b c. 1752 d a. 5-14-1804 m Mary Gass 2Lt PA
James: b 1762 d 8-26-1843 m Mattie Jammeson Pvt NC VA W★
John: b 1725 d 11-23-1802 m Sarah Haffee Pvt NY
John: b 6-14-1760 d 1852 m Margaret Fisher OrdlSgt VA
John: b 3-3-1751 d 3-12-1824 m Elizabeth Cleveland Pvt VA
Wm.: b 1759 d 4-21-1840 m (1)— Boggs (2)Mary Merritt Pvt PA ★
Wm.: b 1739 d 1-11-1819 m Sarah Nichol PS PA
Wm.: b 1751 d p. 11-28-1799 m Dorothea Brayne Benger Maj CS
  VA

MEACHAM, (includes MEACHEM)
Abraham: b 6-24-1753 d 12-24-1822 m Lydia Standish Cpl MA VT
  W★
Asa: b 9-5-1756 d 11-3-1820 m Sarah Truman Pvt CT
Banks: b 1-15-1748 d 2-24-1820 m (1)Jemima Hancock (2)Elizabeth
  (Andrew) Person PS NC
Barnabas, Sr.: b 4-3-1734 d 10-15-1812 m Margaret Owen Cpl CT
Barnabas, Jr.: b 7-21-1759 d p. 1811 m Abigail Weldon Pvt CT
Ebenezer: b 9-30-1721 d p. 1790 m Rachel Hall PS MA
Isaac: b 7-8-1746 d 1828 m Mehitable Terry Pvt CT
Isaac: b 12-25-1748 d 8-16-1838 m Lucy Standish Ens MA VT W ★
Isaac: b 1726 d 11-6-1794 m Ruth Dunnell Sol MA
Jeremiah: b 3-31-1744 d 8-3-1817 m Mary Bartholomew Pvt CT
Jeremiah: b 1-28-1759 d 2-25-1829 m Chloe Jennings Pvt CT ★
Joel: b 8-18-1735 d 12-26-1792 m Priscilla Simons Sgt MA
John: b 5-31-1754 d 10-19-1839 m Tabitha Danniels Cpl MA
John: b 3-22-1750 d c. 1808 m Sarah Hall CS VT
Joseph: b 2-25-1761 d 8- -1838 m Molly West Pvt NC ★
Philip: b 1-9-1761 d 2-15-1835 m (1)Abigail Leland (2)Lydia (Bixby)
  Mathews Pvt CT
Samuel: b 11-15-1739 d 1-22-1811 m Phebe Main Pvt PS NH
Simeon: b 8-30-1766 d 8-26-1836 m (1)Hannah Eddy (2)Lydia
  Calkins Pvt MA ★
Wm.: b 3-1-1742 d 6-17-1775 m Sarah Cook Capt MA

MEAD, (includes MEADE)
Abel: b 7-7-1752 d 8-29-1833 m Phoebe Reynolds Pvt CT
Abner: b c. 1745 d p. 1810 m Mercy Hazen Pvt NY
Amos: b 2-22-1730 d 2-20-1807 m Ruth Bush Dr PS CT
Amos: b 8-4-1760 d 3-22-1827 m Anna Harrison Pvt NY

Amos: b 6-10-1756 d 1846 m Eunice Bates Pvt VT
Andrew: b 12-4-1758 d 5-1-1836 m Elizabeth Bouton QM Sgt NY
Andrew: b 1753 d c. 1800 m Susanna Stith PS VA
Benjamin: b 9-20-1764 d 4-3-1847 m Abigail Wooster Pvt CT
Benjamin: b 2-11-1754 d 4-21-1828 m Susannah Collins Pvt MA
Benjamin: b 10-22-1759 d 3-16-1852 m Elizabeth Mead Pvt MA ★
Caleb: b 10-28-1716 d 1- -1798 m Hannah Rundle Capt CT
Calvin: b 8-1-1760 d 6- -1847 m Deborah Mead Pvt CT NY ★
Darius, Sr.: b 3-28-1728 d 1791 m Ruth Curtice Pvt PA
Darius, Jr.: b 12-9-1764 d 5-19-1812 m Anna Hoffman Pvt PA
David: b 1762 d 5-22-1836 m Sarah Williams Pvt NY ★
David: b 1-17-1752 d 8-23-1816 m (1)Agnes Wilson (2)Janet Finney
  Ens PA
David: b 7-29-1744 d 10- -1830 m Sarah Waters PS VA
Ebenezer: b 12-12-1748 d 2-7-1818 m Nancy (Mead) — Pvt CT
Edmund: b 5- -1752 d p. 1790 m Theodosia Mead Cpl PS CT
Edward: b 9-25-1757 d 1-29-1797 m Mary Finch Sgt CT W★
Elkanah: b 3-6-1746 d 6-20-1816 m Hannah (Mead) — Pvt CT
Enoch: b 4-9-1756 d 9-10-1807 m Jemimah Mead Adj NY
Enos: b 6-3-1761 d 9-5-1838 m Prudence Anderson Cpl CT ★
Ethan: b 6-28-1747 d 8-10-1825 m Elizabeth Keller Pvt NY
Everard: b 10-1-1748 d 9- -1802 m (1)Mary Thornton (2)Mrs Mary
  (Eggleston) Ward Maj VA ★
Ezekiel: b c. 1750 d p. 1787 m Lydia Mead Pvt NY
Ezra: b 10-9-1737 d p. 1790 m Triphena Burton Pvt VT
Henry: b 7-29-1762 d 6-21-1839 m Mary Munson Sct MM VT
Isaac: b 1760 d p. 1791 m (1)Polly Preston (2)— Lindsley Pvt VT
Israel: b 3-18-1760 d p. 3-26-1833 m Mary Ferris Pvt Btm PS CT ★
Israel: b c. 1749 d 1805 m Lydia Cutler Pvt MA W★
Israel: b 8-7-1754 d p. 1837 m Elizabeth Bates MM Pvt MA VT ★
James: b 1743 d a. 9-30-1817 m Hannah — DrmMaj PS MD
James: b 8-25-1730 d 1-17-1804 m Mercy Holmes Col VT
Jared: b 12-15-1738 d 5-8-1832 m Lydia Smith Pvt CT
Jason: b 2-9-1764 d p. 1803 m Silence Atherton Pvt MA
Jasper: b 2-12-1755 d 5-23-1830 m Elizabeth Benedict Lt CT
Jehiel: b 1742 d 7-16-1826 m Deborah — 2Lt CT
Jehiel: b 1744 d 1780 m Mary Newcomb Pvt NY
Jeremiah, Sr.: b 2-13-1727 d 2-5-1815 m Amea Lockwood Pvt CT
Jeremiah, Jr.: b 11-2-1754 d 11-24-1840 m (1)Martha St. John
  (2)Rachel Smith (3)Betty Whitney Pvt CT ★
Jeremiah, Jr.: b c. 1755 d 10-20-1831 m Esther Peck Pvt CT
Jeremiah: b 1747 d 4-2-1831 m (1)Mary Shear (2)Sarah — Pvt NY
Jesse: b 1753 d 11-11-1799 m Sarah Green Pvt NY
Job, Sr.: b 3-4-1735 d 4-23-1819 m Mercy King Capt NY
John: b 1725 d 12-3-1790 m (1)Mary Brush (2)Mrs Mehitable
  (Blackman) Peck BGen PS CT
John: b 10-4-1764 d 12-21-1845 m Elizabeth Bentley Pvt NY ★
John: b 1754 d 6- -1819 m Catherine Foster Pvt PA
John Haile: b 11-20-1755 d 1798 m Elizabeth Crump Ens VA
John P.: b 8-3-1761 d 1-21-1823 m Rebecca Carter Capt NJ
Jonah: b 2-3-1748 d 2-21-1827 m (1)Rachel Mead (2)Mary Husted
  (3)Mary Mead Pvt CT
Jonathan: b c. 1736 d 5-11-1800 m Sarah Guernsey Lt PS NY
Jonathan: b 1755 d 12- -1814 m Molly Brown Pvt Matr CT
Joseph: b 1733 d p. 1790 m Thankful Rockwell Pvt CT
Joshua: b 5-16-1751 d 5-30-1812 m (1)Rachel Knapp (2)Hannah
  Mead Sgt NY
Josiah: b 10-18-1761 d 7-5-1829 m Sally Locke Pvt MA
Jotham: b 1751 d 9-15-1840 m Elizabeth Brown Pvt CT
Levi: b 10-14-1759 d 4-29-1828 m Betsey Converse Sgt MA
Levi: b 3-30-1753 d 11-25-1845 m Esther Bryant Pvt NY
Lewis, Jr.: b 5-10-1764 d 1-15-1842 m Sarah Brown Pvt NY ★
Libbeus: b 1-15-1750 d 7-1-1814 m (1)Mrs Hannah (Benedict)
  Benedict (2)Catharine Peacock Sgt PS NY
Matthew: b c. 1734 d c. 1812 m Mary Bush Capt PS CT
Matthew: b 8-20-1736 d 2-26-1816 m Phebe Whelpley LCol CT
Moses: b 12-2-1754 d 2-26-1818 m Elizabeth Viles Pvt MA
Nathan: b 3-27-1757 d 2-19-1812 m Mary King Pvt CT
Nathaniel: b 8-16-1750 d 3-5-1816 m (1)Hannah Lamb (2)Mary
  Quimby Lt NY
Nathaniel: b 3-7-1746 d 2-2-1814 m Martha Brown PS NY
Nehemiah: b 1721 d 6-16-1791 m Sarah Knapp PS CT
Nehemiah: b 5-27-1747 d 2-17-1822 m Sarah Newcomb Pvt NY
Nicholas: b 2-16-1752 d p. 1817 m Mary (Jones) Bates Sgt VA
Oliver: b 9-2-1751 d 3-20-1836 m Anna Whitney Pvt MA
Peter, Sr.: b 1716 d 7-3-1780 m Hannah Mead PS CS CT
Peter, Jr.: b 1-14-1755 d 12-20-1832 m Hannah Close Sgt CT ★
Peter: b 1720 d 1791 m Jane Van Winkkle PS NJ
Philip: b 8-24-1753 d 7-30-1821 m Susannah Crippen Cpl VT
Richard: b 9-5-1753 d 4-21-1826 m (1)Sarah Mead (2)Rachel Mead
  Sol CT
Richard Kidder: b 7-14-1746 d 2-9-1805 m (1)Jane Randolph (2)Mrs
  Mary Grymes Randolph LCol VA
Robert: b c. 1750 d c. 1825 m Hannah Rhodes CS VA
Rufus: b 10-15-1764 d 11-26-1824 m Betsy Rockwell Pvt VT
Samuel, Jr.: b 6-18-1732 d 2-20-1815 m (1)Amy — (2)Patience
  Whitney (3)Hepsibeth — Pvt MA
Samuel: b 1723 d 6-1-1814 m Hannah Willard Pvt MA
Silas, Sr.: b 5-22-1720 d 10-6-1817 m Mary Mead Sol NY
Silas, Jr.: b 2-27-1748 d 6-8-1813 m Sarah Mead Pvt CT
Solomon: b 10-25-1725 d 9-5-1812 m (1)Hannah Strong (2)Hannah
  Clark PS NY
Stephen: b 1728 d 10-18-1806 m Rachel Sanford Pvt CT

Stephen: b 1731 d 1795 m Mollie Knapp Pvt CT
Stephen: b 3-2-1741 d 4-22-1794 m Elizabeth Hobby Pvt MA
Stephen: b c. 1740 d 7-22-1779 m Mary Inman Pvt NJ
Stephen: b 1-23-1734 d 1825 m Polly White Pvt VT
Sylvanus: b 1-19-1739 d 1780 m Sybil Wood Capt CT
Thaddeus: b 11-16-1730 d p. 1790 m Tamar Hobby Pvt NY
Thomas: b 8-29-1764 d 5-3-1844 m Helen Ressequie Pvt CT ★
Timothy, Sr.: b 4-22-1701 d p. 1790 m Martha Weeks Pvt VT
Timothy, Jr.: b 1-7-1724 d c. 1800 m Phoebe Palmer Pvt VT
Titus: b 9-15-1729 d 9-10-1812 m (1)Rachel Rundle (2)Lucy
    Munford (3)Tamish Brown Pvt CT
Uriah: b 3-27-1759 d 12-12-1846 m Betsy Lyon Sgt CT
Wm.: b 10-10-1727 d 12-13-1805 m (1)Ann Haile (2)Mrs Martha
    (Cowles) Stith Col VA
Wm.: b 10-31-1757 d 1-25-1831 m Sarah — Pvt VA ★
Wm.: b 1720 d 1805 m Ellen — PS VA
Wm. Bingham: b 8-22-1762 d 2-11-1841 m Mildred Esther Davis
    Pvt VA ★
Zebulon, Sr.: b 10-5-1728 d 1-26-1797 m (1)Anna Thompson
    (2)Mercy Carey Pvt Sct VT
Zebulon, Jr.: b 3-4-1753 d 1797 m Anna Wright Pvt VT

MEADER,
Ambrose: b — d a. 9-28-1795 m Franky — PS VA
Daniel H.: b 5-10-1749 d 10-7-1819 m Jerusha Wormwood Pvt MA
Francis: b 3-11-1744 d 1831 m Mary Holley Pvt MA
Jason: b 1736 d 1823 m Ann — PS NC
Jesse: b c. 1750 d a. 9-28-1812 m Martha — Sol PS VA
Joel: b 3-8-1760 d 4-7-1834 m Sally Meador Pvt VA ★
Lemuel: b 1-31-1733 d — m Sarah Worth Pvt NH
Wm.: b 1745 d 1813 m Mary Ann — Sol VA

MEADOWS,
Isham: b 3-20-1762 d 3-2-1840 m (1)Biddy Bradshaw (2)Mrs
    Martha Sullivan Pvt VA
Israel: b 1756 d 9-30-1827 m Barbara Greene Pvt VA ★
James: b c. 1755 d 5-9-1838 m Jane Heryford Pvt NC
James: b 1740 d 1815 m Elinor Shearman PS NC
John: b c. 1750 d 6-9-1812 m — Jester Pvt GA
John: b 3-18-1762 d p. 9-28-1832 m Delila Jones Pvt NC ★
Josiah: b 2- -1758 d p. 1845 m Juda Lilly Pvt VA ★
Thomas: b c. 1760 d 1823 m Alcey (Ayley) Dowell Pvt VA
Wm.: b 2-25-1739 d 1778 m Sarah Haines Pvt MD
Wm.: b 1756 d 10-18-1831 m — Pvt VA

MEALMAN,
Adam: b 1729 d 2-17-1827 m Catherine King Pvt PA

MEALS,
Charles: b c. 1755 d p. 1810 m Mary Van Tassel Pvt NY
Samuel: b 1754 d 9-21-1822 m Margaret Catherine Rieckersin
    Sol PA

MEANS, (or MAINS)
Andrew: b c. 1746 d c. 1826 m Nancy Gray Sol NC
George: b 1748 d 11-19-1833 m Mary — Pvt VA ★
Hugh: b 10-8-1757 d 2-12-1835 m Rosanna Woods Ens PA ★
Hugh: b 10-14-1751 d 6-11-1825 m (1)Prudence Patton (2)Hannah
    Mc Elvan Capt SC
Isaac: b c. 1732 d 3- -1818 m Nancy Gilmer Pvt VA
James: b 1753 d 10-15-1832 m Mary Cox Capt ME
James: b 2-28-1758 d 3-16-1807 m Margaret Mays Ens PA
John: b 7-13-1758 d 4-9-1811 m Mary Ann Milling Sgt MA
John: b 1745 d 10-3-1795 m Martha Ramsey Pvt PA
John: b c. 1744 d p. 1830 m Jemima Scudder Cpl VA
Robert: b 11-2-1750 d 7-15-1837 m Hannah Mc Kee Capt PA
Robert: b 1740 d a. 1-24-1797 m (1)— (2)Elizabeth — Sol PA
Samuel: b c. 1735 d c. 1780 m Elizabeth Clark Pvt PA
Thomas: b 1758 d 1828 m Martha Campbell Cpl PA
Thomas: b 12-13-1757 d 1-26-1830 m (1)Hannah Banks (2)Polly
    Furbish Cpl MA
Thomas, Sr.: b c. 1755 d 1812 m Polly Scotch Pvt VA
Wm.: b c. 1750 d p. 1825 m Sarah Ellerson Sol NC
Wm.: b 1743 d 1815 m Mary Alexander Ens PA
Wm.: b 5-3-1763 d 6-11-1848 m (1)Nancy Mc Elroy (2)Mrs Susan
    Seal Chenowith Pvt SC ★

MEARS,
Alexander: b 1750 d 4-3-1824 m Martha Poland Pvt MA
James: b 1731 d 6-7-1804 m Ann Greaton Pvt MA
James: b c. 1760 d 1806 m Naomi Van Tice Pvt NC
John: b 3-12-1733 d 12-11-1811/12 m Lucy Rockwell Sgt MA
John: b 4-3-1741 d 6-26-1788 m Jane Stickney Pvt MA
John: b 6-4-1738 d 7-10-1819 m Susanna Townsend Capt PA
John: b c. 1760 d a. 1812 m Ann Baldridge Pvt PA
Samuel: b 1757 d 1810 m Margarita — Lt CT
Samuel: b 1725-35 d 4- -1793 m Mary Blair Pvt PA
Thomas: b c. 1740 d 1779/80 m Mary Stuart Sgt MA
Thomas: b 5-2-1738 d 2-17-1807 m Lydia Carleton Pvt MA

MEBANE,
Alexander, Sr.: b 11-26-1716 d a. 2- -1793 m Mary Tinnin PS
    CS NC

Alexander, Jr.: b 11-26-1744 d 7-5-1795 m (1)Mary Armstrong
    (2)Ann Claypoole PS CS NC
David: b 12-28-1760 d 2-15-1844 m (1)Anne Allen (2)Mrs Elizabeth
    Young Sol NC
James: b c. 1742 d p. 5-18-1807 m Margaret Allen PS NC
Wm.: b c. 1728 d p. 5-23-1778 m (1)Mary Nelson (2)Elizabeth —
    CS NC

MECHLIN, (includes MECKLIN & MECKLING)
Dewalt: b 11-11-1731 d 3-29-1816 m Sabilla — Ens PA
Jacob: b 2-28-1747 d 11-8-1824 m Catherine — Capt PA
Philip: b c. 1749 d 1817 m Catherine — Ens PA
Samuel, Jr.: b 4-30-1756 d 7-10-1817 m Maria Bockius Pvt PA
Thomas: b 8-4-1751 d 1785 m Katherine Welch Lt PA

MECK,
Nicholas: b c. 1743 d 4- -1803 m Catherine — Pvt PA
Philip: b 2-27-1757 d 11-21-1844 m Catherine Ament Pvt PA

MECUM,
Wm.: b 6-12-1730 d 3-21-1790 m Eleanor Sinnickson Maj CS NJ

MEDAIRY,
Jacob: b 1735 d 3-9-1785 m Catherine Bauer PS MD

MEDBURY, (includes MEDBERY)
Benjamin: b 12-31-1718 d 12-31-1795 m Sarah — Pvt MA
Isaac: b 10-13-1724 d 12-11-1797 m Lydia — Pvt RI
John: b 8-11-1754 d 11-2-1825 m Abigail Viall Lt MA
Joseph: b 1758 d 1-12-1839 m Mary Potter SgtMaj RI ★
Nathan: b 1751 d 1816 m Rhoda Harris Sol RI

MEDEARIS,
John: b 2-22-1744 d 3-31-1834 m Mrs Sarah (Haywood) Bell
    Dep QMGen NC

MEDLER,
George: b 10-11-1750 d 10-15-1828 m Margaret Ann Quinder
    Pvt PA

MEDLOCK,
Isham: b 1760 d 1825 m Martha — Pvt VA

MEDTART,
Jacob: b 5-14-1752 d 4-19-1821 m Maria Magdalena — Pvt MD

MEECH, (includes MEACH)
Aaron: b 1735 d c. 1800 m Abigail Meach Capt CT
Daniel: b 1-27-1757 d 11-11-1821 m Zerviah Witter Pvt CT
Jacob: b 4-10-1758 d 2-21-1847 m Sarah Plummer Pvt CT
Thomas: b 2-22-1749 d 10-21-1822 m Lucretia Kimball Pvt CT

MEEK,
Adam: b 1746 d 7-8-1828 m Martha Wallace Pvt SC
Alexander: b 12-14-1764 d 1858 m Elizabeth Kase Pvt VA ★
Bazel: b 3-7-1763 d 1-12-1844 m Eleanor Roberts Sol VA
George: b 1741 d 1-10-1801 m Rachel Herron Pvt PA
Isaac: b 10-14-1746 d 12-12-1840 m (1)Mary Robinson (2)Rachel
    Hedges Lt VA
Jacob: b 3- -1755 d 1840 m Nancy Warcins Pvt PA VA ★
James: b 1758 d 1819 m Susannah Byers Drm PA
John: b c. 1750/51 d 1803 m Margaret — Pvt MD ★
John Booker: b c. 1744 d p. 6-5-1800 m Virlinda Thomas PS MD
Joseph: b c. 1744 d 12-15-1807 m Lydia Meek PS VA
Moses: b 1-29-1754 d 12-23-1815 m Agnes Hope Sgt SC
Robert: b 1732 d 11-13-1786 m Elizabeth Alexander Pvt PA
Samuel: b 1732 d 2-12-1799 m Charity — Pvt PA

MEEKER,
Benjamin: b 11-17-1741 d 1-25-1817 m Abigail Burr Grd CT
Caleb: b 1759 d 4- -1817 m Susan Skinner Mus NJ W★
Cory: b 3- -1752 d 1849 m Vannelia Ward Pvt NJ ★
Daniel: b 8-18-1739 d 9-20-1784 m Abigail Gorham Sgt CT
David: b a. 1750 d 1787 m Phoebe Pasel Sgt NJ
Isaiah: b c. 1741 d 2-23-1814 m Deborah Halsey MM NJ
James, Sr.: b 1710 d 1-11-1777 m Mary Crocheron MM NJ
John: b 1758 d 7-3-1840 m (1)Theadosia Skinner (2)Eliza Mosley
    Pvt NY
Jonas: b 3-5-1763/4 d 9- -1852 m Charity — Sol NJ
Jonathan: b 2-11-1744 d 6-10-1805 m (1)Mary Ogden (2)Rachel
    Denman Pvt NJ
Jonathan: b 1758 d 1819 m (2)Eunice Kemp Sol NJ
Jonathan: b 10-16-1761 d 1- -1837 m Persis Carley Pvt NH ★
Joseph: b 3-25-1761 d 11-24-1842 m Sally Hilton Pvt CT
Michael: b 6-10-1753 d 6-27-1834 m Mary Edwards Pvt NJ ★
Nathaniel: b 10-16-1753 d p. 4-14-1792 m Esther Little Pvt NJ
Nathaniel: b 1762 d 5-28-1857 m Esther — Cpl NY
Obadiah: b 1738 d 1829 m Comfort Johnson Capt NJ
Rebert: b 5-22-1752 d 9-27-1835 m (1)Elizabeth Wiltse (2)Catharine
    Vandusen Pvt Spy NY W★
Samuel: b c. 1740 d 5-23-1804 m Sarah — Maj NJ
Seth, Sr.: b 9-12-1731 d 12-1-1798 m Abigail Wakeman Pvt CT
Seth, Sr.: b 1759 d 1793 m Abigail Beers Cpl CT

MEEKER, contd.
Timothey, Sr.: b 1708/9 d 12-22-1798 m (1)Sarah Pierson (2)—
  Munn (3)Desire Cory MM NJ
Timothy, Jr.: b 1748 d 4-24-1834 m Sarah Parcells Sgt NJ ★

MEEKINS,
Thomas: b 1744 d 3-14-1832 m Ruth — Pvt MA

MEEKS,
John: b 8-18-1739 d 2-7-1817 m Susanne Helene Marie de
  Moulinar Capt NY
Joseph: b 12-31-1710 d 10-6-1782 m Sarah Reade PS NY
Samuel: b 8-16-1763 d p. 1794 m Elizabeth Allen Sol VA

MEETCH,
John, Sr.: b 1724 d 1794 m — Pvt PA

MEFFORD,
George: b 1757 d 10-18-1814 m Malinda Masters Pvt PA
Jacob: b 10- -1764 d 12-14-1844 m Eleanor (Mefford) Pvt MD ★
Wm.: b 4-9-1760 d p. 1835 m — Holton Pvt MD

MEGGINSON,
Wm.: b c. 1740 d 8-31-1776 m Elizabeth Cabell Capt VA

MEGQUIRE,
John: b 1762 d 12-27-1825 m Rachel Fogg Pvt MA

MEGRUE,
Andrew: b 3-14-1760 d 8-5-1823 m Hannah Rust Pvt PA

MEHAFFEY, (includes MAHAFFY)
John: b 8-31-1759 d 8- -1848 m Rachel Gordon Pvt PA ★
Martin, Sr.: b 1728 d 1793 m (2)Mary — Cav SC
Samuel: b 5-23-1757 d 1847 m Jemima A. Green Pvt PA

MEHELM,
John: b 1-6-1735 d 10-6-1809 m Joanna Beekman Col PS NJ

MEHL, (includes MAIL)
Frederick: b 11-16-1757 d 9-20-1828 m (1)Maria Thorne (2)Polly
  Foster Pvt PA ★

MEHRING,
Peter: b 3- -1756 d 1- -1800 m (1)Marie Dorothy Friebel (2)Mary
  Wirt Capt PA

MEHURIN,
John: b 1765 d 1805 m Anna — Pvt MA

MEIGS,
Abner: b 6-12-1747 d 1824 m (1)Sarah Church (2)Sarah Labaree
  PS Dr NH
Benjamin Stone: b 10-8-1753 d 8-17-1835 m Roxalanz Chittenden
  Pvt VT
Daniel: b 7-24-1747 d 5-12-1822 m Chloe Scranton Sgt CT
Daniel Bishop: b 1-13-1763 d 12-19-1849 m (1)Huldah Brownson
  (2)Esther — Pvt VT ★
Elias: b 4-15-1735 d 5-22-1819 m Rachel Bishop Pvt CT
Elihu: b 9-21-1749 d 9-9-1827 m Elizabeth Rich CS CT
Giles: b 1744 d 1824 m (1)Experience Allen (2)Anna Pinto LCol CT
Jehiel, Sr.: b 6-11-1703 d 3-23-1780 m Lucy Bartlett MM CT
Jehiel, Jr.: b 7-6-1743 d 12-27-1776 m Abigail Meigs Capt CT
Jesse: b 3-7-1763 d — m Hannah Pritchard Pvt CT
John: b 11-21-1753 d 1826 m Elizabeth Henshaw Lt CT
John: b 11-20-1732 d 1791 m Alice Dexter Pvt MA
Nathan: b 2-1-1758 d 5-7-1810 m Mabel Parmelee Sgt CT W★
Nathaniel: b 1742 d p. 12-21-1790 m (1)Lucy Cushing (2)Hannah
  Holmes (3)Mary Wyatt Cpl MA
Phineas: b 9-21-1708 d 3-19-1782 m Abigail Dudley PS CT
Return Jonathan: b 12-17-1735 d 1-28-1823 m (1)Joanna Winborn
  (2)Grace Starr Col CT
Seth: b 1746 d p. 1784 m Jemima (Von Boskirk) Van Loan Pvt NY

MEILY, (includes MYLEN, MYLIN)
Jacob: b 3-17-1762 d 5-29-1842 m Catharine — Capt PA
John: b 5-13-1739 d 9-3-1823 m Veronica Eshleman Pvt PA
Martin: b 2-21-1747 d 8-21-1820 m Barbara Bear Pvt PA
Samuel: b 3-16-1739 d 8-25-1802 m Catrina — Pvt PA

MEISENHEIMER,
Peter: b 1755 d a. 3-20-1835 m Magdalena — Pvt NC

MEISENHELTER,
Johann David: b 11-3-1753 d 8-10-1819 m Barbara Ginter Pvt PA

MEIXEL, (includes MEIXSELL & MIXSELL)
Jacob: b 11-2-1756 d p. 1832 m Mary — Pvt MD ★
Jacob: b 10-7-1759 d 1-23-1831 m Margaretha — Pvt PA
Martin, Jr.: b 11-19-1756 d 11-20-1823 m Rebecca Reine Pvt PA
Phillip: b 11-23-1731 d 5-13-1817 m Maria Magdalene Illig Maj PA

MELCHOIR, (includes MELCHOR)
Isaac: b 6- -1748 d 7-8-1790 m Mary Caldwell PS PA
John, Sr.: b — d 1787 m Mary — Pvt PA
John, Jr.: b 1-1-1750 d 8-20-1824 m (2)Elizabeth — Pvt PA

MELENDY,
John: b 1757 d 1848 m Sarah Esty Sgt MA ★
Samuel: b 11- -1741 d 9-20-1813 m Sarah Gale Cpl NY
Thomas: b 3-2-1749 d 11-28-1842 m Sarah Patterson Matr Pvt
  NH & MA ★

MELL,
Wm.: b c. 1730 d 1784 m — CS SC

MELLEN, (includes MELLIN)
Abner: b 3-25-1760 d 4-26-1832 m Deborah Homer Pvt MA
Daniel: b 4-6-1749 d 1-7-1847 m (1)Susannah Farwell (2)Hannah
  Goodrich Pvt NH
Gideon: b c. 1750 d p. 1-4-1802 m Joanna — Pvt PA
Henry: b 1735 d 3-22-1813 m (1)Sarah Torrey (2)Jerusha (Burnap)
  Abbe (3)Hannah (Bass) Turner Sgt MA
James: b 6-10-1739 d 9-27-1812 m Elizabeth Russell LCol MA
James: b 12-1-1755 d 6-1-1834 m Deborah Rockwood Adj MA
John: bpt 1-20-1744/45 d 7-25-1784 m Puah Fisher PS Capt NH
Joseph: b 4- -1738 d 11-12-1787 m Mary Parker 1Lt MA
Thomas: b 5-15-1713 d 6- -1782 m Elizabeth — PS MA
Thomas: b 1756 d 1-21-1852 m Janet Mc Collom Pvt NH
Wm.: b 3-29-1756 d 8- -1834 pvt m — Pvt MA ★
Wm.: b c. 1764 d 1- -1826 m Lucretia Marsh Pvt MA ★

MELLET,
Jean de: b 1745 d 1790 m Sarah Sutter Lt VA

MELLICHAMP
St. Lo: b 1757 d 8-19-1827 m Rebecca Stiles Pvt SC

MELLINGER,
David: b c. 1748 d a. 2-18-1800 m Catherine — Sol PA
John Jacob: b 6-2-1756 d 7-25-1819 m Barbara Arnd Cpl PA

MELLISH,
John: b 11-12-1758 d 6-20-1824 m Hannah Holden Pvt Fif MA

MELLUS,
Daniel: b c. 1755 d c. 1795 m Priscilla Stephens Sgt MA

MELONEY,
Samuel: b 1753 d 11-25-1839 m (2)Nancy Berry Pvt PA

MELOTT, (includes MALOTT)
Benjamin: b c. 1734 d a. 9-18-1815 m — PS MD
Jacob: b 1761 d 8-24-1844 m Idee — Pvt PA
John: b c. 1753 d a. 7-18-1835 m Elizabeth Sampson PS Pvt PA
Obediah: b 1755 d 3-28-1828 m (1)Mary Wink (2)Mary Daniels Pvt
  PS PA
Peter: b c. 1745 d p. 1790 m Rachel — 2Lt MD
Theodore: b 12-7-1755 d 3-10-1845 m Millie — Pvt MD ★
Thomas: b 4-15-1753 d 9-4-1846 m Rebecca — OrdlSgt MD ★

MELOY,
Edward: b 5-16-1734 d 9-14-1790 m Mary Parmalee Beecher PS CT
John: b 11-20-1756 d 8-5-1839 m Mary Eyler PS PA

MELSON,
Charles: b 1751 d 3-2-1821 m Frances Shadoun Pvt VA ★
Daniel: b c. 1724 d p. 9-2-1797 m Love — PS MD

MELTON,
Benjamin: b 1756 d 9-15-1845 m (1)Nancy King (2)Elizabeth Coy
  Fowler Pvt NC ★
John: b 1749 d 5-14-1813 m Sarah Melton Pvt VA
Lettice: b c. 1730 d c. 1785 m William Melton PS VA
Wm.: b 7-31-1761 d 6-6-1836 m (1)Polly Bates (2)Lucy (Allen)
  Williams (3)Rebecca (Thompson) Boren Sgt SC ★

MELVILLE, (includes MELVILL)
David: b 1755 d 11-22-1793 m Mary Herrick Lt RI
Seth: b 1753 d 11-26-1836 m Lydia Herrick Smn RI
Thomas: b 1-16-1751 d 9-16-1832 m Priscilla Scollay Maj MA ★

MELVIN, (includes MELVEN)
Amos: b 6-15-1751 d 8-13-1806 m Anna Flat Cpl MA
Benjamin: b 12-9-1733 d 12-29-1802 m Mehitabel Bradley PS NH
David: b 2-24-1720 d 10-27-1787 m Abigail Davis Pvt MA
Ebenezer, Sr.: b 11-10-1725 d p. 1790 m (1)Susannah Densmore
  (2)Mary Bayley (3)Susannah Brown PS NH
Isaac: b 8-29-1724 d 10-8-1842 m Abigail Dearborn Pvt Cpl MA
Jonathan: b 1-14-1752 d p. 8-28-1832 m Beulah Leland Pvt MA ★
Josiah: b 6-14-1727 d 2-23-1809 m Lydia Barrett Pvt MA
Nathan: b 6-25-1730 d 1-6-1807 m Anna — Sgt MA
Reuben: b 11-12-1760 d 8-28-1837 m Achsah Smith Pvt MA
Samuel: b 4-20-1754 d 9- -1825 m Sarah Davis Pvt MA W★
Wm.: b 5-11-1750 d 2-20-1807 m Leah Robertson Pvt PS MD

MELZARD,
John: bpt 9-10-1758 d 5-4-1834 m Susanna Martin Smn MA

MENARD,
Jean Baptiste: b 1735 d *p.* 4-27-1786 m Marie Francoise Ciree Capt CL

MENDALL,
Daniel: b 8-31-1741 d *p.* 1791 m (1)Hannah Mendall (2)Thankful Hammond Cpl MA

MENDELL,
Seth: b 5-5-1732 d 11-14-1797 m Mary Ellis Pvt MA

MENDENHALL,
John: b 4-29-1748 d 11-15-1836 m Tabitha Newlin Pvt PA
Joseph: b 1-14-1741 d 10-12-1840 m Jane Collins Capt PA ★
Mordecai: *c.* 1713 d 11-3-1803 m Charity Beeson PS NC
Moses: b 3-5-1744 d 8-13-1821 m Mary James Pvt PA
Robert: b 7-7-1713 d 6-26-1785 m (1)Phebe Taylor (2)Elizabeth Hatton (3)Esther Temple PS PA
Thomas: b 8-11-1759 d 6-2-1843 m Mary Zane Slr DE

MENEFEE, (includes MENIFE)
George: b — d 1840 m (1)Elizabeth Tatum (2)Nancy Collier Sol GA
Henry: b 10-21-1758 d 8-26-1831 m Mary Roberts Sgt VA ★
Henry: b 2-28-1754 d 3-11-1844 m Sarah Dollins Pvt VA
James: b 1-3-1766 d 6-18-1849 m (1)Nancy Hutch (2)Rebecca Moorhead Pvt VA
Jarrett: b 1721 d 3-7-1811 m — Pvt VA
John: b 12-10-1747 d 2-24-1824 m Frances Rhodes PS VA

MENGEL,
Adam: b 9-9-1752 d 3-16-1842 m Elizabeth Blatt Pvt PA
Peter: b 1750 d 10-25-1805 m Eve Ruth Pvt PA

MENGES, (includes MENGAS)
Charles: b *c.* 1729 d *a.* 3- -1786 m Mary Elizabeth — Pvt PA
Conrad: b 7-9-1744 d 12-27-1789 m Susan Barbara DeWald Pvt PA
John Peter: b 6-10-1731 d 5-30-1806 m Maria Catherine — Pvt PA

MENNIS,
Calonill: b *c.* 1745 d 9-2-1812 m (1)Mary (Macon) Aylett (2)Anne Brooke (3)Martha — BrevMaj VA

MENSCH,
Christian: b 1-31-1745 d 12-26-1826 m Sabina Hess Pvt PA
John Abraham: b 4-3-1754 d 3-16-1826 m (1)Catherin Hess (2)Barbara Huff Pvt PA
John Adam: b 6-9-1747 d *p.* 1797 m Sally Franck Pvt PA

MENTZER,
Japhet: b *c.* 1758 d 9-15-1841 m Barbara — Pvt PA ★
Joseph: b 1757 d 1828 m Barbara Seachrist Pvt PA

MENZIES,
Samuel Peachy: b 1758 d 1- -1833 m (1)Frances Miskel (2)Mrs Hannah Hunt Capt VA ★

MERANDA,
Samuel: b 1-5-1750 d 11-4-1833 m Elizabeth Salt Pvt PS PA ★

MERCEIN,
Andrew: b 1761 d 1835 m Elizabeth Royce (Rice) Pvt NY

MERCER, (includes MERCEER)
Aaron: b 1746 d *p.* 11-17-1800 m Elizabeth — Capt VA
Amos: b 3-8-1755 d 9-15-1802 m Mary Barnes Pvt PA
David: b 6-23-1742 d 10-10-1832 m Sarah Buckingham Sol PA
Hugh: b 1720 d 1-12-1777 m Isabella Gordon BGen VA
Jacob: b 4-12-1753 d 8-6-1837 m Jealy Green Pvt GA ★
James: b — d 1804 m (1)— Hamilton (2)Margaret Patterson LCol PA
Job: b 1733 d *p.* 1790 m Margaret Gordon Pvt PA
John: b *c.* 1712 d 1781 m Rachel — Sol NC
John: b 4-27-1761 d 12-25-1818 m Lydia Barrett PS VA
John: b 5-17-1759 d 8-30-1821 m Sophia Sprigg 1Lt VA
Nicholas: b 1738 d 1816 m Annie Gaddy Sgt SC
Richard: b 1753 d 1816 m Cassandra Tives PS MD
Richard: b *c.* 1740 d 11-25-1812 m Elizabeth — Pvt PA
Robert: b 1746 d 1- 1793 m Sarah Beaston Slr DE
Robert: b 1741-46 d *p.* 5-13-1820 m Elizabeth Brown PS VA
Silas: b 2- -1745 d 8- -1796 m Dorcas — Chp Maj GA
Thomas: b *c.* 1743 d 1818/19 m (2)Mrs Elizabeth (Jackson) Rawlins Sol GA
Thomas: b 1751 d 1833 m Jane E. Nealy Pvt PA
Thomas: b 1-2-1754 d 1-2-1800 m Letitia Wilson Pvt PA
Wm.: b *c.* 1740 d 1788 m Elizabeth Quinn Pvt NC
Wm.: b 1750 d 9-6-1814 m Isabella Maloy Pvt PA

MERCHANT, (includes MARCHANT)
Abel: b 10-26-1756 d 12-25-1820 m Mary Grummond Pvt NY
Chauncey: b 2-25-1753 d 8-25-1804 m Hannah Hambleton Pvt CT
Cornelius: b 1743 d 11-17-1809 m Hepsibah Peas Drm MA

Gamaliel: b 10- -1740 d 1781 m Lydia Ripley Cpl MA
Gurdon: b 2-9-1760 d 2-12-1837 m Hannah Van Duzer Arfr CT W★
Henry: b 4- -1741 d 8-30-1796 m Rebecca Cook CS PS MA
Hezekiah: b 8-28-1749 d 3-22-1806 m Deborah Hamlin CS MA
Jabez: b 4-25-1749 d 1-9-1829 m Rebecca Woodbury Sgt MA
Job: b *a.* 1753 d 1781 m — Pvt CT
Joel: b 5-1-1762 d 3-24-1844 m Molly Sanford Pvt CT ★
John: b 8-31-1755 d 1837 m Tabitha Hamilton Pvt CT ★
John, Jr.: b *c.* 1758 d 7-18-1813 m Matilda Dunham Pvt MA
John: b 1-18-1730 d *p.* 1801 m Prudence Stoddard Pvt PS NY
Joseph: b 8-10-1759 d 5-17-1837 m Dolly Rice Pvt MA
Silas: b 1722 d 11-18-1777 m Hephzibah Jones Pvt MA
Thomas: b 8-4-1755 d 12-17-1829 m Anna — Pvt CT ★
Truman: b 1764 d 1-31-1841 m Margaret Van Rensselaer Pvt NY
Wm.: b 3-3-1751 d 11- -1812 m Rachel Black Pvt SC
Wm.: b 9-6-1751 d 10-15-1802 m Hannah Wheeler PS MA

MERCIER,
Wm.: b 9-24-1717 d 10-24-1797 m Maria Bradford NCapt NY

MERCOM,
Jacob: b 1756 d 1819 m Eva Margaretta Smith Pvt PA

MEREDITH, (includes MERRIDETH)
David: b *c.* 1760 d *c.* 1830 m Elizabeth Wingfield PS VA
Davis: b 1750 d *p.* 5-24-1825 m (3)Ann Pritchard Sol VA
Elisha, Sr.: b 1724 d 1796 m Elizabeth Pleasant Cooke Capt VA
Elisha, Jr.: b 1756 d 1796 m Annie Layne Clopton Capt VA
Henry: b 1757 d *c.* 1843 m — Pvt NC ★
James: b 1747 d 1823 m Mary Crews Sol NC
John: b 1736 d *p.* 1797 m (1)Rachel Pritchett (2)Jane Pritchett PS MD
John: b 6-14-1752 d 1780 m Esther Scrivanor Pvt MD
John: b 1755 d 1784 m Ann Taylor Pvt VA
John Wheeler: b 2-10-1761 d 8-18-1844 m Elizabeth Busby Pvt DE ★
Reese: b 1705 d 11-12-1778 m Martha Carpenter PS PA
Samuel: b 2-10-1741 d 2-10-1817 m Margaret Cadwalader BG PA
Samuel: b 12-25-1758 d 11-29-1841 m Mary Bradley Pvt VA ★
Samuel: b 1732 d 11-22-1808 m (2)Jane Henry Col VA
Thomas: b 1736 d *p.* 3-18-1824 m Sarah — Pvt MD
Thomas: b *c.* 1750 d *p.* 1844 m Ellen Thomas Pvt VA ★
Thomas: b 1745 d *p.* 1790 m Hannah Hutchins Pvt MD
Thomas: b *c.* 1760 d *p.* 9-15-1808 m Abigail — Pvt SC
Wm.: b 1717 d *p.* 1782 m Anne Bushrod Daingerfield PS VA

MEREEN,
John: b *c.* 1730 d *p.* 1812 m Rebecca Pepper 2Lt MA

MERENESS,
John: b 3-12-1762 d 4-21-1851 m Margaret Lawrence Pvt NY
Wm.: b 1754 d 1-23-1816 m Margrettie De Trieux Cpl NY

MERITHEW,
Samuel: b *c.* 1750 d *p.* 1-9-1788 m Polly Potter Pvt RI
Wm.: b — d 5-1-1825 m Sarah Wood Pvt Slr RI

MERIWETHER, (includes MERIWEATHER)
David: b 1755 d 10-13-1822 m Frances Wingfield Lt VA
David Wood: b 1754 d 1797 m Mary Lewis Lt VA
Francis: b 10-31-1737 d 1-2-1803 m Martha Jamison PS VA
James: b 6-4-1755 d 10-25-1817 m Susan Hatcher Capt VA
James: b 6-1-1729 d *p.* 9-26-1800 m (1)Judith Burnley (2)Elizabeth Pollard CS VA
John: b *c.* 1750 d 1820 m (1)Esther McGehee (2)Ann Tinsley PS VA
Reuben: b 12-15-1743 d 1800 m Sarah Dorsey CS MD
Thomas: b 1761 d *c.* 1831 m Rebecca Mathews Sol VA
Thomas: b 4-24-1763 d 9- -1802 m Ann Minor Maj VA
Wm.: b 12-25-1730 d 12-24-1790 m Martha Cox Wood Capt VA
Wm.: b 1760 d 2-10-1842 m Elizabeth Winslow Lt VA ★

MERO,
Amariah: b 5-14-1757 d 8-1-1852 m Susanna Robbins Sgt MA ★
Josiah: b 1-9-1755 d 2-22-1844 m Maria Andrews Pvt MA ★

MERRIAM, (includes MERIAM, MERION)
Aaron: b 6-9-1762 d 9-25-1849 m Esther (Merriam) Pvt CT
Abraham: b 12-23-1734 d 11-26-1797 m Sarah Simonds Pvt MA
Amasa: b 9-27-1757 d 10-7-1840 m (1)Margaret Rice (2)Hannah Douglas Pvt CT ★
Amos: b 8-24-1739 d *p.* 1790 m Elizabeth — 2Lt MA
Amos: b 10-13-1760 d 9-16-1804 m Deborah Brooks Matr MA
Asa: b 10-21-1754 d 5-7-1795 m Mary Lincoln Pvt MA
Asaph: b 3-14-1759 d 7-27-1836 m Damaris Todd Pvt CT
Benjamin: b 12-24-1730 d 2-14-1807 m Mary Berry Pvt CT
David: b 1-28-1760 d 2-15-1849 m (1)Phebe Foster (2)Betsey Conant Pvt MA ★
Ebenezer: b 3-28-1734 d 7-16-1795 m Phebe Locke Pvt MA
Ephraim: b 7-31-1757 d 3-22-1834 m Beulah Galpin Pvt Fif CT ★
Ezra: b 6-15-1760 d 6-21-1827 m Susanna Elliott Pvt MA ★
Ichabod: b 1-7-1755 d 1838 m Desire Burnell Pvt CT
Isaac: b 3-27-1737 d 4-17-1825 m Sarah Scoville Ens CT

MERRIAM, contd.

Isaac: b 8-30-1737 d 12-1-1825 m (1)Eleanor Munroe (2)Rebecca Davis Pvt MA
Jesse: b 1-21-1728 d 8-12-1791 m Mary Johnson Sol CT
Jesse: b 6-4-1755 d 10-31-1838 m Deborah Pratt Pvt MA ★
John: b 1-12-1754 d 10-15-1804 m (1)Martha Putnam (2)Miriam Wheeler 1Lt MA
John: b 1-21-1756 d 12-14-1843 m (1)Mary Baker (2)Gratia Ashley Pvt MA
John, Sr.: b 11-5-1725 d 4-11-1814 m Fannie Goldsmith Pvt NH
John, Jr.: b 2-10-1757 d 10-13-1841 m Esther Brockway Pvt NH
Joseph: b 11-20-1732 d p. 1783 m (1)Sarah Austin (2)Mindwell Rice Pvt MA
Joseph: b 2-3-1763 d 3-4-1849 m Phebe Russell Pvt MA
Joseph: b 9-19-1734 d 7-2-1814 m Sally Wadsworth Pvt MA
Joseph: b 1-26-1744 d 11-6-1826 m Mary Brooks Cpl NH
Jotham: b 8-26-1749 d 8-22-1798 m Sarah Burnap MM MA
Josiah: b 2-13-1725 d 4-23-1809 m Lydia Wheeler PS MA
Nathan: b 5-12-1720 d 11-11-1782 m Abigail Wheeler Pvt MA
Nathaniel: b 1-5-1734 d 8-21-1807 m Martha Berry Lt CT
Nathaniel: b 9-8-1749 d 1797 m Lydia Gay Pvt MA
Nathaniel: b 5-7-1720 d 5-9-1802 m Olive Wheeler CS MA
Samuel: b 12-21-1723 d 1804 m Anne Whitney Pvt MA
Silas: b 3-5-1737 d 1-25-1812 m (1)Abigail Dale (2)Lydia Peabody MM & PS MA
Silas: b 2-6-1762 d a. 4-11-1803 m Mary Elliott Pvt MA
Simon: b 6-3-1749 d 1816 m Phebe Lock Pvt MA
Timothy: b 12-20-1746 d 1829 m Sarah Putnam Pvt MA

MERRICK, (includes MIRICK & MYRICK)

Benjamin: b 11-6-1707 d 8-18-1775 m Mrs Mercy (Morgan) Hoar PS MA
Bezaleel: b 7-20-1758 d 10-30-1841 m Sarah Russell Pvt MA
Constant: b c. 1701 d 3-17-1792 m Sarah Freeman PS MA
Daniel: b 12-19-1757 d c. 1813 m Mrs Underwood Pvt MD
Ebenezer: b 5-23-1722 d 3- -1819 m Hannah Fuller Capt VT
Elisha: b 9-13-1735 d 1-16-1807 m Persis Moore Sgt MA
Gad: b 6-28-1763 d 11-24-1803 m Syble Harrison Pvt MA
Heman: b 4-28-1760 d 4-30-1815 m Sarah Higgins Smn Mar MA
Isaac: b 8-3-1738 d 7-5-1800 m Joanna Libbey Slr Sgt MA
Isaac: b 1740 d 5-14-1812 m Sarah Hazen Pvt NY
James: b 1-6-1732/33 d 12-8-1778 m Dorothy Fairbanks Capt MA
James, Jr.: b 12-22-1729 d 10-30-1813 m Esther Colton Pvt MA
James: b c. 1745 d 3-25-1822 m Elizabeth James Ens NC
James: b c. 1740 d p. 3-26-1814 m Mary — PS SC
John: b 8- -1753 d 11- -1808 m Mary Ann Maynard Cpl CT
John: b 1761 d p. 1813 m Esther Frink Cpl CT
John, Sr.: b 11-18-1722 d 1-1-1782 m Kezia Stratton Pvt CS MA
John: b 4-1-1757 d 8-11-1839 m Thankful Linnell Pvt MA
John: b 5-8-1760 d 7-20-1834 m Lois Cook Pvt NY
John: b 1- -1751 d 8-29-1835 m Amy Goodwin Lt NC
John, Sr.: b c. 1736 d 1803/04 m Ann Thompson PS VA
Jonathan: b 3- -1747 d 3- -1812 m Mary Merrick Pvt MA
Joseph: b 10- -1733 d 4- -1787 m Ann Holt Capt CT
Joseph: b 4-9-1739 d 10-12-1826 m Deborah Leonard Capt MA
Joseph: b 12-30-1749 d 12-29-1823 m Judith Little Sgt MA
Joshua: b 3-5-1745 d 6-19-1833 m Mrs Jane Stocking Capt NY
Matthias: b 8-8-1747 d p. 1781 m Rebekah — Pvt MD
Nathan: b c. 1728 d c. 1-6-1801 m Lydia Jones Pvt MA
Nathaniel: b 9-23-1744 d a. 7- -1815 m Elizabeth Arey PS MA
Phineas: b 3-16-1728 d 1-7-1802 m Margaret Graves Pvt MA
Samuel: b 2-6-1757 d 12-13-1839 m Martha Brown Lt MA ★
Samuel: b 8-9-1761 d 3-18-1828 m Abigail Crosby Pvt MA
Samuel: b c. 1730-35 d p. 1790 m Rachel Heston PS PA
Samuel F.: b 9-13-1751 d 7-22-1836 m Sarah Milkins Pvt SrgnMte MA
Stephen: b 2-2-1759 d 7-8-1841 m (3)Isabell Adams Pvt NY
Thomas: b †738 d p. 1781 m Deborah Lawrence Pvt NY
Tilley: b 9-30-1743 d 8-31-1835 m (1)Parnel Miner (2)Lovisa Colton Cpl MA
Wm.: b 10-26-1734 d 6-12-1795 m Hannah Paine Pvt MA

MERRIFIELD,

Aaron: b 10-28-1738 d 6-19-1821 m Elizabeth Robinson Lt MA
Asaph: b 1741 d 8-29-1820 m (2)Mercy Morse Sgt MA ★
Francis: bpt 11-2-1735 d 4-21-1814 m Hannah Lakeman Sgt MA
John: b 8-13-1749 d 4-24-1828 m Molly Metcalf Pvt MA
Joseph: b 12-9-1712 d 10-18-1796 m Hannah Hill Sgt MA
Richard: b c. 1755 d 1798 m Phoebe — Pvt VA
Samuel, Sr.: b c. 1720 d 1781 m Mary — PS VA
Timothy: b 1-4-1739 d 5-6-1806 m (1)Lydia Cheny (2)Mercy Perry Pvt MM MA

MERRIHEW,

Amos: b 9-2-1738 d 11-19-1794 m Elizabeth Spooner Pvt MA

MERRIKEN,

John: b 12-20-1718 d 3-25-1794 m (1)Anne Sadler (2)Elizabeth Moss PS MD

MERRILL, (includes MERREL, MERRELL, MERRELLS, & MERRILLS)

Aaron: b 3-14-1755 d 9-20-1831 m Annis Humphrey Pvt CT ★

Aaron: b 4-10-1754 d 7-4-1833 m Mercy Levett Cpl MA
Abel: b 3-26-1748 d 12-10-1829 m Elizabeth Page Pvt MA
Abel: b 10-1-1755 d 4-16-1837 m (1)Mehtable Burbank (2)Huldah Fletcher Pvt Mus MA ★
Abijah: b 5-8-1735 d 2-15-1823 m (1)Sarah Barton (2)Hannah Chadwick Pvt MA
Abner: b 11-6-1752 d 5-4-1814 m Elizabeth Royall Cpl MA W★
Adams: b 12-24-1723 d 12-26-1802 m Issabelle Titcomb Pvt MA
Annis: b 6-13-1751 d 1847 m Lydia (Merrill) Pvt NH ★
Asa: b 6-30-1732 d 11-3-1815 m Bethiah Hopkinson Lt MA
Asher: b 2-26-1734/35 d p. 1807 m Delight Sawyer Pvt CT
Benjamin: b 11-1-1755 d 6-10-1834 m Sarah Eastman Pvt MA
Benjamin: b 1740 d 5- -1815 m Elizabeth Dutton Pvt PS NH
Benjamin: b 12-2-1752 d 5-10-1836 m Penelope Merrill Pvt NC SC ★
Benjamin: b 1760 d 5-25-1835 m Mary — Pvt NC VA
Caleb Barker: b 1754 d 7-2-1842 m Sarah Jackson Of MA
Daniel: b 1732 d 9-6-1808 m (1)Sarah Hutchins (2)Mrs Sarah Miller Towne Capt MA
Daniel: b 8-12-1745 d 7-11-1830 m Dorcas Crockett 1Lt MA
Daniel: b 4-27-1723 d 8-19-1809 m Elizabeth Clough Pvt MA
Daniel: b 3-18-1765 d 6-3-1833 m (1)Joanna Colby (2)Susan Gale Pvt MA ★
Daniel: b 8-8-1758 d 8-22-1808 m Huldah Ellis Pvt MA
Daniel: b 5-17-1755 d 3-11-1844 m (1)Elizabeth Lytle (2)Rachel Ward (3)Margaret Thompson (4)Hannah Bishop Pvt NC ★
David, Sr.: b 4-2-1735 d 8-11-1811 m Mary Watson Sol MA
David, Jr.: b 9-5-1757 d — m Martha Taylor Pvt MA
Eleazer: b 11-4-1739 d 12- -1819 m Rebecca Woodruff Pvt CT
Elias: b 1-24-1744 d 2-24-1812 m Lydia Andrews Ens CT
Elijah: b 3-9-1720 d p. 1783 m Rachel Wells Pvt PS CT
Enoch: b 4-21-1731 d 8-28-1778 m Jermima Sprague Ens MA
Enoch: b 1753 d 9-28-1812 m Temperance Little Pvt MA
Enoch: b 11-26-1751 d 5-26-1838 m Mary Ambrose Pvt PS NH
Ezekiel: b 12-9-1747 d 3-16-1830 m Sarah Emery Cpl NH
Ford: b 9-2-1753 d 11-12-1826 m Betsey (Merrill) PS NH
Gideon: b 1749 d 6-27-1803 m Abigail Merrill Pvt CT
Gideon: b 1728 d a- -1811 m Dorothy Wildes PS CS MA
Hosea: b 6-19-1761 d 3-2-1853 m Sarah Phillips Pvt MA ★
Humphrey: b 6-28-1748 d 1-24-1825 m Hannah Lunt Sgt MA
Ichabod: b 9-2-1728 d 6-5-1812 m Mary Merrill Sgt CT
Ichabod: b 6-17-1754 d 12-26-1829 m Sarah Frisbie Pvt CT W★
Jabez: b 8-9-1760 d 1849 m Barbara C. Riggs Pvt MA
Jacob: b 1-27-1755 d 7-18-1835 m (1)Elizabeth Lunt (2)Abigail (Noyes) Dunbar Pvt MA ★
Jacob: b 1750-60 d p. 9-16-1824 m Mary Dow Pvt MA
Jacob: b 1759 d 8-3-1847 m Sarah Huff Pvt MA
Jacob: b 5-31-1732 d 9-19-1812 m Elizabeth Wyatt PS NH
James: b 7-18-1729 d 3-2-1784 m Sarah Ford PS NH
James: b 5-6-1719 d 1-18-1798 m Mary Osgood CS PS NH
James: b 9-21-1751 d 3-16-1807 m Jerusha Seymour Pvt CT
James: b 4-13-1731 d 11-16-1806 m Abigail Brackett Maj MA
James: b 2-10-1751 d 1831 m Sarah Ingram Cpl VT
Jedediah: b 1739 d 9-18-1831 m Martha Lucas Cpl VT
Jeptha: b 12-2-1757 d 1838 m Mary Roice Pvt CT ★
Jerijah: b 7-25-1749 d 6-13-1791 m Tryphena (Merrill) Pvt CT
Jesse: b 4-4-1753 d 1833 m Rhoda Boyle Pvt MA ★
John: b c. 1755 d 4-1-1848 m Elizabeth Shepherd Capt CT
John: b 12-12-1746 d 6-28-1801 m (1)Anna — (2)Ann Whitney Pvt MA
John: b 4-14-1750 d 5-21-1821 m Mary Royall PS MA
John: b 11-19-1751 d 3-28-1828 m Elizabeth Teppet (Tibbetts) Pvt MA
John: b 1-28-1760 d 10-18-1849 m Sarah Henshaw Pvt MA ★
John: b 11-19-1751 d 2-26-1839 m Sarah Rowell Sgt NH ★
John: b 12-11-1750 d p. 1830 m Mary Wiseman Lt NC ★
Jonathan: b 7-8-1738 d 3-15-1777 m Mary (Merrill) Pvt MA
Jonathan: b 11-28-1760 d 8-20-1835 m Anna Gillet Pvt CT ★
Joseph, Jr.: b 1745 d 3- -1821 m Lydia Flower Pvt CT
Joseph: b 3-28-1707 d 1788 m Abigail Stone CS CT
Joshua: b 3-15-1733 d 9-21-1808 m Mary Winslow Capt MA
Lambert: b 10-3-1741 d 10-12-1826 m (1)Tabitha Dunham (2)Mrs Comfort Stiles Wheeler PS NY
Levi: b 1-30-1748/49 d p. 1813 m Hannah Bean Pvt MA
Moses: b 12-10-1744 d 4-18-1834 m (1)Sarah Carl (2)Jane Noyes Hutchinson Lt MA ★
Moses: b 5-18-1741 d 6-6-1832 m Mary True Capt MA
Nathan: b 1-6-1761 d 8-29-1836 m Sarah Merrill Pvt MA ★
Nathan: b 1-21-1763 d 3-13-1846 m Susanna Bacon Pvt MA
Nathaniel: b 3-22-1756 d 10-16-1823 m (1)Honor Doud (2)Mary Pardee Pvt CT
Nathaniel, Sr.: b 2-2-1742 d 3-1-1820 m Hannah Belden Sol CT
Nathaniel, Jr.: b 10-3-1762 d 8-29-1834 m Huldah Hurlbert Pvt CT ★
Nathaniel: b 9-15-1755 d 6-5-1835 m (1)Mary Young (2)Mrs Anna (Smith) Davis Pvt NH ★
Nathaniel: b 6-25-1727 d 1791 m (1)Sarah Peaslee (2)Judith — PS NH
Nathaniel: b 3-2-1747 d 5-3-1825 m Sarah Hazen 1Lt VT
Nehemiah: b 1751 d c. 1779 m Phoebe — Capt CT
Noah: b 1759 d 8-26-1839 m Hepsey Pettibone Pvt CT
Perley: b 9-25-1754 d p. 1796 m Esther Currier Pvt PS NH
Peter: b — d c. 1787 m Mehitabel — PS NH
Phineas: b 2-19-1755 d 3-31-1828 m Anna Buel Capt CT

Richard: b 11-6-1732 d 1791 m Mary Pillsbury Pvt MA
Richard: b 8-29-1738 d 10-14-1795 m Joanna Davis PS NH
Richard: b 10-1-1744 d 2-16-1813 m (1)Elizabeth Johnson (2)Sarah Drake Pvt NJ
Roger: b 8-23-1755 d 1851 m Chloe Merry Pvt CT ★
Roger: b 2-1-1762 d 6-15-1852 m Dorothy Cushing Pvt MA
Samuel: b 12-7-1737 d 12-29-1801 m Abigail Eaton Capt MA
Samuel, Sr.: b 1-8-1728 d 5-4-1822 m Elizabeth Bradbury Lt MA
Samuel, Jr.: b 4-12-1754 d 1838 m Anna Eaton Pvt MA ★
Samuel, Sr.: b 7-20-1711 d 7-12-1801 m Anna Evans PS CS MA
Samuel: b c. 1748 d c. 1803 m Sussanah — PS NC
Simon: b 4-21-1753 d 4-24-1840 m Mary Marston 2Lt NH ★
Spencer: b 8-6-1747 d p. 1779 m Desire Slocum (Greene) Pvt RI
Stephen: b 1-29-1713 d 11-24-1793 m Joanna French Capt MA
Stephen: b 6-5-1748 d 7-30-1828 m Phoebe Clifford Pvt MA
Thomas: b 12-3-1759 d 3-2-1847 m Elizabeth Ensign Pvt MM CT
Thomas: b 10-24-1745 d 2-12-1822 m Hannah Butler 3Lt MA
Thomas: b 3-6-1738 d 12-22-1820 m Mrs Sarah Friend PS MA
Thomas: b 2-5-1723 d 7-2-1788 m (1)Phebe Abbott (2)Mehitable (Harriman) Johnson (3)Mrs Ambrose (4)Mrs Cummings Sol PS NH
Titus: bpt 2-25-1756 d 8-11-1785 m Anna Belding Pvt CT
Wm.: b 4-7-1740 d 6- -1837 m Anstina Whiteman Lt PS NH
Wm.: b c. 1754 d p. 7-28-1803 m Salley Haden Drm NC

MERRIMAN, (includes MARRYMAN, & MERRYMAN)
Abel: b a. 1736 d p. 1790 m Betsy (Mirriman) Capt VT
Amasa, Sr.: b 6-17-1729 d 1829 m (1)Sarah Hart Ives (2)Mrs Tabitha Sexton Adkins Pvt CT
Amasa, Jr.: b 6-2-1767 d 6-7-1843 m Anna Hall Drm CT
Amos: b 12-1-1762 d p. 1795 m Abigail — Sol CT
Amos: b 10-20-1745 d 1805 m (2)Hannah Hawley Pvt MA
Benjamin: b 1739 d 5-30-1814 m Mary Bell PS Capt MD
Charles: b 8-29-1762 d 8-26-1829 m Anna Punderson DrmMaj CT
Charles: b 10-31-1751 d 5-28-1823 m Rachel Cowles Pvt CT
Chauncey: b c. 1752 d p. 1818 m (1)Sarah Ives (2)Sybel Doolittle Pvt CT
Daniel: bpt 1- -1742/43 d 2-19-1825 m Damaris Andrews Cpl MA
Elisaph: b 11-2-1736 d 1815 m Jerusha Mattoon PS CT
Enoch: b 12-7-1755 d p. 1800 m Abigail Bishop Sgt CT
George: b 8-26-1759 d 5-21-1836 m Katharine Johnson Pvt CT ★
James: b 7-18-1761 d 6-20-1813 m Frances Munson Pvt CT
Jesse: b 10-5-1759 d 5-8-1827 m Dolly Ives Pvt CT
John: b 9-12-1728 d 4-13-1801 m — Pvt CT
John: b c. 1757/58 d 6-16-1785 m Mary Flippen Pvt VA
Josiah: b 3-25-1748 d 12-17-1810 m Mrs Lydia (Johnson) Simpson Cpl CT W★
Micajah: b 7-4-1750 d 6-7-1842 m Mary Ensor 1Maj MD
Moses: b 3-10-1748 d 3-17-1800 m Louise Wood Pvt CT
Nicholas, Sr.: b 12-11-1726 d 1801 m (1)Elizabeth Ensor (2)Jane — Capt MD
Nicholas, Jr.: b 1751 d 1832 m (1)Deborah Ensor (2)Nancy Merryman Lt MD
Samuel: b 11-12-1721 d 9-28-1809 m Jane Price PS MD
Samuel, Sr.: b 2-13-1723 d 6-22-1803 m (1)Mary Hawks (2)Lydia (Harwood) Stebbins Capt MA
Samuel, Jr.: b 9-11-1749 d 5-27-1824 m (1)Eunice Hall (2)Thankful Hall Pvt MA
Samuel S.: b 4-2-1762 d 9-19-1847 m Polly Cross Pvt VT ★
Titus: b 8-28-1727 d 12-24-1806 m Dinah Andrews MM PS CT
Walter: b c. 1748 d p. 1788 m Elizabeth Webber CS MA
Wm. Jr.: b 1756 d 1844 m Elizabeth Goodin Pvt PA

MERRISS,
Edward: b 10-31-1763 d 8-16-1826 m (1)Mary Sheffied (2)Lucinda Winne Pvt RI
John: b 1762 d 1808 m (1)Johannah Ellis (2)Elizabeth Austin Sheffield Pvt RI
Wm.: b 7-21-1720 d 7-19-1786 m Susannah Douglass Cpl RI

MERRITT, (includes MARRIOTT, MARYOT, MERRET, MERIT, & MERITT)
Aaron: b c. 1758 d p. 1800 m Prudence Cook Pvt MA
Abraham: b c. 1763 d — m Garthory Brooks Pvt NJ
Amos: b 5-1-1755 d 1-5-1829 m Lydia Bailey Pvt MA
Amos: b 4-6-1758 d 8-10-1842 m Submit Stow Pvt MA ★
Archilas: b 1750 d 1824 m (2)Sarah Harper Pvt VA
Bartholomew: b 1-7-1762 d — m Mary Carter Pvt VT
Caleb: b 2-28-1735 d 11-29-1793 m Martha Purdy Capt NY
Caleb, Jr.: b 2-4-1739 d 1824 m Deborah Lyon 2Lt NY
Consider: b 9-17-1751 d 5-9-1831 m Mrs Sarah Beals Capt MA
Daniel: b 12-12-1761 d 12-22-1833 m Nancy Duncan Pvt PS NC ★
Ebenezer: b 10-1-1762 d 12-13-1826 m Hannah Wheeler Pvt CT
Ebenezer: b 3-28-1764 d 12-31-1819 m Cynthia Willis Pvt NY
George: b 1762 d 6-8-1817 m Abigail Marble Pvt MA
George: b 6-7-1741 d 7-10-1822 m (1)Mary Fowler (2)Mrs Sarah Ecker Pvt NY
Gilbert: b 1754 d 3-4-1824 m Elizabeth Green Sol NY
Henry: b 1-11-1754 d 1821 m Mary Saunders Pvt RI
Humphrey: b 5-17-1737 d 10-28-1806 m — Sol NY
Isaac: b 7-4-1760 d 1-28-1834 m Molly Billings Pvt MA W★
James: b 8-18-1744 d 1821 m Hannah Phelps Pvt CT
James: b 2-12-1734 d 5-20-1818 m Martha Bloomer Pvt PS NY
James: b 3-1-1755 d 1835 m Nancy Coggin Pvt NC ★

James: b c. 1747 d p. 5-20-1837 m Mary Scutchens PS NC
John: b c. 1740 d p. 1798 m Elizabeth Davis 2Lt MD
John: b 1738 d 6-28-1818 m Elizabeth Douglass Capt MA
Jonathan: b 9-16-1715 d 1789 m Sarah Wade Pvt MA
Joshua: b c. 1732 d p. 6-12-1805 m Ann Homewood PS CS MD
Josiah: b 11-17-1752 d 3-12-1817 m (1)Anna Purdy (2)Rachel Sherwood Pvt PS NY
Michael: b 7-27-1738 d 8-18-1815 m (1)Lucy Merritt (2)Sarah (Olney) Hawkins CS VT
Nehemiah: bpt 11-3-1751 d 5-27-1813 m Sarah (Mott) Litchfield Pvt MA
Noah, Sr.: b 10- -1730 d 3-24-1814 m Sarah Lee Pvt MA
Noah, Jr.: b 10- -1758 d 8-21-1843 m Eunice Metcalf Pvt MA ★
Noah: b 2-26-1759 d 5-31-1831 m Elizabeth Bryant Pvt MA
Paul: b 2-4-1761 d 11-30-1850 m Deborah Nash Pvt MA
Reuben: b 6-6-1745 d 5-18-1829 m Mary Anderson Sol CT
Stephen: b 2-20-1755 d 7-27-1852 m Lucenia Waters Pvt NC
Sylvanus: b 4-28-1748 d 6-20-1833 m (1)Elizabeth Devoe (2)Hannah Bea Pvt NY
Thomas: b 1761 d 1839 m Elnora Merritt Pvt NC
Thomas: b 6-17-1744 d — m Elizabeth Curtis Pvt PA
Wm.: b 9-16-1728 d 1793 m (2)Martha Vansant Cpl MD
Wm.: b 1752 d 1795 m Achsah — Pvt MD
Wm.: b 9-10-1739 d 10- -1783 m Elizabeth Barhiter Pvt NY

MERROW,
David: b 1742 d 12-3-1829 m Esther — Pvt NH
Joshua: b 1753 d 5-20-1808 m Peggy Garland Lt NH
Samuel: b 5-9-1710 d c. 1786 m (1)Abigail — (2)Sarah Starbird PS NH

MERRY,
David: b 1741 d 7-8-1815 m Eunice (Chase) Chase Sgt MA
Ebenezer: b 3-27-1748 d 7-3-1809 m Sarah Whiting Pvt CT
Jonathan: b c. 1735 d p. 1810 m Jane Daggett Pvt MA
Prettyman: b c. 1719 d p. 1780 m — Lt VA
Ralph, Sr.: b 1-18-1720/21 d 11-1-1798 m Sarah Knower CS MA
Ralph, Jr.: b 3-16-1753 d 1825 m Sarah Sylvester Pvt MA
Samuel: b 5-3-1739 d 3-8-1799 m Rachel Merry Pvt NJ

MESEREAU, (includes MERCEREAU)
Jacob: b 4-25-1730 d 9-7-1804 m Charity De Groot Col NY
John: b 3-2-1732 d 2-21-1820 m (1)Maria Prall (2)Barbary Van Pelt PS CS NY
John LaGrange: b 1757 d 5-18-1841 m Lois Brookins Spy PS NY NJ
Joshua, Sr.: b 9-26-1728 d 6-10-1804 m (1)Sophie La Grange (2) Ann Roome (3)Mrs Esther Christopher PS NY
Joshua, Jr.: b 1758 d 1-20-1857 m Dinah Garretson Pvt NJ
Paul: b 10-23-1741 d 1-26-1823 m Elizabeth Weston Barnes Slr NY
Peter: b 1-19-1741 d 6-16-1803 m Rebecca Lake PS NY

MERSHEIMER,
Sebastian: b 9-23-1755 d 6-3-1845 m Anna Catherine Wrightmeyer Pvt PA

MERSHON,
Aaron: b c. 1740 d 8-27-1776 m Mrs Mary Gapin Pierson Pvt NJ
Andrew: bpt 8-6-1706 d c. 6-29-1793 m Fransinah — PS NJ
Andrew: b 1764/65 d 3-10-1834 m Mary Yard Wgn NJ W★
Benjamin: b 1736 d 10-12-1802 m Mary — Pvt NJ
Cornelius: b c. 1735 d p. 1784 m Mercy Furness PS VA
Henry: b 1-27-1734 d 11-5-1814 m (1)Mary Burrowes (2)Mrs Rachel (Smith) McCoy 1Lt NJ
Henry: b 1740 d 4-15-1815 m Sarah — CS NJ
Nathaniel: b — d 1813 m Martha Stephens PS NJ
Samuel: b 6-23-1749 d 4-7-1813 m (1)Mary Schenck (2)Susan Height Pvt NJ
Thomas: b c. 1718 d a. 1791 m Susanna Stockton PS NJ
Titus: b 8-22-1756 d 4-11-1841 m (1)Nancy Ann Weedon (2)Elizabeth Davis Pvt NJ ★
Wm.: b 3-20-1761 d 5-22-1834 m Eleanor Bross Pvt NJ ★
Wm.: b c. 1729-31 d 1783 m Sarah Titus PS NJ

MERTZ, (includes MARTZ)
George: b 9- -1761 d p. 3-30-1844 m — Pvt PA ★
George Henry: b 9-4-1755 d 7-23-1827 m Eva Barbara (Guth) B. — Pvt PA
Jacob: b c. 1750 d 2- -1803 m Margaret Miller Pvt PA
Jacob: b c. 1740 d p. 1798 m Catherine — Sol PA
Nicholas: b 8- -1748 d 2- -1802 m Catherine — 2Lt PA
Philip: b 10-14-1738 d p. 12-19-1803 m Anna Eva 1Lt PA

MERWINE, (includes MERVINE)
Andrew: b 1752 d 9-25-1845 m (1)Anne Fisher (2)Catharine Weaver Pvt PA
Wm.: b c. 1740 d a. 1-15-1791 m Christiana Jones Pvt PA

MERWIN,
Andrew: b 4-28-1760 d 3-3-1849 m (1)Tamny Dunning (2)Rhoda Ruggles Starr Pvt CT
Daniel: b 5-30-1746 d 4-18-1820 m Rebecca Seward Pvt CT
David: b 1-7-1743 d 8-13-1816 m Eunice Perry Pvt CT
Fowler: b 7-25-1740 d 2-9-1823 m Amy Nettleton PS CT

MERWIN, contd.
John, Sr.: b 4-3-1707 d 2-17-1792 m Elizabeth Nettleton PS CT
John, Jr.: b 7-25-1735 d 1- -1826 m Elizabeth Buckingham Sol CT
Miles, Sr.: b 3-29-1720 d 12-12-1786 m Mary Talcott Lt CT
Nathan: b 7-11-1757 d 6-22-1837 m Mary Ruggles Pvt CT ★
Samuel, Sr.: bpt 1719 d 1800 m Sarah Camp PS CT
Samuel, Jr.: b 6-20-1742 d 3-6-1828 m Martha Nettleton PS CT

MESCHTER,
Christopher: b 6-4-1734 d 2-12-1791 m Christina Yeakel Pvt PS PA
Christopher: b 12-17-1746 d 5-4-1797 m Rosina Kriebel Pvt PA

MESEROLL, (includes MESEROLE)
Abraham: b 10-27-1758 d 4-2-1842 m Ann Williamson OrdlSgt NJ ★
Charles: b 9-22-1752 d 10-15-1842 m Catherine Wyckoff OrdlySgt NY ★
John I.: b 4- -1753/54 d 2-11-1833 m Elizabeth Titus PS NY

MESERVE,
Clement: b 1716 d 1-15-1800 m Abigail Ham Lt NH
John: bpt 10-13-1728 d p. 1790 m (1)Mary Yetty (2)Sarah Strout Pvt MA
Jonathan: b 1738 d 1812 m Mary Davis PS NH
Nathaniel: b 1-26-1748 d 10- -1815 m Rebecca Martin Pvt MA
Nathaniel: b 4-20-1747 d 1- -1825 m Anna Hunnawell Pvt MA ★
Wm.: b 9-18-1753 d 3-28-1824 m Deborah Bartlett NCapt MA
Wm.: b 10-26-1744 d 2-24-1827 m Margery During Pvt MA

MESERVEY,
Benjamin: bpt 7-4-1744 d p. 1800 m — 1Lt MA

MESICK,
Fiet: b c. 1757 d 9-11-1814 m Catherine Krum Pvt NY
Hendrick: b 1715 d 4-3-1809 m Catherine Dedrick Pvt NY
Jacob J.: b 11-25-1760 d 7-2-1824 m (1)Alida Van Alstine (2)Catharine Ostrander Pvt NY
Peter: b 10-8-1750 d 11-27-1834 m Christina Moul Pvt NY
Thomas, Sr.: b 1- -1734 d 7-26-1782 m Margaret Clough Pvt NY
Thomas, Jr.: b 10-1-1754 d 12-20-1841 m Mary Weissmer Pvt NY

MESSENGER, (includes MESSINGER)
Abner: b 1760 d 1845 m Abigail Pike Pvt CT ★
Abraham: b c. 1760-2 d 9-30-1834 m Catharine — Pvt PA
Bela: b 2-20-1757 d 3-9-1837 m Myranda Ashley Sgt MA
Benoni: b 9-4-1718 d 9-20-1777 m Mary Wood Pvt MA
David: b 1760 d 4-1-1811 m Hannah Higley Pvt MA
George: b 1-24-1745 d 9-12-1825 m Cathrine Brazie Sgt MA
George: b 1755 d 1825 m Catherine Babb Pvt PA
Isaac: b 1745 d 5-8-1839 m Anna Ward Pvt CT
Jehiel: b 1748 d 1798 m Lydia Wilcox Cpl MA
Joel: b 5-26-1760 d 4-28-1850 m Sarah Storrs Pvt MA ★
John: b 5-9-1752 d 3-11-1842 m Lucy Scott Cpl MA
John: b 4-7-1746 d 5-9-1808 m Elizabeth Wilhelm Pvt PA
Joseph: b 1741 d p. 1791 m Jemima Barber Pvt CT
Michael, Sr.: b 11-10-1719 d 10-24-1791 m (1)Catharine Abel (2)Mrs Elizabeth Butz PS PA
Michael, Jr.: b 3-31-1759 d 12-31-1842 m Elizabeth Sichman Pvt PA
Nathaniel: b 6-8-1725 d 2-24-1801 m (1)Joanna Callam (2)Abial — Pvt CT
Philip: b 6-21-1750 d 12-31-1819 m (1)Susanna Elizabeth Abel (2)Margaret — Pvt PA
Reuben: b 1752/53 d p. 1840 m Eunice Lois Bunce Pvt CT ★
Roderick: b 3-11-1741/42 d 8-28-1823 m (1)Tamesia Stephens Pvt MA
Samuel: b 1-29-1733 d 11-17-1795 m Catherine Brown Pvt MA
Simeon: b 1746 d 1821 m Mary Paine Pvt CT
Wiggleworth: b 12-16-1743 d 11-26-1818 m Jemima Everett Lt MA

MESSENKOP,
John: b 11-3-1724 d 1-19-1797 m Ann Elizabeth Sgt PA
John Philip: b 1-16-1761 d 10-30-1828 m (1)Anna — (2)Elizabeth Lauman Fif PA

MESSER,
Abiel: b 3-30-1712 d 6- -1776 m Susan Swan Pvt VT & NY
Daniel: b 1760 d 4-8-1815 m Elizabeth Saunders (Sanders) Pvt NH
James: b 9-26-1754 d 4-14-1832 m Achsah Ladd Pvt MA
Jonathan: b 9-7-1756 d 2-16-1841 m Betsey Brown Pvt MA ★
Nathaniel: b 12-21-1736 d p. 1790 m Ruth Whittier Cpl MA
Nathaniel Smith: b 10-13-1756 d 1-20-1832 m (1)Sarah Clough Pvt MA
Samuel: b 6-30-1736 d 2-27-1811 m Sarah Howe CS NH
Stephen: b c. 1740 d c. 1790 m Nancy Barker Pvt MA
Thomas: b 7-15-1756 d 1-27-1811 m Lydia Merriam Pvt NH

MESSERSMITH,
George: b 12-13-1750 d 10-31-1811 m Elizabeth Hoffman Pvt PA

MESSLER,
Abraham: b 1754 d p. 1796 m Deborah Stevens Pvt NJ
Cornelius: b 2-9-1759 d 11-28-1843 m Maria Stryker Pvt NJ ★
Simon: b 9-16-1756 d 3-22-1838 m Esther Dunham Sgt NJ

MESSMORE,
John: b 1733 d 2-14-1813 m Susan Wise Pvt PA

MESSNER,
Casper: b 1722 d 1781-90 m Anna Barbara Echardt Pvt PS PA
Christian: b c. 1760 d p. 1793 m Catherine Schneder Pvt PA

METAYER,
Wm.: b 1756 d 4-24-1817 m (1)Margaret L'Hercule (2)Abigail — PS PA

METCALF, (includes METCALFE)
Allen: b 8-22-1753 d 2-7-1796 m Margaret — Ens VA
Andrew: b 12-5-1736 d 7-1-1828 m Zeriah Hyde PS CT
Asa: b 5-16-1754 d 8-29-1830 m Melia Ware Pvt MA
Burgess: b 8-28-1741 d 9-26-1816 m (1)Mary Chandler (2)Elizabeth Wait Ens NH
David: b 1758 d 1826 m Anna Champion Pvt CT
Eli: b 10-14-1742 d — m Ruth Hall Drm MA
Ezekiel Shattuck: b 10-13-1759 d 5-31-1831 m Eunice Brooks OrdlSgt MA
George: b 6-2-1730 d 2-10-1816 m Joanna Pond 1Lt MA
Gordon: b a. 1754 d 1799 m Sallie — Capt VA
Jabez: b 4-2-1747 d 4-2-1813 m Mrs Elizabeth Tenney Sgt MA
James: b 8-1-1729 d 8-16-1803 m Abial Haven LCol MA
Joel: b 11-10-1755 d 11-26-1834 m Lucy Gay Pvt MA
John: b 4-17-1754 d a. 3-11-1814 m Sibel Broad Sgt MA
John: b 7-3-1734 d 8-15-1822 m Eunice (Metcalf) Dr MA
John, Sr.: b 1724 d 5-8-1799 m (1)Sybil (Farrow) Farrer (2)Mary Obrine (3)Mrs Rhoda (Dent) Chinn Capt VA
John, Jr.: b c. 1760 d p. 1820 m Amelia Shackleford Ens VA
Jonathan: b 5-18-1729 d 1799 m Bathsheba Pond Pvt MA
Joseph: b 4-3-1734 d 3-19-1793 m Margaret Shattuck Bennett Sgt MA
Joseph: b 1754 d 9-11-1806 m (1)Catherine Neal (2)Jane Brisco (3) Deliverance Pendrick Pvt MA
Levi: b 2-16-1746 d 4-22-1832 m Lois Bigelow Pvt MA
Michael: b — d 8-16-1777 m Anna — Pvt NH
Obed: b 12-11-1763 d 12-27-1836 m Abigail Park Pvt MA
Philemon: b 4-4-1755 d 3-20-1833 m Mary Ide Pvt RI W★
Samuel: b 8-14-1739 d 4-2-1817 m Lois Kingsbury Lt MA
Samuel: b 4-26-1739 d 6-13-1785 m Hannah Richardson Sgt PS MA
Simeon: b 6-14-1759 d 7-22-1827 m Patience Broad Cpl MA
Thomas: b 8-9-1760-4 d 3-16-1827 m Sibyl Chapin Pvt MA
Timothy: b 11-27-1754 d 8-2-1838 m Ruth Chaplin Pvt MA ★
Vachel: b 9-22-1760 d 1857 m Diana Green Pvt VA ★
Wm.: b 1758 d p. 1785 m Elizabeth Barnett Pvt VA
Wm. Haven : b 12-23-1754 d 7-22-1842 m Patty Richardson Pvt MA ★

METTAUER,
Francis Joseph: b 3-16-1755 d p. 12-31-1811 m Gemima (Crump) Gaulding Dr VA

METZ, (includes MATTS, MEETZE & METTS)
Abraham: b 12-18-1755 d 3-20-1843 m Esther — Pvt PA
Christian: b 1750 d 7-27-1827 m Maria Hackman Pvt PA
Frederick: b 10-6-1751 d p. 1830 m Ann Askew Sol NC
John: b 4-23-1726 d 5-8-1830 m Regina Coolger Pvt NY
John: b 1750 d 9-23-1813 m Barbara Seliman Pvt PA
John Yost: b 12-2-1756 d 5-7-1833 m Anna Margaret Gross Sol SC

METZGER, (includes METZGAR, MITSCO)
Casper: b 10-13-1751 d 2-9-1837 m Juliana Elizabeth Best Pvt PA
Conrad: b 1759 d p. 1851 m Margaret Flowers Pvt NJ
David: b 1-15-1765 d 7-26-1840 m (1)Mary Waters Reiser (2)Sarah Groover Sol GA
Frederick: b 3-4-1759 d 10-17-1842 m Anna Schleifer Pvt PA
Jacob: b c. 1729 d 7-8-1790 m Susanna — Capt PA
Jacob: b 1-22-1747 d 8-8-1835 m Mary — Pvt PA ★
John: b 1743 d 1-12-1820 m Christina — Pvt PA
Jonas: b 1735 d 6-18-1800 m Eve — Pvt PA

METZLER,
George: b 12-26-1755 d 11-2-1825 m Margaret Wishaun Pvt PA

MEULLION,
Enemond: b 1737 d 1820 m (1)Anne (Stephen) Desautels (2)Jeannette (Poiret) La Mothe PS LA

MEVERLY,
Frederick: b c. 1742 d 1789 m Anna Margaret Jaeger Pvt PA

MIAL,
Thomas, Sr.: b 3-26-1736 d 9-13-1811 m Pheraby Parker Capt NC

MICHAEL,
Balsher: b 1728 d 2-14-1795 m (2)Ann Osborn PS Pvt MD
Frederick: b c. 1721 d a. 12-15-1786 m Christine PS NC
Ludwick: b c. 1750 d p. 8-22-1803 m Catherine — PS MD
Peter: b 1745 d 3- -1808 m Dorotha — PS MD
Phillip: b — d a. 8-11-1818 m — Sol VA & MD
Philip: b 1736 d 1822 m Catherine — Pvt PA

MICHAU,
Jacob: b *a.* 1758 d *p.* 8- -1784 m Ester Cromwell Lt SC

MICHAUX,
Joseph: b 10-30-1739 d 2-8-1807 m Judith Woodson Capt VA

MICHIE,
George: b 4- -1759 d 6- -1843 m (1)Elizabeth Miller (2)Mrs Judah Hood QMSgt VA
James: b *c.* 1755 d *p.* 4-27-1781 m Sarah Ragland 1Lt VA
Robert: b 1735 d 1793 m Anne Watson 2Lt VA
Wm.: b 1741 d 1811 m (1)Frances Jarman (2)Ann Mills PS Cpl VA

MICK,
John: b *c.* 1749 d *p.* 11-29-1783 m Mary McCubbin Pvt MD

MICKEL,
George: b 7-13-1750 d 4-20-1812 m Margaretha Meintzer Pvt NY

MICKEY,
Daniel: b *c.* 1750 d 1807 m Elizabeth Thompson 1Lt PA
Robert: b 12-21-1746 d 12-3-1827 m Ezemiah Kelly Pvt PA

MICKLE,
Joseph: b 1750 d 8-21-1824 m Hannah Burroughs Pvt NJ
Joseph: b 1720 d 1784 m — Hyde PS SC
Reuben D.: b 1-3-1763 d 1-31-1844 m (1)Violetta Elmer (2)Elizabeth Sharpneck Pvt NJ ★

MICKLEY,
John Jacob: b 12-17-1737 d 12-12-1808 m Susanne Miller PS PA
John Martin: b 3-3-1745 d 3-11-1828 m Eva Catherine Steckel Sol PA
John Peter: b 5-29-1753 d 10-10-1828 m Eva Keck Fif PA

MIDDAUGH, (includes MEDDAUGH, MIDDAGH)
Aurt: b 5-23-1757 d 11-23-1833 m (1)Lena Palen (2)Catherine Pvt NY
Daniel: b 3-15-1735 d 1-27-1837 m — Pvt NJ ★
Garret: b 5-25-1732 d 1810 m Neeltje Van Vleidt Pvt PA
Peter: b 1748 d 10-28-1829 m Mary Moody 1Lt PA

MIDDLEBROOK, (includes MIDDLEBROOKS)
Ephraim: b 1736 d 4-27-1777 m Elizabeth Munson Lt CT
Hezekiah: b 5-18-1740 d 12-1-1832 m (1)Phebe Nash (2)Sarah White (3)Mercy Fitch PS NY
Isaac: b 1755 d 1823 m Elizabeth Perkins Pvt GA
John, Sr.: b 1726 d 12-30-1817 m — Sims Cpl NC
John, Jr.: b 9-20-1755 d 12-30-1830 m (1)Mary Ware (2)Milly Sutton Pvt NC
Michael, Jr.: b 8-9-1741 d 11-19-1806 m Martha Carpenter Lt NY
Stephen, Sr.: b 6-30-1731 d 11-17-1795 m Hannah Hubbell PS CT
Summers: b 12-25-1748 d 2-16-1835 m Susannah Beal Pvt CT
Sylvanus: b 9-13-1743 d 1802 m (1)Jerusha Hubbell (2)Elizabeth Wilson Cpl CT

MIDDLESWART,
Henry: b 5-5-1753 d 4-25-1823 m Sarah Clark Pvt PA
Jacob: b 10-11-1761 d 5-1-1837 m Jane Martin Ens PA ★

MIDDLETON,
Aaron: b 1730 d 12-9-1820 m Elizabeth Clark Pvt VA
Adam: b 1734 d 1792 m Hester Fulton Pvt PA
Arthur: b 6-26-1743 d 1-1-1787 m Mary Izard SDI SC
Charles: b 1750 d *p.* 1780 m Margaret — 2Lt GA
Henry: b 1717 d 6-13-1784 m (1)Mary Williams PS SC
Holland: b *c.* 1719/20 d *a.* 7-23-1795 m (1)Sarah — (2)Mary — Sol GA
Hugh: b *a.* 1740 d 1803 m (1)Martha Heynie (2)Lucy Williams (3)Agatha Garrett LCol PS SC
James: b 1750 d 1798 m Mary James Sol DE
James: b 1736 d 5- -1805 m Mary Nixon Capt NC
John: b 4-26-1743 d *a.* 1825 m (1)Hannah — (2)Mary — Pvt NJ
John: b 1751 d 11-14-1784 m Frances Motte Vol SC
John: b 11-20-1761 d 1-31-1837 m Eleanor Hardy Pvt VA ★
Robert: b *c.* 1752/3 d *a.* 1-9-1816 m (1)Elizabeth Nunnelee (2)Betsy (Blackwell) Williamson Capt GA
Theodore: b 3-3-1758 d 1-28-1844 m Julia Hoxton Capt MD ★
Wm.: b 1767 d 1835 m Panela McPherson Drm VA

MIDLER,
Christopher: b *c.* 1760 d 6-10-1796/7 m Mary Miller Pvt NY W★

MIESSE, (includes MEASE, MEES, MEESE, & MIES)
Baltzer: b 3-20-1756 d 5-15-1838 m Anna Baker Pvt CT ★
Daniel: b 1-28-1743/4 d 4-3-1818 m (1)Miss Ebling (2)Christina Everhardt Pvt PA
Heinrich: b 1-24-1752 d 1-17-1816 m Maria Barbara Faber Pvt PA
John: b 5-11-1738 d 11-21-1825 m Esther Meller Pvt PA
John Michael: b *c.* 1760 d *p.* 1806 m Catherine — Ens PA

MIFFLIN,
Daniel, Sr.: b 1722 d 12-31-1795 m (1)Mary Warner (2)Ann Walker (3)Mary Pusey PS VA
Jonathan: b 1753 d 1840 m (1)Mary Harrison (2)Frances (Mifflin) (3)Susanna Wright DepQMGen PA
Samuel: b 12-13-1724/5 d 5-16-1781 m (2)Rebecca Edgill Col PS PA

MIGHILL, (includes MIGHEL, & MIGHELLES)
Ezekiel: b 1733 d 12-28-1815 m Maragaret Wilson Pvt VT
Nathaniel: b 3-4-1737 d 5-29-1819 m Sarah Bailes Lt NY
Thomas: b 9- -1752 d 12-20-1794 m Ester Arms Pvt MA
Thomas: b 4-2-1722 d 8-26-1807 m (1)Hannah Northend (2)Sarah Northend (3)Mrs Rachel (Rowe) Lane Capt MA
Thomas: b 5-18-1756 d 10-12-1845 m Mary Yaw Pvt MA

MIGHT,
John: b 10-15-1757 d 1-1-1846 m Kereanhappuck Stillwell Pvt Mus SC ★

MIKELL,
Ephraim: b 3-26-1741 d 6-22-1809 m (1)Province Grimball (2)Mary Ann Calder PS SC
John: b 1725 d *p.* 1785 m Ann Ball Maj PS SC

MIKSCH,
Nathaniel: b 9-21-1743 d 11-17-1827 m Anne Marie Fritsch Pvt PA

MILBURN,
John: b 1750-55 d 1814 m Dorcas — PS PA
John, Sr.: b *c.* 1740 d *p.* 6- -1792 m Mary — PS VA
Nicholas: b 1750 d 1830 m Jane — Cpl MD
Wm.: b 1763 d 2-11-1835 m Bethia Hutchison Pvt VA ★

MILCHSACK,
George: b 5-7-1761 d 10-4-1803 m Margaret Barbara Regin Pvt PA

MILEHAM, (includes MILAM)
Bartlett: b 1750 d 9-11-1822 m Elizabeth Guinn PS VA
Benjamin: b *c.* 1750 d 6-19-1781 m Elizabeth Jackson Pvt VA
John, Sr.: b 1725 d *p.* 1788 m Judith — Sol VA
John, Jr.: b 6-12-1753 d 10-26-1838 m (1)Nancy — (2)Polly Allison Pvt VA
Jordan: b 2-26-1750 d 12-31-1851 m Mary Peacock Pvt VA
Wm.: b 1758 d 1825 m Anna — Pvt PA ★

MILES,
Abel: b 9-9-1733 d 12-6-1814 m Lydia Adams Pvt NH
Abel: b *a.* 1750 d 1794 m Elizabeth Kettle 2Lt DE
Abner: b 1-12-1745 d *c.* 1803 m Deborah Underwood 2Lt MA
Aquilla: b 1732-7 d 10- -1801 m Harriet Giroud Pvt PS SC
Benjamin, Jr.: b 3-11-1754 d 10-29-1817 m Hannah Buckminster Lt MA
Benjamin, Sr.: b 11-26-1724 d 1-28-1776 m Mary Hubbard Pvt MA
David: b 3-15-1740 d 10-23-1776 m Sarah Frink Pvt CT
Ebenezer: b 5-20-1758 d 4-8-1827¹m Molly Hudson Pvt MA
Elihu: b 1745 d 4-28-1788 m Hannah St. John Pvt MA
Ephraim: b 12-6-1759 d 9-14-1838 m Zermiah Rugg Pvt MA
George: b 1735 d 11-18-1781 m Sarah — Pvt MD
Henry: b 11- -1752 d *a.* 6-21-1796 m Elizabeth McLamar Capt MD
Isaac: b 1725/6 d 11-15-1780 m Catherine Baldwin NCapt VT
Isaac: b 8-25-1752 d 2-10-1816 m Mary Beach Sgt CT W★
Isaac: b 6-11-1763 d 11-22-1843 m Martha David Pvt CT ★
Jacob: b 1756 d *c.* 1835 m Nancy Rice Pvt NC
Jacob: b — d *p.* 2-10-1800 m Hannah — PS NC
James: b 1743 d 1798 m Susannah Rock Pvt VA
Jesse: b 1756 d 6-13-1833 m Olive Adams Pvt CT
Joab: b 3-13-1741 d 10-28-1832 m Elizabeth Fitch Sgt MA ★
John: b 9-1-1752 d 1830 m (1)Mary Bills (2)Sally Bills Capt CT ★
John: b 8- -1738 d 2- -1815 m Jane Green Sgt CT
John, Sr.: b 10-4-1723 d 10- -1796 m (1)Martha Curtis (2)Mrs Eunice Ives Pvt CT
John: b 1759 d 10-9-1828 m Mary Duval Pvt VA ★
Joshua: b 3-21-1754 d 7-6-1815 m Lucy Cady Pvt CT
Noah: b 4-29-1730 d 10-21-1811 m Huldah Hosmer Capt MA
Oliver: b 9-11-1738 d 11-3-1820 m (1)Martha Stone (2)Lydia — Pvt MA
Richard: b 1760 d *a.* 6-4-1817 m Jane Gardiner Pvt MD
Richard: b 11-28-1738 d 12-6-1823 m Mary Pugh Capt PA
Robert: b 1753 d 1810 m Katherine Watt PS PA
Samuel: b 8-12-1757 d 5-16-1848 m Sylvia Murray Pvt Mar CT
Samuel: b 3-11-1739 d 12-29-1805 m Catherine Wister BGen CS PA
Samuel: b *c.* 1739 d *p.* 3-11-1811 m Sarah James Sol VA
Solomon, Sr.: b 10-13-1744 d 11- -1862 m (1)Lydia Chubb (2)Lucy Chickering (3)Betsy Crane Pvt MA
Thomas: bpt 1-16-1745 d 9- -1806 m Jerusha Hubbard Sgt CT
Thomas: b 1747 d *a.* 11-6-1827 m (1)Polly Pound (2)Elizabeth Treadway Sgt MD
Thomas: b 9-23-1752 d 4-15-1838 m Ann Patterson Lt VA ★
Wm.: b 11-18-1754 d 7-9-1831 m — Cpl PS NH
Wm.: b 1762 d 3-3-1846 m Mary Watts Pvt PA ★
Wm.: b *c.* 1725 d *a.* 1790 m Catharine — PS SC

MILIRON, (or MILLIRON)
Jacob: b c. 1730 d 1785 m Anna Ottilia Christina Pvt PA

MILK,
Benjamin, b c. 1750 d p. 3-6-1813 m Lydia — Pvt NY

MILL,
John: b c. 1736 d p. 1790 m Magdalena — Pvt PA

MILLAN,
Thomas: b 3-1-1750 d 4-28-1828 m (1)Elizabeth Shied (2)Susanna Summers Ens VA

MILLARD, (includes MILLERD)
Abiathar: b 6-22-1744 d 5-24-1811 m Tabitha Hopkins Pvt MA
Charles: b 2-19-1762 d 4-30-1827 m (1)Lydia Pride (2)Sarah Miller Pvt CT
Esquire: b 1-26-1749 d 1820 m Patience Pearse Capt RI
John, Jr.: b 12-21-1736 d 11-22-1812 m Christiana Rust Ens CT
Joseph: b 8-26-1741 d 4-30-1832 m Thankful Gilmore Pvt MA
Joshua: b 10-7-1744 d 7-8-1830 m Mrs Lydia Young CS CT
Leavitte: b 1760 d 11-23-1841 m (1)Lydia Skinner Pvt CT
Nathaniel: b 1-23-1725/6 d p. 1783 m Mary Wheeler Pvt PS MA
Nathaniel: b 1765 d 8-6-1829 m Mary Hunter Pvt NY
Samuel: b 10- -1761 d 8-7-1843 m (2)Sarah Slocum Pvt RI ★

MILLAWAY,
Joseph: b 1750 d 5-11-1778 m Ann Millaway Pvt DE

MILLEDGE,
John: b 1757 d 2-9-1819 m Ann Lamar PS Pvt GA

MILLEN,
John: b 1751 d 3-18-1801 m — Pvt SC

MILLER, (includes MILLAR, MOELLER, MULLER)
Aaron John: b 1-12-1749 d 11-4-1838 m Esther Burr SrgnMte MA ★
Abijah: b 12-20-1745 d 12-24-1824 m Sarah Titus Pvt NY
Abner: b 9-27-1755 d — m Lois Edwards Cpl MA
Abner: b c. 1763 d 9-18-1822 m Sarah Phillips Pvt NJ
Abraham: b 5-1-1749 d 8-19-1824 m (1)Elizabeth Clapper (2)Sevella Lower Pvt MD
Abraham: b 1745 d 1794 m Phebe Hawxhurst PS NY
Abraham: b 4-1-1735 d 7-25-1815 m Winchey McDowell LCol PA
Abraham: b 1745 d 1821 m Catharina — Capt PS PA
Abraham: b 1740 d 1821 m Catharina — Capt PS PA
Abraham: b 1741 d 1805 m Rebecca Epprecht Pvt PA
Abraham: b 1758 d 8-1-1821 m (1)Phoebe Webb (2)Nancy Miller Pvt PA
Abraham: b 1761 d 4-24-1834 m Catherine — Pvt PA
Abraham: b 1762 d 1822 m Elsie Thomas Pvt PA
Abraham: b 9-13-1759 d 2-28-1827 m Elvy (Miller)Pvt SC
Adam: b 5-14-1750 d 2-9-1827 m Rosannah Kershner Pvt MD
Adam: b 2-11-1765 d 5-15-1836 m Anna DeMouth Grd NJ
Adam: b c. 1758 d 7- -1817 m Anna Barbara — Pvt PA
Adam: b 1758 d 1837 m Eve Miller Pvt PA
Alexander: b 1737 d 3-25-1823 m Elizabeth — Pvt MA
Alexander: b 2-22-1758 d 1-13-1843 m — Sgt NY★
Alexander, Sr.: b c. 1720 d p. 2-15-1781 m Mrs Margaret McCartney PS PA
Alexander, Jr.: b c. 1745 d a. 2-7-1804 m Jane Lyle Pvt PA
Amok: b 2-11-1763 d 7-16-1806 m Rachel Bishop Pvt MA
Andrew: b 1732 d 12-4-1803 m Sarah Ann Snyder Ens NY
Andrew: b 1768 d a. 1806 m Anna Abram Pvt NC
Andrew: b 4-12-1717 d 1792 m Anna Maria Ehwald Pvt PA
Andrew: b 1734 d a. 11-24-1778 m Dorothea — Pvt PA
Andrew: b 8-6-1747 d 2-24-1825 m Catherine — Pvt PA
Anthony, Sr.: b c. 1724 d p. 1785 m Hester Davids Capt NY
Anthony, Jr.: bpt 10-22-1762 d 3-22-1812 m Nancy Ward Fif NY
Asa: b 1741 d 9-14-1824 m (2)Eunice Shircoy Lt PA
Barney: b c. 1764 d p. 1840 m — Pvt VA ★
Benjamin: b 4-4-1764 d 9-20-1863 m Martha Allen Pvt MA
Benjamin: b 10-22-1731 d 3-12-1795 m Hannah Halsey Pvt NJ
Benjamin: b 1760 d c. 1828 m Lydia Walling Pvt NJ
Benjamin: b 3-18-1712 d 1785 m Prudence Newman Dr NY
Benjamin: b c. 1757 d p. 6-7-1799 m Hannah Beatty Pvt PS PA
Benjamin: b 3-11-1762 d 3-28-1841 m Elizabeth Parker Pvt VA ★
Charles: b c. 1753 d 9-20-1820 m Barbara — Pvt PA
Charles, Sr.: b 1710 d 1793 m Lucas Armor Pvt SC
Charles, Jr.: b a. 1754 d p. 1795 m Margaret White Armorer SC
Christiam: b 1742 d 1-27-1826 m Barbara Riffel Pvt PA
Christian: b 1704 d 1788 m (2)Susanna — CS Wgn PA
Christian: b 1744 d 4-28-1836 m Catherine Weisman Sgt VA ★
Conrad: b — d 1783 m Hannah — PS MD
Conrad: b 1769 d 1834 m Dorothy — Pvt PA
Conrad: b 6-24-1757 d 4-9-1842 m Anna Margaret Jacoby Pvt PA
Cornelius: bpt 1-11-1746 d 10-20-1819 m Jane Harder Pvt NY
Cornelius S. Sr.: b 8-21-1726 d p. 6-25-1807 m (1)Rachel Hogeboom (2)Cummatie Bronk (3)Gertrude Vandekar Capt NY
Cornelius, Jr.: b 1744 d 4- -1803 m Albertie Van Valkenburg Pvt NY
Cornelius: bpt 4-14-1759 d p. 1820 m Maria Miller Sol NY
Cornelius: b 1754 d p. 1790 m Mrs Tabiatha Covault PS Lt PA
Daniel: b 1-2-1759 d 11-22-1841 m (1)Catherine Caspar (2)Anna Smith Pvt NC
Daniel: b 4- -1741 d 3-7-1812 m Elizabeth Schnebley Pvt PA

Daniel: b c. 1750 d 1816 m Elizabeth — PS PA
Daniel: b 3-23-1755 d 8-22-1836 m Margaret Keesey Pvt PA
Daniel: b 7-15-1713 d 1-26-1798 m Hannah Thayer Sol RI
Daniel: b 5-28-1764 d 4-23-1841 m Susanna Woods Pvt VA
David: b 10-3-1718 d 2-28-1789 m (1)Elizabeth Brainerd (2)Mrs Abigail Ely Capt CT
David: b c. 1740 d 1778/9 m Rachel Blackwood Pvt MD
David: b 12-5-1734 d 5-14-1811 m Catherine Flick PS MD
David: b 1738 d 3-24-1805 m Rebecca Cottrell Sgt MA
David: b 1718 d 2-17-1787 m Sarah — CS NJ
David: b 6-6-1749 d 2-24-1816 m Phebe Huntting PS NY
David: b 1753 d 1845 m (2)Mrs Rachel (Harrison)Snelson PS NC
David: b c. 1760 d 3-18-1832 m Nancy Lamberth Pvt NC ★
David: b 4-20-1725 d 4-20-1803 m Mary Kerr PS CS NC
David: b 5-1-1754 d 11-22-1834 m Mary Souder Pvt PA
David: b c. 1725 d p. 1-18-1782 m Agnes — 2Cpl VA
David Brainerd: b 12-10-1751 d 11-22-1833 m Adah Coe Adj CT
Ebenezer: b 11-27-1734 d 8-30-1814 m Thankful Allen 2Lt CT
Ebenezer: b 5-2-1725 d a. 1809 m Hannah How Pvt MA
Edward: b 1753 d 1-26-1836 m Rebecca Colvell Pvt VA ★
Edward: b c. 1758 d — m Elizabeth Rockwell SgtMaj CT
Eleazer: b 5-20-1759 d 11-3-1793 m Hannah Mills Pvt NJ
Eleazer: b 1797 d 3-13-1788 m Mary Burnett PS NY
Eliakim: b 1-1-1763 d 12-24-1840 m Rhoda Pratt Pvt MA ★
Elias: b 5-4-1763 d 10-8-1848 m Mary Leiberger Pvt PA
Elijah: b 5-8-1728 d 8-21-1776 m Ann Fisher Adj NY
Elisha: b 1730 d 6-12-1807 m (1)Sarah — (2)Abigail (Abernathe) Burrel Pvt CT
Elisha: b 1715 d 1800 m Martha Colson Capt GA
Enoch, Sr.: b 1733 d 1-12-1813 m Elizabeth Ross Pvt NJ
Enoch: b 5-17-1761 d 4-21-1841 m Keziah Ross Pvt NJ ★
Ephraim: b 9-16-1744 d 6-26-1828 m Bulah Wheeler Sgt MA
Ephraim: b 6-4-1744 d 1-14-1834 m Mary Flagg MM Sgt MA ★
Ezekiel: b 1762 d 1836 m Olive Babcock Pvt VT
Francis: b 10-16-1753 d 2-19-1843 m Jane — Capt NC ★
Francis: b 1748 d — m Elizabeth (Miller) Pvt VA
Frederick: b 12-21-1764 d 1-20-1830 m Elizabeth Babcock Pvt MA
Frederick: b 1733 d 9-22-1814 m Euphemia Schaefer Pvt NJ
Frederick: b 11-11-1766 d 2-1-1840 m Margaret Brown Pvt NC W★
Frederick: b 1740 d c. 1783 m Catherine (Miller) PS NC
Frederick: b 3-5-1751 d 4-28-1818 m Sara Doll PS NC
Frederick: b 1754 d 1832 m Katy Story Lt PA
Frederick: b 11-22-1738 d 7-14-1821 m Eva Maria Albright Pvt PA
Frederick: b a. 1760 d p. 1784 m Maria — Pvt PA
Frederick: b 9-14-1762 d 9-9-1843 m Catharine Phillippy Pvt PA
Frederick: b 1758 d 1-3-1815 m Ann Custer Pvt PA
Frederick: b 1-15-1760 d 8-26-1840 m Susannah Zoellner Spy PA ★
Frederick: b 8-8-1760 d 11- -1834 m Ann Elizabeth Sharp Cpl VA ★
Gabriel: b c. 1735 d c. 1787 m Mary — PS VA
Gad: b 1765 d 11-23-1838 m Annie Thomas Pvt MA
Garret, Sr.: b 1737 d 1778 m Patience — Capt NY
Garret, Jr.: b 1758 d 5-2-1824 m Mary Smith Pvt NY
George: b 5-5-1751 d 11- -1840 m Catherine Weir Pvt PA MD ★
George: b 5-4-1749 d 4-26-1828 m Margaret Warburton Sol VA ★
George: b 5-13-1759 d 9-14-1829 m (1)Esther Cleveland (2)Eunice Parsons (3)Mary Lyman Pvt Drm MA ★
George: b 1724 d 1782 m Glory Listler Capt NC
George: b 11-29-1729 d 12-8-1798/9 m Maria Barbara Endt Col PA
George: b 8-2-1754 d 4-10-1815 m Susan Alspach Pvt PA
George: b c. 1760 d 10-1-1850 m Margratha Duck Pvt PA
George: b 3-20-1761 d a. 1820 d 1-18-1844 m (1)Catherine Markle (2)Catharine Moyer Pvt Tms PA ★
George: b 12-2-1750 d 1-13-1829 m (1)Elizabeth Ingleman (2)Mrs Emily Billew Pvt SC
George: b 1755 d 1805 m Keziah Cargill Pvt SC
George: b — d — m (1)Mary — (2)Eve — Pvt VA
George: b 5-24-1762 d c. 1843 m Mary Rector Pvt VA
Giles: b 12-14-1725 d 3-4-1804 m Elizabeth Parsons Capt CT
Giles: b 12-26-1759 d 8-8-1847 m — Pvt NY ★
Hance: b 1745 d 5-17-1809 m Jane — Pvt DE
Hance: b — d p. 4-14-1788 m Susannah — PS SC
Heinrich: b 1728 d 6- -1778 m Susannah Margaret Henkel Cpl PA
Hendrick: bpt 5-5-1728 d p. 10-30-1782 m Arriantje Van Dusen 2Lt NY
Hendrick: b c. 1740 d p. 7-12-1782 m Hanna Joachims Pvt NY
Henry: b 12-5-1725 d 4-22-1817 m Elizabeth Heilman Sgt MD
Henry: b 9-22-1752 d 4-23-1827 m Margaret Kaler Pvt MA
Henry: b 5-22-1728 d 2-9-1819 m Mary C. Melick Pvt VA
Henry: b a. 1749 d p. 1782 m Margaret Weaver Capt NY
Henry: b 8-4-1764 d 1-23-1826 m Lana Van Deusen Pvt NY
Henry: b c. 1750 d 8-6-1820 m Martha — Sgt NC
Henry: b 12-6-1759 d 1-18-1846 m Sarah Pearcy Pvt VA ★
Henry, 1st: b 1727 d c. 1796-1801 m Susannah Sibley Pvt VA
Henry: b 4-5-1760 d 11-24-1832 m Mrs Catharine (Martin)Deshong Pvt PS PA
Henry: b a. 1754 d 1816 m Eliza Lucas Pvt PA
Henry: b c. 1755 d 4-7-1826 m Mary Magdalene Schuman Pvt PA ★
Henry: b 10- -1755 d 4-2-1842 m Anna Maria Lemertine Pvt PA ★
Henry: b 1756 d 12- -1824 m Elizabeth Stayler Matr PA
Henry: b 4-19-1749 d 9-7-1829 m (2)Countess Julian Zebwitz Chp PA

Henry: b 2-13-1751 d 4-5-1824 m Sarah Ann Ursula Rose LCol PA
Henry, 2d: b 1758 d 1-7-1833 m Achusah Margaret Warner Pvt VA
Henry: b 1756 d 5-9-1815 m Cynthia McCarta Sol VA
Henry: b 1757 d 1819 m Rachel Thompson (Liddell) Sol VA
Henry: b a. 1730 d — m Magdalena — Pvt PA
Henry: bpt 11-15-1743 d 1784 m Elizabeth Cooger PS VA
Hezekiah: b 1-2-1755 d 12-24-1821 m Abigal Miller 2Lt NY
Hosea: b 3- -1736 d 12-11-1815 m Mary Stowe Pvt CT
Hosea: b 4-12-1742 d 5-7-1795 m Lydia West Pvt VT
Hugh: b c. 1750 d p. 2- -1803 m — Capt VA
Ichabod, Jr.: b 5- -1739 d 3-12-1824 m Elizabeth Bacon Capt CT
Increase: b c. 1720 d p. 1790 m Anna Sandusky Sgt NY
Isaac: b 1-3-1737/8 d 7-27-1817 m Hannah Coe Capt PS CS CT
Isaac: b 3-31-1754 d p. 1779 m Sarah Bennett Pvt MA
Isaac, Jr.: b 11-12-1752 d 2-14-1826 m Lucretia Knap Sol MA
Isaac: b 5-2-1727 d 1-20-1815 m (1)Hannah Temple (2)Rachel Seal
  Pvt PA
Isaac: b 1730 d p. 1790 m — Pvt PA
Isaac: b c. 1745 d 1799 m Susannah (Thomas) Pvt PA
Isaac: b c. 1755 d c. 1806 m Margaret –– Tms PA
Isaac: b 1755 d p. 2-4-1836 m — Pvt PA
Isaac, Sr.: b 5-7-1708 d 6-18-1787 m Sarah Crosby PS VT
Isaac: b 2-9-1751 d 1-23-1816 m Elizabeth Sea Lt CS VA
Israel: b 3-5-1763 d 1-9-1833 m Mary Henderson Pvt SC
Jacob, Jr.: bpt 4-24-1754 d 12-29-1786 m Elizabeth Filer PS Pvt
  NY
Jacob: b c. 1727 d 12-20-1807 m Maria Anna Daigle PS LA
Jacob: b 1722 d 1779 m — Sgt MD
Jacob: b 1753 d 10-18-1829 m Susanna — Pvt MD
Jacob: b 1732 d 1-17-1812 m Jerusha Wheaton Maj MA
Jacob: b 7-17-1745 d p. 1793 m Deborah Soule Pvt MA
Jacob: b 3-1-1747 d 1-1-1814 m Lucretia Marsh Tms NJ
Jacob: b 3-22-1732 d 5- -1789 m Hilitjie Muller Pvt NY
Jacob: b 10-18-1748 d 8-10-1840 m Maria Agnes Sauer Pvt NC ★
Jacob: b 3-16-1721 d 2-2-1798 m Elizabeth Staud PS NC
Jacob: b c. 1758 d p. 1790 m — Wagoner Ens PA
Jacob: b 12-28-1763 d 11-11-1837 m Hannah Kech Ens PA
Jacob: b 1735 d 1799 m Sophia Mann Ens PA
Jacob: b c. 1718 d 1778 m Anna Barbara Duringale Pvt PA
Jacob: b 1-6-1733 d 7-14-1805 m Elizabeth (Miller)Pvt PA
Jacob: b 1754/5 d 3-4-1824 m Sarah — Pvt PA ★
Jacob: b 1753 d 1802 m Elizabeth Hampton Pvt PA
Jacob: b c. 1760 d p. 1812 m Elizabeth Knerr Pvt PA
Jacob, Sr.: b a. 1740 d 4-31-1782 m Elizabeth Edwards Sct PS PA
Jacob, Jr.: b 8-26-1762 d 8-20-1830 m Anna Mary Leffler Pvt PA
Jacob: b c. 1730 d 1775-92 m Ann Miller Pvt SC
Jacob: b 1755 d 7-25-1839 m Margaret Dick Pvt VA ★
Jacob, Sr.: b 1702 d p. 1800 m Margaret Miller PS VA
Jacob: b 1726 d p. 1799 m (1)Elizabeth Fudge (2)Margaret
  Sullivan PS VA
Jacob: b 1735 d 1815 m Barbara — PS VA
James: b 1-17-1734/5 d p. 1800 m Mary Clark Sgt CT
James: b 1744 d 12-13-1819 m Lois Parkhurst Drm CT
James: b 5-6-1709 d 4-19-1775 m (1)Sarah Lane (2)Sarah Waters
  PS MA
James: b 2-28-1750 d 7-9-1839 m Mercy Livermore Pvt MA ★
James: b 2-9-1758 d 3-31-1839 m Elizabeth Nesmith Pvt MA
James: b 1738 d 11-11-1825 m Catharine Gregg Pvt NH
James: b c. 1734 d a. 11-20-1784 m Susannah Kent CS NJ
James: b 1740 d 6-10-d 6-10-1779 m Eunice — Pvt NY
James: b 1743 d 1812 m Agnes Miller Col NC
James: b 1751 d 1834 m Elizabeth Fuller 2Lt PA
James: b 1739 d 1835 m Anna Sherbley Pvt PA
James: b 1764 d 5-30-1847 m Polly Russell Pvt PA
James: b a. 1765 d 7- -1828 m — Pvt VA
James: b 5-28-1745 d p. 7-16-1809 m Jane Elliott CS PA
James: b 1759/60 d 10-14-1788 m Asenath Strong Pvt Fif RI W★
James: b c. 1750 d p. 7-4-1826 m Lydia — Pvt SC
James: b 1764 d 6-1-1828 m (1)Mary Sargeant (2)Mary Rumsey
  (3)Katherine Keys Lt VA
James: b c. 1755 d p. 12-30-1795 m Esther Dickey Sol VA
James: b — d a. 3-12-1793 m Sarah Hopewell Pvt VA
James (Henry): b 1740 d 1-17-1781 m — Tomson Sol SC
Jeremiah: b 6-23-1714 d p. 1788 m Elizabeth Lassel Pvt MA
Jeremiah, Sr.: b 1-7-1727 d 7-11-1794 m Ruth Huntting PS NY
Jeremiah, Jr.: b 10-9-1748 d 6-28-1803 m Mary Sanford PS NY
Jeremiah: b 12-22-1752 d 3-8-1835 m Elizabeth — Pvt PA
Jeremiah: b 1759 d 7-4-1817 m (1)Elizabeth — (2)Mary Shade Pvt
  PA
Jeremiah Johannes: b 10-6-1741 d 12-4-1824 m Jonacke
  Hogeboom Capt NY
Jesse: b 10-3-1747 d 4-9-1812 m Keziah(Miller)Ens NY
Jesse: b c. 1750-55 d a. 1819 m Martha Rose Pvt SC GA
Joachim: b 1742 d 1804 m Catherine Staats Lt NY
Joash: b 3- -1754 d 2-11-1819 m Anna Stubsch Sgt PA
Job: b 12-16-1746 d p. 1781 m Elizabeth Sherman Pvt RI
Johannes: b 1760 d 12-17-1834 m Eve Mould OrdlSgt NY
Johannes: bpt 5-10-1715 d 1803-7 m Fytie Hallenbeck Pvt NY
John: b 1752 d 1805 m Mary Thomas Pvt DE
John: b — d 11-5-1823 m Rosannah Ulrich Sgt MD W★
John: b 1-1-1764 d 1-6-1841 m Hannah Freese Pvt MD
John: b c. 1730 d 9-15-1813 m (1)Rebecca — (2)Eleanor — Pvt MD
John: b c. 1750 d p. 3- -1795 m Eve Mong Pvt MD

John: b — d 1783 m Catherine — Pvt PS MD
John, 3d: b 12-7-1737 d 12-1-1807 m Zilphia Tinkham Lt MA
John: b 1753 d 11-28-1825 m Mary Sawyer Wood Pvt MA
John: b 12-20-1756 d 12-18-1834 m Polly Davenport Pvt MA
John: b 3-28-1760 d 5-30-1838 m Hannah Root (Worthington) Pvt
  MA
John: b — d p. 10- -1789 m — Lt NJ
John, Sr.: b 1707 d 3-1-1791 m (1)Rebeckah — (2)Mercy Conkling
  PS NY
John, Jr.: b 1740 d 11-11-1808 m Amy Mulford 1Lt NY
John, Sr.: b c. 1732 d 1808 m Hester — Pvt NY
John, Jr.: b 1755 d 3-17-1847 m Elizabeth Banker Pvt NY
John: b 10-26-1739 d 12-16-1821 m Anna Brown Pvt NY ★
John: b 8-3-1758 d 2-15-1819 m Mrs Rachel Newvill Pvt NY
John: b 1760 d 7-28-1808 m Lydia — Pvt NY
John: b 1754 d 1807 m Susan Twitty Ens NC
John: b 12-5-1763 d 3-24-1828 m Christina Bolick Pvt NC
John: b c. 1725 d 1784 m Christiana — Sol NC
John: b c. 1740/1 d 11-17-1776 m Margaret Campbell Capt PA
John: b 1756 d 4-24-1804 m Juleana Stein Capt PA
John: b 1750 d 2-30-1803 m Margaret (Miller)Sgt PA
John: b 10- -1760 d 3-16-1821 m Elizabeth Barbara Snyder Sgt PA
John: b c. 1735 d 4-13-1781 m Margaret Dibert Pvt PA
John: b 8-22-1742 d 4-3-1802 m Mary Wright Pvt PA
John: b 1748 d 1783 m Sarah Cunningham Pvt PA
John: b 1756 d 1840 m Mary Eaton Pvt PA
John: b 12-10-1752 d 12-10-1836 m Margaret Boier Pvt PA ★
John: b 1758 d c. 1840 m Nancy Grimes Pvt PA
John: b 9-16-1739 d 8-12-1810 m Margaret Gonter PS PA
John, Sr.: b 1710 d p. 5- -1780 m Maura — Pvt PA
John, Jr.: b 1729 d 1782 m Ana Kindrick Pvt PA
John: b 1740 d 1791 m Elizabeth Lindsay CS PA
John: b — d p. 7-18-1818 m Mary McCown Lt SC ★
John: b 5-5-1756 d — m Catharine Long Lt SC
John: b 1745 d 179- m Margaret Ott Pvt SC
John: b — d 2-2-1819 m (1)Miss Mary Anderson (2)Sarah Cason
  Sol SC
John: b c. 1745 d 1776 m Margaret Fairbanks PS SC
John: b c. 1746 d 8-25-1832 m Eve Whitener Capt VA
John (Malcolm): b 7-1-1750 d 9-8-1806-8 m Jane Dulaney Capt VA
John: b 1745 d p. 1800 m Nancy Pleasant Lt VA
John: b — d c. 1784 m Martha — Ens VA
John: b 1753 d 1814 m Mary Keene Sol PS VA
John: b 1-10-1749 d c. 1808-12 m Margaret Hicklin PS Sol VA
John: b 3-17-1755 d 8- -1824 m Ruth Bailey Pvt VA
John: b c. 1725 d a. 11-5-1812 m (2)Mrs Mary Moorman Johnson
  PS VA
John: bpt 10-6-1744 d p. 1783 m Mary — PS VA
John: b 9-21-1752 d 9-5-1815 m Annie Mc Clintock PS KY
John A.: b 5-8-1760 d 9- -1850 m Isabel Little Sgt NY ★
John Adam: b 7-25-1743 d 10-12-1831 m Susanna Orth Pvt PA
John Conrad: b 9-28-1752 d 11-23-1823 m Veronica — Pvt PA
John Daniel: b 2-8-1723 d 3-9-1808 m Catherine Fry Lt VA
John Jacob: b 7-31-1731 d 11-25-1810 m Catherine Sponsaler Maj
  MD
Jonathan: b 11-26-1761 d 7-21-1831 m Elizabeth Gaylord Cpl CT
Jonathan: b 2-13-1729 d 7-29-1810 m Sarah (Woodruff) North Pvt
  CT
Jonathan: b 1760 d 2-7-1849 m Mary Hickman Sol VA
Joseph: b 10-21-1727 d 12-10-1801 m Mary Oursler 2Lt MD
Joseph, Jr.: b 9-1-1756 d 4-1-1829 m Mary Wilder Sol MA
Joseph, Sr.: b 6-24-1724 d 4-8-1803 m Catherine Ferry Capt PS MA
Joseph: b 8-5-1723 d 1-31-1785 m Lydia Stowe Pvt MA
Joseph, Sr.: b 7-29-1716 d 5-24-1794 m Mary Williams PS MA
Joseph, Jr.: b 7-27-1741 d 3-3-1818 m Lucy Walker Pvt MA
Joseph: b 1750 d 1-7-1842 m Lucretia Louisa Gauntt OrdlSgt NY ★
Joseph: b 1753 d 11-30-1820 m Mary Johnson Sgt NY
Joseph: b c. 1743 d p. 3-1-1796 m Mary Seeley Lt NY
Joseph: b 1736 d 1793 m Mary Williams Pvt PA
Joseph: b 7-29-1753 d 6-11-1839 m (1) — Montgomery (2)Lillie
  Allen Pvt VA ★
Joseph: b 1756 d 1925 m Ada Gilbert Pvt VA
Josiah: b 1749 d 1817 m Pauline Titus Capt NY
Lemuel: b 3-29-1751 d 8-17-1842 m Anna Burbank Lt MA ★
Leonard: b 4-8-1752 d 1828 m (1)Mary Sikes (2)Sarah Kellogg Pvt
  MA
Levi: b 4-1-1756/57 d 1-18-1843 m Olive Wright Pvt VT ★
Lewis: b 7-31-1739 d 5-20-1793 m Lucy Wadsworth Pvt MA
Lewis T.: b 6-7-1746 d 10-7-1826 m Rachel Pawling Pvt PA
Ludwig: b 1755 d 1-26-1836 m Anna Barbara Meyer Pvt PA ★
Luke: b 9-8-1759 d 1-23-1851 m (1)Esther Thompson (2)Rachael
  Bommel (3)Mary Cook Thompson Pvt NJ ★
Mark: b 1757 d 1820 m Ann Feckley Pvt VA
Marshall: b 9-20-1754 d 6-10-1807 m Abigail Haven Boyden Pvt VT
Martin: b c. 1745 d p. 12-9-1794 m Margaret — Pvt MD
Martin: b 1753 d 8-29-1839 m (1)Sallie Ritchie (2)Elizabeth Gidden
  Pvt NC
Martin: b 4-26-1739 d 5-25-1839 m Mary — Cpl CL
Mary Heath: b c. 1723 d p. 1796 m William Miller PS VA
Mathias: b 10-18-1743 d 12- -1805 m (1)Susanna Catharine
  Mueller (2)Catherine Aulenback (4)Anna Maria (Moyer) Schaeffer
  Pvt PA
Mathias Burnet: b 10-15-1749 d 2-2-1792 m Phebe Smith Dr NY

MILLER, contd.

Matthew: b 6-15-1730 d 5-30-1824 m Mary Morrison MM PS NH
Matthew: b c. 1756 d 1813 m Sarah Price Pvt PA
Matthew: b 1760 d 1824 m Jean Galbraith Pvt PA
Melchior: b 1757 d p. 1796 m Rosanna Wunderlich PS PA
Michael: b 1754 d 1808 m Babara Schaatzlien Pvt PA
Michael: b c. 1750 d p. 2-3-1817 m Ann — Pvt PA
Michael: b 8-14-1757 d 6-20-1825 m Susan Lantz Sol PA
Michael: b 11-7-1742 d c. 1779-90 m Dorothea Dibert Sol PA
Michael: b 1755 d p. 1809 m Margaret Stump Fif PA
Michael: b 1758 d 1815 m Nancy Vernon PS Sol SC
Mordecai: b 12-22-1755 d 2- -1844 m Isabel Adair Pvt SC ★
Moses: b 1741-46 d 9-24-1821 m (1)Azubah Meeker (2)Molly
  Riley (3)Mrs Hannah Bonnell Sgt NJ
Moses: b 1734 d p. 1777 m Esther (Maxwell) Sayre Pvt NJ
Moses: b 8-1-1759 d 3-21-1814 m Phoebe Baker Pvt NY
Nathan: b 8-1-1727 d 10-18-1815 m Robey Salisbury Pvt MA
Nathan: b 1744 d 5-23-1800 m Mary Mulford Pvt NY
Nathan: b 3-26-1740 d 5-20-1790 m Rebekah Barton BGen RI
Nathaniel: b 1738 d 12-15-1834 m Mary Neile Sol GA
Nathaniel: b a. 1758 d p. 5-10-1802 m Sarah — Pvt MD
Nathaniel: b 5-7-1760 d 10-6-1844 m Anna Bartholomew Pvt NY ★
Nelson: b 7-26-1755 d 3-2-1840 m Sarah Allen DrmMaj RI
Nicholas: b 2-4-1760 d 8-22-1835 m Elsie Parker Pvt NY CT ★
Nicholas: b 1740 d c. 1804 m Anna Catherine — Capt PA
Nicholas: b 10-4-1740 d 10-9-1800 m Hannah Resse Capt PA
Nicholas: b 1740 d 10-5-1787 m Dinah — Pvt PA
Nicholas: b c. 1735 d 8- -1786 m Gertrude — PS PA
Nicholas: b — d a. 1789 m Anna Maria Maus PS PA
Noah: b 6-22-1732 d 5-22-1812 m Anneke Buell Pvt CT
Noah: b 1732 d 1821 m Mary Mills Sct MA
Noah: b 8-6-1756 d 9-12-1838 m (1)Mrs Sarah (Ludlum) Marsh
  (2)Mrs Sarah Morrison Pvt NJ ★
Oliver: b c. 1720 d 1782 m Mary Tidball PS VA
Peter: b 3-31-1750 d 3-15-1835 m Kezia Besse Pvt MA
Peter: b 5-15-1759 d 4-20-1838 m Mary (Miller) Pvt NY
Peter: b 1760 d 12-11-1837 m Catherine (Scribner) Pvt NY ★
Peter: b 1742 d 1810 m (1)Sybil Pitzer (2)Polly Howell Pvt NC
Peter: b 1727 d 2-4-1794 m Elizabeth Richardson Pvt PA
Peter: b 1740 d 9-11-1778 m Catherine Rhodes Pvt PA
Peter: b c. 1753 d 1838 m X Pvt PA
Peter: b 1756 d 11-1-1818 m Mary Stutzman Pvt PA
Peter: b 5-4-1757 d 11-10-1824 m (1)Mary Brown (2)— PS PA
Peter: b 3-5-1747 d 4-11-1824 m (1)Barbara (Jung) Young
  (2)Christina (Shirk) Jumper PS PA
Peter: b 6-16-1745 d p. 1784 m Anna Aldrich Cpl RI
Peter, Sr.: b 1741 d 4- -1815 m Catherine Shular Pvt VA
Peter: b 1741 d 1819 m (1)Martha Kropp (2)Rachel Ramsey Sol VA
Philip: b c. 1740 d 8-22-1825 m Christena Elizabeth Windowmaker
  Pvt MD
Philip: b 2-18-1764 d 8-19-1845 m Dorcas Smith Pvt NY
Philip: b 1-1-1742 d 3-22-1815 m Elizabeth — Lt PA
Philip: b c. 1742 d p. 8-22-1822 m Rosanna Fissel Pvt PA
Philip: b 2-3-1750 d 6-6-1809 m Catherine Leydick Pvt PA
Philip: b 10-13-1765 d 10-15-1863 m Catherine Altman Pvt PA
Philip: b 5-6-1750 d p. 1812 m (1)Rhoda Mason (2)Mrs Lurana
  Allen Pvt MA
Phillip: b 8-10-1736 d 6-4-1796 m Joan Potts Pvt NY
Phillip: b 8-31-1756 d 12-26-1824 m Elizabeth Nunn Pvt NC
Reuben: b 1731 d 4-6-1809 m (1)Sarah (Miller) (2)Keziah — Ens CT
Richard: b 1760 d 1845 m Francis Mann Pvt VA
Robert: b 3-19-1714 d 1-21-1790 m Martha Wade Pvt CT
Robert: b 8-28-1740 d 5-16-1798 m (1)Margaret McClellan
  (2)Martha (Smith) Richey Pvt MA
Robert: b c. 1725 d 10- -1797 m Sarah — Pvt PA
Robert: b 1757 d 1-6-1835 m Cassandra Wood Pvt PA
Robert: b 1722/23 d 11-10-1795 m Elizabeth Calhoun PS PA
Robert: b 3-4-1760 d 8-12-1831 m Jennett White Pvt SC
Robert: b 1753 d 6-28-1830 m Mary Perry Pvt VT
Robert, Sr.: b c. 1707 d p. 10-18-1781 m Ann Lynn PS VA
Robert, Jr.: b 5-5-1734 d 10-24-1806 m Margaret Maupin Capt VA
Robert Johnston: b 7-11-1753 d 5-13-1834 m Mary Perkins Pvt VA
Roger: bpt 12-22-1751 d 7-26-1809 m Rebecca Searl Pvt MA
Samuel: b 2-17-1742/43 d 2-26-1817 m (1)Elizabeth Pearce (2)Anne
  Hill Pvt MA
Samuel: b 7-20-1751 d 10-20-1820 m Sara Hale Pvt MA
Samuel: b 1716 d 3-27-1791 m Margaret — PS NH
Samuel: b 1755 d p. 1785 m Magdalen Blattner Pvt NY
Samuel: b 4-12-1761 d 2-12-1829 m Catherine Winfield Pvt NY ★
Samuel: b 1738 d c. 1790 m Magdalena Wiley Pvt PA
Samuel: b c. 1760 d 1806-18 m Ann Brawford Pvt VA
Samuel A.: b 8-7-1753 d 2-13-1818 m Margaret Weiss Pvt NY
Sebastian: b 11-3-1744 d 5-20-1830 m Catharine Gernand Capt PA
Sebastian: b 2-6-1757 d 11-11-1842 m Susan Burdillion Pvt PA
Shadrick: b 2-18-1764 d 8-22-1846 m Martha Parker Pvt MA
Simon, Jr.: b 1742 d 1792 m X CS VA
Simon: b p. 10-2-1740 d p. 7-29-1806 m Jane Hord Pvt VA
Solomon: b 10-9-1731 d 1807 m Desire Smith Pvt MA
Stephen: b 12-19-1749 d 8-28-1838 m Jemima Winston Sgt MA
Stephen: b 5-31-1755 d 1-13-1834 m Priscilla Wolcott Pvt MA
Stephen: b 1755 d 1834 m Jane E. (Miller) Pvt NY
Stephen: b — d 3- -1799 m Rachel — Pvt PA

Stephen: b 4-8-1755 d 1-13-1831 m Elizabeth Miller Pvt PA
Stephen: b c. 1722 d 1776 m (1)Martha Dutarque (2)Mary Roche
  Sol SC
Thomas: b 9-3-1730 d 8-16-1780 m Ellen McGuire Cpl DE
Thomas: b 1764 d p. 1819 m Sally Arche Pvt NY
Thomas: b a. 1742 d a. 2-23-1791 m (1)Elizabeth Patterson
  (2)Margaret Patterson Pvt PA
Thomas: b c. 1746 d 12-29-1807 m Sarah — Pvt PA
Thomas: b c. 1750 d p. 6-24-1808 m Elizabeth — Pvt PA
Thomas: b 1758 d 1820 m Johanna Armistead Lt VA
Thomas: b 10-20-1760 d 7- -1821 m Ann Ball Lt VA
Thomas: b 1749 d 4- -1786 m Anne Langhorne CS VA
Timothy: b 8-22-1753 d 11-28-1837 m (1)Elizabeth Raymond
  (2)Hepzibah Stebings Ens NY
Timothy: b 7-15-1750 d 11-16-1824 m Deborah — Pvt VT
Valentine: b 12-17-1761 d 4-4-1856 m Christiana Meiser Pvt PA
Vespatian: b 6-2-1740 d 7-6-1812 m Abigail Church Pvt VT
Wendell: b c. 1730 d 1804/05 m (2)Christina — Lt NC
Wm.: b 6-30-1759 d 6- -1836 m Margaret Conkey Pvt CT
Wm.: b 10-24-1724 d 10-3-1804 m Eunice Clark PS CT
Wm.: b 1740 d 4-26-1823 m Maria Eva — 2Lt PS MD
Wm.: b 2-22-1732 d 1814 m Rebeckah Bradford PS MD
Wm.: b 12-15-1757 d 12-30-1812 m Paulina Phelps Pvt MA
Wm.: b 4-17-1746 d p. 10-2-1832 m Betsey — Pvt NH ★
Wm.: b 8-13-1735 d 5-9-1799 m Sarah Dennis Ens NJ
Wm.: b 1759 d 2- -1823 m Mercy Brown Cpl NY
Wm.: b 1734 d 11-14-1818 m Mary Haviland PS NY
Wm.: b 1735 d 1784 m Sarah Cooper Pvt NC
Wm.: b 4-8-1759 d 11-27-1837 m Amey Barker Pvt NC ★
Wm., Sr.: b c. 1760 d p. 1-8-1841 m X Pvt NC ★
Wm.: b 5-25-1755 d 6-3-1831 m Margaret Craig Capt PA
Wm.: b 1745 d 1817 m Rachel Art PS Pvt PA
Wm.: b 1762/63 d 8-6-1832 m Margaret Seawright Johnson Sol SC
Wm.: b 10-2-1761 d 4-16-1802 m Hannah Worden Pvt VT
Wm.: b 1720 d 1815 m Mary Heath Capt VA
Wm.: b 1760 d 8-16-1841 m Elizabeth North Capt VA
Wm.: b 3-1-1757 d 11-8-1840 m Elizabeth Lackey Pvt VA ★
Wm.: b 11-2-1744 d 10-22-1790 m Elizabeth Ferree PS VA
Yost: b 7-25-1748 d 8-12-1811 m Mary (Miller) Pvt PA
Zebediah: b 1713 d 1785 m Rebecca Alvord Pvt MA

MILLET, (includes MILLETT)

Daniel: b 5-30-1715 d p. 1786 m Phoebe Jenkins Pvt MA
John: b 6-6-1736 d p. 1778 m Susanna Emons Pvt MA
Johnathon: b c. 1740 d 1801 m Jenny Edmunds Cpl CT
Jonathan: b 12-25-1735 d 6-4-1795 m Sarah Mansfield Cpl MA
Joseph: b 6-21-1737 d 1797 m Elizabeth Bullock Pvt MA
Thomas: b 10-2-1737 d 1823 m Eunice Parsons Pvt Mrnr MA
Thomas: b 8-10-1819 m Alice Low Elwell Pvt MA

MILLHOUSE,

John, Sr.: b c. 1740 d 1795 m Abigail Sleigh PS SC

MILLIGAN,

Edward: b 1734 d 10- -1833 m X Pvt PA
James: b 1741-4 d 1795-8 m Elizabeth McCallister Lt PA
John: b 10-13-1752 d 4-30-1837 m Mary Adams Pvt PA
John: b 8- -1751 d 2-5-1838 m Sarah Robinson Pvt VA PA ★
Joseph: b 1755 d p. 4-1-1836 m (1)Rachael Jeffers (2)Sarah Hopewell
  Pvt PA ★
Wm.: b 1751 d 6-15-1808 m Sarah Rooney Pvt PA

**MILLIKEN, (includes MILLICAN, MILLIKAN, MILLIKIN,
MULLIKEN, MULLIKIN)**

Alexander: b 1720 d c. 1798 m Margaret — PS NH
Amos: b 11-30-1727 d p. 1778 m Mahitable Gage Pvt MA
Andrew: b c. 1755-60 d 1-29-1830 m Lettice Claghorn Sol NC
Archibald: bpt 12-13-1753 d p. 1816 m Elizabeth Vincent Pvt PS
  MD
Belt: b c. 1750 d p. 2-23-1789 m (1)Sophia Hall (2)Mary Duckett
  2Lt PS MD
Benjamin: b 2-7-1763 d 5-13-1849 m Mary Stuart Pvt MA ★
Daniel: b 12-22-1743 d p. 1790 m Bettee — Pvt Sgt MA
Edward: b 3-5-1734 d c. 1812 m Elizabeth Harmon 2Lt ME
James: b 1744 d 3-4-1830 m (1)Elizabeth McKune (2)Elizabeth
  McCoy Pvt NY
James: b 1-5-1752 d 7-20-1821 m Dolly Mc Farland Pvt PA
Jeremiah: b 1-30-1722 d 1788/89 m Margaret Waters PS MD
Joel: b 7-12-1762 d 11-14-1839 m Abigail Carll Pvt MA
John: b — d 1-17-1843 m (1)Pamelia Stiles (2)Mary Campbell Pvt
  PA
John: b c. 1748 d p. 1820 m Mary Price Pvt VA ★
John A.: b 9-13-1738 d p. 4-16-1804 m Abigail Smith 1Lt MA
Joshua: b 4-10-1756 d 11-27-1832 m Margaret Lord Pvt MA ★
Nathaniel: b 1754 d p. 1808 m (1)Mollie Lord Cpl MA
Nathaniel: b 4-11-1750 d 10-6-1777 m Maria — Lt NY
Robert: b 1760 d p. 1784 m Margaret Hogg Pvt NH
Samuel: b 2-25-1746/47 d 7-28-1841 m Susannah Beal Pvt Grd ME
Samuel: b 10-2-1752 d 5-27-1842 m Mary McAllister Pvt NH
Samuel: b 1737 d 10-28-1804 m Margaret Foster Pvt PA
Thomas: b 2-27-1729 d 8-11-1805 m Elizabeth Ellen Williams Capt
  MD
Thomas: b c. 1730 d 1778 m Jane McConnell Pvt PA

Wm.: b 1726 d 3-6-1788 m Mary Mc Knight Pvt MA
Wm.: b 3-15-1762 d 7-8-1850 m Susannah Whitaker Cpl MA
Wm.: b 10-2-1752 d 11-17-1807 m Esther Taggart Pvt NH
Wm.: b c. 1720 d a. 1800 m (1)Jane White (2)Hannah Rowan (3)Jane Rowan PS CS NC
Wm.: b 4-6-1724 d c. 1800 m Eleanor Smith Sol NC

MILLIMAN,
John, Jr.: b 1760 d 9-6-1828 m Elizabeth — Pvt NY

MILLING,
Hugh: b 2-21-1752 d 5-7-1837 m Elizabeth Burney Capt SC

MILLINGTON,
Samuel: b 9-27-1749 d 12-1-1823 m Sarah Reynolds Pvt MA
Solomon: b 6-15-1754 d 2-16-1819 m Lydia Slye Pvt NH

MILLISON,
James: b 5-31-1748 d 11-11-1841 m Abigail Hays Pvt PA

MILLS,
Alexander: b 7-17-1761 d 11-16-1822 m Sallie Knapp Pvt CT ★
Amasa: b 2-27-1736 d 8-24-1821 m Lucy Curtis Capt CT ★
Anthony: b c. 1755 d — m — Green Sgt VA
Benjamin: b 2-13-1738 d 10-24-1829 m Hannah Humphrey Capt CT
Benjamin: b a. 1750 d 11-14-1822 m Elizabeth Collier 2Lt MD
Benjamin, Jr.: b 6-19-1752 d 4-15-1824 m Sarah Loker Cpl MA ★
Benjamin: b 12-30-1755 d p. 7-11-1801 m Dorcas Lovejoy Pvt NH
Cephas: b 6-17-1759 d 3-20-1848 m Hannah Easton Pvt MA ★
Charles: b 1755 d 1853 m Jane Evans Pvt VA
Constantine: b 9-6-1761 d 10-21-1848 m Philecta Way Pvt CT ★
Daniel: b 6-17-1742 d 5-10-1810 m Harriet Humphrey Pvt CT
Daniel: b 1758 d 1808 m Huldah Blackman Pvt CT
Daniel: b 4-1-1746 d 1833 m Nancy McKeen Pvt NH
David: b 1740 d 4-3-1822 m (1)Huldah Edgecomb (2)Jane Hungerford Pvt CT
Edward: b c. 1746 d 9-7-1781 m Hannah Avery Cpl CT
Edward: b 1749 d 1-13-1827 m Phoebe Byram Sgt NJ
Elijah, Jr.: b 9-6-1761 d 11-8-1831 m Huldah Drake Pvt CT
Elisha: b 3-26-1732 d 4-7-1816 m Mary de Forest PS CS CT
Elizabeth Collier: b 1751 d 11-14-1822 m Benjamin Mills PS MD
Elligood: b 8-4-1744 d 1-6-1832 m (1)Mary Dyer (2)Lucy McLucas NOf ME
Ephraim: b 4-19-1752 d 1818 m (1)Rosanna Foote (2)Mrs. Bertha Johnson Pvt CT
Ezekiel: b 4-12-1740 d 1805 m Ursula Phelps PS CT
Frederick: bpt 2-28-1756 d p. 1799 m Roxy Storrs Pvt CT
George: b 5-3-1760 d 1843 m Almira Hoyt Pvt CT
George, Jr.: b 10-3-1743 d 5-18-1826 m Martha Gray Pvt MA ★
George: b 1-17-1765 d 12-1-1858 m Jenny Mills Pvt PA
Gideon: b 10-27-1749 d 1813 m Ruth Humphrey Lt CT
Isaac, Jr.: b 2-18-1727 d 4-25-1783 m Sarah Phillips PS NY
Jacob: b 12-22-1746 d 2-18-1841 m Catherine Denton Pvt NY ★
James: b 1-30-1750 d 1790 m Hannah Mason Pvt MA
James: b 12-9-1755 d 9-4-1838 m J — Baxter Pvt MA ★
James: b 8-1-1753 d 1-5-1819 m Rebecca Lytle Pvt NY W★
James: b 1750 d 3- -1781 m Miss Burwell Capt PS NC
James: b c. 1740 d c. 1-14-1795/4-13-1796 m Rebecca Hicks Sol NC
James: b c. 1733 d a. 7-22-1818 m Joanna — Pvt PA
Jared: b 10-8-1746 d 12-30-1822 m (1)Apphia Higley (2)Mrs Joan (Case) (3)Anna Dyer PS CT
Jedediah: b 2-9-1756 d 3-25-1832 m Sarah Andrews Pvt CT
Jedediah: b 6-6-1744 d 2-1-1820 m (1)Sarah Roberts (2)Mary Goble Pvt NJ
Jedediah: b 11-4-1755 d 12-21-1828 m Elizabeth (Mills) Cpl PS NY
Job: b 9-29-1763 d 12- -1817 m Patsey Higley Pvt CT
John: b 1760 d 2-11-1829 m Eunice Frasier Pvt CT ★
John, Sr.: b c. 1730 d c. 1799 m Elizabeth Rial Capt MD
John: b c. 1745 d 1812 m Keziah Lyon Capt NH
John: b 1-7-1756 d 7-23-1833 m Margaret Caldwell Sgt NH ★
John: b a. 1700 d 5-29-1780 m Ellis Mills PS NH
John: b 1712 d 4-18-1794 m Sarah Beals PS NC
John: b 1758 d 1825 m Perine Marioneau Pvt PA
John: b 1760 d 1829 m Rachel Leonard Pvt PA
John: b 3-23-1757 d 3-19-1795 m Mary Gill Capt SC W ★
John: b 1728 d 1790 m Ellen Crawford Pvt SC
John: b c. 1750 d p. 8-14-1795 m Martha Ewing Capt VA
John: b 3-6-1752 d 11-23-1833 m Ruth Sheppard Lt VA ★
Jonathan: b 10-23-1710 d 10-28-1798 m (1)Ruth Rudyard (2)Dorothy Miller PS NY
Jonathan: b 11-3-1764 d 7-23-1848 m Rachel Canfield Pvt NY ★
Joseph: b 2- -1728 d 7-25-1792 m (1)Susanna Case (2)Mrs. Lucina Holcomb (3)Hannah Remmington (4)Sarah Lewis CS CT
Joseph: b 12-29-1765 d 3-2-1843 m Mary True Pvt MA
Josiah: b 10-7-1763 d 3-23-1833 m Elizabeth Sturdevant Pvt MA
Josiah: b 11-7-1746 d 2-7-1814 m Rachel Miller Pvt PS NY
Justinian: b 4-2-1720 d 3-3-1795 m Mary Dant Pvt MD
Levi: b c. 1740 d p. 5-14-1805 m Elizabeth Dunn PS PA
Lewis: b 10-18-1738 d 1777/8 m Hannah Hall Lt CT
Luke: bpt 2-2-1745 d p. 1790 m Lydia Eydes Pvt MA
Mary Gill: b 10- -1758 d 1841 m John Mills PS SC or NC

Menan: b 1750 d 1838 m Frances Jouett MM Pvt VA ★
Michael: b 1728 d 3-21-1820 m Mercy Lawrence Capt CT
Nasby, Sr.: b 1763 d 1835 m Nancy Elks Pvt NC
Nathaniel, Jr.: b 7-2-1743 d 11-10-1814 m (1)Sarah Corbin (2)Rebecca Robinson Pvt CT
Nathaniel: b c. 1740 d 1813 m Elizabeth — CS NY
Nathaniel: b c. 1750 d 12-27-1815 m Frances Thompson Capt VA
Nehemiah: b 1712 d 9-30-1777 m (2)Mrs Patience Ball Pvt MA
Oliver: b 5-2-1742 d 1- -1827 m (1)Susannah Fisher (2)Mrs. Sibel Pratt Lt MA
Peletiah: b 1-19-1723 d 1786 m Hannah (Higley) Owen PS CS CT
Peter: b 11-14-1741 d 3-9-1829 m Rebecca Marsh Lt CT
Peter: b 8- -1741/2 d 9-30-1830 m Sally Foster Capt NY
Reuben: b 1731 d 12-14-1816 m Mary Howard PS NH
Robert 3d: b 1737 d 10-3-1849 m Margaret Dinsmore PS NH
Roger, Sr.: b 1742 d 8-12-1809 m Mary Webster Sgt CT
Samuel, Sr.: b 3-25-1734 d 1809 m Abigail Cowles CS CT
Samuel, Jr.: b 7-10-1754 d 1-17-1837 m Lucy Coy Pvt CT ★
Samuel: b 9-23-1753 d 3-27-1814 m Jemima Harrington Cpl MA
Samuel: b 1759 d 2-3-1739 m Elizabeth Hammond Matr MA
Samuel: b 9-13-1762/3 d 5-25-1848 m (1)Eunice Comstock (2)Mrs. Phoebe Chappel (3)Priscilla Peters Pvt NH ★
Samuel: b 1758 d 1823 m Mary Weed Pvt NY ★
Samuel: b 1744 d 1806 m (1)Keziah Filley (2)Sarah Humphrey PS NY
Thomas: b 1720 d 1-27-1790 m Elizabeth Hoog PS NH
Thomas: b 1740 d c. 1800 m Lucy — 2Lt GA
Thomas: b c. 1740 d p. 2-17-1799 m Martha Phillips Pvt PS PA
Timothy: b 4-9-1757 d 1-12-1833 m Abigail Ludlow Pvt NJ
Timothy: b 1747 d 9-14-1777 Mary — MM NJ
Timothy: b 6- -1740 d 11- -1781 m Anne Cocalair Pvt NY
Timothy: b 4-14-1748 d 2- -1830 m Mrs. Phebe Oakley Pvt CT
Wm.: b c. 1740 d 7-14-1823 m Elizabeth Cottingham Cpl MD
Wm.: b 1753 d 1842 m Mary Jenkins Pvt PA ★
Wm.: b c. 1749 d p. 1- -1792 m Peggy Swift Capt VA
Wm.: b 8-19-1759 d 12-18-1828 m Phoebe Prindle Pvt NY
Wyatt: b — d 1808 m Sally Starke Pvt VA

MILLSAPS,
Thomas: b a. 1735 d p. 5-23-1783 m Sarah — PS NC

MILLSPAUGH,
Abraham: b 1-10-1759 d 11-6-1814 m Mahetable Dickerson Sgt NY
Adam: b 12-21-1759 d 4-6-1824 m Jane White Pvt NY
Benjamin: b 7-24-1750 d p. 1790 m Maria Mingus Sol NY
Jacob: b 10- -1733 d 1794-6 m (2)Eve Crist Pvt NY
Jacob: b 9- -1733 d 2-5-1806 m Elizabeth Bookstaver Pvt NY
John: b 1-22-1758 d 2-19-1804 m (1)Agnes Rogers (2)Jane Barkley Bbd PS NY
Mathias: b 6-7-1748 d 4-27-1796 m Elsie Kimbark Sgt NY
Philip, Jr.: b 5-20-1745 d 12-5-1800 m Ann Kimbergh Pvt NY

MILNER, (or MILNOR)
Amos: b 7-9-1759 d 9-1-1851 m Hannah Rice Pvt VA
Beverly: b 3- -1756 d 1-18-1843 m Anna Hendrick Sol VA
John: b 5-16-1746 d 5-16-1812 m Elizabeth Godwin Capt SC
John: b c. 1724 d 2-17-1790 m Bathshebar Battoon PS SC
Luke: b 9-20-1750 d 12-25-1835 m Phoebe Wisdome Pvt VA ★
Nathan: b 11-9-1741 d 3-16-1808 m Mary Sharpley Pvt DE
Pate Wells: b c. 1734 d p. 1788 m Jacobina Wilson Pvt NC
Pitt: b 6-22-1769 d 7-21-1839 m Apsyllah Holmes Pvt SC
Solomon: b c. 1728 d p. 1786 m Mrs. Mary Petty Lt PS SC
Wm.: b 1737 d 2-5-1807 m Anna Brientnall PS PA
Wm.: b 1760 d p. 1790 m Christiama Eley Pvt VA

MILROY,
Henry: b 1750 d 1791 m Agnes McCormick Pvt PA

MILTIMON,
Daniel: b 2-23-1753 d 8- -1828 m Agnes Hunter Lt NH

MILTON,
Charles: b 1757 d 9-13-1827 m Sibba — Pvt VA
Elijah: b 12-23-1755 d 10-15-1833 m Catherine Taylor Capt VA ★
John: b c. 1740 d c. 1803/4 m Hannah E. Spencer Capt GA
Richard: b 1715 d 1800 m Margaret Ross PS VA

MILLWEE, (or MILWEE)
James: b c. 1755 d 3-29-1813 m Margaret Hudgins Capt SC
Wm.: b 10-8-1753 d 7-15-1840 m Martha Neal Maj SC ★

MIMS,
David: b 1-2-1734 d 1-6-1820 m Elizabeth Cullen Pvt NC
David: b 1748 d 1786 m Martha Duiguid PS VA
Drury: b 1744 d 1818 m Lydia Jones Pvt SC
John: b c. 1740 d 1810 m (1)Mary Moss (2)Mrs. Elizabeth Howard Sol SC
Wm.: b 1762 d 1825 m Millie — Pvt SC

MINEAR,
David: b 7-31-1755 d 10-20-1834 m Katherine Sailor Pvt VA ★
Phillip: b 3-31-1761 d 10-17-1848 m (1)Winnie Farmer (2)Elizabeth Ritchard Sol VA ★

MINER, (includes MINARD, MINIER, MINNINGER, MINOR)
Aaron: b 3-17-1757 d 3-29-1849 m Hannah Baldwin Pvt CT ★
Abraham: b 5-22-1762 d 3-22-1843 m (1)Mary Collins Pvt PA
Absalom: b c. 1739 d p. 1820 m Ruth Morse Sgt CT
Amos: b 8-5-1755 d 11-11-1836 m Mary Rowley Sgt CT ★
Anderson: b 8-3-1754 d 3-1-1835 m Martha Pitkin Pvt MM MA
Andrew, Sr.: b 5-26-1728 d a. 3-18-1783 m Priscilla Bosworth Pvt CT
Benjamin: b 6-17-174 2 d 1-13-1835 m Anne Champlin Capt NJ
Christian: b 9-30-1747 d 4- -1837 m Christianna Peck Sgt PA
Christopher: b 3-17-1745 d 1-22-1803 m Mary Wheeler Lt CT
Christopher: b 1733 d 3-10-1820 m (1) — Harris (2)Abigail Way Pvt CT
Christopher: b 1-11-1743 d 10-7-1815 m Lucy Avery Pvt MA
Clement, Jr.: b 5-21-1738 d 8-17-1787 m Mary Wheeler Lt CT
Clement: b 11-1-1719 d 8-11-1798 m Mary Barnum Ens CT
Daniel: b 7-27-1735 d 1-15-1791 m Abigail — Pvt CT
Daniel: b 6-21-1749 d p. 1790 m Mercy Denison Pvt CT
Daniel: b 1748 d 8-4-1822 m Polly Shafer Pvt PA
David: b 5-6-1752 d p. 10-11-1832 m — Rogers Pvt CT
David: b 10-15-1760 d 7-19-1826 m Eunice Warner Pvt CT
Ebenezer: b 9-5-1764 d 2-12-1834 m Rhoda McIntosh Pvt CT ★
Elias: b 1748 d 6-12-1800 m (1)Esther Noyes (2)Sarah Ely Pvt CT
Elisha: b 3-17-1764 d 9-19-1860 m (1)Amy Wright (2)Maggie Fox (3)Martha Husted Pvt CT
Elisha: b 7-16-1745 d — m Anna Smith Pvt CT
Ephraim: b 1756 d 6-26-1827 m Thankful Brown Pvt CT
Ephraim: b 7-11-1751 d 1-20-1828 m Lucy Lull Pvt VT
Garrett: b 3-4-1744 d 6-25-1799 m Mary Overton Terrill Maj VA
George: b 1706 d a. 12-14-1779 m (1)Maria Catharina Meyer (2)Marie Elisabeth Stunck PS PA
Ichabod: b 6-1-1766 d 6-25-1861 m (1)Hannah Witheral (2)Elizabeth Brooks Pvt CT ★
Israel: b 7-14-1735 d 5-3-1811 m (1)Anna Lake (2)Mrs Betty Cheravoy Sgt VT
Jacob: b 1761 d 1838 m — Pitman Pvt VA ★
James: b 2-18-1745 d 6-9-1791 m Mary Carr PS VA
Joel: b 1750 d 5-11-1805 m Temperance Ackley Pvt CT
John: b 1762 d 1849 m Rhoda Wood Pvt CT ★
John: b 8-13-1735 d 3-21-1800 m Elizabeth Cosby Maj VA
John: b 1-5-1747 d 12-5-1833 m (1)Seeley Williams (2)Cassandra Williams (3)Jane Hawkins Capt VA
John: b 11-18-1707 d 8-1-1778 m Sarah Carr Pvt VA
John: b a. 1737 d 1782 m Elizabeth Elsey CS VA
Jonathan, Jr.: b 2-22-1740 d 12-24-1798 m Esther Allen Gnr CT
Joseph: b 1756 d p. 1818 m Mary Upson Sgt CT ★
Joseph: b 9- -1760 d 11-19-1835 m Mary Hoskins Pvt VA ★
Joshua: b 8-6-1747 d 2-12-1776 m Rebecca Cotterell Pvt CT
Joshua: b a. 1760 d 1842 m Zipporah Bolles Pvt CT
Justice: b 1-19-1762 d 7-27-1850 m (1)Mable Plum (2)Hanna Moss Pvt CT
Larkin M.: b 8-5-1763 d 11-6-1830 m (1)Rachael Broomfield (2)Anna Harting Pvt VA ★
Manassah: b 1755 d 8-25-1837 m Hannah Haley Sgt CT
Matthew, Sr.: b 9-2-1708 m 11-21-1778 m (1)Sarah Preston (2)Mrs. Mary Sandford (3)Mrs. Mary Minor PS CT
Matthew, Jr.: b 1752 d 7-20-1835 m (1)Phoebe Roots (2)Charlotte Mallory Judson Pvt CT
Nathaniel: b 4-30-1732 d 1-23-1815 m Ann Denison CS CT
Perez: b 7-25-1760 d p. 1808 m Mary — Pvt CT
Richard: b 10-24-1760 d 7-18-1839 m Lucy Griswold Pvt MA ★
Richardson: b 9-10-1753 d 3-19-1847 m Katherine Holman Pvt CT ★
Roswell: b 9-25-1753 d 11-15-1809 m Zibeah Cotton Pvt CT
Samuel: b 11-20-1739 d 1-19-1826 m Anna — Pvt PA
Seth: b 1742 d 1-15-1822 m Ann Charlton Ens CT
Seth: b 11-23-1733 d 11-4-1820 m (1)Eunice Root (2)Rhoda Durkee Pvt CT
Stephen: b 8-25-1754 d 6-8-1831 m Lydia Allen Slr PS CT ★
Thomas: b 3-11-1743 d 1800 m (1)Mary Page (2)Lydia York Pvt CT
Thomas: b 9-17-1751 d 9-6-1781 m Rebecca Perkins Pvt CT
Thomas: b 1743 d 7-12-1827 m Eleanor Lamb Sct Pvt PS CT
Thomas, Sr.: b c. 1720 d 1776 m Alice Taylor Lt CS VA
Thomas, Jr.: b 1751 d 7-21-1834 m Elizabeth Taylor Capt VA ★
Threesivelluss: b 2-28-1759 d p. 1842 m Jane Hemingway Pvt VA ★
Timothy: b 4-22-1743 d 1789 m Elizabeth Down Pvt CT
Timothy: b 4-20-1762 d 3-16-1816 m Polly Ames Pvt CT
Vivian: b 6-4-1750 d 9-29-1791 m (1)Barbara Cosby (2)Elizabeth Dick Capt VA
Wm.: b 12-18-1751 d 2-25-1833 m Abigail Haley Pvt CT
Wm.: b 1735 d 1804 m Frances Phillips Pvt VA
Yost: b c. 1744/5 d 1802 m Rosina Frederick PS PA

MINGE, (includes MING)
David: b c. 1746 d p. 5-16-1779 m Christiana Shields Capt PS VA
George: b c. 1720 d 12- -1781 m Mary Wyatt PS VA
Wolrick: b 6-11-1731 d 9- -1796 m (1)Margaret Jones (2)Sarah Colloday (3)Esther Morris Capt PA

MINGERSON,
John: b a. 1749 d 1784 m Ann Hey Gamble Pvt MA

MINGES,
Jacob: b 1752 d 1- -1827 m Elizabeth — Pvt PA

MINGLE,
John: b 2- -1758 d 8-18-1842 m Martha — Pvt PA
John: b 1761 d 1-15-1848 m Margaret Stout Gnr PA

MINGUS,
Hieronemus: b 1754 d 1823 m Margaret Fitzgerald Pvt NY ★
Moses: bpt 11- -1759 d 5-3-1836 m Elizabeth English Pvt NY ★

MINK, (includes MINCK)
Paul, Jr.: b 1753 d 7-7-1839 m — Gross Pvt MA ★
Philip: b c. 1756 d p. 1804 m — Kaler Pvt MA

MINNERLY, (includes MINNER)
James: b 1742 d 4-6-1823 m Catherine — Pvt NY

MINNICH,
Christopher: b c. 1737 d 1806 m Anna Barbara Holder Sgt PA
George: b c. 1730 d a. 5-3-1784 m Catharine Marg Guthman Pvt PA
Jacob: b c. 1750 d 9- -1806 m Elizabeth Wolf Pvt PA
Michael: b 1-2-1738 d 5- -1800 m Maria Christina Laudig Lt PA
Peter: b 10-28-1761 d 4-25-1826 m Elizabeth Rockel Pvt PA

MINNIS,
John: b c. 1754 d 6-29-1838 m Nancy Susan McCammon Sgt PA

MINOT, (or MINOTT)
George: b 4-23-1741 d 4-13-1808 m Rebecca Barrett Capt PS MA
George: b 11-27-1755 d 9-16-1826 m Eunice Billings Matr MA
Jesse: b 11-5-1759 d 10-19-1828 m Betsey Adams Cpl MA
John: b 12-4-1737 d 1812 m Jemima Bradbury Pvt MA
John: b 12-16-1730 d 9-16-1809 m Rachel Spaulding Capt MA
Jonas: b 4-25-1735 d 3-2-1813 m Mary Hall Capt MA
Jonathan, Sr.: b 9-19-1723 d 2-7-1806 m Esther Proctor Maj MA
Jonathan, Jr.: b 8-23-1749 d 4-3-1833 m Hannah Eastman Sgt MA ★
Samuel, Jr.: b 10-7-1748 d 12-4-1818 m Martha White Sol Adj VT

MINSHALL,
Edward: b 1750 d a. 8-28-1803 m Mary Hughes Pvt PA

MINTER,
Anthony: b — d a. 10-21-1812 m Elizabeth — PS VA
John: b 1755 d 1835 m — Crawford Capt PA ★
Richard: b c. 1750 d a. 1800 m Sarah Ragland Ens PS NC

MINTHORN, (includes MINTHORNE, MINTON & MINTUN)
Ebenezer: b 1760 d p. 1820 m Elizabeth — Pvt VA ★
George: b 1754 d 1820 m Rachel Day Pvt NJ
Jacob: b 1753/4 d 2-8-1817 m Abigail Bonnell Pvt NJ
John: b 7-7-1754 d 7-7-1826 m Rebecca Fairchild SgtMaj NJ ★
John: b 1720 d 1807 m Susannah Rogers PS NY
John: bpt 6-25-1740 d 1802 m Christian Lamorn Capt NY
John: b 1761 d 11-20-1838 m Jane Gillmore Pvt VA ★
Lemuel: b 9-22-1751 d 3-9-1795 m Hannah Howell Ens NJ
Nathaniel: b 1740 d 1822 m Hannah Grant Pvt NY
Philip: b c. 1730 d 12-23-1780 m Abigail — Sgt NJ

MINZES, (includes MINGS)
Joseph: b 4-9-1755 d 4-14-1849 m Margaret Karnatser Pvt NC ★

MIOT,
John: b 5-31-1740 d 11-6-1791 m Frances Harden Pvt SC

MISCAMPBELL,
James: b c. 1760 d p. 1790 m — Sol SC

MISER, (includes MEISER & MICER)
Henry: b c. 1728 d 1801 m Anna Maria — Pvt PA
Henry: b 1733 d 1827 m Dorethea Meyer Pvt PA
John: b p. 1735 d 1795 m Catherine — Pvt PA
John George: bpt 1-25-1749 d p. 1782 m Anna Katherine — Ens PA

MISKILL,
Wm.: b 3-5-1729 d 1789 m Elizabeth — PS CS VA

MISKIMEN,
David: b 1732 d 6- -1823 m Rachael Free Pvt PA

MISSIMER, (includes MISEMER)
Henry Brandt: b 3-9-1754 d 5-16-1837 m Susanna Shultz Pvt PA
Jacob: b c. 1743/4 d p. 7- -1803 m Catherine Mauck Pvt PA
John: b 7-11-1752 d 12-10-1807 m Elizabeth Jost Pvt PA

MITCHELL, (includes MITCHEL)
Abiel: b 1733 d 10-11-1821 m Mary Leonard Col PS MA
Abner: b 10-28-1738 d c. 1795 m Abigail Warren Capt PS MA
Abraham: b c. 1734 d 9-30-1817 m Mary Thompson PS MD
Abraham: b 1-18-1742 d — m Eleanor Mitchell Pvt NC
Abraham: b 8-23-1761 d 4-17-1856 m — Pvt NC ★
Adam: b c. 1745 d c. 1802 m (1)Jennett (Mitchell) (2)Elizabeth McMahan Pvt NC
Alexander: b 1740 d 1808 m (1)Mary Greenlaw (2)Jane Cochran Pvt PA

Amasa: b 5-29-1761 d 1-11-1851 m Mary Frymier Fif MA ★
Andrew: b 5-14-1732 d 10-13-1812 m Maria Van Epps Maj NY
Barnabas: b a. 1764 d 3-14-1813 m Mary Tyler Pvt CT
Benjamin: b 1760 d 9-9-1842 m Jemima Sunderland Pvt CT ★
Benjamin: b 1762 d 3-28-1841 m Sarah Fogg Pvt ME
Benjamin: b 1-9-1755 d 9-24-1840 m Martha Steele Pvt NH
Charles: b 3-13-1759 d 7-24-1842 m Mary Barnett Pvt VA ★
Daniel: b 6-15-1744 d 5-22-1795 m Mary Lewis Pvt MA
David: b 1-20-1749 d — m Desire Barrett Pvt MA
David: b c. 1730 d 10- -1790 m Hannah — CS NC
David: b 7-17-1742 d 5-25-1818 m Martha Brown LCol PA
David: b 6-10-1737 d 6-10-1817 m Margaret (Mitchell) Pvt PA
David: b 4-30-1760 d 1-28-1836 m (1)Martha Black (2)Rebecca
    Nelson (3)Hannah Caldwell Pvt PA
David: b 1733 d 11-1-1803 m Elizabeth Reid Sol PA
Day: b 1-15-1760 d 10-2-1848 m Abigail Parker Pvt MA
Domenicus: b 4-19-1744 d 9-6-1822 m Anna Small Lt MA
Edward, Sr.: b 1716 d 12-25-1801 m Elizabeth Cushing Col MA
Edward, Jr.: b 9-1-1739 d 11-29-1828 m Jane Latham Pvt MA
Edward: b 1757 d 4-16-1798 m Mary Moore Capt SC
Edward: b 8-3-1760 d 12-3-1837 m Nancy Haley Cpl QM VA ★
Eleazar: b 11-27-1732 d 2-3-1819 m (1)Olive Hickock (2)Abigail
    Hicock Capt CT
Elijah: b 10-3-1730 d 11-9-1812 m Elizabeth Miller Pvt MA
Elijah: b 3-6-1761 d 8-1-1847 m Sarah Ireland Pvt NC ★
Ensign: b 1759 d p. 1837 m Lucy Hubbard Pvt NY
Flud: b 2-10-1757 d 12-29-1839 m Sarah Bennett Pvt Spy SC ★
George: b 1762 d 1836 m Betsey Ramsey Pvt NJ
George: b 1738 d 1790 m Elizabeth Hall Capt NC
George: b 1734 d 1822 m Elizabeth Porter Pvt PA
George: b 1749 d p. 7-15-1821 m Elizabeth Thompson Pvt PA
George: b 1761 d 4-3-1817 m Hannah Taylor Wright Pvt PA
George: b 3-16-1763 d 3-5-1848 m Elizabeth Watts Pvt VA ★
Henry: b 1744 d 11-20-1797 m Martha Van Horn Pvt PA
Henry: b 6-10-1749 d 5-17-1839 m Frances Hobbs Sol VA
Hugh: b 1720 d 1822 m Mary Neat PS NY
Isaac: b 1729 d 1787 m Jannett — Ens MD
Issac: b 4- -1761 d 10-14-1848 m Jane Moore Pvt NH ★
Isaac, Jr.: b c. 1760 d a. 10-29-1811 m Anna — Sol SC
Isaac, Sr.: b c. 1735 d p. 10-29-1811 m Sarah — Pvt PS SC
Jacob: b c. 1756 d a. 9-20-1837 m Winnie Duke Pvt NC ★
James: b 3-2-1733 d 6-5-1801 m Hannah Warner Cdr Pvt CT
James: b 12-20-1765 d 11-11-1843 m Mary Craig Pvt NC ★
James: b c. 1710 d 2- -1779 m X PS NC
James: b 9-15-1750 d 1-19-1841 m Mary Lusk Sgt PA
James: b 1719 d 3-15-1793 m Elizabeth McIlhenny PS PA
James: b 9-28-1738 d 6-1-1827 m Ester Gibson Pvt PA
James: b 1745 d p. 1830 m Candis Mercer Capt SC
James: b a. 1751 d 1795 m Sarah W. Hubbard 1Lt VA
James: b 3-27-1727 d 6-11-1819 m Mrs. Molly (Pryer) Berry QM VA
James: b 1737 d 1815 m Jane Wiley Cpl VA
James: b 1750 d 1848 m Catherine Williams Sol VA
James, Jr.: b 11-17-1754 d 5-18-1835 m Elizabeth Bromfield Pvt
    VA ★
James Mills: b 3- -1759 d 2-5-1853 m Hope Lombard Sol MA
Jesse: b 6- -1760 d p. 1792 m Tabitha — Sgt VA NC ★
Joab: b 2-13-1721 d 3-13-1780 m Mary Henderson PS NC
Job: b 5-20-1749 d — m Sarah Stanford Pvt MA
John: b 8-25-1748 d 1-3-1804 m Sarah Thweatt 1Lt GA
John: b 1760 d 10- -1812 m (1)Lucy Stoddard (2)Katherine Barnes
    Capt MD
John: b 3-8-1748 d 2-6-1829 m (1)Anne Byram (2)Susan Lincoln Cpl
    MA
John: b 3-24-1739/40 d 3-17-1830 m Rizpah Richards Pvt MA
John: b 4-22-1762 d 1-17-1850 m Persis Lowell Pvt MA
John: b 4-28-1708 d 4-3-1799 m Lydia Sewall PS MA
John: b 6-30-1738 d 3-10-1830 m Mrs. Mary (Vickery) Weston PS MA
John: b 1714 d 1801 m Elizabeth Wilson CS ME MA
John: b 1744 d 3-19-1816 m Lydia Johnson PS NH
John: b 3-12-1750 d 10-24-1823 m Abigail Billings Pvt NH ★
John: b 12-29-1757 d 2-13-1849 m Sarah Bennett Pvt NY & NJ ★
John: b 1- -1760 d p. 1-7-1832 m X Pvt NC
John: b 1741 d 1-27-1816 m Anna E. H. (Mercer) Col PS PA
John: b c. 1720 d p. 9-2-1780 m Agnes — Col PA
John: b 1760 d 3-2-1842 m Mary Mitchell Pvt PA
John: b 7-29-1758 d 1-11-1851 m Judith Hollinger Pvt CL ★
John: b 1760 d 1838 m Obedience — Fif Maj VA ★
John: b c. 1740 d 1789/90 m Margaret Porter Pvt VA
John: b 5-4-1763 d 4-29-1840 m (1)Margaret Catharine Teter
    (2)Susan Washburn Pvt VA
John: b 1766 d 3-18-1852 m (1)Miss Sisson (2)Elizabeth Gillam
    Pvt VA
John B.: b 1760 d 9-6-1842 m Jemima Sunderland Pvt CT ★
Jonathan: b 10-8-1735 d p. 1800 m Keziah Lucy Libby PS ME
Jonathan, Sr.: b 5-24-1724 d 5-20-1818 m Sarah Loring Col MA
Jonathan, Jr.: b 2-25-1747 d p. 1777 m Rachel Loring 1Lt MA
Jonathan: b 8-31-1736 d 5-1-1810 m Anna Lovitt Cpl MA
Joseph: b 1729/30 d 1-10-1803 m Susannah Paul Pvt MA
Joseph: b 1730 d 1788 m — Capt VA
Josiah: b 3-1-1749 d 11-12-1819 m Eunice (Milbury) Grozier Pvt MA
Josiah: b c. 1735 d p. 1790 m Elizabeth PS NC
Levin: b c. 1754 d 1812 m Mary Ward Pvt MD
Mark: b c. 1756 d 4-18-1838 m (1)Mary Rider Pvt VA ★

Matthew: b 1709 d 1792 m Hannah Preston Cpl CT
Matthew: b 1742 d 5- -1823 m — Ritchie Pvt PA
Morris: b 8-29-1762 d c. 1848 m Elizabeth Pvt PA
Nathan: b 8-9-1739 d p. 1798 m Elizabeth Ross Ens NY
Nathaniel: b 8-23-1757 d 8-31-1837 m Alice Parker Pvt MA ★
Nathaniel: b 1740 d 5-20-1836 m Nancy Stevenson Pvt PA ★
Nathaniel: b 1749 d 3-18-1839 m Janet Burns Pvt PA ★
Nathaniel: b 1753 d 2-21-1814 m Hannah Morris Adj VA
Nazareth: b 1758 d 1-25-1846 m Betsy Griffin Pvt NC ★
Nimrod: b 4-21-1743 d 6-14-1790 m Mary Elizabeth Ann Penn Lt
    PS SC
Randolph: b c. 1760 d 1-11-1821 m Tillitha Wiggins PS NC
Reuben, Sr.: b 1709 d 1815 m Ruth Lee Williams Lt MD
Reuben: b 12-25-1748 d 11-9-1822 m Susannah Judson Lt CT
Richard: b 1758 d — m Eleanor Webster Pvt ME ★
Richard, Jr.: b 9-27-1735 d 1-21-1819 m Hepsabeth Barnard CS MA
Richard: b p. 1738 d 1-12-1798 m Rachael Pierce Pvt PA
Richard: b c. 1740 d 1790 m Mary — Smn VA
Robert: b 12-6-1763 d 11-8-1834 m Rebecca Hilton Pvt NY
Robert: b 1760 d 1830 m Rhoda Burns Cpl VA
Robert: b 5-10-1748 d 7-26-1827 m Eve Aldridge DrmMaj VA
Rotheas: b 3-20-1753 d 10-28-1816 m Hepziba Hayward Lt MA
Samuel, Jr.: b 4-22-1753 d 7-22-1822 m Margaret Swan Sgt MA ★
Samuel: b 4- -1751 d p. 9-9-1835 m — Sgt PA ★
Samuel: b 1740 d 3- -1808 m Mary — 2Sgt PA
Samuel: b 1741 d 4-21-1783 m Ann Elliott Pvt PA
Samuel: b 3-15-1759 d 4-25-1840 m Malinda Cecil Pvt VA ★
Samuel: b 3-23-1764 d 5-6-1855 m Eleanor Metcalf Thomas Pvt VA
Solomon: b 1759 d 1-27-1839 m (2)Nancy Broton Pvt SC W★
Stephen: b c. 1760 d 1825 m Celia Batts Sgt VA
Stephen: b c. 1760 d a. 1834 m Kitura Wade Sgt VA
Stephen: b 1-8-1747 d 1798 m Margaret Maitland QM VA
Thomas: b c. 1755 d 1840 m Mary Barnett Lt GA
Thomas: b 12-25-1727 d 4-1-1776 m Keziah Swift LCol MA
Thomas: b 6-8-1743 d 1830 m Ann Preston PS MD
Thomas: b — d 1824 m Jenny McGinnis Pvt NH
Thomas: b 1754 d 11-1-1831 m Sarah Hyatt Cowell Pvt NJ ★
Thomas: b 8-23-1748 d 1792 m Mary Young 1Lt PA
Thomas: b 8-5-1756 d 7-27-1826 m Ann Raines Pvt VA
Thomas: b 1752 d 1825 m Amelia Berryman Pvt VA
Thomas: b 9-23-1732 d 12-30-1806 m (1)Elizabeth (McClannahan)
    Moor (2)Elizabeth Wales Sol VA
Thomas: b 9-18-1758 d 1-24-1835 m Deborah Parkins Smn VA ★
Timothy: b 8-25-1758 d 7-20-1832 m (1)Hannah Leonard
    (2)Malinda Bradley Sgt MA ★
Uriah: b 10-5-1746 d p. 1794 m Sarah Cornwell Capt NY
Wm.: b 1735 d 7-16-1816 m Sarah Parmlee Cnt CT
Wm.: b 1741 d 1826 m Ruth Jackson Pvt GA
Wm.: b 1748 d 1819 m Harriet Randolf Sol GA
Wm.: b 4-19-1750 d 1837 m Elizabeth Ward Lt MA
Wm.: b 1763 d 1-27-1850 m Elizabeth Curry Pvt NC ★
Wm.: b 1737 d 1816 m Rebecca Anderson Pvt PA
Wm.: b 1756 d 3-8-1822 m Elizabeth Hamilton Pvt PA
Wm.: b — d 1808 m — Pvt PA
Wm.: b 7- -1756 d p. 9-4-1840 m Martha Patterson Pvt PA ★
Wm.: b 10-20-1746 d 7-8-1836 m Chloe Nance Pvt VA
Wm.: b c. 1754 d p. 1791 m — Brown Sol VA

MITCHUM,
Dudley: b 7-2-1754 d 5-19-1831 m Susan Allen PS VA
Susan Allen: b 2-10-1759 d 11-8-1833 m Dudley Mitchum PS VA

MITTEN,
Thomas: b a. 1760 d a. 12-30-1830 m Sophia — Pvt PA

MIX,
Amos: b 2-2-1759 d 10-16-1844 m Clarinda Barns Pvt CT ★
Amos: b 6-10-1764 d 10-16-1847 m Amelia Pennoyer Pvt MA ★
Eldad: b 10-4-1733 d 10-30-1806 m Lydia Beach Sgt CT
Elisha: b 7-1-1761 d 6-12-1818 m Ammy Webster Cpl CT ★
John: b 1755 d 1834 m Martha Hooker Cowles Lt CT
John: b 8-23-1746 d 10-3-1821 m Elizabeth — PS CT
Jonathan: b 4-19-1753 d 1-18-1817 m (1)Anna Sears (2)Elizabeth
    Mary Phipps Capt CT
Joseph, Sr.: b 10-29-1715 d 7- -1789 m (1)Damaris Punderson
    (2)Anna Alcott (3)Sarah Morris PS CT
Joseph, Jr.: b 7-28-1740 d 2-5-1813 m Patience Sperry Pvt CT
Josiah: b 3-7-1754 d 5-13-1845 m (1)Mindwell Rice (2)Keziah Rice
    Pvt CT
Samuel: b 9-24-1759 d 3-29-1828 m Roxana Pelton Pvt CT
Thomas 2d: b 5-3-1755 d 9-1-1810 m Rebecca Wooding Pvt CT
Thomas: b 11-27-1709 d 1794 m Ruth Manross PS CT
Timothy: b 1-20-1740 d 6-11-1824 m Margarette Storer Lt CT

MIXER, (includes MIXTER)
Asa: b 4-5-1746 d 5-12-1849 m Mary Newton Pvt MA
Daniel: b 8-25-1763 d 4-30-1847 m Abigail Allen Pvt MA
Ezekiel: b 6-9-1752 d 1806 m Anne Pepper Pvt NH
Joseph: b 12-14-1705 d p. 1790 m (1)Mary Ball (2)Mrs. Elizabeth
    Ball PS MA
Phineas: b 8-18-1758 d 11-3-1821 m Abigail Fobes Pvt MA
Samuel: b 1-13-1758 d 10-2-1845 m Unity Grout Pvt Drm MA ★

MIXER, contd.
Timothy: b 7-17-1748 d 1792/3 m (1)Molly Eames (2)Mrs. Abigail Sherman Pvt PS NY
John: b 1750 d a. 7-9-1806 m Nancy Goodwyn PS SC

MIXON,
Micah: b c. 1725 d 1805 m Miss Williamson PS SC

MIZELL,
Edward: b 1750 d 1819 m X Pvt NC

MIZNER, (includes MISNER)
Henry: b 9-22-1759 d 9-15-1848 m Barbara Stacker Btm Spy PA ★
Peter: b — d p. 1808 m Maria Bush PS NY

MOAD, (includes MOOK & MUCK)
James: b 1752 d 1826 m Mary — Pvt SC

MOAK,
Andrew: b c. 1754 d 1844 m Elizabeth — Pvt PA
George: b 1760 d 1848 m (1)Barbary Herbster (2)Mrs. Sarah Baker Pvt PA
Jacob: b 1720 d p. 1795 m (1)Frena — (2)Catherina Claus (Classen) Pvt NY

MOALE,
John: b 1-1-1730/1 d 7-6-1798 m Ellin North Col PS CS MD

MOATS,
Jacob: b 4- -1745 d a. 11-20-1820 m Elizabeth — Pvt VA

MOBLEY, (includes MOBBERLY, MOBERLEY)
Benjamin: b c. 1728 d p. 1785 m Mrs. Mary Price (Hill) Sol SC
Clement: b 10-4-1746 d 1834 m X Pvt SC ★
Edward: b 12-25-1735 d 10-17-1783 m Drucilla — Sol SC
Edward, Sr.: b 1700 d 1787 m Susannah DeRuel Sol SC
Jeremiah: b 1744 d 1824 m Sallie Cheves Capt NC
John: b 1755 d a. 1832 m Sarah — Pvt GA
John: b c. 1725 d 1790 m Chloe — PS MD
Samuel: b c. 1739 d p. 12-21-1802 m Mary Wagner Pvt PS SC

MOCK,
De Vault: b 1755 d 1798 m Phebe Clynard PS NC
Hans George: b c. 1735 d p. 1790 m — Pvt PA
Rudolph: b a. 1742 d p. 4-14-1817 m Catherine — PS VA

MOCKERT,
Samuel: b c. 1740 d p. 1807 m (1)Magdalena Buch (2)Catherine — Pvt PA

MODERWELL,
John: b 1745 d 1818 m Nancy Ann Buchanan Pvt PA ★

MOE, (or MOW)
James: b 1740 d 11-16-1798 m Elizabeth Palmer Sol CT

MOFFATT, (includes MAFFITT, MOFFAT, MOFFETT, MOFFITT)
Alexander: b 1753 d 1-2-1826 m Ann Comfort Pvt NY ★
Aquilla: b 5-18-1740 d p. 1796 m Elizabeth — Sgt NH
Archibald, Sr.: b 11-20-1730 d 3-16-1817 m Elizabeth Clark Capt NJ
Charles: b c. 1751 d c. 1800-10 m Mary Cox PS NC
Daniel: b 8-2-1734 d p. 1800 m (1)Rebecca Burt (2)Mary Ann Allen Pvt MA
George: b 1735 d 1811 m Sarah Martha McDowell Col VA
Henry: b 1750 d p. 8-27-1828 m — Pvt SC
Jesse: b 1759 d 12-6-1836 m Elizabeth — Pvt VA ★
John: b 10-5-1760 d 1810 m Abigail Swift Pvt MA
John: b a. 1730 d 1792 m Jane McClung Maj VA
Joseph: b 7-2-1738 d 8-12-1802 m (1)Margaret Bliss (2)Lois Haynes Dr CS PS MA
Josiah: b 1739 d c. 1820 m (1)Martha Gass (2)Elizabeth — (3)Rachel — Capt VA
Hosea: b 11-17-1757 d 8-31-1825 m Elizabeth Hill Lt NY
Robert: b 3-17-1743 d 6- -1816 m Jane McDowell Capt VA
Samuel: b 5-24-1742 d 5-31-1815 m Ann Strawbridge Maj PS MD
Samuel: b 7-18-1704 d 5-17-1787 m (2)Annie Gregg PS NY
Sarah McDowell: b c. 1744 d p. 1811 m George Moffett PS VA
Thomas: -b 2-2-1761 d 3-18-1820 m Abigail Jordon Carpenter Sol GA
Thomas: b 11-19-1742 d 10-10-1805 m Susanna Howell Capt NY
Wm.: b c. 1734 d 9- -1776 m Mary Priest Pvt MA
Wm.: b 1726 d a. 9-16-1806 m Sarah Campbell Capt NJ
Wm.: b c. 1746 d 1816 m Rebecca Elliot Pvt PA
Wm.: b 1738 d 1-20-1794 m Barbara Chesnut Pvt SC
Wm.: b c. 1750 d 10-10-1774 m Mary Gardner Sol VA

MOHLER, (includes MOLER)
Adam: b c. 1735 d p. 11-9-1783 m Eve Horn PS VA
Henry: b 10-21-1754 d 5-12-1833 m — Pvt PA
Jacob: b 10-26-1751 d 3-26-1833 m Marie Bucher Pvt PA

John: b 9-16-1757 d 11-11-1821 m Ann Bollinger 1Lt PA
John: b a. 1743 d 12-19-1813 m Catherine Bowman Sol PA
John: b c. 1744 d p. 1785 m Catherine — Pvt PA

MOLAND,
Wm.: b 11-5-1749 d 4-24-1826 m Hannah Noble Dr CL

MOLL,
Heinrich: b 2- -1734 d 6- -1809 m Elizabeth Faust Pvt PA

MONCRIEF,
Richard, Jr.: b 8-10-1755 d 11-26-1801 m Elizabeth Young Lt PS SC

MONDAY, (includes MUNDAY & MUNDY)
Aaron: b 3-7-1762 d 9-8-1834 m Anne Sinclair Pvt VA ★
Gabriel: b 1-10-1760 d 8-25-1842 m (1)Phebe Kent (2)Margaret Trimback Pvt NJ ★
Henry: b 1752 d 10-1-1807 m Humy Ayres Pvt NJ
Isabel: b 1730 d 2-6-1809 m (1)Stephen Carmen (2)Moses Bloodgood (3)Edward Mundy PS NJ
Jeremiah: b 1760 d 9-12-1835 m Cloe Shelton Pvt VA ★
Nicholas: b 1740 d 3-1-1813 m Sarah — Pvt NJ
Robert: b c. 1750 d 1-13-1777 m Catherine Haney Pvt VA
Samuel: b 1730 d 5- -1801 m Elizabeth Griffith Sol NJ
Samuel: b 10-22-1755 d 11-13-1833 m (1)Elizabeth Barron (2)Abigail Rowland Pvt NJ

MONELL, (or MONNELL)
David: b c. 1754 d p. 1794 m Sally Hill Lt PS NY
James: b 1742-5 d 1790 m Janet Graham Lt NY

MONG,
Nicholas: b c. 1730 d 2- -1792 m Mary Catharine — PS MD

MONIN,
Adam: b c. 1747 d 2-22-1831 m Elizabeth — PS VA

MONK, (or MUNK)
Elias: b 1-2-1726 d a. 1804 m Elizabeth Buck Cpl MA
Elias: b 6-26-1753 d 12-17-1842 m (1)Alice Churchill (2)Louisa Ranson Pvt MA ★
George, Jr.: b 1-15-1764 d 9-27-1834 m (1)Lydia Packard (2)Amy Ball Sol MA
James: b 1760 d 4-29-1854 m Catherine — Pvt NC ★
John: b 1753-5 d 1846 m (3)Nancy (Cahoon) Calligan Pvt NY ★
Jonathan: b c. 1750 d p. 1790 m Mary Popwell Sol SC
Richard: b 1735 d 1805 m (1)Agness Taylor (2)Jane — PS MD
Wm.: b c. 1763 d p. 1815 m Jerusha Parrish Pvt GA
Willis: b 1759 d 1831 m Celia Pool Sol NC

MONNETT,
Abraham: b 3-16-1748 d 12-17-1810 m Ann Hillary Pvt MD
Isaac: b 1726 d p. 1798 m Elizabeth Osborne PS MD

MONROE, (includes MONROW, MUNRO & MUNROE)
Abraham: b 1747 d 3-11-1778 m Lydia Hapgood Sgt MA
Abraham: b 1759-62 d 7-17-1851 m (1)Priscill a— (2)Sarah — (3)Mary — Pvt MA ★
Alexander: b 1736 d 9-5-1807 m (1)Mary McIntosh (2)Mary Hutchinson Sgt MA
Alexander: b c. 1743 d 4-21-1823 m — Pvt NY ★
Alexander: b 1758 d 11-20-1842 m Betsy Chenoworth Sgt VA ★
Amos: b 5-31-1747 d 8-29-1820 m Anna Prouty Pvt MA
Andrew: b 3-30-1764 d 8-7-1836 m Ruth Simonds Sol MA
Andrew: b 1760 d 4- -1847 m Mary Dailey Pvt MA
Archibald: b 11-11-1746 d 1-15-1812 m Rebecca Smith Pvt RI
Benjamin: b 12-13-1752 d 9-24-1824 m (1)Abigail Monroe (2)Mary Washburn (3)Abigail Fullington Pvt MA
Benjamin: b 6-24-1722 d 3-23-1804 m Mary Merriam Capt MA
Benjamin: b 2-5-1735 d 2-22-1818 m Mary Ormsbee Pvt MA
Daniel: b 1758 d p. 1785 m Sarah Frazier Sol MA
Ebenezer: b 4-29-1752 d 5-25-1825 m Lucy Simonds Lt MM MA
Edmund: b 2-2-1736 d 6-28-1778 m Rebecca Harrington Capt MA
Edward: b 5-28-1747 d 3-10-1835 m Sarah Hoar Pvt RI ★
Elijah: b c. 1760 d p. 1790 m — DrmMaj MA
George: b c. 1732 d 6-28-1778 m Anna Bemis Pvt MM MA
George: b 9-26-1760 d 10-16-1837 m Sarah Forrest Sgt VA
Henry, Jr.: b 4- -1749 d 3- -1837 m Mary Miller Pvt MA
Isaac: b 1745 d 8-1-1825 m — Pvt CT ★
Isaac: b 9-11-1737 d 7-17-1791 m (1)Mary Hutchinson (2)Mrs Lydia Caldwell Pvt MA
James: b 1758 d 7-4-1831 m Elizabeth Kortwright LCol PS VA
Jamima Smith: b c. 1725 d 1786 m Wm Monroe PS VA
Jedediah: b 5-20-1721 d 4-19-1775 m Abigail Loring Pvt MA
John: b 6-15-1748 d 4- -1831 m Rebecca Wellington Pvt MA
John: b 1761 d 7-10-1846 m Hannah Gross Pvt MA
John: b 11-10-1749 d 5-25-1837 m Winifred Berryman Lt VA ★
John: b 1733 d 1785 m Sarah Harrison 2Lt VA
Jonas: b 1-25-1757 d 9-21-1840 m Sarah Henry Pvt MA
Joseph: b 1757 d 3-24-1824 m Rebekah — Pvt CT ★
Joseph: b 10-27-1750 d p. 1793 m Sarah Barto Cpl MA W★
Joseph, Jr.: b 1757 d 2-24-1798 m Azuba Henry Pvt MA
Joseph: b 8-20-1763 d 1815 m Hannah Betts Pvt NY

Joseph: b 3-12-1762 d 4-26-1849 m Mary Eddy Pvt Smn RI ★
Joshua: b 3-21-1764 d 5-16-1840 m (1)Hannah Willoughty
(2)Miriam Wales Pvt VT
Josiah, Jr.: b 2-25-1764 d 11-9-1846 m Susanna Andrus Pvt CT ★
Josiah, Sr.: b 9-11-1728 d 2-19-1778 m Sarah Hyde Sgt CT
Josiah: b 2-12-1745 d 9-17-1801 m Susanna Fitch Capt MA
Lemuel: b 3-17-1759 d 4-27-1854 m (3)Martha Rollins Pvt MA ★
Malcom: b 1761 d p. 9- -1832 m Anne Cameron Pvt NC ★
Marrett: b 12-6-1713 d 3-26-1798 m Deliverance Parker Pvt MA
Nathan: b 9-29-1730 d 3-6-1806 m Mrs Hannah Humphrey Allen
Sgt MA
Nathan: b 8-9-1747 d 5-26-1829 m Elizabeth Harrington MM MA
Nathan: b 10-3-1730 d 6-12-1801 m Sarah Kinnecutt NCapt RI
Nathan Benjamin: b 5-31-1760 d 5-20-1823 m Lucy Barritt Pvt MA
Nathaniel: b 1752 d 12-4-1838 m Martha Taylor Pvt RI
Noah: b 1729 d 5-5-1793 m Deborah Younglove Sol CT
Philemon: b 10-30-1753 d 10-17-1806 m (1)Elizabeth Waite
(2)Rhoda Mead Pvt MA
Reuben, Jr.: b 1757 d 1824 m — Bingham Pvt MA
Robert: b 5-4-1712 d 4-19-1775 m Anne Stone Ens MA
Rosbotham: b 2-9-1733/4 d 1831 m Letosia Loid Pvt MA
Samuel: b 9-9-1720 d 1-15-'1777 rn Abigail Read Pvt CT
Simon: b 1740/1 d 12-29-1790 m Elizabeth West PS GA
Shubel, Jr.: b 4-1-1761 d 10-3-1851 m Abigail Stetson Pvt MA
Squire: b 6-27-1758 d 3-31-1835 m Mary Daggett Pvt MA
Stephen: b 1-4-1758 d 9-10-1826 m Susannah Le Baron Pvt Srgn
Mte RI
Thaddeus: b 4-26-1762 d 4-9-1846 m Rebecca Locke MM MA
Thaddeus: b 5-4-1753 d 11-24-1828 m Hannah Richardson Pvt MA
Thomas: b 1748 d p. 1798 m Chloe Carpenter Pvt MA
Thomas: b 5-4-1731 d 9-12-1785 m Sarah Pearse Dr CT
Timothy: b 4-20-1735 d 1808 m Lydia Eaton Sgt MA
Timothy: b 1747 d 2-7-1836 m Lucretia Gates Sgt MA ★
Wm.: b 5-16-1761 d 4-30-1838 m (1)Sallie Barney (2)Rebecca W.
B. Printis Pvt Fif CT ★
Wm.: b 10-28-1742 d 5- -1827 m (1)Anna Smith (2)Mrs Polly Rogers
OrdlSgt MA
Wm.: b 3-29-1756 d 4-30-1837 m Abigail Harrington Pvt MA
Wm.: b 9-25-1741 d 8-14-1827 m Hannah Carey Cpl RI

MONRONEY,
Wm.: b c. 1750 d 1806 m — Lynn Sgt VA

MONTAGUE, (includes MONTIGUE)
Abraham: b 1728 d 12-17-1778 m Elizabeth Corrie CS VA
Adonijah: b 4-11-1757 d 10-8-1828 m Mary Simonds Pvt VT
Caleb: b 7-27-1731 d 11-11-1782 m Eunice Root Capt MA
Clement: b 12-29-1723 d 10-28-1791 m (1)Anna Bartlet (2)Hannah
— PS VA
Daniel: b 1-13-1725 d 8-24-1814 m Lydia Smith PS Sol MA
David: b 3-3-1757 d 1-21-1839 m Sarah Clark Pvt MA
John: b 1755 d 9-20-1831 m Rebecca Brown Sol VA
Jonathan: b 4-26-1745 d 10-19-1823 m Sarah Bidwell Pvt CT
Josiah: b 11-10-1727 d 7-11-1810 m Abigail Montague Pvt MA
Lewis: b — d a. 8-24-1778 m Bettie — PS VA
Medad: b 5-4-1755 d 10-2-1837 m (1)Ruth Dinsmore (2)Mrs Mary
Redding (3)Mrs Eunice Bangs Sol PS MA
Moses: b 11-17-1724 d 12-18-1792 m Sarah Graves Capt MA
Nathaniel: b 7-26-1745 d 11-4-1784 m Sarah Goodrich Pvt MA
Nathaniel: b 6-4-1759 d 1846/7 m (1)Lucy West (2)Leah Burlsils
(3)Mrs — Loomis Pvt VT ★
Peter: b 1732 d 1820 m Elizabeth Henderson Pvt VA ★
Philip: b 4-13-1736 d 1810 m Frances (Montague)Col VA
Rice Daniel: b 1765 d 4-3-1849 m (1)Judith Toler (2)Ann Bransome
(3)Nancy Adams Pvt VA ★
Richard: b 5-7-1729 d 2-21-1794 m Lucy Gunn Cooley Maj MA
Rufus: b 10-28-1762 d 6-14-1834 m Catherine Sandford Pvt VT
Samuel: b 6-30-1720 d 1-17-1777 m Elizabeth Montague PS VT
Samuel: b 1-15-1743 d 3-27-1826 m Lucy Safford Pvt VT
Seth: b 1-28-1756 d 11-15-1830 m Sybil Clark Pvt CT ★
Thomas: b 8-31-1750 d 1805 m Agnes Ellis 2Lt MA
Thomas: b 2-20-1719 d 1777 m Jane Daniel Sol VA
Uriel: b 9-30-1756 d 6- -1812 m Deborah Fay Dr SgtMaj MA
Wm.: b 1-11-1760 d 8-4-1839 m Perses Russell Pvt MA
Wm.: b 1758 d — m Elizabeth Valentine Sol VA

**MONTANYE, (includes MONTAYNE, MONTAGNE & DE LA
MONTAIGNE)**
Abraham: b 1740 d 11-10-1810 m Betsey Sterling Pvt NJ
Benjamin: b 6-26-1745 d 12-25-1825 m Betsy Norris PS NY
John: b c. 1740 d a. 10-19-1802 m — Pvt NY
John: b 1747 d 9-29-1829 m Mary Briggs Pvt NY
John: b 2- -1765 d 12-13-1820 m Mary Weldon Pvt NY
Peter: b 12-25-1757 d 1828 m Gertrude Keator Sgt NY
Peter: b 1-6-1723 d 6-20-1798 m Catherine Van der Hoef Pvt NY

MONTEITH,
Daniel: b 5- -1750 d 5-14-1826 m Sarah Lecky Lt PA
Wm.: b 1743 d 7-18-1820 m Isabel McGilchrist Pvt NY

MONTELIUS,
Marcus: b 10-25-1752 d 5-16-1805 m Christiana Bartholomea Sol PA

**MONTFORT, (includes MONFORT, MONFOORT &
MOUNTFORT)**
Domenicus: b 5-24-1743 d 8-11-1815/6 m Antonetta Van Kleeck
Pvt NY
Ebenezer: b 5-13-1759 d 2-12-1835 m Margaret (Bell)Bass Pvt MA
Elbert D.: b 4-22-1745 d 5-3-1815 m (1)Susannah Hoagland (2)
Susannah Montfort Pvt NY
George: b 1-19-1759 d 10-9-1824 m Phebe Burtis Pvt NY
John Peter: b 1-24-1759 d 11-15-1803 m Jane Bennett Pvt NY
John: b 7-28-1717 d 1796 m Kmerte — Pvt NY
Joost: b 5-25-1724 d 9-15-1779 m Catrina Duryea PS NY
Joseph: b 2-3-1750 d 8-11-1838 m Sarah Gyles Smn MA
Joseph: b 4-2-1728 d 4-27-1792 m (1) — Bower (2)Annie Sheperd
Capt NC
Lawrence: b 3-3-1753 d 7-4-1830 m Elizabeth Cassatt Pvt PA
Peter: b 3-14-1760 d 3-23-1840 m Mary Hoagland Sgt NJ ★
Peter: b 12-15-1759 d 5-11-1824 m Susan Waldron Pvt NY PS NY
Peter: b 1731 d 1791 m (2)Margaret Schenck Pvt PS NY

MONTGOMERY,
Alexander: b 1762 d 4-26-1840 m (1)Rebecca Peabody (2)Mrs Mary
Sarah Porter Pvt MA
Alexander: b 12-21-1743 d 1-9-1837 m (2)Lydia Cox Pvt PA ★
Alexander: b c. 1762 d 11- -1812 m (1)Katherine King (2)Lydia
Swayze Pvt SC
Alexander: b 1750 d 1814 m Elizabeth Robertson CS VA
Alexander: b 1754 d 4-14-1800 m Margaret — Pvt VA
Anne: b 1736 d 1808 m Wm. Lewis PS VA
Archibald: b — d 1789 m Martha Campbell Pvt PA
Burnett: b 12-7-1752-5 d 1-3-1834 m Charlotte Hendrickson Sgt
NJ ★
Charles: b 1748 d 1820 m Margaret Reynolds Pvt SC
Francis: b 9-15-1749 d 7-16-1828 m Mary Smith Ens VA
Henry: b 1-27-1750 d 6-14-1833 m Susannah Beatty Pvt NH ★
Hugh: b 8- -1755 d 3-17-1834 m Anna Sampson Pvt MA
Hugh: b 1760 d 1-6-1842 m Elizabeth Tousley Cpl MA ★
Hugh: b 11-10-1750 d 6-5-1840 m Mary Campbell Pvt NH
Hugh: b 9-10-1752 d 5-27-1819 m Hannah Mack Pvt NH
Hugh: b 1720 d 12-23-1779 m Katherine Sloan Moore PS NC
Hugh: b c. 1736 d 2- -1804 m (1)Janet Johnson (2)Jane Reese Pvt
PA
Hugh: b — d a. 10-22-1785 m X PS Pvt SC
Hugh: b 2-29-1754 d 5-20-1830 m Eva Hartman Pvt VA ★
Humphrey: b a. 1760 d 12- -1798 m Jane Gay Pvt VA
James: b 1736 d 1-1-1808 m (1)Elizabeth McConnell (2)Susannah
Strange 2Lt GA
James: b 11-22-1755 d 6- -1832 m Ellen Reading Lt NJ
James: b 5-15-1739 d 6-20-1825 m Margaret Scott Sgt NY W★
James: b — d 3-4-1810 m (1)Margaret Bowes (2)Hester Griffith
NCapt PA
James: b c. 1730 d p. 8-23-1810 m X Pvt PA
James: b 5-7-1744 d 7-9-1820 m Eleanor Means Pvt PA
James: b c. 1720 d p. 8-17-1791 m Margaret McClelland CS SC
James: b c. 1744 d — m Mary Robertson Capt PS CS VA
James: b 2-12-1757 d 1809 m Cyntha Patsy Dosier Lt VA
John: b 6-18-1760 d 3-2-1846 m Joshan Sedwick Sgt PS MD ★
John, Sr.: b 1730-8 d 3-4-1802 m Mary Knox Pvt MA
John: b 10-4-1763 d 6-16-1854 m Julia Ann Howard Grd MA ★
John: b 1740 d 6-23-1785 m Lydia Winslow Pvt MA
John: b 7-17-1750 d 3-16-1794 m Mary E. Crathome Pvt PA NJ
John: b a. 1758 d p. 1782 m Fannie Green Pvt NY
John: b 1732 d 2-2-1818 m Mary Willcox PS NC
John: b 6-7-1718 d 9-3-1806 m (1)Sidney Smith (2)Sarah Diemer
Rolfe Col PS PA
John: b 1733 d 11-8-1792 m Christiana Foster Pvt PA
John: b 1729 d 12-4-1794 m — Pvt PA
John: b c. 1750 d 1814 m Rosa Roddy Pvt PA
John: b 1751 d 1844 m Jane Beattie Pvt VT
John: b 8-5-1764 d 1-26-1845 m (1)Susanna Porter (2)Elizabeth
Harris Pvt VA ★
John: b 1717 d 1802 m Ann Agnes Crockett PS CS VA
Joseph: b 9-23-1733 d 10-14-1799 m Elizabeth Reed Chp PA
Michael: b 1755 d 2-5-1836 m Nancy — Pvt PA
Neinon, Sr.: b c. 1735 d p. 1810 m — PS SC
Neinon, Jr.: b 1765 d 11-30-1845 m Jane Davis Pvt SC
Robert: b 9-18-1754 d 3-28-1811 m Jean Herdman Lt DE
Robert: b 10-26-1737 d 12-26-1822 m Elizabeth Cooper Pvt MA
Robert: b 7-13-1741 d 10-15-1822 m Mary White Pvt MA
Robert: b c. 1720 d 1797/8 m (1)Rachel Lawrence (2)Phoebe Husted
PS NJ
Robert: b 2-23-1758 d 10-31-1808 m Mary Jones PS NC
Robert: b 1740 d 1806 m Nancy Montgomery Pvt PA
Robert: b c. 1752 d 8-9-1815 m Jane Howard Pvt PA
Samuel: b 1732 d p. 1808 m Elizabeth McElroy Capt PA
Samuel: b 1756 d 10-15-1819 m Jane Spry Pvt PS SC
Samuel: b 1743 d 1815 m Polly McFarland Pvt VA
Samuel: b 1721 d 1797 m Margaret Nichols Pvt VA
Thomas: b c. 1750 d — m Martha — Sgt MA
Thomas: b 1748 d 8-30-1834 m (1)Nancy Johnson Pvt PA
Thomas: b 1748 d 1830 m Mary Patton Pvt PA
Thomas: b 1743 d 1818 m Martha Crockett Lt VA
Thomas, Sr.: b 9-9-1740 d 9-9-1823 m Polly Ann — Pvt VA
Wm.: b 1751 d 1825 m Nancy Nichols Pvt DE

MONTGOMERY, contd.
Wm.: b 1750 d 1815 m Mary Rhea Maj NJ
Wm.: b 8-3-1736 d 6-1-1816 m (1)Margaret Nevin (2)Isabella Evans (3)Hannah Boyd Col PA
Wm.: b 1755 d 1805 m Ann Reid Pvt PA
Wm., Sr.: b 1727 d 3- -1780 m Jane Patterson PS KY
Wm.: b c. 1762 d 4-20-1815 m Agnes Barkley Pvt SC
Wm.: b c. 1756 d 8- -1794 m Margaret Greenlee Pvt VA
Wm.: b c. 1756 d c. 1825 m (2)Mrs Priscilla (Graham) Bryant Pvt VA

MONTROSS,
David: bpt 4-25-1724 d a. 3-5-1807 m — Capt NY
John: b 1752 d 10-12-1797 m Phebe — Ens NY

MONTY,
Francis: b — d 2-8-1809 m Lizzie — Lt NY ★
Francis, Jr.: b c. 1760 d 10-8-1818 m — Pvt NY
John: b 1771 d 1860 m Sarah Clark Mus NY ★

MOOBERRY,
Wm.: b 9-18-1752 d 1-28-1829 m Elizabeth Ramsey PS PA

MOODY, (includes MOODEY & MOODIE)
Asahel: b 7-7-1736 d 8-9-1813 m Beulah Graves Pvt CS MA
Benjamin: b 3-5-1762 d 1-9-1847 m Abigail George Pvt MA ★
Benjamin: b 4-30-1739 d 1-6-1805 m Jace — Pvt MA
Daniel: b 1738 d 1794 m Rebecca Lyon Pvt MA
Daniel: b 12-12-1735 d 2-2-1804 m Esther — Pvt CS NH
Ebenezer: b 1-9-1743/4 d — m Zerviah Seymour Ens CT
Ebenezer: b 9-10-1744 d 6-23-1833 m Lois Smith Sgt MA
Edward: b 10- -1757 d 1834 m Mehitable Brown Pvt NH ★
Elisha: b 1-14-1738 d 1-17-1825 m Elizabeth Nash Pvt MA
Enoch: b 12-23-1713 d 1777 m (1)Dorcas Cox (2)Ann Weeks PS CS MA
George: b c. 1760 d 10-25-1840 m (1)Mary Hughes (2)Rachel (Mitchell) Pvt VA
Gideon: b 1762 d 1849 m Susanna Hathaway Drm Pvt CT ★
Humphrey: b 4-19-1738 d 1793 m Abigail Peaseley Pvt MA
James: b c. 1750 d 1-4-1818 m Elizabeth Shaw Pvt MA
James: b c. 1750 d 1847 m (1)Elizabeth Reed (2)Mary Herron Pvt PA
James: b a. 1760 d p. 1787 m — Whitefield Capt VA
Jeremiah: b a. 1742 d 1783 m Elizabeth — Sol VA
John: b 6-18-1760 d 6-27-1823 m Hannah Copeland Pvt MA W ★
John: b 1-27-1739 d 9-15-1829 m (1)Abigail Swett (2)Mrs Elizabeth Evans White (3)Mrs Hannah Gale Capt NH
Joseph: b 1-13-1712 d 9-15-1803 m Sarah Kellogg PS MA
Joseph: b 9-20-1760 d 10-3-1842 m Bridget Davis Pvt MA W ★
Josiah: b 8-7-1748 d 10-25-1828 m Mary Elmer Pvt MA
Moses: b 1-22-1765 d 5-5-1833 m Elizabeth Buckmaster Pvt MA
Nathaniel Peaslee: b 9-13-1760 d 1832 m (1)Susan Griffin (2)Catherine Tracey Pvt MA
Paul: b 1-20-1743 d 12-30-1822 m Sarah Jewett Capt MA
Phillip, Sr.: b c. 1724 d p. 11-14-1786 m Ruth — PS VA
Philip, Jr.: b c. 1739 d 1783 m Sarah Holleman 1Lt VA
Robert: b 1748 d 4-15-1828 m Mary Hutchinson Lt PA
Robert: b 1752 d 12-13-1838 m Mary (Hutchison)Pvt PA
Samuel: b 10-5-1731 d 2-14-1790 m Jane Dole Lt MA
Samuel: b 4-18-1732 d 1804 m Hanna Severance Pvt MA
Samuel: b 1758 d 1836 m Catherine Quimby Sgt NH★
Seth: b 9-28-1752 d 10-14-1837 m Mary Pomeroy Pvt MM MA
Thomas: b 1-9-1759 d 1856 m Mary Frances Young Pvt PA
Wm.: b 4-2-1710 d p. 1781 m (2)Mary — (3)Elizabeth — PS MD
Wm.: b 4-20-1740 d 1-5-1828 m Rachel (Hodgkins)Gloue Sgt MA
Wm.: b 10-2-1752 d 12-12-1798 m — Moody Pvt VA
Wm. Pepperell: b 11-16-1741 d 8-3-1787 m Elizabeth Scammon Pvt MA

MOON,
Archelaus: b a. 1756 d c. 5-8/7-17-1796 m (1)— Higbee (2)Ann Anderson 1Lt PS VA
Benoni: b c. 1755 d 1810 m (2)Hannah Reynolds Pvt NY
Dake: b 11-29-1759 d p. 1801 m Lydia Waite Pvt RI
Gideon: b c. 1740 d 1790 m Mary — PS CS VA
Henry: b c. 1760 d p. 11-3-1821 m Mrs Sarah Wilson Pvt PA
Jacob, Sr.: b 1727 d p. 1785 m Mildred Cobb Lt PS VA
Jacob, Jr.: b a.1754 d 3-19-1781 m Ann or (Nancy) Ammon Ens PM VA W ★
Thomas: b 3-9-1755 d 4-25-1851 m (1)Lydia Bly (2)Deborah Hoxie (3)Mary — Pvt NY
Wm.: b 5-3-1768 d 3-18-1833 m Martha Knewstep Sol SC
Wm.: b — d 1830 m Martha Glenn Pvt SC
Wm.: b — d 1800 m Elizabeth Martin Smn VA

MOONEY, (includes MONEY)
Benjamin: b 1-6-1740 d 1798 m Hannah Burnham Lt NH
Hercules: b c. 1710 d 4- -1800 m (1)Elizabeth Evans (2)Mary Jones Col PS NH
Johnathan: b 1744 d 7-23-1823 m Patience Gould Pvt MA
Martin: b 7- -1753 d 12-27-1836 m Patsy Gray Pvt NC ★
Nicholas: b 6-14-1727d 1799 m Mary Yeates Sol VA
Nicholas Carroll: b 2-16-1754 d 8-24-1831 m Jemima Reeve Pvt VA

MOORE, (includes MOHR, MOOAR, MOOERS, MOORS, MORE & MORR)
Aaron: b c. 1740 d a. 10- -1782 m Ann — Capt NC
Abigail Hempstead Ledyard (Mrs): b 1728 d 3-7-1805 m (1) John Ledyard (2)Micah Moore PS NY
Abijah: b 4-27-1752 d 4-26-1825 m Abigail Drake Pvt CT
Abijah: b 8-31-1724 d 4-18-1792 m Eunice Gibbs Capt MA
Abner: bpt 12-16-1739 d 3-11-1808 m X Pvt MA
Abraham: b 3-6-1748 d 3-7-1803 m Sarah Johnson Dr MA
Abraham: b 1-14-1728 d 1780 m Martha Allen Pvt MA
Abraham: b 1749 d 2-15-1823 m Esther Walker Sgt NH
Abram: b 9-1-1756 d p. 1833 m Elizabeth — MM Pvt VA MD ★
Alexander, Sr.: b 9- -1704 d 9-5-1786 m Sarah Reeves CS NJ
Alexander: b 1-13-1753 d 11-24-1837 m Elizabeth Robinson Pvt NC ★
Alexander: b 1756 d 1816 m Dorcas Erwin Capt SC
Alexander Spotswood: b 1763 d 1799 m Elizabeth Aylett Lt VA
Alfred: b 5-21-1755 d 10-15-1810 m Susan Eagles Capt NC
Andrew: b 7-17-1743 d 6-9-1776 m Thankful Phelps Lt CT
Andrew: b 4-30-1727 d 1801 m (1)Catherine Elizabeth (2)Mrs Anna Maria Dewald PS PA
Andrew: b 12-1-1733 d 5- -1801 m Rebecca Starr Pvt PA
Andrew: b 10-21-1752 d p. 1793 m Jane Downing Pvt PA
Andrew: b 6-9-1758 d 4-20-1845 m Elizabeth Shepherd PS PA
Andrew: b 5-1-1742 d 1805 m Ruth Birdsall Pvt PA
Andrew: b 1752 d 1821 m Sally Reid Capt VA
Anthony: b 1732 d 11-18-1822 m Margaret Copeland Pvt PA
Apollos: b 1765 d 1-15-1841 m (1)Elizabeth Jackson (2)Deborah Stone Pvt MA ★
Archelaus: b 4-6-1722 d 1795 m Hannah Elkins PS CS NH
Asa: b 1753 d p. 1790 m Abigail — Pvt CT
Asa: b 6-29-1762 d 1-22-1848 m Huldah King Pvt CT ★
Asa: b 1-15-1738 d 8-2-1822 m Eunice Thomas Pvt MA
Augustine: b c. 1750 d p. 1790 m Verlinda Dawson Col VA
Augustus: b 3-3-1746 d p. 1781 m Ruth Plympton Sgt MA
Barton: b c. 1757 d p. 1811 m Priscilla Rawlings Pvt MD
Benjamin: b 4-1-1758 d 2-20-1838 m Hannah Platt Lt MA
Benjamin, Sr.: b 2-18-1715/6 d 11- -1777 m Abiah Hill Pvt MA
Benjamin, Jr.: b 10-28-1743 d 8- -1828 m Hannah Pelps Sgt MA
Benjamin: b 1724 d 1799 m Abigail Hazen Lt MA
Benjamin: b 9-28-1758 d 5-16-1826 m Aphia Baker Ens NH
Benjamin: b 3-22-1754 d 2-4-1836 m (1)Kezia Frazee (2)Mary Smalley (3)Eunice Tingley Pvt NJ ★
Bernard, Sr.: b 1718 d a. 1800 m (1)Anne Catherine Spottswood PS CS VA
Caleb: b c. 1760 d 4-3-1821 m Unicy — Sol NC
Cato: b 1752 d a. 7-24-1797 m Margaret Cooke 1Lt VA
Charles: b 1741 d 9-21-1827 m Esther Bidwell Sgt NY
Charles, Sr.: b 9-30-1732 d 1790 m (1)Mary — (2)Sarah Hunter Maj PS NC
Charles: b 1-11-1763 d 9-19-1839 m Martha Cunningham Pvt NC ★
Charles: b 4-15-1761 d p. 11-30-1834 m Betsey — Pvt NC ★
Charles: b 1727 d 12-31-1804 m Mary — PS SC
Clement: b c. 1762-5 d 1-13-1846 m Elizabeth Morris Sol GA
Cleon: b 1752 d 1808 m Margaret Cooke Capt VA
Comfort: b 8-17-1745 d c. 1785 m Chloe Read Pvt MA
Daniel: b — d 1792 m Mary — Sol MD
Daniel: b 8-18-1755 d 7-28-1832 m Elizabeth Cook Pvt MA
Daniel: b 3-2-1764 d 4-15-1822 m Priscilla Newcomb Pvt MA
Daniel: b 2-11-1730 d 4-13-1811 m Nancy Cox Col PS NH
Daniel: b 6-21-1738 d 7-29-1820 m (1)Margaret White (2)Elizabeth White Capt NH ★
Daniel: b 8-18-1751 d 2-24-1835 m Rebecca Kerenhappuch Pvt NJ
Daniel: b 1752 d 2-4-1817 m Anne Russell Pvt NJ
Daniel: b 1728 d 4-28-1792 m X Pvt NJ
Daniel: b 1708 d 5-10-1791 m Anne Sayre PS NY
Daniel: b 12-12-1764 d 10-11-1845 m (1)Rachel Stone (2)Rachel Carroll Pvt NC ★
Daniel: b 8-30-1750 d 9-22-1827 m Elizabeth Hamilton Cpl PA
Daniel: c. 1758 d 9- -1811 m Martha — PS VA
David: b 6-21-1722 d 4- -1784 m Hannah Parker Capt MA
David: b 10-21-1729 d 2-25-1794 m Ellanor Rice Capt MA
David: b 1762 d 1-30-1847 m Marabah Hatch Pvt Mar MA ★
David: b 11-22-1743 d 11-7-1831 m Jennet — Pvt PS NH
David: b 11-25-1749 d p. 1790 m (1)Bathia Cutler (2)Rachel Haden Pvt NJ
David, Sr.: b 11-25-1713 d 6-18-1789 m Hepzibah Wilmot PS NY
David, Jr.: b 12-9-1734 d 8-4-1805 m Mary Mapes Pvt NY
David: b 1735 d 6-19-1803 m Elizabeth Milton Pvt PA
David: b 10-13-1745 d 1-16-1829 m Martha Williams Pvt PA
David: b 7-25-1752 d 10-31-1839 m (1)Lydia Wheeler (2)Sarah Prentic (3)Keziah Ames Sgt RI
David, Sr.: b 1722 d 8- -1783 m Mary Evans Sol VA
Ebenezer: b 9-7-1751 d 4-10-1817 m Sarah (Moore) Pvt MA
Edward: b 1728 d p. 1790 m Martha Thompson PS NC
Edward: b c. 1755 d 5-7-1806 m Helen McDonald PS VA
Eli: b 10-14-1753 d 12-29-1800 m Anne Welles Adj CT
Eliab: b 1751 d 3-7-1827 m Rebecca Bryant Pvt SC
Elijah: b 1732 d 1806 m Susan Mitchell Capt NC W ★
Elisha: b 12-7-1739 d 3- -1819 m Hannah Moore QM CT
Elizabeth Whitehill: b 1733 d 6-25-1815 m James Moore PS PA
Ely: b 1745 d 10-1-1812 m Elizabeth Hoff Ens NJ

Ephriam: b 8-23-1743 d 3-13-1845 m Priscilla Riggen Pvt DE
Ephriam: b 6-5-1729 d — m (1)Hannah Rogers (2)Jennie Moore Pvt PS NH
Ezekiel: bpt 11-3-1763 d 1789 m Mary Barnard Gould Pvt MA
Ezekiel: b 3-4-1763 d 1840 m (1)Eliza Morril (2)Mary Morrill Pvt NH
Fergus: b 1-18-1751 d 4-20-1806 m Elizabeth Pvt PA
Francis: b — d p. 8-15-1792 m X PS VA
Frederick: b 3-17-1745 d 9-14-1819 m Catherine Bogert Pvt PA
George: b 10- -1749 d 7-18-1848 m Nancy Ball Pvt MD ★
George: b 1716 d 1778 m (1)Mary Ashe (2)Sarah Jones PS CS NC
George L: b c. 1750 d 1818 m Mary Phillips PS NC
Gershom: b 1-14-1752 d 5-7-1820 m Anna Moor Tms NJ
Gideon: b 4-4-1760 d 7- -1814 m Rhoda Smith Pvt PS NY
Goffe: b 12-4-1760 d 9-28-1850 m (1)Betsey Fowler (2)Betsey Gray McKenney Pvt NH
Harvey: b 7-12-1741 d 5- -1801 m Mary Wiggin Lt NH
Henry: b 12-19-1719 d 4-24-1783 m Temperance Conklin PS NY
Henry: b c. 1745 d 1829 m X PS NC
Henry: b 1741 d 9-10-1795 m Hannah — Pvt PA
Henry: b 5-29-1753 d 7-31-1829 m Priscilla Hill Jackson Pvt PA
Henry: b 3-25-1755 d 1835 m Jane Roberson CaptLt SC
Henry: b 10-7-1744 d p. 1802 m Jean Ross Lt SC
Herman: b 3-27-1754 d 2-8-1840 m Anna Margaret Diebert Pvt PA
Hosea: b 12-26-1763 d 4-25-1832 m Isabella Pvt NH
Hugh: b c. 1742 d 3-2-1814 m Margaret Nesmith Pvt NH
Hugh: b 9-15-1750 d 10-24-1833 m Sarah — Lt SC ★
Humphrey: b 8-24-1742 d 12-19-1790 m Mary Sweetser Cpl MA
Isaac: bpt 5-27-1753 d 8-15-1843 m Hannah Studley MM Sgt MA ★
Isaac: b 9-8-1748 d 1-5-1825 m Mary Bigelow Cpl MA
Isaac: b c. 1752 d c. 1833 m Sarah Smalley Pvt NJ
Isaac: b 1745 d 9-20-1803 m Mary — Capt NC
Isham: b 1740 d 4-21-1803 m Nancy Singleton Lt SC
Jacob: b 1730 d 1793 m Hannah Steele Pvt DE
Jacob: b 4-8-1761 d 2-2-1823 m (1)Hannah Shattuck (2)Dorcas Hood Pvt NH
James: b c. 1755 d p. 1830 m — Pvt GA
James: b c. 1750 d a. 10-12-1830 m Bertha Hutchinson Gnr MD
James: b 5-21-1742 d 2-27-1798 m Mary Rider PS MD
James: b c. 1748 d a. 8-19-1794 m Ann Kerby PS MD
James: b 6-20-1741 d 7-15-1820 m (1)Rebecca Jones (2)Lucina Belnap Sgt MA
James: b 1755 d a. 9-16-1834 m (1)Mary Henry (2)Lucy Day Pease Pvt MA
James: b 10-17-1757 d 7-15-1814 m Margaret Anderson Pvt NH W ★
James: b 1761 d 8-27-1835 m Abigail Noyes Pvt NH ★
James: b 4-6-1764 d 2-6-1843 m Molly Brown Tms NH ★
James: b 8-3-1750 d p. 1799 m Mary Carson Pvt NJ
James: b — d p. 1781 m Helena Bogardus Capt NY
James: b 1747 d 1-21-1833 m Isabella Stewart Lt NY W ★
James: b 1725 d 1-23-1787 m Mary Harper Pvt PS NY
James: b 1737 d 4-9-1777 m Ann Ivey BGen NC
James: b 11-14-1729 d p. 1781 m Ann Thomson 1Maj NC
James: b c. 1735 d p. 1790 m (1)Elizabeth Yeaman (2)Elizabeth House Lt NC
James: b c. 1755 d — m Susanne Epperson Lt NC
James: b — d 5-19-1781 m Martha Watkins Pvt NC
James: b 2- -1749 d p. 1-6-1834 m — Pvt NC ★
James: b 1-7-1765 d 12-31-1851 m (1)Martha Williams (2)Sally (Lewis) Lowe (3)Mary Council Smn Sol NC
James: b c. 1740 d p. 1-4-1804 m Mrs Margaret McAden McIntyre CS NC
James: b 1756 d 5-20-1813 m Sarah Sharp Delany BrevetLCol PA
James: b 1755 d a. 10-18-1825 m Sarah —1Lt PA
James: b 5-16-1751 d 3-14-1838 m Mary Carmicheal OrdlSgt PA ★
James: b 1736 d 2-4-1820 m — Pvt PA ★
James: b c. 1751 d p. 1785 m — Robinson Pvt PA
James: b 4-22-1753 d p. 1780 m Mary Wilkinson Pvt PA
James: b 1-8-1760 d 9-17-1834 m Lydia Sharpless Pvt PA
James: b 1760 d 1814 m Mary Lyle Pvt PA
James: b 1757-62 d 1819 m Amy Crow Pvt PA ★
James: b 1730 d 3-31-1802 m Elizabeth Creswell Whitehall PS PA
James: b c. 1750 d c. 1782 m Ann Davis Dep QM Gen SC
James: b 12-10-1764 d 8- -1847 m Mary Moore Pvt SC
James: b 1747 d 7-14-1786 m Martha Poague Capt VA
James: b 2-14-1750 d 1788 m Katherine Briggs Capt VA
James: b 1729 d — m Ellen Carter Cpl VA
James L: b 3-24-1756 d 8-29-1837 m Mary Kirby Pvt NY
Jecemiah: b c. 1760 d a. 11-2-1825 m Nancy — Sol GA
Jeremiah: b 6-7-1746 d 2-23-1815 m Lydia Reno Cpl VA
Jesse: b 4-11-1743 d 3-10-1827 m Alley Johnson PS NC
Jesse: b 1763 d p. 8-18-1840 m (1)Elizabeth Peace (4)Rebecca Matthews Pvt VA
Joel Forbus: b 1758 d 8-24-1814 m Rosanna Phelps Pvt CT W ★
John, Sr.: b 1717 d 5-22-1787 m Sarah Bliss Pvt CT
John: b 1-8-1758 d 1823 m Mary Lewis Pvt GA
John: b 1760 d 1819 m Marcy McCall Sol GA
John: b c. 1754 d a. 6- -1793 m — Pvt MD
John: b 1760 d 1793 m Elizabeth Cadle Pvt MD
John: b 11-28-1738 d 5- -1793 m Esther Bigelow Sol PS MA
John: b — d 1816/17 m Mary Gurnsy Pvt MA

John: b 5-3-1746 d 10-30-1831 m Persis Gates Pvt MA
John: b 12-25-1747 d 3-15-1832 m Hannah Sawtell Pvt MA W ★
John, Jr.: b 1748 d 9-3-1823 m Anna Milliken Pvt MA
John: b 11-28-1731 d 1- -1809 m (1)Margaret Goffe (2)Mrs Eunice Farnsworth Weston Maj NH
John: b 4-9-1696 d 4-10-1786 m Hannah Sias PS NH
John: b 1706 d 1779 m Margaret Jack PS NH
John: b 1748 d 1810 m Abiah Stevens PS NH
John: b 6-6-1746 d 3-27-1815 m Sarah Carpenter Sgt PS NJ
John: b 3-3-1738 d 2-22-1800 m Rachel — Pvt NJ
John: b 2-24-1745 d 1-1-1840 m Betty Taylor Pvt NY
John, 3rd: b 1752 d 3-9-1843 m Leah Groome Pvt NY ★
John: b c. 1735-37 d 2-6-1811 m Mehetabel Havens PS NY
John: b 1752 d p. 1810 m Polly Henry Pvt NC
John: b 1-1-1758 d 4-25-1852 m Mrs Rebecca Fletcher Leslie Pvt NC
John: b 9-5-1761 d 1-6-1842 m Eleanor Marbrey Pvt NC ★
John: b 1759 d 1836 m (1)Annie Adair (2)Mrs Mary Scott PS NC
John: b c. 1740 d a. 11-1-1800 m — Pvt NC
John: b 7-5-1737 d 5-20-1801 m Margaret Colvin Capt PA
John: b 2-1-1761 d 3-17-1854 m Rebecca Curran Capt PA
John: b 7-19-1741 d 2-20-1816 m Hannah Armstrong Pvt PA
John: b 1746 d 1779 m Rebecca Moore Pvt PA
John: b 11-27-1755 d 4-5-1826 m Ann Maria Vogel Pvt PA
John: b 1769 d 8-15-1842 m Nancy Morrow Drm PA W ★
John: b 1738 d 2-10-1811 m Elizabeth Parr CS PS PA
John: b 1756 d 1810 m Priscilla — Capt SC
John: b 1758 d 6-26-1835 m (1) — Wheeler (2)Sarah Sylvester Pvt SC
John: b 1-25-1762 d 12-12-1828 m Jane Patton Pvt SC W ★
John: b 2-22-1752 d 4-16-1830 m (1)Mary Black (2)Elizabeth Kimbro Lt VA
John: b 5-15-1750 d 9-11-1814 m Martha Harvie Lt VA
John: b 1720 d 5-14-1814 m Mary Bullock Pvt VA
John: b 12-22-1763 d 7-2-1815 m Jane — Pvt VA
John: b — d 1798 m Nancy Lee Mstr VA
John George: b 8-3-1761 d 10-18-1817 m Catharine Diefenback Pvt PA
John Johannes: b 1-11-1711 d 1-29-1788 m Miss Peters PS PA
Johan, Sr.: b 3-25-1735 d 11-28-1813 m Mary Ridout Pvt CT
Jonathan: b 11-11-1744 d 2-13-1830 m Mary Freeze Pvt MA
Jonathan: b 4-21-1756 d 3-26-1829 m Relief Nutting Pvt MA ★
Jonathan: b 4-21-1756 d p. 1801 m Deborah Houghton Pvt MA
Jonathan: b 1-12-1754 d 9-25-1853 m Elizabeth Long Pvt NY ★
Joseph: b 8-1-1747 d 1804 m Martha — Sgt MA
Joseph: b 7-21-1720 d 11-3-1776 m Mary Stevens Lt CT
Joseph, Sr.: b 5-30-1738 d 7-25-1820 m (1)Lucy Stone (2)Sarah Ward Capt MA
Joseph, Jr.: b 10-13-1761 d 3-5-1849 m Margaret Lynde Pvt MA
Joseph: b 5-2-1736 d p. 7-26-1777 m (1)Margaret Kellogg (2)Hannah Phelps MM Sgt MA
Joseph: b 1764 d 2-19-1846 m Hannah Miller Pvt MA ★
Joseph: b 5-9-1744 d 8-5-1827 m Zibea Gillett CS MA ★
Joseph: b 10-26-1751 d 1830 m Rachel Tucker Pvt NJ ★
Joseph: b 4-4-1744 d 1-29-1823 m (1)Abigail Fitch (2)Hannah — PS NY
Joseph: b 1756 d 9-27-1838 m (1)Celia Stanford (2)Elizabeth Sheppard Maj NC
Joseph: b 7-13-1736 d 7-13-1805 m Jane Marsh Pvt MA
Joseph: b a. 1746 d c. 1807 m Susan Brown Pvt PA
Joseph: b 7-24-1761 d 4-13-1858 m Sarah Van Dyke Pvt PA
Joseph: b 2-24-1740 d 3-18-1791 m Sarah Ivy Pvt VA
Joshua: b 9-6-1742/3 d 2-15-1816 m Jane Patten Pvt NH
Josiah: b 1737 d p. 1782 m Anna Gillette Lt CT
Josiah: b 4- -1739 d 1812 m Abigail Richardson Pvt MA
Josiah: b c. 1755 d 8-30-1828 m Mercy Wade Pvt MA
Judah, Jr.: b 7-18-1755 d 3-17-1844 m (1)Mary Mac Master (2)Mrs Dorothy Shaw (3)Beulah F Gillett Pvt MA ★
King: b 5-18-1762 d 4-15-1857 m (1)Rebecca Mitchell (2)Susan Tarbox Pvt NY ★
Laurence: b 1753/4 d p. 11-4-1816 m (1)Mary Rutledge (2)Tabitha Lockhart Moore Sol NC
Lawson: b 5- -1756 d 12-20-1847 m Lydia Goodnow Pvt MA ★
Levi: b 5-23-1732 d 1815 m Rebecca Sawyer PS MA
Luke: b 8-21-1736 d 5- -1836 m Lucy Estabrook Sgt MA
Luther: b 1754 d 2-1-1826 m Abigail Maynard Pvt MA
Mark: b 5-4-1749 d 3-28-1832 m (1)Lucy Stone (2)Sarah Briant Pvt MA
Martin: b 1734 d 1785 m Mary Hassinger PS PA
Mary: b 1-23-1733 d 4-10-1798 m James Moore PS NY
Mathew: b a. 1755 d p. 10-6-1824 m Prudence Sol NC
Mathew: b 1738 d 1801 m Letitia Dalton PS NC
Michael: b 1742 d 1785 m Deborah Roseberry Pvt PA
Michael: b c. 1760 d 6-1-1840 m Jane Lewis Pvt PA
Michael: b 1756 d 1849 m Juretter Bohannon Pvt VA
Moses: b 1740 d 1805 m Mary Coryell Lt NJ
Moses: b c. 1751/2 d 1802 m Ann — Pvt NC
Moses: b 1725 d 1807 m Mary Clendennin QMSgt VA
Moses: b 1740 d c. 1810 m — Elliott Pvt VA
Moses Hazen: b 4-26-1756 d 3-8-1813 m Jemima Jackman Sgt MA
Nathan: b 3-10-1762 d 6-3-1848 m Mercey Bruce Pvt MA
Nathaniel: b 1732 d 6-13-1817 m Mary Eaton Pvt CT
Nathaniel: b 5-16-1733 d 1817 m Eliza Morrill PS NH
Nathaniel: b 1735 d 11-4-1798 m Eleanor Van Brunt Sgt NJ

MOORE, contd.

Nathaniel: b 1724 d — m Mary Webb Pvt PS NC
Nathaniel: b 12-10-1757 d 6-23-1829 m Frances Taylor Pvt NC
Nicholas Ruxton: b 7-21-1756 d 10-7-1816 m Sarah Kelso Capt MD
Paul: b 3-31-1711 d 2-20-1799 m Hannah Hubbard Pvt MA
Paul: b 11-22-1731 d 7-2-1809 m Sarah Larrabee PS VT
Peter: b 1750 d *p.* 10-12-1820 m (1)Sarah Littleton (2)Mary Ellis Capt VA
Peter: b 1740 d 5- -1797 m Mary Magdalena Stauffer Pvt PA
Peter: b 1750 d 1827 m Jeany Murtland Pvt PA
Peter: b *c.* 1750 d 7-1-1818 (2)Margaret Love Capt VA W ★
Peterus: b 11-4-1743 d 5- -1813 m Chrystina Bender Pvt NY
Philip, Sr.: b 1726 d 1810 m Eleanor Evans CS NJ
Philip, Jr.: b 1755 d 9-3-1823 m Jemima Roby Pvt NJ
Phineas: b 2-6-1748/9 d 12-15-1839 m Sarah Nurs Sgt MA
Phineas: b 3-6-1729 d 12-15-1807 m Anna Rice Capt MA
Pliny: b 4-14-1759 d 8-18-1822 m Martha Cabot Corbin Lt NY
Randolph: b 1-10-1758 d 7-7-1833 m Elizabeth Stansill Pvt NC
Rescarrick: b 1755 d 4-20-1835 m Sarah Brooks Pvt NJ
Reuben: b 6-10-1755 d 8-6-1803 m Phoebe Harrison Capt VA
Reuben: b 1754 d 6-27-1839 m (1)Catherine Price (2)Elizabeth W Lt VA ★
Reuben: b 1755 d 1- -1803 m Cloe Irby Lt VA
Richard: b *c.* 1750 d *a.* 5-1-1809 m (1)Judith Martin (2)Keturah Austin Sol VA
Risdon: b 11-20-1760 d 1828 m (1)Scarberry Marshall (2)Anna Dent Slr DE
Robert: b 3-21-1757 d 10-11-1811 m Jane Power Pvt MD
Robert: b 4-8-1763 d 2-5-1852 m (1)Mrs Elizabeth (Moore) Hutchings (2)Mrs Abiah Wait Smn ME
Robert: b 5-6-1760 d 10-26-1810 m Dorothy Abbott Sol NY
Robert: b 5- -1741 d 1-21-1829 m Ruhamah Mitchell Pvt NH
Robert: b *c.* 1755 d 1815/16 m Elizabeth McGehee Capt NC
Robert: b *a.* 1752 d 1781 m Bettie Scissom Ens NC
Robert: b 2-10-1743 d 9-29-1800 m Maria Sophia Pvt PA
Robert: b 1753 d 4-24-1831 m Esther Wilson PS PA
Robert: b 3-12-1760 d 4-29-1816 m Mary Hosack Pvt PA
Robert: b *c.* 1732 d *p.* 1805 m Sarah CMmn PA
Robert: b 1759 d 3-23-1834 m Hannah — Sol SC
Robert: b *c.* 1745 d 1800 m Elizabeth Pvt VA
Roger: b *a.* 1740 d *p.* 1793 m Mariam Spencer Capt CT
Roswell: b 5-17-1728 d 12-13-1794 m Desire Dunham Pvt CT
Rufus: b 10-13-1750 d 3-29-1838 m Betsy (Moore) Pvt MA
Rufus: b 8-28-1760 d 12-5-1836 m Rachel Moore Pvt MA ★
Sackett: b 1754 d 1820 m Elizabeth Clifford Pvt NJ
Samuel: b 11-20-1758 d 7-16-1826 m Martha Scott Lt DE
Samuel: b 11-5-1729 d 1793 m Mehitabel Ingalls Sol PS MA
Samuel: b 10-21-1761 d 8-23-1838 m (1)Olive Bent (2)Eunice Goddard Pvt MA ★
Samuel, Jr.: b 6-10-1756 d 2-5-1844 m Jenny Thompson Pvt NH
Samuel: b 9-13-1726 d 1-1-1776 m (1)Joanna Elkins (2)Susannah Webster Pvt CS NH
Samuel, Sr.: b 1727 d 1-28-1793 m Margaret Morrison PS NH
Samuel: b 2-20-1739 d 7-23-1812 m Rebecca Goffe Capt NH
Samuel: b — d *p.* 1792 m Mary Cochran Pvt NH
Samuel: b — d 1794 m (1)Deborah Butterfield (2)Mrs Mary Colburn MM PS NH
Samuel: b *c.* 1747 d 7- -1786 m Elizabeth Cooper Pvt NJ
Samuel: b 1754 d 3-9-1799 m Sarah Green Pvt NJ
Samuel: b 1760 d 1838 m Ann Doane Pvt MA
Samuel: b 1749 d 9-12-1795 m Jane Fulton Capt PA
Samuel: b 1710 d *p.* 1790 m Jane — PS PA
Samuel: b 1756 d 1845 m (1)Elizabeth Romley (2)Blanchard Pvt SC
Samuel: b 1753/4 d 6-22-1838 m Mary Archer Pvt MA
Samuel: b 1760 d 1828 m — Allen Pvt VA
Shadrack, Jr.: b 5-10-1757 d 9-11-1806 m (1)Lovice Selden Nott (2)Marilla — Pvt CT
Shildes: b 1706 d 1777 m (2)Blandana Risdon PS MD
Silas: b 11-14-1759 d 5-5-1854 m Chloe Phillips Pvt RI
Simeon, Sr.: b 1-6-1732 d 1789 m Hannah Barber Pvt CT
Simeon, Jr.: b 3-25-1761 d 6-26-1825 m (1)Hannah Wilson Cooke (2)Elizabeth Andrews (3)Roxaline Phelps Meacham Pvt CT ★
Simeon: b 12-6-1732 d 12-19-1781 m Joanna Thorndike PS MA
Smith: b 1752 d 1804 m Mrs Molly Dent Camel 2Lt MD
Simeon: b *c.* 1734 d 1813 m (1)Mary — (2)Keziah — Sol VA
Stephen: b 12-1-1759 d 1-20-1813 m Parthenia Young Pvt NJ
Stephen: b 10-30-1734 d 7-2-1799 m Grizzy Philips LCol NC
Thomas: b 1745/6 d 11-17-1820 m (1)Elizabeth Coleman (2)Catherine Buckley NCapt MD
Thomas, Sr.: b *c.* 1725 d 1-6-1807 m (1)Ruth Nicholls (2)Mrs Priscilla Holland PS MA
Thomas, Jr.: b 4-12-1751 d 6-12-1842 m Rebecca Harrington Lt MA
Thomas: b 8-3-1738 d 2-15-1801 m Eliza Hill Pvt MA
Thomas: b 9-3-1761 d 4-25-1840 m Rachel (Power) Kerr Pvt MA ★
Thomas: b 2-14-1756 d 10-19-1843 m Mary Whiting Pvt MA
Thomas: b *c.* 1760 d 7-17-1817 m Sarah Dennen Slr MA
Thomas: b 2-6-1761 d — m Comfort Perkins Pvt NH
Thomas: b *c.* 1722 d 6-26-1776 m Maria Ferdon CS PS NJ
Thomas, 3rd: b 1760 d 2-11-1839 m Sarah — Pvt NY ★
Thomas: b 1766 d 1823 m Ann K Goldaborough Pvt NC
Thomas: b 1750 d 6-2-1821 m Rachel Phillis Capt PA
Thomas: b 1741 d 1-6-1793 m Hannah Moulder NCapt PA

Thomas: b 1759 d 7-11-1822 m (1)Martha (Patsey) Price (2)Mary Reagan Pvt SC
Thomas: b 1745 d 10-20-1823 m Mary Harrison Capt VA
Thomas: b 2-12-1755 d 2-25-1835 m Elizabeth Harberson Capt VA ★
Thomas: b 3-3-1756 d 1803-6 m Nancy Walton Capt VA
Thomas: b 9-28-1758 d 9-28-1823 m Nancy Walker Sgt VA
Thomas: b *c.* 1730 d *a.* 1818 m Elizabeth — Pvt VA
Thomas L: b 12-20-1761 d 2-20-1841 m Elizabeth Nelson Slr MD
Timothy: b 2-2-1755 d 7-11-1845 m Sybil Cummings Pvt MA
Tully: b *c.* 1749 d 1794 m Elizabeth — 2Lt VA
Usher: b 3-25-1757 d 8-22-1834 m (1)Patience Vail (2)Phebe Pvt NY ★
Wm.: b 4-10-1744 d 9-5-1796 m — Shultz Pvt GA
Wm.: b 1725 d 2-12-1784 m Rachel Baker Pvt MD
Wm.: b 7-9-1758 d 12-17-1833 m Ann (Twilley) Howard Sol MD
Wm.: b 8-6-1712 d 12-13-1788 m Rachel Ralph PS MD
Wm.: b 6-16-1752 d 8-6-1819 m Patty Campbell Capt MA
Wm.: b 10-12-1747 d 3-29-1836 m Abigail Wheeler Cpl MA
Wm.: b 1740 d 1795 m Sarah Hoskins Pvt MA
Wm.: b 8-19-1720 d 7-3-1804 m Margaret Forrest Pvt NH
Wm., Sr.: b 1733 d 2-13-1812 m Martha Mack Pvt NH
Wm., Jr.: b 8-16-1761 d 4-24-1823 m Sarah McCleary Pvt NH
Wm.: b 2-19-1760 d 5-5-1844 m Isabella McCleary Pvt NH
Wm.: b 1752 d 1803 m Mary Wilson Pvt NH
Wm.: b 9-26-1731 d 9-7-1818 m Jane Holmes PS NH
Wm.: b 1756 d 1836 m Mary — Pvt NJ
Wm.: b *c.* 1730 d *c.* 1800 m — McCord LCol PS NC
Wm.: b 1751 d 11-8-1823 m (1)Mildred Harrison (2)Elizabeth Jarratt Col NC ★
Wm.: b 1726 d 11-11-1812 m Margaret Patton Capt NC
Wm., Sr.: b *c.* 1740 d 1781 m Sarah — Pvt NC
Wm., Jr.: b 12-16-1754 d 4-15-1833 m Rachel — Pvt NC ★
Wm., Jr.: b 12-1-1758 d 7-15-1844 m (1)Olivia Free (2)Anna Inard Pvt VA NC ★
Wm.: b 3-19-1753 d 12-17-1827 m Janet Bell 1Lt PA
Wm.: b 1753 d 9-5-1807 m Mary Henderson Ens PA
Wm.: b — d *c.* 1788 m Isabel Lytle Sgt PA
Wm.: b 2-17-1758 d 5-14-1823 m Dorcas Carr Pvt PA
Wm.: b 5-6-1699 d 5-30-1783 m Williamina Wemys PS PA
Wm.: b 1733 d *p.* 1780 m X Pvt SC
Wm.: b 10-31-1751 d 7- -1797 m Frances Baptist Capt VA
Wm.: b 3-5-1753 d 5-10-1818 m (1)Hannah Ransdell (2)Peggy Lane 2Lt VA
Wm.: b 1751 d 1-20-1820 m Elizabeth Steele Sgt VA
Wm.: b 1740 d 1841 m Nancy McClung Capt VA ★
Wm.: b 11-3-1757 d 2-21-1843 m Drusilla Weatherford Pvt VA ★
Wm.: b 12-5-1759 d 1-31-1822 m Sarah Grimit Pvt VA
Wm.: b 1740 d 1802 m Mary Throckmorton PS VA
Wilson: b 1768 d 12-17-1837 m X Pvt VA ★
Zachariah: b *a.* 1765 d 8-28-1837 m Elsie Bourne Sgt MD
Zachariah: b 1749 d 6-19-1803 m Mary Boggs 2Lt PA

MOORER,

John: b 8-4-1754 d 1814 m (1)Catherine Stroman (2)Mrs Anna Margaret Stroman Bruner Pvt SC

MOORMAN, (includes MOREMAN)

Achilles: b 10-26-1713 d *p.* 5-25-1783 m Elizabeth Adams PS VA
Achilles: b *c.* 1750 d *p.* 1821 m Frances Herndon PS VA
Andrew: b 12-2-1744 d 3- -1791 m Judith Clark PS VA
Charles: b 5-23-1747 d 10-23-1803 m (1)Rebecca Leftwich (2)Nancy Hancock Sol VA
Charles: b 1737 d 6-11-1798 m Mary Venable PS VA
Micajah: b 6-28-1735 d *p.* 11-25-1806 m Susannah Chiles PS VA
Thomas: b 5-9-1746 d 5-25-1835 m Rachel Simmons SgtMaj MD
Zachariah: b 2-2-1732 d *a.* 7-2-1789 m (1)Elizabeth Terrell (2)Elizabeth Johnson PS VA

MOOSE,

George: b 5-1-1745 d 1809 m Christina Dreseray Pvt NC

MORAGNE,

Pierre: b 11-16-1740 d *p.* 8-20-1807 m (1)Mary Bayle (2)Cecila Bayle Pvt SC

MORAN, (or MORRAN)

Gabriel: b 8-30-1730 d *p.* 9-20-1810 m Margaret Wood Pvt MD
Wm.: b 11-23-1748 d 4-3-1824 m Rebecca Barber Pvt MD

MORDECAI,

Samuel: b *c.* 1755 d 1820 m Isabel Andrews Sol SC

MORDOUGH,

Nathan: bpt 1730 d 10-14-1823 m Anna Wingate PS NH

MORECOOK,

Thomas: b *c.* 1747 d 1784 m Mildred Southall Cpl VA

MOREHART,

John: b 1758 d 1-8-1815 m Mary — Pvt PA

MOREHEAD, (includes MOORHEAD)

Alexander: b 1747 d 1839 m Mary Morrow Pvt PA

Charles, Sr.: b a. 1736 d 1783 m Mary Turner Capt PA VA
Charles, Jr.: b 2-3-1762 d 11-20-1828 m Margaret Slaughter Sgt VA
Fergus: b 1742 d 1827 m Jane White Pvt PA
James: b 1723 d 1807 m Lucy — Lt NC
James: b 1732 d 1818 m Catherine Beyers Pvt PA
John: b 5-9-1760 d 9-17-1832 m Obediance Motley Pvt NC
Joseph: b c. 1748 d p. 1-12-1819 m Jane — Pvt VA
Joseph: b c. 1730 d p. 7-11-1806 m Elizabeth Turner PS VA
Samuel: b 1749 d p. 8-18-1814 m Elizabeth Sproul Capt PA
Turner: b 1-7-1757 d 2-23-1821 m (1)Ann Ransdell (2)Mary Hewitt
  Hooe Capt VA
Wm.: b 1747 d 5-27-1819 m Elizabeth Barnett Capt PA
Wm.: b 7-9-1762 d 1844 m Agnes G Gilky Pvt SC ★

MOREHOUSE,
Abijah, Jr.: b 1-23-1748 d 11-9-1809 m Mary Allen Lt CT
Abraham: b 3-26-1758 d 9-12-1841 m Ruth Wilson Pvt CT
Andrew, Sr.: b 3-7-1726 d 1801 m (1)Phebe Hurd (2)Sarah
  Sherrell LCol NY
Andrew, Jr.: b 11-6-1750 d 5-10-1806 m Judith — Lt NY
Benjamin: b 3-14-1752 d 5-29-1823 m Phebe Haines Sol NJ
David: b c. 1741 d 8-19-1808 m Sarah Hanford Sgt CT
David: b c. 1740 d c. 1800 m Thankful Couch Pvt CT
David, Jr.: b 11-25-1764 d 11-16-1839 m Tryphena Bidwell
  Pvt CT ★
David: b 2-2-1761 d 2-1-1833 m Jane Belding Sgt NY
George: b — d c. 1797 m — Densmore QM NY
Gershom, Jr.: b 11-27-1727 d 1-22-1805 m Anna Sanford Capt CT
Isaac: b 6-7-1756 d 8-7-1839 m Thankful Gray MM Pvt NY ★
Jepthah: b 2-14-1759 d 3-15-1824 m Abby Morehouse Pvt NJ
John: b 12-15-1739 d 6-30-1803 m Deborah Brush Pvt CT
John: bpt 8-14-1737 d p. 12-26-1795 m Mrs Eunice Davis PS CT
Joseph: b 6-11-1753 d 6-19-1832 m Molly Buckley Pvt NY
Lemuel: b 12-20-1728 d a. 6-10-1777 m (1)Rachel Osborn
  (2)Sarah Smith PS CT
Samuel: b 3-29-1762 d 2-3-1830 m Anna — Pvt CT
Samuel: b 3-6-1742 d 12-10-1790 m Susanna Ogden Pvt NJ
Sarah Lewis: b 11-17-1748 d p. 1800 m (1)Josiah Morehouse
  (2)Benjamin Chapman PS CT
Seth: b 7-8-1734 d p. 1780 m Ruth — PS CT
Simeon: b 5-3-1751 d 5-4-1836 m Rebecca Meeker Pvt NJ
Solomon: b 11-28-1731 d 5-15-1808 m Mariam Couch Capt CT
Uriel: b 1740 d 1827 m (1)Sarah Wheeler (2)Beulah Lewis Pvt CT
Wm.: b 1-3-1750 d 12-25-1824 m Ann Burr Cpl CT

MOREL,
John: b 1-1-1759 d 6-18-1802 m (1)Sally Powell (2)Henrietta
  Netherclift Capt GA
John: b 1- -1740 d 9- -1782 m Mary Bryan PS GA

MORELAND, (includes MORLAND, MURLAND, MURLIN)
Andrew: b c. 1750 d p. 6-21-1802 m — Pvt PA
James: b — d 1-10-1820 m Susannah Smith Pvt PS NH
John: b 1758 d 1826 m Mary Tucker Cpl VA
John: b 10-1-1752 d p. 1820 m Catherune — Pvt VA ★
Samuel: b 1751 d 1817 m Sarah Notley Pvt MD
Thomas: b 2-27-1764 d 9-14-1864 m Leah Van Campen Pvt PA
Wm.: b c. 1748 d 4-24-1830 m Agnes (Nancy) Huston Pvt PA
Wm.: b a. 1735 d 1810 m Mary — Pvt PA

MORENUS,
Thomas: b 8-7-1756 d 8-27-1826 m Mary Staley Pvt NY
Wm.: b 1755 d 1-23-1816 m Margrette Truax Pvt NY W★

MOREY, (includes MORY)
Asa: b 4-8-1747 d 1- -1808 m Elizabeth — Pvt CT
Benjamin: b 5-18-1732 d p. 1782 m Priscilla — Capt MA
Benoni: b 4-10-1758 d 4- -1821 m Huldah Brown Pvt MA ★
Ephraim: b 12-12-1746 d 9-22-1833 m (1)Anner Goodall (2)Hannah
  Follet Pvt NH ★
Gotthardt: b 3-20-1752 d 5-26-1843 m Magdalena Haarlacher
  Pvt PA
Israel: b 5-27-1735 d 8-10-1809 m Martha Palmer Col NH
Israel, Jr.: b 6-10-1760 d 1-25-1820 m Theodora Phelps Pvt NH
John: b 8-28-1750 d 9-9-1812 m Demis Gillett Pvt NH
Jonathan: b 3-31-1730 d 3-31-1790 m Lydia Campbell Pvt NY
Joseph: b 7-25-1738 d p. 1790 m Martha — Sol PS NY
Robert: b 12-24-1758 d c. 9-3-1834 m Ruth Browning Sgt RI ★
Samuel: b 8-19-1727 d 12-15-1798 m Mary Hodges PS MA
Samuel: b 6-4-1757 d 11-8-1836 m Sarah Palmer Dr MA
Silas: b 6-1-1764 d — m Eunice Donham Sol MA
Silas: b a. 1748 d 9-4-1825 m Elizabeth Benson Sgt NY
Thomas: b 1732 d 1810 m Sarah — Sol NY
Thomas: b 12-5-1760 d 4-7-1829 m Margaret Montgomery Pvt NY
Wm.: b 9-1-1722 d 10-30-1804 m Dorcas Scylla Pvt NH
Wm., Jr.: b 10-1-1758 d 2-9-1838 m Susanna Rowe Pvt NH
Zenas: b 3-28-1740 d 10-11-1821 m Abigail Ellis Pvt NH

MORFIT,
Henry: b 1757 d 1794 m Hannah Porter Lt PA W★

MORFORD,
John: b 5-18-1758 d 5-8-1840 m Mary Cox Pvt NJ ★
Stephen: b 11-10-1756 d 4-22-1833 m Mary Hamilton Pvt NJ

MORGAN, (includes MORGIN)
Aaron: b 3-16-1749 d 8-30-1825 m Abigail Sherman Sgt MA
Abel: b 1-27-1753 d — m Susanna Donahue Pvt PA
Abel: b c. 1759 d p. 1784 m Elizabeth Bedinger Dr PA
Abijah: b 7-6-1715 d 12-7-1778 m Dorothy Williams Pvt CT
Abner: b 1-9-1746 d p. 1782 m Persis (Morgan) Maj MA
Abraham: b 1760 d 1815 m Mary Bedinger Sol VA
Amos: b 11-9-1750 d 7-27-1839 m Sarah Welch Pvt CT
Andrew: b 7-10-1748 d 12-18-1786 m Eunice Bickford 2Mte MA
Ashby: b 3-22-1749 d 10-21-1828 m Hannah Greeley Cpl NH
Asher: b 8-30-1762 d 12-8-1839 m Cynthia Gager Pvt CT
Benjamin: b c. 1750 d 1801 m Sarah Johnson Pvt NJ
Benjamin: b 1750 d 1-30-1834 m Lucy Dunham Pvt VT
Benjamin: b 12-25-1760 d 2-24-1836 m Ann Ellis Pvt VA ★
Benjamin: b 10-6-1762 d 9-29-1841 m Elizabeth Kemper Pvt VA
Charles: b c. 1759 d 1803-6 m Rachel Prest Pvt NJ
Charles: b c. 1740 d 1822 m Susanna Doggett Sgt VA
Charles: b 1750 d 1781 m Nancy Sparks Pvt VA
Christopher: b 10-27-1747 d 7-5-1831 m (1)Deborah Ledyard
  (2)Margaret Gates Ens CT
Consider: b 6-28-1740 d 1802 m Ruth Mosely Pvt NY
Cornelius: b 1-23-1747 d p. 1821 m Mehetabel Preston Pvt VT
Daniel, Jr.: b 9-12-1746 d 5-8-1811 m Elizabeth Lord CS CT
Daniel: b 1736 d 7-6-1802 m Abigail Bailey BG VA
Daniel: b c. 1750 d 1831 m (1)Isabella McAlister (2)Margaret — PS
  VA
David: b 1-25-1745 d p. 1794 m Tabitha Collins Sgt MA
David: b 7-22-1748 d 9-19-1812 m (1)Rebecca Jenkins (2)Mrs
  Margaret Jones Rees Capt PA
David: b 1756 d 7- -1780 m Eunice Tucker Capt PA
David: b c. 1744 d 1798 m Ann — Pvt VA
David: b 3-12-1753 d 10- -1813 m Anna Poteet Pvt VA
David: b 5-12-1721 d 5-19-1813 m Sarah Stephens Pvt VA
Ebenezer: b 6-12-1738 d 3-18-1816 m Miriam Kilbourne Sgt MA
Elijah: b 5-19-1741 d 10-15-1822 m Lucy Avery Pvt CT
Elijah: b 1760 d 1813 m Hessa Pvt DE
Elisha: b 11-9-1748 d 3- -1814 m Olive Coit Lt CT
Elisha: b 3-7-1762 d 4-1-1796 m Abigail Morgan Dr PS CT
Enoch: b 6-20-1752 d 7- -1828 m Susanna Bailey Lt PA ★
Erastus: b 3-29-1764 d 9-7-1857 m Clarissa Chapin Pvt MA
Ester: b c. 1730 d 1805/6 m Thomas Morgan PS VA
Evan: b 3-1-1754 d 3-18-1850 m (1)Mrs Woodfin (2)Camilla Hartley
  Ens PA ★
George: b 2-14/16-1743 d 3-10-1810 m Mary Baynton Col PA
Gideon: b 1751 d 11-15-1830 m (1)Patience Cogswell (2)Elizabeth
  Hardin Cpl CT
Griffey: b 6-22-1742 d p. 4-19-1790 m Rebecca Clement Pvt NJ
Haynes: b 1742 d 1795 m Mary Thompson Col VA
Henry: b 1741 d 1808 m Hannah Whitney Pvt MA
Issac, Sr.: b 3-29-1739 d 5-29-1796 m Alice Spaulding PS CT
Isaac: b 4-24-1734 d p. 2-26-1791 m Lucy Day Pvt MA
Isaac: b 8-23-1741 d p. 1790 m Abigail Tucker PS MA
Isaac: b 5-20-1757 d p. 1839 m Judith Smith Pvt NC
Isaac: b 4-26-1730 d 11-2-1815 m (1)Zilpah Meech (2)Elizabeth
  Tracy PS VT
Israel: b 7-22-1757 d 6-4-1816 m Elizabeth Brewster Sgt CT
Jacob, Sr.: b 11-7-1716 d 11-11-1792 m (2)Rachel Piersol Col PS PA
Jacob, Jr.: b 1742 d 9-18-1802 m Barbara Jenkins Col PA
James, Sr.: b 1730 d 5-16-1792 m (1)Catherine Street (2)Mrs
  Lydia Miner Capt CT
James, Jr.: b 4-20-1759 d 9-14-1824 m Eunice Turner Pvt CT ★
James: b 5-11-1750 d 3-28-1816 m Jerusha Beecher Pvt CT
James: b 1-31-1730 d 10-15-1801 m Grace Smith PS CT
James: b c. 1755 d p. 6-1-1805 m Justina Cremeen Pvt MD
James, Sr.: b 1734 d 2-26-1784 m Margaret Evertson Capt NJ
James, Jr.: b 1-29-1757 d 11-14-1822 m (1)Catherine Van Cortland
  (2)Ann Van Wickle Ens NJ W ★
James: b 8-7-1750 d 3-13-1813 m Phoebe Treadwell PS NY
James: b 3-9-1760 d p. 9-12-1845 m (1)Matilda — (2)Catherine
  Elizabeth Whatley Pvt SC ★
James: b 4-5-1748 d 3-1-1840 m Margaret Joliff Pvt VA ★
James: b 1- -1753 d 1823 m Hannah Cox Pvt VA
Jeremiah: b c. 1738 d 1805 m Elizabeth Connell PS VA
Jesse: b 1-27-1758 d 8-30-1846 m Matilda Fish Pvt CT ★
Jesse: b 7-18-1761 d p. 3-4-1847 m Sarah Tennant Pvt CT ★
Jesse: b c. 1755 d p. 1810 m Albina Carpenter Lt PA
John: b 3-21-1742 d 7-9-1816 m Eunice Crary Capt CT
John: b a. 1752 d 1797 m Sarah Chaffinch Pvt MD
John: b 10-13-1717 d 9-25-1790 m Margaret Bannister Capt MA
John, Jr.: b 10-3-1762 d 12-26-1846 m Mary Pierce Cpl MA
John: b 4-25-1721 d 9-7-1792 m (1)Margaret Larcom (2)Rebeckah
  Corning Cpl MA
John, Sr.: b 1725 d 1787 m Nancy — Pvt NC
John, Sr.: b c. 1737 d 1827 m Jane — Pvt NC
John, Jr.: b 1753 d c. 1830 m Mary Hall Pvt NC
John: b 8-10-1743 d 11-12-1782 m Anna Catharine Comfort Capt PA
John: b 11- -1756 d a. 1819 m Lucy Woods PS VA
John: b 1758 d 1843 m Pricilla Parker Pvt VA
Jonas: b 12-20-1752 d 10-7-1824 m Sarah Mott Ens CT
Jonathan, Sr.: b 1711 d 1-1-1796 m Ruth Miller Sol MA
Jonathan, Jr.: b 4-12-1748 d 4-18-1816 m Elizabeth Thompson Sgt
  MA Heirs ★
Jonathan: b 1761 d 1849 m Anna Woodburn Pvt NJ

MORGAN, contd.

Joseph: b 10-18-1754 d 2-20-1829 m Hannah Stoyell Sgt CT W ★
Joseph: b 12-19-1758 d 9-29-1831 m Eunice Doolittle Pvt CT
Joseph: b 8-10-1706 d 12-1-1785 m Dorothy Avery PS CT
Joseph: b 2-19-1736 d 12-18-1813 m Experience Smith Capt MA
Joseph: b 4-17-1733 d 1-29-1816 m Sarah Mighill Sgt MA
Joseph: b 8-19-1705 d 1-28-1798 m Margaret Cooley Pvt MA
Joseph: b 3-18-1746 d 8-27-1817 m (1)Mary Evans (2)Mary Butcher Pvt NJ
Joseph: b c. 1750 d 1815 m Nancy Curtis Cpl NC
Joseph: b 1748 d 1785 m Anna Thorpe Pvt VT
Joshua: b 9-14-1758 d 3-16-1827 m Welthea Pvt CT ★
Josiah, Jr.: b 7-13-1751 d — m Sarah Dodge Pvt PS NH
Judah: b 3-22-1749 d p. 1786 m Elizabeth Shivoy Pvt MA
Lucas: b 2-26-1743 d 11-12-1817 m Thrphena Smith Pvt MA
Luke John: b — d p. 6-13-1781 m Mary Ecles Sol GA
Mordecai, Jr.: b 6-19-1750 d 8-9-1794 m Mary Davis Lt PA
Morgan: b 5-3-1749 d 2-29-1832 m Ann Roberts Pvt PA
Morgan: b 3-20-1737 d 10-20-1797 m Mary Gossett CS VA
Morgan: b 12-20-1746 d p. 10-31-1826 m Drucilla Prickett Capt VA
Morgan: b 1760 d a. 7-28-1828 m (1)Elizabeth Blades (2)Sally Vaughn Sol VA
Nathan: b 11-29-1744 d 12-23-1790 m Jerusha Benton Pvt CT
Nathan: b 9-6-1758 d 1807 m Abigail Palmer Fif CT
Nathan: b 1755 d 10-16-1842 m Naomi Pool Pvt NC ★
Nathan: b 10-22-1752 d 1733/4 m (2)Elizabeth Williams Pvt VA ★
Nathaniel: b 6-9-1762 d 9-4-1851 m Miriam Pettengill Pvt NH
Nicholas: b 1750 d 12-9-1782 m — Everson Lt NJ
Nicholas: b 1762 d 4-28-1845 m Phebe Avery Pvt CT ★
Noah: b 1736 d 1808 m Mercy — Pvt PA
Peletiah: b 1719 d 1784 m Rachel Bagg Pvt MA
Peter: b 1-15-1758 d 4-21-1830 m Martha Lewis Pvt CT
Phineas: b 2-7-1741 d 5-26-1779 m Syliva Woodbridge Cpl MA
Prudence Avery: b 3-16-1732 d 11-20-1809 m (1)Joseph Morgan (2)Elijah Avery PS CT
Ralph: b 1738 d 1809 m Priscilla Douglas Pvt SC VA
Randal: b 9-9-1734 d 10-3-1780 m Amy Chew 1Lt NJ
Rawleigh: b 9-4-1757 d p. 1820 m Lydia Swearingen Lt VA
Reuben: b c. 1730 d 7-9-1781 m Mary — PS VA
Richard: b 1756/57 d 10-31-1835 m (2)Ann — Drm NC ★
Samuel: b 10-3-1748 d p. 1796 m Judith Dennen Pvt MA
Seth: b 3-29-1755 d 4-2-1821 m Desire Bromley Pvt CT W ★
Shapley: b 2-7-1740 d 1800 m Freelove Hurlburt Pvt CT
Simeon: b c. 1744/5 d 1784 m Lydia — PS NH
Simon: b c. 1755 d 7-6-1810 m Elizabeth Pickett Col VA W ★
Skiff: b 3-7-1761 d 12-25-1847 m Prudence Sackett Pvt NY ★
Solomon: b 2-4-1745 d 9-3-1804 m Eunice Avery Pvt CT
Solomon: b 1735 d 1803 m Jemima Webb Pvt SC
Spencer: b 2-22-1756 d 7-14-1809 m (1)Mrs Susan Kenner (2)Frances Nuckolls Ens VA
Stephen: b 7-19-1765 d 4-19-1843 m (1)Mary Douglas (2)Elizabeth Douglas Pvt CT
Temperance Avery: b 9-14-1725 d 8-7-1801 m William Morgan PS CT
Theophilus: b 2-23-1759 d 9-11-1820 m Mary Hinkley Pvt CT
Theophilus: b 6-26-1732 d 2-17-1788 m (1)Rebecca Shipman (2)Phoebe Merrills PS CT
Thomas: b 6-30-1742 d 9-15-1815 m Sarah Leeds Sgt CT
Thomas: b 9-22-1761 d 9-17-1844 m Polly Baker Pvt MD ★
Thomas: b 7-25-1749 d 7-9-1840 m Hannah — Pvt PS PA★
Thomas: b c. 1752 d c. 1815 m Elizabeth McLin Sol MD
Titus: b 7-17-1740 d 11-22-1811 m Sarah Morgan Pvt MA
Wm.: b 6-1-1746 d 1-17-1824 m Miriam Murdock Pvt CT
Wm.: b 6-17-1723 d 4-11-1777 m Temperance Avery PS CT
Wm.: b 1-6-1766 d 10-30-1850 m Sally Ware Sol GA
Wm.: b 1744 d 11- -1795 m Cassandra Lee Capt MD
Wm.: b 5-13-1729 d 10-11-1809 m Abigail Eliott Gnr MA
Wm.: b 3-22/23-1749 d 6-6-1816 m Agnes Vail Capt VA
Wm.: b 1723 d 10-17-1788 m Drusilla Swearingin Capt VA
Wm.: b a. 1749 d 4-1-1795 m Priscilla — Pvt VA
Wm., Avery: b 11-24-1754 d 3-22-1842 m (1)Lydia Smith (2)Sarah Harris Sgt CT
Youngs: b 1741 d 5-19-1809 m Mary Avery Pvt CT
Zachariah: b 8-13-1760 d 1818 m Abigail Symonds Pvt MA
Zackquil: b 9-8-1758 d 2-27-1834 m Sina West Pvt VA PA ★
Zacquill: b c. 1735 d 1-1-1795 m (1)Nancy Paxton (2)Drusilla Springer Col VA
Zedekiah: b 3-8-1744 d 10-12-1822 m (1)Ruth Dart (2)Rebecca Watson PS CT

MORGANDOLLAR,

John: b 1753 d 3-16-1806 m Elizabeth Strobel PS SC

MORGERT,

Peter: b 4-18-1758 d 1846 m Christina — Sgt VA ★

MORIN,

Edward: b 1745 d 9-15-1841 m Elizabeth Jones Pvt VA ★

MORING, (includes MOURNING)

John: b 1728 d 1800 m Sarah Harris PS NC
John: b 1764 d 9-21-1844 m (1)Nancy Lane (2)Elizabeth Smith Pvt VA
Rodger: b 1752 d 1827 m (1) — (2)Jane Kennedy Pvt PA

MORLEY,

Abel: b 1756 d 6-12-1798 m Rachel Lovering Pvt MA
David: b 3-3-1760 d 12-31-1815 m Hannah Lynde Griswold Pvt MA
Demenick: b 9-12-1750 d 4-1-1834 m Ruth Western Pvt CT ★
Ezekiel: b 1757 d 8-6-1852 m Deliverance Tewsberry Pvt MA
Gideon: b 11-9-1738 d 8-24-1818 m Mary Miller PS MA
Issac: b 2-6-1762 d 5-15-1826 m Beulah Harmon Sgt MA ★
John: b 2-7-1716 d 8-31-1776 m Sarah Greene Pvt CT
John: b 10-25-1753 d 5- m Sarah Stevens Fisher Pvt CT ★
John: b c. 1753 d p. 1781 m Marian Brooks Pvt MA
Thomas: b 3- -1758 d 9- -1844 m Editha Marsh Pvt CT ★

MORRETT,

Hartman: b 11-8-1734 d 11-13-1822 m Gertrude Pvt PA

MORRILL, (includes MORREL, MORRELL, MURREL & MURRILL)

Abel: bpt 9-11-1743 d 1829 m Elizabeth Hibbard Pvt MA
Abel: b 1743 d c. 1810 m Hannah French Sgt NH
Abner: b c. 1751 d p. 1787 m Sarah Hoyt Pvt MA
Abraham: b 8-6-1739 d 7-16-1814 m Sarah Joy Sgt MA
Abraham: b 1-29-1756 d 9-19-1845 m Sarah Hoyt Pvt NH ★
Amos: b 5-9-1748 d 8-6-1810 m Margaret Day Maj NH
Amos: b 12-9-1762 d 2-6-1840 m (1)Anna Osgood (2)Hannah Morrill Pvt MA
Benjamin: b 12-13-1759 d 4- -1837 m Sarah Lowell Swett Pvt MA
Daniel: b 7-4-1760 d 1-28-1830 m Betsey Osgood Pvt MA
Daniel: b 11-1-1724 d 7-19-1805 m Eleanor True PS CS MA
Daniel: b 9-27-1737 d 4-10-1813 m Anna Fitts PS NH
David: b 1-24-1734 d 6-10-1799 m Mrs Abigail Stevens Lt NH
David: b 12-14-1749 d 10- -1816 m Sarah Lewis Pvt NH
Ephraim, Sr.: b 12-9-1717 d p. 1790 m — PS NH
Ephraim, Jr.: b c. 1750 d p. 1799 m — Weed PS NH
Ezekiel: b 1707 d 7-28-1783 m (1)Jemima (Morrill) (2)Joanna Gilman PS NH
Henry: b 6-27-1731 d 10-20-1778 m Eleanor Currier Col MA
Hibbard: b 4-12-1759 d 9-10-1843 m (1)Deborah Tibbetts Pvt VT ★
Isaac: b 12-18-1718 d 8-17-1793 m (1)Mary Ayer (2)Dorothy Ruggles Chp MA
Isaac: b c. 1760 d 1827 m Rebecca Bailey Drm NY ★
Israel: b 8-12-1757 d 7-28-1839 m Elizabeth Jackson Cpl MA ★
Jabez: b 2-15-1745 d 8-26-1800 m Hannah Clough PS Sol MA
Jacon: b 11-23-1733 d p. 1791 m Mary True Pvt MA
Jacob: b 1730 d 2-23-1814 m Mary Harton Pvt NY
Jeremiah: b 4-13-1752 d 12-18-1838 m Hannah Kittridge Sgt MA ★
Jesse: b 4-28-1757 d 1-28-1835 m Mrs Hester Baley Pvt NY ★
John: b 1754 d 12- -1844 m Abigail Knight Pvt NH
John: b c. 1740 d p. 1780 m Lucy Harding QM NJ
John: b 10-21-1733 d 2-7-1816 m Elizabeth Skillman Pvt NY
John: b 1751 d 10- -1805 m (2)Lorano Lockwood Sol NY
John: b 6-8-1750 d 8-4-1812 m Sally Wallace Pvt PA
Jonathan: b 8-4-1754 d 5-18-1839 m Hannah Currier Cpl MA ★
Joseph, Sr.: b 1754 d 1-6-1838 m Olive Morrill Pvt MA ★
Joseph: b 5-13-1755 d 9-6-1837 m Martha Mandeville 1Lt NY ★
Laban: b 9-25-1740 d 5-12-1812 m Sarah Ames Lt PS NH
Micajah: b 2-2-1729/30 d 10-17-1810 m Hannah Hackett PS MA
Moses: b 5-1-1719 d 2-9-1778 m Hannah Jordan PS MA
Moses Sargent: b 3-2-1757 d 7-23-1805 m Abigail Worthen Pvt MA
Nathaniel: b 11-1-1762 d 1-20-1844 m (1)Elizabeth Eastman (2)Mrs Sally Johnson Flanders Pvt NH ★
Oliver: b 8-31-1741 d p. 1790 m Abra Brown Lt NH
Peter: b 9-25-1709 d 11-11-1801 m Sarah Peaslee Matr MA
Robert: b c. 1734 d 1813 m Sarah Cloyd Capt PA
Samuel: b 2-4-1761 d 1- -1808 m Elizabeth Jewell Pvt MA W★
Samuel: b 1-29-1742 d 4-2-1825 m Sally Blunt Lt NH
Samuel: bpt 12-11-1748 d p. 1791 m Rachel Gardenier Pvt NY
Samuel: b 5-24-1766 d 9-8-1836 m Susannah Puryear Ens VA ★
Sargent: b 6-17-1754 d 11-6-1834 m Ruth Hoyt Pvt PS NH
Thomas: b 11-22-1747 d 8-9-1838 m (2)Lydia Frasse (3)Eunice Hamilton Maj NJ ★
Wm.: b 4-21-1736 d 1-28-1812 m Lydia Trask Pvt NH
Wm.: b 1-21-1753 d 3-22-1817 m Sabra Marden Sgt NH
Wm.: b c. 1750 d p. 10-24-1831 m Susan Brinson Sol NC

MORRIS, (includes MARES, MARIUS, MORRISS)

Amos, Sr.: b 1723/4 d 12-30-1801 m (1)Lydia Camp (2)Mrs Louis Clark (3)Mrs Esther Smith Sol PS CT
Amos, Jr.: b 3-13-1750 d 10-11-1823 m Betsey Woodward Pvt CT
Amos: b 8-25-1758-60 d 9- -1847 m Rebecca Tyler Pvt PA ★
Andrew: b 9-22-1749 d 2-20-1820 m Lucretia Russell Mstr CT W ★
Anthony Cadwalader: b 1745 d 1798 m Mary Jones PS PA
Benjamin: b 2-26-1762 d 1- -1804 m (1)Sylvia Carter (2)Lucy Butler Pvt MA
Benjamin: b 1748 d 1833 m Mary Mason Pvt PA
Benjamin: b 1761 d p. 1800 m Sarah Bolton Pvt SC
Charles: b 4-24-1762 d 6-7-1838 m (1)Miriam Nicholas (2)Mrs Sarah Elliott Graves Cpl CT ★
Charles: b — d p. 5-8-1797 m — PS VA
Cornelius: b 10-2-1759 d 8-6-1834 m Sarah Dudley Pvt MD ★
Curtis: b 1757 d p. 3-2-1804 m Elizabeth Wright Capt DE

Daniel, Sr.: b 5-7-1715 d 3-1-1792 m (1)Mrs Sarah Fayerweather Mackard (2)Mrs Prudence Summers Curtis (3)Elizabeth — PS CT
Daniel, Jr.: b 12-17-1750 d 3-15-1828 m Elizabeth Salter Burritt Pvt CT
Daniel, Jr.: b c. 1735 d 1805 m Ann Polk PS DE
David: b 1759 d 1804 m Mary Bartelmy Capt CT
David: b 6-20-1744 d p. 1821 m Phebe McGee Nelson Sgt MA
David: b 12-19-1746 d 1798 m Mary Shotwell Pvt NJ
David: b 2-23-1735 d 1820 m Christiana Mercier Pvt NY
David Hamilton: b 7-11-1769 d 4-3-1843 m Eve Ann Sailor Pvt PA ★
Edmund: b 1758 d 8-27-1833 m Sally — Sol VA
Edward: b 12-12-1756 d 4-29-1801 m Lucy Bliss Pvt MA
Edward: b 1756 d 2-10-1830 m Elizabeth Cary Whittaker Chp VA
Elijah: b c. 1726 d 1803/4 m Mary — PS DE
Ezekiel: b 1744 d 10-24-1822 m Mary Linvill Pvt PA
George: b 1-2-1745 d 1-26-1842 m Margaret Corbley Pvt PA
George: b 1761 d 8-1-1839 m Johanna Thompson Pvt PA ★
Hammond: b 1733 d p. 10-7-1810 m Mrs Mary (Tuttle) Brown PS VA
Henry: b 4-18-1734 d 5-8-1808 m Hannah Frissell Cpl CT
Henry: b 2-24-1744 d 10-24-1812 m (1)Martha Davies (2)Christiana Holm Meredith Sol VA
Henry: b c. 1748 d 1824 m Mary Bird Sol VA
Hugh: b 1727 d 1820 m Anne — Cpl VA
Isaac, Sr.: b 3-26-1725 d 1-10-1778 m Sarah Chaffee Pvt CT
Isaac, Jr.: b 9-10-1753 d 6-26-1805 m Irene Johnson Pvt MA
Isaac: b 4-8-1748 d p. 1808 m Rebecah Van Ette Pvt NY
Isaac: b 1-21-1751 d 10-8-1833 m (1)Hannah Perkins (2)Elizabeth Lewis Pvt PA
Isaac: b 1740 d 1830 m Ruth Henton Pvt VA
Jacob: b 12-28-1755 d 6-10-1844 m Mary Cox Maj ADC NY ★
Jacob: b 1758 d 1841 m (1)Mary Cooper (2)Elizabeth Paynter Pvt PA
James: b 1-19-1752 d 4-20-1820 m Elizabeth Hubbard Capt CT
James: b 1-9-1754 d 10-27-1820 m Lydia Patterson Pvt NJ W ★
James: b 1-2-1740 d 3-5-1810 m Elizabeth Grant Cpl NC
Jan: b c. 1710 d p. 6-22-1779 m Helleyondje Van Ette PS NY
Jesse: b 1769 d 1816 m Elizabeth Pointer Pvt VA
John: b 9-2-1759 d 6-22-1844 m Desire Street Pvt CT
John: b 1738 d 1796 m Hannah Downing Pvt MD
John: b 9-5-1735 d 1790-99 m Rebecca Gore Pvt MA
John: b 5-29-1761 d 10-28-1848 m Sarah Coffin Smn MA
John: b 1763 d p. 1805 m Cynthia Bowers Sgt NY
John: b 1746 d 1827 m Joana Drake Pvt NC
John: b 3-24-1754 d 10-10-1808 m Barbara Myers Dr PA
John: b 4-1-1744 d 2-26/27-1835 m Susannah — Pvt Spy SC
John: b 1740 d p. 11-28-1808 m Rebecca Cox Sol SC
John, Sr.: b 1755 d 1815-18 m Margaret Droddy Capt VA
Jonathan: b 5-13-1735 d 3-8-1813 m Mary Skinner Lt MA
Jonathan: b 1753 d p. 1830 m Anna Maria Barbara Kemball Capt MD ★
Jonathan: b 6-15-1753 d 3-20-1841 m (1)Sarah Davis (2)Hannah Bradford Pvt PS PA ★
Jonathan: b 4-21-1727 d 12-12-1799 m Mary West Pvt PA
Jonathan: b 5-17-1729 d 4-7-1819 m Alice Evans PS PA
Jonathan Ford: b 3-21-1760 d 4-13-1810 m Margaret Smith Euen Lt Dr CL
Joseph: b 1-11-1761 d 8-6-1846 m (1)Mercy — (2)Cathern Havener MM MD
Joseph: b c. 1728 d 1787/8 m Elizabeth Malone Pvt MD
Joseph: b 1732 d 1-5-1778 m Hannah Ford Maj NJ
Joseph: b c. 1760 d p. 1799 m Betsey — Pvt PA
Joseph: b 1752 d 1840 m Jemima — Sol SC
Joseph: b 3-31-1736 d 9-15-1778 m Susan Woodson Pvt VA
Joseph: b c. 1750 d p. 3-3-1796 m Mary Farrer PS VA
Josiah: b 1-10-1746 d 3-9-1825 m Johanna Bolles Pvt CT
Lemuel: b 7-29-1737 d 3-16-1813 m Lydia Wilkinson 2Lt RI
Leonard: b 1747 d 1831 m (1)Mary Price (2)Margaret Likens Sct VA
Lester: b 7-5-1759 d 1853 m Frances Brown Pvt VA ★
Lewis: b 7-17-1726 d 9-15-1801 m Gertrude Montomery Pvt NJ
Lewis: b 4-8-1763 d 6-22-1798 m Mary Beekman Walton BG SDI NY
Lewis: b 1739 d p. 1790 m Rachel Walker Pvt PA
Lewis R: b 11-2-1760 d 12-29-1825 m (1)Mary Dwight (2)Theodosia Olcott (3)Ellen Hunt Ens NY
Major: b 1755 d 9-5-1811 m Elizabeth Hine Pvt CT
Moses: b 1743 d 1827 m Mary Hull Pvt NJ
Nathaniel: b 1734 d 1-21-1813 m Nancy Jeffries Pvt PS VA
Obediah: b c. 1749 d p. 4-11-1820 m Mary Sol GA
Randolph: b c. 1760 d p. 1784 m Mary Pvt NJ
Reuben: b 9-16-1737 d 12-3-1801 m Elizabeth Wetherell Pvt NJ
Richard: b 8-15-1730 d 4-11-1810 m Sarah Ludlow PS NY
Richard: b — d a. 10-25-1816 m (1)Mary Seals (2)Mrs Nancy Seals Vanmeter Pvt PA
Richard: b c. 1735 d c. 1802/3 m Mary — PS VA
Robert: b 1752 d 3-19-1827 m Rachel — Pvt CT ★
Robert: b 1734 d 1836 m (1)Content Dunham (2)Mary Cooker Pvt NJ
Robert: b 1-31-1734 d 5-7-1806 m Mary White SDI VA
Robert: b 1761 d 1807 m Martha — Pvt PA
Robert: b 1759 d 1832 m Patsy — Pvt VA
Samuel: b 1742 d 8-29-1792 m Jerusha Hinman Tms CT

Samuel: b 4-24-1734 d 7-7-1712 m Rebecca Wistar Capt PA
Samuel: b 11-21-1711 d 4- -1782 m Hannah Cadwalader PS PA
Solomon: b 9-5-1755 d 10-26-1840 m Kezziah Moss Sol CT
Thomas: b 1-16-1751 d 2-27-1778 m Sarah (Garner) Stapleton CS MD
Thomas: b c. 1765 d p. 1799 m Elizabeth Chadwick Pvt NJ
Thomas: b 11-8-1745 d 4-14-1814 m Ann Butler Pvt PA
Thomas: b 1756 d 11-30-1826 m (1)Mary Eliot (2)Elizabeth Jones Lt SC ★
Thomas: b 1-16-1761 d 8-4-1842 m Susan Appleton Pvt Grd VA ★
Thomas: b 1740 d 1- -1793 m Joyce Chislon Pvt VA
Wm.: b 11-28-1740 d p. 1794 m Sarah Bowman Lt CT
Wm.: b 11-20-1730 d 2-10-1797 m Nancy Winchester Capt DE
Wm.: b c. 1742 d 1794 m Mary Ann — PS MD
Wm.: b 7-15-1756 d 7-15-1841 m Mary Ann Reed Drm PA ★
Wm.: b 10-30-1758 d 9-8-1824 m Betsey McGinniss Pvt NC ★
Wm.: b 10-30-1755 d p. 12-10-1823 m Sara Terry Pvt NC
Wm.: b c. 1730 d 1- -1806 m Martha — Sol NC
Wm.: b 3-5-1739 d 4-21-1821 m Ann Griffith Pvt PA
Wm.: b 1759 d 10-24-1803 m Margaret McNeilla Pvt PA
Wm., Sr.: b 1724 d 1795 m Abigail Kemp Sol SC
Wm., Sr.: b 1745 d 1785 m Jane Johnson Sol SC
Wm., Sr.: b 1-1-1722 d 12-1-1792 m Elizabeth Stips PS VA
Wm., Jr.: b 12-17-1746 d 12- -1802 Catharine Carroll Sol VA
Wm.: b c. 1760 d 1832 m (1)Ann Freeman (2)Anne Diggs Durrett Pvt VA
Wm.: b c. 1760 d a. 9-3-1836 m — Pvt KY
Zadock: b 1759-61 d 12-18-1842 m Polly — Pvt DE ★
Zephaniah: b 9-20-1744 d p. 5-13-1833 m Mary Daws Pvt NJ

MORRISON, (includes MORISON)

Alexander: b 1749 d 3-8-1826 m Prudence Gamble Pvt PA
Alexander: b c. 1760 d 1839 m (2)Mary Ann Pvt VA
Andrew: b 1733 d a. 3-1-1777 m Mary Organ Pvt VA
David: b 11-4-1752 d 6-28-1837 m Lucy Wells Sgt MA ★
David: b 1732/3 d 4-6-1826 m (1)Kiziah Whittle (2)Huldah Page Pvt NH
David: b 8-29-1750 d 1812 m (1)Hannah Whitaker (2)Mrs Hall (3)Mrs McDonald Pvt NH
David: b 8-27-1763 d 12-9-1831 m Mary Kimball Pvt NH
Ebenezer: b c. 1730 d 3-15-1803 m Agnes Smith PS NH
Ephraim: b 6-5-1759 d 2-2-1806 m Agnes (Foster) Hettick Sol PA
Ezra: b 1756 d 11-1-1844 m Elizabeth Spears Carpenter Pvt GA ★
Francis: b c. 1732 d 1842 m Jane (Morrison) PS PA
Francis: b 1745 d 1800 m Agnes Frew Pvt PA
George: b 1739 d 1785 m Margaret Morrison Pvt PA
Hamilton: b 11-4-1759 d 1808 m Lydia Beemer Sgt NY
Hans: b c. 1725 d 9- -1788 m (1)Ann Holmes (2)Elizabeth — Lt PA
Henry: b 6-30-1752 d 1-18-1835 m (2)Catherine Alyea Sol NJ
Henry: b 1752 d 1834 m Patience Sayers Ens PA
James: b 2-28-1757 d 10-18-1854 m Hannah Gunn Pvt CT ★
James: b 1759 d 1-10-1824 m Agnes Sigler Pvt MD
James: b 1726 d 10-30-1804 m Jennet Morrison Capt NC
James: b 7-23-1748 d 12-22-1810 m — Smith Capt PA
James: b 1755 d 11-14-1813 m Mary Gibson Capt PA
James: b — 1738 d 4-23-1823 m (2)Esterh Montgomery Ens PA W ★
James, Sr.: b 1-4-1744 d 9-4-1839 m (1)Margaret Rice (2) Mrs Martha Guffin Macon Pvt PA ★
James: b 1745 d 2-11-1810 m Charlotte Howell Pvt PA
James: b c. 1758 d 3-3-1842 m — Pvt VA ★
James: b 1761 d 2-7-1858 m (1)Mrs Jane Taylor (2)Elizabeth Callison Pvt VA
James: b 1756 d 2-22-1839 m Catherine Graham Sgt VA ★
John: b 1743 d 10-18-1801 m Elizabeth Griffin Pvt CT
John: b 4-12-1759 d 3-24-1816 m Abigail Libbey Cpl NH W ★
John: b 5-18-1743 d 10-24-1824 m Janet Dinsmore Mil NH
John: b 2-28-1749 d 4-21-1840 m Anne Grey Pvt NH
John, Sr.: b 3-15-1700 d 3-8-1783 m Prudence Gwyn PS NY
John, Jr.: b 5-10-1730 d 7-15-1790 m Elizabeth Scott Pvt PS NY
John, 3rd: b 1753 d 1815 m Jane Storey Pvt NY
John: b 8-16-1722 d 1793 m Elizabeth — CS NY
John: b 1730 d p. 8-30-1777 m Mary Morrison Ens NC
John: b 3-28-1763 d 12-7-1846 m (1)Jane Bradshaw (2)Dorothy Rogers Pvt NC ★
John: b 11-11-1743 d 7-9-1835 m Sarah Potts Pvt NC ★
John: b 8- -1760 d 7-22-1827 m Hannetta Wilhelmina Hoffman SgtMaj PA
John: b 9-21-1748 d 4- -1825 m Elizabeth Huey Pvt PA
John: b 2-25-1756 d 4-14-1824 m Sarah — Pvt PA
John: b 1729 d 4-18-1799 m Rebecca Bryan PS PA
John: b c. 1740 d 1-26-1814 m Martha Campbell Capt VA
Jonathan: b 1758 d 12-23-1841 m Shuah Stevens Cpl NH
Jonathan: b 6-28-1759 d 6-20-1848 m Esther Jane Perkins Pvt NH
Joseph: b 1726 d 1802 m Mary Morrison Pvt PA
Joseph: b 1733 d 10-14-1817 m Hannah Montgomery Sol PA
Joseph: b 1762 d 1839 m Elizabeth McCullough Pvt PA
Joseph: b 1756 d 5-11-1817 m Elizabeth Fletcher Barton PS SC

MORRISON, contd.

Joseph: b 11-30-1759 d 8-25-1835 m Elizabeth Pvt VA ★
Kean: b c. 1740 d p. 2-24-1803 m (2)Nancy Gillis Pvt NC
Malcolm: b 1736 d p. 1790 m — Sol NC
Moses: b 1756 d 1853 m (1)Elizabeth Percy (2)Elizabeth Lowell Pvt MA
Nathaniel, Sr.: b c. 1730 d 1806 m Thankful — Sol VA
Neil: b 1728 d 9-13-1784 m Annabella Houston PS NC
Peter: b 1740 d 1809 m Mary Kirkpatrick Pvt NC
Robert: b 11-29-1744 d 2-13-1826 m Elizabeth Holmes Pvt NH
Robert: b 1728 d 8-12-1810 m Sarah — Sol NC
Robert: b 2-6-1758 d 4- -1808 m (1)Agnes Betton (2)Eunice Dow Pvt NH
Robert: b 1-8-1749 d 9-18-1832 m Elizabeth Culbertson Pvt PA
Roderick: b 12-29-1763 d 8-21-1843 m Charlotte Besse Sgt CT
Samuel: b c. 1760/61 d 9-13-1844 m Margaret Webber Pvt ME ★
Samuel: b 9-28-1748 d 1-2-1816 m (1)Sarah Park (2)Margaret Dinsmoor Armor Sgt NH
Samuel: b 9-11-1754 d p. 1790 m X Sgt NY
Samuel: b 6-23-1762 d 2-10-1812 m Mary Updegraff Pvt PA
Thomas: b 1710 d 11-23-1797 m Mary Smith PS NH
Wm.: b 1754 d 8-5-1845 m (1)Hannah — (2)Margaret — Pvt CT ★
Wm., Jr.: b 8-16-1749 d 8-29-1826 m Hannah Benson Pvt MA
Wm.: b 1759 d 1842 m Keziah Gowan Pvt MA ★
Wm.: b 11-30-1726 d 2-28-1788 m Jane Rogers PS NH
Wm.: b 7-23-1756 d 11-10-1821 m Abigail McEwen Sol NC
Wm.: b 3-25-1765 d 9-16-1839 m Catherine Russell Pvt NC
Wm.: b 1760 d 11- -1806 m Mary Susanna Houston Pvt NC
Wm.: b c. 1740 d p. 5-3-1810 m Elizabeth Mordoch PS NC
Wm.: b 1747 d a. 8-14-1810 m Sarah — Pvt PA
Wm.: b a. 1755 d p. 1818 m Jane — Sgt VA

MORROW, (includes MURROW)

Alexander: b 1743 d 7-5-1812 m Margaret Gardner Cpl NH ★
Alexander: b a. 1745 d 1810 m (2)Margaret Adams Pvt PA
Charles: b a. 1764 d 8- -1813 m (2)Mary Morton Pvt PA
Charles: b — d 8-20-1776 m Mary — Pvt PA
David: b 1762 d 10-17-1843 m Margaret Kelsey Pvt SC ★
George: b c. 1756 d 1815 m Anne — Sol PA
Henry: b 1762 d 1821 m Mary Jane Wilson Sol PA
James: b 6-6-1740 d 10-15-1800 m Elizabeth Frame Pvt VA
James: b 1743/44 d 1826 m Elizabeth Suttle Pvt NC
John: b 11-27-1760 d 8-24-1835 m (1)Elizabeth Pollock (2)Abigail Miller OrdlSgt PA ★
John: b c. 1750 d 11-30-1781 m Mary Kelsey Lt SC
John: b 1750 d 1820 m Mary Peyton Col VA
Joseph: b 1760 d p. 8-2-1831 m Jane Wylie Pvt SC
Rachel Reed: b c. 1733 d p. 8-26-1782 m William Morrow PS NC
Robert: b 1742 d p. 1790 m Margaret Ewing Capt MD
Robert: b 3-21-1755 d 10-28-1810 m Ann Hurley Sol NC
Samuel: b 3-19-1760 d 2-19-1842 m Jennette Nelson Pvt SC ★
Samuel: b c. 1740 d p. 1818 m Mrs Jane (Peden) Morton Pvt SC
Thomas: b 10-1-1740 d 2-2-1824 m Mary Lauthers Pvt PA
Thomas: b 1750 d 8-30-1830 m Ann Zatzinger Pvt PA ★
Wm.: b c. 1730 d 1782 m Rachael Reed PS NC
Wm.: b 1765 d 1835 m Sarah — Pvt SC ★

MORSE, (includes MORS, MORSS, MOSS, MOSSE)

Aaron: b 3-18-1739 d 5-15-1834 m Demaris Garfield Cpl MA
Abiel: b 5-28-1760 d 2-22-1857 m (1)Mary Johnson (2)Lucy Swift Miller Pvt VT CT
Abner: b 10-11-1759 d 3-11-1821 m Millie Leland Drm MA
Adam: b 11-15-1762 d 12-3-1838 m Lydia Bacon Pvt MA
Alexander: b 1730-40 d 1800 m Anne Thurman 1Lt VA
Amos, Jr.: b 11-20-1762 d 11-29-1854 m Susanna Sawyer Pvt MA
Amos, Jr.: b 1-19-1742 d 9-3-1824 m (1)Sarah Clark (2)Susannah Winana Capt NJ
Anthony: b 12-22-1753 d 3-22-1803 m Huldah Taylor Ens MA
Anthony: b 1752 d 11-10-1816 m Susannah Elliot Sgt MA W★
Artemas: b 4-14-1754 d 12-21-1837 m Mary Johnson Pvt MA ★
Asa: b 1-18-1742/3 d 12-10-1818 m Mary Boyden Pvt MA
Asa: b 11-7-1746 d 4- -1813 m Hannah Griggs Pvt MA
Asa: b 2-24-1747 d 2-19-1831 m Susannah Eames Pvt MA
Asa: b 12-30-1748 d 3-1-1815 m (1)Eunice Parker (2)Parthena Weatherbee (3)Betsey Sibley Sol MA
Barachias: b 11-19-1733 d 5-17-1805 m Zuriah Chadwick PS MA
Benjamin: b 3-10-1763 d 11-5-1863 m (2)Elizabeth Onthank Sgt MA ★
Benjamin: b 2-5-1754 d 12-23-1828 m Olive Greenough Pvt MA
Benjamin: b 5-31-1762 d 10-19-1836 m Deborah Sawin Pvt MA
Benjamin: b 3-15-1754 d 8-16-1833 m Nancy Hoar Pvt NH ★
Benoni: b 6-16-1737 d 1817 m Miriam Ware Pvt MA
Caleb: b 7-26-1753 d 12-8-1826 m Lucy Ward Pvt MA
Charles: b 3-20-1754 d 12-19-1830 m Sarah Gay Pvt MA
Chester: b 1-14-1750 d 8-26-1819 m (1)Lydia Putnam (2)Rachel Wood Pvt CT
Cornelius: b 1756-8 d 6-6-1845 m Merium (Mary A) White Pvt MA ★
Daniel: b 4-26-1744 d 1-31-1822 m Rebecca Munson Pvt CT
Daniel: b 4-2-1726 d p. 1800 m (1)Ann Wilcox (2)Mrs Anna (Carpenter) Wolcott PS CT
Daniel: b 2-6-1729/30 d 2-2-1804 m Hannah Eames Ens MA

Daniel: b 6-19-1743 d 12-16-1808 m Freelove Dexter Sgt MA
Daniel: b 2-18-1745 d 2-25-1826 m Miriam Hoyt Cpl MA
Daniel: b 2-8-1755 d 1-19-1824 m Polly (Mary) Gibbs Cpl Gnr MA W★
Daniel: b 8-2-1738 d — m Lois Grouts Pvt MA
Daniel: b 2-2-1750 d 1839 m Mary Wyman Pvt MA
Daniel: b 7-27-1735 d 1808 m Ruth (Morse) PS Pvt NH
David: b 4-18-1754 d 1-8-1831 m Lucy Norton Sgt CT
David: b 3-5-1743 d 11-19-1808 m Ester Sanger Cpl MA
David: b 2-11-1746 d 8-19-1801 m Abigail Bailey Pvt MA
David: b 8-26-1756 d 11-27-1830 m Jemima Wood Pvt MA
David: b 4-23-1761 d 2-29-1844 m Lydia Sutton Pvt NY ★
Elihu: b 4-25-1731 d 2-12-1778 m Esther Clark Lt CT
Elijah: b 6-24-1735 d 1820 m Ann Titus Pvt MA
Elijah: b 3-25-1758 d 3-9-1842 m Abigail Howe Pvt MA
Eliphalet: b 5-11-1734 d p. 2-18-1797 m Martha Mayo Pvt MA
Elisha: b 11-2-1741 d 12-2-1804 m Jemima Tomblin Pvt MA
Elisha: b 11-2-1741 d 5-27-1839 m (1)Abigail Holmes (2)Mrs Sally Littlewood Pvt MA
Enos: b 4-15-1761 d 11-6-1838 m Anna Baldwin Pvt MA ★
Ephraim: b 4-10-1751 d 10-7-1813 m Sarah Clapp Pvt MA
Ezekiel: b 9-12-1749 d 5-5-1823 m Mary Tyler Pvt MA
Ezra: b 9-17-1741 d 5-9-1807 m Susanna Guild 1Lt MA
Ezra: b 11-18-1752 d 6-3-1830 m Agnes Swan Pvt NH
Frederick: b 1735 d 1792 m Sarah Tompkins PS VA
George: b 1742 d 2-17-1808 m (1)Elizabeth Martin (2)Dorothy Phoebe Norton Dr SC
Gershom: b 1-4-1754 d p. 1797 m Thankful Sealy Sgt VT
Henry, Jr.: b 9-5-1754 d — m Lois Crane Cpl MA
Henry: b 12-22-1738 d 3-24-1835 m Mrs Rhoda (Cottle) George Pvt MA
Henry: b 1-22-1734 d 8-24-1787 m Esther Pidge Lt NH
Henry: b 1736 d c. 1810 m Sarah Stevens Capt VA
Henry: b 1755 d 1805 m Sallie Scott Mims Lt VA
Hugh: b 1736 d p. 2-11-1780 m Jane Ford Maj VA
Humphrey: b 12-1-1743 d 10-12-1816 m (1)Elisabeth Lunt (3)Sarah Knight Sgt MA
Isaac: b 4-1-1756 d 5-24-1849 m Charlotte Grant FifMaj CT ★
Isaac: b 3-29-1754 d 1-1-1836 m Sarah Tuttle Trm CT
Isaac: b 1-1-1753 d 1-20-1824 m Elizabeth Morse Pvt MA
Isaac: b 6-24-1762 d 2-21-1840 m Elizabeth — Pvt NH ★
Isaac: b 8-5-1758 d 7-23-1825 m Amy Cundalkin Srgn Mte NJ
Isaiah, Sr.: b 12-5-1715 d 1781 m (1)Phoebe Doolitle (2)Keziah Prindle PS CT
Jacob: b 7-23-1755 d 1-5-1841 m Rebeckah Smith Cpl MA
Jacob: b 9-21-1717 m d 3-30-1800 m Mary Merrifield Pvt MA
Jacob: b 12-24-1745 d 4-4-1818 m (1)Mary Kingsbury (2)Sarah Hawes Pvt MA
James: b 9-21-1760 d 3-13-1845 m Dorice (Lovica) Brewster Pvt CT ★
James: b 8-25-1747 d 9-5-1828 m (1)Mary Lambe (2)Mrs Monica Greenwell PS MD
James, Jr.: b 2-16-1745/6 d 4-7-1805 m Elizabeth Bullard Pvt MA
James, Sr.: b 12-21-1720 d 2-7-1812 m Grace Bullen Pvt MA
James: b 5-6-1746 d — m Hannah Smith Pvt MA
James: b 1-6-1742 d 12-15-1827 m Sarah Ross Pvt PA
James: b 9-6-1760 d 9-20-1846 m Judith — Pvt VA ★
Jedediah: b 7-8-1726 d 1819 m Sarah Child CS Pvt CT
Jeduthan: b 3-9-1730 d 9-18-1776 m Mercy Leonard Pvt MA
Jeremiah, Sr.: b 8-20-1740 d 12-31-1804 m Experience Ware Pvt MA
Jeremiah, Jr.: b 9-27-1762 d 12-17-1836 m Miriam Barrett Pvt MA
Jesse: b 3-10-1729 m 3-20-1793 m Mary (Moss) Capt CT
Jesse, Sr.: b 1-13-1729 d 8-6-1805 m Rachel Allen Sgt MA
Jesse, Jr.: b 8-18-1758 d 4-7-1834 m Mercy White Pvt MA
Joel: b 7-7-1757 d 1794 m Hannah Hall Pvt CT
John: b 11-8-1752 d 1801 m Deborah Lines Pvt CT
John: b 2-25-1736 d 2- -1825 m Joanna Dewey Sol MA
John: b 8-13-1746 d 6-20-1826 m (1)Sarah Sanders (2)Leonice Riggs Pvt MA W★
John: b a. 1750 d 1-1-1811 m Elizabeth — Pvt NY
John: b c. 1740 d 1810 m Charity Hughes Sol SC
John: b 7-15-1746 d 4-7-1822 m Elizabeth Andrews CS VT
John: b c. 1750 d 10- -1809 m (1)Louiza Minor (2)Ann Eliza Minor Capt VA
John, Sr.: b 1705-8 d a. 12-19-1785 m Elizabeth Massie PS VA
Jonas: b 1752 d 12-6-1824 m Abigail Smith Pvt NJ
Jonathan: b 2-8-1731 d p. 1788 m Esther Curtis Pvt CT
Jonathan: b 8-7-1755 d 7- -1836 m Sarah Wyman Pvt MA
Jonathan: b 1-19-1754 d 12-12-1812 m Thankful Smith Pvt NH ★
Jonathan: b 3-3-1757 d 3-3-1840 m (1)Abiah Worth (2)Fannie (Chase) Worthley Pvt NH
Joseph: b 12-17-1742 d 1819 m Esther Lewis Pvt CT
Joseph: b 1-1-1739 d 12-15-1779 m (1)Rebecca Broad (2)Keziah Chickering Maj MA
Joseph: b 9-15-1738 d 9-19-1777 m Jemima Wheat Pvt MA
Joseph: b 1-4-1730/1 d 2-7-1802 m Sarah Ellice Pvt MA
Joseph: b 6-19-1748 d 1835 m Rachel Phillips Pvt MA
Joseph: b 5-3-1757 d 8-1-1833 m Hannah Miller Matr MA ★
Joseph: b 5-12-1753 d 12-25-1811 m Mary Randall PS NH
Joseph: b 9-6-1756 d 9-28-1833 m Anna Coleman Pvt NY MA
Joseph: b 7-19-1749 d 10-22-1841 m Ann Thompson Pvt PA
Joshua: b 1-18-1742 d — m Abigail Hall Pvt CT

Joshua: b 3-5-1751 d 2-6-1829 m Eve (Thorpe)Farrington Cpl MA
Joshua: b 3-29-1728 d 9-13-1819 m (1)Mary Goodenuff (2)Alice Lothrop Chubbock Pvt MA
Joshua: b 11-24-1728 d 4-1-1787 m Unity — Pvt MA
Joshua: b 7-8-1758 d 7-11-1806 m Caroline Matilda Hathaway Pvt MA
Joshua: b 3-8-1752 d 10-1-1828 m Lavinia Holland Pvt VT
Joshua: b 8-5-1744 d 1825 m Sarah Pennington Sgt VA
Josiah: b 1-31-1729 d c. 1779 m (1)Kesiah Clark (2)Dorothea Wood CS MA
Josiah: b 10-23-1762 d 6-2-1824 m (1)Mehitable Carlton Pvt MA ★
Josiah: b 6-17-1763 d 5-21-1839 m Emma Weatherbee Pvt MA ★
Josiah: b 9-28-1721 d 2-8-1795 m Mary Chase PS NH
Levi: b 11-16-1746 d 3-6-1825 m Martha Sherman Sgt CT
Levi: b 1-5-1762 d 2-3-1844 m Polly Gay Bradford Pvt MA ★
Mark: b 12-25-1757 d 3-18-1854 m Lydia Thissell Pvt MA
Mark: b 2-25-1747 d c. 5-12-1826 m Sarah J Sweetsir Pvt MA
Micah: b 10- -1759 d 1840 m Sarah — Pvt NH
Moody, Sr.: b 4-1-1719 d 8-14-1805 m Hannah Carleton PS MA
Moody, Jr.: b 7-7-1746 d 1789 m Abigail Leland Sgt MA
Moses: b 8-15-1751 d 5-7-1847 m Mary Dutton Pvt CT ★
Moses: b 11-3-1752 d p. 1780 m Mary Clark Pvt MA
Moses: b 5-13-1749 d 11-2-1825 m Abigail Lovejoy Pvt MA
Moses: b 6-17-1739 d 4-4-1790 m Lydia Daniels Pvt MA
Moses: b 7-26-1721 d p. 1778 m — PS MA
Moses: b 5-24-1758 d 8- -1837 (1)Elizabeth Day (2)Lucretia Williams Pvt VA ★
Moses: b 2-13-1739 d 6-19-1827 m Mary — PS VA
Nathan: b 2-28-1750 d 10-8-1841 m Mrs Elizabeth Stevens Hills OrdlSgt MA ★
Nathan: b 7-16-1728 d 1783 m Mary Jackson Pvt MM MA
Nathan, Sr.: b 3-23-1734 d 12-12-1812 m Abigail Pond Pvt MA
Nathan, Jr.: b 1-2-1765 d 6-22-1832 m Abigail Smith Pvt MA
Nathaniel: b 10-20-1728 d 6-5-1781 m Mary Morgan Sgt CT
Nathaniel: b 12-14-1722 d 8-21-1804 m (1)Kezia Roys (2)Mary Dorchester Lt CT
Nathaniel: b 12-25-1752 d 11-23-1824 m Joanna Johnson PS VA
Nathaniel Fry: b 12-6-1750 d 3-17-1835 m (1)Hannah Gibbs (2)Rebekah Hall Putnam Pvt MA
Noah: b 4-12-1741 d p. 1796 m Betty Hill Sgt MA
Noah: b 9-16-1734 d 3-11-1813 m Betsy Bonney Pvt VT
Obadiah, Jr.: b 8-16-1730 d 7-21-1776 m Mary Willet Pvt MA
Obadiah: b 3-20-1732/3 d 1-7-1800 m (1)Grace Fairbanks (2)Abigail Death Pvt MA
Obadiah: b 5-7-1763 d 12-20-1818 m Johanna Marsh Pvt MA
Obadiah: b 9-26-1763 d 8-11-1850 m X Pvt MA ★
Obadiah: b 8-15-1738 d p. 1783 m Lydia Myrick Pvt MA
Obed: b 9-13-1763 d 10-26-1832 m Sarah Bunnel Pvt CT
Pain: b 8-13-1747 d 8-20-1830 m (1) — Merrill (2)Martha Sprague CS PS MA
Parker: b 11-16-1751 d 6-23-1805 m Love Knowles Sgt NH
Peter: b 3-5-1722/3 d p. 1790 m (1)Kezia Sabin (2)Sarah Hanes Pvt MA
Peter: b 9-13-1742 d 5-21-1821 m Sarah Ransom PS NY
Philip: b 5-24-1755 d 2-18-1847 m Mary Knowles (2)Irene Briggs Pvt MA NH ★
Phillis: b 10-19-1747 d 3-30-1828 m Abigail Coney Drm MA
Ray: b — d p. 2-26-1804 m (2)Jane Coleman Pvt VA
Reuben: b 7-21-1742 d 8-27-1810 m Abigail Mason Ens NH
Reuben: b 1747 d 1819 m Polly Ann Jorden Pvt NC
Samuel: b 3-3-1749 d 3-19-1807 m Elizabeth Gibbs Cpl MA
Samuel: b 8-6-1762 d 10-20-1844 m Thankful Wheeler Pvt MA
Samuel: b 9-30-1718 d 4-20-1787 m Catherine Clark Capt MA
Samuel, Jr.: b 11-30-1759 d 8-4-1853 m Esther Woodward Pvt MA
Samuel: b 7-30-1750 d 3-8-1848 m Sarah Webster Pvt NH ★
Samuel: b 1721 d 1792 m Elizabeth — PS NC
Seth: b 12-2-1753 d 8-18-1801 m Mary Dean Pvt MA
Seth: b 1-3-1757 d 11-19-1840 m Polly Gibson Pvt MA ★
Seth: b 4-7-1760 d 1833/4 m (1)Ruth Goodrich (2)Elizabeth Young Pvt VT
Silas: b 4-15-1736 d 9-29-1797 m (1)Mehitable Price Pvt MA
Simeon: b 1-31-1751 d 11-9-1831 m Bethia Norris Pvt MA
Simeon: b 4-7-1760 d 8-19-1842 m Azubah Wheeler Pvt MA
Solomon: b 1751 d 3-11-1797 m Hannah Mayo Pvt VT
Solomon: b 1749 d 8-13-1822 m (1)Huldah Coleman (2)Jemima Parker Pvt MA ★
Solomon: b 2-18-1749 d 6-4-1820 m Mary Spellman Pvt CT
Stephen: b 2-16-1747 d 1-31-1826 m Abigail Donnel Cpl PS MA
Stephen: b 5-1-1751 d 4-29-1825 m Sarah Bailey Sgt MA
Stephen: b 5-30-1738 d 10-1-1802 m Lydia Tenney Pvt MA
Stephen: b 12-14-1759 d 9-2-1836 m Rebecca Howe Pvt MA
Stephen 2nd: b 1-28-1757 d 6-14-1843 m Sarah Kay Pvt MA NH ★
Stephen: b 2-17-1723/4 d 3-6-1807 m Abigail Ingalls PS NH
Thomas: b 6-30-1726 d 10-23-1799 m Elizabeth Bartlett PS CS MA
Thomas, Jr.: b 8- -1749 d 6- -1829 m Rebecca Cole PS NH
Thomas: b 12-5-1709 d 1-7-1783 m Mary Treadway PS NH
Thomas: b 11-23-1740 m Mary — Col VA
Thomas: b 1732 d 8- -1812 m (1)Sally — (2)Peggy — Sol VA
Timothy: b 9-3-1759 d 9-22-1824 m Nabby Dean FifMaj MA W ★
Timothy: b 5-10-1756 d 2-26-1828 m Hannah Mixer Fif MA
Titus: b 5-16-1738 d 12-23-1818 m Mary Atwater Lt CT
Wm.: b 2-26-1738 d 6-26-1802 m Phebe Stevens Capt MA
Wm.: b 1726 d p. 1806 m Phebe Bodwell Pvt MA

Wm.: b 11-12-1739 d 1-1-1817 m Frances Sowell PS NC
Wm.: b 1763 d 10-16-1841 m Lydia Glasscock Sol VA
Zeally: b 3-6-1755 d 10-31-1839 m (1)Elizabeth Berry (2)Jennette Glascock Capt Wgm CL ★
Zebadiah: b 8-12-1748 d 8-17-1817 m Mary Sabin Lt MA
Zebulon: b 4-28-1741 d 6-7-1823 m Mary Norris Cpl MA

MORTIMER, (includes MORTIMORE)
Famous: b 1763 d 5-15-1851 m Mary Blue Pvt VA ★
James: b c. 1757 d 4-28-1807 m — Pvt PA

MORTON,
Abner: b 1754 d 11-22-1831 m (1)Sarah — (2)Elizabeth — Pvt CT
Aner: b 1-17-1736 d 2-5-1823 m Sophia Goddard Pvt MA
Agnes Woodson: b 2-27-1711 d 3-10-1802 m Joseph Morton PS VA
Alexander: b 1759 d 4-13-1822 m Ruth Strong Pvt MM CT W ★
Ambrose: b 7-24-1756 d 1-8-1832 m Sarah Tolman Pvt MA
Benjamin: b 11-9-1744 d 10-12-1808 m Lucy Edwards Pvt CT
Bryant: b c. 1705-7 d 1793 m (1)Thankful — (2)Mrs Lucy (White) Chamberlain CS Capt ME MA
Caleb: b 6-5-1758 d 4-11-1822 m Rebecca Wood Pvt MA
Daniel: b 12-23-1720 d 6-20-1786 m (1)Esther Bardwell (2)Eleanor Wait MM MA
David: b 9-17-1747 d 9-8-1826 m Deborah Phelps Sgt MA ★
David: b 9-12-1721 d 2-23-1798 m Christian — CS MA
Deodat: b 1756/7 d 3-24-1812 m Jemima Rockwell Pvt CT
Ebenezer, Jr.: b 1764 d 2-3-1839 m Hannah Ingraham Pvt MA
Edward: b 3-23-1746 d 2-20-1852 m Mary Allison Pvt VA ★
Eleazer: b 1753 d p. 1790 m Jemima Taylor Pvt MA
Elihu: b 2-23-1746 d 6-14-1815 m Lucy Welles Pvt MA
Elijah: b 11-10-1718 d 10-6-1798 m (1)Eunice (Morton) (2)Mrs Martha Barstow CS MA
Elijah: b c. 1705 d p. 1788 m Elizabeth Hawkins PS VA
Elisha: b 6-12-1754 d 7-28-1829 m Elizabeth Sackett Cpl MA
George: b 1746 d a. 7-27-1801 m Jane (Morton) Pvt VA
Hezekiah: b 11-25-1752 d 6-30-1831 m Phoebe Moseley Capt MA
Ichabod: b 1726 d 5-16-1809 m Deborah — Pvt MA
Isaac: b 4-18-1754 d 9-24-1824 m (1)Anna Barber (2)Mrs Mary Folsom Capt MA
Jacob: b 1-29-1751 d 5-22-1829 m Jane Davis Booker Capt VA
James: b 6- -1753 d 4-10-1840 m Susan Dyer Sgt MA
James: b 1743 d 1823 m Mary Gamble Pvt PA
James: b 9-8-1756 d 1847/48 m Mary Smith Lt VA ★
James: b c. 1756 d 1808 m Catherine Wells Lt VA
Job: b 1760 d 1830-5 m (1)Patience Crooker (2)Molly Dunham Pvt MA
John: b 5-10-1753 d 1-15-1820 m Esther Elinor — Pvt CT
John: b 12-25-1763 d 12-23-1857 m (1)Betty Foster (2)Elizabeth Leonard Sol MA
John: b c. 1729 d p. 2-4-1782 m Mary Sophia Kemper PS NJ
John: b 1724 d 12- -1777 m Anne Justus SDI PA
John: b 2-9-1730 d 12- -1796 m Mary Elizabeth Anderson Capt VA
John: b 11-20-1733 d 1794 m (1)Gene — (2)Lucy Blaekley Capt VA
John: b 1747 d c. 1796 m Nancy Ann Smith Capt VA
John: b 8-16-1757 d 5-2-1839 m Talitha Tinsley Pvt VA
Joseph, Jr.: b c. 1735 d 1818 m Nancy — Capt CS VA
Joseph: b 12-10-1760 d p. 1796 m (1)Mary Ann Morton (2)Nancy Baker Sgt VA
Joseph: b 12-27-1709 d 6-28-1782 m (1) — Goode (2)Agnes Woodson PS VA
Josiah: b 2-16-1757 d 5-30-1829 m Phebe Bliss Pvt MA
Josiah: b 3-25-1738 d 11-28-1785 m Elizabeth Venable LCol VA
Livy: b 2-4-1760 d 7-19-1838 m (1)Hannah Daily (2)Cathrine Richmond Pvt MA
Martin: b c. 1735 d 4-24-1782 m (2)Judith Johnson Pvt PA
Moses: b 1751 d p. 9-18-1823 m Mary Dowler Pvt PA
Nathaniel 2nd: b 6-1-1753 d 11-18-1832 m Mary Carey Sgt MA
Nathaniel: b 11-21-1735 d 11-13-1826 m (1)Lucy Washburn (2)Rebecca Morton 1Lt MA
Nathaniel: b 1722/23 d 3-15-1794 m Martha Tupper PS MA
Oliver: b 9-5-1763 d 3-19-1848 m (1)Sarah Everett (2)Mrs Melinda Lary Slr Pvt MA ★
Perez: b 1-4-1725 d 5-19-1795 m Sarah Green 2ndMaj MA
Perez: b 10-22-1750 d 10-14-1837 m Sarah Wentworth Apthorp PS MA
Peter: b c. 1740 d p. 11-1-1795 m Anna — PS NC
Richard: b 6-16-1755 d p. 1790 m Thankful Eaton Sol MA
Samuel P: b 9-23-1745 d 7-19-1834 m Delpha Wade Pvt VA ★
Seth: b 3-11-1732 d 1-30-1810 m Hepsibah Packard Pvt MA
Silas, Sr.: b 4-17-1727 d 10-30-1782 m Martha Morton CS PS MA
Silas, Jr.: b 7-21-1752 d 3-25-1840 m Elizabeth Foster Capt MA
Simeon, Sr.: b 9-26-1723 d 11-3-1798 m Miriam Dickinson Pvt MA
Simeon, Jr.: b 1750 d 4- -1816 m Sibyl Graves Pvt MA
Sketchley: b 1750 d 1-19-1795 m Rebecca Taylor Maj PS PA
Solomon: b 1763 d p. 1806 m Eunice Tower Pvt MA
Thomas: b 1-20-1759 d 6- -1793 m Elizabeth Walling Pvt MA
Thomas: b 1736 d 8-29-1790 m Bettie Paul PS CS SC
Thomas: b c. 1726 d 1802 m Cicily Katherine Moore Pvt VA
Wm.: b 8-18-1761 d 11-12-1837 m Hannah Chambers Pvt MA
Wm.: b c. 1750 d 8-11-1812 m Catherine McIntosh Pvt PA

MORTON, contd.
Wm.: b 3-27-1743 d 11-29-1820 m Susan Watkins Col VA
Zephaniah: b 3-12-1748 d *p.* 1790 m Rebecca Pierce Pvt MA

MOSBY,
Benjamin: b *c.* 1756 d 1819 m Ann Winston 2Lt VA
Hezekiah: b 1-12-1760 d *c.* 1849 m Mary Massie Pvt VA ★
John: b 1749 d *a.* 1809 m Elizabeth — PS VA
Joseph: b 1757 d 11-7-1832 m Martha Owen Sgt VA
Joseph: b 1-28-1758 d 9-15-1848 m Sally Lewis Sgt NC ★
Littleberry: b 1-29-1729 d 1-14-1809 m (1)Elizabeth Netherland (2)Judith Michaux (3)Mrs Martha (Scott) Thomas Col PS VA
Samuel: b 1750 d 1805 m Jean Robards Capt PS NC
Samuel: b *c.* 1710 d *p.* 3-19-1783 m Jerusha Bowles CS NC
Wade: b 1760 d 6-1-1834 m Susanna Trueheart Capt VA W★

MOSELEY, (includes MOSLEY)
Abisha: b 6-6-1736 d 1810 m Lois Dutton Capt VT
Abner: b 5-17-1738 d 2-22-1812 m Ann Clark Capt PS CT
Arthur: b *c.* 1752 d 5- -1803 m (1)Nancy Trigg (2)Pamelia Thorp Crump 2Lt PS VA
Arthur: b 11-9-1760 d 8-21-1835 m Sally Perkins Pvt VA ★
Azariah: b 8-7-1728 d 1815 m Mirriam Parsons Pvt MA
Benjamin: b *c.* 1755 d 1819 m Amey Giles 1Lt VA
Benjamin: b *a.* 1763 d 7-26-1799 m Mary Branch 1Lt VA W★
Blackman: b *c.* 1750 d 1825 m Elizabeth Archer Capt VA
Brantley: b 1755 d 1850-60 m Sarey Phillips Sol SC
Daniel: b 3-27-1714 d 3-6-1777 m Anna Abbott PS MA
David: b 3-7-1735 d 11-5-1798 m Lydia Gay Col PS MA
Ebenezer: b 2-19-1741 d 3-20-1825 m Martha Strong Col PS CT
Edward: b 5-14-1718 d 9-3-1808 m Amey Green Capt VA
Edward Hack: b 2-4-1743 d 2-4-1814 m Martha Westwood Col VA
George: b 4-27-1762 d 12-18-1828 m (1)Lucy Moore (2)Mary Moore Pvt VA
George: b 1757 d 9-7-1835 m Catherine Poulston Pvt PA
Increase: b 5-18-1712 d 5-2-1795 m Deborah Tracy PS CT
Increase, Jr.: b 10-13-1740 d 1811 m Patience Hinman Col CT
Israel: b 8-28-1742 d 6-21-1824 m Abigail Chapin Pvt MA
James Thomas: b 1754 d 1840 m Nancy Jasper Sol SC
John: b 7-25-1725 d 9-1-1780 m Hannah Mandsley Col MA
Jonathan: b 6-10-1749 d 8- -1829 m Esther Clark Pvt NY
Joseph: b 4-13-1735 d 10-25-1806 m Hopeful Robbins Capt CT
Joseph: b 1727 d 9-1-1782 m Sibbillah Dudley PA MA
Joseph: b 1-1-1765 d 4-19-1835 m Mary Robertson Pvt VA ★
Josiah: b 2-29-1748 d 3-3-1826 m Abigail Holt Pvt MA
Nathaniel: b 12-22-1743 d 3-7-1788 m (1)Rosanna Alworth (2)Ester Swift Col CT
Robert: b 1752 d *p.* 6-7-1821 m Mrs Sarah Peak Lt PA ★
Robert: b 1725 d *p.* 1-6-1796 m (1)Sarah Turpin (2)Mary Bransford (3)Penelope Talley Sol SC
Robert: b 2-14-1732 d 1-30-1804 m Magdalene Guerrant Lt VA
Robert Joel: b 9-13-1755 d *p.* 1803 m Mary Ann Stewart Sol PS NC
Samuel: b 9-23-1759 d 12-25-1833 m — Bledsoe Pvt NC ★
Samuel: b 1759 d 1830 m Sarah Ballou Pvt VA
Thomas: b 2-17-1731 d 8-11-1811 m (1)Phoebe Ann Ogden (2)Mrs Rhoda Griswold Troop Dr CT
Thomas, Sr.: b 6-2-1728 d 12-23-1796 m Esther Davis Pvt MA
Thomas, Jr.: b 6-1-1759 d 1-13-1836 m Sarah Withington Sgt MA
Thomas: b 1756 d 1834-41 m Mary — Capt VA
Thomas: b 4-17-1756 d 1830 m Judith Kinney Sgt VA
Thomas: b 1-7-1759 d 1835 m Magdalene Guerrant Pvt VA ★
Thomas: b *c.* 1738 d *a.* 2-19-1795 m Jane Stoner PS Ens VA
Uriel: b 2-1-1756 d 1826 m Sally Hammond Pvt CT
West: b — d 3-23-1821 m Rebecca — PS NC
Wm.: b 1753 d 10-12-1812 m Miss Muse Pvt SC
Wm.: b 1754 d 9- -1808 m Anne Irvine Maj VA W★
Wm.: b 1730 d *p.* 1802 m Mary Watkins Capt VA
Wm.: b 1756 d 1811 m Rachel — Capt VA

MOSEMAN,
Marcus, Jr.: b *a.* 1748 d *p.* 1831 m Phebe Higgins Capt NY
Peter: b 1743 d 10-25-1819 m Thankful Allen Sgt NY

MOSES,
Aaron: b 10-6-1733 d 1809 m (1)Susannah Seymour (2)Rachel Gilbert Sgt CT
Abel: b 6-24-1733 d 6-14-1785 m X Pvt CT
Abraham: b 1754 d 1821 m Esther Sibley Pvt NC
Ashbill: b 1759 d 1-27-1837 m Esther O. — Pvt CT
Daniel: b 6-22-1729 d 9-8-1776 m Mary Wilcox Pvt NY
Darius: b 11-11-1758 d 10-25-1824 m Sarah Adams Pvt MA
Ezekiel: b *c.* 2-3-1762 d 11-15-1834 m Eunice Bogue Pvt CT ★
George: bpt 3-22-1747 d *p.* 1788 m Anna Harmon Pvt MA
Jacob: b 1739 d 1821-23 m Elizabeth Hohlman Pvt PA
Jonah: b *c.* 1759 d 7-2-1804 m — Pvt MA
Joshua: b 2-24-1727 d 1820 m Abigail Terry Mar MA
Joshua: b 1748 d 2-26-1836 m Jane Pleasant Pvt NC ★
Mark: b 1703 d 2-2-1789 m (1)Martha Williams (2)Jane Wallace PS NH
Martin: b 4-12-1761 d 9-21-1849 m Lydia Hale Pvt CT ★

Meyer: b 1735 d 2-15-1787 m (2)Rachel Andrews PS SC
Michael: b 9-12-1737 d 3-14-1797 m Thankful Case Pvt CT
Nadab: b 1749 d 1-21-1792 m Abigail Wallace PS NH
Othniel: b 7-1-1730 d 1822 m Sarah Pinney Pvt CT
Peter: b *c.* 1745 d 1824 m (1)Elizabeth — (2)Mary — Pvt PA
Robert: b 7-16-1735 d 10-9-1832 m Margaret Bradley Pvt MD
Samuel: bpt 8-31-1735 d *p.* 1813 m Anna — PS NH
Samuel: bpt 3-6-1726 d *p.* 1802 m (1)Bridget Weeks (2)Susanna — PS NH
Sylvanus: b 8-25-1745 d 1- -1832 m Mariam Young Sol PS NH
Zebulon, Jr.: b 1754 d 8-3-1808 m (1)Phebe — (2)Hannah Lee Pvt VT

MOSEY,
Christian: b *c.* 1762 d *c.* 4-8-1832 m Eleanor — Pvt PA

MOSHER, (includes MOESIER, MOSHIER & MOSIER)
Abijah: b 8-17-1749 d 12-4-1791 m Hannah Varnum Pvt MA
Cornelius: b 1760 d 1825 m Rosanna Roe Pvt NY
Daniel, Sr.: b 1745 d 2-7-1840 m Elizabeth Macomber Pvt MA ★
Daniel, Jr.: b 5-4-1751 d 3-4-1826 m Susanna Burnham Pvt NY
Ephriam: b 9-21-1726 d 5-28-1823 m Elizabeth Story CS NY
Freeman: b *c.* 1755 d *p.* 1793 m Hephzibah Orton Pvt CT
George: b 1749 d *p.* 1790 m Meribah Beadon Pvt MA
Jacob: b *c.* 1725 d *p.* 10-5-1795 m Magdalina Fritz Sol NY
James: b 7- -1735 d 10-2-1834 m Abigail Frost Cpl MA
James: b 1760 d 1845 m Ann Gray MM Drm MA
Jeremiah, Jr.: b 1-2-1755 d 3-8-1830 m Susannah Thornborough Sgt MA
John: b 2-8-1745 d 3-3-1817 m Hannah Warren Lt MA
John: b 1748-50 d 4-22-1833 m Lois Dibble Pvt MA CT ★
John: b 5-31-1744 d *p.* 1790 m Rebecca Chase Pvt MA
Joseph: b 5-12-1732 d 10-29-1801 m (1)Meriboah Allen (2)Elizabeth Briggs Pvt NY
Josiah: b 5-31-1757 d 8-9-1848 m Rebekah Doolittle Sgt MA
Nicholas: b 3-9-1728 d 5-22-1819 m Elizabeth Crandall Adj VT
Samuel: b 3-9-1742 d 4-23-1815 m Alce Gidley Pvt NY
Stephen: b 1754 d 1-30-1838 m (1) — Cobb (2)Margaret — Pvt CT ★
Thomas: b 1760 d 1-11-1812 m Irene Carpenter Cpl NY
Thomas: b 1758 d 4-9-1832 m Cornelia Barheit Pvt NY ★
Tobias: b 1748 d *p.* 1835 m Nancy Myers Pvt NC ★

MOSMAN, (includes MOSSMAN)
Aaron: b 10-22-1757 d 11-27-1840 m (1)Hepzibah Hosmer (2)Sarah Gardner Pvt MA
Jesse: b 9-8-1754 d 9-22-1840 m Ann Maynard Cpl MA
Mathias: b 3-17-1748/49 d 11-8-1819 m Sarah Haynes Lt MA
Oliver: b 1-19-1760 d 4-30-1835 m Dolly Trowbridge Ens MA ★
Samuel: b 2-27-1740 d 12-29-1828 m Anna Keyes Pvt MA
Silas: b 5-27-1757 d 1-20-1829 m Beulah Heminway Pvt MA
Timothy: b 2-26-1744 d 7- -1826 m Lucy Bond Lt MA

MOSSHOLDER,
John: b *c.* 1750 d 1816 m Johanna Stump Pvt PS PA

MOST,
Jacob: b *c.* 1740 d *a.* 1826 m Ann — Pvt PA

MOTHERAL,
John: b 8-30-1755 d 5-21-1824 m Jane Currier Pvt NC

MOTHERSHEAD,
Nathaniel: b 3-2-1754 d 12-29-1834 m Ruth Burt Sgt VA

MOTLEY,
David: b *c.* 1760 d *a.* 3-20-1826 m (1)Elizabeth Pendleton (2)Jency Wright Sol VA
Edwin: b 1745 d *p.* 10-6-1808 m (1)Catherine Broaddus (2)Elizabeth Gray PS VA
John: b 1740 d *p.* 6-13-1811 m Elizabeth — PS NC
Joseph: b *c.* 1720 d 1806 m (1)Martha Ellington (2)Elizabeth Irby PS CS VA

MOTLOW,
John: b 7-28-1757 d 5-25-1812 m Agnes — 1Lt SC

MOTSINGER,
Felix: b 1727 d *p.* 1791 m (2)Mrs Elizabeth Long PS NC

MOTT, (includes MOTE & MOTTE)
Abel: b 2-22-1736 d — m Rachel Pierce PS CT
Adam, Jr.: b 1735 d 9- -1811 m (1)Abiah Filley (2)Anna Cyrena Filley Pvt CT
Atwood: b 9-18-1736 d *p.* 1790 m Mrs Hannah Whord Lt MA
Christopher: b 7-9-1761 d 12-6-1833 m Elizabeth Mc Clure Pvt NJ
Daniel: b 1741/42 d 6-14-1798 m Mary Dodge PS RI
Edward: b *c.* 1735 d *p.* 1790 m Sarah Kinne Maj PS CT
Gershom: b *c.* 1743 d 5-27-1786 m Elizabeth Williams Capt NY
Isaac: b 12-8-1738 d 5-8-1795 m (1)Ann Smith (2)Katherine Deas (3)Mary Broughton Col SC W★
Jacob: b 10-14-1759-61 d 12-10-1834 m Mary Bishop MM NY
James: b 4-5-1707 d 2-11-1787 m (1)Mary Holmes (2)Amey Herbert PS 2Maj NJ

James: b 1-13-1750 d 7-5-1808 m Mary Denton Ens NY
John: b 1-18-1734 d 1-31-1804 m Eleanor Johnston Alexander Capt NJ
John: b 7-15-1746 d 4-7-1823 m (1)Sarah — (2)Beulah Mann (3)Naomi Dagget Pvt NJ
John: b 3-28-1758 d 8-28-1828 m (2)Jerusha Smith Miller (3)Barbara Skinner Pvt NY
John: b 6- -1747/48 d 5-31-1831 m Mary Rowley Capt VT ★
John: b 1750 d 1818 m (2)Mary Elizabeth Sol VA
Joseph: b 5-8-1752 d 7-20-1843 m Clarinda Marvin Pvt NY ★
Lent: b 8-16-1738 d p. 1828 m (2)Mary Filley Pvt CT
Nathan: b c. 1760-65 d a. 1830 m Keziah Beckham Sol GA
Rebecca Brewton: b 6-15-1737 d 1-10-1815 m Jacob Motte PS SC
Richard: b 1725 d 1791 m Maria Ann — Pvt VA
Samuel: b 10-13-1736 d 5-17-1813 m (1)Abigail Rossiter (2)Abigail Ayer Stanton (3)Mrs Lydia Tyler CS Col CT
Samuel: b 2-5-1736 d 6-14-1819 m (1)Margaret Williams (2)Susannah PS Sol NY
Samuel Jackson: b 2-6-1753 d 8-11-1828 m Glorianna Coles Sol PS NY
Wm., Sr.: b 1735 d 1790 m Jerusha Nash Maj NY
Zebulon: b 9-4-1757 d 2-21-1842 m Rebecca Smith Pvt NY

MOTTER,
Jacob: b c. 1755 d 3-2-1798 m Anna Marie Bene Pvt PA

MOUBRAY,
Anning: b 3-15-1751 d 4-13-1838 m Mary Willetts Ens MM NY

MOUCHET, (or MUSHET)
Samuel Charles, Sr.: b — d a. 5-17-1800 m Barbara — Pvt SC

MOUL, (includes MAUL, MAULL, MAWL & MOULD)
Christoffel: b 6-7-1748 d 4-18-1813 m Rubina Dickerson Pvt NY
Conrad: b 1723 d 1783 m Cadarina — Pvt PA
Frederick: b 9-16-1751 d 4-22-1824 m Mary — PS Sol NY
Jacob: b 1706 d 11-27-1783 m Dorothy — PS NY
James: b 10-3-1744 d c. 1783 m Jane Moulder Mstr PA
Johannes, Sr.: b 7-31-1720 d 3-15-1804 m Maria C. Menges PS NY
Johannes, Jr.: b 5-31-1756 d 4-25-1813 m Maria Lau Pvt NY

MOULDER,
Wm.: b 10-30-1724 d 1798 m Mary Miller 2Lt PA

MOULTHROP, (includes MOLTHROP)
Benjamin: b 7- -1737 d 9-2-1815 m Thankful Allen Grannis Cpl CT
John: b 1757 d 6-10-1822 m Thanks (Moore) Phelps Pvt CT
Reuben: b 1763 d 7-29-1814 m Hannah Street Pvt CT

MOULTON, (includes MOLTON)
Abner: b 6-27-1748 d 8-24-1824 m Anne — Cpl MA
Abraham: b c. 1728 d a. 1791 Sarah Norris Maj NC
Benjamin: b 8-25-1767 d 3-27-1841 m Sarah Johnson Pvt MA
Benjamin, Sr.: b 5-18-1721 d 9-10-1782 m Sarah Rowell PS NH
Benjamin, Jr.: b 5-23-1743 d 12-5-1819 m (1)Mary Sanborn (2)Elizabeth Rowe MM PS NH
Caleb, Jr.: b 1745 d 9-19-1821 m (1)Mary Goodenow (2)Mrs Anna Goldewate Capt MA
Calvin: b 5-10-1753 d 5-8-1825 m Lucy Durkee Pvt MA
Cutting: b 7-25-1748 d 10-23-1809 m (1)Mary Merrill (2)Judith Emery Pvt MA
Daniel: b 3-31-1754 d 1838 m (1)Dorcas Holt (2)Abigail Yong Pvt MA ★
Daniel: b 1762 d p. 1790 m Nabby Blodgett Pvt MA
Daniel: b 3-17-1716 d p. 1790 m Hannah Preble CS ME
David: b 8-13-1754 d 9-13-1838 m Mary Batchelder Sgt NH ★
David: b 4-28-1738 d 1777 m Elizabeth Colby PS NH
Ebenezer: b 1-28-1746/47 d 1816 m Mehitable — Pvt MA
Ebenezer: b 5-18-1751 d 2-15-1807 m Elizabeth Curtis Pvt MA
Edward Brown: b 10-6-1754 d p. 1803 m Anna Smith Sgt PS NH ★
Elijah: b 8-10-1753 d p. 1796 m Ruth Blodgett PS NH
Ephraim: b 5-4-1726 d p. 1790 m Mehitable Godfrey PS NH
Freeborn: b 4-3-1717 d 6-9-1792 m Rebecca Walker Capt CT
Jean: b c. 1754 d a. 12-21-1834 m Marie Marthe Bordat PS LA
Jeremiah: b 1-17-1713 d 7-16-1777 m Hannah Sayward Col MA
Job: b 1752 d 1838 m Anna Way Pvt NH W★
John: b 12-31-1762 d 9-24-1824 m Sarah Webber Springer Pvt MA
John: bpt 10-8-1721 d a. 1801 m (1)Eunice Sawyer (2)Lydia Smith (3)Mary (Moulton) Pettingill PS Capt NH
John: b 6-15-1755 d 2-12-1844 m Ednah Merrill Pvt NH
John, Sr.: b 11-1-1717 d 7-8-1779 m Mary Marston PS NH
John, Jr.: b 11-19-1751 d 4-24-1837 m Huldah Palmer PS NH
John Bound: b 3-29-1744 d p. 1798 m Elizabeth — Cpl MA
Jonathan: b 1-29-1736 d c. 1807 m Mary Tarbox Sgt MA
Jonathan: b 4-19-1729 d 4-22-1821 m Sarah Bow Cpl MA
Jonathan: b 6-30-1726 d 9-18-1787 m (1)Abigail Smith (2)Sarah Emery Col NH
Jonathan: b 2-8-1757 d 7-12-1846 m Martha Gibson Pvt NH ★
Joseph: b 1-15-1738 d 1-15-1816 m (1)Sarah Fuller (2)Hannah — (3)Elizabeth — Sgt MA
Josiah: b 10-31-1739 d 7- -1776 m Rebecca Tarbox Pvt MA
Jotham: b 2-12-1743 d 5-12-1777 m Joanna Tilden BGen MA
Michael: b 3-17-1757 d 12-18-1820 m Dorothy Brown Lt RI
Nathan: b 1721 d 8-7-1776 m Sarah — PS NH

Nehemiah: b 1741 d 8-15-1816 m Sarah — Ens PS NH
Noah: b 11-14-1726 d p. 1779 m Patience Locke Sol NH
Noah, Jr.: b 12-14-1759 d 11-3-1850 m Priscilla Barron Pvt NH ★
Peter: bpt 6-13-1742 d 6-12-1812 m Joanna Shaw 2Lt MA
Redman: b 3-16-1746 d 1-19-1823 m Susanna — Ens NH
Reuben: b 1764/65 d p. 3-4-1849 m Mary Bird Pvt NH
Reuben: b 5-16-1743 d 12-2-1803 m Rebecca Carver Pvt VT
Salmon: b 9-6-1758 d 6-22-1852 m Susannah Johnson PS NY
Samuel: b 1735 d 2-12-1791 m Rachel Loomis Pvt CT
Samuel: b 6-14-1753 d 12-25-1837 m Hannah Noyes Pvt MA
Simeon: b 4-26-1761 d 4-10-1834 m Lydia Pease Pvt NH
Solomon: b 1758 d 3-13-1834 m Prudence Webber Sgt MA ★
Stephen, Sr.: b 3-30-1735 d 3- -1818 m Eleanor Converse LCol CT
Stephen, Jr.: b 7-11-1738 d 2-1-1851 m (1)Hannah — (2)Mrs Nancy Spencer Kmeland Fif Pvt MA CT ★
Stephen: b 7-11-1738 d 1-4-1776 m Hannah Bliss PS MA
Wm.: b 4-17-1754 d 7-5-1830 m (1)Beulah Hubbill (2)Martha Brayton Capt NY CT ★
Wm.: b 5-22-1763 d 10-8-1852 m (1)Molly Page (2)Jennie Cunningham Pvt MA ★

MOULTRIE,
Wm., Sr.: b 11-23-1730 d 9-27-1805 m (1)Elizabeth Damaris de St. Julien (2)Mrs Hannah (Motte) Lynch MGen SC
Wm., Jr.: b 8-8-1752 d 12-12-1796 m Hannah Ainslie 2Lt SC

MOUNCE, (includes MOUNTS & MOUNTZ)
Absalom: b 1760 d 1827 m Martha Ann Mounce Ens VA
George: b 10-22-1732 d 10-22-1800 m X Pvt PA
John: b 1741 d 1813 m Maria Elizabeth Reintzel PS MD
Providence: b a. 1740 d 1784 m Rachel — LCol PA
Richard: b c. 1757 d p. 1812 m Mary Kelly Sol VA

MOUNGER, (or MUNGER)
Henry: b c. 1746 d c. 1795 m Betty Harris PS NC

MOUNT,
Evert: b 3-23-1753 d 2-23-1841 m Effie Dye Pvt NJ
Ezekiel: b 11-22-1758 d 9-21-1834 m Sarah Pritchard Pvt VA ★
George: b 2-8-1757 d 12-7-1832 m Hester Pettinger Cpl NJ
Humphery: bpt 7-13-1746 d 9-27-1801 m Abigail Bayles Pvt NJ
John: b 12-16-1748 d 4-10-1842 m Elizabeth Perrine Lt NJ
John: b 1717 d 12-27-1809 m Elizabeth Brinley PS NJ
Margaret: b 1756 d 5-4-1830 m George Woodward Spy NJ
Mathias: b 1748 d 1828 m (1)— Taylor (2)Mary — Pvt NJ
Matthias: b 4-4-1761 d 11-20-1837 m Elizabeth Chambers Pvt NJ
Mathias: b 8-8-1756 d 6-11-1847 m (1)Elizabeth — (2)Dinah Fortner Pvt VA ★
Richard: b c. 1720 d 11-8-1787 m Lydia — Pvt NJ
Wm.: b 6-11-1743 d 3-11-1818 m Rebecca Cox Pvt NJ
Wm.: b 8-25-1750 d 10-3-1804 m Rebecca Stevenson Pvt NJ

MOUNTCASTLE,
Ann: b — d p. 1783 m Joab Mountcastle PS VA

MOUNTJOY, (includes MONTJOY)
Alvin: b 1-28-1747 d 11-3-1827 m Mary C. — Lt VA ★
George: b 9-9-1748 d p. 1-8-1810 m (1)— (2)Sarah — Capt VA
John: b 10-25-1741 d 3-3-1826 m Mary Anne Garrard Cpat VA ★
Wm.: b c. 1712 d p. 1782 m Phyllis — Sol VA

MOURIS,
Petrus: b 9-17-1749 d 8-19-1833 m Elizabeth Van de Mark Pvt NY

MOUSTON,
Christopher: b 2-18-1744 d 5-17-1837 m (1)Sarah Mitchell (2)Elizabeth Simpson Capt NC

MOWER, (includes MAUER)
John: b 3-26-1759 d 2-4-1854 m Elizabeth Edwards Pvt MA
Peter: b 2- -1738 d 8-4-1851 m Magdalena Vatterlie Pvt NY ★
Samuel: b 10-18-1720 d 1-24-1784 m (1)Comfort Learned (2)Mrs Sarah Leach (3)Esther Locke PS CS MA
Thomas: b 8-27-1726 d 10-9-1788 m Mary Kenney Gnr MA

MOWLAN,
Richard: b 1748 d 2-27-1822 m Rachael Williams Cpl MD

MOWRY, (includes MOWERY)
Abial: b 9-8-1756 d 5-26-1831 m Tabatha Wilbur Cpl RI W★
Christian: b 1747 d 1789 m Margaret Elizabeth Kleinschmidt Pvt PA
Daniel, Sr.: b 8-17-1729 d 7-6-1806 m (1)Anne Philips (2)Mrs Amey Arnold (3)Catherine Steere CS PS RI
Daniel, Jr.: b 4-8-1750 d 7-19-1839 m (1)Alce Aldrich (2)Susannah Steere Capt RI
Elisha: b 3-25-1735 d 6-28-1792 m Phebe Gulley LCol RI
Gideon: b c. 1754 d 5-17-1830 m Nancy Slocum Pvt RI W★
Gideon: b 7-18-1736 d p. 4-26-1793 m Dorcas Smith Pvt RI
Henry: b 11-9-1760 d 9-15-1847 m Thankful Bowen Pvt RI
John: b 1725-30 d 1799 m Lois Potter Pvt RI
John: b 1752 d 8-2-1816 m Phebe Hazard Pvt RI ★
Lewis: b — d p. 9-12-1816 m Christiana — Pvt RI
Uriah: b 10-8-1758 d 10-8-1825 m Joanna Barlett Pvt RI ★
Wm.: b 8-23-1761 d 9-29-1837 m Susannah (Mowry) Sgt RI ★

MOXLEY,
Daniel: b 1755 d 10- -1800 m Betty Muse Sol MD
Jonathan: b 1763 d 1849 m Sarah Woodmansee PS CT
Joseph: b 1736 d 9-6-1781 m Elizabeth Horsford Pvt CT
Nehemiah: b 12-19-1738 d 2- -1836 m — PS MD

MOYE, (includes MAY & MOY)
George: b 1722 d 1800 m Elizabeth Gardner PS NC
George: b 1730 d 1798 m (1) — (2)— Capt PA

MOYLAN,
Jasper: b 1757 d 2-11-1812 m Isabella Mease Ens PA
Stephen: b 1737 d 4-11-1811 m Mary Van Horne QMGen PA

MOZINGO,
Charles: b — d p. 1-21-1793 m Wilmoth — PS VA
George: b 1760 d 1838 m Ann Rogers Pvt VA ★

MUCH,
Jeremiah: b 7-7-1750 d 9-7-1807 m Catherine Fox Matr PA

MUCHMORE,
James: b 1750 d 3- -1834 m Elizabeth — Pvt NH ★
John: b 1742 d 3-22-1802 m Abigail — Pvt NJ

MUCKENFUSS,
Michael: b 1698 d 3-14-1779 m (2)Mrs Susannah Molloson PS SC

MUDD,
Henry, Sr.: b 1727 d 1808 m Blanch Spaulding Cpl PS MD
Richard: b 1759/60 d 5-26-1828 m (2)Mary Berry Sgt MD W★
Wm.: b 1723 d 1804 m Elizabeth Clements PS MD

MUDGE,
Aaron: b c. 1749 d 4-4-1827 m Wealthy Deming PS NY
Abel: b 1744 d 1819 m Elizabeth Anderson Pvt MA
Abraham, Sr.: b 6-16-1728 d 4-30-1804 m (1)Anna Gray (2)Mrs
   Sarah Rexford PS NY
Abraham, Jr.: b 11-3-1753 d 6-27-1833 m Phebe Valentin Lt MA ★
Daniel: b 7-12-1750 d 5-8-1840 m Martha Coles Pvt NY
Ebenezer: b 10-23-1709 d 1802 m (1)Patience Fuller (2)Mary
   (Wilcoxon) Cornish PS MA
Enoch: b 8-1-1754 d 1-30-1832 m Lydia Ingalls Pvt MA
Ezra: b 4-7-1752 d 1-7-1832 m Sarah Munn Pvt MA
Jarvis: b 1724 d 6- -1810 m (1)Prudence Treat (2)Mrs Lucy Root
   Sackett Lt NY
John: b 11-21-1755 d 6-5-1839 m (1)Azebea Benton (2)Sarah
   Chauncey Pvt MA
John: b 12-3-1743 d 11- -1825 m (1)Hannah Hutchinson (2)Mrs
   Phebe Harris Pvt MA
Joseph, Sr.: b 5-23-1716 d c. 1796 m Phebe Green Pvt MA
Joseph, Jr.: b 2-26-1753 d 11-9-1822 m Lois Pratt Pvt Drm MA
Joshua: b 9- -1737 d 3-13-1821 m Mary Cornish Pvt NY
Micah: b 5-15-1742 d 11- -1801 m Abigail Rowley Pvt MA & NY
Nathan: b 9-21-1756 d 2-8-1831 m (1)Hannah Ingalls (2)Mrs
   Elizabeth Burrill Pvt MA
Samuel: b 2-2-1741 d 1820 m Huldah Rowley Pvt NY
Simon: b 4-8-1748 d 8-27-1799 m Elizabeth Whitteridge Pvt MA
Stephen: b c. 1758 d p. 1802 m Nancy Stone Pvt MA

MUDGETT,
John: b — d 4-17-1834 m Tabitha Moody Sgt NH
Joseph: b 1749 d 5-8-1811 m Sarah Rumery Pvt NH

MUFFLY,
Peter: b 1739 d 3-25-1816 m Catharine R. Wanamaker Pvt PA

MUGFORD,
Robert, Jr.: b 12-30-1755 d 2-14-1835 m Lois Graffam Pvt MA
Wm.: b 1-25-1762 d 12-18-1840 m (1)Mary Peele (2)Ruth (Smith)
   Dimon Mrnr MA

MUHLENBERG,
Frederick Augustus: b 1-1-1750 d 6-4-1801 m Catherine Schaffer
   PS PA
Gotthif Henry Ernestus: b 11-17-1753 d 5-23-1815 m Mary Catherine
   Hall PS PA
Henry Melchoir: b 9-6-1711 d 10-7-1787 m Anna Maris Weiser
   PS PA
John Peter Gabriel: b 10-1-1746 d 10-1-1807 m Anna Barbara
   Meyer MGen VA

MUIR,
James: b 10-2-1727 d 9-13-1789 m Sarah Nevitt CS MD

MUIRHEID,
George: b 6-25-1760 d 4-6-1851 m Charity Guild Pvt NJ
Jonathan: b 5-7-1755 d 11-2-1837 m Mary Lott Pvt NJ

MULFORD,
Benjamin: b 1752 d 7-27-1840 m Patience Miller Pvt NJ ★
Christopher: b c. 1750 d 10-30-1824 m Jane Ross Wgn NJ
David: b 1748 d 11-25-1777 m Hannah (Fithian) Barker Lt NJ
David: b 9-10-1722 d 12-18-1778 m Phebe Hunting Col NY

David: b 4-8-1747 d 1826 m Catherine Fanning Pvt NY
David: b 3-15-1723 d 1-31-1778 m Phebe Glover PS NY
Elisha, Sr.: b 1-12-1713 d 5-29-1798 m Joanna Osborne PS NY
Elisha, Jr.: b 1749 d 8-14-1828 m Mrs Damaris (Howell) Sanford
   PS NY
Ephraim: b c. 1740 d p. 4-8-1805 m Elizabeth Brown Capt NC
Ezekiel: b 9-20-1727 d 4-15-1819 m Mrs Amy (Miller) Mulford
   Capt NY
Furman: b 2-5-1756 d 5-6-1827 m Rhoda Lawrence Pvt NJ
Isaac: b 1739 d 11-20-1776 m Mrs Sarah Coffin Lt NJ
Job: b 1749 d 1794 m Hannah Uhl Pvt NY
John: b 1749 d 3-10-1825 m Esther Ball Sol NJ
John: bpt 3-29-1711 d 4-20-1784 m Anna Chatfield PS NY
Jonathan, Sr.: b 9-28-1718 d 10-16-1789 m (1)Esther Conklin
   (2)Aula Powers Bedell Pvt NJ
Jonathan: b 10-20-1749 d 4-22-1826 m Elizabeth Thompson Pvt NJ
Jonathan: b 7-29-1747 d p. 10-8-1776 m Lucy Smith PS NJ
Lewis: b 1744 d 2-17-1830 m Phebe Meeker Pvt NJ
Matthew: b 10-22-1756 d 3-24-1845 m Mary Hutchinson Sgt NY
Nathan: b 7-25-1759 d 5-25-1825 m Sabrina Barker Pvt CT
Thomas: b 11-10-1751 d 12-31-1830 m Phoebe Smith Capt NJ

MULHERRIN,
John: b 1-15-1758 d 2-22/23-1850 m Elizabeth Ruddell Pvt SC ★

MULHOLLAND,
James: b 1733 d 9-20-1820 m Mary Bell Pvt MA

MULKEY,
Jonathan: b 10-16-1752 d 9-5-1826 m Nancy Howard Sol VA
Philip 2d.: b 5-14-1732 d 1-15-1800 m Ann Ellis Pvt NC

MULKS,
Benoni: b 1742 d 10-14-1832 m Nancy Denniston Pvt NY

MULL,
John: b 7-25-1744 d 1-25-1831 m Mary Anne Anthony Pvt NC
Peter: b c. 1735 d 6-10-1814 m Barbara Carpenter PS Capt NC

MULLETT, (or MULLIT)
Robert: b c. 1742 d 6-1-1820 m Ruth Trask Pvt MA

MULLIGAN,
Hercules: b 9-25-1740 d 3-4-1825 m Elizabeth Saunders PS NY

MULLINAX,
Archibald: b 11-10-1756 d 1-1-1820 m Mary Powell Pvt VA
Matthew: b — d p. 1830 m Ruth Kennemore Pvt SC

MULLINER,
Moses: b 1741 d 1821 m Mary Holden Drm & Pvt NJ ★

MULLINS, (includes MULLAN, MULLEN, MULLIN)
Clement: b c. 1750 d p. 1832 m Anna Hunt Pvt NC
David: b 1750 d c. 1820-30 m Mrs Susannah Herndon Pvt VA
Gabriel: b 3-22-1758 d 1841 m Rachel Ballard Pvt VA ★
James: b 1761 d 6-23-1841 m Abigail Jourdan Pvt NH
James: b 1758 d 1824 m Sarah Ayrs Pvt NJ
James: b c. 1759 d p. 1790 m Mary Shannon Pvt PA
James: b a. 1744 d 4-5-1827 m Mary Tombs Pvt VA
John: b 1754 d — m Catherine Haines Pvt NJ
John: b 1-10-1758 d 2-25-1838 m Nancy Gentry Pvt VA ★
Matthew, Sr.: b c. 1720 d p. 1785 m Mary Maupin Sgt VA
Patrick: b 1740 d 10-28-1816 m Sarah Askew Pvt MD
Peter: b — d c. 1782/83 m Eleanor Van Kleeck PS NY
Philip: b 8-24-1763 d 10-29-1840 m Elizabeth Decker Pvt NY ★
Thomas: b 1739 d 3-4-1832 m Elizabeth Garnett Capt VA
Wm.: b c. 1745 d 3-28-1810/11 m (2)Sara Triplett PS NC
Wm.: b 1760 d 1845 m — Wynne Drm Fif SC
Wm. Scott: b — d a. 4- -1806 m Mary — Cpl NC
Wm. Thomas: b 1759 d 1851 m Sallie Potts Pvt VA

MULLOY, (or MOLLOY)
Edward: b 1750 d 1825 m Mary Joyner Sol SC
Hugh: b 12-4-1751 d 7-11-1845 m (1)Priscilla Thompson (2)Jane
   Lt MA ★
John: b 1757 d 12-22-1838 m Effie Smith Pvt NY

MULVANE,
John: b 1758 d c. 1810 m X Pvt PA

MUMBOWER, (or MUMBAEUR)
John Nicholas: b 10-16-1721 d 1-25-1815 m Magdaline — Pvt PA

MUMFORD,
Benjamin: b 12-4-1735 d 2- -1812 m Mary Shrieve PS RI
David: b 3-10-1731 d 1815 m Rebecca Saltonstall PS CT
David: b 4-7-1755 d 7-23-1818 m Abigail — Pvt Sct NJ
Henry: b 10-16-1762 d 7-28-1839 m Sarah Thompson Pvt CT MA ★
Paul: b 3-5-1734 d 7-20-1805 m Mary Maylem PS RI
Robinson: b c. 1740 d p. 8-15-1801 m Sarah Coit Sol NC
Thomas: b 9-10-1728 d — m Catherine Havens Vol NY

MUMMA,
Christian: b c. 1760 d 8- -1831 m Catherine Watts Pvt MD
Henry: b 1758 d p. 1794 m — Hertzler Pvt PA
John: b 3-10-1736 d 6-11-1816 m Mary Longenecker Pvt PA

MUMMERT,
John: b 11-11-1757 d 10-18-1821 m Magalena — Pvt PA
Wm.: b 4-7-1726 d 2-4-1800 m Catherine Malown Pvt PA

MUMMEY,
Christopher: b 4-2-1753 d p. 1832 m Katie Smith Pvt VA

MUNCASTER,
James: b 12- -1735 d -1805 m Rachel Gray Pvt MD

MUNDLE, (includes MUNDELL)
Abner: b 4-21-1758 d 5-8-1845 m Mary Barnhill Pvt PA ★
James, Sr.: b c. 1730 d a. 11-12-1805 m Margaret Garrett PS PA
John: b c. 1758 d p. 8-17-1806 m Jane — Sol VA

MUNFORD,
Edward: b 1-17-1734 d 11-15-1801 m Elizabeth Braudneaux Capt
  VA
Robert: b c. 1730 d 1784 m Anne Beverley Col PS VA
Wm. Green: b c. 1725 d p. 2-8-1786 m Ann Stanhope PS VA

MUNGER, (or MONGER)
Amasa: b 8-27-1762 d 6-23-1827 m (1)Hannah Corbin (2)Nancy
  Powers Pvt MA
Bela: b 1-5-1761 d 8-13-1827 m Tryphena Chittenden Pvt CT ★
Benjamin: b 1737 d 1817 m — Pvt NY
Cyrus: b 3-8-1751 d 5-31-1839 m Prudence Rogers Pvt MA
Daniel: b 8-26-1725 d 2-10-1805 m Eunice Barnes Pvt CT
Daniel: b 4-15-1758 d 12-21-1835 m Elizabeth Worthington Pvt
  MA ★
Ebenezer: b 9-2-1718 d 6-20-1793 m Ann Lee PS CT
Eber: b 3-10-1762 d 6- -1836 m Clarinda Backus Pvt CT ★
Eleizur: b 1760 d 1828 m Rhoda Gaylord Tms CT
Elias: b 2-17-1756 d 9-27-1841 m Elizabeth Austin Pvt CT ★
Elisha Stone: b 11-7-1761 d p. 1790 m Mary Kilbourn Pvt CT
Elnathan: b 7-24-1714 d 10-5-1777 m Deborah Thompson Pvt MA
Ephraim: b 7-22-1749 d 4-21-1825 m (1)Joanna Fay (2)Sally
  Robbins Pvt CT
Ichabod: b 8-11-1756 d 3-27-1827 m Mehitabel Fuller Pvt MA
James: b 2-18-1732 d 2-18-1809 m (1)Submit Hand (2)Prudence
  Dowd Capt CT
Jehiel: b 6-3-1737 d 8-3-1817 m (1)Mary Rogers (2)Elsie Rogers Lt
  MA
John: b c. 1735 d 1797 m Millicent Cox Pvt NY
Jonathan: b 11-30-1755 d 11-9-1837 m Elizabeth Lawrence Cpl CT
Jonathan: b 8-27-1758 d 12-10-1841 m Rachel Chapin Pvt RI CT ★
Jonathan: b 9-5-1741 d 4-7-1808 m (1)Rachel Moulton (2)Elizabeth
  Paul Sgt MA
Joseph, Sr.: b 7- -1719 d 7- -1805 m (1)Jemima Lyon (2)Naomi
  Needham Sgt MA
Joseph, Jr.: b 8-23-1760 d 3-21-1823 m Hannah Fisk Pvt MA ★
Joseph: b 12-28-1758 d 10-15-1815 m Huldah Squier Pvt MA
Josiah: b 10-16-1754 d 8- -1838 m (1)Anne Lee (2)Hannah Coe
  Pvt CT
Lyman: b 12-14-1759 d 7-6-1835 m (1)Elizabeth Coe (2)Eunice
  Parmely Pvt CT
Nathan: b 5-13-1759 d 3-22-1813 m Lovisa Bishop Pvt MA
Nathaniel: b 4-25-1762 d 1798 m Beulah Cox Pvt MA
Nathaniel: b 10-5-1712 d 9-16-1800 m (1)Elizabeth Bullen (2)Fear
  Shaw PS MA
Philip: b 4-6-1735 d 12-6-1809 m Mary — Sgt NY
Timothy: b 9-5-1735 d p. 1790 m Mable Stevens Capt CT
Wait: b 3- -1738 d 1777 m Lydia Kelsey Pvt CT

MUNKS,
Wm.: b 2-2-1762 d 3-9-1841 m Rachel Benn Pvt PA ★

MUNN, (or MUN)
Asa: b 8-24-1759 d 3-17-1792 m Rachel — Pvt MA
Calvin: b 1761 d 2-5-1850 m (1)Hannah Griffin OrdlSgt MA ★
David: b 12-16-1760/61 d 4-22-1843 m Abigail Baldwin OrdlSgt
  NJ ★
Francis: b 1763 d 2-25-1844 m Sarah Wickham Pvt RI ★
Francis Collins: b 2-5-1743 d 8-1-1818 m Rebecca Childs Sgt MA
James: b c. 1754 d 3-11-1839 m Azubah — Capt MD PA VA
John: b 11-16-1741 d 1-18-1820 m Anna Smith Sgt MA
John: b 8-16-1755 d 12-7-1793 m Ruth Harrison Pvt NJ
Joseph: b 5-1-1734 d 1830 m Sally — Cpl MA
Noah: b 4-17-1746 d 5-13-1821 m — Pvt MA
Oliver: b c. 1735 d c. 1810 m Susannah — Fif CT
Reuben: b 4-25-1742 d 10-4-1823 m Hannah — LCol MA
Seth: b 5-5-1754 d 2-12-1808 m Salina Janes Pvt MA

MUNNERLYN,
John: b c. 1742 d 1822 m Sarah Keen Capt SC

MUNSELL, (or MUNSEL)
Alpheus: b 10-12-1749 d 12-1-1807 m Eunice Hayden Pvt CT

Calkins: b 4-10-1761 d 10-15-1852 m Elizabeth Booth Pvt CT ★
Hezekiah: b 1-17-1753 d 4-14-1844 m Irene Bissell Pvt CT ★
John: b 7-16-1735 d 7-17-1819 m (1)Sila Huntley (2)Elizabeth
  McCary (3)Lydia Huntley Pvt CT
Jonathan: b 10-7-1725 d 8-13-1800 m Hannah Pasco Pvt CT
Levi: b 1-26-1764 d 2-15-1849 m Lucretia Oliver Pvt CT ★
Silas: b 3-27-1758 d p. 1821 m Abigail Blodgett Pvt CT
Timothy: b 11-24-1745 d 10-26-1798 m (1)Elishiba Smith Pvt CT

MUNSON,
Almond: b 10-3-1761 d 1831 m (1)Esther Peck (2)Deborah — Pvt
  CT ★
Braszel: b 1-23-1730 d 11-17-1803 m (1)Keziah Stiles (2)Abigail
  Bassett (3)Mary — Capt CT
Benjamin: b 8-23-1744 d 4-30-1813 m Mrs Rosanna (Smith)
  Burgess PS CT
Caleb: b 5-22-1746 d 12-12-1802 m Mary Lee (Leveis) Pvt CT
Caleb: b 1735 d 2-25-1815 m Sussannah Ludlum Pvt NJ
Elisha: b 10-10-1756 d 11-22-1835 m Mabel Homeston Pvt CT ★
Eneas, Sr.: b 6-13-1734 d 6-16-1826 m (1)Susannah Howell (2)Mrs
  Sarah S. Perit PS CT
Eneas, Jr.: b 9-2-1763 d 8-22-1852 m Mary Shepherd Dr CT ★
Ephraim: b 5-1-1763 d 11-27-1834 m Deborah Scott Pvt CT ★
Heman: b 5-29-1761 d 5-4-1798 m Abigale Fenn Pvt CT
Herman: b 10-28-1738 d 2-12-1829 m Anna Bronson Pvt CS CT
Isaac: b 1762 d 1830 m Eleanor Andrews Pvt CT ★
Isaac: b 11-24-1761 d p. 1804 m Elizabeth Phipps Sol CT
Israel: b 10-9-1737 d 12-27-1806 m Anna Griswold Lt CT
Ithiel: b 12-11-1760 d 12-17-1835 m Sarah Ann Finch Pvt CT
Jabez: b 12-17-1728 d p. 12-22-1777 m Eunice Atwater Slr CT
Jared: b 1742 d 7-30-1823 m Annorah Hale Pvt MA
Jesse: b 1741 d 4-27-1813 m Mariam Rowley Lt MA
John: b 8-2-1740 d 1828 m Lydia Todd CS CT
John: b 1755-58 d p. 1826 m Sarah Niles Pvt MA
John: b a. 1743 d 3- -1788 m — LCol NJ
John, Sr.: b 11-27-1731 d 7-22-1808 m Esther Turner PS NY
John, Jr.: b 1-30-1752 d p. 1795 m Mary Mansfield Lt NY
Jonathan: b 6-30-1756 d 3-24-1847 m Mary Taintor Lt CT
Joseph: b 10-8-1727 d 1-9-1793 m Sarah Bishop PS CT
Joseph: b a. 1729 d p. 4-4-1812 m Sarah Morse Pvt MA
Joseph Kirk: b 8-1-1765 d 1-15-1841 m Lucinda Sears Drm CT
Josiah: b 11-21-1765 d 1-1-1843 m (1)Rachel Holloway (2)Ruth
  Hathaway (3)Miriam Young Tms NJ
Levi: b 8-29-1738 d 1815 m Mary Cooley 2Lt CS CT
Medad: b 5-9-1757 d 11-29-1846 m (1)Sybil Carrington (2)Mrs
  Lucretia Ives Humphrey (3)Mrs Mindwell Benham Pvt CT
Moses: b 9-24-1744 d 7-13-1817 m (1)Abigail Munson (2)Lucy
  Morton (3)Mary Truesdale Pvt CT
Nathaniel: b 3-17-1755 d 11-17-1828 m Edatha Noble Cpl NY
Peter: b 11-22-1753 d 2-3-1830 m Elizabeth Hall PS CT
Richard: b 4-28-1741 d 8-13-1813 m (1)Mary — (2)Susannah Cain
  PS NH
Robert: b 6-22-1762 d p. 1850 m Ruth (Scott) Elliott Pvt MA ME
Rufus: b 1763 d 9-13-1797 m Bertha Burton Pvt VT
Samuel: b 7-9-1762 d 2-27-1841 m Martha Barnes Pvt CT PA W★
Samuel: b 1741 d p. 1805 m Susannah Tyler Pvt NY
Solomon: bpt 11-7-1762 d 12- -1810 m Lucy Ball Pvt NJ
Stephen: b 2-10-1759 d 7-9-1824 m Elizabeth Andrews Pvt CT ★
Stephen: b c. 1733 d 11-8-1805 m (1)Letitia Ludlam (2)Keziah —
  Capt NJ
Thaddeus: b 11-22-1748 d 8-23-1814 m Miriam Dibble Lt VT
Theophilus: b 1-4-1747 d 3-30-1795 m Sarah (Read) Hill Capt CT
Thomas Ensign: b 4-3-1742 d 1-20-1820 m Ruth Brockett Pvt CT ★
Timothy: b 7-1-1734 d 10-29-1828 m (1)Sarah Bishop (2)Sarah —
  Sgt CT
Uzal: b 12-11-1754 d 3-26-1826 m Mary Eddy Ens NJ
Waitstill: b 1760 d 3-5-1845 m Elizabeth Frisbie Pvt CT
Waitstill: b 1730 d 2-26-1777 m Mary Wade PS NJ
Wm.: b 5-20-1747 d 2-26-1826 m (1)Martha Hall (2)Elizabeth Collis
  Little (3)Mary Groves Maj CT

MUNSY, (includes MUNCEY, MUNCY & MUNSEY)
John: b 1738 d 8-2-1777 m X Lt NY ★
John: b c. 1764 d p. 1840 m Naomi Muncey Sol VA
Luke: b c. 1763 d 9- -1831 m Mary — Pvt VA
Samuel, Sr.: b c. 1700 d p. 1786 m Mary — Pvt VA
Samuel, Jr.: b c. 1740 d p. 2-9-1811 m Agness — Pvt VA
Skidmore: b a. 1744 d 1797 m Mary Scott Pvt VA

MUNTERBACH,
John: b c. 1755 d p. 6- -1829 m Elizabeth — Cpl NY

MURCH,
Ebenezer: b 1737 d 6-16-1824 m Margery Phillips 1Lt MA
James: b 3-6-1738 d 1827 m (2)Rachel Wright Sgt NH
Joseph: b 1-5-1760 d 1859 m Susan Joy Mid MA
Matthias: b 3-9-1759 d 8-9-1842 m Mary Libby Pvt MA
Wm.: bpt 8-26-1747 d p. 1790 m Thankful Relief Pendexter Pvt
  ME
Wm.: b 1763 d 1846 m Hannah Thompson Pvt MA ★

MURCHEY,
Wm.: b 1760 d c. 1813 m Mrs Barbara Carn Dantzler Pvt SC

MURDAUGH,
James: b 1743 d 1798 m Mary Walke Capt VA
Joseph: b 3-20- 1754 d 1-12-1810 m Mary Ross Pvt PA

MURDOCK, (includes MORDOCK, MUDOCH & MURDAH)
Arial: b 11-18-1763 d 1803 m Eunice Murdock Pvt CT
Asahel: b 4-17-1755 d 1-23-1837 m Elizabeth Starkwather Pvt VT ★
Bartlett:, Jr.: b 1751 d 5-25-1796 m Deborah Perkis Pvt MA
Benjamin: b 1- -1753 d 6- -1834 m Mary Anne Magruder 2Lt MD
Benjamin, Sr.: b 4-1-1736 d 7-21-1776 m Catherine Read Cpl MA
Daniel: b 3-4-1754 d 1813 m Lurana Madison Pvt CT
Eliphalet: b 10-5-1748 d 11-23-1822 m Anna McCall Cpl CT
Elisha: b 11-25-1755 d 12-7-1843 m Hannah Chapin Sgt MA ★
George: b c. 1750 d p. 1814 m Huldah — Pvt VT
George: b 1742 d 5-5-1805 m Eleanor Charlton PS MD
James: b 1720 d 12-17-1808 m (1)Hannah Tilson (2)Faith Sturtevant 1Lt MA
James: b 2-18-1755 d 1-14-1841 m Anna Buckingham Chp VT
John: b 1706 d 1-21-1778 m (1)Phebe Sill (2)Frances Conklin CS CT
John: b 3-29-1741 d 9-17-1817 m Sarah Sampson Lt MA
John: b 12-24-1727 d 7-2-1806 m Bethiah Fuller Pvt MA
John: b 1735 d 10-2-1795 m Sarah Brice Cpl PA
Joshua: b 12-23-1721 d 7-3-1797 m (1)Ester Child (2)Esther Greenwood Sgt MA
Peter: b 10-13-1766 d 3-26-1851 m Bathsheba Dodge PS CT
Samuel: b 3-4-1752 d 11-20-1814 m (1)Beulah Fuller (2)Jane Bacon Cpl MA
Samuel: b 8-27-1729 d p. 1795 m Mary Wight PS VT
Thomas: b c. 1720 d 12-5-1803 m Elizabeth Hatch Maj VT
Wm.: b 1-2-1738 d 10-26-1811 m (1)Mary Pierce (2)Sarah Dean Capt CT
Wm.: b 1-14-1748 d 5-27-1817 m Achsah Woodward Pvt MA
Wm.: b 1746 d 1835 m Elizabeth Thornly Lt MD
Wm.: b 1740 d 1829 m Agnes Wasson Sol NC
Wm.: b c. 1750 d a. 1790 m — Hare Pvt PA
Wm.: b 3-15-1759 d 5- -1840 m Mary Mills Pvt SC ★
Wm. Thompson: b 6-24-1734 d p. 1787 m Isabella Buckalew Sgt NJ

MURFEE,
Richard: b — d 1788/89 m Lucy — PS VA

MURFF,
John: b 10- -1750 d 1781 m Elisabeth Keigler Pvt SC
John: b 1750 d p. 5-16-1789 m Sophia Kinsler Pvt SC

MURFREE, (includes MURPHREE)
David: b 1760 d 2-18-1838 m Jemima Conelius PS NC
Hardy: b 6-5-1752 d 4-6-1809 m Sallie Brickell LCol NC
John: b c. 1735 d 3-6-1798 m Martha — Pvt NC
Mills: b 4-21-1756 d 12-7-1815 m Elizabeth Brack Pvt GA
Wm.: b 1730 d 1778/79 m Mary Moore PS NC

MURPHY, (includes MORPPHEE & MURPHEY)
Archibald: b 12-18-1742 d 10-25-1817 m Jane De Bow Col PS NC
Butler: b 1756 d 1840 m Lydia — Pvt VA
Daniel: b — d 1777 m Mary — PS MD
Darby: b c. 1740 d p. 1830 m — Sol MD
Edmund: b 11-24-1745 d p. 12-16-1826 m (1)Betsey Ann Sullivan (2)Nancy Rhodes Pvt GA
George: b c. 1745 d p. 7-12-1831 m Elizabeth — Sol VA
George W.: b 2- -1759 d 3-27-1842 m Hannah Norwood Hutchins Pvt Sct MA ★
Hugh: b 11-11-1752 d 4-16-1835 m Catherine Mc Millan Pvt SC ★
James: b 1728 d 1825 m Mary Strother Pvt NC
James: b 5-24-1759 d 11-8-1831 m Margaret McDowell Pvt NC
James Jeffrey: b 1747 d 1826 m (1)Magdalin Newland (2)Margaret — Pvt VA ★
John: b 1763 d 5-21-1852 m Phebe Lancaster Pvt NY W★
John: b 6-25-1750 d p. 8-13-1818 m Rachel Cook Lt NC
John: b 1759 d 2-16-1839 m Mary Fitch Pvt NC
John: b — d 7-3-1778 m Lucy Gore Pvt PA
John: b 5-10-1747 d 5-25-1834 m Jane Love Pvt SC
John: b c. 1730 d p. 6-13-1834 m Nancy Ransom Sol VA
John, Sr.: b c. 1725 d 1799 m Catherine PS VA
John: b 1733 d 5-17-1838 m Elizabeth Maling Pvt VA ★
Joseph: b 1760 d 1837 m (1)Elizabeth Williams (2)Sarah (Bell) Williams Pvt MD
Joseph: b 1761 d 2-10-1834 m Sarah Pvt NC W★
Malachi: b a. 1746 d p. 1790 (1)Sally Knight (2)Mary Hicks Capt PS SC
Mark: b 3-8-1753 d p. 2-12-1830 m Holly Duke Sol SC
Martin: b 1-11-1755 d 6-4-1839 m Mary Steadman Pvt RI
Patrick: b 1752 d 1782 m Nancy Moore Pvt MD
Patrick: b 1720 d 7-6-1785 m Elizabeth Kelsoe CS NC
Robert: b 1757 d 5-13-1850 m Martha Mc Neill Pvt VA
Roger, Jr.: b 1767 d p. 2-16-1850 m Nancy Wilson Pvt SC
Samuel: b 5-12-1758 d 10-30-1851 m Elizabeth Power Pvt VA ★
Sarah Duke: b 1733 d 1818 m Simon Murphy PS SC
Timothy: b 3-24-1749 d 5-8-1812 m Mary Garrison Pvt NJ
Timothy: bpt 3-23-1755 d 6-27-1818 m (1)Margaret Feeck (2)Mary — Sol Sct NY
Wm.: b 5-14-1742 d 8-26-1830 m Phebe Sherry Pvt NJ

Wm.: b 1755- 1765 d 3-27-1833 m Eva Dickey Sol PA
Wm.: b 3-12-1759 d 11-12-1833 m Rachel Henderson Ens VA NC ★
Wm.: b 1720-30 d a. 1797 m Lucy Hickman Sol VA

MURRAY, (includes MURREE & MURRY;
Alexander: b 1761 d 9-7-1845 m Isabella Duguid Sgt NY ★
Alexander: b c. 1738 d 1810 m (2)Margaret Adams Pvt PA
Asahel: b 4-16-1745 d 9-11-1784 m Thankful Plum PS CT
Benjamin: b 1756 d 10-31-1834 m Lucretia Ranna Pvt CT W★
Beriah: b 8-19-1746 d 10-1-1820 m Mary Meeker Pvt PS NH
Charles: b 1748 d 4-26-1828 m Jenney Rodman Pvt PA
Daniel: b 11-5-1751 d 12-23-1827 m (1)Lucretia Coe (2)Mrs Hannah Clark Pvt CT
Daniel: b 7-22-1752 d 3-19-1835 m Elizabeth Raymond Pvt NY ★
Daniel: b 1754 d 6-8-1824 m Hannah Nash Pvt PA ★
Daniel: b — d 8-5-1820 m Rachel Horner PS QM IL
David: b 1760 d 11-8-1840 m Mary Walton Pvt GA
Eber: b 1-15-1755 d 11-23-1826 m (1)Azuba — (2)Abigail Dunning Pvt VT
Elihu: b 1-13-1753 d 6-29-1836 m Lydia (Strong) Mc Call Sgt MA
Elijah: b 6-6-1756 d 6-25-1816 m Mercy — Sgt MA
Ezra: b 7-11-1741 d 1815 m Hannah Gould Lt NY
George: b a. 1753 d 1792 m Jane Snyder PS NY
George: b 3-17-1762 d 5-6-1855 m Mary Denny Pvt PA
Henry: b 1744 d 1850 m Elizabeth Coopwood Pvt VA
Ichabod: b 8-16-1755 d 7-16-1831 m Lois Doty Pvt CT ★
Jacob: b c. 1742 d 1824 m Susannah — Pvt PA
James: b 3-18-1747 d 5-20-1808 m Rosannah Prather Pvt MD
James: b 7-4-1736 d 4-1-1817 m (1)Mary Ann Fisher (2)Anne Wind Col PA
James: b c. 1760 d — m — — Pvt PA
James: b 1729 d 3-15-1804 m Rebecca Mc Lean Capt PS PA
James: b 9-10-1747 d 1828 m Susan Cantrall Pvt SC
Jermiah: b 1759 d 9-3-1835 m Ann Montgomery Pvt PA
Jesse: b 1-25-1746 d 4-12-1824 m Rachel Norton Pvt CT
John: b 8-13-1731 d 1-22-1820 m Mindwell Crampton Sol CT
John: b 1759 d 1813 m Tryphena Webb Pvt CT
John: b 1747 d 1833 m Diana Cox Capt MD
John: b c. 1745 d p. 1788 m (1)Anne Montgomery (2)Elizabeth Chapman Pvt MA
John: b 6 - -1745 d 1799 m Mary Kimbrough Sgt NC
John: b 1745 d p. 1790 m Jean — Sgt NC
John: b c. 1731 d 2-3-1798 m Margaret Mayes LCol PA
John: b 1744 d 1782 m Susanna Yates LCol PS VA
John: b 1740 d a. 1801 m Charity — Pvt VA
John: b c. 1740 d p. 7-16-1790 m Abigail Cawson PS VA
John B.: b 1755 d 1828 m Martha Mc Clenachan Pvt RI
Johnathan: b 8-10-1750 d 3-2-1785 m Abigal Hull Cpl CT
Joseph: b 1720 d 6-8-1780 m Rebecca Morris Pvt NJ
Lackey: b c. 1748 d 10-31-1815 m Elizabeth Galbraith Dr PA
Mary Lindley: b 1720-26 d 12-25-1782 m Robert Murray PS NY
Nathan: b 11-4-1756 d 2-6-1808 m Martha Albritton Pvt NC
Neal: b 1742-48 d 5-5-1832 m Elizabeth — Pvt PA ★
Nicholas: b 1754 d 4-10-1812 m Temperance Bond Pvt Matr CL
Noah: b 4-11-1747 d 5-16-1811 m Mary Stowe Sgt CT
Patrick: b 3-17-1755 d 7-23-1854 m Mary Brereton Beatty Pvt PA
Reubin: b 2-17-1743/44 d 11-26-1810 m (1)Sarah Guthrie (2)Mrs Sarah Griffin Lt NY
Samuel: b 9-2-1734 d 1-18-1826 m (1)Elizabeth Berry (2)Hannah Dalton Pvt PS NH
Samuel: b 6-1-1739 d 12-15-1817 m Elizabeth Reese Sol SC
Seth: b 5-21-1736 d 9-16-1795 m Elizabeth White Col MA
Seymour: b 8-30-1754 d 6-9-1813 m (1)Philena Willett (2)Hannah Howe Pvt CT
Solomon: b 1758 d 12- -1822 m Martha Averill Pvt CT
Stephen: b 7-14-1757 d 1-6-1842 m Louisa Rose Arfr PS CT ★
Thomas: b 4-13-1738 d 11-18-1799 m Eleanor Collier LCol PA
Wm.: b 1756 d 1795 m Rosamond Dawson Lt NC
Wm., Sr.: b 1733 d 1797 m Elizabeth — Cpl PA
Wm., Jr.: b 1757 d 1819 m Mary Ann Grace Sol PA
Wm.: b 1754 d p. 1798 m Martha Mc Quillan Pvt Wgn SC
Wm.: b 4- -1747 d 8-9-1805 m Mary Ennalls Lt VA

MUSE,
Battaile: b 4-30-1751 d 3-29-1803 m Margaret Tate Pvt VA
Fauntly: b 1-15-1757 d 9-12-1840 m (1)Mary Jones (2)Margaret Patterson Pvt PA ★
Hudson: b c. 1740 d 1799 m (1)Jemima Chilton Strutman (2)Agnes Neilson NOf PS VA
James: b 11-27-1757 d 1-20-1843 m Nancy (Muse) PS NC
John: b c. 1740 d. 7-14-1811 m Lucy Crenshaw Pvt VA
Richard: b c. 1750 d 1797 m Elizabeth Strother 1Lt VA
Samuel: b c. 1740 d p. 8-26-1794 m (1)Mary Smith (2)Mary Arnold Cpl VA
Thomas: b 3-15-1748 d 6-1-1828 m Elizabeth Fort Capt SC W★
Wm.: b 2-6-1732 d 10-30-1788 m Jane — PS VA

MUSGROVE, (includes MUSGRAVE)
Edward: b 1720 d 1792 m — Adair PS SC
Nathan: b 3-7-1758 d 7-4-1823 m Ann Conner Pvt MD
Samuel: b 1747 d 9-2-1834 m Elizabeth — Pvt PA ★
Samuel: b 6-27-1760 d 4-3-1847 m Elizabeth Critty Pvt VA★
Wm.: b 1735-40 d a. 5-12-1778 m Volinda — PS VA

MUSICK,
Abraham: b c. 1745 d 1832 m Terrell Musick Cnt NC
Elexious: b — d a. 8-28-1798 m — PS VA
John: b c. 1753 d p. 1791 m Mary Berry Pvt VA
Thomas R.: b 10-26-1757 d 12-2-1842 m Mary Neville Pvt NC ★

MUSKETNOUGH,
Henry: b c. 1754-58 d 8-31-1835 m Maria Baer Pvt PA ★

MUSSELMAN,
Christopher: b 1756 d 1-29-1846 m (1)Nancy Jane Young
 (2)Winifred Thornley Pvt PA
David: b p. 1750 d p. 10-21-1812 m Barbar Neff Pvt PA
Henry: b c. 1730 d p. 2-13-1804 m Magdalena Oberholtzer Pvt PA

MUSSELWHITE,
Milbea: b 1750 d 8-31-1835 m Deba Drury Pvt NC ★
Nathan: b 1-19-1743 d 1845 m Elizabeth Rozier Pvt SC
Thomas: b c. 1750 d p. 1815 m — PS NC

MUSSER, (includes MOSER,.MOSIER, MOSSER & MOUSER)
Benjamin: b 7-13-1749 d 11-25-1820 m (1)Barbara Engle
 (2)Magdalene Bossler Pvt PA
Burkhardt, Sr.: b 1736 d 1807 m Mary Agatha Steininger Pvt PS
 PA
Christian: b 2-10-1756 d 12-22-1838 m Margaret — Pvt PA ★
Daniel: b 1764 d 1804 m Magdalena Oswald Pvt PA
Francis: b 1763 d 10-22-1836 m (2)Mary Sipes Sol NC
George: b 3-27-1741 d 7-17-1806 m Christiana Young Capt PA
Henry: b 1757 d 2-21-1825 m Christina Stinsman Sgt PA
Jacob: b 1740 d 12- -1800 m Catherine Shedaker Capt PA
Jacob: b 1758 d 9-23-1822 m Magdalan Thomas Pvt PA
Johannes Nicholas: b 5-19-1738 d 1824 m (1)Catherine Ley
 (2)Margaret Hahn Ruth Pvt PA
John: b 4-16-1741 d 10-11-1810 m Elizabeth Acker 1Lt PA
John: b 1755 d 1848 m Maria Catharina Klein 1Lt PA ★
John: b 7-15-1738 d 1-28-1804 m (1)Margaret Hambright (2)Sarah
 Funk Pvt PA
John: b 1743 d a. 4-28-1804 m Susanna Pvt PA
John: b 11-17-1753 d 6-30-1828 m Barbara Krider Sol PA
John: b 1760 d 7- -1847 m Elizabeth Kleinginny PS PA
John: b c. 1759 d 1844 m — Pvt VA
Joseph: b 7-2-1761 d 2-2-1794 m Huldah Hubbard Sol CT
Michael: b c. 1715 d 1789 m Maria Eva — CS PA
Michael, Jr.: b c. 1750 d 3- -1811 m Mary Ann Shaffer Pvt PA
Nicholas: b 1-12-1750 d 9-25-1826 m Catherine Henninger Pvt PA
Peter: b 1742 d 1829 m — Pvt PA
Peter: b 1740 d 1808 m Margaret — Pvt PA
Philip, Sr.: b 1725 d 1817 m Barbara — Pvt PA
Philip, Jr.: b 7- -1757 d 7-19-1804 m Catharine Shuck Pvt PA
Samuel: b c. 1750 d 2-27-1808 m (1)Elizabeth — (2)Mary — Pvt PA
Sebastian: b 1-3-1760 d 11-29-1829 m Anna Maria Miller Sol PA
Valentine: b 1758 d 2- -1833 m Catherine — Lt PA

MUSTAIN,
Avery: b 2-26-1756 d 8-31-1833 m Mary Shelton Pvt VA

MUSTARD,
James: b 1726 d 8-16-1793 m Charity Reed Capt MA

MUSTOE,
Anthony: b 9-23-1748 d 6-18-1807 m (1)Ann Merchant (2)Mary
 Wright (3)Dorothy Seiler Sgt VA

MUTTER,
Thomas: b 1743 d 8-1-1799 m Elizabeth Moore PS NC

MUZZEY, (includes MUZZY)
Amos: b 5-24-1741 d 12-10-1822 m Abigail Bowers Pvt MA
Amos: b 2-27-1762 d 5-8-1832 m Sarah Snow Pvt MA ★
Benjamin: b 5-13-1747 d 4-24-1820 m Elizabeth Densmore Pvt VT
John, Sr.: b 5-12-1714 d 6-25-1789 m (1)Abigail Reed (2)Eleanor
 Snow PS MA
John, Jr.: b 12-7-1737 d 4-9-1819 m Mary Ball Lt MA
John, Sr.: b 2-7-1716 d 12-16-1784 m (1)Rebecca Reed (2)Rebecca
 Monroe MM MA
John, Jr.: b 1754 d 12- -1824 m Rebecca Monroe Pvt MA
John: b 8-31-1745 d 1-17-1831 m (1)Bulah Butler (2)Rhoda Bartlett
 PS NH
John: b 1743 d 1825 m (1)Mary Waldron (2)Priscilla Johnson Pvt
 NH
Jonas: b 1-2-1748 d 3-17-1819 m (1)Sarah Draper (2) Abigail Lamb
 Sgt MA
Joseph: b 8-26-1740 d a. 1-28-1776 m Hannah Merriam Sgt MA
Robert, Sr.: b 1738 d 9-9-1831 m Martha Cozens Lt MA
Wm.: b 1733 d 10-10-1830 m (1)Mary Clapp (2)Mary Chandler Lt
 MA

MYATT,
Mark: b c. 1750 d 10-25-1821 m Mary Speight Lt NC

MYERS, (includes MAYER, MEYER, MEYERS, MOYER, MYER)
Abraham: b 10-17-1727 d a. 1785 m (1)Margrietje Vanderbilt (2)
 Grietje Van Houten PS NY
Abraham: b 12-31-1742 d 10-30-1826 m Nancy Meyers Pvt PA
Abraham: b — d p. 2-5-1825 m (1)Sarah — (2)Patsy Atterbury 1Lt
 SC
Adolph: b 10-4-1740 d 8-17-1813 m Anna Hoagland Pvt NY
Benjamin: b 3-20-1764 d 1837 m Sarah Riggs Pvt NJ
Benjamin: b 10-21-1730 d 12-12-1819 m Leah Osterhougt Pvt PS
 NY
Charles: b c. 1742 d 3- -1800 m Christina — Capt PA
Christian: b 8-24-1739 d 5-31-1817 m Annatje Wynkoop Sol PS NY
Christian: b 3-14-1688 d 1-5-1781 m Ann Geertruy Theunyes PS NY
Christian: b c. 1750 d p. 1789 m Mary — Capt PA
Christian: b c. 1755 d c. 1826 m Anna L. Bauer Pvt PA
Christian: b 2-25-1761 d 7-12-1843 m Barbara Beachley Pvt PA
Christian Kolb: b 3-27-1763 d p. 1784 m (1)Mary Landis (2)Sarah
 Overholt Pvt PA
Christopher: b 1750 d 1847 m Hannah Harwick Pvt NY ★
Christopher: b 1734 d 8-2-1801 m Anna Maria Schaeffer Pvt PS PA
Christopher: b c. 1740 d p. 2-7-1815 m Susannah — Lt VA
Christopher Bartholomew: b 1-7-1756 d 8-11-1815 m Susan Burkhart
 2Lt PA
Daniel: b 4-15-1757 d 5-8-1835 m Cathrine Van Auken Sgt NY ★
David: b 1768 d 1843 m Nancy Dygart Pvt NY
Egidius: b 1723 d p. 1799 m Eva Barbara — PS PA
Frederic: b 1735 d 1795 m Christina Balch Pvt NY
Frederick: b 3-12-1756 d 12-18-1842 m Gertrude Hoff Sgt NY ★
Frederick: b 5-25-1748 d 7-18-1822 m Anna Margaret Weaver Pvt
 NY
Frederick: b 1748 d 1828 m Magdeline Lichty Pvt PA
Garret: b 10-13-1730 d 4- -1801 m Lammetie Remsen MM NY
George: b 1755 d 1783 m Elizabeth — Pvt MD
George: b c. 1730 d p. 1790 m Elizabeth Sengree PS MD
George: b — d 1803 m Mary — Capt PA
George: b c. 1738 d 12- -1790 m Euphronia Kercher Pvt PA
George, Sr.: b 1723 d 1812 m (2)Hannah Hoover Pvt PA
George, Jr.: b 1757 d 9- -1812 m Maria Langenecker Pvt PA
George: b c. 1740 d p. 1784 m Teany Haymaker Pvt PA
George: b c. 1750 d 10-29-1821 m — Pvt PA
George: b 1745 d — m Mary — Pvt PA
George: b 1742 d 1794 m Mary — PS PA
Heinrich: b 3-13-1752 d 9-2-1838 m Anna Maria — Pvt PA
Henry: b 8-17-1761 d 6-24-1849 m Mary Stroble 2Lt MD
Henry: bpt 4-1-1747 d p. 1790 m Maria Finckel Sol NY
Henry: b 1759 d p. 11-12-1836 m Catherine Weber Pvt PA
Henry: b 8-19-1753 d 10-18-1830 m Catherine Switzer 1Lt PA
Henry: b 12-25-1745 d c. 6-16-1832 m Ann Buffington Pvt PA
Henry: b 1756 d 12-20-1842 m Mrs Hannah Deitch Pvt PA ★
Henry: b a. 1763 d 5-14-1810 m Kathrina Diehl Pvt PA
Henry: b 10-15-1764 d 5-17-1820 m (1)Mary Steese (2)Margaret
 Harper Pvt PA
Jacob: b c. 1730 d p. 10-24-1781 m Anna Maria Hager Lt NY
Jacob: b 1740 d 8-6-1777 m Margaret Weber Pvt NY
Jacob: b 1735 d 1-26-1829 m Christina Schuster Cpl PA
Jacob: b c. 1715 d 1790 m X Pvt PA
Jacob: b 1741 d p. 1790 m Elizabeth Rinehart Pvt PS PA
Jacob: b 1750 d 1817 m Helen Ventriele Pvt PA
Jacob: b c. 1760 d p. 1790 m Barbara Burkholder Pvt PA
Jacob: b 3-2-1753 d 8-3-1812 m Ann Mary Ent Pvt PA
Jacob: b 1-6-1748 d 10-27-1827 m Maria Magdalena Karcher Pvt
 PA
Jacob: b 1-22-1753 d 3-16-1826 m Mary Vau Wunder Sol PA
Jacob: b 9-15-1758 d 10-17-1840 m Hannah Smith Pvt PA
Jacob: b 1758 d 1790 m Rebecca Ann Ent Pvt PA
Jacob: b c. 1730-36 d — m — PS PA
Jacob: b c. 1740 d 3-24-1804 m Catherine Von Enfinger Lt SC
Johannes: b 6-5-1747 d 1817 m Catherine Van Houten Ens NY
Johannes: b 2-19-1746 d 1-5-1829 m Seletje Snyder Sol PS NY
John: b 5-10-1757 d 1826 m Ann Charity Wire Pvt MD
John: b 6-26-1753 d 3-3-1819 m Sarah Shinn Capt NJ
John: b 1748 d 1789 m Rebecca — Sgt NJ
John: b 1747 d 1-17-1829 m Susannah Lambert Sgt NY ★
John: b a. 1758 d 1798 m Elizabeth Lasher Sgt NY
John: b 1757 d 1826 m Elizabeth Bringle Pvt NY
John: b 1760 d 10-5-1848 m Sarah Frimple Lt PA
John: b 1735 d 1785 m Maria Roller Pvt PA
John: b 11-25-1748 d 6- -1833 m Barbara Kauffman Pvt PA
John: b 11-2-1757 d 8-28-1833 m Elizabeth Detwiler Pvt PA
John: b 9-25-1767 d 4-21-1852 m Elizabeth Yehl Pvt PA
John: b 1743 d 1822 m Catherine Smith Pvt VA
John: b c. 1754 d c. 1834 m Sarah Moon Pvt VA
John Jacob, Sr.: b 1732 d 1807 m Susanna See Sgt PA
John Jacob, Jr.: b 1760 d 1813-15 m Julia Morr Pvt PA
John Wilhelm: b 2-13-1714 d 9-12-1794 m Sarah Newkirk Pvt PS
 NY
Josph: b 5-15-1759 d 5-6-1804 m Abigail Harter Pvt NY
Joseph: b 1747 d 4-14-1812 m Elizabeth Clapsaddle PS NY
Josiah: b a. 1755 d 1-26-1797 m Lydia Mudge Cpl NY ★
Lawrence: b c. 1747 d 3-10-1806 m Rachel — Pvt PA
Lawrence: b 1715 d a. 8-25-1778 m Catherine PS PA
Ludwig: b c. 1725-30 d p. 11- -1779 m Sibylla Margaretha PS MD
Martin: b c. 1759 d p. 5-28-1838 m Bregje Akkerman Pvt NJ

MYERS, contd.

Michael: b 2-1-1753 d 2-17-1814 m Catherine Herter Sgt NY W★
Michael: b 2-11-1742 d 5-2-1819 m Barbara Ritter Pvt PA
Michael: b 1745 d 8-11-1852 m Catherine Strickler Sct PA
Michael: b 10-27-1762 d 3-14-1836 m Marie Beeghley Drm PA
Michael: b c. 1754 d 1829 m Elizabeth Maize Pvt PA
Michael: b 1753 d p. 1818 m Margaret Thornbury Pvt VA
Nicholas: b 12- -1759/60 d 6-24-1843 m Cornelia Pvt NY ★
Nicholas: b a. 1728 d p. 1790 m Anna Margreth Pvt PA
Nicholas: b 6-20-1758 d 1841 m Rosina Frederick Pvt PA ★
Oliver, Jr.: b 3-18-1748 d 1788 m Elizabeth Niles Pvt VT
Peter: b 7-4-1732 d 12-30-1813 m Marietje Louw Pvt NY
Peter: b 1760 d 12-23-1819 m Salome Brodt OrdlSgt PA W★
Peter: b 12- -1752 d 10-3-1836 m (2)Elizabeth Conel Pvt PA
Peter: b 6-11-1760 d 9-4-1820 m Mary Hibbs Pvt PA
Peter: b 1723 d a. 5-21-1794 m (2)Barbara Sager Pvt PA
Peter: b c. 1750 d 1798 m Maria — Pvt PS PA
Peter Low: b 11-5-1756 d 10-24-1845 m Neeltje Osterhoudt Pvt NY
Peter T.: b 8-12-1762 d 10-10-1839 m Rachel Low Pvt NY
Petrus, Jr.: b 9-6-1754 d 6-9-1827 m Barbara Langjair Pvt NY
Philip: b 10-4-1759 d 4-8-1835 m Margarette France Pvt NY
Philip: b 11-3-1759 d 4-2-1835 m Martha Bennett Pvt MD
Philip: b c. 1737 d 1811 m Maria Christina Lt PA
Philip: b 11-14-1755 d 4-27-1831 m Margaret Morr Lt PA
Samuel: b 7-20-1765 d 1-30-1859 m Rebecca Waldron PS NY
Samuel: b 12-17-1735 d 12-11-1810 m Caterina Lanin Pvt PA
Simon Johnson: b 12-1-1749 d 7-5-1821 m Cornelia Thorn 1Lt NY
Stephen: b 1740 d 8-27-1819 m Catrina Bernhard Sol NY
Stephen: b 12-27-1760 d 4-4-1841 m Helena Low Pvt NY ★
Stephanus: bpt 8-20-1727 d 5-7-1790 m Grietje Oosterhout Pvt NY
Teunis: b 1755 d 11-22-1831 m Cornelia Legg Pvt NY W★
Tobias: b 2-18-1734 d 1-28-1819 m Catherine Low Lt NY
Ulrick: b c. 1733 d p. 1800 m — PS SC
Valentine: b 1715 d 7- -1797 m (2)Anna Margaret CMman PA

MYGATT, (includes MIGATTS)

Austin: b 3-2-1732 d 2-23-1776 m Lament Blinn Sgt CT
Eli: b 1-25-1742 d 10-26-1807 m (1)Abigail Starr (2)Phebe Judson (3)Mary Boughton LCol CT
Thomas: b 1735 d 10- -1799 m Christian Fairchild Pvt NY

MYNATT,

Richard: b 10-21-1729 d c. 1805 m Sarah Cummins PS VA

MYNDERSE,

Barent: b 2-8-1747 d 8-13-1815 m Jannetje Van Vranken 1Lt NY
Myndert: b 1715 d p. 2-18-1788 m Yannetje Persen Sol PS NY

MYNDERTSE,

Rynier: b 10-6-1710 d 8-6-1788 m Catharina Van der Volgen PS NY

MYRTLE,

John: b c. 1760/61 d c. 1813 m Pheba Field PS VA

MYTINGER,

John Jacob: b 9-19-1750 d 9- -1793 m Elizabeth Mathieu Lt PA

NAFSCAR,

Joseph: b 8-20-1764 d 1828 m Marian — Pvt PA

NAGLE, (includes NAGEL & NAUGEL)

Anthony: b 7-25-1752 d 4-27-1819 m Sarah Foust PS PA
Christopher: b 8-20-1741 d 12-6-1812 m Margaretha Weismanin Pvt PA
Frederick: b 1748 d 11-12-1833 m Elizabeth Dhim Cpl PA
Frederick: b 4-26-1759 d 3-10-1839 m Elizabeth Wildeberger Pvt PA
Henry: b 11-10-1761 d 12-26-1820 m Catherine Warner Sgt PA W★
Joachim: b 2-21-1706 d 7-26-1795 m Catharine PS PA
Joseph: b 4-1-1755 d 10-14-1808 m Maria Magdalena Pvt PA
Leonard: b c. 1750 d a. 12- 1830 m — Pvt PA
Peter: b 10-31-1750 d 11-30-1834 m (1)Barbara Ann — (2)Sarah (Hottenstein) High Capt PA ★
Philip: b 2-28-1752 d 9-30-1843 m Margaret Young DrmMaj PA ★
Richard: b c. 1747 d 2-22-1837 m Mary — Pvt MD ★

NAIL,

Henry: b 1759 d 2-2-1843 m Mary Bates Pvt GA
Henry: b 1755 d 1835 m Mary Tannehill Pvt PA
John: b 1743 d 1824 m Mary Bugg Pvt GA
John: b — d 9-14-1781 m Martha M. — Maj NC

NALL,

Wm.: b c. 1744 d p. 12-26-1791 m Ann Yancey Col VA

NANNY,

David, Sr.: b 8- -1757 d 5-1-1835 m (1)Patience Keeler (2)Anna Whartonby Pvt NY ★

NANTZ, (includes NANCE)

Daniel: b 1745 d 1802 m Patience — Pvt NC
Frederick: b 2-1-1761 d 7-14-1835 m (1)Martha Hughes Watkins (2)Maria Cosby Lt VA ★
Reuben: b 7-12-1745 d 1-13-1812 m (1)Amy Williams (2)Nancy Brown Ens VA
Robert: b — d p. 5-25-1808 m (1)Marshall (2)Faithy Merriman PS VA
Thomas: b c. 1748 d a. 7- -1821 m (1)Sarah Gibbs (2)Mary Cooper Pvt VA
Wm.: b 1730 d 1800 m — Pvt VA
Zachariah: b 5-5-1760 d 12-22-1835 m (1)Jane Wilkins (2)Elizabeth (Morris) Bingley Pvt VA ★

NAPIER, (includes NAPPER)

James: b 1721 d p. 1-30-1798 m Mary Thompson Pvt SC
Patrick: b c. 1746 d 1808 m Elizabeth Woodson Cpl VA
Rene: b 1734 d 1807 m Rebecca Hurt Pvt GA
Richard: b 9-12-1747 d 3-24-1823 m Molly Wills Capt VA
Wm.: b c. 1745 d 1814 m Nellie Wells Pvt VA
Wm. P.: b 10-19-1765 d 11-17-1848 m Elizabeth Cook Pvt VA ★

NARRAMORE,

Asa: b 4-19-1761 d 4-11-1851 m (1)Mary Lake (2)Caty Conger (3)Sally Joslin Pvt MA ★
John: b 1-22-1762 d 6-11-1851 m (2)Nancy Adkins Cpl SC ★

NASH,

Abner: b 8-8-1740 d 12-2-1786 m (1)Mrs Dobbs (2)Mary Whiting Jones PS VA
Abraham: b 10-10-1718 d 6-24-1801 m (1)Rhoda Keeler (2)Mrs Mercy Lynes PS CT
Abraham: b 5-16-1740 d 5-25-1791 m Lydia Smith Pvt MA
Abram: b 11-7-1740 d 11- -1821 m — Olmstead Sgt CT
Asahel: b 12-30-1758 d 8-18-1822 m Betsey Shutts Pvt PA
Benjamin: b 7-3-1750 d 6-17-1897 m Lydia Skinner 1Lt MA
Benjamin: b 9-6-1733 d p. 1790 m Mercy Loud Pvt MA
Caleb: b 4-28-1747 d 1823 m Rachel (Nash) Pvt MA ★
Daniel: b 9-13-1715 d 7-1-1790 m (1)Abigail Stebbins (2)Martha Wells 1Lt PS MA
David, Sr.: b 6-6-1719 d 4-26-1803 m (1)Jemima Boltwood (2)Elizabeth Smith (3)Experience Loomis PS MA
Ebenezer: b 1-20-1744 d 12-8-1823 m Susannah Hills Pvt CT
Ebenezer: b 1729 d c. 1784 m (1)— (2)Phoebe — PS CT
Eleazer: b 2-10-1720 d 5-19-1775 m Phebe Kellogg Lt MA
Elijah: b 2-27-1737 d 1827 m Hannah Thayer Pvt MA
Elisha: b 1750 d 2-6-1801 m Sarah Dammon Sgt MA
Elisha: b 10-8-1729 d 3- -1814 m Lois Frost Drm MA
Enos: b 2-7-1743 d 3-30-1796 m Martha Gaylord Sgt MA
Ephraim: b 3-18-1754 d 12-18-1816 m Hannah Welles Pvt MA W★
Francis: b 5-10-1720 d 10-7-1777 m Sarah Moore ADC BG NC
Isaac: b a. 1746 d 8-16-1777 m Elizabeth Abbott Lt MA
Jacob: b 6- -1750 d 7-11-1779 m Freelove Keeler Pvt CT
Jacob: b 10- -1737 d 5-1-1828 m Margaret Higgins Pvt MA
James: b 11-12-1727 d p. 1778 m Margaret Thompson Pvt MA
James: b 4-16-1756 d 9-10-1823 m Anna Hess Pvt MA ★
Job: b 7-23-1756 d 11-8-1844 m (1)Sarah Wade (2)Nancy Belcher Pvt MA ★
Joel, Sr.: b 6-19-1731 d 12-19-1797 m (1)Zerviah Ladd (2)Sarah Paulk CS MA
John: b c. 1755 d c. 1790 m Ruth Cole Pvt MA
John: b 4-13-1747 d a. 12- -1826 m (1)Sarah — Sgt NY ★
John: b 5-16-1747 d a. 10-20-1794 m Polly Harrison Long Pvt VA
John, Sr.: b 1-1-1711 d 1776 m Anna Owen PS VA
John, Jr.: b 1732 d a. 4-20-1801 m (1)Charlotte Julie Spence (2)Elizabeth Fisher (3)Mary Barksdale Col PS VA
Jonathan: b c. 1750 d 1- -1846 m Ann Bird Sgt MA
Jonathan: b 12-3-1721 d 11-4-1793 m Anna Maria Spoor PS MA
Joseph, Jr.: b 3-3-1760 d 4-8-1834 m Mary Giles Lt CT
Joseph: b 1726 d p. 4-27-1778 m Susannah Shaw Sgt MA
Joseph: b 4-2-1736 d 10-21-1818 m Sarah Damon Pvt MA
Joseph, Jr.: b 2-4-1739 d 6-10-1815 m Lucy Peakes Pvt MA
Moses: b 9-7-1741 d 4-1-1792 m Annie Bliss Lt MA
Moses: b 4-24-1744 d 8-19-1826 m (1)Rebecca Tirell (2)Rachel Cowen Sgt MA
Noah: b 1-23-1734 d 8-6-1775 m Elizabeth Cudworth Pvt MA
Peter: b 7-31-1738 d 3-14-1824 m Sarah Torrey Pvt MA
Phineas: b 10-17-1726 d 1824 m Mary Hamlin Pvt MA
Samuel: b 1-29-1709 d c. 1802 m (1)Margaret Merrill (2)Mrs Dickinson CS CT
Samuel: b 3-14-1749 d 1811 m Chloe Garnsey Parkiss Pvt NC
Samuel: b 6- -1755 d 3-19-1844 m Jerusha Briggs Pvt Slr MA
Samuel: b 2-1-1760 d 9- -1823 m (1)Vashti Pierre (2)Lucy Goodenow Pvt MA
Shubael: b 8-27-1758 d 12-24-1824 m Sybil Alvord Pvt MA
Silas: b 14-1762 d 1-6-1852 m (1)Adri Adams Pvt CT ★
Simeon 2nd: b 2-3-1741 d 1-3-1824 m (1)Betsey Louden (2)Joanna Pope Pvt MA
Simeon: b 5-15-1756 d 2-20-1813 m Eleanor Whipple Cpl MA
Thomas: b 5-21-1743 d 1-29-1815 m (1)Mary Burr (2)Mary Nicholas CS CT
Thomas, Sr.: b — d p. 11-18-1794 m Mary Portlock LCol VA
Thomas, Jr.: b 4-12-1758 d 9-26-1824 m Elizabeth Herbert Sol VA

Timothy: b 10-9-1759 d 3-27-1840 m Martha Porter Pvt MA
Wm.: b 2-5-1763 d 9-1-1834 m Martha — Pvt NC ★

NASON, (includes NASSON)
Abraham: b *c.* 1738 d *p.* 1790 m Anna Erils PS CS MA
Bartholomew: b 6-8-1756 d 2-9-1822 m Elizabeth Hooton Pvt MA
David: b 7-5-1758 d 11-16-1805 m Abigail Stoddard Sgt MA
Edward: b 1756 d 3-14-1847 m Sarah Merrill Pvt MA
Edward: b 3-31-1764 d *p.* 1805 m (1)Abigail Small (2)Susanna
    Small Pvt MA
Jacob: b 11-25-1741 d 11-5-1814 m Ruth Jenkins Pvt MA ★
John: b 9- -1751 d 11-10-1827 m Rebecca Perkins Smn MA
Joshua: b 6-26-1725 d 1809 m (1)Sarah Butler (2)Abigail Curtis
    Capt MA
Nathaniel: b 1754 d 7-27-1818 m (1)Betsey Manning (2)Betsey
    Chapwick Capt MA
Samuel: b 2-14-1744 d 8-28-1800 m (1)Mary Ball Shores (2)Mrs
    Joanna Tilden Moulton Ens MA
Shubael: b 1750 d 5-1-1778 m Sarah Wormwood Pvt MA
Willaby: b 2-21-1750 d 4-9-1838 m Mary Bardens Pvt MA ★

NATHAN,
Simon: b 1746 d 9-8-1822 m Grace Mendes Seixes PS PA

NATION,
Joseph: b *c.* 1750 d 4-12-1803 m Jereter Vickory Pvt NC W★

NAUDAIN,
Cornelius: b 1737-39 d 3-1-1798 m (1) — (2)Mary — PS DE
Elias, Jr.: b *c.* 1745 d 10- -1800 m Elizabeth — PS DE
Elias: b 9- -1751/52 d 3-9-1800 m Catharine Skeer Mc Combs PS
    DE

NAUMAN,
Gottlieb: b 9-19-1747 d 3- -1803 m Anna Margaret Schaffner Sgt
    PA

NAVE,
Abraham: b *c.* 1758 d 1850-60 m Mary Williams Pvt NC
Teter: b *c.* 1735 d 1797-1808 m Ann Vanderpool Sol PS NC

NAY,
Jacob: b 1723 d 1828 m Mary — Pvt VA
John: b 8- -1703 d 2-22-1779 m (1)Mrs Deliverance Leavitt
    (2)Elizabeth Ladd PS NH
John: b 1750 d 1841 m Sarah — Pvt VA ★
Joseph: b 11-25-1753 d *p.* 1792 m Mary Towle Pvt NH
Samuel: b 1739 d 10-1-1817 m (1)Mary Elkins (2)Mercy Wason
    Capt NH
Samuel: b 3-9-1763 d 10-1-1848 m Nancy — Pvt VA
Wm.: b 1764 d *p.* 1833 m Sarah — PS VA

NAYLOR, (includes NAILER)
Batson: b 1748 d *p.* 1797 m Mrs Eleanor Smith Austin PS MD
James: b 1735 d 1779 m Elizabeth Ewing CS PA
Joshua: b *c.* 1745 d *p.* 2-23-1814 m Susannah — PS MD
Ralph: b 4-6-1762 d 8-25-1827 m Nancy Stewart Pvt PA
Wm.: b 12-3-1760 d 12-19-1829 m Eleanor McKean Ens PA

NEAGLES,
Michael: b 12-25-1765 d 4-22-1836 m Sarah Le Bosquet Pvt MA

NEAL, (includes NEALE, NEEL & NEIL)
Adam: b 1735 d 1795 m Jeanette Andrew Pvt PA
Basil: b 10-9-1758 d 10-14-1848 m (1)Milly Briscoe (2)Sarah Hull
    Green Ens PS VA W★
Benjamin: b 1760 d 4-15-1853 m Delilah Barton Pvt VA
Charles: b 8-27-1762 d 8-27-1831 m Ann Miller Pvt VA ★
Charles: b 1730 d 1791 m — Pvt VA
Christopher: b 1737 d 1-11-1811 m Sarah — Pvt VA
Daniel: b *c.* 1745 d 1-3-1777 m Elizabeth Mallam Capt NJ
Daniel: b *c.* 1735 d 8/9- -1804 m Jemima Kitchen Pvt VA
David: b *a.* 1755 d *a.* 5-24-1810 m Mary — Pvt PA
David: b 1-21-1755 d 10-8-1811 m Joyce Mc Cormick Pvt SC
Ebenezer: b 1-18-1726 d 4-15-1805 m (1)Lydia Clark (2)Eliza
    Perkins PS NH
Elijah: b 9- -1740 d 2- -1821 m Sara Nicholson Sol NC
Henry: b 1740 d *p.* 1783 m Eleanor Plowden 3Lt MD
Henry: b 12-2-1736 d 2-28-1788 m Nancy Reid Capt NC
Hubartus, Sr.: b 10-22-1717 d 12-13-1806 m Mary Perkins Pvt PS
    NH
Hubartus, Jr.: b 7-23-1752 d 5-8-1807 m Mary Smith PS NH
James: b 1751 d 4-28-1801 m Rachel McClure Pvt PA
James: b 1738 d 2- -1822 m (1)Hannah Hardin (2)Mary Phelps
    Capt VA
Jeremiah: b 7-10-1757 d 11-8-1827 m Anna Fuller Pvt CT
John: b 1757 d 7-22-1825 m Margaret Miller Pvt NJ MD W★
John: b 1746 d 1801 m Mary Cooper Pvt PA
John: b 1746 d 9-7-1821 m Margaret Warden Pvt PA
Jonathan: b 1-15-1759 d 10-9-1837 m Harriet Preston Capt MA
Joseph: b 1759 d 7-4-1838 m Nancy Perkins Pvt NH
Joseph: b *c.* 1750-53 d *p.* 11-6-1783 m Mary — PS VA

Joshua: b 6-23-1756 d 11-4-1840 m Mary Tarleton Pvt NH ★
Lewis: b 7-4-1760 d 1833 m Pamellia Cox Pvt PS VA ★
Micajah: b 1753 d 2-26-1836 m Mildred Beasley Pvt VA
Philip: b 12-7-1753 d 1-17-1818 m Anna Bragg Sgt NC
Presley: b *c.* 1735 d 1783/84 m Susannah Satchell Smn VA
Presley: b 1747 d *p.* 1-21-1815 m Mary Carter Mid VA
Richard: b *a.* 1747 d *p.* 1801 m (1)Frances Underwood (2)Mary
    (Nelson) Smith Pvt VA
Robert: b 7-17-1755 d 8-17-1822 m Margaret Lear Pvtr PS NH
Samuel: b *a.* 1758 d 12-8-1816 m Mary Mendum Pvt MA
Samuel: b 1729 d *p.* 1778 m Elizabeth Haley PS NH
Samuel: b 1750 d 2-19-1824 m Abigal Conner PS NH
Samuel: b *c.* 1762 d 1803 m Patty Mc Cormick Pvt SC
Thomas: b 1751 d 5- -1806 m Hannah Avery Sgt CT W★
Thomas: b *c.* 1745 d *p.* 9-2-1807 m Sarah — Sol GA
Thomas: b 3-25-1744 d 4-5-1824 m Gresall Penny Lt PA
Thomas, Sr.: b *c.* 1735 d *a.* 2-18-1800 m Susannah Harrell Sol SC
Thomas: b 1730 d 6-20-1779 m Jean Spratt Col PS SC
Thomas: b 1765 d 12- -1836 m Phebe La Rue Pvt VA
Wm.: b 9-15-1763 d 12- -1842 m (1)Abigail Denison (2)Abigail
    Lewis Pvt CT ★
Wm.: b *a.* 1750 d 1786 m — PS MD
Wm.: b 1741 d 1-29-1821 m Sarah Sinclair Pvt NH
Wm.: b *c.* 1736 d 9-9-1813 m Mary Reynolds Pvt PA
Wm.: b 1750 d 1828 m Bathsheba Harrison Capt VA
Wm.: b *c.* 1760 d 3-20-1823 m Sabry Odom Pvt VA
Wm.: b 7-6-1761 d 2-11-1841 m Rhoda Harman Pvt VA ★
Younger: b *c.* 1745 d *a.* 7- -1784 m Sarah — PS NC

NEAR, (includes NEHER)
Charles: b 8-25-1752 d 3-14-1826 m Catherine Hydley Pvt NY
George: b 11-22-1754 d 7-26-1813 m Catharine Feller Pvt NY

NERING,
Asahel: b 5-15-1765 d 9-9-1813 m Molly Loomis Pvt CT
Henry: b 1-29-1758 d 9-15-1845 m (1)Lois Blackman (2)Jane
    (Treat) Baldwin Sgt CT ★
John: b 4-12-1752 d 4-22-1826 m Lucy Wilcox Pvt CT
Joseph: b 1762 d 1-14-1849 m (2)Julia Genung Pvt Tms MA ★

NEASE,
John George, Jr.: b 6-12-1760 d *p.* 1832 m Rebecca — Sol GA

NEBINGER,
George: b 11-1-1744 d 12-7-1796 m Ann Rankin Pvt PA

NEBLETT,
John: b 9-1-1755 d 3-11-1830 m Susanna Hightower PS VA
Wm.: b 1747 d 1835 m (1)Ann Ragsdale (2)Sarah Love (3)Amy
    Williams Sol VA

NEBUCKAR, (or NEBEKER)
John: b 11-26-1756 d — m Mary Senex Pvt DE

NEED, (includes NEET)
George: b *c.* 1740 d *p.* 2-3-1782 m Magdalener — 2Lt MD
Jacob: b *c.* 1755 d *p.* 1811 m — Arnold Pvt PA

NEEDHAM,
Anthony, Sr.: b 5-18-1723 d 1783 m Rebecca Munger Capt MA
Anthony, Jr.: b 11-27-1744 d 9-27-1785 m Catharine Warner Sgt
    MA
Benjamin: b 4-15-1756 d 10-2-1834 m Mary Dowse Pvt MA
Daniel: b 12-10-1760 d 2-7-1844 m Ede Flint Sgt MA ★
David: b 4-22-1755 d 11-22-1815 m Marcilvia Ainsworth Fif MA
Isaac: b 3-4-1746 d 2-19-1830 m (2)Elizabeth Archer Pvt MA
Jasper: b 7-3-1738 d 12-14-1821 m Deborah Fuller Lt MA
Jeremiah: b 6-17-1741 d 8- -1815 m Elizabeth Gardner Sgt MA
John: b 3-22-1742/43 d *p.* 1820 m Phoebe Shattuck Sgt MA ★
John, Sr.: b 1-26-1718 d 2-15-1800 m Prudence Sterns Pvt MA
John, Jr.: b 8-31-1759 d 4-24-1840 m Mary Shedd Pvt MA ★
Joseph: b 1-28-1746 d 12-20-1808 m Mehitable Moulton Pvt MA
Stephen: b 12-6-1763 d 7-4-1836 m Abigail Perry Pvt MA
Stephen: b 10-15-1732 d 12-28-1801 m Elizabeth Moulton Pvt MA
Sterns: b 2-25-1754 d 2-5-1830 m (1)Alice Kidder (2)Hannah Baily
    Pvt MA

NEEDLES,
Wm.: b *c.* 1723 d *p.* 1778 m Ann Blakshear Pvt MD

NEELY, (includes NEELEY, NEELLEY, NEELLY & NELIGH)
Abraham: b 1746 d 2-24-1823 m Hannah Dill Capt NY
Francis: b 10-15-1761 d 11-7-1829 m Mary Holman PS NC SC VA
George: b 1761 d 3-16-1833 m Rebekah Green Pvt SC ★
Henry: b 9-4-1743 d 12-21-1802 m Susannah Nelson Lt NY
Jacob: b *c.* 1762 d 7-16-1845 m — Pvt MM NC
John: b 1756 d *p.* 1832 m Lutetia Black Pvt SC GA ★
John, Sr.: b *c.* 1730 d *p.* 3-21-1781 m — Pvt NY
John, Jr.: b 11-24-1758 d 6-22-1835 m Margaret — Pvt NY W★
John: b 1750 d 5-6-1806 m Isabella Mc Ree Ens NC
John: b 1751 d 1804 m Jane — Pvt PA
John: b 1758 d — m Lucretia Jane Broom Pvt SC
John: b *c.* 1748 d *a.* 11-12-1818 m Susannah Evans Sol VA

NEELY, contd.
Joseph: b 1750 d 8-20-1824 m Susannah Bowdoin Sgt NH
Joseph: b 8-11-1762 d 8-20-1824 m Rachel Shaw Pvt NH ★
Joseph: b 1759 d 5-12-1834 m Nancy Ann Horton Pvt NC ★
Joseph: b 1758 d 10-26-1811 m Martha Johnston Sol PA
Nicholas: b 1730 d 1812 m Anna Margaret Babion Pvt PA
Paul: b 12-21-1759 d a. 9-21-1843 m (1)Frances Shupe (2)Veronica
— Sgt PA
Samuel: b 5-11-1754 d 1-8-1841 m Elizabeth Barnette Pvt Lt SC
Sarah Morgan: b 1730 d 1796 m William Neely PS SC
Thomas, Sr.: b 1723 d p. 11-3-1793 m Hannah — Pvt PS NC
Thomas: b c. 1740 d 1793 m Ann — Pvt NC
Wm.: b c. 1730 d 7/8- -1780 m Margaret Patterson Sol NC
Wm.: b 8-31-1742 d 7-10-1818 m Elizabeth Thompson Capt PA
Wm.: b 1735 d p. 1-19-1819 m Margaret — Pvt PA
Wm.: b — d p. 2-21-1827 m Mary — Pvt VA

NEES, (includes NEASE & NEESE)
John: b 1-8-1757 d 1830 m Elizabeth Rausch Pvt VA
Michael: b — d a. 7-25-1815 m Margaretha Zerkelsen PS Sol MA
Peter: b — d 2-1-1777 m Mary Shoemaker Pvt PA

NEEVLING, (includes NEVELLING)
Jacob: b c. 1754 d 9-11-1777 m Mary — Pvt PA
John Wesley Gilbert: b 1750 d 1-18-1844 m Catherine Steinmetz
Chp NJ

NEFF,
Jacob: b 1-16-1761 d 1-13-1839 m Fanny Kline Pvt NJ ★
Jacob: b 4-3-1726 d 9-3-1793 m Anna Buser Pvt PA
John: b 5-6-1746 d 1822 m Sarah Jennings Pvt CT
Rudolph: b 9-26-1727 d 2-14-1809 m Hannah Morse Capt PA

NEGLEY, (includes NAGLEE)
Alexander: b 1734 d 11-3-1809 m Mary Ann Burkstresser Pvt PA
Eliab: b 1746 d 10-8-1825 m Barbara Poorman Pvt PA
Philip: b 9- -1748 d 10-3-1843 m Elizabeth Hoffer Pvt PA
Wm.: b 1730 d p. 1790 m Margaret — Sgt PA

NEGUS,
John: b 1750 d 9-30-1809/10 m Lydia — Sol VT
Samuel: b 1744 d 5-31-1837 m Mary Gillette Pvt MA
Wm., Jr.: b 10-23-1732 d 1817 m Elizabeth Smith Pvt VT

NEIDIGH, (or NEIDIG)
Leonard: b c. 1750 d a. 5-1-1792 m Margarethe — Pvt PA
Solomon: b 8-17-1744 d 1-28-1797 m Marie Elizabeth Pvt PA

NEIDLINGER,
John Gottlieb: b c. 1760 d p. 1-30-1793 m Mrs Hannah Dasher
(Zettler) Sol GA

NEIGHBOUR, (includes NACHBOR)
Abraham: b 9-12-1737 d 1-12-1815 m Anna Marie Gonsour Ens
PA
Nicholas: b 1742 d 10-29-1821 m Elizabeth Crane Pvt PA
Nicholas: b 6-10-1762 d 7-28-1848 m Elizabeth Catherine Sharp
QM NJ

NEIGHBOURS,
Francis: b 1750 d p. 1806 m Sallie Wheat PS VA

NELLEGAR,
Joseph: b 1758 d 1-7-1831 m Hannah — Pvt NY

NELLIS,
Christian: b 11-2-1731 d a. 1-11-1808 m Christina Keiser Pvt NY
John D.: b 12-10-1755 d 3- -1849 m Nancy (Garlock) Keller Cpl
NY
John L.: b 12-3-1762/3 d 12-27-1841 m Anna Fuchs Cpl NY ★
Joseph: b 4-3-1759 d 2-24-1834 m — Lampman Pvt NY
Ludwig: b c. 1725 d p. 8-8-1809 m Elizabeth Kaiser Lt NY
Peter W.: b 3-6-1760 d 3-9-1818 m (1)Catherine Sevrinus Tygert
(2)Mrs. Rosena (Watts) Flander Dewey Drm NY
Philip: b 12-1-1746 d 11-10-1818 m Elizabeth Dietz MM NY
Wm.: b 1762 d p. 1840 m Isabelle Cloud Pvt NY

NELMS,
Charles: b 1752 d 1838 m — Mott Sgt VA ★
Charles: b 5-18-1750 d 10-10-1834 m Eliza Sydnor Sgt VA
Presley, Sr.: b 10-5-1730 d p. 2-3-1797 m X PS NC
Presley, Jr.: b 1767 d 5-5-1841 m Ann Montgomery Ingram Sol NC

NELSON, (includes NEILSON, NELLSON & NILLSON)
Aaron: b 4-13-1740 d 7-19-1804 m Abigail Williams Cpl PS MA
Alexander: b c. 1755 d10/11- -1799 m Jean — Ens NC
Ambrose: b a. 1756 d a. 8-7-1797 m Rhoda Capt VA
Andrew: b 1762 d 11-1-1850 m — Pvt VA
Asa: b 4-3-1754 d 5-31-1837 m Abigail Harriman Pvt MA
Berryman: b 1760 d 1836-39 m Mary Humphreys Sol NC
Daniel: b c. 1761 d 2-21-1837 m Polly Granville Mar NH ★

Daniel: b 1754 d 9-26-1829 m Relief Pierce Pvt CT
David, Sr.: b 6-4-1737 d 5-12-1827 m (1)Susanna Bacheller
(2)Susanna Bigham Sgt MA
David: b 1725 d 9-8-1807 m (1)Mary Hale (2)Rachael Spofford Pvt
MA
David: b 6-2-1736 d 1808 m Margaret Norton CS PS MA
David: b 7-28-1765 d 4-14-1836 m Elizabeth Hunting Pvt MA
David: b 11-30-1752 d 10-29-1829 m Margaret Logan (Jamison)
1Lt PA
Ebenezer: b 8-1-1723 d 6-29-1809 m Ruth Jackson PS MA
Edward: b 1760 d 7-1,1-1839 m Winifred Johnson Pvt NC ★
Edward: b c. 1745 d a. 1813 m Harriett Morgan Pvt PS VA
Eli: b 8-24-1750 d 8-24-1835/6 m Mary Burling Pvt NY ★
Elisha: b c. 1755 d a. 8-8-1829 m Elizabeth — PS NC
Francis: b c. 1755 d 6-20-1812 m Sarah Lyon Sol NY
Gershom: b 7-29-1729 d 9-23-1813 m (1)Mercy Puffer (2)Lydia
Fairbanks Capt MA
Giles: b 1755 d p. 1840 m — Pvt NC
Harriet Morgan: b a. 1753 d a. 1819 m Edward Nelson PS KY VA
Henry: b 6-20-1754 d 9-13-1805 m Sibble Smith Lt MA
Hugh: b 9-30-1750 d 10-13-1800 m Judith Page Col VA
Jacob: b 11-28-1742 d 10-24-1823 m Anna Harbach Pvt MA
James: b 6-12-1742 d 8-13-1824 m Seibel Allen Pvt MA
James: b 1740 d 7-16-1811 m Rachel Porter Pvt NH
James: b 10-2-1765 d 1-15-1834 m Isabella Louise Richburg Sol
NC
James: b 7-15-1740 d p. 1790 m Margaret — Pvt NC
James: b 2-14-1757 d 11-27-1828 m Martha Sloan Sol PA
Jeremiah: b 3-13-1737 d 11-22-1805 m Rachel Kent MM CT
John: b c. 1750 d a. 9-13-1811 m Elinor Sol GA
John: b 11-19-1757 d — m Frances Lt MD
John: b — d 5- -1806 m Catherine Washington Dr MD W★
John: b 10-25-1737 d 9-11-1803 m Hope Rounsevill Col MA
John: b 3-11-1745 d 3-3-1833 m Catherine Schuyler Voorhess BG
NJ
John: b 1746 d 1816 m Nancy — Ens NY
John: b 1721 d 1-22-1777 m (1)Elizabeth Davenport (2)Rebecca
Scott Pvt NY
John: b 3-23-1753 d 3-3-1833 m Lydia Quitterfield Pvt NY
John: b c. 1750 d p. 1790 m Mollie Howe Pvt NY
John: b 1749 d 1802 m Lavinia McCuiston Maj NC
John: b c. 1762 d c. 6-9-1822 m Jennet Tate Sol NC
John: b c. 1745 d a. 3-7-1822 m (2)Margaret Hamilton 2Lt PA
John, Sr.: b 1732 d 12- -1811 m Mary Gilliland Pvt PA
John, Jr.: b 1755 d 1827 m Martha Archbold Pvt PA
John: b 1761 d 5-21-1826 m (1)Cela Coleman (2)Ruth Stratford Pvt
VA
John: b 1743 d 1-2-1790 m (1)Frances Armistead (2)Rebecca
Woodley Cpl PS VA
John: b 1740 d 2-10-1827 m Ann (Nancy) Carter Maj VA
John: b 7-10-1747 d p. 1829 m Bathsheba Hogan Lt VA
John: b 3- -1751 d 5-31-1838 m (1)Jane Roberson (2)Sarah McGhee
Pvt VA ★
John: b c. 1715 d p. 8-9-1784 m Sarah Whitson PS VA
John: b c. 1745 d — m Mary Young Sol VA
John: b c. 1725 d p. 1777 m Sarah Rising PS VT
Jonathan: b c. 1749 d 9-12-1777 m Sarah Warren Cpl MA
Jonathan: b 7-27-1723 d 6-18-1801 m Hannah Cheney Pvt MA
Joseph: b 1-13-1745 d p. 1789 m Mary Chaplin Pvt MA
Joseph: b 1740 d 5-12-1816 m Isabel Rogers Sgt NY
Joseph: b 1763 d p. 2-6-1834 m (1)Jane Armstrong (2)Anny Pvt PA
Joseph: b c. 1750/51 d 10-6-1837 m (1)Catherine O'Bannon (2)
Jane Bradford Ens VA
Joseph: b 1753 d p. 10-29-1845 m Lucy Tate Pvt VA ★
Joshua: b 9-18-1726 d 12-14-1817 m Sarah Mandeville Maj NY
Josiah: b 8-16-1732 d 1-23-1807 m Elizabeth Thayer Lt MA
Josiah: b 9-13-1726 d 2-26-1810 m (1)Elizabeth Abrams (2)Millicent
Bond MM MA
Justus: b 2-21-1737 d 2-21-1803 m (1)Mary Haight (2)Mrs. Phebe
Budd CS NY
Mary: b — d p. 5-16-1789 m Mathew Nelson PS VA
Moses: b 9-10-1755 d 6-25-1832 m Sally Hovey Pvt NH
Moses: b 1-1-1765 d 8-11-1845 m Dorothy Comstock Pvt NY
Nathaniel: b 4-22-1701 d 1-6-1783 m (1)Deborah Chapin (2)Mrs.
Sarah Thayer PS MA
Nehemiah, Sr.: b 10-4-1716 d 3-16-1782 m Hannah Sheffield Pvt
MA
Paul: b 1752 d 5-4-1832 m Hannah Churchill Pvt NY
Philip: b 6-3-1756 d 9-4-1841 m Hannah Quimby Pvt MA ★
Reuben: b 11-1-1713 d 12-5-1784 m Elizabeth — Sol NY
Robert: b c. 1755 d 4-17-1793 m Mary — QM Sgt NC W★
Robert: b 1725 d 9- -1804 m Martha Patterson PS PA
Robert: b 1747 d 12- -1808 m Rebecca — Cpl Dr VA
Robert: b 1752 d 1802 m Susan Robinson Pvt VA
Roger: b 6- -1759 d 6-7-1815 m (1)Mary Brooke Sim (2)Betsey
Harrison Lt MD
Samuel: b 4-6-1745 d 9-9-1822 m (1)Charity Haskell (2)Anna
Pickens Sgt MA
Samuel: b 9-21-1760 d 2-18-1823 m Sally Torrey Pvt MA
Samuel: b 1756 d 5-22-1837 m Catharine — Ens NC ★
Samuel: b 1748 d 1809 m Rebecca Loughead Pvt PA
Samuel: b 2-7-1742 d 11-8-1802 m Mary Mc Mullin LCol PA
Samuel: b 12-28-1732 d 11-22-1807 m Jean Gamble PS SC

Seth: b 6-22-1735 d 9-10-1811 m Silence Cheney 2Lt MA
Thomas: b 4-9-1727 d 9-4-1807 m Sarah Pope Pvt MA
Thomas: b 3-17-1744 d 11-1-1823 m Sarah Wright PS NY
Thomas: b 1758 d 7-13-1834 m Sarah Pierce Pvt NH & VT ★
Thomas: b 11-25-1745 d 3-27-1846 m Susan Woodward Pvt SC
Thomas, Jr.: b 12-26-1738 d 1-4-1789 m Lucy Grymes BG SDI VA
Thomas: b 1716 d 1786 m Lucy Armistead PS VA
Wm.: b 6-2-1760 d 6-13-1844 m Eunice Young Pvt NY
Wm.: b c. 1735 d a. 1804 m Catherine — Lt PA
Wm.: b 1742 d 1-23-1831 m Jean Stewart PS VT
Wm.: b 6-17-1746 d 11-25-1807 m Lucy Chiswell Col VA
Wm.: b 1754 d 3-8-1813 m (1)— Taliaferro (2)Abigail Byrd LCol VA

NEMONS,
Wm.: b c. 1745 d p. 1782 m Letitia Houston Pvt PA

NEPHEW,
James: b 1758 d 1- -1827 m Mary Gignilliat Capt GA

NESBITT, (includes NESBET, NESBIT, NISBET & NISBIT)
Abram: b 9-12-1763 d 1-2-1847 m Bethiah Wheeler Pvt PA CT
Alexander: b 2-4-1754 d 11-8-1823 m (1)Sarah Ann Davidson (2)Nancy Jane Mc Kay Capt PA
Allen: b 1747 d 3-16-1824 m Margaret Murray Ens PA
Francis: b 1749 d 1802 m Anne Thomson Pvt PA
James, Sr.: b 6-15-1718 m Phoebe Harrison Pvt PS PA
James: b 2-27-1765 d 9-8-1845 m Jane Bratton Sol SC
Jeremiah: b c. 1738-40 d p. 3- -1796 m Sarah — Sol PA
John: b 1738 d 5-18-1817 m Mary Osborn PS NC
John: b 1744 d 12-9-1829 m Sarah Moorehead Pvt PA
John: b c. 1730 d 1801 m (1)Hannah Wickersham (2)Mary Crichton (3)Jean Ewing PS PA
John: b 1759 d 3-21-1829 m Isabel White Pvt PS SC
Jonathan: b 10-5-1736 d 2-11-1832 m Elizabeth — Cmsry SC
Joseph: b c. 1756 d 1825 m Elizabeth Mc Murray PS SC
Moses W.: b p. 1755 d p. 1804 m Elizabeth — PS MD
Nathaniel: b 6-16-1725 d a. 4-13-1805 m Fanny Witmer PS MD
Samuel: b a. 1749 d p. 3-7-1814 m Mary — Sol VA
Wm.: b 1750 d 8-26-1805 m Agnes McClintock Pvt PA
Wm.: b 1755 d 3-2-1831 m (1)Jemima Baker (2)Agnes Freeling Capt SC

NESMITH,
Arthur: b 4-3-1721 d p. 1790 m Margaret Hopkins Pvt NH
Benjamin: b 9-14-1734 d 9-18-1800 m Agnes Gilmore Lt NH
Benjamin: b 8-17-1756 d 1839/40 m Mary Weatherbee Pvt NH ★
James, Sr.: b 8-4-1718 d 7-19-1793 m Mary Dinsmore Pvt PS NH
James, Jr.: b 12-10-1744 d 3-1-1796 m (1)Mary Mc Clure (2)Jane Aiken Pvt PS CS NH
John: b 1728 d 1815 m Elizabeth Reid Lt PS NH
John: b 1750 d p. 1811 m — Brockington Sol SC
Robert: b 3-9-1762 d 5-6-1836 m Elizabeth Britton Sol SC
Thomas: b 11-22-1741 d 10-7-1814 m Jennet Robeson Pvt PS SC

NESSLE,
Conrad: b 1762 d 6-8-1833 m Lavina Neville Pvt NY

NESTLE, (includes NESTELL)
Martin: b a. 1759 d p. 1820 m — Countryman Pvt NY
Peter: b 1750 d 4-30-1817 m Lucy — Capt Lt NY

NETHERLAND, (includes NETHERTON)
Benjamin: b 2-29-1755 d 10-10-1838 m Theadosia Bramlette Brev Capt VA ★
John: b 1747 d 10-31-1834 m (1)Elizabeth — (2)Rebecca Frazier Maj VA ★
John: b 1733 d 9- -1803 m Mary Anne Mosby PS VA

NETTLES,
Jesse: b 6-4-1745 d 2-13-1825 m Ann Stroud Pvt PS NC
Wm.: b 4-2-1734 d 10-15-1832 m (1)Amy Alexander (2)Mary Mathis (3)Mrs Hester Cook Capt SC
Zachariah: b 1-28-1737 d 1803/04 m Lucy Bass 1Lt SC
Zachariah: b c. 1759 d 8-30-1820 m Nancy Scofield Sgt SC

NETTLETON,
John: b 8-31-1744 d 3-31-1831 m Mattaniah Buell Pvt CT
John: b 10-9-1765 d 8-8-1842 m Comfort Hine Pvt CT
Nathan: b 5-4-1734 d 1782 m Sibyl Buckingham Pvt CT
Samuel: b 12-18-1729 d 9-28-1803 m Abigail Burwell Pvt CT
Thaddeus: b 10-24-1734 d 1805 m Hannah Camp Pvt CT

NEUFANG,
Balthaser: b c. 1724-4 d a. 1-12-1788 m (1)Anna Barbara — (2)Elizabeth — PS PA

NEUFVILLE,
John: b 1725 d 7-20-1804 m (1)Martha Rogers (2)Elizabeth Marsden PS SC
John: b 11- -1727 d 7-20-1804 m Elizabeth Moore PS SC

NEVERS,
Samuel, Jr.: b 1742 d 1826 m Anna Wyman Pvt MA

NEVILLE, (includes NEVIL & NEVILLS)
George: b c. 1760 d 2-19-1817 m Mrs Sarah — Sol VA
James: b 1728 d 12-20-1784 m Mary Lewis Col CS VA
James: b 9-1-1741 d 1840 m Sarah Blackburn Pvt VA ★
Jesse: b 7-5-1759 d 1842 m Margaret Mc Carter Pvt NC ★
Jesse: b 9-24-1746 d p. 9-11-1809 m Elizabeth Parke Sol NC
John, Jr.: b 1750 d 7-30-1804 m Frances Ann Nixon Sol VA & SC
John: b 7-26-1731 d 7-29-1803 m Winifred Oldham BG VA
Joseph: b c. 1733-39 d 3-4-1819 m Nancy Brown BG PS VA
Presley: b 9-6-1755/6 d 12-1-1818 m Nancy Morgan Maj ADC VA

NEVINS, (includes NEVENS)
David: b 9-12-1747 d 1-21-1838 m Mary Hubbard Capt CT ★
John: b 1742 d 1832 m Mary Ring Lt MA
Joseph: b 7-20-1748 d 8- -1813 m (1)Sarah Powers (2)Lucy Sawtelle Pvt NH
Samuel: b c. 1758 d 3-1-1837 m Susannah Haskell Pvt MA
Thomas, Sr.: b c. 1720 d 3- -1804 m Bridget Snow Pvt NH
Thomas, Jr.: b 5-25-1748 d 3- -1814 m Rebecca Willoughby Pvt NH
Wm., Sr.: b 1718 d 2-15-1785 m (1)Mary Woolerich (2)Mary Hastings PS NH
Wm., Jr.: b 7-26-1746 d 1776/7 m Rebecca Chamberlain Sgt NH

NEVITT,
James: b 1753 d p. 1800 m (1)Ruth Conn (2)Elizabeth — Pvt PA

NEVIUS, (includes NEAFIE & NEAFUS)
Christian: b 11-1-1759 d 11-1-1815 m Lucretia Chamberlain Pvt NJ
David: b 6-2-1758 d 3-12-1825 m Elizabeth Schureman Sgt PS NJ
Garret: b 1754 d 12-11-1839 m Elizabeth Gano Pvt NJ
John: b 11-4-1730 d 6-9-1802 m Sarah Bilson 1Lt NJ
John: b c. 1740 d 1793 m Helena Dey Pvt NJ
John: b 1742 d 10-26-1816 m (1)Catherine Post (2)Mrs. Martha Hunt Pvt NY
John: bpt 6-27-1742 d 1805 m Sarah Opdycke Pvt PA
Martinus: b 2-21-1751 d 1-10-1820 m Sarah Stoothoff Pvt NJ
Peter: b 3-20-1757 d 11-25-1838 m Ann Voorhees Sgt NJ ★

NEW,
Anthony: b 1747 d 3-2-1833 m (1)Anne Anderson (2)Nancy Wyatt Col VA
Jacob: b 7-13-1761 d 9-7/8-1839 m Mary Coon Pvt VA ★
James Lacy: b 2-20-1764 d 9-21-1842 m Guli Elma Ladd Pvt VA ★
Jethro: b 9-20-1757 d 1825-27 m Sarah Bowman Pvt DE
Wm.: b 11-21-1761 d 4-23-1839 m (1)Elizabeth — (2)Frances — Pvt NC W★
Wm.: b 1759 d 8-8-1847 m Mary White Pvt PS VA ★

NEWAN,
Nehemiah: b a. 1735 d 10-19-1781 m Mary Kepplinger Pvt PA

NEWBECKER,
Martin: b c. 1728 d a. 7-28-1803 m Margaret Spare Pvt PA
Philip: b 1748 d 1826 m Elizabeth Barnett Lt PA

NEWBEGIN,
George: b 1763 d 1851 m Lettice Harding Pvt MA ★

NEWBERRY, (includes NEWBROUGH, NEWBURY)
Amasa: b 10-27-1752 d 1-25-1835 m Ruth Warner Sgt CT
Chauncey: b 1-23-1750 d 3-2-1829 m Mary Ellsworth Pvt CT
Henry: b 1724 d 1789 m Anne Bull Pvt PA
Israel: b 1757 d 1828 m Isabella Pennypacker Pvt PA
James: b 11-19-1749 d 2-22-1830 m Sarah Guess Pvt PA ★
Jeremiah: b 10-1-1740 d 9-25-1825 m Prudence Satterlee Pvt RI
John: b 8-6-1756 d 4-23-1825 m Elizabeth Ellsworth Pvt CT
John: b 1746 d 1-4-1818 m Jemima Benedict Pvt NY
John: b 8-10-1760 d 1-4-1834 m Elizabeth Grist Pvt PA
Noadyer: b 6-18-1765 d 6-20-1846 m (1)Ruth Birge (2)Lucy Terry PS CT
Roger: b 6-19-1735 d 2-13-1814 m Eunice Ely BG CT
Samuel: b 10-26-1746 d 8-28-1809 m Mary Beebe Pvt NY
Samuel: b c. 1725-30 d 1- -1788 m (1)Rosanna — (2)Bethia Begley PS VA
Stedman: b 5-16-1751 d 12-28-1850 m Hannah Chappel Pvt CT ★
Thomas: b 8-1-1740 d 4-5-1804 m Dorothy Mather Ens CT
Wm.: b c. 1732-40 d 7- -1817 m — Sol GA

NEWBERT,
John: b c. 1739 d 1836 m Elizabeth Benner Pvt MA

NEWBOLD,
Brazilla: b 4-18-1728 d 1-8-1798 m J. Paxton Maj NJ
Wm.: b 11-10-1736 d 8-7-1793 m Susanna Stevenson PS NJ

NEWBY,
Ozwald: b c. 1735 d p. 4-9-1786 m Sarahann Davis PS VA

NEWCOMB,
Asa: b 12-15-1759 d 1-27-1827 m Sally Sweet Pvt MA
Bethuel: b 12-17-1751 d 2-2-1826 m Mabel Thomas Pvt CT ★
Bryant: b 10-25-1761 d 11-30-1848 m Jane Glover Sol Matr MA ★

NEWCOMB, contd.

Charles: b 12-19-1754 d 3-14-1821 m Jerusha Adams Sgt MA
Cyrenius: b 1-15-1749 d 1815 m Jane Morris 2Lt NY
Daniel: b 11-29-1729 d *a*. 1789 m Elizabeth May Pvt CT
Daniel: b 11-18-1741 d 9-9-1794 m Irene Field Lt MA
Daniel: b 4-19-1747 d 7-14-1818 m (1)Sarah Stearns (2)Mrs. Hannah Dawes Goldthwaite PS NH
Daniel: b 1756 d 3-10-1832 m (1)Elizabeth Wallace (2)Lucina Woolman Lt NY
David: b 2-13-1763 d 2-28-1819 m (1)Mary Woodworth (2)Submit Spencer (3)Mary Pierce Pvt CT
David: b 1-15-1739 d 1824 m Elizabeth Gross PS CS MA
Ebenezer: bpt 1734 d 1-27-1801 m Jemima Allen Sgt MA
Ebenezer: b 9-18-1754 d 2-13-1829 m Wealthy Willis Pvt MA
Ethan: b 1-1-1763 d 11-19-1849 m Amelia Summers Pvt NJ ★
George Vansant: b *c*. 1754 d *p*. 11-9-1796 m (1)Elizabeth — (2)Rachel — Pvt MD
Hezekiah: b 5-6-1747 d 1-25-1821 m Lydia Hunt CS PS MA
Jacob: b 10-10-1724 d 1777 m Elizabeth Hamilton Pvt CT
James: b 2-7-1732/3 d 12-14-1799 m Mrs. Submit (Downer) Davis Pvt CT
James: b 5-22-1756 d 2- -1813 m Puella Fitch Pierce Pvt CT
James: b 4-11-1759 d 8-19-1794 m Esther Dean Sgt MA
James: b 11-11-1754 d 1-2-1843 m Tabatha Nickerson Smn MA
James: b 1757 d 1835 m Mary Elizabeth Tilden Pvt VA
Jeremiah: b 4-2-1760 d 2-20-1842 m (1)Mary Higgins (2)Sarah Lombard Matr MA ★
Jesse: b 5-26-1756 d 5-16-1832 m Amy Franklin Pvt CT
John: b 5-26-1760 d 4-18-1822 m Theoda Hunt PS CT
John: b 1751 d 9- -1834 m Ann Chase Sgt Slr MA ★
John: b 1733 d *p*. 1796 m Abigail Young Pvt MA
Jonathan: b 8-30-1744 d 6-11-1804 m Elizabeth Copeland Sgt MA
Joseph: b 5-3-1762 d 4-26-1814 m Elizabeth Martin Pvt CT
Joseph: b 3-7-1749 d *p*. 1783 m (1)Phebe Pierce (2)Ann Bullard Pvt MA
Joseph: b 9-17-1718 d *p*. 9-15-1792 m (1)Meriba Bateman (2)Abigail — PS NJ
Lemuel: b 4-7-1757 d 11-4-1843 m Lucy (Harding) Holbrook Pvt MA
Luther: b 6-12-1762 d 6-8-1834 m Pamelia Larrabee (Kennedy) Pvt Slr Dr CT & MA ★
Micah: b 1725 d — m — Sgt MA
Paul: b 3-15-1752 d 8- -1794 m Martha Woodward QM CT
Peter: b 11-28-1718 d 9-26-1779 m Hanna English PS CT
Richard: b 11-18-1728 d 12-5-1804 m Rebecca Brackett Pvt MA
Richard: b 1733 d 6-4-1810 m Margaret — Sol VA
Samuel: b 1750-59 d 7-26-1826 m Nancy Fritz Pvt PA ★
Silas: b 4-17-1723 d 1779 m Bathsheba Dayton BGen NJ
Simon: b 1-9-1736 d 12-26-1819 m Sarah Mead Pvt NY
Simon: b 12-28-1745 d 12- -1776 m Mercy Gore PS Nova Scotia
Simon: b 11-30-1753 d 1841 m (1)Rebecca Norcross (2)Rebecca Banker (3)Mrs — Allen Pvt NY ★
Simon: b 1735 d 5-25-1821 m (1)Elizabeth Harding (2)Sarah Hopkins Pvt MA
Thomas: b 5-12-1761 d 10-11-1853 m (1)Lucretua Webster (2)Mrs Sylvia Bronson Sol Mar CT
Thomas: b 6-15-1730 d 1-11-1800 m Bethiah Copeland Capt MA
Wm.: b 3-19-1752 d 12-29-1822 m Elizabeth Cunnabell Sol CT
Wm.: b 6-21-1751 d 6-6-1821 m Hannah Soles Pvt MA
Zaccheus: b 2-19-1724 d *c*. 1790 m Sarah Tobias Pvt NY

NEWCOMER, (includes NEUKOMMER)

Christian: b 9-26-1756 d 1-31-1832 m Anna Rohrer Pvt PA
John: b *c*. 1718 d *a*. 2-16-1805 m — Pvt PA
John: b 1-8-1733 d 9-24-1812 m (1)Elizabeth — (2)Elizabeth — Pvt PA
Peter: b 5-20-1758 d 5-15-1836 m Annie House Pvt PA ★
Philip: b 6-16-1760 d 11-24-1837 m Susanna Savitz Pvt PA
Ulrich: b 1730 d *p*. 1783 m (2)Magdaline Baumgarrtren Pvt PA

NEWELL,

Abijah, Sr.: b 1-9-1731 d 1807 m Hepsibah Curtis Pvt MA
Abijah, Jr.: b 8-3-1762 d 9-28-1841 m Nancy Gore Pvt MA
Andrew: b 1729 d 1798 m (2)Elizabeth Lee CS Cmsry MA
Daniel: b 9-16-1755 d 12-23-1824 m Nancy Curtis Pvt CT
David: b 1-20-1742 d 7-14-1810 m Susanna Cook Pvt MA
Ebenezer: b 5-13-1745 d 1-14-1831 m Sarah Banister Capt MA
Ebenezer: b 3-18-1747 d 11-20-1791 m (1)Catharine Richards (2)Hannah Sylvester Lt PS MA
Ebenezer: b 10-18-1736 d 2-25-1798 m (1)Elizabeth Wheaton (2)Abigail Allen (3)Rachel Eames 1Lt MA
Ebenezer: b 1-4-1712 d 1-8-1798 m (1)Elizabeth Bullard (2)Elizabeth Allen PS MA
Ebenezer: b 5-7-1757 d 10-24-1830 m Nancy Flower Fif CT ★
Elihu: b 7-14-1730 d 2-14-1814 m (1)Esther Langdon (2)Lucy Paine Sol Arm VT
Elisha: b 5-14-1751 d 11-6-1830 m Phebe Smith Pvt RI
Hugh: b 5-22-1734 d 9-28-1816 m Elizabeth Truax Pvt PS NJ
Hugh: b 1744 d 1810 m Margaret Bentley Pvt PA
Isaac: b 1-31-1753 d 12-23-1831 m Mary Warren Pvt CT
Jacob: b 1760/1 d 3-4-1834 m Keziah Loring Powers Pvt MA
Jacob, Sr.: b 1-21-1732/33 d 1- -1818 m Hepsibah Hart PS NH
Jacob, Jr.: b *c*. 1760 d *p*. 1790 m (1)Anna Finney (2)Rachel Thayer Pvt NH

James: b 1721 d 2-21-1791 m Elizabeth Lawrence Dr NJ
James: b 1756 d 2-14-1840 m (1)Mary Taylor (2)Amy Imlay Sgt NJ ★
James: b 2-24-1749 d 3-2-1823 m Sarah Wood Capt VA
John: b 1-15-1755 d 1828 m Sybil Andrus PS CT
John: b *c*. 1750 d 1-19-1815 m Elizabeth — Sgt MD
John: b 5-7-1745 d *p*. 3-24-1836 m (1)Mary Willard (2)Hannah — Pvt MA ★
Joseph: b 1747 d — m Ruth Wright Sgt MA
Josiah: b 5-18-1749 d 12-27-1818 m Ruth Root Lt MA
Josiah, Sr.: b 12-3-1709 d 12-11-1792 m Sarah MacIntyre CS MA
Josiah, Jr.: b 10-14-1742 d 6-12-1812 m Hannah Whiting Pvt MA
Nathaniel: b 2-8-1757 d 5-19-1835 m Lucy Stanley Pvt CT
Norman: b 8-28-1761 d 4-6-1850 m (1)Rosetta — (2)Lucy Frisbee Pvt CT ★
Oliver: b 2-9-1741 d *p*. 10-28-1781 m Irene — Lt MA
Riverius: b 1756 d 3-28-1835 m (1)— (2)Abigail Teagarden Cpl CT ★
Robert: b *c*. 1744 d *p*. 1790 m Mary George Pvt PS PA
Samuel: b 3-1-1714 d 2-10-1789 m Mrs. Mary Hart (Root) Chp CT
Samuel: b 1751 d 1820 m Rebekah — Pvt MA
Samuel: b 4-29-1757 d 4-26-1836 m Susan Fiske Pvt MA ★
Samuel: b 11-4-1754 d 9-21-1841 m Jane Montgomery Capt VA ★
Seth: b 10-25-1757 d 5-25-1842 m Ruth Holcomb Pvt NY
Simeon: b 2-5-1748 d 1813 m Mercy Hooker Capt CT
Solomon: b 8-27-1752 d 1-22-1799 m Damaris Johnson Pvt CT
Stephen: b 6-7-1758 d 8-28-1848 m Lois Sikes Pvt Fif MA
Theodore: b 10-8-1753 d 9-13-1833 m Hannah (Beardsley) Soper Pvt Mrnr CT ★
Theodore: b 6-1-1744 d *p*. 1782 m Anna Ames Cpl MA
Thomas: b 6-8-1746 d 10-15-1792 m Catherine Swan Pvt GA
Thomas: b 1742 d 11-8-1828 m Margaret Atkinson Sgt PA
Thomas: b 4-16-1765 d *p*. 9-22-1822 m Patience Jenckes Pvt RI
Thomas: b *c*. 1750 d *p*. 10-3-1831 m — Lt VA
Timothy: b 1742 d 2-5-1819 m Miriam Marcy LCol MA

NEWHALL,

Aaron: b 3-26-1740 d 6-28-1811 m Mary Perkins Lt MA
Allen: b -27-1726 d 9-27-1781 m Love Breed Cpl MA
Asa: b 8-5-1732 d 5-1-1814 m Sarah Tarbel Pvt MA
Charfes: b 2-5-1752 d 10-11-1817 m (1)Mary Lewis (2)Lois Newhall Cpl MA
Colley: b 2-4-1754 d 8-2-1833 m Anna Harrington Pvt MA
Daniel, Sr.: b 7-7-1734 d 4-26-1808 m Elizabeth Stebbins Pvt MA
Daniel, Jr.: b 7-9-1760 d 1-14-1849 m Lovina Baker Pvt MA
Daniel: b 2-4-1740 d 11-15-1793 m Hannah Estes 2Lt MA
Ezra: b 5-1-1733 d 4-5-1798 m (1)Sarah Fuller (2)Alice (Breed) Gray LCol MA
Ezra: b 1-5-1729/30 d 5- -1777 m Elizabeth Peck Pvt MA
Henry: b 8-27-1720 d *p*. 1820 m Elizabeth — PS MA
Increase: b 3-31-1725 d 6-22-1815 m Susanna Soudan Adj MA
Jabez: b 12-27-1740 d 5-27-1835 m Lydia Shaw Lt MA
Jacob: b 2-22-1745 d 8-30-1806 m Sarah Berry Pvt MA
Jonathan: b 1757 d 11-15-1799 m Susannah Upton Sol MA
Joseph, Jr.: b 9-23-1743 d 9-23-1843 m (1)Dorcas Barrett (2)Hannah Nourse Pvt MA
Joshua: b 4-20-1755 d 3-20-1820 m Comfort Carrington Pvt NS CT ★
Micajah: b 10-18-1756 d 12-12-1830 m Joanna Farrington Pvt MA
Naphtali: b 6-24-1757 d 9-1-1801 m Sarah Hooper Drm MA
Nathaniel: b 4-27-1740 d 3-17-1806 m Rebecca Harwood CS MA
Samuel: b 8-15-1744 d 3-30-1814 m Anna Reed Pvt MA

NEWHARD, (includes NEWHART)

Frederick: b *a*. 1740 d 8-1-1794 m Mary Susanna — Pvt PA
George: b *c*. 1738 d 1830 m Magdalena Sterner Lt PA
George Jacob: b 7-25-1752 d 9-18-1835 m Anna Maria Kohler Pvt PA
Lawrence: b 1740 d 8-1-1817 m Mary Magdalena Eckert Pvt PA
Michael, Sr.: b 2-9-1713 d 3-10-1793 m Barbara — Pvt PA
Michael, Jr.: b 5-7-1742 d 1814 m Maria Barbara — Pvt PA
Peter: b 11-15-1743 d 9-16-1813 m Catherine Miller Pvt PA

NEWHOUSE,

Anthony: b 1740 d 1780 m X Smn VA

NEWINGHAM,

Daniel: b 1752 d 1777 m Susan — Pvt PA

NEWKIRK, (includes NIEUKIRK)

Abraham: b 6-15-1754 d 1823 m (1)Mary Ann (Brosard) Brock (2)Rachel Rhodes Pvt NC
Abraham: bpt 10-9-1762 d 3-25-1830 m Maria Garritson Pvt NY
Abraham: b 10-29-1724 d 1789 m Keziah Shipman Pvt PA
Cornelius: b 9-2-1733 d 11-8-1795 m Mary Miller Capt NJ
Cornelius: b 11-24-1756 d 11-16-1823 m Abigail Hannah Pvt NJ
Cornelius: b 10-6-1752 d 6-22-1832 m Sarah Kiersted Capt NY Heirs ★
Garret: b 3-23-1726 d 9-9-1786 m Elizabeth DuBois PS NJ
Garret C.: bpt 9-23-1739 d 12-26-1813 m Leah Newkirk Pvt NY
Garret C.: b 2-3-1760 d 12-24-1819 m Maria Vedder Lt NY
Garret Cornelius, Sr.: bpt 1-12-1729 d 12- -1821 m Nellie Quackenbush Pvt NY
Garret Cornelius, Jr.: b 1-22-1760 d 11-12-1839 m Rachel Gardinier Pvt NY ★

Isaac: b 3-23-1754 d 12-24-1825 m Anna Broadhead Pvt PS NY
Isaac: b 1754 d 1823 m Rhoda Carol — Lt PA
Jacob: bpt 9-10-1732 d p. 1790 m Pieterje Philipse Pvt NY
Jacob: b 1760/1 d 2-11-1815 m Margaret Stumph Sgt PA
John, Sr.: bpt 1-12-1724 d p. 1-15-1793 m Rachel Clute Maj NY
John, Jr.: b p. 1762 d 8-2-1839 m Nellie Collier Pvt NY
John: b 1-17-1752 d 6-2-1840 m Sarah Van Keuren Capt NY ★
John: b 9- -1739 d 10-11-1820 m Susanna Bodine Lt NY
John: b 3-10-1743 d 12-25-1813 m Anna Catherine Hugette Pvt PA
Matthew: b 3-3-1734 d 7-10-1811 m Catlyntie Toers Lt NJ
Wm.: bpt 2-3-1764 d 2- -1833 m (2)Rachel Quackenbush Pvt NY

NEWLAND, (includes NEWLIN)

Jacob, Jr.: b 10-19-1740 d 8-26-1823 m (1)Mary Mann (2)Judith
   Newcomb Sgt MA
John: b 1758 d 3-18-1809 m Lydia Thayer Pvt MA
John: b 1743 d 4- -1831 m (1)Margaret — (2)Savina — (3)Elizabeth
   — Pvt NC
John: b 1759 d 4-9-1833 m Catherine Wierman Pvt PA
Joseph: b 7-4-1755 d 1-2-1848 m Sybil Austin Pvt NY MA ★
Nathaniel: b 1734 d 1820 m Rachel Preston PS PA
Ryal: b 1753 d 7-7-1804 m Dorcas Irish Pvt NY
Wm.: b 1727 d 1788 m Hannah Benson Pvt PA

NEWMAN,

Abner: b 3-23-1755 d p. 1824 m Hester Mauzy Pvt VA ★
Abram: b 1-14-1759 d 6-19-1841 m Lucinda Crippen Pvt NY
Alexander: b 10-11-1740 d c. 1788 m Frances Bourne Ens VA
David: b 4-25-1741 d 1-1-1777 m Elizabeth — Cpl MA
Ebenezer: b 6-7-1756 d 9-29-1839 m Sarah Dows Sol MA
Edmund: b 3-19-1762 d 11-8-1850 m Mary Conquest Wyatt Sgt
   VA ★
Ezekiel: b 2-27-1750 d 7-30-1836 m Temperance Stuart Pvt MM
   NY ★
Isaac: b 6-3-1731 d 3-24-1808 m Abigail Webb Pvt NY
Isaac: b 5- -1755 d 1-13-1832 m Sarah Irwin CS Sol NC
Jacob, Jr.: b 1762 d 6-20-1813 m (1)Catherine Freymeyer (2)Susan
   Snively Pvt PA
James: b 10-12-1749 d p. 7-19-1832 m (2)Bethia Rundell 2Lt NY
John: b c. 1745 d a. 2-9-1784 m Sarah — Pvt MD
John: b 9-22-1748 d p. 1775 m Chloe Gill Sgt PA
John: b 1754 d p. 1796 m Keziah Bridger Pvt VA
Jonathan: b 1760 d 2-8-1827 m Elizabeth Willson Pvt MA ★
Jonathan: b 1764 d 7-13-1844 m Rachel McElwee Sol SC
Jonathan: b — d 1823 m — Sol SC
Jonathan: b 1740 d 5-17-1817 m Sarah Carroll CS VA
Joseph: b 1740 d 6-26-1804 m Mary — Capt PA
Joseph: b 1759 d 11-6-1849 m (1)Clary Grady (2)Frankey Padget
   Pvt VA ★
Joshua: b 4-24-1751 d p. 1806 m Rachel De La Mater Pvt NY
Josiah: b 1758 d 11-5-1838 m Abigail Dowse Sgt MA
Leroy, Sr.: b c. 1745 d p. 1798 m X PS VA
Moses: b 9-15-1754 d 10-6-1823 m Susannah Rament Pvt NY
Nathaniel, Jr.: b 4-4-1724 d 1794 m (1)Mary Lounsbury (2)Mrs.
   Martha Hayt Pvt NY
Nicholas: b 11-11-1733 d 9-7-1816 m Elizabeth Keller Cpl PA
Peter: b 1-9-1749 d 2-23-1812/3 m Sarah Seymour Pvt NY
Platt: b 1756 d c. 1840 m Mary Doty Pvt NY
Robert: b 6-10-1755 d 3-23-1806 m Esther Treadwell Pvt MA
Robert: b 3-20-1752 d 5-26-1804 m Mary — PS MA
Samuel: b 5-28-1725 d p. 1790 m Sarah Peck PS CT
Samuel: b 11-28-1739 d 2-27-1829 m Hannah Haskell Pvt MA
Samuel: b 9-9-1749 d 12-9-1821 m Eunice — Pvt NY
Samuel: b 1753-5 d 1808 m Nancy King Sol SC
Shubel: b 6-26-1750 d 11-16-1833 m Elizabeth June Pvt CT
Thomas: b 1755 d 1796 m Mary — Sol GA
Thomas: b c. 1755 d a. 1804 m Elizabeth — Sol MD
Thomas: bpt 11-16-1749 d 5-6-1833 m Abigail Wood Sgt MA
Thomas: b 9-30-1724 d c. 1782 m Hannah Locke Matr MA
Thomas: b 1749 d 1798 m Martha Cosby Pvt VA
Thomas: b c. 1749 d 8-28-1821 m Elizabeth Huffman Pvt VA
Walter: b 2-27-1761 d 4-15-1851 m (1)Catharine Barbara
   Zimmerman (2)Wineford — (3)Elizabeth Wheeler Pvt PA W★
Walter: b 1742 d 7-29-1815 m Catharine Lair Pvt VA
Walter: b 1715 d c. 1815 m Catherine — PS VA
Wm.: b 1749 d 3-8-1840 m Hepzibah — Pvt NH
Wm.: b 10-18-1744 d 2-4-1843 m Nancy Finney Sol VA
Wm.: b — d 3-31-1778 m Elizabeth — Pvt VA

NEWMYER,

Peter: b 5-29-1760 d 3-15-1836 m Susannah Rhodes Pvt PA

NEWSUM, (includes NEWSOM)

Benjamin: b 1752 d 3- -1779 m Elizabeth — Capt SC
Jacob: b 1762 d 11-16-1840 m Lucy Barham Pvt VA ★
James: b 1744 d 1813 m Mary Price Pvt VA
Wm.: b 8-28-1761 d 1837 m Mary Starke Pvt VA ★

NEWTON,

Aaron: b 2-22-1762 d 1825 m Asenath Moss Pvt CT
Abner: b 12-29-1764 d 9-9-1852 m Abigail Fairchild Pvt CT
Abner: b — d 1797 m Alice Baker Pvt NY
Alpheus B.: b 8-17-1734 d 1793 m Elizabeth Claflin Pvt MA

Alvan: b 9-22-1748 d 2-16-1778 m Rebecca Rice Sgt MA
Amos: b 4-17-1727 d 12-23-1814 m Mrs. Jane (Learned) Giles CS
   MA
Asahel: b 6-1-1758 d 5-30-1834 m Versalle Booth Pvt CT
Asahel: b 6-15-1749 d 8-18-1823 m Mary Morse Pvt MA
Barnabas: b 9-18-1733 d 4-10-1812 m Eunice Bond Pvt MA
Benjamin: b 6-20-1763 d 6-22-1848 m Zada Phoebe Mead Pvt NY ★
Benjamin: b 1720 d 10-3-1795 m Mary Satterly PS NY
Benjamin: b 2-3-1748 d 2-20-1835 m Nancy McCall Capt NC ★
Benjamin: b 8-6-1753 d 8-10-1826 m Lucy Sneed Sol VA
Bezaleel: b 7- -1747 d c. 3- -1798/9 m Mollie Ward Pvt MA
Burwell: b 7-20-1729 d 4-16-1807 m Eunice Johnson Pvt CT
Caleb: b 1730 d 8-11-1787 m Anna Blydenburgh PS NY
Cotton: b 11-13-1759 d 4-8-1847 m Abigail Sawyer Pvt MA
Daniel: b 5-20-1749 d p. 1790 m Mary Rice Pvt MA
David: b 3-25-1753 d 12-29-1839 m Mary Hazen Pvt VT
Ebenezer: b c. 1747 d 1798 m Susannah Hubert Pvt PS NH
Ebenezer: b c. 1730 d 1812 m Elizabeth Buchanan PS NC
Edward: b 1-18-1738 d 2-25-1819 m (1)Sarah Winch (2)Elizabeth
   — Capt MA
Elias: b 1756 d 9-17-1811 m Alice Stimson Pvt Mus CT
Elnathan: b 7-5-1724 d 8-12-1792 m Jemima Joslin PS NH
Enoch: b 10-24-1740 d 3-5-1817 m (1)Experience Beecher (2)Mrs.
   Mary (Treat) Woodruff Capt CT
Ezekiel: b 1740/1 d 9-3-1811 m Ann Smith Pvt CT
Ezra: b 7-29-1740 d 10-16-1803 m Elizabeth Hagar Cpl MA
Francis: b 3-21-1731 d 4-18-1781 m Elizabeth Fairfield Pvt MA
Francis: b 11-23-1751 d 4-7-1830 m Eleanor Woodward Pvt MA ★
George: b c. 1742 d p. 1790 m Nancy Ann Moore PS NC
George: b 1745 d 1807 m Polly — Sol VA
Gideon: b a. 1722 d 3-29-1798 m Hannah Lawrence Pvt MA
Gideon: b 6-6-1760 d 11- -1842 m Rebecca Spooner Pvt MA
Hezekiah, Jr.: b 6-25-1755 d 1-6-1848 m Lucy Cogswell Sgt MA
Hezekiah: b 7-28-1719 d 2-4-1786 m Eunice Brigham MM MA
Israel: b c. 1714 d 6-19-1808 m Jerusha Wells PS CT
James: b 8-24-1751 d 2-23-1824 m Bathsheba Nurse Pvt MA
Jason, Sr.: b 2-6-1736 d 4- -1812 m Hannah Warren Pvt MM MA
Jason, Jr.: b 1-7-1762 d 6-7-1842 m (1)Ruth Chase (2)Lydia Collins
   (3)Susannah Hewitt Sgt MA ★
Joel: b 1758 d 1842 m Masey Newton Pvt NJ
John: b 1733 d 1797 m (1)Molly Miles (2)Martha Colbraith Pvt CT
John: b 7-25-1754 d 11-30-1831 m Ruth Bradley Pvt CT
John, Jr.: b 4-8-1758 d 5-24-1854 m Martha Whiting Pvt CT ★
John: b 1-17-1755 d 9-20-1839 m Abigail Parker Sgt MA ★
John: b 1726 d 9-28-1802 m (1)Mary Pickett (2)Huldah — Cpl MA
John: b 7-19-1750 d 9-22-1834 m Elizabeth Arms Pvt MA ★
John: bpt 10-22-1751 d p. 1836 m Mary Ackerly PS NY
John: b 2-20-1759 d 6-17-1797 m Catherine Lowrance Pvt NC
John: b 7-11-1739 d p. 1800 m Sarah Wallace Sgt VT
Jonah: b 1745 d 3- -1816 m Sarah Woodruff Capt PS VT
Jonah: b 1752 d 1831 m Eunice Howe Pvt MA ★
Jonas: b 3-24-1730 d 3-12-1810 m (1)Rebecca Richardson (2)Lydia
   Earle (Wilson) Johnson Lt MA
Joseph: b 1731 d 4-28-1797 m Sarah Hulls Lt CT
Joseph: b 1763 d 3-24-1844 m Mrs. Ann (Stephens) Robinett Pvt GA
Joseph: b 7-15-1728 d 3-8-1795 m Experience Drury Sgt MA
Josiah: b 3-4-1760 d 5-14-1822 m Elizabeth Haynes Pvt MA
Jotham: b 2-27-1751 d 12-8-1817 m Sarah Howard Pvt MA
Lemuel: b 3-17-1718 d 9-27-1793 m Abigail — Pvt CS MA
Levi: b 2-17-1728 d 1814 m Lucy Billings Pvt MA
Levin: b 1760 d 1801 m Sarah — Pvt MD
Liberty: b 5-8-1766 d 10-1-1822 m Asintha North Pvt MA
Luther: b 1760 d 11-19-1829 m Miriam (Newton) Pvt MA
Marshall, Sr.: b 8-25-1729 d 5-5-1758 m (1)Eunice Howe (2)Hannah
   Willard Roberts Pvt MA
Marshall, Jr.: b 1-13-1757 d 12-15-1833 m Lydia (Newton) Pvt MA ★
Matthew: b 12-8-1747 d 5-10-1814 m (1)Elizabeth West (2)Epherina
   Palmer Pvt CT
Moses: b 8-14-1766 d 7- -1826 m Elizabeth Hudspeth Sol Dr SC
Nahum: b 2-16-1752 d 3-20-1816 m Mercy Adams Pvt NH MA
Nathan: b 1-23-1760 d 4-18-1798 m Mary Nicholas Pvt MA
Nathan Brigham: b 3-28-1760 d 12-18-1843 m Mary Stewart
   Fif MA
Patrick: b 1748 d 2- -1793 m Mary Moore Sgt NC
Paul: b 7-30-1751 d 3-2-1837 m Martha Newton MM Pvt MA
Paul: b 1718 d 5-18-1797 m Mary Foster Pvt MA
Peter, Sr.: b 7-25-1731 d 1802 m Hannah Child Pvt MA
Samuel: b 12-7-1737 d 12-31-1814 m Mary Camp Lt CT
Seth: b 9-10-1732 d 2-12-1807 m (1) — Belknap (2)Patience
   Harvey Capt MA
Shadrach: b 1753 d 10-15-1837 m Mary Dike Pvt MA
Silas: b 12-10-1744 d 1-25-1816 m (1)Delia Howe (2)Matilda Gates
   Pvt MA
Solomon: b 6-25-1741 d 5-28-1822 m (1)Hannah Hastings (2)Mrs
   Lydia (Rice)Hemenway Pvt MA
Solomon: b 1-4-1734 d 3-1-1808 m Elizabeth How CS MA
Stephen: b 6-28-1755 d 7-10-1836 m Susanna Davison Sol Sgt MA
Thomas, Jr.: b 11-18-1734 d 3-14-1788 m Chloe Atwater Sol CT
Thomas: b 5-15-1742 d 9-11-1807 m Martha Tucker Col PS VA
Timothy: b 2-23-1727/8 d 7-10-1811 m Sarah Merrick PS CS MA
Timothy: b 9-1-1755 d 7-9-1834 m Abigail Earle Pvt VT ★
Uriah: b 5-17-1736 d 4-25-1805 m (1)Hannah Eager (2)Mrs Johanna
   (Gleason) Gibbs Pvt MA

NEWTON, contd.
Wm.: b 1750 d 1817 m Elizabeth Field Sgt VA
Wm.: b c. 1715 d p. 10-8-1788 m (1)Margaret Monroe (2)Elizabeth Kenyon Sol VA
Winslow: b 4-9-1756 d p. 1790 m Anna Bemis Pvt MA
Younger: b 8-30-1761 d 1847 m Elizabeth Curghill Pvt VA

NEXSEN,
Elias: b 5-30-1740 d 6-10-1831 m (1)Mary Pelse (2)Mary Waldron (3)Jane Waldon (4)Mrs Catharine (Rice) Bailey CS NY

NIBLACK, (includes NIBLOCK)
George: b a. 1755 d p. 8-15-1814 m (2)Frances Morrison PS NC
Wm.: b 1761 d — m Devina Tison Sol NC
Wm.: b 1759 d 1822 m Martha Ann — Pvt VA

NICE, (includes NYCE)
George: b 1739 d 4-10-1812 m Hannah Hall Capt PA
George: b 1725 d 12-5-1789 m (1)Anna Maria Dotterer (2)Elizabeth Fuhrman Pvt PA
Johannes: b 6-3-1767 d 3-7-1844 m Hanna Reinert Pvt PA

NICHOLA,
Lewis: b 1717 d 8-9-1807 m (2)Jane Bishop CS Col Brevet BGen PA

NICHOLAS, (includes NICKEL, NICKELL, NICKLES, NICHOLS)
Flayl: b 1747 d 8-17-1823 m Nancy Hatcher Pvt VA
George: b 1754 d 7-25-1799 m Mary Smith LCol VA
Isaac: b 3-31-1751 d 10- -1839 m Margaret Curry Pvt Spy VA
James: b 6-19-1739 d 4-21-1808 m Sarah Spaulding Sgt MA
Johannes: b 3-21-1756 d 4-19-1813 m Christina — Pvt PS NY
John: b 9-21-1760 d p. 3-27-1816 m Mary Anne Bell Sol VA
John: b 1-19-1726 d p. 12-6-1814 m Martha Fry PS CS VA
John Jacob: b 7-15-1724 d p. 1793 m Anna Barbara Zellars PS VA
Joseph: b 1-10-1750 d 8-18-1829 m Elizabeth Fowler Pvt VA
Robert Carter: b 1-28-1728 d 9-8-1780 m Ann Cary PS CS VA
Samuel: b a. 1750 d c. 1790 m Mary Jenkins Maj PA
Thomas: b c. 1732 d 1807 m Jane King Sol CS VA
Wm.: b 10-6-1758 d 1835 m Rebecca Forscythe Pvt PA ★

NICHOLS, (includes NICCOLLS, NICHOL, NICHOLLS, NICKLES, NICOLL, NICOLS & NUCKOLLS)
Aaron: b 5-6-1757 d 10-13-1821 m Sarah Abbott Pvt NH ★
Adam: b 1754 d 1846 m (1)Ruth Atwood (2)Polly Andrews Pvt NH ★
Andrew: b 4-3-1757 d 9-8-1812 m Eunice Nichols Pvt MA
Benjamin: bpt 6-15-1739 d p. 1790 m Phebe Hard Capt CT
Benjamin: b 10-12-1750 d 1826 m Lucy Fitts Pvt MA
Benjamin: b 8-18-1754 d p. 6-14-1843 m — Pvt Wgn NY
Caleb: b 10-5-1751 d 7-1-1819 m Lydia Kent Pvt MA
Daniel: b 6-13-1759 d 5- -1837 m Elizabeth Banks Pvt CT
Daniel: b 3-16-1711/12 d 6-11-1780 m Abigail Beal Pvt PS MA
David: b 9-21-1741 d 2-25-1823 m Hannah Beach Capt CT
David: b 3-29-1746 d 1-29-1813 m (1)Hannah Alvord (2)Eunice Gilbert Pvt CT
David: b 12-25-1760 d 1840 m Mary Nichols Cpl MA
David: b 9-23-1744 d 6-24-1832 m Anne Hulburt Drm MA
David: b 3-3-1757 d 3-11-1843 m Naomi Newton Pvt MA
David: b 1759/60 d 9-15-1815 m Mary — Pvt RI W★
David: b 1763 d 11-5-1839 m (1)Nancy King (2)Mrs Abigail Brown Pvt RI
Ebenezer: b 5-4-1758 d 3-6-1853 m (1)Sally — (2)Martha Dibble Pvt CT ★
Edmond: b 3-11-1748 d 7-2-1818 m Elizabeth Damon Pvt MA
Eli: b 4-2-1760 d 3-27-1821 m Elizabeth M. Ruggles Pvt CT
Eli: b 8-20-1761 d 9-27-1845 m Sarah Lyon Pvt CT ★
Ephraim: b 4-15-1758 d 1-23-1852 m Miriam Bradley Pvt CT ★
Ephraim: b 12-8-1727 d 1805 m Esther Peet PS NY
Ezra: b 7-6-1763 d 7-31-1827 m Elizabeth Knapp Pvt CT
Fortunatus: b 1-31-1760 d 4-15-1842 m Sarah Clayes Pvt MA
Francis: b 6-17-1765 d 9-30-1808 m (1)Lucy Bishop (2)Martha Jackman Pvt NH
Francis: b 1737 d 2-13-1812 m Anna Maria — Maj PA
George: b 1759 d 1842 m — Deemer Pvt PA ★
Hezekiah: b 4-9-1752 d 11-30-1828 m Hannah Colby Cpl MA
Humphrey: b 1-13-1755 d 10-25-1839 m Margaret Otis Pvt MA ★
Humphrey: b 1-27-1755 d 8-8-1839 m Ruth Sargent Sol NH
Isaac: b 3-9-1753 d 7-23-1825 m Sarah Stevens PS CT
Isaac, Sr.: b 5-13-1737 d 1-6-1822 m Dorcas Sibley Lt MA ★
Isaac: b 4- -1748 d 11-23-1835 m (1)Cornelia VanDeursen (2)Elizabeth Van Deursen Lt NY ★
Isaac: b 7-19-1741 d 10-9-1804 m Deborah Woodhull MM Col NY
Israel: b 10-8-1741 d 12-9-1800 m Rhoba Millard 2Lt MA
Jabez, Jr.: b 7-25-1743 d 3-5-1820 m Sarah Brown Pvt MA
Jacob: b c. 1755 d p. 1791 m Eve Catherine — PS MD
James: b 8-13-1743 d 11-23-1824 m Phoebe Plumb Pvt CT
James: b 1757 d 9- -1790 m Bethiah Clay Pvt CT
James: b 1755 d 1822 m Sally Shaler Pvt CT
James: b 2-1-1732 d 11-16-1811 m Esther Dean Capt MA
James: b 1933 d 5-10-1818 m (1)Dinah Woodburn (2)Hannah Caldwell PS ME
James: b 1732 d 1817 m — (Nancy) Hubbard 2Lt NH

James: b — d p. 1791 m — Todd Pvt PA
James, Jr.: b 1-31-1741/2 d 11-23-1816 m Jemima Morris Sgt VT
James: b c. 1720 d p. 3-17-1810 m — PS VA
Jeremiah: b 8-20-1755 d 2-12-1813 m Lois Damon Pvt MA
Jesse: b 1746 d 1790 m Abigail Resseguie Pvt CT
Jesse: b 4-26-1757 d 9-16-1827 m Mabel Bulkley Pvt CT
Jesse: b 1760 d 1803 m Elizabeth Howard Pvt MA
John: b 5-15-1734 d 5-31-1812 m Jerusha Moore Capt MA
John: b 6-10-1713 d 12-11-1792 m Elizabeth Prince Sgt MA
John: b 9-21-1736 d 8-20-1819 m Bethiah Burnap Pvt MA
John: bpt 8-24-1760 d 2-18-1817 m Lydia Wade Pvt MA
John: b 12-3-1757 d 10-23-1824 m Esther Proctor Sgt NH
John, Sr.: b 3-12-1757 d 1- -1849 m Sarah — Pvt NH
John: b 1759 d 1806 m Deborah Clarkson Cpl NY
John: b a. 1754 d a. 1791 m Elizabeth Knight Pvt NC
John: b 6- -1741 d 2-24-1838 m Hannah Paine Pvt PA ★
John: b 1739 d 7-8-1828 m Susanna Clark Ens CS PS MA
John: b 10-23-1732 d 12-11-1780 m Agatha Bullock Pvt PS SC
John: b 1746 d p. 4-5-1803 m Martha — Sol VA
John: b c. 1748 d c. 1802 m (1)Rachel — (2)Anne Proctor Sol VA KY
Jonas: b 1758 d 4- -1843 m Elizabeth Smith Pvt NY
Jonathan, Jr.: b 6-24-1739 d 1821 m Mollie Sybley Capt CT
Jonathan, Jr.: b 2-23-1758 d 2-13-1829 m Rebecca Swift Pvt CT ★
Jonathan: b 7-25-1754 d 4-26-1842 m Phene Sackett Pvt NH ★
Jonathan: b 3-28-1748 d 3-6-1837 m Rhoba Martin Sgt NJ PA
Jonathan: b c. 1725 d 3-19-1791 m Hannah Godfrey CS RI
Jonathan, Jr.: b 11-15-1755 d 6-11-1830 m Elizabeth Johnson Pvt RI
Joseph, Jr.: b 10-8-1738 d 6-28-1818 m Sally Hemenway Sgt MA
Joseph: b 1744 d 9-3-1828 m Lydia Bisbee Pvt MA
Josiah: b 9-29-1748 d 10-15-1837 m (1)Elizabeth Bouton (2)Sarah Smith Sgt NY ★
Lemuel: b 3-6-1754 d 3-15-1814 m Alice Blackmore Sgt CT
Leonard Dowden: b 5-27-1739 d 6-12-1815 m Ruth Birdsey Capt NY
Levi: b 11-9-1739 d 4-2-1809 m Elizabeth Sawyer PS Pvt MA
Malachi: b 6-29-1747 d 9-26-1819 m (1)Abigail Gale (2)Polly Law Pvt MA
Mansfield: bpt 1744 d p. 4-7-1818 m — Comfort Pvt CT ★
Micah: b 4-14-1737 d 1-26-1809 m Ruth — Pvt MA
Moses: b 2-15-1763 d 11-15-1845 m Susannah Reed Sol MA
Moses: b 6-28-1740 d 5-23-1790 m Hannah Eaton Col NH
Nathan, Sr.: b 12-1-1709 d 2-3-1789 m (1)Patience Hubbell (2)Elizabeth — PS CS
Nathan, Jr.: b 1747 d 5-31-1811 m Phebe Shelton Pvt CT
Nathaniel: b 3-27-1760 d 5-1-1832 m Martha Slafter Pvt CT
Nathaniel: b 7-30-1749 d 6-22-1835 m Zibiah Bates Lt MA
Nathaniel: b 1763 d p. 1795 m Mary — Dr m MA
Nathaniel: b 10-13-1755 d 5-28-1836 m Mehitable Davis Pvt RI W★
Nicholas: b 6-11-1762 d 9-28-1831 m Catherine Sanborn Pvt NH
Noah: b 12-25-1754 d 8-30-1833 m Abigail Lincoln Capt MA
Noah: b 9-12-1746 d 5-22-1824 m Cynthia Curtis Pvt MA
Paul: b 3-29-1746 d 2-25-1806 m Sarah Middlebrook Pvt CT
Peter: b 6-12-1764 d 12-11-1835 m Mary Tower Capt MA
Phineas: b 10-12-1740 d 7-30-1838 m Anne Saunders Pvt MA
Reuben: b 1762 d 7-20-1840 m Freelove Matteson Pvt RI ★
Richard: b 4-10-1715 d 2-1-1791 m Mary Williams Pvt MA
Richard: b 2-26-1762 d 6-20-1835 m Temperance Walton Pvt VA ★
Robert: b 9-6-1735 d 11-13-1814 m Elizabeth Johnson Capt NJ
Samson: b 1752 d 1817 m (1)— Pettigrew (2)Margaret Falconer Ens CA
Samuel: b 1-9-1758 d 12-18-1849 m (1)Hannah Ressegnie (2)Sibel Cranson Sol CT ★
Samuel: b 1738 d 11-16-1802 m Jane Miller PS ME MA
Samuel, Sr.: b 12-20-1720 d 8-19-1806 m Bathsheba — Sol CS MA
Samuel, Jr.: b 1-18-1744 d 11-9-1781 m Lois Dunham Capt MA
Samuel: b — d p. 1809 m — Pvt NH
Samuel, Sr.: b 1728 d 9-31-1777 m Annie Stevens PS VT
Samuel, Jr.: b 1-15-1757 d 2-12-1842 m Rhoda Carpenter Pvt VT
Samuel: b 6-13-1766 d 1853 m Dolly Blodgett Pvt VT ★
Stiles: b 8-13-1761 d 12-28-1844 m Phebe Booth Pvt CT
Theophilus: b 5-13-1748 d 10-23-1785 m Sarah Meeker PS CT
Thomas: b 5-15-1732 d 5-24-1812 m (1)Elizabeth Wells (2)Elizabeth Pierce Lt MA
Thomas: b 5-16-1751 d 6-27-1810 m Hannah Clark Capt MA
Thomas: b 1754 d 4-7-1837 m Bethsheba Marks Pvt MA ★
Thomas: b — d — m Elizabeth Boynton Pvt MA
Thomas: b 1735 d 2-3-1830 m Margaret Campbell Pvt PA
Thomas: b a. 1760 d c. 1818 m Mary Bryson Pvt PA
Thomas: b 6-4-1723 d 1784 m Mrs Welthian (Spencer)Gorton Pvt RI
Thomas: b p. 1723 d 12-23-1798 m (1)Mary — (2)Elizabeth Reynolds Pvt RI
Thomas: b c. 1740 d p. 1790 m Miss — Blair Pvt SC
Walter: b 4-7-1748 d 1-5-1823 m Rachel Stoddard Pvt RI
Wm.: b 3-10-1755 d 7-21-1837 m (1)Anna Edwards (2)Huldah Downs Pvt CT
Wm.: b 1744 d 1- -1792 m Martha Smith Lt MD
Wm.: b 1-11-1751 d 4-20-1784 m Mary Batchelder Cdr MA
Wm.: b 1730 d 12- -1789 m Margaret Breck NOf MA ME
Wm.: b 1721 d p. 1782 m Meriam Ward Pvt MA

Wm.: b 11-1-1739 d *p.* 1795 m Kezia Fitts Pvt MA
Wm.: b 1722 d 8-18-1794 m Mary Wilson Pvt MA
Wm.: b 1-28-1750 d 12-10-1835 m R — Carter MM MA
Wm.: b 1-25-1750 d 4-23-1827 m Susannah — Sgt NJ ★
Wm.: b 5-21-1756 d 4-22-1795 m Frances Smith PS NY
Wm.: b 11-2-1754 d 10-19-1804 m Margaret Hillegas Capt PA
Wm.: b 4-19-1733 d *p.* 1787 m Sarah Hall Pvt MA
Wm.: b 1746 d 1810 m Thankful Barbour PS RI
Zadok: b 5-23-1755 d 10-16-1841 m Calista Danielson Cpl MA ★

NICHOLSON, (includes NICKELSON & NICKOLSON)
Benjamin: b 1745 d 1792 m Mary Ridgely Col CS PS MD
Daniel: b 1754 d 5-6-1806 m Ann Reyburn Pvt NY
David: b *c.* 1738 d 1806 m Rhoda Whitehead Sol SC
Francis: b 1757 d 12-9-1803 m Rachel Loveland Sgt CT
Henry: b — d — m Sarah Hay Cnt VA
James: b 1737 d 9-2-1804 m Frances Witter Commo MD
John: b 5-9-1757 d 8-2-1838 m (1)Mary McComb (2)Catherine
    Stevenson Lt NJ ★
John: b *c.* 1740 d 2- -1799 m Penelope Mann 2Maj NC
John: b 1735 d 3-2-1818 m X Sol NC
John: b 5-1-1762/3 d 12-20-1858 m (1)Nancy Freeman (2)Susan
    Brown Pvt NC ★
John: b 1725 d 1790 m Elizabeth — NCapt VA
John: b 4-3-1752 d 12-31-1827 m Mary Scott Cpl VA
John: b 1756 d *c.* 1820 m Edith Rivers Pvt NGnr VA
Joseph: b *c.* 1709 d *a.* 2-5-1787 m (1)Hannah Smith Scott
    (2)Mary Hopper PS MD
Joseph: b *c.* 1755 d *p.* 1803 m Lillis Jack Sol NC
Josiah: b 1750 d *p.* 1830 m Rhoda Whitehead 2Maj NC
Nathan: b 10-23-1759 d 5-30-1814 m Mary Hibbard Pvt CT
Nathaniel: b 12-3-1751 d 4-13-1825 m Lydia Hillman Pvt MA
Samuel: b 1743 d 12-29-1811 m Mary Dowse NCapt
Samuel: b 12-10-1716 d 6-26-1794 m (1)Sara Dennis (2)
    Hannah Abbott PS NJ
Seth: b 10-21-1737 d 4-11-1801 m (1)Mary Smith (2)Isable
    (Eldridge) Dyer PS CS MA
Thomas: b — d 1835 m Sarah Spinney Pvt MA
Wright: b 1740 d *p.* 1-14-1807 m (2)Mary Douglass Lt SC

NICKERSON,
Caleb: b 4-3-1736 d 12-31-1804 m Elizabeth Mayo Pvt MA
Christian: b 1-25-1750 d *p.* 3-17-1812 m Huldah Bassett Pvt MA
Edward: b 1-3-1761 d 8-8-1841 m Sarah Covel Sgt MA ★
Ensign: b 2-21-1753 d 1-25-1834 m (1)Alice Mayo (2)Mehitable
    Crowell Pvt Slr MA
Hezekiah, Jr.: b 1758 d 9-9-1852 m (2)Jane Kerris Pvt NY ★
Hugh: b 1748 d 1789 m Deborah Hinkley Pvt MA
Judah: b 1761 d 1797 m Tabitha Hinckley Pvt MA
Nathan: b 12-1l-1763 d 7-7-1849 m Sarah Nickerson Smn MA
Phineas: b 1733 d 7-16-1813 m (?)Jane Chase (1)Reliance Taylor
    (2)Ruth Nickerson (3)Jerusha Chase Cpl MA
Salathiel: b 9- -1760 d 10-7-1847 m Sabrina — Pvt MA
Seth: b 5-26-1734 d 9-10-1789 m Martha Atwood Pvt MA
Stephen: b 6-11-1754 d 8-17-1844 m (1)Rebecca Cahoon (2)Levina
    Dunlap Fif MA W★
Thomas: b 2-12-1743 d 3-29-1789 m Hannah Hall Capt MA
Uriah: b 1757 d 3-27-1835 m Patience Small Pvt MA

NICKEY,
John: b 1748/9 d 1788 m Mary — Pvt PA

NICKS,
John, Jr.: b *c.* 1755 d *c.* 1825 m — PS NC

NICODEMUS, (includes NICHODEMUS)
Conrad: b 10-15-1755 d 10-15-1834 m Margaret Hartle PS MD
Conrad: b *c.* 1736-40 d *a.* 9-23-1805 m Anna Maria Pfeiffer Capt
    PS MD
Frederick: b 2-26-1733 d 10-26-1816 m (1)Elizabeth — (2)Catherine
    — (3)Margaret Ripple 1Lt MD

NICOLSON,
Robert: b 11-1-1753 d 8-15-1798 m Elizabeth Diggs Dr VA

NIELD,
John: b *c.* 1746 d *p.* 1780 m Sarah Woodward Pvt VA

NIEMAN, (includes NEIMAN)
Carl: b 2-9-1751 d-2-5-1833 m Elizabeth Leibenguth Sol PA
Charles: b 2-9-1751 d 2-5-1833 m Elizabeth Levengood Pvt PA

NIGHTINGALE,
John: b bpt 3-13-1757 d 3-23-1804 m (1)Mary Brackett (2)Frances
    Brackett Pvt MA
Joseph: b 9-16-1749 d 11-3-1797 m Elizabeth Corlis MGen CS RI
Wm.: b 1750 d *p.* 1799 m Susanna Clark Pvt MA

NIGHTLINGER,
Samuel: b 1761 d 1802 m Elizabeth Schmick Drm Fif Pvt PA

NIHELL,
Lawrence: b — d *p.* 1790 m Nancy Weir Sol PA

NILES,
David: b 3-15-1740 d 10-28-1776 m Sarah Frink Pvt CT
David: b 1756 d *p.* 1784 m Catherine Cronkhite Sgt MA
Ebenezer: b 1-16-1745 d 2-17-1818 m Elizabeth Hunt Sgt MA
Elisha: b 2-29-1764 d 6-18-1845 m Naomi Ackley Pvt CT
Elisha: b 11-23-1764 d 7-17-1840 m Lucy Millington Fif MA ★
Ephraim: b 1755 d *p.* 7-25-1832 m Hannah — OrdiSgt MA ★
Isaac: b 12-4-1731 d 4-4-1816 m Eunice Herrick Cpl MA
John: b 9-11-1759 d 3-18-1840 m Olive Wales Sgt MA ★
Nathaniel: b 1737 d 11-1-1817 m Mary Clark Lt MA
Nathaniel: b 8-18-1735 d 9-16-1825 m Abigail Bentley Pvt NY
Nathaniel: b 4-4-1741 d 10-31-1828 m (1)Nancy Lathrop (2)Elizabeth
    Watson PS CT
Robert: b *c.* 1758 d 1-24-1816 m Tacy Barber Pvt NY
Samuel: b 5-14-1711 d 4-30-1804 m Sarah Niles CS MA
Samuel: b *c.* 1720 d 1778 m Martha — PS RI
Samuel: b 10-4-1755 d 7-10-1838 m (1)Smellage Sisson (2)Lucy
    Roberts Pvt RI
Sands: b 4-19-1727 d *p.* 1795 m Bathsheba Palmer Lt CT
Stephen: b *c.* 1730 d 12- -1810 m Desire Pendleton Capt NY
Thomas: b 7-2-1760 d 12-25-1844 m Rhoda Phelps Pvt CT
Wm.: b 12-11-1737 d 10-18-1826 m Hannah Goodman Pvt PA

NIMMONS,
Wm.: b 3-22-1732 d 11-16-1811 m Margaret — Pvt SC

NIMOCKS,
Richard: b 1744 d 8-23-1803 m Zerviah Noble Sgt MA

NIMS,
Ariel: b 2-25-1751 d 1818 m Anna Brewer Sgt MA
Asa: b 1-12-1760 d 3-5-1840 m Molly Worthington Pvt MA
Daniel: b 11-9-1761 d 11-2-1855 m Lydia Winter Pvt MA ★
David, Sr.: b 3-30-1716 d 7-21-1803 m Abigail Hawkes PS NH
David, Jr.: b 10-29-1742 d 8-30-1826 m Jemima Carter Sol PS NH
Elisha: b 10-22-1749 d 6-14-1809 m Tama Bardwell Sol MA
Hull: b 12-15-1755 d 6-19-1847 m Hannah Newton Pvt MA
Israel: b 2-15-1751 d 9-20-1828 m Bethia Bangs Pvt MA
Jeremiah: b 6-26-1721 d 7-12-1797 m Mary Cooley PS MA
John: b 3-12-1748 d 5-15-1823 m Betsey Rice Pvt MA
Jonathan: b 5-12-1763 d 4-8-1837 m Hannah Dinsmore Pvt MA
Seth: b 1763 d 1833 m Electa Arms Pvt MA
Thomas: b 4-8-1718 d 2-4-1793 m Esther Martindale Pvt MA
Zadok: b 3-27-1754 d 1-31-1842 m Betsey Brown Pvt NH

NISLER, (includes NIESLER)
John: b 6-17-1740 d 2-20-1815 m Susannah —Sol NC

NISWONGER,
John: b 3-17-1754 d 7-13-1821 m Anna Hoffsinger Sgt VA

NIVEN, (includes NEVIN, NIVIN)
Daniel: b 1742 d 11-20-1809 m Jane Wallace Capt NY
Daniel: b 8-28-1744 d 12-6-1813 m Margaret (Williamson) Reynolds
    Pvt PA
John: b 8-28-1736 d 12- -1802 m (1)Martha (Nivin) (2)Sarah English
    2Lt DE
Wm.: b 1761 d 1834 m Jane Hoosac Sol DE

NIVER,
Michael: b 1-2-1746 d 3-5-1826 m Sophia Severson Cpl NY

NIVISON,
John: b 11-21-1756 d 11-24-1794 m Sarah Tyre Pvt Matr PS NJ
Nathan: b 2-8-1760 d 2-11-1806 m Elizabeth Harvey Pvt NJ

NIXDORF,
Johannes: b 12-28-1742 d 7-3-1802 m Elizabeth Grosch Pvt PA
Samuel: b 4-18-1745 d 3-1-1824 m Barbara (Medtart) Pvt PA

NIXON,
Charles: b *c.* 1755 d *a.* 6-25-1796 m Mrs Elizabeth (Pryor) Lockerman
    Capt DE
George, Sr.: b 1752 d 8-5-1842 m (1)Sarah Seeds (2)Martha — Lt
    DE ★
George, Jr.: b 9-30-1751 d *a.* 1818 m Ann Craven Pvt VA
George: b 4-17-1731 d 11-27-1800 m (1)Mary — (2)Mary — PS VA
Hugh Alexander: b 8-10-1765 d 2-21-1825 m Elizabeth Shannon
    Mid SC
John: b *c.* 3-4-1725-7 d 3-24-1815 m (1)Thankful Berry (2)Mrs
    Hannah (Drury) Gleason BGen MA
John: b 1733 d 12-31-1808 m Elizabeth Davis LCol PA
John: b 1755 d 1781 m Mary Adair LCol SC
John: b 1720 d 2- -1777 m Betsey — Pvt VA
John: b 4-7-1750 d 8-7-1833 m Nancy Potts Pvt VA
John: b 3-21-1755 d *p.* 1- -1790 m Rebeckah Todd PS VA
John Bentley: b 2-2-1730 d *a.* 11-7-1797 m Elizabeth Gaden CS SC
Jonathan: b *c.* 1725 d *p.* 10-22-1794 m Mary Bentley PS MD
Robert: b *c.* 1720 d 1777 m Eleanor — Sol NC
Thomas, Sr.: b 4-27-1736 d 8-12-1800 m Bethiah Stearns Col MA
Wm.: b 12-31-1745 d 4-2-1801 m Jane Ayres Pvt NJ

NOAH,
Elijah: b 1755 d 1819 m Eliza Jane — Sol VA

NOAILLES,
Louis Marie Vicomte de: b 4-17-1756 d 1-5-1804 m Louise de Noailles Col FrA

NOBLE, (includes NOBLES)
Aaron: b 11-25-1748 d 3- -1813 m Eunice Bagg Lt MA
Abel: b 1730 d 9-1-1806 m Anne McConn PS NY
Alexander: b 1733 d 2-15-1802 m Catherine Calhound Maj SC
Asa, Sr.: b 1-16-1715 d 3-25-1797 m Bethiah Noble PS MA
Asa, Jr.: b 11-11-1748 d 3-27-1823 m Rhoda Fowler Sgt MA
Asahel: b 10-7-1725 d 3-8-1796 m Catharine Pert PS CT
Bildah: b 5-13-1759 d 4-23-1799 m Esther Garfield Sol MA
Caleb: b 4-1-1741 d 1804 m Mercy Kellogg Lt MA
Clark: b 2-14-1763 d 1830 m (1)Hulda Hill (2)Mrs Sarah Catlin Pvt MA
Constant: b 10-28-1725 d p. 1777 m Elizabeth Hogaboom Pvt MA
Daniel: b 3-5-1734 d 5-22-1818 m Anna Norton Pvt MA
David, Sr.: b 1-25-1732 d 8-5-1776 m Ruth Noble Capt PS MA
David, Jr.: b 3-19-1755 d 11-25-1820 m Sarah Taylor Pvt MA
David: b 12-9-1744 d 3-4-1803 m Abigail Bennett Pvt MA
David: b 4-20-1756 d 9-22-1822 m (1)Sarah Rising (2)Eunice Crane Pvt VT
Eager: b 5-15-1760 d 4-29-1839 m Mary Phelps Pvt MA ★
Eli: b 10-16-1739 d 12- -1827 m (1)Ruth Campbell (2)Mrs Elizabeth Follett Capt VT
Elijah: b 1754 d 8-21-1827 m Maria Humphrey Pvt CT ★
Enoch: b 5-13-1738 d 8-26-1803 m Tabitha Bush Capt MA
Ezekiel: b 5-8-1745 d 10-20-1816 m Eunice Turner Pvt MA
Gad: b 8-25-1739 d 3-9-1823 m Catherine (Noble) PS CS MA
Gideon: b 3-10-1726 d 1785-90 m Martha Prime Sgt CT
Gideon: b 8-3-1763 d 7- -1807 m Lucy Wells Fif CT
Gideon: b 3-6-1728 d 11-6-1792 m Christina Cadwell PS CT
Goodman: b 7-3-1756 d 8-7-1834 m Sarah Tyler Pvt VT ★
Jacob: b 11-28-1759 d 8-2-1828 m Eunice Mosely Pvt MA
James, Sr.: b 7-9-1736 d 2-23-1817 m (1)Anna Cadwell (2) Mrs Agnes Smith (3)Mrs Eunice Crouch (4)Mrs Priscilla Brand Capt PS MA
James, Jr.: b 1-24-1761 d 6-30-1843 m Elizabeth Stevens Pvt MA ★
John: b 8-6-1762 d 8-4-1843 m Jemima Purdy Pvt DE
John: b 9-7-1731 d 9-15-1807 m Lois Sexton Pvt MA
John: b 6-10-1735 d 10-9-1801 m Mary Leavitt PS NH
Jonathan: b 2-15-1759 d 6-1-1839 m (1)Jane Orr (2)Mary (Buckman) Bryant Pvt MA
Joseph: b 6-3-1742 d a. 2-3-1826 m — Ens VA
Josiah: b 11-19-1737 d 5-28-1818 m Olive Hill Cpl VT
Lewis Sanders: b 1758-60 d 11-1-1856 m Esther Robinson Pvt SC
Luke: b 2-7-1751 d 11-1-1780 m Silence Strong Pvt MA
Luke: b 2-24-1761 d 8-9-1848 m Mary McCleary Pvt VT
Mark: b 11-9-1741 d 10- -1822 m Ann Drake Pvt MA
Matthew: b 7-27-1736 d 8-30-1804 m Lydia Eager Lt MA
Medad: b 10-23-1762 d 12-29-1817 m Lydia Frary Cpl MA
Nathan: b 11-20-1747 d 11-11-1820 m (1)Phoebe Austin (2)Mrs Mary Thompson Lt CT ★
Nathan: b 2-4-1722 d 10-7-1777 m Mary Gray Pvt MA
Nathaniel: b 10-23-1736 d 5-28-1824 m (1)Ruth Root (2)Mary Ann Callender Pvt MA
Nehemiah: b 6-6-1756 d 10-31-1836 m Sabra Skinner Pvt CT
Nehemiah: b — d a. 1798 m Rachel — Capt MD
Obadiah: b 9-6-1739 d 2-19-1829 m Mrs Rebecca Rogers White Chp Pvt VT
Oliver: b 9-27-1763 d 12-24-1839 m (1)Sarah Dutton (2)Betsey Callender Pvt MA
Peter: b 5-22-1734 d 10- -1806 m (1)Abigail Eggleston (2)Margaret Webster Sgt MA
Phineas: b 1752 d 5- -1824 m Sarah Humphrey Cpl CT
Reuben: b 6-9-1732 d 1812 m (1)Ann Ferguson (2)Mrs Scovett Pvt VT
Richard: bc. 1750 d p. 1808 m (1)Elizabeth Gough (2)Eleanor Gough Pvt PA
Roger: b 8-3-1748 d 3-7-1813 m Mrs Martha (Foote) Dewey Cpl MA
Roger: b 4-2-1742 d 9-15-1810 m Olive Hunt Pvt MA
Roswell: b 1758 d 9-9-1841 m Susannah Suller Pvt VT
Samuel: b 8-27-1753 d 6-18-1819 m Lovisa Kellogg Pvt MA
Seth: b 4-15-1743 d 9-15-1807 m (1)Hannah Barker (2)Ruhamah Emery (3)Mrs Mary Riddle Pvt MA
Silas: b 8-28-1733 d 7-11-1775 m (1)Bethia Dewey (2)Mary Taylor Sgt MA
Stephen: b 4-16-1727 d 4-2-1791 m Ruth Church PS MA
Thaddeus: b 1-9-1734 d 6-14-1809 m Sarah Peet Capt NY
Thomas, Jr.: b 11-25-1731 d — m Elizabeth Flatt Pvt NJ
Timothy: b 4-8-1758 d 3-3-1827 m Sally Taylor Pvt MA
Wm.: b 9-25-1758 d 7-16-1834 m Mary X Pvt MD
Zachariah: b 4-16-1742 d 3-12-1819 m Phebe Nichols Pvt MA
Zadoch: b 9-17-1723 d 1-13-1786 m Freelove Dibble PS CT
Zenas: b 11-30-1743 d 3-31-1813 m (1)Hannah Jones (2)Margaret Granger Cpl MA

NOBLET,
John: bc. 1734 d 1786 m Elizabeth — Pvt PS PA

NOE,
Lewis: b 1753-9 d 4-5-1838 m Phebe Mundy Sgt NJ ★
Peter: bc. 1720 d 1782 m Hannah — PS NC
Randall: b — d 1808 m (2)Susannah Barker PS VA

NOECKER,
Christian: b 3-3-1744 d 6- -1809 m Catherine Maria Botdorff Pvt PA

NOEL, (includes KNOLL, NOELL, NOLD, & NOLDS)
Cornelius: bc. 1745 d p. 10-14-1820 m Sally — 2Lt PA VA
Elisha: b 7-27-1736 d 1784-1790 m Elizabeth Granger Sgt NY
Jacob: bc. 1742/3 d 1784 m Anna Catharine Reis Ens PA
Jacob: b 8-13-1765 d 3-6-1835 m Susanna Schull Pvt PA
John Y.: b — d 5-18-1782 m Sallie Estes Ens VA
Richard: b 1759/60 d 1-16-1800 m Mary Crutchfield Lt VA Heirs ★
Septimus: bc. 1735 d 5-10-1794 m Ruth — PS MD
Theodorick: b a. 1753 d 1812 m — Sullivan Chp VA
Wm.: b 1750 d 1820 m Sarah Simmons 2Lt NC

NOFFSINGER,
John: b 1751 d 1825 m Catherine Koontz Pvt PA

NOLAND, (includes NOLEN)
James: b 1740 d 12-26-1833 m Barbara Saunders Capt NC W★
James: b 1760 d 1835 m — Emmerson Pvt VA
Jesse: b 1761 d p. 9-9-1836 m (1)Sarah — (2)Abigail Whitacre Pvt NC ★
Ledstone: b 1750 d p. 12-5-1833 m Elizabeth Glascock Pvt PS NC ★
Stephen: bc. 1741 d 1792 m Mary — Sol NC
Stephen: b 1753 d 10-26-1846 m Mary Smith Sol SC
Thomas: b 1748 d 3-12-1811 m Mary Eleanor Luckett Pvt MD
Wm.: bc. 1760 d a. 6- -1850 m Sarah — Pvt NC
Wm.: b 3-10-1759 d 5-11-1857 m Mary Ann Cockrell Pvt SC ★

NOLPH,
Casper: b 1734 d 2-1-1837 m Phoebe — Sol PA

NONES,
Benjamin: b 3-9-1757 d 2-9-1826 m Miriam Marks Sol PA

NOONEY,
James: b 6-4-1748 d 6-2-1829 m Sarah King Sgt CT

NORBURY,
Jacob: bc. 1730 d p. 1782 m Susannah Phillips Pvt PA

NORCROSS,
Daniel: b 10-9-1743 d 6-22-1805 m Abigail Chapin Pvt MA
Daniel: b 3-9-1745 d 7-27-1825 m Thankful Sawyer Cpl MA
Isaac: b 5-23-1739 d 5-2-1817 m Lydia Shepherd Cpl MA
Jacob: b 10-19-1751 d 11-25-1805 m Elizabeth Bannar Drm Pvt MA
John: b a. 1745 d 9- -1804 m Rachel King Pvt NJ
John: bc. 1748 d c. 1825 m Mary Solomon Pvt PA ★
Josiah: b 6- -1734 d 12-13-1801 m Elizabeth Child Pvt MA
Page: b 4-9-1738 d 9-28-1804 m Elizabeth Bailey Sgt PS NH
Philip: b 3-16-1755 d 1821 m Joanna Brackett Sgt MA
Samuel: b 11-12-1745 d 3-16-1812 m Rachel Harvey Sol MA
Samuel: b 12-23-1752 d 12-9-1838 m Hannah — Fif MA
Seth: b 5-21-1744 d 2-25-1795 m Jerusha Learned PS MA
Wm.: b 1-19-1752 d 11-27-1803 m Effie Hennion QM 2Lt NJ
Wm.: b 1720 d a. 6-5-1777 m Martha Mattison PS CS NJ

NORFLEET,
Reuben: b 1-5-1730 d 5- -1801 m (1)Lucy Smith (2)Mrs Mary Exum PS NC

NORGROVE, (includes NORGRAVE)
Nathaniel: bc. 1750 d 1810 m Hannah Devinea Pvt Dr PA

NORMAN,
Benjamin: b 1-14-1751 d 12-13-1837 m Hannah Dunham Pvt NJ ★
Courtney: bc. 1730 d p. 1783 m Frances — Sol VA
Jesse: bc. 1745 d 1793-1821 m Elizabeth Sothard Sol GA
John: b 4-3-1762 d 10-22-1836 m (1)Mary Preston (2)Desire Prentice Pvt CT
John: bc. 1742 d a. 1790 m Elizabeth Bealer Pvt SC
John: bc. 1755 d p. 1842 m (1)Nancy Austin (2)Isabel Ritchie Sol VA
Joseph: bc. 1765/6 d p. 1810 m (1)Ruth Randel (2)Mary Wayson Pvt MD
Nehemiah: bc. 1725 d c. 11-30-1785 m Rachel — CS PS NC
Thomas: bc. 1750 d 10-26-1818 m Mrs Sarah(Williams)Lowe Pvt NC
Thomas: b1760 d 11-2-1838 m (1)Milred Tutt (2)Elizabeth Hare (3)Frances Stewart Pvt VA ★
Wm.: bc. 1744-50 d p. 1817 m X Pvt VA

NORQUA, (includes NORKWAY)
John: b 1748 d 1-25-1810 m (1)Mary — (2)Catherine — Pvt PA

NORRIS,
Alexander: b 12-9-1744 d 1810-20 m Sarah Norrington PS MD
Andrew: b 3-17-1762 d 1852 m — Pvt NH
Aquila: b a. 1750 d 2-6-1812 m Priscilla Temperance Norris PS MD
Aquila: b 6-13-1754 d 1825 m Sarah (Norris) PS Capt MD
Benjamin, Sr.: b 2-24-1731 d 1-31-1799 m Sarah Wiggin Pvt PS NH

Benjamin, Jr.: b 12-13-1757 d 11-9-1836 m Rebecca Hazelton Vol NH
Benjamin: b 6-6-1753 d *p.* 1808 m (1)Betsy Spencer (2)Hannah Colby Pvt VT
Benjamin Bradford: b 8-16-1745 d 4- -1790 m Elizabeth Richardson PS MD
David: b 12-21-1735 d *p.* 1793 m Annie Taylor Sgt PS NH
Eliphalet: b 8-22-1757 d 3-10-1835 m (1)Lydia Rundlett (2)Hulda Brown Sgt Mus NH ★
George, Sr.: b 8-9-1727 d 2-3-1777 m Maria Jones Cpl VA
Isaac: b *c.* 1750 d *p.* 1790 m Susanna Phillip Pvt NY
James: b *c.* 1754 d *p.* 1828 m Sarah — Sol GA
James: b 2-25-1742 d 11-27-1824 m Mary Bradford Lt MD
James: b 4-9-1739 d 11-15-1815 m Mary Fales Maj NH NY
James: b 1761 d 1814 m Ruth Dearborn Lt NH
James: b 11-10-1755 d 11-6-1806 m Lydia Sherriff Pvt NH
James: b — d *a.* 5-6-1833 m Mary Mason Pvt NC
James, Sr.: b — d *p.* 2-20-1807 m Nancy Opie Arms PS VA
Jeremiah: b 12-16-1729 d *p.* 1783 m Hannah Towle Pvt MA
John, Sr.: b 1740 d 1805 m Hopee Benson Pvt CT
John, Jr.: b 10-23-1765 d 5-20-1840 m Ruth Chapman Ladd Pvt CT★
John: b *a.* 1755 d *p.* 1789 m Aggie Cottrell Sol NC VA
John, Sr.: b *c.* 1723/4 d 1792 m X PS Sol NC
John, Jr.: b 1-12-1750 d 5-12-1822 m Patience Pearson Pvt NC
John: b 1750 d 1798 m (1)Mary Brown (2)Jane Swain Sgt SC
John: b 7-4-1760 d 2-12-1836 m Mary Jones OrdlSgt Vt MA
Jonathan: b 9-11-1749 d 3-16-1826 m Thomasine Barker Lt NH
Joseph, Sr.: b 2-6-1725 d *p.* 1780 m Philizana Barton PS MD
Joseph: b 1-11-1729 d 3-18-1813 m Mary Moody PS MD
Josiah: b *c.* 1726 d 4-19-1786 m (1)Katherine Barber (2)Eunice Coffin (3)Anne Chase PS NH
Libbius: b 2-23-1760 d 2-19-1829 m Elizabeth Hedglen Pvt NJ
Nathan: b 1-29-1760 d 7-13-1825 m Jedidah Hammond Pvt MA
Patrick: b 1762 d 1840 m Rachel Calhoun Pvt SC ★
Patrick: b — d 8-27-1835 m (1) — Hurst (2)Martha Wilson Sol SC
Samuel: b 1728 d 1821 m Elizabeth Holmes PS NH
Samuel: b 5-15-1758 d 7-31-1825 m Betsy Brocklebank Pvt NH ★
Stephen: b 8-28-1738 d *p.* 1790 m Abigail Keeler Tms CT
Thomas: b 1-23-1756 d 4-23-1818 m Sarah Ann Billingsley Pvt MD
Thomas: b *a.* 1743 d *p.* 1783 m Hannah Norrington PS MD
Wm.: b 1765 d 1842 m Elizabeth Patrick Pvt GA
Wm.: b 12-8-1760 d 2-6-1853 m Nancy Cornelius Sol MD
Wm.: b 3-26-1749 d *p.* 8-17-1836 m Martha Amos Pvt PS MD
Wm.: b 2- -1758 d 1838/9 m Sarah Ridgon PS MD
Wm.: b 1743 d 6- -1837 m Valeria — Pvt NJ
Wm, Sr.: b *c.* 1720 d 1781 m Agnes Frederick Pvt SC
Wm: b *c.* 1730 d *p.* 12-15-1801 m Hannah Bell 1Lt VA
Wm.: b 1760 d 8-12-1833 m Sarah Graves Pvt VA ★
Zebulon: b 1736 d *p.* 1786 m Margaret Neally Pvt NH
Ziba: b 1-2-1762 d 1-15-1843 m Elizabeth Bower Sgt NJ ★

NORSWORTHY, (or NOSWORTHY)
Tristram: b 6- -1754 d 10- -1810 m Sarah Bridges Col PS VA

NORTH,
Abijah: b 1743 d 5-3-1785 m Triphenia Grant Pvt CT
Abijah: b 2-8-1759 d 3-23-1850 m Sarah Marsh Pvt CT ★
Asa: b 9-10-1745 d 8-21-1801 m Susanna Newell Pvt CT
Benjamin: b 1721 d 3-28-1777 m Margaret Furman 2Lt NY
Caleb: b 7-15-1753 d 11-17-1840 m (1)Ann Hockley (2)Lydia Lewes LCol PA ★
David: b 8-4-1721 d 1791 m Sarah Fuller Sol CT
Ebenezer: b 1703 d 8-5-1789 m Sibyl Curtiss PS CT
Ezekiel: b 8-22-1747 d 9-14-1832 m Abigail Goodwin Pvt CT
Gabriel: b 5-22-1756 d 1-2-1827 m Deborah Carter MM CT NY
George: b 12-30-1814 m (1)Sarah Evans (2)Eliza Keys QM Wgm Gen PA W★
George: b 1802 d 1830 m X Pvt PA
Isaac: b 9-14-1729 d 11-17-1804 m (1)Hepzibah Hart (2)Elizabeth 2Lt CT
Jacob: b — d *a.* 1795 m Ruth — Sgt MD
John, Sr.: b *c.* 1754 d *c.* 1850 m Rachel Nicolas PS SC GA
Joseph: b 4-2-1730 d 11-28-1775 m Sarah Woodruff Fif CT
Joseph, Jr.: b 7-1-1736 d 8-7-1806 m Lucy Cole PS CT
Joseph: b 8-8-1739 d 4-17-1825 m Hannah Flagg Col ME
Joshua: b 11-3-1745 d 1822 m (1)Rebecca Cloyd (2)Mary Murray Pvt PA
Levi: b 4-16-1760 d 10-2-1846 m Rachel White Pvt CT
Lot: b 1-20-1756 d 10-8-1825 m Silence Horsford Sol CT
Martin: b 12-13-1734 d 1806 m Abigail Eno Pvt CT
Noah: b 1-10-1733 d 4-5-1818 m Jemima Loomis CS Mil CT
Phineas: b 1765 d 1808 m Chloe Skinner Pvt CT
Robert: b 1761 d 9-6-1838 m X Pvt NY
Roger, Sr.: b 1704 d *a.* 6-22-1785 m Ann Rambo PS PA
Samuel: b 9-20-1751 d 7-7-1820 m Elizabeth Avery Pvt NY
Samuel: b *c.* 1734 d — m Barbara Hagermood Pvt PA
Simeon: b 2-28-1759 d 3-2-1840 m Ruth Sanders Pvt CT ★
Stephen: b 1-26-1757 d 1-1-1842 m Susanna Savage Cpl CT
Thomas: b 1760 d *p.* 1832 m Sarah McCarthy QM Sgt VA ★
Thomas: b *c.* 1740 d 1794 m X PS Sol VA

NORTHAM,
Samuel: b 1-25-1725 d 5-2-1834 m Hannah Clark QM Tms CT ★

NORTHCUT, (includes NORTHCOTT, NORTHCUTT)
John: b *c.* 1760 d 1-11-1815 m Lincia England Sol VA
Richard: b *c.* 1737 d 10- -1781 m (1)Sally Florence — (2)Frances — Sol VA
Wm.: b 1745 d *p.* 1783 m Sarah Williams Pvt NC
Wm.: b *c.* 1760 d 3-30-1839 m (2)Elizabeth — Pvt SC

NORTHCRAFT,
Richard: b 1740 d 10- -1789 m Virlinda — PS Sol MD

NORTHEN,
Peter: b *c.* 1750 d 8- -1811 m Jane Alderson Ens PS VA

NORTHINGTON,
Jesse: b 1751 d 1828 m Ann Pope Pvt NC
Samuel, Sr.: b 1725 d 1808 m Phillis Edmunds Pvt NC

NORTHRUP, (includes NORTHROP, NORTHROPE)
Aaron: b 11-30-1720 d 3-21-1802 m Rebecca Hyatt Pvt CT
Abijah: b 3-2-1751 d 10- -1779 m Elizabeth Andrus Pvt NY
Abraham: b 9-18-1722 d 11-4-1798 m Abigail — Pvt MA
Amos: b 9-7-1759 d 11-18-1834 m (1) — Pratt (3)Susan Bowman Pvt CT ★
Amos: b 12-19-1742 d 3-19-1779 m Annie Grant 1Lt CT
Amos: b 1730 d 2-9-1810 m Hannah (Calkins) Hatch Pvt MA
Andrew: b 5-30-1753 d 8-15-1825 m Clarina Dunning Pvt CT
Cornwall: b *c.* 1740 d *p.* 1780 m — Pvt MA
Daniel: b 8- -1740 d 10-15-1808 m Sarah — Pvt NY
Daniel: b 6-21-1738 d 11-10-1811 m Ann (Hampton) Collins Sgt RI
Elijah: b 4-10-1750 d 8-31-1832 m (1)Elizabeth — (2)Bertha Parks (3)Lucy (Jones) Hatch Cpl MA
Gideon: b 11-11-1753 d 6-18-1842 m Esther Munson Ens CT ★
Heth: b 5-30-1754 d 8-12-1825 m Ann Newton Pvt CT ★
Isaac, Sr.: b 11-10-1726 d 7-9-1810 m (1)Hannah Gunn (2)Elizabeth Lobdell Sgt NY
Isaac, Jr.: b 12-24-1752 d 4-11-1812 m Hannah Olmsted Pvt NY
Joe: bpt 1755 d 1848 m (1)Sarah — (2)Sarah Bennet Pvt MA
Job: b 9-9-1758 d 2-16-1833 m Chloe Baldwin Pvt MA
Joel: b 4-26-1732 d 2-14-1786 m Abigail Camp Lt CT
Joel: b 7-27-1753 d 2-9-1807 m Mabel Sarah Bird Pvt Dr CT
Joel: b 3-16-1742 d 3-10-1824 m Eunice Marsh Sol CT
Joel: b 7-28-1753 d *c.* 1801 m Phebe Searles Pvt NY
John: b 7-9-1732 d 3-11-1805 m Lois (Northrope) Capt PS CT
John: b 1-16-1735 d 6-2-1781 m (1)Lydia Gardner (2)Phoebe Gardner (3)Mrs Majorty Talford CS PS RI
John: b 1763 d *p.* 1835 m (1) — (2)Hopestill Kelley Pvt RI ★
Jonathan: b 3-3-1715 d 1783 m Ruth Booth PS CT
Joseph: b 3-20-1742 d 4-25-1812 m Mary Jewell PS CT
Joseph: b 1758 d 10-12-1830 m Sarah — Sgt NY
Joseph: b 7-16-1754 d 1-23-1842 m Sarah Hatch CS NY MA
Lebbeus: b 1-24-1740 d 3-10-1815 m Abigail Remington Manton MM RI
Lemuel: b 5-31-1751 d 9- -1843 m Lois Woodward Cpl CT
Nathan: b 5-30-1721 d 1-11-1804 m Eunice — PS NY
Nathaniel: b 1740 d 5-1-1812 m Esther Gould Pvt CT
Nathaniel: b 12-22-1756 d 2-23-1829 m Sarah Hoyt Sol NY
Nicholas: b 10-16-1752 d 2-10-1836 m Lydia Palmer Pvt NY
Samuel: b 11-26-1744 d 8-22-1786 m Phoebe Beecher Pvt MA
Stephen: b 1-22-1759 d 10-17-1831 m (1)Betsey Murch (2)Deborah Robinson Pvt CT
Stephen: b 4-26-1758 d 9-24-1841 m Rhoda Benedict QM Sgt NY
Stephen: b 1745 d 1836 m (1)Lydia — (2)Sarah — (3)Lydia — Pvt MA
Wm.: b 12-8-1732 d 5-27-1827 m Ann Slocum Pvt Drm RI

NORTHWAY,
Francis: b 5-20-1756 d 6-17-1829 m (1)Susannah Owen (2)Elizabeth Woodford Sol CT
Zenas: b 12-29-1764 d 12-29-1843 m (1)Rhoda Phinney (2)Abigail Brown Pvt MA ★

NORTON,
Aaron: b 6-24-1751 d 2-20-1813 m (1)Eunice Rutty (2)Lydia Hutchinson Pvt CT
Aaron: b 3-19-1743 d 11-30-1828 m Martha Foot Ens CT
Abner: b 10-19-1740 d *c.* 1813 m (1)Mary Claghorn (2)Mrs Hannah (Claghorn) Bartlett 1Lt MA
Alexander: b 1728 d 11-13-1790 m — Pvt MA
Bayes: b 3-16-1746 d 1-14-1782 m Dorcas Pease Mstr MA
Benjamin: b 1751 d 1819 m Lois Curtis Cpl MA
Benjamin: b 1-16-1746 d 4-28-1816 m Sarah Wyatt NPvt CT
Beriah: b 1742 d 11-10-1803 m Rebecca Howd Pvt CT
Beriah: b 1-11-1734 d 12-4-1820 m Ann Frances Cosens Col MA
Caleb: b 1-3-1727 d 5-3-1790 m Abigail Hoag PS NY
Charles: b 12-19-1748 d — m Elizabeth Lyman Capt CT
Charles: b 5-12-1742 d 3-19-1818 m Sarah Street Pvt MA
Christophel: b 2-16-1762 d 7-12-1844 m Susana Bettinger Pvt NY
Cornelius, Jr.: b 1739 d 3-26-1811 m Kezia — Fif 2Lt MA
Daniel, Sr.: b 6-17-1733 d 5-25-1813 m Sarah Stone Capt CT
Daniel: b 9-13-1751 d 1-17-1814 m Lucy King Sol CT

NORTON, contd.

Daniel: b 1-17-1707 d 12-4-1789 m (1)Sarah Bradley (2)Mrs Elizabeth Chittenden (3)Submit Benton PS CT
David: b 2-8-1753 d 10-6-1839 m (1)Deborah Phelps (2)Mehitable Ingham Pvt PS MA ★
David: b 3-6-1753 d 9-9-1829 m Lois Ferguson Pvt NY
Ebenezer, Sr.: b 12-30-1715 d 3-15-1785 m Elizabeth Baldwin LCol PS CT
Ebenezer, Jr.: b 8-12-1748 d 9-27-1795 m (1)Experience Lewis (2)Charity Mills Sol CT
Elihu: b 10-31-1760 d p. 6-4-1833 m Sarah Beal Sgt MA
Elijah: b 4-9-1759 d 12-10-1841 m Rebecca Moores Pvt CT ★
Elijah: b 2-16-1740 d 11-6-1816 m (2)Hannah West Pvt MA
Elijah: b 5-28-1759 d 5-19-1838 m Mary Henderson Pvt RI ★
Elon: b 5-29-1758 d p. 1846 m Chloe Page Pvt CT
Freeman: b 8-21-1754 d 2-9-1837 m (1)Martha Chipman (2)Betsy — QM 2Lt Mrnr MA ★
George: b 9-13-1724 d 2-15-1777 m Patience Bell Pvt CT
Giles: b 4-11-1766 d 1862 m Mary Canfield Pvt CT ★
Gould Gift: b 8-18-1751 d 11-21-1813 m (1)Martha (Hitchcock) Hull (2)Sarah Cook Pvt CT
Henry: b 11-11-1756 d 3-12-1827 m Polly Brace Pvt CT
Ichabod: b 1736 d 10-1-1825 m Ruth Strong Maj PS CT
Isaac: b 2-18-1750 d 10-27-1831 m Phebe Lewis Pvt CT
Isaac: b c. 1758 d p. 6-20-1816 m Mary Kennedy PS PA
Isham, Sr.: b c. 1752 d c. 1839 m — Brigman Pvt NC ★
Issachar: b 8-15-1757 d 1825 m Lorana Paine Pvt PS VT
Joel: b 3-13-1753 d 5-6-1825 m Hannah Olcott Pvt CT
John: b 11-29-1758 d 8-24-1828 m Lucretia Buell Pvt CT W★
John: b 1743 d 5-11-1808 m Ede Clark Pvt CT
John: b 12- -1734 d 8-17-1804 m Mary Twitchell 1Ens CT
John: b 9-10-1756 d p. 1809 m Margaret Batchelder Sgt MA
John: b 1758 d 1831 m Sarah Whitmarsh Pvt MA
Jonathan: b 8-15-1739 d 7-27-1830 m (1)Sarah W. — (2)Mrs Mercy Weller 1Lt MA
Joseph: b 11-8-1742 d 9-18-1834 m Martha (Norton) — Capt MA
Joseph: b 5-25-1738 d p. 1805 m Abigail — Pvt NH
Levi: b 5-13-1759 d 1-21-1823 m Olive Wheeler Pvt CT
Medad: b 5-30-1759 d 8-7-1837 m Martha Rice Pvt CT
Miles: b 3-30-1741 d 9-17-1795 m (1)Esther (Norton) (2)Sybil Andrews (3)Anne Agard Capt CT
Nathan: b 1-12-1757 d 1-28-1830 m Experience Howe Pvt CT
Nathaniel: b 8-1-1762 d 3-22-1831 m Hannah Sawyer Pvt MA ★
Nathaniel: b 1762 d — m Lydia Carl Slr MA
Nathaniel: b 8-24-1735 d 4-22-1820 m (2)Meriel (Adams) Burnham CS NH
Nathaniel: b 10-7-1742 d 10-7-1837 m (1)Elizabeth Corwin (2)Mary Corwin (3)Widow Denton NCapt NY ★
Noah: b 5-8-1748 d 5-31-1841 m Jerusha Dunham Cpl MA ★
Noah Uz: b — d 1841 m Rachel Gillett Pvt CT
Obed: b 3-20-1737 d 1788 m Mehitable Pease Pvt MA
Oliver: b 3-15-1757 d 1-7-1838 m Martha Beach Pvt CT ★
Oliver: b 8-10-1763 d 7-19-1838 m (2)Susannah Law Pvt MA
Ozias: b 2-10-1753 d 2-6-1840 m Maria Frisbie Pvt CT ★
Peter: b 3-25-1756 d 7-18-1837 m Elizabeth Athearn Pvt MA
Peter: b 9-9-1718 d 2-3-1792 m Sarah Bassett CS MA
Phineas: b 1-18-1757 d 2-3-1844 m Eunice Sheldon Pvt MA
Robert: b 1756 d a. 6-7-1783 m Love Pease Pvt MA
Roger, Jr.: b 1-20-1750 d — m Hannah Rice Lt CT
Rufus: b 8-9-1756 d 1812 m Hannah Cook Sgt NY
Samuel: b 9-30-1759 d 10-27-1833 m Phebe Edwards Pvt CT ★
Samuel: b 4-16-1743 d 11-22-1801 m Mrs Mary (Davis) Norton Capt MA
Samuel: b 6-3-1748 d 4-20-1817 m Elizabeth Taylor Sgt MA
Samuel, Sr.: b 1727 d 1777 m Sarah — Pvt NY
Seba: b 7-23-1760 d 8-9-1835 m Margaret Wetmore Pvt NY CT ★
Selah: b 2-25-1745 d 10-20-1822 m (1)Chloe Butler (2)Ann Porter Capt CT
Seth: b 1-16-1735 d 4- -1830 m Amy Norton PS MA
Shadrack: b 8-31-1732 d 4-17-1777 m Mercy Smith Pvt CT
Solomon: b 5-12-1757 d 1844 m Sarah Rexford Pvt NY ★
Stephen: b 6-7-1724 d 11-13-1808 m Abigail Graves Capt CT
Stephen: b 1739 d 9-23-1815 m Lydia Woodworth Capt CT
Stephen: b — d — m Lydia Smith Pvt MA
Sylvester: b 1738 d 8-8-1821 m Lydia Jones PS MA
Thode: b 5-27-1763 d 4-20-1852 m Rachel Keeler Pvt NY
Thomas: b 1736 d p. 6-18-1801 m Mary — Pvt GA
Wm., Sr.: b 4-13-1754 d 3-4-1839 m Mrs Lauranah Kimberly Moorehouse Pvt CT
Wm.: b 1744 d a. 1800 m Mary Godfrey Lt GA
Wm.: b 11-20-1718 d 11-11-1799 m — Pvt MA
Wm.: b c. 1750 d p. 10-31-1805 m — Miller PS SC
Zachariah: b 8-28-1754 d 10-3-1830 m Hannah Smith Pvt MA
Zerah: b 7-17-1763 d 10-13-1840 m (1)Ruth — (2)Elizabeth Newman Pvt VT ★

NORVELL, (includes NORVIL, NORVILL)

Aquilla: b c. 1745 d 1795 m Anne Rukard Sgt VA
Benjamin: b 1752 d 1844 m Anna — PS VA
Hugh: b 8- -1759 d 1824 m Margaret Bugg Cpl VA
Lipscomb: b 1756 d 3-2-1843 m Mary Hendricks 1Lt PS VA ★
Spencer: b 1728 d 1806 m Jane — PS VA
Spencer: b c. 1749 d p. 6-26-1829 m Frances Hill Sol VA

NORWOOD,

Benjamin: b 1758 d 1847 m Mary Aiken Capt NC
Charles: b 12-30-1753 d 1832 m (1)Anne Dale (2)Milred Dale Sol VA
Daniel: b — d 8-13-1779 m — Sgt SC
Francis: b 9-18-1755 d 10-23-1842 m Lydia Barney Pvt NH ★
George W.: b 1760 d c. 1840 m Mariah Wall OrdlSgt NC ★
John: b — d p. 11-16-1814 m (1)Patience Barnes ( )Elizabeth — 2Lt MD
John, Sr.: b 4-12-1727 d p. 11-13-1802 m (1)Mrs Lydia Ledbetter (2)Lesey Lenoir (3)Leah (Lenoir) Whitaker CS NC
John, Jr.: b 1749 d 1835 m Clara Ferrall Pvt NC
John: b 3-17-1751 d 6-20-1826 m Mary Warren Capt SC
Moses: b 7- -1761 d 12-9-1833 m Abagail Brooks Pvt MA ★
Nathaniel: b c. 1720 d p. 9-2-1779 m Mary — PS NC
Samuel: b 1753 d 1807 m Martha Hodges Pvt SC
Stephen: b 2-26-1758 d 12-28-1821 m Anna Andrews Pvt MA
Theophilus: b 1725 d p. 1795 m Eliza St. George Capt SC

NOSHULD,

John: b 9-14-1761 d 5-26-1853 m Elizabeth Simmons Pvt NY

NOSS, (includes NUSE, NUSS)

Conrad: b 10-18-1743 d 3-18-1808 m Margaret A. Roeder Sgt PA
George: b 6- -1758 d 3-1-1829 m Elizabeth Wertz Pvt PA
Jacob: b 12-28-1735 d c. 1800 m Elizabeth Catherine Beck Pvt PS PA
Jacob: b 1759 d 7-25-1851 m Phoebe — PS PA

NOTEWARE,

George: b c. 1755 d 8-21-1825 m Huldah Kline Pvt NY ★

NOTHSTEIN,

Peter: b 1755-60 d 1804 m Maria Elizabeth Haus Lt PA

NOTTINGHAM,

Garton: b 2-9-1747 d 1-15-1790 m Margaret Hardenbergh Pvt NY
Severn: b c. 1740 d p. 11-26-1802 m Elizabeth Evans PS VA
Thomas, Sr.: b c. 1730 d 1797 m — Scarburgh CS VA
Thomas, Jr.: b c. 1750 d p. 12-8-1787 m Margaret Johnson Lt VA

NOTZ,

Michael: b 1-31-1740 d 8-31-1800 m Anna — Pvt PA

NOURSE, (includes NURSE)

Abraham: b 7-27-1732 d 1793 m Zerviah Clayes Morse Pvt MA
Asa: b 3-17-1753 d p. 1791 m (1)Sybil Bailey (2)Olive — Pvt MA
Benjamin: b 4-5-1755 d 2-5-1818 m Ruth Tarbell Sol MA
Benjamin, Sr.: b 12-9-1716 d 6-20-1806 m Martha Marble PS NH
Benjamin: b 2-7-1746 d 1840 m Mercy Stevens Pvt NH
Daniel, Sr.: b 6-15-1729 d 5-24-1805 m Sarah — Pvt MA
Daniel, Jr.: b 4-6-1760 d 1-24-1845 m (1)Anna Wilcox (2)Mrs Orinda Wilcox Pvt MA
Daniel: bpt 5-26-1734 d p. 5-20-1816 m Eunice Perley Pvt MA
David: b 1-19-1741/2 d 12-26-1825 m Rebekah Barrett Capt MA
James: b 2-7-1762 d 4-29-1829 m Elizabeth Mansfield Pvt MA ★
James: b 7-14-1731 d 10-10-1784 m Sarah Fouace PS VA
Jonathan: b 1749 d 7-24-1827 m Ruth — Pvt MA
Jonathan: b 4-19-1751 d 9-9-1806 m Hannah Tarbox Pvt MA
Joseph: b 1-6-1724 d 2-8-1812 m Sarah Walkup Pvt NH MA
Samuel: b 1715 d 5-8-1790 m (1)Elizabeth Kellogg (2)Abigail Barnard PS MA
Wm.: b 10-30-1763 d 8-30-1836 m Elizabeth Jameson Mid
Wm.: b — d p. 1798 m Lydia Bruce Pvt NH

NOVINGER,

Dewalt: b 2-7-1737 d 3-10-1826 m Mary Woodside Pvt PA

NOWELL,

Daniel: b 1759 d 1828 m Katharine Nelson Sol NC
Jonathan: b 12-22-1747 d 1-5-1821 m Elizabeth Frost BgdMaj MA
Mark: b 12-26-1762 d 4-3-1836 m Betsey Parker Pvt MA ★
Moses: b 2-4-1737 d 4-11-1829 m Catherine Hill Capt MA
Paul: b 10-24-1753/4 d 1-18-1835 m (2)Emma Horne Pvt MA ★
Peter: b 2-16-1732 d 1801 m (1)Sarah Gray (2)Catherine Hill Pvt MA
Samuel: b 12-18-1744 d 4-18-1833 m Sarah Hanners Pvtr MA ★
Samuel: bpt 12-22-1728 d a. 5-31-1784 m Elizabeth Favor Pvt MA
Samuel York: b 3-4-1754 d p. 11-30-1794 m Mary Hoppin Pvt MA
Thomas: b — d 11-10-1785 m Sarah Lovett Lt MA

NOWLIN, (includes NOLEN, NOWLEN)

Bryan: b 1740 d p. 12-11-1806 m Lucy Wade Sol PS VA
John: b c. 1744 d a. 10-17-1811 m Ann Goolsby Sol NC
Samuel: b 8-16-1739 d 10-19-1805 m Elizabeth Fox Pvt CT

NOXON,

Benjamin: b 1746 d 1-14-1818 m Catherine — Lt PS NY
Pascho: b 3-27-1759 d 1-28-1828 m Eleanor (Lanah) Borgardus Pvt NY
Peter: b 7-27-1755 d 8-13-1797 m Elizabeth Bentley Pvt NY

NOYES,

Aaron: b 11-28-1755 d 3-11-1827 m Betty Ladd Pvt NH

Bela: b 7-20-1757 d 8-21-1833 m Elizabeth Mahan Sol MA
Benjamin: b 4-29-1742 d 3-16-1811 m Hannah Thompson Col CS NH
Caleb: b 3-11-1748 d 11-7-1828 m Hannah Little Pvt NH
Cutting: b 6-2-1745 d *p.* 1793 m Molly Burbank Pvt CS NH
Daniel: b 10-17-1716 d 11-11-1780 m (1)Hannah Thayer (2)Mary Burrill (3)Mrs Mary Reed PS MA
Daniel, Jr.: b 7-19-1749 d 2-11-1832 m Millicent Gibbs Pvt MM MA
Daniel: b 1-30-1722 d 8- -1779 m Anna Chase PS NH
Dudley: b 5-5-1764 d 3-25-1846 m Sally Johnson Pvt MA
Eliab: b 3-31-1744 d 7-6-1822 m Abigail Hersey Pvt MA
Elijah: b 10-2-1758 d 11-8-1809 m Mary Lewis Pvt NH
Enoch: b 3- -1750 d 5-20-1842 m (1)Eunice Kinsman (2)Susanna Parker CS PS NH
Enoch: b 12-11-1717 d 10- -1796 m (1)Lucy Dickinson (2)Elizabeth Chewte PS NH
Enoch: b 3-25-1730 d — m (1)Phebe Harriman (2)Judith Knight (3) Mehitable Simons PS NH
Ephraim: b 2-20-1757 d 6-14-1822 m Sarah Dike Pvt MA
Friend: b 6-26-1763 d *p.* 1796 m (1)Elizabeth Knight (2)Abigail Ilsley (3)Sally Jones Pvt MA
Gershom: b 7-8-1764 d 1843 m Mary Stanton Pvt VT ★
Henery: b 8-1-1740 d — m Mille Hale Drm MA
Humphrey: b 2-11-1717 d 5-21-1790 m Elizabeth Little Sol NH
Isaac: b 5-21-1765 d 9-6-1826 m Sally Haven Pvt MA
James: b 5-7-1738 d 1790 m Jane (Noyes) Pvt NH
James, Jr.: b 3-14-1744 d 8-5-1831 m Eunice Denison PS CT
James T.: b 1757 d *c.* 1814 m (1)Louise Nash (2)Martha Crossman Pvt MA
John: b 3-18-1740 d 5-14-1784 m Mary Wyatt Capt MA
John: b 3- -1741 d 7-18-1778 m Sarah Little Pvt MA
John, Sr.: b 2-8-1729 d *p.* 1795 m Sarah Hersey Pvt MA
John, Jr.: b 11-18-1754 d 1-24-1836 m Zibia Brett Pvt MA
John: b 3-3-1744 d 10-7-1825 m Mary Fowler PS MA
John: b 5-22-1718 d *p.* 1788 m Mercy Breed CS PS VT
Joseph: b 9-10-1758 d 8- -1820 m Jane Lord Pvt CT
Joseph: b 6-18-1747 d 6-28-1824 m Abigail Bailey Lt MA
Joseph: b 7-11-1736 d 1-5-1826 m (1)Hannah Knapp (2)Judith L. Adams PS MA
Joseph: b 1-11-1732 d 7-11-1807 m (1)Mary Flint (2)Mary Darling Pvt NH
Joseph: b 10-9-1727 d 3-13-1802 m Barbara Wells Col RI
Josiah: b 9-8-1712 d 1796 m Mary Lunt CS MA
Lemuel: bpt 8-21-1743 d 8-29-1830 m Sarah Brown Sgt MA
Moses: b 12-9-1753 d 8-1-1838 m Mary Prince Pvt CT
Moses: b 12-16-1743 d 3-12-1824 m (1)Lydia Carter (2)Phebe Richardson Sgt MA
Moses: b 1759 d 12-20-1831 m Abigail Locke Sgt CS MA ★
Moses: b 5-11-1743 d *p.* 1782 m (1)Elizabeth Eaton (2)Dinah Moore Pvt MA
Nathan: b 2-24-1761 d 9-15-1825 m Sarah Thompson Pvt NH
Nathaniel: b 5-23-1740 d *p.* 1790 m (1)Mary Tenney (2)Abigail Newman Fvt MA
Nathaniel: b 12-21-1747 d 4-1-1813 m Sarah Harriman Pvt NH
Nicholas: b 4-14-1761 d 1844 m Rachel Hill Pvt MA
Oliver: b 7-22-1738 d 2-20-1803 m (1)Mary Johnson (2)Rachel Johnson Lt MA
Oliver: b 5-12-1759 d 10-24-1842 m Mehitable Eaton Pvt NH
Oliver: b 5-9-1755 d 12-6-1829 m (1)Thankful Clark (2)Eunice Billings Pvt RI
Peleg: b 5-29-1741 d 1825 m Prudence Williams Capt CT
Peter: b 12-3-1731 d 1803 m Hannah Merrill Col PS MA
Samuel: b 1-30-1740 d 12-10-1775 m Lois Whitmarsh Cpl MA
Samuel: b 4-25-1737 d 4-1-1820 m Rebecca Wheeler Pvt PS MA
Samuel: b 11-12-1759 d 6-7-1816 m Mary Thompson Pvt MA
Samuel: b 3-15-1725 d *p.* 1790 m Mary Merrill Capt PS NH
Samuel: b 9-12-1760 d 2-27-1846 m Sarah Collins Pvt NH
Sanford: b 6-18-1761 d 8-8-1843 m Martha Babcock Pvt RI
Simon: b 11-10-1717 d 1816 m (1)Martha Tappan (2)Elizabeth Eaton Pvt CS MA
Sylvanus: b 2-24-1719 d *p.* 1790 m Phebe Chase Pvt MA
Thomas: b 7-20-1721 d 9-14-1784 m Ann Follansbee Capt MA
Thomas: b 2-4-1762 d *p.* 1813 m Margaret Sutherland Pvt MA
Thomas, Sr.: b 1723 d 1779 m (2)Mary Hale PS NH
Thomas, Jr.: b 6-22-1762 d *p.* 1805 m Mary Reed Pvt NH
Thomas: b 10-3-1754 d 9-19-1819 m Lydia Rogers LCol RI
Timothy: b 10-23-1725 d 2-12-1814 m Sarah Abbott Pvt PS MA
Timothy: b 11-8-1745 d — m (1) — (2)Charlotte Bradish (3)Mary Noyes Pvt MA
Timothy: b 1758 d 7-2-1839 m Sarah Jewett Pvt NH
Wadleigh: b 9-9-1745 d 10-27-1777 m Hannah Smith Lt MA
Wm.: b 1728 d 1807 m Eunice Marvin CS PS CT
Wm.: b 1752 d 4-2-1812 m Rebecca Alling Pvt CT

NUDD,
Simon: b 2-6-1735 d 10-30-1818 m Elizabeth Hook PS NH

NUGENT, (or NEWGENT)
Edward: b 1726 d 1790 m Elizabeth Conway PS VA

NULL, (includes KNULL, NOLL)
George: b 2-12-1764 d 6-28-1834 m Anna Maria — Pvt PA

George: b 1750 d *p.* 1802 m Rachel Richards Capt PA
Philip: b 1752 d 1834 m Margaret Bushong (Beauchamp) Capt NC PA

NUNEMACHER,
Ludwig: b 12-26-1739 d 3-16-1815 m Anna Barbara Weis PS PA

NUNN,
John: b — d *p.* 1827 m — Sol GA
John: b *c.* 1755 d 1828 m Eliza Pratt Sgt PS SC
Thomas: b 3-13-1753 d 4-27-1837 m Sarah — Pvt VA ★
Thomas: b 1748-50 d *p.* 10-20-1805 m (1)— (2)Jane Pace Ens PS VA
Wm.: b 1744 d 1-1-1807 m (2)Elizabeth Copeland Capt NC

NUNNALLY, (includes NUNNALEE, NUNNELEE)
Edward: b 1756 d 4-19-1836 m (1)Sarah Vaughn (2)Mary Ann Reeves Sunderland Sgt VA ★
James Franklin: b 1-3-1760 d 2-12-1838 m Keziah — (2)Jincey Nash Pvt VA
John: b 2-12-1758 d 6-10-1825 m Susan Virginia Burton Sgt Cmsry VA W★
Obadiah: b 1756 d 2-22-1822 m Elizabeth Baldwin Pvt VA W★
Wm.: b 1755 d *p.* 9-17-1839 m — Pvt VA ★
Wm. Womack: b — d *p.* 11-23-1804 m Ann Franklin PS VA

NUSSMAN,
Adolph: b 8- -1739 d 11-3-1794 m Elizabeth Rentilman PS NC

NUTE,
Daniel: b *c.* 1753 d *p.* 1790 m Lucy Tuttle Pvt NH
James: b *c.* 1740 d *p.* 1787 m Leah Pinkham 1Lt NH
Jotham, Jr.: b 11-22-1760 d 2-3-1836 m Sarah Twombly Sgt NH
Paul: b 1741 d 6-2-1812 m Hepzibah Canney Lt NH
Samuel: b 3-11-1750 d 3-21-1828 m Sarah — Lt NH
Samuel: b 3-2-1749 d 1825/6 m Phebe Pinkham PS NH

NUTT, (includes McNUTT)
Aaron: b 1758 d 6-2-1842 m (1)Mary Archer (2)Martha Pedrich Craig Sol Tms Sct NJ
David: b *c.* 1738 d 4-20-1797 m — 2Lt MA
James: b 6-17-1745 d 3-19-1794 m Susannah Cochran Sgt MA
John: b *a.* 1763 d *p.* 1786 m Elizabeth Stewart Pvt NH
John: b 1- -1737 d 1-2-1837 m Hannah — Pvt VA
Samuel: b 12- -1728 d 7-5-1808 m (2)Elizabeth Dickey Pvt PS NH
Wm., Sr.: b 1731 d 4- -1802 m Sarah Elkins James PS NH
Wm.: b 3-14-1760 d 1-20-1833 m Mary Brewster Pvt NH
Wm.: b 7-7-1762 d 2-6-1843 m (1)Hannah Glidden (2)Lucy Avery Pvt NH ★
Wm.: b 12-6-1733 d 1792 m (1)— (2)Sarah — Capt PS VA

NUTTER,
Christopher: b 1-21-1760 d 2-21-1845 m Rebecca Moorhead Pvt VA ★
Ebenezer: b 12-10-1755 d 1847 m Temperance Colbaith Pvt NH
Hatevil: b *a.* 1715 d 3-25-1793 m Hannah Decker PS NH
John, Sr.: b 2-21-1721 d 9-19-1776 m Annie Simes PS NH
John, Jr.: b 3-1-1757 d 11-8-1840 m Elizabeth Dame Pvt NH ★
Robert: b 1738 d 1778 m Sarah Bagwell Pvt DE
Thomas: b *c.* 1735 d *p.* 1785 m — Capt VA
Zadok: b 4-20-1759 d 1839 m Catherine Lynn Pvt DE

NUTTING,
Daniel: b 5-23-1756 d 4-11-1836 m Mollie Lawrence Pvt MA
David: b 3-10-1751 d 4-15-1818 m Tamar — Sgt MA
Ebenezer: b 1749 d 1821 m (1)Hannah Shepard (2)Sally Kidder Cpl MA
Ebenezer: b 7-17-1742 d 12- -1822 m Sybil Stickney Pvt MA
Eleazer: b 9-13-1760 d 1-7-1851 m Anak Parker Pvt MA
Elijah: b 1764 d 10-19-1825 m Suzanne Foster Pvt VT W★
Ephraim, Sr.: b 9-1-1728 d 1-10-1797 m (1)Lydia Spaulding (2)Jerusah Parker Pvt MA
James: b 1738 d 4-19-1822 m Mary Carpenter Pvt MA
John, Sr.: b 6-5-1731 d 5-5-1816 m Martha Blood Capt MA
John: b 4-21-1762 d 7-28-1834 m (1)Esther Smith (2)Catherine Smith Sol MA
Jonathan: b 8-10-1735 d 3-6-1811 m Abigail Bannister Pvt MA
Jonathan: b 1732 d — m Deborah Whipple PS Pvt ME
Josiah: b 2-16-1748 d *p.* 1790 m Zeruiah Lawrence Pvt MA
Samuel: b 4-15-1744 d 1-8-1797 m Elizabeth Farmer Dr MA
Thomas: b 12-10-1758 d 12-28-1813 m Sybel Prescott Sol MA
Wm.: b 1752 d 1832 m (1)Mrs Susanna (French) Danforth (2)Mrs Mary (Barrett) Hubbard Cpl MA

NUTZEL,
Johannes: b 1755 d — m Barbara — Pvt PS MD

NUZUM,
Thomas: b 9-29-1706 d *p.* 4-7-1789 m Elizabeth — CS PA

NYE, (includes NIGH)
Andrew: b *c.* 1754 d 11-30-1816 m Hester Lomison Pvt PA W★
Barnabas: b 1734 d 7-24-1818 m Deborah Tobey Pvt MA

NYE, contd.

Barnabas: b 9-12-1766 d 4-12-1816 m Sally Bennett Pvt MA
Bartlett: b 8-18-1759 d 2-28-1822 m Deborah Ellis Cpl MA
Benjamin: b 5-13-1728 d 8-9-1818 m (1)Phoebe West (2)Mary Crocker PS CT
Benjamin: b 4-18-1725 d 5-27-1816 m Susan Phinney Maj MA
Benjamin: b 6-8-1739 d 9-18-1806 m (2)Mary Hall Pvt MA
Daniel: b 6-8-1758 d 2-16-1844 m Lydia Howe Pvt CT
David: b 9-29-1760 d 9-9-1832 m Honor Tryon Mus Sgt PS CT ★
David: b 7-1-1706 d 4-17-1796 m Elizabeth Briggs Pvt MA
Ebenezer: b 10-10-1750 d 2-27-1823 m (1)Desire Sawyer (2)Mrs Gardner Pvt CT
Ebenezer: b 10-19-1743 d 1798 m Hannah Cotton NCdr MA
Ebenezer: b 7-19-1761 d 12-28-1838 m Lucy Woods Pvt MA ★
Elihu: b 1745 d 12-10-1813 m Sarah Crowell Sgt MA
Elisha: b 4-22-1745 d 5-12-1833 m (1)Lucy Tobey (2)Mehitable Robinson Capt MA
Elisha: b 11-2-1757 d 3-11-1845/6 m Sarah Morey Pvt MA
Elisha: b 1761 d 11-5-1848 m Drusilla Thomas Pvt VT
George: b 1-7-1717 d 1780 m Thankful Hinckley PS CT
George: b 1-21-1755 d 11-16-1830 m Magdalena — PS MD
George: b c. 1717 d 9-22-1805 m (1)Sarah Blackwell (2)Rebecca Marshall (3)Mrs Jane Fenton (4)Mrs Sarah Gilbert Pvt MA
George: b 1-5-1758 d 5-3-1823 m Susan Canote Pvt PA
Ichabod: b 12-21-1762 d 11-27-1840 m Minerva Tupper Pvt MA
Iram: b 1-28-1751 d 6-19-1802 m Eleanor Ellis Cpl MA
Jabez: b 4-11-1749 d 5-5-1828 m (1)Molly Fuller (2)Temperance Crocker Sgt MA
James: b 5-13-1758 d 10-27-1840 m Sarah Clark Pvt MA
John: b 5-12-1758 d 3-13-1840 m Anne Rogers Pvt MA ★
John: b 9-29-1738 d 4-25-1809 m Sarah Dennis Lt MA
John: b 3-1-1741 d p. 8-19-1798 m (1)Abigail Gifford (2)Mrs Phoebe Nobes Lt MA
John: b — d — m Anna Wing Sgt RI
John N.: b 6-6-1745 d 1-14-1826 m Lois West Pvt MA
Jonathan: b 5-22-1748 d 5-28-1832 m Margaret Barr Sgt MA
Jonathan: b 4-3-1731 d 7-8-1806 m Rebecca Freeman Pvt MA
Joseph: b 10-21-1723 d 1-23-1790 m Elizabeth Holmes Pvt MA
Joseph: b 4-18-1735 d 5-11-1804 m (1)Thankful Goodspeed (2)Patience Robinson Pvt MA
Joshua: b 8-31-1733 d 1813 m Lydia Jenkins Pvt MA
Levi: b 4-10-1743 d 3-24-1825 m Sarah B. Freeman Lt MA
Melatiah: b 4-25-1734 d 8-4-1794 m Hannah Hubbard Sgt CT
Nathan: b 2-20-1749 d 5-7-1826 m (1)Hannah Butler (2)Mrs Sarah (Fessenden) Allen Adj MA
Nathan: b 1759 d 9-12-1848 m Lydia — Pvt MA ★
Nathaniel: b 1-18-1754 d 7-23-1799 m (1)Elizabeth C. Smith (2)Celia — Sgt MA
Obed: b 9-15-1736 d 11-10-1815 m Mary Sellers Pvt MA
Oliver: b 4-4-1762 d p. 1809 m Lucinda Houghton Pvt MA
Peleg: b 8-14-1743 d 5-28-1825 m Sarah — Pvt MA
Samuel: b 7-20-1738 d 5-8-1817 m Abigail Benton Pvt CT
Samuel: b 3-15-1746 d 3-15-1814 m Deborah Crowell Pvt MA
Samuel: b 3-24-1749 d 8-31-1834 m Abigail Bachelder Dr NS MA
Seth: b 8-7-1756 d 1-18-1840 m Amy West Pvt MA
Silas: b 1744 d 1812 m Patience Carpenter Sgt MA
Solomon: b 10-22-1763 d 3-1-1857 m (1)Lois Fuller (2)Mary Woods Tms CT ★
Stephen: b 6-6-1720 d 7-6-1810 m Maria Bourne PS MA
Sylvanus: b 8-12-1744 d a. 7-8-1820 m (1)Lydia Freeman (2)Rebecca Parker Pvt CS PS MA
Sylvanus: b 1762 d 7-25-1814 m Mary Bankes Pvt MA
Sylvanus: b 8-1-1753 d 3-5-1841 m Sylvinia Barlow Pvt NY
Timothy: b 6-13-1747 d 2-5-1813 m Keziah (Nye) 2Lt MA
Wm.: b 11-17-1749 d 7-17-1826 m Eunice Handy Pvt MA
Wm.: b 6- -1758 d 12-8-1833 m (1)Mary Purington (2)Anna Adams Pvt MA

OAKES, (includes OAK, OAKE)

Abraham: b c. 1743 d 1778 m Maria Condict Sol NJ
Beriah: b 11-22-1743 d 1781 m Tabitha Fosket Pvt MA
Charles: b c. 1736 d p. 9-4-1795 m Jean — Capt Asst Cmsry VA
Daniel: b 1761 d 1845 m (1)Mourning Blinn Flagg (2)Susan — (3)Deborah Dorcas (Albee) Fletcher Pvt MA
David: b 1-15-1735 d 10-17-1813 m Elizabeth Mead Pvt CT
Ephraim: b 5-24-1753 d 4-21-1846 m Mary Jarvis Pvt NY ★
George: b 2-15-1720 d p. 1777 m (1)Lydia Egar (2)Mercy Bartlett Pvt MA
John: b 9-4-1759 d 3-17-1845 m (1)Patience Mason (2)Susannah P. Staples Pvt MA
Jonathan: b 10-4-1751 d 8-6-1818 m Sarah Nichols NCapt MA
Josiah: b 3-14-1751 d 1-20-1798 m Silence Willcutt Ens MA
Nathan: b 2-4-1747 d 1793 m Esther Peck Pvt CT
Nathaniel: b 5-16-1751 d 3-15-1840 m (1)Susanna Hastings (2) — Gates Pvt MA
Nathaniel: b 1762 d 1830 m Susan Evans Pvt MA
Nehemiah: b 1743 d 11-8-1799 m Esther Buckman Sgt MA
Seth: b 4-8-1733 d 4-24-1810 m Elizabeth Shevally QMSgt MA
Sylvanus: b 1749 d 1800 m Abagail Ball Sgt MA
Urian: b 11-20-1728 d 2-1-1766 m Leah Egree PS MA

OAKLEY,

Cornelius: b 1-1-1737 d 1-15-1825 m Sarah Warner Pvt NY
Elijah: b 1754 d 1836 m Rhoda Janes 1Lt NY
Gilbert: b 5-11-1761/2 d 9-30-1805 m Eleanor Wakeman CG CT W ★
Isaac: b a. 1722 d 1783 m Miriam Hunt 2Lt NY
Isaac: b a. 1724 d 1789 m Sarah — Pvt NY
Jared: b — d 7- -1776 m Mary Wright PS NY
John: b 5-4-1762 d 2-23-1809 m (1)Mary — (2)Catherine Morgan Pvt CT W★
John: b 1743 d 1801 m Martha — Sol VA
Miles: b 4-7-1757 d 1844 m (1)Eunice Bennette (2)Susanna Lyon Pvt Mus CT ★
Richard: b 1751 d 1856 m Winnifred Wheeler Pvt NC
Thomas: b 1739 d 1821 m Ann (Oakley) Pvt NY
Thomas: b 9-8-1749 d 11-7-1825 m Mary — PS NY
Wm.: b 5-27-1753 d 11-2-1834/5 m — Sgt NY ★
Wm.: b c. 1725 d p. 1781 m Phoebe Hunt Pvt NY
Wilmot: b 10-28-1744 d 5-12-1814 m Patience Baylis PS NY

OAKMAN,

Constant Fobes: b 4-5-1759 d 11-18-1833 m Rachel Hatch Pvt MA
Melzar Turner: b 6-29-1750 d 12-23-1795-7 m (1)Persis Rogers (2)Louisa Oakman Adj MA
Tobias: b 5-12-1729 d 6-9-1818 m Ruth Little Sgt MA

OAST,

James: b 1747 d 5- -1833 m (1)Olivè Sharwood (2)Sarah Isham (3)Ann Norris Pvt VA

OATES, (includes OATS)

Jeremiah: b 1757 d 1802 m Jane Sinquefield Pvt GA
Jesse: b 1756 d 8-10-1831 m (1)Mary Caraway (2)Zilpah Mason Pvt NC
Wm.: b 5-20-1734 d 10-12-1818 m Jean Sloan Pvt NC

OATLEY,

Joseph: b c. 1757 d 11-28-1815 m Mary Hazard Pvt RI W★

OATMAN,

Benjamin: b 1755 d 3-1-1816 m Bethia Smith Pvt VT
Isaac: b 9-17-1761 d 8-17-1831 m Anna Brainard Pvt VT

O'BANNON,

John: b 1735 d 1797 m Lydia Duncan Capt VA
Joseph: b 1758 d 12-10-1824 m Jane Martha Welton Sol VA
Thomas: b 1757 d 1834 m Hannah Barker QMSgt VA ★
Thomas: b 1739 d 1801/2 m Frances Jennings Pvt VA
Wm.: b 1730 d 1807 m Ann Neville Sol VA

OBER, (includes OVER)

Benjamin: b 12-29-1752 d c. 1780 m Mary Foster SeaCap MA
Christian: b 9-29-1762 d 11-27-1840 m Elizabeth Huntsberger Pvt PA
Josiah: b 10-18-1739 d p. 1776 m Hannah Butman Pvt MA
Josiah, Jr.: b 8-29-1747 d 2-17-1820 m (1)Phoebe Kimball (2)Abigail Carlton Pvt MA
Richard: b 11-6-1716 d 11-11-1787 m Lydia Chapman Sgt MA
Richard: b 8-11-1741 d 12-4-1817 m Ruth Woodbury Pvt MA
Wm.: b 4-13-1735 d p. 1779 m Hannah Monroe Pvt MA

OBERDORF,

George: b 1755 d 5-24-1828 m Elizabeth Shaffer Pvt PA

OBERLY, (includes EBERLY, OBERLIN)

Adam: b — d 1812 m Eve Ensminger Sgt PA
Adam: b 5-31-1745 d 8-10-1804 m Margaret Stober Cpl PA
Jacob, Sr.: b 1729 d 3-5-1790 m Mary (Eberly) — Pvt PA
Jacob, Jr.: b 3-21-1751 d 2-1-1807 m Anna Shirk Cpl PA
John: b 7-9-1746 d 8-19-1805 m Elizabeth Uhler 1Lt PA
John: b 7-5-1755 d 4-6-1823 m Elizabeth Bricker Pvt PA
Michael: b 1751 d p. 4-28-1814 m Anna — Capt PA
Michael: b 1725 d 1790 m Anna Catrina — Ens PA
Michael: b 9-27-1717 d 10-11-1788 m Christina Barbara Zwecker Pvt PA

O'BLENIS,

Hendrick: b 4-5-1732 d 12-14-1815 m (1)Antje Lydecker (2)Catrine VanOrden Blauvelt (3)Bridget DeClark Pvt NY
Peter: b 12-10-1757 d 5-29-1831 m Maria Breyssent Pvt NY

OBLINGER,

Nicholaus: b 1737 d 5-11-1814 m Salome Driesback Pvt PS PA

OBRIANT,

Dennis: b — d p. 8-7-1790 m Rebecca — Sol PS NC

O'BRIEN, (includes O'BRION, O'BRYAN, O'BRYON)

Daniel: b 3-17-1752 d 10-14-1835 m (1)Eleanor Leman (2)Martha Gay Pvt MD ★
Dennis: b 8-8-1740 d 9-1-1800 m Naomi Lovin Pvt NC
Gideon: b 6-14-1746 d 6-6-1827 m Abigail Tupper Pvt MA
James: b a. 1758 d 1-16-1797 m Elizabeth — Col MD

John: b 9-1-1759 d 9-11-1841 m Abigal Wilson Pvt MA ★
Joseph: b 11-25-1758 d 2-10-1825 m Rebecca Moody Pvt ME
Morris: b 1715 d 6-4-1799 m Mary Cain PS ME
Tillotson: b 5- -1760 d 7-11-1840 m (1)Sarah — (2)Mary Lassiter Pvt NC ★
Wm.: b c. 1759 d c. 1784 m Mrs Lydia (Clarkson) Tappan NLt MA
Wm.: b 2-20-1750 d p. 1833 m Lucinda Walden Pvt RI

OBURN, (or OBORN)
Joseph: b c. 1745 d 1814 m Sarah — Pvt PA

OCHILTREE,
Hugh: b 1745 d 1807 m Nancy McCranie Sol NC

ODELL, (includes ODLE)
Caleb, Sr.: b c. 1730 d 1798 m (1)Alice — Lt CS NC VA
Isaac: b 9-25-1758 d 6-24-1811 m Phoebe Dean Pvt NY
Isaiah: b 1761 d 1847 m Elizabeth Buck Towson Pvt MD
Jacob: b c. 1755 d p. 8-14-1829 m Margaret Butler Pvt NY
Jacob: b 7-25-1756 d 1846 m Ann Devoor Brevoort Pvt NY
Jacob: b 6-20-1744 d 11-10-1814 m Katherine VanRensselaer Capt VT
Jeremiah: b 11-1-1761 d 12-1-1842 m Rachel Walters Sgt VA ★
John: b 12-4-1761 d 11-5-1844 m Edee Nourse Pvt NH ★
John: b 1739 d p. 5-15-1785 m Mary Wiltsea Pvt NY
John: b 2-19-1758 d 12-27-1812 m Enor Schryver Pvt NY
Jonathan: b 12-26-1730 d 9-23-1818 m Margaret Dyckman PS NY
Joseph: b c. 1738 d p. 1793 m Martha Manning Pvt NY
Joshua: b 5-2-1733 d c. 1819 m Mary Vincent Pvt NY
Nathan: b 3-29-1761 d 1-18-1842 m Mary Burrett Pvt CT ★
Nehemiah: b 1743 d 1790 m Mary Julian PS NC
Thomas: b 5-17-1752 d 8-25-1827 m (1)Elizabeth Garrett (2)Gracie Austin 1Lt MD
Wm.: b 1729 d 3-3-1812 m Phebe — PS NH
Wm.: b 12-18-1762 d 2-12-1856 m Johanna Wilsea OrdlSgt NY ★
Wm.: b 1758 d c. 3-28-1839 m Sarah Turney Pvt Mrnr NY

ODEN,
Alexander: b c. 1752 d c. 1834 m (1)Letetia Bussey (2)Mrs Elizabeth (Boyd) Bussey Pvt SC
Hezekiah: b — d p. 8-3-1797 m Luraney — PS SC

ODENWELDER,
John: b 2-12-1756 d 3-12-1842 m Elizabeth Miller Cpl PA
Philip, Sr.: b 1721 d 7- -1795 m (1)Anna Maria Rent (2)Susanna — (3)Catharine — PS PA
Philip, Jr.: b 9-2-1748 d 5-20-1828 m Anna Maria Yeager Pvt PA

ODER,
Joseph: b 8-3-1751 d 1833/4 m Elizabeth — Pvt VA

ODERKIRK,
Frederick: b 1760 d 8-31-1841 m Elizabeth Weygant Cpl NY ★

ODILL,
Thomas: b 7-8-1759 d 3- -1823 m Ann Poole Pvt SC

ODIORNE,
Nathaniel, Jr.: b 2-17-1746 d 10-1-1778 m Mary Grindell Capt NH
Samuel: b 7-6-1758 d 12-13-1835 m Temperance Underwood CS Pvt NH MA
Thomas: b 12-1-1733 d 4-29-1819 m Joanna Gilman PS NH

ODLIN,
Wm.: b 2-17-1738 d 9-6-1787 m Judith Wilson Grd NH

ODOM,
Benjamin: b c. 1745 d a. 1-5-1801 m Thamer — Pvt SC
Jacob: b 1760 d 1835 m Susan — Pvt NC ★
Levi: b 5-1-1759 d 1844 m (3)Patience Bird Pvt NC ★
Seybert: b — d a. 10-4-1824 m — Sol PS SC
Sion: b 1758 d c. 1839 m Martha Snead Pvt SC

O'DONNELL,
John: b 1754 d 2-23-1830 m Sarah O'Brien SgtMaj PA ★

OFFICER,
Wm.: b c. 1738-40 d 1811 m Elizabeth — Pvt PA

OFFNER,
John: b 1742-55 d 1797 m Salome Carpenter Lt PA

OFFUTT,
Alexander: b 5-7-1736 d 1786 m — Perry PS MD
James: b 10-11-1725 d 8- -1802 m Rebecca Magruder CS PS MD
Jesse: b 10-25-1759 d 6-4-1819 m Obedience Bacon Pvt SC
Mordecai Burgess: b 1-25-1744 d 3-7-1814 m Jane — PS MD
Nathan: b c. 1740 d p. 1800 m Rachel — Cpl PS MD
Nathaniel: b 9-20-1737 d c. 1786 m Elizabeth Owen Pvt PS MD
Samuel Owen: b 10-18-1760 d 1-3-1829 m Elizabeth Hite Pvt MD
Thomas, Sr.: b c. 1731 d 1800 m Elizabeth Luckett PS MD
Zephaniah: b 8-14-1754 d 2-3-1796 m (1)Lucy Beall (2)Margaret Butler CS PS MD

O'FLYING,
Patrick: b 1750 d 10-7-1821 m — QMSgt NH ★

OGBURNE,
John: b 1740 d p. 1785 m Selah Tomlinson PS NC

OGDEN,
Aaron: b 12-3-1756 d 4-19-1839 m Elizabeth Chetwood ADC Bgd-Maj NJ
Aaron: b 7-9-1754 d p. 1787 m Esther Preston Pvt PA
Abraham: b 1728 d 5-11-1790 m Susanna — LCol NJ
Benjamin: b 4-16-1764 d 11-20-1834 m Nancy Puckett Pvt NJ ★
Daniel, Sr.: b c. 1710 d p. 1790 m Mercy Marshall Pvt NY
Daniel, Jr.: b 1734 d 11-30-1819 m Eleanor Scoutan 2Lt NY
Daniel: b 9-12-1763 d 2-18-1835 m Phebe Lindsey Pvt NY
David: b 10-14-1760 d 8-23-1828 m Sally Perry Pvt CT
David: b 10-26-1726 d 11-28-1801 m Hannah Woodruff Pvt NJ
David, Jr.: b 1742 d 1790 m Mary Wilkinson PS NJ
David: b 1764 d 10-30-1840 m Susanna Goodrich Pvt NY
Eleazer: b 3-23-1751 d 6-15-1826 m Jemima Harrison MM NJ
Gabriel: b 1730/1 d 12-26-1815 m (1)Mary Shotwell (2)Elizabeth Kinney Pvt NJ
James: b 1-12-1753 d 7-21-1822 m (1)Deborah Church (2)Ruth Ogden Capt NJ
Jason: b c. 1764 d p. 8-10-1801 m Joanna Davis Sol NJ
Jedediah: b 2-17-1750 d 9-5-1840 m (1)Ruth Stratton (2)Mary Whitaker (3)Mrs Judith Harris Sol NJ ★
John: b 1740 d 8-7-1810 m Phebe Howard Pvt NJ
John, Jr.: b 1750 d 2-4-1814 m Deborah Burrows Pvt NJ
John: b 1-12-1755 d 6-27-1832 m Abigail Bennett Pvt NJ
John: b 1753 d 1777 m Nancy — Pvt VA
Joseph: b 2-21-1755 d 7-23-1823 m Rachel Andrus SgtMaj CT
Joseph: b 7-14-1748 d 1826 m Rhoda Baker MM NJ
Joseph: b 7-1-1763 d 5-6-1817 m (1)Comfort Price (2)Mehitable Smith Pvt NJ
Lewis: b 1730 d 9-18-1798 m Margaret Gouveneur PS NJ
Matthias: b 4-25-1742 d 3-7-1818 m Margaret Magie Pvt NJ
Matthias: b 10-22-1754 d 3-31-1791 m Hannah Dayton BGen NJ
Nathaniel: b — d c. 1810 m Elizabeth Collins QM NJ
Richard: b 1760 d 1850 m Lucy Vibbard Pvt NY
Robert, Sr.: b 10-7-1716 d 1-21-1787 m Phoebe Hatfield PS NJ
Robert, Jr.: b 3-23-1746 d 2-14-1826 m (1)Sarah Platt (2)Hannah Platt Cmsry QM NJ
Thomas: b 1720 d 12-23-1785 m (1)Sarah Harris (2)Violetta Harris (3)Mrs Sarah (Austin)(Stratton) Westcott CS NJ

OGIER, (includes OGEAR)
Abraham: b 1723 d 1798 m Mary Cooper Pvt ME
Lewis: b 10-28-1760 d 1-30-1849 m Lucy Thorndike Fif MA
Louis: b 7-16-1726 d 10-8-1780 m Catherine Crewze Capt SC

OGILVIE,
James: b c. 1750 d p. 4-4-1805 m Penelope Parrott Cav SC
Kimbrough Tinsley: b 1-14-1763 d 11-14-1842 m Nancy Harris Pvt NC ★
Thomas: b 9-22-1740 d 10-22-1842 m Jane Taylor Pvt VA

OGLE,
Alexander: b 1726 d 3- -1783 m Marth Ogle PS DE
Benjamin: b 1-13-1747 d 1790 m Rebecca Stilley Maj MD
Benjamin: b 2-7-1749 d 7-9-1806 m (2)Henrietta Margaret Hill PS MD
Hercules: b 4-6-1731 d 1804 m Mary Carson PS VA
James: b 6-1-1753 d p. 1780 m Mary Briggs Capt MD
Joseph: b 6-17-1741 d 2-21-1821 m (1)Drusilla Biggs (2)Jemima Meiggs Capt VA
Thomas: b c. 1749 d p. 1790 m Jane Miller Pvt PA
Wm.: b 4-10-1751 d 1810 m Mary Cresap Pvt PA

OGLEBY,
James: b 1755 d 5-21-1808 m Sarah Crispin 2Lt MD

OGLESBY, (includes OGELSBY, OGILBY)
Elisha: b 12-29-1758 d 3-2-1833 m (1)Mary Bryan (2)Miss Rogers Pvt VA
Jacob: b a. 1734 d 1813 m Mildred (Martin) Clark PS CS VA
Jesse: b 1762 d 3-23-1852 m Celia Witt Pvt VA ★
John: b 10-18-1747 d 4-16-1809 m Anne Thornton 1Lt VA
Richard: b c. 1740 d c. 1811 m Susan — Sol VA
Sabred: b c. 1727 d 4-19-1831 m — Lindsey Gnr Matr SC
Thomas: b c. 1750 d c. 1832 m Martha Bradley Pvt GA
Wm.: b — d 12-28-1802 m Ann Perkins PS VA
Wm.: b 8-22-1751 d 1824 m Martha Ellis 1Lt VA

OGLETREE,
Wm.: b 1-18-1765 d 7-29-1835 m Mary Bird Sol GA

OGSBURY,
John David: b 9-22-1761 d 11-22-1836 m Nancy Apple Pvt NY

O'HAIR,
Michael: b 9-11-1749 d 1813 m (1)Elinor Hawkins (2)Elizabeth Tribett Pvt VA

O'HARA,
Hugh: b 1748 d 1784 m (2)Margaret (Riley) McCombs Pvt PA
James: b 2-10-1750 d 4-14-1813 m Ann Gordon PS SC
James: b 1754 d 12-21-1819 m Mary Carson Asst QMGen VA
Wm.: b 1750 d 1817 m Rebecca Foy Pvt SC

OHL,
Adam: b 1748 d 1788 m Maria Christina Mangolt Pvt PA
Henry: b 12-9-1753 d 3-20-1840 m Margaret Dorothy Sittsman Lt PA ★
Henry: b 3-21-1762 d 9-7-1849 m Abby Lark Pvt PA
Michael, Sr.: b 6-26-1729 d 7-4-1804 m Elizabeth Barbara (Gucker) Capt PS PA
Michael, Jr.: b 1750 d 1823 m Catherine Mosser Pvt PA

OHLEN,
Henry George: b 9-16-1758 d 10-1-1837 m Catherine Henry OrdlSgt NY ★

O'KELLEY,
Charles: b c. 1756 d a. 11- -1810 m Mary Crowder Pvt VA
James: b c. 1734 d 10-16-1826 m Elizabeth Meeks PS Pvt PA

OKELY,
John: b 5-26-1721 d 5-15-1792 m Mary (Okely) PS DepQMGen PA

OKESON,
Nicholas A.: b 3-8-1758 d 4-14-1842 m Susan Silverthorn Pvt Tms Wgm NJ ★

OLCOTT,
Benjamin: b 1732 d 9-26-1813 m Naomi Cumstock Pvt NH
Ezekiel: b 9-19-1735 d 9- -1809 m Dorcas Lyman Capt CT
Hezekiah: bpt 9-30-1759 d 9-17-1825 m Mary Ellis Harris Lt CT
Isaac: b 1762 d 4-23-1834 m Mrs Smith Pvt CT ★
James, Jr.: b 3-20-1740 d 1818 m (1)Mary Rossiter (2)Chloe Wilcox Humphrey Sol CT
Jared: b 7-22-1759 d 7-23-1846 m (1)Mary Cadwell (2)Abigail (Bailey) Smith Pvt CT ★
John Easton: b 7-24-1749 d p. 1790 m Hannah Sands Mar Pvt CT
Josiah, Jr.: b 10-30-1749 d p. 1805 m Mary Babcock Pvt CT
Thomas, Jr.: b 1722/3 d 1788 m Peobe — Pvt MA
Timothy: b 10-11-1739 d 6-24-1832 m Elizabeth Chandler PS CS VT

OLDENBERGH,
Daniel Frederic Augustus: b 1740 d 12- -1786 m Lawyersuyler Dr PA

OLDERFER, (includes ALDERFER)
Jacob: b 1-5-1739 d 7-16-1797 m Elizabeth Kolb Pvt PA
John: b 2-8-1745 d 12-19-1820 m Elizabeth Rosenberger Pvt PA

OLDFIELD,
Wm.: b 2-21-1750 d p. 11-13-1837 m (1)Mary — (2)Elizabeth Taylor Pvt NY ★

OLDHAM,
Daniel: b 1748 d 1808 m Desire Ransom Pvt MA
Edward: b 12-8-1756 d 11-4-1798 m Mary Ensor Capt MD
George: b 1750 d 3-30-1840 m Susannah Hensley 1Maj NC ★
George: b c. 1755 d 1789/90 m — 1Lt VA
Isaac: b c. 1739 d 1821 m (2)Sarah Anderson Pvt PA
Jesse: b c. 1733 d 1814 m Elizabeth Simpson PS KY
John: b 1754 d 6-19-1832 m Elizabeth Chandler Sgt MA
John: b 11-10-1757 d 11-17-1831 m Annis Rice Capt NC Heirs ★
Moses: b c. 1750 d p. 1810 m (1)Mary Rice (2)Mrs Nancy Freeman Sol NC
Richard: b 5-4-1763 d 6-17-1836 m (1)Ursula Williams (2)Patsy Reed Pvt NC ★
Richard: b 3-1-1745 d 4-20-1834 m Annie Pepper Pvt NC ★
Samuel: b 11-31-1749 d 1-31-1823 m (1)Jane Cunningham (2)Ann Lipscomb Smn VA
Thomas: b 8-26-1752 d 4-20-1788 m Hannah Jones Pvt PA
Wm.: b 6-17-1753 d 11-4-1791 m Penelope Pope Capt VA
Wm.: b 11-3-1728 d 6-6-1799 m Anne Howe Ens VA

OLDS, (includes OLD)
Aaron: b 5-28-1751 d 10-19-1825 m Eunice Durkee Pvt CT ★
Benjamin: b 1-21-1732/3 d 4-29-1813 m Via Smith MM Pvt MA
Caleb: b — d p. 1-20-1791 m Anne Tooley Lt VA
Comfort, Sr.: b 5-24-1724 d 7-29-1779 m Abigail Barnes Pvt MA
Daniel: b 4-5-1759 d 9-16-1836 m Lois Stanley Sgt CT ★
Ezekiel: b 5-21-1727 d 3-26-1777 m Elizabeth Gilbert PS MA
Ezra: b 5-25-1747 d 1815 m (1)Sarah Dougherty (2)Mary Thompson Pvt MA
George: b 6-24-1750 d 8-8-1844 m Lucy Ormsby Sgt Sct CS CT ★
Gilbert: b 5-22-1755 d 1835 m Esther Noble Pvt Wgn MA ★
John: b 5-31-1755-57 d 3-10-1825 m Lucretia Clark Pvt VT ★
Jonathan: b 10-19-1726 d 1779/80 m Hannah Jones Pvt MA
Joseph: b 10-19-1761 d 8- -1844 m Bethia Marsh Cpl MA
Josiah: b 3-6-1743 d p. 1790 m Dorothy Smith Pvt MA
Justin: b 8-16-1754 d 4-26-1819 m Mehitable Hixon Pvt MA
Moses: b c. 1755 d 1830 m Keziah Shaw Pvt MA

Reuben: b 10-20-1760 d 8-9-1840 m Azubah Walker Pvt MA ★
Samuel: b 4-1-1747 d p. 1832 m Elizabeth — Cpl MA
Samuel: b 12-29-1748 d 7-8-1813-5 m Persis Rice Pvt MA
Silas: b 11- -1751 d p. 1800 m Hannah Dodge Pvt MA
Thaddeus: b 7-11-1763 d 4-16-1842 m Henlena Mather Sol VT
Thomas, Sr.: b c. 1720 d p. 10-10-1779 m Mary Buck PS VA
Wm.: b 9-6-1714 d 1-22-1805 m Damaria Gilbert Pvt MA

OLDWEILER,
Jacob: b 1739 d 1792 m Anna Leidich Pvt PA

OLENDORF,
Daniel: b c. 1755 d 5-14-1830 m Catharine Hilton Sct NY

OLIN,
Caleb: b 12-8-1753 d 8-7-1838 m Freelove Mitchell Ens VT ★
Gideon: b 10-22-1743 d 1-21-1823 m (1)Patience Dwinell (2)Lydia Myers Pope Maj VT
Giles: b 3-23-1745 d 9-1-1835 m Anna Reynolds Pvt VT
John, Sr.: b 1712 d 9-24-1797 m Susannah Pierce PS RI VT
John, Jr.: b 9-17-1741 d 9-24-1821 m Sarah Card Pvt VT
Jonathan, Sr.: b 6-17-1737 d 1-9-1826 m Anne Gardiner Pvt PS RI
Justin: b 7-17-1739 d 7-7-1821 m Sarah Dwinell Pvt VT

OLINGER,
Christopher: b 2-18-1737 d 2-20-1827 m Eva Margaret Saylor Sol VA
Philip: b c. 1721 d 1787 m Juliana — PS VA

OLIPHANT, (includes OLYPHANT)
Andrew: b c. 1735 d 9-19-1790 m Ann Hughes Sgt PA
David: b 1720 d 4-2-1805 m Ann Vernon PS SC
John: b 1-2-1750 d 1823 m (1)Sarah Pruden (2)Hannah Amos Wgm NJ
John: b 1747 d 10- -1815 m Nancy Ann Frazier Sol SC
Jonathan: b 11-10-1739 d 9-21-1804 m Mary Shinn Capt NJ

OLIVE,
James: b 1723/5 d 1805 m Elizabeth — Pvt NC
John: b c. 1754 d 2-12-1823 m Rachel Partridge Pvt NC

OLIVER,
Alexander: b 10- -1752 d 9-9-1831 m Zeruiah Rice QM MA ★
Alexander: b 11-30-1744 d 9-2-1828 m Mary Warner Lt MA
Alexander: b 1736 d 1816 m Mary Slaughter Pvt SC
Andrew: b a. 1719 d p. 1777 m Ann Brodhead PS NY
Daniel: b 4-4-1753 d 9-14-1840 m Elizabeth Kemble PS MA
David: b 1747 d 3-3-1821 m Elizabeth Boyd MM Sgt MA
Dionysius, Sr.: b 1735 d 1808 m (1)Mary Anne Winfrey (2)Susan Jackson Sol CS GA
Douglas: b 1753-63 d 2-11-1843 m (1)Milly Carnalle (2)Katherine Durrett Pvt VA
Francis: b c. 1740 d 1808 m Sarah Barrow Pvt NC
George: b 1760 d 10-24-1844 m — Pvt NC ★
Henry: b 4-30-1758 d 10-31-1835 m Rebecca McKenny Pvt MA
James: b 2-26-1731 d 2-11-1786 m Mary Buchanan Lt PA
James: b c. 1760 d c. 1802/3 m Mary — Pvt PS SC
James B.: b 4-2-1757 d 4-20-1846 m Jane Spinney Pvt MA ★
James Brush: b 1752 d p. 1834 m Sara McKay Cpl SC ★
John: b 9-10-1763 d — m Milbrey Scott Sol GA
John: b c. 1718 d 12-23-1811 m Lucy — Capt MA
John: b 1-15-1756 d 5-6-1806 m Mary Spinney Pvt MA
John: b 9-5-1761 d p. 8- -1832 m Mary Linnen Pvt MM MA ★
John: b 4-22-1758 d 9-22-1831 m (1)Sarah Pruden (2)Mary Ayers Capt NJ
John: b 9-22-1733 d 4-7-1824 m Mary Carman QM NJ
John: b — d 1791 m Ellen — Pvt NY
John: b 10-6-1738 d 5- -1815 m Maritie Sixberry Pvt NY
John: b 1-12-1762 d 1845 m (1)Mary Hewitt (2)Amey Jones 2Sgt NC
John: b 11-4-1751 d 2-9-1841 m Margaret Lyon Pvt PA
John: b c. 1750 d a. 1840 m Elsie Wade Pvt PA
John: b 1756 d 1-10-1834 m Elizabeth — Pvt VA ★
John: b 1757 d 7-30-1839 m Lucy George Pvt VA
Jonathan: b 11-18-1752 d 6-19-1836 m Silence Bates Pvt MA ★
Joseph: b 1761 d p. 1803 m Catherine — Pvt NJ
Moses: b 1753 d 1790-5 m Lois Wiswell Humphrey Sgt MA
Nicholas: b 11-4-1750 d 6-21-1820 m Anna McKenney Sgt MA ★
Rhesa: b 1756 d 1841 m Mary — Pvt NC ★
Richard: b 2-22-1752 d 11-1-1806 m Catherine Cole Lt PM NY
Richard: b 12-20-1752 d 12-28-1847 m Hannah Conkwright Pvt NC ★
Robert: b 1738 d p. 5-9-1811 m Molly Walker Brev LCol MA
Robert: b — d p. 8-31-1795 m Lydia Gray Sgt MA
Samuel: b 1732 d 8-16-1811 m (1)Sarah Primrose (2)Mary — (3)Mrs Deacon Capt NJ
Samuel: b 9-15-1757 d 6-3-1819 m Lydia — Pvt DE
Stephen: b 1760 d 1857 m (1)Elizabeth Cochran (2)Polly Gracy Sct PA
Thomas: bpt 10-26-1729 d p. 1-1-1800 m Mary Jarvis Pvt MA
Thomas: b c. 1755 d 10-24-1811 m (1)Euphemia Williams (2)Ann Durand PS NC
Thomas: bpt 11-11-1750 d 1790 m Elizabeth Snistrunk Pvt SC

Wm.: b 4-2-1756 d 4-8-1847 m Elizabeth Young Sgt ME
Wm., Sr.: b 1720 d 1782 m Rebecca Sale Pvt MA
Wm., Jr.: b 7-10-1744 d 6-22-1831 m (1)Susanna Sigourney (2)Mary Ann Sigourney 2Lt MA
Wm.: b 1729 d p. 1779 m Hannah Skinner Pvt NH
Wm.: b 1754 d 1830 m Mary Jennings Capt VA
Wm.: b c. 1754 d p. 9-3-1796 m Sarah Holladay Cpl VA

OLIVIER,
Charles Honore: b 6-8-1751 d 4-24-1815 m Marie Madeline Phillipe de Marigny de Mandeville PS LA
Nicholas: b 5-27-1757 d 7-18-1813 m (1)Eulalie Toutant Beauregard (2)Maria Marianne Bienvue PS LA

OLLIFF,
John Shears: b 1752 d a. 12-2-1801 m Johannah Jackson Pvt SC

OLMSTEAD, (includes OLMSTED)
Aaron: b 5-19-1753 d 9-9-1806 m Mary L. Bigelow Maj CT
Abijah: b 8-1-1757 d 2-8-1823 m Miriam Howe Pvt CT
Asahel: b 12- -1749 d 4-28-1804 m Naomi Loomis Sol CT
Ashbel: b 6-15-1763 d 10-6-1847 m Rachel Lusk Pvt CT ★
Daniel, Sr.: b 1731 d 9- -1812 m (1)Anna Cadwell (2)Rachel Hubbard Pvt CT
Daniel, Jr.: b 8- -1749 d 8-11-1836 m Rosanna Tuller Sgt CT
Daniel: b 9-22-1731 d 2-7-1806 m Elizabeth Northrup Grd CT
David: b 11-20-1748 d 2-8-1815 m Abigail Ingersoll Capt CT
David: b 5-10-1755 d 6-11-1824 m Mary Whitlock Capt CT
David: b c. 1745 d 11-29-1829 m Sarah Waller Sgt CT
Ebenezer: bpt 1748 d 7-19-1801 m Esther Ingersol Lt CT
Ebenezer: b c. 1736 d 7-19-1804 m — Pvt NY
Elijah: b 5-1-1743 d p. 1814 m Sarah Terry Lt CT
Elijah: b 4-3-1749 d 9-22-1822 m Sarah Lyon Pvt CT
Ezekiel: b 1730 d p. 1790 m Lydia Hoyt Pvt CT
Francis C.: b 1760 d 1-21-1828 m Chloe Case Pvt CT ★
Gamaliel: b 6-12-1760 d 7-3-1832 m (1)Esther Goodwin (2)Mrs Elizabeth Downer Baker Pvt CT ★
Hezekiah: b 12-16-1750 d p. 1790 m Sarah Gale Cpl CT
Ichabod: b 9-12-1725 d 11-6-1799 m Dorothy Bates PS Cmsry CT
Isaac: b 1745 d 3-27-1825 m Rebecca Forbes Cpl CT
Isaac: b 1-23-1759 d 12-31-1797 m (1)Mary Parsons (2)Sarah Lyon Pvt CT W★
Israel: b 3-24-1716 d c. 1806 m (1)Sarah Bannister (2)Anna Safford Pvt NH
Jabez: b 7-29-1735 d 12- -1777 m Elizabeth — Sgt MA
Jabish: b 1754 d 1813 m Martha Chapman Sol NH
James: b 5-13-1751 d 9-21-1811 m Mary Beaumont Lt CT
Jared: b 7-1-1753 d 5-28-1825 m Hannah Betts Ens CT
Jeremiah: b 1756 d 1816 m Rachel Darling Pvt CT
John: b 1731 d 3-29-1809 m Abigail Lyon Ens CT
Jonathan: b 9-20-1740 d 1835 m Sarah Stanley Pvt CT
Jonathan: b 7-20-1744 d 2-7-1797 m Thankful Crosby Sgt NY
Joseph: b 6-30-1758 d 12-30-1851 m Susan Covit Pvt CT ★
Joseph: b 5-5-1705 d 9-30-1775 m Martha White CS CT
Joseph: b 1745 d 1804 m Sarah Wood 2Lt MA
Lemuel: b 1761/2 d 5-28-1805 m Silence Weed Pvt CT
Matthew: b 3-7-1760 d 2-16-1847 m Sarah Whitney Pvt CT ★
Moses: bpt 4-28-1751 d 1776 m Patty DeForest Cpl CT
Moses: b 1-29-1736 d p. 1790 m Abigail Elwell Lt VT
Nathan: b 11-14-1748 d a. 4- -1802 m Mary Middlebrook Sol CT
Nathan: b 3-7-1716 d 7-30-1805 m (1)Millicent Goodrich (2)Mrs Sarah Smith CS CT
Nathan: b 5-8-1744 d 12-7-1827 m (1)Sarah Ambler (2)Mrs Lorina (Brush) Hoyt (3)Sarah Ann Bush PS Pvt NY
Nathaniel: b 7-19-1751 d 6-9-1792 m (1)Thankful Huntington (2)Eunice Kingsbury Pvt CT
Richard: b c. 1735 d — m Eunice Noble Pvt CT
Roswell: b 3-17-1734 d 2-15-1800 m Elizabeth Stanley Cpl CT
Samuel: b 9-13-1737 d 6-6-1823 m Esther Roberts Ens CT
Samuel: b 8-12-1747 d 8-15-1829 m (1)Ann Dunning (2)Mrs Susanna Fitch Mead Ens CT
Samuel: b 3-27-1715 d 6-10-1788 m Abiah Smith PS CT
Silas: b 2-18-1732 d 4-13-1782 m (1)Abigail DeForest (2)Lydia Sloan Pvt CT
Simeon: b 9-21-1748 d 12-22-1803 m Roxalana Abbe CS CT
Stephen: b 3-20-1720 d 3-9-1814 m (1)Hannah Northrop (2)Abigail Sprague Sol CT
Stephen: b 8-17-1721 d 4-26-1778 m Hannah Fuller Pvt CT
Stephen: b 1742 d 9-9-1776 m Jane — Pvt CT
Stephen, Jr.: b c. 1760 d 9-9-1831 m Jerusha Meacham Pvt MA
Stephen: b 3-8-1748 d 12-25-1836 m Lucy Hatch Pvt NY
Timothy: b 11-19-1743 d 11-20-1812 m Susannah Hillman Cpl NH
Wm.: b 4-5-1750 d 11-30-1812 m Prudence — Pvt CT

OLNEY,
Charles, Sr.: b c. 1751 d 1790 m Phebe Sheldon Capt RI
Charles, Jr.: b 1747 d 1824/5 m Zerviah Olney Ens Lt RI
Christopher: b 12-24-1745 d — m Jemima Potter Capt RI
Ezekiel: b 1740 d 10-21-1826 m (1)Mary Warner (2)Lydia Brown Ens Lt Capt RI
Gideon: b 6-28-1729 d 1798 m Abigail — PS RI
Ithamer: b 1762-5 d 1830 m Anna Cady Pvt CT
James: b 10-5-1761 d 10-11-1840 m Olive Belknap Pvt RI

John B.: b 6-22-1747 d 9-7-1797 m Lydia Steere Capt RI
Joseph: b 7-14-1737 d 1814 m Ann Paget NCapt
Peter: b 11-21-1750 d 2-16-1834 m Tabatha Clark Pvt CT MA W★
Stephen: b 10-12-1755 d 11-23-1832 m Dorcas Smith Capt CT
Stephen: b 12-22-1752 d 12-12-1841 m Martha Aldrich Capt RI

OLP,
Ernst: b 4-3-1728 d 4-12-1798 m Catharine Elisabeth Emig Pvt PA
John: b 1762 d 1842 m Mary Creveling Drm NJ

OMAN,
George: b — d p. 5-5-1790 m Mary — Sgt PA
Henry: b 1742 d 3-4-1800 m Rebecca Marshall Pvtr RI

OMANS,
Thomas: b 4-7-1759 d 5-27-1841 m (2)Mary Peet Sgt MA

OMER,
Daniel: b 1758 d 1835 m (1)Ann Sellinger (2)Elizabeth Meyer Sol PA

OMEY,
John: b 1753/4 d 4-27-1825 m Hannah Clark Pvt MA ★

OMOHUNDRO,
Richard: b c. 1733 d 1811 m Elizabeth Muse Ens VA

ONDERDONK, (includes ONDERDONCK)
Abraham: b 5-9-1743 d 11-25-1823 m Easter Palmer Pvt NY
Abraham: b 5-9-1743 d 10-28-1776 m Femmetje Onderdonk Lt NY
Adriaen: b 1762 d 1-2-1794 m Maria Hegeman PS NY
Adrian: b 2-25-1732 d 10-12-1818 m Willemtje Eckerson Pvt NY
Adrian: b 5-3-1742 d c. 1795 m Nieltje Snedeker Pvt NY
Andries, Sr.: b 1707 d 3-17-1790 m (1)Marretje Remsen (2)Willemyetje VanHouten PS NY
Andries, Jr.: b 4-17-1747 d 9-1-1834 m (1)Wilhelmina Steeveesen (2)Mrs Crawford 2Lt NY
Daniel: b 2-7-1747 d 7-28-1828 m Maria Concklin Lt PS NY
Hendrick: b 12-11-1724 d 3-31-1809 m Femmetie Tredwell PS NY
James: b 7-24-1752 d 8-16-1806 m Rachel Palmer Sgt Maj NY
John: b 9-9-1749 d 2-9-1846 m Margaret VanHouten Pvt NY
Roelof: b 10-29-1739 d p. 1790 m (1)Sara — (2)Annetje Lyons Pvt NY
Thomas: b 1760 d 10-10-1801 m Sarah VanHouten Pvt NY ★

O'NEAL, (includes ONEAL, O'NEALE, O'NEALL, O'NEIL, O'NEILE, O'NEILL)
Barnet: b c. 1751 d 11-29-1777-79 m — PS VA
Barton: b 2-22-1758 d 10-1-1830 m Mary Dyson PS MD
Constantine: b 1753 d 9-16-1834 m Catharine Shepherd Pvt PA
George: b 4-16-1755 d 10-30-1836 m Elizabeth Singleton Pvt VA ★
Henry: b 1750 d 7-30-1835 m Hannah (O'Neil) Pvt NJ ★
John: b 1745 d p. 1815 m Mary Smith Pvt MD
John: b 1719 d 4- -1785 m Margaret — Pvt MD
John: b 1755 d 10-3-1826 m Margaret Osborne Pvt NJ
John: b 1739 d 1-18-1796 m Susannah Johnston Sol PA
John: b c. 1740 d c. 1810 m Mary Mansfield Sol PA
John: b c. 1745 d p. 12-15-1819 m Mrs Ursula Mikell McIntosh Cmsry SC
John: b 1744 d a. 6-14-1832 m (1)— (2)Fannie Hall (3)Margaret Mills Pvt VA
John: b 1760 d 11-7-1832 m Phoebe Scott Pvt VA ★
Timothy: b c. 1756 d 1819 m Mary Highduck Sgt PA
Wm.: b c. 1740 d 2-13-1812 m (1)Sarah Young (2)Sarah (Beall) Adams PS Pvt MD
Wm.: b 11-5-1734 d 11-5-1786 m Mary Frost PS SC
Wm.: b 1760 d 5- -1778 m Sarah — Pvt VA

ONG,
Jacob: b 1-24-1760 d 1847 m Mary McGrew Sol PA

ONION,
Elihu: b 4-19-1760 d 6-15-1848 m Catherine Fisher Pvt MA
Joseph: b 11-17-1755 d 12-6-1792 m Anna Fuller Pvt MA
Zaccheus Barrett: b 1743 d 1781 m Hannah Bond Capt MD

ONSTOTT,
George: b c. 1742 d 1-15-1827 m Mary R. — Pvt VA

ONTHANK,
Wm., Sr.: b 1727 d 5-22-1807 m Elizabeth — 1Lt MA
Wm., Jr.: b 7-1-1757 d 1-6-1820 m Mittie Newton Pvt MA

OOTHOUT,
Abraham: b 1744 d p. 1-12-1811 m (1)Margaret Lansing (2)Lana (Lansing) Zabriski Capt NY
Henry: bpt 5-16-1742 d 5-27-1818 m Lydia Douw Pvt NY

OPIE,
Lindsey: b 1-11-1740 d 1785 m (2)Elizabeth McAdam PS CS VA

OPP,
John Jacob: b 12-14-1740 d 4-16-1805 m Anna Maria Hoffman CS PA

O'QUINN,
Daniel: b 1746 d 9-10-1824 m Elizabeth Singleton Pvt MD
John: b 6-13-1754 d 1-6-1836 m Rhoda Horton Pvt NC

ORAM, (includes ORIM)
Cooper: b 7-13-1759 d 5-7-1832 m Abigail — Pvt PA ★
Robert: b 1761 d 1818 m Jennie — Pvt NY

ORBISON,
John: b 3-27-1750 d 11-22-1821 m Elizabeth Lloyd 1Lt PA
Thomas: b 9-23-1747 d 10-2-1784 m Elizabeth Bailey Capt PA

ORCHARD,
Thomas: b 1760 d 3-26-1844 m Sarah Norman Pvt PA ★

ORCUTT,
Caleb: b 8-19-1743 d 11-7-1804 m Chloe Parker Sgt CT
Daniel, Sr.: b 11-3-1734 d c. 1802 m (1)Lydia Cushman (2)Mary Hurlburt PS CT
Daniel, Jr.: b 2-15-1764 d 11-13-1842 m Betsey Wood PS CT
David: b — d 1790 m (1)Susannah Packard (2)Sarah — (3)Abigail Shaw PS CT
Ephraim: b 6-6-1754 d 11-20-1836 m (1)Olive Lincoln (2)Ruth Worrock Pvt MA
James: b 1-17-1754 d 9-4-1804 m Deborah Cady Cpl MA W★
Job: b 6- -1751 d 12-26-1825 m Mary McClellan Capt PS CT
John: b 1758 d 11-25-1830 m Irene Wales Pvt MA
Moses: b 1-7-1760 d 11-18-1828 m (2)Meribah Jordan Pvt MA
Samuel: b a. 1757 d p. 1780 m Amy Johnson Fif CT
Samuel: b 8-26-1754 d 4-16-1848 m (1)Hepzibah Smith (2)Mary Wood Pvt MA ★
Samuel: b 3-6-1756 d 3-20-1815 m Elsie Brown 2Cpl NH
Solomon: b 1730 d 2-26-1826 m Mary Rockwell 1Lt CT
Stephen: b 5-19-1757 d 3-27-1841 m Molly Washburn Pvt CT ★
Stephen: b 1755 d 1821 m Theodora Scott Pvt MA

ORD,
Robert: b a. 1750 d 3-15-1781 m Ann Leith Pvt VA

ORDWAY,
Enoch: b c. 1760 d p. 1830 m Sarah Abbott Pvt NH
John: b 12-26-1760 d 9-3-1832 m (1)Polly Chase (2)Sarah Rogers Pvt MA★
John: bpt 1-27-1734 d p. 1793 m Mehitable Holms Pvt NH
John: b 9-27-1736 d 4-13-1827 m Mary — PS NH
Nehemiah: b 2-28-1743 d 5- -1836 m Sarah Brown MM MA
Samuel: b 2-10-1763 d 11-20-1841 m Mehitable Silver Pvt NH

O'REAR,
Daniel: b 1758/9 d p. 1839 m Susan Gouch OrdlSgt NC VA ★
John: b 3-21-1749 d p. 8-26-1824 m Sarah — OrdlSgt VA

ORENDORFF, (includes ORNDORF, OHRENDORF, OHRENDORPH, ORENDORF, ORNDORFF)
Christian, 3d: b c. 1750 d 10-1-1824 m Anna Marie Stille Capt MD ★
Christian: b 11-15-1726 d 12-10-1797 m Elizabeth Hoffman 2Maj MD
Christopher: b 11-23-1752 d 9-14-1823 m Mary Thomas 1Lt MD
Frederick, Jr.: b 1758 d 1830 m Lany Fulmer Pvt NY
Lorentz: b 1737 d 1820 m Caroline — Pvt PA

ORGAN,
Cornelius: b 1761 d 10-5-1818 m Rachel Barrett Pvt VA
Isaac: b 1761 d 5-29-1831 m Elizabeth Hallowell DrmMaj MA ★
John: b c. 1735 d 10- -1781 m — Pvt PA
Matthew: b 1758 d 1826 m Mary — Pvt PA ★

ORHENBAUM,
Ludwig: b 1756 d 1818 m Eva Barbara — Pvt PA

ORLOPE, (or ORELUP)
Henry: b c. 1750-9 d p. 1796 m Polly Rino Pvt NY

ORLTON,
Hugh: b c. 1740 d c. 1820 m Rachel Orlton Pvt PA

ORME,
Archibald: b 6-4-1730 d 5-9-1812 m Elizabeth Johns Col MD
Moses, Jr.: b — d 1782 m (1)Verlinda Taylor (2)Priscilla Taylor PS MD
Robert: b 8-12-1744 d 9-13-1820 m Priscilla Edmonston PS MD
Samuel Taylor: b 1750 d 1817 m Martha Ransom Pvt MD

ORMES,
Jonathan: b 10-20-1764 d 8-8-1850 m (1)Eunice Hine (2)Mrs Annah Doyle Gaines (3)Lura Lyman Weston Pvt CT ★

ORMOND, (includes ORMAND)
Benjamin: b 4-22-1745 d 9-2-1829 m Mary Price PS NC
Wm.: b 12-8-1738 d 3- -1815 m Annie Watkins Pvt PS NC

ORMSBEE, (includes ORMSBY)
Abraham, Sr.: b 1-26-1725 d a. 9-7-1802 m Sibbel Cummings Pvt MA

Abraham, Jr.: b 3-20-1759 d a. 11-9-1826 m Bette Perry Pvt MA
Caleb: b 7-24-1763 d 10-31-1812 m Belinda Kingsley Pvt MA
Daniel: b 9-12-1723 d c. 1793 m Keziah Cummings Pvt MA
Daniel: b 11-23-1761 d 11-1-1840 m Hannah Raymond Pvt VT
Ezra: b 1734 d 3-23-1796 m (2)Esther (Smith) Goff Capt RI
Gideon: b 9-24-1736 d 1-21-1804 m Mercy — Maj VT
Isaac: b 6-21-1763 d 10-13-1848 m Patience Chase Pvt RI ★
John: b 3-16-1733 d 6-19-1819 m Sarah Jolls Lt Smn RI CT
John: b 1720 d 12-19-1805 m Jane McAllister PS PA
Joseph: b 1-25-1765 d 1857 m Deborah Stone Pvt NH ★
Joseph: b 7-5-1759 d 2-28-1813 m Elizabeth Barbour Matr RI
Joshua: b 1733 d 3-6-1813 m Rachel Chase Pvt MA
Nathaniel: b 11-7-1734 d 10-25-1777 m Elizabeth Perkins Pvt MA
Stephen: b 1755 d 11-24-1821 m (1)Jemima Snell (2)Phoebe Calkins Pvt CT ★

ORNE,
Azor: b 7-22-1731 d 6-6-1796 m Mary Coleman PS MA
James, Sr.: b 3-29-1734 d 1-17-1804 m Esther Everett Lt MA
James, Jr.: b 3-29-1761 d 10- -1820 m (1)Chloe Hunt Brown (2)Nancy Williams Pvt MA
John: b 11-14-1756 d p. 1790 m Sarah Ashby Pvt MA
Jonathan: b 3-17-1744 d 3-26-1803 m (1)Priscilla Holdgate (2)Mary Collins Matr MA
Joshua, Jr.: b 8-16-1747 d 1-27-1785 m (1)Susanna Trevitt (2)Mary Lee PS MA

ORR,
Alexander: b 1- -1757 d 2- -1832 m Margaret Ramsey Pvt PA
Arthur: b 1753 d 6-20-1814 m Ann Scott Pvt PA
Charles: b 1745 d 1778 m Mildred Hope Cpl NC
Hugh: b a. 1750 d p. 1779 m Sarah Reid CS NH
James: b 1750 d 1834 m Sarah Catherine Snell Maj NC ★
James: b 6-24-1743 d 3-17-1829 m (1)Sarah McConnell (2)Jane Lemmond Sol NC
James: b 1750 d 1840 m Emily Hannah — Pvt NC
James: b 9-30-1755 d 12-11-1819 m Agnes Walker Pvt NC
James: b 1746 d 1809 m Elizabeth Ann — Pvt VA
Jehu: b 8- -1763 d 3-18-1828 m (2)Jane B. Clinkscales Cav NC
John, Jr.: b c. 1760 d 11- -1828 m (1)Rebecca — (2)Mrs Nancy Orr Sol GA
John: b 1763 d p. 1820 m Ruth Freeman Pvt GA or NC
John, Sr.: b c. 1745 d p. 1782 m — Dale Pvt MD
John, Jr.: b 1762-5 d 4-14-1840 m Elizabeth Johns Pvt MD
John: b 1720 d 9-17-1804 m Elizabeth — Sol MD
John: b — d c. 1810 m Eleanor Dennett 2Mte NS
John: b 11-5-1748 d 12-5-1822 m (1)Jane Smith (2)Sarah Houston Lt NH
John: b 1721 d 3-23-1809 m Jane McConnell CS NH
John: b c. 1748 d p. 1820 m Jerusha Wimpsey Sol NC
John: b 1748 d 1829 m (1)— (2)— Pvt PA
John: b a. 1750 d 1795-1803 m Jennie Henderson Pvt PA
John: b 1763 d p. 9-20-1843 m Margaret Wilson Pvt PS PA
John: b 1744 d 1831 m Sarah Mills Pvt VT
Nathan: b 1730 d p. 1790 m Mary Tassey Pvt NC
Robert: b 8-14-1745 d 1811 m Hannah Kingman Maj MA
Robert: b 1744 d 9-4-1833 m (1)Fannie Culbertson (2)Rachel Chambers Capt PA ★
Robert: b c. 1730 d 1800 m Mrs Margaret (Donaldson) Stewart Pvt PA
Samuel: b 4-17-1759 d 6-8-1817 m Charlotte — Pvt VA
Wm.: b 1761 d 1823 m Katie Walker Sol NC
Wm.: b 6-6-1736 d 1820 m Catharine Smith Sol PA
Wm.: b 9-29-1755 d 8-7-1815 m Mary Bailey PS PA
Wm.: b 1733 d 1814 m Margaret — Pvt PA

ORRICK,
Nicholas: b 5-1-1725 d 2-1-1781 m (1)Hannah Cromwell (2)Mary Bell PS MD

ORSOR, (includes ORSER)
Abraham: b a. 1759 d 10-30-1815 m Phebe — Pvt NY W★
Jonas: b 5-20-1744 d 7-7-1834 m Elizabeth Pugsley Capt NY

ORTES,
Jean Baptiste: b 1737 d 11-25-1814 m Elizabeth Barada PS LA

ORTH,
Adam: b 3-10-1733 d 11-15-1794 m Anna Catharine Kucher CS PA
Balzar, Sr.: b 5-5-1703 d 10-20-1788 m Anna Catherine Roehmer PS PA
Balzar, Jr.: b 7-14-1736 d 10-6-1794 m Rosina Kucher Maj CMman PA
Rosina Kucher: b 3-19-1741 d 4-3-1814 m Balzer Orth PS PA

ORTKIES,
Henry: b — d 1821 m Christina — Pvt VA

ORTON,
Azariah: b 9-25-1757 d 1835 m Sybil Cleveland Pvt CT ★
Azariah: b 3-5-1761 d 11-5-1854 m Abigail Jackson Pvt MA
Darius: b 5-18-1760 d 1835 m — Pvt CT ★
Eliada: b 5-29-1748 d p. 1818 m Lucia Hungerford Pvt CT ★

John: b 3-4-1744 d 4-9-1785 m Remember Landers Lt CT
John: b 1742 d p. 1783 m — Pvt VT
Lemuel, Jr.: b 1760 d 9-30-1832 m Sibbel Peck Pvt CT ★
Roger: b 1740 d 1814 m Esther Avery Cpl MA
Samuel: b 12-27-1759 d p. 1790 m — Pvt CT

ORVIS,
Ambrose: b 1-7-1758 d 8-30-1844 m Rebecca — Pvt MA ★
Eleazer: b 11-11-1719 d 2- -1805 m Hannah North Pvt CT
Gershom: b 5-23-1754 d 3-9-1824 m Asenith Parmeter Pvt NY
Roger: b 1-24-1745 d 7-28-1829 m Ruth Howe Pvt CT ★
Waitstill: b 12-2-1755 d 10-11-1823 m Elizabeth Church Ens VT

ORWIG,
George: b 3-11-1758 d 3-2-1841 m Maria Magdalen Gilbert Pvt PA
Gottfried: b 8-24-1719 d 5-26-1804 m Clara — Pvt PA

OSBORN, (includes OSBORNE, OSBURN)
Abraham: b 4-29-1752 d 2-16-1835 m Elizabeth Pintard Allen Lt
    NJ ★
Abraham: b 1755 d 1843 m Lorhetta Finch Pvt NY ★
Adlai: b 1744 d 12-15-1814 m Margaret Lloyd LCol NC
Alexander: b 1709 d 7-11-1776 m Agnes McWhorter PS Col NC
Asa: b — d — m Susan Clarke Pvt CT
Barzilla: b c. 1750 d 1818 m — Pvt NJ
Bennett: b 2-6-1764 d 12-8-1841 m (1)Letitia Redding (2)Rebecca
    Kirtley Lt NC SC ★
Christopher: b 1732 d p. 1-22-1789 m Sarah McGruder PS NC
Cornelius: b 1753 d 9-24-1810 m Hannah Hedges PS NY
Daniel: b 6-23-1736 d 3-18-1818 m Hannah Ely MM CT
Daniel: b 8-17-1748 d 8-13-1826 m Sarah Perry Cpl MA
David: b 4-26-1746 d 5-26-1786 m Mary Talmadge Pvt CT MA
David, Sr.: b 8-4-1730 d 2-16-1813 m Mary Huntling Pvt NY
David, Jr.: b 8-22-1761 d 2-16-1813 m Lucretia Harris Pvt NY
Eleazer: b 4-11-1739 d 5-2-1830 m Sarah Burr Ens CT
Eliada: b 3-15-1761 d 12-26-1847 m (1)Sally Peck (2)Abigail Marsh
    Pvt CT
Elias, Sr.: b 1723 d 10-30-1807 m (1)Hannah Baldwin Ayers
    (2)Phebe Gray (3)Mary Meeker MM NJ
Elias, Jr.: b 1754 d 1828 m Hannah Hayes Pvt NJ
Enoch: b 1750 d 1818 m Jane Hash Capt VA
Ephraim: b 9-24-1731 d 3-12-1779 m Sarah Fisk Sgt MA
Ephraim, Jr.: b 9-5-1763 d 4-8-1851 m Elizabeth Wright Pvt MA
Ephraim, Jr.: b c. 1750 d 1814 m Lydia Wyman PS CS MA
Ethan: b 8-21-1758 d 5-1-1858 m Elizabeth Riley Sol PS CT
Ezekiel: b 1710/16 d 5-30-1779 m (1)Abigail Watson (2)Sarah
    Parsons Pvt MA
Ezra: b c. 1758 d 12-26-1834 m Abigail — Pvt MA CT ★
George: b 1733 d 4-7-1812 m (1)Sarah Wade (2)Deborah Taylor Pvt
    MA
George Jerry: b 3-15-1732 d 8-5-1808 m (1)Olive Pickering
    (2)Elizabeth Walker Capt NH
Henry: b 10-23-1759 d 10-15-1835 m Elizabeth Hayes Pvt NJ ★
Henry: b 1750 d 2-3-1808 m Betsy Pease Pvt MA
Hugh: b 11-10-1763 d 5-25-1847 m Azuba Wade Mar MA ★
Ichabod: b 1760 d 4-13-1825 m Eliza Drummond Pvt NJ
Isaac: b 8-29-1760 d 10- -1853 m (1)Sarah Clark Woodruff (2)Edna
    Ewart Pvt CT ★
Isaac: b 11-31-1756 d 5-15-1837 m Rebeckah Lathrop Sgt NY
Jabez: b 6-23-1757 d 1799 m Hannah Hibbard Pvt CT
James: b 7-20-1738 d 8-31-1810 m Persis Littlefield Lt MA
James: b 1740 d 1825-30 m Lida — Pvt PA ★
James: b — d p. 4-29-1816 m Mary — Sol VA
Jeremiah: b 12-8-1753 d 11-2-1825 m Ann Sherwood Gnr CT
Jeremiah, Sr.: b a. 1715 d 8-24-1775 m Mercy Baker PS NY
Jeremiah, Jr.: b 3-31-1750 d 5-25-1821 m Mary Parsons PS NY
John: b 1728 d 1-7-1814 m Lois Peck PS CT
John: b 6-24-1756 d 3-28-1843 m Jerusha Talcott Bulkley Pvt CT
John: b 1718 d 9-1-1776 m Puah Howel Pvt NJ
John: b 4-16-1763 d 1854 m Sarah Stewart Pvt VA ★
John B.: b 6-6-1764 d 11-30-1848 m Mary Darby Pvt Sgt NJ
Jonathan: b 4-14-1725 d 1-3-1782 m Elizabeth Dibble Pvt PS NY
Jonathan: b 6- -1737 d 11- -1814 m Mary Miller PS NY
Jonathan Howell: b 1743 d 12-2-1792 m (1)Deborah Hart (2)Margaret
    Simpson Lt NJ
Joseph, 3d: b 8-26-1733 d — m Mary Proctor Pvt MA
Joseph: b 12-7-1718 d 3-21-1797 m (1)Esther Mallery (2)Abigail
    Lyman (3)Elizabeth (Clark) Hull Tomlinson Fif CT
Joseph, Jr.: b 12-7-1747 d 1794 m Sarah Smith Sgt CT
Joseph: b 8-17-1751 d 2-19-1831 m Martha Jewett Pvt MA
Joseph: b 1755 d 10-10-1830 m Rosina Dorch Pvt NJ ★
Joseph: b 6-11-1737 d 9-26-1786 m Martha Wright Capt NY
Joseph: b 8-11-1754 d 8-11-1844 m Polly Mulford Pvt NY
Joseph: b 1704 d 11-21-1786 m Hannah Hedges PS NY
Joshua: b 2- -1758 d 9-27-1837 m Diana Warner Pvt CT ★
Josiah: b 4-22-1761 d 8-25-1816 m Hannah Scott Pvt CT ★
Josiah: b 2-20-1746 d 8-27-1830 m Hephzibah Olmsted Pvt MA
Levi: b 6- -1762 d 3-8-1852 m Miriam Dibble Pvt CT ★
Lewis: b 5-20-1747 d 9-14-1783 m Jerushia Gardiner PS NY
Lot: b 4-23-1744 d 1819 m Thankful Doolittle Pvt CT
Nathaniel: b 11-10-1754 d 12-15-1810 m Elizabeth Hawley Sgt CT
Richard: b c. 1752 d 12-12-1837 m Isabel Jones Pvt MA ★
Richard: b 1-24-1714 d p. 4-28-1792 m Phoebe Pearsall PS NJ

Samuel, Jr.: b 2-2-1746 d 2-9-1817 m Hepsibah Scoville Capt CT
Samuel: b 3-5-1738 d 12-21-1776 m Elizabeth Cook Cpl NJ
Samuel: b 9-3-1762 d 4-19-1840 m Mary Johnston Pvt NY ★
Samuel: b 1742 d 4-4-1829 m Susanna Garvin Pvt PA
Samuel: b 1742 d 1-10-1832 m Sarah Holmes Pvt PA
Samuel: b a. 1760 d 1806/7 m Nancy Fowlkes Pvt VA
Samuel Groome, Sr.: b 12-13-1752 d p. 1794 m Mary — Capt MD
Shadrach: b 4-14-1747 d 8-27-1838 m (1)Mary Hinman (2)Alletta
    Blagge QM Cmsry CT
Stephen: b — d — m Apama Gorham Capt CT ★
Thomas: b 3-25-1737 d 3-14-1813 m Lovisa Parsons Pvt CT W★
Thomas: b a. 1750 d 6-28-1778 m — Pvt NJ
Timothy: b 9-2-1720 d 2-3-1807 m Rachel Judd PS CT
Weaver: b 4-17-1756 d 9-1-1820 m Hannah Durfee Ens RI
Wm.: b c. 1-13-1745 d 10-12-1810 m Mary Jackson Pvt CT
Wm.: b 2- -1749 d 3- -1796 m Mary Osborn Pvt GA
Wm.: b 1-10-1764 d 4-5-1835 m Elizabeth Reddin Pvt NC ★
Wm.: b 1763 d p. 5-5-1840 m (2)Mrs Susannah Figley Shrode Fif
    Sol NC
Wm.: b — d p. 1820 m — PS NC
Wm.: b 3-25-1745 d 1816 m Mrs. Mary (Buckles) Hendricks PS PA
Wm., Jr.: b c. 1745 d p. 12-21-1792 m Ann Sterling Clack Capt VA
Wm., Sr.: b c. 1750 d p. 10-22-1786 m Elizabeth Tanner PS VA
Zebedee: b 1-25-1725 d 1-4-1796 m (1)Abigail Osborn (2)Hannah
    Robinson PS CT

OSGOOD,
Aaron: b 3-31-1732 d 2-20-1822 m (1)Mrs Hannah Warner (2)Sara
    Witherby Capt MA
Abraham: b 12-21-1729 d 12-23-1816 m Bethsheba Mayberry PS
    ME
Asahel: b 3-23-1735/6 d 7-21-1812 m Hannah Wilder Sgt MA
Benjamin: b 5-21-1700 d 10-29-1789 m Hannah Divell PS NH
Chase: b 5-13-1729 d 3-10-1817 m (1)Martha Tucker (2)Shuah
    Eastman (3)Phebe Stevens PS NH
David: b 4-21-1734 d 10-9-1812 m (1)Sarah Bailey (2)Martha —
    (3)Mrs — Spencer (4)Mrs — Campbell QM PS CS MA
David: b 7-20-1756 d 2-15-1828 m Ruth Badger Pvt MA
Elijah: b 5-27-1740 d 12-22-1822 m (1)Mary Wallington
    (2)Rebecca Woodward Pvt NH
Enoch: b 1759 d 5-29-1820 m Deborah Fogg Pvt NH
George: b 12-1-1758 d 10-4-1823 m Elizabeth Otis Dr MA
Isaac: b 4-14-1724 d 5-19-1791 m Abigail Bailey Pvt MA
James: b 1757 d 1815 m Abigail Evans Lt MA
James: b 8-27-1738 d 1816 m Anna Webster Pvt PS NH
Jeremiah: b 9-1-1761 d 10-26-1857 m Ruth Hewitt Sol CT ★
Jeremiah H.: b 1732 d 4-5-1816 m (1)Lucy Churchill (2)Mrs Lydia
    Penfield Pvt CT
Joel: b 3-21-1746 d 11-8-1821 m (1)Lois Rugg (2)Mrs Lucretia Rugg
    Thayer Lt MA
John: b 1-22-1749 d 2-1-1816 m (1)Mary Hunt (2)Hannah Hunt
    Cpl MA
John: b 1742 d p. 1797 m Sarah (Hutchinson) Hill Pvt MA
John: b 11-14-1754 d 4-5-1820 m Lydia Newell Pvt MA
John: b 1745 d 1820 m Sarah Danforth Pvt NH
Joseph: b 1743 d 5-22-1822 m Huldah Church Pvt MA
Joseph: b 12-24-1739 d 3-11-1808 m Rebecca Knapp Pvt MA
Joseph: b 11-25-1746 d 6- -1812 m Lucretia Ward Pvt MA
Joseph: b 10-18-1752 d 1786 m Sally Tibbetts Pvt MA
Josiah: b c. 1748 d 2-8-1801 m Margaret Fulton Sol GA
Josiah: b 10-1-1740 d 8-17-1840 m Jane Byington Lt MA
Josiah: b 11-30-1738 d 12-10-1788 m Sarah Stevens Pvt PS MA
Lemuel: b 11-6-1747 d 10-23-1821 m Lydia Merrifield Pvt MA
Manasseh: b 4-30-1745 d 11-26-1830 m Mehitable Clark Pvt MA
Nathaniel: b 8-12-1747 d 12-10-1833 m Sarah Bradbury Pvt MA
Philip: b 7-19-1745 d 3-29-1825 m (1)Elizabeth Flanders (2)Apphy
    Flanders (3)Mehitable Flanders PS NH
Phineas: b 1757 d — m — Cpl MA
Phineas: b 5-19-1753 d 10-31-1836 m Mary Smith Pvt MA
Reuben: b 11-21-1726 d 1-30-1795 m (1)Mary Brown (2)Mary
    True PS NH
Richard: b 1721 d 12-12-1780 m Dorothy Evans Pvt MA
Samuel: b 2-1-1748 d 8-12-1813 m (1)Martha Brandon (2)Mrs
    Maria (Brown) Franklin ADC PS MA
Samuel: b 12-5-1736 d 12-14-1819 m (1)Eleanor Morrill (2)Mrs
    McClary (3)Mrs Lucy — BgdMaj MA
Samuel: b 7-13-1734 d 10-5-1790 m Jane Webster BgdMaj ADC
    MA
Samuel: b 3-29-1749 d 3-23-1834 m Betsey Sanborn Pvt NH
Thomas: b 8-1-1761 d 11-10-1843 m (1)Sarah Kirtland (2)Mrs
    Shepley Pvt NH
Thomas: b 4-3-1734 d 1786 m (1)— (2)— Pvt NY
Timothy: b 7-27-1743 d 7-19-1816 m Chloe Bridges 1Lt MA
Wm.: b 3-25-1740 d 2-8-1804 m Mary Scarborough Lt CT
Wm., Sr.: b 8-20-1732 d 2-5-1801 m Hepsibah Dunton Pvt PS NH

OSLMAN,
John Casper: b — d p. 1-4-1819 m Ruth Hart PS RI

OSMAN, (includes OZMAN)
Abraham: b 11-4-1764 d 11-1-1846 m (1)Sarah Jordan (2)Rachel
    P. Morgan Sol NY
Charles: b 12-12-1761 d 1- -1837 m Matilda Higgins Pvt VA ★

OSTER,
Henry: b 1750 d 1809 m Louisa Schweitzer Pvt PA
Henry: b 1740 d 1810 m Louisa Anna Cresman Cpl PA
Jacob: b 1752 d 1818 m Elizabeth — Pvt PA
Valentine: b 9- -1744 d 2-12-1807 m Maria Elizabeth — Pvt PA

OSTERHOUR, (includes OSTERHOUDT)
Abraham: b 4-22-1748 d 11-3-1817 m Catherine Minklaer Pvt NY
Elias: bpt 4-7-1760 d p. 4-20-1800 m Catherine Carl Pvt NY
Gideon: b a. 1730 d p. 10-2-1798 m Abigail Webster 1Lt NY
Gilbert: b c. 1720 d 1790 m — Sol NY
Henry: b 9-29-1748 d 8-21-1810 m Mrs Catharina Warrant
    Burnside Sgt NY
Henry: b c. 1751 d 10- -1825 m Sarah Crispell Pvt NY W ★
Henry T.: b 5-30-1767 d 10-24-1842 m (1)Mary Bogart ( )Maria
    DeWitt Pvt NY ★
James: b c. 1731 d — m Margaret Davenport Sol NY
Jeremiah: b 10-16-1743 d 5-30-1813 m Juna Reno Pvt NY
John: b c. 1746 d p. 1790 m Catherine Spencer Sgt NY
Joseph: b 1-5-1746 d p. 1790 m Sarah VanGaasbeek Pvt PS NY
Peter: b 5-14-1760 d 2-14-1812 m Anatie Overbaugh Pvt NY
Petrus: b 3-8-1741 d — m Marritje Brink Lt NY
Teunis: b c. 1712/13 d 1785 m Catherine Lek PS NY
Wilhelmus, Sr.: b 1-15-1727 d 10-21-1783 m Mary Decker Pvt NY

OSTERMAN,
Christian: b 1755 d 3-5-1839 m Elizabeth Nukirk Sgt NY

OSTRANDER,
Aaron: b 8-25-1745 d 12-13-1821 m Gertrude Holsapple Capt NY
Abraham: bpt 9-19-1725 d 3-31-1811 m Elizabeth Ostrander 2Lt
    NY
Adam: b 1740 d 12-31-1835 m Catherine Proper Pvt NY
Christopher: b 9-22-1737 d 1813 m Altje Romeyn Pvt NY
Cornelius: b 7-22-1742 d p. 1790 m Mrs Maria Brinkerhoff Pvt NY
Daniel: b 1-21-1751 d a. 3-19-1812 m Sarah Brown Pvt NY
David: b 3-20-1746 d 12- -1809 m Anna Kouwenhoven Capt PS
    NY
Hendrick: b c. 8-12-1739 d 5-10-1825 m Maria VanDenBergh Pvt
    NY
Henry: b 1737 d 1809 m Maria Phillips Pvt NY
Henry: b 10-10-1754 d 1-26-1830 m Martha Nicholson Pvt NY ★
Jacobus: bpt 11-18-1716 d p. 1783 m Margrietjen Heermans Pvt
    NY
John, Jr.: b 1755 d 1- -1800 m Catherine Wetzell 1Lt NY W ★
John A: b 8-8-1761 d 5-4-1840 m Sarah Campbell (2)Sarah
    Carpenter Pvt NY
Marcus: b 12-3-1735 d — m Elizabeth DeGraff Pvt NY
Peter W.: b c. 1756 d 7-28-1836 m Catharine Parsell Cpl NY W ★
Petrus, Sr.: b 2-4-1725 d 12-25-1814 m (1)Debora Dijo (2)Christina
    Ronk Sol PS NY
Teunis: b 2- -1757 d p. 1802 m Maritie VanVliet Sgt NY

OSTROM,
David: b 1753 d 3-17-1821 m Susan — Sol NY
Denee: b 1-14-1730 d 7-20-1812 m (2)Geertruyd Barentsche
    Hegeman Sol NY
Henry: b 11-26-1741 d 1-14-1797 m Abigail Davenport Capt NY
Henry: b 1760 d 12-18-1844 m (1)Elizabeth — (2)Betsy — Pvt NY
Roelif: b 7-4-1758 d p. 1790 m Maria Hegeman Pvt NY

OSWALD,
Daniel: b c. 1740 d a. 1805 m Catharine Everett Pvt PA
Eleazer: bpt 2-22-1750 d 9-30-1795 m Elizabeth Holt LCol PS CT
    NY PA

OTEY,
James: b c. 1755 d p. 1785 m Frances Graves PS VA
John M.: b 1735 d 1817 m Mary Hopkins Capt VA

OTIS,
Araunah: b 1-6-1763 d 2-16-1833 m Elizabeth Adams Pvt NY
Barnabas: b 6-14-1756 d 1-15-1850 m Mehitable Turner Pvt CT ★
Charles: b 3-6-1740 d 1803 m (1)Sarah Ellis (2)Sarah Tilden
    (3)Elizabeth Hammond Pvt MA
Charles G.: b 10-29-1760 d —, m Elizabeth (Gould) Sweetland Dr
    Sol CT
David: b 6-3-1743 d p. 1782 m Mary (Miller) Day Pvt MA
Edward: b 3- -1766 d 6-6-1852 m Mary Merrill Pvt CT ★
Elijah: b 6-10-1749 d 4-8-1838 m Dorothy Locke Pvt NH
Ensign: b 1-9-1747 d 8-25-1830 m Lucy Lapham Capt MA
Ephraim: bpt 6-9-1734 d 10-21-1816 m Sarah Harris PS Dr MA
Ignatius: b 2-2-1731 d 3-21-1802 m Thankful (Otis) PS MA
Isaac, Sr.: b 1699 d 11-11-1777 m Deborah Jacobs PS MA
Isaac, Jr.: b 9-17-1719 d 12-9-1785 m Mehitable Bass Dr MA
Isaac, 3. b 9-24-1752 d 11-2-1838 m (1)Ruth Brown (2)Mrs
    Elizabeth Hopkins Pvt MA ★
James: b 1741 d — m Orphania Randall Smn CT
James: b 6-27-1751 d 9-18-1837 m Sarah Holmes Pvt MA ★
James, Sr.: b 6-14-1702 d 11-9-1778 m Mary Allyne PS MA
James, Jr.: b 2-5-1724 d 5-23-1783 m Ruth Cunningham PS MA
John: b 4-1-1728 d 10-24-1804 m Prudence Taintor PS CT

John: b 3-16-1759 d 6-18-1842 m Hannah Folker Pvt NH ★
John Thatcher: b 10-31-1758 d 9-18-1842 m Lovisa Pomeroy Pvt
    Fif CT ★
Jonathan: b 4-30-1723 d 2-20-1791 m Catherine Coggeshall Cmsry
    CT
Joseph: b 3-6-1725 d 9-24-1810 m (1)Rebecca Sturgis (2)Maria
    Walter BGen MA
Joshua, Sr.: b 1720 d 1810 m Jane Hussey PS NH
Joshua, Jr.: b 3-30-1764 d 3-4-1834 m Lydia Meader Pvt NH
Macajah: b 5-21-1747 d 5-20-1821 m Sara Foss PS NH
Noah: bpt 6-30-1734 d 12-22-1798 m Phebe Cushing Pvt MA
Paul: b 3-4-1755 d 7-17-1848 m Elizabeth Parshley Cpl NH
Richard: b 1744 d 1-5-1825 m Mary Hinckley Cpl NH
Robert: b 3-8-1740 d p. 1790 m Lydia — Pvt CT
Stephen: b 5-14-1738 d 12-29-1776 m (1)Lois Edgerton (2)Sarah
    Lunt Sgt CT
Stephen: b 9-30-1738 d 12-1-1831 m Lucy Chandler PS Sol CT
Stephen: b 11-4-1728 d 1776 m Elizabeth Wade Sol MA
Wm.: b 12-9-1762 d 3-8-1813 m Margaret Jaquin NS CT

OTT,
Abraham: b 11-21-1757 d 6-28-1799 m Ann Green Lt SC
Adam: b 1754 d 8-10-1827 m Julianna — 2 Lt PA ★
Jacob: b 8-14-1755 d 9-12-1820 m Mary Elizabeth Ott Capt SC
John: b 8-14-1754 d 3-26-1820 m Leah Snyder Pvt PA
John George: b 6-24-1745 d 2-13-1814 m Catherine — Pvt PA
Martin: b 2-2-1743 d a. 1-4-1814 m (1)Elizabeth McJoyce (2)Mary
    Ann Gibbs PS SC
Nicholas: b c. 1759 d 1- -1800 m Mary — Pvt PA
Nickolas: b — d p. 1788 m Elizabeth Fielding Sgt PA

OTTERMAN,
Ludwic: b c. 1738 d a. 6-13-1797 m Francenia — PS PA

OTTERSON,
James: b 8-19-1757 d 12-22-1846 m Martha Chase Pvt NH

OTTINGER,
Christopher: b 8-20-1720 d 5-22-1802 m Mary Groathouse PS PA
John: b 7-20-1733 d 3-27-1807 m (1)Elizabeth Williams (2)Margaret
    — Pvt PA

OTTMAN,
Christian: b 1731 d 4-23-1821 m (1)Christiana Schafer (2)Christine
    Bran Pvt NY

OTTO,
Bodo, Sr.: b 1709 d 6-13-1787 m (1)Elizabeth Sauchen (2)Catharine
    Doratha Doehmicher (3)Margaret Parris PS Dr PA
Bodo, Jr.: b 9-14-1748 d 1-26-1782 m Catharine Schweighauser Dr
    Col PM NJ
John Augustus: b 7-20-1751 d 12-16-1834 m Catharine Hitner Dr
    PA

OTTY,
Wm.: b 1748 d 1809 m Hannah — Sgt PA

OUDERKIRK, (includes OUDERKERK)
Abraham: b 11-17-1751 d 10-12-1844 m Alide Ouderkirk Pvt NY
Isaac: bpt 5-3-1724 d 6-18-1824 m (1)Anna Clute (2)Hesje
    VanArnhem Pvt NY
Jacob: b 9-27-1724 d 10-30-1802 m Neeltie Clute Pvt NY
John: b 6-12-1764 d 5-15-1849 m Elizabeth Ramsey Pvt NY ★
Peiter: b 5-8-1735 d 1-9-1827 m Machteldt Takel Heemstraat Pvt
    NY

OURSLER,
Edward: b 1710 d 1789 m Ruth Owings PS MD
Wm.: b 7-31-1753 d 4- -1813 m Mary Parker Sgt MD

OUSBY,
Thomas, Sr.: b a. 1750 d p. 1782 m Mrs Sara (Litchford) Selby Lt SC

OUT,
Mathias: b 1738 d 1813 m Eve Frolick Pvt NY

OUTCALT,
Frederick: bpt 2-8-1736 d 4-26-1818 m Maria Stolts Pvt NJ

OUTHOUSE,
Peter: b 1757 d 8-1-1834 m (1)Georetta — (2)Mrs Nancy Duncan
    Pvt MD ★

OUTLAW,
Alexander: b 1738 d 1826 m Penelope Smith Pvt NC
Benjamin: b 1735 d c. 1800 m Lydia Bentley Sol SC
Edward: b c. 1720 d 1800 m Patience Whitfield Ens NC
James: b 1744 d 4-22-1826 m Elizabeth Grady Sgt NC
Lewis: b 1741/2 d a. 1809 m Milly — Pvt NC
Ralph: b c. 1720 d a. 1790 m — PS NC

OUTTEN,
Isaac: b 9-13-1748 d 9-7-1819 m Sarah Waggomon Pvt MD

OUTWATER,
Francis: bpt 4-28-1727 d 6- -1800 m (1)Marittje DeMaree (2)Deborah Smith (3)Charity Cokefair Pvt NJ
Gillium: bpt 2-17-1751 d 8-17-1811 m Antje VanWagenen PS NJ
John: b 9-17-1746 d 5-18-1823 m Harriet Lozier Capt NJ

OVERACKER,
Adam: b 6-27-1761 d 11-14-1842 m (1)Cornelia Vandercook (2)Patience Adams Pvt NY
Michael, Sr.: b c. 1730 d p. 12-29-1787 m Anna Barbia Stover Pvt PS NY

OVERALL,
Nathaniel: b 1756 d 1835 m Annie Thomas PS TN
Wm.: b 1754 d 1-22-1793 m Susannah Thomas Capt PS NC
Wm.: b 2-17-1750 d 10- -1810 m (1)Sissy Runna Laarite (2)Ann Hilton Sol VA

OVERBAGH, (includes OVERBAUGH)
Abraham: b 12-24-1752 d 11-20-1800 m Rachel Freligh 2Lt NY
Andrew: b c. 1750 d 1805 m — Pvt VA
Clement: b 1-13-1745/6 d 2-25-1825 m Marytje Garrit PS NY
Jeremiah: b 3-24-1759 d 9- -1813 m Sara VanOrden Ens NY
John: b 4-10-1757 d 3-11-1815 m Annaatze Conyn Sgt NY ★
Wilhelmus: b 1-3-1753 d 1826 m Sarah Schutt Cpl PS NY

OVERBOKER, (or OFFENBACHER)
Frederick: b 1730-40 d p. 1-21-1818 m Elizabeth — Pvt VA

OVERFIELD,
Abner: b c. 1750 d p. 3-14-1805 m Mary Desha Pvt PA
Benjamin: b c. 1752 d 10-27-1813 m (1)Maria Gonsalis (2)Margaret Henshaw Pvt PA
Martin: b 1756 d 5-25-1821 m Mary Elizabeth Utt Pvt PA

OVERHISER,
Conrad: b 4-29-1754 d 7-13-1840 m Mary Story Pvt NY

OVERHOLTZER, (includes OBERHOLTZER & OVERHOLT)
Henry: b c. 1774 d 10- -1783 m Catherine Shoemaker Pvt PA
Henry: b 2-5-1739 d 3-5-1813 m Anna Beidler Pvt PA
Joseph: b 11-4-1754 d 2-6-1805 m (1)Susanna Schlichter (2)Anna — Pvt PA

OVERLIN,
John: b c. 1740 d c. 11-1-1800 (1)— (2)Mary — Pvt VA
Wm.: b 1765 d 2-24-1837 m Letitia McKinney Fif Pvt VA PA ★

OVERMYER, (includes OVERMEIER)
Barbara Vogt: b 1741 d p. 1805 m John George Overmyer PS PA
George: b 6-3-1755 d 1811 m Maria Rearick Pvt PA
John George: b 10-27-1727 d 9-22-1805 m (1)Eva Rosenbaum (2)Barbara Faught Capt PA

OVERPECK, (includes OVERPACK)
George, Sr.: b 3-3-1715 d 8-15-1798 m (1)Margaret — (2)Magdalena — Ens PA
George, Jr.: b 3-16-1758 d 1804 m Maria Salome Hausewirt Pvt PA
George: b 12- -1757 d 1799 m Elizabeth Narrowcronk Pvt PA

OVERSTREET,
Henry: b c. 1750 d p. 1-17-1795 m Jane Branch Sol MA
John: b 1760 d 7-8-1848 m Nancy Dabney Pvt VA ★
Sarah: b 12-10-1756 d 12-24-1818 m James Overstreet PS SC
Thomas: b — d p. 12-14-1791 m Agness — PS VA

OVERTON,
David, Sr.: b 1712 d p. 1781 m (1)Anna Hulse (2)Susannah Palmer PS NY
David: b 8-29-1739 d 3-24-1826 m Mary Davis Pvt NY
Elton: b 1733 d 12-13-1810 m Sarah Reeve PS NY
Isaac: b 1735 d 1786 m Phoebe Burnet Maj NY
Isaac: b 25-1740 d 1-10-1799 m Anna Swezey Maj PS NY
John: b 1-12-1747 d p. 11-23-1806 m Lois Hammond PS Pvt NY
John: b c. 1735 d p. 1790 m Ann Booker Clough Capt VA
John: b 1-20-1755 d 4-23-1822 m (1)Susannah Garland (2)Anne Bacon Capt VA
Messenger: b 3-15-1756 d 11- -1803 m Charity Gerard PS NY
Nathaniel: b 1708 d 10-29-1779 m (1)Alathea Way (2)Mary Terry Pvt NY
Nathaniel: b 1753 d 1-10-1803 m Deborah — Pvt NY
Nathaniel: b 1734 d 2-15-1817 m Keziah Coleman Pvt NY
Samuel: b 12- -1760 d 4-30-1836 m Fanny Cosby Pvt Cmsry VA
Seth: b 3-8-1759 d 8-17-1852 m Mehitable White NCapt CT
Thomas: b 8-15-1753 d 2-23-1824 m (1)Sarah Woodson (2)Penelope Holmes Capt VA
Waller: b 11-14-1750 d 10-22-1827 m Martha Ragland CS VA
Wm.: b 1756 d 1820 m Martha Ann Ballard Sgt VA

OVERTUFF,
Martin: b 1756 d c. 1843 m Mrs. Catherine Ditch Pvt PS PA

OVIATT, (includes OVAITT)
Benjamin: b 2-27-1755 d 9-26-1832 m Elizabeth Carter Vol CT
Isaac: b 9-29-1734 d 1814 m Esther Wilson Pvt NY
John: bpt 5-5-1728 d p. 1790 m Abigail Smith Sol CT
Nathan: b 10-27-1764 d 2-10-1855 m Hannah Pardee Pvt CT
Samuel: b 4-10-1763 d 7-31-1851 m Mindwell Smith Pvt CT ★
Wm.: b 3-20-1750 d 5-17-1816 m Sarah Munson Cpl CT

OWEN, (includes OWENS)
Abel: b 4-3-1743 d 6-6-1827 m (1)Anna — (2)Elizabeth Abbott Pvt NY
Asahel: b 7-25-1726 d p. 1790 m Deborah Drake Pvt MA
Asahel: b 10-11-1752 d p. 1807 m Anna Perkins Pvt MA
Bailey: b 1758 d 12-25-1840 m Mary Solomon Pvt NC ★
Benjamin: b 1761 d — m — Capt CT
Benjamin: b 1725 d 12- -1786 m Elizabeth Ferree Pvt PA
Brackett: b 1733 d p. 12-15-1801 m (1)Elizabeth Wooten (2)Elizabeth McGehee PS KY
Daniel: b 1732 d 10-21-1812 m Hannah Angel CS PS RI
Daniel: b 9-14-1751 d 3-24-1825 m Ruth Peet Pvt CT
Daniel: b 1- -1759 d 5-22-1826 m Lydia Rice Pvt CT ★
David: b 1758 d 1846 m Margaret Owen Pvt NJ ★
David: b 1763 d 10-1-1838 m Martha Armstrong Pvt NY ★
David: b 3-13-1713 d 6-15-1790 m Sarah Schmetzer Pvt PA
David: b c. 1735 d 1818 m — PS VA
Ebenezer: b 1737 d 8-28-1800 m Ann — Capt NY
Eleazer: b 4-16-1761 d 3-19-1843 m Abigail Bicknell Sgt CT ★
Elijah: b 1738/9 d 11-13-1815 m Lydia Clark Lt CT
Elijah: b 11-29-1719 d 1802 m — Sgt CT
Elijah: b 1-29-1721 d 6- -1799 m (1)Patience Wright (2)Olive Beeman (3)Abigail — Pvt VT
Elisha: b 1748 d 1832 m Elizabeth Johnson Pvt VA W ★
Ephraim: b 1763 d c. 1802 m Lucina Owens Cpl VA
Frederick: b 2-27-1752 d 4-9-1837 m Margaret Hibbard Pvt CT ★
Gideon: b 4- -1742 d 7-8-1792 m Jane White PS MA
Griffith: b 4-6-1759 d 1829 m Jane Shearman Pvt PA
Hugh: b 9-23-1768 d 1-6-1846 m Mary McFarland Pvt MA ★
Isaac: b 9-24-1736 d 8-2-1816 m Zerviah Griswold Ens CT
James: b c. 1750 d 1824 m (1)Mary Gardner (2)Azubah Brown Pvt RI
James: b 8-6-1763 d 2-19-1833 m Ann Wilkes OrdlSgt VA ★
James: b c. 1755 d 1827 m Elizabeth Russell Pvt VA
Jesse: b 1-24-1740 d 5-12-1828 m Mary — Pvt NY
Jesse: b 1740 d 3- -1793 m Ann Crawford Capt VA
John: 4-16-1741 d 2-24-1843 m (1)Joanna Phelps (2)Lydia Gilson Pvt CT W ★
John: b 1-26-1757 d c. 1845 m Abagail Cullom Pvt PS MD
John: b a. 1749 d 5-15-1826 m Sarah Bradbury Pvt MA
John, Sr.: b 1695 d c. 1795/6 m Mildred Grant PS NC
John, Jr.: b c. 3-25-1753 d 12-8-1824 m Amelia Grant Capt NC
Jonathan: b 5-15-1759 d 11-26-1835 m Polly — Pvt MA ★
Jonathan: b 1749 d 8-21-1814 m Catherine Eleanor Kortright Lt NY
Jonathan: b 3-24-1757 d 5-11-1800 m Mary Dunning Pvt NY
Jonathan: b c. 1750 d 1807/1808 m — Capt SC
Joseph: b 4-12-1759 d 2-5-1827 m Susanna Newell Pvt MA W ★
Joseph: b 1- -1757 d 2-26-1841 m Hannah Button Pvt MA NY ★
Joseph, Sr.: b 9-5-1735 d 5-11-1813 m Milicent Horton Pvt NY
Joseph, Jr.: b 3-30-1763 d 5-6-1818 m Ruth Woolsey Pvt NY
Joshua: b 11-14-1760 d 10-21-1839 m Zippora Winters Pvt NY
Noah: b 2-5-1756 d 1821 m Elizabeth Gilmore Pvt CT
Philip: b 2-18-1756 d 5-28-1849 m Mrs. Joanna (Thompson) Stanwood Sol NY
Richard: b c. 1760 d 1833 m Elizabeth — Pvt NC
Richardson: b 3-4-1744 d 7-24-1821 m Sarah Duty Col Cmdt CS NC
Robert: b 1730/1 d 6- -1779 m Mary Ann Edmonston Maj MD
Solomon: b 1731 d 1797 m Ruth Angel PS RI
Sylvanus: b 1746 d 12-7-1814 m Eunice Roberts Pvt NH
Thomas: b 1750 d 1800 m Sally Farmer Pvt MD
Thomas: b 1735 d 1803 m (1) — Grady (2)Eleanor Porterfield LCol PS NC
Thomas: b 7-21-1742 d 12-31-1825 m Isabell Allen Maj NC
Thomas: b 1743 d 1830 m (1)Jane Musgrave (2)Sarah Matthews Pvt PA
Thomas: b 1711 d — m — PS RI
Thomas: b 1759 d — m Elizabeth Fearne Pvt VA
Timothy: b 11-10-1757 d 8-24-1837 m Lydia Perry Pvt NH ★
Uriah: b c. 1755 d p. 8-23-1820 m Sarah Everet PS VA
Wm.: b 12-29-1764 d 5-16-1833 m (1)Sabrina Olds (2)Lucy Kellogg Pvt NY
Wm.: b 4-8-1740 d 10-17-1805 m Elizabeth Burden PS NY
Wm.: b 1-12-1752 d 1817 m Jane Batchelder Lt VA
Wm.: b 9-3-1748 d 12-22-1821 m Agnes Wilkerson Pvt VA
Zachariah: b a. 1757 d 1822 m — PS MD

OWENBY,
James: b 1-6-1761 d 9-26-1850 m Joannah Sims Pvt NC ★

OWENS,
Caleb: b 1759 d 1842 m Mary Nabors Pvt SC
David: b c. 1733 d p. 6-10-1798 m Mary — PS VA
Isaac: b 5-9-1729 d 9-21-1805 m Priscilla Norman Pvt MD
James: b 1748 d 10-25-1797 m Elizabeth (Owens) — Pvt MD
James: b 1721-3 d a. 4-4-1786 m Eliza — (2)Ann Pritchard PS MD

OWENS, contd.
James: b 1748 d *c.* 1808 m Eleanor Bryesam Pvt SC
James: b 10-19-1763 d *a.* 5-21-1825 m Elizabeth Marrs Sol VA
John: b — d 6-17-1775 m (1) — (2)a widow — Sol MA
John: b *c.* 1740 d 1819 m Sarah Kirk Pvt PA
John: b 11-3-1760 d 2-11-1853 m Nancy — Pvt PA
John: b *c.* 1750 d *p.* 10-20-1798 m Mary — Pvt SC
Jonathan: b 7-9-1755 d 1821 m Abigail — Pvt NY
Joshua: b 4-28-1750 d 5-24-1816 m Amelia Griffiths-Kenton Of VA
Owen: b 10- -1746 d *p.* 8-3-1808 m Sophiah CS VA
Samuel: b *c.* 1730 d *a.* 1803 m Elizabeth — Sol VA
Stephen: b 1752 d 6-8-1837 m Mary Ann Gaunce Pvt MD
Thomas: b 6-20-1745 d 9-6-1821 m Rachel Beall Pvt SC
Uriah: b 4- -1764 d 9-4-1819 m Elizabeth Food Pvt NY W ★
Vincent: b 1740 d 3-20-1834 m Lucinda — Pvt VA
Wm.: b 11-10-1750 d 8-9-1836 m Nancy (Owens) Sgt VA ★
Wm.: b 1763 d *p.* 1840 m Dorcas Stephens Pvt VA ★
Wm.: b 4-5-1763 d 12-15-1840 m Nancy Owens Pvt VA ★
Wm.: b 1762 d 1846 m Nancy Craig Pvt VA ★

OWINGS,
John Cockey: b 2- -1736 d 2- -1810 m Colgate Deye Colgate Capt MD
Joshua: b *c.* 1744 d *p.* 1790 m Elizabeth Howe 1Lt MD
Joshua: b 1704 d 1785 m Mary Cockey PS MD
Richard: b 7-16-1749 d 1-21-1819 m Ruth — Capt MD
Richard: b 1747 d *c.* 1837 m Ruth (Warfield) Pvt SC ★
Samuel: b 8-17-1733 d 6-4-1803 m Deborah Lynch LCol MD
Thomas: b 10-18-1740 d 8-21-1822 m Ruth Lawrence Capt MD

OWRY, (includes OURY & OWREY)
Adam: b 1754 d 4-22-1836 m Mary — Pvt PA ★
George: b 8-10-1757 d 10-20-1844 m Elizabeth Emery Ens PA ★
Windle: b 1747 d *p.* 1784 m Catharine Peterpenner Capt PA

OWSLEY, (includes OSLIN)
Jesse: b 3-31-1729 d 1814 m Winney Lucas Pvt VA
Thomas: b 1731 d 11-1-1796 m Mary Middleton Sol VA
Wm.: b 12-27-1748 d 10-10-1819 m Catherine Bolin 1Lt VA

OX,
Leonhard: b 1742 d 1785 m Maria Catharine Stopf PS MD

OXENHAM,
Richard: b *c.* 1750 d *a.* 3-14-1797 m Elizabeth Rathall Sol MD

OXFORD,
Samuel: b *c.* 1730 d 1811 m Bathsheba Barrett Sol NC

OXX,
Samuel: bpt 3-7-1730 d 11-16-1806 m (1)Mrs. Priscilla Gladding (2)Rebecca Lindsey Pvt RI

OYSTERBANKS,
Moses: b 10-17-1762 d 12-13-1838 m Sarah Bennett Pvt CT

OZIAS,
John: b 1742 d 8-10-1825 m Elizabeth Fall PS NC

OZIER,
Joseph: b 11-7-1745 d 12-30-1838 m Elizabeth Baker 2Lt MA

PACA,
Aquilla: b 6-21-1738 d 2-29-1788 m Ellen Tootle Capt CS PS MD
James: b 10-25-1754 d 10-16-1828 m Ann Reiley Pvt MD
Wm.: b 10-31-1740 d 10-23-1799 m (1)Mary Chew (2)Anna Harrison White SDI MD

PACE,
Barnabas: b *c.* 1747 d 8-3-1831 m (1)Agnes Aycock (2)Mary Casey Sol GA
Drury: b 10-6-1745 d 2-5-1801 m Mary Bussey Capt SC
Joel: b 7-28-1762 d 8-31-1831 m Mary East Pvt VA ★
John: b 5-28-1751 d 4-12-1822 m (1)Elizabeth Nunn (2)Mrs. Polly Stone PS VA
Michael, Jr.: b 6- -1758 d 2-19-1832 m (2)Anne Welsh Pvt NJ ★
Nathaniel: b 7-16-1743 d 10-1-1798 m Amelia Mildred Boykin PS SC
Newsom: b 1754 d 8-19-1845 m Mary Nunn Sgt VA ★
Stephen: b 7-16-1747 d 11-12-1822 m Catherine — Pvt NC
Thomas: b *c.* 1750 d 1795 m Cebell Mathews of PS GA

PACK,
Samuel: b 1760 d 1833 m Mary Farley Pvt VA
Wm.: b 10-16-1758 d 9-23-1838 m Phoebe O'Neale Pvt MD

PACKARD, (includes PICKARD)
Abel: b 4-16-1754 d 4-30-1832 m (1)Mary Bisbee (2)Rachel Porter Ens MA
Abisha: b 4-10-1761 d 7-20-1836 m (1)Esther Fuller (2)Rebecca Preston Pvt MA
Adolph: b 1761 d 7-23-1846 m Catherine Spaulsbury Sgt NY ★

Asa: b 5-3-1758 d 3-20-1843 m Nancy Quincy Fif MA
Asahel: b 3-18-1763 d 6-26-1846 m (1)Maria French (2)Mrs. Priscilla Williams Pvt Drm NH & VT ★
Benjamin: b 6-7-1760 d 9-19-1823 m (1)Mehitable Fobes (2)Abigail Bowman Sgt MA ★
Benjamin: b 10-2-1742 d 2-19-1825 m Asenath Bradford Waters Pvt MA
Caleb: b 3-5-1758 d 12-30-1833 m Lydia Ford Pvt MA
Conrad: b 1740 d *p.* 1790 m Mary Clarissa — Pvt NY
Daniel: b *c.* 1747 d 1836 m Betsey Connery Pvt MA
Ebenezer, Sr.: b 1724 d 1803 m Sarah Perkins Pvt MA
Edward: b 1733 d 1806 m (1)Ruth Bonney (2)Rebecca Pope Cpl MA
Eleazer: b 9-27-1727 d 1803 m (1)Mercy Richards (2)Mary Woodbury Pvt MA
Ichabod: b 1738 d 11- -1813 m Ruth Allen Pvt MA
Ichabod: b 6-15-1760 d 4-8-1814 m Rachel Cole Pvt MA
Isaac: b 9- -1737 d 3-3-1795 m Eunice Rawson Capt MA
Isaac: b 10-7-1762 d 4-26-1843 m Mochtalena Countryman Drm NY ★
Jacob: b 4-12-1728 d *p.* 1781 m Deborah — Capt CT
Jacob: b 2-7-1763 d 8-21-1839 m Tabitha Pearson Pvt MA
James: b 8-5-1758 d *p.* 1800 m Jemima Churchill Pvt MA ★
Job: b 1762 d 1848 m Eunice Babb Pvt MA ★
John: b 1756 d 7-17-1811 m Mary Dodge Pvt MA
John: b 5-28-1760 d 8-30-1827 m Maria Garlock Pvt PS NY W ★
Jonathan: b 9-13-1751 d *p.* 1792 m Susannah Alger 2Lt MA
Jonathan: bpt 5-4-1746 d 5-26-1827 m Mary Kilbourn Pvt MA
Lemuel: b 6-9-1747 d 1-7-1822 m Sarah Hunt Pvt MA
Levi: b 1754 d 2-5-1839 m Martha Fox Pvt MA ★
Mark: b 9-2-1751 d *p.* 7-22-1780 m Hannah Shaw Sgt MA
Marlborough: b 1765 d *p.* 1781 m Mary Ann Blackington Pvt MA
Nathan: b 4-24-1733 d 2-17-1798 m Lydia Jackson Capt MA
Nathaniel: b 1729 d 1809 m Abigail Sterry Cdr RI
Nehemiah: b 10-27-1760 d 1-24-1830 m Lucy Nye Pvt MA
Nehemiah: b 2-2-1762 d 11-1-1851 m Betsey Bradford Drm MA ★
Noah: b 10-3-1752 d 6-9-1830 m Molly Hamlin Cpl MA
Parmenas: b 11-26-1757 d 7-30-1818 m Martha Reynolds Pvt MA
Philip: b 4-24-1763 d 4-14-1842 m (1)Martha Edson (2)Lucinda Stetson Lazelle Pvt MA ★
Reuben: b 11-8-1737 d 12-6-1820 m Anne Perkins Sgt MA
Richard: b 1763 d 2-25-1840 m Mary Coates Pvt MA
Robert: b *c.* 1755 d 5-5-1813 m Elizabeth Hudson Cpl NH
Samuel: b 9- -1751 d *p.* 1788 m Bethia Waters Pvt MA
Seth: b 3-12-1742 d *p.* 1790 m Lois Leach Cpl MA
Thomas: b 9-21-1732 d *p.* 1790 m (1)Mary Howard (2)Martha Packard Pvt MA
Timothy: b 1752 d 1818 m Elizabeth Fairbanks Pvt MA
Wm.: b *c.* 1758 d *c.* 1826 m — Sol NC

PACKER,
Daniel: b 1-31-1731/2 d 12-27-1825 m Hannah Burrows PS CT
Eldredge: b 1-1-1756 d 5-19-1834 m Sabrina (Packer) Pvt CT
Eli: b 9-9-1757 d 5-22-1830 m Elizabeth Vickers Pvt PA
James: b 1734 d 8-24-1803 m Rebecca Walworth Pvt CT
James, Jr.: b 8-17-1760 d 4-22-1831 m Mary Greene CS PS VT
James: b 2-4-1726 d 12-8-1805 m Rose Mendenhall Pvt PA
Job: b 3-27-1754 d 6-28-1836 m (1)Hannah Lamborn (2)Margaret Morris Pvt PA
John 2d: b 2-7-1753 d 2-8-1835 m Hannah Gallup Pvt CT ★
Thomas: b 4-16-1731 d 12-16-1793 m (1)Molly Braughton (2)Molly Tarleton Pvt NH

PACKETTE,
Wm.: b 4-4-1736 d 9- -1792 m (1)Mary Harford (2)Anne Cooper Pvt VA

PACKWOOD,
Joseph: b 1739 d 4-15-1807 m Demise Wright NCapt PS CS CT
Samuel: b *c.* 1750 d *p.* 7-25-1824 m Elizabeth — Pvt VA

PADDOCK,
Apollos: b 9-8-1760 d 1836 m Mary Hudson Pvt MA
Daniel: b 1745 d 1825 m Eleanor Shufelt Pvt NY
David: b 12-12-1734 d 3-31-1794 m Miriam Belden Pvt NY
Ebenezer, Sr.: b *c.* 1740 d *p.* 1830 m Keziah Case Sol MA
Gaius: b 11-2-1758 d 8-11-1831 m Mary Wood Pvt MA
Henry: b 11-10-1751 d 8-12-1835 m Polly Shears Pvt NY
Job: b *a.* 1754 d 1834 m Margaret Tinselaer Pvt NY
John: b 1752 d 4-4-1817 m Mary Loveland Lt CT
John: b 1765 d *p.* 1832 m Hannah Taylor Pvt NY ★
John: b 3-21-1741 d 7-10-1831 m Elizabeth Eastman Pvt VT
Jonathan: b — d *p.* 5-11-1793 m Sarah — Maj NY
Nathaniel: b 10-25-1748 d 3-2-1832 m Mary Crane Pvt NY
Reuben: b 1746 d 11-21-1820/1 m Hannah — Pvt MA
Seth: b 6-3-1756 d 5-19-1839 m Phoebe Johnson Pvt CT
Silas: b 9-17-1739 d 5-4-1795 m Hepsibah Swain PS MA
Stephen: b 10- -1729 d 2-12-1814 m Eunice Coffin PS MA
Stephen: b 1751 d 3-2-1832 m Rebecca — Cpl NY
Thomas: b 5-15-1723 d *p.* 1803 m Hannah Thomas Pvt MA
Wm.: b 11-6-1748 d 6- -1819/20 m Thankful Williamson Pvt MA
Wm.: b 8-31-1752 d 8-31-1834 m Lucy Loveland Pvt MA
Zachariah: b 2-20-1724 d 6-4-1795 m Martha Washburn Pvt MA

PADELFORD,
Benjamin: b 1737 d 1790 m (2)Sylvia Williams Cpl MA
Edward: b 9-8-1740 d 3-8-1813 m Hannah Tichenor Pvt NJ
Jonathan: b 1739 d — m Hannah Flint Pvt MA
Peleg: b 1728 d 7-11-1812 m Sarah Clapp Pvt MA
Philip: b 1753 d 1815 m (2)Elizabeth Macomber Dr MA
Philip Jonathan: b 10-   -1755 d 3-8-1832 m Ruth Bullock Pvt PS NH
Zachariah, Sr.: b 1733 d 12-10-1803 m Rachael Reynolds Pvt MA
Zachariah, Jr.: b 1755 d p. 1790 m (1)Abigail Williams (2)Lydia
  Padelford Pvt MA W ★

PADGET, (includes PADGETT)
James: b 10-1-1746 d 3-15-1830 m Rebekah Floid Ens NY
Thomas: b 9-25-1752 d 4-21-1831 m Sarah Ann Matthews Pvt NC

PAGAN,
David: b c. 1745 d 1-16-1815 m (1)Elizabeth Farrell (2)Mrs. Mary
  (Carter) Harman Pvt VA

PAGE, (includes PAIGE)
Abel: b 6-8-1731 d 1-1-1797 m Mrs. Dorcas Fillmore PS MD
Abijah: b 5-14-1749 d 7-19-1836 m Mary Sawtell Pvt Drm MA
Amos: b 2-24-1727 d 9-5-1788 m Abiah Flanders PS CS MA
Andrew: b 7-30-1751 d 3-9-1821 m Elizabeth — PS NH
Asa: b 12-21-1735 d p. 5-19-1802 m Eunice Page Pvt CT
Asa: b 8-19-1740 d 4-8-1807 m Susannah Johnson Sgt PS NH
Asa: b 1-25-1756 d 12-20-1819 m Lydia Stewart Cpl VT
Benjamin: bpt 11-21-1714 d 12-16-1782 m Mary Sanborn PS CS NH
Benjamin: b 8-7-1738 d 3-26-1816 m Hannah (Shaw) PS NH
Caleb: b 8-16-1705 d 7-   -1785 m (1)Elizabeth Merrill (2)— Carleton
  PS NH
Caleb: b 7-2-1758 d 6-26-1830 m Kiziah Sawtell Pvt MA ★
Carter: b 1758 d 4-   -1825 m (1)Mary Cary (2)Lucy Nelson Capt VA
Charles: b 3-27-1750 d 6-2-1831 m Mary Wales Pvt MA
Daniel: b 4-17-1724 d 7-4-1779 m Dinah Baldwin PS CT
Daniel: b 8-10-1722 d p. 1790 m Ruth Haskell Pvt MA
Daniel: b 4-5-1732 d 5-25-1800 m Abigail Dame Lt PS NH
Daniel: b 3-19-1701/2 d p. 6-5-1777 m (1)Jane True (2)Judith
  Merrill PS NH
Daniel: b 1761 d 12-2-1847 m Anna Towle Pvt NH ★
Daniel: b 3-21-1741 d 12-12-1820 m (1)Betsey Currier (2)Mary
  McClary PS NH
David: b 2-27-1750/51 d p. 1785 m Sarah Cunnable Pvt MA
David: b 11-23-1737 d 4-1-1812 m (1)Betsey Eastman (2)Ruth
  Eastman Col PS CS NH
David: b c. 1712 d 1785 m Priscilla Boynton CS PS NH
David: b 3-26-1735 d p. 1783 m Bethiah — PS NH
David: b 2-12-1748 d 6-10-1812 m Sarah Bradford Capt NJ
Edward Hall: b 8-16-1751 d 3-14-1822 m Hannah Philbrook Sol
  ME MA
Eli: b 2-26-1750 d p. 1750 m Sylvia Thayer Pvt PS NH
Elijah: b 5-1-1764 d 3-24-1855 m Sibil Brooks Pvt NH ★
Enoch: b 12-   -1742 d 11-22-1832 m Elice Cilley Capt NH W★
Enoch: b 9-29-1741 d 10-23-1829 m Mary Davis PS NH
Ephraim: b 3-16-1730/1 d 11-4-1802 m Hannah Currier CS NH
Foster: b 8-29-1761 d 6-22-1843 m Amittai (Page) Pvt MA ★
Gad: b 3-5-1764 d 1-26-1841 m Abigail Loomis Pvt CT ★
George: b 3-9-1768 d 2-8-1823 m Betsey Bicknell Pvt Fif MA
Guillaume: b 10-13-1732 d 1801 m (1)Josette Schabart (2)Marie
  Victoire Huneau PS IN
Jabez: bpt 2-4-1710/11 d 5-4-1782 m Abigail Flanders PS NH
James: b 9-19-1747 d 2-18-1818 m (1)Thankful Raymond (2)Mary
  Lawton Capt MA
James: b 1726 d a. 2-   -1815 m (1)Elizabeth Wall (2)Viney Fowler
  PS NC
Jeremiah: b c. 1740 d 1814 m Polly Ames Pvt CT
Jeremiah: b 10-1-1722 d 6-6-1806 m (1)Sarah Andrews (2)Martha
  Crosby LCol MA
Jeremiah: b 3-28-1708 d 9-18-1786 m Elizabeth Drake PS NH
Jeremiah: b 8-18-1739 d 2-11-1827 m Elizabeth Brown PS Sol NH
Jesse: b 3-4-1752 d 7-3-1818 m Mary Breckenridge Pvt MA
Jesse: b 1741 d p. 1782 m Sarah Sawyer 1Lt NH
John: b 10-17-1704 d 2-18-1782 m Rebecca Wheeler Cnt MA
John: b 7-16-1743 d 10-15-1823 m (1)Abigail Sanders (2)Abigail
  Hazeltine (3)Mrs. Hannah (Rice) Green Pvt NH
John: b 1754 d p. 1784 m Hannah Barnard Pvt MA
John: b 4-17-1744 d 10-11-1808 m (1)Frances Burwell (2)Margaret
  Lowther PS Col VA
John: b 1720 d 1780 m Jane Byrd Col PS VA
Jonas: b 9-2-1750 d 1-26-1822 m Lucy Holden Pvt MA
Jonathan: b 3-13-1734 d 5-11-1811 m Esther Willard Lt MA
Joseph: b 1761 d 2-27-1835 m (1) — (2)Sarah White Smn CT
Joseph: b 9-29-1733 d 1-9-1793 m Dorothy Stockman Maj MA
Joseph: b 4-   -1753 d 2-7-1831 m Anna — PS NH
Joshua: b 5-4-1746 d 5-28-1806 m Anna Runnells MM MA
Josiah: b 1-31-1749 d 9-6-1831 m Sarah Marston Cpl PS NH
Josiah: b 1748 d p. 1789 m Lydia Pettee Sgt VT
Lebbeus: b 6-7-1761 d 7-5-1837 m Susannah Wales Pvt MA
Lemuel: b 12-11-1735 d 9-30-1822 m (1)Sarah Demary (2)Mary
  Paige Fif NH W ★
Leonard: b 9-27-1762 d 3-28-1836 m Jenney Hodges Pvt VA ★
Levi: b 9-21-1760 d p. 1820 m Mrs. Tamar (Gale) Dunnell Pvt MA

Mann: b 1718 d 11-7-1780 m (1)Alice Grymes (2)Anne Corbin Tayloe
  PS VA
Moses: b 7-28-1753 d 8-1-1838 m Sarah Sargent Pvt MA
Nathaniel: b 6-20-1742 d 7-   -1819 m Sarah Brown CS MA
Peter: b 6-2-1739 d p. 1790 m Sarah Farnsworth Capt NH
Phineas: b 4-28-1751 d 3-15-1817 m (1)Sarah La barre Pvt NH
Reuben: b 2-3-1754 d 8-21-1843 m Betsey Stevens Pvt NH
Robert: b 1764 d 1-1-1840 m Sarah Page Sol VA
Robert: b 9-17-1743 d 8-29-1817 m Mary Jane Murrell Pvt VA
Robert: b 1751 d 1796 m Elizabeth Carter PS VA
Samuel: b 8-1-1753 d 9-2-1814 m Rebecca Putnam Capt MA
Samuel, Sr.: b 5-11-1729 d 1789 m Phebe Richardson Pvt MA PS
Samuel, Jr.: b 7-28-1750 d 1796 m Dorothy Perry Pvt MA
Samuel: b c. 1759 d 10-17-1813 m Elizabeth Stacy Pvt MA W★
Samuel: b c. 1729 d 1790 m (1)Eleanor Stevens (2)Mrs. Sallie
  (Osgood) Evans PS NH
Samuel: b 5-11-1729 d p. 1780 m Sarah — Pvt NH
Samuel, Jr.: b 1748 d 1815 m Mary — PS Sol NH
Samuel: b 1730 d 1825 m Susannah Degree Pvt NY
Samuel P.: b 10-10-1743 d p. 1793 m Theodate Drake Pvt NH
Simon: b 6-6-1742 d — m Elizabeth Moors Vol MA
Simon: b 1750 d 1836 m Mary Brown PS NH
Simon: b 4-11-1756 d 12-20-1813 m (1)Anne Bickford (2)Mehitable
  Young (3)Susannah Peary Pvt NH
Stephen: b 1-22-1716 d 3-21-1804 m (1)Ann Perkins (2)Mary
  Burnham PS NH
Stephen: b 4-8-1735 d 6-18-1805 m Mary Dearborn PS NH
Thomas: b 9-6-1730 d p. 1781 m (1)Dorothy Houghton (2)Mary
  Knight Pvt MA
Thomas: b 5-30-1766 d 10-27-1836 m (1)Abigail Duston (2)Polly
  Thayer Drm MA
Thomas: b 4-30-1743 d 6-26-1829 m Mary Elikins QM NH
Thomas: b 2-1-1750 d 5-2-1813 m Betsey Fowler QM Sgt NH
Thomas: b 11-5-1745 d 1828 m Alice Scott Pvt NJ
Timothy, Sr.: b 5-24-1727 d 8-26-1791 m Mary Winslow Foster Capt
  CS PS MA
Timothy, Jr.: b 2-16-1757 d 10-29-1821 m Mary Robinson Pvt MA
Timothy: b 7-24-1763 d 10-30-1840 m Mary Coward Pvt NJ
Wm., Sr.: b 5-2-1723 d 2-14-1790 m Mercy Aiken Capt PS MA
Wm., Jr.: b 5-1-1745 d 1826 m Mercy Raymond Pvt MA
Wm.: b 11-17-1738 d p. 1806 m Martha Parker Pvt MA
Wm.: b 2-21-1749 d 2-14-1810 m Chloe Todd Col QM Dr NH
Wm.: b 11-27-1756 d 1-14-1839 m Sarah Dudley Pvt NH ★

PAGETT,
Frederick: b 1758 d 1846 m Lucia Magan Pvt VA ★

PAINE, (includes PAYN & PAYNE)
Abel: b 6-10-1754 d 1-5-1839 m Cynthia Robinson Sgt RI & VT ★
Abner: b 1-11-1721 d — m Jane Doane Pvt MA
Abraham: b 5-2-1722 d 4-21-1801 m Rebekah Freeman PS Pvt NY
Abraham: b 5-24-1758 d 10-30-1827 m Hannah Lewis Pvt CT
Abraham: b 9-28-1735 d c. 1800 m Lydia Johnson Pvt CT
Alsop: b 1698 d 3-6-1795 m (1)Deborah Bayler (2)Phebe Mary
  Moore PS NY
Amos: b 10-24-1736 d 10-25-1790 m Priscilla Lyon Capt CT
Arnold: b 2-12-1734 d 7-19-1802 m Judith Staples PS RI
Asa: b 2-3-1757 d 5-1-1810 m Patty Bacon Mus MA
Augustine: b 12-11-1761 d 3-16-1844 m Catherine Young Pvt VA ★
Barnabas: b 11-28-1737 d 6-6-1822 m (1)Martha Holbridge (2)Mary
  Burrows PS NY
Benjamin: b 3-14-1727/8 d p. 1790 m Mehitable Dimmock Pvt CT
Benjamin: b 7-3-1751 d 6-12-1838 m Deliverance Wells Sgt NY
Benjamin: b 5-21-1749 d 3-31-1831 m Anna Aldrich Pvt RI W ★
Brinton: b 1737 d 1820 m Hannah Hills Col NY
Daniel: b 4-10-1747 d 5-29-1813 m Elizabeth Wright Pvt CT
Dan: b 1736 d 12-20-1805 m Elizabeth Loomis Pvt CT
Daniel: b 5-12-1716 d 1-25-1785 m Elizabeth Thatcher CS MA
David: b 6-18-1729 d 4-24-1805 m Mrs. Lydia Johnson Fassett
  PS Pvt CT
David: b 3-5-1737/8 d 7-2-1807 m Abigail Shepard Pvt MA
David: b 1762 d 12-11-1842 m Sally Cornell Pvt NY ★
Ebenezer: b 9-27-1762 d 12-19-1834 m Koziah Kinney Pvt MA
Ebenezer: b 1763 d 1852 m Rachel Shaw Pvt MA
Edward: b 1-17-1746 d 8-28-1841 m (1)Elizabeth King (2)Rebecca
  (White) Loomis (3)Lorena Horey Capt CT ★
Edward: b 1-10-1750 d 1-19-1845 m Persis Cleveland Pvt CT
Edward, Sr.: b 4-18-1724 d 1-29-1784 m Elizabeth Tiffany Pvt MA
Edward, Jr.: b 4-8-1761 d 3-26-1827 m Abigail Smith Pvt MA
Edward: b 11-18-1726 d 5-17-1806 m Ann Holland Conyers PS VA
Eleazer: b 1764 d 2-10-1804 m Aurel Ellsworth Pvt CT
Elisha: b 12-13-1762 d 2-4-1843 m (1)Mary Brooks (2)Esther
  Douglas Pvt NY
Elisha: b 3-7-1730 d 7-20-1807 m (1)Ann Waldo (2)Elizabeth
  Spaulding MGen PS CS CT VT
Ephraim: b 8-19-1730 d 8-10-1785 m Mary Thompson PS NY
Ezra: b 1749 d 1803 m Abigail Ellsworth Pvt CT
Francis: b 1743 d 1816 m Susannah Jett Ens VA
George: b c. 1759 d p. 4-19-1794 m (1)Rachel Logsdon (2)Mary
  Sapp Pvt MD
George: b 4-6-1730 d 1795 m Mary Davis Maj NJ
George: b 11-21-1707 d a. 3-15-1784 m Judith Burton LCol VA
George: b 1763 d c. 1798 m Mary Coe Sol VA

PAINE, contd.

Henry: bpt 8-8-1742 d — m Martha Blackler Pvt MA
Henry: b 1-26-1753 d —m Ann Lane 1Lt VA
Isaac: b 3-11-1761 d 11-4-1815 m Anna — Pvt NJ
Isaac: b 8-21-1742 d 5-2-1796 m Hannah Williams Capt RI
Jacob: b 2-7-1750 d 6-5-1836 m Hannah Morse Pvt MA
Jacob: b 1747 d 1810 m Martha Covington Sgt VA
James: b 2-28-1759 d 1826 m Margaret Thomas Pvt MD
James: b 4-23-1763 d 3-2-1835 m Frances Dix Sol VA
Jesse: b 3-18-1757 d 12-13-1848 m Polly Robinson Pvt MA
John: b 7-15-1756 d 3-26-1838 m Olive Martin Pvt CT
John: b 1754 d 8- -1837 m Jane Farabee Pvt DE ★
John: b c. 1750 d 1828 m Milla — Pvt GA
John II: b 10-3-1739 d p. 1790 m Barbara Rice Pvt MA
John: b — d p. 10-3-1781 m Mary Freeman Capt NJ
John, Sr.: b 1737 d 11-1-1813 m Phoebe — Pvt NY
John: b 5-27-1739 d 8-3-1815 m (1)Mary Booth (2)Sarah (Rogers) Halsey PS NY
John: b a. 1750 d p. 1800 m Susanna Satterwhite Maj NC
John: b c. 1745 d p. 1832 m (1) — (2)Mary — Pvt PS NC
John: b 1743-7 d 1784 m Margaret — PS NC
John: b 3-2-1761 d 1-8-1843 m (1)Nabby — (2)Mrs Fanny Stull Pvt RI ★
John: b 1719 d 1794 m Hannah Poole PS RI
John: b 12-4-1713 d 7-28-1784 m (1) — Archer (2)Mrs. Jean Smith Chichester PS VA
John: b c. 1755 d 1831 m Mary Prince Ens VA
John: b 1760 d 12-29-1836 m Ann Burruss Pvt VA ★
John: b 4-8-1764 d 9-9-1835 m (2)Betsey Johnson Pvt VA
John: b c. 1763 d p. 1800 m Elizabeth Litt PS VA
Jonathan, Jr.: b 12-12-1752/3 d p. 6-8-1806 m Martha Davis Pvt MA
Jonathan: b 7-28-1744 d 1-3-1788 m Rebecca Dyer Smn MA
Joseph: b 4-21-1741 d 10-13-1827 m Phebe Rich Sgt MA
Joseph: b 2-28-1758 d 4-5-1826 m Ann Van Clief Ens VA ★
Joseph: b c. 1740 d 1803-5 m Phoebe — PS VA
Joseph Ruggles: b 6-30-1735 d 4-17-1822 m Mehitabel Gittings Pvt MA
Joshua: b 1734/5 d 12-28-1799 m Mrs Mary Moseley Chp MA
Josiah: b 4-8-1760 d 1-21-1825 m Phebe Stone Pvt MA
Josiah: b a. 1735 d 1804 m (1)Elizabeth Fleming (2)Mary Barnett 2Lt VA
Josiah: b 1740 d 12-12-1732 m Elizabeth Fleming Ens VA
Lemuel: b 4-4-1748 d 12-22-1794 m Rachel Carpenter Pvt MA
Michael: b 1740 d 1803 m (1) — Winn (2)Mary Ellett (3) — Judkins Capt NC
Miller: b 11-24-1754 d p. 1830 m Zillah Smith Pvt MA ★
Nathan, Jr.: b 1-21-1755 d 11-23-1794 m Keziah King Sol RI
Nicholas: b c. 1740 d c. 1802 m Elizabeth Towle Capt VA
Noah: b 4-1-1741 d 1820 m Zuriah Humphrey Pvt CT
Noah: b 2-1-1758 d 3-2-1825 m Polly Carley Pvt NH ★
Noah: b 11-24-1729 d 12-14-1806 m (1)Eunice Hawley Lt NY
Oliver: b 12-12-1754 d 12-29-1819 m (1)Abigail Thornton Pvt RI
Peleg: b 5-27-1753 d 8-25-1837 m Joanna Viall Sgt RI
Philip: b 3-29-1760 d 7-7-1840 m Elizabeth Dandridge Sol VA
Reuben: b 1762 d 7-31-1810 m Elizabeth Hamlin Pvt CT
Reuben: b c. 1730 d 1821 m Agnes — Capt PS CS VA
Richard: b 3-2-1757 d 4-21-1847 m Hannah Baker Pvt NH ★
Richard: b 6-18-1763 d 3-18-1843 m (1)Susannah Kelley (2)Mary Major Pvt VA ★
Robert: b 3-3-1748 d 2-27-1808 m Mrs Elizabeth Miller Capt NC
Robert: b c. 1738 d 1791 m Anne Burton Capt CS VA
Robert Burton: b 1752 d p. 3-15-1784 m Margaret Sydenham Morton Lt VA
Robert Treat: b 3-12-1731 d 5-11-1814 m Sarah Cobb PS SDI MA
Roswell: b 2-24-1756 d 3-7-1806 m Sarah Chamberlain Cpl CT
Rufus: b 4-8-1750 d 1-21-1832 m Agnes Findley Pvt CT ★
Rufus: b 1757 d 1827 m Submit Bisbee Arfr CT
Samuel: b 5-11-1744 d 12-13-1834 m Lucy Hall Capt NH
Samuel: b 5-25-1733 d 6-21-1813 m Abigail Graham Pvt VT
Samuel Royal: b 4-23-1757 d 12-26-1838 m (1)Elizabeth — (2)Abigail — (3) Bethia — Pvt VA ★
Sanford: b c. 1728 d 1792 m Abigail Lay PS VA
Seth: b 9-1-1742 d 2-13-1813 m Jerusha Swift Pvt CT
Seth: b 5-21-1719 d 2-24-1792 m Mabel Tyler PS CT
Silvanus: b 11-1-1759 d 4-1-1836 m Susannah Bangs Pvt MA
Solomon: b 9-26-1760 d 8-17-1844 m (1)Eunice Clark (2)Mary Loomis Whitney Sgt CT ★
Solomon: b 3-8-1732/3 d 2-22-1822 m Mary Bacon PS CT
Solomon: b 1745 d p. 10-2-1797 m Mary Haskins Pvt MA
Stephen: b 1-31-1746 d 8-28-1815 m Martha Cogswell Pvt CT
Stephen: b 6-26-1735 d 1810 m Rebecca Bushnell Sgt MA
Stephen: b c. 1739 d 1794 m (1)Mehitabel Whittemore (2)Hannah Sampson Sgt MA
Stephen: b 1731/2 d 1798 m Lydia Cook Sol MA
Stephen: b 8-17-1716 d 12-29-1797 m (1)Sarah Thornton (2)Jemima Martin Lt RI
Tarlton: b 1758 d p. 2-5-1817 m Elizabeth Winston Capt VA
Thomas: b 10-9-1732 d 7-23-1797 m Ann Williams Pvt CT
Thomas: b 4-6-1725 d 1-22-1802 m (1)Phebe Freeman (2)Mrs Sarah S. Mason PS CS MA
Thomas: b 1758 d 10-2-1839 m Hulda Vigil Pvt Matr RI ★
Thomas Jefferson: b 1758 d 6-29-1825 m Elizabeth — Pvt CT

Timothy: b 8-6-1747 d 1-12-1822 m (1)Thankful Cole (2)Azubah Warren Pvt CT
Wm.: b 9-30-1743 d 1-19-1827 m Sarah Mayo Pvt MA
Wm.: b 11-19-1760 d 10-14-1846 m Pamelia Parker Pvt Chp MA ★
Wm.: b 12-19-1751 d c. 1814 m Prudence Bumpass Pvt NC
Wm.: b 1745 d 9-26-1827 m Elizabeth Drury Capt PA
Wm.: b 11-5-1759 d 1-14-1830 m Amy Clark Pvt RI
Wm.: b 3-31-1755 d 9-19-1837 m (1)Elizabeth Susannah Richards (2)Mrs Marian Andrew (Morson) Love Capt VA ★
Wm., Sr.: b 7-31-1724 d 7-15-1782 m Susan Clarke Capt VA
Wm., Jr.: b 2-14-1751/2 d 9-23-1813 m (1)Mary Robinson (2)Mrs Brooks 1Lt VA
Wm.: b 2-10-1732 d 3-2-1822 m (1)Mary Barrett (2)Mary Thomson PS VA

PAINTER,

Adam: b 1736 d p. 1-23-1833 m (1)Elizabeth — (2)Susan Carpenter Pvt VA ★
Christian: b — d a. 9-22-1794 m Mary — PS VA
Christopher: b c. 1750 d p. 1790 m Catherine — Pvt PA
Deliverance: b 8-26-1764 d 9-5-1841 m Urania Hine Pvt CT ★
Deliverance: b 5-31-1701 d 9-1-1781 m Mary Smith PS CT
Edward: b 10-16-1745 d 2-4-1800 m Betty Truesdail Lt NY
Edward: b a. 1738 d c. 1796 m — Pvt NY
George: b 10-30-1743 d 1780/1 m — Bowman Pvt PA
Henry: b 4-8-1759 d 9-19-1845 m Elizabeth — Pvt PA
Jacob: b 1743 d 6-5-1824 m Eve Catharine — Sol PA
John: b 1755 d 1799 m Margarat Altions Pvt PA
John: b 10-8-1752 d 1-7-1837 m Catharine Taggart Lt PA ★
John: b a. 1760 d 4-23-1830 m Ann — Pvt PA
John: b c. 1735 d c. 1807 m Philbena Catherine — Pvt VA
Lamberton: b c. 1740 d 12-22-1795 m Mabel Smith 1Lt CT
Samuel: b 2-29-1752 d 1-17-1802 m Elizabeth Bennett Pvt PA
Thomas: b 1-24-1760 d 10-28-1847 m Hannah Candee Pvt Slr CT
Thomas Welcher: b 9-25-1760 d 3-27-1817 m Lucina Dunbar Pvt CT
Wm.: b 10-9-1760 d 12-28-1842 m Martha Torton Pvt PA

PAISLEY,

John: b 1745 d 10- -1811 m Mary Ann Denny Col NC
John: b 1-19-1752 d 8-25-1800 m Jerusha May Pvt SC
Robert: b 1739 d 8-4-1828 m (1)Margaret Major Capt NC
Robert: b c. 1746 d 3-2-1818 m (1)Sarah — (2)Elizabeth Crocker Capt SC
Robert: b 4-3-1746 d p. 1820 m Sally Forbes PS VA
Wm.: b 12-23-1741 d 9-11-1822 m Deliverance Paine Pvt NC

PALEN,

Ezekiel: b 10-2-1748 d 1-21-1809 m Phebe Thorn Pvt NY
Petrus: bpt 3-21-1742 d p. 1794 m Hilletje Middag Sol NY

PALFREY,

Warwick: b 9- -1739 d 1791 m (1) — (2)Mrs Deborah (Ward) Beckford NOf MA
Wm.: b 2-24-1741 d 12- -1780 m Susan Cazheau LCol CS MA

PALM,

John: b 7-25-1718 d 4-25-1799 m Christina Dorothea Kern Pvt PA

PALMER,

Abel: b 4-4-1756 d 9-27-1822 m Lucy Rice Pvt CT
Abraham: b 2-21-1732 d 11-21-1796 m Rachel Reynolds Pvt NY
Aden: b 1758 d — m Lois — Pvt RI ★
Amaziah: b 1757 d 1-17-1830 m Rebecca Hubble Mrnr NY
Amos: b c. 12-17-1757 d 3-19-1814 m Catharine — Pvt NY
Amos: b 8-27-1729 d 6-4-1797 m Mary York Pvt RI
Andrew: b 10-21-1738 d p. 1780 m (1)Lucy Palmer (2)Hannah Palmer NCapt CT
Asa: b 9-7-1763 d 2-6-1839 m (1)Elizabeth Barker (2)Lucy Brown Pvt CT
Asa: b 6-11-1742 d 1-6-1820 m Lois Stanton Mstr CT
Barnabas: b 5-29-1725 d 11-27-1816 m Elizabeth Robinson CS PS NH
Benjamin: b 5-17-1745 d 10-10-1812 m Sarah Moore Pvt CT
Benjamin: b 1752 d 3-29-1834 m Abigail Gould Pvt CT
Benjamin: b 2-26-1757 d 4-3-1849 m Hannah Woodworth Pvt CT ★
Benjamin: b 10-10-1729 d c. 1789 m Esther Hayward PS Dr CT
Benjamin: b 11-27-1764 d 8-2-1830 m Sybil Ball Pvt MA
Beriah: b 12-25-1741 d 5-20-1812 m Deborah White Pvt NY
Charles: b 1750 d p. 1795 m Jane Colwell Fif Pvt VA
Christopher: b 10-10-1735 d 11-4-1818 m Deborah Brown Pvt CT
Daniel: b 11-9-1740 d 1787 m Barbara — Pvt CT
Daniel: b 4-23-1763 d 10-9-1851 m Joanna Youngs Pvt Pvtr CT ★
David: b 8-30-1739 d 1- -1821 m (1)Grace Plumbe (2)Rachel Coffin Pvt CT
David: b 6-9-1742 d 9-6-1781 m Abigail Gardner Pvt CL
David: b 8-3-1747 d p. 1814 m Vashti Allen Pvt VT
Dudley: b 3-5-1752 d p. 1795 m Rebecca Pingree Pvt MA
Ebenezer: b 4-14-1762 d 4-8-1832 m Dorethy Williams Pvt NH ★
Edmund: b 3-2-1758 d 7-23-1836 m Pamela Anderson Pvt NJ
Elias, Jr.: b 1-4-1762 d 12- -1826 m Mary Caverly Sol CT
Elias: b 9-29-1756 d 11-4-1838 m (1)Huldah Whitney (2)Mrs Mercy Keyes Ens NY W ★

Elias Sanford: b 3-4-1742 d 6-6-1821 m (1)Phebe (Palmer) (2)Mrs Lucy Randell Breed Lt CT

Elijah: b 9-12-1742 d 5-21-1822 m (1)Ann Chesebrough (2)Louise (Fox) Holmes Capt CT

Elisha: b 9-23-1750 d 2-2-1842 m Eunice Billings Pvt CT ★

Elisha: b 5-8-1720 d 8-12-1798 m Jerusha Stetson Pvt MA

Elnathan: b 8-20-1750 d 8-1-1823 m Jemima Strong Pvt NH

Ephraim: b 12-17-1760 d 6-30-1852 m Margaret Force Pvt CT ★

Fenner: b 9-16-1735 d 3-24-1794 m Lydia Buell Capt CT

George: b 6-21-1763 d 1834 m Hannah Harris Pvt CT ★

George: b 1750 d 1820 m Mary Cureton Pvt GA

George: b 9-6-1719 d 12-15-1809 m Hannah Marsh PS NY

Gershom: b 12-5-1738 d 2-9-1815 m Lucy Field Ens CS VT

Gideon: b 4-19-1740 d 5- -1818 m Jane Wilson Pvt NY

Gideon: b 6-23-1751 d 1781 m Abigail Hathaway Mte RI

Gilbert: b c. 1730 d 1810 m Sarah Harmon Pvt NY

Gilbert: b 1-8-1743 d 5-10-1824 m Mary Jackson Pvt NY

Henry: b 8-19-1740 d 7-15-1806 m Hannah Knapp Pvt PS NY

Humphrey: b 12-25-1758 d 7-25-1848 m (1)Wealthy Wheeler (2)Mrs Eunice Tiffany Sol CT

Humphrey: b 1758 d p. 1827 m Mercy — Pvt MA

Ichabod: b 8-8-1730 d 2-17-1819 m (1)Lydia Utley (2)Mary Grant Capt CT

Ichabod Betts: b 7-16-1737 d 11-12-1807 m (1)Anna Noble (2)Mary Wakelee Pvt CT

Isaac: b 11-7-1747 d 7-10-1834 m Ann McAuley Sol VA

James: b 8-2-1754 d 1839/40 m Pamela Miner Sgt Slr CT ★

James: b 1753 d 1808 m Elizabeth (Close) Pvt NY

James : b 1-28-1763 d 1846 m Ann Quarles Sol PS VA ★

Jared: b 6-2-1760 d 11-1-1834 m Jane Chatfield Sgt PS NY ★

Jedediah: b 2-14-1736 d 7-25-1798 m Esther Reed PS CT

Jeffrey: b 1740 d a. 9-27-1819 m Susannah LeGrand Pvt MA

Jesse: b 2-15-1756 d 12-28-1824 m Abigail Brown Pvt NY

Jesse: b 6-28-1763 d 12-13-1850 m Elizabeth Hoffman Pvt NC ★

Job: b 8-15-1747 d 1-30-1845 m Sarah — Pvt SC

John: b 9-12-1757 d 11-25-1822 m Statira Canfield Cpl CT

John: b 6-22-1751 d 7-7-1838 m Ruth Chapman Pvt CT

John: b 3-29-1724 d 10-21-1795 m Elizabeth Longbottom CS PS CT

John: b c. 1748 d 11-11-1799 m Lydia Levick PS DE

John: b 6-6-1754 d 1835 m Sarah Harriman Sol MA

John: b a. 1724 d 6-8-1809 m Mary Howard PS MA

John: b 4-8-1764 d 7-19-1843 m Irena Butler Pvt MA

John: b 1755 d 1-20-1842 m Meribah — Pvt NH ★

John: b 1730 d 1817 m (2)Mary Elizabeth Willett Lt NY

John: b 10-9-1757 d 1-24-1843 m Mary Hill Ens NY

John: b 7-22-1762 d 11-11-1859 m Catherine Frayley Pvt NY

John: b 9-15-1747 d 7-21-1832 m (1)Sarah Jones (2)Ruth Finch Pvt NY

John: b 8-1-1736 d 4- -1793 m Hannah Pyle Pvt PA

John: b 10-12-1756 d 3-27-1829 m Alice Musgrave Bbd PA

John, Jr.: b 4- -1743 d p. 6-7-1811 m Anne Cahusac Capt SC

John: b 6-6-1753 d 1-28-1828 m (1)Martha Williams (2)Hannah — Pvt SC

John: b 1766 d 1839 m Mary Howell Pvt SC ★

John: b 1759 d 1821 m Mary Boatwright Sgt VA

John: b 1-4-1759 d 1850 m Nancy Boyles Pvt VA ★

John Wood: b 4-11-1754 d 10- -1795 m Hannah Ferris CS CT

Jonathan: b 2-12-1753 d 4-20-1832 m (1)Esther Palmer (2)Phebe — (3)Lucy — Pvt CT

Jonathan, Sr.: b 12-23-1720 d 7-5-1801 m Prudence Holmes PS CS CT

Jonathan, Jr.: b 5-5-1746 d 1-10-1810 m Lucinda Smith 1Lt CT

Jonathan: b 6-2-1754 d 1833 m (1)Betsy Quimby Pvt NH

Jonathan: b 3-26-1698 d 11-13-1779 m Anna Brown PS NH

Jonathan: b 12-6-1724 d 1813 m Hannah Rundle Pvt NY

Jonathan: b 3-4-1754 d 1834 m Martha White Pvt CL

Jonathan Wyatt: b 11-11-1739 d 1781/2 m Jemima Satterlee Sgt CT

Joseph, Jr.: b 2-1-1745 d 8-22-1829 m Susanna Kenny Capt CT

Joseph, Sr.: b 8-16-1717 d 4-12-1791 m (1)Zipporah Billings (2)Mrs Elizabeth Stevens Stewart PS CS CT

Joseph, Sr.: b 2-23-1736 d 4-7-1824 m Abigail Lasell Capt CT

Joseph: b 3-31-1716 d 12-25-1788 m Mary Cranch PS BGen MA

Joseph: b 6-12-1739 d 10-8-1808 m Thankful Davis Pvt MA

Joseph: b 9-30-1763 d 4-18-1851 m Christian Churchward Pvt Mrnr NJ ★

Joseph: b 4-21-1759 d 7-30-1838 m Hannah Peters Pvt PA

Joseph: b 2-27-1760 d c. 1832-4 m — Pvt VA ★

Joseph Pearse: b 7-31-1750 d 6-25-1797 m Elizabeth Hunt QMGen MA

Joshua: b 3-12-1750 d 12- -1835 m — Capt SC ★

Joshua: b 1746 d 10-27-1822 m E Amy Smith Mid CT

Joshua, Jr.: b 7-5-1762 d — Lois Sturtevant Pvt MA

Lawton: b 11-24-1727 d c. 1802 m Mercy — PS RI

Levi: b 9-9-1763 d 9-20-1836 m Sarah Rundle Pvt CT ★

Levi: b 6-24-1757 d 4-24-1831 m Dorothy Lee Pvt MA

Luke: b c. 1752 d 1-15-1814 m Mary Foster PS VA

Martin: b 1726 d c. 1790 m (1)Mary Vaughn (2)Milley — Sgt VA

Michael: b 12-25-1755 d 1845/6 m Mary Harp Sol CS MD

Nathan: b 10-24-1711 d 3-28-1795 m Phebe Billings PS Dr CT

Nathaniel, Sr.: b 4-17-1740 d 9-27-1819 m Grace Noyes Vol CT

Nathaniel: b 9-21-1758 d 9-27-1835 m Sarah McGlathry Pvt MA

Nathaniel: b 1753 d 2-15-1826 m Elizabeth — Pvt NY

Nathaniel: b 5-13-1757 d 3-22-1833 m Mary Foster Sgt RI ★

Nathaniel Stanton: b 10-1-1709 d 5-30-1790 m (1)Mary Cheesebrough (2)Anna Way Pvt CT

Nehemiah, Sr.: b 5-2-1738 d 2-5-1829 m Mary Cheesbrough Pvt CT

Nehemiah, Jr.: b 7-2-1764 d 2-5-1835 m (1)Deborah Brown (2)Anna Safford Pvt Smn NY ★

Noah: b 2-9-1756 d 9- -1840 m (2)Tersah Whitney MM Cpl NY

Noah: b 8-25-1759 d 3-13-1838 m (1)Elizabeth Osborn (2)Betsey Sanford Sgt RI ★

Obadiah: b 5-2-1751 d 5- -1836 m Tamer Hadden Pvt NY

Oliver: b 6-25-1763 d p. 1809 m Asenath Barnes Cpl CT

Othniel: b 2-13-1742/3 d 5- -1790 m Silence Stevens Pvt NY

Ozios: b 1757 d 8-30-1839 m Margaret White Pvt CT ★

Peleg: b 1-24-1754 d p. 1810 m Mary Burch Sol CT

Philbrook: b 5-21-1726 d 9-2-1799 m Judith Wadleigh Pvt PS NH

Richard: b 8-16-1747 d 2-10-1783 m Fallie Gray Mstr RI

Roswell Saltonstall: b 8-1-1764 d 3-7-1844 m Derziah (Palmer) NCmsry

Samuel: b 9-23-1723 d 3-25-1791 m (1)Margaret Leonard (2)Mrs Merrick (3)Mrs Lydia Grange Pvt MA

Samuel: b 3-3-1727 d 9-3-1800 m Mary Savory Pvt MA

Samuel: b 1719 d 8-25-1796 m Hester (Rundel) — Pvt NY

Sandford: b 8-4-1763 d 10-14-1828 m Wealthy Grant Pvt CT

Simeon: b 11-13-1763 d 1-13-1829 m Clarissa — Pvt CT

Stephen: b 1737 d 1815 m Susanna Sawyer Lt CT

Stephen: b 8-19-1749 d 5-4-1814 m Hannah Lockwood Grd CT

Stephen: b 1-9-1753 d — m (2)Mary Bemis Pvt MA

Stephen: b 12-27-1760 d 3-1-1845 m Sarah Renne Pvt Fif NY ★

Stephen, Sr.: b 1-10-1723/4 d 11-7-1790 m Priscilla Hoyt PS NH

Stephen, Jr.: b 1754 d 5-23-1831 m Abigail (Brown) Rowe Pvt NH

Stephen: b 8-28-1758 d 12-31-1834 m Dorcas Burdick Pvt Grd RI ★

Sylvanus: b 5-20-1745 d 7-20-1823 m Sarah Finch Pvt NY

Thaddeus: b 6-22-1759 d 9-17-1797 m Thankful Cleveland Sol CT

Thomas, Jr.: b 1760/1 d p. 1840 m (1)Betty Stetson (2)Mary McIntosh Pvt MA ★

Thomas, Sr.: b 1720/1 d 11- -1790 m Love Adams SeaCap PS NH

Thomas, Jr.: b 1740 d 5-27-1825 m Mary Palmer Gnr NH ★

Thomas: b p. 1738 d 1787 m Alenah — Col PS NY

Thomas: b 7-30-1755 d 1828 m Nancy Burton Matr PA

Thomas: b 9-5-1743 d 4- -1803 m Phoebe Shaw Pvt RI

Thomas: b 2- -1763 d 10-17-1811 m (1)Elizabeth Richebourg (2)Amy Amelia Jerman (3)Harriett Jerman Pvt SC

Thomas: b 1-4-1760 d 1852 m Emily Adkins Pvt VA ★

Thomas Kinney: b 8-26-1760 d 10-8-1827 m Margaret (Palmer) Pvt CT W ★

Trueworthy: b 7-20-1749 d 6-25-1830 m (1)Joanna Webster (2)Love Perkins Pvt PS NH

Vaniah: b 2-17-1758 d 2-24-1829 m Cynthia Fitch Cpl RI

Walter: b 7-29-1717 d 11-1-1785 m Mary Hinckley PS CT

Wm.: b 10-15-1759 d 1-13-1838 m Marvil Webb Davis Pvt CT

Wm. III: b 9-11-1731 d 10-10-1807 m Phebe Darrow PS CT

Wm.: b c. 1751 d c. 1831 m Mary Willard Pvt MA

Wm.: b 10-19-1757 d 4-29-1815 m (1)Susannah Twombly (2)Deborah Hamm Pvt NH

Wm.: b 5-17-1726 d 6-6-1786 m (1)Mary Adams (2)Mary Alston CS PS NC

Wm.: b 5-27-1745 d 1813 m Elizabeth Dobyns 2Lt VA

Wm.: b 1752 d 1824 m Caroline Dulaney Cpl VA

PALMERTON,
John: b 1756 d 7-31-1824 m Elizabeth Wilsey Pvt NY ★

PALMES,
Andrew: b 5-6-1755 d 4-11-1846 m Sallie Mattox Mar Sgt MA

Samuel: b 5-6-1755 d 6-23-1849 m Mary Foster Pvt CT ★

PALMETER,
Jesse: b 1745 d 7-19-1819 m Elizabeth — Pvt CT ★

Jonathan: b 9-18-1758 d 10-26-1846 m (1)Eunice — (2)Martha Stillman Pvt CT RI ★

Paul: b 9-5-1754 d 12-13-1831 m Elizabeth Satterlee Cpl RI

Wm.: b 1762 d 1846 m Lurania Meigs Pvt CT ★

PALMIER,
Michel Joseph (Beaulieu): b 4-10-1734 d 1780 m Angelique Chavin Capt IL

PALMORE,
Wm.: b — d p. 9-7-1786 m Judith — PS VA

PALSGROVE,
Henry: b c. 5-14-1755 d 2-13-1838 m Anna Maria Huber Pvt PA

PANCAKE,
Andrew: b c. 1735-40 d a. 9-11-1793 m Elizabeth — PS VA

PANCOAST,
Joseph: b 11-12-1746 d 12-26-1781 m Unity Shinn Capt NJ

PANGBURN,
Richard: b 1749 d p. 8-24-1832 m (1)Cathalyntje Van Etten (2)Hetty Ester Wilson Pvt NY ★

Wm.: b c. 1744 d p. 1790 m Hannah Fitz Randolph Pvt NJ

PANNILL,
David: b c. 1745 d 1794 m Sallie — Capt VA
David: b 1-18-1750 d 3-10-1803 m Drucilla Dove Capt VA
John: b 3-20-1763 d a. 10-21-1793 m Ann Wimbish Lt VA
Wm.: b 10-30-1738 d p. 7-29-1804 m Ann Morton PS VA

PARCELL,
Matthias: b 4-20-1754 d 12-1-1807 m Mary Potter Pvt NJ W ★
Nicholas, Jr.: b 4-6-10-1780 m Esther Baldwin Pvt NJ
Thomas: b 1744 d 7-4-1778 m Lois — Pvt NJ

PARCHER,
Daniel: b 6-14-1745 d p. 1784 m Betsy Seavy Sgt MA
George: b 1750 d 4-16-1831 m Mary Chamberlain Pvt MA ★

PARCHMENT,
Peter: b 1756 d 2-12-1844 m Elizabeth (Mary E) Powell Pvt VA ★

PARDEE,
Aaron: b 11-12-1755 d 2-21-1837 m Jane Perkins Lt CL
Abijah: b 1- -1753 d 9-10-1832 m Rosanna Moulthrop Pvt CT
Benjamin: b 12-9-1714 d 7-4-1782 m Mary Bradley PS CT
Chandler: b 10-30-1760 d 3- -1829 m Lydia Hotchkiss SeaCap CT
Daniel: b 10-19-1762 d 3-28-1852 m Florinda Bray Cpl CT
David: b 5-17-1741 d 5-31-1821 m Phebe Woodruff Sgt CT
Ebenezer, Sr.: b 1732 d 10-20-1776 m Anna Richards Pvt CT
Ebenezer, Jr.: b 1765 d 12-22-1812 m Anna Minor Pvt CT
Eli: b 3-3-1756 d 2-3-1836 m (1)Mrs Martha (Lyman) March
  (2)Sarah Lyman Pvt CT ★
Jacob: b 1727 d 8-10-1807 m Mary Hemingway Pvt CT
James: b 1732 d 2-3-1802 m Sarah Hunter Lt CS CT
James: b 2-1-1757 d 8-18-1810 m Elizabeth Raymond Pvt CT
James: b 12-27-1729 d 1805 m Ann Wheeler Pvt CT
John: b 12-25-1764 d 6-3-1827 m Hannah Gage Pvt NY
John: b 5-28-1737 d 4-26-1808 m Sarah Webb Cpl CT
Jonathan: b 5-8-1744 d 7-2-1788 m Tryphena Beecher Pvt CT
Joseph: b 1757 d 1836 m Sarah Fields Pvt CT
Leavitt: b 3-31-1758 d 1-3-1831 m (1)Elizabeth Hemenway (2)Nancy
  — Pvt CT
Lemuel: b 6-11-1759 d c. 1841 m (2)Mary — OrdlSgt CT ★
Levi: b 1-14-1742 d 1805 m Sarah Chidsey Sol CT
Moses: b 7-24-1744 d a. 1787 m Sarah Wilmot Pvt CT
Samuel: b 3-7-1746 d 4-26-1827 m Faith Brewster Sgt CT
Samuel: bpt 12-7-1760 d 4-14-1847 m (1)Abigail Quick (2)Joanna
  (Kinney) Williams Pvt NY ★
Stephen: b 1737 d 1-31-1795 m Ellen Barnum Capt CT
Thomas: b 10-31-1722 d 8-1-1806 m Weltheon Cook PS CT

PARDUE,
Lilliston: b 1760 d 2-7-1807 m Sarah West Sgt SC W ★

PARHAM,
Drury: b 5-18-1755 d 12-15-1838 m Polly Hinton Pvt NC
John: b 1756 d 1807 m Mary Gee Pvt VA
Kenon: b c. 9-10/19-1762 d 11-3-1843 m Milly Parham Sol NC
Matthew: b c. 1734 d a. 11-5-1795 m Rebecca Maclin PS VA
Wm.: b 1757 d 1-4-1834 m Ruth Merrill Pvt MA
Wm.: b 5-3-1737 d 5-6-1794 m Hester Lillibridge Pvt PA

PARISH, (includes PARRISH)
Booker: b c. 1745 d 1822/3 m Constance Massie Pvt VA
Cyprian: b 4-4-1766 d 5-5-1852 m — Pvt NY ★
Edward: b 8-20-1748 d 4-13-1813 m (1)Ann — (2)Sarah —
  (3)Rachel Evans Pvt MD
Edward: b 1762 d p. 1826 m Susan — Pvt NC
Ephraim: b 3-23-1755 d 2-19-1833 m Eunice Fitch Pvt MA W ★
Henry: b c. 1740 d p. 6-20-1800 m Mary Ann Monk Pvt NC
Humphrey: b c. 1730 d 1-25-1823 m Elizabeth Lane Capt VA
Jacob: b 2-11-1752 d 6-23-1838 m Mehitable Flint Pvt NY
Jeremiah: b 2-17-1765 d 7-16-1851 m Thankful Abbott Pvt CT ★
John: b 5-16-1762 d 11-2-1831 m Sally Osborne Pvt NY
John: b 1751 d 9-12-1843 m Sarah Osgood Pvt Tms NY ★
Jolley: b c. 1715 d p. 1-10-1783 m Ann Powis Col VA
Joshua: b — d 8-2-1799 m Phebe M. — Pvt MA
Josiah: b 1725 d 1806 m Elizabeth Plant Pvt NY
Nathaniel: b 1754 d — m Martha Skinner Pvt VA
Nathaniel: b 10-23-1758 d p. 4-13-1810 m (1)Mary Williams
  (2)Martha Clarkson Pvt VA
Roswell: b 10-18-1759 d 9-6-1807 m Lucy Harris Pvt CT
Stephen: b 1-28-1755 d c. 1830 m Lena Houghtaleing Sol NY
Wm.: b 1750 d 1818 m Patty Goode Pvt VA ★
Zebulon: b 2-12-1726 d 1794 m Hannah Kimball Pvt PS CT

PARISIT,
Nicholas: b 1745 d 11-20-1795 m Sarah Franklin York QM Gen FrA

PARK, (includes PARKE & PARKS)
Aaron: b 1763/4 d p. 1796/7 m (1)Dolly Walker (2)Mrs — (Marion)
  — Pvt VA
Aaron: b 2-2-1758 d 3-13-1832 m (1)Anne Jennison (2)Lucinda
  Nesmith MM Pvt MA ★
Abijah: b 4- -1748 d 8-14-1813 m Mary Dean Pvt MA

Alexander: b 11-27-1753 d 3-5-1837 m (1)Martha Betton
  (2)Rebecca Corliss PS NH
Amaziah: b 1759 d 11-4-1838 m Sabra Barrett Pvt CT W ★
Amaziah, Sr.: b 3-13-1731 d 5-10-1824 m Hannah Mansfield Pvt NY
Amos: b 1729 d 10-2-1804 m Grace Herick Pvt CT
Amos: b 9-19-1745 d p. 1797 m (1)Phebe Farmer (2)Margaret Moore
  Pvt CT
Arthur: b 9-12-1736 d 7-11-1822 m Janet Hope Pvt PA
Benjamin: b 1735 d 6-17-1775 m Hannah Stanton York Capt RI
Caleb: 3-20-1758 d 8-18-1823 m Ruth Woodward Pvt MA
Christopher, Sr.: b c. 1735 d 1798 m Sarah Mansfield Cpl MA
Cornelius: b 6-2-1753 d 12-25-1802 m Abigail Sanger Pvt MA
Daniel: b 8-27-1742 d 3-3-1818 m Lydia Marvin Pvt NY
Daniel: b 4-6-1758 d 10-6-1836 m (1)Esther Ranney (2)Mrs
  Catherine Hulburd Sgt CT ★
David: b 9-29-1740 d 10-28-1825 m Rachel Griffin Pvt CT
David: b 1742 d p. 1-23-1814 m — PS MD
David: b 1-10-1724/5 d p. 1790 m Sarah Gibbs Sol CS MA
David: b 6-28-1766 d 4-26-1845 m Sarah Woodworth Pvt NY
Ebenezer: b 3-2-1750 d 9-22-1821 m Bathsheba Smith PS Pvt NY
Elias: b 9-25-1746 d 10-11-1778 m Lucretia Tracy Sgt CT
Elijah: b c. 1742 d c. 1790 m Anna Beaumont Pvt CT
Elijah: b 11-10-1755 d 1-6-1793 m Lucy Starkweather Pvt CT
Elijah: b 9-25-1756 d 4-6-1821 m (1)Anne Smith (2)Margaret Walker
  Fif CT
Elijah: b 6-8-1744 d 5-16-1795 m Olive Brown Lt NY
Elisha: b 5- -1724 d 4-11-1778 m Mary Ingersoll PS MA
Ezekiel Evans: b 5-10-1757 d 12-31-1826 m Susan Smythe Vol GA
Ezra: b 1-8-1759 d 8-31-1827 m Anna Beebe Pvt CT
George: b 8-5-1759 d 12-7-1837 m (1)Milly Davidson (2)Catherine
  Reed Sgt NC ★
George: b c. 1735 d p. 1810 m Catherine Dunlap Sol PS NC
Gideon: b 4-17-1734 d 7-28-1794 m Hannah Fuller Pvt MA
Henry: b 5-31-1758 d 5-18-1845 m (1)Martha Justice (2)Em
  Cruchfield Pvt GA
Hezekiah: b 4-15-1740 d 11-12-1776 m Martha Kinne Cpl CT
Hugh: b 1754 d 1-12-1830 m Mary Davis Pvt NC
Jacob: b 3-6-1757 d 1845 m Deborah Stevens Sgt NY ★
James: b 9-20-1731 d 4-11-1810 m (1)Mary Grant (2)Mary Barnes
  Pvt CT
James: b 5-6-1763 d 5-6-1836 m Jenny Entrekin Pvt PA
James: b 1756 d 11-27-1823 m (1) — Sankey (2)Phoebe Hogue
  2Lt VA
James: b 2- -1753 d 10-20-1835 m (1)Sarah Ann Stanley (2)Mrs
  Rebecca (Jordon) Hayes 1Sgt NC ★
Jeremiah: b 4-7-1725 d p. 1783 m Hannah — Pvt CT
Joel: b 1761 d 1850 m Chloe Foster Pvt NY VT
John: b 1760 d 1819 m Bethia Smith Sgt CT
John: b 1-12-1752/3 d 9-27-1820 m Sarah Wallen PS CT
John: b3-4-1758 d p. 8-15-1826 m Martha Trahern Pvt MD
John: b 11-3-1739 d p. 1778 m Anna Ferguson Pvt MA
John: b 11-16-1759 d 3-26-1829 m Lucy Richardson Matr MA W ★
John: b 6-1-1759 d p. 1811 m Mary Joslin Pvt MA
John: b 1739 d 3-12-1798 m Mary Gordon 2Lt NJ
John: b 2-22-1751 d 5-21-1795 m Jean Kerr Sol NC
John: b 1726 d 7-23-1780 m Ann Noblett Ens 1 & 2Lt PA
John: b c. 1733 d p. 1788 m Isabella Galbraith Pvt PA
John: b a. 1755 d 1834 m Isabella McMullen Pvt PA
John: b 1758 d 1815 m Rebecca — Pvt PA
John: b 1-18-1758 d 5-31-1832 m Sarah McDowell Sct PA
John: b 1742 d 1812 m (1)Abigail Chapman (2)Abigail Hiscox
  Capt RI
John: b 4- -1762 d p. 1840 m — Pvt VA ★
John: b 9-4-1756 d 3-22-1841 m Ann Ewell Pvt VA Heirs ★
John: b 1-4-1751 d 9-8-1831 m Mary Millslagel Pvt VA
Jonathan: b 2-28-1728 d 12-6-1802 m Polly Washington Pvt NY
Jonathan: b c. 1753 d 1818 m Margery Woodward Pvt PA
Jonathan: b 9-22-1743 d 7-18-1827 m (1)Elizabeth Fletcher
  (2)Sarah Scott (3)Miriam Fiske Lt CS VT
Joseph: b 11-24-1713 d p. 1790 m — CS CT
Joseph: b 10-23-1757 d 7-10-1844 m Martha Ansley Pvt NJ
Joseph: b 8-18-1761 d 4-15-1851 m Abigail R. — Pvt NY
Joseph: b 12-21-1737 d 7-2-1823 m (1)Ann Sinclair (2)Agnes
  Maxwell LCol PS PA
Joseph: b 1746 d p. 1782 m Jean Robinson Pvt PA
Joseph: b 1-19-1735 d 6-6-1808 m Esther Sankey PS Lt VA
Josiah: b 8-9-1757 d 6-13-1841 m Beulah Towet Pvt MA
Leonard: b 10-25-1760 d 6-8-1838 m Elizabeth Buckman Pvt Fif
  MA ★
Matthew: b c. 1760 d 1819 m Martha — Ens PA
Melvin: b 2-13-1751 d 9-5-1804 m Margaret Palmer Pvt CT
Moses: b 4-28-1733 d 1787 m Sarah Brewster Pvt CT
Moses: b 11-23-1738 d 5-10-1828 m Mary Hill Pvt NC
Nathan: b 5-6-1758 d 12-19-1849 m (1)Keziah Doolittle (2)Mary Ann
  Mallery (3)Mrs Mary Bishop Pvt MA ★
Nathaniel: b a. 1747 d 6-6-1815 m Thankful Eccleston Pvt CT
Nehemiah: b 1-7-1735 d 5-31-1805 m Sibbel Douglass Cpl CT
Paul: b 11-18-1720 d 6-25-1802 m (1)Sarah Smith (2)Mary Russ
  PS CT
Reuben: b 1764 d 1856 m Elizabeth Ford Pvt CT
Reuben: b 8-13-1755 d 9-14-1802 m Betsey Clark Pvt MA
Reuben: b 10-2-1746 d 2-20-1813 m Mary Barton Pvt MA
Richard: b c. 1736 d 3-2-1817 m (1)Mary Graves (2)Anne Favor PS VA

Robert: b 12-4-1737 d 1810 m Elizabeth Hall Pvt CT
Robert: b 1759 d 6-17-1841 m Sarah McEwen PS Sol NC
Roswell: b 7-1-1758 d 11-13-1847 m Eunice Starkweather Sol CT
Rufus: b 3-5-1760 d 12-24-1842 m (1)Zerviah Larrabee (2)Lucy
   Wake Fif Maj CT ★
Samuel: b 4-23-1734 d *p.* 1790 m Mary Russell PS MA
Samuel: b 11-6-1749 d 12-18-1832 m Hannah Richardson Ens PS
   NH
Samuel: b 11-28-1757 d 10-23-1844 m — Pvt NC
Samuel: b 1730 d 1794/5 m Margaret Marshall Pvt PA
Samuel: b *c.* 1730 d 1796 m Mary — Sol SC
Silas, Sr.: b 3-10-1726 d 2-23-1802 m (1)Sarah Ayers (2)Deborah
   (Avery) (Park) Brewster CS CT
Simeon: b 3-21-1730 d 7-17-1812 m Anne Button Pvt CT
Smith: b 11-5-1721 d 2-12-1807 m Mary Davis Pvt CT
Smith, Jr.: b 11-13-1749 d *p.* 1805 m Mary Lord Cpl NY
Solomon: b 3-5-1765 d 4-3-1843 m Susannah Burnham PS NY
Squier: b 1759 d 7-10-1847 m Sarah — Pvt NY
Thomas: b 1749 d 2-1-1819 m Abigail (Nesbet)Heady Cpl CT W★
Thomas: b *c.* 1745 d 6-8-1806 m Rosanna Conn Pvt MA
Thomas: b *c.* 1750 d 12-27-1831 m (1) — White (2) — Hornbuckle
   (3)Anne Brockman Pvt NC
Warham: b 3-13-1752 d 1801 m Rebecca Gorham Maj MA
Wm.: b 7-28-1734 d *p.* 1790 m (1)Lydia Hager (2)Sarah (Pierce)
   Holbrook MM MA
Wm.: b 12-22-1749 d 3-5-1840 m Sarah (Read)Potter PS QM
   MA ★
Wm.: b 3-4-1750 d 2-9-1825 m Eunice Stone Sol MA
Wm.: b 9-24-1746 d 8-11-1794 m Rachel Rowland 1Lt NJ
Wm.: b *c.* 1755 d *a.* 5-3-1803 m Mary — Wgn NJ
Wm.: b *c.* 1740 d 5-30-1776 m (1)Tabitha Ware (2)Mary Ann
   Dawson Pvt NC
Wm.: b 5-17-1742 d 7-28-1806 m Frances Boyd Pvt PA
Zebulon: b 1-14-1757 d 7-4-1846 m Jane Burris Sgt NJ

▶ **PARKER,**
Aaron: b *c.* 1760 d *p.* 1827 m Charity Shuffield Sol GA
Aaron: b 4-15-1739 d *p.* 1800 m (1)Lucy Hildreth (2)Lydia Spaulding
   Lt MA
Aaron: b 7-25-1757 d 4-28-1841 m Jerusha Damon Pvt MA
Aaron: b 1759 d 3-17-1857 m Hannah Abbott Pvt MA
Aaron: b — d 7- -1801 m Abigail Covel Pvt MA
Abel: b 1762 d 11-29-1851 m Lydia Wood Pvt CT ★
Abel: b 3-25-1753 d 5-2-1831 m Edith Jewett Lt MA
Abel: b 1744 d 2-10-1834 m Hannah — Pvt VT
Abraham: b 5-30-1751 d 9-10-1837 m Abigail Ingraham Pvt MA
Abraham: b 1720 d 1-12-1796 m Mary Budd PS NY
Abraham: b 1-18-1758 d 1833 m Nancy Love Pvt PA ★
Alexander: b 1728 d 1815 m Nancy Dickey Cpl NH
Alexander: b 1753 d 1792 m Rebecca Blair Capt PA
Amariah: b — d 1788 m Tamor Munson Wgn NJ
Amasa: b 2-28-1751 d 3-12-1805 m Thankful Andrews Sol CT
Amasa: b 11-12-1722 d *p.* 1779 m Sarah (Richardson) Pvt NH
Amos: b 10-30-1757 d 5-1-1836 m Polly Corkins Sgt CT ★
Amos: b 1762 d 1842 m (1) — (2)Mary — Pvt CT
Amos: b 7-24-1723 d 12-23-1790 m Anna Curwen Stone PS MA
Andrew, Jr.: b 4-11-1738 d 5- -1791 m (1)Abigail Jennison (2)Mrs
   Mary Stearns PS MA
Andrew: b 1-15-1759 d 8- -1813 m Lucilla — Cpl MA
Aquilla: b 3-1-1755 d 12-4-1834 m Elizabeth Amos Adj MD
Asa: b 10-7-1757 d 3-28-1841 m — Woodworth Pvt CT ★
Asa: b 5-24-1740 d 8-23-1809 m Hepsibah Nichols Cpl MA
Asa: b 1758 d 5-17-1838 m Lydia Stone Pvt MA
Asa: b *c.* 1736 d *p.* 6-28-1808 m Jemima Smith PS NH
Asa: b *c.* 1765 d 11-12-1853 m Watie Phillips Sol RI
Avery: b 7-19-1743 d 11-21-1794 m Mary Tobey Capt MA
Benjamin: b 2-12-1729 d 2-9-1807 m Mercy Atwater Pvt CT
Benjamin: b 5-27-1755 d 8-3-1823 m Lurenda Curtis Pvt CT ★
Benjamin: b 3-26-1723 d 2-17-1801 m (1)Elizabeth Blodgett (2)Mrs
   Sarah Lane Pvt MA
Benjamin: b 1749 d 12-31-1834 m Rebecca Royall Pvt MA ★
Benjamin, Jr.: b 3-7-1756 d 3-6-1836 m Susanna Nichols Sol MA
Benjamin: b 10-11-1757 d 2-21-1811 m Hannah Guild Pvt MA ★
Benjamin: b 3- -1765 d 11-7-1842 m Mary Davis PS NY
Benjamin: b 2-22-1758 d 3-27-1812 m Rachel Wetherbee Pvt VT
Benjamin: b 2-27-1759 d 10-19-1836 m — Pvt VA ★
Benjamin: b 1723 d 1808 m Margaret Thornton PS VA
Caleb: b 7-14-1760 d 3-4-1826 m Thankful Pratt Pvt MA W★
Charles: b 6-9-1759 d 9-4-1841 m Elly Turner Pvt MA ★
Dan: b 3-1-1762 d 10-18-1839 m Anna Spring Pvt MA
Daniel: b 1756 d 8-14-1844 m Lucy White Pvt GA
Daniel, Jr.: b 5-28-1752 d 3-4-1825 m Sarah Richardson Pvt MA
Daniel: b 10-27-1762 d 4-22-1842 m Nancy Healey Sol NH ★
Daniel: b 1719 d 1784 m Mary Farlee Pvt NC
Daniel: b *c.* 1757 d 12-24-1807 m Elizabeth — Pvt SC
Daniel: b 9-2-1740 d 1814 m Miriam Curtis Pvt VT
David: b 1753 d 1847 m Mary Flint MM Pvt MA ★
David: b 1757 d 7-8-1834 m Martha Carver Pvt MA
David: b *c.* 1740 d *p.* 1832 m Chloe Bertie Sgt VA
David: b 1761 d 1814 m Mrs Elizabeth (Andrews) Hays PS NC
Didymus: b 1-29-1721 d *p.* 1790 m Phebe Johnson Lt MA
Dominicus Jordan,: b 1744 d 12-29-1822 m Mary Rogers Capt MA
Ebenezer: b 3-21-1742 d *p.* 1784 m Lydia Haskell 2Lt MA

Ebenezer: b 8-13-1750 d 10-19-1839 m (1)Dorcas Monroe (2)Mrs
   Mary Rice Sgt MA
Ebenezer: b 1702 d 4-14-1783 m (1)Sarah Stevens (2)Mindwell
   Bird (3)Mary Gollard Pvt MA
Ebenezer: b 11-29-1754 d *p.* 1797 m Lucretia — Pvt MA
Ebenezer: b 6-29-1749 d 12-29-1831 m Experience Hildreth Pvt MA
Ebenezer: b 1756 d 8-31-1848 m Ruby Litchfield Pvt VT ★
Edmund: b 2-7-1731 d 9-13-1813 m (1)Lydia Varnum (2)Elizabeth
   Green Pvt MA
Edmund: b 5- -1761 d 11-18-1836 m (1)Mary Farnsworth
   (2)Margaret — Pvt MA ★
Edward: b 1723 d 5-18-1788 m Mary — PS PA
Eldad: b 9-14-1731 d 7-6-1779 m Thankful Bellamy Sol CT
Eleazer: b 3-10-1753 d 4-8-1826 m Mary Royce Pvt CT
Eleazer: b 3-30-1740/1 d *p.* 1818 m Dinah Fransworth Pvt MA ★
Eli: b 1736 d 11-9-1829 m Elizabeth Hubbard Capt CS MA
Elias: b *a.* 1-30-1735 d 7-8-1794 m Elizabeth — PS VA
Elihu: b 1758 d 4-17-1822 m Mary — Pvt MA
Elijah: b 1761 d *p.* 1830 m Hannah Ashley Cpl MA
Elijah: b 8-4-1750 d 12-25-1804 m Elizabeth Farwell PS VT
Elisha: b *c.* 1725 d 9-22-1799 m Abigail Holmes Sgt CS MA
Elisha: b 10- -1747 d 1841 m Thankful Marchant Sgt MA
Elisha: b 1740 d 3-10-1820 m Eunice Jordon Pvt MA
Elisha: b 4-10-1742 d 2-27-1811 m Martha Jewell Pvt NY
Elisha: b *a.* 1749 d 7-26-1793 m Rebecca Warren Sol NC
Elisha: b 8-6-1746 d 3-19-1813 m Mariah Ellsworth Lt RI
Elvaton: b 11-21-1749 d 10-20-1797 m Mary Beetle Pvt MA
Enos: b 3-12-1744 d 1- -1815 m Damaris (Parker) Capt PS MA
Enos: b 1739 d 7-18-1821 m Anna — Pvt MA
Ephraim: b 4-23-1725 d 1800 m Bathsheba Parsons Pvt CT
Ephraim: b 10-1-1733 d 4-21-1823 m Deborah Sargent PS CT
Ephraim: b 10-20-1738 d 6-27-1811 m Sybil Warren Pvt MA
Ezra: b 12-13-1745 d 7-7-1842 m (1)Sarah Tuttle (2)Elizabeth Perry
   Sgt MA ★
Ezra: b 6-13-1731 d 3-11-1810 m Sarah Pratt PS CS NH
Francis: b 1760 d *p.* 1788 m Priscilla — Pvt MA
Free Groves: b 4-17-1755 d 2-10-1842 m (1)Susanna Hardy (2)Eliz
   (Burbank) Carlton Pvt MA
Freeman: b 10-15-1749 d 9-18-1776 m Desire Davis: Cpl Adj MA
Gamafiel, Sr.: b 6-6-1718 d 12-3-1799 m Elizabeth Blakeslee Pvt
   CT
Gamaliel, Jr.: b 11-2-1756 d 12- -1799 m Martha (Parker) Pvt CS CT
   W★
George: b 1760 d 2-21-1833 m Sarah Dikes Pvt MD
George: b *c.* 1760 d 1820/1 m Prudence Pratt Pvt RI
George, Sr.: b 9-6-1744 d *p.* 1790 m Katherine Parker Lt VT
George, Jr.: b 10-23-1765 d 6-23-1852 m Phebe Pearsall Pvt VT
George: b 10-8-1735 d 1784 m Sarah Andrews PS VA
Green: b 3-24-1736 d *p.* 1790 m Hannah Eaton Pvt MA
Hananiah: b 1735 d 1-1-1793 m (1)Abigail Ward (2)Hepzibath
   Warren Lt MA
Howell: b 3-5-1757 d 10-18-1796 m Elizabeth Loftin Pvt NC
Isaac: b 2-24-1755 d 1821 m Esther Marcy Pvt CT
Isaac: b 5-19-1747 d 7-19-1805 m Elizabeth Walker Lt MA
Isaac: b 7-15-1750 d 1-16-1798 m Margery Maynard Lt MA
Isaac: b 8-17-1760 d 8-27-1825 m (1)Bridget Fletcher(2)Catherine
   (Hyde) Wilson Drm MA
Isaiah: b 11-13-1752 d 1-16-1848 m Sibyl Willard CS MA
Isaiah: b 1743 d 4-29-1820 m Sarah Sturgis Pvt MA
Jacob: b *c.* 1727 d *a.* 10-23-1794 m Mary Teackle Smith Pvt MD
Jacob: b — d *p.* 1790 m Lois Bixby Sgt MA
Jacob: b *c.* 1758 d 1812 m Mary Atkins Sol NC
James: b 8-17-1740 d 8-17-1813 m Mary Conant Pvt MM CT
James: b 11-26-1744 d 9-29-1830 m Sarah Dickerson Lt MA
James: b 1716 d 12-12-1797 m Mary Todd 1Lt PA
James: b 3-5-1731 d 1803 m Mary Eleanor Boyd Pvt PA
James: b *c.* 1732 d *p.* 1780 m Rebecca — Pvt PA
James: b *c.* 1760 d 9-27-1827 m Rachel Douglass Pvt PA W★
James: b 1743 d 4-4-1827 m (1)Elizabeth Shearman (2)Esther
   Whitney (3)Mrs Miriam Gage Hazzard Capt RI
James: b 9-29-1764 d 1-26-1828 m Martha Houston Cpl VT
James: b 5-21-1757 d 11- -1833 m Rhoda — Pvt VA
James: b 7-25-1759 d 4-15-1838 m Rebecca Wolfe Pvt VA ★
Jedediah: b 8-10-1749 d 12-3-1822 m Katherine Horn Cpl MA
Jeremiah, Sr.: b 1719 d 1-8-1778 m (1)Mary Williams (2)Mrs
   Martha White PS MA
Jeremiah, Jr.: b 7-27-1744 d 4-20-1780 m Abigail Peele Pvt MA
Jeremiah, Sr.: b *c.* 1730 d *c.* 1784 m Matilda — PS NY
Jeremiah, Jr.: b 11-16-1760 d 2-19-1830 m Eunice Goodrich Pvt CT
Jeremiah: b 1741 d 1-7-1823 m (1)Lucresha Jenne (2)Deborah
   Dix ( )Releaf Rogers Pvt VT
Jesse: b 1759 d 1838 m Mrs Sallie Guthrie Maddox Pvt GA ★
John: b 2-14-1732 d 7-26-1806 m Sarah Fuller Pvt CT
John: b 2-25-1762 d 10-24-1831 m Mirab — Pvt CT ★
John: b 9-25-1740 d 3-3-1825 m Sarah Gordy Pvt DE
John: b 1-16-1734 d 12-5-1795 m Elizabeth Porter Pvt MD
John: b 7-13-1729 d 9-17-1775 m Lydia Moore Capt MA
John: b 1-22-1752 d 12-27-1823 m Olive Temple Pvt MA
John: b 3-16-1753 d 11-11-1829 m Joanna Bailey Pvt RI
John: b — d 12-15-1814 m Abigail Osgood Pvt MA
John: b 1720 d 5-5-1803 m Abigail Kidder PS MA
John: b 1738 d 1822 m Lydia — Capt NH
John: b 8-15-1760 d 5-27-1825 m Martha Lovejoy Pvt NH

PARKER, contd.

John: b 1747 d 3-4-1781 m Elizabeth Pettit Capt NJ
John: b *a.* 1750 d *a.* 1-10-1808 m Lucy — Pvt NC
John: b *c.* 1740 d 1800 m Mary Weeks PS NC
John: b 9-3-1753 d 5-28-1837 m Isabella Todd Sol Wgn Capt PA ★
John: b — d 4- -1807 m Hannah Pennington Pvt PA
John: b 1757 d 1802 m Agnes Graham Pvt PA
John: b 5-26-1757 d 1842 m Katherine Cole Cpl RI
John: b 11-25-1740 d 1789/90 m Susanna Parker Sgt SC
John: b 1759 d 6- -1845 m Elizabeth Gresham Pvt SC ★
John: b 1-24-1759 d 4-20-1832 m Susannah Middleton PS SC
John: b 1730 d 3-7-1806 m Martha Daniel PS SC
John: b 12-17-1755 d 1801 m Mary Rogers Pvt VA
John: b 9-5-1758 d 5-19-1836 m Sarah White Pvt VA ★
John Riley: b *c.* 1745 d 1800 m Elizabeth Fletcher Capt VA
Jonas: b 1728 d 1800 m Mary Gould Lt MA
Jonas: b 2-6-1722 d 4-19-1775 m Lucy Monroe Pvt MA
Jonas: b 6-15-1750 d 2-15-1794 m Elizabeth Little MM MA
Jonas: b 1753 d 1827 m Susanna Leathe Pvt MA
Jonathan: b 4-26-1736 d 2-26-1824 m Betty Johnson Capt CT ★
Jonathan: b 7-24-1724 d 9-26-1796 m Ruth Boutwell Pvt MA
Jonathan: b 7- -1728 d *p.* 1808 m (1)Abigail Baker (2)Hannah Weld PS MA
Jonathan: b 9-18-1748 d 5-20-1818 m (1)Sarah Osgood (2)Remembrance Fletcher Pvt MA
Jonathan: b 3-20-1751 d 6-6-1822 m Emma Hobart Pvt MA NH ★
Jonatham, Sr.: b 1-1-1722 d 1785 m Eleanor Hunt PS NH
Jonathan, Jr.: b 1744 d 1-16-1808 m Hannah Stanley Pvt NH
Jonathan: b — d *c.* 1-4-1784 m Esther — Pvt SC
Joseph: b 1757 d 5-15-1823 m Hannah Risley Pvt CT W★
Joseph: b 1708 d a. 1800 m Abigail Dutton PS CT
Joseph: b 10-9-1735 d 1-27-1825 m (1)Elizabeth Martin (2)Zeruiah Lincoln Pvt MM MA
Joseph: b 7-1-1736 d 9- -1800 m Hannah Stone Pvt MA
Joseph: b 11-20-1760 d 2-26-1848 m Polly McColister Pvt NH CT ★
Joseph: b 5-20-1742 d 9-22-1807 m Susanna Fletcher Maj NH
Joseph: b — d 1795 m Margaret Shaw Matr NJ
Joseph: b *a.* 1740 d *p.* 1789 m Amelia — Pvt NC
Joseph: b 10-2-1722 d *a.* 10-5-1781 m Catherine Taylor PS PA
Joseph: b 1763 d 2-25-1835 m (1)Judy Watts (2)Lydia Watts Pvt VT ★
Joseph Upton: b 9-9-1762 d 9-22-1828 m Abigail Whittier Pvt MA ★
Joshua: b 12-13-1740 d 1835 m (1)Mary Boynton (2)Hannah Kidder Capt MA
Joshua: b 10-18-1764 d 6-22-1857 m (3)Ruth Paine Pvt MA
Joshua: b 8-28-1749 d 10-10-1832 m (2)Mary Adams Pvt VT
Josiah: b 5-29-1744 d 4-23-1832 m Lydia Beaman Sgt MA
Josiah: b 10-18-1764 d 6-22-1858 m (1)Betsy Walker (2)Ruth Paine (3)prob Sibil Spaulding Ware Sgt MA ★
Josiah, Jr.: b 11-25-1751 d 1-20-1830 m Hannah Gardner Pvt MA
Josiah: b 1-6-1737 d 10-22-1776 m Phoebe — Cpl NY
Josiah: b 1751 d 3-21-1810 m Mary (Pierce) Bridges Col VA
Jotham: b 8-24-1754 d 7-19-1815 m Sarah Seward Wgn CT W★
Kendall: b 4-12-1723 d *p.* 1778 m (1)Mary Harris (2)Prescrilla Austin (3)Mrs Jane Jones MM Cpl MA
Lemuel: b 2-3-1734 d 2-1-1806 m Elizabeth Nichols Sgt MA
Leonard: b 11-10-1745 d 5-25-1813 m Mary Foster Pvt MA
Levi: b 8-21-1757 d 8-29-1835 m Eunice Davis Pvt CT
Levi: b 6-25-1752 d 9-10-1825 m (1)Rebecca Fletcher (2)Abigail Pool Lt MA
Levi: b 9-13-1743 d *c.* 1800/1 m Sarah Blogett Pvt MA
Levi: b 4-16-1762 d 3- -1813 m Mary Lyon Pvt MA W★
Linus: b 5-22-1758 d 6-3-1829 m Elizabeth Gunn Pvt MA
Martin: b *c.* 1765/6 d 1833 m Mary Shumate Pvt VA
Matthew: b 6-24-1712 d 1-10-1800 m Edith Hanes Pvt CT
Matthew Stanley: bpt 10-10-1749 d 9-17-1788 m Ann Rust Pvt CS PS NH
Michael: b 12-24/5-1746 d 10-22-1819 m Phebe Farrington Pvt MA
Moses: b 5-13-1731 d 7-4-1775 m Sarah Parker LCol MA
Moses: b *c.* 1718-20 d 7-13-1797 m Bridget Comings Pvt MA
Moses: b 8-26-1744 d 11-12-1830 m (2)Nancy Thomas Sol SC
Moses: b 1748 d 1798 m Ann — Sol SC
Nahum: b 3-4-1760 d 11-12-1839 m Mary Deeth Cpl MA ★
Nathan: b 6-3-1739 d 1-9-1819 m Mary Wood Capt MA
Nathan: b 9-12-1753 d 8-18-1830 m Ann Barnes Pvt MA
Nathaniel: b 3-23-1746 d 10-17-1802 m Eleanor Robbins 2Lt MA
Nathaniel, Jr.: b 12-2-1741 d 6-5-1813 m Ruth Shattuck Col MA
Nathaniel, Sr.: b 2-25-1717/8 d 3-25-1789 m Eleanor Walker PS MA
Nathaniel, Jr.: b 12-2-1741 d 6-5-1813 m Martha Gilman MM MA
Nathaniel: b 11-28-1760 d 8-11-1820 m Rebecca Dudley Pvt MA
Nathaniel: b *c.* 1803 m (1) — (2)Mrs Bledsoe Sol PA VA
Nathaniel: b 1730 d 1803 m (1)Ann Clayton (2)Mrs Anthony Bledsoe PS VA
Nicholas: b 10-21-1755 d 8-20-1821 m Mary — PS NC
Obadiah: b 4-11-1730 d 10-5-1816 m Ruth Stevens Lt NH
Oliver: b 4-18-1758 d 8-5-1816 m Lydia Bicknell Pvt MA
Pearl: b 8-1-1759 d 1822 m Lydia Marvin Pvt NH
Peter, Jr.: b 1-15-1747 d 3-28-1777 m Mary Butterfield Pvt MA

Peter: b 10-3-1738 d 11-5-1803 m Ruth Eaton PS MA
Peter: b 3-19-1769 d *a.* 3-21-1825 m Mary Dimmitt Pvt VA
Philomon: b *a.* 1750 d *p.* 1786 m Mary Stevens Pvt MA
Phineas: b 7-2-1758 d 10-26-1846 m Lois Southworth Pvt CT ★
Phineas: b 5-11-1757 d 1833 m Elizabeth Swan Pvt NH
Phineas: b 1749 d *p.* 1794 m (1)Hannah Havens (2)Mrs Bethia Havens PS NY
Reuben: b 5-4-1734 d 1-10-1825 m (1)Sarah Wooley (2)Esther Townsend Cpl PS NH
Richard: b *c.* 1759 d 1832 m (1) — (2) — Sol NC
Richard J: b 12-6-1765 d 8-12-1844 m Lydia German Drm NY ★
Richard James: b 1765 d *p.* 1819 m Betty Keigwin Pvt NY
Robert: b 6-20-1720 d 9-30-1775 m Deborah Hubbard Pvt MA
Robert, Sr.: b *c.* 1732 d 4- -1805 m Penelope — PS NH
Robert: b 2-9-1760 d *c.* 8-22-1839 m (1)Sally — (2)Mrs Betsy (Perry) Pratt Pvt MA ★
Robert, Jr.: b 9-3-1759 d 9-11-1834 m Rebecca Carleton Sgt NH
Robert: b 1756 d 5-1-1799 m Mary Smith Lt PA W★
Robert: b *c.* 1735 d *p.* 9-13-1805 m Margaret — PS VA
Samuel: b 1-10/12-1750 d 10-2-1835 m Hannah Bunnell Pvt CT ★
Samuel: b *c.* 1730 d 5-1-1814 m Sarah Babcock PS CT
Samuel, Sr.: b 10-6-1716 d 10-4-1796 m Mary Stevens Pvt MA
Samuel, Jr.: b 6-28-1753 d 6-12-1822 m Anna Greenough Pvt MA
Samuel: b 10-25-1742 d 4- -1822 m Ann Palmer Pvt MA
Samuel: b 1764 d 3-23-1844 m (1)Mary Stockwell (2)Catherine — (3)Submit Cowles Pvt MA ★
Samuel: b 8-17-1745 d 12-5-1804 m Anne Cutter PS MA
Samuel: b 11-14-1754 d 7-5-1841 m Hannah Parker Sgt NH ★
Samuel: b 1745 d *p.* 1790 m Martha Mitchell Fif NH
Samuel: b 4-13-1755 d 1-25-1834 m Candace Hand Matr NH
Samuel: b 4-13-1759 d 7-9-1844 m (1)Lucy — (2)Mary Rhodes Pvt NY
Samuel: b — d *p.* 2-21-1791 m — Pvt NC
Samuel Franklin: b *c.* 1745 d 12-6-1779 m Mary Moore Maj NJ
Scarborough: b *c.* 1750 d *p.* 3-7-1788 m Mary — Ens MD
Silas: b 1748 d 12-7-1832 m (1)Mary Eaton (2)Mrs Mary Herbert Pvt MA
Silas: b 12-13-1758 d *p.* 1803 m Rebeckah (Parker) Pvt MA
Silas: b 8-6-1759 d 9-9-1842 m Martha Foster Pvt MA ★
Simon: b 4-30-1719 d 10-26-1794 m Mary Bodwell Pvt MA
Solomon: b 10-23-1743 d 9-18-1840 m Hannah Melvin PS ME
Solomon: bpt 8-23-1741 d *p.* 1786 m Elizabeth Jones Pvt MA
Solomon, Sr.: b 1723 d 3-18-1798 m Hepsibah Douglas Pvt CS NH
Solomon, Jr.: b 9-30-1753 d 7-9-1843 m Susa Beedle Sol VT
Stephen: b 8-2-1759 d 7-1-1846 m Rebecca Ray Pvt CT
Stephen: b 3-8-1738 d 7-4-1814 m (1)Mary Morse (2)Abigail Morse Hitchcock Capt NH
Stiles: b 1-2-1765 d 9-16-1847 m Dammis Kaple Pvt MA
Thomas: bpt 12-24-1727 d 7-3-1789 m Jane Parrot Sol MA
Thomas: b 10- -1734 d 12-25-1806 m Olive — Pvt MA
Thomas: b 3-29-1754 d 6-29-1829 m Lucretia Johnson Pvt NH
Thomas: b *a.* 1755 d 1825 m Mary Arnold Pvt NC
Thomas: b 4-2-1756 d 1-31-1839 m Laurenia Edwards Pvt RI ★
Thomas: b 10-16-1767 d 9-30-1839 m Sarah Elliott PS RI VT
Thomas: b 1760 d *a.* 1828 m Elsie Marshall Capt VA
Thomas: b 1-8-1757 d 12-18-1819 m Elizabeth Andrews Capt VA
Thompson: b 5-3-1737 d *p.* 1786 m Sarah Milhouse Pvt PA
Timothy: b 1741 d 11-28-1809 m (1)Hannah Curtis (2)Margaret White Capt MA
Timothy: b 5-17-1735 d 5-27-1797 m Deborah Lester Capt CT
Titus: b 2-23-1728 d 6-25-1811 m Martha — Pvt MA
Watts: b 1758 d 1812 m Mary Lightburn Sgt VA
Wm.: b 10-6-1760 d 10-6-1827 m Ruth Smith Pvt CT W★
Wm.: b 1759 d 1861 m (2) — Wren Pvt GA
Wm.: b 1746 d 2- -1797 m Mary — Ens MD
Wm.: b 1-10-1748 d 11-26-1842 m Hannah Hardy Lt MA
Wm.: b 8-29-1755 d 9-7-1842 m Mary Gale Cpl MA ★
Wm.: b 5-45-1745 d 11-26-1825 m Mary Warner Pvt MA
Wm.: b 5-31-1757 d 9-30-1829 m Lucy Spaulding Pvt MA
Wm.: b *a.* 1750 d *p.* 1806 m Elizabeth Parker Pvt NH
Wm.: b 12-9-1703 d 4-29-1781 m (1)Elizabeth Grafton (2)Mrs Abigail Forbes PS NH
Wm.: b 1755 d 12-30-1833 m — Pvt RI ★
Wm.: b *c.* 1720 d *p.* 8-17-1781 m Leah — Capt VA
Wm. Hall: b *c.* 1740-50 d 3- -1838 m (1) — Ferguson (2) — Walker (3)Susannah Hier Sol SC
Wm., Harwar: b 1752 d 1815 m — Sturman Capt VA
Winslow: b 8-2-1755 d 8-12-1812 m Abigail Woods Pvt MA
Wyman: b 1753 d 5-19-1821 m Marcy Gillett Sgt CT ★

PARKHILL,

David: b 1750 d 8-5-1810 m (1)Sibble Blanchard (2)Dorcas Abons Sgt MA
Nathaniel: b *a.* 1745 d *p.* 1791 m (1)Mary Holden Pvt MA

PARKHURST,

Benjamin: b 12-10-1745 d 12-15-1842 m Sarah Shepard Pvt VT ★
Daniel: b 1724 d 1793 m Lydia — Pvt PS PA
Ebenezer: b 8-27-1743 d 9-9-1795 m Marcy Hill Pvt MA
Ebenezer: b 5-8-1746 d 1-12-1831 m (1)Molly Spaulding (2)(2)Charlotte Storrs Capt VT
Ephraim: b 12-27-1743 d 9-20-1798 m Jemima Hayward Cpl MM MA

George: b 8-4-1762 d 6-27-1839 m Rebecca Gitchell Pvt MA
Hugh: b — d 6-6-1776 m Mary Goss Pvt MA
Jabez: b 1766 d a. 8-20-1821 m Lucy Waldo Pvt VT
Joel: b 8-13-1741 d 10-3-1808 m Bettie Cummings Lt MA
John, Jr.: b 5-13-1730 d 11-17-1819 m Phebe Pierce Pvt CT
John: b 5-2-1760 d 11-1-1836 m Sarah Bullard Pvt MA ★
John: b 1752 d 5-13-1832 m Letitia Hathaway Cpl NJ ★
Jonas: b 8-20-1712 d 4-7-1798 m Abigail Bigelow Pvt MA
Jonathan: b 7-23-1725 d 8-22-1787 m Judith Willson Pvt CT
Jonathan: b 1761 d 8-13-1853 m Elizabeth Smith Pvt MA
Jonathan: b 5-12-1725 d p. 1790 m Bridget Butterfield PS NH
Joseph, Sr.: b 8-30-1724/5 d1-31-1803 m Deborah — Pvt MA
Josiah: b 3-8-1736 d 1832 m Elizabeth Bigelow Pvt MA
Leonard: b 4-8-1763 d 5-28-1821 m Hannah Hills Pvt MA
Moses: b 1762 d p. 1820 m — Pvt MA ★
Nathan: b 11-2-1738 d p. 1790 m (1)Elizabeth Shephard (2)Mary
   Eames Pvt MA
Nathan: b 11-29-1758 d 5-17-1815 m Sarah Bradstreet Pvt NH
Nathaniel: b 3-7-1746 d 4-28-1818 m Sarah Brown Sgt MA
Phineas: b 1761 d 10-16-1844 m Lucy Pierce Pvt VT
Pierce: b 11-26-1756 d 1-6-1833 m Hannah Parkhurst Pvt Slr CT ★
Samuel: c. 1756 d 2- -1813 m Rachel Christopher Pvt MA NH W★
Samuel: b 11-4-1759 d 1-15-1849 m Betsy Hutchinson Pvt MA
Simeon: b 9-16-1751 d 12-8-1825 m Polly Briggs Pvt NH
Timothy: b 2-8-1730 d 3-20-1815 m Joannah Cady Pvt CT

PARKINSON, (includes PARKERSON, PARKESON)
Benjamin: b 1750 d 10-26-1834 m Elizabeth Dickey Pvt CS PA
Daniel: b 1754 d 1836/7 m Catherine Overmeir Pvt PA ★
Henry: b 1741 d 5-23-1820 m Janet McCurdy 2Lt NH ★
Jacob: b 3-3-1761 d p. 9-4-1842 m X Pvt NC VA
John: b 1755 d p. 1790 m Anne Parkinson Ens MD
Jonathan: b c. 1750/51 d 2-29-1832 m Nancy Chestney Pvt NJ
Joseph: b 1739 d 4-28-1834 m Margaret Weaver CS PS PA
Peter: b c. 1751 d 3- -1792 m Mary Morgan Sol VA
Reuben: b 8-10-1757 d 9- -1834 m Nancy McCurdy Sgt NJ
Wm.: b c. 1720 d p. 1794 m X PS PA
Wm.: b c. 1720 d p. 1790 m Esther Woods PS NH

PARKMAN,
Alexander: b 2-17-1747 d 4-1-1828 m Keziah Brown 1Lt MA
Daniel: b 1746 d 11-4-1824 m Hannah House Pvt MA
Ebenezer: b 7-20-1753 d 12-21-1838 m (1)Sally Liscomb (2)Phebe
   Harwood Sgt MA
Henry, Sr.: b c. 1730 d p. 1790 m Millie — PS SC
Henry, Jr.: b c. 1755 d p. 1817 m Massey Minter Sol SC
Wm.: b 2-19-1741 d 2-5-1832 m Lydia Adams Sgt MA

PARLIN,
Amos: b c. 1721 d p. 1790 m (1)Esther Conant (2)Mrs Mary Davis
   Pvt MA
John: b 2-8-1719 d 3-25-1806 m Margaret MacCollo Tms MA
Nathan: b 1-1-1749 d 1833 m Lucy — Pvt ME
Oliver: b 9-21-1741 d 3-21-1787 m Rebecca — Pvt MA
Silas: b 8-15-1760 d 3-27-1828 m Lydia Wood Cpl MA

PARLOW,
Thomas: b 8-11-1758 d 12-16-1823 m Sarah Parlow Cpl MA

PARMAN,
Giles: b 1758 d 1832/3 m (1)Elizabeth — (2)Phebe Woolsey Sgt PA

PARMELEE, (includes PARMALEY, PARMELE)
Abraham: b 4-28-1717 d 3-25-1795 m Mary Standley PS CT
Amos: b 7-21-1734 d p. 1779 m Sarah Kilborn Pvt CT
Asahel: b 2-26-1744 d 2-13-1784 m Rhoda Norton Pvt CT
Asaph: b 4-2-1746 d 10-24-1834 m Sarah Everett Sgt CT
Bani: b 12-6-1757 d 2-22-1839 m (1)Temperance Kelsey (2)Mrs
   Charity Peck Pvt CT
Constant: b 5-16-1761 d 3-27-1843 m (1)Esther Farnam (2)Hannah
   — Pvt CT ★
Daniel: b 5-22-1739 d 12-8-1817 m Mary Stevens Ens CT
Elias: b 3-29-1752 d p. 1790 m Thankful Hill Pvt CT
Ezra: b 8-25-1745 d 1-18-1838 m Sybil Hill Capt NH
Giles: b 11-17-1763 d p. 3-4-1846 m Hannah Pomeroy Pvt CT ★
Hezekiah: b 4-20-1737 d 12-3-1794 m Elizabeth Cook Pvt CT
Hezekiah: b 1711/10 d 1796 m (1)Mehitabell Hall (2)Mercy Smith
   PS CT
James: b 11-19-1757 d 7-9-1842 m (1)Caroline Webster (2)Mrs
   Lydia Donelson Pvt CT
James: b 11-27-1762 d 3-4-1846 m Jerusha Coe Pvt CT ★
Jeremiah: b 9-5-1730 d 3-24-1777/8 m Sarah Doolittle Capt CT
Jeremiah: b 3-18-1730 d 1-6-1797 m Temperance Blatchley Pvt CT
Joel: b 3-8-1714 d 4-14-1788 m Rhoda Camp CG CT
Joel: b 8-6-1758 d 1-4-1816 m Esther Hall Pvt CT
John: b 2-12-1755 d 2-14-1828 m Dorothy Scoville Cpl CT
John: b 5-19-1719 d 11-12-1799 m Jane Crittenden Pvt CT
John: b 6-4-1762 d 4-25-1848 m (1)Rebecca Cross (2)Elizabeth
   Pitman Pvt MM NC ★
Mark: b 4-25-1721 d 12-3-1808 m Ruth Brown Pvt CT
Mark Stanley: b 12-4-1722 d 10-25-1815 m Abraham Parmelee PS
   CT
Nathaniel: b 12-2-1710 d c. 1780 m Rebecca — Pvt CT

Oliver: b 10-30-1734 d 8-21-1816 m Abigail Clark Capt CT
Phineas: b 10-16-1734 d 1782 m Eunice Meigs Pvt CT
Reuben: b 11-16-1741 d 11-4-1780 m Lydia Griswold Sgt CT
Roswell: b 8-3-1739 d 1811 m Jerusha Kelsey Lt CT
Samuel: b 7-27-1737 d 1-2-1807 m (1)Sarah Bishiop (2)Widow of
   Wyllys Elliott (3) Wid Ward Capt CT
Simeon: b 8-3-1740 d 5-20-1820 m Jemima Hopkins Sgt MA
Theodore: b 4-3-1751 d 2-21-1824 m (1)Keziah Hudson (2)Mrs
   Sally Roberts Capt CT
Thomas, Jr.: b 7-31-1742 d p. 12- -1826 m (1)Elizabeth Roots
   (2)Olive Curtis Sgt CT ★

**PARMENTER, (includes PALMATEER, PALMATIER, &
   PARMENTIER)**
Aaron: b 6- -1723 d p. 5-3-1794 m Jane Craigie Pvt MA
Abel: b 1756 d 4-12-1834 m Mindwell Briant Pvt MA
Abel: b 1754 d 9-10-1839 m Rebecca Barry Sol MA
Abraham: b 1-27-1760 d 1-19-1842 m Patience Patterson Pvt MA
Caleb, Sr.: b 4-9-1722 d 3-21-1795 m (1)Sarah Richardson
   (2)Elizabeth Blackington Pvt MA
Caleb, Jr.: b 8-29-1758 d 1-22-1852 m Elizabeth Round Pvt
   MA ★
Deliverance: b 12-16-1709 d 1785 m Ruth Hayden CS MA
Deliverance: b 11- -1744 d p. 1780 m Mary Osborne Pvt MA
Edmund: b 1-30-1716 d 4-28-1790 m Millicent — Pvt MA
Elias: b 1746 d 3-9-1811 m Sybil Sheldon Pvt MA
Isaac: b 3-27-1756 d 4-26-1826 m Lydia Furness Pvt MA ★
Isaac: b 1760 d 9-10-1851 m Mary Garington Pvt NY ★
Isaiah: b 7-16-1742 d p. 1790 m Lydia Hayden 1Lt CS MA
Israel: b 11-5-1753 d p. 4-18-1796 m Susanna Stone Pvt MA
Jacob: b 7-26-1752 d 4-7-1776 m Mary Hadley Pvt MA
Jason: b 7-6-1730 d p. 1787 m Abigail Frizzel Pvt MA
Joel: b 5-16-1760 d 7-26-1826 m Zilpah Fay Pvt MA
Jonas, Sr.: b 1-23-1745 d 9-6-1813 m (1)Sarah Buttrick
   (2)Hannah Hunt Pvt MA
Joseph: b 10-7-1753 d 10-14-1824 m Sarah Van Dusen Sol NY
Joshua: b 2-26-1727 d 10-19-1822 m Persis (Parmenter) Pvt MA
Nathaniel: b 5-22-1754 d 10-10-1840 m (1)Lydia Nutting
   (2)Mary Bell MM Pvt MA ★
Reuben: b 3-3-1752 d p. 1820 m Sarah Potter Pvt MA
Thomas: b 3-30-1757 d 10-23-1842 m Mary Walker Pvt MA ★
Wm.: b 7-16-1719 d p. 10-26-1778 m Mary Pepper Pvt MA
Wm.: b 3-18-1761 d 9- -1839 m (1)Sarah — (2)Temperance
   Headington (3)Susanna Mills (3)Mrs Susan Pinkton (5)Mary
   Ann Henry Pvt NY ★

PARR,
Arthur, Jr.: b 7-5-1758 d 3-21-1833 m Mary Morgan Sgt SC ★
Benjamin: b 9-1-1761 d 12-22-1842 m Martha Dincley
   McKinney Pvt NJ ★
John: b 6-14-1759 d 9-7-1850 m — Pvt NJ ★
Matthias: b 9-19-1757 d 4-17-1846 m Mary — Pvt NJ
Moses: b 1-22-1738 d 1-16-1806 m (2)Mary Sweet Pvt RI W★
Stephen: b 1730 d 1800 m Mary Davis Sol VA

PARRAMORE,
John: b — d p. 5-29-1787 m Mary — Capt MD

PARRAN,
John: b 1752 d 1822 m Ann Bourne PS CS MD
Thomas: b c. 1750 d p. 1796 m Jane Mackall Dr MD

PARRIS,
Daniel: b 10-29-1763 d 2-17-1825 m (1)Eunice Lamb
   (2)Drusilla Sherman Pvt MA
Gabriel: b 4-2-1762 d 5-10-1840 m Sarah Jane Olden Arfr PA ★
Samuel: b 8-31-1755 d 9-10-1847 m Sarah Pratt LCol MA

PARROTT, (includes PARROT & PARRETT)
Abraham: b 5-15-1752 d 7-5-1816 m (1)Ruhamah Patchen
   (2)Mrs Esther Wakelee Pvt CT
Benjamin: b 1745 d 9-30-1811 m (1)Elizabeth Ingalls
   (2)Hepzibah Ireson Pvt MA
Christopher: b 3-25-1755 d 10-1-1820 m Martha Clark Sgt MD W★
Daniel: b c. 1737 d 8-5-1810 m Rebecca Inguls Pvt MA
Frederick, Jr.: b 1764 d 5-8-1842 m Elizabeth Keller Pvt VA
George: b 7-8-1712 d 1779 m Ann Bolen Pvt MD
Henry: b 1730 d a. 6-12-1793 m Mary Bettson Pvt VA
Jacob: b 1766 d p. 10-26-1820 m Penelope — Pvt NC
James: b 1756 d 1845 m (1)Katherine Smith (2)Matilda Tharp
   PS MD
John: b 9-13-1745 d 1-13-1830 m Ruth Treadwell Pvt CT
John: b 1747 d 10-15-1806 m Patience Johnson Pvt GA
John: b 1730 d 3-1-1791 m Elizabeth Oxley Pvt NC
John: b 1740 d p. 1798 m (1)— (2)Louise Bean Pvt PA
Joseph: b 1760 d 8-28-1847 m (1)Sara Wendel (2)Ann Hartman
   Lt CS VA ★
Samuel: b 4- -1756 d a. 1835 m Ellen — Pvt VA ★
Wm.: b 9-2-1760 d 3-27-1836 m Catharine Williams Pvt NJ
Wm.: b 1754 d 1853 m Judith Yerby Pvt VA ★

PARSHALL,
David: b 174- d p. 1788 m — Pvt NY

PARSHALL, contd.
Israel: b 10-7-1736 d 2-18-1827 m Ruth Howell 2Lt PA
James: b 9- -1754 d 4-24-1836 n (1)Deborah Clark (2)Mrs Dorothy Longbotham Bostwick OrdlSgt NY
John: b 5-5-1757 d 9-10-1838 m Phebe Coddington Pvt NY
Jonathan: b 11-9-1740 d 10-5-1816 m Jemima Knapp Pvt NY
Samuel: b 3-20-1757 d c. 1827 m (1)Sarah — (2)Rachel Stratton Pvt NY

PARSONS,
Aaron: b 6-2-1712 d 8-4-1795 m Mercy Atchinson CS MA
Aaron, 2nd: b 2-14-1736 d 9-22-1790 m Eunice Warriner Sgt MA
Aaron 3rd: b 1-26-1761 d 2-11-1815 m Rachel Preston Sgt MA
Abraham: b 2-20-1764 d 3-16-1852 m Urana Starr Pvt CT
Abraham: b 3-5-1757 d 8-26-1822 m Leonora Ryder 2Lt NJ ★
Amos: b 8-21-1758 d 6-7-1847 m Abigail Parker Pvt MA ★
Amasa: b 4-8-1764 d p. 1798 m Hannah Bartlett Pvt MA
Andrew: b 12-25-1761 d 9-20-1849 m (1)Rebecca Lee Pvt MA ★
Asahel: b 12-11-1747 d 5-31-1816 m (1)Abigail Kingsbury (2)Hannah Sexton Pvt CT
Asahel: b 1734 d 3-26-1818 m Rebekah Clark Pvt MA
Benjamin: b 1-5-1753 d 10-8-1812 m Miriam Winslow Pvt MA
Charles: b 9-17-1742 d 3-8-1814 m Lucy Baldwin Capt NY
Charles: b 1745 d p. 1820 m (1)Elizabeth Chestnut (2)Nancy Elizabeth Sleith Sol VA
Daniel: b 3-30-1762 d 4- -1841 m Eunice Bartram Pvt CT ★
Daniel: b 6-23-1744 d — m Sarah Davis Pvt MA
David: b 5-24-1732 d 5-22-1803 m (1)Mary Pease (2)Esther Hurlburt Capt CT
David: b 1-17-1748/9 d 3-4-1812 m Lois Thompson Cpl CT
David: b 1735 d 7- -1820 m Rebecca Robinson Lt MA
David: b 10-6-1728 d 11-28-1808 m Mary Winnery Pvt MA
Ebenezer: b 6-23-1746 d 11-16-1818 m Anna Fitch Pvt CT
Eldad: b 8-26-1755 d 7-10-1821 m (1)Experience Bardwell (2)Mrs Asenath (Allen) (3)Mrs Hyocinthia Phelps Pvt MA
Eli: b 1-23-1756 d 11-11-1834 m (1)Rebecah Allen (2)Hulda Kellogg Pvt CT ★
Eli: b 1-29-1748 d 9-25-1830 m Persis Graves Lt NY
Eliezer: b 11-15-1761 d 5-22-1844 m Judith Pote Pvt MA
Elihu: b 1719 d 8-22-1785 m Sarah Edwards Pvt MA
Elijah: b 4-17-1744 d 1796 m (1)Eunice Cadwell (2)Eunice Jennings Pvt MA
Elisha: b 11-16-1731 d 5-22-1805 m Lucy Alvord Pvt MA
Enoch: b 6-18-1739 d 10-1-1827 m Abigail Clogstone Ens CT
George: b 12-16-1734 d 1-4-1809 m Temperance — 1Lt MD
Gideon: b 2-24-1739 d 7-11-1831 m Mary Warner Pvt OrdlSgt MA ★
Hezekiah, Sr.: b 1728 d 9-12-1813 m Mrs Sarah Abbe Chapin Capt CT
Hezekiah, Jr.: b 2-3-1752 d 5-17-1808 m Margaret Kibbee MM CT
Hezekiah: b 6-14-1757 d 5-22-1825 m (1)Anna Webster (2)Ruth Case Ens CT
Isaac: b 4-14-1740 d 10-9-1825 m (1)Anna Merrill (2)Salome Merrill (3)Mrs Deborah (Nash) Hewett (4)Mrs Mary (Noyes) Ellis (5)Mrs Lucy Bacon Capt MA
Isaac: b 10-16-1745 d 9-19-1819 m (1)Mindwell King (2)Martha Bartlett (3)Mrs Rachel Searle Pvt MA
Israel: b 12-12-1748 d 1-29-1818 m Mary Clark Pvt MA
Israel: b 6-11-1762 d 9-20-1846 m Mary Marvin Pvt CS QM MA ★
Ithamar, Jr.: b 10- -1750 d 7-24-1828 m Mehitable Hull PS CT
Jabez: b 7-16-1754 d 12-24-1836 m (1)Martha Terry (2)Sarah Brown 1Lt CT ★
Jacob: b 1719 d 1795 m Lorraine Sedgwick Pvt MA
Jacob: b 10-22-1719 d 1-13-1795 m Beulah Hunt Pvt MA
James: b 10-25-1746 d 8-20-1796 m Deborah Lane Matr MA
James: b c. 1750 d 1813 m (1) — (2)Rebecca Simps Capt VA
Jeffry: b 5- -1746 d 1792 m Mary Vinson Cpl MA
Jesse: b 1758 d 10-29-1828 m Hannah Robinson Pvt CT
Joel: b 1-28-1753 d 8-9-1831 m Tryphena Booth Pvt MA
Joel: b 5-29-1739 d 11-10-1811 m Abigail Ferry Lt MA
John, Jr.: b 4-4-1744 d 1-7-1821 m Ann Osborne Sgt CT
John: b 11-25-1753 d 1848 m (1)Asenath Carrington (2)Elizabeth Munson Pvt CT ★
John: b c. 1735 d a. 11-3-1807 m Rebecca — PS MD
John: b 1- -1737 d 3-2-1821 m (1)Hanna — (2)Mercy Gibson Lt MA
John: b 6-8-1762 d 1-24-1832 m Rebeckah Lee Pvt MA
John: b 11-10-1751 d 5-31-1838 m Lydia Folsom Ens NH ★
John: b 3-12-1748 d 1854 m Louisa Edmonds Pvt NJ ★
John, Sr.: b 1706 d 6-28-1793 m (1)Martha Barnes (2)Abigail Chatfield PS NY
John, Jr.: b 12-18-1738 d 8-16-1799 m Chloe Conklin PS NY
John: b 1705 d 11-5-1775 m Phoebe Miller PS NY
John: b 6-10-1755 d 10-21-1822 m (1)Elizabeth Simcox (2)Sarah Hamilton Pvt PA
Johnathan: b 3-23-1734/5 d p. 1796 m Tryphena Bement PS CT
Jonathan: b 4-25-1735 d 12-29-1784 m Hannah Gyles NCapt MA
Jonathan: bpt 7-19-1713 d 6-25-1823 m Susanna Hadley Pvt MA
Jonathan: b 1735 d 5-2-1810 m Mary Merrick Pvt MA
Joseph: b 6-25-1758 d 1-13-1837 m (2)Mrs Mabel Olmstead Reynolds Maj CT

Joseph: b 6-25-1758 d 2-10-1837 m (1)Anna Hancock (2)Mrs Mabel Reynolds (3)Lydia L — Pvt CT ★
Joseph: b 10-5-1738 d 1-17-1811 m Anna Poor Drm MA
Joseph: b 9-6-1762 d p. 1818 m (1)Lydia Lord (2)Abigail Adams Pvt MA
Joseph: b 12-14-1746 d 2-8-1832 m Mary Langdon Sevev Capt NH
Joseph: b 1760 d 11-28-1737 m Nancy Jordan Capt NC ★
Josiah: b 3-27-1750 d 5-15-1807 m Sarah Sewall Lt MA
Justin: b 7-19-1759 d 4-26-1847 m Electa Frary Pvt VT NY
Lemuel: b 1755 d 1830 m Margaret Colton Sol NH ★
Mahlon: b 7-4-1762 d 3-26-1821 m Mary Wood Pvt PA
Marshfield: b 2-7-1733 d 6-13-1813 m (1)Lois Wait(2)Abigail Marvin (3)Abigail Waterman(4)Phebe Griffin LCol CT
Medad: b 8-22-1754 d 4-24-1818 m (1)Sybil Harmon (2)Wealthy Chase CS VT
Moses, Jr.: b 9-1-1731 d 7-5-1814 m Mahitable Bridgman Pvt MA
Nathan: b 11-27-1734 d 1811 m Ann Smith Capt CT
Nathan: b 12- -1752 d 10-11-1823 m (2)Susanna Dwight Adj MA ★
Nathan: b 9-30-1744 d 6-23-1785 m Sarah Bancroft Cpl MA
Nathaniel: b 5-16-1733 d 11-13-1807 m Sarah Rust Pvt MA
Nehemiah: b 1760 d 8-2-1836 m Lucretia Bray Pvt MA★
Noah: b 2-6-1731 d 1-11-1814 m Phoebe Bartlett Sgt MA
Oliver: b 2-10-1760 d 5-6-1800 m Rhoda Parsons Pvt MA
Paul: b 1-17-1762 d 4-20-1848 m Phebe Coe Pvt CT
Philemon: b 4-3-1737 d p. 1790 m Patty Davis Pvt MA
Reuben: b 1739 d 2-20-1799 m Margaret Granger 1Sgt CT
Richard: b 8-24-1749 d 6-13-1821 m Dorothy Lamphere Pvt MA
Robert, 2nd: b 9-17-1748 d 11-7-1822 m Sarah Mulford 1Lt NJ
Samuel, Sr.: b — d 3-4-1848 m Martha Clark Arfr CT
Samuel: b 1733 d 1812 m Lucy Pomeroy 1Lt MA
Samuel: b 2-22-1758 d 12-25-1821 m Mary Crane Sgt NJ
Samuel: b 4-8-1751 d 11-10-1842 m (1)Mrs Eunice McCord (2)Elizabeth Decker Sgt NY
Samuel, Sr.: bpt 8- -1724 d 1-10-1790 m Mary Merry PS NY
Samuel, Jr.: bpt 8- -1753 d 3-17-1843 m Betsy Conkling Pvt PS NY
Samuel: b 1762 d 1832 m Ann — Pvt VA
Samuel Holden: b 5-14-1737 d 11-17-1789 m Mehitable Mather MGen CT
Seth: b 9-15-1757 d 6-21-1850 m Susan Babcock Pvt CT
Silas: b 9-20-1761 d 12-6-1839 m Sarah Fiske Pvt MA
Solomon: b 8-29-1757 d 5-11-1831 m Rebecca Coburn Pvt MA
Stephen: b 1755 d 1813 m Ellen Mc Ilvaine Pvt NJ
Sylvanus: b 7-26-1758 d 1825 m Mary Webster Pvt MA
Thomas: b 11-29-1718 d 12-22-1811 m (1)Mary Parsons (2)Lydia Booth(3)Mrs Jemima Bailey PS CS CT
Thomas: b 9-18-1735 d 8-10-1811 m (1)Ann Poor (2)Lucy Bradsbury PS NH
Thomas: b 11-11-1730 d 11-1-1804 m (1)Mary Rennick (2)Hannah Taylor (3)Elsie Miles Pvt VA
Timothy: b 6-22-1738 d 2-2-1822 m Martha Hubbard Cpl MA
Warham: bpt 1753 d p. 1- -1809 m Priscilla — Pvt MA
Wm.: b 3-24-1750 d 5-29-1819 m Abigail Wright Pvt CT
Wm.: b 6-11-1746 d 11-12-1828 m Sarah Finson Capt MA
Wm.: b 11-1-1736 d p. 1790 m Sarah Rust PS ME
Wm.: b 10-22-1742 d 8-4-1826 m Abigail Frost Blunt PS CS ME
Wm.: b c. 1742 d 7-6-1829 m Mary Goolsby Sol SC
Wm.: b 9-25-1760 d 9-10-1829 m Catherine Stoker Sol VA
Woodson: b 1747/8 d p. 2-15-1797 m Ann Mosby Pvt VA

PARTHEMORE,
John: b 2-27-1738 d 12-27-1812 m — Shupp Sol PA
Philip: b 4-29-1736 d 1- -1797 m Anna Eve Hypsher Pvt PA

PARTIE,
Charles: b c. 1747 d p. 11-22-1828 m — PS NC

PARTLOW,
John, Sr.: b c. 1735 d p. 12-11-1789 m Sarah Reynolds PS VA

PARTNER,
John: b 1740 d 1836 m Marie Magdalene Auhny Pvt PA

PARTRIDGE,
Amos: b 7-25-1742 d 8- -1821 m Melatiah Ellis Lt MA
Amos: b 4-12-1758 d 1-3-1844 m Sarah Harvey Pvt MA
Asa: b 6-9-1740 d 5-31-1822 m Eliphal Geer Lt CT
Asa: b 1759 d 12-30-1845 m Anna Woodward Pvt CT ★
Calvin: b 3-29-1739 d 11-27-1815 m Mary Alden Capt MA
Daniel: b 1763 d 8-17-1812 m Sarah Ames Pvt MA
Edward: b 5-23-1738 d 10-17-1815 m Hannah Legg Pvt MA
Eleazer: b 4-30-1740 d 3-19-1834 m Lois Rockwood Pvt MA
Elias: b 7-1-1758 d 9-29-1826 m Sarah Brown Pvt VT
Elisha: b 7-8-1734 d 1-1-1787 m (1)Dorcas Pond (2)Sarah Fales Pvt MA
Elisha: b 4-20-1743 d 4-1-1823 m Margaret Murdock Ens VT
Henry: b 9-6-1724 d 3-7-1803 m Mary Chamberlain 2Lt MA
Jasper: b 10-8-1763 d 10-27-1836 m (1)Jemima Bixby (2)Martha Buchanan Kipp Pvt MA
Jesse: b 1742 d 3-29-1838 m Keziah Clapp Cpl MA
Job: b 2-28-1741 d 9-11-1823 m Deborah Fairbanks Pvt MA
John, Sr.: b 1-28-1716 d p. 1790 m Susanna Willcocks CS CT
John, Jr.: b 5-26-1739 d p. 1790 m Hannah Leonard CS MA

John: b 1758 d 1823 m Mary Elizabeth — Pvt NY
John: b 1755 d 1825 m Martha Hirons Pvt SC
Jonathan 2nd: b 7-16-1724 d p. 1790 m Keziah Hastings Pvt VT
Jonathan 3rd: b 2-21-1757 d 1818 m — Harvey Pvt VT
Joshua: b 7-27-1713 d 1795 m Elizabeth Kingsbury Capt MA
Lovet: b 9-13-1750 d p. 1790 m Sarah Hayward Pvt MA
Oliver, Sr.: b 6-13-1712 d 7-21-1792 m Ann Williams CS MA
Otis: b 2-16-1764 d 11-23-1827 m Hannah Smith Pvt MA
Reuben: b 4-14-1744 d p. 1791 m Mary Hill Lt NH
Samuel: b 3-31-1741 d 11-9-1776 m (1)Keziah Hawes (2)Elizabeth — Pvt MA
Sheffield: b 11-2-1752 d 12-14-1830 m Hannah Lyman Cpl MA
Stephen: b 6-17-1747 d 6-6-1826 m Sarah Brookins Sol CT W★
Thomas: b c. 1761 d 9-7-1822 m Sarah — Pvt MA
Thomas: b 12-15-1758 d 1828 m Hannah Wakeman Pvt VT
Timothy: b 1-18-1726/7 d 9-18-1787 m Abigail Barber Pvt MA

PASCAULT,
Louis Charles: b 1755 d p. 1790 m — Schley Col MD

PASCHALL, (includes PASCHAL & PASKIEL)
George: b 11- -1762 d 9-14-1832 m Agnes Brewer Pvt SC ★
John: b c. 1750 d 6-10-1802 m Elizabeth Forester Pvt MA
Thomas: b c. 1750 d a. 11- -1821 m Charity — Sol NC
Wm.: b 1754 d 1829 m Polly Ann Nicholas Pvt NC

PASKO,
John: b 1760 d 10-16-1834 m Abigail Frost Pvt MA ★
Jonathan: b 9-29-1760 d c. 8-2-1844 m Elizabeth Allen Pvt MA ★

PASS,
Holloway: b 3-4-1762 d 9- -1845 m Keziah Roberson Pvt NC ★
Nathaniel: b c. 1735 d p. 1-12-1811 m Alsey Holloway Pvt NC

PASSAGE,
George, Sr.: b a. 1740 d 10-11-1815 m Mary Rutter Lt NY
George, Jr.: b 5-12-1761 d 2-26-1840 m Leah Ostrander Pvt NY
George: b 4-18-1730 d 2-27-1778 m Hortense Lafevre Pvt NY
Henry: b 10-10-1754 d 3-29-1841 m Mary Claus Pvt NY

PASSINGER,
Soverinus: b 8-26-1737 d 5-20-1830 m Maria Young Pvt NY

PASSMORE,
George: b 2-23-1719 d 5-19-1801 m Margaret Stroudt Pvt PA
John: b 7-2-1743 d 3-12-1791 m Phebe Pusey Pvt PA
Thomas: b 3-7-1756 d 1-18-1836 m Esther Dickinson Pvt PA
Wm.: b c. 1760 d p. 1834 m Dinah Elliott PS NC

PASTEUR,
Charles: b c. 1750 d 12-30-1793 m (2)Martha Tarlem Dr NC
John: b c. 1749 d 8-22-1794 m Honor Wilson NCapt VA
Thomas: b c. 1755 d 7-29-1806 m Mary McLannon 1Lt CS NC

PATCH,
Abraham, Jr.: b 3-1-1739 d 1-14-1803 m Anna Banister Pvt MA
Andrew: b 2-16-1752/3 d 5-2-1782 m Anna Dodge PA MA
Benjamin: b 6- -1729 d p. 8- 1779 m Ednah Brown Sol MA
Benjamin: b 5-23-1754 d 9-27-1827 m Persis Lewis Sgt MA
Ephraim, Jr.: b 10-27-1757 d 4-23-1838 m Mary Burnell Pvt MA ★
Isaac, Sr.: b 2-8-1739 d p. 1790 m Elizabeth Avery Cpl MA
Isaac, Jr.: b 10-1-1762 d p. 6-20-1820 m Phoebe Fletcher Pvt MA ★
Jacob: b 4-5-1747 d 12-22-1818 m Mary Hazen Cpl MA
James: b 3-22-1745 d 11-8-1838 m Abigail Foster Pvt MA
John: b 1721 d 12-18-1799 m Abigail Patch PS MA
John A: b 1-4-1761 d 3-7-1813 m Betty Chandler Cpl MA
Jonathan: b 9-28-1744 d 7-17-1825 m Annie Hull Sgt MA
Jonathan: b 5-16-1726 d 4-24-1794 m Hannah — CS MA
Samuel: b 1730 d 2-15-1817 m Lydia Walkut Capt MA
Stephen: b 2-10-1748 d 7-24-1823 m Thankful Bennet Pvt MA
Thomas: b 5-24-1753 d p. 1799 m Desire Cowing Pvt MA
Wm.: b 5-22-1763 d c. 1808 m Mrs Joanna Knowlton Pvt MA

PATCHEN, (includes PATCHIN)
Daniel, Jr.: b 1760 d 4-1-1846 m Elizabeth Pardee Pvt CT
Ebenezer: b 10-29-1759 d 3-2-1830 m Sarah Morehouse Pvt CT ★
Elijah: b 1745 d 1820 m X Cpl CT
Freegift: b 2-20-1758 d 8-30-1830 m Mollie Morehouse Fif NY W★
Isaac, Sr.: b 1730 d p. 2-4-1802 m Betty Stone PS NY
Isaac, Jr.: b 11-20-1761 d 2-23-1834 m Sally Gibbs Pvt Sct NY ★
Jabez: b 4-7-1727 d 2-26-1799 m Hannah Squier Pvt PS NY
Jacob: b 12-26-1764 d 9-20-1844 m Abigail Meeker Pvt CT
Jared: b c. 1750 d 5-11-1826 m (1)Phebe White (2)Mary Stephens Ens CT
Josiah: b 5-3-1764 d 4-1-1809 m Eunice Parrett Pvt CT
Samuel: b 4- -1758 d 3-18-1844 m Mary Elizabeth Hollister Lt NY ★
Walter: b 1764 d 3-20-1854 m (1)Lorany — (2)Sarah Pierson Pvt NY ★
Wolcott: b — d 1799 m — Pvt CT
Zebulon: b 1763 d 4-26-1847 m (1)Miss Butler (2)Polly Cohoon Pvt NY W★

PATE,
Anthony: b — d c. 1815 m Sarah — Capt VA
Jeremiah, Sr.: b a. 4- -1728 d a. 7- -1812 m Christinah Hewman Sol PS VA
John: b 1760 d 1829 m (1) — (2)Nancy Cowart Sol NC
Matthew: b c. 1750 d 2-1-1806 m — Dabney 1Lt VA
Matthew: b 1762 d 11-2-1828m Drusilla Hobson Pvt VA W★
Wm.: b 1750 d 1837 m (1) — Weathersby (2) — Dale(3)Tempty Parkerson Pvt NC

PATMAN
Wm.: b 1760 d 1821 m Susannah Bigger Sgt VA

PATRICK,
Abel: b 5-15-1757 d 5-19-1844 m Elizabeth Hurlburt Pvt CT
Abner: b 1757 d 1802 m Elizabeth Carll Ens NJ
Ebenezer: b 10-14-1753 d 7-8-1834 m (1)Lucy Wheeler (2)Sally Ensign (3)Nancy Nelson Sgt NY
Jacob, Jr.: b 2-13-1764 d 4-28-1850 m Sarah Spicer Pvt CT
Jeremiah: b c. 1738 d 1822 m Sarah Blair CS VA
John: b 1753 d 10-16-1805 m Elizabeth Cummings Capt MD
John: b 1751 d 1789 m Mary — PS NC
John: b 1755 d 1816 m Sarah Allen Pvt VA
Matthew: b 1- -1767 d 7-21-1821 m Zerviah Spicer Cpl VT
Ralph: b 9-16-1764 d 8-8-1846 m Mary — Pvt CT
Robert: b 4-29-1740 d 1811 m Lois Buel Capt CT
Robert: b 8-21-1760 d 9-1-1815 m (1)Elizabeth Pamelia Ives (2)Sally Spaulding (3)Polly Gilbert Pvt NY
Samuel: b 1733 d 8-6-1817 m (1)Jerusha Harris (2)Mrs Relief Oakes Pvt NH
Samuel: b 1732 d c. 1780 m Mary Briggs Pvt NJ
Samuel: b 1750 d c. 1805 m (1)Anna Spicer (2)Isabell Alexander Sgt VT
Wm.: b c. 1760 d c. 1830 m (1)Lucy Hawkins (2)Elizabeth Pharr Sol GA
Wm.: b 1762 d 7-11-1836 m Sabra Hall Pvt MD
Wm.: b 1741 d 5-30-1778 m Deborah Smith Capt MA
Wm.: b 1733 d 1823 m Elizabeth Campbell Pvt NY

PATTEE, (includes PATTIE)
Asa: b 5-14-1734 d 5-24-1825 m (1) — (2)Mehitable Jewett Lt NH W★
Ebenezer: b 2-21-1739/40 d 9- -1825 m (1)Mary Stinson (2)Mrs Sarah Rackliff CS ME
Edmund: b 7-22-1764 d 9-24-1824 m Elizabeth Turner Mus MA ★
Eliphalet: b 3-21-1742 d 1837 m (3)Abigail Ames Pvt MA ★
John: b 7-20-1759 d 1-17-1821 m Deborah Fish Pvt MA
John: b 1750 d 1- -1832 m Ann Sanders Capt VA
Loami: b 11-28-1762 d 11-1-1832 m Priscilla Corliss Pvt NH
Seth: b 3-2-1749 d 1780 m Susanna Savory PS Cpl NH
Wm.: b 12-3-1754 d p. 1778 m Mary Hyde Pvt NH
Wm.: b 1762 d 1842 m Miss — Vaughan MM Arfr VA ★

PATEICHER,
Adam: b 6-30-1755 d 3-24-1827 m Barbara Goodman Pvt PS PA

PATTEN, (includes PATTON)
Actor: b 1-22-1737 d 7-26-1816 m Jane McLellan Capt CS MA
Benoni: b 6-27-1757 d 9-13-1832 m Edith Cole Pvt PS MA ★
David: b c. 1748 d 11- -1830 m Mary — Pvt PA
Edward: b c. 1747 d p. 1822 m Mary Graham Sgt NY ★
George: b 1-17-1759 d 10-14-1813 m Sarah Stringfellow Sgt VA
Henry: b c. 1735 d p. 1806 m Martha — Capt VA
Isaac: b 3-6-1761 d 10-31-1836 m Lydia Keyes Pvt MA ★
Jacob: b 1756 d 8- -1840 m Mary Cooper Pvt VA
James: b c. 1742 d 4-1-1805 m Sarah Bayley Pvt NH
James: b 2-20-1764 d 8-9-1827 m Sarah Cunningham Sol NC
James: b 1733 d 1-5-1821 m Mary — Capt PA
James: b c. 1745 d a. 1818 m Ellen Mitchell Pvt PA
James: b 10-12-1735 d 12-29-1815 m (1)Mary Dougherty (2)Elizabeth Reager (3)Mrs Phoebe (McCausland) Basye Capt VA
John: b 1747 d 8-13-1800 m Hannah Johnson Pvt CT
John: b 1745 d 6-17-1801 m Mary McNabb Maj DE
John: b 8-1-1731 d 12-28-1803 m Abigail Makepeace Pvt MA
John: b 5-26-1740 d 7-14-1828 m (1)Ruth Pillsbury (2)Sarah Clement Sol PS MA
John: b 11-21-1745 d 10-25-1807 m Mary Richardson Pvt PS NH
John: b 1727 d 6-14-1786 m Jane Cochran QM NH
John: b 6-23-1756 d 7-7-1796 m Hannah Wallace Pvt NH
John: b 1730 d 3-3-1812 m Jean Karr PS NH
John: b 7-25-1765 d 12-7-1838 m Jean Eason Pvt PA
John: b 1745 d 9-9-1804 m Jane Bartholomew Davis Col PA
John: b 1728 d 10-31-1809 m Jane Marlin Capt PA
John: b 12-25-1757 d 5-23-1836 m Rebecca Simpson Lt PA
John: b 1749 d 5-10-1832 m Margaret McCown Pvt PA W★
John: b 2-6-1726 d 3-10-1783 m Sarah Latimore Maj SC
John: b 1750 d 1825 m Prudence Nichols Lt SC
John: b c. 1754 d p. 7- -1809 m Martha Sharp Pvt VA
John Mercer: b 1751 d 6- -1797 m Susanna McClintock Col NC
Jonathan: b 8- -1744 d 12-29-1809 m (2)Electa Brown LCol MA
Jonathan: b 1760 d 9-24-1832 m Abigail Blood Pvt NH W★
Joseph: b c. 1760 d p. 1815 m Margaret Houston Ens NC
Mathew: b 1728 d 6-26-1790 m Susanna Dunning LCol MA
Mathew, Jr.: b 5- -1750 d p. 1-6-1834 m Rebecca May Sgt MD

PATTEN, contd.

Matthew: b 5-19-1719 d 8-27-1795 m Elizabeth McMurphy PS NH
Matthew: b 1738 d 8-25-1825 m Jane — Sol NC
Matthew: b 1760 d *p.* 1820 m Margaret — Pvt NC
Matthew: b — d *p.* 3-4-1779 m Rebecca — Lt PS SC
Matthew: b 5- -1730 d *p.* 5-2-1803 m Hester Dyer PS VA
Nathaniel: b 3-19-1733 d 1780 m Grace Walker Pvt NH
Nathaniel: b 1759 d 5-13-1846 m Mehitable Blood Pvt NH
Richard: b *c.* 1760 d 10-4-1823 m Mary — Pvt PA
Robert: b 5-15-1743 d 3-14-1841 m Margaret Hunter Capt MA
Robert: b 8-13-1757 d 12-10-1817 m Jane Shirley Pvt NH
Robert: b 11-10-1746/7 d 3-18-1813 m Elizabeth Dysart Capt NC W★
Robert: b 1736-42 d 11-11-1832 m Rebecca — Sol NC
Robert: b *a.* 1764 d *p.* 1823 m Margaret — PS NC
Robert: b 1755 d 1-3-1814 m (1)Cornelia Bridges (2)Mrs Tace Wallace (Bradford) Dickson Maj PA
Robert: b *c.* 1750 d 9-4-1815 m Isabella Frazier Capt PA
Robert: b 5-1-1754 d 2- -1824 m Mary — Pvt PA
Robert: b 12-25-1762 d 12-10-1827 m Jane Williams Pvt PA
Samuel, Sr.: b 1713 d 4-25-1792 m Mary Bell PS NH
Samuel, Jr.: b 8-10-1752 d 1809 m Deborah Moore Cpl PS NH
Samuel: b 1735 d 1819 m Priscilla Miltmoor PS NH
Samuel: b 1761/2 d 10-18-1851 m Mary Alexander Lt NC ★
Thomas: b 4-4-1734 d 1-1-1805 m Anna Woolson Pvt MA
Thomas: b 1726 d 1808 m (1)Margaret Ervin (2)Mrs Abigail Chambers Sol NC
Thomas: b 6-3-1765 d 10-1-1819 m Margaret Ross Pvt Cav SC
Wm.: b 9-24-1732 d 9-21-1801 m Rebecca Brown Sgt MA
Wm.: b 5-1-1758 d 4-30-1842 m (1)Abigail Turner (2)Abigail Clark Pvt NH
Wm.: b 4-10-1758 d 3-20-1848 m (1)Margaret Silvers (2)Isabella Young Patterson QM PA ★
Wm.: b *c.* 1745 d 5- -1795 m Martha Fullerton Pvt PA
Wm.: b 1758 d *p.* 1791 m Margaretta George Pvt PA
Wm.: b — d *a.* 5-7-1796 m — Pvt Cav SC
Willis: b 11-22-1738 d 9-12-1816 m Hannah Sargent Pvt PS MA

PATTERSON, (includes PADDISON, PATERSON, PATTESON & PATTISON)

Abraham: b *a.* 1760 d 2-16-1832 m Sarah Sawyer Pvt MA
Adam: b 10-27-1754 d 8-6-1823 m Jannet Rinkin Pvt NC
Alexander, Sr.: b 1714 d 1802 m Elizabeth Arbuckle PS NH
Alexander, Jr.: b 1- -1753 d 1-7-1837 m Mary Nelson Pvt NH ★
Alexander: b 1752 d 10-19-1832 m Janet McKenzie Sol NC
Alexander: b 1760 d 5-10-1815 m (1)Elizabeth Patterson (2)Margaret McLaughlin (3)Sarah Mathews Sol NC
Alexander: b 1756 d 7-2-1829 m Jane Gilmer Pvt NC
Alexander: b 1743 d 4-11-1822 m Margaret (Patterson) Capt PA
Alexander: b 1726 d 1812 m Phoebe Carrell Pvt PA
Alexander: b 1751 d 6-8-1839 m Catherine McCaleb Sgt SC ★
Amos: b 1-18-1749 d 3-5-1817 m Anne Williams Pvt MA
Andrew: b 4-7-1750 d 10-13-1812 m Susanna Davis Pvt MA
Andrew: b *c.* 1760 d 5-23-1828 m Margaret Dickson Pvt Arfr PA W★
Andrew: b 1730 d 11-10-1792 m Mary Wilson Pvt PA
Arthur: b *a.* 1747 d 10-7-1780 m — Pvt NJ
Atthow: b *c.* 1720 d *a.* 2-1-1797 m Mary — PS MD
Benjamin: b 9-16-1759 d 7-2-1830 m (1)Jemima Price (2)Mary Taggart (3)Mrs Sarah Shannon Sol PA
Charles: b 9-22-1745 d 5-29-1837 m Martha Hall Pvt MA
Charles: b *a.* 1743 d *p.* 1791 m Elizabeth Duiguid PS VA
Daniel: b 1750-60 d 12-14-1817 m Hannah Sawyer Sol MA
Daniel: b 1731 d 8-5-1809 m Mary McMillan Sol NC
David: b 5-17-1739 d 11-28-1809 m Beulah Clark Pvt MA
David: b 8-7-1743 d 6-21-1827 m Chloe Heath Pvt Tms NY
David: b *c.* 1745 d *p.* 12-19-1819 m (1)Sybel Smith (2)Elizabeth Ann Sol VA
David: b 8-15-1756 d 10-22-1846 m Judith Dibrell PS VA
Ebenezer: b 1-1-1760 d 12-25-1844 m Rebecca Gibbs Sgt MA
Eleazer: b 9- -1716 d 4-8-1801 m (1)Lydia Moore (2)Abigail — Col NY
Elnathan: b 2-11-1726 d 11-27-1811 m Mary Sherman Pvt CT
Ephraim: b 3-22-1739 d 5-3-1809 m Sarah Chandler Lt NH
Francis: b 1721 d 7-9-1801 m (1)Jane — (2)Catharine Perry Pvt PA
George: b 1725 d 7-21-1789 m Margaret Gilmore Pvt MA
George: b 7-24-1760 d 10-31-1814 m Jane Burd PS PA
Isaac: b *c.* 1756 d 9-2-1823 m Marcy Nelson Pvt NH
James: b *c.* 1738 d *p.* 9-5-1787 m Sarah Revel Capt MD
James: b 8-2-1735 d *p.* 1804 m Jean Henry Pvt PS NH
James: b 1733 d *p.* 1794 m Rachael Stout Cpl NJ
James: b 1714 d 1792 m Elizabeth Pattison Pvt NY
James: b 10-16-1755 d 12-30-1829 m Roxanna — Pvt NY ★
James: b 1759 d 12-3-1838 m (1)Miss Nelson (2)Sarah Davidson Pvt NC ★
James: b 1761 d 11-9-1838 m Frances — Sol NC
James: b 1701 d *p.* 12-6-1814 m Emeline McCorcle CS NC
James: b 2-7-1731 d 5-19-1789 m Margaret Agnew 1Lt PA
James, Sr.: b 1708 d 1792 m Mary (Hamilton) Montgomery PS PA
James: b 11-3-1745 d 8-17-1825 m Lettice Gardner Pvt PA
James: b 9-2-1754 d 3-12-1838 m Sarah Edie 1Lt PA ★
James: b 1760 d — m Anna Elizabeth Hull Lt PA
James: b *c.* 1758/9 d *p.* 1792 m Jean Harris Pvt PA

James: b 1752 d 1809 m Annie Dorne Pvt PA
James: b 8-20-1755 d 12-12-1838 m Mary Wiley Capt VA ★
James: b 1745 d 2-19-1815 m Deborah — Pvt VA
Jehu: b 12-14-1765 d 7-22-1851 m Hannah Gordon Pvt NJ
John: b 6-8-1736 d 8-6-1822 m Catherine Mossman Pvt GA
John: b *c.* 1755 d *a.* 8-10-1802 m Ann — Pvt MD
John: b 1744 d 7-10-1808 m Elizabeth Lee MGen MA
John: b 8-4-1742 d 12-16-1829 m Sarah Burns Ens NH
John: b *c.* 1730 d *p.* 9-22-1813 m Isabelle McDuffie Pvt NC
John: b 10-10-1760 d 1-31-1839 m (1)Keziah Horneday (2)Sarah Jamison Pvt NC
John: b *c.* 1730 d *p.* 10-16-1786 m Elizabeth — CS NC
John: b *c.* 1717 d 4-7-1787 m (1)Sarah — (2)Mrs Mary Crouch PS NC
John: b 1754 d 1790 m Miss Edey Capt PA
John, Sr.: b 1732 d 4- -1778 m Sarah Wilson Pvt PA
John, Jr.: b 1745-50 d *p.* 1781 m Isabella Lyon Pvt PA
John: b *c.* 1758 d *p.* 1804 m Margaret — Pvt PA
John: b 10-11-1755 d 4-11-1831 m Betheridge Morrison Pvt VT
John: b 7-2-1760 d 8-1-1824 m (1)Elizabeth Brown (2)Elizabeth Todd Tabb Mid VA
Joseph: b 3-20-1752 d 2-4-1832 m Jane Moak Pvt PA
Joseph: b 8-15-1738 d 1-17-1821 m Jerusha Phelps Pvt MA
Joseph: b 1750 d 1-16-1831 m Susanna Duncan Pvt NH
Joseph: b *c.* 1745 d 1813 m (1)Rebecca Horne (2)Pamela Hall Sol NC
Joseph: b 9-8-1748 d 2-20-1829 m Margaret Laird Capt VA
Josiah: b 10-1-1751 d 12-6-1825 m Margaret Carson Sol SC
Littlebury: b 2- -1754 d 6-23-1825 m Matilda Smith Sgt VA
Littlebury: b 1749 d 1789-96 m Nanney — Pvt VA
Matthew: b 1732 d 2-18-1817 m Sarah Thorpe CS NY
Michael: b 1755-60 d 1-23-1835 m (1)Catherine Ousterhout (2)Nelly Katoe Pvt NY ★
Nathaniel: b 1735 d 1- -1791 m Isabel Ward Sol NC
Nathaniel: b 4- -1729 d 8-9-1795 m Elizabeth Beel Pvt PA
Nicholas: b 1726 d 11-17-1819 m Martha Robinson Capt PA
Obediah: b 5-2-1762 d 3-10-1804 m Ann (Patterson) d Pvt PA
Peter: b 1716 d *p.* 1790 m Grisey C Wilson PS NH
Peter: b 1739 d 1840 m — Montgomery Pvt NH
Richard: b 1759 d 11-13-1823 m Mary McKeel Pvt MD
Robert: b 11-16-1759 d 3-14-1824 m Eleanor Wright Pvt GA
Robert: b 5-30-1748 d 1829 m Betsy — PS ME
Robert: b 1742 d 10-9-1829 m Elizabeth Goodwin CS ME
Robert: b 5-30-1743 d 7-22-1824 m Amy Hunter Ewing BgdMaj NJ W★
Robert: b 1750 d 9-28-1843 m Joanna Allen Sgt NJ
Robert: b 1763 d 11-17-1848 m Rhoda Witt Pvt NC
Robert: b 1742 d *a.* 1802 m Rebecca Edgar Capt PA
Robert: b 3-4-1744 d 9-30-1792 m Mary Millard Ens PA
Robert: b 6-20-1746 d 8-7-1790 m Elenore Porter Pvt PA
Robert: b 12-10-1720 d 1- -1806 m Sarah Carrell PS PA
Robert: b 1757 d *c.* 1853 m Sarah E Sargeant Pvt SC
Robert: b 3-23-1753 d 11-9-1827 m Elizabeth Lindsay Col KY ★
Robert: b 1-27-1763 d 1854 m Jane Anderson Pvt VA ★
Samuel: b 2-1-1743 d 11-11-1822 m Esther Rowland Lt CT
Samuel: b *c.* 1744 d — m Sarah Mellen Pvt NH
Samuel: b 11-23-1727 d 11-15-1820 m Martha Agnew Sgt PA
Samuel: b — d *p.* 1-6-1799 m Cicely Poindexter CS VA
Sherman: b 12-15-1753 d 7-6-1842 m Huldah Beach Sgt CT
Solomon: b 3-1-1763 d 5-21-1842 m Mary Melick Pvt PA
Sunderland: b 1-25-1757 d 2-7-1842 m (1)Sarah Utter (2)Rhoda Worden (3)Amy Gardner Pvt MA ★
Thomas: b 1752 d 4-8-1819 m Elizabeth Ashton Pvt CT
Thomas: b 10-23-1746 d 5-20-1834 m Elizabeth Wallace Lt NH
Thomas: b 2-1-1754 d 3-28-1829 m Mary Tanneyhill Pvt PA
Thomas: b 11-20-1757 d 8-11-1834 m Sarah Lytle Pvt PA ★
Thomas: b 1759 d 1840 m (1)Nancy Blakely (2)Mary McVannan Capt VA
Tilman: b 1761 d 11-30-1849 m Matilda Young Sgt NC
Wm.: b 1760 d 1816 m Lois Ackley FifMaj CT
Wm.: b 9-28-1743 d 6-17-1801 m Nancy Mosman Pvt GA
Wm.: b *c.* 1745 d *a.* 4-18-1796 m (1)Ann Sherwood (2)Sarah Sherwood NCapt MD
Wm.: b 11-1-1752 d 2-7-1835 m Dorcas Spear PS MD
Wm.: b 11-14-1760 d 12-20-1831 m Wealthy Ann Lawrence Pvt MA
Wm.: b 12-24-1745 d 9-9-1806 m Cornelia Bell CS NJ
Wm.: b 9-11-1758 d 1846 m Sally Boyce Pvt NY ★
Wm.: b 1750 d *p.* 2-6-1812 m Margaret Branch Pvt NC
Wm.: b 1762 d 1804 m Elizabeth Brown Pvt NC
Wm.: b 1737 d 1782 m (1)Isabella Galbreath (2)Esther Finley Lt PA
Wm.: b 1740 d *p.* 7-23-1776 m Elizabeth Dysart 2Lt PA
Wm.: b 6-12-1749 d 5-18-1846 m Jane Morrow Ens PA
Wm.: b 1732 d 1800 m Mary McCormick Capt PA
Wm.: b 2-21-1745 d *p.* 1783 m Sarah (Patterson) Pvt PA
Wm.: b 1762 d 3-16-1840 m Mary Ann Hancock Pvt PA ★
Wm.: b 3-14-1733 d 6-29-1818 m (1)Rosanna Scott (2)Elizabeth Brown Pvt PA
Wm.: b 1728 d 1791 m Jane Gregory Pvt PA
Wm.: b *c.* 1760 d 1825 m Agnes Patton Sgt VA
Wm.: b 1760 d 9-1-1847 m Hannah Smith Pvt VA

Wm., Sr.: b 1720 d 1791 m Lucy — Mil VA
Wm., Jr.: b 1743 d 1808 m Polly Oney Pvt VA

PATTILLO, (includes PATILLO)
Henry: b 1726 d 1801 m Mary Anderson PS NC
James: b c. 1750 d 12- -1819 m Elizabeth Floyd Sgt VA
John: b 10-9-1766 d 7-26-1820 m Betsy Harroway Sol VA

PAUL, (includes PAULL)
Amos: b c. 1744 d p. 1795 m Margaret Tetherly Pvt MA
Benjamin: b 1757 d 1-6-1817 m Bethenia Bennett QMSgt NJ W★
Daniel: b 9-30-1760 d 5-6-1828 m Lovisa Ainsworth Pvt CT
David: b 1761 d 1850 m Hannah Paul Pvt ME
Ebenezer: b 5-21-1737 d 9-3-1825 m Ann Williams Capt MA
Ebenezer: b 6-16-1738 d 8-20-1803 m Abigail Talbot Pvt MA
Edward: b 4-10-1749 d 3-23-1810 m Elizabeth Short MM MA
Frederick: b 9-8-1745 d 4-24-1830 m Sophia Bauer Pvt PA
Israel: b 3-6-1762 d — m (1)Olive Farrington (2)Alice Hathaway
   Pvt MA
James: b 5-20-1725 d 5-10-1805 m Abigail Kiles Pvt CT
James: b 2-16-1750 d 6-23-1830 m Zeruah Short Pvt MA
James: b 7-4-1759 d 4-2-1838 m Jemima Myrick Pvt MA
James: b 9-17-1760 d 7-9-1841 m Elizabeth Rogers Lt PA
James: b c. 1748 d 1786 m Sarah Huston Pvt PA
James: b c. 1760 d c. 1852 m Mary McKnight Pvt VA
John: b 5-20-1725 d 1787 m Dorothy V Winthrop Lt PA
John: b 3-17-1751 d p. 1780 m Hannah Newhall Cpl MA
John: b 11-12-1758 d 6-6-1830 m Sarah Thornberry Grover Pvt IL
John White: b 1755 d 1-20-1805 m Anne Smith Sgt RI
Joseph: b 7-25-1739 d 3-18-1799 m Hannah(Paul) — Pvt PA
Lemuel: b 3-6-1761 d 3-9-1815 m Ruth Jones Pvt MA
Nicholas: b 7-8-1748 d 4-16-1820 m Barbara Hess 2Lt PA
Philip: b 1765 d 1825 m Lillie Howell Pvt NC
Samuel: b 4-5-1757 d 4-21-1828 m Lavina Tisdale Pvt MA
Samuel: b c. 1762/3 d 12-17-1793 m Anna Libbey Pvt MA
Seth: b 10-1-1741 d 8-21-1825 m Freelove French SgtMaj MA
Wm.: b 9-24-1744 d 11-19-1816 m Alice C — Pvt PA

PAULDING,
James: b 6-28-1742 d p. 1790 m Elizabeth Beal Pvt MA
John: b 10-16-1758 d 2-18-1818 m (1)Sarah Teed (2)Esther Ward
   (3)Hester Denike Pvt NY
Joseph: bpt 4-22-1733 d 1787 m Sarah Gardinier Pvt CS NY
Wm.: b 1735 d 2-20-1825 m Catharine Ogden Cmsry Gen NY
Wm.: b 3-30-1761 d 7-8-1813 m Elizabeth Sipher Pvt NY W★

PAULETT,
Richard: b 1753 d 1835 m Catherine Smith Lt VA
Thomas: b c. 1750 d a. 1803 m Elizabeth Harvey Capt VA
Thomas: b 1704 d c. 1777 m Semiramis Johnson PS VA

PAULK,
Ammi: b 4-27-1756 d 3- -1843 m Esther Chapman Pvt CT
David: b 3-24-1749 d 2-10-1824 m Margaret Stimson Pvt CT
John: b c. 1745 d p. 6-24-1823 m Caty — Pvt GA
Micajah: b 1742 d 3- -1812 m Sarah — Pvt GA

PAWLING, (includes PAULIN & PAULLIN)
Antoine: b 9- -1737 d 9- -1815 m Theotiste Cottard Capt CAN ★
Benjamin: b 12-27-1751 d 10-9-1800 m Rebecca Lane 2Lt PA
David: b c. 1743 d 1794 m Martha — Pvt NJ
Henry: b 4-30-1756 d 6-14-1825 m Lydia Elwell Pvt NJ
Henry: b 4-22-1764 d 1839 m Anna Brown Capt NY
Henry, Sr.: bpt 6-27-1714 d 9-24-1792 m Eleanor Thomas PS PA
Henry, Jr.: b 7-19-1746 d 10-23-1822 m Rebecca Bull Capt PA
John: b 12-27-1732 d 12-30-1819 m (1)Meltje VanKeuren (2)Maria
   VanDuzen Pvt PS NY
John: b 5-17-1744 d p. 11-10-1813 m Elizabeth Morgan Pvt PA
Joseph, Jr.: b 8-28-1753 d 10-23-1840 m (1)Susannah Lukens
   (2)Mary Shannon Pvt PA
Levi: b 1721 d 3-1-1782 m Helena Burhans Col PS NY
Samuel: b 1753 d 5- -1843 m Mary Yocum Pvt PA
Wm.: b 7-23-1765 d 10-2-1832 m (1)Mary Kelly (2)Sarah E Kelly
   (3)Sarah Hamilton Pvt SC ★

PAXSON,
Abraham: b c. 1749 d p. 7-18-1836 m Elizabeth Brown Pvt PA

PAXTON,
Andrew: b — d 3- -1790 m (1) — (2)Jannet — Pvt PA
John: b c. 1740 d c. 1784 m Mary — Capt PA
John, Jr.: b 1740 d 8-8-1823 m Jane McNeeley Capt PA
John: b 1747 d 8-8-1832 m Sarah Walker Capt VA
John, Sr.: b 1716 d 2-13-1787 m Mary Blair PS VA
John, Jr.: b 1743 d 10-3-1787 m Phoebe Alexander Capt VA
Nathaniel: b 1746 d 9-11-1816 m Jane Gibson Pvt PA
Samuel: b 11-15-1752 d 7-29-1833 m (1)Sara Coulter (2)Jane
   Smiley OrdlSgt VA ★
Samuel: b 1733 d 1806 m — Sol CS VA
Samuel, Jr.: b c. 1754 d 1824 m Margaret Thompson Pvt VA
Thomas: b 1739 d 3- -1813 m (1)Isabella Quaite (2)Martha White
   LCol PA

Thomas, Jr.: b 1761 d 1851 m Jane Crawford Pvt PA
Wm.: b 4-1-1760 d 4-16-1845 m Jane Dunlop Pvt PA
Wm.: b 1732 d 9-30-1795 m Eleanor Hays Maj VA
Wm.: b 1751 d 4-16-1817 m Elizabeth Stuart Capt VA

PAYNTON,
Wm.: b 1757 d c. 1846 m Mary Drum Pvt NJ ★

PAYSON,
Asa, Sr.: b 4-15-1757 d 5-7-1834 m Lucy Bishop Fif Cpl CT
Edward: b 10-21-1757 d 1802 m Eunice Nichols Sgt MA
Ephraim: b 6-16-1754 d 12-15-1834 m Hannah Wentworth Pvt MA
George: b 5-24-1744 d 7-6-1788 m (1)Abigail Blagdon (2)Kezia
   Morse Pvt MA
Joseph: b c. 1740 d 9-14-1823 m Judith — Sgt MA
Samuel: b 3-1-1734 d 6-19-1819 m Sarah Noyes Capt MA ★
Seth: b 9-29-1758 d 2-6-1820 m Greta (Payson) MM MA

PEABODY,
Aaron: b 5-9-1742 d 1817 m — Fitch Pvt NY
Amos: b 2-7-1765 d 8-27-1835 m Rachel Berry Pvt MA ★
Andrew: b 1-20-1747/8 d 3-4-1812 m (1)Mary Morse (2)Hannah
   Kimble Sgt MA
Andrew: b 7-21-1745 d 10-14-1813 m Ruth Curtis Pvt MA
Andrew: b 2-17-1760 d 7-4-1839 m (1)Susannah Gage (2)Mary
   Beadle (3)Hannah Beadle Pvt NS MA ★
Asa: b 1-25-1716/7 d 8- -1788 m Mary Prentice PS CT
Benjamin: b 8-9-1741 d 9-10-1829 m Hannah Black Capt MA
Bimsley: b 9-2-1731 d 1815 m Ruth Marston Pvt MA
Ebenezer: b 1-27-1742 d 1-25-1829 m (1)Elizabeth Pearl (2)Mrs
   Sarah Pearl MM Lt MA ★
Francis: b 1-5-1761 d 1-23-1842 m Lucy Masury Matr MA ★
Isaac, Sr.: b 4-3-1727 d p. 6-3-1776 m Sarah Wilkins PS NH
Isaac, Jr.: b 6-18-1753 d p. 1790 m Miriam Putnam Pvt PS NH
Isaac: b 12-9-1740 d 1826 m — Capt NY
Jacob: b 4-6-1739 d 11-25-1806 m Sarah Potter Pvt MA
Jedediah: b 4-11-1743 d 10-26-1827 m Alice Howlet Pvt MA
John: b 8-9-1732 d 6-12-1820 m Mary Perley Capt MA
John: b 9-10-1730 d 1-29-1802 m Hannah Smith Pvt MA
Jonathan: b 1-27-1763 d 5-7-1849 m Lucy Morgan Pvt MA ★
Joseph: b 4-4-1741 d c. 1815 m Mary — Pvt MA
Moses: b 11-1-1744 d 1-6-1826 m Hannah Foster Pvt MA
Nathan: b 8-31-1756 d 10-30-1799 m Mary Baker Pvt MA
Nathaniel: b 12-18-1727 d 8-17-1778 m Hepzibah Barker Pvt MA
Nathaniel Prentice: b 12-25-1746 d 1-12-1804 m Mary Glover Vol CT
Oliver: b 6-22-1725 d 1796 m Sarah Robinson PS MA
Richard: b 2-11-1734 d 2-17-1811 m Tabitha Child Ens CT
Richard: b 4-13-1731 d 6-7-1820 m Jemima Spofford Capt MA
Samuel: b 9-1-1741 d 8-5-1814 m Elizabeth Wilkins Pvt MA
Samuel: b 1-7-1759 d 2-4-1839 m Abigail Trask Pvt Matr MA ★
Seth: b 11-27-1744 d 1827 m Abigail Kimball Pvt MA ★
Stephen: b 7-22-1753 d 2-6-1838 m Elizabeth Clark Sol MA
Stephen: b 4-25-1735 d 7-7-1815 m Ruth Storer PS MA
Stephen: b 9-3-1742 d 9-19-1780 m Hannah Chandler LCol NH
Stephen: b 11-11-1741 d 5-23-1819 m Polly Hasseltine Chp NH
Thomas: b 1746 d 9-2-1827 m Elizabeth Longley MM MA

PEACE,
John: b 1743 d 4-16-1821 m Margaret Scott PS NC

PEACH,
John: b 5-16-1736 d 6-21-1792 m Elizabeth Conant Pvt MA
Wm.: b 4- -1748 d 8-3-1837 m Elizabeth (Bowden) Messervy Pvt MA

PEACHY,
Benjamin: b 12-26-1756 d 1835 m (1)Annie Abbot (2)Elizabeth
   C Broadus Pvt NJ ★
Wm.: b 4-14-1729 d 1-7-1802 m (1)Million Glascock (2)Elizabeth
   Col VA

PEACOCK,
Adonijah: b 8-5-1724 d 1-19-1777 m Elizabeth Springer PS NJ
Isham: b 1725 d 1791 m Martha — Sol GA
John, Sr.: b 1740 d 8-2-1829 m (1)Priscilla Worrell (2)Elizabeth
   Bishop Pvt NC
John, Jr.: b 1760 d 8- -1828 m Mary Thompson Sol NC
Neil: b c. 1753 d 1827 m Susanna — Pvt MD ★
Richard: b 1745 d 8-21-1796 m Priscilla Covington Pvt MD
Thomas: b 1730 d 7-3-1823 m Margaret Anderson Sgt NY
Uriah: b 1750 d 1830 m Susan — Sol GA

PEAKE, (includes PEAK & PEEK)
Cornelius: bpt 12-1-1729 d 8-22-1802 m Catlyntje Yates Pvt NY
Cornelius C: b 2-21-1763 d p. 1807 m Neeltie Bancker Pvt NY
George: b c. 1720 d p. 1783 m Elizabeth — PS VA
Harmanus: b 12-5-1718 d 8-29-1781 m Sara DeGraff Pvt NY
Henry: b 12-25-1766 d 1857 m (1)— (2)Sarah Jemima Elizabeth
   Phelps Pvt GA ★
Henry: b c. 1750 d 1824 m Polly Lockett PS VA
Humphrey: b c. 1730 d 1-10-1785 m Mary Stonestreet PS VA
James C: b 1752 d 3-7-1826 m Annatje VanVorst Sol NY
Jesse: b 2-9-1752 d 6-3-1810 m Geertruy Bosie Pvt NY
John: b 1744 d p. 1804 m Tabitha Peek Sol GA

PEAKE, contd.
John Comer: b 1744 d a. 1815 m Tabitha Peek Pvt PS GA NC
Joseph: b 2-14-1724 d 4-19-1800 m Sarah Allen PS CT
Samuel: b 1752 d 10-5-1829 m Elizabeth Charter Pvt CT
Wm.: b 1756 d p. 1798 m — Brown QMSgt VA

PEARIS,
George: b 2-16-1746 d 11-4-1810 m (1)Eleanor Howe (2)Rebecca Clay Capt VA

PEARL, (includes PEARLE)
Benjamin: b 11-28-1723 d p. 1790 m Elizabeth Twomly Pvt PS NH
John: bpt 4-30-1738 d 12-17-1825 m Eunice Kimball Pvt MA
Joseph: b 1- -1760 d 1813 m Catherine Clark Pvt NH
Phineas: b 8-2-1753 d c. 1794 m Azubah Heywood Pvt NH VT
Richard: b 5-20-1702 d 12-20-1793 m Sarah Stephens Pvt MA
Simeon: b a. 1740 d p. 1806 m (1)Mary Leighton (2)Abigail Gove Lt MA
Timothy, Sr.: b 10-24-1723 d 10-19-1789 m Dinah Holt PS CT
Timothy, Jr.: b 7-6-1760 d 7-2-1834 m Lois Crocker Sgt CT ★

PEARMAN.
Wm., Sr.: b c. 1730 d 2-9-1788 m (1)Ann — (2)Mary Weldon Pvt VA
Wm., Jr.: b a. 1760 d p. 3-17-1817 m Isabella Weakley Sgt VA

PEARRE,
Joshua: b 12-22-1757 d 10-7-1847 m (1)Margaret Woodward (2)Millie Ann Arnold Capt MD W★

PEARSALL, (includes PIERSALL & PIERSOL)
Benjamin: b c. 1760 d 1792 m — PS PA
Edward: b c. 1730 d 1822 m — Rutledge Pvt NC
George: b 12-3-1739 d c. 12-10-1825 m (1)Magdalene Sears (2)Deborah Killey Pvt NY
Henry: b 1741 d p. 1790 m Elizabeth — PS NY
James: b 2-14-1729 d 1-24-1812 m Mary Seaman PS NY
James: b 1750 d 11-12-1812 m (1)Zilphia Uzzell (2)Feraby Whitfield (3)Anna Dickson Mil NC
Richard: b 3-25-1744 d p. 1841 m — Pvt MD ★
Richard: b 1740 d a. 4-7-1800 m Elizabeth — Pvt PA
Sampson: b 6-7-1764 d 8-8-1842 m Susannah Castor Pvt Spy PA
Wm.: b 1748 d 1848 m Grace Cope Pvt PA
Zaccheus: b 1754 d 11-18-1804 m Margaret Davis Cpl PA

PEARSON, (includes PERSEN, PERSON & PIERSON)
Abraham: b 4-11-1756 d 5-11-1823 m Lydia Redfield Ens CT
Amos: b 12-12-1734 d 1785 m Elizabeth Nichols Sgt MA
Azel: b 1-19-1739 d 10-16-1798 m Philithia Sayre Capt NJ
Bartholmew: b c. 1750 d p. 1830 m Hannah Balch Pvt CT
Benjamin: b 7-5-1754 d 12-7-1825 m Hannah Goodrich Drm Sgt MA
Benjamin, Jr.: b 1736 d 1792 m Phebe Raynor Capt NJ
Benjamin: b 11-25-1757 d 2-10-1832 m Abigail Condit Pvt NJ
Caleb: b 8-25-1761 d 1837 m Mary Locke Pvt MA
Caleb: b 1738 d 1801 m Joanna Baldwin Pvt NJ
Christian: b c. 1755 d p. 5-18-1819 m — PS PA
Cornelius: b 2-18-1744 d 2-7-1827 m Elizabeth Master Pvt NY
David: b 2-10-1737 d 6-26-1790 m Esther Bailey Sgt NJ
David: b 12-30-1754 d 11-6-1801 m Bethia Hallock Cpl NJ
David: b 8-29-1763 d 3-22-1824 m Abigail Thompson Pvt NJ
David: b 1751 d 1829 m Susanna — Capt NY
Dodo: b 1724 d 1-19-1796 m Mary Seward Pvt CT
Ebenezer: b 5-14-1736 d 6-6-1779 m Mary Thompson Pvt NH
Edmund: b 4-26-1758 d 1-23-1842 m Dorothy Swasey Sol NH
Elihu: b 8-1-1734 d 7-12-1812 m Catharine Baldwin Pvt NJ
Elijah: b c. 1736 d p. 1792 m Hannah Morris PS PA
Enoch: b c. 1718 d 1775-79 m Tabitha Jecocks Sol SC
Enoch: b 1760 d 1849 m Hannah Evans Pvt SC
Enoch: b 4-18-1757 d 1-2-1831 m Diana Head PS SC
Enos: b 1762 d p. 1798 m Abigail Cockefair Pvt NJ
Ephraim, Sr.: b 3- -1760 d a. 3-12-1776 m Hannah Barrett Pvt CT
Ephraim, Jr.: b 6-18-1758 d 1804 m Phoebe Cleveland Pvt CT
Henry: b c. 1750 d 3- -1812 m Frances Mary — Capt SC
Isaac: b 10-21-1728 d 3-8-1805 m — PS Pvt NH
Isaac: b 1755 d 8-19-1825 m (1)Hannah — (2)Mary — MM PS NY
Jacobus: bpt 12-26-1747 d p. 1809 m Eva Queen Pvt NY
James: b c. 1735 d p. 1786 m Bathshua — Drm MA
James: b 11- -1735 d 8-21-1813 m Susannah Hart Capt PA
Jesse: b 5-6-1761 d 1-10-1837 m Lydia Stevens Pvt CT ★
Jesse: b 1741 d 1818 m Amy Rush Perry Pvt NC
John: b 4-14-1759 d 11-12-1829 m (1)Martha Hacker (2)Catharine (Clemons)Lusby Pvt DE
John: b 9-20-1759 d 9-27-1836 m (1)Lydia — (2)Mrs Asenath Thwing Sgt MA
John: b 5-24-1758 d 2-11-1827 m Sarah Van Dyke Pvt NJ
John, Sr.: bpt 10-24-1708 d 8-5-1794 m Deborah VanBergen PS NY
John, Jr.: b 7-28-1756 d 1838 m Elizabeth Newkirk Lt NY
John: b 10-17-1740 d 1-22-1829 m (1)Ann Bevan (2)Sarah Johnson Capt PS PA
John, Jr.: b 5-30-1743 d 10-25-1819 m Sara Raiford Maj SC
Jonathan: b 10-1-1754 d 10-6-1805 m Eunice Nourse Pvt MA
Jones: b 1760 d 1850 m Diana Neal Sol GA
Joseph: b 6-8-1759 d 8-15-1840 m (1)Mary Farrar (2)Mrs Martha (Crawford) Wellington Pvt MA ★

Joseph: b 8-17-1755 d 10-28-1828 m Hannah Atkinson Pvt PS NH
Joseph: b 1735 d 1815 m Rebecca Smith Sgt NJ
Josiah: b 6-24-1756 d 3-2-1837 m Sarah Walkup MM Pvt MA ★
Josiah: b 1- -1731 d a. 4-25-1785 m (1)Mary Gilbert (2)Mrs Julianna DeKay Capt NJ
Josiah: b 2-23-1761 d 3-26-1826 m Frances Moffatt Pvt NY
Lemuel: b 1727 d 4-4-1819 m Elizabeth Pierson SgtMaj NY
Mahlon: b 4-7-1761 d 1-28-1839 m (1)Barbara McKenzie (2)Amelia Cain Pvt SC ★
Mary Raiford: b c. 1723 d c. 1800 m John Pearson PS SC
Moses: b 12-18-1744 d 3-31-1840 m Martha Goss Sgt MA ★
Moses: b 11-26-1753 d 8-11-1836 m (1)Hephzibah Jones (2)Lois Holt Sgt NH W★
Moses: b 1730 d 1800 m Rachel — Capt SC
Moses: b 10-11-1733 d 2-28-1805 m Rachel Smith PS VT
Nathan, Sr.: b 8-14-1725 d a. 3- -1788 m (1)Mary Wilson (2)Rebecca Tay Pvt MA
Nathan, Jr.: b 1746/7 d 10-2-1795 m Ann Morrow Pvt CT
Nathaniel: b 3-15-1746/7 d 7- -1830 m Sarah Gerrish Lt MA W★
Paris: b 1761 d 1832 m Mary Gilmore Pvt NC W★
Peter: b 10-14-1756 d 1-12-1836 m Parnel Corey Pvt CT ★
Richmond: b 1750 d 1819 m (1)Miss Hayden (2)Eliza Coit Mumford Capt NC
Robert: b 11-5-1759 d 9-8-1843 m (1)Mary Dalrymple (2)Elizabeth Price (3)Mrs Margaret (Clark) Youngs Sgt NJ W★
Samuel, Sr.: b 4-15-1721 d 1-23-1801 m Lydia Stevens Sol CT
Samuel, Jr.: b 7-29-1750 d 1-23-1801 m Rebecca Parmalee Sgt CT
Samuel: b 8-2-1759 d 6-8-1845 m Betty Dickinson Sol CT
Samuel: b 1745 d 3-7-1835 m Kesiah Richardson Sgt MA
Samuel: b 9-4-1747 d 8-16-1826 m Eunice Jacques Drm MA
Samuel: b 2-22-1759 d 5-12-1852 m (1)Sarah Page (2)Sarah Hill Adj PS NH
Samuel: b 1730 d 1797 m Phebe Harrison Capt NJ
Samuel: b 1762 d 11-6-1839 m Rebecca Demint Pvt NJ ★
Samuel: b 4-10-1748 d 5-4-1790 m Rebecca Garrigas Pvt NJ
Samuel: b 12-28-1754 d p. 8-9-1808 m (1)Prudence Ball (2)Jerusha Woodhall PS NY
Samuel: b 1721 d 5-4-1802 m Mary Simmons Capt NC
Samuel: b c. 1760 d 1801 m Tabitha — Sol NC
Samuel: b 1740 d 1809 m Susannah Bacon PS VA
Shadraak: b 1754 d p. 3-8-1843 m (1)Rachel Clinch (2)Bellany George Pvt VA ★
Silas, Sr.: b 6-27-1724 d 9-2-1804 m (1)Mrs Judith Worth Atkinson (2)Lucy Hidden PS MA
Silas, Jr.: b 7-24-1757 d 3-16-1848 m Mary Little Pvt MA W★
Silas, Sr.: b 1-23-1723 d 2-26-1804 m Elizabeth Gilbert Capt NY
Silas, Jr.: b 4-10-1748 d 2-24-1804 m Rachel Bull PS NY
Stephen: b 1732 d 9-13-1793 m Elishabe Wood Pvt NJ
Stephen: b 2-21-1746 d 1824 m (1)Mary Ludlam (2)Phebe Hand PS NJ
Sullivan: b — d p. 1-20-1797 m Elizabeth — PS NC
Tabitha Jecocks: b a. 7-3-1749 d p. 1-1-1799 m (1)Enoch Pearson (2)John Townsend PS SC
Theodore: b 4-6-1753 d 3-8-1817 m Sarah Wyatt Sgt MA
Thomas: b 2-12-1723 d 8-2-1820 m Martha Woodbridge Pvt MA
Thomas: b 3-25-1728 d 1820 m Ann Powell PS NC
Thomas: b 1758 d 7-10-1826 m Sara Walden 1Lt VA
Thomas: b 1753 d 1835 m Elizabeth Palmer Pvt VA
Timothy Mors: b 5-24-1756 d 2-2-1840 m Deborah Gilman Pvt NH
Uriah: b 1763 d 1843 m Elizabeth Dalrymple MM NJ
Wm.: b 9-20-1756 d 9-22-1836 m Hannah Pearson Pvt NH
Wm., Jr.: b 3-28-1747 d 12-25-1835 m Anna Davis Pvt NJ
Wm.: b 11-30-1731 d 5-8-1797 m (1)Elizabeth Carlisle Holeman (2)Martha Jones PS NC
Wm.: b 1760 d 1844 m Sarah Jones Pvt PA
Wm.: b 4-1-1754 d 4-26-1800 m Ann Stidham PS SC
Wm.: b 1758 d 1799 m Margaret — Lt VA
Wm. Ely: b 1758 d 2-25-1841 m (2)Hannah Hackett Pvt CT ★
Zechariah: b 1750 d 11-15-1827 m Sarah Sanford Pvt NY

PEART,
Richard: b 3-12-1741-5 d 1-13-1822 m Hannah Morgan Pvt MA

PEASE,
Aaron: b 5-4-1726 d 3-13-1828 m Anna Geer Pvt CT
Abner, Sr.: b 3-2-1733 d 1784 m (1)Elizabeth Farrington (2)Lovicy Allen 2Lt PS NY
Abner, Jr.: b 4-24-1763 d 6-26-1836 m Polly Blackman Pvt NY ★
Alpheus: b 4-16-1762 d 4-16-1816 m (1)Olive Anderson (2)Dorothy Spencer Pvt CT
Andrew: b 1763 d 7- -1844 m Mary Engle Pvt PA
Calvin: b 9-14-1757 d 3-2-1815 m Sarah Ives Drm CT
Christopher: b 1719 d 1794 m Hannah Hill MM VT
Cummings: b 11-27-1744 d 6- -1822 m Thankful Cleland Pvt CT
Ebenezer: b 10-16-1742 d 1-11-1789 m Huldah (Pease)Pvt CT
Ebenezer: b 12-23-1748 d 1840 m Rebecca Hills Pvt MA ★
Edward: b 9-7-1744 d 12-30-1817 m Abigail Hale Pvt CT ★
Edward: b 2-22-1763 d 7-21-1840 m (1)Hannah Rogers (2)Rhoda Waldo Pvt CT ★
Eli: b 11-12-1749 d 10-22-1830 m Eunice Bugbee Pvt CT
Eliphalet: b 5-13-1749 d p. 1811 m Mary Pike Pvt NH
Emery: b 5-17-1727 d 7-27-1796 m Mary Horton Capt CT
Ezekiel, Sr.: b 6-25-1710 d 6-19-1799 m Hannah Chandler CS CT

Ezekiel: b 3-22-1756 d 2-8-1838 m Lydia — Pvt CT
Gideon: b 8-8-1744 d *p.* 1793 m (1)Sybil Markham (2)Deborah Meacham Pvt CT
Gideon: b 11-18-1757 d 6-23-1824 m Prudence Sexton Pvt CT
Isaac: b 6-14-1753 d 1-15-1842 m Dorcas Pease Pvt CT ★
James: b 11-26-1749 d 1830 m Sarah Colton Pvt CT
James: b 12-14-1754 d 9-20-1844 m Lucy Meacham Pvt CT ★
James: b *c.* 1725 d 10-6-1798 m Mary Marchant PS MA
Jehiel: b 5-3-1750 d *p.* 5-5-1794 m Hepsah Dodge Pvt MA
Joel: b 11-2-1760 d 10-19-1845 m (1)Lovisa Meacham (2)Aseneth — Pvt MA ★
John: b 12-12-1748 d 1820 m Beulah Booth Sgt CT
John, Sr.: b 5-27-1726 d 11-11-1810 m (1)Bathsheba Jones (2)Mrs Penelope McGregory Pvt CS CT
John, Jr.: b 3-15-1753 d 1843 m Charity Thompson Pvt CT ★
Jonathan: b 9-11-1740 d 2-25-1825 m Mary Bidwell Pvt PS CT
Joseph: b 8-10-1728 d 10-16-1794 m Mindwell King Pvt PS CT
Lemuel: b 12-6-1763 d 10-18-1836 m Mary Parsons Pvt CT
Levi: b 1739 d 1-28-1824 m Hannah Sexton Adj MA
Moses, Jr.: b 10-27-1758 d 10-4-1835 m Lovisa Markham Pvt CT ★
Nathaniel: b 2-21-1737 d 6-5-1799 m Lucy Page Pvt PS NH
Nathaniel: b 6-15-1749 d *p.* 9-2-1807 m Martha Gelman PS NH
Nicholas: b — d 1818 m Hannah — Pvt PA
Noadiah: b 7- -1737 d 3-26-1822 m Tirzah Smith Pvt CT
Noah: b 6-28-1739 d 7-20-1818 m (1)Mary Ward (2)Mrs Dorcas (Hubbard) Arnold Cpl CT
Noah: b 4-14-1754 d 4-18-1841 m Hannah Dunham Pvt MA
Phineas: b 1-9-1756 d 7-11-1836 m Betsy Lawrence Fif CT ★
Robert: b 9-3-1749 d 11-19-1827 m (2)Ann Sexton Pvt CT W★
Samuel: b 3-10-1718 d 6-26-1796 m Zeruiah Chapin Pvt CT
Samuel: b 7-3-1746 d 11-17-1815 m (1)Hannah Booth (2)Elizabeth Sexton Pvt CT
Samuel: b 3-14-1760 d 2-27-1846 m Mrs Lydia Day Pvt CT ★
Samuel: b 3-10-1754 d 9-7-1834 m Comfort Marston DrmMaj NH
Samuel: b 1-31-1750 d 3-21-1838 m Sarah Porter MM VT
Seth: b 8-23-1730 d 12-28-1802 m Sarah Chase PS MA
Sharon: b 6-26-1746 d 5-13-1821 m Mary Prior Pvt CT
Silas: b 1-16-1760 d 3-21-1836 m Rhoda Curtiss Pvt CT W★
Simeon: b 2-7-1758 d 1847 m (1)Mabel Allen (2)Mrs Sybil (Terry) Billings Pvt CT ★
Stephen: b 7-4-1755 d 6-23-1838 m Roxanna Snow Pvt CT
Thomas: b 12-17-1754 d 8-2-1815 m Mary Hall Pvt CT
Thomas, Jr.: b 9-29-1725 d 1-13-1794 m Lydia — Abiah Shaw 2Lt MA
Timothy: b 1713 d 1794 m Mary Chandler CS CT
Uriah: b 11-13-1740 d 11-14-1777 m Naomi Moore Pvt CT
Wm.: b 1746 d *p.* 1787 m Viola Cadwell Pvt CT
Zachariah: b 2-19-1750 d 4-24-1845 m Lydia Crowell Pvt MA
Zebulon: b 11-2-1749 d 2-1-1829 m Hannah Rugg Pvt CT
Zebulon: b 1759 d — m Mary Burleigh Pvt NH

PEASLEE,
Abraham: b 7-20-1756 d 1815 m Martha Bean Pvt NH
Isaac: b 2-18-1751 d 1814 m (1)Mrs Elizabeth Pendegast Wing (2)Mrs Hannah Randall Sage (3)Mary Trowbridge Tubbs Pvt NY
Robert: b 9-4-1735 d 6-2-1796 m Anna Hazen Lt NH

PEAVEY,
Anthony: b *a.* 1765 d *p.* 5-18-1817 m Betsy Hammond Pvt NH
Hudson: b 2-11-1711 d *c.* 1785 m Madeline Brown PS NH

PEAY,
George: b 1-16-1734 d 10-7-1813 m Mary — Sol Grd NC

PECHIN, (includes PECKIN)
Christiana Bright: b 8-12-1747 d 1-7-1835 m Christopher Pechin PS PA
Christopher: b 1737 d 10-26-1779 m Christiana Bright PS PA
Frederick: b *c.* 1735 d 8-15-1778 m Mary — Pvt MA

PECK,
Aaron: b 5-3-1757 d 7-17-1833 m Hannah Ferris Sgt CS CT W★
Abel: b 1745 d *p.* 1-26-1778 m Abigail Gaylord Pvt CT
Abel: b 5-27-1761 d 10-2-1851 m Diadama Phinney Pvt NY ★
Abijah: b 1736 d 2-5-1804 m Rachel Stevens Sol CT
Abijah: b 4-3-1758 d 11-12-1848 m (1)Mindwell Close (2)Mrs Lydia Montgomery Pvt NY
Abner: b 5-4-1759 d 6-3-1842 m Hannah Tinker Pvt MA ★
Adam: b 1753 d 2-13-1817 m Elizabeth Sharkey Ens VA
Allen: b 2-1-1735 d 1-4-1809 m Elizabeth (Randall)Dexter Capt RI
Ambrose: b 11-17-1747 d 1-29-1818 m Polly Lindley Lt RI
Amos, Jr.: b 1-25-1754 d 3-18-1826 m Anna Scovil Fif CT
Ariel: b *c.* 11-17-1745 d *p.* 4-1-1820 m ( )Miss Higby ( )Jerusha — Pvt CT ★
Asahel: b 8-13-1762 d 2-6-1837 m Anna March Pvt CT
Asher: b 1744 d *p.* 1812 Sarah Judson PS CT
Augustus: b 1760 d 6-3-1812 m Elizabeth (Bradley) Potter Pvt CT
Bela: b 7-10-1758 d 12-15-1850 m (1)Betsy Billings (2)Mrs Lydia (Shipman)Spaulding CaptLt CT
Benjamin: b 1722 d 12-4-1788 m Mary Frisbie Capt CT
Benjamin, Sr.: b 11-16-1726 d 1780 m Mary Smith Pvt CT
Benjamin: b 10-10-1740 d 3-12-1806 m (1)Deborah Sackett (2)Hannah Reed PS CT

Benjamin, Jr.: b 1770 d *p.* 1852 m Nancy Buckingham Drm CT NY ★
Benjamin: b 9-4-1760 d 4-3-1829 m Sally Brown Pvt CT
Benjamin: b 1746 d 1827 m Margaret Carper CS VA
Charles: b 3-12-1736 d 8-2-1780 m (1)Hannah Hull (2)Dorothy Hall Sgt CT
Charles: b 1-5-1724 d 4-15-1799 m (1)Rachal Sweeting (2)Lydia Fry Pvt MA
Comfort, Sr.: b 5-26-1731 d 5-29-1814 m (1)Hannah Barney (2)Keziah Peck (3)Ruth Sanders Pvt MA
Comfort, Jr.: b 10-17-1760 d *p.* 1790 m Mary Sanders Pvt MA
Constant: b 1748 d 4-9-1776 m Susan Royal 1Lt NJ
Cyrus: b 8-14-1750 d 8-5-1830 m Clarissa (Kellogg)Wheeler Pvt MA
Daniel: b 5-5-1754 d 5-30-1840 m Mehitable Harvey Pvt MA ★
Darius: b 3-14-1749/50 d 4-30-1804 m (1)Hannah Warner (2)Mary Francis Lt CT
Darius: b 9-11-1733 d 1797 m Elizabeth Beckwith CS CT
David: b *a.* 1760 d *p.* 1805 m Anne Humphreville Pvt CT
David: b 2-14-1754 d 4-23-1834 m (1)Amy Rundell (2)Allathea Honeywell Pvt CT ★
David: b 3-21-1755 d 4-23-1843 m Isabella Nichols Pvt CT
David: b 1727 d 4-5-1796 m Mary Williams Pvt NJ
Ebenezer: b 1-14-1751 d *p.* 1806 m Rebecca Dickerman N2Lt CT
Ebenezer: b 3-12-1743 d 9-8-1833 m Hannah Lockwood Pvt CT
Ebenezer: b 12-11-1762 d 4-20-1816 m Huldah Brown Pvt RI
Ebenezer: b 3-8-1730 d 4-14-1807 m (1)Sarah Carpenter (2)Sarah Brown (3)Sybel Ormsbee Cpl MA
Eliakim: b *c.* 1761 d 5-13-1849 m Polly Starr Sol CT
Elijah: b 10-27-1754 d 1794 m Hannah Harrison Pvt CT
Eliphalet: b 3-19-1758 d 6-8-1842 m Abigail Hawley Pvt CT
Elisha: b 4-3-1762 d 7-15-1829 m Olive Emmons Pvt CT
Elisha: b 9-4-1763 d 12-4-1841 m Huldah Ford Pvt CT
Ephraim: b 5-21-1721 d 1801 m Sarah Porter Pvt CT
Ephraim: b 1-5-1755 d 6-15-1806 m (1)Sarah Classon (2)Margaret Miner PS CT
Frederick: b 2-15-1734 d 9-17-1830 m (1)Elizabeth — (2)Mrs Anna Margaret Barnhart Pvt NC
George: b 1738 d 3- -1834 m ()Phoebe Ballou ()Phebe Whillps LCol RI ★
George: b 1762 d 3-4-1850 m Mary Lancisco Pvt VA
George: b 12-2-1752 d 3-23-1831 m Ann Peck Sgt CT W★
Gideon: b 7-2-1725 d 2-7-1790 m Abiah Smith Pvt CT
Heath: b 1745 d 10- -1780 m Rachel Roselle Pvt CT
Henry: b 1709 d *p.* 1790 m Rachel Whittaker Pvt MA
Hiram: b 1764 d 1-28-1831 m Welthy Kilburn Pvt MA
Ichabod, Sr.: b 2-4-1721 d 12-6-1776 m Lydia Walcott LCol RI
Ichabod, Jr.: b 11-26-1761 d 5-1-1848 m Lydia Dean Sol NY
Isaac: b 1751 d 12-18-1835 m (1)Theodosia Gridley (2)Elizabeth Kilby Pvt CT
Isaac: b 8-2-1758 d 2-21-1856 m Lucy Ferriss PS CT
Israel: b 12-6-1755 d 12-5-1827 m Sarah Marsh Pvt MA
Jacob: b 8-8-1756 d 2-11-1838 m Elizabeth Gibbs Pvt Arfr Ct ★
Jacob: b *c.* 1715 d 1801 m Lydia Borden CS VA
James: b 8-4-1708 d 3-2-1794 m Mary Hitchcock Capt CT
James: b 3-25-1741 d — m Elizabeth Hall Capt CT
James: b *c.* 1760 d *p.* 1790 m Hannah Canfield Pvt NJ
Jasper, Jr.: b 9-20-1737 d 1-16-1821 m Phoebe Dorr Pvt CT
Jathleel: b 1-1-1760 d 6-25-1837 m Olive Hyde Pvt CT
Jedediah: b 1747 d 8-15-1821 m Tabitha Ely Pvt CT
Jesse: b 3-3-1754 d 4-29-1823 m Philomela Cook Lt CT
Jesse, Sr.: b *c.* 1735 d 1-28-1777 m Ruth Hoyt Cpl CT
Jesse, Jr.: b 12-22-1759 d 5-5-1808 m Anna Nickerson Pvt CT
Jesse: b 11-21-1761 d 5-11-1832 m (1)Mary Raymond (2)Sarah Dean Pvt CT
Jesse: b 10-3-1764 d 9-26-1827 m Sarah Carver Pvt CT W★
Job, Jr.: b 7-2-1753 d 2-2-1797 m Martha Wells Pvt CT
Joel: b 8-28-1759 d 11-11-1833 m Lucy Fish Pvt RI
John: b 1-29-1744 d 7-21-1820 m Emily Burrett Cpl CT
John: b 4-21-1758 d 4-21-1788 m Elizabeth Andrews Lt CT
John: b 4-21-1740 d 1-18-1830 m Mary Brooks Ens CT
John: b 4-21-1716 d 4-27-1785 m Catherine Lay CS PS CT
John: b 1733/4 d 3-4-1812 m Mary Drown MM MA
John, Jr.: b 11-12-1742 d 9-19-1819 m Sarah Northrup Pvt NY
John: b 1-8-1729 d 4-9-1812 m Margaret — PS PA
John: b 1750 d 1820 m Susan Hickle Ens CS VA
Jonathan: b 1-17-1734 d 1817 m Ruth Wheeler Pvt MA
Jonathan: b 1-4-1724/5 d 10-7-1797 m Mrs Mary Thropp Maj RI
Joseph: b 5-20-1742 d 5-6-1796 m Mary Castle Pvt CT
Joseph: b 8-26-1757 d 3-3-1829 m Hannah Lambert Pvt CT
Joseph: b 7-5-1762 d 8-9-1845 m Olive Chatterton NS CT
Joseph: b 11-13-1763 d 1840 m Phoebe Vincent Pvt NY ★
Joseph: b 1760 d 6-25-1828/9 m (1)Margaret Carper (2)Nancy Hooks Mrnr VA ★
Josiah: b 10-20-1751 d 5-24-1821 m Helen Birdseye Cpl CT
Josiah: b 5-18-1740 d 1798 m Patience Bosworth Sol MA
Judson: b 5-27-1749 d 11-6-1832 m Mary Blakeman Pvt CT
Justus: b 11- -1737 d 11-3-1813 m Lucy Frisbee Lt PS CT
Lament: b 5-8-1751 d 5-5-1823 m Rachel Tracy Pvt CT
Levi: b 6-23-1748 d 1802 m (1)Rachel Harrison ( )Anna — Sgt CT
Levi: b 1749/50 d 3-4-1815 m (1)Jerusha Starr (2)Sarah Booth Pvt CT
Lewis: b 8-30-1761 d 1- -1825 m Betty Read Capt RI

PECK, contd.

Loring: b 1-19-1744/5 d 7-29-1833 m (1)Sarah Richmond (2)Jane Burke Capt RI

Margaret: b 7-23-1737 d 12-31-1814 m JohnPeck PS PA

Mather: b 4-26-1751 d 6- -1819 m (1)Esther Colt (2)Ruama Howell (3)Azuba Watrauce Tms Cmsry CT

Matthew: b 10-13-1749 d 1819/20 m Hannah Saunders Pvt NH

Michael: b 8-10-1738 d 1825 m Sibyl Merchant CS CT

Moses: b 3-13-1753 d 1-18-1838 m Esther Johnson Pvt CT ★

Nathan: b 1-10-1749 d 5-1-1816 m Huldah Fabrique Fif CT

Nathaniel: b 3-14-1723 d c. 1784 m Lucy Mather Tms CT

Nathaniel: b 4-27-1731 d 11-27-1807 m Mary (Mitchell)Peck Pvt MA

Nathaniel: b 1-9-1742 d 3-28-1787 m Mary Condit Pvt NJ

Nicholas: b 1741 d 4-11-1790 m Catharine — Pvt PS PA

Oliver: b 2-26-1751/2 d p. 1797 m Hannah Bliss Pvt MA

Oliver: b 2-5-1735 d 6- -1796 m Fear Foster Pvt NY

Otis: b 4-10-1750 d 10-9-1805 m Grace Carpenter Pvt MA

Peleg: b 3-6-1736 d 6-22-1807 m (1)Phebe Mason (2)Mary S. Thornton Capt MA

Peleg: b 4-8-1741 d 6-23-1795 m Esther Barney Pvt RI

Peleg: b 9-24-1760 d 11-4-1849 m (1)Betsey Sweet (2)Susanna — . . . .Pvt NS RI ★

Peter: b 1- -1746 d 6-17-1813 m Sarah Terrill Pvt CT

Philip: b 4-25-1747 d 4-6-1805 m Ruth Williams 2Lt MA

Phineas: b — d c. 1830 m Abigail Corbin Lt CT

Phineas: b 7-28-1743 d 9-15-1813 m Elizabeth Barstow Lt CT

Phineas, Sr.: b 4-10-1723 d 1-28-1803 m (1)Deborah Clark (2)Mrs Susanna Hine PS CT

Reeve: b 3-3-1723 d 1803 m Rachel Granger Pvt CT

Reuben: b 10-1-1737 d 4-17-1811 m Charity French Sgt CT

Reuben: b 1758 d 8-20-1843 m Sarah Gridley Pvt CT ★

Reuben: b 1-24-1760 d 12-9-1847 m Sarah Churchel Pvt CT ★

Reynold: b 3-8-1742 d 11-26-1814 m Deborah Beckwith Pvt CT

Richard Augustus: b 8-5-1753 d 10-24-1837 m (1)Sarah Tennant (2)Elizabeth Chamberlain NS CT

Robert: b 6-30-1739 d 7-25-1827 m Ann Reed Ens CT

Samuel: b 8-22-1736 d 6-12-1822 m Mehitable Smith Capt CT

Samuel: b 1753 d 8-9-1796 m Mary Beach Pvt CT

Samuel: b 4- -1720 d 1-29-1793 m Mary Ferris PS Grd CT

Samuel: b 1-4-1734 d 9-28-1815 m Susanna Doolittle PS CS CT

Samuel, Jr.: b 2-27-1734 d 1808 m Sara Jencks Pvt MA

Samuel: b 1761 d 7-3-1825 m Olive Love Pvt RI W★

Seril: b 8-23-1750 d 3-27-1814 m Bethiah Ellis PS CT

Seth: b 11-22-1747 d 2-10-1831 m Hannah Alling PS CT

Silas: b 10-2-1724 d 6- -1808 m Elizabeth Calkins Pvt CT

Simeon: b 8-30-1752 d 10- -1826 m (1)Sarah Merriman (2)Sarah Page Pvt CT

Simon: b 1736 d 7-3-1838 m Eunice — Pvt CT

Solomon: b 10-3-1749 d 11-14-1822 m Anna Wheeler Pvt MA

Solomon: b 10-29-1738 d 8-22-1814 m Abigail Barney Sgt RI

Theophilus: b 3-15-1730 d 6-8-1812 m Rebecca Knapp Pvt CT

Thomas: b 9-1-1750 d 9-30-1781 m Mary Johnson Ferris Sgt CT

Thomas: b 12-27-1757 d 1810 m (1)Lydia Knight (2)Frances Davis Pvt MA

Titus: b 4-7-1742 d 10-29-1776 m Rebecca Hitchcock Lt CT

Ward: b 10-7-1762 d 4-8-1844 m Dorcas Porter Pvt CT

Wm: b 12-15-1755 d 5-10-1832 m Abigail Matthews AdjGen RI

Wm: b 5-10-1759 d 5-8-1814 m Rebecca Spooner Pvt CT

Wm.: b 2-20-1764 d 2-13-1837 m Susanna Glascock Pvt VA ★

Zebulon, Jr.: b 4-15-1743 d 6-23-1820 m (1)Esther Hart (2)Mary (Hawley) Watson (3)Mindwell (Hayden) Chubb Capt CT

PECKER,

Bartholomew: b 6-20-1731 d p. 1789 m Hannah Russel Pvt MA

James, Sr.: b c. 1720 d 9-22-1778 m (1)Hannah Cogswell (2)Ruth Bradley Dr MA

James, Jr.: b 8-9-1756 d 2-14-1842 m Hannah Dalton Pvt MA

Wm.: b 10-10-1758 d 11-22-1820 m Hannah Sawyer Pvt MA ★

PECKHAM,

Abel: b 2-17-1732 d 1825 m Rebecca Burdick Pvt RI

Barber: b 1755 d 5- -1807 m (1)Elizabeth Westcott (2)Sarah Sheffield Capt RI W★

Benjamin: b 1755 d 1-5-1833 m Lucy — Pvt CT

Benjamin: b 3-22-1715 d 3- -1792 m Mary Hazard PS RI

Braddock: b 4- -1758 d 1-9-1833 m (1)Rebecca Johnson (2)Silence Johnson Pvt RI

Daniel: b 9-25-1726 d 1827 m Mary — PS RI

David: b 8-28-1744 d 12-21-1825 m Elizabeth Handy Pvt MA

Enos: b 1733 d 1833 m Ann Hovey Pvt RI

George: b 1720 d 1816 m (1)Hannah Peckham (2)Jerusha Bartlett Pvt RI

George Hazzrd: b 4-14-1739 d 11-29-1799 m Sarah Taylor CS RI

Job: b c. 1692 d 8-13-1779 m Mary Turner PS RI

Jonathan: b 1754 d 2-3-1803 m (1)Susannah West (2)Innocent Wood Pvt MA

Joseph: b 12-10-1735 d 8-15-1812 m Susannah Mumford Lt RI

Joshua: b 6-18-1759 d 6-11-1803 m Rebecca Horsewell Pvt RI

Levi: b 4-17-1758 d 1800 m Sahra Tripp Smn MA

Pardon: b 8-1-1763 d 10-10-1852 m Olive Blodgett Pvt MA

Peleg: b 1739 d 3-12-1833 m Elizabeth Smith PS RI

Peleg: b 5-9-1762 d p. 8-23-1850 m Betsey Stetson Pvt RI ★

Prince: b 1-30-1746 d 3-6-1833 m (1)Mary Jenne (2)Sarah Austin Pvt MA

Samuel: b 12-22-1759 d 10-30-1833 m Hannah Stanton Sgt RI ★

Samuel: b 12- -1756 d p. 1789 m Elizabeth Weaver Pvt RI

Seth: b 10-31-1750 d 4-24-1826 m Mercy Smith Pvt RI W★

Thomas: b 6-20-1747 d 12-18-1825 m Hannah Weaver Capt CS RI

Wm.: b 2-1-1751 d 3-3-1839 m Elizabeth Knapp Pvt MA

PEDDY,

Jeremiah: b c. 1760 d c. 1830 m Louisa — Sol GA

PEDEN,

Alexander: b 4- -1758 d 1-21-1841 m Rebecca Martin Pvt SC ★

David: b 11-1-1760 d 10-25-1823 m (1Eleanor Goodgion (2)Margaret Hughes Sol SC

Hugh: b 1725 d 10-18-1800 m Sarah Boggs Capt PA

Isaac: b c. 1757 d 8- -1809 m Rebecca Garwood Pvt PA

James: b 1734 d p. 1789 m Mary Hemphill Pvt SC

James: b 9-12-1738 d p. 2-15-1784 m (2)Milly — (3) 2Lt PS VA

John: b c. 1738 d 1807 m — Pvt PA

John: b 6-16-1709 d 1792 m Margaret McDill PS SC

Joseph: b 6-30-1758 d 8-5-1850 m (2)Rebecca Driver Arfr PA

Samuel: b 1718 d 1802 m — Pvt PA

Samuel: b 11-10-1754 d 12-26-1835 m (1)Katherine White (2)Margaret — Lt SC ★

Thomas: b 1743 d 3-6-1834 m Elizabeth White Pvt SC

Wm.: b 1749 d 12-23-1817 m Mary Archer Pvt SC

PEDIFORD, (or PEDIGO)

Edward: b 12-24-1732 d 1834 m Mary Elkin Pvt VA

PEDRICK,

Abijah: b 2-13-1762 d 12-27-1852 m Mrs Parmelia Craft Baker Pvt NY

John: b 5-30-1731 d 1-12-1807 m Elizabeth Douglas Matr MA

John: b 1728 d 6-20-1777 m Harriet — Pvt NY

Wm.: b 2-26-1737/8 d 10-24-1803 m Mary Barker Smn MA

Wm.: bpt 9-24-1738 d 10-24-1803 m Elizabeth Lambert Pvt MA

PEEBLES, (includes PEEPLES, PEOPLES)

Alexander: b c. 1740 d 1826 m — Wier Capt PA

David, Sr.: b c. 1730 d 1795 m Elizabeth Cook PS NC

Henry: b c. 1750 d p. 1784 m Sarah — Pvt SC

Hugh: b 1762 d 8-12-1840 m Lydia Seratt Pvt NY

Hugh: b c. 1745 d a. 10-12-1799 m Abigail — PS VA SC NC

James: b 1740 d p. 1790 m Martha Haskell Pvt MA

Jehu, Sr.: b c. 1713 d c. 1803 m Mary — PS VA

John: b 1-31-1763 d 10-6-1849 m (1)Wilmath Owen (2)Martha Johnsy Pvt SC

John, Sr.: b 1720 d p. 11-2-1786 m Agnes — PS NC

John: b c. 1755 d p. 1797/8 m Katherine McBride 1Lt SC

Joseph: b 1735 d 1782 m Mary Robinson Capt VA

Lewis: b c. 1731-5 d a. 1840 m (3)Elizabeth — PS NC

Nathan: b 1750 d a. 12-5-1794 m Rachel Holton PS SC

Robert: b 4-14-1737 d 1778 m Martha Forbush Pvt MA

Robert: b 1740 d 1808 m Rebecca — Maj NC

Robert: b 1736 d 1789-95 m Lucy — Capt NC

Robert: b 1741 d p. 3-5-1813 m Sarah Kleinhoof Capt PA

Wm.: b 1740 d p. 1790 m Elizabeth Edmondson Pvt NC

Wm.: b 1745 d 9-5-1776 m Elizabeth Finley Capt PA

PEELE, (includes PEALE & PEELLE)

Charles Wilson: b 4-16-1741 d 10-22-1827 m (1)Rachel Brewer (2)Elizabeth DePeyster (3)Hannah Moore Capt PA

Edward: b 1750 d 1815 m Sarah — Sol NC

James: b 1749 d 5-24-1831 m Mary Claypole Capt MD

James: b c. 1740 d 1812 m Catherine Carr Pvt PA

John: b 1747 d 1816 m Sarah Gamble Pvt GA

Jonathan, Sr.: b 12-16-1702 d 1-1-1782 m Sarah Willard PS MA

Jonathan, Jr.: b 7-17-1731 d 10-6-1809 m Margaret Mason PS PVT RI

Robert: b 6-29-1709 d 7-13-1782 m Elizabeth — PS NC

PEELER, (includes PEALER)

John Jacob: b 1744/5 d 3 21 1815 m Mary Flagg Pvt VT

Paul: b c. 1740 d 9-1-1796 m Charlotte Speiglemoyer Pvt PA

PEELING,

Joshua: b 1755 d p. 3-6-1837 m Hannah — Sgt PA ★

Joshua: b 1747 d 1824 m Louisa Harland Pvt PA

Robert: b 1751 d 8-2-1839 m Mary Smith Sgt PA

PEERY, (includes PEARY)

George: b 7-12-1755 d 10-9-1830 m Martha Davidson Lt VA

James: b c. 1745 d p. 2-18-1800 m Jane Ferris Pvt VA

James: b 1750 d 10-18-1821 m Ellen Dennis PS VA

Stephen: b 11-14-1759 d 10-7-1837 m Rhoda Boston Pvt MA ★

Thomas: b 1749 d 6- -1820 m Margaret Dennis Ens PS VA

Wm.: b 2-6-1755 d 6-28-1830 m Sarah Evans Sgt VA

PEET,

Abijah: b 6-19-1748 d 2-15-1805 m Bethia Uffoot Pvt CT

Abiram: b 7-20-1737 d 4-22-1786 m Anna Lewis Dr CT
Elijah: b 9-13-1759 d 11-26-1841 m Anna Seeley Pvt CT ★
Gideon: b 2-24-1742 d 7-31-1813 m Bette Burton Pvt CT
Stephen: b. 1744 d 1838 m Elizabeth Gurnee Sgt NY
Wm.: b 1743 d — m Beulah Smith Pvt CT

PEFFLEY,
David: b c. 1740 d 10- -1807 m Maria Sherrick (Casper)Pvt PA
David: b 2-15-1761 d 12-14-1827 m Magdalena Garst Pvt PA

PEGAN,
James, Jr.: b 1754 d 1-20-1834 m Sara Brannon Pvt PA

PEGG,
Elias: b 1759 d 3-5-1839 m (1)Elizabeth — (2)Margaret — Pvt Fif
PA ★

PEGRAM,
Baker: b 1-27-1758 d 10-14-1830 m Mary Manson Sol VA
Edward: b 1-13-1745 d 3-30-1816 m (1)Mary Lile (2)Mrs Anne
Harper Parham Capt VA

PEGUES,
Claudius, Sr.: b 1719 d 1-22-1790 m (2)Henrietta Butler PS CS SC
Claudius, Jr.: b 4-7-1755 d 1820 m Marcia Saunders Capt SC
Wm.: b 5-16-1750 d 3-18-1818 m (1)Elizabeth Saunders (2)Sarah
Hicks CS PS SC

PEIFFER,
John George: b 9-15-1758 d 1-19-1823 m Mary Magdalen Schaeffer
Mil PA

PELHAM,
Charles: b 6-15-1748 d 8-29-1829 m Isabella Atkinson Maj VA ★
Peter: b 5-1-1747 d 8-26-1822 m Parthenia Brown QM VA
Wm.: b 1759 d 2-3-1827 m Penelope — Dr VA

PELL,
John: b a. 1765 d 7-13-1810 m Nancy Harrison Pvt VA

PELLETIER,
Antoine: bpt 2-3-1706 d 9-14-1795 m Marie Doza PS IL

PELLETREAU,
Elias: b 5-31-1726 d 11-2-1810 m (1)Sarah Gelston (2)Sarah
Conkling PS NY
Elias: b 12-20-1724 d 1798 m Rachel Ball Pvt NY
John: b 7-29-1755 d 8-26-1822 m Mary Smith Pvt NY

PELLETT,
Jonathan: b 7-12-1753 d 10-22-1817 m Hannah Palmer Pvt CT

PELLS,
Henry: bpt 5-9-1740 d 1806-8 m Sarah Vanderburgh Pvt PS NY

PELOT,
Charles: b 6-22-1763 d 2-20-1809 m Mary Susannah Postell Sol SC
James: b 1743 d 1824 m Elizabeth Chisholm Sol PS SC

PELTON,
Abner: b 3-4-1755 d 1-17-1846 m (1)Sarah Bidwell (2)Dorothy
Bagley Pvt CT
Benjamin: b 5-17-1752 d 9-8-1830 m (1)Jane Griffith (2)Isabella
Kinley Capt NY
Ebenezer: b 12-28-1762 d 12-23-1824 m Prudence Bogart Pvt CT
Gideon: b 2-23-1747 d 3- -1824 m (1)Margaret Crawford (2)Mrs
Jessup Pvt NY
Ithamar: b 4-1-1744 d 1-22-1806 m (1)Elizabeth Hall Pvt CT
Ithamar: b 11-22-1740 d 3-16-1826 m Asenath Pratt Pvt CT
James: b 7-21-1710 d 1794 m Elizabeth Barb PS CT
James: b 1763 d 1849 m (1)Sarah Lawrence (2)Mrs Abigail B.
McAuley Pvt MA
Joel: b 11-5-1753 d 3-7-1856 m (1)Sally Sloman (2)Anna Cotter
(3)Mrs Ruhamah Beedy Pvt CL ★
Johnathan: b 6-10-1759 d 9-22-1830 m Elizabeth Doane Pvt CT
Joseph: b 11-25-1756 d 6-15-1837 m (1)Prudence Pelton (2)Abigail
Ayers Pvt NH
Moses: b c. 1728 d 4-16-1778 m Mary Whipple Pvt CT
Nathan: b 5-2-1738 d 5-16-1813 m (1)Ruth Thompson (2)Mrs Mary
Waters Pvt CS PS CT
Peleg: b 8-9-1759 d 1-27-1829 m Anna Stoddard Fif CT
Philip: b 3-13-1745 d 1798/9 m Jane VanNostrand Pvt NY
Phineas: b 1712 d 5-24-1799 m Mary KcKay Sol CT MA
Phineas: b 1758 d 1850 m Rebecca Johnson Pvt CT
Samuel: b 12-21-1739 d 12-20-1801 m Rebecca Holmes Sgt CT
Stephen: b 12-10-1768 d 12-10-1843 m Alice Whitney Cpl MA ★
Thomas: b 11-1-1759 d 12-15-1850 m Anna Smith Pvt MA

PEMBER,
Andrew: b 11-25-1753 d a. 1812 m Jemima — Pvt VT
Elijah: b 1729 d 3-15-1812 m Hannah Cross CS CT
John: b 10-31-1751 d 9-1-1827 m Lucretia Bill Sgt CT
Samuel: b 1-4-1750 d 3-14-1826 m Esther Reed Cpl CT

PEMBERTON,
John: b 10-12-1742 d 10-25-1813 m Elizabeth Stanton Capt NC
Patrick Grant: b 9-30-1750 d 1-28-1811 m Mary Johnson Pvt CT
Richard: b 1732 d 1791 m Amy Stith CS NC
Wm.: b 1-30-1749 d c. 1823 m Rhoda Luck Pvt VA

PENCE,
George: b 1750 d 1818 m Margaret Jane Carpenter Capt VA
Jacob: b 12-20-1730 d 2- -1800 m Catherine Persinger Sol VA
Jacob, Jr.: b c. 1742 d 1819 m Elizabeth Trustler Pvt VA
Michael: b c. 1749 d 12-25-1807 m Sybilla Frye Sol VA
Peter: b 1742 d 2- -1812 m Elizabeth — Lt VA
Peter, Sr.: b c. 1732 d 1812 m Mary — Pvt PA

PENDELL, (includes PENDALL)
Benoni: b 1718 d p. 1782 m Mary — Pvt CT
Jonathan: b 6-9-1749 d 6-16-1840 m Mary Powis QMSgt NY ★

PENDERGRASS,
Job: b 1760 d p. 1789 m Mary Reel Pvt NC

PENDLETON,
Amos: b 6-21-1728 d 11-25-1821 m (1)Susan Chesebrough (2)Anna
Foster PS Ens RI
Benjamin: b 9-18-1738 d 12-29-1824 m Lois Burdick NLt PS RI
Caleb: b 12-1-1734 d 3-29-1826 m Hannah Closson Pvt RI
Curtis: b 5-9-1763 d 1-19-1836 m Nancy Wilson Pvt VA ★
Edmund: b 1744/5 d 7-4-1827 m Mildred Pollard Capt VA
Gideon: b 5-15-1759 d 12-17-1809 m Annie Rose Pvt RI
Henry, Sr.: b 1724 d 1818 m Martha Curtis PS VA
Henry, Jr.: b 1-7-1744/5 d 1-6-1800 m Ann Knight Pvt VA
Henry: b 12-4-1762 d 11-1-1822 m (1)Alcey Ann Winston (2)Mrs
Mary B. Overton Burnley Sol VA
Henry, 4th: b 1733 d 1798 m Ann Thomas PS VA
Increase: b 1740 d 7-8-1815 m Phoebe Kingman Ens CT
James: b 6-12-1758 d 12-12-1778 m Sarah Lyon Sol CT
James, Jr.: b 1743 d 1793 m Catherine Bowie Col VA
James: b 4-3-1750 d 7-21-1832 m Sarah Elizabeth Rucker Capt VA
James: b 8-13-1754 d 3-6-1815 m Elizabeth Peachey Capt VA
James: b 1751 d 1827 m Mary Ann Phips Capt VA
John: b 5-22-1735 d 3-31-1812 m Sabra Thompson Ens RI
John: b 1756 d 1828 m Sallie Alsop Pvt VA
John: b 1760 d 1830 m Sarah Banks Sol VA
John: b 1719 d 1799 m (1)Phoebe James (2)Sarah Madison PS VA
Joseph: b 1-17-1747 d 7-9-1822 m (1)Damaris Crandall (2) —
Babcock (3)Nancy Crandall Maj RI
Joseph: b 3-3-1703 d — m Sarah Worden Capt RI
Joshua: b 5-6-1744 d 4-9-1824 m Anna Clark Capt RI
Micajah: b 1758 d 1844 m (1)Miss Breckenridge (2)Mary C.
Horsely Pvt VA ★
Nathan: b 4-2-1754 d 1-26-1841 m (1)Amelia Babcock (2)Rhoda
Babcock Gavitt Grd Ens RI
Nathaniel: b 1-27-1747 d p. 1820 m (1)Cynthia West (2)Sally
Bradford Ens CT
Nathaniel, Jr.: b 1746 d 10-20-1821 m Susan Bard ADC VA
Peleg: b 7-9-1733 d 7-10-1810 m Ann Parks Lt RI
Philip: b 1732 d p. 11-1-1793 m Martha Aubrey Col VA
Philip: b 1752 d 1802 m Agnes Patterson Col VA
Philip: b 8-2-1752 d 7-31-1804 m (1)Martha Hoomes (2)Mary Ann
Fleet PS VA
Reuben: b 1755 d 11-14-1825 m Frances Marie Ann Garland Sol VA
Richard: b c. 1750 d 5-20-1829 m Mary Tinsley Pvt VA W★
Simeon: b 1733 d 10- -1819 m Mercy Palmer Ens RI
Sylvester: b 8-5-1730 d p. 1790 m Sarah Champlain SeaCap NC
Wm.: b 8-13-1740 d 1796 m Abigail Redfield Cpl CT
Wm.: b 7-15-1749 d 1-6-1822 m Martha Brown Ens RI
Wm.: b 3-23-1704 d 8-23-1786 m (1)Lydia Burroughs (2)Mrs
Mary McDowell Cheseborough PS RI
Wm., Jr.: b 2-11-1727 d 8-20-1820 m (1)Judith Carr (2)Lydia
Palmer (3)Priscilla Cheesebrough Capt MA
Wm.: b 1748 d 1817 m (1)Elizabeth Ferguson (2)Elizabeth Daniel
Pvt VA

PENFIELD,
Daniel: b 1759 d 8-24-1840 m Mary Fellows Cmsry CT
Isaac, Sr.: b 1-3-1732 d 1825 m Esther Hurlburt Sol CT
James: b 4-28-1732 d 5-12-1794 m Ellen Burr Pvt CT
James, Jr.: b 2-24-1761 d 12-11-1842 m Mary Tucker Pvt CT
Jesse: b 1759/60 d 12-18-1833 m (1)Sarah Hall (2)Polly Upson Pvt
CT ★
John: b 5-14-1731 d 2-22-1797 m Ruth Stocking LCol CT
John: b 11-5-1747 d 1829 m Eunice Ogden Sgt CT
Jonathan: b 3-25-1719 d 7-23-1794 m Elizabeth Shepard PS CT
Nathaniel: b 11-14-1760 d 2-6-1838 m Eunice Kelsey Pvt CT ★
Peter: b 9-13-1743 d 1-12-1812 m Hannah Lewis Capt CT ★
Phineas: b 6-6-1756 d 3-28-1834 m Lucy Osgood Cpl CT ★
Samuel: b 11-5-1734 d 4-2-1811 m (1)Elizabeth Lewis (2)Hannah
— Lt PS CT
Samuel: b 3-7-1735 d p. 11- -1804 m Rebeckah Scovil Pvt CT

PENGRA,
George: b 5-2-1741 d 1775/76 m Hannah Burnam Sol VT

PENHOLLOW, (includes PENHALLOW)
John: b c. 1723 d 1809 m (1)Sarah Wentworth (2)Ann Wendell CS PS NH
Richard: b 1746 d 5-18-1817 m (2)Huldah Canfield Sgt CT ★

PENLAND,
John: b 11-29-1764 d a. 4-12-1855 m Alice Moore Pvt Spy NC
Robert: b 1742 d 4-16-1826 m Elizabeth Brank Pvt PS N C

PENLEY,
Joseph: b 7-13-1756 d 9-13-1844 m (1)Esther (Fogg)Johnson (2)Thankful Moody Sgt MA ★

PENN,
Abram: b 12-27-1743 d 6-26-1801 m Ruth Stovall Col VA
Benjamin: b 1740 d 1834 m Mary Sargent Pvt MD
Benjamin: b 1753 d 5-10-1827 m Rebecca Ryan Pvt MD ★
Gabriel: b 7-17-1741 d p. 11-21-1794 m Sarah Calloway Col PS VA
George: b 12-2-1737 d p. 2-5-1796 m Elizabeth Douglas Capt VA
John: b — d 1828 m (1)Ann Gartrell (2)Eleanor Dutton (3) — Wingate (4)Jane Dent Pvt MD
John: b 9-2-1741 d 9-14-1788 m Susannah Lyme SDI PS NC
John: b 1759 d 1829 m Elizabeth Thomas Sol VA
Shadrack: b 1-8-1750 d 6-6-1831 m (2)Margaret Holland Pvt MD
Simon: b 1734 d 1798 m Mary Williams Sol VA
Wm.: b 7-31-1762 d 7-26-1836 m Martha Amos Slade Pvt MD

PENNELL,
Abraham: b 3-21-1741 d p. 6-11-1813 m Nancy Smith 2Lt MA
Clement, Jr.: b 4-26-1751 d 1835 m Esther Kunningham Pvt MA ★
Hugh: b 6-1-1763 d 1839 m Elizabeth — Pvt PA
James: b 1740 d 1821 m Elizabeth Wright Pvt VA
John: b 1721 d 10-21-1797 m Elinor Smith Capt VT
Joseph: b 2-14-1747 d 11-1-1833 m (1)Hannah Ward (2)Eunice Nash (3)Bathsheba Buker Cpl MA ★
Nathan: b 7-7-1754 d — m Susanna Talbot Pvt PA
Stephen: b 1- -1752 d 10-10-1832 m Mary Cotton PS MA
Wm.: b 11-27-1725/6 d 9-5-1783 m Mary Dell Pvt PA

PENNEY, (includes PENNY & PINNEY)
Ammiel: b 7-18-1746 d 2-16-1816 m Hannah Heaviland Pvt NY
Caleb: b c. 1745 d p. 11-18-1798 m Sarah — PS NC
David: b 12-5-1757 d 1-20-1830 m Sally Smith Pvt MA
Henry: b 1756 d 4-16-1841 m (1)Hanna Brown (2)Mrs Mary Givans Pvt SC ★
James: b 7-14-1762 d 1845 m Lucy Kennard Pvt PA
John: b 6-10-1740 d 7-21-1826 m Margaret Ann Rutan MM MA
John: b 11-10-1759 d 6-19-1833 m Frances White Pvt NC ★
Jonathan: b 1755 d 1812 m Priscilla Grover Pvt VT
Joseph: bpt 8-22-1762 d 1808 m Mary Gowen Pvt MA
Thomas: b 8-13-1750 d 2-18-1813 m Lydia Herring Pvt MA
Wm.: b 1744 d 8-8-1807 m Sarah Bangs Pvt NY

PENNIMAN,
Adna Taft: b 7-24-1755 d 11-4-1820 m Alice Moulton CaptLt NH
Bethuel: b 1752 d 1827 m Huldah Hollis Pvt MA
Ezra: b 1734 d — m Eunice Thayer Cpl MA
Ezra: b 4-27-1760 d 5-21-1823 m Louisa Eager Pvt MA
Henry: b 10-29-1733 d 12-11-1809 m Experience Wheelock Pvt MA
Peter: b 9-11-1728 d 7-8-1805 m Hulda Wheelock Capt MA
Stephen: b 6-4-1743 d p. 11-22-1823 m Sarah Holbrook Maj MA
Wm., Sr.: b 7-7-1706 d 1779 m Ruth Thayer PS MA
Wm., Jr.: b 1-19-1731 d 7-10-1813 m Sarah Wild Pvt MA

PENNINGTON,
Charles: b 6-6-1758 d 9-5-1845 m Cassandra Swathlander Wgn NJ PA
Daniel: b 11-10-1730 d 3- -1810 m Martha Ball Pvt VA
James: b 7-25-1752 d p. 1833 m Racheal Vick Pvt VA ★
James: b c. 1740 d p. 9-27-1802 m — Pvt VA
John: b 1735 d 9- -1778 m Mary Ryland Pvt MD
John: b 9-3-1761 d 9-21-1841 m — Pvt Tms NJ ★
John: b 1760 d 1-20-1823 m (1)Sally Graves (2)Temperance Parker Pvt VA
Nathan: b 1758/9 d 1810 m Margaret (Wescott)Leonard Pvt NJ
Robert: b 1-17-1754 d 4-22-1826 m Rebecca — Pvt MD
Samuel: b 1725 d 8-6-1791 m Mary Sanford PS NJ
Thomas: b 8-22-1729 d c. 9- -1796 m Deborah — Pvt PA
Wm. Sanford: b 1757 d 9-17-1826 m Phebe Wheeler Maj NJ

PENNOCK, (includes PENICK & PENIX)
Aaron: b 1748 d 1836 m Ruth Lord Pvt VT
Charles: b c. 1743 d 1798 m (1)Agnes Clark (2)Agnes Peek PS VA
James: b c. 1745-7 d 1831 m (2)Elizabeth Faris Sol VA
John: b 9-2-1757 d 9-18-1839 m Martha Walker Pvt PS VA GA
John: b 6-17-1715 d p. 4-25-1784 m (2)Mary Mallory PS VA
Joseph: b 8-19-1753 d 9-30-1821 m Mary Pusey Pvt PA

PENNOYER,
Isaac: b 11-28-1751 d 10-10-1833 m Susannah Bishop Pvt CT
Isaac: b 1751 d 1809 m Catherine Hyatt Adj NY
James: b 5-4-1746 d 5-17-1820 m Sarah Doty Pvt MA

PENNYPACKER, (includes PENNEBACKER)
Dirck: b 1-1-1737 d 1799 m Hannah DeHaven Capt PA
Harmon: b c. 1745 d p. 1792 m Barbara Pennebacker Pvt PA
John: b 2-11-1793 d a. 4-1-1806 m — PS PA
Matthias: b 10-14-1742 d 2-8-1808 m (1)Mary Custer (2)Margaret (Longaker) Maris PS PA
Samuel: b 11-4-1746 d 2-13-1826 m Hannah Gerbert PS PA

PENROSE,
Joseph: b 6-10-1737 d 8-22-1824 m Eleanor DeHaven PS PA
Thomas: b 1-22-1733/4 d 11-28-1815 m Ann Dowding PS PA

PENSEL,
Henry: b — d 7-3-1778 m Sarah Pensel Pvt PA

PENSINGER,
Henry: b 1761 d 1821 m Rosanna — Pvt PA ★

PENTACOST, (includes PENTECOST)
Dorsey: b c. 1739 d 1791-1795 m Catherine Bealer Col CS PS VA
Wm.: b 11-4-1763 d 1-27-1839 m (1)Delilah Wood (2)Mrs Juilanne Brown (3)Mary Bradley Pvt VA ★

PENTON,
Abner: b 3-8-1741 d 1796 m Ann Smith Capt NJ

PEPIN,
Andrew: b c. 1750 d p. 1798 m Judith Dona Lt NY

PEPOON,
Joseph: b 8-2-1749 d 6-15-1812 m Eunice Ayers Sgt CT

PEPPER,
Benjamin: b 10-30-1719 d 9-9-1807 m Abigail Pratt PS MA
Isaac: b 6-15-1756 d 5-15-1819 m Mary Chipman Pvt MA
Jacob, Sr.: b 4-7-1733 d 4-17-1812 m (1)Abigail Foster (2)Mrs Sarah Marrett Pvt MA
Jacob, Jr.: b 1759 d 1832 m Mary Marsh Pvt MA
Joseph, Sr.: b 8-28-1721 d 3-3-1798 m (1)Dinah Cummings (2) Mrs Sallie Cavono Pvt MA
Joshua: b 1-18-1720 d 12-28-1808 m Elizabeth McCauley Pvt MD
Samuel, Sr.: b c. 1725 d p. 1797 m Elizabeth Holton PS VA
Samuel, Jr.: b 2-22-1756 d 3-26-1824 m Milly Connor Pvt VA
Simeon: b 8-8-1754 d 9-19-1822 m Esther Jones Pvt MA
Solomon: b 4-8-1740 d 4-8-1796 m (1)Abial (Pepper) (2)Mrs Phebe (Walker) Knowles Pvt MA

PERCIVAL,
Benjamin: b 1-13-1752 d 4-15-1817 m Lydia Goodspeed Cpl MA
Elisha: b 6-13-1743 d 5-31-1836 m Abigail Smith Sol MA
Gurdon: b 6-13-1749 d 4-17-1825 m Sarah Chapman Sgt CT
Jabez: b 7-16-1760 d 6-28-1841 m Elizabeth Stearns Pvt MA
James: b 2-14-1750 d 9-20-1807 m Eunice Curtis Pvt MA
Jeremiah: b 9-1-1754 d 8-6-1830 m Naomi Hatch Pvt VT
John: b 11-6-1754 d 6-13-1837 m Ruth Crocker Pvt MA ★
Thomas: b 3-14-1759 d 8-21-1816 m Hannah Ryder Pvt MA
Timothy: b 2-4-1733 d 1-15-1815 m Mary Fuller Capt CT

PERCY, (includes PIERCY)
Christian: b 1-1-1744 d 9-25-1793 m Mary Smith Capt PA
Jacob: b 1759 d 8-28-1831 m Abby McDowell Fif PA
John: b 1749 d 10-14-1805 m (1)Hannah — (2)Mary — Capt NY
John: b 1735 d 7-23-1810 m Hannah — Pvt VA
Joseph: b 6-30-1754 d 3-28-1830 m Love Reynolds Pvt CT
Wm.: b 9-15-1744 d 7-13-1819 m Catherine Elliott PS SC

PEREZ,
Manuel Antonio: b 1734 d 11-7-1814 m Jeanne Catherine Dubois PS LA

PERHAM,
Benjamin: b 2-13-1733 d 1-29-1812 m Rachel Clemens Pvt MA
Ezekiel, Sr.: b a. 1744 d 12-14-1807 m Eunice Shattuck Pvt MA
Ezekiel, Jr.: b 5-27-1764 d 4-19-1843 m (1)Hepzibeth Jewett (2)Phebe Oaks Pvt MA ★
Johathan: b 7-28-1735 d p. 1790 m Hannah Wright PS VT
Lemuel: b 1727 d 1795 m Mrs Mary (Butterfield)French Lt MA
Oliver: b 7-5-1762 d 12-5-1846 m Anna Perse Pvt MA ★

PERIAM,
Joseph: b 1742 d 10-8-1780 m Elizabeth (Ogden)Woodruff QM NJ

PERIT,
John: b c. 1738 d 1795 m Ruth Webster Capt CT

PERKINS,
Aaron: b 9- -1744 d 2-16-1823 m Hannah Treadwell 1Lt MA
Abiezer: b 1754 d 9-20-1825 m Irene Loomis Pvt MA ★

Abner: b 4-7-1736 d 1803 m Mary Chick Pvt MA
Abner: b 1762 d c. 1842 m Mary Shay Pvt MA
Abner, Sr.: b 3-14-1749 d 12-4-1828 m Lucy Phelps Pvt CT
Abraham, Sr.: b 1714 d 5-10-1786 m (1)Elizabeth Ely (2)Mrs Mary Ely Sgt CT
Abraham, Jr.: b 8-7-1745 d 4-13-1824 m (1)Elizabeth Ely (2)Anne Fanning OrdlSgt CT ★
Abraham: b 4-15-1744 d 10-24-1803 m Sarah Cogswell Cpl MA
Abraham: b 6-14-1747 d 11-2-1842 m (1)Mrs Mary Spillar (2)Mrs Margaret Elizabeth Lear Pvt MA ★
Abraham: b 4-1-1735 d 8-16-1804 m Mrs Mary Sanborn Fogg Capt NH
Amos, Jr.: b 11-21-1746 d 2-22-1819 m Abiah Downs Ens Lt CT
Andrew: b 1750 d p. 1799 m Rachel Elliott Pvt MA
Archelaus: b 7-17-1760 d 4-17-1849 m Ann Mitchell Lt VA
Archibald: b 1746 d 1840 m Elizabeth Gibbs Sol VA
Benjamin: b 1736 d p. 1790 m Elizabeth Moore Pvt GA
Benjamin: b 6-11-1749 d 10-10-1834 m Lydia Hawkes Cpl MA
Benjamin: b 9-15-1760 d 5-18-1848 m Betsey Swain Pvt NH ★
Benjamin: b 1736 d 12-1-1815 m Mary A. Curd Ens VA Heirs ★
Charles: b 1736/7 d 9-4-1829 m Abigail Waterman Cpl MA
Charles: b 3-26-1742 d p. 1813 m Mary Tate PS NC
Christopher: b 9-15-1758 d 3-25-1813 m (1)Rebecca Palmer (2)Hannah Bishop Carpenter Pvt NY
Daniel: b 1803 m Rebecca Wadsworth Capt PS CT
Daniel: b 6-27-1753 d 3-10-1830 m Abigail Penney Pvt MA
Daniel: b 1757 d 1-26-1853 m Sarah Wilkins Pvt VT
Daniel Buck: b 5-13-1760 d p. 1800 m Sarah Birchard Pvt CT
David: b 12-26-1725 d 4-30-1803 m Mercy Fisk 2Lt MA
David: b 3-3-1739 d p. 1801 m Fear Canedy Pvt MA
David: b 2-11-1739 d 8-28-1825 m Mehitable Swett Pvt NH
David: b 1-15-1739 d 3-14-1805 m Elizabeth Brown Sol NH
David: b 11-3-1740 d 8-15-1816 m Abigail Griffith Pvt NH
David: b 11-26-1733 d 4-17-1797 m Elizabeth — PS NC
David, Sr.: b c. 1729 d 1782 m (1)— Evans (2)Bilzie Stringer Ens SC
David, Jr.: b c. 1760 d p. 1800 m Mrs Margaret Williams Pvt PS SC
Ebenezer: b 10-29-1720 d 12-1-1806 m Sarah Perkins Pvt CT
Ebenezer: b 2-2-1752 d 10-2-1823 m Mary Pratt Cpl MA
Ebenezer: b 5-14-1757 d 12-17-1840 m Sarah Weston Pvt Mar MA
Ebenezer: b 12-14-1740 d p. 3-7-1795 m Hannah Jayne Lt NY
Ebenezer: b 8-20-1736 d 12-25-1827 m Hannah Prosser Pvt RI
Elisha: b 1-28-1743 d 9-6-1781 m Sarah Avery Sgt Vol CT
Elisha: b 11-5-1746 d 2-13-1834 m Lois Smith Pvt CT ★
Elisha: b 7-28-1760 d p. 1820 m Mary Montgomery Pvt CT
Elisha: b 1-16-1741 d 9-6-1799 m Sarah Douglas Dr CT
Elisha: b 5-20-1746 d 1-1-1834 m Phebe Clark Pvt MA
Elisha: b 1750 d 1805 m — Miller Sol NC
Elnathan: b 1717 d 9-6-1781 m (1)Mary Phillips (2)Mrs Freelove Bailey Sol CT
Erastus: b 2-17-1752 d 10-17-1853 m (1)Ann Glover (2)Mrs Mary Hubbard (3)Mrs Lucy Ann Avery PS CT
Francis: b 8-27-1758 d 12-26-1844 m (1)Esther Colburn (2)Saloma Dye Pvt CT ★
Francis: b 5-5-1732 d 6-12-1812 m (1)Hannah Cogswell (2)Martha Low Capt MA
George: b 3-22-1754 d 11-15-1840 m Keziah Manning Pvt SC NC ★
Gilbert: b c. 1730 d p. 1777 m Charity Hartford Pvt MA
Hardin: b c. 1730 d p. 9-9-1794 m Sarah Price PS VA
Isaac: b 8-5-1743 d 1794 m Ann Wallis Col MD
Isaac: b 7-7-1744 d 6-28-1839 m Molly Shurtleff 1Sgt MA
Isaac: b 2-10-1757 d 1834/5 m Olive Leonard Pvt MA ★
Israel: b 9-24-1757 d 4-29-1813 m Lydia Palmer Pvt CT
Israel: b 1-10-1757 d 11-7-1839 m Anna Dodge Pvt MA ★
Ithiel: b 1-10-1734 d 1826 m Esther Fox Sol PS CT
Jabez: b 6-30-1728 d 2-20-1795 m Anna Lathrop NS CT
Jabez: b 1755 d 11-26-1853 m Mrs Joanna (Fernald)Pray Pvt MA
Jacob: b 4-28-1745 d c. 6- -1799 m Martha — Pvt CT
Jacob, Sr.: b 5-22-1709 d 6-3-1776 m Jemima Leonard CS CT
Jacob, Jr.: b 9-14-1731 d 1814 m (1)Mary Brown (2)Abigail Thomas Capt CT
Jacob: b 6-27-1748 d 5-21-1823 m Hannah Andrews Pvt MA
Jacob: b 1731 d 1792 m Elizabeth Hewlings Maj NJ
James: b 1743 d 11-9-1825 m (1)Sally Hovey (2)Hannah Coit Capt MA
James: b 2-23-1731 d 7-6-1776 m (1)Abigail Knowles (2)Jane Moulton Lt NH
James: bpt 1-5-1735 d 11-2-1805 m Abigail Locke PS NH
James: b 11-7-1751 d p. 11-12-1826 m Margaret Chandler Pvt SC
Jenckes: b 9-6-1762 d 3-17-1812 m Elizabeth Wanton Pvt RI
Jesse: b 12-6-1742 d 1-27-1826 m (1)Susanna Field (2)Bliss Phinney (3)Sarah Silvester Capt MA
Joel: b c. 1748 d p. 1790 m Mehitable Brooks Pvt MA
Joel: b 8-6-1761 d 3-26-1841 m Eunice Fuller Pvt MA ★
John: b 1-24-1736 d 10-12-1800 m Bethia (Baker)Kingsley Capt CT
John: b 1728 d 11-7-1778 m (1)Sarah Thompson (2)Hepzibah Griswold Pvt CT
John: b 1751 d 1795 m Mary — Pvt CT
John: b 8-19-1759 d 1854 m Nancy — Cav Grd Capt GA
John: b c. 1712 d p. 3-8-1792 m Eliza Pearce Pvt MA
John: b 1763 d 10-22-1804 m (1)Mehitable Hood (2)Miriam Smith Pvt MA
John: b 12-14-1748 d 2-10-1835 m Hannah Gardner Pvt Mar MA ★
John: b 1727 d p. 1790 m Katherine Lawrence CS NC

John: b 1721 d 6- -1791 m Rachel Martin CS NC
John: b c. 1740 d 11-7-1778 m — PS PA
John: b 1-2-1749 d 11-1-1812 m Elizabeth Herrington Ens RI
John: b 2-1-1746 d 2-20-1776 m Sarah Cozzens PS SC
John Watkins: b 5-31-1752 d 3-17-1803 m Elizabeth Bondurant PS VA
Jonathan: b 1728 d 10-10-1802 m Abigail Packard Lt MA
Jonathan: b 10-16-1748 d 8-11-1824 m Elizabeth Folsom Lt NH W★
Joseph: b 10-25-1704 d 7-7-1794 m (1)Lydia Pierce (2)Mary Bushnell PS Dr CT
Joseph: b 7-16-1744 d 1-28-1821 m Ruth Clark Ens MA
Joseph: b 9-3-1752 d 2-1-1806 m Mary Foster Pvt MA
Joseph: b c. 1761 d 4-30-1843 m Lydia Goodwin Pvt MA
Joseph: b 12-23-1754 d 12-19-1835 m Sarah Cushman Pvt MA ★
Joseph: b c. 1719 d 7-23-1793 m Mary — Pvt CS MA
Joseph: b 1761 d 11-22-1822 m Hannah Woodbury Pvt Smn NH ★
Joseph: b 1750 d 1800 m Sarah Brown Pvt VA
Joseph: b c. 1754 d 1815 m Elizabeth Price Pvt VA
Joshua: b 3-9-1740 d 11-13-1832 m Abigail Bishop Pvt CT
Joshua, Sr.: b 6-6-1729 d 9-30-1797 m Hannah Sampson Lt MA
Joshua, Jr.: b 5-14-1759 d 5-17-1835 m Rebeckah Cobb Pvt MA
Joshua: b 1728 d 1814 m Mary Shirrell Pvt VA
Josiah, Sr: b 1729 d 8-2-1798 m Abigail Edson Pvt MA
Josiah, Jr.: b 1732 d 3-14-1811 m Deborah Soule Pvt MA
Lemuel: b 4-15-1751 d 2-5-1817 m Abigail Foss Sol PS NH
Leonard: b 3-2-1763 d 7-1-1847 m Grace Brewster Pvt CT ★
Lewis: b 1765 d 8-6-1838 m (1)Jannett Scott (2)Martha Gayden Sol SC
Luke: b 1696 d 1-8-1777 m Lydia Davis PS CT
Luke: b 1725 d 1776 m Rebecca Packard Pvt MA
Luke: b 11-17-1733 d 3-2-1819 m (1)Elisabeth Churchill (2)Abigail Soule Little Pvt MA
Moses: b 9-25-1747 d 11-17-1836 m Mary Smith Pvt PS CT
Moses: b 12-17-1732 d 8-7-1807 m Anna Cummings Pvt MA
Moses: b 9-10-1743 d 10-8-1777 m Betty Sherburne Pvt NH
Nathan: b 5-12-1748 d 1-18-1838 m Catherine Pitkin PS CT
Nathaniel, Jr.: b 7-4-1756 d 7-31-1832 m Abigail Haley Pvt MA
Nathaniel: b 6-27-1753 d 11- -1821 m Polly Bryant Pvt NH ★
Nathaniel: b 2- -1754 d 9-5-1842 m Mercy Heath Pvt NH ★
Nathaniel, Jr.: b 7-6-1762 d 7-15-1849 m Martha Johnson Sgt RI ★
Newman: b 7-5-1734 d 1810-20 m Sarah Sawyer 1Lt MA
Nicholas: b 7-7-1745 d 12-8-1800 m Leah Prvor PS VA
Obadiah: b 12-4-1740 d 12-4-1812 m (1)Tabitha Williams (2)Emblem Hood Lt CT
Oliver: b 1744 d 1-30-1826 m Lucy Gould Pvt MA
Pelatiah: bpt 12-8-1754 d — m Eunice Trafton Pvt ME
Peter: b 11-11-1741 d 11-20-1799 m Elizabeth (Perkins) PS CT
Peter: b 1755 d 1816 m Mary — Sol GA
Peter: b 1739 d 2-12-1813 m Agnes Wilson LCol CS PS VA
Phineas: b 10-8-1750 d p. 1806 m — Sgt MA
Reuben: b 11-5-1763 d 4-22-1854 m Anna Steadman Pvt CT ★
Richard: b 1756 d 6-15-1832 m Abigail (Garland)Cook Pvt MA ★
Richard: b 9-29-1725 d 1787 m Susanna Coleman PS VA
Robert: b 1-16-1727 d 11-9-1801 m Hannah Cummings Pvt MA
Simon: b 10-25-1737 d 9-4-1778 m Olive Douglas Lt CT
Solomon: b 7-16-1729 d 11-4-1809 m Deborah Lester Capt CT
Stephen: b 7-6-1732 d 1815 m Susanna Curtis Pvt CT
Stephen: b 3-17-1725/6 d 10-22-1790 m Eunice Boardman Capt MA
Stephen: b — d 3-5-1824 m Sarah Bowles PS VA
Thomas: b 6-2-1724 d 1794 m (2)Susan Hovey Capt MA
Thomas: b 2-8-1724 d 1-5-1801 m Martha (Day)Wildes Pvt MA
Thomas: b 1724 d 7-9-1806 m Hannah Ford Capt PA
Thomas Harden: b 5-3-1757 d 11-17-1838 m Mary Magdalen O'Neal Lt VA ★
Ute: b 7-15-1761 d 3-11-1842 m Sally Gant Pvt NC
Wesley: b 10- -1761 d 5-28-1817 m (1)Sylvania Longbottom (2)Mary Campbell Pvt CT
Wm.: b 1742 d 10-27-1802 m Abigail Cox Maj MA
Wm.: b 11-20-1754 d p. 1800 m Haziah — Ens RI
Wm.: b c. 1750 d c. 1816 m Sarah Walker Sol VA
Wm. Harding: b 1740 d 1- -1806 m Elizabeth Lee Fearn Col VA
Zebulon: b 1-15-1740 d 9-10-1810 m Mary Wildes Pvt MA
Zephaniah: b 4-19-1742 d 5-4-1808 m Patience Ripley Lt MA

PER LEE, (includes PERLEE)

Edmond: b 10-15-1752 d 4-24-1822 m Zada Winans Sgt CS NY
Peter: bpt 1-20-1739/40 d 4-18-1781 m Rebeckah — Pvt NJ

PERLEY,

Allen: b 5-9-1718 d 10-14-1804 m Martha Fowler MM MA
Amos: b 2-4-1749 d 12-7-1830 m (1)Rebecca Stickney Hovey (2)Sarah Smith Cpl MA
Asa: b 10-10-1716 d 4-10-1806 m (1)Susanna Lowe (2)Apphia Porter (3)Mrs Ruth Kimball PS Maj MA
Benjamin: b 2-10-1735 d 1816 m (1)Hannah Clark (2)Apphia Andrews Lt MA
Daniel: b 9-24-1752 d 3-6-1838 m (1)Rebecca Porter (2)Huldah Peabody Pvt MA ★
Dudley: b 11-23-1738 d 12-16-1810 m Mrs Hannah Hale 2Lt MA
Eliphalet: b 11-22-1747 d 4-15-1822 m Anna Porter Sgt MA
Enoch: b 5-20-1749 d 12-23-1829 m Hannah Flint Pvt MA
John: b 12-7-1746 d 12-2-1778 m Hannah Green MM MA

PERLEY, contd.

Nathan: b 1737 d 1816 m (1)Mehitable Mitchell (2)Sarah (Symonds) Rea Sgt MA

Nathaniel: b 10-11-1745 d 1779 m Sarah Dutch Pvt SeaCap MA

Thomas: b 2-22-1704/5 d 9-28-1795 m Eunice Putnam PS MA

Wm.: b 2-11-1735 d 3-12-1812 m Sarah Clark Capt MA

PE'RONNE,

Charles Rene: b c. 1725-30 d 1794 m Marie Aimee Henrietta Nicols de Mouras d'Hercy VAdml FrN

PERRIGO, (includes PERIGO)

David: b 6-30-1761 d 7-2-1826 m Eunice Hurlbut Drm NY ★

Frederick: b 4-10-1765 d 12-6-1850 m Mary Vanornam Pvt VT

James: b 1733 d 12-20-1808 m Elizabeth Pettee Pvt MA

John: b 1767 d 3-7-1820 m Almeria Hitchcock Sol VT

PERRIN, (includes PERRINE)

Abner: b c. 1751 d 9-27-1799 m Sarah Foster QM SC

Asa: b 1733 d 6- -1816 m Olive Bellows Pvt CT

Daniel: b 10-27-1762 d 5-16-1833 m Lydia Cheeseman Pvt NJ

David: b 8-24-1724 d 10-10-1788 m Esther Marcy Sol CT

David: b 10-20-1739 d 2-15-1825 m Abigail Cooper Pvt MA

Elijah: b 3-25-1738 d 8-27-1799 m Milicent Mason Sgt CT

Henry: b 7-19-1758 d 2- -1813 m Catherine Dey Pvt NJ

Henry: b 7-22-1730 d 7-6-1816 m Abigail LaRue MM NJ

Henry: b 1730 d 6- -1788 m Susanna Cole CS PS NY

James: b 10-9-1745 d 4-3-1826 m Hannah Bennett Pvt NJ

James: b 2-8-1747 d 1830 m Mary Smith Pvt NJ

James: b 1752 d 8-12-1835 m Isabel Clayton Pvt NJ

Jesse: b 1-24-1726 d 1-15-1801 m Rachel Ide Capt MA

John: b 2-14-1744 d 6-14-1809 m Eleanor Wyckoff Sgt NJ

John, Sr.: b 10-20-1722 d 4-26-1804 m Mary Rue Pvt MM NJ

John, Jr.: b 3-30-1762 d 11-17-1848 m (1)Anna Nancy Stout (2)Catherine (Perrine) Pvt NJ

John: b 7-22-1760 d 12-7-1831 m (1)Catherine Williamson (2)Mary Ely Pvt NJ

John: b 1-17-1753 d 12-1-1842 m (1)Millicent Bruce (2)Penelope —(3)Anna — Pvt RI ★

John: b 12-6-1740 d 1-15-1800 m Letitica West Pvt VA

Joseph: b 7-16-1748 d 1823 m Elizabeth Wikoff Pvt NJ

Joseph: b c. 1740 d p. 12-7-1791 m Classandra Clopton Pvt VA

Lemuel: b 10-21-1749 d 10-23-1814 m (1)Martha Nash (2)Amelia Dickenson Sgt MA

Lewis: bpt 8-13-1758 d 7-24-1804 m Mary Woolsey Pvt NJ

Peter: b 1-5-1737 d 1817 m (1)Sarah Scanlon (2)Hannah Disbrow (Dey) Capt NJ

Peter: b 7-7-1756 d 9-14-1845 m (2)Sarah Harris Pvt Tms NJ ★

Peter, Sr.: b 1727 d 1787/8 m (1)Catherine Courson (2)Mary — Pvt NJ

Samuel: b 8-20-1725 d 7-12-1805 m (1)Margaret Hyde (2)Molly (Perrin)PS CT

Timothy: b c1-1724 d 1816 m Mary (Perrin)PS CT

Wm.: b 11-20-1753 d 12-17-1838 m Anna Vance Sgt NJ ★

Wm.: b 11-28-1743 d 9-29-1820 m Hannah Mount Pvt NJ

Wm.: b 5-7-1764 d 12-7-1838 m Margaret Rue Pvt NJ ★

Wm.: b 1753 d 7- -1846 m Susanna Craig Pvt NY ★

Wm.: b 1758-60 d 1799 m Letitia West Pvt VA

Zachariah: b 3-18-1748 d 5-28-1838 m Mary Talcott Pvt CT

PERROW,

Daniel B.: b c. 1756 d 7-31-1839 m Elizabeth Fleming Ens VA

Stephen: b 11-20-1735 d 1791 m Elizabeth Fleming PS VA

PERRY,

Aaron: b 4-17-1733 d 11-24-1820 m Mary French PS MA

Abel, Sr.: b 9-16-1736 d 4-7-1808 m Keziah Morse Lt MA

Abel, Jr.: b 6-12-1757 d 4-10-1841 m Asenath Haven Cpl MA

Abijah: b 10-14-1742 d 8-6-1819 m Phoebe Boutel Pvt NH

Abner, Sr.: b 1-17-1728 d 5-21-1813 m Mary Adams Col MA

Abner, Jr.: b 1756 d 9-2-1834 m Anna Phipps Pvt MA ★

Abner: b a. 1760 d 1810 m (1)Peggy Burns (2)Sally Jordon Simons Capt NC

Adam: b 1752 d 8-23-1830 m Elisabeth House Sgt MA

Arthur: b 7-8-1721 d 5-7-1794 m Catherine Gifford CS MA

Asa: b 1746 d 2- -1826 m Lydia Leland Lt MA

Azor: b 1755 d 11-15-1824 m Mary — Pvt VT

Barak: b 8-16-1743 d p. 1782 m Submit Sprague Pvt MA

Benjamin Franklin: b 9-15-1761 d 11-21-1842 m Anna Foster Pvt MA

Caleb, Sr.: b 2-9-1734 d 8-27-1776 m Elizabeth Jacobs LCol PA

Charles: b 1738 d 12-28-1818 m Priscilla Johns PS MD

Christopher Raymond: b 12-4-1761 d 6-4-1818 m Sarah Wallace Alexander Pvt RI

Daniel: b 4-4-1748 d 7-21-1832 m Judith Hunt Sgt MA

Daniel: b 11-24-1724 d 7-6-1804 m (1)Martha (Perry)(2)Thankful Morse CS MA

David: b 6-22-1716 d 9-27-1796 m Mary Perry Pvt MA

David: b 7-5-1737 d 10- -1802 m Mary Burges Pvt MA

David, Sr.: b 8-16-1719 d 5-14-1807 m Margaret Dryer CS MA

David, Jr.: b 1-27-1748 d 7-18-1827 m Sarah Short Pvt MA

David: b 8-18-1741 d 5-4-1826 m Anna Bliss Capt NH

David: b 6-4-1747 d 9-9-1834 m Mary Smith Pvt NY

David: b 5-14-1757 d 6-17-1827 m Mary Farrington Pvt NY

David: b c. 1752 d 1789 m Sarah Dunlap Sol VA

Dimon: b c. 1742 d p. 1798 m (1)Nabby Cushing (2)Susanna Lincoln Pvt MA

Ebenezer: b — d 1787 m Dorcas Moulton Sgt CT

Edward: b 3-28-1731 d 1798 m (1)Dorcas Gardner (2)Ruth (Perry) PS RI

James: b 12-22-1757 d 4-12-1823 m Sarah Johnson Lt MA

James: b 1759 d 2-13-1838 m Mary Perry Sgt MA ★

James: b 5-19-1758 d 1840 m Esther Tinkham Pvt MA

James: b 8-12-1734 d 6-26-1819 m Sarah Littlefield CS MA

James: b 1-18-1759 d 3-15-1843 m Elizabeth Valentine Pvt NC

James: b 1750 d 1816 m Mary Harper Gnr SubLt PA

James: b a. 1745 d 1816 m Hannah Wiggins Pvt PA

James: b 1754 d 1804 m — Pvt PA

James: b — d p. 4-14-1806 m — Sol SC

James: b 1749 d 1-14-1825 m Frances Hunter PS SC

Jasiel, Jr.: b 6-15-1753 d — m Betty Hix Pvt MA

Jeremiah: b 6-20-1754 d 8-6-1843 m Anna Stafford Pvt Mrnr RI ★

Jesse: b 6-27-1758 d 11-27-1835 m Mary Guptail Pvt MA ★

Jesse: b c. 1750 d 1801 m (2)Elizabeth Linder CS NC

Jesse: b 3-15-1755 d 12-31-1845 m Margaret — Pvt SC ★

Job, 2d: b 4-21-1766 d 12-31-1841 m Mary Jordan Pvt MA

John: b 1-10-1749 d 5-13-1835 m Hannah Thorp Pvt CT ★

John: b 8-11-1752 d 11-9-1825 m Jane McMillan Cnt MD

John: b 1753 d 1790 m Fanny Smith Pvt MD

John: b 8-7-1736 d 3-9-1814 m Lepha Walker Capt MA

John: b 11-10-1750 d 1-14-1833 m (1)Lucy Worcester (2)Mrs Perry NCapt MA ME

John: b 4-29-1731 d 12-21-1806 m Silence Battle Sgt MA

John: b 1751 d 1806 m Mary — Pvt NJ

John: b 9-23-1758 d 1-5-1816 m Charity Valentyn Pvt CS NJ W★

Eleazer: b 2-17-1750 d 11-14-1830 m (1)Esther Morse (2)Bethsheba Clapp Pvt MA

Eleazer: b 2-2-1760 d 10- -1819 m Jane Pond Pvt MA

Eliakim, Sr.: b 5-8-1716 d p. 1776 m (1)Sarah Joy (2)Hepsibah Ladd PS NY

Eliakim: b 2-22-1752 d p. 1800 m Lydia Downer Pvt VT

Elijah: b 1-28-1726 d 1-28-1812 m Sarah Crocker Pvt MA

Elnathan: b 3-14-1761 d 6-18-1849 m Christiana McDonald Pvt MA

Erasmus: b 1760 d 5-20-1826 m Elizabeth Harding Pvt MD

Ezekiel: b 6-21-1734 d 1811 m Martha (Smith)Wooster Pvt CT

Ezra: b 5-22-1741 d 5-27-1808 m Jemima Titus Pvt MA

Freeman: b 1-23-1733 d 10-15-1813 m Mercy Hazard Pvt CS RI

Henry: bpt 5-28-1738 d 3-23-1815 m Bertha Baker Pvt MA

Henry: b 1755 d 1816 m — Ellery Pvt VA

Ichabod: b 10- -1758 d 4-20-1839 m Rebecka Sturge Sgt CT ★

Ichabod: b 4-23-1722 d 5-16-1795 m (1)Sarah Haskins (2)Ruth Fisher Pvt MA

Ichabod: b 10-3-1747 d 4-1-1828 m Luranah Burt Pvt MA

Isaac: b 11-3-1754 d 1787 m — Pvt CT

Isaac: b 5-15-1757 d 4-13-1843 m Mary Tiffany Pvt MA

Isaac: b 7-23-1729 d 12-27-1811 m Geritje Haringh QM NY

Jabez: b 2-10-1740 d p. 1790 m Molly Ide 1Lt VT

Jacob: b 8-21-1698 d — m Abigail Smith Cpl MA

James: b 1735 d 1-17-1800 m Jane Davis Pvt DE

James: b 3-5-1746 d 7-3-1806 m Zerviah Wetherell Capt MA

John: b 1755-65 d p. 1810 m Nancy McShaw Colville Sol NC

John: b 1758 d 1820 m Elizabeth McClung Pvt VA

Jonas: b 1759 d 2-28-1827 m Susanna Damon Pvt MA

Jonathan: b 1710 d 1-9-1783 m Martha Morse Pvt MA

Jonathan: b 11-4-1757 d 8-20-1824 m Betty Hill Pvt MA W★

Joseph: b 9-29-1754 d 12-21-1829 m Mary Beers Pvt CT

Joseph: b c. 1755 d 1797 m (1)Mary Wilson (2)Jemima — PS MD

Joseph: b 1752 d 11-20-1819 m Sarah Pollard 2Lt MA ★

Joseph: b c. 1740 d p. 1790 m Rebecca Stephens Sgt MA

Joseph: b 10-3-1724 d p. 1790 m Mary Locke Sol MA

Joseph, Jr.: bpt 4-1-1750 d 3-15-1823 m Susan Tupper Pvt MA

Joseph: b 1761 d 1-18-1853 m (1)Jemima Brown (2)Lucy Holland Pvt MA ★

Joseph: b 11-17-1752 d 1-17-1818 m Mary Stanton Lt RI

Joshua: b c. 1725 d p. 9-11-1792 m Mattie Rush Pvt NC

Josiah: b 2-8-1714 d 10-21-1783 m Hannah Perry MM MA

Josiah: b 1751 d 8- -1799 m Hannah Yeamaus Ens VT

Lewis: b 1753/4 d 4-13-1833 m (1)Mary Burrus (2)Jane Bourne PS VA

Llewellyn: b 1751 d 6-2-1805 m Deborah Perry Pvt PA

Micah: b 12-3-1759 d 9-28-1839 m Susan Woodbury Pvt MA W★

Moses: b 5-19-1741 d 7-26-1826 m (1)Abigail Perry (2)Catherine Haven Lt MA

Moses: b 7-28-1719 d 3-18-1809 m (1)Deborah Ivory (2)Susannah Child Sgt MA

Moses: b 5-28-1758 d 12-7-1843 m Hannah Adams Pvt RI

Nathan: bpt 3-16-1718 d 7-2-1798 m Mary Orsborn Pvt CT

Nathan: b 3-30-1757 d 9-6-1836 m Phebe Braman Pvt MA

Nathaniel: b 9-15-1757 d 1808 m Susannah Hooper Pvt MA

Obadiah: b 7-27-1740 d p. 1785 m Jemima Winchester Sgt CT

Obadiah: b 1-19-1722 d 1803 m Elizabeth Kimball Drm MA

Ozias: b 6-20-1757 d 5-8-1837 m Esther Marvin Cpl VT ★

Peter: b 2-4-1738/9 d 9-16-1804 m Sarah Bradley PS CT

Peter: b 3-24-1752 d 7-10-1827 m (1)Lydia Wilmarth (2)Huldah Miller Pvt MA

Peter: b c. 1760 d 10-5-1827 m (1)Nancy Perry (2)Mrs Elisabeth Carlton (Davenport)(Kidd)Cav VA
Robert: b 1760 d 1836 m Frances Richards Pvt NC
Sam: b 1735 d 1794 m Margaret — Sol VA
Samuel: b c. 1760 d 8-11-1831 m Alice Batty Pvt CT ★
Samuel: b 9-18-1756 d 7-12-1829 m Chloe Lindley Pvt MA
Samuel, Jr.: b 1739 d 9-5-1816 m Alice Baker Lt MA
Samuel: b 6-20-1748 d 5-5-1833 m Joanna Parrot Pvt NJ ★
Samuel: b 1740 d 4-7-1831 m Elizabeth Rowe Pvt MA
Samuel: b 1-23-1763 d 8-24-1824 m Deborah Worden Pvt NY
Samuel: b 1742 d 1810 m Mary McGrew Sol PA
Seth: b 6-8-1750 d 1819 m Ruth Downer Pvt CT
Silas: b 4-14-1763 d 6-3-1852 m Catherine Hale Pvt MA ★
Simeon: b 1-10-1757 d 12-22-1831 m (1)Hannah Barnes (2)Comfort — Pvt MA
Sion: b c. 1760 d p. 1814 m Bertheny Arundell Pvt NC
Swift: b 1750 d a. 1832 m Mrs Ann (Perry)Morehead Sol VA
Sylvanus: b 1741 d 10-5-1821 m (1)Rebecca Bliss (2)Rebecca (Braley)Greenwood (3)Sabra Able Lt CT ★
Thaddeus: b 12-26-1730 d 2-5-1806 m Anna Hayward Pvt MA
Thomas: b 1765 d 3-3-1848 m Rebecca Dunnington Pvt MD
Thomas: b 1720 d p. 1790 m Margaret — PS MD
Thomas: b 1754 d 1833 m Catherine Fisher Pvt NJ PA ★
Wm.,2d: b 8-24-1746 d 1-10-1799 m Sarah Rule QM MD
Wm.: b 4-4-1740 d a. 3-29-1784 m Martha Chase Pvt MA
Wm.: b 2-5-1744 d 11-22-1819 m Ann Mitchell Pvt NH
Wm.: b 1726 d 1830 m — PS NC
Wm.: b 11-3-1745 d 10-25-1793 m Mary Stewart LCol PA
Wm.: b 6-19-1759 d p. 1815 m Elizabeth Segar Pvt RI
Wm. W.: b 1764 d 4-18-1839 m Eleanor Poor Pvt MA
Winslow: b 1758 d 1-16-1830 m Rachel Rice Pvt MA W★
Zadock: b 11-10-1754 d 1-8-1815 m Tabitha Tillman PS SC

PERRYMAN,
Munford: b c. 1755 d p. 9-5-1820 m Elizabeth Travis Sol VA

PERSE,
Silas: b 1756 d a. 10-8-1832 m Elizabeth — PS SC

PERSHING,
Frederick: b 1724 d 1794 m Maria Elizabeth Weigandt PS PA

PERSINGER,
Jacob: b 1-19-1749 d 1840/1 m Mary Kimberlin Cpl VA ★

PERSONIUS,
Jacobus: b 7-11-1749 d p. 1820 m Rachel Kisor Cpl NY ★

PETEET,
Richard: b 12-22-1750 d 9-3-1827 m (1)Isabella Delphy Henderson (2)Susanna Callaway Sol GA

PETERMAN,
Henry V.: b 10-11-1761 d 5-22-1845 m Anna Mary (Fisher) Pvt PA
Jacob: b c. 1732 d 12-8-1814 m Ann Colday Pvt PA
Jacob: b 1729 d 1789 m Ann — Capt PA

PETERS, (includes PETER)
Abijah: b 12-25-1760 d 6-20-1811 m Nancy — Ens PA
Absalom: b 3-25-1754 d 3-29-1840 m (1)Mary Rogers (2)Mrs Mary Gurley Capt ADC CT ★
Adam: b 10-30-1734 d 3-12-1813 m (1)Olive Plimpton (2)Mrs Margaret (Morse)Dunton Capt MA
Andrew: b 12-23-1759 d 2-25-1825 m Sarah Taft CS VT
Andrew: b 1-24-1742 d 2-5-1822 m Beulah Lovett LCol MA
Casper, Sr.: b 8-13-1724 d 6- -1798 m Anna Elizabeth Ribsam PS PA
Casper, Jr.: b 2-11-1753 d 6-28-1811 m Anna Elizabeth Rockel Pvt PA
Christian: b 10-16-1760 d 10- -1837 m Anna Katherine Fudge Sgt VA ★
Daniel: b 5- -1747 d 1816 m Magdalena Romig Pvt PA
George Michael: b 3-14-1752 d 6-7-1825 m Catherine Elizabeth Moser Pvt PA
Jacob: b c. 1720 d 1778 m Elizabeth — Pvt PS PA
Jacob: b 6-5-1761 d c. 1836 m Mary Stokes Pvt PA ★
James: b c. 1750-2 d p. 1-10-1819 m Elizabeth Maury Smn VA
Jesse: b 1753 d — m Martha — Pvt GA ★
John: b 12-28-1717 d 11-9-1804 m (1)Lydia Phelps (2)Elizabeth (Phelps)Murray CS PS CT
John: b a. 1765 d p. 1796 m Mary Eason Pvt GA
John: b 8-9-1741 d 8-20-1821 m Mary (Dyer)Cushing PS MA
John: b c. 1740 d c. 1820 m Martha — Sol SC
John: b 1738 d p. 10-4-1781 m Elizabeth Ashby Lt VA
John: b 1755 d 2-6-1836 m Frances Simms Ens VA ★
John: b 12-28-1762 d 2-17-1833 m Nancy Russon Pvt VA W★
Joseph: b 4-22-1748 d p. 9-4-1834 m Dorothy Owen Cpl CT ★
Joseph Phelps: b 11-7-1761 d 9-21-1843 m (1)Azuba Case (2)Lydia Day Fif Cpl Tms CT ★
Richard: b 1748 d 1809/10 m (1)Jerusha Sutton (2)Jane Huson Sol NY
Richard: b 6-22-1744 d 8-22-1828 m Sarah Robinson Capt PS PA
Thomas: b 8-1-1759 d 12-24-1824 m Rebecca Johnson PS PA

Ulrich: b 11-6-1760 d 3-3-1842 m Katherine — Pvt PA
Wilhelm: b 1756 d 4-1-1813 m Magdalena Hunsicker Pvt PA
Wm.: b 7-17-1746 d p. 1805 m Deborah Strong Pvt CT
Wm.: b c. 1746 d 6-9-1801 m Ann — Sgt MD
Zachariah: b c. 1730 d 1807 m Maria Thompson Ens CT

PETERSON, (includes PETERSEN)
Conrod: b 1759 d 2-3-1847 m Mary Williamson Pvt NS VA ★
Cornelius: b 5-7-1738 d 1820 m Hannah Parsel Capt NJ
Daniel: b a. 1747 d 3-18-1817 m Sarah Carter Dr NH
Gabriel: b 1748 d 2-12-1832 m Margaret C. Heth Lt PA W★
George: b 1735 d 1790 m Rebecca Ann — Pvt NJ
Henry: b 5-13-1761 d 9-9-1821 m (1)Sally Brannon (2)Asenath Powel Pvt NJ ★
Isaac: b 1-5-1762 d 10-13-1835 m Esther — Smn Pvt NY
Jacob: b — d p. 2-14-1815 m — PS VA
John: b 3-22-1735 d 1814 m Mrs Rebecca (Errixon)Goff Capt NJ
John: b 1744 d 7-19-1808 m Elizabeth Lee MGen NY
John: b — d p. 4-5-1808 m Katherine — Sol NC
John Martin: b 5-20-1730 d 1820 m Margaret Teeter PS VA
Jonathan: b 3-26-1754 d 1-19-1843 m Lois Sturtevant Pvt MA ★
Joseph: b 2-1-1749/50 d 1776 m Rebecca Delano Pvt MA
Luther: b 4-19-1746 d 4-1-1822 m Priscilla Chapman Pvt MA
Nathan: b 1734 d 1797 m Amy Tanner Pvt RI
Nehemiah: b 7-29-1736 d 1-23-1811 m Princee Dillingham Pvt MA
Reuben, Jr.: b 4-10-1749 d 5-22-1845 m Abigail Soule Pvt MA
Samuel: b c. 1754 d — m Sarah Armour Pvt PS NJ

PETRIE, (includes PETREE & PETRY)
Daniel: b 1720 d 7-14-1782 m Elizabeth Foltz Capt NY
Dederick Marcus: b a. 1748 d 8-6-1777 m Catherine Bellinger Lt NY
Jacob: b 1740 d 1823 m Maria — Ens NY
Jacob Henry: b 3-18-1758 d 4-7-1837 m Maria Riesser Pvt PA ★
John Marks: b 1751 d 1823 m Dorothea Casler Pvt NY
Marcus: b c. 1754 d p. 10-9-1805 m Margaret Bellinger Pvt NY
Peter: b 1764 d 10-20-1841 m (1)Susan Hardwick (2)—Wilson (3)Mary Franklin Pvt NC ★
Wm.: b 12-7-1733 d 8-20-1806 m Margaret Salome Wolf Dr NY

PETRO,
Henry: b c. 1755 d p. 12-24-1833 m Elizabeth Kittle PS VA

PETTENGILL, (includes PETENGAL, PETTINGALL, PETTINGELL, PETTINGILL)
Abbott: b 2-12-1746 d c. 1797 m Hannah Page Lt CS NH
Andrew: b 1742 d 12-12-1777 m Abigail Greely Lt NH
Benjamin, Sr.: b 2-10-1719 d 10-3-1795 m (1)Mary Kingman (2)Judith Castle Atherton Pvt CS MA
Benjamin, Jr.: b 5-24-1751 d 2-7-1814 m Mary Howard Cpl MA
Benjamin: b 11-10-1756 d 6-16-1837 m Abigail Chase Pvt MA
Benjamin, Sr.: b 3-16-1730 d 3-15-1805 m Mehitable Kimball Pvt PS NH
Benjamin, Jr.: b 9-22-1758 d 2-8-1834 m Lydia Sleeper Pvt NH RI ★
David: b 9-5-1734 d 1-6-1778 m Mercy Lake Pvt MA
David: b a. 1740 d 1807-10 m Betsey Heath Pvt NH
Edmund: b 11-26-1739 d 1830 m Sarah Curtis Pvt MA
Edward: b 9-11-1732 d 3-16-1807 m Elizabeth Clark Pvt ME
John, Sr.: b 7-24-1727 d 10-16-1784 m Judith Huse Pvt MA
John, Jr.: b 1-9-1757 d 4-13-1827 m Hannah Burbank Pvt MA
John: b c. 1744 d 1778-80 m Ann Dorrance Pvt MA
John: b 9- -1763 d 4-23-1864 m Hannah Fox Sol NY ★
Joseph: b 1-9-1741 d 1789 m (1)Sarah Farrington (2)Tabitha — Maj MA
Josiah: b 4- -1753 d 6-30-1827 m (1)Phillipa French (2)Mary Duggan Pvt MA
Matthew: b 10-18-1736 d 4-21-1817 m (1)Sarah Webster (2)Ruth Pillsbury Pvt MA
Matthew: b 6-1-1756 d 1835 m (1)Bethia Ford (2)Rhoda Wing Pvt MA
Nathaniel: b 11-24-1722 d 4-27-1783 m (1)Elizabeth Swan (2)Jane Crow 2Lt PS MA
Oliver: b 8-4-1752 d 1820 m Mary — Pvt CT
Phineas: b 1-28-1745 d — m Rachel Long Pvt MA
Richard: b 8-19-1733 d 3-30-1791 m Joanna Lunt 2Lt MA
Samuel: b 3-16-1732 d 1776 m Mary Holt 2Lt NH
Samuel: b 1742 d 8-6-1777 m Elizabeth Cline Capt NY
Somers, Sr.: b 1-1-1756 d 1-15-1808 m Mary Swanton Pvt MA
Wm.: b 11-29-1759 d 11-16-1846 m Lydia Cobb Sgt MA ★
Wm.: b 8-23-1759 d 10-13-1844 m (1)Rhoda Haggett (2)Sarah Ballard Cpl NH

PETTIBONE,
Abel: b 12-17-1727 d 5- -1815 m Elizabeth Case Capt CT
Abijah: b 5-29-1749 d 4-15-1784 m Dorcas Cornish Pvt CT
Abraham: b 1727 d 1-19-1797 m (1)Jerusha Pinney (2)Mercy (Humphrey)Wilcox Capt CT
Amos: b 4-14-1761 d 9- -1850 m Sarah Barker Cpl CT ★
Daniel: b 1754 d 4-9-1844 m (1)Elizabeth Chittenden (2)Eunice Graham Pvt CT ★
Dudley: b 8-3-1742 d 10-4-1822 m Mary Latimere Sgt CT
Elijah: b 12-22-1748 d 1824 m Martha Field Pvt CT ★

PETTIBONE, contd.
Giles: b 12-11-1735 d 3-17-1810 m (1)Desiah Humphrey (2)Margaret (Holcombe) Case Maj CT
Jacob: b 12-20-1751 d 10-18-1807 m Rosetta Barber Pvt CT
Jonathan, Sr.: b 1709/10 d 9-26-1776 m Martha Humphrey Col CS PS CT
Jonathan, Jr.: b 8-12-1741 d 3-20-1825 m Hannah Owen Lt CT
Noah: b 4-16-1714 d 3-28-1791 m Huldah Williams Pvt PA
Oliver: b 5-13-1762 d 3-17-1832 m Martha Paine PS PA
Ozias: b 5-9-1737 d 9-9-1812 m Sybil Guernsey LCol CT
Samuel: b 11-12-1743 d 12-3-1816 m Mrs Martha Phelps 2Lt CT
Samuel: b 1740 d 8-11-1822 m Rhoda Bridgman Pvt VT
Seth: b 10- -1753 d 6-25-1828 m Deborah Purdy Sgt MA W★

PETTIGREW, (includes PETTEGREW)
Alexander: b 1738 d 1813 m — Alexander Sol SC
Ebenezer: b 1752 d 5- -1795 m (1)Mary McLean (2)Sara McLean Steadman Adj Cmsry SC
George: b 4-14-1746 d 3-7-1818 m Jane Long Pvt PS SC
James: b 1756 d 10-15-1793 m Judith Hart Deshara Lt PA
James: b 1760 d 1841 m Jane Harkness Pvt SC
James, Sr.: b 4- -1713 d 12-24-1784 m Mary Cocheran Pvt PS SC
John: b c. 1736 d 11- -1806 m Sarah Johnson Pvt SC
John: b 12-28-1754 d 7-19-1812 m Nancy McNeall NCapt VA
John: b 3-20-1758 d 9-19-1838 m Elizabeth — Pvt PA ★
Wm.: b 1752-8 d 11- -1816 m (2)Phoebe (Cavendish) Nixon (3)Mary Alden Pvt NH

PETTIJOHN,
Wm.: b 11-3-1751 d 4-27-1796 m Constant Little Pvt VA

PETTIPOOL,
Cadlwell: b c. 1742 d p. 1820 m Mary Marion Pvt VA

PETTIT,
Benjamin: b 1750 d 1827 m Rebecca Larimore Lt VA
Charles: b 1737 d 9-6-1806 m Sarah Reed Asst QMGen CL
Daniel: b 1744 d 1831 m Martha — Pvt PA
James: b 2-18-1762 d 11-5-1833 m Frances Baker Sgt VA ★
Jesse: b 1750 d 4-5-1814 m Anna Quick Johnson Pvt NJ
John: b 11-26-1757 d p. 1797 m Bettsy Kennon Pvt VA
Jonathan: b 6-25-1751 d 3-2-1833 m Agnes Riddell Capt NY ★
Nathaniel: b 1-6-1762 d c. 8-22-1834 m Sarah — Pvt PA
Nathaniel: b c. 1750 d 1810 m Rebecca Owens Pvt VA
Samuel: b 1717 d 1786 m Elizabeth Losee PS NY
Wm.: b 9-12-1754 d 10-27-1813 m Catherine Reidear Pvt NY
Wm.: b 1732 d 1805 m Susanna Ballard Pvt VA

PETTS,
Lemuel: b 1742 d 4-20-1815 m Hannah Butterfield Lt MA

PETTUS, (includes PETTES& PETTIS)
Abigail: b 5-12-1757 d 12-4-1807 m Hannah Morse Sgt NY W★
Abiel: b 9-25-1751 d 3-7-1818 m Eunice Allen Pvt CT
Benjamin: b 3-8-1755 d 1-29-1833 m Temperance Lamb Pvt Pvtr CT VT ★
Ezekiel: b 1755 d 1836 m Anne Hix Pvt MA
John: b 1754 d 7-1-1833 m Martha Reynolds Pvt VA
Joseph: b 7-22-1757 d 12-5-1811 m Charlotte Wales Pvt MA
Joseph: b 1-4-1756 d 1799 m Mary Chapman Pvt NH
Matthew: b c. 1752 d p. 1796 m Ruth — Pvt NY
Samuel O: b 3-11-1751 d 2-12-1819 m Hannah Minor Lt VA
Thomas: b 12-25-1712 d 3-18-1780 m Amy Walker PS CS VA
Wm.: b 1735 d 1803 m Susannah Graves Maj VA

PETTY, (includes PETTE, PETTEE, PETTEY & PITTEE)
Abner: b 4-3-1751 d 2-25-1837 m Catherine Holmes Pvt MA ★
Absolom: b 1750 d 1802 m Mary Clanton Cav SC
David: b c. 1748 d 5- -1804 m (1)Charity Sperling (2)Mary Buckelew Pvt NJ
Davis: b c. 1761 d p. 1816 m Polly — PS VA
Ebenezer: b 5-25-1741 d 5-22-1783 m Rebecca Hartshorn Pvt MA
Ebenezer: b 2-17-1751 d 12-24-1836 m Mary — Pvt Tms NJ
Ezekiel: b 1732/3 d 5-3-1786 m Elizabeth Youngs MM NY
Francis Moore: b — d a. 2-26-1816 m Mary — PS VA
George: b c. 1750 d a. 4-15-1815 m Elizabeth McNeal PS VA
James: b 8-29-1745 d 9-26-1809 m Elizabeth Chandler Drm Sgt MA
John: b c. 1745 d p. 1832 m (2)Mary — PS Pvt NC
Oliver: b 5-31-1760 d 8-3-1831 m Abigail Young Pvt MA ★
Rodham: b 1752 d 1-12-1843 m (1)Catherine — (2)Sarah Steward Pvt VA ★
Simon: b 1-28-1749 d 6-28-1823 m (1)Elizabeth Little (2)Elizabeth Topliff (3)Abigail (Jenkins) Caswell Matr MA
Wm.: b 3-13-1764 d 9-26-1834 m Lucy Wright Pvt NC ★
Wm.: b 6-2-1754 d 4-14-1837 m (1)Mehetabel Clark (2)Mehetable Gould Matr MA ★
Wm., Sr.: b — d a. 5-27-1805 m (1)Elizabeth — (2)Letty — PS VA
Zachariah: b c. 1750 d 10- -1799 m Elizabeth Marshall PS VA

PETTYPOOL,
Seth: b c. 1730 d 1789 m — PS NC

PETWAY,
Micajah: b 1757 d 4-12-1849 m (1)Amy — (2)Elizabeth Skinner Adj NC ★

PEVEARE, (includes PEVEAR)
Joseph: b 1727 d 1798 m Lydia Noyes Pvt NH
Noyes: b 6-20-1751 d 10-1-1833 m Lucy Burnham Pvt NH ★

PEVEY,
Peter: b 4-14-1760 d 7-28-1836 m ()Betsy — ()Lucy Cummings Pvt Pvt MA

PEYTON, (includes PAYTON)
Ephraim: b 8-27-1755 d 1825 m — Jennings Pvt VA
Francis: b 6-27-1748 d 12-13-1808 m Frances Hooe Dade PS Col VA
Francis: b 1764 d 8-26-1836 m Sarah Foushee Lt VA
Henry: b 1-19-1760 d 1843-1848 m Elizabeth Pain Sol VA
Henry: b c. 1730 d c. 1781 m (1)Anne Thornton (2)Margaret Gallagher CS VA
Henry: b c. 1744 d p. 12-7-1814 m Susanna Fowke PS VA
James: b c. 1730 d 6- -1789 m Susannah Threlkeld Capt VA
John: b c. 1720 d 3-25-1790 m (1)Frances Cook (2)Mary Taliaferro Col PS CS VA
John Rowzee: b 10-19-1754 d 1798 m Ann Hooe Sol VA
Lewis: b 3-8-1763 d p. 4-10-1838 m Winifred Followell Pvt VA ★
Robert: b a. 1740 d 1-5-1795 m Ann Guffey Sol VA
Valentine: b a. 1755 d p. 12-20-1785 m (1)Margaret Gwatkin (2)Sally P — BrevMaj VA
Valentine: b 1749 d p. 10-14-1831 m Mary Edwards Lt PS VA
Valentine: b 10-20-1756 d 1802 m Mary Butler Washington Dr VA
Wm.: b 1753 d a. 7-3-1813 m Mary Ross Pvt VA
Wm.: bpt 7-3-1718 d 1792 m Miss Patterson Sol VA
Yelverton: b 11-25-1755 d 1-23-1849 m Anna Guffee Pvt Spy VA ★
Yelverton: b 1735 d 1794 m Elizabeth Heath PS VA

PFLIEGER,
Jacob: b — d a. 4-17-1800 m Maria Catharina — Pvt PA

PFLUGER,
George Frederick: b 8- -1735 d 1791 m Anna Maria Margaretha — Pvt PA

PFRIMMER,
John George: b 7-24-1762 d 9-5-1825 m Elizabeth Senn Slr FrN

PHARES,
Robert: b 10-16-1764 d 11-16-1839 m Mary Willis Pvt NJ
Samuel: b 1- -1761 d p. 4-1-1837 m (1)Miss Smith (2)Elizabeth — Pvt NC ★

PHELAN, (includes PHELAND & PHELON)
Jesse: b 1755 d 1845 m Lydia — Ens PA ★
Joseph: b 12-1-1733 d 11-27-1800 m Elizabeth King Lt MA
Thomas: b 1755 d 2-12-1827 m Mary — Pvt CT

PHELPS, (includes PHELPHS)
Aaron, Jr.: b 1-26-1745 d 1-24-1789 m Ruth Loomis Pvt CT W★
Aaron: b 1-20-1730 d 3-12-1789 m Mary Noble Pvt MA
Aaron: b 3-30-1743 d p. 1780 m Abigail Barber Sgt CT
Aaron: b 1736 d 10-18-1802 m Susannah Wells PS CT
Abel, Jr.: b 7-5-1739 d 10-4-1823 m Lucy Beardsley Lt CT
Abijah: b 3-8-1734 d 4- -1837 m (1)Hulda Hutchinson (2)Mrs Susannah Noble Root Miller Pvt CT
Alexander: b 5-12-1760 d 8-15-1849 m Rhoda Parmelee Pvt CT ★
Amos, Sr.: b 5-30-1736 d 1800 m Anna Filer Pvt CT
Asahel: b 4-4-1762 d p. 1-30-1839 m (1)Agnes Houston (2)Margaret Patterson Abbott Pvt CT
Asahel: b 7-21-1721 d 3-5-1812 m Elizabeth Wilder Pvt MA
Azor: b 10-13-1761 d 4-2-1837 m (1)Mary Tenny (2)Dolly Makepease Dresser Pvt MA
Barret: b 9-22-1722 d 1789 m Hannah Bigelow Pvt NY
Benjamin: b 1-27-1762 d 8-14-1828 m Sarah Smeledge (2)Mrs Sarah Ellithrop Pvt MA
Bethuel: b 4-25-1744 d 8-11-1832 m Caroline Lord CS Pvt CT
Bissell: b 2-16-1754 d 10-27-1845 m (1)Lovina Skinner (2)Sarah Waterman Pvt Tms CT
Cadwell: b 8-14-1765 d 1844 m (1)Rebecca Bush (2)Margaret Hamilton (3)Jane Pratt Pvt MA
Caleb: b 1-11-1708 d 7-5-1781 m Mary Lathrop Henderson PS CT
Charles: b 9-22-1732 d 1-11-1808 m (1)Hannah Dension (2)Sally Swan PS CS CT
Charles: b 8-15-1719 d 1789 m Dorothy Root PS VT
Cornelius: b 1761 d 3-20-1844 m Mary Bishop Pvt CT
Daniel: b 10-11-1753 d 7-28-1828 m Elizabeth Barnard Pvt CT
Daniel, Sr. b 1696 d 9-7-1777 m Mindwell Buckland PS CT
Darius: b 10-15-1752 d 2-11-1818 m Mary Aiken Pvt CT
Davenport: b 8-12-1755 d 6-27-1813 m Catherine Tiffany QM Capt NH
David: b 8-26-1733 d 4-7-1811 m (1)Abigail (Gaylord) Griswold (2)Hannah Humphrey Capt CT
David: b 5-23-1753 d 11-2-1834 m Ann Pease Pvt CT
David: b 8-28-1716 d 1-13-1803 m Margaret Colton Lt CT

David: b 7-8-1735 d 7-8-1783 m Triphene (Phelps) Pvt CT
David: b 4-4-1767 d 8-2-1834 m (1)Mary Sperry (2)Mrs Hannah Olmsted Sol NY
Ebenezer: b 4-30-1741 d 3-27-1806 m Susanna Leavitt 1Lt CT
Ebenezer: b 11-4-1740 d 10-3-1821 m Phebe Wright Pvt MA
Ebenezer: b 11-1-1755 d 1-9-1818 m Polly Russell Jordon Pvt MA
Ebenezer: b 10-21-1759 d 11-1-1832 m Submit Higby Pvt MA NY ★
Edward: b 12-25-1727 d 3-26-1797 m Hannah Marsh Pvt CT
Edward: b 8-27-1759 d 8-10-1840 m Azubah Moore Pvt CT
Eldad: b 5-29-1738 d 10-6-1811 m Jemima Pease Pvt CT
Eli: b 8-8-1743 d 1-28-1829 m (1)Ruth Case (2)Miriam (Case) Adams Pvt CT
Eli: b 10-18-1751 d 5-11-1838 m Rachel Loveland Pvt CT NY ★
Eliakim, Jr.: b 1-5-1755 d 3-13-1824 m Margaret Coombes CS MA
Elijah: b 5-13-1754 d 5-16-1823 m Mary Gibbs Pvt CT ★
Elijah: b 1759 d 7-19-1831 m Zerviah Curtiss Cpl CT ★
Elijah: b 1-13-1748 d 5-25-1819 m Phebe Norton Pvt CT
Elijah: b 7-31-1724 d p. 1783 m (1)Miss Millard (2)Miss Jennings (3)Jemima Wilcox Pvt NY
Eliphalet: b 11-5-1743 d p. 1790 m Mehitable Hyde Pvt CT
Elisha: b 10-17-1737 d 7-14-1776 m Rosetta Owen Capt CT
Elisha: b 3-27-1737 d 1-29-1793 m Elizabeth Clark Cpl CT
Elisha: b c. 1722 d p. 1818 m Elizabeth Holcomb Pvt CT
Elkanah: b 2-3-1742/3 d 12-5-1803 m Abigail (Phelps) Lt CT
Elnathan: b 2-18-1734 d 1-2-1813 m (1)Eleanor Bridgeman (2)Mrs Sarah (Smallage) Elithorpe Pvt MA
Erastus: b 6-13-1763 d 3-11-1833 m Polly Yeomans Sol CT
Ezekiel: b 5-8-1723 d 10-4-1781 m Elizabeth Gillette Lt CT
Francis: b 8-2-1757 d 7-5-1842 m (1)Anna Sophia Pratt (2)Elanor — Pvt Cpl MA ★
Frederick: b 1752/3 d 6-30-1807 m Mary Jones Sol CT
Friend: b 11-1-1745 d 2-6-1826 m Rachel (Phelps) Pvt CT
George: b 1757 d 11-11-1803 m Tabitha Simmons Pvt VA
Homer: b 3-15-1757 d 3-24-1826 m Adah Root SgtMaj CT ★
Ichabod: b 2-11-1738 d p. 1790 m Mary Trumbull Sgt CT
Isaac: b 2-4-1746 d 12-21-1819 m Mary Birge Sgt CT
Israel: b 2-5-1752 d 8-17-1826 m Lovisa Root Pvt MA
Israel: b 8-15-1757 d 5-7-1841 m (1)Sarah Higby (2)Cloey Jewett Owens (3)Sally Lewis Pvt MA NY ★
Jacob: b 6-13-1758 d 8-22-1824 m Prudence White Sgt MA ★
Jared: b 10-3-1760 d 8-13-1827 m Rowena Fuller FifMaj CT ★
Jedediah: b 4-23-1753 d 2-9-1849 m Deborah Crowell Sgt CT
Jeremiah Wilcox: b 1-27-1760 d 1-9-1830 m Anna Humphrey Pvt CT
Job: b 10-5-1727 d 1796 m Lucy Lewis Pvt CT
Joel: b 9-17-1759 d 9-28-1836 m Susannah Holcomb Pvt CT ★
Joel: b 7-16-1755 d 2-27-1838 m Anner Baney Sgt QM MA ★
John: b 2-20-1724 d 2-11-1812 m (1)Thanks Wilcox (2)Anna Northway CS CT
John: b 2-11-1756 d 10-13-1841 m (1)Anna Baker (2)Betsey Bingham Lt CT
John: b 8-10-1759 d 6-15-1812 m Catherine Conine Lt CT W★
John: b 9-7-1731 d 4-5-1814 m Desire Dewey Sgt CT
John: b 7-4-1750 d 1812 m Diana Marshall Cpl CT
John: b 3-3-1756 d 6-25-1833 m Sally Shether Pvt CT ★
John: b 1729 d 7-7-1804 m (1)Mary Richardson (2)Elizabeth — PS CT
John: b 7-6-1709 d 3-23-1787 m Susanna Gates MM MA
John: b 1-30-1758 d p. 3-1-1842 m Anna Buttolph Pvt MA ★
John: b 11-15-1763 d 10-19-1829 m Lucy Cook Pvt MA
John, Sr.: b 3-12-1718 d 12-15-1789 m Deborah — Pvt NH
John, Jr.: b 4-20-1744 d p. 1789 m Mary Lakin Pvt NH
John: b 1-1-1728 d p. 1786 m — Sol PA VA
John: b c. 1740 d 1798 m Katherine — PS VA
John: b 1740 d 1801 m (2)Susanna Younger 1Lt VA
Jonathan: b 2-1-1763 d 9-26-1857 m Charity Beckwith Pvtr Cpl CT ★
Jonathan: b 4- -1729 d 10-23-1800 m Esther Seward Pvt MA
Joseph: b 3-27-1743 d 1-17-1795 m Jemima Post Ens CT
Joseph: b 3-27-1758 d a. 1815 m Cynthia Janes Pvt CT
Joseph: b 12-7-1751 d p. 1790 m Huldah Wilcox Pvt CT
Joseph: b 9-30-1732 d c. 1780 m Cathrine — Pvt MA
Joshua, Sr.: b 1-9-1729/30 d 3-12-1809 m Hannah Tarbox Capt CT
Joshua, Jr.: b 2-5-1750/1 d 3-22-1825 m Elizabeth Fuller Pvt CT
Joshua: b 6-25-1738 d 12-23-1798 m Lois Ballard CS MA
Joshua: b 9-20-1760 d 7-13-1819 m Elizabeth Whittemore Pvt MA
Josiah, Sr.: b 8-24-1708 d 7-24-1791 m Ann Griswold PS RI
Josiah, Jr.: b 11-15-1735 d 11-13-1820 m (1)Ann Denslow (2)Bethiah Meacham PS Capt CT
Josiah: b 2-11-1755 d 6-17-1835 m (1)Elizabeth Patterson (2)Susannah Simmons Pvt VA ★
Judah: b 5-12-1750 d 10-6-1818 m Abigail Bishop Pvt Fif CT
Lancelot: b 11-9-1750 d 11-12-1836 m Jerusha Pinrey Pvt CT
Lemuel: b 2-5-1731 d 9- -1808 m Dorothy Phelps Pvt MA
Luke: b 8-28-1730 d 1-16-1815 m (1)Ann Freeman (2)Prudence Tracy Cpl NY MA
Martin: b 12-24-1723 d 11-12-1795 m Martha Parsons Pvt MA
Moses: b 5-1-1750 d 1-6-1826 m Deborah Munn Pvt MA
Nathan: b 9-1-1749 d 11-19-1812 m Mary Fletcher MM NH
Nathaniel: b 9-19-1703 d 8-13-1781 m (1)Mary Curtis (2)Rachel Sawyer Pvt CT
Nathaniel, Sr.: b 12-13-1721 d 10-29-1789 m (1)Elizabeth Childs (2)Rebecca (Armes) Childs Pvt MA

Nathaniel, Jr.: bpt 6-5-1757 d 3-4-1833 m Lucy Strong Pvt MA
Noah: b 1-22-1740 d 3-4-1809 m Lydia Griswold Col CS PS CT
Noah: b 8-1-1754 d 6-10-1795 m Sarah Adams Pvt CT
Obadiah: b 1-21-1759 d 6-10-1799 m Arminda Phelps Arfr CT
Oliver: b 3-22-1744 d 3-25-1799 m Alice Barber Ens CT
Oliver: b 6-7-1753 d 4-30-1810 m (1)Triphena Johnson (2)Ann Gillette Pvt CT
Oliver: b 3-17-1764 d 11-4-1843 m Sarah Miner Pvt CT
Oliver: b 4-20-1765 d 5-20-1848 m Roxanna Owen Pvt CT ★
Oliver: b 10-21-1749 d 2-21-1809 m Mary Seymore PS MA
Ozias: b 5-1-1756 d p. 1786 m Sally Judson MM Sol CT
Paul: b 4-19-1748 d p. 1780 m (1)Zerviah Calkins (2)Theodosia Root Pvt CT
Reuben: b 9-5-1748 d 7-5-1780 m Mary Hosford Ens CT
Robert: b 5-24-1741 d 8-24-1775 m Rachel Richardson Sgt MA
Roger, Sr.: b 2-24-1738 d 2-22-1809 m Abigail Filer Capt CT
Roger, Jr.: b 10-7-1762 d 9-8-1846 m Anna Jones Pvt CT ★
Roger: b 3-1-1760 d 5-22-1832 m Elizabeth Rice Pvt MA
Samuel: b 12-10-1756 d 1-7-1829 m Margaret Nevins Pvt NH
Samuel: b 9-2-1759 d 10-15-1826 m Lydia Porter Pvt NY
Samuel: b c. 1735 d 1795 m — Felix War Pvt CT
Seth: b 11-17-1751 d 1826 m (1)Lucy Ledyard (2)Sally Pierce Capt CT
Shadrick: b 1748 d p. 1775 m — (Phelps) Pvt NY
Silas: b 1759 d 2-23-1855 m Amitus Phelps Sgt CT
Silas: b 1-27-1720 d 1816 m Hannah Dewey CS CT
Simeon: b 1754 d 12-30-1786 m Submit Holcomb Pvt CT
Solomon, Sr.: b 7-29-1716 d 4-8-1796 m Temperance Barber PS CT
Solomon, Jr.: b 10-3-1743 d 8-25-1817 m Lucy Lord Lt CT
Spencer: b 2-20-1753 d 1-24-1829 m Theodamy Allen Sgt MA
Sylvanus: b 5-28-1729 d 5- -1809 m Zeruiah Swetland PS CT
Thomas: b 7-17-1741 d 2-28-1789 m Dorothy Lamb Woodbridge Lt CT
Thomas: b 8-19-1759 d 7-12-1836 m Tekel Phelps Pvt GA W★
Thomas: b c. 1730 d p. 3-5-1797 m — PS VA
Timothy: b 1722 d 11-7-1816 m Rebecca — Pvt CT
Timothy: b 8-8-1725 d 4-9-1786 m Abigail Edwards Pvt CT
Timothy: b 6-8-1744 d 9-13-1804 m Sarah Skinner Pvt CT
Timothy, Jr.: b 7-14-1748 d 3-11-1827 m Ruth Palmer Wilson Pvt CT
Timothy: b 4-11-1738 d 5-13-1782 m (1)Rachel Ford (2)Sarah Case PS CT
Timothy: b 12-29-1749 d 7-3-1830 m Persis Baxter Pvt CT
Timothy: b 1757 d 1-20-1812 m (1)Janet Broome (2)Henrietta Broome Pvt CT
Timothy: b 1-25-1747 d 7-3-1817 m Ziporah Williams Adj NY
Wm.: b c. 1730 d 4-20-1816 m Anna Ruggles Sol CT
Wm.: b 10-26-1762 d 8-31-1847 m Sally — Pvt CT
Wm., Sr.: b 7-24-1730 d 2- -1802 m (1)Mary Nichols (2)Mrs Mary Flagg Pvt MA
Winslow: b 12-28-1752 d 6-15-1812 m Rebecca Kidder Ens MA

PHETTEPLACE, (includes PHETTIPLACE)

John: b 3-2-1756 d 11-22-1833 m Elsa Weaver Pvt RI
Samuel: b 4-16-1735 d 4-15-1813 m Ruth Philips Pvt RI

PHIFER,

Caleb: b 4-8-1749 d 7-3-1811 m Barbara Fulenwider Col NC
Jacob: b 1757 d 10-9-1846 m Rachel DeGraffe Cpl NY
John: b 3-22-1747 d 1776 m Catherine Barringer PS LCol NC
Martin, Sr.: b 10-18-1720 d 1-18-1791 m Margaret Blackwelder PS NC
Martin, Jr.: b 3-25-1756 d 11-12-1837 m Elizabeth Locke Capt NC ★
Michael: b 1749 d p. 1814 m (1)Katy Bingaman (2)Elizabeth — Lt PA

PHILBRICK, (includes PHILBROOK)

Benjamin: bpt 1718 d p. 1790 m Mary — PS NH
Benjamin: b 5-11-1720 d 1-23-1808 m Sarah Page PS NH
Daniel: b 1-17-1762 d 3-28-1809 m Elizabeth Moody Pvt MA
Daniel: b 9-4-1753 d 4-18-1835 m Ruth Merrill Sgt NH
David: b 4-27-1740 d 2-17-1831 m Katharine MacCausland Cpl MA
George: b 9-18-1752 d 2-8-1821 m Deborah Lombard Pvt MA
James: b 11-29-1739 d p. 1803 m (1)Eunice Hale (2)Elizabeth Cutler Pvt CS PS NH
James: b 2-10-1727 d 2-28-1809 m Tabitha Dow PS NH
Jeremiah: b 1753 d 1819 m Sarah Jane Leadbetter PS MA
Job: bpt 1729 d 9-16-1819 m (1)Mary Trufant (2)Dolly Hinkley (3)Hannah Coombs PS MA
Joel: b 8-14-1759 d 9-15-1820 m Mary Ledbetter Mar MA ★
John: b c. 1709 d 1-30-1779 m Judith Biley Hardy PS NH
Jonathan: b 3-18-1736 d 10-3-1826 m Hannah Brown PS NH
Jonathan: b 1-28-1756 d 5-19-1822 m Esther Dow Drm NH
Jonathan: b 4-27-1749 d 7-29-1818 m Hannah Gilman Pvt NH
Joseph: b 6-17-1755 d 12-21-1814 m Jemima Blake Pvt NH
Joseph: b 8-10-1735 d 9-11-1788 m Anna Towle PS NH
Joshua: b 10-10-1727 d 5-27-1821 m Elizabeth Alexander PS MA
Nathan: b 4-11-1749 d 12-11-1824 m Gertrude Harvey PS NH
Nathaniel: b- -1747 d 8-2-1812 m Tabitha Morse 1Sgt NH W★
Richard: b 10-12-1758 d 5-26-1825 m (1)Shuala Nason (2)Olive Kenniston Pvt NH
Samuel: b 2-11-1739 d 4-4-1779 m Sarah Sanborn Maj PS NH
Samuel: b 7-13-1734 d 12-28-1806 m Phoebe Sanborn Capt NH

PHILBRICK, contd.
Samuel: b 1756 d 2-18-1838 m (1)Elizabeth — (2)Mary Clark Pvt NH ★
Thomas Weld: b 5-9-1760 d 8-6-1814 m Abigail Mason Pvt NY

PHILHOWER,
Christopher: b 10- -1763 d 2-2-1846 m Elizabeth Fox Pvt NJ

PHILIP, (includes PHILLIP)
George: b 8-29-1754 d 3-14-1806 m Jane Ostrander Capt Cmsry NY
Hendrick: b 1- -1755 d 4-30-1847 m Catherine Laudt Pvt NY ★
Henry, Jr.: b 2-6-1726 d p. 1790 m Deborah Roe Pvt NY
Wm.: b a. 1730 d p. 9-7-1791 m (1)Eva Schurtz (2)Anna Schurtz Pvt NY

PHILLEY, (includes FILLEY)
David: b 11-20-1715 d 3-7-1799 m (1)Margery Brown (2)Lydia Center Pvt CT
Mark: b 1745 d 6-28-1828 m Eleanor Bissell Pvt CT ★
Rememberance: b 6-15-1753 d 12-20-1837 m (1)Anne Cyrena Gleason (2)Hannah Hubbard Pvt CT

PHILLIPPI, (includes PHILIPY)
Abraham: b 1-22-1763 d 1-17-1812 m Susanna Kreamer Fif Pvt PA W★
Christopher: b c. 1758 d 10-1-1856 m Elizabeth Hiffey Sol VA
Jacob: b — d 5-20-1822 m Christiana Troutman Pvt PA
John: b 1730 d 1781 m Julianna Ream Sgt PS PA
John: b c. 1736 d 10-21-1800 m Barbara Eichelberger Sol VA

PHILLIPS, (includes PHILIPS)
Abiezer: b 11-13-1730 d 1-25-1806 m (1)Ruth Hathaway (2)Mrs Bathsheba (Walker) Gooding CS PS MA
Abizer: b 11-18-1749 d p. 1790 m — Pvt MA
Abraham: b 2-28-1755 d 10-17-1828 m Hannah Pratt Cpl RI
Abraham: b 3- -1752 d 6-5-1829 m Mary Muckey Pvt NH
Abraham: b 6-25-1755 d 3-23-1836 m Cynthia Lanier Capt NC
Adam: b 1763 d 1859 m Hannah Bailey Pvt NC ★
Andrew, Jr.: b 2-24-1748 d 7-10-1830 m Lettice Fernald 1Sgt MA
Andrew: b 1759 d 10-14-1833 m Susan — Pvt NC ★
Benjamin: b 2-14-1760 d 7-13-1835 m Sarah Anne Cane CS NJ
Benjamin, Sr.: b c. 1725 d 9-29-1795 m Susannah Fisher Pvt VA
Bennett: b 12-27-1763 d 9-20-1842 m Isabella Moore Pvt NC ★
Blaney: b 2-10-1711 d 12-21-1800 m Christian Wadsworth Pvt MA
Caleb: b 1761 d 1829 m Sally Green Pvt PS MA
Daniel: b c' 1740 d p. 1790 m — Pvt NY
Daniel, Sr.: b c. 1705 d 1796 m Hannah Bull Pvt RI
Daniel, Jr.: b 3-22-1745 d 12-21-1818 m Mary Taft Pvt RI
David: b 5-27-1762 d 9-24-1824 m Maria Swartwout Drm NY
David: b 1758 d 3-26-1838 m Nancy Rose Pvt NY ★
David: b 1742 d 6-15-1822 m (1)Ann Barber (2)Mrs — Bell Pvt NJ
David: b c. 1758 d p. 10-3-1819 m Mary — Sgt NC
David: b a. 1750 d p. 1790 m — Pvt NC
David: b 1742 d 1798 m Mary Clark LCol PA
David: b 3-26-1742 d 3-5-1829 m Mary Thomas Capt PA
David: b 1749 d 1836 m — Pvt PA
David: b 1741 d 6-21-1806 m (1)Elizabeth Weaver (2)Olive Walling Pvt RI W★
Ebenezer: b 7-15-1753 d 8-5-1829 m Mary Benedict Lt CT
Ebenezer: b 2-23-1752 d 6-5-1834 m Rachel Gale MM Sgt MA ★
Ebenezer: b 3-27-1726 d p. 1796 m Susannah Manley Pvt MA
Ebenezer: b c. 1728 d p. 12-14-1799 m Sybil Pierce Pvt MA
Ebenezer: b 1759 d 3-11-1854 m (2)Mrs Charlotte Hayden Pvt MA ★
Ebenezer Humphrey: b 7-17-1756 d 12-1-1837 m (1)Ruth Morgan (2)Mrs Ruth (Towne) Wheelock Pvt MA ★
Elihu: b 1761 d 10-16-1799 m Elizabeth Spears Sol NY
Elijah: b 2-14-1759 d 11- -1841 m Cynthia Goodwin Pvt MA
Elijah: b c. 1757 d p. 1798 m Susanna Gates Sgt MA
Elisha: b 2-16-1755 d 6-12-1839 m Mary Meachum Pvt CT ★
Esquire: b 8- -1758 d 3- -1848 m Ann Gates Pvt CT ★
Etheldred: b c. 1738 d 1795 m Sarah Exum PS NC
Exum: b 6-8-1757 d 11- -1802 m Charlotte Exum Capt NC
Ezekiel: b 5-5-1756 d 5-4-1803 m Susannah Scott Pvt CT
Ezekiel: b 2-16-1729 d 12- -1804 m Sarah Arnold Pvt RI
Francis: b 7-29-1720 d p. 1788 m (1)Demis Aylsworth (2)— PS PA
George: b 8-22-1717 d 2- -1778 m Hannah Phillips PS CT
George: b 1758 d 1849 m Sarah Lovell Pvt VA
George: b 1759 d 1839 m Susan Frances Johnston Pvt VA
Gideon: b 4-21-1761 d 7-10-1834 m Rhoda Stone Pvt CT
Gideon: b 11-7-1763 d 6-13-1840 m (1)Chloe Shattuck (2)Mrs Huldah Abbott Pvt MA ★
Henry: b 175- d 1805 m Sarah Phillips 2Maj NJ
Hezekiah: b c. 1740 d p. 1804 m Catherine Lybrook Sol VA
Hugh: b 1759 d 10-4-1842 m Mary Bolen Pvt QM Sgt NJ ★
Ichabod: b 4-9-1765 d 10-13-1830 m Mary Bailey Pvt MA
Isaac: b 3-20-1762 d 7-5-1858 m Lydia — Pvt Grd NY ★
Isham: b 10-10-1741 d 12-14-1837 m Mary Dawson Pvt GA
Israel: b 8-17-1737 d 2-28-1800 m Huldah Towne Lt RI
Jacob: b 1748 d 10-3-1824 m Mary Elizabeth Casper Capt NY
Jacob: b 3-20-1750 d 2-19-1835 m Betsey Mandeville Pvt MA ★

Jacob: b a. 1760 d 1783 m Mary — Pvt PA
Jacob: b c. 1760 d p. 1796 m Hannah Isaacs Sol SC
Jairus: b 1750/1 d 6-4-1828 m Selence — Pvt MA
James: b c. 1722 d 1832 m — Young Pvt CT
James: b 1756 d 1811 m Rachel Frizzell NCdr MD
James: b 1748 d 1807 m Mary Jane — Mar PA
Jenkins: b c. 1745 d p. 11-29-1819 m Hannah Butcher Pvt VA
Jeremiah: b 5-18-1733 d 5-31-1818 m (2)Margaret Stanton Pvt CT
Jeremiah: b c. 1745 d 9-5-1805 m Ann — Pvt NC
Job: b 1741 d 1-22-1835 m — Huff Pvt CT
Job: b 8-5-1763 d 12-23-1833 m Mary — Pvt CT
Joel: b — d a. 10-3-1792 m Elizabeth — Sol GA
John: b 4-2-1762 d 7-1-1836 m (1)Hannah Nicholson (2)Nancy Cornish Pvt CT ★
John: b c. 1745 d 1795 m Sarah Brotherer Pvt DE
John: b 1738 d 9-25-1806 m Sabritta — Pvt MD
John: b 9-4-1756 d 4-3-1833 m Jeanette Young Sgt MD
John: b 5-9-1747 d 11-1-1833 m Sarah Pond Sgt MA ★
John: b 5-21-1734 d 2-14-1805 m Jane Ellis Pvt MA
John: b c. 1750 d 9-15-1833 m (1)Mary Knapp (2)Mrs Priscilla Wilbore Pvt MA
John: b 1750 d — m Abigail Williams Pvt MA
John: b 6-29-1760 d 2-25-1865 m Love Perry Pvt MA
John: b 3-18-1760 d 8-15-1825 m Anna Cummings Pvt NH W★
John: b 1721 d 2-1-1794 m Abigail Tindall Capt NJ
John: b 1760 d 11-13-1847 m Rebecca Fish Pvt NJ
John: b 1-4-1752 d 9-4-1846 m (1)Mary Chamberlain (2)Mrs Lydia Tripp Harding (3)Mrs Bathsheba Green Pvt VT PA NY ★
John: b 3-14-1759 d 11-20-1839 m (1)Polly Johnston (2)Mary Thompson Pvt NC NC SC ★
John: b 1748 d 1790 m Margaret Daus 1Lt PA
John: b c. 1740 d 4-17-1806 m Mary Gallagher Pvt PA
John: b 1-8-1739 d 12-2-1794 m Selah — Pvt VA
John: b c. 1760 d p. 7-20-1815 m Catherine Isner Pvt VA
John R: b 1756 d 12-2-1832 m Elizabeth Canniff Grd NY
Jonas: b 1736 d 1-29-1803 m Rebecca Mendez Machado Pvt PA
Jonathan: b 5- -1722 d 1786 m Jenevereth Branch Pvt PA
Jonathan: b 1744 d 1801 m (1)Mary Phillips (2)Elizabeth Houston Capt NJ
Jonathan: b 1746 d 4-3-1830 m Hannah Cowan Pvt PA
Joseph: b c. 1719 d a. 2-2-1784 m Casander — Capt GA
Joseph: b 1732/3 d 1800 m Sarah Lynde Pvt GA
Joseph: b 1718 d 1788 m Rebecca Griffin Col NJ
Joseph: b 1718 d 1785 m Sarah Leonard Col NJ
Joseph: b 11-1-1754 d 9-3-1832 m Mary (Hall)Laughlin Ens PA
Joshua: b 8-21-1735 d 10-25-1809 m Mary Thayer Lt MA
Joshua: b c. 1723 d p. 1790 m Elizabeth Pits Pvt MA
Joshua, Jr.: b 1748 d p. 1790 m Milicent Anna (Phillips) Pvt MA
Josiah: b 3-29-1751 d 3-1-1817 m (1)Martha Edwards (2)Sarah Thomas Lt PA
Larkin: b 1760 d c. 1816 m Lucy Fleming Pvt VA
Levi: b 9-20-1751 d 1-14-1840 m Jamina — Pvt NC ★
Levi: b 1750 d 2-21-1847 m Barbara Hough Pvt VA ★
Lewis: b 5-15-1741 d 3-5-1820 m Margaret Hatcock Pvt NY
Lot: b 12-13-1754 d 9-12-1812 m Diana Howland Pvt MA
Lot: b 1754 d 12-20-1820 m Elizabeth Titus Pvt NJ
Luck: b 1-1-1759 d 1835 m Martha Bowen Pvt RI ★
Mark: b 6-6-1736 d 9-3-1811 m Mercy Phillips Cpl MA
Mark: b 1755 d 8-5-1839 m Rany Moore Pvt NC ★
Mark: b c. 1740 d p. 5-8-1810 m Nancy — Sol VA
Martin: b c. 1739 d p. 7-26-1781 m Anne — PS VA
Moses: b 3-8-1742 d 9-9-1818 m Sarah Wisner Maj NY
Mourning: b — d 5-21-1831 m (1) — Payne (2)Elizabeth Kendrick Pvt VA
Nathan: b 11-25-1754 d 8-5-1840 m Charity Phillips Pvt NY ★
Nathaniel: b 12-18-1750 d p. 12-19-1827 m Wealthy Williams Sgt CT
Nathaniel: b 8-17-1756 d 6-9-1832 m Rhoby Waterman QMSgt MA ★
Peter: bpt 7-22-1751 d p. 1790 m Ann — Pvt NY
Phillip: b c. 1757 d 1838 m Catherine Survey Pvt PA
Ralph: b — d 1-5-1828 m — Robinson Pvt NY
Richard: b 9-4-1755 d 11-18-1834 m Olive Evans Pvt Mar RI ★
Rufus: b 12-12-1749 d 12-2-1840 m Rebecca Sheldon Pvt RI
Samuel: b 4-8-1760 d 3-29-1842 m Millea Kellogg Pvt CT
Samuel: b 6-22-1758 d 2-4-1810 m Martha Newton Pvt MA
Samuel, Jr.: b 3-8-1745 d 3-5-1827 m Sarah Baker Pvt MA
Samuel: b 2-7-1750 d 2-10-1802 m Phoebe Foxcraft PS MA
Samuel: b 1752 d 1844 m Elizabeth — Pvt NJ ★
Samuel: b 1750 d 1802 m Margaret — PS PA
Samuel: b 12-20-1749 d 8-10-1808 m (1)Margaret Rathburn (2)Thankful Pearce (3)Dorothy Bowyer Maj RI
Seth: b 9-25-1749 d 8-8-1828 m Elizabeth Hamlin Lt MA
Silas: b 7-22-1754 d 1821 m Susannah Drake Sgt MA
Smalley: b a. 1743 d 1816 m Happa Bassett Sgt MA
Smith: b 7-11-1761 d 7-25-1843 m Lydia Leland Pvt MA
Spencer: b 5-11-1755 d 12-24-1840 m Mrs Dorcas Flower Pvt MA
Sylvester: b 6-12-1758 d 2-8-1841 m Rachel Chilson Pvt MA ★
Theophilus: b 5-4-1740 d 12-23-1823 m Abigail — Pvt NJ
Theophilus: b a. 1751 d 1789 m Ann Prater LCol PA
Thomas: bpt 4-19-1761 d 9-9-1801 m Ann Tuttle Pvt CT W★
Thomas, Sr.: b 1-25-1712 d p. 1790 m (1)Elizabeth — (2)Katherine — (3)Rachel Wood CS MA

Thomas, Jr.: b 6-7-1747 d 7-9-1829 m Elizabeth Noyes Sgt MA
Thomas: b 5- -1756 d 1820 m Catherine (Phillips) Pvt NJ
Thomas: b 1739 d 3-6-1806 m Mary Elizabeth Carson Sgt PA
Thomas: b 1740-5 d 10-23-1790 m Jane Blair Pvt PA
Thomas: b 1-13-1735 d 8- -1785 m (1)Dorcas Albro (2)Elizabeth
    Brown Lt RI
Thomas, Jr.: b 1747 d 7-9-1834 m Martha Jones Pvt RI ★
Thompson: b 10-8-1752 d — m Abby Mumford Lt CT
Valentine: b 7-1-1759 d 10-22-1834 m Anna Maria — Pvt PA
Wm.: b c. 1724 d 2-1-1778 m Margaret Lowe Sgt MD
Wm.: b 12-14-1741 d 5-9-1813 m Huldah — Pvt NH
Wm.: b 5-21-1736 d 12-18-1778 m Ruth Titus CS NJ
Wm.: b 1753 d 3-7-1816 m Deliverance Ann Smith PS NY
Wm.: b 1706 d 1-1-1778 m Sybil Smith PS NY
Wm.: b — d p. 11-8-1825 m Mary — Pvt NC
Wm.: b c. 1730 d p. 10-8-1815 m Lussy — Sol NC
Wm.: b 11-1-1744 d 11- -1797 m Elizabeth Fowke Col CS VA
Wm.: b 8-3-1755 d 12- -1836 m Mary Thrasher Pvt PA
Wm.: b 1-8-1731 d 1797 m Elizabeth Robinson Smn VA
Zachariah: b 1-9-1763 d 1836 m — Pvt NC ★

PHILLIS,
Joseph: b 1744 d p. 3-10-1830 m Elizabeth Little Pvt PA

PHILO, (includes FILLOW)
Adams: b 7-6-1768 d 12-22-1836 m Lydia Gregory Pvt CT ★
Isaac: b 5-24-1761 d 11-24-1838 m Ada Waterbury Pvt CT ★
Nathan: b a. 1747 d 3-28-1810 m Elizabeth — Sgt CT

PHILPOT, (includes PHILPOTT)
Benjamin: b 1760 d 1790 m Elizabeth Hackney Capt MD
Brian: b 1749 d 4-11-1811 ,m Elizabeth Johns Ens MD
Charles T.: b 11-20-1753 d 1-3-1828 m Elizabeth — Sgt MD ★
John: b 2-1-1757 d 12-15-1844 m Kezia Wentworth Pvt NH ★
Thomas: b c. 1740 d 1789 m Ann Newman PS SC

PHINAZEE,
John: b c. 1760 d c. 1837 m Sarah Harris Pvt SC

PHINNEY, (includes FINNEY)
David: b 5-1-1726 d 5- -1806 m Ann Thompson CS DE
Edmund: b 7-27-1723 d 12-15-1808 m (1)Elizabeth Meserve (2)Mrs
    Sarah Stevens Col PS CS MA
Eli: b 1-16-1726/7 d 2-3-1777 m Mary (Phinney) PS MA
Ezra: b 1743 d 1780 m Hannah Luce Pvt MA
Isaac: b 5-10-1733 d p. 1790 m Elizabeth Kiney Pvt MA
Isaac: b 12-14-1725 d 10-22-1800 m Hannah — Pvt NY
James, Sr.: b 1726 d 8-3-1802 m Martha Mayes PS PA
James, Jr.: b 1750 d 9-1-1829 m (1)Martha Krunkleton (2)Elizabeth
    Braden (3)Rebecca — Pvt PA
James: b c. 1752 d c. 1810 m Mary Aigell Cpl VA
Jeremiah: b 3-19-1733 d 7-17-1807 m Deborah Loring Pvt RI
John: b 7-17-1717 d 5-31-1832 m (1)Bethiah Carter (2)Nancy
    Hatch (3)Christiana Lee Sgt CT ★
John, Sr.: b 4-8-1696 m 12-29-1780 m Martha Colman PS MA
John, Jr.: b 4-18-1732 d 5-3-1815 m Rebecca Sawyer Sgt MA
John: b 12-18-1760 d 1-20-1839 m Mary Taylor Pvt PA ★
John: b 11-11-1748 d 6-9-1827 m Elizabeth Jackson Pvt PA
John: b 1748 d 1-17-1781 m Sallie Ralston Pvt SC
John: b 1745 d 1790 m Margaret — Pvt VA
Jonathan: b 1749 d 4-26-1822 m Meribah Peirce Pvt MA
Jonathan: b 1759 d 8-10-1843 m Sarah Treadway Sol PS MA ★
Josiah: b 1-6-1756 d 12-18-1844 m Joanna Phelps Pvt CT
Lazarus: b 9-9-1751 d 10-3-1833 m (1)Elizabeth Fulton (2)Elizabeth
    Ocheltree Lt PA
Michael: b c. 1725 d p. 5-7-1787 m Catherine Armstrong Cpl SC
Nathan: b 6-28-1758 d 3-29-1813 m Urania Barney Pvt MA W★
Nelson: b 1729 d 1-22-1781 m (2)Rosamund Thomas Lt MA
Prince: b a. 1756 d 11-8-1824 m Content Fish Drm MA
Robert: b 9-27-1741 d 10-15-1781 m Lydia Clark Capt MA
Robert: b 3- -1753 d p. 1828 m Elizabeth Watson Pvt SC ★
Sylvester: b 3-5-1759 d p. 1838 m Rebecca Rice Pvt CT NY ★
Wm.: b 11-16-1750 d p. 1783 m Elizabeth Sherman Cpl MA
Wm.: b 5-17-1758 d 11-20-1826 m Anne Morton Pvt PA

PHIPPEN,
Jonathan A: b 5-15-1759 d 7-26-1827 m (1)Mary Averill
    (2)Hannah Washburn Cpl VT
Joseph: b 4-21-1745 d 5-17-1825 m Silence Paul Pvt CT

PHIPPS, (includes PHIPS)
Aaron: b 1-12-1729/30 d 10-18-1792 m (1)Zerviah Haven (2)Mrs
    Deborah Day Sgt MA
Benjamin: b 1761/2 d 5-3-1838 m Jean Hash Pvt VA ★
Daniel Goffe: b 7-13-1751 d 7-10-1837 m Anna Townsend Pvtr CT
David: b 8-17-1741 d 3-26-1825 m Mary English NLt CT
Elijah: b 6-7-1727 d 1-2-1805 m Sarah Fletcher Pvt MA
Jason, Jr.: b 7-20-1758 d 4-13-1838 m Mary Healy Pvt CT ★
Jedediah: b 3-11-1725 d 1812 m Sarah Learned PS MA
Jedediah, Jr.: b 8-2-1760 d 1847 m Charlotte Betts Pvt MA ★
John: b 1-26-1757 d 5-5-1831 m Hannah Cooledge Sgt VA ★
John: b c. 1750 d 1810-20 m Levina — Pvt NC
Joseph: b 1740 d 12- -1795 m Margaret Lewis Sol PA

Joshua: b 1746 d p. 1820 m Ester Aston Lt VA ★
Samuel: b 1752 d 2-18-1830 m Mary Maxfield Pvt MA
Samuel: b 12-11-1757 d 8-3-1825 m Sarah Chamberlain Pvt MA
Samuel, Sr.: b 8-1-1735 d 1-5-1841 m Mary Marshall Pvt PA

PHOENIX,
Daniel: b 1742 d 1802 m Elizabeth Platt PS NY
Overton: b 6-5-1760 d 9-22-1838 m Milly Gibson Pvt VA ★

PIATT, (includes PEATT, PYATT, PYEATT, PYEATTE)
Abraham: b 1741 d 11-13-1791 m Annabella Andrews Capt PA
Benjamin: b 1763 d 1851 m Polly Waddell Sgt VA
Daniel: b 12-18-1745 d 4-16-1780 m Catharine Sherrard Maj NJ
Ebenezer: b 1755 d 1835 m Rebecca Milburn Sgt PA ★
Jacob: b 5-17-1747 d 8-14-1834 m (1)Hannah Cook McCullough
    (2)Martha — Capt NJ ★
Jacob: b 1756-60 d 1844 m Margaret Finley Capt NC
John: b 6- -1740 d 1819 m Jane Williamson Capt MM NJ
Joseph: b c. 1755 d 8-25-1838 m Sarah Jane Still Pvt VA
Lemuel: b c. 1745 d 8-29-1795 m Elizabeth Harris Pvt NY
Peter: b c. 1733 d p. 6-15-1779 m — QM Sgt NC
Wm.: b 1745 d 11-4-1791 m (1) — Quick (2)Sarah (Shotwell)
    Smith Capt NJ W★

PICKENS,
Andrew: b 1715 d 3-29-1795 m Elizabeth Reed Pvt MA
Andrew: b 9-19-1739 d 8-17-1817 m Rebecca Floride Calhoun BGen
    SC
Andrew: b 1-6-1753 d 9-15-1844 m (2)Margaret Gillespie Pvt
    Wgn SC ★
James: b c. 1717 d 3-22-1800 m Margaret Strobridge Cpl MA
John: b 1718 d 10-8-1798 m Ruth Cushing Cpl MA
John: b c. 1730 d p. 9-22-1795 m Sarah — Capt SC
Jonathan: b c. 1745-50 d c. 1832 m — PS SC
Joseph Wm.: b 2-1-1737 d 6- -1781 m Elinor — Capt SC
Robert: b 11-26-1747 d 7-19-1830 m Dorcas Hallum Capt SC
Samuel: b 5-4-1752 d 2-12-1830 m Matilda Briggs Cpl MA
Silas: b 10-19-1763 d 10-25-1847 m Susanna Williams Pvt MA
Wm.: b 1749 d p. 1833 m Nancy Craig Pvt Spy SC ★
Wm.: b 10-5-1748 d 5-6-1835 m Jane — Pvt Spy SC ★
Wm.: b 1730 d p. 1790 m Ann Scott PS SC
Wm., Gabriel: b 10-18-1760 d c. 1840 m Rebecca Caldwell Pvt
    SC ★

PICKERILL,
Samuel, Jr.: b 1760 d 5-9-1850 m Mary Lowe Drm Pvt VA ★

PICKERING,
Anthony: b 5-9-1749 d 3-4-1825 m Lovey Hilton Pvt NS NH W★
Ephraim: bpt 1-13-1734 d 1-1-1803 m Lydia Colman Maj NH
Ichabod: b c. 1750 d 12-3-1812 m Margaret Aldrich Pvt MA
Jacob: b 9-4-1750 d 2-28-1832 m Hannah Ellis PS VA
James: b 1750 d c. 10-15-1793 m Jane Casdorp 1Lt PA
James: b 1758 d p. 1791 m Mary Philbrick Pvt NH
John: bpt 1-4-1718 d 1- -1790 m Mary Nutter PS NH
John: b 1727 d — m Elizabeth Pickering PS NH
John Gee: b 8-14-1735 d a. 2-20-1796 m Deborah (Furber) Mills
    PS NH
Samuel: b. 1738 d — m Sarah Ballou Pvt MA
Samuel: b 1727 d p. 1800 m Grace Stackhouse PS VA
Timothy: b 7-6-1745 d 1-29-1829 m Rebecca White QMGen ADC MA
Winthrop: bpt 3-9-1740 d 1783 m Phoebe Nutter Cpl NH

PICKERT,
Bartholomew: b 2-14-1727 d 1-17-1807 m Maria Catharine Pvt NY

PICKETT,
Benjamin: b 10-2-1724 d c. 1795 m Eunice — Pvt CT
Daniel: b 4-17-1742 d 12-14-1794 m Sarah Comstock Pvt CT
David: b c. 1724 d p. 1802 m Abigail (Dickinson) Comstock PS CT
Elizabeth Cooke: b 1712 d 1800 m William Pickett PS VA
James: b 6- -1753 d 6-29-1798 m Martha Terry PS NC
John: b 6-20-1754 d 10-23-1840 m Ruth Boardman Pvt MA ★
John: b 5- -1741 d 1797 m Sarah Abbot Ens NY
John: b 1-14-1744 d p. 7-9-1803 m Hannah Withers Capt VA
Martin: b 12-25-1736 d 4- -1804 m Ann Blackwell Col PS VA
Micajah: b 12-25-1756 d 12-23-1800 m Kizannah Henson PS SC
Phinehas: b 8-22-1757 d 8-10-1841 m (1)Anne Squire (2)Bethiah
    King Sgt CT ★
Reuben: b 1748 d 1825 m (1)Elizabeth Day (2)Elizabeth Wilson PS VA
Wm.: b 7- -1754 d 1- -1822 m Dorothy Skinner Pvt Slr MA
Wm.: b 3-16-1765 d 2-17-1841 m (1)Dorcas Bennett (2)Anna
    Thurlow (2)Hannah Beard Pvt MA
Wm.: b 9-3-1725 d 7-15-1795 m Mourning M Martin Maj PS NC
Wm.: b 1742 d 1814 m Lucy (Blackwell) Green LCol VA
Wm. Sanford: b 2- -1735 d c. 1798 m (1)Elizabeth Metcalfe (2)Lucy
    Young (3)Martha Metcalfe Capt VA

PICKLE,
Baltis: b 12-8-1720 d 11-25-1786 m (1)Sophia VanHorne (2)Anna
    — PS NJ
Matthias: b 5-10-1762 d 4-6-1835 m Adeline Searle Pvt NJ ★
Peter: b c. 1756 d p. 9-6-1821 m Anna Margaret Baughman Pvt PA

PIDCOCK,
Charles: b 7-16-1756 d 8-27-1836 m Martha Hoagland Pvt NJ
Jonathan: b 1729 d 1812 m Ankey — Pvt NJ

PIER,
Oliver: b 5-9-1741 d 1-11-1805 m (1)Elizabeth Webster (2)Phebe
Hayden Howard Pvt MA
Oliver, Jr.: b 11-22-1764 d 5-12-1824 m Caroline Hollenbeck Pvt
MA
Thomas: b 4-6-1730 d 1817 m Rachel Tremaine Pvt MA

**PIERCE, (includes PARCE, PEAIRS, PEARCE, PEARSE,
PEERS, PEIRCE & PERCE)**
Abel: b 1-28-1761 d 1842 m Susanna Spring Pvt MA
Abel: b 9- -1758 d 4;14-1825 m Sally Weeks Pvt Drm MA ★
Abial: b 10-1-1733 d 12-26-1811 m (1)Hannah Canedy (2)Mrs
Theodora Robinson Capt MA
Abner: b 10-4-1761 d 1-28-1851 m Huldah Wilcox Pvt MA
Abraham: b c. 1740 d p. 1799 m (1)Priscilla Reed (2)Mary Russell
Sgt MA
Amos: b 8-8-1761 d 3-11-1845 m (1)Mollie Weston (?)Mary Sterns
Pvt MA
Andrew: b c. 1730 d 1816 m Elizabeth VanMeter Pvt CS VA
Arodi: b 12-29-1750 d 9-3-1825 m Jemima Caswell Pvt MA
Arthur: b 1723 d p. 10-2-1792 m Mary Everett Sol NC
Asa: b 3-21-1754 d 5-1-1820 m Anna Mansfiels Pvt MA
Augustus: b 5-29-1757 d 2-22-1831 m Tamar — Arfr MA ★
Benjamin: b 6-7-1710 d 2-7-1782 m (1)Hannah Smith (2)Naomy
Richards (3)Sarah Mills (4)Sarah Holt Capt CT
Benjamin: b 2-16-1760 d 6-7-1817 m Anna Olmstead Pvt CT
Benjamin: b 12-25-1757 d 4-1-1839 m (1)Elizabeth Andrews (2)Anna
Kendrick Lt PM MA ★
Benjamin, Sr.: b 12-21-1728 d 5-9-1781 m Mary Lamson Pvt PS CS
MA
Benjamin: b 1755 d 11-7-1829 m Rebecca Wright Sgt MA ★
Benjamin, Jr.: b 10-21-1756 d 1-13-1819 m Eunice Jones Pvt MA
Benjamin: bpt 6-25-1738 d 4-19-1775 m Mary Wait MM MA
Benjamin: b 1762 d 1838 m Bathsheba Webster Pvt MA
Benjamin: b 6-22-1763 d 8-11-1840 m Lucy Sage Pvt MA
Benjamin: b — d 10-24-1800 m Tabitha Green Pvt MA
Benjamin: b 5-20-1744 d 11-12-1825 m Phebe Willard Sgt NH
Benjamin: b 5-18-1762 d 5-9-1847 m (1)Dorcas Lovejoy (2)Mrs
Nabby Dodge Pvt NH ★
Benjamin, Sr.: b — d 7-23-1793 m (1)Eliza — (2)Rebecca
Blanding CS NH
Benjamin, Jr.: b 2-13-1761 d 5-23-1847 m Lucinda Cobb Pvt NH
Benjamin: b 1762 d 1842 m Lucinda Sargeant Pvt VT
Benoni: b 1-19-1760 d 4-23-1844 m Elizabeth Waterman Pvt RI ★
Bowen: b 3-7-1762 d 8-9-1853 m Sarah Allen Sgt RI ★
Caleb: b 1759 d 1836 m Mercy Wheeler OrdlSgt MA RI ★
Caleb: b 6-8-1726 d 1776 m Mary Rowland CS MA
Caleb: b 7-12-1752 d 1789 m Hannah Marshall Pvt PA
Caleb: b 2-12-1727 d 10-12-1815 m Hannah Greaves PS PA
Charles: b 10-10-1748 d 8-2-1824 m (2)Susannah Glover Matr MA
Cromwell: b 12- -1732 d 8-4-1794 m Margaret Boggs LCol PA
Daniel: b 1760 d 1830 m Nancy Aunkers Pvt MD
Daniel: b 1746 d 1839 m Mary Hix Pvt MA
Daniel: b 1742 d 7-16-1821 m Mercy Gates Pvt NH
Daniel: b 1742 d 4-12-1812 m Mehitable Carver Pvt NY
David: b 1739 d 1-17-1801 m Phebe Stevens Cpl CT
David: b 3-20-1741 d 3-9-1779 m Abigail Hathaway Lt MA
David: b 8-12-1760 d 9-12-1816 m Sarah Bridges Pvt MA
David: b 10-26-1736 d 3-16-1818 m (1)Bethiah Ingersoll (2)Abigail
Ingersoll (3)Mrs Elizabeth (Baldwin) Gilbert PS MA
David: b 10-3-1742 d 4-6-1821 m Sarah Whitney Maynard Pvt NH
David: b 4-8-1756 d 10-28-1833 m Mary Bell Pvt PA
Delano: b 11-30-1748 d 10-3-1835 m Abigail Hammond Cpl CT
Dixon: b c. 1745 d p. 1800 m — Pvt PS SC
Ebenezer, Sr.: b 9-11-1711 d 3-1-1805 m Mary Stowe PS Dr MA
Ebenezer, Jr.: b 6-9-1745 d 8-1-1802 m Eunice Loomis Lt MA
Ebenezer: b 2-17-1731 d 1804-36 m Elizabeth — Pvt MA
Ebenezer: b 1759 d 6-15-1841 m Sally Gilbert Pvt MA
Ebenezer: b 6-5-1750 d 12-5-1826 m Anna Hussey Pvt PS NH
Ebenezer: b c. 1740 d 10-4-1777 m Elizabeth Gilson Pvt VT
Eli: b 8- -1762 d 12-26-1852 m Polly Lyon Pvt MA RI ★
Eliphalet: b c. 1760 d 3-1-1827 m Tabitha Bryant Pvt MA W★
Elisha: b 1746 d 1839 m Elizabeth Kane Pvt MA
Enoch: b 3-22-1719 d 3-2-1806 m Mary Mason PS CS CT
Ephraim: b 12-13-1745 d p. 1784 m Esther Stone MM MA
Ephraim: b 3-15-1733 d 3-28-1816 m Phebe Mouton Ens RI
Ephraim: b 3-15-1746 d 9-24-1834 m Mary — Ens VT NY ★
Ezekiel: b 3-24-1760 d 5-10-1838 m Sarah Pearce Pvt RI
Francis: b 7-18-1729 d p. 1779 m Lydia Bush Pvt MA
Francis: b 8- -1760 d 2-22-1853 m — Pvt VA ★
Gainer: b 7-1-1740 d p. 1811 m Jane Underwood Pvt PA
George, Sr.: b 1729 d 1800 m Mary Moore LCol PA
George, Jr.: b 1750 d 1-10-1820 m Lydia Buller Pvt PA
George: b 5-5-1714 d 10-2-1775 m Lydia Roberts PS PA
Giles: b c. 1728 d 4-10-1793 m Desire Case PS RI
Giles: b 3-23-1722 d 7- -1792 m Mercy Schruch Pvt RI
Hayward: b 6-22-1753 d 10-18-1826 m Judith Bailey Capt MA
Henry: b c. 1743 d 1-22-1791 m (1)Salome Hinds (2)Deborah
Chase Capt MA

Henry: b 1762 d c. 1812 m Ann Christiana Jacoby Pvt PA
Hezekiah: b 1755 d p. 1800 m Phebe Tibbets Cpl MA
Hilkiah: b 10-19-1727 d p. 1790 m Hannah Briggs Cpl MA
Humphrey, Sr.: b 3-23-1705 d p. 6- -1776 m Lydia Richardson PS
NH
Humphrey, Jr.: b 7-8-1733 d 10-30-1822 m Hannah Ring PS NH
Isaac: b 11-11-1731 d p. 1775 m Martha Graves Pvt MA
Isaac: b 3-24-1738 d p. 1789 m Hannah Mason Pvt MA
Isaac: b 11-17-1757 d c. 1803 m Anna Sanderson Matr MA
Isaac: b 9-22-1763 d 11-26-1849 m (1)Anna Fitch (2)Polly Bowen
(3)Elizabeth Carpenter Pvt MA
Isaac: b 3-8-1749 d 9-7-1821 m Mary Suffield ADC RI
Isaac: b 11-15-1759 d 5-21-1825 m Susannah Stoddard Sol RI
Israel: b 5-19-1760 d 3-25-1838 m Hannah Horton Pvt MM RI MA
Jacob: b 8-2-1751 d 8-9-1826 m Rebecca Whitcomb Sgt NH ★
Jacobus: b 9-28-1748 d 8-18-1812 m Maria VanderBergh Pvt NY
James: b c. 1745-50 d — m Abigail Smith Cpl MA
James: b c. 1720 d 1777 m Phoebe Tottingham Pvt MA
James: b 12-19-1754 d 5-21-1826 m Lydia Clapp Matr MA
James: b 10-14-1760 d p. 12-2-1837 m Esther Kinney Pvt PA
James: b 10-9-1740 d 3-2-1821 m Deborah Hunt Pvt RI
James: b 1764 d 9-17-1830 m Ann Shaw Pvt VA ★
Jeremiah: b 3-7-1760 d 2-20-1835 m Anne (Bowen) Olney Pvt RI ★
Jesse: b 1759 d 5- -1817 m Huldah Thayer Pvt MA
Jesse: b 3-5-1764 d 11-15-1820 m Lydia Gale Pvt MA
Job: b 11-29-1737 d 7-22-1819 m (1)Elizabeth Rounseville (2)Mrs
Elizabeth (Nelson) Strobridge Capt MA
Job, Sr.: b 4-25-1723 d 10-6-1791 m Abigail Pratt Pvt MA
Job, Jr.: b 8-7-1753 d 8-30-1818 m Hannah Bullock Pvt MA
John: bpt 3-13-1718 d 7-26-1788 m (1)Hannah Twitchell
(2)Mary Edmonds Pvt CT
John: b 7-31-1756 d 8- -1829 m Mary Gilmore Sgt MA
John: b 4-20-1754 d 9-20-1832 m Lucy Snow Cpl MA
John: b 3-7-1731 d 1-9-1823 m (1)Sarah Rounsville (2)Lucy Ashley
(3)Elizabeth Reed Sol MA
John, Jr.: b 5-12-1753 d 1- -1827 m Sally Paine Pvt MA
John: b 7-14-1736 d 10-16-1828 m (1)Abigail Demport (2)Abigail
Beard (3)Susanna Beard Pvt MA
John: b 9-18-1758 d 8-19-1837 m Mary Webb Pvt MA
John: b — d 1827 m Elizabeth (Rogers) Doliber Mte MA
John: b 1-26-1743 d 7-7-1812 m Tabitha Porter Capt NH
John: b 8-13-1724 d p. 1790 m — Pvt NH
John: b 1754 d 1856 m (1)Mary Watts (2)Margaret Moon Pvt NC
John: b 2-15-1749 d 6-22-1829 m Eunice Briggs Lt RI
John: b 4-26-1758 d 11-13-1827 m Deborah Hicks Lt RI
John: b 10-4-1756 d 1792 m Freelove Dyer Sgt RI
Jonas: b 7-7-1730 d 6-27-1819 m (1)Sarah Bridges (2)Lydia Gregory
Sgt MA
Jonas: b 2-18-1760 d 12-25-1835 m (1)Lois Clark (2)Susanna Allen
Pvt MA
Jonathan: b 9-17-1757 d 8-19-1808 m Lydia Bowman Cpl MA W★
Jonathan: b 6-10-1736 d 1-22-1800 m (1)Eunice Leathe (2)Mary
Goodale Pvt MA
Jonathan: b 10-27-1747 d 11-20-1824 m Sarah Chapin Pvt MA
Jonathan: b 2-18-1748 d 12-6-1807 m Mary Litchfield Pvt MA
Jonathan: b 4-7-1752 d 10-28-1822 m (1)Hannah Perham (2)Esther
Spaulding (3)Lydia Conant (4)Molly Bachelor Pvt MA
Joseph, Sr.: b c. 1723 d a. 1-20-1789 m Elizabeth — Sol DE
Joseph, Jr.: b c. 1751 d p. 5-7-1827 m Hannah White Sol DE
Joseph: b 3-6-1757 d 3-14-1835 m Elinor Crawford Mus Lt
MA ★
Joseph: b 3-15-1753 d 12-23-1825 m (1)Mary Hadley (2)Mrs
Lucy Parks Sgt Bbd MA ★
Joseph: b 12-1-1759 d 7-21-1840 m (1)Mary Ware (2)Lydia
Horton Pvt MA
Joseph: b 12-25-1745 d 1-1-1828 m Ann Dawes PS MA
Joseph: b 1748 d 1790 m Celia Pitt Lt NC
Joseph: b 4-10-1760 d 4-3-1807 m Susannah Allen Ens PA
Joseph: b 1750-60 d p. 3-22-1836 m Elizabeth — PS PA
Joseph: b 1-2-1763 d 8-6-1836 m (1)Anna Hilliard (2)Priscilla
Palmer Pvt Grd RI
Joseph: b 5- -1741 d 8-12-1827 m Margaret Allen Pvt VT
Joshua: b 1-25-1705 d 3-13-1794 m Hopestill Holloway PS CT
Joshua: b 1-22-1724 d 10- -1803 m Ann Bailey Pvt MD
Joshua: b 5-7-1741 d 11-5-1813 m Lydia Goodrich MM SM MA
Joshua, Sr.: b 1728 d p. 1785 m Mary Horton Pvt MA
Joshua, Jr.: b 3-12-1754 d 11-25-1804 m Susannah Rounds Pvt
MA
Josiah: b 1745 d 8-1-1805 m Lydia Shepard PS CT
Josiah: b 8-27-1756 d 1-23-1830 m Phebe Thompson Sgt NY
Josiah: b 3-30-1720 d 8-18-1799 m (1)Mary Dorr (2)Ruth Simonds
Thompson Sol MA
Josiah: b 10-28-1761 d 10-10-1834 m Azubah Howard Pvt MA
Josiah, Sr.: b 7-13-1708 d 2-10-1788 m Miriam Cooke PS CS MA
Josiah, Jr.: b 3-17-1751 d 5-10-1845 m Miriam Pierce Pvt MA
Josiah: b 2-13-1723 d 1-6-1807 m Sarah Gale PS CS MA
Josiah, Jr.: b 5-7-1752 d 1-4-1820 m Lucretia Bigelow Pvt MA
Justus: b 5-29-1734 d 1789 m Hannah Johnson PS CT
Langworthy: b 12-11-1747 d 8-4-1833 m (2)Eunice Austin
(3)Sarah Sherman Pvt RI ★
Lemuel: bpt 5-22-1737 d p. 1790 m Ruth Paine Pvt MA
Levi: b 5-12-1743 d p. 4-25-1794 m Elizabeth McAlpine Pvt CT
Levi: b 2-26-1739 d 1826 m Bathsheba Babbitt Sgt MA

Levi: b 9-15-1761 d 12-27-1833 m Persis Robinson Sgt MA
Lewis: b 11-21-1748 d 8-23-1825 m Mary Howell Ens PA
Martin: b 2-15-1752 d 1-24-1844 m Keziah Wheeler Pvt MA
Matthew: b 9-6-1755 d 6-16-1835 m (1)Sarah Tainter (2)Ruth
Robinson Sgt Wgn MA ★
Mial: b 9-25-1728 d 9-10-1810 m Hepsibeth Mason Pvt MA
Mial: b 1752 d 3- -1839 m Mehitable Wheeler Pvt MA
Michael: b 10-9-1757 d 3-3-1843 m (1)Sarah Allen (2)Mary Green
Pvt Mar RI ★
Moses: b 8-16-1730 d 1777 m Mehitable Rue Pvt MM MA
Naphtali: b 7-1-1709 d 8-2-1788 m Mary Bird Pvt MA
Nathan: b 1-22-1745 d 5-19-1776 m Sarah Davis Capt MA
Nathan: b 12-15-1732 d p. 1781 m (1)Sarah Reed (2)Mary
Cottonham Pvt MA
Nathan: b 6-24-1758 d 1856 m Anna Hoar Pvt MA
Nathan: b 4-22-1706 d 1790 m Abigail Spink PS NY
Nathaniel: b 9-28-1757 d 3-8-1830 m (2)Tryphena Barbour Pvt
MA
Nathaniel: b 11-23-1708 d 1793 m Mary Lindsay PS RI
Nehemiah: b 12-2-1759 d 8-22-1818 m Phebe Lawerence Pvt NH
Nehemiah: b 1755 d p. 1799 m Mary Hobart Pvt MA ★
Noah: b 2-11-1752 d 3-16-1829 m (1)Patience Rounds (2)Elizabeth
Hail (3)Sabary Wood Pvt MA
Pelatiah: b 3-18-1730 d 10-10-1804 m Anne Cadwell Pvt NY
Phineas: b 1-24-1751 d 10-1-1808 m (1)Ruth Gaines (2)Ruth Beebe
Pvt VT
Reuben: b 3-7-1747 d 12-30-1821 m Mary Wood Cpl MA
Richard: b 1-8-1739 d 12-16-1812 m Susannah Jewett Pvt NH
Richard: b 1-1-1734 d 1822 m Peggy — Capt VA
Robert: bpt 1-27-1751 d 5-15-1827 m (1)Mary Goodwin (2)Mrs
Butman Slr MA
Rouse: b 7-4-1753 d 12-24-1830 m Mary Brownell Lt RI W★
Rufus: b 4-22-1751 d 4-8-1812 m Elizabeth Howe Matr Sgt MA
Samuel: b 9-22-1756 d 3-11-1832 m Hannah White CT ★
Samuel: b 1759 d 6-12-1828 m Dorcas Brooks Pvt CT ★
Samuel: b 1758 d 1-20-1828 m Bridget — Pvt DE
Samuel: b 3-25-1739 d 6-4-1815 m Elizabeth How Col MA
Samuel: b 3-25-1737 d 9-16-1793 m Mary Steward Sgt PS MA
Samuel: b 5-21-1749 d 12-27-1821 m Elizabeth — Pvt NH
Samuel: b 1758 d 7- -1804 m Hannah Amy Pvt NJ
Samuel, Sr.: b 1719 d 9-4-1816 m Esther Wiley Pvt RI
Samuel, Jr.: b 4-13-1752 d 12-7-1827 m Hannah Jerauld Capt
RI
Samuel: — d p. 1786 m Olive Greene Pvt RI
Seth: b 1747 d 2-25-1809 m (1)Huldah Sampson (2)Rebekah Paige
(3)Abigail Hinkley (4)Mary McFarland Capt MA
Seth: b 11-5-1730 d 1790 m Anselette Clark Pvt MA
Shadrach, Sr.: b 7-8-1717 d 5- -1787 m Abigail Hoskins Pvt MA
Shadrach, Jr.: b 1750 d 9-11-1832 m Anna Bridges Cpl MA
Shubael: b 1758 d 6-9-1833 m Abigail Mason Pvt MA
Silas: b 7-25-1744 d 5-1-1816 m Anna Hathaway Pvt MA
Simon: b 1764 d 4-9-1814 m Hepzibah Wood Pvt NH W★
Solomon: b 6-15-1742 d 10-16-1821 m Amity Fessenden MM Lt
MA
Solomon: b 1754 d 1802 m Eunice Farrar Sgt MA
Squire: b 8-27-1758 d 10-24-1840 m (1)Freelove Wood (2)Betsey
Goff Pvt MA
Stephen: b 8-7-1739 d 1-28-1805 m Anna Wheeler Pvt MA
Stephen: b 8-15-1754 d 4-16-1826 m Hannah Marshall Pvt MA
Stephen: b 12-20-1753 d 5-24-1843 m Abigail Taylor Capt RI
Thaddeus: b 5-10-1764 d 7-9-1848 m Susannah Smith Sol MA NY
Thomas: b 2-24-1734 d 1-9-1832 m (1)Lettice Turner (2)Mary
Burtice Capt MA
Thomas: b c. 1757 d a. 3-25-1845 m Mary — Pvt NJ ★
Thomas: b 7-27-1749 d 12-20-1823 m Abigail Wardwell Sol RI
Thomas: b 1-2-1744 d 4-8-1798 m Isabella Steel Sol SC
Timeus: b a. 1759 d 9-27-1802 m Elizabeth Grosvenor Sgt CT
Valentine: b 5-26-1756 d 6-5-1830 m Eleanor Orr BgdMaj VA
Ward: b 1753 d c. 1797 m Sarah Chew Capt NJ
Wm.: b 8-29-1759 d a. 12-12-1866 m Sally Morgan Pvt CT
Wm.: bpt 3-19-1738 d 2-21-1777 m Sarah Bishop Cpl CT
Wm.: b 1754 d 11-6-1813 m Sarah Bray Sol GA
Wm.: b12-4-1727 d 2-1-1793 m Eunice Bent Lt MA
Wm.: b c. 1740 d p. 1790 m Joanna Doggett Pvt MA
Wm.: b 12-31-1741 d p. 1790 m Abigail Walker Pvt MA
Wm.: b 12-6-1760 d 9-4-1825 m Phoebe Manning Pvt MA ★
Wm.: b 12-25-1744 d 10-10-1840 m (1)Charity Brewer (2)Sarah
— PS MA
Wm.: b 12-2-1751 d 3-2-1845 m Tamasin Brown PS MA
Wm.: b a. 1735 d 10-6-1799 m (1)Marah Green (2)Mrs Lydia
Curtis Pvt NJ
Wm.: b 9-12-1745 d 1-17-1813 m (1)Chloe Cary (2)Lydia Birdsall
Capt NY
Wm.: b c. 1730 d 1779 m Chloe McCaskey Sol NC
Wm.: b 1742 d 10- ;1808 m Sarah Mary — Pvt NC
Wm.: b 8-6-1763 d 5-15-1846 m (1)Eleanor (Pearce) (2)Fanny
Wolford Cpl RI ★
Wm.: b 9-18-1716 d 9-13-1788 m Lydia Brown PS RI
Wm.: b 1717 d 1781 m Ursula Lovell PS VA

PIERPONT, (includes PIERREPONT)
Evelyn: b 3-15-1755 d 2-7-1809 m Rhoda Collins Lt CT

James: b 10-2-1732 d 12-27-1815 m Lydia Mansfield Pvt CT
John: b 1753 d p. 1789 m Ruth Stiles Ens CT
John: b 1724 d p. 3-14-1796 m Nancy Ann Morgan Pvt VA
Thomas: b c. 1760 d 10-20-1812 m Hannah Bishop Pvt CT

PIETY,
Thomas: b 1763 d 5-17-1835 m Mary Duncan Pvt PA

PIGEON,
John: b 1725 d a. 1795 m Jane DuMaresq PS NY

PIGG,
John: b c. 1720 d a. 2-21-1785 m Ann Clement PS VA

PIGGOTT,
James: b 1739 d 2-20-1799 m (2)Francies James Capt PA

PIGMAN,
Jesse: b 2-14-1765 d 3-15-1852 m Lurene Newland Ens PA
Mathew: b 1-14-1763 d p. 1803 m Ann Gilmore Pvt VA
Nathaniel: b c. 1735 d 1801 m Ann Waters LCol PS MD

PIKE,
Asa: b 1-24-1739 d 1-27-1813 m (1)Rachel Pike (2)Sarah Blodgett
Pvt MA
Benjamin: b 1-19-1742 d p. 1790 m Abigail Keith Sgt MA
Benjamin: b 1754 d p. 1797 m Dolly Tenny Pvt MA
Daniel: b 7-24-1747 d 12-2-1839 m Lois Underwood Lt MA ★
Daniel: b 2-23-1725 d 4-10-1795 m Sarah Kendall Pvt MA
Daniel: b 12-2-1732 d 5-2-1806 m Anna Carr Sol NH
Dudley: b 9-2-1760 d 7-30-1838 m Celia Weston Pvt NH ★
Ezra: b 3-29-1761 d 4-19-1840 m Mary Garlick Pvt NY ★
George: b 2-13-1755 d — m Mary Severs Pvt MA
Humphrey: b 6-17-1741 d 12-8-1796 m Elizabeth Stevens Maj MA
Israel: b 8-15-1743 d 11-8-1818 m (1)Sarah French Cpl MA
Jacob: b 7-1-1737 d 5-7-1805 m Joanna Marshall CS NH
James: b 6-8-1744 d 10-16-1793 m Mary French Pvt MA
James: b 7-19-1754 d 7-27-1823 m Sarah Parsons Pvt CT ★
James: b 12-26-1751 d 1820 m Ruth Ingalls Pvt MA
James, Sr.: b 5-21-1725 d 1811 m Anna George Pvt MA
James, Jr.: b 12-10-1752 d 11-20-1837 m Alice George Pvt
MA ★
Jesse: b 4-4-1756 d 9-17-1779 m Rebekah Mead Merritt Pvt NY
John: b 1754 d 3-25-1833 m (1)Sarah — (2)Betsey Chamberlain
Pvt CT ★
John: b c. 1734 d 2-5-1799 m Jemima Force Capt NJ
John: b 1762 d 1842 m Beulah Bemis Pvt VT ★
Joseph: b 1760 d 2-19-1842 m (1)Rebecca Hawkins (2)Sally Parker
Pvt MA W★
Joseph: b 6-5-1757 d p. 1802 m Abigail Sawtelle Pvt NH
Moses, Jr.: b 11-27-1750 d 9-1-1845 m Abigail Stevens Sgt MA
Moses: b 5-1-1738 d 11-9-1815 m Sarah Garnsey Pvt MA
Moses: b 1-20-1727 d — m Mary Harriman Sgt NH
Nathaniel: b 8-21-1744 d 10-17-1824 m Sarah Hall Pvt MA
Robert: b 8-25-1746 d 2-3-1819 m Mehitable Perkins Capt NH
Samuel: b 1724 d 4-9-1814 m Ann Allis Pvt CT
Samuel: b 1736 d 2-25-1814 m Mehitable — Sgt MA
Samuel: b 3-1-1730 d 11-6-1815 m (1)Abigail Morse (2)Sarah
Gould (3)Mrs Anna King Pvt MA
Simeon: b 8-16-1747 d 6-17-1775 m Mary — Pvt MA
Thomas: b 9-25-1739 d 9-15-1833 m Joanna Webber Lt MA
Timothy: b 1734 d 1818 m Elizabeth Jones Col MA
Uriah Drury: b 7-8-1761 d 10-18-1822 m Hannah Keyes Pvt NH
Wm.: b 1751 d 4- -1806 m (2)Mrs Molly (Thorp) Darrow Lt CT
Wm.: b 9-23-1748 d 6-7-1804 m Phebe Smith Sgt NH W★
Zebulon: b 9-18-1751 d 7-17-1834 m (1)Anna Parker Jureau Funel
(2)Isabel Brown QM NJ ★

PILCHER,
Robert: b 1758 d 1828 m Eunice Bowen Pvt NC SC

PILLOW, (includes PILLERS)
James: b c. 1760 d 1833/4 m — Pvt VA
Jasper: b 2-11-1760 d 1812 m Sary Willson Cpl VA
John: b a. 1745 d p. 1784 m Mary Johnson Pvt VA

PILLSBURY, (includes PILSBURY)
Benjamin, Jr.: b 12-26-1742 d 2-7-1819 m Anne Plumer Lt NH
Caleb: b 1-26-1717 d 2-7-1778 m (1)Sarah Kimball (2)Mrs
Mehitable Smith PS Capt MA
David: b 1765 d 2-7-1836 m Rhoda Hadlock Pvt NH ★
Edmund: b 3-12-1738 d 8-17-1816 m (1)Sarah Hale (2)Martha Hale
(3)Mrs Hepzibeth T Stiles Pvt NH
Eliphalet: b 1-15-1751 d 12-25-1824 m Elizabeth Cross Pvt MA
Ezra: b 4-18-1740 d 9-15-1820 m Martha Bayley Trm PS NH
John, Jr.: bpt 11-27-1748 d 3-19-1797 m Dorothy Ordway Pvt
MA
Joshua: b 3-23-1738 d 4-1-1798 m Rebeckah Witham Pvt MA
Joshua: b 3-30-1743 d 2-21-1825 m Elizabeth Sawyer Pvt MA
Micajah: b 5-4-1761 d 1801 m Sarah Sargent Pvt MA
Richard: b 2-5-1763 d 7-19-1800 m Miriam Weeks Pvt NH
Samuel: b 11-5-1742 d 1-9-1821 m (1)Mary Kent (2)Anna Jewett
1Lt MA

PILLSBURY, contd.
Samuel: b 7-18-1762 d 3-8-1838 m (1)Anna Swett (2)Hannah Havey Smn Pvt MA ★
Samuel: b 12-22-1752 d *p.* 1796 m Elizabeth Pingree Pvt MA
Stephen: b 1750 d 2- -1816 m Betsey Joy Pvt MA
Tobias: b *a.* 1756 d *p.* 1781 m Hannah Woodbury Pvt MA

PIM,
Wm.: b 11-9-1750 d 1802 m Mary Stalker Pvt PA

PINCKNEY, (includes PINKNEY)
Charles: b 3-7-1731 d 9-22-1782 m Frances Brewton PS SC
Charles Cotesworth: b 10-26-1757 d 8-16-1825 m Mary Eleanor Laurens Col PS SC
Hopson: b 1754 d 12- -1794 m (1)Elizabeth Quash (2)Elizabeth Cannon (3)Mary — PS SC
Israel: b 1735 d 1-7-1829 m Dorothy Rich Pvt NY
Thomas: b 10-22-1750 d 11-2-1828 m (1)Elizabeth Motte (2)Frances Middleton Maj SC
Thomas: b 2- -1729 d 10-6-1815 m Abigail Briggs 1Lt NY
Wm.: b 3-17-1764 d 2-25-1822 m Ann Maria Rodgers Ps MD
Wm.: b 1- -1737 d 3-26-1802 m Freelove Townsend Lt NY
Wm.: b 6/7-11-1739 d *p.* 1780 m Mrs Deborah Miles PS SC

PINDALL, (includes PINDELL)
Jacob: b 1750 d 2-24-1829 m Hannah Roberts Chipps PS MD
John: b 1-15-1735 d 1789 m (1)Eleanor — (2)Eleanor Gill PS MD
Nicholas: b — d 7-31-1779 m Eleanor — Pvt MD
Philip: b 11-20-1731 d 12-6-1804 m Mrs Rachel Shelby McFarland Capt MD
Richard: b 1751 d 3-16-1833 m Eliza Hart Dr MD

PINDER, (or PINDAR)
Wm.: b — d 1793 m Rebecca Huchins PS GA

PINE,
John: b 1745 d *a.* 7-13-1840 m Chatherine Chadeayne Pvt NY
Joseph M: b 9-18-1763 d 6-27-1852 m Sally Hickey Pvt MA ★
Philip: b 1741 d 8-26-1818 m Rhoebe Howard Pvt NY
Samuel: b 10-26-1722 d *p.* 6-6-1786 m Hannah Merritt Pvt NY
Wm.: b 3-14-1759 d 1846 m Judith Lippincott Pvt NJ

PINEO, (includes PINNEO)
Daniel: b 1744 d 6-27-1816 m Jane Hill Pvt CT
James: b 4-5-1734 d 6-14-1824 m Jerusha Strong Capt CT
Jonathan: b 9-8-1747 d 6-20-1821 m (1)Esther Libby (2)Mrs Bridget Doty Sgt MA

PINGREE, (includes PINGREY & PINGRY)
John: b 2-25-1726 d 8-30-1795 m Elizabeth Jewett 2Lt MA
Nathaniel: b 4-15-1763 d 4-23-1850 m (1)Ann Robbins (2)Mrs Rebecca Watkins (3)Mrs Baldwin Pvt MA
Stephen: b 1-22-1712 d 10-21-1794 m (2)Anna Jewett Pvt MA
Steven: b 8-7-1752 d 4-30-1840 m Ruth Hoyt Pvt MA ★
Stephen: b 3-3-1759 d 5-8-1843 m Mary Sanderson Pvt MA
Sylvanus: b 5-22-1737 d 1815/16 m Mary Sawyer Pvt NH
Thomas: b 6-2-1745 d 1814 m (1)Hannah Chapman (2)Molly Burnham Sol MA
Wm.: b 9-25-1757 d 4-3-1814 m Elizabeth Garland Pvt MA

PINKERTON,
David: b *c.* 1737 d 1781 m Mary Fitzrandolph PS NJ
Henry: b 2-16-1754 d 6-1-1816 m Elizabeth Franciscus Pvt PA
James: b 1754 d 8-26-1814 m Sarah Hayes Pvt PA
James: b 1741 d 1823 m — Pvt SC
John: b 1736 d 5-1-1816 m Rachel Duncan Maj NH
John: b 1735 d 9-7-1818 m Rebecca White Pvt PA
Joseph: b — d 4-27-1859 m Jane Robison Pvt PA

PINKHAM,
Abijah: b 2-9-1734 d 3-3-1779 m Rachel Huckins Pvt NH
Daniel: b 11-10-1735 d 5-25-1806 m Eunice Jenkins Smn MA
Daniel: b 1754 d 1787 /8 m Patience Ham Ens NH
Ichabod: b 10-23-1741 d 10-21-1800 m Mercy Catlin Capt MA
Joseph: b 1735 d 8- -1819 m (1)Elizabeth Derring (2)Elizabeth Hayes Lt NH
Nathaniel: b 12-7-1751 d 9-3-1803 m Martha Catland Pvt MA
Paul: b 8-1-1736 d 12-30-1799 m Jemima Gardner PS MA
Solomon: b 1715 d 9-26-1778 m Eunice Gardner PS MA
Thomas: b 6-8-1755 d 5-26-1811 m Sarah Ballard Pvt NH
Tristram: b 6-24-1748 d 6-13-1827 m Lydia Coffin PS MA

PINKLEY,
Peter: b 1745 d *p.* 4-11-1812 m (1)Catherine — (2)Lydia — PS VA

PINKSTAFF,
Andrew: b 1743 d 9-10-1841 m Winnie Owens Pvt VA

PINKSTON, (includes PINKSTONE)
Meshack: b *a.* 1765 d *p.* 4-5-1824 m Susannah — Sol NC
Shadrack: b *c.* 1750 d *a.* 7-21-1795 m Athaliza Carroll Cpl VA
Wm.: b *c.* 1739 d 7-27-1815 m Ann — Pvt NC

PINNELL,
Peter: b 1759 d 6-3-1845 m Nancy Yarber Pvt SC ★
Thomas: b 11- -1740 d 11-12-1812 m Sarah Clopton Pvt VA

PINNEY,
Aaron: b 1743 d 12-26-1812 m (1)Martha Bidwell (2)Susan Phelps Sgt CT
Abner: b 1750 d 11-23-1804 m Ruth Gillet Drm CT
Abraham, Sr.: b 2- -1709 d 9-12-1780 m (1)Elizabeth Butler (2)Sarah Moore PS CT
Abraham, Jr.: b 12-23-1735 d 12-12-1813 m (1)Lucretia Barnard (2)Sarah Clark (3)Mrs Hester (Case) Higley (4)Ruth Cassett Perrin Lt CT
Eleazer: b 2- -1753 d 7-15-1835 m (1)Eunice King (2)Anna McKinney Sgt PS CT
Isaac, Sr.: b 11-5-1716 d 9-2-1791 m Susannah Phelps PS CS CT
Isaac, Jr.: b 12-18-1758 d 2-15-1842 m Mary Parkhurst Sgt CT ★
Isaac: b 1-15-1717 d 1790 m Mary Mansfield Ens CS CT
Isaac: b 7-4-1741 d 7-3-1832 m Sabra Phelps Pvt CT
John: b 1736 d 9-24-1816 m Sarah Lull Sgt CT
Jonathan: b 3-19-1738 d 7-10-1813 m (1)Lydia Case (2)Susannah Pettibone Ens CT
Jonathan: b 1753 d 7-3-1826 m Martha Skinner Sgt CT ★
Levi, Sr.: b *c.* 1755 d 10-5-1805 m (1)Hannah Eno (2)Sabra Freeman Cpl CT
Martin: b 8-31-1747 d 3-8-1831 m Hannah Phelps Sgt CT
Noah: b — d — m Elizabeth Brown Pvt CT
Philaster: b 1755 d 1841 m Rosalinda Humprhey Cpl CT ★

PINSON,
Aaron: b 1754/5 d *p.* 4-12-1838 m Sarah Lycan CS PS NC
Joseph: b 1-30-1754 d 5-26-1838 m Margery — Pvt NC ★
Moses: b 1760 d *p.* 1847 m Margaret Henry Pvt NC

PINTARD,
John: b 5-18-1759 d 6-21-1844 m Elizabeth Brasher Pvt NY

PINTO,
Solomon: b 12-26-1759 d 3-24-1824 m Clarissa Smith Ens CT ★
Wm.: b 12-16-1760 d 12-10-1847 m (3)Lauretta Packard Pvt CT

PIPER, (includes PFEIFFER)
Abel: b 7- -1756 d 6-7-1846 m Sibyl Sawyer Lt MA
Amasa: b 10-26-1760 d 12-13-1829 m Mary — Pvt MA
Andrew: b 1-6-1760 d 6-5-1842 m Elizabeth Fox Ens NY
Caleb: b *a.* 1752 d *p.* 1798 m (1)Keziah Houghton (2) — Pvt MA
Duncan: b — d — m Martha Johnson Sgt Mstr MA
Elisha: b 6-17-1746 d 3-10-1836 m (1)Sarah Barker (2)Olive Dyer (3)Rosanah Dyer PS NH
George: b 11-12-1755 d 11-15-1823 m Eve Sear Pvt PA
Jacob: b *c.* 1740 d 2- -1813 m Elizabeth Catharina Flick Pvt MD
James: b *c.* 1735 d *p.* 8-27-1776 m Lucinda Long LCol PA
James: b 6-11-1762 d 10-15-1837 m Elizabeth Auckney Pvt PA
James: b 2-11-1732 d 9-20-1825 m Margaret Lusk PS CS VA
John: b 4-1-1761 d 9-3-1842 m Sarah Wellington Pvt MA ★
John: b 1-17-1760 d 4-20-1830 m (1)Jemima Hersey (2)Anna Young Pvt NY ★
John: b 12-30-1729 d 1-31-1816 m Elizabeth — Col PA
John: b *c.* 1740 d *p.* 1790 m — Steckel Pvt PA
John: b — d 1811 m Mildred Thomas Lt VA
Jonathan: b 3-27-1752 d 7-21-1807 m Elizabeth Gibson Pvt MA
Jonathan: b *c.* 1755 d 1858 m — Pvt MA
Joseph: b 1718 d 12-19-1802 m Esther Wright CS MA
Josiah: b 3-2-1742 /3 d 6-29-1824 m Sarah Davis Pvt MA
Samuel: b 8-8-1749 d *c.* 1830 m Olive Adams Sgt MA
Samuel: b 9-24-1753 d 1813 m Sarah Norris Lt NH
Samuel: b 1707 d 1788 m Jane Cate PS NH
Samuel: b 7-8-1739 d 4-11-1822 m Jane Elder Pvt MA
Samuel: b 1756 d 1820 m Christiana — Pvt MA
Solomon: b 10-20-1754 d 12-20-1827 m Susannah Pratt Cpl MA

PIPES,
John: b *c.* 1737 d *p.* 8-6-1821 m Mary Morris 1Lt NJ W★

PIPKIN,
Jesse: b *c.* 1753 d *p.* 1810 m Feriba — PS NC
Joseph: b *c.* 1724 d 1789 m Susanna Yeates CS NC
Phillip: b *c.* 1735 d *p.* 1790 m X PS NC
Willis: b *a.* 1751 d 1818 m (1)Sylvia Rhodes (2)Mrs Edith — Sol NC

PIPPEN,
Joseph: b 1752 d 4-10-1833 m (1)Lucretia Knight (2)Mrs Temperance Lee Ens NC W★
Solomon: b *c.* 1745 d *p.* 3-12-1798 m Olive — PS NC

PIRKLE,
John: b 1725 d 1811 m — Dibbs PS NC

PISTOLE,
Charles: b 1757 d 9-6-1839 m Elizabeth — Pvt VA ★

PITCHER,
Abijah: b 7-7-1763 d 2-18-1784 m Sara Ellis Pvt MA
Benjamin: b 1760 d 12-25-1849 m Rosanna — Pvt NY
Ebenezer: b 2-27-1721 d 10-4-1804 m Amy Durgy Sol CT
Elijah: b 1738 d 1794 m Mary Dow Pvt CS MA
Gotlieb: b 9-12-1757 d 7-5-1838 m Mary Pedrick Pvt NY ★
Jabez: b 1745 d 2-28-1816 m Sarah Barrows MM Pvt MA
Jonathan: b 1730 d 9- -1807 m Waitstill Chamberlain 1Lt NY
Nathaniel: b 12-29-1738 d — m Mrs Experience Jones Pvt MA
Reuben: b 1- -1763 d 2-15-1844 m Martha Barrett Pvt MA
Reuben: b 7-20-1759 d 1-23-1814 m Adah Harmon Sol VT
Wm.: b 1725 d p. 1-30-1800 m Magdalena Dunsbach PS NY

PITCHLYNN,
John: b 6-11-1745 d 5-20-1835 m (1) — (2)Sophia Folsom PS MS

PITKIN,
Elisha: b 3-9-1733 d 3-19-1819 m Hannah Pitkin Capt CT
George: b 1729 d 4-18-1806 m Jerusha Church Col CT
John, Sr.: b 12-18-1707 d 6-5-1790 m Elizabeth Olcott PS CT
John, Jr.: b 8-1-1748 d 11-27-1803 m (1)Elizabeth Woodbridge
    Priscilla Hyde Pvt CT
Richard, Sr.: b 3-15-1739 d 8-22-1799 m Dorothy Hills Capt CT
Richard, Jr.: b 10-24-1759 d 5-7-1822 m Abigail Loomis PS CT
Stephen: b 9-19-1754 d 11-1-1833 m (1)Jemima Tyler (2)Mrs Betsey
    Carrington Pvt CT ★
Stephen: b 5-10-1752 d 1807 m (1)Abigail Buckland (2)Mrs Amy
    Butler Pvt VT
Thomas: b 8-29-1724 d 1-25-1818 m Martha White Capt CT
Timothy: b 1-13-1727 d 7-8-1812 m Temperance Clapp Chp PS
    CT
Wm.: b 4-30-1694 d 10-1-1769 m Mary Woodbridge PS CT
Wm.: b 2-11-1724 d 12-12-1789 m Abigail Church PS CT

PITMAN, (includes PITTMAN)
Dempsey: b 1760 d 1824 m (1)Abigail Jones (2)Tabitha Knight PS
    NC
Ebenezer: b 1739 d 3-17-1820 m Sarah Mackrice PS NH
Isaac: b 7-28-1752 d 11-15-1818 m Rebecca Lee Capt RI
James: b 1733 d 11-23-1814 m Abigail Green NS PS CT
James: b 3-4-1756 d 12-25-1850 m Martha Taylor Lt VA GA ★
Joel: b c. 1755 d 1804 m Lurannah — Pvt NC
John: b 4-26-1751 d 7-24-1822 m Rebecca Cox PS OrdlSgt MA
John: b 1750 d 5-5-1823 m (2)Mrs Hawkins (3)Katherine Jones
    Pvt NC
John: b 1755 d 1823 m (1)Ann Whitehead (2)Catherine — Sol
    NC
John: b 6-27-1757 d 5-25-1809 m Nancy Bennett Pvt RI
John: b 1726 d 1785 m Polly Row Matr SC
John: b 1753 d 1839 m (1)Dorothy Peyton Robinson (2)Magdalene
    Irvine Price (3)Mrs — Burns Price Pvt VA
John: b 5-8-1760 d 1818 m Sarah — Pvt VA
Jonathan: b 12-23-1749 d 8-29-1834 m (1)Rebecca Clevenger
    (2)Jane Argardine Capt NJ ★
Joseph: b 1759 d 1820 m Alice Pendexter PS NH
Joseph: b 1742 d 1809 m Eleanor Vail Pvt NH
Joseph: b 1753 d 1829 m Miriam — Pvt PA
Joseph C: b 1762 d 1835 m Nancy Edwards Pvt VA
Joshua: b 1755 d 6-29-1822 m Sally Cox Chamberlain NS MA
Mark: b 1746 d 1792 m Mary Melcher 4Sgt NH
Moses: b 3-27-1743 d 8-5-1801 m Phebe Weedwn Cpl RI
Nicholas: b c. 1725 d p. 1790 m Catherine Snapp Pvt VA
Philip: b 7-7-1765 d 7-14-1839 (1)Epsie Jasper (21Mrs Prince
    (3)Patsy Davis Sol SC
Samuel: b 1740 d 1814 m Lucy Williams Sol NC
Samuel: b c. 1740 d p. 9-6-1811 m Mary Lane PS CS NC
Thomas: b 1750 d 9-21-1825 m Rachel Berry Sol VA

PITNER,
Lambert: b 8-2-1753 d 8-15-1832 m (1)Hannah Bates (2)Elida
    Farley Capt PA

PITNEY,
Benjamin: b c. 1720 d 1798 m Mrs Abigail Byram (Thompson) PS
    NJ

PITRE,
Francois: b c. 1753 d p. 9- -1779 m Maria Josephe Thibodeau PS
    LA

PITTARD,
John: b c. 1750 d 1821 m Franky — PS NC

PITTENGER,
Abraham: b 1762 d 5-1-1837 m Rebecca — Pvt VA

PITTS, (includes PITT)
Ebenezer: b a. 1758 d a. 1779 m Lydia Cudworth Pvt MA
George: b 8-1-1752 d 10-31-1838 m Lydia Stetson Pvt MA ★
Henry: b 1760 d a. 3- -1845 m — Pvt NC ★
Henry, Jr.: b 6-16-1759 d 1-15-1847 m Elizabeth Anderson Sgt SC★
James: b 1710 d 1-25-1776 m Elizabeth Bowdoin PS MA

James: b c. 1745 d p. 2-15-1797 m Martha Rebecca Wells Pvt NC
John: b c. 1740 d c. 1787 m Frances Griffin Capt NC
John: b c. 1755 d 1832 m Elizabeth — Capt NC
John: b 4-25-1746 d 7-6-1823 m Elizabeth — Capt PA
Lunsford: b a. 1758 d p. 6-26-1813 m Elizabeth Crutcher PS VA
Peter: b 9-15-1737 d 12-15-1812 m Abigail Richmond Capt MA
Robert: b c. 1738 d a. 12-20-1806 m Mary Bridger PS NC
Samuel: b c. 1750 d 2- -1833 m Hannah Noble Pvt MA
Samuel: b 12-15-1745 d 3-6-1805 m Joanna Davis CS PS MA
Shubael: b 1766 d 1842 m Sarah Cox Pvt MA ★
Wm.: b c. 1755 d 4- -1834 m Elizabeth Davenport Mid SC

PITTSLEY,
Robert: b 1759 d 12-16-1817 m Mercy Braley Pvt MA W ★

PITZER,
John: b c. 1745 d 1824 m Elizabeth — Pvt VA

PIXLEE, (includes PIXLEY)
Benjamin: b 7-9-1746 d 12-29-1813 m Celia Phillips Pvt MA
David: b 3-27-1741 d 8-25-1807 m (1)Lois Whittlesey (2)Lydia
    Patterson Capt MA
Isaac: b 9-12-1751 d 5-11-1790 m Abigal Hooker Pvt MA
Jonathan: b 7-20-1744 d 10-27-1826 m Mabel Fowler Pvt MA
Wm.: b 5-28-1734 d 5-8-1800 m (1)Betty Judson Lewis
    PS CT
Wm.: b 8-6-1721 d 9-18-1807 m Ruth — Pvt MA

PLACE,
David: b 2- -1741 d 5-18-1821 m Susannah Thompson Capt NH
Enoch: b 4-28-1756 d 10-12-1833 m Elizabeth Milligan Sgt RI ★
Griffin: b 3-16-1763 d p. 1832 m Sylvia Blodgett Pvt VT
James: b 12-13-1760 d 3-14-1826 m Phoebe Winans Pvt PA
John: b— d 4-22-1828 m (1)Patience Downing (2)Lydia Garland
    Pvt NH
John: b 5-23-1745 d 6-23-1832 m Charity Jump Pvt RI
John: b 1763 d 1846 m Lydia Willcox Pvt RI
Joseph: b 1754 d 1829 m Annie Chesley Cpl NH
Philip: b 1-31-1753 d 2-18-1835 m Mary Wightman Pvt RI
Samuel: b 8-10-1762 d — m Clarissa Glagg Pvt RI

PLAISTED,
Roger: b 12-27-1754 d 10-71-1848 m (1)Dorcas Bragdon Black
    (2)Mrs Margaret Haley Pvt Mus MA ★
Samuel: b 1757 d 9-15-1833 m Margarey Huckins Pvt NH

PLANK,
Adam: b 2-29-1736 d 6-7-1815 m Anna Catharine Clyne Pvt NY
John: b 6-25-1748 d 6-3-1825 m Nellie Gardinier Pvt NY
Michael: b 1740 d p. 1805 m Elizabeth Walker Pvt NY

PLANT,
Abraham: bpt 9-23-1727 d p. 1790 m (2)Tamar Frisbie Cpl CT
Solomon: b 5-1-1741 d 5-20-1822 m (1)Sarah Bennett (2)Esther
    Botsford Sol CT
Timothy: b 7-4-1750 d 10-4-1777 m Mary A. Colberth Pvt CT
Williamson: b 1763 d 1830 m Francis Watts Pvt VA

PLANTZ,
Johannes: b c. 1725 d p. 1790 m Margaretga — Sol NY

PLAPPER,
Christian: b c. 1742 d p. 5-1-1818 m Maria — Pvt NY

PLASS,
Coenradt: b 1740 d 1805 m Ann VanHoesen Pvt NY

PLASTERER,
Conrad: b 3-15-1745 d 8-20-1803 m Margaretha Bitner Pvt PA

PLASTRIDGE,
Caleb: b 2-19-1751 d 7-2-1838 m (1)Hannah Manning (2)Susannah
    Lucy Pvt NH

PLATER,
George: b 11-8-1735 d 2-10-1792 m (1)Hannah Lee (2)Elizabeth
    Rousby PS MD

PLATNER,
Christopher: b 1741 d 2-14-1800 m Anna Muller 1Lt NY
Henry: b 1731 d 1804 m Eve Best 1Lt NY
Jacob: b c. 1718 d a. 3-21-1787 m Maria Sibilla Pvt NY

PLATT, (includes PLATTS & PLATZ)
Abel, Sr.: b 2-6-1703 d 7-23-1777 m Mary Varnun PS NH
Abel, Jr.: b 3-28-1738 d 3-6-1819 m Phebe Wetherbee Pvt NH
Abial: b 1745 d 10-8-1825 m Rhoda Hall Sgt MA
Benjamin: b 1756 d 4-25-1808 m Abigail Green Pvt CT
Benoni: b 1718 d 1795 m Elizabeth Lockwood Capt NY
Charles, 3rd: b 1744 d 5-29-1827 m Caroline Adriance QM NY
Dan: b 1739 d 2-16-1826 m Jemima Pratt Lt CT
David: b 3-25-1739 d 7-2-1805 m Lettitia Gilman Capt NJ

PLATT, contd.
Ebenezer: b 8-23-1764 d 11-17-1834 m Anna Hoyt Pvt CT ★
Eliphalet: b 1733 d 1795 m (1)Elizabeth Scudder (2)Hannah Cansten (3)Mrs Bunce 1Lt NY
Epenetus: b 2- -1738 d 1815 m Susannah Merwin Pvt CT
George: b 1763 d 5-15-1843 m (2)Maria Katherine Weisel (3)Rachel — Drm PA ★
Isaac, Jr.: b 1744 d 9-27-1835 m Rachel Chase Pvt MA
Israel: b 1738 d 8-18-1796 m Elizabeth Scudder Capt NY
John: b 2-5-1752 d 1833 m Elizabeth Parmalee Pvt CT
John: b 1746 d 1837 m Lucy Webb PS CT
John: b 8-13-1749 d 12- -1823 m (1)Alice Stevenson (2)Mary Conrow SrgnMte Lt DE
John: b 1-2-1735 d 7-30-1810 m (1)Mary Blydenburgh (2)Phoebe (Hoyt) Husted Pvt NY
John: b 1745 d 1849 m — Pvt PA ★
Jonas, Sr.: b 10-9-1727 d p. 1800 m Elizabeth Sanford PS CT
Jonas, Jr.: b 1756 d 9-15-1840 m Lucy Mills Pvt CT
Jonathan: b 2-14-1740 d 10-5-1795 m (1)Mary Smith (2)Mrs Lounsberry Capt PS NY
Joseph: b 7-29-1741 d 2-19-1792 m Lydia Wilson Pvt CT ★
Joseph, Sr.: b 11-13-1724 d 8-30-1806 m Hannah Buckingham PS CT
Joseph, Sr.: b 1726 d 9-28-1817 m Deborah Page Pvt PS NH
Joseph, Jr.: bpt 8-31-1755 d 3-29-1799 m Abigail Sawtelle Pvt NH
Moses: b 5-17-1746 d 9-18-1819 m Hannah Judson Ens PS CT
Nathan: b 3-3-1761 d 7-20-1845 m (1)Ruby Smith (2)Charlotte Dickerman Pvt CT
Nathaniel: b 9-30-1741 d 5-11-1816 m Phebe Smith Capt NY
Richard: b 3-20-1742 d 1799 m (1)Sarah Camp (2)Ann Rogers PS CS CT
Richard: b 10-7-1762 d 3-20-1832 m Polly Bonnèr Sol NY
Stephen: b 7-26-1762 d 12-12-1800 m Dorcas Hopkins Lt NY
Thomas: b 12-28-1740 d 5-26-1824 m Mary Budd Lt NJ
Zephaniah, Sr.: b 1704 d 1-27-1778 m (1)Hannah Saxton (2)Mrs Anna Smith PS NY
Zephaniah, Jr.: b 5-27-1735 d 9-12-1807 m (1)Hannah Davis (2) Mary Van Wyck Col PS CS NY
Zephaniah, 3rd: b 1-3-1756 d 8-26-1830 m Bethia Ward Lt NY

PLATTER,
Christian: b 11-14-1760 d c. 1830 m Christiana — Pvt MD
Peter: b 9-21-1758 d 1-2-1832 m Sarah Crabbe Pvt PA

PLEASANTS,
John: b 1720 d p. 12-29-1776 m Susannah Woodson Capt VA
Wm.: b 1-5-1756 d 7-19-1836 m (2)Frances Flournoy Pvt VA ★
Wm.: b 1742 d 12-9-1784 m Elizabeth Pleasants Pvt VA

PLEDGER,
Joseph: b 1746 d 12-11-1788 m Elizabeth Gardner 2Lt SC
Philip: b 1710 d 1785 m (1)— (2)Mary Ann Ellis PS CS SC

PLETSCHER,
Henry: b 1756 d 1803 m (1)Anna Stayman (2)Anna Schenck Pvt PA

PLEW, (includes PLOUGH)
Aldert: b 8- -1762 d p. 8-30-1852 m — Pvt NJ
Daniel: b 6-7-1763 d 8-8-1853 m Sarah Ann Driskill Pvt VA
Elias: b 1762 d 5-2-1843 m (2)Lucinda Hall Pvt NY

PLIMPTON, (includes PLYMPTON)
Abner, Sr.: b 5-7-1743 d 5-5-1814 m Esther Mann Sgt MA
Asa: b 1748 d 3-22-1808 m (1)Sarah Dexter (2)Mary Smith Pvt MA
Daniel: b 1-9-1720/1 d 6-10-1777 m Deborah Smith LCol MA
Daniel: b 3-30-1747 d 10-25-1817 m Mary Cheney Lt MA
David: b 9-28-1738 d 4-15-1826 m Sarah Wight Pvt MA
Ebenezer: b 7-4-1752 d 12-9-1834 m Susannah Ruggles Pvt MA
Elias: b 3-2-1749 d 10-30-1814 m (1)Lydia Blashfield (2)Anne Weld Sgt MA
Elijah: b 6-30-1747 d 10-25-1817 m Mary Cheney Lt MA
Elijah: b 9-12-1750 d 6-8-1817 m Mary Pond Pvt MA
Elzaphon: b 9-4-1764 d 9-17-1819 m Sarah Hunt Pvt MA
Ezekiel: b 6-7-1748 d 1-2-1817 m Esther Boyden Capt MA
Job: b 8-12-1746 d 10-16-1814 m Beriah Hawes Cpl MA
Oliver: b 9-7-1758 d 4-26-1832 m Lydia Fiske Cpl MA ★
John: b 7-18-1761 d 8-20-1817 m Molly Marsh Pvt MA
Silas: b 7-30-1738 d 1-14-1818 m Esther Clarke 1Lt MA
Simon: b 2-10-1706/7 d 1- -1798 m Ruth Morse PS MA
Thomas: b 4-17-1723 d 12-9-1789 m Ruth Thompson MM PS MA
Ziba: b 1751 d 12-14-1821 m Tabitha Hart Pvt MA

PLOWDEN,
Edmund: b 1751 d 4-20-1804 m Janet Hammersley Capt MD
Edward: b 6-17-1744 d 5-10-1819 m Susanna Nelson Capt SC

PLOWMAN,
Jonathan: b c. 1725 d 1795 m Elizabeth — PS MD
Jonathan: b a. 1734 d 5-22-1776 m Rebecca Arnold CS MD

PLUMB, (includes PLUM & PLUMBE)
Amariah: b 9-5-1733 d 3-1-1778 m Sarah Aspenwall Pvt CT

Charles: b 6-10-1749 d 1831 m Susannah Starr Mar CT
Daniel: b 4-9-1764 d 1793 m Mary Dowd Pvt CL CT
Ebenezer: b 8-5-1739 d 4-17-1821 m Mary Skeels Pvt MA
Isaac: b 2- -1761 d 6-20-1852 m (1)Sylvia Ward (2)Catherine (VanKeuren) Lane Pvt CT
James: b 9-30-1748 d 7-12-1827 m Lydia Sefford Pvt CT
Jared: b 3-18-1749 d 1821 m Ruth Fowler Pvt MA ★
Jesse: b 7-23-1746 d 11-28-1811 m Mary Churchill Pvt CT
John: b 12-25-1745 d 1822 m Sarah Marsuller Pvt NJ
John, Sr.: b 6-26-1742 d 7-2-1803 m Dorothy Gilbert Pvt NY
John, Jr.: b 1-26-1765 d 11-10-1850 m Tryphena Hunt Pvt NY ★
Joseph: b 1755 d 1820 m Chloe — Pvt CT
Joseph: b 7-2-1755 d 12- -1815 m (1)Deborah Miner (2)Susannah Woodard Pvt CT
Joseph: b 1756 d 1826 m Sybil Edwards Pvt CT
Joseph: b 1759 d 1847 m Lucinda Pratt Pvt CT ★
Nathaniel: b 4-4-1760 d 12-2-1841 m Anna Langworthy Fif Pvt CT

PLUME,
Isaac: b 10-1-1734 d 11-19-1799 m (1)Sarah Crane (2)Annache VanWagenan Ens NJ

PLUMLEY, (includes PLUMLY)
Benjamin: b 4-2-1755 d 9-23-1836 m (2)Anna (McCrea) Fitch Cpl MA ★
George: b 1753 d 1813 m Susannah Nickels Pvt PA

PLUMMER, (includes PLUMER)
Abel: b 8-31-1730 d 6-18-1822 m (1)Mary Early (2)Abigail (Sargent) Hale PS NH
Asa: b 12-27-1742 d 12-20-1800 m (1)Sarah Burpee (2)Betsey Gage (3)Mary Haynes Drm MA
Beard: b 8-12-1754 d 10-7-1816 m Susanna Ham Pvt NH
Benjamin: b 4-29-1750 d 10-19-1817 m Sarah Adams Pvt MA
Francis: b 4-22-1747 d 8-10-1816 m Kezia Kinney Sgt MA
George: b 12-5-1762 d 6-1-1843 m (1)Margaret Lowrey (2)Martha Dean Pvt PA
Jabez: b 9-7-1757 d p. 10-7-1777 m Anne Hunt Pvt NH
Jesse: b 9-18-1740 d 12-26-1824 m Sarah Merrill PS NH
John: b 1752 d 1827 m Susannah Longfellow Pvt MA
John: b 5-16-1760 d 5-14-1841 m (1)Phebe Gould (2)Abigail Gould Pvt MA ★
Joseph: b 1753 d 1858 b Sallie Robbins Pvt NH
Moses: b 1-21-1744 d — m (1)Hannah Hale (2)Phoebe Poor Pvt MA
Moses: b 1748 d p. 3-20-1802 m Lucy Perkins Pvt MA
Nathan: b 1751 d 4-28-1835 m Mary Palmer Pvt NH
Nathaniel: b 3-1-1744/5 d 1-29-1821 m Hannah Walker Lt MA
Paul: b 12-28-1746 d 1-25-1831 m Hannah Woodbridge Sgt MA
Richard: b 1751 d a. 1790 m Patience Neal Sgt ME
Richard: b 1- -1758 d 2-17-1838 m Susannah Moore Pvt RI NC ★
Robert: b 3-7-1761 d 3- -1840 m Zilphia Farr Matr MA
Samuel: b 7-19-1754 d 5-15-1850 m (2)Mrs Nancy McCracken Spy PA MD ★
Samuel: b 9-16-1742 d 3-5-1820 m Sarah Bragdon Sgt MA
Thomas: b 3-30-1735 d 10-10-1786 m (1)Elizabeth Pettingill Muzzy (2)Ruth Dole Pvt MA
Thomas: b 3-10-1756 d 12-21-1836 m Elizabeth Chandler Pvt MA
Thomas: b c. 1735 d p. 4-17-1807 m Phebe Cook Pvt MA
Wm.: b 12-14-1756 d 10- -1840 m Abigail Jordan Pvt MA ★
Wm.: b 12-12-1755 d 7-8-1833 m Catherine McAllister 1Lt PA ★
Wm.: b 1729 d 6- -1798 m Jean (Plummer) Sol PA
Wm.: b 1748 d p. 1785 m Mary Elizabeth Hayes Cpl VA
Wm.: b c. 1755 d p. 7-21-1813 m Elizabeth Cherry PS VA

PLUNKETT,
Benjamin: b c. 1750 d p. 1796 m Frances Ham Ens VA
Reuben: b 1752 d 7-27-1829 m Nancy Purvis Sgt VA
Wm.: b c. 1734 d 1791 m Esther Harris Col PA

PLYLER,
Coonrod: b 1752 d 1837 m Mary Ann Funderburk Sol SC

PLYLEY,
Casper: b 2-11-1763 d 3-28-1849 m Margaret Gossard Pvt PA ★

POAGE, (includes POAGUE & POGUE)
Ann Kennedy (Wilson): b 1735 d 11-11-1815 m (1)John Wilson (2)William Pogue (3)Joseph Lindsey (4)James McGinty PS KY
George: b 3-28-1754 d 9-16-1821 m Ann Allen Capt CS VA
George: b a. 1734 d a. 12- -1786 m Rachel — Col VA
James: b 3-17-1760 d 4-9-1820 m Mary Woods Lt VA
John, Sr.: b 5-16-1726 d p. 2-16-1789 m Mary Crawford PS CS VA
John, Jr.: b 12-23-1757 d 4-10-1827 m Rebecca Hopkins Ens VA
John: b c. 1712-15 d 10- -1802 m Jane Boggs PS VA
Robert: b 10-6-1760-5 d 8-11-1836 m Jane Hopkins Mil Spy Sct VA
Robert: b 1752 d c. 1814 m Mary Hopkins 2Lt VA
Robert, Sr.: b 1730 d 1787 m Jean Wallace CS VA
Thomas: b c. 1740 d p. 11-22-1802 m Agnes McClanahan Sol VA
Wm.: b 1735 d 9-3-1778 m Ann (Kennedy) Wilson PS VA
Wm.: b 5-18-1759 d 9-23-1834 m (2)Elizabeth Franklin Pvt VA ★

POE, (includes POHE)
Adam: b 1747 d 9-23-1838 m Elizabeth Smith Codman Pvt PA
Andrew: b 9-30-1742 d 7-15-1832 m Elizabeth Rutan Lt PA
David: b 1742 d 1816 m Elizabeth Cairnes QM MD
Edward: b 1732 d 1816 m (1)Martha Brittain (2)Catharine — Sgt VA
Elizabeth Cairnes: b 1756 d 7-7-1838 m David Poe PS MD
George: b c. 1741 d 8-20-1823 m Catherine Dawson Capt MD
George: b 3- -1750 d 6-10-1805 m Effie Booth Lt PA
John: b 1758 d 10-9-1834 m Mary Newman Pvt NC
Samuel: b 1738 d 1819 m Margaret King Pvt VA
Thomas: b 1749 d 2-22-1825 m Mary Blakey Pvt VA
Wm.: b 1755 d 1804 m Frances Winslow Sgt PA

POFFENBERGER, (includes POFFENBARGER)
Daniel: b c. 1750 d 7-29-1845 m — Pvt PA
John: b c. 1734 d 1796 m Mary — PS MD
John: b c. 1745 d p. 1782 m Margaret — Pvt PA

POILLON,
John: b 8-12-1723 d 2-2-1803 m Margaret Perine PS NY

POINDEXTER, (includes PENDEXTER)
David: b 3-17-1763 d p. 4-18-1833 m Frances Pope Johnson Pvt VA ★
Eliab: b 4-1-1761 d 11-23-1842 m Mary Thomas Sol MA
Elizabeth Pledge: b a. 1750 d 2-29-1816 m Thomas Poindexter PS NC
Gabriel: b 5-8-1758 d 8-28-1831 m Mary Swift Pvt VA
George Benskin: b 8-26-1739 d p. 5-18-1790 m Sarah Parke Col PS VA
John: b c. 1750 d 9-28-1820 m (1)Nancy Green (2)Elizabeth Johnson (3)Margaret Maer CS VA
Joseph: b 6- -1736 d 6-29-1826 m Elizabeth James Kennerly Capt VA
Mary: b 3-11-1775 d 2-6-1863 m Jesse Ridings PS NC
Thomas: b 1733 d 1-1-1807 m (1)Susan Hughes (2)Elizabeth Pledge Capt NC
Thomas, Sr.: b c. 1718 d p. 1796 m Lucy Jones CS VA
Thomas, Jr.: b 5-25-1759 d 4-10-1843 m Sallie Ragland Pvt VA ★
Wm.: b 1732 d a. 4-19-1808 m Margaret — PS VA

POINTER,
Samuel: b 1752 d 1799 m Elizabeth Ligon Sol VA

POINTS,
Joseph, Sr.: b 8-4-1720 d 7-29-1776 m Felacia — Sgt PA
Joseph, Jr.: b 1760 d 7-22-1837 m Sarah Grainer Pvt PA

POLAND,
Asa: b 1763 d 9-3-1851 m Abigal Poland Pvt MA ★
John: b 1754 d 1-19-1823 m Sarah Smock Bennet Sgt NJ ★
Joseph: b 9-4-1756 d c. 1813 m Hannah Twiss Sgt MA W ★
Joseph: b 1733 d 11-14-1820 m (1)Lucy Woodbury (2)Mrs Sarah Whipple Pvt MA
Samuel: b 1755 d 1822 m (1)Margaret Ullinger (2)Margaret Ritter Pvt PA ★
Seward: b 11-2-1759 d 6-19-1831 m Johanna Thompson Pvt MA ★

POLHEMUS,
Abraham: b 3-20-1755 d 12-25-1831 m (1)Margrietje Lydecker (2)Annatje Smith (3)Rachel (Turner) VanOrden Pvt NY
Cornelius: b 1755 d 2-8-1839 m Mary Ann Meshan Lt NY
Daniel: b a. 1761 d 6-3-1822 m Hannah Osterhout Meyer Sgt NY
John: b 5-25-1738 d 5-25-1831 m Susanna Hart Maj NY
Theodorus: b 1719 d p. 12-23-1781 m Ann Brinkerhoff PS NY
Theodorus: b 3-20-1755 d p. 8-18-1820 m Elizabeth Hendrickse Cpl NY
Tobias: b 6-3-1744 d 8-24-1826 m Mary Schenck Capt NJ

POLING,
Wm.: b 1763 d 1836 m Ann — Pvt MD

POLK, (includes POLKE)
Charles: b 10-26-1740 d 8-28-1795 m Mary Manlove PS DE
Charles: b 7-29-1732 d 3-10-1821 m (1)Mary Clark (2)Philipina Helms Capt NC W ★
Charles: b 1-18-1760 d 10-16-1848 m Margaret Baxter Pvt NC
Charles: b 2-2-1745 d 10-11-1823 m Delilah Tyler Capt VA
Delilah Tyler: b 2-10-1755 d 6-6-1797 m Charles Polk PS VA
Edmund: b 1740 d 1824/5 m Mary Fultz Maj PA
Ephraim: b 11-24-1758 d 11-25-1814 m Rhoda Morris Pvt PA
Ezekiel: b 12-7-1747 d 8-31-1824 m (1)Mary Wilson (2)Bessie Davis (3)Mrs Sophia Neeley Lennard Col SC
George: b 11-15-1746 d 12- -1795 m Miss Rian Capt DE
John: b c. 1739 d a. 4-11-1803 m Eleanor Shelby Capt NC
John: b 4-1-1754 d 1814 m Amelia Hurst Lt PA
Thomas: b c. 1732 d 6-26-1794 m Susan Spratt Col PS NC
Thomas: b 1757 d 5-30-1842 m (1)Mary Shelby (2)Keziah Tarlton Pvt NC
Wm.: b 1705 d 10- -1788 m (2)Mary (Vaughn) Woodgate PS DE
Wm.: b 12-11-1752 d 1814 m (1)Esther Winder (2)Mrs Nancy Purnell Dennis (3)Mary Hubbell Pvt MD

Wm.: b 1733 d a. 1789 m (1)— (2)— Capt NC
Wm.: b 7-9-1758 d 1-4-1834 m (1)Grizelda Gilchrist (2)Sarah P Hawkins LCol SC NC ★
Wm.: b a. 1744 d 1-14-1835 m Sabra Bradford Capt VA

POLLAND, (or POLLAN)
Wm.: b c. 1757 d 1-1-1818 m Feriba — Pvt PS MD

POLLARD,
Absolem: b c. 1760 d 8-29-1835 m Leanna Banks Pvt VA ★
Amos: b 3-2-1737 d p. 2-9-1786 m Miriam — Pvt NH
Benjamin: b 1744 d p. 1777 m (2)Joanna Seely Lt MA
Benjamin: b 2-16-1741 d — m Susannah Tay Sol MA
Benjamin: b 6-23-1753 d 8-6-1845 m Nancy Stevens Capt VA
Braxton: b 12-25-1760 d 9-1-1840 m Anna Guffee Cpl VA ★
Chattin: b 10-10-1762 d 10-23-1843 m Mary Greet Pvt Wgn VA ★
David: b 1745 d 12-30-1830 m Polly — Pvt CT
Edmund: b 11-24-1758 d 6-24-1835 m Sally Herndon Pvt VA ★
James: b 1762 d 7-4-1840 m Annie Rediford Pvt VA ★
John: b 4-20-1729 d 5-10-1814 m Elizabeth Williams Pvt MA
John: b 3-10-1752 d 11-10-1839 m Anna Lockwood Sol MA
John: b c. 1750 d p. 1787 m Sarah (Winans) Jeffers Pvt NJ
Jonathan: b 9-21-1741 d 12-6-1832 m Mary Bowman 2Lt MA
Jonathan: b 3-3-1759 d 4-16-1821 m Kezia Hayward Pvt MA
Joseph, Sr.: b 5-3-1702 d 10-14-1786 m (1)Ann Hill (2)Abigail Hill PS NH
Joseph, Jr.: b 3-4-1737 d 7-23-1820 m Ruth Burge Cpl NH
Joseph: b 3-18-1758 d 9-6-1836 m Catherine Robinson Pvt VA
Oliver, Jr.: b 1-27-1736/7 d 5-28-1831 m Mary Hill Pvt MA
Robert: b c. 1755 d 1820 m — Lt SC
Robert: b 1724 d 1-24-1778 m Elizabeth Camm Pvt VA
Robert: b 1-12-1760 d 7-17-1835 m (1)Anne Talman (2)Mrs Howle (3)Susan Howle Pvt VA ★
Thomas: b 9-30-1741 d 2- -1818 m Sarah Harding Capt VA
Thomas: b 9-30-1741 d c. 1796 m Mrs Mary Thornly Capt VA
Timothy: b 8-24-1745 d 1822 m Sarah Whittemore Pvt MA NH ★
Wm.: b c. 1730 d c. 1795 m Elizabeth Pollard Pvt MD
Wm.: b 8-19-1759 d 7-25-1837 m Keziah Seay Pvt VA ★
Wm.: b 6-3-1737 d 11-2-1802 m (1)Mary Torian (2)Tabitha Collins Pvt VA
Wm.: b 8-27-1761 d 6-6-1841 m Fanny Hampton Pvt VA ★
Wm.: b 1734 d c. 1781 m Mary Anderson CS VA

POLLETT,
John: b 1745 d 1820 m Mrs Mary Skeath Cpl VA

POLLEY, (includes PAULEY, PAULY, POLLY, or POWLEY)
Andrew: b 1740 d 3-8-1825 m Catharine — Capt PA
Edward: b 12-21-1758 d 5-19-1845 m Mary Mullins Pvt VA ★
John: b 12-29-1762 d 10-11-1845 m (1)Abigail Kimball (2)Sally Stone Pvt MA ★
John: b c. 1745 d 4-19-1794 m Sarah McTeer Pvt PA
Jonathan: b 10-26-1759 d 5-31-1840 m (1)Rachel Hubbard (2)Mehitable — Pvt MA VT CT
Joseph: b 9-3-1728 d 1775/6 m Dorcas Colburn Fif MA
Joseph Francis: b c. 1760 d p. 1825 m Anna Maria Shaffer Staff FrA
Robert: b 8-11-1752 d 1828 m Jane Harris DrmMaj MA
Wm.: b 3-2-1762 d 11-22-1838 m Margaret Munsey Pvt MA ★

POLLOCK,
Benjamin: b 1-22-1744 d 3-3-1779 m Mary Ward Pvt NC
Charles: b 1732 d 3- -1795 m Agnes Steel Pvt PA
David: b 1755 d 3-18-1841 m Anne Rowland Pvt MD ★
John: b 9- -1752 d 1806 m Isabella Rowland Pvt PA
Joseph: b 12-13-1750 d 3-11-1828 m (1)Hannah VanDike (2)Margarette Gray Lt PA
Oliver: b 1737 d 12-17-1823 m (1)Margaret O'Kennedy O'Brien PS LA & Cuba
Peter: b 3-21-1751 d 3- -1815 m Mary Poor Sol VA
Samuel: b a. 1750 d 3-20-1812 m Jane — Pvt PA
Samuel: b 1739 d 1822 m Margaret Johnson Pvt PA
Thomas: b 2-16-1749 d 4-8-1803 m Mary Ellis QMSgt VA

POLSLEY,
Jacob: b 5-10-1763 d 5-7-1823 m Margaret Haymond Pvt PA

POMEROY, (includes POMROY — PUMROY)
Abner: b 9-7-1734 d p. 1785 m (1)Mary French (2)Mercy Sheldon Capt MA
Benjamin: b 11-19-1704 d 12-22-1784 m Abigail Wheelock Chp CT
Caleb: b 7-10-1740 d 12-19-1810 m Chloe Strong Pvt MA
Charles: b 4-22-1749 d 1785 m Temperance Watrous Sgt CT
Daniel: b 1728 d 1-23-1785 m Naomi (Kibbe) Phelps Pvt CT
Daniel: b 12-15-1737 d 11-28-1834 m Louise Pomeroy Pvt CT ★
Daniel: b 1751-62 d 4-3-1834 m Mary Loveland Pvt CT ★
Ebenezer, Jr.: b 1-17-1741 d 9-17-1826 m Experience Clark Pvt MA
Elihu: b 1755 d 1834 m Lydia Barber Sol CT
Elijah: b 8-22-1736 d 12-3-1792 m Ruth Phelps CS MA
Elisha: b 8-7-1763 d c. 1860 m (1)Submit Green (2)Lucy Rice Pvt MA NY
Enos: b 1746 d 1813 m (1)Freedom Edwards Clark (2)Miriam (Bartlett) Wolcott Cpl MA
Enos: b 4-23-1761 d 3-26-1826 m Lucy Smith Pvt MA

POMEROY, contd.

Ethan: b 1744 d 1825 m Esther Parsons Sgt MA
Gad: b 4-22-1759 d 2-14-1834 m Lucy Hering Pvt MA
Grove: b 3-13-1763 d 4-15-1813 m Eunice Marsh Pvt MA W★
Ichabod: b 3-9-1757 d 11-13-1843 m Lucy Harris Pvt MA ★
Isaac: b 8-16-1745 d 3-24-1804 m Rhoda Sykes Capt CT
Isaac: b 8-14-1753 d 12-25-1836 m (1)Deborah Torrey (2)Irene
    Parks Pvt MA
Jacob: b 12-13-1751 d 10-1-1842 m Thankful Pomeroy Sgt MA ★
Joel: b c. 1743 d 1777 m Mercy Johnson Pvt CT
John: b 8-12-1733 d 9-21-1810 m Esther Kibbee Lt CT
John: b 3-12-1741 d 5-29-1804 m Elizabeth King Lt CT
John: b 1745 d 2-16-1809 m (1)Isabella Barr (2)Hannah Graham
    LCol PA
Jonathan: b 9-13-1743 d 9-24-1808 m Prudence Austin MM CT
Joshua: b 2-27-1737 d 3-20-1815 m Mary Davis CS CT
Josiah: b 6-18-1745 d 7- -1812 m Mary Cook AsstQM CT
Josiah: b 7-21-1741 d 8-17-1821 m Joanna Wright CS PS Lt MA
Lemuel: b 9-24-1738 d 12-14-1819 m (1)Louise Pynchon (2)Eunice
    Lyman (3)Betsey White Bliss Capt MA
Luther: b 11-8-1757 d 3-27-1855 m Rhoda Burt Pvt MA ★
Medad, Sr.: b 12-17-1730 d 1801 m (1)Eunice Southwell (2)Phebe
    Kent (3)Mary Wilcox Pvt CT
Medad, Jr.: b 10-18-1758 d 1855 m Elizabeth Morrell Pvt CT ★
Nathaniel, Jr.: b 5-23-1734 d 2-12-1787 m Abigal King Capt CT
Nathaniel, 3rd: b 11-29-1758 d 5-17-1831 m Martha Spencer Capt
    CT W★
Oliver: b 1729 d 9-30-1776 m Mary Lyman Lt CT
Phinehas, Sr.: b 4-7-1738 d 12-3-1802 m Thankful Smith Sgt MA
Phinehas, Jr.: b 9-4-1757 d p. 1790 m Rebecca Spaulding Pvt MA
Pliny, Sr.: b 5-19-1734 d 1804 m Sarah Allen CS MA
Pliny, Jr.: b 9-17-1758 d 2-27-1798 m Mehitable Strong Pvt MA
Quartus: b 5-14-1735 d 11-3-1803 m (1)Phoebe Sheldon (2)Rachel
    Pomeroy Pvt PS PA
Seth: b 5-20-1706 d 2-19-1777 m Mary Hunt MGen MA
Simeon: b 6-5-1725 d 6-22-1812 m Abigal Smith Pvt MA
Simeon: b 4-24-1754 d 10-28-1847 m (1)Mary Hastings (2)Mrs
    Hannah Goodale Pvt MA ★
Thomas: b 1733 d 1803 m (1)Margaret — (2)Mary Graham Pvt PA
Timothy: b 1-13-1750 d 1793 m (1)Phoebe Pomeroy (2)Anna Burt
    Cpl MA
Titus: b 10-10-1757 d 1846 m Kesiah Sedgwick Pvt MA

POMPILLY, (or PUMPELLY)

Bennett P.: b 6-16-1761 d 12-5-1834 m Elizabeth Merrill Pvt MA

POND,

Abel: b 10-27-1753 d 12-29-1828 m (1)Eunice Curtis (2)Jerusha
    Gillett Barnes Cpl MA
Abijah: b 10-27-1751 d 1-26-1833 m Molly Ray Pvt MA
Apollos: b 6-12-1764 d 5-29-1831 m (1)Juletta Daniels (2)Phoebe
    Thayer Pvt MA
Barnabas: b 10-29-1755 d 5-9-1841 m Thankful Foote Pvt CT
Bartholomew: b 4-13-1736 d 3-21-1810 m Lucy Curtiss MM Lt CT
Bartholomew: b 8-1-1754 d 3-31-1850 m Elizabeth Dunbar Pvt
    CT ★
Barzillai: b 7-26-1759 d 6-3-1832 m Mellicent Fairbanks Cpl MA
Benjamin: b 3-21-1731 d 12-27-1809 m Lois Partridge Cpl MA
Benjamin: b 6-15-1726 d 2-22-1787 m Mary Park MM MA
Beriah: b 1758 d 3-14-1836 m Sylvia Sandford Pvt CT ★
Charles: b 1744 d 5-18-1832 m (1)Martha Miles (2)Kate DeWitt
    Capt CT
Dan: b 5-4-1751 d 2-7-1838 m Esther Hurd 1Sgt CT ★
Dan: b 11-4-1726 d 5-27-1783 m Mehetabel Munson Pvt MA
Daniel: b 2-9-1726/7 d 11-30-1804 m (1)Sarah Thurston (2)Ede
    Ware Pvt MA
Ebenezer: b 7-4-1728 d 3- -1821 m Freelove Fairbanks Capt MA
Eli: b 2-16-1743 d 5-20-1802 m Huldah Hill Lt MA
Elias: b 9-23-1751 d p. 1824 m Martha Howd Pvt CT ★
Elijah: b 2-3-1738 d 4- -1830 m (1)Margaret Metcalf (2)Mehitable
    Pratt Capt MA
Elisha: b 3-25-1725 d 5-30-1796 m (1)Phoebe Ware (2)Melatiah
    Chever Pvt MA
Enoch: b 4-27-1756 d 8-8-1807 m Peggy Smith Ens MA
Ezekiel: b 1760 d 1-19-1855 m Hannah Fitch Pvt MA ★
Ezra, Sr.: b 3-26-1721 d 12-2-1802/3 m Sarah Morse CS MA
Ezra, Jr.: b 5-28-1758 d 12-16-1843 m Parmelia Hubbell Pvt MA ★
Griffin: b c. 1750-2 d p. 5-25-1813 m (2)Mrs Catherine Schooler PS
    VA
Jared: b 1-27-1762 d 8-12-1817 m (1)Esther Merrill (2)Mary
    (Rogers) Halstead Pvt MA
Joab: b 3-17-1756 d 2-23-1821 m (2)Mary Balch Sgt MA
Jonas: b 10-11-1730 d p. 10-7-1787 m Sarah White Pvt MA
Josiah: b 12-20-1756 d 8-3-1842 m (1)Lydia Belden (2)Olive
    Merrills Pvt MA ★
Moses: b 4-16-1737 d 11-5-1832 m Patience Carpenter Drm Sgt
    MA
Moses: b 2-21-1761 d 10-19-1826 m Anne Davis Pvt MA
Oliver: b 7-29-1737 d 11-8-1822 m Hannah Fisher Capt MA
Paul: b 5-17-1760 d 3-11-1843 m (1)Calley Dexter (2)Mehitable
    Jones Pvt MA
Phineas: b 5-9-1758 d 4- -1846 m Rhoda Wood Pvt MA ★

Robert: b 12-29-1755 d 10-19-1839 m Olive Richardson Pvt MA
Samuel: b 3-2-1742 d 4-12-1808 m Esther Blake MM MA
Samuel: b 6-22-1729 d 4-24-1806 m Hannah Johnson CS MA
Samuel: b 1752 d 8- -1777 m Elizabeth (Sanford) Gibbs Pvt NY
Silas: b 1759 d 11-20-1827 m Lucinda Lee Pvt MA
Simeon: b 2-21-1734/5 d 4- -1825 m (1)Esther or Sarah White
    (2)Ann Hall (3)Mary Harmon Pvt MA
Timothy: b 1731 d 5-22-1801 m (1)Mary Munson (2)Sarah
    Bartholomew Pvt CT
Timothy: b 8-13-1737 d 10-27-1776 m Sarah Cutler Sgt MA
Wm.: b 9-13-1763 d 7-5-1838 m Ruth Wood Pvt MA ★
Zebulon: b 12-5-1765 d p. 1840 m Lucretia Ware Pvt VT ★

PONDER, (includes PANDER & PENDER)

Amos: b 176- d 2-2-1802 m Violet Luckey Pvt SC W★
James: b c. 1750 d 1826 m Rebecca Robins Cmsry Wgm SC
John: b 4-6-1740 d 3-5-1818 m Nancy White PS NC
Joseph: b 1721 d 11-22-1813 m (1)Mrs Bridgers (2)Patience Cobb
    (3)Cecelia Owens Pvt NC
Thomas: b 1757 d 1-14-1833 m (1)— (2)Mrs Ann Atherton Pvt MD
Thomas: b 3-22-1765 d 2-13-1837 m Nancy Henson Sgt NC ★

PONSLER,

Louis: b c. 2-19-1753 d p. 10-30-1779 m Tamar Evans Lt PA

PONTIUS, (includes PONTIOUS)

Henry: b 2-25-1744 d 9-13-1822 m Anna Catharine Wolfe 1Lt PA
John, Sr.: b c. 1718 d p. 1801 m Anna Catherine Zeller CS PA
John, Jr.: b 8-16-1751 d 10-5-1836 m Barbara Catterman Pvt PA
Nicholas: b 10-23-1749 d 1-28-1831 m Maria Appolonia Wilhelm
    Lt PA
Peter: b 10-22-1747 d 3-17-1835 m Catherine — Pvt PA

PONTON,

Joel: b — d p. 6-22-1826 m Hannah — Pvt VA

POOLE, (includes POOL)

Abijah: b 3-26-1753 d 5-9-1830 m Sarah Tirrill Pvt MA
Benjamin: b 1725 d 1796 m Lois Rand Pvt MA
Dudley: b 8-4-1753 d 2-17-1826 m Elizabeth Hyde Pvt GA
Eleazer Flagg, Sr.: b 5-24-1734 d 3-17-1776 m Mary Carter Lt MA
Eleazer Flagg, Jr.: b 1-19-1761 d 1812 m Mary Reed Pvt MA
George: b 2-21-1735 d 5-6-1812 m Mary Herbert Lt NJ
Henry: b c. 1753 d p. 7-10-1813 m Elizabeth Mercer PS MD
Henry: b c. 1765 d 6-25-1852 m (1)Susan Ratlett (2)Mrs Polly
    Wilson (3)Elender Hutchinson Pvt SC
Isaac: b 11-13-1717 d p. 1790 m Sarah Leonard Pvt MA
Isaac: b 4-3-1739 d p. 1790 m Olive Cleaveland Pvt MA
Jacob: b 3-11-1740 d 2-11-1834 m Rachel Beal Capt MA
James: b 1757 d 6-3-1828 m Marcy — Arfr MA
James: b 4-5-1746 d 7-29-1839 m Ursula — Pvt VA ★
Jeptha: b 8-15-1756 d 3-8-1839 m Olive (Whitmarsh) Noyes Cpl
    MA ★
Jeremiah: b 6-8-1750 d 10-19-1818 m Joanna — Wgn NJ
John: b 3-26-1734 d p. 10- -1776 m Zeruiah Sibley CS CT
John, Sr.: b 1733 d 1816 m Sarah Collier PS MD
John: b 1754 d 1828 m Hanna Price Pvt MA
John: b c. 1745 d 3-3-1837 m Jerusha Cade Pvt NJ ★
John: b 1748 d p. 1777 m Barbara Rothermel Pvt PA
John: b 1760 d 1840 m Mahulda Hollaway Pvt SC ★
John E.: b 1- -1761 d 1843 m Sarah Ann Porter PS PA
Jonathan, Sr.: b 1-14-1720 d 9-11-1799 m Mary Leaman Pvt MA
Jonathan, Jr.: b 4-21-1747 d 4-25-1807 m Anne Bancroft Pvt MA
Jonathan: b 9-5-1758 d 7-25-1797 m Elizabeth Hale SrgnMte NH
Joseph: bpt 2-11-1738/9 d 3-25-1823 m Mary Pilsbury Pvt MA
Joseph: b 9-9-1741 d 7-2-1801 m Mehetable Jackson Capt MA
Joshua, Sr.: b 7-15-1734 d 1822 m (1)Mary Burrell (2)Mary Reed
    Pvt MA
Joshua, Jr.: b 12-18-1761 d 8-23-1844 m Lucinda Latham Pvt MA
Mark: b 10-9-1739 d 2-11-1815 m (1)Deborah Tarr (2)Anna
    Jackson Capt MA
Oliver: b 6-16-1748 d 12-25-1813 m Sarah Ramsdell Cpl MA
Peter: b 1758 d 1827 m— Pvt MA ★
Richard: b 10-14-1760 d 2-14-1830 m Elizabeth — Ens NJ
Samuel, Sr.: b 9-18-1713 d 4-28-1795 m Rebecca Shaw Pvt MA
Samuel, Jr.: b 8-27-1736 d 1-18-1831 m Ruth Fullerton 2Lt MA
Samuel: b 1762 d 9- -1853 m Mary Phillips Pvt MA
Samuel: b c. 1760 d p. 10-10-1829 m Nancy Ann Simmons Pvt NC
Thomas: b 10-28-1747 d p. 1790 m Catherine Gardner Pvt MA
Wm.: b 1726 d 10-27-1795 m Hannah Nichols Pvt NH
Wm.: b 1748 d 1820 m Clarkey Morris PS NC
Wm.: b 2-25-1759 d 2-27-1854 m Lois Moore Pvt VT
Wm. P.: b c. 1732 d a. 3- -1813 m Sarah Tynes Ens. VA
Wm. Petty: b 9-12-1755 d 6-10-1848 m Annie Street Pvt NC
Zeginus: b 2-19-1760 d p. 1808 m Rane Lee Pvt MA

POOLER,

George: b 2-21-1757 d p. 1836 m Abigail Stewart Pvt MA ★

POOR, (includes POORE)

Abraham: b 2-23-1742 d 5-2-1819 m Elizabeth Barker Lt MA

Andrew: b 11-30-1740 d 2-28-1814 m (1)Esther Snaw (2)Elizabeth Perley (3)Rebecca Hawe Pvt MA
Benjamin, Sr.: b 3-5-1728 d 1823 m Phoebe Varnum Lt MA
Benjamin, Jr.: b 9-16-1760 d 8-30-1812 m Joanna Batchelder Pvt MA
Daniel: b 1740 d 6-20-1814 m ( )Mary Farnum ( )Hannah Frye Lt MA
Daniel: b 3-13-1716 d 1-9-1792 m (1)Anna Merrill (2)Lydia Bradley PS NH
David: b 1737 d 12-19-1816 m (1)Jane Martin (2)Ellen Mathews Lt MA
David: b 3-18-1748 d 4-20-1817 m Abigail Carleton Cpl MA
David: b 7-24-1745 d 3-20-1834 m Phebe Carlton Lt MA
Eliphalet: b 3-18-1746 d 10-19-1827 m Elizabeth Little Pvt NH
Enoch: b 6-21-1736 d 9-9-1780 m Martha Osgood BGen NH
Jeremiah: b 10-31-1747 d 8-3-1811 m Mary Hasseltine Capt NH
John: b 3-22-1760 d 11-27-1817 m Jane Stratton Pvt VA ★
Jonathan: b 1-20-1737 d 3-19-1807 m Sarah Dole Capt MA
Joseph: b 8-24-1737 d 2-18-1795 m Margaret Boynton Bailey Capt MA
Joseph: b 11-7-1748 d 3-26-1815 m Mary Abbott Pvt MA
Joseph: b 1-17-1758 d 8-1-1782 m Elizabeth Stickney Smn MA
Paul: b 2-24-1762 d 1-9-1837 m Ruth Noyes Pvt MA
Peter: b 7-9-1726 d 12- -1802 m (1)Sara Wood (2)Elizabeth Fry Lt MA
Robert: b 6-18-1763 d 4-3-1801 m Elizabeth Mims Cnt VA
Robert: b c. 1735 d p. 7-10-1791 m Judith Walker PS VA
Samuel: b 12-13-1758 d 8-21-1841 m Anna Bridges Sgt MA ★
Stephen: b 5-24-1744 d 4-18-1823 m Hannah S Dole Pvt MA
Thomas: b 7-19-1732 d 9-24-1804 m Phoebe Osgood Col MA
Thomas: b 1721 d 1788 m Elizabeth Moseley Pvt VA
Timothy: b 1722 d 1-5-1784 m Mary Stevens Cpl MA
Wm.: b 9-15-1750 d p. 1781 m Mary Sampson Capt VA

POORMAN, (includes PURMAN)
Daniel: b 8-31-1744 d 4-18-1825 m Barbara Hufford Pvt PA
Jacob: b 1-7-1742 d 1-10-1784 m Maria Werner Pvt PA
John: b c. 1755 d p. 1794 m Elizabeth Croxon Pvt PA

POPE,
Ansel: b 1751 d p. 1790 m Ann Guile Sol CT
Barnaby: b c. 1728 d p. 1795 m Elizabeth Norman PS SC
Benjamin: b 1740 d 6-12-1816 m Behetherton Foote Ens VA
Burwell: b 1751 d 1-9-1800 m Priscilla Wooten PS NC
Charles: b 1748 d 1803 m Jane Stokesby Capt DE
Christopher: b 12-28-1753 d 11-22-1834 m Mary Ladeau MM Pvt NJ ★
David: b 3-13-1746 d 6-25-1822 m — Clark Pvt MA
Ebenezer: bpt 6-9-1734 d 11-4-1802 m Sarah (Pope) Slr MA
Edward: b 2-15-1739 d 6-10-1818 m (1)Elizabeth Ballard (2)Elizabeth (Greenleaf) Elliot Col MA
Eleazer: b 11-14-1736 d 6-8-1795 m Nannie Ann Putnam Pvt MA
Elijah: b c. 1760 d a. 5- -1798 m Upham — Cav NC
Folger: b 2-14-1756 d 11-7-1828 m Theodate Holder PS MA
Frederick: b 5-15-1735 d 8-20-1812 m Mary Cole LCol MA
Gershom: b 8-22-1743 d 3-22-1810 m Hannah Smith Pvt CT
Henry: b 1-1-1748 d p. 1778 m Charity Hinton Capt NC
Henry: b 5-10-1746 d 9-29-1807 m Delilah Williams Sol NC
Henry: b 8-18-1759 d 10-3-1815 m Elizabeth — Pvt VA
Henry Augustine: b 6-8-1760 d 8-12-1807 m (1)Clara Hill (2)Mary Davis Pvt GA
Humphrey: b c. 1744 d 1815 m (2)Mary Pasquette Pvt VA
Isaac: b 7-3-1744 d 6-21-1820 m Olive Hovey Maj MA
Jeremiah: b 10-17-1749 d 1-11-1813 m Mary VanEmburgh Pvt NJ ★
Jesse: b c. 1730 d p. 12-17-1818 m Mary Fort Sol NC
John: b 1750-6 d c. 1821 m Elizabeth Smith Capt GA
John: b 4-24-1727 d 1781 m Sarah Athearn Sol PS MA
John: b 1757 d 1820 m Ruth Newhall Smn MA
John: b 5-7-1749 d 8-13-1802 m Margaret Hunter Col VA
John: b c. 1761 d p. 1788 m Jane Spears Sol VA
Joseph: b 1761 d a. 1-19-1829 m Sarah Burt Pvt VA
Lawerence: b 1740 d 7-31-1810 m (1)Jane Quisenberry (2)Frances Carter (3)Mrs Penelope (Quisenberry) Vigar PS VA
Lewis: b — d p. 9-20-1803 m Jemima — Sol GA
Louin: b 5-8-1737 d 8-13-1799 m Mary West Capt MA
Nathaniel: b 7-3-1747 d 7-17-1819 m Mary Barstow Lt MA
Nathaniel, Sr.: b 1729 d 11-21-1806 m Lucy S. Fox PS CS VA
Nathaniel, Jr.: b 1761 d 3-13-1809 m Mary Duval Sol VA
Ralph: b 1759 d 4-4-1797 m Abigail Swan Cpl MA
Samuel Ward: b 2- -1763 d 4- -1797 m Mary Wood Pvt MA
Seth: b 3-4-1720 d 6-9-1802 m Abigail Church Col MA
Seth: b 1731 d 1779 m Martha Bacon Pvt MA
Solomon: b 1740 d 10-21-1794 m Susannah Dawkins Capt SC
Thomas: b 4-25-1758 d 7-1-1843 m Huldah Edson Pvt MA ★
Thomas: b c. 1721 d 11-12-1806 m Hannah Austin Pvt PS NH
Thomas: b c. 1745 d 1821 m Ann Duncan Mrnr VA
Thomas: b 11-22-1753 d 5- -1834 m Christiana Johnson Pvt VA
Wm.: b c. 1730 d p. 1-25-1818 m — Sol NC
Wm.: b 1763 d 1823 m Sarah Greene Sol SC
Wm.: b 1745 d 1825 m Penelope Edwards LCol VA
Wm.: b 7-2-1765 d 5-10-1831 m Susan Hardin Lt VA

Willis: b 1754 d 12-23-1795 m Mary — 2Lt NC
Wylie: b 1758 d p. 5-24-1819 m Polly Hill Pvt GA

POPHAM,
Wm.: b 9-19-1752 d 9-27-1847 m Mary Morris ADC Maj DE

POPPINO, (includes POPINO)
John: b 4-27-1726 d 3-7-1828 m Elizabeth Wood Maj NY
Peter: b c. 1750 d 1791 m Elizabeth Martin Pvt VA

POPPLETON,
Samuel: b 12-25-1751 d 11-9-1832 m Caroline Osborn Ens MM VT W★

PORCH,
Henry: b 1758 d 4-3-1849 m Rebecca P Denton Pvt VA ★

PORCHER,
Peter: b 1753 d a. 5-12-1818 m Elizabeth Yonge Wilkinson Pvt SC
Samuel: b c. 1730 d a. 1790 m (1)Martha Gignilliat (2)Mary Sanders CS SC

PORT,
Thomas: b 4- -1713/4 d c. 1780 m Frances — Capt PS SC

PORTER,
Aaron: b 1729 d 1820 m Rhoda Sage Capt CT
Aaron: b 10-24-1757 d 12-3-1848 m Eunice Hathorne Cpl MA ★
Abijah: b 1760 d 1845 m Hannah Deming Fif CT
Abner: b 6-25-1743 d p. 4-20-1814 m Hannah Ingram Lt VA
Adam: b 1750 d 1820 m Ann Tevis PS MD
Alexander: b 12-14-1757 d 4-24-1833 m Zerviah Phelps Pvt CT ★
Alexander: b 10- -1745 d 4-29-1829 m Elizabeth Steadman Pvt PS SC
Amos: b 11-24-1742 d 1807 m Anna Bradstreet Pvt MA
Andrew: b 9-24-1743 d 11-16-1813 m (1)Elizabeth McDowell (2)Elizabeth Parker Col PA
Andrew: b 1734 d 1821 m Jane Ewing Col VA
Asa: b 11-3-1756 d 12-1-1852 m Eunice Williams Sgt MA
Benjamin: b 12-11-1730 d 10-19-1806 m (1)Elizabeth Phillips (2)Mrs Elizabeth (House) Webster Pvt CT
Benjamin: b 1717 d 6-13-1794 m (1)Eunice Nurse (2)Abigail Osborn Sgt MA
Benjamin: b 3-12-1726 d 1810-11 m Mrs Sarah Rae Brown Pvt MA
Benjamin: b 3-9-1739 d 3-28-1817 m Rebecca Tisdale Pvt MA
Benjamin: b 9-29-1754 d 1837 m (1)Polly Sargent (2)Pamelia Barton Pvt MA
Benjamin Jones: b 9-20-1763 d 8-18-1847 m Elizabeth Lydden King SrgnMte MA
Billy Jones: b 8-23-1739 d 11-20-1813 m Mary Woodbury Jones Maj MA
Chandler: b 9-20-1759 d 3-18-1795 m Jerusha Downer Pvt NH
David: b 5-27-1761 d 1-7-1851 m Sarah Collins Pvt CT
David: b 7-5-1757 d 8-27-1815 m Sarah Nimms Pvt MA
David: b 4-6-1754 d 6-24-1808 m Rebecca Henry SeaCap
David: b 1736 d 1810 m (2)Nancy Longwell Pvt VA
Dudley: b 3-13-1753 d 4-7-1841 m (1)Sarah Hay (2)— Hamilton Pvt MA ★
Ebbin: b c. 1748 d a. 1800 m Hannah — Pvt VA
Ebenezer: b 7-16-1732 d 2-24-1827 m Lydia Cummings Pvt MA
Eleazer: b 3-8-1752 d 7-5-1833 m Susannah Rowley Pvt CT ★
Eleazar: b 1-27-1728 d 5-27-1797 m (1)Anne Pitkin (2)Susanna Edwards Maj CS MA
Eli: b c. 1760 d 11-4-1848 m (1)Mrs Nancy Turner Clark (2)— Schley (3)Mary — Pvt VA
Elijah: b 12-4-1757 d p. 1821 m (1)Aurelia Smith (2)Elizabeth Dewey Mus CT ★
Eliot: b 3-31-1757 d p. 1804 m Amelia Wright Pvt VT
Elisha: b 1-29-1742 d 5-29-1796 m Sarah Phillips Jewett Col MA
Elkana: b 7-26-1737 d 1811 m (1)Hepzibeh Allen (2)Anna Talcott Pvt CT
Ezekiel: b 11-10-1762 d p. 1807 m Elizabeth Wyman Cpl MA
Ezekiel: b 10-25-1762 d 7-16-1840 m Elizabeth Horton Pvt CT ★
Ezekiel: b 3-8-1761 d 9-23-1823 m Eunice Grant Pomeroy Pvt MA
Felix: b 1757 d 1830 m Hannah — Pvt NY
Francis: b 9-22-1748 d 3-7-1815 m (1)Martha Gott (2)Priscilla Hall Pvt MA
George: b 1-28-1759 d 7-11-1844 m (1)Experience Hodges (2)Susannah Gray Pvt MA ★
Gideon: b 1721 d 3-23-1805 m Huldah Hart Sol CT
Hezekiah: b 9-9-1735 d p. 1790 m Sarah Carver Pvt CT
Hezekiah: b 11-11-1720 d — m Hannah Hastings Pvt MA
Hugh: b — d 1782 m Elizabeth — Pvt PS SC
Hugh: b 2-7-1715 d 9-5-1795 m Violet Mackey Sol SC
Increase, Sr.: b 2-18-1722 d 6-8-1788 m (1)Mary Niles (2)Abigail Kellogg Pvt CT
Isaac: b 4-27-1755 d 9-27-1839 m Hepzibah North Drm Pvt CT
Isaac: b 7-1-1750 d 3-21-1837 m Mary Kimball Cpl MM MA
Isaac: b — d 1823 m Sarah Hall Pvt MA
Jacob: b 7-23-1737 d 1820 m Rachel Reed Sgt MA
James: b 11-19-1737 d 11-10-1822 m (1)Lucy Bronson (2)Mary Gambel Ens CT

PORTER, contd.

James: b 9-19-1714 d 4-25-1792 m (1)Hannah Wait (2)Eunice Belding PS MA
James: b 4-21-1728 d 1781-85 m Elizabeth — PS NH
James: b 2-4-1742 d 1817 m Mary Traphagen Capt NJ
James: b — d 6- -1786 m Mary — Col PA
James: b 7-16-1741 d 10-12-1793 m Martha Graemes Pvt SC
Joel: b 6-16-1755 d 9-8-1824 m Levina Woods Pvt MA
John: b 1744 d 1791 m Jerusha King Capt CT
John: b 4-30-1723 d 1-5-1783 m Lydia Tarbox MM CT
John: b 3-3-1735/6 d 5-3-1804 m Mary Barnes Pvt CT
John: b c. 1740 d p. 1790 m Susannah — Pvt CT
John: b 1-5-1758 d 3-22-1827 m Hannah Pitkin Pvt CT
John: b 1753 d — m Lydia Kinnamon Pvt MD
John: b 3-29-1741 d 3-16-1834 m Mary Bacon Lt MA ★
John, Sr.: b 7-9-1717 d 3-12-1802 m Mary Kimball Sgt MA
John, Jr.: b 4-18-1742 d 4-23-1834 m Lydia Baker Maj MA ★
John: b 6-24-1740 d 12-13-1823 m Deborah Shaw Pvt MA
John: b 5-11-1754 d 1-27-1838 m Mehitable Flower Pvt MA ★
John, Jr.: b a. 1760 d 1820 m Jane Stuart Pvt NY
John: b c. 1750 d 1785 m Hannah Hamilton Sol NC
John: b 1738 d 1796 m Elizabeth — PS NC
John: b 1737 d 1810 m Ann Mackenzie Sol PA
John: b 1-7-1756 d 5- -1822 m Elizabeth Hosack Sol PA
John: b 1758 d 1840 m Eleanor Kearney Pvt PA
John: b — d 1-8-1815 m (1)Alice Richardson (2)Mary Cox Gnr SC
John: b c. 1755 d p. 1803 m Zilpah Graves Pvt VT
John: b 4-19-1759 d 11-23-1842 m Martha Hutcheson Pvt VA
John, Sr.: b 1715 d 1781 m (1)Mary Anthony (2)Mrs Ann Carson PS VA
John, Jr.: b 1759 d 9-24-1833 m (1)Sally Clark (2)Mrs Roseman Bradley OrdlSgt VA W ★
John: b 10-25-1757 d 1823 m Elizabeth Pendleton Sol VA
John: b 1759 d 11-13-1798 m Jane Smith Pvt VA
Jonathan: b 9-27-1738 d 5-2-1799 m Sarah Brown Pvt CT
Jonathan, Jr.: b 11-24-1748 d 3-25-1825 m Mercy Foote Pvt CT
Jonathan, Sr.: b 3-20-1713 d 3-21-1790 m Sarah Ladd PS CT
Jonathan, Jr.: b 9-17-1737 d 1-19-1819 m (1)Lois Richardson (2)Lydia Williams (Abell) CS PS CT
Jonathan: b 9-28-1746 d 1829 m Hannah Burrill Cpl MA
Jonathan: b 9- -1732 d 6-11-1791 m Mercy Redding Pvt MA
Jonathan: b 4-16-1752 d 4-25-1833 m Ruth Chapin Pvt MA
Joseph: b 1742 d 3- -1776 m Naomi Stoten Cpl CT
Joseph: b 8-17-1732 d 9-27-1824 m Hannah Ripley Sgt MA
Joseph: b 2-27-1729/30 d 7-15-1803 m Elizabeth Burrill Cpl MA
Joseph: b 9-22-1715 d 3-8-1797 m Ruth Towne Pvt MA
Joseph: b c. 1760 d a. 1838 m Martha Noble Pvt PA
Joshua: b 6-26-1730 d 4-2-1825 m (1)Abigail Buel (2)Jerusha Burr (3)Lucy Ashley Col Dr CT
Joshua: b c. 1733 d 4-26-1777 m Elizabeth — Pvt CT
Joshua: b 1742 d 1811 m Rosanna Shipley 1Lt MD
Josiah: b 1759 d 11-18-1798 m Mercy Brown Sol MA
Josiah: b 1-31-1756 d 12-17-1814 m Rachel Gill Pvt SC VA
Landlot: b 2-2-1750 d 1-3-1791 m Winnie Suth Sol SC
Mehitable Hine: d 8-6-1739 d 6-1-1837 m Thomas Porter PS CT
Micah: b 3-21-1742 d 7-7-1811 m Mary Stockbridge Pvt MA
Mitchell: b 4-7-1759 d 4-3-1836 m Penelope West Pvt VA
Moses: b 9-30-1738 d 2-17-1803 m Sarah (Kilham) Part 2Lt CT
Moses: b 7-9-1759 d 5-8-1840 m (1)Mercy Deming (2)Euzubia Perkins Pvt CT★
Moses: b 1-18-1750 d 4-10-1832 m Ann Kay Ens NH
Nathan: b 4-4-1760 d 10-1-1837 m Nancy Adams Pvt MA
Nathaniel: b 1-29-1762 d 9-13-1817 m (1)Anna Dodge (2)Mary Cleves Pvt MA
Nathaniel: b 3- -1762 d 3- -1842 m Sarah F Porter Pvt MA
Nathaniel, Sr.: b c. 8-16-1709 d 11-4-1779 m Elizabeth Storrs PS NH
Nathaniel: b 1-3-1745 d 11-20-1836 m Sarah Stillson Chp NH
Nathaniel: b 1737 d 1818 m Eleanor Gardner LCol PA
Nehemiah: b 11-22-1720 d 2-29-1820 m (1)Rebecca Chipman (2)Elizabeth Raymond Chp MA
Nehemiah, Sr.: b 7-2-1728 d 1780-93 m Sarah Waters PS NH
Nehemiah, Jr.: b 12-14-1756 d 2-20-1846 m Joanna Barbour Pvt NH
Noah: b 1732 d 1-6-1818 m Mary Lewis Lt CT
Noah: b 10-6-1742 d 7-10-1794 m Submit Cook Pvt CT
Noah: b 5-6-1734 d 7-2-1825 m Lois Powers Pvt NH
Oliver: b 10-14-1763 d 8-29-1838 m Margaret Watson Sol VA
Patrick: b c. 1730 d p. 1795 m — PS CS Sol VA
Peter: b 1736 d 3-23-1799 m Abigail Bingham Capt MA
Phillip: b 7-1-1754 d 1852 m Mary Smith Sct Spy MM SC
Phineas: b 12-1-1739 d 3-9-1804 m (1)Esther Clark (2)Miliscent (Baldwin) Lewis Col CT
Reese: b 2-26-1744 d 2-15-1821 m Jane Brown Sol PS NC
Robert: b 1738 d 3-16-1810 m Susannah Buck 1Lt MD
Robert, Jr.: b 6-16-1730 d c. 1800 m Susannah Mercer Capt MD
Robert: b 1739 d 1825 m Susan — Col PA
Robert: b 1-10-1768 d 6-23-1842 m Sarah Williams 1Lt PA
Robert: b 1750 d 1825 m Elizabeth (Watson) Reed Sgt PA ★
Robert: b — d — m Elizabeth E Porter Pvt PA
Robert: b c. 1740 d 1781 m Margaret Ewing Sol VA
Samuel: b 6-14-1750 d 1-28-1838 m (1)Mindwell Griswold (2)Mrs Elizabeth Percival QM CT ★

Samuel: b 10-7-1755 d 8-1-1837 m (2)Lucy Bronson Drm Pvt CT ★
Samuel: b 12-22-1723 d 1-8-1793 m Mary Upson CS PS CT
Samuel: b 5-8-1746 d 5- -1833 m Martha Perley Lt MA
Samuel: b 7-29-1745 d p. 1783 m Sarah Church Sgt MA
Samuel: b 4-18-1750 d 1-22-1822 m (1)Lucy Edwards (2)Prudence Parsons Pvt MA
Samuel: b 5-8-1757 d 8-3-1836 m Miriam Fuller Pvt MA ★
Samuel: b a. 1732 d 10- -1807 m Eve — Pvt VA
Samuel: b c. 1735 d p. 1783 m Elizabeth Duncan Pvt VA
Seth: b 11-24-1752 d 11-25-1834 m (1)Mary Cobb (2)Lois Shaw (3)Elizabeth Leonard Pvt MA
Simeon: b 11-26-1751 d 8-27-1838 m Sarah Patterson Sgt CT
Thomas: b 2-14-1734 d 5-30-1833 m Abigail Howe Capt PS CT
Thomas: b 5-9-1736 d 1-31-1817 m Mehitable Hine PS CT
Thomas: b 9-16-1723 d 1807 m Anne Woodward Pvt PA NH
Thomas: b 1740 d 1795 m — Col PS PA
Thomas: b 1735 d 1791 m Elizabeth DuToy Capt VA
Thomas: b 1734 d 1799 m Sarah Weaver Capt VA
Thomas: b 1755 d 1818 m Polly Mills Capt VA
Thomas: b 11- -1731 d 9-19-1817 m Ann Shropshire Sol VA
Truman: b 7-21-1756 d 6-10-1847 m Deborah Roe Pvt CT
Truman: b 9-8-1763 d 9-27-1838 m Sarah Thompson Pvt CT
Tyler: b 1-23-1735 d 6-27-1811 m Dorcus Emerson Pvt MA
Wm., Sr.: b 10-13-1728 d 1778 m Esther Carpenter Pvt CT
Wm., Jr.: b 11-7-1760 d 3-3-1847 m (1)Phebe Kingsbury (3)Hannah Wright Pvt CT ★
Wm.: b c. 1750 d 2-10-1843 m Deborah Ainsworth Pvt NH ★
Wm.: b 1729 d 1802 m Sarah Pierce Capt PA
Wm.: b 1760 d 8-31-1844 m Mary Moore Ens PA
Wm.: b 10-20-1752 d 4-17-1821 m — Pvt PA
Wm.: b 9-4-1749 d 11-9-1813 m Mary Hodges Pvt VT
Wm.: b 6-15-1739 d 2-7-1824 m (1)Martha Ross (2)Jane (Clark) Coulson 2Lt CS PA
Wm.: b 1746 d 7-8-1828 m Susan A Carson 1Lt VA
Wm.: b c. 1750 d 6-20-1807 m Elizabeth Luke Lt VA W★
Wm.: b 1754 d p. 8-3-1806 m Mary Sandy 1Lt VA
Wm.: b c. 1740 d 1804 m Mary Bowen Sol VA

PORTERFIELD,

John: b 1724 d 1786 m (2)Sarah Cunningham Sgt PA
Josiah: b 1737 d 1828 m Jean McDowell Pvt PA
Robert: b 2-22-1752 d 2-13-1843 m Rebecca Farrar CaptLt ADC VA
Samuel: b 1753 d p. 1799 m Nancy MacGuffen Pvt Cav VA
Samuel: b 1726 d 1789 m — Pvt PA
Wm.: b c. 1715 d 1821 m Martha Alexander Pvt VA

PORTLOCK,

John: b 7-7-1765 d 1-30-1849 m Sarah — Pvt VA ★

PORTMAN,

John: b 1750 d 11-12-1833 m Catherine Gudbling Pvt PA ★
John: b 1758 d 1-30-1857 m Mary Cobb Cav SC

PORTWOOD,

Page, Jr.: b 1758 d 1- -1847 m Sarah — Sgt VA

POSEY,

Belain: b 5-22-1737 d 6-5-1791 m Margaret Corry Capt MD W★
Benjamin Lane: b c. 1749 d p. 1790 m Mary Musgrove Pvt MD
Macajah: b c. 1742 d 3-30-1828 m Rachel Peck Maj PA
Richard, Sr.: b 1734 d 1820 m Elizabeth Wade Mil SC
Thomas: b 7-9-1750 d 3-18-1818 m (1)Martha Matthews (2)Mary (Alexander) Thornton LCol VA
Zephaniah: b 12- -1758 d 1-21-1826 m Mary Jackson Sgt VA ★ʲ

POST,

Aaron: b 10-9-1760 d 11-9-1827 m Elizabeth Maltby Cpl NH
Abraham: b 10-13-1736 d 3-30-1825 m (1)Lydia Palmer (2)Esther — Ens CT
Abraham: b 10-11-1741 d 2-11-1836 m (1)Catherine DeMott (2)Mrs Simon Kinney Lt NJ
Abraham: b 10-2-1708 d p. 11- -1790 m (1)Marietje Schut (2)Anneke Schoonmaker PS NY
Abraham A.: b 12-26-1756 d 1805 m Dosia Schoonmaker Pvt NY
Adrian: b 5-23-1756 d p. 9-13-1825 m Lybetje VanRypen Sol NJ
Adrian: b 2-24-1756 d p. 8-12-1823 m Maria Berdan PS NJ
Anthony: b 3-19-1745 d 5-29-1832 m Petronella Brower Capt NY ★
Cornelius: b 1736 d 2-12-1812 m (1)Marritje Cadmus (2)Anna Maria Kough Sol PS NJ
Cornelius: b 7-5-1755 d c. 1812 m Elizabeth Bikker Sgt PS NY
David: b 1759 d 5-26-1846 m Elizabeth McCollin Pvt NJ ★
Eldad: b 10-5-1733 d 1810 m Hannah Case Pvt MA
George: b c. 1752 d 3-26-1812 m (1)Flora — (2)Esther Lawrence Pvt CT ★
Hendrick: b c. 1740 d — m Margaret Legg PS NY
Hendrick: b 3-30-1749 d 6-17-1830 m Margaret Cock Sgt NJ
Henry, Jr.: b 1740 d c. 1820 m (1)Jannetje Vreeland (2)Esther Dey PS NJ
Henry: b 7-1-1760 d 5-8-1804 m Mersa — Pvt NY
Issac: b 1-3-1742 d p. 1793 m Mary Lawrence Ens NY
Isaac: b 11-26-1760 d 7-31-1812 m Catherine Persen Pvt NY
Isaac: b 1762 d 7-3-1842 m Sarah — Pvt NY

Jacob: b 3-3-1762 d 4-18-1844 m Eunis Genung Pvt NJ ★
Jacob: b c. 1731 d p. 1800 m Rachel Pickney 1 Lt NY
Jacobus: b 6-23-1734 d — m Elizabeth Velie Pvt PS NY
James: b 1741 d 8-13-1813 m Mary Huntting PS NY
Jimmy: b 1760 d a. 3-6-1833 m Tamar Jones Sgt CT ★
John: b 12-25-1726 d 4-10-1809 m (1)Eunice Backus (2)Abigail Leffingwell PS CT
John: b 1759 d 1843 m Catherine Koch Pvt NJ
John: bpt 7-30-1732 d p. 2-11-1783 m Mally Schoonmaker Pvt NY
John: b 12- -1748 d 12-6-1830 m (1)Deborah Conyne (2)Margretta Bellinger Cmsry NY ★
John H.: b 4-10-1760 d 3-7-1847 m Elizabeth Ackerman Pvt NJ ✶
John: b 1758 d p. 1786 m Dorathy Snell Pvt NY
Joseph: b 2-10-1746/7 d 5-28-1828 m Mary Denison Pvt CT
Joseph: b 4-22-1754 d 11-8-1831 m (1)Anna Hoppins (2)Sarah Munson Pvt CT
Joshua: b 5-14-1743 d 6-10-1825 m Anna Jones Cpl CT
Martin: b 1751 d 10- -1815 m Mary Brown PS NY
Oliver: b 10-21-1746 d 3-3-1817 m (2)Experience Submit Hoyt Pvt MA
Peter: b 1743 d 1793 m Margaret Ten Eyck Cpl NJ
Peter: b 7-17-1743 d 3-12-1787 m Deborah Schoonmaker Lt NY
Phineas, Jr.: b 1-3-1743 d 10-15-1814 m Sybil Barber Pvt CT
Reuben: b 10-25-1759 d 8-2-1815 m Esther Harmon Sgt VT
Richard: b 7-17-1735 d 8-8-1813 m Hannah Bedle Pvt NY
Roswell, Sr.: b 5-5-1727 d 1-3-1814 m (1)Mehitable Jones (2)Esther Meeker CS Lt VT
Roswell, Jr.: b 5-10-1753 d 5-5-1827 m (2)Martha Mead Sgt Sct VT
Samuel: b 5-24-1761 d 1-1-1837 m Gertrude Schoonmaker Pvt NY ★
Simeon: b 4-19-1753 d 12-11-1841 m Mary Hull Sgt CT
Stephen: b 4-20-1761 d 6-24-1837 m Mercy Leffingwell Pvt CT
Wm.: b 5-3-1735 d 2-11-1839 m Keziah — Lt VT

POSTELL,
Benjamin: b 2-8-1759 d 12-22-1800 m Mary Skirving Lt SC
James: b 1745 d 3-10-1824 m Susannah Perry Col SC
Jehu G.: b c. 1749 d 12-25-1797 m Hannah Coachman Capt SC
John, Sr.: b c. 1720 d 1782 m Mary Moore PS SC

POSTLETHWAITE,
John: b 1737 d 10-6-1802 m (1)Hannah Wright (2)Susannah Irvin Pvt PA
Samuel: b 1-17-1737 d 8-24-1809 m Matilda Rose AsstQM PA

POSTON, (includes POSTEN)
Elias: b 11-14-1747 d p. 7-4-1802 m Rebecca Cheshire Col PS VA
Jacob: b 10-11-1756 d 8-11-1831 m Annie Burson Pvt Wgm PA
Wm.: b 10-6-1760 d p. 11-17-1821 m Sarah Hamill Pvt MD

POTE,
Thomas: b 2-25-1734 d 1816 m Sarah Merrill Pvt MA

POTTER, (includes POTTERF)
Abel: b 3-13-1760 d 3-13-1846 m Margaret Green Pvt RI
Abijah: b 1-23-1760 d 7-17-1842 m Mary Tower Sgt MA ★
Alexander: b 1711 d 4-14-1800 m Jane — Pvt MA
Amos: b 9-10-1725 d 6-18-1779 m Mary Meeker CS NJ
Anthony: b 2-1-1756 d 3-13-1826 m (1)Mary Shute (2)Dolly Goodwin Pvt NH
Anthony: b 7-10-1749 d 2-9-1822 m Mercy Burlingame Capt RI
Benjamin: b 1763 d 6-18-1837 m Rachel Stone Pvt CT ★
Caleb: b 10-30-1725 d a. 2- -1797 m Welthian Holden PS RI
Caleb, Jr.: b 6-10-1749 d p. 1791 m Elizabeth Tripp Pvt RI
Caleb: b 8-19-1749 d p. 1797 m Catherine Nye PS RI
Casper: b 12-19-1759 d 10-4-1836 m (1)Susanna Ridenour (2)Nancy Jane Longnecker Pvt VA MD ★
Christopher: b 2-17-1762 d 6-2-1842 m Elizabeth Baker Pvt RI
Daniel: b 1-31-1760 d 6-16-1828 m (1)Naomi Crissey (2)Martha Sanders Cpl CT ★
Daniel: b 2-15-1758 d 4-21-1842 m Martha Humiston Pvt CT
Daniel: b 3-1-1735 d 12-11-1814 m Hannah Wallis Pvt MA
David: b 6-26-1760 d 5-13-1838 m Elizabeth Vaughan Pvt CT RI ★
David, Jr.: b 5-28-1761 d 3-13-1846 m (1)Obedience Potter (2)Hannah Hoyt Pvt CT ★
David: b 11-27-1745 d 12-10-1805 m (1)Mary Mason (2)Sarah Boyd Col NJ
David: b 3-31-1763 d 5-13-1841 m Pheobe (Potter) Pvt RI★
Ebenezer: b 8-17-1750 d 4-27-1845 m (1)Sarah Harris (2)Abigail Hardy Sgt NH
Eliakim, Sr.: b 1-6-1744/5 d 3-11-1822 m Temperance Dunbar Blaksley Pvt CT
Elijah C.: b 1743 d 1835 m Ruth Brightman Pvt RI
Elizabeth Williams: b 3-9-1728 d 11-11-1811 m Gilbert Potter NDr NY
Ephraim: b 1752 d 7-15-1830 m Susanna Rice Ens MA ★
Ephraim, Jr.: b 9-17-1755 d 1-18-1825 m Elizabeth Eustis Bbd Sgt MA
Ephraim: b 7-14-1760 d 8-8-1832 m Elizabeth Parker Pvt VT
Esek: b 6-8-1748 d 1777 m Rachel Simmons Pvt MA
Ezra: b 1754 d 4-24-1841 m Lydia Wright Pvt CT ★
Ezra: b 11-30-1730 d 11-25-1802 m Zeriah Chapman PS RI

George: b 1751 d 3-27-1826 m Nancy Willson 2Lt RI ★
George, Sr.: b 1-3-1732 d 8-9-1794 m Content Maxson MM RI
George, Jr.: b 2-10-1757 d 10-25-1801 m Mary Stillman Pvt RI
George: b 3-28-1760 d 1-28-1837 m Phoebe Pitcher Pvt RI ★
George: b 12-3-1753 d 1827 m Martha Matteson 1 Lt RI
Gilbert: b 1-8-1725 d 2-14-1786 m Elizabeth Williams LCol NY
Holliman: b 7-3-1755 d — m Sarah Allen Ens RI
Hugh: b 1763 d 10-6-1841 m Mary Bailey Pvt MA ★
Income: b 7-7-1749 d 2-28-1844 m Elizabeth Arnold MM RI
Isaac: b 11-3-1763 d 1-19-1830 m Johanna Jewett Pvt MA
Israel: b 2-2-1738 d 4- -1815 m Mary Dawson Lt CT
Israel: b 12-7-1759 d 6-26-1842 m Lydia Warner Smith Pvt MA
Israel: b 11-28-1763 d 8-17-1847 m Mary Rice Pvt MA
Jacob: b 8-10-1765 d 4-30-1841 m Susanna Clark Pvt NJ ★
James: b 9-26-1736 d 2-10-1804 m Abigail Boerhave Sol CT
James: b 2-22-1734 d 3-22-1815 m Mary Spear Sgt MA
James: b 1729 d 11-27-1789 m (1)Elizabeth Cathcart (2)Mary Patterson Chambers MGen PA
James: b 1-31-1760 d 1-22-1849 m Amy Steers Sgt RI ★
Jared: b 9-25-1742 d 7-11-1810 m Sarah Forbes Dr CT
Jeremiah: b 3-10-1737 d 1-27-1813 m Sarah Matteson Matr RI
Jeremiah: b 1736 d p. 9-7-1832 m Sally Crosby Pvt RI ★
Joel: b 4-11-1727 d 2-8-1778 m Rhoda — Lt CT
Joel: b 1760 d 7-18-1827 m Thankful Stone Drm CT
John: b 5-17-1760 d p. 1832 m (1)Lydia Harrison (2)Hilda Clark Sgt CT
John: b c. 1750 d 8-11-1832 m Elizabeth Witter Pvt CT
John: b 1706 d 3-10-1784 m Esther Lines PS CT
John: b 9-12-1746 d 10-10-1818 m (1)Lydia Cutting (2)Rhoda Burnap PM Capt MA
John: b 4-28-1736 d 2-11-1792 m Sarah Snipe 1 Lt MA
John: b 11-23-1748 d 11-16-1826 m (1)Hepzibath Allison (2)Sarah Plume (3)Rachael (Thompson) Marsh (4)Elizabeth Callahan Capt NJ
John, Sr.: b 1705 d 1805 m Sallie Tidwell Sol NC
John, Sr.: b 1735 d 1799 m Elizabeth — Sol PA
John, Jr.: b 1762 d 1821 m Barbara Dorewood Pvt PA
John: b 11-17-1734 d 3-25-1811 m Eley Ralph Capt RI
John: b 11-11-1747 d 2-14-1825 m Wait Waterman Ens RI
John: b 1-3-1715 d 3-15-1788 m (1)Mary Perry (2)Elizabeth Hazard PS RI
Joseph: b 5-7-1759 d 2-9-1835 m (1)Lois Guernsey (2)Mrs Evans Pvt MA ★
Joseph: b 9-15-1758 d 9-15-1854 m (2)Jemima Skinner Wgm AsstCmsry NJ
Joseph: b 7-31-1735 d p. 1790 m Dinah Gifford Sol NY
Joseph: b 8-12-1757 d p. 1799 m Anne Brown Capt RI
Joseph: b 11-25-1760 d 8-1-1840 m Diadama Brookens OrdlSgt VT ★
Joshua: b 1755 d 2-10-1837 m Lydia Coit Smn CT
Josiah Isaiah: b 7-23-1746 d 7-5-1817 m Elizabeth Barrett Chp NH
Lake: b 8-13-1759 d 6-13-1834 m Lois Royce Pvt CT
Lemuel: b 11-13-1755 d 2-26-1826 m Lydia Barnes Cpl CT ★
Levi: b 1-1-1757 d 10-8-1835 m Sarah Thompson Pvt CT
Lydia Barnes: b — d 8- -1836 m Lemuel Potter PS PA
Lyman: b 3-14-1747/8 d 7-20-1827 m Abigail Paine Chp VT
Matthias: b 12-27-1741 d 8-25-1819 m (1)Mary Day (2)Rhoda — Capt NJ
Medad: b 2-4-1760 d 8-14-1850 m Mehitable Ball Pvt CT ★
Milton: b 3-6-1763 d 7-2-1840 m Esther Cone Ens CT ★
Moses: b 1759 d 8-8-1801 m Rhoda Osborne Pvt NJ
Mowry: b 1748 d 2- -1785 m Lydia Westcott Pvtr RI
Nathan: b 2-4-1757 d 9-6-1831 m Sarah Knight Pvt RI
Nehemiah: b c. 4-13-1739 d 9- -1812 m (1)Eunice Casey (2)Rhode Castel Sgt RI
Nicholas: b 5-28-1759 d 6-26-1847 m Phoebe Wade Pvt RI ★
Noel: b 8-13-1758 d 11-3-1847 m Anna Roberts Ens VT ★
Noel: b 6-4-1761 d 2-27-1846 m Mercy Arnold Pvt VT
Oliver: b c. 1730 d p. 1775 m Mary Colvin Capt VT
Paul: b 12-7-1764 d 12-6-1853 m (2)Penelope Woodmansie Pvt NJ
Restcome: b 8-1-1762 d 6-21-1846 m Lucinda Strong Pvt NJ
Reuben: b 1717 d 3-25-1799 m (1)Mary Mercereau (2)Deborah — Maj NJ
Richard: b 3-17-1743 d 7-5-1828 m Lydia Averill Pvt NH
Robert: b 5-9-1748 d p. 1820 m — Pvt CT ★
Russell: b 7-23-1754 d 2-15-1814 m Rhoda Maxwell Pvt NJ
Samuel: b 1746 d 6-25-1801 m Elizabeth Dunlap Pvt MA
Samuel: b 1757 d 3-6-1846 m Deborah Rocketson Pvt MA ★
Samuel: b c. 1735 d 9- -1777 m Anne — Pvt NC
Samuel, Sr.: b 1727 d 7-11-1802 m Jemima Baldwin Col NJ
Samuel, Jr.: b 1755 d 12-14-1831 m Sarah Parsons Pvt NJ
Samuel: b 1-22-1746 d 6-22-1808 m Eleanor Pease Pvt NY
Samuel: b 1730 d p. 3-10-1810 m— Pvt PA
Samuel: b 5-24-1745 d 10-1-1777 m Lydia Mattison QMSgt NJ
Samuel J.: b 1-29-1753 d 10-29-1804 m Ann Nancy Seager Capt RI
Silas: b 4-17-1751 d 11-22-1839 m Elizabeth Warren OrdlSgt RI ★
Simeon: b 9-20-1765 d 8-1-1856 m Phebe Beach Pvt NY
Simon: b 1750-5 d 1820-30 m (1)Catherine — (2)Elizabeth Keger Pvt PA
Smiton: b 1736 d 2- -1825 m Lucy Moore Lt RI
Solomon: b 7-29-1749 d 5-25-1800 m (1)Jane Leighton (2)Rachel Bartlett Stl MA

POTTER, contd.

Stephen: b 1-12-1739 d 9-18-1810 m Sarah Lindsley Capt CT
Stephen: b 2-8-1759 d 1846 m Sarah Coon Sgt RI ★
Stephen: b 8-14-1727 d 11-29-1796 m Mary Freeborn CS PS RI
Thaddeus: b 1-4-1763 d 3-4-1836 m Sarah Ferris Pvt CT
Thaddeus: b 5-18-1763 d p. 1833 m Anna Kendall Pvt MA ★
Theophilus: b 1759 d 9-14-1814 m Lois Walker PS MA
Thomas: b 1758 d 6-17-1833 m Lurene Fitch Pvt CT
Thomas: b 7-20-1738 d 6- -1793 m Elizabeth Reynolds LCol RI
Thomas: b 3-25-1735 d 11-13-1795 m Esther Sheldon CS RI
Thomas: b 5-4-1746 d 6-2-1831 m Mary Lawton CS RI
Thomas: b 5-26-1746 d 12-14-1824 m Ann Potter PS VA
Wm.: b 9-3-1750 d 12-9-1815 m Sarah Randall Pvt MA
Wm.: b 1754 d 10-5-1814 m Elizabeth Safford Pvt MA
Wm.: b 8-17-1751 d 8-9-1829 m Lucy Allen Pvt ME
Wm.: b 9-24-1724 d p. 1790 m Lydia Arnold Capt RI
Wm.: b 6-15-1753 d 11-29-1838 m (1)Abby Waterman (2)Amy Pitman Lt RI ★
Wm.: b 1-21-1722 d 1814 m Penelope Hazard PS CS RI
Wm.: b 2-23-1738 d 7-11-1798 m (1)Mary Burlingame (2)Mary Steere (3)Deborah Seamans PS RI
Wm.: b 8-5-1749 d 8-10-1825 m Phebe Woodward Pvt VT
Wm.: b 1744 d 3-4-1800 m Alice Wait Pvt VT
Winsor: b 1-15-1749 d 1815 m Damaris Burlingame Sgt RI
Zurial: b 4-8-1740 d 11-18-1796 m Abigail King Pvt RI

POTTINGER, (includes POTTENGER)

Robert: b 9-23-1729 d 11-24-1780 m Elizabeth Willett PS MD
Samuel: b 4-29-1754 d 1-20-1831 m (1)Jane (Gray) (Withrow) Gilkey (2)Jenny (Caldwell) Logan Pvt MD

POTTS, (includes BATZ)

Alexander: b 1757 d 1833 m (1)Martha Barnett (2)Susan Parsons Pvt PA
Andrew: b 1753 d 1825 m — Zilhart Sol MD
David: b 4-4-1741 d 1798 m Mary Aris PS PA
David: b 1751 d 1823 m (1)Elizabeth Luna (2)Martha Tines-Potts Pvt PA
David: b 11- -1756 d c. 4-30-1839 m Permillia Adams Pvt VA ★
Ezekiel: b 1-8-1843 d 1-16-1809 m Elizabeth Mead Pvt VA
George: b 9-4-1734 d 1818 m Veronica Lescher Pvt NY
James: b 1759 d 1830 m — Pvt GA
James: b c. 1740 d p. 1-27-1810 m Sarah Tinon PS NC
James: b 6-17-1752 d 7-28-1822 m Sarah Wessell 2Lt PA
John: b a. 1734 d 1804 m Maria Hoch CMman PA
John: b 6-25-1752/3 d 1-18-1837 m Christina Potzer Pvt PA
John: b 1751 d 10-20-1820 m Susan Hibbens Pvt VA W★
Jonathan: b c. 1753 d p. 7- -1839 m (1)Elizabeth Stevenson (2)Nancy — Capt PS NC
Jonathan: b 4-1-1745 d 10- -1781 m Grace Richardson Dr PS PA
Jonathan: b 7-5-1758 d 2-22-1840 m Sarah Wright Pvt PA
Jonathan: b 1754 d 7-4-1831 m Elizabeth English Sol VA ★
Joseph: b d 1782 m Hannah Dilworth Capt PA
Joshua: b c. 1740 d p. 1790 m Pattie Moore QM NC
Richard: b 7-19-1753 d 11-26-1808 m (1)Elizabeth Hughes (2)Eleanor Murdoch ADC PS MD
Robert: b 1745 d 9-5-1821 m Elizabeth McKeown PS NC
Samuel: b c. 1750 d 1822 m Amy Baylis Pvt NJ
Samuel: b 11-30-1736 d 7-3-1793 m Johanna Holland PS CS Capt PA
Stacy: b 7-20-1731 d 1816 m (1)Esther Pancoast (2)Margaretta Yardley (3)Mrs Mary (Williams) Boyd PS NJ
Stephen: b 4-18-1740 d 1-12-1801 m Jane Jones Pvt PA
Thomas: b 1729 d 7-29-1777 m Elizabeth Lukens CS NJ
Thomas: b 1764 d 1848 m (2)Mrs Sarah (Wicks) Waterbury Pvt NY ★
Thomas: b 5-29-1735 d 3-22-1785 m Anna Nutt Col PS PA
Thomas: b 1-10-1738 d 1-2-1810 m (1)Margaret Thompson (2)Rebecca Smith Capt SC
Wm.: b 10-18-1759 d p. 1800 m (1)— Talman (2)— West Sol NJ
Wm.: b c. 1721 d 7-25-1783 m Amy Borden PS NJ
Wm.: b 1751 d 11-29-1800 m Lydia McKarahan Capt NC
Wm.: b 6-7-1759 d 1- -1837 m (2)Mary — Pvt NC★
Wm.: b c. 1743 d p. 6-19-1810 m Margaret McKeoun PS NC
Zebulon: b 3-24-1746 d 3-17-1801 m Martha Trotter Capt PA

POTWINE,

George: b 12-28-1759 d 2-1-1835 m Abigail Stoughton Pvt CT

POUDER (also PROUDER & PRUDER)

Jacob: b c. 1755 d 1796 m Margaret Boone Ens PA

POULLAIN,

Antoine: b c. 6-16-1745 d a. 1-26-1795 m Sarah Wingfield Dr GA

POULSON,

John: b 1755 d p. 4-9-1799 m Polly Dix Maj PS VA

POULTNEY,

Joseph: b 9-23-1747 d 1795 m Jane — Pvt PA

POUND,

Hezekiah: b 7-3-1761 d 4-23-1839 m Esther Morris Pvt NJ
John: b 1735 d c. 1790 m (1)Rhoda Cox (2)Sarah Martin Sol NJ

POWE,

Thomas: b 1747 d 5-7-1817 m (1)Rachel Allen (2)Rebecca (Ford) Spencer Lt Cmsry SC

POWELL,

Abraham: b 10-20-1754 d 1-3-1817 m Anna Smith Ens VA
Absalom: b 5-19-1752 d 10-14-1834 m Mary Stephens Ens NC ★
Ambrose: b 9-18-1713 d 10-8-1788 m Mary Bledsoe Capt VA
Ambrose: b 1-18-1761 d p. 7-7-1832 m (1)Sally Britt (2)Nancy Cavender Pvt VA ★
Benjamin: b 5-28-1764 d 8-15-1852 m (1)Betsey Bradley (2)Deborah — Pvt Drm NH ★
Benjamin: b c. 1755 d p. 1806 m Elizabeth Robinson Pvt NC
Benjamin: b 4-2-1747 d 6-1-1820 m Hannah Davis Pvt PA
Benjamin: b 11-25-1716 d 3-21-1787 m Mary Bacon Pvt VA
Benjamin: b c. 1730 d p. 2-10-1800 m Joyce Riddell Pvt VA
Cader: b 1750 d 1835 m Frances Foote Sol NC
Cader: b 4-2-1753 d 1-7-1809 m Honoria Douglas CS NC
Calvin: b 5-1-1764 d 12-7-1839 m Speedy Davis Pvt VT
Charles: b 1740 d 1810 m Sarah Gholson Sol VA
Dempsey: b c. 1730 d 1793 m (1)Nancy — (2)Pleasant — Pvt PS NC
Edward, Sr.: b c. 1720 d p. 11-4-1795 m Mary — PS VA
Elias: b 9-26-1754 d 5-5-1832 m Anna Barbara Albright Ens NC
Elijah: b c. 1738 d c. 1797 m (1)Mary — (2)Mary — Pvt MA
Elisha: b 2-1-1755 d 7-24-1835 m Eunice Woodward 2Lt VT ★
Felix: b 1761 d 2-5-1851 m Lenora Hall Pvt CT VT ★
Francis: b 1737 d p. 3-22-1803 m Rebecca — Mid VA
Henry: b 1738 d 11-22-1781 m Mary Kean PS NY
Isaac: b c. 1732 d 11-5-1781 m Anne — Lt NC
Isaac: b 1749 d 1819 m (1)Hannah Bailey (2)Elizabeth Hutton Pvt PA
James: b 1733 d 8- -1790 m Alse — Lt PS NC
James: b c. 1745 d c. 1825 m Nancy Bailey Pvt PA
James: b 1746 d 9- -1777 m Frances Jane Raymond Pvt VA
John: b 2-13-1749 d 10-29-1796 m Elizabeth King Lt MA
John: b 1-7-1750 d 6-7-1826 m Lois Curtis 1Lt MA
John: b 1750 d 4-23-1801 m Mary Whitehurst Cpl NC
John: b c. 1760 d p. 1827 m Hester — Lt SC
John: b c. 1745 d 1796 m (1)Susanna Bell Brown (2)Boice Gee Capt VA
John: b 1749 d p. 1820 m Polly — Pvt VA ★
John: b a. 1756 d 5-25-1791 m Sarah — Pvt VA
John: b 1744 d 1784 m Sarah — PS CS VA
John Thomas: b 1745 d p. 1796 m Elizabeth Diggs Dr VA
Joseph: b 11-4-1754 d p. 1784 m — McCoy Pvt MD
Joseph: b 1760 d 2-14-1835 m (1)Susan Edwards (2)Ruth Jones (3)Hannah Jewson Pvt NC
Joseph: b 3-6-1734 d 8-28-1804 m Rachel Rose Chp PS PA
Joshua: b c. 1720 d 1781 m Mary — Capt VA
Kedor: b c. 1750 d 1786 m Hester Ingram PS NC
Levin: b 7-19-1738 d 7-23-1810 m Sarah Harrison LCol VA
Levin H.: b 1763 d 11-28-1836 m (2)Elizabeth Cohagan Pvt VA ★
Lewis: b 1763 d 7-14-1857 m Rachel Byrd Sol GA
Lewis, Jr.: b 8-1-1750 d p. 1833 m Martha Thompson Pvt NC ★
Lewis, Sr.: b 1738 d 1790 m Rebecca Field PS NC
Lewis, Jr.: b 1762 d 1810 m Catherine McRae Pvt NC
Lucas: b 1722 d 1811 m (1)Elizabeth Edwards (2)Mrs Elizabeth Row Cowper PS VA
Mark: b c. 1760 d 1826 m — Drm PA
Martin: b 1731 d 8-22-1800 m Rhoda — Lt PS VT
Miles: b 1729 d 9-14-1791 m Jemima Atkinson LCol MA
Morgan: b 1723 d 1815 m Sarah Hays Pvt NY
Moses, Sr.: b c. 1725 d p. 1786 m Mary Williams Sol GA
Moses, Jr.: b 1755-60 d p. 8-23-1821 m Sarah — Sol GA
Moses: b c. 1730 d p. 10-14-1799 m — Pvt NC
Nathan: b 11-5-1754 d 5-13-1831 m Sarah Nickels Pvt PA
Nathaniel: b 1762 d 1-8-1827 m Elizabeth (Cowper) Chamberlayne Pvt VA
Peyton: b 2-28-1760 d 6-23-1844 m (1)Tabitha Harris (2)Elizabeth Briscoe (3)Ann H — Lt VA
Philip: b c. 1743 d c. 1-1-1821 m Julia Ann Miller Pvt PA
Ptolemy: b 1766 d 1840 m Mrs Sidney (Daniel) Leavett Pvt VA
Richard: b 1749 d 12-28-1818 m Ann Cheeseman MM NJ
Richard: b c. 1745 d 1815 m Elizabeth Crews 2Lt PS CS VA
Richard: b 1758 d 7-29-1825 m Sarah Scott Pvt VA ★
Robert: b 1753 d 1828 m Ann West Capt VA
Rowland, Sr.: b 6-9-1730/1 d 1801 m Mary Ann Richardson Pvt VT
Rowland, Jr.: b c. 1750 d p. 1790 m Mary Janes Pvt VT
Stephen: b 5-2-1763 d 7-31-1834 m Lurany — Pvt VT CT ★
Stephen: b 1754 d 9-18-1806 m Mary Barge Pvt NY
Stephen: b 1731 d 2- -1812 m Elizabeth Pettitt PS NY
Thomas: b 1751 d 1-13-1813 m (1)Jane Henry (2)Hannah Smith Fif NJ
Thomas: b c. 1730 d 1781 m Lucy — Lt VA
Thomas: b 1745 d 1815 m Mary Anne Ludwell Lt VA
Thomas: b — d 1796/7 m Elizabeth Digges Dr VA
Thomas: b c. 1736 d 1788 m Sally — PS VA
Truman: b 5-8-1759 d 12-1-1852 m Lucretia Smith Sgt VT ★
Wm.: b 1761 d 9-14-1828 m Rhoda Messenger Pvt MA ★
Wm.: b 4-2-1760 d 11-20-1849 m (1)Charity Brewer (2)Catherine — (3)Nancy Peake Church Pvt NY ★
Wm.: b 3-21-1742 d 9-9-1814 m Ursula Hargrove Pvt NC

Wm.: b 10-20-1759 d 1792 m Mariam Lamb Pvt NC
Wm.: b c. 1711 d a. 6-12-1792 m (1)Elizabeth — (2)Nancy
     PS NC
Wm.: b 1757 d 1835 m Elizabeth Stilley Pvt PA
Wm.: b 1754 d 1835 m Amy Stackhouse Pvt PA
Wm.: b — d 8-27-1776 m Mary Thomas Pvt PA
Wm.: b a. 1715 d c. 1788 m Elenor Peyton Cmsry VA
Wm.: b 1755 d p. 1783 m Mary Cowper Ens VA

POWELSON,
John: b 8-7-1757 d c. 1825 m Ann (Voorhees) Nevins Pvt NJ
Minard: b 6- -1762 d 11-11-1789 m Catherine Voorhees Pvt NJ

POWER, (includes PAUER)
Alexander: b 1745 d p. 1810 m Sallie — QM PA
Benjamin: b 1753 d 1-16-1838 m Elizabeth Keyes Pvt MD PA ★
James: b 9-4-1753 d 9-4-1851 m Mary Rowletter Pvt MD
James: b a. 1754 d 4- -1813 m Mary Marshall Capt PA
John: b 1-6-1757 d 7-20-1805 m Margaret Finley 2Lt PA
Joseph: b 3-14-1764 d 6-14-1849 m Sarah Taylor Pvt VA ★
Michael: b c. 1755 d 1805 m Hannah — Pvt PA
Moses: b 1736 d 1832 m Elizabeth Whitman Pvt NY
Samuel: b c. 1750 d 1787 m Grizell Marshall Pvt PA
Thomas: b 4-12-1753 d 3-2-1823 m Hannah Kelly Pvt MA
Thomas: bpt 11-5-1758 d 9-23-1815 m (1)Mrs Miriam (Russell)
     Sawins (2)Sallie Blackler (3)Mrs Ruthy Main (4)Mrs Margaret
     Millet Mrnr MA
Wm.: b 1759 d 7-3-1835 m (1)Martha Guthrie (2)Sarah McClelland
     Capt PA
Wm., Sr.: b — d 1803 m Polly Neilson Pvt PA
Yost: b 4-23-1731 d 9-15-1794 m Elizabeth Maul PS NY

POWERS,
Aaron: b 1738 d 10-9-1826 m Olive Osborn Pvt MA
Abner: b 12-15-1760 d 9-25-1852 m Sabra Porter Drm Cpl NH
Abraham: b 1743/4 d 9-11-1832 m Phoebe — PS PA
Amasa: b c. 1750 d 9-30-1805 m Lydia Wait Sgt VT W★
Asa, Sr.: b 11-25-1742 d 8-8-1816 m Resinah Wheeler CS MA
Asahel: b 9-29-1759 d 1-8-1846 m Eleanor Bragg Pvt VT
Charles: b 2-1-1762 d 12- -1843 d VA m Solence Rogers Capt MA
Daniel: b 1730 d 1815 m Elizabeth Waller Sol VA
David: b 11-30-1760 d 6-30-1843 m Sarah Pike Pvt MA
David: b c. 1725 d 1778 m Cecelia — Pvt NC
David: b 2-2-1747 d 1815 m Mary Davis Lt VT
Edward: b 9-30-1751 d 6-13-1809 m Deborah Roberts Pvt CT
Edward: b a. 1733 d — m (1)Phillias Bartlett (2)Betty Whately
     Pvt MA
Edward, Jr.: b 9-10-1754 d 9-9-1830 m Priscilla Curtis Pvt MA
Elliott: b 2-12-1732 d 6- -1783 m (1)Sarah Cragin (2)Mary Barker
     Pvt NH
Ephraim: b 2-7-1755 d 5-27-1835 m Abigail Cadwell Pvt MA ★
Ephraim: b 2-11-1757 d 7-15-1835 m Sarah Kentchen 2Sgt VT ★
Esley: b 1740 d 1840 m Mary Waddell Pvt PA
Francis: b 7-15-1742 d 1796 m Elizabeth Cummings Pvt NH
Gideon, Sr.: b 7-28-1731 d 1789 m Ruth Hosmer Pvt NH
Gideon, Jr.: b 9-10-1758 d 9-21-1838 m Ruth (Packard) Lane
     Pvt NH
Henry: b 4-13-1753 d 1825 m (1)Hannah L. Moore (2)Mrs Eunice
     Spofford Sgt MA
Isaac: b 3-26-1735 d 1811 m (1)Phebe Trull (2)Mrs Thankful Stone
     Capt CS MA
Isaac: b c. 1742 d 11-9-1812 m Sarah Clark Pvt MA
James: b 1741 d 3-17-1822 m Lois Clinton Pvt CT
Jerameel: b 2-18-1718 d 5-17-1805 m Eunice Bennett Capt PS VT
Jeremiah: b 1733 d 1801 m Elizabeth Cooley Pvt MA
Jesse: b 1761 d 12-4-1834 m Millie — Pvt MD ★
John: b 8-14-1762 d 2-26-1837 m (1)Susannah Palmer (2)Anna
     Napier Myers Tms Pvt CT ★
John: b 1729/30 d a. 2-28-1786 m Elizabeth Westcott Lt MA
John: bpt 11-21-1756 d 10-26-1813 m Elizabeth Pousland Pvt
     Smn MA
John: b 1744 d 6-12-1826 m Affe Bixby Pvt MA
John: b 1-7-1759 d 3-4-1831 m (1)Elizabeth Hutchins Bonney
     (2)Mary Read Capt NC
John: b c. 1755 d p. 1792 m Frances Bryant Pvt Trm VA
Jonathan: b 1704 d late in 1775 m Hannah More (or Sawyer)
     Pvt MA
Jonathan: b 3-17-1764 d 11-8-1807 m Mary Pickard Pvt VT
Joseph: b 9-7-1748 d 12-1-1826 m (1)Sally Hart (2)Susan Larabee
     (3)Rebecca Stearns Pvt NH
Josiah: b 12-28-1745 d 3-28-1808 m Mary Robbins Pvt NH W★
Lawrence: b 12-31-1751 d 3-5-1811 m Lydia Barber Pvt CT
Lemuel: b 12-11-1714 d 12-11-1792 m Thankful Leland Pvt MA
Major: b 1753 d 1795 m Mary Pettyjohn Pvt VA
Manassah: b 2-7-1754 d 3-18-1839 m Susannah Payne Pvt MA ★
Moses: b 8-27-1764 d p. 1815 m Eunice — Pvt VT
Nahum: b 4-11-1741 d 1826 m Sarah Wheat Pvt MA VT
Nathaniel: b c. 1740 d p. 1794 m — Cpl NH
Nicholas: b 1763 d 3-30-1840 m Hannah — Ens NY ★
Oliver: b 9-6-1741 d p. 1818 m Lydia Winn Pvt MA
Peter: b 4-29-1765 d 4-11-1854 m (1)Lucy Lee (2)Lovisa Liscomb
     Mar MA ★

Simeon: b 12-7-1745 d p. 1820 m Lydia Dwinnell Cpl NH ★
Stephen: b 10-28-1729 d 7-8-1775 m Lucy Cummings Pvt NH
Stephen: b 5-16-1742 d 1813 m Rachel Winter Pvt PS NH
Stephen: b 7-15-1762 d 3-22-1843 m Mary Grow Pvt VT ★
Stephen: b 1736 d 11-27-1809 m Lydia Drew Sol Dr VT
Thomas: b c. 1749 d 7-23-1834 m Mary Hinds 1Lt MA
Timothy: b 1-16-1750 d 4-2-1841 m Elizabeth Gilbert Pvt MA
Wm.: b 2-4-1767 d 8-7-1831 m Mary Dumbolton Pvt MA ★
Wm.: b 12-30-1740 d 3-13-1829 m Elizabeth Gates Pvt NH
Wm.: b 1747 d 4-8-1796 m Rhoda Dean Pvt NY
Wm.: b 1760 d 1827 m Francis Spearman Pvt NC
Wm.: b 9-8-1759 d 12-4-1836 m Elizabeth Spearman Pvt VA
Wm.: b 11-9-1765 d 6-6-1856 m Hannah Stout Spy VA
Wm.: b 11-9-1765 d 3-12-1852 m Rebecca Jones Spy VA ★
Wm.: b c. 1725 d 7-28-1806 m Judith Maddison PS VA

POWLES,
Jacob: b 6-11-1756 d 1836 m Jennetje Verveelen Pvt NJ ★

POYAS,
John Ernest, Sr.: b 1730 d 4- -1786 m (1)Elizabeth Grant (2)Rachel
     Bourget (3)Mrs Mary Magdaline Schwart Koff PS SC
John Ernest, Jr.: b 4- -1756 d 9-17-1821 m Catherine Smith Dr SC

POYTHRESS,
Peter: b 4-2-1733 d 12-19-1787 m Elizabeth Bland PS VA
Wm.: b 1737 d 1783 m Elizabeth — 1Lt VA

PRALL,
Garrison: b c. 1750 d 1792 m Mary Stout Tms Wgm NJ
Peter: b 6-3-1751 d 3-2-1829 m Mary Quick Sol NJ

PRATHER, (includes PRATER)
Aaron: b c. 1739 d p. 11-27-1797 m Mary Swearingen PS MD
Archibald: b 1755 d p. 2-9-1831 m Sarah Fugate Sol PS VA
Baruch: b 1742 d 12-2-1810 m Sarah Higgins PS MD
Basil: b 1742 d 10-7-1822 m Chloe Robinson PS Mil NC
Basil: b 5-10-1740 d 12-18-1803 m Fanny Merriwether 1Lt PA
Bazil: b c. 1745 d p. 12-11-1829 m Priscilla — Pvt PS SC
James: b 1-27-1737 d 11-3-1818 m (1)Sarah Beatty (2)Ruth
     Crownover Capt PS MD
James: b c. 1729/30 d p. 11-1-1783 m Ann Turner PS MD
John: b 1715 d p. 9-8-1795 m Rachel Odle PS MD
John: b c. 1754 d 12-4-1829 m Eleanor Pickens Pvt SC
John Smith: b 4-5-1753 d 1-6-1778 m Jane Deakins Pvt VA
Philip: b c. 1754 d 1796 m Susannah Hubbard Pvt SC W★
Samuel: b c. 1742 d 1785 m Elizabeth Garrett PS MD
Thomas: b 1740 d 1820 m Rachel Gaither Pvt NC
Thomas: b c. 1703/4 d 1785 m (1)Elizabeth Clagett (2)Jeannette —
     PS MD
Thomas, Sr.: b 8-9-1726 d 11-17-1804 m Sarah Jane — PS MD
Thomas: b 12-16-1751 d 7-24-1786 m Mary Phillips PS MD
Thomas: b 3-26-1756 d 8-12-1841 m — Pvt NC ★
Thomas Hicks: b 4-2-1755 d 2-15-1818 m Elizabeth Crunkleton
     Pvt PA
Zachariah: b c. 1752 d c. 1814 m Ruth Allison Pvt PS MD

PRATT,
Aaron: b c. 1760 d 10-9-1813 m (1)Rachel Smith (2)Jerusha Smith
     Brown Pvt MA
Aaron: b 4-8-1734 d 2-11-1811 m Bridget Collier Pvt MA
Aaron, 4th: b 10-15-1760 d 4-14-1843 m Silence Beal Pvt MA ★
Abijah: b 4-25-1758 d 7-28-1800 m (1)Mary Watrous (2)Lucy Dean
     Cpl CT
Abraham: b 1733/4 d 9-29-1797 m (1)Rachel Jones (2)Mrs
     Mahetable Marvin Sol CT
Alpheus: b 9-7-1731 d 12-11-1806 m Lydia Mixer Ens MA
Amos: b 4-11-1734 d 3-14-1821 m Sarah Upham Pvt MA
Asa: b 9-16-1734 d 11-16-1811 m Abigal Denison Pvt CT
Asa: b 3-18-1757 d p. 1833 m (1)Betty Stanford (2)Sarah Bond
     Pvt MA NH ★
Augustus: b 2-24-1751 d 12- -1850 m Esther Burrows Pvt CT ★
Barnabas: b c. 1730 d 1788 m Isabel Downie Pvt MA
Benanuel: b 9-26-1756 d 6-6-1825 m Lucy Hosmer Sgt MA
Benjamin: b 11-7-1743 d p. 1792 m Sybil Stowe NCapt CT
Benjamin: b 7-10-1758 d 9-20-1818 m Betsey Dyer Cpl MA
Benjamin: b 1705 d 6-29-1785 m Mary Turner Pvt MA
Benjamin: b 1764 d 8-27-1826 m Mrs Isabella (Clark) Ham Pvt MA
Benjamin: b 1758 d 6-17-1842 m Mary Smith Pvt RI
Beriah: b 9-30-1750 d p. 1798 m Mary Dudley Pvt MA
Caleb: b 3-26-1745 d 3-8-1831 m Deborah Battles Cpl MA
Chalker: b 1750 d 1827 m Chloe Pratt Pvt MA ★
Cyrus: b 10-31-1760 d 4-20-1821 m Deborah Smith Pvt MA
Daniel, Jr.: b 7-7-1734 d 5-9-1806 m Abigail Bigelow Pvt CT
Daniel: b 2-11-1707 d 11-6-1797 m Mary (Pratt) — Sol MA
Daniel: b 1725 d 6-22-1795 m (1)Abigail — (2)Ruth Burnap Pvt MA
Daniel: b 3-3-1741 d 6-9-1778 m Mary Patten Drm Cpl MA
David: b c. 1725 d 12-20-1803 m Jerusha Chalker PS CT
David: b 1751-7 d 1826-32 m Hannah Hammond Sgt MA
David: b c. 1742 d 9-12-1806 m Lucy Coolidge Sgt MA
David: b c. 1746 d 1-29-1839 m Hepzabeth Fay Pvt MA
David: b 3-8-1751 d p. 1793 m Louise Forbes Pvt MA

PRATT, contd.
David: b 7-13-1762 d 5-30-1844 m Hannah Rockwell Pvt MA
David: b 6-2-1765 d 11-28-1844 m Elizabeth Spaulding Slr NH
David: b 4-20-1738 d 6-7-1828 m (1)Kezia Bill (2)Mrs Elizabeth Burnham (3)Lovisa Hatch LCol NY
David B.: b 1748 d *p.* 1790 m Sarah Banning Pvt CT
Dier: b 1754 d 5-3-1841 m Zilpha Macomber Pvt MA
Ebenezer: b 9-22-1753 d 9-13-1842 m Susannah Bolton Pvt MA ★
Ebenezer: b 3-3-1731 d 10-26-1778 m Abiel Johnson Alger Cpl MA
Edward: b 8-4-1764 d 6-5-1816 m Elizabeth Preble Pvt MA W★
Elam: b 10-5-1751 d 4-18-1836 m Lydia Hunt Sgt MA ★
Eliab: b 1724 d 4-15-1809 m Margaret Ely PS CT
Elias: b 1754 d 12-18-1834 m Patience Clark 2Sgt CT ★
Elias: b 11-7-1743 d 3-14-1816 m Lydia Hill Capt MA
Elisha: b 1728 d 7-3-1807 m Lucy Fletcher Pvt MA
Ephraim: b 8-19-1756 d 11-9-1823 m Keziah Wood Sgt MA
Ephraim: b 1740 d 8-30-1776 m Phoebe — Lt MA
Ephraim: b 5-23-1763 d 3-23-1855 m Anna Ballard Pvt MA
Ethan: b — d — m Mabel Skeel Pvt CT
Ezra: b 12-5-1757 d 8-20-1806 m Temperance Southworth Pvt CT
Ezra: b 1744 d 5-12-1825 m Susannah Barton Sgt MA
Gerard: b 9-22-1739 d 12-24-1826 m Dorcas Ashley Pvt MA
Gideon: b 1741 d *p.* 1800 m (1)Sarah Butler (2)Abigail Buckingham (3)Mrs Mary Williams Pvt CT
Henry: b 2-14-1746 d 8-19-1802 m Elizabeth Murdock Sgt MA
Isaac: b 3-3-1734 d 9-3-1814 m Mary Beckley Lt CT
Isaac: b 10-12-1740 d 12-31-1829 m Mehitable Nickols Cpl MA
Isaac: b 8-26-1732/3 d *p.* 4-11-1808 m Sarah Parmenter Pvt MA
Isaac: b 10-6-1763 d 12-17-1845 m Betsey Bixby Pvt MA W ★
Isaac: b 11-24-1746 d 11-14-1820 m (1)Mary Coney CS MA
Jacob: b 10-3-1735 d 11-23-1811 m Lydia Eames Pvt MA
Jacob: b 2-19-1754 d 5-22-1844 m Phebe Jenkins Pvt MA
James: b 10-14-1753 d 1-3-1820 m Mary Burr Pvt CT
James: b *c.* 1749 d 5-14-1784 m Zerviah Rugg Pvt MA
James: b 3-28-1763 d 9-15-1854 m Sarah Giles Pvt VT ★
Jasper: b 1756 d 7-26-1833 m Abigail Butler Cpl CT
Jedediah: b 5-23-1740 d 4-16-1814 m Ann Wolcott PS CT
Jesse: b 4-12-1761 d 2-4-1841 m Mary Rhodes Drm Pvt MA ★
Joel: b 2-1-1752 d 11-10-1844 m (1)Charlotte Ball (2)Phoebe Hilburn Lt MA
Joel: b 9-26-1745 d 9-30-1821 m Mary Beach Fowler Capt NY
John: b 2-7-1760 d 12-15-1823 m Rebecca Pratt Pvt MA ★
John: b 11-24-1755 d 6-22-1834 m Anna Davis Sgt MA
John: b 10-4-1730 d 6-28-1786 m (1)Martha White (2)Sarah Bayley (3)Deborah Darby Pvt MA
John: b 9-13-1750 d — m Martha Mehurer Pvt MA
John, Jr.: b 1748 d 2-4-1816 m (1)Anna Smith Lt NH
John: b 6-19-1744 d — m Nancy Knapp Lt NH
John: b 1728/9 d *p.* 1800 m — Hampton Pvt NC
John: b 10-12-1753 d 12-27-1824 m Elizabeth Cooper Lt QM PA
John: b *c.* 1760 d 1838 m Elizabeth Gordon Pvt VA
Johnathan: b *c.* 1754 d 4- -1818 m Martha Palmer Pvt VT
Jonas, Jr.: b 4-26-1746 d 1780 m Jenny Foster MM Sgt CS MA
Jonathan: b 3-1-1753 d *p.* 10- -1832 m Margaret Ferdham Pvt CT ★
Jonathan: b 7-25-1734 d 3-28-1808 m (1)Damaris Phillips (2)Susannah Garbett Lt MA
Jonathan: b 1740 d 1813 m (1)Lucy Church (2)Lydia Chamberlain (3)Desire Palmer Pvt MA
Jonathan: b 1763 d 1-13-1850 m Betsy — Pvt MA ★
Joseph: bpt 6-6-1742 d 10-18-1814 m Susannah Caldwell Sgt CT
Joseph: b 8-2-1732 d 7-24-1804 m Hannah Beebe Sol CT
Joseph: b 1745 d 12-12-1832 m Margaret Cheever NCapt MA
Joseph: b 4-1-1748 d *p.* 1790 m Esther Blood Pvt MA
Joseph: b 1712 d 9-16-1796 m (1)Sarah Hunkins (2)Katharine Read PS MA
Joshua: b 9-26-1756 d 9-25-1828 m Lydia Pratt Pvt MA
Josiah: b 2-14-1719 d 2-7-1800 m Abigail Williams Capt MA
Laban: b 10-1-1762 d 7- -1836 m Lucy (Pratt) — Pvt MA
Lemuel: bpt 7- -1760 d 10-18-1834 m (1)Azubah Hutchinson (2)Mary — Pvt CT ★
Levi: b 3-23-1760 d 2-26-1839 m Sally Russell Sgt MA ★
Luther: b 9-29-1763 d 1818 m Theodorah Leonard Pvt MA
Matthew, Sr.: b 12-3-1726 d 10-5-1799 m Mary Lovell CS MA
Matthew, Jr.: b 5-20-1752 d 10-16-1835 m Chloe (Pratt) — Pvt MA ★
Micah, Jr.: b 8-15-1749 d 10-16-1816 m Mary Parkman Cpl MA
Moses: b 6-27-1729 d *p.* 1795 m (1)Jemima Alden (2)Mary Riggs (3)Lucy White PS NH
Nathan: b 11-5-1743 d 2-27-1828 m Mary Pratt Pvt MA
Nathan: b 11-11-1759 d 5-11-1847 m Dolly Parker Drm Pvt MA ★
Nathan: b 1761 d *c.* 1847 m Anna Lay 3Sgt VT
Nathaniel: b 8-6-1757 d *p.* 1790 m Sarah Perkins Pvt CT
Nathaniel: b 7-21-1743 d 12-17-1800 m Zipporah Smith Sgt MA
Nathaniel: b 1757 d *p.* 1810 m Lucy Shaw Pvt MA
Nathaniel: b 11-22-1749 d 4-4-1831 m Lydia Mason Pvt NH
Nehemiah: b 4-11-1749 d *p.* 6-3-1826 m Judith Pratt 2Lt MA
Nehemiah: b — d *p.* 3-16-1812 m Mercy Drake Capt MA
Nehemiah: b 10-22-1732 d 11-9-1793 m (1)Mary Pratt (2)Ruth Torrey Pvt MA
Noah: b 3-5-1748 d 1-4-1807 m Hannah Stearns Lt Adj MA
Noah: b 1731 d 8-11-1807 m Mary Cole Pvt MA

Noah: b 1755 d 1-21-1835 m Desire — Sol MA ★
Noah: b 7-20-1758 d 1825 m Else Jenkins Pvt MA
Obediah: b 9-14-1742 d 3-2-1797 m Jemima Tolles Pvt NY
Oliver: b 1-17-1761 d 7-21-1844 m Jedidah Luce Pvt MA
Paul: b 1713 d 3-19-1798 m (1)Mehetable White (2)Abigail Cobbshares (3)Hanna Lincoln Pvt MA
Paul: b 10-22-1762 d 1-5-1829 m (1)Burredell Hall (2)Lydia Gates (3)Abigail Greggs Pvt MA ★
Peabody: b 10-12-1757 d 10-28-1824 m Sarah Buckingham Pvt CT
Phineas: b 6-27-1747 d 2-14-1813 m Hepsibah Pratt Pvt CT
Phineas: b 1716 d 2-24-1798 m (1)Susanna Wood (2)Mrs Susanna Cody Pvt MA
Phineas: b 8-24-1740 d 6-9-1831 m Elizabeth Sargent Pvt MA
Reuben: b *c.* 1745 d 1809/10 m Lydia Griffin Sgt MA
Reuben: b 1745 d 1-21-1807 m Ruth Williams Sgt NH
Rufus: b 10-2-1737 d 9-19-1777 m Hannah Ball Pvt MA
Samuel: b 7-29-1764 d 8-30-1812 m Esther Wells Pvt CT
Samuel: b 1754 d 12-24-1809 m Mary Fields Newhall Lt MA W★
Samuel: b 12-19-1712 d 12-28-1793 m Betty Bicknell Pvt MA
Samuel: b 9-7-1722 d 4-7-1792 m Althea Cushing Pvt MA
Samuel: b 5-3-1758 d 11-23-1831 m Abigail Caswell Cpl VT
Seth: b 6-24-1741 d 1802 m (1)Abigail Tully (2)Mrs Margaret Smith Pvt CS CT
Seth: b 11-21-1738 d 8-27-1802 m Mindwell Stone Lt MA
Seth: b 3-24-1750/1 d 4- -1829 m Margaret Stacey Pvt MA
Seth: b 9-5-1758 d 3-31-1823 m Elizabeth Kingsbury Pvt MA ★
Seth J.: b 6-28-1762 d 9-27-1838 m Hannah Hunt Cpl MA ★
Simeon: b 9-16-1759 d 9-25-1848 m Sarah Willis Pvt MA
Solomon: b *c.* 1740 d 11-6-1776 m Hannah White Pvt MA
Solomon: b 9- -1751 d 5-2-1838 m Remember Bates Pvt MA ★
Stephen: b 9-11-1751 d 12-20-1835 m Hannah Billings Pvt MA
Stephen: b 6-5-1749 d 6-18-1813 m Phebe Merriam Pvt MA
Stephen: b 12-20-1760 d 6-2-1845 m Lucy Curtis Sol MA ★
Teber: b 1751 d 11-22-1809 m Mary Brockway Pvt CT
Thaddeus: b 1752 d 1843 m Rachel Churchill Pvt MA
Thomas: b 1740 d 8-17-1829 m (1)Caty Cummings (2)Anna Lawrence Pvt MA
Thomas: b 10- -1748 d 1-17-1817 m Sarah Blanchard Pvt MA
Thomas: b 11-14-1736 d 10-18-1818 m Sarah Neal Pvt MA
Thomas: b 1757 d 4-10-1786 m Polly Proud Drm RI
Whitcomb: b 3-23-1761 d 1-13-1839 m Ruth Lovell Pvt MA
Wm.: b 11-22-1750 d 5-18-1850 m Hannah Pratt Lt CT ★
Wm.: b 4-6-1746 d 6-4-1808 m Mary King Capt MA
Wm.: b 9-30-1759 d 2-6-1845 m Mary Lawton Lt RI
Wm.: b 1737 d *p.* 10-2-1817 m Sarah Thomas Sol NC SC
Wm.: b *c.* 1734 d *a.* 3-28-1797 m Mary — Pvt PS SC
Wm.: b *c.* 1760 d 11- -1805 m (1)Lucinda Stage Pvt VA
Zachariah: bpt 2-25-1726 d 10-1-1805 m Abigail Cooke CS CT
Zadock: b 1-16-1755 d 7-27-1828 m Hannah Pickett Pvt CT
Zephaniah: b 3-14-1760 d 9-8-1842 m Rachel — Pvt CT

PRAY, (includes PREY)
Ephraim: b 11-20-1733 d 4-10-1805 m Susannah Sheldon Capt NY
John: b 6- -1754 d 9-12-1812 m Jane Mesier Capt MA
John: b 3-4-1755 d *p.* 8-14-1832 m Mary Cleverly Cpl MA ★
John, Jr.: b 2-4-1749 d 5-10-1830 m Deborah Wade Lt RI
Jonathan: b 1760 d *p.* 1799 m (1)Anne — (2)Patience — Sgt PA
Joseph: bpt 4-27-1743 d 1803 m (1)Mary Libby (2)Mary Hight Capt MA
Joseph: b 1753 d 1-24-1830/1 m (1)Ruth Phettyplace (2)Henrietta Wright Pvt RI
Peter: b *a.* 7-11-1747 d *p.* 7-16-1826 m (1)Peggy — (2)Sarah Libbey Sgt MA
Samuel: b 9-21-1755 d 4-15-1837 m Sarah Fernald Pvt MA ★

PREBLE,
Abraham: b *a.* 1743 d *p.* 1790 m Elizabeth — Capt CS MA
David, 2d: b 1755/6 d 2-21-1802 m — Pvt MM MA
Ebenezer: b 10-20-1758 d 6-22-1837 m Lydia Smith 2Lt MA
Esaias: b 4-26-1742 d 12-22-1813 m Lydia Ingraham Capt MM MA
Jedediah, Sr.: b 1707 d 3-11-1784 m (1)Martha Junkins (2)Mehitable (Bangs) Roberts PS MA
Jedediah: b 12-8-1755 d 8-16-1811 m Isabella Clark Pvt MA
John: b 1742 d 12-3-1787 m Eleanor — Capt MA

PREDMORE,
Daniel: b 1-21-1760 d 7-21-1815 m Sarah Elizabeth Case Pvt NJ

PRENTISS, (includes PRENTICE & PRENTIS)
Amos: b 4-24-1748 d 7-19-1805 m Anna Owen Dr CT
Caleb: b 11-14-1746 d 2-7-1803 m Pamela Mellen MM MA
Daniel: b 1-31-1740 d *p.* 1779 m Mary Billings CS CT
Daniel: b 1-26-1758 d 4-14-1851 m Abigail Standley Pvt MA ★
Eleazer: b 9-26-1735 d 12-18-1805 m Sarah Stanton Capt CT
James: b 8-5-1746 d 5-20-1837 m Mrs Sarah Draper Whitin Lt MA
Jesse: b 1-24-1743 d 8- -1811 m Elizabeth Belcher 2Lt CT
John: b 12-14-1747 d 11-22-1780 m Esther Richards Lt CT
John: b 6-6-1754 d 1-2-1833 m Martha Clemons Cpl CT
John: b 5-13-1733 d 6-21-1810 m (1)Mary Haskell (2)Rebecca Haskell Cpl CT
John: b 8-27-1734 d 6-6-1810 m Dorothy Sexton Pvt CT

John: b 1735 d 1801 m Bridget Rogers Pvt CT
John: b 7-27-1753 d 9-11-1818 m Ann (Kendall) Cook Pvt MA
John: b 12-17-1760 d 2-2-1840 m Hannah Reddington Pvt MA ★
Jonathan: b 5-28-1740 d 1-18-1809 m Mrs Jay Brewster Sgt MA
Joseph: b 2-13-1733/4 d 1804 m Margaret Comstock Pvt CT
Joseph: b 8-24-1727 d 1791 m Abigail Leonard Pvt MA
Joseph: b 1-24-1754 d 6-18-1809 m Margaret Bowdoin PS CS VA
Joshua: b 9-9-1744 d 6-22-1837 m (1)Mrs Grace Bubier
  Brimblecom (2)Mrs Dolly Jean — Lt MA ★
Manassah: b 7-22-1749 d c. 1825 m Asenath Burton Pvt CT
Nathaniel: b 3-14-1764 d 1-23-1839 m (1)Lucy Campbell
  (2)Margaret (Hedden) Boyer Pvt Pvtr CT ★
Nathaniel: b 10-25-1743 d 6- -1817 m Abigail Logan Pvt MA
Nathaniel Sartell: b 12-8-1735 d 1-24-1815 m Martha Howard
  Capt CS PS NH
Samuel, Sr.: b 10-4-1736 d 7- -1807 m Phoebe Billings LCol CT
Samuel, Jr.: b 1759 d 1818 m Lucretia Holmes ADC Dr CT
Solomon: b 5-14-1744 d 1-24-1804 m Rebecca Frost Pvt MA
Stanton: b 11-17-1750 d 7-21-1826 m Mary Fowler Wgm FrA &
  Smn MA
Stephen, Sr.: bpt 12-29-1728 d 2-13-1799 m Ann Starr Sgt CT
Stephen: b 7-28-1752 d p. 1797 m Hannah Babcock Pvt MA
Thomas: b 1-19-1760 d 12-12-1841 m Mary Spencer Pvt CT
Thomas: b 10-25-1719 d 3-30-1783 m (1)Elizabeth Baldwin
  (2)Prudence Denison CS CT
Thomas: b 5-29-1755 d 6-10-1838 m Alice Parker Pvt MA
Valentine: bpt 3-16-1746 d 9-4-1822 m Sarah Bump Sgt MA ★
Wm.: b 9-12-1760 d 1815 m Mary Watson Pvt MA

PRESBREY, (includes PREISBERRY)
John: b 2-25-1760 d 5-24-1845 m Prudence Pratt Pvt MA RI CT ★
Joseph: b 1727 d 1802 m Mary Baker Pvt MA
Joseph: b 1746 d c. 1824 m Patty Perkins Pvt MA
Levi: b 1760 d 1800 m Lina Pratt Sol MA
Seth: b 9-17-1752 d 12-15-1833 m Sarah Pratt Sgt MA RI ★
Wm.: b 3-23-1747 d 3-5-1832 m Lydia Pratt Cpl RI

PRESCOTT,
Aaron: b 4-13-1748 d p. 9-8-1815 m (1)— Glaze (2)Mary Ann
  Flowers Sol SC
Abel: b 12-12-1759 d 9-18-1841 m Hannah Spaulding Pvt Mar
  MA ★
Abraham: b 5-20-1717 d 6-26-1789 m Sarah Clifford PS NH
Benjamin: b 11-28-1777 d 1-1-1831 m (1)Elizabeth Higginson
  (2)Mercy Gibbs (3)Mrs Mary (Pepperill) Frost Coleman PS MA
Benjamin: b 3-15-1754 d 3-7-1839 m Rachel Adams Pvt NH
Benjamin: b 3-18-1708 d 1789 m (1)Dorothy Robie Sanborn
  (2)Abigail Gove PS NH
Charles: b 8-15-1711 d 2-2-1799 m Elizabeth Barrett Col MA
David: b 11-2-1753 d 11-20-1813 m Mary Blood Pvt MA
Dominicus: b 1765 d 5-31-1831 m Hannah Moulton Sol NH
Dudley: b 7-9-1758 d 8-3-1815 m Martha Swain Lt NH
Edward: b 1717 d 1804 m Elizabeth Prescott Pvt NH
Ebenezer: b c. 1720 d 10-15-1776 m Jerusha Matthews Pvt MA
Elisha: b 12-13-1754 d 10-13-1813 m Mary Marston Ens NH
Elisha: b 7-9-1743 d a. 8-26-1828 m (1)Mehitable Swain (2)Hannah
  Belnap Sol NH
Ezra: b 4-30-1756 d 4-29-1789 m Dolly Wright Pvt MA
Henry: b 7-25-1737 d 9-10-1816 m Mary Pepperell Newmarch
  PS NH
James: b 3-15-1749 d 5-25-1842 m (1)Rebecca Barrett (2)Rebecca
  Atwater Pvt CT
James: b 12-5-1733 d 2-27-1813 m Mary Lane Lt NH
James: b 6-15-1743 d 12- -1825 m Jane Hilliard Pvt NH
James: b 10-3-1736 d 1830 m Abagail Lane CS NH
Jedediah: b 9-26-1746 d 3-31-1827 m Sarah Morrill PS NH
Jeremiah: b 12-22-1741 d 4-25-1817 m Jane Sherburne Capt NH
Jeremiah: b 6-3-1760 d 10- -1816 m (1)Mary Rackcliff
  (2)Elizabeth Chase Pvt NH
Jeremiah: b 3-29-1718 d — m (1)Mary Hayes (2)Mary (Shaw)
  Towle PS NH
Jesse: b 3-15-1757 d 12-28-1833 m Judith Johnson Pvt NH ★
Jesse: b 2-7-1729 d p. 1790 m Sarah Dearborn Sgt NH
Joel: b 6-20-1759 d 10-5-1811 m Lucy Reed Pvt MA
John: b 4-25-1752 d 10-30-1842 m Martha Abbott Cpl MA
John: b 1712 d 4- -1791 m Mary White PS MA
John: b 4-23-1743 d 3-12-1821 m Grace Potter Pvt MA
John: b 1746 d 6-17-1775 m Esther Rollins MM NH
John: b 12-2-1723 d 5-2-1785 m (1)Hannah Rundlett (2)Rebecca
  Tilton PS NH
John: b 8-7-1757 d 3-31-1839 m Lucy Clifford Pvt NH
John: b 1744 d 1824 m Molly Carr PS CS NH
Jonas: b 4-7-1727 d 3-23-1813 m Rebecca Buckley Parker Pvt MA
Jonas: b 8-6-1754 d 7-22-1798 m (1)Susanna Wilder (2)Ruth
  Kidder SrgnMte MA
Jonathan: b 6-19-1750 d 11-22-1805 m Mary Brigham Pvt MA
Jonathan: b 1-19-1757 d 2-14-1814 m Catharine Marston Sgt
  NH Heirs ★
Jonathan, Sr.: b 10-8-1723 d 12-10-1809 m Rachel Clifford PS
  Pvt NH
Jonathan, Jr.: b 2-21-1759 d 6-4-1813 m Lydia Tuck Pvt NH
Jonathan: b 12-5-1761 d 2-11-1847 m (1)Sarah Brown (2)Mercy
  Clark (3)Anna Woodman Pvt NH

Joseph: b 11-17-1725 d 4-8-1815 m Molly Norris Maj PS NH
Joshua: b 11- -1740 d 2-22-1829 m Ruth Carr Lt NH
Joshua: b 1713 d 7-12-1785 m (1)Abigail Ambrose (2)Mary
  Moulton PS NH
Josiah: b 7-15-1736 d p. 1776 m Ruth Brown Pvt PS NH
Marston: b 7-25-1739 d 3-14-1824 m Susanna Rowe Pvt NH
Micah: b 10-23-1739 d 2- -1828 m Abigail Brown PS NH
Nathan Gove: b 3-13-1735 d 11-13-1825 m (1)Patience Brown
  (2)Rebecca (Prescott) — (3)Love Rollins PS NH
Oliver: b 4-27-1731 d 11-17-1804 m Lydia Baldwin MGen MA
Oliver: b 5-5-1725 d 1-1-1803 m Bethia Underwood PS MA
Samson: b 11-22-1762 d 5-16-1815 m Lucy Blood Pvt MA
Samuel: b 1-26-1729 d 11-20-1797 m Ruth Smith Pvt NH
Samuel: b 10-30-1755 d 7-4-1819 m Molly Drake Pvt NH
Samuel: b 9-5-1759 d 11-2-1841 m (1)Betsey Whittier (2)Martha
  (Clark) Malloy Pvt NH
Stephen: b 5-16-1731 d p. 6-24-1799 m (1)Debora Weare
  (2)Rebecca Davidson PS NH
Timothy: b 12-1-1728 d 4-30-1808 m (1)Lydia Fletcher (2)Mrs
  Rebecca Boynton Pvt CS MA
Wm.: b 2-20-1726 d 10-13-1795 m Abigail Hale Col MA
Wm.: b 6-21-1728 d 9-28-1811 m Susanna Sanborn Capt NH
Wm.: b 1746 d 1815 m Mary Dearborn Pvt NH

PRESGRAVES, (includes PRESGRAVE)
Wm.: b c. 1735 d a. 12-14-1809 m — PS VA

PRESHO,
Samson: b 1763 d 2-24-1819 m Abi Presho Pvt MA ★

PRESSEY, (includes PRESSY)
Jacob: b 1763 d 1845 m Sarah — Pvt MA
Pasky: b 9-3-1742 d p. 1801 m Judith Blaisdell Sgt NH

PRESSLEY,
David: b 1-2-1764 d 5-11-1834 m Ann Edmeston Pvt SC ★
Robert: b 1735 d 1797 m Mary Elizabeth — Cpl VA

PRESSNAL,
James: b 1736 d 1821 m (1)Sarah Harvey Pvt NC

PRESTON, (includes PRESSON)
Abijah: b 1760 d 1813 m (2)Margaret Simpson Warden Pvt Btm NJ
Abner: b 7-31-1756 d 12-8-1829 m Zerviah Miles Drm NH
Amariah: b 2-7-1739 d 2-28-1834 m (1)Elizabeth Warren
  (2)Susannah Wood (3)Mrs Elizabeth (Hart) Bacon (4)Lucy
  Baker West Cpl MA
Amos: b 1754 d p. 1820 m — Pvt MA ★
Benjamin: b 8-3-1743 d a. 1795 m Thankful Larcom Mrnr MA
Benjamin: b a. 1760 d p. 1793 m Elizabeth Kimball Pvt NH
Benjamin: b 8-31-1762 d 8-17-1827 m Jane Owen Pvt NY
Calvin: b 4-11-1765 d 11-29-1849 m Rachel Rice Pvt CT
Daniel: b 1748 d 3-12-1829 m Deborah Kelhan Pvt CT
Daniel: b 5-4-1762 d 8-27-1849 m Esther Cummins Pvt CT ★
David: b 2-25-1758 d 7-11-1827 m Cynthia Sprague Pvt CT ★
Isaac: b 1757/8 d 6- -1806 m Susanna Fletcher Sgt NH
Isaac: b 11-20-1735 d 3-5-1777 m Hannah Bowed Col NH
Jacob: b 2-24-1733 d 11-5-1806 m (1)Mary Butt (2)Mrs Mehitable
  Knowlton Ens CT
James: b 1760 d 1811 m Catharine Argyle Boone Pvt PA
Jedediah: b 4-27-1749 d 1823 m Esther Burtt PS NH
John, Jr.: b 9-19-1737 d 8- -1799 m Sarah Eastman MM Pvt CT
John: bpt 3-25-1739/40 d 11-14-1804 m Marion Bristol Sgt CT
John: b 5-25-1746 d 7-9-1815 m Rachel Clark 2Lt MA
John: b 9-8-1746 d 12-23-1827 m Mehitable White Pvt MA
John: b 9-22-1738 d 2-18-1803 m Rebecca Farrar PS NH
John: b 5-27-1750 d 1-23-1820 m Rebecca Vicker Pvt PA
John: b 1745 d 1795 m Elizabeth Torrence Pvt VT
Jonathan: b 9-9-1739 d 4- -1783 m Elizabeth Pierce Pvt MA
Lemuel: b 1752 d 12-12-1820 m (1)Lydia Hildreth (2)Anna Lawton
  Temple Sgt MA
Levi: b 10-21-1756 d 1-7-1849 m Mehitable Nichols Pvt MA
Levi: b 1732 d 1790 m Dedamia — Capt NJ
Levi: b 9-6-1736 d 10-14-1777 m Deliverance Mosher PS CS NY
Levi: b 6-13-1760 d 1-1-1849 m Martha Matison Pvt VT ★
Moses: b 1762 d 4-18-1840 m Fanny Arthur Pvt VA ★
Nathan: b c. 1750 d 8-6-1832 m Elizabeth Vaun Pvt VA ★
Nehemiah: b 12-19-1720 d a. 7-4-1795 m Agnes Bradford Pvt MA
Noah: b 2-23-1763 d 4-4-1835 m Anna Rossiter Pvt CT ★
Othniel: b 1734/5 d 9-17-1777 m Anna Love Pvt NY
Othniel, Jr.: b 2-15-1757 d p. 9-4-1840 m (2)Roxanna — Pvt NY ★
Robert: b c. 1750 d 12-16-1833 m (1)Peggy Rhea (2)Sarah G —
  Pvt VA
Samuel: b 10-29-1715 d 1-18-1799 m Typhena Woodbridge CS MA
Samuel: b 1753 d 6-26-1820 m Mary Pugh Ens NJ
Shubael: b 11-20-1758 d 10-17-1846 m — Pvt CT ★
Stephen: b c. 1760 d p. 1803 m (1)Dosha Smith (2)Elizabeth Pullen
  Pvt VA
Tirus: b 10-6-1752 d 5-30-1798 m Esther Eaton Pvt CT
Walter: b 2-25-1756 d 8-9-1834 m Anne Montgomery CS Pvt VA
Wm.: b 7-6-1754 d 1-17-1842 m (1)Elizabeth Clark (2)Mary Herbert
  Sol Sgt NH ★

PRESTON, contd.
Wm.: b 10-26-1737 d 10-6-1802 m Barbara Heisler Lt PA
Wm.: b 12-25-1729 d 6-28-1783 m Susannah Smith PS CS Col VA
Wilson: b 11-18-1744 d *p.* 1790 m Susannah Aldrich Pvt MA
Zera: b 6-30-1759 d 7-16-1821 m (1)Mary Ann Walker (2)Hannah Smith (3)Patience Gould Pvt CT

PRESTWOOD,
Thomas: b 1-16-1762 d *p.* 3-18-1853 m Polly Swilla Pvt SC ★

PRIBBLE,
James: b 1-8-1762 d 6-4-1851 m Margaret — Spy 2Sgt PA ★
Thomas: b 1760 d 1836 m Hannah Enoch Spy PA

PRICE,
Abner: b 7-22-1758 d 1839 m Margery Badgley Pvt NJ ★
Anger: b 2-25-1756 d 12-10-1829 m Jane Price Sgt VA ★
Barret: b 4-17-1749 d 9-4-1794 m Sarah Graves Capt VA
Charles: b 1757 d 9-4-1790 m (1)Ann Hadkins (2)Betsey — Cav VA
Daniel: b *c.* 1761 d 5-17-1854 m — Pvt SC ★
David: b 1759 d *p.* 1807 m Ann Ayres Pvt NJ
Ebenezer: b 9-13-1748 d 6-6-183- m Lois Gray Pvt PS CT
Elijah: b *c.* 1756 d *p.* 1-1-1794 m Nancy — Sol NC
Elisha: b 11-11-1734 d 9-25-1798 m Lydia Barton PS PA
Ephraim: b 1761 d 10-31-1846 m Martha Williams Pvt VA NC ★
Ephraim: b *p.* 1755 d 10-31-1809 m (1)Amey Simpers (2)Sarah Simpers Pvt VA
Farrington: b 7-16-1758 d 12-18-1802 m (1)Joanna Miller (2)Elizabeth Ogden Pvt NJ
Francis: b 9-13-1741 d 4-8-1804 m Esther — Capt NJ
George: b 1736 d *p.* 4-13-1811 m Charity — Pvt NJ
Hyland: b 4-22-1744 d *p.* 1781 m Rachel Benson Lt PS MD
Jacob: b 1750 d 1-28-1841 m Wineford Tillery Pvt VA ★
James: b *c.* 1758 d 1801 m Avarilla Chambers CS MD
James: b — d 4-29-1802 m Susannah Williamson Capt VA
Jerusha Penick: b *c.* 1735 d *p.* 1790 m Pugh Price PS VA
John: b 10-29-1759 d 8-10-1822 m Sarah Bourne QM MD
John: b 4-26-1739 d 9-25-1790 m Eleanor Drew Pvt NJ
John: b 1748 d 1811 m Frances Price Sgt NC
John: b 1744 d 1780 m Sarah Kentee 1Lt PA
John: b *c.* 1740 d *c.* 1784-1809 m Sarah Wilkinson Pvt PA
John: b 12-5-1751 d 9-7-1829 m (1)Elizabeth Weidner (2)Mrs Barbara Oberholtzer Pvt PA
John: b 1765 d 1816 m Jane Boozard Sol SC
John: b — d a. 9-16-1816 m Mary Johnson Capt VA
John: b *c.* 1728 d 10-10-1782 m Sarah Jankens 1Lt VA
John: b 1760 d *p.* 5-19-1832 m (1)Elizabeth Redd Major (2)Susanna Gano Sol VA
John: b 1764 d 4-2-1847 m (1)Frances Branch (2)Judith Womack (3)Anna Fishback Pvt VA
John: b *c.* 1720 d *a.* 3-15-1782 m Mary White PS VA
Jonathan: b 3-2-1760 d 9-17-1822 m Elizabeth Ewart Sol NC
Joseph: b *c.* 1750 d *p.* 4-16-1802 m (2)Lucy — PS VA
Joseph Shores: b *c.* 1740 d 10-20-1801 m Charity — PS VA
Josiah: b 1-7-1757 d 12-17-1825 m Jane Scott 1Lt MD
Levi: b 9-2-1756 d a. 3-23-1846 m Martha — Pvt Fif NJ ★
Meredith: b *c.* 1736 d *p.* 1790 m Elizabeth Fox Lt VA
Michael, Sr.: b — d *p.* 6-11-1802 m Margarette — PS CS VA
Nymphas: bpt 3-29-1741 d *p.* 1790 m Hannah Lothrop Pvt MA
Paul: b 1744 d 5-30-1825 m Sarah (Berry) Vail Sgt CT
Ralph: b 4-24-1749 d 12-2-1815 m Elizabeth Woodruff Pvt NJ
Rice: b 1753 d 9-30-1820 m Phebe Clark Pvt NJ ★
Richard: b *c.* 1750 d *p.* 3-9-1803 m Priscilla Crabtree Sgt VA
Richard: b 2-18-1757 d 7-22-1834 m (1)Nancy Dallas (2)Eleanor Prichard (3)Elizabeth Leggett (Arnett) Pvt VA ★
Rufus: b 8-16-1751 d 9-1-1829 m Ruth Grant Lt CT ★ ,
Samuel: b 6-19-1715 d 1788 m (1)Lucy Blinn (2)Esther Fox (3)Mrs Mary Wheeler PS CT
Samuel: b *c.* 1740 d 4-16-1825 m Rachael Moore Pvt MD
Samuel: b 8-30-1750 d 5-30-1801 m Ann Richards PS Pvt PA
Samuel: b 1748 d 1840 m (1)Margaret Black (2)Margaret Black Sol VA
Stephen: b 12-30-1758 d 6-1-1831 m Elizabeth Hall Pvt NJ ★
Stephen Rickards: b 1757 d 5-22-1832 m Jane Parks Sgt MD ★
Thomas: b 9-3-1732 d 5-9-1795 m Mary — Col MD
Thomas: b *c.* 1735 d 1781 m Sally Llewellyn Capt NC
Thomas: b 1745 d 1830 m Isabella Sharp Pvt NC
Thomas: b 8-29-1754 d 12-21-1836 m Barbara Winston Capt VA ★
Thomas: b 1736 d 11-12-1828 m — Pvt VA
Thomas: b 1752 d 1823 m (1)Elizabeth Taylor (2)Margaret Beard Pvt VA
Timothy: b 3-19-1766 d 9-20-1852 m (1)Rhoda Lewis (2)Polly DeForest Pvt NY ★
Wm.: b 1-20-1745 d *p.* 1795 m Molly Lawson Pvt MD
Wm.: b 12-23-1752 d 12-9-1822 m Susanna Summer Pvt MA
Wm.: b *c.* 1738 d 3-25-1819 m Rebecca Jobs Capt NJ
Wm.: b — d 1794 m Sarah Hall Pvt NJ
Wm., Sr.: b *c.* 1729 d *p.* 1800 m Martha — Pvt NC
Wm., Sr.: b 1720 d 1793 m Mary Morton Capt VA
Wm., Jr.: b 1-4-1756 d 3-26-1816 m (1)Sarah Baulding (2)Catherine Gaines 1Lt VA

Wm.: b 10-20-1755 d 10-10-1808 m Mary Cunningham Lt VA
Wm.: b *c.* 1761 d 9-3-1831 m Nancy Price Pvt VA ★
Wm. H: b 3-31-1755 d 8-25-1835 m Mary — Pvt NC
Williamson: b *c.* 1760 d 6-27-1823 m Susannah Booker Pvt VA W★
Zachariah: b 9-22-1743 d *p.* 1796 m Mary Depue Pvt NJ

PRICKETT,
George: b 1757 d 7-20-1846 m Sarah Anderson Pvt VA
Jacob, Jr.: b 4-15-1758 d 4-14-1826 m Jemimah Kindle Pvt VA
Jacob, Sr.: b *c.* 1720 d *p.* 1782 m Dorothy Springer Capt VA
Jacob: b *c.* 1750 d 1807 m Charity Taylor Pvt VA
Josiah: b 1764 d 12-3-1845 m Sarah Van Camp Pvt Spy PA ★

PRIDDY,
James: b *c.* 1750-60 d *a.* 1803 m Nancy — Sol VA
John: b 4-8-1758 d 4-8-1847 m Martha Rowe Pvt VA ★
Thomas: b *c.* 1745 d 3- -1811 m Mary Snead Capt VA
Thomas: b 1750 d 1809 m Sallie Campbell Mil VA

PRIDE,
Absalom: b 8-20-1756 d 11-21-1844 m Huldah Brewster Pvt CT
Burton: b 1758 d 5-26-1835 m (1) X (21)X (3)Elizabeth (Houston) Millwee Pvt GA NC ★
James: b *c.* 1745 d 9-6-1821 m Mehitable Brainard Sgt NY ★
John C: b 1762 d 4-9-1833 m Phebe Potter Sgt MA
Joseph, Sr.: b 4-12-1728 d 12-3-1810 m Hannah Knight Capt MA
Joseph, Jr.: b 10-19-1755 d 12-4-1843 m Mary Knight Pvt MA ★
Peter: b 5-12-1746 d 1-15-1820 m Elizabeth Thissell Pvt MA
Wm.: b 12-7-1739 d 1-9-1811 m Abigail Stoddard Capt CT

PRIDGEN, (includes PRIDGEON)
Francis: b 12-15-1760 d 8-30-1840 m Mary Sikes Pvt NC ★
Thomas: b *c.* 1740 d *p.* 1794 m Martha Ruffin Pvt NC
Wm.: b 6-27-1732 d 1854/5 m — Taylor MM Pvt NC ★

PRIDHAM,
Isaac: b 9-1-1746 d 1-16-1847 m Catherine Hooper Pvt NH

PRIDMORE,
John: b 1741 d *c.* 1829 m Mary Hull Pvt NJ

PRIES,
George Adam: b 9-29-1757 d 10-23-1824 m Susannah Ruppert Pvt PA

PRIEST,
Abel: b 3-20-1760 d 3-21-1827 m Zerviah Whitcomb Pvt MA
Asa: b 1759 d 2-9-1844 m Mary Pamelia Littlejohn Pvt MA
Benjamin: b 12-12-1738 d 1-4-1814 m Hannah Johnson Pvt MA
Gabriel: b 6-17-1720 d 3-20-1781 m Sarah — Pvt MA
Jacob: b 8-15-1757 d 12-14-1836 m (1)Mary Stone (2)Rhoda Warner Pvt MA ★
Jacob: b 3-17-1757 d 1-28-1824 m (1)Ann Jones (2)Sarah Longley Pvt MA
Jeremiah, Jr.: b 1-10-1746 d *p.* 1787 m (1)Rebecca Houghton (2)Susanna Moore Pvt MA
Jeremiah: b 1755 d 3-4-1840 m Millie Gardner Pvt VA ★
Job: b 3-27-1756 d 8-12-1820 m Martha Butler Pvt MA ★
Joel: b 1748/9 d 1848 m Mercy Goodnow Pvt NH
John: b 12-9-1711 d 9-9-1797 m Bethia Hutchinson Pvt MA
John: b 12-22-1746 d 7-8-1841 m Mary Longly Pvt MA ★
John: b 10-1-1761 d 4-12-1830 m (1)Rebecca Gibson (2)Mrs Phoebe Sherman Pvt MA
John: b 1750 d *p.* 1833 m Elizabeth Brown Pvt VA
Joshua: b 11-21-1744 d *p.* 1818 m Syndona King Pvt VT
Levi: b 3-3-1761 d 9-22-1828 m Mary Brooks Pvt MA
Louden, Sr.: b 10-6-1737 d 8-10-1821 m — Pvt MA
Peter: b 1757 d 1-6-1835 m Sarah McKayor Pvt VA ★
Philemon: b 2-18-1753 d 2-18-1839 m Lois Hartwell Cpl MA ★
Philip: b 6-27-1737 d 1816 m Truba Merritt Pvt VT
Samuel: b 2-18-1756 d 10-24-1826 m Susanna Hastings Pvt MA ★
Wm.: b 11- -1754 d 1-28-1843 m Bethsheba Gilbert Pvt NH ★
Wm.: b 12-1-1754 d 6-2-1821 m Elizabeth Hankey Pvt VA ★

PRILLIMAN,
Jacob: b 1752 d *p.* 1840 m — Sol PS VA

PRIME, (includes PRIMM)
Benjamin: b 12-20-1733 d 10-31-1791 m Mary Wheelwright PS NY
Ebenezer: b 7-21-1700 d 9-23-1779 m (1)Margaret Sylvester (2)Experience Youngs (3)Hannah Carll PS NY
John: b 5-17-1750 d 3-12-1837 m Elizabeth Hansbrough Pvt VA ★
Joseph: b 1739 d 6-30-1789 m Lydia Hobbs Maj ME
Joseph: b 10-13-1736 d 3-17-1811 m Hannah King Pvt MA
Thomas: b 1-11-1748 d 5-8-1793 m Mary Nelson Pvt MA

PRIMMER, (includes BRIMMER)
Jacob: b 1743 d 3-5-1830 m Rosina Brimbus Pvt NY
John: b 1740 d 4-18-1830 m Mary B Simmons Pvt NY
John: b 1760 d 1818 m Mary Permelia Woodward Pvt NY
Joseph: b *c.* 1738 d 1803 m — Shufeldt Pvt NY

PRINCE,
Abel: b 1-1-1757 d 6-9-1838 m Fanny Cowen Pvt NH
Asa: b 2-22-1747 d *p.* 1781 m (2)Mary Roundy Capt MA
Cushing: b 10-29-1745 d 1-8-1827 m Hannah Blanchard Pvt MA
David: bpt 2-19-1737 d *p.* 1790 m Eunice Porter Pvt MA
George: b 1741 d 5-8-1834 m (1)— Henry (Heinrich) (2)Magdalen Shaver Capt VA
Godlieb: b *a.* 1749 d *a.* 10-15-1808 m Magdeline Crumm Pvt VA
Henry: b 6-2-1749 d 8-27-1835 m Jennet McElhenney Pvt SC ★
James: bpt 11-7-1731 d 7-27-1796 m Elizabeth Preston Pvt MA
Job, Sr.: b *a.* 1728 d *p.* 1786 m Elizabeth Allen PS MA
Job, Jr.: b 9-28-1751 d 1790 m Elizabeth Cutler PS MA
John: b 2-2-1710 d 2-16-1782 m (1)Mrs Sarah Berry (2)Mary — PS SC
Joseph: b 8-24-1753 d 11-24-1828 m Sarah Bennett 2Lt MA
Joseph, Jr.: b 1755 d 1800 m Sarah Wyatt Smn MA
Joseph: b 4-10-1719 d 6-1-1804 m Mary Vail PS NY
Joseph: b 5-18-1764 d 7-25-1847 m Priscilla Adams Pvt VA W★
Kimball, 1st: b 5-9-1726 d 4-10-1814 m Deborah Fuller Pvt MA
Kimball, 2d: b 2-29-1753 d 6-6-1824 m Lucretia Hempstead SgtMaj NY ★
Nicholas: b 7-17-1753 d 3-28-1812 m Mary Mitchell Sol NC
Paul, Sr.: b 3-14-1720 d 11-28-1809 m Hannah Cushing PS CS MA
Paul, Jr.: b 11-13-1758 d 1-15-1804 m Sarah Southworth Pvt MA
Robert: b 1-20-1754 d 1-3-1831 m Jemima Bixby MM CT
Samuel: b 11-9-1745 d — m Mary Elliott Pvt CT
Samuel, Sr.: b 5-20-1727 d *p.* 9-28-1778 m Ruth Carmen PS NY
Sylvanus: b *c.* 1740 d *c.* 1808 m Ann — PS Capt VA
Timothy, Sr.: b 8-12-1722 d 7-6-1798 m (1)Mary Putnam (2)Huldah (Prince) Sol CT
Timothy, Jr.: b 11-3-1758 d 5-31-1809 m (1)Deidomia Pierce (2)Prudence Denison Pvt CT
Wm.: b 1735 d 1805 m Mary — Lt CT
Wm.: b 5-19-1752 d *a.* 8-6-1810 m (1)Dulcinea Barry (2)Mrs Elizabeth Ford Capt SC
Wm.: b *c.* 1740 d *p.* 2-22-1801 m Elizabeth — PS VA

PRINDLE, (includes PRINGLE)
Alexander: b 2-20-1749/50 d *p.* 1785/6 m Silence Frisbie Sgt NY
Joseph: b 4-6-1730 d *p.* 1790 m Hulda Glover PS CT
Nathan: b 2-6-1744 d 7-8-1837 m (1)Hannah Frost (2)Mrs Elizabeth Clendening Sgt MA
Peter: b 1-17-1757 d 1-28-1840 m (1)Mary Patton (2)Sarah — Sgt CT ★
Wm.: b 1-22-1745 d 1-22-1829 m Mary Wertz Pvt PS MD
Zalmon: b 1-11-1758 d 8-19-1811 m Mary Williams Pvt CT

PRINTUP
Wm.: bpt 6-19-1735 d *p.* 9-28-1797 m Catrina (Printup) Pvt NY

PRINTY,
Wm.: b 1749 d 2-8-1826 m Rhoda Coleman Pvt NJ ★

PRIOLEAU,
Samuel: b 12-25-1717 d 1-3-1792 m Providence Hext PS SC
Samuel, Jr.: b 8-25-1742 d 1818 m Catherine Cordes Sol PS SC

PRIOR, (includes PRIER & PRYOR)
Abner, Sr.: b 6-2-1732 d *p.* 1785 m Abigail — Maj CT
Benjamin: b 10-23-1740 d *p.* 1776 m Sarah Soule Pvt MA
Christopher: b 1745 d *p.* 1784 m Catherine Clayton PS VA
David: b — d 9- -1804 m Susan Ballow Pvt VA
Eliphas: b 9-11-1733 d 7-9-1806 m Hannah (Howard) CS PS MA
Emory: b 9-27-1756 d 7-18-1795 m Mary McWay 1Lt MD
Haden: b 1745-50 d *p.* 1805 m Elizabeth Wade PS NC
Jesse: b 6-27-1755 d 2-10-1822 m Mary Bunn 2Lt CT ★
John: b 11-5-1744 d *p.* 1790 m Lydia Osier Pvt MA
John: b 4-24-1764 d 8-11-1834 m Margaret Ring Pvt MA
John: b 1750 d *p.* 1790 m — Pvt NJ
John: b *c.* 1735 d *p.* 9-23-1785 m Ann Bland Maj VA
Joseph: b 10-19-1745 d 9-30-1826 m Bethia Peterson Drm MA
Joseph: b *a.* 1750 d *a.* 2- -1813 m Mary Pryor Capt VA
Josiah: b 5-5-1735 d 7-21-1799 m Lucia Tryon Sgt CT
Matthew: b 3-15-1759 d 1834 m Mary Neely Cav NC ★
Nathan: b 1761 d *p.* 10-26-1792 m Abigail Rose Pvt MA
Nathaniel: b 9-20-1702 d 10-19-1785 m Ann Pease PS CT
Samuel: b 1-12-1762 d 12- -1811 m Mary Curd Capt VA
Seth: b 9-30-1734 d 5-4-1811 m Susannah — Pvt SC
Simeon: b 5-16-1754 d 6-29-1837 m Katherine Wright Pvt CT ★
Simon: b 2-19-1760 d 2-10-1842 m Susannah — Pvt NJ
Thomas: b 1733 d 3-23-1786 m Hannah White Pvt NJ
Timothy: b 1-8-1761 d 1803 m Barbara Horter Pvt PA

PRITCHARD, (includes PRICHARD)
Amos: b 8-27-1739 d 11-20-1814 m (2)Mary Tompkins Cpl CT
Amos: b 8-25-1752 d 3-1-1782 m Anna Andrews Pvt NH
Arthur: b *a.* 1760 d *p.* 1812 m Sarah Bell Pvt MD
Benjamin: b 1756 d 4-3-1825 m Anna Vaughn Pvt CT
David: b 1755 d 12-2-1815 m Miriam Jennings Sgt NC
George: b 1747 d 4-14-1805 m (1)— (2)Susannah Milner PS SC
Jabez: b 2-18-1740/1 d 1777 m Eunice Botsford Lt CT
James: b 6-4-1750 d 3-9-1837 m Rachel Warren Sgt CT ★

James: b 1746 d *p.* 5-30-1821 m (1)Elizabeth Hughes (2)Elizabeth Spears Capt MD
James: b 11-1-1763 d 2-6-1813 m (1)Tabitha White (2)Mrs Radinger Pvt MD
Jared: b 5-15-1760 d 3-12-1836 m (1)Anna Beard (2)Elizabeth Smith Pvt CT ★
Jeremiah: b 9-24-1754 d 8-10-1813 m Elizabeth Smith Lt NH
John: b 7-29-1760 d 6-21-1842 m Anne Smar Pvt VA ★
Paul: b 1721 d 1787 m Hannah Perley PS NH
Paul: b 4-9-1716 d 12-5-1791 m Ann Gibson PS SC
Rees: b 9- -1744 d 9-25-1830 m Barthama — Ens VA
Thomas: b 1752 d 6-8-1795 m Lucy Tufts Capt MA
Wm.: b *c.* 1750 d 6-18-1777 m Amelia Kotts Pvt VA

PRITCHETT, (includes PRICHETT, PRICHETTE)
Edward: b *c.* 1750 d *a.* 1-8-1796 m Priscilla (Collison) Minner Lt MD
John: b 4-6-1757 d 6-21-1842 m Elizabeth Hayhurst Capt NC
John: b 1733 d — m Sol NC
John: b *c.* 1740 d 6-2-1803 m — Lt VA
Joseph: b — d *p.* 12-29-1788 m Rachel — PS NC

PRIZER,
Henry: b 1757 d 7-9-1809 m Ann — Pvt PA

PROBASCO,
Garrett: b 9-4-1744 d 1836 m (1)Maake Groenendyck (2)Sarah Smock Pvt NJ ★
Hendrick: b *c.* 1735 d 1801 m Sitie Dumont Capt NJ
Peter: b 1760-5 d 1836 m Martha Probasco MM NJ
Rynear: b 2-20-1743 d *p.* 1785 m Elizabeth Warne Pvt NJ

PROCTOR,
Aaron: b 1757 d *p.* 4-13-1821 m Anna Williams Pvt NC
Azariah: b 9-20-1749 d 11-1-1832 m Azubah Robbins Sgt MA
Benjamin: b 10-20-1704 d 8-3-1794 m Lydia Chamberlain PS MA
Daniel: b 11-20-1744 d 12-5-1803 m Mary Robbins 1Lt MA
Elijah: b 7-6-1736 d 4-19-1819 m Esther Adams Lt MA
Ezekiel: b 8-5-1735 d *p.* 1781 m Elizabeth Proctor Pvt MA
Francis: b 2-28-1758 d 5-24-1832 m Mrs Abigail Edward Obed Pvt MA
Francis, Sr.: b 1705 d 3-12-1792 m Betsy — Capt PA
Francis, Jr.: b *a.* 1756 d 1814 m Ann Henderson Maj PA
Gershom: b 12-3-1753 d 12-17-1813 m (1)Sarah Whipple (2)Mary Hasit Pvt MA
James: b 11-14-1720 d *p.* 1790 m Hannah Nutting Cpl MA
James: b 6-18-1722 d 11-11-1776 m Abigail Whittemore Pvt PS NH
John: b 8-14-1757 d 2-4-1821 m (1)Hannah Cogswell (2)Edna Dean Pvt MA
John: b *c.* 1740 d *c.* 1789 m Catherine Hamilton Col PA
Johnson: b 10-29-1765 d 11-11-1851 m Lydia Waters Sol Drm MA
Jonathan: b 3-15-1751 d 8-14-1831 m Rebecca Pope Pvt MA
Joseph: b 11-2-1746 d 12-8-1818 m Nancy Broughton Sol MA
Joseph: b 8-25-1743 d 1-29-1805 m Elizabeth Epes PS MA
Joseph: b 10-6-1751 d 3-23-1821 m Hannah Brown Smn MA
Leonard: b 8-10-1764 d 2-29-1821 m Experience Hildreth Smn MA
Leonard: b 1-16-1734 d 6-3-1827 m (1)Lydia Nutting (2)Mary Keep Capt MA
Little Page: b 1760 d 11-15-1852 m (1)Sarah Jane Woodruff (2)Sarah Bates Sol PS VA ★
Moses: b 11-25-1747 d 2-27-1805 m Ruth Austin Pvt NH
Nathaniel, Sr.: b 11-5-1723 d 10-30-1806 m Mary Warren Pvt MA
Nathaniel, Jr.: b 7-5-1762 d 8-28-1855 m Mercy Russell Pvt MA ★
Oliver: b 4-25-1745 d 10-30-1815 m Mary Manning Pvt MA
Peter: b 3-26-1735 d 8-31-1822 m Mary Ball Capt MA
Philip: b 3-27-1750 d 11-28-1841 m Hannah Locke Pvt MA
Reuben: b *c.* 1754 d *c.* 1808 m — Pvt VA
Samuel: b 9-12-1764 d 6-8-1844 m Sally Gould Sgt MA ★
Samuel: b 1733 d 1806 m Lucy Wheeler Pvt MA
Silas: b 9-6-1750 d 12-26-1845 m Olive Read 1Lt MA
Steven: b 1755 d 1844 m — Black Sol GA
Thomas: b 1739 d 3-16-1806 m (1)Anna Maria Fox (2)Sarah Ann Hussey Col PA
Thorndike: b 6-2-1698 d 1778 m Abigail Wilson Sol MA
Wm.: b 8-31-1724 d 2-14-1807 m Susannah Hall Pvt MA
Wm.: b 2-20-1748 d 2-19-1846 m Mary (Proctor) Pvt NH
Wm. B: b *c.* 1756 d *p.* 1803 m Elizabeth Epperson Sgt MA

PROFFITT,
David: b 3-1-1746 d *p.* 10-31-1818 m Nancy Haton Capt VA

PRONG, (includes BRONG)
Christopher: b 2- -1757 d 12-12-1809 m Elizabeth — Pvt PA
Sebastian: b *c.* 1755 d 1834 m — Pvt PA

PROSSER,
Daniel: b 1744 d 8-11-1829 m Margaret Mickey Pvt Spy VA ★
Ichabod: b — d *p.* 2-16-1818 m Elizabeth — Sol MA
John: b *c.* 1760 d 1814 m Elizabeth Mastin CS Lt VA

PROTHRO,
Evan: b 1740 d *p.* 12-25-1817 m — Sol SC

PROUDFOOT,
Andrew: b 1728 d 3-30-1807 m Sarah Wallace Pvt PA
David: b 1740 d 1822 m Nancy Livingston Pvt PA
Robert: b 1746 d 1816 m Mary Campbell Pvt PA

PROUT,
Degory: b 5-13-1761 d 9-20-1835 m (1)Jemima Sherwood
  (2)Hannah Ball Pvt Drm NY ★
Harris: b 4-21-1732 d 2-9-1822 m Priscilla Roberts Pvt CT
James: b c. 1747 d 11-11-1836 m Chloe Jordan Pvt CT NJ ★
John: b 9-16-1749 d 4-7-1823 m Rachel Hedges Sgt CT

PROUTY,
Amos: b 3-8-1766 d 10-4-1841 m Phoebe Bartlett Pvt MA
Asa: 2-22-1751 d 3-10-1826 m Lydia Livermore Sgt MA
Caleb: b 7-11-1751 d 9-3-1839 m Sarah Lincoln Pvt MA
Daniel: b 7-15-1759 d 2-1-1837 m Catherine Palmer Pvt MA
David: b 2-23-1753 d 5-28-1831 m Margaret Whiton Pvt MA
Eli: b 9-8-1757 d 6-27-1818 m Rebekah Bemis Cpl MA
Elijah: b 1-27-1759 d 2-8-1792 m Anna Munroe Pvt MA
Isaac: b 12-22-1750 d 6-15-1828 m (1)Anna Dunnell (2)Mrs
  Meribah Hilyard Warner Pvt MA
Joshua: b 5-18-1759 d 3-24-1838 m Molly Muzzey Pvt MA
Wm.: b 7-25-1730 d p. 1784 m Rachel (Damon) Dunbar Pvt MA

PROVANCE, (includes PROVENCE)
John: b 1753 d p. 12-28-1775 m — Pvt MA
John Wm.: b 1742 d a. 1785 m (1)Elizabeth Thomson (2)Sarah
  Yards Wright Pvt PA
Joseph Yards: b 3-31-1764 d 5-16-1842 m Rachel Spencer Pvt PA ★

PROVANDIE,
Louis: b 1757 d 6-30-1834 m Marie Feriole Matr MA

PROVOST,
Daniel: b 5-9-1753 d 12-14-1832 m Elizabeth Bishop Pvt CT ★
David: b 4-10-1750 d 7-9-1841 m Barbara Speaker Sgt NJ
Jasper: b 7-11-1762 d 7-5-1854 m Catharine Gulick Pvt MM NJ
John: bpt 2-22-1762 d 3-8-1832 m Eva Calyer Pvt NJ
Jonathan: bpt 12-17-1745 d a. 5-8-1792 m Abigail — Pvt NJ
Robert, Jr.: b 3-22-1737 d 8-17-1796 m Phoebe Plumb PM QM NY
Samuel: b c. 1740 d p. 1790 m Sarah Bishop Sol CT

PROWELL,
Joseph: b 1753 d 4-3-1805 m Mary Nicholes Maj PA
Wm.: b 3-1-1754 d 9-10-1811 m (1)Margaret Nelson (2)Mrs
  Barbara (Beichler) Singer Capt PA

PRUDDEN, (includes PRUDEN)
Amos: b 1-27-1745 d 9-22-1799 m Damaris Harrison Pvt NJ
Boyce John: b c. 1743 d p. 1789 m Elizabeth Baldwin Pvt NJ
Fletcher: b 8-30-1737 d 1-9-1798 m Sarah Treat Capt CT
Henry: b c. 1755 d 1801 m Mildred Milner OrdlSgt VA
Isaac: b 1738 d 6-20-1798 m (1)Hannah Lum (2)Sarah Keen
  Tms NJ
Joseph: bpt 5-5-1760 d 1830 m Providence Gorden CS NJ
Moses: b 1732 d 1-11-1777 m Mary Morris 2Lt NJ
Newton: b 1754 d 1836 m Elizabeth Northrop Cpl CT

PRUD'HOMME,
Michel: b c. 1750 d p. 1780 m Marie Snaylor PS LA

PRUITT, (includes PREWETT, PREWITT, PRUET, PRUETT,
  & PRUETTE)
Byrd: b 1752 d 1833 m Sarah Hurt Pvt VA ★
David: b c. 1760 d p. 10- -1815 m — Pvt NC
Elisha: b c. 1760 d p. 1808 m Tabitha Collins Sgt VA
Isham, Sr.: b c. 1730 d 1806 m Frances — PS VA
Jacob: b c. 1761 d p. 5-14-1845 m Nancy Agnes Richey Sol NC
James: b c. 1745 d a. 1-9-1811 m (1)Elizabeth Street (2)Mrs Sarah
  Mathews Pvt VA
John: b — d 4-30-1837 m Eady — Pvt VA
Joseph: b 1760 d 1815 m Patsy Elliott Matr VA
Joseph: b — d p. 1-31-1808 m (1)Leah Moss (2)Polly Price PS VA
Joshua: b 1754 d 1840 m Mary — Pvt NC ★
Joshua: b 1765 d 1-27-1843 m (1)Sarah Adams (2)Maria Yeager
  Pvt Matr VA
Martin, Jr.: b 7-15-1752 d 2-4-1841 m Mary Woods Sol NC ★
Micajah: b 1760 d p. 1782 m Betsey Baker Pvt NC
Michael, Sr.: b c. 1722-20 d 4-2-1798 m (1)Elizabeth Simpkins
  (2)Mary Thurston PS VA
Obediah: b c. 1752 d 1801 m Molly Palmer Pvt VA
Robert: b 6-10-1758 d 4-14-1819 m Martha Chandler Pvt VA
Samuel: b 1705 d p. 11-13-1801 m Lucy Owen Pvt VA
Wm., Sr.: b c. 1725 d 1817 m Mary Martin Pvt VA

PRUYN, (includes PRUYNE)
Casparus: b 5-10-1734 d 10-7-1817 m Catharine Groesbeck Lt NY
David: bpt 10-6-1727 d 5-30-1816 m Lenah Snoek Pvt NY
Francis S: b 7-8-1757 d 10-30-1812 m Maria Van Ness Lt NY
Henry: b 1751 d 10-25-1836 m (1)Sarah DeForest (2)Mrs Elizabeth
  Mowers Pvt NY
Henry: b 1765 d 9-14-1851 m Rachel Marenius Pvt NY ★

Rynier: bpt 5-22-1757 d — m Jeannette Goewey Sol NY
Samuel: b 10-15-1728 d 12-14-1785 m Neeltje Ten Eyck Pvt NY

PUCKETT,
John: b 2-26-1764 d 9-30-1844 m Rhoda Lida Pvt VA ★
Richard: b c. 1750 d 1813 m Sarah McConnico Pvt VA
Thomas: b c. 1750 d p. 2-26-1805 m Mary Taylor Pvt VA
Wm.: b 1747 d 1833 m (1) X (2)Phebe Perdue Pvt VA

PUDNEY,
Francis: b 8-14-1755 d 3-13-1826 m (2)Elizabeth Montrose Pvt
  PS NY
Thorne: b 1-2-1723 d 4-18-1813 m Rachel Bogardus Pvt NY

PUFF,
Peter: b 1756 d 6-11-1842 m Marie Embler Pvt NY
Philip: b 6-25-1752 d 1817 m Mary — Pvt PA

PUFFER,
Daniel: b 1-2-1745/6 d 3-13-1829 m Mary Balcom Sol MA
Isaac: b 1763 d 5-22-1838 m Sarah Miriam Pvt MA
Jabez: b 1705 d 1-21-1789 m (1)Thankful Haynes (2)Hannah
  Treadway (3)Mrs Sarah Perry Capt MA
Jabez: b 7-16-1743 d p. 1790 m Rachel Morse PS NH
Jacob: b 4-10-1743 d 4-20-1777 m Sarah Gibson Sol MA
James: b 8-11-1734 d 1814 m (1)Mercy Dakin (2)Submit Goddard
  2Lt MA
John, Jr.: b 5-27-1746 d 4-3-1834 m Silence Jackson Pvt Wgn
  MA ★
Jonathan: b 6-9-1746 d 9-4-1817 m (1)Elizabeth Gibson (2)Jemima
  Taft Pvt MA
Josiah: b 3-21-1736 d 7-9-1806 m Mary Read Sgt MA
Phineas: b 9-23-1741 d 1817 m Molly Stratton CS Pvt MA
Samuel, Jr.: b 5-30-1735 d 5-24-1811 m Olive Rice Sgt MA
Seth: b 3-11-1730 d 1786 m (1)Mercy Bates (2)Patience Tolman
  Pvt MA
Timothy: b 6-6-1756 d 3-28-1828 m Elizabeth Cady Sol MA
Wm.: b 4-24-1734 d 1-15-1809 m (1)Mary Wetherell (2)Anna
  Metcalf (3)Susannah Ellis Sgt MA

PUGH, (includes PEW)
Elijah: o 1760 d 6- -1824 m Ruth Julian Pvt GA
Humphrey: b c. 1757 d c. 1824 m (2)Ann Cheek Sgt MD
Jesse: b c. 1730 d c. 1811 m Elizabeth Stewart Pvt GA
Job: b 1757 d c. 1802 m Ruth Brooke Pvt PA
John: b c. 1745 d 5-4-1799 m Ann Moore Pvt NC
John: b 6-9-1747 d 1840 m Rachel Barrett Ens PA
John: b c. 1741 d 4-19-1791 m Mary Ringberry PS PA
John: b 11-18-1762/3 d 9-20-1848 m — Pvt NC VA ★
Jonathan: b 1732 d p. 9-9-1794 m Margaret — Pvt VA
Joseph: b 6-28-1753 d 11-9-1820 m Elizabeth Hunt Lt VA
Joshua: b 4-25-1743 d 12-28-1808 m Hannah Chandler Pvt PA
Robert: b c. 1735 d 1808 m Mary Edwards PS VA
Ruben: b 12-13-1758 d 8-24-1847 m Fanny Smith Pvt NJ VA ★
Thomas: b 8-6-1726 d 1806 m (1)Mary Scott CS PS Col NC

PUGSLEY,
Samuel: b 1734 d 1804 m Elizabeth Brundage Pvt NY
Wm.: b 9-28-1724 d 4-26-1786 m Deborah Stevenson Pvt NY
Wm.: b 10-1-1752 d 4-1-1810 m Mary Annett Bockee Pvt NY

PULLEN,
James: b 7-16-1749 d 2-1-1829 m (1)Elona Capron (2)Phoebe
  Stanley Cpl MA
John: b 5-7-1763 d 3-29-1810 m Amy Bishop Pvt MA
John: b 1736 d p. 6-25-1808 m Ann — PS NC
Oliver: b 11-1-1760 d 12- -1840 m Abigail Page Pvt MA RI ★
Robert: b 7-6-1756 d 1-12-1854 m Hetty Jewel Pvt VA ★
Stephen: b 9-30-1744 d 9-14-1815 m (1)Mercy Blackington
  (2)Elizabeth — CS MA
Thomas: b 11-21-1752 d 2-6-1828 m (1)Lydia Bowers (2)Mrs
  Linder Sol GA
Thomas: b 12-15-1761/2 d 1-31-1844 m Elizaabeth Abston Pvt VA
Wm.: b 1758 d 4-4-1845 m (2)Mary Haynes Pvt VA W★
Wm.: b a. 1760 d 2-5-1834 m Mary — Pvt VA ★

PULLIAM,
Benjamin: b a. 1758 d 10-27-1817 m Lucy Stuart PS VA
George: b 1747 d 5- -1786 m Frances Price Lt VA
James: b 1736 d p. 4-19-1799 m Elizabeth Allen 2Lt PS VA
John: b 1755 d 12-14-1800 m Elizabeth Wilson Pvt VA
Robert: b 1740 d 1825 m Eleanor Brown Sol GA
Wm.: b 1748 d 1829 m Sara — Capt GA
Zackariah: b c. 1754 d p. 8-10-1844 m Sarah Black Pvt VA ★

PULLING,
John: b 2-18-1737 d 1-25-1787 m (1)Annis Lee (2)Mrs Sarah
  Thaxter McRean Capt MA

PULLMAN, (includes PULMAN)
John: b 1752/3 d 4-26-1811 m Esther — Pvt RI ★
Jonathan: b 3-31-1754 d 9-24-1839 m Sarah Tift OrdlSgt RI
Salter: b 1755 d 12-15-1828 m Orpha Olmstead Pvt NY

PULSIPHER, (includes PULSIFER)
David: bpt 3-4-1716 d *p.* 8-1-1775 m Elizabeth Stowell Cpl NH
Nathaniel: b 5-29-1736 d *p.* 1788 m Abigail Proctor Sgt MA

PULVER,
Henry: b 5-11-1738 d *p.* 1790 m Ann Shaver Capt NY
Jacob: b 1754 d *p.* 1777 m Catherine Brazee Pvt NY
Jacob: b 1734/5 d *p.* 1779 m Christine Burger PS NY
Martin: b 3-3-1763 d 10-21-1832 m Margarita Poplar Pvt NY
Wendel: bpt 8-12-1744 d *p.* 1786 m Anna Barbara Shufelt Lt NY
Wendel: b 11-14-1739 d 8-13-1826 m (1)Charity — (2)Susannah — Pvt NY

PUMMELL,
Francis: b 1-12-1754 d 8-6-1817 m Margaret Sombrecht Jones Pvt VA

PUMYEA,
Peter: b 3-27-1739 d 9-21-1802 m Ida Suydam Capt NJ

PUNCHARD,
James: b 3-14-1737 d 6-6-1812 m (1)Mrs Dorcas Townsend (2)Elizabeth Sprague PS NH

PUNDERSON,
John: b 1-1-1747 d 1-12-1836 m Rhoda Alger Ens NY ★

PUNTENEY,
Joseph: b 1728 d *a.* 8-26-1780 m Sarah — PS MD

PURCELL, (includes PURSELL & PURSLEY)
Daniel: b *c.* 1754 d *a.* 7-8-1813 m Margaret Smith Pvt PA
Edward: b 3- -1759 d *a.* 7-12-1851 m Abigail Williams Pvt VA ★
George: b — d 1804 m (2)Margaret Randolph Ens VA W★
Henry: b *a.* 1740 d 3-24-1802 m Sarah — Chp SC
Jacob: b 3-12-1759 d 11-21-1834 m (1)Rachel — (2)Catharine Bigford Sol NY
James: b *a.* 1748 d 1813 m Miss Dowell Pvt VA
John: b 1735 d 1797 m Katherine — Pvt PA
John: b 9- -1757/8 d 9- -1836 m (1)Sarah Washington (2)Elizabeth Carter Pvt VA
Jonathan: b *c.* 1750 d *c.* 9- -1813 m Catherine — Pvt VA
Thomas: bpt 4-9-1720 d *p.* 6- -1782 m Mary Van Hook PS VA
Thomas: b — d *p.* 1795 m Lydia Vernon PS VA

PURDIN,
Joseph: b *c.* 1730 d *p.* 1790 m Eunity — Drm MD

PURDUM,
John: b *c.* 1739 d *p.* 1-17-1795 m Keziah — PS MD

PURDY, (includes PERDEW, PERDUE, PURDIE)
Aaron: b 1725 d 9-10-1805 m Sallie — PS VA
Abner: b 5-11-1752 d 7-25-1821 m (1)Hannah Fisher (2)Mrs Naomi Rundell 2Lt NY
Alvan: b 1-11-1757 d 7-16-1830 m Lydia Hunt Lt NY
Benjamin, Jr.: b 1743 d 12-11-1828 m Elizabeth Bulleys Pvt VT
Benjamin: b 12-12-1718 d 11-28-1808 m Deborah — Pvt VT
Daniel: b 1-15-1759 d 4-17-1817 m Abigail Lyon Pvt CT
Daniel, Jr.: b 1755 d 3-10-1840 m Martha — 2Lt CT NY ★
Daniel: b 4-26-1752 d 8-25-1825 m Martha Smith Ens VT W★
Deliverance, Jr.: b *c.* 1760 d *p.* 1800 m Susannah Dickens Pvt NY
Elisha: b 3-17-1740 d 3-20-1820 m Mehitable Smith Pvt NY
Francis: b 7-14-1760 d 11-28-1842 m Anna Foreman Sol NY
Henry: b 1751 d 8-16-1816 m Nancy Agnes Richey Pvt Wgn SC W★
James: b *c.* 1756 d 1802 m Susannah Wainwright Capt MD
James: b 11-16-1750 d 11-19-1833 m Phebe (Purdy) Pvt NY
James: b 1760 d 3-8-1835 m Rachel Webb Pvt NY ★
James: b 1732 d 8-7-1813 m Martha McConall Col PA
James: b 1759 d 3- -1822 m Mary Farmer Pvt PA
Jeremiah: b 6-29-1761 d 6-16-1842 m (1)Lydia Thompson (2)Susannah Walworth Pvt NY ★
John: b 11-11-1764 d 10-14-1846 m Esther Barton Pvt NY
John: b 1760 d 2-14-1798 m Nancy Wilson Pvt PA
Mentor: b 12-30-1751 d 10-15-1797 m Jemima Farlow Sol PA
Obediah: b 5-14-1757 d 1-16-1835 m Hannah Smith Lt NY ★
Reuben: b 6-29-1746 d 6-29-1828 m Annah Powel Pvt VT
Samuel: b 11-5-1744 d 5-1-1821 m (1)Phoebe — (2)Glorianna Fowler Pvt NY
Simeon: b 1740 d *p.* 1812 m (1)Elizabeth — (2)Rebecca — Pvt NY
Solomon: b 1732 d 1826 m Ruth Merritt Lt NY
Stephen: b 1736 d 1807 m Hester Bailey PS Cpl NY
Thomas: b 1751 d 5- -1832 m Mary Elizabeth Lipporth Sol NY
Thomas: b 2-3-1769 d 3-9-1813 m Mary Davids Pvt NY
Wm.: b 4-14-1749 d 1824 m Rachel (Purdy) Pvt PS NY
Wm.: b *c.* 1755 d *c.* 1- -1840 m Charity Casteel Pvt PA
Wm.: b 1-13-1745 d 9-13-1825 m Mary Roney Pvt PA

PURINGTON, (includes PURINTON)
Humphrey, Jr.: b 8-16-1759 d 1-28-1832 m Thankful Snow Pvt PS MA
James: b 4-29-1742 d 12-7-1832 m (1)Priscilla Harding (2)Silence Winchel 1Lt MA

Nathaniel: b 1731-6 d 2-9-1788 m Priscilla Woodbury LCol MA
Robert: b 4-21-1751 d 4-1-1833 m Dorcas Eaton Pvt MA

PURKHISER,
Michael: b 1736 d 10-31-1816 m Catharine — Pvt PA

PURKITT,
Henry: b 3-18-1755 d 3-3-1846 m Eunice Wright Sgt MA

PURMORT,
Joseph: b 7-18-1749 d 3-25-1813 m Mercy Dolloff Pvt NH

PURNELL,
Robert: b *c.* 1760 d 3- -1825 m — Sol SC
Thomas: b 2-28-1745 d 5-8-1790 m Sarah Marshall PS CS MD
Wm.: b 1739 d 1795 m Mary Robins Col MD

PURPLE,
Ezra: b 1-16-1747-9 d 7-22-1815 m Mary Pentfield Pvt CT

PURTLE,
John: b *c.* 1750 d *p.* 6-9-1793 m Esther Pyrtle Cpl VA

PURVIANCE,
James: b 1-14-1733 d 4-26-1806 m Sarah Wasson Capt NC
John: b 1743 d 8- -1823 m Jane Wasson Lt PS NC
John: b 6-19-1763 d 9-27-1833 m (1)Nancy Ferguson (2)Elizabeth Lisemby Pvt NC SC ★
John: b 11-30-1742 d 1821 m Elizabeth Thomson Pvt PA
Robert: b — d 10- -1806 m Frances Young CS MD
Wm.: b *c.* 1735 d *c.* 1789 m Eleanor — Col PS NC

PURVIS,
George: b 6-3-1750 d 3-5-1801 m Elizabeth — Capt DE
George: b 11-21-1718 d 12- -1794 m Mary Oldham PS VA
Gilbert: b *a.* 1756 d 1830 m Effica Howell Pvt SC
James: b 1763 d *p.* 1840 m Rhoda Roberts Pvt NC
John: b 1746 d 5-4-1792 m Anne Pritchard Capt SC
Lewis: b 1761 d 1826 m Leeah Purvis Sol PS NC

PURYEAR,
John: b *c.* 1725 d 1785 m Martha — Sol VA

PUSEY,
Joshua: b 9-18-1738 d 3-16-1804 m (1)Mary Miller (2)Lydia Trimble (3)Hannah Canby Pvt PA

PUSHEE,
Davis: b 1760 d 9-21-1840 m Susanna Pierce Pvt MA
Nathan: b 10- -1758 d 10-31-1838 m Jane (Brown) Porter TrmMaj MA ★

PUTNAM, (includes PUTMAN)
Aaron: b 12-15-1733 d 10-28-1813 m Elizabeth Avery Pvt CT
Aaron: b 9-6-1756 d 1801 m Olive Osborn Pvt CT
Aaron: b 1756 d 3-4-1838 m Sally (Coburn) Pvt CT ★
Aaron: b 8-30-1730 d 2- -1810 m Lydia Waters Pvt MA
Aaron: bpt 2-14-1719 d 5-22-1780 m Elizabeth Peek Pvt NY
Aaron J: b 6-12-1745 d 8-1-1830 m Elizabeth DeSpitzer Pvt NY
Allen: b 10-25-1762 d 1807 m Anna Porter Pvt MA
Amos: b 9- -1722 d 7-26-1807 m (1)Hannah Phillips (2)Mary Gott Pvt PS MA
Amos: bpt 8-31-1729 d 7-19-1799 m Lydia Trask Sol MA
Amos: b 5-25-1752 d 10-9-1841 m Lydia Hovey Pvt MA
Andrew: b 5-7-1742 d 1812 m Lucy Parks PS CS MA
Archelaus: b 2-16-1743 d 1-14-1809 m Sarah (Putnam) Sgt MA
Archelous: b 10-15-1749 d 10-22-1816 m Mary Nicholas Pvt PS NH
Archelaus: bpt 5-14-1721 d *c.* 1784/5 m Ruth Flint Lt CS MA
Arent: bpt 7-10-1751 d *p.* 1786 m Rebecca DeGarmo Pvt NY
Asa: b 8-10-1743 d 9-7-1795 m Anna Collins CS MA
Benjamin, Sr.: b 10-12-1718 d 4-26-1796 m Sarah Putnam Sgt MA
Benjamin, Jr.: b 4-28-1757 d 7-9-1812 m Miriam Flint Pvt MA
Caleb: b 10-24-1754 d 1808 m Judith Sibley Pvt MA
Cornelius: b 12-17-1724 d 4-19-1798 m Elizabeth Pruyn Pvt NY
Daniel: b 11-18-1759 d 4-30-1831 m Katharine Hutchinson Maj CT
Daniel: b 10-25-1755 d 10-21-1819 m (1)Elizabeth Oberlock (2)Keziah Pollard Lt MA
Daniel: b 1738 d 11- -1801 m Elizabeth Putnam Lt MA
Daniel: b 4-19-1748 d 4-26-1813 m Rachel Small Ens MA
Daniel: b 3-28-1739 d 5-12-1809 m Anna Chase Pvt CS NH
Daniel: b 1-1-1764 d 7-19-1816 m Prudence Kelton Pvt SC W★
David: b 5-14-1747 d 5-25-1832 m Elizabeth Woodbury Sgt MA
David: b 7-19-1752 d 3-21-1840 m Phoebe Woodbury Cpl MA
David: b 3-6-1753 d 1820 m Abigail Coulton Pvt MA
David: b 1747 d 3-10-1828 m Hannah Van Antwerp Pvt NY
Dirk: b 1744 d 4-14-1833 m Neetje Van Brakle Lt NY
Ebenezer: b 1717 d 8-12-1788 m Margaret Scolley Dr PS MA

PUTNAM, contd.

Ebenezer: b 9-7-1738 d 5-4-1808 m Hannah Dike MM MA
Ebenezer: b 8-8-1719 d 2-2-1782 m Mary Parker PS NH
Edmund: b 6-27-1725 d 1810 m Anna Andrews Capt MA
Edward: b 6-30-1711 d 2-17-1800 m Ruth Fuller PS MA
Eleazer: b 6-5-1738 d 11-23-1804 m Mary Crosby MM 2Lt MA
Elijah: b 6-1-1761 d 8-11-1825 m (1)Betsey Fayton (2)Lucy
   Redington Pvt MA
Elisha: b 12-4-1745 d 5-25-1784 m Abigail Chamberlain Pvt MA
Enoch: b 2-18-1732 d 1796 m (1)Hannah Putnam (2)Elizabeth
   Stratton Col MA
Ephraim, Sr.: b 2-10-1719/20 d 11-13-1777 m Sarah Cram PS NH
Ephraim, Jr.: b 6-15-1744 d 3-2-1799 m Lucy Spalding Pvt PS NH
Ezra: b 11-2-1751 d 7-1-1841 m Rebecca Dyke Pvt MA ★
Ezra: bpt 6-8-1729 d 3-19-1811 m Lucy Putnam Maj MA
Francis: b 9-24-1758 d 10-28-1840 m Joanna Leland Sol MA
Francis: b 5-4-1752 d 11-23-1834 m Maria Fonda 1Lt NY ★
Garret: b 2-22-1752 d 4-13-1826 m Rebecca Garrison Capt NY
Gideon: b 11-25-1750 d p. 1800 m Abagail Holton Pvt MA
Henry, Sr.: b 8-14-1712 d 4-19-1775 m Hannah Boardman MM MA
Henry, Jr.: b 3-6-1737 d 1798 m Sarah Putnam Ens MA
Henry: b 5-7-1755 d 11-27-1806 m (1)Mary Hawkes (2)Lucy Tufts
   Pvt MA
Henry: bpt 9-12-1761 d a. 4-19-1798 m Mariah Quackenbush
   Pvt NY
Henry: b 5-10-1743 d 8-10-1815 m Sarah Williamson Capt PS SC
Howard: b 2-11-1762 d 1-24-1834 m (1)Hannah Greene (2)Caroline
   Jones Pvt MA ★
Isaac: bpt 1763 d 4-23-1808 m Martha Adams Pvt MA
Israel, Sr.: b 1-7-1718 d 5-19-1790 m (1)Hannah Pope (2)Deborah
   (Lothrop) Gardiner Avery MGen CT
Israel, Jr.: b 1-28-1740 d 3-7-1812 m Sarah Waldo Maj CT
Jacob: b 3-9-1711 d 2-10-1781 m Susanna Harriman PS NH
James Phillips: b 4-21-1745 d 4-4-1824 m Mary Herrick Pvt MA
Jeremiah: b 10-31-1737 d 9-16-1799 m Rachel Fuller Capt MA
Jeremiah, Jr.: b 6-26-1762 d p. 1806 m (1)Judith Snow (2)Mary
   Tucker Pvt MA
Jesse: b 10-2-1750 d 11-19-1837 m Rachel Carlton Pvt NH ★
John: b 5-13-1734 d 8-10-1786 m Martha Woodward Sgt CT
John: b 8-25-1735 d 6-13-1809 m Mary Hall Capt MA
John: b 6-13-1746 d 9-9-1838 m Mollie Baker Pvt MA
John, Sr.: b 1720 d 1786 m Ruth Swinnerton Capt MA
John, Jr.: b 12-10-1743 d p. 1779 m Abigail Small 2Lt MA
John: b 7-27-1738 d 12-13-1824 m Mary Cummings Pvt MA
John: b 7-8-1760 d 2-24-1827 m Huldah Waters Pvt MA
John: b 11-2-1762 d 1-13-1821 m Sally Rich Pvt MA
John: b 11-12-1767 d 4-10-1841 m (1)Lucretia Von Duzen (2)Lendy
   Andrus Pvt MA ★
John: b 6-4-1764 d 6-9-1848 m (1)Catharine Case (2)Peggy
   (Glidden) Willard Pvt NH VT ★
John: b 1763 d 11-5-1837 m Olive Barron Pvt NH
John: b 5-10-1761 d 11-17-1849 m Mary Converse Pvt NH
Jonathan: b 1750 d 2-22-1826 m Lucy Lane Cpl PS NH
Jonathan Follansbee: b 5-9-1763 d 10-30-1858 m Philana Leland
   Pvt MA
Joseph: b 4-26-1724 d 1781 m Mary Porter Lt MA
Joseph: bpt 4-21-1746-51 d 9-25-1834 m Anna Putnam MM MA
Josiah, Sr.: b 3-3-1718/9 d 2-4-1795 m Lydia Wheeler Capt MA
Josiah, Jr.: b 6-8-1749/50 d 5-1-1835 m Sibbel Smith Pvt MA
Levi: b 1758 d 4-10-1830 m Hannah Allen Pvt MA
Levi: b 2-11-1757 d 1835 m Rebecca Holden Pvt NH
Lodiwick: b 11-14-1713 d 5-21-1780 m Elizabeth Soets PS NY
Miles: b 9-5-1725 d 4-19-1800 m Rachel Wilkins Pvt MA
Moses: b 1740 d 7-25-1801 m Rebekah Kimball PS NH
Nathan: b 9-19-1749 d 4-10-1823 m Hannah Phillips (Putnam)
   Sgt MA
Nathan: b 10-24-1730 d 8-6-1813 m Betsy Buffington PS NH
Nathaniel: b 5-3-1734 d 1812 m Deborah Towne Lt MA
Nathaniel: b 4-24-1738 d 5-20-1790 m (1)Mary Eastman (2)Mary
   Snow PS NH
Oliver, Sr.: bpt 10-21-1722 d 10-3-1794 m Hannah Brown Ens MA
Oliver, Jr.: b 2-4-1753 d 5-19-1814 m Sarah Perkins Pvt NH
Peter: b c. 1732 d 1797 m Mary — PS VA
Peter: b 5-29-1757 d 11-22-1827 m Sarah Marble Cpl MA
Peter, Jr.: b 1-15-1758 d 10-16-1821 m Susie Osgood Pvt MA
Peter: b 11-29-1763 d 4-21-1856 m (1)Rachel Hills (2)Sally Fuller
   Cpl NH ★
Peter: b 1760 d 10-3-1835 m Sarah Mary Kinnan Pvt NJ W★
Philip: b 3-4-1740 d 11-18-1810 m (1)Abigail Jaquith (2)Hannah
   Jacques Capt NH
Phineas: b 6-10-1728 d 6- -1817 m Mary Whipple Sgt MA
Porter: b 12-7-1758 d p. 1795 m Rebecca Smith Pvt MA
Reuben: b c. 1760 d c. 3-4-1838 m Huldah Cummings Pvt CT ★
Reuben: b 4-9-1757 d 6- -1797 m Elizabeth Mason Pvt MA
Roger: b 10-10-1743 d p. 1790 m — Pvt MA
Rufus: b 4-9-1738 d 5-4-1824 m (1)Elizabeth Ayers (2)Persis Rice
   BGen MA
Samuel: b 5-19-1727 d p. 12-30-1778 m Kezia Hayward Pvt MA
Seth: b 9-16-1756 d 9-3-1827 m Sarah Harden Pvt NH
Solomon: b 7-17-1755 d 4-18-1810 m Miriam Elmer Pvt MA
Stephen: b 4-4-1728 d 3-5-1803 m Mary Gibbs Pvt MA
Stephen: b 2-22-1742 d 6-8-1809 m (1)Ruth Putman (2)Susanna
   Herrick Pvt MA

Stephen: b 9-24-1741 d 6-29-1812 m Olive Varnum PS NH
Tarrant: b 9-2-1732 d 1819 m (1)Mary Porter (2)Eunice Porter Ens
   Adj MA
Tarrant: b 4-3-1716 d 2-8-1794 m Priscilla Baker PS MA
Teunis: b 3- -1716 d p. 1782 m Rebecca Arents VanAntwerp PS NY
Thomas: b 10-22-1728 d 8-20-1814 m Rachel Wetherbe CS PS NH
Thomas: b 7-1-1754 d p. 1790 m Susanna Stone Cpl VT
Timothy, Sr.: b 12-25-1732 d 1-14-1817 m (1)Mehitable —
   (2)Susanna Badger Pvt NH
Timothy, Jr.: b 10-4-1760 d p. 1809 m Sarah Hewit Pvt NH
Victor: b 11-18-1754 d 4-13-1837 m Margaret Putnam Pvt NY ★
Victor A.: b 1747 d 10-12-1800 m Maria Schultes Pvt NY
Victor C.: b 5-31-1756 d 11-9-1816 m Anna Garrison Lt NY
Wm.: b 5-27-1744 d 8-20-1800 m Bathiah Putnam Cpl MA
Wm.: b 1-7-1758 d 7-22-1818 m Submit Fisk Cpl MA
Zadock: b 12-29-1752 d 10-2-1819 m Abigail Elliott Sgt MA

PUTNEY,

Asa: b c. 1752 d 12-8-1834 m — Sgt NH ★
Ebenezer: b 11-19-1739 d 6-18-1802 m Susannah French Lt MA
Eleazer: b 4-23-1732 d 3-27-1809 m Abigail Mixer 1Lt MA
Henry: b 10-4-1722 d 4-13-1807 m (1)Mary Wells (2)Dolly Jewett
   (3)Deborah Austin PS NH
James: b 12- -1754 d — m Mary Ordway Pvt NH
Jonathan: b — d 5-20-1814 m Elizabeth Newhall Sgt MA
Joseph: b 1753 d p. 1840 m Marion Piper Pvt NH ★
Stephen: b 2-12-1765 d 2-18-1847 m (1)Sally Eastman (2)Susan
   Eastman (3)Sally Eastman Pvt NH W ★
Thomas: b 1753 d 3-4-1830 m Lydia Peaslee Pvt NH ★

PYLE, (includes PILE & PYLES)

Benjamin: b 1-13-1766 d 5-29-1824 m Ruth — Pvt VA
Caleb: b 10-8-1741 d c. 1808 m Mary Mattewson Pvt PA
Jacob: b c. 1717 d 1786 m Jane Sharpless Pvt PA
John: b — d 1799-1806 m Sarah Breazier PS NC
Joseph: b c. 1730 d p. 1790 m Alice Smith Pvt PA
Levi: b c. 1745 d p. 1790 m Margaret Johnson Pvt PA
Richard: b 1760 d 3-23-1816 m (2)Rebecca Clifton Sgt VA
Ruben: b 1742 d 1835 m Mary Esther Rochester Pvt SC
Wm.: b a. 1754 d p. 12-28-1814 m (1)Lucretia (Gant) Keys (2)Nancy
   (Keys) Jones 1Lt VA

PYNCHON,

Walter: b 9-5-1744 d 7-24-1818 m Mary Smith Capt MA W ★

PYRON,

Wm. C.: b 1757 d 1-27-1850 m Mary Powell Pvt NC ★

QUA,

Robert: b 1750 d p. 1790 m Margaret Armstrong Sol NY

QUACKENBUSH, (includes QUACKENBOS & QUACKENBOSS)

Abraham D.: bpt 2-5-1730 d 5-20-1812 m (1)Mana Bradt (2)Catharine
   Wemple Lt NY
David: b 1-8-1756 d 1828 m Catharine Terwillergar Cpl NY
Gose: b 1744 d p. 1790 m Susanna Borkit Ens NY
Harmon: b 12-5-1738 d 5-15-1824 m Judith Morrall Pvt NY
Hendrick: b 8-17-1737 d 2-4-1813 m Margareta Oothout Col NY
Hunter Scott: b c. 1745 d 1814/5 m (1)Neylch— (2)Elizabeth Klock
   Cox Pvt NY
Isaac: bpt 5-19-1760 d 1830 m Catherine Gardinier Pvt NY
Jacob: bpt 8-14-1748 d 12-29-1828 m Experience Wilkenson PS
   Pvt NJ
Jacob: b — d 9-17-1822/3 m Mary — Pvt NY
Johannes: b 10-28-1710 m 1794 m Elizabeth Rumbly PS NY
John: b 3-9-1742 d 1824 m Catharine DeWitt Capt NY
Nicholas: b 8-25-1734 d 2-19-1813 m Catharine VanPelt DepQm NY
Nicholas: b 12-9-1750 d 4-21-1830 m Magdalana Collier Pvt NY
Reynier: b 11-30-1730 d 11-18-1807 m (1)Annetje Van Orden
   (2)Sarah Duryea Capt NY
Sybrant: b 9-11-1763 d 5-19-1838 m Elizabeth VanSchoick Pvt NY
Walter: b 8-29-1732 d 8-5-1785 m Cetje Roorbach Asst Cmsry NY
Walter: b 8-11-1735 d p. 1790 m Bata Clute Pvt NY
Wm.: b 1732 d 10-20-1817 m Catarine CanAlstyne Pvt NY

QUAINTANCE,

John: b 1747 d 1836 m Nancy Baker Harford Pvt VA

QUANDRILL,

John, Sr.: b 1734 d 4- -1800 m Deborah Grant Capt PA
John, Jr.: b 1759 d 1808 m Jane Ferguson Pvt PA

QUARLES, (includes QUALLS)

Abner: b a. 1760 d a. 2- -1823 m Anna — Pvt VA
David: b 1759 d 3-5-1807 m Olivia Morgan Sol VA
Dorothy Waller: b — d p. 1794 m Solomon Quarles PS VA
Henry: b c. 1740 d 10- -1810 m — West Capt VA
Isaac: b 3-4-1754 d 1-24-1817 m Elizabeth Southerland Sol VA
James: b 1760 d 1812 m Sarah Belcher Pvt SC
James: b 1737 d 6-24-1824 m Mary Pryor PS Capt VA

John: b 1746 d 1789 m Sarah Winston Col VA
John: b 1755 d 1803 m Mary — Sol VA
Moses: b c. 1755 d 1802 m Constance Fisher Ens VA
Richard: b c. 1732 d a. 1- -1798 m Frances Powell PS VA
Robert: b 7-26-1763 d 8-23-1827 m Martha Minor Ens VA W ★
Roger: b 1720 d 1790 m Mary Goodloe Capt VA
Samuel: b c. 1758 d c. 1819 m Susannah — Pvt SC
Wharton: b 1755 d 1826 m Elizabeth Tandy Lt QM VA
Wm.: b c. 1755 d 11-25-1821 m Nancy Gardner Lt VA
Wm.: b 1735-38 d p. 1-22-1816 m Mary Terry PS VA
Wm. P.: b 1752 d 4-2-1814 m Ann Hawes Lt VA

QUARRIER,
Alexander: b 3-11-1746 d 5-24-1827 m (1)Elizabeth Dannenbury (2)Sally Burns Capt PA W ★

QUARTERMAN,
John: b 1750 d p. 1841 m — Pvt PA ★
Robert: b 1744 d 12-29-1786 m (1)Mary Way (2)Elizabeth Baker Pvt GA
Thomas: b 1738 d 5-31-1791 m (1)Rebecca Bacon (2)Rebecca Smallwood (3)Mrs Rebecca Ball Pvt GA
Wm.: b 9-7-1746 d 12-20-1794 m Sarah Stewart Pvt GA

QUATTLEBAUM,
Johannes: b 2-17-1742 d p. 2-13-1813 m — CS SC
Matthias: b c. 1738 d p. 1803 m Rachel Derrin PS SC
Rachel Derrin: b 1748 d p. 1803 m Matthias Quattlebaum PS SC

QUEEN,
John: b 1755 d 5-12-1842 m Chloe Karick Pvt VA ★
Jonah: b 3-5-1753 d 2-19-1847 m Catharine Marsh Pvt VA
Richard: b c. 1725 d a. 10-7-1794 m — PS MD

QUERY, (includes QUEARY, QUERRE, QUERRY)
Alexander: b c. 1740 d 1803 m Lady Peggy McCord Sol PS NC
Charles: b 1760 d 1819 m Catherine Boyle Pvt PA
Elisha: b 1755 d 6-20-1836 m Sarah Brown Pvt PA ★
John: b 1737 d 1805 m Ellen — PS NC
Pierre: b c. 1740 d p. 1780 m Marie Joseph Peltier PS VA

QUEST,
John: b 12-28-1748 d 4-13-1831 m Eva Maria Anthon Pvt PA

QUICK,
Abraham: bpt 1732 d 5-25-1805 m (1)Joist M. Veighte (2)Charity Bergen Col NJ
Abraham: b 5-18-1746 d c. 1801 m Elizabeth Cortregt Pvt NJ
Cornelius: b c. 1750 d p. 1792 m Anne Covenhoven Pvt NJ
Cornelius: bpt 2-14-1758 d 4-17-1844 m (1)Elizabeth Welch (2)Anna Annis Pvt NY ★
Garret: b 2-2-1761 d 7-21-1821 m Catherine Anna Stryker Pvt NJ
Jacob, Sr.: b 1714 d 9-15-1800 m — Wgn NJ
Jacob, Jr.: b 1749 d 11-7-1816 m (1)Jane Rose (2)Jerusha Rose Pvt NJ
Jacobus: b 6-30-1742 d 1832 m Margaret Bogart Capt NJ
Jacobus, Jr.: bpt 5-16-1725 d 1806 m Annatje Osterhout PS Pvt NY
Jacobus J.: bpt 1-13-1751 d p. 1798 m Christina Cathrina Kloyn Pvt PS NY
James: b 1-5-1753 d 6-27-1847 m Hannah Pelton Pvt PA
Joakim: b 7-23-1734 d 4-6-1816 m Catherine Snedeker Ens NJ
John: b 10-16-1762 d 5-9-1851 m Phebe Smith Sgt NJ ★
John: b 12-8-1738 d c. 1801 m Margaret Pedrie Pvt NY
John: b c. 1760 d 6-16-1831 m Elizabeth Clise Pvt VA ★
Moses: b d a. 12-22-1826 m Elizabeth — Pvt NJ
Peter: b 2-5-1747 d p. 1799 m Hannah DeWitt Pvt PA
Philip: bpt 8-14-1751 d p. 1806 m Polly Campbell Pvt NJ

QUICKSALL,
John, Jr.: b 1742 d 10-10-1783 m Elizabeth Hunt Capt NJ

QUIGLEY, (includes QUIGGLE, QUICKEL)
Christian: b a. 1720 d 1782 m Ann — Pvt PA
Christopher: b c. 1740 d p. 3-30-1811 m (1)Mary Crawford (2)Catherine — 1Lt PA
Isaac: b 2-3-1763 d p. 9-10-1850 m Amy Gale Cpl Tms NJ
Isaac: b 1-22-1734 d p. 6-19-1817 m (1)Jane — (2)Amy — Wgm NJ
James: b 1711 d 11-16-1801 m Isabella Walker Pvt MA
James: b c. 1710 d 1782 m Jeanette Quigley Pvt PA
Michael: b c. 1748 d 1796 m Frances Catherine Cline Pvt PA
Michael: b 7-25-1721 d 12-18-1787 m (1)Barbara Miller (2)Mrs Barbara Bohner Capt CS PA
Nicholas: b 1740 d 1810 m Anna Miller Pvt PA
Peter: b 1732 d 1828 m Ann Sophia Nehemia Pvt PA
Philip: b 1745 d 1800 m Elizabeth Gilfillan Ens PA
Robert: b 1736 d a. 1813 m Marcy Coleman Capt NJ
Robert: b 1744 d 9-1-1815 m Elinor Mary Jacob Lt PA
Samuel: b 4-14-1757 d 4-21-1842 m Rebecca McMasters Pvt PA

QUILHOT,
Jacobus (James): bpt 12-4-1763 d p. 1810 m (1)Catryntje VanderPoel (2)Mrs Eva Van Allen Pvt NY
John: b c. 1735 d 1810-15 m Jannetje VanValkenburg Pvt NY

QUILLIAN,
James: b 3- -1757 d 1838 m Sarah Waggoner Pvt NC

QUIMBY, (includes QUEENBE)
Aaron: b 7-22-1733 d 12- -1810 m (1)Anne Hadley (2)Mary Johnson Capt NH
Daniel: b 1755 d p. 1808 m Abigail Hubbard Sgt NH
James: b1714/5 d 1-11-1802 m Sarah Wiltsey PS NY
John: b c. 1744 d — m Margaret Hewey Cpl NY
Jonathan: b 8-15-1726 d p. 1790 m Ruth Cook MM PS NH
Joseph: b 9-1-1761 d 3-15-1825 m Molly Colby Pvt NH
Moses: b 7-22-1733 d p. 1800 m (1)Esther Hadley (2)Anna Nichols PS Pvt NH
Moses: b 9-29-1755 d p. 9-4-1841 m — Pvt NH ★
Samuel: b 1-28-1759 d 7-1-1833 m (1)Sarah Allen (2)Elizabeth Andrews Pvt NH Heirs ★
Samuel: b 7-5-1718 d 1798 m Elizabeth Stevens PS NH
Wm.: b 6-13-1749 d p. 6-10-1806 m Mehitable Whitaker Sol PS NH

QUINBY,
Benjamin: b 9-15-1746 d 11-6-1810 m Lydia Clements Pvt MA
Ebenezer: b 8-31-1755 d 5-19-1821 m Hannah Colby Pvt NH
Henry: b 5-7-1739 d 1-6-1806 m Susannah Currier 2Lt MA
Joseph: b — d — Azubah Partridge Pvt MA
Josiah, Sr.: b 1726 d 1805 m Martha Harrison Capt NJ
Josiah, Jr.: b 1762 d 3-15-1835 m Phoebe Harrison Fif NJ ★
Samuel: b 1756 d 9-7-1840 m Achsea Park Pvt NJ

QUINCY,
Edmund: b 2-6-1726 d 11-23-1782 m (1)Ann Husk (2)Mehitable Temple (3)Hannah Gannett Pvt PS MA
Edmund: b 6-13-1703 d 7-4-1788 m Elizabeth Wendell CS MA
Josiah, Jr.: b 2-23-1744 d 4-26-1775 m Abigail Phillips PS MA

QUINLEY,
Thomas: b 1754 d 1832 m Lucretia Wells Pvt CT

QUINN, (includes QUYNN)
Allen: b 1724 d 11-8-1803 m — PS CS MD
Benjamin: b 2-5-1747 d 7-7-1823 m Franky Vernon Pvt VA W ★
Daniel: b 1758 d 1844 m Mary Morgan Pvt Tms SC
John: b 1753 d 1813 m Celia Moore Sol NC
John: b 1747 d p. 1805 m Elizabeth Madison Pvt VA
Peter: b 4-11-1750 d 12-29-1824 m Judith Robertson Pvt VA

QUINTARD,
James: b 10-16-1758 d 9-25-1825 m (1)Sarah Raymond (2)Sallie Hilliard Pvt CT
Peter: bpt 7-22-1732 d c. 1795 m (1) — (2)Ruth Stevens PS CT
Peter: b 10-29-1730 d 1813 m Elizabeth DeMill Sgt CT

QUISENBERRY,
Aaron, Sr.: b c. 1720 d 1795 m Joyce Dudley PS VA
John: b 11-6-1756 d 1831 m Rachel — Pvt VA

RABORG,
Christopher: b 5-3-1750 d 6-17-1815 m Catherine DeVorman Pvt MD

RABUN,
Matthew: b 5-15-1744 d 5-14-1819 m Sarah Warren Asst Dep QM Gen NC

RACE,
Philip: b 1747 d 11-14-1820 m — Pvt NY

RACINE,
Francois (de St. Marie): b 10-16-1758 d p. 1790 m Marie Theresa Compagnotte PS IN
Jean Baptiste: b c. 1730 d p. 1790 m Anne Dudevoir Pvt VA

RACKETT,
Noah: b 1757 d p. 1832 m Peny Brown Pvt NY ★

RADCLIFF,
Wm.: b 7-6-1736 d 8-13-1813 m Sarah Kip Maj NY

RADDIN,
Benjamin B.: b 7-5-1741 d 3-25-1825 m Anna Mansfield Pvt MA

RADER, (includes RADAR, RAIDER, ROEDER)
Adam: b 2-4-1761 d 11-28-1817 m Mary Hotzenpeller Pvt VA MD
Anthony: b c. 1745 d p. 1797 m (1)Dorothea — (2)Anna Airy Capt VA
Conrad: b 1765 d a. 7-21-1835 m Mary Wolf Pvt VA ★
George: b c. 1743 d 10- -1815 m (2)Margaret — Pvt VA
Michael: b 3-8-1750 d 6-18-1839 m Catherine Long Maj VA ★
Peter: b 10-10-1749 d 7-7-1828 m Elizabeth Dietz Pvt PA

RADFORD, (includes REDFORD)
Benjamin: b 1747 d 5-21-1820 m Mary Smith Pvt MA ★
Edward: b c. 1740 d a. 2-20-1804 m Ann Curd 1Lt VA

RADFORD, contd.
James: b 1762 d 6-13-1836 m (1)Ann Shelburn (2)Hannah Wilbour OrdlSgt VA ★
Milner: b a. 1750 d 1780 m Sarah Lewis Sol VA
Wm.: b 1759 d 4-4-1803 m Rebecca Winston PS Sgt VA
Wm.: b 9- -1752 d 9- -1832 m Susanna Shelburn Pvt VA

RADLOFF,
John Frederick: b 1749 d 6-13-1808 m Sarah Medbury Dr NS

RAGER, (includes REAGER, REEGER, REGER, &RIEGER)
Anthony: b c. 1755 d 1825 m Mrs Susannah Simmons Ens VA
Jacob: b — d 1825 m Ann Deborah Jones Pvt PA
Jacob: b 8-25-1743 d 5-20-1812 m Margaretha Bay Dr PA
John: b 1-15-1769 d 5-14-1849 m Elizabeth West Pvt VA
John: b 1-25-1742 d 11-1-1844 m Catherine — Pvt PS PA
Philip: b 1767 d 7-18-1846 m (1)Sarah Jackson (2)Mary Jane Fornash (3)Rachel Vandervauter Pvt VA ★

RAGLAND,
Edmund: b a. 1730 d p. 1793 m — Pvt VA
Finch: b 2-1-1763 d 1835 m Nancy Davis Pvt VA ★
Gideon: b 1722 d p. 7-24-1795 m — PS VA
Pettus, Sr.: b c. 1730 d p. 1790 m Elizabeth Davis Cpl VA
Pettus, Jr.: b 7-8-1761 d p. 1827 m Martha Carter Pvt VA
Reuben: b c. 1740 d p. 12-26-1806 m Ann — Lt VA
Samuel: b c. 1720 d 5- -1797 m Elizabeth — CS PS Maj VA
Wm., Sr.: b c. 1715 d p. 3-26-1788 m Sarah Avant PS NC
Wm.: b c. 1756 d 10-31-1823 m — PS NC
Wm., Jr.: b 4-24-1759 d a. 5-2-1836 m Sarah Williams Sol NC

RAGSDALE,
Benjamin: b 1759 d 3-20-1842 m Martha — Pvt NC ★
Daniel: b 5-7-1724 d 1793 m Phoebe — PS VA
Drury: b c. 1745 d 1804 m Barbara Fox Maj VA
Drury: b 1755 d 1820 m Sophia Waller Capt VA
Godfrey: b 1-17-1764 d 2-16-1835 m Elizabeth Mitchell Lt VA ★
John, Sr.: b c. 1725 d p. 1787 m Mary — CS VA
Joshua: b c. 1750 d p. 4-15-1817 m Leniza Maddox Capt VA
Peter: b c. 1730 d 1805 m Sarah Charlton Sgt VA
Wm.: b c. 1732 d 1815-1820 m Lithey — 1Lt VA

RAGUE,
John: b c. 1752 d 10-16-1798 m Hannah Bonnell SrgnMate PA W★

RAHM, (includes RAHN)
Conrad: b — d c. 1782 m Catherine Weiser Cpl PA
Jacob, Sr.: b 8-8-1728 d 6-19-1805 m Margaretha Schafer Pvt CMman PA
Jacob, Jr.: b 7-16-1757 d 10-11-1823 m Elizabeth Schneider Ens PA
John Michael: b 3-7-1755 d 4-20-1795 m Mrs Sophia Ross Pvt PA
Jonathan: b 3-21-1762 d 7-18-1840 m Christina Buntz Cpl PA
Philip: b 12-15-1757 d 3-6-1837 m Catherine — Pvt PA

RAIFORD,
John: b 1730 d 1812 m Lucy Spell 2Maj NC
John: b 6- -1750 d 4- -1812 m Rebecca — Lt NC
Matthew: b 6-18-1710 d 12-29-1789 m Ann Wall CS NC
Maurice: b c. 1755 d p. 4-28-1824 m (1)Polly — (2)Asenath Hodges Lt NC

RAILEY,
John: b 1721 d c. 1784 m Elizabeth Randolph PS VA
Thomas: b 9-22-1754 d 1822 m Martha Woodson Ens VA

RAILSBACK,
David: b 12-12-1768/9 d 10-17-1856 m Sarah Stevens Tms NC

RAINBOLT,
Adam: b 1757 d 11- -1834 m Jane Potter Pvt NC ★

RAINES, (includes RAINE, RAINS, RAYNES)
Anthony: b 10-13-1757 d 3-25-1837 m Nancy Graham Pvt NC
Daniel: b 1747 d 4-25-1828 m Jane Gerrish Pvt MA
James: b 3- -1757 d 3- -1846 m Nancy Owens Pvt VA ★
John: b 1753 d 12-25-1837 m Sarah Eaton Cpl MA
John: b 1753 d 3-26-1834 m Christiana Gowen Capt NC
John: b 7-5-1726 d p. 1790 m (2)Amy Mitchell Capt PS VA
John: b c. 1756 d p. 3-16-1819 m Nancy — Pvt VA
John: b c. 1735 d p. 1783 m Mrs Keziah Cocke CS VA
Nathaniel: b 1735-40 d 1789 m Susanna Parham PS VA
Richard: b 9-18-1755 d 8-21-1847 m Jane Harper Pvt VA
Robert: b 7-11-1766 d 7-31-1816 m Sarah Thweatt Hamilton Pvt GA

RAINEY, (includes RANEY)
Benjamin: b 10-8-1758 d 5-5-1811 m Nancy Sullinger PS NC
Isaac: b 1-12-1763 d 6-17-1836 m Sarah Malone Pvt NC ★
James: b 10-8-1728 d 1789 m Prudence Yarborough Sgt NC
James: b 8-1-1758 d 8-23-1836 m Nancy Samuel Pvt NC
Jeremiah: b 1760 d 1840 m Mrs Mary Joan Sheehan Moore Sgt NY
John: b 3-6-1757 d 2-22-1847 m Elizabeth Stuart Pvt PS NC ★

John: b 5-20-1750 d p. 1833 m — Capt SC ★
Samuel: b 1743 d 5-20-1813 m Mary Fander Pvt SC
Wm.: b c. 1725 d p. 1812 m Mary — Sol NC
Wm.: b 1742 d 11-29-1829 m Jane — Pvt Cav SC

RAINGER,
John: b 1736 d 12-26-1796 m Sarah Hinckley 2Lt MA
Thomas: b 11-30-1739 d 10-6-1827 m (1)Marcy Woods (2)Abigail Brown Pvt MA

RAINSFORD, (includes RANSFORD & RAYNSFORD)
Joseph: b 6-24-1725 d 12-23-1792 m Joanna Gibson Capt CT
Joseph: b 11-13-1752 d 1832 m Anne Waldo Sgt CT ★
Richard: b 1711 d 10-14-1791 m Zerviah Norwood Pvt CT
Solomon: b 12-20-1750 d 10-11-1818 m Persis Hyde Pvt MA
Thomas: bpt 1-13-1740 d 12-13-1826 m Rhoda — Pvt MA

RAKESTRAW,
John: b 4-17-1761 d p. 3-20-1794 m Rhoda Lane Ens VA ★
Wm.: b c. 1760 d 1820-7 m Rhoda — Pvt GA

RALL,
Thomas: b c. 1760 d 1830 m — Pvt SC

RALLS,
Nathaniel Wm.: bpt 1-26-1754 d p. 1-16-1829 m Susanna Stone Sgt VA
Rawleigh: b 1762 d 5-6-1828 m Mary Hansbury Sol VA

RALPH,
Ephraim: b c. 1742 d 1787 m Sarah Melton Lt CL
Nathaniel: b 12-10-1740 d 2-6-1808 m Rebecca Parker Pvt MA
Thomas: b c. 1690 d 5-8-1780 m Patience — PS RI
Wm.: b c. 1748 d 1787 m Mary — Pvt MD

RALSTON, (includes ROLSTONE)
Andrew: b 2-25-1753 d 9-11-1827 m Sophia Waltemyer Pvt PA
David: b 10-20-1760 d 6-5-1849 m Sarah Hinton Pvt VA
John: b 1735 d 2-5-1795 m Christiana King PS CS PA
John: b 11-4-1744 d 9-1-1825 m Catherine Miller LCol PA
John: b 1755 d 1840 m Elizabeth Neely Pvt VA
Robert: b 12-18-1761 d 8-11-1836 m Sarah Clarkson Ens VA
Wm.: b — d p. 1791 m — Ens PA

RALYA,
David: b 12-30-1760 d 1-13-1846 m Sarah Gardner Pvt NY ★

RAMAGE,
Abner: b c. 1762 d p. 1790 m Jemima — Pvt PA
Joseph: b c. 1735 d 1825 m Elizabeth Roberts PS MM SC
Wm.: b 1753 d 9-7-1828 m Mary Cunningham Pvt PA

RAMBO,
Ezekiel: b 1738 d p. 1785 m Elizabeth Matson Pvt PA
Gunnar: b 1723 d 1802 m — Pvt PA
John: b 11-21-1725 d 3-5-1787 m (2)Elizabeth Champney PS NJ
John: c. 1740 d p. 8-28-1822 m Christinah — 2Lt PA
Jonas: b 11-13-1760 d 2-19-1828 m Ann — Pvt PA
Nathan: b 1759 d 7-27-1845 m Hester Reese Pvt PA
Peter: b 10-1-1751 d 4-13-1821 m Nancy Jemes Pvt PA

RAMEY, (includes REMY)
Jacob, Sr.: b c. 1710 d p. 12-4-1784 m Mrs Sara Fryer PS VA
Jacob, Jr.: b c. 1733 d p. 2-9-1808 m (1)Betty Lane (2)Susanna Grigsby PS VA
John: b 11-8-1753 d 7-27-1834 m Edith Browning Pvt VA ★
Lawrence: b 1758 d 4-1-1835 m Ann Nimon Pvt PA
Thaddeus Matthew: b c. 1746 d c. 1840 m Christina Stump Sol VA

RAMSAY, (includes RAMSEY)
Alexander: b 1731 d 12-14-1817 m Martha Dunbar Pvt PA
Alexander: b 7-27-1747 d 3-22-1826 m Mary Egger CS Lt SC
Allen: b 6-12-1764 d 8-15-1845 m (1)Barbara Decker (2)Elizabeth Reedy Pvt PA ★
Andrew: b 1-25-1755 d 12-17-1844 m Mary Wilson Sct Pvt NC ★
Andrew: b 1739 d 1820 m Eva Wright Pvt VA
Andrew: b 1754 d p. 1834 m Margaret Wallace Pvt VA
Ann McCarty: b 1731 d 4-4-1785 m William Ramsay PS VA
Benjamin: b 1-12-1755 d 12-30-1809 m Mary Shields Pvt PA
David: b 4-2-1749 d 5-8-1815 m (1)Sabrina Ellis (2)Frances Witherspoon (3)Martha Laurens Dr PS CS SC
Dennis: b 1756 d 9-1-1810 m Jane Allan Taylor Col VA
Francis A.: b 12-17-1764 d 12-26-1842 m Martha Alen Cav VA ★
Hugh: b 1749 d 3-25-1825 m Jane Thompson PS PA
Hugh: b 1751 d 5-31-1818 m Margaret McHargue Pvt PA
James: b 1725 d 7-11-1797 m Margaret — Pvt PA
James: b 1742 d 1834 m Margaret Steuart Pvt PA
James: b 6-8-1751 d 3-17-1810 m Elizabeth Porter Pvt PA
James: b 10-4-1761 d 6-18-1820 m Frances Ann — Pvt VA
James: b 1753/4 d 1815 m Jane Lyle PS VA
Joel: b 1758 d 11- -1839 m Abigail Freeman Pvt NC ★
John: b 1764 d 1805 m Sarah Allen Pvt GA

John: b 1717 d 10-17-1801 m Jane — Pvt NH
John: b 1760 d 1-31-1849 m Margaret Connell Pvt NY ★
John: b c. 1750 d p. 1801 m Sarah (Birdsong) Drake PS Col NC
John: b — d 11-16-1807 m Elizabeth (Stovall) McBride Pvt NC W ★
John: b 1758 d 1844 m Ruth Donohoe Pvt SC W
John: b 1726 d p. 6-13-1780 m Mary Hutchings Dr VA
Joseph: b 1746 d 7-13-1834 m Rachel Van Syckle Pvt NJ
Josiah: b 1755 d 1835 m Miss Patterson Pvt VA ★
Mathew: b 1-21-1748 d 1-21-1807 m Ann Scurlock Capt NC
Nathaniel: b 5-1-1741 d 10-24-1812 m (1)Margaret Jane Peale
  (2)Charlotte Hall Capt MD
Randolph: b c. 1760 d p. 1820 m Mary — Pvt GA
Reynolds: b 10-24-1736 d 3- -1817 m Naomi Alexander Pvt NJ PA
Robert: b 2-11-1751 d 11-7-1828 m Nancy Agnes McCorkle Pvt VA
Robert: b 1750 d 1825 m Mary Mitchell Capt PA
Robert: b c. 1746/7 d 7-27-1823 m Mary McConkey Capt PA
Samuel: b 1740 d 1804 m Catherine Seawright Pvt MA
Samuel: b 2-5-1751 d p. 1798 m Margaretta Snodgrass Lt PA
Samuel: b 1742 d p. 9-3-1800 m Alice Maxwell Pvt PA
Samuel: b 1740 d a. 1797 m Ealanor — Pvt PS SC
Samuel: b 1739 d 1813 m Mary — Sol VA
Samuel: b c. 1750 d 1814 m Elizabeth Lyle Sol VA
Thomas: b 7-18-1749 d 1-6-1837 m Abigal Craig Pvt NH ★
Thomas: b 1749 d 9- -1833 m Mary Elizabeth Cross (2)Elizabeth
  Myers Pvt PA
Thomas: b 1741 d 6- -1830 m Hannah Lochard 2Lt PA
Thomas: b 1760 d 1847 m Mary Atchison Pvt PA
Thomas: b a. 1734 d 1790 m Frances — PS CS VA
Wm.: b c. 1743 d p. 1805 m Jemima — Pvt GA
Wm.: b 1750 d 3- -1823 m Euphemia Moore Pvt NH
Wm.: b 1755 d 1837 m Jamima — Pvt NH
Wm.: b 1742 d 1824 m Maria Boyd 1Lt NC
Wm.: b c. 1730 d 1804 m Margaret Polk Ens NC
Wm.: b 1748 d 1852 m — OrdlSgt NC ★
Wm.: b c. 1740 d 1822 m — Pvt NC
Wm., Sr.: b 11- -1732 d 1795 m Martha C. Allen Capt PA
Wm., Jr.: b 1-1-1756 d p. 1833 m Martha Allen Ens PA ★
Wm.: b 3- -1747 d 1838 m (1)Elizabeth Lackey (2)Martha Ochiltree
  Lt PA
Wm.: b c. 1745 d 1825 m Margaret Wallace PS VA
Wm.: b 1717 d 2-10-1785 m Ann McCarty PS VA

RAMSBURG, (includes REIMENSPERGER)
Johann George: b 2-19-1736 d 11-24-1820 m (1)Maria Elizabeth
  Brunner (2)Catherine Sulser PS MD
John: b 1741 d 1-29-1806 m Anna Maria Brunner PS MD

RAMSDELL, (includes RAMSDILL, RAMSDALE)
Aquilla: b 2-28-1756 d 4-14-1844 m (1)Esther Brown (2)Mrs Lydia
  Harris Pvt MA
Gershom: b 7-16-1750 d 10-14-1836 m (1)Mary Gary (2)Sarah Delano
  (3)Lydia Bowker Sgt MA
Gideon: b 9-13-1712 d 2-28-1795 m (1)Sarah Farrington (2)Ruth
  Palmer CS MA
Harthon: b 1754 d 10-4-1822 m Caty Burns Pvt MA ★
Isaac: b 1746 d 7-28-1780 m Hannah Dorman Pvt MA
James: b 1762 d 4-7-1829 m Juda Morang Pvt MA ★
James: bpt 9-16-1764 d 6-25-1848 m Margaret Reddan Smn MA
John: b 9-30-1738 d 10-29-1816 m Eunice Cobb Pvt MA
Joseph: b 7-3-1743 d 8-5-1817 m (1)Elizabeth Barker (2)Elizabeth
  Ellis Pvt MA
Joseph: b c. 1750 d 1811 m Mary — Pvt MA
Joseph: b 5-29-1701 d 8-22-1787 m (1)Mary Homer (2)Mercy Delano
  Prior PS MA
Kimball: b 1740 d p. 1781 m Mary Ramsdell Pvt MA
Mesheck: b 3-14-1746 d p. 1790 m Sarah Young Pvt MA
Moses: b 1764 d 5-16-1834 m Nancy Lapham Pvt MA ★
Nehemiah: b 11-13-1738 d 7- -1787 m Rebecca Chamberlain
  MM MA
Robert: b 1765 d 5-21-1825 m Mary Jefferson Pvt MA

RAMSOUR,
David: b 9-22-1733 d 12-14-1785 m Mary Warlick PS NC

RANALDSON,
Archibald: b c. 1755 d 1828 m Mary Allen Pvt NC

RANCIER,
George: b 12-21-1756 d 4-14-1844 m Anna Barbara — Sgt QM NY ★

RANCK, (includes RANK)
George Michael: b 12-8-1729 d 11-10-1813 m Elizabeth Leinbach
  Wgn NC
Jacob: b 1745 d 1827 m Anna Margaret Worst Pvt PA
John: b 1748 d p. 12-31-1825 m (2)Barbara Mattis Pvt PA
Ludwig: b 1748 d 4-8-1842 m Elizabeth — Pvt PA
Michael: b 4-10-1760 d 1826 m Elizabeth Weaver Pvt PA
Samuel: b 7-30-1742 d 5-22-1815 m (1)Maria Salome Wordan
  (2)Margaret Kleinman Cpl PA
Valentine: b 1737 d 1813 m — Pvt PA

RAND,
Abraham: bpt 4-10-1757 d 8-1-1805 m Elizabeth Innis Matr Sgt MA

Barret: b 10-29-1738 d 3-1-1788 m Susanna Hopkins Matr Pvt MA
Caleb: b 3-9-1751 d 10-9-1807 m Hannah Pierce PS MA
Daniel: b 10-15-1742 d 7-3-1811 m Susannah Hemenway Capt
  PS NH
Ezekiel: b 3-24-1747 d 3-17-1826 m Anna Demary Ens NH
Isaac: bpt 1-11-1719 d 4-24-1790 m (1)Margaret Damon (2)Elizabeth
  Appleton (3)Jane Flucker Dr MA
Jasper: b 3-10-1760 d 4- -1838 m Rachel Knowlton Pvt MA
John: b 10-14-1722 d 12-11-1789 m (1)Elizabeth (Shattuck) —
  (2)Tabitha Hart Stedman Col MA
John: b 1-24-1727 d 10- -1805 m Sarah Goffe PS NH
Moses: b 1740 d a. 1825 m Lydia Wentworth Pvt NH
Nathaniel: b 1718 d 9-9-1795 m (1)Frances Phillips (2)Sarah Trowe
  Stacey (3)Hepzibah Larkin Matr MA
Nathaniel: b 3-12-1737 d p. 1784 m Mary Leavitt PS NH
Nehemiah: b 12-9-1734 d 7-15-1794 m (1)Mary Rand (2)Mrs Mary
  (Prentice) Frost (3)Margaret Prentice PS CS MA
Robert: b c. 1750 d 1790 m Emma Avery Sgt VT
Sarah: b 12-30-1755 d 5-26-1842 m Samuel Carter PS MA
Solomon, Sr.: b 3-13-1723 d 7- -1801 m Deborah Dodge PS NH
Solomon, Jr.: b 3-5-1750 d 4-27-1827 m Sally Adams Pvt NH
Thomas: b 1760 d 9-6-1837 m Nabby Dyer Pvt MA
Thomas: b 6-6-1760 d 1839 m Mary Tuck Pvt NH
Thomas: b 5-19-1746 d 10-29-1825 m Elizabeth Carder Sol VA
Waffe: b 12-23-1750 d — m Elizabeth Orne Pvt MA
Walter: b 4-10-1761 d 12-12-1812 m Mary Parker Sgt VA
Wm.: b 1736 d 1811 m Sarah — Cpl NH
Zachariah: b 1751 d 4-23-1827 m Jerusha Sawyer Pvt MA

RANDALL, (includes RANDLES, RANDLE, RANDAL)
Abel: b 1732 d 1792 m Catherine — PS VA
Abraham: b 1740 d 3-3-1815 m Elizabeth Wilkins Lt MA
Andrew: b c. 1738 d 1789 m Phoebe Todd Pvt NY
Andrew: b 1754 d p. 1799 m — Bailey Sgt NC
Aquilla, Sr.: b 5-10-1723 d 1801 m Margaret Browne PS MD
Avery: b 12-18-1762 d 6-11-1823 m Hope Briggs Pvt MA
Benjamin, Jr.: b 7-20-1742 d 9-9-1828 m (1)Amy Avery (2)Eunice
  Smith Sgt MA
Benjamin: b 2-7-1749 d 10-22-1808 m Joanna Oram Sgt NH
Benjamin, Jr.: b 4-13-1736 d 6-17-1816 m Lucy Babcock LCol VT
Charles: b 5-5-1764 d 2-1-1846 m Polly Bradley Pvt CT ★
Christopher: b 9-25-1729 d 4-10-1790 m Elenor Carey PS MD
David: b 1739 d 1-20-1820 m Anna Maxon Lt NY
Dowty: b 1731 d p. 1790 m Elizabeth Tillson Smn QM MA
Elijah: b 10-10-1746 d 5-3-1813 m Judith Coburn Pvt CT ★
Eliphalet: b 4-7-1728 d 1802 m Lydia Rollins Pvt MA
Elisha: b 8-29-1762 d 1-4-1847 m Isabel — Pvt Slr MA ★
Ephraim: b 4-12-1735 d 10-8-1806 m (1)Mary Blake (2)Louise Stone
  Cpl MA
George: b 7-18-1751 d p. 1790 m Sarah Berry Pvt PS NH
George: b a. 1750 d 12- -1823 m Phoeby Roebuck Pvt SC W ★
Gershom: b 1748 d p. 1829 m Judith Kenney Pvt MA
Hezekiah: b 3-28-1745 d p. 1796 m Elizabeth Chesley PS NH
Hopestill: b 7-29-1742 d 4-17-1814 m Submit Bruce Pvt MA
Hugh: b 2- -1758 d 9-7-1825 m Jane McClellan Pvt NY
Ichabod: b 1746 d 3-23-1829 m Elizabeth Titus Pvt MA
Isaac: b 3-4-1725/6 d 4-27-1809 m (1)Ann Coleby (2)Mary Sanborn
  Cpl RI
Isham: b 3-23-1758 d p. 4-18-1838 m Frances Jackson Pvt VA ★
Israel: b 2-27-1743 d 3-22-1829 m Mary Chesley Lt PS NH
Jacob: b 7- -1760 d 4-9-1842 m Elizabeth Call Pvt Smn CT ★
Jacob: b 1759 d 12-14-1840 m Amelia Yoakam Ens VA ★
Jeremiah: b 2-11-1752 d 9-24-1829 m Patience Aborn Matr NY
Jesse: b 2-2-1759 d 12-19-1848 m Mercy Jones Pvt MA
Job: b 4- -1752 d 12-11-1827 m Sarah Ripley Pvt MA
John: b 8-4-1730 d 5-18-1802 m (1)Lucy Brown (2)Thankful Swan
  PS CT
John: b 7-16-1738 d 7-23-1814 m Tamer Phillips Sgt MA
John: b 7-16-1747 d p. 1820 m Anna Roberts Cpl MA ★
John: b 6-21-1758 d 1-19-1837 m (1)Joanna Phoebe Marchant
  (2)Mary Holly Pvt CT ★
John: b 1729 d 1834 m Susan Salles Ens NC
John: b c. 1745 d p. 1790 m Mollie Ware Sol PS VA
John: b c. 1755 d 6-29-1814 m (2)Rebecca Wood Pvt PS PA
John: b — d — m Rebecca Mercer Pvt VA
Jonathan: b 5- -1745 d 11-11-1805 m (1)Amity Morse (2)Lucy
  Waters Pvt RI
Jonathan: b 1706 d 3-26-1790 m Patience Bowen CS RI
Joshua: b 3-3-1743 d 1808 m Rhoda Chesebrough PS CT
Joshua: b 2-29-1756 d 6-12-1837 m Selah Reynolds Sgt NY RI ★
Joshua: b 3-26-1750 d 5-20-1828 m (1)Hannah Randall (2)Keziah
  Hawley Fif Ens VT MA
Mark: b 10-25-1726 d p. 1790 m Abigail Philbrick CS PS NH
Matthew: b 12-25-1747 d 12-4-1801 m Lucy Babcock 2Lt RI
Miles: b c. 1721 d 1791 m (1)Abigail Runnels (2)Deborah — PS CS NH
Moses: b 1757 d 4- -1809 m Agnes Forest Pvt NH
Nathaniel: b 9-30-1759 d 1792 m Rebecca Howard Cpl MA
Nathaniel: b 8-4-1743 d p. 1825 m (1)Grace — (2)Deborah Stetson
  Pvt MA
Nathaniel: b 3-5-1723 d 1814 m Mary Runnels Pvt PS NH
Nathaniel: b 2-29-1764 d p. 1823 m Martha (Field) — Sol NH ★
Nathaniel: b 1756 d 1799 m Mary Bristol Pvt NY
Nehemiah: b 6-6-1730 d p. 1795 m Hope Peterson Pvt MA

RANDALL, contd.

Nehemiah: bpt 9-6-1747 d 5-17-1790 m Rebecca Collamore Pvt MA
Nicholas: b 5-21-1753 d 9-23-1814 m Content Philips Sgt CT
Peleg: b 4-19-1748 d 1-1-1831 m Hannah Palmer Lt CT
Peter: b 6-12-1723 d 8-9-1786 m Frances Barrett PS NC
Reuben: b 4-1-1759 d 4-19-1839 m Elizabeth Hill Pvt CT
Richard: b 8-21-1752 d 4-14-1842 m Polly Rufty Pvt VA NC ★
Robert: b 2-1-1761 d 9-25-1825 m Martha Washington Sol VA
Seth: b 1747 d p. 1790 m Hannah Hafford Pvt MA
Shubel: b 12-1-1754 d 3-19-1843 m Sarah Russeguie Pvt CT ★
Simeon: b 9-11-1755 d a. 1838 m Priscilla Randall Pvt MA
Solomon: b 4-10-1748 d 5-12-1817 m Jerusha Sumner Pvt MA
Stephen: b 1-31-1734 d 4- -1828 m (1)Lydia Patch (2)Sarah
  Fairbanks Pvt MA
Stephen: b 1741 d p. 1801 m Cynthia Wells Lt NY
Stephen: b 1736 d 11-22-1818 m Elizabeth Swezey PS Pvt NY
Stephen: b 8-1-1762 d 3-15-1843 m Lucina Winsor PS RI ★
Thomas: b 12-13-1741 d 1-28-1831 m Molly Chesebrough Sol CT
Thomas: b — d 2-27-1795 m Margaret Husling PS Gnr MD
Thomas: b 6-12-1758 d 8-9-1816 m (1)Jane Lindsay (2)Mary
  Drake Sgt MA
Timothy: b c. 1756 d 11-5-1844 m Eunice Smith Pvt CT W ★
Timothy: b 2-14-1732 d 2-1-1781 m Zeruiah Bruce CS MA
Wm.: b c. 1758 d p. 9-21-1814 m Hannah Briscoe Wgn MD
Wm.: b 1-20-1741 d 6-30-1825 m Jane Patten CS & PS MA
Wm., Jr.: b 5-2-1748 d 1846 m Sarah Morell Pvt MA
Wm.: b 1743 d 6-10-1817 m (3)Jeminia Holly Pvt NY
Wm.: b 9-26-1747 d p. 1790 m Lucy Simmons Lt VA
Zedediah: b 3-20-1758 d 2-22-1844 m Patty York Pvt CT

RANDLEMAN, (includes RENDLEMAN)

John: b c. 1746 d p. 10-24-1806 m Margaret Snap Capt NC
Martin: b 12-25-1761 d 1846 m (1)Mary Fur (2)Mary Holcomb Pvt
  Wgn NC ★

RANDOLPH,

Benjamin: b a. 1745 d 8- -1810/11 m Jane Long Pvt NY
Beverly: b 1744 d 2- -1797 m Martha Cocke PS Col VA
David Meade: b 1758 d 9-23-1830 m Mary Randolph Sol VA
Edmund: b 8-10-1753 d 9-12-1813 m Elizabeth Nicholas ADC PS VA
Edward Fitz: b 2-20-1754 d 3-12-1837 m Anna Julianna Steel Capt PA
Giles: b — d p. 3-3-1792 m (2)Barsheba — PS NC
Harrison: b c. 1748 d c. 1803 m (1)Elizabeth Starke (2)Mary Jones
  CS VA
Henry: b 1-18-1757 d c. 1841 m Polly Peterson Poythress Cpl VA
Henry: b 10-7-1708 d — m Lucy Ward Pvt VA
Hugh: b 5-16-1756 d 1843 m Elizabeth — Pvt SC ★
Ichabod: b 7-19-1760 d 8-29-1840 m Margaret Liggett Pvt PA
James: b c. 1758 d c. 1795 m Sarah — Sgt VA
John: b 4-4-1749 d p. 4-5-1814 m Elizabeth Vance Pvt NJ
John: b 1751 d p. 1790 m Mary G. — Pvt VA
John: b c. 1760 d 1820 m Elizabeth Bland Sol VA
Joseph: b 1750 d 1810 m (1) — Hightower (2)Nancy Turman Sol VA
Joseph Fitz: b 1-16-1750 d 11-11-1801 m (1)Mary Lane (2)Betsey
  G. Mundy Capt NJ
Malachia F.: b 4-5-1718 d 1776 m Sarah Benham Pvt NJ
Matthias: b 8-4-1758 d 3-12-1832 m Mary Myers Pvt NY ★
Nathaniel: b 1734 d 1787-90 m Mary Bolden QM VA
Nehemiah: b 1744 d 1-3-1806 m (1)Phebe Wooden (2)Sarah Wooden
  Vol NJ
Paul: b 1736 d p. 3-19-1806 m Ann Fitz Randolph PS Pvt PA
Peter: b c. 1754 d p. 1790 m Sarah Greenhill 1Lt VA
Peter: b — d p. 5-2-1786 m Frances Parham Lt PS VA
Reuben Fitz: b 3-12-1733 d 8-18-1784 m Elizabeth Moore Capt NJ
Richard, Sr.: b 1715 d 6-6-1786 m Ann Meade PS VA
Richard, Jr.: b 1757 d 1799 m Maria Beverley CavOf VA
Robert: b 1760 d 9-12-1825 m Elizabeth Hill Carter Capt ADC VA
Samuel: b 10- -1748 d 2-25-1825 m Margaret Fitz Randolph Ens NJ
Samuel: b 9-20-1762 d p. 1799 m Sally Harrington Sol NJ
Samuel F.: b 5-2-1762 d c. 1800 m Phebe Brundage MM NJ
Thomas: b c. 1750 d 7- -1801 m Abigail — Pvt NJ
Thomas Mann: b 1741 d 11-20-1793 m (1)Anne Cary (2)Gabrella
  Harvie PS Col VA
Wm.: b 1745/6 d a. 1810 m Miriam Ann Eppes Capt VA
Wm.: b 1754 d p. 1848 m (1)Louisa Bailey (2)Dorothy (Bailey)
  Poindexter Lt VA
Wm.: b c. 1737 d c. 1795 m Sarah Minson PS VA

RANGE,

James: b 7-21-1754 d 7-26-1825 m Barbary Hammer Pvt VA W ★
John: b 1746 d p. 3-7-1827 m Mandlin Shellas 1Lt PA

RANGER,

Joseph: b 10-14-1762 d 9-24-1788 m Eunice Bond Pvt MA
Thomas: b 11-30-1739 d 10-6-1827 m (1)Mercy Woods (2)Abigail
  Brown Pvt MA

RANKIN, (includes RANKINS)

Andrew: b 1758 d 6-11-1829 m Martha — Pvt Mar MA ★
Andrew: b 1759 d 1839 m Dorothy French Pvt NH
Constant: b 4-17-1747 d 12-19-1831 m (1)Patience Dinston (2)Mary
  Tolman Sgt MA
Daniel: b 1752 d 4-30-1833 m Eleanor Tongue Pvt MD

David: b — d — 1802 m Ann Campbell Pvt NC
David: b c. 1726 d a. 10- -1795 m Hannah — Sol PS PA
Hugh: b c. 1754 d 1845 m Mrs Mary (Stewart) Torrence Pvt PA ★
James, Sr.: b c. 1753 d 1800 m Elizabeth Miller Pvt NY
James: b 10- -1747 d 9-23-1823 m Mary Hamilton Pvt VA
James: b 1757 d 12-29-1812 m Martha Stevens Pvt VA
James: b a. 1762 d — 1821 m Jane Russell Pvt VA
Jeremiah: b 1757 d 7- -1803 m Mary Clark Lt PA
John: b 2-12-1749 d 8-1-1830 m Mary Torrance Sgt CS PS MA
John: b 6-15-1744 d 5-2-1828 m (1)Peggy Door (2)Patience Ellis
  Cpl MA ★
John: b 6-27-1736 d 3-27-1814 m Hannah Carson PS NC
Joseph: b 8-19-1756 d p. 1795 m Mehitable Dunnel Pvt MA
Richard: b 11-4-1751 d 5-5-1827 m Jane Steele Pvt PA
Richard: b c. 1730 d p. 3-3-1788 m Mary Douglas PS VA
Robert: b c. 1750 d p. 1790 m Polly Cusack Pvt NC
Robert: b 5-29-1759 d 12-21-1840 m (2)Mary Moody Pvt NC ★
Robert: b 1753 d 11- -1837 m Margaret Berry Lt VA W ★
Samuel: b c. 1734 d 12-16-1814 m (2)Ellen Alexander PS NC
Thomas: b 1724 d 1810 m Isabel Clendennen PS PA
Thomas: b c. 1750 d 1787 m Mary Crawford Capt VA
Wm.: b 1-10-1761 d 12-9-1853 m Mary Moore Pvt NC ★
Wm.: b 1744 d 2-9-1804 m Jane Chambers PS NC
Wm., Sr.: b c. 1725 d 1793 m Abigail Tassie Pvt PS PA
Wm.: b c. 1750 d a. 2-16-1802 m Ann Gillespie Pvt PA
Wm.: b 1-27-1759 d 12-13-1833 m Sarah Moore Pvt Tms QM VA ★
Wm., Jr.: b c. 1760 d a. 2-22-1830 m Rebecca Sutton Pvt VA ★
Wm.: b 1748 d p. 6-10-1823 m Susannah Sinnet Pvt VA ★
Wm.: b 1758 d 4-12-1836 m Mary Ann Reid Pvt VA ★

RANN,

Joseph: b 4-27-1752 d 5-23-1800 m Olive (Howe) Ashley Pvt VT

RANNEY,

Abner: b 3-15-1747/8 d 9-1-1847 m (1)Lovisa Shepard (2)Miriam
  (Shepard) Cook Sgt MA
Comfort: b 1759 d — m Ruth Leona Treat Pvt CT
Daniel: b 2-5-1753 d 1-5-1833 m Eunice Gile Sgt VT
Ebenezer: bpt 4-24-1748 d 10-7-1822 m Lois Blinn Pvt CT
Elijah: b 3-14-1750 d 4-29-1833 m Elizabeth Root Pvt VT
Ephraim, Sr.: b 4-10-1725/6 d 6-9-1811 m Silence Wilcox Capt VT
Ephraim, Jr.: b 10-27-1748 d 5-30-1835 m (1)Lydia Johnson (2)Rhoda
  Harlow 1Lt VT
George: b 4-14-1723 d 2-25-1804 m Hanna Sage PS CT
Nathaniel: b 7-16-1735 d 5-13-1800 m Prudence Willard Pvt CT
Solomon: b 1756 d p. 8-30-1820 m Rebecca Churchill Pvt CT
Stephen: b 5-24-1761 d 1827 m (1)Margery Camp (2)Rhoda Langdon
  (3)Hannah Cooper (4)Elizabeth Hawthorne Sgt CT
Stephen, Sr.: b 1-15-1737/8 d 1807 m Elizabeth Dixon Cpl CT Heirs ★
Stephen, Jr.: b 9-18-1730 d 12-12-1803 m Patience Ward PS CT
Thomas: b 2-17-1723 d 11-8-1809 m Mary Little PS CT
Waitstill: b 1-3-1762 d 7-3-1839 m Abigail Harlow Pvt VT
Willett: b 3-28-1731 d p. 1789 m Mary Butler Pvt MA

RANSDELL,

Thomas: b 1755 d p. 1802 m Mary — Capt VA
Wm.: b c. 1742 d 1823 m Nancy — Ens VA
Wm., Sr.: b c. 1720 d p. 7-3-1776 m Mary Chilton PS VA

RANSOM, (includes RANSONE, RANSOME)

Amos: b 12-4-1760 d 1-28-1834 m Jemima McCarthy Pvt CT
Bliss: b 1739/40 d 1828 m Sarah Mumford Sgt CT
Calvin: b 6-19-1758 d 5-22-1810 m Ruby — Pvt MA CT
David: b 1762 d 3-28-1830 m Elizabeth Tucker Pvt CT ★
David: b 5-26-1748 d 3-1-1813 m Anna Alberton SgtMaj MA CT
  W ★
Edward: b 2-3-1745 d 3-24-1814 m Anna Tooker Pvt CT
Elias: b 2-17-1736 d 12-3-1799 m Sarah Bigelow Pvt MA
Elijah: b 6-12-1752 d 1-22-1828 m Betsy Sears Lt CT
Elisha: b 5-24-1753 d 8-10-1836 m Irene Wells Cpl VT MA ★
Elisha: b 2-26-1746 d p. 1800 m Hannah — PS VT
Ezekiel: b 10-1-1763 d 11-4-1838 m Lucinda Fletcher Pvt CT MA
  W ★
George Palmer: b 1-3-1762 d 9-5-1850 m (1)Olive Utley (2)Elizabeth
  Lamoreux Pvt PA
Hazael: b 1-3-1756 d 5-20-1820 m Zeviah Wills Pvt MA
Henry: b 1764/5 d 3-6-1822 m Sarah Wright Sol VA
Israel: b 7-17-1760 d 9-18-1839 m Lois Newton Pvt CT W ★
James: b 7-16-1738 d 8-12-1823 m Elizabeth Loomis 1Lt CT
James: b 1744 d c. 1800-4 m Priscilla (Jones) Macon PS NC
John: b 11-13-1709 d 12-2-1797 m (1)Bethia Lewis (2)Rebecca
  Baldwin CS CT
John: b 2- -1743 d 8-9-1815 m Deborah Lester MM Cpl VT
Jonathan: b 1731 d 10-1-1805 m Mary Shaw Pvt MA
Joseph: b 9-2-1762 d 1837 m Lois Mitchell Pvt CT
Joshua, Jr.: b 10-21-1744 d 10-26-1829 m Lois Rathburn Ens CT
Luther: b 6-19-1758 d p. 1795 m Mrs Theodosia Bordwell Pvt MA
Newton, Sr.: b 2-21-1722 d 5-31-1796 m Sarah Jones Pvt MA
Pelatiah: b 1752 d 10-11-1807 m Sarah — Sgt CT
Peleg: b 8-5-1735 d p. 1802 m Susanna Griffin Capt NY
Reuben: b c. 1753 d 1847 m Nancy C. ? Sol GA ?
Richard: b 5-13-1740 d 9-5-1811 m (1)Mary Sterling (2)Mrs
  Rosamond (Spooner) Winslow Capt CT

Richard: b 1752 d 7-22-1827 m Kiziah Portiss Capt NC ★
Richard: b c. 1750 d p. 1799 m Ann Whiting Capt VA
Samuel: b 4-10-1738 d 7-3-1778 m Esther Lawrence Capt PA
Stephen: b 5-8-1724 d 2-14-1796 m (1)Lydia Lord (2)Susanna — MM CT
Thomas: b 5-26-1738 d 8-5-1828 m Sarah Alger Lt VT

RANSON,
Jonathan: b 3-17-1751 d — m Esther Baldwin Pvt MA

RANSTEAD,
James: b c. 1762 d 8-20-1836 m (2)Jane McMullen Pvt MA ★
John: b 1747 d 7-7-1777 m Hannah Merrifield Pvt NH

RAPE,
Christopher: b 1734 d 6-25-1820 m (2)Mrs Patience Ann Sayre Capt NJ
Gustavus: b 1764 d 2-27-1852 m Barbary Johnston Pvt NC SC ★

RAPER,
Wm.: b 1725 d 1795 m (2)Rebecca Simmons (3)Elizabeth Hollingsworth PS SC

RAPIER,
Richard James: b c. 1740 d p. 6-8-1815 m Margaret Thompson Capt MD

RAPP, (includes ROPP)
Barnet: b 3-27-1760 d 3-19-1824 m Esther Rositer Pvt PA
Frederick: b 6-20-1754 d 1812 m (1)Elizabeth Ratken (2)Dorothea Wolf Arfr PS PA
Peter: b 4-20-1723 d 8-21-1791 m Christina Reitmeyer PS PA
Philip: b 9-18-1724 d 4-20-1793 m Elizabeth — PS PA

RAPPELYEA, (includes RAPALJE, RAPALYE, RAPELJE, RAPPLYEA)
Daniel: b 1748 d 10-19-1795 m Agnes Bergen Lt NY
Dirick: bpt 5-14-1702 d a. 1-2-1778 m Antje — PS NJ
Jacobus: b 1745 d 10-27-1827 m Sarah Williamson Vol NJ
Jeromus: b c. 1720 d c. 1820 m Anna — Pvt NJ
Jeromus: b 8-23-1751 d 3-10-1831 m (1)Heyltie Bragaw (2)Lanah Folk Pvt NY
John: b 1732 d 1783 m Elizabeth Brinckerhoff Pvt NY

RARDIN, (includes REARDON, RARIDEN & RAREDON)
Dennis: b c. 1732 d 1- -1789 m — Sol VA
Henry: b 11-17-1756 d 10-17-1855 m Elizabeth Hull PS PA
Jeremiah: b a. 1755 d p. 1815 m — Pvt NC
John: b c. 1730 d 3-29-1796 m (2)Nelly Freeland PS PA
John: b c. 1750 d p. 11- -1813 m Hannah — Sol PA
John: b 1754-6 d 1-14-1836 m Massie Hull Pvt VA ★
John: b 1757 d 8-6-1822 m Elizabeth Hall Pvt VA ★

RASBACH,
John: b 1764 d 9-4-1828 m Nancy Moak Pvt NY
Marx: b 6-17-1733 d 8- -1799 m Sophronia Moak 2Lt NY

RASH,
Jacob: b 4-24-1754 d 3-4-1828 m Chloe Lewis Cpl CT

RASIN,
Wm.: b 10-6-1750 d 1-10-1795 m Sarah Freeman Lt MD

RASLEY,
John: b 7-27-1758 d 2-27-1838 m Magdelene Schmell Pvt PA

RATCLIFF, (includes RACKLIFF, RATCLIFFE & RATLIFF)
Francis: b 1757 d 1814 m Rebecca Bridges Cpl VA
James: b 1740 d 1809 m Mary Elizabeth Sol GA
John: b 1762 d 3-6-1842 m Mary Van Dyke Cpl MD
John: b 1760 d c. 1836 m Ann Fields Pvt SC
Joseph Chandler: b 3-26-1737 d p. 1780 m Mary Welch Pvt MA
Nathan: b 1762 d a. 6-5-1835 m Polly Farmer Pvt VA ★
Samuel: b 1753 d 10-17-1823 m Zelinda Spalding Pvt MA
Zephaniah: b 2-25-1753 d 6-8-1831 m (1)Henneretta — (2)Philadelphia Stone PS VA

RATHBUN, (includes RATHBONE & RATHBURN)
Amos, Sr.: b 1-25-1738 d 7-24-1817 m Martha Robinson Capt MA
Amos, Jr.: b 1-31-1761 d 9-22-1823 m Mary Williams Pvt MA
Asa: b 1754 d 12-2-1812 m Ruth Kimball Pvt CT W ★
Benjamin, Sr.: b 1720 d 1778 m Mary Cahoon PS CT
Benjamin, Jr.: b 1-13-1744 d 7-21-1819 m Hulda Williams Pvt CT
Daniel: b 2-27-1731 d 1-17-1823 m Sarah Higbee Pvt MA
Edmund: b 12-8-1737 d 1801 m Hannah Carpenter Pvt MA
Edmund: b 1756/7 d 1-30-1849 m (1)Anna Carpenter (2)Mrs Margaret (Beaple) Warren Pvt MA RI ★
Job: b 7-24-1748 d 5-1-1838 m Debora Welch Sol CT
John: b 6-26-1729 d 8-2-1826 m Content Brown PS CT
John R.: b 10-20-1751 d 8-13-1842 m (1)Eunice Wells (2)Mary Sheffield PS CT
Jonathan: b 1-5-1765 d 2-10-1843 m Hannah Adams Pvt CT ★
Joseph: b 1-28-1763 d 9-28-1854 m Olive Pearson Pvt MA

Joshua: b 11-29-1741 d 3-8-1827 m Elizabeth Kenyon Cpl RI
Josiah: b 2-5-1762 d 2-12-1840 m Catherine Fitch Cpl MA ★
Moses: b 11-12-1754 d 4-19-1823 m Olive Ransom Pvt CT
Nathan: b 1754 d 4-27-1841 m (1)Robie Hopkins (2)Sarah Dalton Pvt RI ★
Samuel: b 6-16-1705 d 1-24-1780 m Elizabeth Dodge PS Lt RI
Solomon: b 3-3-1764 d 8-29-1849 m Eunice Fuller Pvt VT NH ★
Thomas: b 8-5-1730 d 12-29-1793 m (1)Mary Clark (2)Priscilla Baldwin Pvt CT
Valentine: b 12-23-1724 d 2- -1814 m Tabitha Brown PS CS MA
Wait: b 8-18-1744 d 11-14-1832 m (1)Susannah Dodge Westerly (2)Mary Brown Palmer PS CT
Walter: b 6-16-1734 d 1-14-1818 m Hannah Rose CS PS RI

RATHVON, (includes RATHFONG)
George: b 12-7-1747 d 8-7-1799 m Christina Kraemer 1Lt PA

RATTENAUER, (includes RATNOUR)
George: b 1760 d 5-30-1844 m Elizabeth Hess Pvt NY
Jacob: b c. 1758 d c. 1856 m — Robinson Pvt NY ★

RATTS,
Godfrey: b c. 1747 d p. 4- -1780 m Marget — PS NC

RAUCH,(includes RAUSCH, ROUGH)
George: b 1754 d p. 8-13-1834 m (1)Elizabeth — (2)Barbara — PS MD
Heinrich: b c. 1748 d p. 1801 m Maria Dorothea Rever Pvt PA
Henry: b c. 1735 d 1784 m Magdalena Lahr CMman PA
John: b c. 1745 d 1803 m Susannah — Pvt PA
Nicholas: b 1748 d 10-31-1813 m Dorothea Reinefield Pvt PA
Peter: b 1763 d 1819 m Mary Ann Bolenbaugh Pvt PA

RAUDEBAUGH, (includes RADABACH, RODOBACK)
John Nicholas: b 12-4-1752 d 2-5-1850 m Catherine Warner Pvt PA
Joseph: b c. 1755 d c. 1831 m Hannah Walker 1Sgt PA
Peter: b 4-3-1764 d 9-5-1838 m Catherine — Pvt PA ★
Peter: b 1727 d 9-20-1784 m Anna Maria PS PA

RAVEL,
Adam: b 5-15-1752 d 5-16-1827 m Elizabeth Pickering Smn Lt MA

RAVENEL,
Daniel: b 4-11-1762 d 8-15-1807 m Catherine Prioleau Pvt SC

RAVENSCROFT,
Thomas: b 7- -1756 d 5-27-1827 m Margaret Hinkson Lt VA ★

RAWDON,
Ezra: b 1760 d 9-16-1824 m Sarah Lathrop Pvt CT

RAWLEIGH,
Walter: b c. 1747 d p. 1814 m — Ens MD

RAWLINGS, (includes RAWLINS & ROLLINS)
Aaron: b 6-28-1738 d 7-4-1798 m Mary Somers Pvt MD
Asahel: b 3-19-1738 d 12-3-1813 m Margaret Rezin Sol CS NC
Benjamin: b 7-6-1735 d 7-15-1777 m Mary Sandborn Cpl PS NH
Charles: b c. 1750 d 1800 m Anastasia Gregory Sol VA
Edward: b c. 1745 d 7- -1796 m Rebecca Van Meter Pvt VA
Francis: b 1720 d 1- -1794 m Luranah — PS MD
Henry: b c. 1750 d 8- -1807 m Sarah Allen Capt VA
John: b 1738 d p. 1784 m Mary Hays PS MD
John, Jr.: b 2-8-1755 d 3-16-1821 m Mehetable March Pvt MA
Moses: b 1745 d 5- -1809 m Elizabeth McMahon Col MD
Moses: b 1740 d 1787 m Mary Cornwell Pvt VA
Nathan: b c. 1750 d 5-10-1821 m Mary Rankin Capt PA ★
Stephen, Sr.: b c. 1720 d a. 1790 m Abigail Stephenson Pvt VA
Stephen, Jr.: b 11-6-1755 d 9-18-1814 m Margaret Laughlin Pvt VA
Wm.: b 1740 d p. 6-17-1793 m Mary Magdaline Roberts Sol VA

RAWLINSON,
Wm.: b 1759 d p. 10-10-1836 m — Pvt Wgn SC ★

RAWLS,
Benjamin: b 1750-60 d p. 1830 m Elizabeth — Sol NC

RAWSON,
Abner: b 4-24-1721 d 11-14-1794 m Mary Allen PS Pvt MA
Abner: b 11-11-1764 d 7-29-1846 m Mrs Lucretia Jeffords Pvt MA ★
Bailey: b 8-14-1760 d 12-18-1848 m Susanna Brown Pvt Fif MA VT ★
David: b 12-18-1745 d 1-26-1820 m Sybil Beals Pvt CT
David: b 9-14-1714 d 6-7-1790 m Mary Dyer PS MA
Dyer: b 3-17-1747 d 8-21-1807 m Susanna Webb Pvt MA
Edmund: b 7- -1752 d 5-1-1823 m Sarah Hull Pvt MA
Edward: b 7-25-1744 d 6-16-1823 m Sarah Sadler Pvt MA
Edward: b 4-19-1724 d 6-16-1785 m Deborah Green PS MA
Grindal: b 7-13-1719 d 12- -1803 m Elizabeth Boyd Pvt PS RI
John: b — d a. 1810 m Elizabeth Cleavland Pvt MA
Joel: b 12-14-1733 d p. 1780 m Mary Hull Pvt MA
Jonathan: b 12-26-1715 d 11- -1782 m Susanna Stone CS MA

RAWSON, contd.
Jonathan: b 3-17-1751 d 10-28-1828 m Esther Baldwin Pvt MA
Joseph: b 9-21-1756 d p. 1-1-1833 m (1)Lovisa Loveland (2)Rhoda Merrifield Sgt MA ★
Joseph: b 12-24-1759 d 7-19-1835 m Elizabeth Rhoades Lt RI W ★
Josiah: b 1-31-1727 d 2-24-1812 m Hannah Bass PS MA
Levi: b 3-27-1748 d 4-17-1819 m (1)Thankful Warren (2)Nancy Fairbanks Pvt MA
Moses: b 4-26-1753 d 3-31-1833 m Sarah Bussy Cpl MA
Nathan: b 8-4-1724 d 10-15-1809 m (1)Mary White (2)Mary Chase CS MA
Nathaniel: b 5-27-1716 d 8- -1803 m (1)Mary Thwing (2)Rachel Daniels Pvt MA
Paul: b 2-13-1737 d p. 1781 m Sarah Johnson Pvt MA
Samuel: b 5-20-1746 d 2-27-1831 m Mary Thwing Pvt MA
Silas: b 11-17-1739 d 8-26-1819 m (1)Abigail Chapin (2)Rebecca Fellows Pvt MA
Silas: b 7-26-1746 d 3-6-1825 m Sarah Draper Pvt MA
Simeon: b 4- -1753 d 4-30-1834 m Anna Holden Fif MA
Thomas: b 5-2-1733 d 8-27-1776 m Eunice Read Pvt MA
Timothy: b 10-2-1747 d 9-18-1835 m Chloe Fish Sgt MA ★
Wilson: b 2-20-1752 d 11-14-1841 m Experience Hill Pvt MA ★

RAY, (includes RAE, REA, REAUGH, RHEA & WRAY)
Ambrose: b c. 1740 d p. 7-7-1798 m Elizabeth — Pvt GA
Amos: b 10-17-1725 d 1-30-1803 m Prissillah Gates Pvt MA
Asa: b c. 1740 d p. 1784 m Mary — Pvt MA
Benjamin: b 10-17-1725 d 3-27-1787 m (1)Abigail Hawes (2)Sarah Bragg Lt MA
Benjamin: b 9-6-1750 d 7-1-1837 m Lydia Putnam Sgt MA ★
Clement: b 1752 d 11-21-1804 m Abigail Belden Pvt NY
Daniel: b 1754 d 8-15-1825 m Elizabeth McKibben Pvt PA
David: b 9-7-1742 d 12-1-1822 m Eunice Whiting Lt MA
David: b 1728 d 4-3-1805 m (2)Mary Cowden CMman PA
George: b — d p. 10-12-1804 m (2)Catherine — Sol GA
George: b — d a. 2-22-1810 m Diana Mallory Mid VA
Gershom: b 5-20-1760 d 1-25-1842 m (1)Hannah Palmer (2)Sally Breed Sol RI
Gilbert: b 8-18-1764 d 3-17-1829 m Rachael Perry Cpl MA
Hugh: b 11-17-1746 d 2-20-1818 m Margery Knickerbocker Capt NY
Jacob: b 1723 d 12-22-1799 m Mary Ashton PS VA
James: b 5-1-1759 d 1-15-1830 m Mehitable Woodbury Pvt NH ★
James: b 1759-60 d c. 1826 m (2)Sally Morris Pvt MA
James: b 1760 d 5-9-1835 m Elizabeth Talbott Capt VA ★
Jesse: b 1760 d 2-10-1839 m Nellie Baker OrdlSgt NC ★
John: b c. 6-24-1732 d 1811 m Martha Wood Capt MD
John, Sr.: b 1707 d p. 1790 m Sarah Wilson PS MD
John: b 1750 d 9-14-1817 m Frances — 2Lt MD
John: b 9-3-1756 d 3- -1844 m Margaret — Pvt MD ★
John: b 1751 d 1821 m Anna — Pvt MA
John: b 8-4-1728 d 8-29-1818 m Mary Macy CS MA
John: b 1744 d 1-22-1823 m Mary Russell PS NH
John: b 1-10-1748 d 1-28-1796 m Helena Roosevelt PS NY
John: b c. 1760 d 3-4-1816 m Agnes Trousdale Capt NC
John, Jr.: b 8-17-1764 d 11-15-1843 m Nancy Secrest Sol NC SC
John: b 1747 d 1832 m Margaret Campbell Capt PA
John: b 1760 d p. 1788 m Huldah Huddleston Sgt PA
John: b — d p. 3-3-1806 m Jane English Pvt PA
John: b 1747 d 8-9-1822 m (2)Margaret Boyle Pvt PA
John: b 7-6-1755 d 2-6-1829 m Elizabeth Culbertson Pvt PA
John: b 1755 d c. 1781 m Jane Forman Pvt PA
John: b 1741 d 10-13-1820 m (1)Jane Randolph (2)Verlinda — Pvt VA
Joseph: b 5-25-1735 d 5-2-1819 m Mary Sheckel Pvt MD
Joseph: b 7-29-1736 d 6-13-1798 m Mehetable Thorndike Capt MA
Joseph: b 1715 d 9-20-1777 m Elizabeth McElwaine Chp VA
Joseph, Jr.: b — d p. 1803 m Margaret McComb Sol VA
Mark: b c. 1760 d p. 1848 m (1)Rebecca Long Pvt NC
Matthew: b 1755 d 10-5-1816 m Jannette Preston Lt PS VA
Nicholas: b 9-19-1747 d 2- -1819 m (1)Susanna Sheckles (2)Prudence (Peters) Taylor Capt PS MD
Peter: b 12-12-1745 d 2-2-1834 m Mehitable Smith Pvt CT
Philip: b 2-9-1757 d 10-5-1827 m Elizabeth Ragland Sol VA
Robert: b 1756 d 12-14-1845 m Chloe Guild Cpl MA ★
Robert: b a. 1724 d 9-24-1777 m Mary Forman Capt NJ
Robert: b c. 1750 d 7- -1799 m Phoebe — Sgt PA
Robert: b 6-7-1762 d 11-4-1852 m Nancy Patton Pvt NC ★
Robert: b c. 1763 d 2-15-1850 m Mary Stephens Pvt VA ★
Roswell: b 1763 d 1844 m Leah Orser Pvt NY ★
Samuel: b c. 1750 d p. 7-20-1813 m (1)Mary Moore (2)Ann Sims (3)Rebecca — Capt NJ
Samuel: b 4-22-1763 d 1-2-1832 m Martha Wilder Pvt NC
Samuel: b 1732 d 9-19-1813 m (1)Ann McCracken (2)Rebecca Nelson Col PA
Samuel: b 1725-30 d p. 6-13-1807 m (2)Martha — Pvt PA
Stephen: b 9- -1743 d 12-18-1809 m Lucy Hamilton Pvt NY
Thomas, Sr.: b 12-23-1720 d 1-21-1795 m Sarah Edmondson PS CS MD
Thomas: b 1762/3 d 11-16-1829 m Elizabeth Pearce Pvt NC ★
Thomas: b c. 1760 d p. 9-7-1809 m (1)Rachel Arrenton (2)Mary James PS NC
Wm.: b 1705 d 7- -1778 m Anne — PS MD
Wm.: b 1760 d 1836 m Elizabeth Bredon Pvt PA
Wm.: b c. 1753 d 6-1-1826 m Rachel Strout NCapt MA

Wm.: b 5-6-1755 d 10-6-1813 m Hannah Gibb Pvt MA
Wm.: b a. 1746 d 1793 m Maria Wells Pvt PS NY
Wm.: b 11-4-1740 d 7-28-1840 m Anna Brown Lt PA ★

RAYBURN, (includes RAIBORNE, REYBURN)
George: b 1758 d 11-22-1838 m Frances Wallace Fif VA ★
James: b c. 1750 d a. 9- -1814 m (2)Nancy — Ens VA
James: b 1752 d 12-12-1826 m Elizabeth Gordon Pvt Matr PA ★
John: b — d 1808 m Jean McClaren Lt VA
Joseph, Sr.: b 1733 d 1799 m Margaret Woods CS VA
Joseph, Jr.: b 1758 d 3-15-1838 m (1)Frances Wallace (2)Catherine George 2Lt VA
Robert: b 10-23-1761 d 8-16-1836 m (1) — Logan (2)Millie — Pvt VA ★

RAYMER, (includes ROEMER)
Frederick: b 1760 d 11-16-1836 m Nancy LaDue Pvt Tms NY ★
John: b c. 1755 d p. 9-27-1784 m Maria Barbara Whiteman Pvt PA

RAYMOND,
Aaron: b 8-9-1759 d 11-30-1810 m Hannah Weeks Sgt CT
Amos: b 3-23-1757 d 8-22-1852 m Alice Joslin Pvt MA
Asahel: b 1729/30 d 4-19-1782 m Abigail Dunning PS CT
Asahel, Jr.: b 4-24-1760 d 10-17-1830 m Mary Vail Pvt CT
Bartholomew: b 5-7-1742 d 3-28-1827 m Mehitable Mallet Cpl MA
Benjamin: b 1757 d 8-4-1829 m Betsey Andrews Drm MA ★
Clapp: b — d p. 1790 m Rebecca Betts Capt CT
Daniel: b 12-9-1747 d 9-1-1830 m Lucy Richmond Sgt NY
David: b 1739 d 2-4-1835 m Sarah Fountain Pvt CT
Ebenezer: b 11-25-1739 d 5-22-1823 m (1)Ann Perry (2)Mrs Hannah (Gifford) Chadwick Pvt MA
Eliakim: b 2-20-1720 d 1802 m Hannah Street PS CT
Elisha: b 11-9-1761 d 6-11-1842 m Abigail Inman Pvt RI ★
Enoch: b 9-25-1763 d 2-21-1835 m Susannah Lyon Pvt NY ★
Gershom: b 1-18-1725 d 5-18-1806 m Abigail Taylor Sol CT
Hezekiah: b 1-22-1743 d 7-9-1824 m Lydia Lockwood Pvt CT
James: b c. 1745 d 4-3-1817 m (1)Angelica Moore (2)Rachel — LCol DE
James: b 10-2-1729 d 1-11-1798 m (1)Susan St. John (2)Mrs Abigail (Kent) Botsford PS NY
John, Sr.: b 1-18-1725 d 5-7-1789 m Elizabeth Griswold PS CT
John, Jr.: b 1- -1748 d 3-30-1828 m Mercy — Lt CT
John: b 9-5-1731 d 4-19-1775 m Rebecca Tilestone Pvt MA
John: b 7-13-1742 d p. 1784 m Elizabeth Norcot Pvt MA
Jonathan: b 10-21-1735 d 1783 m Susannah White Sol MA
Joseph: b 11-12-1741 d 11-12-1812 m Mercy Chamberlain Capt MA
Joshua, Sr.: b 12-22-1723 d 9-14-1790 m Lucy Jewett CS CT
Joshua, Jr.: b 1753 d 4-5-1806 m (1)Mercy Raymond (2)Elizabeth Prince Lt CT ★
Joshua: b 1-8-1727 d 2-22-1785 m Grace Gurvey Pvt MA
Josiah: b 1738 d 5-26-1824 m Polly Merwine Pvt CT
Lemuel: b 9-18-1762 d 8-8-1849 m Temperance Nichols Pvt CT ★
Lemuel: b 8-15-1759 d 5-18-1829 m Hannah Underwood Pvt MA
Lemuel: b 1761 d 8-28-1803 m Abigail Russell Pvt MA
Moses: b 7-29-1752 d 7-6-1838 m (1)Nancy Benedict (2)Rebecca Boughton Pvt CT ★
Napthali: b 3-26-1764 d 11-23-1844 m Rebecca Stevens Pvt CT
Nathan: b 5-10-1754 d 6-7-1816 m (2)Mary Eaton Sgt MA
Nathan: b 1742 d 6-28-1824 m Mary Morehouse 2Lt NY
Nathaniel: b c. 1735 d p. 8-17-1781 m (1)Rebecca Benedict (2)Mrs Seymour Sgt CT
Nathaniel: b 5-4-1753 d 3-7-1849 m (1)Dorothea Wood (2)Dinah Smith Pvt CT ★
Nathaniel Lynde: b 11-18-1756 d 7-15-1829 m Louisa — Pvt NS CT ★
Newcomb: b 1-20-1763 d 1-26-1852 m (1)Mabel Grey (2)Mrs Lorinda Lyman Pvt CT
Paul: b 6-28-1750 d 1-22-1825 m Elizabeth Reed Sgt CT
Paul: b c. 5-17-1730 d 4-10-1817 m Abigail Jones LCol MA
Paul: b 11-15-1744 d 3-23-1828 m Rachel Stevens Pvt MA
Sands, Sr.: b 1730 d 1791 m Sarah Betts Lt NY
Sands, Jr.: b 9-19-1760 d 9-19-1841 m Esther Olmstead Sgt NY ★
Simeon: b 1711 d 7-7-1795 m Hannah — PS CT
Thaddeus: b 1750 d 4-19-1832 m (1)Tamesin Mead (2)Abigail — Sol NY
Thomas: b 9-17-1754 d 5-21-1803 m (1)Rhoda — (2)Lucretia Shippee Cpl RI
Uriah: b 1744 d 12-6-1821 m Esther Benedict Ens CT
Uriah: b 1- -1746 d 5-17-1810 m Sarah Paddock Pvt NJ
Wm.: b c. 1741 d 1826 m Priscilla Hayden Pvt CT
Wm.: b 1-11-1747 d 1832 m Ruth Hoyt Pvt CT
Wm.: b 4-3-1758 d 9-26-1834 m Sophia Ward Sgt MA ★
Wm.: b — d 11-21-1782 m Lydia Ward Cpl MA
Wm.: b 2-7-1712 d c. 1785 m Hannah Tupper Pvt MA
Wm.: b 7-2-1744 d 9-20-1822 m Phebe Thomas Pvt MA
Wm.: b 7-30-1725 d 12-2-1780 m Mercy Davis Pvt MA
Wm.: b 1748 d 11-1-1803 m (1)Katherine Marshall (2)Mary Jennings (3)Betsey Jackson (4)Lydia Millice Smn MA ★
Wm.: b 1755 d 1820-2 m Annie Holden Pvt NY
Zacheus: b 1- -1766 d 12-9-1844 m Sarah Sears Pvt CT ★

RAYNO,
Elias: b c. 1710 d 9-20-1787 m Mary Severance Pvt NH

RAYNOR,
Amos: b 1-8-1760 d *p.* 8-28-1838 m Hannah — Pvt NC ★
Benjamin: b *c.* 1732 d 1810 m Hannah Smith PS NY
Benjamin: b *c.* 1755 d *a.* 1798 m Jemima Robinson PS NY
Daniel: b 4-16-1745 d 1-28-1815 m Elizabeth Baldwin Pvt NY
Jonathan: b *c.* 1750 d 1816-22 m Triphena Fordham Pvt NJ
Joseph: b *c.* 1723 d 8-16-1797 m (1)Jerusha Hulse (2)Jemima Dayton Pvt MM NY
Josiah: b 2-8-1709/10 d 1796 m Phebe Turner PS NY
Wm.: b *c.* 1740-45 d 1- -1808 m Mary Pierson Pvt NY

RAYSOR, (includes RASOR & RAZOR)
Christian: b 8-14-1760 d 12-16-1848 m Sarah Simms Pvt VA
Daniel: b 1755 d 1816 m Barbara Harshberger Pvt PA
Michael: b 1758-60 d *p.* 1812 m Eleanor Risher Sol SC
Peter: b 10- -1758 d 11-4-1831 m Frances Adair Pvt VA

REABERG,
Andrew: b 9-26-1761 d *p.* 1793 m Sarah York Pvt PA

READING,
Charles: b *a.* 1755 d *p.* 1782 m Abigail Hunt Capt NJ
George, Sr.: b 2-26-1725 d 8-12-1792 m Rebecca Mullen Col PA
George, Jr.: b 12-8-1761 d 8-4-1846 m Nancy McCune Pvt PA VA ★
John: b 1751 d 11-30-1820 m Elizabeth Hankinson Lt NJ
John Mullen: b 2-4-1760 d 6-27-1833 m Mary Porter Pvt PS PA ★
Joseph, Sr.: b 11-23-1730 d 11-15-1806 m Amy Pearson CS NJ
Joseph, Jr.: b 1-28-1760 d 3-11-1810 m Lucy Emley Pvt NJ
Luther: b 8-15-1748 d 9-20-1832 m Experience — Pvt MA
Samuel: b 1758 d 1838 m Sarah Gouverneur Maj NJ
Thomas: b 9-27-1734 d 12-15-1814 m Rebecca Ellis Capt NJ

READY,
John: b 1758 d 1830 m Mary Ann Tobin Lt NY

REAGAN, (includes RAGAN & REGAN)
Charles: b *c.* 1736 d 9- -1815 m Elizabeth — Ens VA
Daniel: b 1750 d 1-7-1812 m Lydia Campbell Capt QM VA W ★
Darby: b 5-20-1755 d 1851 m — Pvt GA ★
Jeremiah: b 1735 d *p.* 1811 m Abigail Harrison PS Wgn Sol VA
John: b 8-8-1766 d 4-30-1830 m Susanna Faucette Battle Pvt GA
John: b 1752 d *p.* 6-18-1814 m Ala (Bennet) Brown Capt NC
Jonathan: b 12-6-1744 d *p.* 4-6-1813 m (1)Rebecca — (2)Ann — Pvt GA
Michael: b 1743 d 1823 m Nancy O'Connell Pvt PA
Philip A.: b 11-5-1756 d 11-25-1848 m (2)Esther Campbell Pvt VA ★
Ralph: b 1745 d *p.* 8-14-1795 m Millie — Capt NC
Richard: b *c.* 1749 d *p.* 11-20-1798 m — Pvt NC
Richard: b 1747 d 5-15-1827 m Cecelia Creppy Capt VA
Timothy: b *c.* 1750 d 1825-30 m — Sol PA

REAM, (includes REAMES, REAMS, REEME, REIM, RIEHM & RIHM)
Abraham: b 5-16-1737 d 7- -1817 m (1)Margaret Zimmerman (2)Magdalene — Pvt PA
Abraham: b 1746 d 1824 m Rosannah Hehn Pvt PA
Andrew: b *c.* 1737 d 1813 m Susanna — LCol PA
Andrew: b 1757 d 1844 m Barbara Schwartzwaller Pvt Drm PA
Daniel: b 9-28-1745 d 1-27-1822 m Mary Elizabeth — Pvt PA
Frederic: b *c.* 1739/40 d *p.* 4-21-1785 m (1)Miss Womack (2)Martha Ann Berry Pvt PS VA
Henry: b 2-7-1759 d 10-5-1840 m Julianna Rupp PS Wgn Lt PA ★
Isaac: b 10-27-1741 d 5-15-1820 m Barbara Mosser Pvt PA
Jacob, Sr.: b 1712 d 10- -1777 m Christina — PS PA
John Frederick: b 10-14-1754 d 2-3-1837 m (1)Magdaline Straus (2)Barbara Ream Pvt PA ★
Matthias: b 25-1726 d 1-15-1789 m Magdalena — Pvt PA
Peter: b 3-3-1764 d 7-1-1833 m Susanna — Pvt PA
Samuel: b 1-4-1749 d 12-23-1809 m (2)Catherine Tudweiler Pvt PA
Tobias: b 1733 d *p.* 1-8-1807 m Julianna Keller Pvt PA
Wm.: b 1-4-1768 d 6-12-1844 m Naoma Vaughn Pvt NC

REAMSCHNEIDER,
Frederick: b 1742 d 8-8-1808 m Margaret Ann Musser Pvt PA

REARICK,
John, Sr.: b *c.* 1730 d 2- -1789 m Mary — Pvt PA

REASIN,
James: b 3-13-1758 d *p.* 1791 m — Pvt PS MD

REASONER,
Jacob: b — d *p.* 9-26-1795 m — PS VA
Peter: b 1740 d 4- -1807 m Molly Spear PS Capt PA

REASONS,
Wm.: b 10-21-1752 d 1827 m Sarah — Pvt NC

REBER,
Adam: b *c.* 1750 d 1794 m Mary Eva — Pvt PA
John: b *c.* 1735 d *p.* 4-28-1793 m Elizabeth Handwerck Pvt PA
John: b 12-16-1736 d 8-27-1821 m (1)Miss Orbengast (2)Miss Haas Pvt Drm PA

RECHER,
Peter: b 8-14-1763 d 6-3-1833 m Elizabeth Protsman Pvt MD

RECKITT,
Wm.: b *c.* 1745 d 1781 m Lucy Stiles Pvt PA

RECKLESS,
Anthony: b 1760 d 1817 m Ann Tallman Lt NJ

RECORD, (includes RECKARDS & RECORDS)
Issachur: b *c.* 1730 d 12- -1776 m Mary Carriel Pvt MA
Jonathan: b 1749 d 1-17-1855 m (1)Rebember Briggs (2)Abigail Cobb Pvt MA ★
Josiah: b 5-1-1741 d 6-1-1809 m Susannah Tully Capt Wgn DE
Seth: b 12-14-1735 d *p.* 1790 m Susanna Packard Pvt MA
Simon: b 1753 d 10-5-1843 m Bethiah Packard Pvt MA ★
Spencer: b 12-11-1762/1 d 2-17-1850 m Elizabeth Elrod Pvt PA

RECTOR,
Charles: b 3-26-1761 d 1-1-1852 m (1)Sarah Chapman (2)Catherine Haynes Marshall OrdlSgt VA ★
Jesse: b 12-26-1759 d 1-22-1843 m Margaret Winford Pvt VA

REDD,
John: b 10-25-1755 d 8-8-1850 m Mary Waller Wgm Lt VA ★
Thomas: b *c.* 1730 d *a.* 6-15-1801 m (3)Frances Anderson Capt VA
Wm.: b 1762-4 d 10-31-1833 m — Pvt NC ★

REDDEN,
John: b *a.* 1760 d *p.* 1790 m Sidney Sevier Pvt VA

REDDING,
Anderson: b 1765 d 2-9-1843 m Elizabeth Delilah Parham Pvt GA
Joseph: b *c.* 1750 d 1-10-1815 m Jane — PS NC
Joseph: b *c.* 1750 d 1815 m Anne Weakley Sol VA
Wm.: b 1736 d 1822 m Patty Parham Pvt VA
Wright: b 10-21-1759 d 4-26-1844 m Elizabeth — Pvt NJ ★

REDDITT,
Josiah: b *c.* 1745 d 1811 m Sarah Williams CS NC

REDFERN,
John: b — d *p.* 1806 m Mary Townley PS NC

REDFIELD,
Ambrose: b 12-13-1750 d 6-31-1830 m Lois Baldwin Ens CT
Constant: b 7-20-1753 d 1-15-1839 m Amanda Buell Pvt CT ★
Daniel: b 2-27-1728 d 1-20-1788 m Margaret Crane PS CT
James: bpt 1-25-1736 d *p.* 1790 m Mary (Hull) Jennings Sgt CT
James: b 3-29-1735 d 4-3-1788 m Sarah Grinnell Pvt CT
Levi: b 8-17-1745 d 9-15-1838 m Sybil Wilcox DrmMaj CT
John: b 5-6-1735 d 5-14-1813 m (1)Amanda Russell (2)Mary Gale PS CT
Martin: b 6-10-1756 d 4-30-1833 m Lydia Griffing Pvt CT ★
Peleg: b 5-14-1762 d 5-26-1852 m Mary Judd Fif CT
Roswell: b 4-27-1763 d 2-15-1838 m Juliana Stearns Pvt CT ★
Samuel: b 9-18-1762 d 1837 m Nancy Fairchild Fif Pvt CT
Seth: b 1-17-1757 d *p.* 1805 m (1)Sarah Pierson (2)Mrs Parmelee Pvt CT
Wm.: b 12-5-1727 d 7- -1813 m Elizabeth Starr Capt PS CT

REDHEIFFER,
Andrew: b — d *p.* 4-17-1786 m Ann Rubicam Capt PA

REDINGTON,
Asa: b 12-22-1761 d 3-31-1845 m Mary Getchell Cpl NH ★
Benjamin: b 3-29-1730 d 8-23-1811 m Ruth Stearns Pvt MA
Eliphalet: b *c.* 6- -1738 d 5-30-1814 m Anna Kingsbury Sgt MA
Jacob: b 7-4-1759 d 8-22-1843 m Eunice King Pvt MA
John: b 9-29-1757 d 4-12-1830 m (1)Miriam Watkins (2)Laura Wales Sgt CT

REDLON, (includes RIDLON)
Ebenezer, Sr.: b 2-13-1723 d 5-5-1777 m Sarah Young Pvt MA ★
Ephraim: b 1758 d 1833 m Betsey Scammon Pvt MA
James: b 12-10-1753 d 9-12-1812 m Hannah Cozens Pvt MA
Matthias, Sr.: b 9-19-1728 d *c.* 1810 m Rachel Edgecomb Sgt MA
Matthias, Jr.: b 2-4-1749 d 1840 m (1)Elizabeth Field (2)Dorcas Field Cpl MA
Thomas: b 12-28-1755 d 1830 m Martha Merrill Pvt MA

REDMOND, (includes REDMAN, REDMAND & REDMON)
Andrew: b 1750 d 1800 m Mary — Lt SC
Benjamin: b 8-3-1750 d *p.* 1799 m Anne — Pvt MD
Conrad: b *c.* 1740 d *p.* 1784 m Anna Catharine Sier Pvt PA
David: b 1758 d 12-9-1838 m Kristian Smydes Pvt NY
George: b 3-24-1757 d 4-5-1837 m Henrietta — Pvt Wgn NC SC ★
John: b 1746 d 1816 m Cloe — Sol MD
Joseph: b 8-30-1730 d *p.* 2-27-1811 m — PS VA
Solomon: b *c.* 1730 d *p.* 1-31-1783 m — Pvt VA
Solomon: b 10-10-1752 d 1789 m Mary Northen Pvt VA
Thomas: b *c.* 1755 d *p.* 1805 m Mary Tapley Pvt VA
Wm.: b *c.* 1755 d 10- -1822 m Martha — Pvt VA

REDSECKER,
George, Sr.: b 5-23-1735 d 3-11-1788 m Anna Maria Andecker Lt PA
George, Jr.: b 6-28-1764 d 5-19-1838 m Susanna Rheim Pvt PA

REDWAY,
Preserved: b 7-14-1764 d 4-25-1827 m Azubah Jones Cpl CT ★

REDWINE,
Jacob: b 10-12-1751 d 2-25-1840 m Rowena Rhinehart Pvt NC

REED, (includes READ, READE, RHEAD, RHEADE, REID, RIETH)
Aaron: b 4-10-1710 d 7-13-1785 m Tabitha Chafee Sgt MA
Abijah: b 8-14-1744 d 6-16-1816 m Sarah Bates Pvt MA
Abijah: b 1755 d 3-27-1844 m Susan Colomon Pvt MA ★
Abner: b 3-11-1757 d 1-19-1829 m Phebe Schuyler Cpl MA
Abraham: bpt 2-3-1756 d 1815 m Thankful Weed Cpl CT
Adam: b 1-17-1750 d 1805 m Martha Shields Pvt MA
Alexander: b 5-9-1752 d 9-11-1826 m Jemima Alexander Pvt MD
Alexander: b 6-11-1755 d 12-10-1851 m Rebecca Thomas OrdlSgt VA ★
Alexander: b c. 1720 d 1804 m — PS VA
Amasa, Sr.: b 5-15-1729 d 2-16-1803 m Mary Heath Pvt CT
Amos: b 4-25-1758 d 11-2-1838 m Mary Bennett Pvt CT
Amos: b 2-15-1762 d 5-11-1847 m Hannah Slade Pvt MA
Andrew, Sr.: b 1725 d 3-4-1807 m Mary Sloss LCol MA
Andrew, Jr.: b 12-12-1755 d 6- -1842 m Phebe (Sawyer) Lt NS MA
Andrew 2d: b c. 175- d a. 1790 m Hannah Davis Mrnr Sgt MA
Andrew: b c. 1743 d p. 1-11-1819 m ( )Esther McBriar Pvt PA
Andrew: b 8-25-1743 d 10-30-1810 m Anna Maria Leidy Pvt PA
Artemas: b 3-1-1747 d 8-6-1826 m Anna — Pvt MA ★
Asa: b 7-29-1748 d 1815 m Jerusha Buddington Pvt CT
Asa: b 10-14-1759 d 2-9-1815 m Elizabeth Bray Capt NJ
Augustus: b 11-30-1761 d p. 1789 m Rhoda Spaulding Pvt MA
Baltzer: b 12-8-1757 d 3-12-1825 m Elizabeth Drake Pvt PA
Bartholomew: bpt 5-14-1727 d 1816 m Mary Harris Pvt MA
Benjamin: b 10-10-1740 d 11-9-1830 m Hannah White Pvt CT ★
Benjamin: b 11-15-1733 d 9- -1802 m Sarah Evans Capt MA
Benjamin: b a. 1750 d 9-19-1777 m Leviner — Lt MA
Benjamin: b 1-29-1746 d p. 1790 m Mrs Abiah Macomber Cpl MA
Benjamin: b 5-3-1752 d 1-10-1835 m Huldah Pratt Cpl MA
Benjamin: b 5-13-1718 d p. 1780 m (1)Mary Kendall (2)Thankful (Stevens) Weeks Pvt MA
Benjamin: b 3-23-1744 d 5-23-1827 m Elizabeth Dotson Pvt MA
Benjamin: b 2-22-1752 d 10-19-1810 m — Powers Pvt MA
Benjamin: b 1756 d 9-28-1842 m Lovina — Pvt MA ★
Benjamin: b 1760 d 1833 m Jemima Edington Pvt PS PA
Benjamin: b 8-21-1730 d 9-7-1778 m Elizabeth — Pvt RI
Bowes: b 1740 d 7-11-1794 m (1)Margaret Johnstone (2)Caroline Moore Col NJ
Casper: b c. 1754 d p. 1790 m Mary E. Bauslock Capt PA
Charles: b 11-12-1760 d 12-12-1843 m Sarah Nail Pvt NJ
Daniel, Jr.: b 12-9-1752 d 9-14-1840 m (1)Sarah Brown (2)Ruth Hudson Tms CT
Daniel: b 6-3-1743 d 1791 m Mary Brown Cpl MA
Daniel: b c. 1744 d 8-22-1819 m (1)Lydia Cook (2)Elizabeth Wilkins Pvt MA
Daniel: b 9-10-1754 d 2-26-1838 m Susannah Richardson Pvt MA
Daniel: b 7-12-1761 d 8-31-1845 m Sarah Brigham Pvt MA ★
Daniel: b 12-6-1713 d 4-5-1781 m (1)Ruth White (2)Sarah (Shaw) Hamlyn PS CS MA
Daniel: b 2-25-1735 d 6-14-1797 m Ephrosina — Pvt PA
David: b 11-14-1744 d 3-23-1827 m Lydia Sabin Cpl MA
David: b 6-1-1755 d 8-18-1831 m (1)Hannah Kinney (2)Hannah Jerold Pvt CT
David: b 5-13-1767 d 8-9-1814 m Sarah Wild Pvt CT
David: b 1736 d 1828 m Waitstill Raynsford Sgt MA
David, Sr.: b a. 1740 d p. 1790 m Diantha Rogers Capt MA
David, Jr.: b 3-7-1767 d 7- -1858 m Nancy Phillips Pvt MA
David: b 7-24-1765 d 2- -1846 m Abigail Belknap Pvt MA ★
David: b c. 1750 d 1-6-1832 m (1)Hannah Raymond (2)Abigail Simonds (3)Martha Simonds Pvt MA
David: b 1729 d 2-28-1803 m Martha Wylie Capt Cmsry MA
David: b 7-9-1740 d 5-10-1808 m (1)Mercy Ford (2)Hannah Reed Bates Pvt MA
David, Jr.: b 11-14-1744 d 3-23-1827 m Lydia Sabin Cpl MA
David: b 11-19-1752 d 6-2-1838 m Rachel Peck Pvt NJ ★
David: b 1748 d 9-20-1824 m Margaret May Capt PA
Dyer: b 7-29-1751 d — m Polly Plant Sgt MA
Ebenezer: b 10-2-1760 d 1- -1845 m (1)Hannah Jones (2)Polly Dickinson Pvt CT ★
Ebenezer: b 11- -1760 d 2-12-1827 m Polly Benton Tms Fif 1Sgt CT W ★
Ebenezer: b 3-22-1734 d 3-11-1818 m (1)Mary Fitch (2)Mrs Elizabeth Barret PS CS CT
Ebenezer: b 8-24-1741 d 5-10-1823 m Mary Chapin PS MM MA
Ebenezer: b 6-21-1759 d 2-7-1840 m Lydia Hoskins Sgt NS MA RI ★
Eleazer: b 1750 d 8-10-1811 m Rachel Cummings Pvt MA

Eli: b 9-24-1743 d 3-23-1811 m Abigail Weed Capt CT
Eli: b 2-11-1756 d 8-29-1831 m Judith Mehitable Ens RI
Eliakim, Sr.: b 9-18-1725 d 10-28-1810 m Sarah Richards Pvt NY
Eliakim, Jr.: b 1752 d 3-15-1830 m Rebecca Fitch PS NY
Elias: b 1756 d 1792 m Hannah Scofield Pvt CT
Elijah: b 2-14-1727/8 d 2-16-1796 m Sarah Reed Pvt MA
Elijah: b 8-16-1745 d p. 1800 m (1)Esther Bates (2)Aarah — PS NY
Elisha: b 1-14-1753 d — m Wealthy Kinney Pvt CT
Elnathan: b 10-12-1758 d 8-15-1841 m Annie Prescott Pvt MA
Enoch: b c. 1741 d p. 1792 m Mrs Phoebe Peck Capt CT
Ephram: b 4-10-1757 d 3-14-1837 m Hannah Carpenter Pvt MA
Ezra: b 11-24-1762 d 5-14-1839 m (1)Mary Lovell (2)Hannah Tillell Pvt MA
Frederick: b 1755 d 4-1-1836 m (1)Lovisa Pease (2)Lavina Bartlett Sgt NH ★
Frederick: b 3-15-1718 d 12-24-1794 m Maria Engel PS PA
Francis: b 1740 d p. 8-2-1819 m (1)Margaret Boyd (2)Florence Blackburn PS VA
Garret: b 1752 d 5-2-1842 m Martha Reed Pvt NY
George: b 11-16-1759 d 2-12-1848 m (1)Experience Blackman (2) — Springer Cpl MA
George: b c. 1755/6 d p. 1820 m Anna — Pvt MA
George: b 9-1-1733 d 9-17-1815 m Mary Woodburn Col NH
George: b 9-17-1733 d 9-21-1798 m Gertrude Ross Till SDI DE
George: b 5-28-1755 d 1820 m Betsey Wright Pvt NJ
George: b 1746 d p. 12-9-1799 m (1)Catherine Chambers (2)Margaret — Sol NC
George: b 6-12-1760 d 1855 m Grace Utterback Sol NC
George: b 1728 d 9-21-1789 m Mary Macelroy PS MA
George: b 8-14-1762 d 3-17-1856 m (2)Catherine Woodworth Pvt RI
George: b 12-23-1719 d p. 11-23-1786 m — LCol SC
George: b c. 1754 d 1844/5 m (1)Miss Renig (2)Margaret Couchman PS VA
Hammon: b — d — m Betsey Simonds Pvt MA
Hankerson: b c. 1740 d p. 1795 m Mary Slaughter Capt VA
Henry: b 1761 d 3-2-1814 m Elizabeth Gregory Pvt VA
Ichabod: b 12-20-1755 d — m Sarah Waughn Pvt MA
Isaac: b 9-7-1743 d 8-29-1845 m Elizabeth Titis Smith 1Lt MD
Isaac: b. 8-9-1756 d 4-20-1848 m Susanna Monroe Pvt MA
Isaac: b 1758 d 7-31-1844 m Rebecca Titus Pvt NJ
Isaac: b 12-26-1754 d 4-11-1844 m Diaderna Shearman (Gray) Pvt Mar RI ★
Isaac: b 1757 d 10-15-1823 m Margaret Baker Pvt PA
Isaac: b 1739/40 d 1776/7 m Sarah Embra Col VA
Isaiah: b 6-7-1759 d 9-25-1794 m Susanna Hedger Pvt NJ ★
Israel: b 6-16-1747 d p. 1786 m (1)Jemima Temple (2)Mary — Pvt MA
J. Frederick: b 3-15-1718 d 12-24-1794 m Maria Engel PS PA
Jacob: b 7-7-1720 d 10-11-1806 m (1)Mary Ford (2)Alice (Reed) (3)Mrs Harden Pvt MA
Jacob: b — d p. 4-7-1795 m Sarah Covert Pvt NY
Jacob: b 4-1-1749 d 6-11-1821 m Ruhamah Benedict Pvt NY
Jacob: b c. 6-25-1735 d 5-29-1819 m Elizabeth Barbara Rominger Sol NC
Jacob, Sr.: b 7-6-1730 d 11-2-1820 m Magdaline Leidy LCol PA
Jacob, Jr.: b 3-28-1762 d 10-28-1846 m Anna Maria Mowery Pvt PA
Jacob: b 11-26-1744 d 9-20-1824 m Maria Magdalena Fisher Ens PA
Jacob: b 6- -1746 d 3-28-1821 m (2)Margaret Emerich Cpl PA
Jacob: b c. 1729 d c. 1797 m (1)Rebecca Claypole (2)Ann Taylor PS Capt VA
James: b 1743 d 12-31-1822 m Susanne Corey Col DE
James: b 10-29-1736 d 9-9-1816 m Mehitable Feno Sgt MA
James: b 1746 d 1826 m Tamer Munn Pvt MA
James: b 4-14-1759 d 6-8-1796 m Olive Johnson Pvt MA
James: b 1-8-1723 d 2-13-1807 m (1)Abigail Hindes (2)Mary Farrar BGen NH
James: b 3-18-1736 d 7-20-1814 m Joanna Castle Maj NY
James: b 1722 d 1803 m Charity O'Connor Capt NC
James: b 1750 d 1820 m Mary McMahan Capt CS NC
James: b 1737 d 4-13-1822 m Ann Hayes LCol PA
James, Sr.: b 1710 d 1-24-1798 m (1)Margaret Floyd (2)Sarah — Pvt PA
James: b 1741 d 1820 m Sarah Speer Pvt PA
James: b c. 1745 d — m Nancy — Pvt PA
James: b 1756 d 7-3-1836 m — Carson Pvt PA ★
James: b c. 1760 d p. 1786 m Mrs Elizabeth Miller Osborne Pvt PA
James: b 1758 d 1- -1800 m Elizabeth Swassick Pvt VA
James: b 1759 d c. 1847 m Sabina Furr Tms VA
James: b c. 1759 d p. 1781 m Martha — Pvt VA
Jesse: b 7-29-1734 d 3-31-1822 m Mercy Weed Pvt CT
Jesse: b 1759 d 5-12-1840 m Elizabeth — Pvt MA ★
Job: b 1761 d 3-27-1842 m Sally Troupe Pvt MA
Joel: b 8-16-1753 d 1-27-1837 m Chloe Stanley Sgt MA
Joel: bpt 11-12-1749 d 12-10-1793 m Eunice Webb Pvt MA
Joel: b 6-18-1757 d 3-19-1830 m Keziah — Pvt NH
John: b 1756 d 1829 m Abigail Whitney Pvt CT
John: b 1701 d 10-30-1786 m (1)Mary Hawley (2)Sarah Bradley CS CT
John: b 1758 d 8-27-1844 m (1)Martha Roland (2)Marian Ashley Pvt MD ★
John: b c. 1730 d p. 10- -1793 m — PS MD

John: b 1747 d 10- -1797 m Rachel Thorne LCol MA
John: b c. 1740 d — m Ann Weaver Capt MA
John: b 1759 d 2-3-1828 m Abigail Chamberlin Sgt MA
John: b 4-20-1758 d 6-3-1840 m Hannah Webster Sgt MA
John, Jr.: b 3-29-1752 d 2- -1841 m Mary Godfrey MM MA
John: b 1-19-1750 d 7-3-1812 m Deborah Holden Pvt MA
John, Sr.: b 8-10-1713 d 1780 m Mary Bates MM MA
John, Jr.: b 2-13-1756 d 2-9-1835 m Rachel Clark Pvt MA
John: b 11-11-1751 d 2-17-1831 m (1)Hannah Sampson (2)Mrs
　　Phoebe Paddock Chp NS MA
John: b 5-28-1731 d 11-20-1805 m Ruhamah Brown PS MA
John, Sr.: b 1722 d 12-17-1788 m Dorothy Pinneo PS MA
John: b 12- -1730 d 2-18-1803 m Thankful Honowell Capt NJ
John: b 7-6-1742 d 6-16-1829 m Leah Golden Ens NJ
John: b 1756 d 7-28-1821 m Sarah Sharpe Capt NC
John: b 1764 d 11-17-1839 m Sarah Bolen Pvt NC ★
John: b a. 1750 d 1778 m Margaret Blythe Capt PA
John: b — d 1789 m Nancy Caldwell Capt PS PA
John: b 10-15-1741 d 1-2-1826 m Sarah — Pvt PA
John: b 10- 26-1754 d 5-3-1832 m Jane Brigham Marshall Pvt PA
John: b 1729 d 1790 m Dorothy Roher Cmsry PS PA
John: b 1739 d 3- -1793 m Elsie Cox Pvt PA
John: b 6-14-1756 d 11-29-1838 m Hester Beyer Pvt PA
John: b 1748 d 1818 m Dorcas Neill Sol PA
John: b c. 1745 d c. 1818 m Elizabeth Gerrard Capt SC
John: b 4-16-1748 d 6-23-1826 m Mrs Keziah Simpson Buchanan
　　Ens QM MA W★
John: b c. 1734 d p. 9-21-1819 m (1)Elizabeth Perkins (2)Eve
　　(Martin) Fishback SgtMaj VA
John, Sr.: b 1735 d 1819 m Mary Hutchinson Pvt VA
John: b 1757 d 1809 m Elizabeth Steppe Pvt VA
John: b 1736 d 1807 m Lettice Wilcox PS VA
John: b a. 1742 d 1785 m Elizabeth — PS VA
John: b 8-25-1750 d 6-29-1816 m Mary Woods PS VA
John Adam: b 1756 d 7-17-1815 m Julianna Braun Fif PA
John I.: b 10-2-1754 d 5-2-1843 m Margaret Taylor OrdlSgt NJ ★
John Nash: b 5-25-1763 d 1-6-1826 m (1)Elizabeth Julia Spencer
　　(2)Elizabeth Fisher Night (3)Mary Barksdale Pvt VA
John Philip: b 1-26-1698 d 9-3-1783 m Veronica Bergey CS PA
Jonathan: b 3-8-1729 d 10-8-1790 m Sarah Lawrence Col MA
Jonathan: b 8-8-1752 d — m Dorothy Blake Capt MA
Jonathan: b 6-15-1740 d 3-26-1820 m Johanna Call Capt MA
Jonathan: b 2-24-1752 d 10-3-1834 m Polly Humphrey Sgt MA
Jonathan: b 11-14-1737 d — m Eunice Weaver Pvt MA
Jonathan: b 1745 d 11-29-1806 m Susannah Shepard Pvt MA
Jonathan: b c. 1762 d 10- -1826 m Rachel Golden Pvt NJ
Jonathan: b 9-6-1752 d 11-5-1801 m Jane Lewis Lt VA
Jonathan Hanson: b 1737 d 2-13-1826 m Lucinda — Pvt CT
Joseph: b c. 1754 d c. 1804 m Deborah (Read) Col MA
Joseph: b 1738 d 3-6-1809 m Sarah Wylie 1Lt MA
Joseph: b 1739 d 1785 m Sybil Proctor Sol MA
Joseph: b 1735 d 1793 m Mary Cornell Pvt MA
Joseph, Jr.: b 12-14-1751 d 7-16-1823 m Abigail Harvy Pvt MA
Joseph: b 6-21-1739 d 1794 m Elizabeth Blood CS MA
Joseph, Sr.: b 6-4-1716 d 11-1-1795 m Ruth Underwood PS MA
Joseph, Jr.: b 10-9-1746 d 7-23-1820 m Martha Fletcher CS NH
Joseph: b 4-16-1739 d 11-19-1814 m Martha Rossell PS NJ
Joseph: b 2-4-1725 d 8-7-1802 m Elsie Lanning PS NJ
Joseph: b 1748 d p. 1832 m Nancy — Pvt NJ ★
Joseph: b 11-27-1733 d 10-19-1804 m Janet Brotherton Capt PA
Joseph: b 8-27-1741 d 3-5-1785 m Esther DeBerdt LCol PA
Joseph: b 1755 d p. 1831 m Shelia — Pvt PA
Joseph: b 6-5-1756 d 10-10-1828 m Isabella Baskin Lt SC ★
Joshua: b 11-19-1739 d 3-9-1805 m Rachel Wyman Capt MA
Joshua, Sr.: b 12-1-1737 d 4-20-1809 m Mary Spaulding Pvt
　　PS MA
Joshua, Jr.: b 3-6-1763 d 1-6-1841 m Rebecca Wright Pvt MA ★
Joshua: b 7-4-1724/5 d 9-8-1795 m Sarah Underwood Cpl MA
Joshua: b 7-21-1728 d p. 1779 m Betsey Barney Pvt MA
Joshua: b 5-15-1730 d 8-11-1798 m Susanna Houghton Pvt MA
Joshua: b 10-29-1757 d 5- -1838 m Hannah McClelland Pvt
　　PA ★
Joshua: b 6-18-1724 d 7-19-1786 m Hannah Proctor Pvt MA
Joshua, Jr.: b 12-14-1742 d p. 1781 m Elizabeth Underwood Pvt NH
Josiah, Sr.: b c. 1732 d p. 1779 m Sybil Baldwin Pvt CT
Josiah: b 12-29-1760 d 10-5-1849 m (1)Rhoda Mitchell (2)Sarah
　　Davis Pvt MA ★
Josiah: b 1763 d 8-28-1849 m Catherine Butler Pvt MA ★
Josiah: b 7-23-1753 d p. 1806 m Betsey Taylor CS MA
Josiah: b 11-18-1750 d 8-20-1845 m Nancy — Pvt NJ ★
Justus: b 10-17-1760 d 10-17-1846 m (1)Sarah Steele (2)Lucinda
　　Elmer (3)Lydia (Tucker) Burnham Pvt CT ★
Ketchel: b 3-8-1754 d 9-11-1842 m Mary Doty Pvt NY
Lemuel: b 1764 d 3-24-1857 m Rebecca Mosher Pvt MA
Leonard: b 4-10-1739 d 8-26-1805 m Anna Maria Zerbe Wgm PA
Lettice Wilcox: b 1740 d 1800 m John Reed PS VA
Lewis: b 3-11-1753 d 11-28-1793 m Rachel Brooks Pvt NJ
Martin, Sr.: b 9- -1742 d 11-26-1815 m Mary Moor Capt CT
Michael: b 1734 d 1782 m Maria Catharine Haag Pvt PA
Moses: b 5-31-1749 d 1-27-1839 m Sarah Whittemore Pvt MA
Nathan, Jr.: b 1-29-1747 d 1827 m Hannah — Pvt MA
Nathan: b 3-3-1753 d 11-6-1830 m Sophia Thorpe Capt VA

Nathaniel: b 1-4-1762 d 8-21-1830 m Sarah Parkes Pvt CT
Nathaniel: b 6-2-1749 d p. 1781 m Hepsibah Bateman Sol MA
Noah: b 9-21-1757 d 4-4-1844 m Mary Robinson Pvt MA
Obadiah: b 3-29-1738 d 10-31-1819 m Elizabeth Shaw Lt MA
Oliver: b 4-11-1746 d 10-21-1778 m Betty Force Sgt CT
Oliver: b 8-21-1734 d p. 1776 m Patience Brayton Lt MA
Paul: b 1761 d 1834 m Martha Shannon Pvt MA
Peter: b 5-19-1701 d 9-19-1791 m (1)Abigail — (2)Mrs Abigail
　　Dudley Pvt MA
Peter: b 2- -1759 d 10-24-1835 m Hannah Martin Pvt NH MA ★
Peter: b 10-8-1735 d p. 1790 m Mary Crom Pvt NY
Philip: b 12-7-1728 d 1798 m (1)Maria Elizabeth Fretz
　　(2)Christiana Schneider Capt PA
Phillip: b 1760 d 11-2-1829 m Hosanah Medford Capt MD
Philip: b 1756 d 3-20-1828 m Margaret Fitch Cpl VT
Reuben: b 2-11-1730 d 5-26-1803 m Tammie Meacham Maj MA
Richard: b 6-6-1759 d 1-28-1835 m Catherine Disbrow Pvt NJ
Robert: b 8-22-1757 d 10-30-1837 m Sarah Stevens Fif MA
Robert: b 8-3-1742 d 4-12-1822 m Catherine Mayers CS PS MA
Robert: b 6-30-1748 d 1-16-1810 m Mary Archer PS NY
Robert: b c. 1730 d 1796 m Mary Pomeroy PS VA
Robert: b 1760 d c. 1800 m Mrs Joanna Garner Pvt SC
Sampson: b 5-13-1754 d 2-22-1777 m Lydia Phelps Pvt MA
Samuel: b 10-18-1761 d 7-25-1851 m Lydia Pierce Pvt CT
Samuel: b 4-12-1730 d 8-24-1798 m Abigail Murdock Capt MA
Samuel: b 4-3-1737 d 3-9-1806 m Hannah Raymond Capt MA
Samuel: b 8-4-1756 d 12-29-1832 m Charity Bourne Pvt MA ★
Samuel: b 8-11-1711 d 3-29-1781 m (1)Abigail Cummings
　　(2)Hannah (Wright) Underwood Pvt MA
Samuel: b 5-4-1722 d 4-28-1809 m Eunice Stone Sol MA
Samuel: b 12-25-1756 d 4-22-1826 m Betsey Smith Pvt MA
Samuel: b 1756 d 2-10-1833 m Mary Winship Smn MA
Samuel: b 1757 d — m Annie Mason Pvt MA
Samuel: b 11-30-1761 d 9-1-1853 m Matilda Doty Pvt MA ★
Samuel: b 2-20-1760 d 2-20-1813 m (1)Mary Fairchild (2)Lucy
　　Towner Cpl NY W★
Samuel: b 7-8-1728 d 1810 m Agnes Kay PS Capt NC
Samuel: b 3-8-1741 d 1-15-1800 m Jane Davis Pvt PA
Samuel: b 1751 d 11-1-1823 m Mary Clark PS SC
Samuel: b 1-26-1749 d 2-5-1843 m — Hampton Lt SC ★
Seth: b 3-6-1746 d 3-19-1797 m Hannah Harwood LCol MA
Seth: b 6-21-1765 d 9-19-1813 m (1)Fanny Harrington (2)Lydia
　　Harrington Pvt MA
Silas: b 10-21-1752 d 1789 m Mary Wallace Cpl CT
Silas: b 5-7-1758 d 11-12-1833 m Bethia Hurd Pvt PS NY W★
Simeon: b 1756 d 1783 m Sarah Cummings Cpl MA
Simeon, Sr.: b 4-17-1733 d 7-4-1804 m Deborah Codding Pvt MA
Simeon, Jr.: b 7-28-1763 d 5- -1830 m (1)Hannah Wheeler
　　(2)Elizabeth Pratt Pvt MA
Simeon: b 3-15-1754 d 7-24-1840 m Abial Rice Pvt NY ★
Simon: b 10-23-1762 d 5-18-1846 m Rocsa Lyon Pvt MA
Squire: b 9-18-1756 d 4-4-1822 m (1)Betty (Reed) (2)Mrs Submit
　　(Preston) Reed Cpl MA
Stephen: b 3-26-1753 d 1-31-1847 m (1)Mary Derimple Pvt MA ★
Supply: b 9-9-1754 d 3-16-1847 m Susanna Byam Pvt MA ★
Thaddeus: b 4-9-1752 d 12-3-1824 m Hannah Taylor Capt MA
Thaddeus: b 1759 d 1- -1824 m Anna Prescott Pvt MA
Thomas, Jr.: b 9-10-1733 d 9-12-1788 m Hannah Nourse Capt MA
Thomas: b 2-6-1732/3 d 12-17-1841 m (1)Susanna Dutton
　　(2)Phebe Proctor (3)Polly Spaulding Lt PS MA
Thomas: b 4-17-1732 d 3-15-1812 m (1)Mary (Howard) White
　　Sarah (Thaxter) Pulling Pvt MA
Thomas: b 5-23-1741 d 1-12-1789 m Martha Park Pvt MA
Thomas: b 3-14-1766 d p. 1820 m (2)Elizabeth Diggins Pvt MA ★
Thomas: b c. 1758 d c. 1811 m Charity Newkirk Lt PA
Thomas: b 1753 d 9-18-1826 m Catharine Adams Dr NY
Thomas: b 9-1-1750 d 10-2-1820 m Stella McKnight Pvt PA
Thomas, Sr.: b c. 1733 d 1802 m Margaret — Pvt PA
Thomas, Jr.: a. 1759 d 1813 m Mary — Pvt PA
Thomas: b 1752 d 1807 m Rachel — Pvt PA
Thomas: b 7-11-1746 d 11-22-1814 m Ruth Carriel Pvt VT
Timothy: b 4-24-1732 d 3- -1808 m Martha Pidge 2Lt MA
Timothy, Sr.: b 3-21-1714 d 4-26-1799 m Mary Cummings Mil
　　PS MA
Timothy, Jr.: b 8-30-1736 d 12-24-1804 m Susanna Taylor Pvt MA
Uriah: b 11-27-1756 d 10-30-1838 m Polly Pratt Sgt MA
Ward: b 1757 d p. 1818 m Abigail — OrdlSgt MA ★
Wm., Sr.: b 1729 d 2-14-1790 m Mary Tuttle Capt MA
Wm.: b 8-22-1730 d 3-10-1808 m Mary Dunning Sgt MA
Wm.: b 1754 d 4-15-1823 m Eunice Flint Pvt MA
Wm. 1st: b 1693 d 2-11-1778 m Sarah Poulter CS MA
Wm. 2nd: b 1-1-1720 d 10-9-1813 m (1)Abigail Stone (2)Lydia
　　Ingalls Col MA
Wm.: b 10-2-1742 d 8-31-1829 m Elizabeth Davis Pvt MA
Wm.: b 9-20-1725 d 12-14-1807 m Silence Nash Pvt MA
Wm.: b 6-4-1744 d p. 1791 m Alice Reckord Pvt MA
Wm.: b 6-8-1755 d 11-16-1809 m Olive Pool Pvt MA
Wm.: b — d — m Prudence Valentine PS MA
Wm.: b 9-24-1739 d 7-12-1817 m Priscilla Emery Capt NH
Wm.: b 8-14-1754 d 9-10-1838 m Bridget Greeley Cpl NH
Wm.: b 2-24-1724 d 1821 m Lucy Spaulding Pvt NH

REED, contd.
Wm., Jr.: b 12-10-1762 d 1-15-1843 m Violet Brown Sgt NC W★
Wm.: b c. 1737 d a. 2- -1800 m Penelope Williams Pvt NC
Wm.: b c. 1745 d 1844 m (2)Elizabeth Walker Pvt NC
Wm.: b c. 1738 d 1815 m Alice Jean — Pvt NC
Wm.: b 1752 d 1812 m Elizabeth Steele Pvt NC
Wm.: b 1751 d 6-15-1813 m Nancy Miller Capt PA
Wm.: b 1745 d 7-15-1830 m Margaret Linn Ens PA
Wm.: b 8-10-1752 d 7-28-1818 m Tabitha Walker Pvt PA
Wm.: b 1748 d 11-18-1831 m Mary — PS PA
Wm., Sr.: b c. 1750 d p. 1794 m — PS PA
Wm., Sr.: b 1730 d p. 1790 m Jane Mitchell PS PA
Wm., Jr.: b 7-4-1753 d 5-14-1831 m Mary Murray Ens PA
Wm.: b 12-12-1751 d p. 4-8-1841 m Rosetta McLean Pvt PA ★
Wm.: b 1761 d 2-11-1845 m Mary Boyd Pvt PA ★
Wm., Sr.: b 1-8-1740 d 9-5-1810 m Edith Shotwell Pvt SC
Wm.: b 1754 d 4-21-1845 m Sarah Harleston Dr SC
Wm.: b 3-7-1761 d p. 1812 m Betsy Cartee Pvt VT
Wm.: b c. 1723 d p. 3-23-1797 m Johanna — PS VA
Zaddock: b 1750 d 1-17-1822 m Lucy Gardner Pvt MA W★
Zadok: b 1752 d 1827 m Lucy McLane Pvt NH
Zalmon, Sr.: bpt 7-23-1738 d 1-15-1801 m Huldah Bradley Capt CT
Zalmon, Jr.: b 4-28-1759 d 10-3-1846 m Huldah Gray Ens CT

REEDER,
Isaac: b 1-27-1754 d 9-25-1784 m Rachel Scudder Pvt NJ
Jacob: b 1742 d 5-8-1826 m Eunice Hazen PS NJ
Jacob: b 1743 d 1798 m Lydia Jayne Mstr Armr NY
John: b 1759 d p. 1790 m Chloe Green Cpl MD
John: b 8-12-1724 d 8-15-1788 m Hannah Mershon Pvt NJ
Joseph: b 5-7-1743-5 d 10-10-1829 m Anna Huff Pvt NY
Joseph: b 5-28-1747 d 12-27-1816 m Isabella McMartin PS NY
Josiah: b c. 1725 d c. 1782 m Sarah — PS NY
Samuel: b c. 1750 d p. 1786 m Amy — PS NY
Simon: b 1724 d p. 1790 m Sarah Green PS MD
Thomas Attaway: b — d 1806 m Katherine Vemere Capt MD

REEDY,
Conrad: b c. 1742 d 8-3-1809 m Catherine Mary Giltner Pvt PA

REEG,
Johann Peter: b 1720 d 3-1-1791 m Eva Elizabeth — PS PA

REEL, (includes RIEL, RIELL, RYEL)
Anthony: b c. 1760 d c. 1795 m Phillipina — Pvt PA
Casper: b 5-11-1742 d 10-10-1824 m (2)Elizabeth Wise Sol PA
John: b 1764 d 3-3-1828 m Catherine Stuckey Pvt NC W★
John Jacob: b — d 1798 m Margaret Arcularius PS NY
Peter: b 7-25-1759 d 12-29-1843 m Mahetable Washburn Sgt NY ★

REESE, (includes REES)
Abraham: b 1750 d 11-6-1822 m Mary — Sol PS NC
David, Jr.: b 1-9-1748 d 3-29-1832 m Elizabeth Keil Capt GA
David, Sr.: b 1710 d p. 2-5-1787 m Susan Ruth Polk PS CS NC
David, Jr.: b 1746 d p. 5-20-1825 m Mary Wilson Sol NC
David: b 1-21-1735 d 6-8-1820 m Jane Ellis Maj PA
Ephraim: b 9-17-1755 d 4-21-1823 m Anne Earle Bgd Cmsry SC
Frederick: b a. 1755 d p. 1792 m Anna Margaret Ulrickson 2Lt MD
George: b 3-11-1752 d 11-11-1827 m Anna Storey Lt NC
George: b 6-16-1762 d 9-29-1841 m Rebecca Pugh Pvt PA
Hugh: b 12-20-1742 d 12-12-1825 m (3)Elizabeth Newsome Sol VA GA
James, Sr.: b 9-14-1745 d 11-17-1828 m Elizabeth Brevard Capt NC
James: b 4-23-1764 d 3-24-1851 m (1)Hannah Betterton (2)Elizabeth Reynolds PS PA
James: b 1747 d 1840 m Elizabeth Brown Sol SC
Jeremiah: b c. 1744 d 11- -1804 m Mary Jacobs Pvt PA
Joel: b c. 1760 d 11-4-1812 m Rebecca — Sol VA
John: b 3-9-1745 d 1-28-1825 m (1)Mary Spoor (2)Martha Lard Pvt NY
John: b 9- -1754 d 4-1-1813 m Barbara Margaretta Wunder Pvt NY
John: b 1752 d 1-2-1827 m Jane (Wetherell) Wetch Pvt VA
Jonathan: b 1752 d 4- -1794 m Priscilla Barnes Pvt PA
Joseph: b 1732 d 3-5-1795 m (1)Ann Reynolds (2)Mrs Sarah (Altum) PS SC
Phillip: b a. 1759 d p. 1794 m Eleanor Callenen Pvt NY
Thomas: b 1742 d 8- -1796 m Jane Harris PS SC

REEVE,
Benjamin: b 1739 d 10-29-1819 m Huldah — Lt MA
Elisha: b 2-21-1750 d 4-25-1837 m Temperance (Reeve) Pvt NY
Isaac: b 1745 d 8-20-1785 m Catherine — Capt NJ
Isaac: b 1735 d 10-5-1814 m (1)Phoebe Tuthill (2)Sarah Cheeseborough Maj NY
James: b 1756 d 3-4-1830 m (1)Parnel Wickham (2)Mehitable Downs Ens NY
James: b 1751 d 8-13-1807 m Parnel Howell Pvt NY
James, Jr.: b 4-24-1760 d 1-15-1837 m Elizabeth Horton Pvt NY
James: b 1709 d 4-27-1781 m Mary Hudson PS NY
Jonathan: b 1743 d 7-6-1823 m Sarah Wells Pvt NY
Joseph: b 1712 d 2-3-1782 m Bethiah Booth PS NY

Joshua: b 1746 d a. 11-16-1812 m (1)Mehitable Howell (2)Mrs Abigail Huff Pvt NY
Luther: b 1760 d 12-13-1843 m Anna Pearson Sgt CT ★
Paul: b 1734 d 1822 m Bethia — Capt PS NY
Selah: b 2-28-1740 d 1796 m Keturah Strong 2Lt NY
Thomas: b 1726 d 5-13-1790 m Keziah Mapes PS NY

REEVES, (includes REAVES & REEVE)
Abijah: b 1750 d 1822 m Mercy Hand Pvt NJ
Abner: b 1738 d 1828 m Hannah Barnes Pvt PA
Asher: b 1757 d 7-31-1845 m Diana Miller Pvt NC VA ★
Burgess: b 1746 d 1823 m Frances Mauldin Sol SC
Daniel: b 1760 d 4-13-1807 m (1)Martha Russel (2)Mary Bowers Pvt NY
Edward: b 1721 d 1826 m Jane Melvin PS NC
Enos: b c. 2-4-1753 d 6-23-1807 m Amy Legare Lt PA
George, Sr.: b 1735 d p. 11-15-1811 m Jean Burton Lt VA
Hezekiah: b 1752 d 11-24-1814 m Mary — Pvt NY
Israel: b 6-5-1757 d 2-21-1837 m (1)Fannie Lord (2)Abia — Pvt NY ★
Jacob: b 8- -1720 d 9-12-1794 m Abigail Ferguson PS MA
James: b 10-13-1762 d 5-19-1838 m (1)Mehitable — (2)Mary Powell Slr NY
James: b 1736 d 11-23-1803 m (1)Hepsibah Moore (2)Mary Corwin PS NY
Jeremiah: b 1738 d p. 7-21-1806 m Jane Brazile PS NC
John: b 8-1-1744 d 2-26-1800 m Mrs Sarah Reeves Patterson Sgt NJ
John: b c. 1720 d p. 1790 m Nancy — Pvt NC
John: b 6-20-1759 d c. 1840 m (1)Sally Locke Elwell (2)Eleanor Howard Lt NC ★
John: b 1745 d 1798 m Elizabeth Puckrindge Slr SC
Joseph: b 1755 d 1816 m Sarah Thompson Lt GA
Joseph: b 6-25-1755 d 5-27-1847 m (1)Abigail Leek (2)Elizabeth Fithian OrdlSgt NJ ★
Joseph: b 1740 d 1833 m Lydia Manning Sgt NJ
Joseph: b 7-5-1753 d 10-26-1801 m Elizabeth Toy Pvt NJ
Joshua: b 9-5-1757 d 6-29-1838 m (1)Catherine Whitecar (2)Mrs Rachel Parvin Pvt NJ
Lazarus: b 1756 d p. 12-11-1847 m Elizabeth — Sgt SC
Manasseh: b — d p. 1797 m (1)Martha Curwin PS NJ
Moses: b 9-1-1752 d p. 1808 m Anne Reeves Pvt NJ
Purrier, Sr.: b c. 1725 d 12- -1782 m Mary L'Hommedieu Pvt NY
Purrier, Jr.: b 3-9-1751 d 1-12-1842 m Mary Fordham Pvt CT
Richard: b 10-15-1759 d 5-19-1846 m Elizabeth Dix Pvt VA
Thomas Henry: b c. 1740 d c. 2- -1809 m (1)Eleanor Neal (2)Mary Edwards PS VA
Wm.: b 1760 d — m Amelia Cook Sgt NY
Wm.: b 4-5-1756 d 1842 m Nettie White Lt VA

REGESTER, (includes REGISTER)
Benjamin: b c. 1740 d p. 1790 m — Pvt NC
Jesse: b c. 1760 d p. 1817 m Mary — Pvt SC
John: b 9-23-1743 d 2- -1802 m (1)Esther Wilson (2)Jane — Pvt MD
Wm.: b c. 1735 d 6-2-1823 m Abigail Hoopes Pvt PA

REHRIG,
Conrad: b c. 1757 d 8-18-1834 m Christina Harter Cpl PA

REICHERLSDORFER,
John: b 12-26-1741 d 8-30-1810 m Anna Elizabeth Hagenbuch Pvt PA

REIFF, (includes RIFE)
Abraham, Sr.: b c. 1735 d p. 8-19-1788 m Barbara Groff Pvt PA
Conrad: b 1750 d 1818 m Catherine Reynolds Pvt PA
Daniel: b 1737 d 1782 m Catharine — Capt PA
George: b 4-9-1740 d 2-25-1808 m Elizabeth Hendricks Pvt PA
Jacob: b 1757 d 10-20-1847 m Mary — Pvt MD
Jacob, Sr.: b 6-18-1734 d 2-25-1816 m Catharine Schneider Pvt PA
Jacob: b c. 1735 d 1786 m Barbara Burkholder Pvt PA

REIFSNIDER, (includes REIFSCHNEIDER)
Peter: b 2-2-1752 d p. 6-3-1828 m (1)Catherine Yost (2)Barbara Lachmund Pvt PA
Sebastian: b 6- -1743 d 9-19-1813 m (1)Anna Maria Ursula Hertzen (2)Catharine — Pvt PA
Wm.: b 10-15-1744 d 1819 m (1)Susanna — (2)Margareth — Pvt PA

REIGART, (includes REIGERT)
Adam, Sr.: b 11-11-1739 d 5-9-1813 m (1)Mrs Catherine Carpenter Yeiser (2)Mrs Susanna Rudisell Metzgar LCol PS PA
Christopher: b 2-24-1731 d 10-14-1783 m Susanna Zimmerman Pvt PA
Jacob: b 1765 d 1821 m Mary — Pvt PA

REIGNER,
John: b 8-27-1755 d 5-14-1832 m Susanna Betz Pvt PA

REIMER,
Isaac: b 2-15-1744 d 11-1-1810 m Margaretha Krotzer Pvt PA

REINACKER,
Caspar: b 7-30-1733 d 7-30-1790 m Anna Maria Carle Capt PA

REINBOLD,
Ludwig: b c. 1740 d c. 1815 m Christina — Pvt PA

REINE,
Etienne: b 4-22-1751 d 1-28-1834 m Marie Chenet PS LA

REINER,
Jacob: b 9-12-1761 d 3-8-1857 m Elizabeth — Pvt PA

REINHARD, (includes REINHARDT, REINHART & RINEHART)
Adam: b 5-15-1724 d 11-14-1806 m Maria Barbara — Pvt PA
Barnet: b c. 1758 d 1822 m (1)Elizabeth — (2)Ruth — Pvt PA
Bernhard: b 2-21-1759 d 5-18-1816 m Elizabeth Kramer Pvt PS PA
Christian: b 1-6-1735 d 3-22-1817 m Elizabeth Warlick Pvt PM NC
Elizabeth Warlick: b 6-17-1754 d 6-17-1806 m Christian Reinhardt PS NC
Frederick: b c. 1735 d p. 1790 m — Pvt PA
George: b 5-2-1752 d 10-12-1807 m Anna Elizabeth Henigman Pvt PA
Godfrey: b 8-24-1744 d 10-7-1814 m Charity Pickel 1Maj NJ
Henry: b 11-5-1751 d a. 10-13-1818 m Catherine Feger Pvt PA
Johannes: b 4-19-1719 d 12-7-1799 m Magdalena — PS PA
John: b 7-7-1743 d 4-21-1823 m Hannah Frick Pvt PA
Lewis: b c. 1740 d 1812 m Catherine Walters Sol VA
Thomas: b 1746 d 8-2-1804 m Hannah Inghram Pvt PA

REINHOLD, (includes REINOEHL)
Christopher: b 4-10-1728 d 3-3-1793 m Sophia Louise Amweg Drm PA
Frederick: b 5-12-1762 d 5-14-1833 m Elizabeth Wenger Pvt PA
Henry: b 12-18-1741 d 2-14-1825 m (1)Juliana Gephart (2)Catherine Matter Pvt PS PA
John George: b 7-10-1752 d 10-12-1832 m Anna Catharine Ritte Pvt PA

REINSMITH, (includes RINESMITH)
John, Sr.: b 1728 d 3-1-1787 m Anna Maria — Pvt PA
John, Jr.: b a. 1753 d c. 1810 m (2)Susanna — Pvt PA

REISE,
Adam: b 1761 d 4-14-1828 m Maria — Pvt PA

REISINGER,
John Martin: b 12-25-1751 d a. 7-23-1814 m Anna Maria Pvt PA
Peter: b c. 1740 d 10- -1801 m Eve Schmahl Pvt PA

REIST,
Abraham: b 2-4-1737 d 2-4-1813 m Elizabeth Metz Pvt VA

REITENAUER, (includes REITENEAUR)
Jacob: b 1-11-1759 d 9-21-1827 m Susanna Barbara — Pvt MD ★
Ludwig: b 1750 d p. 1791 m Rosina Pfueger PS MD

REITER,
Michael: b 1700 d 1770 m Christiana — Pvt PA

REITMEYER, (includes RICHTMYER, RIGHTMEYER & RIGHTMYER)
Christian: b 10-17-1740 d a. 12-2-1803 m Elizabeth Merkel Sgt Sct NY
Conrad: b 7-1-1751 d p. 1800 m (1)Catharine Fiero (2)Antje (Homel) Wells Pvt PS NY
George: b 9-18-1738 d p. 11-9-1800 m Anna Hummel Capt NY
George Wm.: b c. 1724 d p. 10-14-1782 m Anna Hommel Capt PS NY
Henry: b c. 1724 d 1777/8 m Felicitas Friebel PS PA
Johannes George: b 1-4-1742 d 3-4-1818 m (2)Maria Dietz Pvt NY
John: b 1-28-1742 d a. 10-15-1799 m Anna Barbara — Capt PA
Peter: b 5-14-1751 d 9-17-1820 m Hester Hellig 2Lt NY

RELYEA, (includes RELJIE)
David: bpt 12-24-1710 d p. 1798 m Annatje Reynersche PS NY
Dennis, Sr.: bpt 4-17-1723 d 1810/11 m Martje VanVliet PS NY
Henry: b 3-20-1753 d 3-14-1835 m Elizabeth Weismuller Pvt NY ★
Jacob: b 2-27-1756 d 5-8-1829 m Amelia Lodewick Pvt NY
Wm.: b 4-15-1749 d 4-15-1831 m Lena Ostrander PS NY

REMALY, (includes RAMALEY)
Michael: b 1762 d 1834 m Susanna Schaeffer Pvt PA

REMBERT,
Abijah: b 1743 d 12-2-1805 m (1)Jane Reese (2)Elizabeth English PS SC
James: b c. 1740 d 1812 m (1)Mary — (2)Ann — Capt SC

REMER,
David: b 12- -1754 d 9-19-1836 m Nancy Smith Arfr PA ★
John: b 1744 d 1-6-1820 m Leah Anton Pvt NY

REMICK,
Benjamin: b 4-30-1719 d c. 1782 m Elizabeth Deed PS MA

Benjamin, Jr.: b 9-26-1753 d 1-31-1837 m Abigail Fernald Lt NS MA
Enoch: b 4-1-1730 d 5-11-1800 m Abigail Trefethen PS NH
Freeman: b 1755 d 11-30-1826 m Abigail Sears Pvt MA
John: b 8-8-1763 d 8-2-1849 m (1)Elizabeth Evens Cpl NH
Joseph: b c. 1730/1 d 1805 m Sarah Wells Pvt MA
Josiah: b 10-10-1758 d 1-1-1844 m Martha Kelly Parry Pvt MA
Nathaniel: b 12-16-1712 d 6-28-1783 m Jane Libby PS CS MA
Timothy: b 9-7-1755 d 1784 m Mercy Staples Capt MA
Wm., Sr.: b 1726 d 10-10-1813 m (1)Mary Paul (2)Lydia Staples (3)Ruth Staples PS MA
Wm., Jr.: b 1753 d 8-14-1821 m (1)Lucy Hammond (2)Susanna Hammond Pvt MA

REMINGTON,
Abijah: b — d 1832 m Silence Rising Pvt CT
Anthony: b 4-4-1758 d 11-8-1833 m Hannah — Mrnr NY ★
Benedict: b c. 1750 d 12-10-1819 m Ruth Southwick Pvt RI
Benjamin: b 4-7-1733 d 9-30-1820 m Hannah Martin Capt RI
Caleb: b 1748 d 1836 m Roby Warner Sgt RI
Clement: b 1755 d 5-4-1833 m (1)Sarah Hart (2)Sarah Jones Pvt NJ
David: b 6-7-1747 d 1834 m Mary Sheldon Pvt RI ★
Elijah: b 9-18-1743 d 11-24-1804 m Mrs Esther Gunn Pvt CT
Elisha, Jr.: b 5-2-1751 d 12-2-1822 m Margaret Stowell Pvt MA
Enoch: b 1728-30 d 6- -1811 m Molly Watson Sgt RI
John: b 10-21-1761 d 11-11-1849 m Phebe Carr Pvt CT ★
John: b 11-2-1756 d 1-7-1840 m Mary Tillinghast Lt NS RI ★
John: b 11-2-1757 d 1840 m Mary Greene Capt MA
Jonathan: b 9-1-1761 d p. 4-19-1833 m Martha Sprague Pvt VT ★
Joshua, Sr.: b 2-14-1730/1 d p. 1755 m Ruth Clay PS MA
Joshua, Jr.: b 10-4-1760 d 9-4-1855 m Eunice — Pvt MA VT ★
Josiah: b 2-4-1746 d 6-30-1830 m Adah Wait Pvt CT
Peleg: b c. 1757 d p. 11- -1847 m (1)Nancy — (2)Susan Briggs Pvt RI
Seth: b 7-27-1726 d 4-29-1806 m (1)Elizabeth Ball (2)Mary Roberts (3)Lydia — Pvt MA
Simeon: b 1-31-1762 d p. 10-12-1832 m Susanna Pomeroy Pvt CT ★
Stephen: b 1-30-1712 d 1792 m Sarah Barbow Pvt CT
Stephen: b 1750 d 3-13-1813 m Sarah Walton Pvt Ri W★
Thomas: b 8-19-1723 d 4-12-1808 m Abigail Eldred PS RI
Tiddeman H.: b 2-9-1760 d 2-16-1843 m Elizabeth Sheffield Pvt RI ★

REMSBURG,
Henry: b 1752 d 1807 m (1)Susanna Devilbiss (2)Catherine Stickley Pvt MD
Jacob: b 1746/7 d p. 1779 m Anna Elizabeth Develbess 3Sgt MD

REMSEN, (includes RAMSON)
Aart: b 6-4-1748 d 6-4-1819 m (1)Charity Myers (2)Elizabeth Elkerson Pvt NY
Abraham: b 8-23-1730 d 10-12-1807 m Mary Voohees Capt NY
Abraham: b 1-15-1720 d 3-1-1799 m Matildah VanDuyn PS NY
Aris: b 1711 d a. 4-25-1778 m Jannetie Rapalye PS Pvt NY
Auris: b 1758 d 10-26-1839 m Ann Bergen Pvt NY
Christopher: b 7-22-1743 d p. 1781 m Margaritie Hardenbergh PS NY
George: b 3-29-1739 d 6-22-1784 m Cornelia Blauvelt Pvt PS NY
Henry: b 4-15-1736 d 3-13-1792 m Cornelia Dickerson Col NY
Jeromus, Jr.: b 11-22-1735 d 6-7-1790 m Ann Rapelje Col NY
Jeromus, Sr.: b 11-22-1705 d 10-12-1781 m Jane — PS NY
Luke: b 9-1-1749 d 4-20-1839 m (1)Abigail North (2)Judith Titus (3)Lydia Osborn Pvt NY
Remsen: b 1743 d 2-27-1786 m Phoebe Duryea Lt PS NY

RENCH,
Andrew: b 1740 d 9- -1792 m Elizabeth — PS MD

RENDER,
Joshua: b — d p. 4-1-1817 m Susan — Sol VA

RENFREW, (includes RENFRO & RENTFRO)
James: b 11-19-1763 d 7-29-1835 m (1)Charity Huff (2)Dorothy Pvt VA
John: b 4-4-1753 d 10-14-1844 m Sarah Rea Pvt VA
John: b 11-12-1760 d 4-22-1846 m Esther Reach Pvt Drm VA ★
Joseph: b 1700 d 1776 m Mary Randolph CS VA
Joshua: b 7-1-1757 d 9-5-1815 m Jane Hairston 2Lt VA
Mark: b 1760 d 1811 m Naomi Standifore Ens VA
Moses: b 1-2-1728 d 1-14-1824 m (1)Hanna (Renfro) (2)Elizabeth Turpin PS VA TN
Noel: b 1739 d 1819 m Charity Hinnant PS NC
Wm.: b 1734 d p. 8-9-1825 m Jane — Pvt SC

RENNICK, (includes RENICK & RENNOCK)
Alexander: b 1736 d 1-15-1777 m — McKamie Pvt PA
James: b 5-28-1753 d 10-2-1838 m Jane Dyal Pvt SC ★
James: b 1748 d 1807 m Mary — Pvt VA
John: b 10-10-1750 d 1-13-1814 m Mary Heath Ens VA
Samuel: b c. 1755 d p. 11- -1797 m Nancy — Pvt PA
Wm.: b c. 6- -1741 d p. 1784 m Ann Hamilton Of VA
Wm.: b 1746 d 7-15-1807 m (1)Rachel Heath (2)Ann — PS VA

RENNOLDS,
Streshly: b 1760 d 7-25-1822 m Martha Dangerfield Beale PS VA

RENO,
Benjamin: b 2-3-1740 d c. 1803 m Jane Bell Pvt PA
Francis: b 2-7-1758 d 8-12-1836 m Lydia Savers Pvt PA
Francis, Sr.: b — d a. 10-2-1797 m — PS VA
Simeon: b 7-7-1758 d 4-14-1814 m Dorcas Brockway Pvt NY

RENSHAW,
Thomas: b 1718 d 7-31-1785 m Isabella Clark 1Lt PA

RENTCHLER,
Michael: b 10-18-1722 d 1797 m Rosina — Pvt PS PA

REPLEGLE,
Rinehart: b 1724 d 1796 m — Pvt PA

REPLOGUE,
Rynard, Jr.: b c. 1759 d 1813 m Catherine Brown Pvt PA

REQUA,
Abraham: b 11-20-1759 d 11-1-1843 m Bethia Hopkins Pvt NY ★
Daniel: b 6-5-1735 d 10- -1801 m Maritie Martling Sgt NY
Gabriel: b 1753 d 1784 m Elizabeth Oakley Capt NY
Gabriel: b 7-9-1760 d 10-8-1809 m Elizabeth Mattling Pvt NY
Gloda: b 5-4-1727 d 12-9-1806 m Amy Dean Capt NY
James: b 8-10-1729 d 9-9-1817 m (1)Maritia Acker (2)Rebecca Conklin Sol PS NY
John: b 3-11-1763 d 3-24-1827 m Mary Knapp Pvt NY
Joseph: b 8-17-1758 d 1839 m Theodocia Mead Lt NY ★

RESPESS,
Richard: b 7-31-1749 d 1-20-1839 m (1)Martha — (2)Pheriba Dawson Pvt NC

RESSEQUIE, (includes RESSEGUIE)
James: b 1744 d 9-7-1830 m (1)Sarah Rumsey (2)Eunice — Sgt CT
John: b 4-2-1758 d 5-9-1840 m (1)Anna Camp (2)Abigail Brailey (3)Mrs Anna (Thompson) McDonald Pvt CT NY ★

RESWICK,
Joseph: b 8-15-1757 d 1795 m Elizabeth Mattingley Pvt MD

RETTEW,
Aaron, Sr.: b 1721 d p. 7-27-1787 m — PS PA
Aaron, Jr.: b 1753 d 9- -1811 m (1)Rebecca Aston (2)Elizabeth Packingham Capt PA

RETTGE, (includes REDCAY & REDKEY)
Adam: b c. 1763 d 1810 m Mary Davis Sol PA
Elias, Jr.: b 1745 d 1-3-1829 m Elizabeth Hunter Lt PA
Elias: b c. 1716 d 1786 m (1)Elizabeth — (2)Rosina Zigler PS PA
Jacob: b 1722 d 1784 m Catherine — PS PA

REUBACH,
Jacob Borhave: b 174- d 4- -1809 m Sarah Culver Dr VT

REVELLE, (includes REVELL)
Etheldred: b 1758 d c. 1845 m Elizabeth Combs Sol NC
John: b c. 1740 d c. 1806/7 m Elizabeth Poulson Gnr Mte NS VA

REVERE,
Paul, Sr.: b 1-1-1735 d 5-10-1818 m (1)Sarah Orne (2)Rachel Walker LCol MA
Paul, Jr.: b 6-6-1760 d 1-16-1813 m Sally Edwards Capt Lt MA

REVIS, (includes REAVIS)
Isham: b 9-17-1748 d p. 8-16-1824 m (1)Annes — (2)Sally Womack Pvt NC
Joseph: b — d p. 8-17-1804 m Mary — PS NC

REVIS,
Samuel: b 1717 d 1789 m Nancy Jones Sol NC

REW,
Ephraim: b 6-17-1757 d 7-30-1833 m Chloe Adams Pvt CT ★

REWALT,
John: b 5-15-1755 d 2-16-1822 m Ann McMahon Capt DepWgm PA W★

REX,
Abraham: b 1735 d 2-7-1793 m Anna Bastion Pvt PA
Christopher: b c. 1754 d p. 1808 m Hannah Holder Sgt PA
George: b 1750 d 5-1-1821 m Margaret Kepler Pvt PA

REXFORD,
Benjamin, Sr.: b 6-1-1739 d p. 1784 m Esther Hall Pvt CT
Benjamin, Jr.: b 5-15-1761 d 5-29-1839 m Catherine Rice Pvt CT
Ensign: b 1760 d 6-5-1836 m Annis Babbitt Pvt MA
Joel: b 1750 d 3-22-1821 m Rhoda Spencer Pvt CT
Samuel: b 10-12-1750 d 8-24-1816 m Sarah Andrus Lt NY

m Hannah

REYNOLDS, (includes RANNELLS, RAYNOLDS, RENNELLS, RUNNALLS, RUNNELLS & RUNNELS)
Aaron: b 12-1-1753 d 1- -1842 m Martha Davis Pvt VA ★
Abraham: b 5-23-1718 d 7-24-1804 m Hannah Smith Pvt NH
Allen David: b 4-14-1763 d 11-9-1827 m Deborah Branch Pvt NH ★
Ambrose: b 8- -1751 d 12-24-1830 m Mary Knapp Pvt CT
Benjamin: b 1761 d 5-10-1851 m (2)Lydia Bennett Pvt CT ★
Benjamin: b 3-31-1748 d 6-22-1802 m Hepzibah Ayer Pvt MA
Benjamin: b 2-26-1760 d 10-8-1814 m Anne Smith Pvt NY
Benjamin: b 4-18-1756 d 2-19-1820 m Elizabeth Reynolds Pvt RI ★
Benjamin: b c. 1755 d 1826 m (1)Sarah Chaplin (2)Anne Smiley Lt PS SC
Benoni: b 4-8-1755 d a. 2-18-1854 m Anna Harmon Pvt NY
Bernard: b 11-12-1763 d 1-23-1833 m Lucy Johnston Pvt VA ★
Caleb: b 1739 d p. 1790 m Sarah Brown Pvt PS NY
Charles: b 10-30-1762 d 4-12-1816 m Hannah Bidwell Pvt CT ★
Daniel: b 9-15-1742 d 12-13-1795 m Hannah Spofford Col NH
David: b 6-17-1734 d 7-8-1816 m Hannah (Andrus) Gaylord Pvt CT
David: b 1-6-1753 d 8-30-1827 m Margarite Crissey Pvt NY
David: b 1761 d p. 4-6-1827 m Sally Galloway Pvt NY
David: b 9-7-1739 d 4-25-1789 m Mary — MM NY
David: b — d 1809 m Ruth Becket Pvt PA
Dudley: b c. 1750 d 1799 m Fanny Hubert Capt NC
Ebenezer: b 4-8-1726 d 8-4-1795 m (1)Abigail Sallows (2)Hannah Smith PS MA
Eliphalet: b 1753 d p. 1827 m Jemima Tibbets Pvt CT
Elisha: b 4- -1755 d 12-13-1836 m Judith Eddins Lt NC ★
Elisha, Jr.: b 8-29-1763 d 11-15-1840 m (1)Miss Gates (2)Elizabeth Hoxie Pvt RI NY VT ★
Ely: b 1747 d 11-28-1827 m — Pvt NY
Ezekiel: b 10-13-1747 d 11-24-1833 m Mary Mead Pvt CT
Fielding: b 6-1-1763 d 3-8-1862 m (1)Priscilla — (2)Eliza Perry (3)Elizabeth Ducker OrdlSgt SC ★
Francis: b 7-3-1758 d 2-10-1814 m Elizabeth Levering Pvt PA
Gamaliel, Sr.: b 11-4-1725 d 5-7-1805 m (1)Mehitable Beebe (2)Sarah Hazen Pvt CT
Gamaliel, Jr.: b 5-20-1754 d 6-7-1836 m Mary Smith Capt CT ★
George: b 1742 d 1818 m Lenny Wholforth Pvt MD
George: b 10-13-1758/9 d 1821 m (1)Dorothy Landon (2)Mary D Lashmutte Capt NJ ★
George: b c. 1730 d 1795 m (1) — Davis (2)Margaretta Stopp Sol PA
George: b 2-19-1761 d 12-19-1844 m Freelove Northrup Cpl RI ★
George: b a. 1754 d c. 1813 m Susanna Lansford Capt VA
Griffen: b 6-11-1737 d 12-24-1823 m Elizabeth — PS NY
Grindall: b 10-12-1755 d 5-8-1847 m (1)Abigail Rhodes (2)Mehitable Kendall (3)Cynthia Kendall Lt RI ★
Grindall, Sr.: b 7-11-1726 d p. 1790 m Sarah Searles Lt VA
Grindall, Jr.: b 1763 d 11-29-1843 m Dorcas Landon Pvt VT
Hamilton: b 10-7-1761 d 1851 m (1)Rachel Clements Pvt GA
Harman: b 1749-59 d 7-20-1839 m — Howell Sol GA
Henry: b 1742 d 1827 m Mary Fowler MM NY
Henry: b 1-31-1757 d 7-16-1845 m Elizabeth Sidwell Pvt PA
Henry: b — d 1787 m Mahitable Wait Ens RI
Henry: b 10-12-1759 d 3-31-1829 m (2)Elizabeth Mitchel Pvt RI
Horton: b 1732 d 1791 m Lydia Knapp Pvt CT
Israel: b 12-25-1753 d 11-22-1812 m Deborah Hachel Pvt NY
Jacob: b 5-8-1731 d 7-7-1786 m Martha Padelford Pvt CT
Jacob: b 9-14-1728 d 2-6-1799 m Rebecca Daye Pvt PA
James: b 3-17-1732 d 5-8-1818 m Mehitable Blakeslee 1Lt CT
James: b 7-14-1754 d 4-6-1835 m Mary Davis Sgt CT ★
James: b 5-8-1759 d 3-2-1833 m Abigail Knapp Pvt CT
James: b 1-25-1752 d 4-9-1844 m Tamson Ham Ens NH
James: b 1747 d 10-9-1834 m (2)Mrs Phebe Adsit Pvt NY
James: b 1757 d p. 1833 m Sarah Green Pvt NC ★
James: b 12-21-1760 d 1829 m Hannah Webster Pvt PA
James: b 3-4-1757 d 12-3-1846 m (1)Rachel Peckham (2)Eunice Austin Lt RI ★
James: b 1750 d p. 1796 m Susan Lindsay Pvt VA
Jedediah, Sr.: b 1720 d p. 1776 m Abigail Crandall PS NH
Jedediah, Jr.: b 12-15-1744 d 1800 m Hannah — PS NH
Job: b 1-12-1749 d 8-27-1831 m Sarah Ellison Lt NH
John: b 7-6-1743/4 d 5-30-1804/5 m Abigail Bement Sgt CT
John: b 3-16-1761 d 3-3-1840 m Mary Morgan Sgt CT ★
John: b a. 1764 d 10- -1820 m Ann — PS DE
John, Sr.: b 1714 d a. 4-13-1784 m Elizabeth McKee PS MD
John, Jr.: b 1745 d 3- -1779 m Margaret Smith Capt MD
John: b 6- -1749 d 4-23-1829 m Elizabeth Picket Pvt NH
John: b c. 1734 d c. 1827 m Joanna Patterson Pvt NJ
John: b 1738 d 1787 m Rebecca Rundell Sct MM NY
John: b 10-13-1725 d p. 1808/9 m Edith — PS NC
John: b 1728 d 1808 m Miss Hayes Capt PA
John: b c. 1740 d p. 1- -1824 m Mary Campbell Pvt PA
John: b 2-3-1759 d 1-11-1848 m Hannah Faulder Pvt RI ★
John: b 1751 d 7-1-1822 m Rebecca — Sol VA
John: b 1-5-1733 d 1796 m Alcey Reese PS VA
John: b 3-10-1754 d 1795 m Elizabeth Brickey PS VA
Jonas: b 1-28-1741/2 d 8-5-1795 m Anna Perkins Cpl MA
Jonathan: b 4-3-1756 d 8-24-1809 m Mary Brown Pvt CT
Jonathan: b 1726 d 1807 m Keziah Carter PS NH
Jonathan: b 10-3-1740 d 9-14-1840 m Rebecca Day Sgt VT
Joesph: b 5-2-1732 d 12-10-1792 m Phebe Lee PS CT
Joseph: b 11-10-1747 d p. 7-7-1808 m Sarah Smith 2Lt PS MD

Joseph: b 6-21-1751 d 3-15-1831 m Jemima Perkins Cpl MA W★
Joseph: b 8-27-1757 d 11-12-1799 m (1)Ruth Rich (2)Lydia Parker Capt NY
Joseph: b 7-26-1761 d 9- -1847 m Ruth Palmer Pvt NY
Joseph: b 7-9-1749 d 12-25-1823 m Experience Davis Pvt NY
Joseph, Sr.: b 11-15-1719 d 9-11-1789 m Lydia Greenwood CS RI
Joseph, Jr.: b 9-20-1748 d 10-10-1818 m Sarah Cox Lt RI
Joseph: b 1750 d a. 8-7-1821 m Susanna Wright PS VA
Margaret Smith: b 1748 d 1783 m John Reynolds PS MD
Mary: b 1768 d 12-20-1817 m Joseph Clarke PS MD
Moses: b 1752 d 1781-3 m Sarah Crosby Pvt NY
Nathaniel, Sr.: b 1-27-1715 d 4- -1792 m Sarah Lockwood PS CT
Nathaniel, Jr.: b 9-7-1745 d 6-6-1822 m (1)Rebecca Mead (2)Deborah Husted Lt CT
Nathaniel: b 3-19-1718 d 11-26-1807 m (1)Hannah Hartwell (2)Mary Tolman PS MA
Nathaniel: b 10-25-1730 d 1782 m (1)Lydia Raymond (2)Mrs Mary (Chapell) Blaney SeaCap MA
Nathaniel: b 4-26-1757 d 1828 m (1)Bethia Keith (2)Mary Adams Pvt MA
Nathaniel: b 2-22-1754 d 9-21-1843 m Hannah Todd Coley 2Lt NY W★
Nathaniel: b 11-25-1762 d 5- -1844 m Catherine Vernon Pvt VA★
Nehemiah: b 1732-40 d p. 1787 m (1)Mary Armstrong (2)Anstress Southworth Sgt CT
Peter: b 5-17-1730 d 6-15-1780 m Hannah Wells PS CT
Peter: b 4-1-1750 d 4-8-1798 m Elizabeth Lockwood PS NY
Phebe: b 1770 d 1853 m Jeremiah Drake PS NY
Reuben: b 3-14-1735 d 3-8-1819 m Hepzibah — Fif CT
Richard: b c. 1738 d 9- -1787 m Sarah Ann — Sol GA VA
Robert: b 1760 d 5-24-1833 m Sarah Braley Pvt MA ★
Robert: b 9-21-1736 d 9- -1806 m Eunice Waite Capt RI
Robert: b 1760 d 8-29-1844 m Jemima Ross Sgt RI ★
Samuel: b 2-17-1753 d 12-9-1813 m Sarah Foote Pvt CT
Samuel: b — d — m Lucy Pitkin Pvt CT
Samuel: b 7-16-1754 d 3-21-1847 m Mary March Capt NH
Samuel: b 2-12-1752 d 3-24-1828 m Amey Weaver Ens RI
Samuel: b 1757 d c. 10-14-1845 m Mary Gray Pvt SC ★
Sarah: b 2-8-1762 d 8-31-1849 m Josiah Smith PS CT
Silas: b 8-23-1763 d p. 4-1-1837 m (2)Didama Leonard Pvt VT
Solomon: b 8-8-1758 d 10-28-1835 m Elizabeth Green Pvt CT ★
Stephen: b 7-3-1754 d 7-22-1798 m Chloe Thruston Cpl MA
Stephen: b 2-2-1749 d — m Abigail Cottrell Pvt RI
Susanna Lansford: b — d p. 1813 m George Reynolds PS VA
Thomas: b 1752 d 12-6-1836 m Sally Marshall Pvt CT
Thomas: b 1-27-1762 d 12-9-1851 m Tabitha Thayer Pvt MA
Thomas: b 2-25-1719 d c. 10- -1795 m Elizabeth Turner CS MA
Thomas: b 1729 d 1803 m — Col NJ
Thomas: b 11-5-1753 d 4-14-1845 m Mary — Pvt RI
Thomas: b 1752 d 1801 m Sarah Lindsay Pvt VA
Thomas: b 1762 d 6-4-1850 m Catherine Willis Pvt VA
Timothy: b 5-13-1763 d a. 10-2-1781 m Amy Knapp Capt CT
Titus: b 1737 d 12-25-1808 m Sarah Husted Lt NY
Wm.: b c. 1725 d a. 1798 m Mary — PS Pvt MD
Wm.: b c. 1750 d 8-2-1821 m Nancy Griffith PS MD
Wm.: b 7-7-1739 d 7-10-1822 m Rebekah Foster Pvt MA
Wm.: b c. 1734-38 d 2- -1809 m Mary Knapp Pvt NY
Wm.: b 1736 d 1785 m Sarah — Pvt NY
Wm.: b 5-5-1754 d 6-18-1816 m Martha Lamoreax Pvt NY
Wm.: b 12-20-1740 d 4-2-1819 m Ruth Maxwell 1Lt PA
Wm.: b 1700 d 1- -1792 m Deborah Green Pvt PA
Wm.: b 5-2-1739 d 10-4-1841 m Esther Reynolds Pvt RI ★
Wm.: b 10-3-1755 d a. 1785 m Anne Thorton Lt VA
Wm. Whitford: b 5-29-1749 d 4-13-1829 m Mary Lillibridge Pvt NY
Winthrop: b 1754 d 1832 m Hannah Locke Pvt NH

RHINE, (includes RHEIN, RHINES & RHYNE)
Christopher: b 1-20-1742 d 6-12-1826 m Catherine Rue Pvt NY
David: b 1733 d 1801 m Maria Appolonia Moyer Pvt PA
Peter: b 1754 d 7-8-1828 m Anny M Wills Sgt NC

RHODES, (includes RHOADES, RHOADS, ROADS, RODE, RODES & ROTH)
Adam: b c. 1760 d — m Miriam Kibbie Pvt MA
Adam: b 1740 d 1801 m Sarah Jeans Pvt PA
Alexander: b 1739 d 5-6-1805 m Mary Steele Pvt CT
Anthony: b 10-21-1761 d 5-25-1845 m (1)Rehebiah Budlong (2)Mrs Anna Langworthy Pvt RI CT ★
Benjamin: b 3-25-1763 d 3-10-1834 m Phebe Burlingame Smn RI
Benjamin: b 1-13-1754 d 8-24-1791 m Judith Richmond Pvt VT
Charles, Sr.: b 8-12-1725 d 2-14-1800 m Alice Van Kirk PS NJ
Charles: b 2-22-1756 d 2-4-1837 m (1)Isabella — (2)Olivia McGehee Capt NC ★
Clifton: b 11-6-1740 d 10-1-1819 m Sarah Waller CS PS VA
Conrad: b 1743 d p. 1-7-1829 m Catherine — Pvt PA
Daniel: b 1750 d 6-14-1830 m Lydia Rhodes Pvt MA ★
Daniel: b 10-5-1755 d 4-8-1838 m (1)Eva Foust (2)Elizabeth Newman Pvt PA ★
David: b 1755 d 1834 m Jerusha Hitchcock Pvt MA ★
David: b c. 1731 d 12-29-1793 m (1)Mary Mills (2)Susan Anderson PS VA
Ebenezer: b 1745 d 7-4-1825 m Sarah Page PS NH

Eleazer: b 8-24-1738 d 1820/1 m (1)Margaret Bowen (2)Mary Hawkins Pvt MA
Eliphalet: b 2-17-1756 d 12-2-1833 m Mercy Holland Pvt MA ★
Ezekiel: b 1736 d 1-1-1813 m Mary — Pvt PA
Francis William: b 2-1-1746 d 3-25-1811 m Hannah — Capt PA
Frederick: b 3-11-1759 d c. 1841 m (1)Juliana Schweikert (2)Sarah — Pvt PA
Gabriel: b 1751 d 3-28-1818 m Rachel Shedacre Pvt PS PA
George: b c. 1755 d 10-23-1823 m Catherine Storms Pvt PA
Henry: b c. 1735 d 8-7-1812 m (1)Mary — (2)Elizabeth Ward LCol NC
Henry: b 1734 d a. 1-4-1793 m Alice — Pvt NC
Henry: b 6-5-1739 d 5-6-1814 m (1)Elizabeth Stoner (2)Barbara Lauriman Capt PA
Henry: b 1-23-1754 d 1-23-1828 m Catherine — Pvt PA
Issac, Sr.: b 1726 d 6- -1797 m Charity Hill Pvt NY
Jacob: b 9-4-1760 d 9-18-1861 m (2)Susan Edmonds (3)Sarah — Pvt VA
Jacob, Sr.: b c. 1719 d 10- -1798 m X PS PA
Jacob, Jr.: b 9-17-1744 d 4-22-1823 m Susanna Yocum Capt PA
Jacob: b c. 1750 d 1784 m Rebecca Boyer Pvt PA
James: b 3-31-1735 d 10-8-1811 m Mary Ellis Pvt CT
James: b 1-24-1751 d 6-5-1827 m Lydia Woodard Pvt MA ★
James: b c. 7-31-1730 d 6-21-1806 m (1)Ann Crandall (2)Abigail Greenman (3)Mrs Martha Babcock Rhodes Pvt PS RI
Jeriah: b c. 1735 d a. 1812 m (1)Rebecca Lewis (2)Sophronia Ayers Pvt RI
John: b 3-20-1747 d 6-24-1819 m Hannah Graves Pvt MA
John: b 8-8-1760 d 6-10-1826 m Lydia Farrington Pvt MA
John: b 6-7-1759 d 12-4-1828 m Sarah — Pvt NY ★
John: b 8-4-1763 d 5-18-1854 m Sybil Edmunds Pvt NY
John: b c. 1725 d p. 2-8-1799 m Frances — PS NC
John, Sr.: b 6-18-1755 d 12-8-1824 m Eunice Rhoads Pvt PA
John: b 7-8-1709 d 4-15-1791 m Judith — PS PA
John: b 11-4-1756 d 3-14-1835 m Catherine Leib Pvt PA
John: b 1760 d 2-15-1842 m Nancy Fields Cpl RI ★
John: b 11-6-1729 d 7-15-1810 m Sarah Harris Fif VA
Joseph: bpt 3-8-1741 d 6-12-1830 m Emma Chapman Pvt MA
Joseph: b c. 1745 d 11- -1779 m Elizabeth — Mil PA
Joseph: b 9-10-1759 d 12-17-1830 m Nancy Ann Champlin Ens RI
Joseph Thomas: b 1754 d 5-23-1820 m Mary Williams Capt NC
Mark: b 7-17-1753 d 1-25-1830 m Catherine Heiss Sgt PA
Matthias: b c. 1745/6 d 11-11-1804 m Elizabeth Yoder LCol PA
Michael: b 5-1-1749 d 10-11-1820 m Ann Strickler Pvt VA
Moses: b 6-1-1765 d 9- -1856 m Dorothy Stevens Pvt MA ★
Nicholas: b c. 1761 d 1-24-1830 m Elizabeth Taylor Pvt VA ★
Peter: b 4-18-1737 d 12-18-1814 m (1)Sabina Kohler (2)Eva Catherine Miller PS MA
Peter: b 2-24-1741 d 3-16-1823 m Esther Arnold Pvt NOfr RI
Richard: b — d 1777 m — Lewis Pvt NY
Robert: b 3-21-1742 d 3-25-1821 m Phebe Smith Capt RI
Robert: b 5-11-1757 d 11-20-1818 m Eliza Delany Capt VA
Samuel: b 1-30-1737 d 3-18-1823 m Sarah Frothingham Capt MA
Samuel: b 9-25-1758 d 2-9-1832 m Mary Morse Pvt MA ★
Samuel: b 1711 d 1784 m Elizabeth Chandler PS PA
Simon: b 1-24-1716 d 4-27-1784 m (1)Anna Babcock (2)Martha Babcock PS CT
Timothy: b 3-12-1756 d 5-14-1828 m Rowena Hill 2nd Lt MA
Walter G: b 5-19-1738 d 3-12-1813 m Mary Hill Sgt RI
Wm.: b c. 1725 d p. 2-24-1792 m Sarah — PS NC
Wm.: b 3-18-1749 d p. 1-10-1778 m Elizabeth Maginn Lt RI
Wm.: b 9-13-1753 d 8-16-1835 m Sarah Champlin Pvt RI ★
Zachariah: b 3-1-1755 d 1833 m Elizabeth Rea Pvt Mstr RI ★

RIBBLE,
George: b c. 1741 d 1822 m Rachel — Capt NJ

RIBLET,
Christian: b 8-18-1761 d 4-6-1844 m Christiana Magdaline Shull OrdlSgt PA ★
Henry: b c. 1763 d 1-1/16-1839 m Catherine Keiper Pvt PA ★
John: b 1756 d 8-6-1835 m Catherine Keiper Pvt PA ★

RICE, (includes RECE, ROYS & ROYCE)
Aaron: b 1749 d 12-20-1832 m Anna Yale Pvt CT
Aaron: b 1-31-1724/5 d 10-2-1808 m Freedom French PS MA
Aaron: b 1754 d 1-27-1822 m Eleanor Rhoden Sol SC
Abagail Hartman: b 9-4-1742 d 11-6-1789 m Zachariah Rice PS PA
Abel: b 1-26-1760 d 10-6-1827 m Anna Jones Sgt MA
Abiah: b 11-10-1760 d 4-26-1845 m Sarah Sterling Sgt MA ★
Abner: b 1-4-1753 d 2- -1819 m Keziah Hall Sgt CT
Abner C: b 4-20-1746 d 1822 m Tryhena Adams Pvt MA
Adam: b 12-2-1739 d 8-28-1817 m Lois Wood Sgt MA
Adonijah: b 1740 d 6-28-1807 m (1)Anney Brush (2)Deborah Barker Pvt MA
Allen: b 10-7-1759 d 11-29-1837 m Mary Clymer Pvt Wgn PA ★
Amos: b 11-1-1725 d 7-23-1794 m Sarah Moss Pvt CT
Amos: b 2-11-1743 d 12-14-1827 m Sarah Graves Lt MA
Amos: b 9-10-1727 d 5-31-1807 m Martha Hagar Pvt MA
Anthony: b 9-12-1763 d 4-18-1817 m Martha Cook Pvt RI W★
Artemas: b 4-5-1758 d 5-9-1828 m Asenath Adams Pvt MA
Asa: b 10-27-1757 d p. 1805 m Sarah Webber Cpl CT

RICE, contd.

Asa, Jr.: b 9-1-1754 d 1823 m Elizabeth Merriam Pvt CT
Asa: b 3-12-1742 d 8-4-1823 m Miriam Wheeler Col MA
Asa: b 8-8-1726 d 4- -1778 m (1)Elizabeth Livermore (2)Betsy
  Taylor Sgt MA
Asa: b 1747 d 3-23-1833 m (1)Lucy Smith (2)Jemima Greene
  Capt VT
Asahel: b 2-13-1742 d 8- -1811 m Mrs Mary Brownell Sgt MA
Asaph: b 5-9-1733 d 4-30-1816 m (1)Mary Morse (2)Thankful
  Clough (3)Mrs Lucy Shattuck PS MA
Bailey: b 1754-7 d 1851 m Elizabeth — Pvt SC ★
Benjamin: b 6-16-1744 d 5-7-1840 m Ruth Budge Lt MA ★
Benjamin: b 1751 d 11-12-1831 m Levina Wise Cpl MA
Benjamin: b 2-2-1745 d p. 1786 m Sarah Green Pvt MA
Benjamin: b 1753 d 1-17-1821 m Abigail Smith Pvt MA
Benjamin: b 10-24-1764 d 6-21-1837 m Betsey Oliver Pvt MA
Benjamin: b a. 1750 d p. 1789 m Catherine Holt Lt VA
Bezaleel: b 5-19-1721 d 3-13-1806 m (1)Susannah Jennings (2)Sarah
  Brent Pvt MA
Caleb: b 3-20-1753 d 1832 m Mrs Lucy Leland Pvt MA
Caleb: b 11-16-1744 d 5-13-1821 m Freelove Jerauld Sgt RI
Charles: b 1-26-1749 d 1830 m Susanna Moore Pvt MA
Charles: b 1727 d 10-14-1821 m Miriam — Pvt MA NH
Charles: b 1758 d 3-1-1830 m (1) — (2) — Cpl VT
Conrad: b c. 1748 d 1823 m Philipena Dickey Pvt PA
Cyrus: b 12-10-1726 d 8-4-1804 m (1)Mrs Elizabeth Easton
  (2)Elizabeth Wright (3)Mrs Ruth Lamb PS MA
Daniel: b c. 1732 d 7-15-1810 m Keziah Snow Pvt MA
Daniel: b 4-17-1753 d p. 1795 m Lucy Darling Cpl MA
Daniel: b 1758 d 8-28-1834 m Sarah Ball Pvt VT
David: b 9-29-1726 d 5- -1799 m — Tyler Pvt CT
David: b 9-17-1723 d 3- -1802 m Hannah Winch Pvt MA
David: b 9-16-1717 d 4- -1801 m Love Moore PS MA
David: b a. 1765 d 1812 m Susan Newall Sgt NY
David: b 1755 d 6- -1814 m Eunice Cowan Pvt NY
David: b 5-23-1750 d 12-20-1810 m Sara Kincaid Sgt VA
David: b 12-29-1733 d 6-18-1816 m Mary Blair PS VA
Eber: b 10-15-1755 d 11-13-1837 m Mary Alcott Pvt VT
Edmund: b 12-28-1755 d 11-14-1841 m Abigail Cutting Sgt MA ★
Edmund: b 6-10-1725 d 1796 m Margaret Smith Pvt MA
Edward: b 1738 d 1801 m Ann Ryan 2nd Lt VA
Eleazer: b 10-2-1749 d 10-20-1808 m Elizabeth Darling Pvt MA
Eliakim: b 2-27-1709 d p. 6-14-1785 m Mehitabel Livermore Pvt MA
Eliakin: b 4- -1756 d 8-4-1834 m Hannah Kendall Pvt MA ★
Elijah: b 7-26-1756 d 4-22-1834 m Emelia Johnson Pvt CT
Elijah: b 6-4-1760 d 9-26-1843 m Eunice Brigham Pvt CT
Elijah, Jr.: b 9-11-1749 d 1-3-1827 m Relief Williams MM MA ★
Elisha: b 5-14-1761 d 2-12-1831 m Ann Foster Pvt CT
Enoch: b 2-22-1746/7 d 7-12-1843 m Olive Bruce Sol MA
Ephraim: b 1724 d 11-1-1801 m Joanna Wilder Pvt MA
Ephraim: b 10-28-1735 d p. 12-13-1796 m (1)Thankful Walker
  (2)Zerviah Rice (3)Eunice Marks Sol MA
Ephraim: b 1758 d 1-18-1851 m Hannah French Pvt VT ★
Evan: b 1737 d p. 10-15-1783 m Elizabeth Graham CS DE
Ezekiel: b 10-15-1739 d 9-3-1808 m Lydia Hough Sgt CT
Ezekiel: b 12-21-1742 d 1-23-1835 m Eunice Cutting Bbd MA ★
Ezekiel: b 6-20-1752 d 7-25-1829 m Lydia Bullard Pvt MA
Ficher: b c. 1745 d a. 1829 m — Capt VA
Fones: b 4-3-1743 d p. 1783 m Susannah Havens Pvt VT
Frederick: b c. 1741 d 1808 m Catherine — Pvt PA
Frederick: b 9-29-1753 d 1-23-1850 m Catherine Laufer Pvt PA ★
George: b c. 1749/50 d p. 1794 m Eleanor Shelton Pvt PA
George: b a. 1748 d c. 1800 m Elizabeth — Capt VA
Gershom: b c. 1696 d 9-24-1781 m Esther Haynes Pvt MA
Gershom: b 5-2-1710 d 10-11-1790 m Lydia Barrett CS MA
Gideon: b 1760 d 11-21-1838 m (1)Sarah Stone (2)Mrs Elizabeth
  Cummings Pvt MA ★
Henry: b c. 1728 d 1818 m — PS NC
Henry: b c. 1717 d 11-13-1800 m (1)Martha — (2)Phebe —
  CS RI
Hezekiah: b 10-2-1745 d 5-12-1827 m Abigail Eames Pvt MA
Hezekiah, Jr.: b 9-29-1748 d 2-11-1832 m Elizabeth Eames Pvt MA
Hezekiah: b 12-16-1739 d 5-20-1813 m Louisa Rice Pvt NH
Hezekiah: b a. 1739 d p. 1790 m Mary Bullock Capt NC
Hezekiah: b 1758 d 1803 m Mary Saunders Lt VA
Holman: b 2-28-1758 d 1-16-1849 m (1)Jane Morris (2)Mary —
  Capt VA ★
Isaac John S: b 6-8-1756 d 5-20-1836 m Anna Stevens Pvt NH
  RI ★
Israel: b 1757 d p. 1783 m Sarah Maynard Pvt MA
Israel: b 2-22-1761 d 9-27-1843 m Elizabeth — Pvt MA ★
Ithamar: b 11-25-1743 d 10-23-1824 m (1)Susanna Balcom (2)Sarah
  Puffer (3)Eunice Balcom (4)Sally Burbank Sgt MA
Jabez: b 4-7-1728 d 11-4-1809 m Miriam Morse Pvt MA
Jabez: b 7-17-1746 d 11-3-1809 m Alice Howe Pvt MA
Jacob: b 12-9-1756 d p. 1-11-1833 m Anna Hull Cpl CT ★
James: b 12-18-1748 d 2-17-1827 m Mary Tyler MM CT
James: b 6-24-1758 d 4-3-1829 m Sarah Perry Pvt MA
James: b 1760 d 1827 m Elizabeth Mar Sgt NJ
James: b 8-6-1736 d p. 1787 m Alice — PS NC
James: b 1745 d p. 6-21-1825 m Rebecca Norberry Pvt PA
James Brown: b 11-29-1764 d 8-5-1851 m Susan Wallace Pvt VA
Jason: b 5-14-1756 d 12-31-1843 m Sarah Hibbard Pvt MA

Jason: b 5-21-1761 d 11-14-1843 m (1)Dorcas Heald (2)Damaris
  W Smith Pvt PS MA ★
Jedediah: b 4-2-1755 d 5-13-1823 m Jemima Hastings Sgt NH
Jeduthan: b 1-7-1760 d 1842 m (1)Lucinda Merchants (2)Anna Call
  Pvt MA
Jehial: b 8-23-1758 d 1852 m Pernel Sherman Sol CT
Jesse: b 10-3-1746 d p. 1789 m Abigail Waterhouse Sgt MA ★
Joel: b 2-15-1754 d p. 1790 m Eunice Jones Pvt CT
Joel: b 5-3-1733 d 2-4-1819 m Dinah Farnsworth Lt MA
Joel: b 1755 d 9-4-1782 m Hannah Jones Pvt NH
Joel: b c. 1760 d 1833 m Mrs Mary Elizabeth Pryor Hickman Sgt VA
John: b 11-3-1733 d 5-18-1795 m Dessie Goddard Capt CT
John: b 9-22-1736 d 7-17-1800 m Rebecca Fay Pvt MA
John: b 2-2-1758 d 5-18-1829 m Ruth — Pvt MA
John: b c. 1758 d 5-29-1835 m Mehitable Packard Pvt MA ★
John, Sr.: b 1734 d 1809 m Hannah — Pvt NY
John, Jr.: b 9-18-1760 d 9-6-1832 m (1)Elizabeth Crowell (2)Sally
  Hall Pvt NY
John: b 1756 d 1816 m (1) — Hillegas (2)Catherine Hellegas
  Pvt NY
John: b 1755 d 7-22-1837 m Elizabeth — Lt NC ★
John: b 8-6-1744 d 8-8-1823 m Rachel Ball NCapt PA
John: b 1752 d c. 1804 m Mary Finney Capt VA
John: b 1750 d 1806 m Sarah — Lt VA
Jonas: b 6-30-1731 d 1776 m Deborah Force Cpl MA
Jonas: b 8-5-1732 d 11-1-1824 m Mary Parmenter Pvt MA
Jonas: b 2-16-1754 d 4-26-1836 m Zilpah Townsend Pvt MA
Jonas: b 6-26-1755 d 2-17-1839 m Elizabeth Carver Lt VT
Jonathan: b 7-14-1749 d p. 1790 m (1)Eunice Willis (2)Susanna
  Hammond Maj MA
Jonathan: b 10-8-1725 d 1780 m Ruth Eames Pvt MA
Jonathan: b 3-7-1764 d 5-3-1834 m Mary Stevens Pvt MA
Jonathan: b 3-18-1745 d 1826 m Sarah Marvin PS NH
Joseph: b 1748 d — m Ens CT
Joseph: b 7-16-1719 d 4-18-1777 m Mary Merriman Pvt CT
Joseph: b 2-12-1745 d 3- -1826 m (1)Mary Green (1)Huldah
  Wilcox MM MA
Joseph: b 4-7-1760 d 9-11-1826 m (1)Mary — Pvt MA ★
Joseph: b 5-26-1758 d 5-29-1835 m Sarah Bowen Lt RI ★
Josiah: b 3-2-1738 d 10-4-1818 m Lucy Baldwin Pvt CT
Josiah: bpt 2-10-1760 d 10-31-1830 m Betsey Belcher Hooker Fif
  MA ★
Josiah, Jr.: b 9- -1753 d 2-2-1834 m Hannah Marble MM MA ★
Jotham: b 1744 d 3-28-1814 m (1)Harriet Snow (2)Elizabeth Sullivan
  Pvt MA
Justus: b 12-8-1756 d 6-8-1809 m Lois Perkins Pvt CT
Lemuel: b 5-2-1756 d 1-16-1827 m Anna Stone Pvt MA
Lemuel: b 1-14-1749 d 4-28-1853 m (1)Anna — (2)Susan Willard
  Sgt NH ★
Luke: b 10-23-1744 d 5-17-1806 m Prudence Gates Pvt MA
Luther: b 1755 d 11-21-1818 m Betsey Beaman Pvt MA
Martin: b 3-17-1757 d 1833 m Ruth Hastings FifMaj MA
Matthew: b 6-16-1744 d 10-5-1814 m Mercy Porter Pvt CT
Micah: b 7-21-1735 d c. 1804 m Silence Rice Ens VT
Michael: b 1759/60 d 1852 m Rachael Kester Pvt PA VA
Moses: b 9-24-1716 d 10- -1799 m Thankful Austin CS PS CT
Moses: b 4-5-1742 d 9-10-1784 m Ruth Pierce Pvt MA
Nahum: b 3-16-1757 d 9-29-1831 m Ruth Tuttle Cpl MA ★
Nathan: b 8-2-1754 d 4-17-1834 m ( ) Maria Leavith ( ) Sophia
  Blake Maj MA
Nathan: b 12-8-1760 d 5-23-1838 m Hepizbah Allen Pvt MA
Nathan: b 6-18-1762 d 1-18-1841 m Jemima McClure Pvt MA ★
Nathaniel: b 5-20-1734 d 6-3-1793 m Lois Doolittle Ens CT
Nehemiah: b 9-1-1753 d 9-1-1790 m (1)Lucy — (2)Mary Hosford
  Capt CT
Nehemiah: b 1754 d 3-19-1828 m Mary — Pvt NH
Nicholas: bpt 10-26-1765 d a. 12-18-1809 m Mary Ann Marilda
  Elizabeth Hickman Pvt PA
Noah: b 9-10-1751 d 10-1-1820 m Hannah Cole Pvt Fif MA
Obadiah: b 1-19-1746/7 d 1-7-1826 m Hannah Hill Sgt MA
Oliver: b 11-7-1726 d 3-23-1812 m Lucy Rice Pvt MA
Oliver: b 5-3-1717 d c. 1820 m Hannah Barrett Pvt MA
Pelatiah: b 4-1-1753 d — m Mary Dutcher Pvt VT
Peter: b 7-26-1734 d 3-14-1814 m Sarah Brown Pvt MA
Peter: b 3-29-1749 d 12-9-1826 m Levina Howe Pvt MA
Phillip Russell: b 1760 d 4-24-1841 m Martha M Vaughan Mus
  Sgt VA ★
Phineas, Sr.: b 6-16-1715 d 5-11-1787 m (1)Sarah — (2)Thankful
  Merriman (3)Elizabeth Lord (4)Anna Bronson PS CT
Phineas, Jr.: b 4-3-1752 d 9-6-1776 m Lydia Butler Sol CT
Randal: b 1760 d p. 1790 m Elizabeth Russell Pvt MA RI
Reuben: b c. 1732 d 12-1-1826 m Lydia Wilson Pvt MA
Richard: b 10-20-1730 d 1-24-1793 m Sarah Drury Pvt MA
Ruel: b 2-7-1742 d 4-13-1829 m Sarah Pierson Lt NH
Samuel: b 4-20-1757 d 1-26-1847 m Abigail Hawley Sgt CT ★
Samuel: b 10-23-1751 d 8-13-1834 m Hannah Beach Pvt CT
Samuel, Jr.: b 4- -1753 d 12-16-1832 m Dorothy Houghton Pvt VT
  MA ★
Samuel: b 11-17-1752 d p. 1782 m (1)Abigail Underwood (2)Rebecca
  Underwood Fif Pvt MA
Samuel: b 5-9-1742 d 9-5-1805 m Hebzibah Flint Pvt MA
Samuel: b 9-23-1764 d 10-10-1800 m Huldah Edmunds Pvt MA
Samuel: b 5-13-1740 d 6-30-1820 m Rebekah Beckwith Pvt NH

Samuel: b 1759 d *p.* 9-11-1834 m Mary Moore Pvt VA ★
Seth: b 11-9-1737 d 1-2-1815 m (1)Rachel Coolidge (2)Sarah Graham Lt MA
Seth: b 4-24-1748 d 1815 m Sarah Lynde Pvt MA
Silas, Sr.: b 11-7-1719 d 3-24-1800 m (1)Copiah Broughton (2)Lois Pollard (3)Mehitable Goodnow Pvt MA
Silas, Jr.: b 11-4-1749 d 4-19-1830 m Abigail Hagar Pvt MA
Silas: b 1745 d 12- -1820 m Lucy Knapp Pvt MA
Silas: b 1-26-1736 d 1815 m Sarah Wilder Pvt VT
Silas: b 8-17-1749 d 5-31-1835 m Elizabeth Taft Pvt MA
Solomon: b 1-31-1740 d 12-20-1776 m Eunice Miles Pvt CT
Solomon: b 5-13-1749 d *a.* 2-26-1777 m Abigail Cleveland Sgt MA
Solomon: b 6-13-1757 d 9-25-1794 m Mary Binney Pvt MA
Solomon: b 9-11-1763 d 4-14-1858 m (1)Katharine Kyger (2)Sarah Stotts Pvt Spy MD W★
Stephen: b 1749 d — m (1)Ruth Stone (2)Mary Batcheller Pvt MA
Stephen: b 3-15-1737 d 11-24-1831 m Dorothy Woods Col PS MA
Sylvanus: b 1-6-1729 d 3- -1819 m Esther Nims Capt MA
Thomas: b. 1717 d *a.* 10-17-1780 m Elizabeth — PS DE
Thomas: b *c.* 1730 d *p.* 1780 m Abigail — CS Pvt NC
Thomas: b 5-17-1752 d 11-5-1817 m (1)Penelope Justis (2)Eliazbeth Dews Capt PA
Thomas: b 9-1-1745 d 10-8-1833 m Thankful Down Hinckley Mte CT
Thomas: b 10-5-1741 d 6-21-1822 m (1)Hannah Wright (2)Sarah Nurse (3)Abigail Barber 2nd Lt MA
Thomas: b 11-17-1747 d 10-28-1840 m Abigail Hapgood Cpl MA
Thomas: b 11-29-1734 d 4-21-1812 m Rebecca Kingsbury PS MA
Thomas: b *c.* 1725 d 1804 m — CS NC
Tilly: b 11-8-1724 d 11-6-1803 m Mary Buckminster Capt MA
Timothy: b 1-12-1735 d 1813 m Elizabeth Howe Cpl MA
Uriah: b 7-7-1757 d 9-22-1850 m Mary Eames Pvt MA
Wm.: b 11-2-1737 d 12-5-1819 m Sarah Noyes CS MA
Wm.: b 11-25-1755 d 1-10-1815 m Nancy Hager Drm Maj MA
Wm.: b 8-19-1764 d *p.* 9-16-1834 m Roxana Smith Pvt MA
Wm.: b *c.* 1740 d *p.* 1782 m Rebecca Norris Pvt PS PA
Wm.: b 5-23-1748 d 1-18-1836 m Lucy Carpenter Pvt RI
Wm.: b *c.* 1720 d *p.* 2-9-1780 m Sarah — Pvt VA
Wm.: b *c.* 1740 d 3-16-1824 m Frances Grainger PS VA
Wm. B: b 4-27-1744 d 3-1-1838 m Rebecca Ellington Sgt VA W★
Wm., Hickerson: b 3-12-1761 d 8-30-1847 m (1)Sarah Reid (2)Elizabeth M Bowman Lt NC ★
Zachariah: b 1731 d 8-19-1811 m Abigail Hartman PS Pvt PA

RICH, (includes REACH & RITCH)

Appolos: b 9-19-1745 d 4-20-1835 m Abigail Collins Pvt MA
Aquila: b 11-11-1759 d 4-8-1813 m Hannah Thomas Matr PS MA
Benjamin: b 7-20-1737 d 1-13-1815 m Rebeckah Dagget Pvt MA
Calvin: b 7-8-1765 d 8-24-1831 m Martha Billings Pvt MA
David: b 1756 d *p.* 1803 m Mary Eliz Palmer Sgt MA
David: b 1740 d 5-5-1820 m Elizabeth — Pvt MA
Ebenezer: b 4-26-1730 d 12-3-1811 m Ruth Paine Capt MA
Isaac: b 1745 d 5-17-1815 d 6-29-1813 m Sarah Hopkins Pvt MA
Jacob, Sr.: b 1740 d 1780 m Polly Ann — Sol SC
Jacob, Jr.: b 12-16-1762 d 8-14-1838 m (1)Susan Dallas (2)Rosannah Counts Pvt NC ★
Jacob: b *c.* 1735 d 1795 m Annie Craft Capt VA
Joel: b 1753 d 3-22-1838 m Betsey Cates Pvt MA
John: b 1748 d 3-2-1792 m Molly Hyatt Pvt CT
John: b 1729 d 9-31-1813 m Catherine Sophia Whiteman PS NH
Jonathan: b 11-1-1737 d *p.* 1777 m Thankful Newcomb Pvt MA
Jonathan: b 2-14-1735 d 2-27-1814 m Abigail — Pvt VT
Jonathan: b 1740 d 7-11-1825 m Abigail Barton Pvt MA
Joseph: b 11-10-1761 d 10-6-1851 m Hannah Rich Pvt MA ★
Joshua: b 10-14-1752 d 5-28-1810 m Mary Dyer Cpl MA
Moses, Sr.: b 6-4-1730 d 1816 m Lydia Davis Pvt MA
Obediah: b 7-15-1707 d 4- -1788 m (1)Mary Crowell (2)Ruth Dyer Pvt MA
Peter: b 1744/5 d 1801 m (1)Mrs McCracken (2)Prudence Lane Capt MD
Richard: b 9-20-1740 d 12-20-1813 m Betty Smith 2nd Lt MA
Samuel: b 8-30-1735 d 3-18-1832 m (1)Ruth Putnam (2)Sarah Hutchinson Pvt MA
Samuel: b 10-20-1740 d 1796 m Sarah Bracy Vol ME
Stephen: b 6-3-1762 d 1845 m Rebecca Carroll Pvt MA
Thaddeus: b 7-27-1759 d 9-1-1834 m (1)Sarah — (2)Christina Doolittle Pvt CT
Thomas: b 9-29-1738 d 8-22-1828 m Millicent Conant Lt MA
Timothy: b *c.* 1730 d *a.* 5-17-1806 m — Cpl NC
Wm.: b 7-11-1753 d 4-29-1822 m Abigail Peck Gridley Drm CT
Wm.: b 5-26-1764 d 1-10-1853 m Thankful Bowers Pvt NY ★
Wm.: b 1750 d 1792 m Nancy — Pvt VA

RICHARDS, (includes REICHARD, REICHART, RICHAR, RICHARD, & RITCHART)

Aaron: b 5-20-1749 d 1-29-1831 m (1)Dorcas Adams (2)Polly Dickinson Pvt CT
Abel: b 6-6-1738 d 1-18-1832 m Hannah Newell Capt MA
Abiathar, Sr.: b 1730 d 9-30-1839 m Elizabeth — Pvt MA
Abiathar, Jr.: b 4-7-1754 d 7-10-1835 m Elizabeth Smith Pvt MA
Alexander: b *a.* 1751 d 11- -1812 m Sarah Liggett Pvt PA
Amos: b 4-7-1759 d 1848 m Lydia Lewis Pvt CT

Amos: b 1760 d 11-26-1829 m Catherine McCartney Cpl NH ★
Benjamin: b 5-23-1737 d 12-25-1788 m Sarah Judd Col CT
Benjamin: b 1-24-1765 d 10- -1809 m Mary Coit Mid
Benjamin: b 3-20-1738/9 d 1- -1816 m Mary Belcher Pvt MA
Benjamin: b 4-24-1701 d 12-15-1796 m Abigail Bradley PS CS NH
Charles: b 9-27-1755 d 8-17-1852 m Elizabeth Souch Pvt PA ★
Christian: b. 1742 d 10- -1809 m (1)Maria Elizabeth Pence (2)Mrs Timmons Pvt VA
Daniel: b 3-19-1734 d *p.* 1781 m Abigail Warring Pvt PS CT
Daniel: b — d 10-30-1787 m Catherine Carmack PS MD
Daniel: b 9-18-1744 d 6-18-1815 m Elizabeth Richardson Pvt MA
Daniel: b 9-8-1750 d 8-30-1823 m Eunice Somerby Pvt PS NH
Daniel: b 1749 d 3- -1794 m Huldah Fellows Cpl VT
David: b 1-26-1755 d 12-29-1817 m Chloe — Pvt MA
David: b 1756 d 1823 m Martha McCurdy Cpl NH
Ebenezer: b 1-12-1718 d 2-27-1799 m Thankful Stratton Sgt MA
Edmund: b 6- -1756 d 1843 m Ruth Waring Capt CT W★
Edward: b 8-25-1740 d 1799 m Mary Whitney Pvt MA
Edward, Sr.: b 10-16-1724 d *p.* 1790 m Mary Fisher PS MA
Edward, Jr.: b 1-23-1761 d 1791 m Amy Bucklin Pvt MA
Edward: b 1740 d *a.* 4-16-1812 m Elizabeth — Pvt PS VA
Eliphalet: b 6-27-1751 d 10-8-1836 m (1)Sarah — Mary Roby Pvt NH
Elisha: b *c.* 1730 d 7-3-1778 m Sarah — Pvt PA
Guy, Sr.: b 1722 d 1782 m Elizabeth Harris PS CT
Guy, Jr.: b 1747 d 1825 m Hannah Dolbeare PS CT
Henry: b 1735 d 1797 m Ann — Pvt PA
Henry: b 9-12-1737 d 1793 m Jane Gant Sgt VA
Humphrey Hobson: b 11-17-1755 d 5-28-1783 m Sarah Pearson Pvt MA
Jacob: b 12-11-1758 d 2-23-1835 m (1)Hannah Benedict (2)Mary Cross Pvt CT ★
Jacob: b 1720 d 3-19-1802 m Elizabeth Hoover Ens PA
James, Sr.: b 10-29-1723 d 5-12-1810 m Hannah Waring Capt PS CS CT
James, Jr.: b 12-9-1744 d 2-9-1816 m Ruth Hanford Pvt CT
James, Jr.: b 7-28-1709 d 8-3-1778 m (1)Mary Woodward (2)Mary Flagg Pvt MA
James: b 7-5-1737 d 3-28-1820 m Abigail Beal Pvt MA
James: b 1757 d 1842 m Lydia Shaw Pvt MA
James: b 1722 d 1804 m Mary — Sgt PA
James: b *c.* 1750 d *p.* 11-20-1811 m — Sol VA
Jedediah, Jr.: b 5-1-1759 d 1-30-1831 m — Stewart Pvt CT
Jeremiah: b 12-9-1753 d 2-4-1828 m Patience Hawes Pvt MA
Jesse: b 1763 d 12-18-1839 m Lydia Hickock Pvt CT ★
John: b 2-16-1720/1 d 5-5-1790 m Rebecca Fitch Pvt CT
John: b 8-6-1757 d 6-26-1801 m Martha Prentiss Fif CT
John: b 3-31-1731 d 8-12-1821 m (1)Mary French (2)Elizabeth Dickinson (3)Hannah Bear PS CT
John: b 1760 d 10-26-1823 m Catharine Arnold Pvt MD
John: b 9-29-1723 d 12-27-1812 m Keziah Bailey Pvt MA
John: b 4-10-1753 d 11-13-1822 m Sophia Hubner Pvt PA
John: b 1759 d *p.* 1800 m Catherine Litton NLt VA
John: b 11-30-1754 d 6-22-1843 m Ursula Rutherford Pvt VA ★
John: b *c.* 1745 d *p.* 1798 m Sarah Ellisworth Sol VA
Jonathan: b 8-17-1760 d 7-21-1837 m (1)Hepzibah Colburn (2)Sarah Avery Pvt MA
Jonathan: b *c.* 1733 d *p.* 3-15-1803 m Hannah Dutton Pvt PA
Joseph: b 9-25-1753 d 9-28-1824 m Lydia Witt Pvt MA
Joseph: b 12-29-1754 d 2- -1813 m Hannah Snow Pvt MA
Joseph, Sr.: b 9-8-1733 d 3-5-1816 m Sarah Santee PS PA
Joseph, Jr.: b 8-12-1764 d 10-9-1834 m Mary Elizabeth Miller Pvt PA
Josiah: b 11-15-1749 d 1833 m Sarah Shuttleworth Pvt MA ★
Lemuel: b 1-22-1738 d 2-6-1821 m Rebecca Chickering 2nd Lt MA
Leonard: b 10-1-1733 d 4-23-1822 m Sarah Weaver Pvt PA
Lewis: b 1764 d *p.* 9-11-1837 m Lucy Hunton Sgt VA ★
Matthias: b 2-26-1758 d 8-4-1830 m Maria Salome Muhlenberg Maj PA
Moses: b 12-11-1739 d *p.* 1801 m Mehitable Battle Cpl MA
Nathan: b *c.* 1744 d *p.* 2-5-1805 m Mary Snell Sgt MA
Nathaniel: b 9-19-1740 d 2-8-1822 m Deborah Blanchard Pvt MA
Nathaniel: b 5-4-1712 d 3-23-1786 m (1)Mary Colburn (2)Mary Whiting PS MA
Nehemiah: b 1-14-1760 d 1-15-1837 m Hannah Shaw Pvt MA ★
Owen: bpt 9-20-1737 d *p.* 1785 m — Pvt PA
Peter: b 7-21-1755 d 10-21-1822 m Magdelena Schneider LCol PA
Peter: b 4-9-1753 d 12-2-1837 m Susannah Luther Pvt RI ★
Richard: b 1718 d 1811 m Maria Ann Vaughan PS MD
Richard: b 1749 d *p.* 1786 m Hannah Bird Pvt MA
Richard: b 1743 d 1802 m Harriet — Pvt VA
Samuel: b 9-17-1753 d 12-31-1841 m Sarah Welles Lt CT ★
Samuel: b 10-23-1726 d 11-10-1793 m Lydia Buck CS CT
Samuel: b 9-9-1757 d 8-28-1844 m Mary White CS MA
Street: b 12-12-1750 d 7-13-1835 m Eunice Culver Ens PS CT
Thaddeus: b 11-14-1747 d *c.* 1793 m (1)Mary Colburn (2)Mrs Hannah Metcalf MM Cpl MA
Thomas: b 4-16-1764 d 12-8-1844 m (1)Betsy Nurse (2)Mary Chamberlain (3)Lucy Wood Pvt MA
Thomas: b 4-17-1753 d 1-14-1826 m Cynthia Andross Sgt NH ★
Thomas: b 4-11-1754 d 1-3-1823 m Elizabeth Stowe Sgt VA
Tristram: b 1761 d 6-8-1845 m Abagail York Pvt NH
Wm.: b 10-1-1743 d 3-3-1827 m Eunice Wells Col CT

RICHARDS, contd.

Wm.: b 1755 d 1825 m Sarah Sheppard SgnMte CT
Wm.: b 1-17-1756 d 8-28-1812 m (1)Bethia Bixby (2)Monica Frizell Sgt MA
Wm.: b 8-2-1734 d 1-29-1801 m Anna Cummings Pvt MA
Wm.: b 1742 d c. 1820 m Nancy Richards Pvt NC
Wm.: b 9-12-1738 d 8-31-1823 m (1)Mary Patrick (2)Margaret Wood Sol PA
Wm.: b 3-30-1756 d 10-7-1839 m Anne Roberts Pvt PA ★
Wm.: b 1740 d 1817 m Elizabeth Baird PS PA

RICHARDSON. (includes RICHESON)

Aaron: b 10-2-1740 d 10-19-1786 m Ruth Stingley Capt MA
Aaron: b c. 1754 d a. 4-2-1804 m Sarah Bennett PS VA
Abel: b 10-23-1736 d 5-27-1831 m Mary Thompson Pvt MA
Abel: b 1-12-1750/1 d 9-18-1824 m Ann Tufts Pvt MA
Abiatha: b 2-12-1749 d 1-16-1832 m Martha Faulkner Sgt MA
Abijah: b 8-13-1752 d 5-10-1822 m Mercy Daniels Dr MA
Abijah: b 2-22-1749 d 3-15-1822 m (1) — Livington (2)Eunice Thompson Lt MA ★
Abijah: bpt 9-4-1748 d 11-23-1826 m Elizabeth — Pvt MA
Abijah: b 3-20-1761 d 7-12-1840 m Elizabeth Felton Pvt MA ★
Amasa: b 12-29-1761 d 3-17-1838 m Lydia Richardson Pvt CT
Amos, Sr.: b 6-23-1700 d 4-16-1777 m Rachel Torrington PS CT
Amos: b 3-5-1728 d 9-30-1802 m Ruth Stiles Capt CT
Amos: b 5-8-1742 d 4-6-1822 m Phoebe Holbrook Sgt MA
Amos: b 9-8-1764 d 9-15-1847 m Susannah Smith Pvt NC ★
Amos: b 1-10-1741 d 5-28-1815 m Mary Elizabeth Peterson Pvt SC
Andrew: b 8-25-1760 d 1-10-1818 m Hannah Grant Pvt MA
Andrew: b c. 1760 d 10-15-1817 m Elizabeth McKoy Sgt NC
Andrew Crocker: b 12-13-1750 d 2-25-1828 m Mercy Clauson Pvt CT
Anthony: b c. 1750 d p. 9-16-1802 m — PS MD
Arthur: b c. 1730 d a. 3-15-1785 m Mrs Hannah Mitchel PS SC
Asa: b 1757 d 1822 m Jane Wyman Pvt MA
Asa: b 1760 d — m Sarah Tufts Pvt MA
Asa Partridge: b 1-26-1746/7 d 7-2-1837 m Hannah Hill Sol MA
Barnabus: b 3-16-1733/4 d 1-5-1816 m Rebecca Tidd Sgt MA
Bartholomew: b 3-25-1730 d 6-14-1812 m Sarah Converse Sol MA
Bartholomew: b 6-19-1735 d 12-22-1807 m Abigail Marion Pvt MA
Bezeleel: b 1755 d 1825 m Thurzy Priest Sgt VT
Benjamin: b 2-22-1732 d 6-8-1821 m (1)Eunice Swan (2)Mrs Abigail French (3)Mrs Olive Holman (4)Mrs Candace Allen Capt MA
Benjamin: b 8-26-1746 d 1815 m Elizabeth Adeline Somers Sol SC
Bradbury: b 10- -1737 d 10-9-1813 m (1)Judith Blake (2)Abigail Ladd Maj NH
Caleb, Sr.: b 6-26-1739 3-2-1823 m Esther Tiffany Capt MA
Caleb, Jr.: b 12-16-1762 d 4-30-1838 m Huldah Hatch Pvt Fif MA ★
Caleb: b 10-24-1738 d 4-4-1814 m (1)Sarah — Pvt MA
Caleb: b 7-25-1756 d 6-5-1837 m Mrs Martha Libby Pvt NH ★
Daniel: b 3-26-1742 d 12-24-1817 m Sara Read Lt MA
Daniel, Jr.: b 2-10-1752 d 5-19-1831 m Lydia Bacon Pvt MA
Daniel: b 3-11-1749 d 5-23-1833 m Mrs Sarah Merchant Pvt NH W★
Daniel: b 3-28-1722 d 3-23-1799 m Lydia Davis PS NH
David: b 11-28-1757 d 9-9-1843 m Sarah Hudson Cpl CT
David: b 1748 d p. 1790 m Sarah Shackford Pvt PS NH
David: b 8-5-1763 d 5-13-1849 m Polly Dearborn Pvt NH ★
Dudley: b 1713 d 1777 m Martha Cobbs PS VA
Ebenezer: b 11-25-1751 d 6-5-1810 m (1)Catherine Wyman (2)Jerusha Dodge Sgt MA
Ebenezer: b 6-14-1745 d 1825 m Esther Hall Pvt MA
Ebenezer: b 4-1-1754 d 3-18-1827 m Sarah Parker Pvt MA
Ebenezer: b 10-2-1742 d 1808 m Elizabeth Shed PS MA
Ebenezer: b 1761 d 7-11-1832 m Anna Aldrich Pvt NH
Edward, Sr.: b 3-17-1716 d 1797 m Abigail Chenery PS MA
Edward, Jr.: b 2-8-1748 d 7- -1834 m Anne Wilson Capt MA
Edward: b 8-25-1743 d 11-17-1837 m Sarah Tidd Pvt MA
Edward: b 1751 d 1821 m Polly Mason Sol NC
Eleazer: b 6-29-1746 d 2-1-1808 m (1)Catherine Newhall (2)Mary Walker (3)Lydia Upham Grover Pvt MA
Elisha: b 7-5-1743 d 3-5-1798 m Abigail Lawrence Pvt MA
Enoch: b 12-17-1751 d 7-26-1820 m (1)Elizabeth — (2)Phoebe Freeman Sgt NH ★
Ephraim: b 12-27-1745 d 1815 m Molly — Pvt MA
Eri: b c. 1740 d 10-25-1804 m Sarah Durant Pvt NH
Ezekiel: b 3-10-1760 d 12-28-1828 m Betsy Colburn Pvt NH
Ezra: b 3-17-1760 d 2-2-1843 m (1)Jemima Lovell (2)Lavinia Daniels Pvt MA
Francis: b 1763 d 1820 m Martha Gaulden Sol SC
George: b 1762 d p. 1789 m Mary Grizzelle Pvt MD
Godfrey: b 9-13-1759 d 4-21-1854 m (1)Annie Burlingame (2)Martha Vinton Pvt SgnMte NH MA ★
Henry: b 8-7-1752 d 11-4-1827 m Olive Blackinton Cpl MA
Henry: b 9-19-1714 d 1-22-1793 m (1)Priscilla Spauling (2)Ruth Bates PS MA
Herbert: b 10-15-1757 d 12-29-1823 m (1) — (2)Lydia Parker (3)Mary Upham Pvt MA
Hezekiah: b 1-25-1754 d 6-23-1814 m Olive Thompson Pvt CT
Holt: b 7-30-1736 d 9- -1800 m (1)Susanna West (2)Elizabeth Hogg Col VA
Isaac: b 1761 d 4-18-1842 m Elizabeth Henderson Pvt PA
Israel: b 1-24-1736 d 5-8-1800 m Susanna Forbush Capt MA

Jacob: b 12-13-1742 d 9-5-1817 m Sarah Brown Lt MA
Jacob: b 10-26-1726 d 1780 m Judith Lawrence Cpl MA
Jacob: b 7-23-1763 d 3-17-1819 m Ruth Wright Pvt MA
Jacob: b 1748-50 d p. 1784 m Mary Marsh PS NJ
Jacob: b 1750 d 1825 m Mary Hutchinson Pvt PA ★
James: b 1730 d 12-12-1807 m Rachel Gott Pvt MA
James: b 5-5-1730 d 1808 m Ruth — Pvt MA
James: b c. 1740 d 9-27-1810 m Mrs Elizabeth Neal Purdy Col NC
James: b 8-25-1757 d 3-28-1842 m Jemima — Pvt NC ★
James: b 1742 d 3-26-1819 m Molly Dodge Pvt VT
Jeduthan: b 4-16-1738 d 10-11-1815 m Mary Wright CS Lt MA
Jeremiah: b 3-13-1736 d 12-11-1816 m Dorcas Hall Pvt MA
Jeremiah: b 3-25-1757 d 9-12-1834 m Hannah Wright Sgt NH MA
Jeremiah: b c. 1750 d 1826 m Anna Van Zandt Pvt PA
Jesse: b 10-12-1758 d 1840-43 m Annie Jones Pvt CT
Jesse: b 1765 d 1839 m Ruth Jones Pvt GA
Jesse: b 8-20-1761 d 2-12-1837 m Submit Brown Pvt MA
Jesse: b 1760 d 12-17-1839 m (1)Martha English (2)Elizabeth — Pvt VA W★
Jethro: b 6-8-1747 d 8-11-1814 m Hannah — Pvt MA
Joel: b 10-10-1750 d 1-7-1819 m Sarah Wyman Pvt MA
Joel: b 6-22-1758 d 2-20-1827 m Lydia Babb Pvt MA ★
John: b a. 1760 d p. 1827 m Elizabeth Tate Sol GA
John: b c. 1750 d 5-3-1822 m Mary — 2nd Lt MD
John: b 5-26-1748 d 1823 m (1)Christina Lane (2)Rachel Farquhar Ens MD
John: b 2-11-1737 d 11-4-1819 m (2)Rebecca Moore Capt PS MA
John: b 6-19-1735 d 5-4-1809 m Abigail Haven Sgt MA
John: b 9-1-1751 d 5-15-1843 m Sarah Stevens Cpl MA ★
John: b 5-24-1744 d 6-2-1811 m Ruth Woodcock Cpl MA
John, Jr.: b 5-17-1758 d 12-25-1823 m Sarah Wilder Pvt MA ★
John: b 1753 d p. 1810 m Mary L. Stokes Ens IvC
John: b 9-21-1766 d 11-21-1841 m Susan Gardiner Sgt VT
John: b 1756 d 6-30-1822 m Rebeckah Davis 1st Lt VA
John: b 1737 d 1804 m Martha DePriest Sol VA
John: b 1740 d 1766 m Martha Doran Pvt VA
John: b — d a. 6-17-1798 m Mary Johns PS VA
John Crowley: b 3-12-1754 d 1834 m Sarah Bainbridge Hall Ens MD
Jonas: b 1743 d 6-10-1815 m (1)Mary Bailey (2)Lydia Woodbury Pvt MA
Jonathan: b 12-30-1753 d 2-1-1840 m Esther Eaton Sgt MA
Jonathan: b 7-1-1727 d 2-28-1794 m Mary Woodward Pvt MA
Jonathan: b 5-27-1755 d 2-23-1825 m Mercy Richardson Pvt MA W★
Jonathan: b 8-16-1745 d 1-14-1812 m Elizabeth Bunn Pvt NY
Joseph: b 11-20-1748 d 4-8-1819 m (1)Esther Lamond (2)Priscilla Hincher Capt MA
Joseph: b 2-9-1727 d 7-3-1823 m Abigail Felton Pvt MA
Joseph: b 1-5-1754 d 1796-8 m Jerusha Reed Pvt MA
Joseph: b 1756 d 12-22-1824 m Sarah Hanson Pvt NH
Joseph: b 1746 d 8-18-1843 m Hannah Drury Pvt NH
Joseph, Jr.: b 10-27-1761 d 1-25-1818 m Hannah Speachus Pvt NJ
Joseph, Jr.: b 1763 d 2-26-1836 m Molly Carpenter Pvt ME
Joseph, Jr.: b 1760 d 10-29-1843 m Ann Cornish Pvt PA ★
Joseph: b 1762 d 3-24-1842 m Olive Wade Pvt RI ★
Joseph: b 1750-60 d p. 7-1-1815 m Mary DeJarnette Capt VA
Joshua: b 12-20-1755 d 1829 m Mattie Temple Pvt MA ★
Joshua: b 12-19-1762 d 3-14-1844 m (1)Mary Snow (2)Mary Burnett Pvt VA ★
Josiah: b 11-11-1747 d 12-28-1795 m Jerusha Brooks Pvt MA
Josiah: b 11-17-1743 d 11-12-1801 m (1)Mary Richardson (2)Mrs Mary Richardspn Pvt MA
Lemuel: b 7-31-1734 d 4-14-1818 m Anna Preston Pvt MA
Lemuel: b c. 1765 d 1-22-1847 m Jerusha Hedges Pvt NH ★
Luke: b 8-15-1734 d 3-27-1812 m Damaris Carter Lt MA
Luther: b 10-4-1748 d p. 1784 m Sarah Ticknor Capt NH
Lysander: b 3-30-1763 d 4-3-1813 m Lois Ransom PS MA
Martin: b c. 1750 d 9- -1803 m Judith Robertsom 2nd Lt VA
Mathias: b 7-14-1749 d p. 6-17-1827 m Frances — PS NC
Matthew: b 9-7-1757 d 1-2-1838 m Ann Stockton Pvt MD
Matthew: b c. 1762 d 2-7-1818 m Abigail Eaton Sol NH
Moses: b 2-19-1748 d 12-19-1834 m (1)Experience Fisher (2)Miriam Merriam Lt MA ★
Moses: b 2-8-1717 d 4-5-1797 m Abigail Allen Pvt MA
Moses: b 4-8-1722 d 4-19-1775 m Mary Prentice MM MA
Moses: b 6-12-1728 d 1793 m Elizabeth Colburn Pvt MA
Moses: b 11-12-1752 d 3-26-1842 m Sarah Chase PS NH
Nathan: b 3-20-1725 d p. 1785 m Phebe Crocker Pvt CT
Nathan: b 1730-40 d 7-15-1820 m (1)Tamsin Upham (2)Mary Knapp Cpl MA
Nathan: b 1725 d 1817 m Mary Pierce Pvt MA
Nathan, Jr.: b 10-27-1760 d p. 1795 m — Pvt VT
Nehemiah: b 6-28-1759 d 11-14-1839 m (1)Deliverance Worden (2)Kesiah Reeves Sgt MA
Obadiah: b 1-4-1753 d 11-22-1835 m Hannah Hildreth Pvt MA
Oliver: b 9-10-1754 d 4-7-1845 m Vashti Ramsdell Sgt MA
Oliver: b 2-15-1750 d 9-23-1836 m Elizabeth Shed Pvt MA
Reuben: b 12-22-1731 d 11-16-1818 m Jerusha Kendall Pvt MA
Richard: b 9-23-1751 d 11-6 m (1)Mehitable Smith (2)Elizabeth Wyman Park Pvt MA ★
Richard, Jr.: b 12-2-1742 d 1802 m Mary Pierpont PS PA
Richard, Jr.: b 3-4-1741 d a. 3-24-1817 m Dorcas Nelson Col SC
Richard, Sr.: b 1704/5 d 9- -1780 m (1)Mary Cantey (2)Dorothy Sinkler Col SC

Richard: b 6-23-1756 d 5-8-1794 m Sarah Gaines Pvt VA
Rufus: b 9-11-1760 d 9-16-1841 m Ruth Holden Sgt MA ★
Samuel: b 6-15-1750 d 1822 m Susanna Pinney Sgt CT
Samuel: b 2-1-1760 d 1-13-1831 m Catherine Bainbridge Hall Pvt
   MD
Samuel: b 4-25-1734 d 12-25-1803 m (1)Sarah Parker (2)Mrs Sarah
   Holland Lt MA
Samuel: b 10-7-1744 d 4-29-1816 m Mary Walker Pvt MA
Samuel: b 12-5-1748 d 10-16-1839 m Anna Eustis Pvt MA
Samuel: b 2-22-1749 d 7-15-1836 m Lucy Parker Pvt MA
Samuel, Jr.: b 8-18-1741 d 6-21-1823 m Mary McIntire Pvt MA
Sanford: b 1762 d 6-7-1818 m Roxalana Burroughs Sgt CT W★
Seth, Jr.: b 9-15-1755 d 1-29-1824 m Sarah French Cpl MA
Seth: b 2-8-1761 d 2-27-1831 m Hannah Waters Pvt MA
Silas: b 12-28-1748 d 12-23-1803 m Silence Daniels Sgt MA
Silas: b 5-25-1745 d — m — Pvt NH
Simeon: b 6-27-1744 d 5-4-1825 m Elizabeth Jones Cpl MA
Stephen: b 8-6-1737 d 11-18-1808 m (1)Hannah Fuller (2)Mary
   Fuller Col MA
Stephen: b 10-23-1738 d 1812 m Elizabeth Gott PS MA
Stephen: b 3-3-1749 d 12-31-1790 m Rhoda Daniels Pvt NH
Thomas: b 3-26-1723 d 1-1-1820 m Ann Ridgely Capt MD
Thomas: b 1755 d 7-23-1824 m Margaret Sands Pvt MD
Thomas: b 9-3-1747 d p. 1796 m Judith Kendall Sgt Maj MA
Thomas, Sr.: b 10-31-1716 d 1795 m Priscilla Pearson Pvt MA
Thomas: b 6-5-1718 d p. 2-18-1793 m Abigail Merrow Pvt MA
Thomas: b 12-1-1741 d 10-3-1797 m Elizabeth Turner Pvt MA
Thomas: b 10-26-1739 d p. 1788/9 m Margaret Gott PS MA
Thomas: b 1762 d 1-15-1840 m Elizabeth R Crouch Pvt VA
Tilley, Jr.: b 3-22-1759 d 1-14-1852 m Mary Thurston Pvt MA
Timothy: b 1758 d 12-9-1830 m (1)Anna Morgan (2)Mrs Sarah
   Batchelder Philbrick Pvt MA ★
Turner: b 5-1-1739 d 1802 m (1)Anna Allen ( )Catherine — Capt
   VA
Vincent: b — d c. 1776 m Martha Norris Ens MD
Vinton: b 9-20-1744 d 1-4-1820 m Hannah White Pvt MA
Walker: b c. 1757 d 1822 m Prudence Thompson 1st Lt VA
Wiley: b 4-1-1755 d 2-1-1846 m (1)Bridget Farrar (2)Frances Poore
   Pvt VA
Wm.: b 1752 d 1795 m Editha Booth Pvt CT
Wm.: b 12- -1740 d 1833 m (2)Nancy Mercer Pvt GA
Wm.: b 8-17-1735 d 7- -1825 m Elizabeth Green Col MD
Wm.: b 1754 d 1807 m Mary Tennison Sol MD
Wm.: b 5-6-1731 d 12-30-1814 m Esther Joslin Pvt MA
Wm.: b 10-21-1756 d 3-21-1836 m Lydia Messer Sgt MA
Wm.: b 10-9-1758 d 3-23-1833 m Lavina Taft Pvt MA ★
Wm.: b 3-8-1746 d 2-25-1829 m (1)Prudence Morse (2)Esther
   Sawyer 2nd Lt NH
Wm.: b 1756 d 1828 m Martha Hamilton Capt NH
Wm.: b 4-1-1751 d 2-4-1818 m Mary Salome Synder Pvt PA W★
Wm.: b 5-24-1754 d 4-24-1831 m Nancy Montgomery Pvt Slr
   RI ★
Wm.: b 7-13-1743 d 2-28-1786 m Ann Magdalene Guignard PS
   Cmsry Gen SC
Wm.: b 1748/9 d 1-31-1838 m Rebecca Hays Pvt VA
Wm.: b 1759 d 1829 m Polly — Pvt VA
Wm.: b — d p. 1800 m (2)Nancy Roberts Pvt VA
Wm.: b 1-5-1760 d c. 1826 m Ann Sevills Smn VA
Wyman: b 5-13-1746 d 4-6-1839 m Ruth Lane Pvt MA
Zachariah: b 5-21-1720 d 11-22-1804 m Phebe Sawyer Pvt MA
Zachariah: b 1747 d 10- -1829 m Sarah Barnes Pvt NH
Zebadiah: b 3-6-1742 d 1820 m Sarah Snow Pvt NH

RICHBOURGH, (includes RICHBOURG)
James: b 1735 d 1804 m Mrs Levisea Maples PS SC
John: b 8-23-1747 d 11-29-1838 m (1)Mary Long (2)Sarah Abbott
   Capt SC

RICHMOND, (includes RICHMAN)
Abiathur: b 4-13-1762 d 7-4-1850 m Lavinia Deane Pvt MA
Abiezer: b 11-1-1764 d 8-15-1837 m Lydia Eaton Pvt NY VT ★
Abner: b 11-9-1761 d 9-17-1834 m Eunice Dewing Pvt CT
Adam: b 3-24-1737 d 11-17-1817 m (1)Amy Hazard (2)Mary Hall
   CS RI
Amaziah: b 10-14-1761 d 12-30-1843 m Sarah Field Pvt MA ★
Amaziah: b 1745 d 11- -1825 m (1)Zeriah Richmond (2)Abigail Burt
   Pvt MA
Amaziah: b 3-22-1758 d 9-30-1825 m Hannah Throop Cpl MA W★
Benjamin: b 8-7-1747 d 2-20-1814 m Sarah Church Dr MA RI
Daniel: b 5-21-1765 d 1837 m (1)Jane — (2)Bathshaba Dunham
   Pvt NJ
David: b 1748 d 10-14-1818 m Nancy Davis Maj RI ★
Edmund: b 5-7-1738 d 10- -1811 m Abigail Wood Pvt MA
Edward: b 8-13-1724 d 10-14-1802 m Reliance Paddock Pvt MA
Edward: b 8-5-1736 d 1804 m Elizabeth Troop Pvt MA
Edward: b 3-14-1756 d 10-15-1826 m Olive Briggs Pvt MA ★
Edward: b 1760 d 12-20-1856 m Huldah Polly Pvt NY
Eleazer: b 2-25-1737 d 2-27-1802 m Deborah Barrows Pvt MA
Eliab: b 4-9-1751 d 7-31-1831 m Hannah Holmes Pvt MA
Elikam: b 1-28-1724 d 1800 m Sarah Hackett Pvt VT
Elijah: b 1730 d 1809 m Phebe Richmond Pvt MA
Ephraim: b 2-12-1735 d 10-16-1818 m Ann Deane Pvt MA
Ezra: b 1757 d 11-14-1830 m Molly Redding Pvt MA

Gershom: b 9-8-1748 d 8-22-1793 m Susanna Edson Sgt MA
Gideon: b 1735 d 1801 m (1)Hannah Richmond (2)Susannah Busby
   Pvt MA
Gilbert: b 4-27-1754 d 3-19-1780 m Althea Gorham Ens RI
Henry: b 1728 d p. 1790 m Sarah Washburn Pvt MA
Job: b 1737 d 1816 m Jane Washburn Pvt MA
John, Sr.: b 1712 d 1801 m (1)Dighton Mirick (2)Phebe Dunham
   PS MA
John, Jr.: b 1749 d 2-2-1797 m Celia Lincoln Sgt MA
John: b 3-12-1738 d 5-5-1804 m (1)Margaret Lee (2)Mrs — Atwood
   CS MA
John: b c. 1755 d p. 7-23-1830 m (1) — McCracken (2)Mary Currie
   Pvt NC
John: b c. 1759 d p. 1790 m Julia Paden PS Pvt SC
John Rogers: b 3-23-1737 d 4-30-1816 m Hannah Kinnicut Sol RI
Jonathan: b 1-20-1756 d p. 1812 m Amarilles Chambers Pvt CT
Jonathan: b 8-9-1749 d 1-12-1822 m Miriam Walker Pvt MA
Joseph, Sr.: b 7-22-1723 d 6-19-1792 m (1)Elizabeth Hackett (2)Mrs
   Anna Staples Pvt MA
Joseph, Jr.: b 9-7-1756 d 1-23-1821 m (1)Prudence Waldron (2)Mrs
   Phebe Kelt Pvt MA
Joseph: b 12-25-1756 d 1815/6 m Molly Hack Pvt MA
Josiah: b 6-24-1750 d 8-23-1817 m Lydia Babbitt Cpl MA
Josiah: b 5- -1747 d 5-28-1821 m Betsy Hathaway Pvt MA
Josiah: b 10-23-1750 d 12-4-1808 m Charity Haskins Pvt NY
Lemuel: b 2-27-1737 d 4-2-1802 m Molly Richmond Lincoln Pvt
   MA
Nathan: b 1-1-1755 d 1-17-1837 m Mary Steeter Pvt MA
Nathaniel: b 4-15-1765 d 1832 m Azubah Cobb Pvt MA ★
Nathaniel, Jr.: b 3-26-1763 d 9-1-1829 m Susannah Lambert Pvt
   MA ★
Nathaniel, Sr.: b 10-14-1736 d 1813 m (1)Mary Richmond (2)Sarah
   Damon Sol MA
Perez: b 2-1-1741 d 2-22-1803 m Hannah Brightman Pvt MA
Perez: b 10-13-1728/9 d 11-23-1800/01 m Mercy Church PS RI
Philip: b 2-11-1735 d 1-28-1788 m Abilena Cady Sgt CT
Robert: b 4-19-1738 d p. 1782 m Martha Hinde Pvt MA
Samuel: b 11-27-1752 d 2-12-1836 m Mary Booth Pvt MA
Seth: b 3-18-1746 d 10-16-1826 m Hannah Richmond Pvt MA
Seth: b 1757 d 10-9-1822 m Phebe Richmond Pvt MA
Stephen: b 1743 d 6-30-1803 m Hannah Beals Cpl MA
Stephen: b 1-7-1754 d 7-11-1831 m (1)Rebecca Sisson (2)Rachel
   Sisson Sol NY
Sylvester: b 11-20-1729 d 7-11-1797 m Abigail Nightingale LCol MA
Sylvester: b 5-3-1746 d 11-11-1807 m (1)Lucy Weston (2)Elizabeth
   Gardner Pvt MA
Wm.: b c. 1730 d 10- -1832 m Agnes Saunders Sol VA
Wm.: b 11-21-1765 d c. 1809 m Rachel Matteson Pvt RI
Zebulon: b 1757/8 d 2- -1832 m Susanna Beswick Pvt MA

RICKABAUGH, (includes RICKENBACH)
Adam: b 1-3-1761 d 7-23-1836 m (1)Catherine Koontz (2)Mary
   Koontz Pvt VA ★
Jacob: b 9-3-1757 d 1-15-1831 m Barbara Hertzler Pvt PA
Martin: b — d p. 8-29-1801 n Ana — Sol MD

RICKARD, (includes RICHART, RICKART, RICKERT)
Abner: b 9-28-1744 d 7-2-1827 m Susanna Wright Col MA
George: b 9-26-1729 d 10-14-1798 m Eve Staring Sol NY
Jacob: b c. 1747 d 5-1-1803 m Rebecca Tator Pvt NY
Johannes: b 10-9-1746 d 8-31-1792 m Catherine Tator Pvt NY
Lemuel: b 5-29-1757 d 3-17-1826 m Elizabeth — Pvt MA ★
Lodewick: b 9-12-1756 d 1-9-1819 m Catherine Getman Sol NY
Lodowick: b c. 1712 d p. 1790 m Catherine Conrad PS NY
Nickolas: b 9-14-1752 d 3-9-1820 m Lea Hummell Pvt NY
Silas, Sr.: b 4-26-1717 d 3-6-1802 m Elizabeth Raymond PS CT
Wm.: b 1756 d 1811 m Elizabeth Stinson Pvt PA

RICKENBAKER,
Nicholas: b a. 1747 d 7-7-1812 m Mary — Pvt SC

RICKER,
Ebenezer: b 9-12-1739 d a. 12-30-1815 m (1)Patience —
   (2)Temperance Hanscom (3)Judith Witherell Lt NH
Ephraim: b c. 1735 d p. 1820 m Susanna Leighton Pvt NH
Ezekiel: b a. 1757 d p. 1804 m Molly Hanson Pvt MA
Gersham: b 1759 d 12- -1830 m Annie Garland Pvt NH
John: b 1756 d 6-20-1849 m Mary Magdalene Fishburn Pvt PA
Joseph: b 12-9-1746 d 10-18-1825 m Deborah Wentworth Capt MA
Noah: b 1761 d 8-16-1846 m Mary Staunton Mar NH
Reuben: b 1758 d 4-15-1838 m Hanna Gould Smn ME ★
Reuben: b 12-9-1758 d 7-4-1846 m Molly Stiles Cpl NH ★
Stephen: b 3-17-1760 d 2-28-1837 m (1)Sarah Storer (2)Alice
   Goodwin Pvt MA ★
Timothy: b 1758 d p. 1803 m Lois Plummer Pvt NH
Tobias: b 9-13-1762 d 12-20-1847 m Abigail Warren Pvt Smn NH ★
Wm.: b a. 1757 d 1813 m Amy Hobbs Pvt MA

RICKERTSON, (includes RICKERSTON & RICKETSON)
Abednego: b c. 1756 d p. 1810 m Martha Soule Pvt NY
Jesse: b 9- -1758 d 2-31-1835 m (1)Polly Merret (2)Mary — Pvt
   NC ★
Timothy: b c. 1745 d p. 1801 m (2)Mary Wilkins Pvt GA

RICKETTS,
Anthony, Sr.: b 10-4-1725 d *a.* 4-8-1794 m Mary Ricketts PS MD
Benjamin, Sr.: b *c.* 1700 d *c.* 1788 m — Maxwell PS MD
Benjamin, Jr.: b 2-12-1724 d 1788 m (1)Eleanor Maxwell (2)Mary
    Cutchin Pvt MD
Edward: b 4-10-1759 d *p.* 1785 m Millicent Greene Lt PA
John: b 3-2-1754 d *p.* 1790 m (1)Sarah Pennington (2)Jane McKew
    Pvt MD
Richard: b *c.* 1754 d 1830 m Elizabeth Welch Pvt MD
Samuel: b *c.* 1731 d *p.* 9-29-1794 m Hannah Mead PS MD
Thomas: b 1756 d 1814 m Nancy Sipple 1st Lt MD
Thomas: b 11-23-1753 d 8-22-1828 m (1)Ruth Adamson (2)Martha
    Wilson PS MD

RICKEY, (includes REEKIE, RICKY)
Andrew: b 1-31-1749 d 3-5-1817 m (2)Submit McCrory Sgt NY
    W★
Israel: b 1744 d 5-28-1821 m (1)Hannah Roy (2)Nancy Crowell
    (3)Susanna Dennis Capt NJ
Jacob: b *c.* 1753 d *p.* 1795 m Anna — Pvt NJ
John: b 5-23-1750 d 11-30-1836 m Alla Lowe Pvt NY ★
John: b 11-17-1717 d 9-3-1798 m Mary Hutchinson Pvt PA
John: b 1745 d 8-8-1797 m Jane — Pvt VT

RICKS,
Christopher: b *c.* 1740 d 1784 m Dinah Hayes Pvt PA
John: b *c.* 1739 d *c.* 1790 m Mary Holton PS VA
Lewis: b 1741 d 3-15-1781 m Nancy Ann Joiner Sol NC
Wm.: b 1750 d 6-10-1832 m Lydia Brantley Sol NC

RIDDELL, (includes RIDELL & RIDDLE)
Cato: b 3-10-1755 d 8-20-1823 m Martha Tomlinson Capt NC
Edward: b 3-22-1758 d 8- -1826 m (1)Agnes — (2)Margaret
    McMillan Bbd PA
Gawen: b 2-22-1753 d 7-29-1812 m Margaret Taggart Pvt MA
George: b — d *p.* 1786 m — Bird Pvt VA
Hugh: b 1761 d 8-17-1833 m Ann Maria Houston Pvt NH
Issac: b 6-10-1762 d 1-26-1830 m Ann Aiken Pvt NH
James: b 1733 d 1800 m Janet Hall Pvt PS NH
James: b *c.* 1745 d *p.* 1780 m (2)Johannah — PS NJ
John: b *c.* 1745 d 3-17-1782 m Lucy Clark Pvt MA
John: b 1754 d 11-18-1813 m (1)Mary McAffee (2)Sarah Hartshorn
    PS NJ
John: b 12-4-1761 d 6-17-1847 m (1)Phoebe Schmocke (2)Mary
    James (3)Nancy Nutt (4)Jane Marshall (5)Jane Ross Sol Slr NJ
John: b 1761 d 3-11-1818 m Margaret Ann Ross Pvt PS PA
John: b 1-24-1752 d 1818 m Ann McKee PS PA
John Henry, Jr.: b 1741/2 d 6-27-1797 m Polly Clarke Ens MA
Joseph: b 1762 d 3-8-1823 m Mary — Pvt MA ★
Joseph: b *c.* 1755 d *p.* 1808 m Molly Blodget Pvt Fif MA
Matthew: b 11-26-1743 d 11-26-1830 m Elizabeth Gilkey Pvt PA
Robert: b 5-11-1744 d 2-20-1822 m Jane McGee 1st Lt MA
Samuel: b 7-22-1748 d 10-4-1832 m Jane Pinkerton Lt PA
Thomas: b 1739 d 1809 m Rebecca Moulton Pvt MA
Wm.: b *c.* 1720 d *c.* 1777 m Joyce Powell Pvt VA

RIDDICK, (includes REDDICK)
Christopher: b *c.* 1730 d *a.* 5- -1798 m Sarah Hollowell CS NC
Docton: b 1749-52 d *a.* 2- -1781 m Elizabeth Sumner CS NC
Edward: b 1-29-1735 d 9- -1783 m Margaret Temple Col VA
Isaac: b *c.* 1715 d 1788 m Hannah Perry Pvt NC
Jason: b *c.* 1744 d 1785 m — Capt VA
Joseph: b *c.* 1735 d 11-18-1818 m Ann Stallings PS NC
Kedar: b *c.* 1735 d 1784 m Elizabeth Garrett PS NC
Lemuel: b 8-23-1711 d 3-20-1775 m (1)Ann Sumner (2)Esther
    Pugh PS CS VA
Micajah: b 1744 d 11- -1804 m Ruth Parker Pvt NC
Robert: b *c.* 1728 d 1806 m — PS NC
Wm.: b 9-7-1763 d 5-20-1824 m Mary Elizabeth Carver PS VA NC
Wm.: b 1760 d 10-3-1831 m Margaret Trump Pvt PA ★
Willis: b 6-23-1725 d 10-24-1800 m Mary Folk PS VA *Col.*

RIDEOUT,
Abraham: b 1759 d 1-9-1844 m Molly Seavey Pvt MA ★
Benjamin, Sr.: b 6-25-1731 d *p.* 1790 m Mary Getchell PS MA
Benjamin, Jr.: b 7-13-1754 d 8-3-1833 m Miriam Stover Pvt MA ★
James: b 1741 d 12-22-1809 m Mary — Pvt NH
Stephen: b 1760 d 9-15-1843 m (1)Abigail Smart (2)Jane Works
    Pvt MA
Wm.: b *c.* 1759 d 1-23-1831 m Ruth Rideout Pvt MA

RIDER, (includes RYDER & RYTHER)
Benjamin: b 4-15-1724 d *p.* 1790 m Betty Bartlett Capt MA
Benjamin: b 3-2-1760 d 9- -1841 m Mollie Enderly Pvt NY ★
Charles: b 6-18-1752 d 11-27-1801 m Mary Fletcher Pvt MD
Christopher: b 1765 d 12-3-1835 m Mary — Pvt PA
Daniel: b 9-7-1747 d *p.* 8- -1833 m Mary Belding Pvt MA ★
David: b 5-6-1757 d 8-26-1825 m Esther Josleyn Pvt MA
George: b 5-11-1750 d *p.* 1-26-1801 m Maria Catherine Pvt PA
Hophni: b 4-2-1751 d 6-13-1776 m Sarah Connable Pvt MA
Isaac, Sr.: b 1735 d 1776 m Bridget Hatch Pvt MA
Isaac, Jr.: b 5-27-1760 d — m Olive Vaughn Pvt MA
Isaiah: b 3-11-1745 d — m Mary Forbes Pvt MA

John: b 11-18-1739 d 8-25-1820 m Sarah Ruggles Sgt NY
John: b 1732 d 1812 m Sarah Sprague Pvt NY
John: b *c.* 1753 d 1850 m Margaret Engle Pvt PA
John: b 1756 d *p.* 1830 m Elizabeth Bradley Pvt VA
Joseph: b 1737 d 3-1-1814 m (1)Mary — (2)Jane Pool Ens CT
Joseph: b 1728 d 3-30-1794 m Martha Thankful PS MA
Kimball: b 8-31-1750 d 9-26-1834 m Mary Eldredge Sgt MA
Moses: b 1-29-1753 d 10-29-1839 m Mary Twitchell Pvt MA
Nathaniel: b 1747 d *p.* 1783 m Priscilla Bradford Pvt MA
Salma: b 3-14-1758 d 11-28-1822 m (1)Abigail Root (2)Eunice Pierce
    Pvt MA
Samuel: b 5-22-1725 d *p.* 1790 m Hannah Rich Pvt MA
Thomas: b 12-3-1743 d 10-15-1783 m Bethiah Hedge Sgt MA
Timothy: b 6-7-1765 d — m Patience Dennis Pvt NY
Simeon: b 1760 d 5-9-1812 m Sally — Pvt NY

RIDGE,
Daniel: b 9-10-1748 d *p.* 1780 m Mary McLaughlin Pvtr PA
Wm.: b *a.* 1760 d *p.* 1802 m Rebecca Springer Pvt MA

RIDGELY, (includes RIDGLEY)
Charles: b 1735 d 1810 m Ruth Norwood PS MD
Charles Greenbury: b 1-26-1736 d 11-25-1784 m (1)Mary Wykoff
    (2)Ann Moore PS DE
Greenbury: b 1726 d 1796 m Lucy Stringer PS MD
Greenbury: b 7-4-1754 d 3-17-1843 m Rachel Ryan PS MD
Henry: b 1728 d *p.* 1790 m Ann Dorsey Vol CS PS MD
Henry: b 8-3-1755 d 2-26-1824 m Jane Price Capt MD
Richard: b 8-3-1755 d 2-27-1824 m Elizabeth Dorsey CS MD
Westall, Jr.: b *c.* 1741 d 1798 m Sarah Urith PS MD
Wm.: b 1743 d 1822 m Elizabeth Dorsey Lt MD
Wm.: b 1703/4 d 1780 m Mary Orrick PS MD

RIDGEWAY, (includes RIDGWAY)
David: b 6-2-1741 d 7- -1800 m Jane Burr CS NJ
Edward: b 8-15-1713 d *c.* 1780 m Mary Delaplane Pvt PA
Isaac: b 5-27-1758 d 3-4-1840 m Drusilla Lovejoy Sgt MA ★
Jacob: b 7-16-1723 d 1798 m Isabella Schooley Sol NJ
James: b 3-1-1753 d 1-6-1843 m Esther Coburn Cpl MA
Job: b 5-13-1735 d 3-13-1796 m Martha Hilyard CS NJ
John: b 8-14-1755 d 4-12-1845 m Elizabeth Wright PS NJ
John: b 5-2-1738 d 3-4-1800 m Postrema Shinn PS NJ
John: b 1-20-1744 d 1791 m Eliza Ridgway Pvt SC
John: b 1-29-1760 d *p.* 9- -1837 m Fannie Ragsdale Pvt SC VA ★
Lott: b *c.* 1745 d *a.* 11- -1796 m Catherine Frazier CS NJ
Thomas: b *c.* 1744 d *a.* 7- -1801 m Lucy — PS VA

RIDINGS,
John: b 1737 d 1811 m Polly Elizabeth Gentry Pvt NC
Wm.: b 1715 d 1789 m — Pearson Pvt NC

RIDLER,
Isaac: b *a.* 1746 d *p.* 1781 m Elizabeth Hemenway Slr MA

RIDLEY,
Bromfield: b *c.* 1745 d 1796 m Frances Keeling Henderson CS PS NC
Daniel: b 4-4-1759 d 4-1-1837 m Hannah Bridges Pvt MA
David: b 1762 d 6-2-1838 m Mary Lane Pvt ME ★
George: b 1761 d 10-31-1818 m Molly Hopkins Pvt MA
George: b 1-11-1737/9 d 9-29-1835 m (1)Elizabeth Weatherford
    (2)Sally Vincent Pvt VA
James: b 2-6-1718 d 7-14-1797 m (1)Ruth Smalley (2)Mary Bacey
    PS ME
John: b 1751-8 d *p.* 1855 m (1)Abigail Holmes (2)Sarah — Pvt MA ★
Samuel: b 3-4-1752 d 11-18-1842 m Abial Fleming Cpl MD ★
Thomas: b 1740 d 2-15-1815 m Amy Scott Col VA
Wm.: b *c.* 1750 d *a.* 9-1790 m Elizabeth Lewis Dr NC

RIDPATH,
John: b *c.* 1740 d 10-13-1777 m Charlotte Bennett Lt NC

RIEB,
Andrew: b 1740 d 9-9-1816 m Eva Catharine Crumback Pvt PA

RIEGEL, (includes RAIGLE)
Andrew: b *c.* 1748 d *c.* 5- -1815 m Catharine Hoffman Pvt PA
Benjamin: b 1738 d 12-1-1778 m (1)Catharine Rothrock (2)Mary
    Barbara Hass Pvt PA
Daniel: b 1736-40 d *c.* 5- -1786 m Dorothea — PS PA
Jacob: b 1760 d 1825 m Elizabeth Miller Pvt PA
Michael: b 1751 d 1835 m Magdalena Zettelmeir Pvt PA
Simon: b 11-5-1738 d 1-12-1829 m Gertraut Kershner PS PA

RIFFLE,
Nicholas: b 3-16-1752 d 4-18-1808 m — Pvt VA

RIFORD,
Joseph, Sr.: b *c.* 1738 d 1777 m Hannah — Pvt MA

RIGBY,
Joseph: b *c.* 1737 d *p.* 12-15-1775 m Elizabeth Barrea Pvt NY
Wm.: b 1753 d 3-12-1830 m (1)Annie Yeo (2)Ara Lemen Williamson
    QMSgt MD

RIGGIN, (or RIGGAN)
Francis: b 3-7-1764 d 2-20-1847 m Anne Harris Pvt NC ★
Stephen: b a. 1747 d p. 1800 m Sarah Matthews Pvt MD

RIGGS,
Aaron: b 3-18-1749 d 9-25-1827 m Martha Adams Pvt MA
Abner: b 12-24-1760 d 10-1-1818 m Phebe Rowland Pvt CT
Abraham: b 1757 d 8-9-1843 m Elizabeth Bird Pvt VA
Amon: b 4-21-1748 d 3-16-1822 m Ruth Griffith Capt MD
Benjamin: b 1731 d p. 8- -1776 m — PS MD
Bethuel: b 1757 d p. 1832 m Nancy Riggs Capt NC ★
Cyrenus: b 1750 d 10-6-1825 m Esther Crane Pvt NJ
Eleazer: b 12-28-1754 d a. 1855 m — Pvt VA
Elisha: b 10-4-1742 d 6-6-1777 m Caroline Welsh Capt MD
Ezekiel: b 1730 d — m Jane Mifflin Pvt PS PA
Gideon, Sr.: b 1713 d 1-25-1786 m Rebecca — PS NJ
Gideon, Jr.: b 1753 d c. 1830 m Rachel Minthron Pvt CL ★
Greenberry: b 10-7-1757 d 8-30-1844 m Ann Hardy Pvt MD
James: b 11-9-1758 d 9-22-1839 m Sarah Clark Pvt CT
James: b 9-15-1742 d 2-27-1815 m Mary Johnson Pvt PA
Jeremiah: b 7-1-1749 d 5- -1829 m Anna Woodruff Cpl CT
John, Jr.: b 8-31-1735 d p, 1793 m Abigail — Capt CT
John: b 4-10-1742 d 6-18-1814 m Elizabeth Hawkins Capt CT
John: b 8-31-1735 d 5- -1823 m Abigail Peet Sgt CT
John: b 1740 d 6-25-1827 m Catherine Boyer Sol MD
John: b c. 1749 d 7-3-1794 m Sarah Yeaman PS MD
John: b a. 1763 d p. 1782 m Mary Elligan Drm Maj MD
John: b a. 1755 d a. 5-30-1811 m Rachel Huskey Sol NC
Joseph, Sr.: b 2-13-1710 d 3-15-1792 m Mabel Johnson PS CT
Joseph, Jr.: b 7-20-1746 d 5-15-1822 m (1)Rachel Chatfield (2)Elizabeth Johnson Lt CT
Joseph: b 4-24-1740 d 2-26-1829 m Leah Cosad Pvt NJ
Joseph: b 1743 d 5- -1814 m Hannah Cook Pvt NJ
Joseph: b 1720 d 6-25-1799 m Abigail — PS NJ
Miles: b 5-20-1748 d p. 1789 m Patty Bull Pvt CT
Moses: b 4-10-1760 d 9-15-1838 m (1)Susan Tucker (2)Eunice Knapp Pvt CT ★
Preserve: b 1746 d a. 4-5-1821 m Puah Hudson PS NJ
Samuel: b 10-6-1740 d 5-25-1814 m Amelia Dorsey 2nd Lt MD
Shadrack: b c. 1755 d p. 11-23-1807 m — Sol NC
Thomas: b 12-13-1742 d 10-17-1824 m (1)Rhoda Tuttle (2)Sarah Carr Pvt NJ
Timothy: b c. 1723 d p. 1794 m — CS NC
Zebulon: b 1-23-1719 d 12-12-1780 m Elizabeth Brown PS NJ
Zenas: b 1-5-1760 d 8-14-1847 m Jemima Richards Pvt Arfr NJ ★

RIGHTER, (includes RICHTER & RIGHTOR)
Anthony: b 11-20-1756 d 1844 m Catherine Elizabeth Taylor Pvt PA
George: b 1741 d 3-17-1825 m Rebecca — Pvt DE
Jasper: b 1739 d 10-8-1794 m Elizabeth Hopler Pvt NJ
John: b 2-22-1732 d 11-28-1823 m (1)Hannah Tunis (2)Jane McAfee Lt PA
John: b 1762 d 12- -1820 m Sarah Biglar Pvt PA
Michael: b 10-31-1748 d 7-4-1819 m Elizabeth Bower Pvt PA
Michael: d 1777-82 m Christiana — Pvt PA
Nicholas: b c. 1733 d 11-25-1820 m Mary Hanneman Capt NY ★
Nicholas: b 9-1-1754 d 10-5-1851 m Cathrine C McCollam OrdlSgt NY ★
Peter: b c. 1735 d 6-20-1777 m (2)Elizabeth Baker Cpl PA
Wm.: b 11-23-1748 d 1820 m (1)Margaret Kohl (2)Mrs — Turner Pvt NY

RIGHTON,
Joseph: b 9-9-1762 d 1-7-1847 m Elizabeth Fullerton Sgt PS SC ★

RIGHTS,
Matthew: b 12-7-1712 d p. 8- -1782 m (1)Maria Magdalena Bitzman (2)Susanna Durfee PS MA

RIGSBY,
Jesse: b c. 1760 d 10-26-1827 m Elizabeth Pickett Pvt NC ★

RILEA,
Richard: b 3-27-1762 d 8-7-1839 m Rhoda Little Pvt VA ★

RILEY, (includes O'REILY, RALEY, REILAY, REILEY)
Ann: b 1750 d p. 1789 m Patrick Riley PS SC
Ashbel: b 5-3-1760 d 3-5-1797 m (1)Lovina Wells (2)Rachel Springsted Sgt CT
Barnabas: b 1731 d p. 1-20-1782 m Annie Gorral Sol VA
Bennet: b c. 1755 d 12- -1811 m (1)Susanna Drury (2)Frances Frazer Matr MD ★
Daniel: b 1764 d 7-14-1837 m Priscilla Thompson Pvt NJ
David: b 3-12-1743 d p. 1790 m (1)Lois Griswold (2)Rachel Curtis (3)Sarah Goodrich Pvt CT
Dennis: b 11-11-1742 d 8-17-1824 m Elizabeth Price Matr PA
Francis: b 1730 d 1795 m Martha — Pvt PA
James: b a. 1760 d 5-12-1808 m Elizabeth Morris Sgt NJ W★
James: b 6-15-1755 d 1840 m Nancy Yearken Pvt PA VA ★
John: b 2-2-1737 d 1803 m Ruth Williams Capt CT
John: b 10- -1737 d 1776 m Huldah Porter Pvt MA
John: b 1754 d 1778 m Catharine Von Shultze Pvt NJ
John: b 1734 d 1838 m Catherine Vandenberg Capt PS NY

John: b 1760 d 5-30-1852 m (3)Martha Lowell Pvt NY
John: b 4-12-1752 d 5-8-1810 m Elizabeth Myers Capt PA
John: b 9-15-1752-8 d 11- -1838 m Mary McIlvaine Pvt Mus PA
John: b 12-9-1751 d 12-22-1845 m Elizabeth Mc Culloch Pvt PA ★
John: b 11-24-1754 d 2-11-1819 m Sallie Carter Pvt SC
John: b 1757 d 2-23-1804 m Mary Ann — Pvt SC
John: b 1760 d 1854 m — Pvt SC
John: b c. 1756 d p. 12-2-1784 m Ann Robinson Smith Lt VA
John: b 4-10-1763 d — m Nancy Blackburn Hunter Pvt VA
Julius: b 5-22-1750 d 12-1-1838 m Mabel Adkins Pvt CT
Martin: b 1759 d 10-5-1829 m Esther Ewalt Pvt PA
Martin, Sr.: b 11- -1791 m Elizabeth — Pvt PA
Ninian: b 3-18-1726 d p. 1810 m Elizabeth Taylor PS MD
Patrick: b 1740 d 1823 m Ann — PS SC
Richard: b 12-14-1735 d 8-27-1820 m Mary Cheney PS PA
Roger: b 2-6-1737 d 5-22-1822 m (1)Comfort Loveland (2)Sarah Deming Capt CT
Wm.: b — d 7-8-1824 m (1)Rebecca Harvey (2)Barbara Hodgkin Capt MD ★
Wm.: b c. 1745 d a. 1-17-1778 m Elizabeth West Capt VA
Wm.: b 12-25-1760 d 2-14-1837 m Hannah Long Pvt VA ★

RILLIEUX,
Don Vincent: b 1736 d 2-10-1800 m Maria Antonia Troquet PS LA

RIMEL,
John: b 1756 d a. 2-11-1828 m Rebecca Lincoln Pvt PA

RINARD,
John Frances: b 1760 d 1820 m Abigale Thomas Pvt PA

RINDGE,
John: b 1760 d 1830 m Deborah Clarke Sol CT

RING,
Benjamin: b c. 1737 d 8-10-1804 m Rachel James Pvt PA
David: b 9-28-1742 d 4- -1832 m Mehitable Partridge Sol PS ME
Eleazer: b 5-7-1740 d 10-22-1821 m (1)Olive Mitchell (2)Mary Sweetser Sgt MA
Eleazer: b 12-31-1749 d 5-14-1814 m (1)Abigail Joslyn (2)Damaris Johnson Pvt MA
Francis: b 1-28-1738 d 9-27-1820 m Mrs Molly Weston Pvt MA
Issachar: b 12-25-1744 d — m Esther Barnard Pvt NH
Johannes: b 1754 d 8-12-1825 m Barbara Pultz Pvt NY
Jonathan: b 10-4-1736 d 1-9-1815 m Zilpah Adams Lt NH
Joseph: b 11-3-1751 d 4-19-1796 m Penelope Patch Pvt MA
Wm.: b 9-17-1747 d p. 1797 m Abigail Graves Sgt MA

RINGER,
John: b 1752 d 7-7-1827 m Anna Bordenheimer Pvt MD
Mathias, Sr.: b c. 1734 d a. 3-17-1810 m Susanna — Associator MD
Matthias, Jr.: b 1760-3 d 2-11-1843 m (1)Elizabeth Plank (2)Rebecca — Pvt MD
Michael: b 1735 d 1-19-1795 m Margaret — Pvt PA
Michael: b 1755 d 1844 m Mary Catherine Knaup Pvt PA

RINGGOLD,
Thomas: b 12-14-1744 d 10-26-1776 m Mary Galloway PS MD
Wm.: b 2-23-1723 d p. 10-17-1803 m (1)Sarah Jones (2)Mary Wilmer LCol CS MD

RINGLE,
Mathias: b 1742 d 9-3-1811 m (1)Nancy Lovenguier (2)Julia Ann Pohr Ens PA

RINGLER,
Jacob: b 1755 d 8-20-1821 m Agnes Haas Drm PA
John: b 12-5-1728 d 1798 m Anna Mary Nesen Pvt PA

RINGO,
Burtis: b 2-25-1763 d 11-7-1855 m Hannah Rector Sgt VA ★
Cornelius: b 1753 d 9-30-1836 m Sarah Morgan OrdlSgt VA ★
John: b 4-28-1761 d 10-4-1843 m Nancy Ann Harrison Pvt VA ★

RINGWALT,
Jacob, Sr.: b c. 1735 d p. 1790 m Anna Barbara Wagner Pvt PA

RINKER,
Abraham: b 2-28-1756 d 10-27-1820 m Gertrude Stacey Pvt PA ★
Edward: b — d 1813 m (2)Mrs Sarah Wagley Sgt VA
George: b 1752 d c. 1843/4 m Mary Coffman Lt VA ★
Jacob: b 1749 d 1-18-1827 m Mary Keller Col VA

RIPHENBERG,
Petrus: b c. 1745 d p. 1790 m Phebe — PS NY

RIPLEY,
Calvin: b 5-18-1748 d p. 1832 m Peggy Bradford Pvt MA RI ★
Charles: b 2-25-1733 d — m Tabitha Abbe Pvt CT
Cornelius: b 4-3-1736 d 7-9-1815 m Thankful Pease Pvt MA
David: b 12-7-1749 d 2-10-1827 m Jane Ellis Churchill Pvt MA
Epaphras: b 2-13-1759 d — m Anna Webb Cpl VT

RIPLEY, contd.
Gamaliel: b 10-20-1740 d 4-15-1799 m (1)Elizabeth Hebard (2)Judith Perkins Lt CT
Hezekiah: b 9-25-1748 d 11-11-1836 m Mrs Eunice Durmont Lt CS CT ★
Hezekiah: b 2-14-1743 d 11-29-1831 m Dorothy Brientnall Chp CT
Jacob: b c. 1756 d 11-14-1835 m Magdaline — Sgt PA ★
Jepthah: b 4-5-1756 d 11- -1843 m Lois Allen Pvt MA
Jeremiah: b 6-24-1741 d 2-11-1812 m (2)Mary Gove Capt CT
Jerome: b 10-20-1757 d 12-25-1838 m Sarah Franklin Pvt MA
John: b 11-13-1698 d 2- -1781 m Mary Messenger PS CT
John: b 3-31-1738 d 1-27-1823 m Abigail Marsh Maj CT
John: b c. 1754 d c. 1819 m Mary — Sgt VA
Joseph: b 8-1-1757 d 1-26-1830 m Lydia Ripley Pvt MA
Joseph: b 1763 d 12-9-1854 m Salome Phillips Pvt MA ★
Joshua: b 10-30-1726 d 12- -1787 m Elizabeth Lathrop Pvt CT
Kimball: b 12-31-1747 d 11-28-1807 m Sarah Sprague Sgt MA
Nathaniel: b 1743 d — m Elizabeth Bartlett 2nd Lt MA
Nehemiah: b 4-18-1755 d 3-8-1829 m Priscilla Lincoln Cpl MA
Noah: b 9-18-1721 d 9-28-1788 m Lydia Kent Pvt MA
Pelham: b 7-26-1765 d 5-31-1841 m Huldah Austin Pvt MA
Peter: b c. 1712 d 10-17-1782 m Damaris Chase Pvt MA
Phineas: b 8-27-1751 d 1823 m Experience Montague Pvt VT
Piram: b 12-1-1762 d 3-23-1844 m Hannah Plum Pvt NY
Ralph: b 10-25-1751 d 6-19-1827 m Eunice Huntington Cnt QM CT
Thaddeus: b 10-15-1746 d 12-17-1831 m (1)Lydia Ransom (2)Mary Shurtleff Pvt MA
Thomas: b 10-22-1749 d 4-6-1829 m Hannah Bunker Pvt MA
Wm.: b 7-3-1726 d 4-27-1805 m Lydia Ring Pvt MA
Wm.: b 7-5-1765 d 6-27-1823 m Lucy Chipman Pvt MA ★
Wm.: b 1756 d 6-27-1823 m Lucy — Pvt MA
Wm.: b 2-12-1734 d 2-17-1818 m Lydia Brewster Sgt NH

RIPPERDAN.
Frederick: b 1740 d 1825 m Sarah Chiticks PS VA

RIPPETH,
Wm.: b 1748 d 8-19-1843 m Sarah Ross Pvt PA

RIPPEY,
Edward: b 3-23-1764 d 12-9-1853 m Mary Elmore Pvt NC ★
Elijah: b 1740 d 1793 m Elizabeth Thompson Sgt VA
John: b 4-5-1749 d 3-11-1826 m Mary Orson Capt PA
Samuel: b 1754 d 1804 m Mary Finley Pvt PA
Wm.: b 1741 d 9-22-1819 m (1)Margaret Allen (2)Elizabeth McCracken Capt PA

RIPPLE,
Casper: b c. 1748 d 1828 m Anna Regina Pvt PA
Michael: b a. 1755 d p. 1800 m Elizabeth — Pvt PA

RIPSOM,
Mathias: b c. 1740 d 8- -1777 m X Pvt NY

RISDON,
Josiah: b 10-18-1753 d 1830 m Martha Cochran Cpl VT
Onesimus: b 2-18-1760 d 3-4-1848 m Sarah Wheeler Pvt VT ★

RISEN,
Elery: b 1759 d p. 1808 m (1)Elizabeth Rowlett (2)Frances Vasser Sgt VA

RISER, (includes REASOR, REISER, REZER & RISER)
Israel: b 7-30-1757 d 1801 m (1)Hannah Margaret Schubdrein (2)Mrs Anna Barbara Keiffer Pvt GA
Jacob: b 1-16-1725 d 12-27-1815 m Esther Bertolette Cpl PA
Martin: b c. 1745 d c. 1812/3 m Catherine Appel Pvt PA
Michael: b 1746 d 1818 m Hannah Pennypacker Pvt PA
Michael: b 2-3-1760 d 6-11-1843 m Anna Herbert Fif Pvt VA ★

RISH,
Adam: b c. 1751 d p. 1790 m Elizabeth Black Pvt SC
Andrew: b 11-23-1756 d 7-10-1818 m (1)Bertha Elinder Herman (2)Rosanna Barbara Minnick Sol SC

RISHEL, (includes RISHELL)
Ludwig: b c. 1740 d 1815 m (1)Annie Elizabeth Blank (2)Anne Mary Dunmire Pvt PA
Martin: b c. 1753 d 3- -1831 m Elizabeth — Pvt PA
Michael: b 11-28-1750 d 6-18-1826 m — Pvt PA

RISHER,
Benjamin: b 11-14-1752 d 6-16-1812 m Mary DeFontaine Cav SC

RISING,
Aaron, Sr.: b 4- -1733 d p. 1790 m (1)Anna Harmon (2)Mrs Sarah Phelps Pvt VT
Abner: b 1-20-1748 d 1-3-1839 m Abigail Devotion Pvt MA
Benjamin, Jr.: b 9-22-1747/8 d c. 3- -1846 m Mary Barker Sgt MA
James: b 1738 d 1816 m Mary Sheldon Pvt CT
John, Sr.: b 1-22-1724 d 10-15-1793 m (1)Mabel Hall (2)Susanna Mason Cpl CT
John, Jr.: b 4-21-1749 d 11-22-1797 m Philocinda Hatheway Pvt CT

Jonah: b 1761 d 1820 m Mehitabel Brewster Pvt CT
Josiah: b 4-20-1765 d 4-3-1844 m Huldah Miller Cpl CT ★
Nathaniel: b 7-22-1743 d 1-21-1828 m (1)Anne Austin (2)Phebe Munsell Pvt CT

RISLEY, (includes WRISLEY)
David: b 11-23-1766 d 8-24-1834 m Cynthia Gillett Pvt CT ★
Elijah: b 12-25-1756 d 1-11-1839 m Phoebe Bills Pvt CT ★
Jeremiah: b 12-14-1734 d 6-24-1796 m Margaret Doughty 2Lt NJ
Job, Sr.: b 1714 d 8-30-1797 m (1)Mary Bidwell (2)Beriah Fox Sgt CT
Job, Jr.: b 3-3-1743 d 5-23-1786 m (1)— Arnold (2)Mary Webster Sgt CT
Joseph: b 9-1-1754 d 8-6-1827 m Mary Baker Pvt NJ
Levi: b 1760 d 1834 m Lucretia Jones Pvt CT ★
Nehemiah: b 9-28-1762 d 1-31-1813 m Martha Beaumont Pvt CT
Nathaniel: b 3-18-1759 d p. 1831 m Sarah Steelman Pvt NJ
Ruben: b 6-5-1745 d 1811 m Mercy Miller Cpl CT
Samuel: b 10-21-1759 d 4-1-1837 m Mary Huxford Pvt CT
Samuel, Jr.: b 6-11-1761 d 4-3-1838 m (2)Stacy Oliver Pvt PA
Thomas: b c. 1749 d 1799 m Mary Leeds Pvt NJ

RIST,
Joseph: b 9-28-1740 d 10-30-1815 m (1)Rachel Keith (2)Jerusha Cutler Pvt MA

RITCHIE, (includes RICHEY & RITCHEY)
Abraham: b 1737 d 8-15-1830 m — Pvt VA ★
Alexander, Sr.: b 8-20-1739 d 1-11-1818 m Mary Wilson PS SC
Craig: b 12-29-1758 d 6-13-1833 m Mary Price Capt PA
David: b 12-13-1745 d 2-13-1834 m Catharine Trimbell Pvt PA
David: b 1752 d 4-22-1823 m Anne — Pvt PA
Henry: b 1726 d 8-23-1806 m Ann Harrison PS PA
James: b 7-9-1757 d 11-11-1838 m Elizabeth Wilson Smn PA
James: b 1760 d 5-22-1846 m Martha Stanley Pvt PA
James, Jr.: b 1752 d 6-5-1833 m Elizabeth Dunn Pvt SC
James: b 1741 d 9-23-1822 m Jane Arnold Pvt VA
John: b c. 1750 d 1-25-1819 m Helen Crozier Pvt PA
John: b 7-8-1755 d 5-10-1835 m Mary Welch Pvt PA ★
John: b 3-14-1756 d 1833 m Nancy Carmichael Pvt PA
John: b c. 1740 d p. 1800 m — Pvt VA
John: b c. 1760 d 9- -1822 m — Pvt VA
Robert: b 1754 d a. 8-15-1828 m Mary Stewart Pvt SC
Robert: b 1752 d 1828 m Mrs Rosanna Wilson Saltzman Pvt PA
Wm.: b 3-27-1753 d 9-18-1814 m Frances Gilman QM MD
Wm.: b 1756 d 7-3-1842 m Sarah Thomas Pvt PA ★
Wm.: b 12-7-1759 d 8-17-1847 m (1)Catherine O Hale (2)Mary Kane Ens PA
Wm.: b 1-7-1744 d p. 1796 m Elizabeth Scott Pvt VA

RITTENHOUSE,
Abner: b 5-5-1760 d 1833 m Sarah Emmons Pvt NJ
Abraham: b 1723 d 1815 m — Pvt PA
Benjamin: b 1741 d 8-31-1825 m (1)Elizabeth Bull (2)Frances Wade Capt & PS PA
David: b 4-8-1732 d 6-26-1796 m (1)Eleanor Colston (2)Hannah Jacobs CS & PS PA
Elijah: b 1745 d 1831 m Sarah Quick Pvt PA
Elizabeth Bull: b 1753 d 1787-93 m Benjamin Rittenhouse PS MD
Jacob: b c. 1758 d p. 3-8-1847 m Maria Salome Arner Drm Pvt PA
Matthias: b 6-14-1732 d 6-3-1793 m Catherine Van Fosen Pvt PA
Wm.: b 1755 d 7- -1816 m (1)Elizabeth Wilson (2)Rebecca — Pvt NJ
Wm.: b 1756 d 10-3-1819 m Ann Rock Pvt PA

RITTER,
Casper: b c. 1745 d 11- -1822 m Otillia Hertz Cpl PA
Casper, Sr.: b c. 1724 d 1792 m Anna Maria Pvt PA
Casper: b 7-24-1747 d 5-2-1824 m Anna M Germanton Pvt PA
David: b 5-4-1745 d 10-7-1823 m Abigail Lowe 2Lt MA
Elias: b 1748 d p. 1790 m Catherine Ann Young Pvt MD
George: b 2-17-1733 d 11-18-1808 m Maria Elizabeth — Pvt PA
Henry: b 6-16-1760 d 6-17-1847 m Mary — Pvt NY ★
Jacob: b 11-18-1754 d 11-3-1834 m Elizabeth Myrtetus Sol PA
John: bpt 7-29-1759 d 5-14-1824 m Mary — Pvt MA
John: b 3-3-1737 d 3-4-1810 m Elizabeth — Pvt NY
Martin: b 11-10-1749 d 11-2-1827 m Anna Margaret Steininger Sgt PA
Martin: b 8-10-1760 d 2-4-1849 m Barbara Fredericks Fif PA
Moses: b 2-17-1742 d 4-20-1810 m (1)Mary Goodridge (2)Elizabeth Diggins Pvt MA
Wm.: b 1750 d p. 1787 m — Lt MD

RITZ, (or REITZ)
Andrew: b 1-1-1755 d 3-16-1837 m Marie Margaret Brosious Pvt PA
George: b 2-5-1726 d p. 1-30-1793 m — PS PA
Henry: b 1745 d 1814 m Magdalene Herr Capt PA
Lawrence: b 12-1-1761 d 3-9-1844 m Mary Elizabeth Frey Pvt PA

RIVENBARK,
Frederick: b 10-15-1748 d 11-21-1837 m (2)Winnifred Jones Pvt NC ★

RIVERS,

Frederick: b 1740 d 2-20-1820 m Mary Boatwright Pvt SC
John: b — d p. 1-27-1792 m — PS SC
Richard: b a. 1735-40 d p. 1810 m Mary — CS NC
Samuel: b 1747 d 12-29-1834 m Ruth Young Pvt SC
Thomas: b 7-9-1757 d 10-18-1827 m Elizabeth Edmunds Jones PS VA
Wm.: b c. 1718 d p. 1790 m Temple Dempsey PS SC

RIVES,

Benjamin: b 2-4-1752 d 9-14-1839 m (1)Mary — (2)Catherine — Sol SC
Elizabeth Briggs Mason: b 5-10-1742 d 11-5-1803 m Christopher Rives PS VA
Frederick: b 1736 d 1815 m Mary Magdalene Steagall Capt VA
George: b c. 1740 d 3- -1795 m Sarah Eldridge Capt PS VA
Green: b 10-1763 d 10-26-1812 m Mary Ridley Jones Sol SC
Joel: b 4-6-1761 d 1829 m Jemima Bonner Pvt VA
Robert: b 3-11-1764 d 3-9-1845 m Margaret Cabell Pvt VA
Timothy: b 1748 d 6-8-1821 m Priscilla Turner Lt SC
Timothy: b c. 1740 d 1802 m Sarah Gee PS VA
Wm.: b 1737 d 1783 m Lucy Wyche PS SC
Wm.: b c. 1732 d c. 1797 m — PS VA

RIX,

Daniel: b 9-24-1738 d 3-30-1823 m Rebecca Johnson Tms VT
James: b 6-16-1723 d 4-26-1788 m Hannah Safford Pvt CT
Nathaniel: b 4-17-1753 d 10-12-1828 m Esther Clark Sgt NH
Rufus: b 1759 d 1828 m Lydia Rix Pvt NY
Theophilus: b 12-9-1734 d 5-19-1821 m Lydia Kimball Pvt CT
Thomas: b 12-13-1725 d 1809 m Eunice Kimball Sol CT

RIXEY,

Richard, Jr.: b 1744 d 1808 m Elizabeth Morehead Capt PS VA

RIXFORD,

Wm.: b 12-5-1754 d 1-28-1842 m Lucy Wilson Pvt MA

ROACH,

Isaac: b 7-1-1748 d 8-26-1818 m Martha Scanlan Capt PA
John: b c. 1763 d 8-22-1828 m Abigail Jones Pvt MA W★
John: b 1758-60 d p. 1790 m Deborah Howard Sgt SC
John: b 6-10-1760 d 2- -1823 m Pattey McClanahan Pvt VA
Wm.: b a. 1758 d 1780 m Nancy Roach Lt GA
Wm.: b 1732 d 1787 m Martha Jouett Pvt MD

ROANE,

Alexander: b c. 1750 d p. 10-4-1784 m Elizabeth — PS VA
Archibald: b 1759 d 1-4-1819 m Ann Campbell Sol PA
Christopher: b 1732 d 5-1-1837 m — Pvt PA ★
Christopher: b 1756 d 1824 m Elizabeth Temple Royal Capt VA
Henry, Sr.: b 11-11-1731 d 5-17-1795 m Anna Regina Hartman Pvt PA
James: b a. 1750 d p. 1838 m Elizabeth Lytle Pvt NY
James: b 1752 d 1795 m Ann — Sol SC
John: b 4-12-1749 d 12-9-1833 m Elizabeth Howard Cpl MD
John: b 1753 d 1834 m Sarah Hancock Pvt NH
John: b 4-30-1717 d 10-3-1775 m Mrs Ann Leckey Pvt VA
John: b 1733 d 1829 m Eve Catherine — Pvt PS PA
John: b c. 1745 d p. 12-20-1780 m (1)Miss Janes (2)Betsy Taylor PS VA
Peter, Sr.: b 4-1-1763 d 8-21-1834 m Elizabeth — Pvt PA
Thomas: b 1-10-1761 d c. 1846 m (1)Nancy Phelps (2)Jane — Pvt NC ★
Thomas: b c. 1728 d 1799 m Mary Ann Hipkins Col CS & PS VA
Wm.: b 1743 d 1800 m Elizabeth Cooper Capt VA
Wm.: b a. 1740 d a. 12-19-1785 m Judy Ball PS & Col VA

ROBARDS,

George: b 8-5-1760 d 7-13-1833 m Elizabeth Barbara Sampson Capt VA ★
Jesse: b 4-19-1762 d 12-22-1845 m Frances Ann Perkins Sgt VA ★
Lewis: b 12-5-1758 d 4-15-1814 m (2)Hannah Winn Capt VA W★
Wm.: b 2-10-1749 d 8-9-1802 m Phebe Fuller Pvt NY
Wm., Sr.: b c. 1729 d 12- -1783 m (2)Elizabeth Lewis PS VA
Wm., Jr.: b 1750 d 11-18-1823 m (1)Elizabeth Pleasants Cocke (2)Elizabeth Lewis OrdlSgt VA

ROBARTS,

John: b 2-2-1740 d 4-17-1786 m Mary Lambright Sol GA

ROBB, (includes RABB, RAUB, & ROBBE)

Alexander: b 1726 d 2-3-1806 m Elizabeth Cunningham Capt NH
Andrew: b c. 1740 d 9-5-1804 m (1)Mary Scott (2)Catherine Pentacost Capt PA
Andrew: b 4-25-1734 d 9-19-1807 m Maria Magdalina Klinehaus Ens PA
James: b 1735-40 d p. 4-15-1803 m — Pvt PA
James: b c. 1747 d 1825 m Margaret Barr Pvt PA
James: b 1756 d p. 6-18-1806 m Hannah Barnett Sol SC
John: b c. 1733 d 1804 m Barbara — Capt PA
John: b 1725 d 11-17-1793 m Jerusha Craft Capt PA
John: b a. 1758 d p. 1788 m Monica Dunlap Pvt PA
John: b — d p. 1790 m Sarah — Pvt PA

Peter: b 1-30-1742 d 1827 m Maria Dunlap Pvt PA
Robert: b 9-11-1727 d 9-10-1814 m Susannah Fleming PS CS PA
Robert: b c. 1758 d c. 1825 m Nancy Woodward Pvt PA
Samuel: b 10-11-1760 d 11-9-1833 m Abigail Alexander Pvt NH ★
Samuel: b 1738 d 1829 m — Smith Pvt PA
Wm.: b 1762 d 1813 m Mary Rawlston Pvt PA

ROBBINS, (or ROBINS)

Ammi Ruhamah: b 9-5-1740 d 12-31-1813 m Elizabeth LeBaron Chp CT
Aquilla: b 6-19-1736 d 7-24-1816 m Elizabeth Thurston Sgt MA
Asa: b 5-5-1759 11-30-1840 m Olive Clark Cpl MA
Bela: b 5-2-1761 d 4-19-1831 m Margaret Meservey Pvt MA W★
Benjamin: b 1754 d 11-6-1833 m Kezia Titus Pvt MA
Benjamin: b 1758 d 1837 m Huldah Robinson Pvt MA
Brintnal: b 3-22-1756 d 7-25-1836 m (1)Mary Ansley Boardman (2)Mrs Mary Goodlin Ens CT ★
Daniel, Sr.: b 8-17-1722 d 3-4-1803 m Mary Fisher Pvt MA
Daniel: b 2-27-1757 d 4-27-1823 m (1)Mary Clark (2)L — Guile (3)Eunice Wadsworth Pvt MA ★
Daniel: b 11-15-1760 d 11-8-1838 m Mehitable Fish Pvt MA
David, Jr.: b 7-25-1745 d 12-4-1776 m Lucy Knox Sgt MA
David: b 3-21-1752 d 8-12-1831 m (1)Elizabeth Chapman (2)Mrs Marcy Winslow Pvt MA
David: b 1-27-1742 d 1-31-1811 m Mary Ballard Pvt NH
Ebenezer: b 2-24-1748 d 10-6-1849 m (1)Esther Alworth (2)Zeruiah Carpenter Pvt CT
Eleazer: b 6-9-1724 d 10-19-1776 m Rebecca Jackson Pvt MA
Eliphalet: b 1718 d 1795 m Jemima Norcross PS MA
Ephraim: b 12-11-1759 d 6-16-1844 m Lucina Webster Pvt CT ★
Frederick: b 9-12-1756 d 11-1-1821 m (1)Mehitable Wolcott (2)Sarah Deming (3)Abigail Griswold OrdlSgt CT
George: b 8-5-1761 d 12-15-1846 m (2)Phoebe Reed Pvt MA
Jacob: b 7-11-1729 d 11-25-1778 m Anna Whitcomb Lt MA
Jacob: b c. 1725 d p. 1790 m Lydia Heald Pvt MA
Jason: b 5-12-1762 d 1852 m Honor Riley Pvt MA
Jeremiah: b 8-14-1753 d 10-17-1811 m Elizabeth Keels Pvt MA
Job: b 5-27-1743 d 4-23-1828 m (1)Cynthia Cushman (2)Mrs Martha Gates Pvt CT
Job: b 6-7-1764 d 2-22-1839 m Hope White Tms NJ
John: b 3-21-1754 d 6-6-1831 m Alice Williams Pvt CT
John: b 1-5-1716 d 5-31-1798 m (1)Martha Williams (2)Sarah Wright (3)Mary Rupell PS CT
John: b 3-8-1742 d 1832 m Anna Spence CS MD
John: b 9-1-1751 d 12-20-1820 m Lydia Haskell Pvt MA
John: b — d 1855 m Elizabeth Repine Pvt NJ
John: b 1741 d 5-8-1834 m Sarah — Pvt CT
John: b 4-10-1760 d 1840 m Sarah Dailey Lt PA
John: b 1742 d 7-1-1832 m Susanna Teackle Col PS VA
Jonas: b 1-26-1740 d 6- -1790 m Sybil Darant MM MA
Jonathan: b 8-12-1742 d 7-30-1794 m Lunah — Pvt MA
Jonathan: b 1744 d 12-8-1819 m (1)Mary Fletcher (2)Mrs Susannah Fletcher Parker Lt NH
Joseph: b 12-12-1757 d 7-8-1839 m Elizabeth Stevens Pvt MA ★
Joseph: b 1762 d 9-10-1819 m Lucy Cushing Sgt MA
Joseph: b 2-14-1758 d 1-5-1837 m Elenor Miller Pvt MA ★
Joseph: b c. 1745 d p. 5-21-1790 m Meribah Salter Pvt NJ
Joshua: b 10-30-1722 d 7-30-1796 m Mary Welles PS CT
Joshua, Jr.: b 8-7-1763 d 5- -1848 m Hannah Hart Pvt CT
Joshua: b 2-9-1740 d c. 1796 m Elizabeth Hubbard Pvt PS MA
Josiah: b 7-23-1737 d 1-5-1811 m Sarah Smith Pvt MA
Lemuel: b 1758 d 8-28-1822 m Mary Atwood Cpl MA
Levi: b 4-1-1749 d 1826 m (1)Sarah Wolcott (2)Abigail Kilbourn QM CT
Loren: b 6-16-1760 d 12- -1849 m Catherine Langworthy Pvt CT
Luther: b 8-28-1757 d p. 1794 m Anne Barker QM Sgt MA
Moses: b 1729 d 6-23-1794 m Rhoda Fitzrandolph Pvt NJ
Moses: b 1719 d 11-4-1814 m Kezia Miner Pvt CT
Moses: b 1759 d 5-22-1839 m Thirza Dodge Pvt MA
Oliver: b 3-31-1744 d 3-12-1826 m Mary Rose MM CT
Oliver: b 10-1-1727 d 3-27-1792 m (1)Elioenai Shepard (2)Chloe Blackenton PS ME
Otis: b 10-20-1758 d 5-1-1840 m Mary Keene Pvt MA ★
Peter: b 1753 d c. 1849 m Keziah Hallock Pvt Smn RI
Philip: b 8-20-1730 d 3-9-1816 m Jemima Smith Lt MM MA
Philip: b 2-24-1725 d 1804 m Anna Minot Lt MA
Randall: b 5-27-1739 d 4-19-1798 m (1)Abigail Rogers (2)Rebecca Rogers Pvt NJ
Rufus: b 4-13-1748 d 1776 m Sarah Whittell Pvt MA
Samuel: b 8-30-1749 d 9-19-1839 m Zerviah Cook Capt CT
Samuel: b 8-23-1759 d 2-8-1837 m Esther Sears Pvt CT ★
Samuel: b 10-22-1761 d 11-30-1781 m Anna Griswold Pvt CT
Samuel: b 1752 d 7-27-1838 m Sarah Holmes Pvt MA
Samuel: b 1753 d 10-11-1820 m (2)Elinor Wilber Pvt MA ★
Solomon: b 3-3-1756 d 8-23-1798 m Lois Clark Cpl CT
Solomon: b 1720 d 7-26-1801 m Martha — Pvt MA
Solomon: b 3-30-1743 d p. 1792 m Mary Harmon Pvt MA
Stephen, Sr.: b 6-25-1730 d 3-11-1799 m Sarah Wooton Pvt MA
Stephen, Jr.: bpt 2-5-1758 d 10-12-1847 m Abigail Winship MM & Pvt MA
Thomas: b 8-11-1703 d 6-30-1791 m (1)Ruth Johnson (2)Xenia Jackson MM MA

ROBBINS, contd.

Thomas: b 1749 d 8-27-1821 m Tabitha Ireland Pvt MA
Thomas: b 11-3-1759 d 11-6-1838 m (1)Elizabeth Kline (2)Mrs Mary McLaughlin Pvt NJ ★
Thomas: b 10-6-1763 d 10-29-1850 m Elizabeth Smith Pvt RI ★
Thomas: b 1-8-1740 d p. 1816 m Isabella McLenanhant Capt & PS SC
Thomas: b 2-11-1745 d 11-8-1808 m (1)Frances Stubbs (2)Elizabeth Lee Hoomes Pvt VA
Unni: b 2-9-1742 d 6-17-1810 m Mary Kellogg Ens CT
Wm.: b 4-25-1729 d 1786 m Rebecca Miller Pvt CT
Wm.: b 5-4-1746 d 6-13-1819 m Elizabeth Gray Sol DE
Wm.: b 3-22-1734 d a. 6-28-1814 m Hannah Vincent Pvt MA
Wm., Jr.: b 8-20-1740 d 4-16-1824 m (1)Hannah Paine (2)Nancy Leland Pvt NH
Wm.: b c. 1745/6 d 1-11-1831 m (1)Martha Farmer (2)Phebe — Sol NC
Wm.: b 12- -1745 d 1-20-1838 m (1)Sarah — (2)Polly — Pvt NY
Wm.: b 10-21-1761 d 9-11-1834 m Bethiah Vickery Pvt NC ★
Wm.: b 1749 d p. 1784 m Dorothy Boswell Pvt VA
Zachariah, Jr.: b 3-16-1756 d 8-18-1829 m Abigail Hildreth Sgt MA

ROBE,

Andrew: b 2-25-1758 d p. 1790 m Jane Humphrey Pvt CT

ROBERDEAU,

Daniel: b 1727 d 1-5-1795 m (1)Mary Bostwick (2)Jane Milligan BG PA

ROBERTS, (includes ROBBARTS & ROBERT)

Aaron: b c. 1730 d 11-21-1792 m Mrs Hepzibah Shepard PS CT
Aaron: b 8-19-1755 d 5-12-1815 m Elizabeth Hedden Pvt NJ
Abial: b 4-26-1726 d p. 1778 m (1)Martha Hull (2)Susanna Bissell (3)Temperance Beebe Cpl CT
Absalom: b c. 1740 d p. 1816 m Elizabeth — Pvt SC
Alexander Sanders: b 1766 d p. 9-3-1801 m Mary Whyte Pvt VA
Algernon: b 11-24-1750 d 1815 m Tacy Warner LCol PA
Ashbel: b 3-4-1763 d p. 1787 m Elinor Hills Pvt CT ★
Benjamin: b 1724 d 11-13-1817 m Ann Bostwick PS CT
Benjamin, Sr.: b 11-15-1741 d 9-26-1808 m Dorothy Goodwin Pvt CT
Benjamin: b 1750 d 1802 m (1)— Rothwell (2)Elizabeth Benton 2Lt MD
Benjamin: b 1741 d p. 1790 m Mary Weeks Pvt MA
Benjamin: b 1761 d 8-6-1828 m Anna Weller Pvt VT
Benjamin: b c. 1720 d 2-14-1782 m Anne Dulaney PS VA
Benjamin: b 4- -1750 d 3-17-1837 m Anna Field Capt VA ★
Christopher: b 5-4-1753 d 5-16-1832 m Mary Purdy Sgt VT
Cornelius: b — d c. 1788 m — Sol VA
Cyrus: b c. 1754 d 1793 m Mrs Hundley Capt VA
Daniel: b 1750 d 3-4-1827 m Asenath Tucker Pvt CT W★
Daniel: b 1734/35 d 11-17-1779 m Elizabeth Hincksman LCol GA
Daniel: b 1748 d 7-11-1803 m Sarah Yost Pvt PA
Daniel: b 1759 d 1845 m (1)Elizabeth Kiser (2)Widow James Pvt VA
David: b 4-14-1748 d 1-11-1810 m (1)Phoebe — (2)Mary — Sol CT
David: b c. 1760 d 6-28-1804 m Elizabeth Woodberry Pvt MA
David: b 1727 d p. 1790 m Elizabeth — Pvt PA
David: b 12-17-1760 d 5-5-1847 m — Sgt VT
Dudley: b 7-20-1756 d 3- -1782 m Mary Stead Pvt CT
Ebenezer: b 10-11-1758 d 8-29-1840 m (1)Abigail Dobel (2)Mary Higby (3)Rana Cronwell Pvt CT ★
Edmund: b 1757 d 1848 m prob Miss Watts Sgt NC ★
Edward: b 7- -1739 d 3-3-1810 m Alice Rambo Pvt PA
Edward: b 1754 d 6-17-1832 m Christena Bray Pvt VA ★
Eli: b 4-14-1736 d p. 1794 m Abigail Durand PS VT
Elias: b 5-11-1727 d 7-3-1778 m Susannah Ives Pvt CT
Elias: b c. 1750 d c. 1821 m Mary Rue Pvt SC
Elijah: b 8-19-1761 d 9-26-1843 m Phoebe Hubbard Pvt CT ★
Elisha: b c. 1751 d a. 7-1-1822 m (2)Molly — Pvt VA
Ephraim: b 1745 d 1777 m Phoebe Clark Pvt CT
Ezekiel: b 1746 d 3-27-1828 m Frances Baldwin Lt NY
Frederick: b 1733 d c. 5-5-1823 m Angelina Douglass Sol GA
Freelove: b 9-9-1756 d 12-8-1838 m Anna B — Pvt CT
George: b 11-14-1753 d 10-4-1824 m Jerusha Williams Pvt CT
George: b c. 1758 d 1-1-1864 m Polly Hines King Pvt NC ★
Gideon: b 1749 d 6-20-1813 m Folla Hopkins Ens CT
Gideon: b 8-4-1757 d 5-2-1843 m Jerusha Pitcher Pvt CT ★
Giles: b 1756 d p. 11-10-1829 m Catherine Nights Pvt NH ★
Griffith: b 1750 d 6-7-1823 m Rachel Jefferies Sol PA
Isaac: b c. 1750 d p. 1790 m — PS PA
James: b 5-6-1739 d 12-9-1796 m Jerusha Talcott Pvt CT
James: b c. 1744 d c. 1814 m Emily Williamson Lt GA
James: b 3-19-1731 d — m (1)Sophia Thomas (2)Henrietta Tilghman Capt MD
James: b 1755 d 1-6-1819 m — Pvt MD ★
James: b 5-31-1745 d 6-19-1780 m Martha Woodson LCol MA
James: b 11-5-1757 d 5-5-1806 m Martha Goodwin Mar NH
James: b c. 1765 d 1828 m Rachael — PS PA
James: b c. 1734 d p. 11-29-1802 m Amy — Capt SC
James: b 10-10-1754 d 1815 m Nancy McKelvey Cpl VA
James: b — d 7-15-1815 m Elizabeth Lee Pvt PS VA
Jeremiah: b 11-17-1753 d 10-31-1846 m Lucy Conant Pvt NH MA
Joel: b 7-4-1736 d 2-10-1815 m Abigail Foot Pvt CT

Joel: b 10-24-1736 d 1780 m Esther Loomis Pvt CT
Joel: b 1761 d 8-6-1842 m Sarah Goss Cpl NH ★
John: b 1747 d 1830 m Sarah Clapp Pvt CT
John: b 9- -1747 d 6-19-1837 m Sary Merrill Trm CT
John: b c. 1762 d 12- -1812 m Sarah Tomlinson Pvt GA
John: b 8-27-1757 d 8- -1809 m (1)Mary Horney (2)Elizabeth Kemp Norris PS MD
John: b 6-3-1762 d 10-27-1846 m (1)Martha Roberts (2)Sarah Webster PS MD
John: b 10- -1748 d 8- -1823 m Tabatha Leland Sgt MA
John: b 1741 d 1819 m Elizabeth Hodgdon Pvt NH
John: b 10-4-1754 d 1840 m Hannah Roberts Pvt NH
John, Sr.: b 1-3-1742 d 1792 m Elizabeth Haines Pvt NJ
John, Jr.: b 5-5-1767 d 10-13-1850 m Esther Somers Pvt NJ
John: b 1757 d — m Rachel Shatford De Noyelles Col NY
John, Jr.: b 10-4-1759 d 10- -1842 m Edna Hilliard Drm MY
John: b 1757 d 1798 m Sarah — Lt NC
John: b 1756 d 1832 m Susan Magness Pvt NC
John: b c. 1759 d p. 1811 m Phoeby Weeks 2Lt NC
John: b 5-28-1714 d 10-8-1801 m Jane Hank CaptLt PA
John: b 7-1-1731 d 11-11-1780 m Ann Nanna —Pvt PA
John: b 1749 d a. 4-8-1793 m Catharine — Pvt PA
John: b 4-26-1710 d 1-13-1776 m Rebecca Jones PS PA
John: b 7-15-1742 d 2-24-1826 m Elizabeth Dixon Pvt SC
John: b a. 1752 d c. 1808 m — Sol SC
John, Sr.: b 4-21-1727 d 8-6-1796 m Susanna Mayhew Pvt VT
John: b 4-14-1758 d 11-30-1843 m (2)Lucy Ann Blair Pollard Maj VA W★
John: b — d 1826 m Ann Weisiger Dr VA
John: b c. 1735 d a. 1815 m Frankey — Pvt VA
John: b 1-7-1734 d p. 1796 m Mercy Late Pvt MA
Jonathan: b 6-29-1730 d 12-9-1775 m (1)Marcy Whitmore (2)Catherine Doolittle Lt CT
Jonathan: b 1735 d 4-12-1825 m Ruth Judson Capt CT
Jonathan: b 11-8-1743 d 9-8-1797 m (2)Mary Spencer Pvt PA
Joseph: b 1725 d 3-4-1804 m Thankful Forbes Pvt CT
Joseph, Sr.: b c. 1727 d c. 1805 m Hannah Young Sol MA
Joseph, Jr.: b 2-6-1756 d 1-10-1843 m (1)Esther Hamlin (2)Margaret Hall Pvt MA
Joseph, Jr.: b 5-30-1760 d 2-22-1817 m Tamson Huntress Mar PS NH
Joseph: b 12-29-1762 d 1-15-1841 m Elizabeth Dame Pvt NH
Joseph: b c. 1751 d p. 10-28-1832 m (2)Mrs Clarissa Wright PS NC
Joseph: b c. 1740 d 7-16-1780 m Agnes Seabrooks Pvt PA
Joseph: b c. 1760 d 1820-30 m Betsie Suggs Pvt SC
Joseph: b c. 1751 d a. 12-23-1811 m (1)Elizabeth — (2)Mrs Sarah Woods (3)Sally Hardy Ens VA
Joseph: b c. 1762 d 8-24-1823 m Frances Triplett Sgt VA W★
Joseph, Sr.: b 1728-30 d 1-7-1778 m Agnes Seabrook Pvt VA
Joseph, Jr.: b c. 1752/3 d a. 1-29-1804 m (1)Amelia Smith (2)Betsy Baker PS VA
Joshua: b 7-13-1746 d 3-19-1822 m (1)Joanna Wentworth (2)Mrs Elizabeth Nichols Capt NH
Joshua: b 1760 d p. 1840 m Esther Moore Pvt NC ★
Judah: b 9-13-1763 d 6-11-1829 m Mercy Eno Pvt CT
Lemuel: b 10-2-1742 d 12-19-1789 m Ruth Woodford Capt CT
Lewis: b c. 1755 d c. 1824 m Mary — Pvt SC
Love: b 4-21-1721 d p. 1790 m (1)Mrs Mary Roberts (2)Ann Pray Pvt MA
Luke: b 2- -1768 d 5-26-1846 m (1)Annah — (2)Catherine Jackson Fif CT ★
Martin: b a. 1761 d p. 1807 m Sibyl Moses Pvt NY
Martin: b 5-10-1757 d 10-30-1834 m Elizabeth Durburo Pvt VA ★
Mary: b c. 1747 d p. 1790 m Thomas Roberts Jr PS SC
Matthew: b 1756 d 1788 m Eleanor Vanpelt Pvt NJ
Moses: b 1725 d 1804 m Mary Coe Pvt NJ ★
Nathan: b 12-22-1759 d 6-17-1838 m Leah Rich Pvt PA ★
Nathaniel: b 3-24-1745 d 7-31-1800 m Rhoda Woodford Sgt CT
Obediah: b c. 1750 d p. 11-14-1807 m Mary Wood Pvt VA
Owen: b 1720 d 6-20-1779 m Mrs Ann (Frazier) Cattell Col SC
Patrick Henry: b 3-1-1758 d 3-23-1839 m Catherine Austin Pvt MD ★
Paul: b 5-19-1741 d 1825 m Mindwell Hall Pvt CT
Peter: b 1738-40 d a. 1825 m Anne Grimball PS SC
Peter: b 1750 d 1-24-1804 m Jane Baker Lt VT
Philip: b c. 12-4-1763 d 11-24-1854 m (1)Sarah Kirtley (2)Sarah Hall Pvt SC ★
Pleasant: b c. 1745 d p. 9-8-1797 m — Capt VA
Purchase: b 8-20-1764 d 10-21-1834 m Abigail Royce Pvt NY
Reuben: b 1751 d 8-2-1841 m Mary Milly Ashor Pvt NC ★
Reuben: b 1752 d 11-20-1843 m (1)Peggy Hudson (2)Mary Ann — Pvt SC ★
Richard: b c. 1764 d 10-7-1820 m Tobitha Sanderlin Pvt NC ★
Richard: b 1755 d 1-28-1831 m Mary Pettit Pvt VA ★
Richard Brooke: b 1758 d 1-19-1797 m Everarda Catrina Sophie Van Braam Houckgeest Capt SC
Robert: b 1-12-1741 d 6-18-1791 m Catherine Deshler PS PA
Robert: b 1758 d p. 1789 m Agnes Church Dunn Pvt PA
Robert Morgan: b c. 1730 d 2-28-1801 m Mary Richford Sol PS MD
Samuel: b 3-9-1719/20 d 4-17-1792 m Elizabeth — Pvt CT
Sears, Sr.: b 6-14-1754 d 5-9-1847 m Hannah Harrison Matr NJ ★
Stephen: b 1-22-1760 d 9-13-1827 m Rebecca Richards Cpl CT W★
Stephen: b a. 1755 d c. 11-18-1823 m (1)Sarah Grimes (3)Mrs Elizabeth Campbell PS SC

Thomas: b 1755 d 1813 m Mary Sudler 2Lt MD
Thomas: b 1750 d 7-19-1775 m Sarah Allen Pvt NH
Thomas: b 1754 d 1807 m Ann Biddle SgtMaj NJ
Thomas: b c. 1760 d 1818 m Sarah — Sgt NC
Thomas: b 1-11-1735 d 1-6-1815 m Susanna Kirk Pvt PA
Thomas: b c. 1740 d p. 4-3-1816 m Jane Piatt Pvt PA
Thomas: b 10-27-1762 d 1839 m Mary — Sgt VA ★
Thomas: b 1751 d 1845 m — Kelly Pvt SC VA ★
Timothy: b 4-20-1747 d 3-17-1833 m Sarah Furbur Pvt CT ★
Timothy: b 1759 d 8-3-1835 m Elizabeth Hayes Pvt Mar Slr NH ★
Timothy: bpt 5-11-1740 d p. 1832 m — PS NH
Wm.: b 2-26-1752 d 7-12-1833 m Margaret Merrils Pvt CT MA VT ★
Wm.: b 9-3-1754 d 2-5-1838 m Elizabeth Marvin Sgt MA ★
Wm.: b 2-10-1749 d 8-9-1802 m Phebe Fuller Pvt NY
Wm.: b c. 1756 d p. 1799 m Nancy Parish Pvt NC
Wm.: b 3-11-1739 d 1814 m Rachel Griffiths Col PA
Wm.: b c. 1730 d 1797 m (1)Elizabeth — (2)Sarah — Ens PA
Wm.: b 1759 d 1829 m Rachel Andrus Pvt VT
Wm.: b 1762 d 1835 m Hannah Frick Pvt VA ★
Wm.: b c. 1730 d p. 1820 m — CS VA
Zachariah: b c. 1760 d 4-13-1830 m Sarah Netherland Harris Pvt VA

➤ ROBERTSON, (includes ROBERSON)

Alexander: b 11-22-1748 d 8-15-1802 m Margaret Robinson CS VA
Andrew: b 1-27-1740 d 7-8-1823 m Mary (or Mercy) Hall Pvt NH
Andrew: b 1763 d 9-5-1845 m Rosamond Dennis Pvt PA
Andrew: b 1716 d 3-1-1795 m (1)Ann Monroe (2)Ellen Chichester (3)Ann Elizabeth Glasscock PS VA
Archibald: b 1707 d 1803 m Elizabeth Watson PS NH
Archibald: b c. 1748 d 6-18-1814 m (1)Martha Selfridge (2)Rebecca Carswell (3)Elizabeth Bishop Pvt NY
Benjamin: b 7-12-1756 d p. 1840 m Sara Allen Ens NC ★
Charles: b c. 1740 d p. 8-5-1799 m — Maj NC
Charles: b 1740 d p. 8-31-1798 m Susan Nichols Maj CS PS NC
Charles: b 1729 d 1795 m Margaret Lindsay CS NC
Charlotte Reeves: b 1-2-1751 d 6-11-1843 m James Robertson PS TN
Christopher: b c. 1755 d 1805 m Constant Edmundson Capt CS VA
Daniel: b c. 1756 d 10-19-1834 m Esther Nichols FifMaj CT W★
Daniel: b 12-21-1721 d 2-6-1793 m (1)Hannah Hinsdale (2)Susannah Robertson Pvt CT
David, Jr.: b 1752 d 7-17-1823 m Jane Hayden Pvt GA
Donald: b 9-27-1717 d 1-30-1783 m (1)Henrietta Maxwell (2)Rachel Rogers PS VA
Edward: b 4-10-1753 d 4-21-1848 m Catherine Methard Pvt MD ★
Edward: b c. 1750 d 1826 m Mary Pulliam Thompson Pvt VA
Elijah: b 1744 d 4-4-1797 m Sarah Maclin Capt PS NC
Elisha: b 1744 d 1830 m Mary Borrough Pvt VA
Ephraim: b 4-29-1746 d 10-17-1826 m Priscilla Clark Pvt CT ★
George: b 1757 d 10-3-1826 m Lydia Garrett Pvt NY
George: b c. 1740 d 1795 m Michael Archer LCol VA
George: b 1740-50 d 1-2-1819 m Judith Scruggs Pvt VA W★
Henry: b b 8-12-1746 d 4-18-1828 m (1)Sallie Collins (2)Winifred C — Pvt NC
Henry: b a. 1762 d p. 8-13-1791 m Elizabeth — Sol PS SC
Henry: b 1708/9 d 4-24-1782 m Tralucia Stegar PS VA ⟋Amelia
Hugh: b 1762 d 1820 m Elizabeth Campbell Sol NC
James: b 3-8-1741 d 3-19-1830 m (1)Sarah Bancroft (2)Mary (Trowbridge) Snow Lt NH
James: b 6-28-1742 d 9-1-1814 m Charlotte Reeves Col CS PS NC
James: b. 1759 d 1799 m X Pvt NC
James: b 10- -1759 d 4-26-1838 m Sarah Morris Pvt SC ★
James: b 11-16-1738 d 8-18-1836 m Margaret Poage LCol VA
James: b c. 1729 d c. 1789 m Nancy — Pvt VA
James: b 1737 d 1-3-1828/9 m Mary Fuqua Pvt VA
James: b 1744 d 11-29-1819 m Rachel Phair PS VA
James Francis: b c. 1749 d 1778 m Lucretia Townd Adj VA
Jeffrey: b 1709 d 12-16-1784 m Judith Tanner Mills PS VA
Jesse: b c. 1758 d p. 1-7-1830 m Susannah Bryant Pvt NC ★
Jesse: b 1758 d 12-2-1846 m Sarah White Pvt VA ★
John: b 6-8-1732 d 10-11-1816 m (1)Lydia Gale (2)Elizabeth Lovejoy Pvt PS NH
John: b 10-29-1749 d 3-2-1823 m Mary Crane Pvt NJ
John: b c. 1755 d 1799 m Lavinia Thatcher Pvt NJ
John: b 1750 d 1836 m Patsy — Pvt NC
John: b 10-20-1742 d 1808 m Mary Anne Walthall 1Lt VA
John: b 8-12-1749 d 11-23-1820 m Elizabeth Korn Pvt VA ★
John: b 11-6-1763 d 8-30-1845 m Kenyon Pollard Pvt VA ★
John: b 5-6-1750 d 12-18-1832 m (2)Zuriah — Pvt VA W★
John: b c. 1753 d a. 1-11-1809 m Sylvia Wildy 1Lt VA
Joseph: b c. 21-1760 d 10-12-1834 m Margaret Derby Pvt NC
Mathew: b c. 1720 d p. 2-18-1786 m Martha — CS VA
Matthew: b 1-12-1762 d 8-15-1844 m Susan Hogan Pvt Spy VA ★
Nathan: b 1752 d 3-19-1827 m Elizabeth Speaks Pvt PS MD
Norvell: b 5-22-1765 d 9-16-1855 m Sarah Powell Pvt VA
Peter: b 1-1-1743 d 1-31-1807 m Mary Seaton Pvt NH ★
Peter: b c. 1753 d p. 8-5-1837 m Elizabeth Newell Pvt NC W★
Richard: b c. 1750 d p. 1800 m Sarah Rebecca Penn Pvt NC
Robert: a 1744 d p. 1783 m Josephine — Pvt NY
Samuel: b c. 1757 d p. 1-4-1778 m Hannah Crane PS NJ
Seth: bpt 8-11-1754 d 12-6-1811 m Hannah Lyon Pvt CT W★
Thomas: b 1-11-1740 d 5-2-1785 m Mary Bartram Col PS NC

Thomas: b 1740 d 1801 m Lucretia — Pvt NC
Thomas: b 1759 d 1845 m Margaret Smart Pvt NC
Wm.: b 11-12-1748 d 8-19-1828 m Mary Timms Pvt MD
Wm.: b 2-27-1748 d 12-18-1824 m (1)Mary Barnes (2)Nancy Hawley (3)Ellen Woodward Pvt SC
Wm.: b 11-7-1759 d 1-20-1816 m Rhoda Sartin Pvt VA
Wm.: b 1755-60 d p. 1-6-1830 m (1)Elizabeth Collins (2)Ann Grinnan Sol PS VA
Wm.: b 2-5-1750 d 12-11-1829 m Elizabeth Bolling PS VA
Wm.: b 2-2-1754 d 4-9-1833 m Rebecca House Pvt VA
Wm. M.: b 1758 d 1-17-1845 m Nancy Shubert Pvt VA
Zachariah: b 5-6-1760 d 1-16-1839 m (1)Mary — (2)Elizabeth Jones Pvt MD ★

ROBESON, (see ROBERTSON & ROBINSON)

ROBINETT, (includes ROBINETTE)

Allin: b 3-25-1735 d 1777-85 m Ann Collins Pvt DE
George: b 5-10-1745 d 8-5-1804 m Agnes Brandon 1Lt PA
Jesse: b 12-8-1755 d 1832 m Phebe — Pvt NC

ROBINSON,

Abiathar: b — d p. 11-22-1779 m — Parsons Lt MA
Abner: b 2-22-1738 d 11-24-1815 m Mehitabel Palmer Capt CT
Abraham: b 1-5-1741 d 3-4-1787 m Sarah Penrose PS DE
Alexander: b 7-19-1750 d 2-22-1831 m (3)Hannah Oliver Sgt MA
Alexander: b 3-23-1748 d 12-15-1835 m Agner Dickey Pvt PA
Amos: b 8-19-1762 d 3-13-1840 m (1)Bethany Jones (2)Mrs Submit Holden QM VT
Amos: b 9-7-1735 d 8-13-1809 m Hepsibeth Wilmot Sol VT
Andrew: b 8-1-1762 d 6-10-1849 m (1)Olive Hovey (2)Bethiah Church Pvt CT ★
Andrew: b c. 1760 d p. 1810 m Sarah — Sol NC
Andrew: b — d p. 8-25-1812 m Elizabeth Harrison Pvt PA
Andrew: b c. 1750 d 1794 m Margaret Smith Pvt PA
Archibald: b 1-31-1737 d 2-25-1820 m Margaret Watson 2Lt MA
Archibald: b 1-31-1716 d p. 1792 m Mary Field Pvt MA
Asa, Sr.: b 10-17-1726 d 1811 m Mary French Pvt CT
Asa, Jr.: b 6-6-1757 d p. 1799 m Olive Huntington Pvt CT
Asher: bpt 5-4-1740 d 5-4-1808 m Margaret Butcher PS CT
Benjamin: b 4-24-1749 d 1-18-1828 m Sarah Winston Pvt CT
Benjamin: b 5-5-1749 d 3-5-1833 m Ruth Johnson Pvt CT
Benjamin: b 1730 d 12-7-1809 m Mary Connor Pvt MA
Benjamin: b 9-20-1748 d 3-5-1829 m (1)Eve Packard (2)Mrs Keziah (Ames) Packard Pvt MA
Benjamin: b 1755 d 5-31-1848 m Susannah North Sgt VA ★
Benjamin: b 7-2-1758 d 9-4-1840 m (1)Magdalene Webb (2)Mrs Mary Wilkinson Sgt VA
Benjamin: b 12-17-1752 d 1835 m (1)Mrs Mildred (Burbridge) Ellis (2)Agnes Waller Pvt VA KY ★
Caleb: b 5-22-1746 d 7-26-1799 m Mary Waterhouse Maj NH
Chandler: b 12- -1761 d 1848 m Lois Grannis Pvt PA
Charles: b 8-28-1761 d p. 1778 m Chloe Darte Pvt CT
Charles: b a. 1754 d c. 1787 m Amy Holstein Capt PA
Charles: b 1751 d 1813 m Ann — Pvt VA
Charles: b 7-4-1763 d 8-13-1846 m Asseneth Martin Pvt VA
Chase: b 12-15-1738 d 7-27-1829 m Priscilla Pratt PS NH
Christopher, Sr.: b 12-31-1727 d 1807 m Ruhamah Champlain PS RI
Christopher, Jr.: b 11-26-1756 d 1841 m Elizabeth Anthony Capt RI
Christopher: b 5-25-1756 d 8-12-1803 m Hannah Atwood CaptLt RI W★
Clifford: b 1-30-1756 d 7-11-1813 m Lucy Morgan Pvt CT
Comfort: b 6-7-1740 d 1828 m Rachel (Bates) Robinson Pvt MA
Cornelius: b 1735 d 1798 m Elizabeth Pickett CS NC
Dan, Sr.: b 5-16-1725 d 8-12-1810 m Abigail Curtiss CS MA
Dan, Jr.: b 8-29-1758 d 6-12-1833 m Elizabeth Cowdry Pvt MA
Daniel: b 1-18-1732 d a. 10-19-1815 m Mary Flint PS CT
Daniel: b 5-19-1757 d 3-25-1838 m Thankful Sage Pvt CT ★
Daniel: b 5-27-1735 d 1820 m Lucretia Parce Pvt MA
Daniel: b c. 1748 d c. 1819 m Abigail Sayre Pvt PS NJ
Daniel: b 1738 d 8-23-1832 m Rachel Nixon NQM PA
David, Jr.: b 3-4-1721/2 d 3-8-1778 m Esther Cromwell PS CT
David, 3d: b 1749 d 11-15-1826 m (1)Mary Sage (2)Naomi Pease PS CT
David: b 1694 d 2-9-1780 m Rebecca Miller PS CT
David: b 12-13-1752 d 12- -1807 m Elizabeth Hopkins Ens MD
David: b 3-16-1761 d 1851 m Anna Whitaker Pvt MA ★
David: b 3-2-1758 d 6-14-1834 m Elizabeth Eastman Pvt NH
David: b 4-6-1748 d 5-4-1819 m Agnes Moor PS NH
David: b c. 1740 d p. 1793 m Mary Rayner Sol NY
David: b 3-9-1765 d 2-26-1835 m Elizabeth Hunt Pvt NY ★
David: b 1726 d 10-12-1808 m Mary Hayes Pvt CS NC
David: b 11-11-1754 d 12-12-1843 m (1)Sarah Fay (2)Eunice Wallbridge (3)Mary Johnson PS CT
David: b c. 1760 d 1816 m Nancy Mitchell Sol VA
Denison: b 9-18-1746 d 11-17-1827 m Millicent Cutler Capt MA
Ebenezer: b 10-26-1726 d a. 1808 m Mary Bennett PS CT
Ebenezer: b 2-14-1763 d 10-31-1837 m Hannah Ackley Pvt Pvtr MA
Ebenezer: b 1733 d p. 1800 m Anne Stone Maj NY
Eber: b 10- -1759 d 10-28-1838 m (2)Lucinda Converse Ens CT
Edward: b 6- -1763 d 12- -1836 m (1)Wealthy Tracy (2)Eunice Rix Pvt MA

ROBINSON, contd.

Eleazer: b 1736 d 1822 m — Clark Pvt PS NH
Elias: b 4-14-1757 d 2-28-1805 m (1)Sybil Little (2)Annie Luce Lt CT
Elias: b 1761 d 4-23-1838 m (1)Anne Allyn (2)Mrs Betsey Crary Pvt CT ★
Elijah: b 10-1-1735 d 1-25-1809 m Lydia Scripture Capt CT
Elijah: b 7-25-1750 d 8-6-1826 m Mary Dike Pvt CT
Elijah: b 10-3-1727 d 4-14-1799 m Sarah Smith Pvt MA
Elijah: b 8-1-1736 d 1818 m Sarah Blake Pvt MA
Elisha: b 4-24-1764 d 1-26-1846 m Sally Cobb Pvt MA
Enoch: b 11-4-1736 d 11-6-1798 m Mindwell Shepard Capt MA
Ephraim: b 5-13-1760 d 1843 m Mary Upham Pvt CT
Experience: b 4-22-1728 d 9-10-1807 m Zerviah Palmer PS CT
Ezra: b 12-10-1764 d 10- -1849 m Elizabeth Moon Pvt NY
Francis: b 3-2-1765 d 12-31-1840 m Mary Emil Ann Terrill Pvt VA ★
Gain: b 1724 d 1778 m — Dyer Pvt MA
George, Sr.: b 7-23-1726 d 8-19-1812 m (1)Abigail Everett (2)Zipporah Allen Cpl MA
George, Jr.: b 11-23-1754 d 9-15-1847 m Asenath Carpenter Pvt CT
George: b 1727 d 3-6-1814 m (1)Ann Wiley (2)Mary Martin Capt PA
Gideon: b a. 1757 d p. 1802 m Hannah Mead Pvt PS NH
Hanse: b c. 1735 d p. 1790 m Priscilla Hyler Maj MA
Henry: b c. 1740 d p. 1802 m Jenny — Pvt PA
Henry: b c. 1755 d 1826 m Rebecca Wallace Pvt PA
Increase: b 4-26-1756 d 11-21-1816 m Mary Josslyn Cox Lt MA
Increase: b 5-28-1739 d 1-9-1817 m Rebecca Bourne Pvt MA
Isaac: b 1740 d 3-9-1814 m Mary (Robinson) Pvt MA
Isaac: b 1738 d 1818 m Rachel Webb Pvt NC
Isaac: b c. 1735 d 2- -1796 m Jane — Pvt PA
Isaiah: b 5- -1755 d 4- -1838 m Sarah Foote Pvt CT
Isaiah: b 5-20-1729 d p. 1790 m Amy Chappell Pvt NY
Issicar: b 1756 d 1833 m Hulda Millard Pvt NY ★
Jacob: b 2-3-1738 d 6-18-1776 m Elizabeth Draper Pvt MA
Jacob: b 3-9-1765 d 2-26-1835 m Elizabeth Hunt Pvt NY ★
James: b 6-10-1731 d 3-3-1806 m Amy Spellman Capt CT
James: b 1730 d 8-26-1793 m Jerusha Bartlett Pvt MA
James: b 1-30-1732 d 1808 m Sarah Breck Pvt MA
James: b 9-24-1757 d 1-18-1833 m Abigail Hutchings Pvt MA ★
James, Jr.: b 11-26-1761 d 11-29-1836 m Judith Reed Pvt MA ★
James: b — d a. 1-15-1798 m Mary Nelson Sol MD
James: b 1-4-1739 d 12-13-1803 m Dorothy Tyford PS NH
James: b 6-19-1749 d 9-20-1820 m Sarah Drake PS CL NY
James: b 2-7-1741 d 2-1-1815 m Anna Moody Pvt PA
James: b 1750 d 5-15-1799 m Sarah Taylor Capt VA
James: b c. 1757 d 2-20-1801 m Winnefred Fox Capt VA
James: b c. 1745 d 12-5-1792 m Ann Kirkwood Sol VA ★
James: b 1722 d 10-25-1806 m Hannah Rose PS VA
Jared: b 1743 d 9-5-1810 m Mary Thompson Lt CT
Jeremiah: b 4-4-1742 d 7-16-1815 m Susanna Coggswell Pvt MA
Jeremiah: b 1757 d 8- -1836 m Drusilla Lamb Pvt VA ★
Jesse: b 11-25-1760 d 10-30-1840 m (1)Molliana Weidner (2)Mary Ann Mull Pvt NC
Joel: b 5-5-1760 d 2-7-1834 m Mary Wilkinson Pvt MA
John: b 1748 d p. 4-27-1806 m Keziah Elizabeth — PS MD
John: b 7-24-1735 d 1805 m Huldah Putnam Col MA
John: b 9-2-1739 d 1-26-1810 m Rebecca Wood Capt MA
John: b 5-20-1760 d 2-14-1826 m Deborah Cummings Pvt MA ★
John: b 7-26-1761 d 11-19-1835 m Naomi Bliss Pvt NH ★
John: b 5-3-1759 d 3-7-1848 m Lydia Pitman Pvt NH ★
John: b 8-6-1736 d 10-11-1816 m (1)Abigail Whidden Sol NH
John: b 1744 d 6-26-1832 m Eunice Wilcox Sol NY
John: b c. 1753 d p. 11-9-1815 m Lydia Brinn Pvt Mus NC
John: b 3-7-1759 d 9-7-1842 m Abigail Moore Pvt NC W★
John: b 12-8-1755 d p. 1-14-1833 m Margaret Logan Lt PA ★
John: b c. 1750 d p. 1788 m Jean Stuart Ens PA
John: b 7-26-1742 d p. 1780 m Phebe Clapp Pvt RI
John, Sr.: b 1-13-1742/3 d 6-3-1805 m (1)Sarah Pecklaw (2)Hannah Stewart Cpl RI
John, Jr.: b 1754 d p. 1835 m Mary Raymond Drm SC
John: b 12-22-1750 d 5-4-1856 m (1)Elizabeth Piland (2)Polly Webb Capt VA
John: b c. 1740 d 1800 m Gartry Van Lear 2Lt VA
John: b 1755 d p. 9-13-1841 m Sarah — Pvt VA ★
John: b 1736 d 5-12-1815 m Janet Edgar Pvt VA
John: b — d 1814 m Barbara — PS VA
John: b c. 1707/8 d p. 1785 m (1)Anne Reade (2)Frances (Yates) Reade (3)Priscilla Churchill PS VA
John R.: b 5-6-1756 d 12-18-1832 m Jeriah Landers Pvt VA W★
Jonah: b 11-3-1750 d 2-24-1814 m Johannah Daniels Pvt PS PA
Jonathan: b 4-26-1760 d 3-29-1849 m Elizabeth Rouse Pvt CT
Jonathan: b — d c. 1776 m (1)Lucretia Thorp (2)Elizabeth Canfield Pvt PS CT
Jonathan: b 6-25-1753 d 3-17-1838 m Elizabeth Chadwick Sgt MA ★
Jonathan: b 1730 d 11-5-1805 m Sarah Kent Pvt MA
Jonathan: b 4-21-1742 d 1-30-1821 m Anna Batting Pvt MA
Jonathan: b 1741 d 1800 m Abigail Page Capt NH
Jonathan: b c. 1715 d c. 1785 m Mercy Chase PS NH
Jonathan: b 6-15-1752 d 7-11-1834 m Jean Black Capt PA
Jonathan: b 8-24-1756 d 11-3-1819 m Mary Fassett Cpl VT
Joseph: b c. 1750 d 1798 m Elizabeth — Pvt DE

Joseph: b 9-13-1727 d 12-16-1814 m Martha Hedge Pvt MA
Joseph: b 1756 d 12-15-1843 m Sally — Pvt NH ★
Joseph: b — d 11-3-1776 m Freelove Martin OrdlSgt RI W★
Joseph: b 4- -1743 d 9-4-1829 m (1)Ann — (2)Mrs Rebecca Greer Lt SC W★
Joseph: b 2- -1743 d 3-25-1820 m Mary Lucas Pvt VT
Joseph: b c. 1734 d p. 1785 m Rosannah — Pvt VT
Joshua: b 9-24-1748 d 12-13-1834 m Sybil Webb Sgt CT ★
Joshua: b 1738 d 3-25-1813 m Sarah Miller Pvt MA
Lemuel: b 3-4-1736 d 7-29-1776 m Jerusha Minot Col MA
Lemuel: b 1-4-1758 d 3-20-1823 m Comfort Pike Pvt MA
Leonard: b 7-27-1736 d 9-29-1827 m (1)Rebecca Billings (2)Mercy Freeman (3)Eunice Holmes Pvt VT
Levi: b 9-18-1753 d 10-22-1849 m Mary Leavitt Pvt NH ★
Levi: b 6-23-1758 d p. 1-27-1840 m — Pvt NH ★
Littleberry: b 1715 d 1792 m Susanna Rottenberry Capt VA
Maxmillian: b 1752 d 4-22-1831 m Lucinda Gundy Pvt VA ★
McKinney: b c. 1750 d 1829 m Elizabeth Walmesley Pvt VA
Michael: b c. 1732 d a. 2- -1807 m Mary Ray PS NC
Moses, Sr.: b c. 1731 d 11-23-1795 m Mary McFarlane PS MA
Moses, Jr.: b 1757 d 1836 m Jane Burton Sgt MA ★
Moses: b 5-3-1757 d 5-22-1839 m Hannah Smith Pvt MA ★
Moses: b 3-26-1741 d 5-26-1813 m (1)Mary Fay — (2)Mrs Artemas Howe Col VT
Nathaniel: b 3-12-1759 d 4-1-1842 m Susanna Hamblin Pvt CT ★
Nathaniel: b 5-12-1752 d 9-29-1841 m Hannah Woodcock Sgt MA ★
Nathaniel: b c. 1728 d 1777 m Lydia — PS NH
Nathaniel: b 4-4-1724 d 1815 m Kezia Robbins CS PS VT
Noah: b 5-7-1757 d 2-10-1827 m (1)Nancy Wiggin (2)Mrs Elizabeth Walker (Osborne) Brown Capt NH ★
Noah: b 4-16-1758 d c. 1846 m Mary Foote Pvt NY CT ★
Noah: b 3-5-1757 d 11-21-1848 m Abigail Draper Pvt MA RI VT ★
Oliver: b 1766 d 1830 m Elizabeth Johnson Pvt MA ★
Otis: b 6-7-1764 d 3-1-1835 m Hannah Reed Pvt MA ★
Peter: b 7-8-1742 d 9-20-1792 m (1)Sarah Buck (2)Mehitable Sunderland Pvt MA
Peter: b 7-27-1757 d 2-14-1849 m Jane Carlton Pvt MA
Peter: b 4-4-1761 d 5-21-1849 m Phebe Haight Pvt NY ★
Peter: b 1749 d 4-4-1794 m Elizabeth Lord Capt PS NC
Philip: b 11-26-1760 d 12-17-1843 m Mary Perry Sgt MA ★
Ralph: b c. 1748 d p. 3-2-1801 m Elizabeth Rossiter Pvt PA
Randal: b 5-2-1762 d 2-27-1842 m (1)Lydia — (2)Pheriby Hill Pvt SC
Reuben, Sr.: b 1-17-1725 d a. 9-8-1812 m Esther Palmer Pvt CT
Reuben, Jr.: b 1-13-1759 d p. 1834 m Urania Kingsley Pvt CT ★
Reuben: b 8-6-1753 d 1834 m Abigail Burke Sgt VT ★
Richard: b 5-13-1763 d 12-15-1835-38 m Huldah — Pvt CT ★
Robert: b 2-28-1754 d 4-12-1822 m Nancy — PS DE
Robert: b 1-9-1747 d 5-2-1845 m Jane Webb Pvt MA
Robert: b 1762 d 1848 m Deborah Randell Pvt Drm MA ★
Robert: b 1751 d 8-26-1839 m Martha Montgomery Pvt NC SC ★
Robert: b 1739 d 6-23-1836 m Rachel Wier Pvt PA
Robert: b 1763 d 11-19-1815 m Agnes McGuire PS PA
Robert: b a. 1740 d 1803 m Lucretia — Pvt SC
Samuel, Sr.: b 7-26-1726 d 6-11-1792 m Sarah Kimball Pvt CT
Samuel: b 6-7-1752 d 3-2-1815 m Priscilla Metcalf PS NY or CT
Samuel: b 1758 d 8-1-1806 m Elizabeth Emery DrmMaj ME W★
Samuel: b 1744 d 7-12-1811 m Mary Perkins CS ME MA VA
Samuel: b c. 1748 d p. 3-19-1806 m (1)Ruth Raynor (2)Anna Moore PS NY
Samuel: b 1723 d 11-15-1807 m (1)Jean Snoddy (2)Mrs Letitia Montgomery Pvt PS PA
Samuel: b 12-9-1765 d 10-11-1821 m Hannah Krist Pvt PA
Samuel: b 8-15-1738 d 5-3-1813 m (1)Hannah Clark (2)Esther Safford Col CS PS VT
Seth: b 9- -1745 d 11-3-1835 m Rachel Braman Pvt MA
Seth: b 8-21-1750 d 4-25-1835 m Hannah Williams Cpl MA
Shadrach: b 2-7-1758 d 4-6-1842 m Deborah Robinson Pvt MA
Silas: b 11-19-1721 d 9-4-1801 m Susannah Moore Pvt MA
Solomon: b c. 1750 d p. 6-6-1799 m Frances Rice PS VA
Stephen: b 8-25-1760 d 2-19-1843 m Phebe Butler Sgt VT
Stephen, Sr.: b c. 1745 d p. 3-11-1828 m Betty Holland Pvt VA
Thomas: b 1-25-1730 d 1817 m Sarah Richardson NCapt PS CT NY
Thomas: b 7-17-1758 d 9-6-1811 m (1)Elizabeth Jacobs (2)Elizabeth Selby PS MD
Thomas: b 2-10-1753 d 8-31-1815 m Rebecca Paige Sgt MA
Thomas: b 4-20-1718 m 1-4/5-1802 m Mary Warner PS 1Lt MA
Thomas: b 9-18-1753 d 4-22-1839 m Mary Wilson Ens NH
Thomas: b 1754 d 4-22-1839 m Mary Robinson Ens NH ★
ThomasJr.: b 1-11-1740 d 5-2-1785 m Mary Bartram Col PS NC
Thomas: b 1733 d p. 1820 m — Sol NC
Thomas: b 3-30-1751 d 11-21-1819 m Mary (Eyre) Coates Col PA
Thomas: b c. 1754 d 8- -1792 m Catherine Dawson LCol PA
Thomas: b 1729 d 1811 m Jane Simmons Capt PA
Thomas: b 1754 d 7-4-1852 m Nancy McMillan Pvt PA
Timothy: b 4-29-1728 d 4-1-1805 m Catherine Rose Col MA
Wm.: b 10-25-1732 d 2-16-1805 m Anna Blake PS CT
Wm.: b a. 1757 d 4-25-1815 m Anne Duff Capt DE
Wm.: b 1738 d 4-23-1813 m Rebecca (Rea) Minot Sgt MA
Wm.: b 12-26-1757 d 5-2-1830 m Mary Stinson Pvt MA
Wm.: b 1-25-1760 d 6-30-1837 m Sarah Duckworth Pvt NC
Wm.: b 1733 d 6-15-1812 m Martha Houston Pvt NC

Wm.: b 1-8-1743 d 1-16-1814 m Elizabeth — PS NC
Wm.: b c. 1759 d c. 1796 m Margery McNaughton Pvt PA
Wm.: b 1730 d 1810 m Sarah Roseberry Pvt PA
Wm.: b c. 1736 d 1834 m Mrs Sarah Baker Sol SC
Wm., Jr.: b c. 1750 d c. 1804 m Ann Johnston Lt VA
Wm.: b 8-2-1748 d p. 4-27-1837 m — Lt VA ★
Wm.: b 3-25-1709 d 1792 m (1)Agatha Beverly (2)Agness Smith Col VA
Wm.: b 4- -1743 d 10-18-1815 m (2)Margaret (See) Roach PS VA
Winthrop: b 4-22-1761 d 11-5-1836 m Beulah Rice Lt NH ★
Zachaeus: b 3-1-1764 d 1-17-1859 m Bridget Winchester Pvt MA ★
Zebulon: b 2-9-1743 d 1-18-1824 m Mrs Lydia Sears Pvt MA
Zephaniah: b 7-26-1729 d 3-27-1805 m (1)Ann Hatch (2)Jediah West Pvt MA

ROBISON,
Alexander: b 1732 d 1811 m Elizabeth Hardy Pvt PA
George: b c. 1756 d 5-10-1810 m Elizabeth Griffith Pvt PA
George: b 1730 d 1805 m Elizabeth Ann Stewart PS SC
James: b 1753 d 5-5-1839 m (1)Catherine Rummell (2)Sarah Cleland Pvt MD PA NJ CT ★
James: bpt 11-2-1740 d 6-2-1791 m Rachel Brusie Capt NY
James: b c. 1755 d 1804 m Agnes — Ens PA
James: b 8-1-1757 d 4- -1813 m Jane Hardy Pvt PA
John: bpt 10-9-1765 d 2- -1838 m Antje Terwilliger Pvt NY
John: b 1751 d 3-31-1833 m Jannet Thompson Pvt NY
John: b 1745 d 9-7-1818 m (1)Jean — (2)— QMSgt PA
John: b 10-20-1755 d 4-2-1821 m Barbara Dumbaul PS PA
John Decker: b 5-11-1742 d 1-18-1826 m (1)Elizabeth House (2)Lana Scutt PS NY
Robert: b 1737 d 4-21-1821 m Mary Taggart PS PA
Samuel: b 2-27-1764 d 5-10-1830 m Jane Orbison Pvt PA
Wm.: b c. 1735 d p. 1818 m (1)— (2)Sarah Lark PS SC

ROBOSSON,
Elijah: b 2-26-1731 d 9-15-1796 m (1)Elizabeth — (2)Mary — Col MD

ROBY, (includes ROBIE, RUBEY & RUBY)
Ebenezer: b 6-15-1732 d 1786 m Abigail Moffatt Pvt MA
Edward: b 4-23-1746 d 12-26-1837 m Sarah Smith Pvt NH
Henry: b 10-16-1752 d 1788 m Ruth Rowe 3Sgt NH
James: b 1734 d 4-19-1802 m Ann Boynton Cpl NH
John: b 9-9-1757 d 8-9-1830 m Esther Howe Pvt CT
John: b 8-5-1712 d 3-9-1788 m (1)Ann Williams (2)Abigail Varnum (3)Mrs Naomi Long PS NH
John: b 7-23-1743 d 9-11-1824 m Mary Eastman Sol PS CS NH
Joseph: b 5-12-1724 d 1-31-1803 m (1)Rachel Proctor (2)Zerah Marston PS MA
Joseph, Jr.: b 1753 d 4-13-1836 m (1)— Rogers (2)Relief Curtis Capt MA
Philip Abbot: b 9-2-1754 d 7-8-1828 m Lucy Proctor Pvt MA
Samuel: b 12-24-1761 d 11-26-1822 m Dorothy Worthen Pvt NH
Samuel: b c. 1720 d — m (1)— (2)Martha Marshall PS NH
Stephen: b c. 1730 d c. 1790 m Lydia Shaw Pvt NH
Walter: b 5-2-1741 d 6-28-1818 m Susan Hall PS CS NH
Wm.: b 3-15-1742 d 1776 m Hannah Lund Lt NH
Wm.: b 1750 d 1780-82 m Jemima Lewis Sgt VA

ROCHAMBEAU,
Jean Baptiste Donatien de Vimeur, Comte de: b 7-1-1725 d 5-10-1807 m Thérèse de Tellez d'Acosta Cdr FrA

ROCHE,
Edward: b 4-10-1754 d 4-6-1821 m Eliza Brinckle Lt DE
Frederick Franck de la (Baron): b 5-17-1757 d 12-2-1805 m Elizina Marie Merkus-Lespiness ADC FrA
John Philip: b 1756 d 1836 m — Pvt MD
Thomas: b 1723 d 7-30-1777 m Ann Howard Pvt MD

ROCHELLE,
Hinchey: b a. 9-21-1759 d p. 7-10-1832 m Jemima — PS VA
John: b c. 1730 d p. 1784 m Judith Gillan Sol VA
John: b 1748 d 5-16-1802 m Patience Thomas Capt NC W★

ROCHESTER,
Daniel: b 1759 d 7-13-1820 m (1)Hannah Casy (2)Ann Dodson Pvt MD
John: b 1745 d 12- -1794 m (1)Ann Jordan (2)Ann (South) McClannahan Capt VA
Nathaniel: b 2-21-1752 d 5-17-1831 m Sophia Beatty Maj PS CS NC

ROCK,
John: b 1737 d 3-26-1821 m Catherine McClellan Pvt NC

ROCKEFELLER, (includes ROCKAFELLER & ROCKEFELLOW)
David: b 1759 d 7-19-1833 m (1)Hannah Phillips (2)Margaret Risler Pvt NJ
Diel, Jr.: b 8-27-1739 d 11-30-1811 m (1)Anna Maria Maul (2)Elizabeth Sealbeck Capt NY

John: b 11-3-1742 d 12-19-1832 m (1)Margaret Kitchen (2)Catherine La Rue 1Lt NJ
Peter, Sr.: b 3-22-1711 d 1787 m (1)Mary Bellis (2)Elizabeth Peterson Pvt NJ
Peter, Jr.: b 1740 d 1806 m Catherine La Rue Ens NJ
Peter: b 4-6-1732 d p. 1782 m (1)Catherine Blass (2)Eva Christ Lt NY
Philip: b 5-29-1745 d a. 6-3-1813 m (1)Catherine Sharp (2)Catherine Best Adj NY
Simeon: b 1-15-1730 d 1795 m (1)Anna Christina Bahr (2)Eva Blass Pvt NY
Wm.: b c. 1740 d 7- -1785 m Magdalena Quick Pvt NJ
Wm.: b 10-6-1737 d 1786 m Margaret Bahr Lt NY
Wm.: b 1750 d 1793 m Christina Rockefeller Lt NY

ROCKEL,
Balser: b 11-10-1707 d 7-9-1800 m Elizabeth Kehler PS PA
John, Sr.: b 1722 d 1798 m Catherine — PS PA

ROCKEY,
Henry: b 1750 d 1796 m Elizabeth Leonard Pvt PA

ROCKHILL,
Solomon: b a. 1730 d p. 6-28-1795 m Susannah Taylor PS NJ
Wm.: b 1- -1754 d 9- -1814 m Mary Monroe Sgt NJ

ROCKHOLD,
John: b c. 1708/9 d p. 1786 m Mary Maynard PS MD
Maynard: b 2-8-1740 d 5-24-1815 m Sebrah Nelson PS MD

ROCKWELL, (includes ROTHWELL)
Abner: b 10-10-1744 d 6-28-1813 m Sarah Kellogg Sgt CT
Abner: b 1-18-1746/7 d 3-26-1831 m Deborah Carpenter Pvt MA
Amasa: b 2-7-1758 d 12-31-1838 m (1)Olive Morse (2)Mary Stevens (3)Prudence Hutchins Pvt MA ★
Claiborne: b c. 1740 d p. 1-17-1826 m — PS VA
Daniel, Jr.: b 9-4-1746 d 12-20-1831 m Esther Bingham PS CT
Daniel: b 10-14-1742 d 9-14-1806 m (1)Ann Smith (2)Anna Mix Slr CT
David, Sr.: b 10-8-1708 d 5-30-1788 m (1)Elizabeth Hyatt (2)Elizabeth (Whitney) Riggs Pvt CT
David, Jr.: b 1-31-1734 d 7-6-1816 m (1)Mary Atherton (2)Sarah Nickerson (3)Susanna Wooden PS CT
Elijah: b 11-14-1744 d 8-2-1841 m Lucy Wright Lt NY
Enos: b 10-16-1763 d 11-13-1832 m — Sol NY
Ephraim: b 9-15-1703 d 8-1-1826 m Sarah Moore (2)Hannah Coon Sol CT
Jabez: b 7-1-1740 d 1837 m (1)Elizabeth Sperry (2)Phebe Bedicut (3)Elizabeth Andrus Pvt CT
Jabez: b 10-3-1761 d 1-18-1847 m (1)Sarah Rundel (2)Elizabeth Mulford Pvt CT W★
Jabez: b 10-10-1761 d 3-23-1818 m Deborah Bellows Pvt CT ★
James: b 6-9-1750 d 11-25-1808 m Abigail Hawley Lt CT
James: b 4-12-1758 d 1833 m Mercy Smith Pvt MA
Jeremiah: b 7-19-1756 d 8-28-1852 m (1)Anna Stearns (2)Lucy (Eaton) Day (3)Abilene (Stearns) Smith Sgt MA ★
Job: b c. 1760 d 1834 m Hannah Burt Drm NY
Joel: b 9-25-1718 d 1790 m Sarah Drake Pvt CT
John: b 8-25-1743 d 9-10-1823 m Abigail Buckingham Lt CT W★
John, Sr.: b 5-12-1734 d 9-6-1825 m (1)Hannah Scott (2)Mrs Sally Rice Hungerford (3)— Pvt CT
John, Jr.: b 7-11-1755 d 9-2-1825 m Rebecca Ives Pvt MA VT
Jonathan: b 1-10-1738/9 d 1819 m Hannah Bennett Pvt NY
Joseph: b 3-15-1715 d 7-6-1776 m Anna Dodd Capt CT
Joseph: b 2-14-1736 d 4-16-1823 m Sarah (Rockwell) Sgt CT
Joseph: bpt 12-28-1740 d 10- -1825 m Waite Raymond Pvt CT
Joshua: b 10-18-1742 d 3-9-1825 m Rhoda Dowd Cpl PS CT
Josiah: b 5-18-1743 d 11-22-1812 m Lydia Marsh Sgt CT
Matthew: b 1-30-1717/8 d 3-28-1782 m Jemima Cook PS CT
Nathan: b 11-22-1737 d 4-14-1803 m Martha — Pvt NY
Nathaniel: b 11-3-1746 d 8-22-1822 m Sarah Bullen Sol PS CT
Noadiah: b 10-21-1759 d 2-9-1835 m Alice Hall Pvt CT ★
Oswell: b 5-10-1754 d 11-11-1813 m Sarah Witherell Pvt CT
Rebecca Ives: b 1-9-1755 d 10-1-1837 m John Rockwell Jr PS VT
Samuel: b 1-19-1728 d 9-7-1794 m Hepzibah Pratt Capt CT
Samuel: b 1752-56 d 5-27-1855 m Robina Collins Pvt CT ★
Samuel: b 11-28-1727 d 11-24-1794 m (1)Hannah Orcutt (2)Hannah (Johnson) Lee PS CT
Silas: b 8-30-1760 d 6-21-1843 m Hannah Olmstead Pvt NY CT ★
Thaddeus: b 11-23-1753 d 1828 m Mahitable Smith Lt CT

ROCKWOOD,
Ebenezer: b 8-13-1746 d 2-10-1830 m Mary Emerson Dr MA
Elisha: b 6-11-1716 d 12-5-1788 m Elizabeth Adams PS Pvt MA
Elisha, Jr.: b 11-20-1740 d 2- -1831 m Abigail Stone Pvt PS MA
Elisha: b 10-28-1750 d 12-1-1831 m Eunice Clark Pvt MA
Frost: b 11-24-1754 d 3-9-1842 m Sarah Pratt Pvt MA
Joseph: b 2-5-1757 d 4-17-1832 m Martha Shumway Pvt MA
Josiah: b 5-29-1748 d p. 3- -1777 m Lois Olds Pvt MA
Moses: b 5-19-1737 d 2-2-1823 m (1)Lydia Ellis (2)Hannah Ellis Pvt MA
Reuben: b 1-26-1730 d 3-3-1803 m Lydia Green Pvt Wgn MA

ROCKWOOD, contd.
Samuel: b 12-17-1759 d 1-5-1839 m (1)Rhoda Johnson (2)Elizabeth Farrar Platt Pvt MA ★
Samuel: b 12-6-1754 d 5-29-1804 m Lucy Hubbard Pvt MA
Samuel: b 10- -1757 d 5-4-1844 m Sarah Chilson Pvt VT MA
Simeon: bpt 11-22-1752 d 11-20-1823 m Damaris Olds Pvt MA ★
Timothy, Sr.: b 7-5-1727 d 2-21-1806 m (1)Elizabeth Perry (2)Jemima Underwood (3)Alice Littlefield (4)Deborah Fairbanks PS MA
Timothy, Jr.: b 10-14-1751 d 2-19-1831 m Margaret Parker 2Lt MA

RODDYE,
James: b c. 1742 d 1823 m (1)Jane Kathryn Chace (2)Lydia Russell Capt NC

RODEN,
Jeremiah: b 11-3-1754 d 1-1-1851 m Susan Kirkland Pvt SC

RODENHYSER,
John: b c. 1749 d c. 1815 m Maria Margaret Muller Sol PA

RODERFIELD,
Wm.: b 4-29-1760 d 11-4-1793 m Elizabeth Stowe Gnr PA

RODERICK,
Frederick: b c. 1750 d 3-15-1842 m (1)— (2)Elizabeth Phillips PS VA

RODICK,
Daniel: b c. 1744 d p. 1790 m Betty Hamor PS ME
John: b 1730 d p. 1802 m Mary Webber PS ME

RODMAN,
Daniel: b 5-4-1747 d 1799 m — PS RI
Gilbert: b 7-21-1748 d 8-21-1830 m Sarah Gibbs Maj PA
Hugh: b 1756 d 5-7-1815 m Elizabeth Hearst Pvt PA
Joseph: b 3-23-1733 d 1804 m Mary West Pvt NY
Joseph: b 1740 d 3-15-1806 m Mary Allen Pvt PA
Thomas: b 1716 d 2-7-1796 m Elizabeth Pearson CS NJ
Thomas: b 7-1-1740 d 2-14-1825 m Rachel Shaw 1Lt NY
Wm.: b 10-7-1757 d 7-27-1824 m Esther West QM PA

RODNEY,
John: b 9-7-1725 d 11-23-1792 m Ruth Hunn PM DE
Thomas: b 6-4-1744 d 1-2-1811 m Elizabeth Maud Fisher Col DE

RODOCKER,
Frederick: b c. 1750 d p. 1796 m Margaret Sauers Pvt PA

RODRIGUEZ,
John: b 11-7-1762 d 4-12-1803 m Marguerite Delatte PS LA

ROEBUCK,
Benjamin: b c. 1730 d c. 1781 m — PS SC
Wm.: b c. 1750 d 1809 m — Pvt VA

ROESSELL,
John Ludwig Eberhard: b 5-1-1741 d 5-15-1795 m Catherine Fiero Pvt NY

ROFF,
Christopher: b 4-29-1762 d 4- -1850 m Sarah Whelpley Pvt NY ★
Frederick: b 1728 d 8-20-1825 m Maria Elizabeth Tollhamer Pvt NY

ROGERS, (includes RODGERS)
Aaron: b 12-7-1761 d p. 9-11-1832 m Lois (Rogers) Pvt MA ★
Abiather: b 8-23-1758 d 5-9-1833 m Naomi Rose Pvt CT MA ★
Abisha: b 2-1-1762 d 7-18-1831 m Elizabeth Rudd Pvt MA W★
Abraham: b 1755 d 1814 m Mary Hovey Pvt NJ
Abraham Foster: b 10-2-1764 d 10-22-1834 m Martha Faulkner Pvt MA
Achilles: b 1762 d 7- -1854 m Eliza — Sol VA
Alexander: b 10-16-1761 d 2-12-1839 m (1)Catherine Smart (2)Rebecca Emerson Pvt MA
Alexander: b c. 1756 d 1816 m Jerusha Dunnem Pvt PA
Amos: b 1758 d 2-12-1818 m Betsey Ferris Cpl NY
Ananias: b 1750-60 d 1805/6 m Mary Johnson Pvt NY
Andrew: b 7-24-1759 d 8-23-1792 m Elizabeth Congdon (Rogers) Smn CT
Andrew: b 1746 d 9-19-1782 m Jane Henderson 3Lt PA
Aquilla: b c. 1760 d 1838/9 m (1)— (2)Phebe — Pvt VA
Armistead: b 1762 d p. 9-19-1835 m Susannah D Jouett PS VA
Arunah: b 11-5-1758 d 8-12-1838 m Deborah Davis Pvt MA
Asa: b 1755 d 9-30-1836 m Abiah Oakman Sgt MA ★
Benjamin: b 8-1-1736 d 11-18-1824 m Temperance Finney Pvt PS CS MA
Benjamin: b 1747 d 3-7-1825 m Mercy McIntire Pvt MA
Benjamin: b 1-27-1740 d 4-10-1812 m Mary Stevens Mstr MA
Benjamin: b 1730 d 11-28-1819 m Hannah Newcomb Sgt MA
Benjamin: b 12-5-1763 d 11-12-1836 m (1)Margaret McAllister (2)Ann (Shackelford) Wickham Pvt SC
Bolling: b c. 1762 d 11-25-1841 m Naomi Burke Pvt VA ★
Britain: b 10-11-1761 d 4-22-1835 m Elizabeth — Sol GA
Burwell: b 1762/3 d a. 10-29-1832 m Lettice — Sol GA

Byrd: b c. 1735 d a. 10-12-1801 m (1)Mary Trice (2)Martha Trice Sol NC
Caleb: b c. 1750 d p. 1790 m Azubah Foster Pvt MA
Charles: b — d a. 9-16-1793 m (1)Catherine Brent (2)Peggy Chowning (3)Ann Tapscott PS CS VA
Daniel: b 6-2-1727 d 7-9-1801 m Lydia Bartholomew Pvt CT
Daniel: bpt 1-22-1709 d 12-17-1785 m Sarah Mason PS NH
Daniel: b 1762 d 4-14-1832 m Susan Rose Pvt NY
Daniel: b 5-22-1756 d 1-10-1837 m Eliza M Stanley Pvt NC ★
David: b 8-21-1748 d 6-25-1829 m Martha Tennant Dr CT
David: b 3-8-1719/20 d 10-17-1803 m (1)Grace Lester (2)Judith (Maxson) Greene (3)Susanna Truman Pvt CT
David: b 1751/2 d p. 1782 m Jerusha Eldredge Pvt MA
Drury: b c. 1737 d 1791 m Tabitha — Pvt CS GA
Edmund Pendleton: b 5-5-1762 d 8-28-1843 m Mary Shirley Pvt VA
Edward: b 1734 d 7-24-1813 m Hannah Jackson Capt CT
Edward: b 8-26-1763 d 7-26-1813 m Elizabeth Hathaway Pvt VA W★
Elkanah: b 1-1-1760 d 12-1-1835 m Tamsen Snow Pvt MA ★
Ezekiel: b 5-10-1741 d 9-20-1785 m Ache Wilton Pvt PS NY
Ezekiel: b 1764 d 1811 m Rebecca Williamson Mil VA
George: b 2-14-1755 d 2-19-1815 m Mary Wheeler Pvt CT
George: b c. 1720 d 1-29-1801 m (1)Ann Ferguson (2)Sarah Wyman Lt MA
George: b 1740 d 1800 m Elizabeth Losson Mstr VA
George: b 2-6-1764 d 11-28-1858 m Elizabeth Randall Pvt VA W★
George: b 4-6-1735 d 10-6-1828 m — Pvt PA
Gideon: b 2-28-1758-60 d p. 1798 m Sarah Mosher Sgt MA
Gurdon: b 7-28-1760 d p. 1832 m (1)Elizabeth Harris Bliss (2)Lucretia Rogers Pvt CT ★
Hamilton, Sr.: b c. 1726/7 d p. 1796 m Isabelle Mains McCreary PS VA
Hamilton, Jr.: b 12-23-1758 d 3-20-1844 m Mary Gibson Pvt VA
Hannah Ford: b 1726 d 7-10-1778 m Josiah Rogers PS PA
Heman: b 6-22-1757 d 9-6-1844 m (1)Lydia Palmer (2)Eunice Whedon (3)Hannah Baldwin Cpl CT ★
Henry: b 1739 d 1823 m Nancy Linn Pvt MA ★
Henry: b 12-25-1752 d 7-17-1840 m Phoebe Burnett Pvt NJ
Henry: b c. 1741 d 1794 m Elizabeth Lankford PS VA
Hezekiah: b 2-21-1704 d 9-25-1778 m Ruth Scudder PS NY
Hezekiah P.: b 1731 d 9-17-1832 m Mary Yates Sgt MA ★
Hosea: b 10-14-1758 d 1-23-1838 m Caty Clift MM VA ★
Hugh: b 1761 d 10-29-1848 m Nancy Thornton Pvt NC SC
Ichabod, Jr.: b 2-16-1754 d 3-24-1821 m Mary Hobbs Hall Pvt CT
Isaac: b 12-13-1749 d p. 1782 m Mary Howe Mar CT
Isaac: b 6-30-1762 d 5-17-1840 m (2) Mary Griffin Pvt CT ★
Isaac: b 1725 d 4-8-1807 m Anna Halsted PS NY
Isaac: b 8- -1762 d 6-25-1831 m Hannah Conklin PS NY
Israel: b 9-4-1761 d 11-9-1836 m Zerviah Miner Pvt CT ★
James: b 2-8-1739/40 d 9-28-1820 m Zilpha Hyde PS CS CT
James: b 1742 d 4-9-1823 m Eleanor Wakeman CS CT
James: b 1764 d 9-12-1845 m Massey Johnson Fif Sol NJ
James: b 1752 d 2-13-1826 m Amy Bronson Pvt NY
James: b c. 1764 d 6-29-1807 m Nelly McCoy Pvt NC
James: b 10- -1735 d 4-18-1790 m Florence Hutchinson Capt PA
James: b 1740 d c. 1795 m — Dobyns Vol PA
James: b 2-27-1744 d 8-28-1793 m Priscilla — Pvt PA
James: b 3- -1742 d 3-24-1828 m (1)Martha Blackburn (2)Mrs Nancy Flournay Capt VA
Jedediah: b 1751 d 11-3-1827 m Sarah Bush Lt CT W★
Jeremiah: b 9-3-1752 d 1783 m Nancy Forsyth Pvt CT
Jeremiah: b 3-1-1749/50 d 4- -1806 m Lucy Stark PS CT
Jeremiah: b 4-27-1743 d 8-11-1810 m Mary Jones Lt NY
Joel: b 10-14-1729 d 6- -1823 m Sarah Webber PS MA
John: b 6-16-1736 d 5-1-1811 m Patience (Miller) Starr Pvt CT
John: b 7-1-1744 d 8- -1796 m Hannah Smith Pvt CT
John: b 8-5-1727 d 5-7-1811 m (1)Elizabeth Bayard (2)Mrs Mary Grant Chp CT
John: b 7-1-1744-8 d p. 1790 m Mary Larrabee CS CT
John, Sr.: b 10-14-1722 d 1-21-1809 m Thankful Harrison CS CT
John: b 1726 d 1791 m Elizabeth Reynolds Capt MD
John: b c. 1723 d 9-23-1787 m Margaret Lee Clark CS MD
John: b 5-9-1724 d 10-19-1815 m (1)Hannah William (2)Mary (Craft) Trowbridge 1Lt MA
John: b 6-20-1746 d 10-19-1832 m Jane Potter Pvt MA
John, Jr.: b 2-14-1750 d 3-5-1833 m (1)Mary Hall (2)Sarah Hall Pvt MA
John: b 1756 d 4-18-1824 m Rebecca Daggett Pvt MA
John: b 6-25-1729 d 1776 m Jane Ewins Lt NH
John: b 11-13-1747 d 6-4-1827 m Esther Ball Sgt NH
John: b 7-2-1756 d 1-28-1849 m Mary Colbath Cpl NH
John: b 1741 d 12-1-1788 m Prudence Perrigo Pvt NJ
John: b 1747 d 1812 m Mary Bennett Pvt NJ
John: b — d — m Ann Jobes Pvt NJ ★
John, Jr.: b 5-16-1762 d 12-16-1841 m Ruth Titus Sol NY
John: b 1723 d p. 1790 m Martha (Rogers) Pvt NC
John, Jr.: b 1737-9 d 1802 m Mary Clayton Pm NC
John: b 1736 d 12-6-1799 m Mary — Col PS PA
John: b 10-12-1747 d p. 1786 m Ann (Clendennin) McSwain Pvt PA
John: b 1745 d 7-16-1812 m (1)Elizabeth Blackwood (2)Isabelle Ireland PS PA
John, Jr.: b 3-31-1757 d 6-9-1839 m Sarah Ballou Lt RI

John: b 1741 d 5-2-1821 m Sarah — Ens VT
John: b 5- -1740 d 1813 m Elizabeth Courtney NCapt VA
John: b 1-23-1747 d 8-30-1836 m Margaret Ann Daugherty Cpl VA
John R Bayard: b 12-28-1757 d 1-29-1833 m Susannah Ravand Kearney Dr PA
Jonah: b 1743 d 1799 m Deliverance Chaffee Pvt PA
Jonas: b 3-28-1728 d 9-10-1818 m Mary Jarvis PS NY
Jonathan: b 8-3-1750 d p. 1787 m Hannah Mayo Sgt MA
Jonathan: b 4-23-1755 d 7-28-1841 m Phebe Shepard Pvt MA ★
Jonathan: b 1756 d 1838 m (1)Polly Mayes (2)Elizabeth Rogers Pvt NH ★
Joseph: b 8-31-1719 d 7-14-1779 m Diadama Beckwith Sol CT
Joseph: b 8-30-1706 d 2-2-1784 m Elizabeth Clark PS CT
Joseph: b 12-19-1714 d 4-18-1798 m Abigail Bartlett PS NH
Joseph: b 1721 d 11-15-1800 m Margaret Webb Pvt NY
Joseph: b c. 1730-45 d 1798 m Sarah Ludlow PS NY
Joseph: b c. 1735 d 1824 m Elizabeth Burgess CS VA
Joseph: b 3-13-1741 d 7-13-1834 m (1)Anne Early (2)Jane (Ford) Farrar (3)Susan Coons Vol VA
Joshua, Jr.: b 3-30-1746 d p. 1786 m Phoebe Fox Pvt CT
Josiah: b 1749 d 1831 m Catherine — Sgt CT ★
Josiah: b 9-6-1741 d 3-8-1804 m Abigail Arey Capt MA
Josiah: b 1747 d 11-27-1828 m Hannah Woodman Pvt NH
Josiah: b 10-7-1720 d 12-14-1815 m Hannah Ford Pvt PA
Justus: b 3-10-1737 d 11-13-1811 m Naomi Felter Pvt NY
Lot: b 9-12-1755 d 4-2-1828 m Nannie Bethea Pvt VA
Matthew: b 1750 d p. 8-13-1795 m Isabella C Latham PS SC
Matthew: b 11-16-1767 d 1853 m Eleanor Randolph Pvt VA
Michael: b 3-3-1759 d 11-25-1834 m Deborah Rogers Pvt NY
Moses: b c. 1721 d 3-22-1795 m Elizabeth Smith Pvt MA
Nathan: b 5-6-1718 d 3-1-1794 m (1)Martha Davis (2)Hannah Crandall Pvt CT
Nathaniel: b 1725 d 9- -1801 m (1)Theoda Miner (2)Susanna Marvin Pvt CT
Nathaniel: b 5-2-1732 d 5-4-1802 m Zeppora Williams Pvt CT
Nathaniel: b 8-4-1761 d 5-17-1847 m Phoebe Fuller Pvt CT ★
Nathaniel, Sr.: b — d 1786 m Abiah Ingalls Cpl MA
Nathaniel, Jr.: b 11-15-1750 d 10-11-1820 m Eunice Allen Lt NH W★
Nathaniel: b 4-9-1735 d 9- -1792 m Mary — Ens NY
Nathaniel: b 7-25-1755 d 12-22-1804 m Frances Cobbs Pvt SC
Noah, 3d: b 5-8-1732 d 10-17-1810 m Rhoda Leete Vol CT
Noah: b 10-23-1761 d 12-27-1826 m Hannah C Whitney Pvt MA W★
Obadiah: b 1699 d 10-31-1783 m Abigail Herrick PS NY
Oliver: b 4-14-1748 d c. 1822 m Hannah Coburn Mar CT ★
Peleg, Sr.: b 11-6-1725 d 8-13-1820 m Hannah Stevens PS MA
Peleg: b 1747 d 5-15-1811 m Mary Pittman Sol GA
Peter: b 1740 d p. 11-7-1789 m Anna Beraude Lt SC
Peter: b 7-1-1753/4 d 11-5-1849 m (1)Nancy Greene (2)Abigail Darrow FifMaj CT ★
Peter: b 11-21-1752 d p. 1790 m Mehitable Austin Pvt MA
Peter: b a. 1724 d 1785 m Elizabeth Rogers Capt VA
Peter: b c. 1758 d 1832/3 m Hester Colonna Sol VA
Philip, Jr.: b 12-28-1727 d 2-20-1810 m Pheobe Rogers Lt PS NY
Pierre: b c. 1740 d p. 11-7-1789 m Anna Beraude Lt SC
Platt: b 12-30-1739 d 10-7-1798 m Eyda Wiltse Pvt NY
Prince: b 6-29-1738 d 11-17-1822 m Susanna Snow Pvt MA
Ralph: b 3-8-1760 d 4- -1836 m (1)Mary Gilky (2)Judith Lyles Pvt SC ★
Reuben: b 11-1-1735 d 1829 m Temperance James Pvt GA
Reuben: b 1-29-1758 d 1848 m (1)Priscilla Lovell (2)Lucina Stoddard Marchant (3)Resina Hollister MM NY
Rhodam: b c. 1756 d 7- -1843 m Mildred Nelson Pvt VA ★
Richard: b 3-22-1753 d 1-15-1836 m (1)Elizabeth Kenny (2)Ann — Pvt CT ★
Richard: b 1744 d 1819 m Elizabeth Warren Pvt NY
Richard: b 1733 d 9-16-1804 m Rachel Denny 1Lt PA
Richard Carr: b 6-25-1745 d 7-5-1831 m Abigail Cooper Pvt PS NH
Robert: b 1744 d 1800 m Sarah Kyle Pvt PA
Robert: b 7-16-1747 d 1820 m (1)Rose Hanson (2)Sarah Evans (3)Mary — 1Lt NH
Samuel: b 4-16-1738 d p. 1791 m Patience Wood Pvt CT
Samuel: b 1760 d 3-25-1836 m Jerusha Hubbard Pvt CT
Samuel: b 11-24-1739 d 5-4-1777 m Elizabeth Willis Capt MA
Samuel: b 8-7-1740 d 9-5-1825 m (1)Deborah Bassett (2)Amy (Wing) Cooper Pvt MA
Samuel: b 3-19-1762 d 1827 m Phebe — Pvt MA
Samuel: b 2-2-1722/3 d 4-21-1788 m Rebecca Farmer PS MA
Samuel: b p. 1727 d 3- -1802 m Ann — Pvt NH
Samuel: b 8-8-1749 d 5-30-1839 m (1)Deborah Drew (2)Mrs Sarah Morrison Pvt NH ★
Samuel: b 11-13-1766 d 9-9-1830 m (1)Sally Pike (2)Rhoda Harvey Pvt NH ★
Samuel: b 1754 d 1805 m Rebecca Brown Pvt NY
Shadrack: b 1753 d 10-7-1832 m Celia Jordan Pvt SC
Silas: b 11-7-1750 d p. 1821 m Abigail — Sgt MA
Simeon: b 8- -1762 d 3-27-1856 m Mary Allen Barker Pvt CT
Simeon: b 2-1-1762 d 6-18-1848 m Anna — Pvt MA ★
Simeon: b c. 1750 d p. 1820 m Abigail Howard Pvt NJ
Smith: b c. 1753 d 3-19-1817 m Ruth Gage Pvt MA
Stephen: b 3-25-1731 d 11-24-1789 m Lydia Frisbie Pvt CT
Stephen: b 1730 d 11-18-1805 m Lydia Howe Pvt MA
Stephen: b 1754 d 1832 m Rachel — MM NY

Stephen: b 1760 d 11-11-1839 m Permellah Wood Pvt NC
Stephen: b 2-7-1748/9 d 3-17-1826 m Lydia Lapham CS VT
Stephen: b 1755 d 11-30-1845 m (1)Nancy — (2)Nancy McPhearson Todd Pvt VA ★
Theophilus: b 1731 d 9-29-1801 m Penelope — Dr PS CT
Thomas: b 4-10-1757 d 6-2-1842 m Mary Baker Pvt CT
Thomas: b 11-19-1726 d 6-23-1804 m (1)Rebecca Gildersleeve (2)Rebecca Hobart PS CT
Thomas: b 9-4-1762 d 3-30-1830 m Eunice Place Sgt MA
Thomas: b 1-8-1713/4 d 9-18-1794 m Martha Hubbard PS MA
Thomas: b 1759 d 1827 m (2)Sarah Jackson Pvt NC
Thomas: b c. 1750 d — m Eliza Futhey Pvt PA
Thomas: b 3-16-1741 d 1-17-1815 m Elizabeth Kenyon Hoxie (2)Avis Rogers Pvt RI
Thomas: b 12-13-1754 d 3-19-1839 m Rebecca Spahr Pvt VA ★
Timothy: b 12-24-1752 d 1828 m Eunice Beach SrgnMte CT
Timothy: b 6-16-1745 d 2-27-1814 m Hannah Foster Lt MA
Uriah: b 9-21-1737 d 6-13-1814 m Mary Howell Maj NY
Uriah, Jr.: b 6-27-1759 d — m Ruth Wells Pvt CT
Wm.: b 1742 d 3-25-1784 m Sarah — Sol MD
Wm.: b 1739/40 d 9-26-1786 m (2)Abigail Worth Maj MA
Wm.: b 2-8-1760 d 4-28-1810 m (1)Mary Chamberlain (2)Mary Connor Ens NH
Wm.: b 5-27-1732 d 11-28-1796 m Martha Esturgane PS NJ
Wm.: b 7-5-1744 d 11-11-1813 m Mary Halsey Capt NY
Wm.: b 11-19-1741 d c. 1779 m Sarah Potter Capt NY
Wm.: b 11-3-1754 d 4-18-1806 m Esther Hawley QMSgt NY
Wm.: b 1757 d 2-21-1842 m Elizabeth — Pvt NY ★
Wm.: b 1730 d 8-28-1782 m Elleada — Pvt NC
Wm.: b c. 1761 d 12-18-1845 m (1)Hannah McCormick (2)Mary Gourley (3)Mrs Sarah Michael Pvt NC ★
Wm.: b 10-30-1758 d p. 1827 m Mary Hendricks Sol NC
Wm.: b c. 1760 d a. 8- -1809 m Gertra — Ens PA
Wm.: b a. 1750 d 9- -1807 m Margaret Kelly Pvt PA
Wm.: b 8-20-1749 d 12-27-1830 m Susanna Barrett Pvt PA
Wm.: b 7-22-1751 d 4-7-1824 m Susannah Marsh Chp PA
Wm.: b 1750 d — m Edith Adams Lt SC
Wm.: b 1744 d 1828 m (1)Patsy — (2)Nancy Johnson Pvt VA
Wm.: b c. 1750 d a. 1833 m (1)— (2)Elizabeth Grigsby Smn VA
Wm.: b 9- -1754 d 2- -1816 m Neva Williams Sol VA
Wm.: b 5-24-1748 d 5-1-1835 m Letty — Pvt VA
Wm. B.: b 1752 d 9-8-1847 m Cynthia Jones Pvt VA
Willoughby: b 1756-62 d p. 3-22-1828 m Mary — Cpl NC ★
Wing: b 4-14-1740 d 10-28-1800 m (1)Deliverance Chapman (2)Mercy Hatch (3)Rebecca Sherman (4)Hannah Titus PS CS VT
Zabdial: b 5-20-1737 d 3-14-1808 m (1)Elizabeth Tracy (2)Elizabeth Snow Col CT
Zebadiah: b 2-23-1720/1 d 6-25-1803 m Betty Farmer PS MA
Zephaniah: b 3-7-1747 d 10-7-1823 m Elizabeth Rood Pvt CT W★
Zephaniah: b 6-25-1742 d 10-29-1796 m Elizabeth Sayre Capt NY

ROGGEN,
Peter: b 7-23-1752 d 11-4-1804 m Annatje Mosten Lt NY

ROHRER, (includes RORER)
Christian: b c. 1740 d 7-19-1804 m Catherine — Pvt PA
Gottfried: b c. 1725 d c. 8- -1800 m Magdalena Etschberger PS PA
Jacob: b 12-15-1752 d 6-24-1824 m Catharine Bross Lt PA
John: b 5-15-1755 d 11-7-1824 m Margaret Young Pvt PA
John: b c. 1755 d 1835 m Elizabeth Miley Lt PA

ROKES,
Daniel: b 1729 d 5-9-1796 m Abigail Locke Pvt MA

ROLFE, (includes RELFE & ROLPH)
Benjamin: b 5-31-1752 d 1808 m Molly Sweat Pvt NH
Benjamin: b 1751 d 11-19-1832 m Sarah Brush Pvt NY
Enoch: b 12-18-1750 d — m (1)Anna Taylor (2)Anne Pendleton (3)Eliza Watkins Pvt NC
John: b a. 1760 d a. 4-12-1803 m Elizabeth — Pvt MD
Jonathan: b 1734 d 2-6-1828 m Mercy Coons Pvt NJ
Joseph: b 5-14-1730 d 1784 m (1)Esther — (2)Mrs Anna Stickney Pvt Smn MA
Nathaniel, Sr.: b 1-6-1713 d 12- -1808 m Hannah (Rolfe) PS NH
Nathaniel, Jr.: b 8-29-1743/4 d 11-15-1829 m Judith (Walker) Chandler PS NH
Wm.: b c. 1745 d 1798 m Elizabeth — Pvt MD
Wm.: b 3-5-1747/8 d p. 8-27-1832 m Lavinia Harriman Sgt MA

ROLL,
Abraham: b 8-29-1739 d 10-20-1813 m (1)Mary Brooks (2)Caty Veerland Pvt NJ
Abraham: b 1759 d 1827 m Patty Vance PS NJ
Isaac: b 1745 d p. 1809 m Sarah Cauldwell Tms NJ
John: b c. 1755 d 1-16-1816 m Mary Frampton Pvt PA
John, Jr.: b 10-17-1733 d p. 9-11-1807 m (1)Rachel VanWinkle (2)Edith Wick Pvt NJ
Matthias: b 8-22-1762 d 10-7-1831 m Mary Rutan Pvt NJ W★

ROLLER, (includes ROWLER)
Baltzer: b 10-11-1758 d 11-30-1841 m Alse Rose Pvt PA
Jacob, Sr.: b c. 1724 d p. 1781 m Mary Hammer PS PA
John: b 1759 d 1810 m Susana Wildberger Pvt VA

ROLLER, contd.
John: b c. 1725-30 d 6-7-1806 m (1)Anna — (2)Catherine Doser Sol VA
Martin Luther: b c. 1740 d c. 1800 m Sybilla Lotts Pvt VA

ROLLINS,
Aaron: b 1727 d c. 1790 m Elizabeth Ingalls PS NH
Anthony Nutter: b 9-27-1761 d p. 1832 m Abigail Heard Drm NH
Benjamin: b 1734 d 1830 m — Pvt MA
David: b 1760 d p. 1800 m Judith Leach Fif MA
Elijah: b 4- -1759 d 12-19-1809 m (1)Mary Prescott (2)Mary Chase Pvt NH
Eliphalet: b 1758 d 1835 m (1)Mary Hutchins (2)Mary Jones Pvt ME
Eliphalet, Sr.: b 7-23-1734 d p. 12-13-1815 m Abigail Glidden PS NH
Eliphalet, Jr.: b 1756 d 1843 m Elizabeth Bean Sol NH
Hannaniah: b 8-13-1761 d 8-3-1836 m Martha — Pvt CL
Henry: b — d 1812 m (1)Mary Ellen Carson (2)Sarah Harris Pvt PA
Ichabod: b 7-18-1722 d 1-31-1800 m (1)Abigail Wentworth (2)Margaret (Colton) Frost PS NH
James: b 1731 d 1-12-1818 m (1)Abigail Downing (2)Mary Whitney (3)Hannah Ross (4)Martha Muzzy (5)Rebecca Phelps Pvt NH
John: b 1744 d 9-17-1832 m Dorcas Chapman Pvt MA
John: b 2-12-1756 d 12-16-1847 m Elizabeth Leighton Pvt NH ★
John: b 7-17-1756 d 4-14-1843 m — Pvt NH ★
John: b 3-22-1745 d 1-23-1820 m Mary Carr Pvt NH
Jonathan: b c. 1748 d p. 1790 m (2)Mary Barker Pvt PS NH
Joseph: b 1751 d 6-28-1840 m Martha Ames Sgt MA
Joseph: b 12-19-1702 m p. 1776 m (1)Hannah Redman (2)Elizabeth Drake PS NH
Josiah, Jr.: b a. 1754 d p. 1784 m Anna Fogg Pvt NH
Moses: b 3-10-1744 d 1824 m Ann Drew Pvt PS NH
Nathaniel: b c. 1738 d a. 1783 m (1)Lydia Clark (2)Marie Chadbourne Sgt MA
Nathaniel, Jr.: b 1761 d 12-10-1845 m Elizabeth Hussey Pvt MA
Nathaniel: b 1757 d p. 1823 m Mary Allen Pvt NH
Nathaniel: b 1-18-1759 d 2-8-1826 m Mrs Olive (Greely) Harris Pvt NH
Nicholas: b 6-15-1743 d p. 1789 m Abigail Tilton Capt NH
Robert: b 1756 d 4-14-1842 m Mary Greeley Pvt NH ★
Samuel: b 6-8-1740 d 11-19-1831 m Sarah Chapman Lt MA
Samuel: b 1745 d 10-28-1832 m Elizabeth Tucker Pvt NH W★
Simeon: b 1-11-1748 d 1-11-1840 m Mary Rollins Sgt NH ★
Stephen: b 3-28-1750 d 1-27-1842 m Hannah Stanley PS MA

ROLLO,
Joseph: b 1743 d 10-21-1838 m (1)Barbarry Allen (2)Polly Gardner Pvt CT ★

ROMER,
Henry: b 5-11-1755 d 11-5-1830 m Mary Jennings Pvt NY
Jacob: b 1714 d 2-14-1807 m Frena Haerlager PS NY
John: b 11-10-1764 d 5-27-1855 m Leah vanTassel Pvt NY

ROMEYN, (includes ROMAINE & ROMINE)
Abraham: b 8-15-1762 d 3-19-1838/9 m Mary Moore Pvt NY
Benjamin: b 9-24-1762 d 1-31-1844 m Mary Brower Ens NJ ★
Benjamin: b 7-25-1748 d 6-9-1829 m Ragil Vandelinde PS NJ
Nicholas: b — d p. 4-15-1785 m Elizabeth Kipp Pvt PS NJ

ROMIG, (includes ROMICH)
Adam: b 11-27-1744 d 9-27-1798 m (1)Catherine Butts (2)Elizabeth B Newhard Pvt PA
Frederick: b 7-22-1747 d 8-23-1794 m Elizabeth Knauss Pvt PA
Jacob: b 6-1-1765 d 1835 m — Pvt PA

ROMINGER,
Jacob: b 8-13-1743 d 8-30-1816 m (1)Barbara Seidlinger (2)Sabina Krause PS NC
Michael: b 8-9-1759 d 6-5-1818 m Anna Maria Fischel Pvt NC W★

RONALD,
Wm.: b c. 1750 d 2-3-1793 m Katherine Winston PM PS VA

RONEMOUS,
Philip: b 1760 d 3-20-1832 m Jane Thompson Pvt VA

RONEMUS,
Andrew: b — d a. 2-12-1805 m — PS VA

RONEY,
Hercules: b c. 1743 d p. 6-22-1812 m Margaret Buchanan Pvt PA
Thomas: b 1749 d 1826 m Mary Davis Pvt PA

RONQUILLO,
Juan: b 1740 d 2-22-1810 m Graciana Solis PS LA

ROOD,
Azariah: b 1724 d 2- -1795 m (1)Desire Prime (2)Lydia Drakeley PS VT
Daniel: b 1745 d 1805 m Elizabeth Grover Pvt NY
Daniel: b c. 1755 d p. 1783 m Dorothy Robinson Pvt VT
David, Sr.: b 1752 d 6-9-1830 m Lucretia Stowe Pvt CT

David: b 10-11-1762 d 8- -1830 m Sarah Rogers Sol CT
Eli: b 4- -1760 d 10-25-1841 m Mrs Mary Stevens Pvt NY
Elijah: b 9-9-1748 d p. 1815 m Martha Stevens Pvt CT
Ezra: b 11-18-1760 d 3-28-1829 m Parthena Warner Pvt MA
John: b 1754 d 4-4-1827 m Laura — Pvt CT
Joseph: b 5-7-1754 d 3-31-1843 m Lois — Sol CT
Marriner, Jr.: b 4-5-1745 d 1-24-1832 m Mary Keeny Lt PS CT
Moses: b 1753 d 7-11-1830 m Ann Carpenter Pvt MA ★
Robert: b 1743 d 4-5-1815 m Mary Rowe Sgt CT
Simeon: b 12- -1759 d 9-6-1822 m Demaris Munger Fosmerly Pvt CT ★
Thomas Parke: b 5-23-1732 d 10-10-1795 m Dinah Benjamin Pvt VT

ROOF, (includes ROOFF & RUFF)
Jacob: b 1718 d 12-25-1790 m Elizabeth — Cpl PA
John: b 12-7-1730 d 3-7-1798 m Annie Marie Leonhardo Capt NY
John: b 4-28-1760 d 1847 m Gertrude Spraker Pvt NY ★
Peter: b 1- -1753 d 10-25-1834 m Margaret Replogle Pvt PA

ROOKSBERRY,
Jacob: b 1758 d 5-15-1823 m Eleanor — Pvt VA ★

ROOME,
Jacob: b 1730 d 1785 m (1)Sarah Spear (2)Hannah Morse PS NJ
Samuel: b 10-15-1754 d 4-30-1837 m Anna Courter Pvt NJ

ROOSA, (includes ROSA)
Abraham: b 11-5-1721 d 1789 m Elizabeth (Rosendale) Rutz Pvt NY
Egbert: b 2-10-1736 d 8-4-1829 m (1)Elsie Delamater (2)Lena Ostrander Pvt NY
Isaac A.: b 4-19-1751 d 4-22-1803 m Catherine Moule Lt PS NY
Jacob: b 10-14-1739 d 1807 m Jannetje VanWagenen Pvt NY
Jacob: b 10-28-1749 d 12-24-1831 m Catrina Felter Sol NY
Jacob: b 5-12-1754 d 3-31-1808 m Maria Roosa Pvt PS NY
John Egbert: b 1-23-1761 d 1-17-1854 m (1)Elizabeth Houghtaling (2)Maria VanVliet Pvt NY ★
Petrus: b 8-23-1731 d 8-16-1820 m Rachel Orispel PS NY

ROOSEVELT,
Cornelius: b 3-24-1749 d p. 1814 m Miss Wilton Pvt NY
Cornelius C.: bpt 10-29-1755 d 2- -1814 m (1)Alida Fargie (2)Catharine VanAlstyne Ens NY
Isaac: b 12-8-1726 d 10-13-1794 m Cornelia Hoffman PS NY
Jacobus: bpt 8-9-1724 d 10-6-1777 m (1)Annatje Bogart (2)Helen Thompson Capt NY
Jacobus J.: b 10-25-1759 d 8-13-1840 m Maria VanSchaick Pvt NY
Nicholas: bpt 2-16-1715 d p. 1776 m (1)Catharine Comfort (2)Elizabeth Thurman PS 2nd Maj NY
Nicholas: b 12-27-1747 d 7-30-1814 m Lydia Latrobe Pvt NY

ROOT, (includes ROOTE, ROOTES & ROOTS)
Aaron: b 12-20-1720 d 8-31-1809 m (1)Rhoda Ring (2)Jerusha Steele Col MA
Abel: b 3-3-1765 d 4-19-1839 m Princess Lyman Pvt VT ★
Adonijah: b 12-30-1730 d p. 1800 m Ruth Lake Pvt CT
Amos: b 1740 d 1813 m (1)Lydia Webster (2)Mercy Barnes Pvt CT
Amos, Sr.: b 1733 d p. 1784 m (1)Abigail Sheldon (2)Azubah Hubbard Pvt MA
Amos, Jr.: b 7-18-1758 d 2-23-1813 m Anna Baker Pvt MA
Amos: b 8-20-1745 d 10-1-1836 m (1)Mary Burlison (2)Anna Rowe (3)Ruth Tanner Pvt MA
Asahel: b 8-5-1753 d 9-9-1835 m Sarah Sutherland Sgt MA NY W★
Azariah: b 8-23-1728 d 7-3-1717 m Elizabeth Shepard LCol MA
Azariah: b 12-20-1761/2 d 12-31-1851 m Eleanor Barber Pvt MA
Caleb: b 11-3-1738 d 1822 m Patience Porter Sgt CT
Daniel: b 9-29-1764 d 10-13-1834 m Rhoda Coy Pvt CT
Daniel: b 1754 d 7-6-1839 m Lucy Hall Pvt CT
Ebenezer: b 12-17-1760 d 2-12-1842 m Cynthia Whipple Pvt MA ★
Eli: b 2-27-1731 d 1804 m (1)Mindwell Sackett (2)Experience Kellogg Capt MA
Eliazer: b 7-28-1764 d 1-31-1837 m Lucinda Bostwick Pvt CT
Elisha: bpt 2-6-1737 d 9-20-1776 m Lucy Curtiss Lt CT
Elisha: b 9-23-1744 d 6-10-1817 m Mary Cowles Pvt MA
Enoch: b 4-7-1743 d 1-17-1827 m (1)— Barnes (2)Hannah Cory Sol CT
Ephraim: b — d — m Ruth Eggleston Peel PS CT
Ephraim: b 8-16-1751 d 3-21-1832 m Lydia Skinner Cpl NH
Gideon: b 4-26-1735 d 8-1-1804 m Huldah Nelson Lt MA
Isaac: b 9- -1756 d p. 1785 m Tabitha — Pvt CT
Jesse: b 12-28-1736 d 3-29-1822 m Mary Banks AdjGen CT
Jesse: b 10-2-1725 d p. 1790 m Phebe — PS CT
Jeb: b 4-6-1728 d 1807 m Elizabeth Barnes Pvt CT
John: bpt 1-30-1726 d 11-14-1798 m Mabel Root Pvt CT
John: b 3-1-1760 d 7-22-1834 m Polly Eastman Pvt CT ★
John: b c. 1735 d p. 7-1-1795 m Mary — PS NC
John: b c. 1735 d a. 1798 m Sarah Reade Capt VA
Jonah: b 3-3-1744 d 12-21-1831 m Faith Hills Sgt CT
Jonathan: b 12-20-1707 d 8-17-1794 m (1)Ruth — (2)Esther Wadsworth (3)Mrs Susannah Day CS PS CT
Jonathan: b 1745 d 1812 m (2)Anna Gillette PS CT
Joseph: b 4-2-1738 d 11-4-1783 m Martha Moore Cpl MA
Joseph: b 1753 d 9-29-1825 m Elizabeth R Pomeroy Pvt CT

Joseph: b 12-7-1761 d 8-22-1846 m Fannie West Pvt CT ★
Joseph: b 8-23-1715 d 6-7-1789 m Ann Bancroft PS MA
Joseph: b 6-16-1713 d 10-1-1786 m (1)Abigail Bridgeman (2)Mrs
    Mary Bascom PS MA
Joshua: b 7-8-1753 d 1833 m Sarah Bailey Sol CT
Joshua: b 4-28-1715 d 12-8-1791 m (1)Sarah Miles (2)Abigail Olds
    PS MA
Josiah: b 12-17-1752 d 6-6-1841 m Merab Lewis Dr CT
Lemuel: b 7-6-1760 d 10-11-1850 m Mary Magdalene Smith Pvt
    MA ★
Martin, Sr.: b 12-14-1721 d *p.* 1790 m Eunice Lamb PS MA
Martin, Jr.: b 2-20-1753 d 8-19-1822 m (1)Ruth Noble (2)Lois
    Smith Pvt MA
Moses: b 2-29-1758 d 10-10-1810 m Esther Mitchell Pvt CT ★
Nathan: b 6-13-1742/3 d 1839 m Hannah Scripture 1Lt CT
Nathaniel: b 2-27-1766 d 2-9-1846 m Mary Esther Louise
    DeBarnest Pvt CT ★
Nathaniel: b 3-25-1757 d 9-21-1840 m (1)Elizabeth Kingsbury
    (2)Candace Hammond MM Ens CT
Nathaniel Hunn: b 11-6-1747 d 2-16-1837 m Thankful Roberts
    Pvt CT ★
Oliver: b 11-24-1741 d 5-2-1826 m Hannah Ashley Lt MA
Oliver: b 12-16-1744 d 12-5-1807 m (1)Catherine Smead (2)Merab
    Allen CS MA
Orlando: b 7-24-1734 d 1805 m Mary Worthington Cpl MA
Roswell: b 11-29-1759 d 1-27-1827 m Pamelia Dickinson Pvt MA
Salmon: b 1764 d 6-9-1853 m (1)Diademia Byinton (2)Bulah —
    Pvt CT ★
Salmon: b 7-30-1752 d 8-31-1824 m (1)Hannah Bronson (2)Sarah
    Phinney Cpl CT
Samuel: b 1-3-1724 d 4-8-1782 m (1)Sarah Webster (2)Chloe
    Palmer Pvt CT
Samuel: b 1-1-1751 d 8-7-1822 m Miriam Grant Pvt CT
Samuel: b 4-1-1757 d 10-24-1811 m Huldah Hamlin Pvt CT
Samuel: b 7-7-1759 d 1-6-1815 m Dinah Woodruff Pvt CT
Samuel: b 2-11-1763 d 12-18-1829 m Lucy Couch Pvt CT ★
Samuel: b 1713 d 7-3-1800 m Mary Alexander PS MA
Samuel: b 6-3-1748 d 12-5-1830 m Sarah Ingraham Pvt NH
Seth: b 5-18-1762 d 12-20-1821 m Tryphosa Warner Pvt CT ★
Simeon: b 3-25-1760 d 6-8-1813 m Elizabeth Clark Pvt MA
Solomon: b 11-20-1749 d 1809 m Lucrecia Wheaton Sgt MA
Thaddeus: b 6-13-1754 d 7-28-1833 m Sarah Sheldon Pvt
    MA W★
Thomas: b 1757 d 3- -1845 m Azubah Chapin Sgt CT
Thomas: b 3-28-1726 d 1821 m Ann — Pvt CT
Thomas: b 1-26-1736 d 1798 m (1)Elizabeth Field Pvt CT
Timothy: b 10-16-1740 d 1-17-1815 m Mary Langdon Capt CT
Timothy: b 4-9-1719 d 6-21-1794 m Jemima Wood Cmsry CT
Wm.: b 3-15-1759 d 6-29-1848 m (1)Rhoda Fitch (2)Anna
    Messenger Pvt MA

ROPER,
Benjamin: b 1-7-1751 d 11-1-1826 m Azubah Willard Pvt MA
Daniel: b 10-2-1730 d 2-27-1821 m Sarah Greenwood Pvt MA
Ephraim: b 10-21-1716 d 12-5-1793 m Michal Houghton PS MA
George: b 1765 d 2-28-1845 m — Sol NC ★
James: b *c.* 1730 d *p.* 10- -1786 m Mary Peterson PS NC
John: b *c.* 1760 d 4-10-1833 m Dorcas Kilburn Sgt MA
John: b *c.* 1760 d *p.* 1794 m Lucy — Pvt NC
John: b 2-24-1763 d 7-26-1852 m Sarah Lewis Pvt NC ★
Manasseh: b 5-26-1752 d 6-16-1831 m Lucy Livermore Pvt VT
Nathaniel: b 2-23-1758 d 5-28-1800 m Naomi Gibbs Cpl MA
Richard: b *c.* 1735 d 1783 m (2)Ann Lewis PS VA
Silas: b 1-20-1754 d 10-27-1827 m Elizabeth Burpee 1Lt MA

ROPES,
Benjamin: b 7-10-1747 d 11-21-1778 m Margaret Symonds Lt MA

ROQUEMORE,
James: b — d *p.* 1803 m Elizabeth — Sol CL

**ROREBAUGH, (includes ROARBACH, ROHRBACH &
    ROORBACH)**
Christian: b *c.* 1745 d *p.* 10-1-1789 m Christina — PS PA
Henrich: b 2-24-1741 d *p.* 1794 m Cornelia Bresie Pvt NY
John: b *c.* 1738 d 10- -1821 m Elizabeth Harness PS VA
Lorenz: b 10-16-1746 d 1795 m Anna Catherine Grokes Sgt PA
Lorenz: b 1743 d *p.* 11-23-1822 m Christine Frye Pvt PA

RORICK,
Gasper: b 1751 d 4- -1841 m Betsey — Pvt NJ ★

RORIE,
Wm.: b *c.* 1754 d *a.* 12-3-1802 m Judah — PS NC

RORISON,
Alexander: b 4-22-1763 d 12-27-1832 m Mary Wilson PS PA

ROSA,
Isaac: b 2-5-1739 d 10-10-1782 m Maria VanVranken Lt NY
Jacob: bpt 10-14-1739 d *p.* 1790 m Marya Suiderland PS NY
Storm: b 4-1-1756 d 4-17-1834 m Elizabeth Sampman Pvt NY

ROSAMOND, (includes ROSEMAN)
James: b — d *p.* 6-8-1805 m Mary Dohorty Sol PS SC
Robert: b 5-8-1754 d 4-7-1787 m Katherine Forney Pvt VA
Samuel: b 1738 d 8-11-1814 m Sarah Hodges Capt SC W★

ROSBOROUGH,
Alexander: b *c.* 1740 d *p.* 1-23-1812 m Martha Gaston PS SC

ROSCOE,
David: b 1754 d 2-26-1832 m Silphina — Ens CT ★
Wm.: b 1732 d 10-9-1805 m — PS Cmsry NJ

ROSE,
Abraham: b 8-20-1759 d 12-16-1851 m Deziah Fish Pvt RI W★
Alexander: b 1738 d 4-12-1807 m Eunice Lea Maj VA
Allen: b *c.* 1740 d 1803 m Mary Kenton Pvt PA
Amos: b 3-6-1756 d *p.* 1783 m Abigail — Cpl PA
Andrew: b 1754/5 d 1-21-1815 m (1)Sarah Dilworth (2)Hannah
    Chapman PS PA
Benjamin: b 1750 d *p.* 1790 m Lucy Harper Cpl VA
Daniel: b 7-10-1749 d 9-26-1827 m Susanna Arndt Lt PA
David, Jr.: b 1-16-1753 d 1-23-1836 m Mary Rogers Pvt PS NY
David: b 7-2-1757 d 5-15-1845 m (2)Rebecca Carter Pvt NY
David: b 12-11-1736 d 1-1-1799 m (1)Hannah Mulford (3)Mrs
    Sarah Strong Havens PS NY
Edward: b 5-1-1747 d *p.* 1821 m Drusilla Pairpint Lt PA
Elijah: b 1745 d 12-11-1823 m Anna Curtis Pvt MA
Elisha: b 1728 d 2-10-1814 m (1)Abigail — (2)Sybel (Griswold)
    Drake Pvt MA
Erhard: b 2- -1723 d 4-26-1801 m Eve — PS PA
Ezekiel: b 5-13-1745 d 12-5-1824 m (1)Elizabeth Newkirk (2)Mrs
    Elizabeth More Pvt NJ
Ezekiel: b *c.* 1745 d 1814 m Harriet Colson Capt PA
Gad: b 8-24-1756 d 9-24-1837 m Annora Hale Pvt MA ★
Hugh: b 9-18-1743 d *p.* 10-16-1794 m Caroline Matilda Jordan
    Lt VA
Isaac: b *c.* 1748 d 6-7-1822 m Margaret Leyde Sgt MD ★
Isaac: b 1753 d 2-17-1829 m Margaret Forsythe Pvt VA W★
Israel: b 10-13-1734 d 9-10-1807 m Eunice — PS NY
Jacob: b — d *p.* 12-15-1803 m Anna — Pvt NY
Jacob: b 4-21-1761 d 8-20-1839 m Lisa Bowker Pvt NY ★
James: b 12-19-1744 d 5-1-1830 m (1)Thankful Miner (2)Dorcas
    Sherman Pvt RI
James: b *c.* 1755 d *a.* 4-2-1816 m Jane Conover Pvt VA
Jehiel: b 1748 d 6-7-1813 m Mary Ripley Pvt CT
Jesse: b 12-30-1738 d 10-2-1821 m Mary Green PS NY
Jesse: b 1760 d 7- -1852 m (1)Susan Smith (2)Rachel Parshal
    Pvt VA
Joel: b 3-2-1748 d *p.* 1794 m Rachel — Lt MA
John: b 1740 d 12-2-1822 m (1)Rachael Dutcher (2)Katharine
    Wheeler Ens CT ★
John: b 1746 d 1846 m Mary Washington Pvt GA
John: b 3-9-1760 d 1-9-1833 m Eve — Sol PS PA
John: b 1709 d *a.* 10-25-1785 m Elizabeth Eldred Pvt RI
John: b *c.* 1752 d *c.* 7- -1792 m Elizabeth Davis Sol VA
John: b 1- -1760 d 1837 m — Pvt VA
John, Sr.: b *c.* 1720 d 1780/1 m — PA VA
John: b 1735 d 1803 m Catherine Rose PS Col VA
Justus, Sr.: b 3- -1724 d 9-25-1781 m Deborah Barlow Pvt MA
Lemuel: b 6- -1764 d 9-13-1835 m Achsah Hale Pvt VA ★
Lewis: b 10-11-1749 d 2-20-1829 m (1)Barbara Trair (2)Mrs Mary
    McMurtrie Pvt VA
Nathan: b 1731 d 10-21-1793 m Sarah Rumsey Capt NY
Patrick: b 1745 d 12-22-1822 m (1)Jane Lawson (2)Margaret
    Nicholas Col PS CS VA
Peleg: b 9-16-1751 d 11-6-1823 m Mary Spicer Pvt CT
Peter: b 7-25-1738 d 12-29-1788 m Sarah Gates Pvt CT
Peter: b 11-28-1761 d 1-27-1823 m (1)Jemima Day (2)Anna
    Wilcox Pvt MA
Peter Gardiner: b 1-12-1754 d 1834 m (1)Maria Roop (2)Hester
    Thompson Lt PA
Phineas: b 2-29-1760 d *p.* 1800 m (1)Sarah Gillett (2) — Webb
    (3) — Mattoon Pvt MA
Richard: b 1754 d 1843 m Mary — Pvt VA
Robert: b *c.* 1737 d *p.* 5-29-1816 m — PS NC
Robert: b 1745 d 1793 m — Littleton Dr VA
Russell: b 6-10-1753 d 6-1-1830 m Lydia Orvis Pvt MA ★
Samuel: b 1748 d 11-4-1780 m Elizabeth Hale Pvt Dr CT
Seth: b 7-21-1762 d — m Sarah Bates Pvt MA
Sharon: bpt 3-21-1730/1 d 4-4-1821 m Mercy Fowler Cpl MA
Thomas: b 1745 d 1796 m Martha Craig Pvt NJ
Thomas: b — d 12-13-1817 m Clarissa Fish Pvt NY
Thomas: b 9-27-1736 d 4-3-1780 m Deborah — PS NY
Timothy: b 1750 d 1797 m Elizabeth Pomeroy Pvt CT
Timothy: b 6-1-1762 d 11-27-1813 m Lydia Munson Sgt MA
Wm.: b *c.* 1745 d *a.* 4-5-1808 m (1)Elizabeth — (2)Elizabeth
    Martin PS MD
Wm.: b 1757 d 2-12-1835 m Elizabeth Merritt Ens NC W★
Wm.: b *c.* 1735 d *p.* 1778 m Anne Sangston Sgt NC
Wm.: b *c.* 1740 d 10- -1807 m Elizabeth Frost Pvt PA
Wm.: b *c.* 1761 d 1847 m Ann Boyd Pvt PA
Wm.: b 1735 d 1792 m Mary Fielding PS VA

ROSEBERRY,
Alexander: b 1735 d 1803 m — McConnell Pvt PA
John: b 4-28-1761 d 8-20-1855 m Flora Cree Pvt NJ ★

ROSEBOOM,
Garrett: b 9-21-1762 d 5-15-1840 m Frisha Compton Pvt NJ ★
Jacob: bpt 11-23-1740 d p. 4-20-1797 m Hester Lansing Capt NY
John: b 1-20-1760 d 1834 m Phebe VanNest Pvt NJ ★
John: b 10-23-1739 d 4-5-1805 m Susanna Veeder Lt NY

ROSEBROOK,
Eleazer: b 5-28-1747 d 9-27-1818 m Hannah Haynes Sgt NH

ROSEBROOM,
Henry: b 5-27-1757 d 4-1-1843 m Rachel Smawley Sgt NJ ★

ROSEBURGH, (includes ROSBRUGH, & ROSBURGH)
John: b 1714 d 1-2-1777 m Jane Ralston Chp PA NJ

ROSECRANTZ,
Cornelius: bpt 1-2-1763 d 12-16-1824 m Janeke Decker Pvt NY W★

ROSENBERGER, (includes ROSENBERRY)
Benjamin: b c. 1758 d 1824 m Margaret Nash Pvt PA
Erasmus: b — d p. 4-29-1794 m (1)Anna Catarin Baumgaertner
   (2)Regina — Sol VA
John: b 1724 d 1808 m (1)Barbara — (2)Christiana — Pvt PA

ROSENKRANS, (includes ROSECRANS, ROSECRANTS,
   ROSENKRANS, ROSENGRANT)
Benjamin: b 6- -1746 d 3-6-1830 m Hannah — Sol VA
Daniel: bpt 8-24-1737 d a. 10-19-1782 m Catherine Cole Capt NY
Frederick: b 5- -1744 d 1812/3 m Phoebe Bell Pvt NY
Jacobus: b 2-2-1750 d 4-22-1805 m (2)Phoebe Vincent Capt NY
James: b 4-21-1745 d p. 1790 m Maria Hornbeck Pvt PA
Jeremiah: b 1758 d 1842 m Sally Strickland Pvt PA
John: b 7-5-1724 d 6-15-1786 m Margaret De Witt Col NJ
John: bpt 12-23-1744 d p. 1810 m Marie Roosa Pvt NY

ROSENSTEEL,
George: b 4-20-1753 d 10-9-1834 m Susanna — Cpl MD

ROSS, (includes ROUSE)
Adam: b 10-5-1752 d 3-21-1828 m Elizabeth Ramsdell Cpl MA
Adam: b 1760 d 1830 m Catherine Ross Pvt VA
Alexander: b c. 1743 d 4-2-1800 m Sarah Girdler NCapt MA
Alexander: b 1713 d 5-10-1780 m Elizabeth Becket Dr NJ
Alexander: b 1754 d 1809 m Ann Philips Pvt PA
Allen: b 1766 d 4-7-1840 m Rebecca Carpenter Sol PA
Amasa: b 7-5-1750 d 7-30-1807 m (1)Esther Allen (2)Sarah Bartlett
   Pvt MA
Ambrose: b c. 1762 d p. 12-8-1810 m Elizabeth Gordon Pvt VA
Andrew: b 4-23-1741 d 11-9-1819 m Mary Lyon SgtMaj NJ
Andrew: b 1756 d 1816 m Nancy Collins Pvt PA
Arthur Brown: b 8-9-1746 d 8-3-1806 m Hannah Conger PS SC
Benjamin: b 7-23-1749 d a. 1814 m Susanna Lakeman Pvt MA
Benjamin: b 1- -1747 d 7-28-1827 m Prudence Ross Pvt PA
Daniel, Jr.: b p. 1790 m Margaret Burgen Pvt MA
Daniel: b 1735-40 d p. 9-17-1792 m Elizabeth Garth 2Lt PS VA
David: b 2-12-1755 d 1800 m Henrietta Maria Bordley Maj MD
David: b 1733 d 11-19-1796 m Hannah Scudder Wgm Sgt NJ
David, Jr.: b 5- -1746 d 9-22-1824 m Anna Stites Wgm NJ
David: b 1753 d c. 1825 m Susan Sutherland Pvt VA
Edward: b 6-20-1758 d 12-13-1837 m Tacey Ross Mus Ens RI ★
Ezekiel: b 9-7-1766 d 2-13-1845 m Ruth Maxwell Pvt NJ ★
Francis: b 1750 d a. 4- -1824 m Esther Caruthers Lt NC
Francis: b 1744 d 3-31-1779 m Rachel Love Maj SC
George: b 1760 d p. 1827 m (1)Polly Parker (2)Polly Yarbough
   Sol GA
George, Jr.: b 1753 d 1796 m Amy VanCort 2Lt NJ
George: b 5-10-1730 d 7-14-1779 m Ann Lawler SDI CS PA
George: b 11-11-1746 d 3- -1801 m Isabella Montgomery Dr PS SC
George: b 7-15-1760 d 8-21-1846 m Edna Elizabeth Walker Pvt
   SC ★
Henry: b 1758 d 2-7-1847 m Jemimah Robinson Raynor Drm MA ★
Issac: b 5-7-1760 d 1-30-1843 m Elizabeth Pembroke Pvt NJ W★
Issac, Jr.: b 1-15-1760 d 1-19-1836 m Jane Allison Capt SC
James: b 7-22-1744 d p. 1790 m Phoebe Gerry Pvt MA
James: b 6-8-1761 d 1-1-1849 m Lidia Coburn Pvt NC ★
James: b 1752 d 8- -1808 m Maria Sabina Kuhn LCol PA
James: b 1751 d 12- -1805 m Sarah — Lt PA
James, Sr.: b 1732 d 2-22-1780 m Mary McKnight PS PA
James, Jr.: b 1764 d 1842 m Mary White PS PA
James: b c. 1746 d 1797 m Martha Watson Pvt PA
Jesse: b c. 1760 d p. 1841 m Sarah Ann — Sol GA
John: b 4-2-1733 d p. 1784 m Mary Duncklee Pvt MA
John: b 1759 d 10-3-1843 m Mary Barr Pvt MA
John: b 3-2-1752 d 9-7-1796 m Mary Brainerd Bgd Maj NJ
John: b 12-24-1715 d 7-4-1798 m (1)Hannah Talmadge
   (2)Joannah (Miller) Crane (3)Susanna (Miller) Crane PS NJ
John: b 1738 d 9-20-1806 m Sarah Jackson PS NJ
John: b c. 1750 d 1795 m Martha — Pvt NC
John: b 1750 d 1794 m Elizabeth Bennett Pvt NC

John: b 10-3-1754 d 8-14-1815 m Temperance Ferrill Pvt NC
John: b 1751 d 9-8-1833 m Charlotta Bosher QM PA W★
John: b 1730 d 9-10-1802 m (1)Isabella Smith (2)Isabel Wallace
   Pvt PA
John: b c. 1737 d 1779 m Jeames — Pvt PA
John: b c. 1757 d p. 1822 m Jennett Irwin Pvt PA
John: b c. 1725 d 1812 m Deborah Jane Johnston Pvt PA
John, Jr.: b 9-12-1741 d p. 1787 m Lois Taylor PS RI
John: b 7-7-1761 d 10-10-1844 m Elizabeth — Pvt SC ★
John: b 6-8-1730 d 3- -1795 m Allison Sloan Pvt VA
Jonathan: b 4-5-1749 d 11-19-1842 m Joanna Ricker Pvt MA
Joseph: b 1750 d 1838 m Mary Clark Ross Pvt MA ★
Joseph, Jr.: b 1759 d 1811 m Jane — Pvt PA
Joseph: b 1756 d p. 1833 m Margaret Hunt Pvt VA ★
Joseph: b c. 1762 d 1805 m (2)Elizabeth Evans Pvt VA
Kneeland: b 4-3-1748 d p. 1792 m Anna Porter Pvt MA
Lawrence: b 5-15-1722 d 8-8-1818 m Susanne Oldham Pvt PA
Lebbeus: b 3-29-1761 d 8-18-1816 m Rhoda Crandall Pvt RI
Matthias: b c. 1750 d 1826 m Mary Halsey Ens NJ
Moses: b 1749 d — m Abigail Pickering Pvt NH
Nathaniel: b 10-27-1751 d 4-26-1794 m Sarah Lakeman Pvt MA
Nathaniel: b 1748 d 1823 m (1)Rachel Bryant (2)Sarah Badgley
   (3)Nancy Badgley Bbd NJ
Peleg: b 9-9-1733 d p. 12-13-1784 m Hannah Lewis Pvt RI
Perrin: b 7-4-1748 d 7-3-1778 m Mary Otis Lt PA
Reuben: b 1760 d p. 11-16-1832 m (2)Henrietta Biven Pvt Pvtr MD
Reuben: b 1747 d p. 1813 m (2)Sarah Van Tierce Pvt VA
Robert: b 1755 c 10-14-1827 m Hannah — Sgt NJ
Robert: b 1759 d 7-7-1843 m Mary Doak Pvt NC
Robert: b 9-4-1753 d 11-19-1823 m (1)Elizabeth Hamilton (2)Dorcas
   Andrews Cpl PA
Robert: b c. 1736 d c. 1803 m (1)Nancy Reeves (2)Elizabeth — Pvt
   PA
Robert: b 1-13-1740 d 1-23-1825 m Lucy Arnold Pvt PA ★
Roger: b 9-20-1740 d 10-6-1817 m (1)Molly Rugg (2)Hannah
   Robinson Pvt MA
Samuel: b 1-16-1738 d 11-15-1815 m Katherine Gary Sol MA
Seth: b 2-21-1757 d 3-18-1833 m Abigail Fairbank Drm Pvt MA
Seth: b 12-4-1755 d 12-11-1836 m (1)Alice Bowen (2)Rebecca
   Booth Ens RI ★
Thomas: b 4-11-1755 d 10-25-1841 m Hannah Staniford Pvt MA ★
Thomas: b 1760 d 1846 m Deborah Bond Pvt MA
Thomas: b 3- -1738 d 5-20-1813 m Jane Esther Miller Pvt PA
Thomas: b 1740 d 1830 m Margaret Duncan Cpl VA
Timothy: b 7-30-1751 d 1-12-1844 m Mary Burnham Pvt MA ★
Valentine: b 1760 d p. 1820 m Mary Ross Pvt VA ★
Wm.: b 1752 d c. 1798 m Ester — PS DE
Wm.: b 7-25-1759 d 12-4-1839 m Mary Pitman Pvt MA
Wm.: b c. 1736 d a. 1808 m Hannah — Pvt NJ
Wm.: b 4- -1760 d 9- -1813 m Althea Patten Pvt NY
Wm.: b 8-9-1731 d 12-25-1801 m Mary Griffin PS NC
Wm.: b 1-11-1737 d 4-3-1818 m Margaret Evans Col PA
Wm.: b 1755 d 11- -1796 m Elizabeth Goodwin SeaCap PA
Wm.: b 3-29-1761 d 8-9-1842 m Elizabeth Sterling Pvt Sct PA
Wm.: b 11-25-1762 d 8-28-1849 m Esther Reid Pvt PA
Wm.: b 1725 d 1777 m Jean Nesbit CS PS PA
Wm.: b 1739 d 5-14-1834 m Winneford Rector Pvt VA
Wm.: b 1755 d 12-5-1831 m Sally Lamkin Pvt VA
Wm.: b c. 1744 d 4- -1834 m Jane — Tms VA
Williamson: b 1759 d 1840 m Elizabeth Odom Pvt NC ★
Zachariah: b 4-21-1761 d c. 1845 m Elizabeth Davis Pvt NJ

ROSSELL, (includes ROZEL)
Andrews: b c. 1760 d 5-10-1814 m Elizabeth Meyers Pvt NJ
Zachariah: b 1758 d 1830 m Sarah Zilpha Pvt NJ
Zachariah: b 1723 d 2-21-1815 m Mrs Margaret Curtis CS NJ

ROSSER, (includes ROZER)
James: b c. 1740 d 1800 m Alice Worthing PS NC
John: b 1760 d 1830 m Marion — Pvt GA
John: b c. 1750 d a. 1796 m Mary Neavill Sol VA
Jonathan: b c. 10- -1762 d a. 4-2-1795 m (1)Elizabeth Oglesby
   (2)Mrs Nancy Helm PS VA
Joseph: b c. 1760 d 1810 m Nancy Bennett Capt NC
Wm.: b 10- -1762 d 2-24-1835 m Elizabeth Wood Pvt VA ★

ROSSITER, (includes ROSITER, ROSSETER & ROSSETTER)
Bryan: b 9-6-1760 d 1-1-1835 m Sarah Hopper Sgt CT ★
Daniel: b 1736 d 1-31-1821 m Mary — Pvt PA
David: b 1732 d 1810 m — Col MA
Elnathan: b 10-30-1730 d 12-9-1813 m Sarah Baldwin Capt CT
John Cotton: b 7-3-1739 d 2-9-1798 m Phoebe Palmer PS CT
Samuel: b 1753 d 11-16-1823 m Mary Elizabeth Stephens Pvt PA
Stephen: b c. 1732 d p. 1778 m Mary Johnston Pvt CT
Thomas: b c. 1727 d p. 1780 m Elizabeth Bull Lt MD
Timothy: b 5-21-1754 d 2-26-1835 m (1)Mary Ruggles (2)Anna
   Arnold Pvt CT
Timothy: b 4- -1752 d 1845 m Mary Denison Dr MA ★
Wm.: b 2-11-1740 d 12-28-1820 m Submit Chittenden Lt CT

ROSSMAN,
Adam: b 1758 d p. 1790 m Ann Decker Pvt NY
Fite: b 7-20-1743 d 2-19-1831 m Ann Ham 2Lt NY

George, Jr.: b 1755 d 1820 m (2)Ruth Wood Pvt NY
Jacob: b 3-30-1746 d *p.* 1790 m Elizabeth Shufelt 1Lt NY
John: bpt 1-13-1729/39 d 1836 m Magdalena Shufelt Ens NY

ROTH, (includes ROTZ)
Christian: b 12-25-1757 d 4-10-1828 m Catharine Michael Lt PA
Gottfried: bpt 9-24-1759 d 1-10-1829 m Mary Margaret Troxell
      Pvt PA
Jacob: b 1748/9 d 11- -1826 m (1)Veronica — (2)Margaretha
      Bergstresser Pvt PA
John: b *c.* 1730 d 1802 m (1)Sophia Dorothea (2)Mary Eva — Pvt PA
Jonathan: b 3-18-1751 d 9-3-1819 m Dorothea Elizabeth Linn
      Pvt PA
Matthias: b 11-8-1717 d 3-13-1795 m Ann Elizabeth Beyer PS PA

ROTHERAM,
Jacob: b 1752 d 1794 m Mary Pierce Pvt DE

ROTHERMEL,
Daniel: b *a.* 1730 d *p.* 1790 m Elizabeth — CS Capt PA
Jacob: b 9-13-1751 d 4-28-1833 m (1)Mrs Barbara Rothermel
      (2)Magdalena Price Capt PA

ROTHMAHLER,
Erasmus: b 1760 d 1820-30 m Henrietta Wragg Lt SC

ROTHROCK,
George: b 1747 d 5-1-1826 m Elizabeth — Sol PA
Issac: b — d *c.* 1818 m Gertraut — Pvt PA
John: b 2-18-1744 d 8-28-1805 m (1)Dorothy Gump (2)Salome
      Charity Worley 2Lt PA
John: b 1725 d 1794 m Mary Kreiling Pvt PA
Philip: b 8-14-1713 d 2-28-1803 m (1)Catherine Kuntz (2)Mrs
      Elenora Maquinet PS PA

ROTTEN, (or RATTAN)
John: b 1747 d 10-11-1821 m Mary Green Sol NC

ROUDEBUSH,
Daniel: b 1749 d 10-10-1804 m Christina Shively PS MD

ROUNDS, (includes ROUND & ROWND)
Bartram: b 12-22-1741 d 10-1-1833 m Alice Wilkinson Lt RI
Charles: b 1761 d 3-4-1843 m Lydia Pierce Pvt MA ★
George: b 1718/9 d 3-10-1791 m Ruth Horton Pvt MA
George: b 2-12-1746 d 1-2-1842 m Martha Hopkins Pvt VT
Hezekiah: b 12-20-1752 d — m Jemima Perry Sgt MA
Jabez, Sr.: b 9-28-1708 d 3-14-1790 m Renew Carpenter Pvt MA
Jabez, Jr.: b 1-8-1735 d 5-29-1806 m Prudence Crossman Pvt MA
James: b 1758 d 1-3-1843 m (1)Rachel Clay (2)Elizabeth
      Woodruff Pvt MA ★
James: b 1743 d 2-25-1813 m Urania Cole Sgt Sct VT
John: b 11-1-1715 d 1793/4 m Elizabeth Martin Pvt MA
John: b 10-23-1761 d 1812 m (1)Martha Gardner (2)Lavina Horton
      Pvt MA
Joseph: b 1753 d 1-15-1838 m Susannah Mosher Pvt MA
Jotham: b 3-2-1763 d 3-25-1847 m Susan Wilbur Pvt RI ★
Lemuel: b 7-26-1756 d 5-19-1836 m Mary Whitney Pvt MA ★
Nathaniel: b 8-3-1759 d 2-28-1850 m Avis Chase Pvt MA RI ★
Oliver: b 3-27-1759 d *p.* 1841 m Mary — Pvt MA ★
Samuel: b *c.* 1714 d *c.* 1788 m Mary — Pvt MA
Samuel: b 1758 d *p.* 9-12-1836 m — Pvt NY ★
Samuel Hopkins: b *c.* 1744 d *p.* 1801 m (2)Naomi Atkinson Campbell
      Capt MD
Simeon: b 11-18-1761 d 4-8-1840 m Nancy Weaver Pvt RI ★
Sylvester: b 4-10-1762 d 10-26-1824 m Mehetabel Perry Pvt MA

ROUNDTREE, (includes ROUNTREE & ROWNTREE)
Jesse: b 6-27-1765 d 4-12-1831 m Winnie Jenkins Pvt NC
John: b 1765 d 1827 m Lucy — Pvt VA
Randall: b — d *p.* 9-18-1788 m — CS VA
Richardson: b *c.* 1745 d 4-20-1819 m Mildred Hart Sol PS SC
Samuel: b 10-20-1756 d 9-28-1805 m Mary Hughes Pvt VA
Thomas: b 1723 d 1795 m Lydia — PS NC
Thomas: b *c.* 1748 d *p.* 1782 m Letitia Barnard Pvt VA
Wm.: b 2- -1710 d 1791 m Rachel — CS NC
Wm.: b 1747 d 1820 m Mary — Sgt VA

ROUNDY,
John: b 12-3-1726 d 9-25-1799 m Elizabeth Rea PS MA
John: b 10-28-1748 d 4-23-1805 m Ruth Chickerly Sgt VT
Joseph: bpt 9-27-1747 d 6-3-1823 m (1)Elizabeth Vickery (2)Sarah
      Dupar Pvt Arfr MA ★
Samuel: b 6-6-1733 d 9-24-1824 m Anne Huntington PS NH
Uriah: b 10-27-1756 d 5-1-1813 m Lucretia Needham Pvt VT

ROUNSEVILLE, (includes ROUNSEVELL & ROUNSEVILL)
Josiah: b 1728 d 1791 m Sarah — CS NC
Philip: b 7-2-1750 d *p.* 1797 m Mercy Cole Pvt MA
Thomas: b 1746 d 1-31-1826 m (1)Phylena Hathaway (2)Mrs Anna
      Cole Pvt MA

Wm.: b 1735 d 9- -1797 m (1)Rebecca Hoar (2)Gabriella
      DeMaranville Pvt MA

ROURKE, (includes ROARK)
James: b *c.* 1745 d *p.* 1820 m — Pvt NC
Martin: b *c.* 1760 d 6-1-1807 m Elizabeth Lawrence Sgt MA W★
Michael, Sr.: b 9-29-1745 d 1-9-1839 m Letitia Grigsby Lt Spy VA ★
Wm.: b 6-6-1760 d 3-4-1841 m — Pvt Tms NJ ★
Wm.: b 1757 d 1832 m Sarah Dorris Mus NC

ROUSCULP,
Phillip: b — d *c.* 1807 m Mary — 1Lt PA

ROUSE,
Casper: b 3-13-1734 d 4-23-1811 m (1)Rebecca Mead (2)Mrs
      Catherine Kimball PS NY
Jabez: b — d *p.* 2-25-1807 m Margaret Haynes Sgt CT
John: b 1741 d 7-1-1818 m Rebecca Barker Pvt MA
John: b 12-9-1741 d 1-19-1834 m Hannah Smith Capt NY ★
Jonathan: b 1761 d 6-9-1843 m Martha Harden Pvt NY
Joseph: b 2-15-1751 d *p.* 1833 m Susanna Ralsbach Pvt VA
Louis: b 1758 d 11-8-1835 m Elizabeth Garrett Pvt VA ★
Nicholas: b 7-30-1763 d 6-24-1845 m Olive Austin Pvt NY ★
Samuel: b 1752 d 1838 m Elizabeth — Pvt VA ★
Simeon: b 2-11-1757 d 12-21-1832 m (1)Huldah Smith
      (2)Mrs Cheesebrough Pvt MA ★
Wm.: b 1-30-1756 d 6-15-1829 m Mary Stuart Pvt SC

ROUSH,
George: b 8-2-1753 d 1822 m (1)Christian Morr (2)Barbara Potter
      Pvt PA
George: b 10-9-1755 d 8-23-1839 m Mary Margarete — Pvt PA
George: b 1721 d 1815 m Anna Maria Pvt PA
George: b 7- -1761 d 5-31-1845 m (1)Catherine Yerkel
      (2)Mrs Catherine Wolf Pvt VA ★
Henry: b 1752 d 10-26-1831 m (1)Dorothy — (2)Anna — Pvt VA
Jacob: b 7-22-1751 d 12-3-1819 m Mary Elizabeth Whittenmeyer
      Sol PA
Jacob: b 1746 d 1830 m Catharine Fox Pvt VA
John Adam: b 1711 d 10-19-1786 m Susannah — PS VA
Jonas: b 9- -1763 d 1850 m Barbara Fox Pvt VA
Philip: b 1741 d 1820 m Catharine Kelchner Pvt VA

ROUSMANIERE,
Louis: b *a.* 1750 d *p.* 1782 m Ann Davenport CmsryGen FrA

ROUSSEAU,
Nicholas: b *c.* 1752-6 d 3-5-1824 m Maria Gradenigo PS LA

ROUTON, (or ROUGHTON)
Edward: b *c.* 1750 d *p.* 2-25-1797 m Ann — PS NC

ROUTT, (includes ROUT)
George: b 1-6-1750 d 1790 m Winifred Pope Pvt VA
Wm.: b 5-29-1756 d *p.* 10-25-1831 m Anna Staige Cpl VA

ROUZ,
David Lewis Emanuel: b 5-8-1761 d 2-8-1838 m Mrs Ann Buckle Pvt
      SC ★

ROWE, (includes ROE, ROW, ROWE & WROE)
Andrew: b *c.* 1754 d 10- -1821 m (1)Betsy Sell (2)Elizabeth
      Heintzelman (3)Margaret Shuster Pvt PA
Aretas: b 2-20-1753 d 8-21-1825 m Abigail Sargent PS NH
Arthur: b 3-5-1753 d 8-3-1823 m Sarah Ann Row Cpl MD
Austin: b 1749 d 1830 m Catherine — Pvt MA
Benjamin, Sr.: b 10-3-1720 d 3-28-1790 m Susanna Fogg PS NH
Benjamin, Jr.: bpt 7-22-1750 d 11-7-1818 m Joanna Tilton SgnMte
      PS NH
Benjamin: b *c.* 1757 d *a.* 1832 m Catherine Demarest Cpl NY
Benjamin: b 9-28-1759 d 7-25-1825 m Mary Ware Pvt NY W★
Benjamin: b *c.* 1712 d 1790 m Ruth Miller PS NY
Caleb: b 10-15-1755/6 d 2-3-1840 m Priscilla Perkins Ens MA ★
Charles: b 10-15-1755/6 d 2-3-1840 m Catherine Messenger Pvt
      NY ★
Daniel: b — d 5-26-1811 m Thankful — Pvt CT
Daniel: b 5-19-1759 d *a.* 4-7-1813 m Charlotte Griffin Pvt CT
Daniel: b 1-20-1740 d 1-11-1820 m Deborah Brewster PS NY
Ebenezer: b 8-25-1749 d 12-21-1838 m (1)Martha Sheldon (2)Mrs
      Sally Thurston Grover Sol MA ★
Ebenezer: b 1759 d 1825 m Deborah Davis Pvt MA
Elizabeth Eltinge: b 1-8-1745 d 9-28-1793 m James Roe PS NY
Ezra: b 4-5-1752 d 9-17-1834 m Huldah Chidsey Pvt CT ★
George: b 1750 d 1818 m Margaret Weaver Lt PA
George: b *c.* 1753 d *p.* 1820 m Rachel — Pvt VA
Henry: b 5-20-1754 d 11-26-1834 m Ann Jaggard 2Lt NJ
Isaac: b 1-1-1762 d 1-20-1852 m Elizabeth Butler Pvt MA ★
Isaiah: b 5-25-1743 d 9-18-1810 m Sarah Healey Sgt PS NH
James: b 3-2-1738 d 3-26-1819 m Elizabeth Sanders Pvt MA
James: b 4-9-1744 d 10-31-1815 m Elizabeth Eltinge QM NY
Jeremiah, Jr.: b 1-1-1743 d 3-20-1829 m Sarah Hoyt Pvt NH
Jesse: b 1-21-1755 d 11-14-1845 m Mary Jane Ferris Pvt VA

ROWE, contd.
John: b 9-18-1737 d 6-13-1801 m (1)Sarah Pool (2)Mrs Elizabeth Adams Maj MA
John, Sr.: b 6-28-1714 d 10-2-1781 m Mary Baker CS MA
John: b 1744 d 1-25-1825 m Susanna Scribner Pvt NH
John: b 1751 d 1810 m Charity Row Capt NY
John: b 1757 d 1831 m Sarah Harris Pvt NY
John: b 1705 d 11-17-1782 m Joanna (Miller) Helme PS NY
John, Sr.: b c. 1748 d 12-23-1812 m Elizabeth — Pvt SC
John: b 3-17-1760 d 12- -1828 m Jane — Ens PA
John: b 1759 d 2-11-1835 m Susanna Sperau Pvt PA
John: b c. 1750 d 1790 m (1)Mary — (2)Betsey — Pvt VT
John: b 10-21-1721 d p. 6-14-1783 m Sarah — Cav VA
Jonas, Sr.: b c. 1727 d a. 4-12-1798 m Phoebe — Pvt VT
Jonathan: b 10-6-1729 d 7-1-1795 m (1)Rachel Parsons (2)Mrs Alice Escob Hoole Sgt MA
Joseph: b 11- -1743 d p. 1792 m Anna (Hodgkins) Carter Pvt MA
Joseph, Jr.: b 1744 d 1784 m Lydia Palmer 2Lt RI
Joshua: b 7-8-1758 d 4-30-1814 m Mary Ayer Pvt MA W★
Lazarus: b 1725 d 10-14-1829 m Molly Webber Pvt NH ★
Michael Christopher: b c. 1715 d c. 1788 m (1)Margaret Hesse (2)Mrs Ann Chivilette LCol SC
Nathan: b 6-25-1725 d 5-17-1809 m Lydia Page Pvt NH
Nathaniel: b 8-11-1761 d 5-23-1833 m Mary Satterly Pvt NY
Nathaniel, Sr.: b 5-2-1734 d 10-13-1814 m Susanna Roe Capt NY
Nathaniel: b c. 1702 d p. 5-3-1785 m Mary — Pvt NY
Nathaniel, Sr.: b 1-17-1701 d 4-16-1789 m Elizabeth Phillips PS NY
Nicholas: b 1719 d p. 4-25-1786 m Susanna Winnegar PS NY
Phillips: b 10-20-1729 d 9-10-1815 m (1)Submit Strong (2)Martha Hawkins Adj PS NY
Richard: b 4-3-1738 d 9-18-1813 m Rebecca Chancellor PS VA
Robert: b 12-11-1726 d 1-25-1804 m Abigail Tilton PS NH
Shadwrick: b 5-11-1762 d 9- -1853 m (1)Elizabeth Hudson (2)Mrs Mary Moultrie Bynum Pvt NC
Stephen: b 1-31-1758 d 11-9-1838 m Rebecca Lewis Pvt NY ★
Simon: b 12-15-1751 d p. 1789 m Mary Morrison Pvt NH
Thomas: b 1737 d 1825 m Mary Welles Pvt MA
Thomas: b 3-7-1754 d 2-23-1840 m Rachel Keeling Pvt VA
Timothy: b c. 1759 d 9-1-1830 m Martha Sayre Cpl NY
Wm.: b — d c. 8-13-1787 m Juliana — Sgt MD
Wm.: b 4-1-1744 d 8-29-1830 m Mary VanDeusen Lt NY
Wm.: b 1739 d p. 1811 m Mary Feake Sgt NY
Wm.: b 9-15-1729 d 1781 m Grace Chancellor Sgt VA
Zebulon: b 7-9-1749 d 5-9-1843 m Prudence (Rowe) Cpl MA ★

ROWELL,
Abraham: b 1743 d 1-29-1815 m Elizabeth Eastman PS NH
Christopher: b 10-29-1732 d 1812 m Ruth Morse PS NH
Daniel: b 12-1-1745 d 11- -1831 m Judith French Lt NH
Daniel: b 1763 d 1847 m Nancy Neal Pvt NH ★
Eliphalet: b 1729 d c. 1801 m Sarah King Pvt MA
Enoch, Jr.: b 7-3-1756 d 8-2-1840 m Rachel Worthen Sgt NH ★
Jonathan: b 10-1-1753 d 12-26-1831 m (1)Mehitable Wells (2)Hannah Newman Sol VT W★
Lemuel: a. 1750 d 1806 m Mary Sevrance Pvt MA
Peter: b 8-13-1758 d 4-6-1819 m Betsey Marsh Fif MA
Philip: b c. 1750 d p. 1798 m Dorcas Reddington Pvt NH
Samuel: b 1754 d 6-11-1830 m Sarah Dustin Pvt NH
Thomas: b 4-9-1702/3 d 9-21-1790 m Abigail Stevens CS PS MA
Thomas: b 4-21-1737 d 8-27-1816 m Mary — PS MA
Wm.: b 9-1-1740 d 9-27-1816 m (1)Mary Brown (2)Hannah Sargeant Brevt Maj NH
Wm.: b 1755 d 9-30-1810 m Mrs Ruth Matthews Tenant Pvt NH
Wm.: b 1749 d p. 1840 m Hannah Duty Pvt PS NH

ROWLAND, (includes ROLAND)
Andrew: b 1-17-1737 d 7-26-1802 m Elizabeth Fitch PS CS CT
Daniel: b 4-21-1750 d 5-3-1823 m Hester Beers Pvt CT
David: b 2- -1762 d 2-5-1843 m Zuviah Whipple Pvt CT ★
George: b 1736 d 1793 m Rachel — PS NJ
Henry, Jr.: b 10-15-1742 d 1816 m (1)Phebe Huntley (2)Martha — Pvt CT
Henry: b 5-7-1748 d 1821 m Mary — Pvt PA
Hezekiah: b 1-9-1759 d 4-29-1819 m Grace Wildman Pvt CT ★
James: b 5- -1783 d 1840 m Elizabeth — Pvt NC ★
James: b a. 1745 d 1805 m Margaret Kyle Pvt VA
John: b 1744/5 d 3-18-1850 m Mary Osborne Pvt DE
John: b 1735 d 1791 m Ann — Capt PA
John: b 1716 d 2-8-1793 m (1)Grace Paschall (2)Ann Smith PS PA
Jonathan: b 12-18-1751 d 4-9-1783 m Sarah Maxwell Capt PA
Jonathan: b 4-15-1739 d 4-12-1807 m Catherine Huber PS PA
Joseph: b 10-20-1760 d 9-21-1856 m Christina — Sgt PA
Michael: b 1755 d 1814 m Elizabeth Hairston Pvt VA
Thomas: b 9-8-1750 d 4-3-1836 m Mildred McCoy Lewis Sol NC
Thomas: b 10-10-1758 d p. 1785 m (1)Elizabeth Weaver (2)Mary Stark Pvt PA
Thomas: b 1744 d 1814 m Mary Russell LCol VA
Thomas Wood: b 4-5-1758 d 3-18-1836 m Mary Hubbard Hand Pvt NY ★
Wm.: b 1722 d 1794 m Mary Womach Arfr NC

ROWLANDSON,
Wilson, Sr.: b 9-30-1733 d 7-1-1775 m Anne Bunce Pvt CT

ROWLES,
John: b 1756 d 1818 m Mary Whippo Pvt PA
Wm.: b 1759 d 3-9-1846 m Ann Brierly Pvt MD ★

ROWLETT,
Wm.: b 1753 d p. 1831 m Nancy Hudson Ens VA
Wm.: b 8-13-1755 d 6-2-1839 m (2)Mrs Rebecca Short Pvt VA ★

ROWLEY, (includes ROWLEE & ROLEY)
Aaron, Sr.: b 9-2-1739 d 3-1-1799 m Anna Richmond LCol MA
Aaron, Jr.: b 1762 d 2-27-1824 m Sarah — Pvt MA
Abijah: b 4-27-1758 d 7-23-1850 m Elizabeth Culver Pvt Arfr CT ★
Daniel: b 4-20-1759 d 4-1-1840 m Phebe Miller Pvt NY ★
Daniel, Sr.: b 3-12-1720 d p. 1790 m (1)Bethia Langwell (2)Jemima Parsons (3)Rachel — Sol NY
Ebenezer: b 10-20-1727 d 2-7-1811 m Susan Anable Sol CT
Ebenezer, 3d: b 1-10-1756 d — m Abigail Knowlton Fif CT
Heman: b 11-14-1746 d 12-26-1818 m (1)Lydia Seely (2)Mrs Graham Lt NY
Hopkins: b 12-18-1758 d 9-1-1831 m Elizabeth Stuart Pvt VT
Ithamar: b 10-1-1753 d p. 1798 m Dimmis Gates Pvt CT
John: b c. 1748 d 1822 m (2)Margaret — Pvt PA
Jonathan: b 11-18-1729 d p. 10-13-1798 m Esther Hopkins PS VT
Joseph L.: b 1752 d 12-23-1835 m (2)Hannah Loveland Pvt MA
Nathan C.: b 1756 d 7-11-1830 m Lucy Lament Pvt MA
Nathaniel: b 8-20-1763 d 1-6-1850 m Jerusha Rood Lt NY
Reuben: b 1750 d 7-6-1833 m Susan Campbell Pvt VT ★
Roger: b 8-24-1750 d 2-11-1822 m (1)Anne Bunce (2)Anna Moore Pvt CT
Roswell: b 5-25-1761 d 1812-15 m Lucinda Tinker Pvt MA
Seth: b 2-19-1762 d 1-19-1851 m Innocent Salsbury SgtMaj NY CT
Shubel: b 5-10-1765 d 7-1-1839 m Elizabeth Wright Pvt NY
Thomas, Sr.: b 3-24-1721 d 1803 m Lois Cass PS VT
Thomas, Jr.: b 1746 d 9-11-1828 m Eunice Cooper Ens VT
Timothy: b 1745/6 d 3- -1829 m (1)Naomi Rute (2)Mrs Mary Purdy Pvt NY ★

ROXBURY,
Reuben: b 1760 d 5-14-1825 m — Pvt VA ★

ROY,
Andre: b c. 1750 d 1795 m Frances Nicolet Chapart PS VA
Beverly: b c. 1760 d 1820 m (1)Anne Currie (2)Janet Bird Capt VA
John: b 2-11-1711 d p. 5-9-1779 m Margaret Insley PS NJ
Joseph: b 12-16-1741 d 6-17-1823 m Lucretia Perrine Pvt NJ

ROYALL, (includes ROYALL & ROYALS)
David: b c. 1760 d p. 8-4-1807 m Ruth — Pvt NJ
John: b 2-25-1755 d p. 1792 m Elizabeth Townes 1Lt VA
Jonathan: b 12-22-1762 d 2-3-1840 m Rebecca Godbee Sol GA
Joseph: b 2-23-1726 d 3-6-1778 m Susie Lockett Pvt NC
Thomas, Jr.: b 3-27-1754 d 8- -1834 m (1)Hannah Cooper (2)Rebecca Matthews (3)Mrs Ellen Brunk Pvt PA
Wm.: b a. 1749 d 1834 m Elizabeth Crosskeys Pvt SC
Wm.: b 3-11-1754 d 1-28-1821 m Elizabeth Bedford Capt VA

ROYER,
Christian: b 5-4-1749 d 1814 m Anna Stoler Pvt PA
Christopher: b 1739 d p. 2-26-1803 m Anna Landis Pvt PA
Daniel: b 1741 d 10-3-1784 m Catherine Kemper Pvt PA
Daniel: b 4-27-1762 d 3-26-1838 m Catharine Stoner Sol PA
Phillip: b 4-8-1752 d 8-29-1813 m (1)Christian Magaretha Freyern (2)Margareth Melcher Pvt PA
Philip: b 9-1-1733 d 9-12-1804 m Elizabeth Hernley PS PA
Samuel: b 1738 d 1823 m (1)Catharine Laubscher (2)Mary Lampshear Capt PA

ROYSTER,
David: b c. 1750 d p. 3-4-1816 m Mary Daniel 2Lt VA
Nathaniel: b c. 1752 d 9-24-1810 m Elizabeth Phelps 2Lt VA

ROYSTON,
James: b 11-22-1756 d 1780 m Mary Goan Matr Cpl MD

ROZIER,
Reuben: b c. 1742 d c. 1815 m Mary Lee Sol NC

RUARK,
Elgate: b c. 1756 d p. 5-3-1816 m Margaret — Pvt MD

RUBB,
Johannes Jonas: b 10-23-1729 d 5-21-1801 m Anna M E Borst PS PA

RUBBELEE,
Thomas: b 6-6-1740 d 1-16-1808 m Lydia — Pvt VT

RUBINCAM,
Peter: b c. 1760 d 7-2-1799 m Hannah Potts Pvt PA

RUBLE,
Mathias: b c. 1740 d p. 1790 m — Pvt PA
Owen: b c. 1730 d a. 12-6-1824 m (1)Helena White (2)Mrs Alley Wade Capt PS VA

RUBLEE,
Wm.: b 1732 d 3-26-1792 m Catherine Baker Pvt MA

RUCH,
Christian: b 1-1-1748 d 12-2-1827 m Anna Rosina Freeman Ens PA
Lorentz: b 11-14-1744 d 10-27-1825 m Charlotte Knouse Pvt PA

RUCKER,
Ambrose: b c. 1725 d 1807 m (1)Mary Clifton Headley (2)Mary
      Tinsley Capt VA
Augus: b c. 1752 d 9-2-1836 m Jane Allen Capt VA
Anthony: b a. 1742 d 1821 m Rebecca Burgess Capt CS VA
Benjamin: b c. 1730 d p. 11-20-1808 m Elizabeth — PS VA
Colby: b 10-10-1760 d 1-20-1852 m Sarah Roberts Sol NC
Elliott: b 1755 d 3-19-1832 m Nancy Smith Lt VA ★
Ephraim: b c. 1722 d p. 9-24-1796 m Margaret Vawter LCol VA
George: b 1754 d 1818 m Martha Tucker Pvt VA
George: b 1740 d p. 9-5-1810 m Catherine Ehart PS VA
Isaac: b a. 1742 d c. 1798 m Mildred (Hawkins) Plunkett Lt VA
John: b 1759 d p. 8-26-1806 m (1)Mrs Fielding (2)Elizabeth
      Tinsley (3)Mrs (Garr) Hudson Ens VA
John, Sr.: b 1720-5 d a. 9-4-1780 m Eleanor Mildred Warren Sol VA
John, Jr.: b 1752 d 4-24-1814 m (1)Sally Plunkett (2)Patsy — Pvt VA
John: b c. 1728 d 1794 m Mary Burton PS VA
Lemuel: b 4-15-1754 d 3-4-1842 m Anna Booton Pvt VA ★
Reuben: b 12-26-1755 d 1-27-1782 m Margaret McDaniel Pvt VA
Thomas: b c. 1739 d 1-7-1805 m Elizabeth — PS VA
Wm.: b 9-28-1744 d 11-22-1834 m Elizabeth — Pvt VA ★

RUCKS,
Josiah: b 8-3-1754 d 8-15-1836 m Elizabeth Taylor Sol VA NC

RUDD,
Benjamin: b c. 1759 d 1808 m Susan Jennings Smn VA W★
Bezaleel: b 7-24-1751 d 8-25-1846 m Ruth Brush Lt CT★
Daniel, Sr.: b 3-12-1710 d p. 1775 m (2)Mary Metcalfe Sol CT
Daniel, Jr.: b 6-10-1754 d 5-13-1820 m Abigail Allen Pvt CT
Increase: b 9-21-1734 d 1801-3 m Bathsheba Johnson Sgt VT
James: b 11- -1752 d 9- -1824 m (1)Sarah Higley (2)Olive
      Manning (3)Althea Manning (4)Elizabeth Vining Sgt MA
John: b 1748 d 1840 m Clara Hill Sgt VT
John: b 9-4-1748 d 10- -1834 m Hannah Woodward Smn VA
Jonathan: b 4-29-1743 d 4-3-1823 m (1)Mary Tracy (2)Amy Tyler
      Ens CT
Joseph: b 3-26-1740 d 5-25-1818 m Sarah Story Lt VT
Joseph: b 10-31-1708 d 1-8-1787 m Sarah Mosely PS CT
Nathaniel: b 11-2-1731 d 11-15-1819 m Alice Kingsley Pvt MA
Silas: b 2-25-1756 d p. 12-28-1803 m Phebe Davis Pvt VT
Wm.: b 1-20-1746/7 d 8-21-1835 m Eunice Waldo Cpl CT ★
Zebulon: b 7-6-1717 d 7-26-1795 m Jerusha Brewster PS NY

RUDDER,
Charles: b 1760 d 11-27-1837 m Lucretia Mathias Sol VA
Edward: b c. 1760 d 10- -1825 m Jane Chambers Pvt VA W★
John: b 2-13-1757 d 1840 m Martha Garrett Sgt VA ★

RUDDEROW,
John: b 2-17-1759 d 5-1-1840 m (1)Jerusha Inskeep (2)Brina
      (Welch) Leconey Pvt NJ

RUDDLE, (includes RUDDEEL & RUDDELL)
Cornelius: b 1730 d 3-6-1798 m Ingabo Allen Sgt VA
George: b 1740 d 1805 m Elizabeth Preston Capt VA
Isaac: b 1738 d 1812 m Elizabeth Bowman Capt IL
James: b 8- -1758 d p. 8-20-1835 m Jane Mulkerine Pvt VA ★
Stephen: b c. 1725 d 8- -1800 m (1)Mary — (2)Sarah (Barnes)
      Beggs PS CS VA

RUDDOCK,
Ebenezer: b 1-28-1747/8 d p. 1779 m Mollie Ingerfield Smn MA

RUDE, (includes ROOD)
Caleb: b c. 1737 d c. 1800 m Ann Wade Pvt NJ
Ezekiel: b 12-25-1754 d 9-8-1836 m Phebe Rix Pvt CT
Stephen: b 4-25-1746 d p. 1792 m Elizabeth — Cpl CT

RUDISILL,
Jonas: b a. 1734 d 9- -1799 m Maria Elizabeth Moul Pvt PA
Melchion: b 10-11-1738 d 8-10-1805 m Anna Christian Metzgar
      Pvt PA
Michael: b c. 1730 d p. 8-4-1792 m — PS NC
Philip, Sr.: b c. 1715 d p. 8-4-1794 m Mary Costner PS NC
Philip, Jr.: b 1755 d 5-6-1812 m Elizabeth Lowe PS NC
Weirich: b c. 1728 d p. 1780 m Magdalena Emig Pvt PA

RUDOLPH,
Jacob: b 9-8-1726 d 9-23-1793 m Rachel Johnson PS MD
Jacob: b 5-28-1744 d 3-14-1795 m Ann Yocum Capt PA
John: b 1760 d 1838 m Anna Brand Matr Pvt PA
John G.: b 1748 d p. 1836 m Christena Meyers 2Lt PA
Michael: b 1-15-1758 d 1793 m Sarah Baker GA VA

RUDY,
Andrew: b 1757 d 1834 m Catherine Baer Pvt PA

Frederick: b 1-8-1737 d 4-20-1817 m Scharlotta Braun Pvt PA
Jonas: b 1751 d 1811 m Barbara — Sol PA

RUE,
Benjamin: b 1755 d 1820 m Mary Taylor Capt PA
John: b c. 1750 d p. 1804 m Elizabeth — Pvt NJ
John: b 3-20-1755 d 10-4-1844 m (1)Ann Combs (2)Rebecca
      Perrine Pvt NJ ★
Matthew: b 4-27-1752 d 6-22-1820 m Phoebe Combs PS NJ
Richard: b —d 1785 m Elizabeth — Pvt PA
Richard: b 1760 d 12-12-1844 m Elizabeth Holman Pvt VA ★

RUFFCORN,
Simon: b 1749 d 2-13-1841 m Mary — Pvt PA ★

RUFFIN,
Edmund: b 1-2-1744 d 1807 m Jane Skipwith PS VA
Francis: b 5-13-1750 d 3-13-1805 m (1)Hannah Cocke (2)Susan
      Harris PS VA
Frederick: b 1749 d 1778 m Mary — PS NC
James: b c. 1754 d 9-11-1802 m Mary Roane Capt VA
Robert: b c. 1720 d 1778 m Mary (Clack) Lightfoot PS VA
Thomas: b c. 1730 d 9-11-1777 m Mary Roane Capt VA
Wm.: b c. 1735 d p. 1781 m Sarah Hill Sol VA

RUFFNER, (includes RUFNER)
Benjamin: b 8-14-1743 d p. 1795 m (1)Miss Burner (2)Elizabeth
      Heistand Pvt VA
Christian: b c. 1740 d 1826 m Mary Odilia Kuhn PS PA
Emanuel: b 3-13-1757 d 6-4-1848 m (1)Magdaline — (2)Elizabeth
      Groves Tms VA
Phillip: b a. 1751 d 1794 m Eve Hoenig Pvt PA
Simon, Jr.: b a. 1751 d 12-19-1819 m Catherine Griffin Sgt PA

RUGAN,
John: b 1750 d 10-26-1837 m Elizabeth Waine Sgt PA ★

RUGER,
Gideon: b 1752 d 4-16-1808 m Mary Ferris Pvt NY

RUGG,
Amos: b 9-13-1716 d p. 1787 m Mary Burpee PS MA
Asa: b 3-23-1752 d 11-20-1821 m Millicent Harris Pvt MA
Daniel, Jr.: bpt 3-29-1743 d 4-11-1830 m Elizabeth Woods Divoll
      Capt MA
Daniel: b 4-19-1751 d 1-15-1834 m Sarah Bancroft Pvt MA
Daniel: b 1714 d 11-12-1792 m Sarah Wilder PS MA
Elijah: b 4-4-1753 d p. 1797 m Lois Wilder Pvt MA
Elisha: b 4- -1755 d 1-7-1805 m Amy Clark Sgt MA W★
Isaac: b 2-25-1765 d 1-30-1853 m (1)Dorcas Gates (2)Polly Mattoon
      (3)Abigail Skinner Pvt VT ★
Jonathan: b 5-6-1753 d 11-20-1833 m (1)Hepzibah Haven
      (2)Rachel Tucker Sgt MA
Joseph: b 10-28-1733 d 12-27-1825 m Elizabeth Meacham Pvt MA
Levi: b 12-3-1752 d 2-22-1824 m Relief Whitcomb Pvt NH
Moses: b 1759 d 4-21-1832 m (2)Mrs Isabella L Nicholson McKillip
      Pvt MA ★
Reuben: b 10-19-1746 d 1830 m Elizabeth (Stevens) Warfild
      Pvt MA
Solomon: b 1737 d 1817 m Margaret Hudson Pvt CT
Thomas, Sr.: b 2-17-1743 d 12-29-1811 m Eunice Stickney Pvt MA
Thomas, Jr.: b 5-28-1765 d 11-8-1846 m Elizabeth Norcross
      Pvt MA

RUGGLES,
Ashbel: b 7-19-1739 d p. 1790 m Rebecca Bostwick Ens CT
Benjamin: b 8-18-1747 d 7-10-1794 m Elizabeth Durkee Lt CT
Benjamin, Sr.: b 5-19-1713 d 10-11-1790 m (1)Alice Merrick
      (2)Mary Smith PS MA
Benjamin: b 3-5-1753 d 12-22-1820 m Betsey Ruggles Pvt MA
Benjamin Abijah: b 9-7-1758 d 11-30-1828 m Betsey
      Trowbridge Pvt CT ★
Daniel: b 1-5-1755 d 2-26-1838 m Lucy Paige Sgt MA ★
Edward, Sr.: b 6-22-1724 d 12-25-1797 m Ann Sumner Pvt CT
Edward, Jr.: b 8-3-1750 d 1-17-1805 m Anna Dean Sgt MA
Edward, Sr.: b 8-23-1723 d 5-21-1778 m Lucy Spooner Pvt MA
Ephraim: b 3-20-1757 d 4-21-1836 m Olive Powers Pvt MA
John: b 1-6-1741 d 8-28-1800 m Mary Caldwell Pvt MA
Joseph: b 1-30-1701 d 1791 m Rachel Tolls PS Fif CT
Joseph: b 7-30-1725 d 1-3-1819 m Rebecca Curtis Lt MA
Lazarus: b 8-29-1730 d 5-6-1797 m — Lt CT
Lemuel: b 2-26-1735 d 10-22-1806 m Lydia — Pvt MA
Nathaniel, Sr.: b 1712 d 10-16-1794 m Anna Bartlett PS CT
Nathaniel: b 5-4-1755 d 3-2-1827 m Druscilla Briggs Pvt MA
Robert Bostwick: b 2-10-1762 d 5-13-1823 m Lucy Northrop Pvt CT
Samuel: b 1751 d 1795 m Huldah Wakelee Pvt CT
Samuel: b 2-25-1751 d 10-23-1778 m Lucy Robison Pvt CT
Thomas: bpt 6-24-1750 d 5-12-1808 m Hannah Winslow Cpl MA
Timothy: b 4-22-1748 d 7- -1831 m Rachel Ward Capt MA

RUGH,
Jacob: b 2-15-1761 d 2-6-1845 m Sabilla Mecklin Pvt PA
Michael: b 1724 d p. 1788 m Anna Francena Markle CS PA

RUICK,
Owen: b 1748 d 5-13-1820 m Elizabeth — Pvt CT ★

RULAND, (includes RULON)
Benjamin: b 1758 d 5-19-1845 m Olive Fuller Pvt NY ★
David: b 1730 d 1820 m Rebecca Soper Pvt NY
Joseph, Sr.: b 1727 d 1798 m Mary — Pvt PS NY
Joseph, Jr.: b 2- -1757 d 4-12-1823 m Susan Gerard Pvt PS NY

RULE, (includes RUHL)
Henry: b 1754 d 1789 m Peggy LeRoy Pvt VA
John: b 9-27-1739 d 1-23-1825 m Helena Schenck Pvt PA
Wm.: b a. 1743 d c. 1782 m — Frederick Pvt PA
Wm.: b c. 1750 d 12- -1814 m Anna Maria — Pvt PA

RULOFSON, (includes ROELOFSON & RULIFSON)
Harmon: b 9-15-1760 d 3-24-1851 m Susannah Beemer Pvt NJ
Herman: b 7- -1719 d 3- -1805 m Margaretta VanHorn PS NJ
Lowroe: b 11-28-1740 d 4-8-1814 m Elizabeth Barnhart Pvt NY

RUMBLE, (includes RUMMELL)
George: b 1740-5 d 1808-10 m — Pvt PA
Jacob: b 1743 d p. 10-11-1824 m Elizabeth Gans Cpl PA

RUMERY,
Dominicus: b 1765 d 10-26-1835 m Pamelia Fountain Matr MA ★
Thomas: b 12-27-1733 d 6-21-1813 m Charity Edgecomb Capt MA

RUMFIELD,
Casper: b 4-15-1754 d 11-26-1829 m Catherine Schautzenbach
    Sgt PA

RUMFORD,
Jonathan: b 4-28-1743 d 8-24-1790 m Sarah Way Capt DE

RUMNEY,
Benjamin: b 5-29-1762 d 1789 m Nancy — Slr MA
Edward: b 8-25-1745 d 1-13-1808 m Seeth Beath Lt MA

RUMPH,
Abraham: b 7-30-1760 d 3-4-1816 m Ann Rumph Pvt SC
David: b c. 1725 d 1783 m Mary Ann — PS SC
Jacob: b — d 1785 m Anne Detwyler Capt SC
Jacob: b 7-9-1752 d 10-10-1812 m Ann May Hergersperger
    Capt SC

RUMRILL,
Aaron: b a. 1742 d 3-31-1800 m Elizabeth Clapp Pvt MA
David: b 6-21-1740 d 5-10-1818 m Priscilla Corey Pvt NH
Ebenezer: b 7-16-1745 d 12-17-1801 m Eleanor Cooley Pvt MA
Joseph, Sr.: b 1726 d 1799 m Lucy Stevens Pvt MA
Joseph, Jr.: b 5-1-1756 d 2-24-1844 m (1)Abigail Lawson
    (2)Rebecca Lawson Pvt MA
Nehemiah: b 8-23-1733 d 1-14-1805 m Alice Parsons MM Pvt MA
Thomas: b 11-30-1762 d 11-10-1849 m (1)Abigail Richardson
    (2)Sally Dudley Mus MA

RUMSEY,
Charles: b 1736 d 1780 m Abigail Jane Caner Col PS MD
David: b 10-22-1738 d p. 3-30-1810 m Anna Lovell Capt NY
David: b 1-28-1759 d 6-2-1849 m Hannah Bronson Pvt CT ★
Jeremiah: b 7-2-1763 d 5-29-1842 m Areneth Doud Pvt CT ★
John: b 1726 d 12-28-1796 m Esther Jones Pvt CT
John: b 1753 d 7-26-1826 m — Pvt NY
Joseph: b 10-29-1743 d 8-11-1803 m Mary Gorham Cpl CT
Moses: b 7-20-1758 d 1816 m Lydia Ann Miller Pvt NY
Wm.: b 6-22-1750 d 2-22-1836 m Elizabeth Walker Cpl CT ★

RUNDIO,
Peter: b c. 1755 d p. 7-19-1814 m Susanna — Capt PA

RUNDLE, (includes RUNDALL & RUNDEL)
Abraham: b 1716 d 3-14-1799 m Mercy Reynolds Cpl NY
Ezra, Sr.: b 6-10-1726 d 9-21-1807 m Hannah — Pvt NY
Ezra, Jr.: b 1761 d 12-20-1839 m Hannah Hoyt Pvt NY
Jared: b 4-23-1750 d 3-10-1812 m Abijah Allen Pvt NY
Jeremiah: b p. 1734 d p. 1790 m Lydia Reynolds Pvt CT
Joseph: b 8-20-1762 d p. 1793 m Polly Olmstead Sol CT
Nathaniel, Jr.: b 1760 d p. 1786 m Hannah Ferris Pvt CT
Reuben, Sr.: b 7-14-1735 d 2- -1815 m Amy — Lt CT
Reuben, Jr.: b 3-10-1757 d 10-25-1848 m Sarah Holly Fif NY ★

RUNDLETT,
Charles: b 1720 d 1803 m Dorothy — PS NH
James: b 6-10-1744 d 12-28-1800 m Dorothy Stevens Drm NH
Jonathan: b 10-13-1759 d p. 1786 m Mary Huntoon Pvt NH
Reuben: b 6-21-1763 d 7-8-1840 m Hannah Elsworth Cpl NH

RUNEY,
John: bpt 10-1-1758 d a. 8-10-1829 m — Pvt MA

RUNK,
Samuel: b 6- -1753 d 4-21-1847 m Margaretta Synder Pvt NJ

RUNKLE, (includes RUNKEL)
Henry: b c. 1754 d a. 11-1804 m Catherine Smith Pvt PA
Jacob: b 4-12-1749 d 7-21-1813 m Anna Christina Weber PS PA
John: b 3-28-1756 d 2-17-1813 m Helena Van Woert Pvt NY
Samuel: b c. 1743 d 1802 m Catherine Eteris Pvt VA

RUNYON, (includes RUNYAN)
Absalom: b a. 1749 d p. 7-20-1809 m Ann — Wgm NJ
Benjamin: b 1739 d 2-7-1830 m Rebecca McGill Pvt NY ★
Elias: b 6-7-1749 d 3-8-1793 m Deborah Clark Tms NJ
Enoch: b 1755 d p. 5-5-1819 m Rachel Blackford Pvt NJ
George: b 1756 d 1-14-1846 m Margarett Davis Pvt NJ
Hugh: b 1738 d 7-11-1823 m Sarah Hill QM NJ
Job: b 11-14-1759 d 2-12-1835 m Grace — Pvt NJ
John: b 8-7-1743 d 10-27-1792 m (1)Violet Layton (2)Sarah
    Wheaton Pvt NJ
John: b 11-26-1756 d 9-14-1836 m Mary Conkling Pvt NJ
Reune: b 11-29-1741 d 11-21-1811 m Anna Bray PS NJ
Richard: b 11-30-1758 d 8-16-1845 m Jemima Hoagland Pvt NJ

RUPERT, (includes RUPPERT)
Adam: b 1756 d p. 4-27-1829 m — Margaret Gotzen Pvt
    PA ★
Dietrich: b 12-5-1740 d 9- -1820 m (1)Mary Margaret Schultz
    (2)Mrs Elizabeth Haltgapfel Pvt PA
George: b 12- -1758 d 9-2-1846 m Elizabeth — Pvt VA ★
John Philip: b 1-17-1738 d 8-6-1829 m Catharine Rosch 1Lt PA
Leonard: b 10-11-1763 d 3-11-1848 m Sarah Bright Fif PA
Peter: bpt 3-30-1755 d 11-1-1824 m — Cpl PA

RUPLE,
Martin: b 1720 d 1789 m Betsey — Wgn PA

RUPLEY,
Jacob, Sr.: b 6-9-1724 d 1-12-1793 m (1)Barbara Longhman (2)Mary
    Schoff Lt PA
Jacob: b 11-16-1753 d 6-5-1806 m Anna Marie Rupp Ens PA

RUPP, (includes ROOP & ROUP)
Adam: b c. 1720/1 d 12-29-1803 m Catherine — Pvt MA
Adam Hermanus: b 11-7-1756 d 8-30-1831 m Barbara Bever Pvt PA
George: b 8-11-1721 d 9-13-1807 m Ursula VonPeter Holtz PS PA
Jacob, Sr.: b 7-21-1717 d 8-10-1793 m Barbara — PS PA
Jacob, Jr.: b 7-22-1750 d 3-22-1826 m Ada Poorman Sol PA
Jonas: b 10-26-1760 d 4-30-1857 m Abigail Horr Pvt PA
Jonas: b 10-23-1729 d 5-21-1801 m Anna Maria Elizabeth Borst
    PS PA
Matthias: b c. 1750 d 1803 m Lydia Keiser Pvt PA

RUSCOE, (or RUSCO)
John: b 1737 d p. 1778 m Joanna Arnold Pvt NY

RUSH, (includes ROSCH)
Benjamin: b 1715 d 5-23-1801 m (1)Alice Grisby (2)Elizabeth — CS
    PS NC
Benjamin: b 12-24-1745 d 4-19-1813 m Julia Stockton Dr SDI PA
Charles: b c. 1730 d p. 4-4-1806 m Elizabeth — PS VA
Conrad: b 1740 d 1796 m Susanna — Capt PA
Daniel: b 1744 d 1822 m (2)Susannah Sheetz Pvt PA
David: b c. 1760 d 9-26-1839 m Margaret Rosena Adolph PS SC
George: b 1710 d 1820 m Christina Rush Pvt VT
George: b c. 1755 d 2-11-1831 m (1)Mary Bushong (2)Mrs
    Elizabeth Harry Pvt VA
Henry: b 8-17-1745 d 12-18-1815 m Sarah Steed Capt PA
Jacob: b 1738 d 1820 m Lydia Bell Pvt PA
Jacob: b 10-3-1752 d 10-30-1810 m Martha Kendig Pvt PA
Jacob: b 3-19-1755 d 1-14-1850 m (1)Mary Skinner (2)Ann McNeal
    Pvt PA ★
John: b 10- -1758 d 3-10-1838 m Rebecca — Pvt NJ ★
John: b — d 1800 m Martha — Pvt PA
Michael: b 1747 d 2- -1835 m (1) — Bisset (2)— Johnson
    (3)Betsy Dickinson Pvt NJ
Michael: b 2-27-1703 d 11-3-1796 m Catherine Fischer PS PA
Nathaniel: b 5-5-1755 d 3-6-1822 m Sarah Robbins Pvt MA
Peter, Jr.: b 1752 d 1819 m Susanna Fordyce Pvt NJ
Wm.: b 1-1-1765 d 2-27-1839 m Jane — Pvt NJ ★
Wm.: b 2-1-1755 d 1-25-1827 m Abigail Terrell PS VA

RUSHING,
John: b 7-6-1764 d 2-25-1843 m Rachel Renfroe Lt SC
John Paul: b 1754-6 d 1812 m Temperance J May Sol SC

RUSHTON, (or RUSTON)
Wm.: b 1730 d 1779-90 m Elizabeth Coon Sol NY

RUSK,
James: b 1754 d 7-1-1839 m Ann Robb Pvt PA ★
Margaret: b c. 1720 d p. 1790 m John Rusk PS VA

RUSS,
John: b 10-6-1748 d 1804 m Abigail Stevens Pvt NH
Jonathan: b 5-6-1731 d c. 1790 m Lucy Kendall Cpl NH
Samuel: b 1759 d 4-11-1841 m Margaret Rightmyre Pvt NY
Sempronious: b 7-6-1767 d 10-19-1816 m Amelia Potter Gnr CT

RUSSELL, (includes ROUSSELLE & RUSSEL)
Abel: b 9-3-1751 d *a.* 1822 m Mrs Sarah (Bryan) Frost Pvt MA
Adonijah: b 2-25-1713 d 7-21-1775 m Mary Sherman PS MA
Albert: b 5-25-1755 d 6-27-1818 m (1)Miss Russell (2)Miss
   Ellzey (3)Ann Frances Hooe (4)Mrs Henderson Lt VA
Alexander: b 2-25-1758 d 4-15-1836 m Mary McPherson Lt PA
Andrew: b 3- -1732 d 6-20-1814 m Isabel Mayes Pvt PA
Andrew: b 5-17-1738 d 1789 m Margaret Christian Maj VA
Andrew: b 1739 d 5-5-1803 m Elizabeth Mitchell Pvt VA
Anthony: b *c.* 1738 d 1779 m — PS VA
Aquila: b *c.* 1756 d *p.* 1798 m Abigail Glazier Pvt NH
Armistead: b 1756 d 1801 m Elvira Clayton PS VA
Ashur: b 10-27-1753 d 7-6-1836 m — Pvt CT ★
Benjamin: b 9- -1761 d 1-4-1845 m Esther Rice Pvt MA
Buckner: b 1751 d *p.* 1-15-1834 m Rachael — Pvt NC
Caleb: b 8-9-1713 d 2-20-1804 m Rebecca Borden PS MA
Calvin: b 2- -1762 d 5-1-1852 m Hannah Bailey Pvt MA ★
Cornelius: b 4-3-1750 d 8-3-1823 m Huldah Pember Lt CT ★
Daniel: b 3-18-1755 d 2-25-1837 m (1)Rachel Gould (2)Betsy
   Crocket Pvt NH ★
Daniel: b 12-25-1758 d 5-10-1824 m Sarah Susannah Cross NC
   SC W★
David: b 12-10-1742 d 7-28-1813 m (1)Sally — (2)Sarah Horton
   Sgt MA
David: b *c.* 1750 d 1792 m Susan — Sgt NC
Ebenezer: b 1732 d 12-6-1836 m Elizabeth Stark Pvt NY
Edward: b 8-13-1732/3 d 12-26-1819 m Sarah Maltby Col CT
Edward: bpt 11-10-1734 d 4-19-1785 m Hannah Clark Capt CS MA
Edward: b *c.* 1729 d *p.* 3-31-1797 m Mary Page PS NH
Elmore: b 1761 d 3-19-1835 m Asenath Hotchkiss Pvt CT ★
Emanuel: b 9-9-1743 d 9-18-1812 m Esther C Heavilo Sgt DE
Enoch: b 10- -1760/1 d 8-29-1848 m (1)Ruth — (2)Martha
   McQuaid Pvt VA ★
Ephraim, Sr.: bpt 8-8-1731 d 1793 m Miriam Wheeler Pvt CS
   PS MA
Ephraim, Jr.: b 11-6-1755 d 11-11-1831 m Mary Porter Sgt MA
Evan: b 8-24-1760 d 2-3-1838 m (2)Mary Benson Sgt PA ★
George: b 1720 d 1797 m Elizabeth — Capt CS TN
Gideon, Jr.: b 12-25-1760 d 1838 m Jemima Alvord Pvt CT ★
Giles: b 11-8-1729 d 10-28-1779 m Prudence Coleman Col CT
Henry: b *c.* 1754 d 12-10-1836 m Chloe Smallwood Pvt PS MD
Hezekiah: b 3-18-1745 d 1-3-1823 m (1)Lydia — (2)Eleanor
   Osborne Pvt CT
Hezekiah: b 2-13-1739 d 8-2-1816 m Abigail Clarke Capt MA
Isaac: b 1758 d 3-23-1836 m Mary Green Pvt MA ★
Isaac: b 5-11-1750 d 2-26-1821 m Hannah Fairbanks Capt QM NY
Jabez: bpt 8-4-1728 d 3-9-1818 m Hannah Wheeler Pvt MA
Jacob: b 4-15-1746 d 8-29-1821 m Esther Dunham Pvt CT
James: b *c.* 1760 d *p.* 5-5-1810 m Lydia Brown Pvt CT
James: b 5-10-1725 d 8-17-1801 m — Potter Capt MA
James: b 1-7-1753 d 4-24-1830 m Rebecca Peabody Sgt MA ★
James: b 8-5-1715 d 4-24-1798 m Catherine Graves CS MA
James: b 1746 d 10-1-1821 m Mary French Capt NH
James: b — d 1798 m — Lt NH
James: b *c.* 1747 d 1820 m Elizabeth Gower Sol NC
James: b 1733 d 2-25-1799 m Jean Carson CS NC
James: b 1744 d 4-21-1836 m — Pvt PA ★
James: b 1754 d 1824 m Rosannah Rutherford 2Lt VA
James: b 1754 d 12-12-1831 m (1)Sarah Osborne (2)Ann Heath Sgt
   VA
James: b *c.* 1763 d 9-9-1849 m Margaret Wilson Sgt VA
Jason, Sr.: b 1-25-1716/7 d 4-19-1775 m Elizabeth Winship PS MA
Jason, Jr.: b 3-18-1742 d 9-25-1825 m Elizabeth Locke Pvt NH
Jason: b 1-16-1718 d *a.* 9-11-1775 m Mary Robbins Pvt NH
Jeduthan: b 1744 d 5-13-1813 m Hannah Glazier Sgt NH
Jeffery: b *c.*1734/5 d 1805-10 m Sarah Brown Pvt VA
Jeremiah: b 1-5-1752 d *p.* 1785 m Martha Barker Cpl NH
Jeremiah: b *c.* 1750 d *a.* 1810 m — Pvt SC
Jesse: b 1731 d 1799 m Sarah Cornish Pvt CT
Joel: b 8-2-1716 d 1780 m Hulda — PS NH
John: b 1-27-1749 d 11-2-1826 m Lovica Cooley Ens CT
John: b 1-3-1754 d 8-31-1820 m Mary Woodruff Drm CT
John: b *c.* 1753 d *p.* 1783 m — Sol CT
John: b 4-12-1737 d 7-8-1813 m Martha Martin Cmsry MA
John: b 4-7-1759 d 5-13-1836 m Miriam Graves Pvt MA
John: b 6- -1760 d 1829 m Abigail Godding Pvt MA
John: b 1761 d 6-22-1844 m Martha Thrall Pvt MA ★
John: b 4-12-1727 d 11-23-1824 m Abigail Hildreth CS MA
John, Jr.: b 10-17-1761 d 5-22-1843 m Charity Evarts Sgt NY ★
John: b 4-13-1758 d 8-3-1838 m Rachel Hobbs Capt NC
John: b 1- -1728 d 9-26-1816 m Betsy Swink Pvt PA
John: b 1735 d 11-14-1815 m Hannah Fincher Pvt PA
John: b 1757 d 1- -1814 m Clara Ann Stansel Pvt SC
John: b 1755 d *p.* 1844 m Mary Ward Sol SC
John: b 1755 d 12-31-1820 m Hannah Storr Lt VA
John: b 1760 d 11-18-1832 m Elizabeth Pfaff Pvt VA
Jonathan: b 7-25-1731 d 2-3-1813 m Lydia Barker Sol CT
Jonathan, Sr.: b 8-2-1714 d 4-8-1777 m Mary Smith PS MA
Jonathan, Jr.: b 6-24-1746 d 2-17-1829 m Anne Ashley Cpl MA
Jonathan: b 1732 d 1-22-1819 m Elizabeth Daniels Pvt MA
Jonathan: b *p.* 1726 d 1810 m Mary — MM PS NY
Joseph: b 7-4-1740 d 2-20-1826 m Abigail Grannis Pvt CT

Joseph: b 1757 d 6-26-1837 m Margaret Browning Sgt MA ★
Joseph: b 5-16-1743 d 12-1-1799 m Sarah — Pvt MA
Joseph: b 1-5-1745 d 3-27-1829 m Susanna Upham Pvt MA
Joseph: b 1763 d 12-27-1855 m Betsey Goodrich Pvt MA
Joseph: b *c.* 1757 d 5-27-1817 m Margaret Campbell Pvt VA
Joseiah: b 1756 d 6-19-1820 m (2)Joanna Spaulding Pvt CT ★
Josiah: b 9-5-1736 d *a.* 7-30-1817 m Lydia Kingsbury Capt NH
Levi: b *c.* 1749 d 8-22-1834 m Hannah Simmons Pvt MA ★
Lewis: bpt 10-4-1747 d *p.* 1782 m Abigail Martin NLt MA
Mark: b 4-24-1754 d 4-22-1831 m (1)Mary — (2)Mrs Elizabeth
   (Moore) Wilkinson Sol PS MC
Matthew: b 1760 d *p.* 5-17-1831 m Jane Henderson Pvt VA
Moor: b 10-30-1757 d 8-29-1851 m Elizabeth Webster Pvt NH ★
Moses: b 10-16-1756 d 10-30-1825 m Mahitable Nolan Pvt VA ★
Nathaniel: b 5-5-1741 d 12-18-1810 m Elizabeth Willard Cpl CT
Nathaniel: b 12-27-1733 d 1-1-1812 m (1)Abigail Goldsmith (2)Mrs
   Anna Thayer Pvt PS NH
Nathaniel Prentice: b 1744 d 3-17-1812 m (2)Patience Robinson Pvt
   MA
Noadiah: b 1747 d 5-18-1832 m Lydia Weston CS VT
Noah: b 3-8-1763 d 11-6-1824 m Eunice Bemis Pvt MA
Oliver: b 10-27-1753 d 10-28-1820 m Betty Howe Pvt MA
Philip: b 4-5-1727 d 1-19-1816 m (1)Lydia Eaton (2)Lydia Doge Pvt
   CS PS MA
Philip: b 3-18-1752 d 4-11-1821 m Miriam Hubbard Pvt MA
Philip: b 11-14-1765 d 8-17-1842 m (1)Elizabeth Stuart (2)Mary
   Williams Wgm Pvt VA ★
Philip M.: b 7- -1747 d 8-11-1830 m Esther Mordecai SgnMte PA ★
Riverius: b 3-13-1755 d 4-7-1834 m Charity Hotchkiss Pvt CT
Robert: b 1730 d 1798 m Elizabeth Carson PS NC
Robert: b 1748 d 6-22-1819 m Eave Kuzblek Ens VA
Robert, Sr.: b *c.* 1728 d 1791 m Ann Bard PS VA
Robert, Jr.: b 1760 d 1- -1804 m Jane Rutherford Sgt VA
Robert Spotswood: b 3-28-1762 d 1-16-1842 m Deborah Allen Cpl
   VA
Samuel: b 12-30-1759 d 7-2-1834 m Lucy Monson Pvt MA
Samuel: b 1730 d 3-14-1794 m Ruth Whitmore PS CT
Samuel: b 1729 d 8-11-1807 m Eunice Snow Pvt MA
Samuel: b 5-31-1753 d *p.* 1795 m Abigail Russell Pvt NH
Seth: b 3-31-1734 d 9-30-1798 m Dinah Harrington PS MA
Seth, Sr.: b 1729 d 1821 m Keziah Walker PS MA
Silas: b 10-10-1742 d 1822 m — Pvt NH ★
Solomon: b 10-3-1748 d 10-18-1829 m Anna Nichols Pvt MA
Solomon: b 1-29-1758 d 12-30-1851 m Bulah Bancroft Sgt MA ★
Stephen: b 12-7-1756 d 6-4-1817 m Asenath Peck Pvt CT
Stephen: b 1722 d 6-3-1800 m Abigail Gage Capt MA
Thomas: b 8-24-1740 d 5- -1827 m Elizabeth Goodrich Pvt CT
Thomas: b 10-16-1727 d 3-2-1803 m Mary Patterson Dr CS PS NH
Thomas: b 7-31-1743 d 8-20-1777 m Bethiah Penfield CS CT
Thomas: b 11-13-1719 d 5-7-1792 m Hepzibah Nichols Pvt MA
Thomas: b 6-5-1732 d 3-30-1818 m Bethia Holt Pvt NH
Thomas: b 10-22-1751 d 11-27-1845 m Eunice Alexander Pvt NH
Thomas: b — d *p.* 6-21-1813 m Charity Hopkins 1Lt NY
Thomas: b 6-7-1761 d 7-11-1850 m Tabitha Jenkins Pvt NC ★
Thomas: b 1760 d 3-20-1837 m Martha Rallston Pvt PA
Thomas Commander: b 4-28-1754 d 9-28-1819 m Mary Starnes Lt
   SC ★
Timothy: b 6-23-1755 d 1-16-1840 m Elizabeth Gildersleeve Pvt CT
Uriah: bpt 5-14-1743 d 11-19-1822 m Lydia Abbott Pvt MA
Walter: b 1-24-1737 d 5-5-1782 m Hannah Adams Pvt MA
Wm. Sr.: b *c.* 1720 d *c.* 1800 m (1)Bethia Curtis (2)Hannah Brinsmaid
   Pvt CT
Wm., Jr.: bpt 11- -1753 d *p.* 1793 m Jerusha Hawley Pvt CT
Wm.: b 1759 d *p.* 9- -1848 m Syble Maria Crosby Pvt CT ★
Wm.: b 12-23-1760 d 10-14-1838 m Kezia Pierce Pvt NH ★
Wm.: b 3-19-1756 d 11-25-1832 m Jane Sewell Pvt NJ
Wm.: b 1741 d 4- -1824 m Jennette Roberson Sol NC SC
Wm.: b 11-12-1748 d 1-9-1785 m Mary Ann Stewart Pvt PA
Wm.: b 1759 d 1820 m Sallie Moreland Pvt SC
Wm., Sr.: b 1735 d 1-14-1793 m (1)Tabitha Adams (2)Elizabeth
   Henry Campbell BGen VA
Wm., Jr.: b 1758 d 7-3-1825 m Anne Price Lt VA
Wm.: b 1746 d 1813 m (1)Ruth Russell (2)Edith Smith PS VA
Wm.: b *c.* 1750 d 11- -1813 m (2)Tabitha (Barnes) Drake Matr VA

RUSSEY,
James: b 1755 d 3-30-1835 m (1)Sarah — (2)Nancy Scott Pvt VA ★

RUSSWURM,
Wm. Alexander: b *a.* 1757 d *p.* 1793 m Eleanor Sumner Lt NC

RUST,
Abel: b 1759 d 1854 m Lydia Sprague Pvt CT ★
Aloney: b 2-19-1766 d 6-29-1857 m Esther Dowd Pvt CT
Amaziah: b 6-4-1733 d 7-8-1801 m Mary Marsh CS CT
Ebenezer Kingsley: b 11-8-1763 d 8-2-1819 m (1)Lydia Lyman
   (2)Mary Sheldon Pvt MA
George: b *c.* 1756 d 1-23-1850 m Elizabeth (Rust) Dunbar Lt VA
Gersham: b 3- -1738 d 10-8-1823 m Mary Cooley Sgt MA
Henry: b 8-23-1737 d 9-28-1812 m Lydia Janes Pvt MA
Henry, Jr.: b 5-14-1755 d 11-2-1844 m Hannah Horne Pvt NH
Henry: b 1-22-1726 d 3-17-1807 m Ann Harvey CS NH
Israel, Jr.: b 12-4-1741 d 10-21-1816 m Esther Bartlett Pvt MA

RUST, contd.
John: b 1755 d 1842 m Sarah Clement Ens VA ★
Joseph: b 1749 d 10-24-1844 m Mary Reed Pvt MA
Lemuel: b 2-22-1741 d 7-31-1813 m Azuba Kingsley Lt MA
Levy: b 9-28-1750 d p. 9-30-1795 m Rebecca Booth Pvt CT
Matthew: b c. 1758 d 1824-30 m Martha Triplett 2Lt PS VA
Moses: b 6-19-1740 d 10-10-1827 m Sarah Choate Pvt MA
Nathaniel: b 5-5-1755 d 3-26-1822 m (1)Sarah Robbins (2)Mrs
    Mary (Sutton) Kimball Pvt MA
Nathaniel: b 8-21-1739 d 5-27-1814 m Hannah Burroughs Pvt NH
Nathaniel Wilson: b 4-25-1751 d 3-25-1828 m Rachael Babcock Pvt
    CT
Peter: b 1760 d 3-4-1829 m Elizabeth Ballew Pvt VA NC W★
Peter: b 1762 d 10-23-1828 m Mrs Elizabeth Hickman Sgt VA
Phineas: b 7-7-1754 d 4-27-1831 m Mary Powers Pvt VT
Wallis: b 1-8-1741 d 12-1-1792 m Abigail Jones Dr MA

RUTAN, (includes RUTON)
Abraham: b c. 1734 d 1792 m Anna — Ens NJ
Abram D.: b 8-5-1763 d 7-11-1848 m (1)— Kasine (2)Lydia
    Vanderbeek Pvt NJ ★
John: b a. 1762 d 3-17-1803 m Jane Blauvelt Pvt NJ W★
Paul: b 3-30-1763 d p. 1837 m Metje Spier Pvt NJ ★
Samuel: b 9-19-1754 d 1-4-1840 m Eleanor — Pvt NJ
Wm.: b 10-9-1760 d 2-23-1828 m Rachel (Bower) VanWort Pvt NY
    W★

RUTGERS,
Anthony: b 8-22-1742 d 1775-8 m Gertrude Gouverneur Capt PS NY

RUTH,
Adam: b 1730 d p. 1793 m Christina Britinger PS SC
Christian: b 12-16-1729 d 8-24-1793 m (2)Marie Barbara (Epler)
    Heister Pvt PA
David: b 1761 d 1828 m Mary McLachlin Pvt PA
Francis: b a. 1746 d 1809 m Elizabeth Taylor Adj PA
Francis: b a. 1749 d 1809 m Elizabeth Deator Sol PA
George: b — d p. 3-14-1809 m Barbara Krum Pvt PA
Henry: b 6-12-1748 d 2-28-1826 m Elizabeth Shepler Pvt PA
Jacob: b 9- -1726 d 9-24-1797 m Catharine Krick Pvt PS PA
Jacob: b 6-14-1760 d 11-17-1832 m Barbara — Pvt PA
Peter: b 1753 d 1833 m Mary Ann Fluck Pvt Ens PA

RUTHERFORD,
Absalom: b 1763 d 6-28-1841 m Mary McBride Pvt VA ★
Archibald: b 1755 d 7-31-1838 m Elizabeth — Pvt VA ★
Griffith: b 1721 d 8-10-1805 m Elizabeth Graham BGen PS NC
James: b 1736 d 12-19-1797 m Drucilla Brooks Maj SC
James: b 4-26-1757 d 4-9-1838 m Elizabeth Cartwright Pvt VA ★
John: b 1762 d 11-17-1840 m Mary Wadleigh Pvt Smn MA
John: b 2-16-1737 d 10-1-1804 m Margaret Parke Capt PA
John: b 1759 d 10-31-1833 m Mary Hubert CS Sol SC
Robert: b 4- -1734 d 1-23-1814 m (1)Dorothy Ann Brooks (2)Mrs
    Frances (Birt) Harrington CS PS NC
Robert: b 10-20-1728 d 10- -1803 m Mary (Dobyn) Howe PS VA
Samuel: b 12-13-1749 d 5-2-1785 m Susannah Collier Capt PA
Thomas: b 1700 d 8-11-1804 m Mary Rush PS VA
Wm.: b 1761/2 d 6-19-1838 m Sarah Potter Pvt MA
Wm.: b c. 1720 d p. 3-8-1808 m Sarah — Pvt PA
Wm.: b — d a. 1-13-1801 m Ursula Parrish PS VA

RUTHRAUFF, (includes RODROFF)
John: b 1727 d 1792 m Anna Barbara Hoffman Pvt PA
John: b 1756 d 12-12-1824 m Anna Maria Krank Pvt PA

RUTLAND,
Reading: b c. 1755-60 d 2- -1834 m Martha — Pvt NC
Thomas: b c. 1743 d p. 8-15-1781 m (1)Margaret Howard (2)Comfort
    — PS MD

RUTLEDGE,
Edward: b 11-23-1749 d 1-23-1800 m (1)Henrietta Middleton
    (2)Mary (Shubrick) Eveleigh SDl Col SC
Edward: b 1761/2 d 6-30-1836 m Anne Gillespie Pvt VA ★
George: b 4-13-1761 d 7-1-1813 m Annis Armstrong Of NC
George: b 1746 d 4-29-1821 m — Brown Pvt SC
James: b 9-5-1749 d 2-25-1825 m (1)Sarah Gilkie (2)— Cherry
    (3)Anne Rankin Pvt NC
James: b c. 1745 d p. 7-26-1822 m Ann Hicks Pvt SC
John: b 9- -1739 d 7-18-1800 m Elizabeth Grimke PS SC
John: b 10-17-1738 d 2-8-1803 m (1)Hannah — (2)Elizabeth — PS
    Sol SC
Joshua: b 1760 d 9-15-1825 m (1)Augustina Biddle (2)Elizabeth
    McComas Lt MD ★
Peter: b 2-16-1760/1 d 5-29-1844 m (1)Mary E Sanford (2)Ruth
    Robinson Pvt MD
Sarah Hext: b 1724 d 1792 m John Rutledge PS SC
Thomas: b c. 1729 d p. 8-10-1801 m (2)Mrs Catherine Pearsall
    CmsryGen CS PS NC
Wm.: b 1728 d 1790 m Elenor Caldwell Lt NC

RUTTER,
Joseph, Sr.: b 1703 d 1781 m Mary Willard Pvt MA

Joseph, Jr.: b 3-28-1753 d 1821 m Eunice Maynard Pvt MA
Joseph: b 1755 d 1839 m Margaret Besore Pvt PA
Philip: b 3-23-1750 d 3-1-1842 m (1)Kezia — (2)Sarah Maynard Pvt
    CS VT
Thomas: b 1731 d 5-7-1795 m Martha Potts PS PA
Wm.: b 6- -1754 d 1805 m Evaline Ray Pvt PA

RUTTY,
Ezra: b 9-14-1741 d 1812 m Mary Simons Ens NY
John: b 2-26-1748 d p. 1790 m Tamar Brooker Pvt CT
Samuel: b 2-7-1713/4 d 4-30-1777 m Patience Wright Sol MA

RYALS, (includes RIAL, RIALE & RYAL)
Arthur: b c. 1740 d 7- -1798 m Ann Bailey Pvt GA
Isaac: b 7-12-1760 d 3- -1837 m Phoebe Ann DeVore Pvt NJ ★
John: b 3-1-1759 d 4-2-1846 m Rachael Evans Pvt PA
Richard: b — d 1810 m Milly Baggett Pvt NC
Wm.: b 1748 d 2-1-1828 m Edith Childs Pvt NC

RYAN, (includes RINE & RYON)
Edward: b 3-6-1756 d p. 1795 m Lena Huyck Pvt NY
James: b 2-13-1738 d 3-19-1832 m Dorothea Henderson Pvt PA
Jeremiah: b 1753 d 9-10-1837 m Mary Wilkes Pvt Bbd CT ★
John: b 3-10-1748 d 1-5-1832 m (1)Sarah Goodale (2)Mrs Sarah
    (Walker) Inman (3)Isabelle — Sgt CT ★
John: b c. 1757 d 1808 m Priscilla Kerr PS MD
John: b c. 1745 d p. 7-8-1822 m Susanna — PS MD
John: b 1749 d 12- -1819 m Ruth Burwell Pvt NJ
John: b 1750 d 6-30-1836 m Elizabeth — Pvt PA ★
John Isaac: b 11-14-1758 d 4-15-1830 m Hannah Townsend Sgt PA
Lacon: b 6-6-1748 d 11-4-1785 m Margaret — Lt PS SC
Michael: b 1744 d 10-30-1818 m (2)Mary Agnes White Pvt MD
Michael: b 1758 d p. 1821 m (1)Eleanor Smith (2)Elizabeth Bucy Pvt
    MD
Philip: b c. 1755 d 1822 m Obedience — Sol PS VA
Robert: b 1763 d 6-5-1837 m Elizabeth Mars Pvt NY ★
Samuel: b 12-26-1750 d 12-17-1816 m (1)Mercy Stoddard (2)Eunice
    Evans Pvt MA
Thomas: b 1747 d 1780 m Catharine — Sol PS VA
Wm.: b 1750 d p. 6-18-1801 m Sarah — 1Lt VA

RYANT, (or RIANT)
Joseph: b 10-13-1757 d 9-13-1849 m Sally Powers Pvt MA

RYCKMAN, (includes RICKMAN)
Garret: b a. 1748 d p. 1776 m Elizabeth VanBuren QM NY
Jesse: b 5-2-1770 d 3-10-1860 m (1)Mary Trantham (2)Mrs Rhoda
    Radd Pvt NC
John: b 11-4-1759 d 11-1-1834 m Mary Allen Pvt Arfr NY ★
John: b c. 1740 d p. 1800 m — Sol VA
Mark: b 1762 d 8-14-1805 m Mary Harper Pvt NC

RYER,
John: b 1745 d 1832 m Levinia Tippetts Pvt NY
John: b c. 3-4-1759 d 11-10-1827 m Sarah Browers Pvt NY
John: b 1-22-1766 d 4-7-1850 m Elenor Myers Pvt NY
Peter: b 1737 d 1825 m Catharine Stump Pvt PA
Tunis: b 2-17-1744 d c. 1793 m Elizabeth Bussing Pvt NY
Tunis: b a. 1754 d 1824 m Sammy Myer Pvt NY

RYERSON,
George: bpt 4-5-1713 d 4-1-1789 m Mary R White MM Lt NJ
Luke: b 1-9-1739 d 8- -1808 m (1)Abigail Ellery (2)Sarah Coombs
    PS ME
Richard G.: b 5-26-1755 d 5-17-1833 m Martha Vreeland Pvt NJ ★
Ryer: b 10-2-1743 d 9-24-1817 m Elizabeth Bertholf Sol NJ
Stephen: b 2-9-1763 d 12-10-1849 m Mary Kinne Pvt NY
Thomas: b 11-12-1753 d 10-2-1835 m Mary Turner Lt PA

RYKER, (includes RIKER)
Abraham: b 11-25-1721 d 2-9-1820 m Elizabeth Conkle 1Lt NY
Abraham: b 5-22-1753 d 5-21-1825 m Elizabeth VanValen Pvt NY
Abraham: b 5-10-1756 d 1-28-1843 m Mary Delanoy Arfr NY
Gerardus: b 11-16-1740 d 1-12-1784 m Rachel Demarest Ens NJ
John: b 1-18-1764 d 11-2-1848 m Mary VanCleve Pvt NJ
Matthew: b 9-10-1756 d 9-8-1837 m Ann Nagle Pvt NY
Samuel: b 4-8-1743 d 5-19-1823 m Anna Lawrence Lt NY

RYLAND,
John: b 1738 d 1821 m Rachel Sylvester AsstWgm PA
John: b 1759 d 1826 m Eleanor — Pvt PA

RYNDERS,
Evert: b c. 1747 d c. 1791 m Anna Finehout Pvt PS NY

RYNEARSON,
Isaac: b 9-8-1758 d 9-14-1840 m Catharine LeGrange Pvt NJ ★

RYNO,
John: b 11-16-1749 d 8-14-1819 m Prudence Stites Pvt NJ

RYTHER,
David: b 8-15-1719 d 6-6-1804 m Martha Shattuck CS PS MA

SAAM,
Adam, Sr.: b 1- -1735 d 9-22-1809 m Mary Magdalena Bell PS PA

SABIN, (includes SABINE & SABINS)
Elihu: b 1750 d 11-10-1828 m Hannah Bacon Pvt CT ★
Elijah: b 3-17-1755 d 8-26-1843 m Mary Salmon Pvt NY ★
Elisha: b 10-12-1733 d 4-14-1798 m Maria Dickerman Pvt MA
Gideon: b 3-20-1743 d p. 1794 m Freelove Searl Pvt MA
Hezekiah, Sr.: b 9-5-1720 d 3-7-1791 m Mercy Power LCol CT
Hezekiah, Jr.: b 4-15-1750 d 4-5-1822 m Sarah Munson Capt CT
Ichabod: b 5-25-1726 d 4-23-1783 m Sarah Cole Pvt CT
James: b 7-17-1732 d 4-27-1806 m (1)Phebe Hammond (2)Anne
    Bicknell Pvt RI
Jonathan: b — d 1816 m Mary — Cpl Mid Cnt CT
Joseph: b 5-31-1729 d 2-10-1803 m Mary (Sabin) Cpl CT
Joshua: b 6-6-1740 d 3-3-1825 m Ruth Wiswall Sgt CT
Joshua: b 1760 d 2-1-1825 m Desire Niles Pvt NY
Josiah: b 3- -1742 d 2-1-1833 m Lydia Cady Pvt MA ★
Nehemiah: b 4-8-1741 d p. 1782 m Mary Rice Cpl CT
Noah: b 10-17-1714 d 3-10-1811 m Mary Perren CS VT
Peter, Jr.: b 8-6-1744 d 2-20-1811 m (1)Lydia Turtlott (2)Sarah
    Allen Pvt CT
Samuel: b 1758 d 12- -1847 m (1)Sarah Hill (2)Lillas Soule Pvt RI ★
Wm.: b 10-5-1754 d 4-15-1832 m Maria Cady Pvt MA
Zebediah: b 7-23-1737 d 1777 m Anna Dwight 1Lt MA
Ziba: b 8-10-1749 d 1825 m Lydia Welsh Pvt MA

SACIA,
David: b 1736 d 3-8-1828 m Susannah Bratt Pvt PS NY W★

SACKETT, (includes SACKET)
Adnan: b 12-5-1745 d 4-28-1813 m (1)Jerusha Pomeroy (2)Mercy
    Bush (3)Mrs Fernard Lt MA
Ananias Rogers: b 1-23-1760 d 9-2-1838 m Eunice Meeker Pvt NY
Benjamin: b 1730/1 d p. 1790 m Deborah Buell Pvt NY
Benjamin: b 2-28-1762 d 7-14-1844 m (1)Betsey Eldred (2)Mercy
    Gaylord Pvt CT
Benjamin: b 1752 d 1826 m Phoebe Davis Pvt NY
Buell: b 7-28-1763 d 1-18-1840 m Sally E Beach Pvt CT
Daniel: b 3-6-1734 d 1824 m (2)Mrs Mahitable Cadwell Dewey Capt
    MA
Elijah: b c. 1751 d 8-29-1837 m Catherine Gibson Pvt PA
Erastus: b c. 1728 d p. 1810 m Elizabeth Leonard Pvt MA
Ezekiel: b c. 1737 d p. 1786 m Mary Atherton Pvt NY
Gad: b c. 1757 d p. 1788 m Lucy Williams Cpl MA
John, Jr.: b c. 1743 d 1811/2 m Jane — Sol NY
John: b 1755 d 1819 m Elizabeth Gibbs Pvt NY
John: b 8-18-1747 d 7-25-1805 m Prudence Atherton Sol NY
Justus: b 3-9-1730 d 3-16-1815 m Lydia Newcomb Capt PS CT
Justus: b 1740 d 1-15-1827 m Anne Lyon Sgt CT
Nathaniel: b 4-10-1737 d 7-28-1805 m Mary Rogers PS NY
Ozem: b 1-24-1736 d 1801 m Mercy Weller Sgt MA
Peter: b 11-4-1757 d p. 1779 m Esther Palmer Adj NY
Reuben: b 6-17-1732 d 6-5-1805 m Mercy Finney CS PS CT
Richard: b c. 1745 d 1799 m Rachael Holmes Capt NY
Richard: b 7-15-1749 d 1789 m Martha Benedict Pvt VT
Samuel: b 4-5-1754 d 2-13-1833 m Sarah Manning Dr CT PA ★
Samuel: b 3-7-1702 d 3-5-1781 m (1)Elizabeth Todd (2)Lydia Todd
    (3)Hannah (Russell) Pierpont CS CT
Samuel: b 6-23-1724 d 4-15-1780 m Mary Betts Capt NY
Samuel: b 1747 d 8-20-1816 m Thankful Wood Pvt NY
Skene Douglas: b 5-1-1765 d 6-9-1852 m Hannah Saxton Pvt CT ★
Wm.: b 11-16-1753 d 1-20-1841 m (1)Eunice Bowman (2)Parthena
    Patterson OrdlSgt CT ★
Zaven: b 4-28-1751 d 10-26-1840 m Abigail Bills Pvt MA ★

SACKRIDER, (includes SAIKRYDER)
Moses: b 8-29-1746 d 4-1-1825 m Hannah Wright Pvt PS NY
Solomon: b 10-24-1748 d 9-14-1835 m Mary Ogden PS NY

SADD,
Thomas: b 3-29-1748 d 7-10-1823 m Delight Warner Lt CT

SADLER,
Christopher: b 1758 d 3-23-1789 m Sophie Orts Cav CL
David: b 8-31-1762 d 2-13-1848 m Elsie Bratton Pvt SC ★
Isaac: b 5-14-1760 d 6-20-1843 m Jennie Hunt Maj PA
John: bpt 10-31-1762 d p. 1830 m Lavina Porter Pvt MA
John: b 5-11-1766 d p. 1818 m Lydia Bond Pvt MA ★
Richard: b 1- -1733 d p. 1785 m Jane — PS SC
Robert, Sr.: b c. 1735 d p. 1834 m (1)Sarah Jarrot (2)Margaret
    Atherton Pvt VA
Seth: b 11-8-1752 d a. 1820 m Olive Battle Cpl MA
Stephen: b 8-20-1723 d 10-18-1811 m Elizabeth Taintor Capt MA
Thomas: b 1730 d 1796 m Rebecca — PS VA

SAFFELL,
Charles: b 1748 d 3-3-1837 m Sophia Segar Mus MD ★

SAFFORD,
Benjamin: b 1717 d 4-25-1810 m Prudence — Pvt NH
Benjamin: b 12-1-1734 d 11-28-1827 m (1)Shuah Longee (2)Susan
    Malone Pvt NH

Challis: b 1765 d — m Sarah Jones Pvt VT
Daniel: bpt 9-1-1734 d 6-24-1818 m Mrs Lydia Caldwell Pvt MA
David: b 2-8-1743/4 d p. 1824 m Anna Brewster Pvt VT
Elisha: b 3-27-1748 d 9-18-1788 m Sylvina — Pvt MA
Erastis: b 1763 d 12-5-1849 m Clarissa Hopkins Capt VT
Gideon: b 11-4-1754 d 3-7-1838 m Lucy Freeman Pvt CT ★
Jesse: b 2-9-1755 d 8-3-1834 m Abigail Damon Capt MA ★
John: b 1709-11 d 5-2-1782 m Martha Haskell Lt PS MA
Jonas: b 7-23-1763 d 9-27-1834 m Joanna Merrill Pvt VT
Joseph, Sr.: b 3- -1705 d 6-15-1775 m Ann Bottom PS VT
Joseph: bpt 10-25-1730 d 1-19-1798 m Martha Powers Col VT
Joseph, Jr.: b 1742 d 12-4-1807 m Marcy Robinson Capt VT
Josiah: b 2-21-1740 d 1825 m (1)Deborah Sprague (2)Polly
    Leffingwell Pvt VT
Nathan: b 6-5-1760 d 12-27-1823 m Elizabeth Foster Pvt MA
Philip: b 1739 d 4-14-1814 m Elizabeth Bigelow Lt VT
Samuel: b 4-27-1737 d 3-13-1813 m Mary Lawrence BGen VT
Silas: b 9-14-1757 d 5-12-1832 m Clarinda Hawley Pvt VT
Thomas: b 6-13-1738 d 3-1-1788 m Elizabeth Phelps Cpl MA

SAFLY, (or SAFLEY)
Henry: b 11-15-1759 d 11- -1838 m Margaret — Pvt VA MD ★

SAGE,
Abel: b 1758 d 1827 m Tryphena Turrill Pvt MA
Allen, Jr.: b 6-9-1751 d p. 1837 m (1) X (2)Elizabeth Beacraft Cpl
    MA
Allen, Sr.: b 2-14-1729 d p. 1790 m Abigail Willard 2Lt MA
Benjamin, Sr.: b 1-17-1725 d 12-8-1813 m Abigail Blinn PS NY
Benjamin, Jr.: b 1754 d 1784 m — Pvt NY
Comfort: b 8-22-1731 d 3-14-1799 m ( ) Sarah Hamlin ( )Hannah
    Coleman Col PS CT
Daniel: b 6-30-1756 d p. 1-31-1814 m Freelove — Pvt MA
Daniel: b 12-5-1756 d 12-17-1852 m Sybil Jewett Pvt NY ★
David: b 1703 d p. 1796 m Bathsheba Judd CS CT
David: b 1760 d 7-20-1834 m Thirza — Pvt MA ★
Elias: b 4-17-1759 d 3-12-1823 m Sarah Reed Pvt MA
Elisha: b 8-20-1755 d 5-30-1801 m Martha Montague Pvt CT
Enos: b 1757 d 7-16-1839 m (1)Rhoda Chamberlain (2)Eunice
    (Smith) Clark Pvt MA ★
Epaphras: b 1757 d 5-28-1834 m Elizabeth Wells Ranney Pvt CT ★
Giles: b 7-28-1742 d a. 12-8-1788 m Esther Hall NCapt CT
Giles: b 2-24-1742 d 6- -1797 m (1)Hannah Sheldon (2)Ann Wright
    Cpl CT
Harleigh: b 1764 d 1-8-1828 m Lucinda Pratt Pvt CT ★
James: b 8-26-1754 d 3-17-1820 m Lovisa Utt Pvt VA
John: b 11-6-1747 d 5-20-1807 m Mary Nash Pvt VA
Miles: b 1758 d p. 1785 m Hannah — Pvt NJ
Nathaniel: b 4-6-1707 d 2-4-1780 m Rebecca Hart PS CT
Samuel: b 6-11-1755/6 d 4-8-1824 m Judith Callivan Sgt PA ★
Selah: b 12-18-1752 d 5-3-1813 m Mary — Pvt MA
Simeon: b 1759 d 1840 m Mary Holden Pvt MA ★
Solomon, Sr.: b 3-24-1720 d 6-7-1795 m Hannah Kirby Capt CT
Solomon: b 8-18-1737 d 8- -1805 m Lois Wilcox Capt CT
Stephen: b 1752 d 3-25-1842 m Esther Hollister Pvt CT ★
Timothy: b 1743 d a. 1796 m Abigail Riley SeaCap CT
Wm.: b 1-1-1748 d 11-8-1833 m (1)Bathsheba Hollister (2)Abigail
    Eells Ens CT

SAILOR, (includes SAHLER, SAILER, SAYLER & SAYLOR)
Abraham, Jr.: b 9-14-1747 d 1-14-1800 m Tryntje VanWagener
    Pvt NY
George Michael: b 1-17-1752 d 6-3-1835 m (1) — Benraught
    (2)Elizabeth Miller Pvt PA
Jacob: b 6-10-1752 d 2-25-1833 m Amelia Neff Pvt PA
Jacob, Sr.: b 1735 d 1779 m Elizabeth — PS SC
Jacob: b 1748 d 9-21-1800 m Mary Elizabeth Steele Pvt PA
Jacob: b a. 1752 d 6-19-1816 m Frances Weir Ens PA
John: b c. 1736 d p. 1815 m (2)Marietta — Pvt PA
John: b — d a. 4-23-1786 m Franny — Sol PS PA
Matthias: b 1760 d 1785 m — PS MD
Peter: b 9-26-1721 d 1-8-1803 m Anna Margaretha Maurer LCol PA
Peter: b 1753 d a. 2-29-1836 m — Pvt PS MD
Philip: b — d p. 10- -1818 m Elizabeth Coyle Capt PA

ST AMAND,
Michel: b 1757 d 12-10-1827 m Francosie Zeringue Sol LA

ST JOHN,
Abijah: b 5-16-1742 d — m Ruth Hoyt Pvt CT
Abraham: b 3-25-1759 d 1803 m Anna Hoyt Pvt CT
Adonijah: b 1754/5 d 3-2-1836 m (1)Abigail Weed (2)Mrs Olive
    Strong Curtis Pvt CT
Caleb: b 1732 d 2-20-1805 m Mary Seely Capt CT
Daniel: b 7-16-1748 d c. 1796 m Abigail Holmes Pvt CT
Daniel: b c. 1736 d 8-1-1781 m Ruth Benedict PS CT
Daniel: b c. 1750 d 7-8-1778 m — PS PA
David: b 1730 d 4-14-1796 m Jemima Penoyer 1Lt CT
David: b 10-7-1758 d 9-1-1844 m Elizabeth Waring Sgt CT
David: b 1763 d 6-6-1840 m Mary Camp Pvt CT
Gideon: b c. 1757 d p. 1803 m Phebe Staples Smn Pvt CT
James: b 10-27-1736 d 2- -1829 m Jerusha Thomas Pvt NY
Jesse: b 1759 d 8-13-1843 m Anna Weed Cpl CT ★

ST JOHN, contd.
John: b 4-11-1753 d 10-22-1825 m Hannah Fitch Capt CT
John: b 4-2-1737 d — m Martha Northrop CS PS CT
John: b 2-2-1750 d 7-5-1819 m Anna Lockwood Pvt NY
Josiah: b 1744 d 5-22-1830 m Mary Fitch PS CS CT
Lydia: b — d 1829 m Williams Seymour N CT
Matthew: b 7-7-1754 m 1849 m Eleanor Pelm Pvt NY
Matthias Sr.: b 1732 d 3-20-1819 m (1)Naomi Weed (2)Anna Bishop Cpl CT
Matthias, Jr.: b 7-25-1762 d 1-4-1836 m (1)Esther Raymond (2)Esther Abbott (3)Sarah Bishop Pvt CT ★
Moses: b 11-8-1739 d 4-7-1822 m Anna Clark Capt NY
Nathan: b 1720 d 6-10-1795 m Lois — Capt CT
Nehemiah: b 1742 d 7-23-1803 m Ruth Wheeler Cpl CT
Nehemiah: b 1719 d 4-5-1804 m Lois Cornell PS CT
Peter: b 1-11-1726 d 1-4-1811 m (1)Mary Cook (2)Rebecca Crofoot MM CT
Samuel: b 2-5-1747 d 2-19-1790 m Gloriany St John Gregory Pvt CT
Samuel: b 6-15-1753 d 10-6-1785 m Lois Hamilton 1Lt MA
Samuel: b 8-12-1760 d 3-8-1819 m Thankful Lockwood Sol NY
Stephen: b 1736 d 5-9-1785 m Ann Fitch LCol PS CS CT
Stephen: b 1733 d 1801 m Mary Platt Betts CG CT
Thomas: b 10-12-1738 d 6-12-1816 m (1)Susanna Northrup (2)Betty Thomas Sgt CT
Wm.: b 4-7-1744 d 6-19-1800 m Mary Esther Beldon CS CT

ST JOHN DE CREVECOEUR,
Michel Guillaume: b 2-1-1735 d 11-13-1813 m Mehitable Tippet PS NY

SALE,
Cornelius: b 1749 d 1808 m Jane Dawson PS VA
John, Sr.: b 1727 d 4-20-1803 m Sarah Floyd PS MA
John, Jr.: b 8-3-1757 d 9-1-1835 m (1)Deborah Hobart (2)Hannah Butterfield Pvt MA
John: b 12-30-1729 d 3-30-1815 m (1)Elizabeth Willis (2)Frances Saunders Capt VA

SALISBURY, (includes SALSBURY)
Abraham: b 12-5-1744 d 2-22-1808 m Elsie Hasbrouck Pvt NY
Ambrose: b 3-2-1742 d 12-16-1804 m Sarah Whitman Lt MA
Anthony: b 9-18-1756 d 1809 m Hannah Dedman Pvt RI
Barent Staats: b 4-3-1743 d 4-11-1797 m Sarah Dubois 1Lt NY
Benjamin: b 2-27-1756 d 1-23-1852 m Lydia Baker Pvt RI
Caleb: b 6-25-1710 d p. 1781 m (1)Prudence West (2)Elizabeth Luther Pvt CT
Edward: b 9-6-1733 d 3- -1829 m Abigail (Hawkins) MM RI
Francis: b 10-8-1742 d p. 1789 m Elsie Staats Lt NY
George: b 1736 d 1-22-1818 m Abigail — Sgt RI ★
Henry: b 1733 d 4-1-1821 m Catharine Head PS NY
John: b 7-15-1757 d 2-18-1837 m (1)Freelove Herendean (2)Mary Dean Pvt RI ★
Jonathan: b 11-18-1735 d 3-27-1817 m Mary Child NCapt VT
Joshua: b 1757-9 d 10-9-1800 m Elizabeth Owen Pvt RI
Martha Saunders: b 4-22-1704 d 2-18-1792 m Nicholas Salisbury PS MA
Nathan: b 2-27-1756 d 1-23-1842 m Lydia White Pvt NY
Nathan: b 12-1-1751 d 5-4-1817 m Abigail Stone Pvt RI
Richard: b 1750 d 1798 m Polly Milton PS CT
Samuel: b 10-11-1744 d 1-25-1835 m Sarah — 2Lt MA
Samuel: b 11-18-1739 d 9-29-1818 m (1)Elizabeth Sewall (2)Abigail Freeman Snow PS MA
Sylvester: b 1-27-1741 d 4- -1815 m Neeltje Staats Pvt NY
Sylvester: b a. 1743 d 4-10-1785 m Eljen Eltinge Capt NY
Wm.: b 9-29-1731 d 1-22-1821 m Elizabeth Beals Dep Cmsry MA
Wm.: b 1758 d 1843 m Elizabeth — Pvt MA ★

SALKELD,
Issac: b 1743 d a. 11-11-1782 m Marya Bockee Lt NY

SALLADA, (includes SALLADAY & SALLADE)
Daniel: b 1758 d 4-20-1820 m Mary Waste Pvt PA ★
Jacob: b 1-22-1748 d 4-15-1815 m Barbara Loux Pvt PA
John: b 4-12-1755 d 1-19-1842 m Elizabeth — Pvt PA
John: b 1739 d 1827 m Margaret Everhart Pvt PA

SALLEY, (includes SALLEE)
John: b 1740 d 11-2-1794 m Mrs Mary Keziah Wright Moss Capt SC
Joseph: b 3-9-1746 d a. 7- -1814 m — PS VA

SALMON,
Absalom: b 6-14-1761 d 3-27-1831 m Lydia Wilbur Pvt NY
Edward: b 8-19-1743 d 6-29-1809 m Elizabeth Keller Capt MD
George: b 2-4-1754 d 8-18-1827 m Elizabeth Young Lt SC
John: b 1-8-1730 d p. 1790 m Jerusha Coval Pvt NY
John: b 4-22-1760 d 11-12-1837 m Sarah Wilson Pvt PA ★
Joseph: b 11-12-1754 d 7-26-1824 m Ann Wheeler Ens PA
Peter: b 11-25-1740 d 2-19-1825 m Margaret Stark Capt NJ
Solomon: b c. 1762 d 7-14-1837 m Rozilla — Pvt DE

SALTER, (includes SALTAR & SELDERS)
Alexander: b 4-2-1718 d 11-1-1801 m Elizabeth Sanborn Sgt PS NH
Edward: b 1740 d 1805 m Abigail — PS NC

James: b 1-1-1754 d 2-5-1829 m Agnes Housel Tms NJ
James: b p. 1760 d p. 1830 m Nancy Gainor Sol NC
John: b 9-19-1748 d 5-22-1804 m Abiah Webster Pvt NH
John: b c. 1763 d 10-10-1834 m (1)Celia Phillips (2)Christian McCorvey Mus NC
Joseph: b 1732 d 8-28-1820 m (1)Sarah Holmes (2)Huldah Mott (3)Rachel (Hartshorne) Robinson LCol PS NJ
Michael: b 1754 d 3-7-1846 m Osee Read Mus NJ ★
Peter: b 3-17-1759 d 7-30-1834 m Susanna Nelson Sgt MA ★
Titus: b 10-19-1722 d 9-20-1798 m Elizabeth Bickford Capt NH
Wm.: b 1-18-1732 d 1-9-1802 m Sarah Lloyd PS NC

SALTMARSH,
Thomas: b 3-2-1736/7 d 1826 m Betsey Abbott Pvt NH ★
Wm.: b 1-20-1735 d 1-13-1811 m Elizabeth Patterson Pvt NY

SALTONSTALL,
Dudley: b 9-8-1738 d 1796 m Frances Babcock Commo CT
Gurdon: b 12-22-1708 d 9-19-1785 m Rebecca Winthrop BGen CT
Gurdon F.: b 5-18-1760 d 1-30-1836 m Hannah Hempstead Fif CT
Nathaniel: b 1727 d 8-1-1807 m (1)Mrs Rebecca (Flower) Young (2)Lucretia Latimer Capt CT
Winthrop: b 6-10-1737 d 1811 m Anne Wanton PS CT

SALTSMAN, (includes SALTZMAN)
Anthony: b 1745 d 1-2-1778 m Rosanna Wilson Sgt PA
George: b 12-13-1763 d 2-14-1838 m Weena Lepper Pvt NY ★
Henry: b 12-6-1752 d p. 1800 m Fanny Cook Pvt NY

SALTZGABER,
John: b 9-14-1747 d 3-30-1829 m Maria Margaret Eisenmengeon Pvt PA

SALYER,
John: b c. 1763/4 d 1810-20 m Elizabeth Scott Pvt SC

SAMFORD,
Wm.: b a. 1762 d 1795 m Elizabeth Samford PS VA

SAMMIS,
Jonathan, Sr.: b 1715 d 1781 m Abigail Ketcham PS NY
Jonathan, Jr.: b 4-8-1748 d 4-1-1794 m Rebecca Ketcham PS NY
Joseph: b 10-30-1748 d 12-1-1818 m Abigail Mott Pvt NY
Silas, Jr.: b 9-13-1731 d 1779 m Ruth Rogers Pvt NY
Timothy, Jr.: bpt 7-29-1739 d c.10-10-1813 m Elizabeth Scudder Sgt NY
Wm.: b 6-9-1745 d 1790 m Sarah Conklin Pvt NY

SAMPLE,
Ezekiel: b 5-26-1749 d 6- -1829 m Elizabeth McBride Cpl PA
James: b 3-25-1756 d 11-24-1830 m Christiana Taggert Capt PA
James: b 1750 d 1799 m Sarah Jane — Pvt VA
John: b 12-25-1757 d 6-13-1843 m Mary — Pvt PA ★
John: b c. 1759 d 1836 m — Pvt SC ★
Moses: b c. 1730 d p. 1-24-1824 m (1)Ruth Wood (2)Mary Rutherford Sol VA
Nathaniel: b 1750 d 1838 m Betsy Little Sol VA
Robert: b 9-20-1735 d 8-19-1808 m (1)Lydia Steele (2)Elizabeth Young Capt PA
Robert: b c. 1760-5 d 1797 m Barbara Blain Pvt SC
Wm.: b 1736 d 9- -1791 m Elizabeth Alexander Sol NC
Wm.: b c. 1762 d 5- -1785 m Ann Brackney Sol PA

SAMPSON, (includes SAMSON)
Abishai: b 3-7-1752 d 9-28-1828 m Phebe Wheeler Sgt MA
Amos: b 9-24-1756 d 8-3-1843 m Joanna French Pvt MA ★
Beriah: b 11-1-1728 d — m Alice Howland Sgt MA
Caleb: b 1760-2 d 1823 m Rebecca Stanford Pvt MA
Croade: b 12-12-1763 d 10-4-1836 m Bethany Dawes Pvt MA
Daniel: b 11-10-1758 d 5-27-1842 m Mary Howe Pvt NH
David: b 6-28-1736 d — m Lucy Warner Pvt MA
Edward: b 12-13-1746 d 2-25-1816 m (1)Mary Catherine Sharrow (2)Mrs Sarah Cannon Pvt MA
Elijah: b 10-25-1757 d 8-21-1834 m Hannah Sprague Pvt MA
Ezekiel: b 8-8-1744 d 5-5-1811 m (1)Sarah Fause (2)Mary — Lt MA
Francis: b 11-27-1747 d p. 9-2-1832 m Drucilla Siller Sol VA
Henry: b 2-23-1767 d 3-3-1852 m Sarah Whitaker Arfr NY ★
Howland: b 1756 d 7-4-1840 m Elizabeth Samson Pvt MA ★
Isaac: b 1760 d 1838 m — Merrifield Pvt NY
Isaiah: bpt 6-24-1759 d 11-15-1841 m Betsey Samson Pvt MA ★
Jacob: b 1737 d 1834 m Ruth Bradford Sgt MA
James: b 11-17-1754 d 4-15-1825 m Sarah Smith Pvt MA
James: b 4-11-1761 d c. 9-4-1851 m Jemima Stetson Pvt MA ★
John: b 8-8-1727 d 7-23-1805 m (1)Rebecca Brewster (2)Abigail Stetson Pvt PS MA
John: b 1751 d 5-20-1830 m Deborah Torey Pvt MA
Jonathan, Sr.: b 10-25-1733 d 1820 m (1)Mary Oaks (2)Sarah Osborne Pvt PS MA
Jonathan, Jr.: b 5-7-1759 d 12-8-1846 m Susan Rice Cpl MA ★
Joshua: b 1750 d p. 1781 m (1)Rachel French (2)Susannah Parkhurst Cpl MA
Judah: b 8-10-1735 d 11-29-1797 m Mary Delano Pvt MA

Luther: b 3-26-1760 d 8-31-1847 m (1)Abigail Ford (2)Lydia — Pvt MA ★
Micah: b c. 1735 d p. 1790 m Hannah Poole Cpl Matr Gnr MA
Peter: b 10-16-1747 d p. 1790 m Elizabeth Perry Sgt MA
Richard: b c. 1755 d a. 12-30-1808 m Mary — Pvt MD
Samuel: b 2-24-1764 d 7-30-1850 m Lydia Holmes Pvt MA
Simeon: b 8- -1736 d 6-22-1789 m Deborah Cushing Capt MA
Stephen: b 1730 d a. 8-16-1816 m Sarah Johnson Capt PS VA
Thomas: b 12-14-1737 d 3-7-1824 m Ruth Bryant Capt MA
Thomas: b a. 1764 d 8- -1833 m — Duff PS PA
Wm.: b 1749/50 d 6-12-1815 m Deborah Randal Pvt MA
Wm.: b 1-3-1763 d 1815 m Mary (Neal) Blazell PS PA
Wm.: b 9-15-1761 d 8- -1833 m Sarah Coleman Pvt VA ★
Wm.: b 1765 d 11-4-1833 m Betsy Povall Pvt VA ★
Zabdiel: b -4-26-1727 d 9-16-1776 m (1)Abigail Cushman (2)Abiah Whitmarsh Pvt MA

SAMUEL,
John: b c. 1745 d p. 5-3-1803 m Catherine — PS VA
Reuben: b — d p. 1785 m Sally Slaughter Lt VA
Thomas: b 3-24-1742 d 10-7-1821 m Ann Brooking PS VA

SAMUELS,
Gilbert: b 8-5-1755 d 2-11-1835 m Cathren — Pvt PA

SANBORN, (includes SANDBORN & SANBURN)
Aaron: b 2-8-1742/3 d 6-9-1790 m (1)Molly Barter (2)Susanna Gale Ens Capt NH
Abijah: b 3-4-1748 d p. 2-13-1790 m Molly Morrill PS NH
Abner: b 5-14-1746 d 12-31-1841 m (1)Eunice Brown (2)Mrs Sarah Johnson Cpl PS NH ★
Abner: b 8-3-1726 d 4-18-1811 m Lucy Lowell CS NH
Abraham: b 5-25-1732 d p. 1776 m Rachel Hilliard Lt NH
Abraham: b 4-2-1717 d 2-21-1780 m Abigail Clifford PS NH
Abraham: b 12-28-1735 d 11-26-1808 m (1)Mary Choate Jewett (2)Mrs Mary Parsons PS NH
Abraham: b 4-7-1729 d a. 8-23-1798 m Mary — Pvt NH
Abraham: b 12-24-1744 d 10-5-1820 m Deborah Wilson PS NH
Benjamin: b 8- -1747 d 1829 m (2)Sarah — Pvt MA
Benjamin: b 8-24-1760 d 3-19-1803 m Rhoda Folsom Pvt NH
Benjamin: b 4-4-1762 d 10-9-1850 m (1)Polly Mason (2)Hannah Dorman Pvt NH ★
Caleb: b 7-25-1716 d 7-4-1794 m Mehitable Weare PS NH
Daniel, Jr.: b 5-17-1731 d 7-26-1800 m Lucy Hobbs Maj CS PS NH
Daniel: b 5-6-1742 d p. 1785 m (1)Hannah Folsom (2)Priscilla Sanborn (3)Nabby Giles Sol NH
Daniel: b 5-28-1728 d 5-25-1812 m (1)Anna Tilton (2)Mary Collins Pvt NH
Daniel: b 2-17-1702 d 2- -1798 m Catherine Rollins PS NH
Daniel: b 10-8-1708 d 9-22-1782 m Abigail Prescott PS NH
David: b 4-19-1753 d 3-13-1826 m Sarah Fuller Pvt PS NH
Dudley: b 5-22-1742 d p. 1790 m Molly Green Ens NH
Ebenezer: b 10-15-1745 d 2-13-1829 m Lydia Way Capt NH
Edward: b c. 1732 d p. 1784 m Elizabeth Rundlett PS NH
Elijah: b 9-22-1761 d 1836 m (1)Elizabeth Tilton (2)Sarah Gordon Pvt NH
Eliphalet: b 7-8-1730 d 7-17-1794 m Margaret Wallace Sol NH
Enoch: bpt 6-28-1724 d 1778 m (1)Mary Morrill (2)Sarah (Greene) Sanborn (3)Phebe Sanborn (4)Mrs Hannah Day Pvt MA
Ezekiel: b 7-29-1748 d 12-19-1818 m Abigail Burleigh CS PS NH
James: b 9-1-1760 d 10-10-1841 m (1)Sarah Dearborn (2)Sarah Elkins Pvt NH
Jeremiah: b 11-12-1764 d 3-5-1837 m (1)Theodate Sanborn (2)Sarah Page Pvt NH
Jeremiah: b 8-18-1741 d 10-18-1818 m Betsy Beverly Sgt NH
Jeremiah, Sr.: b 2-12-1703 d 8-17-1783 m Lydia Dearborn PS NH
Jeremiah, Jr.: b 7-7-1739 d 2-13-1823 m Meriam Dearborn Ens NH
Jeremiah, Jr.: b 11-5-1757 d 10-6-1839 m (1)Lydia Tilton (2)Susan Greely (3)Mrs Huldah Avery Pvt NH
Jethro: b 11-15-1755 d 1-22-1829 m Elizabeth Rand Ens NH
John: b 9-1-1723 d 12-6-1802 m (1)Lucy Sanborn (2)Susanna Pierce Pvt MA
John: b 12-28-1743 d 1828 m Jane Deban Pvt MA
John: b 1-28-1736 d 8-29-1814 m Tabitha Page Sgt NH
John: b 1-25-1742 d 10-30-1832 m (1)Lydia Rollins (2)Mary Green (3)Anna Sanborn Cpl NH
John: bpt 8-24-1745 d c. 1778 m Hannah Eastman Pvt PS NH
John: b 11-23-1747 d 4-4-1826 m Susanna Simpson Pvt NH
John: b 2-16-1747 d 9-23-1826 m Ruth Rand 1Lt Pvt NH
John: b 7-16-1730 d 10-4-1812 m Mary Glidden PS NH
John: b 2-9-1741 d 4-10-1797 m Elizabeth Sargent PS NH
John Pearson: b 1-28-1733 d 1- -1783 m Jane Beverly Pvt NH
Jonathan: b 4-11-1754 d 6-19-1796 m Sarah Shaw Cpl NH
Jonathan: bpt 2-4-1739 d 5-25-1809 m Lydia Severance PS PS NH
Jonathan: b 3-16-1718 d 2- -1804 m Mary Batchelder PS NH
Jonathan: b 5-3-1759 d 1813 m Sally Miles Pvt NH
Jonathan: b 4-13-1733 d 10-11-1789 m Anna Marston Mus PS NH
Joseph: b 5-14-1726 d 1812 m (1)Sarah Lane (2)Anna Philbrick Marston PS NH
Joseph Clifford: b 11-30-1737 d 1787-90 m Elizabeth French PS NH
Josiah: b 8-19-1738 d 1-18-1809 m (1)Anna Dalton (2)Mrs Prudence Haines Lt NH ★
Josiah: b 7-8-1764 d 1-24-1841 m Hannah Rundlett Pvt NH

Josiah: b 6-19-1747 d 5-7-1817 m Lucy Swain PS NH
Mark: b 3-4-1750 d 7-27-1821 m Esther Cleveland Sol NH
Mathew Neally: b 6-28-1757 d 4-21-1853 m (1)Phebe Roby (2)Elizabeth Barnard Sgt NH ★
Moses: b 6-8-1740 d 1778 m Judith Brown Sgt NH
Moses: b 3- -1717 d — m Elizabeth Mitchell Pvt NH
Moses: b 7-12-1717 d 6-8-1807 m (1)Priscilla (Sherburne) James (2)Lydia — PS NH
Moses: b 12-25-1757 d 3-14-1812 m Sarah Marden Pvt NH
Nathan: b 10-28-1737 d 8-13-1813 m Jemima French Capt NH
Nathan: b 6-27-1709 d 1784 m Catherine Sattalee PS NH
Nathaniel: b 2-6-1757 d 6-25-1814 m Hannah Goold Pvt MA
Nathaniel: b 12-17-1737 d — m Polly French Pvt PS NH
Paul: b 12-21-1752 d 1833 m (1)Mrs True (2)Rachel Sweetser Pvt MA
Peter: b 7-9-1751 d 8-6-1827 m Lydia Richardson Pvt MA ★
Peter: b 8-18-1752 d 12-22-1832 m (1)Martha Dow (2)Abigail Dow Pvt NH ★
Peter: b 5-25-1713 d 1-15-1810 m Mary Sanborn PS NH
Reuben: b 9-8-1754 d 12-29-1833 m Sarah Worthen Pvt NH ★
Reuben: b 12-25-1728 d 6-2-1828 m Elizabeth Ward PS NH
Richard: b 2-1-1736 d p. 1780 m Abigail Kelly Pvt MA
Shurburn: b 7-10-1756 d 5-18-1836 m Polly Hoyt Sgt NH
Simeon: b 2-2-1752 d 1812 m (2)Anna Randall Sol NH
Theophilus: b 10-24-1753 d 3-4-1829 m Mary Sleeper Sgt NH
Thomas: b 5-17-1738 d 11- -1807 m Anna Marston PS NH
Timothy: b 6-9-1733 d 6- -1813 m Elizabeth Leach Pvt NH
Wm.: b 5-1-1723 d 5-23-1810 m (1)Mary Sleeper (2)Betsey Weare (3)Elizabeth Chase PS NH
Zadock: b 4-19-1733 d p. 1790 m Susanna Judkins Pvt PS NH

SANDERS, (includes SAUNDERS)
Alexander: b 3-12-1760 d a. 1832 m Ann Carpenter Sol VA
Andrew: b — d p. 1-31-1816 m Mary — Sol SC
Benjamin, Sr.: b 8-28-1736 d 1-16-1808 m Mary Davis Sgt MA
Daniel: b 12-24-1738 d 12-24-1819 m Joanna Barney Lt CS NH
George: b c. 1740 d 1820 m Elizabeth — PS SC
Hardy: b 1747 d 1812 m Lucy Utley Capt NC
Henry: b 5-15-1744 d 8-19-1832 m Elizabeth Moyer? Pvt NY
Henry: b 10-26-1751 d 2-13-1834 m Dicy Blake Pvt SC
Jacob: b c. 1742 d 8-28-1797 m Susannah — Pvt PA
Jacob: b 1734 d 1792 m Elizabeth Whiting Cpl RI
Jesse: b c. 1754 d 4-14-1841 m Rebecca A Strange Pvt VA
John: b 1762 d 3-20-1823 m (1)Esther Griffin (2)Zane Lazzelle Sol DE
John: b 12-1-1756 d 1-27-1841 m Esther Chapman Sgt NH
John: b 4-6-1759 d 1817 m Judith Fore Pvt VA
John: b c. 1738 d p. 5-18-1803 m Jane Craig PS VA
Joshua: b c. 1730 d 1800 m Patricia Williams PS GA
Moses: b 1742 d 1816 m (1)Sallie Hamilton (2)Mary — Sol NC
Nathaniel: b 1741 d 10- -1826 m Sallie Pattie Spy Pvt VA
Solomon: b 8-31-1745 d 12-19-1809 m Lydia Levistone Pvt MA
Thomas: b c. 1750 d c. 1826 m Jane — Sol SC
Timothy: b 1748 d 5-15-1827 m Mary Rose Pvt NJ ★
Wm.: b c. 1755 d c. 1806 m Elizabeth — Sol NC
Wm.: b 2-20-1760 d 3-15-1847 m Patience Benthal Sgt NC
Wm.: b c. 1740 d p. 12-31-1802 m Sarah — Sol Cav SC
Zachariah: b 1759 d 9-10-1842 m (2)Sarah Kitchen Pvt VA ★

SANDERSON, (includes SAUNDERSON)
Abner: b 4-9-1739 d 11-6-1822 m Mrs Mary Child Hager Pvt MA
Abraham: b 2-23-1735/6 d 3-14-1828 m Sarah Wheeler Pvt MA
Abraham: b 6-10-1748 d 2-6-1824 m Lydia Smith Sgt MA
Amaziah: b c. 1760 d — m — Sol MA
Asa: b 4-11-1756 d 12-12-1842 m Lucy Scott Cpl MA ★
Benjamin: b c. 1746 d 9-25-1826 m Esther Lawrence Pvt NH
Ebenezer: b 6-8-1752 d 4-29-1800 m (1)Lucy Bragg (2)Sarah Stone 1Lt MA
Elijah: b 10-10-1751 d 2-13-1825 m Mary Mulliken Pvt MA
Henry: b c. 1744 d 8- -1782 m Hannah Popham Pvt PA
Hezekiah: b 3-4-1750 d 10-4-1820 m Elizabeth Pain Cpl MA
Issac: b 10-9-1757 d 2-10-1849 m (1)Submit Montague (2)Mercy Allen Pvt MA ★
Israel: b 12-14-1754 d 3-1-1806 m Relief Rice OrdlSgt MA
Jacob: b 8-3-1741 d 2-9-1829 m Mrs Elizabeth Child Pvt MA
James: b 4-7-1744 d 8-4-1818 m Sara Parker Cpl MA
Jeduthan: b 3-17-1755 d 6-13-1824 m Persis White Pvt MA
John: b 12-13-1731 d 4-28-1791 m Submit — Pvt NH
John: b c. 1754 d p. 2-15-1831 m — Pvt PA
John: b 10-17-1744 d p. 1778 m Elenor Sanderson Sct VT
Jonathan: b 9-5-1740 d 12-26-1832 m — Pvt MA
Joseph: b 3-8-1741 d — m Lois Fuller Pvt MA
Moses: b 2-22-1721 d 8-11-1798 m (1)Mary Flagg (2)Anna (Jewett) Pingry MM Pvt MA
Nathan: b 4-9-1755 d p. 10-22-1807 m (1)Elizabeth Bond (2)Mrs Sarah Hastings Pvt MA
Phineas: b 4- -1751 d 12-11-1840 m Lucy Burke Pvt VT
Rufus: b 8-10-1758 d 3- -1847 m Mercy Nason Pvt MA ★
Samuel: b 9-8-1748 d c. 1800 m Mary Munroe Sgt MA
Stephen: b 8-24-1758 d 6-9-1839 m Mary Dudley Pvt MA ★
Thomas: b 3-16-1746 d 3-12-1824 m (1)Miriam Wait (2)Lucy Wright Lt MA
Wm.: b 1761 d 11-13-1808 m Rebecca Randolph Maj PA

SANDIDGE,
Clayborne: b 1761 d 1843 m Jane Higginbottom Pvt VA
James: b c. 1726 d c. 1810 m Jane Shelton Sol VA
John: b 11-25-1760 d 7-27-1832 m Mary Wood Pvt VA
Larkin: b 1757 d 1820 m Mary Holliday Sol VA
Wm.: b 1754 d 1786 m Susannah — PS Sol VA

SANDIFER,
James: b 1750 d 6-22-1825 m Martha Coleman Pvt VA ★

SANDLIN,
Nicholas: b 1755 d 1834 m Nancy Brooks Pvt NC ★

SANDRIDGE,
Joseph: b 1760 d 2-14-1826 m Mary Shelton Pvt VA

SANDS, (includes SAND)
Adam: b 12-14-1731 d 4-7-1793 m Elizabeth Christina (Seip) Chumber Pvt PA
Andrew: b 1754 d 1849/50 m — Sgt PA ★
Benjamin: b 11- -1735 d 10-24-1824 m Mary Jackson PS NY
Comfort: b 12-29-1740 d — m Sarah Dodge PS NY
Edward, Sr.: b 1-17-1712 d 10-21-1778 m Hannah Tredwell Dr RI
Ephraim: b 1-25-1720 d 7-8-1817 m — Pvt MA
George: b 4-17-1733 d 8-8-1816 m Jemima Smith PS NY
John: b 2-22-1737 d 6-25-1811 m Elizabeth Jackson Col NY
John: b 1761 d 1846 m Anna Palmer Pvt NY
John: b 11-30-1736 d 7- -1789 m Hannah Trump PS PA
John: b 8-2-1745 d 12-27-1820 m (1)Elizabeth Paine (2)Phebe Littlefield Capt PS RI
Joshua: b 10-12-1757 d 9-12-1835 m Ann Askew PS NY
Joshua: b 3-22-1725 d 3-28-1787 m Mary Smith PS RI
Othniel: b 1-27-1733 d 1-5-1823 m Martha Ketchum Pvt NY
Ray: b 1-16-1737 d 2-15-1808 m Ann Niles LCol RI
Samuel: b 1744 d p. 1790 m Mary Bradbury Pvt MA
Samuel: b 1723 d 6-20-1792 m Mercy Gedney PS NY
Samuel: b 12-6-1756 d 10-16-1832 m Sarah Dean Pvt NY
Samuel: b 1736 d 1792 m Catharine Bechtel Capt PA
Simon: b 7-12-1727 d 4-5-1782 m (1)Catharine Tredwell (2)Sarah Sands PS NY

SANFORD, (includes SANDERFORD, SANDFORD, SANTFORD)
Aaron: b 5-26-1757 d 2-8-1849 m Lydia Hawley Sgt CT
Amos: b 12-29-1740 d — m Eunice Bradley Pvt CT
Augustine, Sr.: b c. 1745 d 1785 m Henrietta Randall PS VA
Caleb: b 8-22-1761 d 6-6-1822 m Lucinda Pike Pvt CT
Daniel: b 1-6-1729 d 8-5-1793 m Thankful Toles Lt CT
Daniel: b 1737 d 11-8-1807 m Phebe Sandford Pvt NY
David: b 11-16-1739 d 6-15-1787 m Abial Lacy Pvt CT W★
David: b 12-11-1737 d 4-7-1810 m Bathsheba Ingersoll Chp MA
David: bpt 2-6-1737 d 1790-1808 m Patience Sullivan Pvt NY
Ebenezer: b 1739 d 5-1-1778 m Esther Hotchkiss Pvt CT
Edward: b 1753 d 6-5-1814 m Margaret Ann Washington Lt VA
Ellada: b c. 1755 d 11-4-1820 m Nancy Todd Pvt CT
Elihu, Sr.: b 5-6-1731 d 5-28-1808 m Hannah Sanford Sol CT
Elihu, Jr.: b 4-26-1759 d 10-9-1839 m (1)Sarah Thorpe (2)Mrs Nancy (Atwood) Carrington Sgt CT ★
Elisha: b 7-11-1750 d 7-12-1841 m Rhoda Johnson Pvt CT
Elnathan: b 10-11-1727 d 4-19-1803 m (1)Deborah White (2) Hannah — PS CT
Ezekiel: bpt 7-4-1742 d 3-8-1809 m (1)Sarah Sturges (2)Abigail Starr Capt CT
Ezekiel: b 12-21-1745 d 1-9-1833 m (1)Sarah Cook (2)Rebecca (Barker) Foote Cpl CT ★
Ezekiel: b 9-7-1754 d 10-17-1826 m Hannah Halsey PS NY
Ezra: b 4-15-1747 d 4-22-1822 m Ann Hopper Pvt NY
George: b 1726 d 3- -1820 m Mercy Phillips Pvt MA
Halsey: b 10-10-1766 d 5-13-1845 m (1)Lydia Dimock (2)Miriam Lamphear Pvt CT ★
Henry: b 1-22-1752 d 12-25-1830 m Rhoda Perkins Pvt CT
Jairus: b 11-21-1762 d 9-9-1851 m Lucy Cook Pvt CT ★
James: b 1753 d 4-14-1842 m Sarah Beach Pvt CT
Jeremiah, Sr.: b 11-4-1739 d 8-11-1825 m Mary Modesett (Motley) Pvt VA
Jesse: b 1-3-1764 d 2-18-1827 m Martha Goodwyn Mitchell Sol VA
John: b c. 1737 d 1784 m Mary Esther — Col GA
John: b 1724 d 11-26-1785 m Esther — Capt PS NY
John: b 1743 d 1815 m Rebecca DeBow Capt NY
John: b 9-1-1759 d 2-15-1851 m Catherine DeBow Pvt NY ★
John M: b 1761/2 d 1844 m (2)Sarah Race Sol NY
Jonath: b 8-1-1735 d 1-21-1817 m Rhoda Woodruff Ens CT
Jonah: b 1749 d 11-15-1824 m (1)Mary Dunbar (2) — West Pvt CT
Jonathan: b 3-15-1757 d 12-2-1836 m Jerusha (Sanford) Pvt CT ★
Joseph, Jr.: b 7-28-1745 d 12-13-1813 m Mehitable Young Capt CT
Joseph: b 10-6-1726 d 8-13-1791 m Ann Hickock Ens CT
Joseph: b c. 1720 d 11-13-1784 m Bethia Lothrop Pvt CT
Joseph: b 6-20-1736 d 11-25-1776 m Hepsibah Griffith Pvt CT
Joseph: b 4-7-1735 d 8-26-1802 m Mahitabel Clark Pvt CT
Joseph: b 6-24-1761 d 1843 m Eleanor Macomber Pvt MA ★
Kingsbury: b 9-14-1753 d 2-20-1834 m Lavinia Edgerton Pvtr 1Sgt CT ★
Lemuel: b 4-18-1740 d 3-12-1803 m Mary Russell PS CT

Liffe: b 8-30-1750 d 12-3-1815 m Hulah Blackman Sgt CT
Moses: b 5-7-1725 d p. 1781 m Mary Robinson Pvt CT
Nehemiah: b 10- -1763 d 12-20-1844 m Hannah Beach Pvt CT
Oliver: b 9-20-1741 d 3-14-1814 m Rachel Coley Pvt CT
Oliver: b 5-24-1744 d 12-18-1817 m (1)Phebe Newton (2)Mrs Robert Green Pvt VT
Peleg: b 2-28-1739/40 d 6-8-1804 m Alice — Pvt MA
Peleg: b 10-23-1751 d 5-13-1789 m Lilias Wilcox Pvt RI
Peter: b 2-17-1738 d 1-2-1830 m Eleanor Turner 1Lt NJ
Philo: b 9-7-1761 d 9-8-1835 m Lydia Whiting Pvt MA
Raymond: bpt 9-13-1752 d 3- -1805 m Rebecca Chatfield Capt CT
Restcome: b 3-3-1759 d 3-15-1823 m Sarah Coggeshall Pvt RI
Richard: b c. 1755 d 1795 m Winnifred Redmond Sgt VA
Robert: b 1735 d 1782 m Susannah Kerenhappuch Turner PS VA
Robert: b 3-12-1745 d 3-18-1792 m Jean Sanders PS VA
Royal: b 5-17-1760 d 12-30-1834 m Rhoda Wilds Pvt RI ★
Samuel, Sr.: b c. 1739 d 3-17-1804 m Parthena Baldwin Capt CT
Samuel, Jr.: b 4-15-1766 d 9-18-1857 m Rhoda Atwater Pvt CT ★
Samuel: b 8-27-1760 d 12-24-1834 m Ruhamah Wheeler Sgt Grd CT ★
Samuel: b 1721 d 5-12-1794 m (1)Abigail Beaumont (2)Mrs Deborah Williams CS CT
Seth: b 8-23-1735 d 7-3-1805 m (1)Rebecca Burr (2)Abiah — (3)Abigail — Ens CT
Stephen: b 4-17-1740 d 8-13-1790 m Sybil White Pvt CT
Strong: b 10-9-1760 d 5-3-1846 m Temperance Hotchkiss Sgt CT ★
Thomas: b 7-26-1739 d 3-3-1810 m Keziah Brackett Sgt CT
Thomas: b 3-3-1732 d 3-24-1814 m Lydia Clark Pvt CT
Thomas: bpt 4-18-1736 d p. 1800 m Susannah Palmer PS VT
Thomas: b c. 1750 d 1809 m — Artl VA
Timothy: b 2-8-1734 d 1784 m (1)Mary Meeker (Sanford) (2)Mrs Esther Whitney PS CT
Wm.: b 2-9-1757 d 10-26-1837 m (1)Abigail Simmons (2)Susan Brigham Howe Sgt MA ★
Wm.: b 11-12-1752 d 3-13-1842 m Ann Chapman OrdlSgt NJ
Wm.: b 1732 d 5-31-1828 m Jerusha Arnel Pvt NJ W★
Wm.: b 4- -1734 d 12-12-1806 m Rachel Medford Mar Capt VA
Wm.: b 10-30-1750 d 1801 m Penelope Thornton Capt VA
Zachariah: bpt 5-29-1737 d 1-14-1807 m Ann Hills Sgt CT ★

SANGER,
Daniel: b 2-13-1739 d 9-27-1807 m (1)Oliver Hooker (2)Esther Goodman PS MA
Eleazer: b 1735 d 1800 m Hannah Sherwood Pvt NH
John: b 12-20-1733 d p. 1790 m Eunice Davis Pvt PS NH
Jonathan: b 8-24-1755 d 8-21-1819 m Lucy Sawyer Pvt CT
Noadiah: b 12-12-1738 d 8-7-1808 m Priscilla Russ Pvt CT
Richard: b 11-4-1706 d 5-14-1786 m Deborah Rider PS MA
Samuel: b 6-1-1736 d 10-27-1775 m (2)Grace Harrington Sgt MA
Samuel: b 7-7-1735 d 10-6-1822 m (1)Mary Fairbanks (2)Abigail Whiting PS MA
Wm.: b 7-20-1730 d 4-21-1798 m Abigail Jennison Pvt MA

SANKEY,
Ezekiel: b c. 1750 d 5-8-1807 m Catherine Dennett Pvt PA W★
Richard: b c. 1745 d 1814 m Bridget E — Pvt PA
Richard: b c. 1712 d 1789 m Sarah Thomson PS VA
Wm.: b c. 1750 d 12- -1794 m Elizabeth Doe Pvt PS PA

SANOR, (includes SANNER & ZEHNER)
Adam: b 1726 d 1809 m Maria Mertz Pvt PA
John, Jr.: b c. 1760 d c. 1842 m Elizabeth Abell PS MD
Michael: b 1745 d 11-18-1829 m Mary Schrader Pvt PA ★

SANSBURY,
Thomas: b 1740 d 1781 m Eleanor — PS Sol MD

SANTEE,
John: b 10-20-1730 d 4-28-1807 m (1)Catharine Smith (2)Regina — Capt PA
John: b 8-8-1757 d 3-5-1840 m Maria Magdaline Gross Pvt PA ★
Valentine: b 1748 d 1808 m Margaret Funston Pvt PA

SAPP,
George: b 1726 d 1811 m Christina Texter PS MD
Joseph: b 1760 d 9-15-1837 m Sarah Pride Pvt DE ★
Wm.: b 1755 d 1840 m Polly Wilson Pvt GA

SAPPENFIELD,
Michael: b 12- -1761 d 4-14-1837 m Sarah Myres Sgt NC ★

SAPPINGTON,
Hartley: b 1758 d 5-11-1840 m Mary Pursel Pvt PA ★
James: b 1754 d 1838 m (1)Sarah Durbin (2)Margaret Brown Sol PA
John: b 1758 d 1816 m Elizabeth — PS MD
John: b 9-3-1750 d 9-10-1815 m Jemima Fowler Sgt VA
Mark Brown: b 1746 d c. 1-1-1805 m Rebecca Boyce PS Dr MD
Richard: b 9-27-1749 d 4-21-1824 m Cassandra Frances Durbin Dr MD ★
Richard: b c. 1758 d 1810-28 m Nancy Jones PS MD
Thomas: b 6-25-1755 d 11-7-1830 m Mary Keating MM MD

SARGENT, (includes SARGEANT, SEARGENT, SERGEANT & SERGENT)

Aaron: b 2-13-1726 d 1797 m (2)Submit Esterbrook PS NH
Abel: b 9-10-1734 d p. 1790 m Sarah Hadley PS NH
Amos: b 11-23-1758 d 8-12-1836 m Alice Buckman Sol Smn MA
Benjamin: b 1763 d 1846 m Olivia Mary Bodwell Pvt MA ★
Benjamin: b 3-27-1760 d 3-19-1818 m Eunice Sendel Pvt NH
Charles: b 3-30-1760 d 4-14-1833 m Sarah Green Pvt NJ
Christopher: b 5-18-1740 d 1-10-1830 m Anna (Sargent) Pvt CS PS MA
Christopher: b 8-4-1704 d 3-20-1790 m Susannah Peasley PS MA
Daniel: b 9-9-1750 d 5-17-1838 m Mary Lycett Pvt MA
Daniel: b c. 1753 d 10-8-1800 m Charity Grover Smn NH
David: b 3-22-1723/4 d 6-2-1803 m Mehitable Green Pvt MA
David: b 10-24-1750 d 1- -1816 m (1)Anna Everden (2)Sukey — Pvt MA
David: b 4-8-1737 d 4-12-1808 m Janney Eastman Pvt NH
David: b 3-14-1752 d 2-11-1821 m Anna Chittenden GnrMte MA
David: b 1-1-1733 d 4-12-1812 m Martha Wells PS NH
Diamond: b 11-18-1761 d 1847 m Prudence Parker Pvt NH
Ebenezer: b 11-10-1753 d 4-18-1831 m Lydia Williams Pvt MA
Ebenezer: b 10-26-1756 d 11-8-1838 m Mary Marsh Pvt MA ★
Ebenezer: b 1754 d c. 1828 m (1)Esther Quimby (2)Phoebe Flanders Pvt MA ★
Elijah: b 2-2-1750 d 6-15-1798 m (2)Dorcas Fox Sgt MA
Eliphalet: b 5-24-1749 d p. 5- -1776 m Deborah — Sol NH
Enoch: b 12-11-1751 d 12- -1836 m Molly Wells Cpl NH
Erastus: b 7-27-1742 d 11-14-1814 m Elizabeth Partridge Dr 2Maj MA
Ezra, Sr.: b 3-21-1729 d 6-29-1810 m (1)Deborah (Sargent) (2)Mrs Phoebe Sprague PS MA
Ezra, Jr.: b 12-6-1752 d 9-25-1839 m Sarah Oakes Pvt MA
Isaac: b 11-1-1738 d 11-26-1818 m Ruth Blaisdell Pvt PS NH
Jacob: b 2-28-1761 d 1843 m — Arfr CT ★
Jacob: b 2-18-1759 d 4-9-1804 m Lydia Paine Pvt MA
James, Sr.: b 1717/8 d 1794/5 m Eleanor Taylor PS MD
James, Jr.: b 1-25-1747 d 1826 m Philena Pigman PS MD
James: b 1764 d 1821 m (1)Polly Roach (2)Susan Cheney Pvt NH
Jeremiah: b 1757 d 1837 m (1)Armalee Enoch (2)Katharine Bennett Pvt VA ★
John: b 11-6-1720 d 1-13-1776 m Susanna Chamberlain Sol MA
John: b 9-13-1749 d 4-1-1822 m Mrs Ann Taylor Miller Pvt MA
John: b 10-24-1759 d 2-7-1829 m (1)Sarah Gates (2)Mrs Isaac Denny Pvt MA
John, Sr.: b 1727 d 11-14-1797 m Susanna Harriman PS NH
John, Jr.: b 12-26-1764 d 1828 m Nancy Y Burgin Pvt NH
John: b a. 1750 d p. 1790 m Mehitable Smith PS NH
John: b 12-4-1732 d 7-30-1798 m Mary Kathan Col VT
John, Sr.: b 12-16-1739 d 12-6-1827 m Fear Gibbs Pvt VT
John: b 6-30-1761 d 10-30-1843 m Delight Bell Sgt VT ★
Jonathan: b 8-30-1746 d 2-4-1830 m Lydia (Sargent) 3Sgt MA
Jonathan: b 10-2-1723 d 2-24-1806 m Mary Earle Pvt PS MA
Jonathan Dickinson: b 1746 d 10-8-1793 m (1)Margaret Spencer (2)Elizabeth Rittenhouse PS PA
Joseph: b 10-13-1758 d 11-13-1814 m Mrs Lucretia Williams Campbell Pvt CT
Joseph: b 10-6-1732 d 3-22-1797 m Elizabeth Wheeler Capt MA
Joseph: b 7-17-1740 d 9-16-1809 m Anna Loring Pvt MA
Joseph: b 1716 d 1802 m Hannah Whittemore PS MA
Joseph: b 8-20-1751 d 1-5-1841 m Judith Harvey Pvt NH
Joshua: b 1757 d 1844 m Abigail Ladd Pvt MA ★
Lemuel: b c. 1745 d 1823 m Sarah Hall Pvt VT
Mara: b 10-9-1762 d 8-30-1844 m Joseph Grace PS MA
Moses: b 1-12-1757 d 8-11-1839 m (1)Sarah Cram (2)Ruth Burroughs Sgt MA NH ★
Moses: b 5-23-1738 d p. 1775 m Elizabeth — Pvt MA
Moses: b 11-2-1743 d 1826 m Sarah Varnum PS Cpl NH
Nathan: b 8-27-1718 d 6-15-1799 m (1)Mary Sargent (2)Mary Denny Pvt MA
Nathan: b 4-10-1738 d 9-16-1818 m (1)Jemima Bradbury (2)Hannah — Pvt PS NH
Nathaniel: b 5-15-1740 d 12-1-1821 m Hannah Wheeler Lt MA
Nehemiah: b 1737 d 2-29-1822 m Mary Hoyt Pvt MA
Paul Dudley: bpt 6-23-1745 d 9-15-1827 m Lucy Sanders Col PS MA
Peter, Sr.: b 11-2-1736 d 3-8-1816 m (1)Ruth Nichols (2)Abigail Homans (3)Ruth Hills Chase PS NH
Philip: b 5-9-1731 d 3-3-1809 m Hannah Hadley PS NH
Phineas: b 6-9-1746 d 1776 m (1)Mary Edson (2)Abigail Dunbar Cpl MA
Phineas: b 7-3-1750 d 7-8-1843 m (1)Rebecca Wells (2)Hannah Colby Pvt NH
Rueben: b 4-27-1745 d c. 1777 m Lydia Barrett Sgt MA
Robert: b 10-10-1716 d 1-28-1808 m Anna Coffin Pvt MA
Rufus: b 6-15-1740 d 11-23-1826 m Susanna Houghton Sgt VT
Samuel: b 2-2-1730 d 4-30-1804 m Hannah Baldwin Pvt CT
Samuel: b 5-18-1761 d 10-1-1830 m Patty Johnson Cpl MA
Samuel: b 1-7-1764 d 7-11-1825 m Mary Washburn Pvt MA
Samuel: b 2-26-1752 d 1817 m Mary Hunt Pvt MA
Snowden: b 2-27-1742 d 1814 m Mary Heathman PS MD
Stirling: b 5-25-1731 d 1796 m (1)Lydia Coffin (2)Mehitable Davis (3)Mary Andrews PS NH
Thomas: b 9-29-1723 d 5-6-1812 m (1)Mary Waite (2)Elizabeth Bridge (3)Hannah Comee Pvt MA

Thomas, Jr.: b 11-30-1729 d 3-16-1794 m Sarah Clements Pvt MA
Thomas: b 3-31-1750 d 3-10-1809 m Abigail Balisdell Pvt NH
Thomas: b 2-23-1734/5 d 4-19-1783 m Anna Stebbins CS VT
Timothy: b 2-1-1755 d 3-24-1836 m (1)Asenoth Tillotson (2)Elizabeth Chase Pvt NH ★
Timothy: b 8-17-1747 d 5-2-1823 m (1)Anna Whittier (2)Deborah Smith PS Sol NH
Timothy: b 1751 d 1827 m Ann Horton Pvt VT
Wm.: b 1760 d 8-28-1844 m (1)Margaret Tucker (2)Mary McNeal (3)Mrs Charlotte Ford Ambrose Pvt Grd MA ★
Wm.: b 6-22-1752 d 1823-1826 m Susanna Allen Pvt MA
Wm.: b 9-7-1756 d 4-5-1835 m Rachel Todd Pvt MA
Wm.: b 3-28-1760 d p. 1840 m — Foster Pvt MA
Winslow: b 2-26-1749/50 d 9-8-1819 m (1)Mary Burditt (2)Mrs Tabitha Bill (3)Hannah Sargent (4)Mrs Martha Barrett Drm MA
Winthrop: b 3-6-1727 d 12-3-1793 m Judith Saunders PS MA
Winthrop: b 5-1-1753 d 6-3-1820 m (1)Rowena Tupper (3)Mrs Mary Williams ADC MA
Winthrop, Sr.: b c. 1741 d 1835 m Mary Lord Pvt MA
Winthrop, Jr.: b 10-20-1761 d 8-1-1839 m Sarah Lane Pvt MA
Winthrop: b 10-28-1711 d 12-7-1788 m Phoebe Healey PS NH

SARTOR,

Wm.: b 3-11-1760 d 6-11-1829 m Rebecca Hughes Pvt SC W★

SARVENT, (includes SARVANT, SARVEN, SERVEN SERVENT)

Abraham: b 9-27-1719 d 1806 m Brechje Smidt Pvt NY
Adrian: bpt 8-4-1751 d p. 1790 m Mary Simmons Pvt PS NY
Garret: b 1-10-1756 d 1840 m Elizabeth VanHouten Pvt NY
Henry: b 11-6-1752 d p. 6-18-1809 m Gertrude Myers Pvt NY
Phillip: b 8-15-1721 d 8-15-1786 m Maria Knapp Pvt NY

SARVIS,

John: b 3-10-1751 d 10-29-1834 m Lora Hamah Floyd Sol SC

SASS,

Jacob: b 1750 d 2-12-1836 m Ann D Villiaur 1Lt SC

SASSAMAN,

Henry: b c. 1755 d 9- -1794 m Catherine — Pvt PA
Jacob: b c. 1747 d 5- -1789 m Catharine Pearson Pvt PA

SASSER,

Joseph: b 1725 d 1806 m Mary (Sasser) PS NC

SATCHWELL,

John: b 1750 d 3- -1820 m Elizabeth Clark Pvt MD

SATER,

Henry: b 4-27-1745 d a. 1790 m Hannah Stansbury PS MD

SATTERLEE, (includes SATTERLY)

Benedict: b 8-11-1714 d a. 1778 m (1)Elizabeth Crary (2)Rachel Parks Pvt PA
Elisha: b 5-12-1760 d 8-25-1826 m Cynthia Stevens Pvt PA
Elnathan: b 12-21-1734 d 12-15-1800 m Mary Topping Reeve PS NY
James: b 3-21-1763 d 8- -1844 m Desire Thompson Fif CT ★
John: b 1745 d 2-13-1829 m Hannah Hyde Cpl CT W★
Jonas: b 1743 d 1778 m Lydia Geer Pvt CT
Nathaniel, Sr.: b 1709 d 1795 m (1)Sarah Wood (2)Mary (Sell) Tooker PS NY
Nathaniel, Jr.: bpt 2-4-1743/4 d p. 4- -1795 m (1)Elizabeth Seely (2)Elizabeth Sweasy Pvt NY
Samuel: b 3-7-1746 d 2-4-1804 m (1)Sarah Seeley (2)Margaret — PS NY
Sylvester: b 1752 d 1825 m Bethany Coon Pvt NY
Wm.: b 1-10-1740/1 d 12-6-1798 m Hannah Sherwood Capt MA

SATTERWHITE,

Ann: b c. 1715 d p. 1787 m John Satterwhite PS VA
Francis: b c. 1758 d p. 5-5-1803 m Elizabeth — Sol GA
James: b — d 1823 m Franky Childs PS NC
John: b 1734 d 1808/9 m (1)Frances — (2)Mary — PS SC
Thomas: b c. 1750 d a. 1797 m Annie Keeling Capt NC

SAUL,

Joseph: b 1751 d 8-14-1825 m (1)Elizabeth Heather (2)Mary Standley Slr MA

SAUNDERS, (includes SANDERS)

Abraham, Sr.: b 10-14-1749 d 4-26-1824 m Keziah Thorpe Sgt PA ★
Caleb: b 9-14-1751 d 5-12-1821 m (1)Eunice Burdick (2)Esther Harkness Pvt Grd RI
Celey: b 1745 d — m Anne Blackburn NCapt
Charles: b 3-4-1755 d p. 1795 m Martha Hall Lt RI
Daniel: b 9-8-1744 d 12-31-1824 m Sarah Peal SeaCap Pvtr MA
David: b 1760 d 9-28-1842 m Lockey Leftwich OrdlSgt VA ★
Edward: b 1725 d 1786 m Sarah Hiscox PS RI
Ezekiel: b 1743 d 5-6-1814 m Abigail Angell Ens RI
George: b 1756 d 1812 m Ruth Page Pvt MA
George Berry: bpt 9-11-1748 d 7-25-1805 m Anna Perkins Page Pvt NH

SAUNDERS, contd.
James: b 1729 d 1794 m Susanna Ricketts PS MD
James: b 12-29-1733 d *p.* 1790 m Sarah Tully Sol NC
James, Sr.: b *c.* 1733 d 1794 m Rachel Saunders PS RI
James, Sr.: b *c.* 1720 d *p.* 2-28-1776 m Cassandra Hayden CS VA
Jesse: b 7-21-1743 d *p.* 1779 m Ann Yancey Capt NC
John, Jr.: b 2-7-1756 d *p.* 1-5-1784 m Sybil Yeomans Pvt CT
John: b 1736 d 1826 m Ann Margaret Speight Pvt NC
John: b — *p.* 12-16-1783 m Mary — Pvt NC
John: b 5-22-1751 d *p.* 12-7-1790 m Elizabeth Palmer Lt SC
John: b *c.* 1762 d *p.* 1830 m Elizabeth Faulconer Pvt VA
John M.: b 6-9-1748 d 4-20-1827 m (1)Hannah Hustead (2)Rheuama
     Jones Pvt CT
Jonathan: b 1743 d 1827 m Elizabeth Woodworth Pvt MA
Joshua: b 1749 d *p.* 1817 m Mary Taylor Pvt RI
Julius: b 1-12-1758 d 8- -1821 m — Hughes Sol VA
Luke: b 4-12-1758 d 7-14-1839 m Sarah Dewey Pvt RI
Nathaniel: b 3-15-1740 d *p.* 9-10-1804 m Mercy Murfee Lt SC
Peleg: b 9-5-1759 d *p.* 1820 m Sarah Vars Cpl RI
Peleg: b 3-4-1737 d 1-26-1822 m Mary Clarke Lt RI
Peter: b 1740 d 1823 m — PS SC
Peter: b 9-20-1748 d 8-14-1813 m Mary Sparrel PS VA
Philemon: b *c.* 1763 d *p.* 1-31-1837 m Jemima Greer Pvt VA ★
Reuben: b *c.* 1763 d 10-26-1842 m Fanny Jones Pvt VA ★
Richard: b 9-25-1762 d 6-19-1838 m Leanah Gravett Pvt VA ★
Robert Hyde: b 1759 d 3-5-1834 m Lucy Mayo Lt VA
Samuel: b 1745 d 1796 m Edith — CS NC
Stephen: b 4-28-1749 d 9-30-1839 m Tacy Stillman Lt RI
Stephen: b 5-22-1747 d 12-16-1830 m Isabella Campbell Capt VA
Thomas: b *c.* 1728 d *p.* 1790 m Mary Mitchell Sol NC
Thomas: b 6-18-1739 d *a.* 1808 m Ann (Turner) Harper Pvt VA
Thomas: b 1-22-1748 d *p.* 1782 m Elizabeth Nelms Sol VA
Tobias: b 3-28-1732 d 5-31-1809 m Martha Hall CS Pvt RI
Wm.: b *c.* 1712 d *p.* 1776 m Esther Peaslee PS NH
Wm.: b 1735 d 1803 m (1)Elizabeth Mitchell (2)Miss Cunningham
     Capt NC
Wm.: b 4-25-1749 d 1810 m Sarah Ragin Pvt PS SC
Wm.: b *c.* 1755 d 5-11-1819 m Sarah Jones Capt VA
Wm.: b *c.* 1750 d 1-1-1797 m Ann Briscoe Capt VA

SAURMAN,
Peter: b *c.* 1740 d 1830 m Margery Yerkes Pvt PA

SAUSSURE,
Henry, Wm., de: b 8-16-1763 d 3-26-1839 m Eliza Ford Pvt SC
Victor Daniel de: b 4-10-1736 d 7-2-1798 m Mary McPherson PS SC

SAVAGE,
Abel: b *c.* 1725 d 1797 m (1)Leah — (2)Elizabeth Dunton (3)Susanna
     Dixon Clegg Pvt VA
Abijah: b 7-2-1744 d 6-9-1825 m Martha Torrey Capt CT ★
Abraham: b *c.* 1750 d 4-18-1812 m Sarah Sprague Drm Pvt MA
Abraham: b *c.* 1750 d *p.* 1796 m Ann Bowman PS VA
Amos: b 9-25-1733 d 2-4-1783 m Sarah Montague Ens CT
Caleb: b *c.* 1760 d *p.* 5-29-1809 m (1)Elishe Johnson (2)Elizabeth
     Ewing Jenny Cpl VA
Caleb: b *a.* 1755 d 1809 m Elizabeth — PS VA
Daniel: b 1729 d 1-1-1795 m (1)Elizabeth Robinson (2)Mrs Anna
     Johnson 1Lt MA
Edward: b 12-13-1745 d 10-13-1833 m Mary McNaughton Pvt MA
Elisha: b 12-9-1728 d 1-24-1807 m Thankful Johnson 2Lt CT
Gideon: b 5-31-1751 d 2-26-1833 m Sara White Sgt CT ★
Henry: b 1730 d 2-12-1803 m — Pvt NY
Jacob: b 1756-8 d 11-7-1826 m Hannah Gray Mrnr MA
James: b 1715 d 10-12-1805 m Mary Lord Hilton Pvt MA
James: b *c.* 1745 d 1831 m Anne — Sol NY
James: b 1749 d 3-4-1784 m Margaret McClaughry Pvt NY
Joel: b 9-25-1761 d 5-13-1835 m Abigail Smith Pvt MA NY W★
John: b 1707 d 1-27-1792 m Eleanor Hamilton PS NY
John: b 6-11-1739 d 10-28-1798 m Mary Greenough 2Lt MA
John: b — d 1816 m Sarah Doliver Pvt MA
John: b 9-29-1744 d 10-25-1821 m Mary Jackson Pvt NH
John: b *c.* 1750 d *p.* 1820 m Sarah Parmer Capt SC
John: b 1750 d *p.* 4-24-1787 m Lydia — Pvt VA
John: b *c.* 1700 d 1792 m Margaret Parker PS VA
Joseph: b 6-14-1756 d 1-20-1814 m (2)Catharine Hubbard Capt MA
Joseph: b 6-17-1755 d 1-31-1805 m Jane Murray Dr VA
Josiah: b 10-17-1735 d 7-6-1804 m Sarah Stowe Ens CT
Josiah: b 1-11-1761 d 4-14-1831 m Mary Roberts Pvt CT
Levin: b *c.* 1750 d *p.* 1837 m — Pvt NC ★
Nathan: b 12-25-1752 d 9-27-1814 m Elizabeth Sawin Sgt RI CT
Nathaniel: b 10-27-1745 d 11-11-1823 m Mary Stow Pvt CT
Nathaniel Littleton: b 1722-36 d 1780-6 m Ann Reynolds Lt VA
Samuel: b 1722 d 8-2-1786 m Sarah Kirby Pvt CT
Samuel Phillips: b 4-27-1718 d 12- -1797 m (1)Sarah Tyler
     (2)Bathsheba (Thwing) Johnston (3)Mary Meserve PS MA
Samuel Stow: b 3-1-1743 d 7-12-1813 m Mary Cole Capt VT
Selah: b 1-9-1759 d 14-15-1846 m (1)Elizabeth Porter (2)Roxy
     Galpin Pvt CT
Seth: b 9-8-1755 d 10-25-1842 m Esther Prudence DeWolf Cpl CT
Seth: b 1732 d 8-21-1807 m Lydia Craige CS Sol MA
Seth: b 10-6-1756 d 9-13-1829 m (1)Rhoda Bacon (2)Miriam Smith
     Richards Pvt VT

Solomon: b 1762 d *p.* 1820 m (1)Lydia Bulkeley (2)Mrs Jane
     Bingham Pvt CT
Stephen: b 10-26-1737 d 1824 m Triphena Riley Sol CT
Thomas: b 1730 d *p.* 12-19-1795 m Elizabeth Bell Pvt VA
Timothy: b 1-24-1769 d 11-1-1847 m Sarah Collins PS CT

SAVILLE,
Abram: b *a.* 1763 d *p.* 1810 m Martha Keebler Pvt PA

SAVITZ,
George: b 1753 d 1826 m Catherine Frederick Pvt PA
Joseph: b 1735 d 9-27-1794 m Gloy Dicter Pvt PA

SAVORY, (includes SAVARY & SAVERY)
Benjamin: b 10-2-1762 d 3-26-1850 m Judith Burbank Pvt MA
Hiram: b 1-5-1761 d 5-28-1839 m Sally Milliken Cpl MA
Isaac: b 9-5-1743 d 1-23-1825 m Deliverance Clifton Cpl MA
John: b 5-21-1736 d 4-5-1805 m Sarah Wood Capt MA
Nathan: b 1748 d 1826 m (1)Elizabeth Nye (2)Deidamia Sabin
     Pvt MA
Samuel: b 3-15-1749/50 d 9-9-1821 m Elizabeth Sargent Pvt MA
Samuel, Sr.: b 8-18-1718 d 1-23-1812 m Elizabeth Bumpus PS MA
Samuel, Jr.: b 2-14-1747 d 11-28-1836 m Ruth Gibbs Lt MA
Thomas: b 7-1-1736 d 3-13-1822 m Zilpha Barrows Pvt MA
Wm.: b 12-6-1743 d 7-22-1800 m Mary Gage Sgt MA

SAWIN, (includes SAWEN)
Benjamin: b 8-8-1748 d 2-9-1817 m Martha Howe PS MA
Daniel: b 1759 d 8-27-1834 m Lucy Byam Pvt MA
Eliphalet: b 1722 d 1801 m (1)Rachel Thayer (2)Sarah — Capt MA
Ezekiel: b 12-25-1751 d 7-21-1817 m Mary Parker Pvt MA
John: b 1721 d 1800 m Abigail Babcock Pvt RI
Jonathan: b 1-12-1735 d 1-17-1822 m Mary Whitney Pvt MA
Levi: b 1760 d 2-9-1856 m Lurana Morse Pvt MA
Munning: b 1720 d 6-28-1807 m Rebecca Munroe CS PS MA
Reuben: b 1753 d 10-25-1797 m Annis Robbins Pvt MA
Samuel: b 1737 d 10-23-1822 m (1)Molly Wasson (2)Martha Miller
     (3)Abigail Bowers Capt MA
Samuel: b 5-7-1762 d 1-12-1849 m (2)Sarah Webb Cpl MA
Thomas, Sr.: b 10-12-1717 d 2-3-1790 m Abigail Morse Capt MA
Thomas, Jr.: b 10-15-1752 d 12-7-1826 m Abigail Bacon Ens MA
     W★

**SAWTELLE, (includes SARTELL, SARTELLE, SARTWELL &
     SAWTELL)**
Benjamin: b 5-3-1760 d 12-28-1831 m Sybbel Patt Pvt MA
Elnathan: b 9-14-1753 d 8-31-1836 m Ruth Patch Cpl MA ★
Ephraim: b 1-18-1734 d *c.* 1800 m Abigail Stone PS NH
Hezekiah: b 2-26-1761 d 10-1-1824 m Sarah Russell Pvt MA
John: b 4-18-1729 d 12-23-1790 m Susanna Farnsworth Capt MA
John: b 5-2-1754 d 4-25-1822 m Elizabeth Gleason Pvt NH
Jonas: b 7-26-1734 d *p.* 7-29-1778 m (1)Elizabeth Albee (2)Eunice
     Kemp Pvt MA
Jonathan, Sr.: b 6-6-1724 d 8-12-1801 m Mary Holden Sgt PS NH
Jonathan, Jr.: b 1-31-1753 d 12-29-1830 m Hannah Whitaker Pvt
     NH ★
Joseph: b 5-8-1764 d 3-21-1842 m (1)Hannah Kemp (2)Lucy Parker
     Pvt MA ★
Nathan: b 2-14-1758 d 1-24-1843 m Sarah Butterfield Pvt MA
Nathaniel, Sr.: b 11-8-1737 d 1- -1822 m (1)Catherine — (2)Abigail
     — Lt MA
Nathaniel, Jr.: b 10-27-1760 d 9-1-1847 m (1)Sybil Shattuck (2)Mrs
     Hannah Green Pvt MA ★
Nathaniel: b 10-6-1743 d 5-7-1825 m Abigail Wyman Sgt MA
Nathaniel: b 2-12-1729 d 8-5-1816 m Hannah Gunn Lt MA ★
Oliver: b 6-1-1743 d 11-2-1807 m (1)Mary — (2)Hannah Taylor
     Pvt VT
Richard: b 7-20-1751 d 7-31-1838 m Sarah Grout Sgt MA ★
Simon: b 6-25-1749 d 5-30-1791 m Dolly — Capt NH
Sylvanus: b 11-10-1757 d 11-21-1842 m (1)Lydia Searls (2)Lucy
     Hosley Fif MA ★

SAWYER,
Aaron: b 6-30-1729 d 8-30-1805 m Rachel Sargent PS MA
Abel: b 1-24-1753 d 3-29-1845 m Mary Strong Cpl NH ★
Abner: b 5-9-1742 d 9-4-1779 m Hannah Piper Lt MA
Aholiab: b 5-27-1742 d 4-1823 m Bathsheba Barrett Pvt MM MA
Azariah: b 9-11-1755 d 12-12-1824 m Esther Sessions Sol CT
Benjamin: b 12-2-1739 d 10-10-1821 m Molly March Pvt MA
Benjamin: b 1760 d 2-7-1834 m Rebecca Hardy Pvt MA ★
Benjamin: b 11-24-1721 d *p.* 1785 m Phebe Jones PS MA
Benjamin: b 2-3-1762 d 8-12-1843 m Sallie York Sol VT
Benjamin: b 1758 d 3-18-1846 m Tabitha Kittredge Pvt NH ★
Benjamin: b 1735 d 2-5-1792 m Margaret Haynes Pvt PA
Caleb: b *c.* 1730 d *p.* 1790 m Mary Griffin Sgt MA
Caleb: b 1737 d *c.* 1822 m Sarah Patch Sgt MA
Calvin: b 10-29-1760 d 10-4-1834 m (1)Relief Houghton (2)Mary
     Britton Pvt MA W★
Conant: b 4-8-1756 d 4-18-1838 m (1)Deborah Robinson (2)Roxalina
     Miller (3)Ruth Boardman (4)Mary McAllister (5)Margaret
     McAllister Pvt CT ★
Cornelius: b 2-20-1749 d *p.* 1790 m (1)Anna Williams (2)Caroline
     Ellis Pvt CT

David Francis: b 1761 d 1832 m Judith Bodill Pvt MA
Deliverance: b 12-11-1746 d 1835/6 m Mercy Nash Cpl NH VT
Ebenezer: b 1-27-1734 d 4-7-1795 m (1)Susannah Yeaton (2)Hannah Small Cpl MA
Ebenezer: b 12-30-1755/6 d p. 1840 m Hannah Whitter Cpl MA ★
Edmund: b 9-2-1759 d 2-20-1827 m Mehitable Morrill Pvt NH
Elisha, Jr.: b 2-9-1743 d 3- -1809 m Mary Belknap Lt MA
Ephraim, Sr.: b 4-20-1729 d 1813 m (1)Mrs Sarah Richardson (2)Susannah Richardson Col MA
Ephraim: b 9-19-1756 d 1827 m Abigail — Sgt VT
Ezekiel: b 9-27-1742 d 1-13-1817 m Mary Payson Sgt MA
Ezra: b 8-18-1730 d 3-7-1776 m Keziah Sawyer Ens MA
Francis, Sr.: b 2-21-1728 d 12-31-1827 m (1)Elizabeth Richardson (2)Tamar Barker Pvt MA
George: b 12-6-1757 d 4-30-1842 m Lucy Merritt Sgt MA ★
Isaac: b 7-14-1720/1 d c. 1786 m (1)Susanna Gillette (2)Hannah McFarland PS NY
Israel: b 9-9-1751 d 1-18-1832 m (1)Beulah Wilson (3)Catherine — (4)Anna Thompson Cpl MA ★
Jabez: b 12-24-1759 d 12-21-1841 m Hannah Brooks Pvt MA
Jacob: b 6-4-1755 d 12-10-1832 m (1)Sarah Hatch (2)Hannah Roberts (3)Esther Hibbard Pvt MA W★
James: b 8-28-1747 d 2-4-1828 m Sarah Jones Pvt CT
James: b 12-3-1737 d 1801 m Lydia Flint Capt MA
James: b 7-7-1753 d 6-16-1807 m Deborah Newrnan Pvt MA
James: b 1755 d 11-23-1834 m — Sol NH
James: b 11- -1738 d 11- -1782 m Elizabeth Bradner Maj QM NY
James: b 1762 d 3-27-1827 m Lydia Foster Ens VT
Jesse: b — 1829 m Catharine White Capt VT
Joel: b 1750 d 2-11-1825 m Elizabeth Stone Cpl MA
John: b 6-16-1746 d 1-15-1821 m Abigail Kilbourne Cpl MA
John: b 12-24-1745 d 12-3-1805 m Isabella Martin Pvt MA
John: b 3-20-1748 d 11-9-1833 m Elsa Couch Pvt NH MA ★
John: b 9-5-1721 d 7-7-1801 m Elizabeth Kelly MM MA
John: b 8-31-1716 d 6-29-1784 m Abigail Thompson PS MA
John: b 1729 d 1812 m Jean Allen Pvt PA
John: b 1745 d 11-20-1831 m Rebecca Crawford Capt VA
Jonathan: b 10-22-1736 d 11- -1789 m Martha Rich Capt MA
Jonathan: b 1728 d p. 1786 m Elizabeth Lenney Lt MA
Jonathan: bpt 1739 d 5-3-1823 m Susannah Flint Sgt MA
Jonathan: b 11-6-1742 d p. 1779 m Tabitha Palmer Sgt MA
Jonathan: b 10-6-1756 d 12-11-1829 m Jemima Webster Pvt NH ★
Joseph: b 3-8-1756 d 3-12-1828 m Ruth Walcot Pvt MA
Joshua: b 9-9-1732 d 1-6-1812 m Thankful (Sawyer) Pvt MA
Josiah: b 1757 d 1838 m Susannah Green Ens MA
Josiah: b 11-8-1752 d p. 1800 m (1)Bathsheba Moore (2)Persis Baker (3)Prudence Johnson Pvt MA
Josiah: b c. 1763 d p. 1820 m Elizabeth Brown Pvt MA ★
Josiah, Sr.: b 8-10-1721 d 3-14-1813 m Hannah Gowing PS NH
Josiah, Jr.: b 9-7-1744 d 10-2-1829 m Lydia Barnard Sgt NH
Josiah: b — d 6-19-1812 m Miriam Eastman Pvt NH
Lemuel: b 1749 d 8-25-1830 m Anna Pratt Pvt MA
Lemuel: b 12-24-1734 d 1784-8 m (1)Mary Taylor PS NC
Luke: b 6-24-1760 d 4-8-1840 m Rachel Greenleaf Pvt Sct Spy MA ★
Manasseh: b 6-1-1729 d 12-24-1808/9 m Lydia Fairbanks Pvt MA
Manassah: b 3-27-1759 d 3-24-1842 m Beulah Howe Sgt NH ★
Moses: b 1750 d 5-5-1805 m Mary Sawyer Lt MA
Nathaniel, Sr.: bpt 3-16-1716 d 1805 m Mary Houghton Lt MA
Nathaniel 3d: b 2-21-1744 d p. 1796 m (1)Catherine Ellis (2)Lucy (Whitney) Whitcomb Capt MA
Nathaniel: b c. 1737 d 7-26-1797 m Jerusha Flint PS MA
Peter: b 8-10-1763 d 1827 m (1)Nancy Stark (2)Chloe — Pvt MA
Samuel: b 1-2-1739 d p. 1783 m Phoebe Cooper Capt MA
Samuel: b c. 1745 d 8-3-1779 m Mary Littlefield Capt MA
Thomas: b 9-7-1757 d 4-23-1825 m Susanna Wilder Pvt MA
Thomas: b 7-14-1758 d 4-11-1833 m Mary Davis Pvt MA ★
Thomas: b 1710 d 3-31-1797 m Elizabeth Osgood Pvt MA
Thomas: b 8-3-1760 d 3-11-1818 m (1)Elizabeth Damon(2)Betsey Stone Pvt MA
Wm.: b 9-26-1749 d 1822 m Kezia Moor Lt MA
Wm.: b 9-20-1754 d 7-1-1817 m (1)Hannah Snow (2)Mrs Hannah Snow (3)Mrs Bethiah Wyman Cpl MA
Wm.: b 8-8-1758 d 1817 m Hannah Upton Pvt MA
Wm., Sr.: b 1703 d 10-18-1784 m Sophia Clemson PS PA

SAXE,
Jacob: b 1754 d 1820 m — Rice Sgt NY ★

SAXTON, (includes SAXON)
Charles: b 1743 d 1808 m Mary — Capt SC
Charles: b 1744 d p. 6-2-1816 m — Sol PS SC
David: b 1734 d 9-21-1800 m Rebecca Barnard PS MA
Ebenezer: b 1-1-1754 d 9-10-1828 m Hannah Loomis Sol NY
Frederick: b 5-22-1748 d 4-28-1796 m Rhoda Messenger Sgt MA
George: b a. 1748 d p. 1788 m Sarah Harlan Pvt PA
Gilbert: bpt 2-18-1738/9 d p. 1790 m (1)Tjatje Bevier (2)Sarah Armstrong Sgt NY
James: b 4-17-1757 d 8-24-1831 m Huldah — Pvt MA
John: b 11-17-1761 d 1862 m Elizabeth Evans Pvt NY ★
Lewis: b 12-10-1765 d 12-31-1813 m Sally Allen Capt SC W★
Wm.: b 12-25-1755 d 3-12-1832 m Mary Betts Pvt MA

Wm.: b c. 1740 d c. 1815 m Lottie Moore Pvt SC
Wm.: b 12-16-1749 d 12-31-1830 m Leah Free Pvt VA ★

SAYE, (includes SAY)
James: b c. 1742 d c. 1810 m Mary Reed Cpl PA
Richard: b c. 1740 d 1779 m Mary Hodge Sol SC

SAYERS, (includes SAYER, SAYRE & SAYRES)
James: b c. 1745 d c. 1815 m (1)Rachel Sheppard (2)Mrs Hannah (Stretch) Sayre (3)Mrs Sarah Smith Pvt NJ
John Thompson: b 7-18-1758 d 3-25-1816 m Susan Crockett Lt VA
Joseph: b 1748 d 1830 m Rebecca Neely MM NJ
Joshua: b 2-10-1746 d 9-4-1781 m Rebecca Sanford Lt RI
Josiah: b 8-3-1763 d 2-12-1857 m Rhoda Drake Pvt PA
Samuel: bpt 9-21-1746 d 8- -1779 m Mary Littlefield Maj MA
Stephen: b 3-9-1745 d 4-9-1820 m Anna Smith Pvt NY
Wm.: b 1729 d 9-16-1796 m Mary Fithian Lt PA

SAYGER,
Philip: b 9-20-1754 d 4-9-1837 m Rebecca Covert Tms NJ

SAYLES,
Ahab: b 10-10-1756 d p. 1790 m — Pvt NY
Ahab: b 10-17-1760 d 4-17-1849 m Lillis Steere Pvt RI
Daniel: b 1-18-1758 d 1-18-1844 m Eunice Ballou Ens RI ★
David: b 5-17-1755 d 1-9-1820 m Silence Whipple Capt RI
Israel: b 3-17-1726 d 4-22-1801 m Mercy Whipple Pvt RI
John: b 1-6-1713 d 3-1-1822 m Martha Arnold Col RI
John: b 6-14-1753 d 1-22-1838 m Abiah Paine Pvt RI ★
Jonathan: b 5-12-1730 d 2-28-1806 m Elizabeth Paine PS RI
Richard, Jr.: b 8-5-1723 d a. 10-17-1807 m Abigail Hawkins Lt RI
Smith: b 8-31-1759 d 2- -1841 m Abigail Scott Pvt RI ★
Sylvanus: b 3-29-1724 d 1809 m Ann Sayles CS RI
Wm.: b 2-22-1744 d 10-15-1832 m Ann Mowry Pvt MA

SAYRE, (includes SAYRES & SAYRS, SEARS)
Abbott: b 1750 d 10-9-1797 m Elizabeth Bacon Sol NJ
Abraham: b 2-5-1745 d 4-16-1810 m Mehitable Howell Sol NY
Anannias, Sr.: b c. 1703 d p. 11-26-1785 m (1)Mary Gibbons (2)Patience Reed CS NJ
Benjamin: b 12-21-1740 d 5-7-1815 m Susan Jennings Pvt NY
Benjamin: b 2-3-1743 d 8-10-1810 m (1)Rachel (Frazier) (2)Sarah (Littell) Frazier Pvt NJ
Daniel: b 9-17-1760 d 9-11-1824 m Sarah Hall Pvt NJ
Daniel: b 1-13-1743 d 11-26-1823 m Lydia Burt Sct Grd NY
David: b 5-30-1736 d 7-11-1826 m Hannah Frazier Pvt NJ
David: b 5-1-1747 d 9-11-1830 m Jane Gelston Capt NY
Ebenezer: b 10-29-1747 d 7-27-1822 m (1)Lois Potter (2)Charity Cooper Pvt NJ
Ebenezer: b 7-20-1760 d 8-24-1840 m Elizabeth Seeley Pvt NY
Ephraim: b 3-8-1746 d 10-24-1819 m Hannah Meeker MM NJ
Ephraim: b 1738 d 7-22-1804 m (1)Mary Meeker (2)Jane — PS NJ
Ezekiel: b 1726 d p. 1800 m — Lt NJ
Isaac: b 1762 d 1-22-1842 m Abigail Hunt Fif NJ ★
James: b 7-3-1748 d 9-21-1807 m Elizabeth Howell Lt NY
James, Jr.: b 3-2-1750 d 6-4-1826 m Mercy Seeley Pvt NY
Jeremiah: b — d c. 1786 m Elizabeth Fripp Green Ens NJ
Job: b 2-28-1738 d 11-18-1845 m Hannah Tuttle Cpl NY ★
John: b 1742 d 9- -1779 m Sarah Townley MM NY
John: b c. 1736 d 10-12-1814 m Abigail Goldsmith Capt NY
Jonathan: b 3-29-1752 d 9-4-1829 m Mary Monell Pvt NY
Joseph: b c. 1760 d p. 1806 m Sara Little Pvt NJ
Joshua: b 8-8-1755 d 1845 m Dency Harlow Ens NY ★
Matthew: b 7-17-1731 d 7-8-1819 m Mehitable Herrick 2Lt NY
Nathan: b 6-30-1748 d 4-16-1841 m (1)Sarah Ann Mann (2)Abigail Haxton Lt NY NJ ★
Nehemiah: b c. 1717 d 8-5-1784 m Bethia Cooper PS SeaCap NY
Samuel: b c. 1761 d 4-7-1788 m Betsey Hedden Pvt NJ W★
Seely: b 5-7-1751 d 1-3-1815 m (1) — Carr (2)Mary Thompson Davis Sgt NJ
Thomas, Jr.: b 1739 d 1-17-1819 m Abigail Lupton 2Lt NY
Wm.: b 1749 d c. 1830 m Sarah Young Pvt NJ ★

SAYWARD,
George: b 5-27-1753 d 5-9-1836 m Susannah Palfrey Lt MA

SCAGEL,
Jacob: b 1759 d 3-15-1826 m Betsey Dalton Pvt NH ★

SCALES,
Abraham: b 9-1-1718 d 1796 m Sarah Thompson PS NH
Henry: b — d 1827 m Mary — Sol NC
James: b 1754 d 9-8-1833 m Maria Phillips Pvt MM NC ★
Joseph: b 1742 d 1820 m Anne Perkins PS VA
Nathaniel: b 4-13-1756 d 9- -1824 m Ann Allen Sol NC
Nathaniel: b 4-13-1758 d 1834 m Mary France Pvt NC ★
Samuel: b 8-25-1757 d 3-13-1844 m (1)Susanna Southworth (2)Anna Moody (3)Sarah Moultin Pvt Smn MA ★
Samuel: b 9-9-1754 d 3- -1778 m Hannah Langley Pvt NH
Thomas: b c. 1760 d a. 8-9-1797 m Anne — Sol NC

SCAMMON,
Samuel: b 9-3-1738 d 12-10-1825 m Sarah Dennett Lt MA

SCANLAND,
John Fielding: b 1752 d — m Sophia Spiller Pvt VA

SCARBOROUGH, (includes SCARBURGH)
Americus: b *c.* 1750 d *p.* 3-24-1818 m (2)Rachel Watson Capt VA
Euclidus, Sr.: b 1714 d 1808 m Mary Dean Pvt MD
Isaac: b 1745 d 1825 m (1)Susan Dean (2)Rachel Lewis Pvt PA
James: b 11-29-1748 d 3-1-1836 m (2) Grace King (3)Penelope
　Eason (4)Martha Tartt Eason (5)Martha — Maj NC SC ★
James: b 3-15-1755 d 2-12-1809 m Rachel Wood Pvt VA
James: b 9-1-1750 d 1818 m Mary Moore Sol VA
John: b 11-28-1734 d 1813 m (1)Margaret Kirk (2)Mrs Johanna
　Cahoon PS PA
John: b — d *c.* 1-2-1794 m Mary Jacobs Pitts Lt VA ★

SCARFF,
William: b 1749 d 1778 m Elizabeth Harrison 2Lt MD

SCARLETT,
Newman: b 10-24-1740 d 6-4-1799 m (1)Betty Peacock (2)Mary
　Merrill Lt MA
Thomas: b *c.* 1755 d 4-15-1834 m Anna James Pvt NC ★

SCARRITT,
Nathan: b 1753 d 1828 m Abigail Atkins Pvt CT ★

SCATES,
John: bpt 11-3-1726 d 3-12-1822 m Abigail Hayes Cpl MA

SCATTERGOOD,
Thomas: b 1765 d 1844 m Lydia Sankey Pvt NJ

SCHALL, (includes SHALL)
George: b 8-24-1735 d 12-2-1802 m Catherine Newhard 1Lt PA
George Frederick 2nd: b 9-6-1756 d 10-24-1837 m (2)Margaret
　Krebs Pvt MD ★
John: b *a.* 1760 d 1820 m Sarah — Pvt PA
Michael: b 1739 d 1830 m Anna Maria — Lt PA
Nicholas: b 1735 d *a.* 9-13-1808 m Margaret Beck PS VA

SCHAMP,
David: b 6-21-1755 d 4-3-1839 m Lenah Hoffman Capt NJ ★
George, N: b 1751 d *p.* 1844 m Mary Smock Pvt PA

SCHANTZ,
Jacob: b 4-26-1761 d 9-11-1816 m Maria Bortz Pvt PS PA

SCHATT, (or SCHADT)
Johannes: b 10-14-1760 d 3-23-1829 m Elizabeth Clader PS PA

SCHAUB,
Johannes: b 5-4-1744 d 12-18-1803 m Anna Johanna Leinbach Pvt
　PS CS NC

SCHEIBEL,
Theobald: b 8-16-1725 d 1-10-1786 m Agnes Goeb Lt PA

SCHEIBLER,
Frederick: b 7-28-1763 d 2-28-1843 m Salome Leichty Sol VA

SCHELL, (includes SHELL)
Henry: b 1738 d 1804 m Maria Margaretta Cunrad Pvt PA
Jacob Frederick: b 10-16-1740 d 10-9-1824 m Maria Heanes Pvt NY
John: b 1734 d 8-1-1802 m Barbara Raspach Pvt NY
John: b 1-6-1749/50 d 11-　-1796/7 m Catharina Feigly PS Lt NC
John Christian: b 1725-30 d 7-　-1781/2 m Maria Schell Mil NY
Maria: b 1735 d 1790 m John Christian Schell PS NY
Nicholas: b 1746 d 1803 m — Dr PA
Wm.: b *c.* 1740 d 8-19-1807 m — Pvt PS VA

SCHELLINGER, (includes SCHELLENGER)
Abraham: b 1748 d 12-23-1821 m Jane Johnson Sgt CT ★
Enos: b 1752 d 1809 m Sara Coxe NS NJ
Jacob: b 12-22-1758 d 4-6-1821 m Elizabeth Edwards Pvt NY
Jonathan: b 1733 d 1814 m Elizabeth Stratton PS NY

SCHELLMAN, (includes SHELLMAN)
John, Sr.: b 1724 d 1816 m Margaret Fout PS MD
John, Jr.: b 5-5-1756 d 4-17-1838 m Clarissa Montfort Lt MD ★

SCHENCK, (includes SCHANCK)
Abraham: b 8-6-1720 d 1790 m Elsie Vandervoort Maj NY
Abram: b 3-3-1749 d 12-12-1810 m Eva VanBeuren Pvt NJ
Cornelius: b 10-12-1744 d 1790 m Margaret Taylor Pvt NJ
Garret G: b 4-30-1758 d 8-24-1839 m Jane Vankink Pvt NJ ★
Garret: b 5-23-1719 d *a.* 10-9-1794 m (1)Mary VanSicklin (2)Mary
　VanMater (3)Anne Ten Eyck Lt NJ
Garret, Jr.: b 10-24-1743 d 9-29-1797 m Sarah Conover Pvt NJ
Henry: b 7-30-1743 d 1-8-1799 m Hannah Brett Maj PS NY
Henry H.: b 8-9-1760 d 11-25-1838 m Ellen Hardenbergh Pvt Dr
　NJ ★
Jacob: b 4-6-1761 d 2-6-1825 m Eleanor Vanmater Pvt NJ
John: b 2-5-1740 d 10-10-1794 m Maria VanDorn Capt NJ

John: b 8-28-1745 d 8-28-1834 m Maria Denise Capt NJ ★
John: b 5-26-1750 d 8-22-1823 m Ida Sutphen Capt NJ
John H: b 10-16-1758 d 3-5-1845 m (1)Sarah Denton ( )Mrs Eliza
　Roberts Maj NY ★
Josiah: b 6-13-1762 d 5-　-1824 m Alche Wycoff Pvt NJ
Koert: b 2-24-1745 d *p.* 1786 m Rebecca Rogers 1Lt NJ
Koert: b 5-27-1751 d 12-25-1837 m Sarah Pieterse VanVoorheese
　Pvt NJ ★
Martin: b 9-27-1743 d 7-10-1792 m Ida Suydam Ens NY
Peter: b 5-27-1763 d 1837 m Anna Rhoda Ogborn Pvt NJ
Peter: b *c.* 1710 d *p.* 1779 m (1)Jannetze Van Nostrand (2)Jannetze
　(Hendrickson) Covenhoven PS CS NJ
Ralph: b 3-23-1755 d 9-5-1836 m Ann Taylor Pvt Wgn NJ ★
Ralph: b 7-13-1762 d 6-27-1831 m Aleta Sebring Pvt NY ★
Stephen: b 1743 d 8-　-1782 m Geertje Cook Pvt NY
Wm.: b 10-13-1740 d 9-1-1823 m Anna Cumming PS NJ

SCHEPMOES,
Wm.: b 6-21-1752 d *p.* 12-27-1784 m Jannetje Turk Pvt NY
Wm.: b 12-8-1745 d *p.* 1785 m Lena Ten Broeck PS NY

SCHERDEL, (includes SCHERTEL)
Jacob: b 4-29-1741 d 2-18-1819 m Elizabeth Glasin Capt PA
John: b 1-17-1738 d 7-7-1800 m Maria Catherina Riegel Pvt PA

SCHERMERHORN,
Bartholomew: b 8-24-1757 d 7-16-1845 m Annatje Teller Pvt NY ★
Bernardus: b 10-14-1739 d 7-14-1799 m Anentye VanDerBogart
　Pvt NY
Cornelius: bpt 2-2-1738 d 1798 m Annatje Planck Sol NY
Cornelius: b — d 1832 m Matilda Dayton Pvt NY
Daniel: bpt 3-23-1745 d 5-5-1818 m Maria Vanderpoel Capt NY
Henderick: bpt 9-25-1726 d 8-27-1794 m Cornelia Lansing Sol NY
Jacob: b 11-21-1729 d 1812 m (2)Maria Vedder LCol NY
Jacob C: b 5-25-1743 d 5-5-1822 m (1)Gerritge Schermerhorn
　(2)Cornelius Gardenier (3)Sarah VanDerPoel Maj NY
Jacob H: b 9-10-1763 d 5-8-1813 m Alida Schermerhorn Sol NY
Jacob R: b — d *p.* 1790 m Maria — Sgt NY
Jacob R: b 1761 d *p.* 1798 m Tysje Covert Pvt NY
Johannes: bpt 5-13-1727 d 1798-1807 m (1)Jannetje Vosburgh
　(2)Elizabeth Dederick Pvt NY
John: b 1758 d 1845 m Lois Daly PS NY
John C.: b 12-28-1744 d 1-22-1832 m Annatie Osterhout PS NY
John Winne: b 1747 d 1-5-1817 m (1)Catalyntje VanValkenburgh
　(2)Abigail Everett Capt NY
Laurens: b 2-12-1749 d 3-26-1836/7 m Gesina Viele Pvt NY
Leonard: b 10-12-1758 d 1841 m Mary Doty PS NY
Lucas Jacob: b 10-15-1732 d *p.* 9-19-1787 m Wyntje Fitzgerald Capt
　NY
Maus: b 3-9-1753 d 1-26-1830 m Catharine Swits Pvt NY
Phillip: b 1-28-1750 d *p.* 1794 m Dorothy Miller Pvt NY
Ryer: b 9-24-1716 d 3-6-1795 m Marcia VanVranken Pvt NY
Ryer: b *c.* 1736 d *p.* 1792 m Maria Teller Pvt NY
Simon: bpt 1-3-1723 d 5-6-1808 m Hillegarda VanVranken Pvt NY
Wm.: b 1766 d 10-18-1824 m Mary VanHoesen Pvt NY

SCHEURER, (or SCHIRER)
Adam: b 1749 d 1806 m (1)Elizabeth Luther (2)Catharine Elise
　Herzog Tms CMman PA

SCHICK, (includes SHICK)
John: b 1726 d 1797 m Margaret Ritter Lt GA
Ludwig: b 1735 d 1805 m Anna Maria Frederick Pvt PA

SCHIDTLER, (includes SHIDLER)
Henry: b 1-28-1744 d 2-13-1830 m Margaret Barkley Pvt PA
Jacob: b 1742 d — m Katrine Hoonen Pvt PA
Ludwig: b 7-29-1731 d 3-7-1798 m Anna Barbara Kalb Pvt PA
Peter: b 1751 d 7-9-1830 m Susannah — Pvt PA

SCHIESLE,
Christoph: b *c.* 1756 d *p.* 11-30-1822 m Anna Catherine Deibler
　Pvt PA

SCHILLINGER,
George: b 1735 d 1809 m Elizabeth Horning Pvt VA .

SCHILP,
Peter: b *c.* 1717 d 4-　-1782 m Catharine — PS PA

SCHLEASMAN,
Nicholas: b *c.* 1730 d 7-24-1787 m Barbara — PS PA

SCHLEICH,
Frederick: b *c.* 1740 d 1-　-1801 m Christina — Lt PA

SCHLEIFE, (includes SLIFE & SLIFER)
Frederick: b *c.* 1751 d 1816 m Ann Marie — Pvt PA
John: b 5-14-1743 d 10-17-1822 m Assenate — Sol MD
John: b 1757 d 1820 m Sarah — Pvt PA

SCHLENGER,
John: b 1748 d 5-　-1808 m — PS PA

SCHLEPPI,
Johannes Ulrich: b 6-9-1720 d 7-30-1789 m Juliana — Lt PA

SCHLEY, (includes SCHLEIGH)
George Jacob: b 1735 d 5-27-1811 m Marguerite Fortenay PS MD
Peter: b 1761 d 1801 m Mary Doane Pvt PA
Thomas: b 8-31-1712 d 11-24-1790 m Margaret Wintz VonWinz PS MD

SCHLOTT,
John Adam: b 12-26-1761 d 8-3-1833 m Catharina Holder Pvt PA ★

SCHLOTTERBACK,
George: b 1755 d 9-4-1826 m — Pvt PA ★

SCHMEISSER, (includes SCHMEISER & SMYSER)
Jacob: b 1742 d 1794 m Elizabeth Eichelberger PS PA
Matthias, Sr.: b 2-17-1715 d 4-12-1778 m Anna Cath Koppenhofer PS PA
Matthias, Jr.: b 11-1-1744 d 2-21-1829 m Louisa Slagle Pvt PA
Michael: b 11-21-1740 d 7-7-1810 m Anna Maria Hoke LCol PA

SCHMELTIZER,
Peter: b 9-29-1724 d 5-29-1799 m Anna Magdalena — Pvt PA

SCHMEYER, (includes SCHMEIER & SMYARS)
Daniel: b 12- -1738 d 1812 m (1)Elizabeth Scherer (2)Catherine Barbara Keiser Pvt PA
John: b 1739 d 1835 m Othello Bost Sol NC
Michael: b 1-1-1745 d 11-5-1800 m Maria Kuchel Pvt PA

SCHNEBLY, (includes SCHNABLE)
Henry: b 12-7-1728 d 7-2-1805 m (1)Elizabeth Shafer (2)Catherine — CS PS MD
Jacob: b 7-20-1760 d 2-24-1834 m Elizabeth Arner Sol PA

SCHNERR,
Casper: b 4-21-1732 d 3-30-1790 m Madlen Deringher Pvt PA

SCHOBER,
Gottlieb: b 11-1-1756 d 6-29-1838 m Maria Magdaline Transon PS NC

SCHOCK, (includes SCHOCH, SHAUCK, SHOCH & SHOCK)
George: b c. 1740 d 1826 m (1)Mary — (2)Mrs Esther Regina (Sharp) Bickel Pvt PA
Jacob: b 1745 d a. 6-14-1813 m — Pvt PA
John: b c. 1730 d 1804 m Mary Margaret Wagner Pvt PA
John: b 5-24-1754 d 7-23-1839 m Mary Epaugh Pvt PA
Meichel: b 12-16-1738 d 5-10-1812 m (1)Maria Margretta Marquette (2)Catherina Lips Gruber Pvt PS PA
Michael: b 1757 d 1814 m Susanna — Pvt PA

SCHOENER,
Wm.: b 1749 d 10-19-1808 m Elizabeth Klinger Sgt PA

SCHOFF, (includes SHOFF)
Frederick: b 10-19-1732 d 11-20-1800 m (2)Margaret Fieldenberger Pvt PA
Jacob, Sr.: b 1725-30 d p. 1806 m Elizabeth Darrow CS NH
Jacob, Jr.: b 5-2-1756 d 1-17-1848 m Anna French Lt NH
Phillip, Sr.: b 1744 d 1778 m Elizabeth Saenger Sol PA
Philip, Jr.: b 4-2-1770 d 11-15-1855 m Elizabeth Ramsey (McGrew) Sol PA

SCHOFFSTALL,
Peter: b c. 1740 d 1815 m — Pvt PA

SCHOLL, (includes SHOLL & SHULL)
Abram: b 12-15-1765 d 1851/2 m (1)Nellie Humble (2)Tabitha Noe Pvt VA
Elias: b 2-3-1755/6 d 5-3-1838 m (1)Catherine Gruver (2)Charity Gruver Pvt PS PA
Frederick, Sr.: b c. 1730-2 d c. 1790 m Anna Katrina — Pvt PA
Frederick: b 2-27-1759 d c. 1832 m (2)Catherine Chrisman Pvt PA
John: b 8- -1749 d 1827 m Merilanina Schmidt Lt NY
John David: b c. 1738/9 d 1795 m Christina Ehro Pvt PA
John Nicholas: b 1735 d 8-11-1796 m Johanna Magdalina Ehro Pvt PA
Joseph: b c. 1755/6 d a. 1- -1830 m Levina Boone Sgt KY
Miachael: b 4-8-1742 d 9-16-1825 m Margaret Gerhart Pvt PA
Peter: b 1745-50 d 5-24-1834 m (1)Barbara Weikert (2)Catherine — Lt PA
Peter: b 4-7-1738 d 3-18-1814 m Anna Susanna Dorothea Scholl Pvt PA
Peter: b 1-11-1761 d 11- -1834 m Anna Dorothea — Pvt PA ★
Peter: b 9-15-1754 d 9-11-1821 m Mary Boone Lt VA
Philip: b 1751 d 6-22-1814 m Magdalena Letch Sol PA
Tobias: b c. 1740 d 3-29-1818 m Anna Hess Pvt PA
Wm.: b c. 1731 d p. 10-14-1794 m (1) — VanMetre (2)Reah Morgan PS VA

SCHOLLENBERGER,
Lorenz: b — d c. 1800 m Elizabeth Mertz Pvt PA

SCHOOLCRAFT,
Jacob: b 12-18-1761 d 8-12-1834 m Marie Catrina Zimmer Sgt NY ★
Lawrence: b 9-4-1738 d 12- -1820 m Maria Synder Adj NY
Lawrence: b 2-28-1759 d 6-7-1840 m Margaret Ann Barbara Rowe Pvt NY

SCHOOLER,
Wharton: b c. 1743 d a. 5- -1824 m Margaret Gatewood PS VA
Wm.: b 1760 d 5- -1833 m Elizabeth Harrison Sgt VA ★

SCHOOLEY,
Benjamin: b 4-24-1733 d c. 1809 m — PS NJ
John: b 4-15-1739 d 1-20-1787 m Mary Coleman Pvt NJ
John: b 11-28-1761 d 9-3-1834 m Mary Earl Pvt NJ
Samuel: b 2-16-1743 d 4- -1832 m (1)Margaret (Brown) Gibbons (2)Elizabeth Wilson Capt NJ

SCHOONMAKER,
Abraham: b 4-26-1752 d 1-18-1814 m Sarah Adriance Adj NY
Cornelius: b 1740 d 1805 m Helena Bassett Pvt NY
Cornelius C: b c. 1740 d 1796 m Sarah Hoffman PS NY
Daniel: bpt 2-22-1713 d 1791 m Magdalena Jansen PS NY
Edward: bpt 3-14-1736 d a. 4-30-1816 m Elizabeth Whittaker Pvt PS NY
Edward: bpt 9-14-1735 d p. 5-1-1776 m (1)Cornelia Wynkoop (2)Lydia Shepmoes 1Lt NY
Egbert: b 9-15-1723 d p. 1800 m Gertruy Schoonmaker Capt NY
Frederick: b 1-13-1738 d 12-2-1819 m Elizabeth (Schoonmaker) Capt NY
Hezekiah: b 6-24-1733 d 1-6-1793 m Deborah Schoonmaker Ens PS NY
Hezekiah: b c. 1724 d a. 1806 m Johana Wolfin PS NY
Jacobus: b 1740 d 1820 m (1)Annatje Sleight (2)Mrs Catherine DePuy PS NY
Jochem, Sr.: bpt 10-12-1710 d p. 7-14-1789 m Lydia Rosekrans PS NY
Jochem, Jr.: b c. 1731 d p. 1790 m Catharine Schoonmaker Capt PS NY
Jochem D: bpt 2-13-1737 d 1804 m Helena DePuy Pvt NY
Johannis: bpt 2-5-1744 d 1782 m Geertruy Brodhead Pvt PS NY
John: b 1760 d 1839 m Delano Hanson Sgt NY
Martinus: b 9-15-1759 d p. 1797 m Maria Smith Drm NY
Martinus: b 3-1-1737 d 5-20-1824 m Mary Bassett PS NY
Samuel: b 3-8-1692 d 1-11-1778 m Nelly Finney PS NY

SCHOONOVER,
Rodolvis: b 4-20-1753 d 3-20-1828 m Hannah Hyndshaw Pvt PA

SCHORTZ,
Frederick: b 2-9-1755 d 4-24-1835 m Gertraut Gradwohl Pvt PA
Michael: b 1728 d 9- -1791 m Margaret Scholl Pvt PA

SCHOTT, (includes SHOTT)
Frederick: b 1729 d 1786 m Maria Esther Odeman Pvt PA
John Paul: b 10-25-1744 d 7-18-1829 m Naomi Sill Capt PA
Ludwig, Sr.: b c. 1725 d 1786 m Barbara — Sol PA

SCHOTTS, (or SHOTTS)
Henry: b c. 1760 d 2-2-1807 m Eve Froelig Sol PS PA

SCHOUTEN,
Andris: b 1738 d p. 1790 m Elizabeth Linneebeek Pvt NY
Daniel: b 9-9-1764 d p. 1808 m Lydia Ladue Pvt NY

SCHRACK,
Abraham: b 10-26-1759 d 10-12-1820 m Catharine — Pvt PA
David: b 12-24-1752 d 10- -1825 m Sarah Hamer Capt PA

SCHRAMBLING,
David: b 1759 d p. 2-14-1824 m Susannah Young Pvt NY
Henry: b a. 1745 d p. 1784 m Sarah Leonardson Lt NY

SCHREFFLER,
Henry, Sr.: b — d 9- -1784 m Magdalena — PS PA
Henry, Jr.: b c. 1739 d 1826 m Anna Maria Weber Pvt PA

SCHRIEBER, (includes SHRIEBER & SHRIBER)
Herman: b c. 1752 d p. 1800 m Barbara Maurer Pvt PA
Philip Jacob: b 6-13-1735 d 4-5-1813 m Catherine Elizabeth Kern Pvt PA

SCHRONCK,
Godfrey: b a. 1758 d 1830 m Elizabeth Williams Pvt PA

SCHROPP,
John: b 10-11-1750 d 7-4-1805 m (1)Elizabeth Tannenberg (2)Elizabeth Krogstrup Pvt PA

SCHROYER,
Conrad: b 12-19-1761 d 8-31-1825 m Catherine — Pvt PA

SCHUCKER,
Tobias: b 1752 d 1803 m Anna Maria — Pvt PA

SCHUHART, (or SUGART)
Hartman: b 1754 d 1842 m Sarah Moll Pvt PA

SCHUMPERT,
Jacob: b c. 1726 d p. 5-8-1786 m Ann Christian Pvt SC
Peter: b 1753 d p. 1-26-1821 m Elizabeth Schaeffer Pvt SC

SCHUREMAN,
James: b 2-12-1756 d 1-22-1824 m Eleanor Williamson 2Lt PS NJ
John: b 1757 d 1-1-1833 m (1)Miss Valentine (2)Catherine Leonard (3)Catherine (Scott)Loder Pvt NJ ★
John: b 2-27-1729 d 7-6-1795 m Antje (Reimer)Strycker PS NJ

SCHUYLER,
Abraham: b 4-8-1741 d 11-3-1815 m Altje Voorhees Capt NJ
Abraham: b 12-25-1735 d 5-27-1812 m Eva Beekman ILt NY
Arent: b 10- -1746 d 10-28-1803 m Swan Schuyler PS NJ
Catherine VanRensselaer : b 11-4-1734 d 3-7-1803 m Philip John Schuyler PS NY
Harmanus: b 4-2-1727 d 9-1-1796 m Christina Ten Broeck DepAsst Cmsry Gen NY
Jacob: b 4-29-1734 d 11-3-1807 m Effie Swackhammer 2Maj NJ
Jacob: b 1754 d 9- -1824 m Delilah Kerkimer PS NY
John: b 6-4-1751 d 4-16-1811 m Jannetje Vrooman Sgt NY
John: b 5-15-1745 d 1806 m Mary Hunter Pvt NY
Peter: b 1756 d 1845 m Ann Richardson Pvt NJ
Peter P.: b 3-10-1723 d — m — Maj NY
Philip: b 11-22-1733 d 11-18-1804 m Catharine VanRensselaer MGen NY
Philip P.: b 4-22-1736 d 6-3-1808 m Annatje Wendel Col NY
Stephanus John: b 8-14-1737 d 12-24-1820 m Lena TenEyck Col NY

SCHWAB,
John George: b c. 1730 d p. 1819 m Anna Maria — PS PA

SCHWALM,
Johannes: b 5-31-1752 d 12-24-1834 m Odilla Robb PS PA

SCHWARTZ, (includes SWARTZ)
Conrad: b 3-10-1744 d 4-24-1820 m Anna Maria Loeser Pvt QM PA
Frederick: b 1731-5 d 1-17-1787 m Abigail Chester Pvt PA
George: b 10-29-1761 d 8-28-1824 m Margaret Bruner Sol PA
Jacob: b 8-28-1760 d 7-26-1842 m Catharine Kimmel Pvt PA
Ludwig: b 4-4-1761/2 d 4-14-1843 m Mary Katherine Lesher Pvt PA
Michael: b a. 1746 d p. 11-24-1801 m — Froney or Frone Pvt PA
Peter: b a. 1750 d 10-16-1804 m (2)Mrs Magdalena Weyland PS PA
Philip: b 1729 d 1811 m — Pvt PA
Phillip Michael: b 1758 d 4-9-1805 m Margaret Schlusher Pvt PA
Samuel: b 1739 d 1-1-1821 m Catherine — Sol MD
Samuel: b c. 1753 d 1811 m Maria Grickry Pvt PA

SCHWARTZBACH,
Adam: b 1723 d p. 6-11-1792 m Magdelena Weiss PS PA

SCHWARTZLANDER, (includes SWARTZLANDER)
Conrad: b 1753 d c. 1845 m — Pvt PA
Gabriel: b 3-31-1747 d 7-17-1814 m Salome (Stout)Freed Pvt PA

SCHWEITZER, (includes SWEITZER)
Casper: b 12-10-1715 d 5-6-1783 m Anna Maria — PS PA
John, Sr.: b c. 1728 d 1801 m Catharine — PS PA
John, Jr.: b 8-15-1755 d 11-29-1839 m Mary Freeman Pvt PA
Leonhard: b 2-11-1757 d 12-14-1833 m Elizabeth Kolpin Pvt PA
Rudolph: b 2-1-1753 d 12-12-1822 m Maria Barbara Biesecker Pvt PA

SCHWENCK, (includes SCHWENK)
Abraham: b 5-24-1759 d 8-6-1843 m Veronica Bauer Sgt PA
George: b c. 1730 d 2-24-1803 m Frances Veronica Markley Pvt PA

SCHWEYER, (includes SCHWOYER)
Nicholas, Sr.: b 10-18-1721 d 3-23-1800 m (1)Maria Barbara Kuntz (2)Mrs Catherine — PS PA
Nicholas, Jr.: b 1764/5 d 8-28-1828 m Mary Magdalena Reifschnider Sol PA

SCHWONGER, (or SWANGER)
Abraham: b 1733 d 8-10-1838 m Elizabeth Wagner Mil PS PA

SCLATER,
Wm. Sheldon: b 1749 d 1811 m Katherine Nutting Capt VA

SCOBEY,
James: b 1745-9 d p. 1819 m Catherine Brown 2Lt NJ

SCOFIELD, (includes SCHOFIELD & SCHOLFIELD)
Abram: b 2-17-1736 d 5-17-1812 m Sarah Lockwood Pvt CT
Benjamin: b 11-5-1751 d — m Rebecca Howe Pvt CT
David: b 1756/7 d 1789 m Hannah Lockwood Pvt CT
Ebenezer: b 5-22-1754 d 9-26-1846 m Thankful Scofield Pvt CT ★
Elisha: b 8-30-1757 d 9-10-1807 m Mary Weeks Pvt CT
Elisha: b 5-21-1764 d 9-6-1859 m Abigail Ingerson Pvt CT

Elnathan: b 2-21-1746/7 d 1826/7 m Mary Sanford Pvt NY
Ezra: b 11-27-1756 d 6-29-1840 m Mellicent Amelia Smith Pvt CT
Gershom: b 7-4-1751 d 3-10-1825 m Lydia Bell Sgt CT ★
Gideon, Jr.: b 1-17-1765 d 5-7-1807 m Abigail Kennedy Sol CT
Hait: b 6-1-1756 d 7-16-1840 m Abigail Weed Sgt CT ★
Hezekiah: b 1723 d 1804 m Mary Waterbury Pvt NY
Isaac: b 6-13-1720 d p. 6-2-1783 m Joanna Weed Pvt CT
Israel: b 1754 d 6-10-1833 m Mary Selleck Pvt NY ★
Jacob: b 10-27-1741 d 1781 m Hannah Knapp Pvt CT
Jared: b 3-17-1764 d 7-11-1843 m (1)Dorcas Weed (2)Mrs Sally Brown Weed Pvt CT ★
John: bpt 5-27-1753 d 1- -1805 m Hannah Turner Sgt NY
Joseph: b 1739 d 1836 m Anna Brown Pvt CT
Joseph: b a. 1739 d p. 1787 m Mary Rex Pvt NY
Josiah: b 11-21-1735 d 10-2-1824 m Mary Smith Cpl CT
Michael: b 1-24-1741 d 1-23-1786 m Annah Lockwood Pvt NY
Peter: b 10-21-1743 d 4-28-1830 m Hannah Bates Pvt CT
Samuel: b 6-21-1712 d 1786 m Elizabeth Ambler Pvt CT
Samuel: b 1734 d 9-4-1801 m Edith (Newlin)Marshall Pvt PA
Seely: b 7-6-1759 d 6-15-1843 m Hannah Crissy Cpl CT
Silas: b 4-2-1758 d 11-1-1837 m Charity Finch OrdlSgt NY ★
Silvanus: b 6-26-1733 d 1830 m Sarah Weed Pvt CT
Silvanus, Sr.: b 5-1-1729 d p. 1790 m Hannah Seely Pvt CT
Silvanus, Jr.: b 5-19-1751 d p. 1782 m Mary Griffin Pvt NY
Smith: b 10-1-1756 d 5-8-1803 m Susanna Wood Sgt NY W★
Uriah: b 1752 d 7-17-1824 m Elizabeth — Pvt CT
Wm.: b 5-15-1744 d 9-26-1851 m (1)Patty Seely (2)Hannah Abbott Pvt CT NY ★
Wm.: b 1753 d 2-3-1823 m Elizabeth Lane Lt PA ★

SCOTT,
Aaron: b 10-1-1750 d 4-9-1839 m Phoebe Story Pvt VT
Abraham: b c. 2-17-1733 d 11-1-1796 m (1)Mehetable — (2)Abigail Latham Pvt PS NH
Abraham: b 1750 d 8- -1798 m Sarah McQueen Maj PS PA
Abram: b 1757 d 3-1-1834 m (1)Margaret McClean (2)Jean Kerr (3)Margaret McMillan Ens PA
Adam Calhoun: b 1746 d 1831 m Elizabeth Thornton 2Lt PA
Alexander: b c. 1740 d p. 1810 m (1)Mrs Hannah (Barksdale)Miller-Polhill Stark (2)Mrs Elizabeth Grimball Chp GA
Alexander: b c. 1715 d 6-20-1787 m Margaret — Pvt NC
Alexander, Jr.: b 5-19-1754 d 12-17-1831 m Elizabeth McEntire Pvt PA
Alexander: b 10- -1762 d 1844 m Sarah — Spy Pvt VA ★
Amos: b 8-3-1751 d 8-29-1822 m Miriam Eastman Cpl VT
Andrew: b c. 1735 d p. 1813 m Elizabeth Ritter PS NC
Archibald: b c. 1745 d p. 12-7-1804 m Margaret McClelland Pvt PA
Archibald: b c. 1750 d 3-4-1799 m Frances Ramsey PS VA
Arthur, Jr.: b 6- -1761 d 7-24-1843 m Ann Hamilton Pvt PA
Barakiah: b 12-30-1751 d 12-8-1810 m Allis Shumway Pvt MA
Benjamin: b 1724 d 10-27-1809 m (1)Lydia Johnson (2)Azubah Cheeny Sgt MA
Benjamin: b 5-31-1708 d 8-1-1792 m Jamima Tuttle PS MA
Benjamin: b 4-24-1757 d 2-5-1841 m Margaret VanTuyl Pvt NY VT ★
Benjamin: b 1765 d p. 2-9-1812 m (1)— Shaver (2)Seveleah Ruff Sol SC
Benjamin: b 5-29-1754 d 10-5-1840 m Nancy — OrdlSgt VA ★
Caleb: b 7-11-1758 d 1832 m Phoebe Webb Pvt NY ★
Cason: b c. 1755 d 3-3-1807 m Tabitha Dixon Sgt SC
Charles: b — d 11-3-1827 m Mary Shurtleff Pvt NH
Charles: b 1759 d 2-12-1838 m Amie Briggs Pvt RI W★
Charles: b 7-21-1763 d 10-22-1818 m Priscilla Read Cnt VA W★
Charles: b 1733 d 10-22-1813 m (1)Frances Sweeney (2)Mrs Judith Gist BGen VA
Cornelius: b 2-17-1741 d 7-5-1804 m Hannah VanTassel Sgt NY
Cornelius: b 2-20-1723 d 1800-4 m Julia Benson Pvt NY
Daniel: b 1759 d 7-3-1824 m Ann Radford Poindexter Pvt VA ★
David: b 2-25-1727 d 5-21-1809 m Hannah Smith Lt CT
David: b 8-2-1742 d 1-18-1833 m Susanna Bolton Lt MA
David: b 9-19-1748 d 5-31-1812 m (1)Esther Frary (2)Sarah Field Cpl MA
David: b 1753 d 12-28-1821 m Bethiah Easterbrook Pvt MA W★
David: b c. 1750 d p. 1820 m (1)Jane McLelland (2)Jane Walker Capt PA
David: b c. 1760 d c. 1800 m (1)Sarah McCreary (2)Jane Ramsey Lt PA
David: b c. 1750 d 1811 m (2)Rachel Smith Pvt PA
David: b 1737 d 1818 m (1)Judith Cunningham (2)Clary (Byrne) Buckner (3) — Bells Capt VA ★
Ebenezer: b 8-2-1723 d p. 1790 m Susannah Webster Sgt CT
Ebenezer: b 4-18-1735 d p. 1790 m Mary Weed CS PS CT
Ebenezer: b 9-18-1743 d 3-3-1826 m Love Fairman Cpl MA ★
Ebenezer: b 4-22-1750 d 10-11-1821 m Susannah Parker Sol MA
Ebenezer: b 9-25-1748 d 3-11-1820 m Celia Brett Pvt PS NH
Eleazer: b 1746 d 1840 m Lois — Pvt CT
Eleazer: b 12-28-1749 d 2-20-1826 m Experience Severance Pvt MA
Elisha: b 7-26-1732 d 1-18-1821 m Mercy North Capt CT
Elizabeth Harrison: b 2- -1740 d 11-9-1823 m James Scott PS VA
Ethiel: b 7-24-1762 d 3-1-1845 m Eunice Barber Pvt CT ★
Francis: b 8-16-1756 d 5-6-1813 m Nancy Wyatt 2Lt VA
Francis: b 1758 d 12-14-1840 m Margaret Smith Pvt VA ★
George: b 1758 d 1826 m Jane Ray Capt VA

George: b 11-30-1755 d 12-20-1807 m Betsy Walker Pvt VA
Gershom, Jr.: b 6-9-1744 d 2-4-1778 m (2)Sarah Morris Sol CT
Gideon: b 12-12-1755 d 3-28-1826 m Anna Burt Pvt CT
Gustavus: b 1753 d 1801 m Margaret Hall Caile PS MD
Henry: b 11-24-1763 d 3-27-1834 m Christiana Rowley Sgt NY W★
Henry: b a. 1741 d p. 1782 m Mary — Pvt PA
Hugh, Sr.: b 1726 d 10-11-1819 m Janet Agnew Maj PS PA
Hugh, Jr.: b 8-7-1763 d 10-17-1849 m Jean Latta Pvt PA
Isaac: b 1766 d 1802 m Sarah Curtis Pvt NY
Israel: b c. 1755 d 1830 m Mary — Pvt NJ
Jacob: b 1748 d 10- -1808 m Catherine Morgan Pvt Spy VA
James: b c. 1725 d 1-20-1781 m (1)Sarah — (2)Mary — Pvt PS MD
James: b 1735 d 10-28-1776 m Rhoda Rockward Cpl MA
James: b 4-16-1749 d a. 1818 m Hannah Croft Cpl MA
James: b c. 1755 d 11-19-1828 m Hannah Parkhurst Pvt NJ
James: b 1760 d 8-30-1823 m Jane Adams Pvt VA NC
James: b c. 1750 d 1807 m Jane Cleghorn Pvt NC CL
James: b 1752 d 1825 m Mary Pearson Lt PA
James: b 1755 d a. 1 -1814 m Jenet — Ens PA
James: b c. 1718 d p. 1777 m Rebekah — Pvt PA
James: b c. 1739/40 d p. 1787 m (2)Elizabeth — Pvt PA
James: b 1741 d 1819 m (1)Margaret Powers (2)Rachel Forbes Pvt PA
James: b 1736 d 10-18-1817 m Rachel Holmes PS VA
James: b c. 1746 d 1- -1813 m — Pvt PA
James: b c. 1754 d 1808 m Sarah Bell Pvt PA
James: b 1755 d 10-23-1842 m Jane McClure Pvt PA
James: b a. 1750 d 1808 m Hannah Beale Cpl VA
James: b c. 1728 d 1799 m Frances Collier Capt VA
James: b 1-8-1742 d 1779 m Elizabeth Harrison Capt VA
James: b c. 1751 d 1-11-1833 m Rebeckah Duval Capt VA
James: b 1744 d 1781 m Elizabeth — Lt VA
James: b 1756 d p. 11-6-1834 m — Pvt VA ★
James: b 1757 d 1830 m (3)Temperance Rawls Pvt VA
James: b 1764 d 7-5-1848 m Amelia Dougherty Mus VA ★
James: b — d 2-5-1705 m (1)Elizabeth Osborne (2)Elizabeth Cunningham CS VA
Jeremiah: b 1726 d 3-1-1795 m Rebecca Jenckes Sgt RI
Joel: b 10-29-1751 d 11-8-1836 m Mary Bacon Cpl MA
John: b — d 1779 m Rose — PS MD
John: b 3-2-1757 d 3-2-1828 m Mehitabel Todd Pvt MA
John: b 2-14-1743/4 d 1-13-1816 m Mrs Frances Boyd Pvt MA
John: b 3-23-1765 d 12-27-1847 m Bethia Ames Pvt NH
John, Sr.: b 3-18-1731 d p. 1805 m (1)Mary Trott (2)Joanna Brown (3)Chloe Daniels PS NH
John, Jr.: bpt 10-5-1760 d 1790 m Freelove Boyden Pvt NH
John: b 2-9-1760 d 7-9-1851 m — Tms Lt NJ ★
John: b 12-15-1736 d 7-8-1832 m Eunice Wilson Pvt NY
John: b 1742 d 2- -1807 m Mehitable Cary Pvt NY
John: b c. 1745 d 5-10-1818 m Jane Raymond PS Pvt NY
John: b 1742 d 10-14-1815 m Bettie Machen Pvt NC
John: b 1756 d 1826 m Drucilla Hilliard Pvt NC
John: b c. 1725 d p. 10-16-1816 m Letitia — PS NC
John: b 1724 d p. 2-22-1798 m (1)Agnes McElroy (2)Janet Mitchell Cmsry Lt PA
John: b 1739 d 1802 m Jane Reed Pvt PA
John: b c. 1748 d 1816 m Catherine — Pvt PA
John: b c. 1758 d p. 1779 m Mary McBride Sgt SC
John: b 1745 d 10-17-1788 m Sarah Frierson Sol PS SC
John: b 1718 d 1801-5-m Mary Hacket PS Capt VA
John: b 5-29-1763 d 3-13-1847 m (1)Ann Craytin (2)Nancy Keith Pvt VA ★
John: b 6-26-1748 d 11-20-1815 m Hannah Early Capt VA
John: b 1761 d 3-24-1843 m Sophia Murray Pvt VA ★
John Baytop: b 9-26-1761 d 2-15-1814 m (1)Elizabeth Coleman (2)Patsy Thompson Lt VA
John Morin: b 1730 d 9-14-1784 m Helena Rutgers BGen PS NY
Jonathan: b 1-28-1737 d 11-23-1784 m Abigail Clifford Lt VT
Joseph: b 5-5-1761 d 7-31-1841 m (1)Catharine Upham (2)Betsey Wilkins Sgt MA
Joseph: b 1-7-1751 d 12-23-1818 m Hannah Fearson Smn NY
Joseph: b 1742 d c. 1800 m Cornelia Osterhout Pvt NY
Joseph: b 1-2-1757 d 1821 m Mary Steen Pvt PA
Joseph: b 8-18-1747 d 7-5-1805 m Janet McCrae Lt SC
Joseph, Jr.: b 1759 d 4-23-1828 m Elizabeth Booker Capt VA ★
Joseph: b 8-12-1736 d 10-18-1817 m Rachel Holmes Lt VA
Joseph: b 1757 d 10-17-1833 m Mary — Pvt VA ★
Josiah: b 1735 d 2-20-1819 m (1)Violet Foster (2)Jane Gordon Ens PA
Joyce Jane Calliham: b — d p. 1780 m Samuel Scott PS SC
Levi: b 1762 d 1-16-1844 m Nancy Carter Pvt NC ★
Mark: b 6-11-1763 d 1834 m Mehitable Scott Pvt MA
Mathew: b c. 1755 d 1815 m Lucretia Ogle Ens VA
Matthew: b 1739 d 5-20-1796 m Elizabeth Thompson Capt PA
Moses: b 1749 d 1-7-1817 m Eunice Woods Pvt VA W★
Moses: b 1761 d 2-3-1853 m Hannah Wilkinson Pvt CT
Moses: b 3-22-1742 d 12-8-1817 m Mary Todd 2Lt MM MA
Moses: b 2-3-1713 d 7-23-1799 m (1)Miriam Nash (2)Henry — CS MA
Moses: b 1737 d 12-28-1821 m Anna Johnson Dr NJ
Moses: b 2-22-1740 d 1797 m Mary Ballard Pvt VT
Nathan: b 1-5-1743 d p. 1789 m Ruth Allen Cpl NH
Nathaniel: b 1-16-1761 d 1-21-1846 m Lydia Arnold PS RI

Obediah: b 2-15-1764 d 11-3-1840 m Mary — Pvt VA
Oliver: b 12- -1762/3 d 3-19-1845 m (1)Ruth Kingsbury (2)Rosanna Hanna Burt Pvt CT ★
Oliver: b 2-27-1739 d p. 3-30-1782 m Bethsheba Eastman Sgt VT
Peter: b c. 1733 d p. 1793 m Susanna Green Sgt NY
Philip: b 6-20-1760 d 1-18-1838 m Martha Foster Pvt MM MA ★
Phineas: b 1745 d 6-6-1819 m Thankful Kinsley Pvt VT
Robert: b 5-24-1754 d 4-27-1838 m Sara Gardner SgtMaj PA ★
Robert: b — d 1816 m Mary Blackwood Sol VA
Robert S.: b 10-17-1734 d 9-16-1776 m Betsey Scott Pvt MD
Samuel: b 3-12-1746 d p. 11-3-1776 m Lois North Sol CT
Samuel: b 1761 d 2-10-1834 m Elizabeth — Pvt MD ★
Samuel: b 6- -1723 d 1793 m Susan Perry PS Pvt MA
Samuel: b 9-12-1724 d 11-27-1793 m Mary Thompson Pvt MA
Samuel: b c. 1740 d c. 1794 m Abigail — Pvt PS NH
Samuel: b 5-9-1759 d 4-8-1835 m (1)Mary Rugg (2)Sarah Roberts Pvt NJ NY ★
Samuel: b 8-5-1762 d 12-12-1820 m Martha McCorkle MM Mil NC
Samuel: b c. 1739 d c. 1818 m — Fisher Pvt PA
Samuel: b c. 1740 d 9-13-1823 m Rachel Tidball Pvt PA
Samuel: b 1751 d 12-27-1819 m Elizabeth Wilson Pvt PA
Samuel: b — d p. 5-22-1796 m — Pvt PA
Samuel: b 1763 d 3-2-1829 m Sarah Matthews Pvt SC
Samuel: b c. 1729 d p. 1809 m Joyce Jane Calliham PS SC
Samuel: b 1754 d 1-20-1822 m Ann Roy Maj VA
Samuel: b 12-7-1760 d 4-17-1810 m Jane Hutton Capt VA
Samuel: b 1750 d 8-8-1833 m Alice Muncie Sol PS VA ★
Samuel: b 3-3-1707 d 1787 m Elizabeth Richardson PS VT
Selah: b 11-19-1753 d 10-9-1826 m Mary Dickinson Pvt MA
Stephen: b 9-14-1738 d 1794 m Freelove Hikcox Sgt CT
Sylvanus: b 5-22-1743 d p. 6-9-1824 m Jerusha Browne Pvt MA
Sylvanus, Jr.: b 1736 d 8-5-1784 m Sarah Andrews Pvt MA
Thomas: b 2-9-1749 d 1899 m (2)Mrs Sarah Embra Read Capt GA
Thomas: b c. 1750 d p. 1-21-1819 m Margaret — Ens PS MD
Thomas: b 1761 d 1852 m Olive Proctor Pvt MA ★
Thomas: b 7-19-1755 d 3-1-1834 m Lettice Russel Pvt NC ★
Thomas, Sr.: b c. 1705 d p. 1778 m Annie Baytop PS VA
Thomas: b c. 1759 d 2-13-1817 m Elizabeth Tucker Pvt PA W★
Thomas, Jr.: b 1727 d 1804 m Catherine Tomkies Capt VA
Thomas: b 1730 d 1801/2 m Elizabeth Wingfield Capt VA
Thomas: b 1762 d a. 2-8-1854 m — Sol VA
Waitstill: b 1742 d 3-6-1824 m Lydia — Capt NH
Wm.: b 12-25-1757 d 12-17-1838 m Susanna Stewart Sgt CT ★
Wm.: b 1756 d 1-16-1824 m (1)Phylena Hawley (2)Abigail Barnard Pvt CT
Wm.: b 8-26-1754 d 3-26-1806 m Jane Thomas Capt GA
Wm., Sr.: b 1744 d p. 1788 m Margaret — Pvt GA
Wm., Jr.: b 12-25-1762 d 10-4-1826 m Deborah Sell Sol GA
Wm.: b c. 1763 d 12-23-1823 m Mary Haller Sol MD
Wm.: b 5- -1743 d 9-19-1796 m Phoebe Woods Capt MA NH
Wm.: b 9-28-1744 d 2-6-1803 m Ann Boise MM MA
Wm.: b 1743 d 7-14-1815 m (1)Rosanagh Tait (2)Charity Gilliard Col NH
Wm.: b 1713 d 11-20-1795 m Margaret Gregg Pvt PS NH
Wm., Jr.: b 1-8-1756 d 10-10-1829 m (1)Catherine Ames (2)Dorcas Pulcifer Pvt NH
Wm., Jr.: b c. 1750 d a. 10- -1829 m Eleanor Ward Sol NC
Wm.: b 1750 d 1801 m Rebecca — Pvt NC
Wm.: b 9-8-1747 d 5-6-1833 m Jenny Allison PS Pvt PA
Wm.: b 5-8-1754 d 7-19-1824 m Susannah Hamilton Pvt PA
Wm.: b d 6-17-1786 m Jane — Pvt PA
Wm.: b 1725 d 5-4-1807 m Mary Waring LCol SC
Wm.: b 12-3-1760 d 6-19-1830 m Mary Miller Sgt SC ★
Wm.: b c. 1760 d p. 4-20-1806 m Mary — Pvt SC
Wm., Jr.: b 1755 d 1790 m Rebecca Rogers Pvt SC
Wm.: b 1759 d 1- -1818 m Mrs Elizabeth (Roddy)Moore Pvt SC
Wm.: b 1747 d 1791 m Ann Mason Capt VA
Wm.: b 12-15-1756 d 10-16-1817 m Anne Jones Capt VA W★
Wm.: b 5-17-1745 d 1828 m Mary Scott Lt VA
Wm.: b 1-30-1744 d 1-1-1797 m Elizabeth Abbott Wade Lt VA
Wm.: b c. 1702 d 1804 m Grizzell Caruthers Sgt VA
Wm.: b 12-3-1757 d 9-13-1842 m Mary Baker Pvt VA ★
Wm.: b c. 1735-8-1804/5 m Helen Montgomery PS KY
Zebediah: b 11-22-1741 d 5-5-1794 m Hannah — Pvt CT

SCOUT,
Aaron: b — d 12-16-1809 m Sarah Gilbert Ens PA

SCOUTEN,
Jacob: b 1-25-1755 d 1-7-1842 m Charity Roberts Pvt NJ ★

SCOVELL, (includes SCOVEL, SCOVIL, SCOVILL & SCOVILLE)
Amasa: b 12-22-1759 d 3-30-1844 m Esther Merrill Pvt Mus CT ★
Benjamin: b 1-3-1763 d 5-6-1826 m Eunice — Pvt CT ★
Daniel: b 5-25-1756 d 1-9-1813 m Elizabeth Granger Pvt CT
Elijah: b 7-15-1738 d 4-27-1810 m (1)Jemima Shaler (2)Hannah Frary Pvt CT
Elisha: b 1734 d c. 1797-9 m Eliphal Bliss Lt CT
John: b 4-19-1758 d 2-15-1833 m Mary Smith Pvt CT
Jonah: b 9-1-1750 d 4-1-1831 m Sarah Spencer Pvt CT
Joseph: b 3-31-1757 d 3-1-1839 m Sarah Spencer Pvt CT
Josiah: b 6-12-1740 d 11-27-1821 m Frances — Pvt CT
Levi: b 6-29-1762 d 1828 m Content Dunbar Pvt CT

SCOVELL, contd.
Moses: b 12-6-1762 d 7-24-1836 m Rachael Baker Pvt CT ★
Nathan: b 5-8-1758 d 6-19-1813 m Ruth Harris Pvt CT
Samuel: b 9-6-1731 d p. 1803 m Abigail Yale Ens CT
Samuel: b 10-14-1757 d 6-3-1824 m Lydia Hitchcock Sgt CT
Samuel: b 9-29-1731 d p. 1790 m (1)Ruth Squiers (2)Mary Rowland Pvt CT
Selah: b 6-20-1757 d 7-22-1822 m Mary Roberts Pvt CT
Solomon: b 9-16-1759 d 11-27-1833 m Molly Dewey Pvt Tms CT ★
Stephen: b 3-1-1728 d c. 1820 m Elizabeth Eggleston Pvt CT ★
Thomas, Sr.: b 6-16-1722 d 5-25-1791 m (1)Jerusha (Scovell) (2)Bathsheba — PS NH
Thomas, Jr.: b 2-20-1753 d 4-7-1813 m Mrs Rachael (Boardman) Wilcox Pvt NH
Timothy: b 9- -1762 d 12-25-1845 m Chloe — Pvt CT ★

SCOWDEN,
Theodorus: b 2-10-1754 d 2-11-1833 m Sarah Reed Sol PA ★

SCRAFFORD,
George: b 11-19-1759 d 1-11-1840 m Eve Rosanna Kaley Sgt NY ★

SCRANTON,
Abraham, Jr.: b 12-13-1749 d 1-28-1836 m (1)Hannah Camp (2)Louisa Fairchild Lt CT ★
Abraham: b 9-10-1754 d 2-24-1844 m Lucy Stone Sgt CT ★
John: b 11-13-1741 d 8-22-1832 m Anna Blatchley Pvt CT ★
Nathan: b 9-15-1739 d 1828 m (1)Mrs Mary Fields (2)Sarah Crampton PS CT
Thomas: b 2-11-1760 d 11-17-1834 m Davaris Seward Pvt CT
Timothy: b 4-1-1761 d 2-11-1848 m (1)Deborah Chittenden (2)Sarah Wright Pvt CT ★
Torry: b 4-6-1756 d 12-17-1840 m Rachel Hall Sgt CT ★

SCREVEN,
James: b 1738 d 11-25-1778 m Mary Esther Odingsell BG PS GA
John: b 11-23-1750 d 9-2-1801 m (1)Patience Holmes (2)Elizabeth Bryan Lt GA
Thomas: b 1741 d 5-14-1804 m Eleanor Hart Col SC

SCRIBER,
Peter: b 1755 d 10-5-1850 m Clara Van Etten Pvt NY

SCRIBNER,
Asa: b 10-29-1757 d 10-30-1790 m Rachel Olmstead Sgt CT
Daniel: b 7-31-1748 d 1-1-1812 m Elizabeth Taylor Pvt MA
Edward: b 12-16-1742 d p. 1791 m (1)Shuah Bean (2)Eunice Stevens Pvt PS NH
Enoch: b 8-29-1750 d 9-21-1816 m Betty Benedict Ens CT
Esther: b 8-3-1763 d 7-4-1840 m Hezekiah Dikeman PS CT
Ezra: b 6-19-1761 d 9-17-1825 m Nancy — Pvt CT W★
Iddo: b 11-11-1752 d 2-5-1831 m (1)Judith Brown (2)Mrs Huldah Jewett Pvt PS NH
Jonathan: b 9-5-1759 d 4-7-1841 m Deborah Gildersleeve Pvt NY
Josiah: b 1750 d 8-13-1821 m (1)Webster (2)Mary Ann Farmer Pvt CS NH
Matthew: b c. 1720 d 4-20-1801 m Martha Smith Pvt CT
Nathaniel: b 12-23-1743 d 11-5-1800 m Phebe Kellogg Capt CT
Samuel: b 1-28-1755 d 11-28-1818 m Abigail Hill Pvt MA
Samuel, Sr.: b 4-29-1716 d 2-5-1794 m Hannah Webster Pvt NH
Samuel, Jr.: b 12-28-1743 d p. 1810 m Mary Rayno Pvt NH
Samuel: b 1745 d 8-19-1825 m Lydia Baker Pvt NY
Thaddeus: b 7-26-1761 d 12-20-1845 m Lydia Wescott Pvt NY
Zaccheus: b c. 1723 p. 1799 m Mary — PS NY

SCRIPTURE,
James: b 1-11-1749 d 6-19-1810 m Sibbel Shepley Sgt NH
Samuel, Sr.: b 4-27-1727 d 1817 m Mary Green Pvt NH
Samuel, Jr.: b 12-9-1760 d 1-16-1852 m Betsey Barrett Pvt NH

SCRIVENS,
Wm.: b 2-23-1756 d 4-19-1822 m Mary Saunders Sgt RI ★
Wm., Sr.: b 6-6-1727 d 1826 m (1)Mercy Lewis (2)Elipha — (3)Mary Mosher Pvt RI

SCROGGIN,
John: b 11-13-1743 d 12-14-1812 m Eunice Jane Polk Sgt MD

SCROGGINS,
Humphrey: b 1763 d 7- -1845 m Sarah Kirby Pvt VA

SCROGGS,
James: b 1746 d 1820 m (1)Margaret Jack (2)Margaret Cowden Pvt PA

SCROGGY,
Thomas: b 3-20-1751 d 6-27-1835 m Ann Jones Pvt NJ ★

SCROGIN,
Robert Caldwell: b 3-1-1753 d p. 1790 m (1)Ann Culber (2)Sarah Ann Richardson Ens MD

SCRUGGS,
Drury: b — d p. 4-29-1782 m Mary Carter PS VA
George: b — d 1778 m — Spencer Capt VA
Gross: b 1748 d p. 1796 m (1)Annie Ruth Hale (2)Margaret Eearle Pvt PS GA
Richard: b a. 1755 d p. 10-2-1816 m Prudence Hicks Pvt NC
Richard: b 1758 d 1832 m Sarah Jones Sol Pvt VA
Samuel Scott: b 1758 d p. 3-26-1830 m Jane — Pvt VA ★
Timothy: b 1761 d 8-29-1853 m Mary Welch Pvt VA ★
Wm.: b 1765 d 1833 m Elizabeth Buford Pvt VA

SCUDDER,
Amos: b 2-14-1739 d 8-11-1824 m Phebe Rose Ens NJ
Benjamin: b 6-6-1733 d 3-6-1822 m (1)Sarah Cory (2)Lydia Chandler (3)Jemima Young Pvt NJ
Daniel: b 8-6-1736 d 1811 m Mary Snowden PS NJ
Edmund: bpt 7-19-1747 d p. 1795 m Elizabeth Higbe Pvt CS NY
Ephraim: b c. 1748 d 1788 m Martha Spinning Pvt NJ
Eleazer: b 2-12-1737 d 1812 m Mary Lewis Pvt MA
Ezekiel: b 1763 d 3-20-1853 m Cynthia Gould Pvt NY
Henry: b 8-5-1742 d 1-21-1822 m Phebe Carll 2Lt PS NY
Jedediah: b 1742 d 8-21-1821 m Anna Roberts Pvt NJ
Joel: b 11-8-1746 d p. 1776 m Sarah Brush Capt PS NY
John: b 3-22-1740 d 1-14-1790 m Mary Budd Sgt NY
John: b 1-29-1738 d 2-12-1786 m Susanna — 1Lt PA
John Anderson: b 3-22-1759 d 11-6-1836 m Elizabeth Wyckoff Forman Dr NJ ★
Jonah: bpt 2-24-1744 d p. 1790 m (2)Sarah Taylor PS NY
Lemuel: b 9-30-1741 d 7-9-1806 m Margaret Longstreet Pvt NJ
Nathaniel: b 5-10-1733 d 10-15-1781 m Isabella Anderson Col NJ
Richard: b 5-9-1745 d 12-24-1785 m Rebecca Stiles Pvt NJ
Robert: b — d 1806 m (1)Esther Jennings ( )Rachel Buckley Pvt CT
Timothy, Sr.: b 1696 d 4-25-1788 m Mary Whitehead PS NJ
Wm.: b 4-6-1739 d 10-31-1793 m (1)Mary Skelton (2)Sarah Van Dyke LCol NJ
Wm.: b 7-25-1747 d 1798 m Mary Torf Ens NJ
Wm.: b 1739 d 3-7-1804 m Elizabeth Wood Pvt NY

SCULL,
Abel: b 6-3-1760 d 11-8-1809 m Alice Collins Pvt NY
Benjamin: b 11-13-1744 d 7-22-1828 m Elizabeth Barry Pvt PA
John: b 1-7-1752 d 3-31-1826 m (1)Sarah Somers (2)Catharine Steelman Capt NJ
Joseph: b 1731 d 9-13-1810 m Sarah — Pvt NJ
Peter: b 12- -1753 d 11-4-1779 m Miss Biddle Maj PS PA

SCURLOCK,
James: b 6-25-1749 d 1-11-1805 m Lydda Poore Lt NC
Mial: b c. 1730 d c. 5-7-1785 m Sarah — Maj NC
Wm.: b 7-19-1763 d 10-12-1840 m Rhoda Simmons Pvt NC ★

SCURRY,
Thomas: b 1763 d 1837 m (1)Susan Morgan (2)Sarah Ross PS SC

SCUTT,
Wm., Sr.: b 6-14-1735 d 12-23-1780 m Anna VanNess Pvt NY
Wm., Jr.: b 5-23-1761 d 5-13-1825 m Ruth Crandall Pvt NY ★

SEABOURN,
Jacob: b 1762 b 1762 d 5-16-1840 m (1)Annie — (2)Ann — Pvt VA ★

SEABROOK,
John: b 1731 d 11-26-1783 m Sarah Lawton Lt SC
Thomas: b 2-28-1738 d 2-22-1805 m Martha Tallman LCol NJ

SEABURY,
Gideon: b 3-1-1747 d 10-29-1827 m Betsey Pearce Pvt RI
John: b 11-26-1727 d 1799 m Mary Manchester PS NY
Philip: b 12-6-1740 d 5-30-1819 m Sarah Pierce Sgt RI
Samuel: b 6-3-1741 d 11-28-1822 m Sarah Rackley Pvt MA

SEAGRAVES,
Edward: b c. 1722 d 5-18-1793 m Lois White Capt MA
Jacob: b c. 1763 d 6-7-1835 m (2)Alinair — Pvt NC ★
John: b 11-6-1757 d 2-3-1842 m Sarah Dorrington Cpl MA
John: b c. 1738 d 7-28-1823 m (1)Sarah Priddy (2)Phebe Cook Pvt NC ★

SEAHORN,
John, Jr.: b 6-21-1748 d 5-23-1831 m Elizabeth Cathey Pvt PA
Nicholas: b c. 1745 d p. 2-1-1791 m Polly — Sol SC

SEAL,
Joseph: b c. 1738 d 9-1-1834 m Mary Montgomery Pvt PA
Wm.: b c. 1756 d 1821 m Mary Hunt Pvt PA

SEALE,
Charles: b c. 1734 d c. 1798 m Lydia Muse Sol NC
Jarvis: b 3-23-1759 d 4-12-1838 m (1)Nancy Ann (2)Loucretia O'Neal Pvt VA ★
Thomas: b 7-7-1759 d 11-12-1825 m (1)Rachel Baxter (3)Levy Mosely (4)Sallie Holloway (5)Lucretia O'Neal PS NC

SEALS,
James: b 11-14-1755 d 11-6-1832 m Sarah Elizabeth Brown Pvt Spy MD ★

SEAMAN,
Andrew: b 8-15-1763 d *p.* 1832 m (1)— Van Vleck (2)Sarah H. McLain Pvt NY ★
Andrew: b — d 1845 d Sarah Knight Pvt PS CT
Benjamin: b 1738 d 1820 m Letitia Allen PS NY
Eberhart: b 7-30-1752 d 8-6-1827 m Catherine Bossler PS PA
John: b 11-25-1753 d 9-9-1820 m Elizabeth Schlabbig Pvt PA
John Ludwig: b 1722 d 12-12-1797 m Anna Maria — PS PA
Jonah: b 1742 d 1811 m (1)Jane Dunlap (2)Margaret Van Meter (3)Elizabeth Harris PS VA
Jonathan: b *c.* 1738 d *p.*1780 m Elizabeth Baldwin PS VA
Joseph: b 1760 d 1822 m Lydia Sol NY
Micah: b 12-1-1748 d 1834 m Jemima Ball OrdlSgt NY
Samuel, Sr.: b 1-11-1738 d 2-19-1828 m Mary Birdsall PS CS NY
Thomas: b 7-4-1734 d *a.* 12-24-1819 m Rhoebe Hinton PS NY
Thomas: b 4-12-1739 d — m Martha Rowland PS NY
Willet: b 12-11-1737 d 5-4-1807 m Mary Searing Pvt NY
Zebulon: b 3-17-1718 d 2-9-1784 m Phoebe Valentine PS NY
Zebulon, Jr.: b 11-22-1747 d 4-1-1806 m Jane Jackson Lt NY

SEAMANS,
Hezekiah: b 4-29-1763 d 3-15-1835 m Annis Eastman Pvt RI ★
John, Sr.: b 10-4-1728 d 5-10-1813 m Patience Hopkins Pvt RI
John, Jr.: b 1748-50 d 1838 m Sarah Wescott Pvt VT
Josiah: b 9-30-1752 d *p.* 1796 m Penelope Baker Pvt MA
Thomas: b 4-11-1746 d 12-8-1824 m Mary Whitman Sol RI

SEARCH,
James: b 10-7-1759 d 10-3-1819 m Elizabeth Moore Pvt NJ ★
Lot: b 3-8-1762 d 12-11-1851 m Sarah Davis Pvt NJ ★
Wm.: b 1736 d 1806 m Mary McMasters Pvt NJ

SEARCY,
Reuben: b 1729 d 1815 m (1)Susan Henderson (2)Susannah Jett PS CS NC
Reuben: b *c.* 1760 d *a.* 1817 m Elizabeth Mason Sol VA
Richard: b 8-21-1738 d 10-26-1824 m Molly — Capt NC

SEARING,
Christian: b 10-5-1753 d 6-5-1832 m (1)— Umberger (2)Anna Maria Rauch Pvt PA
Daniel: b 1-31-1741 d 1800 m Elizabeth Davenport 2Lt NY
Daniel: b 1-28-1759 d 11-16-1833 m (1)Elizabeth (2)Martha — Pvt NY
Henry, Jr.: b 3-20-1760 d 1-24-1798 m Mariah Elizabeth Rupp Sol PA
Jacob: b *c.* 1759 d 6-24-1824 m (1)Anna Williams (2)Elizabeth — Pvt NJ
Samuel: b 8-5-1756 d 3-31-1838 m Phebe Seaman Pvt NY
Simon: b 1754 d 1-2-1795 m Mary Hudson Pvt NJ

SEARLE,
Aaron: b 6-16-1727 d 9-27-1810 m Hannah Pomeroy Pvt MA
Benjamin B.: b 1765 d 1828 m Eunice Scott Pvt NH
Bildad: b 12-16-1733 d *p.* 1790 m Mary Hannum Pvt MA
Constant, Sr.: b 6-17-1728 d 7-3-1778 m Hannah Miner Pvt PA
Constant, Jr.: b 10-7-1759 d 8-4-1804 m Lucinda Miller Pvt PA
David: b 11-24-1736 d 4-19-1792 m Judith Sayward Pvt MA
Eliphaz: b 1722 d *p.* 1790 m Abigail Pomeroy Pvt MA
Gideon, Sr.: b 11-13-1742 d 2-4-1798 m Cynthia Sweetland Sol VT
Gideon, Jr.: b 3-11-1763 d 9-26-1830 m (1)Hannah Woodard Lucy Osgood Pvt VT
Job: b 1739 d 4-6-1788 m Dorcas Strong Pvt PS MA
John: b 5-14-1721 d 7-5-1787 m Mehetable Dunbar Chp MA
John: b *c.* 1760 d 1820 m Sarah — Sol GA
John Ruggles: b 4-17-1744 d 5-11-1837 m Mary Brown Sol CT
Jonathan: b 11-16-1746 d 12-2-1818 m Margaret Toppan Pvt PS NH
Joseph: b 1757 d — m Molly Coleman Pvt MA
Lemuel: b 9-21-1758 d 10-30-1835 m Deborah Owen Pvt PS MA ★
Lot: b 5-26-1745 d 12-16-1822 m (1)Margaret Moseman (2)Thankful — Pvt NY
Moses: b 3-3-1729 d 2-3-1783 m (1)Rebekah Danks (2)Sarah Kingsly Pvt MA
Nathaniel, Sr.: b 1- -1715 d 12-26-1801 m Mary Pomeroy PS MA
Nathaniel, Jr.: b 1748 d 1812 m Mrs Experience Loomis Sgt MA
Reuben: b 1-17-1747 d *p.* 1813 m Mary Allis Sgt VT
Rogers: b 8-13-1762 d 5-19-1813 m Catherine Scott Sol CT
Stephen: b 1759 d 1830 m Hannah Wade Pvt MA
Wm.: b 5-12-1764 d 12-30-1834 m Anna Fifield Pvt PS NH
Wm.: b 12-2-1751 d 1-21-1817 m Philena Frink Sgt CT
Zophar: b 1735 d 3-10-1817 m Anna Clark Pvt MA

SEARS,
Alden: b 2-24-1738 d 3-25-1803 m (1)Hannah Bassett (2)Phoebe Walker Pvt MA
Barnabas: b 1745 d 6-29-1821 m Hannah Gove Pvt MA ★
Benjamin: b 7-11-1725 d 1816 m Sarah Mallet Pvt NY
Benjamin, Jr.: b 5-2-1738 d 3-12-1827 m Mary Hall Pvt NY

Christopher: b 8-16-1756 d 2- -1809 m (1)Deborah Manter (2)Mary Snow Pvt MA
David: b 11-27-1757 d 4-29-1842 m Lucy Hall Pvt Tms CT ★
David: b 4-14-1753 d 12-22-1846 m Martha Cole Sgt MA
David: b 5-10-1744 d *c.* 1782 m (1)Abigail Gerry (2)Susannah Handy Pvt MA
Ebenezer: b 10-11-1755 d 9-17-1835 m Hannah Gray Cpl MA
Ebenezer: b 12-15-1754 d 1-24-1849 m Jane White Pvt MA
Edmund: b 8-6-1712 d 8-12-1796 m Hannah Crowell PS MA
Edmund: b 1-3-1743/44 d 3-16-1832 m Hannah Taylor Pvt MA
Eleazer, Jr.: b 1728 d 9- -1810 m Ruth Lewis Pvt MA
Elisha: b 6-6-1748 d 6-28-1820/21 m Hannah — OrdlSgt MA W★
Elkanah: b 4-12-1734 d 11-24-1816 m Ruth White NCapt & PS CT
Enos: b 6-11-1752 d 7-17-1822 m Rebecca Kelley Pvt MA
Freeman: b 7-29-1740 d 6-30-1807 m Mehitable Haskell Pvt MA
Hezekiah: b 12-30-1728 d 5-7-1801 m Deborah Spencer PS CT
Holmes: b 7-13-1757 d 11-5-1836 m Mercy Bradford Pvt MA
James, Jr.: b 1747 d *p.* 1784 m Abigail Sherwood Pvt MA
John: b 1752 d 9-29-1802 m (1)Teresa Cilison (2)Mary Dutton Lt MD
John: b 1712 d 12-5-1791 m Debora Crowell PS MA
John: b 5-2-1759 d 3-26-1834 m (1) — Bodine (2) — White Pvt NY ★
John: b 1750 d 1831 m Matilda Hobson Pvt NC
Jonathan: b 5-7-1750 d 2-18-1808 m Abigail Hall Sgt MA
Joseph: b 7-20-1756 d 5-30-1836 m Thankful Howes Pvt MA
Joshua: b 7-1-1753 d 3-31-1825 m (1)Sarah Sears (2)Olive Clark Sol & Slr MA
Judah: b 11-10-1734 d 1782 m Molly Crowell Lt MA
Knowles: b 1732 d 6-17-1817 m (1)Susanna Townsend (2)Charity Haviland Capt CT
Micajah: b 4-25-1738 d 2- -1823 m (1)Anna Crowell (2)Huldah Bangs Lt MA
Moody: b 5-6-1734 d 11-27-1795 m Elizabeth Lewis Sol MA
Nathan: b 6-18-1741 d 2-27-1825 m (1)Rebecca Crowell (2)Thankful Bassett 2Lt MA ★
Nathaniel: b 9-1-1738 d 4-28-1816 m (1)Elizabeth Winslow (2)Mehitable Thomas Pvt MA
Nathaniel: b 2-15-1758 d 11-26-1834 m Rachel Rules Pvt MA
Paul, Sr.: b 10-18-1740 d 8-19-1832 m (1)Elizabeth Slawter (2)Lydia Lyon Knight Cpl MA
Paul: b 6-20-1750 d 9-3-1808 m Eleanor Smith Pvt MA
Peter: b 11-29-1753 d 5-17-1821 m Susa Collamore Capt-Lt MA
Richard: b 1748 d 1841 m Charity Bennett Sgt MA
Richard: b 1748 d 8-6-1814 m (1)Mary Lee (2)Miss Edgcombe Sgt MA
Richard: b 6-8-1747 d 5-30-1788 m Sarah Bumpus Cpl MA
Robert: b 1740 d *p.* 1812 m Eleanor Dallas Capt VA
Roland: b 8-23-1750 d 1-18-1833 m Thankful Crowell Cpl MA
Roland: b 2-3-1744 d *p.* 1796 m Jedidah Conant Pvt MA
Seth, Jr.: b *c.* 1751 d *p.* 1790 m — Pvt NY
Seth: b 10-3-1736 d 8-2-1809 m Sarah Sears Pvt NY
Silas: b 2-11-1719/20 d 2-29-1780 m Deborah Buck Pvt MA
Silas: b 11-26-1762 d 1-23-1838 m (1)Elizabeth West (2)Betsy Newton Pvt MA
Simeon: b 1-14-1742 d *p.* 1781 m — Pvt VT
Stephen: b 9-5-1736 d 12-9-1806 m Elizabeth — Pvt PS MA
Stephen: b 5-20-1738 d 1791 m (1)Sarah Hunter (2)Elizabeth Hyde (3)Sybil Hunt Pardee Pvt NY
Thomas: b 4-30-1745 d 4-26-1804 m Deborah Baldwin 2Lt NY
Willard: b 9-8-1760 d 8-23-1838 m (1)Rhoda Bailey (2)Betsey Strong Pvt CT ★
Willard: b 1746 d 12-12-1832/31 m (1)Lois Oaks (2)Mrs Lucy M. Russell Pvt MA ★
Wm.: b 1762 d 2-9-1828 m — Pvt MD
Wm.: b 1732 d 4-27-1818 m Elizabeth Whaley Pvt VA

SEATON,
Benjamin: b *c.* 1760 d 1846 m Elizabeth Bird Pvt PS PA
Francis: b *c.* 1756 d *p.* 6-8-1820 m Rebecca Gregg Ens PA
George: b *c.* 1756 d *c.* 1826 m (1)Nancy Amberson (2)Martha James Pvt PA
George: b 2-8-1739 d 1791 m Elizabeth Watson CS VA
James: b 7-19-1751 d 3-2-1830 m Mary Clark CS PA
John: b 1724 d 1793 m Ismenia — PS MA
Wm.: b 10-4-1743 d *p.* 5-8-1782 m Mary Kenner Ens PS VA

SEAVER, (includes SEVER)
Calvin: b 1758 d 10-2-1840 m Mary Hovey Pvt Sgt MA ★
Daniel: b 1753 d 7-21-1831 m Martha Nutt Pvt MA ★
Ebenezer: b 4-26-1721 d 3-26-1785 m (1)Mary Weld (2)Tabitha Davenport Lt MA
Ebenezer: b 1745 d 1800 m (2)Mary Beebe QM MA
Joseph: b 12-1-1752 d 12-31-1832 m Abial Rich PS MA
Nathaniel: b 1750-2 d *p.* 1806 m Mary Bush Ens VT
Norman: b 1734 d 1787 m Sarah Reed Lt MA
Peter: b 1749 d *p.* 12-22-1777 m Hanah Cookus PS VA
Robert: b 1743 d 11-3-1828 m Joanna Parmenter Lt NH
Robert Whitmore: b 7-3-1762 d 7-31-1836 m Anna Edson Sgt MA
Shubael: b 8-11-1740 d 1-20-1827 m Deliverance Hyde Sgt MA
Thomas: b 2-19-1745 d 4-13-1832 m Hannah Wood 2Lt MA
Wm., Sr.: b 9-2-1721 d 3-4-1783 m Patience Trescott Pvt MA
Wm., Jr.: b 5-8-1743 d 7-28-1815 m (1)Rebecca Hunt (2)Mary Foster (3)Thankful Stetson BG MA
Wm., Jr.: b 1763 d 9-22-1822 m Mary Everitt Pvt MA
Wm.: b 10-12-1729 d — m Sarah Warren PS MA

SEAVEY, (includes SEAVERY, SEVERY & SEVEY)
Isaac: b 1753 d 3-31-1839 m Abigail Gardner Matr NH ★
Jonathan: b 8- -1758 d 8-26-1846 m (1)Priscilla Philbrooke (2)Sarah Towle Sol NH
Joseph: b c. 1717 d p. 1790 m Sarah Scott Capt MA
Joseph: b 8-24-1727 d 1779 m Almina McKenney Pvt MA
Joseph: b c. 1746 d p. 1790 m (1)Sarah Locke (2)Susannah Kennison Sgt PS NH
Joseph: b 6-12-1747 d 10-15-1826 m Elizabeth Knight Pvt NH
Moses: b 1734 d p. 4-15-1794 m Hulda Locke PS NH
Nicholas: b 8-4-1717 d p. 1790 m Hannah Leach PS CS MA
Paul: b c. 1740 d c. 1800 m Sarah Wallis PS NH
Reuben: b 1757 d p. 1789 m Lucy — Sgt MA
Reuben: b 1760 d 6-29-1811 m Elizabeth Burnham Sgt MA
Stephen: bpt 3-3-1751 d p. 1802 m (1)Elizabeth Wilde (2)Jane Chism Pvt NH
Wm.: b 1745 d 3-15-1829 m Anna Trefethern LT NH
Wm.: b 1-31-1724 d p. 1790 m Ruth Moses PS NH

SEAWRIGHT,
Gilbert: b 9- -1740 d 1815 m Esther Seawright Lt PA
James: b c. 1745 d 4-6-1790 m Elizabeth McCullough Pvt PS SC

SEAY,
Abraham: b c. 1729 d a. 2-23-1829 m Miss Loving Pvt PS VA
Austin: b 12-25-1759 d 2-1-1836 m Elizabeth Weaver Sgt VA ★
Jacob: b 12-6-1758 d 1850 m Rebecca Davis Pvt VA ★
James: b 4-6-1752 d p. 1840 m Elizabeth Crank Pvt VA
Joseph: b c. 1753 d 4-2-1847 m — Pvt VA ★
Joseph: b 1767 d 1845 m Nancy Harvey Sol VA

SEBASTIAN,
Benjamin: b 6-29-1739 d 11-20-1832 m Amelia Broadwater Pvt VA

SEBREE,
John: b 1749 d 1781 m Mildred Johnson Pvt VA
Richard: b 3-29-1752 d 9-5-1835 m Esther Watts Pvt VA ★

SEBRELL,
Frederick: b 1761 d 5-10-1811 m Catharine — Pvt MD

SEBRING,
Abraham: b 6-23-1758 d 4-16-1839 m Nancy Ann Harris Pvt NJ ★
Fulkard: b 1745 d 1822 m Sophia Hourning Pvt PA
John: b 1725 d 1796 m (1)Abby — (2)Nancy Ann Harris Capt NJ
Roelof: b 1-19-1729 d 4-25-1782 m Catharine Auten Capt NJ
Thomas: b 11-4-1744 d 5-31-1815 m Rachel Lee Capt PA

SECHLER,
Andrew: b c. 1748 d 9- -1830 m Elizabeth Bankes Pvt PA
John: b 3-2-1739 d 12-24-1831 m Christiana Goodman Sgt PS PA
Michael: b 1762 d 2-26-1847 m Rebecca Love Pvt PA

SECOR,
Daniel: b 1755 d 3-21-1829 m Margaret VanHorn Drm NY
David, Jr.: b 11-27-1749 d 8-6-1818 m Bridget Ferguson PS NY
Isaac: b 1739 d 5-1-1810 m Mary Gedney Pvt NY
Isaac: b 1756 d p. 1790 m Maria Semen Pvt PS NY
Isaac: b 1751 d 1818 m Eleanor Scouten Sol NY
James: b 3-29-1745 d 1832 m Rachel Taylor Pvt NY ★
James: b 1751 d p. 1813 m Abigail — Sgt NY
John: b 1-13-1764 d 9-27-1845 m Mary — Pvt NY

SECRIST,
Frederick: b c. 1750 d c. 1822 m (2)Catherine — Pvt PS VA
Jacob: b 1754 d p. 12-21-1835 m (1)Barbara — (2)Nancy — PS NC
Jacob: b 1760 d 2-28-1831 m Christina Foulk Pvt PA
John: b 8-8-1764 d 4-3-1841 m Veronica Raymond Pvt PA
Melker: b 1754 d 1835 m Mary Earlhart Pvt PA ★

SEDGWICK, (includes SEDWICK)
Abraham: b 4-27-1721 d p. 1790 m Abi Brace Capt CT
Benjamin: b a. 1742 d — m Christiana — Sol VA
John: b 3-7-1742 d 8-28-1820 m (1)Abigail Andrews (2)Mrs Sarah Lewis LCol CT
John: b 1742 d p. 1781 m Elizabeth Lander Cook PS MD
Joshua: b 1744 d 4- -1794 m — Manning Pvt CT
Samuel: b 4-11-1725 d 1794 m (1)Deborah Higgins (2)Hannah K. Barker Sgt CT
Samuel, Jr.: b 3-14-1754 d 8-20-1828 m Anna Steele Capt CT ★
Theodore: b 5- -1746 d 1-24-1813 m (1)Pamela Dwight (2)Abigail Williams (3)Penelope Russell LCol MA
Timothy: b 12-7-1763 d 9-13-1833 m (1)Lucy Sedgwick (2)Annie L. Barber Pvt CT
Wm.: bpt 6-6-1762 d p. 1818 m Lucy Merrill Pvt CT ★

SEE,
Abraham: b 10-1-1753 d 1-4-1813 m Sarah Storms Pvt NY
George: b 1756 d p. 1835 m Martha George Pvt VA
John: b c. 4-14-1752 d 6-26-1828 m Rachel Martling Pvt NY
John: b 1757 d 1836/7 m Margaret Jarret Pvt VA ★
Michael, Sr.: b c. 1730 d p. 1784 m Barbara Harness PS VA
Michael, Jr.: b c. 1751 d 8- -1791 m Elizabeth Morris Sol VA

SEEBER, (includes SEBER, SIEBER & ZIEBER)
Christian: b c. 1754 d a. 1-18-1797 m Catharine — Pvt PA
Henry: b 3-15-1741 d 5-15-1845 Veronica Barleth Pvt NY ★
Jacob: b 1738 d — m Polly Forbes Capt NY
Johannes Wilhelm: b 11-15-1721 d 9-1-1777 m (1)Maria Catherine Walbrathin (2)Mary Elizabeth Goeblin LCol PS NY
John: b 11-17-1750 d 11-23-1829 m Elizabeth Markley Pvt PA
Philip: b 11-15-1757 d 7-25-1825 m Catharine Schultz Pvt PA
Saffreness: b c. 1750 d 8-6-1777 m Sally P Yates 1Lt NY
Wm.: b 6-15-1747 d 1828 m Elizabeth Schrierrin Lt NY

SEEBOLD,
Christopher, Sr.: b 1743 d 1813 m Barbara Spade Pvt PA
Christopher, Jr.: b 9-3-1763 d 5-6-1839 m Anna Eva Hocklander Pvt PA
Leonard: b c. 1728 d 4- -1807 m — Pvt PA

SEEDS,
George: b 1753 d 4-9-1780 m Sarah Mitchell Pvt NY
George: b 1750 d 11-25-1836 m Margaret Hoopes Pvt PA

SEEGER,(includes SAGER, SAGARE, SEAGER, SECOR, SEGAR SEGER & SEGOR)
Caleb: b 6-14-1758 d p. 1798 m Sally Hannah Goodenow Pvt Matr MA
Elijah: b 1754 d 2-11-1851 m (1)Esther Beach (2)Eunice Hawley Pvt CT ★
Evert: bpt 5-29-1720 d p. 1780 m Sarah Orchert Pvt NY
Ezekiah: b 11-13-1753 d 7-12-1851 m Abigail Bixby Pvt MA ★
Garret: b 6-4-1753 d 9-1-1840 m Catharine Shaver Pvt NY ★
George: b 1-19-1744 d 1842 m Maria Elizabeth Schutz Pvt PA
Gideon: b 10-4-1749 d 2-26-1839 m Keziah Huggins Lt VT
John Christian: b 1-26-1731 d 11-30-1800 m Maria Susanna Kern Pvt PA
Joseph: b 10-13-1757 d 6- -1845 m — Morgan Arfr CT ★
Malaechia: b 11- -1737 d 3- -1810 m Hannah Vandenburg Pvt NY
Nathaniel: b 1750 d 5-10-1847 m Mary Russell Sol MA
Nicholas: b 5-16-1759 d 1-7-1835 m (1)Eva Balliet (2)Maria Stofflet Lt PA
Thomas: bpt 1-16-1726 d 3-25-1809 m (1)Seintje Wieler (2)Judith Hogeland CS NY

SEEKEL,
Abiather: b 11-26-1763 d 9-28-1835 m Martha Parks Pvt RI MA ★

SEELEY, (includes SEELYE & SEELY)
Abel: b 10-1-1739 d 1806 m Betsy Briggs Pvt CT
Abner: b 2-17-1739/40 d p. 1784 m Hannah Thayer Capt CS VT
Bezaleel: b 8-20-1725 d p. 1792 m Zerviah — PS NY
David: b a. 1751 d p. 1796 m Lucy Owen Pvt NY
Denton: b 2-4-1758 d 2-1-1837 m Charity Wells Pvt CT
Ebenezer: b 8-17-1755 d p. 8-13-1833 m Mary Bell Fif CT ★
Ebenezer: b 3-26-1756 d 6-23-1837 m Mabel Todd Pvt CT
Ebenezer: b 1-10-1761 d 5-21-1842 m (1)Anna Coley (2)Mrs Betsey Hill Pvt CT ★
Ebenezer: b 9-27-1761 d 11-30-1840 m Mary Clark Pvt NJ
Eli: b 10-9-1764 d 9-20-1850 m (1)Zipporah Worden (2)Sally Lyon Cpl NY ★
Eliphalet: b 8-20-1701 d 5-3-1784 m Sarah Holly Lt CT
Enos: b c. 1721 d 6-22-1801 m Naomi Petty LCol NJ
Ephraim, Sr.: b 1717 d 1777 m Keziah — Pvt CT
Ephraim, Jr.: b 12-30-1748 d 3-20-1840 m (1)Electa — (2)Eleanor — (3)Hannah Harshorn Lt NH VT ★
Ezra: b 1746 d 8-14-1827 m Mary Sherwood Sgt CT
Gideon, Sr.: b 9-7-1729 d 12- -1804 m Deborah Lockwood Capt NY
Gideon, Jr.: b 5-15-1764 d 2-15-1844 m (1)Mabel Todd (2)Esther Owen (3)Patience Jermaine Pvt NY
Isaac: b 1751 d 2-4-1844 m Elizabeth — Pvt CT ★
Israel: b a. 1750 d 1810 m Peggy Bromley Pvt VT
James: b 7-29-1722 d 12-5-1809 m Hannah — PS CT
James: b c. 1760 d 1848 m Mary Smith Pvt CT
Jedidiah: b c. 1752 d 3-17-1813 m — PS NJ
John: b 1758 d 7-30-1838 m Mercy Harding Pvt MA ★
John: b 9-21-1759 d 4-19-1809 m Elenora Pease Pvt NY
John: b 1749 d 1835 m — Ens PA ★
John: b c. 1710 d 2- -1792 m Jean — PS SC
Jonas: b 5-13-1752 d 12-13-1814 m Elizabeth Sayer Pvt CT
Jonathan: b 9-11-1758 d 10-30-1839 m (1)Elizabeth Bromley (2)Martha Freelove Bromley Pvt VT ★
Jonathan S.: b 1740 d 1805 m Deborah Barker Pvt VT
Joseph: b 3-25-1751 d 5-4-1812 m Hannah Hoyt Sgt CT
Josiah: b 1755 d 1832 m Rebecca Gibbon Lt NJ
Josiah: b 9-22-1736 d 9-29-1803 m Abigail Smith 1Lt NY
Justus: b 1712 d p.10-25-1795 m (1)Elizabeth Gibbs (2)Phebe Bissell Tms CT
Justus, Jr.: b 9-18-1751 d 1795 m Sarah Stuart Pvt CT
Michael: b 4- -1750 d 5-11-1823 m Sarah De Pue Pvt NJ
Nathan: b 1743 d 6-24-1787 m Deborah Gregory Lt CT
Nathaniel, Sr.: b 1726 d a. 2-1-1810 m Rebecca Hubbell Capt PS CT
Nathaniel, Jr.: b 10-16-1748 d 4-30-1806 m Rhoda Bennett Pvt CT
Nehemiah: b 9-18-1743 d 6-17-1802 m Mary Hopkins Capt NY
Nehemiah: b 3-6-1757 d 6-11-1821 m Deborah Wood Pvt NY
Peter: b c. 1740 d 12- -1811 m Sarah — Pvt SC
Samuel: b 1740 d 4-27-1777 m Sarah Silliman Pvt CT

Samuel: b 1761 d 1-10-1827 m Mercy Bartlett Cnt NY ★
Samuel: b 6-10-1756 d 9-28-1819 m Patience Morrell Capt NJ ★
Seth: b 1739 d 5-23-1817 m Joanna Odell Ens CT
Sylvanus: b 11-17-1738 d 11-4-1797 m (1)Sarah Jones (2)Rebecca
  Tuttle Pvt CT
Sylvanus: b 12-19-1745 d 4-17-1821 m Jane Williamson Col NJ
Thaddeus: b 7-18-1758 d 3-24-1830 m Sarah Scofield Cpl NY ★

SEEM,
George: b 10-4-1742 d 11-12-1826 m Margaret Newhard Pvt PA

SEES,
George: b 1754 d 7-11-1783 m Mrs Margaret — Lt PA
Melchior: b 2-16-1759 d 6-27-1835 m Sophia Lint Sol PA

SEFTON,
John: b c. 1734 d 12- -1799 m Elizabeth Giles Wootton PS MD

SEGENDORPH, (includes SAGENDORF)
Adam: bpt 7-7-1754 d p. 1790 m Elizabeth Meyer 2Lt NY

SEGHNER,
John Paul: b c. 1740 d p. 3-23-1786 m Maria Elizabeth Eiseman Cpl
  NY

SEGURA,
Francisco: b c. 1756 d 9-18-1831 m Maria de Prados PS LA

SEIBERLING,
Christian: b 1733 d 1820 m Ernestine Louisa Hobben Pvt PA

SEIDEL, (or SIDLE)
Henry: b 3-31-1732 d 8-21-1801 m Anna Catharine Rodmacher Pvt
  PS PA
Nicholas: b 1734 d 6-27-1798 m Anna Maria — Arfr PA
Peter: b 1760 d 9-12-1838 m (1)Katherine — (2)Mary Roan Mus PA

SEIFERT, (includes SEYFERT, SIFRID, SIFRITT & SYFRED)
Andrew: b 3-16-1755 d 10-16-1847 m (1)Susanna Shrock
  (2)Hannah Marrle Pvt VA ★
Conrad: b 1760 d 7-8-1822 m Sarah — Lt PA
Daniel: b c. 1755/6 d c. 1850 m Barbara Sheumer Matr PA
Jacob, Sr.: b c. 1738 d 4- -1786 m Elizabeth — Pvt PA
Jacob, Jr.: b 1758 d 10- -1826 m Susan Marg. Spahr Pvt PA
Johann Michael: b 9-26-1753 d 1818 m Maria Magdalene Wilt PS PA

SEIGLER,
David: b c. 1740 d 1806 m Rachel — Pvt PS SC
George: b 7-10-1750 d 5-11-1822 m Ruth Brooks Pvt SC

SEIP, (or SIPE)
Christopher: b 1732 d 1801 m Margaret Phillips Pvt PA
George: b1759 d 8-21-1843 m (1)Catherine Klein (2)Mary
  Magdalena PS PA
Henry, Sr.: b a. 1734 d p. 5-29-1821 m Mary — PS PA
Henry, Jr.: b 1762 d 1839 m Martha — PS PA
Jacob: b 9- -1741 d 4-7-1831 m Anna Rosina Mertz Pvt PA
Manuel: b 1758 d 1823 m Annie Cline Pvt PA
Peter: b 6-8-1735 d 2-19-1809 m Anna Maria Erb Pvt PA
Wilhelm: b 4-10-1747 d 9-13-1794 m (1)Margaret Schaefer
  (2)Suzanna Gildner Pvt PA

SEITZ, (or SITES)
Charles: b c. 1754 d p. 1790 m Charlotte Gerber 2Lt PA
George: b 1755 d 10-6-1824 m Catherine Burkhart Pvt PA
Henry: b c. 1767 d 1814 m Mary Shultz Pvt PA
Henry: b — d p. 12-18-1802 m Nancy — Pvt PA
Jacob: b c. 1740 d 1822 m Elizabeth Witmer Pvt PA

SEITZINGER,
Michael: b 9-29-1763 d 9-18-1838 m Margaret Vanderslice Pvt PA
Nicholas, Sr.: b 12-25-1725 d 12-19-1786 m Anna Maria Filsmeyer
  PS PA
Nicholas, Jr.: b 12-27-1758 d 7-5-1834 m (1)Barbara Setley
  (2)Catherine Printz OrdlSgt PA ★

SEIXAS,
Benjamin Mendez: b 1-17-1747 d 8-16-1816 m Zipporah Levy 3Lt
  NY
Gershom Mendez: b 1-14-1745 d 7-2-1816 m Elkalah Cohen PS NY

SELBY,
James: b 1760 d 1801 m (1)Elizabeth Selby (2)Mary Hickman Bell
  Pvt MD
Mordecai: b 1736 d 1835 m Hannah — PS MD
Nicholas: b c. 1750 d 8-11-1825 m Lucretia Evans Pvt PS MD
Wm.: b 6-8-1717 d 6-6-1804 m (1)Hannah Brainard (2)Dorothy
  Booge (3)Mrs Anna Sparrow PS CT
Wm. Atkinson: b 11-28-1757 d 8-2-1809 m Sarah White Townsend
  Pvt MD

SELDEN,
Asa: b 1760 d 12-2-1840 m Siley Leland Pvt MA ★

Calvin: b 3-14-1763 d 10-28-1820 m Phoebe Ely Lt CT
Cary: b 1723 d 1792 m Elizabeth Jennings PS VA
Charles: b 11-23-1755 d 1-1-1820 m Abigail Jones Capt CT
Elias: b 8-27-1758 d 7-1-1817 m Ruth Kirby Pvt CT
Ezra, Sr.: bpt 11-5-1727 d 12-20-1814 m (1)Elizabeth Rogers
  (2)Amy Ely PS CT
Jonathan: b 6-15-1740 d 3-17-1808 m Mehitable Cady Pvt MA
Miles Cary, Sr.: b 1726 d 3-20-1785 m Rebecca Cary PS VA
Miles Cary, Jr.: b c. 1750 d 5-19-1811 m Elizabeth Armistead Col VA
Samuel: b 1-11-1723 d 10-11-1776 m Elizabeth Ely Col CT
Samuel: b 11-1-1748 d 1819 m Deborah Colt Lt CT
Thomas: b 9-22-1732 d 10-31-1821 m Jane Ferrand Pvt VT
Wilson Cary: b 1761 d 3-14-1835 m Mary Mason Page (2)Eleanor
  Love (3)Mary Bowles Alexander Dr VA

SELEE,
Nathan: b 1733 d 8-24-1815 m Love Penny Pvt MA

SELF,
John: b 3-4-1759 d 1836 m Sarah Harris Ens VA

SELFRIDGE,
John: b 10-12-1758 d 11-4-1849 m (2)Sarah — Pvt NY ★
Oliver: b 9-15-1759 d 11-27-1845 m Elizabeth Selfridge Pvt NY ★
Wm.: b c. 1733 d p. 1790 m Katharine McMaster Pvt NY

SELHEIMER,
Nicholas: b 1740 d c. 1822 m Elizabeth Powell Pvt PA W★

SELIN,
Anthony: b — d 2-3-1792 m Catherine Snyder Maj PA

SELKIRK,
James: b 11-22-1757 d 12-2-1820 m Elizabeth Henry Sgt NY

SELKRIGG,
Jeremiah: b 5-25-1756 d p. 11-4-1851 m Olive Stoddard FifMaj CT

SELL,
Abraham: b 1734 d 11- -1812 m Magdalene Pvt PA
Jacob: b 1756 d 2-5-1807 m (1)Hannah Levering (2)Hannah Bow-
  man Pvt PS PA
John: b c. 1733 d 10-2-1796 m Margaret Jones Pvt PA
Jonathan: b 3-17-1739 d 12-7-1800 m Nancy — Sol GA

SELLARD,
James: b 1758 d 9-6-1824 m Lydia De Wolf Pvt CT

SELLECK,
Daniel: b 1745 d 1-23-1819 m Mary Brown Pvt CT
Ebenezer: b c. 1733 d 5-1-1828 m Mary Hinman Pvt CT
Frederick: b 1755 d c. 1814 m Esther Hanford Cpl NY
Gershom: b 7-10-1730 d p. 1786 m Puella Gorham Pvt NY
James: b 1752 d 3-21-1809 m (1)Sarah Weed (2)Joanna Morgan
  Pvt CT
Joseph: b 2-14-1759 d 3-16-1846 m Phebe Clock Pvt CT
Nathan: b 5-26-1759 d a. 1840 m (3)Amy Holmes Pvt NY
Nathaniel: b 5-26-1759 d 9-25-1843 m Millicent Betts Pvt CT
Peter: b 12-8-1756 d 9-16-1840 m Mary Lockwood Pvt CT ★
Samuel: b 2-4-1734 d 1776 m Hannah Weed Pvt CT
Samuel: b c. 1750 d 8-5-1814 m Nancy Vance Pvt PA
Uriah: b 10-3-1762 d 9- -1822 m Hannah Smith Drm CT

SELLERS, (or SELLER)

Abraham: b 6-30-1758 d 9-27-1831 m Sophia Bodder Pvt PA
Christian: b c. 1747 d 1834-39 m Susannah Hill PS VA
Elisha: b c. 1744 d p. 11-16-1801 m (1)Sarah — (3)Mary Willis
  Pvt NC
Howell: b 3- -1762 d p. 10-17-1832 m Margaret Conner Pvt SC ★
Isaac: b 1747 d 1792 m Elizabeth Blackmore Sgt PA
Isham: b 1754/55 d p. 12-1-1827 m (1)Eunice — (2)Lydia — Pvt
  NC ★
James: b 1756 d 3-27-1793 m Pamelia Randell Sol Smn MA W★
John: b 8-19-1728 d 2-2-1804 m Ann Gibson CS PA
Jordan: b 2-16-1763 d 9-9-1838 m (1)Elizabeth Hunchy (2)Mary
  Osborne PS NC
Nathan: b 9-15-1751 d 7-14-1830 m Elizabeth Coleman Ens PA
Nathan: b 1762 d 1826 m Sarah Finley Pvt PA
Philip: b 1724 d 10-6-1808 m Barbara — Pvt PA
Samuel: b c. 1744 d p. 8-29-1794 m Zilpha Sellers Sol NC
Samuel: b 1752 d 2-2-1830 m — Pvt PA ★
Thomas: b c. 1745 d 1820 m — Pvt NC
Ulrich: b 1740 d p. 1782 m Elizabeth Giesi Ens PA
Wm.: b c. 1745 d p. 1790 m Tabitha Banks Pvt MA

SELLEW,
John: b 1746 d 12-21-1820 m Hannah Lombard Lt MA
Philip: b 1743 d 6-12-1828 m Elizabeth Smith PS CT

SELLMAN, (includes SELMAN)
James: b 12-27-1770 d 9- -1847 m (1)Martha Foster (2)Elizabeth
  Covington PS SC

SELLMAN, contd.
Jeremiah: b c. 1748 d 9-4-1817 m — Mil SC
John: bpt 5-6-1744 d 5-30-1817 m Deborah Girdler Capt MA
Jonathan: b 3-2-1753 d 5-21-1810 m (1)Rachel Lucas (2)Ann Elizabeth Harwood Maj MD
Jonathan: b 1751 d 9-9-1815 m Elizabeth Dawson PS MD
Thomas: b 11-29-1727 d 1794 m Ruth Shipley PS MD
Wm.: b c. 1720 d 1796 m Charity Sparrow PS MD

SELLON,
John: b c. 1754 d 10-4-1820 m Martha Moseley Pvt MA

SELLS,
John: b a. 1720 d 10-14-1781 m Sarah Haak Pvt PA
Ludwick: b 2-15-1743 d 10-13-1823 m Catherine Deardorff Sol PA

SELOVER, (includes SLOVER)
Abraham: b c. 1753/54 d 1834 m Martha Anderson Pvt VA
Andrew: b 5-16-1756 d p. 3-4-1845 m Maria Ebberts Pvt NY ★
Isaac: b 9-30-1759 d 12-25-1829 m Mehitable Betts Pvt NJ
Isaac: bpt 11-3-1734 d 1808 m Marie Johnson Pvt NJ
John: b 9-11-1765 d 12-5-1838 m Margaret Scobie Pvt Mar NJ ★
Luke: bpt 3-21-1731 d 1776 m — Neettje Lt NJ

SELTZER, (includes SELSER)
Christian: b 2-16-1749 d 2-3-1831 m (1)Marie Diewing (2)Elizabeth — Pvt PA
George: b 1756 d 2-24-1826 m Rachel Newman PvtPA
Jacob, Sr.: b 10-31-1732 d 10-18-1788 m Maria Catharina Heister CMman PA
Michael: b c. 1750 d p. 1811 m Barbara Caffery Pvt PS PA
Weyrich: b 1728 d 1799 m Elizabeth Lint Cpl PA

SEMMES,
Thomas: b 1758 d 6-14-1824 m (1)Mary Ann Branner (2)Mary Semmes Lt MD
Thomas: b 1748 d 6-14-1832 m Ann Queen PS MD

SENDERLING,
Christopher: b c. 1740 d p. 1790 m Anna Maria Detrick Pvt PA

SENEY,
John: b c. 1733 d 4- -1795 m Ruth Benton LCol MD

SENSEMAN,
John: b 7-17-1754 d 3-11-1817 m Justina Kimmell 2Lt PA

SENSENY,
Abraham: b 5-19-1761 d 2-23-1844 m Margaretta Huber PS PA

SENTELLE,
Samuel: b 1759 d 2-20-1844 m Nancy Stephens Sgt NC ★
Wm.: b 10-14-1756 d c. 5-7-1836 m Elizabeth Stevens Sol NC

SENTER,
Asa: b 1-19-1756 d 1-15-1835 m Mary Tufts Capt NH
Benjamin: b — d 7-9-1811 m Lydia Taylor Pvt NH
Isaac: b 1753 d 12-10-1799 m Elizabeth Arnold Dr RI
Joseph, Sr.: b 3-2-1723 d 5-27-1798 m Elizabeth Johnson LCol NH
Moses: b 1733 d 3-2-1813 m Priscilla — Pvt NH
Moses: b 4-25-1763 d 1854 m Sally Smith Pvt NH
Samuel: b 2-15-1752 d 2-11-1833 m Hannah Reed Pvt NH
Thomas: b 5-4-1753 d 3-25-1834 m (1)Esther Greeley (2)Mercy Jackson (3)Eunice White Sgt MA ★

SENTMAN,
Lawrence: b 1-13-1759 d 4-17-1815 m (1)Elizabeth Slyhoff (2)Mary Eliza Henry Pvt PA

SERRILL,
Jacob: b 11-13-1747 d p. 1790 m Hannah Pearson Pvt PA

SERVISS, (includes SERVIS)
George: b 2-23-1753 d 2-9-1812 m Mary Overbaugh Pvt NY
Philip: b c. 1750 d p. 5-26-1818 m — Lt NJ

SERVY,
Wm.: b c. 1760 d 11-6-1798 m Elizabeth Ward Pvt MA

SESSIONS,
Abijah: b 6-2-1753 d 5-22-1834 m Hannah May Ens CT ★
Abner: b 5-4-1722 d 2-18-1781 m Mrs Mary Wyman PS CS CT
Alexander, Jr.: b 12-26-1751 d 11-9-1823 m Sarah Grosvenor Lt MA
Amasa: b 8-10-1715 d 4-7-1799 m Hannah Miller CS PS CT
David: b 5-11-1749 d 9- -1824 m Rachel Stevens Pvt MA
Ebenezer: b 3-6-1748 d 8-28-1824 m Huldah Hayward Ens CT
John: b 5-27-1758 d 7-4-1836 m Mary — Pvt NC ★
John: b 1-9-1741 d 5-1-1820 m Ann Warstley PS VT
Joseph: b c. 1745 d 1-7-1836 m Delilah Whitley PS NC
Nathaniel: b 6-10-1750 d 10-5-1824 m (1)Irene Wales (2)Frances Chandler Pvt CT

Robert: b 3-15-1752 d 9-27-1836 m Anna Ruggles Lt PS MA
Samuel: b 11-26-1746 d 1818 m Abigail Ruggles Lt CT

SESSUMS,
Jacob: b 1752 d 4- -1792 m (1)Elizabeth Newsone (2)Frances — PS NC
Solomon: b 10-12-1746 d 2-12-1818 m Elizabeth Lloyd PS NC

SETH,
Wm. C.: b 1757 d 12-27-1815 m Martha Chamberlain Sgt MD

SETTLE, (includes SETTELE, SITTLEY & SUTTLE)
Edward: b 9- -1764 d 7-23-1839 m Elisabeth Hubbard Pvt VA
George: b c. 1732/3 d a. 7- -1820 m Mary Morgan PS VA
Henry: b 2-10-1721 d 2-19-1784 m Marie Barbra Kaepple PS PA
Johannes: b c. 1745 d a. 1802 m Maria Schieterlin Pvt NY
Neuman: b c. 1761 d a. 1- -1833 m Elizabeth — Pvt VA
Thomas: b c. 1760 d 1816 m (1)Mary — (2)Polly Brown (3)Mrs Priscilla Jefferson Pvt VA
Wm.: b a. 1761 d 1827 m — Cpl VA
Wm.: b c. 1720 d 3-25-1782 m Sarah — PS VA

SETTLEMEYER,
Godfrey: b c. 1753 d 4-27-1842 m Rosanna — Pvt PA ★

SETZER,
John: b 4-9-1760 d 12-13-1836 m Mary Schwartz Pvt VA

SEVERANCE,
Benjamin: b 1761 d 6-8-1845 m Mrs Rebecca Sweet Holcomb Pvt MA ★
Daniel: b 1751/52 d 3-10-1817 m Betsy — Pvt NH
Ebenezer: b 7-24-1709 d 3-24-1791 m Hannah — PS CS MA
Ebenezer: b 9-8-1752 d — m Lucy Nutting Sol NH
Ephraim: b 1759 d 3-6-1825 m Ruth Gould Pvt PS MA ★
John: b 12-15-1720 d 12-25-1805 m Esther Arms Pvt MA
Jonathan, Sr.: b 1725 d 1822 m Thankful Stebbins CS PS MA
Jonathan: b 1758 d 2-15-1835 m Mehitable Brown Pvt NH ★
Martin, Sr.: b 4-10-1718 d 4-8-1810 m Patience Fairfield PS CS MA
Martin, Jr.: b 3-8-1755 d 12-29-1843 m Lucy Whitney Pvt NH
Peter: b 1754 d 5-30-1817 m Sarah Hall Pvt NH
Samuel: b 6-12-1761 d 8-28-1833 m Azubah Smith Pvt MA

SEVIER, (includes XAVIER)
Abraham: b 2-14-1760 d 6-18-1841 m Mary Little Spy & Sol NC ★
Catherine Sherrill: b 8-3-1755 d 10-2-1836 m John Sevier PS NC
John: b 9-23-1745 d 9-24-1815 m (1)Sarah Hawkins (2)Catherine Sherrill Col PS NC
Robert: b p. 1747 d 10-7-1780 m Keziah Robertson Capt NC
Valentine, Sr.: b c. 1702 d 12-30-1803 m (1)Joanna Goad (2)Jemima — PS NC
Valentine, Jr.: b 1747 d 2-22-1800 m Naomi Douglas Maj PS CS VA W★

SEWALL, (includes SEAWALL & SEWELL)
Benjamin: b 1742 d 7-16-1821 m (1)Mary Booker (2)Susan Brown Tullocks Col PS NC
Clement: b c. 1758 d 1-7-1829 m Helen Carberry Ens MD ★
David: b 1746 d p. 1801 m Mary Tullis PS VA
Dummer, Sr.: b 12-12-1737 d 4-5-1833 m Mary Dunning LCol ME
Dummer, Jr.: b 1-15-1761 d 2-11-1846 m Jenny Dunning Pvt MA
Henry, Jr.: b 10-24-1752 d 9-4-1845 m (1)Tabitha — (2)Rachel Crosby (3)Elizabeth Lowell Capt MA
Henry: b 2-23-1740 d 1-24-1795 m Mary Stinson Capt PS MA
James: b 1738 d p. 1790 m Mrs Rachel Gassaway Pvt MD
John: b 1740 d 1805 m Mary Warfield Marriott PS MD
John: b c. 1758 d p. 1790 m Eliza Young Sgt MD
John: b 2-6-1760 d 1806 m Fanny Hobday Capt VA
Joseph: b 1753 d p. 1847 m — Pvt NC ★
Joshua: b 1755 d 1834 m Jennie Willis Sol NC
Jotham: b 1-1-1760 d 10-3-1850 m Jenny — Sol MA
Lewis: b 2-2-1760 d p. 7-4-1832 m Elizabeth Howard Wailes Pvt MD
Samuel: b 1-15-1750 d 2-18-1815 m Kitty White Sol NC
Samuel, Sr.: b — d p. 4-6-1789 m (1)Mary — (2)Elizabeth — PS NC
Thomas: b 1751 d 10-13-1834 m Hannah — QM Sgt CS VA ★
Thomas: b 1757 d 1822 m Mary Brown Sgt VA

SEWARD, (includes SEAWARD)
Aaron: b 2-24-1732/3 d p. 1779/80 m Elizabeth Clark Pvt NY
Benjamin: b — d c. 1805 m Ann Blake Pvt VA
Brotherton: b 7-28-1724 d 9- -1776 m Abigail Crane Sgt CT
Carter: b 1734 d 1-22-1814 m Rebecca — Pvt VA
Daniel: b 2-28-1758 d 1-15-1794 m Mary Lee MM NJ
David, Jr.: b 10-9-1748 d 5-29-1813 m Mabel Field Cpl CT
Enos: b 7-13-1735 d 8- -1820 m Sarah Gosse Pvt MA
George: b 10-2-1759 d 6-14-1834 m Mary Spencer Cpl NH
James: b c. 1760 d 1781 m — Pvt SC
Jedediah: b 1763 d 3-10-1830 m Susan Hodgkins Pvt CT ★
John: b 1740 d 1810 m Mary Lee Pvt MD
John: b 5-22-1730 d 12-29-1797 m Mary Swazy Col NJ
Josiah: b 2-22-1756 d 7-10-1828 m Sarah Osgood MM MA

Nathan: b 10-11-1758 d 11-9-1815 m Martha Gridley Cpl CT
Noadiah: b 2-14-1742 d 3-29-1825 m Sarah Swain Pvt MA
Richard: b 1- -17— d 10- -1832 m (1)Mollie Deering (2)Sarah
  Deering (3)Olive Fowler Mid PS NH MA★
Samuel: b 1-30-1734/5 d 1-30-1817 m Abigail Hull Pvt CT
Samuel: b 4-12-1757 d 12-8-1833 m Olive Adams Sgt MA
Samuel: b 1752 d 8-11-1829 m Sara Jobe Pvt NJ★
Samuel: b 9-18-1754 d 4-22-1828 m (1)Abigail Pitney (2)Ann Van
  Blear Pvt NJ
Silas: b 1760 d 1841 m Charlotta Seward Mus MA & CT★
Wm.: b 11-19-1747 d 1822 m Thankful Parmelee Chp CT
Wm.: b a. 1750 d p. 1783 m Nancy Lee Pvt MD

SEXTON,
Aaron: b c. 1764 d 8- -1827 m Jane Jameson Sgt VT★
Charles: b 1755 d 1803 m Rebecca — Pvt NJ
Elijah: b 10-15-1754 d 3-29-1839 m (1)Sybil Spencer (2)Thankful
  Sprague Pvt CT★
Ezra: b 1-25-1758 d p. 1834 m Patty Chapin Sgt CT★
George: b 9-2-1744 d 6-29-1815 m (1)Mary Stebbins (2)Chloe
  Chapen Pvt MA
George: b 11-14-1756 d 10-15-1815 m Lois Bostwick Capt VT★
Jared: b 1737 d 5-10-1785 m Anna Larison PS CS NJ
Jonathan: b 5-30-1754 d 1-14-1817 m Susannah Montgomery Sol
  CT
Joseph: b 9-21-1743 d 3-3-1807 m Rachel Richardson Pvt CT
Joseph: b 8-25-1753 d 4-20-1823 m Hannah Cadwell Sgt MA
Noah: b 3-2-1764 d 6-7-1838 m Martha Watt Pvt MA
Oliver Chapin: b 10-25-1760 d 12-30-1845 m Jerusha West Pvt MA
Samuel: b 2-9-1748 d 4-15-1826 m Theda Hastings Pvt CT
Samuel: b 6-22-1726 d 3-22-1816 m Sarah Chapin Lt MA
Wm.: b 1760 d 1821 m Nancy Reid Pvt VA

SEYBERT, (includes SEIBERT, SIBERT & SIVER)
Charles Frederick: b 1738 d 1777 m Mary — Pvt VA
Christian: b c. 1740 d p. 1800 m Catherine Holstein PS PA
Christian: b 1744 d 1838 m Mary — Pvt VA★
David: b 1760 d 10- -1836 m Susannah Stall Pvt PA★
Henry: b c. 1755 d p. 3-21-1795 m Rachel Thrah Pvt VA
Jacob: bpt 9-23-1760 d p. 1796 m Martha Radley Pvt NY
Jacob: b 2-3-1751 d 4-18-1830 m Sophia Keller Pvt PA
John: b 1760 d 1825 m — Wilmore Pvt SC
John Frederick: b 1759 d 1825 m Martha Curtis Pvt PA
Peter: b 8-18-1753 d p. 8-15-1828 m Elizabeth— Pvt PA
Sebastian: b a. 1750 d 1809 m Anna Maria Bowman Sgt PA
Wendel: bpt 5-15-1721 d 1801 m Catherine Rice Sgt PA

SEYBOLT,
John, Sr.: b 1727 d 2-11-1797 m Mary Kneizer Pvt NY

SEYMOUR, (includes SEMOUR)
Aaron: b 3-4-1749 d 8-20-1820 m Anna Phelps Pvt CT
Aaron: b 3-11-1744 d 11-26-1795 m (1)Abigail — (2)Jerusha
  Alvord Pvt CT
Abel: b 5-5-1760 d 8-26-1823 m Ann Van Meter Sol VA
Abijah: b 7-12-1754 d 3-26-1847 m Elizabeth Hine Pvt VA
Allyn: b 7-12-1757 d 7-15-1828 m Amelia Stanley Pvt CT
Asa: b 9-16-1756 d 2-12-1837 m Abigail Deming Pvt CT
Asa: b 3-5-1760 d 10-28-1810 m Elizabeth Denison Pvt CT
Ashbel: b 1-25-1748 d 7-31-1814 m (1)Lucy Abigail Welles
  (2)Honor Willard Sgt CT
Charles: bpt 1-29-1738 d 5-16-1802 m Lucy Whitman Capt CT
Daniel, Sr.: b 7-19-1730 d 11-8-1815 m Lydia King Capt CT
Ebenezer: b a. 1757 d 1808 m Achsah Woodruff Pvt CT
Eli: b 11-1-1761 d p. 1838 m (1)Amy Marsh (2)Mrs Salome Sexton
  Pvt CT
Elias: b 8-23-1738 d p. 1782 m Tryphena Hurlbut Pvt CT
Elias: b 2-28-1746 d 10-6-1828 m Elizabeth Wolcott Pvt CT
Elisha, Sr.: b 1722 d 1790 m Abigail Sedgwick Sgt CT
Elisha, Jr.: b 1-27-1744 d 10-20-1776 m Rhoda Sedgwick Sgt CT
Ezra: b 6-29-1748 d 1815 m (1)Abigail Waterbury (2)Sarah Hanford
  Pvt CT
Freeman: b 1-17-1756 d 4-29-1800 m Mary Carter Pvt CT
Hezekiah: b 7-11-1745 d 8-28-1815 m Ruth Kellogg Pvt CT
Horace: b 1760 d — m Hope Jones Capt CT
James: b 5-26-1752 d 12-11-1835 m Rebekah Keeler QMSgt CT
Jesse: b 6-30-1754 d 1829 m Mercy Fancher Ens NY
Joash: b 1742 d p. 1789 m (1)Margaret Lathrop (2)Phoebe Bronson
  Pvt CT
John: b 11-22-1726 d 2-2-1814 m Lydia Wadsworth Lt CT
John: b 1711 d 9-8-1796 m Ruth Belden Pvt CT
Jonathan: b 8-27-1759 d 7-26-1819 m Abigail Hart Pvt CT
Joseph: bpt 2-23-1751/2 d 1828 m — Sol CT
Josiah: b 10-11-1759 d 12-20-1804 m Dinah Doolittle Sol CT
Levi: bpt 3-19-1764 d 1850 m Huldah Bevans PS CT
Moses: b 7-25-1742 d 9-17-1826 m Molly Marsh Capt CT
Nathan: b a. 1760 d p. 1796 m Elizabeth Warner Pvt CT
Nathaniel: b 2-18-1757 d 9-12-1846 m (1)Mercy Carter (2)Marion
  Dickson Pvt CT★
Noah: b 11-10-1759 d 3-6-1832 m Miriam Kellogg Pvt CT
Phelix: b 1725 d 2- -1798 m Margaret Renick PS VA
Richard: b 1758 d 1848 m Margaret McCoy Pvt GA
Samuel: b 10-20-1759 d 7-25-1821 m Lydia Hanford Sol Fif CT

Samuel: b 9-21-1756 d 1-23-1834 m Anna Whitney Pvt CT★
Samuel: b 1730 d 4- -1818 m Sarah Betts PS CT
Seth: b c. 1740 d 1777 m Anna Benedict Capt CT
Stephen: b 7-21-1718 d 11-13-1807 m (1)Mehitable Hickox (2)Mary
  Elwell Capt CT
Thaddeus: b 8-25-1737 d 1- -1811 m Mrs Molly Smith Pvt PS NY
Thomas: b 3-17-1735 d 7-30-1829 m Mary Ledyard LCol CT
Thomas: b 1727 d 2-16-1812 m Sarah Rockwell Pvt CT
Thomas: b 1756 d 4-16-1831 m Catherine Hider Pvt VA
Thomas Young: b 6-19-1757 d 5-16-1811 m (2)Susan Bull Capt CT★
Truman: bpt 11-9-1760 d 7-27-1812 m Zibiah Packard Pvt CT
Uriah: b 9-9-1735 d 1800 m (1)Elizabeth Andrus (2)Mary Hopkins
  Capt CT
Wm.: b 1730 d 1821 m Lydia St John Lt CT
Wm., Sr.: b 8-18-1728 d 11-18-1782 m Mehitable Merrill PS CS CT
Wm., Jr.: b 11-15-1754 d 12-22-1841 m Sarah Patrick Pvt Fif CT★
Wm.: b 4-13-1758 d 4-18-1811 m Esther Sands Fif CT
Zachariah: b 1-4-1759 d 7- -1822 m Elizabeth Colt Pvt Cpl CT★
Zachariah: b 9-24-1712 d 8-27-1777 m (1)Sarah Steele (2)Elizabeth
  Pvt CT
Zadock: b 4-30-1757 d 11-2-1845 m Naomi Munger Pvt CT
Zebulon: b 9-12-1736 d 7-27-1807 m Ann Marsh Ens CT

SEYNOR, (or SEHNER)
Jacob: b 1-23-1757 d 1798 m Magdelene Neff Pvt PA
Michael: b 1754 d 11-18-1829 m Mary Schrader Pvt PA W★
Peter, Jr.: b 11-13-1749 d 5-9-1823 m Catherine Schafer Sol NC

SHACKELFORD, (includes SHACKLEFORD)
Benjamin: b 12-10-1733 d 1817 m Martha Jones Capt VA
Edmond: b c. 1746 d 1821 m Judith Eastin Capt VA
Francis: b 3-18-1739 d 5-5-1823 m Rebecca Ballard PS NC
George: b 1-19-1759 d 1- -1802 m Mary Shine Pvt NC
Henry: b 1750 d p. 1778 m Elizabeth — Sol VA
James, Sr: b 1728 d p. 1800 m (1)Elizabeth Scott (2)Mrs Mary
  Allen PS VA
James, Jr.: b 2-17-1763 d 1824 m Elizabeth Clarke Pvt VA
John: b 1745 d 1-4-1808 m (1)Rebecca Warren (2)Mary Mason
  Pvt VA★
John: b 1736 d 4-13-1800 m Frances Wade Butler Pvt VA
John: b 1758 d 1827 m Mary Hickman Pvt VA★
Lyne, Sr.: b c. 1731 d p. 1782 m Elizabeth Taliaferro CS PS VA
Roger: b 1744 d 11-24-1825 m (2)Nancy Carter (3)Sally Laird Sgt VA
Roger, Sr.: b c. 1700 d p. 12-24-1779 m (1)Carey Baker (2)Mrs
  Drucilla Hendrix PS VA
Stephen: b 9-23-1756 d 10-18-1834 m Susannah — Lt PS NC
Wm.: b 1738 d 11-23-1777 m Rebecca Cook Lt VA
Wm.: b c. 1745 d p. 1785 m Elizabeth — Sol VA
Zachariah: b c. 1745 d 1810 m Dolly — Lt VA

SHACKFORD,
John: b 10-28-1754 d 12-28-1840 m (1)Esther Woodwell (2)Mrs Elsie
  Olmstead PVT MA
Paul: b — d 1-27-1787 m Rebecca Hudson Pvt MA
Samuel: b 6-8-1728 d 4-12-1812 m (1)Elizabeth Ring (2)Mrs Eleanor
  Jackson Marshall Pvt NH
Theodore: b 9-9-1733 d 10-18-1809 m Mary Bartlett PS NH

SHACKLETT, (or SHACKLETTE)
Edward: b 10-17-1758 d 4-23-1826 m Elizabeth Rector Sgt VAW★
John 2nd: b 1743 d 10- -1809 m Barbara Juich Pvt PA

SHAD,
Solomon: b 1759 d 4-23-1833 m Mary Garbet 2Lt GA

SHADDAY,
John: b 2-26-1754 d 2-21-1859 m Mary Fogleman Pvt NC★

SHADDEN, see CHADEAYNE

SHADDOCK, (or SHADDUCK)
James: b c. 1735 d p. 1-10-1793 m Hannah Samuel Pvt VA
Thomas: b c. 1750 d 8-18-1815 m Eveline Frank Sgt NY W★

SHADE, (includes SCHADE)
Andrew: b c. 1725 d 9-3-1786 m (1)Marie Elizabeth Kraft (2)Maria
  Eva Ketner PS PA
Boston: b 1757 d 1817 m — Pvt PA
John: b 6-11-1756 d 1816 m Mary Catherine Pvt PA

SHADEL,
Henry, Jr.: b 5-24-1761 d 11-22-1828 m Eve C Liesering Pvt PA

SHAFF,
Frederick: b 5- -1753 d 5-17-1860 m Mary Purine Pvt NY★

SHAFFER, (includes SCHAEFFER, SHAFER, SHAVER)
Abraham: b 12-17-1754 d 1-11-1820 m Sarah Armstrong Capt NJ
Abraham: b 1749 d 3-8-1816 m Barbara — Pvt PA
Adam: b 4-5-1740 d 9-5-1794 m Susanna — PS MD
Adam, Sr.: b 5-9-1724 d 11-8-1800 m Maria M Hiltz Pvt NY
Adam, Jr.: b 8-15-1762 d 9-25-1838 m (1)Magdelina Frantz
  (2)Helena Schaefer Pvt NY

SHAFFER, contd.
Adam: b 3-3-1755 d 12-15-1807 m Laura Shufeldt Pvt NY
Adam: b 1746 d 10-6-1812 m Anna Elizabeth Leidner Pvt PA
Adam: b 1751 d 11-19-1840 m Catherine Trope Pvt PA ★
Adam: b 1754 d 2-29-1848 m (1)Elizabeth Swartwood (2)Sarah
   Baker Pvt PA ★
Adam: b 1755 d 6-1-1846 m Susannah — Pvt PA
Alexander: b 1-8-1712 d 4-10-1786 m (1)Anna Engle (2)Catharine
   Unger PS PA
Andreas: b 1737 d p. 1-10-1824 m Gertrude — Sol PA
Andrew: b 11-1-1759 d 12-2-1853 m Martha Mary Stroup Pvt MD ★
Andrew: b 1757 d 1827 m Elizabeth Chambers Pvt PA ★
Anthony: b 1744 d 1825 m Maria Catherine Reeg Pvt PA
Belschazzer: b 4-1-1742 d 5-4-1811 m Magarette Eppinger Sol GA
Casper: b 1712 d 12-17-1784 m Maria Catrina Bernhardt PS NJ
Charles: b 6- -1742 d 1- -1812 m Elizabeth Smith Lt NY
Daniel: b 2-11-1760 d 3-21-1835 m Mary Magdalene Kobessen
   Pvt PA
DeWalt: b 12-3-1756 d 6-18-1834 m Elizabeth Bouhal Pvt NY
Elizabeth Warner: b 1760 d p. 6-4-1839 m Henry Shaffer PS NY
Frederick: b c. 1738 d a. 3-5-1830 m — Pvt PA
Frederick: b a. 1738 d p. 1790 m Barbara Zimmerman Pvt PA
Frederick: b 1738 d 1832 m Margaretha Rebmonnin Pvt PA
Frederick: b a. 3-7-1729 d a. 5-10-1786 m Elizabeth — PS SC
Frederick: b 12-14-1755 d 12-19-1855 m Barbara Ann Fry Pvt VA ★
George: b 1759 d 3-4-1828 m Charity Becker Pvt NY W★
George: b 1725-27 d 7-11-1796 m (1)Elizabeth — (2)Margaret
   Eidenauer (3)Barbara Stucky 2Lt MD
George: b 11- -1755 d 8- -1826 m Katherine Margaret Coons Maj
   PA
George: b c. 1728 d 1-30-1792 m Maria Catharine Ruhlin 2Lt PA
George: b 1763 d 3-1-1837 m Susan Pifer Pvt PA
George 2d: b 4-25-1757 d p. 1817 m Catharine Strubel Pvt PA
George Lewis: b 1755 d 12-27-1829 m Catharine — Sol PA
Henricus: b 9-25-1758 d 8-27-1832 m Sophia Hilts Gnr NY
Henry: b 6-1-1757-9 d 4-15-1839 m Elizabeth Warner OrdlSgt
   NY W★
Henry: b 6-5-1749 d 10-12-1803 m (1)Anna Eva Schweitzer
   (2)Margaret Hoffman Capt CS PA
Jacob: b 2-3-1725 d 2-4-1800 m Dorthea Broscher Pvt MD
Jacob: b 10-21-1762 d 8-15-1858 m (1)Engelge Van Slyck (2)Sally
   Priscilla Handy Pvt Tms NY ★
Jacob: b 9-3-1735 d 11-17-1809 m Anna M Bellinger Pvt NY
Jacob: b 1-6-1754 d 12-6-1813 m Margaret Feltzmeyer Cpl PA
Jacob: b c. 1757 d 8-9-1814 m Nancy Allen Pvt PA W★
Jacob: b c. 1714 d 5-11-1789 m Mary Barbara PS PA
John: b 1-11-1753 d 8-11-1823 m Ann Maria — Pvt PS MD
John: b c. 1750 d a. 3-10-1835 m Mary Blackwelder Pvt NC
John: b 2-20-1735 d 11-17-1804 m Anna Sophia Lesh Capt PA
John: b 9-11-1762 d 10-16-1829 m Mary Glass Maj PA
John: b 1726 d 1801 m Anna Catherine Slack Pvt PA
John: b 4-27-1744 d 10-9-1816 m Barbara Maunasmith Pvt PA
John: b c. 1758 d 10-25-1823 m Margaretta Yungin Pvt PA
John: b 11-1-1756 d 1798 m Leah Norris Pvt VA
John: b 6-13-1755 d 4-27-1847 m Eve Kelknar Pvt VA ★
John Adam: b 10-31-1752 d 1-14-1840 m Elizabeth Klinefelder
   Capt PA
John Conrad: b 6-15-1751 d 11-21-1784 m Dorothy Crim Lt NY W★
John Peter: b a. 1757 d 1818 m Catherine Magdaline Hoefflich Pvt PA
Joseph: b 1731 d 12-2-1776 m Mary McClure Capt PA
Lambert: b 2-11-1753 d p. 7-27-1832 m Sarah Frymyer Pvt NY ★
Martin: b 8-30-1724 d p. 1808 m Elizabeth Catherine Laudensghlager
   PS PA
Michael: b 1735 d 1806 m Justina Haack Capt PA
Michael: b c. 1735 d 8-15-1780 m Catherine — Ens VA
Nicholas: b 1730 d 1797 m Maria Susanna Haag Capt PA
Nicholas: b 1-31-1736 d 6-20-1796 m Sussana De Turk Pvt PA
Nicholas: b c. 1750 d 1-7-1827 m (1)Juliana — (2)Regina — Pvt PA
Nicholas: b 1723 d 11-3-1780 m Juliana Margaretta Michael PS PA
Peter: b 1754 d 9-27-1826 m Caty Koolbach Pvt NJ
Peter: b 1763 d 9-6-1834 m Angelica Noman Pvt NY
Peter: b 4-5-1740 d p. 1794 m (1)Esther — (2)Margaret Kuntz
   Capt PA
Peter: b 1755 d 2-13-1840 m Catherine Trough Ens PA ★
Peter: b c. 1755 d p. 1810-12 m C Piper Pvt PA
Peter: b 2-4-1760 d 4-11-1846 m Susan Gussman Pvt PA
Peter: b c. 1750 d 1781 m Catherine Lorisch Pvt PA
Peter: b 2-2-1751 d 3-5-1848 m Catharine Albert Pvt PA ★
Peter: b p. 1750 d 4- -1781 m Sarah Riffle PS Spy VA
Philip: b 3-27-1761 d 11-6-1851 m Ann Maria Lore Pvt PA
Philip: b 9-29-1758 d 5-18-1847 m Sarah — Pvt PA
Peter Bernhardt: b 7-28-1744 d 4-6-1799 m Elizabeth Simpson Capt
   NJ
Simon: b 1- -1753 d 6-10-1824 m Susanna Hanna Pvt PA
Thomas: b 8- -1755 d 1850 m Mary — Pvt PA ★
Valentine: b 1740 d 1800-1810 m Cathrin Ruth Pvt PA

SHAFFNER, (includes SHAFNIR)
Charles: b 3-17-1762 d 5- -1845 m Maria Elizabeth Stoy Pvt PA
Martin: b 9-27-1759 d 2-28-1826 m Veronica Haldeman Pvt PA

SHAFTER,
James: b 9-15-1759 d 1-9-1816 m Abigail Johnson Sgt NH VT

SHAILOR, (includes SHAILER)
Asa: b 3-1-1736 d 12-13-1805 m Susanna Cone Pvt CT
Ezra: b 1-17-1739/40 d 12-17-1829 m Jerusha Brainerd Pvt CT
Hezekiah: b 2-2-1747 d 12-6-1834 m Hannah Dickinson CS CT
Joseph: b 1737 d 3-4-1816 m (1)Rachel Hough (2)Mrs Armstrong
   Lt CT
Rufus: b 5-4-1764 d 11-18-1861 m Hannah Cole Mil CT
Samuel: b 10-13-1758 d 5-25-1807 m Susannah Hazelton Capt CT

SHAINHOLTZ, (or SHOENHOLTZ)
Martin: b c. 1737 d 1807 m Ruth — Pvt PA

SHAKES,
George: b c. 1750 d c. 1789 m Mary Tanner Pvt MD

SHALLCROSS,
Leonard: b 9-7-1757 d 10-6-1826 m (1)Mary Livesey (2)Sarah
   Wilson Pvt PA

SHALLUS,
Jacob: b 1750 d 4-18-1796 m Elizabeth Melchoir Ens CS PA

SHAMBACK,
Daniel: b c. 1750 d p. 1797 m Catherine Hendricks Ens PA
George 2d: b c. 1755/6 d 1827 m Katherine Reger Pvt PA
Philip: b 3-22-1761 d 9-24-1844 m Hannah — Pvt PA

SHANAFELT, (or SHENAFELT)
John: b 1766 d 1832 m Elizabeth Shenefelt Pvt PA
Nicholas: b 3-11-1758 d 11-5-1826 m Anne — Pvt PA ★

SHANDS,
Wm.: b 9-5-1757 d 9-25-1844 m Lucy Oliver MM OrdlSgt VA ★

SHANE,
James: b 1745 d 6-27-1804 m Elizabeth — Pvt PA
Timothy: b 1751 d 3-21-1814 m Hannah Blunk Pvt MD

SHANER,
Henry: b 12-7-1757 d 1-6-1832 m Mary Magdalene Starner Pvt PA
   W★
Mathias: b c. 1740 d 2-10-1828 m Fannie Poe Sgt VA ★

SHANK,
Christian: b 10-10-1752 d 3-23-1832 m Mary Ann Elizabeth Baker
   Pvt PA
Christian: b 1-1-1751 d 3-21-1836 m Juliana Schmitin Cpl MD ★
George: b 1750 d 3-27-1826 m Maria — Pvt PA
Jacob: b 1750 d a. 7-27-1836 m Mary Steiwig Pvt PA
John: b 1761 d p. 10-27-1834 m — Pvt VA ★
Wentle: b c. 1742 d p. 1787 m Charlotte — Pvt PA

SHANKLAND,
Alexander: b 5-3-1756 d 2-20-1833 m Vintintia Willson Pvt NY W★
Rhoads: b 3-12-1740 d 10-12-1816 m (1)Ann May (2)Mary
   Emory (3)Elizabeth Wolfe Capt DE
Robert: b 1726 d 1796 m Sarah Beaty PS NY
Wm.: b 8-15-1762 d 4-17-1859 m Margaret Henry Pvt Spy NY ★

SHANKLIN,
Andrew: b 1760 d p. 1782 m Abigail Herring Lt VA
James: b 1737 d p. 1790 m Sarah Yearsley Pvt PA
Thomas: b 1750 d 1829 m — Pvt Lt SC

SHANKS,
Holden: b 3-22-1757 d p. 8-19-1831 m (1)Eloner Sample (2)Jane
   — Sol NC
John: b 12-25-1740 d 11-22-1825 m Mary Morris 1Lt CS MD
Matthew: b — d p. 6- -1810 m Ann — PS SC
Wm.: b 8-25-1747 d 7-27-1817 m Sarah Hanley Pvt PA

SHANKWEILER,
Jacob: b 1735 d 8- -1787 m Anna — Pvt PA

SHANNAHAN,
John: b a. 1740 d 6-17-1806 m Elizabeth — 1Lt MD

SHANNON,
David: b 1757 d 7-18-1811 m Jane Sample Pvt PA
George: b 1758/59 d 1-18-1803 m Jane Milligan Pvt PA
George: b 3- -1759 d 12-5-1840 m Ann Read Pvt PA ★
John: b 1-20-1743 d 1825 m Susan Alexander Sgt PA
John: b 1755 d 4-19-1836 m Jane Dunlap Sol PA
John: b 1758 d 9-3-1816 m Martha Reed Pvt PA
Nathaniel: bpt 4-20-1740 d 9- -1792 m (1)Ann Card (2)Elizabeth
   Kitson PS NH
Robert, Jr.: b c. 1763 d 1808 m Nancy MacGregor Pvt NY W★
Robert: b c. 1725 d 2- -1796 m Jean — Capt PA
Robert: b 1-23-1753 d 1-22-1827 m Catherine Davidson Lt NC
Samuel: b c. 1727/8 d a. 3-20-1813 m Martha — Capt PA
Samuel: b 1746 d c. 10-15-1781 m Elizabeth McGee Capt PA
Samuel: b 4-15-1750 d 5-14-1813 m Martha Bracken Lt PA
Thomas, Sr.: b c. 1735 d 1793 m Eleanor — Sol GA

Thomas: b 1760 d 4-16-1846 m (1)Sarah Pillsbury (2)Mrs Dolly Moore Pvt NH
Thomas: b 1-30-1749 d 5-28-1800 m Lillian Watson PS NH
Thomas: b 3-25-1753 d 11-12-1841 m Agnes Crowe Capt VA
Thomas: b 1742 d 1800 m Mary Reid Pvt PA
Wm.: b c. 1730 d 7-5-1784 m Mary — Cpl PA *Scott & eliot?*

SHAPLEIGH,
Dependence: b 3-5-1744 d 12-17-1812 m Catherine Leighton PS MA
Elisha: b 3-10-1749 d 2-11-1822 m Elizabeth Waldron Capt MA
James: b 3-5-1741 d 1-30-1806 m Hannah Bartlett Lt MA

SHAPLEY,
John: b 11-19-1756 d 3-16-1817 m Hannah Bartlett PS CT

SHARKEY,
Patrick: b c. 1720 d 1786 m Anne — Pvt PS VA

SHARON,
Samuel: b c. 176- d 1815 m Sarah Russell Lt PA
Wm.: b a. 1753 d 1809 m Sarah Whittaker Pvt PA

SHARP,
Abraham: b c. 1755 d p. 5- -1842 m Rebecca Armstrong Pvt Spy VA
Alexander: b 1756 d 1824 m Margaret McDowell Pvt PA
Andrew: b 1750 d 7-3-1794 m Mary Ann Wood Pvt PA
Anthony: b 1746 d 6-9-1812 m Margaret Nelson Capt NC
Asa: b 2-10-1746 d 1-12-1840 m Sarah Sabin Pvt CT
Benjamin: b — d 9-18-1787 m Ruth Foster Sol CT
Benjamin: b 1-22-1762 d 1842 m Hannah Fulkerson Pvt Spy VA ★
Caleb: b 11-8-1753 d 10-22-1833 m Alica Sanger Pvt CT ★
Daniel: b 6-12-1754 d 8-21-1840 m Jemima Eastman Pvt CS CT ★
David: b 6-12-1746 d 3-14-1836 m Chloe Holt Pvt CT
Edward: b c. 1740 d 1789 m Mary Graham CS NC
Eliakim: b 2-6-1761 d 9-5-1829 m Hannah Guthrie Sol NY
Elijah: b 8-22-1735 d 8-2-1794 m Lois Hammand Capt CT
George: b c. 1735 d 1813-15 m Catharine Fliegerty Capt NY
George: b 4-24-1748 d — m Rebecca Teator Lt NY
George, Sr.: b 1732 d 6-7-1812 m (1)Mary — (2)Mrs Rachel Johnson Capt PA
George, Jr.: b 1757 d 1840 m Mary Officer Pvt PA
George: b 1757 d 8-2-1826 m — Ens PA
Gershom: b 5-15-1720 d 9-29-1802 m Hannah Dana PS CT
Gibeon: b 7-4-1736 d 1822 m Thankful Hayford Pvt MA
Jacob: b 8-18-1734 d 1811 m Francina Skatts Pvt NY
Jacob: b 9-9-1725 d p. 5-9-1813 m Catherine Huyser PS NY
James: b 1754 d 1811 m Rachel Cannon Pvt NC
John: b 3-2-1762 d 10-4-1835 m Betsey Wynn Pvt GA ★
John: b 1756 d p. 1802 m Harriet Short Pvt NY
John: b 4-28-1753 d 11-1-1824 m Martha Young Lt NC
John: b — d p. 1-20-1830 m Phillis Efland PS NC
John: b 8-30-1745 d 1823 m Elizabeth Laughlin Ens NC
John: b 6-15-1744 d 5-17-1818 m Lilly McCoy Pvt NC
John, Sr.: b 1720 d p. 7- -1776 m Jane Hamilton Sol VA
John: b 1-2-1746 d 12-27-1815 m (1)Susan — (2)Mary Bridges Pvt PA
John: b 1755 d p. 1820 m Sarah Higgins Pvt PA ★
John: b c. 1757 d p. 7-2-1816 m Anne Boyd Pvt PA
John: b 1740 d 1830 m Anne Dooley Pvt VA
Jonathan: b c. 1750 d p. 1782 m Margaret Herriot Pvt NJ
Josiah: b 3-26-1761 d p. 1832 m — Pvt VA ★
Matthew: b 1751 d 1796 m Elizabeth Lindsay Pvt PA
Moses: b 5-2-1757 d 6-25-1820 m Elizabeth Walker Pvt PS VA ★
Richard: b 1-1-1735 d p. 9-17-1785 m Mary — Pvt VA
Robert: b 5-2-1742 d 6-30-1825 m Sarah Davis Ens CT
Robert: b 1748 d 9-12-1815 m Margaret Boyd Pvt PA
Robert: b 1752 d 1809 m Nancy — PS VA
Samuel: b 5-2-1736 d 12-29-1804 m Sophia — PS MD
Samuel: b 1745 d 6-8-1838 m Susanna Nowlin Pvt NC
Samuel: b 8-30-1734 d 10-15-1819 m Mary Harlow Starr PS PA
Solomon: b 2-29-1762 d 1847 m Katharine Sharp Pvt VA ★
Spencer: b 2-13-1762 d 12-29-1851 m Anna Arnold Sol VA
Starkley: b 1-1-1741 d 3-2-1791 m (1)Sarah Winborne (2)Jamima Hare CS NC
Thomas: b 5-28-1746 d 3-4-1805 m Mary Treadwell Pvt PS CT
Thomas: b 8-1-1742 d 9-6-1813 m Jean Maxwell Ens VA
Walter: b 1-5-1747 d 1788 m Elizabeth Harden Lt NC
Wm.: b 3-27-1740 d 2-23-1828 m Sarah Farrington PS CT
Wm.: b 12-13-1742 d 7-6-1818 m Catherine Reese Capt PS NC
Wm.: b 1750-60 d 10-6-1832 m Elizabeth James Pvt NC MD
Wm.: b c. 1760 d 1804 m Abrilla Johnson Sol NC
Wm.: b 1760 d 1806 m Jane McClintock Pvt VA
Wm.: b 1745 d 1833 m Lucy — Sgt VA
Wm., Sr.: b 1744 d 4- -1833 m Mary Meeks Pvt VA
Wm.: b 1737 d 9-20-1839 m Betsey Johnson Pvt Fif VA
Wm.: b c. 1760 d 12-17-1842 m (2)Elizabeth Massey Pvt VA ★

SHARPLESS,
Caleb: b 3-12-1750 d 7-4-1821 m Ruhaney Jordon Pvt DE
Daniel: b 3-30-1745 d 12-25-1822 m Elizabeth Dick Pvt PA
Joel: b 11-28-1759 d 9-25-1795 m Hannah Mendinhall Pvt PA
John: b 9-28-1749 d 10-29-1834 m (1)Elizabeth Yearsley (2)Hannah Smith Pvt PA

Nathaniel: b c. 1750 d 6-9-1789 m Elizabeth Wilkinson Pvt PA
Thomas: b 8-29-1733 d 1796 m Martha Preston Pvt PA

SHARPLEY.
Daniel, Jr.: bpt 6-4-1772 d p. 1786 m Isabel Weldon Pvt DE

SHARPNACK,
Henry: b 1760 d 1848 m Mary Rice Pvt PA

SHARPSTEEN,
Jacob: b — d c. 1802 m Mary Bush Pvt NY
John: b 9-6-1762 d 5-3-1822 m Rachel Wilbur Pvt NY

SHARTS,
Nicholas: b 11-8-1732 d 12-4-1828 m Mariah Sheetz Pvt NY
Nicholas, Jr.: b 1760 d p. 1800 m Margaret Cooper Pvt NY

SHATTUCK,
Abel: b 1759 d 7-1-1816 m (1)Mary Marble (2)Lydia Oak Pvt MA
Abiel: b 8-8-1762 d 4-29-1834 m Phoebe — Pvt MA ★
Abraham: b 10-12-1759 d 3-17-1841 m (1)Mary Wright (2) — Gray (3)Mrs Creigton Eunice Jefts Pvt MA ★
Asa: b 5-21-1762 d 3-28-1851 m Anna Wright Pvt RI
Daniel: b 4-11-1727 d 4-7-1809 m (1)Mary Smith (2)Mrs Lucy Smith Capt MA
David: b 9-12-1758 d 1-23-1840 m Dorothy Alcott Pvt CT ★
David: b 2-19-1735 d 1-2-1820 m (1)Sarah Burt (2)Lucy Sawtell Pvt MA
Ebenezer, Sr.: b 12-25-1760 d 7-30-1840 m Lucy Woods Sol MA
Ebenezer Lakin: b 9-8-1756 d 3-2-1823 m Hannah Tarbell Pvt MA
Eleazer: b 10-26-1751 d 8-19-1844 m Mary Blood Pvt MA
Ephraim: b 3-8-1728 d 5-5-1817 m (1)Elizabeth Jackson (2)Hannah Jordon Cpl MA
Ezra: b 8-5-1751 d 8-8-1816 m Rebecca Cunnable Cpl MA
Jeremiah, Sr.: b 6-11-1703 d 8-2-1798 m (1)Sarah Parker (2)Ruth Bixby CS MA
Jeremiah, Jr.: b 4-11-1726 d 3-26-1815 m (1)Lydia Lakin (2)Keziah Shattuck Cpl MA
Job: b 2-11-1736 d 1-13-1819 m (1)Sarah Hartwell (2)Elizabeth Grigg Capt MA
John: b c. 1751 d c. 1821 m Ruth Phelps Lt MA
John: b 2-7-1722 d 1785 m (1)Abigail Morse (2)Mary — CS MA
John: b 3-12-1724 d 12-31-1807 m Elizabeth — CS MA
John: b 7-7-1757 d 4-26-1816 m Elizabeth Miles MM MA
John: b 1-21-1711 d 12-15-1785 m (1)Sarah Hobart (2)Lydia Hobart MM MA
Jonas: b 12-2-1756 d 1-27-1847 m Anna Robbins Cpl MA
Jonathan: b 3-16-1747 d 3-18-1835 m (1)Abie Chamberlain (2)Mrs Elizabeth Parker PS MA
Joseph, Sr.: b 11-27-1731 d 4-9-1778 m Anna Johnson Cpl MA
Joseph, Jr.: b 7-27-1757 d 1847 m (1)Hannah Chandler (2)Phebe Abbott Cpl MA ★
Joseph: b 3-5-1744/5 d p. 1779 m Abigail Fairbanks CS MM MA
Joseph: b 9-22-1749 d 12-29-1819 m Chloe Scott Sol MA
Moses: b 1-24-1752 d 7-24-1830 m Abigail Woods Pvt MA
Nathan: b 10-19-1760 d 6-28-1808 m Hannah Mason Pvt MA
Nathaniel: b 8-3-1760 d 7-15-1835 m Mary Barnes Pvt MA ★
Nathaniel: b 4-3-1749 d 1-30-1828 m Catherine Andrews Pvt NH
Oliver: b 7-29-1751 d 8-27-1797 m Lucy Parker Capt MA
Philip: b 1-18-1745 d 7-11-1806 m Mercy Butterfield Pvt MA
Randall: b 6-11-1748 d 1804 m Comfort Tyler Pvt CT
Robert, Sr.: b 6-3-1721 d 2-12-1802 m (1)Ruhama Cook (2)Mrs Hannah Blake PS CT
Robert, Jr.: b 10-1-1756 d 3-8-1813 m Anna Loomis Pvt CT
Samuel: b 9-8-1741 d 9-1-1827 m Chloe Field Sgt MA ★
Sarah Hartwell: b 3-19-1738 d 5-5-1798 m Job Shattuck PS MA
Silas: b 8-21-1738 d 3-3-1825 m Sarah Jackson Pvt MA
Simeon: b 9-12-1738 d 4-6-1832 m Lydia Jewett CS MA
Stephen: b 2-10-1710 d 6- -1801 m Elizabeth Robbins Pvt MA
Stephen: b 2-5-1760 d 6-5-1833 m Lucy Richardson Pvt MA ★
Thomas: b 7-1-1752 d 5-23-1835 m (1)Olive Phelps (2)Mrs Ruth Wells Sgt MA ★
Wm.: b 8-13-1750 d 2-7-1840 m Hannah Spencer Pvt CT
Wm.: b 1-1-1718 d 1- -1806 m Abigail Reed CS NH
Wm.: b c. 1755 d 1777 m Mary Duston Sol MA ★
Wm.: b 8-31-1747 d 1810 m Lydia Allis Maj NY
Zachariah: b 11-24-1747 d 6-7-1819 m Elizabeth Farley Pvt NH

SHAUCK,
Jacob: b 11-15-1759 d 1843 m (1)Anna Dorothea Kiester (2)Elizabeth Brady Pvt Spy PA ★
John: b 5-24-1754 d 7-23-1839 m Mary Epaugh Pvt PA
Michael: b c. 1752 d p. 1800 m Katherine Hetrick Pvt PA

SHAUL,
John: b 2-18-1760 d 6-18-1844 m Elizabeth Bronner Pvt NY ★

SHAW,
Abiathar: b 1762 d 12- -1853 m — Pvt Fif MA
Abner: b 6-11-1751 d 6- -1803 m Abigail Eaton Cpl MA
Abraham: b 8-10-1757 d 4-8-1813 m Hannah Miller Capt MA
Abraham: b 12-17-1744 d 5-5-1813 m Priscilla Beal Sgt MA
Abraham: b 8-18-1762 d 6-12-1824 m Mary Haley Pvt MA ★

SHAW, contd.

Abraham: b 3-1-1729/30 d 7-8-1808 m Sarah Barrows CS MA
Alexander: b 1765 d 5-19-1843 m Catherine Conner Pvt PA
Amos: b 2-25-1742 d 5-9-1807 m (1)Hannah Whitman (2)Mrs Bethiah Burrell Lt MA
Amos: b c. 1739 d c. 1800 m Catherine Shaw Pvt PA
Anthony: b 1-29-1750 d 8-7-1820 m (1)Susanna Remington (2)Dinah Smith Pvt NY
Archibald: b 1755 d 6-22-1845 m (1)Mary — (2)Priscilla — (3)Agnes — Pvt PA ★
Asahel: b 11-25-1751 d 5-3-1844 m Sarah Alden Pvt MA
Basil: b 1761 d 1843 m Katrina Ecke Sgt MD ★
Bela: b 2-19-1764 d 5-9-1825 m Lorena Smith Pvt MA ★
Benjamin, Sr.: b 5-2-1734 d 1788 m Jerusha Brown Ens MA
Benjamin, Jr.: b 9-29-1758 d 8-29-1811 m Mehitable Porter Lt MA
Benjamin, Jr.: b 3- -1758 d 1-21-1836 m Sarah Richmond Pvt PS MA ★
Benjamin: b 10-19-1753 d 8-5-1838 m Elizabeth Cushing Sgt MA ★
Benjamin: b 3-26-1756 d 4-1-1825 m Mary Sanborn Pvt NH
Benjamin: b 1758 d 1825 m Sarah Sanborn Pvt NH
Benjamin: b 10-5-1720 d 1794 m Elizabeth — Pvt RI
Caleb: b 5-9-1719 d 12-20-1791 m Abigail Batchelder Pvt PS NH
Christopher Columbus: b 10-25-1765 d 2-23-1832 m Mary Butler Sol SC
Comfort, Sr.: b 1738 d 10-20-1819 m Elizabeth Carey Lt NY
Comfort: b 1759 d 1799 m Mary — Drm Fif NY
Dan: b 11-15-1758 d 11-14-1814 m Joanna Perkins Pvt MA
Daniel: b 1743 d 9-20-1830 m Olive Lillie Cpl MA W★
Daniel, Sr.: b a. 1732 d p. 1789 m Mary Gardner Pvt NY
Daniel, Jr.: b 1754 d 4-23-1828 m Lucretia — Pvt NY
Daniel: b — d c. 1825 m Hannah Wells Pvt NY
David: b 1749 d 6-23-1824 m Mary Kellogg Terry Sol CT
David: b 12-28-1750 d 12-4-1837 m Elizabeth McMaster Sgt MA
David: b 4-2-1757 d 11-11-1825 m Abigail Smith Pvt NH
David: b 5-21-1761 d 1834 m Jane Ekin Pvt PA
Ebenezer, Sr.: b 4-23-1718 d 11-21-1796 m Anne Colson 2Lt MA
Ebenezer, Jr.: b 12-25-1742 d 7-18-1818 m Sarah Porter PS Pvt NH
Edward: b 3-2-1724 d 7-16-1787 m Ruth Fellows PS NH
Elijah: b 6-22-1736 d 7-24-1806 m Phebe Sampson Pvt MA
Elijah: b 8-26-1745 d 6-26-1824 m Hannah Smith Ens MA
Erwin: b 12-29-1752 d 4-26-1832 m Anna Gardner Cpl MA
Francis, Jr.: b 7-28-1748 d 4-17-1785 m Hannah Nickels Maj MA
Francis, Sr.: b 3-29-1721 d 10-18-1784 m Sarah Burt PS MA
George: b c. 1727 d 6-23-1809 m Mercy Thomas Lt MA
George: b 1763 d 9-2-1841 m Betsy Vaughan Pvt MA
George: b 1755 d 11-11-1844 m Betsy Townsend Pvt Smn NH ★
George: b 3- -1750 d 3-30-1793 m Mary Toplin Pvt PA
Gideon: b 9-18-1746 d 11-17-1825 m Abigail Fobes Pvt MA
Henry: b c. 1741 d 1781 m Elizabeth Gordon PS NJ
Ichabod: b 5-10-1734 d 3-25-1821 m Priscilla Atwood Sgt MA
Ichabod: b 5-28-1733 d — m Zilpah Balcom Pvt NH
Isaac: b 1738 d 7-19-1805 m Betsey Beals Sgt MA
James: b 11-19-1739 d 4-8-1831 m Leah Shaw Capt MA
James: b a. 1741 d 1786 m Rebecca Butler Lt MA
James: b 5- -1742 d 5-8-1831 m Faithful Vaughn Pvt MA
James: b 6-24-1758 d 3-16-1825 m Susannah McElwain Sol MA
James: b a. 1755 d 1811 m Polly — Pvt NC
James: b 1757 d 10-18-1823 m Anna Jolly Pvt Spy PA
Jedediah: b 1763 d 5-15-1800 m Martha Gore Pvt NY
Jeremiah: b 7-26-1747 d 10-20-1834 m Hannah Moulton PS NH
Jeremiah: b 2-2-1730 d 5-29-1815 m (1)Esther Southworth (2)Abigail Campbell PS Sol NY
John: b 1745 d 1805 m — Turner Pvt MD
John: b — d p. 1793 m Elizabeth Barnette Pvt MD
John, Jr.: b 6-15-1754 d 4-30-1835 m Abigail Perkins Pvt MA
John: b 1726 d 7-28-1802 m Elizabeth Lucas Lt MA
John: b 5-19-1729 d 12-20-1815 m (1)Hannah White (2)Molley Hudson Pvt MA
John: b 5-7-1761 d 4-9-1834 m Polly Eaton Cpl MA ★
John: b 1724 d 5-12-1810 m Hannah White 2Lt MA
John: b c. 1730 d 3-17-1811 m Martha Studley Sgt PS MA
John: b 1733/4 d 11-12-1796 m Sarah Cox Pvt NJ
John: b 1-29-1763 d 1- -1848 m Mary — Pvt NC ★
John: b 1730 d 1788 m Mary Donaldson Pvt NC
John: b 10-27-1745 d 5-27-1823 m Hannah McDowell Pvt PA
John: b 4- -1745 d 3-30-1818 m Agnes Ferguson PS PA
John: b 5-5-1737 d 5-11-1816 m Elizabeth Allen Pvt RI
John Baptist: b c. 1750 d p. 9-16-1815 m Frances McKelroy Capt PS NC
Jonathan: b 2-14-1732 d 11-26-1896 m Bethia Hall Maj MA
Joseph: b 4-15-1729 d p. 1785 m Mary Cheney Pvt CT
Joseph: b 5- -1738 d 1826 m (1)Catherine Chandler Hamill (2)Elizabeth — Sgt MD
Joseph: b 11-6-1751 d 5-2-1845 m Sylvia Wade Pvt MA
Joseph: b 2-17-1742 d 2-5-1798 m Mary Bates Pvt MA
Joseph: b 1760/61 d 8- -1844 m Susan Mason Pvt MA ★
Joseph: b 5-10-1760 d 8-24-1830 m Eunice Bean Pvt NH
Joshua: b 1737 d 4-20-1813 m (1)Mary Pratt (2)Naomi Bates Lt MA
Joshua: b 5-18-1726 d 12-22-1805 m Abigail Williams Pvt MA
Joshua: b 4-28-1728 d 4-28-1793 m Lucy — Pvt MA
Joshua: b 1725 d 9-14-1807 m Elizabeth Dickenson CS MA
Joshua: b c. 1749 d c. 1805 m Anne Furman CS NJ

Josiah: b 1757 d 11- -1842 m (1)Rebecca — (2)Mary Bundy MM MA ★
Josiah: b 6-23-1751 d 11- -1804 m Rebecca Cox Cpl MA
Jotham: b 9-25-1764 d 4-18-1832 m Sarah Young Roberts Pvt MA W★
Knowles: b 5-18-1757 d 1-6-1831 m (1)Margaret Hungerford (2)Sophia — Cpl MA
Mason: b 1-15-1737 d 9-26-1815 m Mary King Adj MA
Moses: b 4-12-1745 d 6-6-1817 m Dorothy Sanborn 2Lt NH
Nathan: b 5- -1753 d 6-17-1797 m Sarah Witherell Pvt MA
Nathan: b c. 1740 d 6-24-1820 m (1) Mary VanMeter (2)Juliana Miller Lt NJ
Nathaniel: b 9-26-1703 d 8-26-1778 m Temperance Harris PS CT
Nathaniel: b 6-13-1717/18 d 8-25-1800 m Hannah Perkins Capt MA
Nathaniel: b 1757 d 8-16-1831 m Polly Thomas Cpl MA ★
Nathaniel: b 7-12-1762 d 6-27-1846 m Betsey House Pvt MA
Nehemiah: b 1753 d — m Molly Hill Pvt MA
Noah: b 2-2-1758 d 2-8-1844 m (1)Rhoda Palmer (2)Esther Potter Pvt RI
Peter: b 12-29-1731 d 1823 m Elizabeth Meachem Lt MA
Peter: b 9-3-1738 d 1-10-1795 m Lydia Briggs Pvt RI
Phillip: b 1748/49 d 10-22-1818 m Susannah Lane Pvt MA
Richard: b 1754 d 3-4-1847 m (3)Eliza Pitts OrdlSgt CT ★
Richard: b c. 1757 d 1809 m Catharine Vanaman Pvt NJ
Richard: b 10-7-1751 d p. 1793 m Mary McDowell Capt PA
Robert: b 1760 d 1829 m Martha Hodges Pvt NC
Samuel, Jr.: b 8-17-1735 d 1823 m Fear Thomas Pvt MA
Samuel, Jr.: b c. 1752 d p. 1790 m Thankful Williams Pvt MA
Samuel: b 7-4-1748 d p. 1800 m — Whitcher Pvt NH
Samuel: b 4-11-1745 d 7-9-1834 m Zerviah Herrick Capt NY
Sargent: b 10-23-1745 d 12-3-1823 m (1)Sarah Knight (2)Mrs Salome Dorsett (3)Anna Thompson Pvt MA
Seth: b c. 1760 d 6- -1839 m (1)Caty Mason (2)Catherine MacDougall Pvt MA
Sylvanus: b 1753 d 5-20-1847 m Rebecca Donham Pvt MA ★
Sylvanus: b 5-28-1766 d 1-18-1852 m Persis Wilder Stoddard Pvt MA
Thomas: b 1738 d 7-6-1778 m Mary Atwood Pvt MA
Thomas: b 5-1-1753 d 7-30-1829 m Joanna Vaughn Pvt MA
Thomas: b 9-16-1753 d 12-29-1835 m Polly McCoy Pvt PA NC ★
Wm.: b 12-3-1757 d 6-1-1815 m Charlotte Trimble Pvt MD
Wm.: b 1745 d 1802 m Priscilla Fearson PS MD
Wm.: b 1730 d 1809 m Hannah West Pvt MA
Wm.: b 1754 d 11-27-1821 m Eda Edwards Sgt NY
Wm.: b 1827 m Mary Wade Ens NC
Wm.: b 2-5-1758 d 8-25-1842 m Sarah Job OrdlSgt NC ★
Wm.: b 5- -1748 d 8-7-1811 m Esther Taylor Pvt PA
Wm.: b c. 1760 d 3-20-1821 m Isabella — Pvt PA
Wm.: b 5-29-1739 d 12-27-1802 m Ann Elizabeth Sample PS PA
Wm.: b 1759 d 2- -1863 m Frances LeGette Pvt SC
Zechariah: b 6-28-1711 d 1-22-1790 m Sarah Packard Pvt MA
Zephaniah: b 4-16-1751 d 12-29-1828 m Hannah Pratt Cpl MA

SHAWHAN,

Daniel: b 12-1-1738 d 5-11-1791 m Margaret Bell Pvt MD
Darby: b 1748 d 1-21-1824 m Priscilla — Pvt VA
Frederick: b 8-12-1760 d 8-8-1840 m (1)Elizabeth Allen Pvt MD ★
Robert: b 3-5-1764 d 2-25-1833 m Mary Williams Pvt PA

SHAY,

Daniel: b 1747 d 9-29-1825 m (1)Eunice Hayden (3)Abigail Gilbert (3)Mrs Rhoda Havens Capt MA
Timothy: b 9-9-1756 d 10-13-1838 m Hannah Fairchild Pvt CT ★
Timothy: b 10-26-1756 d 7- -1837 m (1)Mary Drake (2)Mrs Mary Emery Pvt CT
Wm.: b c. 1755 d 6-11-1832 m (1)Lydia — (2)Rebekah Babcock Ens CT

SHEAFE,

Jacob: b 9-6-1745 d 7-25-1829 m Mary Quincy PS NH

SHEAFF,

Philip: b 7-8-1741 d 8-2-1829 m Mary Tanger Pvt PA

SHEAHEY, (includes SHEA, SHEHEE, SHEHI & SHEHY)

Daniel: b 1754 d 1824 m Alifair Green Cpl MD
Daniel: b 1749 d 1-20-1831 m Jane McLain Cpl PA
John: b 1753 d p. 1811 m Mary Smith Pvt PA

SHEAKLEY, (or SHAKLY)

George: b 1760 d 1812 m Margaret McCurdy Ens PA
John: b 1-29-1755 d 9-25-1816 m Margaret Jenkins Ens PA
Wm.: b 1720 d 1810 m Jennet Moor PS PA

SHEAR,

Lodewick: b 1746 d 2-4-1831 m Margaret Gance Pvt NY

SHEARER, (includes SHERER & SHERRED)

Archibald: b 1734 d 3- -1800 m Sarah Prather Capt VA
Christopher: b 4-14-1752 d 3-14-1830 m Juliance Phillipi Sgt PA
David: b 5- -1759 d 11-7-1846 m Hannah Yougman Pvt NH ★
Frederick: b 1763 d 2-20-1817 m Barbara Smith Pvt NC
Henry: b 1727 d 1- -1812 m (2)Catharine Dorothea Heller (3)Anna Mary Pvt PA

SHEARIN,
Henry: b c. 1738 d 1-4-1812 m Barbara — Pvt PA
Jacob: b 4-14-1755 d 2-27-1837 m Sarah Northrope Sgt PA ★
Jacob: b 1744 d 1-29-1823 m Elizabeth Deal Pvt PA
Jacob: b c. 1755 d p. 1790 m Elizabeth Beakley Pvt PA
John, Jr.: b 3-22-1746 d 12-18-1817 m Jane White Cpl MA
John, Sr.: b 1710 d 1-12-1802 m Jane — Pvt MA
John, Sr.: b 8-22-1737 d 5-30-1810 m (1)Elizabeth Fleming (2)Mrs Mary Baille QM NJ
John: b 1750 d 4-22-1809 m Mary Cathcart Pvt PA
John Jacob: b 9-14-1759 d 3-20-1845 m Catey Smith Pvt NC PA
Joseph: b 1731 d 12-1/2-1776 m (2)Mary McClure (3)Mary McCracken Capt PS PA
Noah: b 9-4-1764 d 6-24-1849 m (1)Tirza Merrick (2)Betsey Heald Pvt MA
Philip: b 1758 d 1819 m Rosanna Helphenstine Pvt PA
Philip: b 1761 d 1835 m Susanna Christman Pvt PA
Samuel: b 1755 d 12-26-1821 m Elizabeth Barnett Ens PA
Valentine: b 9-14-1736 d 12-1-1818 m Mary — Pvt PA
Wm.: b 1756 d 11-6-1826 m Elizabeth Morton Pvt MA
Wm.: b — d 4-16-1834 m Elinor Kenfield Pvt MA
Wm.: b 3-1-1752 d 3-5-1847 m Lutitia Langdon Pvt NY ★

SHEARIN,
Joseph: b c. 1735 d a. 12-29-1790 m Amey — CS NC

SHEARS, (or SHARE)
Andrew: b 1763-5 d 1-9-1847 m Polly — Pvt NY
Zachariah: b 1747 d 3-16-1814 m Eunice Bush Pvt MA

SHECKLER,
Frederick: b 1754 d 7- -1829 m Mary Catherine Monrow PS PA

SHEDD, (or SHED)
Abel: b 3-9-1743 d 9-21-1819 m Ruth Haskell PS NH
Daniel: b 6-12-1715 m Mary Tarbell Pvt MA
Daniel: b 3-30-1735/36 d 8-30-1810 m Hannah Lakin Pvt MA
Daniel: b 4-15-1749 d 4-10-1820 m Lucy Nutting Pvt NH
David: b 3-19-1759 d 4-11-1841 m Sarah Putnam Cpl MA ★
Ebenezer: b 10-23-1753 d 3-1-1829 m (1)Mary Blood (2)Lucy Hartwell Sol CS MA
Jacob: b 10-23-1752 d 6-29-1790 m Mary Goodhue Cpl MA ★
Joel: b 2-16-1760 d 1841 m Dolly Farmer Pvt MA
John, Sr.: b 1-27-1731 d 12-2-1797 m Martha Hosley Lt MA
John, Jr.: b 3-17-1759 d 11-18-1838 m (1)Rachel Danforth (2)Lucy Farley (Jewett) Cpl MA
John: b 8-3-1756 d 12-8-1830 m Sarah Sprague Pvt MA
John: b 8-10-1762 d 9-29-1842 m Betsey Hall Pvt MA ★
Jonas: b 8-24-1750 d — m Hannah — Pvt NH
Joseph: b 6-17-1732 d 10-18-1812 m Rebecca Gair PS MA
Oliver: b 2-11-1738 d p. 1791 m Mary — Pvt MA
Reuben: b 7-27-1748 d 4-30-1781 m Sibel Bullard Pvt MA
Samuel: b 12-26-1764 d 4-12-1829 m Hannah Brooks Pvt MA
Samuel: b 1748 d 1-20-1830 m Rhoda Kellogg Pvt MA
Simon: b 4-14-1765 d 3-3-1813 m Lucy Dole Pvt MA
Wm.: b 6-16-1748 d 7-18-1815 m (1)Elizabeth Parker (2)Martha Jefts Pvt MA
Wm.: b 4-15-1735 d 3-18-1806 m Lydia Farnsworth Pvt MA
Zachariah: b 2-7-1745 d 1-15-1813 m Lydia Spring Pvt MA

SHEE,
Bertles: b 1742 d 2-18-1787 m Cecilia Parke LCol PS CL
John: b 1740 d 8-5-1808 m — Col PA
Walter: b c. 1722 d 10-12-1782 m (1)Catherine Benter (2)Mrs Ann Vernon Thompson CS PA

SHEED,
Wm.: b c. 1725 d 5-27-1795 m Martha Coats PS PA

SHEEHAN,
Cornelius: b c. 1758 d p. 1794 m — Pvt PA

SHEETS, (or SCHITZ, SHITZ)
Adam: b c. 1734 d 1789-96 m Catharine Schell PS PA
Adam: b c. 1740 d 1822 m Mary — Pvt VA
Conrad: b c. 1758 d 1812 m Christine Pfluger Pvt PA
Henry, Sr.: b 4-30-1742 d 10-7-1793 m Catherine Rubicam Pvt PA
Henry, Jr.: b 12-9-1764 d 9-4-1848 m (1)Elizabeth Hocker (2)Mrs Dager Pvt PA
John: b 1755 d p. 1832 m Elizabeth — Pvt VA
John Adam: b 2-22-1760 d 7-30-1825 m Susanna Tiffenbach Pvt PA

SHEFFIELD, (or SHUFFIELD)
Acors: b 1740 d 12-20-1801 m Lois Cobb Lt CT
Arthur: b 9-12-1750 d 12-26-1824 m Lucretia Hogan Capt NC
Isham: b 1750 d 1784 m Barbara Boney Pvt NC
John: b 12-13-1728 d 1790 m (2)Mrs Elizabeth Grady Pvt GA
John: b c. 1727 d c. 1796 m Hannah — Pvt NC
Joseph: b 1760 d 1848 m (2)Polly Bowers Pvt CT ★
Robert: b 8-10-1753 d 2-20-1838 m Temperance Doty Drm NY
Robert: b c. 1758 d 1795 m Sarah — Smn VA
Samuel: b 8-13-1750 d 5-1-1832 m Anna Browning PS RI
Stanton: b 3-27-1761 d 3-18-1833 m Anna Crandall Pvt PS RI W★
Thomas: b 11-25-1740 d 1- -1822 m Wealthia Pendleton Maj RI

West: b 12-13-1747 d 9-22-1830 m (1)Susannah Sherrard (2)Elizabeth — (3)Mrs Dill Pvt GA

SHEFFY,
George: b 6-8-1755 d 1-1-1831 m Anna Margaret Weinerich Mus PA

SHEFTALL,
Levi: b 12-12-1739 d 1-20-1809 m Sarah DeLaMotta PS Sol GA
Mordecai: b 12-12-1735 d 7-6-1797 m Frances Hart Col GA

SHEIDY,
Peter: b 6-15-1719 d 7-20-1783 m Catharine Leiby PS PA

SHEIVE,
George: b 2-4-1763 d 4-5-1836 m Catherine Hoover Pvt PA

SHEKELL,
John: b 1742 d 3-4-1823 m (1)Anna Rachel Simmons (2)Mary Burgess Pvt MD

SHELBURN,
Augustine: b 1754-56 d 9-8-1817 m Jane Bush Sol VA

SHELBURNE,
James: b 11-29-1738 d 3-6-1820 m Anne Pettus PS VA

SHELBY,
David: b 1763 d 1822 m Sarah Bledsoe Pvt NC
Evan, Sr.: bpt 10-31-1719 d 12-4-1794 m (1)Letitia Cox (2)Mrs Isabella Elliott BGen VA NC
Evan, Jr.: b 2-27-1754 d 2-18-1793 m Catherine Shelby Col VA
Elvan: b 1754 d 1813 m Susan Polk Alexander PS NC
Isaac: b 12-11-1750 d 7-18-1826 m Susanna Hart Col VA NC
John, Sr.: b 1724 d 12-4-1794 m (1)Louisa Looney (2)Sarah Davis Capt CS VA
Joshua: b 1750-60 d 7- -1830 m Susanna — Sol VA
Moses: b 10-31-1760 d 9-17-1828 m Mellicent Renfro Capt NC
Moses: b 5- -1728 d 1776/7 m (2)Isabel — PS NC
Rees: b c. 1724 d p. 1810 m Mary — Sol NC
Thomas: b c. 1756 d p. 1793 m Sarah Helms Pvt NC

SHELDON, (or SHELDEN)
Abner: bpt 4-5-1752 d 3-3-1823 m Rebecca Frary Sgt MA
Abraham, Sr.: b 6-17-1717 d 5-15-1790 m (1)Sarah Gowing (2)Mrs Phebe Russell Holt Sol MA
Abraham, Jr.: b 5-23-1740 d 2-5-1796 m Sarah Haward Pvt PS NH
Amasa, Sr.: b 8-27-1726 d 3-8-1808 m Sarah Bardwell Capt MA
Amasa, Jr.: b 1748 d 1780 m Sibyl Holton Pvt MA
Arad: b 1754 d 3-26-1813 m Elizabeth Gibbs Sgt MA
Asa, Jr.: b 1750 d 1-24-1727 m Rhoda Catlin Pvt MA
Asher, Jr.: b 1-30-1756 d 4-27-1780 m Hannah Rogers Sol CT
Benjamin: b 1728 d 10-1-1803 m Elizabeth Hunt PS MA
Benjamin: b 1-27-1751 d 7-18-1816 m Sarah Smith Lt RI
Cephas: b 5-12-1754 d 7-24-1848 m Abigail Foster Pvt MA
Christopher: b 2-29-1732 d 11-14-1799 m Rosamond Arnold Gnr RI
Daniel: b 1715 d 12-23-1798 m Mary Harmon Pvt CT
David: b 1756 d 2-15-1832 m Sarah Harmon Pvt CT
Ebenezer: b 2-20-1764 d 7-24-1825 m (1)Huldah Hanchett (2)Love Davis Pvt CT
Ebenezer: b 12-10-1737 d 1-19-1804 m Esther Strong Capt MA
Elijah: b 9-1-1738 d 7-2-1812 m Rachel Hanchett Pvt CT
Elijah: b 11-1-1733 d p. 1783 m Mrs Anna McClaren PS CS MA
Elisha, Sr.: b 9-2-1709 d 9-1-1779 m Elizabeth Ely PS CT
Elisha, Jr.: b 3-6-1740 d 1805 m Sarah — Col CT
Epaphras: b 8-2-1753 d 1-31-1850 m Hannah Lyman Col CT
Ephraim: b 5-21-1754 d 4-22-1840 m Miram Warrener Pvt CT ★
Ephriam, Jr.: b 1745 d 12-30-1806 m Eunice Felt Pvt MA
Ezekial: b 2-11-1758 d 1-27-1846 m Amy Potter Pvt RI ★
George: b 10-11-1757 d 1840 m Lucy Niles Pvt NY ★
Isaac: b 7-22-1755 d 5-6-1844 m Esther Carpenter OrdlSgt RI ★
Isaac: b 1752 d 1810 m Mindwell Phelps Pvt CT
Israel: b 5- -1715 d 6-8-1791 m (1)Naomi Warner (2) Mrs Miriam Strong Pvt PS MA
James: b 1743 d 8-19-1806 m Abigail Fenner Capt RI
James: b 4-11-1743 d p. 1784 m (1)Hannah Beard (2)Elizabeth — CS RI
James, Sr.: b 12-19-1728 d 10-5-1819 m Diadama Perry PS RI
James, Jr.: b 4-9-1757 d 6-18-1819 m Mary Cheesboro Lord Ens RI
Job: b 1758 d 4-1-1832 m Joanna Crawford Trippe Sgt RI
Joel: b 1746 d 12-25-1829 m Mary Hanchett Sgt VT
John: b 8-9-1710 d 12-4-1793 m Mercey Arms PS MA
John: b 1747 d 8-26-1823 m Rebecca — Sol NY
John: b 1749 d 1845 m Abigail Phillips Pvt RI ★
John: b 2-27-1749 d 12-20-1812 m Sybil Spear Pvt VT
Jonathan: b 1744 d 10-2-1802 m (1)Mehitable Field (2)Naama Fox Pvt PS MA
Jonathan: b 1-23-1757 d 11-9-1849 m Lizzie Ann Rider Smn MA
Josiah: b 1754 d 2- -1843 m Chloe Bixby Pvt MA ★
Martin: b 2-1-1762 d 9-4-1848 m Abigail Gillette Sol CT
Palmer: b 1-28-1745 d 1794 m Penelope Brown PS CT
Pardon: b 4-20-1755 d 1825 m Sarah Warner Ens RI
Phineas: b 6-27-1717 d 9-18-1807 m (1)Debor Hatheway (2)Mrs Ruth Smith PS CT

SHELDON, contd.
Remembrance: b 10-16-1717 d 4-3-1787 m Mehitable Burke PS MA
Reuben: bpt 9-11-1749 d p. 1797 m — Pvt MA
Roger: b 3- -1756 d 3-23-1823 m Elizabeth Marsh Pvt CT W★
Samuel: b 3-10-1766 d 7-31-1856 m Mary Hanchett PS CT
Samuel, Jr.: b 1734 d 8-26-1818 m Beulah Jackson Pvt MA
Samuel: b c. 1740 d 12-24-1832 m Sarah Wellman PS NH
Seth: b 1738 d 4-24-1810 m Hannah Mary Hanchet Pvt CT
Simeon: b 3-22-1726 d 2-1-1813 m Grace Phelps Capt CT
Whiting: b 1758 d 7-7-1839 m Sarah Hubbard Pvt MA
Wm.: b 1736 d 1816 m Hannah Noble Pvt MA
Wm.: b 1-27-1758 d 12-26-1831 m Elizabeth — Pvt MA
Wm.: b 7-12-1759 d 2-8-1826 m Hannah Page Pvt MA ★
Wm.: b 1751 d 1818 m Ruth Bishop Pvt NY
Wm.: b 1756 d 7-27-1805 m Abigail Udall Pvt NY
Zachariah: b 1754 d 1815 m Polly Mary Jones Pvt MA

SHELDRAKE,
David: b 1723 d 3-29-1803 m Christina Young Arfr PA
Wm.: b 1744 d 5-21-1837 m Fanny Barr Pvt PA

SHELLABARGER,
Martin: b c. 1748 d p. 12-5-1807 m Anna Bear Pvt PA

SHELLENBERGER, (or SHALLENBERGER)
Christian: b 1751 d 1828 m Catherine — Pvt PA
Conrad: b 11-16-1753 d 4-18-1839 m Eva Christena Leydi Pvt PA
Jacob: b 1724 d 1812 m (1)Magdaline — (2)Ann — Pvt PA
John Michael: b c. 1736 d c. 1826 m Margaret Fredline Pvt PA

SHELLER,
Daniel: b 2-13-1762 d 3-10-1829 m Elizabeth — Pvt PA

SHELLEY, (includes SHEALEY, SHEELY & SHELY)
Abraham: b c. 1726 d 1792 m Barbara — Pvt PA
Christopher: b a. 1749 d 4-3-1800 m Catharine — Pvt PA
Conrad: b 10-15-1753 d 12-8-1836 m Elizabeth Hornbeck Pvt NY
Daniel: b 1737 d 6- -1802 m (2)Catherine — (3)Elizabeth —
    (4) Barbara — Pvt PA
David: b 5-27-1750 d 12-13-1823 m Mary Hurst Of VA
Jacob: b c. 1742 d 1790 m Hester Clearwater Pvt PS NY
John: b 1723-27 d 1820-22 m Margaret — PS VA
Jonathan: b 4-4-1738 d 10-22-1811 m Sarah Andrews Pvt MA
Libbeus: b c. 1756 d p. 1790 m (1)Bethany (2)Phebe Pvt MA
Martin: b 2-28-1756 d 3-12-1840 m Margaret Jackson Pvt NY
Samuel: b 1-20-1765 d 3-17-1838 m Catharine Pride Pvt Fif CT
Thomas: b c. 1745 d a. 9-17-1782 m Lucy — Ens VA

SHELLHAMMER,
Abraham: b 8-24-1748 d 3-28-1815 m Anna Maria Pvt PA
George: b 5-14-1750 d 6-14-1817 m Marcia Margaretha Ehrs Pvt PA
Philip Jacob: b 1759 d 1836 m Elizabeth — Pvt PA ★

SHELMIRE,
George: b 6-1-1746 d 4-21-1826 m Rachel Acuff Pvt PA
John: b 1755-60 d 4-6-1818 m Catharine Lashan Capt PA

SHELOR,
Daniel: b 3-5-1750 d 2-13-1847 m Mary Wickham Capt MD ★

SHELP,
Christian: b 1760 d 1825 m Jane Freeman Pvt NY

SHELTON, (includes CHELTON, & SKELTON)
Abraham: b c. 1735 d 1789 m Chloe Robertson Maj PS VA
Armstead: b 1753 d 6-16-1844 m Susan — Capt VA
Clough: b 11-11-1752 d 1833 m Mildred — Capt VA
Crispen: b 4-1-1713 d a. 2-17-1794 m Lettice — PS CS VA
Daniel: b 5-17-1729 d a. 9-18-1809 m Lettie — Maj VA
David: b a. 1736 d a. 1801 m (1)Elizabeth Matlock (2)Susan
    Vaughn Matr VA
Eliphaz: b — d p. 7-4-1818 m Anne — Capt PS VA
Gabriel: b 1740 d 1803 m (1)Elizabeth Shepphard (2)Mary Buford
    Capt PS VA
Godfrey: b 1760 d p. 10-24-1825 m Mary Williams Pvt VA
Henry: b c. 1760 d p. 1791 m Ann Flowers Pvt VA
Henry: b c. 1735 d 1799 m Mary Mildred Long PS VA
James: b c. 1760 d 11-8-1817 m Fannie S Allen Capt VA
Jeremiah: b — d p. 7-10-1826 m Nancy — PS VA
John: b c. 1760 d 9-7-1843 m Susannah Bradley Sol NC
John: b c. 1751 d 10-31-1798 m Ann Randolph (2)Nancy Williamson
    (3)Nancy Southall Capt VA
John: b c. 1740 d 11- -1805 m Susan Hord PS VA
Joseph: b 5-8-1754 d 1826-32 m Mary Carey Pvt PA
Leroy: b 1763 d 1-2-1847 m Nancy Lanier Sol VA
Malbon: b c. 1754 d 1784 m Alice — PS VA
Medley: b 1760 d 3-10-1839 m Elizabeth Ward Pvt VA
Peter: b a. 1737 d p. 10-27-1803 m Frances Nuckolls PS 2Lt VA
Richard: b 8-14-1728 d 1-5-1821 m Mary Wright PS VA
Samuel: b 11-3-1758 d 5-28-1833 m Jane Henderson Sgt VA W★
Samuel: b 1703 d 1793 m Judith Clough Anderson PS VA
Spencer: b c. 1743 d p. 6-18-1799 m Clary Sheldon Capt VA
Thomas, Sr.: b 1742 d 1846 m (1)Jane Clopton (2)Cousins (3)Crump
    1Lt VA

Thomas, Jr.: b 1763 d 1857 m (1)Barksdale (2)Pheobe Hulett
    (3)Phoebe Hatcher MM VA
Thomas: b c. 1750 d c. 1826 m (1)Cicely Dabney (2)Sallie Farrar
    (3)Sally Miller Mus VA
Thomas: b c. 1730 d 1808 m Jane — PS VA
Vincent: b c. 1750 d p. 1802 m Susan Robertson Ens VA
Wm.: b c. 1750 d 8-4-1827 m Ann Lomax Pvt PS VA W★
Wm.: b 1-7-1763 d 8-6-1825 m Elizabeth Chaney Johnston Pvt VA
Wm., Jr.: b 1709 d 1789 m (1)Patience — (2)Elizabeth Rogers PS VA
Wm., Jr.: b c. 1731 d p. 7-13-1802 m (1)Lucy Harris (2)Sarah — PS VA
Wilson: b 1747 d p. 3-30-1839 m — Pvt VA ★

SHEMWELL, (or SHAMWELL)
Joseph: b c. 1762 d 12-9-1823 m Ann Billingsley Pvt MD
Wm.: b c. 1755 d 10- -1824 m Ann Billingsley Pvt MD

SHENKEL, (includes SCHENCKEL & SHINKLE)
Christian: b 7-10-1756 d 1833 m Maria Magdalena Pvt PA
Philip: b 10-25-1753 d 5-29-1829 m Barbara Walderin Pvt PA
Philip Jacob: b 3-5-1747 d p. 3-28-1805 m Julia Ann Bolender Pvt PA
Philipp Carl: b 8-6-1717 d p. 1778 m Maria Elisabetha Zimbel PS PA

SHEPARD, (includes SHEPHERD, SHEPPARD & SHEPPERD)
Abner: b 5-28-1750 d 3-12-1824 m (1)Mary Dowdney (2)Ruth
    Pauline (3)Mary McGear (4)Elizabeth Fithian Pvt NJ
Abraham: b 1744 d 6-13-1832 m Rhoda Ferriss Pvt CT
Abraham: b c. 1745 d 7-22-1779 m Temperance Cory Lt NY
Abraham: b 1740 d p. 11-16-1790 m — Haywood Col PS NC
Abraham: b 11-10-1754 d 9-7-1822 m Eleanor Strode Capt VA
Alexander: b c. 1720 d 1785 m Mary Willard PS MA
Asa: b 9-10-1754 d 9-10-1836 m Hannah — Sol CT
Augustine: b c. 1730 d p. 11-21-1795 m Sarah Shelton PS VA
Benjamin: b 2-27-1760 d 1837 m — Pvt NJ ★
Benjamin: b 2-24-1710 d 1791 m Sara Ruffin PS NC
Catharine: b 6-1-1763 d 12-6-1863 m George Shepard PS NJ
Charles: b 1744 d 12-22-1820 m (1)Agnes Wool (2)Elizabeth Dyer
    Pvt PA
Charlton: b c. 1740 d p. 2-9-1785 m Hannah — Capt NJ
Daniel: b 1753 d 10-24-1850 m (1)Phebe Strickland (2)Ruth
    Penfield Wilcox Sgt CT
Daniel: b 9-16-1723 d 8-22-1798 m (1)Sarah Cornwall (2)Grace
    Savage Pvt CT
Daniel: b 9-8-1747 d 7-3-1829 m Sarah Adams Pvt MA
Daniel: b 1758 d p. 7-7-1820 m Anna Forest Pvt NH
Daniel: b 2-22-1725 d — m (1)Mary Challis (2)Mrs Eliz Ashe PS NH
David: b 1-10-1732/3 d 2-9-1790 m Phoebe Cady Capt PS CT
David: b 10-23-1744 d 12-12-1818 m (1)Margaret Class (2)Lucinda
    Mather Capt Dr MA
David: b 1755 d 11-1-1822 m Diadamer Hopkins Pvt MA ★
David: b 10-30-1721 d 5-12-1792 m Sarah Brooder PS NY
David: b 1734 d 2-2-1795 m Rachel Teague Col CS VA
Dubartin: b c. 1740 d 1823/4 m Elizabeth Woods Pvt CS VA
Ebenezer: b 1-13-1742 d 4-12-1811 m Mrs Jane McCordy Lt MA
Elijah: b 3-27-1763 d 2-17-1848 m Elizabeth Adkins Pvt MA ★
Elisha: b 7-16-1750 d 8-11-1834 m Alletta Smock Capt NJ
Enoch: b 10-23-1742 d 9-17-1821 m (1)Esther Dewey (2)Margaret
    Gass Capt MA
Furman: b 7-6-1756 d 12-21-1832 m (1)Mary — (2)Hannah Maskell
    Ens NJ ★
George: b 1750 d 6-13-1838 m (1)Jemina Gough (2)Elizabeth Crane
    (3)Mrs Abigail Mix Crane Goodwin (4)Nancy Tripp Pvt CT
George: b 2-5-1759 d 3-26-1843 m Catharine VanWinkle Pvt NJ
George: b 1-2-1757 d 7-13-1819 m Eunice Makepeace Pvt Smn MA
Gideon: b 1-6-1747 d 12-28-1790 m Silence Noble 2Lt MA
Henry Lenox: b 5-8-1753 d 12-12-1816 m Phoebe Brown Sol MA
Isaac: b 1731/2 d 5-13-1802 m Jemima Smith CS MA
Isaac: b 12-8-1755 d p. 1797 m Comfort Dam Sgt NH
Israel: b 1746 d 2-21-1836 m Hannah Pitcher Cpl NY
Jacob: b 11-30-1741 d 9-18-1816 m Lydia Clapp Lt MA
Jacob: b 4-17-1738 d 1798 m Bathsheba Puffer Pvt MA
Jacob: b 1757 d 1-21-1838 m Isabella Ileff Jones Pvt NJ ★
Jacob: b 1735 d a. 2- -1808 m Pamelia Pines PS NC
James: b 8-6-1749 d 12-28-1816 m Roxanna Merritt Cpl CT
James: b c. 1741 d 1810-20 m Mary Cashion Lt MD
James: b 9-13-1731 d 1801 m Abigail Morrill Capt NH
James: b 2-16-1763 d 5-20-1856 m Persis Hutchinson Pvt NY ★
James: b 10-1-1759 d 10-15-1828 m Pheobe Mastin 1Lt NC
James, Jr.: b 3- -1760 d 3-7-1823 m Susanna Haynie Pvt SC
James, Sr.: b 1737 d 1791 m Jannett Riddle Pvt SC
Jared: b 11-6-1738 d 3-10-1811 m Abigail Edwards Capt CT
Jesse: b 7-6-1744 d c. 1800 m Sarah White Pvt CT
John: b 4-17-1765 d 5-15-1837 m (1)Anna Gore (2)Deborah
    Hawkins Ens CT
John: b 10-27-1743 d 4-4-1811 m Elizabeth Bradley Ens CT
John: b 5-25-1757 d 1-29-1822 m (1)Millicent Edsall (2)Sally —
    Capt NY ★
John: b 11-8-1733 d 1817 m Elizabeth Sackett Capt MA
John: b 6-17-1752 d 8-27-1816 m Abigail Eaton Pvt MA
John: b 12-25-1730 d 12-4-1802 m Mercy Wilkins PS NH
John: b 2-8-1764 d 10-14-1857 m (1)Huldah — (2)Mrs Sarah
    Warren Pvt NH ★
John: b 1756 d 1824 m — Capt NY ★
John: b c. 1745 d c. 1793 m Miriam Wallis Pvt NC

John: b 3-16-1723 d 1-3-1846 m Elizabeth Gould Pvt PA
John: b *c*. 1730 d 1803 m Virginia — Pvt VA
John: b 1749 d 7-31-1812 m Martha Nelson Pvt VA
John: b 1738 d *p*. 12-16-1796 m Mary Ann Lilly PS VA
Jonadab, Jr.: b *c*. 1737 d 11- -1807 m Hannah Sheppard Capt NJ
Jonas, Jr.: b 5-29-1722 d 1809 m Esther Reed Pvt VT
Jonathan: b 1758 d 4-17-1825 m Martha — Pvt MD ★
Jonathan, Sr.: b 3-23-1732 d 1-10-1800 m Miriam Strong Pvt MA
Jonathan, Jr.: b 2-6-1757 d 6-22-1838 m Abigail Boise Pvt MA
Jonathan: b 9-24-1737 d *p*. 5-10-1795 m (1)Susannah Bacon (2)Mrs
    Mary Abbott Pvt MA
Jonathan, Sr.: b 8-6-1709 d 3-26-1798 m (1)Love Palmer (2)Polly
    Underwood PS NH
Jonathan, Jr.: b 1-6-1739/40 d 1781 m Hannah Benjamin PS NH
Jonathan: b 4-23-1764 d 12-17-1844 m Louise Marvin PS NH
Joseph: b 3-15-1754 d 10-23-1840 m Sybil Kirby Pvt CT
Joseph: b 4-11-1746 d 1-4-1832 m Abigail Hodges Cpl MA
Joseph: b 9-8-1728 d 1-8-1782 m Mary Sayre CS NJ
Lawrence: b 9-9-1758 d 10-5-1822 m (1)Hannah Cushing (2)Mrs
    Hannah Pedrick Pvt NJ
Lemuel: bpt 1763 d — m Lorana Mallory Pvt CT
Levi: b — d 1849 m Elizabeth Moore Pvt MA
Mace: b 5-28-1759 d 2-14-1821 m Deborah Haskins Pvt RI
Morrill: b 1763 d 10-23-1844 m (1)Azuba Hancock (2)Elizabeth —
    (3)Olive Sawyer Frye Sgt NH ★
Moses: b 10-25-1743 d 11-16-1818 m Rebecca Stillwell Capt NJ
Moses: b 2-28-1744 d 2- -1828 m (1)Lydia Stevens (2)Truelove
    Hutchins (3)Ruth Cotton Pvt VT
Nathaniel: b 8-29-1760 d 5-4-1822 m Hannah Roberts Pvt CT
Nathaniel: b 2-4-1741 d 1-20-1828 m Lydia Graham Pvt MA
Oliver: b 1743 d 8- -1830 m Zerviah Hatch Ens NH
Philip: b 1720 d 1-5-1797 m Mary — PS NJ
Phineas: b 6-19-1757 d 11-22-1842 m (1)Deliverance Smith (2)Mrs
    Flora Mac Intyre Pvt CT ★
Samuel: b 5-4-1754 d 2-15-1803 m Thankful Mallory Pvt CT
Samuel: b 1740 d 9-21-1821 m Sobriety Hill CS NH
Samuel: b 6-3-1762 d *p*. 1832 m Anne Margaret Boyd Pvt VA
Samuel: b 6-3-1762 d 12- -1846 m Jane Guill Pvt VA ★
Samuel: b 2-3-1730 d *p*. 1792 m Ann Burwell Sol VA
Seth: b 1-21-1750 d 11-5-1812 m (1)Rachel Dunham (2)Esther
    Carrell Pvt MA
Simeon: b 8-13-1750 d 11-15-1832 m (1)Lois Morse (2)Mrs Betsey
    Reynolds Pvt PS MM MA
Stephen: b 4-17-1740 d 8-13-1819 m Ame Grannis Pvt CT
Stephen: bpt 3-24-1730 d 6-30-1799 m Susannah Blanchard Pvt CT
Stephen: b 2-13-1750 d 7-4-1831 m Prudence Adams QM Sgt MA
Thomas: b 1-4-1730 d 5-22-1819 m (1)Mary Kellogg (2)Ann Rowley
    Burr Capt CT
Thomas: b 6-20-1731 d 11-23-1823 m (1)Mercy Sears (2)Mrs Ann
    Washburn Pvt CT
Thomas: b 1757 d 6-7-1840 m Lydia Goodsell Pvt CT ★
Thomas: b 1740-50 d 1805 m (1)Catherine Palmer (2)Sarah
    Castleman (3)Martha Humphrey PS VA
Thomas C: b *c*. 1743 d 1793 m Susanna Hulse Sol VA
Timothy: b 3-22-1718 d 5-22-1776 m Susannah Stillson Lt CT
Wm.: b 10-26-1737 d 11-16-1817 m Sarah Dewey Col MA
Wm.: b 1759 d 9-13-1843 m Anagail — Pvt NY ★
Wm.: b 1746 d 2-8-1822 m Elizabeth Haywood Col NC
Wm.: b *c*, 1732 d *p*. 2-2-1807 m Mary Booker Capt NC
Wm.: b 1745 d 1810 m Elizabeth Ashe Pvt NC
Wm.: b 7-9-1755 d 11-12-1825 m Nancy Pvt PA
Wm.: b *c*. 1755 d 7- -1805 m Isabel Pvt VA
Wm.: b *c*. 1747 d 1824 m Mary Clark Pvt VA

SHEPARDSON,
John: b 2-16-1729 d 1-3-1802 m Anna Blanchard CS Pvt VT
Joseph: b 10-27-1760 d 11-2-1821 m (1)Zurvier Packer (2)Lucy
    Stedman Pvt VT
Nathaniel: b 6-18-1731 d 4-23-1817 m (1)Sarah — (2)Elizabeth
    Tingley Jackson PS RI
Samuel: b 2-10-1757 d 2-28-1813 m Anna Barney CS VT
Zephaniah: b 5-6-1733 d 10-16-1804 m (1)Ruth Hills (2)Damaris
    Church (3)Lucinda Chase PS CS VT
Zephaniah, Jr.: b 3-21-1755 d 8-19-1837 m (1)Rachel Wilkins
    (2)Lettice Barney (3)Mrs Sarah Stedman Pvt NH ★

SHEPLER,
Henry: b 8-1-1737 d 10-18-1781 m Justina Catherine Kraft Capt
    PA

SHEPLEY,
John, Sr.: b 12-20-1727 d 11- -1785 m Abigail Greene Sol MA
John: b 1757 d 1809 m Mary Gibson Sol MA
Jonathan: b 9-14-1731 d *p*. 1790 m Abigail Blood Pvt MA

SHERARD,
John: b 2-16-1746 d 2-2-1823 m Dorothy Holmes PS NC

SHERBURNE,
Andrew, Sr.: b 5-22-1730 d 1780 m Susanna Knight Pvt MM NH
Andrew, Jr.: b 9-30-1765 d 11-27-1831 m (2)Betsy Miller Slr NH ★
Benjamin: b 8-31-1832 d 1808 m Mary Cavendish Pvt NH
Henry: b 1-15-1745 d 8-25-1783 m Anne Van Leuvan Maj NY

Jacob: b 12-4-1753 d 8-11-1837 m Dorcas Holden Sol NH
James: b 1743 d 1824 m Martha Sias Cpl NH
James: b 1751 d 1813 m Betsy Gibson Pvt NH
Job: b 5-28-1754 d 5-20-1847 m Hannah Elliot Pvt NH
John Samuel: b 1757 d 8-2-1830 m Submit Boyd Maj NH
Joseph: b 1745 d 9-1-1807 m Olive Pitman Pvt NH
Samuel: b 1744 d 1824 m Phebe Chapman Pvt PS NH
Samuel: bpt 6-9-1754 d 4-21-1827 m (1)Sarah Smith (2)Nancy
    Randall (3)Sarah Stevens Pvt PS CS NH

SHERERTZ,
Ludwig: b — d . 1-7-1792 m Margaretta Kiesterin Pvt PS PA

SHERIDAN,
James: b 3-17-17-- d 3-17-1803 m Mary Armstrong Pvt Canada
Patrick: b *c*. 1756 d *c*. 1808 m Mary Spence Todd PS PA

SHERLOCK,
Ichabod: b 1762 d 1870 m Aura Welch Pvt MA

SHERMAN, (includes SHARMAN & SHEARMAN)
Aaron: b 8-25-1748 d 12-9-1806 m Sarah Kimball Pvt MA
Abel: b 1744 d 8-15-1794 m Lucy Foote Pvt MA
Abiel: b 3-7-1744 d 7-31-1834 m Mary Bouton Pvt NY W★
Abiel: b 3-11-1761 d 7-31-1837 m Johanna Howland Pvt NY ★
Abner: b 5-6-1748 d *p*. 1790 m Abigail Maynard Pvt MA
Adam: b *c*. 1740 d 5-3-1797 m Catherine Pvt VA
Amos Plumb: b 5-12-1759 d *p*. 12-24-1819 m (2)Patience Cpl MA ★
Anthony: b 9-13-1758 d 1830 m — MM Pvt NY ★
Asaph: b 9-13-1758 d 4-7-21-1810 m Lucy Whitney Lt MA
Batcheldor: b 8-27-1761 d 1828 m Waite Allen Pvt NY
Benjamin: b 1761 d 7-10-1810 m Lydia Ray Pvt CT ★
Benjamin: b 2-3-1736 d 1805 m Deborah Dilnoe CS Pvt NY
Benjamin: b 1719 d 1783 m Ruth Fish Ens RI
Beriah, Sr.: b 9-15-1705 d 4-1-1792 m Mary Crooks Pvt MA
Beriah, Jr.: b 10-7-1747 d 9- -1832 m Elizabeth Brown Pvt MA
Bezaleel: b 3-31-1703 d 1779 m Abigail Graves PS MA
Caleb: b 5-14-1762 d 9-18-1847 m Eunice Bacon Pvt MA
Caleb: b 1743 d 4-14-1814 m — Sol NY
Christopher: b 11-1-1759 d 1-12-1835 m Patience Childs Pvt MA ★
Conrad: b 1740 d 4-3-1821 m Hellen Clay Capt PA
Cornelius: b 5-15-1756 d *p*. 1802 m Delia Handy Cpl MA
Daniel: b 8-14-1721 d 7-2-1799 m Mindwell Taylor PS CT
Daniel: b 3-1-1728 d *p*. 1790 m Hannah Eddy Pvt MA
Daniel: b 8-28-1736 d 3-18-1829 m Rebecca Palmer Capt RI
David: b 12-20-1755 d 10-30-1836 m Mabel — Pvt CT
David: b 3-15-1721 d 11-10-1799 m Hannah Judson PS CT
David: b 1724 d 1778 m Rebecca French Sol NY
Ebenezer: b 11-10-1748 d 12-23-1834 m Mary Simmons Pvt MA
Eber: b 1747 d *p*. 3-4-1836 m Penelope Bentley Ens RI ★
Edmund: b 11-2-1755 d 3- -1839 m Hannah Wise Sgt CT ★
Edward: b 1726 d 11-26-1804 m Lucee Hathaway Pvt MA
Elijah: b 1-10-1746 d 4-1-1817 m Elizabeth Claghorn Pvt MA
Elijah: b 1754 d 1-5-1844 m Nannie Northrop Pvt CT
Enoch: b 9-5-1762 d 3-31-1849 m Catherine Seely Pvt CT ★
Fortunatus: b 9-24-1728 d *a*. 4-11-1803 m Sarah Delano PS NY
George, Sr.: b 11-10-1719 d 1825 m Rebecca Russell Capt VT
George, Jr.: b 7-17-1749 d 4-20-1821 m Chloe Mason Sgt MA
Gideon: b 1732 d — m Abigail Eddy Pvt MA
Henry: b 3-31-1759 d 4-8-1830 m (1)Mary Elizabeth Gardner
    (2)Sarah — Capt RI
Humphrey: b 1760 d 4-12-1812 m (1)Mary Durfee Capt RI
Humphrey: b 10-27-1755 d 1797 m Mercy Lapham Capt RI
Jacob: b 1748 d 1826 m Elizabeth Williams Pvt MA
James, Sr.: b 8-12-1716 d 1789 m Mrs Mary Stebbins Capt MA
James, Jr.: b 1750 d 7-14-1813 m (1)Hannah Gleason (2)Nancy
    Correl Cpl MA
James, Jr.: b 1-16-1747 d 12-31-1789 m Peggy Dennison Sgt MA
James: b 7-17-1762 d 1-12-1839 m Ruth Brewster Pvt RI
Jason: b 9-13-1745 d 8-6-1815 m Anna Bigelow Sgt MA
Jeremiah: b 6-12-1751 d 8- -1836 m Eunice Belknap Cpl MA
Job: b 9-30-1746 d 2-24-1837 m Elizabeth Holmes Pvt MA
Job: b 6-24-1760 d 7-24-1838 m Lucy Thomas Pvt MA
Job: b 1747 d 2-23-1836 m May Conger Sol NY ★
Job: b 1-7-1742 d 1777 m Eunice Briggs PS NY
Job: b 2-3-1757 d 7-12-1842 m Margaret Havens Pvt RI
John: b 7-19-1750 d 8-8-1802 m (1)Rebecca Austin (2)Nancy Tucker
    1Lt CS CT
John, Sr.: b 7-19-1720 d 12-17-1800 m Elizabeth Dingley Pvt MA
John, Jr.: b 6-9-1762 d 4-25-1840 m Lydia Doten Pvt MA ★
John: b 11-20-1683 d 11-28-1774 m Abigail Stone PS MA
John: b 1763 d 11-28-1833 m Chloe Dickenson Pvt MA ★
John: b 12-12-1753 d 3-23-1837 m Margaretha Ruth PS PA
John: b 4-11-1756 d — m Amy Gardner Pvt VT ★
John Higginbotham: b 10-24-1750 d 7-19-1816 m Lydia Whitford
    Sol RI
Jonathan: b 12-3-1716 d 1785 m Susanna Gifford Pvt MA
Joseph, Jr.: b 6- -1742 d 3-8-1777 m Abigail Muzzy Pvt MA
Josiah: b 4-2-1729 d 11-24-1789 m Martha Minot PS CT
Jotham: b 2-27-1733/4 d 3-12-1817 m (1)Grace Peck (2)Amy
    Beers (3)Cynthia Beers (4)Rhoda — CS PS CT
Lemuel: b 8-19-1756 d 7-10-1842 m Sarah Carswell Cpl MA
Lemuel: b 9-14-1750 d *a*, 1-4-1791 m Rose Blashfield Pvt MA

SHERMAN, contd.
Levi: b 6-29-1742 d c. 1810 m Thankful Tripp Pvt MA
Michael: b 12- -1719 d a. 4-3-1784 m Deborah Briggs Pvt MA
Nathan: b 3- -1736 d 5- -1805 m Mary Wheeler Capt CT
Nathan: b 3-18-1762 d 1851 m Bethiah Thomas Pvt MA ★
Nathan: b 6-4-1761 d 6-5-1820 m Mercy Madison Pvt VT
Nathaniel: b 8-15-1759 d 8-30-1838 m Polly Carp Nichols Pvt CT
Nathaniel: b 2-9-1748 d 7-11-1829 m Mariah Clark Cpl MA
Peleg: b 8-31-1747 d 11-20-1811 m Mary Heath Col MA
Philo: b 9-16-1760 d 1812 m Hannah Wilcox Pvt CT
Phineas: b 11-10-1719 d 10-1-1806 m (1)Elizabeth Morgan
    (2)Rachel Marsh 2Lt MA
Phineas: b 1733/4 d 7-10-1806 m Elizabeth Wheeler Capt CT
Reuben: b 12-1-1759 d 8-14-1824 m Betsey Whitcomb Pvt MA
Reuben: b 7-22-1763 d 5-3-1843 m Ruth E Sherman Pvt RI W★
Robert: b c. 1745 d 1-1-1816 m Catherine — Fif Maj VA
Roger: b 4-19-1721 d 7-23-1793 m (1)Elizabeth Hartwell (2)Rebecca
    Prescott SDI CT
Samuel: b c. 1723/4 d 2-23-1815 m (1)Experience Branch (2)Betty
    Sears Pvt MA
Samuel: b c. 1736 d p. 10-2-1807 m (1)Mary Crary (2)Hannah —
    Pvt MA
Samuel: b 10-23-1756 d 11-19-1834 m Abigail — Pvt Cav RI ★
Samuel: b 12-28-1756 d 6-10-1822 m Sarah Sawyer Pvt RI
Samuel: b 4-8-1740 d 6-22-1811 m Molly Clark CS VT
Stiles: b 2-22-1763 d 1-27-1841 m Mary Wright Cpl MA
Thomas: b 4-18-1754 d 2-8-1846 m Betsey Keith Pvt PS MA
Thomas: b 8-16-1746 d 4-1-1828 m Zerviah Lumbard Cpl MA
Thomas: b 9-6-1722 d 11-22-1803 m Anna Blodgett Pvt MA
Thomas: b 11-12-1760 d 1840 m Catherine — Sgt NJ
Timothy: b 8-30-1748 d 12-31-1819 m Mary Maynard Pvt MA
Timothy: b 9-7-1759 d p. 1820 m Polly Curtis Pvt MA ★
Wm.: b 11-12-1751 d 6-26-1789 m Sarah Law PS CT
Wm.: b 8-8-1750 d 12-28-1823 m Hannah Stevens Pvt NY
Wm.: b 1- -1752 d 9-29-1841 m Margaret Stewart Matr RI ★
Wm. Bisil: b 1759 d 1846 m Sarah Gardiner Pvt VT ★

SHERRICK, (includes SHARROCK & SHEIRICH)
James: b 1750 d 3- -1826 m Jane Everard Pvt NY
Joseph, Sr.: b 1734 d 4- -1807 m Susan Strickler Pvt PA
Joseph, Jr.: b 12-26-1757 d 12-21-1811 m Anna Musser Pvt PA
Nicholas: b 1-6-1758 d 7-28-1832 m Anna Catherine Russing Pvt PA

SHERRILL,
Abraham: bpt 4-2-1754 d 11-18-1844 m Anna Huntting Pvt NY ★
Adam: b 1758 d 6-22-1812 m Mary McCormick Pvt Sct NC
David: b — d 11-2-1818 m Elizabeth McLean Sol GA
George Davison: b 1763 d p. 1840 m Elizabeth Hunt Pvt NC ★
Henry: b 9-29-1753 d 12-8-1813 m Lois Chidsey Cpl MM NY
Jacob: b 1722 d 7- -1801 m (1)Abigail Conkling (2)Clemens
    Huntting PS NY
Jeremiah: bpt 12-10-1750 d 1-14-1840 m Elizabeth Hand Pvt NY ★
Joshua: b 6-4-1752 d 9- -1817 m Susanna Osborne Sol NC
Lewis: b 4-14-1761 d 12-16-1840 m Mary Mason Sol NC
Moses: b 8-8-1742 d 1-15-1813 m Anna Simpson PS NC
Recompence. Sr.: b 1706 d 2-7-1786 m (1)Sarah Leak (2)Puah
    Parsons PS NY
Recompence, Jr.: b 5-11-1741 d 6-7-1839 m Naomi Burnham PS
    Capt NY
Samuel: b 10-1-1725 d p. 1780 m — Sol NC
Samuel Wilson: b 3-21-1758 d 10-12-1823 m Elizabeth — Sol NC
Uriah: b 2-12-1757 d p. 1790 m (1)Betsy Clark (2) — Sol NC
Wm.: b 5-1-1723 d 12-31-1786 m Agnes White Sol NC

SHERROD,
Arthur: b 1755-65 d 5-11-1831 m Sarah Boykin PS NC
Thomas: b 1730 d 1818 m (2)Elizabeth — CS Col NC

SHERWIN,
Ahimaaz: b 8-7-1759 d 12-31-1839 m Ruth Day Fif MA CT
Asa: b 12-16-1744 d 2-6-1812 m (1)Mehitable Porter (2)Mercy
    Kimball Lt NH
Daniel, Sr.: b 2-15-1730 d 6-24-1804 m Susanna Proctor Lt MA
Daniel, Jr.: b 5-3-1757 d 4-17-1834 m Abigail Manning Pvt MA ★
Ebenezer, Sr.: b 3-12-1728 d p. 12-15-1786 m Sarah Hovey PS MA
John: b 10-27-1758 d 10-5-1830 m (1)Kezia Adams (2)Lucretia
    Smith (3)Eunice Farwell Pvt MA W★
John: b 5-15-1732 d p. 1781 m Mary Gould Pvt NH
Jonathan: b 9-6-1729 d 2-23-1804 m (1)Mary Crumbie (2)Content
    Lapham CS PS NH
Joshua: b 10-9-1737 d p. 1779 m Esther Badger Pvt MA
Nathaniel: b 1760 d 1834 m Mary Bement Pvt MA

SHERWOOD,
Abel, Jr.: b 1750 d 10-14-1819 m Kesiah Hodge Pvt CT
Adiel: b 12-25-1749 d 12-14-1824 m Sarah Sherwood Capt NY ★
Albert: b 11-18-1733 d 11-12-1803 m Anna Buckingham Lt CT
Amos: b 1745 d 12-17-1808 m (2)Mollie Fanton Pvt CT
Andrew: b 2-4-1746 d 9-29-1831 m (2)Judah Richmon Sgt NY ★
Asa: b 7-4-1762 d 6-18-1834 m Mary Philips Pvt CT ★
Benjamin: b 4-13-1760 d 1820 m Anna Hull Cpl CT
Benjamin: b 4-10-1753 d 4:11-1840 m Sarah Olmstead Pvt CT
Daniel: b 11-1-1759 d 7-24-1834 m Polly Hill Cpl CT ★

Daniel: b 11-20-1735 d 4-5-1819 m Abigail Andrews Pvt CS CT
Daniel: b 2-28-1752 d 6-1-1826 m Pruella Lyon Pvt CT
Daniel: b 5-20-1749 d 3-18-1838 m (1)Frances Linthicum (2)Rachel
    — Pvt MD
David: b 5-21-1745 d 4-22-1817 m Abigail Ogden Pvt CT
Eleazer: bpt 10-21-1733 d 2-15-1808 m Mary Squires Cpl CT
Eliphalet: b 1758 d 11-21-1831 m Abigail — Pvt CT
Gershom: b 1734 d 2- -1805 m Mary Auser Lt NY
Isaac: b 1731 d 8-19-1814 m Mary Martha Holmes Pvt CT
Isaac: b 1754 d 5- -1803 m Rebeckah — LCol NY
Isaac: b 1758 d 8-8-1844 m Drusilla Moorehouse Pvt CT
Jabez: b 7-4-1744 d 7-17-1825 m Damaris Cable Pvt CT
Jabez: b 12-28-1719 d 3-15-1788 m Hannah Disbrow PS CT
James: b c. 1755 d 5-27-1838 m Sarah Roberts Pvt NY
Jehiel: b 3-1-1739 d p. 1795 m Sarah Squire Ens CT
Jeremiah: b 1738 d 1792 m Abigail Bishop Pvt NY
Job: b 1725 d 4-4-1800 m Sarah Drake Pvt NY
John, Sr.: b 1705 d 1779 m Mary Walker Pvt CT
John, Jr.: b 1739 d 6-30-1810 m Eunice Lacey Capt PS CT
John: b 12-13-1749 d 1790 m Ann Thomas Sgt NY
Jonathan: b 1757 d 8-7-1825 m Martha Bruce Cpl MA
Joseph: b 1-15-1754 d 1-22-1838 m (1)Sarah Bradley (2)Mrs
    Hannah Gregory Lt CT
Joseph: b 5-16-1712 d — m Mary — Pvt NY
Lemuel: b — d — m Elizabeth Gibbs Pvt CT
Moses: b 1762 d 2-17-1837 m Apolona Rosecrans Pvt NY
Nathan: b 1-16-1738 d 2-17-1824 m Johanna Noblet Pvt NY
Nathan: b 1759 d 4-20-1822 m Lucy Hollister Pvt NY ★
Nehemiah: b 1762 d 7-10-1819 m Mary Shelly Pvt NY ★
Nicholas: b a. 1746 d 1794 m Susannah — Cpl MD
Samuel: b 9-19-1731 d 9-10-1802 m Ann Nichols Sol CT
Samuel: b 1732 d 2-9-1788 m Ruth — Lt NY
Samuel: b 7-8-1761 d 5-11-1838 m Priscilla Burr Pvt CT
Samuel: b 2-10-1729 d 5-25-1783 m Rachel Hyde PS CT
Seth: b 6-18-1720 d — m Sarah Petcher Capt NY
Seth: b 1747 d 5- -1820 m Elizabeth Bronson Capt NY
Solomon: b — d p. 4-10-1798 m Elizabeth Forshay Pvt NY
Wm.: b 12-2-1758 d 2-12-1821 m Rebecca Sherwood Pvt NY

SHETHAR,
John: b 12-14-1752 d 6-19-1835 m (1)Sarah Smith (2)Nancy
    Nelson Capt CT ★

SHETZLINE
Adam: b 6-25-1744 d 12-23-1826 m Hannah Baker Pvt PA

SHEW,
Godfrey: b a. 1710 d p. 1782 m Catherine Frey Pvt NY
Jacob: b 4-15-1763 d 1-23-1853 m Hannah Putnam Pvt NY
Stephen: b 1761 d 3-27-1841 m (1)Rachel Sammons (2)Susannah
    Wells Pvt NY ★

SHEWELL,
Robert: b 1-27-1740 d 12-28-1825 m Sarah Sallows LCol PA

SHIBE,
Matthew: b 5-14-1736 d 4-9-1807 m Ann Catherine Pheiffer Pvt PA

SHIELDS, (or SHIELD)
Daniel: b 2-14-1766 d 10-17-1835 m Elizabeth Fenn Pvt NY
David: b 7-19-1764 d 1844 m Nancy McChord Pvt PA ★
David: b 1752 d 7-21-1841 m Elizabeth Henry Pvt VA ★
David Lombard: b 1-23-1757 d 5-8-1843 m (1)Miriam Cannon (2)
    Abigail Burnham Sgt MA ★
George: b c. 1755 d 5-4-1813 m Mary — PS Ens PA
James: b 7-21-1757 d 8-23-1840 m Jane Gilliland Pvt MD
James: b 1745 d 4- -1847 m Margaret Douglas Pvt PA ★
James: b 10-27-1739 d 1794/5 m Susannah Page Capt VA
James: b 1751 d p. 8-3-1779 m Elizabeth Graham Pvt VA
James: b a. 1752 d p. 1791 m Elizabeth Higginbotham Pvt VA
James: b c. 1754 d 7-10-1824 m Nancy Ann Brown Pvt VA
James: b — d p. 1783 m Nancy Brown Pvt VA
John: b c. 1720 d p. 1-29-1777 m Margaret — Maj GA
John: b 2-21-1740 d 11-3-1821 m Jean Kirkpatrick Maj PA
John: b 8-22-1759 d 10-26-1840 m (1)Mary Elizabeth Marshall (2)
    Elizabeth Carson Cpl PA W★
John: b 1732 d 1783 m Rebecca Childs Capt VA
John: b 1750 d 1-16-1779 m Mary McMullen Capt VA
Joseph: b c. 1719 d p. 1790 m — Fortque Lt PA
Luke, Jr.: b c. 1740 d c. 1805 m Rebecca Robinson PS DE
Matthew: b 1730 d 1785 m Sarah — Pvt PA
Matthew: b c. 1738 d 10- -1809 m Mary McKane Pvt PA
Robert: b c. 1745 d 1804 m Anne — Pvt PA
Robert: b 1738-40 d p. 1802 m Nancy Stockton Pvt VA
Robert: b 4- -1759 d 3-31-1804 m Martha Hansford Ens VA
Wm., Sr.: b 7-14-1728 d 1797 m Jane Bently Williams PS Capt MD
Wm.: b c. 1740 d p. 2-10-1791 m — Pvt NC
Wm.: b 1760 d 10-5-1823 m Mary Houston Pvt NC W★

SHIELL,
Hugh: b c. 1760 d 11- -1785 m Ann Harris PS Dr PA

SHILL,
Jacob: b — d 2-5-1829 m Elizabeth Smidt Cpl NY

SHILLABER,
Robert: b 5-20-1736 d 6-20-1808 m Elizabeth Proctor Pvt MA

SHILLIDEAY,
George: b c. 1750 d p. 11-15-1796 m Esther Baker CS VA

SHILLING,
George: b — d 3- -1798 m Bridget Shrader (Blackstone)Pvt VA
John: b c. 1753 d 9- -1804 m Barbare Oberlin Pvt PA

SHILLINGFORD,
James: b 1731 d 11-10-1793 m Mary — PS PA
John: b 1-1-1760 d 5-23-1839 m Jane Quinn Pvt PA

SHILLITON,
George: b 1759 d 12-7-1845 m Nancy Miller Pvt PA

SHIMER,
Abraham: b 1724 d 1805 m (1)Lena Westbrook (2)Mrs Margaret Van Etten Willson Capt NJ
Edward: b 2-28-1741 d 2-16-1815 m Rosina Shimer PS PA
Peter: b 1-20-1760 d 10-22-1828 m (1)Anna Maria Lerch (2)Mrs Elizabeth (Kratzer) Lerch Pvt PA
Samuel: b 1738 d p. 1790 m Elizabeth Johnson Of PA

SHIMP,
Andrew: b c. 1759 d 2- -1838 m Elizabeth Miller Pvt PA
Casper: b c. 1756 d 1821 m Catherine Elizabeth Guyer Lt PA
John: b 5-20-1758 d p. 7-5-1836 m Eve Speck Pvt PA

SHINDEL,
Frederick G.: b 8-27-1760 d 11-19-1815 m Gertrude Windemeyer Pvt PA
Lutwig: b 5-22-1759 d 2-23-1830 m Elizabeth Millin Pvt PA
Peter, Sr.: b 2-28-1732 d 5-29-1784 m Anna Margretta Gephart Sgt PA
Peter, Jr.: b 8-21-1766 d 12-17-1829 m Anna Maria Menges FifMaj PA

SHINE,
John: b 11-25-1725 d 12-12-1783 m Sarah Shelweain Capt NC
John: b 5-5-1759 d 3-11-1832 m Clarissa Williams Pvt NC

SHINER,
Andrew: b 1749 d 4-4-1841 m Margaret Smith Pvt PA

SHINGLER,
George: b 1761 d 6-8-1808 m Mary Shingler Pvt SC

SHINN,
Benjamin: b c. 1733 d 1791 m Anne Reese PS VA
Buddell: b 1745 d 1787 m Sarah Bispham QM NJ
George: b 1-1-1737 d 9-23-1782 m Rachel Wright Pvt VA
Isaac: b 10-9-1760 d 9-7-1844 m Agnes Drake Sct Spy VA
John: b 1767 d 1801 m Jane Herbert PS NJ
Joseph: b 11-27-1751 d 12- -1804 m Jane Ross Capt NC
Samuel: b 1743 d p. 1779 m Elizabeth Starkey Pvt NJ
Vincent: b 1745 d 10-6-1784 m Elizabeth Budd Wgm NJ

SHIP, (includes SHIPP)
John: b 1757 d 1817 m Elizabeth Cannon Pvt NC
Laban: b 5-5-1757 d 6-26-1828 m Elizabeth Allen Pvt VA
Richard: b 11-12-1747 d p. 1828 m Elizabeth Doniphan Ens VA
Richard: b c. 1740 d p. 2-9-1781 m (1)Elizabeth — (2)Isabel Martin Sol VA
Thomas: b 10-26-1757 d 4-26-1853 m Hannah Joyce Pvt NC ★
Thomas: b 1750 d p. 1808 m Jedediah Moore Pvt VA
Thomas: b c. 1727 d 1777 m Rachel — CS VA

SHIPE, (or SHIEP)
George: b 8-10-1744 d 7- -1815 m Ann Elizabeth Shellenberger Pvt PA
Peter: b c. 1750 d 1829 m Elizabeth Walker Pvt VA

SHIPLEY,
Able: b c. 1742 d a. 1806 m Lucy Farley PS NH
Adam: b 8-17-1759 d 3-8-1840 m Rachel Frost Capt PS MD VA ★
Benjamin: b 1750 d 7-27-1828 m (1)Rachel Frost (2)Amelia Hobbs PS MD
Henry: b 1759 d 2-11-1828 m Ruth Howard Pvt MD W★
John: b c. 1743 d a. 1-12-1815 m (1)Keziah Porter (2)Eleanor Purnell Lt MD
Richard: b 1730 d 1787 m Christina — Ens VA
Samuel: b 1751 d p. 1831 m (1)Violota — (2)Ketura Sutton Pvt MD
Wm.: b c. 1729 d p. 10-10-1794 m Sarah Rumford Pvt PS DE

SHIPMAN,
Aaron: b 7-16-1760 d 1-22-1840 m Phebe Tuttle MM NJ
Daniel: b 1747 d 1810 m Elizabeth McMin Capt NC
David: b c. 1735 d 2-28-1813 m — Pvt NY
Edward: b 1734 d 12-19-1804 m Joanna — Maj CT
Herman: b 1717 d p. 9-3-1798 m Elizabeth Howe PS NJ
Jabez, Sr.: b c. 1730 d 1781 m Phoebe Rogers Pvt NJ

Jacob: b 1750 d 1-23-1833 m Maria — Capt NJ
Jacob: b c. 1746 d p. 11-19-1794 m Sarah — Pvt NC
James: b 5-10-1855 d 6-21-1821 m Philena Ingraham Sgt CT ★
John: b 1-20-1717 d 11-21-1786 m Margaret Bushnell CS CT
John: b 8-11-1763 d a. 1832 m Jane Ewing Sol VA
Jonathan: b 7-28-1723 d 12-3-1806 m Abigal Fox Pvt CT
Joseph: b 5-8-1757 d 1828 m Anne Gillam Pvt NJ
Matthias: b 7-12-1726 d 1-12-1812 m Margart Sharpenstein LCol NJ
Nicholas: b 1758 d 9- -1827 m Catharine Fisher Pvt NJ
Samuel, Sr.: b 5-21-1726 d 9-3-1801 m (1)Sarah Doty (2)Hannah Bushnell NCapt CT
Samuel, Jr.: b 9-3-1750 d 3-12-1826 m Sarah Stanclift Sgt CT
Silas: b 8- -1759 d 2-4-1832 m Sarah Sanders Tms CT W★
Stephen: bpt 7-25-1762 d 1804-14 m Deborah Percel Pvt VA
Stephen, Jr.: b 2-20-1750 d 2-8-1834 m Eunice Rea Pvt CT
Timothy: b 12-31-1748 d 10-20-1828 m Rachel Ackerman Sol NY

SHIPPEN,
Edward, Sr.: b 7-9-1703 d 9-25-1781 m (1)Sarah Plumley (2)Mary Knowland PS PA
Edward, Jr.: b 2-10-1728 d 4-16-1806 m Margaret Francis PS PA
Wm.: b 1750 d 1777 m Benjamina Fisher Capt PA
Wm., Sr.: b 10-1-1712 d 11-4-1801 m Susannah Harrison PS PA

SHIPPEY,
Caleb: b 8-23-1747 d 6-12-1838 m Alice Collins Pvt RI ★
Christopher: b 1748 d 1835 m Hannah Harrington Pvt RI ★
Joseph: b 2-8-1717 d p. 1777 m Bethiah Herendeen Sol RI
Thomas: b 1747 d 3-20-1823 m Hannah Matthewson Pvt RI ★
Wm.: b 8-26-1755 d 4-26-1841 m Catherine — Pvt NY ★

SHIRA,
John: b 1757 d 1822 m Maria Anna Frifugle Ens PA

SHIRK,
Andrew: b 9-7-1753 d 1-14-1829 m Martha Hamilton Pvt PA
Michael: b 5-26-1758 d 4-4-1827 m Barbara Flickenger Pvt PA
Ulrich: b 5-16-1751 d 5-14-1842 m Mariah Eberly Pvt PA

SHIRLEY,
Edward: b 1743 d 10-31-1816 m (1)Elizabeth Hutchins (2)Abigail Kelley Sol MA
George: b c. 1761 d p. 5-8-1824 m Ruhannah Norris Fif PA
James: b 1700 d 5- -1796 m Janet Shirley PS NH
James: b 1739 d 1815 m Judith Garriott Pvt VA
Job: b — d 8-25-1842 m Mary Wilbur MM MA
John: b 1-1-1755 d 11-23-1848 m Submit Bogle Pvt MA ★
John: b c. 1735 d 1826 m Hannah Stevens Sol NH
John: b 4- -1760 d 3-12-1840 m Francis Yates Pvt VA★
Michael: b c. 1740 d p. 7-23-1784 m Katie Franz Lt VA
Samuel: b 12-25-1748 d 12-7-1832 m (1)Margaret Graham (2)Anna Hazard (3)Betty McDuffee Pvt NH ★
Thomas: b 1728 d 2-27-1808 m Margaret Shirley Pvt NH
Thomas: b c. 1740 d p. 1810 m Nelly — Sol PS SC
Thomas: b 3-21-1761 d 4-17-1820 m Mollie Yates Pvt VA
Valentine: b c. 1751 d 9- -1811 m Catherine Baer Ens PS VA
Wm.: b — d 4-4-1807 m Annis Mayley Pvt MA
Wm. Stubley: b 8-31-1757 d 6-3-1799 m Elizabeth Maxwell Pvt GA

SHIRTS,
Christian: b — d p. 9-20-1783 m Anna Barbara Christ Pvt PA
John: b c. 1750 d p. 8-1-1813 m Dellj — Wgm NJ
Mathias: b 2-13-1753 d 1-14-1845 m Susannah McGehan Cpl NY NJ
Michael: b 7-4-1760 d 5-23-1840 m (1)Anna Haver (2)Mary Taylor Sgt PS NJ ★
Peter: b 1752 d 1824 m Sarah Houser Pvt NY

SHISSLER,
Conrad: b 1758 d c. 11-6-1821 m Anna — Pvt PA
Godfrey: b c. 1750 d c. 1786 m Hannah — Lt PA

SHIVE,
George: b 2-5-1763 d 4-5-1836 m Katherine — Pvt PA
Lewis: b 1-26-1760 d 11-29-1848 m Magdalena — Pvt PA ★
Philip: b 4-19-1756 d 10-4-1836 m Anna Catherine Goodman Pvt PA ★

SHIVEL,
Frederick: b 1755 d p. 2-14-1747 d Margaret — Pvt PA

SHIVELY,
Christian: b 1751 d 12-12-1842 m Sophia Catherine Smith Pvt PA
Henry: b 6- -1760 d 6-14-1842 m Mary Banta Pvt PA
Jacob: b 2-22-1751 d 1-1-1824 m Barbara Linder Pvt PA
John: b 3-15-1761 d 1834 m — Sgt NJ ★
Peter: b 4-10-1742 d 9-7-1823 m (1)Anna Elizabeth Heinsin (2)Christina Linn Pvt PA

SHIVERICK,
David: b 9-1-1727 d 12-31-1811 m Martha Robinson Pvt MA
Joseph: b 8-16-1756 d 3-29-1838 m Elizabeth Price Cpl MA

SHIVERS,
Jesse: b *a.* 1760 d *p.* 9-18-1819 m Sallie — Mus NC ★
John, 2d: b 1738 d 6-13-1802 m Zipporah Cheesman Pvt NY
Jonas, Jr.: b 10-14-1750 d 11-12-1825 m Lilory Godwin Pvt GA

SHOBE,
Martin: b *c.* 1727 d 1792 m Elizabeth Hier PS VA
Rudolph: b *c.* 1755 d *a.* 3-30-1821 m — PS VA

SHOCKEY, (includes SHOCKEN)
Abraham: b — d 11-1-1782 m Elizabeth — Pvt MD
Christian: b 4-18-1756 d 4-18-1829 m Mary Welch Pvt PA ★
George Philip: b *a.* 10-17-1807 m (1)Elizabeth Shockey
    (2)Anna Barbara Crist PS PA
Jacob: b *c.* 1750 d 1803 m Anna — Pvt PA

SHOCKLEY, (includes SHORKLEY)
Samuel: b 1753 d 10-11-1798 m Susanna Cushman Pvt MA
Solomon: b *c.* 1760 d *a.* 2-15-1822 m — Pvt MD
Thomas: b 9-15-1755 d 9-18-1843 m Elizabeth — Pvt VA ★

SHOCKNEY,
Patrick: b 1752/3 d 2-6-1827 m Mary Nash Pvt PA ★

SHOECRAFT,
Jacob: b 5-10-1759 d 2-17-1836 m Caroline Sammon Pvt NY
John: b 12-13-1755 d 4-14-1833 m Elizabeth McKee Sgt NY

SHOEMAKER, (includes SCHUMACHER & SHUMAKER)
Abraham: b 6-10-1758 d 7-2-1845 m Margaret Melick Pvt PA ★
Charles: b 12-28-1742 d 4-27-1820 m Maria Kepner PS PA
Christopher: b 7-19-1759 d 5-19-1831 m Elizabeth Eder Pvt NY
Conrad: b 9-22-1751 d 9- -1832 m Anna Maria Meixsell Pvt PA
Daniel: b 11-22-1751 d 8-13-1836 mAnna McDowell Lt PA
Elijah: b — d 7-4-1778 m Jane McDowell Lt PA
George: b *.c.* 1759 d *p.* 1805 m Mary Magdalena Frantz Pvt VA
Gottfried: b 5-19-1731 d 1781 m Anna Maria Henrich Stahl Pvt NY
Hanyost: b 8-29-1747 d *c.* 1800 m Mary Smith Maj NY
Henry: b 1758 d 11-15-1833 m (1)Phebe Peck (2)Hannah More (3)
    Rachel Moore Tms NJ
Henry: b 1731 d 7-18-1797 m Barbara Kepner LCol PA
Henry: b *c.* 1755 d 10- -1821 m (1)Barbara Raube (2)Sarah Slutter
    Capt PS
Henry: b 1750/1 d 1826 m (1)Blandina VanCampen (2)Sarah
    Chambers Lt PA
Isaac: b 1753 d 9-8-1829 m Cathrerine E Carpenter Pvt PA
Jacob: b 1744 d 10-5-1810 m (1)Elizabeth Arndt (2)Elizabeth
    Eberhard Lt PA
John: b 1759 d 8-11-1815 m Mary Ann Baker Pvt PS PA
John George: b 3-31-1731 d 1-2-1801 m Susanna Weiss Pvt PA
John Henry: b — d 8-13-1832 m Christine Margaretha Hirsch Pvt PA
Jonathan: b 5-10-1756 d 12-12-1837 m (1)Hannah Lukens
    (2)Elizabeth Deaves CS PA
Leonard Claybourne: b 5-19-1757 d 1837 m Eunice Ritchey Pvt
    VA ★
Matthias: b 12-14-1736 d 1-17-1816 m Hannah Kenderdine Sol
    PA
Peter: b 8-28-1748 d 9-11-1834 m Maria Wolver Pvt NY ★
Peter: b 11-9-1749 d *c.* 1814 m (1)Elizabeth Magdalene Maurer (2)
    Elizabeth Domblasser Pvt PA
Peter: b 1758 d *a.* 12-5-1821 m — Pvt PA
Peter: b *c.* 1750 d *p.* 7-1-1799 m Elizabeth Sea PS VA
Rudolph: bpt 10-9-1756 d *p.* 1790 m Mary Rosencrans Capt NY
Simon: b 10-24-1757 d 8-29-1830 m Barbara Ballou Pvt PA
Thomas: b *c.* 1760 d 2-1-1821 m Frances Shepherd Sol PS VA
Zedekiah: b 1753 d 4-18-1839 m Elizabeth Peters Pvt VA ★

SHOFNER,
Henry: b 1755 d 1845 m Nancy — Pvt NC
Martin: b 12-8-1758 d 9-30-1838 m Catherine Cook Pvt NC

SHOLES,
Abel: b 4-15-1735 d 10-4-1789 m Lucy Mallerson Sol CT
Cyrus: b 2-21-1758 d 1790 m Bridget Latham Pvt CT
Miner: b 12-31-1760 d 12-15-1842 m Abigail Pvt CT ★
Stanton: b 3-14-1772 d 3-7-1865 m Abigail Avery Sol CT

SHOMO,
John: b 5-1-1752 d 5-5-1836 m (1)Anna Marie — (2)Barbara —
    Pvt PA ★

SHONNARD,
Frederick: b 8-24-1720 d — m Elizabeth Fairchild Pvt NY

SHOOK,
Jacob: b 4-19-1749 d 1839 m Isabella Wysel Pvt NC ★
John: b 1754 d 7-10-1829 m Sophia Kessler Pvt PA

SHOOTS,
John: b 1755 d 1816 m Mary Wilson Pvt VA

SHOPBELL,
Daniel: b 1760 d 1806 m — PS PA

SHOPF,
Henry: b 8-18-1733 d 3-16-1804 m Ann — Pvt VA

SHOPPEE,
Anthony: b 9-11-1760 d 10-19-1817 m Phoebe Spear Pvt MA

SHORES,
Benjamin: b 1731 d *a.* 1784 m Jemima Pratt Crossman 1Lt MA
Henry: b 2-13-1735 d *p.* 9-16-1819 m Barbara Mueller PS NC
John: b *c.* 1710 d 1785 m Elizabeth Smith PS VT
Richard: b *c.* 10-16-1755 d 1840 m Susannah Simpson Ens VA
Thomas, Sr.: b 1733 d 1795 m Sarah Woodson Capt CS VA
Thomas, Sr.: b *c.* 1730 d 1815 m Susanna Woodson CS VA
Thomas, Jr.: b 1755 d 10-15-1841 m (1)Susanna Buggs (2)Elizabeth
    Putney Pvt VA ★

SHOREY,
Abel: b 9-12-1766 d 1-18-1858 m Nancy Fuller Tms Pvt MA
John: b 3-30-1736 d 1-25-1816 m Patience Read Pvt MA
John: b 2-2-1755 d 9-3-1842 m Mary Piper MM Pvt MA ★

SHORT,
Daniel: b 1741 d 9-30-1817 m (1)Hopestill Wheeler (2)—
    Phillips Cpl MA
John: b 1757 d 8-25-1822 m Betsey Short Pvt RI
John: b 2-15-1756 d 5-15-1836 m Mary Hansford Pvt VA ★
Joshua: b 1752 d *c.* 2-9-1841 m Parthena — Pvt VA ★
Moses: b 7-22-1760 d 7-6-1841 m (1)Lydia Emery (2)Abigail IIsley
    Pvt MA
Petrus: b *c.* 1732 d 1806 m Annatje Bakker Pvt NY
Philip: b 5-24-1746 d 2-25-1810 m Margart Col Pvt MA
Philip, Sr.: b 1728 d *p.* 1790 m Lydia — PS MA
Richard: b 1745 d *p.* 1786 m Anne — Cpl PA
Samuel: b 4-8-1762 d 3-21-1847 m Mary Cross Pvt CT
Samuel: b 1755 d 1836 m Eleanor Chace Pvt Drm RI
Shubael: b *c.* 1763 d 5-29-1842 m Mary Barney Pvt MA ★
Siloam: b 7-10-1752 d 6-10-1835 m Mary Day Sgt CT ★
Thomas, Sr.: b 1720 d *p.* 1790 m Mary Lee Sol VA
Thomas, Jr.: b *c.* 1760 d 8-8-1810 m Dorothy Jones LCol VA
Thomas: b 1763 d 9- -1815 m Martha Jones Pvt VA
Wm.: b 4-8-1730 d 2-8-1805 m Winifred Richardson Capt PS VA
Wm.: b 11-23-1763 d 6-15-1849 m (1)Theodosia — (2)Susannah
    Crump (3)Jemima Jones Pvt VA

SHORTRIDGE,
Richard: bpt 12-13-1762 d 6-5-1811 m Mary Pitman Capt NH
Richard: b 10-20-1734 d 7-8-1776 m Lois Ham Pvt NH
Samuel: b *c.* 1756 d *p.* 8-20-1822 m Sarah — Sol KY VA

SHOTWELL,
Caleb: b 12-1-1749 d 1796 m Phoebe Hickston Pvt NJ
Jacob: b 8-29-1746 d 12-15-1815 m Bathsheba Pound Pvt NJ
James: b 1-23-1752 d 6-4-1795 m Elsa Smalley Runyon Pvt NJ
Jasper: b *a.* 11-17-1757 d *p.* 5-3-1816 m Clarry Lines Pvt NJ
John: b 3-6-1753 d 12-19-1826 m Abigail Shipman Pvt NJ
John: b 7-7-1712 d *c.* 1779 m (1)Elizabeth Smith (2)Grace Webster
    PS NJ

SHOUP, (includes SHOOP, SHOOPE, SHOPE, SHUPE & SHUPP)
Abraham: b 1752 d *p.* 1791 m Maria Catharine Pvt PA
Bernard: b — d 1813 m — Maeder Pvt PA
Henry, Sr.: b — d 11-27-1833 m Elizabeth Selson Sol PA
Jacob: b *c.* 1755 d *p.* 8-4-1810 m (1)Sarah Rebecca Lightcap (2)Ann
    Elizabeth — Capt PA
John D.: b 5-19-1750 d 4-2-1835 m Mary Messer Pvt PA
John: b 3-13-1756 d *a.* 10-27-1852 m Sara Gragg Pvt PA ★
Michael: b 1762-65 d *p.* 6-8-1810 m Christine Royer Pvt PA
Sebastian: b 1735 d *p.* 1792 m Margaret — CMman PA

SHOUSE,
Henry: b 1754 d 9-26-1825 m (1)Elizabeth Rose (2)Elizabeth Jones
    Pvt PA

SHOVER,
Henry: b *c.* 1755 d 6- -1831 m Rosanna Baker PS MD
Peter: b *a.* 1755 d *p.* 1795 m — Lt MD

SHOWALTER,
Jacob: b *c.* 1744 d 3-25-1809 m Barbara — Pvt PA
John, Sr.: b *c.* 1732 d 1806 m Esther — PS PA
John, Jr.: b *a.* 1758 d *p.* 1813 m Barbara Falley Pvt PA
Ulrich: b *c.* 1743 d *p.* 1816 m Susannah Watterson Pvt PA

SHOWER,
Henry: b 7-14-1751 d 11-21-1818 m Barbara Gerben PS PA
John: b 7-25-1730 d 4-10-1810 m Anna Mary Born Pvt MD
Nicholas: b 5-2-1755 d 7-15-1829 m Maria Gehrigin Cpl PA

SHRADER, (includes SCHRADER, SHRADAR, SCHREEDER
    SHREDER)
John: b 1745 d 12-13-1825 m Elizabeth Hack Pvt NY ★
Philip: b 1750 d 1822 m Catherine Schrawder Capt PA
Philip: b *c.* 1749 d 10-1-1778 m — Byre Cpl PA

Wm.: b 3-6-1755 d 8-4-1828 m Mary Sechrest Pvt PA
John J.: b 3-14-1756 d *p.* 1820 m Anna Barabara Eplin Pvt NY

SHREFFLER,
Henry: b 3-15-1751 d 1833 m Christine — Pvt PA ★

SHREIBER,
Steffan: b *c.* 1750 d *p.* 1-12-1820 m (1)Rebecca Rachall (2)Mrs
   Brant Sol NY

SHRENK,
Andrew: b *c.* 1760 d 7- -1809 m Elizabeth Lichty Pvt PA

SHREVE,
Caleb: b 8-25-1734 d 4-21-1792 m Grace Pancoast Pvt PS NJ
Caleb: b 8-13-1721 d 9-27-1786 m Abigail Antrum PS NJ
Isaac: b *c.* 1750 d 1829 m Abigail Thorn PS NJ
Israel: b 12-25-1739 d 12-14-1799 m (1)Grace Curtis (2)Mary
   Cokely Col NJ
Joshua: b 1740 d 1819 m Rebecca Lamb Pvt NJ
Richard: b 9-25-1760 d 9-12-1822 m Margaret Newbold Capt NJ
Samuel: b 1-25-1750 d 1815 m Mira Trout LCol NJ
Samuel: b 9-15-1747 d *c.* 1790 m Sophia — Sol NJ
Wm.: b 8-4-1737 d 1812 m (1)Anna Ivans (2)Ann Reckless Col NJ
Wm.: b 8-26-1761 d 1-26-1837 m (1)Mary Laurence (2)Mrs
   Ann Wake Cav VA ★

SHREWSBURY,
Samuel: b *c.* 1740 d *p.* 4-2-1782 m Elizabeth Dabney CS PS VA

SHRINER, (includes SCHREINER & SHREINER)
George Michael: b *c.* 1740 d 1812 m Anna Barbara Schreiber Pvt PA
Martin: b 11-11-1715 d 1-28-1807 m Anna Margaretha
   Shoufberger PS PA
Michael: b 1749 d 1827 m — Pvt PA
Philip: b 12-18-1758 d *c.* 1830 m Susanna — Pvt PA
Philip: b 8-25-1724 d 3-5-1791 m Eva Catherine Boltz PS PA

SHRIVER, (includes SCHRIVER & SCHRYVER)
Adam: b 1740 d *p.* 1803 m Christianna — PS VA
Albartus: b 1-8-1760 d *p.* 1805 m Marie van Wagenen Pvt NY
David: b 3-30-1735 d 1-30-1826 m Anna Rebecca Farrie LCol PS
   MD
Henry: b 4-17-1727 d 1794 m (1)Anna Maria Solmes (2)Mary — PS
   MD
John Peter: b 5-19-1748 d *p.* 1793 m Neeltjen VanBenschoten Pvt
   NY
Peter: bpt 5-15-1720 d 1798 m Anna Barbara Shever Pvt NY
Stephen: b 5-20-1750 d 6-4-1822 m Sara Stynberg Pvt PS NY

SHROCK,
Henry: b 1755 d *p.* 1790 m Catherine Housman Pvt PA

SHRODE,
John: b — d *p.* 1798 m — Pvt PA

SHRODLE,
Andreas: b 7-24-1722 d 11-1-1804 m Sabina Klein CS PA

SHROPSHIRE,
Abner: b 5-13-1761 d 12-13-1841 m Susanna Foster Pvt VA

SHRUM,
Peter: b 1762 d *p.* 12-1-1835 m Margaret Espey Pvt NC ★

SHRYOCK,
Henry: b 10-2-1734 d 12-10-1809 m Catherine Soloday LCol MD
John: b 9- -1747 d 10- -1831 m Mary Teagarden Pvt PS MD
Leonard: b 1-2-1738 d 1/2-12-1782 m Marie Magareta Streiter 2Lt
   MD

SHUBERT,
Christopher: b 1-8-1756 d 11-25-1836 m Elizabeth Beils Pvt PA

SHUBRICK,
Richard: b 10-9-1751 d 11-8-1777 m Susan Bulline Capt SC
Thomas: b 12-27-1756 d 1810 m Mary Branford Maj SC

SHUCK,
Jacob: b 1748 d *p.* 4-30-1832 m Ann Barbara Way Lt PA

SHUEY,
Christian: b 10-10-1760 d 8-30-1814 m Magdalena Edris Pvt PA
Daniel: b 1743 d 8-23-1804 m Eva Rosanna Sample Cpl PA
John Henry: b 3-9-1748 d 10-15-1804 m Barbara Tice Pvt PA
John Ludwick: b 5-6-1755 d 1-22-1839 m Mary Lash Pvt PA
Ludwig: b 10-12-1726 d 2-25-1775 m Elizabeth — PS PA
Martin: b 6-20-1750 d 2-2-1829 m Margaret Elizabeth Conrad Pvt
   PA

SHUFELT, (includes ZUFELT)
Peter: b 4-18-1755 d 5-29-1834 m Maritje Coon Sgt NY ★
Philip: bpt 4-15-1740 d 1807 m Sarah Shaeffer Pvt NY

SHUFORD,
John, Sr.: b 1718 d 6-18-1790 m (1)Sarah — (2)Mary Clare — PS
   NC

SHUGART,
Eli: b 9-10-1755 d 1-4-1832 m (1)Phoebe Lodge (2)Elizabeth — Pvt
   PA ★
Zachariah: b *c.* 1738 d *p.* 1790 m Mary Elizabeth Mulholland Lt PA

SHULER,
Lawrence: b 3-12-1735 d 2-14-1813 m Mrs Sarah Du Bois Overbaugh Lt NY

SHULTSBACH,
Philip: b *c.* 1749 d 10-12-1784 m Margaret — Pvt PA

SHULTZ, (includes SCHULTZ, SHOULTES, SHOULTZ, SHULTES)
Abraham: b 12-15-1738 d *p.* 1782 m Deborah Kilburn Lt NY
Andrew: b 1-29-1753 d 2-5-1802 m Charlotte Yeakel Pvt PA
Christian: b 10-27-1746 d 11-15-1817 m Hannah Gardner Sol NY
Christian: b *c.* 1762 d *p.* 8-23-1817 m Maria Elizabeth Schmidt Pvt
   PA
Christopher: b 1-12-1743 d 5-2-1823 m Rebecca Churchill Pvt NY
Christopher: b 3-27-1718 d 5-9-1789 m Rosina Yeakel PS PA
David: b *c.* 1738 d *p.* 1790 m Elizabeth Cooper Pvt NY
George: b 3-16-1752 d 10-6-1827 m Elizabeth Shoemaker Pvt PA
George: b 1751 d 6-18-1810 m Christianna — Pvt VA
Henry: b 4-1-1750 d 1846 m Mrs Empie Pvt NY ★
Jacob: b *c.* 1720 d *p.* 1784 m Dorrity — Pvt NY
Jacob: b 7-23-1752 d 11-24-1830 m Ursula Schryver PS Pvt NY
Jacob: b 2- -1739 d 1810 m Elizabeth Barndoller Pvt PS PA
John: b 1728 d 1789 m Mary Hess SgtMaj NY
John: b 2-18-1755 d 6-7-1801 m Anna Van Streuburg Pvt NY
John: b 7-27-1761 d 2-26-1840 m Sarah Fullweiler Sol NY
John: b 12-2-1753 d 11-5-1840 m Katherine Otto Sol VA
Lawrence: b 1739 d 8-27-1827 m Maria Catherine Hollander Sol PS
   PA
Mathias, Sr.: b 10-7-1740 d 1-9-1812 m Anna Eve Engle 1Lt NY
Mathias, Jr.: b 8-10-1764 d 1-4-1849 m Charity Post Pvt NY
Michael: b *c.* 1750 d 1804 m (1)Deborah Fries (2)Maria Rush (3)
   Mary Way Pvt NJ
Peter: b 3- -1737 d 12- -1784 m Maria Elizabeth — 1Lt PA

SHUMAN,
Adam: b *c.* 1752 d 5-16-1832 m Elizabeth Curts Pvt PA

SHUMATE,
Daniel: b 6-14-1749 d 7-19-1826 m Milly — 2Lt VA
Wm.: b 1745 d 1810 m Lee Pvt VA

SHUMWAY,
Abijah: b 1-2-1738/9 d 7-25-1808 m Lucy Weld Sgt MA
Abisha: b 10-3-1754 d 2-9-1844 m Abial Stone Pvt MA
Abner: b 1-9-1748 d 9-13-1813 m Lucy Howe Drm MA
Amasa: b 3-1-1756 d 8-19-1830 m (1)Sarah Gleason (2)Sarah
   Gleason (3)Mary Witherill (4)Betsy French Cpl MA ★
Amos: b 9-11-1750 d 12-18-1816 m Miriam Hovey Pvt MA
Asa: b 10-16-1738 d 1811 m Eunice Bardwell Pvt MA
Benjamin: b 11-27-1752 d 9-22-1749 m Eunice Putnam Cpl MA ★
Cyril: b 5-14-1752 d *p.* 1792 m Sarah Harding Pvt MA
David: b 5-12-1742 d 4-9-1818 m Rhoda Eddy Sgt MA
Ebenezer: b 6-25-1743 d 1833 m Comfort White Sgt MA
Elijah: b 4-24-1754 d 5-26-1819 m Zilpha Gilbert Pvt MA
Isaac Whitney: b 10-12-1761 d 12-30-1849 m Patience Elizebeth
   Pratt Pvt MA ★
Jabez: b 8-4-1746 d 6-13-1821 m Olive Penniman Pvt MA
John: b 7-29-1738 d 4- -1829 m Judith Mills Capt CT
Joseph: b 10-25-1743 d *p.* 1793 m (1)Bathsheba Owens
   (2)Mehitable Kidder Pvt CT
Peter: b 4-29-1735 d 8-30-1829 m Rebecca Leavens Drm MA
Peter: b 2-13-1757 d 1-8-1832 m (1)Lydia Sleeman (2)Dorothy
   Nichols Pvt MA ★
Reubin: b 12-28-1759 d 12-20-1827 m Mariam Towne Pvt MA
Samuel: b 6-10-1748 d 10-3-1842 m Polly Hooker Pvt MA
Solomon: b 1745 d 3-8-1826 m Ruth Trask Pvt MA
Stephen: b 11-30-1756 d 11- -1840 m Abigail Billings Pvt MA

SHUNK,
Peter: b 8-5-1746 d 6-19-1834 m Barbara Iden Pvt PA
Simon: b 5-3-1749 d 10-7-1828 m Susannah Harmon Pvt PA

SHURTLEFF,
Abiel: b 3-11-1733 d 1-6-1826 m Mary LeBaron Sgt MA
Asahel: b 5-25-1757 d 3-24-1830 m Sarah Dewey Pvt CT
Barnabas: b 6-3-1750 d 3-23-1837 m Phebe Harlow Pvt MA
Benjamin, Jr.: b 10-14-1748 d 7-8-1821 m Abigail Atwood Pvt MA
Benoni: b 5-15-1757 d 2-7-1841 m (1)Nancy Farrar (2)Lucy Selfridge
   Pvt Mar MA ★
David: b 11-20-1756 d *p.* 1832 m Mercy Atwood Pvt MA
Francis: b 1739 d 8-14-1794 m Mary Shaw Lt MA
Gideon: b 10-21-1762 d 9-24-1845 m Lucy Shaw Pvt MA ★
Ichabod: b 1764 d 6-9-1820 m Betsy Pettingill Pvt MA

SHURTLEFF, contd.
Lathrop: b 12-21-1735 d 4-1-1810 m Submit Terry Pvt CT
Silas: b 3-12-1737 d 8-15-1816 m Fear Merifield Pvt MA
Wm.: b 4-22-1743 d 5-15-1790 m Ruth Shaw Pvt MA
Wm.: b 11-2-1756 d 7-3-1825 m (1)Mehitable Thomas (2)Lydia
    Flagg Pvt MA W★

SHUSTER,
Daniel: b 6-13-1752 d 6-12-1818 m Mary Margaret — Pvt PA
Martin: b c. 1750 d c. 1810 m (1)Catharina Shumacker (2)Catharine
    Klein Pvt PA
Paul: b c. 1752 d 4-22-1788 m Margarethe — Pvt PA

SHUTE,
Aaron: bpt 9-19-1767 d c. 10-16-1817 m Margaret Schilman PS NY
Benjamin: b 6-6-1734 d 1-18-1807 m Elizabeth Stowers Capt MA
Daniel: b 1-30-1756 d 8-19-1829 m Betty Cushing Dr MA
Enoch: b — d — m Mary DuBois Pvt NJ
Frederick: b — d — m Polly — Pvt NY
Henry: b — d p. 7-21-1790 m Lydia Barber Capt PS NJ
James: b 5-30-1754 d 7-6-1837 m Billiche Hill Lt NY ★
John: b 3-26-1693 d 9-20-1780 m Mary Waite PS MA
John: b 1732 d 2-1-1829 m Anna Colby Pvt PS CS NH
John: b c. 10-10-1731 d p. 1780 m Margaret Schouten Capt PS NY
John: b 1756 d 5-2-1848 m Mary Asher Lt PA ★
Peter: bpt 3-13-1715 d p. 6-3-1778 m Gertrude Oosterhoudt Pvt NY
Richard: b — d 8-11-1803 m Mary Hoyt Capt CT
Richard: b 7-25-1729 d 1-27-1818 m Mary Green Pvt MA
Samuel: b 2-27-1717/18 d 4-16-1786 m Elizabeth Pratt Pvt MA
Solomon: b 5-1-1752 d 2-6-1834 m Eulalie Pvt MA ★
Wm.: b 1726 d 4-5-1784 m Hope Moore Col PS NJ
Wm.: b 3-9-1750 d 8-12-1841 m Ann Hatfield Blanchard Ens PS
    NJ ★
Wm.: b 8-31-1730 d 2-6-1783 m (1)Elizabeth Jackson (2)Mrs Edith
    Warner 1Lt PA

SHUTS,
Hendrick: b a. 1760 d p. 1789 m Mary Head Pvt NY

SHY, (or SHI)
Samuel: b 8-15-1765 d 12-13-1830 m Jane Patterson Pvt GA

SIAS,
Benjamin: b 6-14-1747 d 12-21-1799 m Abigail Moore Capt NH
Charles: b 1742 d 3-7-1837 m Jane — Pvt PS NH
Joseph: b c. 1718 d p. 1815 m Ruth Mathis PS CS NH

SIBLEY,
Abner: b 4-9-1744 d 5-5-1822 m (1)Betty Lillie (2)Mary Studley Pvt
    MA
Daniel: b 4-14-1757 d 6-25-1840 m Phoebe Prince Drm Maj MA ★
Elijah: b 10-30-1728 d 1812 m (1)Mary Carriel (2)Mrs Abigail
    Stone Pvt MA
Elisha: b 2-21-1746 d 1812 m Lydia Carriel Pvt MA
Elisha: b 1751 d 1809 m Elizabeth Twitchell Pvt MA
Ezra: b — d p. 1828 m Martha Fuller Sgt CT ★
Gideon: b 11-20-1750 d 8-21-1846 m (1)Tamar Fitts (2)Ziphorah
    Cummings Pvt MA
Jacob: b 5-2-1746 d 6-25-1831 m Anna George Sol NH
John, Sr.: b 8-2-1711 d 11-27-1778 m Hannah Marsh CS MA
John Jr.: b 11-5-1740 d p. 177 8 m Elizabeth — Capt MA
John: b 11-13-1714 d 3-4-1790 m Abigail Towne CS MA
Jonathan: b 2-10-1740 d 1810 m Eunice Perkins Capt MA
Moses: b 3-5-1762 d 1846 m Patience Yeaman Pvt Tms CT ★
Nathan: b 10-26-1760 d p. 1805 m Rachel Studley Pvt MA
Peter: b 5-13-1751 d 9-10-1825 m Mary — Pvt MA
Reuben: b 2-20-1743 d 11-17-1810 m Ruth Sibley Capt MA
Rudolph: b c. 1735 d 1804 m Elizabeth Kern Pvt PA
Samuel, Sr.: b 1724 d 8-31-1801 m Abigail Park Capt MA
Samuel, Jr.: b 4-26-1756 d 1-30-1840 m Sarah Leland Pvt MA
Samuel: b 2-23-1751 d 9-16-1838 m Sarah Dow Pvt NH ★
Stephen: b 7-12-1741 d 8-25-1828 m Thankful Taft Pvt MA
Tarrant : b 9-1-1754 d 7-26-1823 m Hannah Putnam Cpl MA
Timothy: b 11-2-1727 d 12-6-1818 m (1)Mary Wood (2)Anne
    Saite (3)Hannah Amidon PS MA
Wm.: b c. 1740 d 1790 m (1)Sarah Shaw (2)Lydia Hopkinson Sgt NH

SICKLER,
Christopher: b — d 1781 m Susannah — Lt NJ

SICKLES,
Garret: b 8-12-1758 d 12-12-1822 m Rachel Beach Crane Sgt NY
Gerret: b 1732 d 1830 m Hilletje Klaeuw Pvt NY
James: b 1759 d 11-11-1836 m Ann — Sgt NJ Heir ★
Thomas: b 1749 d 1811 m Mary Norwood Maj PS NY
Wm.: b 7-4-1742 d 9-6-1819 m Marretje Cuyper Capt NY

SIDDALL, (or SIDDELL)
Stephen: b 1765 d 7-24-1852 m (1)Polly Head (2)Rebecca Landrum
    Pvt VA

SIDNEY,
Hemanus: b 9-9-1719 d 10-4-1798 m Catharine Elisabeth Dietz
    Sol NY

SIDWAY,
James: b 5-8-1759 d 5-18-1836 m Rebecca Wilks Sol NY

SIEBACH,
Christopher: b c. 1740 d p. 1782 m Catherine Swartz Pvt PS PA

SIEG,
Paul: b 11-14-1753 d 9-22-1817 m Susanna Fauber Pvt PA

SIEGFRIED, (includes SIGFRIED)
Andreas: b 1740 d 6-29-1810 m Mary Agatha Zweyer Pvt PS PA
Jacob: b 1755 d 12- -1823 m Maria Barbara Lt PA
Jacob: b 8-19-1762 d 3-28-1829 m Dorothea LeVan Pvt PA
John: b 10-27-1745 d 11-27-1793 m Catharine Heist LCol PA
Joseph: b 1749 d 5-21-1825 m Elizabeth — Capt PA

SIEGLE, (or SIEGEL)
Frederick: b 1733 d 1798 m Catherina Miller Pvt PA
Frederick: b c. 1750 d 9- -1776 m Elizabeth — Dr VA
Henry: b 1756 d 7- -1839 m Elizabeth Snyder Pvt PA
Peter: b 10-3-1757 d 5-15-1835 m Catherine — PS Sol PA

SIEGRIST,
Lorentz: b 1-15-1731 d 5-18-1825 m Magdalena Noll Pvt PS PA

SIEVELY, (or SIVLEY)
Joseph: b — d p. 11-28-1782 m Catharine — PS VA

SIGERSON,
Patrick: b c. 1750 d 3-28-1819 m Mary Hall Pvt PA

SIGLER,
George: b — d p. 1824 m Elizabeth Serrault Pvt PA

SIGMAN,
Dieterick: b 11-25-1744 d 3-12-1809 m Barbara Miller Pvt PA
George: b 2- -1756 d 10-20-1841 m Catharine — Pvt NC
Jacob: b 7-29-1754 d 5-11-1819 m Elizabeth Miller Pvt PA

SIGNOR,
John: b 1737 d 4-12-1823 m Hannah Schaffer Pvt NY

SIGOURNEY,
Andrew: b 11-30-1752 d 4-15-1838 m Elizabeth Wolcott Pvt PS MA
Anthony: b 5-12-1751 d 7-10-1825 m (1)Ruth Chase (2)Mrs Mary
    White Philips Sol MA

SIGSBEE,
Nicholas: b 7-18-1744 d 8-4-1820 m Cornelia Cooper Pvt NY

SILER,
Plikar Dederic: b 5-27-1719 d 12-15-1784 m Elizabeth Hartsoe PS
    NC
Welmar: b 2-28-1755 d 2-4-1831 m Margaret Rafferty Pvt SC

SILKMAN,
John: b 1720 d 1805 m Marcy Randall Sol NY

SILKNITTER,
Henry: b c. 1746 d c. 1831 m Elizabeth — Pvt PA

SILL,
Andrew, Jr.: b 4-20-1745 d 10-29-1835 m Helen T. Dorr Ens PS CT
Bennett: b 1760 d p. 1804 m Chloe Barnes Pvt CT
David F.: b 4-24-1733 d 1-8-1813 m Sarah Griswold LCol CT PA
Elisha: b 4-6-1730 d 1808 m Mary Heaton Dr. CT PA
Elisha Noyes: b 1-15-1761 d 5-24-1845 m Chloe Allyn Dr Pvt CT
Ezra: b 1753 d a. 1790 m Charity Pratt Pvt CT
George: b 1733 d 7-18-1813 m Dolly Holsman Of PA
George: b 1740-50 d 1831 m Isabella Kennedy Pvt MA
Isaac: b 4-20-1749 d 12-22-1806 m Sarah Harvey Pvt CT
Jaboz, Sr.: b 8-4-1722 d 1-20-1790 m Elizabeth Noyes CS PA
Jabez, Jr.: b 3-6-1763 d 7-29-1838 m (1) — Haight (2)Mary Osborn
    Pvt CT
Micah: b 12-25-1751 d 12-10-1786 m Auzubah Harvey Pvt CT
Michael: b a. 1755 d p. 1816 m Abigail Ottey Sol PA
Michael: b c. 1735 d a. 2-19-1813 m Barbara Rhodes CS PA
Richard: b 7-18-1755 d 6-4-1790 m Elizabeth Nicoll Maj CT
Shadrack: b 8-12-1758 d 11-3-1813 m Eytje Van Loon Pvt CT
Thomas: b 3-16-1747 d 10-11-1780 m — Capt CT
Wm.: b c. 1760 d 1820 m Mary Holstein PS PA
Wm.: b 1757 d 1841 m Jane — Pvt PA
Zachariah: b 5-19-1758 d 10-12-1812 m Prudence Comstock Pvt
    MA

SILLCOCK,
Joseph: b 3-11-1757 d p. 11- -1832 m Eliza — Lt NJ

SILLIMAN, (includes SILLYMAN)
Alexander: b 4-17-1764 d 9-18-1846 m Mary Brown Pvt PA
Daniel: b 1-15-1752 d 9-18-1818 m Sarah Brinsmade Sgt CT
David: b 10-2-1737 d 8-29-1810 m Lydia Penfield PS CT

Deodate: b 12-13-1749 d 10-11-1825 m (1)Katharine — (2)Hannah Martin Lt CT
Ebenezer: b 9-21-1707 d 10-11-1775 m Abigail Selleck PS CT
Gold Sellick: b 5-7-1732 d 7-21-1790 m (1)Martha Davenport (2)Mary Noyes BG CT
Isaac: b 8-6-1756 d 9-28-1803 m Mary Hall Sgt CT
Jonathan: b 8-31-1742 d p. 6-23-1777 m Anna Morehouse Lt CT
Seth: b 1742 d 3-30-1808 m Lois Silliman Capt CT
Thomas: b 12-27-1755 d 5-29-1843 m Nancy Neilson 1Lt PA ★
Thomas, Sr.: b c. 1734 d 1810 m Margaret — CS PA
Thomas, Jr.: b 9-12-1756 d 10-6-1835 m Maritje Middagh Pvt PA

SILLOWAY,
Hezekiah: b 1742 d 4-16-1822 m Esther — Lt VT

SILSBY,
Eliphaz: b 4-22-1758/9 d 9-29-1802 m Esther Scovell Pvt NH
Henry: b 5-6-1718 d 5-15-1789 m Mrs Bethiah Lassell Pvt CS NH
Jonathan: b — d 9-28-1787 m Rachael Blood Ens NH
Julius: b 10-7-1752 d 1830 m Rebecca Putnam Cpl CT
Lazell: b 3-30-1755 d 3-25-1846 m Huldah Scoville Pvt NH ★
Samuel, Sr.: b 4-4-1726 d 1812 m Elizabeth Woodard PS CS NH
Samuel, Jr.: b 11-4-1755 d 2-10-1825 m Hannah Goodell Pvt NH

SILVA,
Joseph De: b 1749 d 1836 m Margaret — Vol NY

SILVER,
Benjamin: b 1753 d 2-6-1818 m Euphemia Smith Pvt MD
Daniel: b 1- -1761 d 3-7-1847 m Mrs Rebeckah Harriman Cpl MA
Francis: b c. 1740 d 1815 m (1)Lucy Semple (2)Mary Hackett Pvt PA
George: b c. 1751 d 7-11-1839 m Ann Nancy Griffin Pvt MD ★
James: b 1763 d 9-12-1807 m Jane Morton PS PA
John: b 1762 d 1813 m Eliza Emanuel Pvt VA
Zebediah: b 9-14-1760 d 9-30-1821 m Sarah Shilly Pvt MA ★

SILVERS,
John: b c. 1755 d a. 3-13-1815 m (1)Nancy Springer (2)Mary Whitesides Pvt VA

SILVERTHORNE,
Wm.: b 1748 d 3-15-1813 m Jane Bartlow Tms NJ
Wm.: b c. 1725 d 1795 m Mrs Mary Youngs PS NJ

SILVEY,
Stephen: b 1754 d p. 1832 m Frankey Dear Pvt VA ★

SILVIUS, (or SILVIS)
Henry: b c. 1752 d p. 9-20-1834 m Elizabeth — Pvt PA
John: b 1759 d a. 1831 m Anna Maria Yeager Pvt PA
Nicholas: b 2-13-1723 d 12-13-1802 m Catherine — Ens PA

SIM,
Joseph: b c. 1725 d 11-27-1793 m Catherine Murdock PS MD

SIMCOCK,
John: b 1742 d 1800 m Rebecca Jennes PS NC

SIMLER,
John Henry: b 1751 d 10-6-1829 m Letitia Morrow Pvt PA

SIMMERMAN,
Earhart: b 1762 d 8-31-1827 m Marry — Pvt VA
Stophel: b c. 1757 d 2-4-1813 m Anna Margaret Reinhardin Pvt VA

SIMMONS, (or SIMONDS, SIMONS & SYMONDS)
Aaron: b c. 1758 d 2-16-1795 m Mary Call Pvt MA
Aaron: b 3-24-1736 d 2-14-1811 m Abigail Church Pvt RI
Abel: b 10-24-1753 d 12-27-1815 m Hannah Holmes Drm CT
Abraham Bassett: b 4-2-1737 d 1-28-1807 m (1)Mrs Rachel Bryan (2)Lucy Gunter Sol NC
Adriel: b 2-2-1756 d 10-12-1829 m Sarah Bingham Pvt CT
Allen: b 1-11-1757 d 7-24-1809 m Silence Rice Smn Pvt MA W★
Arad: b 8-27-1754 d 11-19-1836 m Bridget Arnold Pvt Mar PS CT ★
Asael: b 4-1-1736 d 2-2-1806 m Jane Fletcher Maj NC
Barnabas: b 6-20-1756 d p. 1809 m Lydia Wade Pvt MA
Benjamin: b c. 12-8-1731 d 10-30-1805 m Edith Markham Pvt CT
Benjamin, Jr.: b 11-5-1754 d p. 1795 m (1)Ann McGregory (2)Martha Nooney Pvt CT
Benjamin: b 2-23-1726 d 4-11-1807 m (1)Mary Davis (2)Mrs Anna Putnam Col MA
Benjamin: b 1761 d 1826 m Mary Averill Pvt NH
Benjamin: b 12-5-1758 d 11-26-1843 m Hannah Mintline Pvt NY ★
Benjamin: b 10-4-1751 d 9-3-1836 m Anne Alexander Sgt NC
Benjamin: b 1757 d 6-2-1840 m Susanna Briggs Sgt Wgm PS RI ★
Benjamin: b 9-10-1737 d 9-7-1789 m Catherine Chicken PS SC
Benoni: b 8-4-1755 d 6-15-1835 m Nancy Bailey MSgt RI ★
Caleb: b 8-27-1720 d 1-4-1811 m (1)Susanna Converse (2)Mrs Munroe Pvt MA
Caleb, Jr.: b 2-17-1755 d c. 6-15-1819 m Abigail Cummings Pvt MA
Calvin: b 10-16-1752 d 7-30-1840 m Abigail — Pvt MA
Charles: b 1730 d a. 9-4-1794 m Mary Wainwright Pvt VA
Charles: b c. 1753 d p. 1833 m Elinor Cummins Pvt VA

Cornelius: b 9-25-1750 d 6- -1836 m Margaret Potter Pvt NY Heirs ★
David: b 11-23-1767 d 2-3-1854 m Margaret Van Deusen Pvt NY
Easterling: b c. 1730 d p. 1778 m — PS MD
Ebenezer: b 8-15-1758 d 8-23-1845 m Anne Bradbury Pvt MA
Edward: b 3-16-1730 d 9-5-1803 m (1)Mary Robinson (2)Amey — PS RI
Eli: b 2-1-1736 d 4-12-1828 m Abigail — Pvt CT ★
Elijah: b 1756 d 8-13-1832 m Margaret Canada Pvt CT
Elijah: b 1750 d 3-18-1832 m Abigail Roff Pvt MA
Frederic: b 1762 d 11-20-1849 m Barbara Reid Pvt MD ★
Frederick: b 7-4-1760 d 5-22-1836 m Ruth Schotenkirk Sct NY
George: b 10-7-1731 d 3-26-1809 m (1)Deborah Taylor (2)Lucy Davis (3)Sarah Wilbor Capt RI
Gideon: b 12-14-1744 d 8-25-1840 m (1)Patience Ellis (2)Ruth Sawyer Capt RI ★
Henry: b 1740 d 1826 m Barbara Castleman Pvt PA ★
Ichabod: b c. 1720 d p. 1781 m (1)Lydia Soule (2)Mercy Sprague Pvt MA
Ichabod: b 9-20-1761 d 10-17-1841 m Anna Thomas Pvt RI ★
Isaac, Sr.: b 1721 d 1792 m Margaret — PS MD
Isaac, Jr.: b 1745 d 1806 m Elizabeth — PS MD
Isham: b 1-16-1763 d 6-17-1845 m Deborah White Halbert Pvt CT ★
Jacob: b 4-23-1752 d 11-4-1815 m Eva Veeder Lt NY
James: b 6-20-1741 d 9-5-1829 m Rebecca Shekells Gnr MD
James: b 4-30-1763 d 8-15-1842 m Lydia Morrison Pvt NH
James: b 1762 d 1852 m Sarah Quimby Pvt NC
James: b 2-20-1761 d 12-30-1815 m (1)Sarah De War (2)Sarah Hyrne (3)Sarah Tucker Harris Maj SC
James, Jr.: b 1762 d p. 1782 m Betty Anne Pvt VA
Jehazel: b 12-28-1752 d 7-3-1835 m Mary Tidd Pvt MA
Jeremiah: b 4-5-1748 d 1-16-1798 m Elizabeth Crossman Capt PA W★
Jesse: b — d p. 2-15-1819 m Rachel Wells PS VA
Joel: b 3-17-1744 d 1821 m Patience Hall Pvt VT
Joel: b 6-10-1757 d p. 9-4-1838 m — Pvt VA ★
John: b 1-17-1761 d 3-5-1849 m Rachel Bissell Pvt CT ★
John: b 1746 d 10-15-1824 m Lydia Dixon Pvt DE
John: b 1-5-1730 d 12-6-1812 m Mary Tufts Pvt MA
John: b 7-6-1749 d 4-22-1790 m Hannah Bullock Pvt MA
John: b 3-25-1759 d 8-23-1807 m Susanna Webb Pvt MA W★
John: b 10-24-1761 d 5-19-1843 m (1)Mary Nelson (2)Lucy Cunningham Pvt NY ★
John: b — d c. 8-15-1795 m Catherine Salter Pvt NY
John: b c. 1720 d 1785 m — PS NY
John: b c. 1744 d p. 1-7-1839 m Ann — Pvt NC
John: b 1763 d 11-15-1836 m Dicey Gore Pvt SC NC ★
John: b 1740 d a. 12-7-1798 m Catherine — Pvt PA
John: b 1720 d 1795 m Ann Butler CS NC
John: b 2-11-1761 d a. 5-6-1836 m (1)Barbara — (2)Mary Elizabeth Luzenby Pvt PA
John, Jr.: b 3-19-1724 d 4-22-1797 m Miriam Jones Capt CS CT MA
John: b 1712 d 1800 m Rebecca — PS VA
Jonas: b c. 1732 d 1848 m Elisa Strunck CaptLt NY
Jonathan: b 11-8-1750 d 2-10-1827 m Mary Edwards Cpl MA
Jonathan: b 9-19-1742 d 1779 m Ursula Knapp Drm Pvt MA
Jonathan: b 1755 d 8-14-1803 m Elizabeth Smith Lt RI
Joseph: b 1757 d 1843 m Elizabeth — Pvt MA CT ★
Joseph: b 10-1-1739 d 3-18-1813 m Elizabeth Stone Lt MA
Joseph: b 9-19-1744 d 5-24-1816 m Elizabeth Chamberlain Pvt MA
Joseph: bpt 10-29-1749 d 10-10-1820 m Mary Martin Pvt MA
Joseph: b 8-6-1754 d 6-18-1823 m Susanna Hale Pvt MA
Joseph: b 1-30-1746 d 10-15-1820 m Mittie Cummings Pvt NH
Joseph: b 8-22-1732 d 3-30-1809 m Lucy Kimball PS NH
Joshua: b 8-3-1762/3 d 1-28-1840 m Ruth Andrews Pvt MA
Joshua: b 5-26-1736 d 7-25-1805 m Martha Bowers Sol MA
Keating: b 1-6-1753 d 9-18-1834 m (1)Sarah Lewis (2)Eleanor Wilson Maj SC
Lemuel: b 2-22-1749 d p. 1794 m Abigail Pierce Lt MA
Leonard: b c. 1730 d 1808 m Mary A. — Pvt MA
Levi: b 6-6-1741 d 7-3-1798 m Lydia Lewis Pvt MA
Libbeus: b 8-28-1749 d 3-13-1835 m Mary Douglas Sgt MA W★
Maurice: b 1-23-1744 d 11-12-1785 m Mary Mitchell Col SC
Michael: b 2-2-1741 d 5-20-1839 m (1)Anna Otila Smeltzer (2)Mrs Althans (3)Gertrude Schmidt Pvt PA
Moses: b 1740 d 8-17-1824 m (1)Desire Penny (2)Lois — Pvt PS NY
Nathan: b 4-12-1749 d p. 1833 m Prudence Broughton Sgt CT ★
Nathaniel: bpt 8-18-1754 d 12- -1803/4 m Elizabeth Gardner Pvt MA
Nathaniel: b 1763 d 1-29-1827 m Mary Swift Pvt MA ★
Noah: b 1-15-1739 d 5-30-1824 m (1)Lydia Howland (2)Diana Keene (3)Molly Sherman 2Lt MA
Paul: b 9-11-1729 d 5-24-1778 m Mary Isham PS CT
Peleg: b 6-17-1764 d 10-1-1854 m Amia Barrett Pvt CT
Peleg: b 5-7-1755 d 1-4-1829 m Eliphal Sanford Capt RI
Phillip: b 7-22-1728 d p. 1790 m Anna Catharina Eisenhardin Pvt PA
Reuben: b 8-28-1726 d 5-22-1798 m Sarah Lincoln Pvt MA
Reuben: b 1736 d 5-5-1810 m Elizabeth Stewart Pvt NY
Robert: b 12- -1757 d 1840 m Sarah George Sgt MD ★
Sampson: b 12-2-1720 d 10-17-1796 m Rachel Shoonmaker Lt PS NY
Sampson: b 1714 d 1785 m Mary — PS NC
Samuel: b 1754 d p. 1820 m Elizabeth Williams Cpl CT ★

SIMMONS, contd.

Samuel: b 12-9-1712 d 1799 m Mary Hooper Smn MA
Samuel: b 1743 d 1824 m Hannah — Cpl NC
Silas: b 9-11-1758 d 1-4-1840 m Rachel Spaulding Pvt NH
Spratley: b 7-23-1759 d 1812 m Anna Drewry Sgt VA
Sterm: b c. 1743 d p. 1820 m Grace Nagel Sol SC
Susanna: b c. 1710 d p. 11-7-1793 m Henry Simmons PS VA
Thomas: b — d p. 1790 m Mary Chapman Pvt MA
Thomas: b 10-29-1762 d 11-20-1838 m Mary Wood Pvt NY
Thomas: b 9-9-1740/1 d p. 1790 m Elizabeth Manchester Pvt RI
Wm.: b 1745 d 3- -1828 m (1)Mary King (2)Anne King Pvt GA
Wm.: b 1-8-1750 d 7-26-1830 m Eunice Gardner Pvt MA
Wm.: b 6-5-1756 d 1845 m Mary Fuller Pvt NH ★
Wm.: b 1759 d 4-15-1825 m Josephine Bertrand De La Point Pvt PA
Wm.: b 2-24-1745 d 3-3-1838 m Anna Richmond Ens RI ★
Wm.: b 1-15-1724/5 d 6-2-1817 m Susanna Gardner Capt VT
Wm.: b — d 1778 m Rebekah Holt Maj VA
Wm.: b 1757 d p. 1820 m Tabitha Hobbs Sgt VA

SIMMS, (or SIMS)

Augustin: b 5-27-1763 d 2-10-1851 m Nancy Farmer Pvt VA ★
Charles: b 11-8-1737 d 4-17-1827 m Sybella Bowles Capt SC
Charles: b 1755 d 8-29-1819 m Nancy Douglas LCol VA
Edward: b 9-2-1761 d 6-20-1833 m Frances Taylor Pvt VA ★
Edward: b 10-12-1762 d c. 1825 m Amy — Sol VA
Elisha: b c. 1748 d p. 1810 m Anna Howard PS NC
Isabella: b 1740 d 1818 m Charles Sims PS SC
James: b a. 1753 d 1809 m Sarah Eleanor Ann Lee Pvt MD
James, Sr.: b c. 1712 d a. 2-26-1787 m Mary Simpson Pvt MD
James: b a. 1766 d 10-16-1781 m Lydia — Pvt NJ
James: b c. 1735 d a. 2- -1804 m — PS VA
Jeremiah: b 7-7-1760 d 5-17-1846 m (1)Elizabeth Sanders (2)
    Catherine Madden Pvt PS VA ★
John: b 8-16-1755 d 6-24-1834 m Elizabeth Wright Pvt MA W★
John: b c. 1755 d p. 1791 m Fannie Tucker Pvt SC
John Cleves: b 7-21-1742 d 2-26-1814 m (1)Anna Tuthill
    (2)Mrs Halsey (3)Susannah Livingston Col PS CS NJ
Joseph: b 2-22-1731 d 12-28-1891 m Catherine Culver Pvt PS MD
Leonard: b 7-2-1739 d 8- -1804 m Sallie Swepson PS NC
Martin: b 12-16-1754 d p. 4-7-1822 m Anna Jane Howard Pvt GA
Matthew: b c. 1745 d 1810 m (1) — Emory (2)Elizabeth Night Sol
    NC
Nathan: b a. 1741 d 1802 m (1)Agnes — (2)Mary — Pvt SC
Pariss: b 1750-60 d 1825-30 m Keziah — Sol NC
Presley: b 1758 d 1852 m Nancy Bridewell Pvt VA★
Rhodam: b 1756 d 1853 m Mary Stark Pvt VA ★
Richard: b 3-13-1753 d 10-21-1850 m Betsy Ashby Pvt VA ★
Robert: b 1731 d 4- -1791 m Mary — Sol CS NC
Robert: b 1755 d 2-15-1815 m Sarah Dickinson Pvt NC
Sherrod: b 1730 d 1825 m Sarah Ashburn Pvt VA
Smith: b c. 1755 d p. 10-23-1828 m — Pvt MD
Thomas: b 4-24-1758 d 5-9-1831 m Amy Wall Sgt VA
Thomas: b — d p. 4-21-1784 m — PS VA
Timothy: b 4-10-1744 d 2-20-1797 m (1)Abigail Tuthill Randolph
    (2)Marcy Harker CS NJ
Wm.: b c. 1715 d p. 3-5-1813 m Susanna Bullock Sol GA
Wm.: b 11-15-1755/6 d 12-20-1825 m Mehitabel Moulton MM MA
    NJ NH W★
Wm.: b c. 1745 d p. 1830 m Triphena — PS NH
Wm.: b 1757 d 1822 m Elizabeth Howard Sol NC
Wm.: b 2-25-1732 d 1797 m Agatha Step Capt VA
Wm., Sr.: b 1735 d 1778 m Martha — PS VA
Wm., Jr.: b 5-14-1760 d 8-7-1845 m (1)Amelia Russell (2)Mrs
    Sturdevant Pvt VA ★
Wm.: b 5-7-1751 d 1814 m Judith Cross PS Pvt VA

SIMONSON,

John: b 10-20-1743 d 6-20-1804 m Elizabeth Stryker Pvt NJ

SIMONTON, (includes SIMINGTON & SIMISON)

Adam: b 1-29-1744 d 1810-20 m Margaret — Pvt NC
Alexander: b 1734 d 7-3-1821 m Mrs Hughes Sgt PA ★
James: b 1735 d 3-4-1813 m Ann Lane Pvt MA
John: b c. 1736 d 1796 m Katherine — 2Lt PA
John: b 1754 d 9-29-1828 m — Pvt PA ★
John: b 1760 d 1-31-1841 m Margaret Strong Mil SC
Robert: b 12-1-1757 d 12-8-1841 m Elizabeth Jacoby Pvt PA
Thomas, Jr.: b 11-17-1762 d p. 1795 m Mary Alden Pvt MA
Thomas: b 10-10-1757 d 6-11-1830 m Mary Clark Pvt PA ★

SIMPERS,

John: b 1722 d 1806 m Ann Nash PS MD

SIMPKINS, (or SIMKINS)

Arthur: b 12-10-1742 d 9-29-1826 m Mrs Margaret Dalby PS Capt
    SC
Ephraim: b 3-10-1756 d 1-22-1855 m Rebecca Chandler Pvt NJ ★
John: b 11-12-1740 d 12-11-1831 m (1)Elizabeth Grant
    (2)Mehitable Torrey Capt MA
John, Sr.: b 1717 d 1801 m Anne Badeau Pvt NY

SIMPSON, (or SYMPSON)

Aaron: b c. 1758 d 12-11-1832 m Charlotte Wiseheart Pvt VA W★

Alexander, Sr.: b 1721 d 12-12-1788 m Janet Templeton PS NH
Alexander, Jr.: b 12-9-1756 d c. 1834 m Mary Rogers Pvt NJ ★
Alexander: b 5-2-1763 d 1834 m Elizabeth Caldwell Drm Pvt NJ ★
Alexander: b — d p. 1790 m — Lt PS NY
Andrew: b 1731 d 9-11-1799 m Agnes Ayers Ens NH
Andrew: b 6-14-1761 d 8-11-1845 m (1)Lucy Reynolds (2)Rebecca
    McWhorter Pvt NY
Andrew, Sr.: b c. 1728 d 1789/90 m — PS PA
Archibald: b 3- -1750 d 11-4-1829 m Catharine Nelson Pvt GA
Benjamin: b 12-25-1754 d 9- -1839 m Sarah Shattuck Pvt MA
Benjamin: b 1742 d 11-27-1828 m (1)Sarah — (2)Mrs Mary
    Eastman Pvt PS NH
Charles: b 7-11-1744 d 1-24-1834 m Abigail King Drm MA
David: b 3-4-1757 d 2-19-1823 m Rebecca Price Pvt NJ
Ebenezer: b 1725/6 d p. 1790 m Mary Nowell Capt MA
Francis: b c. 1721 d a. 8-12-1804 m Thomasine Warfield PS MD
Frederick: b c. 1754 d 1820 m Martha Jones PS NC
George: b 12-12-1759 d 11-30-1822 m Eleanor Day AsstCmsry PA
Henry: b 1757 d 1841 m Mary Pettit Pvt NJ
Ignatius: b 1760 d 1793 m Ann Semmes Sgt PS MD
Isaac: b 1757 d 7-14-1829 m Rachel Drake Pvt NJ
James: b 1720 d 1791 m Mary Elizabeth — Pvt GA
James: b 8-28-1751 d 1847 m Jane Van Syckle Pvt NJ
James: b 4-30-1750 d 9-20-1819 m Margaret Conier Sol PA
James: b c. 1756 d 6- -1813 m Hannah White PS Pvt PA
James Henry: b 1725 d 1801 m Francina Bayard PS Sol DE
Jeremiah: b — d 3-22-1822 m Elizabeth — PS VA
John: b 1741 d 1817 m Jean Douglas Pvt GA
John: b 1750-55 d p. 1786 m Elizabeth Perkins Lt MD
John: b 12-1-1748 d 10-28-1825 m Mary Langdon Whedden Maj
    PS NH
John: b 11-8-1754 d 11-18-1824 m (1)Mary Hennessey (2)Margaret
    Smith (3)Jane Wilson Pvt NH
John: b 2-14-1722/3 d p. 7-27-1791 m Sarah Sheafe CS PS NH
John: b 1726 d 5-9-1786 m Sarah Carle Sol NY
John: b 7-3-1758 d 1-18-1812 m Deborah Coleman Pvt NY
John: b 3-8-1729 d 3-1-1788 m Elizabeth Hardee Col NC
John: b 11-22-1735 d p. 1-29-1780 m — Sol NC
John: b 1747 d 8-9-1800 m Margaret — CS NC
John: b 1-10-1744 d 2-3-1807 m Margaret Murray Lt PA
John, Sr.: b 1738 d 8-16-1804 m Hannah Roberts Pvt PA
John: b 6-10-1757 d 3-2-1800 m Mary Schenck Pvt PA
John: b 1740 d 2-14-1808 m Mary Remer Chp SC
Joseph: b c. 1760 d 1810-20 m Mary Ann Montgomery Cpl MD
Joseph: b 1730 d 1795 m Charity — Pvt VA
Josiah: b 10-4-1750 d 12-25-1819 m (1)Elizabeth Spear (2)Martha
    Potter CS MA
Josiah: b 12- -1765 d 2-18-1837 m Bathiah Sweat Pvt NH ★
Lewis: b 1747 d 11-24-1830 m Martha Skofield Pvt MA
Patten: b 1737 d 1807 m Jane McClure Pvt NH
Peter, Jr.: b 5-25-1758 d 1847 m Anna Waite Pvt NY ★
Rezin: b 1758 d 1816 m Jane Burgess Sgt MD
Robert: b 1763/4 d 2- -1844 m Mary Forte Daily Pvt NH ★
Samuel: b 1706 d 1791 m Hannah — PS PA
Southy: b c. 1725 d p. 10-15-1778 m Comfort — Col VA
Stephen: b 8-19-1749 d 5-30-1842 m (1)Sarah Conger (2)Mary —
    Pvt NJ ★
Thomas: b 2-25-1755 d 1-28-1802 m (1)Mary Marona (2)Mary
    Clifton Pvt DE
Thomas: b c. 1744 d 8- -1825 m Anna Magdalena Pvt PA
Thomas: b 6-27-1757 d 8-10-1825 m Abigail Moore Pvt PA
Thomas: b 1760 d 1822 m Margaret Reed Sgt VA
Thomas: b c. 1755 d p. 8-28-1815 m Mary Coleman Pvt VA
Wm.: b 1754 d 10-31-1819 m Mary Blanchard Pvt MA ★
Wm.: b 2-5-1748 d 10-15-1830 m (1)Ruth Dow (2)Grizzell Wilson
    (3)Sarah Morgan Pvt NH
Wm.: b 1742 d 1823 m Mehitable Sherburn CS NH
Wm.: b 1764 d 11-22-1828 m Elizabeth Hanson Drm NH
Wm.: b 1741 d 5-1-1825 m Esabella Wilson Pvt PA
Wm.: b 1740-50 d a. 10-7-1788 m Lavicia — Sol NC
Wm.: b 10-25-1766 d 2-27-1843 m Rebekah Clendennin Pvt NC ★
Wm.: b c. 1740/41 d 11-21-1796 m Rhoda Tadlock PS NC
Wm.: b 1732 d 1816 m Nancy Hines Pvt PA
Wm.: b 1729 d 1806 m Mary — Pvt SC
Wm.: b c. 1741 d c. 1797 m Elizabeth Campbell Pvt VA
Wm.: b c. 1757 d 3-11-1818 m Polly Ann — Pvt VA ★
Wm.: b 10-14-1755 d 3-21-1839 m Elizabeth Cheshier Pvt VA
Zebadiah: b 10-10-1756 d 1-8-1833 m Lucy Jacobs Pvt MA

SIMRALL, (includes SIMRELL & SUMRALL)

Alexander: b 1748 d 7-7-1834 m Martha McGrew Lt PA★
James, Sr.: b 3-2-1740 d 7-1-1798 m Sarah Ferguson Lt VA
Moses: b 8-25-1761 d a. 12-28-1848 m — Sol NC
Wm.: b 5-5-1743 d 7-2-1814 m Bethiah Ownes Pvt Tms NY

SINCLAIR, (includes SINKLER, ST. CLAIR & ST. CLARE)

Alexander: b — d 1804 m Jane McClanahan PS VA
Arthur: b 3-23-1736 d 8-31-1818 m Phebe Bayard MajGen PA
Benjamin: b 1750 d c. 1810 m Hannah Sanborn Pvt NH
Daniel: b 3-17-1759 d 2-28-1835 m Isabella Auchmuty DrmMaj
    PA ★
Duncan: b 1753 d 1-5-1833 m Hannah Templeton Pvt PA
Edward: b c. 3-3-1726 d p. 1790 m Martha Shaw Pvt NH

George: b 1730 d *p.* 1-27-1787 m Mary — Pvt NJ
George: b 1754 d *a.* 1833 m Eunice — Pvt NJ
George: b 1754 d 7-23-1845 m (1)Betsy Miller (2)Ogden Sarah Barber Slr Pvt NJ ★
Jacob: b 12-27-1752 d 9-5-1830 m Rachel Clifford Pvt NH ★
James: b 2-14-1737 d 1811 m (1)Rachel Folson (2)Abagail Veasey (3)Elizabeth Blake Capt MA
James: b 12- -1757 d 1-27-1836 m Sarah Hunt Sgt NJ ★
James: b 1741 d 1806 m Sara Miller Pvt PA
James: b 1764 d 9-9-1849 m Anna Morehead Pvt SC
James: b 1736 d *p.* 2-20-1806 m Mary Patterson PS VA
Jeremiah: b 1765 d 11-19-1822 m Abigail Glines Pvt NH
John: b 1738 d 7-19-1803 m Mary Folson Capt CS NH
John: b 12-11-1743 d 1-9-1821 m Ann Albaugh Wgn NJ
John: b 1743 d 9-18-1797 m Sarah — Lt VA
John: b 1755 d *p.* 8-18-1815 m (1)Elizabeth Wilson (2)Mary Mackie Ianson Mstr VA
Joshua: b 4-16-1760 d 11- -1845 m Abigail Pattee Pvt Fif NH
Peter: b 1719 d 1784 m Elizabeth — Pvt NJ
Richard, Sr.: b 12-3-1731 d 7-27-1813 m Polley Cilley Maj CS PS NH
Richard, Jr.: b 10-6-1756 d 1820 m Elizabeth Hodgdon Ens NH
Robert: b 1755 d1817 m Lucy Patterson Pvt VA
Samuel: b *c.* 1740 d *p.* 1791 m Miss Ford Capt MD
Samuel: b 5-10-1762 d 2-8-1827 m (1)Sally Perkins (2)Mrs Fanny Edson Pvt NH
Samuel: b *c.* 1750 d *p.* 8-26-1793 m Jane — Ens PA
Thomas: b 1721 d 12-7-1796 m Sarah — Pvt NH
Wm.: b *c.* 1705 d 1795 m — PS MD
Wm.: b 1765 d 9- -1830 m Mary Drake Sgt NC

SINEX,
Henry: b 5-4-1732 d *c.* 1815 m (1)Ann Stalcop (2)Rachel Peterson Sol PS DE

SINGER,
John, Jr.: b *c.* 1750 d *p.* 4-18-1810 m Mary — Pvt PA
Michael: b 9- -1756 d 4- -1831 m Hannah Schaeffer Pvt PA
Simon: b *c.* 1750 d *p.* 1810 m Mary Clouser Pvt PA

SINGLETARY,
Amos: b 9-30-1721 d 10-30-1806 m Mary Curtis PS MA
Benjamin: b *c.* 1734/5 d *p.* 10-15-1807 m — Mil SC
Ebenezer: b 1753 d 1820 m Agnes McNeeley Sol PS SC
James: b *c.* 1750 d *p.* 1810 m Nancy — Sol SC

SINGLETON,
Anthony: b *c.* 1750 d *c.* 1795 m Lucy Harrison Capt VA CL
Daniel: b 1720 d 1792-4 m Susannah — Sgt VA
Edmund: b 1755 d *p.* 9-6-1845 m Elizabeth — Pvt VA ★
John: b *c.* 1750 d *a.* 1800 m Francis Terry Pvt NC
John: b 9-1-1754 d 12-5-1820 m Rebecca Cooper Capt SC
John: b 1759 d 9-10-1799 m Jane Miller Pvt SC
John: b 7-2-1758 d 8-12-1824 m Anne Armistead Sol VA
Manoah: b 1740 d 9-3-1818 m Sarah Craig Lt VA
Matthew: b 1730 d 9-20-1787 m Nancy Mary James Capt PS SC
Richard: b 1750 d *p.* 1800 m Ann Whiteside Maj NC
Richard: b 1758 d *p.* 1796 m Margaret Darquier Pvt SC
Ripley Nicholson: b 1- -1754 d 1-26-1799 m (1)Isabel Miller (2)Mrs Mary Butler Pvt SC
Robert: b 3-16-1763 d 1800 m Margaret Van Nuyes Pvt SC
Sarah Craig: b *c.* 1747 d *p.* 1810 m Manoah Singleton PS KY
Spyers: b 1745 d 2-18-1814 m Elizabeth Blackledge PS CS NC
Thomas: b 1721 d 10-22-1798 m Mary Black PS SC

SINGLEWOOD,
Stephen: b *c.* 1760 d 3-1-1803 m Ann Stroup Sgt PA

SINK, (or ZINK)
Abraham: b 5-26-1760 d 1828 m Ann Keys Pvt PA
Gottlieb: b *c.* 1731 d 1802 m (1)Catherine — (2)Rosanna — Pvt PA
John: b 6-6-1758 d 12-30-1798 m Elizabeth Wilson Sol PA CL

SINKINS,
George: b 1740-45 d 6- -1777 m Mary Aldridge Mstr RI

SINNETT,
Michael: b 1730 d 9-15-1800 m Molly Ward Pvt MA
Patrick: b 3-17-1752 d 12-19-1850 m Katherine Hefner Pvt VA ★

SINNICKSON,
Andrew, Sr.: b 1719 d 8-23-1790 m Sarah Gill Johnson PS NJ
Andrew, Jr.: b 3-2-1749 d 7-23-1819 m Margeth Bilderback (2)Margaret Johnson (3)Sarah Sinnickson (4)Elizabeth Norris Capt NJ

SINQUEFIELD,
Francis: b — d *p.* 12-4-1780 m — Capt SC

SINSABAUGH,
Christian: bpt 9-5-1731 d 5- -1799 m (1)Catherine Weber (2)Hannah — Pvt NY

SIPPELL,
Caleb: b 7-2-1750 d 11-30-1822 m (1)Alice Walker (2)Elishe Laws (3)Mrs Jane Darrell 1Lt DE

SIPPELL, (or SIPPEL)
Peter: b 1757 d 8-6-1841 m Hannah Bates Pvt RI ★
Thomas: b 9-8-1760 d 1825 m (1)Susanna Harrington (2)Jemima Molleston PS DE

SIPPY,
Joseph Tremau: b 1764 d 1-22-1819 m Lucretia Johnson Smn

SIRJACQUES,
Henry: b 12-11--1754 d 1835 m Marie de Villeneuve Sol FrA

SISCO,
Jacob: b 12-7-1758 d 11-22-1836 m Mary McNeal Pvt NJ
Nathaniel: b 1759 d 1-12-1845 m Susan Jennings Pvt NJ
Wm.: b 1748-50 d 1-12-1832 m Abigal Rand Pvt NH

SISK,
Daniel: b — d 10-7-1780 m — Sol NC
Timothy: b 1763 d 9-2-1835 m Ann Jenkins Pvt VA ★

SISLER,
Michael: b 10-9-1740 d 7-8-1807 m Rachel Pence Pvt PA

SISSON,
Caleb: b *c.* 1740 d 9-17-1807 m (1)Milly Branham (2)Sarah Roach Ens VA
George: b 9-30-1753 d 3-26-1813 m Rhoda Sherman Sgt MA
John: b *c.* 1742 d 7-17-1840 m Sarah — Sol VA
John: b 4-21-1749 d 10-21-1818 m Alcha Crandall Pvt NY
Peleg: b 5-22-1754 d 8-11-1836 m Polly Van Valkenburg Sgt NY ★
Thomas: b 4-4-1754 d 10-2-1841 m Abigail Cottrell Pvt RI
Wm.: b 7-12-1744 d 10-15-1798 m Mercy Noyes Pvt CT

SITGREAVES,
John: b *c.* 1740 d 3-4-1802 m Mrs Martha Green Lt NC

SITHIN,
John: b 2-5-1760 d 3-14-1838 m Ruth Dare Fif NJ

SITLINGTON,
Robert: b 11-17-1749 d 9-18-1838 m Mary Feamster Pvt VA ★

SITZ, (or SITS)
Hendrick: b 8-29-1754 d 12-3-1846 m Elizabeth Garlick Pvt NY

SIX,
John: b 8-18-1758 d *p.* 1825 m Mary Duvall Pvt VA ★

SIZER,
Anthony: b 3-12-1763 d 10-17-1840 m Lucretia Ward Pvt CT ★
Daniel: b 3-31-1754 d 3-24-1826 m Marey De Wolf Sgt CT ★
Jabez: b 9-10-1757 d *p.* 9-24-1784 m Hannah Butler Sgt CT
John: b *c.* 1730 d 1818 m Ruth Mason Pvt CT
Lemuel: b 3-9-1759 d 10-19-1831 m Elizabeth Sears Sgt CT ★
Wm.: b 11-12-1746 d 12-1-1826 m Abigail Wilcox Capt CT

SKAGGS, (or SCAGGS)
Charles: b — d *p.* 2-9-1815 m Lucy — PS VA
James: b *c.* 1760 d *a.* 4-23-1822 m Mary Brinker Pvt PS VA
John: b *c.* 1762 d 1829 m Cathrine Hicks Spy Sct VA
Wm.: b 12-20-1757 d 8-20-1848 m (1)Mary Simpson (2)Polly Pierce Spy VA ★

SKEEL, (includes SKEELE)
Amos: b 5-6-1750 d 3-3-1843 m Mercy Cone Otis Capt CT
Belden: b 4-10-1751 d *p.* 1821 m Mabel Hill Pvt CT
John: b 12-9-1747 d 2-6-1837 m Phoebe Webster Pvt NH ★
Jonathan: b 11-16-1749 d 1833 m Joanna Wood Pvt MA ★
Nathan: b 10-5-1748 d 5-19-1829 m Lucy — Pvt NY
Wm.: b 3-17-1744 d *p.* 3-2-1798 m Rhoda Coggswell Sgt MA

SKEELS, (or SKEELES)
David: b 3-11-1746 d 1833 m Lydia Powell Pvt MA
Samuel: b 5-29-1755 d 1812 m Rachel Martin Pvt CT
Truman: b 2-11-1753 d 1811 m Chloe Hill Cpl CT

SKEEN, (or SKEAN)
James: b *c.* 1759 d 9- -1828 m Elizabeth — Pvt PA
Samuel: b 1746 d 10-3-1813 m Jerminah Newberry 2Lt PA

SKELLINGER,
Daniel, Jr.: b 1734 d 11-27-1815 m Lois Pain Pvt NY

SKELLY, (or SKELLIE)
Alexander: b *c.* 1735 d 3-25-1816 m — Sol NY
John: b *c.* 1760 d 1842 m Catherine Whitstone Pvt PA
Wm.: b 12-11-1761 d 5-9-1843 m Janet McLaren Pvt NY ★

SKELTON,
Daze: b 12-21-1742 d *p.* 1794 m Ruth Hartwell Pvt MA
John: b *c.* 1762 d 1842-43 m Rebecca Harbour Sol SC

SKERRETT,
Joseph: b 9-17-1752 d 1-11-1804 m Mary Eve Humbert 2Lt PA

SKERRY,
Samuel: bpt 12-7-1747 d 11-21-1829 m Lydia Chever CS MA

SKIDMORE,
Andrew: b 11-8-1750 d 11-15-1827 m Margaret Johnson Pvt VA
Hubbard: b 12-1-1767 d 5-28-1841 m (1)Caroline Avery (2)Hannah McConn Cpl NY
John: b 1738 d 5-7-1804 m (1)Mary Denton (2)— Helicke Maj NY
John: b 1736 d 10-12-1809 m Magdalena Hinkle Capt CS VA
Joseph: b 7-31-1761 d *a.* 2-8-1847 m Hannah McKinney Pvt VA
Joshua: b *c.* 1755 d *p.* 1785 m Catherine — PS PA
Peter: bpt 1734 d 1800 m (1)Elzabeth Tucker (2)Mary Dayton PS NY
Richard: b 10-30-1738 d 10-26-1820 m Rachel Wilkins Sgt MA
Samuel: b 9-28-1743 d 4-29-1787 m Abigail Whitehead PS NY
Solomon: b 1758 d 1791 m Mary Mosher Cpl NY
Zophar: b 1744 d 10-31-1822 m Mary Titus Cpl NY

SKIFF,
James: b 7-15-1722 d *c.* 1815 m Ann Stewart Pvt MA
John: b 1-14-1762 d 1834 m Mary Makepiece Pvt MA ★
Nathan, Jr.: b 8-22-1751 d 1-3-1833 m Abigail Fuller Pvt CT
Obadiah: b 12-26-1755 d 2-18-1835 m Lucy Bartlett Pvt MA
Prince: b 12-27-1747 d 7-5-1834 m Jane Jones Cpl MA ★
Saunders: b 7-9-1765 d 1812 m Lovina Smith Pvt MA
Stephen: b 1742 d 9-20-1816 m Dimmis Puller Pvt CT
Stephen: b 2-29-1760 d 6-7-1835 m Ada Bates Pvt CT ★

SKILES,
Henry: b — d *p.* 1790 m — Pvt PA
James: b 1741 d 1814 m Margaret Devers Pvt PA

SKILLEM,
George: b 2-19-1728 d 8-11-1806 m Anna Brown LCol VA

SKILLING,
John: b 1756 d 1835 m Betsy Campbell Pvt PA ★
Josiah: b 5-22-1752 d *p.* 1800 m (1)Sarah Blackstone (2)Susanna Noyes Cpl ME

SKILLINGS,
John: b 1-4-1741 d 4-2-1777 m Hannah Hasty Capt MA
Samuel, Sr.: b 2-4-1706 d 3-12-1799 m Rebecca Sawyer Capt ME
Samuel, Jr.: b 3-25-1736 d 1799 m Mary Mitchell Pvt Sct ME
Simeon: b 12-17-1747 d 12- -1804 m Mary Pvt MA

SKILLMAN,
George: b 1747 d 1837 m (1)Rebecca Gracie (2)Catherine Parker Pvt NJ
Geradus: b 9-20-1754 d 1-2-1810 m Jane Van Dyke Pvt PS NJ
Jacob: b 8-28-1764 d 4-13-1854 m (1)Eleanor Ten Broeck (2)Mary Hageman Tms NJ
Jacob: b 1708 d 1783 m Jennetje Van Alst PS NJ
John: b 2-15-1733 d *c.* 1817 m Nancy Paynter PS NJ
John T.: b 1-10-1753 d 12-2-1835 m Mary Stryker Pvt NJ ★
Thomas: b 1739 d *c.* 1794 m Sarah — Cpl NJ
Thomas: b 1727 d 12- -1809 m Mary Beekman Pvt NJ
Thomas: b 3-13-1736 d 3-3-1814 m (1)Jane Tutus (2)Jemima Wells Lt NY

SKILTON,
Henry: b 11-19-1718 d 6-7-1802 m Tabitha Avery Dr Chp CS CT

SKINKLE, (or SCHINKLE)
Jonas: b 1728 d 12-3-1819 m Elizabeth Opham Pvt NY

SKINNER,
Abner: bpt 5-4-1735 d 1806 m Keziah Dustin Pvt PS NY
Abraham: b 1755 d 1-14-1826 m Mary Ayers Pvt CT
Apollos: b 2-17-1756 d 6-6-1828 m Sarah Putnam Sol NY
Ashbel, Sr.: b 3-16-1716 d 6-6-1792 m Marah Holcomb CS CT
Ashbel, Jr.: b 12-25-1751 d 5- -1829 m Rhoda Bradley Cpl CT W★
Benjamin, Jr.: b 5-2-1756 d 1842 m (1)Lois Lane Pvt MA ★
Benjamin: b 1754 d 3-25-1813 m Sarah Manning Fif VT ★
Benjamin F.: bpt 2-20-1743 d 10-30-1846 m Mary Foster PS CT
Calvin: b 10-5-1746 d 7-15-1777 m Eleanor Porter Cpl CT
Daniel: b 6-29-1743 d 6-3-1841 m (1)Abigail Briggs (2)Mrs Miriam Grover Sgt MA
Daniel: b 1728 d 1838 m Mary Smith Pvt NY
Daniel: b 9-22-1748 d 3- -1846 m Mary Smith Pvt NY ★
David: b 12-22-1743 d *p.* 4-30-1794 m (1)Sarah Lord (2)Jerusha Lord Pvt CT
David: b 5-21-1707 d 1788 m Elizabeth Ellsworth PS CT
David: b 5-13-1737 d 9-10-1824 m Phebe Grover 2Lt MA
Ebenezer: b 1731 d 10-18-1804 m Eunice Culver Sgt PA
Eli: b 7-30-1760 d 7-2-1851 m (1)Lucinda Nims (2)Eleanor — Pvt MA ★

Elias: b 2-1-1735 d 3-5-1825 m Rhoda — PS CT
Elisha: b 9-13-1753 d 3-2-1823 m Achsah Webster PS CT
Evan: b 3-15-1719 d 8-14-1789 m Sarah Stacey PS NC
Gershom: b 4- -1749 d 2-13-1824 m Maria Margaret Getman Sgt NY
Gideon: b 2-5-1738 d 3-26-1813 m Abigail Patridge Pvt MA
Isaac, Sr.: b 10-7-1717 d 6-13-1799 m Dorcas Drake Pvt CT
Isaac, Jr.: b 3-11-1746 d 10-30-1816 m Mabel Olcott Pvt CT W★
Isaac: b 7-24-1759 d 4-19-1843 m Lucy Shaw Pvt CT
Isaac: b *c.* 1758 d *a.* 1-4-1805 m Jane — Capt GA
Israel: b 3-2-1757 d 5-29-1796 m Lovisa Pratt Wgm CT
Israel: b 10-26-1754 d 5-14-1837 m Sally Douglas Pvt MA ★
James: b 1-1-1752 d 8-9-1841 m (1)Rachel — (2)Mary — Pvt NJ
James John: b 6-18-1731 d 12-27-1894 m Mary Hastings Capt MD
John: b 2-23-1734 d 8-29-1819 m Elizabeth Merrill Capt CT ★
John: b 1-15-1760 d 2-9-1824 m Patience Hennessay Pvt NJ
John: b 1757 d 1849 m Susan Story Pvt VA
Jonathan: b 1759-63 d 8-8-1848 m — Pvt NY ★
Joseph: b 3- -1741 d 11-13-1830 m Anna Day Cpl CT
Joseph: bpt 5-5-1751 d *p.* 1790 m Sarah Brooks Pvt MA
Joseph, Sr.: b 6-23-1723 d 9-16-1809 m Ruth Strong PS NH
Joseph: b 8-12-1749 d 5-11-1779 m Mary Bromley PS NY
Josiah: b 7-25-1754 d 11-27-1835 m Elizabeth Green Lt NY ★
Luther: b 1-8-1753 d 7-21-1827 m Sarah De Wolf Pvt CT ★
Oliver, Sr.: b 5-29-1736 d 8-9-1820 m Mary Rockwell Pvt CT
Priscilla: b 1737 d *p.* 1781 m Reuman Skinner PS MD
Reuben: b 11-26-1761 d 5-12-1812 m Mary Chase Pvt PA
Richard: b *c.* 1764 d 2-12-1842 m Martha Bailey Pvt CT ★
Richard: b 11-17-1761 d *p.* 1790 m Eleanor Glover Smn MA
Richard: b 1740 d 7-1-1779 m Sarah Britton Capt NJ
Richard: b *c.* 1746 d *p.* 1799 m Adaline Vandeventer Pvt VA
Roswell: b 2-20-1754 d 2-4-1831 m (1)Mary Gay (2)Lurana — Pvt CT
Salmon: b 5-7-1763 d 2-4-1813 m Catherine — Sol CT
Samuel, Sr.: b — d *p.* 2-2-1798 m — PS NC
Samuel, Sr.: b 5-20-1728 d 1-4-1800 m Mary Drake Pvt PA
Samuel, Jr.: b 11-20-1757 d 10-10-1840 m Agnes Crutchfield Pvt PA
Stephen: b 1-14-1755 d 1842 m (1)Mary Foote (2)Mary Chamberlain Pvt CT ★
Thomas: b 5-31-1741 d 8-7-1796 m Jerusha Christopher Dr CT
Thomas: b 5-24-1759 d 1843 m (1)Maria — (2)Anne Caton Pvt DE
Timothy: b 2-10-1761 d 7-17-1843 m Ruth Warner Pvt MA
Truman: b 4-13-1737 d 1780 m (1)Priscilla — LCol MD
Uriah: b 12- -1759 d 1847 m Azuba Brainerd Pvt Tms CT ★
Wm.: b 7-16-1720 d 1-30-1807 m Thankful Mascraft CS CT
Wm.: b 7- -1743 d 12-30-1835 m Elizabeth Church Sol CT
Wm.: b *c.* 1737 d *p.* 3-27-1792 m (2)Elizabeth Smith (3)Rebecca — Sol DE
Wm.: b 1741 d 2-28-1813 m (1)Elizabeth Jones (2)Elizabeth Fookes PS MD
Wm.: b 12- -1756 d 12-24-1800 m Sarah Mansfield Pvt MA
Wm.: b 2-24-1748 d 7-25-1829 m Sarah Green Pvt MM MA NY
Wm.: b 1-25-1730 d 2-26-1798 m Sarah — BGen NC
Wm.: b 11-15-1757 d 5-8-1856 m Martha Duncan Pvt PA

SKIPWITH,
Henry: b 1751 d 1815 m (2)Tabitha Wayles LCol VA

SKIRVEN,
Francis: b — d 1810 m Sarah Ann Beck Pvt MD

SKIRVING,
James, Jr.: b 3-29-1745 d 6- -1778 m Sarah Vinson Capt SC
Wm.: b 1745 d 1-2-1812 m (1)Mary Scheverell (2)Ann Holland Hutchinson Col SC

SKOFIELD,
Thomas: b 1707 d 1-6-1796 m (1)Mary Orr (2)Martha McPatrick CS PS ME

SLABACK,
Wm.: b 5-2-1759 d 10-31-1837 m — Pvt NJ ★

SLACK,
Abraham: b 12-26-1755 d 1833 m (1)Elizabeth Torbert (2)Mary Huddleston Pvt PA
Cornelius: b 1751 d 10-15-1835 m Sarah Hellings Pvt PA
Henry: b *c.* 1738 d 1820-25 m Sarah — Sgt MD
Israel: b 10-10-1764 d 12-25-1849 m (1)Lucinda Bond (2)Mrs Sarah Perkins Pvt MA
James: b 1756 d 1-31-1832 m Alice Torbert Pvt PA
Jesse: b 1758 d *p.* 1793 m Elizabeth Burke Cpl VT
John: b 1757 d 6-3-1847 m Maria Margaret Aurman Cpl MD ★
John: b 1- -1755 d 2-28-1823 m Mary Fuller Pvt MA
John: b 7-30-1730 d 4-15-1788 m Elizabeth Ruggles PS MA
John, Sr.: b *c.* 1755 d *p.* 12-15-1832 m Rhoda — Pvt VA
John: b 8-20-1754 d 4-17-1838 m (1)Sarah Lapose (2)Elizabeth Swank Fif PA ★
Joseph: b 1759 d 11-15-1838 m Jerusha Fairman Pvt NH
Philip: b 1751 d 1837 m Rosanna — Pvt Lt PA
Samuel: b 5-10-1738 d 6-5-1806 m Ruth Stearns Pvt MA
Thomas: b 1753 d 2-4-1816 m Sarah Jobe Pvt PA
Uriah: b 3-19-1761 d 9-10-1835 m Jane Job Pvt NJ
Wm.: b 1753 d 1830 m Margaret — Pvt VA

SLADE,
Abner: b 5-5-1756 d 1-8-1846 m (1)Olive Stanclift (2)Clarissa —
  Sgt CT ★
Job: b 6-15-1745 d *p.* 1830 m Prudence Chase Capt MA
John: b 1725 d 3-17-1797 m Martha Gleason PS NH
Nicholas: b 1755-57 d *p.* 3-24-1799 m Martha Amos PS MD
Peleg: b 12-8-1729 d 12-28-1813 m Mary Mason Chase LCol MA
Samuel: b 9-16-1747 d 8-4-1826 m Sarah Durkee Sgt NH
Samuel: b 2-2-1762 d 9-28-1860 m Hannah Thomas Sgt NH ★
Thomas: b *c.* 1724 d *p.* 4-10-1798 m Hannah Miles PS NC
Wm.: b 10-26-1753 d 11-24-1826 m (1)Rebecca Plumb (2)Mercy
  Bronson (3)Sarah Ann Clarke Cpl CT
Wm.: b 11-25-1756 d 10-25-1857 m Anne Root Pvt Tms CT ★
Wm.: b *c.* 1726 d *p.* 1790 m Elizabeth Dulany PS MD
Wm.: b 1746 d 2-27-1795 m Elizabeth Stansbury PS MD
Wm.: b 3-29-1742 d *p.* 1788 m (1)Ruth — (2)Ruth Pearce Pvt MA
Wm.: b 1-7-1745 d 2- -1791 m Anne Gainor Lt NC

SLADER,
Samuel: bpt 6-4-1732 d 4-14-1790 m Mehitable Lewis Pvt CT

SLAGLE, (or SKAGLE)
George: b 1- -1761 d 4-21-1820 m Catherine Koiner Drm PA
Henry: b 8-19-1735 d 2-14-1811 m Dorothy Kefanfre Col PS CS PA
Jacob, Sr.: b 6-10-1723 d 4-9-1790 m (1)Mary Catherin Kline
  (2)Barbara — Pvt PA
John Jacob, Jr.: b 8-19-1751 d *a.* 12-15-1800 m Hannah Burrell Pvt
  MD

SLAPP,
John: b 10-27-1715 d 12-2-1790 m Elizabeth Bosworth PS NH

SLAPPEY,
Henry: b 10-5-1753 d 3-20-1820 m Anne Rutherford Sgt SC

SLARROW,
Joseph: b 3-31-1731 d 8-18-1784 m Mary Thomas Capt MA
Samuel: b 2-4-1759 d *c.* 9-30-1839 m Nancy Morrison Pvt NY MA ★

SLATE,
Daniel: b 12-17-1738 d 2-15-1817 m Abigail — CS MA
Ezekiel: b 12-26-1719 d 1-9-1792 m Mehitable Hall Pvt CT
Jonathan: b 1-27-1744 d 12-27-1831 m Mehitable Burke Pvt MA
Joseph: b 2-12-1734 d 11-26-1818 m Mary Strong White Capt CS
  CT
Zebulon Zebadiah: b 1756 d 10-12-1833 m (1)Mary Atherton
  (2)Rebecca — Pvt MA

SLATER, (or SLAFTER)
Benjamin: b 2-22-1750/1 d *p.* 1790 m Lydia Stephens Pvt CT
Benjamin: b — d *p.* 1800 m Mary Simpson Chamberlain Mstr 1Lt MA
Benjamin: b 8-28-1758 d 1812 m Mrs Waite Bennet Pvt CT
Giles: b *c.* 1752 d — m Susanna Taft Sgt MA
John: b 1757 d *c.* 1810 m Nancy Herlack Pvt SC
John: b *c.* 1750/1 d 2-14-1815 m Lois — Sgt MA
John: b 5-26-1739 d 10-8-1819 m (1)Elizabeth Hovey (2)Priscilla
  Whitaker Pvt VT
Joseph: b 10-10-1745 d 3-21-1828 m Lois King Pvt RI
Peter: b 5-2-1760 d 10-13-1831 m Zilpah Chapin Matr MA
Silas: b 11- -1754 d 8- -1825 m (1)Beulah Adams (2)Sarah Coomer
  Pvt RI ★
Thomas: b 6-6-1740 d 1-24-1815 m Eleanor — Pvt PA

SLATTERY,
John: b 8-5-1763 d 1-18-1854 m Ocey Teeples Smn CT

SLAUGHTER, (or SLAUTER)
Cadwallader: b 1735 d 1798 m (1)Margaret Ransdell (2)Lucy
  Slaughter Sol VA
Cadwallader C: b 1748 d 1816 m (1)Miss Yancy (2)Sarah Hampton
  Sgt VA
Charles: b *c.* 1751 d 1812 m Elizabeth Poindexter Pvt VA
Ephraim: b 5-6-1755 d 7-28-1843 m (1)Lydia Fuller (2)Mrs Sophia E.
  Woodward (3)Mrs Ruth Horsford Sgt CT ★
Ezekiel: b 1720 d 8-20-1792 m Sallie Butler Pvt VA
Francis: b 1730 d 1805 m Sarah Coleman QMSgt VA
Francis: b *c.* 1730 d *p.* 9-2-1774 m Jemima Suggett PS VA
Francis Lightfoot: b 5-22-1765 d *p.* 1833 m Dorothy — Pvt VA
George: b 1-6-1764 d 1-25-1840 m (1)Martha Smith (2)Mrs
  Copeland Pvt VA ★
Isaac: b 1755 d 1838 m Jane McBride Pvt NY
Jacob: b 1730 d *p.* 8-24-1821 m — Sol NC
James: b 1732 d *p.* 11-30-1799 m Susan Clayton LCol PS VA
James: b 1754 d 11-17-1833 m (1)Elizabeth Hampton (2)Nancy
  Johnson (3)Mildred Bocock Capt VA
John, Sr.: b 1732 d *p.* 7- -1796 m (1)Millie Coleman (2)Elizabeth
  Suggett LCol PS VA
John, Jr.: b 11-2-1759 d 1-16-1830 m Susan Brown 2Lt VA
John: b 1731 d 1783 m Roberta Bland Capt VA
John: b *c.* 1753 d 8-5-1798 m Frances Brothers Pvt VA
John: b 1745-50 d 1805 m Mary Hendricks CS VA
Joseph: b 10-20-1760 d 8-3-1822 m Rachael Harper Lt VA
Lawrence: b *c.* 1735/36 d *p.* 7-5-1796 m (1)Elizabeth Field
  (2)Susannah Winston Sol VA

Nathan: b 1750 d *p.* 1800 m Margaret Sherwing PS MD
Philip: b 12-3-1758 d *p.* 12-4-1849 m (1)Margaret French Strother
  (2)Elizabeth Towles Capt VA
Reuben: b 1733 d *p.* 8-13-1821 m Ann Poindexter Capt VA
Robert: b 4-16-1758 d *p.* 1820 m Lucy — Lt VA
Robert: b 1724 d *p.* 1790 m Susannah Harrison Sol VA
Samuel: b *a.* 1760 d 1821 m Fanny Slaughter Sol GA
Thomas: b *c.* 1755 d *c.* 1794 m Elizabeth Bash PS MD
Thomas: b 8-19-1734 d 6-10-1804 m Mary Robertson QM VA
Walter: b *c.* 1750 d *p.* 1790 m (1)Margaret Webb (2)Susannah — Pvt
  NC
Wm.: b 4-19-1761 d *p.* 1-2-1821 m Lucy Brown Lt VA

SLAUSON, (includes SLASON & SLAWSON)
David: b 8-29-1735 d 5-15-1805 m (1)Mary Ferris (2)Christie — Pvt
  CT
Deliverance: b 12-17-1710 d *p.* 1790 m Hannah Hoyt Pvt CT
Ebenezer: b 7-2-1736 d 1821 m (1)Catherine Ann Sellick (2)Rachael
  Hayes Maj NY
Eleazer: b 4-24-1726 d 1790 m Sarah Raymond Sol NY
Henry: b 1745 d 5-24-1804 m Mary Dutcher Capt NY
John: b 1-29-1764 d 3-7-1851 m Rhoda Slauson Sgt NY ★
Jonathan: b 2-28-1736 d 8-31-1825 m Lydia Lockwood Pvt CT
Nathan: b 1-30-1738 d 10-5-1821 m Elizabeth Hubbell Capt CT
Nathan: b 1-9-1753 d 12-18-1844 m Hannah Ferris Pvt NY CT ★
Nathan: b 8-29-1764 d 10-9-1826 m Hannah Slawson Pvt NY
Nathaniel: b 1-13-1745 d 5-1-1835 m (1)Lydia Bates (2)Hannah
  Whitney Capt CT
Nathaniel: b 1696 d 1787 m Margaret Belden CS CT

SLAVEN, (includes SLAVIN & SLAVINS)
Isaiah: b 6-14-1762 d 9-8-1848 m (1)Martha Stuart (2)Mrs Barbara
  Leston Pvt VA ★
John: b 12-25-1757 d 12-16-1851 m Eliza Graham Pvt NC ★
John, Sr.: b 1725 d *p.* 7-18-1802 m Elizabeth Stuart Pvt VA
John, Jr.: b 4-5-1760 d 1851 m (1)Sarah Wade (2)Elizabeth Warwick
  Pvt VA ★

SLAYBACH,
George: b — d *p.* 1820 m Rosina — Pvt PA
Solomon: b *c.* 1753 d *p.* 1798 m — Hoagland Sol NJ

SLAYDEN,
Daniel: b *c.* 1758 d *a.* 11-17-1817 m Sarah Isbell Pvt VA

SLAYMAKER,
Amos: b 3-11-1755 d 1835 m Isabella Fleming Ens PA
Daniel: b *c.* 1738 d 1801 m Agilis Young Pvt PA
Henry: b 8- -1734 d 9-25-1785 m Faithful Richardson Pvt PS CS
  PA
John: b 1732 d 3-27-1798 m Elizabeth White Capt PA
Mathias: b *c.* 1727/28 d 1-9-1804 m Barbara Smith Lt PA
Wm. Mathias: b 1761 d 1826 m Jane Slaymaker Ens PA

SLAYTON,
Arthur: b *c.* 1705 d *p.* 6-18-1787 m Rachel — PS VA
David: b 6-2-1740 d *c.* 1794 m Martha Thayer CS VT
Ebenezer: b 4-12-1759 d 12-20-1841 m Rebecca Hamilton Pvt MA
Jesse: b 2-25-1762 d 8-26-1846 m Betsy Bucklin Pvt MA
Joshua: b 12-16-1744 d 11-14-1785 m Desire Felton Pvt VT
Phineas, Sr.: b 9-4-1737 d 9-13-1825 m (1)Eleanor Morey
  (2)Roxanna — Cpl MA
Phineas, Jr.: b 1761 d 1811 m Experience Gleason Pvt MA
Reuben: b 5-30-1748 d 1811 m Mary Moore Capt MA
Thomas: b 2-20-1733 d 12-28-1822 m Judith White Pvt MA

SLEDD,
Wm.: b *c.* 1761 d 1812 m Lucy Hogg Sol VA

SLEDGE,
Daniel: b *a.* 1731 d 1-10-1798 m Winifred Isham PS NC
John: b 1730 d 1798 m Amy Chappell PS NC

SLEEPER,
Benjamin: b 4-18-1746 d 10-15-1820 m Judith Clough PS NH
David: b 11-26-1721 d 10-18-1780 m (1)Margaret Scribner (2)Ruth
  Jeness PS NH
Jacob: b 9-17-1761 d 1816 m Dorothy Clough Pvt NH
Jedediah: b 5-17-1753 d 6-28-1833 m Margaret — Pvt NH
John: b 4-17-1741 d *p.* 1784 m Hannah — Pvt PS NH
John Blaisdell: b 8-31-1752 d 8-7-1830 m Mary Brubank Sgt NH
Moses: b 9-4-1755 d 5-14-1838 m Betty Colby Cpl NH ★
Peter: b 4-28-1746 d 9-11-1826 m Mary Sanborn Sgt PS NH
Richard: b 4-17-1738 d *p.* 1786 m Martha Fifield 2Lt NH
Robert: b 1762 d 6-5-1850 m Catherine Fox Pvt NH
Samuel: b 2-19-1752 d 5-4-1801 m Hannah — PS NH
Stephen: b 2-23-1729 d 9-4-1801 m Elizabeth French PS NH
Thomas: bpt 8-7-1748 d 6-23-1828 m Mary Davis Pvt NH

SLEET,
James: b 1752 d 7-26-1834 m (1)Nancy Ford (2)Rachel White Ens
  VA

SLEETH,
Alexander, Jr.: b 8-20-1750 d 5-14-1820 m (1)Mrs Montgomery (2)Ann Smith PS Sct VA
John, Sr.: b c. 1727 d 9-20-1794 m Mary Ann Wallace Sol VA

SLEIGHT, (or SLEGHT)
Abraham: b 7-27-1755 d 7-25-1842 m Ruth Roe Pvt NY
Jacobus: b 4-19-1753 d 9-2-1833 m Elsie de Reimer Lt NY
John, Sr.: b c. 1731 d 7-14-1794 m Mary H Pvt NY
John, Jr.: b 10-7-1753 d p. 1789 m Fanny Simonson Pvt NY
Petrus Jansen: b 6-25-1732 d p. 1790 m Cornelia Cantine Pvt NY

SLEMONS, (includes SLEEMAN & SLEMMON)
Peter: b c. 1737 d 1777-85 m Lydia Drury Cpl MA
Robert: b 1754 d 1814 m Hannah Donelly Pvt PA
Thomas, Jr.: b 1733 d 12-21-1791 m Margaret Brown Pvt PA
Wm.: b 1717 d 1786 m Catherine Porterfield PS ME
Wm.: b 1761 d 1-27-1827 m (2)Jane Osburn Pvt PA

SLEMP,
Frederick: b c. 1735 d p. 2-17-1807 m Mary Metz Pvt VA

SLICER,
John: b 1739 d 3-29-1828 m Elizabeth Wollaston Pvt MD

SLICK,
Wm.: b 11-10-1754 d 4-7-1844 m (1)Barbara Winhuls (2)Rebecca Metler Pvt MD ★

SLIGH,
Philip: b 1755 d 12-21-1818 m Christianna — Pvt SC

SLINGERLAND,
Albert: b 1733 d 1814 m Elizabeth Moak Pvt NY
Gerrit: b 1723 d 1816 m Egie Van Derzee Pvt NY
Tenuis: b 3-4-1722 d 3-5-1805 m Agnes Witbeck Pvt NY

SLITER,
John: b 12-15-1760 d 6-18-1842 m Mary Sornburger Pvt NY
Wm.: b 5-12-1763 d 9-3-1847 m Hannah Slouter Pvt NY ★

SLOAN, (or SLOANE)
Alexander: b 5-10-1742 d 2-15-1812 m — Lt MA
Alexander: b 1744 d 1- -1812 m Jean Mower Pvt PA
Alexander: b 2-2-1760 d 1844 m Agnes Dobson Pvt PA
Brian: b 1762 d 12-15-1845 m (1)Betsy — (3)Nancy King Pvt VA ★
David: b c. 1753 d p. 1787 m Elizabeth Scott Pvt MA
David: b 1753 d 10-9-1826 m Susan Majors Capt NC
David: b 1723 d 1784/5 m Margaret Jones Sol NC
David: b c. 1744 d 8-27-1776 m Mary — 2Lt PA
Fergus: b 1725 d 1812 m Ann Elizabeth Robinson Pvt NC
George: b 9-28-1749 d 1-15-1840 m Huldah Foote Lt MA
Hugh: b — d p. 8-5-1793 m Esther Harsha Pvt NY
Israel, Sr.: b 8-30-1759 d 7-9-1836 m Rebeckah Wilson Pvt MA
James: b c. 1720 d 6-18-1775 m Jane Wilson Pvt MA
James: b 12-24-1759 d 1813 m Phebe Stratton Pvt MA
James: b 9-27-1756 d 9-27-1818 m Elizabeth Gibson Sgt PA
John: b 3-5-1736 d 10-22-1778 m Mary Dewey Pvt MA
John: b c. 1740 d a. 2- -1780 m Mary Green Capt PS NC
John: b 1759 d 7-23-1835 m Lavinia Scott Capt PS PA
John: b 12-13-1759 d 5-10-1840 m Margaret Pinkerton Cpl PA
Joseph: b 6-24-1760 d 3-15-1835 m Temperance Waterman Sgt NH ★
Peter: b 5-15-1750 d 5-25-1794 m Dorcas Niles Pvt MA
Robert: b c. 1750 d 6-20-1780 m Margaret Shipley Capt NC
Robert: b 1752 d 11-1-1839 m Mary Greer Pvt NC
Robert: b 1761/2 d 12-16-1823 m Nancy Agnes Curry PS NC
Robert: b 1738 d p. 4-20-1812 m Mary McBrayer Sol PA
Samuel: b 1740 d 4-12-1813 m Hannah Douglas Capt MA
Samuel: b c. 1758 d 1-17-1840 m Elizabeth Paterson Pvt NC ★
Samuel: b 1756 d 7-4-1846 m (1)Margaret Thompson (2)Elizabeth Van Horne Sgt PA
Samuel: b c. 1735 d 12-20-1791 m Agnes — Pvt PA
Wm.: b 6-5-1755 d 7-12-1828 m Sarah Nelson Sgt NH VT ★
Wm.: b 1736 d p. 11-10-1803 m Frances Nesbit Pvt PS PA
Wm.: b c. 1764 d 1-16-1849 m Elizabeth Prickett Pvt PA
Wm. Alexander: b 1753 d 6-22-1827 m Jane Stevenson Pvt NC

SLOAT,
Cornelius: b 12-22-1741 d 1-1-1816 m Eleanor McKinney OrdlSgt NY
David: b 12-25-1730 d 8-2-1814 m Sarah Wooley Pvt NY
John: b 1-31-1736 d p. 12-30-1783 m Trainor Loundsbury Sgt NY

SLOCOMB, (includes SLOCUM & SLOCUMB)
Benjamin: b 1751 d 1837 m Sarah Mowry Pvt MA
Benjamin: b 1-18-1751 d — m Rebecca Willcox Ens NY
Ebenezer: b 1-5-1756 d p. 1799 m (1)Sarah Wood (2)Mehitable Norton Pvt NY
Ebenezer: b 11-2-1747 d — m Sarah Casey Sgt RI
Edward: b c. 1748 d 3-2-1822 m Phoebe Kelpe Capt RI ★
Eleazer: b 5-15-1744 d 12- -1826 m Anstace Viail Pvt NY
Ezekiel: b 2-7-1760 d 7-4-1840 m Mary Hooks Capt NC
Ezekiel: b 6-18-1760 d 1835 m Elizabeth — Sgt NC ★

Giles: b 12-20-1750 d p. 1796 m Susannah Brownell CS PS RI
Giles: b 1-5-1759 d 11-14-1829 m Sarah Ross Sol PA
Job: b 1757 d p. 1790 m Susanna Keene Capt MD
John: b 1720 d 1817 m Experience Healy Pvt MA
John: b 7-1-1755 d 10-8-1828 m Sarah Callam Beard Pvt RI
John Charles: b 5-24-1761 d 10-23-1845 m Lydia Reaves Pvt NC★
Jonathan: b 5-1-1733 d 12-16-1778 m Ruth Tripp PS PA
Joseph: b 1-30-1766 d 10-8-1815 m Elizabeth Wright Pvt NY
Joshua: b 1759 d 5-28-1816 m Lucy Dunn Pvt MA
Mary Hooks: b 2-11-1760 d 7-4-1840 m Ezekiel — PS NC
Peleg: b 1751 d 1-18-1827 m Elizabeth Underwood Sgt RI W★
Samuel: b 6-24-1738 d 11-8-1829 m Miriam Richardson Pvt MA
Samuel: b 11-4-1736 d 11-4-1826 m Ruth Hall Sol RI
Samuel: b 7-25-1756 d 12-22-1827 m Margaret Spike Pvt VT
Simon: b 1-13-1748/9 d 6-11-1816-8 m Esther Plymton Pvt MA
Thomas: b 1740 d 1825 m (1)Mary Carder (2)Margaret Greene Pvt MA
Wm.: b 4-22-1750 d 1-11-1842 m Jerusha Richardson Pvt MA ★

SLONECKER,
George Adam: b 1740 d p. 8-5-1812 m Frederica Dorothea Barbara Wistar Pvt PA
John: b 2- -1752 d p. 1832 m Elizabeth Kootzer Pvt PA ★
J. Michael, Sr.: b 7-29-1727 d 7-8-1812 m Anna Marie Heilig Pvt PA

SLOO,
Thomas: b c. 1761 d p. 1814 m Elizabeth Roe PS NY

SLOPER,
Ambrose: b 1734 d 4-13-1822 m Sarah Root Capt CT
Daniel: b 1-5-1727 d 9-9-1799 m (1)Rachel Langdon (2)Hannah Newell Capt CT
Henry: b 1759 d 4- -1841 m Hannah — Pvt NH

SLOSS,
Joseph: b — d p. 11-11-1800 m — PS NC

SLOT,
Daniel: b 4-27-1740 d p. 1800 m Martha Van Duzer Arfr NY
John: b 10-24-1754 d 4-4-1781 m Ruth Drake Pvt NY
Jonas: b 6-25-1738 d p. 1791 m (1)Phebe Clark (2)Abigail Longsberry Pvt NY
Steven: b 3-25-1726 d 10-11-1806 m Marretje Van Deusen Capt NY

SLOUGH,
Matthias: b 1733 d 9-15-1812 m Mary Gilson Col PS PA
Nicholas: b 1-8-1757 d 8-16-1834 m Maria Gouldy Pvt PA

SLOUT,
Philip: b 8-27-1756 d 11-23-1839 m Elizabeth — Pvt NJ ★

SLOUTER,
John: b 12-15-1761 d 6-18-1842 m Mary Seruberger Pvt NY ★

SLUSSER, (includes SCHLOSSER & SLOSSER)
George Ernest: b 10-27-1714 d 2-5-1802 m (1)Fredericka Rudhardt (2)Anne Mary Peter PS PA
Peter: b 1710 d p. 1790 m Mary Elizabeth — Pvt PA
Phillip: b 9-20-1760 d 9-26-1829 m Sarah Anna — Cpl PA
Tobias: b 5- -1762 d 6-8-1823 m Mariah C — Pvt PA

SLUTHOUR,
Anthony: b 1751 d c. 1832 m — Pvt PA ★

SLUYTER,
Wm.: b 1763 d 1840 m Hannah Slouther Pvt NY

SLY, (or SLYE)
John: b 2-16-1748 d 3-12-1831 m Ruth Brown Pvt RI
Nathan: b 1762 d 5-7-1845 m Elizabeth Mansfield Pvt MA
Samuel: b 1710 d 9-4-1786 m Letitia Hamilton PS NY
Wm.: b c. 1760 d p. 1820 m Ann — Cpl MD

SLYFIELD,
Andrew: b c. 1740 d 12-30-1801 m Elizabeth Tucker Smn MA

SMALL, (includes SCHMELL & SMEAL)
Adam: b a. 1755 d p. 3-12-1828 m — Pvt PA
Andrew: b 2-17-1756 d 3-1-1840 m Mary Long Ens PA ★
Daniel: b 1757 d c. 1847 m Betsey Tucker Pvt MA ★
Daniel: b 11-17-1759 d 3-22-1844 m (1)Nancy Tyler (2)Mrs Sarah D Libby Pvt MA ★
Edward: b 8-18-1751 d 1826 m Sarah Mitchell Cpl MA
Elisha: b 1756 d 8-5-1844 m Priscilla Strout Sgt MA
Henry: b 10-29-1757 d 11-9-1826 m Elizabeth Damm Pvt MA ★
Jacob: b c. 1745 d 1783 m Susanna Beltzer Capt NY
Jacob: b 10-14-1759 d 1-4-1817 m Catherine Elizabeth Welsh Pvt PA
Jacob: b 1752 d 9-18-1835 m Barbara — Sol CS VA
James: b 8-4-1734 d 12-9-1812 m Hannah Delano Pvt MA
James: b 1736 d p. 1788 m (1)Abigail Swett (2)Rebecca Gilkey Pvt MA

James: b 1749 d 8-13-1827 m Ann Beveridge Pvt NY
James: b 2- -1757 d 4-23-1842 m Margaret Mitchel Pvt PA ★
Jeremiah: b 4-15-1750 d p. 8-18-1845 m Jerusha Woodbury Pvt
   MA ★
John: b 6-27-1748 d p. 1800 m Hannah Preble Sgt MA
John: b 8-9-1747 d 8-9-1819 m Anna Catherine — Maj PA
Joseph: b 8- -1748 d 2-18-1831 m Mindwell Purington Pvt MA
Joshua: b 2-26-1725/6 d 1803 m (1)Susanna Kennard (2)M Libby
   PS ME
Joshua: b 1-5-1749 d 11-25-1836 m Keturah Hopkins Pvt MA
Killian: b 10-7-1735 d 9-28-1815 m Eva Welschhance Pvt PA
Nicholas: b c. 1752 d 1827 m (1)Elizabeth Volck (2)Catherine Kline
   Pvt PA
Peter: b 1756 d 1821 m Magdalena Bonbrake Pvt PA
Samuel: b 6-30-1748 d 8-1-1814 m (1)Molly Waters (2)Deborah
   Pierce 2Lt MA
Samuel: b 10-14-1757 d 12-2-1851 m Noami Blaisdell Pvt MA ★
Samuel, Sr.: b 4-17-1700 d p. 1786 m Anna Hatch PS CS MA
Samuel, Jr.: b 5-26-1718 d 12-21-1791 m Dorothy Hubbard PS CS
   MA
Thomas: b c. 1741 d 3-23-1827 m Sarah Roberts 2Lt MA
Wm.: b 6-8-1759 d c. 1833 m (1)Mary March (2)Sarah March Sgt
   MA ★
Wm., Sr.: b 4-14-1714 d 9-10-1781 m Sarah Clark PS NH
Wm., Jr.: b 10-21-1743 d 1-8-1834 m Patience Lovejoy Pvt PS NH

SMALLCORN,
Samuel: b 1735 d 12-21-1793 m (1)Margaret Kitchener (2)Jane
   Moore CS Pvtr MA ME NH

SMALLEY,
Daniel: b 10-28-1740 d p. 1782 m Martha Owen Cpl CT
David: b 5-10-1745 d 9-8-1816 m Hannah Roff Capt NJ
David: b c. 1737 d 1796 m Mercy Clark Pvt NY
Elijah: b c. 1742 d p. 1790 m Ruth Porter Pvt VT
Francis: b p. 1734 d p. 1811 m (1)Sarah Hutchinson (2)Rachael
   Woodward (3)Mary Wright Pvt VT
Jacob: b 1756 d 8-22-1836 m (1)Tabitha Moore (2)Elizabeth
   Willett Sgt NJ
James: b c. 1742 d 2-21-1812 m Abigail Jennings Pvt NJ
James: b 1750 d 9-7-1784 m Sarah Bartlett Lt VT
John: b 1-26-1747 d 3-23-1838 m (1)Amy Sutton (2)Rachel
   Clawson (3)— Babcock MM NJ
John: b 1762 d 9-29-1831 m Margaret Randolph Pvt NJ
Joseph: b 1711 d 11-27-1783 m Jemima Ordway PS CS VT
Lewis: b 9-9-1760 d 10-9-1822 m Margaret Cookson Pvt PA

SMALLIDGE,
Samuel: b 1750 d 1789 m Elizabeth Tucker Sgt MA
Timothy: b a. 1747 d p. 1800 m Jemima Black Cpl ME

SMALLING,
George: b 6-8-1735 d 7-9-1780 m Anna Maria — Pvt PA
Jacob: b 5-16-1760 d 3-20-1835 m Mary Gillett Pvt NY

SMALLMAN,
Thomas: b 1710 d 1785 m — PS PA

SMALLWOOD,
Wm. Marbury: b c. 1741 d p. 3-19-1806 m (1)Elizabeth Caroline
   Moore (2)Mrs Grace Harmon PS MD

SMART,
Caleb: b c. 1730 d p. 3-10-1792 m Rebecca — PS NH
Caleb, Jr.: b 5-3-1760 d 10-9-1833 m Catherine Black Pvt NH ★
Elisha Carter: b 8-15-1756 d 4-15-1832 m Ann Glover PS VA
Laban: b 11-9-1758 d 11-28-1840 m Susannah Simmons Pvt NC ★
Moses: b 1-13-1756 d 8-18-1849 m Annie Haynes Pvt NH
Nathan: b 3-15-1749 d p. 11-25-1792 m Nancy Rowell Pvt SC
Peter: b 2-7-1730 d p. 1790 m — Sol NC
Winthrop: b 10-22-1742 d 1814 m Rebecca Nickerson Ens NH

SMEAD, (or SMEED)
Asa: b 2-3-1751 d p. 1810 m Mehitable Currier Sgt NH
Darius: b 1766 d 6-5-1846 m Sarah Naughton Pvt NH ★
John: b 12-28-1749 d p. 1790 m Irena Arms CS MA
Lemuel: b 1740 d 1-29-1812 m Sarah Nims Pvt MA

SMEDES,
Abraham: bpt 1-27-1745 d p. 1-16-1804 m Catherine Decker Pvt NY
Aldert: b 9-3-1750 d 1844 m Elizabeth Mancieus Pvt NY ★
Matthew: b 4-17-1740 d 12-8-1810 m Elizabeth Graham Pvt NY
Petrus: b 12-4-1701 d 3-15-1783 m Catrina Du Bois PS NY

SMEDLEY,
Ephraim, Sr.: b 1713 d 8-21-1785 m Concorrence Hurd PS CT
Ephraim, Jr.: b 7-14-1742 d 5-20-1821 m Anne Gibbs PS CT
Gideon: b 3-30-1745 d 1-11/3-16/1827 m Sarah Gibbs Capt CT
Jedediah: b 1734 d 3-14-1823 m Ruth Grover Pvt MA W★
John: b 1-4-1731 d a. 1779 m Deliverance Humphries Pvt MA
John: b 10-22-1755 d 8-23-1815 m Mary Baker Pvt PA
Nehemiah: b 1732 d 1789 m Mary Harwood Capt MA

SMICK,
Christian Carl: b 11-7-1761 d 12- -1844 m Elizabeth Mattern Pvt
   PA ★
Peter: b 5-23-1750 d 5- -1786 m Mary Hiede Pvt PA

SMILEY, (includes SMILIE & SMYLY)
Alexander: b 1760 d 1848 m (1)Zermiah Moore (2)Mrs Catherine
   Hastings Harlow Pvtr MA
David: b 4-10-1760 d 10-3-1855 m Rachel Johnson Pvt MA ★
Hugh: b 1723 d 4-10-1818 m Mary Park CS ME
James: b 1743 d p. 5-20-1803 m Elizabeth-Luffram Pvt PA
John: b 2-14-1730 d 2-10-1811 m Anne Houton Stuart Pvt PA
John: b 1746 d 5-5-1840 m Margart Mehaffie Pvt PA
John: b 1745 d 1806 m Christiana Robeson Pvt PA
John: b 5-18-1763 d p. 1840 m Mary Mott Pvt Tms PA ★
Pierce 2Lt MA: b 1742 d 12-31-1813 m Jane Porter PS PA
John: b c. 1755 d 1807 m (1)Margaret Caldwell (2)Charity
   Tuchstone Pvt SC
Robert: b 1732 d 1811 m Rhoda Boyd Pvt PA
Robert Porter: b 7-6-1767 d 10- -1851 m Mary Ann Beatty Sol PA
Samuel, Sr.: b 1739 d 8-15-1825 m (2)Rachel — Pvt PA ★
Samuel, Jr.: b 1760 d 1831 m Elizabeth Ann Gehringer Pvt PA
Thomas: b 5-27-1759 d 1-12-1832 m Nancy Tucker Pvt PA
Thomas: b 2-28-1753 d 9-25-1804 m Margaret Ross Pvt PA
Wm.: b a. 1760 d 1- -1825 m Hannah Wilcox Pvt CT
Wm.: b 8-19-1747 d 11-25-1804 m Hannah Nelson Pvt MA
Wm.: b 1725 d 3-4-1813 m Sarah Robinson CS NH

SMITH, (includes SCHMIDT, SMYTH, SMYTHE)
Aaron: b 4-16-1738 d 11-25-1825 m Eunice Clark Pvt CT ★
Aaron: b 3-28-1730 d 12-4-1795 m Beulah Woodward Capt MA
Aaron, Jr.: b 10-5-1756 d 4-26-1833 m Lydia Pratt Sgt MA ★
Aaron: b 6-22-1736 d 5-9-1825 m Dinah Wheeler Pvt MA
Aaron: b 4-6-1760 d 6-19-1824 m Huldah Webb Pvt MA ★
Aaron: b 2-23-1760 d 9-23-1838 m Lydia Bass Pvt MA ★
Aaron: b 1720 d 7-4-1776 m Elizabeth Carraway Capt SC
Aaron: b 1758 d 3-23-1817 m — Wilde Lt SC
Aaron: b 7-25-1752 d 7-31-1840 m Abigail Kendrick Pvt VT
Aaron: b 3-28-1751 d 10-11-1826 m Sarah Allen Pvt VA
Abel: b 4-26-1757 d 8-21-1849 m Sarah Dunning Sgt CT ★
Abijah: b c. 1758-60 d 12-9-1831 m Judith Whiton Pvt CT
Abijah: b 10-29-1740 d 11-13-1786 m Abigail Wheelock Capt NH
Abner: b 2-5-1729/30 d 5- -1812 m (1)Mehitable Knowles
   (2)Deborah (Brainerd) Brainerd (3)Mrs Roxanna Rush Lt CT
Abner: b 8-27-1730 d 1814 m Anna Sanford Pvt CT
Abner: b 1757 d 11-23-1838 m (1)Alma Moor (2)Lovina Cary Pvt
   CT ★
Abner: b 8-16-1747 d 2-15-1843 m Sibyl Rose Pvt MA
Abner: b a. 1749 d p. 1780 m (1)Maria Hutchins (2)Molly Hutchins
   Pvt MA
Abner: b 3-30-1762 d 4-7-1833 m Hannah Prentice Pvt MA ★
Abner: b 12-8-1766 d 1846 m (1)Sally Straw (2)Sally Waterhouse
   Pvt MA
Abraham: b 5-17-1734 d 2-13-1796 m Sarah French Lt CT
Abraham: b 5-3-1735 d p. 1780 m Mary Gales Sol CT
Abraham, Sr.: b 10-16-1730 d p. 1790 m Mary Hawkes Sol MA
Abraham, Jr.: b 4-12-1762 d 3-30-1829 m Delilah Willey Sol MA ★
Abraham: b 1755 d 1848 m Kezia Stiles Pvt MA ★
Abraham: b 11-20-1705 d 1795 m (1)Mary Page (2)Dorothy Rowell
   PS NH
Abraham, Sr.: b 6-9-1733 d 3-20-1784 m Mary Baxter Lt NY
Abraham, Jr.: b 1754 d 1808 m Sarah Crane Pvt NY
Abraham: b 4-11-1755 d 7-15-1837 m Isabella McKinley Pvt PA ★
Abraham: b 1722 d 1806 m Mary Guyton PS SC
Abraham: b 9-20-1730 d 11-4-1809 m Lucy Allen Pvt VT
Abraham: b 1722 d 1781 m Sarah Caldwell Col CS VA
Abram: b 1762 d 1-2-1824 m — Pvt NJ ★
Adam: b 1761 d 6-17-1838 m Elizabeth Carman Pvt NY
Adam, Sr.: b 9-29-1738 d 12-24-1824 m (1)Mary Elizabeth Cassel
   (2)Elizabeth Barbara Miller Ens PA
Adam: b 2-2-1734 d 12-16-1799 m Maria Barbara Grauel Pvt PA
Adam: b c. 1745 d 12-19-1822 m Catherine — Pvt PS PA
Adam: b 1720 d 1785 m — Chp VA
Albert: b 3-22-1763 d 5-28-1823 m Anne Lenthal Eells Pvt MA
Albertson: b c. 1758 d 1836 m Dinah Skaden Pvt NY
Alexander: b 2-14-1762 d 1-17-1844 m Hepzibah Hobbs Pvt MA
Alexander: b 10-11-1717 d 9-21-1787 m Rebecca Warner PS MA
Alexander: b 5-30-1747 d 9-8-1825 m Keziah Lamar Pvt NC
Alexander: b 10-15-1761 d 6-25-1836 m Rebecca Aikman Pvt PA
Alexander: b c. 1756 d p. 1790 m Diana Felps Sol VA
Alexander: b 1752 d p. 1814 m Racheal Douglas Drm VA
Alexander Gordon: b c. 1752 d p. 1804 m — Cpl PS NH
Alexander Lawson: b 1740-45 d 1801 m Mary — LCol MD VA
Allyn: b 8-23-1742 d 12-13-1816 m Eunice — Pvt CT
Alpheus: b c. 1744 d 1791 m — Bennett Pvt NY
Amos: b 1747 d 1- -1823 m Deborah Knapp Capt CT
Amos: b 10-7-1755 d 4-10-1843 m Lucinda Miller Cpl CT
Amos, Sr.: b 1759 d 1850 m Lydia Gillett Pvt CT ★
Amos: b 1743 d 1-11-1820 m Mary — Lt MA
Amos: b 1742 d 9-9-1789 m Rachel Bassett Pvt MA
Amos: b 10-23-1747 d 10-6-1807 m (2)Christiania Phelps Pvt MA
Amos: b 4-28-1750 d 1-21-1821 m Nabby Farr Pvt NH
Amos: b 1757 d 1843 m — Cpl VT ★

SMITH, contd.

Amos: b 4-9-1757 d 10-15-1835 m Nancy Hazard Pvt RI ★
Ananias: b 3-7-1729 d 9-21-1797 m Desiar Swezey PS NY
Anderson: b — d p. 9-27-1834 m Elizabeth Mary Ann Avary Sol VA
Andrew: b 8-14-1762 d 9-3-1836 m Sarah Fowler CG CT
Andrew: b 9-4-1749 d p. 1790 m Nabby Woodberry Pvt MA
Andrew: b 1-1-1752 d 5-2-1812 m Margaret Mitchell Sol PA
Andrew: b 5-5-1761 d 5-16-1836 m Mary Gresh Pvt PA
Anning: b 12-25-1742 d 10-30-1802 m Eleanor Clark Lt NY
Anthony: b 3-15-1752 d 3-3-1838 m Esther Hodge Pvt CT
Anthony: b 9-10-1753 d 8-11-1835 m Hannah Sooy Pvt NJ ★
Archibald: b 1749 d 12-2-1821 m Jane McArthur Capt NC
Archibald: b c. 1756 d 7-3-1824 m Mary Hammond Ens MD
Arent: b 10-15-1738 d p. 1794 m (1)Catarina Veling (2)Maria Hanson Pvt NY
Arthur: b c. 1740 d 1808 m Sarah — PS NC
Asa: b 2-8-1761 d p. 1-6-1834 m Sarah Goodrich Pvt CT ★
Asa: b 7-24-1745 d 8-19-1775 m Hannah Bowen Pvt CT
Asa: b 5-7-1752 d 2-13-1835 m Submit Severance Sgt MA
Asa: b 1740 d 9-19-1815 m Lydia Lynds Cpl MA
Asa: b 8-6-1743 d 9-30-1823 m Ruth Averell CS MA
Asa: b 9-16-1758 d 10-25-1841 m Margaret Traver Pvt MA ★
Asa: b 9- -1760 d 8-30-1815 m Sarah Lettice Leonard Pvt RI
Asa: b 1723 d 1807 m Syble Flagg Pvt VT
Asahel: b 4-20-1742 d 1-4-1796 m Althea Tracy Tms CT
Asael: b 3-1-1744 d 10-30-1830 m Mary Duty Pvt NH
Asahel: b 1750 d 3-20-1831 m Esther Harrison Pvt MA
Asahel: b 11-26-1739 d 6-26-1794 m Agnes Gillette Ens VT
Asher: b 1757 d 1-26-1838 m Sarah Calkins Pvt CT W★
Augustine: b a. 1725 d a. 10-22-1781 m Ann Marshall PS VA
Aurie: b 10-30-1736 d 8-13-1820 m (1)Geertje Onderdonck (2)Neeltje (Snedeker) Onderdonk Capt NY
Austin: b 12-20-1753 d 12-9-1846 m (1)Elizabeth Newman (2)Rebecca Reynolds Sgt CT ★
Austin: b 1728 d 1817 m Sarah Knapp Pvt CT
Austin: b 10- -1760 d 11-27-1810 m Elizabeth Hubbard Cpl VA
Baltzer: b 1729 d 1802 m Magdalena Koch Pvt NY
Barnett: b c. 1747 d c. 1819 m Jane — PS VA
Bartholomew: b — d p. 12-29-1818 m (2)Margaret — Sol VA
Benajah: b 1749 d 5-18-1823 m Mary — Matr CT
Benajah: b 1750 d 1818 m Anna Tibbals Pvt CT
Benjamin: b c. 1740 d — m Marcsy Maker Ens PS CT
Benjamin, Sr.: b 1726 d 6-26-1795 m Abigail Sprague Cpl CT
Benjamin: b 5- -1734 d 10-8-1786 m Abigail Prout Sol CT
Benjamin: b 12-6-1753 d 9-12-1822 m Lois Chase Pvt CT ★
Benjamin: b 1743 d 1-19-1816 m (1)Welthea Ann York (2)Zurviah Gallup Pvt CT
Benjamin: b 2-26-1740 d 5-4-1821 m Love Coffin Capt MA
Benjamin: b 10-29-1741 d 7-2-1819 m Lucy Maynard Cpl MA
Benjamin: b 12-23-1749 d 5-15-1814 m Elizabeth Sparrow Lt MA
Benjamin: b 11-3-1728 d 2-6-1793 m (1)Abigail Smith (2)Elizabeth Smith MM PS MA
Benjamin, Sr.: b 3-3-1724 d 2-10-1796 m Ruth Snow Pvt MA
Benjamin, Jr.: b 12-8-1751/2 d 4-19-1826 m Phoebe Smith Pvt MA
Benjamin: b 1753 d 4-19-1832 m Sarah Paul Pvt MA ★
Benjamin: b c. 1754 d 2-5-1831 m Sarah Peterson Pvt MA
Benjamin: b 2-8-1765 d 6-18-1863 m Mary Elizabeth Graves Pvt Mus MA
Benjamin, Sr.: b 1728 d 1827 m Sarah Hoit Pvt NH
Benjamin: b 5-25-1754 d 10-26-1827 m Lois Bacon Pvt NH
Benjamin: b 10-21-1757 d 6-29-1842 m Judith Pottle Pvt NH
Benjamin: b 4-15-1759 d 12-3-1837 m Mrs Elizabeth (Wedgewood) Dudley Pvt NH ★
Benjamin: b 5-1-1760 d 4-26-1836 m Elsie Woodman Pvt NH
Benjamin: b 3-22-1709 d 10-13-1791 m (1)Jemima Hall (2)Anna Veazie (3)Sarah Clark PS NH
Benjamin: b 1731 d 2-21-1825 m Meribah Tilton PS NH
Benjamin: b 10-15-1736 d 3-29-1821 m Johannah Lund PS NH
Benjamin: b 8-1-1746 d 1-20-1785 m Mary — Pvt NY
Benjamin: b 1753 d 8-2-1815 m Catharine Dockstader Pvt NY
Benjamin: b 5-12-1754 d 5-29-1833 m Abigail — Pvt NY
Benjamin: b c. 1745 d c. 1790 m Freelove — PS NY
Benjamin: b 1759 d 2-23-1840 m Pheobie Smith Pvt NC ★
Benjamin: b 1745 d 9-5-1806 m Nancy Ann Burch Pvt NC
Benjamin: b 9-15-1735 d 7-22-1790 m (1)Elizabeth Ann Harleston (2)Catherine Ball (3)Sarah Smith (4)Mrs Rebecca Coachman Sol SC
Benjamin: b 5-25-1761 d 8-18-1812 m Elizabeth Cravens Lt VA
Benjamin: b c. 8-18-1756 d 7-2-1826 m Sarah Owen Pvt GA VA ★
Benjamin: b 9-24-1729 d 3-24-1843 m Marcia Hazleton Ens NJ
Benoni: b 10-6-1740 d 7-17-1799 m (1)Elizabeth Hall (2)Elizabeth Smith Capt CT
Beriah: b 2-23-1745 d 1-13-1817 m Penelope Montague Sgt MA
Bethia Doolittle: b 8-17-1746 d 1842 m Jonathan Smith PS CT
Bezaleel: b 2-10-1762 d 3-3-1848 m (1)Lydia Allis (2)Lavina Munson Pvt MA ★
Biley: b 1752 d 7-17-1831 m (1)Martha Dudley (2)Lydia Elkins Pvt NH W★
Bill: b 2-15-1753 d 8-4-1834 m Mary Ranney Sgt CT NY ★
Bruten: b c. 1740 d 1809 m Catherine Maggart Pvt VA
Byrd: b 9-27-1761 d 2-19-1815 m Rhoda Ingles Pvt VA
Caleb: bpt 4-26-1740 d 12-5-1815 m Sarah (Hawley) PS CT
Caleb: b 4- -1739 d 10-13-1813 m Submit Morton 1Lt MA

Caleb: b 9-24-1760 d 11-1-1818 m Olive Hibbard Pvt MA
Caleb: b 6-1-1745 d 1810 m Martha Mason Pvt NJ
Caleb: b 10-24-1762 d 1-13-1839 m Hannah Drake Pvt NY
Caleb: b 6-24-1724 d 10-23-1800 m Martha Smith PS NY
Caleb: b 1749 d 2-10-1808 m Roxana Mallory Sgt VT
Cephas: b 8-5-1736 d p. 1793 m Sarah Bulkeley Pvt VT
Charles: b 2-24-1737 d 3-10-1815 m Martha Rogers Maj MA
Charles: b 6-28-1755 d 12-17-1831 m Mary Gould Pvt MA ★
Charles: b — d p. 9-19-1823 m Pleasant — Pvt NC
Charles: b 1749 d 8-30-1832 m Anny Spitler Pvt PA
Charles: b 6-15-1742 d 4-7-1824 m Catherine Rhodes Cmsry SC
Charles: b c. 1755 d c. 1860 m — Sol SC
Charles: b 1763 d a. 7-6-1833 m (1)Vicey Ann Ellis (2)Rebecca Lane Sol SC
Charles: b 1762 d 1846 m Elizabeth England Pvt VA ★
Charles: b 4-15-1735 d 10-26-1821 m Patsy Jones PS VA
Charles Somerset: b 10-13-1733 d p. 11-17-1780 m Ann Hine Capt MD
Chileab, Sr.: b 5-21-1708 d 8-19-1800 m (1)Sarah Moody (2)Rebecca Butler PS MA
Chileab, Jr.: b 10-16-1742 d 5-25-1743 m Elizabeth Sawyer Pvt MA
Christian: b 1755 d p. 1804 m Catharine Fress 1Lt MD
Christian: b 3-4-1754 d 5-2-1794 m Elizabeth Stoffer Pvt PA
Christopher: b 1734 d 8-18-1820 m Abigail Harger Chatfield Pvt CT
Christopher, Jr.: b 1-26-1762 d 3-9-1826 m Hannah — Pvt MA
Christopher: b 10-11-1736 d 12-7-1814 m (1)Mary Page (2)Abigail Cilley Lt NH
Christopher: b 1740 d 11-10-1825 m Abigail Mann Pvt NH
Clemence Mills: b 5-18-1733 d 3-14-1828 m John Smith PS CT
Clement, Sr.: b 1724 d 1792 m Barbara Sim DepCmsry MD
Clement, Jr.: b 1756 d 1831 m — Brooke Dr NJ
Colesby: b 1765 d c. 1840 m Anna Henry Sol NC
Comfort: b 10-31-1746 d 2-15-1815 m Lucy Kendell Pvt CT
Coomer: b 2-18-1755 d 8-17-1793 m Freelove Barnes Capt RI
Cornelius: b 5-16-1730 d 5-19-1814 m Marya Peeck Pvt NY
Cotton Mather: b 10-25-1730 d 11-27-1806 m Temperance Worthington Chp CT
Daniel: b 1752 d 1813 m Susan Jones Pvt CT
Daniel: b 6-25-1722 d 11-27-1814 m (1)Elizabeth Rich (2)Mary (Brown) Rich (3)Mary Blinn Pvt CT
Daniel: b 8-16-1727 d 8-29-1783 m Hannah Atwater Pvt CT
Daniel: b 9-21-1756 d 5-2-1839 m Amelia Sholl Capt MD ★
Daniel: b 9-1-1761 d 3-15-1826 m Mary Bliss Pvt MA
Daniel: b — d 11-6-1702 m Joannah Jordan Pvt MA
Daniel: b 1716 d 1800 m Abigail Sacket QM MA
Daniel: b 12-24-1745 d 11-30-1836 m Roanna Cutler Pvt NH
Daniel: b 10-24-1740 d 6-16-1818 m Sarah Michie Col CS NC
Daniel: b 1757 d 5-17-1824 m Mary Davidson Capt NC W★
Daniel: b 10-7-1753 d 10-24-1843 m Ruth Pebodie 2Sgt RI CT ★
Daniel: b 1-14-1755 d 6-5-1836 m Elizabeth Shute Pvt NS PA
Daniel: b 1-22-1752 d p. 1793 m Elizabeth Mastin Dr. SC
Daniel: b 1763 d 4-2-1813 m Hannah Atwood Sol VT
Daniel: b 1724 d p. 9-24-1781 m Jane Harrison Col VA
Daniel: b 1748 d p. 1811 m — Reeves Pvt VA
Darius: b 1746 d 8-10-1820 m Lydia White Pvt MA
David: b 12-2-1747 d 11-16-1814 m Ruth Hitchcock MGen CT
David: b 1740 d 9-13-1798 m Mrs Lydia Orvis Hawley Maj CT
David: b 7-20-1744 d 1811 m Betsey Stark Ens CT
David: b 11-20-1755/6 d 11-7-1841 m Mary Sanford Sgt CT ★
David: b 11-13-1744 d 2-7-1825 m Abigail Lewis Cpl CT
David: b 6-16-1757 d 5-31-1835 m Lois Taylor Pvt Fif CT ★
David: b 1758 d 3-23-1840 m Mary Seabury Pvt CT ★
David: b 3-15-1764 d 10-30-1837 m Olive Talcott Pvt CT ★
David: b 1763 d 11-19-1852 m Lucy Prindle Pvt CT W★
David: b 9-18-1746 d 11-15-1809 m Huldah Beecher PS CT
David: b 7-9-1752 d p. 1794 m Martha Green Cpl MA
David: b 1756 d 10-1-1818 m (1)Sarah Skiff (2)Maria Allen Pvt MA
David: b 6-15-1758 d 3-3-1826 m Jane Gregg Pvt MA
David: b 1-1-1758 d 1-8-1839 m Clarissa Day Pvt MA
David: b 10-4-1758 d 3-11-1816 m (1)Mary Martha (Newell) Daggett (2)Lucy Tyler Pvt MA
David: b 6-21-1757 d 7-24-1814 m Naomi Howard Fif MA
David: b 1760 d 1840 m (1)Eunice Thurston (2)Betsy Gross Pvt NH ★
David: b 2-23-1743 d 12- -1835 m Lydia Ball PS NJ
David: b 1750 d 1800 m Hannah Petitt Pvt NJ
David: b 11-25-1750 d — m Ruhama Hull Lt NY
David: b 1759 d 1809 m (2)Fanny Ludlow Pvt NY
David: b 1763 d 10-1-1843 m Persis — Pvt NY ★
David: b 10-9-1753 d 12-3-1835 m (1)Sarah Terry (2)Obedience Fort Pvt NC W★
David: b 9-7-1746 d p. 1789 m Charity Whitfield Maj PS NC
David: b c. 1740 d a. 1784 m Anna Barbara — Lt NC
David: b 1751 d 1823 m Susanna Freesor Capt PS NC
David: b c. 1745 d 10-2-1821 m Barbara Shively Pvt PA
David: b 12-25-1761 d 9-16-1837 m Mary — Pvt RI ★
David: b c. 1760 d 3-27-1833 m Rebecca Lindley Pvt SC W★
Deborah Knapp: b 9-2-1739 d c. 1826 m Amos Smith Grd CT
Deliverance: b 3-6-1757 d 10-18-1838 m (2)Sarah (Daly) Conger Pvt NY ★
Dennis: b 1738 d 8-29-1829 m Elizabeth Sook Pvt PA ★
Dow: b 3-17-1737 d 2-26-1841 m (3)Clarissa Cook Pvt Smn CT ★
Drury: b 1748 d 1809 m Martha Peyton Pvt VA
Dudley: b 1750 d 2-18-1814 m Mary Baker Cpl MA

Duncan: b c. 1730 d p. 1790 m Sallie McLean Adj NC
Ebenetus: bpt 7-25-1745 d p. 1778 m Susannah Scudder 2Lt NY
Ebenezer, Sr.: b 4-4-1730 d 10-9-1808 m Thankful Candee Capt CT
Ebenezer: b 3-25-1720 d 7-6-1796 m Jane Clark Pvt CT
Ebenezer, Jr.: b 1756 d 1832 m Sarah Candee Pvt SC
Ebenezer, Jr.: b 10-3-1761 d 4-25-1844 m Elizabeth Bostwick Pvt CT
Ebenezer: b 4-19-1747 d 8-13-1832 m Naomi Gray Pvt CT W★
Ebenezer: b 7-17-1758 d 5-4-1835 m Lucy Stevens Pvt CT
Ebenezer: b 1- -1730 d 1799 m Mehitabel Buck Pvt CT
Ebenezer: b 8-12-1741 d p. 1791 m Martha — Pvt CT
Ebenezer: b 1-11-1746 d 9-8-1816 m Sarah Dean Capt MA
Ebenezer: b 1751 d 9-4-1824 m (1)Susanna Stinson (2)Jennet McKown Capt MA
Ebenezer, Sr.: b 8-18-1708 d 9-1-1778 m Abigail (Fessenden) Wellington Pvt MA
Ebenezer, Jr.: b 9-20-1740 d 1815 m Priscilla Diamond Pvt MA
Ebenezer: b 2-4-1756 d 6-27-1821 m Ruth Smith Pvt MA
Ebenezer: b 11-8-1719 d 1798 m Lydia Hartshorn Pvt MA
Ebenezer: b 1730 d 1796 m (1)Mary Green (2)Hepzibeth Damon Pvt MA
Ebenezer: b 10-4-1734 d 7-6-1824 m (1)Remember Ellis (2)Lucy Shepardson (3)Esther Harny Pvt MA
Ebenezer: b 11-10-1734 d 5-23-1794 m (1)Jean Marchant (2)Jane Claghorn Means Pvt MA
Ebenezer: b 10-13-1740 d 1821 m Anna Rice Pvt MA
Ebenezer: b 2-26-1747 d 2-21-1819 m Catharine Richards Pvt MA
Ebenezer: b 4-2-1751 d 1825 m Mary Gould Pvt MA
Ebenezer: b 2-27-1748 d 9-3-1779 m Elizabeth Kellogg Pvt MA
Ebenezer: b 1760 d 3-16-1844 m (3)Sally Aplin Pvt MA
Ebenezer: b a. 1720 d 5-26-1793 m Thankful Claghorn PS CS MA
Ebenezer, Sr.: b 1734 d 8-22-1807 m Sarah Spiller LCol PS CS NH
Ebenezer, Jr.: b 1765 d 7-23-1831 m Elenor Hilton Pvt NH
Ebenezer: b 1-31-1739 d 2-1-1832 m Rhoda — Cpl NY
Ebenezer: b 1-4-1751 d 1-19-1834 m (1)Martha Bentley (2)Mary Robinson Pvt PA
Ebenezer: b 1740 d 1830 m Nancy — Pvt VT
Edmund: b 8-13-1761 d 1812 m Patience Sumner Pvt MA
Edward: b 1762 d 8-20-1834 m Annis Blood Pvt MA ★
Edward: b c. 1754/5 d 1-6-1833 m Abigail Kelley Pvt NH
Edward: b 11-25-1727 d 1-15-1815 m Ruth Porter PS CS NH
Edward: b c. 1738 d 1806 m Eve — Pvt NY
Edward: b 1720 d 1807 m Catherine (Stonecipher) Pvt NC
Edward: b c. 1740 d p. 1792 m Sally Rice Capt VA
Edward: b 1754 d 1828 m Nancy Black Lt VA
Edward: b 1761 d 12-6-1852 m Hannah Crabtree Pvt VA ★
Elam: b 4-14-1756 d 9-30-1813 m Elizabeth Dows Pvt CT
Eldad: b 1740 d 1805 m (1)Sarah Easton (2)Hannah Case Pvt CT
Eleazer: b 11-22-1761 d 3-30-1809 m Hannah Richmond Pvt CT
Eleazer: b 1-27-1725 d 1-4-1816 m Lydia Thomas PS MA
Eli: b 11-8-1751 d 3-29-1824 m Deborah Phelps Ens CT W★
Eli: b 11-10-1751 d 6-16-1816 m Jemima Denton Pvt NY
Eli: b c. 1760 d 4-19-1836 m Jane Denny Pvt Spy VA
Eliakim: b 1735 d 8-29-1775 m Mehitable Smith Capt MA
Elias: b 8-8-1731 d 10-17-1791 m Catherine Blanchard Chp MA
Elihu: b 7-11-1734 d 2-9-1830 m Oner Slade Ens CS CT VT
Elijah: b 12-29-1735 d p. 1790 m Elizabeth Benedict Pvt CT
Elijah, Jr.: b 5-30-1753 d 12-31-1824 m Susanna Judd Pvt CT
Elijah: b 1761 d 1851 m Martha Jenkins Pvt MD
Elijah: b 3-1-1737 d 1802 m Mary — Cpl MA
Elijah: b 1745 d — m Sybil Worthington Pvt MA ★
Elijah: b 1754 d p. 1832 m Esther — Pvt NH ★
Elijah: b 9-1-1751 d 1-27-1830 m Mary Sutton Lt NJ
Elijah: b 8-15-1755 d 1836 m (1)Elizabeth L Litten (2)Lucretia Jones Sgt NJ VA ★
Elijah: b 4-24-1761 d 6-23-1852 m Mary Smith Pvt RI ★
Elijah: b 5-29-1763 d 1840 m Polly Nichols Sol VT
Eliphalet: b — d p. 1797 m (1)Beriah Leland (2)Susanna Pratt Pvt MA
Eliphalet: b 11-16-1759 d 4-15-1849 m Elizabeth Bartow Pvt MA ★
Elisha: b 12-31-1758 d 4-23-1846 m Mary Samson Lt MA ★
Elisha: b 3-14-1749 d 3-25-1823 m Ursula Billings Pvt MA
Elisha: b 1749 d 8-10-1841 m Susannah Wing PS ME
Elisha: b 2-15-1759 d 8-8-1837 m Keturah Edson Pvt MA
Elisha: b 5-2-1755 d 6-28-1834 m (1)Sarah Huse (2)Mrs Thyng Pvt NH
Elisha: b 1723 d 3-12-1811 m Lydia Norris PS MA
Elisha: b 5-18-1755 d 6-26-1849 m Rachel Hughson Pvt NY
Elizabeth Carraway: b c. 1722 d 7- -1776 m Aaron Smith PS SC
Elizabeth Chamberlain Lanier: b c. 1717 d c. 1786 m (1)Sampson Lanier (2)Cuthbert Smith PS VA
Elnathan: b 11-23-1738 d 3-6-1826 m Chloe Lee Cmsry CT
Elnathan: b 1758 d 7-25-1834 m Mary Thorp Sgt CT
Enoch: b 1753 d 3-19-1833 m Lydia Crocker Pvt Tms CT ★
Enoch: b 6-21-1750 d 4- -1825 m (1)Nancy (Belfield) Lane (2)Frances Wren Sol KY
Enoch: b 1760/1 d 3-10-1852 m (1)Betsy Reed (2)Abigail Glazier Pvt MA ★
Enoch: b c. 1752 d p. 10-6-1802 m Elizabeth O'Bannon Gnr VA
Enos: b 2-16-1759 d 2-11-1840 m Anna Minor Cpl CT
Enos: b 7-24-1749 d 3-8-1836 m Hannah Drake Sgt MA ★
Enos: b 6-28-1745 d 3-14-1836 m Mary Dickinson Pvt MA
Enos: b 11-14-1754 d 10-5-1818 m Phebe Vail Sol NY
Enos: b 3-4-1739 d 8-29-1803 m Keziah Brown 2Lt RI

Epenetus: bpt 7-25-1745 d p. 1778 m Susannah Scudder 2Lt NY
Epenetus: b 1-11-1723 d 8-8-1803 m (1)Deborah Smith (2)Mrs Mary (Arthur) Blydenburgh CS PS NY
Ephraim: b 1715 d 1806 m Sarah Newton Pvt CT
Ephraim: b 9-24-1740 d 10-7-1839 m Abbey Higgins Pvt CT
Ephraim: b 1743 d 5-1-1830 m Elizabeth Bingham Pvt CT
Ephraim: b 9-5-1762 d 8-21-1837 m Deborah Sanford Pvt CT ★
Ephraim: bpt 8- -1744 d 6-17-1796 m Susan Hotchkiss PS CT
Ephraim: b 1744 d 6-30-1827 m Thankful Goodman Pvt MA
Ephraim: b 6-23-1758 d 1839 m (1)Elizabeth Clark (2)Jerusha Clark Pvt MA W★
Ephraim: bpt 5-19-1758 d p. 1835 m Phebe Porter Sol MA
Ephraim: b 4-8-1761 d 6-11-1815 m Miriam Thurston Pvt NY
Ephraim: b 1756 d 5-9-1817 m — Pomeroy Pvt VT
Ethan: b 12-19-1762 d 8-29-1849 m Bathsheba Sanford Pvt MA
Ezekiel: b 2-7-1756 d 3-7-1847 m Anna — Pvt CT ★
Ezekiel: b 8-21-1740 d 2-10-1795 m Ruth Childs PS NH
Ezekiel: b c. 1742 d 1821 m Lurania Phelps Pvt SC
Ezra: b 10-6-1711 d p. 1784 m (1)Zurviah Russel (2)Judath Bosworth (3)Catherine Spring (4)Alice — PS CT
Ezra: b 1-13-1754 d 2-22-1834 m Phebe Walcott Cpl MA W★
Felix: b 10-27-1732 d p. 11-23-1778 m Esther Cordery Pvt NJ
Fergus: b 1735 d 1815 m Elizabeth — 1Lt PS MD PA
Fleming: b 12-5-1745 d 8-27-1847 m Nancy Goode Pvt SC ★
Floyd: b 1720 d 1812 m Clarisa Helme Pvt PS NY
Frances: b — d 1783/4 m John Smith PS VA
Francis: b c. 1749 d 1814 m Lucy Wilkinson Pvt GA
Francis: b 1760 d 8- -1821 m — Pvt GA
Francis: b 2-21-1733 d 6-14-1812 m Eunice Smith Cpl MA
Francis: b 6-4-1733 d 5-1-1785 m Elizabeth (Smith) Capt NY
Francis: b 1742 d 1833 m Catherine Markham Lt VA
Francis: b 11-18-1757 d p. 1785 m Martha Allen Capt VA
Francis Joseph: b c. 1752 d 1802 m (2)Elizabeth Brodhead Ens PA
Frederick: b 3-1-1760 d 7-17-1852 m Sarah Brainard Mrnr CT ★
Frederick: b 5-19-1750 d 6-11-1822 m Christina Leather Myers Cpl NY ★
Frederick: bpt 12-6-1752 d p. 5-6-1806 m Helen — Pvt NY
Frederick: b 12-25-1755 d 1845 m Elizabeth McGee Capt NC SC ★
Frederick: b 12-20-1743 d 9-11-1832 m (1)Miss Williams (2)Sarah (Sloan) Grant Lt VT W★
Gad: b 1-23-1749 d 1-9-1827 m Irene Wait Sol MA
Gaius: b 7-8-1795 d 5-18-1827 m (1)Rachel Allen (2)Olive Fisher Pvt MA
Gasper: b 1723 d p. 1784 m Margaret — PS NC
George: b 6-19-1761 d 6-17-1844 m Polly Bent Pvt MA ★
George: b 3-12-1762 d 11-12-1840 m Lydia King Smn MA
George: b 1748 d 3-15-1816 m Hannah Hall Sgt NY
George: b — d 3- -1803 m Mary Tyler Pvt NY ★
George: b 5-8-1756 d 3-11-1818 m Elizabeth Taylor Sgt NC
George: b 12-23-1763 d 11- -1842 m Phoebe Ellis Pvt NC
George: b 1730 d 1799 m Rhoda Allen PS NC
George: b 8-10-1745 d 6-22-1825 m Effie Drake Lt CS PA
George: b 1750 d 8-17-1831 m Anna Barbara Beyschley Pvt PA
George: b 3-15-1747 d 8-9-1820 m Judith Guerrant Lt VA
George: b c. 1730 d 3-20-1804 m Rebecca Bowen Pvt VA
George: b a. 1753 d 12-30-1822 m Kezea — PS VA
George Bernard: b c. 1744 d 4-27-1793 m Dorothea — Pvt PA
George Stovall: b 4-11-1750 d 1810 m Frances Sandifer Ens VA
George W.: b 2-15-1742 d 1-21-1797 m Deliverance Frost Capt MA
Gideon: b 7-29-1743 d 12-3-1815 m Mehitable Tuttle Pvt CT
Gideon: b 1759 d p. 10-15-1832 m Hannah Currie Pvt NY ★
Gideon, Sr.: b 3-19-1736 d 4-23-1813 m Rebecca Smith Sgt CS NH
Gideon: b 5-28-1752 d 3-31-1841 m Elizabeth — Pvt PA ★
Gilbert: b 1-20-1756 d 3-13-1795 m Delia Bundy Cpl CT
Gilbert: b 4-2-1742 d 4-7-1814 m (1)Eunice Denison (2)Phebe Chesebrough Sol CT
Godfrey: b 1-3-1765 d 11-5-1820 m Elizabeth Howard Cav VA ★
Gold: b 10-14-1752 d 1835 m Esther Smith Pvt CT
Granville: b 1758 d p. 10-24-1806 m Ann Pasteur DepQM VA
Griffith: b 1764 d 1-3-1843 m Mary Brand Drm PA ★
Gulielmus: b c. 1735 d 1814 m — Sol NC
Guy, Sr.: b 1728 d 1787 m — PS NC
Guy, Jr.: b c. 1755-60 d 8-17-1830 m (1)Cornelia — (2)Mrs Sarah (Walker) Stallings Sgt NC
Guy: b c. 1730 d p. 1-10-1781 m Ann Hopkins CS VA
Hardy: b 1757 d 1852 m (2)Rebecca Thompson Pvt NC ★
Harlock: bpt 4-27-1746 d p. 1790 m Jedidah Smith Sgt MA
Heman: b 6-7-1747 d 7- -1812 m (1)Miriam Moody (2)Lucy (Taylor) Cutler (3)Almira Messenger Capt MA
Heman: b c. 1745 d 6-7-1820 m Sarah Ann Myrick Sgt MA ★
Hendrick: b 1-21-1733 d p. 7-7-1798 m Sarah VanWagenen PS NY
Henry: b — d 10-12-1870 m Melissa Davis Pvt PA
Henry: b 9-29-1738 d 12-12-1827 m Sarah Colburn Capt MA
Henry: b 4-24-1724 d a. 12-5-1805 m Lucretia Moore Pvt MA
Henry: b 4-24-1711 d 7-2-1875 m Abigail Clark PS MA
Henry: b 1-17-1740 d 10-19-1815 m Maria Crist Lt NY
Henry: b 1748 d 10- -1829 m — Ens NY
Henry: b 1755 d 1-9-1828 m Hulda Olmsted Pvt NY
Henry: b c. 1744 d p. 7-18-1802 m Sarah Grover PS NY
Henry: b c. 1755 d 7-17-1845 m Sarah Adams Pvt NC
Henry: b 12-25-1741 d 8-28-1835 m Mary Barbara Hison Maj NC ★
Henry: b 2-25-1752 d 3-10-1838 m (1)Elizabeth Grovenstadt (2)Margaret (Sheeter) Staugh Pvt Sct PA ★

SMITH, contd.

Henry: b 1761 d 11-29-1835 m Elizabeth Powell Sgt VA
Henry: b 1753 d 1838 m Margaret Lyon Pvt VA
Henry: b c. 1715 d 1780-9 m Sarah Crosby PS VA
Hezekiah: b 1726 d 1800 m Eunice Morris Maj PS MA
Hezekiah: b 4-18-1753 d 4-26-1824 m Mary Ann Rector Pvt MA
Hezekiah: b 4-21-1737 d 1-28-1805 m Hephzibah Kimball Chp MA
Hezekiah, Sr.: b 6-3-1714 d 4-6-1801 m Sarah Hull Sol NJ
Hezekiah, Jr.: b 4-6-1755 d 11-3-1817 m Mercy Fitz Randolph Pvt
　　NJ
Hezekiah: b c. 1747 d — m Sally — Pvt NJ
Hiram: b 12-22-1756 d 4-27-1833 m (1)Eleanor Parrott (2)Mrs
　　Susan (Ten Eyck) Darbe Lt NJ ★
Hugh: b c. 1750 d 1812 m Mrs Mary Miller Pvt PA
Humphrey: b 6- -1760 d c. 1847 m Eleanor McElhaney Pvt VA
Ira: b 9-11-1757 d 4-22-1835 m (1)Elizabeth Judson (2)Mrs Chloe
　　Stevens OrdlSgt CT ★
Isaac: b 3-18-1730 d 12-4-1789 m Lucy Clark PS Lt CT
Isaac: b 12-16-1735 d p. 1790 m Ruth Hollister Pvt CT
Isaac: b 1-16-1757 d 2-16-1805 m Abigail Warring SrgnMte CT
　　W★
Isaac: b 1758 d 1834 m Hannah Swift Pvt CT ★
Isaac, Jr.: b c. 1761 d p. 1827 m Sarah (Webb) Nichols Sol PS CT
Isaac: b 4-9-1754 d 3-14-1835 m (1)Hannah Heywood (2)Mrs Sarah
　　(Whitman) Dexter PS ME
Isaac: b 5-7-1721 d 11-29-1799 m Eunice Adams Col MA
Isaac: b 1724 d 3-4-1811 m (1)Abigail — (2)Rachel — (3)Esther
　　Morgan Pvt MA
Isaac: b 7-5-1744 d 12-12-1795 m Dorcas Barrett Pvtr MA
Isaac: b 1737 d 2-9-1823 m Sarah Meeker Capt NJ
Isaac: b c. 1741 d c. 1824 m Mary English Pvt NJ
Isaac: b 3-19-1751 d 2-7-1823 m Rachel — Pvt NJ
Isaac: b 1738 d 6-11-1820 m Fanny Mead Capt SrgnMte NY
Isaac: b 3-10-1763 d 1855 m Hannah Hawley Pvt NY
Isaac: b 3-1-1731 d 2-6-1789 m Martha — PS NY
Isaac: b 1763 d 1811 m Sary Hampton Pvt NC
Isaac: b 1760 d 4-4-1834 m Sarah Brown Pvt PA
Isaac: b 1761 d 1828 m Eunice Whitney Pvt VT MA ★
Isaac: b 8-17-1758 d 7-20-1834 m Ann Rebecca Gilman OrdlSgt
　　VA W★
Isaac: b c. 1730 d p. 8-18-1801 m Margart Rucker Sol VA
Isaac: b 1760 d 1845 m Sarah Handcock Pvt VA ★
Israel: b 12-8-1748 d 6-4-1791 m Mary Hasbrouck Capt NY
Israel: b 1741 d 1809 m Jamima Payne Maj VT
Israel: b 4-13-1731 d 11-13-1811 m Mary Morse Capt MA
Israel, Sr.: b 4-2-1739 d 6-7-1811 m Abigail Chandler PS VT
Ithamar: b 7-4-1761 d 11-11-1834 m Deborah Gorham Pvt CT
Jacob: b 1738 d 4-14-1807 m Mary Lewis Sgt CT
Jacob: b 1740 d 1822 m — Dugger Pvt MD
Jacob: b 9-17-1739 d 1816 m Dorothy — Capt NH
Jacob: b — d 10-27-1807 m Betsy Cass Lt PS NH
Jacob: b 9-18-1762 d 12-1-1836 m Rachel Ferris Pvt NY
Jacob: b 1725 d — m Elizabeth — Pvt PA
Jacob: b 1-11-1741 d 8-17-1811 m Anna Margaret — Pvt PS PA
Jacob: b c. 1737 d 1805 m Sarah Butler Pvt SC
Jacob: b 7-7-1742 d 7-8-1831 m (1)Elizabeth Blanchard (2)Mrs
　　Hannah Ketchum Lt VT ★
Jacob: b 1749/50 d 2-3-1835 m — Pvt VA ★
Jacob: b 1753 d 12-12-1819 m Patience — Pvt VA
James, Sr.: b 5-19-1738 d 1-11-1831 m Mary Hubbard Capt CT
James, Jr.: b 8-25-1762 d 8-2-1844 m Elizabeth Shalor Pvt CT ★
James, Jr.: b 3- -1732 d 9-6-1798 m Abigail Hempstead Sgt CT
James: b 1704 d 1787 m — Pvt CT
James: b 8-22-1764 d 4-16-1838 m Martha Howard Sol CT ★
James: b 7-18-1765 d 8-2-1827 m Mercy Johnson Fif CT W★
James: b 3-6-1755 d 1817 m Elizabeth Cowan Pvt GA
James: b 1751 d 1779-80 m Mary Graham PS MD
James: b 10-27-1728 d 1817 m Patience Wood Lt MA
James: b 7-13-1751 d 5-19-1808 m Hannah Field Sgt MA
James, Sr.: b 4-28-1721 d 3-13-1810 m Margaret McLeland Pvt
　　MA
James, Jr.: b 2-22-1751 d 10-9-1835 m Dolly Watson Pvt MA
James: b 5-2-1730 d 1789 m Hannah Barlow Pvt MA
James: b 2-8-1740 d 10-27-1805 m (1)Mrs Lydia Warner
　　(2)Jemima Foster Pvt MA
James: b 1-25-1763 d 6-28-1844 m Polly Taylor Pvt MA
James: b 1-9-1755 d 4-30-1823 m Mary Browning Pvt MA
James: b 11-1-1753 d 12-6-1838 m Sarah Pitcher Pvt MA ★ .
James: b 1750 d 4-5-1825 m Hannah Wilbur Pvt MA
James: b 1-6-1744 d 5-8-1817 m Elizabeth Mack Lt PS NH
James: b 1-10-1763 d 10-8-1844 m Ruth Weeks Pvt NH
James: b 1-29-1756 d 8-11-1842 m Sarah Ames Pvt NH
James: b 1740 d 11-16-1784 m Eleanor Harrison Pvt NJ
James: b — d2- -1810 m Cornelia McKee Pvt NJ
James: b 1749 d 8-23-1843 m Elizabeth Shyble Pvt NJ ★
James: b 4-2-1749 d — m Esther — Sgt NY
James: b 7-7-1746 d 9-30-1779 m Sarah Hewlett MM Pvt NY
James: b 5-1-1757 d 9-11-1841 m (1)Deborah Reynolds (2)Ruth
　　Hoffman Pvt Sct NY ★
James: b 1725 d 12-26-1799 m Sarah — Maj NC
James: b 1735 d 1782 m Clara Smith PS Maj NC
James: b c. 1754 d 12-7-1817 m (1)Constantia Ford (2)Mrs Lucy
　　Marshall Turner Sgt NC ★

James: b 1737 d 1812 m (1)Anne Wilson (2)Mrs Margaret Irvin Col PA
James: b 1759 d 1-14-1835 m Jemima Russell CaptLt PA ★
James: b 1747 d 11-28-1837 m Flora Erskine Pvt DE PA ★
James: b c. 1759 d 1843 m Nannie (Nair) Hunt Pvt PA
James: b 1749 d 1829 m Nancy Waterman Lt RI
James: b 5-3-1745 d 6-30-1826 m Phebe Wardwell Sol Grd PS RI
　　W★
James: b 1736 d 12-5-1795 m Lillis Patton PS SC
James: b 2-18-1758 d 2-3-1823 m Amy Pomfret Lt VA
James: b 1760 d 1812 m Ellinor Hicks Lt VA
James: b c. 1742 d p. 1793 m Magdalene Woods Ens VA
James: b 1754 d 1837 m Margaret Truax Pvt VA
James: b 1745 d 1778 m Lucy Lane Pvt VA
James: b 9-17-1757 d p. 7-12-1794 m Elizabeth Porter Pvt VA
James: b c. 1762 d p. 1810 m Hannah Parker Pvt VA
Jared: b 7-25-1741 d 3-13-1813 m (1)Dorcas Beecher (2)Mary
　　Johnson Pvt CT
Jared: b 4-2-1741 d c. 1796 m Rebecca Wood Lt MA
Jarius: b 6-22-1759 d 7-3-1803 m Sarah Paine Cpl CT
Jasiel: b 3-25-1734 d 10-12-1810 m Anna Crosman Ens MA
Jedediah: b c. 1760 d p. 1793 m Lydia Crane Cpl CT
Jedediah: b c. 1725 d 1782 m Hannah Leach Sol CT
Jedediah: b 1738 d 2-25-1847 m Esther Fuller Pvt CT ★
Jedediah: b 4-5-1752 d 2-4-1819 m Rhoda Smith Sgt CS MA
Jeffery: b 1762 d 2-1-1846 m Dorothy Hubbard Pvt CT
Jeffrey: b 3-17-1734 d 1812 m Prudence Smith Maj NY
Jehiel: b 1761 d 11-15-1825 m Rachel Hine Pvt CT ★
Jehiel: b 4-21-1757 d 3-26-1813 m Mercy — Cpl VT
Jeremaih: b 12-24-1746 d 7-19-1835 m (1)Mary (Smith)
　　(2)Elizabeth Beecher Cpl CT
Jeremaih: b 6-29-1758 d 12-20-1837 m Temperance Comstock
　　Cpl CT ★
Jeremiah: b 8-1-1762 d 8-25-1851 m Anna Kellogg Pvt CT ★
Jeremiah: b 7-23-1729 d 9-1-1789 m Mary Roads Capt MA
Jeremiah: b 4-14-1753 d 5-26-1821 m Mary Loker Pvt MA
Jeremiah: b 1733 d 5-29-1794 m Hannah Lock Pvt NH
Jeremiah: b 1752 d 1831 m Naomi Babcock Capt NJ
Jeremiah: b 1753 d 1793 m Elizabeth Harris 1Lt NJ
Jeremiah: b 5-5-1755 d 11-27-1810 m Eva — Pvt PA
Jeremiah: b 1711 d p. 3-25-1786 m — PS VA
Jesse: b 1758 d 5-24-1841 m Susannah Nichols Pvt CT
Jesse: b 1758 d 1831 m Annie Thomas Sgt CT ★
Jesse: b 4-13-1756 d 6-4-1844 m Sarah Grant MM MA
Jesse: b 3-15-1761 d 11-21-1829 m Lucy McDonald Pvt MA NH ★
Jesse, Jr.: b 2-1-1736 d 11-12-1777 m Lydia Gregory Pvt NY
Jesse: b 6-3-1747 d 8-23-1830 m Hannah Carll PS Pvt NY
Jesse: b 10-17-1758 d 1-6-1829 m Elizabeth Ansley Pvt NY
Jesse: b — d 1802 m — Pvt NJ
Jesse: b 12-29-1762 d 2-27-1837 m Nancy Hendricks Byers Cpl VA
Joab: b 1760 d 2-8-1840 m Elizabeth Lennon Pvt CT
Job: b 1725 d 2-16-1795 m Hannah Barney PS MA
Job: b 2-4-1754 d 12- -1821 m Diadema Booth Pvt MA
Job: b 9-26-1745 d 8-6-1776 m Sarah Ogdon Pvt NY
Job: b c. 1740 d 4-15-1813 m Eunice McClure CS MA
Joel: b 8-5-1757 d 4-15-1844 m (1)Hannah Griswold (2)Lydia
　　Stanley Ens CT
Joel: b 4-20-1763 d 9-30-1827 m Laura Roena Franklin Pvt VT
Johannes: b 1735 d p. 2-22-1798 m (1)Margarita Weltman
　　(2)Margaretha Peesinger Sol NY
Johannes: b 4-8-1730 d 4-18-1813 m Elizabeth Zapperlie PS NY
Johannes: b 2-2-1750 d 3-9-1818 m Christina Miller Pvt PA
John: b 11-1-1735 d p. 1-18-1786 m Mehitable Smith Lt CT
John: b 7-27-1736 d 1- -1811 m (1)Sarah Tyler (2) Abigail Smith
　　1Lt CT
John: b 2-2-1744 d 12-26-1819 m Mary Ford Lt CT
John: b 7-13-1752 d 3-23-1798 m Martha Shailer NLt CT
John: b 7-19-1755 d 5-8-1834 m Anna Burr Matr CT ★
John: b c. 1755 d 1805 m Abigail Chapel Pvt CT
John: b 1739 d 2-15-1807 m Matilda Catlin Pvt CT
John: b 6-24-1730 d 2-28-1779 m Clemence Mills PS CT
John: b 1745 d 1- -1795 m Sarah — Pvt GA
John: b 1747 d 6-23-1832 m Martha VanCleve Capt MD
John, Sr.: b 1722 d 6-9-1794 m Mary Buchanan PS MD
John, Jr.: b 5-3-1754 d 4-5-1804 m Elizabeth — Pvt MD
John: b 2-2-1753 d 7-22-1835 m Elizabeth Mulliken Pvt MD ★
John: b 8-29-1716 d 3-28-1793 m Elizabeth Smith Col MA
John: b 12-12-1744 d p. 1787 m — Capt MA
John: b 4-4-1743 d 1816 m Sarah Doolittle Lt MA ★
John: b 1-17-1744 d 2- -1818 m Marah Cooke Cpl MA
John: b 11-12-1752 d 8-11-1840 m Ruth Cook Cpl MA
John: b 6-11-1757 d 9-3-1835 m Keziah Pease Cpl MA
John: b 1729 d 1790 m Abigail Dillingham Pvt MA
John: b 1736 d 5-16-1822 m Sarah Burnell Pvt MA
John: b a. 1753 d p. 1786 m Mary Morton Pvt MA
John: b 3-21-1740 d 5-25-1796 m (1)Abigail Hamblen (2)Desire
　　Fuller Pvt MA
John: b 1747 d 6-7-1828 m Anna Eaton Pvt MA ★
John: b 1753 d 12-8-1821 m Abigail Wilson Pvt MA ★
John: b 11-16-1755 d 8-5-1830 m Caroline Smith Pvt MA W★
John: b 10-9-1758 d 8-4-1838 m Sarah Mastick Pvt MA ★
John: b 1753 d 1-19-1835 m Elizabeth McLellan Pvt MA ★
John: b 9- -1760 d 7-18-1836 m (1)Betsy Banks (2)Anna Banks
　　Pvt MA

John: b 1760 d 6-12-1845 m (2)Mary Cummings Pvt MA
John: b 9-3-1761 d 10-2-1840 m Dolly Crary Pvt MA ★
John: b 11-18-1761 d 2-6-1798 m Susanna Newhall Vol MA
John: b a. 1756 d 7-11-1811 m Lydia Graves Smn MA
John: b 12-22-1716 d 6-19-1803 m Margaret McMarras PS MA
John: b 6-6-1752 d 6-5-1826 m Lucy Whitman Ens NH W★
John: b 11-13-1749 d 11-30-1832 m Mary Pike Pvt NH ★
John: b 1-20-1760 d 7-17-1842 m Martha Drake Pvt NH
John: b 6-9-1759 d 8-24-1824 m (1)Elizabeth Campbell (2)Lucretia Colby Sol NH
John: b 1715 d 1801 m Mary Harkness Pvt MA
John: b 1744 d 1808 m Anna Hovey PS NH
John: b 1715 d 1785 m Sarah Freeman Cpl NJ
John: b 12-27-1761 d 5-24-1836 m Elizabeth Dunham Adj NJ
John: b c. 1712 d 1790 m Ann Test or Sarah Hill Pvt NJ
John: b 3-4-1756 d 3-3-1833 m Jane Robertson Pvt NJ ★
John: b 2-21-1735 d 1-5-1806 m Sarah Higbee Pvt NJ
John: b 1742 d 5-23-1814 m Sarah Snider Pvt NJ
John: b 4-1-1735 d 7-25-1825 m Meribah Ayers Pvt NJ
John: b 6-4-1762 d 3-19-1851 m (2)Rebecca Griffin Pvt Tms NJ ★
John: b 4-23-1763 d 4-23-1855 m Sarah Gould Wgn NJ
John: b 10-8-1743 d 1-12-1833 m Jemima DeWindt Maj NY
John: b 8- -1741 d 2- -1796 m Sarah — Pvt NY
John: b 11-12-1760/1 d 5-12-1836 m Esther Little Sol NY ★
John, Jr.: b c. 1724 d 12- -1790 m Sarah — Col NC
John: b 1749 d 1806 m Katherine O. — Sol NC
John: b 1740 d 1782 m Mary Flake Pvt NC
John: b 3-4-1752 d 4-17-1808 m Margaret Withrow Pvt NC
John, Sr.: b a. 11-20-1710 d 2- -1793 m Elizabeth Whitfield PS CS NC
John: b 1756 d p. 1783 m Margaret Patterson Cpl PA
John: b 4-8-1743 d 4-20-1832 m (1)Catharine Odenwalder (2)Barbara Odenwalder Pvt PA
John: b 1749 d 3-29-1818 m Ann Craig Pvt PA
John: b 1755 d 4-6-1834 m Catherine Farling Pvt PA ★
John: b 8-26-1753 d 1842 m Martha Wallace Pvt PA ★
John: b 1-29-1756 d 8-25-1825 m Anna Christiana Schreiber Pvt PA
John: b 12-27-1758 d 2-11-1826 m Agnes Hume Pvt PA
John: b c. 1750 d 1800-10 m Molly Templeton PS PA
John: b 12-6-1759/60 d 7-16-1810 m Lydia Sheffield Pvt RI W★
John: b 12-14-1735 d 3-23-1817 m Elphal Arnold PS RI
John: b 6- -1739 d 1802 m — Polk Capt SC
John: b 8- -1754 d 4-7-1841 m Mary — Sgt SC
John: b c. 1715 d p. 6-10-1797 m (1)Abigail Commander (2)Jane Ford (3)Mary — PS SC
John: b 1730 d 7-24-1806 m Phebe — Capt CS VT
John: bpt 6-1-1729 d 12-14-1790 m Hannah Goodhue Cpl VT
John: b 2-13-1758 d 10-28-1851 m Sarah Kaincaid Pvt NH VT ★
John: b 5-7-1750 d 3-3-1836 m Amimus Bull Col VA
John: b 1737-40 d p. 1785 m Elizabeth Taylor Lt VA
John: b 11-30-1752 d 12- -1781 m Margaret Davis Lt VA
John: b 1755 d 1815 m Mrs Mary Jane (Smith) Hart Ens VA
John: b 1733 d 1809 m Elizabeth — Ens VA
John: b c. 1720 d p. 1809 m — Pvt VA
John: b 10-1-1742 d p. 3-3-1837 m — Pvt VA ★
John: b a. 1755 d 10- -1802 m Julia Phillips Pvt VA
John: b 11-2-1760 d 3-23-1812 m Sarah Spencer Pvt VA
John: b 6-30-1760 d 4-4-1833 m Nancy Wilson Pvt VA ★
John: b 6-25-1764 d 9- -1820 m (1)Mary English (2)Ann — Pvt VA
John: b 6-25-1764 d 1821 m (1)Mary Byrd (2)Anna — Pvt VA
John: b 1740 d 3-12-1804 m Mary Fosque CS VA
John: b c. 1727 d a. 11-15-1784 m Martha — PS VA
John: b c. 1748 d p. 12-12-1825 m Jane — PS VA
John Andrew: b 4-7-1754 d 11-22-1836 m (2)Margaret Broadway Pvt VA ★
John Blair: b 6-12-1756 d 8-22-1799 m Elizabeth Fisher Nash Sol PS VA
John Duncan: b 1730 d 2-28-1822 m Ann — Maj NY
John (Frederick): b 1758 d 10-29-1812 m Elizabeth Paul Sol PA
John Gottleib Israel: b 8-4-1755 d 6-4-1820 m Christina Keiffer Pvt GA
John Kilby: b 12-17-1753 d 8-7-1842 m Polly Webb BgdMaj MA
John L.: b 3-16-1744 d 8-22-1797 m Elizabeth Remsen Maj NY
John P.: b 1749 d 10-25-1840 m Gertrude Herder Pvt NY ★
Jonas: b 2-21-1748 d 5-9-1814 m Mary Parker Lt MA
Jonas, Sr.: b 6-17-1719 d 11-4-1802 m Thankful Fiske Pvt MA
Jonas: b 12-30-1754 d 12-7-1845 m Susanna Bruce Pvt MA
Jonas: b 11-3-1762 d 1852 m Elizabeth Perry Sol NY
Jonas: b 1763 d 10-16-1828 m Mary LaBar Pvt PA
Jonas: b 4-11-1750 d 7-16-1839 m (1)Mary Kincannon (2)Annabel Bates Pvt VA
Jonathan: b 1-24-1746 d 4-29-1840 m Hannah Witter Sgt CT
Jonathan, Jr.: b 1762 d 5-2-1824 m Mary Summer Pvt Matr CT W★
Jonathan, Jr.: b 1761 d 8-6-1812 m Rebecca Ventres Pvt CT ★
Jonathan: b 1741 d 9-9-1802 m Esther Bacon LCol CS MA
Jonathan: b 8-9-1741/2 d c. 1814 m Elizabeth McDougle Cpl MA
Jonathan: b 8-21-1744 d 8-13-1821 m (1)Elizabeth Drury (2)Abigail — Cpl MA
Jonathan: b 3-17-1717 d 6-1-1809 m Ruth Hunting Pvt MA
Jonathan: b 5-15-1727 d 1-2-1803 m Charity Hooper Pvt ME
Jonathan: b 8-18-1742 d 2-9-1809 m Abigail Chauncey Pvt MA
Jonathan: b 10-16-1749 d 12-19-1809 m Bathsheba Chapin MM MA

Jonathan: bpt 12-14-1760 d p. 4-1-1814 m Lucy Hobart Pvt MA
Jonathan: b 3-10-1761 d 1-3-1855 m (1)Lydia Harding (2)Patience Green Pvt MA ★
Jonathan, Sr.: b 10-16-1713 d 3-23-1801 m Mrs Abigail Stratton Pvt PS MA
Jonathan, Jr.: b 10-4-1748 d 11-29-1819 m (1)Mrs Lydia (Reed) Muzzy (2)Abigail Marrett (3)Ruth Fiske PS MA
Jonathan: b 1-7-1755 d 3-22-1830 m Jemima Merrill Pvt NH ★
Jonathan: b a. 1754 d 1- -1777 m Mary Golden Capt NJ
Jonathan, Jr.: b 1-30-1758 d 3-10-1850 m (1)Mary Furman (2)Lydia Kercheval Pvt Fif NJ ★
Jonathan: b — d p. 3-18-1786 m Catherine — PS NY
Jonathan: b 3-27-1760 d 1843 m (1)Esther Bryan (2)Miss McCullers Capt NC
Jonathan: b 2-28-1746 d 5-2-1841 m Freelove Boss Capt RI
Jonathan: b 1762 d 9-14-1829 m (1) — Guyton (2)Elizabeth — Sol SC
Jonathan: b 9-10-1757 d 12-7-1847 m (1)Anna Holland (2)Nancy—Lt VA ★
Jonathan: b 1750 d 1781 m Elizabeth Evans 2Lt VA
Jonathan Warren: b 1748 d 8-14-1833 m Catherine Keys Cpl MA
Joseph: b 3-15-1730 d 8-10-1810 m Jemima Bostwick Capt CT
Joseph: b 7-6-1755 d 3-6-1834 m Hannah Hewett 2Lt CT
Joseph: b 10-1-1747 d 10-24-1794 m Anna Bradley Pvt CT
Joseph: b 1751 d 10-8-1846 m Sybil Wardell Pvt CT
Joseph: b 7-18-1746 d — m Mary Waterbury Pvt CT
Joseph, Jr.: b 1756 d 4-7-1814 m Sarah King (Smith) Pvt CT
Joseph: b 1-19-1734/5 d 8-4-1784 m Eunice Williams Grd CT
Joseph, Jr.: b 10-11-1744 d p. 7-1-1806 m Elizabeth Dew Capt MD
Joseph: b a. 1755 d 1801 m Lucy — PS CS MD
Joseph, Sr.: b 1716 d 3-9-1803 m Abigail Wallis Capt MA
Joseph: b 11-1-1745 d 9-1-1809 m Rhoda Parker Ens MA
Joseph: b 11-22-1740 d 8-11-1811 m (1)Lucia Wadsworth (2)Bathsheba Torrey N2Lt MA
Joseph: b 1736 d 7-3-1796 m Abigail Butler Sgt MA
Joseph: b 4-19-1751 d 9-13-1842 m Nancy Day Cpl MA W★
Joseph: b 1720 d 1803 m Eunice Bascom Pvt MA
Joseph: b 5-24-1720 d 11-15-1799 m Experience Talbot Pvt MA
Joseph: b 5-21-1743 d 8-19-1805 m (1)Lucy Stone (2)Abigail Ingoldsby Sgt PS MA
Joseph: b 3-12-1758 d 6-27-1844 m Sally Cooley Pvt MA
Joseph: b 1-22-1740 d 1-25-1816 m (1)Hannah Harriman (2)Mary Sawyer (3)Phebe Runnels Lt NH
Joseph: b 6-30-1738 d 3-12-1802 m Naomi Johns Lt NH
Joseph: b c. 1738 d p. 12-29-1799 m Elizabeth (Smith) Pvt NH
Joseph: b 1746/7 d 7-4-1790 m Margery Rogers Pvt NH
Joseph: b 1754 d 1800 m Sarah Drew Pvt NH
Joseph: b 1754 d 10-20-1838 m Hannah Durkee Pvt NH ★
Joseph: b 9-7-1701 d 3-29-1782 m Sarah Glidden CS NH
Joseph: b 1736 d 10-13-1805 m Isabella Wason PS NH
Joseph: b 4-25-1742 d 1-21-1816 m Esther Stockbridge PS NH
Joseph: b c. 1735 d 5-9-1815 m Jennie McClure Pvt PA
Joseph: b 1737 d 1804 m Mary Fell Sol PA
Joseph: b 2-14-1761 d 7-20-1846 m Mary Donohoe Pvt PA
Joseph: b 1722 d p. 1-6-1793 m — Capt PS VA
Joseph: b 1758 d 1-4-1824 m Lindsey Spinks Pvt VA ★
Joseph: b 1763 d 7-9-1842 m Basha Humphrey Pvt VA ★
Joseph: b 1718 d p. 1-6-1793 m Kitty Anderson PS VA
Joseph: b 8-2-1762 d p. 3-26-1855 m — Pvt Spy PA ★
Joseph S.: b 1758 d 9-5-1822 m Elizabeth Price 2Lt MD
Joshua: b 1-31-1729 d 10- -1798 m Elizabeth Pomeroy Capt CT
Joshua, Jr.: b 1750 d 7-17-1790 m Elizabeth Smith Pvt CT
Joshua: b 3-2-1754 d 4-3-1836 m Olive Shailer Pvt CT
Joshua: b 9-19-1724 d 2-15-1804 m (1)Joanna Redway (2)Elizabeth (Perren) Walker Pvt MA
Joshua: b 1313 d 1814 m Hannah Smith Capt NY
Joshua: b c. 1750 d 1795 m Freelove Kibbe Pvt MA
Joshua: b 12-5-1751 d 6-3-1809 m Hepzibah Patch Pvt MA
Joshua: b 3-18-1759 d 6-10-1839 m Polly Shepard Pvt NH
Joshua: b 1732 d 5-11-1799 m Ann Tripp PS RI
Josiah: b 8-23-1750 d 11-29-1830 m Sarah Reynolds Lt CT
Josiah, Jr.: b 2-18-1744 d 9-28-1824 m Elizabeth Merrill Lt CT
Josiah: b 1750 d 3-18-1838 m Hannah Brown Pvt CT ★
Josiah: b 12-20-1747 d 1834 m Eunice Palmer Cpl CT ★
Josiah: b 12-17-1757 d 11-17-1833 m Thankful Hitchcock Pvt CT
Josiah: b 2-26-1738 d 4-4-1803 m Mary Barker Lt MA
Josiah: b 3-1-1757 d 7-20-1848 m Mercy Shaw Lt MA
Josiah, Sr.: b 7-6-1724 d 1-18-1784 m (1)Sarah Francis (2)Hannah Brown Pvt MA
Josiah: b 11-26-1753 d 11-20-1826 m Polly Barber Pvt MA
Josiah: b 1756 d 2-23-1823 m Persis — Pvt MA ★
Josiah: b 4-7-1736 d p. 1790 m Esther Pool PS MA
Josiah: b 10-31-1723 d p. 1790 m Jemima Jewett PS NH
Josiah: b 11-28-1723 d 5-15-1786 m (1)Susannah Gelston (2)Mary Howell Col NY
Josiah: b 6-7-1742 d 3- -1837 m Eleanor Taylor Pvt RI
Josiah: b 9-15-1731 d 2-12-1827 m Mary Stevens PS SC
Justin: b 6-2-1755 d 3-27-1835 m Mary Fox Sgt VA ★
Justus: b 10-11-1754 d p. 1808 m Eunice Matthews Pvt CT
Lamberton: b 11-28-1734 d 4-28-1791 m Abigail Kimberly CS CT
Larkin: b 7-10-1745 d 9-28-1813 m (1)Mary Eleanor Hill (2)Mrs Sophia A. Tazewell Taliferro Capt VA
Larkin: b 3-6-1760 d 10-20-1834 m Avey Bradley Pvt VA

SMITH, contd.

Leighton: b 1756 d 12-12-1840 m Elizabeth Roberson Pvt VA ★
Leavin: b 1759 d 10-26-1851 m (2)Charlotty Gann Pvt GA
Lemuel: b 2-14-1752 d 9-18-1841 m Sarah Hawley Sgt CT ★
Leonard: b 1734 d 3-25-1794 m Elizabeth Neale PS MD
Leonard: b 1-16-1718 d 7-16-1787 m Ruth Mobury PS NY
Levi: b 1761 d 9-11-1828 m Hannah Holland Fif Maj MA
Lewis: b 4-26-1753 d 5-21-1841 m Anna Hubbard Sgt CT ★
Lewis: b 3-2-1758 d 2-21-1812 m Lucy Have Pvt MA
Lewis: b 2-7-1763 d 3-15-1838 m Eunice Judd Pvt NY ★
Manassah: b 12-25-1748 d 5-21-1823 m Hannah Emerson Chp MA
Manuel: b 1741 d 9-30-1821 m Sarah Raymond 1Lt MA
Mark: b 10-24-1755 d 6-24-1840 m Mary Pence Pvt VA ★
Marshall: b c. 1755 d p. 7-21-1815 m Nancy Timmons Sol MD
Martin: b 1-25-1762 d 3-20-1853 m Sarah Kellogg Pvt CT
Martin: b 12-20-1756 d 9-4-1840 m Charity Rodenbaugh Fif NJ ★
Martin, 5: b 10-15-1747 d 2-27-1811 m Mary Mowry Lt RI
Mary: b 1729 d 1844 m Stephen Smith, Sr. PS SC
Mary: b 8-5-1737 d 8-17-1829 m W Robert Smith PS SC
Matthew: b 9-11-1740 d 7-1-1824 m Thankful Ackley Pvt CT
Matthew: b 11-1-1722 d 10-9-1804 m Sarah Church PS CT
Matthew: b c. 1739 d 8- -1797 m Elizabeth — 2Lt CS MD
Matthew: b 5-12-1753 d 7-13-1833 m Asenath Anable Pvt CT ★
Matthew: b 1758 d p. 1821 m Rachel Tallman Pvt NJ
Matthew: b 1740 d 7-22-1794 m Agnes — LCol CS PA
Matthew: b 2-21-1750 d 1816 m Sallie Wallace Cpl SC
Matthew: b 1-6-1758 d 1822 m Kerren Happuch Waits Pvt SC
Matthew: b 1745 d 1795 m Permelia Greene Capt VA
Matthias: b 5-22-1728 d c. 1806 m Comfort Carpenter Pvt MA
Maurice, Sr.: b 2-26-1736 d p. 1795 m (1)Mary Jackson
  (2)Obedience Babbitt Pvt NY
Melancton: b 5-7-1744 d 7-29-1798 m Margaret Mott Capt NY
Melchoir: b c. 1720 d — m Mary Margaret — Pvt PA
Melchoir: b c. 1753 d 5-6-1816 m Sybilla — Pvt PA
Meriwether: b 1730 d 1-24-1794 m (1)Mrs Alice (Lee) Clarke
  (2)Elizabeth Dangerfield PS VA
Michajah: b 1-25-1742 d 4-6-1807 m (1)Sarah Owen (2)Rebecca
  — Capt NJ
Michael: b c. 1735 d p. 1783 m Dorathea Hunt Pvt CT
Michael, Sr.: b a. 1740 d 5- -1787 m Mrs Sipps Sgt MD
Michael: b 1752 d 11-24-1842 m (1)Ragina Fruit (2)Nancy Levits
  Pvt MD
Michael: b c. 5-3-1760 d 4-24-1846 m Mary Barrett Sgt NY ★
Michael: b 5-28-1748 d 1842 m Mary Crouce Pvt NY
Michael: b c. 1740 d c. 1791 m Elizabeth — Gnr NC
Michael: b c. 1760 d c. 1828 m Sarah — Pvt PA
Michael: b 1732 d 3- -1801 m Mary — Sgt VA
Moses: b 7-12-1756 d 4-12-1822 m Lydia Browne Sgt CT
Moses: b 10-15-1756 d 6-19-1846 m Lucy Dole Pvt MA ★
Moses, Jr.: b 2-22-1748 d 3-19-1829 m Ruth Jewett Pvt MA
Moses, Sr.: b 12-10-1733 d 10-27-1781 m Sarah Catlin PS MA
Moses: b 1-22-1756 d 6-6-1837 m Ann Cullom Sol SC
Nathan: b 9-16-1702 d 12-4-1794 m Mary Denison CS CT
Nathan: b 9-24-1724 d 3-13-1810 m Elisabeth Denison PS CT
Nathan: b 3-9-1751 d 4-30-1816 m Sarah Foster Pvt GA
Nathan: b a. 1762 d p. 1783 m Sarah — Ens MD
Nathan: b 1732 d 11-15-1805 m Parnell Cathcart Capt MA
Nathan: b 2-4-1741/2 d p. 10-17-1780 m Susanna Livermore
  Lt MA
Nathan: b 1731 d 8-21-1811 m Eunice Smith Pvt MA
Nathan: b c. 1746 d 5- -1826 m Jane — Pvt MA
Nathan: b — d 5-9-1799 m (1)Joanna — (2)Phoebe Gay Pvt MA
Nathan: b 12-11-1728 d 1791/2 m Mary (Benedict) Stoddard Sol NY
Nathan: b 3-27-1763 d 5-1-1835 m Abigail Eldridge Sol VT
Nathan: b 3-30-1746 d 9- -1798 m Susan Mackintosh CS NY
Nathan: b 4-1-1757 d 3-15-1843 m Jemima — Pvt MA
Nathan, Sr.: b 1740 d 1795/6 m Hannah Whelpley Maj CS PS VT
Nathan: b 4-16-1752 d 2-13-1835 m Mrs Wait (Allen) Trask Pvt VT
Nathan: b 10-8-1754 9-27-1821 m Ann Johns Chew Lt MD
Nathaniel: b 8-8-1724 d 1- -1802 m Sarah Burphee Pvt MA
Nathaniel: b 7-9-1745 d 5-11-1835 m Mary Thompson Pvt MM MA
Nathaniel: bpt 10-15-1752 d p. 1791 m Judith Morse Pvt MA
Nathaniel: b 4-8-1758 d 5-1-1833 m (1)Mary Parsons (2)Anna
  — Pvt NH
Nathaniel: b 1-31-1765 d 10-8-1839 m (2)Catherine Porter Pvt NJ
Nathaniel: b 9-16-1729 d 1- -1783 m Margaret Smith Cpl NY
Nathaniel: b 11-6-1763 d 9-18-1843 m Lydia Talbot Pvt RI
Nathaniel: b 1-7-1747 d 3-11-1823 m Lillie Humphrey Sgt RI
Nathaniel: b a. 1757 d p. 4-14-1820 m Jenny — Sol NC
Nathaniel: b 5-5-1762 d p. 10-25-1838 m Mary Hanby Sol VA
Nathaniel: b c. 1718 d 1- -1799 m Elizabeth Temple (2)Sarah —
  PS VA
Nehemiah: b10-30-1733 d 5-4-1810 m Abagail Avery Lt CT
Nehemiah: b 12-5-1764 d 12-20-1836 m (2)Polly Steward Pvt MA
Nehemiah: b 6-25-1741 d 7-24-1827 m Lydia Warrington Pvt VT
Neil: b 1756 d 1822 m Mary Little Sol NC
Nicholas: b c. 1750 d p. 9-2-1803 m Barbara — PS MD
Nicholas: b c. 1755 d 1790 m Abigail Boughton Cpl MA
Nicholas: b 7-9-1764 d 3-16-1823 m Mary Marston Pvt NH
Nicholas: b 1723 d 1814 m (2)Elizabeth Jenness PS NH
Nicholas: b 4-26-1736 d 3-15-1778 m Elizabeth Lampman Pvt NY
Nicholas: b —d 5-10-1779 m Margaret Bellinger Pvt NY
Nicholas: b a. 1758 d p. 1786 m Julenah Feagle Pvt PA

Nicholas: b 6-15-1756 d 6-15-1839 m Mary Jones Pvt VA ★
Noah: b 3-7-1737 d p. 3-8-1794 m Eunice Hoyt Cpl CT
Noah: b 10-8-1742 d 2-22-1830 m Mary Elmer Pvt MA
Noah: b c. 1730 d 12- -1790 m Rebecca Risley Pvt NJ
Noah: b 1734 d p. 1790 m Keziah Man PS RI
Noahdiah: b 9-26-1751 d 9-23-1799 m Sarah Lee Pvt MA
Noble: b 8-22-1737 d p. 8-4-1795 m Mehitable Calender Pvt MA
Obadiah: b 3-1-1720 d 6-20-1794 m (1)Elizabeth Chichester
  (2)Sarah — PS NY
Obadiah: b c. 1749 d 1810 m Lucy Harris 1Lt VA
Oliver: b 4-27-1739 d 8-1-1811 m (1)Mary Denison (2)Mary Noyes
  Eggleston Col CT
Oliver, Jr.: b 4-24-1761 d 12-11-1807 m Elizabeth Martin Pvt CT
Oliver: b 2-8-1730 d 10-17-1797 m Margaret Bingham Pvt CT
Oliver: b 9-23-1726 d 8-22-1808 m Elizabeth Eastman Capt MA
Oliver: b 8-24-1761 d 8-1-1844 m (1)Hannah Fales (2)Sarah Gay
  Pvt MA
Oliver: b 9-26-1757 d 8-16-1843 m Eleathear Herendeen Pvt RI ★
Oliver: b 1752 d — m Betsey Rood Pvt VT
Oren: b 3-21-1749 d 5-14-1823 m Keziah Shepard Sgt MA
Othniel: b 12-7-1723 d p. 1782 m Deliverance Longbotham Ens NY
Oziel: b 1746 d 9- -1818 m Margaret Walton Lt RI
Patrick: b 12-23-1760 d 8-30-1823 m Nancy Bishop Sol MD
Patrick: b 6-17-1750 d 7-14-1816 m Ann Clark Pvt NC
Paul: b 6-21-1734 d 8-31-1798 m Elizabeth Smith PS MA
Peregrine: b 8-22-1737 d p. Zerviah Eddy Pvt RI
Perez: b 4-7-1763 d 4-13-1837 m Sally Brown Pvt MA
Peter: b 8-2-1755 d 7-15-1837 m Nancy Lintworth Pvt CT
Peter: b 10-10-1742 d c. 1832 m Lucy Willard Pvt MA ★
Peter: b 6-22-1765 d 1-21-1834 m Nelly Parmenter Pvt MA
Peter: b 2-15-1760 d 3- -1837 m Hannah Sanborn Pvt NH
Peter: b 1741 d 7-1-1814 m Eve — Pvt NJ
Peter: b 12-23-1753 d 12-31-1816 m Catherine Stout Pvt NJ
Peter: b 12-25-1742 d 1-15-1843 m Abigail Bathrick Sgt NY
Peter: b 2-3-1729 d 11-16-1820 m Sarah Winans Pvt PS NY
Peter: b 6-28-1761 d 6-28-1838 m Hannah Bess Pvt NC
Peter: b c. 1736 d p. 4-18-1793 m Jemima Simpson PS NC
Peter: b 9-27-1753 d 1831 m Huldah Fordham Lt PS PA ★
Peter: b c. 1730 d 9- -1795 m Catherine — Pvt PA
Peter: b c. 1750 d p. 1790 m Anna Maria Steininger Pvt PA
Peter: b 6-15-1736 d 11-30-1816 m Louise — Pvt VA
Peter T.: b 6-24-1760 d 11-7-1841 m Rhoda Cornish Pvt MA ★
Petrus, Jr.: b c. 1757 d p. 1790 m Maria Hotler Pvt PS NY
Peyton, Jr.: b a. 1745 d p. 6-29-1809 m Judith Wadlow CS PS VA
Philemon: b 12-8-1747 d 6-22-1808 m Rebecca Sherman Sgt CT
Philemon: b 10-1-1760 d 2-25-1834 m Hannah Reynolds Pvt NY ★
Philetus: b 10-24-1730 d 12-22-1800 m Phebe Tredwell Capt NY
Philip: b 2- -1756 d 9- -1826 m Charity Kinder Lt NY
Philip: b c. 1715 d p. 1790 m Magdalena — PS MD
Philip: b 7-2-1730 d 8-30-1806 m Elizabeth Graves Pvt MA
Phillip: bpt 5-11-1738 d 1823 m Elizabeth Hoff Capt NY
Philip: b 1-8-1755 d 6-23-1842 m Ellenor Fismire Pvt PA
Philip: b c. 1727 d 9-1-1787 m Ann — Sol Grd VT
Philip: b 1745 d 12- -1811 m Olive Crocker Pvt VT
Philip: b 6-1-1715 d 1789 m Elizabeth Bushrod PS VA
Philip: b 3-25-1729 d 3-29-1801 m Bathsheba Hartt PS NY
Philip: b c. 1745 d a. 1-14-1809 m Margaret Armel Pvt PA
Phineas: b 6-7-1759 d 11-7-1839 m Deborah Ann Judson Pvt CT ★
Phineas: b 6-5-1717 d 2-6-1787 m (2)Elizabeth Smith Capt MA
Phineas: b 5-7-1728 d p. 7-18-1786 m Ruth Doane Pvt MA
Phineas: b 1761 d 12-5-1846 m Betsy Downing Pvt CT MA ★
Phineas: b 4-12-1719 d 9-26-1805 m Eleanor Bell PS CS VT
Pliny: b 12-19-1761 d 7-5-1840 m Sarah Porter Pvt VT ★
Polycarpus: b c. 1737 d 9- -1807 m (1)Dorothy Skinner (2)Dorothy
  Otis 1Lt NY
Preserved: b 6-25-1759 d 8-15-1834 m Eunice — Pvt MA ★
Press: b 9-15-1754 d 10- -1777 m Elizabeth Miles 2Lt SC
Rainsford, Sr.: b 8-12-1722 d 6-10-1811 m Elizabeth Lambert PS
  MA
Ralph: b 3-15-1742 d 2-6-1807 m Hannah Hollister Pvt MA
Ralph: b 1-11-1758 d 11-13-1825 m Anna Treat Pvt CT ★
Ralph: b 1-11-1761 d 1-26-1838 m (1)Hannah Smith (2)Honor
  Duning (3)Mary (Brainard) Pvt CT ★
Ralph: b 10-18-1743 d 8-12-1812 m Sarah Ruggles Pvt MA
Ralph: b 8-28-1725 d 4- -1784 m Mercy Penquite CS Pvt SC
Ranson: b 4-11-1761 d 8-12-1855 m Elizabeth Moss Pvt NC ★
Redman: b 1-13-1760 d 12-3-1742 d Hannah Hamlett Pvt VA ★
Remembrance: b — d — m Bathsheba Stebbins Drm MA
Reuben: b 2-2-1757 d 8-13-1820 m Hannah (Swift) Bird PS CT
Reuben: b 1740 d 8-24-1832 m (1)Catherine Wright (2)Mrs Elizabeth
  (Lane) Partridge Alvord Capt MA
Reuben: b 4-2-1721 d 8-6-1798 m Miriam Moody Pvt MA
Reuben: b 10-21-1759 d 3-20-1842 m Miriam Goodman Pvt MA
Reuben: b c. 11-25-1758 d p. 1834 m Mary Williams Pvt Mrnr RI ★
Reuben: b c. 1750 d 9-22-1810 m Silvia Hawkins Lt SC
Reuben: b 8- -1750 d 8-29-1834 m Lois Everest Pvt VT
Reuben: b c. 1768 d 1843 m Mary — Cpl VA ★
Reuben: b 1761 d 12-2-1731 m Elizabeth Rice Smith Pvt VA ★
Richard: b 1731 d 1-20-1807 m Annie Hurd Capt CT
Richard: b 9-24-1736 d 12-19-1819 m (1)Sarah Sherman
  (2)Hannah Bostwick (3)Ruth Wheeler Barlow Capt CT
Richard: b 1746 d 2-7-1836 m Elizabeth Allen Pvt CT
Richard: b 12-6-1750 d 7-14-1838 m Lois Rogers Pvt CT

Richard: b 1750 d 1788 m Mary Peters Capt MD
Richard: b 11-9-1750 d 2-4-1809 m Mehitable Jacques Pvtr MA
Richard: b 3-22-1735 d 9-17-1803 m Elizabeth Rodman PS NJ
Richard: b 1-19-1748 d 1817 m Mary Miller Sgt NY
Richard: b 4-16-1753 d 10-17-1832 m Susanna Treby Sgt PS RI W★
Robert: b 1735 d 10-16-1800 m Rachel — Capt MA
Robert: b 11-5-1752 d 1-3-1793 m Lovina Cook Pvt MA
Robert: b a. 1748 d 11-11-1801 m Sarah Eaton PS Lt NH
Robert: b 10- -1736 d 11-2-1831 m Irene — Adj NH
Robert: b 7-10-1729 d 3-13-1816 m Abigail Case Pvt NH
Robert: b 11-17-1752 d 4-8-1838 m Rebecca Hobart Potts Capt NY
Robert: b 7-15-1754 d 1-8-1830 m Grace Braitwaite Sgt NY
Robert: b c. 1745 d p. 12-15-1829 m (2)Mary — Col NC
Robert: b 1740 d c. 1800 m Mary Gist Capt NC
Robert: b 4-1-1750 d 1-3-1838 m Elizabeth Lee Lt NC ★
Robert: b 1720 d 12- -1803 m Margaret Vaughn Capt PA
Robert: b 1740 d 1802 m Mary — Capt PA
Robert: b 1725 d 8-19-1789 m Elizabeth Buchanan 1Lt PA
Robert: b 1753 d 3-9-1813 m (2)Susan Line Pvt PA
Robert: b 9-29-1757 d 8-16-1837 m Mary Starret Pvt PA ★
Robert: b 2-20-1760 d 6-19-1853 m Ferguson Wilson Pvt SC
Robert: b 6-18-1749 d 9-30-1822 m Mary Jarrett Ens VA
Robert: b 2-7-1749 d 12-9-1834 m Hannah Andrews Pvt PS VA
Robinson: b 1761-3 d 8-27-1828 m Miriam Glidden Pvt NH ★
Roger: b 4-9-1759 d p. 4-20-1833 m Anna Bradford Buck Pvt Mar
    CT ★
Roger Moore: b 8-4-1745 d 7-30-1805 m Mary Rutledge LCol SC
Roswell: b 10-19-1753 d 11-14-1835 m (1)Sarah Nash (2)Lucy —
    Pvt VT
Rowland: b 8-27-1761 d 3-27-1840 m Nancy Clark Pvt MA ★
Rowley: b 5-5-1752 d 5-21-1823 m Elizabeth Woodword Lt VA
Rudolph: b c. 1725 d p. 3-1-1777 m Barbara — PS PA
Rudolph: b 1732 d 1810 m Jenny — Pvt PA
Samuel: b 4-9-1730 d 4-15-1811 m Abigail Higley Lt CT
Samuel: b 12-26-1744 d 2-13-1830 m Abigail Woodmancy Ens
    PS CT
Samuel: b 1762 d 5-13-1835 m Sarah Lewis Sgt CT ★
Samuel: b 12-14-1749 d 8-18-1833 m Anna Moulthrop Pvt Matr
    CT ★
Samuel: b 1746 d 11-9-1802 m Abigail Bennett Pvt CT
Samuel: b 5-20-1753 d 12-1-1829 m Sarah Buell Pvt CT
Samuel: b 9-7-1732 d 5-16-1802 m Mary Goodrich PS CT
Samuel: b 7-27-1752 d 4-22-1839 m Margaret Spear MGen MD
Samuel: b 9-4-1758 d 11-8-1834 m Sabra DeBell 2Lt MA
Samuel: b 5-28-1734 d 1-25-1842 m Anna Hartshorn Sgt MA
Samuel: b 10-22-1757 m Abigail Standley Pvt MA
Samuel: b 2-21-1729 d p. 1792 m — Pvt PS MA
Samuel, Sr.: b 1-26-1714 d 11-14-1785 m (1)Priscilla Gould
    (2)Priscilla Gould PS MA
Samuel, Jr.: b 10-28-1737 d 1792 m Rebekah Towne Pvt MA
Samuel: b 7-22-1757 d 6-6-1841 m Sally Bayley Pvt MA
Samuel: b 1705 d 12-21-1799 m (1)Sarah Morton (2)Abigail Holton
    PS MA
Samuel: b 6-28-1714 d 10-25-1778 m Mary Gove PS MA
Samuel: b 6-17-1742 d 12- -1815 m Sarah Fay Pvt MA
Samuel, Jr.: b 1728 d 10-27-1796 m Anna Wass CS MA
Samuel: b 1751 d 1830 m Deborah Dart Sgt NH
Samuel: b 3-11-1751 d 9-14-1777 m Rachel Hunt Sgt NH
Samuel, Jr.: b 2-19-1735 d 6-17-1777 m Sarah Homans Sol NH
Samuel: b 1749/50 d 1837 m Betty Gilman Pvt NH
Samuel: b 12-21-1757 d 1-10-1853 m Margaret — Pvt NY NH ★
Samuel: b 2-8-1749 d 4-20-1817 m Jane Burd QMSgt NJ
Samuel: b 1740 d 1798 m (1)Susanna Holmes (2)Sarah Lloyd
    Pvt NJ
Samuel: b 8-14-1736 d p. 4- -1786 m Hannah Stringham Capt NY
Samuel: b 6-25-1753 d 1-27-1791 m Susannah Blydenburg 1Lt
    NY NY★
Samuel: b c. 1735 d p. 1812 m Betsy Toby Lt NY
Samuel: b 8-2-1755 d p. 1802 m Margaret Litcholt Pvt NY
Samuel: b c. 1755 d 1836 m — PS NY
Samuel, Sr.: b 5-27-1709 d 9-14-1783 m Edith Whitfield PS NC
Samuel, Jr.: b 6-12-1744 d p. 1800 m Sally McCullers 1Maj NC
Samuel: b c. 1730 d p. 3-1-1797 m Christina — Sol NC
Samuel: b 1744 d 1839 m Sally Farrar Pvt NC
Samuel, Jr.: b 11-16-1758 d 5-6-1839 m Martha Nance Pvt NC ★
Samuel: b 1762 d 1-16-1837 m (1) — Dodson (2)Sallie W Williams
    Pvt NC ★
Samuel: b c. 1749 d 9-17-1836 m Ann Lacey Wilkinson Capt PA
Samuel: b c. 1749 d p. 2-12-1799 m Agnes — Pvt PA
Samuel: b 6-13-1759 d 7-8-1854 m Hope Doten Pvt RI ★
Samuel: b 5-1-1753 d 4-4-1843 m Mollie Rice Lt SC
Samuel: b 1761 d 1819 m Elizabeth Huey Pvt SC
Samuel: b 1744 d 1828 m Hannah Stevens PS SC
Samuel: b 9-3-1749 d 3-25-1820 m (1)Sarah Grant (2)Mary — Capt PS
    VT
Samuel: b 4-19-1763 d 1839 m Sally Catlett Pvt VA ★
Samuel Bryan: b 1755 d 7-27-1842 m Sarah Somers Sgt CT ★
Samuel Webb: b 12-3-1729 d 10-6-1800 m Mary Webb Col CS NC
Selah: b 1-17-1762 d 3-23-1830 m Mary Taylor Pvt MA W★
Seth: b 1-14-1753 d 3-19-1840 m Mrs Hannah (Lay) Murdock
    OrdlSgt CT ★
Seth: b 5-6-1733 d 3-16-1804 m Sarah Tyler Pvt CT
Seth: b 9-13-1734 d 9-9-1813 m Sarah Cobb 1Lt MA

Seth: b 9-25-1734 d 7-6-1829 m Rebecca Sheldon 2Lt MA
Seth: b 8-22-1743 d 11-17-1802 m Elizabeth Eldridge Lt MA
Seth: b 6-19-1736 d 5- -1786 m Drusilla Lyon Sgt Drm MA
Seth: b 8-21-1736 d 10-13-1820 m (1)Thankful Jones (2)Eunice —
    Pvt MA
Seth: b a. 1739 d 1804 m Sarah Manley LCol VT & NY
Sihon: b c. 1760 d 3-19-1832 m Sarah Page Pvt NC W★
Silas.Jr.: b 11-30-1754 d 3-23-1813 m Asenath Chapin Pvt MA
Silas: b 11-22-1758 d 1790 m Molly Stearns Sol MA
Simeon: b 11-10-1744 d 1-16-1799 m (1)Annie Byles (2)Lucy
    Waldron Capt CT
Simeon: b 11-14-1753 d 3-4-1843 m Mary Colton Sgt MA
Simeon: b 2-29-1756 d 1840 m (2)Elizabeth Hayes (3)Lois — Pvt
    MA NY ★
Simeon, Sr.: b c. 1735 d 1814 m (2)Mary Betsy Gilman Pvt PS NH
Simeon, Sr.: b 1718 d 1786 m — Of NJ
Simeon: b 1-16-1730 d 11-27-1807 m Catherine Servis Pvt NJ
Simeon: b 3-4-1746 d 3-3-1843 m Martha Peck Pvt MA ★
Simon: b 2-17-1759 d 6-20-1849 m Abigail Fowler Sgt CT ★
Simon: b c. 1758 d p. 9-19-1826 m Mary — Sgt GA
Simon: b 9-20-1741 d p. 1-7-1814 m — Pvt MA
Simon: b 1737 d 10-17-1831 m Elizabeth Sayles Lt RI
Simon: b 1748 d 1780 m Rachel Tiffany Ens RI W★
Skelton: b 1-19-1762 d 7-9-1838 m (1)Dianah (Wood) Dandridge
    (2)Jane Cosby Yancey Pvt VA W★
Solomon: b 8-21-1749 d 9-22-1830 m Rebecca Crane Pvt CT
Somon: b 1764 d 2-27-1846 m (1)Avis Stickney (2)Eunice Griswold
    Sgt MA ★
Solomon: b 11-3-1741 d 1-20-1829 m Deborah Kibbee Pvt MA
Solomon: b 12-25-1753 d 11-17-1818 m Tabitha Briggs Pvt MA
    W★
Solomon: b 1754 d 5-27-1838 m Esther Porter Pvt MA W★
Solomon: b 1704 d 6-20-1782 m Hannah Conklin PS NY
Solomon: b 1-23-1745 d 3-17-1807 m Hannah Lane Pvt NY
Sparrow: b 8-14-1760 d 7-14-1842 m Eunice Clark Pvt CT ★
Steele: b 9-20-1729 d 4-5-1812 m (1)Lois Spooner (2)Elizabeth
    Andrews Curtis Capt VT
Stephen: b 11-23-1724 d 1-22-1816 m (1)Jemima Parmalee
    (2)Sarah Dawson Capt CT
Stephen: b 1747 d 1817 m Sarah Loomis Pvt CT
Stephen: b 4-18-1749 d 4-16-1834 m Esther Church Pvt CT ★
Stephen, 2: b 1756 d 2-2-1827 m Theoda Medelle Pvt CT
Stephen: b 5-30-1739 d 9-29-1806 m Deborah Ellis Maj NS MA
Stephen: b 1750 d 5-30-1836 m Mercy Andros Pvt MA ★
Stephen: b 12-6-1754 d 1-8-1830 m Achsah Foster Pvt MA ★
Stephen: b 6-26-1749 d 1794 m Dorcas Way Sgt NH
Stephen: b 1760 d 10- -1801 m Martha Ladd Pvt NH
Stephen: b 9-15-1756 d 11-11-1845 m Elizabeth Martin Pvt NY ★
Stephen: b 2-27-1752 d 7-25-1803 m Abigail Goldsmith PS NY
Stephen: b 1746 d p. 7-2-1784 m Joanna Council Sol NC
Stephen: b c. 1750 d 1802 m Mary Troup Pvt PA
Stephen: b 4-22-1741 d 11-4-1799 m (1)Mrs Mary Gorham (2)Ruth
    — Capt RI
Stephen: b c. 1725 d a. 8-21-1802 m (1)Sarah Coman (2)Ruth —
    PS RI
Stephen: b 1758 d 1822 m Mary Eve Hamiter Pvt SC
Stephen: b c. 1740 d 10-17-1788 m Martha Newman CS SC
Stephen: b 1745 d 7- -1829 m Martha Whelpley Lt VT
Stephen: b 1755 d 9-11-1835 m Anna Munson Pvt VT
Sylvanus: b a. 1749 d p. 1782 m (2)Mary Shipman Capt CT
Sylvanus: b 1740 d 1830 m Agnes Moore Maj MA
Temple: b 4-26-1745 d 2-3-1818 m Lydia Lane PS VA
Thaddeus: b 5-6-1742 d 4-12-1839 m Anne Hise Pvt NJ ★
Thaddeus: b 9-25-1753 d 7-5-1825 m Silence Jones Pvt MA
Theophilus: b 5-15-1741 d 2-26-1805 m Sarah Gilman PS CS NH
Theophilus Miles: b 11-9-1757 d 9-8-1849 m Abigail Grace Nettleton
    Sgt CT ★
Thomas, Jr.: b 1-21-1738 d 9-17-1821 m Mary Green Cpl CT
Thomas: b 5-16-1754 d 12-1-1844 m Thankful Bennett Pvt CT ★
Thomas: b a. 1743 d 1785 m Pheoby — Pvt GA
Thomas, Sr.: b 4-3-1729 d 3-19-1819 m (1)Sarah Gresham
    (2)Margaret Hands PS MD
Thomas, Jr.: b 4-30-1757 d 1-3-1819 m (1)Mary Sudler (2)Anna
    Maria Garnett Maj MD W★
Thomas: b — d 1803 m Elizabeth Reynolds Pvt MD
Thomas: b 1740 d 1800 m — Barbour Matr MD
Thomas: b 1721 d p. 4-11-1791 m Hannah — PS MD
Thomas, Sr: b 1722 d 1809 m Rebekah Moulton Sgt MA
Thomas, Jr.: b 3- -1750 d 4-17-1837 m Lydia Wheeler Pvt MA
Thomas: b 1724 d 8-1-1805 m Mary Chase Pvt MA
Thomas: b 1- -1742 d 1-21-1784 m Mrs Elizabeth (Merrifield)
    Goldsmith Pvt MA
Thomas: b 6-26-1744 d 4-21-1833 m Hannah (Shurtleff) Bunker
    Pvt MA
Thomas: b 1751 d 6-1-1827 m Lucretia Featherton Pvt MA ★
Thomas: b 7-24-1760 d 8-11-1807 m Sarah Taylor Pvt MA
Thomas: b 5-10-1702 d 5-23-1795 m (1)Sarah Tyng (2)Olive
    Plaisted (3)Elizabeth Wendell PS ME
Thomas: b 10-11-1751 d 11-21-1834 m Lettie Hamilton Pvt NJ ★
Thomas: b 1717 d c. 1783 m Sarah Cresse Capt NJ
Thomas: b — d 10-13-1791 m Mary — PS NY
Thomas: b c. 1754 d 1798 m Rebecca (Smith) Sgt NC
Thomas: b c. 1740 d p. 1790 m Rachel — Pvt NC

SMITH, contd.
Thomas: b 1745 d 1809 m (2)Jerucia Jane Post Col PA
Thomas: b 6-13-1728 d 10-20-1813 m Mary Ross Pvt PA
Thomas: b *c.* 1750 d *a.* 1821 m Sarah Campbell Pvt PA
Thomas: b 1756/7 d 1844 m Mary Williams Pvt Spy PA ★
Thomas: b 6-3-1757 d 11-21-1821 m Edith Smith Lt SC
Thomas: b 1744-9 d *p.* 12-17-1787 m Elizabeth Cunningham Capt VA
Thomas: b 6-13-1747 d 10-13-1796 m Elizabeth Adams Lt VA
Thomas: b *c.* 1760 d *p.* 5-6-1831 m Molly Fugua Cpl VA ★
Thomas: b 10-12-1751 d 1822 m Nancy Lennard DrmMaj VA
Thomas: b 1733 d 6-20-1797 m Mary Jackman Pvt VA
Thomas: b *c.* 1750 d 2-27-1829 m Cuzzy Bundrant Pvt VA ★
Thomas: b 1739 d 11-29-1801 m Elizabeth Keith Pvt VA
Thomas: b 1757 d *p.* 1832 m Nancy Tupeway Pvt VA
Thomas: b 1739 d 1790 m Mary Smith PS VA
Thomas: b *c.* 1750 d *p.* 1798 m Ann Smith Sol VA
Thomas Gibson: b 1756 d 4-10-1837 m Jemima Allen Lt NY
Timothy: b 7-3-1725 d 7-1-1803 m (1)Esther Dewing (2)Abigail Bacon Lt MA
Timothy, Sr.: b 1-24-1728 d 6-25-1818 m Hannah Hall Pvt MA
Timothy: b 8-28-1752 d 10-11-1818 m Mehitable Newell Pvt MA
Timothy, Jr.: b 1-10-1759 d 1835 m Prudence Pratt Pvt MA
Timothy: b 1752 d 4-27-1809 m Fanny Little PS NY
Timothy: b 1747 d 4-3-1822 m Sarah Willetts Tms NJ
Titus: b 11-25-1759 d 9-1-1805 m Atarah Hamant Pvt Fif MA ★
Titus: b 1722 d 12-10-1799 m Mehitable Trowbridge Capt CT
Titus: b 1753/4 d 12-3-1813 m Zipporah Hubbard Sgt MA
Tunis: b 1-4-1727 d 9-27-1810 m Tobidah Ham Pvt NY
Uriah: b 8-11-1745 d 3-4-1829 m (1)Lydia Keyes (2)Susanna (Cram) Bridges Sol NH
Uriel: b 9-1-1743 d 5-20-1818 m Alice Fuller Pvt MA
Walter: b 1744 d 8-29-1796 m Esther Belt Dr PS MD
Walter: b 12-15-1733 d 10-14-1820 m Hannah Baldwin Wgn NJ
Warham: b 3-19-1735 d 10-30-1802 m Martha — Pvt PS MA
Weathers: b 1741 d 12-7-1813 m Jane Lane Lt VA
Weedon: b *c.* 1750 d *a.* 1823 m Sarah Reed Pvt VA
Wells: b 1-8-1762 d *p.* 1799 m Elizabeth Shaler Pvt CT
Willard: b 12-23-1746 d 5- -1820 m Mary Stafford Pvt CT
Willard: b 10-30-1761 d 10-18-1835 m Jerusha Cook Pvt MA
Wm.: b 1746 d 5-20-1824 m Esther Brainerd Lt CT
Wm.: b 1754 d 7- -1825 m Elizabeth Campbell Pvt DE ★
Wm.: b 3-16-1765 d 7-16-1841 m (1)Mary T. Platt (2)Neter Stephens Pvt GA
Wm.: b 1757 d 1-27-1829 m Margaret Williams Pvt MD
Wm.: b 1712 d 11- -1782 m Mary Elizabeth — PS MD
Wm.: b 1728 d 1814 m Elizabeth Buchanan PS MD
Wm.: b *c.* 1737 d 1815 m Agnes — PS MD
Wm.: b 2-18-1752 d 1818 m Lydia Houston Capt MA
Wm.: b 6-16-1743 d 2-21-1834 m (1)Catherine B Williams (2)Elizabeth Allen Sgt MA
Wm.: b 1756 d 1838 m Mary Eliza Boutler Sgt MA
Wm.: b 10-25-1754 d *p.* 1804 m Hannah Albee Cpl MA
Wm.: b 1-16-1736 d 1811 m Abigail — Pvt MA
Wm.: b 1741 d 1831 m Thankful Phillips Pvt MA
Wm.: b 1-30-1742 d 1-21-1832 m Rebecca Parmenter Pvt PS MA
Wm.: b 6-2-1746 d 5-30-1797 m Prudence Shaw Pvt MA
Wm.: b 1-17-1751 d 9-22-1831 m Thankful Butler Pvt MA W★
Wm.: b 11-7-1747 d 7-2-1816 m Annie True Lt NH
Wm.: b 1750 d *p.* 1799 m Peggy Allison Pvt NH
Wm.: b 1723 d 1-31-1808 m Elizabeth Morrison PS NH
Wm.: b 12-10-1742 d 4-28-1820 m (1)Sarah Stretch (2)Hannah Stretch Capt NJ
Wm.: b 3-10-1754 d 9-7-1832 m Martha Scull Capt NJ
Wm.: b 1740 d 3-24-1806 m Abigail — Pvt NJ
Wm.: b 12-3-1755 d 2-15-1790 m Alice Stewart Sgt NY
Wm.: b 5-2-1760 d 5-22-1752 m Ursula — Pvt NY ★
Wm.: b 10-21-1760 d 4-4-1843 m (1)Magdalena Auchmoody (2)Catherine Woodlsey Pvt PS NY ★
Wm.: b 9-9-1760 d 3-26-1837 m Catherine Denton Pvt NY ★
Wm.: b 6-28-1720 d 3-17-1799 m (1)Mary Smith (2)Ruth Woodhull PS NY
Wm.: b 2-17-1762 d 1840 m Miss Cox Capt NC ★
Wm.: b 12-1-1753 d 6-17-1833 m Susan — Pvt NC ★
Wm.: b *c.* 1755 d 3- -1845 m Elizabeth Bailey Sol NC
Wm.: b — d 1793 m Sarah Harry Capt PA
Wm.: b 5-23-1732 d 02-4-1806 m Dinah Edwards Lt PS PA
Wm.: b *c.* 1736-8 d 7- -1778 m Margery Kellogg Pvt CT
Wm.: b 1745 d 1822 m (2)Eliza — Pvt PA
Wm.: b 12-3-1760 d 3-4-1836 m Catherine Robinson Pvt PA ★
Wm.: b 9-7-1727 d 5-14-1803 m Rebecca Moore PS PA
Wm.: b 1752 d 1807 m Hannah Carr Pvt RI W★
Wm.: b 9-20-1751 d 6-22-1837 m Mourning Bearden Maj SC
Wm.: b *c.* 1750 d 1817 m Katy — Lt SC
Wm.: b 10-19-1764 d 1-30-1843 m Elizabeth Wilson Pvt SC
Wm.: b 11-15-1752 d 12-26-1800 m Elizabeth Mayo LCol VA
Wm.: b 10-28-1742 d 11-11-1816 m (1)Joice Humphrey (2)Mary Elanor Halley Capt VA
Wm.: b *c.* 1730 d 1796 m Sarah Harrison Capt VA
Wm.: b *c.* 1741 d *p.* 9-17-1818 m Mary Rodes Lt PS VA
Wm.: b 11-18-1720 d 1-15-1790 m Mary Smith Lt VA
Wm.: b 1755 d 1823 m Ann Ashby Lt VA
Wm.: b 2-5-1741 d 1-22-1803 m Elizabeth Doniphan Ens VA
Wm.: b 1752 d 1845 m Elizabeth Parker Ferguson PM VA

Wm.: b 1759 d *a.* 1-2-1830 m Mary Smith Sgt VA
Wm.: b 5-5-1756 d 4-15-1834 m Elizabeth Via Pvt VA ★
Wm.: b 1746 d 1824 m (1)Anne Ashley (2)Mary Richards Sol VA
Wm.: b 1-6-1731/2 d *p.* 1806 m Ann Williams PS VA
Wm.: b *c.* 1730 d *p.* 11-29-1815 m Hannah Jackson PS VA
Wm.: b 12-14-1755 d *p.* 3-20-1833 m (1)Catherine Bibb (2)Anne Bibb PS VA
Wm. Hooker: b 3-25-1725 d 7-17-1815 m (1)Sarah Brown (2)Mrs Margery Smith Capt Dr PA
Wm. Peartree: b 1723 d 11-20-1801 m Mary Bryant PS NJ
Wm. Stephens: b 11-8-1755 d 6-10-1816 m Abigail Adams ADC LCol NY
Wm. Sterling: b 12-20-1758 d 3-18-1829 m Judith — Sol VA
Wyatt: b 1740 d 1800 m Elizabeth Sanford Sol VA
Zachariah: b 9-30-1716 d 1793 m Lydia Hastings Pvt MA
Zachariah: b 5-29-1759 d 1829 m (1)Mary (Smith) (2)Elizabeth Davis Pvt MA
Zachariah: b *c.* 1742 d 1815/6 m (1)Anna Elizabeth Fishback (2)Sarah Anne — Pvt VA

SMITHERS, (includes SMITHER & SMOTHERS)
Gabriel: b 9-29-1717 d *p.* 12-30-1784 m Wilmoth Sydnor PS VA
Jacob: b 1749 d 1826 m (1)Rosannah Klinetub (2)Rebecca Aborn Hoff Pvt PA
Nathaniel: b 1753 d 11-2-1820 m (1)Isabell Patton (2)Esther Beauchamp PS DE
Wm.: b 1762 d *p.* 1825 m (1)Cecelia Fitzpatrick (2)Mary Winters Pvt VA

SMITHPETERS,
John Michael: b 1753 d 4-5-1836 m (1)Mary Kyle Fletcher (2)Christina Miller Pvt VA NC ★

SMITHSON,
Daniel: b 1723 d 2-22-1798 m (2)Susannah Taylor CS MD
John: b *c.* 1739 d *a.* 1783 m Ann Walker Pvt VA

SMOCK,
Barnes: b 10-5-1738 d 1829 m (1)Sarah Williamson (2)Nellie Covenhoven Capt PS NJ
Barnes: bpt 3-27-1743 d *p.* 1812 m Antje Cosyn PS PA
George: b 11-24-1754 d 12-7-1834 m (1)Sarah Conover (2) Margaret Van Deventer (3)Anna Lane Pvt NJ
Hendrick: b 10-25-1749 d 3-25-1814 m Sarah Lane Capt NJ
Henry: b — d 4-24-1814 m Margaret Brunt Pvt VA W★
Jacob: b 5-20-1744 d *p.* 1792 m Catherine Demaree Sgt VA
John: b 2-13-1727 d 2-26-1808 m Elizabeth Conover Col NJ

SMOKE,
Andrew: b 1753 d 8-15-1834 m (1)Catherine Stroman (2)Harriet Gilbert Pvt SC

SMOOT,
Edward, Sr.: b 1724 d *p.* 10-2-1794 m (1)Ann Chandler (2)Mary Magdalene Stoddert PS MD
Hendley: b *c.* 1748 d 1811 m Eleanor Wilson Briscoe Ens MD
Henry: b 1761 d 2-24-1820 m Elizabeth Douglass Lt MD
John: b 1748 d 1-15-1793 m (1)Elizabeth Douglass (2)Elizabeth Parker Capt PS CS MD
John: b 12-25-1755 d 7-15-1842 m Elizabeth Jenifer (2)Lucy Buckner Thornton Pvt MD
John: b 1707 d *p.* 10-26-1789 m (2)Mrs Sarah Crane PS MD
John: b 5-11-1755 d 5-23-1845 m Elizabeth Grant Pvt VA ★
John Nathan: b 1744 d 1812-5 m (1)Anna Hanson (2)Mary Briscoe PS MD
Samuel: b *c.* 1720 d *p.* 10-8-1792 m Elizabeth Davis PS MD
Thomas: b 12- -1742 d 1783 m Elizabeth — Pvt MD
Thomas: b 1697 d 1782 m Abigail — PS MD
Wm.: b *c.* 1750 d *p.* 5-13-1815 m — Jenifer Pvt MD
Wm.: b 8- -1751 d 11-1-1821 m Susan Hayden Pvt PS MD
Wm. Barton: b 1750 d 1794 m Rachel Smoot Capt MD
Wm. Barton: b — d *p.* 10-6-1816 m Margaret Dodson Cpl MD

SMULLER,
John: b *c.* 1756 d 5-20-1783 m Margaret Dellinger Capt PA

SNAPP,
George: b 2- -1752 d 1843 m Margaret — Pvt VA ★
John: b 1-10-1748 d 11-2-1798 m Christiana Fry Pvt PA
John: b — d *p.* 10-9-1818 m Mary — Ens VA
Lawrence: b *c.* 1725 d 1782 m Margaret — PS VA
Philip: b *c.* 1748 d 1812 m (1)Catherine — (2)Sallie — Sol VA

SNAVELEY, (includes SNAVELY, SNEVELY & SNIVELY)
Andrew: b 1-4-1751 d 2-25-1813 m (1)Susannah Funk (2)Mary Magdalena Shenk Pvt PA
Christian: b 9-13-1731 d 3-16-1795 m Margaret Washbaugh Pvt PA
George: b *c.* 1750 d *p.* 8-31-1813 m — Pvt PA
Henry: b 1739 d 12-7-1802 m Barbara Whitmore Cpl PA
Henry: b 1758 d 1825-35 m — Flickener Pvt PA
Isaac, Sr.: b *c.* 1720 d *p.* 1798 m — PS PA
Isaac, Jr.: b 6-18-1753 d 9-12-1801 m Anna (Snevely) Pvt PA
John: b 1-1-1763 d 10-11-1842 m Elizabeth Long Pvt PA

John Ulrich: b 1730 d 5-20-1816 m Eve Brandt Pvt PA
Joseph: b 1748 d 10-30-1833 m Magdalena Stoner Pvt PA

SNEAD, (includes SNEED)
Benjamin: b c. 1740 d a. 1800 m Mary — Lt VA
Israel: b 1730 d p. 7-3-1788 m Johanna Hendley Pvt NC
John: b 2-2-1755 d 12-21-1855 m Sarah Sneed Sgt VA ★
John: b 1759 d 1822 m Sarah Weaver Pvt VA
John: b 6-27-1739 d 9-6-1793 m Mary Gooch Pvt VA
Philip: b 12-11-1754 d 2-25-1834 m Ann Stone Sgt VA ★
Robert: b 5-23-1762 d 1-19-1841 m Sophia Harris Pvt VA
Samuel: b 1711 d p. 1790 m Ruth Dudley Capt NC
Stephen: b c. 1756 d 1821 m Mary Williams PS VA NC

SNEDEKER, (includes SNEDICOR & SNEDIKER)
Garrett: b 4- -1751 d 1840 m Euphemia McWright Pvt NJ ★
Isaac: b c. 1740 d 1809 m — Pvt NJ
Isaac: b 1750 d p. 1818 m Eleanor Story Pvt VA
Johannes: b 1721 d 9-28-1779 m Affie Martyne PS NY
John: bpt 10-27-1737 d — m Sarah Willemson Pvt NJ
Samuel: b 1751 d 5-16-1820 m Hannah Harrison Pvt NY

SNEEDEN,
John: b 1740 d p. 1778 m Rebecca Archer 2Lt NY

SNELGROVE,
Henry: b c. 1747 d c. 1800 m Sarah Duke PS SC
Sarah: b 3-15-1753 d p. 1800 m Henry Snelgrove PS SC

SNELL, (includes SCHNELL)
Adam: b 1742 d 1820 m Lucy Epsy Sgt SC
Charles: b 2-4-1753 d 8-15-1813 m (1)Mary Kingman (2)Rebecca
    Packard Pvt MA
Daniel: b 7-19-1733 d p. 1790 m (1)Abigail Packard (2)Mary — Pvt
    RI
Ebenezer: b 10-1-1738 d 8-2-1813 m Sarah Packard Pvt MA
Elijah: b 1734 d 12-24-1815 m (1)Susanna Howard (2)Ann (Perkins)
    Reynolds (3)Polly Linds Lt MA
Elisha: b 1740 d 1820 m Deborah Dunton Pvt MA
Frederick: b — d 8-6-1777 m — Sol NY
Issachar: b 5-25-1732 d 6-30-1820 m Sarah Hayward Ens MA
Jacob: b 12-15-1761 d 8-28-1838 m (1)Maria Markell (2)Elisabeth
    Dockstaeder Sgt NY ★
Jacob: b 8-11-1744 d 9-29-1790 m Anna Margaret Oziah Mus PA
Jacob: b 12-31-1743 d 8-6-1777 m Margaretha (Snell) Pvt NY
Job: b 4-17-1763 d 7-17-1821 m Abigail Winslow Pvt MA W★
John: b 1744 d 3-10-1824 m (1)Elizabeth Dengler (2)Maria
    Gottschall Pvt PA
John: b a. 1760 d 1833 m Ann — Pvt PA
John: b c. 1740 d p. 4-19-1820 m Elizabeth Watts Pvt VA
John, Sr.: b — d p. 5-20-1785 m Philadelphia — PS VA
Joseph: b 6-3-1755 d 10-30-1755 m Lydia Franham Pvt CT
Joseph: b 6-5-1750 d p. 1802 m Mrs Hannah Cook Cpl MA
Joseph: b 1743 d 8-6-1777 m Catherine Groot Pvt NY
Lewis: b c. 1760 d 2-19-1820 m Mary Kirtley Sgt VA W★
Moses: b 7-9-1741 d p. 1790 m Hannah Washburn Sgt MA
Nicholas: b 4- -1750 d 3- -1811 m Elisabeth Zimmerman Sgt NY
Peter: b 6-24-1730 d 7-24-1804 m Anna Kiltz Pvt NY
Robert: b 1-12-1765 d 3-29-1857 m Joanna King Pvt MA ★
Samuel: bpt 4-14-1754 d 8-11-1837 m Mary Bondley Pvt Drm MA
Thomas: b c. 1745 d p. 1790 m Abigail Frost PS NH
Wm., Sr.: b 12-25-1737 d p. 1790 m Sarah Barney Sol CL
Wm., Jr.: b 8-29-1762 d 12-14-1827 m Polly Chaffee Pvt CT
Zebedee: b 12-9-1736 d p. 1789 m (1)Martha Howard (2)Mary
    Hayward Capt MA

SNELLING, (includes SNELLINGS)
George: b 1760 d p. 10-4-1818 m Rebecca Hudson Pvt VA
John Wm.: b c. 1760 d a. 5-1-1815 m Hannah Nelson Sol GA
Joseph: b 12-6-1741 d 2-6-1741 d 2-6-1816 m Rachel Mayer
    PS MA

SNIDOW,
Christian: b 3-15-1760 d 9-17-1836 m Mary Burke Lt VA ★
Jacob: b 11-15-1763 d p. 7-5-1847 m (1)Clara Burke (2)Sara
    Pickelsimmer (3)Mary Ann Hankey Pvt VA

SNIFFIN,
James: b 6-10-1720 d 1-7-1797 m Hannah Purdy Cpl NY

SNIPERS,
Wm.: b c. 1740 d 1787 m Sarah — Pvt NC
Wm. Clay: b 1742 d 2-16-1806 m Miss Sanders Maj SC

SNOODY,
John: b 2-23-1758 d 3-22-1848 m (1)Nancy Niblick (2)Mary Nancy
    McNeil Pvt NC ★
John: b 1-11-1746 d 2-2-1815 m Ealse Johnston Pvt PA
John: b 1730 d 11-11-1808 m Jane Cowen Pvt SC
John: b 1740 d 12-12-1814 m Margaret Walker Capt VA
John: b 1720 d 1784 m Agnes Glasgow CS VA

SNODGRASS,
David: b — d p. 1-6-1814 d Margaret — PS VA
James: b 10-31-1762 d 7-3-1828 m Ann Long Lt VA
James: b 1734 d 3-5-1809 m Anna Wilson Pvt PA
James: b 1743 d 1796 m Catherine — Pvt PA
James: b 8-2-1732 d 8-12-1800 m Jane Greenlea Pvt VA
Joseph: b 9-26-1741 d 8-15-1809 m Mary Bartley Ens VA
Joseph: b c. 1730 d 1782 m Hannah — PS VA
Robert: b 9-11-1758 d 9-30-1834 m Jane Reed Pvt PA ★
Robert: b 10-14-1742 d 8-7-1823 m Susanna Rawlings PS VA
Thomas: b 3-28-1748 d 2-29-1808 m Mary Woods Pvt PA
Wm.: b 5-10-1760 d 9-18-1849 m Mary Elder Pvt VA ★
Wm.: b 1758 d 1814 m Eleanor Beggs Pvt PA

SNOKE,
Christian: b 8-18-1740 d 2- -1786 m Catharine — Pvt PA

SNOOK,
Coonrad: b 4-11-1757 d 5-6-1813 m Elnora Scutt Pvt NY
George: b c. 1742 d p. 10-15-1803 m Anna — Lt NJ
Martinus: b c. 1754 d p. 1805 m — Pvt NY
Peter: b 9-25-1758 d 9-4-1837 m Katherine Heavender Cpl NJ ★
Peter: b c. 1750 d p. 1799 m Keturah Laish Pvt PA
Phillip: b c. 1745 d 11-12-1816 m Margaret Heivener Capt PS NJ
Wm.: b c. 1752 d 9-11-1837 m Catherine Spangenberg Capt NJ
Wm.: b 1730 d a. 2-6-1815 m Catherine Cline Capt NY

SNOVER,
Frederick: b 9-11-1743 d 1-14-1830 m (1)Anna Margaret —
    (2)Margaret — (3)Susan King PS CS NJ

SNOW, (includes SCHNEE)
Aaron: b 11-10-1759 d 1-10-1832 m Abigail Smith Pvt MA
Abijah: b 12-15-1754 d 1-26-1819 m (1)Sarah Porter (2)Rebecca
    Whiting (3)Keziah Thomas Pvt MA
Abner: b 7-31-1759 d 9-27-1833 m Hannah Watson Pvt MA
Amaziah: b 4-21-1764 d 4-5-1823 m Sally Watson Pvt CT
Benjamin: b 12-15-1754 d 6-17-1817 m Elizabeth Payson Ens MA
Daniel, Jr.: b 4-2-1756 d 1812 m Dorothy Flint MM MA
David: b 7-17-1732 d 5-25-1793 m (1)Sarah Hatch (2)Hannah
    Collins Lt MA
David: b 3-22-1739 d 1808 m Mary Cole Pvt MA
Ebenezer: b c. 1750 d 1-21-1832 m Anna Crowell PS CT
Ebenezer: b 1-5-1734/5 d p. 1791 m (2)Elizabeth Chase (3)Sarah
    — Pvt MA
Edward: b 1741 d — Sarah Turning PS MA
Eleazer, Sr.: b 10-30-1734 d 2-1-1797 m Mary Wood Lt MA
Eleazer, Jr.: b 4-5-1759 d 11-5-1843 m Hannah Dunbar Pvt MA ★
Eliab: b 1759 d p. 1793 m (1)Lydia Snow (2)Dorcas Churchill Pvt MA
Elisha: b 3-26-1739 d 1-30-1832 m Betsey Jordon Pvt MA
Elnathan: b 5-2-1734 d 1806 m Phoebe Sparrow Pvt MA
Ephraim: b 5-3-1754 d 12-27-1833 m Martha Godfrey Rogers Pvt
    MA
Harding: b 12- -1755 d 10-15-1846 m Betsy Cobb Pvt NS MA
    RI ★
Isaac: b 10-8-1758 d 3-12-1855 m Hannah Freeman Pvt Smn CT ★
Isaac: b 2-4-1719/20 d 8-19-1812 m Thankful King Pvt MA
Isaac: b 3-21-1714 d 1799 m Appiah Atwood CS PS MA
Jacob: b 3-10-1750/1 d — m Betty Marble Pvt MA
James: b 8-1-1763 d 2-24-1810 m Elsie Green Pvt MA
James: b 3-7-1732 d 6-28-1783 m Persis Grey Pvt MA
James: b 9-21-1756 d 8-19-1839 m (1)Ruth Hall (2)Anna Powers
    Sgt NH
James: b 12-30-1730 d 10-8-1812 m Hannah Searle Capt RI
Jeremiah: b 4-20-1735 d 2-24-1803 m Mary Brewer NS MA
Jesse: b 2-19-1731 d 6-28-1825 m Mary Eaton Pvt MA
Johannes: b 5-18-1758 d 11-25-1826 m Anna Marie Renninger
    PS PA
John: b 1733 d 7-6-1808 m Hepzibah Hall Pvt CT
John: b 7-25-1734 d a. 1790 m Hannah Larrabee Capt MA
John: b 3-18-1760 d 1-28-1841 m (1)Hannah Parker (2)Caroline
    Perry Pvt MA
John: b 1705 d 5-12-1777 m Abigail — PS NH
Jonathan: b 12- -1755 d 3-27-1810 m Hannah Burgess Pvt MA
Joseph: b 10-2-1740 d p. 1777 m Hannah Bailey Pvt MA
Joseph: b 9-27-1740 d 4-19-1793 m Priscilla Berry PS MA
Joseph: b 3-26-1741 d 9-7-1808 m Johannah Jewett Cpl NH
Joshua: b 9-27-1729 d p. 1790 m Ruth Bolles Pvt MA
Joshua: b 1760 d 1839 m (1)Molly Roberts (2)Sarah Harpswell Sgt
    NH ★
Josiah: b 1732 d 4-5-1807 m (1)Azubah Dickinson (2)Lucy Judd
    Sgt MA
Lemuel: b 12-7-1758 d 9-3-1824 m Lydia Hodges Pvt MA ★
Levi: b 11-5-1760 d 12-18-1840 m Lydia Rudd Pvt CT ★
Mark: b 8-6-1731 d 9-2-1799 m (1)Hannah Sears (2)Mrs Susannah
    Whelden Pvt MA
Michajah, Jr.: b 12- -1716 d 6-10-1798 m Elizabeth Freeman CS MA
Moses: b 4-22-1755 d 8-16-1818 m (1)Thankful Thwing (2)Eunice
    (Shaw) Branch Brown Pvt MA
Nathan: b 7-9-1725 d 8-2-1803 m Mary Mansfield Capt MA
Nathan: b 12-10-1759 d 10-18-1835 m Thankful Pettibone Cpl
    MA ★
Nathaniel: b 12-8-1736 d 12-23-1831 m Rebecca Doane Pvt MA

SNOW, contd.
Nathaniel: b 4-19-1743 d 1820 m (1)Thankful Hopkins (2)Mercy Webber Pvt MA
Nehemiah: b 4-16-1759 d 4-5-1840 m Miriam Herriman Pvt NH
Nicholus: b 6-6-1745 d 3-17-1790 m Hannah Dexter Pvt MA
Oliver: b 3-14-1748 d 8-5-1841 m (1)Rebecca Wadsworth (2)Roxcylana Taylor Pvt MA
Prince: b 6-1-1746 d 4-23-1828 m Content Doty Pvt MA
Reuben: b 5-20-1748 d 12-17-1795 m Reliance King 1Lt MA
Reuben: b 1740 d 4-5-1814 m Mercy Sears Pvt MA
Robert: b 12-19-1732 d 1810 m Sarah Chub Pvt CT
Robert: b — d 8-18-1806 m Anna Peck Pvt CT ★
Samuel: b 7-28-1745 d 7-21-1791 m (1)Sarah Dean (2)Abigail Jordon Lt MA
Samuel: b 6-6-1733 d p. 1790 m Mary White Pvt MA
Samuel: b 5-21-1752 d 9-28-1822 m Elizabeth Perkins Pvt MA
Samuel: b 8-10-1758 d 5-13-1838 m Frances Wanton Capt RI
Seth: b 7-15-1744 d 11-25-1815 m Ruth Holden Cpl MA
Seth: b 4-28-1755 d c. 1854 m Mary Snow Gnr Matr MA
Silas: b a. 1760 d 1793 m Elizabeth Paxton Lt DE
Silas: b 4-15-1732 d 9-16-1806 m Anna Farwell 2Lt MA
Solomon: b 2-21-1755 d 1-26-1848 m Lavinia Guild Sgt MA ★
Sparrow: b 4-12-1748 d 8-21-1815 m Lucretia — Pvt MA
Sylvanus: b 3-17-1731/2 d 1-19-1828 m Rebecca Crary Pvt CT
Sylvanus: b c. 1760 d 1824 m Sybil Buckland Pvt CT
Sylvanus: b 3-8-1742 d 9-17-1806 m Jerusha Henckley Pvt MA
Thomas: b 1734 d 1825 m Jane Mague Pvt MA
Thomas: b — d 9-20-1830 m Rachel Bennett Pvt VA
Timothy: b 9-8-1762 d 4-9-1830 m Hannah Briggs Pvt MA
Warren: b 2-12-1734 d 1824 m Anne Harvey PS NH
Wm.: b 1750 d 7-23-1715 m Mary Johnson Pvt CT
Wm.: b 1738 d 1828 m Lydia Wixon Sgt NY
Zerubbabel: b 1741 d 4-12-1795 m Mary Trowbridge Capt NH

SNOWDEN,
Ann: b a. 1747 d p. 1776 m Wm. Snowden PS PA
David: b 1759 d 6-2-1739 m Nancy Hazelrigg Pvt Spy PA ★
Isaac: b 4-14-1732 d 12-26-1809 m (1)Mary Parker (2)Mrs Mary (Cox) McCall QM PA
Samuel: b 11-2-1728 d 6-27-1801 m Elizabeth Thomas PS MD
Thomas: b 1751 d 1803 m Ann Ridgely Maj PS MD
Wm.: b 6-19-1741 d — m Anna Maugridge Seacap PA

SNOWMAN,
John: b 8-6-1755 d 7-16-1829 m Comfort Horn Pvt MA

SNUFF, (includes SCHNORF)
Jacob: b c. 1755 d 1827 m Mary — Pvt PA

SNUFFER,
George: b c. 1750 d p. 1798 m (1) — Wirts (2)Amy Margrave CS VA

SNYDER, (includes SCHNEDER, SHEYDER & SNIDER)
Abraham: b 8-9-1750 d 5-11-1830 m Mary Fraeligh Sgt PS NY W★
Abraham: b 1754 d 6- -1828 m Mary Ann — Pvt PA
Adam: b c. 1728 d 1795 m Doortje Herzeele PS NJ
Adam: b c. 1730 d p. 1-5-1787 m Catherine Klom Pvt PS NY
Adam: b 12-31-1747 d 2-6-1826 m Catharine Putman Pvt PA
Adam: b 1750 d 1830 m (2)Margaret Hartzel Schaeffer Pvt PA ★
Adam: b c. 1760/1 d p. 1809 m Christina Fetter Pvt PA
Andrew: b 8-17-1732 d 11-4-1845 m Barbara Metzgar Pvt PA ★
Andrew: b 1- -1739 d 10-26-1815 m Margaret Jacobi PS PA
Anthony, Sr.: b c. 1724 d 1803 m (1)Ann Mary Dui (2)Elizabeth Reffert (3)Mrs Judith Hartzog Pvt PA
Baltzer, Sr.: b 2-16-1738 d a. 4-15-1800 m (1)Sophia Vogel (2)Barbara — (3)Eve — Pvt PA
Benjamin: b 11-24-1742 d p. 1790 m Anna Brink Pvt PS NY
Benjamin: b 12-21-1748 d 10-26-1816 m Esther Herbein Pvt PA
Casper: b 5-2-1745 d 9-3-1821 m Elizabeth Farst Lt PA
Christian: b 4-22-1743 d 3-15-1810 m Susanna Horlacher PS Sol PA
Christopher: b 10-14-1747 d 3-30-1797 m Sarah Luyster Pvt NJ
Christopher: b 2-24-1756 d 7-3-1842 m Deborah Lowe Sgt NY ★
Christopher: b c. 1758 d 1811 m (1)Rachel Davis (2)Hanna Zimmerman (3)Elizabeth — 1Lt PA
Conrad: b c. 1737 d 4-28-1802 m Catharine Stautz Capt PA
Conrad: b 1762 d p. 1840 m Catherine Gehr Drm PA
Cornelius: b 4-21-1762 d 8-31-1822 m Mary Felter Pvt NY
Daniel: b 1717 d 1-25-1799 m Anna Margrit Nees Pvt NY
Daniel, Sr.: b 5-1-1731 d 8-3-1778 m Dorothea Burkhalter Capt PA
Daniel, Jr.: b 1757 d 4- -1814 m Catherine Bechler Pvt PA
Daniel: b 8-27-1749 d 5-21-1804 m Barbara Schenkel CMman PA
Dewald: b 11- 2-1755 d 12-7-1828 m Anna Clara Feathers Pvt PA
Elizabeth Catherine Mann: b 12-1-1722 d 10-17-1790 m Peter Snyder PS NY
Frederick: b c. 1740 d c. 1789 m Maria Steer Sol PS MD
George: b 3-19-1754 d 2-20-1841 m Christiana — Pvt MD ★
George: b a. 1751 d 1- -1810 m Maria Elizabeth Rehrer Pvt PA
Hendrick: b — d 6-3-1782 m Barbara — Pvt NJ
Hendrick: bpt 11-13-1759 d 11-4-1806 m Maria Terwilliger Pvt NY
Hendrick: b 1710 d 1802 m Marget Eckert Pvt NY
Henry: b 1736 d 1820 m Sarah Lake Pvt NJ
Henry: b 11-5-1760 d 2-12-1841 m Charlotte King Pvt NJ
Henry: b 1760 d 1845 m Mary Smelker 2Sgt PA

Henry: b c. 1735 d p. 1-7-1812 m Elizabeth — Pvt PA
Henry: b 7-15-1753/6 d 4-17-1828 m Elizabeth Baker Pvt PA ★
Henry W.: b c. 1758/9 d 1837 m Elizabeth Foenck Pvt NY
Herman: b 1-27-1756 d 3-31-1833 m Gertjen Dekker Pvt NY
Jacob: b 1731 d p. 7-30-1804 m (1)Elizabeth Fisher (2)Esther Corwin Pvt NJ
Jacob: b 1745 d 1786 m (1)Elizabeth Mann (2)Sarah (Vrooman) Schuyler Capt NY
Jacob: b c. 1753 d p. 1790 m Elizabeth Abel Sol NY
Jacob: b a. 1755 d p. 1791 m Rebecca — Lt PA
Jacob: b 1755 d 1835 m Maria Elisabeth — Cpl PA
Jacob: b 1727-30 d p. 1782 m Maria Hershey Pvt PA
Jacob: b 3-8-1735 d 7-10-1829 m Anna Maria — Pvt PA
Jacob: b 1737 d p. 6-15-1790 m Margaret Studebaker Lt VA
Jeremiah: b 8-8-1738 d 6-10-1828 m Catherine Holley Capt NY
Johann Conrad: b 7-17-1759 d 7-16-1787 m Elizabeth — Cpl PA
Johann Jacob: b 10-26-1752 d 10-27-1840 m Magdalena Gerhart Pvt PA ★
Johannis: b 1-4-1720 d 8-22-1794 m Rachel Swart LCol NY
John: b 1757 d 12-24-1730 m Mary — Pvt MD
John: b 1750 d 8-11-1811 m Elizabeth Armstrong Pvt MD
John: b c. 1753 d 11-15-1825 m Margaretha Countryman Cpl NY W★
John: b c. 1740 d 1818 m Bathena Horton Pvt NY
John: b 1753 d 10-14-1835 m Lois Cash Pvt NY
John: b 10-18-1757 d 7-31-1850 m Mary Bachman Pvt PA
John: b 7-15-1766 d 8-30-1828 m Catherine Maria Rimon Pvt PA
John: b 3-25-1745 d 11-22-1814 m (1)Margaret Hilman (2)Christena — Pvt PA
John: b 1755 d 1787 m Mary — ADJ PA
John: b 4- -1743 d 5-13-1830 m Dorcas Evans Pvt PS VA
John Ludwig: b 8-5-1746 d 3-23-1860 m Anna Maria Gilman Pvt PA
John Peter: b 1-18-1729 d 6-18-1807 m Mary Catharine Elizabeth Stautz Cpl PA
Joseph: b — d a. 2- -1783 m Margaret — Lt NJ
Leonard: b 1739 d 3-16-1800 m Catharine — Pvt PA
Lodewyck: b 8-12-1756 d 6-3-1841 m Hannah Sommers Sgt NY ★
Ludwig: b 10-4-1740 d 10-16-1810 m Sarah Hagadome Pvt NY
Martin: b 1728 d 11-7-1810 m Catherine Amon Pvt PA
Martinus: b 2-22-1748 d 2-2-1831 m Trineke Newkirk Pvt NY
Michael: b 1755 d 1-27-1815 m Martha Stigler Pvt VA
Nicholas: b c. 1757 d 1830 m (1)Hannah Hice (2)Elizabeth Hartzog Pvt PA
Nicholas: b 9-10-1749 d 10-28-1821 m Anna Maria Bordner Pvt PA
Nicholas: b 1-19-1732 d 3-20-1786 m Maria Catherine Fischer Pvt PA
Peter: b 12-26-1752 d 7-23-1832 m Mary Shaver Pvt NJ
Peter: b 3-25-1743 d 5-29-1803 m Anna Maria Catarina Sternberg Capt NY
Peter: b 10-14-1721 d 5-29-1803 m Elizabeth Catherine Mann Capt NY
Phillip: b 4-27-1757 d 10-20-1793 m Jane Rasor Ens PA
Phillip: b c. 1730 d 1779 m Maria Elizabeth Knecht PS PA
Samuel: b c. 1746 d 10-17-1822 m Regina Carnright Pvt NY
Samuel: b 11-22-1753 d 5-15-1816 m Catharine Schmidt Pvt PA
Simon, Sr.: b — d a. 12-27-1784 m — Lt PA
Simon, Jr.: b 1747 d 1794 m Catherine — Cpl PA
Wm.: b 5-7-1720 d 9-9-1806 m Anna M. Kline Pvt NY
Wm.: b 1751 d 4-19-1801 m Anna Warner Pvt NY
Wm.: b 1757 d 1799 m Mary — Pvt PA

SOBER,
George: b 1755 d 10-17-1849 m Anna Margaret Erdman Pvt PA
Jacob: b 8-30-1764 d 11-23-1848 m Mary Catherine Hahn Pvt PA
John: b c. 1729 d a. 8-2-1790 m Barbara — Pvt PA

SOCKMAN, (includes SACKMAN)
John: b 2-2-1754 d 12-12-1827 m (1)Catherine Franckenberger (2)Catherine Eichner Pvt PA ★

SODAN,
Jonathan: b c. 1740 d c. 1790 m Mrs Gorman Matr NJ

SODER,
John: b 1740 d 3-27-1817 m (2)Eva Margaret Aldstar Capt PA

SODOWSKY,
Jacob: b 1750 d 1832 m (1)Jemima Voss (2)Elizabeth Evans Pvt KY
James: b 1748 d p. 1-18-1819 m Mary Ball Brown Pvt VA

SOEY,
Joseph: b — d p. 1800 m Ann — (2)Dorothy Leeds Pvt NJ

SOLLERS,
James: b c. 1735-40 d 1800-10 m (2)Anne Dare PS MD
Thomas: b c. 1730 d 1-3-1783 m Arianna Dorsey Maj PS CS MD
Thomas: b 5-17-1759 d 6-30-1835 m Elizabeth — Sol MD

SOLLEY, (includes SOLEY)
Thomas: b 8-14-1759 d 6-1-1829 m Eunice Duffee Pvt CT W★

SOLOMON, (includes SALOMON)
Hyman: b c. 1740 d 1-6-1785 m Rachel Frank PS NY PA
Lazarus: b 1765 d 4-20-1833 m Elizabeth Bedgood Pvt NC
Wm.: b c. 1751 d p. 4-16-1814 m Diana — Pvt NC

SOLSBEE,
Daniel: b 4-15-1755 d 3-4-1841 m Racheal Burcham Pvt PA

SOLT,
John: b 1722 d 1-8-1803 m Maria Catherine — PS PA
Paul: b 3-17-1758 d 1-21-1749 m Eva Schaffer Ens PA ★

SOMERBY,
Daniel: b 5-28-1728 d p. 1790 m Mary Bartlett Pvt MA
Henry: b 9-5-1738 d 4-5-1804 m Mrs Joanna (Cheney) Allen Sgt MA
Moses: b 1-13-1760 d 10-20-1844 m Bethiah White Pvt MA ★

SOMERSET,
Thomas: b 6-15-1754 d 11-6-1834 m Mary Shulenberger Pvt VA

SOMERVILLE, (includes SOMERVELL & SOMMERVILLE)
Alexander: b 1734 d 3-22-1783 m Rebecca Dawkins LCol MD
David, Jr.: b 1749 d 9- -1794 m Martha Irvine Ens PA
James: b 4-19-1758 d 5-4-1815 m Anna Trueman Capt MD
Wm.: b 3-4-1756 d 3-18-1826 m Margaret Brown Capt PA

SOMES,
Abraham: b 3-17-1732 d 9-7-1819 m Hannah Herrick 1Lt MA
Isaac: b 9-24-1741 d 1782 m Hannah Davis Cdr MA
Samuel: bpt 4-27-1728 d p. 1790 m Elizabeth Conklin PS NY

SONES,
Peter: b 11-23-1755 d 11-3-1850 m — Pvt PA ★

SONNER,
Philip: b c. 1736 d c. 1814 m Tena Windle Sol PS VA

SOOY,
Joseph: b 2-27-1738 d 1801/2 m Mary Leak Pvt NJ
Nicholas: b 5-4-1747 d 12-22-1822 m Sarah Sears Pvt NJ
Samuel: b 1745 d 4-28-1825 m (1)Christiana Doughty (2)Sophia Ireland OrdlSgt NJ ★

SOPER,
Alexander: b 1723 d 4-6-1801 m Mary Cox Pvt MA
Amassa: b c. 1740 d 1809/10 m — Capt MA
Brutis: b 12-29-1753 d 10-19-1827 m Rebecca Soper Sol NY
Edmund, Sr.: b 12-26-1731 d 9-27-1776 m (1)Bethiah Fobes (2)Eunice Curtis Maj PS MA
Edmund, Jr.: b 1-24-1759 d 4-14-1811 m Rebecca Miller Thayer Lt MA
Joseph, Sr.: b 1721 d p. 1797 m (1)Mary Wright (2)Sarah — Pvt NJ
Justus: b 8-3-1760 d 3-30-1851 m Elizabeth Viles Pvt MA
Mordecai: b 12-31-1746 d 8-6-1824 m Naomi Owens Pvt VT
Oliver: b 3-17-1740 d 8-8-1821 m Ruth Staples Capt MA
Timothy: b 8-12-1742 d p. 1793 m Rhoda Lee Sgt CT
Timothy: b 1745 d 8-2-1845 m Sarah Adsit Sgt NY
Zadock: b 2-15-1749 d 1796 m Ann — Pvt PS MD

SORBER, (includes SORVER)
Christ: b c. 1759 d 1815 m — Pvt PA
Henry: b 10-13-1756 d a. 10-15-1814 m (1)Susanna Ceimm (2)Catharine Schmidt Pvt PA
John: bpt 1-27-1758 d p. 1795 m Margaretta — Drm PA

SORINE,
Charles: b c. 1756 d c. 1843 m Polly Smith Pvt NY

SORNBORGER,
George: b 6-15-1759 d 9-27-1841 m (1)Margaret Manson (2)Catherine Woolcott Pvt NY

SORRELL, (includes SORREL)
Elisha: b 1754 d 1825 m Elizabeth — Pvt VA
John: b c. 1710 d 1783 m (1)Mary — (2)Mary Coleman PS VA
Samuel: b c. 1753 d 1811 m Nancy Newberry Sol NC

SORSBY,
Benjamin: b 1750 d 9-13-1811 m Susan Davis Pvt NC
Samuel: b c. 1745 d p. 1790 m Elizabeth — PS NC

SORTER, (or SORTORE)
Henry: b 7-5-1758 d 12-14-1823 m Charity Stout Pvt NJ

SOUDER, (includes SOWDER)
Christian: b c. 1750 d 1822 m Mary Oberholtzer Pvt PA
Jacob: b 1749 d 12-24-1804 m Sarah Felton Cpl PA
Jacob: b 1734 d 1819 m — Pvt VA
John: b 1726 d 10-10-1787 m Anna Bowman Pvt PA

SOULE,
Abner: b 3-27-1748 d 12-17-1814 m Dorcas Seabury Pvt RI
Amasa: b 11-2-1761 d 8-30-1853 m Susanna Holbrook Pvt MA
Asa: bpt 5-1-1753 d p. 9-2-1830 m Olive Southworth Sol MA
Asa: b 1765 d 7-17-1838 m Ruth Stetson Pvt MA
Asaph: b 9-20-1739 d 6-13-1823 m Mary Hudson Pvt MA
Benjamin: b 2-1-1730/31 d 3-30-1816 m Mehitable Bonney Pvt MA
Benjamin: b 8-12-1728 d p. 1777 m Abigail Howland PS NY

Beza: b 2-26-1750 d p. 1778 m Zerviah Cushing Pvt MA
Charles W.: b 3-21-1762 d 7-3-1831 m (1)Dorothy Clark (2)Chloe — Ens MA ★
Constant: b 1744 d 7-10-1790 m Jemimia — Pvt MA
Daniel: b 11-16-1757 d 1-16-1840 m Sarah Cushman Pvt MA ★
Dorcas: b 1-9-1748 d 2-6-1824 m Abner Soule PS RI
Ebenezer: b 1710 d 1792 m Susannah Comers Cpl MA
Ebenezer: b 5-14-1750 d 7-9-1812 m (1)Mercy Foote (2)Mrs Mary Lord Pvt NY
Ephraim: b 5-4-1729 d 1-24-1817 m Rebekah Whitemarsh Sgt MA
Gideon: b 1-26-1739 d 9-15-1792 m (1)Marcy Sylvester (2)Ruth Harden Cpl MA
Jacob: b 2-5-1736 d 8-19-1823 m Mary Thomas Pvt MA
Jacob: b c. 1733 d 6-5-1822 m Meribah Lewis Ens RI
James: b 4-4-1754 d 5-3-1846 m Martha Custis Sol MA
James: b 5-25-1761 d 11-8-1821 m Patience Macomber Pvt MA
James: b 7-23-1761 d 2-2-1845 m Eunice Thompson Sol RI
John: bpt 3-12-1740 d p. 1814 m Elizabeth Mitchell Lt MA
John: b 12-23-1748 d 1-29-1815 m Joanna Perkins Lt MA
Jonathan: b 1756 d 10-18-1841 m Mary Soule Pvt MA ★
Jonathan: b 1758 d 1-6-1832 m Honor Southworth Pvt MA W★
Joshua: b 11-14-1743 d 5-8-1808 m Mary Cushman PS CS MA
Micah: b 4-12-1711 d 11-4-1778 m Mercy Southworth PS CS MA
Moses: bpt 4-2-1738 d a. 4-4-1796 m Eleanor Williams Capt MA
Moses: b 2-19-1738 d p. 1790 m Nancy Hewes Pvt MA
Nathan: b 7-12-1725 d a. 5-23-1783 m Sarah Southworth Capt MA
Wm.: b 9-16-1739 d 12-6-1777 m Sarah Briggs Sol MA
Wm., Sr.: b 12-25-1759 d 1-7-1826 m Priscilla Sampson Pvt MA

SOUSLEY,
Henry: b 3-5-1728 d 1792 m Susan Cooper Pvt PA

SOUTH,
Benjamin: b c. 1747 d a. 10-20-1809 m Elizabeth — PS MD
Benjamin: b 1758 d 5-2-1839 m Elizabeth Slack Pvt NJ
Elijah: b 5-20-1753 d 1836 m Rachel Hartupoe Pvt NJ
John: b c. 1730 d 1819 m Margaret Weldon Drake Lt VA
Samuel: b c. 1768 d 1833 m Patsy Glover Pvt VA

SOUTHACK,
Cryprian: b 1743 d 11-19-1805 m Ann Gibbs Cpl MA

SOUTHALL,
Furney: b 5-23-1763 d 9-3-1850 m Mary Ann Wagginor Sgt NC
Henry: b 1740 d 5-16-1791 m Elizabeth Holman Lt VA
James: b c. 1751 d 1801 m Elizabeth — PS VA
Stephen: b — d — m Martha Wood Lt VA
Turner: b 7-25-1736 d 4-27-1791 m Martha Vanderwall Col PS VA

SOUTHARD,
Abraham: b 8-5-1758 d 3-20-1855 m Elizabeth Hull Pvt NJ
Benjamin: b 1740 d 3-26-1813 m Hannah — Ens NJ
Constant: b 8-20-1764 d 11-19-1826 m (1)— Pettengill (2)Lucy Ford Pvt MA
Henry: b 10- -1747 d 6-2-1842 m Sarah Lewis Wgn NJ ★
Henry: b 1752 d 9-24-1842 m Ruth Gosline Pvt NY ★
Richard: b 6-11-1707 d 7-10-1797 m Jane Smith Pvt NY
Thomas: b 1-22-1741 d 6-4-1794 m Martha Lane Pvt NY
Zebulon: b c. 1735 d p. 3-11-1788 m Jannetje Van Voorhis Capt NY

SOUTHER,
Daniel: b 2-11-1758 d 7-23-1809 m Grace Sprague Pvt MA
John: b 2-13-1755 d 8-19-1807 m Deborah Leavitt Pvt MA
Joseph: b 12-31-1745 d 4-3-1827 m Esther Town Worriell Pvt MA
Samuel: b 11-29-1730 d 11-15-1814 m Mary Goodwin Pvt MA

SOUTHERN, (includes SOTHORON)
Gipson, Jr.: b 12-25-1748 d 4-3-1833 m Mary — Pvt GA
Richard, Sr.: b c. 1740 d 1782 m Elizabeth Letchworth Sol MD
Richard, Jr.: b 1763 d 1794 m Catherine Tubman Sol MD

SOUTHGATE,
Isaac: b 1744 d 10-13-1800 m (1)Rebecca Brown (2)Eunice White Pvt MA
Richard, Sr.: b 7-11-1714 d 1798 m Eunice Brown PS MA
Richard, Jr.: b 2-20-1742 d 2-25-1822 m Sarah Sprague Pvt MA
Stewart: b 9-10-1748 d p. 1800 m Deborah Raymond Sgt MA

SOUTHMAYD,
Daniel: b 11-11-1738 d 2-5-1827 m Hannah Tryon SrgnMte CT
Wm.: b 6-27-1740 d 7-31-1778 m Irena Todd Sgt CT
Wm.: b 6-14-1735 d 8-23-1811 m Elizabeth Green Sol CT

SOUTHWELL,
Phineas: b 1731 d 7-5-1809 m Mary (Stiles) Birch Pvt MA

SOUTHWICK,
David: b 1756 d 1841 m (1)Betsy Stacy (2)Mrs Mary Stacy Pvt MA ★
George, Jr.: b 1750 d 4-19-1775 m Hepsibeth Bussell MM MA
Jacob: b 4-5-1751 d 8-19-1833 m Sarah Fowler Pvt MA
Jonathan: b 7-10-1738 d p. 1790 m Judith Mussey Pvt MA
Joseph: b 1738 d 3-23-1813 m Hannah Hunt CS MA
Solomon: b 1731 d 12-23-1797 m Mrs Ann (Gardner) Carpenter PS RI
Wm.: b c. 1742 d p. 1793 m Elizabeth Allen Pvt NJ

SOUTHWORTH, (includes SOUTHWARD & SUTHARD)
Abiah: b 3-6-1760 d 12-27-1835 m Keziah Boltwood Pvt MA
Alden: b 8-6-1758 d 9-15-1794 m Lydia Taylor Sgt RI
Asa: b 8-28-1756 d — m (1)Hannah Allen (2)Phebe Ketchum Sgt CT
Constant: b 4-15-1730 d 11-19-1813 m Mary Porter PS CS CT
Edward: b 1747 d 2-8-1833 m Mercy Thomas Sgt QM MA
Ephraim: b 7-27-1760 d 1828 m Rebecca Simmons Pvt MA
George: b 1731 d 1815 m Anne Phelps Pvtr MA
Gideon: b 5-16-1750 d 1-13-1827 m Mary Haskell Pvt MA
Isaac: b 1-25-1759 d 5-4-1846 m Martha Boland Pvt Drm CT VT ★
Jedediah: b 1-6-1745 d 1810 m (1)Mary Atherton (2)Eunice Mills Capt MA
Job: b 10-24-1763 d p. 1803 rn Ruth Shipman Pvt CT
John: b 10-22-1733 d 5-17-1814 m Joanna Mitchell Lt MA
John: b 1-4-1743 d 11-30-1832 m Elizabeth Whitman Pvt NY
Joseph: b 3-12-1760 d 4-15-1828 m Lydia Barrows Pvt CT
Lemuel: b 6-11-1758 d 2-4-1841 m Elizabeth Stoddard Pvt CT
Lemuel: b 4-27-1728 d p. 1790 m Patience West Sol MA
Nathan: b 12-1-1735 d 8-16-1811 m Hannah Wheeler Pvt CT
Perez: b 4-11-1754 d — m Eunice Kingman Sol PS RI
Samuel: b 1-25-1756 d 9-23-1812 m (2)Marabah — Sgt CT
Samuel Wells: b 6-4-1757 d 8-17-1837 m Marcey Allen Pvt CT ★
Stephen: bpt 5-18-1755 d 1815 m Rebecca Jenney Ens MA
Thomas: b 4-1-1722 d 1-12-1805 m Anna Hatch Pvt MA
Uriah: b 12-2-1752 d 3-13-1814 m Patience Goodspeed Sgt MA
Wilbur: b 1735 d 1807 m Lois (Winslow) Roper Pvt MA
Wm.: b 10-18-1741 d 1815 m Susanna Antice Pvt CT
Wm.: b 1758 d 2- -1849 m Charlotte Bicknell Pvt CT ★
Wm.: b 7-27-1753 d 10-30-1808 m Mary Throope Maj RI

SOWASH, (or SAUVAGE)
Henry: b c. 1731 d 1799 m Anna Esther Schneider Pvt PA

SOWELL,
John: b 1762 d 10-8-1825 m Elizabeth — PS NC

SOWERS, (or SOURS)
Daniel: b c. 1750 d a. 7-28-1821 m Cathrine — PS VA
George: b a. 1765 d 2-22-1836 m Elizabeth — Pvt PA
John: b 3-10-1760 d 8-22-1834 m Agnes Owens Pvt NC ★
John, Jr.: b 3-4-1757 d 7-23-1820 m Mary Ann Kramer Sol PA
Michael: b 10-9-1762 d 10-16-1853 m Dorothea Cox Pvt MD ★
Paul: b — d p. 8-20-1832 m Magdalena Throne PS PA

SOYARS,
James: b c. 1760 d 10-20-1838 m (1)Francis Rogers (2)Jane Oaks Cpl VA ★

SPACE,
John: b 1757 d 9-16-1813 m Abigail Mott Pvt NJ

SPACH,
Adam, Sr.: b 1-20-1720 d 8-23-1801 m Maria Elisabeth Huter PS Wgn NC
Adam, Jr.: b 10-3-1753 d 6-19-1816 m Catherine Tesch PS NC

SPADER,
Bergen: b 12-5-1762 d 5-17-1847 m Elizabeth Rynearson Pvt NJ ★

SPAHR,
Matthias: b 1740-50 d 1785 m Mary — PS VA

SPAIGHT,
Richard Dobbs: b 1760 d 9-5-1802 m Mary Leach ADC NC

SPALDING, (includes SPAULDING)
Aaron: b 1752 d 3- -1843 m (1)Nellie Mattingly (2)Mary Moore Pvt MD ★
Aaron: b 7-12-1762 d 3-7-1820 m Phebe Bryant 2Lt MA
Abel: b 5-12-1755 d 5-29-1849 m Lucy Wetherell Pvt MA
Abel, Sr.: b 7-10-1728 d 1808 m Mary Anderson Capt NH
Abel, Jr.: b 9-30-1756 d p. 1800 m Elizabeth Chase Pvt NH
Abel: b 12-28-1764 d 6-16-1844 m Hannah Chase Pvt VT ★
Amasa: b 12-11-1753 d 3-22-1836 m Mary Roberts Pvt NY
Andrew: b 1-6-1729 d p. 1790 m Abigail Martin Pvt MA
Asa: b 10-6-1751 d 2-21-1811 m Lucy York Dr CT
Asa: b 10-5-1754 d c. 1832 m Mary Ross Pvt MA
Azel: b 11-30-1754 d p. 1793 m Alice Cole Pvt VT
Barzillia: b 1757 d 4-21-1838 m Elizabeth Spalding Pvt Drm MA
Basil, Sr.: b c. 1718/9 d 9-26-1791 m Catherine — PS MD
Benedict: b 1748 d 1813 m Alethia Abell Pvt MD
Benjamin: b 8-14-1743 d 5-27-1832 m Mary Heald Sgt MA
Benjamin: b 1-6-1741 d 8-6-1806 m Mary Spaulding Pvt MA
Benjamin: b 6-6-1757 d 2-28-1843 m Hannah Haskins Pvt MA ★
Benjamin: b 2-5-1738/9 d 10-14-1811 m Patty Barrett Pvt MA
Benjamin: b 3-15-1738 d 1810 m (1)Sarah Chandler (2)Betty (Whitcomb) Flood Capt NH
Benjamin: b 3-24-1762 d 5-11-1838 m Azubah Gates Pvt NH ★
Benjamin: b 2-29-1720 d 3-19-1807 m Rachel Crary Pvt VT
Bennett: b 1750 d 1820 m — Pvt MD
Benoni: b 12-18-1760 d 9-25-1839 m Lydia Duren Pvt MA
Champion: b 9-23-1753 d 9-7-1846 m Ruth Stevens Pvt CT

Charles: b 12-12-1735 d 3-15-1807 m Abgail Gates Pvt NH
Daniel: b 7-21-1758 d 1818 m Esther Austin Sol CT
Daniel: b 8-13-1754 d — m Rebekah Osgood Pvt MA
Daniel: b 11-5-1737 d 4-17-1808 m Phebe Dustin Pvt NH
Daniel: b 4-15-1758 d 1839 m (1)Mary Broadwater (2)Sinai Tapman Mrnr VA ★
David: b 12-23-1728 d 8-23-1803 m Elizabeth Barrett Pvt CT
Davis: b 6-16-1740 d 3-16-1817 m Sarah Denison CS CT
Dywer: b 11-14-1732 d 4-27-1814 m Elizabeth Parkhurst QM NH
Ebenezer, Sr.: b 6-24-1717 d 6-19-1794 m Mary Fassett PS CT
Ebenezer, Jr.: b 7-13-1751 d 1-2-1838 m Molly Payne PS CT
Ebenezer: b 3-27-1750 d 7-1-1808 m Amy Roundy Pvt NH W★
Edward: b 1765 d — m Mehitable Goodrich Mil NH ★
Edward: b 6-13-1761 d 2-25-1813 m Abigail Salisbury Pvt NY
Eleazer: b 11-12-1728 d 11-1-1812 m Elizabeth Procter 1Lt MA
Eleazer, Sr.: b 5-26-1733 d 6- -1813 m Mary Shepley Lt MA
Eleazer, Jr.: b 1-21-1759 d 4-19-1850 m Sarah (Spaulding) Pvt MA ★
Elijah: b a. 1750 d p. 1793 m Deborah Scribner Sgt NY
Ephraim: b 5-24-1747 d 1811 m (1)Esther Snow (2)Hannah Stowell Pvt CT
Ezekiel: b 3-18-1734 d 1809 m Jane Mather Sgt MA ★
Ezekiel: b 9-30-1731 d — m Sarah Morgan Pvt MA
Ezra: b 11-5-1754 d 1-1-1828 m Hannah Eaton Pvt CT
Ezra: b 1752 d 1840 m Lydia Fitch Pvt NH ★
Henry: b 1747 d 1816 m Ann Elder Pvt MD
Henry, Jr.: b 11-22-1704 d 4-29-1792 m (1)Lucy Proctor (2)Marah Adams Pvt Cnt VT
Henry: b 7-8-1744 d 2-12-1808 m Ruby Bishop Pvt VT
Isaac: b 7-30-1757 d — m Mercy Knapp Sol CT
Isaac: b 10-1-1735 d p. 1782 m Susanna Lawrence Pvt MA
Jacob: b 11-14-1729 d 9- -1805 m (1)Martha Gerould (2)Thankful Burgess Pvt CT
Jacob: b 12-17-1732 d 4-30-1814 m Rachel Knapp PS CT
Jacob: b 5-6-1764 d 8-29-1823 m (1)Sarah North (2)— Gildersleeve Pvt VT
James: b 10-9-1746 d c. 1831/2 m Hannah Neff Pvt CT
James, Sr.: b 10-27-1714 d c. 1790 m (1)Anna Underwood (2)Eunice Fassett Pvt MA
James, Jr.: b 8-31-1748 d 6-8-1832 m (1)Hannah Barron (2)Mrs Abigail Wilkins Pvt MA
Jeptha: b 11-10-1754 d 1-10-1834 m Rebecca Barron Pvt MA
Jeremiah: b 5-14-1761 d 5-2-1847 m (1)Elizabeth Dwelle (2)Mrs Eunice Howard Sgt MA
Jesse: b 12-30-1748 d 5-28-1813 m (1)Mary Sentor (2)Hannah Clark Cpl MA
Job: b 5-1-1737 d 10-1-1806 m Abigail Pierce Sgt MA
Joel: b 3-12-1742 d 7-26-1823 m Phebe Tyler Sol MA
John: b 11-14-1765 d 2-19-1828 m Wealthy Ann Gore Fif CT ★
John: b 7-20-1742 d 6-18-1801 m Sarah Newell PS CT
John: b 9-15-1747 d 9-30-1832 m Mary Marsall Pvt MA
Jonathan: b 9-15-1747 d 9-30-1832 m Mary Marsall Pvt MA
Jonathan: b 3-4-1747 d 5-20-1798 m Abagail Hoar Pvt MA
Joseph, Jr.: b 6-7-1745 d 8-31-1832 m (1)Eunice Shepard (2)Mrs Ann Snell Ens CT
Joseph: b 9-30-1744 d 2-25-1840 m (1)Huldah Hubbard (2)Thankful Mehurin Adj VT ★
Joseph: b 4-26-1739 d 6-17-1775 m Phebe (Spalding) Lt MA
Joseph: b 5-1-1737 d 8-14-1796 m Bridget Crosby Pvt MA
Joseph: b 11-2-1760 d 5-2-1852 m Mary Collins Pvt NH ★
Josiah: b 2-7-1729 d 12-18-1809 m Priscilla Paine Lt CT
Leonard: b 10-28-1728 d 7-17-1788 m Margaret Love Capt VT
Levi: b 10-23-1737 d 3-1-1825 m (1)Anna Burns (2)Lois Goodrich Capt NH
Nathaniel: b 9-19-1742 d 2- -1823 m Abilene Grover Sgt CT
Nathaniel: b 7-15-1752 d 7-16-1838 m Thankful Whipple Pvt RI
Nehemiah: b c. 1757 d 8-19-1830 m Bettsey Tubbs Sgt NY
Noah Billings: b 1-10-1751 d — m Eliza Ripley Dr PA
Oliver: b 9-30-1739 d — m (1)Mary Witter (2)Rebeckah Bottom Pvt CT
Philip: b 11-22-1755 d 1-29-1847 m (1)Thankful Waterman (2)Mrs Dorcas Baker Sgt CT ★
Philip: b 2-26-1726 d 3-22-1810 m (1)Parnel Champion (2)Deborah Woodward PS CT
Philip: bpt 3-21-1736 d p. 1779 m Elizabeth Obert Pvt MA
Phineas: b 6-4-1759 d 11-5-1838 m (1)Rebecca Jaquith (2)Susannah Hotchkiss Sgt MA
Phineas: b 2-19-1760 d 1-8-1842 m (1)Elizabeth Bryant (2)Sarah Rice Pvt MA ★
Phineas: b 5-8-1745 d 1-14-1809 m Elizabeth Bailey Pvt NH
Phineas: b 1-23-1721 d 2-28-1784 m Sarah Summers PS VT
Reuben: b 12-15-1759 d 9-15-1849 m (1)Jerusha Carpenter (2)Polly Parkhurst Sgt VT ★
Reuben: b 7-26-1728 d 2-12-1809 m Sarah Chandler PS NH
Robert: b 1-28-1729 d 1776 m Hasadiah Johnson Lt MA
Sampson: b 4-18-1754 d 9-19-1807 m Temperance Nott Sgt CT
Sampson: b 11-19-1745 d 1- -1832 m Experience Merrill Sgt MA
Samuel: b 3-26-1749 d p. 1786 m Joanna Kee Sgt CT
Samuel: b 3-3-1737 d 3-16-1819 m Leafe Duren Pvt MA
Samuel: b 7-30-1764 d 5-2-1854 m Sarah Brooks Pvt MA ★
Samuel, Sr.: b 1-31-1727 d 9-11-1797 m Sarah Woods Lt NH
Samuel, Jr.: b 3-22-1754 d 3-1-1825 m Sarah Heald Pvt NH
Silas: b 10-30-1746 d 3-7-1827 m Sybil Pierce Sgt MA

Silas: b 3-25-1757 d 2-29-1812 m Hannah Brown Pvt MA
Simeon: b 8-4-1713 d 4-7-1785 m (1)Sarah Fletcher (2)Mrs Abigail
    (Johnston) Wilson Col PS MA
Simon: b 1-16-1742 d 1-24-1814 m Ruth Shepard Capt CT
Solomon: b 9-28-1748 d 8-2-1826 m Jemima Reed Sgt MA
Stephen: b 7-23-1748 d p. 1787 m Dinah Brown Pvt CT
Stephen: b 5-28-1717 d 3-30-1796 m Martha Foster Pvt PS NH
Stephen Greeley: b 10-28-1764 d 10-19-1853 m (1)Phebe
,   Lawrence (2)Lucy Parker Pvt NH ★
Thomas: b 10-7-1743 d 11-12-1802 m Lydia Shipley Lt MA
Timothy: b 11-15-1741 d p. 1777 m Lucy Skillion Pvt CT
Timothy: b 2-15-1737 d 3-5-1822 m Margaret Mathews Pvt MA
Uriah: b 2-27-1745 d 1805 m Elizabeth Adams Sgt MA
Wm., Sr.: b 3-17-1711 d 6-21-1790 m Hepsibeth Blood Pvt MA
Wm., Jr.: b 4-4-1732 d a. 9-25-1790 m Mary Green Pvt MA
Wm.: b 9-11-1737 d 6-28-1805 m Esther Dutton Cpl MA
Wright: b 2-5-1757 d 5-17-1830 m (1)Olive Warren (2)Mrs Martha
    (Smith) Reid Pvt CT MA ★
Zachariah: b 1741 d p. 1812 m Rachel — Pvt MA
Zebulon: b 3-2-1744 d 2-26-1816 m Lydia Wright Pvt MA
Zebulon: b 9-3-1753 d 5-26-1840 m Rhoda Dewey Pvt MA

SPANGENBERG,
John: b a. 1748 d 11- -1814 m Elizabeth — Adj PA W★

SPANGLER, (includes SPENGLER)
Baltzer, Jr.: b 4-16-1735 d 8-1-1798 m Christina Messersmith Lt PA
Bernhard: b 9-30-1745 d 1802 m Mrs Eve Richard Pvt PA
Bernard: b 1719 d 1804 m Anna Margaretha Brauns PS PA
Charles: b c. 1747 d 9-22-1832 m (1)Susanna Diehl (2)Anna Welsh
    Ens PA
Christopher: b 1720 d 1792 m Anna Catherine Riefele PS PA
George Christian, Sr.: b 1728 d p. 6-27-1800 m Anna Maria Krider
    Pvt PA
George Christian, Jr.: b 11-2-1755 d 3-2-1829 m Catherine — Pvt
    PA
George Michael: b a. 1751 d 1823 m (1)Ann Elizabeth Probst
    (2)Christiana Vogelsong 2Lt PA
Henry: b 11-10-1747 d 3-12-1826 m Margaretha Hagenbuch Pvt
    PA
Henry: b 1750 d 1791 m Maria Clara Hoke Pvt PA
Henry: b 8-3-1753 d 8-9-1826 m Catherine Mohr Pvt PA
Henry: b 1-2-1761 d 8-17-1837 m Susannah Lightner Pvt PA
John: b 6-29-1747 d 10-11-1796 m Margaret Beard Pvt PS PA
John Peter: b 1-27-1764 d 9-17-1850 m Maria Spang Pvt PA
Jonas: b 1741 d 9-19-1821 m Catherine — Pvt PA
Joseph: b 1745 d 1802 m Elizabeth Gardner Maj PA
Mathias: b c. 1739 d 3- -1781 m Juliana — PS MD
Michael: b 1750 d p. 1786 m Mary Catherine Wurdman Pvt PA
Michael: b 10-13-1758 d 7-2-1842 m Catharina Schweisgood Pvt
    PA
Peter: b 1740 d 1808 m Anna Maria (Poger) PS Pvt PA
Philip, Sr.: b 1730 d 1786 m Margaret Salome Dinkel Pvt PA
Philip, Jr.: b 3-17-1761 d 1823 m Regina Stover Pvt PA
Rudolph: b 8-8-1738 d 8-8-1811 m Mary Dorothea Dinkel Capt PA
Rudolph: b 5-10-1748 d 1-4-1816 m Anna Sophia Roth Pvt PA
Rudolph: b c. 1752 d 8- -1830 m Christena — Sol PA

SPANKNABLE, (or SPONABLE)
Johannes: b 1747 d 12-25-1825 m Elizabeth King Pvt NY

SPANN, (includes SPAIN)
Charles Stuart: b 12-7-1755 d p. 5-16-1833 m Mary Russell Sol PS
    NC ★
Frederick: b c. 1730 d 1798 m Mary Roberts Pvt PS NC
Frederick: b 1760 d 1827 m Elizabeth — PS NC
James: b 8-15-1757 d 1-29-1833 m Anna Jennings Pvt NC ★
James: b 1754 d 1796 m Elizabeth Fox Lt SC
Jesse: b 10-17-1766 d 1848 m Mary Leighton Sct SC
Thomas: b 2-15-1753 d c. 1804 m Betsy Hall Pvt NC
Willis: b 6-7-1755 d 2-26-1802 m Anna Mabry Pvt NC

SPARE,
Daniel: b 2-3-1760 d 10-24-1812 m Rosina — Pvt PA
George: b 1765 d p. 1792 m Lettice McFee Pvt PA
John: b 10-17-1737 d 6-6-1820 m Elizabeth Barber Pvt MA
Leonard: b 4-22-1750 d 6-18-1811 m Catherine Vanfossen Pvt PA

SPARHAWK,
John: b 11-8-1745 d 1787 m Mary Bacon PS MA
Nathan: b 10-28-1727 d 10-1-1777 m Hannah Murdock PS MA
Thomas: b 3-24-1737 d 10-31-1802 m Rebecca Stearns PS PM NH
Timothy: b 3-13-1751 d 12-24-1838 m Mary Conant Cpl MA

SPARKMAN,
Lewis: b c. 1757 d p. 10-5-1822 m Theresa Eure CS NC

SPARKS,
Benjamin: b c. 1754 d 1801 m Rachel — Pvt PA
Daniel: b 1740 d 1810 m (1) — Stephens (2)Martha Pearce Capt SC
Ebenezer: b 1758 d 6-11-1832 m Margaret — Pvt CT W★
George: b 1760 d 12-31-1829 m Mary Inskip Sgt NJ
George: b c. 1750 d 1802 m Rachel Norris Pvt PA

George: b c. 1730 d p. 7-9-1803 m Mary Bostwick PS VA
Henry: b 6-16-1753 d 8-14-1836 m Lucy Clark 3Cpl VA ★
John: b 7-12-1750 d 6-5-1814 m Bethia Burrows Sol CT
John: b 1755 d 2- -1831 m Mary Parmely Lt NC ★
John: b 2-25-1753 d c. 6-1-1840 m Sarah Shores Pvt MM PS NC ★
John: b 1755 d 1806 m (1)Elizabeth — (2)Joyce Putnam Sol SC
Matthew: b 1-20-1759 d p. 9-19-1840 m — Pvt NC ★
Richard: b 1757 d 7-1-1815 m (1)Frances Nash (2)Ruth Seiver PS PA
Stephen: b 1759 d 6-9-1827 m Sarah Holt MM VT
Wm.: b 1739 d 4- -1789 m Rachel — Capt PA

SPARLING,
Isaac: b 10-1-1758 d 5- -1825 m Elizabeth Gilliland Pvt NJ

SPARR,
John: b 1748 d 1835 m Mary Maria Neathawk Sol PA

SPARROW,
Edward: b 4-2-1745 d 1-29-1817 m Rhoda Bumpus BgdMaj MA
Isaac: b 4-4-1725 d 6-19-1808 m Rebecca Knowles Pvt MA
Josiah: b 2-10-1759 d 1849 m Mercy Smith Pvt MA
Thomas: b c. 1750-60 d a. 11-23-1840 m X Pvt VA ★

SPATZ, (includes SPOTZ)
Christian: b 1758 d 1796 m Sarah — Pvt PA
Frederick: b 9-10-1760 d 10-2-1828 m Catherine — Pvt PA
John Frederick: b 12-26-1755 d 9-19-1790 m Elizabeth Shreyer Sgt
    PA ★

SPEAKE,
Francis: b c. 1750 d p. 1790 m Margaret Massey NCapt MD
Richard: b 1753 d 1834 m Margaret Tate Pvt SC
Wm.: b 8-2-1756 d 2-8-1820 m Sarah Shoebridge Pvt MD VA

SPEAKMAN, (includes SPACKMAN)
Hannah Carver: b 6-21-1754 d 12-27-1833 m Townsend Speakman
    PS PA
Thomas: b 12-18-1728 d 10-24-1810 m Jane Wollerton Pvt PA

SPEAR, (includes SPEARE, SPEER & SPIER)
Allen: b 1749 d 9-15-1801 m Elizabeth Scott Pvt NH
Cornelius: b 1711 d c. 1780 m Susanna Vincent Capt NJ
David: b 8-15-1725 d 4-11-1800 m Hannah Shaw PS CS MA
Edward: b a. 1745 d 11-4-1791 m Jane Holliday 1Lt PA
Henry: b 1-17-1760 d 6-29-1846 m Metje Martha Vreeland Capt NJ
Jacob: bpt 11-24-1745 d — m Marriegrietje Vrederixse Pvt NJ
James: b 12-18-1749 d 1826 m (1)Rachel King (2)Hannah Grimes
    2Lt NJ
John: b 1738 d 6-10-1811 m Agnes Lamb Pvt PS ME MA
John, Sr.: b 4-19-1724 d 3-12-1797 m Magdalena VanDyck PS NJ
John, Jr.: b 3-7-1754 d 9-24-1818 m Margaret Joralemon 1Lt NJ
John: b 12-22-1759 d 6-12-1833 m Elizabeth Terhune 2Lt NJ
John: b c. 1754 d 1811 m Margaret Cloyd Sgt VA
Jonathan: b 6-18-1724 d 10-10-1811 m (1)— Dexter (2)Hannah
    Brown (3)Margaret McDougal Capt PS MA
Joseph: b 9-19-1741 d 6-9-1822 m Sarah Wales Sgt MA
Lemuel: b 2-9-1747 d 8-3-1809 m Ruth Hayward Sgt MA
Luther: b 8-21-1758 d 8-20-1843 m (1)Rebecca Tower (2)Abigail
    Marcy Pvt MA
Moses: b 1-5-1734 d 8-11-1813 m Catherine Jones Lt MA
Nathaniel: b 3-26-1751 d 1-13-1826 m Keziah Stevens Bbd MA
Samuel: b 5-4-1761 d 5-6-1824 m Elizabeth Baxter MarSgt MA W★
Samuel: b 12-3-1745 d 5-17-1814 m (1)Relief Thayer (2)Lois
    Bartlett Sol MA
Samuel: b 5-14-1755 d 3-10-1813 m Lydia Walker Pvt NH
Seth: b 1-19-1741 d 8-28-1818 m (1)Judith Adams (2)Abigail
    Marsh (3)Frances Nightengale Lt MA
Stephen: b 6-13-1764 d 1-9-1844 m Mehitable Ball Pvt MA ★
Wm.: b 8-24-1720 d 11-24-1804 m (1)Esther Thomson (2)Elizabeth
    Murdock (3)Mary Thompson Fox PS CT
Wm., Jr.: b 8-22-1739 d 12-6-1805 m Hannah Brackett Pvt MA
Wm.: b 1758 d 1859 m Milley — Ens NC ★
Wm.: b 4-25-1760 d 1-11-1840 m Barbra White Pvt PA
Wm.: b 1747 d 4-17-1830 m (1)Eleanor Norris (2)Mrs Martha
    McBride Pvt SC

SPEARMAN,
John: b c. 1758 d 1836 m Martha Jopson Sol MD
John: b 3-31-1764 d 1827 m Ann Dawson Toombs Sol VA
Thomas: b c. 1740 d 1800 m (1)Miss Catlett (2)Margaret — (3)Jane
    (Wright) PS VA
Wm.: b c. 1735 d 4- -1824 m (1)Ann Blackiston (2)Molly — Pvt MD

SPEARS, (includes SPEARE & SPEERS)
Christian: b c. 1755 d p. 7- -1811 m Ann Mary Burger Pvt PS VA
George F.: b 1731 d p. 1807 m Christine Neely Sol VA
Henry: b 7-8-1756 d 1-2-1840 m Rebecca Frye Pvt PA
Jacob: b 1-2-1754 d 9-28-1825 m Elizabeth Kellar Pvt VA
John: b 1757 d p. 1840 m Mary Ann — Pvt VA ★
John: b 2-12-1759 d 10-4-1842 m (1)Mary — (2)Susan Womack
    Pvt VA ★
John: b 4-14-1771 d 1-14-1866 m Margaret Chrisman PS VA
Wm.: b c. 1745 d 7-1-1844 m Ann Holliday Sgt VA ★

SPEAS, (includes SPIS)
Barnhard: b c. 1745 d 11- -1779 m Anna Maria — PS PA
Victor: b c. 1720 d 1791 m Anna Margaret PS PA

SPECHT, (includes SPECK & SPECT)
Adam: b 1749 d 10-4-1824 m Eva Elizabeth Hauser Pvt PA ★
Christian: b 12-27-1758 d 3-9-1837 m (1)Barbara Sensenderfer Pvt PA ★
Michael: b c. 1754 d c. 1854 m Margaretha — Sol PA

SPECKLER,
Frederick: b 1764 d 6-18-1833 m Mary Burgner Pvt PA

SPEDDEN,
Robert Brannock: b 4- -1760 d 8-10-1843 m Elizabeth Taylor Slr MD

SPEED,
James: b 3-4-1739 d 9-3-1811 m Mary Spencer Lt VA
John: b 8-3-1738 d 1784-6 m Sarah Baird Sol VA
Joseph: b 5-27-1750 d p. 1796 m Anne Bignall PS VA
Matthias: b 6-18-1754 d p. 5-25-1829 m — CS VA

SPEES,
Benjamin: b 5-26-1740 d 1-27-1816 m Jane Treat Lt CT

SPEIGHT,
Robert: b 1739 d p. 1790 m Elizabeth — PS MD

SPELMAN, (includes SPELLMAN, SPILMAN, & SPILLMAN)
Aaron: bpt 1-22-1734/5 d 10-18-1821 m Elizabeth Rose Pvt MA
Charles: b 12-24-1743 d 7-13-1827 m Lucina Kent Pvt MA
Eber: b 10-27-1753 d 8-15-1829 m Lucy Thrall Pvt MA
Elihu: b 7-12-1738 d 4-17-1829 m Mary Carpenter DrmMaj MA ★
Francis: b c. 1755 d a. 9- -1828 m Rebecca Erskine Sgt VA
James: b 1763 d 1833 m Sarah — Pvt VA ★
John: b 3-5-1740 d 9-22-1826 m Damaris Rose Cpl MA
Oliver: bpt 2-25-1738 d 1815 m (1)Jane Ball (2)Mrs Mercy Cornwell Sgt MA
Phineas: b 2-7-1736 d 12-31-1783 m Elizabeth Griswold PS CT
Richard: b 12-3-1758 d 2- -1805 m Rhoda Camp Pvt CT
Samuel: b 2-15-1716 d 6-26-1778 m — Pvt CT
Stephen: b 12-5-1745 d 12-5-1800 m Deborah Rose Sgt CT
Thomas, Sr.: b c. 1740 d 1782 m Elizabeth — Pvt VA
Thomas, Jr.: b 1763 d 1802 m Mary Massey Pvt VA
Thomas: b c. 1754 d 1822 m Frances Bowmer Sol VA
Timothy: b 1-15-1756 d 4-21-1828 m Hannah Hayes Pvt MA

SPENCE,
Andrew: b c. 1740 d p. 3-1-1799 m Hanna — Pvt PA
Burwell: b 1763 d 3- -1844 m (1)— (2)Nancy Thomas Pvt VA ★
David: b 1758 d 1839 m Mary McElyea Pvt PA
James: b 1748 d p. 1793 m Jane Bluford Pvt VA
Nathan: b 3-20-1743 d p. 7-15-1833 m Elizabeth Quindley MM Spy DE

SPENCER,
Abner: b 1735 d 1802 m (2)Deborah Clarke Pvt CT
Amaziah: b 4-14-1752 d p. 1795 m Elanor Harvey Pvt CT
Amos: b 4-26-1759 d 7-13-1843 m Dorcas Woodcock Pvt NY
Ansel: b 10-21-1765 d 9-6-1850 m Loly Benham Pvt CT
Asa: b 1735 d 3-7-1778 m Deborah Patterson Pvt NH
Ashbel: b 5-25-1750 d 8-14-1821 m Dorcas (Spencer) Pvt CT
Ashbel: b 11-27-1737 d p. 5-30-1808 m Abigail Burdell PS CT
Benjamin: b 3-31-1728 d 7- -1781 m (1)Sarah Low (2)Sarah Johnson Sgt MA
Benjamin: b 1760 d 12-18-1843 m Mary Winkler Pvt NC SC ★
Caleb: b 12-27-1750 d 12-6-1806 m Jerusha Scovil Pvt CT
Caleb, 2d.: b 12-8-1724 d 9-30-1783 m Mrs Hannah Stokes (Goodrich) Cpl CT
Calvin: b 1754 d 1-19-1801 m Rebecca Ford Capt SC
Charles: b 3-10-1749 d 11-17-1838 m (1)Zeruiah Wright (2)Prudence B — Pvt VT
Corey: b 2-28-1760 d 3-20-1839 m Matilda Bull Pvt MA
Daniel: b 5-14-1764 d 11- -1843 m Chloe Wilson Tms CT
Daniel: b 10-28-1733 d — m Elizabeth Stiles Sol CT
Daniel: b 1763/4 d 7-3-1854 m Catherine Cramer Pvt CT ★
David: b 1761 d 6-29-1848 m Mary Fuller Pvt CT ★
David: b 1- -1753 d 8- -1824 m Sarah — Pvt NJ
Ebenezer: b 2-1-1721 d 8-2-1796 m Hannah Gates PS CT
Edward: b 5-7-1753 d 12-29-1829 m Mary Finch Pvt PA
Elam: b 1764 d 10-20-1840 m Hannah Deming Pvt CT ★
Elihu: b 2-12-1721 d 12-27-1784 m Joanna Eatton Chp NJ
Elijah: b 2-14-1758 d 3-18-1838 m Hannah Farnham Pvt Smn CT ★
Eliphalet: b 1-1-1757 d 4-10-1832 m Tryphena Austin Pvt CT
Ephraim: b 1-31-1759 d 1828 m Sarah Stoddard Cpl CT ★
Gideon: b 9-20-1741 d 10-15-1819 m Zerviah Buck 1Lt VT
Gideon: b 5-21-1760 d 5-8-1822 m (1)Catherine Clements (2)Ann Porter Capt VA
Hezekiah, Sr.: b 12-16-1740 d 8-3-1797 m (1)Olive Natt (2)Deborah Easton Pvt CT
Hobert: b c. 1742 d c. 1806/7 m Eunice Barnes Pvt NH
Humphrey: b 1728 d 12-14-1808 m Sarah Airley PS ME

Ichabod: b 9-27-1747 d 9-27-1821 m Hannah Jane Jewett Lt CT
Ichabod S.: bpt 10-19-1755 d — m Rhoda Merwin Pvt CT
Isaac: b 6-10-1745 d 6-25-1818 m Elizabeth Hungerford Lt CT
Isaac B.: b 9-28-1766 d — m Polly Waugh Fif NH
Israel: b 1-30-1732 d 11-18-1813 m Elizabeth Marsh Capt CT
Israel Selden: b 8-1-1762 d 3-5-1837 m Temperance Brockway Pvt CT
Israel Brainerd: b 9-28-1765 d 4-5-1832 m Polly Waugh Fif NH ★
Ithamar: b 1733 d 4-1-1825 m (1)Matilda Houghton (2)Rebecca (Spencer) Capt NY
Jabez: b 3-18-1764 d 5-2-1839 m Joanna Ives Pvt CT
James: b 1756 d 2-10-1825 m Elizabeth Golding Pvt CT ★
James: b 1735 d 1805 m Anna Spencer Pvt NY
James: b 1743 d 9-18-1783 m Margaret Armstrong Ens NC
James, Jr.: b 1767 d 12-9-1825 m Mary Abrams Pvt PA
James: b 3-16-1734 d 3-19-1813 m (1)Sarah Walton (2)Elizabeth Lukens (Marple) Pvt PA
James: b 1762 d 10-22-1843 m Mary McClure Pvt VA
Jared Wilson: b 2-24-1760 d 5-21-1809 m Margaret Wiggins OrdlSgt CT W★
Jedediah: b 1-30-1725/6 d 8-27-1789 m Mary Fuller PS CT
Jeduthan: b 8-29-1753 d 8-17-1812 m Abigail Brown Pvt CT
Jehiel: b 1748 d 2-24-1816 m Anna Patience Tomlinson Pvt CT
Jeremiah: b 3-25-1749 d 7-11-1825 m Tirzah Ashley Lt NH
Jeremiah: b 5-8-1727 d a. 7-14-1813 m Ruth Briggs Pvt RI
Joel: b 1762 d 10-16-1858 m Anne Mitchell Pvt CT ★
John: b 6-21-1750 d — m Susanna White Sgt CT
John: b 8-7-1749 d 9-12-1812 m Mary — Pvt CT
John: b 10-18-1762 d 2-14-1826 m Abigail Marshall Pvt CT
John: b 7-12-1758 d c. 1830 m Eunice Phelps Pvt CT
John: b 5-24-1758 d 8-25-1826 m Rebecca (Spencer) Lt NY
John: b 12-16-1745 d p. 1-1-1798 m Sallie Watkins Lt VA
John: b a. 1760 d 6-20-1817 m Mollay Clopton 2Lt VA W★
John: b c. 1742 d 1789 m Rosannah — Pvt VA
John, Jr.: b 3-11-1763 d 7-9-1816 m Lydia Phillips Pvt VA
Jonathan: b 5-24-1705 d 1-3-1788 m Content Platts Pvt CT
Jonathan: b 1734 d 1813 m Elizabeth Rogers Pvt CT
Jonathan: b 1743 d 6-1-1821 m (1)Ruth Mudge (2)Martha Keech Pvt NY
Joseph, Sr.: b 10-3-1714 d 1-13-1789 m (1)Martha Brainard (2)Mrs Hannah (Brown) Southmayd MGen CS CT
Joseph, Jr.: b 5-11-1750 d 5-11-1824 m Deborah Selden Dr CT
Joseph: b 4-14-1720 d 2-18-1810 m Lydia Grinnell PS CS CT
Joseph: b 1745 d 8-27-1829 m Sarah N Moore LCol VA ★
Michael: b 1766 d 2-26-1846 m (1)Rebecca — (2)Lucinda (Kinne) Fletcher Pvt MA ★
Michael: b 1-6-1744/5 d 1805 m (1)Martha Fones (2)Hannah Boyd Pvt RI
Moses: b c. 1744 d 3-27-1826 m Elizabeth Tinsley Pvt VA ★
Moses: b 1-3-1760 d 8-20-1842 m Judith Ayers Pvt VA W★
Nathan: b 1734 d 1-30-1809 m Hannah Lufborough PS VA
Noah: b 1-13-1762 d p. 1840 m Persis Cobb Pvt CT ★
Obediah: b 10-6-1745 d 2-22-1798 m Mindwell Griffin Sol CT
Oliver: b 10-6-1736 d 1-22-1811 m Anna Ogden Col NJ
Orange: b 7-30-1765 d 1-10-1843 m Sarah Bostwick Mus NY ★
Perry: b 1-16-1756 d 11-15-1822 m (1)Mary Hopkins (2)Eliza Hayes Pvt PS MD
Peter: b 8-29-1763 d 5-29-1842 m Jerusha Post Capt CT
Philip: b 4-30-1724 d 5-8-1815 m Abigail Moore PS CT
Phineas: b 7-14-1746 d 1-24-1817 m Anna Holland Pvt NY
Randall: b 2-28-1753 d 1-16-1813 m Rhoda Green Ens RI
Reuben: b 6-14-1741 d 3-2-1808 m Ruth Nelson Sol CT
Reuben: b 9-3-1751 d 8-25-1804 m Alice Ainsworth Pvt NH
Reuben: b 8-13-1739 m 4-14-1806 m Elizabeth Snyder Capt NY
Richard: b 1743 d 1820 m Eleanor Hopkins Pvt MD
Samuel: b 1713 d 1806 m Mary — Pvt CT
Samuel: b 10-31-1730 d 12-27-1792 m Experience Olds Pvt CT
Samuel: b 9-28-1740 d 3-31-1784 m Deborah Spencer Pvt CT
Samuel: b 1761 d 4-2-1838 m Eunice Griggs Pvt CT ★
Samuel: b — d — m Sarah Read Pvt Arfr CT
Samuel: b 1739 d 1794 m (1)Sybil Pegues (2)Sarah Daniel Col PS CS NC
Simeon: b 1749 d p. 1799 m Abigail Dart Pvt CT
Simeon: b 6-21-1752 d 1840 m (1)Lydia Goodwin (2)Susanna Hamilton PS ME
Simeon: b 1740 d 3-23-1808 m Esther Gould 3Sgt VT
Sharp: b c. 1738/9 d 4-19-1814 m Sarah — Lt VA
Stephen: b 1745 d 1803 m Rhoda Squire Pvt CT
Taylor: b 3-18-1745 d 1812 m Mary Davis Ens VT
Theodore: b 1-13-1758 d 6-29-1845 m Abigail Jones Pvt CT ★
Thomas: b 8-29-1755 d 8-22-1840 m (1)Dorkas — (2)Huldah Oakes Sgt CT ★
Thomas: b 2-27-1725/6 d 1800/1 m (1)Ann — (2)Thankful Ackley Sol CT
Thomas: b 11-26-1744 d a. 4-6-1832 m (1)Dorothy Hills (2)Hannah Symonds (3)Lavinia Latimer MM Pvt CT
Thomas: b 1-16-1736 d 5-1-1807 m Phebe Grenell Pvt CT
Thomas, Sr.: b c. 1721 d 1793 m Elizabeth Julia Flournoy PS VA
Thomas, Jr.: b 6-16-1750 d 7-23-1806 m (2)Lucy A Watkins Maj VA W★
Timothy: b c. 1740 d a. 10-18-1779 m Lois — Lt VT
Truman: b 1764 d 4-14-1840 m (1)Lois Pattison (2)Martha Wheeler Cpl NY

Wm.: b 1760 d 1834 m Eleanor Cooper Drm MA
Wm.: b 10-21-1743 d 8-12-1821 m Eleanor Woodberry Sgt MA
Wm.: b 1757 d 12-3-1841 m Susanna — Sol PA
Wm.: b 4-10-1742 d 1-4-1815 m — Maj VA
Wilson, Jr.: b 2-22-1762 d 12-3-1835 m Elizabeth Waite Pvt RI ★

SPERING,
Henry: b 1763 d 1-6-1823 m Mary Richards Fif PA
John: b 1755 d 9-17-1846 m Sarah Clackner Pvt NJ PA

SPERLING, (includes SPURLIN & SPURLING)
Benjamin: b 9-19-1752 d 12-30-1836 m Fanny Cuptill Cpl MA
John: b c. 1740 d p. 1790 m Myally — PS NC
Wm.: b c. 1760 d 8-20-1829 m Nancy Ann Cary Pvt VA

SPERRY,
Ambrose: b 5-6-1755 d 9-23-1817 m Patience Wheeler Pvt CT
Benjamin: b 8-26-1703 d 2-23-1791 m Mary Taylor Pvt CT
Caleb: b 3-10-1728 d 3- -1799 m Mary Downs Pvt CT
Darius Bradley: b 11-29-1758 d p. 1807 m Mary Hall Pvt CT
Ebenezer: b 11-25-1749 d 1-4-1843 m Hannah Pardee Sgt CT ★
Elihu: b 1722 d 6-15-1779 m (1)Mary Mansfield (2)Martha Payne Pvt CT
Gilead: b 1728 d 4-14-1788 m Mercy Boardman PS CT
Jacob: b 6-29-1748 d 1834 m Sarah Perkins Sgt CT ★
Jacob: b c. 1750 d 1807 m Catherine Elizabeth Louch Pvt VA
James: b 10-26-1718 d 2-20-1789 m Mary (Sperry) Pvt CT
Job: b 1754 d 10-26-1833 m Rebecca Russell Cpl CT ★
Joel: b 8-23-1752 d 2-2-1826 m Abigail Wheeler Pvt CT
Joseph: b c. 1754 d 3-12-1801 m Abigail Paine Pvt CT W★
Moses: b 5-17-1743 d 5-17-1812 m Aene Dillah Beardsley Pvt VT
Nathan: b 11-5-1750 d 1793 m Mary Johns Pvt MA
Peter: b 1- -1740 d 5-29-1838 m Mary Hammock Pvt VA★
Simeon: b 3-16-1738 d 1825 m Patience Smith Sol CT

SPESSARD,
Michael: b 12- -1750 d 4- -1825 m Christieana — Pvt MD

SPETH,
Henery: b c. 1748 d p. 1790 m Elizabeth Shriptein Pvt PA

SPICELY,
James: b 3-22-1761 d 3-18-1855 m (3)Martha H Edwards Trm VA★

SPICER,
Abel: b 6-1-1760 d 7-7-1849 m (1)Sarah Parke (2)Elizabeth Morse (3)Sarah Rose Pvt CT
Asher: b c. 1751 d 1811/12 m Rebecca Adderson Pvt CT
Edward: b 11-17-1755 d 1-6-1823 m (1)Esther Ames (2)Deborah Brown Pvt CT
Edward: b 4-4-1722 d 1-8-1797 m (1)Hannah Bill (2)Abigail Allen CS CT
Jabez: b 9-11-1753 d 1- -1823 m Faith Ripley Cpl NH
Jacob: b 1757 d 5-9-1824 m Sarah Meeker Pvt NY ★
Jeremiah: b 8-28-1761 d 8-14-1825 m Rhoda Brownell Sol NY
John: b 4-20-1749 d 10-8-1826 m Mary Park Sgt CT
John: b 1744 d 8-6-1838 m Catherine — Pvt NJ ★
Michael: b 1766 d 4-12-1842 m Sarah Atwood Pvt NY W★
Nathan, Sr.: b 9-10-1735 d 7-27-1811 m (1)Leah — (2)Abigail Mayhew PS NY
Nathan, Jr.: b 1759 d 8- -1843 m Catherine Philkins Pvt NY
Oliver: b 5-28-1726 d 2-11-1804 m Alethea Allyn Capt CT
Samuel: b c. 1737 d 1836 m Rebecca Fowler Pvt PA★

SPICKARD,
George: b 6-10-1757 d 2-15-1848 m (1)Mary Barr (2)Eleanor Gardner Pvt VA★

SPICKERMAN,
Andrew: b 1764 d 1843 m Savale — Pvt NY
Philip: b 1762 d 5-1-1822 m Annie Simmons Pvt NY

SPICKET,
Daniel: b 1749 d 1-4-1823 m Abilene Coburn Trm MD

SPICKNALL,
Leonard: b 1752 d 1834 m X PS MD

SPIGHT,
Simon: b 1741 d 1-12-1816 m Mary Harrison PS NC

SPIGNER,
Frederick: b c. 1754 d p. 10-7-1820 m Martha — Sol SC

SPILLER,
Benjamin C.: b c. 1746 d 1801 m Ann Frazer Capt VA
Henry: b 11-5-1732 d 1-3-1817 m Mary Hodgkins Pvt MA
John: b 1741 d 1829 m (1)— Jackson (2)Catherine Marquis Pvt PA
Micajah: b c. 1740 d a. 1782 m X Pvt VA
Samuel: b 8-17-1759 d 3-12-1824 m Agnes Vining Pvt MA ★
Samuel: b 3-27-1757 d 8-10-1822 m Molly (Spiller) Pvt NH
Wm.: b 1750 d 1800 m Catherine George (?) Capt VA

SPINK,
Nicholas: b 12-6-1763 d 3-17-1849 m Susanna Carr Mus RI★
Robert: b 11-10-1738 d p. 11-5-1799 m (1)Ruth Matteson (2)Susanna Warren Pvt MA
Shibnah, Jr.: b 8-1-1757 d 1846 m Delight Clothier Pvt MA

SPINKS,
John: b c. 1747 d p. 11-28-1799 m Sarah Baker PS NC

SPINNER,
Jacob: b 3-3-1740 d p. 1788 m Maria Catherine Stoudt Ens PA
Jesse: b c. 1762/3 d 11-27-1836 m (1)Celia Cheatwood (2)Nancy (White) Robinson (3)Lucinda (Douglas) Clayton Smn VA

SPINNEY,
Jeremiah: bpt 4-18-1742 d 10-30-1812 m Mehitable Hinckley Pvt MA

SPINNING, (or SPINING)
Isaac: b 10-3-1759 d 12-24-1825 m Catherine Pierson MM NJ
John: b 8-23-1753 d 7-6-1816 m Jerusha Frary Pvt MA
Mathias: b 1-17-1750 d 12-4-1830 m Hannah Haines Pvt NJ

SPIRES,
Zachariah: b c. 1745 d p. 4-22-1806 m (1)Dinah — (2)Rhoda — PS SC

SPITLER,
Jacob: b 9-29-1749 d 4-16-1829 m Nancy Henry Sol VA
John: b 8-12-1760 d 1840 m Catherine Lytle Pvt PA

SPITZER,
Gerret: b 6-20-1758 d 6-2-1801 m Nancy Sixby Pvt NY

SPIVEY,
Aaron: b 9-18-1753 d 9-2-1834 m (1)— Pearce (2)Charlotte Nixon PS NC
Moses: b 1756 d 6-2-1829 m Rebecca Gladdish Pvt SC
Wm.: b c. 1750 d c. 1817 m Molly — Sol NC

SPLANE,
Thomas: b 2-9-1758 d 1831 m Mildred Rigby Pvt VA ★

SPOCK,
James: b 2-22-1741 d 5-14-1804 m Mary Smith Pvt NY

SPOFFORD, (includes SPAFFORD)
Abijah: b 4-22-1736 d 10-19-1811 m Mary Town PS NH
Amos: b 8-28-1765 d 1838 m Mary Taggart Pvt NH
Andrew: b 3-22-1743 d p. 1790 m Molly Chamberlain Sgt MA
Asa: b 8-4-1725 d 3-12-1808 m Huldah Flint Armr CT
Asa: b 6-2-1759 d 1-2-1800 m Persis White Pvt NH
Bradstreet, Sr.: b 9-2-1731 d 12-2-1808 m Mary Page Lt NH
Daniel: b 4- -1721 d 4-26-1803 m (1)Judith Follansbee (2)Mrs Betty Emery (3)Mrs Phoebe Jewett Col MA
David: b 12-4-1738 d — m Elizabeth Fales Pvt NH
David: b 12-4-1710 d p. 1790 m (1)Hannah Cheney (2)Mary Bailey PS NH
Eldad: b 1-2-1745 d 1-6-1806 m Lucy Spaulding Sgt NH
Eleazer: b 8-12-1739 d 1825 m Mary Flint Cpl MA
Elephalet: b 2-4-1744 d p. 1790 m — Capt VT
Jacob: b 2-22-1754 d 8-2-1841 m Abigail Deane Pvt MA
Job: b 1-29-1757 d p. 1843 m Hannah Chipman Pvt VT
John: b 2-20-1742 d 1800 m Susanna Dow Sol MA
John: b 7-31-1752 d 4-24-1823 m Mary Baldwin Capt VT
John: b 2-19-1758 d 3-18-1803 m (1)— Newton (2)Elizabeth Kendall Pvt VT
Jonathan: b 5-28-1740 d p. 5-12-1787 m (1)Dorcas Frost (2)Mary Cochran PS ME MA
Jonathan: b 4-26-1751 d 1835 m (1)— Sanderson (2)Mrs Esther Ruddock MM MA
Joseph: b 7-13-1720 d 3-13-1803 m (1)Sarah Eames (2)Mary Marble Pvt MA
Moody: b 6-24-1744 d 12-23-1828 m (1)Huldah Spofford (2)Mrs Mirriam (Flint) Sgt MA
Moody: b 4-19-1755 d 3-31-1833 m Dolly Farnham Pvt MA W★
Moses: b 1-3-1723 d 3-9-1825 m Abigail Bibbins Pvt CT
Moses: b 4-6-1747 d 9-17-1820 m (1)Elizabeth Morse (2)Hannah Kimball Pvt MA
Moses: b 1-19-1732 d p. 1783 m Caroline Sherman Sgt NH
Nathan: b 5-25-1761 d a. 1817 m Hannah Barnett Pvt NH
Solomon: b 1764 d 2-2-1837 m Sarah Sheldon LCol VT
Thomas, Sr.: b 6-10-1726 d 1787 m Roxbee Moody CS MA
Thomas, Jr.: b 1751 d 5-23-1833 m Esther Pearl Sgt CS NH

SPOHN,
Conrad: b 4-7-1755 d 7-2-1831 m Dorothea Bolich Pvt PA
Henry: b 3-10-1729 d 1-21-1813 m Maria Catherine — CMman PA
John: b 1-19-1754 d 4-19-1822 m Maria Beidler Capt PA
Nicholas: b 1758 d 1833 m Catherine Kilts Pvt NY
Philip, Jr.: b 9-24-1737 d 9-13-1807 m Maria Krick 1Lt PA

SPONG, (or SPANG)
Frederick: b 12-25-1762 d 1-14-1826 m Margaret Seltzer Ens PA
Peter: b 8-3-1758 d 6-5-1829 m Elizabeth Sherman Pvt PA

SPONSELLER,
John: b *c.* 1755 d *c.* 1804 m Christina — Pvt MD

SPOONER,
Benjamin: b 10-23-1743 d 1827 m (1)Mary (Hoskins) Peirce (2)Tryphenia Booth Sgt MA
Benjamin: b 1748 d 1-9-1845 m Mary Lanksford Cpl RI ★
Bigford: b 12-18-1743 d 8-5-1814 m (1)Mary Babbitt (2)Mary Peters Pvt MA
Charles: b — d 11-14-1847 m Charity Curtis Pvt MA
Charles: b 1738 d 1779 m (1)Patience Allen (2)Mrs Mary Mendell Gardiner Lt RI
Clapp: b 6-13-1760 d 12-7-1826 m Mary Church Pvt MA
Daniel: b 2-28-1694 d 1797 m Elizabeth Ruggles PS MA
Daniel: b 12-10-1741 d 11- -1828 m Abigail Monroe Lt VT
Ebenezer: b 5-29-1724 d 1800 m Sarah Robinson Slr MA
Eleazer: bpt 11-15-1734 d 3- -1813 m Mehitable Allen Pvt MA
Eliakim: b 4-6-1740 d 1-3-1820 m Bathsheba Warner Pvt MA
Gardner: b 6-21-1745 d *p.* 1834 m Deborah Shaw Pvt MA ★
Isaac: b 1-9-1716 d 5-14-1800 m Ruth Gardner Pvt MA
James: b 10-5-1739 d 10-3-1815 m Susan De Moranville Cpl MA
Jeduthan: b 11-12-1755 d 5-16-1817 m Hannah Crowell Cpl MA
John: b 12-29-1745 d 1811 m Mrs Sarah (Gilbert) Whitlock Pvt MA
Judah Paddack: b 11-5-1748 d 2-11-1807 m Deborah Douglass Smn CT
Micah: b 5-22-1754 d 10-9-1822 m Patience Crapo MM MA
Philip: b 12-13-1733 d 9-30-1826 m Elizabeth Winslow PS MA
Samuel: b 1-20-1763 d 4-18-1840 m Hannah Williams Pvt MA
Shearjashub: b 8-16-1735 d 4-25-1785 m Sarah Whipple Pvt MA
Thomas: b 3-15-1751 d 3-8-1837 m (1)Mary Haven (2)Martha Smith Pvt MA
Ward: b 4-23-1751 d *p.* 1777 m Abigail Pease Pvt MA
Wm.: b 5-8-1752 d 2-3-1831 m (1)Hannah (Spooner) (2)Jerusha Lumado Pvt CT
Wing: b 12-29-1738 d 12-7-1810 m Eunice Stevens Capt MA
Wing: b 1749 d 12-28-1802 m Frances Burroughs Capt RI
Zoeth: b *a.* 1765 d *p.* 6-6-1856 m (2)Nancy — Pvt MA

SPOOR, (includes SPORE)
Abraham: b 1-29-1749 d *p.* 1789 m (1)Sophia (Fytie) — (2)— Robinson Pvt MA
Abraham: b 9-11-1757 d 1820 m Rebecca Betts Pvt MA
Abraham: b 7-28-1759 d 12-17-1829 m Maria Wells Pvt NY
Cornelius: bpt 1-19-1736 d *p.* 1790 m Leah Van Hoesen PS NY
Dirk: b 6-2-1741 d 9-12-1826 m Judith Severson Pvt NY
Isaac: bpt 8-16-1741 d 4-19-1789 m Christina Van Deusen Pvt NY
Isaac: bpt 8-15-1753 d *p.* 1790 m Magdalena Van Valkenburg Pvt NY
Isaac Derrick: b 9-22-1752 d 7-15-1827 m Diadamia Smith Pvt MA
Johannes: bpt 10-8-1733 d *p.* 1790 m Catherine — Pvt NY
John: bpt 1-29-1750 d 7-1-1834 m Rachel Freese Ens NY ★
John: b 7-21-1760 d 7-12-1849 m Elizabeth Von Wormer Pvt NY
Nicholas: b 1-21-1733 d *p.* 1782 m Maria Van Vechten Pvt NY

SPOTSWOOD, (includes SPOTTSWOOD)
Alexander, Jr.: b 1746 d 12-10-1818 m Elizabeth Washington Col VA
John: b *c.* 1748 d *p.* 1801 m Sarah Rowsie Capt VA

SPRAGUE,
Abel: b 1-27-1737/8 d *c.* 1792 m Mercy Harvey Pvt NY
Abiel: b *c.* 1745 d *c.* 1810-17 m Martha Bryant Pvt MA
Amasa: b 9-23-1758 d 9-7-1806 m Sarah Evans Pvt NY
Amos: b 6-20-1747 d 12-2-1838 m Desire Stodder Cpl MA
Anthony: b 6-29-1742 d 11-20-1831 m (1)Sarah Harper (2)Cloah — Sgt MA
Asa: b 7-24-1748 d 2-2-1830 m Martha Wilson Sgt MA
Barnabas: b 9-5-1754 d 8-16-1828 m Lydia Ransom Pvt MA
Benjamin: b 3-10-1711 d 4- -1788 m Sarah Comstock Pvt CT
Benjamin: b 9-28-1752 d 6-22-1839 m Hannah Barnes Sgt MA ★
Beriah: bpt 8-11-1754 d *c.* 1805 m Elizabeth — Pvt CT
Caleb: b 7-17-1755 d 3-20-1828 m Lillie Smith Pvt MA
Calvin: b 5-29-1744 d *p.* 1800 m Elizabeth Wright Pvt MA
Dan: b 5-29-1758 d 9-15-1840 m Lucy Crocker Pvt CT ★
David: b 5-15-1754 d 8-7-1832 m Jane Burrell Cpl MA W★
David: b 3-14-1731/2 d 12-22-1821 m (1)Amey Sweet (2)Peace Chase Sol NY
David: b 5-15-1742 d 7-25-1789 m Lydia Lamb Pvt NY
Dyre: b *c.* 1754 d 7-9-1822 m Faith Williams Pvt CT W★
Ebenezer, Jr.: b 1-18-1753 d 10-2-1838 m Mary Chamberlain Pvt NY
Ebenezer: b 8-2-1740 d 1-21-1811 m Melicent Sheldon PS RI
Ebenezer: b 8-16-1747 d 9-17-1837 m Lydia Sprague CS VT
Elijah: b 5-10-1748 d 1808 m Hannah Golder Capt NY
Elijah: b 1759 d 2-26/7-1841 m Mrs Nancy Palmer Smith Pvt NY
Elkanah, Sr.: b 1-25-1732 d *p.* 1781 m Mehitable Moulton Capt VT
Elkanah, Jr.: b 12-19-1760 d 3-17-1846 m Charlotte Johnson Pvt VT
Eseck: b 5-29-1756 d 9-4-1824 m Lucy Rublee Sgt MA
Frederick: b 10-12-1762 d 1-4-1839 m Rebecca Nichols Pvt CT
Gideon: b 4-4-1758 d 7-1-1817 m Abigail Terrill Pvt MA
Gideon: b 7-15-1747 d *c.* 1807/8 m Chloe Spaulding Ens RI
Hezekiah: b 1-12-1704/5 d *p.* 5- -1785 m Sarah Smith PS RI
Hosea: b *c.* 1759 d 11-20-1843 m Elizabeth Charles Pvt MA ★
Isaac, Sr.: b 3-28-1709 d 12-12-1789 m Leah Stodder Drm MA

Isaac, Jr.: b 9-28-1743 d 8-27-1800 m Hannah Jacob Sgt MA
Israel: b 10-19-1741 d 11-21-1823 m (1)Pheobe Hosey (2)Ruth (Larned) Fisk Pvt MA
Jacob, Sr.: b 1709 d 1- -1785 m Sarah Stodder Cpl MA
Jacob, Jr.: b 6-25-1737 d 1778 m Alice Tower Pvt MA
James: b 1761 d 9-23-1845 m (1)Mary Spooner (2)Susanna Rice Pvt CT ★
James: b 3-16-1749/50 d 4-4-1838 m (1)Mary Bartlett (2)Nancy Richards Pvt MA ★
James: bpt 3-4-1753 d 6-18-1832 m Persis Huse Pvt NH
James: b 1742-5 d — m Rachel Perkins Cmsry NJ
Jesse: b 7-22-1745 d 3-28-1818 m Elizabeth Joy Pvt MA
John: b 3-1-1720 d 4-1-1801 m Margaret Webb Sgt MA
John: b 8-23-1743 d 5-15-1813 m Mary Everett Pvt MA
John, 3d.: b 1-13-1754 d 10-21-1803 m (1)Susanna Fowle (2)Elizabeth Poole Dr MA
John: b 12-4-1718 d 1797 m (1)Elizabeth Delhonde (2)Mrs Esther Harrison PS MA
John: b 7-20-1746 d 3-4-1843 m Rebecca Alden Ens NH
John: b 4-2-1727 d *p.* 1776 m Elizabeth Titus PS NH
John: b 4-25-1755 d *p.* 1810 m Polly Kennedy Sgt NY
John: b 9-25-1742 d 2-26-1809 m Mary Valentine Sol NY
John: b 1757/8 d 4-29-1811 m Deliverance Pearce Pvt RI
Jonathan: b 4-30-1716 d 1-17-1807 m (1)Lydia Barrows (2)Mrs Mary (Chamberlain) Smith Pvt CT
Jonathan: b 1761 d 5-9-1813 m Phoebe Lonsberry Lt VT
Joseph: b 1-15-1739/40 d 1808/9 m (1)Deborah Brown (2)Phillis Jillson Capt RI
Joseph: b *c.* 1717 d *p.* 1790 m Martha Benson PS CS VT
Joshua: b 7-3-1729 d 10-1-1816 m (1)Amey Darling (2)Abigail Wilber Maj MA
Knight, Sr.: b 10-12-1711 d 1804 m (1)Mary Lewis (2)Mary Beal PS Pvt MA
Knight, Jr.: b 3-25-1740 d 8-9-1835 m (1)Lucy Sprague (2)Rhoda Marsh 2Lt MA
Moses: b 4-25-1749 d 10-3-1828 m (1)Mary Lincoln (2)Mary Lincoln Sgt MA
Nathaniel: b 11-15-1747 d 9-12-1802 m Hannah Ford Cpl MA
Nicholas: b 12-29-1722 d 2-10-1800 m Sarah Walker Pvt MA
Philip: b 1-9-1760 d 4-1-1856 m (1)Clarice Dutton (2)Mrs Olive C Hovey Pvt VT ★
Phineas, Sr.: b 9-15-1751 d 10-4-1777 m Sarah — Pvt CT
Phineas, Sr.: b 1-13-1700/1 d 6-13-1775 m Rebecca Lynde Pvt MA
Phineas, Jr.: b 9-25-1725 d 12-29-1805 m (1)Hannah Gould (2)Sarah Fowler Sgt MA
Reuben: b 3-10-1748/9 d 1822 m Silence Lasell Pvt MA
Rufus: b 6-7-1745 d 7-27-1795 m Rosannah Leech PS RI
Samuel: b 9-27-1712 d 4-15-1783 m Martha Hills Capt PS MA
Samuel: b 12-22-1753 d 6-20-1844 m Joanna Thayer Gnr MA
Samuel: b 8-5-1753 d 4-7-1835 m (1)Elizabeth Humphries (2)Mary Smith Pvt MA ★
Samuel: b 1753 d 1832 m Mary Benner Pvt MA
Samuel: b 9-2-1724 d 9-18-1797 m Elizabeth Wade PS MA
Seth: b 7-4-1760 d 7-8-1847 m Deborah Sampson Pvt MA
Silas, Sr.: b 1727/8 d 9- -1808 m (1)Hannah Binney (2)Abigail Hill Capt MA
Silas, Jr.: b 2-18-1762 d 3-8-1841 m Polly Leonard Sol MA
Terah: b 2-17-1711/2 d *c.* 1777-82 m Love — Pvt MA
Thomas: b 4-26-1752 d 5-12-1828 m Thankful Hatch Pvt MA
Timothy: b 1752 d 1-8-1815 m Mary Sergent Bbd MA
Wm., Sr.: b 11-19-1740 d 3-25-1829 m Mrs Miriam (Day) Blethen Lt MA
Wm.: b 3-22-1738 d 2-6-1782 m Tryphena Blackman Pvt MA
Wm.: b 3-3-1759 d 6-26-1828 m Anna Marrow Pvt MA ★
Wm.: b 4-23-1763 d 7-31-1842 m (1)Abiah Hubbell (2)Mary Gregory Pvt RI ★

SPRAKE, (includes SPRAGUE)
Nicholas: b 12-29-1722 d 7-11-1784 m Margaret — Pvt MA
Samuel, Sr.: b 2-2-1725 d *a.* 1789 m (1)Judith Pollard (2)Mrs Ruth Dunckle Pvt MA
Samuel, Jr.: b 9-9-1750 d 12-10-1836 m Anna Sprake Cpl MA ★

SPRAKER, (includes SPRECHER)
George: b 8-16-1724 d 7-15-1800 m Maria House Sgt NY
George: b 1762 d 1823 m Catherine — Pvt PA
John: b 1757 d 6-13-1837 m Margaret Ansley Pvt NY ★
Joseph: b 8-14-1765 d 8-19-1848 m Katherine Frasier Pvt NY

SPRATLEY,
Wm.: b 8-14-1742 d 9-16-1800 m Mary — PS VA

SPRATLING,
James: b *c.* 1750 d 7-18-1812 m Winnifred Monday Pvt VA

SPRATT,
James: b *c.* 1748 d 1799 m Mary Jackson Sol VA
Thomas: b 1731 d 1807 m Elizabeth Bigger Lt SC

SPRIGG,
Frederick: b 1749 d 10-15-1791 m Deborah Woodword Maj MD
Joseph: b 1736 d 1800 m (1)Mrs Hannah (Lee) Bowie (2)Mrs Margaret (Weems) Elzey (3)Mrs Magruder CS PS MD

Levin: b 3-13-1762 d *p.* 3-4-1836 m Mary Fowler Cpl VA ★
Zachariah: b 5-12-1751 d *p.* 5-26-1828 m Elizabeth Stephenson Pvt PS VA

SPRING,
Amos: b 1-7-1734 d 9-19-1777 m̃ Phebe Asenath, Pvt MA
Amos: b 12-4-1752 d 2-24-1814 m Rebecca Curtis Judd Pvt MA
Converse: b 12-30-1734 d 4-14-1812 m (1)Mercy Learned (2)Mary Fuller Pvt MA
Ebenezer: b 11-8-1748 d 1831 m Naomi Sedgwick Pvt MA
Ephraim: b 7-21-1750 d 9-23-1834 m Eunice Taft Adj MA
Jedediah: b 4-16-1730 d *p.* 1790 m Elizabeth Saltmarsh Sol PS NH
Nicholas: b 1730 d 1-22-1824 m Margaret — Pvt VA
Samuel: b 2-27-1746 d 3-4-1819 m Hannah Hopkins Chp MA
Thaddeus: b 8-29-1739 d *p.* 1790 m Lydia Traine Cpl CS MA
Thomas: b 6-3-1737 d 3-24-1825 m (1)Mary Gossard (2)Abigail Hawley Cpl CT
Thomas: b 9-16-1756 d 7-27-1842 m Mary Osgood Cpl MA

SPRINGER,
Benjamin: b 6-14-1740 d *p.* 1778 m Henrietta Oliver Pvt NY
Charles: b 9-3-1732 d 11-19-1817 m Margareta Springer 2Lt DE
Charles: bpt 8-21-1735 d 3-6-1802 m Mary Baal Pvt DE
Charles: b — d *c.* 4-29-1777 m Susannah Seeds 2Lt PS MD
Daniel: b 1744 d 6-8-1825 m Elizabeth — Capt PA
Dennis: b 6-23-1748 d 4-6-1823 m Elizabeth Small Lt PA
Durfee: b 1758 d 9-4-1839 m Desire Lake Pvt RI★
Edward: b 3-27-1752 d *p.* 1802 m Edith Merihew Sgt MA
Jacob, Sr.: b *a.* 1745 d *a.* 5-2-1831 m Elizabeth — PS MD
Jacob: b *c.* 1746 d 4- -1817 m Margaret Gregg Pvt PA
Jacob: b 4-28-1741 d 9-23-1818 m Mary Snyder Pvt NY
Jacob: b 1759 d 1808 m Catharine Arvine Lt VA
John: b 9-12-1753 d 10-6-1823 m Catherine Hanson Wgm DE
John: b 1758 d 8-17-1818 m (1)Sarah Ann Butler (2)Mrs Elizabeth Ingram Pvt MD
John: b 1724 d 6-12-1783 m Hannah Trufant Vol ME MA
John: b 1743 d 9-3-1798 m Ann Green Sol VA
John: b 4-5-1756 d *p.* 12-23-1816 m Bathsheba Merrifield Pvt VA
Knight: b 1759 d 1850 m (1)Betsy Rounds (2)Sarah Manchester Pvt RI★
Levi: b 5-4-1744 d 3-26-1823 m (1)Annie Gaddis (2)Mrs Sarah (Shepherd) Duke PS Pvt VA
Michael: b 9-1-1756 d 3-15-1839 m Susana Sunderland Pvt PA
Nathan: b 12-2-1752 d 1-2-1831 m (1)Hannah McDaniel (2)Lydia Watson (3)— Rice Pvt VA
Nathaniel: b 1732 d 8- -1780 m Sarah Hodgskins Capt ME
Nicholas: b 8-5-1743 d 3-30-1792 m Elizabeth McIlvaine PS DE
Phillip: b 1734 d 5-3-1791 m Mary — Pvt PA
Robert: b 3-5-1754 d 10-15-1814 m Rebecca — Pvt RI
Samuel: b 1750 d 3-7-1826 m Amy Smith 1Lt NJ
Stephen: b 10-27-1757 d *p.* 11-13-1815 m Sarah Macy PS NC SC VA
Stukley: b 3-10-1755 d 4-23-1829 m Mary Badcock Pvt Smn PS MA
Wm.: b 11-29-1754 d *p.* 7- -1816 m Mary Norcross Vol ME

SPRINGS,
John: b 10-27-1751 d 6-25-1818 m Sarah Alexander Capt NC
Richard: b 10-22-1754 d 12-22-1833 m Jane Baxter Capt NC
Sedgwick: b 4-2-1756 d 12-3-1837 m (2)Lucy Crocker Pvt CS NC W★

SPRINGSTEEN,
Jacobus: b 4-27-1746 d *p.* 1790 m Rachael Cole Pvt NY

SPRINKLE, (includes SPRENCKEL)
George: b 1756 d *p.* 1790 m Barbara Millison Pvt PA
Michael: bc. 1732 d *p.* 5-25-1816 m (1)Margaret Oyster (2)Elizabeth — Pvt PA

SPRONG,
John: b 1730 d *p.* 1790 m — Pvt NY

SPROUL,
James, Jr.: b 1760 d 1-13-1842 m Mary Greenlaw Pvt MA
James: b 1756 d 6-26-1777 m Zilpah McChesney Ens NJ
Wm.: b 2-7-1746 d 1795/6 m Rebecca Fossett Pvt MA

SPROUT, (includes SPROAT)
Ebenezer: b 2-9-1752 d 2- -1805 m Katherine Whipple Col MA
Ebenezer: b 1757 d 9- -1822 m (1)Mary Thayer (2)Miriam Barnes Pvt MA
James: b 1722 d 10-18-1793 m Sarah Smith Chp PA
Michael: b *c.* 1752 d *c.* 1795 m Lydia Warner Pvt NH
Nathan: b 6-5-1763 d 1-1-1845 m Lucinda Dana Pvt MA ★
Nathaniel, Jr.: b 1753 d 1824 m Azubah Cummings Pvt MA
Robert: b 1-1-1715 d 6-11-1797 m (1)Hannah Sampson (2)Hannah Southworth Pvt MA
Thomas: b 10-1-1756 d 2-3-1833 m Mary Briggs Fif MA★
Wm.: b d-1757 d 10-11-1793 m Maria Thompson Maj PA MD
Zebedee: b 3-1-1742 d 1810 m (1)Elizabeth Robinson (2)Mrs Hannah Walker (3)Joanna Pierce Sgt MA

SPRUILL,
Benjamin: b 1752 d 1812 m (2)Lois Blount PS NC
Hezekiah: b 1-22-1732 d 3-20-1804 m Rhoda — Capt PS NC

SPRY,
Wm.: b 1-1-1756 d 6-10-1836 m (1)— (2)Ruth — Pvt MD

SPURGEON,
Mary Jane: b 6-20-1736 d 8-3-1803 m William Spurgeon PS NC

SPURLOCK,
John, Jr.: b *c.* 1750 d *p.* 8-25-1816 m Frances Turman PS VA

SPURR, (or SPUR)
John: b 6-27-1724 d 1-18-1781 m (1)Ruth Blake (2)Rebecca — Cpl MA
John: b 1758 d 3-3-1816 m Mercy Dunbar Pvt MA
Lemuel: b 10-4-1747 d 10-8-1808 m Lois Bullard Pvt MA
Redman: b 9-4-1747 d *c.* 1816 m Rebecca Stone Cpl MA
Richard: b *c.* 1750 d *p.* 5-7-1790 m Frances Cotton Capt VA

SPURRIER,
Thomas: b — d *p.* 9-20-1797 m Sarah — PS MD

SPYKER,
Benjamin: b 3-16-1747 d *p.* 1790 m Catherine Lauer Capt PA MD
Henry: b 8-29-1753 d 7-1-1817 m Maria Weiser Col PA
Peter: b 10-7-1711 d 7-18-1789 m Maria Margareta Seidel CS PA

SQUIRE, (includes SQUIER & SQUIRES)
Abiather: b 11-15-1740 d 3-20-1803 m Mary Dudley Pvt CT W★
Andrew: b 8-27-1732 d 1-2-1823 m Huldah Brownson Pvt MA
Asa: b 5- -1764 d 4-3-1852 m Eunice — Pvt CT ★
Daniel: b 1756 d *p.* 1822 m Elizabeth Wood Pvt CT ★
David, Jr.: b 10-8-1762 d 7- -1843 m Lurana (Gilbert) Pvt CT
David: b 12-24-1743 d 1821 m Mary Bunker Pvt CT
Ebenezer: bpt 10- -1730 d *p.* 1790 m Ann Pierce Pvt CT
Eli: b 7-11-1764 d *p.* 1802 m Sarah Willmarth Pvt MA
Elijah: b 11-21-1738 d 9-6-1808 m Elizabeth — Capt NJ
Ellis: b 9-17-1746 d 8-10-1824 m Rebecca Purcel Pvt NJ
Ephraim: b 2-9-1748 d 8-17-1841 m Priscilla Sibley Pvt CT★
Ezra: b 3-8-1761 d 5-17-1836 m Betsey Pangman Pvt VT ★
James: b 6-9-1756 d 1-21-1848 m Lydia Reynolds Pvt NJ★
James: b 6-25-1730 d 11-12-1785 m Ruth Baldwin Pvt VT
Jesse: b 1725 d 10-1-1804 m (1)Lydia Clothier (2)Mary Whitney Pvt CT
Jesse: b 11-11-1760 d 3-25-1835 m Amy Cole Cpl NY★
John: b 12-10-1730 d 7-25-1777 m Hannah Clark Pvt NJ
Jonathan, Sr.: b 10-6-1739 d *p.* 1782 m (1)Elizabeth Morehouse (2)Mary Gray (3)prob A Reaves Lt CT
Jonathan, Jr.: b 3-6-1763 d 3-10-1842 m (1)Esther Truesdale (2)Catee Holmes Sol PS CT
Jonathan: b 1733 d 1- -1800 m (1)Eunice Crane (2)Hannah Dixon Cpl NJ
Joseph: b *c.* 1762 d *p.* 3-4-1830 m Phebe Crane Pvt NJ★
Meeker: b 11-24-1750 d 6-21-1818 m Rachel Meeker Pvt NJ
Nathaniel: b 1727 d 10-28-1789 m Mary Beach Capt NJ
Noble: b 10-2-1760 d 5-11-1837 m X Pvt Smn MA ★
Phineas: b 4-13-1761 d 11- -1839 m Katherine Bates Sgt CT ★
Samuel: b 1736 d 9-1-1807 m Ann Bishop Pvt NJ
Saxton: b 6-4-1758 d 7-25-1828 m (2)Sylvia Newell DrmMaj CT
Thomas: b 2-4-1700 d 2-14-1778 m Rachel Ludlum Pvt NJ
Wm.: b 9-17-1762 d 8-27-1826 m Esther Gould Pvt CT
Wm.: b 4-15-1753 d 6-27-1832 m Sarah Conklin Sgt NJ

STAATS,
Abraham: b *c.* 1735 d 10-12-1786 m Amy Barber Capt DE
Abraham: b 1743 d *a.* 5-10-1821 m Margaret DuBois CS NJ
Barent: b 6-3-1739 d — m Anatje Winne LCol NY
Barent G.: b 5-16-1762 d 8-25-1849 m Catharine Cuyler Pvt NY
Gerrit: b 6-3-1722 d *p.* 1781 m Deborah Beekman 2Lt NY
Jacob: b 11-20-1756 d 10-14-1819 m Elizabeth Low QM NY
John: b 1740 d 1805 m Gertrude Quick CS NJ
John: b *c.* 1757/8 d 3-12-1813 m Jane McClellan Ens NY W★
Nicholas S.: b 10-2-1743 d 5-7-1816 m Maria Salisbury Capt NY
Peter: b 7-6-1738 d 8-14-1825 m Susanna Middleswert Pvt NJ
Philip: b 7-26-1755 d 8-22-1821 m Anna Van Alstine Lt NY
Rynear: bpt 4-14-1747 d 2-13-1826 m Sietje Van Nest Capt NJ
Wm.: bpt 5-2-1736 d 5-22-1825 m Annetjie Yates Sol NY

STABLER,
Adam: b *c.* 1764 d 1791 m Christina — Pvt PA
Christian: b *a.* 1731 d 1783 m Anna — Pvt PA

STACKER, (or STACHER)
Christopher: b 1737 d 1830 m Elizabeth Breitzman PS Capt PA
Lewis: b 1745 d 1822 m Catherine Doll PS Capt PA

STACKHOUSE,
Isaac: b 1751 d 5-1-1838 m Bethia — Pvt VA★
John: b *c.* 1738 d 1800 m Elizabeth Buckingham Sol PA
Samuel, Jr.: b 11-15-1756 d 9- -1787 m Esther Penquoit Tms PA
Wm.: b 1736 d *p.* 1805 m Mary Rogers Sol SC

STACKPOLE,
Charles: b 1745 d 1780 m Rachel Pray Pvt NH
Ebenezer: b *c.* 1750 d *p.* 1779 m Mary Ham Cpl NH

STACKPOLE, contd.
James: b 1762 d 11-10-1804 m Dorcas Holt Pvt PA
John: b 8-4-1749 d 6-26-1829 m Elizabeth Dunning Pvt NH
Joseph Young: b 8-28-1747 d 2-26-1823 m Anna Fletcher Pvt MA
Joshua, Jr.: b c. 1743 d — m Lydia Plummer Lt NH
Samuel: b 10-17-1740 d 7-18-1823 m Zervia Watson Lt NH ★

STACY, (or STACEY)
Abel: b c. 1758-60 d c. 1815 m Sarah Willis Pvt MA
Amos: b 1758 d 3-9-1812 m Abigail Burt Pvt MA
Benjamin: b 1762 d 1-10-1844 m Anna Heminway Pvt MA
Ebenezer: b 12-7-1760 d 6-9-1826 m Mercy Foster Pvt MA ★
Isaac: b 1-17-1756 d 2-28-1829 m Abigail Averill Pvt MA
John, Sr.: b c. 1740 d a. 1-7-1788 m Sarah (Dunham) Way PS Sol GA
John: b 10-23-1754 d 8-4-1804 m Ann Goodwin Pvt MA
John: b 10-16-1760 d 12-4-1846 m Mary Baldwin Sgt MA
John: b 9-12-1761 d 5-4-1835 m Mary McNeal Pvt MA ★
Molton: b 5-10-1765 d 4-1-1844 m (1)Mary Chapel (2)Abigail — Pvt MA
Nathaniel: b 9-16-1752 d 4-1-1827 m Mabel Beach Pvt CT
Nymphas: b 1764 d 2-4-1837 m Sarah Gibbs Pvt MA
Philemon: bpt 5-17-1741 d 12-17-1784 m (1)Mary Richardson (2)Mrs Molly Fairbanks 2Lt MA
Rufus: b 3-1-1734 d 2- -1824 m (1)Elizabeth Allen (2)Anna Day Pvt MA
Samuel: b 8-2-1750 d 2-4-1788 m Alice Shapleigh Mstr ME MA
Thomas: b — d 1776-1803 m Sarah Jarsey Mstr RI
Wm.: b 2-15-1733/4 d 1804 m (1)Sarah Day (2)Hannah Sheffield LCol MA
Wm.: b c. 1742 d p. 1781 m Deborah Varnum Pvt MA
Wm.: b 1746 d p. 1790 m — Pvt PA

STADDEN,
Thomas: b 1750 d 1800 m Margaretta Jones Pvt PS PA
Wm.: b 5-25-1760 d 3-3-1835 m Mary White Pvt PA ★

STAFFORD,
Amos: b 2-20-1757 d 3-27-1813 m Sarah Wagaman Sol NY
Arnold: b 2-22-1746 d 9-20-1794 m Phebe Sprague Pvt RI
Benjamin: b 4-25-1761 d 1-13-1836 m Lydia Lockwood Pvt RI
Ichabod: b 6-17-1762 d 7-30-1804 m Humility Green Fif RI ★
James: b c. 1750 d 1816 m Sarah — PS NC
James: b 8-28-1754 d 10-7-1826 m Lucretia — Sol PA
James Bayard: b c. 1758 d 8-19-1838 m Abigail Smith Mid MA NY ★
Joab: b 11-14-1729 d 11-23-1801 m Susannah Spencer Col MA ★
John: b 1755 d 8-15-1828 m Hannah Collings Matlack Pvt PA ★
John: b 8-25-1759 d 2-18-1833 m Anna Letson Pvt RI
John: b — d 1802 m — CS VT
Joseph: b 4-25-1759 d 1855 m Orpha Sweet Cpl RI ★
Joseph: b 1-16-1719 d 1-30-1791 m Rebecca Arnold Pvt RI
Joshua: b 3-6-1749 d 1809 m Susannah Cory PS RI
Joshua: b a. 1743 d a. 8-20-1795 m Martha — PS SC
Laban: b c. 1745 d p. 5-16-1811 m — PS NC VA SC
Richard: b 9-24-1763 d 10-19-1826 m Susan Brown Pvt MA
Robert: b c. 1760 d 1829 m Jane Blair Pvt SC
Samuel: b c. 1760 m Dorcas — Sol GA
Samuel: b 8-2-1759 d 11-25-1830 m Dora Wells Sgt MA
Seth: b c. 1750 d 1803/4 m Amanda Maner Sol SC
Stephen: b 7-19-1756 d 8-26-1823 m Abigail Durfee Sgt RI
Stukeley: b 5-25-1759 d 1-13-1830 m Ruth Kingsbury Pvt NH
Stukeley: b 5-20-1759 d 2-12-1826 m Rebecca Irish Ens RI
Stukeley: b 11-8-1758 d 11-12-1839 m Patience Yaw Pvt RI
Thomas: b 1763 d p. 1797 m Eunice Grinsman Pvt MA
Thomas: b c. 1740 d p. 10-11-1809 m Eve — Pvt PA
Thomas, Sr.: b 4-20-1723 d 7-20-1779 m Deadema Carpenter Pvt RI
Thomas, Jr.: b 1-19-1755 d 7-20-1805 m Lydia Corey Cpl RI MA
Wm.: b 1750 d a. 9-4-1819 m Christiana — Col PS SC
Wm.: b 1753 d 1846 m — Relph Pvt RI ★
Wm.: b 1748 d 1809 m Hulda Gordon Ens VA

STAGE,
Benjamin: b 6-4-1756-65 d 7-12-1838 m Mary Norcross Pvt NY ★

STAGER, (includes STEGER, STEIGER & STIGER)
Adam: b 1734 d 9-9-1808 m Sophia — Pvt NJ
Baltus: b 4-6-1762 d 7-28-1830 m Mary C Miller MM NJ
Frederick: b 8-28-1760 d 2-18-1824 m Elizabeth Yiengst Pvt PA
Henry: b 1759 d 7-19-1841 m (1) — Stager (2)Barbara Sweitzer Fif PA
Jacob: b 5-16-1746 d 8-13-1818 m Elizabeth Titelson Sgt PA
Peter: b 5-12-1760 d p. 3-10-1851 m Barbara Durst Pvt PA
Samuel: b c. 1752 d p. 9-26-1818 m (1)Agnes McLaurine (2)Nancy Moore PS VA

STAGG,
Cornelius: bpt 4-2-1734 d 11-13-1824 m Margreta (Banta) Demarest Pvt NJ
James: b 9-18-1737 d 5-4-1825 m Leah Brewer Capt NJ
James: b — d 1826 m Huamah Moore Sgt NJ
John: b 10-22-1754 d — m Martytge Spier Pvt NJ

John, Sr.: b 1732 d 8-23-1803 m (1)Rachel Conklin (2)Anneka Dolly Stoutenburgh CmsryGen NY
John, Jr.: b 10-26-1758 d 1803 m (1)Phebe Wood (2)Margaret DePeyster Maj NY

STAGNER,
Barney: b a. 1759 d p. 5-18-1820 m Sally — Pvt VA

STAHL, (includes STAHLE, STALL & STEELE)
Dietrich: b c. 1727 d 9- -1796 m Anna Margaret Wever 1Lt NY
George: b 1750 d 11-23-1803 m Dorothea Shoemaker Pvt NY
Henry: b 2-3-1752 d 4-1-1816 m Rosina Stemple Pvt PA
Isaac: b c. 1750 d p. 1787 m Elizabeth — Sgt PA
Jacob: b 8-21-1754 d 11-19-1833 m Barbara Stahle Pvt PA ★
Peter: b 1762 d 1856 m — Bereker Pvt NY ★

STAHLER,
Ludwig: b 1750 d a. 9-17-1815 m Catrina — Pvt PA

STAHLMAN,
John: b c. 1758 d p. 9-31-1823 m Elenor Crorey Pvt PA

STAINS,
Thomas: b 7-4-1750 d 11-3-1837 m Prudence Ann Perigo Pvt PA

STAKE,
Frederick: b c. 1755 d 4- -1805 m Barbara Halderman Pvt PA
George: b — d 11-9-1789 m Catherine — Pvt PA

STALCUP,
Wm.: b 5-27-1740 d p. 11-22-1815 m Margaret Anderson Pvt NC

STALEY, (includes STEHELEY & STEHLEY)
Balthaser, Jr.: b 8-21-1754 d c. 3- -1820 m Barbara — Pvt PA
George: b 7-6-1753 d 3-26-1839 m Janet McCall Pvt NY W★
Henry: b 2- -1746 d 7-24-1835 m Rachel VanHoesen Pvt PS NY ★
Jacob: b 1745 d 1801 m Mary Elizabeth House Pvt NY
Jacob: b 1749 d 4-18-1824 m Susanna Reybex Pvt NY
Martin: b a. 2-25-1826 m (1)Margaret — (2)Elizabeth Thompson Sol VA
Melchior: b 6-5-1719 d 3-21-1791 m Anna Barbara — PS MD
Peter: b 2-6-1753 d 7-16-1837 m (2)Margaret Munson Pvt PA ★

STALKER,
Jonathan: b 1742-4 d c. 1782 m Mary May Pvt PA

STALLARD,
Randolph: b 1757 d p. 1832 m Mary Bullitt Lt VA ★
Walter: b — d p. 7-13-1803 m (1)— (2)Hannah — PS VA

STALLINGS,
Frederick: b c. 1752 d p. 6-15-1781 m Hannah Kilgore Capt GA
John: b c. 1730 d 12-2-1787 m Elizabeth Ward PS VA
Shadrack: b c. 1750 d p. 1821 m — Capt NC

STALLWORTH,
Wm.: b 1745 d 9-9-1806 m Jemima Trippe Pvt SC

STALNACKER, (or STALNAKER)
Jacob: b c. 1740 d p. 1834 m — CS VA
Valentine: b 1758 d 11-28-1833 m (1)Catherine — (2)Lucy Jenkins PS VA

STAM,
Peter: b 1726 d 1795 m Catharine Graef Pvt PA

STAMBACH, (includes STAMBAUGH & STOMBAUGH)
Daniel: b 3-12-1748 d 1784 m Catharine — Pvt PA
Jacob: b 4-18-1761 d 5-29-1837 m Catherina Weitzel Pvt PA
Philip, Sr.: b — d p. 1790 m — Pvt PA
Philip, Jr.: b c. 1760 d p. 1798 m Barbara — Pvt PA
Philip: b a. 1748 d a. 4-18-1801 m — Pvt PA

STAMM,
George: b c. 1738 d — m Eva Bellin Pvt NY

STAMPER,
Joel: b 5-17-1755 d p. 4-30-1833 m Nancy Canady Pvt NC ★
Joshua: b c. 1760 d a. 1850 m Mary Blevins Pvt VA

STAMPS,
John: b c. 1740 d 1812 m Eleanor Dodson Ens PS VA
John: b 1763 d 12-1-1845 m Mary McGrew Pvt VA

STANAGE,
Thomas: b 1759 d 1832 m Sarah Green Sgt VA ★

STANBROUGH, (or STANBRO)
John: b 3-22-1758 d 5-24-1844 m Hannah Whittlesey Cpl RI ★
Lemuel: b 1764 d 2-28-1842 m (1)Ruth — (2)Jane Osborn Pvt CT ★
Thomas: b 11-25-1749 d 11-12-1801 m Catherine Goldsmith MM NY

STANCLIFF, (or STANCLIFT)
Lemuel: b 4-9-1764 d 4-3-1848 m Mehitable Goff Pvt CT ★

STANDART,
Oliver: b 3-17-1766 d 8-7-1841 m (1)Nancy Jane Hancock (2)Sally Way Pvt MA★

STANDEFER, (includes STANDIFER, STANDIFOR & STANDIFORD)
Benjamin: b 5-17-1764 d 3-18-1839 m (1)Rachel Forrest (2)Nancy Echols OrdlSgt NC ★
David: b 9-23-1758 d 1-27-1822 m Frances Ashby Ens VA
Luke: b c. 1758 d p. 1810 m Mary Ann Price Lt VA
Wm.: b 3-30-1757 d 6-21-1826 m Jemimah Jones Lt VA

STANDIN,
Henderson: b 3-19-1725 d 3-29-1781 m Frances L Blount PS NC

STANDISH,
Amasa: b 1-8-1756 d 10-11-1847 m Zerviah Smith Pvt CT
Asa: b 9-28-1763 d 9-1-1828 m Rebecca Sherwood Pvt MA
David: b 4-9-1723 d 6-4-1795 m Hannah Magoon Pvt MA
Ebenezer: b 9-6-1760 d 6-27-1834 m Lydia Cushman Pvt MA ★
Hadley: b 2-4-1759 d 11-10-1813 m Abigail Garnet Pvt MA
Israel: b 4-22-1738 d a. 4- -1806 m Sarah — Pvt MA
Lemuel: b 6-24-1746 d 1-9-1824 m (1)Rachel Jackson (2)— Crawford Pvt MA
Miles: b 1748 d 7-22-1819 m Naomi Keith Cpl MA
Moses, Jr.: b 4-20-1733 d 3-22-1778 m Mary Eddy Pvt MA
Nathan: b 9-27-1753 d p. 1779 m Esther Smith Pvt CT
Samuel: b 5-8-1753 d 5-18-1841 m Lois Curtis Sgt MA ★
Shadrach: b 5-12-1746 d 11-29-1837 m Mary Churchill Drm MA
Thomas: b 5-12-1724 d 3-3-1798 m Sarah Tracy Pvt MA
Wm.: b 6-24-1737 d 11-1-1828 m Abigail Stetson Pvt MA
Zacharia: b 5-30-1739 d 3-26-1780 m (1)Rebecca Wood (2)Olive Pool Pvt MA

STANFIELD,
James: b 2-4-1753 d 11-3-1840 m Fanny Gwinn Sgt NC ★
Thomas: b. 1747 d p. 12-19-1796 m Elizabeth — PS Lt VA

STANFORD,
Abner: b 5-12-1747 d 5-27-1821 m (1)Jemima Green (2)Sarah McIntyre Pvt MA
Caleb: b 8-31-1716 d p. 1776 m Ruth Cozens PS NH
John: b c. 1760 d 1825 m Rachel — Pvt GA
John: b c. 1746 d 1-16-1842 m Elizabeth Thorndike McCaffery Pvt MA★
Joshua, Sr.: b 1740 d 5-1-1826 m Mary Rookes Sol MD
Josiah: b 10-3-1724 d p. 1780 m Sarah Woodbury Pvt MA
Moses: b 8-3-1753 d 11-2-1827 m Jemima Flagg Pvt MA ★
Richard: b 12-19-1740 d p. 1784 m Elizabeth Winch Pvt MA
Samuel: b 10-1-1764 d 5-16-1833 m Margaret Torrence Pvt NC ★
Stephen: b c. 1742 d p. 9-24-1805 m (1)— (2)Nancy — Pvt MD
Thomas: b 12-28-1756 d 3-2-1795 m Milly Disharoon Sgt MD
Thomas: b c. 1756 d p. 1843 m Martha Brown Pvt SC ★
Wm.: b — d a. 9-4-1810 m — Sol GA

STANHOPE,
Peter: b 11-29-1759 d 1845 m Elizabeth Pramenter Pvt MA
Samuel, Jr.: b 10-15-1756 d 10-22-1839 m Mary Goodenow Pvt MA★

STANIFORD,
Jeremiah, Jr.: b 9-28-1751 d 2-29-1816 m Mary Fowler Pvt MA

STANLEY, (includes STANDLEY & STANDLY)
Comfort: b 1751 d 8-26-1818 m Marcy Viall Sgt RI
Daniel: b 3-21-1748 d 2-9-1798 m (1)Anna Daggett (2)Catherine Pond Gould Pvt MA
Dennis: b 4-23-1749 d 3-17-1813 m Sally Bishop Ens NH W★
Elisha: b 1-13-1762 d 1848 m Esther Merwin Sol CT ★
Frederick: b 1-20-1754 d 1-9-1795 m Martha Bigelow Pvt CT
Gad: b 3-21-1735 d 1-10-1815 m Mary (Burnham) Judd Col PS CT
George: bpt 10-18-1741 d 8-17-1817 m Hannah Porter Lt PS CT
Hezekiah: b 7-15-1749 d 2-7-1778 m Jerusha Marther Pvt CT
James: b c. 1744 d p. 1792 m Esther Gridley Pvt CT
James: b 2-1-1725-35 d 4-19-1793 m Winnifred — Pvt NC
James: b 1765 d 10-9-1845 m Mary Bradberry Pvt NC
John: b 1749 d 9-30-1806 m (1)Mary Fuller (2)Sarah Danic (3)Anna Anterrel Pvt VT
John Wright: b 4-9-1742 d 6-4-1789 m Annie Cogdell PS NC
Jonathan: bpt 4-12-1747 d 10-13-1810 m Lydia Preston Pvt MA
Jonathan: b 8-18-1733 d 5-5-1811 m Hannah Shepherd PS MA
Jonathan: b 8-26-1748 d 7-12-1789 m Lois Moors Pvt NH
Jonathan: b 5-2-1711 d p. 1791 m Abigail Gould PS NH
Joseph: b 1745 d 3-18-1833 m Martha Rogers Pvt NH W★
Kenny: b 9-17-1750 d 4-4-1816 m Elizabeth Biggs Pvt MA
Marshall: b 1730 d 11- -1796 m Thamer — Lt PA
Matthew: b 6-22-1718 d p. 1785 m Mary Putney PS NH
Moses: b 1757 d — m Mary Mills Allen Mar VA ★
Noah: b 4-16-1759 d 5-4-1829 m (1)Lucy Lewis (2)Experience Wells (3)Naomi Burritt Cav CT

Oliver: b 10-10-1743 d 2-22-1813 m Desire Yale Capt CT
Pentecost: b 1739 d p. 1-1-1785 m Experience Fairbanks Pvt NH
Rial: b 3-17-1759 d 5-9-1841 m Abigail Fairbanks Pvt MA ★
Richard: b 12-5-1750 d 1816 m Diana Covington Pvt VA
Samuel: b 1719 d 12-13-1790 m Jerusha Roberts CS MA
Samuel: b 1732 d 1792 m Sibyl Sage Pvt NH
Samuel, Jr.: b c. 1742 d 8-10-1818 m (1)— Peasley (2)Mrs Martha (Hendricks) Dukes Pvt VA
Sands: b c. 1742 d p. 2-26-1796 m Zilphah Edwards PS NC
Solomon: b 5-13-1740 d 3-9-1819 m Patience Perry Lt MA ★
Theodore: b 10-8-1752 d 12-14-1830 m Elizabeth Pitkin Pvt CT
Thomas: b 9-27-1762 d 3-14-1816 m (1)Anna Ford (2)Miranda Nott Cpl CT
Thomas: b 5-12-1757 d 10-31-1800 m Edith Stanley Sol VA
Thomas: b a. 1760 d 1-11-1799 m Susannah Gurnell Pvt VA
Timothy: b 6-8-1729 d 6-9-1793 m Mary Bailey Capt CT
Timothy: b 3-8-1727 d 4-28-1817 m Lydia Newell PS CT
Timothy: b 8-29-1730 d 12-26-1776 m Mary Hopkins Pvt CT
Wm.: b 4-5-1745 d 1- -1827 m Mary — Pvtr MA
Wm.: b 6-4-1729 d 11-11-1807 m Elizabeth Walker PS NC

STANNARD, (or STANARD)
Eliakim: b 8-31-1752 d 6-28-1838 m Bethia Kelsey Pvt CT ★
Elijah: b 1752 d 1841 m Peggy Divall Pvt CT ★
Ezra Peabody: b 3-13-1766 d p. 1847 m Margaret Norton Pvt CT ★
Jasper: b 1747 d 1839 m Abigail Post Pvt CT ★
John: b 1-27-1760 d 5-26-1843 m Azubah — Pvt CT
Larkin: b 5- -1760 d 1840 m Elizabeth Beverley Chew Cadet VA
Lemuel, Jr.: b 4-25-1750 d 6-27-1821 m Christian Spencer Pvt VT
Libbeus: b 12-7-1756 d 9-5-1846 m Eunice — Pvt VT CT ★
Peter: b 1731 d 8-3-1778 m Jemima Parmele CG CT
Samuel: b 1749 d 4-8-1815 m Jemima Wilcox Sgt CT
Wm.: b 1750 d 1820 m Mindwell Buel Pvt NH
Wm. b c. 1750 d 10-23-1807 m Elizabeth Carter QM VA

STANSBURY, (includes STANBERY, STANBURY, STANSBERY)
Caleb: b c. 1760 d p. 3-15-1843 m (1)Rebecca Cook (2)Mary—PS MD
Dixon, Sr.: b 12-6-1720 d 1806 m Penelope Body PS MD
Edmund: b 10-6-1746 d 1801 m Belinda Slade Talbot 1Lt MD
Luke: b 1758 d 10-13-1848 m Nancy Haddox Pvt NC
Recompence: b 10-9-1710 d 5-20-1777 m (1)—(2)Margaret—PS NJ
Samuel: b 6-26-1754 d 5-20-1823 m (1)Mary — (2)Mary Andrews Baxter Pvt NJ
Solomon: b 9-26-1755 d 4-1-1842 m Jane Lewing Pvt NC MD ★
Thomas: b 1741 d 12-3-1816 m (1)Ruth Ghant (2)Deborah — 2Lt MD
Tobias Emerson: b 1758 d 10-25-1849 m (1)Mary Buffington (2)Ann Dew (3)Mrs Anna D. Steinbeck NCdr MD ★
Wm.: b 1-20-1716 d 11-3-1788 m Elizabeth Ensor PS MD

STANSILL, (or STANSELL)
George: b 2-25-1760 d 1-7-1832 m Leah Pickard Pvt NY
Nicholas: b 9-11-1755 d 12-11-1819 m Margaret Featherly Pvt NY

STANTON,
Abel: b 1-9-1749 d 1821 m Olive Reede Pvt CT
Amos: b 11-29-1750 d 9-6-1781 m Thankful Billings Capt CT
Amos: b c. 1740 d 8-14-1806 m Marcy Davis Pvt MA
Asa: b 3-2-1760 d 11-12-1817 m Keziah Kimball Pvt CT
Augustus: b 3-22-1745 d 4-10-1822 m Eunice Crandall Capt RI
Benjamin: b 1756 d 5-10-1838 m (1)Elizabeth — (2)Sarah Rood Pvt NY W★
Ebenezer: b — d 7-24-1811 m Mary Palmer Pvt CT
Edward: b 6-10-1761 d 7-27-1832 m — Page Vol CT
Elijah: b 12-28-1750 d 1833 m Jemima Beach Pvt CT
Elijah: b 1754 d 5- -1847 m Lucy Goodell Pvt CT MA ★
Enoch: b 9-15-1745 d 9-6-1791 m Waity Dyer Lt CT
George: b 1-29-1733 d 10-27-1809 m Agnes — Pvt NY
Isaac Wheeler: b 1-14-1743 d 1831 m Ruth Ayers Lt CT
Jason: b 8-25-1760 d 2-1-1842 m (1)Kezia Brumbly (2)Sabra Olen (3)Sally Beckwith Pvt CT ★
John: b 11-16-1746 d 3-16-1818 m Huldah Freeman Sgt CT
John: b 1761 d 5-24-1851 m Elizabeth Fish Sgt CT
John, Sr.: b 5-13-1736 d 1819 m Susanna Champlin Sol CT
John: b 6-22-1758 d 9- -1819 m Huldah Pomeroy Pvt MD
John: b 1756 d 9- -1832 m Elizabeth Short Sgt NC
John: b 2- -1722 d 9-1-1814 m Dorothy Richardson Adj VT
Jonathan: b 1716 d 1814 m Hannah — Pvt DE
Joseph: b 7-19-1739 d 9-11-1807 m — PS RI
Joshua: b 2-2-1752 d — m Sarah Cross Sgt Smn RI
Joshua: b 6-21-1721 d 10-25-1819 m (1)Hannah Cottrell Randall (2)Molly — Capt CT
Joshua: b 4- -1740 d p. 1803 m Abigail Sackett Capt CT
Ludovick: b 5-22-1749 d 1829 m (1)Nancy — (2)Thankful (Stanton) Pvt NY
Nathan: b 12-15-1749 d 9-26-1835 m Anna Stanton Ens CT
Nathan: b 4-3-1732 d p. 1790 m Elizabeth Billings Sol CT
Peleg: b 3-13-1758 d 4-28-1799 m Lydia Hewitt Pvt CT
Phineas: b 10-28-1719 d 2-3-1790 m Elizabeth — PS CT
Robert: b 1751 d 5-1-1811 m Rachel Reeve Pvt NY
Rufus: b 1751 d 2-13-1832 m Rachael Reeve Pvt NY
Samuel: b 6-26-1726 d 3- -1803 m Mary Palmer Sgt CT
Samuel: b 4-16-1760 d 2-4-1838 m Hannah Palmer Pvt CT

STANTON, contd.
Samuel: b 4-17-1759 d 4-15-1816 m Martha Carpenter Morse Pvt CT
Samuel: b 12-2-1745 d p. 6-18-1822 m — Lt RI
Thomas: b 12-20-1729 d 7-30-1799 m Sarah Chesebrough PS CT
Wm.: b 3-5-1745 d 8-12-1828 m Hannah Williams Capt CT
Wm.: b 8-19-1744 d 2-23-1811 m Eunice Palmer PS CT
Wm.: b 1730 d 2-10-1777 m Elizabeth Brock Pvt NH
Wm.: b c. 1750 d p. 1811 m Lucy Blackwell Pvt VA

STANWOOD,
Isaac: b 5-2-1755 d 10-15-1821 m Eunice Hodgkins Pvt MA
John: b 7-23-1748 d — m Sarah Burgin Pvt MA
Joseph: b 9-13-1740 d 2-1-1813 m (1)Lydia Lunt (2)Mrs Sarah Ela
   Pvt MA
Joseph: b 1-12-1764 d 9-5-1833 m Sarah Dodge Pvt MA
Samuel: b 11-6-1719 d 3-22-1790 m (1)Mrs Janet (Lithgow)
   McFarland (2)Mary Woodside PS CS MA
Solomon: b 4-18-1736 d 11-4-1784 m (2)Susanna Wheeler Goss
   Cdr MA
Wm.: b 4-17-1727 d 7-17-1797 m Elizabeth Reed Capt ME MA
Wm.: b 4-5-1752 d 6-24-1829 m (1)Mary Orr (2)Hannah Thompson
   (3)Ruth Thompson 1Lt ME MA
Wm.: b 9-12-1744 d 2-11-1800 m (1)Hannah Moody (2)Hannah
   Chase PS CS Sol MA

STANYAN, (or STANYON)
Jonathan: b c. 1740-42 d 11-11-1777 m Martha Hook Lt NH

STAPLEFORT,
Edward: b 9-30-1745 d 1805 m Sarah Tubman Capt MD

STAPLER,
John: b 1755-8 d 1794 m Jean Welch Sol GA
Thomas: b 1740 d 2- -1826 m Ruth Story Pvt GA

STAPLES, (or STAPLE)
Abraham: b 4-4-1731 d 10- -1792 m (1)Mary Harvey (2)Ruth D.
   Wheelock 1Lt MA
David: b — d p. 4-30-1821 m Frances — Sol GA
Ebenezer: b 1759 d 4-14-1856 m Charity Caswell Pvt MA
Elias, Sr.: b 5-27-1738 d 1825 m (1)Lydia Hamilton (2)Abigail
   Nichols Pvt MA
George: b 3-9-1756 d 9-23-1827 m Lois Aldrich Cpl MA
George: b 1750 d 1820 m Harriet Satchwell Pvt RI
Hezekiah: b 1734 d p. 1777 m Mary Paul Sgt NH MA
Isaac: b 11-29-1764 d 5-29-1848 m Esther Benson Pvt MA ★
Jacob: b 1730-5 d 3-20-1818 m Lois Edson Pvt NH
John: b 10-4-1737 d 8-10-1813 m (1)Elizabeth Sherwood (2)Mrs
   Esther Burr Hill Pvt CT
John: b 1743 d 2-16-1804 m Susanna Perkins Pvt CT
John: b 5-18-1754 d 2-2-1843 m Margaret Teeple Sgt MD ★
John: b 9-14-1757 d 6-28-1837 m Betsey Upsher Pvt VA W★
Jonathan: b 4-29-1753 d 12-28-1832 m Rachel Holbrook Sol MA
Joseph: b 1746 d 6-21-1832 m Louisa Smith Pvt ME
Joshua: b 3-15-1757 d 1-20-1840 m Hope Pierce Sgt MA
Josiah: b 3-18-1742 d 1799 m Eunice Fogg Capt MA
Mark: b 1761 d 4-3-1830 m Sarah Rackley Slr Pvt MA ★
Moses: b 1753 d 1846 m Judith Eaton Pvt MA
Nahor: b 2-3-1756 d 2-9-1820 m Prudence Darling Cpl MA
Nathan: b 5-28-1733 d 2-3-1804 m (1)Jemima Comstock (2)Martha
   Comstock Ens RI
Nathaniel: b 8-16-1753 d 9-24-1827 m Elizabeth Leighton Pvt MA
Nathaniel: b 5-3-1727 d 11-4-1800 m Margery Frost Pvt PA
Robert: b c. 1760 d 6- -1820 m Annis Perkins Pvt NC
Samuel: b 4-19-1733 d p. 1789 m (1)Sybil Winslow (2)Mrs Lydia
   Wells Pvt MA
Samuel: b 3-23-1762 d 3- -1825 m Lucinda Penn Maj VA
Seth: b 1749 d 10-20-1801 m (1)Iseballa Babson Collins
   (2)Asenath Soule Cpl MA
Stephen: b 1749/50 d 3- -1805 m Mary Starke Pvt GA
Stephen: b 3-27-1739 d 12-5-1798 m (1)Jude Merrill (2)Susannah
   Hobbs PS ME MA
Thaddeus: b — d c. 1815 m Miss Nichols Pvt CT
Thomas: b c. 1758 d p. 11-12-1827 m Mary — Pvt NC

STAPLETON,
Edward, Sr.: b c. 1715 d p. 5-12-1780 m Rachel — PS MD
George Lawson: b 12-21-1760 d 5-30-1832 m Margaret Downer Pvt
   VA GA
John: b 9-29-1751 d 5-17-1820 m Rosena Miller Lt PA
John: b c. 1745 d 1809 m Maria Magdalena Hagenbuch PS PA
Tobias: b 1715 d 1805 m — PS PA

STAPP,
Achilles: b 12-22-1755 d 9-4-1849 m (1)Margaret Vawter (2)Mrs
   Ann Milbank Delph Pvt VA

STARBIRD, (includes STARBARD)
John: b c. 1756 d 11-4-1824 m Chloe Bradford Ens MA ★
John: b 1754 d 12-14-1839 m Hannah Stroud Pvt MA NY ★
Moses: b 7-9-1743 d p. 1777 m Martha Atwood Pvt MA
Simeon: b a. 1750 d p. 1793 m — Pvt NH

STARBUCK,
Matthew: b 3-6-1750 d 1815 m (1)Rose Barnard (2)Lydia Barney
   (3)Anna Swain (4)Dinah Macy Smn MA
Sylvanus: b 6-6-1727 d 5-9-1813 m Mary Howes CS MA

STARING, (or STARIN)
Adam A.: b 1752 d 1812 m Mrs Hannah Harter Myers Bellinger
   Ens NY
Adam: b 1756 d 6-6-1812 m Nelly Qackenbush Sgt Btm NY W★
Adam: b 1762 d c. 1859 m — Sterling Pvt NY
Henry: b 1743 d 5-27-1808 m Elizabeth Hess Capt NY
Henry: b c. 1730 d p. 1790 m (1)— (2)— Pvt NY
John: b 8-31-1754 d 2-19-1832 m Jane Wemple Pvt NY
Nicholas: b 5-11-1749 d p. 1809 m (1)Catherine Reichtmyer (2)Mary
   Cunningham 2Lt NY
Nicholas: b 1712 d 1802 m Anna — Sol NY
Nicholas Henry: b 1766 d — m Jane Dygert Pvt NY
Nicholas N: b 1753 d 11-12-1816 m — Pvt NY
Peter Joseph: b c. 1750 d p. 1793 m Maria Dedrick Pvt NY
Philip: b 1757 d — m Margaret — Pvt NY

STARK, (or STARKE)
Aaron: b 1755 d c. 1835 m (1)Mary Bennett (2)Elizabeth Evans
   (3)Rebecca Griffin (4)Tacy Adelaide Wilson Sol CT
Aaron: b 11-3-1732 d 7-3-1778 m Margaret — Pvt PA
Amos: b 3-23-1750 d 11-10-1832 m Polly Vantele Ens NJ ★
Archibald: b 1740 d 1-17-1819 m Mary Anderson Lt NH
Bolling: b 9-20-1733 d 1788 m (1)— Burwell (2)Elizabeth
   Bellefield (3)Mrs Ann Orr PS VA
Christopher: b c. 1750 d p. 11-9-1807 m Margaret Vineyard Pvt PS
   VA PA
Daniel, Sr.: b 1725 d 11- -1787 m Jemima Colver Pvt CT
Daniel 3d: b 1762 d 8-14-1800 m Elizabeth Frink Pvt CT
Elizabeth Page: b 2-16-1737 d 6-29-1814 m MGen John Stark PS NH
Henry: b 4-19-1762 d 1-22-1807 m Elizabeth Kennedy Pvt PA
Israel: b 6-20-1753 d 5-7-1830 m (1)Anna Webster (2)Sarah Buell
   Cpl CT
James: b 5-22-1734 d 7-20-1777 m Elizabeth Carey Pvt CT
James: b 12-12-1760 d 6-10-1812 m (1)Sarah Pearce (2)Susanna
   Crandall Pvt NY
James: b 2-7-1757 d c. 1819 m (1)Jane Fristoe (2)Susanna Hart
   (3)Rachel Brice Pvt VA
James: b 12-21-1747 d p. 10-13-1822 m Elizabeth — PS VA
John: b 1721 d 1800 m Sarah Hough Pvt CT
John: b 8-28-1728 d 5-8-1822 m Elizabeth Page MGen NH
John: b 1753 d 12-14-1825 m Tryphena Cary Sgt NH
John: b 4-1-1733 d 5-8-1825 m Mary Dilla LCol NJ
John: b c. 1743 d 9-26-1806 m Eunice Adams Capt VT
John, Sr.: b a. 1715 d p. 1783 m Ann Wyatt PS Col VA
John, Jr.: b 4-27-1742 d 10- -1800 m Elizabeth Shepherd Sol PS VA
John C: b 11-6-1748 d 5-16-1814 m Sarah English Capt VA
Joseph: b 12-17-1750 d 3-17-1841 m Phebe Pitney Sgt NJ PA
Joseph: b 1753 d 1821 m Sarilda Guthrie Dr VA
Moses: b 6- -1716 d p. 1790 m Elizabeth Holdredge Pvt NH
Nathan: b 1743 d 1830 m (1)Olive Morgan(2)Esther Gallup Pvt CS VT
Nathan: b 12-25-1763 d 5-23-1837 m Dorcas Dixon Pvt NY
Robert, Jr.: b 1-10-1752 d 9-4-1830 m (2)Mary Hay Adj SC
Samuel: b 10-8-1736 d 12-12-1794 m Elizabeth Powers PS CS NH
Wm.: b 1723 d 7-5-1795 m Ann Appleton Pvt CT
Wm.: b 5-8-1745 d 1795 m Polly Cary Pvt NY
Wm.: b 5-20-1763 d 3-4-1826 m Martha Morgan Sol NC
Wm.: b 12-14-1754 d 12-20-1838 m Mary Kendall OrdlSgt VA

STARKER,
Aaron: b c. 1755 d p. 1789 m Charity — Capt NJ

STARKEY,
John: b c. 1745 d p. 7-19-1818 m Elizabeth — Sol VA
Joseph: b 2-12-1755 d 7-6-1823 m Waitstill Morse Pvt NH
Peter: b 1-29-1750 d 10-25-1821 m Lona Grosvner Pvt NH
Timothy: b 11-26-1739 d 11-1-1817 m (1)Rachel Bushnell (2)Hepsibah
   Pratt (3)Chloe — Capt CT
Wm.: b 1742 d 3-23-1788 m Sarah Martin Pvt MA

STARKWEATHER,
Amos: b 2-7-1763 d 3-20-1844 m Elizabeth Benjamin Pvt CT
Asa: b 11-25-1753 d 6-11-1811 m Amy Kimball Pvt CT
Belcher: b 1-23-1755 d 3-1-1831 m Mary Leonard Pvt CT
Charles: b 4-29-1759 d 7-9-1843 m Martha Kingsley Pvt CT
Ephraim: b 5-24-1757 d 5-10-1840 m Rachael Clark Pvt CT RI ★
Ezra: b 12-8-1759 d 11-12-1822 m Mary Cary Pvt CT
Jabez: b 1-9-1734/5 d 4-1-1815 m Martha Cole PS CT
Jesse: bpt 2-9-1739 d 11-7-1825 m Mary Kinne Capt CT
John: b 8-14-1752 d 1-26-1837 m Hannah Stimson Leonard Sgt CT ★
Roger: b 12-9-1752 d 5-12-1812 m (1)Jerusha Parker (2)Mariam
   Griswold Pvt VT
Samuel: b 3-19-1719 d 3-26-1786 m Sarah Purple Pvt CT
Thomas: b 6-25-1749 d 11-4-1837 m (1)Sybil Anderson (2)Anna
   Hayes Pvt CT ★

STARLING, (includes STERLING)
Roderick: b 1760 d 2-15-1828 m Esther Hill Pvt VA

Wm.: b 1755 d 2- -1830 m Sarah — Sol NC
Wm.: b 9-4-1756 d 12-5-1826 m Susanna Lyne Col VA

STARNER,
Michael: b 1758 d 1822 m Katharine Durst Pvt MD

STARR,
Benjamin: b — d 9-3-1775 m Christiana Church Pvt CT
Caleb: b 1739 d 9- -1800 m Bulah Gregory Sol CT
Comfort: b 8-10-1731 d 11-30-1812 m Judith Cooper Capt VT
Daniel: b 1724 d 4-27-1777 m Rachel Starr Maj CT
Daniel: b 12-26-1741 d 6-5-1780 m Lucy Douglass Lt CT
Daniel: b 4-8-1759 d 3-23-1809 m Rachel Buell Fif CT
David: b 3-21-1738 d 8-11-1813 m (1)Ruth Moore (2)Hannah
  Goodwin Capt CT
David, Sr.: b 12-7-1724 d 2-11-1810 m Abigail Beebe PS CT
David, Jr.: b 12-2-1755 d 3-13-1814 m Lucy Sanford Maj CT
Eleazer, Sr.: b c. 1720 d 4-26-1777 m Rebecca — Sol CT
Eleazer, Jr.: b 1758 d 12-23-1810 m Rebecca Raymond Pvt CT
Elijah: b 1751 d 7-19-1806 m Mary Smith Pvt CT
Ezra: b 8-9-1753 d 5-8-1805 m Elizabeth Codwise Maj CT
George: b 11-26-1740 d 1-28-1820 m Anna Catharine Carnell
  Capt CT
Henry: b c. 1752 d p. 1827 m Mary — Sol MD
James: b 5-2-1740 d 11-20-1830 m Mary Winter Sol MA
Jared: b 1-14-1748 d 10-26-1838 m (1)Mary Cook (2)Abigail Hazard
  (3)Esther (Hazard) Niles Capt PS CT
Jehosaphat: b 1-31-1759 d 9-17-1814 m Mary Warne Ens CT
Jesse: b 11-13-1753 d 5-21-1798 m Mary Brown Dewey Sgt CT ★
John: b 1-16-1743 d 8-10-1824 m Mary Sharp Pvt CT
Johnathan: b 4-20-1733 d 11-21-1793 m (1)Sarah Leffingwell
  (2)Mary (Perkins) Bishop Pvt CT
Jonathan: b c. 1738-40 d 2- -1823 m Elizabeth Ruggles PS CT
Jonathan: b 3-18-1764 d 5-6-1838 m Mary Dibble Pvt CT
Joseph: b 1726 d 4-3-1802 m Mary Benedict Pvt PS CT
Josiah: b 1740 d 10-15-1813 m Sarah Mygatt Col CT
Josiah: b 1-27-1751 d 4-12-1837 m Mary Warner OrdlSgt CT
Levi: b 4-9-1759 d 9-3-1810 m Mabel Read Cmsry CT
Micajah: b 4-2-1746 d 3-2-1820 m (1)Anna Betts (2)Mrs Anna
  Clark Tms PS CT
Nathan: b 4-14-1755 d 7-29-1821 m Polly Pomeroy Sol CT
Nicholas: b 1-10-1741 d 9-6-1781 m Hannah Street Sgt CT
Noah: b 3-24-1753 d 1-6-1782 m Sarah Keeler Pvt CT
Richard: b 5-14-1718 d 2-25-1805 m Priscilla Smith Pvt CT
Samuel Moore: b 11-1-1765 d 8-21-1844 m Abigail Rockwell Pvt
  CT ★
Thaddeus: b 12-14-1759 d 5-3-1840 m Lydia Trowbridge Pvt CT
Thomas: b c. 1720 d 4-27-1806 m Mary Sherman Capt CT ★
Thomas: b c. 1722 d 1787 m Elizabeth Closson Pvt CT
Timothy, Sr.: b 12-24-1730 d 1-3-1802 m (1)Eunice Parsons (2)Mrs
  Abigail Hamlin Mstr CT
Timothy, Jr.: b 4-16-1753 d 3-30-1797 m Mary Fosdick Cpl CT
Vine: b 1-19-1716 d 1-1-1799 m Mary Street Sgt CT
Wm.: b 4-3-1747 d 1-24-1825 m Hannah Tallman Capt CT
Wm.: b 4-20-1745 d 12-31-1816 m (1)Freelove Bailey (2)Mary Stark
  Lt CT ★

STARRETT, (includes STARRITT)
David: b 12-27-1736 d 3-19-1813 m (1)Mary McClincock (2)Elizabeth
  Thorndike Langdell PS CS NH
James: b 1751 d 1849 m Nancy Cooper 2Lt NC
John: b 3-14-1757 d 1-24-1840 m Mary — Pvt Mar PA ★
John: b 1748 d 1810 m Mary Webb Pvt PA
Thomas: b 1738 d 1-31-1822 m Rebecca Lewis Capt MA
Wm.: b 5-4-1743 d 8-3-1829 m Abagail Fisher Pvt NH

START,
George: b — d — m Mary Tucker Pvt NH
Wm.: b 3-24-1746/7 d 2-11-1781 m Keziah Bullard Sgt NH

STARTZMAN,
Henry: b 5-5-1748 d 4-23-1811 m Eve — PS MD

STATHAM,
John: b a. 1760 d 1823 m — PS Pvt VA

STATON,
Ezekiel: b c. 1760 d p. 2-25-1815 m Mary Taylor PS NC
Jesse: b c. 1750 d 1813 m — Sol NC

**STATTLER, (includes STADLER, STATLER, STETLER,
STETTLER, STITELER & STOTLER)**
Christian: b 2-3-1741 d 12-5-1813 m Catharine Elizabeth Kurtz
  Pvt PA
Daniel: b 1730 d 10- -1788 m Catharine — Pvt PA
Heinrich: b 1754 d p. 1812 m Eva Barbara Sternenger Pvt PA
Henry: b 10-2-1763 d 2-12-1840 m Sarah Hass Pvt PA
Jacob: b 1731 d 1780 m Elizabeth — Pvt PA
Jacob: b c. 1751 d c. 2-19-1790 m Nancy Stites Lt PA
John Jasper: b 1724 d 12-3-1796 m Maria Elizabeth Scansbrook
  Col VA
Peter: b c. 1744 d 3-23-1811 m Eve — Pvt PA
Rudolph: b a. 1750 d 5-5-1825 m (1)Barbara Scroogs (2)Fanny
  Bush Capt PA

STAUBER,
Christian Gottlieb: b 1761 d 2-1-1837 m Anna Maria Baumgarten
  Sol NC

STAYNER,
Jacob: b a. 1762 d 1798 m Elizabeth — Pvt PA
Roger: b 1-15-1753 d 5-17-1839 m (2)Sarah Hough Capt PA
Wm.: b 5-4-1759 d 4-5-1840 m Mary Renelds Pvt PA

STEARLY, (or STAIRLEY)
Jacob: b c. 1754 d 1789 m Mary Ursula — Sol SC

STEARNS, (includes STARNS, STARNES, STERN, STERNS)
Aaron: b 2-2-1746 d 9-11-1807 m Esther Glazier Cpl NH
Abraham: b 4-2-1757 d 1825 m Esther Warren Pvt MA
Asa: b 7-30-1758 d 2-2-1852 m (1)Lucy Cady (2)Mrs Phoebe
  Dunham Pvt MA NH
Asahel: b 1755 d c. 1806 m Mary Smith Pvt MA
Bartholomew: b 8-4-1742 d p. 1786 m Mary Raymond Pvt MA
Benjamin: b 9-12-1757 d 5-24-1836 m Susannah Frye Cpl MA
Benjamin: b 12-27-1728 d 5-26-1801 m Hannah Seger Pvt MA
Benjamin: b 12-3-1754 d 11-10-1808 m Mehitable Holt Sol NH
Charles: b c. 1756 d 1818 m Susannah Waller Sgt VA
Daniel: b 8-3-1729 d 8-21-1779 m Hannah Fuller Pvt MA
Daniel: b 12-17-1760 d 6-19-1824 m Elizabeth Knowlton Pvt MA ★
Daniel: b 1756 d 5-4-1849 m (1)Jerusha Clarke (2)Lois Rice Pvt NH ★
David: b — d p. 1789 m (1)Lois Crouch (2)Miriam Walker Pvt MA
David, Sr.: b 3-25-1729 d 2-28-1788 m Hannah Burnell CS MA
David, Jr.: b 7-26-1757 d 9-5-1836 m Susanna Beal Pvt MA
Ebenezer, Jr.: b 1-19-1747 d 10-8-1833 m (1)Rachel Jones (2)Anna
  (Hyde) Griswold Sgt MA
Ebenezer: b c. 1749 d 1801 m Thankful Alvord Pvt MA
Ebenezer: b 1-26-1745 d 6-30-1834 m Rebecca Lackey Pvt MA
Ebenezer: b 12-25-1744 d 1816 m Rachel Ames Pvt VT
Edward: b 5-9-1726 d 6-11-1793 m Lucy Wyman Capt MA
Eleazer: b — d 1809 m Aurelia Castle Pvt VT
Elias: b 6-21-1754 d p. 1795 m Sarah Hutchins Lt CT
Elias: b 9-30-1753 d 4-2-1845 m Sarah Keyes Pvt MA ★
Elijah: b 6-15-1735 d 10-3-1801 m Lucy Lane Lt MA
Elijah: b 8-19-1762 d 1-25-1823 m (1)Lucretia Johnson (2)Catherine
  Clisbee Pvt MA
Eliphaz: b 8-19-1736 d 4-3-1803 m Hannah Clark Lt MA
Elisha: b 8-8-1756 d 8-30-1789 m Judith Peirce Pvt MA
Ephraim: b 1-10-1739 d 9-2-1808 m Prudence Wilder Capt MA
Ezekiel: b 2-20-1743 d p. 1779 m — Pvt MA
Ezra: b c. 1756 d p. 1835 m Desire Baker Pvt MA
George: b 4-18-1745 d 8-25-1795 m Sarah West Pvt DE
George: b 4-16-1741 d 1-1812 m Keziah Palmer Pvt MA
George: b 4-25-1762 d 7-13-1845 m Ruth Watson Pvt MA
Increase, Jr.: b 7-1-1763 d 11-30-1830 m Mercy Bassett Pvt MA
Isaac: b 6-13-1750 d 4-29-1807 m Mary Crosby Sgt MA
Isaac: b 1736 d 1818 m Rebecca Jewett Pvt MA
Isaac: b 6-16-1722 d 3-23-1808 m Sarah Abbott CS PS MA
Jacob: b 1750-60 d p. 1-14-1812 m Elizabeth — Sol KY VA
John: b 1-11-1736 d 9-11-1788 m Elizabeth Willis Mil PS CT
John: b 1743 d p. 1780 m Elizabeth Willard Pvt MA
John: b 4-11-1751 d 12-25-1841 m (1)Mary Baldwin (2)Lucy Merrill
  Pvt MA ★
John: b 7-23-1712 d 8-15-1792 m Rebecca Dean CS PS MA
John: b 10-15-1750 d 7-1-1823 m (1)Lucy Shedd (2)Sarah Hamlin
  2Lt NH VT ★
John: b 2-17-1728 d 10-2-1810 m Rachel Codman Pvt NH
John: b 1-16-1762 d 1-23-1843 m Sarah Lane Pvt NH
Jonas: b 2-27-1738 d 9-13-1782 m Submit Davis PS NH
Jonathan: b 1758 d 1822 m (1)Molly Wright (2)Betsey — Pvt MA
Jonathan: b 9-26-1762 d 7-20-1845 m Joanna — Pvt MA ★
Jonathan: b 5-22-1750 d 12- -1833 m Mary Bigelow Pvt MA
Jonathan: b 1-10-1759 d 1-3-1804 m Hannah Thayer Pvt PS MA
Joseph: b 10-7-1751 d 6-2-1829 m Rhoda Tingley Sgt MA ★
Joseph: b 4-3-1755 d 1844 m Rachel Rice Pvt VA ★
Joshua: b 1748 d 10-7-1829 m Hannah Hewes Pvt MA
Josiah: b 7-18-1747 d 4-6-1822 m Mary Corey Capt PS MA
Josiah: b 5-16-1760 d 3-23-1831 m Sarah Davis Pvt MA ★
Josiah Howe: b 1-20-1732 d 7-25-1788 m (1)Sarah Abbott (2)Sarah
  Ruggles PS NH
Levi: b 1-1-1755 d 8-5-1839 m Louise Stoddard Pvt CT ★
Nathaniel: b 3-29-1754 d c. 1791 m (1)Sarah Carlton (2)Lydia
  Wilson Pvt MA
Nathaniel: b 9-19-1763 d 8-27-1848 m Mary Turner Pvt MA
Nathaniel: b 3-11-1751 d 9-27-1812 m (1)Dorcas Sanger (2)Polly
  Monroe (3)Grace Wheat PS NH
Nicholas: b 11-6-1756 d 5-22-1835 m (1)Mary — (2)Sophia Cress
  (3)Barbara Winters Sgt VA ★
Peter: b 1734 d 1813 m (1)Abigail Wheat (2)Judith Bartlett Lt NH
Phineas: b 2-28-1737/38 d 10-7-1792 m Mary Wellington Pvt MA
Reuben: b 2-6-1759 d 1-29-1845 m Anna Stewart Pvt MA
Samuel: b 11-14-1739 d 1-18-1817 m Mary Bigelow Lt MA
Samuel: b 1720 d 3-17-1776 m (1)Jemima Hoyt (2)Sarah Ann
  Grover Pvt MA
Samuel: b 6-21-1726 d 7-23-1801 m (1)Elizabeth Hutchinson
  (2)Hannah Trask Pvt MA
Samuel: b 5-14-1759 d 1-15-1844 m (1)Sarah Davis (2)Lydia
  Preston (3)Mrs Hannah (Farr) Hildreth Pvt NH

STEARNS, contd.
Samuel: b 7-17-1760 d 11-6-1833 m — Pvt NH
Samuel, Jr.: b 1732 d 1787 m Hepsibah Bryant PS CS NH
Silas: b 3-6-1734 d 12-31-1804 m Elizabeth Wellington Pvt PS MA
Thomas: b 7-4-1710 d 9-28-1784 m Mary Heald Pvt MA
Thomas: b 2-12-1724/5 d 12-18-1811 m Bette Manning CS MA
Timothy: b 11-30-1738 d 1-15-1831 m Lydia Walton Pvt MA
Timothy: b 9-25-1763 d 8-8-1816 m Sarah Lane Pvt MA
Wm.: b 10-16-1745 d 1-10-1838 m Mary — Pvt MA ★
Wm.: b 8-5-1754 d 2-14-1834 m Anna Duncan Pvt MA
Wm.: b 8-4-1752 d 7-12-1826 m Lydia Davis Pvt MA
Wm., Sr.: b 4-27-1734 d 4-22-1804 m (1)Elizabeth Lawrence
    (2)Elizabeth Burt Lt PS VT
Wm., Jr.: b 10-24-1755 d 1-12-1842 m Lydia Glazier Sgt NH NY
    VT ★

STEBBINS, (includes STEBBENS & STEBBINGS)
Abner, Sr.: b 5-3-1724 d 11-19-1810 m Martha Smith Pvt MA
Abner, Jr.: b 11-2-1757 d 11-7-1846 m Abigail Bacon Pvt MA
Asahel: b 5-30-1750 d 7-26-1822 m Susanna Field Cpl MA
Benjamin: b 1727 d 9-7-1803 m Sabra Miner Pvt MA
Benjamin: b 6-25-1744 d 1814 m Mercy Aiken Pvt VT
Bethuel: b 1-30-1742 d 11-26-1811 m Mary Shapleigh Pvt MA
Darius: b 4-17-1759 d 8-2-1819 m Louisa Merick Pvt MA W★
David: b 4-20-1741 d 9-30-1816 m Rhoda Sheldon Lt MA
Ebenezer: b 2-2-1733 d p. 4-27-1785 m (1)Hannah Day (2)Margaret
    Ball Pvt MA
Ebenezer: b 10-25-1734 d 10-3-1830 m Diadama Burt Pvt MA
Edward: b 9-26-1729 d 4-10-1816 m Elizabeth Burt Pvt MA
Eldad: b 8-13-1737 d 12-1-1811 m Ann Badger CS MA
Enos: b 7-26-1740 d 4-12-1798 m Mary (Stebbins) Sgt MA
Ezra: b 8-16-1731 d 2-5-1796 m Margaret Chapin Pvt MA
Francis: b 10-28-1754 d 12-23-1795 m Mrs Rebecca (Lloyd) Davies
    Capt MA
Gad: b 5-31-1748 d 9-5-1826 m Sarah Buckminster PS MA
Gideon: b 3-13-1739 d 1829 m Mary Hinsdale Capt MA
Hasadiah: b 10-25-1754 d 1-12-1824 m Betty Sessions Babcock
    Pvt MA
Jabez: b 5-17-1728 d 1798 m Sarah Turner CS CT
James: b 4-29-1740 d 1-21-1821 m Deborah Hoar Pvt MA
James: b 10-6-1760 d 3-14-1846 m Rachel Wright Pvt MA
Jesse: b 1-25-1744 d 1-25-1834 m (1)Beula Munn (2)Elizabeth
    M. Squiers Pvt MA
Joel: b 3-11-1752 d 6-30-1800 m Mrs Sarah Beebe Pvt MA
John: b 1-20-1712 d 1784 m Margaret Brooks Pvt MA
John: b 6-4-1759 d 9-8-1840 m Sarah Ball Pvt MA ★
Jonathan: b 10-24-1709 d 7-11-1788 m (1)Margaret Bliss (2)Sarah
    Moseley (3)Abigail Hale CS MA
Joseph: b 7-4-1735 d 12-13-1794 m Joanna Smith Capt CT
Joseph: b 10-20-1718 d 5-30-1797 m Mary Stratton PS MA
Joseph, Jr.: b 10-15-1749 d 12-15-1816 m Lucy Frary Capt MA
Joseph: b 3-1-1761 d 1-21-1829 m Betsy Eddy Lt MA
Joseph: b 1-13-1720 d 2-6-1784 m Thankful Belding PS NH
Jotham: b 4-21-1761 d 3-20-1850 m (1)Phoebe Ellenwood
    (2)Hannah Sewell Pvt MA W★
Moses: b 5-3-1750 d 1825 m (1)Hannah Hale (2)Catherine Chapin
    Pvt MA
Moses, Sr.: b 12-4-1718 d p. 1787 m Dorcas Hale PS MA
Nehemiah: b 11-12-1729 d 11-24-1807 m (1)Sarah Jessup
    (2)Abigail Brooks Pvt NY
Nehemiah M. Hoyt: b 11-1-1752 d 9- -1784 m Elizabeth Hoyt Pvt NY
Noah: b 10-13-1741 d 9-24-1818 m Margaret Stebbins Lt MA
Phineas: b 5-19-1739 d 3-21-1837 m Anne Chaffee Capt MA
Samuel: b 8-4-1725 d 1-20-1783 m Martha Bradwell Sgt MA
Thomas: b 10-1-1727 d 1-20-1807 m Phoebe Burt 2Maj MA
Thomas: b 3-11-1730 d c. 1776-83 m Anna Chamberlain Pvt
    MM MA
Thomas: b 10-10-1698 d 1793 m Mary Munn PS MA
Zadok: b 8-12-1741 d 4-20-1832 m Elizabeth Pease Cpl PS MA

STECK,
Baltser: b 7-6-1759 d 3-29-1821 m Elizabeth Fague Pvt PA
Philip: b 4-18-1762 d 7-29-1839 m (1)— (2)Sarah — Pvt PA

STECKEL,
Henry: b 1756 d 5-30-1826 m Maria Schneider Pvt PA
Jacob: b 11-1-1753 d 6-15-1836 m Eva Catherine Saeger Pvt PA

STECKER, (or STECHER)
Christopher: b 1750 d 1828-31 m Elizabeth Doll Pvt PA
George: b 1-23-1737 d 1- -1808 m Elizabeth Ehrich Lt PA
Lewis: b 1747/8 d 1-5-1821 m Margaret Dull Capt PA

STEDDIFORD,
Gerard: b 1752 d 4-3-1820 m Jane Bicker Lt PA

STEDHAM, (or STIDHAM)
Cornelius: b 3-16-1737 d p. 1795 m Christina Justis 2Lt DE
John: b 1-21-1729 d 1795 m Anna Ford Pvt DE
Jonas: b 2-24-1720 d 1795 m Anna Mary Colesbery Pvt DE
Jonas, Jr.: b 10-17-1744 d 8-2-1811 m (1)Ellinor Derickson
    (2)Ingeborg Sinnex Pvt DE
Joseph: b 7-5-1744 d 4-22-1791 m (1)Sarah Hedges (2)Elizabeth
    Bouldin (3)Rebecca — Capt DE

STEDMAN, (includes STEADMAN & STEEDMAN)
Ebenezer: b 9-17-1744 d 3-27-1813 m Eunice Morse Pvt MA
Ebenezer, Sr.: b 1- -1709 d 9-13-1785 m (1)Lydia Moore (2)Mary
    Austin PS MA
Ebenezer, Jr.: b 5-16-1743 d 10-17-1815 m Eunice (Monroe)
    Winship Pvt MA
Enoch: b 1760 d 6-17-1833 m Hannah Ball Sgt RI ★
James: b 3-6-1726 d 9-7-1788 m Hannah Griffin Capt CT
James: b c. 1740 d 1801 m — Pvt PA
James: b 3-3-1738 d 12- -1822 m Isabel Babcock PS RI
James: b 5-21-1748 d 5-21-1798 m Elizabeth Kelsey Pvt SC
John: b 1715 d 1795 m (1)Elizabeth Barton (2)Jane Calhoun Sol SC
Lemuel: b 1758 d 1828 m Eunice Smith Pvt CT
Levi: b 11-3-1758 d 10-26-1834 m Anna Percival Pvt PS CT W★
Nathan: b 7-11-1762 d 11- -1847 m Ann Clark Pvt CT ★
Nathaniel: b 4-18-1746 d 10-16-1812 m Ruth Boyden Pvt VT
Philemon: b 1756 d 1-17-1823 m (1)Anna Crosby (2)Lucy Brooks
    (3)Sarah Babcock Pvt CT ★
Stephen, Jr.: b 8-28-1749 d c. 1790-1803 m Jerusha — Pvt CS CT
Thomas: b 9-10-1732 d 1814 m Mehitable Griffin Sol CT
Thomas: b 1730 d p. 1796 m Mary Perry Pvt RI
Timothy: b 11-3-1743 d 1821 m Hannah Gilman Pvt CT
Wm.: b c. 1765 d p. 1801 m Rebecca Cooke Pvt PA
Wm.: b 5-31-1741 d 4-6-1815 m Hannah Scranton Ens RI ★

STEED,
John: b 1724 d 1798 m Mary Randolph Capt VA

STEELE, (includes STEALE & STEEL)
Aaron: b 12-4-1731 d 11-28-1777 m Sarah Rumrill 1Lt MA
Aaron: b c. 1740 d 1795 m (1)Violet Alexander (2)Mrs Elizabeth
    Crosby Sol SC
Adam: b c. 1740 d p. 12-21-1796 m (1)Catherine Krantz (2)Anna
    Eve Staring Pvt NY
Alexander: b a. 1730 d p. 8-9-1783 m — PS MD
Alexander: b 12-25-1757 d 2-14-1820 m Nancy Scudder Pvt NJ
Alexander, Sr.: b 1735 d 6-25-1808 m Sarah Helm 1Lt VA
Allyn: b 7-21-1757 d 6-17-1802 m Joanna Cadwell Pvt CT
Andrew: b 1750 d 1808 m (1)Jane Lindsay (2)Anne Carr Pvt KY
Andrew: b c. 1743 d 1801 m Mary Ramsey Pvt VA
Archibald: b 1741 d 10-19-1832 m Miss Vance Deputy QM Gen PA
Archibald: b 1728 d 10-28-1805 m Agnes Edwards Pvt SC
Ashbel: b — d — m Eunice Thompson Pvt QM CT
Benajah: b 1-2-1760 d 8-28-1854 m Sarah Bundy Pvt NC
Benjamin, Sr.: b 2-6-1748 d 11-14-1817 rn Hannah Lovejoy Pvt NH
Bradford, Sr.: bpt 9-22-1734 d 4-10-1804 m (1)Mary Perkins
    (2)Sarah Wheeler Capt PS CT
Bradford, Jr.: b 8-31-1762 d 12-23-1841 m Ruth Wheeler Pvt CT ★
David: b 1-17-1759 d 11-2-1832 m Hannah Kelsey Pvt CT
David: b c. 1763 d 5-20-1804 m Margaret — Pvt PA
David: b 9-16-1748 d 2-4-1819 m Jane Welsh Capt VA ★
David: b 1759 d p. 1838 m Mary Moore Pvt VA ★
David: b c. 1730 d 12-12-1812 m Mary (Steele) CS VA
Dietrich: b ¡0- -1764 d 5-29-1840 m Anna Cunningham Pvt NY
Ebenezer: b 5-18-1727 d 1-21-1821 m Sarah Sage Pvt CT
Ebenezer: b 8-5-1753 d 11-8-1805 m Rachel Seymour MM CT
Eldad: b 2-15-1763 d 10-20-1841 m Sybal Bates Pvt VT ★
Elijah: b 1-22-1758 d 8-21-1830 m Hannah Scovill Pvt CT ★
Elisha: b 11-23-1726 d 10-16-1811 m Susanna Strong Sgt CT
Elizabeth Maxwell, Mrs: b 1733 d 11-22-1790 m (1)Robert Gillespie
    (2)William Steele PS NC
Ephraim: b 1740 d 9-21-1814 m Esther Smith Mil PA
Francis: b 3-11-1759 d 12-18-1840 m Elizabeth Neal Pvt PS VA
Frederick: b 6-16-1762 d 7-8-1825 m Sabra Shephard Pvt CT
George: b 1730-40 d 1801 m Margarite Dalman Pvt PA
Henry: b c. 1720 d 2-5-1782 m Ann Billings PS CS MD
Isaac: b 10-14-1752 d 8-24-1835 m (1)Dorothy Pitkin (2)Lavinia
    Goodwin Pvt CT ★
Isaac: b 1765 d 1850 m Elizabeth Galloway Pvt PA
Jacob: b c. 1754 d 2- -1794 m Martha Thomas Lt PA
James, Sr.: b 2-6-1737 d 4-5-1813 m (1)Abigail Huntington
    (2)Dorothy Converse (3)Abagail Makepeace Lt CT
James, Jr.: b 10-13-1756 d 1-15-1819 m Jemima Wolcott Sgt CT
James: b 1740 d 18- -1807 m Susanna Knopf Pvt PA
James: b 3-1-1724 d 2-19-1819 m (1)Peggy Ramsay (2)Margaret
    (Parker) Cochran PS NH
James: b c. 1750 d p. 5-6-1795 m Edith Pyle PS NC
James: b 1732 d 11-2-1840 m Mrs Mary Peterson Pvt PA
James: b c. 1741 d 9-10-1823 m (1)Elizabeth McMasters (2)Elizabeth
    Donaldson PS CS PA
James: b 1735 d 1802 m Sarah Wright 2Lt VA
Jesse: b 8-18-1755 d 5-6-1815 m (1)Mehitable Sager (2)Lucinda
    Adams Sol CT
John: b c. 1725 d 2-4-1785 m Christian — MM CT
John: b 10- -1759 d 2- -1829 m Lucy (Saxton) Smith Pvt CT ★
John: b c. 1732 d 3-3-1784 m — Allen Pvt DE
John: b 12-25-1755 d 5- -1846 m Mary Eoff Sgt NJ ★
John: b 6-9-1758 d 1837 m Elinore Webster Capt NY
John: b 1758 d c. 1792 m Nancy Jane Shaw Ens NC
John: b 6-5-1758 d 2-27-1828 m Abigail Bailey Capt PA
John, Sr.: b 1715 d 8- -1779 m Margaret Hutchinson Capt Chp PA
John, Jr.: b 7-15-1744 d 12- -1812 m Agnes Moore Capt PA
John: b 1737 d 9-11-1820 m Mary — Capt VA

John: b c. 1760 d 8-6-1826 m Lucy Moon Sol VA
Joseph: b 1750 d 1-16-1816 m Olive Churchill Pvt CT W★
Joseph: b 1760 d 8-28-1795 m Rebecca Anderson Capt SC
Josiah, Jr.: b 8-24-1760 d 10-22-1836 m Phebe Smith Sgt CT ★
Josiah: bpt 6-11-1758 d 3-25-1825 m Susan Lewis Pvt CT ★
Katherine Fisher : b a. 1725 d 1785 m Thomas Steel PS SC
Levi: b 1728 d 8-18-1819 m Chloe — Pvt MA
Luke: b 6-   -1739 d 1789 m Esther Kasson Pvt CT
Moses: b 12-10-1757 d 3-30-1832 m Amanda Steele Cmsry CT
Nathaniel, Jr.: b 8-23-1747 d 8-6-1823 m Bethea Centre Pvt CT
Ninian: b 12-24-1738 d 12-30-1813 m Elizabeth Chambers Pvt NC
Ninian: b 6-14-1763 d 3-10-1831 m Jane Armstrong Sol NC
Perez: b 5-1-1758 d 2-28-1836 m Hannah Simmons Pvt CT
Peter: b 8-7-1743 d 11-10-1825 m (1)Hannah Norman (2)Jane
    Bell Pvt PA
Robert: b c. 1750 d 2-18-1822 m Elizabeth Booth Pvt PA
Robert: b c. 1758 d c. 1816 m Elizabeth Pickerd Pvt NC
Robert: b 1753 d 9-7-1836 m Esther Rowe Pvt PA
Samuel: b 1751 d 12-13-1811 m Rachel Putnam Cpl MA
Samuel: b 6-24-1749 d 1816 m Mrs Anna Sargent Garfield Gnr MA
Samuel: b 1745 d 10-27-1833 m Jennet Knox PS NC
Samuel: b c. 1733 d p. 1789 m Agnes Lindsay Pvt NC
Samuel: b 1730 d 4-   -1803 m Margaret Campbell Capt VA
Solomon: b 11-18-1728 d 1786 m Mary Guernsey Pvt VT
Stephen, Sr.: b 9-29-1724 d 10-20-1802 m Hannah Chapman CS
    PS CT
Stephen, Jr.: b 9-11-1752 d 12-27-1831 m Chloe Hubbard Fif CT
Thomas: b 1731 d 5-22-1808 m Jean Lowrie Pvt NC
Thomas: b 1740 d 1798 m Susanne Parquette Slr NY
Thomas: b 3-   -1757 d 12-17-1838 m Sarah — Pvt NC ★
Thomas: b 1752 d 1846 m Margaret Maxwell Pvt PA
Wm., Jr.: b 5-27-1742 d 5-9-1806 m Hannah Webster Ens CT
Wm.: b 1757 d 3-28-1825 m Rebecca Rena Penfield Pvt CT
Wm.: b c. 1726 d c. 1787 m Mary — Cpl NC
Wm.: b 1763 d 10-19-1849 m Mary — Pvt NC
Wm., Jr.: b 7-30-1750 d 5-4-1822 m Elizabeth Bailey Capt PA
Wm.: b 1739 d 8-17-1805 m Mary Trimble Fif PS PA
Wm.: b 1740 d 5-13-1827 m Mary Gault Pvt PA
Wm.: b 12-3-1763 d 7-21-1821 m Esther Love Sol SC
Wm.: b 6-21-1764 d 11-   -1827 m Betzey Hanger Pvt VA
Zadoc: b 12-17-1758 d 3-23-1845 m Hannah Shurtleff Pvt VT CT ★

STEELMAN,
Daniel: b 4-15-1750 d 1-24-1823 m Eleanor Edwards CS Pvt NJ
Frederick, Sr.: b 1718 d a. 4-29-1778 m Sara Somers Sol NJ
Frederick, Jr.: b a. 1755 d 1782 m Sophia Risley MM NJ
Frederick: b 3-25-1752 d a. 8-19-1807 m Naomi Edwards Pvt NJ
James, Sr.: b c. 1750 d 10-7-1817 m Sophia Covenover MM NJ
John, Sr.: b a. 1735 d 4-7-1796 m Abigail Adams Capt NJ
John: b 1756 d 1799 m Margaret Leeds Maj NJ
John: b 1757 d 4-10-1836 m (1) — Carson (3)Elizabeth Smith
    Pvt NJ ★
John: b 1755 d 1778 m Jane Cashion Sol NC
Jonathan: b c. 1735 d 2-22-1781 m Hannah Corson Smn CS NJ
Matthias: b c. 1723 d 10-   -1793 m Ruth — PS NC
Zephaniah: b 12-25-1759 d 4-3-1834 m Sybilla Albertson Pvt NJ ★

STEEN,
Frederick: b 1755 d c. 1815 m Katherine Rector Pvt PA
James: b 1756 d 1832 m Margaret Reynolds Pvt PA
James: b 1734 d 10-7-1780 m — Bogard LCol SC
Matthew: b 1755 d 4-23-1835 m Jane Taylor Pvt PA
Robert Moses: b c. 1740 d p. 1790 m Elizabeth Boyd Pvt PA
Wm.: b 1738 d p. 1804 m Nancy Lusk Pvt SC

STEENROD,
Cornelius: b — d c. 1805 m Mary Elizabeth Caldwell Capt NY

STEEPER,
Wm.: b 1724 d 1786 m Mary Moser Pvt PA

STEER,
John: b — d a. 8-22-1787 m Magdalene — Pvt PA

STEERE, (includes STEER & STEERES)
Hugh: b 5-6-1758 d 1-12-1846 m Mary Fowler Pvt PA ★
Jeremiah: b 2-22-1722 d 1803 m (1) — Burlingame (2)Mary (Wade)
    Thornton (3)Mary Wade (4)Jemima Lee PS RI
Jonah 6th: b 1-   -1720 d 4-14-1798 m Lydia Whipple PS RI
Richard: b 6-3-1707 d 10-16-1797 m (1)Anna Comstock (2)Jean
    Aldrich PS RI
Samuel: b 11-12-1731 d 8-2-1814 m Martha Colwell Pvt RI
Sebastian: b c. 1730 d 1793 m Eve — Pvt PA

STEES,
John: b 9-13-1760 d 6-5-1840 m Barbara Frantz Pvt PA

STEEVER,
Daniel: b 1757/8 d p. 10-18-1820 m Ann Zell Ghasslin Pvt PA ★

STEIDINGER,
Frederick: b 4-12-1726 d 12-29-1790 m Magdalena — Sol PS MD

STEIGERWALT,
Abraham: b 1756 d 2-4-1824 m Catharina — Pvt PA ★

STEIN, (or STINE)
Abraham: b 10-1-1724 d 5-30-1807 m Anna Maria Ebe Lt PA
Leonard: b 7-26-1754 d 8-   -1834 m Magdalena — Capt PA
Michael: b c. 1745 d 2-   -1814 m Catherine Brobst Pvt PA

STEINBERGER,
John: b 1760 d 1821 m Elizabeth Norman Pvt VA
Jost: b c. 1757 d p. 1786 m Magdalena Ruch Lt PA
Lorenz: b 1756 d 10-14-1826 m Catharine Dietrick Pvt PA

STEININGER,
George: b 4-12-1738 d 9-29-1790 m Anna Barbara Stettler Pvt PA

STEINMETZ,
Charles: b 3-7-1756 d 11-25-1832 m Margaretta Beaver Pvt PA
John: b 1740 d 9-6-1803 m Maria Catharine Keppele PS PA
Philip: b c. 1762 d — m Mary Becker Pvt NY
Philip: b 1749 d 7-   -1807 m Catharine Goodekunst Pvt PA

STELLE, (or STELL)
Abel: b 11-4-1748 d 11-4-1829 m (1)Sarah Dunham (2)Mrs
    Providence Webster Pvt NJ
Isaac: b 2-6-1718 d 10-9-1781 m Christiana Clarkson Pvt NJ
John: b 1746 d p. 1788 m Hannah DeBon Repos Sol NJ
John: b c. 1725-30 d p. 1790 m Susan Malone Pvt SC
Thompson: b 1745 d 6-   -1812/3 m Sarah Langstaff Capt NJ W★

STELLY,
George: b c. 1722 d 1792 m Marie Christine Edelmayer Pvt LA

STELTZ,
Peter: b 10-24-1745 d 5-24-1833 m (1)Gertraut — (2)Susanna
    Grub Pvt PA

STEMAN,
John: b 1730 d 1785 m Maria Breneman Pvt PA

STEMPLE,
Frederick: b 1745 d 11-16-1840 m Esther Catherine Leutertin
    Lt MD
Godfrey: b c. 1718 d 1798 m Margaret — PS MD

STENGER,
Conrad: b c. 1725 d 4-5-1798 m Catherine — Capt PA

STEPLETON,
Andrew: b 1752 d p. 1820 m Barbara — Pvt VA ★

STEPTOE,
James: b 7-6-1750 d 5-30-1826 m Frances Callaway CS VA

STERINGER,
Peter: b 1760 d 1-5-1806 m Ann Elizabeth Haubt Pvt PA

STERLING, (or STIRLING)
Abijah: b 1745 d 3-17-1802 m Eunice Sherwood Capt CT
Alexander: b 1753 d 1-6-1808 m Ann Alston PS LA
Ephraim: b c. 1758 d 1845 m Esther Polk Pvt MD
Jacob: b 3-3-1744 d 10-9-1818 m Edez Tucker Pvt CT
James: b c. 1745/6 d 7-13-1829 m Hannah May Pvt CT
James: b 1-6-1742 d 1-6-1818 m (1)Mary Shaw (2)Rebecca Budd
    Maj NJ
Joseph: b 1738 d 9-17-1814 m Lydia Ransom Cpl CT ★
Josiah: b 1-29-1762 d 12-28-1832 m Mary Trefethan Pvt ME
Samuel: b 10-14-1732 d 5-16-1823 m (1)Elizabeth Perkins (2)Anna
    Dudley (3)Mrs Lucretia Champion Pvt CT
Samuel: bpt 6-21-1746 d 4-4-1834 m Mary Gregory Pvt CT
Seth: b 3-18-1763 d 4-27-1846 m Polly Brewster Pvt CT ★
Sylvanus: b 3-18-1763 d 1-6-1781 m Esther Sherwood PS CT
Thaddeus: b 6-4-1749 d 3-8-1837 m (1)Lydia Dunning (2)Mary
    St. John Pvt CT ★
Travers: b 3-4-1740 d p. 12-21-1825 m Grace — Pvt MD
Wm.: b 5-28-1743 d 7-22-1805 m Jemima Sill Ens CT

STERNBERGH, (or STERNBERG)
David: b 9-12-1743 d 6-8-1828 m Cathern Bergh Pvt NY
(John) Jacob: b 12-11-1714 d 2-17-1777 m (1)Anna Eva Fuxin
    (2)Margaret Brown Pvt NY
Joseph: b 1-24-1751 d 1836 m Eunice — OrdlSgt NY ★
Lambert: b 3-8-1757 d 9-4-1829 m (1)Gertrude Snyder (2)Anna
    Enders Pvt NY
Nicholas: b 1-13-1723 d 12-12-1809 m Catherine Rickart Pvt PS NY

STERNER,
Abraham: b 1750 d 4-14-1835 m Elizabeth Merkem Pvt PA
Casper: b 1742 d 1-24-1793 m Margaret Hunsicker Sgt PA
John: b 11-12-1760 d 3-17-1843 m Barbara Waltman Drm PA

STERRETT, (includes STERETT & STERRET)
Alexander: b c. 1738 d 1786 m Mary — Pvt PA

STERRETT, contd.
David: b 1736 d 1790 m Rachel Innis Pvt PA
James, Sr.: b 1723 d 3-30-1808 m Sarah Montgomery Pvt PA
James, Jr.: b 1747 d 6-18-1812 m (1)Mary Hanna (2)Margaret McClure Pvt PA
James: b 1755 d 10-15-1822 m Ann McKnight Ens PA
John: b 2-1-1751 d 1-1-1787 m Deborah Ridgely Capt MD
John: b 8-5-1766 d 1-15-1837 m Margaret McClelland Pvt PA
Joseph: b 6-5-1756 d 6-22-1809 m Mary Elliott Pvt PA
Robert: b 8-2-1763 d 3-12-1834 m Rosannah Green Pvt PA
Wm.: b 1724 d 1801 m Jean Morrow Pvt PA
Wm.: b 1762 d 7-28-1818 m Sarah Woods Pvt PA

STERRY,
David: b 8-12-1754 d 4-4-1843 m Catherine Gray Pvt MA ★
Roger: b 1-22-1730 d 4-19-1780 m Abigail Holmes CS PS CT

STETSON, (or STUTSON)
Amos: b 5-19-1730 d 1779 m Experience — Pvt MA
Amos: b 6-9-1741 d p. 1786 m (1)Elisabeth Pray (2)Mrs Lydia Richardson Pvt MA
Benjamin: b 7-7-1736 d p. 1775 m Mercy Turner Lt MA
Benjamin: b 4-7-1740 d 4-8-1819 m Bradbury Eells Lt MA
Benjamin: b 4-12-1737 d 12-30-1821 m Zebiah Ellmes Pvt MA
Benjamin: b 7-3-1741 d 8-18-1817 m Mary French Pvt MA
Benjamin: b 7-19-1757 d 11-16-1831 m Mary Johnson Pvt MA ★
Charles: b 5-24-1755 d 3-12-1816 m Jane — Sgt MA
Ebenezer: b 3-8-1761 d p. 1847 m Olive Hale Mar Sgt MA ★
Elisha: b 3-8-1759 d 2-4-1848 m Rebekah Curtis Cpl MA
Elisha: b 1-30-1719 d 8-28-1803 m Sarah Adams Pvt MA
Ephraim: b 1744 d 10-27-1840 m Ruth Ford Sgt MA
Ezra: b 9-22-1729 d 4-25-1805 m (1)Sarah Rider (2)Susanna Gibbs PS MA
Gideon: b 1-18-1762 d 10-14-1835 m Anne Thayer Sgt MA ★
Gideon: b 7-17-1745 d 11-4-1808 m Hannah Holbrook Cpl MA
Hezekiah: b 12-2-1752 d 3-4-1833 m Elizabeth Tilson Pvt MA
Job: b 3-22-1733 d 6-10-1794 m Hannah Munroe MM MA
John: b 1710 d 12-12-1802 m (1)Abigail Crooker (2)Deborah Tower Pvt MA
John: b 10-27-1731 d 1-30-1811 m Rachel Paine Pvt MA
Jonah: bpt 7- -1721 d 12- -1782 m Elizabeth Hatch Pvt MA
Lot: b 9-21-1751 d 12-17-1811 m Joanna Soule Cpl MA W★
Matthew: b 8-24-1731 d 1-25-1807 m Mary Randall MM MA
Micah: b 11-21-1754 d 12-27-1838 m Sarah Copeland Cpl MA
Nathan: b 12-15-1757 d p. 1786 m Bethiah Crooker Pvt MA
Nathaniel: b 3-4-1746 d 12-10-1815 m Ruth Mitchell Cpl MA
Oliver: b 11-9-1757 d 11-10-1839 m Jennette Anderson Pvt MA
Prince: b 8- -1741 d p. 1790 m (1)Eunice Sylvester (2)Mrs Jane (Grant) Carver PS MA
Samuel: b 12-30-1713 d 5-13-1782 m Ann Dimmock PS CT
Samuel: b c. 1725 d 2-5-1791 m Alice Rogers Pvt MA
Seth, Jr.: b 6-4-1735 d 1815 m Lucy Studley PS MA
Silas: b 3-1-1759 d 6-10-1828 m Martha Milton Pvt CT W★
Stephen: b 5-17-1747 d c. 1779 m Dorcas Hall Pvt RI
Thomas: b 3-9-1752 d 1820 m Elizabeth Cook Cpl MA
Thomas: b 7-23-1741 d 12-24-1821 m Olive Mann Pvt MA
Timothy: b 1-23-1743/4 d 1806 m Zeruiah Church Pvt CT

STEUBEN,
Jonathan Arnold: b 2-27-1757 d 1-1-1839 m Lucy Porter Pvt CT

STEVENS, (Includes STEFFEN, STEFFY & STEPHENS)
Aaron: b 4-25-1736 d 8-29-1820 m Sarah Willcocks Capt CT ★
Aaron, Jr.: b 4-29-1761 d 11-12-1831 m Phebe Post Pvt CT
Aaron: b 1710 d 2-2-1796 m Deborah Stevens PS NH
Abel: b c. 1750 d c. 1816 m Eunice Buck Pvt VT
Abiel: b 3-24-1749/50 d p. 1785 m (1)Tabitha Holt (2)Elizabeth Holt Sgt MA
Abijah: b 9-24-1756 d 5-9-1844 m Esther Ruth Codner Hurlbut Pvt MA ★
Abijah: b 2-22-1732 d 11-21-1802 m Priscilla Thomas PS PA
Abram: b 2-20-1737 d 3-7-1826 m Lucy Collens Pvt VT
Adam: b 1718 d 1791 m Anne — MGen VA
Adams: b 11-10-1751 d 5-4-1849 m (1) — (2) Mrs Rena Rumsey Sgt CT Ri ★
Albert: b 8-31-1743 d 2-28-1824 m Grietje Van Houten Pvt NY
Alexander: b 3-17-1726 d 3-15-1814 m Catherine Baskins Capt PA
Amasa: b 4-27-1750 d 5-22-1780 m Margaret Putnam Cpl NY
Amos: b 1763 d 10-22-1830 m Rachel Pratt Pvt CT W★
Amos: b 7-16-1749 d 2-4-1832 m Mary Whiting 2Cpl PS ME
Amos: b c. 1740 d 1785 m Rosanna Ricomb PS PA
Asa: b 6-26-1761 d 1843 m (1)Sarah Hodgman (2)Nancy Draper Pvt MA
Asa: b 5-3-1734 d 7-3-1778 m Sarah Adams Lt PA
Benjamin: b 6-25-1754 d 4-3-1838 m Esther Rowlson Sgt CT
Benjamin: b 2-20-1737 d 3-21-1797 m Elizabeth Murphy Pvt MD
Benjamin, Jr.: b 1-20-1748 d 9-14-1826 m Mehitable Harris Pvt MA
Benjamin: b 5-14-1734 d 2-16-1800 m Hannah Varnum CS MA
Benjamin: b 12-29-1751 d 10-1-1811 m Anna Brazer PS MA
Benjamin: b 3-8-1756 d 12-11-1823 m Elizabeth Stevens Cpl NH
Benjamin: b 8-29-1751 d 6-22-1810 m Sarah Fogg Sol NH
Benjamin: b 1735 d 1814 m Rebecca Caldwell Pvt PS GA
Benjamin, Sr.: b 1733 d 6-9-1803 m Hopestill Shaw Sol VT

Benjamin: b 4-15-1754 d 9-7-1839 m Dorothy Jemima Waller Grd VA
Caleb: b 3-20-1744 d p. 1784 m Elizabeth Wilson Pvt MA
Calvin: b 2-17-1753 d 2-22-1833 m (1)Esther Wilkins (2)Mrs Hannah (Brown) Wilkins Pvt MA ★
Christian: b 10-31-1763 d 10-30-1837 m Elizabeth Wise Pvt PA
Clark: b 10-15-1764 d 11-20-1853 m Huldah Foster Pvt MA
Cutting: b 7-18-1749 d 12-17-1837 m Annie Green Pvt PS NH
Cyprian: b 8-18-1747 d 11-22-1838 m (1)Sarah Gale Pierce (2)Abigail Blashfield Sgt MA
Daniel: b 5-7-1746 d 11-7-1810 m Anne Bent Pvt MA
Daniel: b 11- -1747 d 10-10-1824 m Mehitable Heath 2Lt NH
Daniel, Sr.: b c. 1740 d 1811 m Hannah Hills Sgt NH
Daniel, Jr.: b 7-19-1764 d 1-19-1851 m Martha Bedell Pvt NH ★
David: b 5-23-1755 d 12-23-1819 m Judith Spofford Pvt MA
David: b 1-25-1736 d 11-20-1820 m Ruth Benton Pvt MA
David: b 2-3-1761 d 1-29-1834 m Sarah Abbot Pvt MA
David: b 2-15-1755 d 8-19-1845 m Eleanor Fulton Pvt NY ★
Dudley: b c. 1760 d p. 1790 m Nancy Cornell Pvt VA
Ebenezer: b 4-4-1713 d p. 7- -1798 m Lucy Griswold Pvt CT
Ebenezer: b 8-22-1752 d 9-2-1823 m (1)Rebecca Hodgdon (2)Lucretia (Ledyard) Sands LCol PS MA W★
Ebenezer: b c. 1785 m Mrs Lydia French Lt MA
Ebenezer: bpt 6-20-1725 d 2-27-1801 m Sophia — Pvt MA
Ebenezer: b 5-12-1759 d 1-13-1839 m Rachel Squirrel Pvt NY ★
Edward: b 1723 d 4-9-1788 m Phebe Harlow Pvt MA
Edward: b c. 1744 d a. 6-25-1792 m Mary — PS NC
Elias: b 9-20-1764 d 6-6-1852 m (1)Lucilla Chapman (2)Lucretia Snow Pvt CT ★
Elihu, Sr.: b 4-8-1731 d 1-8-1814 m (1)Rachel Meigs (2)Mrs Jerusha (Smith) Leonard PS CS NH
Elihu, Jr.: b 3-21-1755 d 4-2-1798 m Lucretia Mathews Pvt NH
Elijah: b 10-15-1740 d p. 1780 m Jane — Cpl CT
Eliphalet: b 1731 d 8-31-1814 m Elsa Holloway Pvt PS NY
Elisha: b 10-1-1748 d 3-8-1813 m (2)Agnes Kimberly Pvt CT
Elisha: b 1739 d 1814 m Lois Fuller Pvt MA
Elisha: b 2-28-1759 d 1814 m Rachel DeMott Pvt NY
Elnathan: b 1753 d 10-17-1846 m Sarah Prout Pvt CT ★
Ephraim: b 9-1-1730 d 9-17-1806 m Sybil Gay Sgt MA
Ephraim: b 6-29-1758 d 7-4-1837 m Sybil Foster Lt NH ★
Ephraim: b 4-5-1758 d 2-5-1846 m Dorcas Farmer Pvt NH
Ezekiel: b 1736 d 4-11-1820 m Elizabeth Godfrey CS PS NH
Ezra: b 5-25-1724 d 2-25-1823 m (1)Ann Barnum (2)Elizabeth (Coe) Burt Lt CT
Forward: b 5-1-1762 d 9-1-1847 m Rachel Knapp Pvt CT ★
Gershom: b 6-11-1741 d 1825 m Phebe Henry Arfr PS CT
Giles: b 1747 d 1836 m Nancy Tipton Sgt PA
Henry: b 9-2-1764 d 4-16-1851 m Ruth Page Pvt CT
Ira H.: b 7-18-1759 d 9-20-1803 m Sybil Ransom Pvt CT
Isaac: b 9-17-1748 d 10-25-1820 m Sarah Brackett Ens MA
Isaac: b 1752 d 6-1-1840 m Elizabeth Rich Pvt NH ★
Isaac: b 1754 d 1818 m Elizabeth Spalding Pvt VT
Isaac: b 12- -1760 d 6-28-1833 m Rebecca Havens Pvt VA ★
Isaac: b c. 1762 d 1831 m (1)Mary J. Wright (2)Catherine (Cummins) Briggs Sol VA
Israel: b 12-21-1752 d 5-15-1834 m Love Benedict Pvt CT ★
Israel 2d: b 9-7-1747 d p. 1787 m Sarah Kelsey Pvt CT
Jabez: b 2-13-1758 d c. 1849/50 m (1)Sarah Ellis (2)Esther Bemis Pvt MA
Jacob: b 10-7-1747 d p. 1790 m Mary Prindle Sgt CT
Jacob: b 1755 d 8-15-1826 m Martha Sawyer Pvt MA
Jacob: b 9-2-1756-9 d 1-10-1841 m Ann Warren Pvt VA ★
Jacob: b c. 1750 d 6-6-1849 m Rachel English Pvt VA ★
James: b 8-10-1757 d 7-8-1847 m (1)Honor Talcott (2)Mrs Esther Darrow Pvt CT ★
James: b 7-21-1753 d 12-18-1836 m (2)Elizabeth Tompkins Sgt NY
James: b 3-17-1750 d 4-29-1836 m Lydia — Lt VT CT ★
James: b 7-2-1757 d 1822 m Susana Kimball Pvt NH
Jared: b 1-19-1738 d 3-4-1814 m Elizabeth Tyler Pvt CT
Jared: b 9-28-1739 d 1800 m Lucy Stewart Pvt NY
Jedediah: b 5-11-1757 d 1-26-1830 m Abigail Cory Pvt NY
Jeduthan: b 6-22-1769 d 9-28-1844 m Roxanna Church Pvt MA ★
Jeremiah: b 12-23-1750 d 5-30-1835 m Patience Holmes Pvt CT ★
Jesse: b 4-4-1764 d 10-4-1852 m Molly Spaulding Pvt MA
Jesse: b 1-22-1757 d 1829 m Elizabeth Heath Pvt NH
Joel: b 1747 d 4-2-1842 m Mary Webber Cpl ME
John: b 10-19-1737 d 11-20-1801 m Phoebe Howe Capt CT
John: b c. 1727 d 1788 m Lydia Barnum Pvt CT
John: b 1737 d 11-13-1777 m Margaret McCarty PS GA
John: b 1728 d 1797 m Ann Burton Pvt MD
John: b 1740 d 1834 m Mary Burgess Pvt MA
John: b 1761 d 5-16-1838 m (1)Elizabeth Deland (2)Lucy Cutter Dickson Pvt MA
John: b 6-17-1755 d p. 1790 m Sarah French Pvt MA
John: b c. 1746 d p. 1789 m (1)Sarah Skillens (2)Mary Dove Pvt MA W★
John: b 8-19-1737 d 11-22-1826 m Huldah Wilcox Pvt CT
John: b 1749 d 3-6-1838 m Rachael Cox Mag PS NJ
John: b c. 1708 d 5- -1792 m Elizabeth Alexander PS CS NJ
John: b 1-15-1743 d c. 1790 m Agnes Guion Cpl NY
John: b 4- -1743 d 1-1-1808 m Elizabeth DeBow Pvt NY
John: b 1750 d p. 1796 m Pheby Faile 2Maj NC

John: b *c.* 1765 d 1851 m Elizabeth Matthews Pvt NC
John: b 1760 d *c.* 1792 m Susannah Speece Pvt VA
John: b 1748 d 3-17-1819 m Jeanette Vance Sol VA
John: b 1-30-1763 d 3-30-1842 m Martha Faulkner Sol VA
John: b 10-31-1763 d 3-3-1836 m Mary Christine Elizabeth Wise Pvt VA
John Adam, Sr.: b *c.* 1736 d 1822 m Agnes Pfrang Cpl PA
Jonas: b 4-26-1727 d 11- -1804 m Ruth Farrar Capt MA
Jonas: b 7-5-1751 d 2-9-1833 m Mary Crandall Sgt MA ★
Jonathan: b 7-16-1764 d 6-13-1850 m (1)Eleanor Adams (2)Mrs Elizabeth Shipley Pvt CT ★
Jonathan: b 9- -1741 d 1-9-1822 m Mary Tracy Sgt MA
Jonathan: b 6-12-1758 d 4- -1847 m (1) — Hobart (2)Sarah Shattuck Sgt MA ★
Jonathan: b 1726 d 1777 m Lydia Felch Pvt MA
Jonathan: b 1746 d 6-25-1832 m Thankful Foster Pvt MA
Jonathan: b *c.* 1725 d 12-28-1794 m Jamima — PS NY
Jonathan: b 4-8-1747 d 4-3-1834 m Susanna Bragg Pvt MA ★
Joseph: b 10-29-1733 d — m Rachel Goodrich PS Pvtr CT
Joseph: b 11- -1753 d 8-14-1830 m Elizabeth Hobbs Sgt MA ★
Joseph: b 5-17-1725 d 1793 m Elizabeth Rushnell Cpl MA
Joseph: b 10-17-1720 d 10-4-1791 m Elizabeth Sawtell PS MA
Joseph: b 6-14-1752 d *c.* 1830 m (1)Naomi Matthews (2)Desire (Stevens) Waterhouse Cpl NY
Joseph: b 6-28-1758 d 7-18-1843 m Hanah Cox Sol NC
Joseph Lawrence: b 4-17-1764 d 1848 m (1)Nancy Shackleford (2)Lucy Garrard Pvt VA
Joshua: b 10-28-1743 d 5-7-1800 m Susannah Sawyer Lt MA
Joshua: b 3- -1733 d 3- -1823 m Priscilla Humphreys Pvt PA
Joshua: b 2-2-1735 d 9-6-1824 m Elizabeth Dyer Sol SC
Josiah: b 5-4-1738 d 8-4-1793 m Abagail Nye Pvt MA
Josiah: b 1743 d 3-12-1817 m Mary Lawrence Sgt MA
Josiah: b 8-12-1752 d 4-10-1827 m (1)Abigail Dudley (2)Mrs Matilda Cooke Brewer LCol NH
Josiah: b 10-21-1743 d 7-2-1804 m (1)Mary Gray (2)Mrs Abigail Giles Ens NH
Lawrence: b 1755 d 5-3-1847 m Joanna Herbert Cpl VA ★
Lemuel: b 1-10-1753 d 7-31-1818 m Hannah Green Pvt VT
Levi: b 6-5-1748 d 3-15-1829 m Anna Snow Pvt MA
Levi: b 7-14-1744 d 2-21-1808 m Elizabeth Brown Pvt PA
Lewis: b *c.* 1713 d 1805 m Mary — PS VA
Loammey: b — d 2-21-1815 m Mary — Pvt NC
Mary Bowman: b 11-9-1735 d 1- -1820 m Lawrence Stephens PS VA
Mary Elizabeth: b 4-14-1761 d 8-1-1839 m Samuel Rossiter PS PA
Matthew: b 2-28-1745 d 8-29-1811 m (1)Hannah Crosby Rebecca Alsworth Pvt NY
Moses: b 1-23-1725 d 7-28-1814 m Esther Lovett Capt PS CT
Moses: b 1750 d *p.* 1800 m Sallie — Pvt GA
Nathaniel: b 10-18-1739 d 7-27-1808 m Lois Camp Ens PS CS CT
Nathaniel: b 1-5-1729 d 5-7-1817 m Jerusha Bennett Pvt MA
Nathaniel: b 11-22-1754 d 11-20-1837 m Mary Francis Pvt ME MA
Nathaniel Gove: b 1750 d 1830 m Lois Stone Pvt MA
Oliver: b 1759 d 1813 m Nancy Crittenden Pvt CT
Oliver Willard: b 8-10-1761 d 5-15-1846 m Elizabeth Lang Pvt MA
Otho: b 1765 d 8-26-1821 m Sarah Bayley Pvt VT
Parker: b 6-3-1743 d 1-26-1827 m Concurrence Hull Pvt MA
Peter: b 5-6-1759 d 1838 m Mercy House Sgt VT CT ★
Peter: b 12-16-1731 d 8-6-1779 m (1)Sarah Hurd (2)Lucy Anne Jackson (3)Truelove Barnum Pvt CT
Peter: b 3- -1741 d 5-26-1821 m Lois Glass Pvt CT ★
Peter: b 9-24-1746 d *p.* 1783 m Nabby Johnson Pvt MA
Peter: b 4-6-1748 d 12-8-1824 m Molly Pillsbury Pvt PS NH W★
Peter: b 1735 d 1812 m Mary Joanna Chrisman Sgt PA
Priscilla Thomas: b *c.* 1735 d *p.* 1782 m Dr. Abijah Stephens PS PA
Reuben: b 1758 d 2-13-1822 m Jerusha Barce Pvt CT
Reuben: b 8-17-1734 d 8-3-1804 m Hannah Brookins Pvt CT
Reuben: b 2-16-1738 d *p.* 1795 m — Pvt NH
Reuben, Jr.: b 3-29-1761 d 6-6-1842 m Molly Fancher Pvt NY
Rezin: b 9-9-1748 d 4-10-1826 m Sarah Hold PS MD
Richard: b 1750 d 1847 m Esther Ward Cpl MA
Richard: b 2-22-1732 d 5-18-1792 m Dorothy Landon Pvt NJ
Richard: b *a.* 1762 d 2-3-1808 m Mary Beverly Carter Capt VA W★
Richard: b 9-7-1755 d 7-2-1831/2 m Elizabeth Jennings Pvt VA
Roger: b 1759 d 6-7-1840 m Esther Snow Pvt NH ★
Safford: b 4-26-1742 d 6-19-1822 m Hannah Wells 2Lt CT NH ★
Samuel, Sr.: b 4-11-1708 d 12-21-1792 m Ruth Wright PS MA
Samuel, Jr.: b 11-14-1734 d 12-10-1805 m Tabitha Parker Lt PS MA
Samuel: b 8-27-1730 d 8-10-1810 m Hannah Shattuck Pvt MA
Samuel: b *c.* 1740 d *c.* 1806 m Rebecca Stiles Pvt NH
Samuel: b *c.* 1755 d 8-2-1777 m Ruth Fry Lt RI
Silas: b 12-27-1733 d 2-10-1825 m (1)Lydia Prouty (2)Persis Adams Pvt MA
Silas: b 5-20-1755 d 11-18-1848 m (1)Lucy Simons (2)Mrs Deming Pvt MA★
Simeon: b 1711 d 5-3-1786 m Mercy Cotts Pvt CT
Simeon: b 2-7-1729/30 d *p.* 1790 m Mercy Bennett Pvt CT
Simeon: b 10-4-1747 d 9-5-1799 m Mariah Ingalls SgtMaj MA W★
Simeon: b 1736 d 7-6-1788 m (1)Sarah Hadley (2)Mrs Susanna (Chamberlain) Shepard Capt NH VT
Simon: b 12-5-1736 d 2-18-1817 m (1)Isabella Taylor (2)Lydia Silsby (3)Anne Field Maj VT

Simon, Jr.: b 2-27-1765 d 1-21-1844 m Anna Woodward Sol CT
Simon: b 2-25-1760 d 8-15-1824 m Lois Willard Dr MA
Simon: b 3-14-1755 d 6-19-1825 m Elizabeth Boynton Pvt NH
Solomon: b 2-22-1725 d 11-11-1807 m Phebe Walker 1Lt PS MA
Solomon: b 1749 d 7-21-1812 m Martha Littlefield Matr NH
Solomon: b *c.* 1758 d *a.* 9-11-1786 m Milly Britt Pvt VA
Stephen: b 1753 d 1-1-1779 m Mary Matthews Pvt NJ
Sylvanus: b 7-8-1760 d 2-24-1835 m Sylvia Fuller Pvt MA ★
Theophilus: b 1-31-1732 d 10-10-1818 m Eleanor Tucker Sol NH
Thomas: b 7-5-1739 d 1-22-1824 m Mary Tryon 1Lt CT
Thomas: b 5-5-1760 d 12-3-1841 m Lucy Miller Pvt CT
Thomas: b 3-13-1720 d 7-20-1791 m Esther Waite CS CT
Thomas, Jr.: b 2-7-1741 d 2-17-1823 m Sarah Redfield CS CT
Thomas: b *c.* 1745-50 d *a.* 1814 m Jane Jefferson Pvt MD
Thomas: b *c.* 1750 d *p.* 9-9-1806 m Barbara — PS MD
Thomas: b 6- -1755 d 6-19-1815 m Sarah Stowell Cpl MA
Thomas: b 1765 d — m Elizabeth Perkins Pvt MA ★
Thomas: b 8-9-1737 d 6-23-1795 m Anna Rea PS MA
Thomas: b 2-23-1756 d *J*-28-1843 m Sarah Hart Howard Sol NY
Thomas: b *a.* 1750 d *p.* 1796 m Martha Davis Pvt NC
Thomas: b *c.* 1722 d 3-3-1801 m Rachel — Armr RI
Thomas: b *c.* 1755 d *p.* 1826 m Agnes Perkins Cpl VA
Timothy: b 9-17-1744 d 2- -1810 m Mary Ware Sol CT
Timothy: b 2-4-1729/30 d 1775-80 m Mary Sanders Smn MA
Timothy: b 5-10-1748 d 1-8-1834 m Dorothy Pettibone OrdlSgt NY
Uriah, Jr.: b 1-26-1761 d 2-8-1849 m Elizabeth Jones Pvt PA
Vincent: b 1745 d 1843 m X Pvt PA ★
Wm.: b 4-20-1757 d 11-26-1839 m Abigail Smith Sgt CT ★
Wm.: b 1-22-1753 d 9-27-1828 m (1)Abigail Green (2)Sarah (French) Harkness Cpl MA
Wm.: b 2-20-1752 d 2-28-1801 m (1)Elizabeth Gurney (2)Hannah Frisbie Capt NY
Wm.: b 1743 d 6-13-1827 m Eunice — Ens NY
Wm.: b 9-10-1732 d 12-7-1793 m Gertrude Van Epps Sgt NY
Wm.: b *c.* 1755 d 1806 m Esther Burling Sgt NY
Wm.: b 1757 d 1805 m Catrine Mennel Pvt NY
Wm.: b 1721 d *a.* 1783 m Mary — Pvt NY
Wm.: b 1745 d 1829 m (2)Elizabeth Leachman PS NC
Wm.: b 1711 d 1780 m Mary Sampson Sol NC
Wm.: b 1748 d 1828 m — Sol PA
Wm.: b 3- -1754 d 1-10-1838 m Margaret Stultz Pvt PS PA ★
Wm., Jr.: b 1751 d 12-28-1825 m Isabella Rountree Lt VA ★
Zachariah: b 11-13-1763 d 8-30-1846 m (1)Elizabeth Lowe (2)Betsey Rogers Smn Pvt MA
Zebulon, Jr.: b *c.* 1755 d 7-5-1814 m Sarah Herrick Cpl CT

STEVENSON, (includes STEPHENSON)
Abiather: b 1754 d 12-26-1829 m Olive Lombart Of MA ★
Abraham: b *c.* 1750 d *p.* 1810 m Mary Jenkins Sol NC
Augustine, Sr.: b 4-22-1744 d 1-3-1794 m Caroline Willett PS NJ
Benjamin: b 7-23-1749 d 10-27-1832 m Mary Cox Ens MD
Briant: b 6-15-1759 d 1835 m Deborah Turner Slr MA
Calvin, Sr.: b 3-23-1760 d 12-29-1831 m Roxey Russell Pvt MA ★
Daniel: b 2-2-1737 d 9-3-1827 m Ruth Stevenson Pvt PA
George: b 10-30-1760 d 1829 m Mary Holmes Lt SrgnMte PA
Hugh: b 3-16-1743 d 3-15-1822 m Rebecca Debolt Pvt PA
Hugh: b *c.* 1735 d *p.* 3-3-1776 m Ann — Col MD VA
James: b *c.* 1725 d 1816/7 m (2)Jane Buchanan CS MD
James: b 1755 d 1835 m Mary Colley PS NJ ★
James: b 1747 d 4-19-1798 m Margaret Brown Pvt NY
James: b *c.* 1750 d 1830 m Sarah — Capt NC
James: b 12-10-1754 d 5-23-1845 m Mary Guess Capt NC ★
James: b 5-27-1746 d 9-3-1828 m Jane Stevenson Pvt NC
James: b 1-8-1755 d 1834 m (1)Hannah Bull (2)Catherine Moore Sgt PA ★
James: b 11-4-1749 d 8-15-1810 m Elizabeth Caldwell Cpl PA W★
James: b 3-7-1743 d 9-16-1821 m Jane — Pvt PA ★
James: b 7-25-1755 d 12-20-1815 m Catherine Bonar Pvt PA
James: b *c.* 1740 d 9-6-1804 m Mary Reed Pvt PA
James: b 10-1-1744 d 5-12-1822 m Elizabeth Tompson 2Lt SC
James: b 1744 d 8- -1817 m Elizabeth — Pvt SC
James: b 1740 d 5- -1813 m Rachel McKeevers PM VA
James: b *a.* 1740 d 6- -1809 m Frances Littlepage PS VA
James White: b 1-17-1756 d 1-6-1832 m (1)Elizabeth James (2)Mary (Frierson) Fleming Pvt SC
John: b 3-17-1757 d 9-11-1831 m (2)Mary Havenor Lt MD
John: b 7-6-1755 d 1-8-1842 m Margaret Majors Ens MD ★
John: b 1750 d 7-17-1807 m Rachael — Dr NY
John: b 6-12-1761 d 4-17-1831 m Hannah Phelps Sgt NY
John: b 7-23-1758 d 11-2-1836 m Elizabeth Moffitt Pvt NC ★
John: b — d *p.* 11-11-1793 m Hannah — CS NC
John: b 1746 d 12-14-1821 m Margaret Huston Sgt PA
John: b 1740 d 1823 m — Bond PA
John: b 1735 d 1785 m Mary McCown CS PS PA
John: b 1751 d 1813 m Sarah Nye Pvt PA
John: b 1761 d 6-13-1847 m Mary McCombs Sol PA
John: b *c.* 1710 d 1778 m (2) Mrs Sarah Waite Taylor Capt PS VA
John: b 1758 d 12-20-1827 m Nancy Ewing Pvt VA
John: b 1720 d 1798 m Martha Warwick Maj VA
Jonas: b 1751 d *a.* 3-9-1801 m (1)Rebecca — (2)Rachel Hughes PS MD
Jonathan: b *c.* 1747 d *p.* 3-10-1796 m (2)Nancy Mills Ens MD
Joseph: b 1757 d 1820 m Mary Espy 1Lt PA

STEVENSON, contd.
Marcus: b 7- -1748 d 1- -1810 m Mary Holman Ens VA
Nathaniel: b 1751 d 3-19-1839 m Mary Allen Cpl PA W★
Robert: b 3-25-1759 d 7-23-1835 m Elizabeth Baird Pvt PA ★
Robert: b c. 1762 d 1816 m Mary Teeters PS Pvt PA
Samuel: b 1748 d 4-6-1814 m Mary Riley Pvt PA
Samuel: b 3-11-1744 d 12-17-1825 m Jane Gay Pvt VA
Silas Sears: b c. 1748 d 1793 m Dorothy — Capt CS NC
Thomas: b 11-17-1740 d 10-8-1776 m Hannah Taylor Lt CT
Thomas: b 1754 d 9-25-1829 m Sarah Evens Pvt MD
Thomas: b 1720 d 3- -1812 m Mary Hawkins Pvt VA
Thomas: b c. 1759 d 1782 m Frances McConnell Sol KY VA
Wm.: b 1737 d 1780 m Elizabeth — Pvt NC
Wm., Sr.: b 1725 d 1809 m Mary McClelland Sol NC
Wm., Jr.: b 1763 d c. 1840 m Prudence Hall Sol NC
Wm.: b — d p. 7-12-1814 m Rebecca Tanner Pvt PA
Wm.: b 1733 d p. 1798 m E T Mills Pvt PA
Wm.: b 1764 d 3-17-1836 m Margaret — Pvt PA ★
Wm.: b 1744 d 1809 m (1)R — Green Beattie (2)Elizabeth Wylie
    Sol SC
Wm.: b 1720 d 10-3-1793 m Jane Newton Sol VA

STEVER,
Jacob: b 12-17-1759 d 1-18-1848 m Dorthea Schmit Sgt NY
Phillip: b c. 1735 d 1807 m Maria Elizabeth Keller Capt PA

STEVES,
Jeremiah: b 1-23-1762 d 10-25-1840 m Sarah Thorp Cpl NY ★

STEWART, (includes STEUART, STEWARD, & STUART)
Abraham: b 10-16-1762 d 4-4-1840 m Sarah McKechnie Pvt MA
Alexander: b 11-8-1727 d 8-5-1805 m (1)Sarah Bogue (Booge)
    (2)Mrs Zurviah Wright Pvt CT
Alexander: b 9-6-1744 d 10-1-1829 m Thankful Denison Pvt CT
Alexander: b c. 1750 d 5-26-1833 m Thankful — Cpl MA
Alexander: b c. 1744 d c. 1823 m Elizabeth Barron Pvt SC
Alexander: b 8-27-1734 d 1822 m (1)Mary Patterson (2)Mary (Moore)
    Paxton Maj VA
Alexander: b c. 1755 d 1835 m (1) — (2)Catherine Sheets Pvt VA
Allan: b 1755 d 1-28-1846 m Mary Barry Pvt NH
Andrew: b 2-11-1750 d 5-24-1833 m Lucretia Hancock Cpl CT ★
Archibald: b 1736 d 5- -1795 m Phoebe Helm PS NJ
Archibald: b c. 1735 d p. 9-3-1792 m Isabella Jordan Sol PA
Benjamin: b 1756 d 6-4-1820 m Damaris Rice Sgt MA
Benjamin: b 1736 d 12- -1808 m Eleanor Tate Pvt VA
Benjamin: b 1-26-1727/8 d 2-26-1815 m Rebecca Taylor Pvt MA
Charles: b 7-5-1763 d 12- -1841 m (1)Mary Hulbert (2)Hannah Gates
    Pvt MA
Charles: b 5-18-1733 d 8-17-1796 m Sarah Hoyt Lt PS NY
Charles: b 3-9-1729 d 6-24-1800 m Mary Oakley Johnson Cmsry
    Gen NJ
Charles: b 1719 d 9-16-1794 m Sarah — Pvt PA
Charles, Sr.: b 1743 d 9-25-1809 m Elizabeth Hunter Pvt PA
Charles: b 10-15-1759 d 1840 m Frances Stockton Pvt PA
Charles: b c. 1730 d 2- -1801 m Martha Foreman 2Lt PA
Christopher: b 1748 d 5-27-1799 m Elizabeth Bull LCol PA
Daniel: b 4-4-1745 d 4-28-1826 m Elizabeth Stewart Capt CT
Daniel: b 11-18-1762 d 2-20-1858 m Ruth Fulford Pvt CT ★
Daniel: b 10-20-1761 d 5-17-1829 m (1)Martha Pender (2)Susanna
    Oswald Pvt GA
Daniel, Sr.: b 11-24-1734 d 6-2-1802 m Mary Ireland Pvt MA
Daniel, Jr.: b 10-3-1758 d 9-15-1840 m Rachel Kemp Pvt MA
Daniel, Sr.: b 10-14-1722 d a. 1790 m Lydia Cutting CS MA
Daniel, Jr.: b 1756 d 1834 m Dorothy Maynard Pvt MA
Daniel: b 10-23-1756 d 12-29-1843 m Dorothy (Stewart) Pvt MA ★
Daniel: b c. 1758 d p. 3-5-1816 m — Pvt PA
David: b c. 1760 d 10-25-1810 m Ann Ridgely Sol MD
David: b 1-16-1744 d 1788 m Mrs Abigail (Thorndike) Davidson Pvt
    NH
David: b 1752 d 2-2-1828 m Barbara — Pvt NC
David, Sr.: b c. 1733 d p. 9-1-1788 m Elizabeth McQueen Pvt SC
Edward: b a. 1763 d p. 1793 m Sarah Evans Pvt MD
Edward: b 2- -1759 d 4-7-1844 m Mary Callaghan Ens VA ★
Elias: b 3-24-1742 d p. 2-6-1792 m Sarah Stewart Pvt CT
Elijah: b 1754 d 11-7-1827 m (2)Jedidah Butler Pvt MA
Elijah: b c. 1743 d 1807 m Mary Patterson Pvt PA
Eliphalet: b 8-15-1759 d 11-3-1837 m Mercy Coates Lt RI NY ★
Elisha: b 6-29-1757 d 6-19-1837 m (1)Sarah Witter (2)Sabra —
    Pvt CT ★
Enoch: b c. 1743 d 2-26-1805 m Elizabeth — PS NJ
Finley: b 12-17-1730 d 2-18-1809 m Prudence Shaw PS NC
George: b 1739 d 9-9-1801 m (1)Sarah Whitehall (2)Susannah
    Wilson Col PA ★
George: b 5-10-1758 d p. 11-21-1850 m Elizabeth Crawshaw Pvt VA
Grovener: b c. 1756 d 1831 m Jane Fields Sol GA
Henry: b 11-1-1766 d p. 1790 m Mary Nelson PS NC
Hugh: b 2-22-1751 d 8-5-1835 m Mary Marchant Pvt MA ★
Hugh: b 8-19-1761 d a. 3-17-1842 m Rhoda — Pvt MA ★
Hugh: b 12-19-1757 d 5-1-1824 m Margaret Roxburgh Smith Pvt PA
Isaac: b 1754 d 1837 m Helen Dodson Pvt MD ★
Jacob: b 4-22-1743 d 5-14-1813 m Elizabeth Pierce Ens MA
James: b 1761 d 4- -1843 m Lydia Morehead Pvt DE
James: b 1746/7 d 8-22-1781 m Elizabeth — Capt PS MD

James: b 11-11-1729 d 1809 m Agnes — Pvt MA
James: b 6-8-1743/4 d 11-5-1816 m Sarah Rawlings PS NH
James: b a. 1732 d 1811 m Jane — Pvt NY
James: b 1737 d 1794 m Elizabeth — Pvt NC
James: b 4-16-1765 d 2-6-1854 m Margery McGhee Pvt NC ★
James: b 1752 d 1792 m Eleanor McElwain 2Lt PA
James: b c. 1756 d c. 1848 m Catherine Shaeffer Pvt PA
James: b c. 1758 d 1805 m Margaret Armstrong Pvt PA
James: b a. 1765 d a. 9-13-1823 m — Sol PA
James, Sr.: b 1708 d 11- -1783 m Margaret Stewart Pvt PA
James, Jr.: b c. 1737 d 1783 m Priscilla Espy PS PA
James, Jr.: b 6-8-1743 d 12-29-1811 m Rebecca Marchant Pvt PA
James: b 1-2-1757 d 1840 m (1)Barbara Taylor (2) — Montgomery
    Pvt VA ★
Jehiel: b 10-22-1750 d 3-18-1813 m Rachel Williams Pvt MA W★
Jehu: b 8-24-1750 d 6-30-1827 m (1)Sarah Stanley (2)Sarah
    Guyer PS NC
Jeremiah: b c. 1750 d 7-22-1830 m Priscilla Chisholm Sol VA
John: b 1761 d 8-12-1834 m Mahitable Burdick Pvt CT ★
John: b 5- -1747 d p. 1784 m Elizabeth Jackson CS MD
John: b 1735 d 8-28-1818 m (1)Ann McClellan (2)Jean Love (3)Mrs
    Morse Lt MA
John: b 9-22-1743 d 1-9-1819 m Rebecca Stewart Lt MA
John: b 6-26-1747 d a. 1813 m Elizabeth Dresser Pvt MA
John, Sr.: b c. 1733 d 1789 m (1)Elizabeth Arvin (2)Soviah Smith Pvt
    NJ
John: b 2-9-1749 d 8- -1807 m Lydia Douw Pvt NJ
John: b 1757 d 4-11-1827 m Rhoda Shinn Pvt NJ
John: b 1-15-1763 d 7-15-1848 m Phebe Castle Pvt NY
John: b c. 1760 d p. 1850/1 m Margaret Roach Pvt NC
John: b 1725 d 1810 m Mrs Mary Culbertson Pvt PA
John: b c. 1730 d a. 8-27-1817 m — Pvt CS PA
John: b 1740 d 3-4-1820 m Elizabeth Henry Pvt PA
John: b 9-28-1752 d 8-12-1809 m (1)Ann Herr (2)Rachel (Davis)
    Johnston Pvt PA
John: b 1753 d 8-10-1837 m Mary Robeson Pvt PA ★
John: b 10-16-1755 d 4-26-1826 m — Graham Pvt PA
John: b 3-25-1755 d 7-17-1829 m Mary Kennedy Pvt PA ★
John: b c. 1760 d p. 1790 m — Pvt PA
John: b 1745 d 1828 m Huldah Hubbell Vol MA
John: b 2-14-1755 d 8-27-1831 m Susan Smith Sgt VT W★
John: b 3-27-1749 d 8-23-1823 m Agatha (Lewis) Frogge Capt VA
John, Sr.: b 10-16-1734 d 1784 m Ann Haw Capt VA
John, Jr.: b 1740 d 1831 m Elizabeth Walker Of VA
John: b 1761 d 9-25-1845 m Mary Arnold Pvt VA ★
John: b c. 1751/2 d 1808/9 m Tryphena — 2Lt MA
Joseph: b 6-23-1753 d 4-8-1823 m Anne Preston Pvt CT ★
Joseph: b 2-11-1762 d p. 1837 m Elizabeth — Pvt CT ★
Joseph: b 1759 d 8-19-1842 m Lydia Stuart Pvt CT ★
Joseph: b 1757 d 5-5-1811 m Beatrice Coburn Pvt MA
Joseph, Jr.: b 5-13-1746 d 1-14-1813 m Ann Robbins Pvt NJ
Jotham: b 1-7-1764 d 6-16-1816 m Hannah Burham Sol ME
Lazarus: b 1734 d 7-3-1778 m Martha Espy LCol PA
Lazarus: b c. 1755 d 7-3-1778 m Dorcas Hopkins Lt PA
Lemuel: b a. 1750 d 11- -1807 m Lydia — Capt MA
Lemuel: b 4-6-1759 d 3-8-1829 m Rebecca — Pvt CT RI W★
Luther: b 4- -1762 d 1815 m Ester Smith Pvt MA
Luther: b 1748 d 8-29-1823 m Kezia Carpenter Sol NY
Martha: b — d p. 1-6-1792 m James Stewart PS VA
Matthew: bpt 4-21-1765 d 12-16-1814 m Sarah Bryant Pvt CT
Matthew: b c. 1720 d 1808 m Elizabeth — Capt NC
Nathan: b 6-27-1739 d p. 1819 m (1)Martha Shaw (2)Eunice — Sol CT
Nathan: b 6-22-1745 d 1814 m Barbara Palmer Pvt CT
Nathaniel: b 1749 d 4-5-1830 m Sarah Bronson Pvt CT
Nathaniel: b 1739 d 3-26-1832 m Mercy Lockwood Sgt MA
Oliver: b 10-30-1763 d 6-28-1847 m (1)Sarah Steward (2)Rebecca
    Snifen Pvt CT
Oliver: b 3-2-1761 d 3-21-1858 m (1)Cynthia Jacques (2)Mrs
    Margaret Spoor Pvt NY ★
Paul: b 1764 d 1851 m Olive Munger Pvt MA ★
Peter: b 6-1-1750 d p. 2-3-1826 m Juliana Boyle Cochran Sol PA
Philip: b 1760 d 8-14-1830 m (1)Mary Marshall (2)Mary Fell
    Baynes Lt VA
Phineas: b 8-17-1748 d 11-2-1812 m Mary E — Pvt CT NY
Ralph: b 12-17-1752 d 11-18-1835 m (1) — Elliott (2)Mary Clay
    Capt VA ★
Richard: b 1743 d 1798 m Anne Stuart Sol VA
Robert: b 1749 d 12-8-1835 m Nancy Holloway Sol GA
Robert: b c. 1727 d 1826 m Susannah — Pvt MD
Robert: b 9-30-1743 d 6-27-1819 m Ruth Currier Lt NH
Robert: b 1749 d 1828 m Margaret Edie 2Lt PA
Robert: b c. 1750 d p. 1790 m — Pvt PA
Robert: b c. 1720 d c. 1770-89 m Mary — Sol VA
Sampson: b c. 1752 d p. 1-28-1828 m Catherine Wiley PS Sol NC
Samuel: b c. 1746 d p. 1783 m (1)Sarah — (2)Agnes Calhoun Sgt MA
Samuel: bpt 6-5-1748 d p. 1810 m (2)Lucy (Foss) Harmon Pvt MA
Samuel: b 1760 d 7-12-1832 m Hannah Brown Pvt NH ★
Samuel: b c. 1734 d 9-16-1803 m (1)Nancy Templeton (2)Agnes
    Calhoun Pvt PA
Silas: b 7-1-1739 d 3-19-1812 m (1) — (2)Abigail — Fif CT
Silas Silvanus: b 8-1-1756 d 3-5-1839 m (1)Mabel Wright
    (2)Nancy Hubbell Pvt CT

Simpson: bpt 2-5-1749 d 6-13-1841 m Hannah — Pvt PS NH
Solomon: b 2-9-1748 d 5-19-1835 m Elizabeth Moors Capt MA
Solomon: b 1-14-1730 d 1804 m Elizabeth Taylor PS CS MA
Stephen: b 7-25-1758 d *p.* 1796 m Hannah — Pvt CT
Thomas: b 3-17-1752 d 10-12-1836 m Rachel Farmer Dewees Lt PA
Thomas: b *c.* 1741 d 2-17-1828 m Nancy Chambers Pvt PA
Thomas: b 5-26-1757 d 10-18-1817 m Polly Fleming Pvt PA
Walter: b 1755 d 6-14/15-1796 m Deborah McClenachan BGen PA
Walter: b *c.* 1748 d *p.* 1780 m Catherine — Adj VA
Wentworth: b 10-20-1731 d 4-17-1776 m Susanna Lombard Capt MA
Wm.: b 2-18-1752 d 9-19-1844 m (1)Desire Crary (2)Mary Whitney
    Pierce Lt CT ★
Wm.: b 3-15-1751 d 1-23-1843 m (1)Anna Coates (2)Amanda Darrow
    Pvt CT ★
Wm.: b 1760 d 7-17-1846 m Mary Scott Lt MD
Wm.: b 6-20-1760 d 2-21-1849 m Mary Knox Pvt MA
Wm.: b 1745 d 6-28-1788 m Sarah Blackler Matr Pvt MA
Wm.: b 1738 d 2-17-1810 m (1)Frances Todd (2)Mrs Bethany Dunn
    Pvt NJ
Wm.: b 6-23-1738 d 3-10-1788 m Catharine Rowe Capt PS NY
Wm.: b *c.* 1741 d 1832 m Lurena — Pvt NC
Wm.: b 1-10-1763 d 11-19-1856 m Mary Newel Pvt NC ★
Wm.: b *c.* 1738 d *p.* 4-2-1805 m Mary Gass 2Lt PA
Wm.: b 1759/60 d 2-5-1831 m Elizabeth Clinton 2Lt PA
Wm.: b *c.* 1739 d 3-7-1821 m Elizabeth Leeper Pvt PA
Wm.: b 1757 d 1837 m Jane Armstrong PS PA
Wm.: b 10-21-1757 d 5-29-1829 m Martha Walker Ens PA
Wm.: b 6-2-1758 d 6-27-1841 m Anna Catharine Kleppinger Pvt PA
Wm.: b *c.*1732 d 7-29-1784 m Elizabeth Wilson Pvt PA
Wm.: b 8-4-1739 d 8-4-1830 m Sarah Calhoun Pvt SC
Wm.: b 10-21-1761 d 6- -1818 m Mary Parker Pvt SC
Wm.: b 1736 d 1820 m Jennett Caldwell Sol SC
Wm.: b 11-8-1762 d 6-17-1848 m (1)Mary Penn (2)Martha B Wilson
    Sgt VA ★
Wm.: b 1727 d 2-10-1811 m Elizabeth Given Pvt VA
Wm.: b 1732 d 1797 m Margaret Usher Pvt VA
Wm.: b 1-5-1756 d 12-12-1833 m Mary — Pvt VA ★
Wm.: b 1724 d 1799 m Sarah Foote PS VA
Wm. Gibbons: b 11-25-1749 d 1796 m Mary Fitzhugh PS Lt VA

STHRESHLEY,
Thomas: b 1739 d *p.* 1798 m Margaret Hipkins Capt PS VA

STICHTER,
Peter: b 8-9-1761 d 12-18-1843 m (1)Catharine Hoff (2)Elizabeth
    Lybrand (3)Rebecca Sheufelter Pvt PA

STICKLE,
Johannes: b 10-10-1743 d 10-3-1816 m Elizabeth Bohm Pvt NY
Nicholas N: b 9-27-1755 d 6-9-1842 m Jemima Wheeler Pvt NY ★

STICKLEY,
Benjamin: b *c.* 1750 d 1796 m Ann Stover Sol VA

STICKNEY,
Abraham, Sr.: b 11-2-1733 d 3-19-1803 m Sarah Kittredge Lt MA
Abraham, Jr.: b 5-30-1758 d 11-22-1821 m Abigail Bell Pvt MA ★
Amos: b 5-16-1746 d 1-27-1839 m Lucy Searle Pvt MA
Amos: b 6-19-1749 d *p.* 1823 m Mrs Elizabeth Thomas PS NH
Asa: b 12-10-1742 d 1-18-1826 m Molly Richardson Pvt MA
Benjamin: b 3-5-1739/40 d 1-1-1801 m (1)Sarah Metcalf
    (2)Elizabeth (Stickney) Lt MA
Daniel: b 1760 d 11-17-1843 m Sarah Morse Pvt NH ★
Daniel: b 8-9-1737 d 1803 m Susannah Head Pvt MA
Daniel: b 4-5-1730 d *p.* 1813 m Sarah Good PS NH
Eleazer: b 8-30-1740 d 1-5-1824 m Martha Brown 2Lt MA
Eliphalet: b 1-10-1747 d 12-12-1821 m Joanna Wright Pvt VT
James: b *c.*1761 d *p.* 1807 m Susannah Beadle Pvt NH
James: b 8-6-1742 d 1823 m Mary Belknap Lt NY
Jedediah: b 4-1-1735 d 4-8-1809 m Margaret Tarlar Lt MA
Jeremiah: b 10-10-1758 d 2-21-1837 m Elizabeth Flanders Pvt MA
    W★
John: b 5-31-1744 d 4-23-1827 m (1)Elizabeth Howard (2)Lucy
    Nash Alvord Sgt MA
John: b 5-16-1744 d 8-12-1807 m Rachel Farnum Pvt MA
John: b 2-1-1760 d 10-7-1825 m Mary Evans Pvt NH
Jonathan: b 8-17-1736 d 4-30-1802 m Silence — Capt MA
Jonathan: b 12-26-1746 d 4-16-1810 m Abigail Stickney 2Lt MA
Jonathan: b 9-25-1736 d *p.* 1785 m Martha March Sgt MA
Jonathan: b 7-29-1763 d 9-12-1839 m Sarah Abbott Pvt MA
Jonathan: b 8-3-1739 d 11-19-1792 m (1)Sarah Webster (2)Anna
    Clark CS PS NH
Joseph: b 11-25-1758 d *p.* 1796 m Mehitable Sawyer Pvt MA
Joseph, Jr.: b 4-13-1762 d 4-3-1848 m Anna Hosmer Pvt NH
Lemuel: b 2-7-1745 d 5-10-1824 m Rebecca Kimball Pvt MA
Levi: b 1788 d 9-30-1824 m Molly Leach Pvt NH
Moses, Sr.: b 2-11-1729 d 8-11-1819 m Abigail Pickard Hale Pvt RI
Moses, Jr.: b 11-21-1751 d 3-2-1852 m Mary Hastings Pvt MA
Nathan: b 8-7-1760 d 5-20-1812 m (1)Rachel Phelps (2)Amelia
    Phelps (3)Hepsibah Burpee Pvt MA W★
Oliver: b 2-22-1739 d 4-24-1811 m Hannah Stiles Sgt MA
Peter: b 4-7-1761 d 3- -1815 m Eunice (Willard)Carlton Pvt MA
Reuben: b 1-24-1761 d 8-7-1827 m Sarah Cleveland Sgt NH ★

Richard: b 1-26-1730 d 5-31-1790 m Lydia Atkinson Pvt MA
Samuel: b 1743 d 1826 m Elinor Butman Lt MA
Samuel: b 8-9-1741 d 3-23-1802 m Rebecca Raymond Cpl MA
Simon: b 12-9-1753 d 1- -1831 m Zeruiah Rice Pvt MA NH W★
Solomon: b 2-5-1737 d 1815/6 m Abigail Pitcher Sgt MA
Sylas Richard: b 4-7-1751 d 10-22-1825 m Sarah Upton Pvt NH
Thomas: b 10-24-1734 d 11-8-1808 m Sarah Tenney Lt MA
Thomas: b 4-7-1748 d 7-28-1791 m Abigail Blodget Pvt PS MA
Thomas: b 6-15-1729 d 1-26-1809 m (1)Anne Osgood PS NH
Thomas: b 1-6-1755 d 2-15-1839 m (1)Priscilla (Cole) Wilkins (2)Mrs
    Eunice (Davis) Wilson Pvt NH ★
Wm., Sr.: b 10-14-1704 d 8-27-1781 m (1)Anna Whiting (2)Mrs
    Hannah Abbot PS MA
Wm., Jr.: b 4-3-1743 d 10-26-1831 m Abigail Walker Sgt MA
Wm.: b 8-27-1726 d 1808 m Mary Sawyer PS MA

STIEGEL, (includes STEGAL)
Anthony: b 9-2-1739 d 1-9-1785 m (1)Maria Elizabeth Gleassner
    (2)Christina Neip Pvt PS PA
Henry Wm.: b 5-3-1729 d 1-10-1785 m (1)Elizabeth Huber
    (2)Elizabeth Holz PS PA
Wm.: b *c.* 1740 d *p.* 9-25-1815 m (2)Sina Stokes PS VA

STIELS,
Jacob: b 9-26-1737 d 1829 m Abigail — Pvt MA

STIFF,
Jacob: b — d —m Jenny Smith Pvt VA
James: b 1758 d 5-19-1837 m Mary — Pvt VA ★
Wm.: b 1-28-1729 d 1804 m Sarah Meacham PS VA

STIFFLER,
Jacob: b 1733 d 1807 m Catharine Meyer Pvt PA
Peter: b *c.* 1735 d *p.* 3-1-1808 m Catherine — Pvt PA

STIGLEMAN,
Philip: b 1758 d 1845 m Margaret Weaver Pvt PA

STILES,
Aaron: b 6-4-1741 d 9-7-1807 m (1)Margaret Miller (2)Prob Abigail
    Beard Pvt MA
Aaron: b 8-18-1761 d 6-24-1843 m Catherine Conklin Pvt NJ ★
Abraham: b *c.* 1745 d *c.* 1814 m Patience — Pvt PA
Asa: b 3-21-1768 d 8-14-1838 m Olive Rood Pvt CT
Asahel: b 5-2-1753 d 11-29-1833 m Tryphena Chaplin Pvt CT
Asahel: b 5-21-1759 d 4-13-1854 m Bissell Gleason Vol MA
Asahel: b 1745 d *p.* 1787 m Sarah Dutton Sol NH
Ashbel: b 9-11-1735 d 10- -1810 m Hannah (Stiles) Pvt CT
Benjamin: b 5-31-1750 d *p.* 1787 m Elizabeth Cutler Sgt MA
Benjamin: b *c.* 1730 d 9-22-1805 m Sarah Staples Capt SC
Benoni: b 7-15-1763 d 1-1-1820 m Hannah Harper Pvt CT
Caleb, Jr.: b 6-19-1737 d 10- -1824 m Mary Elizabeth Townsend Sol
    NH
Cyrus: b 5-13-1753 d 8-24-1831 m (1)Hannah Curtice (2)Hannah
    Berry Pvt MA
David: b 1760 d 12- -1839 m Elizabeth Kitchell Pvt NJ
Elijah: b 5-21-1743 d 1-21-1826 m Betsey Price Kitchell Pvt NJ ★
Ezra: b 11-29-1727 d 5-12-1795 m Elizabeth Hubbard PS NH CT
Ezra: b 12-18-1749 d *p.* 1826 m Hannah Cutter Pvt MA
Gideon: b 8-10-1731 d *p.* 1781 m Sarah Taylor Lt MA
Gould: b 3-12-1750 d 2-5-1840 m (1)Delight Boughton (2)Delia
    Clark (3)Anna — Cpl CT ★
Henry: b 1730 d 4-20-1810 m Ruth (Wells) Kellogg Capt MA
Isaac: b 9-5-1729 d 3-13-1783 m Mabel Clark Sol CT
Jacob: b 9-26-1737 d 1828 m Abigail — Capt MA
James: b 11-4-1743 d 10-16-1830 m (1)Altje Henricus Cavalier
    (2)Mary Benner (3)Mrs Sarah Stevens Pvt NY
Jeremiah: b 2-23-1744 d 12-6-1800 m Mary Sanger Capt PS MA
John: b 8-21-1738 d *p.* 1780 m Betsy Olds Pvt CT
John: b 10-23-1750 d 10-19-1835 m Ruth Roberts Sgt MA
John: b 7-27-1749 d 4-25-1818 m Keziah Divoll Cpl NH
John, Jr.: b *c.* 1753 d 10-23-1830 m Mary Sanford QM NJ ★
John: b *c.* 1755 d 1825 m (1)Agnes Franklin (2)Clarissa — Sgt VA
Jonah: b 1-1-1759/60 d 3-10-1840 m Sophia Brooker Pvt MA
Joseph: b 1737 d 3-18-1820 m Eunice Wilkins Ens PS NH
Joseph: b 5-7-1706 d 11-30-1777 m Comfort — PS NJ
Joshua: b 4-6-1758 d 5-14-1828 m Abigail Gale Pvt MA
Josiah: b 5-26-1755 d 12-15-1822 m (1)Lydia Gale (2)Elizabeth
    Wadsworth Pvt MA
Levi: b 2-18-1733 d 12-21-1810 m Patience Smith 1Lt MA
Lincoln: b 8-17-1765 d 10-31-1857 m (1)Patience Johnson
    (2)Ruth — Pvt MA ★
Martin: b 11-20-1761 d 7-26-1841 m Candace Cone Pvt CT ★
Martin: b 7-17-1728 d 12-9-1808 m Dorcas Adams Lt MA
Nathan: b *c.* 1760 d *p.* 1811 m Betsey Wagner Pvt CT
Samuel: b 6- -1736 d 4-11-1819 m Phebe Brooks Pvt CT
Samuel: b 1-1-1758 d 1813 m Sara Rose Pvt MA
Shubael: b 1-7-1762 d 11-17-1845 m Eunice Owen Pvt MA
Silas: b 6-3-1750 d 1809 m Sarah Ayres Pvt NJ
Simeon: b 5-12-1726 d 3-10-1808 m Experience Pvt MA
Stephen, Jr.: b 11-5-1757 d *c.* 1785 m Irena Bliss Pvt CT
Stephen: b *c.* 1738 d *p.* 10-27-1815 m (1)Elizabeth Taler (2)Bithena
    — (3)Deborah — Sgt PA

STILES, contd.
Timothy: bpt 1743 d *p.* 1791 m (1)Phebe Kimball (2)Naomi McMillion Sgt MA
Timothy: b 1-3-1755 d 1822 m (1)Anna Carter (2)Damaris Cramer Pvt NJ
Zebediah: b 9-15-1723 d 6-14-1814 m Experience Wells Pvt MA

STILL,
Murphy D.: b 1-10-1758 d 8-4-1831 m Phoebe Rives Pvt SC

STILLE, (includes STILLEY)
John: b 11-17-1743 d *p.* 1790 m Mary — PS NC
Peter: b 1748 d 11-2-1803 m Elizabeth Orendorff 1Lt MD

STILLMAN,
Allyn: b 3-20-1731 d 7-20-1803 m (2)Prudence Kingsbury NCapt CT
Amos: b 4-24-1762 d 10-7-1807 m Mrs Naomi Kenyon Davis Ens RI
Elisha: b 2-14-1731 d 9-23-1803 m Abigail Nash PS MA
Elisha, Sr.: b 4-25-1722 d 7-26-1796 m (1)Hannah Rogers (2)Mary Davis (3)Betsy Burdick PS RI
George: b 3-7-1751 d 11-4-1804 m Rebecca Crocker Maj MA
George: b 5-19-1739 d 6-15-1817 m Esther Stillman Capt RI
John: b 8-9-1717 d 7-15-1789 m Rachel Robbins Pvt MA
John: b 3-13-1752 d *p.* 1782 m Mary Potter Pvt RI
Joseph, Sr.: b 10-21-1739 d 1-17-1794 m (1)Sarah Wright (2)Mrs Huldah (Brainard) Meeks Pvt CT
Joseph, Jr.: b 1761 d 1-3-1844 m Rhoda Boardman Sol CT ★
Joseph, Sr.: b 12-5-1716 d 8-10-1792 m Mary Maxson PS RI
Joseph, Jr.: b 2-29-1743 d 3-27-1825 m Eunice (Stillman) PS RI
Joseph: b 8-30-1752 d 12-9-1825 m Elizabeth Maxson Pvt RI
Josiah: b 9-16-1737 d 1808 m Comfort Robbins Lt MA
Nathaniel: b 1752 d 1838 m Martha Hanmer Pvt CT
Roger: b 7-4-1754 d 12-8-1832 m Mehitable Hurd Pvt CT ★
Samuel: b 9-7-1763 d 9-27-1821 m Lydia Doty Pvt CT
Waite: b 11-27-1758 d 2- -1833 m Welthy Maxson Pvt RI ★

STILLSON, (includes STILSON)
Abel: b 2-13-1754 d 8-28-1824 m Mary Hine Pvt CT
Joseph: b 1726 d 4-26-1811 m Margaret Clinton MM CT
Josiah: b 1753 d 4-23-1815 m Rebecca Clark Pvt CT

STILLWAGON, (includes STILWAGON)
Jacob, Sr.: b *c.* 1730 d *p.* 1790 m (1)Joanna Shean (2)Judith Shegan Pvt PA
Jacob, Jr.: b *c.* 1753 d 1-26-1840 m Elizabeth Zearfoss Pvt PA ★
John: b 10- -1718 d 8-24-1785 m Anna Maria — PS PA
Peter: b *a.* 1755 d 12-1-1831 m Elizabeth Pool Pvt NJ W★
Phillip: b 1757 d 7-28-1839 m Barbara — Pvt PA ★

STILLWELL, (includes STILWELL)
Azariah: b 9-30-1752 d 11- -1812 m Elizabeth Brooks Pvt NJ
Daniel: b 6-8-1747 d 9-3-1805 m Lydia Sheldon Lt RI
James: b 8-17-1755 d 4-14-1836 m Catherine Lounsberry Sgt NY
Jeremiah: b *c.* 1750 d *p.* 12- -1780 m X Pvt PA
John: b 3-15-1716 d 5-28-1800 m Ann Wall PS NJ
John: b 12-26-1738 d 9-26-1813 m Elizabeth Watson QM NJ
John: b 1730 d 8- -1825 m Sarah Stevenson Pvt NJ
John: b 1735 d 1- -1799 m Mary Mulliner Pvt NJ
John: b 2- -1760 d 4-22-1837 m Rebecca Pembroke Sol NY
John: b 12-1-1746 d 10-3-1823 m Sarah Warford Lt PA
John: b 1753 d 1833 m Josephine — Pvt VA
Joost: b 10-22-1742 d 2-21-1827 m Ann Williamson Capt NY
Joseph: b 9-28-1739 d 3-10-1805 m Mary Ogborne Capt NJ
Joseph: b 3-3-1752 d 9-10-1822 m Sarah Winters Pvt NJ
Joseph: b 3-12-1747 d 3-31-1813 m Jemima Throckmorton Pvt NJ
Joseph: b 1757 d — m Lydia Luther Pvt RI
Nicholas: b 9-20-1742 d 6-23-1792 m Rhuhamah Hand Col NJ
Nicholas: b 12-2-1709 d 10-1-1776 m Altie VanBrunt Ditmas Sol NY
Obadiah: b 7-21-1744 d 4-13-1777 m Mary — Pvt NJ
Richard: b 5-25-1742 d 3-26-1826 m Ann Ten Eyck Capt NJ
Richard: b 11-17-1739 d 3-4-1801 m Mary LaRue Capt PA
Thomas: b 12-3-1751 d 12-17-1834 m Amy Shaw Pvt MA
Thomas: b *c.* 1720 d 10- -1777 m — Pvt NY
Thomas: b *c.* 1754 d 12-2-1794 m Eveline Smith Pvt NY
Wm.: b *c.* 1745 d *p.* 1778 m Sarah Ogborne Pvt NJ

STILPHEN,
Cornelius: b 1757 d 9-1-1835 m (1)Bettie Allen (2)Martha — Sol MA

STILTS,
Philip: b *c.* 1740 d *a.* 3- -1811 m Rachel — Capt PS MD

STIMPSON, (includes STIMSON & STINSON)
Ebenezer: b 8-24-1749 d 10-31-1829 m Esther Hartshorn Sol MA
Elijah: b 5-15-1762 d 3- -1835 m Rachel Cobb Sgt NC ★
Elijah: b *c.* 1751 d 3-5-1840 m Mary Henderson Sgt PA ★
George, Sr.: b 11-5-1726 d 11-8-1796 m Abigal Clark MM Sol MA
George, Jr.: b 1764 d *p.* 1807 m Sarah Westlake Pvt MA
James: b 3-21-1745 d 4-5-1827 m Janet Allison Pvt NH ★
James: b 1762 d *p.* 9-13-1845 m Mary Parker Pvt NJ ★
James: b 1746 d *p.* 1781 m Nellie — Sol NC
Jeremiah: b 10-15-1751 d 1821 m Anne Jones Pvt MA
Joel: b 8-10-1751 d 5-15-1813 m Susanna Grow Fif CT

John: b 1756/7 d 3-26-1812 m Agnes Nancy Stinson Sol NH
John: b *c.* 1700 d *p.* 1776 m Mary Hogg PS NH
John: b 8-14-1714 d 11-11-1801 m Jane Huston PS ME MA
John, Sr.: b 10-22-1732 d 1818 m Naomi Orme Pvt MA
John, Jr.: b 5-28-1733 d 1-29-1819 m Patience Pattee PS ME MA
Joseph: b 1-12-1746 d 7-1-1810 m Rebecca Williams Pvt CT
Josiah: b *a.* 1758 d 7-6-1813 m Molly Hubbard 1Lt MA
Josiah: b *c.* 1732 d 6-23-1792 m Sarah Phillips PS MA
Lemuel: b 7-11-1758 d 9-22-1840 m Phoebe Felton Pvt MA ★
Luther: b 8-22-1764 d 10-2-1801 m Sarah McElwain Pvt MA
Samuel: b 1747 d *c.* 1800 m Martha Russ Pvt MA
Samuel, Jr.: b 1762 d 1841 m Mary Godfrey Mil MA
Stephen: b 11-5-1740 d 3-23-1815 m (1)Keziah Paulk (2)Rebecca Nye PS CT
Stephen: b *c.* 1730 d *p.* 1790 m Hannah Havin Pvt MA
Wm.: b 2-8-1756 d 1838 m Catherine Rappalye Pvt MA
Wm.: b 1-23-1756 d 1828 m Mary Fullerton Adj MA
Wm.: b 5-7-1763 d 3-9-1823 m Abiah Macomber Pvt MA ★
Wm.: b 10-14-1732 d 12-8-1812 m Catherine Nichols Dr MA

STINCHCOMB,
Thomas: b 9-19-1757 d 10-3-1827 m Ruth Owings Ens MD

STINCHFIELD,
Ephraim: b 2-11-1761 d 8-18-1837 m Sarah Herring Pvt MA
John: b 10-20-1738 d 2-21-1801 m Mehitable Winship Pvt MA
Thomas: b 12-29-1747 d 10-25-1837 m (1)Mrs Sarah (True) Paul (2)Hannah Lindsey Sol MA
Wm.: b 1-9-1741 d 5-2-1781 m Mary Bodge Pvt MA

STINGLEY,
George: b 9-12-1763 d 1838 m Klorie Hagler Sgt VA ★

STIPP,
George: b 4-22-1757 d *p.* 1835 m — Pvt VA PA

STITCHER,
Wm.: b — d *p.* 11-18-1778 m Ann — Lt NJ

STITES,
Benjamin: b — d 1791 m Rhoda — PS NJ
Benjamin: b 1748 d 8-30-1804 m (1)Rachel — Capt PA
Elijah: b 3-22-1758 d 1-6-1843 m Rhoda Brown Pvt NJ ★
Hezekiah: b 8-13-1761 d 1842/3 m (1)Deborah Ferris (2)Elizabeth Ferris MM Sgt NJ ★
Humphrey: b 4-3-1754 d 11-1-1829 m Priscilla Leaming Capt NJ
Jacob: b *c.* 1755 d 1787 m Silvithia Flower PS NJ
John: b 5-5-1706 d 4-21-1782 m (1)Abigail Rushmore (2)Margaret Hampton PS NJ
John: b 1750 d 9-24-1797 m Sarah Townsend PS NJ
Richard: b 11-8-1747 d 9-16-1776 m Sarah Cutler Dennis Capt NJ
Wm.: b 1750 d 1778 m Margarette Hush Pvt NJ

STITH,
Buckner: b 1722 d 1791 m Susanna — Capt VA
Griffin, Jr.: b 8-24-1753 d *p.* 1808 m (1)Frances Townsend Washington (2)Mary Dent Alexander (3)— Watkin PS VA
John: b 3-24-1755 d 1808 m Ann Washington Maj VA
Joseph: b 9-6-1759 d 11-3-1837 m Nancy Cocke Ens VA ★
Richard: b 9-30-1727 d 11-16-1802 m Lucy Hall PS CS VA
Wm.: b 1736 d 3-17-1799 m Katherine (Stith) PS VA

STITT,
James: b 1733 d 9-9-1817 m Amy Head Pvt NY
John: b 7-14-1752 d 1-14-1814 m Mary Mackley Sgt NY

STITZER,
David: b 3-12-1752 d 7-3-1821 m Barbara Ann Elizabeth Pofenhouser Pvt PA ★
Henry: b 7-10-1753 d 8-17-1838 m Mary Klunk Pvt PA ★
John: b 9-28-1749 d 1818/9 m Elizabeth Stimel(Stemmel) Gnr PA

STIVER,
Michael: b *c.* 1748 d 8-13-1814 m — Pvt PA

STIVERS,
Daniel: b 1763 d 4-19-1842 m Margaret Hobart Pvt NJ ★
Edward: b — d *p.* 1810 m Rebecca — Mus VA
John: b 1765 d 1841 m Martha Neel Pvt VA ★
Reuben: b 5-5-1759 d 11-25-1827 m Elizabeth Rozelle Pvt VA ★

STOBO,
James: b 1705 d 1784 m Elizabeth Scot PS SC
Richard Park: b *c.* 1735 d 3- -1785 m Mary Harvey CS PS SC

STOCK,
John: b 1746 d *p.* 1787 m Phoebe Cothrell Pvt MA
John: b 2-21-1757 d 7-7-1821 m Margaret Mumma Pvt PA
Michael: b 9-26-1754 d 3-25-1832 m (2)Barbara Ried Pvt PA

STOCKARD, (or STOCKART)
James: b 1741 d 7-26-1826 m Ellen Trousdale PS NC

STOCKBERGER,
Matthias: b c. 1750 d c. 1822 m Sarah Salome Dumbauld PS PA

STOCKBRIDGE,
Benjamin: bpt 12-11-1757 d 9-15-1832 m Elizabeth Dresser 1Lt MA
David: b 2- -1749 d 3-11-1832 m (1)Patience Bartlett (2)Mary (Nash) Wood Cpl MA
John: b 8-11-1757 d 8-23-1820 m Mary Dillingham Pvt MA ★
Joseph: b c. 1760 d c. 1836 m Sarah Mitchell Cpl MA ★
Samuel: b 5-13-1711 d 6-27-1784 m Sarah Tilden Capt MA

STOCKER, (includes STUCKER)
Adam: b 2-15-1736 d 6-27-1814 m Maria Magdalena Beisel Capt PA
Andreas: b 1746 d 1823 m Julianna Marie Watuert Pvt PA
Ebenezer: b 2-9-1749 d 1-16-1807 m Mary Potter Lt MA
George: b c. 1733 d p. 8-15-1782 m Margaret — Lt PA
George: b 8-21-1760 d 3-21-1811 m Catherine Walter Pvt PA
Michael: b 12-26-1762 d 12-21-1846 m Ann Catherine Barbara Knecht Pvt PA
Thaddeus: b 5-10-1742 d 2-25-1838 m Irene or Minerva Stone Pvt CT ★
Thomas: b 8-19-1741 d 4-20-1798 m Susanna Newhall Pvt PS MA

STOCKETT,
Thomas Noble: b 7-12-1747 d 5-16-1802 m Mary Harwood Dr MD

STOCKHAM,
George: b 1765 d 1849 m Elizabeth Biss Pvt PA

STOCKING,
Abner: b 4-1-1730 d 1-1-1816 m Ruth Higgins Capt PS CT
Abraham: b 9-26-1754 d 1832 m Abigail Smith Pvt MA
Amos: b 1756 d 1834 m (2)Deborah Henry Pvt MA
Eber: b 1-15-1755/6 d 8-26-1828 m Olive Sage Sgt CT ★
Elijah: b 12-30-1728 d 1-19-1807 m Hannah — PS CT
Elisha: bpt 4-21-1734 d 3-10-1825 m Susanna Hamlin Pvt CT
George, 1st: b 8-16-1705 d 1790 m Mercy Savage PS CT
George, 2nd: b 5-11-1728 d 8-23-1777 m Eunice Cobb Sgt CT
George, 3rd: b 5-15-1750 d 8-23-1777 m Lois Hubbard Pvt CT
John: b 1756 d 12-9-1794 m Sarah Winchell Cpl CT
Joseph: b 6-28-1723 d 1819 m Mrs Sarah (Shepherd) Cornwall Sgt CT
Reuben: b 2-12-1744 d 10-25-1828 m Sarah Hurlbut Lt CT
Samuel: b 1759 d a. 1790 m Mrs Young Pvt CT
Wm.: bpt 6-26-1757 d 7-3-1795 m (1)Elizabeth — (2)Anna Olcott Sgt CT

STOCKLEY, (includes STOCKLY & STOKELY)
Charles: b 1757/8 d p. 3-16-1805 m (1)Margaret Allen (2)Anne Taylor Lt VA
Thomas: b 3-27-1755 d 7-24-1824 m Elizabeth Mountford Capt PA

STOCKMAN,
John: b 1760 d c. 1803 m Abigal Freeman Pvt NJ
Jonathan: b 8-15-1761 d 1845 m (1)Emeline — (2)Sarah Moody Cpl MA
Roland: bpt 8-19-1744 d 9-2-1797 m (1)Bathsheba Moulton (2)Mrs Sarah Doran Pvt MA

STOCKSLAGER, (includes STOCKLEGER & STOCKSLEGER)
Adam: b 4-11-1746 d p. 1794 m Catherine Godner Pvt PA
Philip: b c. 1744/5 d 2-26-1824 m Magdalena Bauman PS PA

STOCKTON,
Abraham: b 9-19-1749 d 11-9-1827 m Susanna Kemble CS NJ
Benjamin Briarly: b 8-14-1754 d 6-9-1829 m Sarah Howell Arnett Dr NJ
Daniel: b 2-17-1727 d 4-18-1804 m Mary Clayton PS NJ
David: b c. 1735 d p. 1800 m Ann — Capt PA
Ebenezer: b 1760 d 12-9-1837 m Mrs Elizabeth (Story) Duncan SrgnMte NJ
George: b 7-20-1745 d 4-9-1818 m Rachel Dorsey Pvt VA
James: b — d 2-25-1807 m Mary Searles 1Lt NJ W★
John: b 2-26-1756 d 5-8-1832 m Mary Gardiner Pvt NJ
John: b 1733 d — m Mary Withrow Capt PA
John: b c. 1750 d p. 1790 m — PS VA
Richard: b 10-1-1730 d 2-28-1781 m Annis Boudinot SDI NJ
Robert: b 1730 d 4-24-1805 m Helen McComb QM NJ
Robert: b 10-13-1737 d 6-3-1821 m Mary Makemie Pvt PA
Robert: b 12-12-1743 d 9-21-1825 m Katherine Blakey Chp VA
Samuel Witham: b 2-4-1751 d 6-26-1795 m Catharine Cox PS NJ
Thomas, Sr.: b 1709 d 5-31-1795 m Margaret Fleming PS PA

STOCKWELL,
Abel: b 9-23-1708 d 9-7-1777 m Sarah Selden CS PS VT
Abel, Jr.: b 4-24-1744 d 11-11-1805 m (1)Patience Thomas PS VT
Daniel, Sr.: b 1719/20 d p. 1777 m Miriam — PS MA
Daniel, Jr.: b 5-13-1744 d 2-13-1817 m Rebecca Warren Sgt MA
David: b 5-14-1750 d 7-16-1824 m Abigail Giles Pvt NH
Eli: b 2-26-1759 d 3-8-1849 m Eunice Hill Pvt MA
Emmons: b 1740 d 1819 m Ruth Page Pvt CS NH
Ephraim: b 1734 d 7-13-1802 m Sarah Grout Capt MA

Jacob: b c. 1757 d 7-7-1777 m — Pvt VT
Jonas: b 1755 d 11-23-1812 m Susanna Wheeler Pvt VT
Jonathan, Jr.: b c. 1730 d 1776 m Mary Kenney Pvt MA
Stephen: b 1731 d 11-1-1807 m Mehitable Holman Pvt MA

STODDARD, (includes STODDER & STODDERT)
Aaron: b 7-15-1739 d 1-12-1777 m (2)Philena Long Pvt CT
Abijah: b 2-28-1718 d 5-6-1776 m Eunice Curtiss Pvt CT
Anthony: b 10-21-1734 d 1785 m Phebe Reed Pvt MA
Benjamin: b 1751 d 12-18-1813 m Rebecca Lowndes Maj MD
Bryant: b 11-16-1737 d 2-17-1824 m Phebe Barnes Capt CT
Daniel: b 9-6-1761 d 12-14-1840 m Lucretia Bellows Mus CT
David: b 10-17-1741 d 6-18-1818 m Sybil Leavitt Pvt MA
David: b 11-27-1726 d 8- -1777 m Joanna Kingsley Sgt NH
David, Jr.: b 10-23-1754 d 5-1-1838 m Sarah French PS NH
Ebed: b 3-15-1759 d 9-6-1836 m (1)Deborah Marsh (2)Lydia Waterman Pvt MA ★
Eli: b 2-24-1739 d 4-24-1777 m Abigail Atwood Pvt CT
Eli: b 6-17-1748 d — m Abigail Hurlburt Pvt CT
Elijah: b 12-14-1730 d 10-14-1800 m Mabel Gillett Pvt VT
Elisha: b 11-4-1735 d 1806 m Mary Ann Hunt Pvt CT
Enoch: b 1-10-1746 d p. 1785 m Dinah Fuller Pvt CT
Ezekiel: b 8-15-1762 d 3-6-1822 m Lucy Foristall Sgt MA
Gideon: b 5-27-1714 d 5-21-1780 m Olive Curtis PS CT
Hezekiah: b 5-20-1747 d 7-2-1825 m Lydia Farrow Pvt MA
Hosea: b 8-16-1756 d 9-8-1797 m Lucy Stowell Cpl MA
Ichabod: b 1-10-1741/2 d 4-20-1825 m Tabitha Billings Sgt PS CT
Jacob: b 4-2-1751 d 4-8-1810 m Mollie Stowell Pvt MA
Jacob: b 5-17-1761 d 2-12-1817 m Mary Salisbury Pvt MA ★
James: b 9-13-1747 d 3-2-1835 m Minerva Bird Capt CT
James: b 9-24-1756 d 3-11-1833 m Susannah Lincoln Arfr MA
John: b 7-12-1736 d 3-20-1818 m Eunice Kilbourn Capt CT
John: b 1-26-1730 d 1-22-1795 m Mary Atwood Lt CT
John: b 7-18-1767 d 9-15-1849 m Phebe Northrup Pvt CT
Jonathan: b 1-18-1738 d 3-13-1811 m (1)Sabra Andrus (2)Candice Gilbert (3)Charity Grannis Ens CT
Kenelm Truman: b 9-11-1739 d c. 1778-84m Letitia Dent Maj PS MD
Laban: b 7-16-1744 d 11-18-1826 m (1)Persis Wilder (2)Celia Sprague Smn MA
Lemuel: b 5-15-1760 d 3-18-1851 m Mary Thomas Pvt NH
Mark: b 10-10-1742 d 3-8-1829 m Lucy Allyn Sgt CT
Melzar: b 1752 d 4-19-1831 m Lucy W Turner Pvt MA
Nathan: b 8-8-1742 d 11-15-1777 m Eunice Sanford Capt CT
Nathaniel, Sr.: b 5-8-1727 d 2-24-1803 m Elizabeth Sprague Pvt MA
Nathaniel, Jr.: b 6-18-1758 d 10-20-1828 m (1)Sarah Garner (2)Hannah Todd Pvt MA
Obadiah: b 7-4-1760 d p. 1797 m Celia Vining Pvt MA
Obed: b 4-5-1743 d 12-3-1777 m Mary Harrison Pvt CT
Orange: b 5-29-1742 d 10-3-1824 m Experience Nash Capt MA
Othniel: b 8-13-1754 d 4-8-1803 m Ruth Vinal Pvt MA
Ralph, Sr.: b 7-30-1723 d 8-30-1811 m Susannah (Elderkin) Avery Capt CT
Ralph, Jr.: b 1750/1 d 12-31-1831 m Mable Newton Sgt CT
Robert: b 6-2-1757 d 6-27-1842 m Sarah Lee Sgt CT ★
Robert: b 8-26-1729 d 4-20-1802 m (1)Lucy Billings (2)Sarah Rogers Cpl CT
Samuel: b 7-1-1759 d 4-9-1838 m Susanna Mansfield Pvt & Smn MA ★
Stephen: b 2-9-1736/7 d 1797 m (2)Grace Whiton Sgt MA
Stephen: b 9-5-1756 d 10-6-1835 m (1)Lucy Stoddard (2)Mary Waterman Sgt MA
Thomas: b 4-2-1751 d 3-19-1822 m Molly Lewis Sgt MA
Thomas: b c. 1745 d 5-19-1816 m Abigail Culver CS PS PA
Vine: b 2-27-1749 d 1-29-1834 m (1)Jemima Fish (2)Abigail Avery Ens CT
Zenas: b 9-23-1758 d 1793 m Ruth Beal Gnr MA

STOEHR,
Christopher: b 2-8-1750 d 7-22-1821 m Maria Dorothy Doudel Lt PA

STOFFT, (includes STUFF)
Jacob: b 1-13-1754 d 2-1-1798 m Anna Maria Bockritter Pvt PA
Nicholas: b 1-31-1750 d 12-26-1827 m Catharine Mowan Pvt PA

STOKELL,
John: b 1744 d p. 1788 m (2)Elizabeth Briard Mstr NH

STOKER,
Edward: b 1757 d 5-7-1846 m Anna Ricker Pvt VA ★
John: b 4-3-1754 d 11-7-1833 m Elizabeth Critton Pvt VA
Thomas: b a. 1747 d 1-12-1778 m Elizabeth — Pvt VA

STOKES, (includes STOAKES)
Allen: b — d p. 1-10-1781 m (2)Mrs Ann Freeman PS VA
Christopher: b 11-5-1755 d 10-6-1806 m Mary Dunford Sgt VA
David: b 3-18-1745 d 1797 m Mary Marable PS VA
Jeremiah: b 6-19-1736 d p. 6-12-1811 m Elizabeth Hughes PS MD
John: b 4-8-1764 d 4-28-1840 m Sarah Hall Pvt NC ★
Joshua: b 4-6-1716 d 1779 m Amy Hinchman PS NJ
Montfort: b 3-12-1762 d 11-4-1842 m (1)Mary Irwin (2)Rachel Montgomery Sol NC
Peter: b 10-25-1758 d p. 1779 m Sallie Smith Ens VA

STOKES, contd.
Richard: b 1-20-1764 d 11-7-1848 m Jerusha Lay Pvt CT ★
Sylvanus: b c. 1737 d 1798 m Sarah Walker Allen Pvt VA
Wm.: b 1735 d a. 7-1-1811 m Lucretia Ellis PS VA
Zachariah: b 1757 d 1803 m Rhoda Robertson Pvt VA

STOLP, (includes STALB)
Peter: b 1741 d 9-5-1826 m Catherine Chrysler Pvt NY
Ulrich: b 1747 d 1823 m Elisabetha Derr Ens PA

STOLTZ,
John: b 1754 d 7-30-1865 m Magdeline Caplinger Cpl PA

STONE,
Aaron: b 10-21-1741 d 1-7-1821 m (1)Lois Dudley (2)Mrs Abigail
  Coe Cpl CT
Aaron, Sr.: b 1747 d 1814 m Betsey Ray Pvt NY
Abel: b 4-20-1742 d 6-15-1835 m (1)Lydia Whittaker (2)Mrs
  Patience Elliot Ens NH ★
Abner: b 2-2-1751 d 10-1-1829 m Persis Moore Pvt MA
Abner: b 1755 d 1821 m (2)Anna B Powers Pvt NY
Abraham: b 5-8-1748 d 1838 m Mary Osgood Cpl MA
Ambrose: b 1743 d 8-12-1813 m Mary Everden Pvt MA
Ambrose: b 4-21-1757 d 3-18-1850 m Katherine Partridge Pvt MA
Amos: b 9-28-1759 d 1842 m (2)Elizabeth Holiday Pvt MA ★
Archibald: b 10-19-1740 d c. 1811 m Rhoda Dewey Sgt VT
Benajah: b 1758 d 1-29-1825 m Phoebe Hotchkiss Capt CT
Benjamin: b 10-17-1739 d 9-10-1830 m Ann Tolls Capt CT
Benjamin: b c. 1732 d p. 1790 m Susannah Buckman Pvt MA
Benjamin: 2-27-1727 d 1806 m Rebecca Littlefield CS PS ME MA
Benjamin: b 6-13-1738 d p. 1784 m Prudence Farnsworth PS MA
Benjamin: b 1-14-1756 d 7-14-1843 m Rachel Grandy Pvt NH
Benjamin: b c. 1733 d p. 1778 m — Pvt NC
Benjamin: b 1743 d 6-4-1833 m Anna Asbury Sgt SC
Carder: b 1763 d p. 12-21-1849 m — Pvt RI
Clark: b 5-31-1757 d 7-6-1825 m Chloe Kelley Pvt MA
Cudbeth: b c. 1758 d 6-24-1844 m Sally — Pvt MD
Daniel: b 6-21-1751 d 11-15-1834 m Penelope Sperry Pvt CT
Daniel: b 10-25-1752 d 1-22-1792 m Abigail Jones Capt MA
Daniel, Jr.: b 1739 d p. 1809 m (1)Hannah Town (2)Hannah Gould
  Pvt MA
Daniel: b 4-11-1727 d 4-3-1816 m Persis Haynes PS MA
David: b 12-6-1750 d 12-9-1827 m Sarah Treadwell Cpl MA
David: b 9-24-1728 d 11-19-1802 m Mary Herring Pvt MA
David: b 10-12-1761 d 7-24-1833 m Lucy Sampson Pvt MA ★
David: b 2-26-1736 d 7-26-1834 m (1)Anny Moffitt (2)Alice Smith
  PS VT
Ebenezer: b 3-8-1756 d 2- -1803 m Jerusha — Cpl CT
Ebenezer, Sr.: b 9-8-1722 d 10- -1807 m Sarah Crowell Pvt MA
Ebenezer, Jr.: bpt 8-23-1747 d p. 1786 m Hannah Hathorne Pvt VT
Edmund: b 4-24-1743 d 3-13-1829 m (1)Susanna Whitney (2)Lavina
  Reed Sgt MA
Eliah: b 5-5-1737 d 8-31-1822 m Sarah Hubbard PS MA
Elias, Sr.: b 4-2-1728 d 1801 m Sarah Sawyer PS MA
Elias, Jr.: b 10-3-1757 d 8-16-1816 m Sarah Boardman Arms Pvt
  MA
Elijah: b 1-21-1749 d 6-20-1831 m Eunice Savage Pvt MA
Eliphalet: b 12-5-1735 d 2-9-1817 m Lydia Goddard Lt PS CS NH
Enoch: b c. 1760 d 8/9- -1823 m Nancy Anthony PS NC
Enos: b 8-5-1744 d 1822 m Sarah Stoddard Capt MA
Ephraim: b 1-11-1765 d 1- -1841 m Sarah Ames Pvt MA
Ezekiel: b 1751 d — m Lovely Esther Pvt NH
Ezekiel: b 11-24-1756 d 9-15-1855 m Jane Wood OrdlSgt NC ★
Francis: b 1-13-1740/1 d 12-12-1802 m (1)Martha Chase (2)Sarah
  Witt Capt MA
Francis: b c. 1750 d 2-24-1817 m Ann — Pvt NC
Frederick: b 11-11-1734 d 12-19-1792 m Mary Hambright Pvt PA
George: b 3-21-1760 d 12-8-1834 m (1)Hannah Lovering (2)Abigail
  Currier Sol MA ★
Gregory: b 2-5-1754 d 4-12-1807 m Lucy Jones Pvt MA W★
Henry: b 1745 d 12- -1830 m Mollie Brown Pvt CT
Henry: b c. 1735 d 1810 m Susannah Zorn PS VA
Henry: b 1762 d p. 1833 m — Pvt VA ★
Isaac: b 2-25-1743 d 4-15-1826 m Parthenia Dudley Capt MA
Isaac: b 2-22-1731/2 d p. 1790 m Sarah Lyon Pvt CT
Isaac: b 6-30-1766 d 4-21-1844 m Chloe Mosey Sol MA
Isaac: b 1731 d 12-3-1794 m Martha Monroe Sol MA
Isaac: b 2-17-1723/4 d 1776 m Keziah Pierce 1Lt NH
Israel: b 4-15-1749 d 7-3-1808 m (1)Lydia Barrett (2)Mary
  Broadhurst Corner Pvt MA
Israel: b 1-2-1751/2 d 1-3-1844 m Tryphena Boyden Pvt MA
Ithiel: b a. 1733 d 1799 m Martha Baldwin PS CT
Jabez: b 4-1-1764 d 10-3-1849 m Freelove Manchester Pvt RI
Jacob: b 7-25-1756 d 1825 m Abigail Howe Pvt NH
Jacob: b 1758 d 1838 m Eva Cooper Pvt SC ★
James: b 8- -1722 d 12-2-1800 m Hanna Holloway LCol MA
James: b 12-15-1744 d — m Sarah Billings Sgt MA
James: b 2-23-1755 d 1-5-1841 m Elizabeth Haven Pvt MA
James, Sr.: b 1-23-1701/2 d 2-27-1783 m Mary Farwell PS MA
James: b 8-11-1727 d 6-24-1788 m (1)Deborah Nutting (2)Susanna
  Fosgate CS PS MA
James: b c. 1749 d 5-15-1790 m Lydia Abbott Pvt NH

James: b 3-27-1751 d 3-27-1836 m Rebecca Sheldon Pvt RI
James: b c. 1760 d p. 1830 m Mary — Sol SC
Jeduthun: b 1-14-1748 d 3-8-1829 m Elizabeth How Pvt MA
Jeremiah: b 1745 d 1825 m (1)Dinah Knight Ens RI
Jeremiah: b c. 1742 d p. 9-17-1823 m Susannah — Pvt VA
Jesse: b 9-28-1737 d 7-26-1803 m Elizabeth Livermore Capt MA
Joel, Sr.: b 5-1-1742 d 8-19-1806 m Eunice Holden Sgt MA
Joel: b 1751 d 1-21-1825 m (1)Sarah Stone (2)Hannah Adams Pvt
  MA
John: b 12-18-1732 d 7-30-1819 m Lucy Fletcher Capt MA
John: b 6-21-1732 d 8-1-1817 m Mary Haven Capt MA
John: b 10-15-1728 d 1791 m (1)Eunice Cutts Raynes (2)Martha
  Greenough QM MA
John: b 6-12-1736 d 1797 m Martha Craft Sgt MA
John: b 7-6-1751 d 12-6-1814 m Lydia Byam Pvt MA
John: b 2-11-1757 d 8-18-1844 m Ann Hunt Pvt MA ★
John: b 3-7-1755 d 5-29-1819 m Mary Tufts Pvt MA
John: b 5-15-1763 d 2-20-1849 m Nancy Rice Pvt MA
John: b 3-7-1765 d 4-13-1849 m (1)Elizabeth Stanley (2)Mrs
  Rebecca (Cooledge) Ward Pvt NH
John: b 1714 d p. 8-6-1775 m (2)Mrs Mary (Warren) Musgrove PS
  MD
John: b 6-30-1761 d 11-25-1831 m Hannah Stratton Sol NH
John: b 1750 d 1827 m Polly Russell Pvt NC
John: b 1761 d 1841 m Maria Magdalena Seibold Pvt PA ★
John: b 11-25-1754 d 7-10-1824 m (1)Dollie Hoskins (2)Lucy
  Hoskins Pvt CS PS VA
John Evarts: b 11-28-1760 d 1-29-1852 m Eunice Goldsmith Pvt CT★
John H.: b 1745 d 10-5-1804 m — Cowden Col MD
Jonas: b 9-5-1722 d 9-13-1804 m Anna (Stone) Pvt MA
Jonas: b 8-12-1725 d 3-23-1809 m (1)Rachel Stow Rice (2)Anna
  Parker Pvt CS MA
Jonas: b 11-1-1737 d 4-26-1816 m Rebekah Fletcher Pvt PS MA
Jonas, Jr.: b 6-13-1749 d 2-4-1835 m (1)Martha Winchester
  (2)Abigail Winchester Pvt MA
Jonas: b 12-3-1710 d 10-29-1790 m (1)Elizabeth Adams PS
  MA
Jonas, Jr.: b 1741 d 4-24-1814 m Sarah Buckman Pvt MA
Jonathan: b c. 1756 d 4-19-1834 m Damaris Elder Cpl ME
Jonathan: b 3-4-1752 d 3-24-1801 m Susanna Mathews Capt MA
Jonathan, Sr.: b 11-17-1725 d 12-21-1806 m (1)Ruth Livermore
  (2)Mary Gates (3)Martha — Pvt MA
Jonathan, Jr.: b 3-8-1750 d 11-24-1809 m Sarah Hall Lt MA
Jonathan, Jr.: b 3-14-1725 d 10-3-1805 m Martha Cutter Pvt MA
Jonathan, Jr.: b 5-7-1748 d 1776 m Hannah Gates Pvt MA
Jonathan: b 5-7-1732 d 1-7-1799 m (1)Hannah Griffin (2)Phebe
  Downing (3)Sarah Washburn Pvt MA
Jonathan: b 7-4-1755 d 3-27-1837 m Philisa Cooke OrdlSgt NC ★
Joseph: b 7-12-1750 d 11-19-1825 m (1)Lydia Rice (2)Mrs Mary
  (Keyes) Field Sgt MA
Joseph: b c. 1750 d p. 1837 m (1)Susanna Gates (2)Betsey
  Williams Drm MA
Joseph: b 10-13-1761 d 1-8-1833 m Mary Bowen Pvt RI W★
Joshua: b c. 1725 d c. 5- -1822 m Mary Coleman Capt VA
Josiah: b 7-29-1730 d p. 1790 m Mary Sanford Pvt MA
Josiah, Sr.: b 12-23-1724 d 4-12-1785 m Anne Haven PS CS MA
Josiah: b 2-22-1762 d 9-3-1820 m (1)Elizabeth Fiske (2)Ann
  (Nancy) Stone Pvt MA
Josiah: b 5-1-1758 d c. 1792-1805 m Abigail Cheney Pvt MA
Josiah: b 2-6-1750 d 5-23-1833 m (1)Hannah Weld (2)Margaret
  Williams Pvt NH ★
Josiah: b 2-10-1759 d 5-20-1845 m Millicent Wheeler Pvt NH
Josiah: b c. 1755 d p. 1817 m Mary Washington Donaldson Pvt VA
Josias: b 1725 d 1789-1793 m Mary Coleman Sgt PS VA
Julius: b 2-27-1754 d 3-10-1835 m Esther (Sperry) Wheaton Pvt CT
Leonard: b 4-13-1746 d 4-18-1818 m Mrs Catherine Wyman
  Kendall Lt MA
Levi: b 7-1-1753 d 1832 m Bettie Clarke Pvt CT
Levi: b 5-16-1750 d 2-4-1830 m Lydia Ward Pvt MA
Marshall: b 1748 d p. 1791 m (1)Sarah — (2)Betty Harris PS MD
Matthias: b 10-23-1723 d 1814 m (1)Susanna Chadwick (2)Huldah
  Fletcher PS CS NH
Micah: b c. 1729 d 9-6-1813 m (1)Rachel Haynes (2)Mrs Sarah
  Tilton Batchelder LCol MA
Micah: b 4-10-1735 d 11-7-1806 m (1)Mary Whitney (2)Elizabeth
  Lawrence Sgt PS MD
Moses: b 6-26-1734 d 1-26-1804 m Hannah Moore Capt MA
Moses, Sr.: b 12-16-1723 d 12-2-1796 m Hannah Taintor Pvt MA
Moses, Jr.: b 6-16-1749 d 7-25-1803 m (1)Elizabeth Stone
  (2)Abigail Learned Sgt MA
Nahum: b 11-25-1752 d 9-7-1821 m Hannah Haven Cpl MA
Nathan: b 8-9-1746 d 12-19-1827 m Freelove Phillips Sol MA
Nathan: b 8-14-1746 d 7-3-1793 m Eunice Stone Pvt MA
Nathan: b 1750 d 3-27-1833 m Mercy Matterson Lt VT
Nathaniel: b 9-8-1753 d 4-11-1835 m Rebekah Woodward Sol MA
Nathaniel, Sr.: b 5-7-1714 d 5- -1793 m Ruth Stone PS MA
Nathaniel, Jr.: b 7-21-1760 d 4-5-1843 m Jerusha Learned Pvt MA
Nathaniel: b 4-11-1732 d p. 1779 m (1)Thankful Morse (2)Mrs
  Rhoda (Goddard) Goddard Sol NH
Nathaniel: b c. 1759 d 8-2-1833 m Mercy Gorton Sgt RI W★
Nathaniel: b 11-15-1761 d 1-24-1837 m Lucretia Fox Pvt VT ★
Nehemiah: b c. 1750 d 2-20-1809 m Mary Hutson Pvt MA
Nehemiah, Jr.: b 10-11-1759 d 1856 m Lucy Bartlett Pvt MA

Nimrod: b 10-1-1764 d 1841 m Sarah (Craig) Russell Pvt VA
Oliver: b 1757 d 2-23-1835 m (1)Margaret Boughton (2)Lydia Price Pvt CT
Peter: b 8-25-1741 d 10-18-1820 m Abigail Fassett Sgt MA
Philip: b 1742 d 3-6-1813 m Submit Ward CS PS VT
Reuben: b 1-18-1740 d *p.* 1790 m Rachel Stone PS CT
Reuben: b 3-13-1726 d 10-5-1804 m Elizabeth Chittenden Capt CT
Reuben: b 1755 d 2-9-1849 m Polly Stone Pvt SC ★
Richard: b 1762 d 1-1-1830 m — Lupfer Pvt PA
Richard: b — d *p.* 9-7-1795 m Mary — PS VA
Rowland: b 8-1-1764 d 1844 m Elizabeth Miller Pvt SC ★
Russell: b 1-26-1759 d 12-11-1803 m Lois (Stone) Grd CT
Salmon: b 4-17-1744 d 10-4-1831 m Susanna Page Capt NH
Samuel: b 1764 d 10-2-1854 m (1)Caroline — (2)Fanny — Pvt CT ★
Samuel: b 6-8-1727 d 12-15-1806 m (1)Martha Earle (2)Mrs Eunice Smith Capt MA
Samuel, Sr.: b 10-31-1714 d 1776 m Dorothy Monk Cpl MA
Samuel, Jr.: b *c.* 1737 d *p.* 1784 m Katharine Hewets Cpl MA
Samuel, Jr.: b 12-14-1750 d 12-12-1841 m Anna Stacy Cpl MA ★
Samuel: b 11-7-1751 d 11- -1831 m Martha Wilder Drm MA
Samuel: b 9-15-1754 d 5-23-1820 m Hannah Craig Pvt MA W★
Samuel, Sr.: b 9-30-1716 d 1787 m Rebecca Clarke MM MA
Samuel: b 11-24-1756 d 6-9-1837 m Anna Thompson Pvt VT
Seth: b 1761 d 4-22-1826 m Lucy — Pvt CT ★
Seth, Jr.: b 1-20-1754 d 6-10-1822 m (1)Anna Evarts (2)Abigail Bradley Pvt CT
Seth: b 12-26-1752 d 5-27-1827 m (1)Mary Tufts (2)Polly Hopkins 2Lt MA
Shubael: b 12-14-1766 d 6-21-1823 m Polly Rogers Pvt MA ★
Silas: b 2-11-1742 d 7-31-1827 m Eunice Fairbanks Pvt MA
Silas, Jr.: b 1757 d 1837 m Polly White Pvt MA
Silas: b 4-5-1755 d 7-12-1820 m (1)Jennet Twitchell (2)Mrs Caroline (Jones) Leland Pvt MA NH
Silas: b 4-29-1728 d 1777 m Elizabeth Russell Pvt NH
Simeon: b 1722 d 5-12-1785 m Hannah Kendall Pvt MA
Solomon: b 10-23-1740 d 7-13-1814 m Thankful Stone Pvt CT
Spencer: b 6-3-1755 d 1-1-1813 m (1)Sally Smith Pvt VA
Stephen 2: b 8-13-1721 d 9- -1792 m (1)Rebecca Bishop (2)Deliverance Chapman Pvt CT
Stephen: b 1750 d *p.* 3-28-1838 m Kezziah A. — Pvt VA ★
Sylvannus: b 10-17-1713 d 12-13-1785 m Lydia Wright Pvt CT
Sylvanus: b 1-11-1761 d 2-27-1852 m (1)Asenath Lyon (2)Mehitable Kellogg Pvt MA
Thomas, Sr.: b 3-16-1731 d 1778 m Leah Norton Pvt CT
Thomas, Jr.: b 1755 d 9-10-1843 m Mary Parmelee Sgt CT ★
Thomas: b 1742/3 d 10-5-1787 m Margaret Brown SDI MD
Thomas: b 1751 d 3-21-1819 m Rachel Marsh Pvt MA
Thomas.: b *c.* 1720 d 10-7-1807 m Rebecca Johnson PS NH
Thomas, Jr.: b *c.* 1735-40 d 11- -1811 m Elizabeth Carder Sgt RI
Thomas: b *c.* 1760 d *p.* 1830 m Elizabeth Corder Cpl VA
Thomas: b *c.* 1740 d *p.* 7-21-1812 m Sally — Pvt VA
Thomas: b 2-23-1720 d 4-16-1795 m (1)Phebe Price (2)Margaret Wells PS VA
Uriah: b 5-16-1713 d 10-24-1797 m Mary Blount PS MA
Uriah: b 12-1-1748 d 4-7-1807 m Hepzibah Hadley Cpl PS NH
Valentine: bpt 4-30-1751 d 9- -1822 m (1)— Evans (2)Keziah French Madden Pvt VA
Warren: b 7-22-1766 d 10-28-1849 m (1)Martha Bedell (2)Mary — (3)Silvey — Sol NC
Wm.: b 7-10-1759 d 3-20-1840 m Tamson Graves Pvt CT
Wm.: b 5-3-1760 d 2-7-1839 m (1)Sarah Clark (2)Mrs Hannah (Perry) Jenney Cpl MA ★
Wm.: b 1-16-1726/7 d *p.* 1790 m (1)Hannah Briggs (2)Hannah Tolman Pvt MA
Wm.: b 1-29-1730 d 12-8-1804 m Anna Woodbury Pvt MA
Wm.: b 1744-6 d 5-22-1836 m Martha Gray Pvt MA ★
Wm.: b 10-6-1750 d 5- -1808 m Hannah Barnard Pvt MA
Wm, 2d: b 1733 d 9-18-1821 m Lydia Westcott (Westcott) PS CS RI
Wm. 3d: b 12-24-1757 d 12-3-1839 m Lucy Scott Sgt RI ★
Windsor: b 5-30-1764 d 1-15-1838 m Betsey Mellen Pvt MA
Zachariah: b 10-2-1731 d 2-20-1786 m Susanna Foster Pvt MA
Zedikiah: b 3-4-1710 d 11- -1796 m Mrs (Shrivers) Hobson PS NC

STONEBACK,
Baltser: b *c.* 1736 d 11- -1823 m Anna Maria — Pvt PA

STONEBRAKER,
Sebastian: b 1757 d 7-6-1836 m Susanna Yeagle Pvt PA ★

STONECYPHER,
Henry: b 2-4-1755 d 7-12-1841 m Elizabeth Hoffheinze Pvt PA
John: b 1756 d 12-16-1850 m Nancy Curtis Pvt NC ★

STONEHAM,
Henry: b — d 1-18-1815 m Jane Dillard Cpl VA
John: b 1715 d 1784 m Elizabeth Markam PS PA

STONER, (includes STEINER)
Abraham: b *c.* 1745/6 d 9- -1824 m Mary — Pvt VA
Augustus: b 1765 d 1826 m Sara Whittington Drm PA
Christian: b 1754 d 12-12-1811 m Barbara Shank Pvt PA
David: b 1-25-1758 d 11-6-1843 m Elizabeth Stover PS MD
David: b *c.* 1736 d 1820 m Margaret — Pvt PA

David: b *c.* 1750 d 1806 m Anna Phyfer Pvt PA
George Michael (Holstein): b 1748 d 9-3-1813 m Frances Tribble Pvt KY VA
Henry: b *c.* 1750 d 9- -1780 m Elizabeth Link Pvt PA
Jacob: b 3-10-1732 d *a.* 3-8-1804 m Adrain Ferguson PS MD
John: b *a.* 1737 d 9- -1798 m Catherine Elizabeth Ramsburg Capt MD
John: b 1756 d 2-5-1827 m Mary Jack Pvt MD
John: b 1748 d 3-24-1825 m Ann Coffman Capt PA
Nicholas: b 12-15-1761 d 11-24-1853 m (1)Anna Scarborough Mason (2)Mrs Hannah Frank Pvt NY ★
Peter: b 6-6-1764 d 4-7-1851 m Eva Cotner Pvt NC ★

STONEUM,
Henry: b *a.* 1760 d 1-18-1815 m Jane Dillard Sol VA

STONEY,
John: b 1749 d 10-12-1821 m Elizabeth Caulfield Pvt SC

STONG,
Henry: b *a.* 1760 d *c.* 1826 m Elizabeth Schweitzer Pvt PA

STOOPS,
Eliakim: b 2-11-1756 d 3-26-1815 m Margaret — Pvt NJ
James: b 1754 d *c.* 1813/14 m Jean Sherer Pvt PA
Philip: b 8-20-1754 d *p.* 1791 m — Spence Pvt DE ★
Robert: b *c.* 1744 d 1797 m (1) — (2)Rachel Milar Sgt PA

STOPHLET, (or STOFFLET)
John Michael: b 1730 d 1782 m Elizabeth Engel Capt PA

STOPPLEBEEN,
Valentine: b *c.* 1745 d 12-12-1794 m Mary Ashley Pvt NY

STORER,
Amos: bpt 9-13-1729 d *p.* 1800 m (1)Joanna Penney (2)Susanna Bennett PS ME
Ebenezer: b 1752 d 9-12-1801 m (1)Eunice Brewster (2)Mary Bellows Smn CT
Ebenezer: b 7-9-1758 d 1-23-1846 m (1)Eunice Titcomb (2)Catherine Stephenson Lt MA ★
Ebenezer, Jr.: b 1-2-1730 d 6-1-1807 m (1)Elizabeth Green (2)Mrs Hannah Lincoln CS MA
Elias: bpt 5-5-1765 d 9- -1824 m Sarah (Hamilton) Grant Pvt MA
Jeremiah: b *a.* 1740 d *c.* 1797-1820 m Abigail Wells PS MA
John: b *c.* 1750 d *c.* 1816 m Catherine — Mstr NJ
Joseph: b *c.* 1744 d 10- -1777 m Joanna Graves Cpl ME
Matthias: b *c.* 1754 d 8-11-1806 m Elizabeth Mitchell Pvt MA
Nathaniel: b — d 1811 m Polly Augusta Boutecore Sol Mar CT
Thomas: b *c.* 1730 d 1801 m Elizabeth — Pvt NJ
Wm.: b 5-11-1765 d 5-2-1843 m (1)Deborah Beman (2)Mary Street Pvt CT ★

STORM, (includes STRUM)
Garret: b 9-18-1722 d 1801 m Mary Stickles PS NY
Isaac: b 9-2-1762 d *p.* 1840 m Rebecca Wilsey Pvt NY ★
Isaac: b 1730 d 1813 m Elizabeth Losee Pvt NY
Isaac, Jr.: b 1767 d *p.* 1812 m Jane Salisbury Pvt NY
Jacob: b 5-12-1754 d 10-4-1799 m Julian Herr Pvt MD
Jacob: b 1756 d 3- -1830 m Mary Margaret — Wgn MD
Jacob: b 1762 d 4-6-1842 m Catherine Frushour Pvt MD
John: b 8-10-1765 d 3-27-1835 m Susanna Brinkerhoff Pvt NY
John: b *c.* 1750 d *c.* 1810 m Jemima Chancy Mil NY
John: b 1735 d 1793 m Elizabeth — Pvt NY
John: b 1725 d 1790 m Catherine — Sgt VA
John: b 2-3-1760 d 12-13-1835 m Anne Parsons Pvt VA ★
Leonard: b 5-22-1736 d 7-12-1819 m Catherine — Sol MD
Thomas: b 4-10-1740 d 7-9-1829 m Catherine Hogeboom PS NY
Thomas: b 1749 d 8-4-1833 m Elizabeth Graham Capt PS NY

STORMS,
Abraham: b 6-6-1759 d 6-27-1838 m Aeltje Snedeker Pvt NY ★
John: b 9-10-1752 d 11-30-1845 m Elizabeth Sidman Pvt NY ★
Nicholas, Sr.: b 1722 d *a.* 1790 m (1)Rachel — (2)Maritje Dutcher Pvt NY

STORRS,
Benjamin: b 5-21-1752 d 2-25-1805 m (1)Olive Mackall (2)Mrs Margaret (Tracey) Lathrop Sgt CT
Dan: b 2-7-1748 d 1-5-1831 m (1)Ruth Conant (2)Mary Southworth QM CT
Ebenezer: b 8-26-1744 d 10-9-1838 m Lois Southworth Pvt NY
Eleazer: b 1744-8 1738 d 12-24-1810 m Anna Phelps PS MA
Huckins: b 11-6-1732 d *p.* 1780 m Mrs Jerusha (Bicknell) Allen Pvt PS NH
John H. Jr.: b 12-1-1735 d 10-9-1799 m (1)Eunice (Conant) Howe (2)Hannah Moore Chp CT
Joseph: b 3-8-1711 d 10-5-1785 m (1)Hannah Porter (2)Experience Gurley CS CT
Joshua: b *a.* 1751 d 1779 m Susanna Pleasants PS VA
Josiah: b 11-3-1755 d 1845 m Diadamia Woodworth Pvt CT
Justus: b 9-22-1756 d 12-3-1818 m Sarah Wright Dr NY CT
Nathaniel: b 1-27-1751 d 1829 m Martha Burrows Pvt CT
Nathaniel: b 6-21-1747 d 8-25-1813 m Ruth Hall Pvt NH

STORRS, contd.
Rodger: b 1758 d 1819 m Charlotte Moore Pvt CT
Thomas: b 1-16-1716 d 5-14-1802 m Eunice Paddock PS CT

STORTS,
John Jacob: b 10-7-1763 d 1-12-1852 m (1)Christina Keller (2)Mary Ann (Burkhead) Notestine Cpl MD

STORY, (includes STOREY & STORRY)
Andrew: b 1756 d 10-22-1825 m Molly Brown Pvt MA
Anthony: b 1746 d 9-12-1783 m Sarah Faris Sol Cav SC
Asa: b 9-1-1748 d 2-1-1828 m Abiah Giddings Lt CT
Daniel: b 7-23-1749 d 12-6-1823 m Ruth Burnham Sgt NH
David: bpt 10-6-1745 d 3-20-1834 m Thankful Burnham PS CS NH
Ebenezer: b 6-26-1749 d 1781 m Mehitable Webb Slr CT
Elisha: b 1752 d 10-21-1817 m Lois Perkins Pvt MA
Elisha: b 12-3-1743 d 8-27-1805 m (1)Ruth Ruddock (2)Mehitable Stacey Pedrick Dr MA
Enoch: b 2-5-1757 d c. 1850 m Polly — Pvt MA ★
Francis: b 9-15-1761 d 5-30-1830 m Ruth Beeman Pvt VT
George, Sr.: b c. 1725 d 1- -1805 m Nancy Cantor PS SC
George, Jr.: b 1758 d p. 1805 m Susie Elder Pvt SC
Henry: b 7-9-1753 d 10-6-1821 m Hannah Tewksbury Pvt MA
Henry: b 6-21-1757 d 3-19-1837 m Elizabeth Cunningham Sgt SC ★
Jacob: b 1714 d 5-12-1796 m Mary Butler Lt MA
Jacob: b 1762 d 1835 m Susanna Merrill Pvt VT
James: b 9-10-1760 d 1840 m Deborah Avery Pvt CT ★
James: b 10-17-1762 d 12-16-1851 m Sarah Woodbury Pvt MA ★
James: b 1763 d 1785 m Sarah Schenck Pvt NJ
John: b 1-8-1739 d 10-14-1785 m Hannah Perkins Sgt MA
John: b 7-13-1746 d 4-1-1802 m Sarah Lake Dep QMGen NJ
John: b 1761 d 9-12-1845 m Martha Caughey Pvt VA ★
John: b 1762 d 1-20-1840 m — Pvt VA ★
Jonathan: bpt 10-6-1745 d 5-21-1822 m Lydia Saunders Sgt MA
Joseph: b 10-1-1752 d 1-6-1826 m Rachel Low Pvt PS NH
Nehemiah, Sr.: b 9-29-1720 d 7-4-1802 m Sarah Gold Pvt MA
Nehemiah, Jr.: bpt d 2-26-1748/9 d 1784 m Lucy Allen Mstr MA
Samuel: b 3-2-1755 d 6-24-1806 m Olive Catlin Pvt MA
Solomon: b 1739/40 d 8-17-1820 m (1)Elizabeth Thomas (2)Dorothy Rude 1Lt CT
Solomon: b 1726 d 5-22-1816 m Dorcas Branch Pvt MA
Stephen, Jr.: bpt 8-22-1762 d 10-9-1825 m Mary Boyd Sgt MA
Thomas: b 4-20-1746 d 4-1-1816 m Hannah Burnham Sgt MA
Wm., Sr.: bpt c. 1720 d p. 11- -1787 m Mary Giddings PS MA
Wm., Jr.: b 1749 d 1-9-1800 m (1)Mary Choate (2)Lydia Giddings Capt MA
Wm.: b 3-17-1748 d 12-17-1806 m Bathsheba Gray Pvt MA

STOTTLEMEYER,
Davalt: b c. 1756 d 4-9-1841 m Barbara Bossert Pvt MD

STOUGH,
George: b 1717 d 8-11-1803 m (1)Ann Margaretta Deish (2)Christina Bauman PS PA
Jacob: b 1753 d 1820 m Mary Ann — Sol PA
Jacob: b 1753 d 1-3-1823 m Catherine — Pvt PA
Nicholas: b 1730 d 1790 m Katharine Elizabeth — Pvt PA

STOUGHTON,
Augustus: b c. 1759 d 3-25-1837 m Cylinda Bissell Pvt CT ★
Elisha: b 1-9-1750 d 7-5-1823 m Lucretia Rockwell Grd CT
Henry: b 1755 d 1821 m Mary Ann — Sol PA
John: b 11-23-1735 d 6-9-1809 m Ann Lewis Pvt CT
John: b 1-18-1746 d 3-19-1823 m Bridget (Fitch) Skinner Pvt CT
Joseph: b 7-31-1738 d 2-5-1815 m Martha Wolcott PS CT
Lemuel: b 8-9-1731 d 3-4-1793 m Anne Ellsworth Maj CT
Nathaniel: b 3-6-1746 d 2-6-1815 m Abigail Potwin PS Ens CT
Oliver: b 5-19-1727 d 1-23-1815 m (1)Eleanor Burbank (2)Mrs Elizabeth Gillett Pvt CT
Samuel: b 12- -1740 d 1-25-1814 m (1)Mary — (2)Sarah Mun Lt CT
Shem: b 1-15-1757 d 2-5-1837 m Flora Gillett Sol CT
Wm.: b 1716 d 12-27-1781 m Abigail Wolcott PS CT
Wm.: b 6-6-1750 d 11-29-1831 m Eleanor Prior Pvt CT

STOUT, (includes STAUDT, STOUD & STOUDT)
Abel: b 1740 d 8-24-1797 m (1)Williampy Wycoff (2)Elizabeth Armstrong Pvt NJ
Abraham: b 5-14-1754 d 7-10-1821 m Jane Pettitt Capt NJ
Abraham: b 8-17-1740 d 6-8-1812 m Mary Magdalene Hartzel PS PA
Andrew: b 9-2-1728 d 3-28-1807 m (1)Anna (Stout) (2)Mrs Sarah Stout Morgan Pvt NJ
Benjamin: b 11- -1756 d 6-9-1827 m Mary Hutchinson Pvt NJ
Daniel (Godfrey): b c. 1750 d p. 9-26-1843 m Catherine Boltzen PS MD
Daniel: b 11-14-1758 d 4-2-1843 m Anna Chadwick Pvt NJ W★
Daniel: b 2-28-1754 d 4-1-1820 m Sophia Merkle Lt PA
Daniel: b 7-20-1760 d 11-19-1840 m Maria Salome Sgt PA
David: b 1732 d 12-27-1827 m (1)Sarah Parke (2)Mrs Drake Pvt NJ
Elisha: b 1756 d 5-28-1838 m Huldah Robbins Pvt NJ ★
Emanuel: b a. 1727 d 1781 m (1)Luraney Owen (2)Mary Griffin PS DE
George: b 1753 d 2-28-1818 m Margaret Wolf Ens PA

George Wilhelm: b 1748 d 1820 m Christina Weidenhammer Pvt PS PA
Harmon: b 1745 d 1803 m Anna Hall Capt PA
Isaac: b 8-12-1749 d 8- -1821 m Barbara Bachman Pvt PA
James: b c. 1732 d 5-4-1810 m Catherine Stout PS NJ
James: b 3-4-1758 d 1815 m Rachel Bryant Capt NJ
Jediah: b 4-10-1757 d p. 1789 m Mary (Stout) — Pvt NJ
Jesse: b 9-7-1751 d 1825 m Abigail Lott Pvt NJ
Job: b 2-21-1763 d 2-28-1833 m Rhoda Howell Cpl NJ PA ★
John: b 1728 d 1791 m Ruth Ellison Capt NJ
John: b c. 1720 d 1798 m Mable Sexton Pvt NJ
John: b 6-12-1760 d 9-26-1838 m Eunice Evans Pvt NJ ★
John: b 1-8-1701 d 8-6-1783 m Margaret Taylor PS NJ
John: b 6-6-1737 d 10-13-1801 m Maria Anna Kershner 2Lt PA
John: b 10-4-1762 d 9-6-1847 m Mary Jarrett Pvt PA
Jonathan: b 1726 d 7-25-1808 m Rachel Burroughs Pvt NJ
Jonathan: b c. 1750 d 1778 m Mary Compton Pvt NJ
Joseph: b 1717 d p. 9-11-1803 m Mary Hixon Pvt NJ
Joseph: b c. 1750 d 1807 m Sarah Hancock Pvt NJ
Joseph: b c. 1752 d 8-26-1776 m Catherine — Pvt PA
Moses: b 6- -1751 d 3-2-1833 m Abigail Hart Ens NJ
Nathan: b 1-31-1748 d 3-10-1826 m (1)Esther Ketcham (2)Catherine (Holmes) Hageman Capt NJ
Peter: b 1721 d 2-7-1807 m Mary Catherina Capt PA
Saint Leger: b c. 1760 d 1806 m Anna Buckalow Pvt NJ
Samuel: b 4-22-1730 d 9-24-1803 m Anna Van Dyke Capt NJ
Samuel: b 1756 d 4-22-1795 m Helena Cruser Pvt NJ
Thomas: b 10-30-1734 d 4-30-1827 m Jeannette Van Stoy Cmsry NJ
Thomas: b 1751 d 10-27-1837 m (1)Margaret Phillips (2)Mary Stewart Spy VA ★
Timothy: b 8-2-1753 d 1831 m (1)Sarah Shrieve (2)Sarah Jane Reed Pvt NJ

STOUTENBURGH, (or STOUTENBURG)
Abram: b 1-8-1755 d 2-8-1794 m Rebecca Watson Pvt NY
Isaac: bpt 3-12-1739 d 12-10-1799 m Elizabeth Will LCol PS NY
Jacobus: bpt 4-15-1727 d — m Jesyntje Teller Pvt NY
James W.: b 1-23-1756 d 1807 m (1)Mary Moss (2)Hannah Marshall (3)Comfort Bell Sol NY
Luke: bpt 6-5-1736 d 12-21-1789 m (1)Rachel Teller (2)Mary Van Vleck Capt NY
Peter: bpt 6-13-1731 d p. 1777 m (1)Rachel Vansteenburg (2)Sarah Snediker Capt NY
Tobias: b 2-12-1718 d c. 1778-80 m Catherine Van Vleck Col NY
Wm.: bpt 6-3-1722 d p. 1780 m Maria Van Vleck Pvt NY
Wm., Jr.: b 5-19-1759 d 8-19-1829 m Elizabeth Conklin Pvt NY

STOVALL,
Bartholomew: b c. 1743 d p. 12-22-1802 m Ann — Pvt VA
Bartholomew: b 8-23-1759 d 3-9-1841 m (1)Sarah Webster (2)Mrs Betsey Evitts Pvt VA ★
Bartholomew: b c. 1732 d p. 7-16-1796 m (1)Tabitha Moss (2)Sally Brackett PS VA
George: b c. 1760 d 1833 m Rebecca — Sol GA
George: b 1743 d 1785 m Mary Hairston Sol VA
George, Sr.: b c. 1705 d p. 4-18-1786 m (1)Elizabeth — (2)Elizabeth — PS VA
James: b c. 1762 d 1791 m Mary Bradley Pvt VA
John, Sr.: b a. 1721 d 1781 m Dorcas — PS NC
Josiah: b 1749 d 11-20-1798 m Mary Hicks PS NC
Thomas: b 1755 d 9- -1806 m Elizabeth Cooper Pvt VA

STOVELL,
Stephen: b c. 1718 d 4-12-1787 m Mary Cole CS CT

STOVER, (includes STAUFFER, STOBER, STOEVER & STOFER)
Abraham: b 1-17-1747 d 3-11-1809 m (1)Barbara Hershey (2)Elizabeth Boyer Pvt PA
Abraham: b 1752 d 9-3-1826 m Anna Nissley Pvt PA
Adam: b 1751 d 1829 m Pauline Troutner Pvt PA
Alcot: b 1741 d 11-1-1823 m Elizabeth Ashe Pvt ME
Christian: b 12-18-1728 d 7-14-1797 m Susanna — Pvt PA
Christian: b 1761 d 1845 m Barbara Weller Pvt PA
Christle: b a. 1755 d 1805 m — Pvt PA
Daniel: b 1757 d 1822 m Barbara Benedict Pvt PA
Emanuel: b 1761 d 1833 m Susanna Price Pvt PA
George: b 1748 d 7-12-1826 m Katherine Price (2)Margaret Beaver Sgt PA
George: b 1740 d 12-27-1827 m Catherine — Lt PA
George: b 1735 d 9-20-1779 m Sarah — PS PA
Henry: b 8-26-1739 d 5-18-1796 m Catarina — Lt PA
Jacob: b 5-2-1754 d 3-20-1839 m Susanna Huff Pvt PA
Jacob: b c. 1754 d p. 3-28-1807 m Eve — Sol PA
Jacob: b 3-13-1757 d 4-28-1844 m (1)Elizabeth Swartz (2)Catherine Stover Tms PA
Jacob: b 1735 d 1820 m Elizabeth Witwer Pvt PA
Jacob: b 7-19-1761 d 1-24-1839 m Barbara — Sol PA
Jacob: b c. 1753 d a. 1-13-1817 m Elizabeth Ruffner PS VA
Johannes: b 7-5-1753 d 7-20-1823 m Anna Engle Kisseckern Pvt PA
John: b 10-1737 d 1-19-1808 m — Pvt PA
John: b 12-24-1758 d 3-5-1845 m Elizabeth Yerger Pvt PA

John: b c. 1760 d 1836 m (1)Nancy Shelenburger (2)Esther — Pvt PA
John Casper, Sr.: b 12-21-1707 d 5-31-1779 m Maria Caterina
    Merkling PS PA
John Casper, Jr.: b 3-10-1736 d 7- -1821 m Anna Marie Barbara
    Nagel Capt PA
Matthias: b — d 1826 m Anna Clemens Pvt PA
Michael: b 1755 d 1834 m Christina Hess Pvt PA
Nathaniel: b c. 1725 d 1794 m Mary — Pvt MA
Ralph: b 1-10-1760 d 11-7-1811 m Catherine Funk Pvt PA
Samuel: b 1-7-1757 d 6-7-1825 m Elizabeth Haldeman Pvt PA

STOW, (includes STOUGH & STOWE)
Abijah: b 8-26-1763 d 3-11-1826 m Lucinda Adams Fif Maj NY ★
Abner: b 9-5-1743 d — m (1)Elizabeth Meriam (2)Eunice Goldsbury
    Cpl MA
Amos, Jr.: b 11-29-1750 d 10-16-1829 m Sarah Carley Pvt MA
Andrew: b 10-11-1748 d 9-4-1838 m Mary — Pvt NC ★
Ebenezer: b 4-4-1745 d 1824 m Content Tillotson Pvt MA
Ebenezer: b 12-15-1753 d 5-19-1841 m Mary Hartwell Pvt MA
Elihu, Sr.: b 5-27-1736 d 11-13-1812 m (1)Jemima Paine (2)Mrs
    Mary Griffin PS CT
Elihu, Jr.: b 12-4-1760 d 4-19-1839 m Mary Parsons Pvt CT ★
George: b 1-10-1737 d 6-5-1812 m Hannah Davis Pvt VT
Ichabod: b 1757 d — m Ruth — Sol MA ★
Jabez: b 4-13-1716 d 12-4-1785 m Anna Lord Lt CT
Jedediah: b 1757 d 12-11-1848 m Sarah Clark Pvt CT ★
John: b 3-10-1760 d 6-27-1839 m Sally Gillette Pvt CT
John: b 7-25-1763 d 11-9-1837 m (1)Patty Gibbs (2)Sarah Healy
    Pvt MA
Jonah: b 3-31-1746 d p. 1786 m Lydia Powers Cpl MA
Jonathan: b 2-4-1740 d 9-11-1803 m Elizabeth Warren Lt MA
Joseph, Jr.: b 3-31-1745 d p. 1790 m Lydia Hubbard Sgt CT
Joseph: b 3-8-1711 d 10-5-1785 m Experience Gurley PS CS CT
Nathan: b 4-27-1746 d 1810 m Abigail Merriman Sgt MA
Peter: b 1733 d 1817 m Mary Cotton Pvt CT
Quartus: b 8-26-1755 d 6-20-1798 m Hannah Ray Cpl MA
Samuel: b 8-22-1761 d a. 11-30-1831 m Elizabeth Benedict Sgt CT
Samuel: b 3-10-1733 d 5-9-1814 m Lucretia Rockwell Pvt CT
Samuel: b 8-13-1744 d 4-12-1780 m Naomi Olmstead Mid CT
Stephen: b 5-22-1726 d 2-8-1777 m Freelove Baldwin PS CT
Timothy: b 10-21-1745 d 1-18-1832 m Prudence Battelle Capt
    MA W★
Timothy: b 5-5-1759 d 7-19-1802 m Mary Kendall Pvt MA
Warren: b 1755 d p. 1-20-1823 m Sally — Pvt CT

STOWELL, (or STOEL)
Abijah: b 5-12-1745 d 9-6-1800 m (1)Rhoda Packard (2)Mary
    Stowell Pvt MA
Asa: b 1760 d 11-3-1826 m Hannah Bixby Pvt VT
Benjamin: b 1-12-1726/7 d 2-18-1786 m Susanna Hersey Pvt MA
Benjamin: b 5-4-1730 d 8-6-1803 m Elizabeth Parker PS MA
Daniel: b 8-2-1737 d 12- -1778 m Anna Bugbee Pvt CT
Daniel: b 8-19-1750 d p. 1778 m Susannah Sherran Artl MA
Daniel: b 12-8-1757 d 9-20-1828 m Lucretia Houghton Pvt MA
David: b c. 1750 d 4-27-1826 m Betsey Thomas Pvt MA ★
David: b 3-30-1740 d 6-3-1816 m Mary Larrabee Capt VT
David: b 7-7-1736 d 12-7-1786 m Sarah Royse Pvt PS VT NH
Ebenezer: b 12-14-1758 d 4-27-1837 m Pamelia Whitney Cpl VT ★
Elias: b 4-5-1762 d 10-26-1839 m Polly Barnard Pvt MA
Elisha: b 2-9-1740 d 2-21-1814 m Jerusha Sabin Sgt CT
Enoch: b 7-16-1740 d 1829 m Sarah Field Cpl NH
Hezekiah: b 12-25-1732 d p. 1793 m Hepzibah Persis Rice PS MA
Israel: b 12-25-1753 d 3-30-1844 m Lydia Mansfield Pvt MA ★
Israel: b 11-16-1732 d 2-21-1801 m (1)Mary Butler (2)Sarah Carpenter
    (3)Mary Leonard CS PS NH
John: b 3-25-1759 d 5-1-1842 m Susanna Todd Pvt MA
John: b 1726 d 4-5-1791 m Sarah Parmenter CS MA
Joseph: b 2-1-1736 d 2-29-1812 m Martha Page PS NH
Josiah: b c. 1750 d p. 1788 m Mary Leavens Capt CT
Lemuel: b 3-25-1747 d 3-29-1832 m Rebecca Fisher Pvt MA
Nathaniel: b 1755 d 12- -1823 m Aurelia Bancroft Sgt CT ★
Nathaniel: b 12-7-1734 d 3-23-1814 m Lois Bugbee Pvt MA
Samuel, Sr.: b 9-2-1742 d 1-30-1824 m Ann Russ Sol CT
Samuel, Jr.: b 7-28-1762 d 1-27-1850 m (1)Eunice Crocker
    (2)Hannah Whiton Cpl CT ★
Stephen, Sr.: b 1-5-1722 d 1-24-1795 m Lydia Sprague Pvt MA
Thaddeus: b 8-7-1751 d 5-28-1786 m Deborah Fisher Pvt MA
Wm.: b 8-8-1756 d 1-8-1829 m Kate Nixon Pvt MA
Wm.: b 1759 d a. 3-23-1822 m Phoebe Sawtell Pvt NH

STOWERS,
John: b 12-3-1751 d 10-11-1821 m Abigail Fullerton Lt MA ★
Lewis: b 1764 d 11-22-1844 m Joyce Shifflett Pvt VA
Nicholas: b 4-13-1745 d 5-13-1816 m (1)Miss Butler (2)Fanny Bright 2Lt VA
Samuel: b 11-15-1764 d 12-16-1843 m Mary Oaks Pvt MA ★
Samuel: b c. 1738 d p. 3-21-1785 m Ann — Lt VA

STOWITS,
Philip George: b 9-9-1739 d 8-6-1777 m Mary Ecker Pvt NY

STOY,
Daniel: b 5-3-1738 d 1-12-1835 m Sarah Hickens (Higgins) Sgt PA ★
Wm.: b 3-14-1726 d 9-14-1801 m Marie Elizabeth Maus PS PA

STRACHAN,
Alexander Glas: b 7-29-1748 d 1812 m (1)Lucy Pride (2)Sarah Feild
    PS VA

STRADER,
Christopher: b 3- -1745 d 12-21-1825 m Elizabeth — PS VA

STRAIL,
John: b c. 1740 d 1805-7 m Margaret Demper Cpl NY

STRAIN, (or STRINE)
David: b 1730 d 1780 m Eliza — Pvt PA
David: b — d 1824 m (1)Nancy Montgomery (2)Sarah Watts Pvt SC
George: b c. 1745-50 d a. 12- -1796 m — Pvt PA
Peter: b c. 1749/50 d p. 1830 m — Pvt PA
Thomas, Jr.: b 1756 d 5-14-1833 m Elizabeth — Pvt PA ★

STRAIT, (includes STRAAT & STRAIGHT)
Anthony: b 12-26-1732 d 1-11-1813 m Elizabeth Bise Pvt NY
Jacob: b a. 1741 d 1796 m Elizabeth — Sol VA
Job: b 9-17-1750 d p. 1790 m Mary Moon Capt RI
John: b 3-18-1744/5 d 6-22-1818 m Patience — Pvt RI MA
John: b 8-31-1758 d 1-7-1860 m (2)Elizabeth Downing (3)Sarah
    (Blake)Phelps Pvt RI ★
Nathan: b 2-14-1755 d 7-22-1840 m Prudence Hastings Cpl RI ★
Samuel: b 7- -1742 d 12- -1839 m (1)Mary Mattison (2)Muncy
    Dunning (3)Jerusha Burton (4)Sybil Satterlee Pvt RI

STRALEY,
Christian: b 9-21-1742 d 8-14-1818 m Christena Lantz Pvt PA

STRANG,
Francis: b 1727 d 1-2-1815 m Elizabeth Hyatt Sol NY
Garbiel: b — d 1812 m (1)Katherine Chichester (2)Deborah Sely Pvt
    NY
Gilbert: b 7-5-1753 d 1-3-1825 m Hester Haviland Pvt NY
Henry: b 1739 d 7-22-1802 m Margaret Hazzard Capt NY
John: b 10-18-1753 d 3-23-1809 m (1)Drusilla Oakley (2)Jane
    Fowler Pvt NY
Joseph: b 2-27-1725 d 8-2-1794 m (1)Jemima Budd (2)Anna Haight
    Maj NY
Wm.: b 1752 d 10-23-1831 m Abigail — Pvt NY

STRANGE,
Abner A.: b 3-14-1761 d 8-27-1834 m (1)Elizabeth — (2)Mary —
    Pvt VA ★
Amos Bradford: b 1759 d 6-1-1842 m Frances Bayley Pvt NC ★
Charles: b 10-11-1758 d 3-17-1834 m Esther Babbitt Pvt MA
John: b 2-2-1743 d 11-28-1830 m Martha — Sol VA
John M.: b 1719 d 1806 m Fanny Smith Pvt VA
Lot: b 5-10-1720 d — m Abigail Hathaway Pvt MA
Lot, Jr.: b 1745 d 1829 m Mary Douglass Pvt MA

STRASSER,
Conrad: b 1744 d 1799 m Christina — PS PA

STRATTON,
Asa: b 1-17-1758 d 3-17-1816 m Lucy Woodbury Pvt MA
Benjamin: b — d 6-28-1781 m Mary — PS NY
Cornelius: bpt 4-3-1737 d 8-11-1810 m Abigail Hull Pvt CT
Daniel: b 5-9-1748 d 10-13-1816 m Martha Fuller Pvt MA
Daniel: b 10-13-1743 d 7-23-1832 m (1)Sarah Start (2)Sarah
    Warner MM NH
Daniel: b 1758 d 1824 m — Pvt NJ
David: b 12-26-1742 d 6-13-1819 m Dinah Wheeler Pvt MA
David: b 1755 d 3-8-1836 m Polly Leland Cpl MA ★
Ebenezer: b 11-2-1751 d 3-22-1837 m Tabitha Davis Pvt MA
Elisha: b 10-2-1753 d 11-19-1817 m Mehitable Russell Pvt MA
Henry, Sr.: b 1735 d 1799 m Sarah Hampton Lt VA
Hezekiah: b 1-7-1724 d 1-5-1800 m Molly Smith PS MA
Hezekiah: b 1746 d 1834 m Eunice Haywood PS MA ME
Isaac: b 6-26-1739 d 4-3-1789 m Mary Fox Maj MA
James: b 9-28-1751 d 1-27-1809 m Lydia Tower Pvt MA
Joel: b 10-16-1757 d 1-7-1847 m Rhoda Beeman Pvt MA
John: bpt 10-22-1727 d 2-2-1817 m Grace Osborn Sgt CT
John Handley: b a. 1745 d p. 4-6-1805 m Susan Ann Douglass
    Artl VA
Jonathan: b 9-29-1742 d 1794 m Abigail Barnes Pvt MA
Jonathan: b 1-20-1764 d 8-23-1823 m Ruth Forster Pvt MA
Jonathan, Sr.: b 6-29-1716 d p. 10-21-1801 m Dinah Bemis Pvt MA
Jonathan, Jr.: b 3-20-1747 d 11-30-1819 m Sarah Child Pvt MA
Joseph: b 7- -1751 d 1827 m Eunice Middlebrook Sgt CT
Josiah: b 6-7-1741 d p. 1790 m Mary Davis Pvt MA
Nehemiah: b 1-15-1759 d 11-25-1843 m (1)Sarah Prichard
    (2)Lois Newell Sgt NH ★
Peleg: b 1748 d 1833 m Elizabeth Kendall Pvt MA
Samuel: b a. 1760 d 9-8-1807 m (1)Eleanor Dickinson (2)Mary
    Hollister Smn CT
Samuel: b 1755 d 1838 m Grace Darrow Pvt CT ★
Samuel: b 11-2-1752 d 8-7-1810 m (1)Mehitable Hollister (2)Mrs
    Sarah Bidwell Pvt CT MA
Samuel: b 6-28-1739 d 8-26-1801 m Beulah Parker Pvt MA

STRATTON, contd.
Samuel: b 12-2-1763 d 1-12-1838 m Martha Davis Pvt MA
Samuel: b 7-6-1765 d c. 1823 m (1)Beulah Jones (2)Tabitha
    Simmons Pvt MA
Samuel: bpt 7-8-1760 d 10-5-1789 m Sarah — Pvt NJ
Seth: b 10-15-1762 d 12-29-1845 m Mary Greenway Pvt VA ★
Solomon: b c. 1745 d c. 1810-20 m — Pvt VA
Stephen: b 1743 d 3-31-1814 m Martha Graves Sgt MA
Stephen: b 1-23-1754 d 1-26-1842 m Sarah Darrow Sgt CT ★
Thomas, Sr.: b 3-13-1723 d 1787 m (1)Sarah Barlow (2)Ann (Curtiss)
    Smith Sol CT
Thomas, Jr.: b 9-11-1756 d 1-7-1850 m Martha Edwards Pvt CT
Thomas: b 1760 d 1846 m Elizabeth Chandler Pvt NJ ★
Wm.: b 1- -1735 d 5-9-1805 m Mrs Elizabeth (Lombard) Smith Pvt
    MA
Wm.: b c. 1708 d p. 8-30-1780 m — PS VA
Zebulon: b 5-15-1753 d 8-18-1842 m Jerusha Bradish Pvt MA

STRAUB,
Peter: b 11-8-1724 d 9-15-1804 m Maria — Sol PA

STRAUCH,
Henry: b c. 1753 d p. 1811 m Elizabeth Rothermel Capt PS PA

STRAUSS,
Jacob: b 5-5-1737 d 3-31-1781 m Elizabeth Drecht Pvt PA
Philip: b 11-9-1754 d 7-20-1816 m Susanna Wennerich Pvt PA
Samuel (John): b 5-13-1756 d 3-25-1835 m Catherine Elizabeth
    Umbenhauer Pvt PA

STRAW, (includes STROH & STROW)
Ezekiel: b 1-15-1730 d 1811 m (1)Martha Gould (2)Betty (Hoyt)
    Colby Pvt NH
Jacob: b 1758 d 3-13-1839 m Betty Burbank Cpl NH
Jacob: b 5-21-1733 d 11-5-1807 m Lydia Ordway PS NH
Jacob: b 1735 d 5- -1808 m Maria Catherine — PS PA
John: b 5- -1762 d p. 1806 m Elizabeth Strumpf Pvt PA
Jonathan: b 1-28-1725 d 1-25-1791 m Mary Carr Pvt NH
Nicholas: b 1753 d 8-20-1833 m Mary Catherine Dale Lt PA ★
Thomas: bpt 1754 d — m Judith Richardson Pvt NH

STRAWN, (includes STRAHAN, STRAUGHAN & TRAHAN)
Gregory: b 1752 d 9-21-1811 m Margaret Bourke Pvt PA W★
Isaiah: b 10-28-1758 d 8-12-1843 m Rachel Reed Tms PA
Jacob: b 1717 d 1801 m Christina Percell PS PA
John: b 5-13-1733 d a. 1-3-1785 m Tamzin — Pvt NC

STRAYER, (or STRAER)
Jacob: b 1753 d 11-24-1834 m Catherine — 2Lt PA
John: b 1744 d 10-24-1800 m Mary Shultz Pvt NY

STRAYHORN,
Gilbert: b 1715 d 2-6-1803 m Margaret Roan PS NC
John: b 8-3-1742 d p. 1817 m Elizabeth Johnston Pvt NC
Wm.: b 1756 d 5-17-1834 m (1)Mary Tate (2)Mary Hunter Pvt NC

STREEPER,
John: b 1759 d 1-24-1790 m Barbara — Pvt PA
Wm.: b 1724 d 1786 m Mary Moser Pvt PA

STREET, (includes STREETS & STREETT)
Anthony: b 10-16-1741 d 1-22-1809 m (1)Molly Stokes (2)Mary
    Gray Capt CS VA
Anthony: b 8-24-1757 d 2-24-1836 m Trephenia Stirman Pvt VA ★
David: b 1754 d 1814 m Miss Bailey Pvt VA
Elisha: b 12-17-1745 d p. 1784 m — Pvt MA
Jacob: b a. 1760 d 12-25-1821 m Elizabeth Harman Pvt DE
James: b 2-10-1708 d 3-6-1799 m (1)Kesiah Haynes (2)Mrs Emblem
    (Latham) Hood CS CT
Jesse: b 4-24-1741 d 3-22-1784 m Lois Cook MM CT
John, Sr.: b 7-22-1728 d 8-27-1776 m Hannah Jarvis Pvt CT
John, Jr.: b 10-2-1759 d 9-13-1833 m Silvia Bessey Pvt CT ★
John: b 12-17-1735 d 1-18-1801 m Frances Parke QM PS VA
John: b c. 1713 d p. 4- -1800 m Hannah Waddy QM VA
Nicholas: b 2-21-1730 d 10-8-1806 m (1)Desire Thompson (2)Hannah
    Austin PS CT
Richard: b 9-22-1740 d 1793 m Margaret — 1Lt VA
Thomas, Sr.: b 8-20-1737 d 1822 m (1)Mary Fox (2)Sarah James PS
    MD
Thomas, Jr.: b 1765 d p. 1802 m Jemima McClure PS MD

STREETER, (includes STREATOR & STREETOR)
Asa: b 7-31-1762 d 12-16-1821 m (1)Polly Bolton (2)Hannah Cotton
    Pvt MA
Barzilla: b 5-1-1759 d 4-6-1839 m Mary Brown Cpl RI
Benjamin: b 1753 d 1846 m Atathea Morse Pvt MA ★
Benjamin: b 12-5-1737 d 1835 m Jemima Moss Pvt NH
Comfort: b 9-3-1743 d c. 1786 m Bethia Rich Pvt MA
Daniel: b 3-23-1739 d 3-28-1814 m Mary Jones Pvt MA
Ebenezer: b 1678 d 5-30-1835 m Penelope Caswell Pvt MA
Ebenezer: b 2-22-1730/1 d 1794 m Jemima Streeter Sol NH
George: b 3-21-1752 d 11-19-1808 m Rhoda Ballou Lt RI
James: bpt 10-17-1734 d p. 1801 m Susanna Sloper Sgt NH

John: b 10-20-1738 d 2-23-1812 m (1)Keziah Morse (2)Anna
    Robinson Cpl MA
John, Sr.: b 2-28-1732 d 8-24-1810 m (1)Margaret Hemingway
    (2)Elizabeth Rowlee (3)Hannah Walker Pvt MA
John, Jr.: b 11-17-1761 d 1813 m Elizabeth Kibbee Pvt MA W★
Jonathan: b 7-2-1741 d p. 1779 m Abigail Vinton Pvt MA
Joseph: b 7-5-1719 d 8-8-1777 m Mrs Mary Inman Pvt RI
Naphtali: b 6-30-1762 d 9-15-1839 m (1)Susanna Howell
    (2)Elizabeth Reynolds Pvt RI NH ★
Nathaniel: b 3-1-1747 d p. 1797 m Sarah Dix Pvt MA ★
Rufus: b 2-21-1754 d 10-13-1816 m Nancy Ballou Capt RI W★
Samuel: b 8-24-1754 d 9-7-1844 m Bathsheba Barton Pvt MA ★
Samuel: b 7-9-1730 d 10-13-1812 m Joanna Morse CS MA

STREGLER,
Nicholas: b c. 1760 d 12-21-1835 m Sarah O'Bryan Pvt GA ★

STREIT, (or STRITE)
Christian: b — d 1823 m (1)Mary Myers (2)Barbara Sharer Pvt PA
Christian: b 6-7-1749 d 3-10-1812 m (1)Anna Maria Hoff (2)Salome
    Graff (3)Susan Barr Chp VA
Frederick: b 3-8-1742 d 5-21-1800 m Anna Catrina Moul Capt NY

STREMBECK,
Jacob, Sr.: b 11-24-1755 d 7-11-1841 m Mary Steinmetz Mus PA ★

STREVE,
Paul: b 1755 d 1829 m Mary — Pvt PA ★

STRIBLING, (or STRIPLIN)
Clayton: b 1-9-1762 d 3-11-1831 m Mary Beckhan Pvt SC ★
Thomas: b c. 1730 d p. 9-24-1818 m Nancy Kincheloe Sol SC
Wm.: b c. 1754 d c. 1795-1800 m Juliatha Oliver Pvt SC

STRICKER,
George: b 1732 d 11-29-1810 m (1)Catherine Springer (2)Mrs
    McMahon LCol PS MD

STRICKLAND, (or STRICKLEN)
Jacob: b 1741 d 4- -1804 m Priscilla Young PS NC
James: b 1759 d 3-8-1837 m Naomi Needham Pvt MA ★
Jonathan: b — d p. 6-4-1812 m Eleanor — Pvt NJ
Joseph: b 1722 d 11-29-1802 m Mary — Pvt MA
Joseph: b c. 1755 d p. 1816 m (2)Rachel Quick Pvt NJ
Samuel: b 1744 d 11-8-1826 m Amy Cogswell Capt CT
Samuel: b c. 1740 d a. 7-25-1786 m Diadema — Pvt NJ
Seth: b 3-8-1758 d 7-15-1828 m Anna Shepard Pvt CT
Solomon: b c. 1735 d 1818 m Amy Pace Pvt GA
Wm.: b 9-22-1755 d 6-25-1823 m Patience Wright Webster Pvt MA

STRICKLER, (or STRICKER)
Andrew, Sr.: b a. 1728 d 1794 m Anna Margaret Graff PS PA
Benjamin: b c. 1721 d 1791 m Mary Beidler PS CS VA
Henry, Jr.: b c. 1750 d 1816 m Anna Rhodes Pvt PA
Henry: b 1763 d 1-14-1840 m Frances Stewart Pvt PA
Jacob: b 12-5-1749 d 10-29-1828 m Elizabeth Stewart Pvt PA
Jacob: b 1755 d 1837 m Elizabeth Miller Pvt PA
Jacob: b 1731 d 4-26-1803 m (1)Martha Shirk (2)Catherine Forry PS
    PA
Jacob: b c. 1710 d 1784 m (1)Nancy Kauffman (2)Magdalena
    Moomaw PS VA
John: b c. 1740 d a. 4-11-1795 m Elizabeth Sprenckle Pvt PA
Joseph: b 5-20-1764 d 5-15-1813 m Elizabeth Neiswanger Pvt PA
Leonard: b 2-12-1738 d 7-31-1815 m Catharine Stump Pvt PA
Ulrich: b a. 1753 d 1804 m Elizabeth — Pvt PA

STRINGER,
Leonard: b 1760 d 2-15-1843 m (2)Dolly Stringer Pvt GA
John: b 1755 d c. 1795 m Hannah Henley Sgt MA
Noah: b 1760 d 8- -1836 m Celia Stringer Pvt NC
Samuel: b 3-30-1734 d 7-11-1817 m Rachel Van Der Heyden PS NY
Wm.: b c. 1740 d 4-27-1834 m Jane McKeown Pvt PA

STRINGFIELD,
James: b 12-19-1735 d p. 1810 m Mary Ann Ray PS NC
John: b 2-13-1762 d 1-5-1822 m Sarah Boydston PS NC

STRITZEL,
John: b 5-26-1755 d 8-12-1809 m Margaret Levering Pvt PA

STROBECK,
Adam: b 1733 d 4-15-1811 m Hannah — Pvt NY

STROBEL,
Daniel: b 1733 d 12-7-1806 m Mary Elizabeth Martin Lt SC
Daniel: b 8-21-1765 d 2-26-1827 m Elizabeth Aberly Pvt SC

STRODE,
James, Sr.: b c. 1700 d 12- -1789 m — PS VA
James, Jr.: b 12-26-1727 d 3-7-1795 m (1)Anna Hamilton (2) —
    (3)Elizabeth Fryatt Capt VA
Jeremiah: b 7-4-1732 d 1785 m Margaret Forman PS VA

John, Sr.: b 1-11-1729 d 8-18-1805 m Mary Boyles PS VA KY
Richard: b 1745-50 d 1795 m (1)Hannah Batton (2)Ruth Shields Pvt PA
Samuel: b 12-16-1754 d 8-15-1842 m Nancy Ann Watson Sgt VA

STROHECKER,
Gottlieb: b 11-1-1724 d 11-17-1805 m Wilhelmina Rosina PS PA
John: b 1-5-1755 d 1-8-1835 m Juliana Wunder 2Lt PA ★

STROHL,
Jacob: b 1761 d 5-3-1830 m Mary Bloodgate Pvt PA ★

STROHM,
John: b 1757 d 1820 m Elizabeth Brubaker Pvt PA

STROMAN,
Jacob: b c. 1751 d c. 1795 m Elizabeth Tyler Pvt SC
John: b 3-5-1756 d 2-27-1843 m Mary Catherine Von Sitler Pvt PA ★
John: b 1728 d 1781 m (1)Ann Margareth Schaumloffel (2)Eva Catherine — Pvt SC
Paul: b 1751 d 9-2-1844 m Anne Baltziger Pvt SC

STRONG,
Aaron: b 10-2-1736 d 10-16-1777 m Sarah Burt Pvt MA
Adino: b 4-5-1750 d 12- -1824 m Anna Scott Pvt CT
Adonijah: b 5-21-1749 d 5-18-1824 m Mary Kellogg Pvt CT
Adonijah: b 7-5-1743 d 2-12-1813 m (1)Abigail Hale (2)Mary Pierce (3)Abigail Bates 1Lt CT
Alexander: b 1749 d 2-25-1826 m Abigail Rice Pvt CT
Amasa: b 7- -1749 d 5-25-1825 m Sarah Noble Pvt MA
Ambrose: b 11-1-1750 d —m Mrs Lydia Holdridge CS CT
Ariel: b 2- -1763 d 12-9-1813 m Jane Grant Dickson Pvt CT
Asahel, Sr.: b 1715 d 11-25-1776 m Hannah Lyman PS CT
Asahel, Jr.: b 4-28-1750 d 1-6-1831 m Martha Barber Sol CT
Bela, Sr.: b 10-4-1719 d 5-5-1803 m Eunice Alvard Pvt MA
Bela, Jr.: b 1- -1760 d 12-14-1814 m Sarah Parson Pvt MA
Benajah: b 2-22-1740 d 5-22-1836 m (1)Jane Cochrane (2)Abigail Powers Lt CT
Benajah: b 6-30-1717 d 1-12-1783 m Mabel Bartlett Pvt MA
Benajah, Jr.: b 5-9-1749 d 12-29-1795 m Hannah Thompson Capt NY
Benajah: b 1-30-1735 d 1815 m (1)Mary Bacon (2)Mrs Elizabeth Wilson Pvt VT
Benjamin: b 2-15-1759 d 1818 m Susan Trowbridge Pvt CT
Caleb, Jr.: b 6-20-1749 d 11-27-1815 m Amy Lee Pvt CT
Caleb, Sr.: b 3-27-1710 d 2-13-1776 m Phebe Lyman Sol MA
Charles: bpt 7-6-1735 d 1812 m (1)Betsy Hinman (2) X (3)Eunice Hawley Pvt CT
Charles: b 1-18-1763 d 10-15-1848 m Sarah Thompson Pvt VA ★
Christopher: b 1-20-1760 d 11-22-1850 m (1)Frances Elizabeth Dunn (2)Rosannah McColloch Pvt SC ★
Daniel: b 9-17-1719 d 1- -1808 m Esther Chapel Pvt CT
Daniel: b 1749 d 2-2-1805 m Tryphosa Bush DrmMaj MA
David: b 7-6-1743 d 8-19-1801 m Chloe Richmond Capt CT
David: b 6-4-1736 d 10-8-1811 m (1)Sarah Warner (2)Jane Grover Capt CT
David: b 5-23-1725 d 1807 m Rebecca Swift (2)Deborah Terry Pvt CT
David: b 7-27-1748 d 4-1-1821 m (1)Amy Carver (2)Leah Bissell Pvt CT
David: b 11-25-1758 d 10-13-1838 m Esther Thayer Cpl MA
Ebenezer: b 1754 d 1824 m (1)Lucy (Kilbourne)Lawrence (2)Abigail Smith Pvt CT
Eli: b 12-13-1755 d 1825 m Lament Sheldon Pvt CT
Eliakim: b 10-6-1751 d 5-13-1804 m (1)Remembrance Wright (2)Ruth Camp Sgt CT
Elijah: b 8-11-1833 d c. 1775 m Ruth Loomis Pvt CT
Elijah: b 11-11-1752 d 7-25-1838 m Elizabeth Morton Pvt MA
Elisha: b 12-1-1747 d 2-28-1826 m Mary Beebe CS CT
Elnathan: b 9-23-1736 d 12-16-1806 m (1)Rachel Warner (2)Mary Marsh Sgt PS CT
Ephraim: b 7-11-1754 d 9- -1843 m Hannah Platt Sgt CT
Ezra: b 3-4-1733 d 8-7-1804 m Temperance Phelps Pvt MA
Horatio: b 5-16-1758 d 7-14-1831 m Patience Stevens Cpl MA
Isaac: b 1-28-1765 d 2-18-1829 m Miriam Bacon Pvt VT
Israel: b 1756 d 2-19-1836 m Mary Bronson Lt CT
Ithamar: b 4-1-1721 d 6-28-1805 m Experience King Cpl MA
Jabin: b 8-12-1734 d c. 1816 m (1)Betsy Curtis (2)Mrs Grover Sgt CT
James: b 1743 d 8-22-1818 m Margaret Brainard Artl PA
James: b 1760 d 1806 m Letticia (Strong) Sol PS SC
Jedediah: b 10-23-1751 d 2-25-1832 m Ruth Harper Pvt CT
Joel: b 3-2-1764 d 2-9-1857 m Amelia — Pvt NY ★
John: b 6-24-1733 d 11-15-1816 m (1)Sarah Strong (2)Mary (Newell) Root (3)Annie Beecher LCol CT
John: b 11-10-1752 d 4-19-1843 m Sarah Walker Lt CT
John: b 12-7-1743 d p. 1790 m Rachel Curtis Pvt CT
John: b 4-10-1755 d 1- -1836 m Lydia Thomas Pvt CT
John: b 3-2-1759 d 3-30-1838 m Hepzibah Roberts Fif CT
John: b 1743 d 1804 m Susan — Pvt MD
John: b 10-13-1742 d 1815 m Martha Knowles Capt MA

John: b 8-16-1738 d 6-16-1816 m Agnes McCure PS VT
John: b 9-5-1723 d c. 1806 m (1)Elizabeth Crouch (2)Mrs Mary Hoisington Capt PS CS VT
John: b 2-6-1763 d 9-25-1838 m Mary Gibson Sol VA
John: b 1734 d 1815 m — PS CS VA
Johnson: b 10-28-1758 d a. 12-7-1844 m Mary Ann — Pvt VA ★
Jonathan: b 6-7-1741 d 11- -1814 m (1)Mary Brewster (2) X Pvt CT
Jonathan, Sr.: b 12-15-1708 d 4-19-1797 m Elizabeth Clapp MM MA
Jonathan, Jr.: b 1737 d 12-18-1803 m Rachel Lyman Pvt MA
Joseph: b 11-6-1741 d 3-23-1816 m Comfort Nichols Pvt CT
Joseph: b 3-19-1728 d 1-1-1803 m Jane Gelston Chp CT
Joseph: b 3-13-1765 d 3-31-1835 m (1)Chloe Cogswell (2)Lucy Elderkin Cpl MA
Joseph: b 9-23-1766 d 11-25-1840 m Margaret (Strong) Pvt NY
Josiah: b 9-18-1729 d p. 1776 m Eleanor White Pvt CT
Josiah: b 1-28-1740 d 9-8-1814 m Mary Harris Pvt PS CT
Josiah: b 6-17-1758 d 11-14-1841 m Martha Green Pvt CT ★
Judah: b 11-28-1738 d 12-15-1783 m Martha Alvord PS CT
King: b 12-4-1744 d 4-7-1839 m Hannah Noble Sgt MA
Nathan: b 7-13-1755 d 2-7-1848 m Naomi Lee Pvt MA ★
Nathaniel: b 11-18-1737 d 11-6-1810 m Amy Brewster Maj NY
Noah, Jr.: b 7-2-1736 d 8-3-1819 m Hannah Searls Lt MA
Oliver: b 7-7-1739 d 1-9-1815 m Lois Lawrence Fif CT
Ozem: b 1760 d 1830 m Mary Hopkins Pvt MA
Ozias: b 9-3-1734 d 11-21-1807 m Susannah West Pvt MA
Philip: b 2-9-1735/6 d 9-13-1787 m Rhoda Payne Pvt CT
Phineas: b 6-6-1756 d 3- -1827 m Anna Filer Cpl CT
Return: b 8-1-1717 d 4-5-1794 m Elizabeth Andros Pvt CT
Return: b 12-30-1755 d 3-1-1807 m Hannah Harman Pvt CT
Reuben: b 11-2-1762 d 9-12-1796 m Elizabeth Farrand Pvt VT
Samuel: b 7-16-1705 d 1-13-1789 m Martha Stoughton PS CT
Samuel: b 7-14-1744 d 10-20-1806 m (1)Abigail Brewster (2)Experience Reeve Brewster 2Lt PS NY
Selah: b 9-6-1734 d 3-7-1807 m Esther Weed Pvt CT
Selah: b 1-6-1759 d 3-11-1837 m Eunice Baldwin Pvt CT ★
Selah: b 12-25-1737 d 7-4-1815 m Anna Smith Capt PS NY
Seth: b 5-8-1761 d 11-18-1818 m Rachel Robinson Pvt CT
Solomon: b 9-26-1741 d 9-14-1791 m Mary Hogeboom Capt PS CT
Solomon: b 12-25-1746 d 12-21-1829 m Mindwell Clapp Pvt MA
Solomon: b 10-6-1730 d 12-12-1799 m (1)Mary White (2)Mrs Mary (Wilson) Hutchinson Pvt CS VT
Thomas: b 11-17-1722 d p. 1790 m Phoebe Seward PS CT
Timothy: b 5-29-1719 d 8-19-1803 m (1)Sarah Stricklin (2)Abi Gowdy (3)Editha Richestone Pvt CT
Titus: b 5-15-1756 d 6- -1789 m Mary Burrill Pvt MA
Uriel: b 9-10-1754 d 1-15-1819 m Phebe Minor Pvt CT
Waitstill: b 12-15-1764 d 12-20-1822 m Sarah Phillips Pvt MA
Warham: b 1-31-1753 d 2-21-1816 m Martha Crofoot Cpl MA
Wm.: b 6-12-1754 d 9-25-1823 m Susan Nelson Cpl VA
Wm., Jr.: b 4-17-1758 d 8-18-1810 m Margaret Stokes Sgt VA

STROPE, (includes STROOP, STROUP & STRUPE)
Adam: b c. 1755 d 1797 m Magdalena — Pvt PA
Henry: b 1753 d 2-16-1843 m Susannah George Lt PA ★
John: b 4-16-1719 d 7-30-1789 m (1)Elizabeth Taudy (2)Elizabeth Loliger PS NC
John: b 4-24-1748 d 9-2-1826 m Mary Fitzgerald Pvt PA ★
Malchor: b c. 1749 d 6-11-1833 m Mary — Pvt VA ★
Peter: b 3-8-1728 d 1-20-1793 m Catharine Armin Pvt PA
Sebastian: b 1735 d 6-4-1805 m Lydia Van Valkenberg Pvt PA

STROTHER,
Anthony: b 5-10-1736 d 1790 m Frances Kenyon CS VA
Benjamin: b 6-22-1750 d 10-22-1807 m Kitty Price Mid VA
Christopher: b c. 1749 d p. 1790 m Ann Kemp Sol NC
French: b 1733 d 7-3-1800 m Lucy Coleman CS Col VA
George: b c. 1750 d 1812 m Jane Ellerbe Lt SC
George: b a. 1746 d p. 1781 m Ellen Kinnerley CS SC
John: b c. 1743 d 1796 m Jane Fussel Pvt PS NC
John, Sr.: b 1721 d 3-31-1795 m Mary Willis Wade Capt VA
Joseph: b 1740 d 1808-10 m Nancy Stuart Capt VA
Robert: b a. 1760 d c. 1836 m Martha Radcliffe Sol VA
Wm.: b a. 1750 d 1805 m (1)Miss Rogers (2)Lucy Hicks CS PS SC

STROUD,
Adam: b c. 1745 d 1804 m Eve — Sol VA
Jacob: b 1-15-1735 d 7-14-1806 m Elizabeth McDowell Col PA
James: b c. 1728 d p. 5-16-1788 m (1)Elizabeth Beene (2)Anna Coulston Pvt PA
James: b 1745 d 1813 m Mary Margaret Dozier Pvt VA
Jesse: b 1758 d 1832 m (1)Naomi Stroud (2)Tabitha Hicks PS NC
John: b 7-15-1749 d 2-1-1840 m (1)Elizabeth Smith (2)Mrs Bates Pvt NH ★
John: b 10-1-1758 d 1831 m Delilah Bryant Pvt NC W★
John: b 1- -1732 d p. 1-1-1805 m Sarah Connelly Pvt NC
Mark: b 2-27-1763 d 7-2-1798 m Martha (Strother)Thompson Pvt NC
Richard: b c. 1744/5 d 6-18-1819 m Elizabeth Billings Sol PS CT
Wm.: b 1759 d 1829 m Nancy Stubblefield Sol SC

STROUT,
Daniel: b 1729 d 6-11-1804 m Mary Delano Capt ME
Elisha: b 1-13-1746 d 9-29-1811 m Eunice Freeman Cpl MA

STROUT, contd.
Enoch: b 12-25-1761 d 4-1-1832 m Mercy C. Small Pvt MA
Joseph: b 1730 d 1818 m Sarah Mayo Sgt MA
Prince: b 1754 d 7-3-1834 m Christiana Dyer Pvt MA ★

STROWBRIDGE, (or STROBRIDGE)
George: b 4-23-1760 d 3-20-1837 m (1)Julia Tuttle (2)Bathshua
    Crawford Pvt MA
John: b 7-4-1756 d 5-5-1825 m Patience Tyler Pvt MA
Robert: b 1752 d 8-14-1790 m Elizabeth Nelson Sgt MA
Wm.: b 10-19-1756 d 3-9-1843 m (1)Suzannah Hinds (2)Hannah
    Tuttle Sgt MA ★
Wm.: b 8-21-1724 d 4-1-1797 m (1)Jean Thompson (2)Sarah
    (Montgomery) Morrison Pvt MA

STROZIER,
Margaret Dozier: b 9-18-1740 d 1842 m Peter Strozier PS GA
Peter: b c. 1740 d 1-18-1807 m Margaret Dozier Pvt GA

STRUB,
Samuel: b 7-19-1757 d 10-25-1832 m Susanna Elizabeth Stoltz
    Mil PS NC

STRUBING,
Philip: b a. 1758 d p. 1791 m Sarah Deamer Lt PA

STRUBLE,
Daniel: b 1749 d 9-8-1829 m Mary Ann Couse Ens NJ
Leonard: b 1740 d 1805 m (1)Catherine — (2)Margaret Longcor Pvt
    NJ

STRUDWICK,
Samuel: b c. 1732 d 1794 m — PS NC

STRUNK,
Henry: b 1743 d 1823 m Elizabeth Ace Pvt PA
Henry: b a. 1730 d p. 1798 m Anna Elizabeth Harwish Pvt NY
Wm.: b c. 1757 d p. 1840 m (1) — Rhine (2)Rebecca Brush Pvt PA

STRUTHERS,
John: b 2-11-1759 d 12-31-1845 m Mary Foster 1Sgt PA

STRYKER,
Abraham, Sr.: b 8-4-1715 d 4-4-1777 m (1)Ida Ryder (2)Katriena
    Cornell (3)Katriena Hogeland Sol NJ
Abraham, Jr.: b 1-10-1752 d 11-2-1827 m (1)Cornelia Beekman
    (2)Ann Terhune Pvt NJ
Abraham: b 11-30-1747 d 9-25-1784 m Anna Stoohoff Pvt NJ
Christopher: b 4-19-1756 d 6-27-1826 m Judith Lorn Pvt NJ
Dominicus: b 6-24-1734 d 1821 m (1)Maria D. — (2)Jean
    Vanderveer Pvt NJ
Hendrick: b c. 1737 d a. 4-20-1786 m Catrina — PS NJ
Isaac: b 9-11-1751 d 9-24-1817 m Jane Veghte Pvt NJ
James: b 9-18-1755 d 12-16-1831 m Mary Horn Pvt NJ
John: b 3-2-1740 d 3-25-1786 m Lydia Cornell Capt NJ
John: b 10-18-1744 d 11-29-1776 m Maria Veghte Pvt NJ
Peter: b 2-17-1765 d 6-6-1838 m Sarah Lowe Pvt NJ
Peter: b 12-31-1755 d 9-20-1801 m Elanah J. Low Pvt PA
Peter: b 12-23-1763 d 3-6-1847 m Sarah Barkaloo Fif NJ
Peter: b 10-19-1749 d 2-12-1828 m Maria Van Nortwick Pvt NJ
Peter: b 1761 d 5-11-1830 m Nelly Voorhees Pvt NJ
Simon: b 1750 d 3-25-1838 m Aletta Blue Pvt NJ ★

STUBBLEFIELD,
Beverly: b 11-8-1742 d 12-23-1823 m Mary Shelton Capt VA
George: b c. 1740 d p. 2-9-1801 m (1)Sarah — (2)Mrs Sally (Lowry)
    Daingerfield Maj PS VA
Wyatt: b a. 1755 d a. 10- -1824 m Anne Challis Sol NC

STUBBS,
Benjamin: b c. 1750 d p. 11-23-1794 m Rebecca Dunbar Pvt ME
James: b 6-10-1746 d 5-12-1822 m Mary Eliza Scott Pvt GA
Jeremiah: b c. 1753 d 12-2-1833 m Jane Bradbury True Cpl MA
John, Sr.: b — d p. 10-21-1786 m Rebecca Conner PS SC
Joseph: b 5-16-1756 d 8-25-1791 m Ruth Atwood Pvt Smn MA
Lawrence Smith: b 1738 d 1797 m Ellis Duval PS VA
Lewis: b c. 1758/9 d 1845 m Elizabeth Bridges Pvt SC ★
Peter: b 6-1-1744 d 1821 m Mrs Mary Barradall Palmer Tyler Pvt SC
Thomas: b c. 1753 d p. 12-16-1795 m (1)Hannah Swinson (2)Mrs
    Margaret Jones PS NC
Wm.: b c. 1748 d p. 9-7-1820 m Mary — Pvt NY
Wm.: b 12-22-1748 d 6-26-1839 m (1)Elizabeth Hubbard (2)Mrs
    Ann F. McDaniel Stubbs Pvt SC ★

STUCK,
Jacob: bpt 11-3-1751 d 12-31-1828 m Catherine — Pvt GA
John: b 1749 d 6-18-1833 m (2)Elizabeth — Pvt PA

STUCKER,
Eve (Anna Eva Maria): b c. 1745 d 1795 m Jacob Stucker, Sr. PS VA
Jacob, Sr.: b a. 1745 d 1782 m Eve (Anna Eva Maria) — Pvt VA
Jacob, Jr.: b 8-11-1764 d 6-11-1820 m (1)Elizabeth Rogers
    (2)Catherine Utter Pvt VA

STUCKY, (includes STOOKEY & STUCKEY)
Abraham: b c. 1755 d 1816 m — PS VA
John: b 1742 d 8-9-1818 m Salome Zimmerman Pvt PA
John: b 1759 d 1855 m Barbara Stump Pvt PA

STUDEBAKER,
Joseph: b 1745 d 4- -1813 m Molly — PS Pvt PA
Philip: b 1747 d p. 3-11-1826 m Christiana Miller Pvt PS PA

STUDER,
Philip: b 1752 d p. 5-20-1836 m (1)Elizabeth — (2) — Pvt MD ★

STUDLEY,
Anthony: b 1736 d p. 1793 m (1)Mary Marchent (2)Mrs Priscilla
    (Chase) Baker Pvt MA
Benjamin: b 1745 d a. 7-7-1812 m Hannah Litchfield CS PS MA
Consider: b 11-2-1760 d 12-28-1832 m Olive Mann Cpl MA ★
David: b 10-13-1748 d p. 1820 m Ruth Damon Cpl MA
Eliab, Sr.: b 9-10-1706 d 12-13-1785 m Mary Briggs Pvt MA
Eliab, Jr.: b 1754 d 8-14-1826 m Betsey Stetson Pvt MA
Gideon: b 5-15-1738 d 8-14-1816 m Rosamond Church Pvt MA
Wm.: b 2-6-1752 d 8-23-1833 m Mrs Ruth Hatch Pvt MA

STUDWELL,
Anthony: b 1738 d 1824 m Hannah Whelpley Pvt CT
Joseph: b c. 1743 d c. 1784 m Mrs Deborah Lockwood Pvt CT

STULL, (or STOLL)
Daniel: b 1755 d 1811 m Mary Beatty Capt MD
David: b c. 1728 d 1785-90 m Mrs Rebecca (Dixon) Reese PS SC
Jacob: b 1741 d 11-14-1809 m Sarah Pipenger (Tipinger) Capt NJ
John: b 1733 d 4-9-1791 m (1)Sarah — (2)Mercy (Williams)Ross
    Col PS MD
John Adam: b 1754 d 1821 m Elizabeth — Sol PA
Wm.: b — d 7-18-1825 m Christina Elizabeth — Pvt Matr PA

STULTS,
Henry: b 2-24-1755 d 10-3-1832 m Ellen Cortelyou Pvt NJ
Jacob: b 1761 d 1-14-1841 m Margaret Outcalt Pvt NJ

STUMP, (includes STUMM & STUMPFF)
Adam: b c. 1740 d c. 1805 m Isabella — Pvt PA
Christopher: b 1720 d 1778 m Anna Margaretta — PS PA
Daniel: b 9-9-1761 d 10-4-1832 m Mary Ramey Pvt VA
George: b 1740 d p. 1791 m Barbara — Pvt PA
George: b 4-8-1744 d 4-22-1805 m Elizabeth Wilson PS VA
John: b 2-22-1735 d 9-28-1827 m Mary Magdalena Howell
    Freeman Pvt NY ★
Leonard: b 11-21-1748 d a. 2-10-1829 m Catherine — PS VA
Mathias: b 1730 d 10- -1784 m Margaret — Pvt PA
Michael: b c. 1744 d a. 6-2-1799 m Sarah Hughes LCol VA

STUNTZ,
Conrad: b 1738 d 7-24-1810 m Margaret Anna Briefling Pvt PA

STUPP,
Leonard: b 6-26-1756 d 3-25-1827 m (1)Anna Maria Rohrer (2)Mrs
    Maria Glass PS PA
Martin: b c. 1733 d 5- -1811 m (1)Christina Walborn (2)Magdalena
    Gebel PS PA

STURGEON,
Henry: b 1745 d 1839 m Jane Dickson 1Lt PA
Jeremiah: b c. 1708 d p. 12-5-1792 m Mrs Lydia Lee PS PA
Peter: b 12-15-1756 d c. 1830 m Rebecca McClure 1Lt PA
Robert: b 1740 d a. 1787 m Margaret — Pvt PA
Robert: b 1740 d 6-30-1805 m (1)Jean Robinson (2)Jane Snodgrass
    Pvt PA
Samuel: b 6- -1741 d 10-2-1801 m Margaret Rogers Pvt PA
Thomas, Sr.: b 12-1-1731 d 5-18-1813 m Margaret Corbett Lt PA
Thomas, Jr.: b 9-15-1762 d 5-19-1849 m Sarah Hume Lt PA

STURGILL,
Francis: b 1758 d 1807 m Rebecca Hash Sol VA

STURGIS, (or STURGES)
Aaron: b 6-20-1760 d 10-23-1842 m Sarah Morehouse Pvt CT ★
Amos: b 5-17-1757 d 4-17-1826 m Rachael Randall Capt PA
Andrew: b 11-12-1741 d p. 4-18-1809 m Abigail Finch Pvt CT
Aquila: b 1761 d p. 1838 m Sarah Little Pvt VT
Augustus: b 10-19-1759 d 7-18-1826 m Mercy Conger Pvt CT W ★
Benjamin: b 8-23-1757 d 6-12-1846 m Nancy — Pvt NJ PA ★
Dimon: b 10-29-1754 d 1-16-1829 m Sarah Perry Sol CT
Edward: b 7-27-1737 d — m Mary Bassett Pvt MA
Hezekiah: b 11-23-1725 d 4-27-1792 m Abigail Dimon PS CT
Isaac: bpt 8-22-1742 d 8-22-1782 m Rhoda Banks Pvt CT
James: b 9-10-1754 d 2-5-1816 m Mary Ogelby Pvt PA
John: b 1749 d 2-14-1822 m (1)Leah Phillips (2)Mrs Fannie West Pvt
    PA
Jonathan: b 8-25-1740 d 10-4-1819 m Deborah Lewis CS PS CT
Jonathan: b 4-9-1743 d 5-11-1834 m Temperance Hawes Gorham
    Pvt MA
Jonathan: b a. 1751 d 10-27-1824 m Elizabeth Smith Pvt MA
Joseph: b 6-25-1739 d 1779 m Sarah Dimon Sol CT

Joseph: b 1738 d 1817 m Margaret Stoehr Pvt PA
Judson: b 2-21-1748 d 12-12-1782 m Abigail Squier Pvt CT
Lewis: b 7-14/15-1756 d c. 6-1-1838 m Mary Porter Cpl CT
Miner: b 1-26-1759 d 3-23-1786 m Anne Mayes Pvt KY VA
Nathan: b 1750 d 8-22-1827 m Catherine Phillips Pvt PA
Nathaniel: b 1742 d 1-24-1816 m Phebe Burnett Pvt NJ
Seth: b 4-28-1735 d 5-9-1804 m Mary Burr PS CT
Solomon: b 5-15-1698 d 7-8-1779 m Abigail Bradley PS CT
Thaddeus: b a. 1749 d p. 1780 m Mary Comstock Pvt CT
Thomas, Sr.: b 7-22-1722 d 1785 m Sarah Payne Pvt MA
Thomas, Jr.: b 4-5-1755 d 9-16-1821 m Elizabeth Jackson Pvt MA

STURMAN,
Hannah Chilton: b 1-4-1720 d p. 12- -1792 m Foxhall Sturman PS
  VA

STURTEVANT, (includes STURDEVANT, STURDIVANT or STURTIVENT)
Andrew: b 1760 d 7-10-1848 m Diana Besse Pvt MA ★
Asa: b 1760 d 1839 m (2)Eunice Morse Pvt MA
Caleb: b 8-25-1759 d 10-17-1837 m Merriam Howe Pvt CT ★
Caleb: b 3-16-1716 d 10-7-1793 m Mrs Abigail Bearse Pvt MA
Church: b 4-4-1730 d 1814 m Sarah Leach Pvt MA
Consider: b 1733 d 2-10-1805 m Ann Bessee Pvt MA
David: b 6-16-1742 d 11-30-1808 m Marcia Perkins Pvt MA
Dependence: b 11-30-1739 d 7-28-1803 m (1)Hannah Waterman
  (2)Abigail Smith Sgt MA W★
Francis: b 8-20-1756/7 d 5-6-1833 m Lois Barrows Sgt MA ★
Hosea: b 2-14-1762 d 4-20-1850 m Sarah Paine Pvt MA ★
James, Sr.: b c. 1735 d 6- -1807 m Hannah Knapp Sol CT
James, Jr.: b 1- -1757 d 8-4-1843 m Lucy Butler Pvt CT ★
John: b 12-15-1757 d 4-7-1839 m Nancy Hollinsberry Lt VA
John: b 8-22-1717 d 12- -1816 m Martha Hobbs NLt VA
Joseph: b 8-21-1734 d 12-26-1808 m Mary Gibbs Sgt MA
Justus: b 1741-8 d 12-28-1825 m Sarah Hastings PS VT
Lemuel: b 3-5-1710/11 d 12-2-1789 m Deborah Bryant Pvt MA
Lemuel: b 11-9-1756 d 11-5-1839 m Priscilla Thompson Pvt MA ★
Lot: b 7-25-1759 d 1-4-1848 m Elizabeth Bessie — Pvt MA ★
Nathan: b 1750 d 10-1-1777 m — Pvt CT
Nehemiah: b 9-19-1749 d 1-27-1819 m Huldah Fuller Pvt MA
Noah: b 7-4-1758 d 3-10-1828 m Ruth Bishop Pvt MA ★
Peleg: b 2-25-1736 d 11-11-1803 m Abigail Swift Capt CT
Samuel: b 1740 d 4-9-1828 m (1)Ruth Benedict (2)Sarah Morris
  (3)Mrs Lucy Cooley Sol CT
Samuel: b c. 1750 d 8- -1831 m — Cushman Pvt MA
Simeon: b 5-11-1742 d 3-2-1822 m Ruth Thompson Cpl MA

STUTZBAUCH, (or STOTSENBURG)
Christopher: b 1762 d 1827 m Mrs Eliza Alice (Cannon)Wilder Pvt PA

STYMETS,
Frederick: b 3-7-1751 d 10-21-1795 m Ann Barrea Lt NY
Jakob: b 8-14-1720 d 11-5-1789 m (1)Jannette Requa (2)Mary
  Dean Pvt NY

STYRON,
John: b c. 1720 d p. 9-16-1785 m Abigail — PS NC
Wm.: b 1745 d 3-7-1825 m Ann (Wallace) CS NC

SUBLETT, (or SUBBLETT)
Benjamin: b 4-23-1733 d p. 9-19-1809 m Elizabeth Jordan Cpl VA
James: b c. 1758 d p. 1795 m Elizabeth Ford Sol VA
Lewis: b 1759 d 1830 m (1)Mary Trabue (2)Sally Samuel PS VA

SUDDUTH, (includes SUDDARTH, SUDDATH & SUDDERTH)
Benjamin: b 1722 d 1792 m Silent (Simpson?) PS VA
James: b c. 1720 d — 1800 m Patience Sumter PS VA
Wm.: b 1753 d 4-13-1830 m Sarah — Pvt VA ★
Wm.: b 2-2-1756 d 11-18-1832 m Martha Pleasants Pvt VA

SUDLER, (or SADLER)
Thomas: b 1745 d 1794 m Ann Long Pvt MD
Thomas Seon: b 10-15-1760 d 11-19-1832 m Eleanor Waters Pvt MD

SUFFERN,
John: b 11-23-1741 d 11-11-1836 m (1)Mary Meyers (2)Mrs Elizabeth Berthol Bogart Sol PS NY

SUGGETT,
James: b c. 1712 d p. 3-5-1786 m (2)Jemima Spence PS KY
John: b 6-20-1751 d 12-12-1834 m Mildred Davis Pvt KY
Mildred Davis: b 3-5-1756 d 7-11-1834 m John Suggett PS KY

SUGGS, (or SUGG)
Aquilla, Sr.: b 1706 d p. 5-8-1780 m Elizabeth Battle CS PS NC
Aquilla, Jr.: b 4-1-1730 d 1-10-1791 m Lucy Reading PS NC
George: b a. 1748 d p. 1792 m Mary Sanders 1Lt NC
George Augustus: b a. 1758 d a. 10-5-1810 m Mrs Patience (Jones)
  Sugg CS NC
Joel: b c. 1748 d a. 4-3-1781 m Sarah Patience Jones PS NC
John: b c. 1732 d p. 1790 m Elizabeth Murphrey Pvt NC
Noah: b c. 1740 d 1- -1800 m Murphree Howell CS NC
Thomas: b 1761 d 9-5-1829 m Zerah Spencer Sol NC

SUISSHOLTZ,
Lorenz: b 10-21-1739 d 11-26-1808 m Elizabeth Zimmerman Pvt
  PA

SUITS, (or SUTS)
Peter: b 3-3-1764 d 4-24-1853 m Elizabeth Gaster Pvt NY

SULLENGER,
Thomas: b c. 1756 d 1795 m Fanny Shipp PS VA

SULLINGS,
John: b 1746 d 10-14-1824 m Ruth Spooner Sgt MA ★

SULLIVAN,
Charles: b 1728 d 1808 m Mrs Mary Charlton Johnson PS SC
Charles Craven: b 3-27-1760 d 1-12-1813 m Susanna Johnson Pvt
  VA
Cornelius: b 1749 d 9-10-1816 m Catharine Bohn PS MD
Daniel: b 1- -1730 d 2- -1792 m Margaret — Pvt NC
Daniel: b c. 1738 d 4- -1782 m (1)Amey Paul (2)Abigail Bean
  Capt MA
Darby: b c. 1761 d 1841 m — Pvt MD
David: b 3-31-1751 d 9-18-1845 m Hannah Huyk Sgt NY ★
Ebenezer: b 10-3-1753 d 6-3-1799 m Abigail Cotton Capt MA
George: b c. 1750 d 1815 m Sally Perrin Sol SC
Hewlet: b 12-28-1763 d 7-11-1830 m Mrs Mary Dunklin Pvt SC
James: b 4-22-1744 d 12-10-1808 m Mehetable Odiorne CS PS
  MA
James: b 1754 d 8-27-1825 m Mary Cox Sgt NC
James: b c. 1763/4 d p. 1809/10 m Elizabeth Wood Cpl NC
James: b c. 1722 d 8- -1809 m (1)Matoaka Bolling (2)Sarah
  Harrison Choice Lt SC
James: b 9-24-1765 d 2-12-1817 m Eleanor Wilson Pvt VA
Jeremiah: b 1735 d c. 1780 m Zilpah Ramsey Pvt NC
WJohn: b 2-17-1740 d 1-23-1795 m Lydia Wooster MGen PS NH
John: b 1756 d 1839 m Sarah Roberts Sgt SC ★
Mary (Charlton)Johnson: b 6-1-1722 d 12-20-1837 m (1) —
  Johnson (2)Charles Sullivan PS GA SC
Patrick: b 1-1-1759 d a. 1819 m Mary Hannah Roots Pvt NC
Patrick: b 1751 d 1841 m Henrietta Connors Pvt PA
Patrick: b 3-17-1754 d 12-17-1821 m Barbara Bauser Pvt PA

SULLIVANT,
Hampton: b a. 1756 d a. 3-24-1794 m Elizabeth — PS SC

SUMMERALL,
Jesse: b 1740 d 2-10-1792 m Sarah — PS NC

SUMMERLIN,
Winburn: b 11- -1762 d 4-24-1842 m Milly Pearson Pvt NC

SUMMERS, (includes SOMERS, SOMMER & SUMMER)
Andrew: b 1742 d 1-26-1806 m Hannah Myers Capt PA
Bartholomew: b 1744 d — m Susanna Carr Cpl VT
Benjamin: b c. 1737 d 1783 m Grace Letton Ens PS MD PA
David: b 1750 d 1820 m Sarah Treat Pvt CT
David: b 1758 d 1838 m Judith Scull MM NJ
Francis: b 1752 d 1810 m Christina Hipp Mil SC
Francis: b 3-3-1732 d 9-10-1800 m Jane (Watkins) Charlton CS VA
George: b 4-23-1721 d 8-8-1785 m Barbara Longstreet Ens NJ
George: b 4- -1764 d 10-25-1841 m Prudence Gross Drm PA
George: b 1735 d 9-11-1806 m Elizabeth Henderson Col VA
Jacob: b 1762/3 d 1838 m — Pvt PA
Jacob: b 4-29-1749 d 5-27-1817 m Anna Mary Dauber Capt PA
James: b 7-2-1739 d 6-4-1779 m Rebecca Steelman Capt NJ
James: b 12-6-1761 d 10-12-1850 m (1)Lettice Finley (2)Aner
  Blackman (3)Martha Wiley Pvt NJ
John: b 10-14-1727 d 8-23-1799 m (2)Mrs Hannah Spicer Ludlum
  Capt NJ
John: b 12-30-1723 d 6-23-1783 m Esther Risley Pvt NJ
John: b 1760 d 8- -1844 m (1)Deborah Batton (2)Deborah Lippin-
  cott (3)Edith — Sol NJ
John: b 7-22-1763 d 2-1-1838 m Gertrude (Charity) Meriness Pvt NY
John: b 1750 d 1818 m Catherine Arden Capt NC
John: b 9-6-1752 d 11-6-1838 m (2)Elizabeth Snyder (3)Sarah Hahn
  Pvt PA
John: b 12-31-1749 d 12-7-1821 m Elizabeth Dulin Sgt VA
John: b 12- -1746 d 1806 m — Sol VA
John Adam, Sr.: b 1716 d 1794 m — Jostin PS SC
John Adam, Jr.: b 9-29-1744 d 10-1-1809 m Mary Reuss Capt PS
  SC
Leonard: b 4-23-1759 d 2-18-1836 m Elizabeth Phillippe Pvt PA
Martin: b 1740 d p. 3- -1804 m Anna Barbara Geiss Pvt PA
Peter: b 1757 d 1812 m Elizabeth Busby 1Lt PA
Phillip: b 10-2-1728 d 5-2-1814 m Salome Reibel Pvt PA
Simon: b 11-23-1747 d 12-2-1836 m Elizabeth Ferguson Adj VA
Stephen: b 3-19-1743 d 7-16-1811 m Mary Holberton PS CT
Thomas: b 1750 d 1826 m Alice Higby Pvt NJ
Wm.: b 5-12-1750 d 10-19-1820 m Ann White Pvt MD
Wm.: b 5-26-1758 d 9-20-1840 m (1)Frances Lewis (2)Mary Haven
  Cpl VA
Wm.: b 1764 d 1832 m Mrs Eve Margary (Sease)Summer Sol SC

SUMNER,
Benjamin: b 8-15-1764 d 3-8-1808 m Ruth Palmer Pvt PS CT
Benjamin: b 12-29-1724 d 1-27-1803 m Bridget Perry CS CT
Benjamin: b 1734 d 4-25-1798 m Hannah Bemis Pvt MA
Benjamin: b 1-7-1744 d 7- -1829 m Martha Clark Pvt MA
Clap: b 1750 d 11-30-1817 m (1)Keziah — (2)Mehitable Tassel
 (3)Mary Stevens Pvt CT
Clement: b 2-2-1752 d 3-16-1839 m Elizabeth Randall Pvt MA ★
Daniel: b 5-26-1759 d 11-23-1838 m (1)Lucy Cook (2)Hannah
 Watson Pvt MA
Daniel: b 6-26-1739 d 7-31-1819 m Lydia Fairbanks Pvt VT
Darius: b 9-28-1756 d 5-2-1847 m Anna Daniels Sgt MA ★
David, Sr.: b 1-6-1717 d 11-11-1789 m Deborah Houghton Pvt MA
David, Jr.: b 6-6-1749 d 1821 m Ruth Cane Pvt MA
Davis: b 7-22-1761 d 12-12-1826 m (1)Lydia Sewall (2)Dorothy Vose
 Drm MA
Dempsey: b 1725 d a. 11- -1779 m Martha Baker CS NC
Ebenezer: b 8-14-1737 d 10-12-1784 m Person Pease Capt CT
Ebenezer, Jr.: b 5-1-1758 d 8-16-1844 m Jemima Hall Pvt Mar CT ★
Ebenezer: b 4-16-1749 d 4-22-1823 m Catherine Smith Sgt MA
Edward: b 6-14-1746 d 10-28-1829 m Elizabeth Clapp PS MA
Ezra: b 8-7-1752 d p. 1791 m Mrs Mary Kane Davis Pvt MA
Hezekiah: b 12-4-1724 d 1802 m (1)Desire Higgins (2)Mary — Pvt
 MA
Hopestill: b 9-9-1746 d 12-25-1826 m Mary Rhodes CS ME MA
James: b 12-10-1718 d 8-29-1795 m (1)Mary Bigelow (2)Mary
 Jones PS MA
Jethro: b 3-15-1758 d 4-6-1830 m Elizabeth Turner Capt NC
Joel: b 7-31-1761 d 4-3-1813 m Elizabeth Warren Everett Cpl MA
John: b 1736 d 8-6-1804 m Mehitable Perry Capt CT
John: b 1747 d 1796 m — Cpl MA
John, Jr.: b 4-26-1760 d 3-19-1839 m Hannah Evans Pvt MA ★
John, Sr.: b 8-1-1705 d 1787 m (1)Susanna Stevens (2)Jedidah
 Smith PS MA
Joseph: b 1761 d 12-30-1827 m Mary Kight Sol GA
Joseph: b 7-29-1760 d 12-7-1846 m Ruth Legg Pvt MA ★
Joseph: b 1-19-1740 d 12-9-1824 m Lucy Williams PS MA
Joseph: b c. 1748 d 4- -1795 m Martha Philip Sol NC
Robert: b 9-18-1761 d 11-19-1845 m Jemima Younglove Sgt CT ★
Samuel, Sr.: b 11-13-1695 d 2-8-1782 m Elizabeth Griffin CS CT
Samuel: b 12-29-1732 d 10-11-1813 m (2)Elizabeth Williams PS
 MA
Seth: b 7-8-1735 d 5-2-1814 m (1)Elizabeth Davis (2)Mary Gay
 Capt MA
Shuball: b 11-11-1759 d 4-1-1841 m Lucy Grover Pvt CT ★
Thomas: b — d 12-22-1791 m Anna Baker Sol GA
Thomas: b 6-2-1757 d 4-19-1825 m Elizabeth Holland Pvt MA
Wm.: b 7-9-1757 d 11-19-1846 m Rebecca Arnold Sol CT
Wm.: b 1-9-1761 d 7-21-1850 m Saviah Udall Pvt MA
Wm.: b 8-6-1748 d 1-30-1836 m Mary Pond Lt MA

SUMNEY,
Jacob: b a. 1762 d 1807 m Margaret — Pvt PA

SUMPTER, (or SUMTER)
George, Sr.: b — d 1806 m Elizabeth Gross PS VA
John: b 1740 d p. 12-12-1809 m Catherine — Pvt VA
Thomas: b 12-15-1761/2 d 1-15-1846 m Lydia Kirkpatrick Pvt NC ★
Thomas: b 8-14-1734 d 6-1-1832 m Mary Cantey Jameson BGen
 SC
Wm.: b a. 1741 d c. 1828 m Judith Randall Capt NC

SUNDAY,
Adam: b 7-5-1759 d 4-14-1855 m Mary — Pvt PA ★

SUNDERLAND,
Joseph: b 1762 d 4-30-1838 m Elizabeth Smith Pvt PA ★
Peter: b 1737 d 8-1-1827 m Catherine Holman Sol NJ
Samuel: b 5-4-1752 d 7-28-1842 m Thankful Clark Pvt CT ★

SUNDERLIN,
Samuel: b 8-26-1758 d — m Elizabeth Minegar Pvt PA ★

SUPLEE, (or SUPPLEE)
Andrew: b 9-13-1734 d 1806 m (1)Mary Zimmerman (2)Rachel
 Davis Sol PA
Jacob: b 1759 d 3-18-1825 m Rebecca Ramsey Ens PA
John: b 1730 d 1805 m Sarah Roberts Pvt PA
Peter: b 9-2-1745 d 1-24-1778 m Susana Wagoner Pvt PA

SUPLER,
John: b 11-3-1757 d 6-14-1835 m Rachel Kirk Pvt PA ★

SURBER,
Joseph: b 1749 d p. 1802 m (2)Mary Ann Stevens Pvt VA

SUSONG,
Andrew: b c. 1737/8 d 1826 m Barbara — Pvt PA

SUTER, (includes SUDER)
John: b 1-16-1744 d 11-12-1794 m Sarah Williams 2Lt MD
John: b 1755 d c. 1820 m Elizabeth Stringfellow Matr VA

SUTHERLAND, (includes SOUTHERLAND)
Alexander: b c. 1730 d 10-12-1777 m Maria McDanielis PS NY
Andrew: b 3- -1728 d p. 9-11-1794 m Elizabeth Board Pvt PS NY
Daniel: b 5-9-1755 d 1-5-1792 m Ann McDowell Matr NC
Daniel: b 1749 d 6-14-1831 m — Newkirk Sol NC
David: b 9-20-1735 d 9-6-1799 m Hannah McDonnell PS NY
David: b 8-31-1757 d 9-23-1828 m Lucretia Smith PS NY
David: b 1722 d 4-10-1794 m Judith Griffin Col NY
George: b 8- -1761 d p. 1-1-1846 m (1)Jane (Johnson)Shores
 (2)Mary Herndon Drm VA NC
John: b c. 1738 d 1797/8 m Cecil Brickell Pvt NC
John: b 1747/8 d 1-2-1842 m Susannah — Pvt MD
John: b 7-8-1735 d 6-10-1817 m (1)Marie Germaine (2)Jerusha
 Stanley Lt PS VT
Lawrence: b 6-12-1763-5 d 10-9-1846 m Elizabeth — Grd NY
Ransom: b c. 1740 d 9- -1822 m Charity Kimbrough Col PS NC
Robert, 2d: b 8-30-1747 d 8-12-1835 m Patience Tonille Pvt NC
Roger, Sr.: b c. 1720 d 1798 m (1)Abigail — (2)Mary Scofield PS CT
Roger, Jr.: b 3-16-1743 d 10-7-1828 m Hannah Barton Capt NY
Samuel: b 1-27-1747 d 5-11-1810 m Rachel Prudy Sgt VT
Stephen: b 4-5-1753 d 1813 m Sarah Mead Pvt NY
Thomas: b 1733 d 10-1-1816 m Jane Chambers LCol PA
Wm.: b 1745 d 1826 m — Sol NY
Wm.: b c. 1746 d 6-22-1803 m Mary — Pvt VA

SUTLIFF, (includes SUTLIEF & SUTLIFFE)
Abel: b 8-23-1751 d 5-15-1799 m Charity Barber Pvt CT
Gad: b 1-1-1756 d 3-4-1842 m Catherine Squires 2Sgt CT ★
Janner: b 3-11-1762 d 12-28-1826 m Hepzibah Beulah Story Pvt CT
John: b 3-8-1713/14 d 1-27-1790 m (1)Anna Ives (2)Martha
 Bassett (3)Esther — PS CT
John: b 3-23-1744 d 4-12-1816 m Lois Curtiss Pvt CT
John: bpt 10-16-1757 d p. 1832 m — Sol NY
Joseph, Jr.: b 1-1-1733 d 11- -1801 m Mrs Zerviah (Webster)Cobb
 PS CT
Samuel, Sr.: b 9-18-1733 d 5-6-1799 m Eunice Curtiss Pvt CT

SUTPHEN, (includes SUTFIN & SUTPHIN)
Abram: bpt 6-9-1745 d 1827 m Deborah Nickols Pvt NJ
David: b 3-17-1760 d 9-17-1845 m Lydia Smith Pvt NJ ★
Derick: b 7-14-1743 d 1-27-1831 m Ann Chamberlain Pvt NJ
Derrick: b 1712/13 d 6-27-1796 m Mary Howell PS NJ
Guisbert: b 8-28-1720 d 11-16-1796 m Ariontje Van Pelt Pvt NJ
James: b 1735 d a. 5-8-1811 m (1)Elizabeth — (2)Elizabeth
 Voorhees Pvt NJ
John: b 7-14-1756 d 7-27-1823 m Lydia — Pvt NJ
John: b 3-31-1759 d 10-3-1832 m Anna Snedecar Pvt Pvtr NJ ★
Peter: b 8-17-1762 d 2-4-1839 m Catherine Hunt Pvt NJ
Richard: b 12-23-1757 d 12-22-1835/6 m Isabel Clayton Pvt NJ ★

SUTS, (or SUITS)
John I.: b 4- -1759 d 1-31-1817 m Catharine Wauffel Pvt NY W ★
John P.: b 11-22-1758 d 1-8-1836 m Nancy Nellis Fif NY ★

SUTTER,
Daniel: b 9-19-1744 d 10-19-1828 m (1)Anna Catherine Gardener
 (2)Susannah — Pvt PA
George: b c. 1730 d c. 1800 m — Pvt PS PA
James: b 4-17-1751 d 9-21-1791 m Elizabeth Whitton Lt PA

SUTTLES, (or SUTTLE)
George: b 10-25-1766 d 2-15-1816 m Nancy Byers Pvt NC
Isaac: b c. 1730-40 d p. 1812 m Sarah Bushrod Sol VA
Wm.: b 1-4-1731 d 1-23-1839 m Margaret Harbin Sol GA

SUTTON, (or SITTON)
Abner: bpt 5-31-1730 d 5-4-1805 m Ann Hayden Pvt MA
Abraham: b c. 1739 d p. 1790 m Mary Chenoweth Pvt PS PA
Andrew: b 1754 d c. 1824 m Elizabeth Montross Pvt NY
Arod: b 1758 d 1793 m Hannah Okeman Pvt PA
Benjamin: b 1745 d p. 1820 m Molle Jacobs Pvt CT VT
Benjamin: b 1-29-1741 d p. 1793 m Martha — Sol NY
Benjamin, Sr.: b 1735 d 1796 m Mary Jennings Cpl PA
Benjamin, Jr.: b 9-20-1759 d 9-4-1840 m Sarah Tingley Pvt PA ★
Edward: b 1750 d 9- -1776 m Abigail Burrell Dr CT
Elisha Kent: b 1756 d 1831 m Hannah Voght Pvt NJ
Henry: b 11-5-1758 d 4-20-1841 m Nancy Sutton Pvt NJ
Jacob: b c. 1755 d 3-20-1838 m Louise Rene Cotte Pvt NC
Jacob: b 1758/9 d 5-28-1836 m Ann (Nancy) — Pvt SC ★
James: b 3-7-1744 d 9-19-1824 m Sarah Smith Pvt PS NY
James: b 1747 d 1815 m Martha Elizabeth Brown 2Lt NC
James: b 1750 d 1795 m (1)Frances Powell (2)Elizabeth Taylor Capt
 VA
Jeremiah: b 10-29-1738 d c. 1814 m Elizabeth — Sol NJ
John: b 1734 d 1820 m Rachael Collier MM NJ
John: b 7-25-1748 d 10-3-1795 m Dinah Bonham Pvt NJ
John, Sr.: b 12-25-1736 d 2- -1818 m Deborah Bennett 2Lt NY
John: b c. 1750-2 d 1815 m Dorothy — Pvt PA
John, Sr.: b c. 1735 d 6-14-1810 m Temperance Lane Sgt VA
John, Jr.: b 5-25-1759 d 4-22-1826 m Mary Coleman Pvt VA
John: b c. 1725 d 1800 m Sarah — PM VA
John Pell: b c. 1747 d 1807 m Winifred Montross Pvt NY
Jonas: b 4-18-1721 d c. 1797 m Elizabeth Runyon Pvt NJ

Jonathan: b 3-23-1735 d 2-2-1818 m Rachel Colyer Sgt NJ
Jonathan: b 8-29-1749 d 2-8-1830 m Hannah Hayden Tms NJ
Joseph: b 7-9-1747 d 11-8-1822 m Mrs Martha Pierson Sgt NJ
Joseph: b c. 1760 d 2-25-1836 m Mary Betson Pvt NJ
Joseph: b 10-15-1745 d 2-8-1832 m Diannah Beck Pvt NC
Moses: b 1745 d 12-7-1827 m Susanna Cox Capt NJ PA
Nathaniel: b 1735-40 d p.-11-12-1818 m (1) X (2)Sarah — Sol VA
Peter: b c. 1743 d 4- -1829 m Phoebe Kennan Pvt NJ
Richard: b 12-12-1736 d 12-12-1825 m Elizabeth Foster Lt MA
Robert: b 7-19-1741 d 11-15-1811 m Rhoda Lloyd Sgt MA
Samuel: b 6-10-1733 d — m Ruth Cantwell PS MD
Thomas: b c. 1756 d 1805 m Elizabeth Madison Sol NC
Thomas: b 1759 d 6-21-1840 m Lucretia Blackman Pvt NC
Uriah: b 7-21-1741 d 2-2-1840 m Elizabeth Bockover Capt NJ
Wm.: b 5-19-1749 d 6-29-1830 m — Pvt MD
Wm.: b c. 1746 d 1794-7 m Anne Hawkins Pvt NJ
Wm., Jr.: b 10-31-1727 d 6-28-1778 m Sarah Turner Pvt PA
Wm.: b c. 1745 d p. 4-18-1796 m Sarah Carter 2Lt VA
Zebulon: b 11-12-1752 d 2-25-1840 m: Sarah Hull Pvt NJ

SUYDAM, (includes SEDAM & SWIDAM)
Cornelius: b 1757 d 5-23-1827 m Anne Rappleye Pvt NJ
Cornelius: b 4-6-1761 d 3-17-1851 m Margaret Perrine Pvt NJ
Cornelius R.: b 1759 d 5-9-1823 m (1)Elizabeth Winton (2)Nancy Highner Ens NJ
Hendrick: b 6-4-1751 d 12-15-1819 m Phoebe Bedell Sol NY
Hendrick: b 3-20-1732 d 7-9-1805 m Rebecca Emmans PS NY
Jacob: b 4-4-1751 d 11-19-1804 m Sophia Boyce Pvt NJ
John: b c. 1755 d p. 1817 m (1)Jane Piatt (2)Sally Rose (3)Jane Tate Pvt NJ
Lambert: b 7-30-1743 d 4-1-1833 m (1)Sarah Hageman (2)Anna Johnson Capt NY
Ryke: b 10-30-1757 d 9-6-1847 m Rachel Merrill Pvt NJ ★

SWACKHAMER,
Conrad: b 11-30-1753 d 9-19-1831 m Mary Roelofsen PS NJ

SWAILS,
John: b 1742 d 10-30-1788 m Eleanor — Pvt MD

SWAIM,
Isaac: bpt 7-28-1751 d 2-2-1829 m Hannah — Pvt NJ
John: b 4-26-1748 d 1827 m Elizabeth Vickory PS NC

SWAIN, (or SWAINE)
Abishai: b 12-8-1746 d 9-22-1832/3 m Jedidah (Swain) PS MA
Abraham: b a. 1748 d 1-21-1790 m Sarah Woolston Pvt NJ
Benjamin: b 11-3-1754 d 8-18-1820 m Phebe Meader Pvt MA
Daniel: b 9-1-1729 d 9-13-1787 m Elizabeth Wyer PS MA
Dudley: b 11-17-1763 d 1-8-1854 m Molly Chase Pvt NH ★
Edward: b 5- -1752 d 9-8-1798 m Elizabeth Smith Pvt MA
Hezekiah: b c. 1757 d 4-9-1812 m Miriam York Pvt NH
Jacob: b 1762 d 7-16-1849 m Elizabeth Bloom Pvt PA
Jeremiah: b 6- -1751 d 2-21-1841 m (1)Elizabeth Calley (2)Sarah Rawlings Pvt NH ★
John: b 5-2-1751 d 8-24-1815 m Lois Walton Pvt MA
John: b 1759 d p. 3-7-1821 m (1)Mary Smith (2)Anna Maine Pvt SC
Jonathan: b 4-15-1728 d 8-23-1803 m Margaret Folger CS MA
Joseph: b 8-15-1754 d 3-4-1831 m Melicent Barrett Arfr MA
Luke: b c. 1753 d 11- -1801 m Rebecca Peyton NPilot SC
Phineas: b 1761 d 1842 m Jane Carr Pvt NH ★
Reuben: b 1725 d 1807 m Hannah Macy CS MA
Robert: b 1726 d p. 10-2-1812 m Elizabeth Ward Pvt SC
Silas: b 1722 d 5-8-1795 m Judith Somers PS NJ
Stephen: b c. 1746 d 1796 m Ann Elizabeth — Ens NC

SWALLOW,
Amaziah: b 11-22-1732 d 1-21-1803 m Elizabeth Kendall Lt MA
Andrew: b 4-17-1760 d 9-30-1843 m Catherine — Pvt PA VA NC ★
John: b 2-22-1729/30 d 11-23-1815 m (1)Mary Lawrence (2)Mary Hall Pvt NH
Peter: b 10-9-1743 d 4-7-1813 m (1)Prudence Stiles (2)Sybel Blood Pvt MA

SWAN, (or SWANN)
Adin: b 5-13-1764 d 12-26-1842 m Hannah Gardner Pvt CT
Benjamin: b 4-15-1735 d 5-11-1830 m Sarah Howe Pvt MA
Caleb, Sr.: b 4-12-1718 d 12-20-1808 m Dorothy Fry PS MA
Caleb, Jr.: b 7-2-1758 d 7-10-1798 m Dorcas Ingalls Capt MA
Charles: b 5-24-1746 d 3-29-1833 m Eunice Barnes Pvt CT
Charles: b 8-22-1749 d 12-5-1832 m Sarah Van Meter Pvt PA
Charles: b 8- -1753 d 8-4-1841 m Catharine Goyer Pvt VA ★
Ebenezer: b 1750 d 3-18-1820 m Tamasin Ballou Dr NH
Elias: b 1759 d 1797 m Anne Andros Sgt Mar CT RI
Francis: b 8-2-1752 d 3-25-1817 m (1)Martha Tasker (2)Abigail Elliot Ens MA
Francis: b 3-31-1710 d 1-13-1797 m Lydia Frye CS MA
George: b 8-26-1750 d 1-3-1798 m Abigail Randall Pvt CT
George: b 7-1-1750 d 3-28-1803 m Prudence Swan Pvt MA
Hugh: b c. 1742 d a. 8- -1796 m Martha — Pvt PA
James: b 1754 d 1831 m Hepzibah Clarke Maj MA
John, Sr.: b 12-28-1700 d 1780 m Lucy Denison PS CT

John, Jr.: b 9-24-1731 d p. 1790 m Mary Prentice Capt PS CT
John: bpt 11-27-1750 d 8-21-1821 m Elizabeth Trippe Maj MD
John: b 5- -1721 d p. 11-3-1800 m Elizabeth Lucas PS MD
John: b 1755 d 7-8-1843 m Ann Mitchell Cpl MA ★
John: b 1739 d c. 1836 m Sarah Taggart Pvt NH ★
John: b 1759 d 1811 m Judieth Woodson 1Lt VA
Joseph, Sr.: b 3-12-1734 d p. 1783 m (1)Elizabeth Smith (2)Mary Miner Pvt CT
Joseph, Jr.: b 12-3-1758 d p. 1800 m Deborah Alderman Cpl CT
Joseph: b c. 1732 d 1800 m Catherine Denny Pvt MA
Joshua: b 7-12-1755 d 3-25-1845 m Deborah Burbank Arfr MA ★
Matthew: b 1743 d 1-6-1795 m Ann McKean PS MA
Nathan: b 2-27-1753 d p. 1792 m (1)Lydia Tyler (2)Sarah Tyler 2Lt MA
Nathan: b 5-31-1747 d 11-6-1799 m Phoebe Wilson Pvt MA
Richard: b 1755 d 4- -1808 m Catherine Boggs QMSgt PA
Robert: b 1725 d 1802 m Rachel Draper Maj MA
Samuel, Jr.: b 1-17-1750 d 11-14-1825 m Hannah Lamson PS MA
Samuel: b 6-19-1747 d 7-11-1787 m Mildred Lyon Maj NC
Thomas: b 3-18-1742 d 12-27-1830 m Amy Denison Ens CT
Thomas: b a. 1749 d a. 2-2-1796 m Catherine — Sol NC
Thomas: b 1749 d 7-30-1805 m Elizabeth Bosworth Lt RI
Timothy: b 1723 d 9-1-1829 m Jane Watson Cpl PA ★
Wm.: b 9-4-1737 d p. 1802 m Lucy Robbins Pvt MA
Wm.: b 1746 d 1835 m Mercy Porter Pvt MA
Wm.: b c. 1745 d 5-19-1829 m Sally Oldfield Matr NY W ★
Wm.: b 1745 d 9-25-1782 m Martha Renick Lt QM PA
Wm.: b 2-28-1753 d 8- -1826 m Eleanor Chestnut Pvt PA

SWANDER,
Jacob: b c. 1754 d p. 1784 m Barbara Gerster Pvt PA

SWANGO,
Abraham: b c. 1727 d p. 1785 m Ailsie Pyles Pvt VA

SWANSEY,
Robert: b c. 1740 d 6-22-1795 m Rosannah — Lt SC
Wm.: b 1746 d 8-8-1825 m Anna Lusk Capt PA

SWANSON,
Edward: b 12-28-1759 d 9-26-1840 m (1)Mary Carvin (2)Polly Allen Pvt PS CS NC
Nathan: b c. 1748 d c. 1805 m Mary (prob. Graves) PS VA
Wm.: b 1720 d 1784 m Mary McGuire PS VA

SWANTON,
Wm.: b 1711 d 1810 m Rachel Browne Lt ME MA

SWARR,
John: b 1736 d 1823 m (1)Veronica Shirk (2)Magdalena Nissley Pvt PA

SWART,
Adam: bpt 9-23-1716 d 1801/2 m Helena Burhans PS NY
Benjamin: b 3-14-1750 d 7-18-1815 m Catalina Wemple Sgt NY
Jacobus: b 10-19-1740 d 1-27-1812 m Sarah Vedder Pvt NY
James: b c. 1758 d 5-10-1813 m (1)Jane Rogers (2)Mrs Margaret Thomas Cav VA W ★
John: b 3-3-1760 d 5-18-1826 m Eleanor (Neeltje)Van Epps Sol NY
Lawrence: b 11-16-1753 d 10-12-1830 m (1)Engeltie Lamb (2)Anna Borst Pvt NY
Nicholas: b 10-19-1749 d 3-25-1825 m Anganistje Vedder Sgt NY
Peter: b 6-13-1752 d 11-3-1829 m Cornelia Becker Ens NY
Philip: b c. 1736 d p. 1790 m Maria Salanica Van Steenburgh Capt NY
Teunis: b 11-4-1744 d 2-21-1830 m Margareta Mynderts 1Lt NY
Teunis: bpt 10-14-1748 d 11-5-1822 m Annatje Zielie Pvt NY
Walter: b 4-29-1753 d — m Eva Quackenbush Pvt NY

SWARTLEY,
John: b 1754 d 1817 m Magdalena Rosenberger Pvt PA

SWARTS,
Tewalt: b 1755 d 7-8-1850 m (1)Elizabeth Corselius (2)Abigail — Pvt NJ

SWARTWOOD,
Barnardus: b 11-27-1759 d 3-21-1843 m Rima (Rymerick)Etten Pvt PA
Peter: b 1-16-1747 d 5-22-1841 m (1)Elisabeth Schoonmaker (2)Sarah Beaker Pvt NJ

SWARTWOUT, (includes SWARTHOUT & SWARTOUT)
Abraham: b 2-13-1743 d 10-15-1799 m Mary North Capt NY
Alexander: bpt 5-13-1764 d 1824 m Catherine Schoonmaker Pvt PA
Anthony: b 7-4-1759 d 10-11-1842 m Elizabeth — Pvt NY ★
Barnardus, Sr.: b 9-12-1731 d 11-18-1794 m (1)Maria Van Steenbergen (2)Elizabeth (Van Steenbergen) Snyder Capt NY
Barnardus, Jr.: b 9-26-1761 d 10-8-1824 m Mary Brower Ens NY
Barnardus: b 2-13-1742/3 d 6- -1807 m Neeltje Hoogteyling PS NY
Cornelius: b 7-12-1757 d 9-22-1831 m Sarah Ter Bush Sgt NY ★
Cornelius: b 12-24-1751 d 3-21-1838 m Sarah Bedell Sol NY

SWARTWOUT, contd.
Derick: b 8-21-1762 d 4-24-1852 m (1)Lucretia Polhemius (2)Elizabeth Polhemius Cpl NY
Jacobus: b 11-5-1734 d 1-16-1827 m Aaltje Brinckerhoff BGen PS NY
Jacobus: b c. 1750 d 1822 m Mary Barry Ens NY
Jacobus: bpt 12-4-1758 d 9-3-1817 m Huldah McLean Perkins Ens NY
Johannes: b 1-15-1753 d 9-17-1823 m Aaltje Bedell Cpl NY
Johannes: bpt 4-29-1716 d 12- -1805 m Neeltje van der Bogaerdt PS NY
John: b 3-4-1754 d 12-12-1837 m Sarah Decker Lt NJ
Phillip: b 1-28-1728 d 10-13-1778 m (1)Antje Wynkoop (2)Deborah Schoonover PS CS NY
Rudolphus: bpt 5-6-1724 d 12-11-1782 m (1)Gerrardina Brinckerhoff (2)Sarah Polhemus PS NY
Samuel: b 1-23-1726 d p. 1787 m Phoebe Poedne Pvt PS NY
Wm.: b 8-25-1753 d 10-31-1848 m Hannah Ladue Capt NY ★

SWARTZEL,
Mathias: b 1739 d 1820 m — Sol PA

SWAZEY, (includes SWASEY & SWAYZE)
Benjamin: b 1754 d 1783 m (Mary) Jane Bond PS NH
Daniel: b 10-18-1756 d 8-27-1843 m Bethia Horton Pvt NJ
David: b 3-4-1762 d 3-2-1838 m Alice Milligan Pvt NJ ★
Ebenezer: b 2-14-1727 d 11-27-1801 m (1)Sarah Knight (2)Abigail Pearson Pvt NH
Jerathmel: b 5-10-1752 d 1829 m Sarah Hellon Lt MA
Joseph: b 5-13-1750 d 4-1-1816 m Susannah Wise Maj MA

SWEARINGEN, (includes SWEAREGEN, SWEARINGIN & VAN SWEARINGEN)
Andrew: b 1747 d 6-26-1824 m Elizabeth Chaplin Capt PA
Charles: b 8-21-1735 d 6-21-1818 m Susannah Stull Col PS MD
Frederick: b 1758 d 5-29-1822 m Sarah Bettis Pvt SC
John: b 11-9-1751 d 1830 m (1)Eleanor Dawson (2)Fannie Baker Lt PA
John, Sr.: b 2-15-1720 d p. 9-6-1786 m Catherine Stull PS PA
John, Jr.: b 1744 d 1829 m Jennie Barkley Pvt PA
John: b 1745 d p. 1800 m Betty Fisher Pvt SC
Joseph: b 7-10-1754 d 8- -1821 m Hannah Rutherford Capt VA
Josiah: b 3-28-1744 d 8-9-1795 m Phoebe Strode Capt VA
Richard Cheek: b 9-18-1760 d 9-4-1852 m Mary Penley Pvt NC ★
Samuel: b c. 1732 d c. 1820 m Catherine Condell Capt MD
Thomas: b c. 1730 d 1794 m (1)— (2) Mary — PS Pvt MD
Thomas: b 5-13-1761 d 10-3-1837 m Margaret Bettis Pvt SC
Thomas: b 12-14-1735 d c. 1786 m Mary Morgan PS VA
Van: b 11-3-1754 d 7-18-1839 m (1)Susannah Greathouse (2)Sarah — Lt MD PA ★
Van, Sr.: b 1692 d 1801 m Elizabeth Walker PS MD
Van, Jr.: b 1725 d 1784 m Margaret Stull Capt MD
Van, Sr.: b 1743 d p. 1-22-1808 m Rachel — Lt SC
Van: b c. 1735 d 1796 m — Dr SC
Van: b 5-22-1719 d 4-20-1788 m (1)Sarah (Swearingen) (2)Priscilla Metcalf Col VA

SWEENEY, (includes SWANEY, SWEENY & SWINNEY)
Benjamin: b a. 1753 d p. 5-3-1814 m (1)— (2)Keziah — Sol PS VA
James: b a. 1753 d 1783-7 m Rebecca Worthington Lt PA
Moses: b 1746 d p. 5-27-1813 m Lizzie Johnson Pvt VA
Moses: b 1762 d — m Elizabeth — Pvt VA★
Timothy: b 2-14-1761 d 12-7-1846 m Elizabeth Newcomb Drm DE
Wm.: b c. 1757 d 10- -1812 m Mourning — PS VA

SWEET, (includes SWEAT, SWEATT & SWETT)
Abraham: b 7- -1742 d 4- -1817 m Sarah Poor Lt MA
Abraham T.: b 11-18-1760 d 5-25-1850 m Priscilla Eastman Cpl NH ★
Amos: b 3-9-1734/5 d p. 1795 m Hannah Richardson Pvt MA
Amos: b c. 1740 d 1-19-1793 m Elizabeth Straight Pvt NY
Angell: b 1754 d 7-19-1820 m Marcy Field Lt RI
Benjamin, Sr.: b 10-17-1707 d 11-2-1787 m Abigail Darling PS NH
Benjamin, Jr.: b 9-31-1736 d p. 1777 m Mary Eliot Pvt NH
Benjamin: b 1740 d 1805 m Martha — Pvt PA
Benjamin: b 3-25-1722 d a. 3- -1789 m Elizabeth — Pvt RI
Benoni: b 7-25-1765 d 3-16-1848 m Jerusha Halstead Pvt NY
Caleb: b 2-7-1743 d 11-3-1798 m Geritze Newkirk Dr NY
Enoch: b 2-14-1748 d p. 1790 m (1)Mary Perkins (2)Sally Smith Pvt MA
Freeborn: b 1-17-1757 d 12-3-1845 m Martha Tibbetts Cpl RI ★
Gideon: b 5-6-1748 d 11-29-1827 m Experience White Cpl MA
Gideon: b 4-11-1758 d p. 1802 m Silence Williams Pvt RI
Jabez: b 8-20-1744 d 1-3-1817 m Harriet Kimball Pvt MA
James: b 11-14-1764 d 7-24-1823 m (1)Mrs Joanna O'Neal (2)Susanna Anderson (3)Mrs Margaret Hogg Pvt SC
Jeremiah: b 4-25-1731 d 1806 m Mary Ellis Pvt NY
Jeremiah: b 2-3-1757 d 1-6-1845 m Dorcas Darling MM Pvt RI ★
Job: b 12-1-1724 d p. 1790 m (1)Jemima Sherman (2)Sarah Kingsley PS RI
John: b a. 1746 d 6-7-1830 m Anna Stevens Pvt CT ★
John: b 12-22-1765 d 1-20-1853 m Abagail Witham Pvt MA
John: b 3-11-1753 d 8-11-1836 m Mary Albro Pvt NY ★

John: b c. 1753 d 10-3-1837 m Joanna Casey MM NY RI ★
John Barnard: b 6-1-1752 d 1796 m Charlotte Bourne Dr MA
Jonathan: b 12-25-1749 d 6-15-1828 m Anna Lyne Pvt MA★
Jonathan: b 4-15-1755 d 2-11-1836 m (1)Elizabeth Jones (2)Mary Brimmer Pvt NY
Joseph: b 8-16-1739 d c. 1787 m Jemima — Pvt MA
Joshua: b 8-29-1764 d 5-2-1849 m Mary Hawks Pvt MA
Josiah: b 12-20-1741 d 12-28-1808 m Prudence Dodge Pvt MA
Lebbeus: b 12-2-1730 d a. 4-27-1816 m Catherine Collins Sgt PS RI
Luke: b 6-20-1742 d 3-18-1817 m Hannah Dole 2Lt MA
Moses: b 11-5-1738 d 12-17-1819 m Hannah Plummer PS MA
Nathan: b 1760 d 3- -1840 m Sarah — Sol SC
Palmer: b 1744 d 3- -1822 m Lucy Bidwell Sol CT
Peleg: b 1758 d 12-9-1825 m Mary Wilkinson Pvt CT
Reuben: b 6-3-1753 d 9-2-1804 m Mary Palmer Pvt CT
Rufus: b 9-3-1753 d 8-5-1820 m Elizabeth Clarke Pvt RI W ★
Samuel: b 12-26-1744 d 9-21-1792 m Mary Jones Ens NH
Simeon: b 1750 d 4-29-1816 m Mary — Sol NH
Solomon: b 1742 d 12-11-1811 m Jemima Bickford Pvt MA
Stephen: b 1-3-1733/4 d 1-6-1807 m Sarah Adams Dr MA
Stephen: b 1760 d 1845 m Anna Sweet Pvt RI
Sylvester: b 1741 d 1810 m Patience Congdon Ens RI
Sylvester: b 1-5-1725 d — m (1)Wait Brown (2)Mary Johnson Pvt RI
Theophilus: b 12-16-1736 d 6-11-1811 m Elizabeth Bosworth Lt NY
Thomas: b 8-16-1741 d 8-14-1830 m Margaret Foster Sgt MA
Thomas: b c. 1763 d 7- -1828 m Mary Neely Pvt PA
Thomas: b 1732 d 3-26-1813 m Frances Congdon Sol RI
Thomas Rogers: b 5-2-1761 d 10-9-1849 m (2)Betsey Knowlton Pvt NH MA
Timothy: b 10-24-1753 d 3-7-1837 m Eunice Woodworth Pvt RI
Wilbur: b 1760 d 8-19-1857 m — Pvt VT
Wm.: b 4-3-1730 d 12-9-1808 m (1)Miss Merrill (2)Anna (Morgridge) Hackett 2Lt MA
Wm.: b c. 1755 d 2-10-1840 m Patience Maxon Pvt NY
Wm.: b c. 1748 d 11- -1832 m Sarah (Hayes)Turner Pvt NC

SWEETING,
Eliphalet: b 6-15-1756 d 6-15-1828 m Lavina Benton Luce Sol MA
Lewis, Sr.: b 1-20-1723 d 2-9-1804 m Abiah Cobb MM Dr MA
Lewis, Jr.: b 1-17-1752 d 4-2-1842 m Naomi Hoskins Lt MA NY ★
Nathaniel: b 12-1-1758 d 6-9-1841 m Mary Tyrrell Sgt MA RI
Whiting: b 1756 d 1791 m Sarah Kilbourn Pvt MA

SWEETSER, (or SWITZER)
Cornelius: b 12-10-1749 d 11-10-1845 m Sarah Smith Sol MA
Henry: b 10-21-1739 d 6-18-1827 m Lucy Johnson Capt MA
Henry: b 5-12-1756 d 10-7-1804 m Ann Summers Pvt SC
Henry: b — d p. 1783 m Cloe — PS VA
Jacob: b c. 1745 d p. 1800 m Barbara — Pvt PA
John: b 1-7-1760 d 5-25-1847 m (1)Elizabeth Green (2)Rebecca — Pvt MA ★
Michael: b 9-18-1737 d 7-22-1819 m Mary Pool Pvt MA
Nathan: b c. 1764-66 d 1841 m Elizabeth Chenowith Pvt VA
Nathaniel: b 10-17-1748 d p. 1790 m Martha Mills Pvt PS CS NH
Philip: b 5-5-1756 d 7-3-1835 m Nancy Bridgeman Pvt VA★
Phineas: b — d 7-3-1823 m Rebecca — Pvt MA
Richard: b 11-17-1749 d 1-12-1844 m Sarah Matthews Sgt MA
Samuel: b 9-24-1750 d 12-23-1831 m Elizabeth Wells Pvt MA
Thomas: b 5-5-1752 d 10-26-1818 m Sarah Pratt MM MA
Valentine: b c. 1736 d p. 11-7-1809 m Mary Hotzenbella — PS VA
Wm.: b 4- -1755 d 2-22-1849 m Alice Prince Cpl MA

SWEEZY, (includes SWEESEY & SWEZEY)
Abel: b 1750 d 1798 m Jerusha Hedges Pvt NY
Daniel: b 1725 d 9-1-1777 m Hannah Tuthill Pvt PS NY
Daniel: b 8-30-1753 d 10-26-1825 m (1)Sarah Beal (2)Mrs Howell Sol PS NY
David: b 3-9-1747 d 3-20-1835 m Abigail Wells Capt NY ★
Joseph: b 3-28-1740 d 3-31-1811 m Mary Tuthill Wright Pvt NY
Stephen, Sr.: b 1717 d 1781 m (1)Phebe Tuttle (2)Mary Horton PS NY
Stephen, Jr.: b 9-28-1756 d 5-6-1833 m Sophia Jayne PS NY

SWEINHART, (or SWINEHART)
Adam: b 6-30-1760 d 4-8-1852 m Margaret Leslie Pvt PA
John: b 3-26-1758 d 1778 m Sarah — CMman Pvt PA

SWENTZEL,
Frederick: b 6-10-1743 d 11-19-1834 m Eve Barbara Knull Pvt PA

SWEPSTON,
John: b 1761 d 1-21-1853 d Dolly Ashfurd Fif VA

SWETLAND, (includes SWEATLAND & SWEETLAND)
Aaron: b 7-29-1753 d 3-6-1819 m Lois Allen Sgt CT
Benjamin: b 9-29-1756 d 9-29-1819 m Rosanna Hancock FifMaj MA★
Bowen: b 1-14-1756 d — m Nancy Bates Sgt MA
Hannah: b 4-22-1738 d 1-8-1809 m Luke Swetland PS PA
Israel: b 1-12-1736 d p. 1796 m (1)Dorcas Dewey (2)Mary Miner Pvt CT

John: b 1751 d 10-23-1823 m Sarah Wood Sgt MA ★
Luke: b 7-26-1729 d 1-30-1823 m Hannah Tiffany Pvt CT
Nathan: b 11-27-1754 d *p.* 1799 m Rebecca Tarr Sol MA
Noah: b 10-1-1742 d 10-8-1793 m Molly Cushman Pvt VT
Samuel: b *c.* 1750 d *p.* 1788 m (1)Hannah Gay (2)Mrs Elizabeth
    Matthews Pvt MA
Stephen: b 1757 d 1853 m Mabel Hayden Pvt MA

SWICKHART,
Martin: b 1745 d 5-22-1840 m Christena Page Pvt PA

SWIFT,
Abraham: b 10-19-1762 d 11-19-1841 m Olive Lawrence Pvt MA ★
David: b 1704 d 1797 m Lydia Savery Pvt MA
Elisha: b 5-16-1731 d 7-2-1777 m Mary Ransom Capt CT
Enoch, Sr.: b 7-25-1735 d *p.* 1776 m Esther Sampson Cpl MA
Enoch, Jr.: b 11-29-1758 d 8-21-1837 m (1)Olive Wing (2)Elizabeth
    Wyman Pvt MA
Flower: b 1750-55 d *p.* 1810 m Mary Bedsaul Capt PS VA
Foster: b 1- -1760 d 8-18-1835 m Deborah Delano NDr MA
Heman: b 10-14-1733 d 11-12-1814 m (1)Mary Skiff (2)Mrs
    Eleanor (Marvin)Johnson (3)Mrs Sarah (Robinson)Fay (4)Mrs
    Hannah (Hopson)Pratt Brevet BG CT
Heman: b 11-15-1757 d 2-26-1813 m Rebecca — Ens CT
Isaac: b 2-27-1753 d 7-29-1802 m Patience Case Dr PS CT
James: b 1-29-1739 d 4-6-1802 m Mehitable Merwin Pvt CT
Jirah: b 8-20-1738 d 7-28-1776 m Sarah Delano Capt CT
Jireh: b 5-31-1740/1 d 7-16-1817 m Elizabeth Haskell Sgt MA
Job, Sr.: b 10-3-1711 d 2-14-1801 m Sarah Blackwell PS Pvt MA
Job, Jr.: b 9-5-1746 d *p.* 1791 m (1)Rebecca Cummings (2)Elizabeth
    Guild Pvt MA
Job: b 6-17-1743 d 10-20-1804 m Mary Ann Sedgwick Chp NY
John: b 8-23-1760 d 3-10-1838 m Anna Throop Sgt CT ★
John: b 6-17-1761 d 7-13-1814 m (1)Rhoda Sawyer (2)Hepzibah
    Treat Davidson Pvt CT
John: b 1-14-1714 d *p.* 1790 m Jerusha Clark PS CT
John: b 9-15-1746 d 1835 m Elizabeth Gibbs Cpl MA
Judah: b 9-3-1716 d 1-17-1807 m Elizabeth Morton Pvt NY
Lemuel: b 10-31-1752 d 8-30-1822 m Betty Briggs Cpl MA
Lot: b 3-13-1758 d 8-10-1840 m Elizabeth Barlow Pvt NY ★
Moses: b 3-13-1737 d 4-9-1838 m Hannah Hurd Pvt NY
Nathaniel, Jr.: b 9-18-1749 d 12-4-1825 m Sarah Thomas Lt CT ★
Nathaniel: b 6-12-1764 d 11-19-1831 m Mary Baker Cpl MA
Nathaniel: b 3-19-1747 d 2-23-1833 m Deborah Smith Sol PS NY
Philetus: b 6-26-1763 d 7-24-1828 m (1)Sally Deane (2)Faunia Cole
    Swift Sgt CT W★
Phineas: b 2-25-1731 d *a.* 11- -1793 m Rebecca Phillips Pvt MA
Rowland: b 3-24-1721 d 2-13-1795 m Mary Dexter Pvt CT
Rowland, Jr.: b 12-15-1753 d 1-20-1849 m Betsey Larned Pvt MA ★
Samuel: b 1754 d 5-18-1821 m Susannah (Hannah)Green Pvt CT
Samuel: b 6-9-1715 d 8-30-1775 m (1)Eliphael Lilley (2)Ann Foster
    PS MA
Seth: b 10-30-1749 d 2-13-1807 m Lucy Eliot Seaman CT
Seth: b 3-16-1757 d 11-12-1823 m Mary Wells Pvt PS NY
Silas: b 3-15-1743 d 1-12-1803 m Deborah Tobey Pvt MA
Thomas: b 8-14-1747 d *p.* 1792 m Mehitable Barrows PS CT
Thomas: b *c.* 1732 d 1803 m Abigail Phillips Pvt MA
Thomas, Sr.: b 1-11-1724/5 d 4-17-1795 m Rebecca Clark Pvt MA
Thomas, Jr.: b 5-3-1753 d 1-30-1818 m Margaret Aiken Pvt MA NY
Thomas, Jr.: b 1755 d 1816 m (1)Margaret Patterson (2)Mary
    Burnett PS NC
Thomas, Sr.: b *c.* 1724 d 1792 m Amediah Duke PS VA
Thomas, Jr.: b 7-4-1760 d 8-25-1830 m Frances — Pvt VA ★
Ward: b 8-29-1735 d 6-15-1805 m Remember Toby Capt MA
William, Jr.: b 2-17-1747 d 2- -1829 m Martha Eldred Pvt MA
William: b *c.* 1735 d 9- -1808 m Frances Waddy CS NC

SWIGER,
John: b 4-25-1759 d 6-26-1844 m Elizabeth Tetrick Spy PA ★

SWIGERT, (includes SWEIGART & SWEIGERT)
George: b *c.* 1730 d *p.* 11-9-1805 m Elizabeth — Pvt PA
Jacob: b 11-9-1761 d 11-30-1850 m Margaret — Pvt PA
John: b 1762 d *c.* 1861 m Maria Wolford Pvt PA
Philip: b 4-13-1757 d 12-16-1832 m Sarah Gerber Pvt PA
Sebastian: b 11-15-1736 d 3-16-1808 m Agnes Maria Swank Pvt
    PA

SWINDLE,
John: b 1746 d 8-20-1839 m Hannah Weaver Pvt VA ★

SWING, (or SCHWING)
Godfrey (John): b — d *p.* 1802 m Margaret Danecker 2Lt PA
Samuel: b 9-15-1729 d 3-13-1801 m Sarah Diament Pvt NJ

SWINK, (or SWANK)
John (Lewis): b 1735 d 3-15-1781 m Mary Neace Pvt NC
John Wm.: b 1742 d 1821 m Mary — Pvt PS MD

SWINNERTON, (or SWINERTON)
James: b 8-13-1757 d 12-6-1824 m Eleanor Guilford Pvt MA ★
John: bpt 6-13-1746 d *a.* 5-8-1824 m Elizabeth Phippen Pvt MA
Joseph: b 10-5-1761 d 1847 m Lucy Guilford Pvt MA ★

SWINSON,
Jesse: b 1759 d 4-17-1834 m Nancy Winders Pvt Mus NC

SWINT,
John: b 1763 d 1802 m Elizabeth — Pvt GA

SWINTON,
Alexander, Sr.: b 1732-37 d 1814 m Elizabeth Potts LCol SC
Hugh: b 1737 d 1-19-1809 m Susannah Hayne Splatt PS SC
Wm.: b 6- -1735 d 3-13-1780 m (1)Mary Slade (2)Mrs Sarah Baron
    CS SC

SWISHER,
Abraham: b 1741 d 11-12-1828 m Hannah Christine — Capt NJ

SWISSHELM,
John: b 3-8-1752 d 10-18-1838 m Mary Elizabeth Miller Lt PA ★

SWITCHER,
Henry: b 1724 d 9-1-1818 m Rebecca Livermore Pvt MA

SWITS,
Abraham: b 10-1-1730 d 8-17-1814 m (1)Neeltje Van Antwerpes
    (2)Elizabeth Vrooman (3)Margaret De la Mont Maj NY
Walter: b 11-10-1754 d 10-31-1823 m Sarah Peck Lt CT

SWOPE, (includes SCHWOOB & SWOOPE)
Adam: b 5-21-1756 d 2-7-1821 m Sarah Grabill Pvt PA
Benedict: b 9- -1732 d 3-30-1811 m Susannah Welker PS MD
George: b 9-1-1758 d *c.* 1830 m Margaret Huffheins PS MD
Henry: b 3-10-1747 d 9-11-1808 m Barbary Weidler PS PA
Jacob: b *c.* 1740 d 7- -1788 m Elizabeth — Sol PA
Joseph: b 8-7-1751 d 3-3-1819 m Catherine Sullivan CS VA
Lawrence: b 1742 d 8- -1794 m Ann — PS PA
Michael: b *c.* 1725 d 1792 m (1)Anna Maria Spangler (2)Eva Barbara
    Kuhn Col PA
Michael: b 9-29-1753 d 4-25-1839 m Mary — Spy Pvt VA
Nicholas: b 12-14-1752 d *p.* 1815 m Anna Maria Hagerin Pvt PA
Peter: b *c.* 1745 d — m Eva Knorr Pvt PA

SWORDS,
Francis Dawson: b 1731 d 1800 m Amity Graves Pvt CT

SYDEBOTHAM,
John: b 12-11-1759 d 4-28-1823 m Jane McCarthy Pvt VA ★

SYDNOR, (or SIDENOR)
Christopher: b 1756 d *p.* 11-7-1825 m Catherine — PS MD
Elizabeth Taylor: b 3-2-1722 d 1785 m Anthony Sydnor PS VA
Joseph: b 10-17-1749 d 1787 m Ann Chowning PS VA
Martin: b 1733 d 4-1-1806 m Margaret Mira Schotte PS MD
Wm.: b 2-24-1738 d *p.* 12-20-1815 m Judith Armistead Williams
    2Lt VA
Wm.: b 1740 d 1810 m Bessie Ann (Garland) Thompson PS VA

SYKES, (or SIKES)
Abner: b 10-12-1729 d 1-24-1800 m Mercy Parsons Pvt MA
Amos: b 10-17-1744 d 1776/7 m Agnes Austin MM CT
Ashbel: b 2-24-1756 d 12-13-1840 m Esther Sheldon Pvt VT
Benjamin: b 8-18-1704 d 8-2-1781 m Hannah Chapin Pvt MA
David: b 1-9-1756 d 12-28-1833 m Lucy (Sikes) — Pvt CT ★
Gideon: b 5-26-1753 d 4-13-1846 m (1)Silence Granger (2)Keziah
    — (3)Mercy Leonard Pvt CT
Increase: b 9-5-1760 d 1-17-1837 m Lucy Wright Pvt MA
Jacob: b 1758 d 1797 m Elizabeth Edwards PS NC
Jacob: b 1-21-1758 d 9-18-1840 m Michal Kent Pvt VT
James: b 8-13-1719 d 2-11-1795 m Dinah Hitchcock PS MA
John: b 8-25-1753 d 7-26-1839 m Lucy Harvey Pvt CT VT ★
John: b 1750 d 3-27-1851 m Lucy — Pvt VA ★
John Jones: b 1759 d 1807 m Sarah Soules Pvt MA W ★
Nathaniel: b 1-28-1734 d 9-30-1820 m (1)Lois Cooley (2)Mrs Anna
    Shattuck Taft Pvt MA
Reuben: b 9-8-1730 d 12-24-1804 m Thankful Buell Fif PS CT
Rufus: b 8-11-1756 d 11-14-1815 m Azubah Champion Pvt MA
Thomas Aldrich: b 1760 d 9-5-1835 m Sarah — Pvt VA ★
Victory: b 10-19-1758 d 10-25-1838 m Lucy Burbank Pvt CT
Wm.: b 1760 d 3- -1813 m Burchett L Turner Pvt VA

SYLVESTER, (or SILVESTER)
Caleb, Jr.: b 10-5-1754 d 1844 m Abigail Jacobs Sgt MA ★
Edmund: b 6-17-1762 d 5-25-1828 m Deborah Cushman Pvt MA
Job: b 5- -1742 d 10-6-1832 m Margaret Stetson Pvt MA
Joseph: b 7-6-1735 d 3-1-1818 m Lucy Sampson Pvt MA
Joseph: b 1755 d 7- -1828 m (1)Mrs Dameron (2)Mrs Winn (3)Mrs
    Amelia (Seely)Filkins Pvt MA ★
Nathaniel: b 1740 d 3-1-1813 m Sarah Bartlett Sgt MA
Nathaniel: b *c.* 1755 d 2-2-1804 m Rebecca Johnston Pvt NC
Obadiah: bpt 1-19-1755 m Mary Walling Pvt NJ
Peter: b 1-12-1713 d 1801 m Deborah Torrey CS MA
Peter: b 1734 d 1808 m Jane Van Schaack PS NY
Samuel: b 12-20-1743 d 1791 m Mary Horner 2Lt MA
Seth: b 1740 d 9-12-1814 m Febe White Sgt MA
Seth: b 2-12-1762 d 1801 m Hannah Eddy Pvt MA
Wm., Sr.: b 2-22-1709 d 6-17-1799 m Mary Barstow PS ME
Wm., Jr.: b 4-25-1757 d 1778 m Mary Springer Low Pvt MA

SYME,
John, Sr.: b c. 1729 d 12-10-1793 m (1)Mildred Meriwether
　(2)Sarah Hoopes Col PS VA
John, Jr.: b a. 1740 d 2-　-1793 m Sarah Overton Capt VA

SYPHER,
Abraham: b 12-17-1753 d — m Eve Hollman Pvt PA

TABB,
Elizabeth Elliot: b c. 1740 d a. 9-23-1799 m (1)Robert Tabb
　(2)James Kearney PS VA
George: b 11-14-1750 d 8-23-1829 m (1)Anna White (2)Anne
　Eliason Sol VA
Robert: b 1-23-1737 d 9-11-1775 m Elizabeth Elliott CS VA

TABBS,
Barton: b c. 1735 d 10-30-1818 m Elizabeth Bond Dr MD

TABOR, (includes TABER & TABLER)
Amaziah: b 8-14-1758 d 8-1-1843 m Silence Babcock MM MA
Amon: b 1745 d 3-12-1828 m Sibil Terry PS Pvt NY
Church: b 11-15-1754 d 1-27-1835 m Elizabeth Steele Sgt MA ★
Frederick: b 6-　-1747 d 12-10-1802 m Esther Vail PS Sol NY
George: b a. 1761 d 10-10-1827 m — PS VA
Gideon: b 1762 d 2-　-1824 m Hannah Carpenter Pvt RI ★
Ichabod: b 3-8-1755 d 3-1-1835 m Elizabeth Lawton Cpl RI ★
Jeduthan: b 3-15-1743 d 1799 m Patience Jenne Pvt MA
Job: b 3-16-1741 d a. 5-3-1791 m Lydia Tripp Pvt MA
John: b c. 1762 d 1825-32 m Elizabeth — Sol GA
John: b 10-9-1735 d 2-18-1819 m (1)Elizabeth Bennett (2)Amie
　Cook (3)Hannah Tripp Pvt MA
John: b 8-8-1715 d 1787 m (1)Mary Taber (2)Sarah Walker Pvt RI
Jonathan: b 10-5-1712 d p. 5-22-1790 m Robe Brown PS MA
Lemuel: b 12-20-1748 d 4-18-1833 m Sarah Brightman Sgt RI ★
Pardon: b 7-16-1739 d p. 1790 m Mary (Taber) Capt MA
Phillip: b 1-6-1747 d 5-4-1827 m Mary Gibbs Sgt RI
Stephen: b a. 1737 d p. 1782 m Ruth — Pvt RI
Thomas: b 3-　-1747 d 10-14-1820 m (1)Mary Bennett (2)Hannah
　Davis Pvt MA
Thomas: b 10-28-1717 d 3-14-1802 m Mary — Pvt RI
Water: b 10-24-1731 d 1806 m Hannah Taber Sgt RI
Wm.: b 1-4-1761 d 6-4-1844 m Susannah Tubb Lt NC ★

TACKELS,
Alexander: b 6-15-1755 d 8-7-1842 m Philena — Pvt MA ★

TACKETT,
Lewis: b c. 1730 d p. 1823 m Mary — PS VA

TADLOCK,
John: b — d 1820/1 m (1)Sally Keel (2)Mrs Ann Harrod (3)Mrs
　Nancy Rochester Sol VA

TAEGER,
John: b 3-8-1751 d 5-10-1830 m Jacobina Catharina Miller Pvt CL

TAFFE, (includes TAFF)
James: b 12-4-1755 d 6-13-1832 m Elizabeth Reed Radcliffe Pvt
　VA ★
Peter: b 1753 d 1824 m Mary Edmundson Pvt VA ★

TAFT,
Aaron: b 4-12-1727 d 11-5-1803 m Marcy Arnold Sgt MA
Aaron: b 5-27-1761 d 5-14-1831 m Temperance — Sol VT
Abner: b 12-28-1736 d 5-30-1809 m Trial White Lt MA
Artemas: b c. 1746 d c. 1837 m Abigail Staples Sgt MA
Bezaleel: b 11-3-1750 d 6-21-1839 m Sarah Richardson Capt MA
Daniel, Jr.: bpt 7-22-1751 d a. 5-12-1810 m (1)Molly Sibley
　(2)Rhoda Ellis QMSgt MA
Ebenezer: b 1758 d 10-3-1836 m Mary Howard Pvt MA ★
Eleazer: b 3-29-1759 d 1-4-1836 m — Pvt MA NH ★
Elisha: b 5-8-1728 d 3-3-1791 m Experience (Taft) PS MA
Frederick: b 6-19-1759 d 2-10-1846 m Mrs Abigail Wood Sgt
　MA ★
Gershom: b 12-29-1739 d 4-29-1813 m Abigail Reed Pvt MA
Grindal: b 11-28-1753 d 5-31-1823 m Abigail Partridge Pvt MA
Henry: b 2-17-1736/7 d 2-2-1812 m (1)Sarah How (2)Azuba
　Thompson Cpl MA
Israel: b 3-1-1761 d 4-24-1842 m Submit Read Cpl MA
Jacob: b 12-3-1750 d 5-30-1823 m Mary Taft Sgt MA
Jesse: b 4-5-1731 d 4-7-1800 m (1)Lydia Sibley (2)Hannah (Taft)
　PS MA
Joseph: b 1724 d 2-1-1803 m Elizabeth Cummings Pvt MA
Josiah: b 5-27-1758 d 1-8-1846 m (1)Margery Green (2)Mrs Mary
　Parmenber Cpl MA ★
Lovett: b 1-30-1756 d 3-23-1837 m Lydia Post Pvt MA
Lyman: b 3-14-1762 d p. 1790 m Daborah Wood Pvt MA
Marvel: b 2-6-1763 d 11-3-1832 m (1)Ruth Murdock (2)Molly Taft
　Pvt MA
Matthew: b 3-13-1762 d 1838/39 m Mary Crocker Pvt MA ★

Moses: b 9-29-1760 d 12-4-1848 m (1)Nancy (Taft) (2)Judith
　Cummings Cpl MA ★
Moses: b 1-30-1712/3 d 7-13-1788 m Priscilla Thayer CS MA
Nathan: b 3-27-1754 d 1-21-1809 m Judith Sibley Pvt MA
Nathaniel: b 10-15-1747 d 8-12-1827 m Abigail Holbrook Pvt MA
Noah, Sr.: b 1731 d 9-2-1814 m Margaret Keith 2Lt MA
Noah, Jr.: b 1-14-1758 d 2-25-1828 m Charlotte Arnold Pvt MA
Robert: b 2-14-1729 d 11-12-1810 m Jane Crag Capt MA
Robert: b 7-21-1749 d 11-21-1821 m Chloe (Taft)Sgt MA
Robert: b 1724 d 9-22-1787 m Deborah Lovett Pvt MA
Samuel: b 9-3-1736 d 8-2-1816 m (1)Mary Murdock (2)Experience
　Humes Pvt MA
Seth, Sr.: b 10-27-1729 d 2-15-1794 m Anna (Read)Taft Lt MA
Seth, Jr.: b 8-23-1754 d 9-15-1816 m Lydia Staples Cpl MA
Silas: b 6-10-1744 d p. 1786 m Elizabeth Cruff Pvt MA
Silas: b — d c. 1811 m (1)Mary Farnum (2)— Twitchell PS NH
Stephen: b 4-16-1710 d 2-3-1803 m Mary Lewis 2Lt MA
Thaddeus: b 12-13-1757 d 9-5-1831 m Silence Holbrook Pvt MA
Thomas, 3d: b 10-30-1753 d 6-8-1835 m (2)Betsey Britten
　Fletcher Sol MA
Zadok: b 8-15-1763 d 11-15-1843 m Abagail Bennett Pvt MA

TAGGART, (includes TAGGARD & TAGGERT)
Charles: b 11-1-1753 d 7-16-1831 m Mary Darby Capt PA
James: b 5-11-1742 d 1-25-1828 m Elizabeth Nay Lt NH
James: b 1-12-1748 d 1833 m Margaret Ferguson Lt NH
John, Sr.: b 1755 d 1817 m Rebecca Cooper Pvt MD
John, Sr.: b 1720 d 1813 m Barbara — Capt NH
John, Jr.: b c. 2-11-1750 d 11-15-1832 m Anna Eames Ens NH ★
John: b 1735 d 9-5-1806 m Elizabeth Jameson CS NH
John: b 8-12-1756 d 8-23-1830 mSarah McCartney Pvt PA
Joseph: b 12-4-1756 d 1-1-1833 m Lydia Jones Cpl NH ★
Patrick: b 1723 d 11-15-1815 m (1)Marianne Stevenson
　(2)Hannah Haeltzel Sgt PA W★
Robert: b a. 1746 d 11-26-1786 m Margaret — PS PA
Thomas: b c. 1738 d c. 1787 m Jean/Jane — PS CS NH VT
Wm.: b 12-1-1751 d 3-20-1830 m Sarah Mead 2Lt NH ★
Wm.: b 9-25-1733 d 1-9-1798 m (1)Mary Clarke (2)Almy
　Clark Maj RI
Wm., Jr.: b 5-7-1755 d 11-10-1833 m Elizabeth Macomber Capt
　RI ★

TAINTER, (includes TAINTOR & TAYNTOR)
Abijah: b 6-7-1744 d 4-1-1828 m Sarah Small Sgt MA
Benjamin: b 1-3-1733 d 1798 m Sarah Brigham Pvt MA
Benjamin, Sr.: b 1725 d 8-　-1810 m Hannah Wood Pvt VT
Benjamin, Jr.: b 5-27-1753 d 6-24-1844 m Margaret Hinds Pvt MA
Charles: b 2-8-1723 d 3-　-1807 m Mary Skinner PS CT
Eaires: b 7-20-1741 d 7-24-1824 m Elizabeth Coolidge Pvt MA
John, Jr.: b 8-12-1732 d p. 1790 m Mary Shedd Cpl MA
Jonathan: b 6-26-1755 d 7-31-1801 m Jemima Root Pvt VT
Medad: b 11-13-1757 d 2-21-1823 m Anna Linsley Cpl CT
Michael: b 3-14-1748/9 d 4-14-1831/2 m Lydia Loomis Pvt NH
Nahum: b 2-23-1751 d 7-6-1816 m Huldah Sibley Cpl MA
Stephen: b 10-13-1760 d 7-11-1847 m (1)Elizabeth Gorham
　(2)Mercy Winslow Pvt MA ★

TALBEE,
Edward, Sr.: bpt 7-26-1730 d 3-19-1807 m (1)Anstis Waldron (2)
　Nancy Newman Pvt RI
Stephen: b 9-14-1756 d 10-17-1842 m Mary Smith Pvt RI

TALBOT, (includes TALBERT, TALBIRD, TALBOTT & TALBUT)
Ambrose, Sr.: b 1720/1 d 5-2-1804 m Mary Clark Bayley Pvt MA
Ambrose, Jr.: b c. 9-7-1760 d 6-2-1819 m Olive Carter Pvt MA
Ambrose: b 6-19-1746 d 2-　-1838 m Elizabeth Johnston Pvt MA
Benjamin: b 2-11-1750 d 1-5-1816 m Sarah Wilmott Capt MD
Benjamin, Jr.: b 4-3-1763 d 6-3-1838 m Mary Gilkey Pvt PA
Benjamin, Sr.: b 4-26-1713 d p. 1790 m Elizabeth Ball PS PA
Benjamin R.: b 1750 d a. 10-21-1805 m Martha Deavers Sol MD
Charles: b 11-6-1723 d 8-　-1779 m Drusilla Gwynn CS VA
David: b 11-19-1748 d c. 1800 m (2)Margaret Winslow Pvt MA
Demoville: b 7-25-1754 d 4-16-1839 m (1)Leana (Talbott)
　(2)Margaret Williams PS VA
Drusilla: b 12-20-1727 d 1785 m Charles Talbot PS VA
Ebenezer: b 1740 d 6-21-1832 m Lucy Starkweather Pvt CT
Edward: b 7-15-1723 d 8-29-1797 m Temperance Merryman PS MD
Edward: b 1744 d p. 1783 m Margaret Slade PS MD
Henry: b c. 1745 d p. 1-22-1816 m (1)Hannah King (2)Barbara
　Whaley PS MD
Isaac: b 6-21-1744 d 1-27-1822 m Susannah Turner Pvt MA
Isham, Sr.: b 11-3-1738 d p. 1785 m Elizabeth Davis Lt VA
Isham: b 1759 d 7-30-1839 m Jane (Talbot) Pvt VA
James Smith: b 1763 d 1853 m Unity DeWitt Pvt VA
Jared: b 12-3-1738 d 11-30-1818 m Deborah Joy Pvt CT
Jeremiah: b — d 1-19-1791 m Mary Chambers Maj PA
Jesse: b — d p. 8-23-1822 m (2)Mrs Elizabeth Burnham Jackson Sol
　GA
John: b 7-13-1748 d p. 4-15-1825 m Hannah Bosley Capt MD
John: b 1724 d p. 1799 m Margaret Webster Pvt MD
John: b 7-13-1735 d p. 8-15-1798 m (1)Sarah Anthony (2)Phoebe
　Mosely Col PS VA

John Lawrence: b c. 1750 d 1825 m (1)Henrietta Phillips (2)Mary
    Porter PS MD
Joseph, Sr.: b 1710 d 1783 m (1)Hannah Baker PS PA
Joseph: b 11-13-1738 d 1-6-1814 m Ruth — Lt PA
Josiah: b 10-10-1756 d 7-13-1841 m Susanna Morse Pvt MA
Matthew, Sr.: b 11-27-1729 d 10-12-1812 m (1)Mary (Hale)Day
    (2)Agness — PS NC
Matthew, Jr.: b 1756 d 1804 m 1)Lucy Bailey ( )Jane Quarles Pvt GA
Nathaniel: b 6-11-1748 d 10-17-1829 m (1)Sarah Wilson
    (2)Martha Davenport Sgt MA
Peter, Sr.: b 2-17-1716 d 10-18-1793 m (1)Abigail Wheeler
    (2)Mary Bailey Capt MA
Peter, Jr.: b 11-15-1745 d 4-28-1836 m Lucy Hammond Capt MA
Richard: b 12-25-1753 d 12-22-1821 m (1)Achsah Wells
    (2)Temperance Wells Lt MD ★
Samuel: b 2-24-1746 d 11-29-1821 m Mary Fisher Capt MA
Silas: b 1-11-1750 d 6-30-1813 m (1)Anna Richmond (2)Rebecca
    Morris (3)Madam Pinlard Cdr MA
Thomas: b 6-12-1755 d 1804 m Christine Crawford Capt SC
Thomas: b 4- -1760 d 1-28-1831 m (1)Ruth Greer (2)Mrs Elizabeth
    Paw CS VA
Wm.: b a. 1728 d p. 1790 m Leana Mason Pvt VA
Williston: b 8-1-1750 d 10- -1827 m (1)Elizabeth,Cock (2)Nancy
    Keesee Lt VA
Zephaniah: b 5-9-1737 d 12-20-1811 m Hannah Richmond Ware
    Pvt MA

TALCOTT, (includes TALLCOTT)
Benjamin, Sr.: b 6-27-1702 d 3-9-1785 m (1)Esther Lyman
    (2)Deborah Gillet CS CT
Benjamin: b 6-10-1725 d 4-18-1811 m Elizabeth Lyman Pvt PS CT
Daniel: b 4-1-1759 d 8-28-1843 m Lydia Ellis Pvt Tms CT
Eleazer: b 4-19-1759 d 1-4-1835 m Sarah Baxter Sol CT
Elizur: b 12-31-1709 d 11-24-1797 m Ruth Wright Col CT
Gad: b 7-26-1745 d 10-3-1830 m (1)Abigail Root (2)Susannah
    Wells Pvt CT
George: b 9-30-1755 d 6-13-1813 m (1)Virginia Bradford (2)Abigail
    Goodrich Pvt CT
Isaac: b 8-29-1740 d 8-6-1815 m (1)Sarah Goodrich (2)Rhoda
    (House)Stratton Sgt CT
Jonathan: b 5-12-1754 d 7-28-1847 m Sarah Hubbard MM CT
Joseph, Sr.: b 6-31-1728 d 6-10-1789 m Eunice Lyman Lt CT
Joseph, Jr.: b 8-6-1755 d 6-8-1826 m Rebecca Porter Sgt CT W★
Joseph: b 1753 d 1826 m Mary Thomas Pvt MA
Nathaniel: b 1720 d 2-26-1783 m Sarah Hale Pvt CT
Samuel: bpt 3-28-1711 d 3-6-1797 m Mabel Wyllys Col CT
Wm.: b 6-8-1742 d 3-28-1807 m Mary Carter Lt CT

TALEMA,
Theunis: b 10-27-1734 d p. 1787 m Annetje Vanderbilt Pvt NY

TALIAFERRO, (includes TOLIVER & TALLIAFERRO)
Benjamin: b 1-4-1754-6- d 9-3-1821 m Martha Merriweather Capt
    VA
Charles: b 7⋅16-1735 d 4-12-1798 m Isabella McCullough Pvt VA
Francis: b 11-15-1743 d a. 3-9-1815 m Jane Taliaferro Capt VA
Francis: b 3-12-1750 d 2-18-1826 m Letitia Hughes Sgt VA
Harry: b c. 1745 d p. 1-21-1803 m Elizabeth — PS VA
Jesse: b 1756 d 1838 m Franky Stamper Pvt NC ★
John: b 1760 d 1863 m Tobitha Howell Pvt NC
John: b 4-7-1733 d 4-7-1821 m (1)Mary Hardin (2)Lydia Howard
    Capt VA
John: b 3-23-1764 d p. 3-4-1840 m (1)Nancy Brooke (2)Nancy
    Catlett Sol VA
Lawrence: b 12-9-1734 d 4-8-1798 m (1)Mary Jackson (2)Sarah
    Dade Col PS VA
Nicholas: b 10-30-1757 d 2- -1812 m (1)Ann Champe (2)Frances
    Blasingame Lt VA
Philip: b 1745 d p. 1791 m Sarah Baytop Capt PS VA
Richard: b 1756 d 3-15-1781 m Dorcas Perkins Sol VA
Richard: b 5-25-1757 d 4-15-1806 m Mildred Powell Capt VA
Richard: b 9-24-1763 d 11- -1836 m (1)Sarah Jones (2)Rebecca
    Riddle Pvt VA
Richard, Sr.: b 1706 d 1779 m Elizabeth Eggleston CS VA
Richard, Jr.: b 1732 d 1789 m Rebecca Cocke PS VA
Samuel: b c. 1727 d 1798 m Ann — PS VA
Wm.: b c. 1750 d 1805-10 m Margaret Aylett LCol VA
Wm.: b 1710 d 2-1-1778 m — LCol VA
Zachariah, Sr.: b 8-29-1730 d 1811 m Mary Braxton Boutwell PS
    CS VA

TALL,
Anthony: b c. 1741 d p. 1783 m Mrs Mabelle Ross Harrington PS MD
James: b 1755 d p. 12-13-1795 m Anne Young PS MD

TALLEY,
Charles: b c. 1750-60 d p. 1815 m Sarah — PS VA
Elisha: b c. 1751 d p. 1833 m Susan — Pvt PS VA
Henry: b 1760 d 6-4-1836 m Edith Hubbard Pvt VA ★
Nicholas: b. 1738 d 1795 m Mary — PS NC
Wm.: b 1- -1747 d 5-9-1812 m Diana Stilley Pvt PA
Wm.: b 1- -1714 d 8-1-1790 m (1)Hannah Grubb (2)Rebecca —
    (3)Magdalena — Pvt DE

TALLMAN, (includes TALEMAN, TALMAN & TAULMAN)
Douwe Harmonsen: b c. 1689/90 d 5-11-1779 m Maritie Haring
    PS NJ
Garret: b 11-23-1740 d p. 1783 m Catharine Blauvelt Pvt NY
Harma: b 1-30-1737 d 3-29-1811 m Elizabeth Blauvelt Ens NY
Hermanus: bpt 4-6-1731 d 1-22-1796 m (1)Antie Voorhis (2)Katrina
    Blauvelt Pvt NY
James: b — d 2- -1811 m (2)Mary Holland Pvt VA
Peleg: b 1-24-1764 d 3-8-1841 m Eleanor Clarke Petty Of NS
Peter: b 3-3-1757 d 12-16-1835 m Mary Neal CaptLt CL
Peter: b 10-23-1759 d 11-17-1826 m Margaret Cobham Pvt NY
Rescom: b 1-7-1759 d 11-13-1832 m Mary Gorum Pvt MA ★
Timothy: b 1740 d 1823 m Mary Townley Lawrence Pvt NY
Wm.: b c. 1750 d p. 1797 m Rhoda Akin Cmsry MA
Wm.: b 1760 d 11-17-1833 m Sarah Mount Pvt NJ ★

TALMAGE, (or TALLMADGE)
Abram: b 2-16-1736 d 11-16-1815 m (2)Phebe Fairchild Sol NJ
Benjamin: b 2-25-1754 d 3-7-1835 m Mary Floyd LCol CT
Daniel: b 12-22-1746 d 1831 m (1)Thankful Eaton (2)Mrs Rebecca
    (Bradley) Sgt CT ★
Daniel: b 1745 d 7-22-1779 m Loisa Allen Pvt NJ
David: b 8-5-1731 d 5-13-1809 m Lydia Pike PS NY
Dayton: b c. 1760 d 6-12-1826 m Charity Stiles Sol NJ
Elisha: b 10-18-1750 d 1-2-1814 m Maria Brazee Pvt NY
Enos: b 11-12-1725 d 11-12-1815 m Mary Hand PS NY
Ezra: b 3-31-1759 d 3-18-1830 m Anna Polley Pvt NY
Ichabod: b 10-1-1747 d 11-15-1805 m Hannah Minor Pvt CT W★
James: b 9-11-1743 d 12-21-1821 m Anna Sutherland Capt NY
Joel: b 11-25-1756 d 1-26-1834 m Rhoda Potter Pvt NY ★
John: b 5-20-1752 d 1-14-1815 m Sarah Lyon Pvt NY
Jonathan: b 3-30-1742 d 1813 m Mary Wilsey PS NY
Joseph: b 4-4-1739 d 11- -1818 m (1)Martha Marks (2)Rachel
    Bliss Sgt MA
Joseph: b 9-22-1754 d 2- -1832 m Mary Barnes Pvt NY
Josiah, Sr.: b 4-19-1713 d 10-22-1792 m (1)Phoebe Dibble
    (2)Hannah Williams PS CT
Josiah, Jr.: b 11-25-1736 d 6-3-1784 m Sybil Todd Pvt CT
Josiah: b 2-10-1749 d 8-21-1802 m Margaret Hoffman Pvt NY
Noah: b 1761 d 8-10-1837 m Elizabeth Chamberlain Pvt NJ ★
Samuel: b 11-23-1755 d 4-1-1825 m Mary Hilton Lt NY
Seymour: b 5-28-1755 d 7-6-1840 m Sarah Hoyt Pvt CT ★
Thomas: b 10-24-1755 d 10-2-1834 m Mary Goyn-McCoy Maj NJ

TALTON,
James: b — d a. 8-19-1817 m — Pvt NC

TAMBLIN,
Seth: b 1709 d 2-23-1797 m Susannah Thompson Pvt MA
Timothy: b 11-11-1756 d 8-31-1845 m Susanna Webster Arfr
    Sgt MA

TANDY, (includes TANDAY)
Achilles: b 1758 d 1820 m Nancy Ferguson Lt SC
Henry: b 3-6-1741 d 7-1-1809 m Ann Mills PS VA
Roger: b c. 1720 d 6-27-1778 m Sarah Quarles Pvt VA
Smyth: b 1741 d 10-12-1823 m (1)Joyce — (2)Susannah Williams
    Pvt PS VA
Wm., Sr.: b c. 1725 d p. 1790 m Mary Morgan Drm PS NH
Wm., Sr.: b 1720 d a. 3- -1794 m Jane Quarles PS VA

TANEY,
Joseph: b 2-5-1755 d 11-24-1844 m Dorothy Brooke Ens MD
Michael: b 1-2-1756 d 2-12-1796 m Monica Brooke 1Lt MD

TANKARD,
John: b 1752 d 4-24-1836 m (1)Mrs Zillah (Turner) Downing
    (2)Sarah Townsend Dr VA W★

TANKERSLEY,
George: b 1740 d 1784 m Elizabeth Bouldin Pvt VA
John: b — d a. 6-20-1808 m Susanna — Capt VA
John: b 1757/8 d 3-14-1840 m Frances Muse Mar Pvt VA ★
Joseph: b c. 1760 d p. 1830 m Catherine Buckner Pvt VA
Richard: b 3-13-1738 d 1810 m Mary Wood Pvt VA
Wm.: b 1742 d p. 1790 m Martha Nelson Pvt NC

TANNEHILL,
John: b 1746 d 1814 m Catherine Acheson Pvt PA
Josiah: b 6-7-1753 d 3- -1811 m Margaret Wilkins PM PS MD VA
    W★
Ninian Bazel: b 1747 d 11-16-1776 m Agnes Coulter Lt MD

TANNER,
Abel: b 6-22-1762 d 6-2-1830 m Lydia Sweet Pvt NY
Abel: b 9-17-1740 d p. 8-23-1787 m Phebe Bent PS RI
Benjamin: b 12-1-1758 d 1804 m Thankful Stafford Pvt NY
Benjamin: b 8-20-1730 d 6-5-1777 m (1)Hannah Perkins Pvt RI
Benjamin: b c. 1744 d 1792 m Sarah Ann Aylesworth Pvt RI
Ebenezer: b 1-20-1757 d 1819 m Lydia Hatch Lt CT W★
Francis: b 1762 d 1847 m Elizabeth Peterson Pvt RI ★
Frederick: b c. 1750 d p. 4-1-1833 m Maria — Pvt VA

TANNER, contd.
George: b 1757 d 9-19-1820 m — Pvt MA
George: b 11-9-1723 d 1791 m Mary Wilcox Pvt RI
Isaac: b 9-9-1736 d 9-10-1822 m (1)Lydia Sherman (2)Hannah
  Boss (3)Mary Bentley Ens RI
Jacob: b 12- -1745 d 9-1-1835 m Maria Lewis Sgt NY ★
James: b 1755 d 7-17-1818 m Mary Emigh PS NY
Job: b 4-5-1740 d 3-19-1829 m Annie Sherman Lt NY
John: b 5-15-1741 d 1-14-1794 m Ann Schenck Pvt NY
John: b 2-19-1760 d 2-19-1832 m Esther Childs Pvt RI ★
Joseph: b 9-17-1750 d 6-6-1825 m Ruth (Duel)Briggs Capt NY
Joshua: b 3-23-1748 d 4-10-1828 m Lois Thorpe Pvt NY
Joshua: b 7-27-1757 d 9-12-1807 m Thankful Tefft Ens RI
Josiah: b 6-10-1734 d 3-14-1810 m (1)Anne Blackman (2)Phebe
  Brownell Pvt RI
Josiah: b 10-10-1754 d 11-1-1807 m Martha Wooten Lt SC ★
Matthew, Sr.: b 1730-40 d p. 1806 m Lucy Creed PS VA
Nathan: b 9-27-1755 d 3-22-1830 m Sarah (Bailey)Devoe Pvt MA
Nathan: b 1738/9 d 1828 m (1)Patience Austin (2)Bertheno Briggs
  Pvt RI
Nathan: b 9- -1737/8 d p. 1790 m Elizabeth Thurston PS RI
Palmer: b a. 1760 d — m Amy Thomas Pvt NY
Palmer: b c. 1740 d 4-21-1813 m Phebe Wood Pvt RI
Samuel: b c. 1753-5 d c. 12-17-1800 m Mary Gorton Cpl RI
Thomas, Jr.: b 8- 1743 d 1817 m Anna Baldwin 2Lt CT
Thomas, Sr.: b c. 1738 d p. 11-16-1802 m Mary — Ens PS VA
Tryal: b 12-20-1751 d 11-22-1833 m (1)Huldah Jackson (2)Polly
  Doud Lt CT ★
Wm.: b 2-5-1761 d 6-4-1835 m Lois Johnson Pvt RI ★
Wm.: b 8-6-1760 d p. 1-5-1793 m Hannah Utter Cpl RI
Zebulon: b 1751 d 11-9-1806 m Mary Kent Pvt RI

TAPLEY,
Amos: b 10-15-1748 d 9-6-1835 m Hannah Putnam Preston Lt MA
Asa: b 9-11-1761 d 7-22-1836 m Elizabeth Smith Pvt MA
Gilbert: b 5-6-1722 d 5-6-1806 m Phoebe Porter Putnam Lt MA
Joseph: b 4-11-1756 d 3-11-1820 m (1)Mary Smith (2)Rowena
  Page Pvt MA

TAPLIN,
Elisha: b 1758 d 1795 m Martha Newton Pvt MA
John, Jr.: b 7-14-1748 d 11- -1835 m (1)Catherine Lovewell
  (2)Lydia Gove Capt VT

TAPP,
George: b 1732 d p. 1820 m (2) — Fowler Pvt NC
Vincent, Sr.: b c. 1729 d 12- -1790 m Mollie Jett Pvt VA
Vincent: b 4-2-1757 d 3-20-1824 m Susanna Gambill SgtMaj VA
Wm.: b 12-22-1750 d 1796 m Mary Smith Lt NY
Wm.: b 1755 d 1823 m Jemima Hoper Pvt VA

TAPPAN, (includes TAPPEN, TAPPIN & TOPPAN)
Abraham: b 10-14-1744 d 4- -1782 m Mary Hunt Mstr MA
Abram: b 1756 d 9-29-1799 m Margaret Montgomery Pvt NJ
Benjamin, Sr.: b 2-28-1720 d 5-6-1790 m Elizabeth Marsh PS MA
Benjamin, Jr.: b 10-21-1747 d 1-29-1831 m Sarah Homes Pvt MA
Christopher: b 1725 d 1806 m Sarah Eaton PS NH
Christopher: b 6-2-1742 d 8-3-1826 m Annatje Wynkoop PS NY
David: b c. 1747 d c. 1821 m Martha — Pvt NJ
Ebenezer: b 7-16-1761 d 5-16-1849 m Betsey Forster Sgt MA ★
James: b 1750 d 12-9-1809 m Nancy Dunham Pvt NJ
John: b 1742 d 9-6-1818 m Abigail Weare PS CS NH
John: b 2-4-1756 d 11-22-1818 m Sarah Munson Cpl NJ
John: b 10-18-1753 d 3-4-1846 m Rachel Van Benschoten Arfr Adj
  NY ★
Petrus, Jr.: b 6-24-1748 d p. 1791 m Elizabeth Crannell 1Lt Srgn
  NY
Stephen: b 12-6-1756 d 10-7-1839 m Edna Little Cpl MA
Teunis: b 11-3-1728 d 1809 m Hester Concklin Capt PS NY

TAPSCOTT,
George: b 1748 d 1787 m — PS VA
Henry: b c. 1730 d 1781 m Mary Shearman PS VA
James: b 11-17-1750 d 11-3-1815 m (1)Sarah Baird (2)Ann (Baird)
  Barcalow Pvt NJ

TARBELL,
Benjamin: b 2-19-1762 d 2-28-1838 m Lydia Hodgman Cpl MA ★
Cornelius: b 3-27-1722 d c. 1788 m Elizabeth Giles Sgt MA
David: b 8-21-1732 d 1- -1826 m Bathsheba Woods Pvt MA
David : b 9-15-1726 d 1805 m Hannah Fitch PS NH
Edmund: b 4-4-1747 d 4-3-1800 m (1)Mary Hildreth (2)Beulah
  Hildreth Pvt NH
James: b 10-11-1725 d 6-17-1805 m Esther Fletcher Pvt MA
John: b 1710 d 11-28-1804 m Esther Grovenor Pvt MA
Jonathan: b 9-15-1726 d 4-9-1788 m (1)Mary — (2)Mrs Anna
  (Gilson) Patch Lt VT
Nathaniel: b 4-19-1745 d 11-22-1831 m Ruth Elliott Pvt NH
Peter: b c. 1761 d 1-22-1816 m Frethal Spofford Cpl VT
Thomas, Sr.: b 2-2-1719 d 2-9-1796 m Esther Smith Cpl NH
Thomas, Jr.: b 10-8-1751 d 1-10-1827 m Sarah Barrett Pvt NH ★
Wm.: b 10-3-1752 d p. 1799 m Elizabeth French Pvt MA

Wm.: b 10-19-1764 d 8-2-1851 m (1)Mary Simons (2)Suza —
  (3)Susan Blood Pvt MA
Wm. Cox: b — d 1823 m Ann Chapman Cpl CT

TARBOX,
Daniel: b 1733 d 1818 m Agnes Hooper Pvt MA
David: b 3-26-1728 d 6- -1810 m Abigail Taylor Capt CT
Eleazer: b 5-11-1753 d 2-6-1831 m Phebe Stackpole Pvt MA
Jonathan: b 12-27-1754 d 1-29-1837 m Lydia Bill Pvt CT
Samuel: b 9-25-1736 d 1789 m Lois Matteson Pvt CT
Solomon: b 4-29-1733 d p. 1810 m Asenath Phelps Lt CT
Thomas: bpt 12-23-1753 d a. 6-24-1799 m Sarah Nason Pvt MA
  ME
Wm.: b 9-23-1755 d 1829 m Lydia Atwell Pvt MA ★

TARLETON, (includes TARLTON)
Elias, 1st: b 8-13-1693 d 6-3-1785 m Mary — PS NH
Elias, 2d: b 1720-21 d 12-2-1811 m Hannah Ackerman PS NH
Elias, 3d: b 10-14-1749 d 12-15-1828 m Mary Randall Pvt NH
Jeremiah: b 2-11-1755 d 7-6-1826 m Eleanor Medley Cpl MD W★
Jeremiah: b 1761 d 1833 m Mary Herbert Briscoe PS MD
Richard: bpt 10-24-1724 d p. 1790 m Mary Cotton PS NH
Wm: b 11-23-1752 d 3-26-1819 m (1)Betsey Fisk (2)Polly Melvin
  Capt NH

TARPLEY,
Thomas: b 10-28-1734 d 1798 m — Valentine Slr VA

TARR,
Benjamin: b 12-25-1726 d 1814 m Mary Barber Lt MA
Benjamin: b 8-25-1749 d 1810 m Lucy Sayward CG MA
Benjamin: b 10-10-1751 d 5-11-1826 m Elizabeth Smith CS ME
Daniel Barber: b 5-12-1754 d 4-16-1840 m Rachel Davis OrdlSgt
  MA
Henry: b 2-5-1750 d 7-11-1816 m Catherine Sink PS NC
Henry: b c. 1740 d p. 1784 m Mercy Sayward Pvt MA
Jabez: b 8-19-1759 d 11-25-1844 m (1)Sally Saward (2)Peggy
  Somes Sgt MA
James: b 3-13-1729 d 1804 m Lucy Pool Pvt MA
John, Sr.: b 1732 d 1776 m Elizabeth Goss Pvt MA
John, Jr.: b 9- -1756 d 5-29-1838 m Annis Thurston Pvt Smn MA ★
Joseph: b 12-20-1748 d 3-30-1817 m Sarah Brown Pvt MA
Joseph: b 1759 d 1-5-1845 m Deborah Toothaker Pvt MA ★
Peter: b 10-1-1764 d 8-25-1836 m (1)Mary Houser (2)Mary
  McConnell Ens PA
Wm.: b 1760 d 4-10-1817 m Elizabeth Clark Cpl MA

TARRANT,
James: b 11-30-1753 d 7-5-1840 m Jane Birch Capt VA
Leonard: b c. 1730 d p. 7-3-1777 m Mary — PS VA
Mary: b c. 1735 d p. 1782 m Leonard Tarrant PS VA
Thomas: b 2-14-1764 d 8-11-1832 m Mary Flower Smn

TARRY,
George: b 6-12-1740 d 1814 m Sarah Crawley Capt VA

TART,
Thomas: b 2-7-1761 d a. 5- -1850 m — Pvt NC ★

TARVER,
Absalom: b 1757 d 8-27-1831 m Ursuala Smith Pvt GA
Samuel: b 1763 d 2-8-1845 m Charlotte Goff Pvt NC ★

TARWATER,
Jacob: bpt 4-26-1761 d 1789-98 m Maudlin Wolford Pvt PA

TASH,
John: b 1- -1729 d 8-3-1801 m Mary Ham Sol PS NH
Thomas: b 7-5-1722 d 10-1-1809 m (1)Mrs Ann Freeman Parsons
  (2)Martha Crummet Col NH

TASKER,
John: b c. 1718 d 1797-1800 m Mary Young PS Pvt NH
Jonathan: b 1752-4 d c. 1806 m Comfort Seavey Sgt NH

TATE, (includes TAIT)
David: b 1759 d 8-1-1838 m Comfort Knox Sgt VA ★
Edward: b — d a. 4-30-1794 m Barbara Gast Pvt VA
Henry: b 1725 d 9-5-1793 m Sarah — Pvt PS VA
James: b 12-18-1738 d 3-5-1799 m Margaret Bradley Chp NC
James: b 1741 d 3-15-1781 m Sarah Hall Capt VA
James: b 1746 d 6-8-1798 m Rebecca Hudson Sgt VA
Jesse: b p. 1746 d p. 9-25-1804 m Margaret Miller 1Lt VA
John: b 5-4-1758 d 12-24-1838 m Anne Oliphant Pvt PA ★
John: b 1743 d 12-15-1828 m Mary Bracken BgdMaj VA
John, Sr.: b 1722 d 3- -1801 m Mary Doak Pvt VA
John, Jr.: b 2-26-1749 d 12-13-1802 m Jane Steele Sol VA
John: b 8-6-1761 d 8- -1836 m Susanna Mayse Pvt VA
Nathaniel: b c. 1740 d 1810 m (1)Rhoda Tarry (2)Susan Gilliam Capt
  VA

Robert: b c. 1746 d 1814 m — 2Lt MD
Robert: b 1754 d p. 1798 m Nancy Campbell Ens PA
Robert: b 3- -1753 d 7-9-1832 m Margaret McClung Pvt VA
Samuel: b 5-21-1730 d 3-23-1815 m Elizabeth Caldwell Pvt PA
Samuel: b a. 1751 d p. 1-6-1831 m Nancy Johnson Pvt PA
Thomas: b 6-11-1743/4 d 2-9-1833 m Jane Campbell Lt VA
Waddy: b c. 1751 d 1789 m Anne — Capt NC
Wm.: b 7-19-1738 d 1-1-1781 m Isabella Traill 1Mte MA
Wm.: b 1740 d 4- -1782 m (1)Martha Dixon (2)Mrs Ann (Nichols) Dixon PS PA
Wm.: b — d p. 2-7-1792 m Elizabeth — CaptLt SC
Wm.: b 11-20-1753 d 2-11-1830 m Dorcas Mitchell Capt VA

TATLOW,
Joseph: b 1741 d 1-26-1808 m (1)Mary Janvier (2)Mrs Eleanor Rankin Pvt DE

TATNALL,
Joseph: b 9-6-1740 d 8-3-1813 m Elizaeth Lea PS DE

TATUM, (includes TATEM & TATOM)
Haley: b c. 1760 d p. 3-20-1819 m — Pvt NC
Henry: b 9-22-1755 d 7-22-1836 m Dorothea Claiborne Lt VA
Howell: b a. 1753 d 1823 m Henrica Organ Ens Capt NC
Isham: b 3-12-1756 d p. 1850 m (1)Rachel — (2)Savannah — (3)Mary — (4)Sarah — (5)Fannie Stypes PS VA
James: b c. 1750 d 9-10-1821 m — Sheppard Lt PS NC
John: b c. 1762 d 8-3-1824 m Mary Wright Pvt NC ★
John: b c. 1720 d 1794 m Ann Wright Pvt NC
Joseph: b 12-9-1711 d a. 1-20-1779 m Mary Bright PS NJ
Peter S.: b 1-27-1742 d p. 7-20-1791 m (1)Ann Chappell (2)Rebecca — PS NC
Richard: b — d a. 8- -1790 m — PS NC
Thomas: b 1750 d 10-27-1813 m Margaret Dagnell Pvt VA W★
Wm.: b 6-23-1737 d 5-1-1820 m Susannah Ashbrook Pvt NJ

TAUL,
Arthur Thomas: b 4-12-1749 d 2-24-1812 m Mary Anne Johnson PS MD

TAUNT,
John: b a. 1738 d p. 1780 m Hepzibah Kenny Pvt MA

TAVENNER,
George: b 1743 d a. 3-14-1826 m Tabitha Roach PS VA

TAWS,
David: b 12- -1748 d p. 10-12-1832 m Jeanette Youll Pvt NY ★

TAY,
Aaron: b 1749 d 12-15-1794 m Phoebe Locke Pvt MA
John: b 3-29-1732 d 1782 m Susanna Pierce Pvt MA
Wm., Sr.: b 10-25-1700 d 12-8-1780 m Abigail Jones Pvt MA
Wm., Jr.: b 7-11-1726 d 3-17-1795 m Susanna Jones Pvt MA

TAYLOE,
Abraham: b 1740 d p. 11-7-1801 m Ann — Sol NC
John: b 5-28-1721 d 4-18-1779 m Rebecca Plater PS VA
Richard: b — d p. 6-16-1786 m — PS CS NC

TAYLOR,
Aaron: b 5-21-1740 d 1791/2 m Phoebe — Pvt MA
Abel: b 6-9-1730 d p. 1811 m Martha Conant Pvt MA
Abraham: b 5-17-1765 d 6-9-1839 m Mary Stone Pvt CT ★
Abraham: b 1-3-1738 d 11-12-1806 m Rachel Howe Sgt MA
Abraham: b 8-11-1739 d 5-2-1811 m Sarah Prescott Pvt MA
Abraham: b 4-3-1763 d 11-9-1833 m Frances Blood Pvt MA
Abraham: b 4-12-1743 d p. 1779 m Mary Leland MM MA
Adonijah: b 1730 d 1810 m Rachel Sawtell Lt MA
Alexander: b 1756 d 3-8-1815 m Mary McKisson Sgt PA
Alexander: b 1-6-1762 d 9-5-1835 m Phebe — PS VA
Andrew: b 1730 d p. 5-22-1787 m (1)Elizabeth Wilson (2)Anne Wilson Sol NC
Andrew, Jr.: b 1765 d 10-22-1847 m Isabella Cooper Pvt Spy NC
Anthony: b 3-26-1749 d 1-2-1826 m (1)Priscilla Clark (2)Mrs Joanna (Paige) Reed Cpl PS NH
Archibald: b 1735 d 11-22-1785 m Mary Ferguson CS VT
Archibald: b c. 1760 d 5-27-1813/4 m Rachel Chinalt Pvt VA
Benjamin: b 3-5-1732 d 1-10-1803 m Sarah Birge Sgt CT
Benjamin: b 1739 d 5-26-1814 m Sarah Whelden Pvt MA
Benjamin: b 1733 d 11-17-1787 m Martha Lyon Capt NH
Benjamin: b 3-8-1759 d 2-2-1839 m Anna Lowe Pvt NH ★
Benjamin: b 10-24-1751 d 7-12-1832 m Elizabeth Burroughs Pvt PA
Benjamin: b 3-31-1756 d 4-23-1842 m Catherine — Pvt PA ★
Billington: b 1748 d a. 10-4-1836 m — Pvt SC ★
Charles: b 1-13-1755 d 1-27-1821 m Sarah Conway Dr VA
Chase: b 3- -1728 d 8-13-1805 m (1)Phoebe Hayes (2)Sarah Put-Putnam Elkins Capt NH
Childs: b 9-5-1756 d 12- -1829 m Rhoda Bates 1Lt NJ
Christopher: b 1746 d 9-10-1833 m Mary Edwards Capt NC ★
Clark: b 4-1-1759 d 7-27-1846 m Elizabeth Whitehead Pvt VA
Dan: b 10-16-1756 d 10-1-1813 m Sibyl Ely Pvt MA
Daniel: b 9-23-1714 d 9-23-1791 m Elizabeth Bouton Capt CS CT

Daniel: b 1- -1757 d 2-16-1831 m Ruhamah Ellis Pvt MA W★
Daniel: b 2-1-1758 d 5-3-1844 m (1)Margaret Thatcher (2)Sarah Larue Sgt NJ ★
Daniel: b 9-15-1760 d 8-19-1834 m — Pvt NJ ★
Daniel: b 11-7-1748 d 10-19-1826 m Elizabeth Rouse Capt NC
Daniel: b 6-17-1739 d 9-20-1807 m Elizabeth Lydia — PS VT
Daniel: b 8-3-1761 d 11-25-1835 m Jane Rowland Pvt VA ★
David: b c. 1756 d c. 1830 m Anna Landon Pvt CT
David: b 10-22-1753 d 12-10-1822 m Mercy — Cpl MA ★
David: b 6-10-1763 d 12-7-1840 m Hannah King Pvt MA
David: b 11-17-1750 d 10-2-1839 m Roseanna Gilbert QMSgt NY ★
David: b 1723 d 1809 m Hannah Taylor Pvt MA
David: b 8-5-1742 d 7-2-1822 m Hannah Hannaford Dr NH
David: b 8-10-1735 d p. 1790 m Margaret Kelsey Pvt PS NH
David: b 12-25-1759 d 4-17-1840 m Cornelia Vanbrockle Pvt NJ
David: b 1752 d 9-11-1828 m Elizabeth Henry Pvt NY W★
David: b 1759 d 1844 m Nancy Hingston Pvt Wgn VA ★
David: b c. 1755 d 12- -1824 m Margaret Taylor Pvt VA
Ebenezer: b 7-14-1721 d p. 8-25-1775 m Zerviah Culver Pvt CT
Ebenezer: b 3-24-1723 d 1-3-1809 m Experience — Pvt MA
Ebenezer: b 9-28-1737 d 1-3-1799 m Ruth — Pvt MA
Edmond: b 8-16-1741 d 1-28-1822 m Ann Day Pvt VA
Edmund: b 10-21-1744 d 7-1-1786 m Sarah Stubbs Capt VA
Edmund: b 5-12-1723 d 1808 m Ann Lewis PS VA
Edward: b 1-25-1743 d 6-11-1817 m Sarah Ingersoll Pvt MA
Edward: b 5-29-1750 d 1801 m Hannah Haskell Pvt MA
Eldad: b 4-10-1708 d 5-21-1777 m (1)Rhoda Dewey (2)Thankful Day PS MA
Eleazer: b 6- -1755 d 3-1-1836 m Hannah Starr Pvt Tms CT ★
Eleazer: b 8-26-1728 d 1807 m Sarah Keyes Lt MA
Eli: b 10-8-1759 d 12-4-1840 m Hannah Platt Pvt CT ★
Elias, Sr.: b 1-16-1727 d 5-29-1777 m Mary Johnson Arfr MA
Elijah: b 10-3-1763 d 8-25-1841 m Rachel Hulbert Pvt MA
Eliphalet: b 12-15-1716 d 6-19-1782 m (1)Ruth Flint (2)Elizabeth Sibley Pvt MA
Eliphalet: b — d p. 1792 m Abigail Runnels Sol PS CS NH
Elisha: b 1748 d 8-26-1822 m Jerusha Hutchins Cpl MA
Elisha: b 8-7-1760 d 6-9-1836 m Anna Kimball Cpl MA
Eliud: b 1757 d 4-10-1850 m Mary Hall Cpl CT ★
Elnathan: b a. 1754 d 1- -1781 m Elizabeth Odell Pvt NY
Enos: b 2-3-1751 d 3-25-1831 m Eunice Longley Pvt MA
Ephraim: b 8-22-1758 d 8-24-1847 m Deborah Otis Pvt MA ★
Erasmus: b 9-5-1715 d 7-19-1794 m Jane Moore PS VA
Ezra: b 8-20-1760 d a. 12-15-1790 m Meriam Eaton Pvt MA
Gad: b 1760 d 3-13-1841 m Abigail Hill Pvt CT ★
Gamaliel: b 1-9-1735 d 10- -1815 m Abigail Cabel Lt CT
Gamaliel: b 1758 d 7-28-1840 m Anna Losee Sgt NY ★
George: b 1-7-1746 d 10-11-1793 m Mary Bauman Capt PA
George: b 1741 d 2-4-1820 m — Pvt PA
George: b 1762 d 1826 m (1)Hannah Jennings (2)Margaret Hall Lt VA
George: b c. 1745 d 1823 m Elizabeth Anyon Ens VA
George: b 2-11-1711 d 11-4-1792 m (1)Rachel Gibson (2)Mrs Sarah Taliaferro Conway PS VA
George: b c. 1758 d 1787 m Letitia Wade Pvt VA
George: b 1716 d 2-25-1781 m Anne Savage SDI PA
Gilbert: b 1-20-1744 d 10-25-1805 m Dorothy Crawford Lt NY
Harrison: b 8-11-1735 d 11-25-1811 m Jane Curlett PS VA
Henry: b 1757 d 4-5-1825 m Elizabeth Taylor Pvt NJ ★
Henry: b 1738 d 10-8-1801 m Jane White Maj CS PA
Henry: b 1733 d 11-22-1813 m Rhoda Williamson Capt PA
Henry: b c. 1730 d a. 6-14-1781 m Temperance Peterson Col VA
Henry: b 11- -1752 d 7-18-1838 m (1)Mary Blackburn (2)Elizabeth Dill Pvt PA ★
Hezekiah: b 11-28-1748 d 8-23-1814 m Sarah Frost MM VT
Hubbard: b 1760 d 1840 m Clarissa Minor Pvt VA
Ignatius: b 9-11-1742 d 9-21-1807 m (1)Anne Wilkinson Parran (2)Mrs Jordan (3)Mrs Barbara (Bowie) Hall Maj MD
Isaac: b 6-13-1753 d 1817 m Sarah Taylor Pvt MA
Isaac: b 2-27-1758 d 2-27-1828 m — Pvt NY
Isaac: b 3-7-1756/7 d 12-4-1842 m (1)Jane Cunningham (2)Elizabeth Brown Lt NC ★
Isaac: b 1-20-1734 d 1-16-1813 m Hannah Arnold LCol PA
Isaac: b 5-7-1747 d 1805 m Elizabeth Townsand CS PA
Isaac: b a. 1757 d p. 1790 m Phebe McIntire Pvt SC
Isaac: b c. 1730 d 1801 m Emeline — Capt VA
Isaac: b 2-13-1753 d 2-26-1815 m (1)Martha Street (2)Margaret Elizabeth Irwin Capt VA W★
Isaiah: b 3-17-1725 d 11-1-1801 m Marcy — Sgt PS NH
Israel: b 8-1-1733 d p. 3-8-1796 m Esther King Gunn Pvt MA
Israel: b 1750 d 1820 m Huldah — Pvt NY
Ithamar: b 1752 d 5-16-1818 m Thankful — Pvt MA
James: b 1755 d 7-19-1817 m Penuel Fletcher Pvt CT
James: b a. 1743 d 3-24-1798 m Abiah Moore Lt MA
James: b 3-13-1750 d 1-5-1836 m Sarah Wright Sgt MA ★
James: b 1762 d 1832 m Salome Partridge Pvt MA
James: b c. 1748 d 1814 m Lois Butterfield Sol NH
James: b 1750 d 1-8-1832 m Elizabeth Thompson Pvt NY
James: b 1-30-1760 d p. 3-19-1846 m — Ens NC ★
James: b 1753 d 1817 m (2)Winnefred Best SgtMaj NC
James, Jr.: b c. 1750 d c. 1815 m Nancy Collins Maj PA
James: b 1753 d 5-24-1844 m Mary Ann Cully Sgt PA ★
James: b 2-28-1731 d 4-4-1815 m Nancy Owen Pvt VA

TAYLOR, contd.

James, Sr.: b 3-20-1703 d 3-1-1784 m (1)Alice (Thornton) Catlett (2)Mrs Elizabeth McGrath Lewis (3)Mrs Gregory PS VA
James, Jr.: b 12-27-1732 d 3-12-1814 m (1)Anne Hubbard (2)Sarah Taliaferro (3)Elizabeth (Fitzhugh) Conway Col PS VA
James; b 12-16-1738 d p. 6-13-1808 m Ann Pendleton Sgt VA
James: b 3-2-1740 d 1801 m Ann Paul Cpl VA
Jasher: b 1-22-1753 d p. 1800 m Dolly Carr Pvt MA
Jasher, Sr.: b 10-6-1719 d 11-28-1795 m Thankful Sears Pvt MA
Jasher, Jr.: b 3-12-1761 d 2-17-1806 m Susannah Kelley Pvt MA
Jedediah: b 10-27-1752 d 11-8-1833 m Abigail Fowler Fif Pvt MA
Jeremiah, Sr.: b 1758 d c. 1858 m Leah — Sol GA
Jeremiah: b 9-19-1754 d 10-28-1828 m Elinor Greene Pvt MA
Jeremiah: b 1759 d 8-3-1813 m Mrs Helen Eleanor (Wood)Gibson Pvt NY
Jesse: b 1753 d — m Polly Owen Pvt CT ★
Jesse: b 1755 d 1830 m Sarah Emory Slr VA
Job: b 1750 d 1841 m Anna Ross Pvt CT
Job: b 8-21-1756 d 5-19-1842 m Mercy Phelps Pvt CT ★
Joel: b 3-4-1764/5 d 1-19-1846 m Hannah Farrar Pvt MA ★
John: b 1738 d 5-18-1812 m Sybil Bidwell Pvt CT
John: b 1-4-1757 d 8-23-1840 m Rebecca Jones Sgt CT ★
John: b 1753 d 7-2-1829 m Mary Pratt Pvt CT
John: b 1-12-1754 d 2-3-1817 m Sarah Benedict Pvt CT
John: b 1760 d 1-25-1839 m Deborah Chambers Pvt CT ★
John: b c. 1755 d — m (2)Hannah Hodge Cav CT
John: b — d 1795 m Lorena Stanford PS DE
John: b 2-8-1757 d 5-12-1827 m Ruth Bailey OrdlSgt MD ★
John: b 2-13-1755 d 7-25-1841 m Elizabeth Chapman Lt MA
John: b 2-16-1752 d 5-1-1826 m Sally Rider Cpl MA
John: b 1739 d 1822/3 m Phoebe Clark PS MA
John: b 8-24-1762 d 3-25-1840 m Comfort Burley Pvt NH ★
John B.: b 1757 d 9-19-1834 m Jerusha Spencer Pvt MA NH ★
John: b 1751/2 d 4-26-1840 m Hannah — Pvt MA ★
John: b 5-8-1761 d 12-8-1832 m Mercy Burgess Pvt MA W★
John: b 1-17-1722 d 3-8-1799 m Mary Nims PS MA
John: b 1734 d 4-27-1794 m (1)Mrs Rebecca Prescott (2)Mrs Anna Dole (3)Ruth Hunt PS Dr MA
John: b 2- -1715 d 1-16-1795 m (1)Abigail Drake (2)Mary (Dearborn) Hobbs Sgt NH
John: b 1762 d 1840 m Susannah Thompson Sgt NH
John: b 1-12-1712 d 2-28-1796 m Sarah Dearborn PS NH
John: b c. 1740 d c. 1830 m (1)Lydia Kerr (2)Mrs — Lindley Col NJ
John: b 8-1-1751 d 11-5-1801 m Janet Fitz Randolph LCol NJ
John: b 1738 d 1795 m Jane Collins Pvt NJ
John: b 8-26-1749 d 4-26-1829 m Chloe Cox Lt NY
John: b 1748 d 4-16-1813 m Margaret Livingston Pvt NY
John: b — d — m Jane Smedes Pvt NY
John: b 7-10-1747 d 5-28-1826 m Winifred Horton Capt PS NC W★
John: b — d — m Sarah Day Ens NC
John: b 11-18-1696 d 3-22-1780 m Catherine Pendleton PS NC
John: b 1744 d 1824 m Mary Franks Pvt SC NC
John: b 7-2-1743 d 1-24-1812 m Dinah Bailey Sgt PA
John: b 1748 d 6-7-1832 m Nancy — Sgt PA
John: b 1746 d 2-1-1781 m Sarah Hirons Capt SC
John: b 3-20-1760 d 9-20-1847 m Triphena Smith Pvt VT ★
John: b 1736 d 3-21-1813 m Elizabeth Campbell Maj VA
John: b 6-3-1749 d 9-8-1824 m Lucy Penn Col VA
John: b 10-26-1760 d 8-6-1826 m Anne Gilbert Capt VA
John: b 1756 d 1847 m Elizabeth — 1Lt VA
John: b — d a. 2-20-1793 m Blanche — Ens VA
John: b a. 1750 d 1805 m — CS VA
John: b 1764 d 1-21-1843 m Blanche Buckner Pvt VA ★
Jonas: b 11-30-1739 d 12-15-1823 m Mary Danforth Cpl MA
Jonathan: b 2-11-1758 d 4-15-1834 m Nancy (Taylor) Pvt CT ★
Jonathan: b 2-27-1729 d 10-29-1811 m Mary Jones Pvt MA
Jonathan, Jr.: bpt 11-11-1759 d 8-6-1835 m Nancy Phelps Pvt MA
Jonathan: b 7-29-1762 d 5-16-1820 m Rhoda Root Pvt MA
Jonathan: b 5-3-1757 d 3-19-1839 m (1)Phebe Howes (2)Eunice (Baker) Matthews (3)Jemima (Shepherd) Lyon Pvt MA ★
Jonathan: b 2-18-1726 d 12-28-1792 m Thankful Phinney PS MA
Jonathan, Sr.: b 10-2-1739 d 3-2-1816 m Rachel Moore Cpl NH
Jonathan: b 12-8-1750 d 5-13-1832 m Dorothy French Pvt NH
Jonathan: b 8-5-1764 d 10-11-1846 m Judith Badger Pvt NH ★
Jonathan: b c. 3-10-1716 d 8-4-1784 m Susanna Smith PS NH
Jonathan: b 2- -1752 d 12-28-1837 m Annie Halstead Pvt NY
Jonathan: b c. 1710-20 d a. 1795 m Mary — PS SC
Jonathan: b 12-3-1742 d a. 9-5-1803 m Ann Berry Lt VA
Joseph: b 11-8-1739 d 1-17-1816 m Sybil Northam Pvt CT
Joseph: b 11-29-1753 d 1802 m Ann Wilson Pvt CT
Joseph: b c. 1750 d 10-23-1793 m — PS DE
Joseph: b 11-20-1737 d 1-5-1818 m Thankful Clarke Pvt MA
Joseph: b 1730 d 3-17-1813 m Elizabeth Sumner Capt NH
Joseph: b 10-20-1748 d 3-27-1824 m (1)Mary Lovering (2)Margaret Nason Pvt PS NH
Joseph: b c. 1723 d 1795 m — Pvt NJ
Joseph: b 12-19-1743 d p. 1790 m Frances Anderson Col NC
Joseph: b 2-19-1742 d 12- -1788 m Mary — Pvt NC
Joseph: b 1751 d 3-22-1818 m Sarah Best Pvt NC
Joseph: b 11-17-1754 d p. 1812 m Esther Hewes Sgt PA
Joseph: b 12-3-1731 d 5-7-1810 m Ruth Stoddard Pvt RI

Joseph: b 1-27-1726/7 d 9-1-1802 m Experience Sherman PS RI
Joseph: b c. 1755 d p. 1790 m Sally Eaton Pvt VT
Joseph: b 1747 d c. 1834 m Susan Wooden Pvt Wgn VA ★
Joseph: b 1750 d p. 1782 m (1)Judith Gilliam (2)Sarah Moseley Pvt VA
Joshua: b 8-29-1751 d 8-29-1804 m Eunice Seeley Sgt CT
Joshua: b c. 1745 d 1827-30 m Hannah — Pvt NC
Joshua: b c. 1730 d a. 10-8-1782 m Ann — PS VA
Josiah: b 10-17-1720 d 2-11-1781 m Thankful French Pvt CT
Josiah: b 11-13-1754 d 2-2-1838 m Anna — Pvt CT ★
Lemuel: b 2-11-1749 d 7-28-1834 m Abigail White Sgt MA
Leonard: b 6-6-1759 d 7-14-1837 m Eunice Parker Pvt MA ★
Leonard: b 12-22-1757 d 9-4-1841 m Sarah Blackgraves Pvt VA W★
Leroy: b 7-25-1758 d 3-20-1834 m Nellie Wilson Capt NC ★
Levi: b 12-17-1733 d — m Martha Seymour Lt CT
Levi: b 1764 d 6-1-1832 m Sarah Smith Pvt MA
Lewis: b 12-19-1761 d 4-27-1831 m Jemima Ford Cpl MA
Lewis: b 8-11-1744 d 5-26-1812 m Sarah Davis Pvt PA
Mahlon: b 10-22-1759 d 9-26-1823 m Mary Stokes Sol PA
Matthew: b 1707 d p. 1-3-1784 m Mary — PS MD
Matthew: b 1747 d 11-12-1828 m Mrs Sarah Sample Mayes Pvt PA
Matthias: b 5-15-1724 d — m Desire Harding Pvt Mar MA
Meredith: b 1764 d 3-31-1837 m Anna Duke Pvt SC ★
Moses: b c. 1730 d p. 1817 m Elizabeth Prevatt Pvt VA
Nathan: b 7-7-1760 d 9-25-1838 m (1)Hannah Gilbert (2)Mehitable Watkins Sgt CT ★
Nathan: b 2-11-1761 d 1-27-1832 m Lydia Ann Harris Pvt MA W★
Nathan: b 10-29-1754 d 3-28-1840 m (2)Abigail (Elkins) Ward Lt NH
Nathan: b 11-19-1748 d 12-4-1831 m Prudence Wilcox Lt RI W★
Nathaniel: b 1756 d 12-1-1810 m Chloe Bloss Pvt CT
Nathaniel: b 8-27-1722 d 12-9-1800 m Tamar Boardman Chp CT
Nathaniel: b 1730 d 8-7-1795 m Esther Burge Pvt MA
Nathaniel: b 10-15-1756 d — m Sarah Fuller Pvt MA
Nimrod: b 1756 d 7-16-1834 m Mary Lotz Pvt VA
Obadiah: b 1763 d 10-27-1830 m Rhoda Wilcox Pvt CT
Obadiah: b 1762 d 1839 m Abigail Williams Pvt MA
Oliver: b 6-12-1748 d 5-12-1826 m Lilley Beals Lt CS MA
Oliver: b 3-30-1754 d 3-10-1840 m Betty Wetherbee Cpl PS CS MA
Oliver: b 11-29-1760 d 6-8-1812 m Tamar Eaton Pvt VA
Oliver: b 1747 d 4-29-1789 m Sarah Hillyer Pvt NY
Othniel, Sr.: b 4-16-1719 d 12-27-1788 m Martha Arms Capt MA
Othniel, Jr.: b 10-1753 d p. 1818 m Dorothy Wilder Capt MA ★
Ozias: b 3-13-1760 d 1814 m Amelia Humphreys Pvt CT
Parmenas: b 4-11-1753 d 2-28-1827 m Betty White Sol NC
Peter: b 1746 d 7-10-1812 m Nancy Crossthwaite Sol VA
Philip: b 3-25-1759 d 1795 m Sarah Fauntleroy Lewis Capt NC
Philip: b 7-10-1737 d 2- -1819 m (1)Mary Gray (2)Elizabeth (Simmons) CS PS RI
Philip W: b 6-15-1765 d 2- -1856 m Elizabeth Poor Sol VA ★
Phineas: b 4- -1760 d 10-7-1837 m Molly Sherwood Pvt CT
Reuben: b 1732 d 4-10-1807 m — Pvt CT
Reuben: b 2-8-1759 d 3-9-1833 m Anna Skinner Pvt CT ★
Reuben: b 1761 d 7-14-1845 m Lucretia Bowers Pvt MA ★
Reuben: b 3-8-1736 d 1813 m Lucy Kendall Capt NH
Reuben: b 1726 d a. 1824 — Pvt NY
Reuben: b c. 1745 d p. 10-12-1829 m — PS NC
Reuben: b 1-14-1757 d 11-30-1824 m Rebecca Moore Capt VA
Richard: b 1753 d 3-26-1807 m Mary Bennett Pvt DE
Richard: b 3-21-1752 d 1-31-1842 m Hannah Campernell Pvt NH ★
Richard: b 1-17-1753 d p. 11-9-1826 m Lucy Byne Capt NC
Richard: b 4-3-1744 d 1-19-1829 m Sarah Dabney Strother LCol VA
Richard: b 1-6-1749 d 8-30-1825 m (2)Catherine Davis Capt VA ★
Richard: b 12-10-1760 d 12-9-1843 m (1)Sarah Ann Cornett (2)Darcus Thomas Pvt VA
Richard Squire: b c. 1730 d 1806 m Ann Meaux PS VA
Robert: b 1730-40 d 1789 m Susanna Tonkin Col NJ
Robert: b c. 1720 d 1790 m Mary — Maj PA
Robert: b 1740 d 8-6-1824 m (2)Anna — PS PA
Robert: b 1736 d 9-30-1801 m Jane Alexander Maj RI
Robert: b 7-28-1758 d 12-11-1851 m — OrdlSgt VA ★
Robert Dennison: b 4-23-1763 d 1-26-1798 m Pathenia Alvord Pvt CT
Rufus: b 8-15-1740 d 2- -1783 m (1)Mary Goddard (2)Susannah Goddard Pvt MA
Samuel: b 7- -1733 d 1805 m Mary Jesup Sturgis Pvt CT
Samuel: b 12-1-1761 d p. 1833 m Lovina Donaldson Pvt CT
Samuel: b c. 1750 d 11-20-1813 m — Pvt CT
Samuel: b 4-1-1740 d 1-1-1789 m Patience Tipton PS MD
Samuel: b 9-21-1744 d 9-5-1837 m Esther White Capt MA
Samuel: b 10-17-1757 d 4- -1785 m Lydia Brownell Sgt MA
Samuel: b 11-20-1755 d 4-30-1841 m Lucretia Taylor Pvt MA ★
Samuel: b 1722 d 12-29-1787 m Mehitable Ryder Pvt MA
Samuel: b 1757 d 10-1-1826 m Hannah Low Pvt MA
Samuel, Sr.: b 12-26-1718 d 1-22-1798 m (1)Sarah Stebbins (2)Martha Lamb CS MA
Samuel, Jr.: b 6-4-1768 d 4-10-1813 m Sarah Jagger Pvt MA
Samuel: b 12-1-1708 d 12-23-1792 m Susannah Perham PS MA
Samuel: b c. 1742 d p. 1798 m (2)Sarah — Pvt NC
Samuel: b c. 1740 d 4-20-1798 m Eleanor (Cannon) Hudgins Capt SC
Samuel, Jr.: b c. 1747 d 1812 m Elizabeth Hughes 2Lt VA
Samuel: b c. 1721 d 1803 m Sophia Creed PS VA

Samuel: b 1742 d 1786 m Sarah — PS VA
Seth: b 8-6-1732 d 2-15-1810 m Martha Stetson Pvt MA
Silas: b 1743 d 9-19-1814 m Mary Wilkins Capt MA
Simeon: b 2-14-1749 d 4-26-1820 m Sibella Hotchkiss Pvt CT ★
Simeon: b 7-12-1752 d 9-17-1824 m Tabitha Howes Pvt MA ★
Simon: b 3-11-1728 d p. 3-10-1784 m Anna Maria Hite CS VA
Skelton: b 2-12-1752 d 10-7-1831 m Sallie DeMoss 1Lt VA
Solomon: b a. 1754 d 1-27-1812 m Anna Whitman Cpl MA
Solomon: b c. 1760-65 d a. 1810 m Jerusha Smith Pvt NY
Stacey: b 2-23-1757 d 1836 m (1)Euphemia Hoff (2)Ruth Beans Pvt PA
Stephen: b 3-29-1760 d 8-24-1844 m Aimee Maynard Pvt MA
Stephen: b 1755 d 1844 m Sarah Power Sol VA
Tertius: b 7-25-1754 d 12-22-1822 m Elizabeth Carter Lt MA
Theophilus: b 1759 d 10-4-1845 m — Pvt NC
Thomas: b 1744 d 11-27-1826 m Lucy Dexter Pvt CT
Thomas: b 1752 d 4-5-1815 m Experience Freeman Pvt CT
Thomas: b 9-30-1758 d 2-14-1826 m Mary Morehouse Pvt CT
Thomas: b 1753 d p. 1778 m Elizabeth Evans Pvt MD
Thomas: b 4-13-1753 d 8-6-1806 m Hannah Wheeler Sgt MA
Thomas: b 12-14-1751 d 12-31-1775 m Susannah Ewer Cpl MA
Thomas: b 11-11-1759 d 3-20-1820 m Abigail Piper Sol NH
Thomas: b c. 1759/60 d 9-20-1824 m Hannah Johnson Pvt NJ
Thomas: b 1760 d 9-14-1851 m (1)Mary Thompson (2)Grace Spencer Pvt NJ ★
Thomas: b c. 1764 d p. 4-19-1821 m Elizabeth Bird Pvt NJ
Thomas: b 1756 d 1-26-1849 m (1)Elizabeth Purdy (2)Elizabeth — Pvt NY MA ★
Thomas: b c. 1740 d 2- -1798 m Meriam — CS NC
Thomas: b 5-15-1732 d 3-24-1782 m Martha Woodward Col PA
Thomas: b 1760 d c. 1832 m Nancy Lee — Pvt PA
Thomas: b 9-10-1743 d 11-16-1833 m Anne Wyche Col PS SC
Thomas: b 12-13-1744 d 11-11-1822 m Elizabeth Eddings Pvt VA
Thomas: b 10-27-1745 d 10-23-1817 m Cynthia Corse Pvt VT
Thornton: b — d 1832 m Elizabeth Minor Lt VA
Timothy: b 8-13-1753 d 5-3-1802 m Elizabeth Cooke Capt CT
Timothy: b 1735 d 1820 m Prudence Belden Seacap CT
Timothy: b 9-18-1754 d 2-26-1851 m Esther French Pvt NH
Timothy: b 1729 d 1788 m (1)Letitia Kirkbride (2)Sarah Yardley CS PA
Timothy: b 10-11-1761 d 6-8-1838 m Achsah Johnson Pvt VA
Titus: b 12-14-1757 d 4-3-1825 m Rebecca Hunt Pvt PA
Walter: bpt 1763 d 10- -1830 m Anna Bradt Pvt NY W★
Wm.: b 7-13-1757 d 3-23-1835 m Abigail Case Sgt CT
Wm.: b c. 1760-2 d a. 3-17-1825 m Anna Eckles Pvt DE
Wm.: b 7-13-1725 d 3-15-1784 m (2)Mary Baker (3)Mary Lovett Pvt MA
Wm.: b 4-18-1735 d p. 4-26-1790 m Lois Smith Pvt MA
Wm.: b 3-25-1753 d 4-7-1827 m Priscilla Loveland Pvt MA ★
Wm.: b 3-23-1733 d 12-10-1795 m Betsey Grimes Sol NH
Wm.: b 12-27-1744 d 4-24-1830 m Lucy Embly Pvt Wgn NJ
Wm., Jr.: b c. 1750-60 d -1812 m Mary Billingsley Pvt NC
Wm.: b c. 1750 d 5-19-1803 m Sarah Scroggs Pvt NC
Wm.: b 1761 d 1829 m Nancy Gavin Pvt NC
Wm.: b 1747 d 12-25-1836 m Jane — Wgn NC
Wm.: b 3- -1743 d 6-16-1819 m Mrs Celia Edwards CS NC
Wm.: b 1740-3 d c. 1800 m — Smart Pvt NC
Wm.: b 6-8-1753 d 6-4-1849 m Catherine Askey Pvt Smn PA ★
Wm.: b 1752 d 3-24-1815 m Elizabeth Card Capt RI
Wm.: b 1755 d p. 1827 ,m Sarah Wheeler Sol PS SC
Wm., Sr.: b 1719 d 6-20-1779 m Nancy Johnson Pvt SC
Wm., Jr.: b 1765 d p. 1794 m Mollie Clark Sgt SC
Wm.: b 1-23-1753 d 4-14-1830 m (1)Lucy Norval Hord (2)Elizabeth Courts Maj VA
Wm.: b c. 1740 d p. 7-23-1789 m Hannah — Pvt VA
Wm.: b 1745 d 1798 m Camilla Ridenay Pvt VA
Wm.: b c. 1745 d p. 8-22-1815 m Anne — Capt VA
Wm.: b 5- -1754 d 3-31-1838 m Sarah — Pvt VA W★
Wm.: b 4-3-1754 d 3-31-1841 m Ann Hensley Pvt VA ★
Wm.: b 1758 d 6-10-1843 m (1)Sisly Palmore (2)Agnes Royalty Sol VA
Wm.: b c. 1750 d 1815 m Hannah Guilliam Pvt VA
Wm.: b 1732 d 9-11-1820 m Martha Waller CS VA
Wm.: b c. 1730 d p. 3-27-1782 m Sarah — PS VA
Wilson: b c. 1745-50 d 1-29-1827 m Sarah Moore Lt NC
Woolerick: b a. 1761 d p. 1-7-1806 m Margaret — Sol VA
Zachariah: b 1760 d 8-16-1845 m Susannah Jarrell Pvt VA ★
Zachery: b 2-26-1735 d 6-15-1815 m Alice Chew Capt PS VA
Zalmon: b 2-12-1757 d 5-11-1815 m Hannah Benedict Pvt CT
Zeeb: b 8-18-1750 d 8-5-1825 m Lydia (Taylor) Pvt MA

TAZEWELL,
Henry: b 11-15-1753 d 3-3-1799 m Dorothea Elizabeth Waller PS VA
John: b 1747/8 d 4-7-1787 m Sarah Bolling CS PS VA

TEA,
Richard: b — d 2- -1809 m Mrs Ann Manbrey (Mayberry) PS PA

TEACHEY,
Daniel: b 1750 d 3-15-1826 m Mary James Lt NC

TEACHOUT,
Jacob: b 4-23-1754 d 8-16-1843 m Sabra Teachout Pvt NY

TEACKLE,
John: b 7-3-1753 d 9-8-1817 m Elizabeth Dennis Pvt VA
Severn: b 10-25-1756 d 1-25-1794 m Lucretia Edmondson Capt VA
Thomas: b 4-11-1734 d 8-15-1784 m Elizabeth Upshur PS CS VA

TEAGARDEN, (includes TEAGUARD, TEEGARDIN & TEGARDEN)
Aaron: b 1754 d 3-21-1823 m Margaret Dibel Pvt PA
Abraham: b c. 1750 d .1783 m Mrs Mary Elizabeth Parker Capt VA
George: b 6-29-1744 d 7-24-1815 m Rachel Pribble Pvt PA
Wm.: b 7-17-1746 d p. 1796 m Bethia Craig Pvt PA

TEAGUE,
Jesse: b 1752 d p. 1818 m Margaret — Pvt MA ★
John: b 1759 d 1839 m Elizabeth — Pvt SC
Joshua: b — d 1808 m — PS SC
Moses: b c. 1725 d p. 3-31-1785 m Rachel — PS NC
Wm.: b 11-23-1761 d 9-23-1845 m Elizabeth Miller Pvt SC ★

TEAM,
Adam: b 10-3-1760 d 6-12-1844 m Catherine Plyler Pvt NC SC ★

TEARSE,
Peter Bailey: b 5-10-1751 d 1803 m Mary Hunter Maj NY

TEAS,
Wm.: b 3-4-1750 d 2-16-1824 m Sarah Loving Cnt VA

TEASLEY,
John: b 1755 d p. 3-8-1816 m Lucy Hunt Sol GA

TEATE,
Anthony: b 1710 d 4-4-1781 m Elizabeth Torbet Sol PS PA

TEBBS,
Daniel: b — d a. 3-26-1776 m Elizabeth Foushe PS PA
Wm.: b 5-5-1732 d 9-3-1813 m (1)Judith Heath (2)Victoria (Haislip) Johnson Capt VA

TEDFORD,
Alexander: b c. 1754 d 3- -1781 m Sarah Edmondson Capt VA
John: b 1750 d 7-14-1832 m (1)Mary Paxton (2)Jane Henderson Capt VA ★
Joseph: b 9-27-1763 d 6-30-1825 m Mary McNutt Pvt MA
Robert: b 1-9-1759 d 9-15-1849 m Agnes Dickson Sgt VA ★

TEDROW,
Michael: b 7-29-1760 d 2-12-1818 m — King Pvt PA
Reuben: b 9-29-1759 d 1843 m Jane Leech Pvt MD

TEED,
John: b 12-26-1753 d p. 1833 m Mary Collins Cpl NJ ★
Wm.: b 1-15-1727 d 6-1-1812 m Anna Seville Pvt NY
Wm., Jr.: b 4- -1750 d p. 10-2-1846 m (1)Catherine Gregory (2)Anna Knox Pvt NY
Zephaniah: b 6- -1763 d 6-3-1838 m Hannah Thorne Pvt NY

TEEL, (includes TEAL, TEALL & THIEL)
Ezekiel Hand: b 12-2-1769 d 9-28-1846 m Rebecca Tucker Pilot NJ
Gershom: b 6-29-1755 d 12-8-1822 m Susanna Adams Cpl MA
John: b — d — m Sarah Hand NS PS
John: b 1751-2 d 7-4-1835 m (2)Catherine Vendermark Sgt PA ★
John: b 1755 d 1-1-1803 m Maria Rosina Stout Pvt PA W★
Jonathan: b 1-30-1754 d 6-7-1828 m Lydia Cutter Pvt MA
Joseph: b 4-29-1762 d 1-12-1837 m Anna Griswold Pvt CT ★
Oliver: b 1-1-1759 d 9-18-1842 m Susan Paine Pvt CT
Samuel: b 1748/9 d 2-25-1832 m Ruth Walker 2Lt MA
Timothy: b 5-27-1754 d 6-11-1820 m (1)Phoebe Hull (2)Dorothy (Alcott) Foote Pvt CT

TEEPLE,
George: b c. 1760 d 5-27-1810 m Hannah Montanye Pvt NJ
Jacob: b 6-19-1763 d 7-7-1835 m (1)Penelope — (2)Hannah Martin Fif Pvt PA ★

TEERS,
Jacob: b a. 1746 d p. 1784 m Anna Butters Pvt NY

TEETER, (includes TEATER, TEATOR & TETER)
Abraham: b — d 1827 m Shively — Sol PA
Conrad: b 8-1-1757 d 10-11-1843 m Elizabeth — Pvt NJ ★
George: b 1739 d 8-8-1815 m (1)Sarah Phares (2)Hester — Ens VA
George: b c. 1740 d 1798 m Anna Margaret Henkel Mil VA
Henry: b 1743 d 12-10-1804 m Elizabeth Bidelman PS Pvt PA
John: bpt 3-2-1742 d p. 8-15-1794 m Margaretha Rifenberg Pvt NY
John: b c. 1753 d 8- -1818 m Eve Turney CS VA
Paul: b c. 1730 d 1784 m Rebecca Henkel Capt VA
Samuel: b 10- -1737 d 10-8-1823 m Mary Doddridge Capt PA
Zachariah: b 10-2-1743 d p. 1800 m Elizabeth Whalen Pvt NY

TEETSELL,
Johannes: b c. 1760 d p. 4-16-1797 m Rosina Fierer Pvt NY

TEFFT,
David: b 4-19-1760 d 3-13-1843 m Ruhama James Sgt RI ★
Gardner: b 5-5-1746 d 11-23-1826 m Waity Eldred Lt RI
Jeremiah: b 5-29-1747 d p. 1806 m Rhoda Hoxie Ens RI
John: b 2-19-1758 d 4-26-1813 m Anna Vallett Pvt RI
Joseph, Sr.: b 1-10-1710 d p. 1790 m Esther Brownell CS PS RI
Joseph, Jr.: b 3-19-1737 d p. 1790 m (1)Sarah Maxson (2)Alice Albro PS RI
Samuel: b 8-29-1749 d p. 1793 m Amy Gardiner PS RI
Stanton: b 7-9-1744 d 7-28-1811 m Mehitable Rogers Pvt NY
Wm.: b 2-29-1732 d 11-28-1822 m Mary Kenyon Cmsry RI

TEISLEY,
Michael: b 5-12-1730 d 9-1-1808 m Catherine Teisley Pvt CT

TELFORD,
Alexander, Sr.: b c. 1713 d a. 2-5-1793 m (2)Mary — CS VA
Alexander, Jr.: b 6-1-1760 d 5-22-1844 m (1)Mary — (2)Elizabeth McClung Pvt VA ★
Robert: b 9-28-1762 d 9-23-1829 m Esabella Sterratt Pvt VA

TELLER,
Abraham: b 4-16-1744 d 1-26-1803 m Margaret Wayman Dr CL
Isaac: b c. 1735-8 d 1775-1783 m Rebecca Remsen Pvt NY
Jacobus: b 3-17-1738 d 9-27-1784 m Maria Yates Pvt NY
John: b c. 1735 d p. 1781 m Jane Delamont Pvt PS NY
John: b 1741 d 6-23-1830 m Sarah Hanes Pvt NY
Luke: b 1740 d p. 1789 m Sarah Snediker Pvt NY
Pierre: b 1747 d 2-19-1783 m Margaret Haines Pvt NY
Tobias: b 1745 d 10-30-1834 m Isabella Neely Pvt NY
Wm.: b 1740 d — m Helena VanEps Pvt NY

TEMPEST,
Robert, Jr.: b 12-25-1746 d 6- -1809 m Deborah Shelley Pvt PA

TEMPLE,
Aaron: b 8-18-1739 d 12-28-1816 m Elizabeth Smith Cpl MA
Archelaus: b 12-10-1735 d 4-15-1815 m — PS NH
Benjamin: b 7-23-1748 d p. 1806 m (1)Sarah Saunders (2)Mary Fletcher PS NH
Benjamin: b c. 1734 d 1800-2 m Molly Brooke Baylor Col VA
Ebenezer: b 3-15-1754 d 10-7-1805 m Olive Gibbs Pvt MA
Elijah: b 7-2-1732 d p. 6-8-1781 m Abigail — Cpl MA
Enos: b 2-10-1764 d 3-4-1846 m Anna Burt Pvt NH ★
Isaac: b 2-8-1704 d 5-31-1791 m Elizabeth Holland PS MA
John: b 10-7-1756 d 1-13-1842 m Mary Mason Lt MA ★
John: b 3-17-1738 d 4-5-1821 m Hannah Nichols Cpl MA
John: b c. 1752 d c. 1812 m Fannie — Pvt VA
Jonas: b a. 1736 d p. 1789 m (1)Olive Keys (2)Mrs Keziah Howe (3)Mrs Zellah Howe Lt MA
Jonas: b 2-8-1716 d 3-8-1803 m Sarah Woods PS MD
Jonathan: b 2-17-1752 d 3-4-1796 m Rebecca Howe Sgt MA
Jonathan: b 5-5-1735 d 3-30-1813 m Dorothy Morse MM MA
Joseph: b 11-20-1747 d 11-22-1825 m Jerusha Treat Pvt NCapt CT
Joseph: b 8-30-1732 d 1796 m Mary Whittimore Pvt MA
Joseph: b 12-23-1743 d 3-23-1832 m (2)Lois Hubbard Taylor Pvt VT
Joseph: b c. 1730 d 12-15-1819 m Mary Hill PS VA
Levi: b c. 1751 d c. 1821 m Rachel Nutting Cpl MA
Liston: b c. 1755 d p. 1810 m Agnes Elliott Capt VA
Nathaniel: b c. 1747 d c. 1848 m Mary Blaker 2Lt NJ
Peter: b c. 1756 d a. 4-24-1802 m Ann — Pvt SC
Samuel: b 10-17-1752 d 4-7-1826 m Jerusha Hager Pvt MA
Samuel: b c. 1730 d a. 1-15-1784 m — PS CS NC
Samuel Francis: b c. 1745 d p. 1795 m Fannie Redd Capt VA
Seth: b 2-21-1753 d 1-22-1824 m Martha Hunt Pvt MA
Solomon: b 7-23-1746 d 3-7-1825 m Abigail Hayden Pvt MA
Stephen, Sr.: b 1734 d 1809 m (1)Sarah — (2)Rhoda — Sgt MA
Stephen, Jr.: b 1- -1764 d 1852 m Susannah Wood Pvt MA
Thomas: b 1-29-1739 d 1775 m Martha Brewer Pvt NH
Thomas, Jr.: b 1-8-1756 d p. 12-19-1807 m Wilmarth Doty 2Lt PA
Timothy: b 3-31-1742 d 1804 m Deborah Ball Pvt MA
Urijah: b 7-6-1757 d 9-14-1808 m Margaret Spear Sgt NH
Wm.: b 11-8-1742 d p. 1790 m Jemima — Pvt MA
Wm.: b 1746 d 11-29-1825 m Sarah Aldrich Shaw Pvt NH

TEMPLEMAN,
James: b 1760 d 10-11-1814 m Cavey Bridwell Sol VA

TEMPLETON,
Alexander: b 1-22-1759 d 3-25-1853 m Jane Smith Pvt PA
David: b c. 1755 d p. 3-10-1813 m — Pvt NC
James: b 1748 d 2-9-1824 m (2)Jane — Cav SC
James: b 3-20-1765 d 6- -1863 m (1)Lucy Billups (2)Ann Frazier PS VA
John: b c. 1760 d 1820 m Nancy Hawkins Sol NC
Nathaniel: b c. 1750-54 d 5- -1782 m Isabella Caldwell Pvt PA
Robert: b 9-6-1762 d 11-10-1845 m Mary Hanna — Pvt SC ★
W. David: b c. 1750 d 4-20-1817 m Mary — PS SC

TEMPLIN,
James: b — d p. 1795 m Mary Salmon Pvt PA

TEN BROECK, (includes TEN BROOK)
Abraham: b 5-13-1734 d 1-19-1810 m Elizabeth VanRenselaer BG NY
Adam: b 7-24-1759 d 5-30-1826 m (1)Lydia Maria Monson (2)Hannah Morrison Ens NY
Benj: b 5-2-1724 d 12-9-1793 m Catherine Jansen PS NY
Cornelius: b 5-31-1719 d 8-4-1790 m Margaret Louw PS NJ
Dirck Wesselse: b 5-1-1715 d p. 1783 m (1)Catharine Conyn (2)Dorothy Vosburg PS NY
Jacob: b 5-2-1724 d 8-21-1798 m Gerritje Smedes PS NY
Jeremias: b 10-18-1724 d 10-24-1802 m Maria VanAllen Pvt NY
John: b 12- -1780 d 1820 m (1)Katie Lough (2)Katie Emmons LCol NJ
John: b 1764 d 3- -1854 m Livina Miller Pvt NY
John: b 9-20-1719 d 1- -1790 m Patience Williamson Col NJ
John Cornelius: b 3-15-1755 d 8-10-1835 m Antje (Ten Broeck) Capt NY
Leonard: b 11-12-1752 d 11-11-1836 m Gertrude Schermerhorn Capt NY
Samuel J: b 3-28-1757 d 4-25-1830 m Christyntije — Lt NY W ★

TEN EYCK, (includes TEN E ICK)
Abraham: b 1734 d p. 1790 m Sarah Smith PM QM Lt NY
Abraham J: b 11-29-1743 d 11-14-1824 m Annatje Lansing PS NY
Andrew J.: b 9-8-1758 d 4-27-1842 m Sarah Berger Pvt NJ ★
Anthony: bpt 9-26-1749 d c. 1817 m Maria Egberts Pvt NY
Barent: b 1740 d 1810 m Jeanette Concklin QMSgt NY
Barent: bpt 8-27-1739 d 1810 m Marytje Schermerhorn Pvt NY
Conrad: b 5-31-1758 d 10-30-1844 m (1)Elizabeth Thompson (2)Jane Thompson Sgt NJ ★
Conrad T.: b 2-12-1757 d 1-27-1846 m (1)Charlotte — (2)Garitje (Ten Eyck) 2Lt NY
Jacob, 2: b 9-25-1733 d 11-7-1794 m Margaret Hagaman Capt NJ
Jacob, 3: b 4-29-1759 d 5-23-1828 m Jane Lane Ens NJ
Jacob Conraedt: b 4-21-1705 d 9-9-1793 m Catharina Cuyler PS NY
Jeremiah: b 2-6-1755 d 5-7-1841 m Jane VanArsdalen Capt NJ ★
John: bpt 9-30-1750 d 1811 m Elizabeth LaGrange Capt NJ
John: bpt 9-7-1732 d 1795/6 m Maria Field Pvt NJ
John DePeyster: b 1758 d 4-6-1798 m Mary DePeyster Doww QM NY
Matthew: b 2-22-1728 d 6-11-1809 m Cornelia Wynkoop PS NY
Richard: b 2-1-1762 d 2-15-1851 m Jennette Baker Pvt NY

TENNANT, (includes TENANT & TENNENT)
Caleb: b c. 1740 d p. 1783 m (1)Sarah Wightman (2)Eunice Culver Morgan Cpl CT
Daniel: b 1762 d 1850 m Martha Hale Pvt CT
James: b c. 1763 d 4-11-1839 m Mary Chapple Sgt RI ★
Joshua: b c. 1750 d c. 10-9-1777 m Ruth Mathews Pvt MA
Richard: b 1744 d p. 12-18-1822 m Elizabeth Haught Drm VA
Thomas: b 10-3-1755 d 3-11-1808 m Elizabeth Hauth Pvt MA W★
Wm.: b 3-4-1740 d 8-11-1777 m Susannah Vergereau PS SC

TENNELL,
George: b 1757 d 1-22-1831 m Hannah Tennell Sgt VA

TENNEY, (includes TENNY & TINNEY)
Benjamin: b 1-17-1743 d 6-23-1811 m (1)Jane Smith (2)Susannah Jewett Sol MA
Benjamin: b 11-8-1746 d 9-2-1790 m Ruth Blanchard Pvt NH
Benjamin: b 1-9-1761 d 1826 m Lydia Jackman Pvt MA
Daniel: b 5-22-1721 d 10-23-1812 m Rebecca Dickinson Cpl MA
Daniel: b 3-16-1734 d 1- -1815 m Joanna Cheney Pvt MA
Daniel: b 6-25-1748 d 1825 m Patty Morse MM MA
Daniel: b 2-23-1732 d 11-4-1815 m Elizabeth Dole Pvt MA
David: b 5-15-1759 d 3-14-1851 m (1)Susanna Durkee (2)Anna Jacobs (3)Mrs Priscilla (Smith) Dole Pvt NH ★
Edmund: bpt 9-6-1741 d 10-10-1831 m Hannah Wood Pvt MA
James: b 12-21-1765 d 12-30-1841 m Thankful Shippee Pvt MA ★
Jesse: b 4-20-1741 d 1-8-1815 m Hannah Griswold Pvt VT
John: b 4-7-1723 d 7-1-1808 m (1)Rose Chandler (2)Mrs Hannah Hall Lt MA
John: b 9-2-1729 d 2-19-1810 m Olive Armstrong Pvt NH
Jonathan: b 2-24-1758 d 11-17-1826 m Betty Willard Pvt MA
Jonathan: b 7-25-1736 d 1-12-1806 m Mehitable Peaslee Pvt PS NH
Joseph: b 1750 d 10-29-1819 m (1)Ruth Hills (2)Sarah Pearson Pvt MA
Josiah: b 9-24-1734 d p. 1795 m Mary Shearer Pvt MA
Josiah, Jr.: b 5-15-1760 d 9-4-1837 m (1)Levinah Keyes (2)Susannah Hines Pvt MA
Moses: b 3-31-1751 d 1- -1797 m (2)Anna Knight Pvt MA
Nathaniel: b 1-29-1723 d 6-22-1810 m (1)Elizabeth Boynton (2)Sarah Pike PS MA
Oliver: b 9-12-1736 d 12-30-1787 m Sarah Reed Pvt MA
Oliver: b 8-21-1762 d 1-13-1826 m Bathsheba Watkins Pvt MA
Reuben: b 7-29-1760 d 2-26-1827 m Rebecca Hopson Pvt NH
Richard: b 10-2-1736 d 1-23-1802 m Abigail Perley Pvt MA
Samuel: b 1-7-1752 d 4-23-1790 m Esther Parmenter Drm MA
Samuel: b 6-2-1764 d 6-28-1841 m Deborah Wilbur Sol MA
Silas: b 4-15-1757 d 4-16-1827 m Temperance Woodward Cpl NH W★
Wm.: b 5-6-1740 d 5-4-1826 m Rebecca Eames Pvt MA
Wm.: b 3-17-1755 d 6-16-1806 m Phebe Jewett Cpl NH
Wm.: b 7-3-1749 d 9-14-1823 m Mehitable Jones Pvt PS NH

TENNILLE,
Benjamin: b c. 1750 d 6-30-1811 m Mrs Rachel Deeson Sgt VA
Francis: b 1747 d 12- -1812 m (2)Mary (Elizabeth)Bacon Dixon Lt GA

TENNIS,
Israel: b 1750 d 8-9-1790 m Jane Meredith Pvt PA
Samuel: b c. 1745 d c. 1820 m Eleanor Sacheverell Pvt PA
Wm.: b 1747 d 6-30-1831 m Mary — Pvt PA

TENNISON,
John: b 1745-50 d p. 8-19-1790 m Elizabeth — PS VA

TER BUSH, (includes TER BOSS)
Benjamin: bpt 9-2-1743 d 1777/8 m Mary Ann Fox PS NY
Peter: b 1749 d 8-29-1831 m Sarah Griffin MM OrdlSgt PS NY W★
Simeon: b 1737 d 1814 m — Cooper Sgt NY

TERHUNE, (includes TERHONE)
Abraham: b 8-15-1760 d 1-12-1854 m Moycay Williamson 1Lt NJ
Albert, Sr.: b 9- -1733 d 1820 m Elizabeth — PS NY
Daniel: b 12-29-1758 d 1842/3 m Anne Williamson Pvt NY NJ ★
Garret: b 12-1-1737 d 8-10-1819 m Eleanor Hoagland Pvt PS NJ
Jacob: bpt 7-22-1739 d 11-3-1829 m Elizabeth Nagel Capt NJ
John: b 4-15-1759 d 1-6-1839 m Sarah Vreeland Sgt NJ ★
John: b 6-4-1753 d 1-14-1805 m Catharine Lutkins CS NJ
John: b 7-10-1757 d 1-22-1839 m Mary McCreedy Sgt NY
Nicholas: b 2-22-1733 d 12-18-1807 m (1)Leah Powelse (2)Rysie Haring Capt NJ
Stephen: b 11-27-1735 d 4-23-1814 m Margrietje Cornel Cpl NJ
Wm. S: b 10-13-1757 d 6-18-1828 m Maria VanNuys Pvt NJ

TERPENNING, (includes TEERPENING & TEERPENNING)
Boudewyne: bpt 8-31-1735 d p. 1792 m Elizabeth (Terpenning) Capt PS NY
Gerrit: b 12-15-1723 d p. 1790 m Annetje Beem Pvt NY
Henricus: bpt 12-24-1732 d 1783-5 m Maria VanAaken Lt NY
Jacobus: b 1725 d 1779 m Marreitje Beem PS NY
Simon: bpt 4-11-1756 d p. 1787 m Gritje Smit Pvt NY

TERRELL, (includes TERRAL, TERRILL, TIRRELL, TIRRILL, TURRELL, TURRILL & TYRELL)
Aaron: b — d p. 7-29-1814 m Hannah — PS Sol NC
Abraham: b 1-30-1735 d 4-7-1791 m Mary Dunham Pvt NJ
Adam: b 9-19-1742 d p. 3-19-1788 m Mary — 2Lt NJ
Asahel: b 9-20-1739 d 10-8-1777 m Hannah Hoyt Pvt CT
Benjamin: b 10-15-1731 d — m Elizabeth Derby Pvt MA
Charles: b 8-3-1748 d 1828 m Ann Tyler PS VA
David: b 1729 d 2-14-1805 m (1)Sarah Johnson (2)Sarah Goode (3)Patty Johnson PS VA
Ebenezer: b 4-3-1742 d 7-18-1825 m Lois Hill Pvt MA
Ebenezer: b 2-5-1729 d 8-10-1807 m Lydia Wild Pvt MA
Edmund: b 2-12-1753 d p. 1802 m (1)Margaret — (2)Jane Johnson Sgt VA
Edmund: b 3-21-1740 d p. 6-1-1784 m Margaret Willis Capt VA
Edward Young: b 7-10-1765 d 11-6-1833 m Artalissa Stephens Pvt SC
Eliakim: b 2-10-1760 d 3-16-1807 m Elizabeth Twitchell Pvt CT
Ephraim: b 12-15-1713 d 8-13-1786 m (1)Phebe Winans (2)Phebe Wood (3)Ann Heard Capt NJ
George: b 1- -1728 d 4-7-1806 m Sarah Sherman Capt PS CS CT
George: b 6-28-1753 d 12- -1817 m Elizabeth Tyler 1Lt VA
Gideon: b 6-5-1753 d 2-26-1823 m Mary Loring Cpl MA
Henry: b 3-29-1735 d 1-29-1812 m Mary Tyler PS VA
Isaac: b 5-22-1749 d p. 1783 m Sarah Prince Pvt CT
Isaac, Sr.: b 3-23-1718 d 2-22-1791 m Mary Whitmarsh Pvt MA
Isaac, Jr.: b 7-28-1745 d 9-18-1823 m Hannah Porter MM MA
Israel: b 3- -1737 d 9- -1811 m (1)Zeruah Beebe (2)Lois Upson 2Lt CT
James, Sr.: b 5-10-1719 d 4-10-1812 m (1)Abigail Buck (2)Elizabeth — PS CT
James: b 3-11-1763 d 10-8-1857 m Susan Payne Sol NC
Jared: b 10-18-1762 d 9-27-1833 m Hannah Buck Pvt CT
Joel, Jr.: b 4-16-1762 d 12-26-1819 m Martha Williams Pvt NC ★
Joel: b c. 1750 d 1815 m Elizabeth Rush Sol NC
John: b 3-16-1756 d 2-19-1827 m (1)Elizabeth Buck (2)Polly Stilson Pvt CT
John, Jr.: b 10-16-1752 d 8-28-1807 m Lydia — Pvt MA
John: b 1752 d 1822 m Jane — Pvt PA ★
Jonah: b c. 1756 d 1840 m Joanna Lincoln Pvt NH
Joseph: b 1-28-1745 d 4-9-1787 m Elizabeth Mills Pvt VA
Joseph: b c. 1761 d p. 4-11-1826 m Elizabeth Chisholm Pvt VA
Josiah: bpt 11- -1732 d 7-17-1795 m Eunice Hoadley Capt CT
Mathew: b 1762 d 1830 m — Hughes DrmMaj VA
Micajah: b 4-22-1746 d 11-10-1805 m Hannah Goodman PS NC
Micajah: b a. 1734 d 1805 m Sarah Lynch PS VA
Nathan: b 1755 d 1-24-1834 m Dorothy Phelps Pvt CT ★
Oliver: b 6-2-1755 d 1-17-1823 m Huldah Barnum Pvt CT
Oliver: b 1730 d 1816 m (1)Mrs Lidda Lewis (2)Mrs Damaris Lewis Pvt CT
Peter: b 1745 d p. 1785 m Mary Wingfield Capt VA
Philemon: b 1750 d a. 12-9-1816 m Elizabeth — Pvt NC

Richmond: b 1760 d 1856 m Cecelia Darracott Pvt VA
Robert, Sr.: b 12-25-1797 d 1786 m Mary Foster PS VA
Robert, Jr.: b c. 1730 d c. 1786 m Judith Towles Pvt VA
Samuel: b 1749 d 8- -1800 m Mary McInnis Pvt MA
Simon: b 3-27-1755 d 1840 m Sarah Thompson Cav Lt NC
Solomon: b 11-27-1755 d 12-28-1816 m (1)Amelia Robertson (2)Nancy Wall PS NC
Stephen: b c. 1740 d 2-28-1848 m Hepsibah — Sol CT
Thomas: b 2-27-1748/9 d 1-31-1832 m Susannah Colson Pvt MA ★
Thomas: b 1-3-1761 d 1-17-1822 m Sarah Shelton 2Lt VA
Thomas: b 8-20-1736 d 1804 m Rebecca Peatross PS VA
Vinson: b 12-16-1755 d 2-28-1816 m Salome Hunt Pvt MA
Wm.: b 2-22-1754 d 9-3-1827 m Jane — Pvt Drm NY
Wm.: b 2-11-1732 d 8-6-1812 m Frances Wingfield 2Lt VA
Wm.: b c. 1745 d c. 1812 m Martha Winston PS VA
Wm.: b 11-27-1757 d 10-31-1829 m Martha Patterson Lt VA
Wm.: b 1735 d p. 1780 m (1)Mary Mallory (2)Ann Daniel Pvt VA
Wm.: b 6-27-1764 d 3-24-1830 m Malinda Bernard Pvt VA

TERRETT,
Wm. Henry, Jr.: b 11-21-1752 d c. 1820 m Amelia Chapman Hunter PS VA

TERRY,
Asaph: b 11-15-1756 d 5-10-1839 m (1)Penelope McGregory (2)Nancy Atwell Mus CT ★
Benjamin, Jr.: b — d p. 6-2-1817 m Elizabeth — PS Capt VA
Brewster: b 9-29-1732 d 8-23-1796 m Elizabeth Davis PS NY
Caleb: b 10-10-1762 d 8-10-1805 m Sarah Horton Pvt NJ
Daniel, Sr.: b c. 1736 d 2-3-1814 m (1)Rachael Young (2)Mrs Betsey Parshall Pvt PS NY
Daniel, Jr.: b 1758 d 4-28-1828 m (1)Phoebe Howell (2)Mrs Mary Albertson Pvt PS NY
David: b 1737 d 6-8-1828 m Susan Allen Pvt MA ★
David: b 8-24-1720 d 6-17-1779 m Mehitable Aldrich PS NY
David: b c. 1740 d a. 1-2-1797 m Elizabeth — PS VA
Ebenezer: b 8-27-1748 d 10-3-1838 m Sarah Hurlburt Pvt CT
Eliphalet: b 12-24-1742 d 11-2-1812 m Mary Hall Ens PS CT
Elisha: bpt 8-8-1743 d 1810/11 m Phoebe Granger Pvt MA W★
Elnathan: b 4-17-1758 d 12-31-1840 m Mary Kinyon Pvt RI
Ephraim: b 10-24-1701 d 10-14-1783 m Mary Ann Collins PS CS CT
Gamaliel: b — d 3-24-1806 m Susanna Moore Sgt CT ★
Gershom: b 1710 d 4- -1777 m Mary Wells PS NY
Isaac: b 10-16-1755 d 4- -1845 m Huldah Taber Sol MA
James: b 10-6-1758 d 12-13-1840 m (1)Rachel — (2)Bethiah Reeve Pvt NY
Jeremiah: b 1739 d 4-25-1823 m Elizabeth Morris 1Lt NY
Job: b 8-11-1753 d p. 1801 m Rebecca Winslow Pvt MA
John: b 8-5-1760 d 5-2-1835 m Susannah Holland Smn MA ★
John (Cleves): b 2-18-1744 d 9-6-1823 m (1)Temperance Conkling (2)Abigail King Pvt NY
John: b 10-28-1753 d 9-25-1843 m Mary Griffing Pvt NY
John: b 1750 d 1817 m Mary Virginia — Pvt VA
John: b 1760 d 2-11-1845 m Sarah Hudnett Ens VA ★
Jonathan: b 1714 d 6- -1775 m Lydia Tuthill PS NY
Jonathan: b 6-17-1758 d 2-16-1833 m Abigail Terry Pvt PA
Joseph: b 1717 d 1782-85 m Judith Crawford PS VA
Joshua: b 1764 d 11-11-1827 m Elizabeth Parshall Pvt PA
Julius: b 10-21-1761 d 7-17-1843 m Sarah King Pvt CT
Nathaniel: b 6-3-1730 d 2-27-1792 m Abiah Dwight Col CT
Nathaniel: b 6-2-1752 d 6-28-1847 m Esther Woodward Pvt NY
Nathaniel, Sr.: b c. 1726 d p. 6-10-1778 m Sarah Royall PS VA
Nathaniel, Jr.: b 12-2-1746 d 2-8-1837 m Ann Thompson Capt VA W★
Parshall, Sr.: b 8-8-1734 d 5-15-1811 m (1)Deborah Clark (2)Sarah (Lee) Horton Pvt CT
Philip: b 5-31-1755 d 1819 m Elizabeth Mason Pvt MA
Robert: b c. 1750 d p. — 1790 m Susannah Sanders Sol PS NC
Samuel, Sr.: b 10-18-1725 d 5-8-1798 m Mary Kellogg Pvt CT
Samuel, Jr.: b 7-29-1750 d 11-11-1838 m (1)Huldah Burnham (2)Dorcas — PS CT
Samuel: b 2-28-1753 d 7-28-1838 m Elizabeth Phelps Pvt CT
Samuel: b c. 1750 d 2-28-1813 m Sarah Ogden Pvt NY
Stephen: b 1758/9 d 8- -1820 m Mildred Bagby Sgt VA
Stephen: b a. 1750 d 10- -1797 m Sarah Fuqua PS VA
Thomas: b 10-6-1759 d 2-3-1842 m Sarah Tanner Pvt MA ★
Thomas: b 1746 d 4-24-1832 m (1)Mary Littell (2)Susannah Frazee (3)Anne Shaw (4)Abigail Conklin (5)Catherine Spinning Sol NJ
Thomas: b 1724 d 12-24-1776 m (1)Sybil King (2)Abigail Havens (3)Mrs Mary Moore Col NY
Thomas: b 7-27-1761 d 3-6-1833 m Lucy Lax Pvt VA
Thomas: b c. 1740 d 10-8-1804 m Ann — Pvt VA
Thomas: b 2-16-1762 d 7-23-1845 m Sarah Hendrick Pvt VA
Urbane: b 1-15-1760 d 9-29-1840 m Huldah Tiff Pvt NY
Uriah: b 11- -1725 d 6-29-1804 m Abigail Cleveland PS PA
Wm.: b 1720 d a. 1- -1777 m Mary Raiford PS NC
Wm.: b 1761 d p. 1799 m Mary Elizabeth Gideon Sol SC
Wm.: b 5-1-1732 d 11-7-1797 m Susanna Johns Maj VA
Wm. Nathan: b 1760 d 1-20-1840 m Eleanor Lewis Pvt PA ★
Zeno: b 8-20-1755 d 1-7-1838 m Tabitha Abbe Pvt CT ★

TERWILLIGER,
Hugo, Sr.: b 10-4-1724 d 6- -1804 m Jannetze Freer Pvt NY
Hugo, Jr.: b 8-29-1757 d p. 1799 m Elizabeth Decker Pvt NY
Jacob: b 1-4-1747 d c. 9-28-1805 m Elizabeth VanWagenen Lt NY
James: b 1755 d 8- -1835 m Elizabeth — Pvt NY
James P.: bpt 2-17-1754 d 1829 m (1)Rachel Teerpenning
  (2)Cassandana Goldsmith Cpl NY
John: b 1753 d 1846 m Margaret — Pvt NY
John: b 9- -1722 d 3-29-1797 m Maria VanWagenen PS NY
Jonathan: b 8-18-1734 d p. 2- -1803 m Maria Freer Lt NY
Simon: b 10-10-1738 d p. 1790 m Maria Terwilliger Pvt NY

TESCH,
Heinrick: b 9-30-1733 d 6-24-1804 m Margaretha Jaeger PS NC

TESHO,
Peter: b — d — m — Pvt Smn QM MA

TEST,
Francis, Jr.: b 4-4-1747 d 3-4-1832 m (1)Mary Morgan (2)Rachel
  Greene Pvt NJ
George: b 5-20-1759 d 6- -1795 m Margaret Wogan Pvt PA

TETHERLY,
Wm.: b 11-28-1729 d p. 1790 m Anna Tetherly Pvt MA

TEVIS,
Robert: b 3-9-1752 d 8- -1848 m (1)Martha Crow (2)Elizabeth
  DeBois (3)Lucy Crow Ens MD
Robert, Sr.: b c. 1709 d p. 10-25-1796 m Elizabeth Curry PS MD

TEW,
Benjamin: b 175- d 1798 m Abigail Hathaway Pvt MA
Daniel: b 8-12-1737 d p. 1790 m Keziah Hathaway Pvt MA
Henry: b 1735 d 1780 m Elizabeth Hathaway Capt MA
Thomas: b 1737/8 d 12-10-1821 m Ann Clark Capt RI
Wm.: b 4-5-1745 d 10-31-1808 m Sarah Wilson Capt RI

TEWKSBURY, (includes TEWKESBURY)
Andrew: b 2-21-1740 d 10-24-1814 m Susannah Hasey Sol MA
Henry: b 1741 d 11-28-1806 m Sarah Calfe 2Lt NH
Isaac: b 8-17-1747 d 3- -1813 m Judith Sargent Sol PS NH
James: b 9-26-1744 d 11-5-1800 m Mary Sargent Pvt MA
James, Sr.: bpt 1727/8 d p. 1787 m Sarah Grushee Pvt MA
James, Jr.: b 9-21-1760 d 1812 m (1)Mary Paine (2)Mrs Nancy
  Goodwin Pvt MA
John: b 7-20-1735 d 3-11-1816 m Anna Bill Pvt MA
John, Sr.: b 5-25-1728 d 11-12-1775 m Elizabeth Hilton Pvt MA
John, Jr.: b 11-11-1753 d p. 1797 m Sarah Lendall Pvt MA

TEXTER,
Adam: b 1746 d 4- -1813 m Elizabeth — Pvt PS PA

THACKER,
James: b 1748 d 1810 m Mary Armistead Pvt VA
Nathaniel: b 1750-2 d 1838 m — Pvt VA ★
Stephen: b 10-24-1745 d p. 1783 m Zulima — Matr NY

THACKRY,
Amos: b 1759 d p. 1797 m Sarah — Pvt PA

THARIN,
Daniel: b c. 1750 d 10-1-1788 m (1)Elizabeth Long (2)Mrs
  Susannah Witten Sol SC

THATCHER, (includes THACHER)
Amasa: b 3-26-1742 d 12-15-1828 m (1) — Hyde (2) — Hawley
  Pvt VT
Amos: b 5-29-1755 d 6-25-1834 m Jerminia Corwin Pvt PA ★
Anthony: b 8-28-1744 d 1-18-1806 m Betsy Taylor Pvt MA
Asa: b 9-5-1755 d 1-22-1833 m (1)Hannah Hunt (2)Hannah
  Haynes Pvt CT
Benjamin: b 8-5-1764 d 5-17-1835 m Sybel Foster Pvt CT ★
Benjamin: b 1724 d 1807 m Desire Yerrington Pvt NH
David: b 3-14-1730 d 11-9-1801 m Abigail Russell PS CS MA
Ebenezer: b 6-2-1754 d 4-1-1831 m Tamsen Taylor Sgt MA
Edward: b c. 1750 d 9- -1785 m Sarah Snyder Pvt PA
Eliakim: b 3-30-1763 d 1-14-1848 m Deborah Swift Trns CT ★
Elisha: b 8-31-1760 d 12-24-1835 m Temperance Sholes Pvt NH
George: b 4-12-1754 d 4-6-1824 m Sarah Savage Pvt MA
James: b 2-14-1754 d 5-26-1844 m Susanna Hayward Dr MA
John: b 7-25-1742 d 1-16-1805 m (1)Ann Perry (2)Mehitable
  (Ufford) Thompson Capt CT
John: b 2-22-1739 d 10-7-1805 m Abigail Swift Pvt CT
John: b 10-25-1759 d 1-8-1841 m Sally Richardson Pvt MA ★
John Oxenbridge: b 8-3-1764 d 4-8-1843 m Lucy Richmond Pvt
  MA ★
Joseph: b 1756 d 1802 m Rebecca Gould Pvt NH
Josiah: b 2-15-1728 d 3-9-1807 m (1)Mary Fitch (2)Wait Burwell
  Pvt CT
Josiah: b 2-2-1732 d 1-19-1802 m (1)Desire Crowell (2)Mary
  (Miller) Hedge 1Lt MA
Levi: b 2-6-1740 d 2-12-1817 m Adosha — Pvt VT
Lot: b 6-3-1757 d 3-4-1833 m Abigail Fearing Pvt MA

Obadiah: b 7-31-1757 d p. 1803 m Elizabeth Richardson Pvt MA
Peter, Sr.: b 1-14-1715 d 9-13-1785 m Bethiah Carpenter Chp MA
Peter, Jr.: b 10-21-1753 d 12-4-1814 m Nanny Tyler Pvt MA
Roland: b 3-13-1745 d 3-29-1813 m Elizabeth Nye Pvt MA
Samuel: b 11-24-1754 d 3-10-1846 m Rebekah Durkee Pvt CT
Samuel: b 6-10-1717 d 3-21-1795 m Mrs Sarah Kent Cpl MA
Thomas: b 1-20-1757 d 2-24-1806 m Mary Churchill Sgt MA
Wm.: b 5-30-1743 d 5-24-1829 m Thankful Hedge Cpl MA

THAXTER, (includes THACKSTON)
Gridley: b 4-9-1756 d 2-13-1845 m (1)Sarah Lincoln (2)Mary
  Shattuck Dr MA
Joseph: b 4-23-1743/4 d 7-18-1827 m (1)Ann Smith (2)Mary
  Allen Chp MA

THAXTON,
James: b a. 1749 d 1799 m Mrs Sarah Elebank PS VA
Thomas: b 1744 d 8-29-1824 m (2)Hannah Williamson Pvt NC
Wm.: b c. 1767 d 4-5-1850 m Sarah Gravitt Pvt PS NC

THAYER, (includes THAYR)
Abel: b 7-28-1741 d 5-24-1805 m Dorothy Curtis Capt MA
Abiah: b 6-25-1729 d 12-12-1789 m Elizabeth Hunt Pvt MA
Abraham, Jr.: b 4-30-1757 d 1-12-1819 m Lydia (Thayer) Sgt MA
Amasa: b 3-26-1764 d 10-18-1813 m Elizabeth Miller Hilger Pvt MA
Amos: b 1745 d 1819 m Hannah Damerell Pvt MA
Amos: b 8-19-1757 d 7-11-1837 m Lois White Pvt MA
Asa: b 10-4-1761 d 4-9-1828 m Mary Murdock Cpl MA
Asa: b 2-9-1752 d 4-2-1828 m (1)Molly Hunt (2)Mrs Mercy Taylor
  Pvt MA
Ashel: b 10-17-1737 d 2-2-1808 m Esther Daniels Pvt MA
Barnabas: b 10-23-1759 d 1-12-1833 m Lucy Nash Pvt MA
Baruch: b 3-2-1752 d 3-15-1826 m Mary Bingham Pvt MA W★
Bartholomew: b 7-15-1757 d 1826 m Elizabeth Blanchard Lt MA ★
Benjamin: b 4-16-1. '4 d 6-29-1826 m (1)Sarah Bosworth (2)Ruth
  Allen Cpl MA
Benjamin: b 1-11-1720 d 10- -1807 m (1)Ruth Capen (2)Bethia
  Thayer Pvt MA
Benjamin: b 12-11-1738 d 3-1-1802 m (1)Hannah Howland
  (2)Chloe — Pvt MA
Benjamin: b 1746 d 1815 m Jane Clark Pvt MA
Caleb: b c. 1760 d 9-5-1831 m Judy Hayden Pvt MA
Caleb: b 1736 d p. 1790 m Elizabeth Daniels Sol MA
Christopher: b 4-27-1741 d 9-28-1823 m Bethiah Hunt Sgt MA ★
Cornelius: b 12-14-1723 d 10-23-1790 m Abigail Jones CS MA
Daniel: b 1756 d 9-20-1835 m Beulah Corbett Pvt MA W★
David: b 1745 d 12-30-1843 m Molly Sprague Pvt CT ★
David: b 3-29-1725 d 3-13-1795 m Mary Eagers Pvt MA
David: b 2-8-1729 d 6-20-1785 m Hannah Thayer Pvt MA
Ebenezer: b 7-31-1721 d 2-7-1794 m (1)Susanna Niles (2)Rebecca
  Miller Col MA
Ebenezer: b 7-16-1734 d 9-6-1792 m Martha Cotton PS NH
Elias: b 6-22-1741/2 d 9-10-1806 m Hannah Ellis Lt MA
Elijah: b 1-24-1760 d 7-11-1820 m Mehitabel Pratt Pvt MA
Elijah: b 1738 d 10-21-1810 m Lydia Cobb Pvt MA
Eliphaz: b 3-14-1762 d 12-31-1848 m Deliverance Thayer Pvt MA
Elisha: b 11-27-1721 d — m Anna Grover Pvt MA
Ellis: b 9-10-1752 d 1840 m Polly Shafter Pvt PS NH
Enoch: b 5-15-1751 d 5-18-1847 m (1)Catherine Sherman
  (2)Joannah Darling (3)Mary Higgins Pvt MA
Enoch: b 11-17-1728 d 6-12-1830 m Rebecca Curtiss Pvt MA
Gideon: b 11-5-1753 d 2-20-1836 m Meribah Wilcox Pvt RI
Grindel: b 6-14-1744 d c. 1820 m (1)Sarah Parkhurst (2)Lydia
  Comstock PS NH
Hezekiah: b 9-30-1730 d p. 1778 m Mary Stetson Cpl MA
Ichabod, Jr.: b 3-6-1745 d 3-22-1820 m (1)Mary Marsh (2)Meriam
  Jones (3)Matilda Gould Capt MA
Isaac: b 5-9-1742 d 11-29-1814 m Abigail — Capt MA
Issac: b 11-23-1744 d 2-22-1805 m (1)Mary Spear (2)Rachel
  Sawin (3)Hannah Joyce Lt MA
Jacob: b 2-27-1726 d 1802 m (2)Bathsheba Bates (3)Molly Pratt
  Pvt MA
Jeremiah, Sr.: b 6-18-1729 d p. 1778 m Tabitha Leavitt Pvt MA
Jeremiah, Sr.: b 3-11-1725 d p. 1805 m Alice Holbrook PS NH
Jeremiah, Jr.: b 11-14-1757 d 3-15-1832 m Katherine Pratt Matr
  Fif MA ★
Jeremiah, Jr.: b 9-30-1750 d p. 1787 m (1)Anna Page
  (2)Elizabeth (Cook) Man PS NH
Jerijah: b 4-22-1762 d 6-15-1857 m Cynthia Case Pvt CT ★
Joel: b 8-23-1761 d 3-5-1840 m Sabra Cheney Sgt MA
John: b 11-26-1745 d 2-15-1808 m (2)Eunice West Pvt MA
John, Sr.: b 3-1-1725 d p. 1775 m Rachel Skinner Pvt MA
John, Jr.: b 1759 d 4-5-1819 m Achsah Power Pvt MA
John: b 11-4-1734 d 3-10-1823 m Deborah Briggs Pvt MA
Jonah: b 12-14-1751 d 7-25-1820 m (1)Agnes Cannon (2)Esther
  Cutler (3)Mary Putnam Cpl MA
Jonathan, Sr.: b 2-11-1726 d 1-18-1805 m Dorcas Hayden Pvt MA
Jonathan, Jr.: b 4-10-1760 d 11-10-1836 m Betsy Faxon Pvt MA ★
Jonathan: b 11-6-1733 d 11-5-1823 m Betsy Britton Pvt MA
Jonathon: b 4-7-1753 d 2-24-1827 m Martha Smith Capt MA
Joseph: b 5-4-1754 d 5-17-1838 m Abigail Sackett Pvt CT W★
Joseph, Sr.: b 1715 d p. 1787 m (1)Sarah Balcom (2)Rachel
  Richardson Pvt MA

Joseph, Jr.: b 1742 d p. 1787 m Rachel Jepherson Pvt MA
Joshua: b 2-11-1743 d 4-23-1822 m Sarah Hunt Sgt MA
Josiah, Jr.: b 6-28-1752 d 2-9-1814 m (1)Avis Howard (2)Lois
　　Knight Pvt MA
Leavitt: b 1761 d 1838 m Abigail Snell Pvt MA
Lemuel: b c. 1740 d 2-14-1842 m Lucy Bronson Cpl CT
Lemuel: b 7-14-1744 d p. 1822 m (1)Charity Manley (2)Clarissa
　　Davis Pvt MA
Levi: b 1752 d 3-4-1816 m Hannah Parkhurst Cpl MA
Micah: b 1726 d p. 1790 m (1)Sarah Emerson (2)Urana Thayer Pvt MA
Nathan: b 1756 d 9-24-1827 m Catherine Draper Ens MA ★
Nathaniel: b 2-11-1829 m Dorcas Faxon Pvt MA
Nathaniel: b 4-11-1752 d 2-8-1829 m Dorcas Faxon Pvt MA
Nathaniel: b 5-27-1755 d 3-27-1818 m Phebe Crossman Pvt MA ★
Nehemiah: b 8-11-1748 d 1785 m Sarah Hobart Cpl MA
Nicholas: b 3-7-1758 d 4-12-1818 m Judith Cook Pvt MA
Obadian, Jr.: b 1755 d 10-18-1825 m Elizabeth (Theyer) Cpl MA ★
Oliver: b 6-7-1752 d 8-5-1823 m Jerusha Hunt Pvt MA
Pelatiah: b 10-3-1739 d 3-23-1797 m (1)Hannah Thayer (2)Hannah
　　Blake Pvt MA
Peter: b 10-2-1755 d 1820 m Abigail Green Pvt MA
Reuben: b 1-21-1741 d 1- -1839 m Sarah Lindfield Pvt MA
Reuben: b 1758 d 7-4-1834 m (1)Rachel Stetson (2)Betsey
　　(Howard) Wales Pvt MA
Reuben: b 5-15-1747 d 1839 m (1)Experience White (2)Mary
　　Carrier (3)Sarah Bundy Pvt MA
Richard: b 1-26-1727 d 9-21-1800 m Susanna Wild Pvt MA
Richard: b 2-18-1731 d 3-23-1823 m Esther French Pvt MA
Samuel: b 6-10-1721 d 10-24-1794 m (1)Sarah Farmer (2)Judith
　　Walker Pvt MA
Samuel: b 9-6-1762 d 12-26-1833 m (1)Rachel Nelson (2)Dinah
　　Johnson Pvt MA ★
Samuel White: b 6-4-1757 d 1-3-1816 m Esther French Pvt MA
Seth: b 7-27-1725 d 5-24-1803 m Judith (Thayer) Lt MA
Simeon: b 5-25-1765 d p. 1809 m Experience Nelson Pvt MA
Stephen, Sr.: b 12-31-1732 d 1781 m Rachel Davis Pvt MA
Stephen, Jr.: b 12-29-1765/66 d 8-31-1821 m Anna Twichell Pvt
　　MA W★
Timothy: b 1755 d 12-11-1823 m (1)Hannah Thayer (2)Phebe
　　Kingman Sgt MA W★
Timothy: b 6-8-1757 d 1-15-1824 m Rachel Spear Sgt MA W★
Uriah, Sr.: b 10-15-1724 d 3-10-1797 m Deborah Copeland Pvt MA
Uriah, Jr.: b 12-22-1750 d 4-22-1805 m Phebe Hayden Pvt MA
Wm., Sr.: b 1732 d 2-2-1779 m Mary (Leonard) Tisdale Lt MA
Wm., Jr.: b 4-3-1764 d 5-18-1830 m Susannah Lincoln Pvt MA
Wm.: b 3-8-1759 d 3-17-1822 m Sarah Jones Pvt MA
Zaccheus: b 12-27-1742 d 11-27-1825 m Deborah Mann Lt MA
Zachariah: b 12-26-1719 d 1- -1812 m Lydia Pray Pvt Mus MA
Zephaniah: b 7-15-1736 d 2-11-1818 m (1)Prudence Loomis (2)Mrs
　　Rachel Noyes Pvt CT
Zephaniah: b 5-13-1760 d 1809 m Polly Church Pvt CT

THEALL,
Charles: b 1704 d 9-29-1778 m Jemima Lyon PS NY

THEOBALD,
John: b c. 1735 d p. 12-8-1810 m Anna Christine — PS PA

THEUS,
Christian: b c. 1715 d p. 1789 m — PS SC
John: b 1-31-1744/5 d 12- -1784 m Mrs Simmons Sol SC
Randolph: b c. 1757 d 1785 m Sarah — Cmsry PS SC
Simeon: b 1750 d 1821 m Rebecca Legare Capt SC

THEW,
John: b — d p. 2-28-1784 m (1)Aeltje Cuyper (2)Elizabeth Blauvelt
　　Pvt PS NY

THIGPEN,
Gilead: b 11-10-1760 d 4- -1829 m Elizabeth Victoria Hemby Pvt
　　NC ★
James: b 4-25-1743 d 12-12-1825 m Lydia Grey Mayo PS NC
Joshua: b 2-27-1736 d 10- -1803 m (1)Sarah Norwood (2)Katherine
　　— PS NC
Travis: b 6-19-1747 d 1848 m (1)Mary Dennis (2)Lydia Mayo (3)Mrs
　　Hannah Hall Sol NC

THISSEL, (includes THISSEL & THISTLE)
Jeffrey, Jr.: b 9-27-1755 d 9-24-1829 m Jemima Morse Pvt MA
Paul: b 9-6-1747 d p. 6-2-1779 m Hepsebath Ellenwood Pvt Smn
　　MA
Thomas: b 10-16-1759 d 1846 m Bathsheba Richardson Pvt MA

THOM,
Isaac: b 3-1-1746 d 7-13-1825 m Persis Sargeant PS CS NH
John: b 7-21-1730 d p. 1783 m Mary — Sgt MA
Joseph: b 1743 d 11-23-1829 m Elizabeth Craig Pvt PA

THOMAS,
Aaron: b c. 1733 d p. 1-21-1812 m Ruth Bailey Cpl CT
Abraham: b 1755 d 4-5-1843 m (1)Susana Smith (2)Polly Swailes
　　Pvt VA ★
Adam: b 1756 d 1845 m Catherine Landis Pvt PA
Alexander: b c. 1748/9 d 2-14-1802 m — Sgt PA

Alexander: b 11-25-1743 d 10-1-1812 m Ursula Oldridge Capt RI
Amos, Jr.: b c. 1735 d — m Betty Brewster QM CT
Anthony: b 7-4-1759 d 4-17-1825 m Lucy Cecil Pvt MD
Anthony: b 3-25-1719 d 7-14-1781 m Abigail Alden Col MA
Asa: b 12-25-1759 d p. 12-17-1834 m Mary Green Pvt NJ ★
Benjamin: b — d 1834 m Asenath Hanchett Pvt CT
Benjamin: b 1760 d 1823 m Mary Turner Sol GA
Benjamin: b 1741 d 6-29-1816 m Eleanor Wells 2Lt MD
Benjamin: b 9-9-1721 d 1-18-1800 m Elizabeth Churchill Pvt MA
Benjamin: b 7-18-1756 d 1-1-1833 m Melinda Gurley Pvt NC
Benjamin: b 1737 d 1814 m Susanna Dyer Capt RI
Briggs: b 10-28-1751 d p. 1788 m Abigail Thomas Lt MA
Caleb: b 1-10-1764 d 4-16-1825 m Lucy Thomas Pvt NY
Charles: b 1758 d 2-16-1842 m Deborah Brewster Pvt MA RI ★
Charles: b 1739 d 12-17-1832 m Judith Ripley Pvt VA SC ★
Christian: b 1748/9 d p. 7-9-1798 m Susannah Baer PS MD
Daniel: b 11-16-1757 d 7-10-1836 m Eunice Baker Cpl CT ★
Daniel: b 11-21-1754 d 4-23-1825 m Eunice Foster Pvt CT
Daniel: b 5-5-1750 d 1820 m Mercy Bartlett Pvt MA
Daniel: b 1763 d 8-2-1846 m Eunice Barrett Pvt NH
Daniel: b — d p. 10-23-1809 m Sarah — Pvt NC
David: b 1743 d 2-19-1820 m Deborah Howland Lt MA
David: b 11-4-1743 d 2-9-1823 m Rebecca Tinkhans Pvt MA
David: b 6-11-1762 d 1834 m Jennette Turner Sgt NY
David: b 8-16-1732 d 1809 m Sarah Allison Pvt PS PA
David: b c. 1750 d 1828 m — PS SC
Ebenezer: b 1728 d 4-28-1805 m Abigail Brooks Sgt CT
Edward: b 10-14-1713 d 12-26-1802 m Rachel Cushing 1Lt MA
Edward: b 1750 d 6-25-1797 m Prudence Kirkbride Capt NJ
Edward: b 7-15-1736 d 2-29-1794 m Mary Terrill Col NJ
Eleazer, Jr.: b 3-4-1755 d p. 1790 m Rizpah (Arispay) Bryant Cpl MA
Elias: b 1-20-1747 d 2-24-1820 m Sylvia Thompson Sct Pvt VT
Elijah: b 7-9-1758 d 5-5-1845 m — Mindwell PS CT ★
Elisha: b 7-25-1760 d 12-25-1834 m Alice Glasscock Pvt VA ★
Ellis: b 1755 d 11-13-1839 m Mary Harris Pvt MD
Enoch: b 8-10-1748 d p. 1811 m Mary Howland Pvt MA
Enoch: b 8-4-1754 d 1830 m Mary Coleman Capt VA
Evan: b 1-31-1739 d 1826 m Rachel Hopkins PS MD
Evan: b 2-10-1743 d 1836 m Rebecca Green Pvt VA
Evan: b 2-22-1757 d 2-1-1840 m (1)H Nixon (2)S Booth (3)Mary
　　Everton Pvt VA ★
Ezekiel: b 10-25-1747 d 1790-1808 m Susannah Russell Pvt PA
Foxel: b 9-12-1746 d p. 1790 m Martha Holmes Lt PA
Gabriel: b 6-12-1721 d 1-18-1794 m Anna Margaret — PS MD
Garret: b c. 1730 d 7- -1797 m Mary Magdalena — Pvt PA
George: b 1753 d 7-5-1824 m (1)Hope Thomas (2)Hannah Tinkham
　　Cpl MA
George: b 10-25-1747 d 1793 m Margaret Huling Arfr PA
George: b c. 1756 d p. 1787 m Mary Green PS VA
Giles: b 11-30-1763 d 3-21-1842 m Anne Wheeler Pvt MD
Harrison: b c. 1760 d 1809 m — (2)Elizabeth Downing Capt VA
Henry: b c. 1737 d 1817 m (1)Ann Ditch (2)Mary Ditch (3)Rachel —
　　Pvt PA
Henry: b 2-17-1758 d 1837 m Rachel Stillwell Pvt VA ★
Holmes: b 6-12-1755 d 3-26-1836 m Susanna Churchill Pvt MA
Isaac: b 4-21-1721 d p. 1790 m Mary Townsend Pvt PA
Isaac: b 6-20-1746 d 2-23-1815 m (1)Eleanor Miller (Milner)
　　(2)Mrs Eleanor Williams Taylor Pvt PA
Isaac: b c. 1756 d p. 1798 m Margaret (Thomas) Pvt PA
Isaac: b 1735 d 10-30-1818 m Elizabeth Massengale Sol Sct NC
Isaiah A.: b 1-19-1749 d 4-4-1831 m (1)Mary Dill (2)Mrs Mary
　　Fowle (3)Rebecca Armstrong PS Sol MA
Israel: b 1-27-1713 d 6-29-1778 m Phebe Lyon Pvt MA
Israel: b 5-9-1741 d 10-1-1805 m (1)Mary Gates (2)Amy Casivel
　　Pvt NY
Jacob: b 4-14-1747 d 9-10-1811 m (1)Elizabeth Smith (2)Susannah
　　— PS MD
Jacob: b 1-31-1763 d 12-20-1835 m Ruth Perkins Fif NH ★
Jacob: b 1752 d 3-26-1824 m Louisa Shultz Pvt PA
James: b 1753 d 7-19-1842 m Jerusha Clark Pvt CT ★
James: b 1737 d 6-22-1794 m Hannah McCall Dr CT
James: b 5-8-1753 d 4-17-1826 m Martha — Pvt MA
James: b 1762 d 9-9-1832 m (1)Molly Standley (2)Dillie Mitchell
　　Pvt NC
James: b c. 1757 d 11- -1803 m Elizabeth Calaham Capt SC
James: b 1-5-1739 d 11-8-1799 m Mary Morris Rhea Pvt SC
James: b 1764 d 1851 m — Pvt VA ★
James: b 3-10-1756 d 9-25-1819 m Matilda Glover Pvt VA
James: b c. 1745 d p. 9-4-1799 m Mary White PS VA
Jane Black: b c. 1720 d p. 1780 m John Thomas PS SC
Jeremiah: b 2-18-1736 d 12-12-1798 m Susanna — Pvt MA
Jeremiah: b c. 1737 d 1805 m Mary Harper Pvt VA
Jesse: b a. 1750 d a. 7-22-1805 m Mary Howell Pvt VA
Job: b a. 1730 d p. 3-6-1787 m Elizabeth Hoggatt Pvt VA
John: b 2-28-1760 d 6-16-1843 m Mary Hotchkiss Cpl CT W★
John: b 2-2-1746 d 7-24-1807 m (1)Martha Grigsby (2)Elizabeth
　　Jones Col GA
John: b 6-21-1728 d 1801 m Catherine Getzendanner PS MD
John: b 1724 d 6-2-1776 m Hannah (Thomas) Col MA
John: b 1725 d — m Hannah Brown Pvt NY
John, Jr.: b 6-16-1751 d 1834 m Lydia Bayley Pvt MA
John: b 1705 d 5-2-1777 m Abigail Sands CS NY
John: b 8-15-1754 d 1829 m Mary Jetton Ens NC

THOMAS, contd.

John: b 10-11-1710 d p. 4-21-1788 m Christiana Roberts CS NC
John: b 12-9-1713 d 10-3-1790 m Sarah James Pvt PA
John: b 2-22-1723 d 1795 m (1)Joanna Marshall (2)Jane Evans Pvt PA
John: b 1745 d 1818 m Margaret — Pvt PA
John: b 4-10-1763 d 10-16-1838 m (1)Susannah Hodgen (2)Rebecca Keith Sol PA VA
John, Sr.: b c. 1720 d p. 5-2-1811 m Jane Black Col SC
John, Jr.: b 5-26-1751 d 7-29-1819 m Margaret McElwayne Col SC
John: b 6-16-1743 d 11- -1814 m Molly Clark PS Sol SC
John: b 1756 d 9-13-1849 m (1)Miss Roberts (2)Sally West (3)Mrs Susan Nowlin Capt VA ★
John: b c. 1736 d p. 8-29-1801 m Mary Moody Ens VA
John: b 4-8-1757 d 6-8-1847 m Frances Lewis Pvt PS VA
John: b 11-25-1760 d 1-25-1843 m Catherine Burd Pvt VA
John: b 1698 d 9- -1791 m (1)Mrs Harrison Taylor (2)Hannah Meade PS VA
John: b 4-16-1725 d p. 11-23-1788 m Jemima Miller PS CS VA
John: b 1730 d 1801 m (2)Caty Watkins Sol VA
John: b 4-29-1759 d a. 1787 m Catharine Wirt Pvt VA
Jonathan: b a. 1735 d 1784 m Catherine Burch PS MD
Jonathan: b c. 1760 d p. 5-8-1820 m (1)Letitia Evans (2)Catherine — Pvt PA
Jonathan: b 11-29-1762 d 12-13-1838 m Patience Bourne Pvt NC
Joseph: b 5-22-1764 d 7-14-1829 m Esther Sanford Pvt CT W★
Joseph: b 1743 d 8- -1825 m Temperance Drew Lt NH
Joseph: b — d 2-8-1796 m Huldah Tickery Lt MA
Joseph: b c. 1750 d 3- -1786 m Mary Bryant Cmsry SC
Joseph: b 8-3-1759 d 8-1-1839 m Rebecca Tindal Pvt VA ★
Joshua: b 1751 d 1-10-1821 m Isabella Stevenson Capt MA
Joshua, Jr.: b 8-3-1759 d 9-15-1819 m Mary Burgess Pvt MA ★
Josiah: b 9-10-1735 d 4-1-1807 m Rachel (Thomas) Pvt MA
Josiah: b c. 1739 d 1814 m Hannah Custard Pvt PA
Lemuel: b 10-8-1727 d 9-30-1775 m Mary Foot PS CT
Levi: b 7-22-1755 d 8-12-1824 m Hannah Weston Pvt MA
Liverton: b c. 1740 d 1814 m Mary — Sol PA
Mark: b — d 5- -1813 m — Capt VA
Martin: b 3-15-1737 d 7-15-1802 m Ursula Muller Ens PA
Massey: b 3-23-1760 d 3- -1818 m Dicey Talbot Pvt VA W★
Michael: b 1765 d p. 12-3-1816 m — PS NC
Michael: b 1730 d 1799 m Susanna Margaret — Capt VA
Michael, Sr.: b a. 1724 d 1802 m (2)Elizabeth Station CS VA
Michael, Jr.: b c. 1760 d 1826 m Elizabeth Snyder Pvt VA
Morris: b c. 1727 d p. 2-10-1793 m Mary — PS VA
Moses: b — d 7-22-1779 m Hannah Tyler Lt NY
Moses, Jr.: b c. 1750 d 7-22-1779 m Abigail Tyler Pvt PA
Moses: b 1756 d a. 12- -1818 m (3)Elizabeth Whaley Pvt VA
Nathan: b 1757 d 7-24-1822 m Margaret Metts Pvt MD ★
Nathan: b 12-7-1757 d 10-11-1834 m Elizabeth Lyford Pvt MA
Nathan: b 1718 d 6-27-1790 m Hephzibah Farr Pvt PS NH
Nathaniel: b 9-16-1750 d 5-1-1811 m Betty House 1Lt MA
Nathaniel: b 11-23-1756 d 3-21-1838 m Priscilla A Shaw Pvt MA
Nehemiah: b 7-26-1712 d 5-30-1802 m Abiah Winslow PS MA
Nicholas: b 3-22-1738 d — m (1)Lucy Somes (2)Jane Richardson (3)Lucy Hadley Sol MA
Nicholas: b 12-31-1755 d 5- -1845 m (1)Phebe Knight (2)Freelove (Knight) Fiske (3)Mrs Sarah Hopkins Pvt RI ★
Noah: b 7-11-1759 d 10-20-1842 m Sarah Howland Cpl MA VT ★
Owen: b 7-9-1754 d 8-26-1799 m Martha Davis Pvt PA
Owen: b 5-12-1754 d 1838 m Elizabeth March Pvt PA VA ★
Peleg: b 2-1-1736 d 4-17-1834 m Mary Bartlett Lt CT
Perez: b 1757 d 1828 m Sarah Wood Pvt MA
Philip: b 1753 d 1821 m Elizbaeth Covington Wailes Cpl MD
Philip: b c. 1744 d 3-14-1799 m Mary LaFevre Capt MA NH
Philip: b 4-8-1752 d 1 -1822 m Annamary — Pvt PA
Prince: b 1751 d 6-4-1797 m Abigail Pratt Pvt MA
Recompense: b 11-2-1709 d 4-18-1793 m Elizabeth — PS CT
Recompense, 2d: b 1-28-1734 d a. 1797 m Sarah Lawrence PS CS CT
Richard: b 10-19-1758 d a. 11-13-1843 m Elizabeth Bowles Pvt NC ★
Richard: b 12-30-1744 d 1-19-1832 m Thomasine Downing Col PA
Robert: b c. 1763 d 1810 m Margaret Warwick Pvt NC
Robert: b 9-26-1735 d 1817 m Mary Sands PS SC
Robert: b — d — m Mary Woodbury Pvt NC
Samuel: b 1735 d p. 1796 m Ann Richardson 1Lt MD
Samuel: b 12-2-1753 d a. 1808 m Mary Cowman Pvt MD
Samuel: b 6-12-1725 d 7-17-1784 m Mary Thomas PS MD
Samuel: b c. 1753 d p. 1790 m — Pvt NY
Samuel: b 3-10-1759 d p. 9-17-1850 m — Pvt NC ★
Samuel: b 1767 d 1842 m Rachel Hampton Pvt NC
Samuel: b c. 1733 d 1822 m Rachel — Capt PA
Samuel, Jr.: b 8-1-1748 d 1-14-1839 m Hope King Capt RI
Samuel: b 8-12-1743 d 9-25-1815 m Ann — Pvt VT
Samuel Wright: b 6-2-1742 d 3-23-1821 m ( )Ann Bags ( ) — Clayton 2Lt MD
Simeon: b 12-13-1753 d 7-2-1834 m Lucretia Deshon Pvt CT
Stephen: b 1765 d 5-10-1825 m Mary Covington Pvt NC ★
Stephen: b 8-19-1750 d 6-19-1839 m Mary Frazil Sol SC
Sylvanus: b 1-22-1740 d 8-30-1814 m Susanna Tomson Sgt MA
Theophilus: b 3-8-1739 d 1803 m Mary Gibble PS NC
Thomas: b 1-30-1761 d 11-17-1839 m Mary N Grimes Pvt NJ ★

Thomas: b 2-13-1752 d 2-16-1836 m Rebecca — 2Lt VA
Timothy: b 12-18-1747 d 4-23-1832 m Bathsheba Gardiner Pvt PA
Tristram: b 7-28-1752 d 9-3-1811 m (1)Ann — (2)Mary Hollingsworth Col SC
Wm.: b 4- -1754 d 6- -1821 m Huldah Cook Mar CT
Wm.: b 1734 d 1785 m (1)Sarah Canley (2)Mary — Mar Mstr MD
Wm.: b 1757 d 1807 m Mrs Elizabeth Woodall Jury Pvt MD
Wm., Sr.: b 1714 d 3- -1795 m Elizabeth Reeves PS MD
Wm., Jr.: b 1757 d 1815 m Catharine Boarman Adj MD
Wm.: b 12-18-1751 d p. 1790 m Martha Rowe Pvt Mte MA
Wm.: b c. 1745 d c. 1789 m Mehitabel Whittemore Mstr MA
Wm.: b 1718 d 9-20-1802 m (1)Mary Papillion (2)Mrs Mary (Bridgham) Logan Dr MA
Wm.: b 8-6-1743 d 3-2-1805 m Abiel Collins Dr MA
Wm.: b 1734 d 2-3-1812 m Mary Smith Pvt PS NH
Wm.: b 1-20-1763 d 11-27-1835 m Agnes Carruthers Pvt NC ★
Wm.: b c. 1726 d p. 1814 m Celia — Pvt NC
Wm.: b 1741 d 1800 m (2)Rachael Roe Pvt PS NC
Wm.: b 12-31-1736 d 4-12-1815 m Ann Foulke PS PA
Wm.: b c. 1760 d 1812 m Eleanor Booth Cpl SC
Wm.: b c. 1755 d 10-27-1828 m Mary Loftin Pvt SC
Wm.: b 2-1-1741 d 5-3-1835 m Keziah Thomas Cpl VA
Wm.: b 1740 d p. 1783 m Ann Upton Cpl VA
Wm.: b 1758 d 1-28-1828 m Margaret Marshall Pvt VA ★
Wm.: b 1730 d 1784-1795 m (1)Mary Woodson (2)Joice — PS VA
Winslow: b 1763 d 11-7-1813 m Abigail Delano Pvt MA
Zadock: b 4-23-1734 d 12-20-1810 m Averick Standish Pvt MA

THOMASSON,

Wm. P: b 2-4-1763 d 1-31-1818 m Mary — Pvt NC W★

THOMES, (includes THOMBS, THOME & THOMS)

Charles: b 2-23-1750 d 11-25-1833 m Anna Gray Pvt MA ★
Ebenezer Scot: b 1758-60 d 1829/30 m Mary Plummer Pvt MA
John: b — d p. 1791 m Anna Maria Reiss PS CS PA
Joseph: b 1758 d 1833 m (1)Nancy Scott (2)Abigail — Cpl MA
Joseph: b 1760 d 5-13-1835 m Elizabeth Austin Pvt MA

THOMPSON, (includes THAMASON, THOMASON, THOMASSON, THOMSON & TOMSON)

Aaron: b 3-20-1759 d p. 1793 m Annis Martin Pvt CT
Abel, Sr.: b 2-2-1717 d 5-14-1798 m (1)Comfort Porter (2)Mary Merwin PS CT
Abel: b 5-26-1755 d 6-19-1811 m Sarah Martin Pvt MA
Abijah: b 4-11-1739 d 1-11-1811 m (1)Esther Snow (2)Abigail Wyman (3)Sarah (Stanley) Burlt Armr MA
Abner: b c. 1740 d 7- -1815 m Mary Ross Pvt NJ
Abner: b 4- -1761 d 3-7-1839 m Mary Whipple Pvt RI
Abraham: b 7-15-1752 d 7-4-1822 m Sarah Blackman Pvt CT ★
Alexander: b 8-27-1757 d 2-23-1820 m Lydia Wildes Pvt MA
Alexander: b 5-17-1758 d 10- -1830 m (1)Hannah Baker (2)Mrs Cushman Pvt MA
Alexander: b c. 1722 d 2-26-1800 m Elizabeth Edmondston 2Lt PA
Alexander: b 9-3-1758 d 9-25-1840 m Sarah Scroggs Pvt PA ★
Alexander: b 3-14-1759 d 9-16-1843 m (1)Ann Scott (2)Elizabeth Duncan Lt PA
Alexander: b 1739 d 1815 m Elizabeth Hodge Pvt GA
Alexander: b 1760 d p. 1794 m Lucy Fontaine Pvt SC
Alexander Ramsey: b 8-17-1759 d 9-28-1809 m Abigail Amelia DeHart 2Lt NY
Alpheus: b 1-12-1758 d p. 1785 m Beulah Blodgett Pvt MA
Amherst: b 5-20-1762 d 5-21-1858 m Sarah Clark Pvt MA
Amos: b 9-3-1749 d 6-6-1835 m Hannah Wooster Pvt MA
Anderson: b 9-4-1755 d 1- -1836 m Anne C Anderson 2Lt VA ★
Andrew 3d: b 5-29-1739 d 8-17-1782 m Grace Nicholson Pvt NJ
Andrew: b 6-15-1728 d 8-21-1804 m Margaret Maxwell Capt NY
Andrew: b 1767 d 1819 m Mary McBride PS SC
Andrew: b 1750 d p. 1839 m Anne — Ens CS VA
Andrew: b c. 1753 d p. 1827 m Elizabeth — Sol VA
Anthony: b 3-19-1759 d 5-22-1834 m Rachel Handley Sgt PA ★
Anthony: b c. 1735 d 1794 m Ann Bibb PS VA
Archibald: b 1749 d 7-27-1777 m Sally Smith Pvt NY
Archibald: b 1-24-1740 d 11-1-1779 m Hannah Bartholomew Col PA
Archibald: b 6-24-1755 d a. 1803 m Ann Andrews Pvt PA
Archibald: b 9-3-1760 d 9-5-1833 m Mary McBride Sol SC
Archibald: b 6-6-1763 d 8-4-1846 m Rebecca Peery Grd VA
Asa: b 5-14-1743 d 1783 m Esther Keith Pvt MA
Asa: b 1-25-1764 d p. 10-2-1841 m Diana Quarles Pvt NC
Benajah: b — d 1780 m Prudence — Capt NJ
Benjamin, Sr.: b c. 1725-30 d 5-12-1796 m Ann — Sol GA
Benjamin, Jr.: b 1758 d 1841 m Lustacia — Pvt GA
Benjamin: b 3-30-1764 d 9-30-1851 m Mary Bourne Pvt MA
Benjamin: b 9-20-1735 d — m Mary Thompson Pvt PA
Benjamin: b 1751 d 1845 m Abigail Whitney Pvt NH
Benjamin: b 5-22-1753 d 2-6-1839 m Elizabeth Lord Pvt NH ★
Benjamin: b 9-13-1757 d 10-13-1830 m Melicent Burnet OrdlSgt NJ W★
Benjamin: b 1749 d 1795 m Sarah — Pvt NC
Bennett: b c. 1758 d c. 1828 m (1)Margaret — (2)Rhuame Curtis Pvt MD
Caleb: b 11-4-1712 d 1-19-1787 m Argail Crossman Pvt MA
Caleb: b 10-18-1752 d 2-9-1821 m Mary Perkins Pvt MA

Caleb: b 11-7-1758 d 11-16-1830 m Mehitabel Knowles Pvt MA
Caleb: b 2-24-1732 d p. 12-4-1809 m (1)Lydia Hoskins (2)Mrs
    Dorothy Curtis Reynolds Sol NY
Charles: b 4-14-1748 d 5-1-1803 m Sarah Childs Chp RI
Charles: b c. 1735 d 1811 m Sarah Thompson Pvt NC
Cornelius: b 8-2-1756 d 3-28-1835 m (1)Judith Browne (2)Peggy
    Thomas Mstr Pvt MA ★
Cornelius: b c. 1745 d 12- -1813 m — Pvt PA
Daniel: b 1-28-1758 d 5-19-1799 m Lydia Mills Pvt CT
Daniel: b 1725 d 2-1-1811 m Hannah — Pvt MA
Daniel: b 3-9-1734 d 4-19-1755 m Phebe Snow MM MA
Daniel: b 1737 d p. 1790 m Sarah Linscott Sol MA
Daniel: b c. 1755 d p. 1800 m Euphemia Badgley Pvt NJ
Daniel: b 3- -1754 d 3-3-1835 m Elizabeth — Pvt NY
Daniel: b 1731 d 2-27-1815 m Ann Bucher Pvt PA
Daniel: b 1755 d 1835 m Sarah Blundon Pvt VA
David, Jr.: b 12-3-1749 d 8-4-1817 m Sarah Curtis Capt CT
David: b 4-20-1751 d 7-24-1828 m Jane Wright Sgt CT ★
David: b 5-28-1729 d 9-19-1798 m Priscilla Chesebrough Leeds
    PS CT
David: b 5- -1766 d 1847 m Sally Fisk Drm CT
David: b 1755 d 1795 m (2)Frances Aiken Dr DE
David, Jr.: b 1-14-1736 d 8-5-1836 m Sarah Osgood Pvt MA
David: b 3-21-1740 d 10-1-1819 m (1)Lucy Blake (2)Eunice —
    Pvt MA
David: b 10-4-1737 d 12-28-1824 m Hannah Cary Pvt NJ
David: b 10-6-1758 d 7-4-1840 m (1)Frances Longmire (2)Nancy
    Sojourner Sol VA
David: b c. 1763 d p. 1804 m Elizabeth Brockman Pvt VA
Ebenezer: b 3-11-1726 d 9-10-1813 m Mary Wright Pvt MA
Ebenezer: b 10-27-1751 d 1800 m Sarah Aplin Pvt NH
Ebenezer: b 3-5-1737 d 8-14-1802 m Mary Torr PS NH
Ebenezer: b 1-15-1735 d 12-10-1805 m Elizabeth Kinnicutt Maj RI
Edward: b 5-7-1741 d 1810 m (1)Hannah Cook (2)Mary Aldrich
    (3)Urana Paine Mowry (4)Thamer Allen (5)Sarah Harris LCol RI
Elias: b 11-14-1708 d c. 1780 m Thankful Stanton PS RI
Elihu: b 9-5-1741 d p. 1784 m Desire Palmer Ens CT
Elijah: b 12-16-1751 d 10-8-1825 m Mabel Alling Cpl CT
Elijah: b 2-8-1762 d 12-14-1846 m Keziah Tucker Fif Pvt MA
Elisha: b 10-23-1729 d 2-24-1812 m Dorcas Wright Sol PS CS CT
Epaphras: b 1756 d p. 1832 m Margaret Horner Pvt CT ★
Francis: b 3-15-1735 d 12-17-1798 m (1)Rebecca Snow (2)Mary
    Bumpus Sgt MA
Francis: b 1763 d 7-15-1827 m (1)Jemima Parker (2)Achsa Lincoln
    Pvt MA
Frederick: b 9-16-1763 d 4-24-1842 m (1)Nancy Coker (2)Frances
    Mitchell Pvt NC ★
George: b 1753 d 1826 m Sally Bunker Pvt MA
George: b 1719 d 1-17-1782 m Elizabeth (Wells) Yelverton Capt NY
George: b 1763 d 11-28-1849 m Mrs Smythe Pvt Drm NC ★
George: b 1750 d 12-8-1776 m Sarah Taggart Pvt PA
George: b 2-12-1748 d 3- -1834 m Rebecca Burton Maj ADC VA ★
Gideon: b 1750-60 d 8-2-1831 m Hannah Wooley Pvt NY
Gideon: b 1764 d 1841 m (1)Jane Vance (2)Nancy Gallaher Pvt NC
Hambleton: b c. 1750 d p. 8-23-1803 m Hannah — Sol NJ
Hezekiah: b 1735 d 3- -1803 m Rebecca Judson PS CT
Hezekiah: b 1740 d a. 7-4-1796 m (1)Jane Ross (2)Jane
    Woodruff Pvt Wgn NJ
Hiram: b 5-17-1743 d 1-15-1812 m Bridget Snow Pvt MA
Hugh: b 9-15-1763 d 2-13-1843 m (1)Jane Miller (2)Mrs Lamb Pvt
    MA
Hugh: b c. 1735 d p. 1798 m Margaret Keen PS NH
Hugh: b 5-9-1748 d 5-9-1812 m Jane Boyd Sgt PA
Hugh: b 1720 d 9- -1797 m Sarah — Pvt PA
Hugh: b c. 1740 d p. 1781 m — Pvt PA
Isaac: b 2-1-1746 d 12-21-1819 m Lucy Sturtevant Pvt MA
Isaac: b 5-29-1749 d 12-6-1782 m Huldah Sturtevant Pvt MA
Isaac: b 1-18-1743 d 1-30-1816 m Mary Gardiner Lt NY
Isaac: b 1751 d 4-25-1823 m (1)Martha Larimore (2)Mrs Martha
    Jane (Evans) Wells 1Lt PA ★
Isaiah: b 1753 d 7-28-1791 m Lydia Norton Capt CT
Isham: b c. 1740 d 1795 m Mary Ann Oliver Pvt GA
Jabez: b 7-3-1727 d 9-15-1776 m Sarah Gunn LCol CT
Jabez: b 5-24-1746 d 1-15-1804 m Keziah Wyman Sol MA
Jabez: b 11-19-1759 d 3-31-1835 m Mary Jones Pvt NJ ★
Jacob: b 3-28-1738 d 11-30-1806 m Freelove Finney Pvt MA
James: b 3-17-1741 d 11-8-1817 m Ruth Benton Lt CT
James: b 1724 d 6-20-1790 m Elizabeth McKnight Pvt CT
James: b1743 d 4-10-1819 m Rachel (Enos) Hovey Pvt CT
James: b 1753 d 7-8-1844 m Elizabeth Brumbley Pvt CT ★
James: b 5-16-1747 d 9-16-1818 m Anna Perry Sgt MD
James: b 3-24-1748 d 12-1-1837 m Elizabeth Davis 2Lt MA ★
James: b — d 3-18-1812 m Mary Vorce Pvt MA
James: b 2- -1707 d 9-22-1891 m (1)Reliance Hinckley (2)Lydia
    (Brown) Harris (3)Mary Higgins PS MA
James, Sr.: b 11-14-1696 d 5-25-1776 m Mary Hancock PS MA
James, Jr.: b 1753/4 d 10-28-1819 m Mary Sellon Pvt MA
James, Jr.: b 5-7-1724 d — m Mary Hitchcock Pvt MA
James: b 11-14-1758 d p. 1824 m Isabella Bean Pvt NH ★
James: b 1748 d 2-27-1804 m Sarah Falconer QM NY
James: b c. 1740 d p. 1778 m Elizabeth Gill Pvt NY
James: b c. 1735 d 3- -1792 m Elizabeth Stump PS NC
James: b 1-27-1755 d 1834 m Lucy Ivey Pvt NC ★

James: b 12-18-1752 d 5-6-1832 m Rachel Baldwin Pvt NC
James: b 11-25-1755 d 1838 m Mildred Williams Pvt NC
James: b 2- -1745 d 1807 m Lydia Bailey Col PA
James: b a. 1757 d p. 1803 m — Patterson QM PA
James: b c. 1726 d p. 10-31-1805 m (2)Elizabeth — Pvt PA
James: b 1730 d 1817 m Mary Henry Pvt PA
James: b c. 1750 d p. 1835 m Susannah Skelton Pvt PA
James: b 1757 d 8-9-1825 m Elizabeth — Pvt PA ★
James: b c. 1758 d 8-10-1805 m Mary Carmichael Pvt PA
James: b 2-20-1758 d 10-8-1835 m Mary Ann Jackson Sol PS PA
James: b c. 1745 d p. 1790 m Elizabeth Ball LCol PS SC
James: b c. 1738 d p. 1809 m Sarah Thompson Pvt VA
James: b 5-5-1742 d 9-20-1803 m (1)Nancy Larkin (2)Phoebe —
    Capt VA
James: b a. 1749 d 1800-1811 m Catherine Shelby Capt VA
James: b 5-11-1745 d 11-14-1812 m Nancy Townsend Lt VA
James: b 1756 d 1840 m (1)Rebecca Gay (2)Elizabeth Shingtafer
    Ens CS VA
James: b 1750 d 4-26-1825 m Ruth Peyton CS Mil KY
James: b 1760 d 12-11-1843 m Senior Temperance Moonye Pvt VA ★
James: b 1739 d 2- -1812 m Mary Ann Farrow PS VA
James Hampden: b — d 3-3-1795 m Elizabeth Martha Trezevant
    PS SC
Jeduthan: b a. 1745 d 7-7-1779 m Thankful Beardsley Pvt CT
Jesse: b 2-20-1757 d 1833 m Elizabeth Pugley Lt NY
Jesse: b c. 1754 d c. 1819 m Nancy Clarke Pvt VA
Job: b 11-24-1728 d p. 3-9-1790 m Rhoda Crane Pvt CT
Joel: b 10-23-1753 d 5-1-1841 m Martha Cottom Sgt MA
Joel: b 10-3-1760 d 2-8-1843 m (1)Catherine Root (3)Amy Weeks
    Pvt NY ★
John: b 11-15-1743 d 4-24-1801 m Rebeckah Curtis Pvt CT
John: b 10-9-1764 d 12-30-1840 m Mary — Trm CT
John: b 2-27-1757 d 8-8-1832 m Pamelia Cowles Pvt CT ★
John: b 7-17-1763 d 7-16-1836 m Alice Benjamin Pvt CT ★
John: b 4-7-1753 d 9-10-1838 m Dorcas (Smith) Andrews Cpl CT ★
John: b 4-27-1753 d 1833 m Abigail — Cpl CT ★
John: b 4-21-1762 d 6-1-1847 m (1)Katherine Hanford Smith
    (2)Elizabeth Raymond (3)Mrs Mary Johnson Fif CT ★
John: b 1727 d 1790 m (1)Mary Sands (2)Letitia McKean PS DE
John: b — d p. 1780 m Prudence Clark Capt MA
John: b 9-3-1753 d 10-16-1823 m Juda Merritt Sgt MA
John: b 10-23-1755 d 1830 m Janet Allen Sgt MA
John: b 1751 d p. 1792 m Margaret Striker Drm MA
John: b 6- -1741 d c. 1808 m (1)Lucy Sabin (2)Mrs Sarah Guild
    Pvt NH
John: b 7-17-1746 d 4- -1822 m Jane Stryker 1Lt NJ
John: b 3-20-1748 d 11- -1823 m Fanny McFarland Capt NY
John: b — d p. 1783 m — Sgt NY
John: b c. 1746 d c. 1820 m Sophia — Pvt NY ★
John: b 1758-61 d 6-25-1841 m Rhoda Hull Pvt NY ★
John: b 1751 d 1830 m Polly Mosher Pvt NY ★
John: b c. 1747 d 1831 m Eleanor Dimond Cpl NC
John: b 1-12-1760 d 5-28-1813 m Mary Knapp Pvt NY
John: b 1722 d p. 11-3-1784 m Rachel Peacock Pvt NC
John: b 1749 d 1811 m Susannah Lea PS NC
John: b c. 1720 d c. 1827 m Grizell Ellis Sol NC
John: b 8-17-1754 d p. 1803 m (1)Catherine Arkley (2)Mrs Mary
    Fine Capt PA
John: b 11-16-1726 d 7-18-1799 m Mary Huston Ens PA
John: b c. 1720 d 1779 m (1) — Greenleaf (2)— Slocum (3)Sarah
    Patterson Pvt PA
John: b 11-26-1751 d p. 1808 m Abigail — Pvt PA
John: b 12- -1755 d 7-23-1828 m Rebecca Edwards Powell Pvt PA
John: b 12-17-1761 d 1-10-1854 m Jane Reed Pvt PA
John: b 2-28-1761 d 11-24-1840 m Margaret Mitchell Pvt PA ★
John: b — d 1801 m — CS PA
John: b 4-15-1730 d 6-9-1778 m Juda Bodine PS PA
John: b 1744 d c. 1781 m Margaret Ann Wallace Capt SC
John: b 1750 d 1826 m Margaret Baldridge Pvt SC
John: b 1756 d 7-1-1833 m Susan Burton Lt VA ★
John: b 1753 d 1-2-1846 m Mary McCraw Pvt VA ★
John: b 2-27-1764 d 7-16-1850 m (1)Louise Bowen (2)Mary Walker
    Pvt VA
John: b 1762 d 1829 m Sarah McMullan Pvt VA
John: b 1759 d 1826 m Mary Wilson Pvt VA ★
John: b1758/9 d 3-27-1843 m Winney Brickey Pvt VA ★
John: b 1731 d p. 12-3-1810 m Mary — Pvt VA
John, Sr.: b — d p. 1-5-1791 m Margaret — PS VA
Jonathan: b 5-23-1727 d 11-3-1824 m Elizabeth Warriner 1Lt MA
Jonathan: b 9-6-1731 d 1-5-1793 m Jemima Baxter Pvt MA
Jonathan: b 5-1-1748 d 10-5-1825 m Lucy McIntyre Pvt MA ★
Jonathan: b 3-3-1750 d 1845 m Prudence Osgood Pvt MA
Jonathan: b 4-26-1760 d 11-20-1836 m Mary Richardson Pvt Fif
    MA ★
Jonathan: b 1-23-1758 d 12-9-1803 m Abigail Runnels Pvt NH
Jonathan: b — d 1803 m (2)Elizabeth Jewell Pvt NH
Jonathan: b 1718 d 1792 m Susannah (Runnells) Thompson PS NH
Jonathan: b 12-22-1734 d 12-20-1817 m (1)Abigail Haines
    (2)Rhoda (Crane) Pierson Lt NJ
Jonathan: b 10-25-1710 d 6-5-1786 m Mary Woodhull Pvt PS NY
Jonathan: b c. 1740 m Hannah (Brooks) Thompson Pvt NY
Joseph: b 1-31-1730-1 d p. 3-5-1791 m Lydia Gilbert Col CT
Joseph: b 8-6-1755 d 12-29-1829 m Ruby Rust Pvt CT

THOMPSON, contd.
Joseph: b *c.* 1753 d *p.* 12-9-1809 m Elizabeth Middleton PS MD
Joseph: b 3-25-1733 d 1795 m Abigail Sherman LCol MA
Joseph: b *c.* 1720 d 4-9-1803 m Jeannette McClellan Pvt MA
Joseph: b 3-6-1722 d *p.* 1777 m Elizabeth Andrews Pvt MA
Joseph: b 2-2-1755 d 5-26-1827 m Happy Proctor Pvt MA
Joseph: b 8-11-1765 d 9-13-1835 m Olive Junkins Pvt MA ★
Joseph: b 11-29-1737 d 2-6-1805 m Hannah Chesley PS NH
Joseph: b 12-11-1743 d 8-5-1808 m Sarah Conover Pvt NJ
Joseph: b *c.* 1765 d *p.* 12-27-1851 m — Sol NC
Joseph, Sr.: b 1730 d 1793 m Elizabeth — Sol PA
Joseph, Jr.: b 1755 d 1819 m Rachel — Pvt PA
Joseph: b 1765 d 7-1-1802 m Jane Dill Pvt SC
Joseph: b 1747 d *p.* 2-25-1810 m Mary M. Jolly PS SC
Joseph: b 1763 d 4-19-1843 m Susanna (Thompson) Pvt VA ★
Joshua: b 1758 d 6-20-1829 m Hannah Catlin Pvt CT W★
Joshua: b 2-2-1713 d 1795 m Sarah Smith Pvt NJ
Joshua, Jr.: b 6-25-1749 d 1791-1800 m Mary Cobb Pvt RI
Josiah: b *c.* 1737 d *c.* 1802 m Mary Swann Lt VA
Lawrence: b 1755 d 1863 m Martha — Sgt NC ★
Leonard: b 1750 d 1810 m Emma Napier 2Lt VA
Levi: b 9-3-1755 d 12-12-1813 m Lucy Woodford Sgt CT
Loring: b 4-25-1756 d *p.* 1795 m (1)Mary Whiten (2)Elizabeth Hall Swinnerton (3)Rachel Whitten Pvt NH
Lydia Punderson : b *c.* 1710 d 1802 m Gideon Thompson PS CT
Mark: b1739/40 d 12-14-1803 m Anne Breckenridge Col NJ
Mathew: b 7- -1763 d 3-4-1828 m Betsey Collins Pvt CT ★
Matthew: b 1746 d 1803 m (2)Rachel Allen Pvt PS SC
Matthew: b1719/20 d 9-30-1787 m Mary — PS CT
Moses: b 12-23-1728 d 6-24-1794 m Keziah Partridge Lt MA
Moses: b 7-1-1762 d 12-2-1858 m Abigail Sampson Pvt MA
Moses: b 1734 d 1819 m Jane Page Pvt NH
Moses: b 9- -1749 d 10-11-1816 m (1)Mehitable Crockett (2)— Piper Norris PS NH
Moses: b 11-3-1758 d *c.* 1827 m Sarah Winans Sgt NJ
Moses: b *c.* 1764 d 7-14-1809 m (1)Esther Bonnell (2)Polly Winans Pvt Tms NJ
Moses: b 10-27-1754 d 5-20-1816 m (1)Nancy Culbertson (2)Lydia Adams Pvt PA
Nathan: b 1726 d 9-4-1804 m Hannah Dodge Pvt CT
Nathan: b 1712-3 d 10-22-1799 m Hannah Lewis Pvt CT
Nathan: b1762/3 d 8-14-1826 m Mary Cutler Pvt MA
Nathaniel: b 3-15-1752 d 9-9-1826 m Anna — Sgt CT ★
Nathaniel: b 9-13-1750 d 1-31-1833 m Hannah Thomas Pvt MA
Nathaniel: b 5-29-1726 d 6- -1785 m Elizabeth Stevens PS NH
Nelson Anderson: b 1757 d 2-13-1798 m Sarah Kerr Pvt VA
Noah: b 3-20-1747 d 3-5-1813 m Priscilla Holmes Pvt MA
Peter: b 11-18-1735 d 1-25-1801 m Elizabeth Badger Pvt MA
Peter: b 1756 d 12-19-1845 m Susannah — Pvt NH ★
Peter: b 7-3-1746 d 4-17-1823 m Mary Potts Sol NC
Phillip Rootes: b 3-26-1760 d 7-27-1837 m (1)Susanna Davenport (2)Sarah Slaughter PS VA
Phinehas: b 1740 d 3-6-1815 m Martha Willard Pvt CS MA
Price: b 3-22-1755 d 3-1-1842 m (1)Molly Thompson (2)Martha Morrison Cpl NJ ★
Reuben: b 1-11-1765 d 12-31-1855 m Rachel Chambers Sol GA
Reuben: b 9-5-1762 d 6-16-1844 m Chloe Dodge Pvt Fif MA ★
Richard: b 3-7-1749 d 10-25-1806 m (1)Rebecca Eaton (2)Rachel Barnes Pvt NH
Richard: b *c.* 1742 d *p.* 9-16-1822 m Margaret — Sol NC VA
Richard: b 1741 d 1836 m Rebecca Lee Mus VA
Robert: b — d *a.* 1-3-1807 m Elizabeth — PS MD
Robert: b 8-28-1748 d 5-6-1824 m Hannah Berry Pvt MA
Robert: b *a.* 1756 d *p.* 1782 m Margaret Smith Pvt PS NH
Robert: b 6- -1759 d 1-27-1848 m (2)Susan Hue Pvt NJ Heirs ★
Robert: b 1742 d 6-15-1818 m Mary Jackson Sol NY
Robert: b *c.* 1750 d 2- -1839 m Ruth McQuistain Pvt NC
Robert: b 9-3-1760 d *p.* 1840 m — Sgt PA ★
Robert: b *c.* 1745 d *p.* 4-1-1823 m Sarah Robison Pvt PA
Robert: b *c.* 1760 d 12- -1838 m Jane — Pvt PA
Robert: b 1759 d 1809 m Margaret McElhaney Pvt PA
Robert: b -1722 d 11-8-1804 m Hannah (Delaplaine) Simpson PS PA
Robert: b 1757 d 6-29-1831 m Sarah Watkins Pvt VA ★
Roger: b 12-13-1744 d *p.* 1791 m Elizabeth — Pvt PS NH
Roger: b 12-5-1750 d 12-30-1838 m Mary White Pvt VA ★
Rufus: b 1765 d 1-6-1841 m Sarah Burley Pvt CT
Samuel: b 1730 d 1-5-1793 m Abigail Eldredge Capt CS CT
Samuel: b 8-1-1737 d 2-14-1817 m Desire Moulthrop Sgt CT
Samuel: b *c.* 1745 d 8-2-1798 m Mary Baker Rogers Pvt CT
Samuel: b 1691 d 2-23-1782 m Elizabeth McKinney PS CT
Samuel: b 3-22-1735 d 5-16-1797 m Abial Purington BG MA
Samuel: b 10-13-1731 d 8-17-1820 m (1)Abigail Tidd (2)Lydia Jones (3)Esther Wyman Pvt MA
Samuel: b 3-8-1755 d 11-4-1837 m Sarah Hewins Pvt MA ★
Samuel: b 1756 d 6-5-1812 m Jane Bray Pvt Slr MA
Samuel: b 6-30-1754 d 12-13-1833 m Mary Reed Pvt MA
Samuel: b 10-2-1738 d 9-17-1811 m (1)Phebe Satterley (2)Ruth Smith Capt NY
Samuel: b 1744 d 8-13-1808 m Elizabeth — 1Lt NY
Samuel: b 6-23-1750 d 10-24-1837 m Elizabeth Debow Pvt NC ★
Samuel, Sr.: b 1722 d 5-29-1799 m Sarah Holcomb PS NY

Samuel, Jr.: b 1753 d 12-6-1815 m (2)Mary Barnet (3)Rebecca — Pvt NY
Samuel: b 1746 d *p.* 4-10-1800 m Mary — PS PA
Samuel: b 1754 d 1-8-1839 m Martha Hoosong Sgt VA NC ★
Samuel: b 1734 d *p.* 1784 m Nancy A. Jennings Capt VA
Samuel: b — d *a.* 1-25-1791 m Susanna Grayson Sol PS VA
Sanford: b 1746 d 11- -1819 m Sarah Camp 1Lt MA
Seth: b 5-28-1747 d 3-5-1828 m Elizabeth Thompson Pvt NH
Seth: b 6-18-1760 d 10-23-1828 m Mary Waterman Pvt NH ★
Silas: b 3-16-1735 d 4-25-1806 m Abigail Bancroft PS NH
Stanley: b 1758 d 7-3-1833 m Susanna Cable Pvt NY ★
Stephen: b 12-25-1723 d 11-10-1808 m (1)Hannah Rowe (2)Mary Foote Pvt CT
Stephen, Sr.: b 4-20-1734 d 2-25-1823 m Mary Walter Pvt PS CT
Stephen: b 2-13-1764 d 9-1-1859 m Phebe Chapin Pvt MA
Stephen: b 1750 d *c.* m Elizabeth — Pvt VA
Stith: b *c.* 1738 d *p.* 11-5-1795 m (1) — Reeves (2)Elizabeth Parks Lt VA
Swan: b *c.* 1745 d 1801 m Susannah — Pvt NC
Thaddeus: b 3-5-1762 d 6-16-1829 m (1)Hannah Perkins (2)Rhoda Sperry Bbd CT
Thaddeus: b 7-2-1751 d *p.* 1823 m Betty Whitlock Dr MA ★
Theopholis: b 12-7-1759 d 4-10-1826 m Mary Newcome Sol NC
Thomas: b 8-4-1719 d 3-10-1802 m Elizabeth Mallory PS CT
Thomas: b 10-21-1741 d *p.* 1812 m Mehitabel Hinckley Capt MA
Thomas: b 1742 d 2-21-1811 m (1)Elizabeth Frye (2)Sarah Scott Pvt MA
Thomas: b 5-27-1762 d 3-3-1827 m Ruhama Barrows Pvt MA W★
Thomas: b 8-4-1749 d 4-5-1834 m Jane Forman Pvt NJ
Thomas: b 1741 d 10-24-1823 m Elizabeth Berry Pvt NY
Thomas: b 6-7-1762 d 3-14-1848 m (1)Experience Hopkins (2)Ruhama Grandy Drm Pvt CT ★
Thomas: b *c.* 1750 d *p.* 3- -1818 m — PS NC
Thomas: b *a.* 1755 d 2-17-1817 m Mary Harper Lt PA
Thomas: b 1754 d 1823 m Jane Fifer Pvt PA
Thomas: b 5-6-1721 d 1782 m Martha Finley PS PA
Thomas: b 1734 d 10-31-1825 m Mary Anne — Pvt VA
Thomas: b *c.* 1755 d *p.* 1826 m (1)Elizabeth — (2)Jemima Tracy Pvt VA
Thomas A.: b *c.* 1750 d *p.* 1829 m Elizabeth — Sol MD
Timothy: b 1-14-1750 d 2-4-1834 m Mary Frothingham Sgt MA
Timothy: b 5-15-1735 d 4-20-1778 m Mrs Rachel Draper PS NH
Waddy, Sr.: b 1730 d 1801 m (1)Elizabeth Anderson (2)Mary (Lewis) Cobb PS VA
Waddy, Jr.: b 1759 d *p.* 6-29-1827 m (1)Elizabeth Anderson (2)Susan Ormsby Capt VA
Wm.: b 10-29-1742 d 4-27-1777 m Mehitabel Ufford PS CT
Wm.: b *c.* 1743 d 11-10-1809 m Polly Fassett Pvt DE
Wm.: b *c.* 1717 d 10-13-1811 m Mary Wells Sol GA
Wm., Jr.: b 7-24-1760 d — m Abigail Cruft Mar Lt MA
Wm.: b 2-15-1748 d 3-14-1816 m Deborah Sturtevant Lt MA
Wm.: b *c.* 1752 d *c.* 1827 m Anna Wood Sgt MA ★
Wm.: b 10-19-1723 d 5- -1808 m (1)Abigail Jones (2)Mary Baldwin CS MA
Wm.: b 1728 d 9-7-1811 m Ann Thompson PS MA
Wm.: b *c.* 1750 d 1- -1827 m Betsey Ayer PS Cpl NH
Wm.: b 6-30-1754 d 10- -1830 m Dorcas Eaton Pvt NH
Wm.: b 1758 d 5-26-1797 m Mary Prescott Pvt NH
Wm.: b 1722 d — m Catharine Mason PS NH
Wm.: b 6-15-1746 d 11-24-1831 m Mary DeKay Ens NY
Wm.: b 1730 d *p.* 1790 m Mary — Pvt PS NY
Wm.: b 7-29-1756 2-29-1836 m Submit Hudson Pvt NY
Wm.: b 5-10-1749 d 1792 m Martha Drake PS NY
Wm.: b 1727 d 1788 m Hannah — 2Lt NC
Wm.: b *a.* 1765 d 1813 m Milbrey — Sol NC
Wm.: b *c.* 1759 d *a.* 12-31-1808 m Mary — Sol NC
Wm.: b 1736 d 9-3-1781 m Catharine Ross BG PA
Wm.: b 1-2-1752 d 1-3-1813 m Jane Mitchell Capt PA
Wm.: b *a.* 1753 d *p.* 1790 m Mary Reed Capt PA
Wm.: b — d *p.* 1785 m Sarah Fall Lt PA
Wm.: b 1721 d 1800 m Jane Hanna Cpl PA
Wm.: b 1751 d 1797 m Betsey — Pvt PA
Wm.: b *c.* 1752-4 d — m Sarah — Pvt PA
Wm.: b 1757 d 8-16-1815 m Elizabeth Huston PS PA
Wm., Sr.: b *c.* 1723 d *c.* 1812 m — PS PA
Wm., Jr.: b 1746 d *c.* 1836 m Elizabeth Turner PS PA
Wm.: b 9-5-1746 d *p.* 1796 m Hannah Lewis Pvt RI
Wm.: b 1-16-1727 d 11-22-1796 m Eugenia Russell Col SC
Wm.: b 1760 d 2-5-1811 m Mary Tabor Sgt SC ★
Wm.: b 1762 d 1842 m Elizabeth Martin Pvt SC
Wm.: b 1750 d 1830 m Mary Perry Capt VA
Wm.: b 1727 d 4-27-1778 m Anne Rodes Ens VA
Wm.: b 1722 d 12- -1798 m (1)Margaret — (2)Lydia Ward Lt VA
Wm.: b 1749 d 1797 m Frances Mills Capt VA
Wm.: b 3- -1751 d 1844 m Betsey — Pvt VA
Wm.: b *a.* 1739 d *p.* 3-31-1780 m Rachel Coleman Sgt PS VA
Wm.: b 1760 d 1838 m Mary Shirley Pvt VA
Wm.: b *c.* 1722 d 1815 m Rachel Allen Sol VA
Zachariah: b *c.* 1760 d *a.* 2-3-1824 m Eleanor Davis Sol PS MD
Zebadiah: b 12-15-1758 d 11-4-1840 m Phebe Curtis Pvt MA

THORNAL,
Israel: b 1745 d 5-19-1819 m Rachael Manning Pvt NJ

THORNBURGH, (includes THORNBERRY, THORNBOROUGH, THORNBROUGH, THORNBURG & THORNBURY)
Benjamin: b c. 1735 d a. 1-22-1795 m Mary Brooks PS VA
John: b c. 1734 d a. 9-23-1799 m Elizabeth — Pvt VA
Joseph: b 7-22-1739 d 1809 m Sarah Clayton Pvt PA
Joseph: b 1752 d 1821 m Rebecca Miller LCol PA
Thomas: b 9-9-1752 d 5-10-1793 m (1)Ruth Hunt (2)Mrs Prudence Collins Lt VA
Walter H.: b 11-15-1782 d 1852 m Mary Baldwin PS NC

THORNDIKE,
Ebenezer: b 7-9-1719 d 2-4-1819 m Lydia Herrick 1Lt PS MA
Israel: b 4-30-1755 d 3-8-1867 m (1)Mercy Trask (2)Anna Dodge (3)Anne Dickey NCapt MA
Joshua: b 3-12-1755 d 12-25-1823 m Hannah Nutting Pvt MA W★
Larkin: b 6-22-1730 d 12-19-1797 m Ruth Woodbury Col MA
Robert: b 4-22-1761 d 1-20-1843 m Abagail Hadley Fif Smn ME ★

THORNE, (includes THORN)
Benjamin: b 3-19-1755 d 4-1-1819 m Frances Estes Pvt NY
Edward: b c. 1735 d 1805 m Hannah Tripp 2Lt NY
George: b 3-11-1746 d 9-17-1794 m Christiana Miller Pvt PA
James: b 1734 d 1824 m Mary Cocks Pvt NY
John: b 5-18-1736 d 9- -1807 m — PS NH
John: b 5-4-1730 d 8-22-1807 m Diadamia Ivins PS NJ
John: b 1750 d 1800 m Martha — Sol VA
Joseph: b 1730 d 11-19-1819 m Isabella Cheeseman Capt NJ
Nathan: b 7-19-1759 d 4-9-1851 m Elizabeth James Pvt NH
Richard: b a. 1751 d 1816 m Anne — Pvt NJ
Samuel: b 1754 d 8-12-1823 m Helen Van Slyck 2Lt PS NY ★
Thomas: b 1735 d p. 9-9-1815 m Mary Williams PS NC
Wm.: b c. 1747 d p. 8-11-1811 m Leah — PS NC

THORNHILL,
Henry: b 1757 d 1835 m — Pvt VA ★
Jesse: b 10-13-1763 d 1-5-1837 m Elizabeth Stevens Pvt VA ★
John: b 1754 d 12- -1778 m Mary Thornhill Pvt VA
Reuben: b 1730 d 1797 m Margaret Thornhill Sol VA
Thomas: b c. 1715 d p. 1785 m Elizabeth Walker PS VA
Wm.: b 1758 d p. 9-4-1839 m — Pvt VA ★

THORNLEY,
Robert: b c. 1745 d 5-5-1805 m Mary R. — Maj PS SC

THORNTON,
Anthony, Sr.: b 11-15-1727 d 1782 m (1)Sarah Taliaferro (2)Susanna Fitzhugh PS SVA
Anthony, Jr.: b 2-1-1748 d 12-21-1828 m Mary Rootes Col VA
Borden: b 3-14-1761 d 2-15-1838 m (1)Phebe Carpenter Chafee (2)Hope Greene Trm RI ★
Daniel: b 11-11-1733 d 7-14-1793 m Susanne Pearce Pvt RI
Dozier: b 4-14-1755 d 9-12-1843 m (1)Lucy Elizabeth Hill (2)Mrs Jane Pulliam Pvt GA
Elizabeth Dozier: b — d a. 1-6-1794 m Thomas Thornton PS VA
Francis: b 1762 d 1819 m Maria Meacham Cnt VA
Francis: b 7-21-1725 d 8-3-1784 m Sarah Fitzhugh PS VA
Francis: b 5-17-1734 d 3- -1795 m Ann Thompson PS VA
Francis: b 8-22-1747 d p. 11-18-1808 m (1) — Lacy (2)Lucy Ligon 2Lt PS VA
George: b 11-18-1752 d 8-30-1853 m (1)Margaret Stanley Lt VA
George Washington: b 12-6-1737 d 4-30-1781 m Mary Alexander Maj PS VA
Gilbert: b 5-23-1732 d 10-8-1802 m Keziah Kitchell Pvt NJ
James: b c. 1761 d p. 1810 m Sarah Jackson Pvt Drm PA
James: b 3-7-1744 d 2-22-1815 m Antje Schermerhorn Pvt NY W★
Jesse: b 1756 d 5-22-1824 m Johannah Hill Pvt NH
John: b c. 1720 d a. 1787 m Elizabeth — PS NC
John: b c. 1730 d 1798 m Ann Reifsneider Cpl PA
John: b 3-1-1734 d 1786 m (1)Sarah Ashburn (2)Sarah Walker Palmer Pvt PA
John: b a. 1749 d 1822 m Jane Augusta Washington Col VA
John: b c. 1764 d 1822 m Polly — Sol VA
Joshua: bpt 5-6-1764 d 7-27-1843 m Hannah Nevins Fif Maj NH
Mark: b 1725 d 1809 m Susannah Dozier Sol VA GA
Mathew: b 1714 d 6-24-1803 m Hannah Jack SDI NH
Presley: b 1736 d 1812 m (2)Mary — Pvt VA '
Presley: b 1760 d 11-5-1811 m Alice Thornton Capt VA
Reuben: b 1758 d 1800 m Prudence Ward Sgt VA
Samuel: b — d p. 1-27-1786 m (1) — (2) — Pvt MA
Samuel: b 1712 d 8-10-1796 m — Pvt SC
Solomon: b c. 1745 d 1809 m Sarah — Pvt GA
Stephen: b 1744 d 2-20-1836 m Lydia Waterman Pvt RI ★
Stephen: b 4-30-1759 d 3-13-1834 m Elizabeth Rogers Pvt RI ★
Sterling Clack: b 8-12-1753 d 8- -1832 m Mrs Mary (Jones) Jones PS VA
Thomas: b 1751 d — m Elizabeth Richardson Pvt NY
Thomas: b 1755 d 1840 m Elizabeth Robertson Pvt NC
Thomas: b 1762 d p. 1789 m Mary Whatley Pvt VA
Wm.: b c. 1755 d 1820 m Diana Griggs Pvt GA
Wm.: b 1742 d 1800 m Martha Stuart Col VA
Wm.: b 1764 d 1842 m Ann — Pvt VA
Wm.: b 12-20-1717 d a. 11-23-1791 m Jane Clack PS VA

THORP, (includes THARP, THARPE & THORPE)
Aaron: b 6-12-1745 d 1819 m Mary Curtis Ens CT
Abner: b 2-22-1731 d 12-4-1812 m Eunice Brown Sol NJ
Abner: b c. 1753 d 3- -1819 m Jerusha Cook Pvt CT
Baker: b 1752 d 6-27-1799 m Elizabeth Wager Pvt NJ
Benjamin: b 1745 d 12- -1814 m Sarah Lyon Pvt NJ
Charles: b 1743 d 4-11-1835 m Elizabeth Depreace Pvt VA ★
Daniel: b 5-30-1761 d 4-10-1838 m Sarah Moorehouse Cpl CT ★
David: bpt 7-4-1714 d c. 1793/4 m (1)Mary — (2)Naomi Williams (3)Rebecca Hall CG CT
Eliphalet: b 2-3-1740 d 9-1-1795 m (1)Eunice Perry (2)Mrs Sarah Ogden Capt PS CT
Eliphalet: b 6-10-1738 d 8-9-1812 m Hannah Lewis Capt MA
Ezekiel: b 12-28-1744 d 1-15-1797 m Nellie Voorheis Pvt NJ
Jacob: b 8-3-1745 d 7-5-1779 m Eunice Bishop Sgt CT
James: b c. 1748 d p. 1791 m Sarah Collins Cpl NC
Jehiel: b 4-27-1746 d 5-11-1828 m Eleanor Burr Ens CT
Joel: b 9-11-1741 d 11-3-1790 m Mary Miles Stanley Pvt CT
John: b 3-15-1746 d c. 1785 m Abigail Gilbert Pvt VA
John: b 4-28-1751 d 3-19-1819 m Hannah Hurin Lt NJ
Paul: b 1748 d 1837 m Isabella — Pvt PA ★
Perry: b 1757 d 11-13-1845 m Margaret Shuck Pvt PA ★
Peter: b 1757 d 10-2-1823 m Jemima Turner Pvt NJ
Reuben: b 1-16-1755 d 2-8-1848 m Hannah Lobdell Pvt NJ ★
Reuben: b 1743 d 11-23-1824 m Hannah Bucklin Pvt RI
Samuel: bpt 5-10-1747 d 3-30-1820 m Huldah Burton Sgt CT
Stephen: b 3-5-1737/8 d 7-15-1807 m Sarah Gould Capt CT
Thomas: b 1756 d c. 10-12-1849 m (1)Sabina Emerson (2)Nabby Barker (3)Mrs Lucy Tufts Sgt MA ★
Thomas: b c. 1752 d 1818 m (1)Elizabeth Holliday (2)Eleanor Jackson PS VA
Timothy: b 1746 d 1829-31 m Alice (Ellis) Bates Pvt CT
Timothy: b 1759 d 1823 m Jennie Worley Ens VA
Vincent A.: b 11-18-1760 d 9-23-1825 m (1) — Rogers (2)Sarah Pierson Pvt SC

THOYTS,
Thomas: b 10-8-1732 d 6-20-1795 m Honor Khan Pvt MA

THRALL,
Benjamin: b 1744 d 1793/4 m Anne — Lt CT
David: b 9-23-1749 d 12-7-1822 m Zulima Denslow Pvt CT
Ezekiel: b 9-30-1742 d p. 1781 m Elizabeth McMarren Pvt CT
Jesse: b 5-7-1765 d 12-16-1843 m Mabel Rose Pvt CT
John: b 7-22-1728 d 1791 m (1)Rebekah Davis (2)Elizabeth — Lt CT
Lemuel: b 2-5-1748/9 d 1-31-1831 m (1)Lydia King (2)Lydia Skinner Cpl CT
Noah: b 4-3-1754 d a. 1-20-1808 m Hannah Fowler Pvt CT
Richard: b 4-23-1753 d p. 1833 m Anne Johnson Pvt MD ★
Samuel, Sr.: b 7-11-1737 d 12-3-1821 m Lucy Winchell QM NY MA
Samuel, Jr.: b 8-31-1760 d 5-8-1815 m Triphosia Cooley Pvt CT

THRASH,
Valentine: b 1749 d 3- -1835 m Barbara Yountz Pvt NC ★

THRASHER,
Bezaleel: b 7-16-1758 d 1-19-1841 m (1)Sarah Woodhouse (2)Elizabeth Curtiss Pvt CT
John: b 1753 d 12-2-1833 m Bathania Stephens Cpl MA ★
John: b 1761 d 6-5-1844 m Susan Barton Pvt NC
John: b 1730 d 1806 m Elizabeth Hooker Pvt PA
Jonathan: b 1761 d 1837 m Nancy Swift Pvt MA
Thomas: b 10-29-1725 d a. 6-26-1804 m Martha Lee — PS MD

THRELDKELD, (includes THREADGILL, THRELKELD & TRAILKILL)
Elijah: b 1744 d 1-20-1798 m Mary (Bronough) Waugh Capt VA
James: b c. 1740 d a. 1814 m (1)Mary — (2)Ann Kelly Pvt VA
John: b a. 1740 d a. 1780 m Nancy Johnson Pvt VA
John: b 11-17-1750 d 9-22-1835 m Mary Cob Pvt VA ★
John: b c. 1725 d p. 1-23-1798 m Margaret — PS VA
Joseph: b 1731 d 1782 m Jane Orme PS MD
Stephen: b 1740 d c. 1792 m Ann Duncan Sol PS VA
Thomas: b 1752 d 1835 m Tabitha Ingram Capt VA

THRESHER,
Aaron: b 8-20-1760 d 1833 m (1)Mercy Bullock (2)Zilpha Hix Pvt MA ★
Ebenezer: b 10-22-1756 d 10-23-1832 m Hannah Blodget Pvt CT ★

THREWITZ, (includes THREEWIRTZ & THREEWITZ)
John: b 1754 d 1842 m Eleanor Fitzpatrick Bgd Maj SC
Llewellyn: b c. 1758 d 1814 m (1)Emily Geiger (2)Catharine Daniel Adj SC

THRIFT,
Charles: b 1753 d 8-13-1826 m Elizabeth Offutt Pvt VA
Isham: b c. 1762 d p. 1805/6 m Mary — PS NC
Wm.: b 1760 d 1821 m Hanna Moffitt Pvt VA

THROCKMORTON,
Albion: b c. 1760 d p. 1808 m Mary Webb Cnt VA
Holmes: b 4-22-1759 d 10-4-1821 m Susanna Forman Pvt NJ ★

THROCKMORTON, contd.
James: b 6-20-1754 d 12-17-1838 m (1)Frances Barbarie (2)Mary Chasey Pvt NJ ★
James: b 5-23-1726 d *p*. 1780 m Rosina VanNote Pvt NJ
Job, Jr.: b 5-27-1761 d 4-5-1839 m Mary Robinson Pvt NJ ★
Joseph: b 1720 d 1786 m Mary Forman Sol NJ
Lewis: b 2-9-1745/6 d *c*. 1798 m Rachel Dumas Pvt VA
Richard: b 1763 d 12-25-1839 m (1)Caroline — (2)Sally Dunkley Pvt VA ★
Robert: b *c*. 1756 d 1796 m Catherine Robinson Pvt VA
Samuel: b 1723 d 12-27-1786 m Catherine Franses Sgt NJ
Thomas: b 1739 d 4-27-1826 m (1)Mary Throckmorton (2)Mary Ann Hooe Sol VA
Wm.: b 6-27-1730 d 10- -1796 m Sarah Gillet Pvt VA
Wm.: b *c*. 1755 d 1- -1812 m Mary Rootes Dixon Sol VA

THROOP, (includes THROOPE)
Benjamin: b 3-9-1744 d 5-16-1822 m Susannah (Throop) Maj CT ★
Benjamin: b 10-8-1754 d 1-17-1842 m Rachel Brown Cpl CT
Benjamin: b 9-13-1752 d 10-8-1833 m (1)Mary Burgess (2)Mary Bateman Smith Pvt CT
Billings: b 5-31-1735 d 1-27-1776 m Hannah Morton Capt RI
Dan: b 11-8-1748 d 11-1-1833 m Amy Barnes Lt CT
Dan: b 4-27-1768 d 5-18-1824 m Mary Gager Fif CT ★
Daniel: b 4-19-1740 d *p*. 1790 m Rachel Terry Capt CT
John: b 9-11-1733 d 1-25-1802 m Frances Dana Pvt CT
Joseph: b 12-25-1748 d 9-13-1836 m Zerviah Bissell Sgt CT
Wm.: bpt 6-13-1739 d 2-26-1817 m (1)Alethea Fales (2)Mary Healy Capt RI

THRUSH,
Leonard: b 1760 d 1842 m Catherine — Pvt PA

THRUSTON,
Charles Mynn, Sr.: b 11-6-1738 d 3-21-1812 m (1)Mary Buckner (2)Anna Alexander Col VA
John: b 10-15-1761 d 2-19-1802 m Elizabeth Thurston Whiting Cnt VA
Robert: b 1-14-1759 d 1826 m Frances Jones Lt VA

THUM,
Adam: b 12-17-1735 d 4-24-1814 m Dorothy Shepperman Capt NY

THURBER,
Benjamin: b 6-12-1749 d 5-3-1834 m Esther Allen PS MA
David: b 10-16-1734 d 10-27-1818 m Mary Bullock PS VT
James: b 6-28-1726 d 9-19-1805 m Lydia Harding Pvt MA
John: b 3-3-1718 d 7-4-1797 m (1)Ann — (2)Mary Thresher (3)Elizabeth Coomer Pvt MA
Nathaniel: b 4-13-1761 d *p*. 1842 m Polly Shores Pvt MA ★
Samuel: b 2-15-1757 d 9-11-1832 m Elizabeth Wilson Pvt RI
Samuel: b 2-15-1757 d 11-6-1839 m Mehitabel Dexter PS RI
Squire: b 2-7-1759 d 6-22-1837 m Catherine Fowle Pvt RI ★

THURLOW, (includes THURLO)
Abraham: b 7-14-1743 d 8-31-1786 m Lydia Boynton Pvt MA
Joseph: b 1-2-1757 d 8-18-1837 m (1)Ruth Adams (2)Joanna (Lunt) Chase Pvt MA ★
Thomas: b 9-25-1752 d 12-27-1828 m Deliverance Owen Cpl MA ★
Tristram: b 3-22-1739 d 2-13-1777 m Elizabeth Carr Pvt MA
Wm.: b 12-4-1744 d 12-8-1784 m Mary Gibson Capt MA

THURMAN,
Benjamin, Jr.: b 1755 d 1840 m Julia Shumate PS SC
John: b 1755 d *p*. 1800 m Mary Little Sol VA
Philip: b 11-15-1757 d 9-2-1840 m Kesiah — Pvt SC ★
Richard: b 12-18-1743 d 8-14-1830 m Ann Brown Pvt VA
Wm.: b *c*. 1745 d 1800 m Mackie Norvel Pvt VA

THURMOND, (includes THURMAN)
Absalom: b *c*. 1740 d *p*. 10-3-1800 m Mary — Pvt GA
Benjamin: b *c*. 1750 d 5-22-1824 m Nancy Carr PS VA
John: b *c*. 1742 d *p*. 9-13-1793 m Elizabeth — Sol GA
John: b 1747/8 d *c*. 1827 m (1)Sarah Goolsby (2)Mrs Nancy Gregory Pvt VA
Philip: b *c*. 1720 d *p*. 9-5-1803 m Judith Tucker PS VA
Wm.: b 2-28-1766 d 3-24-1831 m Lucy Wills Sgt Maj VA ★

THURSTON,
Abijah: b 7-5-1751 d 7-10-1812 m Rachel Johnson Pvt MA
Abner: b 1729 d 1778 m Martha Piper Cpl NH
Benjamin: b 10-21-1746 d 12-11-1807 m Jane Knight Pvt MA
Daniel, Sr.: b 3-1-1719-20 d 7-14-1805 m (1)Hannah Parker (2)Judith Gerrish (3)Elizabeth Rolfe Pvt PS CS MA
Daniel, Jr.: b 6-12-1757 d 1-11-1831 m Susannah Crombie Pvt MA
Daniel: b 6-1-1722 d 6-25-1785 m Elizabeth Whiting PS MA
Daniel, Jr.: b 9-11-1749 d 11-7-1802 m Susan Johnson Pvt MA
Daniel: b 9-18-1737 d 1-23-1829 m Sarah Curtiss Pvt NY
David: b 3-19-1745 d 8-26-1821 m (1)Mary Bacon (2)Chloe Reddington Pvt MA
David: b 7-9-1736 d 8-6-1826 m Eunice Whitney PS NH
David: b 3-20-1762 d 10-22-1842 m Esther Taylor Pvt NJ ★
Ephraim: b 3-25-1753 d — m Annie Marsh Pvt MA

George: b 1741 d 11-30-1827 m (1)Dolly Cottrell (2)Mrs Sarah Rathburn LCol RI
Joel: b 2-9-1739 d 3-10-1833 m Miriam Blakely Pvt NY
John: b 4-19-1723 d 8-5-1807 m (1)Hepzibah Burpee (2)Lydia Kimbal Pvt MA
John: b 6-30-1737 d 6-25-1814 m Eunice (Gott) StockbridgeMstrMte MA
John: b 4- -1741 d 3-16-1824 m Susanna Wheeler Pvt MA
John: b 11-15-1754 d 12-1-1838 m Rebeckah Gates Pvt MA ★
John, Jr.: b 1755 d 9- -1830 m Elsie Leavitt Pvt NH
John: b 7-9-1736 d *p*. 1790 m Sarah — Pvt PS NY
John: b 2-28-1703/4 d *p*. 1776 m Grace Olive Lucretia — PS NY
John: b 11-14-1759 d 5-10-1847 m Lydia Fletcher Pvt RI ★
John: b 6-12-1750 d 8-12-1819 m Sabra Smith PS CS RI
Jonathan: b 12-21-1745 d 6-8-1832 m Elizabeth Hovey Pvt NH
Joseph: b 1724 d 11-28-1782 m Rachel Montross Pvt NY
Joseph: b 12-29-1739 d 8-13-1822 m Thankful Wood Lt MA
Joseph: b *a*. 1758 d *c*. 1806 m Sarah Taylor Lt RI
Moses, Sr.: b 1721 d 4-6-1800 m (1)Hannah Sewall (2)Katherine Emerson Pvt MA
Moses, Jr.: b 6-7-1744 d 6-29-1809 m Esther Bigelow Pvt NH
Moses, Sr.: b 6-10-1730 d 8-23-1812 m Elizabeth Clifford Lt NH
Oliver: b 1738 d *p*. 1783 m Sarah French Sgt NH
Peter: b 1739 d 12-22-1812 m Dorothy Gates Sgt MA
Richard: b 10-16-1710 d 7-12-1782 m Mehitable Jewett PS MA
Samuel: b 6-7-1727 d 3-26-1806 m Priscilla Burpee Sgt MA
Samuel: b 2-1-1744 d 9-11-1810 m (1)Sarah Townsend (2)Sarah Harrington Pvt MA
Samuel: b 1-21-1751 d 1795 m Elizabeth Brown Pvt NH
Stephen: b 1-24-1750 d 5-26-1846 m Kezia Cheney Pvt MA
Stephen: b 4-8-1760 d 1-23-1861 m Betsey Wiggin Pvt NH
Thomas: b 1-9-1752 d 1830 m Lucy Fenderson Pvt MA
Thomas: b 2-2-1755 d 10-31-1825 m (1)Lydia Davis (2)Mehitable Upton Pvt MA
Thomas: b 2-16-1750 d 6-21-1833 m Patience Beers Pvt RI ★
Wm.: b 3-8-1747 d *p*. 1782 m Priscilla Norman Mte
Wm.: b *c*. 1740 d 1817 m Jennie Jones Drm VA
Wm.: b 1742-3 d 1833 m Phoebe Rhodes Pvt NY

THWEATT,
Thomas: b *c*. 1752 d *c*. 1812 m (1)Susannah Barksdale (2)Jane Coleman Williamson Capt VA
Wm.: b *c*. 1755 d *a*. 1820 m Fannie Daniels Lt VA

THWING, (includes TWING)
James: b 11-28-1753 d 3-6-1834 m (1)Hannah Carpenter (2)Mrs Nancy Carpenter Pvt MA
John: b 3-11-1732 d 1811 m Sarah Chamberlain Sgt MA
John: b 7-7-1756 d 6-13-1836 m Chloe Packard Pvt MA ★
John: b 1-27-1761 d 6-19-1844 m Ruth Beebe Pvt MA
Nathaniel: b 6-26-1731 d 4-6-1817 m Abigail Greenough NOf ME
Nathaniel: b 3-18-1760 d 8-13-1817 m Aseneth Billings Pvt MA
Nicholas: b 7-16-1761 d 11-10-1841 d Lydia Stratton Cpl MA
Timothy: b 9-9-1744 d 2-17-1836 m Mary Rawson Pvt CS MA

TIBBALS, (includes TIBBILS)
Abel: b 3-4-1750 d 4-6-1822 m (1)Jane Kelsey (2)Anna Alvord Pvt CT
Abner: b 1757 d 1-15-1830 m Clara — Arfr CT
Arnold, Sr.: b 8-16-1725 d 6-1-1795 m Dorothy Thompson PS CT
Arnold, Jr.: b 7-28-1755 d 5-3-1825 m Mary C. Whiting Pvt CT
Ebenezer: b 1-19-1730 d 5-25-1819 m Submit Seaward Pvt PS CT
Joseph: b 11-10-1750 d — m Sally Dimmock Pvt CT

TIBBETTS, (includes TEBBETTS, TIBITS)
Abner: b 3-1-1759 d 4-17-1843 m (1)Sarah Davis (2)Mrs Mary (Fisher) Crane Pvt MA
Caleb: b 4-7-1751 d *a*. 3-4-1828 m Elizabeth Power CS MA
Ebenezer: b 10-10-1747 d 3-19-1804 m Rebecca Fisher PS 2Maj CS NH
Edmund: b 7-4-1747 d 3-6-1817 m Mary White Pvt NH
Ephraim: b 2- -1754 d 11- -1840 m Tamson Pinkham Sol NH
Giles: b 6-9-1757 d 7-13-1832 m Hannah Alley Pvt MA
Henry: b 1-7-1756 d 5-19-1818 m Sarah Bunker Sinclair Pvt NH
Ichabod: b 12-17-1749 d 1842 m Elizabeth Hutchins Sgt MA ★
Jacob: b 1738 d 1818 m Judith Berry Pvt NH
Jeremiah: b 5-4-1713 d 1804 m Martha Bickford CS NH
John: b 9-25-1737 d 1-27-1817 m Waite Brown Pvt MA
John: b 2-1-1755 d 6-12-1826 m Lydia Lamson Cpl RI ★
Jonathan: b 2-21-1738/9 d 12-27-1798 m Sarah Emery MM Pvt NH
Jonathan: b 5-6-1745 d 11-30-1815 m Assa Tiffany Pvt NY
Nathaniel, Sr.: b 8-30-1727 d 1804 m Elizabeth Giles 1Lt MA
Nathaniel, Jr.: b 8-9-1752 d 9-23-1845 m Elizabeth Alley Pvt MA ★
Obadiah: b *a*. 1746 d 1818 m — Wing Pvt CT
Richard Salter: b 5-10-1761 d 10-5-1821 m Sarah Frost Mrnr NH
Samuel: b 1740 d 5-2-1824 m (1)Margaret — (2)Mrs Abigail (Thompson) Coombs 2Lt MA
Samuel: b 3-18-1763 d 3-27-1850 m Sobriety Drew Pvt MA
Simeon: b 12-14-1752 d 3-27-1845 m (1)Bethany — (2)Abigail Burnham Ens NH ★
Wm.: b 4-21-1731 d 1807 m Laurana Young Pvt MA

TICE, (includes TEIS)
Elias: b 7-7-1760 d 11-20-1841 m Sarah Horn Pvt NJ ★
Henry: bpt 5-27-1759 d p. 2-17-1793 m Lydia Coddington Pvt NY
Henry: b 7-16-1762 d 10-7-1851 m Huldah Van Gorder Pvt NY ★
Jacob: bpt 2-24-1751 d 11-17-1805 m (1)Euphreme Francis (2)Ann
    Ellen Carney 1Lt NJ W★
Jacob: b c. 1750 d p. 1787 m Susannah Querie Pvt MD
John: b 11-13-1756 d 6-30-1830 m Eleanor Anderson MM NJ
John: b 1735/6 d c. 1815 m Elizabeth Pease Pvt NY
Joseph Henry: b 1720 d p. 1790 m Anna Senseback Sol NY
Michael: b 2-2-1728 d 3-20-1804 m Elizabeth Ried Maj PS PA
Richard: b 9-28-1762 d 8-27-1850 m Letitia — Pvt NJ ★
Wm.: b 1760 d 5-22-1844 m Ruth Johnston Pvt VT

TICHENOR,
Aaron: b 1743 d 4- -1826 m Elizabeth — Pvt NJ
Caleb: b 4-10-1758 d — m Martha Dickerson Pvt NJ
Daniel: b 1742 d 4-12-1804 m (1)Elizabeth Wade (2)Mrs Anna
    Byram Condict Pvt NJ
Daniel: b 5-9-1748 d 10-16-1831 m Abigail Coe Lt NJ
Daniel: b 1754 d 1814 m Jemima Walton Pvt NJ
David: b 1731 d 8-5-1788 m Catharine Sampson Lt NJ
Jabez: b 1-6-1752 d 3-10-1825 m Mary Darcy Pvt NJ
John: b 1751 d 7-27-1810 m Mary Freeman Pvt NJ
Joseph: b a. 1755 d 1817 m — Pvt NJ
Zenas, Jr.: b 1762 d 11-27-1838 m Electa Pierson Pvt NJ
Zopher: b 10-22-1759 d 4-4-1821 m Elizabeth — Pvt NJ

TICKNOR, (or TICKNER)
Daniel: b 2-23-1740/1 d c. 1796-1802 m Mehitabel Tobey Sgt MA
Elisha: b 12-26-1736 d 6-13-1822 m (1)Ruth Knowles (2)Deborah
    Davis Capt PS NH
John: b 5-7-1750 d 1796 m Tabitha Strong Pvt CT
Joseph: b 1-27-1756 d 5-9-1839 m Hannah Reid Pvt NY ★

TIDD,
John: b a. 1760 d 5-10-1813 m Abigail Goodard Cpl MA W★
John: b 10-26-1749 d 3-29-1812 m Elizabeth Reed MM MA
Jonathan, Jr.: b 8-3-1757 d 2-17-1842 m Rhoda Thompson Pvt MA ★
Jonathan, Sr.: b 11-7-1724 d 8-16-1785 m Serviah Baker Lt MA
Joseph, Jr.: b 5-11-1734 d 7-12-1815 m (1)Sarah Munroe (2)Grace
    Mason Lt MA
Martin: b c. 1740 d p. 1820 m Betsy Marvin Pvt PA ★
Samuel: b 1-12-1741 d 10-7-1791 m Rebecca Simonds Pvt MA
Wm.: b 7-11-1736 d 12-25-1826 m Ruth Munroe Lt MA

TIDMORE,
Dorothy: b c. 1738 d 1814 m — PS SC

TIDWELL,
Wm.: b c. 1750 d 1780 m Mary de Graffenreid Lt SC

TIEBOUT,
George: b 6-9-1760 d 9-17-1826 m Margaret Cayler Pvt NY

TIFFANY,
Benjamin: b 4-9-1741 d 10-28-1825 m Sarah Carr Sgt Dr NH
Benjamin: b 1745 d 4-12-1801 m Mary Olin 2Lt NY
Daniel: b 2-28-1739 d 5-4-1817 m (1)Mary Woodcock (2)Phoebe
    Adams Cpl MA
Daniel: b 5-8-1736 d c. 3- -1785 m Mary Bolkom Pvt MA
Ebenezer: b 6-26-1734 d 10-3-1807 m Mary Carpenter Pvt MA
Ebenezer: b 6-10-1753 d 4-4-1826 m Mary Anne Bullock Pvt RI
Gideon: b 9-19-1737 d p. 1785 m Mrs Sarah (Dean) Farrar Pvt
    PS NH
Hosea: b 7-22-1754 d 4-22-1833 m Ann Wilmarth Sgt MA W★
Humphrey: b 1-19-1750 d p. 1807 m (1)Phebe Browne (2)Rhoda
    Ann Sherman Pvt MA
James: b 11-10-1760 d 3-18-1823 m Mary Howe Pvt MA
John: b 1711 d 1-10-1788 m Deliverance Parmiter PS MA
John: b 10-16-1747 d 1- -1825 m Ruth Clapp Sgt MA ★
Lemuel: b 1763 d 3-18-1847 m Sarah Aldrich Pvt MA
Noah: b 7-7-1752 d 7-19-1818 m (1)Hannah Carpenter (2)Mary
    Olney Sgt MA
Philemon: b 1760 d p. 1818 m Catherine Goldsmith Pvt CT ★
Samuel: b — d 9-3-1817 m Hannah Balkam Cpl MA
Simeon: b 5-29-1751 d 8-17-1806 m Esther Clark MM CT
Thomas: b 5-31-1756 d 5-12-1835 m Melatiah Tingley Sgt MA ★
Timothy: b 11-24-1755 d 1841 m Mary Davis Pvt CT

TIFFT, (includes TIFT)(see also TEFFT)
John: b 1744/5 d p. 1790 m Mrs Mary Lewis Pvt RI
Joseph: b c. 1732 d 1812-3 m Lydia Gallup Pvt CT
Solomon: b 3-27-1758 d 12-2-1850 m Eunice Burrows Pvt CT

TILDEN,
Calvin: b 9-23-1744 d 3-26-1822 m Lydia Fuller Sgt MA
Charles: b c. 1753 d 1798 m Catharine Kennard Ens MD
Daniel: b 11-5-1743/4 d 12-8-1833 m Esther Mason Capt CT ★
David: b 10-5-1741 d 1777 m Joanna Thwing Maj MA
Ebenezer: b 12-19-1757 d 3-20-1823 m Elizabeth Brown Pvt CT
Elijah, Sr.: b 3-18-1719 d 3-7-1799 m Ruth Wadsworth Pvt MA
Ezra: b 6-7-1751 d 11-1-1819 m Sarah White Pvt MA W★

John Bell: b 12-9-1761 d 7-31-1838 m Jane Chambers 2Lt PA
Joseph: b 4-1-1753 d 1800 m Sarah Parker Capt MA
Joshua: b 6-19-1749 d 11-7-1819 m Eunice Carpenter Ens CT
Josiah: b 4-19-1760 d 1-31-1849 m (1)Elizabeth Tracy (2)Susannah
    Clark Pvt VT
Nathaniel: b 7-23-1730 d — m Susanna Britt Pvt MA
Samuel: b 9-14-1739 d 5-29-1834 m (1)Mercy Hatch (2)Grace
    Hatch Pvt PS MA
Stephen: b 1757 d 1837 m Dorothy Goodrich Pvt CT ★
Thomas Turner: b 8-11-1744 d p. 1791 m Martha Stillman Cpl MA
Wales: b 8-29-1756 d 10-7-1850 m Abigail Little Pvt MA

TILESTON,
Cornelius, Sr.: b 1756 d 2-20-1843 m Sarah Ludden Cpl MA
Ezekiel: b 4-6-1731 d 5-5-1799 m Sarah Belcher Pvt MA
Ezekiel: b 11-12-1754 d 3-7-1812 m Waitsill — Pvt MA
James: b 10-2-1761 d 5-21-1817 m Hannah Vose Pvt MA
Nathaniel: b 11-29-1736 d 12-5-1797 m Prudence — Pvt MA
Timothy: b 2-24-1727/8 d 4-20-1819 m Hannah Clapp Pvt MA

TILFORD,
Wm.: b 1750 d 1835 m Isabelle Weir Sgt VA ★

TILL,
George: b 12-22-1752 d 3-3-1808 m Rachael Hugh Pvt PA

TILLARD,
Edward: b 1756 d 9-15-1830 m Sarah Estep Col MD

TILLERY,
Joshua: b — d p. 7-22-1820 m Susanna Zeigler Sol VA

TILLEY, (or TYLEE)
Edmund: b 3-6-1740/41 d 1835 m — Pvt NC ★
Henry: b 1754 d 8-13-1833 m Elizabeth — Pvt NC ★
James: b 1748 d p. 9-4-1840 m (1)Elizabeth Dorrington (2)Sarah
    Smith Pvt Smn MA
Samuel: bpt 1736 d a. 6-11-1781 m Hannah Emmons Cdr CT

TILLINGHAST,
Benjamin: b 9-13-1746 d 9-8-1819 m (1)Anna Northrup (2)Ann
    Cole LCol RI
Benjamin: b 9-20-1726 d 7-18-1817 m Sarah James CS RI
Charles: b 1748 d 9-17-1795 m Catherine Lamb Capt NY ★
Charles: b 4-5-1729 d 11- -1776 m (1)Mercy Green (2)Abigail
    Allen PS RI
Daniel: b 6-2-1732 d 9-18-1806 m (1)Hannah Gibbs (2)Lydia
    Hopkins PS Col RI
Daniel: b 1-5-1757 d 3-22-1839 m (1)Penelope Holly (2)Mary
    Weaver Capt RI ★
John: b 12-9-1745 d 5-6-1810 m Elizabeth Tillinghast Capt RI
John: b 1756 d — m Phoebe Tillinghast Capt RI
Pardon: b 6-3-1718 d 1810 m Hannah Stafford PS RI
Stuckeley: b 11-24-1741 d 1826 m Honor Hopkins Pvt RI
Thomas: b 4-27-1732 d 10-21-1827 m (1) — (2)Mary — (3)Mary
    Casey CS RI
Thomas: b 8-21-1742 d 8-26-1821 m Mary Hill Maj PS RI

TILLMAN, (or TILGHMAN)
Edward: b 1760 d p. 7-30-1814 m (1)Molly Johnston (2)Sarah
    (Davis) Smarr Lt PS SC
Frederick: b 9-11-1755 d 3-1-1809 m Ansabell Miller Pvt SC
James: b 8-2-1743 d 4-9-1809 m (1)Susanna Stewart (2)Elizabeth
    Jones PS MD
Jesse: b 1755 d p. 1798 m Frances Taylor Sol SC
John: b 1751 d 1830 m Sarah Eggerton Pvt NC
John: b 1736 d 1787 m Millicent White PS VA
Joshua: b 1-16-1753 d p. 9-4-1818 m (1)Patsy Taylor (2)Chloe
    Taylor PS NC
Littlebury: b 1754 d 1825 m Polly Lowry PS SC
Matthew: b 2-17-1718 d 5-4-1790 m Anne Lloyd PS MD
Richard: b 1-28-1746 d 5-28-1805 m (1)Margaret Tilghman
    (2)Mary Tilghman 1Maj MD
Richard: b c. 1727 d 1800 m Anne Randle PS VA
Tench: b 12-25-1744 d 4-18-1786 m Anna Maria — LCol MD
Thomas, Sr.: b a. 1720 d 1813 m Lucy Hix PS VA
Tobias: b 6-15-1751 d 2-6-1845 m Catharine Sharp Pvt NC ★
Wm.: b c. 1748-50 d a. 1786 m Mary Farrow PS SC

TILLOTSON,
Abraham, Sr.: b 7-25-1726 d p. 1791 m Cybil Brooker Pvt CT
Abraham, Jr.: b 5-6-1755 d 5-6-1821 m Abagail Backus Pvt CT ★
Daniel: b 1-12-1760 d 12-21-1848 m Hildah Gridley Pvt CT ★
Daniel: b 5-6-1744 d 6-27-1803 m Sarah Barnard 2Lt NY
Elias: b 1-25-1758 d 3-10-1812-4 m Experience Hosford Arfr CT
George: b 11-14-1754 d 10-4-1838 m Sila Munsell Pvt CT ★
Isaac: b 5-25-1765 d 4-4-1849 m (1)Rachel Mann (2)Sarah Robins
    Pvt CT ★
John: b 6-9-1756 d 7-12-1826 m Elizabeth Brockway Sol CT
Samuel: b 10-4-1758 d 12-3-1848 m Sarah Partridge Pvt MA
Simeon: b c. 1735 d 3-4-1834 m Martha Webb Pvt CT ★
Thomas: b 1751 d 5-5-1832 m Margaret Livingston Dr 1Lt MD

TILLSON,
Ephraim, Sr.: b 11-21-1728 d 3-27-1808 m Mercy Sears Pvt MA
Ephraim, Jr.: b 5-23-1760 d 6-20-1833 m Fear Waterman Pvt MA
Ichabod: b 4-25-1750 d p. 1797 m Azubah Thomas Drm MA ★
Isaiah: b 10-5-1744 d 5-13-1822 m Phoebe Crocker Drm MA
Jacob, Sr.: b 12-28-1736 d p. 1779 m Elizabeth Barden Pvt MA
Job: b 7-29-1766 d 1854 m Esther Freer Pvt NY
John: b 12-31-1742 d 11-25-1820 m Ruth Barrows Cpl MA
John: b 11-7-1725 d 3-28-1790 m Mercy Sturtevant Pvt MA
Timothy: b 8-28-1738 d 3-16-1800 m (1)Silence Whiting (2)Mrs
   Anna Lamb Adams PS NY
Wm.: b 4-25-1754 d 6-28-1841 m Anna Haskell Sgt MA ★
Wm.: b 3-15-1741 d c. 1825 m Mary Ransom Pvt NC

TILT,
Thomas: b — d p. 1790 m Eva Forshea PS NY

TILTON,
Caleb: b 6-19-1742 d 7-6-1816 m Mary Prescott Lt NH
Daniel: b 10-20-1754 d 4-8-1826 m Mary Lowd Pvt NH
Daniel: b a. 1750 d 12-31-1800 m Sarah — Pvt NJ
David: b 10-27-1735 d 8-27-1825 m Jane — PS NH
Ebenezer: b 4-11-1752 d 1- -1835 m Leah Lovering Pvt NH
Ebenezer: b 4-23-1751 d 9-25-1800 m Mary — Dr NH
Green: b 9-9-1759 d 3-8-1810 m Judith Favor Pvt NH W★
Jacob: b — d 12-14-1822 m Mary Hayes Pvt NH
Jeremiah: b 1764 d 4-10-1822 m Mehitable Hayes PS NH
Jethro Bachelder: b 10-9-1736 d p. 1790 m Bridget — PS NH
John, Jr.: b 12- -1746 d 1-4-1825 m Mary Williams Pvt MA
John: b 9-7-1736/7 d 1-18-1818 m Hannah Clifford Ens NH
John: b 3-3-1755 d 1-8-1846 m Mary Risley Ens NJ ★
John: b 10-27-1759/60 d 8-12-1849 m Mariah Sutphen Sgt NJ ★
Joseph: b 9-4-1759 d 3- -1847 m Betsey Russell Pvt MA ★
Josiah, Sr.: b 4-1-1709 d 10-15-1796 m Sarah Flanders PS NH
Josiah, Jr.: b 10-22-1743 d 2-13-1820 m Sarah True Ens NH
Michael: b 9-27-1750 d 2-15-1825 m Lucy Burnham Cpl NH
Nathan: b 2-2-1755 d 12-28-1805 m Susanna Gale Pvt NH
Nathaniel: b 1-22-1745 d c. 1776-90 m Ann Safford Cpl MA
Nehemiah: b 1747 d 8-31-1814 m Lydia Hanson LCol DE
Philip: b 4-10-1741 d 1-26-1835 m (1)Molly Batchelder (2)Eunice
   Dodge Capt NH
Samuel: bpt 1-11-1740 d 4-14-1805 m Elizabeth — Pvt MA
Sherburne, Sr.: b 11-19-1699 d 2-11-1785 m Anne Hilyard PS NH
Sherburne, Jr.: b 7-31-1735 d 9-20-1813 m Hulda Prescott Pvt
   PS NH
Sylvester: b c. 1747 d 1813 m Mary — Pvt NJ
Timothy: b 1-2-1748 d 1-11-1831 m Sarah Prescott Ens NH
Timothy: b 10-4-1718 d 10-1-1785 m Martha Boynton PS NH
Uriah: b 11-15-1713-15 d 1-1-1788 m Jedidah Mayhew Maj MA
Wm.: b 7-28-1759 d 7-7-1820 m Hannah Putnam Pvt MA ★

TIMBERLAKE,
Francis: b 1758 d 6-10-1830 m Nancy Poindexter Pvt NC ★
Henry: b 1760 d 10-3-1829 m Elizabeth R. Wilson Sgt VA
Henry: b 1740 d p. 2-2-1805 m Nancy Austin Sgt VA
John: b 1753 d 4-18-1825 m Mary Lynch Johnson Pvt VA ★
John: b 7-24-1748 d 10-14-1832 m Christiana Thomasson 2Lt VA
Joseph: b 1752 d 10- -1841 m Anna Douglas Sgt VA ★
Richard: b 1736 d 1811 m Mary — Pvt NC
Richard: b 1738 d 1807 m (3)Mary Mundon Sol VA

TIMMERMAN, (or ZIMMERMAN)
Abraham: b 1754 d p. 1795 m Bernice Werley Pvt PA ★
Adam: b 5-18-1763 d 7-8-1808 m Margaretha Mathias Cpl NY
Bernard: b c. 1745 d 1- -1818 m Eva — 1Lt PA
Chris: b 8-27-1764 d 1839 m Elizabeth Miller Pvt VA
Christopher: b 1735 d 5-8-1782 m Deborah Supplee Pvt PA
Christopher: b a. 1750 d 3- -1832 m Mary Tanner Pvt VA
Conrad: b 1748 d 4-23-1827 m Margaret Snell Ens NY
Frederick: b c. 1740 d 12-10-1804 m Judith Bourke Pvt VA Heirs ★
George: b 3-7-1714 d 1795 m Catherine — PS MD
George: b p. 1730 d p. 1782 m Salome — Pvt PA
Gottfried: b 12-15-1763 d 1-8-1853 m Anna Mary Yoder Pvt PA
Henry, Sr.: b 1-31-1738 d 5-18-1807 m (1)Anna Margaretha Maarin
   (2)Catherine (Fox) — (3)Margaret Elizabeth Petrie (4)Margaret
   Bellinger Lt NY
Henry: b 1-1-1750 d 10-11-1834 m Elizabeth Keller Pvt NY ★
Henry: b 1758 d 1834 m Mary Ann Lingenfelder Pvt PA
Henry: b 2-20-1762 d 8-5-1831 m Maria Koller Pvt PA
Jacob: b 9-1-1757 d 1-18-1835 m Magdalena Failing Pvt NY ★
Jacob: b 3-18-1740 d 3-6-1819 m Elizabeth Supplee Pvt PA
John: b 1-1-1760 d 4-26-1834 m Sarah House Lt NY
John: b 11-11-1747 d 1829 m Christiana Clacum Pvt PA
John: b c. 1740 d p. 1790 m Susanna — Pvt VA
John: b a. 4-5-1726 d p. 9-4-1799 m Ursula Blankenbaker PS VA
Leonard: b c. 1740 d p. 9-12-1812 m Sophia — Lt PA
Michael: b 5-22-1732 d p. 1795 m Maria Magdalene Santes Pvt PA
Michael: b 8-21-1752 d 6-3-1789 m Barbara Boyer Pvt PS PA
Peter: b c. 1710 d 1790 m Elizabeth — Pvt PA
Peter: b 1752 d 10-22-1823 m Maria Shirk Pvt PA
Peter: b 3-4-1763 d 1810 m Mary Magdalene Beane Pvt PA
Wm.: b 12-24-1754 d 4-21-1830 m Catharine Failing Pvt NY

TIMMONS,
Edward: b c. 1750 d p. 1790 m Sarah Smith PS MD
George: b 1760 d a. 5- -1845 m — Pvt VA ★
John: b c. 1757 d p. 3-3-1834 m — Sgt VA

TIMMS, or TIMS
John: b 1745 d 1828 m — Hough Pvt VA
Joseph: b 1751 d p. 1820 m Susan Douglas Pvt MD ★
Joseph: b 12-2-1747 d 8-16-1801 m Mary Glover PS SC

TIMSON,
Samuel: b 1740 d a. 6-17-1782 m (1)Sarah Ann Thornton (2)Mary
   — Capt VA

TINDALL, (or TINDELL)
Benjamin: b c. 1732 d p. 1782 m Ann — PS VA
John: b 1754 d 11-5-1837 m (1)Hannah — (2)Mary L. Taylor Ens
   Sgt NJ W★
Obediah: b 9- -1763 d 1-1-1852 m Jemima Everett Pvt VA
Wm.: b 1738 d c. 1812 m Elizabeth Ann Bryan Sol GA
Wm., Sr.: b 1717 d 7-22-1804 m Betty Ann Booker Pvt GA
Wm.: b 1745-7 d 1-14-1838 m Elizabeth — Pvt NJ ★

TINGEY,
Thomas: b 9-11-1750 d 2-23-1829 m (1)Margaret Murdoch
   (2)Hannah Craven (3)Sarah Dulaney Commo NJ

TINGLEY,
Araunah: b 10-14-1744 d 8-13-1775 m Keziah Pitcher Pvt MA
Benjamin: b 4-24-1741 d 5-29-1828 m (1)Sabula Fuller (2)Elizabeth
   (Cole) Philbrook Lt MA
Ebenezer, Sr.: b c. 1730 d 1783 m Annice Jennigs Capt NJ
Ebenezer, Jr.: b 3-27-1763 d 6-14-1824 m (1)Elizabeth Runyan
   (2)Rebecca Steele Pvt NJ
Elkanah: b 3-26-1760 d 8-12-1838 m (1)Priscilla Aldrich
   (2)Keziah Mason (3)Mrs Hall Pvt MA
Jeremiah: b 9- -1755 d 6- -1803 m Esther Leddel MM NJ
Joseph: b c. 1720 d p. 1780 m Christiana Manning Tms NJ
Nathan: b 12-16-1750 d 11-10-1798 m Lucy Barrows Pvt MA
Samuel: b 10-17-1752 d 3-27-1846 m (1)Rebekah Cushman
   (2)Amey Vial Pvt MA ★

TINGUE, (or TINKEY)
John: b 1740 d 1812 m Eliza Scrafford Pvt NY

TINKER,
Elihu: b 5-6-1739 d 8-29-1816 m Lydia Huntington Pvt MA
Jehiel: b 11-11-1741 d 9- -1780 m Temperance — Mstr CT
John: b 1755 d 1845 m Mary Haslem Pvt CT
Martin: b 6-26-1739 d 12-20-1811 m Mary Peck Capt MA
Nathan: b 1759 d 11-22-1833 m (2)Lucy Smith Pvt CT ★
Nehemiah: b 5-18-1740 d 3-17-1783 m Mary Huntington Capt CT
Samuel: b 12-5-1752 d 1-12-1838 m (1)Lucy Moore (2)Sally Smith
   Pvt CT ★
Silas: b 11-25-1748 d 11-9-1840 m Lois Wade Cpl CT

TINKHAM,
Amos, Jr.: b 5-21-1765 d p. 1819 m Susan Thomas Pvt MA
Caleb: b 3-20-1738 d 7-5-1798 m Deborah Babbitt Pvt MA
Daniel: b 1-26-1746 d 8-6-1807 m Martha LeBaron 2Lt MA
Ephraim: b 1750/1 d 1795-7 m Elizabeth Jones Pvt MA W★
Hazeal: b 4-20-1763 d 5-9-1839 m Susanna Pratt Pvt MA
Hezekiah: b c. 1720 d 1812 m — Pvt RI
Isaac: b 3-18-1754 d a. 8-11-1802 m (1)Sylvia Sturtevant
   (2)Bethiah Emons Cpl MA
Isaac: b 11-26-1741 d 4-18-1818 m Lucretia Hammond Pvt MA
Isaiah: b 9-19-1757 d 9-29-1842 m Susan Ellis Pvt MA
James: b 5-8-1745 d 7-22-1836 m Chloe Rickard Pvt MA
Jeremiah: b 10-27-1740 d 12-25-1812 m (1)Molly Wood (2)Zermiah
   Richmond Pvt VT
John, Sr.: b 5-18-1719 d 8-22-1793 m Jerusha Vaughn Sgt MA
John, Jr.: b 4-16-1754 d 4-5-1829 m (1)Mary Leach Wood (2)Mrs
   Lydia Wood (3)Mrs Jerusha (Sparrow) Lovell Pvt MA
Nathan: b 4-18-1725 d 1790 m Sarah Soule Pvt MA
Peter: b 1722-4 d p. 1790 m Eunice Clark Pvt MA
Seth: b 11-13-1734 d 2-13-1808 m Eunice Soule Pvt MA

TINNEN,
James: b 5-23-1758 d p. 10- -1844 m Hannah — Pvt NC ★

TINSLEY,
Edward: b c. 1700 d c. 1783 m Margaret — PS VA
Golding: b 1756 d 5-9-1851 m Mary Foster Pvt SC VA ★
James: b c. 1759 d 1844 m (2)Susan Hooker Pvt SC ★
John: b — d p. 5-5-1816 m — PS CS VA
John: b c. 1735 d p. 9-1-1797 m Sarah — PS VA
Thomas: b 9-4-1755 d 12-17-1822 m Susanna Thomson Pvt VA
Wm.: b 1763 d 2-28-1835 m Sarah Samuel Pvt VA ★
Wm.: b 3- -1735 d 8-2-1800 m Jane Geese Pvt VA

TINSMAN,
Adam: b c. 1746 d c. 1813 m Anna — PS PA

TIPPEY,
Uriah: b 7-16-1759 d 6-27-1848 m — Pvt PS PA ★

TIPPINS,
Philip: b 1754 d 1820 m (1)Mary Underwood (2)Nancy Phillips Pvt SC

TIPPLE,
Adam: b *c.* 1735 d *p.* 1792 m Catherine — Pvt NY

TIPTON,
Benjamin: b 1755 d 2- -1807 m (1)Rebecca Ray (2)Rebecca Cusick Lt VA
Jabez Murray: b 11-17-1754 d 12-25-1818 m (1)Rebeckah Lemmon (2)Elizabeth Mitchell PS MD
John: b 7-6-1726 d 11-18-1808 m Martha Murray PS MD
John: b 8-15-1730 d 8- -1813 m (1)Mary Butler (2)Mrs Martha (Denton) Moore PS VA
Jonathan: b 1750 d 1-18-1833 m (1)Frances Perlina Daugherty (2)Keziah Robertson Sevier (3)Lavinia Stephens Maj NC ★
Luke: b 5-14-1760 d 10-8-1855 m — Pvt MD ★
Samuel: b *c.* 1755 d 1817 m Ruth Bowen Ens MD
Samuel: b 6-7-1752 d 7-21-1833 m (1)Mrs Jemima Little (2)Susanna Reneau Sol VA
Shadrach: b *c.* 1755 d 1822 m (1)Drusilla — (2)Elizabeth — Pvt PA
Thomas: b 1733 d 10-7-1841 m Nancy — Sgt VA ★
Wm.: b *c.* 1754 d *c.* 1834 m Sallie Spawn Pvt VA ★
Wm.: b 2-13-1761 d 11-3-1849 m (2)Phebe Moore Pvt VA ★

TISDALE,
Cudbud: b 11-23-1750 d *c.* 1838 m Martha — Pvt VA ★
Ebenezer: b 1-24-1723 d 1-24-1791 m Priscilla Drake Capt MA
Edward: b 2-13-1755 d 11-13-1826 m Ruth Harlow Pvt MA
John: b *c.* 1758 d 8-21-1814 m Jane — PS SC
Joseph: b 1-16-1755/6 d 1-20-1840 m Phebe Clarke Pvt RI ★
Reuben: b 4-29-1757 d *p.* 1798 m Rachel Crane Sgt MA
Seth: b 1716 d 8-3-1788 m Rebecca Hodges Pvt MA

TISHEW,
John: b *c.* 1751 d 3-20-1838 m Mrs Sarah Rhodes Lear Pvt MA

TISSERAND,
Francois De Moncharveaux: b 12-20-1748 d 9-4-1810 m Anna Guinault PS LA

TITCOMB,
Benjamin, Jr.: b 1-4-1726 d 10-15-1798 m Anne Pearson PS MA
Benjamin: b 6-12-1743 d 1-28-1793 m Hannah Hanson LCol NH
Edmund: b 5-20-1736 d 9-8-1818 m (1)Martha Swett (2)Mary Whittier Pvt MA
Enoch: b 12-6-1752 d 8-13-1814 m Anne Jones BMaj MA
John: bpt 8-3-1760 d 8-9-1816 m Sarah Ham Pvt NH
Jonathan: b 9-12-1727 d 3-10-1817 m (1)Mary Dole (2)Sarah Stedman MGen CS PS MA

TITLAR,
George: b 3-3-1753 d 3-28-1839 m Mary Cargill Pvt NY ★

TITTERMARY,
David: b 1759 d 5-10-1800 m Ann Van Dyke Ens PA
John: b 1723 d 5-1-1808 m (2)Eleanor Porter Matr PA

TITTLE,
George: b *c.* 1761 d 1819 m Mary Cooper PS VA
John: b 1735 d 12-8-1800 m Lydia Tuck Capt MA
Peter, Jr.: b 10-20-1746 d 3-26-1834 m Sarah Whiteside Pvt PA

TITUS,
Abel: b 8-12-1761 d 4-25-1841 m Mary Cotton Place Pvt MA ★
Benjamin: b 1729/9 d 12-17-1849 m (2)Rachel Gapen (3)Rachel Mercer Pvt NJ ★
Comfort: b 10-22-1741 d *p.* 1790 m Dorothy Gore PS Sgt CT
Francis: b 1728 d 1802 m (1)Cornelia Duryea (2)Mrs Catherine Voortman PS NY
Harmen: b 6-10-1738 d 5- -1822 m Susanna LaRue Pvt PA
James: b 1724 d 1805 m Mary Morgan Pvt NY
Joel: b 1740 d *c.* 1820 m Mary Treat Pvt CT
John: b 10-28-1763 d 3-4-1858 m Mehetable Fuller Pvt CT VT
John: b *a.* 1738 d *p.* 4-2-1784 m Anna Smith PS NJ
Johnson: b *c.* 1754 d — m Ann Stout Sgt NJ
Jonathan: b 1724 d 6-12-1808 m (1)Martha Ketcham (2)Mrs Sarah Brush Capt NY
Joseph: b 4-2-1758 d-2-25-1845 m (1)Elizabeth Ann Givens (2)Tamor Givens Sol CT ★
Joseph: b — d *p.* 8-14-1828 m Elizabeth Mathews Sol PS VA
Lenox: b *a.* 1748 d *p.* 1778 m — Morey Pvt MA
Michael: b 10-24-1746 d 6-15-1827 m Susanna Wood Pvt MA
Noah: b 3-25-1739 d *p.* 9-4-1789 m Lydia Batcheller Pvt MA
Robert: b 5-20-1719/20 d 1784 m (1)Esther Wilmarth (2)Elizabeth Foster Pvt MA
Samuel: b 3-13-1734/5 d 1817/8 m Ann Bigelow Capt NH
Samuel: b *c.* 1751 d 1825 m Elizabeth Baldwin Pvt NJ
Serick: b 1751 d 1792 m Deborah Vandegrift Pvt PA

Solomon: b 10-8-1757 d 12-19-1833 m Susanna Read Pvt NJ
Timothy: b 1746 d 1831 m Patience Hoff Capt NJ
Timothy: b 9-26-1732 d *c.* 1783 m Mary — Pvt NY
Timothy: b 10-7-1726 d 10-31-1802 m Charity Losea PS NY
Uriel: b 6-20-1760 d 10-26-1834 m Hannah Ege Pvt NJ
Wm.: b 8-17-1751 d *p.* 4- -1792 m Bathsheba Fisher Pvt MA

TOADVINE,
Wm.: b *c.* 1760 d *p.* 10-20-1804 m Priscilla Toadvine Pvt MD

TOBEY,
Eliakim: b 10-11-1711 d 1780 m Abigail Bassett, Jr. PS MA
Elisha: b 1-2-1739 d 2-23-1809 m Susannah — Capt CT
Elisha: b 7-14-1723 d 5-10-1781 m Desire Newcomb PS MA
Isaac: b 7-20-1749 d 6-5-1845 m (1)Lydia Williams (2)Deborah Williams Lt MA
Jessey: b 1-26-1740 d 1788 m Anne — QM Sgt CT
John: b 7-29-1732 d *p.* 3-28-1811 m Mary Bennett Pvt MA
John: b 1-23-1803 m Mercy Howes Lt MA
Joseph: b 1-26-1759 d 2-15-1830 m Elizabeth Pope Pursell Pvt MA W★
Joshua: b 1729 d 1794 m Maria (Tobey) Capt MA
Lemuel: b 2-27-1748/9 d 11-7-1820 m Elizabeth Pope Lt MA
Nathaniel: b 3-1-1743/4 d *p.* 1794 m (1)Mary Tobey (2)Deborah Finney Cpl MA
Nathaniel: b 8-17-1747 d 1-11-1802 m Abigail Burt Pvt MA
Noah: b 3-8-1745 d 1812 m (1)Elizabeth Butler (2)Mrs Elizabeth (Sears) Howes Sol MA
Prince: b 6-7-1741 d 7-7-1810 m Jane Delano Pvt MA
Richard: b 6-26-1740 d 10-8-1827 m Jemima Haskell PS NH
Samuel, Jr.: b 2-20-1740 d 1804 m Mary — 1Lt MA
Samuel: b 6-5-1743 d 12-17/18-1823 m Experience Paull Pvt MA
Samuel: b 1715 d 1781 m Bathsheba Crocker PS MA
Seth, Sr.: b 1716 d 8-31-1801 m (1)Zipporah Young (2)Betsey (Sears) Howes PS MA
Wm.: b 9-9-1759 d 8-22-1835 m Mary Sylvester Pvt MA ★
Zaccheus: b 12-2-1734 d 3-3-1833 m (1)Anna Sampson (2)Rhummah — Pvt MA
Zoeth: b 12-30-1758 d 8-21-1838 m Abigail Keene Pvt MA

TOBIAS,
Isaac: b *c.* 1757 d 1808 m — Thurston Ens NY
Ludwig: b 6-24-1739 d 9-27-1810 m Sophia Emrich Pvt PA

TOBIN,
Isaac: b 6-23-1750 d 1836 m Phebe Thomson Pvt NJ ★
Samuel: b 1762 d 12-30-1834 m Margaret Legro Pvt MA ★

TOCK,
John: bpt 12-25-1744 d *p.* 1814 m Martha Bunnell Pvt PA

TODD, (or TOD)
Abraham: b 12-21-1738 d 4-19-1797 m Lydia Husted Lt NY
Adam: b 6-2-1746 d 1798 m Margaret Dodge PS NY
Adam: b 1751 d 10-4-1844 m Esther Barr Sol NC
Alexander: b 9-7-1736 d 1808 m Rachel — PS MD
Alexander: b *c.* 1738 d 7-3-1811 m Mary Sharp Pvt PS PA
Andrew: b 1752 d 5-5-1833 m Hannah Bowyer Sol PA
Asa: b 1756 d 7-16-1847 m Abigail Bishop Pvt CT
Asa, Sr.: b 3-24-1723 d 7-5-1779 m Mary (Tuttle) Alling PS CT
Asa, Jr.: b 8-5-1750 d 11-1-1805 m Sarah Potter Sgt CT
Benjamin: b 1756 d 1-7-1828 m Phoebe Tuttle Sgt CT ★
Bernard: b 1750 d 1814 m Elizabeth Pollard Capt VA
Charles: b *c.* 1740 d *p.* 6-20-1814 m Mary (Burke) Capt VA
Daniel, Sr.: b 3-5-1724/5 d *p.* 9-16-1777 m Sybil Carrington PS CT
Daniel, Jr.: b 9-9-1751 d 1827 m Eunice Hitchcock PS CT
Daniel: b 3-17-1757 d 8-31-1839 m Hannah Bradstreet Sgt MA
Daniel: b 1753 d *p.* 1790 m Susan Wilson Pvt NH
David: b 10- -1746 d 11-7-1827 m Rachel Kent PS CT
David: b 4-8-1723 d 2-8-1785 m Hannah Owen Pvt PA
benezer: b 1757 d 3-7-1811 m Patience Jacobs Pvt CT
Eliel: b 2-20-1746 d 1793 m Anne Stafford 2Lt MA
Enos: b 1729 d 6-17-1803 m Sarah Blakeslee MM CT
George: b 1710 d 3-11-1790 m — PS VA
Gideon: b 11-3-1737 d 3-22-1817 m (1)Prudence Tuttle (2)Eunice Brockett Capt CT
Henry: b *c.* 1745 d 1788 m Mary — Pvt PA
James: b 1763 d 3-7-1840 m Katrina Mellick Pvt NJ
James, Sr.: b 1712 d 9-9-1783 m Mary — PS PA
James, Jr.: b 1748 d 9-14-1794 m Mary Wilson Pvt PA
Jehiel: b 11-3-1761 d 1-28-1843 m Hannah Street Pvt CT ★
Job: b *c.* 1740 d *p.* 5-11-1798 m Mary Insley Ens MD
John: b 1-8-1731 d 8-29-1814 m Jemima Hait Drm CT
John: b *a.* 1747 d *p.* 1780 m Susanna Rolfe Capt MD
John: b 1750-55 d 8-16-1777 m Molly Jameson Pvt NH
John: b 4-9-1757 d 10-27-1846 m (1)Rachel Duncan (2)Mrs Sarah Annan Pvt NH ★
John: b 1739 d 10-27-1823 m Sarah Ismay Lt NJ
John: b 1755 d 9-4-1820 m Jane Todd Pvt NJ
John: b *c.* 1755 d *p.* 1812 m — Pvt NC
John: b 4-18-1756 d 10-29-1829 m Jane Caldwell 2Lt PA
John: b 1757 d 6-3-1838 m Jane Snodgrass Pvt PA
John: b *c.* 1745 d *p.* 10-14-1809 m Mary — Sol VA

TODD, contd.
John: b 1719 d 7-27-1793 m Margaret Thompson PS VA
John: b *c.* 1763 d *p.* 1840 m Sarah Sterrett Pvt VA
Jonah: b 4-28-1731 d 8-8-1803 m (1)Esther Lowly Harrison (2)Mrs Abigail Heaton Crittenden (3)Mrs Johnson PS CT
Jonathan: b 8-12-1734 d 3-17-1783 m Jane Welch Sol SrgnMte PS CT
Jonathan: b 3-2-1752 d 12-2-1801 m Sarah Prichard Pvt MA
Joseph, Sr.: b *c.* 1745 d *p.* 1792 m Julianna Johnson 2Lt PS NY
Joseph, Jr.: b 2-11-1765 d 8-4-1848 m (1)Julia Johnson (2)Patty Lee Pvt NY ★
Joseph: b 1748 d *p.* 1782 m Ann Cross Pvt PA
Levi: b 10-4-1756 d 9-6-1807 m (1)Jane Briggs (2)Mrs Tatum Maj VA
Nelson: b 11-15-1744 d 12-20-1821 m (1)Hannah Jewett (2)Hannah Bailey Pvt PS MA
Paul: b 11-24-1758 d 9-3-1815 m Sarah Brown Sgt MA ★
Peter: b 6-23-1751 d *p.* 4-18-1840 m Hannah — Pvt NC ★
Robert: b *a.* 1750 d *p.* 1815 m Elizabeth Verveeler Lt NY
Robert: b 6-20-1732 d 2-22-1816 m Elinor McFarland 2Lt PA
Samuel, Sr.: b 3-6-1716 d 6-10-1789 m Mercy Evans PS MA
Samuel, Jr.: b 11-19-1752 d 3-18-1852 m (1)Mary Dudley (2)Jane Rosecrans Pvt CT
Samuel: b 7-24-1742 d 5-29-1840 m Mary Martin MM MA ★
Thaddeus: b 2-19-1757 d 2-26-1826 m Peninah Brockett Pvt CT
Thelus: b 5-12-1760 d 2-1-1846 m Irene Rogers Pvt CT
Thomas: b 11-27-1738 d 9-1-1798 m Sarah Wilkinson PS MD
Thomas, Jr.: b 11-17-1760 d 11-20-1848 m (1)Betty Dagget (2)Mrs Eunice Millard Sol MA ★
Thomas: b 6-3-1761 d 4-5-1843 m Zipphora Conger Pvt NC ★
Thomas: b 1-23-1765 d 2-7-1826 m (1)Elizabeth Harris (2)Lucy Payne Pvt VA
Timothy: b 5-16-1753 d 12-3-1805 m Phebe Buel Sgt CT
Timothy: b 3-3-1722/3 d 1-3-1779 m Abigail Crain PS CT
Wm.: b 1755-60 d 9-21-1845 m — Pvt NJ ★
Wm.: b *c.* 1739 d 11-8-1810 m Ann Rembow PS CS PA
Wm.: b 1750 d *a.* 4- -1815 m Phoebe Ferguson PS CS VA
Yale: b 8-25-1754 d 1-25-1807 m Phoebe Brown Pvt Matr CL

TODHUNTER,
Abram: b 6- -1750 d 12-24-1796 m Margaret — Pvt PA
Jacob: b 6-2-1760 d 11-26-1832 m Elizabeth Parker PS PA

TOLAND,
Hugh: b *c.* 1751 d 11-27-1805 m Rebecca — Pvt PA

TOLER, (includes TOWLER)
Benjamin: b 1752 d 1837 m Martha Darby Pvt VA ★
Joseph: b 9-15-1743 d 11-10-1819 m Frances — Sol VA
Wm.: b *c.* 1720 d *p.* 10-21-1785 m Ann — Pvt NC

TOLFORD,
John: b 1-2-1750 d *p.* 1798 m Sarah — PS NH

TOLLES,
Amos: bpt 2-12-1744 d 12- -1805 m Elizabeth Cummins Pvt NY
Clark: b 8-24-1758 d 7-19-1832 m Sally Proctor Pvt VT
Henry: b 8-8-1736 d 1810 m Hannah Clark Pvt VT
Jared: b 8-3-1752 d 5-12-1841 m Mabel Ball DrmMaj CT ★
Lamberton: b 8-5-1750 d 7-25-1821 m Abigail Briscoe Sol CT

TOLLEY,
Walter: b *c.* 1711 d 9- -1782 m (1)Mary Garretson (2)Martha Hall PS MD

TOLMAN, (includes TALLMAN, TOLLMAN)
Benjamin: b 1755 d 3-9-1840 m Hepsibeth Newell Pvt NH ★
Benjamin: b 1-9-1745 d 6-4-1820 m Dinah Boone Pvt PA
Benjamin: b 9-15-1743 d 6-10-1836 m (1)Rhoda Church (2)Lucretia Williams Col RI ★
Charles: b 12-4-1749 d 11-16-1814 m Mary Sylvester Sgt MA
Curtis: b 5-12-1762 d 2-24-1852 m Ann Harrington Pvt MA
Daniel: b 7-25-1759 d 3-8-1829 m Chloe Bozworth Sgt MA
Desire: b 3-19-1748 d 1-20-1834 m Sarah Howe Pvt Lt MA
Ebenezer: b *a.* 1751 d *p.* 1790 m Dorcas Ayres Pvt MA
Ebenezer: b 5-31-1748 d 12-27-1838 m Mary Clark Pvt NH
Ezekiel: b 10-24-1740 d 12-31-1827 m Sarah Harrington Lt MA
Jeremiah: b 2-8-1753 d 11-28-1827 m Martha Calderwood Pvt MA
John: b 3-18-1753 d 5-20-1839 m Elizabeth Fisher Capt MA
Jonas: b 6-9-1744 d 2-18-1815 m Mary Pierce Sol MA
Joseph: b 10-28-1750 d 7-3-1831 m Bethia Turner Pvt MA
Samuel: b 5-5-1740 d 9-9-1804 m Elizabeth Tolman Pvt MA
Samuel: bpt 6-30-1754 d *p.* 1820 m Hannah Rogers Pvt MA
Samuel: b 11-13-1754 d 11-30-1835 m Elizabeth (Wales) Hammond Pvt MA
Thomas: b 1757 d 9-8-1842 m Lois Clark Lt VT ★

TOLSON,
Wm.: b 1-9-1760 d 8-31-1844 m Sarah Wright Pvt VA

TOMAN,
Draper: b *a.* 1747 d 12-18-1782 m Mary Cahoone 2Lt RI

TOMB,
David: b 5-15-1763 d 9-13-1839 m Sina — Sgt SC ★
Jacob: b *c.* 1750 d 1818 m (1)Mrs Elizabeth (Campbell) Ross Dickerson (2)Christine Jane Schneider Pvt PA

TOMBAUGH,
George: b 8-15-1761 d 11-5-1822 m Elizabeth Gardner Pvt PS PA

TOME,
Henry: b 1754 d 1- -1846 m Veronica Kirchfort Pvt PA ★

TOMKIES,
Charles, Sr.: b *c.* 1720 d *p.* 1778 m Sarah — Capt VA
Charles: b *c.* 1750 d 12-12-1801 m Anne Dixon Capt VA W★
Francis: b — d *a.* 1808 m (2)Mildred — PS Col VA

TOMLIN,
Jacob: b *c.* 1740 d 3-4-1777 m Elizabeth Franklin Pvt NJ
James: b 1755 d 1836 m Mary Morgan OrdlSgt NJ
Wm.: b — d 1804 m Martha — Pvt NJ

TOMLINSON,
Aaron: b 1748 d 1828 m (1)Letita — (2)Mary Matilda Josey Pvt GA
Abraham: b 7-20-1738 d 12-29-1816 m (1)Mary Gibson (2)Esther Benjamin Dr CT
Agar: b 11-10-1713 d 2-7-1800 m Sarah Bowers PS CT
Agur: b 12-1-1756 d 10-31-1843 m Sarah Curtiss Pvt CT
Beach: b *c.* 12-3-1726 d 11-11-1817 m Charity Shelton Capt CT
Benjamin, Jr.: b 8-30-1752 d 4-4-1833 m Mary Harger Pvt CT
Benjamin: b 12-11-1752 d 9-30-1838 m Rachael Greathouse PS Lt MD
Benjamin: b *c.* 1728 d *p.* 9-29-1787 m Jane Harris Col VA
Curtis: b 8-31-1752 d 4-25-1835 m Lucy (Atwood) Martin Pvt CT ★
Dan: b 7-30-1749 d 12-24-1832 m Susanna Hotchkiss PS CT
David: b 1742 d *p.* 1783 m Ruth Hawkins Sgt CT
Eliphalet: b 1764 d 1-12-1839 m Polly Chase Pvt CT
Henry: b 4-1-1755 d 6-13-1843 m Abigail Welles Pvt CT

TOMLINSON,
Henry: b 4-18-1712 d 1790 m Patience Tomlinson PS CT
Hugh: b 1752 d *p.* 1790 m Mary — Pvt Cpl PS MD
Humphrey Becket: b 11-24-1744 d *p.* 3-1-1825 m (1)Tabitha Wheat (3)Cassander (Ellis) Summers Pvt MD
Isaac: b 4-7-1749 d 1-5-1817 m Mary Hawkins Pvt CT
Jabez Huntington: b 12-24-1760 d 1-14-1849 m Rebecca Lewis Ens CT ★
James: b 1735 d 5-31-1811 m (1)Barbara Brown (2)Dorothy Furness Lt NJ
John: b 9-23-1725 d 1-18-1817 m Deborah Bassett PS CT
John: b 1752 d 11-7-1775 m Phebe — Lt NJ
John: b *c.* 1750 d 1801 m Rebecca Luertia Hardeman Sol SC
John: b *c.* 1755 d *a.* 10-17-1826 m — Sol PS SC
Jonah: b 4-6-1712 d 10-2-1796 m Mary Moss PS CT
Joseph: b 1760 d — m Sallie Curtiss Pvt CT
Joseph: b *c.* 1750 d *p.* 1810 m Catharine — Pvt PA
Joseph, Sr.: b 10-12-1712 d 12-1-1797 m Rebecca Swearingen PS VA
Joseph, Jr.: b 10-12-1745 d 5-30-1825 m Elizabeth Hartness Capt VA
Levi: b 2-15-1752 d 3-4-1831 m Amelia (Beard) Worden Ens CS CT
Nathaniel: b 1762/3 d 1840 m (1)Rebecca Anderson (2)Mary — Pvt SC
Noah: b 3-6-1727 d *p.* 1790 m Abigail Beers PS CT
Richard: b 1748 d 1832 m Anne — 2Sgt NC ★
Samuel: b 2-16-1762 d *p.* 1793 m Ann Garrison Pvt NJ
Victory: b 1760 d 1840 m (1)Eunice Dunbar (2)Martha Warner Pvt CT
Webb: b 2-28-1743 d 8-12-1803 m Jerusha Beers PS CT
Wm.: b 11-9-1761 d 9-29-1807 m Jane Treat Pvt CT
Wm. T.: b 3-27-1749 d 3-17-1813 m Martha — PS VA

TOMPKINS, (or TOMKINS)
Christopher: b 8-10-1739 d 4-5-1823 m Mary Anne Fleet Capt VA
Enoch: b 1745 d 1815 m Lucretia Husted Pvt NY
Gideon: b 12-25-1761 d 1-3-1837 m Cynthia Brownell Pvt RI ★
Gilbert: b 5-24-1753 d 10-1-1835 m (1)Lucy Brownell (2)Mary Brownell Sgt RI ★
Humphrey: b 1749 d *p.* 1808 m Amelia Eubanks Sol VA
Isaac: b *c.* 1735 d *p.* 1790 m Hannah Pressler (2) — (Tompkins) PS Pvt NY
James: b 9-19-1755 d 10-28-1845 m Jane Snyder Fif NY ★
James: b 1-22-1757 d 3-20-1832 m Mary Richmond Sgt RI ★
John: b 1739 d 3-2-1825 m Sarah Barker Pvt NY
John: b 12-2-1760 d 9-8-1834 m Comfort Seabury Pvt RI ★
Jonathan Griffin: b 7-18-1736 d 5-22-1823 m Sarah Hyatt PS NY
Joseph: b *c.* 1745 d 11- -1818 m Bethiah Freeman Pvt NJ
Lawrence: b 4-5-1764 d 3-23-1826 m Margaret Carmen Drm Matr NY W★
Nathaniel: b 1742 d 4-7-1822 m Polly Tompkins Pvt NY ★
Nathaniel: b 12-15-1756 d 3-10-1833 m Sarah Snell Pvt RI
Philip: b 5-6-1748 d *p.* 1821 m Esther Blakesley PS CT
Robert: b 1730 d 6-7-1796 m Ann Dickenson Capt VA
Stephen: bpt 4-21-1741 d 11-25-1794 m (1)Hannah — (2)Sarles — Pvt NY

Stephen: b 5-9-1730 d 2-4-1801 m Puggy Franklin Capt NC
Sylvanus: b 1725 d 1822 m Mary Fields Pvt NY
Thomas: b 1730 d 3-   -1805 m (1)Phebe Evans (2)Ruth Jones Pvt NY
Uzal: b 10-26-1747 d 4-12-1831 m (1)Martha Reeve (2)Susannah
    Benjamin (3)Elizabeth Osborn Pvt NJ

TOMS,
James: b 1755 d 11-4-1834 m Lucina Cook Pvt NY ★
John: b 10-9-1714 d 5-   -1786 m Helena Johnson Lt NJ
Michael: b 12-6-1736 d 5-7-1798 m Hannah Seaman Cpl NJ

TONDEE,
Peter: b 1723 d p. 10-22-1775 m Lucy — PS GA

TONE,
John: b 10-11-1719 d p. 6-9-1791 m Margaret Harvey Pvt NJ
John F: b 1752 d 7-6-1830 m Sarah — Pvt CT ★
Wm.: b 7-30-1756 d 5-13-1815 m Naomi Sutphen Pvt NJ

TONEY,
Carey: b 10-10-1763 d 9-6-1859 m Elizabeth Doren Pvt VA ★
John: b 1758 d p. 1825 m Mary — Pvt VA

TONGUE, (or TONG)
Thomas: b 6-9-1746 d 2-6-1826 m Elizabeth Roberts 1Lt MD
Wm.: b 8-9-1763 d 2-8-1848 m (1)Eleanor Ford (2)Elizabeth Thomas
    Pvt MD ★

TOOK, (or TOOKE)
John: b c. 1748 d p. 1798 m Mary Burt Sol NC
Joseph: b 1750 d p. 12-8-1805 m Mary — Sol NC

TOOKER,
Charles: b 1712 d c. 1785 m Hannah Smith PS NY
John: b — d p. 12-30-1794 m Sarah — PS NJ
Reuben: b 1730 d 1788 m Mary Tuthill Ens NY
Reuben: b 2-19-1744 d 9-15-1807 m Martha Fowler Pvt NY

TOOLE, (or TOOL)
Edward: b c. 1750 d 1785 m Judith — PS NC
Henry Irwin: b 1750 d 1791 m Elizabeth Haywood Capt NC
John: b 1756 d 3-13-1791 m Ruth Rankin Pvt PA
Stephen: b c. 1756/7 d p. 1812 m Tacy — Pvt PA

TOOLEY,
Salmon: b 1732 d 1789 m Mary — Pvt CT

TOOMBS,
Andrew: b 1745 d — m Elizabeth — Pvt NH
Robert: b — d p. 8-1-1815 m (1) — Sanders (2)Sarah Catlett
    (3)Catherine Huling Maj VA

TOOMER,
Henry: b 1738 d 1799 m (1)Sophia (Edwards) Clerk (2)Mary Nesbett
    (3)Mary Granger (4)Magdalene Mary deRosset Capt PS NC
Joshua: b 10-25-1740 d 4-25-1796 m (1)Mary Vanderhorst (2)Mary
    Sabina Vanderhorst Capt SC

TOOPER,
Wm.: b 6-8-1760 d 6-28-1811 m Maria Hilton Pvt NY

TOOT,
David: b 1726 d 2-15-1792 m Catherine — PS PA
George Fred: b 8-5-1759 d 1-25-1815 m (1)Mary — (2)Catharine
    (Stetler) Shulze (3)Ann Eve Parthemore Pvt PA

TOOTHAKER,
Abraham: b 8-15-1747 d 8-2-1829 m Mary Wilson Pvt MA
Roger: b 9-5-1744 d p. 1779 m Mary Wright Pvt MA

TOPHAM,
John: b 1742 d 9-26-1793 m Ann Tew Col RI

TOPPING,
Charles: b c. 1756 d p. 1805 m (1)Jerusha — (2)Sarah — PS NY
Daniel, Sr.: b c. 1720 d 4-15-1787 m Elizabeth — PS NY
Daniel, Jr.: b 1741 d 10-12-1830 m Keturah Howell Sgt NY ★
Edward: b 1728 d 3-   -1819 m Susanna Sayre Lt NY
Garret: b 1745 d 9-   -1817 m Scarborough Snead Cpl VA
Henry: b 5-15-1750 d 3-25-1812 m Mary (Sanford) Pvt NY
Josiah: b 1726 d p. 1790 m Susanna Holcomb Sol CT
Matthew: b 1753 d 9-5-1837 m Jane Baker Sol PS NY
Stephen: b c. 1720 d 1782 m Abigail — PS NY
Wm.: b 1764 d 9-17-1840 m Lucy Hall Pvt CT

TORBERT,
James: b 3-14-1760 d 12-16-1831 m Margaret McNair Lt PA
John: b — 1800 m Susannah Siddons Cav PA
Samuel: b c. 1730 d p. 2-27-1795 m Susannah — Sol PS SC

TORR,
Andrew: b 8-25-1744 d 3-8-1817 m (1)Molly Jones (2)Mrs Deborah
    Hicks PS CS NH

Simon: b 11-5-1749 d 3-14-1821 m Sarah Ham SgtMaj NH
Vincent: b 1758 d 5-29-1829 m Mehitable Morse Pvt NH

TORRENCE, (or TORRANCE)
Adam, Sr.: b c. 1732 d 6-20-1780 m Ann Bona Pvt NC
Andrew: b a. 1755 d 7-1-1812 m Hester Howard QM VA
George: b 1761 d 7-24-1843 m Margaret A McKnight Sol NC
Hugh, Sr.: b 10-10-1701 d 7-22-1784 m (1)Elizabeth — (2)—
    (3)Mrs Sarah Marjory Cunningham CS PA
Hugh, Jr.: b 11-5-1745 d 6-23-1830 m (1)Mary Fenton (2)Mary
    (Borland) Gray Ens PA
James: b 2-12-1744 d 5-12-1826 m (1)Mary McConnell (2)Margaret
    Stewart Capt PA
James: b 7-26-1736 d 6-   -1810 m Jennet (Torrence) Pvt PA
John: b 1750 d 7-4-1827 m Jemima — Pvt PS GA
John: b 10-6-1757 d 6-29-1840 m Jane (McConnell) Jolly Sgt PA ★
Joseph: b 12-2-1751 d 2-23-1831 m Mary Paull Lt PA
Robert: b 1736 d 10-9-1816 m Lucy Peck PS CT
Samuel: b 4-5-1752 d 12-5-1843 m Anne Mitchell Pvt CT
Thomas: b 1-   -1751 d 5-14-1842 m Eunice Lacey Pvt CT ★
Thomas: b c. 1730 d a. 1790 m Elizabeth Kenan Lt NC

TORRENTINE, (or TURRENTINE)
Samuel: b 1717 d a. 5-   -1801 m (2)Mary Bryant PS NC

TORREY, (or TORRY)
Abner: b 12-12-1736 d 1826 m Lydia Beal Cpl MA
Caleb: b 12-23-1758 d 3-16-1808 m Mary Miller Pvt MA
Daniel: b c. 1740 d c. 1794/5 m Keziah Stockbridge Sgt MA
David: bpt 4-21-1743 d p. 1795 m Susannah Rogers Drm MA
David: b c. 1750 d 1-29-1827 m (1)Anna McDuffie (2)Margaret
    McPaul Sol NC
Elijah: b 8-2-1755 d 2-8-1833 m Anna Trask Fif MA ★
James, Sr.: b 4-22-1738/9 d 12-7-1777 m Lydia Wallbridge Pvt CT
James, Jr.: b 7-18-1763 d 5-29-1813 m Miriam Dimick Pvt CT
James: b c. 1732 d c. 1785 m (1)Mrs Mary (Sheffield) Partridge
    (2)Mary White (3)Rhoda Lathe Pvt MA
James: b c. 1753 d 12-16-1817 m Mrs Deborah (Fitch) Wheeler
    Dr Srgn Mte MA
John: b 9-5-1754 d 3-9-1821 m Abigail Richardson Pvt CT W★
John: b c. 1720 d p. 1790 m Margaret — Sol NC
John: b 2-3-1754 d 8-23-1833 m Eleanor Arnold Sgt MA
John: b 1-14-1741 d 1823 m Ruth Tyrell Cpl MA
Jonathan: b 10-2-1711 d 4-9-1784 m Sarah Smallpiece Pvt MA
Jonathan: b 12-28-1758 d 6-14-1837 m Abigal Stowell Pvt MA ★
Joshua: b 1-14-1725 d 2-8-1796 m Mirriam Terrell Pvt MA
Luther: b 5-26-1733 d 4-9-1825 m Dorothy Green Pvt MA
Nathaniel Brown: b 1758 d p. 1810 m (1)Abigail — (2)Sarah Hall Pvt
    MA
Noah: b 2-1-1756 d 10-24-1826 m Abigail — Pvt MA
Samuel: b 2-19-1762 d 1-25-1819 m Hannah Carpenter Pvt MA W★
Samuel: b 6-23-1753 d c. 1838 m Olive Ganes Sgt VT CT ★
Stephen: b 6-30-1732 d 9-14-1812 m Elizabeth Mellen Pvt MA
Timothy: b 6-3-1765 d 3-9-1841 m Chloe Kibby Pvt MA ★
Wm.: b 10-6-1761 d 4-4-1852 m Mehitable Baldwin Pvt CT ★
Wm.: b 9-15-1759 d 10-8-1831 m Margaret Nichols Lt MA
Wm.: b 1-21-1744 d 10-30-1820 m Hannah Wheeler Pvt MA
Wilson: b 1-24-1733 d 1793 m Ruth Ormsbee Pvt MA

TOTMAN,
Ebenezer: b 1731 d 1781 m Grace Turner Pvt MA
John: b 1732 d 8-2-1815 m Sarah Vining Cpl MA
Joshua: b 1751/2 d c. 1787 m Elizabeth Sutton QM MA W★
Stephen: b 4-5-1756 d 9-27-1830 m Mrs Hannah Damon Pvt MA

TOTTEN, (or TOTTIN)
Jacob Brinkerhoff: b 10-18-1761 d 1818 m Lydia Van DenBerg Pvt
    NY
John: b 1749 d 5-   -1812 m Nancy McNair Pvt PA
Lovina: b 3-7-1761 d 10-13-1857 m Benjamin White PS NY

TOTTINGHAM,
Elisha: b 10-18-1713 d 1-19-1802 m Sarah Lawrence Pvt MA

TOUGAS,
Joseph: b c. 1740 d c. 1793 m Jeanne Cardinal PS VA

TOUP,
Caleb: b 6-25-1757 d 2-23-1835 m Mototana — Pvt PA NC ★

TOUPS,
Gaspard: bpt 3-27-1755 d p. 10-10-1805 m Genevieve Heidel PS
    LA

TOURJE,
Philip: b 1746 d 5-8-1826 m Desire (Tourje) Pvt RI MA ★

TOURTELLOTTE, (or TOURTELLOT)
Abraham: b 2-27-1725 d 5-6-1779 m Phoebe Thornton PS CT
Abraham , Sr.: b 1744 d 12-6-1820 m (1)Hannah Coombs
    . . . .(2)Mallason Walling (3)Mrs Lea (Mansell) Burley Capt RI ★
Daniel: b 3-26-1751 d 8-2-1826 m (1)Urania Keech (2)Anne
    Burlingame Pvt CT

TOURTELLOTTE, contd.
Isaac: b 1-30-1752 d 6-6-1837 m Serviah Brown Pvt CT
Wm.: b 6-6-1747 d 11-9-1833 m Phoebe Whitman Pvt RI

TOUSEY,
Thomas: b 12-5-1735 d 1783 m Mercy Platt PS CT

TOUSLEY, (or TOWSLEY)
David: b 5-22-1757 d 1827 m Abiah — Cpl VT
Nathaniel: b 10-10-1749 d 1-18-1834 m Olive Warters Cpl NY ★
Samuel: b 12-25-1744 d a. 1788 m Ann Peck Pvt CT
Wm., Sr.: b 2-5-1731/2 d p. 1799 m Sybble Spencer Pvt VT
Wm., Jr.: b 8-4-1761 d 8-18-1827 m Sally Reed Pvt VT ★

TOUSSIGER,
James: b 1744 d 1800 m Elizabeth Lamberth Pvt PS SC

TOWBERMAN,
Henry: b 7-30-1757 d 6-3-1827 m Sarah Towberman Pvt PA ★

TOWER,
Abraham: b 4-18-1752 d 9-26-1832 m Hannah Kent Sgt MA
Asahel: b 10-9-1760 d 8-3-1833 m Milicent Wyman Pvt MA
Benjamin: bpt 3-8-1738/9 d 7-24-1790 m Ann Vose Pvt MA
Benjamin: b 7-4-1756 d 5-10-1829 m Lucy Totman Pvt MA ★
Bethiah: b 5-20-1724 d 4-27-1813 m Daniel Tower Jr PS MA
Enoch: b 12-20-1737 d 4-16-1807 m (1)Lucy Lovett (2)Ellis White (3)Ruth Kirby PS RI
Gideon: b 2-29-1752 d 4- -1825 m Elizabeth Cox Cpl MA
Gideon: b 1723 d 10-16-1803 m Lydia Sylvester MM MA
Gideon: b 4-30-1753 d 9- -1847 m Abigail Perkins OrdlSgt RI VT
Issac: b 5-10-1744 d 3-7-1826 m Mary Sprague Sgt MA
Isaac: b 2-2-1752 d 2-13-1823 m Elizabeth Wheeler Sgt MA
Isaiah: b 9-2-1731 d 2-2-1811 m Lydia Gill Pvt MA
James: b 2-16-1722 d 10-4-1796 m (1)Mary Day (2)Lucy Dunbar Pvt MA
James: b 12- -1746 d 4-26-1828 m Elizabeth Whitmarsh Pvt MA
Jeduthan: b 5-17-1756 d 8-27-1817 m Mary Smith Pvt MA
Jesse: b 7-13-1755 d 12-20-1812 m Rebecca Cushing Pvt MA
Job: b 9-8-1726 d 1790 m (2)Mary Pratt Capt MA
Joseph: b 1731 d 9-7-1801 m Rebecca — Capt MA
Joseph: b 7-28-1745 d 4-20-1823 m Sarah Hersey Pvt MA
Joseph: b 4-28-1746 d 9-6-1822 m (1)Ellen Mason (2)Mrs Zereviah (Eddy) Smith Pvt VT
Laban: b 8-3-1751 d 7-30-1824 m Esther Cushing Cpl MA
Levi: b 7-25-1756 d 8-12-1823 m (1)Priscilla Nichols (2)Ruth Beale Stoddard Pvt Mstr MA
Levi: b 7-19-1742 d 8-4-1826 m (1)Mary Whipple (2)Mrs Hannah Emerson Capt RI
Lunde: b 12-10-1746 d 4-21-1805 m Rebecca Bowker Sgt MA
Malachi: b 3-1-1737 d 4-21-1806 m (1)Ruth (Hayward) Wilder (2)Susannah Ward (3)Susannah Harris Pvt MA
Malachi, Jr.: b 4-1-1761 d 12-15-1833 m Bathsheba Wetherbee Pvt MA ★
Matthew: b 12-1-1755 d 3-3-1831 m Jerusha Hatch Pvt MA ★
Nathaniel: b 10-7-1744 d 4-9-1810 m Leah — Cpl MA
Nathaniel: b 6-23-1748 d 4-17-1836 m Lucy Tingsley Sgt VT ★
Peter: b 1-19-1729 d 8-4-1814 m (1)Deborah Stowell (2)Joanna Baker Pvt MA
Peter: b 6-1-1761 d 1799 m Sarah Putnam Sgt MA
Reuben: b 11-9-1745 d p. 1790 m — Sgt VT
Richard: b 9-10-1733 d 1813 m Hannah Tower Sgt MA
Samuel: b 3-17-1728/9 d 10-7-1811 m Hannah Collamore Pvt MA
Stephen: b 5-24-1755 d 4-25-1826 m (1)Anna Bowker (2)Mary — Pvt MA

TOWLE, (or TOLL, TOWLES & TULL)
Amos: b 5-6-1749 d 8-29-1825 m Abigail Dow Cpl NH
Benjamin: bpt 12-8-1745 d 11-4-1831 m Abigail Edgerly Pvt NH
Brackett: b 1736 d 5-5-1827 m Nelly Richardson Lt NH W★
Daniel: b 10-27-1751 d 1831/2 m Susannah Swits Lt NY
Elisha: b 9-23-1739 d 1-7-1820 m Ann Sanborn Pvt NH
Henry: b 12-18-1738 d 11-18-1799 m Judith Haynes Col PS VA
Henry: b 1755 d 5-10-1829 m Elizabeth Weatherall Capt VA W★
Jabez: b 4-5-1747 d 6-20-1837 m Sarah Garland Pvt NH
Jacob: b 6-16-1744 d 6-18-1814 m Mary Moulton PS NH
James: b 10-28-1737 d 11-28-1815 m Tryphenia — PS NH
John: b 1762 d p. 1853 m Sarah — Sol PS SC
Jonathan: b 8-23-1747 d 3-21-1822 m Miriam Marston Pvt NH
Jonathan: b 1755 d 6-13-1841 m Betsy Tuttle Pvt NH W★
Josiah: b c. 1752 d 9-18-1836 m (1)Mary — (2)Mrs Jane (Powell) Lane Cpl NH
Karl H: b 2-10-1745/6 d 8-26-1832 m Elizabeth Ryley Adj NY
Levi: b 1757 d 5-24-1827 m (1)Mary Lock (2)Lucy Hobbs (3)Perna Judkins Pvt NH
Oliver: b 9-1-1736 d 1825 m Mary Beverly Chew Smith LCol VA
Oliver: b 1734 d 11- -1781 m Jane — Capt SC
Phineas: b c. 1758 d 9-12-1819 m Sarah Leavit Sgt MA
Reuben: b 10-24-1762 d 9-15-1849 m Sarah Clough Pvt NH ★
Samuel: b 11-20-1737 d 1793 m Mary Dearborn PS NH
Simeon: b 8-18-1745 d 183- m Mary Page Pvt PS NH
Simeon: b 11-13-1752 d 1-3-1823 m Elizabeth Marden Sgt NH
Simon: b 5-22-1759 d 12-11-1808 m Eleanor Hall Pvt NH

Stokley: b a. 1750 d 1811 m Elizabeth Porteus Downman Capt VA
Thomas: b 2-21-1750 d 5-22-1800 m Mary Chew Smith Maj VA
Wm.: b c. 1760 d p. 1801 m Elizabeth — (2)Abigail Welch Ens NH
Wm.: b 1740 d 3-28-1825 m Elizabeth Prescott Pvt NH

TOWNE, (or TOWN & TOWNS)
Amasa: b 5-18-1755 d 12-27-1820 m Margaret Smith Pvt MA
Amos: b 10-17-1737 d 9-8-1793 m (1)Jane Smith (2)Sarah Miller Lt MA
Archaelaus, Sr.: b 1734 d 12-1-1779 m Martha Abbott Capt NH
Archaelaus, Jr.: b 7-10-1760 d 7-8-1818 m Esther Weston Pvt NH W★
Daniel: b 7-9-1760 d 5-25-1813 m Hitta Brown Pvt MA
David: b 3-17-1744 d 2-26-1815 m Susannah Averill Sgt MA
David: b 8-7-1756 d a. 4-5-1802 m Elizabeth Southworth Pvt MA
David: b 6-25-1762 d 9-5-1828 m (1)Lydia Slade (2)Olive — Pvt MA ★
David: b 7-17-1734 d 1- -1792 m Kezia Shumway Cpl MA
Ebenezer: b 9-22-1744 d 2-11-1778 m Huldah Wheelock Ens MA
Edmund, Sr.: b 8-19-1724 d 1779 m Abigail Brewer Pvt MA
Edmund: b 8-6-1764 d 1843 m Anna Fisher Pvt MA
Eli, Sr.: b 3-3-1731 d 10-14-1800 m Elizabeth Gould Pvt MA
Elijah, Sr.: b 2-16-1719 d p. 1793 m Lydia Locke Capt MA
Elijah, Jr.: b 7-18-1754 d 2-22-1825 m Sarah Holton Pvt VT
Elijah: b 9-11-1740 d 1803 m Eunice Dwinnel Pvt NH
Ezra, Sr.: b 4-30-1736 d 12- -1795 m Elizabeth — Capt NH
Francis: b 7-27-1737 d 8-11-1811 m Phoebe — Capt PS NH
Francis Alonzo: b 11-18-1757 d 8-24-1827 m Eunice Warner Drm MA ★
Israel, Sr.: b 3-24-1705 d 1791 m Grace Gardner PS NH
Israel, Jr.: b 11-16-1736 d 4-28-1813 m Lydia Hopkins CS NH
Jabez: b 6-15-1704 d 4-1-1783 m Tryphena Dwinnell PS NH
Jacob: b 3-7-1728 d 9-18-1807 m Elizabeth Perkins Pvt MA
Jacob: b 9-25-1738 d 7-29-1829 m (1)Susannah Brown (2)Mrs Sarah Bridge PS Pvt NH
James: b 12-15-1757 d 8-1-1837 m Lucy Bettis Pvt MA W★
John, Jr.: b 12-5-1729 d 1-9-1820 m Mary Thomas Capt MA
John: b 9-22-1740 d 3-8-1830 m Ann Cummings Sgt MA
John: b 5-12-1758 d p. 10-19-1829 m Mrs Margaret (George) Hardwick 1Lt VA
Jonathan: b 12-24-1756 d 9-25-1824 m (1)Mary Holbrook (2)Miriam Warner Pvt MA ★
Joseph: b 2-22-1761 d 1-18-1824 m Hannah Coleman Pvt MA
Joshua: b 9-23-1721 d 1-31-1788 m Sarah Ball Pvt MA
Moses: b 4-1-1747 d 4-3-1781 m Sarah Lawson Cpl MA
Nathan: b 7-11-1744 d 9-3-1810 m (1)Mary Poole (2)Hannah Gould (3)Mrs Lydia Hall Sgt MA
Nehemiah: b 10-15-1748 d 5-2-1820 m Lucy — Pvt MA
Peter: b 8-10-1749 d 5-20-1830 m (1)Lydia Abbott (2)Rebecca Sheldon Pvt MA
Reuben: b 7-29-1746 d 1775 m Sarah Dodge Pvt MA
Robert: b 5-11-1754 d 6-26-1820 m Elizabeth Hawes Pvt MA
Salem: b 10-21-1746 d 7-22-1825 m (1)Elizabeth Mayo (2)Ruth Moore (3)Mrs Comer Maj MA
Sylvanus: b 2-15-1750 d 4-8-1818 m (1)Margaret Watson (2)Ruth Hovey Lt MA
Thomas: b 12-25-1759 d 12- -1819 m (1)Ruth Burton (2)Mary Coleman Pvt MA
Thomas: b 2-8-1743 d 5-1-1824 m (1)Elizabeth (Towne) (2)Sarah Burton Pvt NH
Thomas: b 1751/2 d 1848 m Sarah Wade Pvt VA ★
Wm.: b 9-3-1758 d 12-25-1846 m (1)Lucy Prince (2)Alteda Newell Pvt CT ★
Wm.: b a. 1753 d 1826 m Obedience Allen 2Lt VA

TOWNER,
Daniel: b 1- -1723 d 4-4-1809 m Jane — PS CT
Daniel: b 3-25-1731 d 1796 m Mercy Barnes Capt PS CT
Elijah: b 8-21-1759 d 10-7-1840 m Mary Knapp Pvt CT
Samuel: b 1746 d 4-1-1814 m Mary Birdsall Pvt NY
Zacheus: b 4-3-1729 d 2-14-1814 m Sarah Vaughn PS CT

TOWNLEY,
Charles: bpt 4-21-1751 d 1-14-1802 m (1)Hannah Thompson (2)Mrs Sarah Earl (3)Mary Hannah Miller Capt NJ
Charles: b 3-30-1762 d 1-31-1817 m Betsy Lewis Pvt NJ
Edward: b 11-29-1740 d 3-3-1823 m Abigail Price Pvt NJ
Effingham: b 12-11-1729 d 4- -1818 m Mrs Jemima Earl Pvt NJ
Evetts: b 8-8-1751 d 7-2-1826 m Sarah Lyon Pvt NJ
George: b 6-20-1755 d 9-28-1840 m (1)Martha Baldwin (2)Elizabeth (Parsons) Cory Pvt NJ
James S: b 8-7-1760 d 9-7-1837 m Catherine Brown Pvt NJ
Matthias: bpt 2-10-1750 d 12-23-1831 m (1)Nancy Searing (2)Johannah Smith Pvt NJ
Richard: b 8-22-1736 d 8-4-1801 m (1)Rachel Carpenter (2)Rhoda Clark Capt NJ

TOWNSEND, (or TOWNSON)
Abraham: b 11-5-1717 d p. 1717 d p. 1790 m Elizabeth Libby Sol ME
Absalom: b 11-21-1744 d 6-4-1817 m Helena DeKay Pvt NY
Amasa: b c. 1730 d p. 1804 m Phebe Ingham Pvt MA
Andrew: b c. 1712 d a. 7-20-1781 m Mrs Ann (Wilkins) Clark PS SC

Barkley: b *c.* 1737 d 4-3-1795 m Mary — 1Lt MD
Bela: b 2-6-1758 d 1-28-1832 m Hannah Burrill Drm MA ★
Benjamin: b 8-30-1759 d 1825 m Patsy — Sgt MD
Benjamin: b 11-11-1753 d *c.* 1- -1803 m Sarah Mitchell Fif MD
Benjamin: b 1741 d 7-18-1783 m Elisabeth Stratton Lt MA
Benjamin, Sr.: b 5-5-1711 d 11-23-1810 m Sarah Petty MM MA
Benjamin, Jr.: b 10-8-1751 d 1-11-1798 m Eunice Stoddard Pvt MA
Caleb: b 10-27-1743 d 8-2-1817 m Joanna Kelly PS NY
Daniel: b 12-26-1738 d 4-19-1775 m Zerviah Upton Pvt MA
Daniel: b 1740-43 d 1778 m Sarah Butterfield Pvt MA
Daniel: b 8-13-1747 d 7-3-1833 m Lydia Sawens Pvt PA
Daniel: b 9-21-1756 d 1812 m (1)Hannah Lord (2)Priscilla
   Peterson Pvt NJ
Daniel: b 1756 d 1799 m Rebecca Ward Pvt NY
Daniel: b 12-3-1759 d 7-26-1815 m Millicent Benedict Fif NY
David: b 1725 d 1815 m Sarah Irena Loomis Pvt CT
David: b 1-7-1763 d 4-13-1829 m Elizabeth Davis Dr MA
David, Jr.: b 11-13-1755 d 6-22-1841 m (1)Tamesin Wiley (2)Mrs
   Esther Fiske Sol NH
Dennis: b 1760 d 2-21-1812 m Alice Baldwin Pvt MA
Eber: b *a.* 1763 d 1826 m Sarah Drew Pvt NY
Elijah: b 6-8-1751 d 4-3-1824 m Mary Tredwell Capt NY
Evan: b 8-14-1748 d 12-24-1824 m Abi Croasdale Pvt PA
Frances: b 4-15-1740 d 1789 m Rachel Talbot Pvt PA
George: b 11-12-1713 d 5-14-1802 m Rosanna Youngs PS NY
Henry: b 1739 d 1789 m — Barrett Pvt GA
Henry: b 2-17-1752 d 2-28-1815 m Mary Bennett Capt NY
Henry Young: b 5-7-1744 d 5-13-1789 m (2)Edith (Stites) Swain
   Capt NJ
Isaac: b 2-4-1765 d 11-5-1841 m Rhoda Atwater Pvt CT
Isaac: b 1- -1757 d 11-1-1832 m Nancy Goodwin Pvt MA ★
Isaac: b 3-31-1742 d 9-10-1803 m Hannah Wixon Lt NY W★
Isaac: b 2-28-1756 d 6-20-1826 m Kesia Paddock Lt NY
Isaac: b 11-6-1763 d 1853 m Elvira Cain Pvt NC
Isaac: b 12-27-1760/1 d 11-2-1837 m Rachel King Pvt PA
James: b 1754 d 1-15-1840 m Catharine Allen Pvt VA ★
Jeremiah: b 12-28-1758 d 2-14-1841 m Sarah Pettengill Pvt Slr
   RI MA ★
Job: b 1748 d 5-5-1842 m Peace Hammond Sgt MA
John: b 12-22-1758 d 4-9-1841 m Mary Kingsbury Sgt CT ★
John: *c.* 1745 d 3- -1789 m Sarah Liston 2Lt DE
John: b 5-16-1742 d 4-14-1827 m Eunice Fairbanks Sgt MA
John, Jr.: b 5-8-1755 d 3-26-1832 m Sarah Swain PS NJ
John: b 1743 d 9-17-1821 m Jemima Travis Pvt NY
John: b 9-8-1757 d 8- -1847 m Sarah Birdsall Pvt NY
John: b 11-6-1763 d 8-25-1853 m Elvira Cain Sol NC
John: b *c.* 1760 d 7-7-1843 m Kesiah Hayes Pvt SC
John: b *c.* 1761 d 8-4-1834 m Elizabeth Bachelor Pvt VA
Joseph: b 1745 d 1797 m Ann — Pvt PA
Joshua: b 1731 d 1812 m Susannah — Pvt MA
Jotham: b 9-10-1746 d 10-22-1815 m Deborah Kirk Capt NY
Lawrence: b 3-13-1740 d 8-29-1821 m Phoebe Green Capt NY
Micah: b 5-13-1749 d 4-26-1832 m Mary Wells Capt NY
Nicholas: b 10-2-1738 d 1810 m Philadephia Doughty PS NY
Noe: b 10-19-1746 d 6-15-1812 m Elizabeth Palmer Capt PA W★
Platt: b 1-25-1733 d 10-11-1816 m (1)Elizabeth Hubbard(2)Martha
   Dickerson Dr NY
Reuben: b 8-23-1758 d 2-11-1837 m Margaret Metcalf Pvt MA
Robert: b 12-2-1760 d 9-9-1845 m Susanna Dennison Pvt MA
Robert: b 1756 d 4-10-1846 m (1)Ruth Sawtell (2)Rachel—Pvt RI ★
Roger: b — d 7-22-1779 m Kesiah Gale Pvt NY
Samuel: b 12-25-1725 d 1793 m Rachel Godfrey PS NJ
Samuel: b 8-7-1744 d 9-15-1792 m Sarah Horton PS NY
Samuel: b 4-9-1751 d 5-14-1849 m Mary Criswell Pvt SC
Solomon, Jr.: b 6-24-1748 d 3-22-1818 m Martha Bourne QM RI
Solomon: b 10-27-1716 d 12-25-1796 m Rebecca Baker PS RI
Stephen: b 7-18-1727 d 7-20-1787 m Deborah Smith PS NY
Thomas: b 8-23-1736 d 7-27-1814 m Susanna Green 1Lt MA
Thomas: b 10-10-1722 d *p.* 1790 m Mariam Poak Pvt MA
Thomas: b 1725/6 d *p.* 1796 m Lettice McConkey PS NC
Thomas: b 11-10-1730 d 1784 m Sarah Hall Pvt PA
Thomas: b 1732 d 1796 m Anphilida Watson Sol SC
Timothy: b 11-10-1755 d 2-10-1832 m Hannah Alling Pvt CT
Wm.: b 4-5-1760 d *c.* 1837 m Mary McGraw Pvt NC ★
Wm.: b 1750 d 7-21-1830 m Sarah Thompson Sol NC
Wm.: b *c.* 1750 d 1801 m — Hall Pvt NC

TOWNSLEY,
Adam: b 6-7-1752 d 9-16-1788 m Azubah Lumbard Sgt MA
Dan: b 10-6-1763 d 12- -1851 m Rachel Bullard Pvt MA ★
John: b 9-12-1757 d 12-27-1827 m Hester Martin Pvt PA
Reuben: b 11-18-1718 d 7-25-1776 m Sarah Blodgett Pvt MA
Thomas: b 5-2-1841 m Sarah Patterson Pvt Wgn PA ★

TOWSON,
John: b 1746 d 9-17-1832 m Penelope Buck Capt MD

TOZER,
Elishama: b *a.* 1750 d *p.* 1790 m Mary — Lt NY
Jared: b 4-4-1764 d 1850 m Sarah Ives Pvt CT ★
John: b 1754 d 2-5-1835 m Mary Frye Pvt NH ★
Julius: b 6-16-1764 d 12-7-1852 m Hannah Conklin Pvt CT
Richard: b 9-3-1754 d 1- -1837 m Ann Middleton Sol PA

TRABUE,
Daniel: b 3-31-1760 d 9-10-1840 m Mary Haskins Capt VA ★
Edward: b 1762 d 7-6-1814 m (1)Martha Haskins (2)Jane E Clay
   Pvt VA
James: b 1750 d 1804 m Jean Porter Lt Comsry Gen VA
John, Sr.: b 8-28-1735 d 1791 m (1)Elizabeth Elmore (2)Magdaline
   Baskerville Lt VA
John, Jr.: b 12-3-1762 d 4-5-1828 m Priscilla Pendleton Pvt VA
Olympia: b 11-12-1729 d 1822 m John James Trabue PS VA
Wm.: b 3-13-1756 d 3-2-1786 m Elizabeth Haskins Sgt VA

TRACY, (or TRACEY)
Andrew, Jr.: b 3-17-1749 d 12-26-1819 m Anna Bingham Pvt PS CT
Andrew: b 8-1-1754 d 8-26-1802 m Sarah Bliss Grd Sgt CS VT
Asa: b 8-4-1760 d 12-23-1831 m (1)Dorcas Leighton (2)Dorcas
   Bunker Pvt ME
Asaph: b 1723 d 1799 m Mary Jacobs Matr Gnr MA
Benjamin: b 8-2-1742 d *p.* 1785 m Olive Killam Drm CT
Charles: b 11- -1759 d 3-19-1834 m Sallie Noe Pvt MD
Christopher: b 10-2-1758 d 11-12-1839 m Anna Getchell Pvt MA
Cyrus: b 8-6-1757 d 5-31-1845 m (1)Elizabeth Palmer (2)Hannah
   Lillie Pvt CT ★
David: b 4-10-1755 d 4-19-1814 m Electa Sheldon Capt MA
Ebenezer: b 4-20-1744 d 3-10-1803 m (1)Mary Freeman (2)Thankful
   Ayres (3)Anna Vera Kirtland Sgt CT
Ebenezer: b 11-5-1762 d 9- -1835 m Electa Howard Pvt MA ★
Eleazer: b 1765 d — m Hannah Rogers Pvt CT CL ★
Elias: b 4-6-1763 d 4-24-1848 m Lydia Gates Pvt CT ★
Elijah: b 7-31-1741 d 9-15-1821 m Lois Smith Pvt MA
Elisha: b 5-17-1712 d 1783 m Lucy Huntington Dr CT
Ezekiel: b 1754 d 2-24-1822 m Patience Kimball Sgt CT W★
Frederick: b 8-3-1749 d 6-21-1803 m Deborah Thomas PS CT
Gamaliel R: b 2-17-1759 d 2-5-1853 m Sally Lewis Pvt CT ★
Gilbert: b 17-1761 d 6-9-1841 m Deborah Woodworth Sol CT ★
Hezekiah: b 1736 d 6-23-1817 m Elizabeth Pettis Lt CT
Hezekiah: b 4-5-1746 d 7-14-1837 m (1)Eunice Reed (2)Sarah Peck
   (3)Mrs Hannah Hull Pvt VT
Isaac: b 5-25-1706 d 1-25-1779 m Elizabeth Bushnell PS CT
Isaac: b 1706 d *a.* 4-5-1784 m Mehetable Rude PS NY
Jabez: b 3-24-1760 d 11-15-1825 m (1)Zipporah Hibbard (2)Hannah
   Edgerton Pvt CT
James: b 1759 d 12-30-1839 m Agnes — Pvt SC
Jeremiah: b 8-9-1744 d *p.* 11-11-1786 m Sarah Leighton Pvt MA
Jesse: b 12-21-1745 d 11-16-1828 m (1)Faith Bingham (2)Hannah
   Aspewall Pvt CT
John: b 12-21-1755 d 1-14-1821 m Ester Pride Pvt CT
Joshua: b 8-13-1745 d 3-20-1777 m Naomi Bingham Pvt CT
Lucy Sprague: b 7-28-1725 d 3-6-1826 m Thomas Tracy PS MA
Moses: b 4-3-1728 d 11-9-1813 m Esther Richmond Tracy Cpl CT
Nathaniel: b 10-31-1750 d 12-9-1831 m Susannah Bingham Lt MA
Nathaniel: b 1743 d 1818 m Mrs Mary (Tidwell) Hill Sol NC
Nehemiah: b 3-23-1744 d *p.* 2-4-1778 m Miriam Waterman Pvt MA
Perez: b 6-18-1744 d 1814 m Diadama Dimmick Cpl CT
Perez: b 11-13-1716 d 2-12-1801 m Elizabeth Hyde Pvt CT
Rufus: b 12-9-1749 d 8-27-1776 m Mary Reed Sgt CT
Samuel: b 2-28-1731 d 1783 m Ame Partridge Pvt CT
Samuel: b 9-9-1723 d 6-3-1798 m Sybel Lathrop CS PS CT
Seth: b 10-18-1759 d 7-31-1829 m Sylphina Holly Cpl MA
Silas: b 7-17-1759 d 10-27-1823 m (1)Elizabeth — (2)Susanna
   Baldwin Pvt CT
Solomon: b 3-4-1750 d *p.* 1777 m Mary Getchell Pvt MA
Solomon: b 6-1-1756 d 4-4-1835 m Mary Wells 1Lt NY
Thomas: b 9-3-1724 d 5- -1777 m Lucy Sprague Pvt MA
Thomas: b 8-19-1725 d 1-28-1821 m Elizabeth Warner Pvt VT
Uriah: b 2-2-1755 d 7-19-1807 m Susannah Bull Sol CT

TRADER,
Arthur, Sr.: b *c.* 1725 d *a.* 1801 m Sarah Connor Pvt VA
Arthur: b 1747 d *p.* 8-20-1835 m Sarah — Pvt VA
Moses: b 1754 d *c.* 1803 m Elizabeth Wade Pvt VA

TRAFFARN, (or TRAFFAN)
Cromwell: b 1764 d 12-9-1851 m Nancy Wescott Pvt RI
Philip: b 1737 d 6-28-1787 m Elizabeth Stetson Capt RI

TRAFTON,
Benjamin: b 6-14-1739 d 1825 m Eunice Fisher Lt MA
Benjamin: b 1757 d 1829 m (1)Hannah Sayward (2)Katherine Lewis
   (3)Susanna Piper Pvt MA
Gardner: b 12-31-1760 d 9-2-1830 m Lovey McPherson Pvt MA
Joshua: b 6-6-1746 d 5-22-1834 m Ruth Wilson Capt MA ★
Jotham: b 8-28-1760 d 1-20-1857 m Hannah (Johanna) Spinny
   Pvt MA

TRAILL, (or TRAIL)
David: b 1726 d *c.* 1781 m Margaret — Pvt PS MD
Robert: b 4-29-1744 d 7-31-1816 m Elizabeth Grotz Maj PA

TRAIN,
George: b 2-12-1750 d 1-19-1800 m Adeline Weld Capt PA
Isaac: b 5-22-1759 d 8-19-1843 m Elizabeth Cummings Pvt MA ★
Oliver: b 6-8-1760 d 7-10-1820 m (1)Mariam Waite (2)Rachel
   Bardwell Pvt MA
Samuel: b 1711 d 1806 m Rachel Allen CS MA

TRAINOR, (or TRAYNOR)
David: b c. 1750 d 1831 m (1)Martha Booth (2)Margaret Morton Pvt PA
John: b 1754 d 1824 m Catherine King Pvt PA

TRAMMELL,
Thomas: b 1747 d 9-22-1823 m Mary Turner Pvt SC W★
Wm.: b c. 1752 d 12-17-1843 m — Lynch Pvt NC

TRANSUE, (or TRANSOU)
Abraham, Sr.: b 6-6-1731 d 4-13-1813 m Maria Magdalena Long Pvt PA
Abraham, Jr.: b 1757 d 1790 m Sophia Hess Pvt PA
Elias: b 6-1-1756 d — m Catharine Miller Pvt PA
Jacob: b 1759 d p. 1820 m Mary Yeates Pvt PA
John: b 1755/6 d p. 12-2-1830 m — Pvt PA
Philip: b 10-2-1724 d 4-19-1793 m Magdaline Gander PS NC

TRANTHAM,
Martin: b 1720 d 1800 m — Sol SC

TRAPHAGEN,
Jonathan: b 1743 d a. 1-19-1807 m Catherine Doremus Pvt NJ

TRAPP,
Philip: b 1715 d a. 4-23-1787 m Dorothea Toffen PS PA

TRASEL,
Jacob: b 9-12-1748 d 12-15-1822 m Hannah Matlack Pvt PA

TRASK,
Benjamin: b 4-25-1716 d 1776 m Mary Elliott Pvt MA
David: b 9-24-1758 d 7-21-1806 m Anna — Pvt MA
Ebenezer, Jr.: b 6-12-1741 d 3-9-1814 m Betty Dodge Pvt MA
Ebenezer: b 1761 d 11-19-1842 m Hannah Pierce Pvt MA
Ebenezer: b 1733 d 2-26-1795 m Sarah — Capt RI
John, Jr.: b 1747 d 4-17-1822 m Mary Wier Lt MA
John: b 1752 d 2-21-1829 m Elizabeth — Drm MA
Noah: b 1757/8 d 10-15-1830 m Deborah Walbridge Pvt MA
Peter: b 5-22-1746 d 10-7-1808 m Rachel Colburn Pvt MA
Retire: b 4-18-1757 d 9-14-1832 m Lydia Foster Pvt Smn MA ★
Rufus: b 8-6-1758 d 1830 m Hannah Stacey Pvt MA
Samuel, Sr.: b 12-17-1721 d 3-7-1790 m (1)Bethiah Sibley (2)Anna Bond (3)Hannah Park Sgt MA
Samuel, Jr.: b 8-25-1749 d 1-2-1826 m Ruth Tenney Sgt MA
Thomas: b 11-8-1737 d 2-1-1823 m Lydia Sylvester Sol MA
Thomas, Jr.: b 10-22-1759 d 7-19-1844 m Alice Hodge Pvt RI ★
Wm.: b a. 1738 d 4-4-1808 m Sarah — Pvt MA

TRAUGER,
Christian: b 5-30-1726 d 1-8-1811 m Anna Lumborn Stein Pvt PA

TRAUTMAN, (or TROUTMAN)
Christian: b 10-16-1742 d 3-27-1789 m Elizabeth Falkrod Pvt PA
George: b 5-17-1733 d 3-17-1791 m Christine Eckert CS PA
George: b 1757 d 2-2-1813 m Margaret — Pvt PA
Michael: b 1732 d 1815 m (1)— Baird (2)Elizabeth Shrader Capt MD
Peter: b p. 1727 d p. 1790 m Elizabeth — Capt MD
Peter: b 1-13-1741 d 12-15-1820 m Anna Maria Muller Cpl MD
Peter: b 12-18-1756 d 3-6-1846 m (1)Mary Barbara (2)Catherine Cassell OrdlSgt PA ★
Valentine: b 1-7-1752 d 4-19-1822 m Anna Margaret Pvt PA
Wm., Jr.: b c. 1763 d 1844 m Catherine Uhl Pvt PA
Wm.: b c. 1730 d p. 1-18-1790 m Elisabeth — PS PA

TRAVER, (or TREBER)
David: b c. 1734 d p. 1790 m Catherine Lewis Pvt NY
Johannes: b 10-17-1736 d 10-18-1808 m Catherine Becker Pvt NY

TRAVIS, (TRAVERS & TRAVISS)
Abraham: b 8-7-1757 d 3-26-1836 m Hannah Van Ostrandt Pvt Drm NY NJ ★
Amos: b 5-16-1746 d p. 1834 m Zeporah Turner MM NY
Asa: b 5-28-1729 d 1806 m Sarah Dunton Pvt MA
Champion: b 1747 d 8-22-1810 m Elizabeth Boush Col PS VA
Daniel: b 10-13-1742 d 10-24-1800 m Thankful Watkins Pvt MA
Edward: b c. 1750 d 3-28-1784 m (1)Betsy Tate (2)Clara Waller Capt VA
Elijah: b 1758 d 2-3-1824 m Lydia Pierce Pvt MA
George: b 1-3-1760 d 6-24-1843 m Abigail Owens Pvt NY
Gilbert: b 1740 d 9-6-1814 m Jemima — Sol NY
Jacob: b 1-15-1742 d p. 1801 m Sarah — Lt NY
Oliver: b 5-14-1761 d 5-8-1838 m Milly Gooding Pvt MA ★
Philip: b 1761 d 1848 m Eatchie Wixon Pvt CT NY ★
Robert: b 1732 d 1807 m Phebe L'Estrange Pvt MD
Robert: b 4-16-1757 d 4-16-1839 m Susan Burkdoff Pvt NY
Silvanus: b 1755 d 1840 m Rhoda Bennett Pvt NY ★
Titus: b 11-11-1739 d 2-25-1815 m Elizabeth French Pvt NY
Wm.: b c. 1740 d p. 1812 m Rebecca — Col MD
Wm.: b 4-1-1728 d 4-26-1805 m Abigail Denmark PS NC
Zebulon: b 10-10-1755 d 6-29-1826 m Martha — Pvt NY

TRAYLOR,
Humphrey: b 1730-40 d 1802 m Sarah Cousins PS VA

Jesse: b c. 1745 d 1795 m Sandall — PS VA
Thomas: b 1737-9 d p. 2-14-1817 m (1)Jane Travis (2)Betsy Bagley Sol NC
Wm., Sr.: b 6-12-1733 d 1803 m Judith Archer Pvt VA
Wm., Jr.: b 1750-5 d 1829 m Esther — Pvt VA
Wm., Jr.: b 1750 d 1812 m Mary Williams Pvt VA

TREADWAY,
Amos: b 2-19-1738 d 12-11-1814 m Elizabeth Blake PS CT
Benjamin: b 5-15-1748 d 1824 m Hannah Stacey Pvt MA
David: b 4- -1743 d p. 9-27-1833 m Sarah Gustin Pvt CT ★
Elijah: b 1753 d c. 1837 m — Sgt CT ★
John: b 5-11-1755 d 4-26-1800 m Hester Camp Lt CT
Jonathan: b 4-18-1755 d 11-17-1843 m Hannah Rood Sgt CT ★
Josiah: b 1707 d 1790 m Eunice Foot PS CT

TREADWELL, (or TREDWELL)
Benjamin: b 6-3-1763 d 8-1-1851 m Ruhama Wheeler Cpl CT
Benjamin: b 5-11-1735 d 6-19-1830 m Elizabeth Seabury PS NY
Daniel: b 3-23-1758 d 4-15-1822 m Mrs Sarah (Wheeler) Hoyt Pvt CT W★
James, Sr.: bpt 9-16-1733 d 11-22-1777 m Sarah — Pvt RI
John: b 11-23-1745 d 8-18-1823 m Dorothy Pomeroy PS CT
John: b 9-20-1738 d 1-5-1811 m (1)Mehitable Dexter (2)Dorothea (Ashton) Goodhue (3)Hannah Austin PS MA
John: b 1735 d c. 1821 m — Maj NC
Moses: b 9-20-1746 d 1-24-1831 m Susanna Cogswell 1Lt MA
Nathaniel: b 1753 d 1-7-1822 m Mary Hovey Cpl MA
Reuben: b 1751 d 5-29-1833 m Amelia Dawsey Pvt SC NC ★
Samuel: b 4-19-1752 d 1-29-1835 m Susanna Edwards Sgt MA ★
Samuel: b 1728 d 12-20-1803 m Hannah Sands Lt NY
Stephen: b 2-2-1748 d 1-13-1833 m Rachael Walker Lt NC
Thomas: b 4-20-1735 d 7-13-1805 m Ruth Bradley Pvt CT
Thomas: bpt 10-20-1745 d 5-7-1796 m Jane Jewett Sgt MA
Thomas: b 8-3-1732 d 2-11-1779 m Peggy Kissam Pvt NY
Thomas: b 2-6-1743 d 12-25-1832 m (1)Anne Hazard (2)Mary Conklin Hedges PS NY

TREAT,
Amos: b 10-23-1757 d 11-6-1788 m (1)Mary Wilcox (2)Rebecca Stow Pvt CT
Ashbel: b 5-13-1764 d 4-14-1842 m Sarah Bell Pvt NY ★
Ashbel: b 3-22-1762 d 8- -1848 m Elizabeth Carpenter Pvt NY
Bethnel: b 3-5-1738 d 3-25-1820 m (1)Anna Camp (2)Keziah Hurd Capt CT
Charles: b 6-13-1756 d 9-4-1841 m Hopeful Robbins Sgt CT ★
Cornelius: b 10-30-1766 d 10-21-1847 m (1)Esther Parker (2)Mrs Alcy Palmer Cpl MA ★
Gershom: b 9-15-1740 d p. 1790 m Jane — Pvt CT
James: b 3-3-1763 d 4-17-1852 m Mary Stanton Pvt CT
John: b 10-29-1752 d 11-18-1822 m Elizabeth Lancton Pvt CT ★
John: b c. 1740 d 1801 m Esther Barber PS MA
Jonathan: b 7-6-1762 d 1-24-1817 m Keturah Weir Tms CT W★
Joseph, Sr.: b 11-28-1722 d 7-27-1791 m Mary Merwin PS CT
Joseph, Jr.: b 1-1-1747 d 10-24-1828 m Rebecca Downs Pvt CT
Joseph: b 4-21-1734 d 1797 m Elizabeth (Bryant) Woodruff Chp NY
Joseph Canning: b 6-1-1758 d 12-19-1836 m Mary Fairbanks Pvt CT ★
Joshua: b 9-22-1729 d 8-12-1802 m (1)Catherine James (2)Mrs Polly Lancaster Armr ME
Matthias: b 12-3-1750 d 6-15-1827 m Tryphena Risley Pvt CT
Nathaniel: b 12-15-1747 d 4-13-1824 m Anna Rich Pvt MA
Philosebius: b 1727 d 5-3-1798 m (1)Mercy Hull (2)Elizabeth Baldwin (3)Sarah Atwater PS CT
Robert: b 7-14-1752 d 5-27-1824 m (1)Mary Partridge (2)Mary Gale 2Lt MA
Samuel, Sr.: b 8-6-1728 d 8-17-1787 m Frances Bryan Maj CT
Samuel, Jr.: b 8-16-1760 d 5-3-1813 m (1)Sarah Nettleton (2)Clarissa Wetmore Pvt CT
Samuel: b 8-13-1714 d p. 1795 m (1)Beulah Jennings (2)Mehitable — CS CT
Samuel: b 1750 d 5-1-1806 m (1)Elizabeth Brewer (2)Ann May (3)Helen Merlino de St Pry 1Lt MA
Samuel: b 6-18-1745 d 11-22-1820 m Elizabeth Lombard Pvt MA★
Samuel Peet: b 9-29-1754 d 7-5-1837 m Sarah Thompson Pvt CT ★
Stephen: b 5-26-1747 d p. 1789 m Grace Sage Pvt CT
Theodore: b 8-15-1754 d 3-28-1828 m Mary Williams Pvt CT
Thomas: b 9-4-1761 d 3-11-1847 m (1)Jerusha — (2)Rachel Welsh Pvt CT ★
Thomas: b 9-11-1758 d 10-6-1832 m (1)Jemima Calkins (2)Mrs Betsy (Blair) Pvt MA ★
Timothy, Sr.: b 1731 d 4-21-1776 m Ruth Hamlin Cpl MA
Timothy, Jr.: b 4-5-1756 d 1810 m Beulah Strong Pvt MA

TREAUX,
Pieter: b 1725 d 1797 m Jacoba Van Santvoord Pvt NY

TREBERT,
Michael: b 8-15-1756 d 11-27-1818 m Eve Margaret — Vol PS PA

TREEN,
William: b 6-22-1748 d 1814 m (1)Phoebe Bow (2)Rebecca Golding (3)Ruhamah Golding Pvtr PA

TREES,
John: b 1756 d 3-4-1826 m Barbara — Pvt PA ★

TREFRY,
John: b 2-11-1759 d 1800 m Susanna Stacey Pvt MA
Wm.: b 7-12-1730 d 3-4-1824 m Tabitha Powsland Pvt MA

TREGO,
Wm.: b 8-11-1725/6 d 10-3-1793 m Rachel Thomas Pvt PA
Wm.: b 9-18-1754 d a. 2-22-1814 m Elizabeth Stubbs Pvt PA

TREMAIN, (or TREMAINE)
Abner: b 12-25-1761 d 8-18-1823 m Mary McLallen Pvt NY W★
Daniel: b 1759 d 12-21-1853 m (1)Mary — (2)Sabrina — Pvt MA ★
Joseph: b 1750 d 4-13-1814 m (1)Margaret — (2)Lucy Winchael Cpl MA
Nathaniel: b 9-14-1757 d 12-29-1844 m Olivia Lyman Pvt MA
Philip: b 1-22-1744 d 1805 m (1)Althea Warren (2)Anna Chapman Cpl MA

TREMBLEY,
Peter: b c. 1734 d 5-20-1797 m Sarah Cox Tms NJ

TREMPER,
George: b 3-1-1751 d 8-6-1827 m Mary Ten Eyck Pvt NY
John: b 11-24-1736 d 12-25-1784 m Cathrine Fippel Pvt NY
Michael: bpt 3-13-1745 d 1786 m Leah Van Deusen Pvt NY

TRENCH,
James: b 12-24-1744 d 6-26-1822 m Elizabeth Strong OrdlSgt SC ★

TRENCHARD,
George: b 1714-1720 d 1776 m Jane Wood PS NJ

TRENOR,
James: b 3-24-1757 d 7-3-1834 m Elizabeth Goggin Sgt PS VA ★

TRENT,
Alexander: b 3-29-1759 d 5-17-1841 m Jane Burton Pvt VA
James: b 3-13-1763 d 1-23-1823 m Catherine Falcner Pvt PA
Lawrence: b c. 1750 d 1791 m Sarah — Capt VA
Thomas: b 2-6-1757 d 6-29-1820 m Elizabeth Edwards Sgt VA ★

TRESCOTT, (or TRISCOTT)
Ebenezer: b 1-2-1751 d 2-1-1830 m Patience Firman Pvt MA
Jeremiah: b 4-14-1749 d 11-6-1824 m Sarah — Pvt VT
Samuel, Sr.: b 8-31-1715 d 5-1-1786 m Hannah Purchase CS MA
Solon: b 6-26-1750 d 4-15-1826 m Margaret Lewis Pvt MA

TRESTER,
Wm.: b 1761 d 1814 m Elizabeth Hesler Pvt PS PA

TRETABOUGH,
Conard: b 1740-50 d a. 4-29-1831 m Mary — Sol VA

TREUTLEN,
John: b 1726 d 4-10-1782 m (1)Margarethe Dupuis (2)Mrs Anne Unselt PS GA

TREVETT,
John: b 1747 d 11-5-1823 m (1)Sarah Graves (2)Elizabeth Gardner 1Lt RI
Samuel Russell: b 11- -1751 d 1- -1832 m Sarah Wormstead Capt MA
Samuel: b 1756 d p. 1792 m Isabel Mellen Fif MA

TREVILLE,
John la B. de: b 1-26-1742 d 1790 m Sarah Wilkinson Capt SC

TREVILLAIN,
Thomas: b — d p. 10-4-1787 m Sophia Terry Capt VA

TREWORGY,
Spencer: b 2-19-1743 d 12-12-1777 m Judith Townsend 1Lt MA

TREXLER,
Emanuel: b c. 1760 d p. 5-20-1822 m Catherine — Sol PA
Jeremiah: b 7-9-1748 d 2-5-1827 m Elizabeth Reiss Drm PA
Jeremiah: b 1708 d 1783 m Mary Catherine — PS PA
John, Sr.: b 1729 d 1795 m (1)Elizabeth — (2)Susanna Bauer Hasler Maj PA
Jonathan: b 5-1-1762 d 5-11-1846 m Elizabeth Horlacher Pvt PA
Peter, Sr.: b 2-11-1721 d 8-25-1798 m Catherine Winck CS PA
Peter Jr.: b 8-15-1748 d 3-13-1828 m Catherine Grim Col PA
Peter: b 12- -1727 d 11-7-1784 m Maria Katherine Albright Capt PS PA

TREZEVANT,
John Timothy: b 2-16-1758 d 9-10-1816 m (1) — Wells (2)Catherine Cocke Wyatt (3)Anna Bell Dr VA ★
Theodore: b 4-20-1722 d 5-14-1801 m (1)Elizabeth Wells (2)Catherine Timothy (3)Catherine Crouch PS SC

TRIBBLE,
Andrew: b 3-22-1741 d 12-22-1822 m Sarah Ann Burris Pvt VA
George, Sr.: b a. 1715 d 1792 m Betty Clark PS VA

TRIBBY, (or TREBY)
John Sr.: b 1725-30 d 1794 m Sarah Richardson Pvt RI
John Jr.: b 1758 d 5- -1819 m Abigail Hazard Slr CT

TRIBOU,
Amasa: b 4-14-1760 d 6-22-1842 m Mary Pratt Pvt MA ★

TRICE,
Edward: b c. 1737 d 1800 m Tabitha Harrison Sol NC
James: b 1762 d 4-2-1840 m Mary Smith Pvt VA ★
John: b c. 1740 d 1812 m Mary — Sol VA
Thomas: b c. 1720 d p. 8-24-1801 m Sarey — Sol NC

TRICKEY,
John Sr.: b c. 1720 d 1782 m Rebecca Chamberlain PS NH

TRIGG,
Daniel: b 8-14-1749 d 4-3-1819 m Anne Smith Col VA
John: b 1748 d 6-28-1804 m Dinah Ayers Capt VA
Stephen: b 1742 d 8-19-1782 m Mary Christian Col VA
Wm., Jr.: b 1742 d p. 9-5-1817 m Sarah Saunders LCol PS VA

TRIGLETH,
Richard Spingler: b 1752 d 11-17-1776 m Elizabeth (Spingler) Trigleth Cpl NY

TRIM,
Ezra: b 12-16-1750 d 5-25-1834 m Rosannah — Pvt NY

TRIMBLE, (or TRUMBLE)
Alexander: b 11-28-1726 a 8-5-1785 m Sarah McCloughy QM NY
Archibald: b c. 1758 d p. 1817 m Jennet Dennison PS PA
George: b 1746 d 4-25-1810 m Janet Mearns Pvt PA
George: b 1-1-1756 d 12-14-1814 m Jane Armstrong Pvt VA
Issac: b 4-6-1747 d 3-28-1824 m Elizabeth Walters Pvt PA
Isaac: b 1760-65 d — m Mary Graham Pvt VA
Jacob: b 2-2-1753 d 5-31-1819 m Phoebe Dunham Pvt NJ
James: b 4-24-1707 d 11-21-1792 m Mary Palmer PS PA
James: b 7-19-1755 d 1-26-1836 m Clarissa Sidney Claypoole CS PA
James: b 1735 d 1815 m Jean Young Capt VA
James: b 2-25-1753 d 1804 m (1)Martha McNair (2)Jane Allen Capt VA
John: b 1738 d 1822 m Susannah Woods Capt NC
John: b 1756 d p. 1838 m Charity — Pvt SC ★
Joseph: b c. 1743 d p. 9-20-1808 m (1)Elizabeth — (2)Mrs Martha Bowles Pvt SC
Lewis: b 1742 d 4-14-1821 m Margaret Edwards Capt PA
Moses: b a. 1765 d 1828 m Catherine Lewis Lt PS SC
Thomas: b 1755 d c. 1806 m Elizabeth Crow Sol PA
Wm.: b 1736 d 1798 m Jane Sterrett Pvt PA
Wm.: b 10-1-1735 d 4-30-1819 m Mary McMillan Pvt VA
Wm.: b 1760 d 6-6-1840 m Mary Fleming Pvt VA ★

TRIMMER,
Andrew: b 10- -1728 d 10-26-1795 m Eliza Deardorff 1Sgt PA
Andrew: b 3-8-1753 d 10-10-1832 m Susanna — Pvt PA
Obadiah: b 11-1-1759 d 1-22-1829 m Lucy Stribling Ens VA

TRINDLE,
Alexander: b 9- -1739 d 8-5-1785 m Sarah Lamb Capt PA

TRINE, (or TREIN)
George: b 1752 d 1-7-1843 m Barbara Saeger Pvt PA ★
Peter: b a. 1759 d p. 3-23-1812 m Margaret — Pvt PA

TRINKLE, (or TRENKEL)
Christopher: b c. 1751/2 d 1829 m Elizabeth Hickman Pvt VA ★
John: b 1754 d 8-28-1822 m Susanne — PS PA

TRIPLETT,
Daniel: b 10-15-1763 d 9-27-1845 m Susannah Botts OrdlSgt VA ★
Enoch: b a. 1761 d p. 1-22-1823 m Mary — Pvt VA
Francis: b 1756 d 1786/7 m Rachel Brock Sol GA
Francis: b 1728 d 1794/5 m Benedite Hedgman Sennett Col PS VA
Hedgman: b a. 1758 d 9-22-1837 m Nancy Popham Maj VA ★
Hedgman: b 1756 d 1826 m Mary Marshall McClanahan PS VA
Peter: b c. 1752 d 6-19-1851 m Catherine — Pvt VA ★
Simon: b 1740 d 1810 m Martha Lane PS Col VA
Thomas: b c. 1769 d 2- -1833 m Elizabeth Hedgman Capt VA
Wm.: b 11-15-1763 d p. 10-30-1832 m Nancy — Pvt NC
Wm.: b 1-20-1719 d 5-3-1822 m (1)Annie Miller (2)Elizabeth Moorehead Capt VA
Wm.: b 1730 d p. 1785 m Sarah Peake Lt VA

TRIPP, (includes TRIPE & TRIPPE)
Anthony: b 1-5-1762 d 5-7-1846 m Mary Brown Pvt NY ★

TRIPP, contd.
Benjamin: b 3-3-1746 d *p.* 1790 m Eunice Wakefield Lt MA
Benjamin: b *c.* 1745 d *p.* 1802 m Elizabeth — Pvt RI
Calvin: b 8-15-1758 d 2-20-1841 m Martha Record Pvt MA
David Jr.: b 7-19-1758 d *p.* 1790 m Lucy Potter Pvt MA
Edward: b *c.* 1715 d 3-19-1780 m Susanna — CS RI
Everett: b 1754 d 1834 m — Pvt NY ★
Francis: b 1759 d *p.* 10-2-1832 m Betsey Wilson Pvt RI ★
Gideon: b 1737 d *p.* 11-23-1793 m Amy Shippee CS RI
Isaac: b 1700 d 12-26-1778 m (1)Sarah Sweet (2)— Spencer
    (3)Sarah Dow PS CT
Job: b 1741 d 1808 m Hannah Carver Drm MA
Job: b 1731-6 d *p.* 1790 m Hannah Rice Cpl NY
John: b 1756 d 1796 m Sally — PS GA
John: b 3-25-1761 d 9-16-1847 m Jedidah Smith Pvt MA
Peleg: b 12-1-1755 d 9-5-1838 m Mary Samist Pvt MM NY
Peleg: b 6-13-1723 d — m Sarah — Pvt RI
Richard: b 1720 d 1811 m Ann McClary Cpl NH
Robert: b 11- -1744 d 8-30-1845 m Mercy Woodward Pvt MA ★
Robert: b 1722 d 12-30-1800 m Grace Caw PS NC
Robert: b 6-9-1758 d *p.* 1797 m — Pvt RI
Stephen: b 1725 d 4-4-1785 m Sarah Topham Ens RI
Wm.: b 12-24-1749 d 3- -1828 m (1)Dorcas Low (2)Keziah
    Thompson Cpl MA
Wm.: b 1759 d 1851 m Leah Van Buskirk Pvt NY ★

TRITT, (or DRITT)
Jaco: b 1-10-1746 d 12-19-1818 m Elzabeth Beyer Capt PA
Peter, Jr.: b 3-5-1755 d 2-24-1839 m Elizabeth Le Fevre Pvt PA

TROGDON,
Solomon: b 1760 d 5-14-1826 m Tabitha York Sol NC
Wm.: b 3- -1722 d *c.* 1781 m — PS NC

TROLINGER, (or TROLLINGER)
Henry: b 3-10-1762 d 2-29-1844 m Mary Thomas Pvt PS VA ★
Henry Jacob: b 1718 d 1798 m Barbara — PS VA

TRONQUET,
Nicholas: b 11-13-1760 d 5-2-1825 m Mary Ganiard Sol FrA

TROTT,
Benjamin: b 8-14-1741 d 1829 m Mehitabel Sewall Sgt MA
John: b 1738 d 2-6-1820 m (1)Ann Motherwell (2)Phebe Reed
    Sgt MA
Lemuel: b 1743/4 d 1-23-1832/3 m Martha Motherwell 2Lt MA
Thomas: b 1730 d 1821 m Sarah Knapp Capt MA

TROTTER,
Anne Hannis: b *c.* 1742 d 11-22-1825 m (1)Richard Trotter
    (2)James Bailey Sct PS VA
Christopher: b 10- -1758 d 1828 m Prepare Mc Clintock Pvt VA ★
George: b 12-23-1746 d *p.* 5-16-1806 m Catherine Crook PS VA
Isham: b *c.* 1744 d 1791 m Jennie Burch PS VA
James: b 5-1-1753-5 d 7-13-1827 m Margaret Downey LCol VA
James: b *a.* 1745 d *c.* 1790 m Mary Beard Capt VA
James: b *c.* 1725 d *p.* 8-17-1782 m (1)Ann — (2)Hannah Wilson
    Pvt VA
Joseph: b *c.* 1745 d *p.* 9-5-1808 m Nancy — Pvt VA
Richard: b *c.* 1738 d 10-10-1774 m Anne Hennis Sol VA

TROTTI,
Gaspar Joseph: b 11-1-1740 d 1-3-1813 m (1)Clarissa Koronius
    (2)Mary Keller (3)Mrs Dougherty Sol SC

TROUGH,
Adam: b *c.* 1749 d *p.* 12-27-1813 m Eva — Pvt PA

TROUP,
Jacob: b *c.* 1750 d *a.* 1782 m Mary — Pvt VA

TROUT, (or TRAUT)
Anthony Daniel: b 12-24-1751 d 2-21-1844 m Mary Catherine
    Grubb Pvt GA ★
Baltus: b 6-27-1758 d 1810 m Hannah L D Hoffman Gnr PA
Baltzer: b *c.* 1743 d *p.* 12-27-1782 m Eve Moser CMman PA
Baltzer: b 1757 d 7-5-1837 m Elizabeth Ritinour Pvt MA ★
Christian: b 1753 d 6-16-1847 m Elizabeth Geerhart Pvt MD ★
Daniel: b *c.* 1758 d 1826 m Anne Maria Kline Pvt VA
Henry: b 2-12-1757 d 10-11-1812 m Catherine Bossart Ens MD
Michael: b *c.* 1734 d *c.* 1798 m Elizabeth Basgal PS MD
Michael: b *c.* 1740 d 1822/23 m Elizabeth Baer Ens VA
Wendel: b 10-29-1743 d 9-9-1820 m Elizabeth Druckenbrod Pvt PA

TROVINGER,
Christopher: b *c.* 1753/4 d 12-17-1820 m Barbara Kimmel Pvt PA

TROW,
Bartholomew: bpt 7-25-1736 d 9-20-1806 m Mary Call Lt MA
Israel: b 1737 d 2-17-1825 m (1)Mary Clapp (2)Prudence Leonard
    Capt MA
John: b 10- -1745 d 11-28-1806 m Hannah Dodge Pvt MA
Joseph: b 1740 d 5-8-1833 m Martha Dodge Pvt MA

TROWBRIDGE,
Aaron: b 3-25-1765 d 1-7-1831 m Kezia Jacob Pvt MA ★
Abel: b 9-28-1751 d 9-23-1815 m Anna Mosier Pvt CT
Billy: b 11-25-1748 d 2-16-1798 m Rhoda Beardsley Lt CT W★
Caleb: b 8-7-1747 d 12-14-1799 m Anna Sherman Capt CT
Caleb: b 1745 d *p.* 1800 m Bethia Russica Pvt MA
Daniel: b 7-1-1757 d 3-14-1814 m Mary Taylor Pvt CT
Daniel, Sr.: b 4-6-1711 d 10-1-1795 m (1)Hannah Spring
    (2)Jerusha (Prentice) Bowen PS CT
Daniel, Jr.: b 7-20-1738 d 10-2-1776 m (1)Phebe Paine (2)Mary
    Pearl Sgt CT
Daniel: b 8-25-1726 d 1792 m Deborah — PS CT
Daniel: b 2-1-1764 d 3- -1825 m (1)Prudence Badger (2)Hetty —
    Pvt MA
Ebenezer: b 6-4-1757 d 6-2-1836 m Parnel Wheeler Pvt CT ★
Edmund: b 10-3-1752 d 6-30-1812 m Elizabeth Wiswall Sgt MA
Isaac: b 1788 d 1822 m Rachel Hodges Pvt MA
James: b 1753 d 5-5-1821 m Elizabeth Harris Sgt NY W★
Job: b 3-6-1764 d 8-12-1821 m Martha Doty Wgm NJ W★
John: b 6-1-1748 d 9-7-1791 m Thankful Doolittle Lt CT
John: b 4-11-1742 d 3-5-1831 m Anne Kinne Sgt CT
John: b 4-7-1746 d 2-28-1825 m Abiah Stevens Sgt CT ★
John, Sr.: b 5-22-1732 d 5-22-1807 m (1)Margaret Farrar
    (2)Martha Fisher (3)Elizabeth (Upham) Fiske Col PS MA
John, Jr.: b 2-12-1752 d 7-29-1825 m Mary Bent Lt MA
John: b 4-8-1739 d 6- -1794 m Elizabeth Parker Pvt MA
Levi: b 5-25-1753 d 12-14-1843 m Hannah Smith Pvt CT
Luther: b 6-3-1756 d 2-19-1802 m Elizabeth Tillman Capt MA W★
Newman: b 9-7-1738 d 4-29-1816 m (1)Elizabeth Bills (2)Mrs
    Rebecca (Dodd) Cable PS CT
Oliver: b 12-11-1759 d 1800 m Anna Noble Pvt CT
Philemon: b 1-13-1751 d 3-9-1812 m Eunice Hicock PS CT W★
Ralph: b *c.* 1737 d *c.* 1800 m Hannah — Pvt NY
Rutherford: b 2-3-1744 d 4-6-1825 m (1)Dorcas Hitchcock (2)Mrs
    Thankful Alling Mix PS Sol CT
Samuel: b 12-22-1761 d 7-21-1827 m Lydia Johnson Sol CT
Samuel: b 6-24-1757 d 9-23-1843 m Elizabeth Bond Capt MA
Samuel: b 2-23-1742 d 1824 m (1)Jane Ruble (2)Christiann Dumira
    PS VA
Seth: b 6-24-1729 d 2-16-1798 m (1)Mary Hayt (2)Mrs Mable
    Barnum Sgt CT
Seth: b 6-1-1763 d 5-10-1836 m Lucretia Spore Pvt MA ★
Shubel: b 9-3-1739 d 3-12-1782 m Mary Bayles Pvt NJ
Stephen, Sr.: b 1-30-1726 d 6-6-1812 m Lydia Crofoot Ens PS CT
Stephen: b 1-18-1756 d 11-5-1841 m Elizabeth Barnum Pvt CT ★
Wm.: bpt 12-30-1747 d 10-30-1837 m Hepzibah Weller Pvt CT
Wm.: b 5-1-1748 d 1-12-1834 m (1)Susann Sessions (2)Cynthia
    Child (3)Dorcas Bartholomew Pvt CT
Wm.: b 3-20-1751 d 9-30-1833 m (1)Sarah Rice (2)Acsah Hearsay
    Sgt MA W★

TROWER,
Solomon: b 1734 d 1840 m — Givens Pvt VA ★

TROXELL, (includes TRAXELL & TROXEL)
Daniel: b 1754 d 1814 m Maria Veronica — Pvt PA
George: b — d 1790 m Catharine — Pvt PA
Jacob: b 12-23-1750 d 10-2-1836 m Elizabeth — Pvt PA
John: b 1748 d 12-11-1835 m Margaret Harpole Pvt MD
Peter, Sr.: b 12-28-1723 d 2-28-1811 m (1)Anna Maria — (2)Hanna
    Zirckel Pvt PA
Peter, Jr.: b 3-28-1751 d 4- -1816 m Helena Catharine Schoener
    Cpl PA

TRUAIR,
Manuel: b 11- -1759 d 9-24-1841 m R— Pvt Wgn CT ★

TRUAX,
Abraham I: b 1-2-1743 d 6-27-1833 m Annatje Peck Ens NY
Abraham Jacobse: b 4-4-1737 d *p.* 1790 m Elizabeth Van Antwerp
    Ens NY
David: b 2-9-1756 d 2-11-1855 m Mary — Pvt VA ★
Isaac, Sr.: b 1-13-1715 d *p.* 1790 m Engeltie Beck Pvt NY
Isaac, Jr.: b 7-19-1755 d 12-22-1854 m Elizabeth Clute Pvt NY ★
Isaac Jacobse: b 5-26-1726 d 4-17-1808 m Marytje Wyngard
    Pvt NY
Jacob W: b 1761 d 12-7-1841 m Anna Barbara Bell Pvt NY
John: b 3-23-1762 d 1-3-1840 m (1)Sarah Catherine Goodenough
    (2)Mary Sutton Pvt NJ
John: b 8-29-1749 d 5-25-1825 m Nancy Van Hyden Pvt NY
John Phillip: bpt 7-27-1755 d 8-12-1817 m Cornelia Barheyt Pvt NY
John W: b 10-7-1752 d 9-29-1808 m Magdalena Huysen Pvt NY
Joseph: b 6-15-1758 d 1-25-1839 m — Pvt PA
Peter: b 8-27-1725 d 8-29-1797 m Jacoba Van Santvoord Pvt NY
Samuel: b 7-15-1715 d 10-5-1790 m Elizabeth Walton Pvt NJ

TRUBY,
Christopher: b 1736 d 2-20-1802 m Isabella Bowman Maj CS PA

TRUCKENMILLER,
Lewis: b — d 10- -1826 m Rachel Pawling Pvt PA
Jacob: b 8-29 1756 d 8-23-1823 m Anna Maria Kirchner Ens PA
Sebastian: b 8-1-1715 d 2-1-1795 m Catarina Schmuckbrucken
    Pvt PA

TRUE,
Abraham, Sr.: b 5-28-1721 d 3-30-1812 m Sally French PS NH
Abraham, Jr.: b 7-15-1755 d 7-15-1828 m Anna Batchelder OrdlSgt NH W★
Benjamin, Sr.: b 1730 d 5-25-1817 m Mehitable Osgood Pvt PS NH
Benjamin, Jr.: b 5-6-1762 d 12-6-1843 m Mary Locke Pvt NH ★
Benjamin: b 4-11-1759 d 1826 m Abigail Sanborn Pvt NH
Benjamin: b 5-2-1760 d 8-22-1806 m Mary Batchelder Pvt NH
Bradbury: b 7-29-1738 d a. 1-5-1777 m (1)Sarah Parsons (2)Sarah Pettingill Lt MA
Elijah: b 7-14-1744 d 7-31-1821 m Susan Clifford PS NH
Ephraim: b 12-21-1756 d 8-17-1835 m (1)Mary Eaton (2)Elizabeth Amlin Pvt MA
Ezekiel: b 5-16-1755 d 7-24-1842 m Mary True Pvt MA
Henry: b 10-4-1759 d 6-8-1803 m Martha Mc Keen Pvt NH
Jacob: b 4-6-1748 d 9-20-1826 m Lydia Dow Pvt NH
John: b 3-11-1762 d 3-4-1843 m (1)Mehetable Cram (2)Jemima (Eastman) Dodge Cpl MA ★
Jonathan, Sr.: b a. 1725 d 2-2-1791 m Ann Stevens (Bradbury) Pvt MA
Jonathan, Jr.: b 4-30-1758 d 11-10-1844 m Mehitable Worthley Pvt MA W★
Moses: b 11-30-1751 d 5-12-1838 m (1)Mary Page (2)Dolly Moulton Pvt MA
Obadiah: b 12-5-1760 d 11- -1844 m (1)Grace Garey (2)Mary Boston Cpl MA ★
Reuben: b 6-26-1732 d 6-30-1799 m Hannah Osgood Lt NH
Robert: b 1758 d 8-7-1833 m Nancy Crookshank MM Pvt VA ★
Samuel: b 10-4-1728 d 11-10-1815 m Mrs Hannah (Kimball) Hazeltine Pvt MA
Thomas: b 5-7-1728 d p. 1790 m Sarah Clough Pvt PS NH
Wm.: b 1-20-1730/31 d 2-2-1825/6 m Sarah Tuttle Pvt MA
Wm.: b 8-1-1737 d 11-1-1818 m (1)Miriam Clough (2)Mary True CS 2Lt MA
Wm.: b 1-11-1752 d p. 1800 m Susanna Brown Pvt MA
Zebulon: b 5-21-1765 d 2-4-1830 m Martha Kennedy Pvt MA

TRUEBLOOD,
Abel: b 1745 d 1807 m Jemima Scott PS NC

TRUESDALE, (includes TRUESDALL, TRUSDALE & TRUSDEL)
Darius: b 1-7-1752 d 5-6-1808 m Rhoda Chaffee Pvt CT
Gamaliel: b 1741 d 7-3-1778 m Anne Whitney Pvt NY
Gershom: b 1723 d 1796 m Elizabeth — Capt NY
Hiel: bpt 6-13-1762 d 1-5-1847 m (1)Jane Walker (2)Martha de Wolf Pvt NY
Hugh: b 1730 d 1814 m Mary Lytle Pvt PA
Jabish, Jr.: b 1759 d 2-11-1838 m Bethiah Paddock Sol NY
James: b 1736 d 12-24-1818 m Elizabeth Furgison (2)Elizabeth Dobbins Capt NC W★
Jesse: b c. 1734 d p. 1790 m — Maj NY
John: b c. 1704 d 1784 m Elizabeth — PS NC
John: b 10-3-1762 d 12-11-1837 m Elizabeth Stockard Pvt NC
John: b 1745 d 3-20-1819 m Hannah Robinson Pvt PA
John: b c. 1743 d p. 7-24-1803 m Mollie Hollingsworth Pvt SC
Johnathan: b 2-6-1762 d 11-11-1838 m Phebe Mead Pvt NY
Richard: b 1744 d 1839 m Rachel Keeler OrdlSgt NY ★
Samuel: b 4-8-1760 d 10-3-1839 m Sybil Phillips Lt NY ★
Stephen: b 1751 d 6-25-1852 m Nellie Winfield Pvt NJ
Thomas: b 4-19-1740 d p. 1793 m Rhoda Curtis Pvt MA

TRUFANT,
David: b 5-22-1743 d — m Mary Turner Sol CS MA
David: b 2-27-1761 d 4-21-1836 m Lydia Beals Pvt MA ★

TRUITT,
James: b c. 1740 d 3- -1787 m — Pvt MD
Purnall: b 2-26-1757 d a. 9- -1838 m (1)Polly Godfrey (2)Rachael Render Pvt DE

TRULL, (or TRUELL)
David: b 12-17-1738 d 1-20-1822 m Jemima Hawes Pvt MA
David: b 2-22-1731 d 6- -1796 m Mary — Pvt MA
David: b 7- -1754 d 7-19-1829 m Mary Wilson Pvt MA
John: b 2-3-1737 d 10-5-1797 m (1)Hannah Trull (2)Esther Wyman Capt MA
Samuel: b 1-7-1731 d 9-27-1810 m Elizabeth Johnson Pvt MA

TRULOCK, (or TRULUCK)
Sutton: b c. 1760 d p. 1-27-1818 m Mary (Hines) O'Donnell Pvt NC

TRUMAN,
John: b 8-26-1739 d 10-22-1828 m Rachel Moore Pvt PA
Jonathan: b 10-6-1745 d 3-25-1826 m Anna Mackey MM NY
Shem: b 1760 d p. 1818 m (1)Abigail Spellman (2)Sarah Barto Rose (3)Lucy Remington Pvt CT
Solomon: b 2-13-1757 d 12-18-1836 m Lodema Chapman Pvt MA
Thomas: b 5-17-1752 d 8-7-1786 m Sarah Jencks Dr RI

TRUMBULL,
Asaph: b 3-1-1738 d 2-5-1821 m Zilpah Phelps Lt CT
Benjamin: b 12-19-1735 d 6-21-1825 m Martha Phelps Capt CT

David: b 11-10-1744 d 1-27-1800 m Sarah Harper PS CT
John: bpt 4-23-1715 d 12-13-1787 m Sarah Whitman PS CT
John: b 4-24-1750 d 5-12-1831 m Sarah Hubbard PS CT
Jonathan, Sr.: b 10-12-1710 d 8-17-1785 m Faith Robinson PS CT
Jonathan, Jr.: b 3-26-1740 d 8-7-1809 m Eunice Backus PS CT
Nathan: b 9-12-1762 d p. 1804 m Hannah Pickett Pvt MA
Robert: b 1754 d 8-24-1840 m Lucy Babcock Sgt CT
Wm.: b 1747 d 11-2-1797 m Allitheah Williams Cpl CT

TRUMP, (or VAN TRUMP)
Abraham: b 1-5-1743 d 6-27-1832 m Jemima Heaton Pvt PA
Jesse: b 3-29-1753 d p. 1798 m Margaret Loofburrow Pvt PA
Michael: b 1724 d 1790 m Susanna — PS PA

TRUMPBOUR,
Jacob: bpt 12-26-1748 d 4-11-1824 m Margaret Dederick Pvt NY
Johannes: b 4-5-1719 d 1785 m Christina Fiero Pvt NY
Nicholas: b 7-26-1741 d p. 1790 m Elizabeth Smith Pvt NY

TRUNDLE,
John: b 3-6-1753 d 3-10-1797 m Ruth Lewis Ens MD
Thomas: b 1-16-1746 d 1795 m Rachel Lewis PS Sol MD

TRUSLER,
James: b 11-7-1755 d 9-5-1844 m Susannah Wilson Pvt VA W★

TRUSSEL,
Joshua: bpt 8-10-1743 d 11-15-1807 m Betty Blasder Pvt MA

TRUXTUN,
Thomas: b 2-17-1755 d 5-5-1822 m Mary Von Drieull NCdr PA

TRY,
Jacob: b 2-6-1757 d 7-31-1832 m Justiana Bernhard Pvt PA

TRYAR,
Andrew: b 2-8-1749 d 3-31-1822 m Elizabeth — Sgt PA ★

TRYON, (or TRION)
Amos: b 1735/6 d 8-18-1790 m Mary Hubbard PS CT
Caleb: b 4-15-1743 d 1835 m Lydia Hubbard Pvt PS CT
Edward: b 3-14-1738/9 d p. 1800 m — Mrnr CT
Elijah: b 5-17-1861 d 9-8-1853 m Truba Priest Pvt MA ★
Eliod: b 7-28-1740 d 10- -1791 m Bethiah Aldrich Lt NY
Ezra: b 1760 d 5-26-1847 m Anner Tryon Pvt CT ★
Isaac: b 4-23-1742 d 12-26-1823 m Elizabeth Kimberley Arfr CT
Michael: b a. 1751 d a. 1799 m Anna Maria Elizabeth — PS PA
Samuel: b 3-9-1743 d 8-21-1808 m Prudence Brown Pvt CT
Simeon: b 2-26-1746 d a. 9-28-1778 m Bethiah Harding Brown 1Lt Dr NY
Thomas: b 3-18-1758 d 1-3-1843 m Sarah Curtis Pvt CT
Wm.: b c. 1757 d 9-17-1839 m (1)Susanna Spofford (2)Hannah Hopkins Sgt MA ★

TUBBS, (or TUBB)
Abisha: b 3-11-1740 d p. 1790 m Hepsibah Mack CS Sgt NH
Ananias: b 1747 d 1828 m Hannah Hill Pvt NH ★
Enos: b 1750 d 4-15-1838 m (1)Molly Earl (2)Mrs Sarah Jackson Pvt CT ★
George: b — d p. 1800 m Mary — PS NC
Joel: b 2-7-1746/7 d 1- -1820 m Dorcas Babbitt Ens MA
John: b c. 1752 d 1778 m Sarah Sims Pvt CT
John: b 8-6-1758 d 9-9-1836 m (1)Karenhappuck Tabar (2)Ferraby —|Pvt SC ★
John M: b 8-30-1760 d 2-23-1843 m Elizabeth Bush Pvt CT
Lebbeus: b 9-15-1730 d 1800 m Bathsheba Hamilton Lt PA
Morris: b 10-23-1749 d 7-29-1830 m Betty Randall Cpl MA
Samuel: b 1755 d 9-7-1841 m Sarah Susannah Dorrance Pvt CT

TUBBS,
Simon: b 1-16-1755 d 4-2-1824 m Rozina Lawrence Pvt CT ★
Zephaniah: b 1763/4 d 1-29-1835 m Katharine Eliza Bradford Sol RI

TUBMAN,
Richard, Sr.: b 1717 d 1-27-1786 m Sarah Keene PS MD
Richard, Jr.: b 1752 d 8-26-1813 m Nancy Traverse Lt MD

TUCK, (or TUCKE)
Edward: b 12-10-1762 d 6-22-1840 m Nancy Winfry Pvt VA ★
Jesse: b 1-16-1743 d 12-20-1826 m Hannah Garland Pvt NH
John: b 8-1-1740 d 2-9-1777 m Mary Parsons Chp NH
Jonathan, Sr.: b 9-28-1742 d 2-3-1781 m Tabitha Towle PS NH
Jonathan, Jr.: b 10-10-1736 d 7-20-1780 m Huldah Moulton PS NH
Samuel: b 9-13-1738 d 11-12-1777 m Anna Moulton Lt NH
Samuel: b 3-20-1731 d 1739 m Martha Blake PS NH
Wm.: b 1738 d 1796 m Elizabeth Johnston PS MD
Wm.: b 6-22-1740 d 3-5-1826 m (1)Mary Lee (2)Elizabeth Lee (3)Sarah Hager Mstr MA

TUCKER,
Aaron: b 12-4-1758 d 7-28-1794 m Tamison Stacy Pvt MA
Abijah: b 6-1-1735 d 1792 m Lucy Lyon Sgt MA
Alexander: b c. 1755 d 11-26-1811 m (1)Mary Day (2)Elinor Berry Pvt MD

TUCKER, contd.
Ashbel: b *c.* 1752/3 d *p.* 1789 m Nabbie — Pvt VT
Benjamin: b 1759/60 d 2-19-1828 m Anna Fox Ens MA ★
Benjamin: b *c.* 1738 d 1815-18 m Mary Thomas Pvt Dr MA
Benjamin: b 1744 d 11-23-1832 m Jane Babcock Lt MA
Benjamin: b 1-23-1734 d 9-13-1806 m Martha Daviess PS MA
Benjamin: b 3-15-1704 d 5-20-1785 m Mary Warren PS NH
Daniel: b 10-22-1758 d 4-18-1810 m Eunice Christie Cpl CT
Daniel: b 3-14-1760 d 1823 m Lydia Crabtree Pvtr ME
Daniel: b 11-9-1756 d — m Rachel Noyes Drm MA
Daniel: b *c.* 1746 d *a.* 1807 m Judith Harris Coleman Ens VA
Daniel: b 2-14-1740 d 4-7-1818 m Frances — Ens VA
David: b 1734 d 1814 m Mrs Athaliah Deland (Wright) Hunt Pvt VA
Drury: b 9-24-1719 d *p.* 2-24-1798 m (1)Susanna Douglas (2)Frances Penn PS VA
Ebenezer: b 12-5-1729 d 1802 m Elizabeth Atherton Pvt MA
Ebenezer, Sr.: b 8-31-1707 d *p.* 1776 m Deborah Blake PS NH
Ebenezer, Jr.: b 1-27-1742 d 8-6-1824 m Mrs Mary Hawke Cilley Pvt NH
Elijah: b 4-14-1737 d 6-3-1810 m Violet Hills Sol & PS CT
Ephraim: b 5-12-1745 d 4-25-1823 m Mehitable Chandler Pvt CT
Ephraim: b *c.* 1744 d *p.* 7-29-1805 m (1)Sarah Miller (2)Mrs Rhoda (Price) Valentine Sol NJ
Ezra: b 2-11-1750 d 4-3-1845 m Abigail Moulton Cpl MA ★
Ezra: b 5-3-1738 d 10-26-1804 m Hepsibeth Pressey Lt NH
George: b 1762 d 2-1-1834 m Mary Hutchingson Pvt MD ★
George: b *c.* 1740 d *a.* 1-22-1805 m Maria Dorothea PS NC
George: b *c.* 1750 d 1800-1809 m Mary Merrifield Pvt VA
Gideon: b 1746 d *p.* 1790 m Eunice — Ens CT
Godfrey: b *c.* 1744 d *p.* 2-7-1827 m — Sol GA
Harbert: b 1761 d *p.* 1833 m (1)Frances de Jarnette (2)Helena Vaughn Pvt VA ★
Isaac: b 10-7-1756 d 12-27-1837 m Nelly McKendry Pvt MA
Jacob: b 5- -1745 d *c.* 1814 m Dorcas Danforth Pvt NH
Jacob: b 9-22-1717 d 7-24-1804 m Lydia Hoyt PS NH
Jacob: b 1742 d 5-21-1807 m Hannah Lines 2Lt NJ
James: b 6-3-1741 d 2-27-1827 m Elisabeth Bean Tms NJ
Jedediah, Jr.: b 9-26-1744 d 12-3-1821 m (1)Lucy Mixer (2)Mrs Elizabeth Goulding Pvt MA
Jesse: b 1760 d 3- -1817 m Nancy Lane Pvt VA W★
John: b 1763 d 1845 m Elizabeth Thomas Pvt CT ★
John: b 1750 d 11- -1807 m Nancy Wofford Pvt MD
John: b 4-21-1750 d 1-11/15-1831 m Elizabeth Elwell Lt Pvtr MA ★
John: b 10-26-1748 d 12-12-1826 m Rachel Thompson Pvt MA
John: b 1741 d 11-15-1809 m Leah Morris Pvt PA
John: b *c.* 1750 d 2- -1808 m Phoebe Beal Pvt PA
John: b 12- -1755 d 3- -1821 m Fannie Wood Pvt VA
Jonathan: b 5-27-1707 d 11-22-1789 m (1)Martha Jackson (2)Lucy — PS MA
Joseph: b 2-14-1754 d *p.* 1796 m Mary Stone Lt ME
Joseph: b 5-20-1736 d *p.* 1790 m Abigail Nason Pvt MA
Joseph: b 10-22-1748 d *p.* 1791 m Abigail Hurd Pvt NH
Joseph: b 6-9-1753 d 1841 m Elizabeth Rollins Pvt NH ★
Joseph: b 1-3-1757 d 2-3-1840 m Debora Line Pvt NJ
Joshua: b 7-4-1738 d 1821 m Elizabeth Davis PS VT
Josiah Pascal: b 8-5-1766 d 11-9-1845 m Lucy Dougherty Pvt NH ★
Martin: b 11-4-1759 d 1817-27 m Ann Elam Pvt VA
Matthew: b *c.* 1728 d *p.* 3-3-1786 m Esther Stumps PS Sol VA
Moses: b 1734 d 1792 m Mary Start Lt NH
Nathaniel: b 9-18-1732 d *p.* 1776 m Elizabeth Hall Pvt PS NH
Nathaniel: b *c.* 1740 d 1797 m Mary Lyon Lt NY
Nicholas: b 7-8-1745 d 12-1-1801 m Susan Chadwell Pvt MA
Reuben: b *c.* 1760 d 1-7-1821 m Lucy Daniel Pvt VA ★
Richard: b 7-28-1754 d 10-20-1797 m Johanna Cunningham Pvt Bosn Mte MA
Robert: b 1760 d 1844 m Elizabeth Jordon Pvt MA
Robert: b *c.* 1760 d 2-15-1843 m Charity Phillips Pvt RI ★
Robert: b 9-8-1739 d *p.* 3-31-1795 m Mary Gilliam PS VA
St. George: b 7-10-1752 d 11-10-1828 m Frances (Bland) Randolph LCol VA
Samuel: b 11-1-1747 d 3-10-1833 m Mary Gatchell NCapt ★
Samuel: b 7-8-1719 d 3-17-1796 m Abigail Sheperd Pvt MA
Samuel, Sr.: b 9-25-1719 d 5-27-1776 m Elizabeth Haywood Matr MA
Samuel, Jr.: b 1750 d 1841 m Abigail Vose Pvt MA
Samuel: b 5-10-1760 d 10-24-1832 m Annie Logan Pvt MA
Samuel: b 10-8-1735 d 9-2-1818 m Elizabeth White PS NJ
Silas: b 1740 d 1777 m Mary Histed Pvt MA
Stephen: b 11-25-1732 d 11-8-1808 m Lois Lyon Lt QM CT
Stephen: b 1733 d 11-28-1811 m Abigail Newell Pvt MA
Swallow: b 8-26-1742 d 4-22-1809 m Lucretia Carter Pvt NH
Thomas: b *c.* 1717 d *c.* 1785 m Mary — PS MD
Thomas: b 10-14-1750 d *p.* 8-7-1837 m Nancy Anne — Pvt PS MD ★
Thomas: b *a.* 1755 d *p.* 1800 m Mary — Pvt PS MD
Thomas: b 2-11-1757 d 5- -1840 m — Pvt NC ★
Thomas Tudor: b 1745 d 5-2-1828 m — Dr SC
Wm.: b 1757 d 1816 m Mildred Beale Lt MD
Wm.: b 1747 d 2-18-1780 m Margery — Sgt MD
Wm., Sr.: b 10-19-1734 d 1-15-1815 m (1)Annis Thompson (2)Elizabeth Hammond Capt MA
Wm., Jr.: b 2-28-1763 d 3-26-1817 m Sarah Coburn Pvt MA
Wm.: b 12-21-1760 d 3-6-1849 m Mary — Pvt MA
Wm.: b 2-13-1735 d — m Mary Tucker Capt NJ

Wm.: b 1756 d 5-23-1829 m Jemimah Lewis Lt VA ★
Zephanian: b 10-28-1759 d 9-18-1848 m Sarah Clark Drm CT

TUCKERMAN,
Edward: b 12-29-1740 d 7-17-1818 m Elizabeth Harris PS MA

TUDOR, (or TUDER)
Henry: b 8-8-1733 d 1787 m Eleanor Du Shane PS PA
John, Jr.: b 10-10-1754 d 1-10-1838 m (2)Martha Searcy (2)Frances Phillips Pvt NC ★
Samuel: b 6-22-1737 d 11-19-1822 m Naomi Diggins Lt CT
Valentine: b *c.* 12-4-1764 d *p.* 1851 m Elizabeth Hicks Pvt NC ★
Wm.: b 3-26-1750 d 7-8-1819 m Delia Jarvis LCol MA

TUELL,
Wm.: b — d 10-4-1777 m Rachel — Pvt MD

TUELS,
Barnard: b *c.* 1733 d *p.* 1778 m Experience Taylor Pvt MA

TUFTS, (or TUFFS)
Anne Adams: b 7-8-1729 d 2-13-1813 m Peter Tufts PS MA
David: b 6-17-1763 d 7-6-1823 m (1)Mary Massy (2)Elizabeth Mansfield (3)Eunice Hart Cpl MA ★
Ebenezer: b 4-19-1761 d 11-27-1830 m Elizabeth Travis Pvt MA ★
Eliakim: b 9-14-1767 d *p.* 1810 m Sarah Ross Pvt MA
Francis: b 7-21-1744 d 10-2-1833 m (1)Sarah L. Blunt (2)Mrs Lydia Blunt Blackstone Pvt MA ★
Francis: b 5-9-1756 d 8-20-1823 m Hannah Greenleaf Lt Adj MA
James, Jr.: b 5-24-1755 d 11-10-1810 m Elizabeth Hay Cpl MA
John: b 11-24-1754 d 9-10-1839 m Elizabeth Perry Cpl MA
John: b 3-15-1739 d 2-23-1799 m (1)Rebecca Hawkes (2)Lois Taylor Pvt MA
John, Jr.: b 1743 d 11-29-1828 m Mary Show Pvt MA
Joseph, Sr.: b 2-21-1731 d 12-6-1778 m Hannah — PS MA
Joseph, Jr.: b 2-17-1755 d *c.* 1794 m Esther Dickson PS MA
Peter 2nd: b 4-24-1728 d 3-4-1791 m Anne Adams PS MA
Peter, Jr.: b 1-9-1753 d 11-4-1833 m Hannah Adams Pvt MA
Samuel: b 11-24-1737 d 10-24-1828 m Martha Adams Pvt MA
Timothy: b 1-20-1734 d 2-18-1805 m Anna Adams PS MA
Wm.: b 1738 d 10-14-1783 m Margaret Browning Lt MA
Wm. 4th: b 3-27-1736 d 4-27-1782 m Susanna Dix Pvt MA

TUGGLE,(or TUGWELL)
Henry: b 1755 d 1781 m Drusilla Boteright Pvt VA
John: b 1759 d *p.* 1785 m Sarah Anderson Pvt VA
Reuben: b 8-10-1724 d 12-12-1805 m Jane Morton Sol VA
Wm.: b 4-27-1759 d 7-5-1834 m Nancy Harrison Pvt VA ★
Thomas: b 3-29-1752 d 7-24-1831 m Nancy Penick Pvt VA

TUKEY,
Benjamin: b 1755 d 10-30-1777 m Hannah Stanford Pvt MA
Houchin: b 2-26-1759 d 12-15-1787 m Rhoda Blaisdell Pvt MA
Stephen: b 7-6-1754 d 7-8-1826 m Hannah Cushing Sgt MA

TULEY,
Charles: b *c.* 1747 d *c.* 1787 m Elizabeth Floyd Sol VA

TULL,
Charles: b 12-2-1753 d 10-8-1836 m Sarah Hardy Pvt NC ★
Handy: b — d *a.* 8-1-1796 m Eleanor — Sol MD
James: b 4-19-1754 d *a.* 10-16-1795 m Elizabeth Porter Sgt MD
John: b *c.* 1748 d 3-2-1792 m Hannah Collins Lt MD
Joshua: b 7-13-1747 d *p.* 1788 m Mary Sharp PS MD
Wm.: b 4-12-1756 d *p.* 8-10-1819 m Susanna — Pvt NC

TULLER, (or TULLAR)
Eli: b 2-14-1740/1 d 3-12-1839 m — Pvt CT ★
Elijah, Sr.: b 2-22-1727 d 2-7-1814 m Sarah Case PS CT
Elisha: b 7-13-1744 d 9-1-1817 m Sarah Case Cpl CT
Isaac: b 4-24-1720 d 1-4-1806 m Phebe Case Ens CT
Jacob: b 8-18-1724 d 10-6-1818 m Mary — Cpl CT
Joel: b 11-15-1758 d 1-22-1826 m (1)Mary Case (2)Anna Woodruff MM CT
Joel: b 4-14-1757 d 5-1-1835 m (1)Mercy Loomis (2)Abigail Humphrey Pvt MA
Reuben: b 8-3-1755 d 10-10-1828 m Mary Cole Pvt NY

TULLIS, (includes TELLIS, TILLIS & TULLOSS)
Aaron: b 8-20-1751 d 10-29-1840 m Sarah Thomson Pvt VA ★
John: b 1751 d 1825 m Nancy Dork Pvt VA
Joshua: b 11-17-1735 d 12-16-1827 m Mrs Gladys McDonald Lt VA
Michael: b 1749 d 3-2-1832 m Elizabeth Jones Pvt VA W★
Moses: b 1730 d 1805 m Mary VanDyke Cpl NJ
Rodham: b *c.* 1740 d 1815 m Ann James Finnie PS VA

TULLOCH,
Magnus: b 1763 d 1845 m — Logan Fif SC ★

TULLY,
Elias: b 7-30-1752 d 8-30-1848 m (1)Azubah Kirtland (2)Lydia Buckingham CG Pvt CT ★

TUMEY,
John: b 8-25-1749 d 2- -1838 m Margret Howard Pvt NJ

TUNISON,
Garrett: b 11-12-1751 d 7-18-1837 m Sarah Ten Eyck Dr NJ

TUNNELL, (includes TUNNEL)
Wm.: b 7-12-1731 d 3- -1776 m (1)Arlantoo Howard (3)Elizabeth
     Evans Capt DE
Wm.: b 12-27-1760 d 12-8-1806 m Leah McCloud Sol NC
Wm.: b 1751 d 8-16-1814 m Mary Maysey Pvt VA

TUNNICLIFF,
Wm.: b 12-30-1756 d 6-30-1827 m Mary Spoor Pvt NY

TUNSTALL,
Edmund: b 1762 d 9-22-1818 m Ann Eliza Tunstall Sgt VA
John: b 1734 d a. 1796 m Sally Temple PS VA
Richard: b 11-30-1700 m 11-14-1781 m Ann Hill PS CS VA
Wm.: b 1736 d 1795 m Elizabeth Barker LCol CS VA

TUPMAN,
John: b c. 1745/6 d c. 1795 m Patsy Thomas Mstr VA

TUPPER,
Absalom: b 4-22-1761 d 12-9-1816 m Polly Fisk Pvt VT
Benjamin: b 3-11-1738 d 6-7-1792 m Huldah White BGen PS MA
Benjamin: b 6-10-1743 d 1778 m Diadame Smith Col MA
Benjamin: b 10-4-1721 d 3-27-1794 m (1)Elizabeth Ellis (2)Abigail
     (Woodberry) (Calif) Starbuck PS MA
Benjamin: b 3-10-1749 d 10-8-1825 m Eunice Raymond CS VT
Darius: b 6-15-1754 d 1828 m Sarah Lyman Pvt MA
Ezra: b 3-31-1763 d 9-30-1849 m Huldah Spencer Pvt MA ★
Ichabod: b 1-21-1752 d 4-27-1825 m Rebecca Ripley Pvt MA ★
Joseph: b 8-25-1739 d 7-14-1797 m (1)Joanna Cole (2)Lydia
     Tinkham Lt MA
Peleg: b 4-1-1731 d p. 1790 m Deborah Fish Pvt MA
Wm.: b 1750 d p. 1810 m Phebe Tupper QM Sgt CT
Wm.: b 7-6-1735 d 1802 m Margaret Gates Sol MA
Wm.: b 9-14-1735 d 11-25-1824 m Susannah Clapp LCol MA
Zuriel: b 3-21-1758 d 1800 m Jerusha Goodrich Pvt MA

TURBERVILLE, (includes TURBYFILL)
George: b c. 1742 d p. 6-29-1790 m Martha Corbin PS VA
George Lee: b 9-7-1760 d 3-26-1798 m Bettie Tayloe Corbin ADC VA
John: b 1742 d 4-6-1838 m Nancy — Sol VA

TURBETT,
Thomas: b 1-20-1741 d 6-12-1820 m (1)Janet Taylor (2)Jean
     Wilson Col PA

TURK,
Hendrick: b 10-31-1756 d p. 1802 m (1)Jannetje Brink (2)Mrs
     Catherine Wittaker Pvt NY
John: b 10-21-1744 d p. 11-29-1790 m Annatje Mol Pvt NY
Thomas, Sr.: b 1710 d p. 8-3-1808 m (1)Margaret Grove (2)Mary
     Woolman PS VA
Wm.: b 1744 d 4-10-1795 m Margaret Archibald Pvt Cmsry SC

TURLEY,
James: b 1754 d a. 3-15-1838 m Betsy — Pvt VA ★
James: b 1761 d 6-4-1836 m (1)Agnes Kirby (2)Mrs Sarah (Hoblett)
     Lucas Pvt VA ★
Thomas: b — d p. 1781 m Lucy Halliday PS VA

TURMAN,
Benjamin, Sr.: b 1741 d 10-12-1784 m Frances — PS VA
James : b 5-8-1752 d 6-3-1804 m Martha Seals Pvt VA

TURNAGE,
Wm.: b 1747 d 1823 m Mary — PS SC

TURNBULL,
Charles: b 9-4-1753 d 12-19-1795 m Phebe Bloom 2Lt PA
George: b c. 1752 d 12- -1807 m Abigail — 1Lt VA
Wm.: b 3-10-1751 d 7-25-1822 m Mary Nisbet Lt PA

TURNER, (includes TOURNEUR)
Aaron: b 3-4-1757 d 4-17-1845 m Cynthia Simmons Sgt NS MA
     RI ★
Abel: b 8-22-1758 d 12-27-1829 m Olive White Pvt VT
Abiel: b 5-3-1741 d 9-30-1836 m Lurana Sylvester Pvt MA
Abisha: b c. 1750 d 1-2-1826 m — Sol GA
Abraham: b 6-3-1734 d 1796 m Rebecca (Seeley) Gosling Arfr CT
Abraham, Jr.: b 8-23-1752 d 1817 m (1)Sarah Penfield (2)Esther
     McAllister Pvt MA
Adam: b 7-24-1743 d 7-24-1782 m Chloe Bonney Sgt MA
Adam: b — d 1784 m Mary — Pvt PA
Alexander, J.: b 1763 d 1806 m Sarah McCrea Pvt NY
Alexander W.: b c. 1759 d 10-19-1783 m Elizabeth Blanchard Sol NJ
Amos: b 9-24-1763 d 4-1-1847 m Thankful Allyn Pvt CT
Amos: b 7-16-1741 d 3-14-1822 m (1)Betsey Perry (2)Mary R.
     Stetson Capt MA

Andrew: b 3-10-1751 d 12-7-1840 m Ann McDonald LCol MD
Andrew: b 4-5-1762 d 8-8-1842 m (1)Comfort Turner (2)Mary
     Samples Pvt NC ★
Arthur: b 1740 d 1787 m Mrs Young Pvt NC
Asa: b 6-14-1765 d 11-27-1847 m Isabel Ketcham Pvt CT ★
Asa: b 2-20-1743 d 8-25-1821 m Abigail Mann Sgt MA
Benjamin: b 1-15-1758 d 1836 m — Pvt NH ★
Berryman: b 1755 d 1806 m Susannah — Capt NC
Bethuel: b 1762 d 7-9-1829 m Abigail Austin Pvt MA
Charles: b 4-21-1745 d 1-4-1796 m Mary — Pvt MD
Charles, Jr.: b 8-5-1733 d p. 1805 m Hannah Jacob Pvt MA
Charles: b 1763 d p. 1820 m (1)Hepsibah Rose (2)Irene Abbott
     Pvt MA ★
Daniel: b 6-1-1755 d 2-17-1835 m Hannah Welch Pvt PA
David: b 8-16-1753 d 9-6-1826 m Rhoda Porter Pvt MA
Edward: b 11-17-1739 d 12-26-1777 m Hannah Fisher Lt MA
Edward: b c. 1705 d a. 8-2-1803 m Ann Davies PS NC
Elisha: b 10-8-1756 d 1840 m Nancy Smith Pvt NY ★
Ezekiel: b 1-27-1734 d 4-7-1826 m Rebecca Allyn Pvt CT
Ezra: b 2-6-1743 d c. 1828 m (1)Abigail Cook (2)Ruhamah
     Jefferies Pvt MA
Francis: b c. 1750 d p. 10-19-1803 m — Pvt VA
George: b 1731 d 7-17-1821 m Elizabeth Coute Capt NH
George: b 1738 d 1804 m (1)Hannah Middleton (2)Ann Anderson
     Capt SC
Gordon: b 8-9-1746 d p. 1799 m Sarah Humiston Pvt CT
Henry: b a. 1757 d 10-23-1729 m Rachel Stoval Capt VA
Hezekiah: b 1752 d 1842 m Elizabeth Mills Pvt MA ★
Hezekiah: b 7-23-1739 d c. 1817 m Henrietta Chunn Capt PM VA
Hugh: b c. 1752 d 1808 m (1)Elinor Moffatt (2)Mary Stettler Sgt NY
Ichabod: b 12-3-1725 d 11-13-1809 m Susannah Fisher Pvt MA
Isaac: b 8-20-1744 d 5-9-1807 m Anne Wentworth Lt CT
Isaac: b 4-2-1754 d 11-13-1829 m Anna Comstock Lt CT
Isaac: b 1756 9-17-1840 m Molly Hanscom Pvt MA
Isaiah: b 1757 d 1828 m Judith Partridge Cpl MA
Jabez: b 1-31-1756 d 12-12-1846 m Rebecca Wolcott Pvt CT ★
Jacob: bpt 9-17-1732 d p. 8-29-1808 m Elise McClean Pvt NY
Jacob: b c. 1754 d 10-4-1777 m Mary Edwards Capt NC
James: b 10-27-1752 d 1-31-1839 m Ann Ford Pvt DE
James: b c. 1739 d 2- -1778 m Susan Thomas Pvt NY
James: b 12-20-1766 d 1-15-1824 m (3)Mrs Elizabeth Johnson
     Pvt NC
James: b c. 1745 d c. 1800 m Nancy Porter Pvt NC
James: b 1-24-1758 d 2-12-1856 m Rebecca Clendenin Pvt NC ★
James: b 10-9-1756 d 1835 m (1) — (2)Catherine White Pvt NC ★
James: b 1737/8 d 12-11-1803 m Rebecca Armstrong 1Lt PA
James: b c. 1753 d 1825 m Margaret Heydon Sct SC
James: b 1732 d p. 1803 m (1) — Wyatt (2)Sarah Irby Capt VA
James: b c. 1744 d p. 7-8-1785 m — Capt VA
James: b 5-7-1759 d 1-8-1828 m Sallie Leftwich Pvt VA
Jedediah: b 5-27-1733 d p. 1788 m (2)Rachel Tompson Pvt CT
Jesse: b 5-14-1744 d 3-13-1821 m Bethsheba Lapham Pvt MA
Jesse: b 10-7-1746 d 4-19-1834 m Phebe Humaston Pvt MA
Job: b 4-2-1751 d 2-17-1823 m (1)Sally James (2)Sylvia Sampson
     (3)Nabby Clift Pvt MA
John: b 1-10-1757 d 2-6-1843 m (1)Elizabeth Berry (2)Margaret
     Young Pvt DE
John, Sr.: b 1712 d 2-6-1894 m (1)Mary Randall (2)Anna King
     (3)Deborah King PS MA
John, Jr.: b 1739 d 12-22-1820 m Mary Little Capt PS MA
John, Sr.: b 1714 d 1798 m Patience Gardiner Pvt Dr MA
John: b 10-2-1758 d 1-14-1839 m Unity Boyden Armsby Pvt MA
John: b c. 1750 d 1808 m Rebecca Learnard Pvt NJ
John: b 12-28-1751 d 10-18-1811 m Hannah Bugbey Sgt NY
John: b 1-25-1740 d 9-12-1803 m Sarah VanHosesen Pvt NY ★
John: b a. 1737 d p. 10-2-1793 m Phebe Sadly PS NY
John: b 1738 d 12-5-1813 m (1)Rebecca — (2)Jane Barnett Sgt NC
John: b 1745 d 5-26-1823 m Mary Clark Ens PA
John: b 1750 d 8-19-1807 m (1)Margaret Adger (2)Jean —
     Capt SC
John: b 9-25-1749 d 8-3-1811 m Ruth Rawlings Lt VA
John: b c. 1740 d 1796/7 m Priscilla Blount Ens VA
John: b 1750 d p. 1813 m Elizabeth — Pvt VA
John: b c. 1747 d c. 1816 m Elizabeth Price PS VA
Joseph: b 9-2-1759 d 5-23-1829 m Sarah Knap Cpl MA
Joseph: b 10-28-1718 d 1779 m Abigail Smith Pvt RI
Joshua: b 7-14-1741 d 3-27-1825 m (2)Mrs Mary Ann (Maddox)
     Corley Pvt MD
Joshua: b 12-13-1757 d 12-21-1820 m Lydia Drury Pvt MA
Kerenhappuch Norman: b 1692 d 1807 m James Turner PS NC
Lewis: b 7-30-1761 d 10-10-1834 m Nancy — Pvt SC ★
Lewis: b 12-3-1756 d p. 1807 m (1)Mary — (2)Elizabeth — Sol VA
Lewis Ellzey: b 9-14-1754 d 10-9-1823 m Theodosia Payne PS VA
Matthew: b 10-12-1733 d 3-10-1824 m (1)Mary Fargo (2)Elizabeth
     Smith Pvt CT
Micah: b 5-31-1752 d 9-28-1810 m Mary Pratt Sgt MA
Micah, Sr.: b 7-8-1710 d 4-25-1797 m Bethiah Allen PS MA
Moses: b 11- -1755 d 1844 m Elizabeth Bean Pvt NH
Moses: b 5-6-1745 d 3-4-1816 m Abigail Child Capt RI
Nathaniel: b 8-5-1717 d 1-25-1796 m Mary Bailey Pvt MA
Nathaniel: b 1750 d p. 1784 m Mary — Sol VA
Noel: b 5-11-1764 d 1-21-1837 m Sarah Turner Pvt SC ★
Peter: b 9-2-1751 d 2-14-1822 m Eliza Child Dr RI ★

TURNER, contd.

Prince: b 1753 d 3-29-1800 m Rebecca Keep Cpl MA
Robert: b 10-8-1760 d 10- -1838 m Ann Carlisle Tms NJ
Samuel: b 2-4-1721 d 8-2-1808 m Mary Stocker Pvt NY Canada
Samuel: b 1704 d 1800 m Mary — MM MA
Samuel: b 10- -1724 d 6-15-1784 m Ruth Smith Pvt MA
Samuel: bpt 12-15-1728 d a. 7-10-1782 m Hannah Devereux Pvt MA
Samuel: b 1758 d 4-17-1847 m Sarah Spencer Pvt VA ★
Seth, Sr.: b 4-7-1727 d 1-29-1806 m Rebecca Vinton Maj MA
Shadrack: b c. 1720 d 1783/4 m Ann — PS VA
Simon: b 1720 d 4-9-1783 m Ann Smith Maj NC
Simon: b 1738 d 1- -1817 m Martha Ann Person CS VA
Solomon: b 1760 d 4-14-1820 m Cassandra Harvey Pvt MD ★
Stephen: b c. 1757 d 1841 m Amy Bennett Pvt NY
Stephen: b c. 1750 d 1800-10 m Mary Roundtree Pvt VA
Stephen: b 1750 d p. 4-19-1802 m Susan Hamner Sol VA
Stephen: b — d p. 4-27-1799 m (2)Sarah — PS VA
Terisha: b — d p. 5-7-1793 m Sarah — PS VA
Thomas: b 6-12-1740 d — m Eunice Coffin Smn NS
Thomas: b 10-15-1764 d 11-17-1847 m (1)Catherine Patterson
    (2)Anna Berry (3)Elizabeth Holden Pvt NC
Thomas: b 8-27-1734 d 7-1-1822 m (1)Catherine Smith (2)Nelly
    Dell PS NC
Thomas: b 1742 d 1806 m (1)Sally Van Swearingin (2)Mary
    McQuillan Capt VA
Thomas: b 1751 d 1834 m Sarah Lyons Pvt VA
Timothy: b 8-18-1757 d p. 1790 m Rachael Carpenter Pvt CT
Wm.: b 1753 d 3- 1841 m Mrs Phebe Marie DeWolf Pvt CT ★
Wm.: b 1-7-1756 d p. 1779 m Hannah Williams Pvt CT
Wm.: b 12-14-1737 d p. 1784 m Rhoda Dent PS MD
Wm.: b 1-16-1745 d 1807 m (1)Betty Oakman (2)Eunice Clapp
    PS MA
Wm.: b 5-2-1760 d 3-2-1829 m Joanna Pettingill Pvt MA
Wm.: b 1738 d 1-5-1799 m Jane Wright Lt NH
Wm.: b 8-12-1698 d 12-8-1796 m (1)Abigail Church (2)Sarah
    Colby PS NH
Wm.: b 8-6-1755 d 3-14-1839 m Hannah — Sgt NJ
Wm.: b 3-31-1753 d 5-17-1807 m Action Howard Pvt NC
Wm.: b c. 1760 d a. 3-3-1813 m Frances — Sol NC
Wm.: b c. 1756 d a. 12- -1816 m Nancy (Turner) Pvt SC
Wm.: b 1760 d 9-30-1834 m Sarah — Sgt VA W★
Wm.: b 1740 d p. 1830 m Lucy — Pvt VA
Wm.: b 1-19-1753 d 12-11-1845 m Jane Hunter Pvt PS VA
Wm.: b 11-30-1757 d 9-27-1817 m Elizabeth Thurmond Pvt VA
Wm. Henry: b 1764 d 6-25-1810 m Mercy Risley Pvt CT
Winslow: b 1762 d 1826 m Molly Standish Slr MA
Zackariah: b a. 1760 d p. 1815 m — Pvt MD
Zadoc: b 9-3-1729 d 10-12-1819 m (1)Sabia Hicks (2) — Parker
    (3)Anna Blizzard Pvt MD
Zadock: b 1762 d 2-11-1828 m Hannah Hott Pvt MA ★

TURNEY,

Aaron: b 6-28-1754 d 11-15-1833 m (1)Miss Ellen (Gold) Chapman
    (2)Sarah Staples 1Lt NS CT ★
Abel: b 9-25-1762 d 4-7-1841 m (1)Deborah (Couch) Bulkley
    (2)Molly — Pvt Slr CT
Asa: b 10-15-1759 d 4-5-1833 m Polly Downs Pvt CT ★
Daniel: b c. 1730 d c. 1804 m Margaret — Lt PA
Daniel, Jr.: b c. 1755 d 1803 m Margaret — 2Lt PA
Henry: b c. 1760 d 1843 m Elizabeth — Pvt VA
John: b 1749 d 3-6-1823 m Magdalena Grove Pvt PA
Peter: b c. 1734 d 1804/5 m Frances Haines Pvt VA
Stephen: bpt 5-28-1721 d p. 1-24-1786 m (1)Hester Middlebrook
    (2)Sarah Squires (3)Abiah (Treadwell) Mitchel PS CT

TURNHAM,

Thomas: b 1749 d 1830 m (1)Nancy — (2)Eve Liston Pvt VA ★

TURNIPSEED,

Jacob: b c. 1760 d a. 12-9-1819 m Catherine Kinsler Pvt SC

TURNLEY,

Francis: b 12-31-1762 d 12-18-1836 m Susan Walls Pvt VA ★
George: b 8-30-1762 d 9-3-1848 m Charlotte Cunnyngham SgtMaj
    NC VA ★
John: b 1730 d 10- -1808 m Mary Handy Pvt VA
John: b 2-7-1757 d 12-7-1832 m Elizabeth Spindle Pvt VA

TURPIN,

Francis: b 9-9-1759 d 11-2-1829 m (1)Nancy (Smith) Reed (2)Nancy
    Ann Chance (3)Ann Nancy Dill Capt MA
Henry: b c. 1725 d p. 10-18-1782 m Anna Williamson PS VA
Horatio: b 4-13-1755 d 10-8-1826 m Mary Bancroft Ens VA
John: b 11-22-1745 d a. 1-19-1795 m Sarah Dixon 1Lt MD
Luzby: b c. 1730 d p. 1-2-1791 m Sarah Redford CS VA
Obediah: b 1761 d p. 3-4-1844 m — Pvt VA
Thomas: b 5-9-1748 d 6-20-1790 m Mary Jefferson PS VA
Wm.: b c. 1728 d 1-19-1782 m Constance Cannon Capt MD
Wm.: b c. 1750 d 1824 m Sarah Harris Ens VA

TURTELOT,

Isaac: b 11-20-1752 d 6-6-1837 m Zerviah Brown Pvt CT

TUSSEY,

Wm.: b 7-22-1743 d 8-6-1815 m Hannah Wright PS DE

TUSTEN,

Benjamin: b 1716 d 6-9-1796 m (1)Mary Horton (2)Abigail Conkling
    (3)Ruth — PS NY
Benjamin, Jr.: b 12-11-1743 d 7-22-1779 m Anna Brown LCol NY

TUTEN,

Wm.: b 1748 d 3-25-1826 m Anne Hill Pvt MD ★

TUTHILL,

Barnabas: b 1733 d 10-9-1782 m (1)Lydia King (2)Amy King Maj NY
Benjamin: b 1725 d 6-12-1785 m Clementine Woodhull Pvt PS NY
Christopher: b 1726 d 1798 m Phebe Youngs Sol NY
Daniel, Sr.: b 1700 d 10-19-1785 m (1)Prudence Goldsmith (2)Mrs
    Jemima (Paine) Petty PS NY
Daniel, Jr.: b 1732 d 3- -1822 m Sarah Thurston PS NY
Daniel: b 11-5-1757 d 1842 m Elizabeth Davis Pvt NY ★
Daniel: b 3-13-1749 d 7-17-1830 m Ruth Terry PS NY
Francis: b 1-28-1757 d 10-8-1799 m Fanny Conklin Cpl NY
James, Jr.: b 1-7-1753 d 5-26-1826 m Temperance Wells Pvt NY
John: b 1750 d 1806 m (1)Mary Bull (2)Fanny Brewster Pvt NY
John 6th: b 1747 d 9-13-1828 m (1)Elizabeth Downing (2)Anna
    Evans Lt NY
John: b 9-8-1742 d 1-30-1821 m Phoebe Corwin Adj PS VT NY
John: b 1730 d p. 1783 m Abigal Terry Pvt NY
John, 5th: b 1709 d 3- -1795 m Abigail Lambert PS NY
John: b 1728 d 11-4-1805 m Sarah Wells Lt NY
John Woodhull: b 1744 d 11-8-1818 m Mary Brewster Lt NY
Jonathan: b 10-6-1727 d 2- -1802 m Anne Brewster Capt NY
Joshua: b 10-25-1732 d 1795/6 m Mary Conklin Pvt NY
Nathan: b 3-9-1742 d 1-18-1803 m Elizabeth Hudson Pvt NY
Nathaniel: b 1-17-1730 d 9-16-1803 m Margaret Herod Pvt PS NY

TUTT,

Benjamin: b — d p. 1810 m Elizabeth (Clayton) Pendleton QM VA
Gabriel: b 2-11-1758 d 3-29-1838 m Elizabeth Tutt 2Lt VA SC ★
James: b c. 1732 d p. 6-20-1786 m Anna Hansford PS Capt VA
James: b c. 1755 d p. 1821 m — Mid VA
John: b 1745 d 1812 m Mary Tutt Capt VA
Richard, Sr.: b 1736 d 2-23-1785 m Mary Merrifield PS MA
Richard, Jr.: b 2-11-1759 d 1786/7 m Hannah Girdler Pvt Slr MA
Richard: b 6-17-1749 d 9-15-1807 m Elizabeth Perrin Col SC
Thomas: b c. 1762 d 1804 m Sallie Parks Sol VA

TUTTLE,

Aaron: b 1-9-1760 d 9-15-1836 m Rebecca Wooster Pvt CT
Abraham: b 1758 d 5-21-1846 m (1) — Benham (2)Clarissa Bebee
    (3)Abigail — Pvt CT ★
Andrew: b 3-25-1739 d 1-18-1824 m Lydia Sturgis Pvt CT
Ayers: b 9- -1837 m (1)Rhoda Bassett (2)Hannah Barnes
    (3)Jerusha Brown Grd CT
Benjamin: b 1760 d 1833 m Elizabeth Hammond Pvt CT
Caleb: b 11-9-1758 d 3-27-1836 m Phineas Fairchild Pvt NJ ★
Caleb: b 12-7-1760 d 3-20-1845 m Mary Masters Pvt CT
Charles: b 1-26-1753 d 4-5-1818 m (1)Anna Finch (2)Sarah
    Cooly Bliss Pvt CT
Charles, Jr.: bpt 12-6-1741 d 10-29-1820 m Lucy Dodge Cpl MA
Chatfield: b 3-10-1758 d 5-7-1815 m Deborah Carman Pvt NJ
Clement: b 6-29-1756 d 6-13-1840 m Abigal Dutton Pvt CT ★
Daniel: b 7-11-1747 d 4-16-1825 m Esther Hoar Pvt MA
Daniel: b 1-13-1725 d 10-9-1805 m (1)Jemima Johnson (2)Catherine
    McDowell (3)Mary Plum Pvt NJ
Daniel: b 7-15-1760 d 8-30-1841 m Phebe Case Pvt NJ
Ebenezer: b 11-17-1750 d 1-15-1834 m Rebekah Broadwell Pvt NJ
Edmund: b 8-9-1764 d p. 8-2-1832 m Salome Phillips Pvt CT
Elijah: b 1-4-1747 d 9-1-1823 m Esther Johnson CS NH
Enos: bpt 6-15-1740 d a. 8-24-1792 m Abigail Penyor Pvt CT
Enos: b 8-11-1762 d 2- -1843 m Candace Hotchkiss Pvt CT ★
Gershom: b 8-23-1738 d 1-15-1818 m — Mitchel PS CT
Henry: b 11-24-1733 d 1-3-1820 m Phebe Beach Pvt NY
Hezekiah: b 4-3-1736 d 1-2-1796 m Martha Bradley Sgt CT
Hezekiah: b 5-20-1747/8 d 2-19-1834 m Mary Turner Drm CT
Ichabod: b 6-23-1748 d 7-3-1778 m Elizabeth Matthews Pvt PA
Ichabod: bpt 6-1-1729 d 2-7-1799 m Sarah Prime Pvt VT
Isaiah: b 5-5-1757 d p. 1802 m (1)Hannah Jones (2)Sarah Yale
    Sol CT
Ithamar: b 10-26-1737 d 11-8-1817 m Rhoda Barnes Ens CT
Jabez: b 7-30-1753 d 6-11-1799 m Mary Todd Pvt CT
Jabez: b 6-22-1732 d 10-4-1777 m Hannah Scoville Pvt CT
James: b 7-2-1760 d 1832 m Lovica Wolcott Pvt MA ★
Jared: b 6-2-1760 d 3-17-1837 m Roxana Ward Pvt CT ★
Jedediah: b 11-24-1753 d 9-9-1833 m Lucy Smith Cpl MA
Joel: b 1755 d 1830 m ( )Vincy Tuttle ( )Rebecca Jennings Pvt CT ★
John: b 10-20-1728 d 1781 m Mary Burrill Pvt MA
John: b 4-8-1763 d 1829 m (1)Abigail—(2)Sarah Broad (3)Polly
    Parker Pvt MA
John: b 4-30-1746 d 8-13-1825 m Lois Austin Pvt NY
Jonathan: b 1756 d 8-20-1822 m Sibly Cooper Pvt CT
Jonathan: b 9-30-1753 d p. 1807 m Catherine Gray Sgt MA
Joseph: b 7-18-1734 d 1-18-1813 m Mary Granger Grd CT

Joseph: b 8-23-1755 d 12- -1798 m Elizabeth Pratt Pvt MA
Joseph: b 3-10-1728 d 9-16-1800 m (1)Joanna — (2)Jemima
 Haines MM NJ
Josiah: b 9-4-1762 d 6-20-1833 m Eveely Gates Pvt CT
Jothan: b 5-14-1752 d 5-11-1817 m (1)Keziah Munson (2)Elizabeth
 Perkins Pvt CT
Jotham: b 3-29-1729 d p. 1810 m Molly Worthley Pvt PS NH
Levi: b 5-5-1751 d p. 1790 m Huldah Allen Pvt CT
Lucius: b 4-29-1749 d 6-27-1846 m (1)Hannah Hull (2)Mary Atwater
 Lt CT ★
Moses, Sr.: b 12-18-1723 d 1-17-1809 m Sibyl Thomas Sol CT
Moses, Jr.: b 10-24-1753 d 1-17-1835 m Damaris Hitchcock Sol
 CT ★
Moses: b 11-9-1732 d 7-11-1819 m Jane Ford PS NJ
Moses: b 2-22-1760 d 2-24-1837 m Anna Tuttle Pvt NY CT ★
Nathaniel: b 10-1-1721 d 7-7-1796 m Currence Squier Capt CT
Nathaniel: b 5-29-1714 d — m (1)Mary Todd (2)Abigail Ingham
 Capt CT
Nicholas: b 1759 d 1849 m (1)Nancy — (2)Annie Burk Pvt VA
Oliver: b 12-28-1739 d p. 1830 m Hannah Tuttle PS Pvt NH
Peter: b 2-10-1735 d 2-10-1802 m Anna Jeliff Pvt CT
Reuben: b 3-3-1739 d 1803 m Hannah Tyler Cpl CT
Samuel: b 1741 d 5-20-1817 m Bethaia Miles Pvt CT
Samuel: b 1760 d 7-6-1802 m Chloe Todd Sol CT
Samuel, Sr.: b 5-19-1709 d 12-11-1780 m Martha Shattuck Lt MA
Samuel, Jr.: b 6-5-1736 d 1-18-1813 m (1)Mary Russell (2)Rebecca
 Robbins Pvt MA
Simon: b 12-19-1733 d 4-21-1814 m Rebecca Holden Lt PS MA
Solomon: b 9-3-1757 d 11-30-1830 m (1)Deborah Strong (2)Amy
 Pugsley (3)Sarah (Lowe) Seamans Pvt VT
Stephen: b c. 1730 d a. 1790 m Rebecca — CS PS MA
Stoten: b 9-30-1739 d 9-7-1812 m Lydia Stevens CS PS NH
Sylvanus: b 5-12-1761 d 1-1-1846 m Mary Brown Pvt NJ
Thaddeus: b 8-18-1757 d 1836 m Amelia Atwater Pvt CT ★
Thomas: b 4-21-1733 d 7-31-1803 m Sarah Hanson Pvt NH
Thomas: b 11-30-1730 d p. 1796 m Lydia Owens Capt VT
Timothy: b 5-17-1746 d 1820 m Mehitable Royce Sgt CT
Timothy: b 6-12-1756 d 6-14-1814 m Hannah Winslow Sgt CT
Timothy: b 9-18-1746 d 6-16-1816 m Mary Ward Capt NJ
Titus: b 9-18-1731 d 1-17-1820 m Lois Atwater MM CT
Turell: b 7-25-1759 d 11-27-1831 m Mary Wilkinson Pvt Matr MA
Wm.: b c. 1757 d a. 1-8-1818 m Phebe Bradley Pvt CT
Wm.: b 1-14-1744 d p. 1810 m Taphar Castle PS NY

TUTWILER, (includes TUCKWILLER, TUTWILLER)
John: b 1752 d 1832 m Catherine Riffe Sol VA
Jonathan: b 8-22-1753 d 7-20-1819 m Barbara Wagner Pvt MD ★

TWADDELL,
Robert: b c. 1727 d p. 1-12-1779 m Hannah Chadwick Cpl MA

TWAY,
John: b c. 1753 d 1828 m Sarah Hempstead Pvt NJ

TWEED,
Joseph: b 1750 d 11-2-1839 m Jane Wilson Lt PA

TWEEDY,
David: b 1763 d 1779 m Susannah — Pvt DE
Thomas: b — d 1821 m Jane — Gnr PA ★

TWIGGS,
John: b 6-5-1750 d 3-29-1816 m Ruth Emanuel BGen GA

TWILLEY,
George: b 1743 d 3-13-1801 m Ann Bradley Pvt MD

TWINING,
Barnabas: b 7-7-1737 d 1829 m (1)Abigail Nickerson (2)Abigail
 Knowles (3)Mrs Hannah Smith Lt MA
David: b 6-17-1722 d 12-12-1791 m Elizabeth Lewis PS PA
Elijah: b 11-4-1741 d 10-2-1802 m Lois Rogers Pvt CS MA
John: b 1-1-1761 d 3-25-1849 m Becca Bennett Tms NJ
Nathan: b 3-8-1755 d 1850 m Sarah Clayton Pvt RI ★
Thomas: b 7-5-1733 d 4-23-1816 m (2)Anna Cole (Doane) Pvt MA

TWISS,
Daniel: b c. 1750 d 1775-8 m Rebecca Cressey Pvt MA
Ebenezer, Jr.: b 11-14-1750 d 8-3-1837 m Mrs Mary Nichols Pvt MA
John: b 5-25-1722 d 5-11-1796 m (1)Sarah — (2)Sarah Hopkins
 MM MA
Joseph: b 4-13-1761 d 5-16-1842 m Lois Austin Arfr CT ★

TWIST,
David: b 1740 d 9-12-1828 m Esther Town Pvt CT

TWITCHELL,
Abel: b 6-28-1751 d 3-8-1837 m (1)Sarah Adams (2)Elizabeth
 Clark Pvt NH MA ★
Benjamin: b 3-7-1748 d 9-13-1824 m Hannah Tucker Pvt MA
Daniel: b 4-10-1757 d 7-10-1800 m Eunice Child Sgt MA ★
Eli: b 2-17-1759 d 11- -1845 m Rhoda Leland Sgt MA ★
Enos: b 1-1-1749 d 7-25-1812 m Relief Fairbanks Pvt MA

Ezra: b 6-23-1746 d 6-26-1821 m Susanna Rice Pvt MA W★
Gershom, Sr.: b 10-6-1725 d p. 10-2-1779 m (1)Hannah Sawin
 (2)Priscilla Holt PS NH
Gershom, Jr.: b 9-13-1748 d — m Prudence Adams PS NH
Jonas, Jr.: b 3-31-1748 d 11-14-1821 m Olive Tucker Pvt MA
Joseph: b 2-13-1718 d 3-12-1792 m (1)Deborah Fairbanks (2)Mrs
 Deborah Sanger Fassett CS PS MA
Joshua: b 11-13-1750 d 1811 m Sarah Miller Pvt MA
Moses, Sr.: b 3-18-1723/4 d 11-15-1777 m Mary Sheffield Foster
 Pvt MA
Moses, Jr.: b 11-14-1758 d 7-13-1839 m Dorcas Dolly Pvt MA
Stephen: b 6-25-1753 d 9-12-1845 m Lucy Norcross Pvt PS NH
Thomas, Jr.: b 7-2-1757 d 12-27-1831 m Phebe Pond Pvt MA
Timothy: b 6-11-1736 d 2-15-1835 m (1)Sarah Adams (2)Ruth
 Fowle Pvt CS MA

TWITTY,
Susan: b 1763 d 4-14-1825 m John Miller PS NC
Wm.: b 7-13-1761 d 2-2-1816 m Frances Rhodes Lewis Pvt NC SC

TWOMBLY,
John: b 11-25-1755 d 10-2-1835 m Anna Hurd Cpl NH ★
John: b 1730 d 1795 m Mary — Cpl NH
Wm.: b 6-10-1753 d 9-20-1828 m Mehitable Baker Ens NH ★

TWYMAN,
George: b 3-29-1731 d a. 6-2-1818 m Mary Walker PS VA
James: b 6-17-1761 d 2-22-1834 m Tresa James OrdlSgt Spy VA ★
Reuben: b 10-23-1758 d 2-26-1839 m Margaret Griffen Sgt VA ★
Wm., Sr.: b 5-20-1727 d 10- -1811 m (1)Winifred Cowherd (2)Anna
 Smith PS VA
Wm., Jr.: b 1754 d 1843 m Elizabeth Garnett OrdlSgt VA ★

TYDINGS,
John, Sr.: b c. 1730 d p. 1800 m (1)Ann — (2)Mary — PS MD
Keeley: b 8-12-1759 d 1814 m Mary Beard Pvt MD
Richard: b 12-4-1754 d p. 1800 m Sarah — PS MD

TYE,
John: b 1737 d 3-16-1833 m (1)Mollie Wheeler (2)Elizabeth Powers
 Sgt VA

TYLER, (includes TYLOR)
Aaron: b 1756 d 4- -1826 m Elizabeth — Sol NC
Abner: b 1738 d 1819 m Bethiah Muzzy 2Lt MA
Abraham: b 11-12-1733 d 11-12-1804 m Jedidah Thomas LCol CT
Abraham: b 6-9-1733 d 1823 m Tirzah (Tyler) Sgt CT
Abraham: b 6-9-1735 d 4-2-1815 m (1)Abigail Stickney (2)Jerusha
 (Coburn) Mersay (3)Annie Stickney Peabody Sgt MA
Asa: b 12-21-1748 d 4-9-1808 m Martha Dodge 2Lt MA
Asa: b 10-23-1743 d p. 1803 m Elizabeth Tyler PS NH
Benjamin: b 5-17-1721 d 4-7-1805 m Elizabeth Page Pvt MA
Bezaleel: b 2-26-1745 d 7-22-1779 m Abigail (Calkins) Bush Capt
 NY
Bishop: b 1-22-1767 d 1844 m Alice Morgan Cpl CT ★
Bradstreet: b 8-27-1745 d 4-5-1842 m (1)Mary Foster (2)Eunice
 Adams (3)Mrs Mary Bacon Pvt CS MA
Charles: b 3-5-1762 d -1826 m (1)Rachel Cronklin (2)Isabel
 Young Pvt NY
Charles: b 1740 d p. 1800 m Ann Moore Ens VA
Charles: b c. 1758 d 1815 m Sarah Brown Sgt VA
Daniel: b 3-17-1738 d p. 1779 m Jerusha Barker PS CT
Daniel: b 5-21-1750 d 4-29-1832 m (1)Mehitable Putnam (2)Sarah
 (Edwards) Chaplin Capt CT
Daniel: b 9- -1756 d c. 1838 m Mary Carter Pvt MA ★
Daniel: b 2-18-1758 d 3-10-1845 m Sarah Cash Pvt VA
David, Jr.: b 1-4-1749 d p. 1789 m Judith — Pvt MA
Dudley: b 1700 d p. 3-5-1788 m (1)Phoebe Coleman (2)Mary Willson
 PS MA
Ebenezer: b 4-5-1740 d 1-29-1811 m Hannah Read Lt MA
Ebenezer: b c. 1744 d p. 1790 m Jerusha — Pvt NH
Edward: b 1719 d 5-20-1802 m Nancy Langley PS VA
Elnathan, Sr.: b 4-19-1711 d p. 1777 m Lucy Bissell PS CT
Elnathan, Jr.: b 3-30-1755 d 10-19-1817 m (1)Elizabeth —
 (2)Phoebe Atwater Cpl CT
George: b 1755 d a. 1-4-1833 m Judith Terrell Lt VA
Henry: b 1755 d a. 5-11-1813 m Anne — Sol VA
Jacob: b 2-20-1760 d 2-19-1847 m Abi Wheeler Sgt CT ★
Jacob: b 3-18-1754 d 7-3-1832 m Julia Newell Fif Maj CT W★
Jacob, Sr.: b 4-16-1728 d 10-4-1795 m (1)Abigail Bridges (2)Lydia
 Varnum Capt MA
Jacob, Jr.: b 5-27-1752 d 3-6-1810 m Ruth Marsh Pvt MA
James: b 1763 d 1843 m Sarah Cushman Cpl CT
James: b 10-12-1736 d 3-22-1813 m Mary Place Ens RI
Jepthah: b 1741 d 1-6-1782 m Molly — 1Sgt NH VT
Jeremiah: b — d 9-2-1835 m — Pvt MA ★
Jeremiah: b 4-9-1776 d 1- -1844 m Irene Heaton Pvt NH ★
Job: b 6-18-1727 d 2-24-1800 m Martha Chaffee Lt CT
John, Sr.: b 12-29-1721 d 7-4-1804 m Mary (Spalding) Coit BGen CT
John, Jr.: b 7-22-1755 d 4-6-1836 m (1)Mary Boardman (2)Esther
 Moss Sgt CT
John: b 8-26-1759 d 4-8-1829 m Mabel Bradley Arfr CT W★
John: b 1759 d 11-5-1837 m Anna Rogers Pvt CT ★

TYLER, contd.
John: b 9-26-1764 d 3-10-1840 m Waitstill Fuller Pvt CT ★
John: b 9-27-1731 d 9-27-1788 m (1)Anna Morse (2)Mrs Urana (Thayer) Bates Capt MA
John, Sr.: b 9-19-1724 d 1-11-1794 m Anne Blackington Capt MA
John, Jr.: b 4-25-1746 d 5-27-1822 m Mercy Thacher Sgt MA
John: b 2-28-1747 d 1-6-1813 m Mary Marot Armistead Capt VA
John: b c. 1730 d a. 9-2-1793 m Margaret — 1Lt VA
John: b c. 1761 d 8-19-1830 m Elizabeth Dillard Pvt VA W★
John Steel: b 3-1-1754 d 10-1-1813 m Sarah Whitwell LCol MA
Jonathan, Jr.: b 7-6-1742 d 2- -1794 m Mercy Hackett Pvt MA
Jonathan: b 6-14-1760 d 2-14-1833 m Rhoda Bruce Sol MA
Jonathan: b 1-1-1752 d 1848 m Sarah McConnell Pvt NH ★
Joseph: b 3-29-1752 d p. 11-25-1825 m Jane March Small Pvt MA
Joseph: b 5-21-1737 d 7-28-1815 m Ruth Read Maj CS PS VT ★
Joseph: b 8-12-1758 d 6-11-1807 m Judith Ayers Pvt MA
Major: b 10-14-1754 d 8-17-1833 m Hannah Brown OrdlSgt CT NY ★
Moses: b 5-4-1722 d 10-9-1804 m (1)Patience Ide (2)Thankful Read Lt MA
Moses: b 2-25-1730 d 2-8-1776 m Mrs Tryphena (Keyes) Hinds Pvt MA
Moses: b 9-18-1738 d 2-11-1824 m (1)Hannah (Tyler) (2)Sarah Lindall Pvt MA
Moses: b 8-8-1763 d 5-13-1806 m Sarah Patrick Pvt MA
Moses: b 6-27-1766 d 5-11-1854 m Sarah Cook Pvt MA
Moses: b a. 1745 d p. 2-7-1781 m Miriam Bayley PS NH
Moses, Jr.: b 11-26-1734 d 9-16-1811 m Elizabeth Adams PS RI
Moses: b 2-19-1707 d 2-5-1787 m Mary Belcher PS CT
Nathan: b 4-26-1736 d 10-13-1805 m Experience Smith Ens CT
Nathan: b 10-31-1729 d 2-25-1784 m Mary Salisbury Col MA
Nathaniel: b 10-4-1747 d 1829 m Abigail Andrews Pvt MA
Nehemiah: b 1760 d 1840 m Prudence Brainerd Pvt CT ★
Oliver: b 1-2-1754 d 9-18-1834 m Abigail Warren Pvt CT ★
Parker: b 1-31-1752 d 10-13-1737 m (1)Hannah Flint (2)Ludy Giddings Pvt MA ★
Phineas: b 5-17-1738 d p. 1800 m Lucy Hyde Pvt CT
Phineas: b 11-22-1736 d 8-6-1817 m (1)Hannah Foster (2)Elizabeth Barker Pvt MA
Robert: b 1727 d 1777 m (1)Eleanor Bradley (2)Henrietta — Col MD
Robert: b 8-19-1751 d 4-6-1815 m Margaret (Tyler) Pvt VA
Robert Bradley: b 1759 d 1791 m Dryden Belt Pvt MD
Roger: b 1-25-1740 d p. 1783 m Martha Stent CS PS CT
Royall: b 7-18-1757 d 8-16-1826 m Mary Palmer MGen MA
Samuel: b 8-21-1734 d 3-20-1820 m Judith Brown Maj CT
Samuel: b 9-16-1733 d 8-17-1816 m Abigal Dickenson Pvt CT
Samuel: b 1755 d 11-13-1832 m Dimmis Isham Cpl MA
Samuel Page: b 6-15-1753 d 5-10-1839 m Esther Hamilton Sgt MA ★
Silas: b 8-28-1742 d 10-13-1841 m Hoshea Scott Pvt NY ★
Silas: b 1752 d 1812 m Lucy Drake Pvt CT
Simeon: bpt 6-27-1754 d 9-21-1840 m Hannah (Merrill) Wright Sgt MA
Solomon: b 9-23-1757 d 11-1-1810 m (1)Mary Archer (2)Mrs Jerusha Newell Pvt MA
Stephen: b 5-27-1755 d 7-15-1836 m Polly Collier Cpl CT ★
Stephen: b 6-10-1754 d 4-27-1833 m Anne Stevens Pvt MA
Theodore: bpt 1-22-1758 d 4- -1799 m Susannah Hunt Pvt MA
Wm.: b 3-29-1734 d 5-12-1787 m Jermina Cooper Pvt CT
Wm.: b 8-4-1764 d 2- -1844 m Hope Brown Pvt MA ★
Wm.: b 4-26-1758 d 8-28-1834 m Mary Vail Pvt NY ★
Wm.: b c. 1748 d a. 2-10-1823 m Lydia Reynolds CS RI
Wm.: b 12-27-1747 d 3-17-1843 m Lettie George Pvt VA ★
Wm.: b 6-6-1755 d p. 11-11-1834 m Sally Williams Pvt VA ★
Wm.: b c. 1753 d c. 1799 m — Pvt VA
Zelotes: b 4-8-1760 d 6- -1840 m Mary Robinson Pvt MA ★

TYNER,
Joshua: b 7-21-1767 d 12-26-1838 m Winifred Teasby Pvt GA ★

TYNES,
Flemming: b c. 1750 d c. 1830 m Miss Watkins Pvt SC

TYNG,
John: b 1-28-1705 d 4-7-1797 m Mary Morse PS MA

TYRE,
Thomas: b 1720 d 1790 m Ann — Capt NC

TYREE,
James: b 3-20-1743 d 1-3-1785 m (1)Matilda Ballard (2)Lucy — Lt VA
Wm.: b c. 1750 d p. 1783 m — Sol VA

TYSON, (includes TISEN & TISON)
Benjamin: b 2-16-1751 d 1812 m Margaret — Pvt PA
Cornelius: b c. 1720 d 1789 m Mary Sherrod Grd NC
Henry: b 10-5-1742 d 3-24-1817 m Sarah — Pvt PA
Isaac: b 8-20-1718 d p. 1783 m Esther Shoemaker Pvt PA
Jehu: b c. 1750 d p. 3-4-1800 m Mildred Moye Sol NC
John: b 11-7-1731 d 5-7-1808 m Cornelia Bergen Pvt NY
John, Sr.: b 5-6-1737 d p. 1785 m Mary May Pvt SC
Mathias: b 7-20-1754 d 3-25-1829 m Jane Lewis Pvt MA
Nathaniel: b c. 1740 d p. 9-11-1792 m Judith Wilkins PS VA

Noah: b 9-12-1757 d 1805 m (1)Elizabeth Moore (2)Nice Moore PS NC
Thomas: b 9-1-1754 d 10-6-1813 m Margaret Siler Sol NC
Wm.: b 11-26-1722 d 1-28-1810 m Alyce Nash PS PA

TYSOR,
Lewis: b 1-18-1755 d 12-27-1832 m Susannah Harris Pvt NC ★

TYUS,
Lewis: b — d p. 6-28-1794 m Amy Gilliam PS VA

UBIL,
Peter: b 1742 d 1-6-1825 m Ruth — Pvt PA

UDALL,
John: b 2-10-1748 d p. 3-31-1778 m Ann Stevens Pvt NH
Samuel: b 4-17-1739 d 12-11-1805 m Lydia Chapman CS PS VT
Wm.: b 2-19-1759 d 4-3-1849 m Margaret Hogan Pvt NY VT ★

UFFORD,
Benjamin: b 3-10-1743 d 3- -1810 m Elizabeth Wells Pvt CT
John: b c. 1750 d c. 1824 m Mary Goodrich Pvt CT
Samuel: b 2-27-1749 d 12-10-1822 m Abigail Gold Capt CT
Samuel Morse: b 6-8-1761 d 11-8-1848 m Faustina Hawley Sol CT ★

UHL, (includes UHLL)
Charles: b 8-7-1761 d 1-20-1827 m Catherine Close Cpl PA
Christian: b 12-21-1718 d 10-12-1793 m Christiana Catherine Ritchour Pvt PA
Daniel: b — d 1812 m (1) — Storms (2)Mary Emigh Lt PS NY
Frederick: b 9-25-1765 d 10-12-1822 m (1)Huldah Mulford (2)Sarah Lines Horton Pvt NY
Michael: b c. 1730 d 1803 m Catherine — Pvt PA

UHLER,
Christopher: b 1741 d 1804 m (1)Barbara Sprecher (2)Judith Blocher Pvt PA
Erasmus: b 9-21-1751 d 9-15-1814 m Mary Neace PS MD
Jacob: b 12-27-1748 d 4-14-1807 m Margaret Messer Pvt PA
Martin: b 9-24-1744 d 3- -1810 m Ann Eliza Yeagley Pvt PA

ULERY, (or ULARY, ULLERY)
Henry: b 3-2-1737 d 6-1-1831 m — Sol PA

ULLMAN,
Frederick: b 6- -1755 d 8-14-1841 m (2)Magdalena Keller Pvt NY ★

ULMER,
Adam: b c. 1756 d p. 9-7-1794 m Ann — Pvt SC
George: b 7-8-1760 d 2-24-1840 m (1)Mary Beckett (2)Miriam Townsend Pvt MA ★
George: b 2-25-1756 d 12-23-1825 m Mary Tanner Capt MA
John: b 1736 d 8-1-1809 m Catherine Remilly Pvt MA
John Jacob: b 7-3-1758 d 1830 m Matilda Baumgartner Pvt SC
Philip Martin: b 1751 d 10-3-1816 m Christiana Young Maj MA

ULRICH,
Adam: b — d 1795 m Catherine — Pvt PA
Christopher: b 8-23-1746 d 8-6-1790 m Juliana Umberger Pvt PA
George: b 2-3-1753 d 4-16-1825 m Maria Catharine Laudenslager Lt PA
John: b 10-14-1764 d 8-23-1838 m Christena Brombaugh Pvt MA

UMBENHAUER,
Balthaser: b 2-19-1730 d 1779 m — PS PA
Francis: b 10-23-1751 d 3-31-1812 m — Capt PA
Samuel: b 2-3-1754 d p. 1795 m Christiana Greim Lt PA

UMBENHEN,
Jacob: b 1753 d 8-20-1811 m Susannah Fried Pvt PA

UMBERGER,
Henry: b 1745 d 1820 m (1)Anna Margaret Baurin (2)Margaret Catherine Neff Pvt PA
John, Sr.: b 1728 d 1799 m Margaret — Pvt PA
Michael: b c. 1718 d a. 7-16-1785 m Ann Maria Ramler PS PA

UMHOLTZ,
Henry: b c. 1745 d 1829 m (1) — Rouch (2)Magdalena Seidensticker Pvt PA

UMSTEAD, (includes UMSTED)
Harman: b 1745 d 1822 m Barbara Kiter Pvt PA
Herman: b 3-16-1726 d 4-4-1806 m Ann — Pvt PA

UNANGST,
Bernhardt: b 8-23-1748 d 12-5-1819 m Anna Rosina Hering Sol PA
George Heinrich: b 12-29-1752 d 12-10-1827 m Rosina Frankenfield Pvt PA

UNCLES,
Benjamin: b 1742 d 6-9-1826 m Margaret Plaister Pvt MD ★

UNDERHILL,
Abraham: b 1730 d 1796 m Mercy Paddock Capt VT
Ann Elizabeth Bowne: b 5-13-1722 d 8-16-1786 m John Underhill PS NY
Augustine: b 3-24-1736 d 1-17-1819 m Jerusha Bloomer CS VT
Hezekiah: b 9-17-1727 d 3-8-1800 m Mrs Tabitha (Sargent) Foss PS NH
Israel: b 9-7-1731 d 9-23-1806 m Abigail Lispenard Ens NY
John: b 3-16-1720 d 7-31-1792/3 m Johanna Healey PS NH
John: b 1-25-1729 d 10-22-1798 m Rebecca Frost PS NY
John: b c. 1740 d 1825 m Mary White PS NC
Nathaniel: b 1755 d 2-2-1849 m Esther Carr Pvt NH
Thomas: b 1748 d p. 7-12-1796 m Susanna Evans NCapt VA

UNDERWOOD,
Alpheus: b 1750 d 6-18-1834 m (1)Hannah Willcocks (2)Polly — Pvt MA
Amos: b 10-14-1757 d p. 1832 m Mary Lamb Pvt MA ★
Asa: b 1754 d 10-3-1834 m (1)Elizabeth Littlehale (2)Mercy Durant Pvt MA ★
Benjamin: b c. 1736 d 1781-90 m Mary Hull Capt CS PS RI
David: b 11-24-1742 d 2- -1817 m Bathsheba Adams Drm Maj MA
George: b c. 1742 d p. 1785 m Elizabeth Curd PS VA
Isaac: b 1-26-1723 d 6-1-1793 m Grace Greenwood Sgt MA
Isaac: b 10-25-1764 d 1847 m Zilpha Castle Pvt MA ★
Israel: b 4-4-1746 d 6-15-1817 m — Pvt CT
James: b 12- -1731 d 10-25-1808 m Mary Lund Adj NH
James: b 5-2-1752 d 5-20-1834 m (1)Margaret Campbell (2)Ruth Winter Pvt NC
John, Sr.: b c. 1734 d 1785 m Margaret — Pvt DE
John: b 9-16-1756 d p. 1800 m Sarah Agnes Sloan Capt PA
John: b 10-14-1739 d 9-1-1827 m (2)Sarah Morrison Pvt PA
John: b c. 1740 d p. 1811 m Margery Price Pvt PA
John: b 10-3-1755 d 3-9-1819 m Jeanne McAllister Sol VA
Jonas: b 1733 d 9-26-1800 m Naomi Pike Pvt MA
Jonas: b 1765 d 1842 m Sally Pine Pvt MA ★
Jonathan, Sr.: b 1-22-1716 d 10-1-1794 m Hannah Richardson PS VT
Jonathan, Jr.: b 1744 d 12-21-1801 m Deborah Morgan Pvt MA
Joseph: b 4-30-1749 d 2-27-1829 m Mary Munroe Pvt MA
Joseph: b 1745 d p. 11-25-1821 m Winifred Henderson Sol VA
Joshua: b 1-10-1755 d p. 10-7-1834 m Martha — PS DE
Nathan: b 8-3-1753 d 5-1-1841 m Susanna Lawrence OrdlSgt MA W★
Nicholas: b 5-23-1759 d 8-22-1800 m Phoebe Brownell Mstr RI
Samuel: b 1-29-1756 d 1-22-1830 m (1)Susan Tripp (2)Mary Hill Smn RI
Samuel: b 4-20-1765 d 2- -1864 m (1)Lovisa Spelman (2)Jemima Fletcher Cpl MA
Silas: b 3-2-1762 d 1844 m Amelison — Pvt MA ★
Thaddeus: b 9-17-1758-60 d 9-8-1840 m Mary Farr Pvt VT
Theophilus: b 2-21-1757 d 6- -1805 m Elizabeth Joyner Pvt VA
Thomas: b 1760 d — m Mehitable Gage Pvt NH
Thomas: b 11-6-1740 d 1-29-1815 m Ann Taylor Col VA
Timothy: b 1724 d 3-27-1804 m Rachel Russell Capt MA

UNGER,
Michael: b c. 1738 d 1785 m Christina — PS PA

UNSELL,
Henry: b 1750 d 1820 m Katherine Scowell Pvt VA

UNTHANK,
Sarah Hunt: b 1747 d 1843 m (1)John Unthank (2)Solomin Hiatt N NC

UPCHURCH,
Moses: b 2-13-1755 d 1855 m Mary Simms Pvt NC ★
Nathan: b 1759 d 1835 m Mackey — Pvt NC ★

UPDEGROFF, (includes UPDEGRAFF)
Nathan: b 9-3-1750 d 2-3-1827 m (1)Ann — (2)Ann Lupton Pvt PA
Samuel: b 1744 d c. 1797 m Mary Low Pvt PA

UPDIKE, (includes OPDYCKE & OPDYKE)
Albert: b 1750 d 1790 m Martha Hendrickson Capt NJ
Benjamin: b 1721 d 1807 m Joanna — CS PS NJ
George: b 1743 d 4-15-1795 m Sophia Baker Pvt NJ
Isaac: b 1762 d 8-25-1825 m Nancy — Pvt NJ
Jacob: b 1752 d 9- -1827 m Anna Savage Pvt NJ
John: b 1710 d 8-10-1777 m Margaret Green PS NJ
John: b 1708 d 1794 m Mary Bragaw PS NJ
John: b 1726 d 1804 m Ann Crawford PS RI
Lawrence: b 5-11-1739 d 1813 m Alteye Lanning Pvt NJ
Luther: b 3-29-1750 d 1838 m (1)Gertrude Hall (2)Ruth Sinclair (3)Mary Dalrymple Ens NJ
Richard: b 1740 d 1825 m (1)Grace Thatcher (2)Mrs Diana Bonham Sutton CS NJ
Thomas: b 1756 d 1805 m Anne Cowel Pvt NJ
Wm.: b 1746 d 1839 m Naomi Johnson Pvt NJ
Wm.: b 1755 d 1822 m Sarah Palmer Pvt NJ ★

Wm.: b 1759 d 1847 m Alchea Voorhees Pvt NJ
Wm.: b 1751 d p. 12-10-1779 m Nancy Carpenter Wgn NJ

UPHAM,
Abijah, Sr.: b 5-1-1726 d 1-2-1802 m Jemima Bailey Mus MA
Abijah, Jr.: b 5-17-1752 d a. 11-8-1785 m Rebecca Gill Fif MA
Amos: b 9-29-1718 d 1-23-1786 m Lois Green CS PS MA
Chester: b 6-2-1764 d 8-27-1829 m Dolly Childs Pvt CT ★
Daniel: b 12-18-1743 d 10-5-1812 m Sarah Sprague Pvt MA
Ebenezer, Jr.: b 6-13-1764 d 8-17-1834 m Tamar King Pvt MA ★
Isaac: b a. 1722 d — m Hannah Barns Pvt MA
Isaac: b 10-3-1741 d 3-10-1800 m Hepzibah Sharpley MM MA
Ivory: b 9-27-1724 d 2-14-1791 m Jerusha Stone Pvt CT
Jabez: b 5-6-1735 d p. 1781 m Hannah Burgess Sgt MA
James: b 7-13-1755 d 10- -1827 m Elizabeth Barnard Sol MA
Jesse: b 3-18-1745 d 8-23-1825 m Sarah James Pvt MA
John: b 4-6-1734 d 5-30-1800 m Damaris Wilder Sol MA
John: b 1732 d 4-16-1777 m Wintje Esselstyne 1Lt NY
Jonathan, Jr.: b 2-7-1759 d 4-3-1840 m Sarah (Upham) Pvt MA ★
Joseph: b 4-14-1712 d 10-12-1792 m (1)Martha Green (2)Elizabeth Richardson (3)Mrs Abigail Amsden PS MA
Joseph, Jr.: b 12-10-1740 d 10-12-1792 m Eunice Kidder PS MA
Luke: b 6-1-1733 d 11-7-1815 m Lois Sabin Cpl CT
Nathan: b 7-13-1750 d 4-17-1828 m Eleanor Gilbert Pvt MA
Nathan: b 1-18-1760 d 12-1-1828 m Rhoda Fisher Pvt MA
Nathaniel: b 6-22-1745 d 3-21-1833 m (1)Abigail Ward (2)Phebe Kimball Pvt MA ★
Phineas: b 25-1764 d 8-6-24-1810 m Susanna Buckminster Col MA
Phineas: b 4-26-1747 d 2-1-1789 m Lydia Myrich Sol MA
Samuel: b 12-27-1749 d 1824 m Abigail Porter Pvt CT
Samuel, Sr.: b 9-28-1722 d p. 1790 m Martha Tenney PS MA
Samuel, Jr.: b 9-15-1762 d 5-12-1848 m Patty Livermore Pvt MA ★
Simeon: b 5-11-1757 d 12-26-1840 m Miriam Larned Pvt MA
Thomas: b 8-25-1747 d 4-24-1835 m Mary Lewis Pvt NH
Wm.: b 10-29-1738 d 12-20-1812 m Elizabeth Wood Capt VT

UPP,
Jacob: b 1751 d 1822 m Elizabeth Sprinkle Pvt PA

UPSHAW, (includes UPSHUR)
James: b 1755 d a. 2-16-1807 m Mary Martin Capt VA
John: b 2-22-1755 d 1834 m Amey Gatewood Pvt VA ★
John: b 1741 d 9-5-1779 m (1)Ann Emerson (2)Margaret (Downing) Michael (2)Rosy Robins CS VA
John: b 7-24-1715 d 7-23-1801 m Mary Lafon PS VA

UPSON,
Asa: b 11-30-1728 d 2-5-1807 m (1)Mary Newell (2)Mehitable Wetmore Capt PS CT
Ashbel: b 4-25-1762 d 6-30-1831 m Mary Munson Pvt CT W★
Ashbel: b 3-19-1764 d 12-10-1834 m Mehitable Castle Pvt CT
Benjamin: b 8-4-1720 d 11-23-1792 m Mary Blakeslee Pvt CT
Ezekiel: b 10-7-1748 d 1836 m Mary Bronson Sgt CT ★
James: b 10-9-1756 d 1-22-1803 m Mary Cowles Pvt CT
Jesse: b 9-10-1754 d 3-25-1833 m Elizabeth Smith Cpl CT
Joseph: b 5-5-1750 d 12-21-1835 m (1)Anne Beder (2) — Sheperd Pvt MA ★
Noah: b 9-27-1758 d p. 12-2-1780 m Rachael Frisbie Pvt CT
Samuel: b 3-8-1737 d 2-25-1816 m Ruth Cowles Capt CT
Thomas: b 12-20-1719 d 1798 m Hannah Hopkins PS CT

UPTON,
Amos, Sr.: b 10-30-1717 d 10-6-1780 m Sarah Bickford Capt MA
Amos, Jr.: b 10-3-1742 d 4-3-1838 m (1)Edith Upton (2)Joanna Bruce (3)Hannah Haskell OrdlSgt MA ★
Amos, Jr.: b 5-6-1738 d 1-21-1822 m Ruth Upton Capt MA
Asa: b 1734 d 10-4-1824 m Elizabeth Webber Sgt MA
Benjamin: b 5-7-1745 d 8-12-1827 m (1)Rebecca Putnam (2)Elizabeth (White) Cowley Sgt MA
Benjamin: b 1754 d 5- -1829 m (1)Deborah Goodell (2)Hannah Hixon (3)Sarah Owen Trask Pvt MA
David: b 1741 d 1845 m Elizabeth Wilkins Pvt MA
Ebenezer: b 12-22-1730 d 4-3-1799 m Mary Girdler Pvt MA
Elisha: b 5-18-1732 d 1805 m (1)Margery Wilkins (2)Sarah Guilford Pvt MA
Jacob: b 12-10-1739 d 6-4-1804 m Mary Clark Pvt MA
Jacob: b 6-12-1726 d 1800 m Rebecca — MM MA
Jeduthan: b 4-12-1752 d 5-30-1823 m (1)Mary (Brown) Austin (2)Rachel Gage Pvt MA
John: b c. 1745 d 1845 m (1) — Baxley (2)Ozisia Shaw Cpl NC
Josiah, Sr.: b 8-24-1735 d 12-10-1791 m (1)Susanna Emerson (2)Catherine Hartwell CS MA
Nathaniel, Jr.: b 11-28-1753 d 5-29-1841 m (1)Sarah Flint (2)Jerusha (Upton) Pvt Smn MA
Paul: b 8-12-1751 d — m Jerushia Richardson MM MA
Robert: b 5-21-1758 d 1824 m Anna Wheelock Sgt MA
Wm.: b 8-25-1728 d 1790 m (1)Sarah Goodell Herrick (2)Hannah Stanley (3)Mehitable — Pvt MA

URANN, (includes URAN)
Daniel: b 4-10-1750 d 1-20-1827 m Sarah Keniston Pvt NH
John: b 8-10-1718 d p. 1796 m (1)Sarah Duty (2)Abigail Layton Pvt PS NH

URANN, contd.
Jonathan: b c. 1732 d p. 1785 m Abigail Hodgkins PS VT
Thomas: b 2-3-1723 d 10-8-1792 m Mary Sloper PS MA

URICH, (includes UHRICH)
John: b 1751 d p. 1790 m (1)Jeseba Fahnestock (2) — Heinike
    Pvt PA
Michael: b 8-7-1751 d 8-14-1817 m (1)Catharine Koeber
    Borroway (2)Susannah C Rouse Pvt PA
Valentine: b 9-27-1740 d 9-27-1812 m Susanna Hoehn Pvt PA
Valentine: b 7-4-1757 d 1-1-1821 m Elizabeth Sweigart Pvt CL

URIE,
Samuel: b 2-19-1759 d 1821 m Ann Templeton Pvt PA
Thomas: b 1718 d 7-15-1804 m Sarah Reed PS CS PA

URTON,
Peter: b 4-22-1765 d 9-23-1835 m Hannah — Pvt VA ★

USHER,
Abijah: b 2-15-1757 d 8- -1836 m (1)Mary Weld (2)Rebecca
    Kidder Pvt MA
Robert: b 1-31-1742/3 d 3-27-1820 m (1)Susanna Gates (2)Anna
    Cone Dr CT
Robert: b 3-7-1761 d 9- -1838 m (1)Lydia Scolly (2)Lydia Harris
    Pvt NH

USILTON,
Francis: b 4-16-1753 d 9- -1824 m Catharine — Pvt MD

USSERY,
Thomas: b c. 1740 d p. 6-10-1811 m Sarah — Pvt NC

USTICK,
Thomas: b 8-30-1753 d 4-18-1803 m Hannah Whitear PS MA

UTLEY,
Elijah: b 1765/6 d 1820-30 m Lois Swan Pvt CT
Jacob: b c. 1750 d 1796 m Phoebe — CS PS Sol NC
John: b 11-21-1753 d 12-10-1839 m Thankful Kinney Pvt CT
John: b 1749 d 1807 m Mary Cook CS NC
John: b c. 1746 d a. 11-12-1824 m Nancy Clarkson PS VA
Stephen: b 3-28-1736 d 9-15-1807 m (1)Sipporah Hastings
    (2)Sarah Love Pvt CT
Wm., Sr.: b 1715 d 1794 m Elizabeth — PS Pvt NC
Wm., Jr.: b 7-3-1750 d 8-6-1808 m Dorcas — Pvt NC
Wm.: b 2-5-1724 d 3-17-1790 m Sarah Peabody PS VT

UTT,
Adam: b c. 1762 d 12- -1837 m — Pvt PA
Elias: b c. 1749 d 4-13-1833 m Lucretia Solomon Pvt PA

UTTER,
Abraham: b 5-9-1765 d 1-14-1851 m Martha Lycan Pvt PA ★
Ebenezer: b 10-1-1759 d 2-9-1837/8 m Ruth — Pvt NY ★
James: b 11-14-1759 d 7-23-1839 m Hannah Spencer Pvt CT ★
Jesse: b 1757 d 10-26-1847 m Sarah — Fif Pvt NY CT ★
Joseph: b 1733 d 11-6-1818 m Margaret Doty Pvt NY
Joseph: b 3-25-1750 d 6-11-1796 m Sarah Mead Pvt NY
Josiah: b 1755 d 3-19-1812 m Mary Ketcham PS CT

UTTERBACK, (includes OTTERBACK)
Harmon: b 10-16-1755 d 1854 m Elizabeth Crose Pvt VA ★
Harmon: b 1746 d 1829 m (1)Elizabeth Crump (2)Margaret
    Strumatt PS VA
Jacob: b 8-3-1743 d 4-7-1842 m (1)Anna Elizabeth Martin
    (2)Quency Hanks PS VA
Joseph: b c. 1742 d p. 1810 m — Sol VA

UTZ, (includes OUZTS)
Ephraim: b 1764 d 1848 m Christena Blankenbaker Sol VA
George: b c. 1730 d p. 1810 m Margaretha — Pvt VA
Peter: b 3-25-1757 d 1829 m Elizabeth Harling Pvt SC

UZZELLE, (includes UZZELL)
Elisha: b c. 1740 d 1798 m Dorcas Stanley Pvt NC
Thomas: b 12-6-1740 d 6-10-1818 m (1)Mary Parr (2)Polly James
    PS NC

VACHER,
John Francis: b 1751 d 12-4-1807 m Sarah Potter Dr NY

VADEN,
Burwell: b 9-2-1733 d c. 1824 m Sarah — PS VA
George: b c. 1740-7 d p. 7-24-1798 m Sarah — PS VA

VAIL, (includes VAILL & VAILS)
Abram: b 3-15-1742 d 10-30-1814 m Elizabeth Lee PS NY
Alexander: b c. 1750 d p. 4-17-1809 m — PS DE
Alsop: b 1-3-1761 d 12-11-1840 m Frances Seybolt Pvt NY

Asa: b 7-20-1755 d 3-6-1813 m Sarah Smith Pvt NY
Benjamin: b 1731 d 5-16-1814 m Mary Horton Capt CT NY
Benjamin, Sr.: b 1709 d 1784 m Mary Paine Pvt NY
Benjamin, Jr.: b c. 1740 d 7-22-1779 m Elizabeth Stillwell Capt NY
Daniel: b 2-19-1745 d 2-23-1832 m Elizabeth Smith Ens NY
Edward: b 10-20-1746 d 9-22-1831 m Mary Oberton Pvt MA
Edward: b 8-6-1717 d a. 6-5-1777 m (1)Mary Benners (2)Susanna
    Vail BGen NC
Edward: b 1756 d 1837 m Margaret Allen CS VT
Elisha: b c. 1749 d 6-22-1797 m Rhoda Moore Pvt NY
Gilbert Townsend: b 1739 d 7-22-1779 m Hannah Arnot Pvt NY
Isaac: b 2-27-1747 d 10- -1808 m Hester Buckhout Capt NY
Isaac: b 10-29-1754 d 3-21-1839 m Eleanor Ferguson Lt NY
Isaac: b 1740 d 8-1-1801 m Livinia Ketchum PS NY
Isaiah: b 9-28-1731 d 1-1-1810 m Abigail Meeker Capt NY
Israel: bpt 12-15-1728 d 11-7-1796 m Rebecca Hubbard Capt NY
John: b 8-29-1734 d 1-13-1814 m Catherine Fitz Randolph PS NJ
John: b 10-22-1744 d 2-2-1815 m Mary Youngs Pvt NY
John: b 1750 d 1790 m (2)Catherine Weller Capt VT
Jonathan: b 9-16-1736 d 10-3-1801 m (1)Hannah Horton (2)Mrs
    Clayton Capt NY
Jonathan: b 10-1-1758 d 5-4-1835 m Grace Beebe Sol NY ★
Joseph: b 1721 d 8-10-1800 m Jerusha Peck PS CT
Joseph Alexander: b 1765 d 1828 m Julia Smith Sol NY
Micah: b 11-16-1750 d 10-21-1809 m Rhoda Brush Smn PS NY
Micah: b 9-29-1730 d 6-8-1777 m Mary Briggs PS CS Capt VT
Moses: b 1747 d 12-31-1793 m Hannah Benedict Sgt CT
Moses: b 1721 d 1788 m Mary Gildersleeve PS NY
Nathaniel: b 1755 d 10-6-1801 m Mary Hall Pvt CT
Peter: b 1726 d 1-30-1782 m Bethiah Landon Capt PS CT
Platt: b 3-27-1757 d p. 1798 m Keziah Vail PS NY
Samuel: b 1741 d 12-27-1776 m Sarah Beebe Pvt CT
Samuel: b 5-15-1754 d 5-19-1823 m Mary Rogers Sgt NY
Stephen, Jr.: b 1743 d 11-26-1806 m Ruth Terry PS NY
Thomas: b 8-18-1734 d 10-21-1806 m Hannah Hanks Brown Lt NY
Wm., Sr.: b 1734 d 1790 m Phebe Vail Pvt PS NY
Wm., Jr.: b 6-27-1761 d 7-27-1838 m Ruth Mapes Pvt NY ★

VALENTINE, (includes VALLENTINE, VOLENTINE & VOLLINTINE)
Alexander: b 8-25-1760 d 10-29-1828 m Sarah Woods Pvt NY
Ananias: b 1769 d 1-16-1825 m Elizabeth Meeker Pvt NY
David: b 4-15-1762 d p. 1847 m Elizabeth Satterwhite Pvt VA ★
Elvin: b 6-25-1744 d p. 1779 m Abigail Oakley Wgn NY
Gabriel: b 10-7-1767 d 9-11-1836 m Deborah Jennings Pvt NY
George: b 1-2-1752 d 11-27-1839 m Mary Grove Pvt Tms MD ★
Henry: b 1732 d 11- -1792 m Anna Maria Weik PS PA
James: b c. 1726/7 d c. 1807 m (1)Martha Mott (2)Mrs Dorothy
    Baldwin Pvt NY
John, Sr.: b 1720 d c. 1790 m Charity Dean Sgt NY
John, Jr.: b 1761 d 5-14-1838 m Hannah Wiltse Pvt NY
Jonas: b 3-10-1730 d 3-10-1786 m Susanna Bedell Pvt NJ
Jonathan: b 1730 d 1811 m Lydia Pusey Baldwin Pvt PA
Joseph: b 1-6-1750 d 1-29-1814 m Esther Athersan Pvt NY
Obediah: b c. 1730 d 5-19-1788 m (1)Mary Mulford (2)Elizabeth
    Baker Maxwell (3)Elizabeth Roberts Day Pvt NJ
Obadiah: b a. 1735 d 1807/8 m Ann Vollentine Pvt NY
Peter: b 12-29-1735 d 4-22-1810 m Mary Wiltsee Pvt NY
Peter: b 6-8-1763 d p. 1794 m Rachel Hazen Pvt NY
Richard: b 8- -1742 d 6-26-1807 m Mary Oakley PS CT
Samuel: b 12-7-1745 d 3-10-1834 m Elizabeth Jones Pvt MA
Stephen: b 1758 d 1817 m — Hooper Pvt NY
Thomas, Sr.: b 3-8-1713 d 4-17-1783 m Elizabeth Gooch PS MA
Thomas, Jr.: b 8-31-1736 d a. 7-9-1779 m Rebecca Ingraham Capt
    MA
Wm.: b 3-17-1741 d 12-2-1801 m Sybil Winslow PS MA

VALLANDINGHAM, (includes VALLANDIGHAM)
George: b 1737 d 10- -1810 m Elizabeth Noble Col PS PA
George: b 9-12-1761 d p. 1830 m Peggy Frier Pvt VA ★
Lewis: b 3-10-1761 d 2-2-1845 m Betsy Drake Pvt VA ★
Wm.: b c. 1753/4 d 5-4-1842 m Sarah Middleton Pvt NC ★

VALLE,
Francois: b 1-2-1716 d 9-29-1783 m Marianne Billeron PS IL

VALLERCHAMP,
Simeon Peter: b 6-29-1751 d 7-12-1825 m (1)Hannah Dodson Of
    FrA

VALLETTE,
David: b 1739 d 7-27-1821 m Phoebe Hopkins Sol RI

VALLOTTON,
David Moses: b 7-6-1745 d a. 1-21-1795 m Mary DuBois Pvt PS GA
James: b 1754 d 5-25-1805 m Elizabeth (Knott)Fengins Sol GA

VALPEY,
Abraham: b c. 1730 d p. 12-21-1776 m Lydia Clough Pvt MA

VAN ALEN, (or VAN ALLEN)
Abraham: b c. 1735 d c. 10-23-1791 m Mary Freyenmoet Pvt NY
Harmanus: b c. 1761 d c. 1816 m Martha Northrup Pvt NY

Johannis: b 3-14-1748 d 7-21-1835 m Marie Luke Pvt NY
Peter: b 11-5-1749 d 1816 m Ann Van Buren 2Lt NY
Peter: b 8-15-1735 d 9-9-1806 m Elizabeth Dixon Pvt NY

VAN ALSTYNE, (includes ALSTYNE, VAN AALSTEYN & VAN ALSTINE)
Abraham: bpt 6-25-1738 d 10-29-1808 m Maria Van Alen Col NY
Jacob: b 5-28-1749 d 5- -1844 m Annetie Lansing QM NY ★
Jeronemus: bpt 2-11-1736 d 7-23-1807 m Eyda Beekman Sol NY
John M.: b 7-12-1745 d p. 12-6-1780 m Dirckje Winne Lt NY
Lambaert: b c. 10-4-1724 d 3-29-1797 m (1)Alida Conyen (2)Aletteka Osterhout Pvt NY
Leonard: bpt 9-18-1743 d p. 1795 m (1)Elizabeth Gose (2)Hannah Sluyter Steves Pvt NY
Martin Goshen: b 3-25-1755 d 12-20-1830 m Anna Margaret Schrembling Pvt NY
Nancy Quackenbush: b 1743 d 1831 m Martin Van Alstyne PS NY
Nicholas: b 12-26-1749 d 8-28-1836 m Cornelia VanAlstyne Pvt NY
Philip: b 9-16-1735 d 12-24-1814 m Maritje (Van Alstine)LCol NY
Phillip: b 2-2-1752 d 1805 m (2)Barbara Roof Pvt NY
Wm.: b 11-10-1721 d 5-22-1802 m (1)Christina VanAlen (2)Catherine Knickerbocker Pvt NY

VAN ANDEN,
Paul: b 1-1-1736 d p. 1787 m Sarah Hageman 2Lt NY

VAN ANTWERP,
Jacobus: b 1724 d 1785 m Margaret Bogert PS NY
John, Sr.: bpt 2-6-1732 d p. 5-24-1785 m Annetie Veeder Pvt NY
John, Jr.: b 2-6-1759 d 4-10-1827 m Rachel Allen Cpl NJ
John Lewis: b 1-12-1765 d — m Catlyne Yates Ens NY
Lewis Simonse: b 2-25-1731 d 12-11-1824 m Hendrikje Fonda Van Buren PS NY
Margaret Collier: b 5-18-1733 d 5-16-1811 m Abraham Van Antwerp PS NY
Nicholas: b 8-27-1760 d 12-23-1825 m Mary Lawrence Sol NY
Peter: bpt 5-15-1745 d 1824 m Susanna Bond Ens NY
Simon Johannes: b 2-2-1751 d 1-18-1839 m (1)Magdalena Vedder (2)Elizabeth Viele OrdlSgt Sct NY ★

VAN ARNUM, (includes VAN AERNAM, VAN AERNUM, VAN ORNAM)
Abraham: bpt 11-19-1749 d p. 1785 m Anneke Bogart Sgt NY
Abraham: b 3-24-1744 d 6-5-1830 m Margaret Cole Pvt NY
Abraham: b 10-29-1762 d 2-12-1835 m Hannah Newcomb Pvt NY
Hendrick: b 7-2-1738 d 5-23-1816 m Susanna Winne Pvt NY
Jacob: b 10-27-1732 d 5-5-1813 m Catherine Banker Capt NY
Johannes: b 11-21-1756 d p. 1789 m Jannetje Van Loon Pvt NY
Luykas: bpt 8-22-1738 d p. 1780 m Sarah Pean Cpl NY

VAN ARSDALE, (includes VAN ARSDAL, VAN ARSDALEN, VAN ARSDOLL, VAN ORSDOLL, VAN ORSDOL, VAN OSDOL, VANARTSDALEN)
Abraham: b 1760 d 8- -1849 m Mary Eoff Sgt NJ
Abraham: b 12-2-1750 d 4-10-1821 m (1)Elsie Baird (2)Margaret Kennedy Cpl NJ
Christopher: b 4-20-1760 d 2-19-1833 m Sarah Dumont Pvt NJ
Christopher: b 1760 d 1840 m Mary — Pvt NJ
Cornelius: b 7-5-1747 d 2-24-1843 m (1) — Baxter (2)Elizabeth — 1Lt NJ W★
Cornelius: bpt 11-14-1762 d 2-24-1843 m Elizabeth — Pvt Spy Wgn NJ ★
Garrett: b 1725 d a. 1787 (1)Lucretia Voorhees (2)Mariah — CS NJ
Garret: b 5-8-1757/8 d 10-21-1848 m Euphemia Hogeland Pvt PA
Hendrick: 7-25-1731 d 3-24-1820 m (2)Catherine Brokow Pvt NJ
Hendrick: b 5-10-1729 d 1-2I-1811 m (1)Jannet Detmars (2)Mary Terhune Cortelyou Pvt NJ
Isaac: b 3-30-1734 d 7-27-1776 m Margaret Stryker 2Lt NJ
Jacob: b 2-18-1745 d 10-24-1803 m Mary Sutphen PS NJ
Jacob: b 5-11-1762 d 3-5-1839 m Sarah Barnes Smock Sgt DrmMaj PA ★
James: b 1761 d 1824 m (1)Frances Haines (2)Elizabeth — Pvt NY
John: b 1-5-1756 d 8-14-1836 m Mary Crawford Sgt NY ★
John: b 1722 d 1798 m (1)Deborah Van Pelt (2)Catherine Mills PS NY
John: b 11-30-1752 d 2-21-1826 m Sarah Monfort PS VA
Myndert: b 12-28-1760 d — m Caty Hoagland Drm NJ ★
Oakey: b 12-25-1757 d 7-7-1849 m Mary South Pvt NJ ★
Philip: b 3-16-1760 d 10-3-1804 m Margaret Wortman Pvt NJ
Simon: b c. 1750 d 1802 m Ellen Cozine Maj PA
Tunis: b c. 1745 d 4-13-1813 m Jennie Wear Ens NY

VAN AUKEN,
Abraham: b 4-27-1746 d — m Maria Low PS NY
Abraham G.: bpt 9-2-1750 d c. 1801 m Maria Louw 1Lt NY
Benjamin: b 2-13-1756 d 9-18-1835 m Margaret Chesney Pvt PA ★
Elijah: b 10-23-1759 d 8-27-1837 m Catherine Cole Lt NY
Gideon: bpt 10-12-1755 d 9- -1834 m Elizabeth Masten Pvt PS NY ★
Henry: b 2-5-1755 d 9-1-1825 m Maria Terpenning Pvt NY
Jacobus: bpt 6-1-1734 d 1812 m Elizabeth (Van Benscoten) Middaugh Pvt PA
John: b 1765 d 3-19-1854 m Margaret Westfall Drm PA ★

Levi: b 1756 d c. 1830 m Elizabeth Terpening Lt NY
Nathaniel: b 12-19-1764 d 1-26-1835 m Mary Westbrook Pvt NY ★
Pieter: bpt 11-29-1741 d p. 1790 m Annatien Ecker Pvt NY

VAN BENSCHOTEN, (includes VAN BENSCOTEN & VAN BUNSCHOTEN)
Aaron: b 4-27-1746 d 1-18-1836 m Margaret Hoffman Pvt NY ★
Anthony: b 1763 d 5-23-1850 m Catherine Hover Pvt PA
Cornelius: bpt 6 7-1741 d p. 1796 m Heyltje Quick Sol NJ
Egbert: b 12-14-1755 d 12-28-1822 m Catherine Van DeBogart Pvt NY
Egnos: b 1-2-1754 d 10-29-1841 m (1)Jacomyntje Freer (2)Phoebe Mass 2Lt NY ★
Elias, Sr.: b 1-24-1717 d 7-25-1783 m Jacomynte Van Covenhoven PS NY
Elias, Jr.: b 10-3-1749 d c. 1805 m Catalyntje Leydt Maj NY
Elias: b 7-14-1751 d 1-24-1841 m Hannah VanKeuren Pvt NY ★
Garritt: b 7-15-1756 d 6-3-1832 m Rebecca Totten Pvt NY
Hermanus: b 8-9-1757 d 3- -1835 m Maria Stoutenburg Sgt NY
Isaac: bpt 9-11-1723 d p. 1786 m Nellie VanVliet Pvt NY
Jacob: b 11-28-1756 d 8-18-1823 m Catherine DuMond Cpl NY
Jacob: b 1-21-1722 d 1784 m Maria Lossing Pvt NY
John: b 7-11-1751 d 3-29-1817 m Jane Low Capt NY
John: b c. 1730 d p. 1784 m Sarah Rappelye PS NY
Solomon: b 10-8-1749 d 1825 m Margarete VanAuken Pvt NY
Teunis, Jr.: b 10-9-1755 d 12-22-1835 m Eliz Van der Burgh Pvt NY
Teunis: b 9-22-1706 d 1-31-1788 m Antje Sleght PS NY

VAN BENTHUYSEN, (includes VAN BENTHUSEN)
Jacobus P.: b 1711-1717 d a. 9-27-1790 m Sarah Cooper PS NY
Obadiah: b 6-17-1744 d 1816 m Annatia Rumley PS NY
Wm.: b 5-28-1759 d 1-23-1845 m (1)Margaret Ann Conklin (2)Mary — Sgt NY ★

VAN BERGEN,
Anthony: b 11-1-1729 d 11-23-1797 m Maria Salisbury Col NY
David: b 1760 d 4-27-1819 m Catherine Newkirk Pvt NY
Henry: b 11-6-1731 d 3-16-1817 m Neeltje Salisbury Capt NY
Pieter: b 6-16-1753 d 8-16-1833 m Anneatje Schermerhorn Ens NY

VAN BIBBER,
Isaac: b p. 1725 d 10-10-1744 m Miss Davis Pvt VA
John: b 1740 d 1820 m Chloe Standiford Capt VA
Peter: b a. 1723 d a. 7-3-1797 m Margerey Bounds Sol VA

VAN BLARCOM, (includes VAN BLARIGAN)
Anthony: b 12-16-1760 d c. 1812 m Elizabeth VanHorn Pvt NJ
Hendrick: bpt 5-18-1740 d — m (1)Sophronia VanWinkle (2)Elizabeth Goetschius Capt NJ
Martin: b 5-12-1755 d 1836 m Antje VanVeght Pvt NJ

VAN BRAMER,
Peter: b 7-20-1754 d p. 1800 m Magdelena Ackerman Pvt NY

VAN BROCKLIN, (includes VAN BRACKELEN & VAN BRACKLE)
Gerrit: b c. 1740 d.p. 1802 m Anna Kitts 2Lt NY
Gysbert: b c. 1750 d p. 2-18-1817 m Barbara — Pvt NY
Matthias: b 2-17-1766 d 7-26-1831 m Eleanor Vanderbilt Pvt NJ
Stephen: b 3-2-1758 d 1-2-1811 m Elizabeth Himes Pvt NJ

VAN BRUNT,
Adrian: b 11-17-1735 d 9-18-1785 m Engletie Rapalje Capt NY
Cornelius: bpt 1-28-1754 d p. 1799 m Margaret — Pvt NY
Jacob: b 10-1747 d 7-27-1813 m Phebe Woodhull PS NY
Jacques: b 9-24-1746 d 8-20-1811 m Mary Johnson PS NY
Nicholas: b 4- -1738 d 1802 m (2)Catherine Conover CS PS NJ
Nicholas: b 8-27-1749 d 9-5-1802 m Mary Wyckoff PS NY
Rutger: b 1-16-1733 d 5-18-1812 m Altie Cortleyou Col NY

VAN BUREN, (includes VAN BEUREN)
Abraham: b 11-11-1761 d 8-11-1823 m (1)Mary Swift (2)Sarah Holme Pvt NJ
Abraham: b 2-27-1737 d 4-8-1817 m Maria Goes Capt NY
Beekman: bpt 11-5-1732 d 6-1-1812 m (1)Hyltje DePeyster (2)Elizabeth Gilbert (3)Angenetje Vreeland Dr NJ
Francis: b 11-16-1728 d 5-6-1815 m Johanna VanSlyck Pvt NY
Harmon: b 1736 d 1819 m (1)Eva VanSlyck (2)Elizabeth Veeder Maj NY
Hendrick: b 2-2-1752 d — m Annatie Van Schaick Pvt NY
Johanes: bpt 11-12-1758 d 6-11-1821 m Catharine VanValkenburg (2)Elizabeth Sharp Pvt NY
John A.: b c. 1759 d 3-31-1808 m Maria Van Deusen Ens NY
Maas: b 10-28-1733 d 10-17-1783 m Catlyntje Van Valkenburgh Pvt NY
Peter: b 2-18-1733 d p. 1782 m Dorothy Fryenmost Pvt NY
Phillipus: bpt 12-4-1743 d p. 10-24-1794 m Christina VanGaasbeck Pvt PS NY
Wm.: b 5-2-1759 d 2-11-1830 m Catharine Putman Pvt NY

VAN BUSKIRK, (includes BUSKIRK & VAN BOSKERCK)
George: b 1755 d 12-9-1831 m Rachel Brower Pvt NJ
George: bpt 10-8-1721 d 5- -1798 m Sarah — Pvt PA

VAN BUSKIRK, contd.
Isaac: b 10-7-1760 d 10-27-1843 m Jerusha Little Pvt VA ★
Jacobus: b 2-11-1739 d 8-5-1800 m Anna Maria Holleback PS PA
Johannis: b 11-28-1739 d 4-5-1820 m Truntje Van Lone Pvt NJ
John: b 9-26-1757 d 12-1-1840 m — Little Lt VA PA ★
Joseph: b c. 1750 d 6- -1821 m (1)Mary Strawn (2)Mary Levers Pvt PA
Lawrence: b 9-10-1749 d 2-14-1842 m Catherine Johnson Pvt PA
Martin: b 2-18-1755 d 5-18-1823 m Maria Van Ness Pvt NY
Moses: b c. 1750 d p. 10-6-1819 m Margaret — Pvt PA
Peter: b 8-29-1762 d 12-18-1861 m Sally Baldwin PS NJ
Thomas: b — d 3-10-1811 m Maryette — CS NJ

VAN CAMP,
Cornelius, Sr.: b 11-14-1761 d 11-21-1839 m Barbara Diefendorf Sgt NY ★
Isaac: b 12-27-1749 d 3-2-1833 m Mary — Pvt PA
Moses: b c. 1757 d 8-11-1838 m (2)Anna Riggs Sgt NY
Thomas: b 5-30-1746 d 12-23-1831 m Catherine VanMiddlesworth Pvt NJ

VAN CAMPEN,
Abraham: b 2-22-1736 d 5- -1811 m (1)Maria Depue (2)Elizabeth (Schoonmaker) Depue PS NJ
Cornelius: b 1-24-1727 d 3-28-1780 m Winnefred Depue PS PA
John: b 8-15-1755 d 5-24-1835 m Susanna VanGorden Mus NY ★
John: b 5-15-1726 d 1801/2 m Sarah Depue PS Maj PA
Moses: b 1-25-1757 d 10-15-1849 m Margaret McClure Lt PA

VANCE,
David: b 1748 d 1813 m Priscilla Brank Capt NC
David: b — d 1-7-1801 m — Pvt NC
David: b 1-20-1737 d 10-4-1819 m Margaret Colville Maj PA
David: b 1749 d 12-19-1816 m Sarah Quimby Pvt VA
Edward: b 1754 d 1-23-1808 m Sarah Pierson Pvt NJ
Handle: b c. 1730 d c. 1797 m Elizabeth — Sol VA
Isaac: b 2-11-1754 d 11-5-1837 m (1)Mary Cotton (2)Mrs Anne Yerty Sgt PA
James: b 8-3-1753 d 3-9-1833 m Amy Slack Pvt NJ ★
James: b 1759 d 1837 m Bethia Kinkade Pvt VA
John: b — d p. 1778 m Annie Hogg Pvt MA
John: b c. 1725 d p. 1803 m — CS Pvt VA
John: b 1730 d 8-13-1796 m Isabella — Pvt VA
John Carlow: b 1752 d 1806 m Sarah — 2Lt NC
Joseph: b c. 1750 d 5-6-1832 m (1)Anne — (3)Mary Moore Pvt PA
Joseph: b 10- -1759 d 8-5-1809 m Sarah Wilson Pvt VA
Kennedy: b 1728 d 1785/6 m Mrs Phoebe (Potter) Pettit Pvt NJ
Nathaniel: b 1753 d 11-4-1812 m Mary Dunbar McTeer Pvt NC
Philip: b c. 1740 d 1790-3 m Mary — Pvt PA
Robert: b c. 1728 d 8-18-1818 m Jean White Capt VA
Samuel: b 6-18-1762 d 3-1-1843 m Mary Ann Waters Pvt MD
Samuel: b 10-22-1737 d 6-24-1804 m Sarah Riggs PS NJ
Samuel: b 1734 d 1807 m Sarah Byrd Col VA
Samuel: b 1749 d 12-8-1838 m Margaret Laughlin CS VA
Wm.: b 1746 d 1833 m Barbara Grider Pvt PA
Wm.: b 1740-2 d 10- -1792 m (1)Nancy Gilkerson (2)Mary Colville (3)Ann Glass Ens VA
Wm.: b 1718 d 4-18-1788 m Mary Gilkerson PS VA

VAN CLEVE, (includes VAN CLEAF, VAN CLEAVE, VAN CLEEF, VAN CLIEF)
Benjamin: b 2-28-1747 d 7-27-1836 m Mary — Capt NJ ★
Benjamin: b 11-15-1741 d 7-27-1819 m Ruth Munson CS NC
Isaac: b 1742 d 6-30-1804 m Dorcas Pumyea Cpl NJ
Isaac: b 8-15-1754 d 5-18-1801 m Antje Conklin 2Lt NY
Ishi: b 2-9-1759 d 8-30-1827 m Mary Hart Pvt NJ
John: b 5-16-1749 d 6-1-1791 m Catherine Benham Capt NJ
John: b 2-6-1757 d 1814 m Elizabeth Moore Pvt NJ
John: b c. 1739 d 5-28-1812 m (1)Mary Shepherd (2)Mrs Rachel Demaree Ryker Pvt VA
Joseph: b 2-6-1760 d 7-20-1843 m Eleanor Schenck Pvt NJ ★
Laurence: b 4-15-1754 d 1-15-1830 m Sarah Angevine Pvt NY ★
Peter: b 1763 d 3-5-1816 m Mary Ann — Pvt NJ
Wm.: b 8-15-1737 d 4-23-1813 m (1)Deborah Smith (2)Anna Clutter Sgt PA

VAN CORTLANDT,
Philip: b 9-1-1749 d 11-'5-1831 m Catharine DePeyster BGen NY
Pierre: b 1-10-1721 d 5-1-1814 m Joanna Livingston Col NY

VAN COTT,
Gabriel: b c. 1748 d p. 1783 m Phoebe Brass PS NY
Nicholas: bpt 10-22-1727 d p. 1788 m Jannetze Wortman Cpl NY

VAN COURT,
Michael: bpt 3-4-1739 d 1814 m Elizabeth Brown Asst QMGen NJ

VAN DALFSEN,
John T.: b c. 1757 d 6-11-1823 m Charlotte Amelia Bronck Pvt NY

VAN DALSEM, (or VAN DALFSEM)
Henry: b 8-12-1757 d 3-10-1835 m Eunice Zabriskie Sgt NY ★

VANDAMAN,
Frederick: b 1762 d 7-8-1813 m Susannah Hillicost Pvt VA ★

VAN DE BOE,
Jacob: b 5-24-1760 d 8-24-1830 m Comeche — Pvt NY

VAN DEMAN,
John: b 10-12-1757 d 1-18-1840 m Mary Magdalene Hester Pvt VA ★

VAN DE MARK, (includes VANDEMARK, VANDE MARK & VANDERMARK)
Benjamin: b 2-10-1734 d 11-3-1805 m Sarah Brink Pvt PA
Frederick, Jr.: bpt 2-25-1733 d p. 1793 m Mary Oosterhout PS NY ★
Jeremiah, Jr.: b 12-4-1748 d 10- -1823 m Esther Courtright Pvt PA
Joseph: b 7-11-1762 d 3-28-1841 m (1)Ann Burnett (2)Elizabeth Smith Pvt NY ★
Lodewick: b 2-18-1760 d 1-6-1813 m Charity VanAuken Pvt NY ★
Sylvester: b 1740 d p. 1784 m Margaret Rapalie Pvt NY

VAN DEN BERG, (includes VANDENBERG, VANDENBERGH, VANDENBURGH, VANDERBERGH, VANDERBURGH)
Benjamin: b 1718 d p. 1777 m Jozannah Zuyland Pvt NY
Cornelius: bpt 5-13-1727 d p. 4-18-1790 m (1)Maria Viele (2)Eva (Van Petten) Bratt Capt NY
Evert: b 6-12-1738 d 1-3-1785 m (1)Annattie Lansing (2)Janette VanSchaick Pvt NY
Garret: b 6-3-1736 d 10-13-1793 m Adaleda (VanDenBergh) Pvt NY
Gerrit: b 9-26-1725 d a. 5-11-1809 m Agnietje Lieverson Col NY
Gysbert: b 8-7-1748 d 9-12-1836 m Jane Whitbeck Sol NY
Henry: b 1760 d 4-12-1812 m Marie Frances Connoyer Capt NY
Henry: b 2-28-1756 d 5-15-1841 m (1)Yetmercy Carey (2)Abigail — Seaman Capt NY
Henry: b c. 1743 d p. 1790 m Margaret Field Lt NY
Henry: b 1722 d c. 1794 m Mary Green Sol NY
James: b 9-4-1729 d 4-4-1794 m (1)Margaret Noxen (2)Helena Clark Col PS NY
James: b 10-26-1758 d p. 1834 m (1)Jane Rosencrans (2)Margaret Vanderburgh Pvt NY ★
Maas: bpt 4-11-1742 d p. 1792 m Catherine Scheer Pvt NY
Reynier: b 1-6-1751 d — m Elizabeth Vonhagen Pvt NY
Richard: bpt 6-24-1753 d p. 1789 m Annatje Brandow Lt NY
Rutger: bpt 8-28-1726 d 6-1-1781 m Maria VanDenBergh Pvt NY
Winant: b 1760 d 5-11-1745 d Sarah Fort Sgt NY ★

VAN DER BECK, (or VANDERBECK)
Abraham: b 4-14-1757 d 2-22-1834 m Margaret Godwin Pvt NJ ★
Andrew: b 1760 d 1828 m Althea Barcalow Pvt NJ

VAN DER BILT, (includes VANDERBILT)
Cornelius: b 3-11-1731 d 8-18-1800 m Margaret Lamberse PS Pvt NJ
Cornelius: a. 1760 d 11-7-1824 m Catherine Vredenburgh Pvt NY W★
Derick: b 12-25-1728 d p. 1810 m Gritje Hogelant PS NY
John: b 2-26-1744 d 1814 m Isabella Beaty Lt NJ
John, Jr.: b 1-19-1757 d 10-23-1812 m Anna Conover Pvt NJ ★

VAN DER BOGART, (includes VANDEBOGART)
John: b 1718 d 1811 m Christine Fero Sgt NY
Tecarus: bpt 3-23-1717 d 1799 m Nealtje de Graaf PS NY

VAN DER COOK, (includes VANDERCOOK & VANDER COOK)
Cornelius: b 1754 d c. 1791 m Mary Mandeville Pvt NY
Isaac: b 1-3-1755 d 7-3-1821 m Sarah Teachout Cpl NY
Michael: b 11-10-1715 d 11-2-1786 m Cornelia VanNess PS NY
Simon: b 8-17-1749 d 11-28-1829 m Levina VanderHoof Ens NY

VANDEREN,
Godfrey: b 1722/3 d 1792 m Geertje VanHorn Pvt PA

VANDERFORD,
Charles: b c. 1757 d p. 7-11-1820 m Sarah English Smn Pvt MA

VANDERGRIFT, (includes VANDEGRIFT)
Folkhard: b a. 1739 d 10-10-1795 m Elizabeth Watson Pvt PA
Jacob: b 2-28-1729 d 5-10-1800 m (1)Catrintje Hufte (2)Sarah Titus Capt PA
John, Sr.: b 3-25-1723 d 1805 m (1)Mary Praul (2)Katrine — Pvt PA
John: b 1754 d p. 1791 m — Weiser Pvt PA
Leonard: b 4-4-1756 d 2-5-1821 m (1)Elizabeth Dushane (2)Ruth Sankey (3)Mrs Martha Pennington Sol DE

VANDERHOF, (includes VANDERHOEF & VANDERHOOF)
Cornelius: b 6-6-1745 d 4-22-1793 m Margaret Keyser Pvt NJ
Cornelius: b 5-7-1752 d 4-22-1844 m (1)— Henderson (2)Mary Patterson Pvt NJ ★
Cornelius: b 1750 d 1790 Marie Bougarel Matr NY
Cornelius P.: b 11-1-1762 d 5-10-1816 m Phebe Hunn Pvt NJ
Hendrick: b 10-3-1725 d 9-3-1797 m Sarah Doremus Capt NY
Peter: b 6-21-1742 d 10-21-1822 m (1)Mary Dorsett (2)Margaret — Ens NJ

VANDERHULE,
Abraham: b 7-29-1757 d 5-18-1837 m Catherine Smith Pvt NJ

VANDER HORST,
Arnoldus: b 2-22-1723 d — m Elizabeth Simons Capt SC

VANDERLIN,
John: b 1760 d 1856 m Elizabeth Kimes Pvt PA

VAN DER POEL, (includes VANDERPOEL & VANDERPOOL)
Andries: b 12-9-1754 d 6-9-1812 m (1)Catharine A. Van Valkenburg
  (2)Elizabeth Smith Ens NY
David: b 2-1-1735 d 1-26-1821 m Deborah Lane Pvt NJ
Jacobus: bpt 7-3-1737 d 7-9-1804 m (1)Lena VanAllen (2) Lucretia
  Van Vleck (3)Jannetje Fryemnoet Adj NY
John: b 2- -1744 d 2-27-1781 m Elizabeth Crane Pvt NJ
John: b 1-26-1755 d 1-26-1843 m (2)Isabella Douglas Pvt NY ★
John: bpt 4-17-1758 d p. 1802 m Gerritje VanValckenburgh Pvt NY
Thomas: b 1733 d 1789 m Rachel Campbell Pvt NJ

VANDERSLICE,
Anthony, Jr.: b 10-23-1743 d 5-17-1803 m Elizabeth Pannebecker
  Sgt PA
Henry, Sr.: b 3-9-1726 d 2-10-1797 m Catherine Sassamenhaussan
  CS Wgn PA
Henry, Jr.: b 4-17-1755 d 2-12-1825 m Ann — Pvt PA ★
Thomas: b 10-4-1756 d 8-14-1817 m Tacy Richardson Cav PA

**VAN DER VEER, (includes VAN DERVEER, VANDERVEER,
  VANDIVER, VANDIVIER)**
Cornelius: bpt 1758 d 1-1-1827 m Aeltie Vanderveer Pvt NJ
Cornelius: b 12-5-1731 d 2-13-1804 m Leah VanKerk Capt NY
Edward: b c. 1748 d 1837/8 m (1)Helena Turley (2)Catherine Pool
  Pvt SC
Garret: b 12-4-1731 d 1-31-1803 m Jane Voorhees PS NJ
Jacob: b 1726 d1806 m Alche Wyckoff PS NJ
John: b 4-4-1763 d 1-3-1844 m Ann Bowne Pvt NJ
John: b 10-3-1752 d 6-16-1841 m Jane VanPelt Pvt NJ ★
Joseph: b 3-4-1761 d 5-1-1841 m Sarah Tice Pvt Gnr NJ ★
Lawrence: b 1741 d 12-8-1815 m (1)Maria Sckenk (2)Maria
  Onderdonk Dr NJ
Peter: b 1760 d 3-12-1823 m Anna LaGrange Pvt NJ
Peter: b 1-5-1745 d 10-24-1778 m Jane Schank Pvt NJ
Tunis: bpt 4-22-1739 d c. 10-13-1801 m Jannetje Van Nostrand Lt
  NJ
Tunis: b 10-20-1760 d 1-20-1835 m Martha Saybrook Pvt NJ
Wm.: b 3-19-1762 d 7-17-1833 m Mary G. Johnson Pvt VA ★

VANDER VOLGEN,
Cornelius: b 7-25-1731 d 1-15-1786 m Rebecca Fort Pvt NY

**VAN DER VOORT, (includes VAN DERVOORT &
  VANDER VOORT)**
John: b 3-30-1755 d 7-3-1836 m Mary Elizabeth — Pvt Gnr NY
Paul: b 3-29-1751 d 1827 m Jane VanHorn 2Lt NY
Paul: b 1753 d p. 1790 m — Pvt NY
Peter: b 3-29-1751 d 9-24-1798 m Ann Kovenhoven Ens NY

VANDERWERKER, (includes VANDERWACKER)
Isaac: b 2-23-1750 d 1-25-1824 m Elizabeth Sybrandt Pvt NY
Martin: b 12- -1744/5 d 12-16-1843 m Mary Winne Cpl NY

VAN DER ZEE, (includes VAN DERZEE & VANDERZEE)
Albert: b 1716 d p. 1790 m Antje VanWie Capt NY
Albert: bpt 6-28-1738 d 1-23-1822 m Hester Houghtaling Pvt NY
Cornelius: b 10-5-1740 d p. 1786 m Annetie Veder Pvt NY
Cornelius: bpt 8-10-1740 d 3-19-1823 m Aginitz Whitbeck Ens NY
Tunis: b 8-24-1746 d p. 1791 m Geertruy — Pvt NY

VANDEURSEN, (includes VAN DUERSEN)
Ann: b 4-5-1745 d 1-6-1834 m Wm. VanDuersen PS NJ
Peter: bpt 7-3-1762 d 4-11-1809 m Lydia Brewster Pvt NY
Wm.: b 4-11-1736 d 10-17-1816 m Ann Stryker Pvt NJ

VAN DEUSEN, (includes VAN DUESEN & VAN DUSEN)
Abraham: b 1737 d p. 1797 m Elenor VanBrunnall Pvt NY
Abraham: b 1756 d 6-22-1835 m Annata VanSise Pvt NY ★
Abraham: b 9-28-1742 d 7-17-1795 m Sarah Chipman Pvt VT
Abraham: b 5-19-1742 d 1819 m Gertje — Pvt NY
Cornelius: b 1-8-1758 d 10-8-1787 m Rachel Elting Ens NY
George: b 11-13-1757 d p. 1803 m Eva Brazee Pvt NY
Gilbert: bpt 11-4-1739 d 7-15-1832 m Neeltje VanAntwerp Sgt NY
Gloude: b 9-6-1754 d 7-18-1845 m (1)Elizabeth Muller
  (2)Angelica VanSlycke Pvt NY ★
Hartman: bpt 1-7-1722 d p. 1782 m Margrieta Dyckman Pvt NY
Hendrick: b c. 1758 d c. 1801 m Eleanor Brumjum Pvt NY
Jacob: b 7-15-1741 d 5-26-1812 m Mary Laird PS MA
Jacob: b 9-21-1748 d 8-10-1814 m Elsie Lansing Ens NY
Jacob: bpt 5- -1710 d 1797 m Lena Vosburgh Pvt NY
Johannes: bpt 4-14-1728 d p. 1795 m Fytje Roorbach Pvt NY
Johannes: b 5-30-1728 d 10-14-1803 m (1)Christyntje De La Mater
  (2)Maritje Bronck Pvt PS NY
John: bpt 5-16-1740 d 6-8-1824 m Lydia Slye Pvt NY
John: bpt 8-12-1759 d 10-16-1841 m Christina Spoor Pvt NY
John: b 3-19-1737 d 1-13-1826 m Catherine Hollenbeck Pvt MA

Martin: bpt 1-29-1737 d 5-28-1815-1825 m Elizabeth Ostrander
  Mil NY
Matthew: b 8-12-1740 d 3-7-1807 m Elizabeth Van Wormer PS CS
  MA
Matthew: b 1739 d c. 1806 m Jane Belden Pvt PS NY
Matthew: b 9-2-1759 d 11-30-1812 m Lydia Brehaut Pvt NY
Matthias: bpt 2-16-1746 d 9-4-1795 m Cornelia Van Wie Pvt NY
Melchert: b 12-27-1719 d 1789 m Neeltje Quackenbosh PS NY
Robert: bpt 2-7-1727 d p. 1784 m Cathrina VanHam Pvt NY
Robert T.: b 2-15-1765 d 2-17-1864 m Christina Decker Van Tacknick
  Pvt NY
Tobias R.: bpt 8-16-1696 d 10-17-1781 m Arriantje Muller PS NY
Tobias: b 1-13-1737 d p. 1817 m Cornelia (Van Deusen)Pvt NY
Tobias R.: bpt 4-12-1747 d p. 1795 m Catharina — Pvt NY

**VAN DE VENTER, (includes VANDERVENTER, VAN DERVENTER,
  VANDEVANTER & VAN DEVENTER)**
Abraham: b 5-7-1758 d 5-20-1820 m Elizabeth P. Johnston Pvt NJ
Barnabas: b 3-24-1761 d 1-4-1851 m Elizabeth Siler Pvt VA ★
Christopher: b 10-12-1755 d 1-23-1840 m (1)Rachael Vreeland
  (2)Elizabeth Lambison Pvt NJ
Isaac: b 12-7-1762 d 10-24-1826 m Ann Willett Pvt NJ
Isaac: bpt 2-8-1747 d 7-12-1803 m Elizabeth McGeath 2Lt VA
Jacob: b 1743 d 1815 m Mary Slater Capt NJ
Jeremiah: b 3-12-1741 d 12-22-1806 m Elizabeth Cooper Pvt NJ
John: b 2-10-1756 d 8-27-1846 m Ann Charters Fif NJ ★
Peter: bpt 7-27-1742 d 1821 m Margaret Miller PS PA
Peter: b 7-3-1755 d 6-25-1837 m Mary Durham Capt NJ ★

VANDEWATER,
Abram: b 1757 d 1829 m Eliza Smith Pvt NJ

VAN DOREN, (includes VAN DOORN & VAN DORN)
Aaron: b 9-14-1744 d 7-14-1830 m (1)Ghacy Schenck (2)Mrs
  Margart Hurd Pvt NJ
Abraham: b 1-30-1743 d 1-21-1813 m (1)Neeltje — (2)Mary
  Covert Lt NJ
Abraham: b 10-28-1750 d 4-17-1823 m (1)Charity Bennet
  (2)Elizabeth Bowman (3)Catherine Nevius (4)Rachel Babcock
  Pvt NJ
Abraham: b 12-30-1738 d 12-29-1805 m Anne Van Dyke PS CS NJ
Anne Van Dyke: b 11-28-1749 d 2-29-1820 m Abraham Van Doren
  PS NJ
Anthony: b 2-19-1736 d 12-1-1786 m Ruth Ingraham PS RI
Bergun: b 3-22-1759 d 10-5-1850 m (1)Neltje Voorhees
  (2)Margaret (Wortman) VanArsdale Pvt NJ ★
Christina: b 10-30-1757 d 6-3-1831 m Nuel Suydam Pvt NJ
Christianus: b 7-12-1752 d 3-13-1828 m Johanna Hoagland Pvt NJ
Cornelius: b 6-15-1758 d 1825 m Sophia Snedeker Pvt NJ
Cornelius: b 9-25-1746 d 12-28-1834 m Elizabeth Wyckoff Pvt NJ ★
Hezekiah: b 1757 d 1800 m Lydia Balser Pvt NJ
Isaac: b 11-12-1744 d 12-25-1828 m Sarah Opie Ens NJ
Jacob, Sr.: b 12-11-1724 d 9-12-1811 m (1)Phebe Vanderveer
  (2)Jane Ditmars Capt NJ
Jacob, Jr.: b 5-4-1760 d 8-5-1824 d Maria Mellick Pvt NJ
Jacob: b 8-24-1745 d 2-18-1813 m Jane Voorhees Ens NJ W★
John, Sr.: b 4-23-1726 d p. 9-18-1811 m Martha Lott PS NJ
John, Jr.: b 1-9-1757 d 7-28-1832 m (1)Catrynje Voohees (2)Ellen
  Lott Pvt NY
Joseph: b 6-15-1748 d 2-5-1801 m Sarah Vanderbilt CS NJ
Martha Lott: b 1728 d 4-27-1805 m John VanDoren PS NJ
Nicholas: b 1724 d 2-6-1796 m Sarah Smith Pvt NJ
Peter: b 7-4-1755 d 4-18-1834 m Janilfe Williamson Pvt NJ ★
Wm.: b 11-13-1727 d 8-9-1786 m (1)Catherine Hoff (2)Maria
  Wyckoff Pvt NJ

VAN DRIESEN,
John: bpt 3-11-1744 d p. 1778 m Margarita Truax Adj NY

VAN DUYNE, (includes VAN DINE)
Cornelius: b 1714 d 12-30-1782 m Ann Vanderveer PS NY
John: b 10-3-1762 d p. 10-28-1836 m Rachel Cole Pvt NJ

VAN DUZER,
Adolphus: b 9-19-1762 d 12-26-1844 m Unice Coleman Pvt NY
Christopher: b 1743 d 9-28-1812 m (1)Julianna Strong (2)Julia
  Tusten Capt NY
Henry: b 2-15-1759 d 11-10-1845 m Frances Mandeville Pvt NY
Isaac: b 10-17-1755 d 10-17-1814 m Martha Tusten Ens NY
Isaac, Sr.: b 2-6-1698 d 3-20-1792 m (1)Angenetie Laroe
  (2)Elizabeth Rosenboom PS NY
Isaac: b 9- -1721 d 7-20-1798 m Jane — PS NY

VAN DYKE, (includes VAN DIKE, VANDIKE & VAN DYCK)
Abraham: b 4-11-1753 d 3-7-1804 m Ida Stryker PS NJ
Andrew: b 1-11-1744 d 9-3-1814 m (1)Martha — (2)Mary Cook Pvt PA
Cornelius: b 6-24-1748 d 2-24-1840 m Mary Brokaw Sgt NJ ★
David: b 5-11-1742 d 11-20-1835 m Lovina — Pvt NJ
Hendricus: b 8-29-1731 d p. 1787 m Engeltje Mebie Pvt NY
Hendrick: b 12-25-1743 d 1817 m Margaret — Col NJ
Henry: b 1-1-1753 d 12-8-1815 m Elizabeth — Pvt NY
Henry: b 6-11-1700 d 1784 m Elizabeth Campbell PS PA
Jacob: b c. 1755 d 10-7-1805 m Milcah Ann Bostick Maj DE

VAN DYKE, contd.
Jacob: b 1760 d 10-3-1844 m Charlotte Lawrence Sgt NY
Johannis: b c. 1745 d p. 1790 m Annatie Couenover Cpl NJ
John: b 11-7-1709 d 6-28-1778 m (1)Margaret Barcolo (2)Gerretje Bergen Pvt NJ
John: b 1-31-1753 d 2-28-1840 m (1)Sarah Clark (2)Ann Gentner Lt NY
John: b c. 1739 d 8- -1821 m Martha — Pvt PA
John: b 3- -1755 d 9-12-1835 m Martha Moore Pvt PA ★
Lambert: bpt 4-29-1750 d 12-7-1794 m Margaret McMichael Pvt PA
Laurens: b 11-6-1738 d 7-14-1814 m Maria Vanderpoel Pvt NY
Matthew: b 1-8-1752 d 9-18-1832 m Lydia Longstreet Ens NJ
Matthyas: b —d 8-27-1799 m Sarah Vanderbilt 1Lt NY
Nicholas: b 9-25-1738 d 2-19-1789 m (1)Elizabeth Nixon (2)Charlotte Stanley Maj PS DE
Nicholas: b c. 1745 d p. 1790 m Elizabeth VanBrunt Ens NY
Petrus Douw: bpt 5-5-1760 d p. 1794 m Alida Barhydt Pvt NY
Roelof: b 5-18-1711 d 1788 m Catharine Emmons PS NJ
Stephen: b 12-13-1726 d p. 2-16-1776 m Eytje VanLoon Pvt NY
Wm.: b 5-12-1756 d p. 1803 m Mary Labryteaux Pvt NJ

VANDYNE,
Matthew: b 8- -1752 d p. 7-3-1837 m — Sgt NJ

VAN EMBURGH,
John: b 10-17-1736 d 8-18-1803 m (1)Antje — (2)Lenk — Pvt NJ

VAN EMMON,
George: b 9-12-1753 d p. 1810 m Rebecca Scott Pvt PA

VAN EPPS, (includes VAN EPS)
Abraham: b 9-20-1764 d 8-7-1840 m (2)Sarah Underhill Pvt NY
Abraham: b 10-15-1738 d 3-19-1812 m (1)Margarita Veeder (2)Deborah Viele Capt NY W★
Charles: b 2-16-1724 d p. 1800 m Cathrina Winne Pvt NY
Evert: b 1740 d 12-19-1813 m Polly Minthorn Capt NY W★
Johannes: b 12-27-1764 d 8-29-1847 m Jane Van Vleck Pvt NY
John B.: b 4-28-1706 d 3-7-1788 m Janetze Lansing PS NY
John Baptist: b 5-30-1731 d 12-24-1814 m Anna Vedder Pvt NY

VAN ETTEN,
Anthony, Sr.: bpt 6-12-1726 d a. 11-25-1778 m Annetje Decker PS NY
Jacob: b 1738 d p. 1785 m Sarah Decker Lt NJ ★
Jacob: bpt 6-17-1740 d — m Janet Louw Pvt NY
Jacob: b 12-25-1696 d 1779 m Antjen Westbroek PS NY
Johannes, Sr.: b 1730 d 2-15-1815 m (1)Marie Gonzales (2)Rachel (Williams) Decker Capt PA
Johannes, Jr.: b 1759 d 8- -1808 m Cornelia Decker Ens PA W★
John: bpt 1-1-1744 d p. 1782 m Maregreta — Pvt NJ
John: b 5-31-1759 d 8-3-1836 m Maria VanValkenburgh Pvt NY
John: b 4-17-1720 d a. 3-20-1786 m (1)Maritje Westfael (2)Margaret LeFever CS NC
Levi: b 7-12-1757 d 10-25-1843 m Jane Westbrook Pvt NY

VAN EVERA, (includes VAN EVERY)
Cornelius: b 12-12-1730 d 1815 m (1)Janettje Van Alstine (2)Cornelia Schermerhorn Ens NY
Martinus: bpt 12-25-1741 d 3-26-1813 m Cornelia Van Schaick Pvt NY
Rynier: b 5- -1729 d 5-22-1811 m (1)Neeltje Van Epps (2)Elizabeth Doxtater Capt NY

VAN FLEET, (includes VAN VLEET, VAN VLEIT)
Abraham: b 1760 d 1834 m Sarah Brown Cpl NY ★
Charrick: b 10-17-1748 d 1823 m Barbara LaBar Pvt PA
Cornelius: b 3-6-1757 d 12-7-1841 m Sarah Shipman Pvt NJ ★
Daniel: b 1756 d 5-19-1840 m Martha Brown Sgt NY ★
Jan: b 11-16-1694 d 7- -1775 m Jesyntje Swartwont PS NY
Johannes: b 11-26-1721 d p. 1-27-1788 m (1)Cornelia Swart (2)Seletje Schneider Sol NY
Joshua: b 8-22-1764 d 1-8-1848/9 m (1)Sabra — (2)Elizabeth — Pvt NY ★
Petrus: bpt 1-1-1737 d p. 1790 m Johanna VanWormer PS NY
Wm.: b c. 1724 d p. 1777 m Adriantje Wyckoff Pvt NJ
Wm.: b 5-9-1725 d 5-4-1798 m Marytje Aten Pvt NJ

VAN FOSSEN,
Jacob: b — d p. 5-5-1840 m Rose Shiniker CS PA
John: b 1740 d 12-27-1818 m Rachel Elizabeth — Pvt PA
Levi: b 1-29-1762 d 11-11-1811 m Elizabeth Hanna PS PA

VAN GAASBEEK, (includes VAN GAASBECK)
Abraham, Jr.: bpt 8-19-1753 d c. 5-10-1823 m Annetje Ten Broeck Lt Cnt NY
Abraham: bpt 5-30-1758 d 5-11-1811 m Elizabeth Hasbrouck Pvt NY
Jacobus: b 2-27-1737 d 1-23-1825 m Deborah Kiersted 1Lt NY
John: bpt 2-8-1756 d p. 1801 m Maria Van Steenberg Pvt NY

VAN GIESON, (includes VAN GIESEN)
Henry: b 12-22-1745 d a. 1805 m Henrietta Banta Pvt NJ
John: b 9-23-1731 10-5-1809 m Metje Van Houten Sol NJ

VAN GILDER,
Abraham: b c. 1736 d a. 1809 m Martha Ann Hand Pvt NJ
Isaac: b c. 1750 d 3-25-1813 m Mary — Pvt NJ
Jacob: b 1752 d 7- -1846 m Margaret Gibler Pvt PA

VAN GORDER,
Jacob: b 1761 d 5-17-1836 m Margaret — PS PA
Samuel: b 1763 d c. 1840 m Catherine Sheriden Pvt PA ★
Wm.: b 10-17-1758 d c. 1840 m Lena Sherred Pvt NJ ★

VAN GORDON, (includes VAN GORDEN)
Alexander, Sr.: b 10-10-1728 d p. 1801 m Annetje Kortrecht Pvt NY
Alexander, Jr.: b 3-16-1752 d 1820 m Hannah Pomeroy Lt PA W★
Jacobus: bpt 6-17-1740 d p. 1789 m Antje VanEtten Pvt NY
Moses: b 10-14-1753 d 10-9-1838 m (1)Elizabeth Van Etten (2)Mrs Elsie Middaugh Pvt NJ ★

VAN GUYSLING,
Jacob: b 1-18-1736 d 11-19-1803 m Jannetje Feling Pvt NY
Peter: b 1-22-1745 d 11-30-1824 m Annatje Beck Pvt NY

VAN HARLINGEN,
John Martin: b 12-18-1755 d 4-25-1825 m Eleanor Schureman Pvt NJ

VAN HEINING, (or VAN HYNING)
Henry: b 1738 d 12-25-1839 m (2)Hannah Braver (3)Patience Taylor Pvt NY

VAN HOESEN,
Albert: b 10-13-1750 d 2-22-1839 m Sophia Delyn Pvt NY
Garret: b 5-24-1742 d 1815 m Elizabeth Van Hoesen Pvt NY
Jacob: b 11-17-1722 d p. 1804 m Annatje VanLoon Pvt NY
Jacob F.: b 2-13-1740 d 11-13-1820 m Rachel — Pvt NY
Jacob Jurry: b 2-28-1756 d p. 1787 m Geertruy Bakkers Pvt NY
Jans Casperus: bpt 12-10-1710 d p. 1789 m Hendrike VanLoon PS Pvt NY
John: b 10-10-1728 d p. 1788 m Cornelia Becker Pvt NY
John: b 1757 d 3-24-1829 m Elizabeth (Van Hoesen)Pvt NY

VAN HOEVENBERG,
Eggo T. H.: b 3-7-1764 d 5-29-1842 m Eva Conyes Pvt NY ★
Henry: b 3-30-1758 d 8-12-1839 m Esther Dumond Lt QM NY ★
Rudolf: b 1-22-1752 d 3-16-1808 m Lydia VanDyck Lt NY

VAN HOOK,
Jacob: b 1761 d p. 1833 m (1)Lucretia — (2)Elizabeth — Sgt NC ★
Lawrence, Sr.: b 6-23-1723 d a. 1- -1801 m (1)Bridget — (2)Vittory Rankin (3)Mary Kernol CS NC
Lloyd: bpt 2-12-1751 d 1815/6 m Margaret Johnston CS NC
Samuel: b 11-15-1733 d p. 11-13-1809 m (2)Hannah Wilson Williams PS Sol VA

VAN HOOSEAR,
Rinear: b c. 1756/7 d 4-17-1819 m Mercy Taylor Sgt CT ★

VAN HORN,
Abram, Sr.: b 3-1-1740 d 3-5-1817 m Gertrude Wycoff PS NJ
Abraham, Jr.: b 12-31-1763 d 1-5-1840 m Anne Covenhoven PS Pvt NJ
Abraham, Sr.: b 8-28-1738 d 3-5-1810 m Hannah Hoff QM PS NY
Benjamin: b 7-14-1759 d p. 8-26-1833 m (1)Nancy Young (2)Rachel Dailey Pvt PA ★
Bernard: b 6-13-1730 d 1-11-1778 m (1)Sarah VanPelt (2)Jane Slack Lt PA
Cornelius: b 3-5-1739 d p. 2-16-1783 m Geesje VanOrden Pvt NJ
Cornelius: b 12-16-1750 d 7- -1847 m Sarah Dunn Lt PA
Cornelius: b 11- -1747 d p. 5-19-1824 m Sarah Blauvelt PS NJ
Cornelius: b 3-10-1745 d 2-6-1823 m Eve Frederic MM NY
Daniel: b 1729 d 1822/3 m Anna Parlman Sol NY
Gabriel Peterson: b — d a. 4-20-1815 m Mary VanSant Col PS MD
Gabriel: bpt 3-3-1716 d 1789 m Martha Brelsford Pvt PA
Garret: b c. 1725 d p. 10-14-1801 m (1)Mary Neal (2)Ann — PS PA
Henry: b 10-2-1734 d 1777 m Elizabeth VanZandt Capt PA
Isaac: b 1-13-1754 d 2-2-1834 m Mrs Dorothy Johns Marple Capt PA ★
Isaiah: b 11-12-1750 d a. 4-16-1793 m Catherine Rue Pvt PA
Isaiah: b 10-24-1760 d 8-26-1844 m Dorcas Logan Drm PA ★
James: b 4-3-1740 d 2-8-1794 m Elizabeth Sleght Lt NJ
Johannis: b 6-8-1742 d 10-10-1786 m Beelitje VanRiper PS NJ
Samuel: b 1753 d 10-25-1850 m Katharine Evans Pvt PA ★
Thomas: b 1745 d 2-26-1841 m Maria Frederick Lt NY ★
Wm.: b 1750 d 1820 m Elizabeth Ellis Pvt NJ ★
Wm.: b 7-18-1747 d 10-13-1807 m Lavinia Budd PS PA

VAN HOUTEN,
Adrian: b 10-9-1755 d 10-24-1782 m Elizabeth (Van Houten) Pvt NJ NJ
Clause R.: b 11-13-1749 d 10-1-1818 m Catharina Blauvelt Sol NY
Garret: b 1-13-1764 d 8-23-1826 m Cornelia VanNess Pvt NY
Gerrit: b 11-7-1718 d p. 6-7-1786 m Jannetje Blauvelt PS NY
Hendrick: b 3-25-1747 d p. 4-21-1810 m Catherine Sandford Pvt NJ

Resolvent T.: b 4-10-1742 d *p.* 1790 m Elizabeth Hogencamp 1Lt NY
Resolvert: b 12-14-1743 d 5-24-1837 m Maria Blauvelt Lt NY ★
Richard: b 7-12-1742 d 12-1-1810 m Marretje VanRipen PS NJ
Richard: bpt 11-21-1746 d 1819 m (1)Ragel New Kerck (2)Ragel Post Pvt NJ
Roelif: b 10-9-1748 d 3-2-1802 m (1)Antje Hennion (2)Antje Berdan Pvt NJ
Roelof: bpt 3-11-1721 d 1790 m Catherine Nagel PS NY

VAN HUYSEN,
Harmanus: b 10-23-1751 d 11-26-1833 m Rachel Bogert Capt NJ ★

VAN INGEN,
Dirk: b 9-20-1738 d 2-27-1814 m Margariet VanSeysen Dr NY

VAN INWEGEN,
Cornelius: bpt 10-17-1743 m 1823 m Lena Westbrook PS Pvt NY
Harmanus: b 5-10-1730 d 7-16-1814 m Margrietje Cole Pvt NY

VAN KEUREN, (includes VAN KUEREN)
Abraham, Sr.: b 9-20-1711 d 10-12-1776 m Garritje Niukerch PS NY
Abraham: bpt 2-20-1737 d *p.* 1797 m Margaret Storm 2Lt NY
Gerrit: b 11-2-1747 d 1-21-1800 m Margreitje Slejt Pvt NY
Hendrick: b 1737 d 12-8-1802 m Margaret Miller Capt NY
Jacobus: bpt 5-17-1719 d *p.* 6-8-1802 m Lea Van Hoogteeling Pvt NY
Johannes: b 11-29-1741 d 12-22-1826 m (1)Elizabeth Zuylandt (2)Anna M. B. (Sieperlez) Franklin Pvt NY
Mattheus: bpt 1-29-1743 d *p.* 1783 m Elizabeth Bras Pvt NY
Matthew: b 12-15-1760 d 4-15-1845 m Mary — Pvt NY
Matthew: b 1706 d 1781 m Seletje Delamater PS NY
Matthew: bpt 2-10-1751 d *p.* 1802 m Maria Ekkert PS Sol NY
Tobias: b 12-4-1757 d *p.* 1792 m Lewa Lewis Pvt PS NY

VAN KIRK,
Barnard: b 9-15-1748 d 9-10-1817 m Agnes Pennington Pvt PS PA
Benjamin: b 11-5-1747 d 9-2-1815 m Sarah Armitage Cpl PS NJ
Henry: b 1-9-1742 d 4-3-1797 m Sarah VanKirk CS NJ
Jemson: b 1758 d 12-8-1836 m Elizabeth — Pvt NJ ★
John: b 4-20-1751 d 9-18-1834 m Elizabeth — Pvt NJ ★
Josiah: b 6-5-1743 d 8-20-1821 m Achsah Hunt Pvt NJ
Peter: b 1-8-1759 d 3-10-1824 m Esther Drake Tms NJ
Samuel: b 12-15-1757 d 1-9-1836 m Mary Price Pvt NJ
Wm.: b 2-1-1758 d 2- -1826 m (2)Deborah Waters Pvt NJ

VAN KLEECK, (includes VAN KLEEK)
Baltus: b 10-10-1725 d 1794 m (1)Sara Kip (2)Josyartha Curson (3)Gertrude Crannell (4)Rhoda Dutcher Pvt NY
Barant: b — d *p.* 1782 m Hannah DuBois Pvt NY
Hugh: b *c.* 1741 d *p.* 1810 m (1)Marie Everitt (2)Rachel Brinkerhoff (3)Ariaantje Palamtier Capt NY
Jeremiah: b — d *p.* 1795 m Antje VanBomel Pvt NY
Peter: bpt 6-1-1725 d *p.* 5-25-1793 m Antoinette Freer Sgt NY
Peter Baltus: b 1749 d 11-3-1800 m Chatje Tappen Pvt NY
Peter P.: b 8-21-1757 d *p.* 1829 m (1)Miss Meddaugh (2)Emily Sabin (3)Charlotte Sickles Pvt NY

VAN LEER, (includes VAN LAER, VAN LEAR, VON LEER & VON LOHR)
Benjamin: b *c.* 1733 d 11-17-1820 m (1)Hannah — (2)Kesiah Tonkin PS NJ
George: b 1735 d 4-22-1807 m Elizabeth Roberts PS NJ
Isaac: b 1754 d 7-31-1799 m Sarah Davis Pvt PA
John Wm.: b 8-17-1745 d 11-8-1833 m Nancy Allison 1Lt PA
Samuel: b 1747 d 9-14-1825 m Hannah Wayne Capt PA
Wm.: b 1757 d 1-11-1815 m Sarah Sargent BgdMaj PA

VAN LEUVEN,
Peter: b 1-31-1714 d 12-29-1776 m (1)Angenietje Van Slyk (2)Jannetje Bekker PS NY

VAN LIEW, (includes VAN LEW & VAN LIEUW)
Denice: b 3-25-1729 d 10-17-1777 m Eidea Wyckoff Pvt NJ
Dennis: b 5-10-1761 d 9-19-1811 m Dinah Duryee Pvt NJ
Frederick: b 6-12-1756 d 11-28-1791 m Elisabeth VanDike Sgt NJ
Frederick: b 7-12-1760 d 7-30-1820 m Ann Rappleyea Pvt NJ
Frederick: b 2-5-1755 d 12-31-1838 m Penelope Stout Sgt NY ★
Hendrick: b 7-30-1743 d *p.* 1785 m Margaret Cornell Pvt NJ
Johannes: b 4-16-1736 d 10-10-1794 m Dorothy Lot Pvt PS NJ
John: bpt 12-19-1756 d 5-18-18— m Magdalena Wyckoff Pvt NJ
Peter: b 8-28-1759 d 9-4-1813 m Sytie Wyckoff Pvt NJ

VAN LOON,
Evert: b 3-7-1756 d — m Anaatje VanDyke Pvt NY
John: bpt 9-17-1723 d 1823 m (1)Jane Valkenburgh (2)Maria (Van Loon) Pvt NY
Matthias: bpt 1-31-1736 d 1804 m Rebecca Everts Pvt PA

VAN METER, (includes VAN MATER, VAN MATRE, VANMETER, & VAN METRE)
Abraham: b 1721 d 1783 m (1)Ruth Hedges (2)Martha Wheeler Pvt VA

Abraham: b 6-13-1744 d 1787 m Rebecca Cline Sol VA
Benjamin: b 10-1-1744 d 10-15-1826 m Bathsheba Dunlap Sgt NJ
Cyrenius: bpt 7-29-1737 d *p.* 10-13-1800 m (1)Anna Van Dorn (2)Cobanche Conover Pvt NJ
Garrett: b 2- -1732 d 4-17-1788 m Ann (Markee) Sibley Col VA
Gilbert: b 6-7-1762 d 7-6-1832 m Margaret Spragee Pvt NJ
Henry: b *c.* 1717 d *c.* 1793 m (1)Eva — (2)Hannah Pyle (3)Elizabeth Pyle PS VA
Isaac: b 2- -1759 d 11-4-1840 m (1)Martha Hubbard Hoagland (2)Jane Carson Pvt VA ★
Isaac: b 12-10-1757 d 12-13-1837 m Elizabeth Inskeep Pvt VA
Isaac: b 1750 d 1798 m Hester Beck CS VA
Jacob, Sr.: b 1723 d 11-16-1798 m Letitia Strode PS PA
Jacob: b 1745 d 1-24-1838 m Catharine DeMoss Ens VA
Jacob: b 1752 d 4-12-1838 m (1)Nancy Covenhaven (2)Rebecca Rawlings Capt VA ★
Jacob: b 1745 d 1806 m Isabel Evans PS VA
John: b 1751 d 6-12-1825 m Sarah Hendricks Sgt NJ ★
John, Sr.: b *c.* 1745 d *p.* 1814 m Elizabeth — Capt PA
John: b 1738 d 1806 m (2)Jemima (Dunn) Bukey Maj VA
Johonnes: b 9-9-1735 d 9-26-1818 m (2)Josinah Taylor Capt VA
Joseph: b *c.* 1728 d *a.* 11-12-1790 m (1)Hannah Vial (2)Hannah Beryman Pvt NJ
Joseph: b 1747 d 1779 m Margaret Morgan Ens VA

VAN MIDDLESWORTH,
Andrew: b 10-11-1752 d 2-23-1833 m Sarah Bogart Sgt NJ

VANN,
Edward: b 3-24-1763 d 6-26-1854 m Elizabeth Walls Sol SC
Jesse: b *c.* 1746 d *p.* 5-6-1815 m Sarah Arline PS CS NC

VAN NAMEE,
Abner: b 7-30-1752 d 2-17-1835 m Polly Denton Lt NY ★

VANNEMAN, (includes VAN EMAN, VANEMAN, & VANEMON)
Andrew: b 12-25-1759 d 1-4-1847 m Elizabeth Riddle Pvt PA ★
Garrett: b *c.* 1751 d *c.* 1812 m Martha Liddell Pvt PA
Wm.: b *c.* 1756/7 d 1821/2 m Susan Ann — Pvt NJ

VAN NESS, (includes VAN NEST & VAN NESTE)
Abraham: b 4-2-1750 d 11-18-1833 m Katharine Sebring Capt NJ ★
David: b 8-3-1745 d 10-3-1818 m Cornelia Heermance Maj NY
David: b — d 2-14-1849 m Elizabeth Boget Maj NY
David: b *c.* 1745 d *p.* 1792 m Annatje VanBuren 2Lt NY
Garret: b 1-21-1750 d 8-13-1831 m Effie Sharp 1Lt NY W★
George: b 8-17-1735 d 11-2-1821 m Cataline Williamsen Pvt NJ
Hendrick: b 2-18-1754 d 1816 m Susanna — Pvt NJ
John: b 11-20-1731 d 1781 m Susan Bodine Lt NJ
John: b 1- -1741 d 9-17-1778 m Dinah Hoagland 2Lt NJ
John: b 1732 d 1776 m Jane Bradt Col NY
John: b 9-18-1723 d 3-18-1802 m Sarah Jane VanAllen Lt NY
Peter: b 1737 d 1816 m Jane Brokaw 1Lt NJ
Simon: b 1734 d 1831 m Catherine DeBow Lt NJ
Wm.: b 3- -1737 d 9- -1821 m Elizabeth Cantine 1Lt NY

VAN NICE, (or VAN NUIS)
John: bpt 6-30-1754 d 1822 m Lucretia VanDeRipe Pvt NJ

VAN NORDEN,
David: b 1757 d 1-14-1837 m Mary — Pvt NJ ★
John: b 3-2-1732 d 1810 m Rebecca Eaton Pvt NJ
Tobias: b 1715 d 3-28-1800 m Jannetie Campbell CS PS NJ

VAN NORMAN,
Joseph: b *c.* 1745 d 1817 m Elizabeth — Pvt NJ

VAN NOSTRAND, (includes NOSTRAND & VAN NORTHSTRAND)
Aaron: bpt 8-5-1731 d *p.* 1790 m — PS NY
Albert: bpt 11-5-1749 d 11-9-1822 m Sarah Hegeman PS NY
Crisparius: b 1745 d 8-14-1828 m Eva Frelinghuysen MM NJ
Jacob: b 4-16-1756/8 d 7-11-1819 m Phoebe McDonald Pvt NJ
John: b 11-2-1730 d 1787 m Maria Brokaw Pvt NJ
John: bpt 6-27-1731 d 6-23-1784 m Sarah Flower Pvt PS NY
Matthew: b 3-13-1759 d 1835 m Mary Phillips Pvt NJ
Peter: b 5-29-1724 d *p.* 4-11-1784 m Elizabeth Ammerman Pvt NY
Peter: b 8-26-1745 d 11-4-1816 m Mary Seaman Capt NY
Wm.: b 10-1-1764 d 5-5-1849 m Phoebe Sherwood Pvt NY ★

VANNOY,
Andrew: b 8-12-1742 d *p.* 1796 m Sarah Owens Capt NC
John: b *c.* 1716 d 1778 m Susanna Anderson PS NC
Joseph: b *c.* 1735 d 1826 m Anna Hornbeck Pvt NJ
Nathaniel: b 2-16-1749 d 7-26-1835 m Elizabeth Ray CS NC

VAN NUYS,
Isaac: b 12-30-1745/6 d 12-28-1815 m Nelly Quick PS NJ
Jacobus: b 4-16-1753 d 5-27-1836 m Catharine Ditmars Pvt NJ

VAN OLINDA,
Jacob: b 2-20-1739 d *p.* 1790 m Elizabeth Schermerhorn Pvt NY
Pieter: b 1-17-1748 d *p.* 1796 m Eva Spoor Lt NY

VAN ORDEN,
Andreas: b 8-27-1741 d 3-16-1811 m Martha VanBlascom Pvt NY
Andrew: b 5-3-1756 d *p.* 1801 m Elizabeth Towne Pvt NY
Ignatius: bpt 2-4-1731 d 7-9-1807 m (1)Annatje Oosterhoudt (2)Sara Loveridge 1Maj NY
Jacobus: b 5-24-1741 d 5-18-1808 m Maria Blauvelt Pvt NY
Jacobus: b 1711 d *p.* 10-16-1784 m Lea Christie PS NY
John: b 1733 d *p.* 1790 m Sarah Van Evre Pvt PS NY
John: b 5-16-1727 d 2-8-1813 m Trentje DuBois PS NY
Mary Koning: b *c.* 1740 d *p.* 11-27-1783 m Stephen Van Orden PS NJ
Peter: b 2-19-1761 d 7-15-1841 m (1)Neeltje Dumond (2)Rebecca Freligh (3)Mrs Mary Crooker Carbine Sgt NY
Peter: b 10-26-1761 d 10-2-1838 m Mary Warner Pvt NY NJ ★
Peter S: b 8-14-1763 d 11-8-1846 m (1)Margrietje Haring (2)Mrs Maria Haring Sgt PS NJ NY ★

VAN PATTEE,
John: b 4-29-1739 d 1-10-1809 m Nieltje Vedder Capt NY

VAN PATTEN, (includes VAN PETTEN)
Adam: b 11-17-1757 d *p.* 1832 m Lydia Van Alstyne Pvt NY ★
Dierck: b 1725 d *p.* 1801 m Rebecca Van Antwerpen Pvt NY
Frederick Simon: bpt 1-20-1760 d — m (1)Alida Fairly (2)Sally Bartlett Sgt NY
John: b 3-26-1749 d *p.* 10-16-1824 m Margaret Hemstradt Capt NY
John: b 1-4-1753 d 10-24-1835 m Wintie Clute Pvt NY
Nicholas, Sr.: b 1716 d 1790 m Sarah Clement Pvt NY
Nicholas, Jr.: b 9-23-1745 d 10-30-1816 m Margaret Ecker Pvt NY
Nicholas: b 4-14-1748 d *c.* 1816 m (1)Maria Van Natta Le Roy (2) — Bradt Pvt NY
Peter: bpt 5-5-1751 d *p.* 1803 m Annatje Ecker Pvt NY
Philip: b 1-18-1743 d *p.* 9-2-1809 m Deborah Viele Pvt NY
Simon: b 3-24-1722 d *a.* 1790 m Jannetje Vrooman Pvt NY

VAN PELT,
Abram: b 1757 d 7-25-1848 m Ellen Williamson Sol NJ
Daniel: b 10-12-1752 d 8-27-1776 m Mary Sutton Pvt NJ
Garret: bpt 11-3-1716 d *a.* 6-24-1797 m Mayke Sutphen Sol NJ
Isaac: b 1750 d 1816 m Abigail — Pvt NJ
Jacob: b *c.* 1754/5 d *p.* 11-16-1824 m Mary — Pvt NJ
Jacob: b 8-12-1759 d 8-23-1831 m Sarah Ryan Pvt NJ
John: b *c.* 1730 d 1808 m Jemima — Pvt NJ
John: b 4-8-1758 d 5- -1829 m Sarah Platt Pvt NY
John: b 8-31-1749 d *p.* 1805 m Susanna — Capt PA
Joseph: b 1742 d *p.* 1782 m Charity Bennett Lt PA
Petrus A: b — d 9-6-1781 m Antje Dorland PS NY
Rem: b 4-17-1738 d 3-18-1829 m Ida Lefferts PS NY
Rulif: b 10-8-1758 d 6-2-1854 m Catherine Ten Eyck Pvt NJ ★
Walter: b 1763 d 2-28-1814 m Nancy Roberts Pvt NJ ★

VAN PRADELLES,
Benedict Francis: b 8-31-1753 d 12-12-1808 m Cassandra Owings Lt FrA

VAN REED,
Henry: b 1722 d 1790 m (1)Agnes Vanderslice (2)Anna Eastered PS PA
Jacob: b 3-15-1758 d 1839 m Anna Elizabeth Hiester Pvt PA
John: b 12-15-1747 d 4-18-1820 m Eva Elizabeth Yost Pvt PA

VAN RENSSELAER,
Henry J: b 10-23-1742 d 3-22-1814 m Rachael Douw Gen NY
Henry Killian: b 7-25-1744 d 9-9-1816 m (1)Alida Bradt (2)Nancy Simmons LCol NY
James: b 1747 d 2-1-1827 m Catherine Van Cortlandt Capt NY
Killian: b 11-25-1717 d 12-28-1781 m (1)Ariantje Schuyler (2)Maria Low Col NY
Philip: b 5-19-1747 d 3-3-1798 m Marie Sanders LCol NY
Robert: b 12-16-1740 d 9-11-1802 m Cornelia Rutson BGen NY

VAN REYPEN,
Daniel: b 6-26-1736 d 7-23-1818 m Elizabeth Terhune CS NJ

VAN RIPER,
Cornelius: b *c.* 3-10-1755 d *c.* 4-5-1829 m Elizabeth Davenport MM NJ
Harmon: b 1761 d 1841 m Margrietye Jacobusse Pvt NJ ★
John: b *c.* 1745 d 5- -1827 m Catharina Post Ens NJ
John: b 2-12-1753 d *c.* 1835 m Lea Winne Pvt NJ
Richard: b 6-9-1734 d 4-24-1807 m Elizabeth Mead Capt NJ

VAN SAEN, (or VAN SAUN)
Samuel: b 12-25-1743 d 4-5-1809 m Leah Zabriskie PS NJ

VAN SANT, (includes VANSANT, VAN ZANDT, & VAN ZANT)
Bernardus: b *c.* 1759 d 4-14-1817 m Mary — Cpl NJ
Cornelius: b *c.* 1751 d 3- -1816 m Ann Larzalere 2Lt PA
Garbriel: b *c.* 1740 d 4-23-1798 m Joyce Brelsford 1Lt PA
Garrett: b 10- -1746 d 4-13-1797 m Elizabeth Larue 1Lt PA
Jacob: b *c.* 1750 d *p.* 10-9-1815 m Catherine Moon Capt CS NC
Jacob: bpt 7-7-1754 d 5-6-1802 m Mary Vansciver Pvt PA

James: b 1731 d 1-31-1798 m Jane Bennett Pvt PA
Johannes: b 12-8-1728 d *p.* 1790 m Margarita Wilkinson Pvt NY
John: b 1726 d 1820 m Rebecca — Capt PS NJ
John: b *c.* 1762 d 1836 m Rachael — Pvt NJ
John, Sr.: b 3-16-1765 d 1835 m Esther Van Vorse Pvt NY ★
Nicholas: b 12-25-1737 d 1805 m (1)Gesya — (2)Lucretia Van Brunt PS NJ
Nicholas: b 1-1-1711/12 d 5-1-1801 m Mary Britian Pvt PA
Peter: b *a.* 1750 d 1820 m Elizabeth Wollard Capt PA
Rykert: b 11-2-1735 d 6-6-1814 m Sara Hilton Pvt NY

VAN SANTVOORD, (includes VAN SANVOORD)
Cornelius, Sr.: b 3-3-1723 d *p.* 1779 m Ariantje Bratt Capt NY
Cornelius: b 12-31-1749 d *p.* 1790 m Cornelia VanWie Pvt NY

VAN SCHAICK, (includes VAN SCHAACK, VAN SCHOICK & VAN SKIEHAWK)
Arent: b 1727 d 12-18-1811 m Barbary — Pvt PS NY
Cornelius: bpt 9-13-1734 d 3-18-1797 m (2)Angelica Yates Maj NY
David: b 4-13-1730 d *p.* 1794 m Hannah Holmes Pvt NJ
Gerret G: b 10-6-1760 d 4-18-1842 m Christine Barringer Cpl NY
Goosen: b 9-5-1736 d 7-4-1789 m Marie VanTenBrooke Col NY
Hendrick: b 2-19-1763 d 9-15-1837 m Cathalina VanBuren Pvt NY ★
Jacob: b 5-17-1723 d *c.* 8- -1797 m Geertie DeRidder 2Maj NY
John: b 4- -1752 d 9- -1838 m Elizabeth VanArnum Ens NY ★
Stephanus: b 2-4-1730 d *p.* 1800 m Jane Bratt 2Lt PS NY
Stephen: b *c.* 1748 d *c.* 1805 m (2)Rachel Bales Pvt PA

VAN SCHOONHOVEN,
Hendrick: b 4-7-1727 d 9-11-1781 m Altije VanNess Pvt NY
Jacobus: b 3-2-1744 d — m Elizabeth Clute Col NY

VAN SCOTER,
Anthony: b *c.* 1725 d 1824 m Margaret Decker Pvt PA

VAN SCOY, (includes VANSCOY)
Abraham, Jr.: b 1-7-1760 d 9-1-1844 m Hannah Bostwick Pvt NY ★
Isaac, Sr.: b 4- -1732 d 1817 m (1)Mary Edwards (2)Elizabeth (Dibble) Osborn PS NY
Isaac: b 7-9-1758 d 2-4-1846 m Temperance Pain PS NY

VAN SICE,
Cornelius: b 3-29-1737 d *p.* 1780 m Maria Vedder Pvt NY
J Cornelius: b 10-30-1756 d 10-28-1849 m Deborah Murray Sol NY
John: b 1-16-1726 d *p.* 1798 m Margarita Fort Pvt NY

VAN SICKLE, (includes SICKLE, SICKLIN & VAN SICKELEN)
Andrew: b 4-8-1761 d 3-4-1822 m Magdalene Lane Pvt NY
Andrew: b 1751 d 1840 m Nancy Lowe Sgt NJ
Cornelius: b — d 3- -1850 m Catherine Johnson Pvt NY
Garret: b 2-2-1740 d 2-2-1810 m Ann Cannan Pvt NJ
Jacob: b 1733 d *p.* 1784 m Sarah — Cpl NJ
Peter: b *c.* 1749 d 1-27-1843 m Catherine Hoffman Pvt NY ★
Reinier: b *c.* 1723 d 12-12-1803 m Mercy Longstreet PS NJ

VAN SICKLER,
David: b 8-20-1764 d 6-29-1828 m Mary Dunlap Pvt NY

VAN SLYKE, (includes VAN SLYCK & VAN SLYOKE)
Adam: b 1721 d *p.* 1790 m Katherine Van Epps Cpl NY
Adam: b 1758 d *c.* 1830 m Margaret Seber Pvt NY
Baltus: b 2-26-1749 d 9-19-1827 m Annatje Lewis Pvt NY
Cornelius: b 12-1-1736 d *p.* 1779 m Catherine Veeder Lt NY
Dirck: b 3-1-1713 d *p.* 1790 m Christina TenBroeck Pvt NY
George: b 1762 d 9-14-1832 m Margaret Pickard Sgt NY ★
Harmanus: b 6-14-1724 d 8-6-1777 m Elizabeth VanPetten Maj PS NY
Harmanus: b 6-3-1750 d 12-2-1847 m Maria Vrooman Pvt NY
Jacobus: b *a.* 1748 d *p.* 1814 m Gertrude Windecker Pvt NY
Martinus: b — d 11-30-1813 m Anna Bikkert Pvt NY W★
Nicholas: b — d *p.* 1789 m Elizabeth (Johan) Leder Sol NY
Nicholas: b 9-30-1739 d 2-16-1792 m Catherine Luthers Fif NY
Tobias: b 10-17-1738 d *p.* 12-26-1779 m Josyna Wieler Pvt NY
Wm.: b 2-26-1759 d 6-2-1851 m (1)Magdalena Mareness (2)Elizabeth Adair Cpl NY ★

VAN STEENBURGH, (includes STEENBERGH, STEENBURGH, & VAN STEENBERGH)
Benjamin: bpt 11-7-1736 d *a.* 7-1-1790 m Sara Burhans Lt NY
Benjamin: b 3-21-1759 d 6-20-1832 m — Pvt NY Chn★
Elias, Sr.: b 6-30-1734 d 3-11-1817 m Catharine Hoffman Capt NY
Elias, Jr.: b 9-27-1759 d 7-28-1836 m (1)Mary Brouse (2)Mary Taylor Ens NY ★

VAN SURDAM,
Anthony: b 12-18-1754 d 12-14-1841 m Sybil — Pvt NY
Samuel: b 1753/4 d 12-8-1801 m Caziah Pvt NY

VAN TASSEL, (includes VAN TASSELL)
Abraham: b 1754 d 3-15-1806 m Hester Devoe Pvt NY
Cornelius: b 4-11-1735/6 d 3-6-1820 m Elizabeth Storms Lt NY
Cornelius: bpt 5- -1748 d 4-28-1830 m Elcey Brewer Pvt NY ★

Cornelius: b 1739 d 1816 m Carstiena — Pvt NY
David: bpt 6-28-1743 d *a.* 1801 m Margaret Brush Pvt NY
Isaac: bpt 6-2-1752 d 1-10-1814 m Lena (Van Tassel) Sgt NY
Isaac: b 6-22-1745 d *p.* 8- -1777 m Lea Duyster Pvt NY
Jacob: b 11-10-1744 d 1837 m Hester Van Tassel Lt NY ★
John: b 1743 d 5-26-1779 m Sarah Ackerman Pvt NY
John: bpt 4-21-1734 d 1813 m Mary Bartine Pvt NY
Nicholas: b 12-23-1747 d 5-24-1832 m Mary Whittaker Pvt NY
Stephen: b 1758 d 1846 m Mary DeRevere Pvt NY

VAN TILBURG,
Henry: b 1756 d 1842 m (1)Jane Holman (2)Jane Sunderland Pvt NJ

VAN TINE,
Cornelius: b 12-25-1747 d 1831 m Nellie Ames Pvt NY
Ephraim: b 1-4-1762 d 12-5-1831 m Ann Pumyea Pvt NJ
Robert: b 10-15-1757 d *p.* 1802 m Sarah Carpenter Pvt NY

VANTRESSE,
Joseph: b 8-11-1750 d 1838 m Ann — Pvt MD ★

VAN TUYL, (includes VANTUYL, VAN TYLE)
Abraham: b 5-21-1745 d 11-22-1837 m Catharine — Ens NJ ★
Isaac: b 1740 d 2- -1803 m Mary (Seabring) Ens NJ
John, Jr.: b 10-1-1760 d *p.* 1834 m Mary Birgit Pvt NY
Otto: b *c.* 1752 d 1829 m Elizabeth — Pvt NJ

VAN VALKENBURGH, (includes VAN VALKENBURG)
Barent: b. 1755 d 1844 m Maria — Pvt NY
Bartholomeus: b — d *p.* 1788 m Sarah VanEtten Pvt NY
Bartholomew Jacob: b 5-25-1753 d 8-4-1831 m (1)Elizabeth Moore (2)Catherine Pryne 1Lt NY ★
Bartholomew Thomas: b 10-21-1753 d *p.* 7-18-1790 m Engeltje VanSlyck Pvt NY
Hendrick: b *c.* 1790 m Margaret VanderBogart Pvt NY
Henry: bpt 3-12-1732 d *p.* 1790 m (1)Annetje VanderPoel (2)Catharine Head Pvt NY
Isaac: b 2-12-1710 d 1785 m Jannetje Clements PS NY
Isaac Peter: bpt 9-3-1735 d 1802 m Annatje Van Ostrander Capt NY
Jacobus: b 3-1-1753 d *p.* 1812 m Catharina Sixby Pvt NY
Jochem Lambertse: bpt 1-15-1710 d 9-19-1801 m (1)Susan Magdalena Werner (2)Maria Berri PS NY
Johannes: b 1742 d *p.* 3-17-1791 m Elizabeth Meinderssen Pvt NY
John Joseph: b 1-10-1744 d 3-28-1815 m Magdalen Brown Pvt NY
Lambert: b 10-18-1745 d 8-1-1826 n Mary — Pvt NY
Lambert: b 12-3-1758 d *p.* 1791 m Freelove Attley Pvt NY
Lambert: b 5- -1731 d *p.* 6-12-1782 m Catarina VanVechten PS NY
Lawrence: b. 1750 d 1828 m Gertrude Sharp Pvt NY
Pieter: b 1-19-1707 d *p.* 1790 m Maria Vosburg Pvt NY

VAN VALZAH,
Robert: b 4-17-1764 d 4-18-1850 m Elizabeth Sutherland Pvt NY

VAN VARICK,
Effie Ten Eyck: bpt 12-25-1718 d 1782 m Andrew VanVarick PS NY

VAN VECHTEN, (includes VAN VEGHTEN, VAN VEGHTON)
Anthony: bpt 1-24-1748 d 10-14-1812 m Mary Fonda Lt NY
Derrick: b 6-1739 d 8-8-1777 m Alida Maria Knickerbocker Maj NY
Derrick: bpt 2-17-1745 d — m (1)Cathelyntje Van Ness (2)Petertie (Caroline) Yates (3)Catherine Spoor Ens NY
Derrick: b 10-24-1758 d 11-17-1847 m Rachel Spoor Ens NY ★
Dirck: b 7-15-1699 d 11-29-1781 m (1)Judith Brochols (2)Barbara Antonides Wichaut (3)Sarah Middah PS NY
Dirck: b 9-22-1695 d *a.* 2-8-1782 m Helena Sybrant PS NY
Samuel: b 9-28-1742 d 2-12-1813 m Sarah VanOrden Capt NY
Teunis Teunisson: b 4-24-1749 d 12-7-1817 m Elizabeth DeWandelaer Ens NY

VAN VLACK,
Abraham: b 2-22-1755 d 11-19-1836 m Margaret Wiltsie Pvt NY ★

VAN VLECK,
Abraham Kipp: b 3-19-1743 d 3-3-1785 m Margaret Cantine Pvt NY
Abram T: b 12-19-1740 d 2-19-1821 m Jannette Phillips Pvt NY
Isaac: b 1744 d 5-19-1801 m Bata Goes Pvt NY

VAN VLECKREN,
George: b 8-20-1757 d 3-14-1828 m (1)Mary Balding (2)Martha Balding Pvt NY

VAN VOORHEES, (includes VAN VOORHIS, VOORHEES, VOORHES, VOORHIES, VORHEES, VORIS, & VORYS)
Aaron: b 2- -1760 d 11-27-1841 m Hannah Morris Pvt NJ ★
Abraham: b 5-2-1753 d 2-19-1808 m Willempie Wyckoff Drm NJ
Abraham: b 9-16-1730 d 1812 m Maria VanDoren Pvt NJ
Abraham: b 11-6-1751 d 3- -1811 m Marretje Phillips Pvt NY
Abraham: b 5-17-1748 d 1-4-1818 m (2)Sarah De Mond PS NY
Albert: b 4-6-1727 d 3-24-1784 m Adrionna VanDerwort Pvt NJ
Albert: b 1-1-1738 d 8-25-1825 m Jannetje VanHouten Pvt NY
Albert: bpt 8-28-1748 d *p.* 1800 m Rachel Bogart Pvt NJ
Albert: b 12-26-1757 d 12-25-1834 m Margaret Workman Pvt NJ

Albert: b *c.* 1742 d *c.* 1820 m — Sol NJ
Albert: b 3-25-1753 d 2-18-1830 m Anna Banta Pvt PA
Albert P: bpt 11-27-1743 d *p.* 2-17-1791 m Mary Doremus Pvt NJ
Coert, Jr.: b 6-2-1756 d 3-9-1821 m Ann Updike Pvt NJ ★
Coert: bpt 10-4-1761 d 1816 m Jane Hogeland Sgt NJ
Court: b 1741 d 1800 m Mary Johnson Pvt NJ
Daniel: b 12-18-1737 d *p.* 11-16-1783 m Maria Tallman Pvt NJ
Daniel: b 3-9-1749 d 1782 m (1)Sarah Gordan (2)Eve Covenhoven Lt NJ
Daniel: b 1759 d — m Rebecca Imlay Pvt NJ
Daniel: b 7-8-1738 d 2-21-1819 m (1)Mrs Sarah (Van Voorhis) Brit (2)Mary Newton (3)Nancy Meyers Pvt PS NY
David: b 9-6-1758 d 10-9-1841 m Eve Oakley Pvt NJ
Folkhard: bpt 5-7-1756 d 5-10-1822 m Margaret Gottery Sol NJ
Garret: b 1-30-1748 d *p.* 1784 m Elizabeth Burr Pvt NJ
Garret: b 1739 d 10-18-1816 m Ann Beekman Pvt NJ
Garrett: b 6-9-1763 d 12-14-1861 m Jerusha Keurig Tms NJ
Garrett, Sr.: b 5-1-1720 d *c.* 1785 m (1)Meltje Nevius (2)Sarah Strothoff PS NJ
Garrett, Jr.: b 3-4-1750 d 10-18-1823 m Matilda Ditmar Sgt NJ
Hendrick: b 1760 d 7-26-1827 m Elizabeth Williams Pvt NJ ★
Hendrick: b 5-12-1740 d 11-12-1827 m Jane Lesley MM NJ
Henry: bpt 11-18-1759 d *p.* 1802 m Elizabeth Letson Pvt NJ
Henry: b 4-21-1735 d 9- -1801 m Hannah Flagler Pvt NY
Isaac: bpt 8-17-1755 d 4-14-1833 m Jane VanDerveer Sgt NJ
Isaac: b 4-3-1758 d 10-4-1844 m Sarah Nevius Pvt NJ
Isaiah: b 8-5-1750 d 3-16-1834 m (1) — (2)Charlotte — Ens NJ
Jacob: b — d — m Lammetie Simonson Pvt NJ
Jacob: b 10-21-1748 d 9-22-1814 m Sarah Cockaver Pvt NJ
Jacob: b 1742 d 2-2-1828 m (1)Hannah Sickles (2)Sarah Sickles (3)Agnes — Pvt NJ
James: b 1751 d — m Maria Doty Pvt NJ
James: b 12-23-1748 d 10-31-1810 m Anna Harris Wgn NJ
Jerome: b 4-8-1743 d *p.* 1797 m Ann Townsend Pvt NY
John: b 11-5-1745 d 4-28-1819 m Rebecca Williamson Pvt NJ
John: b 9-1-1757 d 9-25-1796 m Ann Schenck Pvt NJ
John: b 1-18-1763 d 3-5-1817 m Maria LeQuier Pvt NJ
John: b 6-7-1738 d *a.* 9-28-1804 m Johanna Rowe Pvt NY
John C: b 12- -1747 d 1807 m Margaret Van Zandt Capt NJ
Koert: b 3-15-1749 d 1822 m Rachel — PS'NJ
Lucas: b 5-2-1753 d 8-24-1812 m Johannah Dumont Pvt NJ
Martin: b 8-28-1763 d 7-31-1825 m Alice Van Dyke Wgn NJ
Peter: b 10-10-1750 d 10-10-1823 m Elizabeth Talman Pvt NJ
Peter: b 2-12-1756 d 6-21-1842 m Maria Ditmars Pvt NJ ★
Peter: b 5-7-1759 d 4-17-1833 m Mary Boice Pvt NJ W★
Ralph: b *c.* 1742 d *p.* 1800 m Elizabeth Nevius Pvt PS PA
Rem: bpt 1-30-1757 d *p.* 1793 m (1)Hilletje — (2)Elizabeth — Pvt NJ
Roelef: bpt 9-19-1742 d 10-16-1799 m M Rebecca Pease Pvt NJ
Stephen: b 1-21-1739 d 6-12-1815 m Margareta Van Dyke Pvt NJ
Stephen: bpt 2-5-1748 d *p.* 1778 m Maria Blauvelt Pvt PS NY
Stephen: b *c.* 1730 d 11-23-1796 m (1)Maria Leek (2)Elizabeth Mathewman PS NY
Wm.: b 1727 d 1784 m Ann Conenhoven Capt NJ
Zachariah: b 3-25-1748 d 7-3-1811 m (1)Anna Lawrence (2)Nancy Springsteen Pvt NY

VAN VORST,
Cornelius: b 11-25-1728 d 9-30-1818 m Annetje Van Horn PS LCol NJ
John: b 1-19-1742 d 5-23-1844 m Sarah Kittel PS Pvt NY ★

VAN VOST,
Gillis: b 1735 d 9-4-1823 m Anna Barrett Pvt NY
Jacobus: b 1762 d 1838 m Williampie Treaux Pvt NY

VAN VRANKEN, (includes VAN VRAKEN)
Claus: b 8-3-1749 d 1835 m Maria Vedder Lt NY
Derrick: b 12-3-1750/1 d 8-19-1837 m Anne Failing Sgt NY ★
Garrit A: b 7-16-1760 d 3-20-1835 m Mary Bell Pvt NY
Gerrit R: b *c.* 1730 d *p.* 7-9-1796 m (1)Susanna Egbertse (2)Alida Reyly Pvt NY
Jacob: b 6-22-1729 d 1817 m Margarite Pootman Pvt NY
Nicholas: b 2-15-1761 d 7-20-1837 m Eva Peek Pvt NY
Nicholas P: bpt 8-3-1749 d 9-10-1835 m Mariah Vedder 2Lt NY ★

VAN WAGENEN, (includes VAN WAGENIN)
Aart, Jr.: b 9-11-1709 d 1789 m Rebecca Van Wagenin PS NY
Abraham: b 2-5-1699 d 6-7-1787 m Hillegond Crispel PS NY
Benjamin: b 1-23-1726 d *p.* 1786 m Margaret Burger Pvt NY
Benjamin: b 1790 d 1810 m Lydia Depuy Pvt NY
Conrad: b 1-16-1753 d 9-20-1842 m Sarah (Bogert) Stryker Pvt NY W★
Evert: bpt 5-9-1740 d *p.* 12-31-1824 m Annatje Westfal PS NY
Gerrit: b 4-6-1712 d 1791 m Marytje Freer PS NY
Hendrik: bpt 3-18-1711 d — m Catharine Schoomaker QM NY
Jacobus: b 2-16-1729 d 5-3-1790 m Rachel Brodhead Pvt NY
John: b 3-27-1761 d 12-24-1839 m Margaret Schryver Pvt NY

VAN WAGONER,
Nicolas: bpt 5-15-1748 d 1-7-1811 m Eltsy Ostrander Pvt NY

VAN WART,
Isaac: b 1750 d 7-13-1840 m Mrs Amy Bishop Lt NY ★
Isaac: b 4-25-1758 d 5-23-1828 m Rachel Storm Pvt NY
Jacob: bpt 6-20-1730 d c. 1800 m Engeltic Acker Pvt NY
Martinus: bpt 6-26-1733 d 1784 m Rachel Williams Pvt NY
Rachel Storms: b 6-4-1760 d 3-4-1834 m Isaac VanWart PS NY

VAN WAY,
Henry: b a. 1765 d 2-28-1814 m Mary Lewis Pvt NJ

VAN WICKLE,
Simon: b 2-22-1732 d 5- -1806 m Anna Johnstone Capt NJ

VAN WIE,
Andries: b 11-20-1720 d — m Lena Van Arnhem Pvt NY
Casparus: b 12-5-1742 d 3-17-1818 m Jannetje Winne Pvt NY
Garrit: b 2-20-1739 d p. 1780 m Catharina Lansing Pvt NY
Isaac: b 7-14-1755 d 5-19-1843 m — Pvt NY ★
John A.: b 10-25-1747 d 4-14-1797 m Alida (Van Wie) Capt NY W★
Peter: bpt 2-27-1737 d a. 3-24-1788 m Ebbetje VanDenBergh 1Lt NY
Wm.: b 10-19-1740 d 7-29-1816 m Jannetje Lansing Pvt NY

VAN WINKLE,
Elias: b 3-29-1759 d 12-11-1847 m (1)Lucy Price (2)Hannah Tuttle
    Pvt NJ ★
Evert: b c. 1740 d p. 1835 m Ann Johnstone Pvt NJ
Francis: b 12- -1749 d 1830 m Isabel Archibold PS NJ
Jacob: b 12-17-1727 d 12-18-1778 m Rachel Comingear 1Lt NJ
Johannes: b 12-6-1733 d 8-13-1829 m Naomie Dickerson Ens PA
Michael: b 4-6-1736 d 5-22-1808 m Phebe Carter Cpl NJ
Peter: b 12-25-1754 d 5-28-1837 m Deborah Berry Pvt NJ
Simeon: b 4-4-1752 d p. 1807 m Annetje Marselis Pvt NJ
Waling: b c. 1718/19 d 1784 m Jannetje VanHouten Ens NJ
Wm.: b 5-1-1759 d 4-20-1845 m Mary Ross Pvt NJ

VAN WOERT,
John: b 5-13-1750 d 10-5-1836 m Cathalyna Lansing Lt NY
Nicholas: b 3-3-1735 d 8-13-1792 m Mary Staats Sol NY

VAN WORMER, (includes WORMER)
Arent: bpt 10-7-1740 d p. 1790 m Maria Van Schaick Pvt NY
Cornelius: b a. 1764 d 3-17-1824 m Catherine Hendricks Pvt NY ★
Jacob: b 1753 d 8- -1829 m Polly Oller 2Lt NY
Peter: b 5-16-1749 d 1808 m Rachel VanHoesen Pvt NY

VAN WYCHE,
John Brinckerhoff: b 1-15-1762 d 6-5-1841 m (1)Gertrude
    Brinckerhoff (2)Susan Schenck Pvt NY

VAN WYCK,
Abraham: b 3-22-1733 d 2-5-1809 m Elizabeth Wright Capt NY
Cornelius: b 1744 d 10-31-1776 m Sarah Carmen Capt NY
Cornelius: b c. 1748 d 7- -1784 m Sarah Hicks PS NY
Cornelius R: b 1-6-1753 d 10-20-1820 m (1)Anna Duryee
    (2)Magdalena Monfort Capt NY
Richard: b 12-28-1729 d 4-5-1810 m Barbara VanVoorhees Maj NY
Theodorus, Sr.: b 10-15-1697 d 9-15-1776 m (1)Elizabeth Creed
    (2)Mrs Jenetje Hasbrouck PS NY
Theodorus, Jr.: b 12-21-1730 d 12-7-1789 m (1)Altje Brinckerhoff
    (2)Mrs Mary DuBois Lt NY
Theodorus: b 11-30-1718 d 11-6-1776 m Helena Santford PS NY
Wm.: b 7-13-1727 d 11-24-1793 m Martha Carmen PS NY

VARDEMAN,
John: b 1718 d 1827 m Elizabeth Morgan Sol VA KY
Peter: b c. 1754 d 1811 m Prudence — Capt VA

VARIAN,
Isaac: b 9-8-1740 d 5-29-1820 m (1)Hannah VanDenBerg
    (2)Alletta Harsen (3)Jane Betts Cmsry NY
James: b 1-10-1734 d 12-11-1800 m Deborah Dibble Capt NY
Michael: b 12-9-1738 d 1825 m Cornelia Harsen PS NY
Richard: b 12-25-1736 d 12-20-1822 m Susannah Gardinear Sol NY

VARICK,
John: b 12-25-1723 d 11-7-1809 m Jane Dey PS NJ

VARLEY,
Peter Bernard: b 4-15-1766 d 10-28-1847 m Rachel Bolson Mus NY ★

VARNADO,
Henry: b 10- -1749 d 9-6-1840 m Elizabeth — Sol SC

VARNUM,
Bradley: b c. 8-19-1750 d 10-15-1799 m Rachel Butterfield Pvt MA
Daniel: b 6-15-1741 d 7-10-1814 m Lydia Porter Pvt MA
Ebenezer: b 2-23-1744 d 4-7-1815 m (1)Sarah Butterfield
    (2)Hannah Fox (3)Eunice Brown Lt MA
Enoch: b c. 1760 d p. 1840 m Mary Mechling Pvt PA ★
James: b 9-8-1747 d 12-2-1832 m (1)Prudence Hildreth (2)Eleanor
    Bridges (3)Martha McAdams Capt MA
John: b 9-8-1721 d 7-26-1786 m Ann Staule Pvt MA
John: b 2-6-1705 d 7-28-1785 m Phoebe Parker PS MA

Jonas: b 1752 d 1834 m Mary Parker Sgt MA
Joseph Bradley: b 1-29-1750 d 9-11-1821 m Molly Butler Capt MA
Molly Butler: b 6-4-1750 d 4-17-1833 m Joseph Bradley Varnum
    PS MA
Parker: b 2-7-1764/7 d 12-18-1824 m Dorcas Osgood Brown Sgt MA
Samuel, Sr.: b 2-21-1715 d 4-17-1797 m (1)Mary Prime (2)Hannah
    Mitchell PS MA
Samuel, Jr.: b 2-17-1746/7 d 1- -1828 m Mary Parker Pvt RI ★
Thomas: b 5-5-1743 d 7-1-1805 m Polly Atkinson MM MA
Wm.: b 10-19-1746 d 1- -1814 m Sarah Colburn Pvt MA

VARS,
John: b 1735 d 4-29-1811 m Martha Saunders Capt RI
Joseph: b 11-7-1760 d p. 1832 m Hannah Maxon Pvt RI ★

VASQUEZ,
Benito: b 1750 d p. 1810 m Julie Papin PS MO

VASTINE,
Jonathan: b 1742 d 4- -1830 m Elizabeth Lewis Pvt PA

VAUDRY,
Jean Baptiste: b c. 1722 d 9-24-1792 m Agnes Richard PS VA

VAUGHAN, (includes VAUGHN)
Almond: b 4-19-1756 d 5-22-1842 m Joanna Harris Pvt VA ★
Benjamin: b 8-15-1757 d 2-12-1839 m (1)Sarah Beaman
    (2)Sylvina Averill (3)Mary Reynolds Pvt CT VT ★
Benjamin M P: b 4-19-1751 d 12-7-1835 m Sarah Manning PS ME
Benjamin: b 11-4-1730 d 1818 m Catherine Godfry Pvt RI
Caleb, Jr.: b 2-10-1750 d 9-9-1797 m Abigail Sweet Pvt RI
Daniel: b 6-17-1746 d 5-29-1810 m Dinah Watkins 1Lt NJ
Daniel: b 3-30-1736 d 12-12-1812 m Ruth Hayes Pvt NY
David: b 1750 d p. 1809 m Catherine Anderson Sol VA
Frederick: b 11-26-1766 d 8-10-1845 m (1)Lucy Blodgett
    (2)Catherine Cornet Pvt CT ★
Jabez: b 5-25-1740 d 1817 m Lois Soul Capt NH
Gist: b 1718 d 6-27-1800 m Rachel — Maj MD
James: b 11-16-1741 d 7-21-1819 m Jane Whitman Ens VT
James: b 1745 d 7-22-1811 m Susanna — Sgt VA
James: b c. 1750-2 d 1803 m (1)Ann Hill (2)Mary Jeter Pvt VA
Jesse: b 10-30-1735 d 4-23-1815 m Margaret Shaw Ens MA
John: b 10- -1733 d 6-9-1820 m Ann Beebe Capt CT
John: b 2-20-1745 d 1827 m Mary Chapman Sgt MA ★
John: b 1753 d 11- -1795 m Nancy Cahill Pvt NJ
John: b 3-29-1751 d 9-9-1837 m (1)Eunice Kellogg (2)Lydia
    Pettibone Pvt NY ★
John: b 4-10-1760 d 4-5-1845 m Sarah Rogers Sol NC
John: b 5-28-1761 d p. 1803 m Margaret Sweet Pvt RI
John: b c. 1745 d 6-12-1818 m Lucy — Lt VA
John: b c. 1760 d 1796 m (2)Mary Patton Sgt VA
John Daniel: b 3-13-1762/3 d 4-16-1860 m Rhoda Effingham
    Pvt MA
Jonathan: b — d a. 1790 m Richard Gould Sol RI
Joseph: b 1746 d 1802 m Ann — LCol DE
Joseph: b 3-21-1761 d 3-31-1795 m Mary Waples Pvt DE
Obadiah: b 2-21-1748 d p. 1821 m Elizabeth — 2Lt NY ★
Reuben, Sr.: b 10- -1732 d 5-8-1817 m Elizabeth Ingram Capt
    PS VA
Richard: b 1752 d 7-25-1821 m Diana Wilson Pvt PA
Richard: b 8-16-1755 d 8-26-1791 m Ellen Race Pvt PA
Robert: b 11-11-1732 d p. 1782 m Prudence Stone PS RI
Robert: b c. 1735 d p. 1800 m Elsie Motley 2Lt VA
Samuel: b 1-2-1747 d 3-10-1837 m (1)Waitstill Cole (2)Huldah
    Thompson (3)Mrs Sarah (Faunce) Parker Sgt MA
Shadrach: b 7-3-1733 d 8-11-1806 m Mary Meriwether Sgt VA
Thomas: b 1751 d 12-28-1827 m Agness — Pvt PA ★
Thomas: b c. 1757 d 2-12-1842 m Mary Bryan Pvt PA
Thomas: b 8-11-1758 d 9-9-1835 m Sarah Long Pvt VA ★
Thomas: b 1756 d 1834 m (1)Abigail Franklin (2)Sallie Farthing
    Pvt VA
Thomas: b c. 1725 d c. 9-15-1788 m Dorothy Jones CS PS VA
Thomas: b c. 1750 d 10-1-1804 m (1)Anne Smith (2)Martha Lewis
    (3)Mary A Blackburn CS VA
Wm.: b 1750 d 5-1-1835 m Catherine Broughton PS NH
Wm.: b 1750 d 1806 m Sarah — Pvt NC
Wm.: b 1750 d 3- -1824 m Martha Billups Capt VA
Wm., Jr.: b 11-18-1760 d 3-22-1841 m Elizabeth Fielder Pvt VA ★

VAWN,
Richard: b 1752 d 4- -1834 m Katherine Pears Pvt NY

VAWTER,
David: b 1720 d a. 3-24-1785 m Mary Rucker Pvt VA
Jesse: b 12-1-1755 d 3-20-1838 m Elizabeth Watts Pvt VA
Wm.: b 1760 d 11-27-1823 m Mary Rucker Lt VA

VEALE, (includes VEAL)
James Carr: b 3-17-1763 d 1-14-1839 m Levina Towne Pvt SC ★
John: b 1749 d 1818 m Sarah Vance Pvt DE

VEAZIE, (includes VEASEY, VEAZY & VESEY)
Benjamin: b 4-11-1740 d a. 12-31-1777 m Abigail Brackett Pvt MA

Eleazer, Sr.: b 1748 d 2-21-1826 m Mary Brown Pvt CT
Elijah, Jr.: b 5-31-1754 d 3-6-1827 m Bulah Weston Pvt MA
James: b c. 1745 d 1795 m Ann — Pvt GA
James: b 8-17-1725 d 12-17-1789 m Mrs Elizabeth Hollingsworth
　　Johnston Pvt MD
John: b 11-12-1750 d 1820 m Martha Talcott Ens MA
John Ward: b c. 1732 d p. 1790 m (1)Sarah — (2)Mary Wilmer
　　CS Capt MD
Jonathan, Jr.: b 4-18-1756 d 11-15-1833 m Anna Morrill Pvt NH
Joshua: b 11-23-1753 d 12-23-1850 m Mary Fifield Pvt NH
Lemuel: b 1743 d 1825 m Sarah Abbott Pvt MA
Samuel, Jr.: b 1750 d 1828 m Phebe Holbrook Sgt MA
Simon: b 6-8-1756 d 6-23-1845 m Susanna Ham Pvt NH
Thomas: b c. 1750 d 9-23-1829 m Lydia Wiggin Pvt NH ★

VEDDER,
Aaron: b 12-27-1761 d p. 1798 m Agnes Van Epps Pvt NY
Albert: b 7-27-1730 d 11-18-1805 m Hester VanderBogart Pvt NY
Albert: b 2-17-1734 d 3-20-1805 m Anna Quackenbush Pvt NY
Albert Alexander: b 3-17-1737 d 6-21-1800 m Neeltje Bancker
　　Pvt NY
Arent: b 10-25-1714 d c. 1780-90 m (1)Sara Vander Bogart
　　(2)Catrina VanPatten PS NY
Francis: b 12-14-1753 d 5-20-1827 m Rebecca VanPetten Pvt NY
Frederick: b 4-28-1761 d 7-2-1851 m (2)Maria VanPatten Sgt NY ★
Philip: b 1738 d 5-6-1822 m Margarita VanderBogart Lt NY
Simon: b 10-3-1707 d 5-17-1791 m Maria Truax Groot PS NY

VEECH, (includes VEACH, VEATCH, & VEITCH)
Elias: b 5-5-1759 d 9-13-1839 m Jean Brown Pvt SC ★
James: b 1741 d p. 7-29-1822 m Rebecca Jamison Pvt PA
James: b 4-22-1701 d 1781 m Sarah Prow PS PA
James: b 1725 d 10-29-1780 m Eleanor Raymer Sol SC
Jeremiah: b c. 1760 d 1-13-1836 m Priscilla — Pvt PA MD ★
John: b 1732 d 9-11-1784 m Mary Conn Pvt PS MD
John: b c. 1743 d 3-2-1820 m Sara — Pvt PA
Nathan: b 8-15-1752 d 9-5-1829 m Elizabeth Cragg Sol NC

VEEDER,
Abraham: b 11-11-1745 d 1-25-1814 m (1)Sarah (Vedder)
　　(2)Annetje Fonda Capt NY
Cornelius: b 9-14-1764 d 11-9-1848 m Harriet Zeeley Pvt NY
Elizabeth Margareta Shannon: b 1755 d 1808 m Simon B Veeder
　　N NY
Garret S: b 7-4-1751 d 2-18-1836 m Jenneke TenEyck Capt NY
Gerrit: b 4-2-1716 d p. 1790 m (1)Hester Slingerland (2)Anneke
　　DeGraaf Pvt NY
Johannes: bpt 4-8-1714 d 6-11-1798 m (1)Catherine Mebie
　　(2) Elizabeth Wallace PS NY
John: b 6-29-1734 d 9-26-1793 m Lena Vrooman Pvt NY
John J: b 5-31-1766 d 11-20-1836 m Maria Fonda Pvt NY
Nicholas Gerrit: b 12-25-1761 d 4-7-1862 m Anne Hetherington
　　Pvt NY ★
Nicolas: bpt 2-3-1734 d 11-11-1807 m Catarina VanEps PS NY
Peter V.: b 11- -1760 d 10-9-1814 m Jannetje Van Eps Sgt NY W★
Pieter Symonse: b 12-28-1746 d — m (1)Maria Van Slyke (3)Alida
　　Fairly Sol NY
Simon: b 6-11-1748 d 12-18-1836 m Margaret Terwilliger QM NY
Simon B: b 1-25-1753 d 8-10-1810 m Elizabeth Margaret Shannon
　　Pvt NY
Simon H: b 1723 d p. 1784 m (1)Elizabeth Bancker (2)Margarita
　　Pootman Pvt NY
Volkert: b 12-14-1740 d 2-22-1813 m (1)Elizabeth Smith (2)Mrs
　　Maria Hardenburgh LCol NY
Volkert: b 9-30-1736 d 5-20-1807 m Susanna Myndertse LCol NY

VEGHTE,
Henry: b 3-6-1745 d 9-5-1833 m Dorothy Polhemus Pvt NJ
John: b 1754 d 1799 m Mary E Oppie Pvt NJ
John: b 1739 d 12-23-1825 m Catharine Vanderbuilt Pvt NJ
Reynier: b 2-19-1754 d 2-27-1833 m (1)Catlintie TenEick
　　(2)Catherine VanWagener Lt NJ W★

VENABLE, (includes VENABLES)
Charles: b 4-12-1730 d 11- -1815 m Elizabeth Smith Capt VA
Elizabeth Michaux Woodson: b 6-6-1740 d 9-27-1791 m Nathaniel
　　Venable PS VA
Hugh Lewis: b c. 1727 d a. 12-28-1801 m Mary Martin PS VA
James: b 1757 d p. 1808 m Agnes Dean CS VA
John: b 9-1-1762 d 6-1-1839 m Mary Curry Ens NC ★
John: b c. 1740 d 1811 m Agnes Moorman PS VA
Joseph: b 1753 d 1803 m Lucy Davenport Sol SC
Nathaniel: b 10-21-1733 d 12-27-1804 m Elizabeth Woodson PS VA
Samuel Woodson: b 9-19-1756 d 9-7-1821 m Mary Scott
　　Carrington Lt VA

VENARD,
Thomas: b 1756 d 4-2-1839 m Ann — Pvt VA ★
Wm.: b 3-16-1759 d c. 9- -1840 m Dorothy — Sol VA ★

VENTON,
Wm.: b 11-10-1730 d 6-30-1809 m Annatje Egmont Pvt NY

VENTRES,
John: b 3-7-1729/30 d 6-30-1818 m Elizabeth Arnold Capt CT

VERANO,
Peter: b 2-28-1759 d 3-4-1846 m Emabel Blean Pvt Canada ★

VERBRYCK,
Wm.: b 3-17-1737 d 1-31-1824 m Rebecca Low Maj NJ ★

VERDIER,
James: b c. 1730 d 9- -1785 m Susannah — PS VA

VEREEN,
Jeremiah, Jr.: b 7-4-1748 d 7-4-1808 m Susanna Blanchard Sgt SC
Wm.: b 11-3-1729 d 9-20-1789 m Elizabeth Lewis Sol PS SC

VERMEULE,
Cornelius: b 4-2-1716 d 3-15-1784 m Mary Marselis PS NJ
Eder: b 1-4-1748 d 4-5-1828 m Elizabeth Myer Lt NJ

VERMILLION,
Jessee: b 10-25-1752 d 11-2-1840 m Mary Scott Pvt NC ★

VERMILYEA, (includes VERMILLIA, VERMILYA,
　　VERMILYE)
David: b 1740 d 18— m Patience — Pvt NY
Gerardus: b 1740 d p. 1-1-1799 m Jane Valentine Pvt NY
Jacob: b 1740 d 1814 m (1)Susanna Dyckman (2)Mary Dyckman
　　Lt NY
Jacob: b 1757 d c. 1793 m Phebe Vail Lt NY W★
Philip: bpt 9-6-1758 d p. 7-9-1819 m Rebecca Elliott Pvt NY
Wm.: b c. 1759 d 1803 m Phebe Husted Pvt NY

VERNER, (includes VARNER & VERNOR)
David: b 2-20-1760 d 6-10-1852 m Ester — Sgt SC ★
Henry: b 1740 d 9-9-1784 m Rebecca — Pvt NC
John: b 9-18-1746 d 12-1-1825 m Eva Van Valkenberg QM NY
John: b 1757 d 11-21-1846 m Mary — Pvt PA ★
John, Sr.: b 1725 d 1800 m Mary Pettigrew Pvt SC
John, Jr.: b 3-5-1763 d 8-17-1853 m (1)Jane Edmonson
　　(2)Rebecca Dickey Pvt SC
Matthew: b 1760 d p. 1845 m Susannah Henley Pvt NC ★
Peter: b c. 1730 d p. 1790 m Mary Eve Roth Pvt PA
Thomas: b 1760 d 1828 m Emeline — Sol GA

VERNON, (includes VARNON)
Alexander: b 1-24-1732 d 1-7-1787 m Margaret Chesnee PS SC
George W: b 1752 d 8-9-1828 m Susanna Ashbridge Pvt PA
Jacob: b c. 1732 d p. 1781 m Sarah Frazer Lt PA
Job: b c. 1750 d c. 1810 m Isabella — Ens Capt PA
John: b 1744 d 2- -1825 m Mary West Pvt PA
Joseph: b 1746 d 1-26-1834 m Sarah — Ens PA
Richard: b 10-18-1756 d 7-24-1840 m Betty Wooten Capt NC ★
Richard: b 1746 d p. 1810 m Patsy Tinsley PS VA
Samuel: b 1755 d 1817 m Ann Hall Pvt PA
Samuel: b 9-6-1711 d 7-6-1792 m Amey Ward PS RI
Thomas: b 1758/9 d p. 1794 m (1)Margaret Hayes (2)Hannah Evans
　　(3) — Malcaub Pvt PA
Thomas: b 5-23-1752 d c. 1839-41 m Nancy Hicks Pvt VA ★
Wm.: b 1-17-1719 d 12-26-1806 m Judith Harwood PS RI

VERNOOY,
Peter: b 12-25-1739 d 6-11-1813 m Mary Clearwater PS NY

VERONE,
Joseph: b 6-14-1755 d 1-12-1825 m Mary Kelly Pvt VA ★

VER PLANCK,
Isaac: b 2-19-1759 d 2-4-1836 m Elena Houghtaling Pvt NY

VERRET,
Augustin: bpt 6-7-1755 d 1840 m Marie Madelaine Bisot PS LA
Jacques: b 11-28-1752 d 1833 m (1)Isabelle Elizabeth Duverges
　　(2)Marguerite Schwitzel PS LA

VERRILL, (includes VARRELL)
Edward: b c. 1744 d 10-13-1819 m (1)Elizabeth Saunders (2)Mary
　　Berry Pvt NH
Samuel: b 4-20-1734 d 5-4-1821 m Eunice Bray Pvt MA
Samuel, Jr.: b 1757 d 12-15-1838 m Sarah Prince Pvt MA ★

VERRY, (includes VERY)
Francis, Jr.: b 2-7-1745 d c. 1820 m Rebecca Simonds PS NH
Samuel: b 1759 d 1-20-1832 m (1)Abigail Crowninshield
　　(2)Martha Cheever Pvt MA
Wm.: b 9-28-1760 d 5-17-1819 m Marcy Wiswall Pvt MA

VERTEE,
John: b c. 1751 d p. 1790 m Elizabeth Widger Pvt MA

VERTREES,
Isaac: b 4-15-1755 d 4-5-1822 m (1) — (2)Elizabeth Barkhimer
　　Pvt PA

VERTREES, contd.
John: bpt 1741 d 1803 m (1)Rebecca Burris (2)Mrs Elizabeth McNeil Capt VA

VER VALEN, (includes VAN VALIN & VER VALIN)
Cornelius: b 5-14-1762 d 4-19-1820 m Ann VanOrden Sol NY
Gideon: b 2-10-1742 d p. 1797 m Jane Low 2Lt NY
Jeremiah: b 10-26-1749 d 4-23-1811 m Margaret McNeel Pvt NY
John: b 1754 d 1794 m Maria Banta Pvt NJ
John: b 10-22-1747 d 11-28-1840 m Sarah Bloodgood Pvt PS NY
Samuel: b 5-8-1760 d 12-10-1837 m Mary Perry Pvt NJ W★

VESTAL,
Wm.: b c. 1750 d p. 1800 m Sarah — Capt NC

VIA,
Wm.: b 1761 d 6-27-1836 m Mary Craig Pvt VA ★

VIALL,
John: b 11-26-1759 d 4-7-1833 m (1)Esther Peck (2)Mrs Elizabeth (Barnes) Coy Sgt MA
Nathaniel: b 3-28-1762 d 10-6-1846 m Betsey Clark Pvt MA ★
Nathaniel: b 12-23-1748 d 8-2-1833 m Patience Bennett Pvt RI ★
Samuel: b 1730 d 4-2-1777 m Ruth Allen 1Lt MA
Samuel: b 6-4-1759 d 12-22-1851 m Susannah Stocker Sgt MA ★
Sylvester: b 1751 d 5-2-1816 m Abigail Adams Pvt RI

VIBBERT,
Jesse: b 1-30-1759 d 9- -1830 m Martha Abbey Pvt CT ★

VIBBIRD,
David: b 4-2-1760 d 8-24-1792 m Sarah Hill Cpl CT ★

VICK,
Joshua: b 5-20-1762 d 2-25-1833 m — Pvt VA ★

VICKER,
Solomon: b 1730 d 1798 m Sarah Ann Pvt PA

VICKERY, (includes VICKORY & VICORY)
Benjamin: b 1749 d 1809 m Rhoda Holbrook Pvt MA
David: b 1734 d 11-14-1823 m Sarah Stone Pvt MA ★
John: b 1750 d 1834 m Rebecca — Cpl MA ★
John: b 1738 d a. 10-1-1808 m Eleanor Martin Pvt MA
Joseph: c. 1735 d p. 1827 m — Sol GA
Joshua: b 1731 d p. 1795 m (1)Mollie Haley (2)Elizabeth Flood Pvt NH
Marmaduke: b c. 1715 d p. 12-26-1787 m Elizabeth Swaim Pvt NC
Matthias: b 7-19-1743 d 11-21-1812 m (1)Ruth Horton (2)Elizabeth Wagg Sol MA
Merrifield: b 1763 d 3-16-1840 m Joanna Nye Pvt NH ★
Roger: b c. 1721 d p. 1790 m Mrs Susanna Hines Northey Pvt MA

VICKROY,
Thomas: b 10-18-1756 d 6-9-1845 m Sarah Ann Atlee Cmsry PA

VICTOR,
John: b a. 1756 d 4- -1791 m Hannah Bruington 2Lt MD
John: b 1757 d 2-10-1817 m Sarah Tankersley Lt VA W★

VICTORY,
John: b 1764 d 1857 m (2)Persis Russell Pvt NY

VIELE, (includes VELIE & VEARS)
Cornelis: bpt 6-11-1718 d p. 1790 m (1)Rachel Swartout (2)Arriaantje Palmenter Pvt PS NY
Jacob: b 6-21-1719 d p. 1797 m Eva Fort Pvt NY
Jacobus: b 1761 d 12-22-1843 m Catharine Palmentier Pvt NY
John: b 7-30-1758 d 2- -1840 m Wyntie Sickles Pvt NY
Lewis: b 8-30-1751 d p. 1790 m Anna Quackenbos Pvt NY
Lodervecua: b 10-17-1742 d 12-27-1800 m Eva Toll Pvt NY
Mindert: b c. 1752 d p. 6-30-1800 m Johanna Palmatier Pvt NY
Peter: b 1-12-1745 d 7-8-1819 m Elizabeth Fonda Pvt NY
Philip: b 7-7-1745 d 8-7-1797 m Rachel Fonda Pvt NY
Philip: b 10-4-1747 d 1807 m (1)Maria Bradt (2)Mary Vandenburg Pvt NY
Stephen: b 8-3-1753 d 10-8-1803 m Sarah Toll QM NY

VIERS,
Wm.: b 1735 d p. 6-25-1811 m Mary — LCol PS MD

VIETS,
Abner: b 2-15-1747 d 7-27-1826 m Mary Viets Lt PS CT
John: b 11-3-1712 d 4-8-1777 m Lois Phelps CS CT
Jonathan: b 9-26-1750 d 2-17-1837 m Caroline Munsell Pvt CT

VIGNERON,
Charles: b c. 1750 d p. 11-1-1777 m Mary Taylor PS RI

VIGNES,
Lorenzo: b 1737 d 1780 m Marguerite Verge PS LA

VILAS,
Noah: b 11-2-1733 d 9-17-1799 m Abagail Baker Pvt MA
Noah: b 2-1-1763 d 10-31-1820 m Lovina Cady Pvt MA

VILES,
Joel: b 12-14-1743 d 1814 m Mary Reed Bowman Sgt MA
John: b 6-12-1750 d 9-19-1820 m Hannah Warren Pvt MA
Jonas: b 7-3-1746 d 10-8-1799 m (1)Susanna Hastings (2)Irene Hastings Pvt MA

VILLERS,
John: b 1734 d 5-20-1826 m (1)Victory Muskelroy (2)Mary Dakens (3)Elizabeth Ewart PS PA

VINAL,
Francis: b — d — m Mary Ewell Pvt ME MA
Israel: b p. 1723 d 1794 m Mercy Cushing PS MA
Issachar: b 3-27-1718 d 1-15-1799 m (1)Mary Chittenden (2)Patience Judith Bailey PS MA
Wm.: b 7-25-1751 d 10-24-1813 m Lucy Mann Lt MA

VINCE,
Joseph: b 1745 d 2-19-1811 m Lucy Robison Capt SC
Richard: b c. 1740 d c. 1806-13 m Flora Ann Strickland Pvt SC

VINCENT, (includes VINSON)
Aaron: b a. 1747 d 1791 m Sarah Ogburn CS NC
Benjamin: b 1749 d 12-2-1800 m Relief Ellery PS MA
Bethuel: b 6-3-1762 d 4-30-1837 m (1)Martha Himrod (2)Margaret Hayes Pvt PA ★
Cornelius: b 4-15-1737 d 7-12-1812 m Phoebe Ward QMSgt PA
Daniel: b 1-17-1760 d 1-26-1827 m Angelica Huff Pvt PA
David: b 6-30-1762 d 11-1-1848 m Elizabeth Hall Pvt MA
Drury: b c. 1740-9 d a. 6- -1816 m (2)Anne Durham Sgt NC
Gilbert: b 1756 d 3-26-1842 m Phoebe Vail Pvt NY
Isaac: b c. 1754 d p. 1827 m (1) — Hart (2)Martha Bradford (3) — Smith Pvt GA
Isaac: b 4-23-1727 d 8-19-1808 m Hannah Pope Pvt MA
Jeremiah: b 10-18-1741 d 6-8-1833 m Mary Merritt Capt NY W★
John: b 2-13-1730 d 12-17-1824 m Sarah Colson Pvt MA
John: b c. 1720-5 d 1787 m Emelia — PS Sol VA NC
John: b 1-26-1709 d 2-24-1801 m Elizabeth Doremus Pvt PA
John: b 8-24-1750 d 1-26-1837 m Sarah Johnson Lt VA ★
Jonathan: b 11-20-1753 d 7-13-1824 m Sarah Germond Sol NY
Joseph: b 1737 d 2-2-1823 m Anna Dunbar PS CT
Joshua: b 4-24-1757 d 12-8-1845 m (2)Phebe Negus Pvt MA ★
Joshua: b 9- -1764 d 8-24-1837 m Susannah Willard Pvt RI ★
Phoebe Ward: b 4-8-1740 d 2-25-1809 m Cornelius Vincent PS PA
Thomas: b 4-14-1761 d 10-25-1840 m Mary Ayres Matr NH ★
Wm.: b 3-31-1729 d 7-19-1807 m Zeruiah Rudd Dr RI

VINER,
John: b 12-21-1754 d 9-24-1826 m Sarah Chard Pvt MA W★

VINEYARD,
Christian: b — d p. 2-27-1798 m Christiana Tabler PS VA
Christopher: b 1741 d p. 11-3-1807 m — PS VA
John: b 1750-60 d a. 7-21-1834 m Mary — Sol VA

VINING,
Benjamin: b 11-16-1738 d 8-2-1812 m (1)Mehitabel Brooks (2)Lydia Turner (3)Bathsheba Davis PS CS MA
David: b 9-25-1740 d 7-1-1830 m Lydia Torrey Pvt MA
Ebenezer: b 10-5-1753 d 1843 m Abigail Eason Pvt MA ★
George: b 12-24-1754 d 4-8-1822 m Abigail Alden Sgt MA
Israel: b 1760 d 4-16-1840 m Abi Dunbar Pvt MA ★
Jesse: b c. 1760 d a. 6-20-1800 m Phoebe Pledger Pvt SC
Joseph: b 6-6-1744 d 10-25-1828 m Olive Torrey Cpl MA

VINSONHELLER,
John: b c. 1735 d p. 1-22-1825 m — PS VA

VINTON,
Abiathar: b 9-18-1732 d p. 1800 m (1)Rhoda Wheelock (2)Rachel Caswell (3)Mrs Sarah Smith Pvt MA
Abiathar: b 10-11-1758 d 1-22-1850 m Sarah Paine Pvt MA ★
Benoni: b 9-2-1756 d 1-25-1837 m Rebecca Dix Pvt MA
David, Sr.: b 3-7-1725 d 1791 m Ruth Dorman MM MA
David, Jr.: b 3-18-1759 d 3-18-1825 m Persis Newton Pvt MA
David: b c. 1746 d 12-3-1778 m Mary Gowen Pvt Smn MA
Ezra: b. a. 1-8-1754 d 11-11-1817 m Sarah Green Pvt MA
John: b 2-2-1760 d 3-19-1838 m Susanna Manning Pvt CT
John: b 2-11-1734 d 12-6-1803 m Hepzibah French Capt MA
John: b 8-8-1752 d 9-24-1781 m Mary Traill 2Lt PS MA
John: b 8-9-1732 d 12-19-1800 m (1)Sarah Swain (2)Lydia Nichols Sgt MA
John: b 3-1-1743/4 d 6-18-1778 m Sarah Thayer Sgt MA
John: b 2-14-1742 d 7- -1814 m (1)Mary Sabin (2)Dorothy Holmes Cpl MA
Joseph: b 3-2-1758 d 5-19-1839 m Mary Allard Pvt MA
Josiah: b 4-25-1755 d 12-27-1843 m Anne Adams Pvt MA
Levi: b 6-5-1760 d 9-20-1820 m Jerusha Fenton Pvt MA

Pelatiah: b 10-27-1738 d 12-25-1798 m Zipporah Jackson Pvt MA
Ralph: b 10-17-1740 d 4-14-1832 m Phebe Holmes Pvt MA
Seth: b 6-6-1756 d 5-25-1846 m (1)Ruth Hatch (2)Dorcas Rider
   (3)Polly Rider Pvt MA
Thomas: b 6-2-1739 d 8-9-1798 m Jemima Mills Pvt MA
Timothy: b 2-14-1749 d 6-27-1823 m Dolly Shumway Pvt MA
Timothy: b 11-22-1765 d 12-20-1803 m Brucy McLeod Pvt MA

VIOLET, (includes VIOLETT)
John: b 1756 d 1-1-1848 m (1)Mary Taylor (2)Mrs Constance
   (Trembly) (Philips) Welty Pvt VA ★
Sampson: b c. 1755 d p. 6-7-1817 m (1)Sarah Boydston (2)Eve
   (Hoover) Phillips Pvt VA

VIRDEN, (includes VARDEN)
Marnit: b 1745 d 4-1-1796 m Mrs Lydia Mustard Cpl DE
Steven: b 6-6-1754 d 1821 m — Drm VA
Wm.: b — d a. 5-6-1803 m Anne — Sol DE

VIRGIN,
Ebenezer: b 5-25-1735 d p. 1783 m Dorcas — PS NH
Rezin: b — d 1819 m Jemima Arnold Capt VA
Wm.: b 7-4-1737 d 8-26-1803 m Mehitabel Stickney PS NH

VIRMILLION,
Wilson: b c. 1750 d 1827 m Nancy McNeil Tms NC

VISSCHER, (includes VICHER)
Bastian T: b 3-31-1728 d 5-9-1809 m Engeltie Van Den Bergh
   Capt NY
Eldert: bpt 2-11-1753 d c. 1840/1 m Geertruy Fort Pvt NY
Frederick: b 2-21-1741 d 6-9-1809 m Gazena De Graff Col NY
Gerrit T: bpt 2-5-1737 d 1-5-1805 m (1)Alida Fonda (2)Rachel
   Van den Bergh Pvt NY
John: bpt 4-23-1739 d 10-24-1821 m Elizabeth Bradt Col NY
John T: b 2-12-1744 d 9-18-1834 m Annatie Pearce PS 1Lt NY ★
Matthew: b 12-15-1751 d 8-8-1793 m Lydia Fryer Capt NY
Nanning: bpt 9-26-1736 d 8-19-1813 m (1)Catharyntje Wendell
   (2)Helena Lansing (3)Abigail (Van Denbergh) McIntosh Capt NY
Teunis: b 6-17-1740 d p. 1804 m (1)Maria Tymessen (2)Elizabeth
   Groot Capt NY

VITTUM,
Wm.: b 9-16-1750 d 9- -1834 m (1)Elizabeth Jewell (2)Mrs Sarah
   Page Pvt NH ★

VIVES,
Don Juan: b c. 1750 d p. 1813 m Marguerita Bujol PS LA

VIVIAN,
John, Sr.: b 8-10-1714 d c. 1783 m Jane Smith PS VA

VLIET,
Daniel, Sr.: b 1726 d 11-22-1810 m (1)Geertrudje Springsteen
   (2)Charity Blackwell Capt NJ
Daniel, Jr.: b 7-1-1752 d 2-26-1841 m Margaret VanNess Pvt
   NJ ★
David: b 10-1-1748 d 2-2-1842 m (1) — (2)Ann Wyckoff Lupardus
   (3)Jane — Capt NJ ★
Jasper: b 8- -1757 d 12- -1830 m Polly Black Sgt NJ
Wm.: b 1756 d 1839 m Anne Wilson Pvt NJ

VOGAN,
James: b 1744 d 5-13-1824 m Margaret Riley Ens PA

VOGDES,
Jacob: b 4-13-1744 d 3- -1827 m Elizabeth Hampton Pvt PA

VOGLER,
George Michael: b 9-5-1759 d 8-1-1795 m (1)Anna Maria Kunzel
   (2)Elisabeth Beroth Pvt NC

VOILES, (includes VOILS)
Wm.: b 1741 d 1804 m Hannah Bundi Pvt NC

VOINARD,
Joseph: b — d p. 1799 m — Deweiss Pvt FrA

VOLLANDT,
Wilhelm: bpt 1-23-1737 d p. 1800 m Elizabeth Felton`PS NY

VOLLUME,
Leonard: b c. 1742 d 1777 m Elizabeth Perry Pvt VA

VONDERAU,
Adam: b 1756 d 1819 m Margaret (Rupley) Snyder PS PA

VON DER LINDE,
Jacob: b 9-13-1736 d 1-2-1830 m Anna Maria Essig Pvt PA

VONDERSMITH,
Valentine: b 6-6-1746 d 10-12-1820 m Elizabeth Le Fever Pvt PA

VON EFFINGER,
John Ignatius: b 12-4-1756 d 9-1-1839 m (1)Catherine Spatzer
   (2)Barbara Cook Sgt PA ★

VON GACHNAT, (includes VON GOOCHNAT)
Johan Eberhardt: b 2-2-1736 d 6-13-1810 m Elizabeth Ruport
   MM NY

VON NEIDA,
Jacob: b c. 1755 d 1835 m Catherine — Pvt PA

VON PHUL,
Wm.: b 11-14-1739 d 1792 m Catharina von Graff Capt PA

VON PLANK, (see PLANK)

VON STEDINGK,
Count Curt Bogislaus Ludvig Christoffer: b 10-26-1746 d 1-7-1837
   m Countess N F Ekstrom Col GermanA

VON ZOLL,
Wm.: b 1755 d 1800 m Margaret Riter Pvt PA

VORE,
Peter: b c. 1750 d p. 1800 m Elizabeth Huckle Pvt PA

VORSE,
Charles: b 12-14-1766 d 1-13-1856 m (1)Lucretia (Fancher)
   (2)Elizabeth (Olcott) Holcomb Pvt CT ★

VOSBURGH, (or VOSBURG)
Abraham: bpt 5-19-1745 d p. 2-17-1799 m Johanna Spoor 2Lt NY
Abraham: b c. 1760 d 7-12-1821 m Chloe Wood Pvt NY
Abraham I: b 11-4-1757 d p. 11-6-1846 m Deborah Hanson Pvt
   NY ★
Cornelius: dc. 1729 d p. 1796 m Lytje Hallenbeck Sol NY
David: b 11-6-1753 d 3-6-1820 m Elizabeth Snider Pvt NY
Martin: bpt 7-29-1738 d 5-6-1801 m (1)Hannah Ashley
   (2)Cornelia Gilbert Pvt PS NY
Peter Isaac: b 1753 d 1830 m Elizabeth Van Alstyne Lt NY

VOSE,
Daniel: b 2-20-1741 d 12-7-1807 m Rachel Smith Lt MA
Ebenezer: b 3-4-1710 d 1-15-1784 m Phebe Williston PS RI
Elijah: b 2-24-1744/5 d 3-29-1822 m Ruth Tufts LCol MA
George: b 1-29-1754 d 7-17-1798 m Mary Glover Sgt MA
James: b 3-2-1734/5 d 10-3-1808 m Abigail Richardson PS CS NH
Jeremiah: b 4-19-1747 d 5-31-1823 m Hannah Holmes Cpl MA
Jesse: b 3-3-1742/3 d 11-6-1824 m Mary Durfee Sgt MA ★
John: b 5-21-1746 d 9-30-1825 m Militiah Davenport Fif MA
John Blake: b 6-24-1759 d 4-4-1848 m Sarah Sharpe Pvt MA ★
Jonathan: b 5-15-1732 d 4-22-1790 m Mary Gulliver Cpl MA
Joseph: b 11-26-1738 d 5-22-1816 m Sarah How BGen MA
Joshua: b 5-16-1742 d 9-28-1775 m Lydia Babcock Pvt MA
Joshua: b 3-15-1737/8 d 1-28-1812 m Mary Lamphere CS RI
Josiah: b 1741 d 6-6-1823 m Ruhamah Vose Capt MA
Lemuel: b 4-30-1753 d 3-2-1827 m Prudence Cady Pvt CT
Nathaniel: b 4-25-1737 d 11-30-1803 m Ruth Miller Pvt MA
Oliver: b 2-10-1734/5 d 8-31-1810 m (1)Elizabeth Badcock
   (2)Keziah (Whiting) Draper Capt MA
Samuel: b 5-13-1730 d 1799 m Phebe Vickery PS CS NH
Thomas: b 5-8-1753 d 12-28-1810 m Sarah George Capt MA
Thomas: b 1758 d 4-18-1818 m Mary Stoddard Golden Pvt RI
Wm.: b 1-20-1752 d 5-19-1828 m Judith (Briggs) Drew 2Lt MA
Wm.: b 12-9-1751 d 4-29-1813 m (1)Mary Howe (2)Hepzibah
   Crehore Sgt MA
Wm.: b 8-12-1718 d 3-17-1778 m Hannah Peake Pvt MA

VOSSELLER,
Jacob, Sr.: b 1730 d 1812 m Mary Teeple Pvt NJ
Luke: b 3-18-1757 d 1-17-1843 m Anne Smith Pvt NJ

VOUGHT, (includes VAUGHT, & VOIGT)
Godfrey: b 4- -1761 d 4-15-1849 m Polly Croft Pvt NY
Henry: b 1743 d 2-7-1814 m Margaret — PS PA
John: b 12-15-1761 d p. 1810 m Elizabeth Martin Pvt PA
Joseph Christian: b 1741 d 1799 m Catherine Rhinehart Pvt NY
Matthias: b 1759 d 1833 m Martha — Pvt SC

VREDENBURGH, (includes VAN VREDENBURG & VREDENBURG)
Benjamin B: bpt 4-14-1759 d p. 1793 m Lidia Beem PS NY
Isaac: b 1757 d 2-15-1844 m Marie — Pvt NY
Johannes: b 1740 d 2-9-1821 m Annatje Morris Pvt NY
John: b 3-6-1730 d 9-13-1794 m Maryetje VanWagenen Sgt NY
Wilhelmus: b 9-16-1733 d c. 1800 m Elizabeth Van Garden Pvt NY
Wm., Jr.: b 4-18-1760 d 5-9-1813 m Elizabeth Platt Townsend
   Pvt NY

VREELAND, (includes VREELANDT)
Abraham: b 6-9-1759 d 8-17-1826 m Racheal Ackerman Cpl NJ
Garret: b 12-1-1751 d 11- -1825 m Jannetje Cadmus Cpl NJ

VREELAND, contd.
Hartman Michael: b c. 1720 d 1785 m Maritje Gerbrants Tms NJ
Isaac: b 1747 d 1-11-1836 m Myntje Romyn Pvt NJ
Jacob: b 3-11-1737 d 1780 m Fitze Deryee PS NJ
Johannes: b 3-2-1742 d 7-30-1823 m Keetje Hoagland Capt NJ
John M: b 10-17-1758 d 1821 m Ann Speer Sol NJ
Michael: b 6-24-1739 d 12-5-1804 m Annatje (Vreeland) Tms NJ
Michael: b 7-31-1758 d 1814 m Gertje Sickles Pvt NJ

VROOM,
Elizabeth De Mott: b 1758 d 1835 m Hendrick D Vroom PS NJ
Hendrick D: b 1743 d 1810 m (1)Jamima — (2)Elizabeth DeMott Pvt NJ
Hendrick P: b 1757 d 8-7-1845 m Sarah Lane Sgt NJ

VROOMAN, (includes VROMAN)
Abraham: b 11-15-1715 d c. 1800 m Marytje Verplanck PS NY
Abram: b 1-24-1759 d 1-29-1813 m Matilda Vischer Pvt NY
Adam: b 9-25-1740 d 10-31-1823 m Anatia Zelia Pvt NY
Adam: b 10-25-1737 d 11-8-1820 m Janett Zeiley Sol NY
Adam J: b 11-5-1707 d 10-28-1790 m Dinah Larroway PS NY
Barent, Jr.: b 3-10-1754 d p. 11-23-1808 m Catherine Ziele Cpl NY
Bartholomew: b 4-24-1762 d p. 1788 m Santje — Pvt NY
Cornelius: b 2-10-1722 d 1806 m Margareth Bratt Sol NY
Cornelius: b 7-3-1742 d p. 6-25-1817 m Magdalena Huyck Cpl NY
Ephraim: b 3-4-1738 d 3-9-1811 m (1)Anna Christiana Swart (2)Maria Sidney Lt NY
Hendrick: b 7-4-1722 d 1786 m Neeltie Veeder Lt NY
Hendrick B: b 5-16-1742 d p. 1799 m (1)Margaret Vander Werken (2)Alida Conyne Lt NY
Hendrick Johannes: b 10-23-1757 d 1-30-1813 m Sarah Gonzalis (Consaulis) Pvt NY
Henry H: b 3-3-1754 d p. 1790 m Elizabeth Simmons Lt NY
Isaac: bpt 4-8-1721 d 6-9-1807 m Anna Dorothy Van Buskirk PS NY
Jacob: b 1-5-1737 d 1815 m Catharine — Pvt NY
Jacob A: b 12-30-1747 d 7-21-1831 m Helena Swits Pvt NY
Johannes: b 12-25-1734 d 5-1-1785 m Jannetje Swits Pvt NY
Johannes B: bpt 1-13-1745 d p. 1790 m Margarita (Vrooman) 1Lt PS NY
Johannes Jacob: b 1-8-1726 d p. 10-13-1805 m Clara VanSlyck Pvt NY
Jonas: b 4-9-1735 d 4-16-1804 m Delia Hager Pvt NY
Martynus: b 12-6-1745 d 3-6-1821 m (1)Santje Swart (2)Cornelia Becker Lt NY
Marytje Ackerson: b — d 8-9-1780 m Tunis Vrooman PS NY
Peter A: b 5-12-1763 d 11-23-1838 m Angelica (Vrooman) Pvt NY ★
Peter B: b 1-7-1736 d 1794 m Angelica Swart Col NY
Peter C: b 9-12-1760 d p. 1785 m Effie VanEvery Pvt NY
Samuel: b 10-16-1734 d 12-6-1805 m Catrina VanZiele Pvt NY
Simon Jacob: b 8-3-1760 d 1-3-1844 m Sarah Clark Lt NY ★
Tunis, Sr.: b 6-27-1738 d 8-9-1780 m Martyje Ackerson Capt NY
Tunis, Jr.: b 10-2-1770 d 6-30-1865 m Elizabeth Fretts PS NY
Walter: bpt 6-21-1750 d p. 1785 m Jacomyentje Barheyt Capt NY

VUNCK,
Hendrick: b 3-6-1757 d 11-28-1840 m Christina Hagaman Pvt NJ ★

WADDELL, (includes WADDILL, WADDLE, & WEDDLE)
Alexander: b 2- -1732 d 9-8-1834 m (2)Elenor Roush Sol VA
Benjamin: b c. 1742 d a. 4- -1807 m Mary — Sol VA
Edmund: b 1748 d 1815 m Lucy Birdsong Sol NC
George: b a. 1729 d 1796 m Mary — PS PA
Jacob: b c. 1755 d 2-26-1815 m Frances Rush Sgt NC
James: b 3-17-1733 d 8-20-1806 m Mary Courtney 2Lt PA
James: b 1739 d 9- -1805 m Mary Gordon PS VA
John: b 1736 d 7-4-1827 m (1)Margaret McCoy (2)Rachel Quee (3)Susan Green Sol NC
John: b 4-10-1729 d 1812 m Mary Dickey Pvt PA
Peter: b 1741 d 10- -1786 m (1)Rebecca Prichard (2)Sarah Martin 1Lt PA
Peter: b 1766 d 6-1-1841 m Malinda — Pvt VA
Richard: b c. 1728 d c. 6- -1806 m Frances — PS VA
Robert: b c. 1750 d 12-16-1816 m Bathia Orbison Ens PA
Wm.: b 11-17-1758 d 11-15-1831 m Nancy White Pvt VA
Wm.: b c. 1760 d 7-24-1830 m Hannah — Sol VA

WADDEY,
John: b c. 1743 d 10-13-1805 m Elizabeth Wise Rodgers CS VA

WADE, (includes WAID)
Abner: b 11-14-1746 d 10-24-1827 m Mrs Hopestill Delano Bradford Capt MA
Abner: b 1755 d 1801 m Phoebe Beach Pvt NJ
Abraham: b 1740 d 1802 m Elizabeth — CS NC
Alverson: b 10-28-1761 d 1828 m Naomi Munger Pvt MA
Amasa: b 3-16-1751 d 8-30-1838 m Anna Hale Pvt CT
Benjamin: b 1749 d p. 1818 m Tabritha Harrison Matr NJ

Daniel: b 1718 d 7- -1793 m (1)Elizabeth — (2)Temperance — Pvt NJ
Daniel: b 1768 d 6-20-1820 m Jane Brown Ross PS SC
David: b 1732 d — m Mary Littlefield Cpl MA
David E: b 2-22-1763 d 1842 m Mary Jones Pvt NJ
Dudley: b 12-1-1734 d — m Katherine Alverson Pvt MA
Ebenezer: b 1745 d 1838 m (1)Phebe Wyman (2)Elizabeth Leathe (3)Mrs Jerusha Brooks Richardson Pvt MA
Edward: b 5-24-1754 d 12-8-1845 m (1)Susan Florence (2)Elizabeth Trumbull Cpl NH
Edward, Sr.: b c. 1727 d 1790 m Mary — PS Sol VA
Elisha: b c. 1759 d a. 9-19-1849 m Mary Ann — Pvt NC
George: b 9-15-1759/60 d 10-30-1842 m Nancy Howard Pvt PA ★
George: b 5-29-1747 d 11-24-1824 m (1)Mary McDonald (2)Mrs Martha Taylor Lt SC
George, Sr.: b c. 1725 d p. 1814 m Ann — Pvt VA
Hampton: b 1760 d 1808 m Elizabeth — Sgt PS VA
Henry: b 1762 d 1833 m Deboroh — Sol SC
Henry: b 6-6-1748 d 2-24-1825 m Margaret Ward Cpl NJ
Hezakiah: b 4-13-1754 d 11-23-1834 m Rebecca Joseph Pvt Spy VA W★
Ichabod: b 1742 d 1-5-1810 m Mary Peck Capt MA
Increase: b 1757/8 d c. 3-10-1832 m Freelove Nettleton Pvt CT W★
Isaac: b 1753 d 1-1-1834 m Lucy Harding Drm MA
Isaac: b a. 1758 d 8-9-1823 m Mary (Gibbs) Stevens Pvt VA W★
Jacob: b 5-2-1756 d p. 4-16-1818 m (1)Ann — (2)Mary Branch Pvt VA ★
James: b 7-8-1750 d 5-9-1826 m Mary Upham Pvt MA
John, Sr.: b 11-16-1735 d a. 1781 m Abigail Brawner Pvt MD
John, Jr.: b 1760 d 1840 m Elizabeth Offutt Pvt PA
John: b 9-10-1755 d 6-18-1843 m (1)Abigail Bates (2)Rosanna Gitchel Pvt MA ★
John: b 1759 d 1830 m Mary Holmes Pvt NC
Joseph, Sr.: b 1715 d 2-12-1777 m (1)Sarah Searing (2)Phebe — Wgm NJ
Joseph, Jr.: b 10-16-1761 d p. 3-3-1818 m (1)Sarah Beach (2)Hannah (Beach) Allen Pvt NJ
Joshua: b c. 1762 d 2-17-1800 m Anne Boatright Pvt VA ★
Jotham: b 4-21-1763 d 12-1-1804 m Margaret Tilden Pvt MA
Martin: b 3-22-1745 d 4-6-1792 m Lucy Mack Pvt CT
Matthias: b 8-10-1742 d 5-25-1820 m Johanna (Stewart) McGee Pvt NJ
Nathaniel: b 2-27-1749 d 10-26-1826 m Mary Foster Capt MA
Nathaniel, Sr.: b 6-13-1753 d 5-18-1793 m Sarah Wade Pvt NJ
Nathaniel: b 3-17-1744 d 12-28-1821 m Molly — Capt RI W★
Nathaniel: b p. 1-27-1708 d 5-1-1799 m Ruth Hopkins MM RI
Nehemiah: b 1736 d 10-19-1776 m Abigail Mulford Maj NJ
Noadiah: b 1746 d 1830 m (1)Unis Cory (2)Anna Braisted Capt NJ
Obadiah: b 10- -1761 d 1838 m Abigail — Pvt NC
Peyton: b 12-25-1755 d 1831 m Martha Perkins PS Sol VA
Richard: b 10-26-1752 d 2-7-1844 m Judith Handcock Pvt VA ★
Simon: b 9-15-1749 d 9-21-1817 m Abagaile Beardslee Pvt NJ
Snell: b 3-25-1762 d 1795 m Charlotte Otis Pvt MA
Stephen: b 1720 d 2-8-1817 m Maria Abigail Hoadley Pvt CT
Stephen: b 4-17-1755 d 1792 m Marcy Peirce Sgt MA
Sylvanus: b 8-28-1764 d 8-19-1826 m Mary Chase Pvt MA ★
Thomas: b c. 1722 d a. 6-2-1786 m Jane Boggan Col PS NC
Wm.: b 3-4-1757 d 12-29-1841 m Sarah Allen Cpl VA

WADERMAN,
Daniel: b 1762 d 6- -1837 m Hannah Dolph Pvt NY

WADHAM, (includes WADHAMS)
Abraham: b 9-24-1756 d 10-31-1834 m Tryphena Collins Pvt CT
Caleb: b 1735 d 1816 m Dorothy Hubbard Pvt MA
Caleb: b 1-14-1754 d 5-18-1835 m (1)Eunice Furr (2)Mrs Mary (Rude) Hammond Arfr NY ★
John: b 4-25-1728 d 8-5-1812 m Eunice Porter Pvt MA
Jonathan: b 10-18-1730 d 4-12-1812 m Judith Howe Vol CT
Noah: b 5-17-1726 d 5-22-1806 m (1)Elizabeth Ingersoll (2)Diana Ross PS PA
Seth: b 11-3-1743 d 4-18-1817 m Anne Catlin PS CT

WADLEIGH, (includes WADLIA & WADLIN)
Benjamin: b 6-16-1759 d 11-4-1807 m Sarah Patton Pvt NH
Daniel: b 2-2-1753 d 5-26-1832 m Margaret Thompson Pvt MA ★
Daniel: b — d 1780 m Patience — Pvt MA
Elijah: b 3-18-1757 d 10-9-1800 m Sarah (Patton) Saunders Pvt NH
James: b 1753 d 2- -1830 m Molly Blake Pvt NH
John: b 8-10-1753 d 8-11-1842 m Molly Fox Pvt NH
Jonathan: b 3-26-1751 d p. 9-7-1787 m Abigail Eastman Pvt NH
Joseph: b 9-3-1752 d 6-21-1808 m Elizabeth Morrill Pvt MA
Joseph, Sr.: b 1712 d 1792 m Anna Swaine PS NH
Joseph, Jr.: b 11-3-1743 d 4-5-1821 m Elizabeth Dole Pvt NH
Joseph: b 7-21-1752 d 5-18-1818 m Betty Longfellow Pvt NH
Nathaniel: b 1759 d 4-4-1834 m (1)Mary Robinson (2)Nancy Pickering Pvt NH MA ★
Simeon: b 10-3-1762 d 8-25-1843 m Abigail Hayes Pvt NH
Thomas, Sr.: b — d 10-9-1787 m Margaret Rowen PS NH
Thomas, Jr.: b 3-29-1755 d 2-25-1827 m Merriam Atwood Pvt NH

WADLINGTON,
James: b 1-2-1745 d p. 1790 m — Sol SC
Thomas: b c. 1740 d 1784 m — PS SC

WADSWORTH,
Asa: b 1735 d p. 1810 m Sarah Hills Pvt MA
Asabel: b 12-20-1743 d 5-5-1817 m (1)Marcy Woodruff (2)Hannah
  Wadsworth PA CT
Cephas: b 8- -1743 d 9-12-1819 m Molly Cook Pvt MA
Daniel: b 1-7-1761 d 1-7-1806 m Azuba Pearl Pvt CT
Daniel: b 10-14-1762 d 3-22-1849 m Mercy Eells Pvt CT
Ebenezer: b 1-9-1745 d 10-24-1817 m Lucy Brooks Pvt MA
Elijah: b 1746/7 d 1817 m Rhoda Hopkins Capt CT
Elisha: b 1746 d a. 1790 m Elizabeth Wells Pvt NY
Epaphras: b 1754 d 10-26-1841 m Desdemona Marshall Fif CT
Gad: b 1743 d 1820 m Elizabeth Hulbert 1 Lt CT
Hezekiah: b 1724 d 10-23-1810 m Lois Judd PS CT
Hezekiah: b 12-13-1759 d 10-23-1845 m Mary Noble Pvt CT ★
Ichabod: b 1741 d 3-31-1815 m (1)Chloe Webster (2)Lydia Porter
  Sgt CT
James: b 7-7-1742 d 7-7-1821 m Irene Palmer Pvt CT
James: b c. 1763 d p. 1838 m Nancy Davie Sol GA
James: b 6-28-1752 d 7-10-1801 m Mary Brace MM CT
Jeremiah: b 7-12-1743 d 4-30-1804 m Mehitable Russell
  CmsryGen CT
John, Sr.: b 12-12-1735 d — m Jerusha White Sol MA
John, Jr.: b 9-11-1762 d 4-18-1834 m (1)Hannah Clapp (2)Mrs
  Sarah Fales Pvt MA ★
John, Sr.: b 1737 d 1788 m Sarah Webster Pvt NY
John, Jr.: b 4-4-1762 d 1840 m Rachel Wheeler Pvt NY
John Noyes: bpt 7-26-1732 d 1786 m Esther Parsons PS CT
Jonathan: b 5-9-1739 d 9-19-1777 m Abigail Flagg Capt CT
Jonathan: b 1722 d 1798 m Rebecca Davenport PS MA
Joseph: b 1738 d 7-4-1824 m Jerusha Marsh Cpl CT
Joseph: b 7-7-1750 d 7-4-1824 m Anna Drew Capt MA
Joseph: b 5-20-1759 d 5-25-1845 m Chloe Barrett Pvt MA ★
Peleg: b 1715 d 1799 m Susannah Sampson PS MA
Peleg, Jr.: b 5-6-1748 d 11-12-1829 m Elizabeth Bartlett BGen MA
Recompense: b 2-12-1730 d 8-8-1798 m (1)Hannah Pain
  (2)Abigail Lyon Pvt MA
Reuben: b 1753 d 7-19-1836 m Elizabeth Stevens Sgt CT
Roger: b 3-19-1756 d 5-17-1810 m Ann Prior 1 Lt CT
Samuel: b 10-25-1716 d 12-29-1798 m Millicent Cook PS CT
Samuel: b 1732 d p. 1790 m Thankful Dewey Pvt MA
Seneca: b 4-9-1753 d 8-29-1825 m Drewsbury Soule Lt MA ★
Theodore: b 10-5-1752 d 6-2-1808 m (1)Elizabeth Allen (2)Asenath
  Carter Clark Dr CT
Thomas: b 1716 d 12-21-1783 m Sarah Arnold Sgt CT
Thomas: b 1763 d p. 1832 m Harriet Seymour Pvt CT ★
Timothy: b 2-18-1745 d 9-22-1826 m Lucretia Marsh Sgt CT
Timothy: b 6-4-1727 d 1810 m (1)Mary Cowles (2)Hepsy Kilburn
  Pvt CT
Wait: b 10-7-1754 d 1840 m (1)Jerusha Robinson (2)Mrs Priscilla
  Stetson Weston Capt MA
Waite: b 10-23-1714 d 6-5-1799 m Abigail Bradford Pvt PS CS MA
Wm.: b 1742 d 1816 m Marcy Clark Cnt CT
Wm.: b 1762 d p. 1832 m Catherine — Pvt NC

WAGE,
Thomas: b 3-25-1759 d 1838 m Caroline Green Pvt MA

WAGENSAILER,
John: b 6-24-1739 d 9-29-1799 m Margaret Honnetter Pvt PA

WAGER,
Henry: b 1769 d 8-9-1840 m Latetia Isim Asmond Pvt NY
Leonard: b 1729 d 1796 m Barbara — Pvt NY
Philip: b 1748 d 5-14-1813 m (1)Maria Keller (2)Hannah Wirtz
  Pvt PA

WAGERMAN, (includes WAUGAMAN)
John: b 4-2-1768 d 12-28-1822 m Anna Elizabeth Hall Drm PA
Philip: b 8-5-1744 d 1809 m Mary Greisher Pvt PA

WAGG,
James: b 8-26-1754 d 3-31-1845 m (1)Dorcas Strought (2)Mrs
  Rhoda Gould Pvt MA ★

WAGGAMAN,
Henry: b a. 1755 d 5-26-1809 m Sarah Ennalls PS MD

WAGLE,
Abraham: b 12-12-1755 d 5-17-1846 m Christina Briney Pvt PA
Isaac: b 4- -1758 d 10-8-1835 m (1)Mary C Kepple (2)Barbara —
  Pvt PA

WAGLOM,
Abraham: bpt 8-8-1731 d p. 3-10-1804 m (1)Sary Liddell (2)Rachel
  Ann Winant (3)Rachel Johnson 1 Lt NY

**WAGNER, (includes WAGGERNER, WAGGONER &
  WAGONER)**
Adam: b 9-29-1754 d 1-27-1806 m Margaretta Michael Capt PA W★

Andrew: b 1743 d 5-27-1813 m Mary Chapman Maj VA
Christopher: b 1733 d 1801 m Elizabeth — Pvt PA
Daniel: b 1756 d 7-30-1838 m Mary Rowe Pvt PA
Edmon: b 1755 d 6-28-1842 m Nancy — Sol VA or NC (?)
Frederick: b 12-14-1758 d 7- -1846 m Anne Wrightmyer Pvt PA
George: b 1744 d p. 1781 m Susanne Mans 1 Lt NY
George: b 1-17-1752 d 3-18-1832 m Elizabeth Nellis Ens NY ★
George: b 1756 d 1827 m Mary Connor Ens NY
George: b 1721 d 4-8-1784 m Susanna Yeakle Lt PA
George Frederick: b 12-19-1752 d 2-10-1827 m (1)Katherine
  Koons (2)Margaretta Wagner Sgt PA
Isaac: b 9-11-1761 d 8-24-1838 m Emsey Holyfield Pvt SC ★
Jacob: b 2-19-1762 d 5-5-1833 m Salomma Bronner Pvt NY
Jacob: b 7-6-1725 d 11-30-1802 m Louisa Huber Pvt PA
Jacob, Sr.: b 10-4-1729 d 5-13-1800 m Catharine Magdalena
  Gerhard PS PA
Jacob, Jr.: b 12-12-1757 d 5-27-1833 m Eva Catharine Rentschler
  Pvt PA
Jacob: b 1743 d 12-4-1790 m Grace Menan Pvt PA
Johan Peter: b 1-18-1722 d 5-23-1813 m Barbara Elizabeth
  Dockstader PS Col NY
Johan Peter, Jr.: b 11-6-1750 d 8-1-1816 m Anna Bell Lt NY
John: b c. 1745 d 8- -1794 m Elizabeth Weir PS MD
John: b 1734 d 7-16-1808 m Mary Crouse Pvt MD
John: b 1758 d 12-15-1842 m (1)Elizabeth Leach (2)Sarah Minich
  Pvt MD ★
John: b 3- -1763 d 10-24-1850 m Johanna Burnet Pvt NY
John: b 1751 d 1831 m Susannah Lees 1 Lt PA
John: b 5-28-1760 d 9-4-1837 /8 m Sarah Gault Ens PA ★
John: b 5-11-1762 d 4-21-1834 m Catharine Moses Sgt PA
John: b 11-20-1764 d 7-11-1841 m (1) — Miller (2) — Leymaster
  (3) — Conrad Pvt PA
John M: b 1752 d 1834 m (2)Hannah Kyles PS Spy VA ★
Joseph: b 3-6-1759 d 8-15-1848 m (1)Catherine Abeel
  (2)Catharine Gibson Pvt NY ★
Labrecht: b c. 1739 d a. 9-15-1823 m Diana Huling Sgt PA
Martin: b 3-13-1760 d 1-8-1841 m Susan — Pvt PA
Melchior: b 1725 d 10-22-1784 m Gertrude Steyer PS PA
Michael: b c. 1748 d 2-28-1842 m Maria Sabold Pvt PA
Michael, Jr.: b 11-6-1752 d 2-21-1839 m (1)Barbara — (2)Sophia
  — PS MD
Peter: b 1730 d 1797/8 m Sinah McCarty Col VA
Philip: b 1720 d 1788 m (2)Catherine Leshorn 2 Lt PA
Rueben: b c. 1755 d 1818 m Catherine — Pvt VA
Thomas: b 11-15-1762 d 10-16-1842 m Mary Garnett Sgt VA
Tobias: b 1760 d p. 1848 m Priscilla — Pvt NY

WAGNON,
Thomas: b 1727 d 1810 m Frances Vaughn Sol GA

WAHAB, (includes WALKUP)
Francis: b 3-30-1754 d 3-3-1831 m Ruth Rice Pvt MA
Henderson: b 9-4-1735 d 10-30-1825 m Susan Congdon Pvt MA
James: b 1724 d 2-1-1798 m Margaret Pickins Capt NC SC
John: b a. 1758 d 1784 m Margaret Blair 2 Lt VA
John: b 12-6-1760 d 4-12-1823 m Rebecca — Tms SC
Joseph: b c. 1724 d 1787 m — Graham PS VA

WAIGHT,
Isaac: b 5-30-1746 d p. 1797 m Mrs Elizabeth Tucker Ens SC

WAINWRIGHT,
Cannon: b c. 1745 d p. 1820 m — Pvt MD
Thomas: b 2-8-1737 d 1785 m Rebecca Halsted Capt NJ
Vincent: b c. 1740 d 3-12-1782 m Elizabeth Williams MM NJ

WAIT, (includes WAITE, WAITT & WAYTE)
Aaron: bpt 8-20-1758 d 3-21-1821 m Elizabeth Mansfield Pvt MA
Asa: b 3-23-1747 d 7-7-1827 m (1)Submit Smith Pvt MA
Benjamin: b 12-8-1759 d 2-5-1814 m Zilpha Howard Pvt MA
Benjamin: b 9-3-1753 d 1830 m Ann Waldo Pvt NY
Benjamin: b 2-13-1736/7 d 6-28-1822 m Lois Gilbert Col VT
Beriah: b 4- -1756-8 d 11-6-1820 m (1)Asa Baker (2)Hannah
  Arnold CS Lt RI
Consider: b 3-25-1762 d 12-4-1829 m (1)Sarah Lull (2)Elizabeth
  Weaver Pvt MA
Daniel: b 3-21-1753 d 10-15-1829 m Phoebe Manchester Pvt MA
Elihu: b 8-15-1757 d 7-19-1828 m Rebecca Graves Pvt MA
Elisha: b 10-10-1725 d 6- -1816 m Martha Wells Pvt MA
Ezra: b c. 1755 d 7-2-1831 m Sarah Hutchinson Matr Pvt MA
Ezra, Sr.: b 1768 d 3- -1815 m Elizabeth Chandler Sol VT
Gardner: b 7-30-1759 d 8-10-1847 m Lucretia Filmore Pvt NY ★
George: b 10-16-1722 d 8- -1782 m Sarah Tripp Pvt NY
Gideon: b 3-3-1745 d 4-1-1808 m Lois Tripp Sgt RI
Jacob: b 2-24-1751 d 1-11-1826 m Abigail Trefry Pvt Smn MA
Jeduthan: b 6-7-1754 d 4-2-1829 m Naomi Sterling Pvt MA
Jenks: b 1756 d 2-21-1824 m Sarah Brown Smn Pvt RI ★
Joel: b 9-9-1754 d 7-4-1835 m Deborah Blood Pvt MA
John, Jr.: b 4-11-1745 d 1-9-1825 m Ruth Lynde Pvt MA
John: b 1750 d 3-16-1834 m Sally Buxton PS ME MA
John: b 7-10-1732 d 1-20-1820 m Hannah Jones CS PS MA
John: b 11-20-1730 d c. 1815 m Martha Wolcott Capt PS MA

WAIT, contd.
John, Sr.: b 12-3-1703 m 3-4-1776 m Submit Hastings MM MA
John, Jr.: b 11-25-1743 d 9-28-1801 m Mary Smith Pvt MA
John: b 12-29-1757 d 2-6-1841 m Lydia Chase Pvt NY
Jonathan: b 1-12-1764 d 1-12-1821 m Betsy Brown Sol MA
Joseph: b 11-14-1751 d 5-6-1807 m Sarah Dane Pvt MA
Joseph: b 3-1-1754 d 7-26-1819 m Hepzibath Sherman Pvt MA
Joseph: b 1732 d 9-28-1776 m Martha Stone LCol NH & Canada
Joseph: b 1-27-1759 d a. 10-1-1828 m Abigail Clark Pvt NH
Joshua: b 12-30-1749 d 8-28-1827 m Mary Burnap Cpl MA
Josiah 2d: b 4-25-1743 d 9-16-1776 m Mary — Sol MA
Nathaniel: b 12-21-1761 d 6-15-1834 m Mercy Jenks QMSgt MA
Nathaniel: b 1738 d 2-2-1815 m Anna Sweetser Pvt MA
Nathaniel: b 1-23-1758 d 1826 m Hannah Frye Pvt MA ★
Oliver: b 1-15-1742 d 3-14-1817 m Sybil — Ens NY
Payn: b 12-23-1745 d 1849 m Keziah Crandall Pvt RI ★
Peleg: b 10-22-1761 d 10-17-1847 m Mary Greene MM RI
Phineas: b 11-12-1736 d 11-29-1802 m (1)Sarah Pierce (2)Ede Fossett (3)Ruth — Cpl MA
Remick: b 4-10-1758 d 9-20-1830 m Susannah Matson Pvt CT
Reuben: b 10-23-1757 d 1831 m Mary (Waite) Pvt RI
Richard, Sr.: b 6-11-1711 d 12-29-1790 m (1)Elizabeth Marvin (2)Rebecca Higgins CS CT
Richard, Jr.: b 11-28-1739 d 6-16-1810 m (1)Lucy Griswold (2)Mary (Lay) Wood Maj CT
Richard: b 10-6-1745 d 12-8-1831 m Submit Thomas Lt VT
Samuel: bpt 10-21-1722 d a. 1808 m Mrs Sarah Day Pvt MA
Stephen: b 1734 d 1782 m (1)Abigail Wheeler (2)Mary — CS PS ME
Thaddeus: b 5-26-1755 d 4-3-1823 m Sally Moss Pvt MA
Thomas: b 10-6-1749 d 8-13-1828 m (1)Lydia Hitchens (2)Phebe Parker Pvt MA
Thomas: b 11-2-1757 d 8-14-1822 m Hannah Gould Pvt MA
Wm., Sr.: b 9-24-1725 d 1807 m Ruth Lovell Pvt MA
Wm., Jr.: b 1-8-1754 d 5-29-1840 m Sarah Cummings Cpl MA ★
Wm.: b c. 1738 d p. 1790 m (1)Mary — (2)Sarah Ingraham Pvt CS MA
Wm.: b 1-9-1730 d 3-20-1826 m Mary Nickols Pvt NY
Wm.: b 1731 d 3-20-1826 m Mary — Pvt VT
Yelverton: b 9-14-1743 d 2-29-1816 m (1)Margaret Whitford (2)Zipporah Colvin Maj RI W★

WAKEFIELD,
Aaron: b 2-6-1744 d 1826 m Olive Wight Pvt MA
Benjamin: b — d — m Elinor Littlefield Sgt MA
David: b — d p. 1794 m Mary — PS PA
Ebenezer: b 11-15-1753 d 4-28-1835 m Abigail Damon Sgt MA ★
Ezekiel: b 11- -1753 d 7-7-1837 m Hannah Larrabee Sgt MA
Henry: b 1752 d 11-13-1850 m (1)Elizabeth Alexander (2)Mary — Pvt NC ★
Isaiah: b 1-1-1749/50 d 1-16-1808/9 m Eunice Burdon MM MA W★
John: b 1727 d 1793 m Martha — Lt PA
John: b 11-3-1757 d 1812 m Elizabeth Alexander Lt PA
Jonathan: b 8-16-1736 d 3-9-1776 m Anne Wheeler Pvt MA
Joseph: b 5-9-1752 d 6- -1827 m Relief Kendall Pvt NH
Pattishall: b 3-6-1746 d 12-5-1829 m (1)Margaret Phelps (2)Sarah Barnard Pvt CT
Peter: b 8-7-1764 d 1- -1847 m Keziah Burns Pvt NH ★
Samuel: b 1737 d p. 1810 m (1)Ruth Burbank (2)Mrs Small Sgt MA
Samuel: b 5-11-1745 d 1820 m Mary Davenport Pvt MA
Samuel: b 1753 d 4-13-1840 m (1)Ollive — (2)Elizabeth Wheat Pvt MA ★
Thomas, Sr.: b 8-5-1727 d 9- -1791 m Dorcas Pratt PS NH
Thomas, Jr.: b 1-12-1751 d 1-11-1839 m Elizabeth Hardy PS NH
Thomas: b 10-5-1762 d 9-17-1846 m (1)Lucy Johnson (2)Nancy Johnson (3)Jemima Griffin Pvt NC ★
Thomas: b 10-2-1757 d 11-20-1844 m Elizabeth Morton Pvt PA
Timothy: b 2-15-1756 d 4-19-1849 m (1)Susanna Bancroft (2)Hannah B Emerson MM Pvt MA ★
Wm.: b — d p. 1790 m (1)Mary Holmes (2)Dorcas Hayward (3)Kesia — PS NH

WAKELEY, (includes WAKELEE & WAKELY)
Abel: bpt 10-7-1759 d 4-13-1850 m Annis Hurd Pvt CT
David: b 10-4-1739 d 5-18-1822 m (1)Mary Burton (2)Naomi Hawley Ens CT
David: b 1754 d 10-1-1821 m Mary Parker Wgn CT ★
Wm.: b 1738 d a. 9-6-1819 m Jane Elliott PS PA

WAKEMAN,
Andrew: b 12-22-1745 d 8-22-1821 m (1)Hannah Allen (2)Eunice Smedley Capt CT
David: b 1-14-1730 d — m Mary Jennings Pvt CT
Ebenezer: b 7-20-1737 d 3-31-1823 m (1)Elizabeth Webb (2)Sarah Shelton MM CT
Gershom: b 11-8-1731 d 5-30-1781 m (1)Elizabeth Down (2)Huldah Williams Pvt CT
Gideon: b 11-23-1761 d 4- -1853 m Clara Stratton Pvt CT
Jabez: b 5-10-1762 d c. 1836 m Clarissa Banks Pvt CT
Jeremiah: b 4-16-1856 d 1801 m Phebe Hendricks Pvt CT
Jesup: b 9-25-1748 d 1-2-1780 m Amelia Banks PS CT
John: b 1-29-1731 d 7-24-1809 m Esther Bradley Pvt CT
Joseph: b 2-25-1740 d 9-2-1784 m (1)Rebecca Adams (2) — Kent PS CT

Samuel: bpt 3-10-1734 d 8-9-1809 m Mabel Burr PS CT
Seth: b 4-12-1766 d 8-31-1835 m Mary Stratton Pvt CT ★
Squier: b 6-29-1738 d p. 1790 m Dammarais Bradley Cpl CT
Stephen, Sr.: b 9-19-1744 d 1789 m Mary Adams Capt CT
Stephen, Jr.: b 9-19-1761 d 9-16-1852 m Sarah Whitehead Pvt CT ★
Timothy: b 12-2-1749 d 3-28-1822 m Anna Sherwood Pvt CT
Wm.: b 4-1-1730 d 3-22-1802 m Sarah Hill Ens CT

WAKLEE,
John: b 1-15-1759 d 2-4-1838 m Elisabeth Cummings Pvt CT ★

WALBORN,
Martin: b 4-15-1733 d 2-3-1816 m Maria Margaret Ley Sol PA
Peter: b 2-20-1759 d 3-27-1832 m Catherine Kehler Pvt PA

WALBRIDGE, (includes WALLBRIDGE)
Ames: b 12-15-1727 d 10-24-1793 m Margaret — Maj MA CT
Asa: b 10-12-1766 d 1-15-1850 m Relief Dickenson Pvt VT
Ebenezer: b 12-20-1738 d 10-3-1819 m Elizabeth Stebbins Col PS VT
Eleazer: b 1748 d 10-31-1815 m Abigail Washburn Cpl CT
Gustavus: b 10-4-1755 d 9-23-1828 m Anna Sanford Pvt CT
Henry: b 1-23-1727 d 9-17-1809 m Anna Safford Pvt CS VT
Henry: b 11-10-1738 d 1818 m Martha Read Sgt MA
John, Jr.: b 4-13-1740 d 1823 m Mary — Pvt CT
Joshua: b 10-4-1758 d 3-8-1846 m Priscilla Blackmer Sgt CT ★
Silas, Sr.: b 6-27-1759 d 5-11-1840 m Rhoda Gun Sol VT
Solomon: b 1-8-1755 d 9-15-1814 m Mary Holmes Pvt VT

WALDEMEYER, (includes WALTEMYER)
David: b c. 1730 d 5-20-1790 m Eve — Pvt PA
George: b c. 1736 d c. 1810 m Elizabeth — Pvt PA
Ludwig: b c. 1700 d 1-10-1783 m (2)Anna Margaretta — Grd PA

WALDEN,
Ambrose: b 1-3-1752 d 3-18-1840 m Elizabeth Taylor Lt VA
Ebenezer: b 3-8-1739 d 10-1-1822 m Elizabeth Watson Drm MA
Elijah: b 1761 d 2-17-1833 m Mary Phillips Pvt VA ★
Jacob: b 5-8-1751 d 12-24-1831 m Abby Lowd Mrnr NH ★
John: b 8-24-1754 d 4-12-1824 m Lydia Palmer Pvt CT
John: b c. 1756 d 12-22-1835 m Mary Collins Pvt VA ★
John: b 1763 d 1832 m Lily Ann Gatewood Sgt VA ★
John: b 1762 d 4-25-1848 m Elizabeth Pitts Pvt VA ★
Joseph: b 1760 d 8-4-1831 m Nancy — Pvt VA
Nathan, Jr.: b 1-14-1762 d 5-23-1855 m Mercy Eggleston Pvt MA ★
Richard, Sr.: b c. 1730 d 1790 m Candace Hubbard PS VA
Richard: b c. 1750 d 1792 m Patty Davenport Ens VA
Wm., Jr.: b 9-13-1762 d p. 5-13-1804 m Elizabeth McFall Pvt CT
Zachariah: b c. 1760 d p. 1834 m Martha Winfree Cpl VA

WALDHAUER, (includes WALTHOUR)
Andrew: b — d 1824 m (1)Ann Hophmire (2)Mrs Elizabeth Johnson Pvt GA
Christopher: b c. 1728 d 1802 m Barbara Koch Pvt PS PA
Jacob Casper: b a. 1734 d 1803/4 m (1)Agnes Ziegler (2)Mary Dobbins PS Capt GA
Michael: b 1752 d 6-10-1810 m Amy Hawk Pvt PA

WALDO,
Beulah: b 1-16-1749 d 3-31-1833 m Amy Benjamin Sgt VT
Daniel: b 1-30-1744 d 12-18-1825 m Hannah Carlton Pvt PS NH
David: b 9-26-1764 d 8-10-1854 m (1)Catherine Weatherbee (2)Saloma Skiner Pvt NY ★
Edward: b 5-14-1742 d 12-22-1829 m Jerusha Thompson Lt NH
Gamaliel: b 8-28-1755 d 4-29-1829 m Mrs Mary (Campbell) Gardner Pvt PS VT
Jesse: b 9-6-1736 d 2-28-1823 m (1)Bridget Thomson (2)Hannah Welsh Lt CT
Jesse, Jr.: b 2-17-1761 d 11-22-1826 m Martha Hovey Pvt CT
John: b 4-22-1750 d 5-9-1786 m Lucy Lyman Dr CT
John: b 10-18-1728 d 8-23-1814 m Jemima Abbott PS Pvt NY
John J: b 2-16-1762 d 12-10-1840 m Peace Bull Pvt NY
Johnathan: b 3-22-1728 d 12-21-1788 m (1)Abigail Whittmore (2)Mrs Johannah Mighiel PS CT
Jonathan, Sr.: b 8-17-1738 d 7-17-1821 m Ann Palmer Pvt NY
Jonathan, Jr.: b 4-11-1763 d 2-5-1833 m (1)Lucy Mattison (2)Diadama (Porter) Pvt NY ★
Joseph: b 10-5-1755 d 2-13-1840 m Ann Bliss Pvt Dr MA ★
Samuel: b 8-28-1747 d 2-14-1810 m Molly Putnam CS CT
Samuel: b 9-18-1731 d 9-10-1793 m Hannah Waters PS NY
Zachariah: b 2-1-1734 d 2-8-1811 m (1)Elizabeth Wight (2)Cynthia Parke Pvt CT
Zachariah: b 12-26-1764 d 8-3-1818 m Abigail Corbin Pvt CT W★
Zacheus, Jr.: b 11-20-1756 d 10-3-1834 m Esther Stevens Sgt CT

WALDRON,
Aaron: b 8-1-1749 d 12-9-1820 m Hannah Boodey PS NH
Abraham: b 6-27-1737 d 1810 m Sarah Waldron Pvt MA
Adolph: b 3-3-1729 d 1802 m Catherine Phoenix Capt NJ
Benjamin: b 2-15-1759 d p. 1799 m Maria Brinkerhoff Pvt NY
Cornelius: bpt 4-13-1740 d p. 1789 m Sarah Vantine Pvt NJ
Cornelius: b 6-5-1743 d p. 1829 m Alida Goewey Sol NY

Daniel: b 9-13-1758 d 4-1-1832 m Catherine Covenhoven PS NY
David: b 9-11-1754 d 1812 m (2)Fanny Morgan Pvt NY
Gerret: b 5-31-1738 d 1829 m Catherine Vandenberg Pvt NY
Isaac, Jr.: b 6-18-1746 d 2-6-1795 m Sarah Currier Sol NH
Isaac: b 3-16-1747 d 5-3-1841 m (1)Sarah Boody (2)Tirzah Noble PS NH
Jacob: b 3-2-1743 d p. 1780 m Sarah Abbott Lt NH
James: b 9-14-1737 d 12-26-1828 m Elizabeth Holland Capt NY
Jerome: b 11-1-1760 d 1-15-1848 m Elizabeth Van Fleet Sgt NJ
Johannes: b 1721 d 1813 m Wyntie Terhune Pvt NY
John: b 1740 d 8-31-1828 m (1)Joanna Shapherd (2)Polly Winn (3)Margaret (Frost) Wentworth (4)Mrs Pamelia Millen Prentiss Col NH
John: b 12-13-1760 d 7-24-1842 m Altia Onderdonk Lt NY
John: b 2-13-1760 d 9-29-1818 m Elizabeth Howland Pvt RI
Joseph: b 2-7-1753 d 6-19-1822 m Rhoba Pierce Pvt MA
Joseph: b 1765 d 1810 m Miriam Blaisdell Pvt NH
Nathaniel: b 6-10-1756 d 6- -1829 m Lydia Salisbury Pvt RI
Peter: b 1720 d p. 1785 m (1)Neeltie Lansing (2)Antje Ouderkerk Pvt NY
Peter: b 9-5-1723 d 1806 m Maria Ackerman Pvt NY
Richard: b 1749 d 1811 m Elizabeth Clements Pvt NH
Robert: b 4-21-1762 d 1-2-1838 m Sarah Barrows Pvt MA
Samuel V.: b 8-19-1752 d 1-24-1849 m Magdalena Simpson Pvt NJ
Samuel: b 5-10-1723 d 1806 m Lydia Salsbury Pvt MA
Thomas: b 1-16-1762 d 9-11-1821 m Lucretia Gladding Pvt RI
Thomas Westbrook: b 7-26-1721 d 4-3-1785 m Constance Davis CS NH
Wm.: b 6-8-1756 d 9-18-1793 m Susannah Ham Pvt NH
Wm.: b 3-3-1746 d 3-22-1832 m Margarita VanDerwerken Ens NY
Wm.: b 10-22-1752 d 4-8-1824 m Mary Waldron Pvt NY

WALDROUP,
James: b 2-8-1751 d 12-3-1846 m Mary Morrison Pvt VA ★

WALDSCHMIDT,
Johannes: b 8-6-1724 d 9-14-1786 m Marie Elizabeth Grube PS PA

WALDSMITH,
Christian: b 3-23-1755 d 3-30-1814 m (1)Catherine Bollender (2)Magdalena Kern Custard Pvt PA

WALES,
Benjamin: b — d 1788 m Susanna — Capt MD
Benjamin: b 1-2-1727 d 1789 m Sarah Howard PS CS MD
Benjamin: b 2-14-1756 d c. 1810-12 m Anne Handy PS MD
Benjamin: b 6-5-1759 d 1837 m Susanna Ludden Pvt MA
Eleazer: b 1748 d 1803 m Sara — Lt CT
Eleazer: b 7-30-1755 d 8-21-1842 m (1)Deidameia Chaffee (2)Mary Whiting Pvt CT
Eliel: b 6-29-1761 d 3-24-1821 m Anne EdgertonSol CT ★
Elijah: b 1-28-1748 d 3-2-1826 m Rachel Needham Sol PS CT
Elisha: b 3-10-1728 d 4-6-1788 m Mary Abbe PS CT
Elisha: b 5-14-1753 d 1811 m Lydia Thayer Fif MA
Ephraim: b 5-9-1746 d 4-7-1805 m Mary Beale Dr MM PS MA
Jacob: b 2-19-1747 d 2-2-1821 m Phoebe Hayward Capt MA ★
John: b 3-17-1757 d p. 1811 m Jerusha Derby Pvt CT
Jonathan: b 9-23-1756 d 2-23-1839 m Beulah Clark Sgt MA ★
Joshua: b 2-21-1752 d 1-25-1829 m Elizabeth Porter Cpl MA
Nathaniel, Sr.: b 5-23-1694 d 11-5-1782 m (1)Mercy West (2)Prudence Denison PS CT
Nathaniel, Jr.: b 6-1-1733 d 11-13-1810 m Grace Brewster Capt CT
Nathaniel, Sr.: b 4-11-1717 d 6-26-1790 m (1)Anna Wild (2)Mrs Ann (Waldo) Fitch Pvt PS MA
Nathaniel, Jr.: b 2-8-1757 d 12-26-1825 m Mary Hayden Pvt MA W★
Oliver: b 2-23-1744 d 3-23-1816 m (1)Elizabeth Lawrence (2)Martha Hyde Pvt PS CT
Roger: b 2-7-1759 d 12-18-1806 m Esther Brewster Pvt CT
Solomon: b 11-19-1729 d 3-20-1805 m (1)Lucy Strong (2)Dorothy Perrin Capt CT
Timothy: b 12-17-1723 d 4-8-1777 m Hannah Davenport Pvt MA
Wm.: b 3-1-1762 d 4-15-1813 m Sarah Tinker Mil CT
Wm.: b 8-23-1759 d 3-22-1838 m Mary Noyes Pvt MA

WALFORD,
John: b 1763 d 2-20-1814 m Lucy Pearce Pvt RI

WALKE,
Anthony: b 1-3-1726 d 10-17-1779 m (1)Jane Randolph (2)Mary Moseley PS VA

WALKER,
Aaron: b 10-19-1728 d 10-19-1775 m (1)Esther Carpenter (2)Hulda Whitaker Lt MA
Aaron Forman: b 3-29-1759 d 12-29-1849 m Mary Hubbard Drm NJ
Abel: b 5-11-1736 d 2-13-1819 m (1)Lois Read (2)Bathsheba Read Pvt MA
Abel: b 4-20-1734 d 3-11-1815 m Elizabeth (Parker) Graves LCol NH
Abraham: b 1753 d 6-1-1834 m (1)Sarah Gray (2)Nancy — Pvt RI ★
Adam: b a. 1759 d p. 1796 m Priscilla Terry Pvt SC

Alexander: b c. 1720 d p. 9- -1777 m (1)Sarah — (2)Peggy Kennedy PS NH
Alexander: b 5-19-1716 d 1784-85 m Jane Hammer PS VA
Alexander: b 1725-30 d p. 8-6-1799 m Frances Scott Pvt SC
Alexander: b 1744 d 8-1-1799 m Eleanor White Lt SC W★
Alexander: b 1- -1761 d 1809 m Esther Gaston Pvt SC
Alexander: b c. 1720 d 1786 m Jean — Lt VA
Alexander: b 1718 d a. 3-25-1775 m (2)Elizabeth — Sol VA
Allen: b 2-14-1758 d 1817 m Esther McCrory Sgt NC
Andrew: b 3-18-1742 d 11-2-1826 m Damaris Cross Pvt MA
Andrew: b 12-5-1756 d 9-20-1845 m Elizabeth Moore Capt NC ★
Andrew: b 1754 d 1823 m Sarah Donaldson Pvt PA
Andrew: b c. 1764 d 1837 m Jane — Pvt PA
Asa: b 3-19-1737 d 12-27-1800 m Sarah Burbank Pvt MA
Asa: b a. 1760 d p. 1790 m (1)Prudence — (2)Lydia Haskell Pvt MA
Asa: b 3-28-1752 d 10-5-1809 m Hannah Dudley Pvt MA
Azariah: b 6-24-1722 d 1798 m Abigail Seaver Sgt MA
Benjamin: b 10- -1758 d 8-5-1847 m (1)Ann Crawford (2)Mary Criswell Sgt MD ★
Benjamin: b 1742 d 8-15-1775 m Abiel Abbott Capt MA
Benjamin: b 8-14-1751 d 5-14-1822 m (1)Margaret Rawson (2)Eunice (Willard) Carvl Lt MA
Benjamin: b 10-26-1757 d 9-1-1821 m Sophia Van Horn Pvt PA W★
Benjamin: b 11-25-1762 d 12-1-1843 m Margaret Cunningham Pvt PA
Bruce: b 5-17-1760 d 7-27-1840 m Mehitable Currier Pvt NH ★
Buckley: b a. 1742 d a. 6- -1812 m Anne — PS MA
Calvin: b 1-5-1754 d 3-25-1835 m Phebe Cole Sol RI
Catherine: b — d 1786 m James Walker PS VA
Charles: b c. 1757 d p. 1790 m Mrs Sarah Wilson Ryon Pvt MD
Charles: b 11-9-1744 d 11-15-1825 m Ann Cradock PS MD
Charles: b 8-15-1759 d 6-20-1843 m Eunice Berry Sgt MA ★
Charles: b a. 1758 d p. 1778 m — Pvt MA
Charles: b 9-28-1760 d 1-3-1835 m (1)Ann Johns (2)Frances Roper Pvt VA ★
Christopher: b 1757 d 5-6-1841 m Patience Foster Pvt MD
Daniel: b 1762 d 7-3-1839 m Hannah Pearson Pvt GA
Daniel: b 11-30-1759 d 4-20-1850 m Sybil Roper Sgt MA
Daniel: b 1761 d 3-21-1834 m Martha Kilgore Sol NC
David: b 1762 d 7-29-1826 m Eunice Woodruff Pvt CT
David: b 5-24-1717 d 1781 m (1)Mary Wilmarth (2)Sarah Richmond PS MA
David: b 7-20-1752 d 9-7-1831 m Annie Banks Pvt PA
David: b 12-11-1752 d 8-16-1840 m Johanna — 1Lt VA
David: b 3-6-1731 d 1792 m Peletiah Jones Lt VA
Ebenezer: b 1738 d 1801 m Hannah Farmer Pvt CT
Ebenezer: b 10-17-1731 d — m Sarah — Sgt MA
Ebenezer: b 10-13-1749 d 4-20-1820 m Elizabeth Carpenter Cpl MA
Ebenezer: b 11-2-1732 d p. 1786 m Hannah Woodward Pvt MA
Ebenezer: b 12-9-1716 d 9- -1799 m (1)Bethiah Brown (2)Mrs — PS MA
Ebenezer, Jr.: b 10-30-1759 d 6-1-1816 m Molly Wood Pvt MA
Edmund, Jr.: b c. 1746 d p. 1793 m Mary Williamson Capt VA
Edward: b 10-10-1739 d 6-10-1802 m Abigail Lovell Lt PS MA
Edward: b 1-3-1754 d 9-25-1821 m Abigail Reed Pvt MA
Edward: b 1761 d 11-5-1832 m Susan Scribner Pvt MA ★
Edward: b 1745 d 1799 m Nancy Larned OrdlSgt VA SC
Edward: b 1755 d 8-26-1838 m Jane Horne Pvt NC ★
Edward: b 1758 d p. 8-9-1781 m Priscilla — Capt & PS VA
Eleakin: b 5-8-1740 d 12-28-1812 m Eunice Nicholas PS CT
Eleanor: b 1759 d 10-10-1839 m Alexander Walker PS SC
Eleazer: b 6-22-1745 d 9-23-1817 m Caty Carpenter MM MA
Eliakim: b 3-23-1753 d 4-14-1842 m Ruth Annis Sgt MA ★
Elijah: b 11-15-1730 d 8-31-1804 m Hannah Piggsley Capt MA
Elijah: b c. 1762 d a. 4-26-1833 m Dorcus — Sol SC
Elisha: b c. 1767 d 1802 m Elizabeth Bowers Pvt GA
Elnathan, Sr.: b 1706 d 6-6-1775 m (1)Hannah Crossman (2)Bethiah Tisdale (3)Mrs Phoebe King PS MA
Elnathan, Jr.: b 2-9-1727/8 d 11- -1815 m (1)Hannah Works (2)Hannah Bugbee PS CT
Enos: b 12-9-1730 d 5-3-1789 m Patience Peck MM MA
Ephraim: b 3-8-1735 d 3-29-1815 m Priscilla Rawson PS MA
Esther Gaston: b 1761 d 1809 m Alexander Walker PS SC
Ezekiel: b 1743 d 3-9-1797 m Abigail Coolidge Pvt MA
Ezekiel: b 2-22-1745 d 2-24-1805 m Abigail Maxon Sgt NH
Felix: b 7-19-1753 d 1828 m Isabella Henry CS NC
George, Jr.: b 11-14-1763 d 12-4-1830 m Betsy (Walker) Sol GA
George: b 9-7-1761 d 10-13-1844 m Thankful Burt Pvt MA ★
George: b 11-20-1745 d 10- -1833 m Eleanor Hicks Capt NC ★
George: b 1740 d 4-16-1812 m (1)Lydia — (2)Mary Onstine Pvt PS PA
George: b c. 1753 d 12-29-1839 m Margaret Heefner Pvt PS PA
George: b c. 1750 d 1800 m Priscilla — Col VA
George Reynolds: b 4-3-1760 d 3-4-1822 m (1)Judith Haynes (2)Lucy West Lt VA
Gideon: b 10-8-1737 d 5-14-1800 m Mrs Hannah (Billings) Olds Lt MA
Gideon: b — d 1-1-1779 m Mary Alvord Sgt MA
Gideon: b 2-25-1756 d 9-9-1825 m Mary Carrial Pvt MA
Gideon: b 11-20-1738 d 11-2-1793 m Rachel Foster Ens VT
Gordon: b c. 1762 d p. 1818 m Dorcas Walker Pvt MA ★
Henry: b 1-25-1742 d 1-4-1792 m Martha Bolling Eppes Col VA

WALKER, contd.

Henry: b 1735 d 1791 m Mary — Pvt VA
Henry: b c. 1760 d 1803 m Martha Woods Pvt VA
Hezekiah: b 4-18-1746 d 2-18-1831 m Jerusha Ames Pvt CT
Hezekiah: b 2-14-1750 d 12-13-1837 m Lucy Raymond Pvt MA
Hezekiah: b 1760 d 1845 (1)Polly Rhodes (2)Deborah Gleason Pvt MA
Hugh: b c. 1740 d 11-27-1800 m (1)Mary Thurston (2)Mrs Catherine (Montague) Morgan PS VA
Ichabod: b 12-23-1749 d 3-21-1832 m (1)Abigail Logia (2)Mrs Penelope Ring Pvt VT
Isaac, Sr.: b 1707 d 1781 m Mary Morgan PS GA
Isaac, Jr.: b c. 1730 d c. 1810 m Ida Wolf Pvt & PS GA
Isaac: b 1721 d 1807 m Elizabeth Stuart 1Lt PS MD
Isaac: b 6-17-1742 d 11-21-1807 m Jerusha Garfield Pvt MA
Isaac, Sr.: b 7-12-1707 d 1790 m Sarah Breed PS NH
Isaac, Jr.: b 10-26-1741 d c. 1800 m Sarah — Pvt NH
Isaac: b 2-13-1763 d p. 1790 m Patience Bell Sol NY
Isaac: b 1746 d 1812 m Mrs Mary Richardson Sol PA
Isaac: b 9-21-1754 d 11-3-1822 m (1)Mary Pugh (2)Mrs Sarah Conard PS VA
Jacob: b 1742 d 5-24-1783 m Elizabeth — 2Lt PA
James, Sr.: b 7- -1715 d 6-9-1796 m Jerusha Nichols Sol CT
James: b 11-2-1753 d 11-1-1828 m Mary Benjamin Sol CT
James: b 1762 d 1849 m Percy Walker Sol CT
James: b 1744 d 6-30-1796 m Ann — Pvt DE
James: b 1760 d 1852 m — Pvt GA
James: b 1753 d 6-24-1849 m Charity Smith Sol GA
James: b 11-15-1732 d 11-21-1806 m (1)Esther Shumway (2)Mrs Anna Saxton Lt MA
James: b 1-19-1721 d 1812 m Abagail Wood Pvt MA
James: b 11-23-1759 d 6-29-1849 m Deborah Holmes Pvt MA ★
James: b 1760 d 2-17-1837 m (1)Hannah Woodbury (2)Lucinda Boman Pvt MA ★
James: b 1-1-1752 d 6-23-1841 m Sarah Shapley Pvt NY NH ★
James, Sr.: b c. 1711 d 1786 m Esther Goffe PS NH
James, Jr.: b 10-6-1758 d 9-3-1822 m Mary Wallace Pvt NH
James: b 1759 d 1849 m Deborah Thomas Cpl NY
James: b c. 1760 d p. 7-1-1825 m Rachel White Pvt NC
James: b 2-20-1754 d 7-26-1825 m Isabella McCormick Wgm QM PA
James, Jr.: b 1757 d 1832 m Mrs Editha Smith Pvt PA
James, Sr.: b a. 1730 d 1815 m Catherine — Pvt PA
James: b 5-21-1731 d 1-3-1791 m — Adams Ens VT
James: b c. 1740 d a. 1783 m Katherine — PS VA
James: b 4-5-1726 d 12-18-1801 m Sarah Jane Ware PS VA
James: b 6-29-1751 d 4-12-1800 m Margaret Gray PS VA
James Reuben: b 1757 d 1836 m Sarah McHerd Pvt NC
Jedediah: b 8-25-1762 d 1-19-1841 m (1)Polly Goss (2)Olive Squire Pvt MA
Jeremiah: b 1732 d 8-20-1811 m Elizabeth Small Sgt MA
Jesse: b 6-26-1748 d 2-19-1839 m (1)Fannie — (2)Elizabeth — Pvt NC ★
Jesse: b 2- -1760 d 6-3-1832 m Sarah Emerson Pvt NH
Joel: b 1-28-1745 d 8-25-1822 m (1)Rhoda Taft (2)Eunice Rogers Sgt MA
Joel: b 1756 d p. 1800 m Holly Berry Persons Sol NC
Joel: b 3-1-1764 d 5- -1834 m Margaret A. Armstrong Pvt VA
John: b 11-10-1743 d 11-11-1776 m Mary Ann Gilborn Pvt CT
John: b 9- -1754/5 d 10-14-1844 m Nancy Stewart Pvt GA W★
John: b 1739 d 5-2-1816 m Elizabeth Burbank 2Lt MA
John: b 6-9-1759 d c. 1790 m Olive Johnson Sol MA
John: b 10-3-1721 d 4-22-1809 m Molly Bosworth Sgt MA
John: b 6-5-1749 d 5-7-1809 m Mary Gibbs Sgt MA W★
John, Jr.: b 8-31-1737 d 3-12-1782 m Ruth Childs Pvt MA
John: b 2-28-1743 d 12-17-1809 m Deborah Rickard Pvt MA
John: b 5-4-1750 d 7-21-1827 m Hannah Emerson Cpl NH ★
John: b 1755 d 3-17-1834 m Jemima Downer Pvt NY ★
John: b 1733 d — m Hannah Brower Pvt NY
John: b 1736 d 12-2-1809 m Nancy Ashford LCol NC
John: b c. 1730 d 1795 m Ann — Capt NC
John: b c. 1750 d 1820 m Ursula Covington Sol NC
John: b 12- -1755 d 1841/42 m — Sol NC ★
John: b 1-15-1728 d 1-25-1796 m Elizabeth Watson PS NC
John, Sr.: b 1727 d 10-24-1802 m (1)Jane — (2)Martha (Smyth) Lemant PS NC
John: b — d a. 11-30-1811 m — PS PA
John: b 1750 d 8-6-1837 m Mary — Pvt PA ★
John: b 2-20-1754 d 7-26-1825 m Isabella McCormick Pvt QM PA
John: b c. 1747 d 1806 m Eva Christina — Pvt PA
John: b 4- -1766 d 5-17-1853 m Mary Walker Pvt PA ★
John, Sr.: b 1706 d 8-13-1782 m (1)Sarah Wilson (2)Jane Wilson PS PA
John, Jr.: b c. 1715 d p. 2-15-1796 m Elizabeth Banfield Capt VA
John, Jr.: b 1740 d 6- -1796 m Elizabeth Stewart Ens VA
John: b 10-5-1755 d 2-2-1830 m Margaret Paul Pvt VA ★
John: b 2-13-1744 d 12-2-1809 m Elizabeth Moore ADC VA
John: b 11-1-1747 d 1-16-1814 m (1)Margaret Hudson (2)Margaret Kelso Pvt VA
John: b c. 1755 d 6-13-1835 m Susannah Givens Pvt VA
John: b 10-1-1764 d 9-3-1841 m Rachel Cochran Pvt VA ★
John: b 12-7-1766 d 10-10-1826 m Martha Smith Pvt VA
John: b a. 1757 d a. 2- -1796 m Mary — CS VA

John H.: b 12-25-1763 d 6-19-1836 m (1) — Loftin (2)Elizabeth Johns (3)Mariah Leverett Pvt VA ★
Jonas: b 1750 d 2-13-1817 m Sarah Davis Ens VT
Jonathan: b 7-3-1754 d 1-19-1832 m Betsey Weymouth Pvt MA
Jonathan, Jr.: b c. 1760 d p. 1805 m Anna Pierce Pvt MA
Jonathan, Sr.: b 7-19-1719 d 1808 m (1)Elizabeth Hathaway (2)Deborah Burrel Pvt MA
Jonathan Hoge: b 1756 d 1- -1824 m Lucretia Duncan Pvt PA
Joseph: b 2-13-1731 d 6- -1816 m — Capt CT
Joseph: b 12-29-1761 d 9-12-1843 m Sela Cooley Cpl CT ★
Joseph: b 11-3-1761 d 2-25-1818 m Elizabeth Goold PS ME
Joseph: b 12-26-1760 d 1-9-1852 m Mehitable Gibbs Pvt MA ★
Joseph: b 8- -1754 d 6-25-1826 m Asenath Mills Pvt MA ★
Joseph: b 8-29-1742 d 10- -1814 m Mary — Capt NC
Joseph: b 1740 d 9-12-1822 m Mary — Pvt PA
Joseph: b 1742 d 5- -1832 m (1)Rebecca — (2)Jane Alexander Capt PA
Joseph: b 1744 d 1790 m Rachel Johnson Pvt PA
Joseph: b 5-25-1731 d 11-1-1818 m (1)Sarah Thomas (2)Mrs Jane Rankin PS PA
Joseph: b 1-5-1738/9 d 1- -1789 m Lydia Shippee Pvt RI
Joseph: b 7-15-1722 d 1806 m (1)Nancy McClung (2)Grizelda McCrosky Pvt CS VA
Joseph: b c. 1748 d p. 1815 m Jane Moore PS VA
Joshua, Sr.: b 10-5-1728 d 10-2-1798 m Mary Proctor Capt MA
Joshua, Jr.: b 11-24-1751 d 1825 m (1)Mary Whittemore (2)Hannah Wyman Sgt MA
Josiah: b 2-11-1741 d 1-22-1812 m Jerusha Bardwell PS Cpl MA
Learned: b 1760 d 10-10-1834 m Sally Corey Pvt MA ★
Lemuel: b 1769 d 1845 m (1)Hannah Allen (2)Sophia Cleaves Pvt Mrnr MA ★
Lewis: b 12-13-1745 d 5-21-1813 m Hannah Cooper Lt MA
Marshall: b 6-20-1757 d 2- -1816 m Hannah Dunbar Pvt MA
Matthew: b 9-12-1727 d 3-11-1821 m (1)Milly Bowen (2)Abigail Nichols (3)Lydia Woodward Pvt CT
Merry: b 4-21-1760 d 1811 m Elizabeth Kirtley Lt VA
Micah: b 1-22-1727 d 2-10-1823 m (1)Buelah Wooster (2)Elizabeth Stinchfield 1Lt Capt MA
Mordecai: b 8-17-1742 d 4-1-1830 m Rachel Barrett PS VA
Moses: b 10-5-1726 d 5-3-1806 m (1)Sarah Bowen (2)Deliverance (Carpenter) Read (3)Jemima Bishop Lt MA
Moses: b 1761 d 11-8-1822 m (1)Tabitha Barton (2)Esther Smith Pvt MA
Moses: b a. 1763 d p. 1790 m — English Pvt NC
Nathan: b 1756 d 12-28-1842 m (1)Nancy Baggerly (2)Elizabeth Thomas Sol MD
Nathan: b 5-4-1744 d 1823 m Catherine Johnson Pvt MA
Nathaniel, Sr.: b 2-8-1708 d 2-8-1783 m Submit Brewer PS MA
Nathaniel, Jr.: b 2-12-1734/5 d 6-15-1815 m Basinith Hament Lt MA
Nathaniel: b 12-19-1748 d 3-16-1834 m Dorothy Bailey Pvt MA
Nathaniel: b 1-30-1757 d 6-13-1843 m Abigail Charles Sol NH
Nathaniel: b c. 1728 d 1778 m Hannah — Pvt PA
Nathaniel: b 1751 d 1822 m Mary Young Pvt PA
Nathaniel, Sr.: b 5-12-1724 d 12-23-1794 m Marian — Pvt SC
Obadiah: b 6-8-1721 d a. 1790 m Abigail Gary Pvt MA
Obed: b 1762 d 1850 m (1)Asenath Hamant (2)Zerviah Allen (3)Sarah Adams Pvt MA
Oliver: b 5-24-1739 d 1-22-1805 m Elizabeth Olds Pvt MA
Perez: b 1737/8 d 2-3-1801 m Elizabeth Tisdale Pvt MA
Peter: b 5-13-1750 d 12-24-1788 m Annis Miner Pvt CT
Peter: b 1-29-1747 d 9-26-1824 m (1)Deborah Gooding (2)Deborah Lincoln Lt MA
Peter, Sr.: b 11-11-1739 d p. 1783 m Eunice Sever Pvt MA
Peter, Jr.: b 12-13-1765 d 4-17-1838 m Diana Brower Mus MA W★
Peter: b 1753 d 1803 m (1)Charlotte C. Bevoil (2)Anna — PS LA
Philip: b 8-3-1751 d p. 1802 m (1)Abigail Knapp (2)Hannah Hall (3)Mrs Mott Lt MA
Philip: b 1740 d p. 1790 m Esther Gray Pvt SC
Phineas: b 3-25-1738 d 7-22-1829 m Susanna Hyde Lt CT W★
Phineas: b 8-20-1722 d 10-16-1792 m Beulah Clapp Capt MA
Phineas: b 3-18-1753 d 9-9-1834 m Tryphena Hines Sol MA
Reuben: b 5-27-1742 d 2-24-1825 m Mary Read Pvt MA
Richard: b c. 1755 d 1830 m Mary Gilpin PS MD
Richard: b 3-10-1758 d 2-24-1841 m (1)Abagail Eastabrooks (2)Sarah Ormbee Pvt MA
Richard: b 1745 d 1801 m — Pvt VA
Robert: b 1757 d 1842 m — Pvt MD ★
Robert: bpt 2-25-1753 d p. 1784 m Dorothy Leighton PS NH
Robert: b c. 1760 d p. 1823 m — Pvt NC
Robert: b 1733 d c. 1790 m Margaret — Pvt PA
Robert: b 10-10-1729 d 1797 m Elizabeth Starke Capt VA
Robert: b 1738 d 6-19-1812 m Elizabeth — Sol VA
Samson: b 4-4-1751 d 4-23-1828 m Thankful Pierce Sgt NH ★
Samuel: b 3-29-1753 d 2-3-1841 m Abia Judson Pvt CT ★
Samuel, Sr.: b 8-30-1721 d 12-15-1817 m Mary Stratton Pvt MA
Samuel: b 5-24-1745 d 10-22-1823 m Hannah Hazeltine Pvt MA
Samuel: b 9-30-1759 d 1804 m Elizabeth Parkhurst Pvt MA
Samuel: b 5-11-1747 d 1795 m Joanna Rice Sol NH
Samuel, Jr.: b 3-23-1753 d 2-8-1830 m Elizabeth Hartwell Pvt NH
Samuel: b 3-5-1753 d 5-18-1808 m Mary Noble Lt PA
Samuel: b a. 1753 d 1793 m Isabel Brice 2Lt PA
Samuel: b 1743 d 1825 m Elizabeth Springer Pvt PA
Samuel: b c. 1745 d 9- -1813 m Martha — Pvt SC

Samuel: b 7-9-1750 d 9-19-1826 m Phoebe Green Cav SC
Samuel: b 8-23-1748 d 7-5-1830 m Susan McDonald Capt VA
Samuel: b 1758 d 1834 m Rebecca Dryden Pvt VA ★
Samuel: b 3-21-1762 d 6-13-1842 m Jane Simpson Pvt VA
Sanders: b 3-16-1741 d p. 10-11-1805 m Sarah Lamar Chp GA
Sarah: b 3-25-1734 d 3-12-1792 m Joseph Walker PS PA
Seth: b 4-16-1717 d 1-4-1794 m (1)Abigail Holden (2)Jemima
— Pvt NH
Seth, Jr.: b 4-15-1747 d 11- -1804 m Eunice Stevens Ens NH
Seth: bpt 10-9-1726 d —m Annie Tripe Pvt NH
Seth: b 8-29-1756 d 10-8-1838 m Temperance Peverley Capt NH
Simonds: b 4-4-1749 d 1839 m Elizabeth (Walker) Pvt CT ★
Solomon: b 1720 d 7-21-1790 m Miriam — Capt MA
Solomon: b 6-3-1739 d p. 6-24-1792 m (1)Sarah Bullard (2)Ann
Levering Sgt MA
Solomon: b 1753 d 1791 m Martha Mitchell Lt PS NC
Solomon: b 1755 d 1837 m Gooden Cox Pvt NC
Solomon: b a. 1760 d 8-1-1822 m Frances Taylor Sgt VA W★
Stephen: b 1755 d 11-22-1816 m (1)Mary Williams (2)Lucy Bates
Pvt VA
Sylvanus: b c. 1750 d p. 7-16-1827 m Alice — Sol GA
Sylvanus: b 4-8-1728 d 1-9-1797 m Mary King Capt PS MA
Sylvanus: b 8-4-1728 d 1786 m Susannah Wade Capt VA
Thomas: b 9- -1742 d 10-18-1818 m Descretion Sater N2Lt PS MD
Thomas: b 10-13-1736 d p. 1790 m Elizabeth Hayden Sol PS MA
Thomas: b c. 1761 d a. 2-5-1805 m Agnes — Capt VA
Thomas, Sr.: b 1-25-1715 d 11-9-1794 m (1)Mrs Mildred Thornton
Merriwether (2)Elizabeth Thornton PS VA
Thomas, Jr.: b 3-17-1748/9 d 1810 m Margaret Hoops Capt VA
Thomas Reynolds: b c. 1730 d a. 4-11-1788 m Sarah — LCol PS VA
Timothy: b 7-26-1718 d 12-26-1796 m (1)Elizabeth Carpenter
(2)Mrs Patience — Col MA
Timothy: b 5-22-1751 d 4-2-1814 m (1)Molly Wilmarth (2)Lucy
Redaway Capt MA
Timothy: b 7-25-1732 d 5-9-1809 m Eunice Brewster Capt MA
Timothy: b 7-27-1758 d 3-26-1841 m Hannah Gleason Sgt MA ★
Timothy: b 2-12-1753 d 11-20-1834 m Lois Gibbs Pvt MA ★
Timothy, Sr.: b 3-17-1711 d 1790 m Martha — Capt NH
Timothy, Jr.: b 1742 d 1790 m Sarah — Sol NH
Timothy: b 6-26-1731 d 5-5-1822 m Susannah Burbeen PS NH
Timothy, Jr.: b 2-6-1752 d 7-3-1819 m Betsey Barros Pvt VT
Wm.: b 12-17-1762 d 2-7-1818 m Elizabeth Bostick Pvt GA
Wm.: b 1750 d 1820 m Marie Siegfried Pvt MD
Wm.: b 7-3-1751 d 10-31-1831 m (1)Sarah Woodruff (2)Mary
(Hutchinson) Parmalee Lt MA
Wm.: b 12-14-1743 d 3-20-1816 m Elizabeth Read Pvt MA
Wm.: b 1746 d 10-2-1819 m Elizabeth — Pvt MA
Wm.: b 3-22-1742/3 d 5-2-1825 m (1)Dorothy Osgood (2)Love
Smith Capt NH
Wm.: b 12-29-1763 d 12-19-1844 m Phebe Ordway Pvt NH
Wm.: b 1759 d 2-3-1832 m Elizabeth Shackford Pvt NH ★
Wm.: b 6-20-1761 d 1857 m Margaret Neeley OrdlSgt CS NY ★
Wm.: b 1759 d 1822 m Sarah — Pvt NC
Wm.: b c. 1760 d 2- -1808 m Ann — Pvt NC
Wm.: b 9-3-1721 d 10-15-1803 m Elizabeth Hoge Pvt PA
Wm.: b 1-11-1759 d 12-13-1843 m Cynthia Hopping Pvt RI
Wm.: b 1757 d 1807 m Sarah Hand Capt SC
Wm.: b 1764 d 1-25-1841 m Jane Lemant Sol SC
Wm., Sr.: b 12-19-1735 d 12-7-1807 m Ann Merry Capt VA
Wm., Jr.: b 3-3-1765 d 1836 m (1) — Bohannon (2)Catherine
Williams Sgt VA
Wm.: b 3-25-1744 d 12-24-1806 m (1)Ann Harrison (2)Jane Cato
2Lt VA
Wm., Sr.: b c. 1720 d p. 1784 m — Pvt VA
Wm., Jr.: b 2-26-1757 d 7-20-1840 m Mary Ann Smith Sgt VA★
Wm.: b 2-10-1761 d 1815 m Polly Logan QM Gen VA
Wm.: b c. 1725 d c. 7-28-1810 m Mary — PS VA
Wm. Needham: b 8-1-1756 d 9-5-1846 m Mrs Jerusha Bethea Pvt
NC ★
Wm. Richmond: b 2-9-1760 d 1790-2 m Margaret Bowers Sgt MA
Wm. T.: b 1757 d 9-28-1833 m (1)Frances Williamson (2)Mary
Dupuy Pvt VA★
Zaccheus: b 3-12-1749 d 2-2-1832 m (1)Martha Danforth (2)Mrs
Rachel Pitts Bigelow 1Lt MA ★

WALKLEY,
Jonathan: b 3-8-1736 d 4-1-1816 m Anna Bates Pvt CT
Solomon: b 8-20-1745 d 7-14-1824 m Rebekah Hazelton Sgt CT

WALL,
Charles: b a. 1742 d 1802 m Elizabeth Bates Capt VA
Francis: b 1760 d 1835 m Sally Thurston Pvt NH
George, Jr.: b 6-12-1745 d 5- -1803 m Sarah Kitchen Capt PA
Howell: b c. 1750 d p. 9-21-1822 m Rebecca Vernon Cav SC
James: b 6- -1739 d 12-11-1819 m Sarah Brown Smn CT
James: b 3-13-1753 d 3-23-1791 m Mary Dorsett 2Lt NJ
James: b c. 1740 d 5-7-1811 m Catherine Vanemin Pvt PA
James: b c. 1715 d 1788 m Sarah — PS CS VA
John: b a. 2-28-1831 m (1)Frances Mooreman (2)Martha
Cole CS NC
John: b 4-27-1742 d 6- -1814 m (1)Agnes McDuffee (2)Hannah
Ketchum Capt PA
John: b 5-15-1743 d 11-28-1788 m Nancy Carter Pvt VA

John: b 2-3-1759 d 3-28-1849 m Sally Ricker Pvt & Pvtr CT ★
Jonathan: b 1744 d 1836 m — Kilbee Pvt NC ★
Richard: b 12-25-1754 d 1-5-1842 m Anne Parham Mid SC ★
Samuel: b 1738 d 5- -1813 m (1)Elizabeth Coggeshall (2)Mary
Tatton Maj CS RI
Wm.: b 1-11-1758 d 11- -1835 m (1)Betsey Houtersheldt (2)Nancy
Elkins Pvt VA
Wright: b c. 1754 d a. 1825 m Mary Bradley 2Lt SC

WALLACE, (Includes WALLES, WALLICE & WALLIS)
Abijah: b 8-25-1748 d 1-9-1832 m Elizabeth Keeler Pvt NY
Andrew: b 9-25-1748 d 7-2-1829 m Catherine Parks Maj VA
Bartholomew: b 8-25-1753 d 11-25-1828 m Edith Wood Sgt MA
Benjamin, Sr.: b 1723 d 12-25-1814 m Lydia Dudley Capt MA
Benjamin, Jr.: b 3-4-1751 d 2-28-1838 m Sarah Thayer Sgt MA
Benjamin: b c. 1745 d p. 1805 m — Van Ornam Pvt NY
Benjamin: b 1-12-1758 d 8-24-1838 m Mary — Pvt NC ★
Benjamin: b 10-17-1727 d 12-9-1803 m (1)Lettice Rolston
(2)Elizabeth Culberton Capt PA
Benoni: b c. 1728 d 3-15-1792 m Rebecca Brown Pvt MA
Caleb: b 1742 d 1814 m (1)Sarah McDowell (2)Rosanna Christian
(3)Mrs Mary Brown PS VA
Charles: b 9-15-1760 d 5-15-1842 m (1)Anna Truman (2)Abigail
Hollowell Pvt PA ★
Cornelius: b 4-20-1765 d 3-6-1858 m Elizabeth Brundage Pvt NY ★
David: b 9-13-1758 d 7-11-1843 m Persis Rosebrooks Pvt MA
David: b 1730 d 1811 m Mary — CS NC
Ebenezer: bpt 1-2-1742/3 d 2- -1797 m Mary Butman Pvt MA
Ebenezer: b 4-11-1765 d 11-8-1835 m Anna Snow Pvt MA
Ebenezer: b 1765 d 11-13-1842 m (1) — (2)Fanny Cole Pvt MA ★
Ebenezer: b 1746 d 1790 m Sarah McGaffey Pvt NH
Elijah: b 8-12-1756 d 4-5-1832 m Dorcas Burdick Pvt NY
Ephraim: b 1747 d 3- -1817 m Janet McCulloch Pvt PA
Francis: b 10-15-1749 d a. 12-17-1787 m (1)Sophia Brooks
(2)Elizabeth Cooper 2Lt MD
George: b 9-5-1761 d 10- -1840 m (1)Miss Bland (2)Jane Drake
FifMaj VA
Henry: b 9-23-1758 d 2-1-1840 m Sara Dodge Pvt MA ★
Hugh: b 1741/42 d 1-11-1820 m — Bruce Pvt PA
James: b 1733 d p. 1800 m Mollie McClellan Pvt MA
James: b 11-11-1735 d p. 1800 m Molly Linn Pvt PS NH
James: b 1736 d 9-3-1822 m Hannah — Pvt NY
James: b 8-8-1760 d 5- -1848 m Jennett Walker Pvt VT
James: b 1720-25 d 1777 m Isabel Miller PS PA
James: b 1744 d 6-23-1784 m Sarah Rose Hank Ens VA
James: b 1735 d 8-24-1777 m Elizabeth Westwood PS VA
Jesse: b 10-4-1767 d 2-13-1854 m Martha George Sol NC
John: b 9-11-1750 d 9-2-1833 m Betsy Wight Sgt CT ★
John, Sr.: b 1736 d p. 1797 m Agnes Lindsey Pvt MA
John, Jr.: b 9-2-1762 d 1-8-1851 m Hannah Parsons Pvt MA ★
John: b 12-15-1746 d 4-27-1837 m Isabella Witherspoon Pvt NH
John: b 3-20-1766 d 7-23-1835 m Mary Bradford Pvt NH ★
John: b 4-12-1727 d 1802 m Sarah Woodburn PS CS NH
John, Sr.: b 1695 d 3-29-1777 m Annis Barnet PS NH
John: b c. 1745 d p. 1790 m — Sct PS NY
John: b 12-22-1758 d 6-18-1847 m Margaret Thompson Pvt NC ★
John: b 1721 d 1799 m Leticia Butt PS NC
John: b 1750 d 8-25-1834 m (1) — (2)Mrs Frances (Alsop)
Meadows Pvt NC ★
John: b 12-18-1748 d 1814 m Jane Finley Ens PA
John: b 1725 d p. 1782 m Mary Madden Pvt PA
John: b 7-5-1726 d 5-9-1808 m Mary Likens Pvt PA
John: b 1750 d 8-8-1808 m Mary Alexander Pvt PA
John: b 1760 d 5-1-1832 m Margaret Anderson Pvt PA
John: b 2-7-1763 d 6-25-1844 m Esther Patton Pvt SC
John: b 1754 d 1822 m Eleanor Morgan Pvt VA
John: b 1-19-1761 d 5-4-1829 m Elizabeth Hooe Sol VA
John: b 1748 d 1837/8 m (1)Jane Miller (2)Rebecca Norton Ens VA
John: b 5-19-1736 d 1814 m Mary Whorry PS VA
Joseph: b 1722 d p. 5-20-1784 m Elizabeth — PS MD
Joseph: b 4-1-1736 d 6-3-1826 m Lucy Thorndike Capt MA
Joseph: b 8-6-1751 d 10-15-1820 m Mary Meek Sol NC
Joseph: b a. 1753 d p. 1795 m Elizabeth Weaver Pvt PA
Joshua: b 1761 d 2-27-1847 m (1)Mary Smith (2)Elizabeth Brewer
Onan PS SC W★
Josiah: b 10-15-1733 d 1780 m Abagail White Pvt ME
Josiah: b 9-19-1749 d 1811 m Susan — Pvt VA
Levi: b 1755-60 d 5-2-1825 m Jennett Hodge Pvt SC W★
Michael: b 12-21-1732 d p. 1807 m Ann Allen Capt VA
Michael: b 6-8-1753 d p. 1797 m Lettice Smith Wishart Pvt VA
Michael: b 1752 d 8-2-1809 m Jane Bratton PS VA
Moses: b 1730 d 1792 m Mary Tidball Pvt PA
Nathaniel: b 1753 d 3-31-1837 m (1)Mrs Lucy Pelton Jackson
(2)Elizabeth Hyde Pvt NY
Peter: b 1719 d 9- -1784 m Martha Woods PS VA
Richard: b 1-16-1757 d 8-30-1797 m Mary Peck Cpl CT
Richard: b 1742 d a. 10-5-1795 m Mary (Simpson) PS QM PA
Richard: b 2-24-1753 d 1-16-1833 m Bethsheba Rich Pvt Sct VT
Robert: b 1758 d 9-4-1835 m Amy Witherell Pvt MA ★
Robert: b a. 1758 d p. 1810 m Esther — Pvt VA
Samuel: b c. 1720 d 1793 m Sarah Moses PS NH
Samuel: b 11-17-1755 d 4-19-1826 m Rachel Morehouse Pvt NY
Samuel: b 1730 d 10-2-1798 m Margaret Patton Capt PA

WALLACE, contd.

Samuel: b 1745 d 3- -1786 m Rebecca Anderson Capt VA
Thomas: b *c*. 1740 d 12- -1799 m (1)— (2)Mrs Sarah Percy Lt DE
Thomas: b 1747 d 9-4-1815 m Elizabeth Walton Pvt MD
Thomas: b 1748 d 3-31-1812 m Esther Patterson PS MD
Thomas, Sr.: b 1745 d 4-28-1830 m Rebecca Milligan Capt NC W★
Thomas: b 4-19-1746 d 5-21-1804 m Nancy Haslet 1Lt PA
Thomas: b 1730 d 2-27-1778 m Mary StClair (2)Ann Black (3)Jane
    Bell Pvt PA
Thomas: b 8-18-1744 d 7-24-1824 m Margaret Lynn Pvt SC
Thomas: b 1-19-1761 d 6-6-1818 m Mary Hooe Lt VA
Uriah: b 1753 d 2-24-1812 m Frances Drake Lt NY W★
Weymouth: b 1752 d *c*. 1842 m — Doe Pvt NH ★
Wm.: b 10-10-1748 d 2-24-1832 m Eleanor Drake Pvt CT
Wm.: b 10-15-1750 d 2-28-1847 m Sarah Thele Dickerson Pvt CT
Wm., Sr.: b 1736 d 1806 m Susannah Young Pvt MD
Wm., Jr.: b 1758 d *p*. 1800 m (1)Margaret Magruder (2)Ferabe
    Brinson Pvt MD
Wm.: b 7- -1720 d 5-25-1815 m Mary Burns PS NH
Wm.: b *c*. 1740 d 1812 m Mary Brown PS 1Lt NH
Wm.: b 1746 d 2-25-1837 m Catherine Miller Lt NY
Wm.: b 1737 d 1799 m Mary Wallis CS NC
Wm.: b *c*. 1750 d *p*. 1783 m Margaret Paintre 2Lt PA
Wm.: b *c*. 1750 d 4-24-1821 m Elizabeth Hopkins Pvt PA MD
Wm.: b 1-16-1753 d 12-28-1805 m (1)Sarah Wallace (2)Jean Gray
    Pvt PA
Wm.: b 1756 d 7-18-1842 m Mary Miller Pvt PA
Wm.: b *a*. 1755 d *p*. 1782 m Hannah Carleton Pvt VT
Wm.: b 1-4-1740 d 3-17-1809 m Mary Pilson Lt VA
Wm.: b 1731 d 1800 m Betty Ferguson Pvt VA
Wm. Brown: b 7-26-1757 d 1833 m Barbara Fox Capt VA

WALLEN,

Jonathan: b 11-6-1751 d 6-21-1819 m Betsey — Capt RI
Thomas: b 1723 d 1792 m Ann — CS VA

WALLER, (includes WALLAR)

Benjamin: b 10-1-1716 d 5-18-1786 m Martha Hall CS VA
Benjamin: b 1749 d *p*. 7-31-1826 m Jean Curtis PS VA
Benjamin Carter: b 12-24-1757 d *p*. 1788 m Catherine Page CS VA
Edward: b 1-12-1754 d 12-2-1791 m Sarah Calas Maj VA
George: b 2-8-1731 d 11-18-1814 m Anne Winston Carr Col VA
Handy: b 12- -1768 d 1845 m Martha Teasley Sol MD
Jesse: b 4-22-1758 d 2-27-1837 m Mary Farley Pvt VA ★
John: b *c*. 1752 d 1822 m Mary Small Sgt VA ★
John: b 3-13-1749 d 1808 m Elizabeth Rhodes Pvt MD
John: b 1751 d 1791 m Mary Matthews Pvt VA
John: b 1753 d *p*. 10-24-1819 m Garnet Routt Pvt VA
John: b *c*. 1737 d 1782-1787 m Mary Ann — PS VA
John: b 12-21-1741 d 7-4-1802 m Elizabeth Curtis PS VA
John: b *c*. 1735 d *a*. 2-20-1809 m Lydia — PS VA
Joseph: b 1745-50 d 1818 m Elizabeth Flint Sol GA
Nathan: b 3-7-1753 d 7-11-1831 m Elizabeth Weeks Pvt CT
Nelson: b 1759 d 9- -1796 m Fanny McIlvain Pvt DE
Peter: b 1745 d 3-13-1831 m Hannah Baldwin PS CT
Thomas: b 7-29-1732 d 2-10-1788 m Sarah Dabney Sgt VA
Thomas: b *c*. 1750 d *p*. 2-6-1817 m Sophia Gaither Pvt VA
Thomas: b 1758 d 8-3-1819 m (1)— (2)Lydia Chandler Pvt VA
Trueman: b 1760 d 7-3-1846 m Patty — Pvt NY VT ★
Wm.: b 11-5-1752 d 9-21-1832 m Sarah — Cpl VA MD ★
Wm. E.: b 1747 d 8-17-1830 m Mildred Smith Pvt VA
Zephaniah: b *a*. 1761 d *a*. 2- -1797 m Sarah — Sol NC

WALLING,

Daniel: b 1-1-1761 d 5-6-1851 m Helena Hoff Pvt NJ ★
James: b 7-1-1753 d 10-20-1811 m Mary Mercy Stull Capt MD
James: b 1-6-1751 d 8-2-1829 m Diana Culver Pvt NY
James: b *a*. 1750 d 3-28-1786 m — Smn VA
John: b *c*. 1738 d *p*. 1796 m Ann Mayhew Sgt & PS MD
John: b 2-3-1725 d 1-31-1815 m Elizabeth Roberts Pvt NJ
John: b 7-27-1750 d 4-18-1836 m (2)Elizabeth Roberts Pvt VA ★
Ladis: b *c*. 1745 d *p*. 11-18-1787 m Ruth Brewster Maj NJ
Simeon: b 1761 d 8-22-1828 m Sarah Whitmarsh Pvt RI ★
Thomas: b 4-2-1755 d 8-12-1819 m Ruth Carmon Capt NJ
Thomas: b 1759 d *a*. 10-19-1831 m Mary Roberts Pvt NJ

WALLINGFORD, (includes WALLINGSFORD)

David: b 9-25-1744 d 3-12-1791 m Elizabeth Leeman 2Lt MA
Jonathan: b 7-7-1762 d 8-5-1847 m Elizabeth Bunker Pvt NH ★
Thomas: b *c*. 1729 d *p*. 1790 m Abigail Hill Pvt NH

WALLOWER,

Leonard: b 7-22-1762 d 5-22-1822 m Susan — Pvt PA

WALLS,

George: b 1730 d 1786 m Mary — QM Gen VA
John: b 4-4-1762 d 11-21-1837 m Mary Patterson Drm PA ★
Samuel: b 1740 d 10- -1784 m Mary — 1Lt MD

WALMSEY,

Wm.: b *c*. 1760 d *c*. 1830 m Prudence Weed Ens CT

WALN,

Joseph: b 6-4-1764 d 1814 m Mary Bonard Pvt PA

WALRATH, (includes WALRADT)

Henry: b 4-3-1760 d *p*. 3-22-1795 m Maria G H Bell Sgt NY
Jacob: b 2-21-1723 d 2-1-1790 m Magadalena Fox Pvt NY
John Adam: b 2-20-1750 d 7-15-1822 m Lana Klock Pvt NY
Nicholas: b 1750 d — Barbara Schultz Ens NY
Peter J.: b 6-9-1764 d 9-17-1849 m Elizabeth Bauder Sol NY
Wm.: b *c*. 1750 d 1802 m Catherine Lipe Pvt NY

WALSER,

Frederick: b 12-25-1760 d *p*. 9-4-1836 m — MM NC ★

WALSH,

Thomas: b 1746 d 6-22-1813 m Margaret Madison Pvt VA
Thomas: b 1751 d 3-19-1819 m Margaret Brush Sol PA

WALSTON,

Boaz: b 1757 d 1823 m Bathsheba — Pvt MD
Henry: b *c*. 1740 d 1796 m — Pvt MD
Wm.: b 1733-35 d 1778 m Mary Pryor Pvt VA

WALTERS, (includes WALTER & WELTER)

Adam: b *c*. 1750 d 1830 m (1)Sophia Gilbert (2)Catherine Donad Pvt
    PA
Christopher: b 1753 d 1834 m Mary Stutts Pvt PA ★
David: b 1741 d *p*. 11-5-1802 m (1)Ann — (2)Elizabeth Allison Ens
    PS MD
David: b 1760 d 1823 m Susan Hassinger Pvt PA
David: b 7-15-1761 d 12-9-1838 m Susana Eberhart Pvt PA ★
Elijah: b 7-27-1757 d 11-10-1836 m Mary Field Pvt CT
Frederick: b 3- -1743 d 10-15-1787 m Martha Saunders Pvt PA
Henry: b 1735 d 5-25-1835 m — Drm NJ ★
Henry: b 1735 d 1798 m Mary Elizabeth — Pvt PA
Henry: b *c*. 1735 d 2- -1781 m — Pvt PA
Henry: b *c*. 1750 d 1823 m Catherine Dull Pvt VA
Jacob: b 1-15-1729 d 6-10-1803 m Maria Kaufman Pvt PA
Jacob: b 1758 d *p*. 1834 m Rebecca Brooks Pvt PA ★
Jacob: b 1759 d 1834 m (3)Elizabeth Miller Pvt PA
Jacob: b 7-17-1760 d 12-12-1827 m Eleanor Walter Artl PA
James: b 3-31-1744 d 1797 m Sarah — Capt VA
James: b 2-17-1752 d 5-10-1838 m Margaret — Sol VA
John: b 3- -1748 d 9- -1848 m Sally Gleason Pvt CT
John: b 3-27-1742 d 10-15-1814 m Priscilla Rathbone Pvt NY
John: b 4-17-1760 d 11- -1819 m Anna Bettinger Sol NY
John: b 1733 d 1818 m X Pvt PA
John: b 1740 d 1802 m Rebecca Rambo Pvt PA
John: b 1-20-1758 d 3-31-1846 m Catherine Friend Pvt PA ★
John: b 1764 d 1829 m Katherine Huffman Pvt PA ★
John: b 1753 d 1836 m Ellinor Spiers Capt VA
John Nicholas: b 6-6-1757 d 5-20-1835 m Barbara Raub Cpl PA
Michael: b 2-8-1750 d 2-21-1820 m Anna Maria Buss Pvt PA
Michael: b *c*. 1750 d 8- -1798 m Catherine Krieger Pvt PA
Paul: b 11-9-1755 d 7-13-1835 m Catharine — Pvt NC
Peter: b *c*. 1755 d 1819 m Mary Geiger Ens PA
Peter, Sr.: b *a*. 1730 d 1786 m Anna Maria — Pvt PA
Peter, Jr.: b 9-1-1753 d 10-30-1793 m Charlotte Maria Hause Pvt
    PA
Peter: b 4- -1760/1 d 2-15-1834 m Isabella Huston Pvt VA ★
Philip: b 6-4-1756 d 5-19-1811 m Susan Baer Lt PA
Richard: b *c*. 1743 d 4- -1784 m Harriet Cantey PS SC
Robert: b *c*. 1708 d *p*. 11-2-1793 m — PS VA
Robert, Jr.: b 1752 d *p*. 4- -1827 m Mary — PS 2Lt PA
Robert: b *c*. 1750 d 2- -1834 m Leathia Magby Sol VA
Thomas: b 2- -1757 d 2- -1837 m Mary E Sibley Sol VA
Thomas, Sr.: b 1732 d 1796 m Lucy Walker PS VA
Wm.: b 1752 d 4-21-1824 m (1)Theodosia Pierpont (2)Mrs Kirby Sol
    CT
Wm.: b 1717 d 3- -1796 m Patience Clark PS CT
Wm.: b 1741 d 1802 m Ann Shank Sol MD
Wm.: b 1750 d 1840/41 m Selah — Pvt NC

WALTHALL,

Christopher, Jr.: b *c*. 1746 d *p*. 12-6-1798 m Patience Marshall PS
    VA
Edward: b 1758 d 1816 m Nancy Featherston Pvt VA
John: b — d *p*. 1799 m Grace Booker 1Lt VA
Wm., Sr.: b 11-19-1757 d *p*. 4-3-1832 m Martha Wooldridge Sgt VA
Wm.: b 1735 d 1798 m Betty Baugh PS VA

WALTMAN, (includes WALDMAN)

Andrew: b 1760 d 1829 m Anna Marie Marguerite Zerfass Pvt PA
Conrad, Jr.: b 2-7-1759 d 12-3-1785 m Catherine Bieber Pvt PA
Michael: b 1754 d 8-24-1829 m Mary Prutzman Pvt MD ★
Peter: b 5-9-1741 d 11-9-1817 m Mary Elizabeth Boyer Pvt PA
Valentine: b 1742 d *p*. 1790 m Catherine Brucker 2Lt PA

WALTON,

Amos: b 1749 d 1826 m Mercy Laycock Pvt VA
Andrew: b 1733 d 6- -1813 m Mary Bachelor Pvt MA
Benjamin: b 1-15-1760 d 10-1-1851 m Mary Westcott Pvt MA ★
Boaz: b *c*. 1740 d 1823 m (1)Rebecca Leach (2)Hannah Ashton
    (3)Mary Ashton Pvt PA
David: b 1730 d 1793 m Elizabeth — Pvt VA
Edward: b 12-3-1758 d *p*. 1820 m Sinia Davis Pvt PA

Elisha: b 9-8-1746 d 1-18-1813 m Mary Forman Maj NJ
George: b 11- -1725 d p. 1783 m Jean Black Pvt DE
George: b 1740 d 1806 m Elizabeth Jennings 2Lt GA
George: b 1740 d 1804 m Dorothea Camber SDI GA
George: b 2-17-1724 d 11-17-1796 m (1)Elizabeth Hughes
    (2)Martha Hughes PS VA
Henry: b 1753 d 9- -1813 m Rebecca Brewer Capt VA
Jacob: b 8-24-1720 d 3-4-1789 m (1)Eunice Hawkes (2)Elizabeth
    Wait (3)Mrs Thankful Brown Pvt MA
Jacob: b 1750 d 1830 m Malissa — Pvt NY
Jesse: b c. 1748 d p. 6-13-1789 m Mary Walker Lt GA
Jesse: b 11-10-1739 d a. 5-21-1821 m Ann Pleasant Lt VA
John: b 8-9-1716 d 10-17-1795 m Martha Burnap Capt MA
John: b 1723 d p. 11-27-1794 m X 1Lt VA
John, Sr.: b c. 1715 d 1780 m Mary Sims Pvt VA
John, Jr.: b 1-7-1838 d 1793 m Mary Baker Pvt VA
Josiah: b 3-8-1736 d 6-21-1831 m Elizabeth Woodward Pvt NH
Josiah: b c. 1760 d p. 1838 m Sarah Clarke Pvt NC
Mark: b 1754 d 5-14-1808 m Ann — PS NJ
Martha Cox: b c. 1712 d p. 1783 m Thomas Walton PS VA
Martin: b 10-1-1761 d 11-13-1844 m Eliza Johnson Pvt VA
Moses: b 1-2-1747 d 2-25-1831 m Martha French Pvt MA
Nathaniel: b — d — m Mary Pattridge Pvt NH
Newell: b 12-13-1763 d 1834 m Agnes Woolfolk Pvt VA ★
Oliver: b 8-2-1758 d 11-3-1845 m Rebecca Tarbell Pvt MA ★
Robert: b 9-25-1749 d 7-24-1837 m Mary Hobson Ens VA
Robert: b 2-4-1754 d 9-9-1800 m Blanche Glascock Pvt PS GA
Silas: b 8-1-1755 d p. 1818 m (1)Elizabeth Deming (2)Rosetta
    Belding Pvt CT ★
Thomas: b c. 1739 d 1805 m (1)Sarah Hill (2)Jean Sudduth Sol GA
Tilman: b 1-9-1760 d 2-3-1831 m Judith — Sgt VA ★
Wm.: b 1-12-1751 d 3-22-1835 m Susannah Mansfield Pvt MA
Wm.: b 1725 d 6-13-1797 m Elizabeth Smith Capt NC
Wm.: b 2-11-1754 d 8-1-1818 m Sarah Grinage Pvt NC
Wm.: b 1760 d 3-6-1816 m Sarah Jones Capt NC ★
Wm.: b 1758 d 1829 m X Pvt PA
Wm.: b 1758 d 1811 m Ellen — Sol PA
Wm.: b 1759 d p. 1802 m Hannah Shoemaker PS PA
Wm.: b 10-25-1749 d 1-29-1845 m Mary Leftwich 2Lt PS VA
Wm., Sr.: b 12-24-1736 d 1-31-1806 m Elizabeth Tilman Sol NC VA
Wm., Jr.: b 1-12-1767 d 5-18-1844 m (1)Jennie McEntire (2)Justina
    Louisa Smith Gennerick Pvt VA NC ★

WALTZ, (includes WALTS & WOLTZ)
Frederick: b 1749 d 1799 m Mary Seltzer PS PA
George: b 10-12-1743 d 6-15-1813 m Charlotta — 2Maj MD
Jacob: b 1763 d 1825 m Jane — Pvt NY ★
Michael: b c. 1755 d 3-6-1839 m Elizabeth Gower Pvt PA ★
Peter: b 1749 d 11-5-1847 m Hannah Davis Pvt NY
Peter: b 1751 d 4-26-1832 m (1)Miss Moon (2)Eva Milliron Pvt MD

WALWORTH,
Benjamin: b 11-11-1746 d 2-26-1812 m Mrs Apphia Cardell QM PS
    NY
Charles: b 1745 d 7-12-1782 m Lucy Harris PS NH
Elijah: b 1-15-1762 d p. 1840 m Jemima Gallop Pvt VT MA ★
James: b 9- -1734 d p. 1795 m Eunice Packer Pvt VT
Wm.: b 9-17-1755 d 5-24-1838 m Ester Packer Pvt NY
Wm.: b c. 1740 d 1810 m Sarah Coville Ens VT

WAMBOLD, (includes WAMPOLE)
Abraham: b 4-5-1750 d 8-3-1832 m Louisa Rentschlium Pvt PA
Elias: b c. 1753 d p. 1813 m Barbara Crey Pvt PA
Frederick: b 2-15-1717 d 2-13-1800 m (1)Eva Elizabeth —
    (2)Catherine Magdalena Roth PS PA

WAMSHER,
Peter: b 3-31-1752 d 5-11-1826 m (1)Anna Catharine Geiger
    (2)Lydia Griffith PS PA

WAMSLEY, (includes WALMSLEY)
David: b 11-19-1755 d 3- -1849 m Sarah Delay Spy VA ★
James: b 1763 d p. 1789 m Barbara Bland Pvt VA
John: b 2-10-1762 d 3-15-1815 m Mary Robinson Sgt VA

WANDELL, (includes VANDALL & WANDEL)
Abraham: b 10-18-1758 d 1848/9 m Mary Dillon Pvt NY ★
Daniel Thurston: b 10-3-1754 d 2-18-1828 m Hannah VanHouten
    Pvt NJ
David: b 12-22-1759 d 9-16-1825 m Lydia Finch Pvt NY
Jacob: b 5-30-1747 d 11-5-1828 m Catherine Stillwell Sol NY ★
John: b 1740 d 9-20-1797 m Letitia Swan Cpl NY
John: b 1745 d 2-2-1826 m Mary Mertel Fish Pvt PA

WANDS,
Ebenezer: b 1736 d 1790 m Maria Hunter Sol NY
John: b 1740 d p. 8-23-1822 m Margaret Burnside Ens NY

WANN,
John: b c. 1754 d 8-14-1824 m Susanne — Pvt PA ★

**WANNAMAKER, (includes WANAMAKER &
    WANNEMACHER)**
George: b a. 9-21-1731 d c. 1795 m Elizabeth Catherine — PS PA

Jacob, Sr.: b 1714 d 1798 m Maria Barbara — Pvt PA
Jacob, Jr.: b 3-28-1754 d 10-31-1828 m Anna Maria — Pvt PA
Jacob: b c. 1750 d 1795 m Ann Rumph Lt SC
Peter: b 3- -1743 d p. 1805 m Easter Pulis Pvt NY

WANNER,
Peter: b 10-15-1739 d 7-21-1831 m (1)Catherine Rothermel
    (2)Anna M Schwartz (3)Magdalena Rothermel Dreibilbis Capt
    PA

WANSLEY,
John: b 1738 d 1842 m Amelia Barber Pvt VA ★

WAPLES,
Joseph: b 1750 d 1826 m (1)Hester White (2)Mrs Leah Prettyman
    (3)Mary Burton Capt DE
Nathaniel: bpt 7-13-1745 d 2-27-1798 m Agnes — Col DE
Samuel: b 6-9-1755 d 8-11-1834 m (1)Ann Custis (2)Mrs Sabra P
    Scarborough Lt VA ★

WARBURTON,
Benjamin: b 1755 d p. 1783 m Mary Cary Higginson Sol VA
John: b c. 1732 d 1806 m Elizabeth Barrell PS VA

WARD,
Aaron: b 8-23-1749 d 9-7-1838 m Elizabeth Wendell Sgt NY ★
Abijah: b 10-2-1759 d 12-15-1835 m Rachel Burgett Pvt NY ★
Abner: b 7- -1757 d 10-7-1838 m Hannah Gaffield Cpl MA ★
Abner: b 9-2-1742 d 7-27-1806 m Elizabeth Fay Pvt MA
Abner: b 4-12-1761 d 5-26-1841 m Polly Davis Pvt MA ★
Andrew: b 11-19-1727 d 1-10-1799 m Siana Hubbard BGen CT
Andrew: b 10-6-1742 d 1- -1816 m Sarah Henfield Pvt MA
Artemus: b 11-27-1727 d 10-27-1800 m Sarah Trowbridge MajGen
    MA
Artemas: b 4-23-1757 d 1827 m Hannah Perry Pvt MA
Asael: b 11-24-1726 d c. 1777 m Esther Franklin PS VT
Benjamin: b 1745 d 4-18-1812 m Mary Shaw 2Lt PS MA
Benjamin: b 4-23-1763 d 1-15-1840 m (1)Mary Clough (2)Adah
    Bump Pvt MA
Benjamin: b 12- -1764 d 1849 m Sarah Richardson Pvt MA
Benjamin: b — d 1824 m X Sol NC
Benjamin: b 1717 d 10-24-1788 m (1)Martha Lyle (2)Elizabeth Hill
    PS NC
Benjamin: b c. 1750 d p. 4-18-1820 m Selah — Sgt NC
Benjamin: b 1747 d a. 8-8-1783 m Catharine Crawley Capt VA
Bernard: b 11-4-1764 d 12-10-1844 m Rachel Strong Pvt VT ★
Bethuel: b 1752 d 3-29-1830 m Hannah Dodd Pvt NJ
Caleb: b 11-22-1748 d 6-20-1813 m Rebecca Foster Pvt MA
Caleb: b 5-17-1749 d 1-18-1839 m Ruth Lane Pvt Tms NJ ★
Caleb: b 12-12-1760 d p. 1833 m Mary Wood Pvt Arfr NJ ★
Christopher: b 11-5-1757 d 10-14-1840 m (1)Sarah Morgan
    (2)Sarah Newell (3)Mrs Betsey Blodgett (4)Mrs Sybil Bond Pvt
    MA ★
Cotton: b 9-29-1734 d 5-4-1802 m Hannah Nudd Lt PS NH
Daniel: b 1732 d 9-12-1812 m Hannah Harroon Pvt MA
Daniel: b 1-30-1764 d 8-19-1841 m Bridget French Cpl NH
Daniel: b 1763 d 1825 m Ruth Bigelow Pvt NY ★
David: b 1753 d 5-14-1806 m Mary Austin Pvt CT
David: b c. 1733 d p. 10-23-1799 m Abigail — CS NC
David: b 11-30-1761 d 12-17-1821 m (1)Abigail Pray (2)Mehitable
    Rider Pvt NY
David: b c. 1751 d p. 1810/11 m Elenor Cecil Capt CS VA
Edward: b a. 1755 d 1820 m X Pvt MD
Edward: b 1757 d 8- -1840 m Lucy Wiggins Pvt MD ★
Edward, Sr.: b 1709 d 5- -1791 m Cassandra Talbot PS MD
Edward, Jr.: b 9-25-1736 d 1783 m Mary Griffith PS MD
Edward: b 1744 d 7-29-1812 m Ruth Oliver 1Lt PS NC
Elijah: b 12-1-1748 d 8-22-1809 m Rachel Nichols Pvt MA ★
Elijah: b 5-21-1761 d 8-11-1832 m Marano Colburn Pvt MA ★
Elijah: b 3-15-1753 d 6-7-1823 m Pheruba Knight Pvt NC
Elisha: bpt 4-16-1758 d 6-6-1813 m Abagail Churchill Mar Pvt CT
Enoch: b 7-4-1749 d 7-29-1825 m Mary Carter CS MA
Enoch: b c. 1743 d 9-20-1785 m Mary Cumberlow Capt PS NC
Ephraim: b 1733 d 5-20-1820 m Eliza Priest Pvt MA
Francis: b c. 1740 d 1800 m X PS NC
George: b 1751 d 5-30-1807 m (1)Annie Middleton (2)Edith Wood
    PS NJ
George: b c. 1759 d 1788 m Margaret Swacsac Pvt VA
Henry: b 1759 d p. 1783 m Martha Barbour Cmsry QM VA
Hezekiah: b 10-6-1725 d 5-11-1802 m (1)Hannah Bellows (2)Mrs
    Martha Earle CS PS MA
Hezekiah: b 1724 d 1804 m Jane — Pvt NY
Humphrey: b 11-16-1764 d c. 1795 m Martha Grice Pvt MA
Ichabod: b 5-1-1750 d 2-23-1824 m (1)Lydia Towner (2)Mrs Mary
    Mitchell Sgt CT ★
Ichabod: b 8-22-1759 d 5-26-1848 m Mary Cady Pvt CT ★
Ichabod: b 5-25-1743 d 12-20-1822 m Mehitable Marcy Capt NY
Isaac: b 3-16-1758 d 2-27-1816 m Polly Thurlow Pvt NH
Isaiah: b 4-25-1762 d 3-22-1834 m Abigail Tatem Pvt NJ
Israel: b 1737 d 4-4-1793 m Betsey Bonnell Capt NJ
Israel, Jr.: b 5-4-1763 d 6- -1846 m Sarah Cook Pvt NJ ★
Ithamar: b 4-24-1752 d 7-2-1828 m (1)Phebe Parker (2)Anna
    Powers (3)Mrs Sarah Parker Pvt MA

WARD, contd.

Jabez: b 2-22-1760 d 3-26-1825 m Eleanor Warner QMSgt MA
Jabez: b 2-10-1734/35 d 8-29-1786 m Jemima Allen Pvt MA
Jacob: b 1- -1756 d 11-12-1843 m Mary Kibby Pvt CT ★
Jacob: b 1738 d 9-27-1811 m Mary Davis Pvt NJ
James: b 2-8-1729 d 4-12-1804 m (1)Mary Wilcox (2)Amy Crane Sgt CT
James: b c. 1720 d 11- -1780 m Martha — Sol NC
James: b 8-3-1723 d 3-1-1818 m Mary A Kent Pvt NC
James: b a. 1729 d 10-10-1774 m Phoebe Lockhart Capt VA
James: b 3-25-1758 d 7-15-1848 m Elizabeth Williamson Pvt VA W★
Jedediah: b 4-1-1760 d 10-28-1847 m Elizabeth Cheedle Pvt CT ★
Jedediah: b 6-6-1741 d 4-19-1805 m Esther Post 2Maj MA
Jesse: b 7-20-1763 d 12-18-1839 m (1)Olive Nye (2)Ruth — Pvt MA
Jesse: b 6-8-1762 d 8-10-1809 m Susan Booth Pvt PA
John: b 9-16-1739 d 11-1-1831 m Elizabeth Miller Pvt CT
John: b 9- -1759 d 4-21-1834 m Abigail Phelps Pvt CT ★
John: b 3-13-1730 d a. 12-18-1787 m Elizabeth Wilson Lt MD
John: b c. 1750 d 2-18-1824 m Elenor Ward PS MD
John, Sr.: b 11-9-1716 d 1800 m (1)Abigail Walker (2)Abigail Heath PS CS MA
John, Jr.: b 1749 d 1820 m Bethiah Fuller Cpl MA
John: b 8-12-1720 d 1805 m Molly Torrey Pvt MA
John: b 12-6-1748 d 4-29-1828 m Martha Shed Pvt MA
John: b 7-26-1752 d 5-15-1839 m Pamelia Bridge Pvt NJ ★
John: b 6-9-1760 d 10-13-1831 m Deborah Hinkley Pvt NY ★
John: b 8-20-1756 d 7-20-1840 m Jane Daniells Pvt NY
John: b a. 1760 d p. 1789 m Elizabeth Whitley Pvt PA
John, Sr.: b 1725 d 1779 m Mary Daniel PS NC SC
John, Jr.: b 3-25-1756 d 4-5-1837 m Winifred Horn Pvt NC ★
John: b — d p. 1797 m Mary Boyd Lt PS PA
John: b c. 1755 d p. 1809 m Nancy — Pvt SC
John: b 3-5-1751 d 12-8-1808 m Christina Cory Pvt VT
John: b 1716 d p. 1-23-1807 m (1)Ann Chiles (2)Sarah (Clark) Lynch Maj CS PS VA
John: b 6-28-1766 d 10-25-1846 m Theodocia Anderson Pvt VA
John: b a. 1759 d p. 1805 m Nancy Bowen Pvt CS VA
Jonas: b 11-17-1744 d 1812 m (1)Percis Stow (2)Mrs Sarah Stow Sgt MA
Jonas: b 1-21-1720 d 9- -1792 m Abigail Child Pvt MA
Jonas: b a. 1748 d 2-22-1801 m Cloe Smith Capt NJ
Jonathan: b 4-30-1760 d 9-15-1838 m Mary Louk Pvt CT
Joseph, Jr.: b 8-15-1750 d 9-6-1834 m Elizabeth Treadway Pvt CT
Joseph: b 7-2-1737 d 2-14-1812 m Prudence Bird Col ADC MA
Joseph, Sr.: b 9-21-1706 d 12-23-1784 m Experience Stone Sol MA
Joseph: b 8-24-1734 d 1824 m (1)Phebia — (2)Rachel Muchmore Pvt NJ
Joseph: b 1760 d 3-8-1826 m Jane Campbell Pvt PA
Joseph: b 1753 d 1836 m Sarah Thompson Pvt RI ★
Joshua: b 10-25-1752 d 9-14-1825 m Sarah Lander PS MA
Joshua: b 1-9-1758 d 6-21-1833 m Mary Forman Sol NY
Joshua: b 1736 d p. 1777 m Sarah McCall PS SC
Josiah: b 3-10-1725 d a. 1786 m Leah Webb Pvt MA
Josiah: b 5- -1763 d 1-18-1845 m (1)— Sherman (2)Elanor — Pvt Slr MA ★
Josiah: b 1-20-1748 d 9-25-1780 m Polly Wiswall Pvt MA
Josiah: b 1756 d 4-20-1824 m Hannah Morse Pvt MA
Josiah: b 9-4-1741 d 2-27-1795 m Sarah Goodell Capt NH
Kerley: b 2-17-1752 d 5-19-1835 m Catherine Graham Cpl MA
Levi: b 11-26-1745 d 2-27-1838/9 m (1)Mary Meigs (2)Mrs Jemima Hubbard Ens CT
Luke: b 4-16-1763 d p. 1808 m Mary Davis Pvt MA
Luther: b 10-1-1761 d 7-10-1848 m Anna Tenney Pvt MA CT
Macock: b 10-16-1745 d 8-2-1836 m Elizabeth Squire Pvt MA
Moses: b 3-23-1753 d 12-3-1812 m Ann Sherwood Pvt NY
Nahum: b 3-26-1744 d 2-6-1812 m Anna Wood Sgt MA
Nancy: b c. 1735 d 1824 m (1)"Kingfisher" (2)Bryan Ward PS NC
Nathan: b 4-11-1721 d 6-15-1804 m (1)Tamasin Ireland (2)Lydia Clough PS NH
Nathan: b 1742 d 1807 m Amy Cattell Sol NJ
Nathan: b 1756 d 10-17-1839 m Mary Churchill Pvt NY
Nathaniel: b 5-12-1734 d 3-17-1793 m Hannah Bachellor Cpl MA
Nehemiah, Sr.: b 1738 d p. 1790 m Hannah Hennery Sgt MA
Nehemiah, Jr.: b 3-4-1764 d 1846 m Mary Stover Pvt MA
Nehemiah: b 9- -1759 d p. 10-4-1839 m Elizabeth — Pvt NY ★
Nicholas: b 6-8-1760 d 2-18-1845 m Elizabeth Sanford Pvt RI ★
Obadiah: b 12-17-1752 d 8-12-1840 m (1)Priscilla Eaton (2)Lydia Johnson Pvt MA
Peter: b 1-29-1751 d 1- -1831 m Sarah Gaffield Pvt MA
Peter: b 1755 d 3-15-1812 m Nancy Mead Capt NJ
Phineas, Jr.: b 4-27-1744 d p. 1796 m Dorothy Osgood PS NH
Reuben: b 12-28-1746 d 1-8-1800 m Sarah Kendall PS NH
Richard: b 4-5-1741 d 12-14-1824 m Mehitable Curwen Capt MA
Richard: b c. 1730 d c. 1785 m Mary Daniel Pvt SC
Richard: b 9-9-1739 d 12-27-1794 m Margaret Chandler Pvt VT
Robert B.: b 1749 d a. 10-25-1793 m Mary Peaue Pvt VA
Rowland, Sr.: b 1730/1 d 1800 m Rebecca Jones Maj VA
Rufus: b 1-6-1759 d 9-4-1834 m Elizabeth Barnes Cpl MA ★
Samuel: b 3-11-1743 d 8-18-1822 m Anne Johnson Cpl CT
Samuel: b 7-20-1739 d 8- -1828 m Hannah Lee Pvt CT
Samuel: b 9-17-1754 d 1-7-1835 m Zeruiah Ward Pvt MA

Samuel, Sr.: b 5-27-1725 d 3-26-1776 m Anne Ray PS RI
Samuel, Jr.: b 11-17-1756 d 8-16-1832 m Phoebe Greene LCol PS RI
Samuel: b 1753 d 1842 m (1)Sarah — (2)— Eady Pvt VA ★
Samuel Lawrence: b 7-1-1748 d 7-9-1814 m Margaret Farrand Pvt NJ
Simon: b 1762 d 2-15-1857 m (1)Chloe Thorp (2)Elizabeth N Moore Pvt NH ★
Stephen: b 1742 d 7-7-1828 m Abigail Pratt Pvt CT
Stephen: b 9-17-1757 d p. 1792 m (1)Patience Cook (2)Sarah Cook Pvt MA
Stephen: b 2-27-1730 d 12-8-1797 m Ruth Gedney PS NY
Stephen: b 1757 d 1799 m Polly Griffin Sol NY
Stephen: b c. 1750 d p. 1833 m Elizabeth Harrison Pvt VA
Sylvester: b c. 1739 d p. 1-22-1793 m Mary Cunningham Capt VA
Thelus: b 4-24-1737 d 4-24-1804 m (1)Sarah Shelley (2)Lydia Franklin Meigs Pvt CT
Thomas: b 1754 d 10-5-1824 m Anna Wakely Pvt CT ★
Thomas: b c. 1758 d 1800 m Mary Zachery Pvt MD
Thomas, Sr.: b 1716-18 d 6-30-1806 m Jemima Pinckney Pvt NY
Thomas, Jr.: b 4-5-1756 d 8-6-1827 m (1)Hannah — (2)Elizabeth Requa (3)Phebe Ireland Sgt NY
Thomas: b 5-3-1759 d 2-11-1839 m Margery Piggott Pvt NC
Timothy: b 3-10-1760 d 6-3-1845 m Elizabeth Zeluff NonCom NJ ★
Uriah: b 12-8-1745 d 3-12-1813 m Jemima Harrington Lt MA
Uriah: b 1746 d 1-7-1820 m Prudence Wood Clark Pvt MA
Wm., Sr.: b 10-29-1720 d 2-25-1786 m Martha Bow PS CT
Wm., Jr.: b 9-17-1744 d 11-26-1819 m Mary Miller Pvt CT
Wm.: b 12-15-1736 d 11-6-1829 m Anna Palmer Arfr CT
Wm.: b 8-12-1757 d 3-12-1850 m Sarah Vernon Sol GA
Wm.: b 3-20-1733 d 9-25-1798 m (1)Elizabeth Mower (2)Sarah Trowbridge Capt MA
Wm.: b 1755/6 d 5-16-1836 m Hannah Appleby Pvt NY
Wm.: b c. 1760 d 1840 m Alise Parker Sol NY
Wm.: b — d 1791 m Sarah Lightfoot CS NC
Wm.: b 4-3-1756 d 8-18-1837 m Catherine Frazer Sgt PA
Wm.: b 1750 d 1836 m Mary Ward Lt SC
Wm.: b 9-12-1743 d 8-3-1819 m Lucy Church PS Lt VT
Wm.: b 6-29-1753 d 12-21-1817 m Jean Watson Capt PS VA
Wm.: b 12-25-1743 d 11-28-1814 m Nancy Ann — Pvt VA
Wm.: b 3-15-1758 d 5-25-1833 m Verlinda Harrison Pvt VA
Wm.: b a. 1750 d p. 1808 m Mildred Adams Capt PS VA

WARDER,

Joseph: b 12-5-1752 d p. 1798 m Esther Ford Pvt MD

WARDLAW,

Hugh: b c. 1740 d 11-14-1802 m (1)Elizabeth Coalter (2)Mary Logan Capt SC
John: b c. 1737 d 1791 m (1)Peggy Moore (2)Mrs Lydia Heard Sol PS SC
Robert: b 1752 d 1824 m Janette Downey Pvt VA
Wm.: b 9-2-1764 d 10- -1839 m (1)Miss Margaret Hall (2)Miss Margaret McCully Pvt SC ★

WARDNER,

Frederick: b 4-1-1754 d 12-17-1825 m Rebecca Waldo PS NH
Jacob: b 7-20-1752 d 12-10-1822 m (1)Sarah Hatch (2)Olive Richardson Cpl NH
Philip: b 6- -1727 d 5-12-1819 m Katherine Eidel Pvt NH

WARDWELL, (includes WARDELL)

Eliakim: b 6-16-1749 d 6-26-1819 m Sarah Huxley Pvt CT
Eliakim: b 1764 d 6-20-1823 m (1)Catherine — (2)Susan Russell Pvt NY
Ezekiel: b 1750/51 d 1834/35 m Mrs Damaris Wardwell Pvt MA
Isaac: b c. 1750 d p. 1790 m Hannah Trawl Pvt CT
Isaac: b 12-28-1766 d 2-22-1841 m Hannah Knapp Pvt CT
Jacob: b 8-19-1744 d p. 1818 m Hannah Whitney Pvt CT ★
Jeremiah: b 12-17-1748 d 8-9-1817 m Mary Lovejoy Pvt PS NH
Jonathan: bpt 12-16-1711 d 1-31-1788 m Rachel Pevey CS MA
Joseph: b 1-29-1760 d 3-5-1849 m Sarah Hemmenway Lt MA ★
Josiah: b 7-20-1757 d 11-1-1820 m Martha Smith Cpl RI
Samuel: b 4-25-1755 d 11-23-1819 m Lydia Wardwell Cpl RI
Simon: b 5-17-1762 d 7-25-1827 m (1)Ruth Church (2)Mrs Sarah Dole Pvt MA ★
Solomon: b 1743 d 9-20-1825 m Bethia Holt Pvt MA
Wm.: b 2-11-1760 d 2-12-1848 m (1)Sarah Scofield (2)Patty Jones (3)Catherine Ray Pvt CT ★

WARE, (includes WEARE, WEIR & WIER)

Andreas: b c. 1728 d 11-2-1804 m Mary Weyer Pvt PA
Andreas: b 1733 d 1804 m Sophia Elizabeth Wolf Pvt PA
Anthony: b — d 4-2-1829 m Mary Kurtz Pvt PA
Asa: b 1759 d 5-9-1832 m Phoebe Ware Pvt MA
Asa: b 6-21-1751 d 6-6-1831 m Mary Metcalf Pvt MA
Asaph: b 11-20-1755 d p. 1809 m (1)Mercy Clark (2)Anna Park Pvt MA
Benjamin: b 1-8-1759 d 2-2-1814 m Mehitable Leland Pvt MA
Daniel: b 1750 d 5-30-1797 m Tabatha Collins Cpl VT
Daniel: b 3-19-1755 d 10-20-1819 m Abigail Newell MM MA
David: b — d 3-10-1796 m Jean McClurkin Pvt SC
Edward: b 10-18-1760 d 11-3-1836 m Sallie Thurmond Sgt VA ★
Eli: b 5-31-1748 d 11-1-1835/6 m Tamar Wight Pvt MA

Elias: b 5-30-1754 d 6-29-1841 m Deborah Groves Pvt MA
Elijah: b 10-29-1739 d — m Susannah Bangs Pvt MA
Elisha: b 3-21-1715 d 7-18-1796 m Phoebe Clark Pvt MA
Ephraim: b 1-14-1725 d 9-30-1792 m Martha Parker Pvt MA
Ezra: b 7-6-1741 d 2-2-1815 m Hannah Pratt Lt MA
Frederick: b 9-3-1760 d 12-16-1832 m (1)Eunice Emerson
 (2)Jermima Manning Pvt MA
Frederick: b 2-22-1762 d 2-2-1848 m Elizabeth Detter Arfr PA
George: b 5-29-1755 d 1-10-1839 m Priscilla Harden Pvt Smn MA ★
George: b 9-5-1761 d 1-7-1805 m Mary Andrews Pvt MA
Henry, Sr.: b c. 1730 d p. 11-1-1801 m Martha Garrett Sol GA
Hezekiah: b 11-27-1740 d 6-19-1779 m Molly Hall 1Lt MA
Isaac: b 10-1-1757 d p. 1789 m Mahitable — Pvt MA
James: b 11-19-1745 d — m Mary Veal Lt VA
James: b 1759 d 1833 m Susannah Miller Sgt VA
James: b 12-27-1756 d 1818 m Elizabeth Miller 2Lt VA
James, Sr.: b 11-15-1714 d p. 9-25-1790 m Agnes Todd PS VA
James, Jr.: b 3-13-1741 d 1820 m Catherine Todd Sol VA
James R.: b 5-25-1752 d 5-26-1839 m Mary Stiles Sgt MA ★
Jeremiah, Sr.: b 3-28-1729 d 5-4-1821 m Sarah Preble PS CS MA
Jeremiah, Jr.: b 6-3-1757 d 7-26-1842 m Lucy Webber Cpl MA ★
Jesse: b 7-31-1750 d 10- -1829 m (1)Anna Woods (2)Eunice Scott
 Sgt MA
Jesse: b 3-10-1736/7 d 7-13-1813 m Kezia Mills Pvt MA
John: b 7-4-1753 d 9-14-1833 m Hannah Leland Pvt MA
John: b 1757 d 2-26-1826 m Mary Mallett Pvt MA
John, Sr.: b c. 1745 d 1819 m Sarah Marple Sol NJ
John: b 1742 d 3-5-1826 m (1)Nancy Green (2)Rebecca Wilson Sgt
 NY
John: b 1743 d 8-11-1819 m Elizabeth McKelvey Capt NC
John: b 1-12-1741 d p. 1833 m Nancy Blackburn Pvt NC ★
John: b 1753 d 1839 m Anne Janson Pvt PA ★
John: b c. 1756 d 9-28-1786 m Elizabeth Campbell Cav SC
John: b 12-12-1736 d p. 2-24-1816 m Anne Harrison PS Capt VA
Jonathan: b 8-4-1738 d 10-24-1819 m Hannah Battles Pvt MA
Jonathan: b 6-28-1724 d — m (1)Sarah Lane (2)Mary French CS NH
Jonathan: b 1755 d — m Nancy Wortte CS NH
Joseph: b 4-30-1751 d 6-11-1833 m Grace Coolidge Pvt MA
Joseph: b 10-15-1753 d 11-12-1805 m Esther Smith Sgt MA
Josiah, Sr.: b 3-21-1707 d 7-3-1798 m (1)Lydia Mackentyre
 (2)Dorothy Dewing (3)Mrs Mehitable Whitney (4)Mrs Sibel
 Robinson Pvt MA
Josiah, Jr.: b 9-15-1742 d 10-23-1836 m Lois (Ware) Pvt MA
Mesheck: b 6-1-1713 d 1-25-1786 m (1)Elizabeth Shaw
 (2)Mehitable Wainwright PS NH
Michael: b 12-5-1725 d 1814 m (1)Abiel Metcalf (2)Lucy Grant Pvt
 MA
Moses, 5th.: b 11-16-1739 d 8-23-1812 m Rebecca Puffer PS NH
Nathan: b 12-29-1754 d 2-1-1835 m Hannah Everett Pvt MA ★
Nathaniel: b 8-6-1697 d 3-4-1781 m Priscilla Grant Sol MA
Nathaniel: b 1734 d — m Elizabeth Swain Sol MA
Nicholas: b c. 1758 d 1827 m Mary Heard Sol CS GA
Nicholas: b — d p. 6-11-1799 m Dolly Garrett PS VA
Paul: b c. 1760 d p. 1777 m X Pvt MA
Peter: b 12-3-1760 d 1-20-1828 m Hannah Nason Pvt MA
Reuben: b — d 5- -1803 m Susanna — Pvt VA
Robert: b 10-10-1759 d 5-6-1827 m (1)Jane Stokes (2)Judith
 Green Pvt GA
Robert: b 6-2-1733 d p. 1785 m Martha Hutcheson Sgt NC
Robert: b c. 1752 d 1817 m Margaret Bassell Capt VA
Samuel: b 1765 d 12-23-1827 m Eunice Gould Pvt CT
Samuel: b 2-8-1716/17 d 1-5-1806 m (1)Anna Goodale (2)Mrs
 Hannah Belding Billings PS MA
Samuel: b c. 1725 d c. 1790 m Jane — Pvt PA
Samuel: b 2-26-1750 d 4-3-1817 m (1)Mary Lyle Thompson
 (2)Mary Gilliland Capt VA
Thomas: b 1762 d 12-26-1851 m Mildred Bryant Pvt VA ★
Timothy: b 11-20-1746 d 5-30-1798 m Abiel Ray Pvt MA
Wm.: b 6- -1757 d 2-24-1824 m (1)Martha Miller (2)Mary Ann —
 Sgt CT
Wm.: b 10-17-1756 d 6-14-1784 m Sarah Williams Sgt MA
Wm.: b 8-20-1728 d 9-15-1809 m Elizabeth — Pvt PA
Wm.: b 1752 d 1800 m Susannah Miller Pvt SC
Wm.: b 11-1-1768 d 10-12-1856 m Mary Agnew Pvt SC
Wm.: b 3-29-1750 d 9-10-1829 m Sarah Samuel Pvt VA
Wm.: b 1760 d 3-28-1833 m Pricilla Gregory Pvt VA

WARFIELD,
Azel: b 4-3-1726 d 1787 m Sarah MacCubbin Griffith PS MD
Benjamin: b 1740 d 1814 m Catherine Dorsey Capt MD
Brice: b 1-12-1760 d 6-17-1835 m Sarah Dickerson Sol MD
Charles: b 8-30-1738 d 6-23-1790 m Elizabeth White Warfield PS
 MD
Charles Alexander: b 12-14-1751 d 1-29-1813 m Elizabeth Ridgely
 Maj MD
Elisha: b 3-29-1741 d 7-16-1818 m (1)Eliza Dorsey (2)Ruth
 Burgess PS MD
John: b c. 1740 d p. 8-14-1787 m Mary Chaney 2Lt MD
Joseph: b 2-9-1755 d 1830 m Elizabeth Dorsey Lt MD
Joshua: b 4-15-1757 d 7-21-1835 m Prudence Buck Pvt MA ★
Lancelot: b c. 1740 d 5-1-1804 m (1)Mary Robosson (2)Rachel
 Marriott 2Lt MD
Philemon: b — d a. 3-19-1794 m Assantha Waters Capt MD

Samuel: b c. 1705 d p. 9-2-1778 m Sarah Welch PS MD
Samuel: b 1-13-1757 d 2-20-1845 m Margery Gay Pvt MA
Seth, Sr.: b 1-15-1723 d p. 3-14-1805 m Mary Gaither PS MD
Thomas: b c. 1753 d 3- -1819 m (1)Sarah Anderson (2)Elizabeth
 Hollyday (3)Elizabeth Marriott Ens MD
Walter: b 1760 d 3-10-1826 m Sarah Winston Christian Dr MD

WARING,
Abraham: b 1754 d 4-28-1819 m Love Graham Ens NY ★
Basil: b 11-16-1740 d c. 1800 m Anne Gantt Lt MD
Basil, Sr.: b 1711 d 4-17-1793 m Susannah Darnall PS MD
Ephraim: b 5-4-1764 d 12-18-1804 m Huldah Hickox Pvt CT
Henry: b 10-6-1744 d 11-6-1830 m Hannah Ferris Capt CT ★
James: b 4-23-1759 d 2-18-1838 m Sarah Dibble Pvt CT ★
James: b 1755 d 12-18-1813 m Elizabeth Hilleary Cpl MD
James Haddock: b 1755 d 1839 m Anne Boone PS MD
John: b 1736 d 2-17-1809 m (1)Joanna Smith (2)Mary (Elwell)
 Chapman Pvt NY
Joseph: b 1-1-1753 d 1-14-1842 m (1)Abigail White (2)Prudence
 Smith Pvt CT
Robert Payne: b 10-13-1746 d a. 6-17-1799 m (1)Katherine
 Robinson (2)Mrs Ann Clements (3)Sarah Upshaw PS CS VA
Thaddeus: b 4-18-1746 d 1-1-1825 m Deborah Frost Pvt CT W★
Thaddeus: b 7-28-1744 d 5-2-1822 m Tryphena — Pvt NY
Thomas: b 1752 d 1-18-1818 m Lydia Walton 2Lt MD

WARLEY,
Felix: b 1750 d 1814 m Anne Turquand Maj SC
Paul: b 1752 d 3-17-1807 m Mrs Mary Caldwell Lt SC

WARLICK,
Barbara: b c. 1720 d p. 6- -1784 m Daniel Warlick PS NC

WARNALL,
James: b 1764 d 10-28-1835 m Charlotte Jinkins Sgt VA ★
Roby: b c. 1740 d 1784 m Edey — PS MD

WARNE,
George: b 4-13-1713 d 10-13-1789 m Abigail Warford PS NJ
Jacob: b c. 1739 d 1814 m Phoenix Clark Pvt MA
John: b 1730/1 d 1790 m (1)Zehiah — (2)Mary Brown Pvt NJ
Joseph: b c. 1743 d 3-16-1788 m Dorcas Miller Pvt PA
Joshua: b 12- -1740 d 2-10-1814 m Meleny Disbrow Pvt NJ
Margaret Vilet: b 10-10-1746 d 10- -1840 m (1)Joseph Warne
 (2)Elijah Warne PS NJ

WARNER, (includes WERNER)
Aaron, Sr.: b 3- -1717 d a. 12-6-1787 m (1)Ruth Selden (2)Esther
 — PS MA
Aaron: b 6-30-1751 d 2-12-1777 m Mary Stow Pvt MA
Abel: b 4-29-1763 d 2-12-1837 m Sarah Cooke Pvt MA
Abijah: b 7-15-1753 d p. 1803 m Elsea Fuller MM MA
Alpheus: bpt 3-18-1753 d 1-28-1800 m Meribah Hilyard Sgt MA
Amos: b 8-11-1761 d 11-14-1838 m Ruth Gilbert Pvt CT ★
Anthony: b 1744 d 1798 m Rachel Evans Pvt PA
Asa: b 10-1-1743 d 1819 m Eunice Camp PS CT
Benjamin: b 10-10-1762 d 12-27-1853 m Polly Hibbard Pvt CT
Benjamin: b 6-26-1757 d 1-30-1846 m Anna Sperry Pvt NY
Calvin: b 9-7-1763 d p. 1800 m Anna Houghton Pvt MA
Charles: b 1-18-1736 d 8-12-1803 m Martha Warner Pvt CT
Charles: b 11- -1762 d 11-26-1837 m Sarah Stockwell Sol CT
Consider: b 5-19-1762 d — m Peggy Thorpe Pvt MA
Cuthbert: b 1700 d 1838 m (1)Rachel Hill (2)Anna Smith PS MD
Daniel: b 6-30-1729 d 9-1-1814 m (1)— Winchell (2)Martha Case
 Lt CT
Daniel: b 1756 d 12-12-1840 m Grace Warters Sgt MA ★
Daniel: b 12-22-1734 d 7-19-1823 m Mary Wright PS MA
Daniel: b 6-25-1745 d 3-20-1813 m Elizabeth Boardman Lt NH
Daniel: b 7-10-1714 d p. 1790 m Bethia Gining PS PA
Daniel: b 4-21-1741 d 8-16-1777 m Patience Norton Pvt VT
David: b 8-7-1730 d 11-6-1800 m (1)Sarah Ward (2)Eunice Prout
 Pvt CT
David: b 11-27-1731 d 3-18-1794 m Abigail Garrison Pvt CT
David C.: b 7-12-1758 d p. 1799 m Mary Russell Pvt MA
Deliverance: b 11-22-1747 d 5-22-1813 m Esther Karr Pvt CT W★
Demas: b 1746 d 1804 m Rhoda Gridley Pvt CT
Ebenezer: b 12-14-1732 d 2-19-1811 m Susanna Tuttle Sgt CT
Eleazer: b 2-8-1738 d 6-2-1821 m Johanna Hale Capt CT
Eleazer: b 1-15-1729 d 6-19-1810 m Mary Chapin Capt MA
Eleazer: b 9-20-1755 d 12-8-1829 m Elizabeth Belden Pvt MA
Eleazer, Sr.: b 1733 d 10-26-1817 m Elizabeth Kirtland Sol NY
Eleazer, Jr.: b 4-3-1764 d 11-16-1851 m Irinda Skiff Sgt NY ★
Elias: b 1764 d 4-13-1843 m Abigail Priest Pvt MA ★
Elihu: b 10-28-1758 d 1-16-1851 m Elizabeth Freeman Pvt MA
Elijah: b 12-14-1738 d 1-24-1819 m (1)Submit Wells (2)Rachel
 Sampson (3)Sarah Wheeler Capt MA
Eliphaz: b 9-1-1742 d 3-12-1816 m Mercy Drinkwater Pvt MA
Ezra: bpt 2-19-1758 d 3-26-1849 m Parnel — Pvt NY
Frederick Wilhelm: b 12-12-1761 d 6-15-1849 m Catherine Bens
 Pvt PA
George: b 6-20-1758 d 4-30-1836 m Elizabeth Wagner Vol MD
George, Sr.: b 6-24-1720 d 6- -1815 m (1)Lana Mattice (2)Dorsa —
 Pvt NY

WARNER, contd.

George, Jr.: b 10-6-1757 d 3-28-1844 m Anna Bellinger Pvt NY ★
George: b 3-24-1750 d 3-4-1825 m (1)Magdeline Walgrave
　　Goodwin (2)Ann Kepple PS NY
George: b 1759 d 1820 m Eliza Swogord Cpl PA
Gideon: b 8-15-1762 d 1-14-1836 m Eunice Castle Tms CT
Gideon: b 5-15-1721 d c. 1789 m Mary Parsons Pvt MA
Henry: b c. 1750 d a. 1-1-1816 m Susannah (Bostetter) Pvt PA
Henry: b 3-5-1751 d 12-22-1830 m Elizabeth Miller Pvt PA
Henry: b 1746 d 9-5-1820 m (1)Magdalena Meyer (2)Mrs
　　Magdalena Stub PS PA
Ichabod: b 3-1-1738 d 11-16-1815 m Mary Lazell PS CT
Isaac: b 5-1-1750 d 5-6-1807 m Beulah Hobbs 2Lt MA
Isaac: b c. 1737 d 11-29-1794 m Lydia Coulton Col PA
Isaac: b 11-27-1741 d 11-27-1829 m Martha Janney Pvt PA
Jabez Ichabod: b 5-17-1761 d 1-14-1849 m (1)Ann Wakeley
　　(2)Mary Young Pvt CT ★
Jacob: b 6-14-1741 d 2-23-1820 m Elizabeth Abel Sol PA
James: b 12-11-1737 d 5-27-1819 m Eunice Dutton 1Lt CT
James: b 1736 d 12-11-1812 m (1)Abigail — (2)Elizabeth Bates Pvt
　　NY
Jason: b 4-2-1760 d 9-5-1841 m Abigail Whiting Sol NY
Jesse, Sr.: b 5-6-1718 d 5-10-1793 m (1)Miriam Smith (2)Mrs Mary
　　VenHorn MM MA
Jesse, Jr.: b 2-1-1747 d 8-14-1834 m Sarah Warriner 2Lt MA
John: b 10-27-1739 d 3-11-1800 m (1)Hannah Westover (2)Eunice
　　Waller Capt CT
John.: b 10-14-1749 d p. 1792 m Anne Sutliff Capt CT
John: b 9-22-1752 d 1830 m Eunice Darrow Sol CT
John, Jr.: b 1760 d 2-30-1808 m Patience Hall Pvt CT
John: b 4-20-1756 d 12-24-1807 m Mary Ward MM MA
John: b 11-2-1747 d 7-1-1827 m (1)Priscilla Adams (2)Sarah
　　Eastman Pvt NH
John: b 10-13-1754 d 2-13-1806 m Sibyl Sawtelle Pvt NH
John: b 8-23-1752 d p. 1809 m (1)Mary Marden (2)Mrs — Webster
　　PS NH
John: b 6-10-1737 d 6-23-1829 m Elizabeth — Capt NY
John: b 5-14-1754 d p. 1790 m Catherine Hunder Pvt PA
John: b 5-29-1745 d 7-2-1819 m (1)Mrs Hurlbert (2)Joanna Ames
　　Capt VT W★
John Joost, Sr.: b 9-14-1726 d 10-18-1810 m (1)Margaret Bellinger
　　(2)Anna Dorothea Huls Pvt NY
Jonathan: b 3-17-1750 d 3-20-1810 m Mary Griffin Pvt CT
Jonathan: b 10-1-1728 d 2-22-1810 m Elizabeth Selden PS CT
Jonathan: b 7-14-1744 d 1-7-1803 m Hannah Mendall BGen PS
　　MA
Jonathan: b 7-16-1743 d 10-15-1826 m Eglah Sheldon Capt MA
Jonathan: b 1751 d 1782 m Mary — Pvt MA
Jonathan: b 11-3-1759 d 1-14-1845 m Margaret Elizabeth Zuill PS
　　MA ★
Jonathan: b 12-4-1747 d 4-8-1823 m (1)Mary Wright (2)Clarina
　　Eliot (3)Lucina Tilden Adj NY
Joseph: b 10-23-1735 d 9-20-1808 m Huldah Nicholls Capt CT
Joseph: b 10-26-1743 d 3-1-1807 m Bridget Hosley Lt MA
Joseph, Sr.: b 6-18-1710 d 4-20-1794 m (1)Mary Hubbard
　　(2)Rebecca (Alden) Spooner PS MA
Joseph, Jr.: b 7-2-1743 d 6-8-1818 m Mary Whipple Capt MA
Joseph: b 12-25-1751 d 4-13-1836 m Jerusha Edwards Pvt MA
Joseph: b 3- -1738 d 9-5-1842 m Ruth Troat Pvt VA
Josiah: b a. 1770 d p. 1813 m Deborah Warner Sgt MA
Josiah: b 3-13-1745 d 7-6-1832 m Olive Jackson 1Lt NY
Lemuel: b 9-6-1731 d 2-20-1814 m Sarah Gaylord PS CT
Levi: b 1750 d 7-25-1813 m Joanna Joslin Sgt MA
Mark: b 11-15-1762 d 2-1-1839 m Lovisa King Pvt MA
Martin: b 1-11-1735 d 7-15-1807 m Mary Ruggles Ens PS CT
Martin: b 9-2-1735 d p. 1791 m (1)Deborah — (2)Mary — Pvt PS
　　NH
Moses: b 2-25-1758 d 8-17-1840 m Rachel Rider Pvt CT ★
Moses: b 1754-8 d 8-1-1828 m Mary King Pvt MA
Moses: b 4-4-1760 d 7-11-1837 m (1)Molly Ward (2)Abigail
　　Colton Pvt MA ★
Nathan: b 10-31-1756 d 5-12-1844 m (1)Jerusha Webb (2)Amy
　　(Witter) Cook Cpl MA
Nathan: b 1710 d 1-7-1792 m Dorothy Goodenough CS MA
Nathan: b 6-6-1744 d 8-26-1802 m Mary Silvernail Pvt PA
Nathan: b 1743 d 2-28-1821 m (1)Sarah Hambleton (2)Rebecca
　　Talhot (3)Elizabeth Rhude 2Lt RI
Nathaniel: b 1760 d 7-28-1843 m Ruth Colyer Tms Pvt CT ★
Nathaniel: b 8-9-1731 d 8-27-1818 m Esther Rice Pvt CT
Nathaniel: b 12-25-1718 d p. 1790 m Abigail — Pvt CT
Nicholas: b 10-31-1747 d 7-27-1838 m Maria Shaver Ens NY
Noahdiah: b 1749 d 10-16-1824 m Martha Hunt 2Lt NY
Oliver: b 10-12-1729 d 2-21-1814 m Lois Ruggles PS CT
Oliver Ring: b 3-16-1729 d 9-28-1799 m (1)Elizabeth Wyatt
　　(2)Elizabeth Read PS RI
Omri: b 5-1-1762 d 7-28-1841 m (1)Prudence Hollister (2)Catherine
　　Evans Pvt MA ★
Peter: b 1745-50 d 1842 m Judith Shoemaker Pvt VA
Philip, Sr.: b c. 1726 d p. 1796 m Barbara — Fif PA
Phineas: b 7-27-1740 d 10-25-1804 m (1)Lydia Whitney (2)Mrs
　　Elizabeth Willard Cpl MA
Robert: b 1745 d 1-9-1826 m Mary Tule Maj CT ★
Samuel: b 1754 d 9-16-1834 m Deborah Snow Sgt CT

Samuel: b 1-9-1760 d 9-3-1840 m Lydia Hitchcock Pvt CT
Samuel, Sr.: b 10-14-1708 d 9-10-1783 m (1)Mary Gilling (2)Mrs
　　Hannah Skinner PS MA
Samuel, Jr.: b 1-1-1733 d 12-4-1823 m Ann Steel Pvt MM MA
Seth: b 1-28-1743 d 1790 m Hannah DeAngelis Mstr CT
Seth: b 12-2-1760 d 7-5-1845 m Polly Painter Pvt MA ★
Seth: b 5-17-1743 d 12-26-1784 m Hester Hurd Col VT
Solomon: b 1761 d 8-10-1839 m Rachel Ruggles Pvt CT ★
Stephen: b 10-4-1731 d 11- -1812 m Phebe Baldwin Pvt PS CT
Stephen: b 12-16-1726 d 9-16-1796 m (1)Mary — (2)Rachel
　　Montague Pvt MA
Stephen: b 1744 d 12-15-1812 m (1)Lois Goss (2)Mary (Norton)
　　Porter 1Lt MA
Thomas: b 1748 d 2-7-1818 m (2)Huldah Blodgett Sgt CT W★
Thomas: b 11-8-1722 d 12-17-1778 m Abigail Prentice Pvt PS CT
Thomas: b 1756 d 3-26-1840 m Belinda — Pvt CT
Thomas: b 12-14-1761 d 8-16-1815 m Alida Fitchett Pvt NY
Thomas: b 7-26-1757 d 3-10-1815 m Mary Hill Pvt RI W★
Timothy: b 11-13-1763 d 2-15-1852 m (1)Sarah Harcourt (2)Huldah
　　Raymond Pvt CT
Tobias: b c. 1744 d 1788 m Agnes Caldwell PS NH
Warham: b 11-2-1730 d 12-4-1817 m Hannah Ware Pvt MA
Wettenhall: b 12-12-1736 d a. 1-25-1819 m Elizabeth Cargill CS
　　SC
Wm.: b 1747 d 1821 m Sarah Dow Mte CT
Wm., Sr.: b 10-1-1715 d 5-1-1790 m (1)Elizabeth Mitchell
　　(2)Prudence May PS CT
Wm., Sr.: b 12-4-1717 d 10-24-1776 m Rebecca Lupton PS NY
Wm., Jr.: b 5-13-1740 d 8-28-1795 m (1)Abigail Hawley (2)Rhoda
　　Treat (3)Elizabeth Norton (4)— Lt NY
Wm.: b 1760 d 1- -1822 m Nancy Wharton Pvt PA

WARNOCK,

Andrew: b 1755 d 1819 m Mary — Lt SC
John: b 1757 d 5-28-1842 m Eleanor Dowdle Pvt SC ★
Joseph: b 1750 d 1810 m Ann Motheringham Pvt SC
Micheal: b 1751 d 8-30-1823 m Nancy Walker Pvt SC

WARREN, (includes WARRIN)

Aaron: b 1758 d 3-25-1821 m Keziah Huntress Pvt MA
Aaron: b 6-3-1762 d 4-21-1849 m (1) X (2)Abigail Nelson Cpl NH ★
Abijah: b 10-15-1762 d 10-26-1842 m Sally Gray Pvt MA
Abraham: b 9-25-1747 d p. 1820 m Isabel Jerome Pvt CT ★
Asa: b 11-9-1725 d p. 1790 m (1)Tabitha Johnson (2)Huldah
　　Hale Pvt MA
Ashbel: b 5-8-1762 d 9-17-1843 m Penelope Pratt Pvt CT ★
Benjamin: b 1740 d 1822 m (1)Jane Sturtevant (2)Lois Doten
　　(3)Mrs Patience Dimon (4)Phebe (Parsons) Doty Capt MA
Benjamin: b 7-30-1720 d 1-11-1802 m Jedidah Tupper Pvt MA
Benjamin: b 11-20-1728 d — m Hannah Lewis Pvt MA
Benjamin: b 2-2-1730/1 d 1776 m Elizabeth Hayward Sol MA
Benjamin: b 7-21-1745 d p. 1788 m Lucretia How Pvt MA
Benjamin: b 12-9-1750 d p. 1799 m Abigail Philpott Sol MA
Caleb: b 1764 d 1846 m Rachel Webster Pvt VT ★
Cornelius: b 1746 d 3-21-1806 m Patience Hoar Pvt NH
Daniel: b 8-11-1765 d 4-16-1845 m (1)Jane Hodgdon (2)Sally
　　Smith (3)Sarah Lord Pvt MA ★
Daniel: b 2-28-1764 d 6-23-1845 m Hannah (Randall) Manchester
　　Pvt MA
Daniel, Jr.: b 3-15-1758 d 1-13-1833 m Abigail Drury Pvt MA
David: b 11-17-1760 d 8-27-1847 m Mary Knight Pvt MA
David: b 5-24-1742 d 1820 m Prudence Whipple Lt PS NH
David, Sr.: b 1751 d 3-22-1827 m Mary — Pvt VT
Ebenezer: b 9-14-1748 d 1-1-1824 m Ann Tucker PS MA
Edward: b 9-18-1761 d 12-10-1814 m Mary Steele Pvt CT
Eleazer: b 11-19-1707 d 4-28-1800 m (1)Mary Day (2)Mrs Olive Day
　　(3)Zerviah Russell PS CT
Elijah: b 8-27-1758 d 7-18-1843 m (1)Elizabeth Wheeler (2)Mary
　　Belcher Wheeler Pvt MA
Eliphalet: b 1734 d 7-16-1815 m Marion Rice Pvt MA
Elisha: b 1754 d 12-24-1831 m Hannah Marble Pvt MA
Ephraim: b 5-3-1737 d 2-21-1819 m (1)Sarah Kezer (2)Ruth
　　Alexander Cpl MA
Ephraim: b 1-9-1743 d 4-26-1813 m Susannah Hubbard Capt CT
Ephraim, Sr.: b 12-16-1731 d 11-10-1812 m Marah Parker Cpl MA
Ephraim, Jr.: b 4-8-1759 d 3-10-1812 m Sarah Proctor Cpl MA
Ezra: b 4-24-1755 d 11-12-1842 m Rebecca Dean Pvt CT ★
Ezra: bpt 12-13-1730 d p. 1790 m (1)Mary Phillips (2)Mercy Packard
　　(3)— Tirrell Cpl MA
Gamaliel: b c. 1755 d a. 2-14-1811 m Meribah — PS NJ
George: b c. 1739 d 7-3-1792 m Mary Hodgdon Pvt NH
Gideon: b 12-12-1730 d 4-4-1803 m (1)Eunice Chapman (2)Ann —
　　Col NY
Gilbert: b 9-6-1739 d 1-10-1809 m Lydia Jellison 2Lt MA
Isaiah: b 1749 d p. 9-4-1846 m (1)— (2)Nancy McDougall Sol NC
Jabez: b 1754 d 4-29-1810 m Hannah Sumner Sgt VT
Jacob: b 4-16-1719 d p. 1813 m (1)Elizabeth Cooper (2)Mrs Abigail
　　Waters (3)Mrs Polly Pike Pvt MA
Jacob: b c. 1743 d 1831 m Rebecca Mount PS PA
James: b 8-2-1757 d 9-15-1803 m Polly Suard Pvt CT
James: b 9-28-1726 d 11-27-1808 m Mercy Otis MGen CT MA
James: b 1710 d 1790 m Mary Terry PS MA
Jeduthan: b 11-24-1757 d 10-28-1841 m Joanna Moore Pvt MA ★

Jesse: b 5-12-1759 d 11-7-1841 m Hannah Bates Pvt CT ★
Jesse: b c. 1750 d 1794/5 m Martha Thompson 2Lt VA
John: b 1755 d 9-27-1838 m (1)Mary St.John (2)Sally Webb Pvt CT ★
John: b 11-22-1757 d 12-2-1803 m Elizabeth Griffith Pvt DE
John: b c. 1742 d 5- -1811 m Elizabeth Warren Sgt CT
John: b 12-18-1752 d 5-27-1821 m Elizabeth Perkins Sol GA
John: b 12-25-1753 d 12-25-1823 m Elizabeth Belknap Lt MA
John: b 3-5-1731 d 1-30-1807 m Jane Johnson Pvt MA
John: b 1745 d 6-21-1816 m Catherine Cooper Pvt MA
John: b 12-23-1749 d 4-25-1806 m Abigail Wright Pvt MA
John: b 1752 d 5-27-1837 m Annah Forbush Pvt MA
John: b 5-20-1756 d 6-4-1807 m Elizabeth Buck Pvt MA
John: b 7-27-1753 d 4-15-1815 m Abby Collins Dr MA
John: b 3-7-1713 d 9-24-1790 m Mary Myrick PS MA
John: b c. 1749 d 10-31-1779 m Sarah Merriott CS Lt VA
Jonas: b 6-19-1752 d 10-26-1821 m Mary Ober Cpl MA
Jonas: b 1719 d 3-26-1806 m Lydia — Pvt MA
Jonathan: b 12-3-1751 d 5-17-1826 m Mrs Elizabeth Weston Wright Pvt MA
Jonathan: b 6-11-1750 d 10-4-1822 m (1)Huldah Winchester (2)Sarah Sawtell Capt VT
Joseph: b 6-11-1741 d 6-17-1775 m Elizabeth Hooton MGen MA
Joseph: b 4-22-1745 d 7-19-1808 m Lois Lyon Capt MA
Joseph: b 1760 d 5-26-1849 m (1)Elizabeth Woodward (2)Hannah Groyer Pvt MA ★
Joseph: b 5-6-1744 d 6-11-1840 m Mary Davis Sol MA
Joshua: b 4-14-1758 d 2-27-1849 m Annie Young Pvt MA ★
Josiah: b 2-18-1759 d 1809 m Nancy Dotey Capt GA
Josiah: b 4-5-1724 d 5-28-1801 m Sarah Katherine Pratt Pvt MA
Josiah: b 4-27-1745 d 6-29-1826 m Jane Livingston Pvt NH
Josiah: b 7-10-1756 d 11-24-1840 m Fanny Hemenway Pvt RI
Levi: b 3-29-1741 d p. 11- -1780 m Deborah Partridge 2Lt MA
Martin: b 8- -1763 d 8-19-1852 m (1)Sally Dunbar (2)Ruth Cole Pvt VA
Mercy Otis: b 9-14-1728 d 10-19-1814 m James Warren PS MA
Moses, Sr.: b 1-19-1725 d 4-19-1805 m Judith (Bailey) Brand Capt CT
Moses, Jr.: b 9-5-1762 d 1-10-1835 m Mehitabel Raymond OrdSgt PS CT
Moses: b 1755 d 10-3-1833 m Mary Besse Pvt CT
Moses: b 8-2-1760 d 9-27-1851 m Priscilla Nourse Pvt MA ★
Nathan: b 1757 d 5-28-1807 m Keziah Weston Sgt MA
Nathan: b 9-27-1762 d 9-4-1843 m Lucy Terrill Pvt MA W★
Nathan H: b 2-5-1761 d 1843 m (1)Betsy Smith Pvt MA
Nathaniel: b 1-15-1755 d 3-8-1836 n (1)Susanna Johnson (2)Mary Wedge Pvt CT ★
Obed: b 3-18-1760 d 8-29-1823 m Mary Blood Pvt MA
Oliver: b 2-10-1752 d 3-20-1813 m Lucy Winslow Pvt MA
Peletiah: b 1754 d 10-5-1841 m Sarah Parker Pvt MA
Peter: b 1751 d 1825 m (1)Thankful Briggs (2)Ann Proctor (3)Eunice Libby Capt MA
Phineas, Sr.: b 6-21-1717 d 6-30-1797 m Grace Hastings Pvt MA
Phineas, Jr.: b 5-29-1741 d 2-11-1820 m Eunice Hammond Pvt MA
Phineas: b 1700 m Betsy Collier Pvt MA
Richard: b 11-1-1754 d 2-14-1847 m Lydia Beal Sgt MA ★
Robert: b 7-14-1745 d 10-7-1826 m (1)Parmelia Love (2)Mary Law Pvt VA
Samuel: b 4-20-1730 d 1812 m Eunice Corbett Capt MA
Samuel: b 1765 d 10-14-1820 m Elizabeth Alexander Pvt MA W★
Samuel: b 11-9-1729 d 1802 m (1)Grace Wood (2)Mrs Elizabeth Bowen 1Lt NH
Shubael: b 1749 d 11-8-1820 m Hannah St John Pvt MA
Solomon: b 1748 d 4- -1778 m Mary Tilgham Pvt MD
Stephen: b 10-5-1752 d p. 1790 m Mary Hooker MM Pvt MA
Stephen: b 10-10-1757 d 9-10-1833 m Mary Giles Pvt MA
Stephen: b 1735 d 1800 m Joanna Read PS NY
Sylvanus: b 5-9-1746 d 5-14-1809 m (1)Huliah Pierce Booth (2)Sarah Washburn Sgt MA
Thadeus: b 1-17-1735 d 2-20-1829 m (1)Abigail Whipple (2)Hannah Gould Pvt MA
Thomas: b 4-5-1743 d 1818 m Sarah Dodge Capt MA
Thomas: b 4-5-1743 d 1-1-1819 m (1)Tabitha Dustin (2)Sarah (Marsh) Myrick Sol PS NH
Thomas: b 3- -1757 d 8- -1838 m Margaret Milner Pvt PA
Thomas: b c. 1751 d p. 1790 m Hannah Jackson Capt VA
Thomas: b 1744 d 1823 m (1)Hannah Powell (2)Elizabeth — Sgt VA
Timothy: b 9-14-1715 d 8-3-1803 m Rebecca Taintor Pvt MA
Timothy: b 1761 d p. 1820 m — Pvt MA ★
Wm.: b 1745 d p. 1794 m Abigail Emmons Pvt CT
Wm.: b 9-17-1751 d 7-29-1831 m Rebecca Hathaway Capt MA
Wm.: b 5-29-1740 d 11-20-1822 m Elizabeth Fletcher Sgt MA
Wm.: b 1724 d p. 1775 m (1)Hannah Boynton (2)Sarah Stevens MM MA
Wm.: b 1740 d 9-3-1819 m Anne Wilcox PS VA
Wm.: b 10- -1761 d 5-10-1842 m Rhoda — Pvt SC ★
Wm. Cotton: b 1752 d p. 7-11-1820 m Dorcas Smith Cpl MA ★
Zenas: b 3-22-1758 d 2-9-1835 m Susanna Weston Pvt MA ★

WARRINER,
Abner: b 12-1-1752 d 4-14-1828 m Elizabeth Wright Cpl MA
Benjamin: b 3-3-1751 d 5-8-1823 m Rachel Tolles Pvt MA ★
James: b 9-2-1723 d 6-20-1793 m Miriam Parsons Capt MA

Lewis W.: b 12-13-1759 d 11-11-1805 m Elizabeth Remington Sgt MA
Reuben: b 11-17-1756 d p. 1800 m Sarah Colton Cpl MA
Samuel, Jr.: b 5-24-1760 d 8-21-1813 m Keziah Pease Pvt MA
Samuel: b 4-30-1744 d 9-25-1808 m Chloe Nash Pvt VT
Willard: b 2-17-1755 d 3-9-1835 m Lois (Stebbins) Hancock Pvt MA ★
Wm.: b 1-2-1744 d p. 1787 m Lois Morgan PS MA

WARRINGTON,
John: b 1751 d — m Eunice Johnson Pvt DE
Wm.: b 4-10-1755 d 5-25-1851 m (1) — (2)Leah Townsend (3)Nancy Holland (4)Mrs Nancy Littell Sgt VA ★

WART,
John: b 1712 d 1790 m Mary Putnam Pvt NY
Matthias: b 1714 d 8-9-1798 m Hannah — Pvt NY

WARTERFIELD,
Peter: b 1760 d 8-4-1849 m Mildred Martin Pvt VA ★

WARTH,
George: b 2-28-1747 d 5-24-1812 m Hannah Berry Pvt VA

WARTHEN,
Richard: b 1742 d 1806 m Elippia Burrow Pvt MD
Wm.: b 1749 d p. 1795 m Esther Whitter PS MD
Wm.: b 1761 d 1823 m (1)Mary Mott (2)Rebecca Beckham Pvt GA

WARWICK,
Abraham: b 5-19-1739 d 4-28-1808 m Amy Campbell Sol VA
Andrew: b c. 1735 d p. 4-5-1802 m X PS NC
Jacob: b 1743 d 1-10-1826 m Mary Vance Lt VA
James: b 2-19-1764 d 1840 m — Martin Pvt VA
Wm.: b — d p. 1-7-1784 m Martha — Pvt MD

WASGATT,
Davis: b 3-11-1751 d 11-27-1843 m Rachel Richardson Sgt MA ★

WASH,
John: b 12-23-1751 d 1839 m Nancy Frazier Gatewood Capt NC VA ★
Wm.: b c. 1753 d 4-7-1837 m Amelia Jones Sgt VA ★
Wm.: b 4-4-1752 d 7-24-1835 m Anee Lipscomb Sgt VA ★

WASHBURN, (includes WASHBURNE)
Abiel: b 11-21-1757 d 9-7-1848 m Abigail Briggs Pvt MA
Abner: b 10-12-1757 d 12-27-1848 m Olive Standish Sgt MA ★
Abraham: b a. 1733 d 6-9-1803 m Mary Weston Pvt MA
Abraham: b 1742 d 7-8-1785 m Rebecca Leonard Capt MA
Alden: b 1759 d 4-14-1826 m Sarah Gannet Pvt MA ★
Amos: b 4-8-1742 d 10-14-1794 m Prudence Haskins Capt MA
Barzaleel: b c. 1737 d 10-5-1813 m (1)Barsheba Hammond (2)Hannah Griffith (3)Patience Sollard Pvt MA
Benjamin: b 7-6-1735 d 1-5-1796 m Desire Sears Pvt MA
Benjamin: b 1752 d 4-5-1822 m Alice Shaw Pvt MA
Benjamin: b 1752 d p. 5-21-1847 m Mary Beason Pvt VA ★
Bildad: b 1762 d 9-18-1832 m Lucy Adams Drm MA
Daniel: b 11-13-1754 d 4-24-1841 m Eleanor Matthews Pvt NY
Ebenezer: b 9-14-1736 d 1-28-1810 m Sarah Waterman Capt MA
Ebenezer: b 7-30-1734 d 1-24-1795 m Dorothy Newhall Lt QM MA
Eliab: b 4-15-1740 d 5-27-1818 m Anna Edson Pvt MA
Elijah: b 10-8-1758 d 6-7-1836 m Elizabeth Watson Pvt NH W★
Ezra, Jr.: b 1745 d 4-16-1793 m Lucy Fuller Pvt MA
George: b c. 1759 d 3-9-1850 m (1)Azuba Robbins (2)Mrs Eleanor Rankin Spy KY
Hosea: b 6-9-1765 d 8-23-1817 m Hannah Dotem Pvt MA
Isaac: b 2-1-1755 d 11-2-1832 m (1)Mary Phillips (2)Eunice Carey (3)Elizabeth Richmond Pvt MA
Isaac: b 1760 d p. 1791 m Huldah Allen Pvt MA
Isaac: b 3-11-1760 d 8-23-1823 m Sarah Egglestone Pvt NY
Isaiah: b 1750 d 2-21-1839 m Patience Wood Pvt MA ★
Isaiah: b 1754 d 1-5-1840 m Priscilla Wood 2Sgt MA
Israel, Sr.: b 8-11-1718 d 1-21-1796 m (1)Leah Fobes (2)Hannah Keith Capt PS MA
Israel, Jr.: b 1-30-1755 d 1-8-1841 m Abiah King Sgt MA
James: b 1746 d 1797 m (1)Ruth Rice (2)Mariah — Sgt MA
Japheth: b 9-11-1746 d 9-6-1828 m Priscilla Coombs Pvt MA
Jesse, Sr.: b c. 1724 d p. 1800 m Silence — Lt PA
Jesse, Jr.: b 7-25-1759 d 4-2-1810 m Catherine — Pvt PA
John: b c. 5-8-1730 d 1812 m Lydia Prince Lt MA
Jonah, Sr.: b 2-16-1733 d 3-12-1810 m Huldah Sears Capt MA
Jonah, Jr.: b 1-3-1760 d 11-7-1836 m Sally Eddy Pvt MA
Joseph: b 4-8-1755 d 3-27-1807 m Ruth Davis Lt MA
Joseph: b 1-30-1763 d 5-24-1841 m Sarah Gay Pvt MA ★
Joseph: b 5-29-1752 d 12-2-1831 m Freelove Matthews Pvt NY
Judah: b 7-10-1746 d 5-8-1824 m Priscilla Sampson Cpl MA
Lettice: b 6-9-1758 d 4-3-1844 m (1)Mercy Spooner (2)Sarah Spooner Pvt MA W★
Luther: b 3-25-1757 d 3-25-1837 m Sarah Spinning Pvt MA
Manassah: b c. 1765 d p. 6-12-1824 m Sylvia Caswell Pvt MA
Moses: b 1750 d 1830 m Eunice Ellithorpe Drm CT MA
Nathan: b 6-25-1758 d 10-9-1837 m (1)Annah Ellithorpe (2)Elizabeth Marsh Pvt NY

WASHBURN, contd.
Nathan: b c. 1725 d 1785 m Mary Mahurin Pvt MA
Nathaniel: b c. 1740 d 1810-1820 m Christeneh — Sgt NJ
Oliver: b 1755 d c. 1850 m Hannah Gannett Pvt MA
Robert: b a. 1756 d 6- -1797 m Elizabeth Harwood Pvt MA W★
Samuel: b 1753 d 3-31-1818 m Hannah Haven Pvt MA
Seth, Sr.: b 5-19-1723 d 2-12-1794 m (1)Mary Harrod (2)Mrs Sarah
    Sargent Col MA
Seth, Jr.: b 1751 d 10-8-1799 m Elizabeth Brown Sgt VT
Solomon: b 9-1-1734 d 12-20-1816 m Mary Warner Ens CT
Solomon: b 10-25-1754 d 1824 m Anne Mitchell Pvt MA
Wm.: b 5-9-1767 d 7-26-1851 m Huldah Clark Sol MA

WASHER,
Stephen: bpt 8-25-1736 d 8-20-1806 m Sarah Wilkins Pvt NH

WASHINGTON,
Augustine: b 1720 d a. 1799 m Ann Aylett PS VA
Bailey: b 1730 d 1803 m Catherine Storke PS VA
Charles: b 5-21-1738 d 1799 m Mildred Thornton Col VA
Edward, Sr.: b c. 1715 d p. 6-30-1791 m X Pvt VA
Edward, Jr.: b 1750 d 5-16-1813 m Elizabeth Hough Sanford PS VA
George: b 1737-40 d p. 10-2-1800 m Esther — PS VA
George Augustine: b c. 1763 d a. 1-24-1793 m Frances Bassett
    2Lt VA
John: b c. 1704 d 8- -1782 m Mary Massie PS VA
John: b c. 17- - d 1787 m Nancy Constant PS VA
John: b c. 1735 d 3-14-1777 m Elizabeth Buckner Capt VA
John Augustine: b 1-13-1736 d 2- -1787 m Hannah Bushrod Col VA
Joseph: b c. 1745 d 1803 m Zillah Branch Ens VA
Lawrence: b 3-31-1727 d 1804-09 m Elizabeth Dade PS VA
Martha Custis: b 5- -1732 d 5-22-1802 m (1)Daniel Parke Custis
    (2)Gen George Washington PS VA
Mary Ball: b 1706 d 8-25-1789 m Augustine Washington PS VA
Samuel: b 11-16-1734 d p. 9-9-1781 m (1)Jane Champe (2)Mildred
    Thornton (3)Lucy Chapman (4)Ann Allerton (5)Mrs Susannah
    Holding Col VA
Thomas: b 5-24-1731 d 1794 m Ann Muse Lt VA
Thomas: b c. 1759 d p. 3-20-1818 m Janet Love PS VA
Thornton: b 1760 d p. 6-26-1787 m (1)Mildred Berry (2)Frances
    Thornton Washington Ens VA
Warner, Sr.: b 9-22-1722 d 6-23-1790 m (1)Elizabeth Macon
    (2)Hannah Fairfax PS VA
Warner, Jr.: b 4-15-1751 d c. 1808 m (1)Mary Whiting (2)Sarah
    Warner Roote PS VA
Wm.: b 2-28-1752 d 3-6-1810 m Jane Riley Elliott LCol VA SC
Wm. Augustine: b 11-25-1757 d 10-2-1810 m (1)Jane Washington
    (2)Molly Lee (3)Sarah Tayloe LCol VA

WASS,
David Moore: b 1744 d 1-29-1827 m Rebecca Allen Sgt MA
John: b c. 1746 d p. 1790 m Catherine Norton PS CT

WASSON, (includes WASON)
James: b 1711 d 8-22-1799 m Hannah Caldwell PS NH
James: b 9-18-1762 d 7-7-1826 m Elizabeth Dinsmore Pvt NH
James: b c. 1749 d 1789/90 m Margaret Baird PS NY
James: b 11-15-1763 d 2-4-1848 m Margaret Dorne Pvt NY
James: b c. 1758/9 d 12-29-1810 m Mary Orr Pvt PA
John: b 1759 d 10-11-1839 m Annie Turner Pvt CT ★
Joseph: b 12-25-1744 d 6-23-1822 m Sarah Smith Pvt NC
Robert: b 1735 d 3-28-1805 m Elizabeth Wason Pvt NH
Thomas: b 12-26-1748 d 11-18-1832 m Mary Boyd Sol NH
Thomas: b c. 1701 d 1- -1801 m Ann Wright PS NH
Wm.: b a. 1762 d p. 1852 m Elizabeth Lorrance Pvt NC

WATERBURY,
Daniel: b 2-15-1742 d 3-15-1798 m Ann Bouton Lt NY
Daniel, Jr.: b 7-25-1764 d 10-5-1847 m (1) — Bishop (2)Mary
    Stevens Pvt NY
David: b 2-12-1722 d 6-29-1801 m Mary Waterbury BG CT
David: b 12-26-1735 d 1-20-1808 m (1)Mary Prue Smith (2)Martha
    Hoyt Capt NY
Deodate: b 4-23-1763 d 9-22-1830 m Mary Wardwell Pvt CT W★
Ebenezer: b 7-27-1760 d 1795 m Sarah — Pvt CT
Enos: b 6-19-1762 d 3-1-1846 m (1)Sarah — (2)Anna Wicks Sol CT
James: b 11-28-1754 d — m Elizabeth Mead Sgt CT
John: b 2-21-1752 d 8-6-1829 m X Lt CT
John: b 12-5-1711 d c. 1780 m Hannah Ferris Ens CT
John: b 12-21-1718 d 1788 m Mary Slosson Pvt CT
Jonathan: b 3-6-1756 d 3-24-1824 m Sally Maria Travis Pvt CT
Josiah: b 7-31-1732 d p. 1782 m Sarah Hunter Pvt CT
Peter: b 5-29-1750 d 1818 m Mary Slosson CG CT
Phineas: b 6-1-1739 d — m Elizabeth Lounsbury Pvt CT
Samuel: b 2-24-1745 d 12-8-1832 m Lydia Webster Sgt NY

WATERMAN,
Abraham: b 11-29-1733 d 3-16-1818 m Anna Brown Capt CT
Abraham: b 5-9-1766 d 12-30-1842 m (1)Hannah Spalding (2)Mary
    Boardman (3)Hepsibah Perry Pvt CT
Adonijah: b 3-12-1738/9 d 6- -1806 m (1)Mary Elwell (2)Rachel
    Bagg (3)Mrs Dorcas Treat Pvt MA

Andrew: b 1724 d 3-6-1812 m (1)Sarah Wilkinson (2)Margaret
    Foster Capt RI
Anthony, Sr.: b 12-3-1736 d 9-27-1799 m Deborah Foster Lt PS MA
Anthony, Jr.: b 2-3-1763 d 6-20-1825 m Mrs Deborah Waterman Pvt
    MA
Arannah: b 4-24-1749 d 8-27-1838 m Hannah Leffingwell MM CT
Asa, Sr.: b 11-15-1706 d 11-14-1783 m Lucy Hyde PS CT
Asa, Jr.: b 5-1-1743 d 2-26-1789 m Anne Sterry Capt CT W★
Asa, Sr.: b 7-25-1736 d 11-9-1817 m Ruth Beebe LCol NY
Asher: b 7-31-1759 d 5-2-1827 m Sally Lockhart Pvt CT
Benjamin: b 2-20-1740 d 11-30-1832 m (1)Mary Knight (2)Sarah
    Sheldon Pvt RI
Benjamin: b 1730-5 d a. 1817 m (1)Anne Manton (2)Catherine
    Latham Pvt RI
Calvin: b 1-17-1755 d 10-16-1840 m (1)Nancy Remmington
    (2)Priscilla Peck Pvt CT ★
Charles: b 1762 d 11-12-1823 m Anna Waterman Pvt CT
Charles: b 11-17-1761 d 2-9-1840 m Sarah Aplin Pvt CT
Daniel: b 1-21-1745 d 9-17-1832 m (1)Lydia Waterman (2)Susan
    Hammond (3)Esther Hammond Pvt RI
Daniel, Sr.: b 5-6-1724 d 10-27-1798 m Ann Ford Pvt CT
Daniel, Jr.: b 5-24-1749 d 5-1-1825 m (1)Phoebe House (2)Hannah
    Fellows Pvt VT
Darius, Sr.: b 3-17-1735 d p. 1790 m Mary Barker 2Lt CT
Darius, Jr.: b 8-12-1760 d 1-26-1846 m (1) — (2)Mrs Rhoda Pratt
    Pvt Smn CT ★
David: b 6-11-1760 d p. 1796 m Nancy Brown Pvt RI
Ebenezer: b 3-10-1733 d p. 1781 m Sybil — Pvt CT
Elijah: b 3-4-1756 d 4-29-1828 m Ruth Clark Cpl VT ★
Elisha: b 10-18-1735 d 4-10-1813 m — Sgt NY
Ephraim: b 10-20-1725 d p. 1820 m Betty Delano Pvt MA
Ephraim, Jr.: b 1757 d 9-27-1824 m Jerusha Palmer Pvt MA ★
Gladding: b 9-17-1759 d 10- -1834 m Charlotte Dean Pvt Smn
    CT ★
Issac: b 2- -1755 d 6-23-1813 m Lucy Sampson Pvt MA
John: b 1739 d 4-7-1810 m Mary Lord Lt CT
John: b c. 1748 d 12-16-1825 m Elizabeth — Ens CT ★
John: b 1-22-1745 d 12-23-1830 m Molly Fitch Pvt CT
John: b 7-3-1718 d 4-26-1790 m Fear Sturtevant Pvt MA
John: b 5-18-1755 d 5-28-1830 m Anna Hall Pvt MA
John: b 6-25-1760/1 d 5-30-1847 m Mary Harris Pvt MA
John: b c. 1728 d 2-7-1777 m Mary Olney PS RI
John: b 8-25-1730 d 6-11-1812 m Sarah Potter Col RI
John: b c. 1728 d 8-19-1812 m (1)Sally Fenner (2)Alice Stephen Col
    RI
Jonathan: b 2-20-1748 d 7-19-1842 m (1)Abigail Washburn
    (2)Hannah Bartlett Cpl MA
Joseph: b 10-29-1738 d 1-15-1818 m Deborah Winslow Capt MA
Joseph: b 1750 d 1833 m Susanna — Sgt MA ★
Joseph: b 11-12-1750 d 3-7-1837 m Lucy Joscelyn Monroe Pvt MA
Josiah: b 4-20-1735 d 1-6-1795 m Thankful Humphrey Pvt MA
Laban: b 1754 d 4-25-1795 m Esther Eddy Capt NY
Luther: b 3-25-1753 d 9-9-1807 m Phoebe Barker Srgn Mte Dr CT
Nathaniel: b 1743 d 5-27-1785 m Mercy Otis Pvt PS MA
Nehemiah: b 10-2-1736 d 1802 m Susannah Isham Capt CT
Noah: b 3-3-1754/5 d 3-31-1838 m Esther Ellis Pvt MA ★
Olney: b c. 1760 d p. 1836 m Mary Pitcher Sgt RI ★
Perez, Sr.: b 10-8-1713 d 8-9-1793 m Abigail Bryant Pvt MA
Perez: b 6-19-1739 d 1821 m Abigail Coffin Hussey Lt RI
Richard: b c. 1743 d p. 8-26-1826 m Elizabeth Smith Pvt RI
Robert: b 3-12-1759 d 3-4-1838 m Rebecca Cushman Pvt Mar MA ★
Samuel: b 1-6-1743 d 1799 m Hulda Sawyer Pvt VT
Seth: b 2-1-1740/41 d 9-1-1824 m Hannah Perkins Pvt MA ★
Stephen, Jr.: b 8-22-1752 d 5-5-1794 m Mercy Thornton Pvt RI W★
Theophilus: b 5-7-1752 d 3-11-1826 m Lydia Chadwick Pvt MA
Thomas: b 5-4-1731 d 8-9-1797 m Lydia Lincoln Pvt MA
Thomas: b 6-7-1731 d 9-14-1807 m Lydia (Waterman) Lt RI
Wm.: b 6- -1763 d 2-25-1847 m Miriam Thorpe Mar CT
Wm.: b 8-13-1749 d 4-1-1809 m Deborah (Lobdell) Bryant Pvt MA
Wm.: b 3-6-1745 d 12-23-1839 m Phebe Arnold Lt RI ★
Zenas: b 12-29-1762 d 10-6-1852 m Eunice Dean Fif Pvt MA

WATERS, (includes WATTERS)
Abner: b 4- -1758 d 12-11-1838 m Anna Brewster Pvt MA ★
Abraham: b 4-3-1743 d 8-12-1798 m Mehitable (Waters) Sgt PS MA
Andreas: b 9-21-1752 d 1777 m Betty Goodell Pvt MA
Asa: b 1-27-1742 d 11-12-1813 m Sarah Goodale Lt MA
Asa: b 2-11-1760 d 1845 m (1)Lydia Smith (3)Susan B Sheppard Pvt
    MA ★
Boardwine: b 1761 d 1820 m Jane Lynch Sol SC
Daniel: b 3-13-1735 d — m Lucy Spauling Lt CT
Daniel: b 6-20-1731 d 3-26-1816 m (1)Agnes Smith (2)Mary
    Mortimer (3)Sarah Sigourney Mstr MD
David: b 4-15-1748 d a. 9-11-1834 m Phebe Thurston Pvt NY ★
Hezekiah: b 4-12-1739 d 5-23-1813 m Mary Bliss Pvt NH
Ignatius: b 10-13-1753 d 9-27-1809 m Sarah Squier Pvt CT
Israel: b 10-13-1753 d 9-27-1809 m Sarah Squier Pvt CT
James: b 12-8-1737 d 1808 m (1)Anne Dement (2)Dradin King
    PS MD
John: b 1735 d p. 2-19-1784 m Elizabeth Hutchkins Pvt MD
John: b 1748 d 6-17-1775 m Hannah Pike Pvt NH
John: b a. 1755 d 1811 m Margaret Morah Pvt PA
John Cartwright: b — d p. 1-16-1812 m — Pvt PS MD

Jonathan: b 1758 d 5-3-1823 m Mrs Sarah Ann Thornton Mar MD ★
Jonathan: b c. 1750 d 9- -1800 m Mary Snyder Tms NJ
Joseph: b 1745 d 1811 m Lydia Gillett Sgt CT
Joseph: b 5-28-1759 d p. 3-15-1800 m Sarah Collins Sol GA
Joseph: b 4-16-1744 d 10-9-1804 m Elizabeth Dwight Cpl MA
Josephus: b 1742 d p. 1800 m Mary Edwards PS MD
Josephus Burton: b 1753 d 1837 m Margaret Lancaster Lansdale
    Pvt MD
Judah: b 4-12-1758 d 2-23-1838 m Olive Fuller Pvt MA ★
Philemon: b 6-1-1734 d 1796-99 m Mary Berry Col SC
Philemon, Jr.: b 1762 d 3-1-1818 m Ruth Llewellyn Pvt SC
Richard: b 1756 d 8-25-1829 m (1)Debora Slifer (2)Eliz Jane
    Boyle Capt MD ★
Richard: b 1759/60 d 1810 m Margaret Hamilton Smith Dr MD
Richard, Sr.: b 1715 d 1797 m Elizabeth Williams PS MD
Samuel: b 5-29-1719 d 4-24-1782 m Jemima Howard PS NY
Stephen: b 4-13-1735 d 1-10-1819 m Huldah Flagg Pvt MA
Thomas: b c. 1753 d p. 1820 m Elizabeth Storms Pvt VA ★
Thomas Willoughby: b 11-14-1763 d 1806 m Fanny Davis Pvt SC
Wm.: b 2-11-1740 d 5-13-1804 m Sarah Hayward 2Maj MD
Wm., Sr.: b 1716 d 1788 m Mary Harris PS MD
Wm., Jr.: b 12-25-1751 d 1-2-1817 m Susannah Magruder PS MD
Zebulon: b 1- -1735 d 1790 m Allis Bradford Pvt MA

WATHEN,
Henry Hudson: b 5-11-1766 d 6-22-1851 m (1) — Snowden (2)Mary
    Spalding Sol MD
John: b c. 1740 d 12-12-1810 m Henrietta Biney Sgt MD
Leonard: b c. 1740 d p. 5-1-1782 m Ann Mattingly Pvt MD

WATKINS,
Abner: bpt 9-9-1744 d c. 1829 m (1)Ruth Annis (2)Rebecca Wells
    Pvt NH
Abner: b 1758 d 1835 m (1)Obedience Tucker (2)Mrs Sebella Hatchett
    Pvt VA
Alexander: b 8-2-1756 d 1-24-1824 m Hannah Ruggles Pvt CT
Benjamin: b 1738 d 8-18-1807 m (1)Margaret — (2)Esther Winans
    Pvt NJ
Benjamin: b 1748-58 d 1808 m Mildred (Whitlock) Sol VA
Benjamin: b 1725 d 2-12-1781 m Elizabeth Cary PS VA
Benjamin: b 7-5-1755 d 10-10-1831 m Agness Hatcher PS VA
Claiborne: b 1744 d 1804 m Elizabeth Craig Capt VA
David: b c. 1760 d p. 2-1-1810 m Temperance Kemp Sol VA
Edward: b c. 1764 d — m Keturah Denison Sol NH
Elias: b 1754 d 3-16-1813 m Rebecca Larrabee Pvt NH
Ephraim: b 1748 d 1821 m Susannah Watkins Pvt CT ★
Evans: b c. 1749 d a. 1820 m Theressa — Pvt VA
Francis: b 7-15-1745 d 1826 m Agness Woodson PS CS VA
Gassaway: b 1752 d 7-14-1840 m (1)Sarah Jones (2)Ruth Dorsey
    (3)Eleanor Bowie Clagget Capt MD
Gilbert: b 1765 d 3- -1824 m Sarah — Pvt MA ★
Henry: b 1759/60 d 11-24-1829 m Elizabeth (Hudson) Clay PS VA
Israel: b 8-8-1762 d 6- -1831 m Mary Tucker PS NC
James: b 1730 d 1800 m Ann — Pvt NC
James, Sr.: b 2-5-1728 d 12-21-1800 m Martha Thompson PS VA
Jedediah: b 1740 d 7-29-1833 m Abigail Gould Sgt CT
Jeremiah: b 3-8-1743 d 5-3-1833 m Elizabeth Waugh PS MD
Joel: b a. 1745 d 1-2-1820 m Agness Woodson Morton LCol PS VA
John: b 1753 d 1818 m Margaret Tydings Ens MD
John: b 1755 d 1825 m X Pvt MD
John: b 1740 d 6-11-1831 m Mary Scarborough Pvt NH VT
John: b 3-1-1758 d 5-2-1847 m Ruth Guyton Pvt MD
John: b 9-23-1753 d 5.14-1814 m Elizabeth McFarren Chp NS
John: b 6-7-1756 d 2-19-1841 m Cynthia Loftis Pvt VA NC ★
John: b c. 1740 d 11- -1821 m Mary Moore 1Lt VA
John: b 1745-50 d p. 1782 m (1)Phoebe (Watkins) (2)Mary — Pvt VA
Jonathan: b 1740 d 1844 m (1)Elizabeth Haning (2)Mrs Deborah
    Dennis Pvt PA ★
Joseph: b 2-23-1734 d 1788 m Ann Brown PS MD
Joseph: b c. 1745 d 1803 m Lucy Herington Sgt MA
Joseph D.: b 3-12-1762 d p. 9- -1833 m Martha Mayo Pvt VA ★
Leonard: b 1754 d 10-10-1828 m Mary Eleanor Higdon Sgt MD ★
Levin: b c. 1740 d 11-3-1812 m (1)Edith Hilliard (2)Mrs Sarah Becton
    Fonville Sol MD
Mark: b 12-6-1763 d 6-21-1836 m Esther Legg Pvt Drm MA W★
Micajah: b a. 1745 d 1780 m Mary Boyd PS VA
Mitchell: b c. 1740 d p. 1830 m Penny Coleman Sol NC
Moses: b 3-8-1745 d 1814 m Margaret — Pvt VA
Nathan: b 3-3-1736 d 5-30-1815 m Sarah Whitney Capt MA
Oliver: b 11-29-1760 d 2-11-1833 m Lucy Loomer Pvt MA ★
Peter: b 4-12-1742 d 1778 m Mary — Pvt MD
Richard: b 1-26-1751 d 1-15-1836 m — Spencer Pvt VA
Robert: b — d 1803 m Frances Morton Sgt VA
Samuel: bpt 10- -1736 d 1794 m Submit Reeves Capt NY
Samuel: b 1750 d 1795 m Elizabeth Goode 2Lt VA
Samuel: b 1-21-1748 d 1830 m Mary McClure Pvt VA
Seth: b 1755 d 1834 m Abigail Cheney QM MA ★
Silas: b 1748 d 1821 m Elizabeth Sanders Capt VA
Stephen: b 1753 d 2-12-1838 m (1)Frances Hanslip Warnam (2)Alice
    Woodward (3)Sarah Miller Pvt MD
Stephen: b 7-18-1765 d 5-5-1852 m (1)Susannah Rice (2)Eunice
    Crane Pvt MA
Thomas: b c. 1738 d p. 1822 m Mary V. — Capt MD

Thomas: b 1746 d 1787 m Lucy Belt Capt MD
Thomas: b 11-19-1759 d 6-4-1806 m Lydia Eager Pvt NY
Thomas: b 1761 d 1797 m Betsey Ann Venable Capt VA
Thomas, Jr.: b 1740 d 10-2-1846 m (1)Rebecca Vaughn (2)Catherine
    Jenkins Pvt VA
Wm.: b 2-29-1752 d 11-17-1828 m Lois Jennings Pvt CT
Wm.: b c. 1740 d 1822 m Rachel Mullen Pvt MD
Wm.: bpt 8- -1742 d p. 1810 m Lydia Kibbe Capt MA
Wm.: b 11-12-1762 d 1840 m Anne Rowlin Pvt VA
Wm.: b c. 1730 d 1794 m (1)— (2)Winifred — PS VA
Wm.: b 1753 d 1820 m Betsy Jearingan Pvt VA

WATLINGTON,
Armistead: b 12-27-1730 d 10-29-1803 m Susannah Coleman Col VA
John: b c. 1753 d 2-6-1812 m (1)Elizabeth Allen (2)Elizabeth
    Donoho Capt VA W★

WATROUS,
Abraham: b 3-12-1732 d 5-11-1817 m Elizabeth Chapman Capt CT
Ambrose: b 2-26-1757 d 12-18-1843 m Elcy Bushnell Pvt CT ★
Austin: b c. 1750 d 1834 m Jerusha Buck Pvt CT
Benjamin: b 1748 d 6-27-1827 m Sarah Buck Pvt CT
Benjamin: b 2-8-1762 d 1-21-1843 m Elizabeth Lester Pvt NY ★
Edward Allen: b 9-11-1753 d 1802 m Susannah Pierson PS NY
George: b 6-21-1750 d 10-9-1835 m Dorcas Libby Pvt MA
George: b 3-15-1746 d 4-2-1840 m (1)Elizabeth Garland (2)Mrs
    Sallie Tucker Capt NH ★
James: b 3-13-1744 d 8-5-1824 m Ann Jewell QM CT
John: b 1732 d 2-27-1814 m Temperance Wright Capt CT
John: b 1-19-1748 d 1802 m Hulda Scott PS CT
John R: b 3-16-1754 d 12-13-1842 m Lydia Wright Dr CT
Jonathan: b 6-2-1758 d 9-23-1841 m Abia Webster Pvt Mar CT ★
Joseph: b 4-11-1711 d 7-6-1796 m (1)Mary Libby (2)Mrs Rachel
    Norman Smith Pvt MA
Joseph: b 2-12-1754 d 8-2-1837 m Lydia Harmon Pvt MA ★
Lazarus: b c. 1739 d 7-8-1800 m Lois Loomis Pvt CT
Nathaniel: b 2-6-1762 d 3-27-1845 m Elizabeth Cane Pvt ME
Samuel: b 1730 d p. 1781 m Mary Howd Ens CT
Samuel: b c. 1755 d 4-24-1824 m Patience Gillpatrick Sgt MA W★
Samuel: b c. 1730 d 1795 m Mary Whitten 2Maj MA

WATSON,
Abraham, Sr.: bpt 2-21-1696/7 d 10-7-1775 m Mary — PS MA
Abraham, Jr.: b 3-21-1728 d 12-11-1781 m Lucy Prentiss PS MA
Abraham: b 3-5-1752 d — m Lucy — Dr MA
Amariah: b 2-18-1752 d 1835 m (1)Eleanor Burr (2)Catherine
    Pettibone Pvt CT ★
Andrew: b 8-31-1755 d 10-27-1823 m Margaret Thomson Pvt PA
Benjamin: b 4-3-1734 d 12-29-1785 m Lydia Hanson Pvt NH
Caleb: b 12-17-1761 d 4-28-1832 m Lydia Howlett Pvt NH
Cyprian: b 6-1-1737 d 9-11-1807 m Dorothy Benton Pvt NY
Daniel: b 2-14-1731/2 d 4-30-1805 m Anna Tainter Sol MA
Daniel: b 2-17-1735 d 6- -1823 m Eunice Woodman PS NH
David: b 2-20-1758 d 9-20-1855 m Hannah Croxford Pvt NH ★
David: b 1741/2 d 1803 m Anne Bremer Pvt PA
David: b 1732-4 d 12-16-1805 m (1)Mary Hamilton (2)Sarah
    Patterson CS PA
David: b 10-23-1766 d 1822 m Mary McCord Pvt SC
Douglass: b — d p. 4-20-1791 m Margaret Park Lt VA
Drury: b 1740 d 1829 m Sally — Lt VA
Ebenezer: b 1744 d 9-16-1777 m (1)Elizabeth Seymour (2)Hannah
    Bunce Ens CT
Edward: b 10-14-1746 d 11-20-1839 m Annie Noble Pvt VA
Eleazer: b a. 1758 d p. 1779 m X Pvt NH
Eliphalet: b 6-8-1717 d 3-14-1812/14 m Elizabeth Phinney Pvt MA
Elkanah: b 1-22-1758 d 12-5-1842 m Rachel Smith Pvt RI
Hezekiah: b 2- -1767 d 1818 m Mary Hollman Pvt SC
Hugh: b 3-1-1743 d 5-16-1822 m Isabella Craig Pvt VA
James: b 1746 d p. 1789 m Sarah Ann Lee Pvt MD
James: b 7-20-1754 d 4-17-1823 m Lucy Browning MM MA
James: b 5-23-1746 d 9-16-1823 m Margaret — Pvt NC
James: b 1743 d 7-2-1831 m Elizabeth Long Col PA
James: b 9-29-1746 d 10-15-1800 m Mrs Martha Keys Capt PA
James: b 1-15-1742 d 4-26-1822 m Mary Evans (2)Agnes Graham
    Pvt PA
James: b a. 1746 d p. 1818 m Jeane Craig Sol SC
Jesse: b a. 1760 d 10-22-1812 m Mary Meredith Capt VA ★
Job: b 8-7-1744 d 10-12-1812 m Sarah Hazard Pvt CS RI
John: b 12-9-1740 d 10-4-1795 m Sarah Douglass Capt CT
John: b 1-28-1763/4 d p. 2-4-1834 m Eunice Fox CT ★
John: b 9-23-1741 d 10-26-1834 m Tabitha Whitney Sgt MA ★
John: b 9-26-1729 d 4-12-1789 m Dinah Viles Pvt MA
John: b 1750 d 7-19-1827 m Lucy Bukford Pvt MA
John: b 1753 d 5-2-1823 m Eunice Caswell Pvt MA
John: b — d 1-29-1815 m Elizabeth Lowry Sol NC
John: b 6-10-1765 d 10-3-1838 m Mary Lassiter Kittrell Pvt NC
John: b 10-15-1755 d 6-11-1839 m Jennie Torrance Sgt PA
John: b c. 1745 d 1829 m Mary Greenland Pvt PA
John, Jr.: b 5-23-1737 d p. 1782 m Desire Wheeler Pvt RI
John: b 1753 d 1848 m Charity Hillen Pvt SC
John: b 7-7-1718 d 8-17-1791 m Anne Murphy PS SC
John: b 1751 d 1841 m Jane Howard Price QM VA
John: b 11-18-1763 d 7-31-1849 m Elizabeth — Pvt VA ★

WATSON, contd.

John: b 1752 d 7-1-1823 m Mary Brannon Sol VA
John: b c. 1758 d p. 1836 m Mary Gillum Sol VA
John, Sr.: b c. 1720 d p. 2-3-1797 m Anne Allen PS VA
John, Jr.: b c. 1740 d 1828 m Mary Smith PS VA
Joseph: b 1760 d 1836 m Christian Ressler Fif PA
Joseph: b — d 8- -1798 m X PS CS VA
Joshua: b c. 1760 d 1827 m X Sol GA
Jude: b 3-19-1759 d 8-19-1846 m Mary Jenks Pvt MA
Larner: b 1-1-1763 d 1-16-1840 m Margaret Eahart Pvt VA ★
Levi, Sr.: b 1726 d 5-27-1798 m Abigail — Ens PS Cpl CT
Levi: b 10-9-1760 d 2-21-1842 m Lucy Olmstead Cpl CT ★
Luke: b c. 1740 d p. 1816 m Mary Ann — 2Lt PS VA
Marston: b 5-25-1756 d 8-7-1800 m Lucy Lightfoot Lee 2Lt Mstr MA
Matthew, Sr.: b 3- -1696 d 1-17-1803 m (1)Bethiah Reed (2)Sarah (Howland) Lawton PS RI
Matthew, Jr.: b 4-9-1741 d 3-15-1801 m Alice Adams Pvt RI
Michael: b 4-10-1726 d 5-5-1782 m Martha Watson Capt SC
Nathaniel: b 1735 d 5-23-1818 m Rosamond — PS NH
Nicodemus: b 1-3-1726/7 d 1812 m Elizabeth Harriman PS NH
Oliver: b 1718 d 10-31-1804 m Elizabeth Blair PS MA
Oliver: b 1760 d 7-31-1839 m Dorcas Gardiner Pvt RI
Parmenas: b 1739 d 8-23-1826 m Miriam Savage Pvt NH
Patrick: b c. 1751 d p. 11-20-1809 m Ann — 2Maj NC
Patrick: b 1745 d 3-5-1801 m Abigail Blythe Capt PA
Richard: b 4-6-1754 d 11-14-1812 m Ann Anderson PS VA
Robert: b 5-28-1746 d 1-20-1806 m Tamer Whittemore Pvt MA
Samuel: b 3-8-1749 d 10-8-1818 m Ruth Baldwin Sgt MA
Samuel: b 1-8-1748 d 10-8-1830 m Mehitable Reynolds Cpl NH
Samuel: b 1747 d 12-19-1834 m Abiah Young Pvt RI
Samuel: b 1731 d 11-25-1810 m Elizabeth McDowel PS Col SC
Samuel: b 1740 d 1-17-1781 m Frances Lewis Lt SC
Samuel: b — d a. 1809 m X PS VA
Thomas: b 10-15-1763 d 1-23-1850 m Melescent Wetmore Pvt CT
Thomas: b 1756 d 6-20-1822 m Christina Clelland Pvt MD
Thomas: b 12-25-1754 d 10-11-1840 m Rhoda Brewster Pvt VA ★
Thomas: b 12-20-1750 d p. 1779 m Sally Withers Lt NC
Thomas: b c. 1743 d 1840 m Catherine Locke Pvt VA
Thomas: b c. 1740 d 1811 m Alcy Justice PS CS VA
Titus: b 2-8-1744 d 12-14-1820 m Mercy Merrill Capt CT ★
Walter: b 1761 d 1822 m Rachel Stone Pvt MD
Walter: b 1761 d a. 9-20-1855 m Nancy Naylor Pvt MD ★
Wm.: b 6-25-1744 d 4-13-1828 m Susannah Bullock Capt MA
Wm.: b 1745 d 2-3-1813 m Phebe Garfield Sgt MA
Wm.: b 8-14-1751 d p. 1786 m Thankful Bowman Sgt MA
Wm.: b 12-11-1756 d 1817 m Sarah Ackley Capt NJ
Wm.: b 7-12-1759 d 1-9-1854 m Rebecca Robertson Pvt NC ★
Wm.: b 1718 d 1-27-1804 m Sarah Ann — PS SC
Wm.: b 1758 d 8-16-1832 m Mary Jane Ellington Cpl VA
Willis Murphy: b 4-4-1741 d 1-5-1811 m Elizabeth C Middleton Lt SC

WATTERSON,

Henry: b c. 1744 d 1791 m Agnes Reaburn Capt VA
James: b c. 1747/8 d p. 1821 m Catherine DeTar PS PA
John: b — d 1781 m Catherine Spees Pvt VA

WATTLES,

Charles: b 11-19-1758 d c. 1800 m Olive Williams Pvt CT
Dennison: b 7-12-1754 d 7-18-1830 m (1)Elizabeth Alden (2)Anne Hyde PS CT
Mason: b 1752 d 7-23-1819 m (2)Catharine Noughton Capt MA ★
Nathaniel: b 3-7-1750 d 1-2-1798 m (1)Lucinda Pettus (2)Ruth Dewey PS MA
Wm., Jr.: b 12-19-1739 d 1787 m Sarah Seabury Starr Mstr CT
Wm.: b 3-14-1757 d 4-8-1841 m (1)Eunice Parke (2)Levina — Pvt NY ★

WATTON,

John: b 1761 d 12-12-1824 m (1)Laura Smith (2)Elizabeth (Bigeloe) Green Pvt MA

WATTS, (includes WATT)

Arthur: b 10-29-1733 d 10-9-1809 m Sarah Falwell PS PA
Benjamin: b 10-5-1764 d 3-7-1840 m Elizabeth Hey Pvt VA
Caleb: b a. 1751 d p. 12-14-1825 m Susannah — Sol PS VA
David: b 1752 d 8-30-1804 m (1)Sarah Davis (2)Mary Cressey 1Lt MA
David: b 1720 d 1793 m Susannah — Pvt PA
David: b c. 1753 d p. 1809 m Lydia Swayne Pvt PA
Francis: b 1755 d 1808 m Jane Means 2Lt PA
Frederick: b 6-1-1719 d 10-3-1795 m Jean Murray BG PA
Garrett: b 1-8-1756 d 2-6-1838 m Anna Self Pvt NC ★
George: b 1-11-1762 d 1-4-1835 m Mary B Walker Sgt SC ★
Hugh: b — d 4-17-1813 m Mary Read Pvt PA
Jacob: b 1731 d 1821 m Elizabeth Durrett Pvt VA
James, Sr.: b 7-30-1733 d 7-28-1779 m Ann Walker Sgt PA
James: b c. 1764 d 7-19-1808 m Sophia Ann Bruner Pvt PA W★
James: b 1754 d 9-8-1828 m Anna — Lt SC
Jesse: b 11-23-1746 d 6-23-1830 m Eleanor Hildreth Pvt NH ★
John, Jr.: b 1737 d 12-3-1810 m Martha Brewer Pvt MA
John: b 11-8-1742 d 8-10-1817 m Eliizabeth McNeil Pvt MA
John: b 7-6-1746 d 3-1-1823 m Martha Wright Sgt NY ★

John: b 1748 d p. 1787 m Hannah — Pvt PA
John: b 1756 d 1817 m (1)Elizabeth Colvin (2) — McCully Pvt PA
John: b 1765 d 4-11-1843 m Jane Orr Pvt PA
John: b 1764 d 10-13-1812 m Margaret Pollard PS SC
John: b 1730 d 1796 m Sarah Barnet Non Com VA
John: b 1760-65 d p. 6- -1828 m Elizabeth — Pvt VA
John: b 12-14-1741 d p. 1830 m Mary Johnson Sol VA
John: b 1-24-1756 d 9- -1836 m Lucy Dalton Pvt VA
John A: b c. 1751 d p. 10-3-1818 m Judith — Pvt NC
Nicholas: b 11-30-1749 d 3-27-1824 m Eunice Newton Pvt MA
Peter: b 7-10-1756 d 5-5-1833 m Margaret Fisher Pvt NC ★
Richard: b c. 1755 d p. 1820 m Susannah — CS VA
Richard: b c. 1740 d a. 1817 m Elizabeth Townsend PS VA
Robert: b c. 1744 d 2-16-1790 m Elizabeth — Pvt NY
Samuel, Sr.: b 8-29-1716 d 1788 m Elsie Bean Pvt MA
Samuel, Jr.: b 2-4-1756 d 3- -1849 m Polly Noyes Pvt MA ★
Samuel: b 1741 d 11-25-1802 m Janet Lesley Pvt SC
Stephen: b 1-12-1750 d 9-13-1832 m (1)Elizabeth Farrar (2)Martha Christian Capt VA
Thomas, Jr.: b 2-14-1747 d p. 11-25-1797 m Hannah Rust Bogges Lt VA
Wm.: b 1730 d p. 1790 m Lydia Shute Pvt MA
Wm.: b 4-1-1736 d 9-9-1777 m Winnie Redmond Pvt NC
Wm.: b c. 1740 d p. 3-4-1808 m (1)Jane Hord (2)Lucy Wood (3)Mrs Sarah Ellis Sol VA
Wm.: b c. 1749 d 1795 m Mary Wood Pvt PS VA
Wm.: b — d p. 1776 m Mary Scott PS VA

WAUFFLE, (includes WAFEL)

George: b — d p. 1787 m Maria Esther Seeber Pvt NY
Henry: b 1-1-1758 d 5-24-1841 m Margaret Warmouth Pvt NY

WAUGH,

Alexander: b 1729 d p. 1800 m Elizabeth Throop Capt CS CT
Alexander: b c. 1716 d p. 1- -1793 m X PS VA
George: b c. 1760 d 12-29-1814 m Elizabeth Boston Capt VA ★
James: b 1752 d 1816 m Henrietta Maria Turley Capt PA
James: b 1720 d p. 9-13-1783 m Mary Douglas Capt PA
John: b 1745 d 6-1-1828 m Jane McKee Sol PA
John: b c. 1755 d p. 1795 m (1)Martha Kennedy (2)Sarah Muchmore Pvt PA
John, Sr.: b c. 1725 d p. 1782 m Martha — PS PA
Joseph: b 12-4-1763 d 1-12-1849 m Mary Hopkins Pvt CT ★
Richard: b c. 1750 d 1805 m Mrs Margaret Brown Maj VA
Robert: b 2-2-1739 d 1-2-1821 m Elizabeth White MM Cpl MA
Robert: b 11-5-1759 d 12-5-1856 m Anna Dodge Pvt NH
Samuel: b 1758 d 10-12-1838 m Elizabeth Goodwin Sgt CT
Thaddeus: b 1759 d 11-9-1810 m Ruth Farnham Cpl PA W★
Thomas: b 1727 d 2-24-1801 m Rosannah Watson PS CT

WAX,

Henry: b 1747 d 11-6-1796 m (1)Margaret Geschwind (2)Mrs Catherine Kern Sgt PA

WAY,

Caleb: b 1739 d p. 1810 m Rebecca Mendenhall Pvt PA
David: b 1751 d 5-14-1821 m — Churchill Pvt NY
Duren: b 12-22-1759 d 1-8-1833 m Sarah A Beckwith Pvt CT ★
Elisha: b 6-13-1757 d 4-14-1842 m Eunice Crocker Sgt CT ★
Francis: b 5-27-1719 d a. 10-18-1797 m Elizabeth Gosline PS NY
Isaac: b 12-22-1757 d 5-5-1847 m Mercy Baldwin Pvt CT
James: b 1721 d c. 1783 m Hester Hilliard PS NY
John: b 10-6-1740 d 4-11-1831 m Lucy Lord Lt CT
John: b 1-28-1720/1 d 3-13-1785 m (1)Dorcas Bronson (2)Mary Stebbins (3)Abigail Spofford Sgt NH
Joseph: b 5-11-1764 d a. 9-13-1816 m (1)Sarah Armstrong (2)Effitha Anderson Sol GA
Martin: b 3-9-1738 d — m Hannah Sterling Pvt MA
Moses: b 1749 d 4-7-1813 m Sarah Miles Pvt CT
Moses: b 1734 d 1786 m (1)Lydia Mitchell (2)Mrs Ann Winn Capt GA
Parmenas: b c. 1712 d p. 1778 m Sarah — Sol PS GA
Reynold: b — d — m Irene Beckwith Pvt CT
Selah: b 1764 d 11-15-1835 m Lucy Cross Pvt CT ★
Thomas: b 6-14-1731 d 11-26-1815 m Amy Merick Lt CT
Thomas: b 10-25-1729 d p. 1779 m Zillah — Sol NY
Timothy: b 8-7-1746 d — m Molly Baker Pvt CT
Wm.: b 1-4-1750 d 1-22-1808 m (1)Elizabeth Warner (2)Elizabeth Bennett (3)Drucilla Hines Sol SC

WAYLAND,

Adam: b — d p. 5-16-1775 m (1)Elizabeth Blankenbaker (2)Mary — PS VA
Edward: b 5- -1763 d 5-9-1833 m Molly Bennett Pvt CT
James: b 1733 d 1828 m Sarah — Pvt CT ★
John: b c. 1730 d 3-22-1804 m Catherine Broyle Sol VA
Joshua: b 3-23-1760 d 8-18-1823 m Rachel Utz Fif VA ★
Herman: b 8-19-1750 d 1-20-1837 m (1)Elizabeth Clore (2)Frances Clore Pvt VA ★

WAYMIRE,

John Rudolph: b c. 1725 d 7-26-1801 m (1) — Lough (2)Elizabeth Louck Sol NC

WAYNE,
Anthony: b 1745 d 4-30-1832 m Sarah Johnson Pvt NY
Anthony: b 1-1-1745 d 12-15-1796 m Mary Penrose Col PA
Benjamin: b c. 1752 d c. 1832 m Mary — Pvt VA
Wm.: b 1754 d p. 10-1-1847 m Barbary — Pvt PA
Wm.: b 1734 d 1818/20 m (1)Mrs — Way (2)Esther Trezevant Sol SC

WEAGER,
John: b 12-12-1760 d p. 1790 m Elmira Steele Pvt NY

WEAKLEY,
Edward: b 1-19-1743 d 5-29-1817 m Margaret Lightcap Pvt PA
James: b 2-27-1740 d 1-20-1820 m Rebecca McKinley Lt PA
Robert: b 1722 d 1801/2 m Elizabeth Gillespie Pvt PA
Robert: b 7-2-1764 d 2-4-1845 m Jane Locke Pvt VA
Robert, Sr.: b — d 1-27-1798 m Eleanor — PS VA
Samuel: b 10-11-1755 d 2-10-1829 m Hester Luck Pvt PA
Thomas: b a. 1760 d 1818 m Elizabeth Redding Pvt VA
Thomas: b 1750-55 d 1830-40 m Prudence Chappell Pvt VA
Wm.: b c. 1742 d 4-22-1813 m Jane Elliott PS PA

WEASNER, (includes WESNER)
David: b 1760 d 2-14-1834 m Margaret — Pvt PA
George: b 2-29-1728 d 1-29-1796 m Gertrude Braeuning Pvt PA
Henry: b 8-23-1758 d 1815 m Catherine Yerger Pvt PA
Henry Philip: b c. 1755 d p. 1790 m Barbery — Sgt GA SC

WEATHERHEAD,
Daniel: b 8-25-1717 d 1-16-1794 m (1)Berthia — (2)Susannah Gould (3)Mrs Lydia Ramsdell Pvt RI
Jeremiah: b 1-22-1715 d 5-5-1789 m Rachel Franklin Pvt RI
John: b 12-27-1740 d 1-28-1817 m Tabitha Kempton Pvt RI
Levi: b 9-15-1759 d p. 1849 m Joanna Ray Pvt MA RI ★

WEATHERHOLT,
Jacob: b 1758 d 4-23-1837 m (1)Catherine Wilson (2)Sarah Jane Miller Pvt VA ★

WEATHERLY,
Thomas: b 1734 d 1785 m Rachel — Drm Fif VA

WEATHERWAX, (includes WITHERWAX)
Andreas: b 5-16-1742 d a. 5-10-1784 m (1)Catherine Reisdorp (2)Anna — Pvt NY
Johannes: bpt 1-13-1741 d a. 3-11-1818 m Hannah Primer Pvt NY
Peter: b 1752/53 d 5-1-1805 m Catherine Appley Pvt NY

WEAVER,
Aaron: b 1736 d 1787 m Mary Douglas Pvt SC
Andrew: b 11-5-1758 d 3-11-1836 m (2)Mrs — French (3)Lois Chapel Pvt NY
Benjamin: b 5-25-1755 d 4-23-1838 m Amy Brownell Pvt MA
Benjamin: b 1760 d 5-20-1816 m (1)Miss — Drewry (2)Elizabeth Daniel Pvt NC
Benjamin: b — d 2-28-1785 m Susannah Hammett Sgt RI
Benjamin: b 5-28-1748 d 8-5-1806 m (1)Susannah Spencer (2)Prudence Lewis Lt RI
Caleb: b c. 1754 d 4-15-1836 m Freelove Cammett Pvt RI
Caspar: b c. 1720 d 1780 m Catherine LeFevre Sgt.PA
Christian: b 1728 d 5- -1783 m Barbara — Drm Fif PA
Christian: b 12-25-1731 d 2-13-1820 m Magdalena Rutt Pvt PA
Christopher: b 3-20-1762 d 9-13-1835 m Mary Smith PS NY
Christopher: b 9-6-1760 d 3-17-1820 m Phoebe Greene Ens RI
Constant: b 1757 d 2-8-1838 m Molly Spalding Pvt RI ★
David: b 1745 d 1813 m Massenburg Shoemaker Sol VA
David: b 9-25-1758 d 6- -1813 m Eve Wolf Pvt PA
Edward: b 6-10-1746 d 1-29-1828 m Mary Smith Ens NY ★
Frederick: b 1763 d 1-22-1807 m Polly Morse Pvt PA
George: b c. 1725 d 8-2-1811 m Elizabeth DuBois 2Lt NY
George Michael: b 11-17-1763 d 12-4-1832 m Catherine Harter Pvt Mus NY
Hartwell: b c. 1750 d p. 1822 m X Sol SC
Henry: b 4-15-1761 d 8-17-1829 m (1)Miss Meeker (2)Susan Ross Crane Pvtr NY
Henry: b 1750 d 1- -1808 m (2)Mary Rives Pvt NC
Henry, Sr.: b 5-28-1735 d 4-10-1815 m Elizabeth Filbert Capt PA
Henry: b 2-22-1732 d a. 11-9-1807 m Elizabeth Smith Capt PA
Issac, Jr.: b 3-1-1756 d 5-22-1830 m Abigail Price Pvt PA
Jabez: b 2-26-1756 d 4-29-1823 m Ruth Smith Sgt VT
Jacob: b c. 1740 d p. 1790 m Margaret Cooke 1Lt NY
Jacob: b 6-7-1732 d 6-2-1812 m Anna Martha Walter Capt PA
Jacob: b 1746 d 12-27-1820 m (1)Hannah Harrison (2)Sophia Spader Sgt PA
Jacob: b 9-8-1748 d 10-6-1820 m Magdalina Oberholtzer Pvt PA
Jacob: b 7-4-1750 d 7-25-1824 m Esther Neff Pvt PA
Jacob: b 1720 d p. 1797 m Susan Eitner Pvt CL
Jacob: b 3-22-1757 d 8-2-1844 m Margaret Stake Pvt PA
James: b c. 7- -1759 d 1-25-1799 m Mary — Pvt RI
James: b 1745 d 1-21-1825 m Nancy — Pvt VA ★
John: b c. 1750 d p. 11-5-1799 m Martha Sherrod Sol NC
John: b c. 1760 d 9-8-1840 m Hannah Mager Pvt VA

John: b 4-4-1741 d 1784 m Susannah Carr Sol RI
John: b 1761 d p. 12-28-1784 m Judith — Pvt PS VA
John: b 1749 d p. 1-13-1831 m Catherine—Pvt VA
John: b 175- d 1837 m Keziah Grinnan Pvt VA
John, Sr.: b c. 1732 d p. 5-28-1804 m Barbara Kaffer PS VA
John, Jr.: b 2-10-1761 d p. 5-28-1804 m Elizabeth — Sol VA
Jonathan: b 7-27-1747 d 10-6-1823 m Anna Weaver Pvt RI
Joseph: b 7-4-1742 d 11-9-1821 m Rachel Robinson Capt NJ
Joseph: b 5-7-1744 d 1822 m (1)Abigail Lewis (2)Betsy Stafford Lt RI
Joshua: b 3-3-1753 d 6-4-1811 m Anna Davis Pvt CT
Joshua: b 12-28-1753 d 6-2-1827 m Mary Trego Vol PA
Josiah: b 6-16-1748 d 1-30-1841 m Elizabeth L — Pvt NY
Langford: b 5- -1749 d 8- -1819 m Margaret Greene Capt RI
Lodowick: b 5-18-1763 d 1-31-1848 m Polly Brown Pvt CT ★
Martin: b 5-24-1739 d 8-28-1803 m Anna Maria Grubb Capt PA
Michael: b c. 1739 d 7- -1821 m Margaret Hess Capt PA
Nicholas: b 1736 d 1-10-1824 m Mrs Catherine Edick Pvt NY
Nicholas: b 1758 d 7-27-1805 m Lillis Matteson Pvt VT
Nicholas George: b 8-5-1762 d 3-11-1838 m Gertrude Dygert Pvt NY
Peter: b 1755 d 1826 m Mary Weaver Pvt PA
Peter: b c. 1759 d 1845/6 m Elizabeth Hisband Pvt PA ★
Philip: b 10-19-1764 d 1835 m Ann Schwartz Pvt VA ★
Reuben: b 8- -1757 d 12-31-1832 m Hannah Baker MM Pvt RI ★
Richard: b 5-18-1751 d 6-5-1842 m Judith Reynolds Sgt NY ★
Samuel, Jr.: b 9-9-1759 d 2-28-1851 m Nancy — Pvt NC ★
Samuel: b 11-26-1755 d 11-14-1842 m Mary Ann Bollinger Pvt VA ★
Shadrach: b 1762-1766 d 1849 m Lucy Greene Pvt NC ★
Sheffield: b 1764 d 7-26-1839 m (1)Rhoda Gibbs (2)Lydia Reade (3)Hannah Durfee Pvt MA ★
Thomas: b 1749 d p. 1820 m Mary — Sgt CT ★
Thomas, Jr.: b 2-23-1760 d 1822 m Jane Holmes 2Lt RI
Thomas: b 1754 d 4-18-1832 m Amey — Pvt RI W★
Thomas: b 10-11-1763 d 11-9-1813 m Lois Greene Pvt RI
Thomas Dell: b 9-27-1751 d c. 1804 m Jane Hinkson Pvt PA
Wendal: b c. 1746 d p. 2-20-1802 m (1) — (2)Ann (Hitron) Houts Capt PA
Wm.: b c. 1760 d 1816 m Ann Hackett Pvt Mar MD
Wm.: b 1742 d c. 1782 m (1)Lucy Godfrey (2)Elizabeth Loveland 1Mte MA
Wm.: b 1761 d p. 1845 m Mary Ashley Pvt NC ★
Wm.: b 12-24-1759 d 6- -1836 m Mary Kiger Pvt VA ★

WEAVERLING,
John Peter: b 3-4-1754 d 1796 m Ann Maria Price Sgt NJ

WEBB,
Aaron: b c. 1750 d 1807/8 m X PS VA
Abner: b 6-26-1759 d 6-26-1848 m Prudence Jenkins Baker Pvt CT
Andrew: b 8-31-1755 d a. 10-12-1808 m Agnes — Pvt SC
Andrew: b 6-10-1759 d 5-8-1834 m Hannah Whitmore Pvt VT ★
Armiger: b c. 1744 d c. 1791 m Sarah — Sol VA
Augustine: b 1-6-1763 d 10-9-1827 m Lucy Crittenden Pvt VA
Austin: b 2-14-1757 d 7-31-1839 m Ailsey Waters Pvt GA ★
Azariah: b 10-23-1750 d 4-12-1846 m Lucy Andrews Capt NH ★
Banks: b c. 1764 d p. 8-14-1820 m Mary Bull Pvt MD ★
Barnabas: b 8-20-1753 d 11-21-1832 m Anne Stetson Pvt MA
Benjamin: b 8-2-1730 d c. 1790 m Sarah Weed Ens CT
Benjamin: b 3-16-1756 d 8-16-1840 m Anna H DeAngelis Cpl CT ★
Benjamin: b 3-2-1754 d 10-13-1815 m Mary King Pvt MA
Benjamin: b 11-17-1747 d 2-9-1812 m X Pvt VT
Calvin: b 7-31-1757 d 11-15-1853 m Mary Porter Sgt VT
Charles, Sr.: b 2-13-1724 d p. 1780 m Mary Holly Col CT
Charles: b 4-3-1753 d 5-9-1843 m Martha VanVactor Pvt NY
Charles: b 1755 d 1806 m Mary Todd Ware Lt VA
Christopher: b 6-14-1755 d c. 1837 m (1)Olive Brown (2) — Davenport (3)Sally Branch Sgt CT ★
Claborn: b c. 1760 d c. 1813 m Margaret — Sol VA
Constant: b 1752 d 5-1-1834 m Molly Dennison Sgt CT ★
Daniel: b 7-1-1738 d 5-8-1821 m Hannah Wilkinson CS MA
David: b 11-5-1758 d 3-23-1829 m Sarah Davenport Sgt CT
Ebenezer, Jr.: b 5-29-1757 d 8-14-1846 m Abigail Rood Pvt CT ★
Ebenezer: b 5-27-1764 d 1834 m Phebe Todd Pvt CT ★
Edward: b c. 24-1760 d 11-18-1846 m Sarah Bolton Pvt MA
Eli: b 11-7-1737 d 10-26-1826 m Sarah Cloutman Pvt MA
Epenetus: b 8-2-1740 d p. 1790 m (1)Sarah Judson (2)Prudence Scofield Sgt CT
Ezekiel: b 8- -1747 d 5-26-1828 m (1)Cordelia Jones (2)Elizabeth Hollingsworth Pvt PA
Foster: b 10-16-1735 d 10-26-1795 m Sarah Shore CS VA
Foster: b 1-13-1756 d 12-9-1812 m Theodosia Cocke Pvt PS VA
Francis: b 1759 d 1811 m Frances Walker Mid VA
George: b 1740 d 8-25-1825 m Ann Sears Capt MA
George: b 1758 d 1836 m Elizabeth Spurgeon Pvt NC ★
George: b — d 1820 m Lucy Wells Pvt VA ★
Hugh: b 1763 d 1824 m Sara Madison Cpl VA
Isaac: b 7-28-1761 d 5-11-1840 m Mary Weed Pvt CT ★
Isaac: b 1758 d 1833 m Lucy Ware Capt VA
Jabez: b 4-18-1753 d 1830 m Elizabeth Smith Pvt CT
Jacob: b 1748 d 10-18-1795 m Hannah Thompson Pvt DE
James: b 4-14-1754 d 10-20-1823 m Elizabeth Douglass Pvt CT
James: b 1755 d 9-1-1825 m (1)Nancy Conney (2)Mary (Thomas) Peaks Ens MA ★
James, Sr.: b 11-19-1708 d 10- -1785 m Martha Webb PS PA

WEBB, contd.

James: b 6-12-1729 d 8-6-1813 m Edith Harford Pvt VA
Jehiel: b 1-23-1745 d 2-6-1813 m Mary Eastman Pvt VA
Jeremiah: b 11-29-1748 d 11-22-1830 m Deborah LeJeune Pvt CT
Jesse: b 4-29-1756 d 10-3-1837 m Mary Lucretia Taylor Pvt NC ★
Joel: b 11-29-1748 d 3-4-1825 m Caroline Wales Cpl CT
John, 2d: b 11-12-1749 d c. 4-1-1842 m Zipporah Robinson Smn CT
John: b 2-18-1759 d 4-18-1826 m Elizabeth Curtis Capt ADC CT ★
John: b 1739 d 1798 m Rachel Giles Pvt GA
John: b 4-24-1761 d 9-17-1841 m Susan Ann Boothe Pvt GA ★
John: b 8-10-1733 d 5-17-1811 m Judith Phelps Pvt MA
John: b 11-12-1758 d 10-23-1843 m Elizabeth Hayward Pvt MA
John, Jr.: b 5-19-1754 d 7-8-1846 m Sarah Leighton Pvt MA
John: b c. 1745 d 6-14-1781 m Rebecca Edwards PS NC
John: b 1-18-1747/8 d 8-29-1826 m Amy Booker Lt VA
John: b 1743 d p. 6-9-1801 m Lucy Hardiman PS VA
John: b 7-3-1739 d 11-25-1808 m Rachael — PS VA
Jonathan: b 10-2-1747 d 7-14-1830 m Abigail Curtiss Pvt CT
Jonathan: b 5-16-1723 d 1801 m Penelope Bennett Sgt NY
Joseph: b 1-26-1701 d c. 1791 m (1)Sarah Blachley (2)Elizabeth Starr QM CT
Joshua: b 2-19-1722 d 4-17-1808 m Hannah Abbe PS VT
Josiah: b 2-9-1751 d 1-23-1842 m Rhoda Page Pvt NY ★
Lewis: b 7-14-1759 d 7-12-1841 m Lucy R Carey Capt VA ★
Lewis: b 4-19-1731 d 1785/6 m Elizabeth Beckerton PS VA
Luther: b 10-24-1763 d 8-2-1860 m Dorothy Wheelock Pvt VT
Mary Edmondson: b c. 1715 d p. 1782 m James Webb PS VA
Michael: b — d 7- -1832 m Rebecca Sears Pvt MA W★
Moses: b 2-18-1756 d 1-2-1850 m (1)Polly Street (2)Abigail Jarvis Pvt CT ★
Moses: b 1756 d p. 1832 m X Sgt VA ★
Nathaniel, Jr.: b 2-3-1734/5 d p. 1790 m Hannah White Cpl CT
Nathaniel: b 8-5-1737 d 1-25-1814 m Zerviah Abbe Adj CT
Nathaniel: b 11-29-1754 d 11-10-1797 m Margaretje Deyo SgtMaj NY
Nathaniel: b 4-20-1752 d 12-25-1832 m Mrs Lydia Stanford Tukey Cpl ME W★
Nathaniel Coit: b 1748 d p. 7-8-1784 m Martha (Needham) Archer N1Lt MA
Orange: b 1728 d 8-18-1805 m Frances Sandford Sol PS NY
Reuben, Sr.: b 1745 d 1813 m Hannah Arnold Pvt VT
Richard, Sr.: b c. 1748 d p. 6-24-1831 m (1)Elizabeth Burgess (2)Mrs Mary Maulsby Pvt PA
Samuel: b 1737 d 5-24-1790 m Naomi Warner Pvt CT
Samuel: b 4-8-1746 d 8-1-1813 m Sarah — Ens MD
Samuel: b 2-3-1762 d 7-4-1846 m Sarah Haller Pvt NC
Samuel Blachley: b 12-15-1753 d 12-13-1807 m (2)Catherine Hogeboom BG ADC CT
Seth: b 4-15-1763 d 10-18-1816 m Ann Nichols Pvt CT
Seth: b 1732 d 1785 m Hannah Winship Pvt MA
Stephen: b 10-4-1742 d 12-10-1819 m Content Hewitt Pvt CT
Stephen: b 9-21-1756 d 2-11-1831 m Sarah Hodges Putnam NCapt MA
Theodoric: b 1733 d 1816 m Mary — PS NC
Theodrick: b 1749 d 1807 m Sarah Huff Sol VA
Thomas: b 11-17-1746 d 11-13-1827 m Jane Reed Drm MA
Wm.: b 4-24-1758 d 4-6-1824 m (1)Lois Strong (2)Mrs Hannah Clapp Eaton (3)Esther Curtiss Pvt Slr CT
Wm.: b 9-19-1746 d 9-23-1832 m Elizabeth Hudson MM NY
Wm.: b 4-21-1741 d 6-15-1827 m Mary Powell Pvt VA
Wm.: b 5-1-1745 d 4-11-1809 m Frances Young Pvt VA
Wm.: b 11-16-1758 d 6-8-1830 m Mary Morse Pvt VA
Wm.: b 1-2-1739 d 3-19-1818 m Miss Oney Sol CS VA
Wm., Crittenden: b 1732 d 12-20-1815 m (1)Jane Vivian (2)Jane Buckner (3)Mrs Fanny (Smith) Wortham PS VA

WEBBER, (includes WEBER & WEBBERS)

Benjamin: b 7-30-1748 d p. 1795 m Hannah Parker Pvt MA
Benjamin: b 6-5-1747 d 1815 m Mary Barbara Fisher Pvt PA
Bradley: b 1760 d 5-9-1833 m Sibbel Allen Pvt MA ★
Charles: b 1- -1741 d 11-20-1819 m (1)Hannah Call (2)Sarah Smiley 2Lt MA
Christian: b 2-22-1743 d 1815 m Elizabeth Weidner Capt PA
Christopher: b 5-25-1739 d 2-28-1803 m (1)Hannah Sumner (2)Lucy — Maj NH
Ebenezer: b 1743/44 d 5-8-1807 m (1)Keziah Kinney (2)Mrs Rebecca Breckenbridge Capt MA
Ezekiel: b 11-11-1751 d 11-11-1842 m Hannah Wakefield Pvt MA ★
George: b 1760 d 4-27-1838 m Abigail (Webber) Sgt MA ★
Henry: b 2-13-1729 d 10-26-1795 m Elizabeth Brandow PS NY
Ignatius: b 7-6-1733 d p. 1780 m Elizabeth Stewart Mstr MA
Isaac: bpt 6-23-1756 d a. 9-11-1819 m Mary Dayton Pvt NY
Jacob: b a. 1754 d 1779 m Margarette Myres Pvt NY
Johannes: b 9-21-1751 d 1823 m Eva Margaret Braun Sol PA
John: b c. 1733 d p. 1790 m Mary Redding Drm MA
John: b 11-25-1732 d 4-29-1808 m (1)Sarah Fasset (2)Mrs Susannah (Simonds) Pvt MA
John: b 1735 d 1816 m Alice Hasty Pvt MA
John: b 4-2-1762 d 4-5-1841 m Lydia Littlefield Pvt MA
John: b 5-4-1766 d 6-26-1794 m Margaret Kiger Pvt NJ
John Peter: b 3-7-1737 d 4-7-1822 m Eve Thomas Pvt NJ
John Wm.: b 5-3-1735 d 7- -1816 m (1)Maria Agnes Born (2)Maria (Sarver) Robinson PS PA

Noah: b 1754 d 9-30-1828 m Nancy Quinn Pvt MA ★
Peter: b c. 1733 d p. 1790 m Margaretha — Lt NY
Prince: b 3-20-1753 d 9-12-1831 m Sarah Cash Pvt MA
Rinaldo: b 8-28-1761 d 8-31-1853 m Elizabeth Webber Pvt MA ★
Stephen: b c. 1722 d p. 3-10-1794 m Sarah Durell Pvt MA
Stephen: b 3-18-1756 d 3-21-1836 m Elizabeth Thompson Pvt MA
Wm.: b 5-4-1749 d 4-23-1823 m Anna Porter Pvt MA
Wm.: b 3-9-1750 d a. 10-16-1810 m Catherine Mighall Pvt MA

WEBSTER,

Aaron: b 2-25-1717 d 3-21-1783 m Lydia — Pvt CT
Aaron: b 9-4-1748 d p. 1791 m Mary Shepard Pvt CT
Abel: b 7-2-1726 d 2-14-1801 m (1)Hannah Emerson (2)Mrs Jemima Eastman PS NH
Abigail Marsh: b 5-28-1705 d 8-5-1790 m Thomas Webster PS MA
Abijah: b 1762 d 9-8-1832 m (1) — Webster (2)Sarah Warren (3)Olive (Kingsley) Ward Pvt CT
Abner: b c. 1759 d 1803 m Elizabeth — Pvt GA
Abraham: b 9-17-1751 d 8-30-1831 m (1)Rachel Merrill (2)Dorothy Seymour (3)Eunice W Childs Pvt CT ★
Alexander: b 1734 d 9-21-1810 m Elinore Burney Col NY
Allen: b 12-7-1765 d 12-27-1851 m (1)Cynthia Carney (2)Rebecca — Pvt CT ★
Amos: b 7-12-1740 d 10-12-1827 m Theodosia Bull Sgt CT
Amos: b 3-10-1762 d 1841 m Polly Curtis Pvt CT
Amos: b 1-5-1748 d 10-7-1777 m Elizabeth Webber 1Lt NH
Amos Andrews: b 8-30-1752 d 1-10-1827 m Mabel Andrus Pvt CT
Ashbel, Sr.: b 3-12-1733 d 8-1-1801 m Rachel Price Pvt CT
Ashbel: b 8-8-1756 d 11-13-1838 m Mercy Swetland Pvt CT ★
Benjamin: bpt 7-6-1760 d 11-19-1840 m Lydia Kingsley Pvt CT
Benjamin, Jr.: b 12-8-1736 d 10-29-1782 m Lucretia Buell Pvt CT
Benjamin: b 12-29-1759 d 1-20-1832 m Eva (Melius) Ross Pvt CT ★
Benjamin: b 4-22-1744 d 10-19-1827 m (1)Susan Webster (2)Judith Heath Cpl NH
Benjamin: b 8-24-1701 d 2-5-1781 m (1)Elizabeth Stuart (2)Mary Standian PS NH
Caleb: b 7-12-1752 d 11-13-1796 m (1)Sarah Davis (2)Joanna Smith (3)Mary Smith (4)Lydia — Pvt NH
Charles: b 3-18-1743/4 d 6- -1796 m Rhoda Kilbourn Fif CT
Charles: b 3-22-1745 d 5-2-1802 m Hannah Phelps Pvt CT
Charles Richard: b 9-30-1762 d 7-18-1834 m (1)Rachel Steele (2)Cynthia Steele Pvt CT
Constant, Sr.: b 12-7-1741 d 7-9-1826 m (1)Lois Kinne (2)Mrs Chloe (Atherton) Sackett Capt MA
Constant, Jr.: b c. 1763 d 2- -1830 m Chloe Daniels Pvt MA
Cyrenius: b 7-18-1747 d 6-26-1830 m Prudence Skinner Pvt CT
Cyprian 2d: b 1732 d 4-12-1809 m Sarah Haden PS CT
Daniel: b 4-29-1740 d 4-4-1835 m (1)Bridget Holdbridge (2)Temperance Culver Pvt CT
Daniel: b 1748 d 8-9-1834 m (2) — Whittler 2Lt MA
Daniel: b 1-10-1758 d p. 1793 m Martha Vaughn Pvt CT ★
Daniel: b 11-7-1761 d a. 6-1-1802 m Anne Clark Pvt MA
Daniel: b 12-6-1730 d 9-22-1813 m Hannah Vosburgh Cpl NY
David: b 2-14-1754 d 10-15-1819 m (1)Jerusha Berge (2)Nancy Randall Pvt CT
David: b 12-10-1738 d 5-8-1824 m (1)Elizabeth Clough (2)Susanna Chase Col NH
David: b 8-12-1758 d 9-1-1847 m Sarah Carr Sgt NH ★
Ebenezer: b 2-1-1744/5 d 3-13-1823 m (1)Rebecca Baldwin (2)Martha Barker (3)Elizabeth Bradford Pvt NH
Ebenezer: b 4-22-1739 d 4-22-1806 m (1)Mehitable Smith (2)Abigail Eastman CS PS Capt NH
Ebenezer: b 10-10-1714/15 d 1792 m Susannah Batchelder PS NH
Elijah: b 3-29-1755 d 7-13-1843 m Martha Clark Pvt CT
Elijah: b 3-19-1761 d 10-26-1791 m Lois Coe Pvt CT
Elizur: b 9-30-1743 d 3-26-1791 m Ruth Densmore Pvt CT
Ephraim: b 11-26-1747 d 5-17-1833 m (1)Hopeful Cloutt (2)Prudence Smith (3)Eunice Olmstead Pvt CT
Ephraim: b 6-30-1762 d 10-16-1824 m Hannah Danks Pvt MA
Ephraim: b 1730 d 8-18-1803 m Mrs Sarah Wills Pvt VT
George: b 6-1-1749 d 8-1-1801 m Deborah Dewey Pvt CT
Isaac: b c. 1714 d p. 1775 m Aliceanna Calwell PS MD
Isaac: b 10-1-1759 d 1848 m Clarissa Dinsmore Capt NY ★
Isaac: b 1-7-1755 d 1-28-1827 m Anna Robinson Sgt VT
Israel: b 7- -1753 d 9-8-1835 m Elizabeth Rolfe Pvt NH
Jacob: b 3-31-1746 d 1-6-1808 m (1)Naomi Dunham (2)Lois Baxter Pvt MA
Jacob: b 2-12-1748 d 10-3-1776 m Abigail Goodrich Pvt MA
Jacob: b 1744 d 4-21-1836 m Elizabeth George Capt NH ★
James: b 12-22-1752 d 4-24-1829 m Ann Marsh Pvt CT
James: b 8-17-1759 d 2-2-1850 m Mollie Rossiter Pvt CT
James: b c. 1737 d p. 1790 m Mary Ann Phoebe PS MD
James: b 3-27-1742 d 9-5-1824 m Mehitable — Lt NH
John: b 9- -1733 d p. 1806 m Lucy Colburn Pvt CT
John: b 4-3-1747 d 5-2-1839 m Anna — Pvt CT ★
John: b 8-9-1714 d 9-16-1784 m (1)Hannah Hobbs (2)Mrs Sarah Smith Col PS CS NH
John: b 11-14-1730 d 1827 m Phebe Hazeltine Maj NH
John: b 1743 d 11-20-1810 m Abigail Haselton Lt NH
John: b 11-12-1703 d — m Hannah Haines PS NH
John: b 2-10-1710 d 4-29-1788 m (1)Ruth Clough (2)Susannah (Snow) Gale Lt PS NH

John: b 2-10-1712 d 2-11-1780 m Elizabeth Lunt PS NH
John: b 1-18-1751 d 9-22-1823 m Dolly Chapman PS NH
John: b 12-16-1751 d 3- -1808 m Hannah Plummer Pvt PA
John: b 1759 d 7-31-1833 m Maggie Walker Pvt VA ★
John: b 1765 d 9-6-1839 m X Pvt VA ★
John Bateman: b 3-4-1753 d 3-19-1834 m Eleanor Graham Capt
   Lt PA
Jonathan: b 2-26-1727 d — m (1)Dorothy Hills (2)Ruth Holdridge
   PS CT
Jonathan: b 10-5-1705 d 11-14-1781 m Mabel Risley PS CT
Jonathan: b 5-17-1767 d 4-25-1845 m (1)Polly Williams (2)Sarah
   Jossey Pvt GA
Jonathan: b 2-12-1732 d 6-6-1797 m (1)Eunice Shalor (2)Elizabeth
   Wilcox Pvt MA
Jonathan: b 11-22-1761 d 8-21-1811 m Betty Fanning Pvt NH
Jonathan: b 2-22-1739 d 5-29-1823 m Rebeckah Hall PS NH
Jonathan Lad: b 8-16-1745 d 5-19-1830 m Judith Currier Sol PS NH
Joseph: b 5-20-1720 d 2-28-1788 m (1)Martha Adams (2)Hannah —
   Pvt CT
Joseph: b 3-30-1739 d 3-16-1817 m Mary Sawyer Pvt NH
Joseph: b 1763 d 4-22-1835 m Elizabeth Scribner Pvt NH ★
Joseph: b 9-15-1724 d 9-13-1810 m Maria Goss PS NH
Joseph: b 4-3-1743 d 11-29-1799 m Rebecca Kester Pvt PA
Joshua: b 1749 d 6-10-1798 m Abigail Booth Sgt CT
Joshua: b 4-16-1750 d 9- -1830 m (1)Beria Risley (2)Prudence Smith
   (3)Ellinor Squires Sgt CT ★
Joshua: b 2-12-1732 d 1825 m Mary — Pvt MA
Joshua: b 11-24-1754 d 11-9-1840 m Susanna Bailey Pvt MA
Justus: b 4-2-1740 d 2- -1779 m Sarah Talcott Sol VT
Levi: b c. 1745 d 1790 m Rachel (Goodhue) Morse PS NH
Medad: b 1-5-1723 d 4-7-1793 m Elizabeth Holton PS CT
Michael: b 5-8-1748 d 2-27-1850 m Elizabeth Clark Pvt CT ★
Moses: b 5-25-1743 d 1-28-1815 m Elizabeth Bennett Pvt CT
Moses: b 1754 d 10-11-1844 m Elizabeth Woods Pvt NH
Nathan: b 8-29-1752 d c. 1838 m (1)Mary Andrus (2)Mrs
   Elizabeth (Pitcher) Fish Pvt CT ★
Nathan: b c. 1758 d p. 1835 m (1)Sarah Russell (2)Elizabeth — Pvt
   CT ★
Nathan: b 7-12-1745 d 1787 m Hannah Bailey Pvt NH
Nathaniel: b 11-23-1753 d 4-29-1836 m Mehitable Smith Pvt NH
   W★
Noah, Sr.: b 3-25-1722 d 11-9-1813 m (1)Mercy Steele (2)Sarah
   Hopkins Capt CT
Noah, Jr.: b 10-16-1758 d 5-28-1843 m Rebecca Greenleaf Sol CT
Oliver: b 5-6-1735 d 1816 m Patience Wright Pvt MA
Pelatiah: b 11-17-1725 d 9- -1795 m Ruth — PS PA
Peter: b 1-29-1750 d 1-25-1835 m Polly Webster Pvt NH
Philologos: b 4-24-1759 d 5-28-1824 m Sarah Scott Pvt CT
Ransford: b 12-5-1765 d p. 1810 m Tryphena Vaughn Pvt CT
Reuben: b 5-12-1757 d 8-2-1833 m Anne Buel Pvt CT
Richard: b 1-1-1754 d 1-16-1836 m Elizabeth Randall Pvt NH ★
Robert: b 1730 d 1778 m Molly Burt Capt CT
Samuel: b 5- -1764 d 12-11-1834 m Margaret Keeney Sgt CT ★
Samuel: b 1737 d 6-2-1799 m Lucy Bissell Pvt CT
Samuel: b 9- -1749 d 3-25-1813 m Huldah Skinner Pvt CT
Samuel: b 4-18-1750 d 4-9-1804 m Lydia Bradley Sgt NH
Samuel: b 2-15-1757 d 1832 m Anna Roby Pvt NH
Samuel: b 9-24-1753 d 9-1-1826 m Elizabeth Pillsbury Pvt NH ★
Simeon: b 2-13-1760 d 7-28-1842 m Sybil Converse Pvt CT ★
Skinner: b 11-10-1736 d 6-9-1825 m Jane Hambleton Pvt PA
Stephen: b 5-21-1739 d 11-28-1823 m Honor Killborn Cpl CT
Stephen: b 1713 d 11-19-1782 m Bathsheba Bryant Pvt MA
Stephen, Sr.: b 6-11-1728 d 2-4-1818 m (1)Rebecca Williams
   (2)Elizabeth (Kilbourne) Fox (3)Patience Johnson PS MA
Stephen, Jr.: b 10-20-1759 d 6-6-1829 m Eunice Loomis Sol MA
Stephen: b 1-1-1754 d p. 1808 m (1)Susanna Pettengill (2)Mrs
   Sarah (Ellison) Parsons Sol NH
Stephen: b 3-11-1758 d 3-24-1845 m Cloa Wheeler Pvt MA
Stephen, Sr.: b 2-18-1717/8 d 1798 m (1)Rachel Stevens (2)Sarah
   (Baker) Clough PS NH
Stephen, Jr.: b 7-7-1741 d 1788 m Hannah Dolbier Sgt NH
Thomas: b 3-23-1747 d 12-17-1807 m Margaret Clark Sol DE
Thomas: b 9-11-1760 d 9-1-1821 m Mary Quarles Drm GA
Thomas: b 2-14-1712 d 12-13-1781 m (1)Ruth Haseltine (2)Abigail
   (Webster) Emery PS MA
Thomas: b 12-2-1726 d 12-12-1804 m Sarah Kimball PS MA
Timothy: b 1-12-1747 d 4-30-1803 m Mabel Bidwell Pvt CT
Wm.: b 8-19-1758 d 1-10-1841 m Anna Hodge Pvt CT ★
Wm.: b c. 1740 d 12-19-1808 m Jane (Little) Yeaton 2Lt MA

WEDDING,
Thomas, Jr.: b 1758 d 1838 m X Pvt MD

WEDERSTRANDT,
Conrad Theodore: b 7- -1736 d 10- -1801 m Mary Blake Cmsry MD

WEDGE,
Daniel, Jr.: b 11-3-1736 d 10-2-1809 m Hannah Wiswall Sgt MA
Isaac: b 2-12-1744 d 4-12-1812 m Ruth Parmalee Pvt CT
Jepthah: b — d 6-18-1823 m Esther Marshall Pvt MA
Stephen: b 1759 d 2-15-1831 m (1)Temperance Alger (2Sarah —
   Pvt NY ★

Thomas: b 7-29-1761 d 7-13-1831 m Rhoda Smallidge Pvt MA
James: b 3-1-1746 d 5-18-1826 m (1)Olive Dearborn (2)Anna (Veasey)
   Dearborn Lt NH ★

WEDGEWOOD, (includes WEDGWOOD)
John: b 8-4-1762 d 1845 m Polly Towle Pvt NH
Jonathan: b 11-9-1716 d 6-11-1806 m Mary Marston Sol PS NH

WEED,
Aaron: b 5-24-1742 d p. 1780 m Elizabeth Penoyer Pvt CT
Alexander: b c. 1769 d 1849 m Elizabeth Irish — Pvt CT ★
Amos, Jr.: b 3-30-1753 d — m Hetty Sutherland Pvt CT
Ananias: b 11-20-1752 d 1-8-1820 m Sally Brown Sol CT
Asahel: b 12- -1765 d 12-7-1812 m Hannah Hoyt Sol CT
Bartholomew: b 8-4-1730 d p. 1790 m Sarah Benedict PS CT
Benjamin: b 2-3/14-1743 d 5-8-1812 m Catherine (Raymond) Smith
   Sgt CT
Benjamin: b 12-19-1759 d 1-11-1846 m (1)Mary Waterbury
   (2)Hannah (Husted) Hoyt Pvt CT ★
Benjamin: b 12-16-1707 d 5-28-1786 m (1)Mary Smith (2)Sarah
   Smith PS CT
Charles: b 10-25-1764 d 4-29-1833 m Mary Platt Pvt CT ★
Charles: b 1749 d 4-10-1832 m Dorothy Goodwin Lt MA ★
David: b 1721 d 10-18-1801 m Abagail Judkins PS NH
Ebenezer: b 10-25-1751 d 9-6-1790 m Hannah Ambler Lt CT
Elijah: b 8-19-1743 d 10-21-1793 m (1)Anne Shreve (2)Mary
   Mitchell Capt PA
Elnathan: b 4-14-1758 d 4-11-1844 m Lydia Bouton Cpl NY
Ezra: b 1764 d 1831 m Rachel Roselle Jones Pvt NY
Frederick: b 4-1-1765 d 9-17-1845 m Nancy Hoyt Pvt CT
Gideon: b 1743 d 1-17-1820 m Abigail Slason Pvt CT
Gilbert: b 12-1-1767 d 8-14-1841 m Margaret Lawrence Pvt CT ★
Gilbert: b 8-1-1740 d 9-22-1823 m Abigail Hoyt Pvt NY
Henry: b 1764 d 5-8-1852 m Rebecca Weed Pvt CT
Hezekiah: b 1755 d 3-25-1840 m Rebecca Knap Pvt CT ★
Isaac: b 7-5-1757 d 5-20-1834 m Hannah Talmadge Pvt CT ★
Isarel: b 4-12-1725 d p. 1785 m Abigail Waterbury PS CT
Jacob: b 1737 d 2-1-1813 m Sarah Kittersfield Pvt MA
James: b 1726 d 1-17-1789 m Keturah Belding Lt CT
Jared: b 12-8-1761 d 7-3-1842 m Mary Weed Pvt PS CT
Jesse: b 1746 d 4-9-1830 m Anna Rice Cpl CT
John: b 1747 d c. 1845/6 m Hanna Knapp Pvt CT
John: b 4-27-1752 d 10-11-1829 m Emily Fray Sgt NY VT
John, Jr.: b 3-26-1742/3 d 5-21-1803 m Hannah Mann 1Lt NH
Jonas: b 3-2-1760 d 4-4-1826 m Abigail Knapp Pvt CT ★
Jonathan: b 2-5-1755 d 3-13-1829 m Elizabeth Mead Pvt MA
Josiah, Jr.: b 1751 d 1812 m Sarah Seeley Cpl CT
Nathan: b 9-28-1760 d 10-20-1819 m Mary Scofield PS CT
Peter: b 4-9-1745 d p. 1799 m Esther Bouton Sgt CT
Reuben: b 1760 d 6-30-1845 m Elizabeth Dale Pvt SC
Reuben: b 1765 d 2-21-1848 m Judith — Pvt CT ★
Samuel: b 2-13-1759/60 d 3-31-1841 m (1)Abigail Gardner
   (2)Martha Gardner Pvt NY ★
Seth: b 1-13-1752 d 12-26-1822 m Hannah Andros Lt CT
Smith: b 1-6-1754 d 7-11-1839 m (1)Mary Skelding (2)Sarah
   Fitch Sol PS CT
Timothy: b 5-22-1758 d 10-20-1800 m Sarah Silabee Pvt CT

WEEDON, (includes WEEDEN)
Augustine 2d: b 9-14-1751 d 5-5-1833 m Jane Wroe 1Sgt VA ★
Elijah: b — d 10-29-1816 m Evy Rude Sgt CT
Henry: b 1755 d p. 1807 m — Thomas Pvt MD
John: b 2-10-1756 d 10-1-1839 m (1)Isabel Watson (2)Anna Chase
   Lt RI W★
John: b 1755-60 d 9- -1823 m Lucy Wroe Pvt VA
Thomas: b 1730 d 6-11-1824 m Molly Weeden Ens MA ★

WEEKS, (includes WEEKES)
Absolom: b 1740 d — m — Van Tassel Pvt NY
Ammiel: b 2-15-1743 d 2-15-1832 m (1)Susanna Chamberlain (2)Sarah
   (Johnson) Mandell Pvt MA
Andrew: b 1757 d 12-20-1825 m Anna Dorothy Shaver Pvt NY
Benjamin: b 2-28-1749 d 1829 m Sarah Weed PS NH
Benjamin: b 6-17-1755 d 8-2-1815 m Rebecca Prescott Pvt NC
Braddock: b 1761 d 10-11-1811 m Bethia Jones Fif Pvt MA
Charles: b 1759 d 3-27-1842 m Jane — Sol VA
Cole: b 1737 d 4-6-1801 m Hannah Chapman PS NH
David: b 1-1-1740 d 1788 m Eunice Rockwood Pvt VT
Ebenezer, Jr.: b 8-5-1741 d 7-6-1813 m (1)Eunice Griswold (2)Olive
   Keyes Pvt CT
Ebenezer: b 9-11-1755 d 5-8-1815 m (1)Dorothy Smith (2)Barbara
   Godfrey Small (3)Hannah Fessenden (4)Mehitabel Tripp Pvt MA
Ebenezer, Sr.: b 4-17-1704 d 5-6-1781 m Anna Holland CS CT
Elijah: b 8-23-1764 d 6-24-1834 m Sarah Bachelder Pvt MA ★
Gilbert: b 4-27-1741 d 3-12-1799 m Jemima Van Amburgh Lt NY
Hezekiah: b c. 1739 d 4-22-1819 m Ruth Cole Pvt MA
Holland: b 1-19-1743 d 11-22-1812 m Hannah Moseley Pvt PS CT
Holland: b 8-14-1742 d 1833/4 m Mary Peirce Pvt MA
Isaac: b 4-11-1747 d 7-12-1792 m Thankful Nickerson Pvt MA
Jabez: b 7-14-1731 d a. 7-20-1789 m (1)Lydia Hammond (2)Mehitable
   Campbell Pvt MA

WEEKS, contd.
James: b 1761 d 3-10-1843 m (1)Priscilla — (2)Margaret — Pvt
   MA ★
James: b 2-11-1753 d 3-17-1847 m Freelove Brundage Pvt NY ★
John: b 1737 d 7-21-1814 m Thankful Slade Pvt CT
John: b 1732 d 3-20-1804 m Abigail Piper Lt MA
John: b c. 1740 d 6-10-1782 m Mercy Gifford Pvt MA
John: b 2-17-1749 d 9- -1818 m Deborah Brackett 2Lt NH
John: b 10-26-1762 d 1-3-1841 m Esther Spencer Sgt NH
John: b 9-8-1762 d 1852 m Hannah Moody Pvt NH
Jonathan: b 12-8-1705 d 11-21-1781 m Abigail — PS MA
Jonathan, Jr.: b c. 1740 d 7-3-1778 m Jerusha — Pvt CT
Jonathan: b 12-14-1741 d 4-5-1805 m Lucy Newton Lt MA
Jonathan: b 1707 d 1794 m Esther — Pvt NH
Joseph: b 1-6-1746 d 12-11-1836 m (1)Hannah Willis (2)Elizabeth—
   (3)Rebecca — Cpl MA
Joshua: b 12-6-1748 d 1800 m Martha Rust 2Lt NH
Matthias, Sr.: b 1708 d 1777 m Mrs Sarah Ford PS NH
Matthias, Jr.: b 6-5-1740 d 3-20-1821 m Judith Leavitt PS NH
Micajah: b 12-31-1749 d 3-27-1826 m Bathsheba Barber Sgt CT ★
Philip: b 1742 d 7-3-1778 m Abigail Beers Pvt PA
Samuel: b 4-3-1756 d 3-9-1841 m Taphath Ball (2)Amy — Pvt MA ★
Samuel: b 1764 d 3-15-1843 m Lydia Williams Pvt MA ★
Samuel: bpt 1728 d p. 1790 m Martha Haines Pvt PS NH
Stephen: b 1-14-1755 d 1835 m Esther Dann Pvt PS NY
Sylvanus: b 1759-61 d p. 1804 m Elizabeth Cook Cpl MA
Thomas: b 4-21-1735 d 4-20-1817 m Mercy Hinckley Lt CS MA
Thomas: b c. 1740 d 1805 m — Pvt NC
Wm.: b 4-18-1762 d 4-4-1810 m Martha Barnes Cpl MA
Wm.: b 4-28-1755 d 1843 m (1)Abigail Rogers (2)Sarah Cotton Capt
   NH
Zephaniah: b 5-12-1758 d 3-3-1831 m Mary Meyers Pvt NJ

WEEMAN,
Joseph: b c. 1750 d p. 1789 m Mary Richards Pvt MA

WEEMS,
David: b 1706 d 5-5-1779 m (1)Elizabeth Lane (2)Ester Hill PS MD
James: b 5-5-1731 d 11-4-1784 m Sarah Isaac Sol MD
John: b 1727 d 11-28-1794 m (1)Mary Dorset (2)Catherine Cromptos
   Col MD
Thomas: b c. 1744 d p. 5-11-1796 m X Pvt PA
Wm.: b c. 1743 d c. 1815 m (1)Mrs Chapman (2)Ann Ewell PS MD
Wm., Lock: b 1735 d p. 1782 m Amelia Chapman PS CS MD

WEGGANDT,
Jacob, Sr.: b 12-13-1741 d 7-11-1828 m X Capt PA

WEIDEL,
Frederick: b 1756 d 1811 m Susanna Schreiber Pvt PA

WEIDENHAMER,
John: b 11-14-1726 d 8-3-1804 m Margaret Magdelina Eblinger 2Lt
   PA

WEIDLER,
Michael: b 2-10-1740 d p. 12-2-1804 m Magdalena Wybright Pvt PS
   PA

WIEDMAN, (includes WIDEMAN)
Adam: b 1761 d 7- -1842 m Millie Harris Mil SC
Jacob: b 1749 d p. 1789 m Maria Margaret Zimmer Pvt NY
Jacob: b 1750 d 1816 m Elizabeth Speigle SgtMaj PA
John: b 6-7-1756 d 6-9-1830 m Catharine Mason Lt PA

WEIDNER, (includes WIDENER)
Henry: b c. 1755 d p. 1813 m Mary (Clackner) Widener Pvt NJ
Johann Christopher: b — d p. 1794 m (1)Anna Katherine Kinneman
   (2)Anna Margaretha Engelhardt Sol PA
John: b 11-15-1750 d 11-13-1830 m Eve — Lt PA

WIEGLE, (includes WEIGEL)
Christopher: b c. 1755 d 12-11-1821 m Catherine Poole Pvt PA ★
Daniel: b c. 1745 d c. 1810 m Anna Weibler Pvt PA
Jacob: b 11-19-1739 d 1804 m Maria Margaret Ruppert Pvt PA
Martin: b 9-11-1735 d 11- -1822 m (1)Anna Catharina Schultz
   (2)Christina — (3)Margaret Opp Pvt PA

WEIKEL,
John: b 2-4-1748 d 9-15-1830 m Elizabeth Baker Pvt PA

WEIKERT,
George: b 2-2-1760 d 7-20-1823 m (1)Margaret Spitler (2)Anna Maria
   (Lightner) Colestock Pvt PA
John: b 1735 d 1797 m Mary Eva — Pvt PA

WIEL,
Peter: b 9-29-1736 d 3-2-1806 m Elizabeth — Pvt PA

WEINLAND,
David: b 3-1-1760 d 10-24-1844 m Catherine Elizabeth Luckenbach
   PS PA
John Christian: b 9-3-1750 d 10-28-1829 m Philippine Boemper Pvt
   PA

WEIRICH, (includes WIRICK)
Jacob: b 1754 d 9-17-1822 m Margaret — Pvt PA
Valentine: b 1750 d 1819 m Catherine — Pvt PA
Wm.: b c. 1747 d p. 3-9-1807 m Elizabeth Simons Capt PA

WEISEL, (includes WISEL)
George, Sr.: b 1730 d 8-10-1802 m Anna Mary — PS PA
George, Jr.: b 1754/55 d 1- -1850 m Margaret Rohr Pvt PA
Henry: b 4-6-1760 d 5-26-1830 m Eva Shellenberger Pvt PA
Jacob: b c. 1725 d 4-26-1797 m Anna Margaret — PS PA
Michael, Sr.: b 1720 d 6-24-1796 m Madalena Drach Ens PA
Michael, Jr.: b 7-17-1750 d 4-29-1818 m (1)Catherine Geres (2)Mrs
   Mary Sorver Pvt PA

WEISER, (includes WYSOR & WYZER)
Conrad: b 8-30-1749 d 2-1-1803 m Barbara Boyer Capt PA
Conrad: b 4-16-1753 d 9-19-1804 m Elizabeth Klinger Pvt PA
Frederick: b 12-24-1728 d 1798 m Amelia Zoeller Sol PA
Henry: b 4-15-1755 d 1-12-1844 m Barbara Ann Ripseed Sgt VA ★
Jabetz: b 6-27-1753 d 5-14-1829 m Maria Elizabeth Wenger Pvt PS PA
Jacob: b 9-24-1736 d 1-1-1808 m Anna Elizabeth Kurr CS Cpl PA
John: b 1757 d 9-16-1827 m Justina Kehl Pvt PA
Martin: b 10-15-1751 d 11-3-1822 m Maria Catherine — Pvt PA
Peter: b 4-26-1751 d p. 1790 m Catherine Muhlenburg 1Lt PA

WEISIGER,
Daniel: b a. 1735 d 1784 m X PS VA

WEISS, (includes WEIS & WEISE)
Adam: b 12-23-1751 d 10-5-1833 m (1)Margaret E Wingard (2)Mrs
   Mary Kuchly (3)Mrs Catharine Patton Ens MD ★
Henry: b 2-12-1750 d 3-2-1827 m Margaret Burgen Pvt PA.
Henry: b 8-29-1745 d 9-30-1805 m Barbara Siegrist Pvt PA
Jacob: b a. 1768 d 5-16-1784 m Maria Elizabeth — Dep QM Gen NJ
Jacob: b 9-1-1750 d 1-9-1839 m Elizabeth Robinson Dep QM Gen PA
Johan Erhard: b 3-12-1758 d 10-26-1833 m Magdalene — Pvt
   PS PA
John: b a. 1752 d 7-21-1803 m Catherine — Pvt PA
Matthias: b 3-12-1752 d 4-5-1831 m Rachel (Bonham) Ball Pvt PA

WEISSENFELS,
Frederick H: b 1728 d 5-14-1806 m (1)Mary Shurman (2)Elizabeth
   (Williams) Bogart Col NY

WEIST, (includes WIEST)
Henry: b 1-1-1754 d 11-18-1845 m Elizabeth Reister Pvt PA
Jacob: b 5-6-1730 d 12-14-1806 m Mary Roshon Pvt PA
Jacob, Jr.: b 1-29-1738 d 1- -1808 m Catharine Hoch Pvt PA

WEISTER,
Jacob: b 1741 d 6-25-1803 m X Pvt PA

WELCH, (includes WELSH)
Aaron: b 1744 d 1780 m Margaret Carmel Lt MD
Aaron: b 1755 d p. 1790 m Elizabeth Franklin 1Lt MD
Alexander: b 2-10-1752 d 1-11-1810 m Frances (Hunter) Lawrence
   Arbuckle PS VA
Calvin: b 1758 d 1825 m Eunice Rogers Pvt MA
Casper: b c. 1746 d p. 4-28-1817 m Mary Bracer Pvt PA
Constant: b 1755 d 7-3-1830 m (1)Lucy Anna — (2)Abigail Barton
   Booth Sol PS CT
David: b 1-3-1725 d 3-26-1815 m Irene Marsh Capt CT
Ebenezer: b 10-27-1766 d 5-29-1837 m (1)Patience Mentor (2)Lois
   Merrill Pvt NY W★
Edmund: b c. 1752 d 7-13-1829 m Hannah Annis Pvt MA
Eleazer: b 12-12-1750 d 1-30-1827 m Athea Manning Pvt CT
George: b 1750-57 d 6- -1837 m Nancy Cannon Pvt MD
Henry: b 1748 d 8-21-1827 m Christianna Hubert 2Lt PA
Hezekiah: b 8-26-1734 d c. 1797 m Elizabeth Woods Mid MA
Hopestill: b 1741 d 3-9-1828 m Alice Woodward Sgt CT ★
Isaac: b 1754 d 12-10-1836 m Nancy Ayres Pvt VA
Jacob: b c. 1752 d p. 4-3-1787 m Barbara — Pvt PA
Jacob: b a. 1757 d p. 9-8-1831 m Catherine Martz Pvt PA
James: b 1754 d 10-27-1806 m Nancy — Pvt PA
Jared: b 1-24-1749 d 7-18-1828 m Mary Brooks Pvt PA
John: b 9-23-1759 d 12-26-1844 m Rosanna Peebles Lt CT
John: b 2-11-1758 d 1-13-1839 m (1)Jemima Morgan (2)Jemima
   Fletcher Cpl CT
John: b 1745 d 5- -1831 m Deborah Monroe Pvt CT
John, Sr.: b 2-2-1719 d 12-16-1784 m Hannah Hammond PS MD
John, Jr.: b 1742 d a. 10-12-1820 m (1) — Hammond (2)Lucretia
   Dorsey PS MD
John: b 8-19-1711 d 2-9-1789 m (1)Sarah Burrington (2)Dorcas
   Gatcomb (3)Elizabeth Hall Sgt MA
John: b — d p. 1820 m Mary Armstrong Cpl NY
John: b 3-17-1753 d 1-25-1830 m Mary Clute Pvt NY ★
John, Jr.: bpt 11-29-1761 d 12-8-1853 m Annatjen VanWagner Pvt
   NY
John: b c. 1740 d 1812 m Hanner — Capt NC
John: b 1728 d 2- -1785 m Susannah — Pvt PA
John: b 6-6-1738 d 4-15-1811 m Eleanor Hill Pvt PA
John: b 1749 d 3- -1831 m Mary Livingston Pvt PA ★
John: b c. 1760 d p. 6-2-1834 m Jane Blakeney Sol SC

John: b 11-18-1750 d *p.* 1834 m — Pvt Wgn VA ★
John: b *c.* 1755 d 11- -1780 m Sarah Hewlitte Drm VA
Joseph: b 1738 d 2-15-1825 m Eunice Brooks 1Lt MA
Joseph: b 2-20-1734 d 7-9-1729 m Hannah Chase LCol PS CS NH
Lemuel: b 1752 d 12-16-1824 m Jerusha Gaylord Maj CT
Leonard: b *c.* 1748 d 1786 m Elizabeth Roose Cpl PA
Nathaniel: b 1-17-1755 d 11-20-1815 m Elizabeth Terrell Capt VA
Paul, Sr.: b 1696 d 8-26-1778 m (1)Jeusha Bronson (2)Rachel (Buel) Grant CS CT
Paul, Jr.: b 1-19-1759 d 9-15-1815 m Abigail Crane PS CT
Robert: b 1731 d 1786 m Mrs Frances Peacock Dr MD
Robert: b *c.* 1725 d 1788 m Mary — Pvt PA
Samuel: b 11-7-1763 d 12-30-1842 m Jane Cunningham Drm Pvt PA
Samuel: b 4-16-1730 d 1800 m Jerusha — Pvt VT
Solomon: b 1-16-1758 d 11-27-1837 m Orpha Sweet Pvt CT
Sylvester: b 5-15-1764 d 4-19-1834 m (1) — Jackson (2)Anne Glascock Pvt VA
Thomas: b 10-12-1753 d 3-18-1837 m Lovey Elliott Pvt NH ★
Thomas: b 1743 d 1789 m Nancy Alexander Sgt NC
Thomas: b 5-11-1749 d 3-2-1846 m Mary Ann — Pvt NC ★
Thomas: b 2-17-1755 d 1821 m Sarah Grigsby Pvt VA
Wm., Sr.: b *c.* 1721 d 11-25-1789 m Anna Bliss PS CS CT
Wm., Jr.: b 3- -1753 d 3-6-1838 m Deborah L Jewett Pvt CT
Wm.: b *c.* 1757 d 1800-10 m Jane Thompson PS MD
Wm.: b 8-21-1755/6 d 4-5-1845 m Mary S Hunter Pvt MA ★
Wm.: b 1747 d 1821 m Dorothea Scharpenstein Capt NJ
Wm.: b 10-28-1763 d 5-16-1841 m Mary Eichelberger Pvt PA
Wm.: b 1760 d 1820 m Sarah Allen Pvt SC
Wm.: b 1744 d 5-25-1781 m Bridget Addison Pvt VA
Wm.: b 1758 d 1825 m Elizabeth Brewster Pvt VA

WELD,
Aaron: b 9-30-1726 d 7-18-1794 m Esther — Lt MA
Caleb: b 8-31-1759 d 2-12-1846 m Phebe Clemons Pvt MA
Calvin: b 4-14-1761 d 8-8-1830 m Eunice Rogers Pvt MA ★
Eben: b 1744 d 1827 m Rebecca Mayo Sgt MA
Eleazer: b 2-19-1737 d 5-16-1800 m Mary Hatch LCol MA
Habijah: b 9-2-1702 d 5-14-1782 m Mary Fox PS MA
Isaac: b 6-13-1754 d 4-22-1808 m Elizabeth Farrell 2Lt MA VT
Jacob: b 1752 d 1819 m Sarah McClellan Cpl MA
John: b 1-4-1752 d 1-22-1834 m Deborah Plympton Pvt CT ★
John: b 9-23-1730 d 3-20-1816 m Chloe Perrin CS CT
Joseph: b 1728 d 4-28-1806 m Lucy Fowler Ens CT
Moses, Jr.: b -15-1757 d 11-22-1834 m Miriam Harding Sgt MA
Walter: b 4-24-1761 d 12-18-1813 m Lucy Carpenter Pvt MA

WELDON, (includes WELDEN, WELDIN, WHEALDON, WHEELDEN, & WHILLDIN)
Abraham: b 7-5-1757 d 1831 m (1)Sarah — (2)Anna — Pvt CT
Alexander: b *c.* 1755 d *p.* 1791 m Margaret — Pvt PS NJ
Andrew: b *c.* 1762 d 1836 m (1) — (2)Mary Peacock Sol GA
Benjamin: b *c.* 1720 d *p.* 1787 m Mary McKinde PS VA
Ebenezer: b 4-24-1739 d *p.* 1787 m Rebecca Young Pvt MA
Elijah: b 7-5-1753 d *p.* 2-12-1811 m Ruth Wesscoat Pvt CT
George: b 12-29-1753 d 12-24-1796 m Elizabeth Allmond Pvt DE
Isaac: b 1754 d 9-11-1777 m — Pvt DE
Jacob: b 1755 d 6-26-1817 m Jane — Pvt DE
James, Sr.: b 1714 d 11-5-1780 m (1)Jane Hand (2)Jane Izard (3)Susannah Hand PS NJ
James, Jr.: b 8-20-1742 d *p.* 1801 m (1)Rhoda Mulford (2)Martha Hand PS NJ
Jesse: b 10-10-1759 d 6-8-1837 m (1)Sarah Babb (2)Elsie Henderson Pvt DE ★
Jesse: b 3-6-1735 d 1795 m Ruth — Pvt VT
Joshua: b 6-5-1757 d 1842 m Mary Vincent Pvt MA ★
Matthew: b 1749 d 7-16-1828 m (1)Phebe Hildreth (2)Ruhama Hand PS NJ
Samuel: b *a.* 1725 d 1782 m Penelope Short PS NC
Seth: b 1750 d 1778 m Rebecca Goldin Capt NJ
Wm.: b *c.* 1755 d 1806 m Mary Hutchinson PS DE
Wm.: b — d 1785 m Betsy Plummer Maj NC

WELKER,
Daniel: b 1759 d 3-8-1824 m Susan Conrad Pvt PA ★
Michael: b *c.* 1733 d 1799 m (1)Anna Marie Reed (2)Mrs Elizabeth Wagoner Pvt PA

WELLBORN, (includes WELBORN, WILBURN, & WILLBURN)
Curtis, Jr.: b 1760 d 1816 m (1)Drucilla Thurmond (2)Rhoda Robertson Pvt GA
Elias: b 9-9-1759 d 3- -1836 m Mary Marshall Pvt NC ★
Isaac: b 1-30-1758 d 1-25-1839 m Mary Barton Lt NC ★
James: b *c.* 1731 d *p.* 2-15-1811 m Isabelle — PS SC VA
John: b 1757 d 11-9-1825 m Jane McGee PS NC
Joshua: b 4-20-1758 d *p.* 1833 m Elizabeth — Pvt NC ★
Thomas: b 11-8-1760 d 4-13-1826 m (1)Mrs Sarah Wellborn Cloud (2)Mary Cooke Pvt GA
Thomas: b *c.* 1750 d 1796-1800 m Martha — Sol GA
Wm.: b 1733 d 2- -1792 m Hepzibah Stearns Pvt NC
Wm.: b 1762 d 10-20-1839 m — Pvt VA ★

WELLER,
Amos: b 1755 d 6-4-1836 m Dimis Rowley Sgt VT ★
Daniel: b 1754 d 3-23-1824 m Elizabeth Mechie Pvt PA
Daniel: b 5-19-1760 d 6-19-1829 m Lucinda Treat Sgt MA W★
Frederick: b 12-5-1757 d 5-18-1850 m Elizabeth Sebastin Sgt NY ★
Frederick: b 7-5-1761 d 9-18-1829 m Maria Barbara Shafer Pvt PA
John: b 5-24-1716 d 3-11-1792 m Catharine — PS MD
Philip: b 1754 d 2-15-1828 m Gertrude Herb Pvt PA
Wilhemus: b 1- -1745 d *p.* 3-20-1777 m Eleanor Bull Pvt NY
Wm.: b 1763 d 9-3-1843 m Anna Root Pvt MA

WELLING,
John: b 1757 d 11-7-1834 m (1)Zilpah Roberts (2)Mary Hart Sol NJ

WELLINGTON,
Benjamin: b 8-7-1743 d 9-14-1812 m Martha Ball 2Lt PS MA
Benjamin: b 4-22-1738 d 8-28-1817 m Lucy Smith CS MA
Ebenezer: b 2-25-1763 d 3-3-1851 m Rebecca Leavins Pvt MA ★
Elijah: b 2-28-1750 d 12-15-1828 m Phebee Brown Sgt MA
Elisha: b 7-20-1758 d 1-12-1799 m Lucy Cutler Lt MA
Enoch: b 9-1-1756 d 1817 m (1)— Colman (2)Sarah Richardson (3)Sally Wood Pvt MA
George: b 10-21-1749 d *p.* 1801 m Lucy Peirce Pvt MA
Jeduthan: b 9-4-1750 d 11-25-1838 m (1)Susanna Reed (2)Elizabeth (Loring) Winneck Sgt MA
John: b 10-3-1736 d *p.* 1785 m Bette Warren Pvt MA
John: b 10-24-1737 d *p.* 1783 m Susanna Brown Pvt MA
Jonathan: b 6-5-1736 d 1803 m Lydia Fiske Pvt MA
Jonathan: b 9-12-1760 d 1-2-1810 m Anna Garfield Drm MA
Joseph: b 1710 d 12-18-1777 m Dorcas Stone CS MA
Samuel: b 11-28-1757 d 4-10-1836 m (1)Hannah Pickering (2)Experience Kendrick Bemis Pvt MA ★
Thaddeus: b 4-5-1758 d 1-11-1816 m Ruhamah Brown Pvt MA
Thomas, Sr.: b 8-6-1714 d 11-4-1783 m Margaret Stone PS MA
Thomas, Jr.: b 12-12-1734 d 1-19-1818 m Elizabeth Dix Capt MA
Timothy: b 4-15-1747 d 4- -1809 m Hannah W Abbott Sgt MA

WELLMAN,
Abraham: b 1-12-1762 d 10-21-1829 m Rebecca Pearson Sgt MA ★
Barnabas: b 8-15-1756 d 3-7-1847 m Lois Page Drm Maj CT ★
Bennett: b 1754 d 9-15-1830 m May Mulligan Pvt PS MD
Benoni: b 7-28-1765 d 6-1-1840 m Rebeka Lawton Pvt MA ★
Caleb: b 5-3-1761 d 4-23-1822 m Mary Mason Wormsted Pvt MA
Darius: b *c.* 1761 d *p.* 1800 m — Cpl VT
Jacob: b 12-6-1742 d 1830 m Rebecca Chase Pvt MA
Jacob: b 5-13-1746 d 1834 m (1)Hannah Boffee (2)Elizabeth Moore Pvt NH
Jacob: b 7-22-1761 d 1-17-1829 m (1)Abigail Wellman (2)Betsey Barney Pvt MA ★
Jedediah, Jr.: b 12-11-1762 d 2-3-1858 m (1)Betsey Jarvis (2)Mrs Jane Jackson Slr MA
John: b 6-9-1761 d 5-25-1841 m Phebe Tuttle Pvt CT W★
John: b 1759 d 12-18-1829 m Lydia Blandin Sgt VT
Joseph: b 12-28-1747 d 8-24-1831 m Mary Gilbert Sgt MA ★
Oliver K: bpt 7-31-1763 d *a.* 1790 m Sarah Chapman Slr MA
Paul: b 4-15-1758 d 4- -1829 m (1)Phebe Eastman (2)Abigail Wheeler (3)Mrs Mary Thayer Pvt CT ★
Reuben: b 8-3-1743 d 3-2-1798 m Mary Grover Pvt PS MA
Rudolph: b 11-1-1758 d 12-27-1836 m Agnes Archer Pvt PA
Samuel: b 3-13-1751 d 12-7-1835 m Martha Hilton Pvt MA ★
Thomas: b 5-13-1742 d 12-25-1818 m (1)Martha Follet (2)Hannah Bolles Pvt MA
Timothy, Sr.: b 1724 d *p.* 1790 m Rachel Newland Pvt MA
Timothy, Jr.: b 4-27-1757 d 3-8-1842 m Lucy Skinner Pvt MA ★
Zadock, Jr.: b 9-2-1760 d 1849 m Martha Chatfield Pvt VT

WELLS,
Aaron: b 1743 d 2- -1819 m Mary Wallis MM NH
Abraham: b 10-9-1757 d 12-22-1850 m Sarah Blackamore Pvt RI ★
Alexander: b *c.* 1742-27 d 12-9-1813 m Leah Owings PS PA MD
Amos: b 2-28-1735 d 8-24-1801 m (1)Lydia Treadway (2)Rebecca — PS CT
Asa: b 9-16-1755 d 12-10-1829 m Martha Goodrich Pvt CT
Asa: b 12-15-1763 d 1842 m (1)Elizabeth Smith (2)Dollie Allis Pvt MA
Ashbel, Sr.: b 8-25-1734 d 12-14-1806 m Abigail Kellogg Sol CT
Ashbel, Jr.: b 9-1-1758 d 9-4-1819 m (1)Bridget Chancer (2)Mary Hopkins CS CT
Austin: b 2-14-1759 d 12-8-1849 m Sarah Cowan Sgt NY ★
Barker: b 5-16-1750 d 5- -1780 m Rebecca Clarke Capt RI
Bayze: bpt 8-5-1744 d 10-24-1814 m Ruth Gaylord Lt CT ★
Benjamin: b 9-17-1745 d 6-8-1818 m Elizabeth Curtiss Sgt CT
Benjamin, Sr.: b *c.* 1735 d 5-9-1804 m Lucy Talcot Sgt CT
Benjamin, Jr.: b 2-9-1758 d 1811 m Mary Warner Fif CT
Benjamin: b 4-25-1755 d 2-12-1842 m (1)Mary Rice (2)Polly Aultz Mar MD ★
Benjamin: b 1724 d *p.* 11-26-1794 m Temperance Butler PS MD
Benjamin: b 11-22-1756 d 4-19-1813 m Sarah Nelson SrgnMte PS MA★
Benjamin: b 7-12-1756 d 6-4-1828 m Anna Chapin Lt MA
Benjamin: b 8-23-1729 d 3-1-1802 m Lucy Graves PS MA

WELLS, contd.

Benjamin: b c. 1746 d 7-20-1820 m Sarah Reynolds Sgt NY
Benjamin: b 11-28-1750 d 11-6-1834 m Rachel Hall Pvt VT ★
Charles: b 4-6-1745 d 4-16-1815 m (1)Michal Owens (2)Elizabeth Prather PS VA
Charles D.: b 5-23-1758 d p. 1832 m (1)Mary Williamson (2)— Pvt VA MD ★
Chester: b 3-22-1739 d 4-17-1815 m Hannah Belden Maj CT
Daniel: b c. 1739 d 5-23-1817 m Susanna — Pvt MD
Daniel: b 10-2-1760 d 7-26-1815 m Rhoda Newton Pvt MA
Daniel: b 11-7-1754 d 5-6-1840 m Hannah Lathrop OrdlSgt NY
Daniel: b 5-13-1731 d 8-18-1793 m Joanna Youngs PS NY
David: b 9-20-1723 d 1-10-1814 m Mary Taintor LCol MA
David: b c. 1754 d 1777 m Mary Hand Pvt NY
David: b 1744 d 7-26-1828 m (1)Bethiah Parshall (2)Abigail Youngs PS Pvt NY
Duckett: b 3-22-1752 d 4-13-1833 m Sarah Lakin Pvt PS MD ★
Ebenezer: b 4-10-1756 d 2-22-1810 m Margery Stocking Pvt CT
Ebenezer: b 5-16-1723 d 1-11-1787 m (1)Elizabeth Field (2)Mary Whipple PS MA
Ebenezer: b 3-24-1729/30 d 7-23-1783 m Mercy Bardwell PS CS MA
Edmund, Sr.: b 12-24-1721 d 6-1-1805 m Mary Howell Sgt NY
Edmund, Jr.: b 1746 d 1824 m Wealthy Ann Goodrich Pvt NY
Edward: b 2-23-1726 d 1798 m Elizabeth Sheffield PS RI
Elias: b 11-30-1756 d 1-19-1826 m Peninah Wheeles Pvt CT
Elijah: b 1-10-1751 d 12-23-1796 m Sarah Balch Pvt CT
Elijah: b 1-4-1760 d 1-8-1834 m Phebe Tillason Pvt CT
Elijah: b 7-20-1740 d 3-10-1786 m Ruth Faunsworth Pvt MA
Elisha: b 3-12-1758 d 5-18-1843 m Mary Griswold Sol CT
Elisha: b 11-12-1731 d 10-5-1792 m (1)Abigail Brooks (2)Mehitable Mattoon (3)Rhoda Graves Cpl MA
Elisha: b 1-2-1759 d 12-17-1836 m Tirzah Severance — Sol MA
Enos: b 1754 d 1807 m Anna Ballard Pvt MA
Ezekiel: b 1746 d 12-7-1818 m Phoebe Meacham Pvt NH
Fregitt: b 4-21-1714 d 11-26-1785 m Anna Booth PS NY
George: b 2-13-1755 d 6-21-1813 m Prudence Talcott Capt CT
George: b 1749 d p. 1791 m Caroline Hooker Pvt CT
Gershom: b c. 1753 d 1805 m Phoebe Armstrong Pvt NY
Gideon: b 11-12-1720 d 10-19-1805 m Eunice — Pvt CT
Gideon: b 7-15-1764 d 3-19-1810 m Emily Hart Pvt CT
Gurdon: b 2-28-1758 d 12-27-1824 m Sarah Burnett Pvt NY
Henry: b 12-11-1740 d 3-1-1824 m Margaret Burhans Sol NY
Henry: b 4-20-1763 d 9-6-1829 m Rebecca Collins Pvt NY
Henry: b 1740 d 1802 m Elizabeth Holmes Pvt PA
Henry: b 6-14-1742 d 8-24-1814 m Hannah Stout PS VT
Henry: b 9-7-1754 d 8-27-1814 m Jemima Coe Pvt VA
Hezekiah: b 12-9-1725 d 1-1-1804 m (1)Mary Boardman (2)Hannah Wells Capt CT
Hezekiah: b 6-25-1736 d 3-8-1817 m Sarah Trumbull Capt CT
Hezekiah: b 1738 d p. 1790 m Phoebe Talcott Pvt MA
Hubbel: b 1735 d p. 1789 m Zerviah Chandler CS PS VT
Issac: b 12-16-1750 d — m Unice Burritt Cpl PS CT
Isaac: b 4-17-1761 d 1-31-1839 m Anna Elsworth Adj PS CT
Isaac: b 11-10-1745 d p. 9-7-1784 m Jemima — Pvt NY
Israel: b 7-3-1757 d 4-3-1831 m Chloe Wilcox Pvt CT ★
Israel Wyatt: b 12-17-1714 d 1797 m (1) — (2)Mary Worthington PS CT
James: b 2-10-1748 d 3-25-1825 m (1)Lucy Wells (2)Abigail Gaylord Peck Lt PS CT
James: b 1760 d 2-23-1806 m Lucy Bull Lt MA
James: b 10-21-1760 d 6-16-1811 m Lydia Taylor Pvt NY
James: b 1751 d 1-29-1814 m Rachel Brown Capt PA
James: b 1-10-1732 d 7-3-1778 m Hannah Loomis Lt PA
James: b 12-23-1750 d 6-27-1839 m (1)Jane Westbrook (2)Kate VanAuken PS PA
James: b 3-27-1734 d 9-4-1823 m (1) — Slocum (2)Freelove Aylesworth Lt RI
James: b a. 1755 d p. 1800 m Ammy — Sgt VT
Jediah, Jr.: b 1751 d 3-9-1827 m Hannah Odell Pvt CT
Jeremiah: b 2-26-1737 d 3-5-1814 m Hannah Cleaves PS NY
Jesse: b 10- -1749 d 5-17-1844 m Elizabeth — Pvt NC ★
John, Jr.: b 8-23-1739 d 9-10-1806 m Mrs Lois Merrill Pvt CT
John: b a. 1742 d 1- -1806 m Sarah Hinton Pvt GA
John: b 2-6-1757 d 2-25-1835 m Mary Ann Sudler Pvt MD ★
John: b 2-16-1733 d 4-23-1806 m Tamar Rice Capt MA
John: b 9-8-1754 d 5-21-1813 m (1)Mary (Wells) (2)Elizabeth May Cpl MA
John: b 11-21-1744 d 7-17-1813 m Frances Brown Pvt MA
John: b 1729 d 12-15-1797 m Mary (Wells) PS NY
John: b a. 1750 d 1799-1813 m Rebecca — Sol SC
John Calvin: b 6- -1761 d 4-19-1810 m Amy Homans Pvt NY
John Howell: b 2-23-1744 d 3-7-1826 m Mary Bill Capt CT
John Jordan: b 10-30-1761 d 6-10-1808 m Mary Carter Pvt GA
Jonathan, Sr.: b 2-20-1732 d 7-13-1816 m Esther Hills LCol CT
Jonathan, Jr.: b 5-19-1757 d 1-6-1816 m Jemima Treat Pvt CT
Jonathan: b 9-8-1732 d 1-27-1792 m Catherine Saltonstall Maj PS CT
Jonathan: b 4-13-1718 d 4-29-1780 m Abigail Dickinson Pvt PS MA
Jonathan: bpt 12-20-1741 d 4-2-1793 m (1)Martha Hodgkins (2)Hannah (Hovey) Smith CS MA
Joseph: b 4-14-1746 d 8-13-1809 m Jerusha Hurlburt Sol CT
Joseph: b 12-24-1751 d 9-28-1815 m Ruth Thompson Cnt CT
Joseph: b 10-8-1731 d 12-22-1804 m Eunice Field Pvt MA

Joseph: b 7-24-1748 d 2-22-1808 m Mary Burham Pvt MA
Joseph: b 8-28-1726 d 1817 m Thankful Shaler 2Maj NY
Joseph: b 1746 d 1804 m (1)Martha Corey (2)Ellice Conkling Pvt NY
Joseph: b 1765 d 1823 m — Sol PS NC
Joseph: b 10-25-1766 d 2-6-1852 m Mary Scott Pvt PA
Joshua: b 9- -1726 d — m Experience Dinckinson Pvt CT
Joshua: b 2-7-1744 d 8-3-1803 m Elizabeth — Sol NH
Joshua: b 5-2-1747 d 12-23-1820 m Rhoda Boothe Pvt NY
Joshua, Sr.: b 1742 d p. 1776 m — PS NY
Joshua, Jr.: b 1-19-1763 d 10-20-1855 m Hannah Finch Pvt NY
Joshua: b 1-22-1728 d 1780 m Joanna Parshall PS NY
Josiah: b 7-20-1756 d 7-21-1821 m Mary Tucker Pvt CT
Josiah: b 1756 d 1839 m Prudence Leavenworth Sgt CT
Lemuel: b 5- -1745 d 2-22-1822 m Lydia Scott Sgt MA
Levi: b 1734 d 1803 m Jerusha Clark Col CT
Lewis: b 1750 d 8-12-1846 m Elizabeth Bates Sol SC
Manly: b 1746 d 5-8-1802 m (1)Joanna Young (2)Mary Benjamin PS NY
Matthew: b 2-17-1735/6 d 7-28-1818 m Bridget Burdick CS MA
Miles: b c. 1744 d a. 9- -1829 m Frazanna — PS NC
Moses: b 9-17-1716 d 12- -1794 m Anna Colby PS NH
Moses: b c. 1747 d 1830 m Polly Bowman Sol PA
Nathaniel: b c. 1730 d 1804 m Polly Thurston Pvt CT
Nathaniel, Jr.: bpt 5-26-1734 d 1-24-1810 m Lucy Goodhue Pvt MA
Nathaniel: b 8- -1759 d 10-3-1831 m Anna (Bean) Wells Pvt NH W★
Nathaniel: b 3-27-1740 d 3-26-1803 m Jerusha Wickham Pvt NY
Nathaniel: b 1705 d 9-26-1781 m Mary Parshall PS NY
Nathaniel: b 10-19-1763 d 1-20-1813 m Alinda Swain Pvt NY
Nathaniel: b c. 1755 d 4-4-1817 m Esther — PS NC
Noah: b 9-25-1718 d 12-31-1776 m Abigail Woolsey Chp CT
Obadiah: b 6-27-1712 d p. 1776 m (1)Judith Straw (2)Jemima Wiburn PS NH
Obadiah: b 11- -1716 d 5-27-1800 m Mary Conklin PS VT
Oliver: b 6-19-1732 d 10-25-1810 m Azubah Fitch Ens CT
Oliver: b 11-11-1757 d 8-16-1837 m Rebekah Ranney Pvt VT ★
Paul: b 1750/51 d 6-6-1827 m Rachel Webster Lt NH ★
Peter: b c. 1734 d c. 1824 m — Carpenter Pvt NY
Peter: b c. 5-4-1713 d 1813 m (1)Elizabeth Arnold (2)Elizabeth Sweet PS RI
Philip: b 11-23-1753 d 12-23-1818 m Elizabeth Tomlinson PS NY
Phineas: b 1742 d 3-9-1825 m (1)Prudence Kittle (2)Jane Clark Pvt PA
Randall: b 9-30-1747 d p. 1790 m Lydia Crandall Capt RI
Richard: b 2-11-1760 d 3-28-1838 m Susanna Hutcherson OrdlSgt GA ★
Richard, Sr.: b 3-15-1722 d 9-12-1816 m (1)Nancy Brown (2) — Capt PS VA
Richard, Jr.: b 1752 d 1812 m (1)Honor Holmes (2)Jane Brown Pvt PA
Richard: b — d 2-13-1801 m Rachel Hill PS PA
Richard: b — d — m Mary Haynesworth Drm SC
Robert: b 9-7-1710 d 2-3-1786 m Abigail Burnham Pvt CT
Robert: b 2-17-1740 d 7-3-1812 m Abigail Hurlburt Capt CT
Robert: b c. 1756 d p. 8- -1832 m Anna Wheeler Pvt CT
Robert: b 2-6-1743 d 2-17-1820 m Abigail Jeffords 2Lt MA
Roger: b 12-29-1753 d 5-27-1795 m Jemimah Kellogg Capt CT
Samuel: b 1727 d 12-29-1800 m Lucy Kilbourn Capt CT
Samuel, Jr.: b — d — m Ann Hale Pvt CT
Samuel: b 12-10-1753 d 2-10-1815 m Anna Griswold Pvt CT
Samuel: b 10-28-1729 d 5-25-1801 m Margaret McCrellis 2Lt MA
Samuel: b 1752 d 11-21-1830 m Margaret Scott Ens NH ★
Samuel: b 1750 d 1819 m Mary Glenn Sol PA
Samuel: b 2-10-1835 m (1)Rebecca Pope (2)Margaret Andrain Capt CS VA
Samuel: b 1759 d 11-20-1830 m Elizabeth Slimp Pvt VA ★
Selah: b 4-1-1750 d 3-3-1842 m Mehitable Tuthill PS NY
Seth: b 8-13-1749 d 4-23-1828 m (1)Judith Robbins (2)Lydia Benton Pvt CT
Silas: b 9-10-1752 d 5-14-1831 m Mary Taggert Pvt NH
Simeon: b 6-10-1754 d 8-10-1806 m Sara Snow Pvt MA
Solomon: b 10-6-1721 d 9-28-1802 m Sarah (Welles) LCol CT
Stephen: b 4-4-1754 d 6-14-1838 m (1)Love Ford (2)Caroline King (3)Elizabeth Butler Griffith Pvt MA
Stephen: b 8-2-1751 d 1834 m Mehitable Worthly Pvt NH
Stephen: b 1-28-1753 d 11-19-1835 m Mary Sanborn Pvt NH ★
Styles, Jr.: b 1748 d 11-14-1828 m Rebecca Ayres Cpl CT
Thomas: b 6-12-1741 d p. 1795 m Lucy Belden Sgt CT
Thomas: b 3-28-1752 d 2-1-1826 m Anne (Grant) Northrop Sgt CT
Thomas: b c. 1750 d 10-30-1799 m Ruth Harrison Capt MA
Thomas: b 9-12-1753 d 1848 m Phebe Eggleston Pvt CT ★
Thomas, Sr.: b 1709 d 5-20-1804 m Elizabeth Howard PS MD
Thomas: b 1-10-1758 d 5-6-1839 m (1)Sarah Scott (2)Nancy Davis Pvt PA
Thomas, Sr.: b c. 1699 d p. 1780 m Phoebe Green PS RI
Thomas, Jr.: b 4-5-1723 d 1795 m Sarah Thompson CS RI
Thomas 3d: b 1750 d 1788 m Mary Robinson Capt RI
Thomas: b c. 1757 d 1780 m Anna Bailey Pvt SC
Timothy: b 1746 d 1820 m Easther Clark Sgt CT ★
Wait: b 5-3-1724 d 5-24-1819 m Anna Strickland Pvt CT
Wait: b 1-4-1708 d 6-3-1789 m Jerusha Treat PS CT
Will: b c. 1750 d p. 1800 m Martha — Sol NC
Wm.: b 3-8-1725 d 4-19-1778 m Ann Shelton Pvt CT
Wm.: b 1-16-1741 d p. 1790 m Rebecca Stoddard Sgt MA

Wm.: b 1746 d 4-11-1827 m Martha Bridges Pvt MA
Wm.: b 1755 d 2-5-1818 m Elenor Hickey Pvt MA W★
Wm.: b 12-26-1763 d p. 1788 m Chloe Thresher Pvt MA
Wm.: b 12-13-1760 d 1839 m (1)Elizabeth Skinner (2)Milly Wilson
    Sgt NY ★
Wm.: b a. 1727 d p. 1790 m Maria Bronk PS NY
Wm.: b 1767 d p. 4-15-1840 m (1)Catron Selmon (2)Margot Ankrom
    Pvt VA
Winthrop: b 8-21-1726 d 1797 m Dorothy Healey PS NH
Youngs: b 1760 d 1831 m Anna Corwin Pvt NY
Zachariah: b c. 1739 d p. 1825 m — Osborne Pvt NC

WELTON,
Aaron: b 2-19-1752 d p. 1786 m Zerah Bronson PS CT
Ard: b 8-19-1752 d 7-9-1803 m Elizabeth Warner PS CT
Daniel: b 5-19-1731 d p. 1-10-1792 m Ann Brewster Pvt CT
David: b 7-27-1752 d 7-3-1827 m Sarah Tuttle Pvt CT
Eben: b 1764 d 1859 m Sally Barnes Pvt CT ★
Elijah: b 8-13-1742 d — m Hannah Tyler Pvt CT
George: b 11-12-1761 d 5-21-1837 m Elizabeth A Botsford Pvt CT ★
Job: b 1-28-1744 d 1820 m Mary McQuire Lt VA
John: b 1-1-1727 d 1-22-1816 m Dorcas Hickox PS CT
Peter: b 9-28-1718 d 6-20-1790 m Abigail Porter CS CT
Samuel: b 11-2-1744 d 5-10-1777 m Jerusha Hill Cpl CT
Thomas: b 11-22-1751 d 1834/5 m (1)Abigail Hickox (2)Ruth
    (Hopkins) Norton (3)Hannah Hill Pvt CT

WELTY, (includes WELDE)
John: b 9-15-1722/3 d 1-16-1817 m Barbara — Pvt MD
John: b 4-21-1760 d 12-20-1837 m Catherine Weaver Pvt PA
Philip: b 1745 d 2- -1796 m Anna Margaretha Schmitt Pvt PA

WELTZHEIMER, (includes WELSHIMER)
Philip, Sr.: b c. 1730 d p. 1780 m — PS PA
Philip, Jr.: b 3-11-1757 d 1811 m (1)Catherine Hull (2)Mrs Ellen
    McCoy Wade Melton Pvt PA

WELTZHOFFER,
Jacob: b 1737/8 d 5-28-1805 m Anna Maria Basler Pvt PA

WEMPLE,
Abraham: b 1728 d 1799 m Antje Vandenbergh Col NY
Barent: bpt 10-29-1704 d 2-16-1791 m Debora Wemple PS Pvt NY
Barent, Jr.: b 8-3-1733 d 3-13-1813 m Sarah Smith Pvt NY
Ephraim: bpt 2-16-1724 d p. 6-27-1782 m Agnietje Brouwer Pvt NY
Hendrick: b 1730 d p. 1790 m Aefje VanEpps Sgt NY
John Barent: b 12-1-1745 d 3-1-1787 m (1)Maria Veeder (2)Alida
    Wemple Capt NY
John R: bpt 4-18-1732 d 9-14-1814 m (1)Maritie Fisher (2)Voljke
    Wemple (3)Esther Van Arnham Sgt NY
Margaretta: b 11-20-1733 d 3-12-1825 m Barent Wemple PS NY
Myndert: b 12-26-1737 d 12-18-1821 m Sarah Veeder Pvt NY
Myndert B: b 7-7-1763 d 7-10-1838 m Catherine Veeder Pvt NY ★
Myndert M: bpt 11-20-1738 d 1789 m Gertrude Mynders Maj NY
Myndert Reyer: b 9-30-1742 d p. 1787 m Alida Wemple Ens NY
Ryer: b 9-10-1703 d 1796 m Debora (Vedder) Wemple Sol NY

WENDELL,
Ahasuerus: b 12-21-1755 d 2-22-1848 m Eva Peck Pvt NY ★
Harmonus: b 1756 d 1832 m Deulah Leland LCol NY
Henderick: b 10-15-1733 d 10-1-1795 m Maria Lansing Pvt NY
John: b 9-10-1731 d 4-26-1808 m (1)Sarah Wentworth (2)Dorothy
    Sherburne PS CS NH
John: b 8-15-1757 d 3-6-1824 m Hannah VanDenberg Pvt NY
Thomas, Sr.: b 1738 d 1777 m Abigail Taylor Sol MA
Thomas, Jr.: b 7-13-1770 d 11-19-1862 m Elizabeth Eaton Smn ME

WENDOVER,
Hercules: b 11-3-1732 d 10-7-1786 m Jane Ruger PS NY
Thomas: b 1695 d c. 1784 m Elizabeth Elsworth PS NY

WENDT,
Frederick: b 1752 d 1824 m Susanne — PS PA

WENGER, (includes WANGER)
John: b 12-10-1726 d 1-5-1803 m Margaret — CMman PA
Martin: b 1741 d 9-23-1815 m (1)Anna Gingrich (2)Katherine Funk
    Pvt PA

WENNER, (includes WENER)
Christian: b c. 1760 d p. 1822 m Barbara — Cpl PA
George: b 12-21-1756 d 2-12-1833 m Eva Kummel Fif PA

WENRICH,
John: b 7-7-1727 d a. 6-27-1793 m Christina Mountz Pvt PA
Mathias, Sr.: b — d a. 1-5-1785 m Judith — PS PA
Mathias: b 5-1-1729 d 3-18-1808 m (1)Eva Rosina Shauer (2Maria
    Margaret Eisenmenger Ens PS PA

WENTWORTH,
Alpheus: b 1760 d 1-10-1840 m Mary Tubbs Pvt CT ★
Amaziah: b 3-30-1760 d 1813 m Sally Davis Pvt NH
Andrew: b 12-2-1761 d 6-25-1823 m Sally Weeks Pvt MA ★

Bartholomew: b 11-28-1737 d 5-23-1813 m Ruth Hall Sgt NH
Benjamin: b 7-31-1731 d 11-4-1813 m Rebecca Hodsdon Sgt NH
Benjamin: b 5-24-1732 d 4-19-1818 m Rachael Wentworth Pvt NH
Benning: b 10-2-1763 d 3-3-1852 m Phoebe Sawyer Pvt Drm MA ★
Caleb: b 10-20-1754 d 4-7-1830 m (1)Sarah James (2)Mrs Lydia
    Stanton (Brackett) Pvt NH
Daniel: b 10-16-1756 d 1840 m Susanna Turner Pvt CT ★
David: b c. 1750 d c. 1797 m Christiana Tucker PS NY
David: b 8-30-1765 d 5-24-1827 m (1)Anna Marks (2)Mrs Rebecca
    (Dyer) Payne Pvt VT
Drisco: b 6-15-1756 d 10- -1810 m Anna Libbey Pvt NH
Ebenezer: b 12-7-1748 d 2-6-1820 m Jane Merrill Pvt MA
Edward: b 1-13-1735/6 d c. 1812 m Mary Lord Pvt CT
Elihu: b 10-27-1751 d 6-28-1829 m Lois Pinkham PS NH
Elijah: b 4-17-1758 d 8-13-1826 m (1)Ruth Griswold (2)Lydia
    Griswold Pvt CT ★
Elijah: b 12-30-1744 d 7- -1810 m Rebecca Capen Sgt MA
Ephraim: b c. 1736 d 1-23-1795 m Phebe (Wentworth) PS NH
Ezekiel: b 1761 d p. 1832 m Ruanna Ganoung Sol CT
Ezekiel: b 1743 d 5-6-1811 m (1)Betsey Pike (2)Patience
    Pike (3)Molly Wooster Pvt ME
Foster: b 7-24-1765 d 8-23-1861 m Catherine Jordon Pvt MA ★
George: b 1-11-1740 d 9-20-1820 m Rebecca (Wentworth) PS CS
    NH
Gershom: b c. 1740-2 d p. 1820 m Deborah Wentworth Ens NH
Henry: b 2-11-1740 d 1810 m Hannah Romer Pvt MA
Hunking: b 12-19-1697 d 9-21-1784 m (1)Elizabeth Wibird
    (2)Elizabeth — (3)Margaret Vaughan PS NH
Isaac: b 2-17-1745 d 6- -1803 m Jerusha Wentworth Cpl MA
Isaac: b 8-29-1752 d 1807 m Abigail Nutter Pvt NH
James: b 4-13-1727 d 1800 m Letitia Tilden PS CT
Jedediah: b 11-2-1748 d 10-7-1821 m (1)Eunice Clark (2)Shore Hodson
    Pvt NH
John: b 1753 d 9- -1834 m (1)Elizabeth Webb (2)Mrs Wheeler Pvt
    CT
John: b 2-23-1736 d 6-9-1781 m (1)Hannah Fernald (2)Sarah
    Bartlett CG Capt MA
John: b 1761 d 6-18-1824 m (1)Sarah Young (2)Lydia Fletcher Pvt
    MA ★
John: b 9-21-1761 d 9-19-1825 m Hannah Elwell Pvt MA ★
John: b c. 1740 d 10- -1806 m (1)Hannah Hodgdon (2)Ann Blazo
    Pvt NH
John: b 3-30-1719 d 5-17-1781 m (1)Joanna Gilman (2)Abigail
    Millet (3)Elizabeth (Wallingford) Cole CS NH
John: b 1746 d p. 1790 m Hannah (Leach) Roroback Pvt NY
Jonathan: b 9-8-1741 d 11-16-1790 m Betsy Philpot Maj NH
Joshua: b 1-4-1741 d 10-19-1809 m Sarah Pierce Col NH
Josiah: b 3-21-1753 d 1-24-1841 m (1)Mary Hanford (2)Mrs Frances
    Atwood Pvt CT ★
Lemuel: b 1752 d 1-18-1802 m Elizabeth Sanger Pvt CT
Lemuel: b 5-28-1754 d 1-15-1844 m Susanna Whittemore Pvt MA
Moses: b 11-8-1740 d 3-12-1812 m (1)Judith Grant (2)Mrs Elizabeth
    (Swett) Smith Sol PS MA
Nathaniel: b 1743 d 1788 m Patience Abbott Lt NH
Nicholas: b 9-7-1748 d 6- -1840 m Patience (Wentworth) Pvt NH
Paul: b 1758 d 1833 m Mary Coffin Pvt MA ★
Paul: b 5-5-1737 d 4-18-1783 m Hannah Smith Pvt CS NH
Reuben: b 1730 d 5-18-1826 m Eleanor James PS NH
Richard: b 5-16-1746 d 6-15-1825 m Joanna Clark Sgt MA
Samuel: b 2-19-1742 d 5-19-1798 m Lydia Gowell MM ME
Samuel: b 4-24-1728 d 12-23-1783 m Sarah Puffer Pvt MA
Samuel: b 7-1-1760 d 1831 m Sarah Stone Pvt MA
Samuel Shackford: b 8-12-1756 d 7-27-1850 m Mary Berry Pvt NH ★
Shubael: b 1-29-1759 d 7-28-1837 m Lavinia Vozer Sol MA
Spencer: b 10- -1739 d 6-20-1816 m (1)Sarah Stiles (2)Sarah
    (Welch) Bryant Sol NH
Stephen: b 6-1-1749 d p. 1783 m Abigail Tolman Pvt MA
Timothy: b 1-22-1747 d 11-29-1842 m Amy Hodgdon 1Lt MA
Tobias: b 1752 d p. 1796 m Elizabeth Roberts Pvt NH
Wm.: b 10-20-1730 d 10-20-1798 m Hannah Hayes Pvt NH

WENTZ,
Jacob: b 1740 d 1783 m Barbara Alsentz Sgt PA
Johannes Jost: b 12-13-1749 d 5-22-1812 m Anna Elizabeth Horn
    3Sgt PA
John: b c. 1751 d 8-3-1827 m Miss Starns (2)Miss Boman
    (3)Catherine Caraker Pvt NC √
John: b 7-20-1743 d 4-18-1804 m Susanna Dickensheed Capt PA
John: b 3-23-1760 d 3-11-1818 m Hannah Nana Pvt PA
Peter: b 11-19-1719 d 9-13-1793 m Rosanna Magaretha PS PA

WENTZEL, (includes WENZEL)
Henry: b 1731 d 1-24-1786 m Mary Tinges Pvt MA
Philip: b c. 1731 d 1818 m Anna Maria Lauffer Pvt PA

WERFELL,
Henry: b — d p. 2-22-1815 m Christina Steinbrecher Pvt PA

WERKHEISER,
Charles: b 1733 d 1782 m Anna — PS PA
John: b 11-1-1759 d 10-11-1831 m Anna Margaret Diehl Pvt PA
Peter: b 12-16-1764 d 11-9-1843 m Anna Margareta Miller Pvt PA

WERTZ, (includes WERT, WERTS, WERTY, WIRT, WIRTZ, & WURTS)
Christian: b 1727 d 4- -1813 m Margaretha Houser CS PA
Christian: b 1760 d 1813 m Catherine Bretz Pvt PA
Conrad: b 1735 d 1793 m Mary — Pvt PA
George: b 6-5-1746 d 4-20-1802 m Esther Hasbrouck PS NY
George: b 1750 d 1812 m Mary — Lt PA
George: b 1-31-1745 d 11-27-1798 m Catharine Stoner Sol PA
George: b 6-4-1752 d 1-21-1837 m Nancy Cristy Pvt PS PA
Henry: b 5- -1765 d 11-27-1840 m Mollie Singley Pvt SC
Jacob: b 1742 d 1815 m — Pvt PA
Jacob: b 9-1-1756 d 9-22-1823 m Eve Marks 1Lt PA
John: b 1757 d 4-15-1842 m Anna Catherine Hair Pvt SC
John Adam: b 1727 d 1800 m Eva Elizabeth Snoke Pvt PS PA
Martin: b c. 1745 d 7- -1815 m Catherine Homan Pvt PS PA
Nicolas: b c. 1760 d a. 9-29-1823 m Margaret Sidel (2)Mrs Ann (McKearns) Ronsail Mus PA
Paul: b 11-19-1745 d 3-30-1825 m Catherine Stiffler Pvt PA
Peter: b 2-3-1748 d c. 1783 m Eleanora Roelaffson PS NJ

WESSELS,
Andries: b 2- -1756 d 1-25-1813 m (1)Gertrude Clute (2)Catherine Colyer Pvt NY
Hercules: b 9-7-1754 d 11-10-1833 m Elizabeth Addington Cpl NY ★
Luke: b — d a. 11-4-1825 m Jannetje Hugenor Sol NY

WEST,
Aaron: b 6-3-1763 d 5-15-1840 m Susannah Kellogg Pvt CT W★
Abel: b 5-6-1747 d 1-12-1836 m Hannah Chapman PS MA
Abner: b 1-1-1737 d 12-7-1828 m Mary Hatch Pvt MA
Alva: b 9- -1754 d 8- -1820 m Susan Davis Cpl CT
Asa: b 10-7-1757 d 7-11-1812 m Phebe Cranston Pvt RI
Basil: b 4-10-1745 d 2-2-1836 m Phoebe Ann Stockett PS MD
Benijah: b 9-17-1752 d 12-30-1832 m Annah Younglove Pvt NY
Benjamin: b 1729 d 1820 m Virlinde Hilleary PS MD
Benjamin, Sr.: b 1759 d 11-25-1842 m Nancy — Pvt NC ★
Benjamin: b 1747 d 5-12-1780 m Jean West Capt SC
Benjamin: b 1767 d 1830 m Sarah Dinkins Pvt SC
Cato: b c. 1750 d 1819 m (1)Miss Winn (2)Martha Green 1Lt SC
Clement: b 5-20-1760 d p. 1832 m Prudence Dailey Pvt NY
Ebenezer: b 1732 d 1822 m Jane — Ens CT ★
Ebenezer: b 11-23-1757 d p. 1800 m Mehitable Nye Pvt MA
Edward: b 10-29-1766 d 4-8-1849 m (1)Lydia Stanfield (2)Elizabeth Humphreys Sol NC
Edward: b 6-16-1729 d 6-14-1812 m Elizabeth McComis Pvt PA
Elias: b 7-5-1744 d 2-9-1835 m Mary Lathrop Lt CT
Elisha: b 5-31-1714 d 1-8-1790 m (1)Abigail Gibbs (2)Mrs Mary Smith PS MA
George: b 8-27-1749 d 5-1-1837 m Mary Ann Dillahunty Ens Spy NC ★
George: b 1758 d 6-28-1810 m Mary Clark NOf NC TN
Hezekiah: b 6-13-1754 d 1-16-1805 m Experience — Pvt CT
Hezekiah: b 11-7-1763 d 7-29-1845 m Priscilla Osborn Pvt SC ★
Ignatius: b 12-13-1750 d 6-1-1831 m Elizabeth Meachan PS NC
James: b 1735 d 1820 m Mary Chadwick Sgt PS GA
James: b 10-8-1768 d 6-6-1844 m Nancy Walls Pvt MD
James: b c. 1740 d 1815-17 m (1)Mary — (2)Martha — Sgt VA
James: b 1740 d p. 1784 m Ann — Sol VA
Jeremiah: b 7-20-1753 d 1806 m Martha Williams Dr CT
Jeruel: b 10-12-1753 d 6-30-1810 m Deborah Shaw Cpl MA
John: b 1740-5 d p. 1786 m Amy Wilcox Sgt CT
John: b 4-22-1762 d 1-31-1836 m Polly — Pvt NC ★
John: b c. 1741 d 1778 m — Pvt SC
John: b 1757 d p. 1843 m Mary West King Sgt VA ★
John: b 1748 d 8-11-1833 m Susannah Robinson Pvt VA ★
John: b 1756 d 1818 m Sallie — Pvt VA
John: b 1735 d 1806 m (3)Elizabeth West Sol VA
John: b p. 1715 d 1777 m Mary — PS VA
John: b 1758 d 8-8-1808 m Eleanor Laws Edwards Pvt VA
John: b c. 1738 d p. 11-23-1791 m Rachel Perry PS VA
Jonathan: b 12-30-1737 d 9-17-1795 m Elizabeth Hamilton Pvt MA
Joseph: b 10-22-1766 d 8-21-1847 m Sally Phelps Pvt CT
Joseph: b 11-2-1728 d 1805 m (1)Dorcas Reddington (2)Lois Strong CS CT
Joseph: b 11-28-1731 d 12-22-1797 m Sarah Hilleary Sol MD
Joseph, Sr.:b c. 1718 d p. 1798 m Jane Owen PS VA
Joseph, Jr.: b 1747 d 9- -1845 m Judith Ballinger Pvt VA
Joseph: b c. 1760 d 10-9-1809 m Eleanor Batson Pvt VA ★
Joshua: b 7-30-1715 d 1-9-1782 m (1)Sarah Wattles (2)Elizabeth Williams PS CT
Judah: b 9-11-1765 d 4-9-1825 m Mary Todd Pvt MA ★
Leonard: b 8-12-1760 d 10-13-1842 m Phoeby Morgan Pvt NC SC ★
Levi: b a. 1751 d p. 1830 m (1)Wealthy Bruton (2)Sarah Jackson (3) — White Pvt NC
Nathan: b 3-22-1763 d 4-1-1835 m Martha Titus Pvt RI ★
Nathaniel: b 9-5-1748 d 2-12-1815 m Lucretia Woodbridge Lt CT
Nathaniel: b 1-31-1756 d 12-19-1851 m (1)Elizabeth Derby (2)Julia Houghton Pvtr Capt MA
Nathaniel Hicks: b 11-23-1751 d 1-31-1836 m Rebecca Sheldon Pvt RI
Oliver: b 10-2-1733 d 4-23-1816 m Thankful Nye Pvt MA
Osborne: b 10-2-1749 d 1819 m Dorcas Trail Sol MD

Peter: b 8-6-1746 d 2-25-1828 m Hannah Cottle Cpl MA
Peter: b 1-1-1749 d 4-30-1829 m Elizabeth Reichtmeyer Ens NY
Prince: b 10-30-1735 d 6-4-1828 m Hannah Gibbs Pvt MA
Samuel: b 8-23-1743 d 1-10-1835 m Sarah Hunt Sgt CT
Samuel: b 3-30-1732 d p. 1790 m Sarah Lathrop CS CT
Samuel: b 3-3-1729 d 9-24-1807 m (1)Experience Howland (2)Mrs Louisa Jenny PS MA
Solomon: b 3-15-1723 d 8-9-1810 m Abigail Strong Pvt CT
Solomon: b c. 1720 d 12-1-1830 m (1)Isabella Boyd (3)Martha Norton PS NC
Thomas: b c. 1750 d a. 4-12-1802 m Rachel — Pvt DE
Thomas: b 1-28-1760 d 7-12-1848 m Tabitha Dale Sol MD
Thomas: b 1-12-1748 d 1-4-1822 m Sarah Butler Cpl MA
Thomas: b 2-28-1737 d 1-11-1819 m Deborah Freeman Pvt MA
Thomas: b 1733 d 3-12-1782 m Mary Simons PS MA
Thomas, Sr.: b c. 1735 d p. 1795 m — Oliphant Sol NC
Thomas: b c. 1735 d 1807-1821 m Lucy — PS NC
Thomas: b c. 1747 d 1795 m Elizabeth Hibbs Sgt PA
Thomas: b 1741 d 3-12-1828 m Molly Jay Pvt VT
Thomas: b c. 1750 d 1828/9 m Elizabeth Blair Bolling Capt VA
Thomas: b c. 1730 d p. 1785 m Sarah Trammel Pvt VA
Timothy: b 1750 d 2-24-1833 m Lois Dexter Sgt MA ★
Wilkes: b 3-1-1736 d 4-10-1830 m (1)Phebe Dearborn (2)Hannah Forsaith Pvt PS NH
Wm.: b 6-2-1756 d 3-15-1836 m Hannah Throckmorton Pvt NJ ★
Wm.: b 1750 d 1830 m Anne Stout PS NJ
Wm.: b 1750 d 11-15-1823 m Susannah Lancaster Pvt NC W★
Wm.: b 1752 d 1842 m Angeline Clendennen Pvt NC ★
Wm.: b 3-7-1724 d 12-6-1808 m (1)Sarah Ennis (2)Ann Shaw Maj PA
Wm.: b 1732 d c. 1816 m Ellen Brown BGen PS RI
Wm.: b c. 1730 d — m Mary Jane — Pvt SC
Wm.: b 1763 d 3-15-1841 m (1)Bersheba — (2)Margaret White Pvt SC ★
Wm.: b 11-27-1762 d 4-27-1830 m Alice Egmon Pvt VA
Wm.: b 10-25-1735 d p. 1784 m Letitia Martin Sol VA
Wm. Blay: b 1-21-1747 d 5-24-1813 m Patience Webber Hammond Cpl MA ★
Willis: b 1755-60 d 11-23-1837 m (1)Miss Gainey (2)Sylvia — Pvt NC

WESTALL,
George: b — d p. 1801 m — Drm VA

WESTBROOK,
Cherick: b c. 1760 d 1817-19 m Rachel — Pvt CT
Cornelius b: b 1760 d p. 1829 m Jane — Pvt PA ★
Dirck: b 1751 d p. 1785 m Gertrude Brodhead Capt NY
Gideon: b 9-20-1761 d 12-28-1840 m — Pvt NY ★
Jacob: b 7-1-1722 d 9-19-1784 m Lydia Westfall PS NJ
James: b 1-6-1767 d 1-26-1839 m Charity — Pvt NJ
James: b c. 1750 d p. 4-1-1816 m Mary Lee PS NC
Johannis: bpt 2-4-1725 d p. 6-3-1787 m Maria (Westbrook) Tms NJ
Jonathan: bpt 1711 d 1785 m Jannetje Vandermerken PS NY
Joseph: b c. 1730 d 1-4-1804 m (1)Elizabeth Kuykendal (2)Deborah Krom Pvt NJ
Leonard: bpt 1-28-1759 d p. 1790 m Margaret Brinck Pvt CT
Martinus: bpt 3-24-1754 d a. 11-9-1813 m Margaret Louw Capt NJ
Peter: b 5-30-1738 d 4-19-1780 m Lydia Vredenburg Capt NJ
Richard: b 5-24-1760 d 8-30-1833 m Lydia — Pvt PA ★
Samuel: b 2-25-1746 d 7-10-1833 m Katrina Frettenburg Maj NJ
Wilhelmus: b 10-3-1748 d 5-2-1805 m Aeltje Jobe Ens NJ

WESTCOE, (includes WESCOE)
Francis: b a. 1730 d a. 4-26-1809 m (1)Esther Shaist (2)Eva Margaret Christman Pvt PA
Matthias: b 3-15-1755 d 5-27-1827 m Susanna Laros Pvt PA

WESTCOTT, (includes WESCOAT, WESCOTT & WESTCOT)
Abraham: b 3- -1716 d 3-21-1791 m Elizabeth Kellum Pvt NY
Amos: b 9-9-1761 d 3-17-1840 m Abigail Keth Fif RI CT
Daniel: b 7-17-1754 d 8-5-1840 m Mrs Sally Lockwood Pvt CT ★
Daniel: b 8-4-1751 d 3-9-1823 m Marcy Warner Sgt RI
David: b 7-28-1717 d 7-30-1806 m Mary Slawson Pvt CT
Ephraim: b 1735 d 1795 m Freelove Stone PS RI
Ford: b 1750 d 2-20-1794 m (1)Freelove Burkell (2)Sally Field Sgt RI ★
George: b 1762 d 12-21-1799 m Phoebe Salisbury Pvt RI W★
George: b 4- -1730 d 1814 m Phebe — Pvt RI
Gideon: b 1740-6 d p. 1781 m Robe Edmonds Capt RI
James: b 3-25-1740 d 3-17-1814 m Martha Tillinghast Pvt RI
John: b 1741/2 d 11-25-1813 m Sarah Diament Capt NJ
John: b 1757 d 6-2-1825 m Mary Sanford Ens RI
John: b 3-26-1745/6 d 12-12-1831 m Amey Clarke CS RI
Jonathan: b 3-26-1759 d 3-7-1824 m Nancy W Casey Pvt RI
Joseph: b 8-19-1763 d 1-10-1857 m Olive Knight Pvt MA ★
Nathan: b 1711 d 1791 m (1)Anne Greene (2)Mary Rutenberg Mstr RI
Reuben: b 4-29-1751 d 4-29-1818 m Hannah Greene Pvt RI
Richard: b 10-5-1733 d 3-9-1825 m Margaret (Brazier) Lee Maj NJ
Samuel, Sr.: b a. 1736 d 1792 m Hannah Shaw Capt NJ
Samuel, Jr.: b 1-26-1757 d 3-18-1834 m Mary Buck Sgt NJ ★

Samuel: b 6-6-1745 d 12-2-1795 m Mary Hoppin 1Lt RI
Stukely: b 1723 d 8- -1802 m Anna Wells Sgt RI
Thomas: b 7-16-1758 d 9-22-1838 m Marcy Arnold Sgt CL RI
Thomas: b 1743 d 1778 m Mary Iten Pvt SC
Uriah: b 3-19-1757 d 2-8-1800 m Susannah Butts Lt RI
Wm.: b 3-10-1734 d p. 1790 m Elizabeth Perkins Smn MA
Wm., Jr.: b c. 1728 d p. 1777 m Christina — Pvt RI
Ziba: b 1763 d 9-18-1829 m — Harmon Pvt RI ★

WESTER,
Fulgam: b 1757 d 1810 m Edith Knolly Pvt NC

WESTERMAN,
Peter: b c. 1743 d p. 1790 m Maria Elizabeth Dunkel Pvt NY

WESTERVELT,
Abraham: b 9-11-1720 d 7-28-1796 m Hendrickjen Van Boscerck PS NY
Albert: b 3-5-1754 d 11-6-1829 m Maria VanZaun Pvt NY
Benjamin: bpt 2-14-1748 d 1834 m Sarah Bordet Pvt NJ
Benjamin: b 11-12-1754 d 1838 m Jane Short Pvt NY
Casparus: bpt 8-11-1734 d 11-15-1810 m (1)Martintje Durie (2)Rachel Zabriskie Pvt NJ
Casparus: bpt 9-29-1728 d 10-27-1796 m (1)Sarah Durie (2)Wyntje Terheun Pvt NY
Casparus: b 9-15-1752 d 1-18-1836 m (1)Nancy Campbell (2)Jane Ryder Pvt NY
Casper: b 1-25-1757 d 5-7-1821 m Deborah Fort Pvt NY
Cornelius: b 3-4-1726 d 9-19-1785 m Wyntje Berritt Pvt NY
Cornelius Petrus: b 6-12-1760 d 1-23-1839 m Maria Conklin Sgt NJ ★
Daniel: b 2-26-1748 d 10-23-1777 m Margrietje Christi Lt NJ
Derick: b 6-24-1759 d 10-7-1819 m Catherine VanBenschoten Pvt NY
Jacobus: b 3-28-1761 d 4-12-1834 m Rebecca DuBois Pvt NY
James: b c. 1757 d a. 6- -1826 m Phoebe Cosine Pvt NY
John: b 7-3-1761 d p. 1790 m Hannah VanKleeck Pvt NY
Joost: b 10-16-1747 d 2-21-1825 m Maria VanKleeck PS NY
Peter: b 5-5-1759 d 1801 m (2)Catherine Blauvelt Pvt NY
Roelof: b 12-4-1723 d 1800 m Dirkjen Taelman CS NJ

WESTFALL,
Abraham: b 11-18-1755 d 9-5-1829 m Blondina VanEtten Capt NY ★
Abraham: b 1758 d 1- -1833 m Massey Harvin Pvt VA W★
Benjamin: b 3-19-1740 d 7-27-1820 m Catharine VanDuesen Pvt NY
Jacob, Sr.: b 1730 d 1801 m Sidney — Capt VA
Jacob, Jr.: b 10-10-1755 d 3-5-1835 m Mary King 1Lt VA
Jacob: b 1761 d 1801 m Elizabeth Pugh Sgt VA
John, Sr.: b c. 1725-30 d p. 2-9-1789 m Sarah — PS VA
Peter: bpt 6-15-1740 d 12-15-1825 m Sophia Vanauken Pvt NY
Samuel: b 1-31-1749 d 1787 m Margaret Liskert Pvt NJ
Simeon, Sr.: b 7-30-1721 d 1805 m Jannetje Westbrook PS NY
Simeon, Jr.: b 2-3-1749 d 1812 m Sarah Cole Lt PA
Wilhemus: b 7-8-1753 d 10-26-1796 m Margaret Haynes Capt Grd NY W★

WESTGATE,
Joseph Earl: b 6-10-1761 d p. 1834 m (1)Rebecca Brownell (2)Lydia Westgate (3)Polly Beal Ordl Sgt RI ★

WESTHOFER, (includes WESTHEFFER)
Conrad: b 11-19-1737 d 10-25-1804 m Catherine Heil Pvt PA
John: b c. 1759 d 11- -1852 m (1)Elizabeth Ellis (2)Catherine Falch (3)Mary — Cpl PA

WESTLAKE,
Benjamin: b 4-15-1756 d 9-15-1835 m ( )Catherine Dusenbury ( )Sarah — Pvt PS NY ★
George: b 1747 d 5-22-1831 m Mary Smith PS NY
Samuel: b 1743 d 10-13-1818 m Sarah — Pvt NY

WESTLAND,
Joseph: b 8-2-1763 d 3-22-1812 m Lucina Rowley Pvt CT

WESTMORELAND,
Joseph: b c. 1740 d a. 1790 m Martha Shores Pvt VA
Robert: b c. 1762 d 9-8-1791 m Martha — PS VA

WESTON, (includes WESSON & WESTERN)
Abner: b 3-28-1760 d 9-26-1836 m Huldah Washburn Cpl MA W★
Abraham: b 8-20-1755 d 8-29-1837 m Naomi — Drm CT
Arunah: b 2-4-1746 d 1-17-1831 m Sally Martin 2Lt MA
Benjamin: b 2-15-1747 d 5-7-1818 m Mary Woodhouse Ens CT
Daniel: b 6- -1758 d 9- -1832 m Lydia Brown Pvt MA
David: b 1754 d 2-4-1836 m Keziah Eaton Pvt MA
Ebenezer: b 2-10-1731 d 12-22-1805 m Esther Kendall CS PS NH
Edmund: b 2-23-1731 d 4-4-1814 m Mary Tinkham Pvt MA
Edward, Sr.: b — d a. 2-23-1788 m Mary — PS VA
Ephraim, Sr.: b 9-8-1722 d 3- -1814 m Lydia Proctor CS PS NH
Ephraim, Jr.: b 7-27-1751 d 1834 m Judith Morse Pvt NH
Hannah Watts: b 11-22-1758 d 12-12-1855 m Josiah Weston PS MA
Isaac: b 3-15-1733 d 4- -1779 m Lucy Dean Pvt NH

Isaac: b 8-22-1756 d 12-5-1835 m Sally — Pvt VA
Jacob: b 1729 d 11-4-1822 m Deborah Simmons PS MA
James: b 4-2-1734 d 10-15-1809 m Lydia Ann White Col MA
James: b 10-31-1723 d 10-26-1786 m Abigail Dunham Ens MA
James: b 6-11-1755 d 5-23-1840 m Sarah Witherell Ens MA ★
James: b 3-3-1760 d 1-25-1834 m Ann Hayford Pvt VT ★
John: b 11-19-1755 d 9-11-1837 m (1)Sarah — (2)Margaret Dean Sgt CT
John: b 1711 d 9-30-1786 m Ruth Death Pvt MA
John: b 8-12-1736 d 4-3-1801 m (1)Joanna (Weston) (2)Martha Farmer Pvt MA
John: b 11-12-1731 d p. 1800 m Mary Atwood CS MA
Jonathan: b 11-17-1744 d p. 1805 m Anna Gillett Pvt MA
Jonathan: b 4-19-1753 d 3-31-1828 m Mary — Pvt MA
Jonathan, Sr.: b 12-26-1731 d 2-22-1794 m Ruth Flint Pvt MA
Jonathan: b 3-1-1757 d 1839 m Mary Parker Pvt MA
Joseph, Sr.: b 3-7-1732 d 10-16-1775 m Eunice Farnsworth PS MA
Joseph, Jr.: b 1-17-1757 d 3-22-1838 m Sarah Emery Pvt MA ★
Joseph, Jr.: b 1750 d 11-21-1813 m Rebecca — Pvt MA
Josiah: b 7-22-1756 d 8-2-1827 m Hannah Watts Pvt MA
Levi: b 5-27-1753 d 5-14-1853 m Olive Lock Pvt MA
Nathan: b 7-14-1745 d 11-29-1829 m Hannah Mansfield Pvt MA
Nathaniel: b 11-3-1737 d 3-11-1822 m Mary W Upton CS VT
Robert: b 1762 d 1840 m Mary Ogelvie Sgt SC
Rogers: b 9-30-1758 d 3-9-1843 m (1)Deborah Lawrence (2)Anna Frost (3)Rebecca Keyes (4)Mrs Lydia Buttrick (5)Mrs Betsy Wright Sgt NH ★
Samuel: b 1754 d 3-12-1829 m Abigail Bisbee Pvt MA
Simeon: b 9-16-1728 d 12-3-1808 m Honor Hunt Fif MA
Sutherick: b 11-19-1751 d 5-11-1831 m Mary DeLancey Cpl NH
Wm.: b 5-14-1732 d 6-27-1820 m Mary Weston Capt PS CS MA
Wm.: b 1755 d 5-25-1838 m Elizabeth Sampson Pvt MA
Wm.: b 5-10-1760 d 9-10-1834 m Hannah Key Pvt NJ
Wm.: b c. 1750 d p. 1820 m Grace Hirons Lt SC
Zachariah: b 6-25-1762 d 3-19-1836 m (1)Anna Silla (2)Nancy Frost Pvt MA
Zachariah: b 1762 d 12-15-1819 m Sarah Wood Pvt MA

WESTOVER,
Job: b 4-23-1742 d 4-18-1813 m Rachel — Pvt MA
Moses: b 3-24-1744 d p. 1782 m Elizabeth Holmes Pvt MA
Oliver: b 10-11-1739 d p. 1792 m Jerusha — Pvt MA

WESTWOOD,
Wm.: b 1738 d 1782 m Ann Stith Pvt VA

WETHERBEE, (includes WEATHERBEE, WEATHERBY & WEATHERSBY)
Abijah: b 8-26-1761 d 4-20-1840 m Mehitable Trowbridge Pvt MA ★
Abraham: b 6-5-1752 d 1-22-1828 m Joanna Sawtell Pvt NH
Benjamin: b 1732 d 1803 m Susanna Aldridge Pvt MA
Benjamin: b 4-12-1747 d 4-20-1812 m Edith Smith Capt NJ
David: b 4-22-1747 d 4-29-1812 m Mary Cavalier Capt NJ
Edward: b 12-20-1752 d 1-12-1813 m Eleanor Davis Pvt MA
Ephraim: b 6-3-1756 d 1-31-1852 m Olive Gates Sgt MA
Hezekiah: b 6-20-1757 d 3-31-1823 m Lucy Hale Pvt MA
Isaac: b 9-2-1760 d 1844 m Sarah Wetherbee Pvt MA ★
Joab: b 4-26-1759 d 4-4-1843 m Abigail Houghton Pvt MA
John: b 9-14-1746 d 3-31-1838 m Susannah Page Pvt MA
Joseph, Sr.: b 1725 d 4-14-1809 m (1)Elizabeth Whitney (2)Hannah Forbush PS Sol MA
Joseph, Jr.: b 5-22-1751 d 3-24-1829 m Hannah Pettengill Pvt MA ★
Judah: b 4-13-1755 d 12- -1835 m Catherine Windham Cpl MA
Lewis: b 1-1-1762 d 9-16-1843 m Mary Culpepper Pvt NC
Nathan: b 6-3-1742 d 9-22-1786 m (1)Patience Baker (2)Elizabeth Dunton Cpl MA
Nathaniel, Sr.: b 4-9-1738 d 3-22-1791 m Submit How Sgt MA
Nathaniel, Jr.: b 2-10-1764 d 6-10-1835 m Elizabeth Crane Pvt MA
Oliver: b 4-9-1743 d c. 1820 m Rachel Willard Pvt MA
Paul: b 2-1-1749 d 4-24-1834 m Dorcas Hovey Cpl MA
Phinehas: b 2-4-1744/5 d p. 1790 m Hannah Whitney Pvt MA
Samuel: b 4-3-1745 d 10-29-1819 m Susannah Johnson Capt NH
Shadrach: b 1740 d 1815 m Elizabeth Stackpole Pvt MA
Thomas: b 8-7-1757 d — m Abigail Maria Sawtell Pvt MA
Timothy: b 1750 d 1832 m Lydia Parker Pvt MA

WETHERINGTON,
Solomon: b 10-4-1761 d 1840 m Mary Moore Pvt NC ★

WETHERN,
Micah: b 10- -1761 d 12-2-1856 m (2)Hannah Parker Pvt MA

WETMORE,
Amos: b 10-14-1740-1 d 7-28-1808 m Rachel Parsons Capt CT
Bela: b 6-1-1764 d 10-15-1839 m (1)Elizabeth Trescott (2)Mehetable Livermore Pvt MA
Elihu: b 7-23-1757 d p. 1819 m Lucy — Grd CT
Increase: b 6-2-1726 d 10-4-1807 m Sarah Chilson PS CT
Izarahiah: b 8-30-1729 d 8-3-1798 m Phoebe Walker PS CT
John: b 3-27-1734 d 2-17-1814 m Marcy Bacon Capt CT
John: b 10-27-1727 d 8-27-1795 m Elizabeth Leming PS CT
Oliver: b 5-24-1752 d 12-6-1798 m Sarah Brewster Lt CT

WETMORE, contd.

Prosper: b 5-14-1722 d 10-15-1787 m Keturah Cheesborough Pvt CT

Reuben: b 3-30-1733 d 1829 m (1)Hannah Foster (2)Chloe Johnson Sol NY

Seth: b 1744 d 4-15-1810 m (1)Mary Wright (2)Mrs Lucretia Scott PS CS CT

WETZEL, (includes WEITZEL, WETSEL, WETZELL, WHETSALL, WHETZEL & WHITESELL)

Adam: b 1749 d 1827 m Mary Davis PS Pvt PA

Andrew: b 8-18-1723 d 3-18-1813 m Margaretha Green PS NJ

Christopher: b c. 1757 d 7-30-1825 m Margaretta Groberger Pvt NY

George: b 1723-31 d 4-6-1824-7 m Maria — Pvt NY

Jacob: b 1754 d 7-17-1809 m Catherine Markle Pvt PA

Jacob: b 2-11-1747 d 6-9-1785 m Worthy Maria Basler Lt PA

John: b 1733 d 6-11-1786 m Mary Bonnet Capt VA

John: b 12-30-1752 d 1799 m (1)Tabitha Morris (2)Elizabeth Lebo PS CS PA

Martin: b 1762 d 1830 m Mary Coffee Pvt VA

Philip: b 12-19-1751 d 9-4-1826 m — Sgt PA

WEYBERG,

Casper Dietrich: b c. 1742 d 9-26-1790 m — PS PA

WEYBRIGHT,

Martin: b c. 1758 d p. 1-3-1824 m Mary Eliz Geiger Capt PA

WEYBURN,

Samuel: b 1746 d 1825 m (1)Jane Bratton (2)Livia — Pvt PA

WEYMAN,

Edward: b 8-11-1730 d 1- -1793 m Rebecca Breintnall PS Capt SC

WEYMOUTH,

Benjamin: b c. 1755 d 3-19-1811 m Catherine Abbott Pvt MA

George: b 9-4-1749 d 8-18-1811 m Huldah Folsom PS NH

James: b 3-13-1759 d 2-16-1852 m Polly Barber Mrnr Pvt NH ★

Stephen: b 1742 d 1788 m Olive Earle Pvt MA

WHALEY,

Alexander: b 7-27-1746 d 1833-40 m (1)Abigail Leverich (2)Maria Shute Pollard PS NY

Benjamin: b 1760 d 9-7-1833 m Jane Vance Capt VA ★

Hezekiah: b 1755 d — m Sarah Whaley Pvt CT ★

James, Jr.: b c. 1742 d p. 3-25-1785 m Virginia — 2Lt VA

James: b 1727 d p. 1-13-1783 m Ann Talbot PS Sol VA

James: b 12-10-1750 d 12-4-1840 m Elizabeth (Page) Hall Pvt VA ★

Jeremiah: b c. 1728 d c. 1795 m Tamson Purchase Sol RI

Job: b 6-28-1749 d 8- -1834 m (1)Elizabeth Greene (2)Rachel Colgrove Sgt PS RI ★

Joseph: b 1758 d 1835 m Waitey Holly Pvt RI ★

Reynolds: b 10-5-1762 d 10- -1844 m Elizabeth Odell Pvt RI ★

Samuel: b 1-2-1754 d 2-3-1813 m Olive Darrow Sgt CT

Seth: b c. 1754 d a. 9-19-1823 m Hester — Pvt MD

Theophilus: b 1759 d 9-6-1827 m Mary Burdick Pvt VT ★

Thomas: b 1751 d 1806 m Mary Ann Seabrook Pvt SC

WHALLEN,

Patrick: b 1738 d 1826 m Susanna Leach Pvt VA

WHALLON, (includes WHALEN)

Abel: b 1750 d 11-30-1813 m Lydia Bixby Lt NY

James: b c. 1730 d c. 1785 m Mrs Smith Lt NJ

WHAN,

John: b 11-22-1761 d 4-4-1826 m Mary — Pvt PA

WHAPLES,

Eli: b 3- -1739 d 1804 m Elizabeth Foster Cpl CT

WHARRY, (includes WHERRY)

Daniel: b 1764 d 3-2-1842 m Eunice Golden Pvt NY ★

David, Jr.: b 4-8-1755 d 1827 m Nancy Forbes Ens PA

David: b 1717 d 7-7-1800 m (1)Isabelle Sharp (2)Margaret Mackey PS PA

David: b 12-8-1757 d 5-16-1834 m Ann Hall Pvt PA

Evans: b 1749 d 4-17-1831 m Phebe Belknap Lt NY ★

James: b 3-6-1762 d 2-15-1803 m Abigail Ball Sgt NY

James: b a. 1765 d 3- -1807 m Sarah McConel Pvt PA

WHARTNABY,

John: b c. 1735 d p. 1783 m Elizabeth Keeper Pvt PA

WHARTON,

John: b 1746/7 d 2-28-1816 m Rhoda Morris Lt VA

Revil: b 3-18-1746 d 1776 m Mary Scroggin Mstr MD

Robert: b c. 1750 d 4-10-1822 m Sarah Farley Sol PA

Samuel: b 1742 d 8-18-1823 m Sarah Wilson Pvt PA

Samuel: b 9-13-1740 d 3-4-1824 m Maudaline Sullivan Capt SC

Samuel: b 7-27-1761 d 12-11-1841 m Letitia Hutcherson Pvt VA ★

Thomas: b 4-15-1758 d 6-28-1831 m Susanna Dill Pvt PA

Thomas: b 1735 d 5-23-1778 m (1)Susannah Lloyd (2)Elizabeth Fishbourne PS PA

WHEADON, (includes WHEDON)

Abraham: b 6-6-1761 d 8-31-1848 m Lydia White Sol Arfr CT

Ansel: b 2-24-1765 d 1826 m Rachel — Pvt NY

Daniel: b 5-6-1726 d p. 1790 m Abigail Granger Pvt NY

David: b 4-28-1731 d a. 4-22-1802 m Zillah Shelley Pvt NY

Denison: b c. 1760 d p. 1825 m Mary Parish Pvt MA

Rufus: b 1759 d 12-6-1842 m Annie Norton Sgt CT

WHEAT,

Benjamin: b 1-31-1734/5 d p. 1780 m Elizabeth Grant Sol CT

Benjamin: b 4-1-1743 d 8-18-1817 m Sarah Wright Pvt MA

Daniel: b 1755 d 1-17-1827 m Betty — Pvt MA

Samuel: b 3-13-1747 d 2-13-1835 m Jerusha Allen Pvt MA ★

Thomas, Sr.: b 5-12-1723 d 2-12-1820 m (1)Mary Ball (2)Sarah Temple Pvt NH

WHEATON,

Charles: b 2-20-1762 d 9-12-1823 m Abigail Miller QMSgt RI

Isaac: b 10-25-1748 d 12-15-1802 m Judith Ludlam 2Lt NJ

James: b 3-3-1747/8 d 1-21-1834 m Sarah Child Sol MA

Jonathan: b 4-10-1725 d 12-25-1811 m Phoebe Pierce Pvt MA

Jonathan, Jr.: b 5-28-1758 d 9-30-1841 m (2)Serepta Martin Pvt MA

Jonathan: b 6-26-1755 d 4-23-1828 m Penelope Lacy Pvt CT ★

Joseph, Jr.: b 3-1-1745/6 d 1776/7 m Esther Sperry Sol PS CT

Joseph: b 10-8-1752 d 7-24-1843 m Bethiah Carpenter Sgt QM RI ★

Joseph: b 2-20-1745 d c. 1803 m Esther Willets 2Lt NJ

Joseph: b c. 1755 d 11-23-1828 m Sarah — Lt RI ★

Levi: b 2-6-1761 d 8-29-1851 m Martha Burrill Dr MM RI

Lucas: b 9-25-1748 d 5-7-1833 m Elizabeth Short Pvt MA

Nathaniel: b 12-30-1732 d 1795 m Hannah Burr PS RI

Reuben: bpt 10-2-1763 d 1840 m Maria McGee Pvt NY ★

Roswell: b 1757 d 9-24-1842 m (2)Elizabeth Bassett Pvt CT NH ★

Seth: b 11-15-1759 d 10-26-1827 m Abigail Wheaton Lt RI

Wm.: b 5-16-1757 d 8-4-1847 m Susanna Willcoks Pvt RI ★

WHEELAND,

Michael: b 1748 d 4-24-1832 m Elizabeth Hildabiddle Pvt PA ★

WHEELER,

Aaron, Sr.: b 1-17-1722/3 d 3-19-1800 m Hopestill Daggett Pvt MA

Aaron, Jr.: b 7-29-1752 d 11-2-1829 m Mary Knap Lt MA

Abel: b 5-25-1748 d 1820 m Mary Hosmer Cpl MA

Abijah: b 9-18-1751 d 12-28-1812 m (1)Mary Hayward (2)Hepsibah Blood (3)Mrs Catherine Wyman 1Lt NH

Abner: b 1-20-1752 d 8-11-1815 m Sarah Stickney Drm NH

Abraham: b 5-12-1746 d 7-20-1817 m (1)Jemima Walker (2)Mrs Catee Munro Pvt MA

Abraham, Sr.: b 9-29-1711 d 9-23-1795 m (1)Martha Blood (2)Hannah — PS CS NH

Abram: b 12-17-1735 d 6-20-1778 m Sarah Baker Capt MA

Adam: b 4-29-1732 d 8-24-1802 m Mary (Wheeler) Capt MA

Agur: b 12-20-1754 d 12-12-1802 m Anne Tuttle Cpl MA

Amos: b 10-15-1759 d 10-8-1843 m Lucy Holmes Sol CT

Amos: b 2-26-1741 d 6-21-1775 m Rhoda Stearns Sgt MA

Amos: b 7-12-1754 d 4-7-1817 m Eunice Gates Pvt MA

Amos: b 7-28-1756 d 9-15-1839 m Catherine Locke Pvt NH

Artemus: b 12-5-1748 d p. 1811 m Lucretia Howe Cpl MA

Asahel: b 3-1-1741 d 10-31-1820 m Jerusha Haynes Capt MA

Benjamin: b 4-15-1756 d 7-22-1830 m Lolly Mallory Cpl CT ★

Benjamin: b 1758 d 1862 m — Pvt MD ★

Benjamin: b 1726 d 1-7-1807 m — Mar MD

Benjamin: b 2-7-1764 d 2-6-1836 m Celia Buffington Sgt MA ★

Benjamin, Sr.: b 3-1-1728 d p. 1790 m Charity Pike Pvt MA

Benjamin: b 3-5-1758 d 11-16-1844 m Sarah Harris Pvt NH

Benjamin: b c. 1765 d p. 1819 m Penelope Spencer Pvt VA ★

Caleb: b 11-17-1757 d 1824 m (1)Jerusha Dorr (2)Mrs Rebecca Maynard Sgt MA

Caleb: b 1752 d 5-28-1824 m Elizabeth Morris Capt NJ

Charles: b a. 1755 d p. 1806 m Sarah Woolford Cpl PS MD

Clement, Jr.: b 3-13-1737 d 12-12-1796 m Jane Stonestreet Capt MD

Comfort: b 3-13-1764 d 5-1-1855 m (1)Betsey Wilbur (2)Esther P. Keniston (3)Amelia Ainsworth Pvt CT ★

Daniel: b 7-10-1752 d a. 8- -1811 m (1)Eunice Hobart (2)Mary Fuller Pvt NH

David: b 1741 d 1-13-1818 m Hannah Pease Capt MA

David, Sr.: b 7-22-1730 d 11-10-1803 m Rebecca Jones Capt MA

David, Jr.: b 6-30-1758 d 10-5-1806 m Martha Brooks Pvt MA

David: b 12-26-1707 d 3-24-1784 m Sarah Merriman PS MA

David: b 12-8-1744 d 10-6-1813 m Rebecca Hoar Capt NH

Ebenezer: b 7-15-1748 d 3-15-1817 m Azubah Taylor Pvt MA

Edward: b 11-18-1743 d 4-24-1824 m Thankful Daniels Capt NY

Edward: b 1745 d 2-10-1824 m Mary Dutcher PS NY

Elisha: b 3-20-1710 d 7-17-1785 m Mary Loring Lt MA

Elisha, Jr.: b 2-21-1750 d 1-26-1794 m (1)Sarah Goodenow (2)Mary Adams Sol MA

Elizur: b c. 1758 d 11-5-1815 m Olive Kasson Pvt Fif CT

Elnathan: b 5-20-1740 d 2-14-1809 m Charity Frost Pvt CT

Ephraim: b 12-16-1764 d 1-9-1806 m Martha Buckley Pvt CT

Ephraim: b 6-7-1751 d 5-12-1803 m Sarah Wells Sgt CT

Ephraim: b 5-15-1738 d c. 1795 m Mehitable Spaulding Pvt CT

Ephraim: b 12-11-1734 d 9-23-1809 m Sarah Heywood Lt MA
Ephraim: b 3-12-1734 d p. 1778 m (1)Azubah Eager (2)Mrs
   Elizabeth Temple Pvt MA
Ephraim: b 4-3-1738 d 6-13-1798 m Sylvia Briggs Pvt MA
Ephraim: b 6-7-1754 d p. 1795 m Hannah Goodell PS NH
Ezekiel: b 1748 d 10-26-1826 m (1) — (2)Charity — Pvt NH
Francis: b 6-31-1728 d 6-25-1778 m Mary Heywood Lt MA
Gideon: b 4-13-1764 d 4-23-1830 m (1)Ruth Barton (2)Samantha
   (Blackman) Johnson MM CT
Gideon: b 7-27-1745 d 12-5-1822 m (1)Anne Lyman (2)Anna — Pvt
   MA
Gilbert: b 7-5-1740 d — m Elizabeth Bryan Pvt NY
Henry: b 1-10-1745 d 9-23-1832 m Esther Williams Capt RI
Hezekiah: b 4-13-1762 d 10-21-1833 m Meribah Bishop Pvt CT ★
Hezekiah: b 1750 d 1-8-1828 m Mary Wood PS RI
Ignatius: b 1744 d 8- -1793 m Henritta Maria (Neale) Smith Col
   CS MD
Ignatius: b c. 1744 d p. 7-20-1821 m Elizabeth — PS MD
Ignatius: b 1760 d 1809/10 m Ann Morris 2Lt MD
Isaac: b 12-26-1746 d 12-31-1831 m Ruth Swan Lt CT
Isaac, Jr.: b 6-6-1768 d 5-11-1856 m (1)Hannah Holmes (2)Olive
   Burdick Fif CT
Isaac: b 3-24-1734 d 4-22-1817 m Elizabeth Stone Sgt MA
Isaac: b 1754 d 2-26-1833 m (1)Miriam Rugg (2)Bethena — Capt
   CT
Isaiah: b 9-21-1761 d 1-9-1880 m (1)Elizabeth Woodbury (2)Anna
   Jones Pvt NH
Israel: b 1-7-1745 d 12-13-1830 m (1)Lucy Ingersoll (2)Susanna
   Carter Sol MA
Jabez: b 3-25-1721 d 1810 m (1)Charity Beach (2)Mary (Wheeler)
   Capt CT
Jacob: b c. 1740 d a. 7-9-1799 m Ann — PS MD
Jacob: b 3-17-1750 d 12-27-1841 m Mary Flint Pvt MA
Jacob: b 6-4-1747 d 2-16-1824 m (1)Phoebe Wheeler (2)Temperance
   Blydenburg PS NY
James: b 5-18-1759 d 12-24-1847 m (1)Ellen Wakely (2)Elizabeth
   Field Phelps Pvt CT ★
James: b 12-22-1756 d 2-15-1828 m Vashti Bigelow Pvt MA
James, Jr.: b 5-6-1731 d 1785 m Mary Butterfield Pvt NH
James: b 1740 d 3-12-1777 m Rhoda Lyon Capt NJ
James: b c. 1735 d 1804 m Abigail — Pvt VA
Jeremiah: b 3-23-1731 d 2-26-1811 m (1)Submit Horton (2)Eliza
   Pearce Throop (3)Hannah Slade PS MA
Jeremiah:b 1747 d 10-17-1827 m Keziah Blanchard PS NH
Jeremiah: b 2-11-1765 d 5-29-1819 m Mary Joslin Pvt VT
Jesse: b 11-24-1757 d p. 1808 m Hannah Dwinnell Pvt NH
Joel: b 6-2-1761 d p. 1792 m Mary Proctor Pvt MA
Joel: b 1-27-1743 d 12-10-1814 m Mary Dudley Cpl MA
Joel: b c. 11-24-1748 d 10-22-1807 m Dorcas Davis Pvt MA
John: b 3-15-1738 d 3-15-1801 m Esther Mallett Pvt CT
John: b 7-13-1740 d 12-28-1797 m Lydia Warner Pvt CT
John: b 8-6-1744 d p. 1776 m Mary Miner Fif CT
John: b 6-2-1756 d — m Sybil Todd Pvt CT
John: b 1755 d 1820 m Amelia Williams Pvt CT
John, Jr.: b 3-20-1765 d 6-19-1840 m Ann Borodel Denison Sol CT
John: b 1760 d 1832 m Tabitha Warrington Sgt MD
John: b 2-5-1731 d 6-12-1815 m Deborah Gleason Capt MA
John: b 1742 d 11-20-1788 m Mrs Elizabeth (Partridge) Richardson
   2Lt MA
John: b 12-22-1756 d 6-8-1794 m Mary Paige QMSgt MA
John: b 5-7-1726 d p. 1790 m (1)Freelove Goff (2)Rebekah Haskins
   (3)Susanna Luther Dr MA
John: b 11-11-1747 d 3-11-1824 m Joanna Crow Pvt MA
John: b 9-4-1752-5 d 9-22-1844 m (1)Dolly Coombs (2)Anna
   Thompson (3)Jenny Townsley Pvt MA ★
John: b 1756 d 3-24-1840 m Hannah Lawrence Pvt MA W★
John: b 3-16-1761 d 1-28-1845 m (1)Abigail Flint (2)Sally White
   Read Pvt MA ★
John: b 1750-60 d 4-23-1843 m (1)Mollie — (2)Betsey — NS NH★
John: b 4-12-1747 d 10-4-1814 m Elizabeth Longworth Dr NJ
John: b 1757 d 11-24-1838 m Susanna Clark Lt NC ★
John: b 9-9-1735 d p. 1790 m Jedidah Bigelow CS VT
John: b 1755 d a. 5- -1823 m Betsey Emerson Sol VA
Jonas, Sr.: b 5-18-1720 d 4-2-1815 m Persis Brooks Pvt NH
Jonas, Jr.: b 1-25-1745/6 d — m (1)Rebecca Maynard (2)Kate
   Koburn Pvt NH
Jonas: b 2-23-1755 d p. 10-25-1777 m Lucretia Smith Pvt MA
Jonathan: b 5-11-1743 d 10- -1794 m Beulah Fiske Pvt MA
Jonathan: b 8-8-1735 d 7-9-1815 m (1)Patience Cole (2)Priscilla
   Hicks Pvt MA
Jonathan, Jr.: b 2-9-1762 d 2-23-1848 m Mary Sage Pvt NY
Jonathan: b 1750 d 5-11-1811 m Chloe Wilson Pvt NH
Jonathan: b 1733 d 1788 m Esther Kimball PS MA
Joseph: b 11-2-1734 d 2-27-1818 m Keziah Botsford Pvt CT
Joseph: b 1-23-1747 d 11-7-1836 m Prudence Palmer Pvt CT
Joseph: b 9-24-1727 d p. 1806 m Mary Southwick Pvt MA
Joseph: b 3-13-1735 d 2-10-1793 m Mary Greenleaf Sol PS MA
Joseph: b c. 1720 d a. 2- -1787 m Maria Holmes Sol PA
Josiah: b 7-13-1743 d 8-9-1817 m Rhoda Bowker Capt MA
Josiah: b 11-14-1742 d 3-23-1823 m (1)Lucy Graves (2)Calla
   Smith Sgt MA
Josiah: b a. 1754 d 4-11-1827 m (1)Elizabeth — (2)Hannah W Howe
   Sgt VT

Lemuel: b 11-17-1743 d 8-30-1801 m Jerusha Summers Dr CT
Lemuel: b 6-6-1709 d 7-29-1782 m Bethia Bronson SrgnMte CT
Lemuel: b 3-8-1757 d 1832 m Katherine Whitney Sgt MA ★
Lester: b 7-24-1757 d 5-15-1835 m Eunice Bailey Pvt CT
Levi: b 11-6-1754 d 1798 m Elizabeth Taylor Pvt MA
Moses: b 1717 d 1792 m Elizabeth — MM CT
Moses: b 7-28-1750 d 8-24-1823 m Lucy Hecock PS CT
Moses: b 8-29-1752 d 4-12-1832 m Pamela Putman Cpl NH
Nathan: bpt 10-11-1747 d 4-11-1817 m (1)Charity Beach (2)Betty
   Hawley (3)Eunice Edwards Sol CT
Nathan: b 5-7-1751 d p. 1790 m Abigail Oakley Pvt CT
Nathan: b 2-9-1726/7 d 1812 m Mary Hunt 1Lt MA
Nathan: b 1751 d 7-15-1823 m Abigail Whitmore Ens PS MA ★
Nathan: b 4-6-1752 d p. 7-6-1792 m Cynthia — Pvt MA
Nathan: b 8-12-1744 d 11-16-1812 m (1)Jemima Benjamin
   (2)Barsheba — Pvt VT
Nathaniel: b 12-7-1733 d 5-19-1819 m Rachel Lewis Capt CT
Nathaniel: b 4-10-1754 d 7-2-1840 m Mehitabel Haven Cpl PS NH
Nathaniel: b c. 1750 d 11-5-1825 m Mrs Averilla Worrell Pvt MD
Nehemiah: b c. 6-29-1796 m Sarah (Hunking) Meserve PS NH
Noah: b 1-25-1750 d 2-23-1834 m Sarah Meriam Pvt MA
Noah: b 6-6-1743 d 6-4-1823 m Eunice Newcomb Capt NY
Obadiah: b 6-27-1730 d p. 11-22-1814 m Mary Manville PS CT
Oliver: b 11-13-1748 d 4-9-1833 m Hepzibah Monroe Pvt MA
Paul: b 9-11-1728 d 10-25-1787 m Lucy Swan PS CT
Peter: b 4-16-1744 d 7-3-1778 m Annis Martin Pvt PA
Peter: b 10-29-1763 d 7-13-1847 m (1)Abigail Tuttle (2)Mrs Abigail
   Tuttle (3)Mrs Beulah Rule Pvt Drm MA ★
Peter: b 2-22-1732 d — m Mehitable Jewett Pvt NH
Phineas: b 7-2-1757 d 6-1-1836 m Mary McCobb Sgt MA ★
Phineas: b 4-3-1745 d 6-18-1814 m Lydia Merriam Pvt MA
Randall: b 4-8-1758 d p. 6-2-1837 m Experience Alden Pvt MA ★
Rufus: b 11-21-1740 d 1-21-1823 m Lydia Pike 1Lt MA
Rufus: b 10-9-1759 d 3-16-1835 m Tamer Joy Pvt MA
Russell: b 3-27-1766 d 12-3-1825 m Elizabeth Hix Pvt MA ★
Salisbury: b 5-27-1764 d 10-2-1856 m Phoebe Peck Pvt MA
Sampson: b 1737 d p. 9- -1832 m Sarah Parlin Pvt NH
Samuel: b 1-22-1761 d 10-27-1819 m Julia Odell Cpl CT ★
Samuel: b 1752 d 7-20-1833 m (1)Sarah — (2)Esther Parrock PS CT
Samuel: b 10-18-1734 d 4-5-1817 m Martha Hosmer Pvt MA
Samuel: b 1-27-1748 d 10- -1812 m Lydia Munroe Pvt MA
Samuel: b 1- -1764 d 5-23-1847 m Ruby Dewey Pvt MA
Samuel: b 7-18-1755 d 1832 m Anna Todd Pvt NH
Samuel: b 1758 d 5-8-1808 m Elizabeth Daniels Pvt NY
Samuel: b 1- -1757 d 6- -1818 m Elizabeth Drake Pvt PA
Samuel: b 10-5-1752 d 12-27-1836 m (1)Eleanor Wheeler (2)Mary
   Handly Pvt VA ★
Seth: b 1747 d 7-6-1817 m (1)Betty Hinman (2)Elizabeth Powell
   Pvt MA
Seth: b 7-13-1756 d 1827 m Rebekah Elliott Cpl NH
Seth: b 5-25-1750 d 1822 m Rachel Butterfield Capt NH
Seth: b 2-22-1749 d 2-3-1818 m Mary Treadwell PS NY
Shepard, Sr.: b 3-22-1726 d 4-9-1790 m Hannah Hewitt Pvt CT
Shepard, Jr.: b 12-5-1756 d 12-9-1798 m Lucy Wheeler Cpl CT
Shubael: b 9-19-1757 d 2-20-1812 m Chloe Martin Cpl MA
Silas: b 3-7-1752 d 11-28-1828 m Sarah Gardner 3Cpl RI
Simeon: b 1-10-1761 d p. 1840 m Anna Sanford Pvt CT ★
Simeon: b 11-25-1733 d p. 1793 m Chloe Way Pvt MA
Simeon: b 9-14-1760 d 12-24-1833 m (2)Sarah Turner Pvt RI ★
Solomon: b 2-22-1747 d 8-5-1822 m Zipporah Harrington Pvt NH
Solomon: b 1756 d 1824 m Elizabeth Ward Winthrop Lt NY
Stephen: b 1756 d 1815 m Jerusha Hawley Sgt CT
Stephen: b 3-8-1749 d 12-19-1806 m Rhoda Spinning Pvt NJ
Stephen: b 1761 d 3-18-1831 m Roxanna Bishop Pvt NY ★
Thaddeus: b 12-16-1742 d 5- -1826 m Elizabeth Farmer Pvt NH
Thomas: b 10-12-1745 d 6-8-1810 m (1)Lucy Prentice (2)Mary Swan
   Wheeler Capt CT
Thomas: b — d 1816 m (1)Molly Ross (2)Mary (Beckwith) Eccleston
   2Lt MD
Thomas: b 5-19-1755 d a. 3-16-1809 m — Sol MD
Thomas: b 5-6-1749 d 1823 m Mary Child Pvt MA
Thomas: b 3-22-1738/9 d 7-10-1804 m Sarah Anna Warner PS MA
Timothy: b 3-18-1696/7 d 5-7-1782 m (1)Abigail Munroe
   (2)Mehitable Whittemore CS MA
Truman: b 11-26-1741 d 4-19-1815 m Huldah Caldwell Capt MA
Uriah: b 1-26-1747 d p. 1787 m Anne Smith Cpl MA
Valentine: b 2-14-1725/6 d 1791 m (1)Sarah Goff (2)Anna
   Bennett Capt NY
Wm.: b 1738 d 8-18-1782 m Hannah French PS CT
Wm.: b 7-20-1755 d a. 4-1-1825 m — Ens MD
Wm., Sr.: b 1731 d 3-1-1804 m Sarah — PS NH
Zaccheus: b 9-9-1749 d 3-31-1836 m Silence Leland Pvt MA
Zadock: b 5-17-1753 d 12-24-1834 m Martha Hall Cooper Pvt CT
Zadock: b 1749 d 7-21-1830 m Lois Wellman Sgt NH
Zebulon: b c. 1755 d p. 1800 m Jemima Keeler Pvt NY

WHEELES,
Amos: b c. 1760 d c. 1826 m Charlotte Tindall Pvt NC

WHEELOCK,
Adam: b 1-24-1763 d 9-27-1846 m (1)Lucy Lamb (2)Chloe Green
   (3)Mrs Ruth Morey Pvt MA ★
Asa: b 10-2-1741 d 3- -1816 m Rachel Drury Sgt MA

WHEELOCK, contd.
Asa: b 6-26-1758 d 5-23-1842 m (1)Lucy Maynard (2)Abigail Read Pvt MA ★
Benjamin: b 1730 d 4-16-1776 m Hannah Chapin Sgt MA
Calvin: b 5-5-1754 d a. 5-24-1808 m Mercy White Pvt MA
Eleazer: b 7-15-1756 d 3-16-1841 m Thankful Maynard Sgt MA
Eleazer: b 4-22-1711 d 4-24-1779 m (1)Sarah Maltby (2)Mary Brinsmead CS PS NH
Eli: b 7-7-1760 d 9-18-1797 m Hannah Streeter Fif MA
Ephraim: b 1733 d 1826 m Mary Clapp LCol MA
James: bpt 1746 d p. 1779 m Lois Starkey Pvt NH Canada
Jesse: b 9-8-1731 d 1781 m Phebe White Pvt MA
John: b 12-23-1756 d 1824 m Dorothy Wilder Drm MA ★
John: b 1759 d 6-13-1816 m Lydia Davis Fif MA
Jonathan: b 5-5-1737 d 7-16-1790 m Thankful Haskell Pvt MA
Jonathan: b 1-11-1759 d 9-5-1845 m Lucy Beaman DrmMaj MA
Jonathan: b 9-18-1727 d 1797 m Ann Drury PS NH
Joseph: b 2-14-1729/30 d 3-10-1778 m (1)Allice Page (2)Olive — Pvt MA
Joseph: b 1765 d 1820 m Sally Slater Pvt MA
Josiah: b 3-30-1725 d 12-20-1794 m Experience Clark Pvt MA
Moses: b 1-11-1738 d 4-15-1801 m (1)Abiel Haws (2)Lydia Bond LCol MA
Nahum: b 5-12-1761 d p. 1804 m Betty Steele Pvt MA
Paul: b 4-26-1727 d 1824 m Thankful — Sol MA
Peter: b 7-23-1724 d 2-18-1802 m Sarah Taft PS MA
Ralph: b 1726 d 1822 m — Capt MA
Samuel: b 9-2-1743 d p. 1790 m Dinah Leland Pvt MA
Seth: b c. 1752 d c. 1806 m (1)Mrs Elizabeth Weld (2)Lucy Johnson Sgt MA
Silas: b 3-10-1718 d p. 5-4-1791 m Hannah Albee Col PS MA
Simeon: b 3-29-1741 d 1786 /7 m Deborah Thayer Lt MA
Timothy: b 6-24-1724 d 4-14-1812 m (1)Sarah Rand (2)Abigail Muzzy Sherman MM NH

WHEELWRIGHT,
Abraham: b 7-26-1757 d 10-14-1850 m Rebecca Knight Pvt Pvtr MA

WHELAN, (includes WHELEN)
Israel: b 12-13-1752 d p. 10-21-1806 m Mary Downing PS PA
John: bpt c. 1736 d p. 6-7-1792 m Rebecca — PS VT

WHELCHEL,
Davis: b 1752 d 9-4-1833 m Nancy Barnes Sol SC
Francis, Sr.: b c. 1730 d 8-7-1796 m Ann Stockton PS SC
Francis, Jr.: b 9-16-1754 d p. 1804 m Judith Davis Sol SC
John: b 10-11-1756 d 3-14-1837 m Abigail Davis Pvt SC

WHELPLEY,
Isaac: b a. 1737 d p. 1781 m Hester Clark Pvt VT

WHERREN,
Wm.: b 1751 d 3-31-1816 m Peggy Paul Pvt MA

WHERRITT,
John: b 1740 d 6- -1779 m Ann Watts Pvt MD
Thomas: b c. 1754 d 1811 m Margaret King Pvt MD

WHETSONE, (includes WHITSTONE)
Henry: b 1751 d 3-10-1816 m Hannah — Pvt PA
Jacob: b 1738 d 1833 m Anna Maria Schaeffer Capt PA

WHETTEN,
Margaret Todd: b 1736 d 3- -1809 m Wm. Whetten PS NY

WHICKER, (or WHICKEAR)
Wm.: b 8-27-1760 d 11-2-1851 m Sarah Eliza Bingamon 1Sgt NC ★

WHIDDEN, (includes WHIDDON)
Ichabod: b 1714 d 3-20-1798 m (1) — Uran (2)Elizabeth Small (3)Mrs Eunice Mason PS NH
Joseph: b 1736 d 1-5-1794 m Mary Seavey PS NH
Samuel: b 9-22-1738 d 3-17-1813 m Sarah Skellions PS RI
Wm.: b c. 1755 d a. 1819-20 m Mary Davis Pvt GA

WHIGHAM,
Wm.: b c. 1755 d p. 1810 m Catherine Smith 3Sgt PA

WHINERY,
Thomas, Sr.: b c. 1750 d p. 1785 m Phoebe Mills Pvt PA

WHIPPEN,
George: b c. 1751 d 10-12-1835 m Eunice Bowden Pvt Smn MA ★

WHIPPLE,
Aaron: b 3-23-1761 d 1838 m Matilda Cooper Pvt NH
Abraham: b 9-26-1733 d 5-29-1819 m Sarah Hopkins Commo RI
Asa: b 1753 d 5-24-1831 m Sylvia Staples Pvt RI
Benajah: b 6-17-1734 d 1812 m Tabitha — Capt RI
Benedict: b 10-13-1739 d 6-16-1819 m Elizabeth Mathewson Pvt RI
Benjamin: bpt 7-2-1727 d 4-1-1824 m Sarah Tuttle Pvt MA ★
Benjamin: b 11-17-1754 d 4-30-1819 m Susanna Hall Mar RI or NY

Benjamin: b 1-5-1726 d 10 -1803 m (1)Anna (Brown) (2)Deborah Dammon Capt CS RI
Benjamin, Sr.: b 4-23-1727 d 4-30-1806 m Hepzibah Crosby PS VT
Benjamin, Jr.: b 4-23-1727 d 3-8-1813 m Silence Bimby Drm VT
Caleb: b 7-23-1764 d 10-15-1851 m Polly McIntyre Pvt CT ★
Christopher: b p. 5-20-1745 d 1-27-1808 m — Lt RI
Christopher: b 11-26-1754 d 8-12-1787 m Sarah Cushing Ens RI
Daniel: b 8-19-1716 d 12-22-1783 m Mary Razee Ens RI
Daniel Peck: b 1751 d 5-19-1814 m Hannah Weatherhead Dr RI
David: b 1759 d 1842 m Arthusia Brooks Pvt MA
Eleazer: b 1734 d 9- -1776 m Abigail Chamberlain Pvt MA
Eleazer: b 1-20-1733 d p. 1781 m Anna Brown Pvt RI
Elijah: b 5-22-1752 d 10-8-1834 m Elizabeth Dennison Pvt CT
Ethan: b 2-13-1758 d 12-18-1836 m (1)Elizabeth Green (2)Abigail Hawkins (3)Mrs Lydia Babcock (Church) OrdlSgt RI ★
Ezekiel: b 5-15-1759 d 4-16-1829 m Mary Olney Ens RI
Ezra: b 5-2-1741 d 11-20-1829 m (1)Lydia Dow (2)Abigail Harwood Barnum Capt MA
Ibrook: b c. 1716 d 1799 m Mary — Pvt RI
James: b 11-23-1737 d 7-28-1808 m Elizabeth Hall 1Lt MA
Jesse: b 9-16-1744 d 2-10-1823 m Freelove Olney Sgt RI
Job: b 5-1-1755 d 2-6-1838 m (1)Mrs Patience Stafford Pratt (2)Ruth Stone Pvt RI ★
John: b 10-11-1743 d 5-28-1832 m (1)Martha Cogswell (2)Mrs Susanna Cogswell Sgt PS MA
John: b 5-21-1742 d 8-18-1811 m Ruth Adams Sgt MA
John: b 12-9-1751 d 5-11-1824 m Lydia Irons Pvt RI
Jonathan: b c. 1750 d p. 1788 m Susan Burnham Cpl MA RI
Jonathan: b 12-8-1723 d 11-5-1805 m Anna Smith PS RI
Joseph: b 12-26-1733 d 1777 m Eunice Fairfield PS Dr MA
Joseph: b 1742 d p. 1781 m Ellen Wellwood Capt MA
Matthew: b 3-20-1754 d 1783 m Mercy Giddens Lt MA
Moses: b 5-13-1733 d 1814 m Catherine Forbush Capt CS PS MA
Moses: b 1-21-1729 d 9-3-1807 m Patience Mathewson MM PS RI
Nathan: b 7-7-1761 d 1-7-1832 m Mary Hill Pvt VT
Nehemiah: b c. 1750 d 1809 m Sarah Roberts Pvt VT
Peter: b 3-7-1747 d 11-20-1820 m Sarah Sly Pvt RI
Preserved: b 9-6-1746 d 5-25-1812/3 m Olive Ballou Pvt RI
Rufus: b 1-14-1747 d 1831 m Mary Comstock Ens PS NH
Samuel: b 12-7-1751 d p. 1792 m Sarah Leonard Pvt MA
Samuel: b 8-28-1749 d 12-8-1782 m Lucy Brown Cpl NH
Simon: b 4-9-1745 d 1-16-1829 m Mary Sibley Pvt MA
Simon: b 9-28-1738 d p. 1790 m Mary Miller LCol RI
Simon: b 6-15-1760 d 5-12-1829 m Abigail Verry Ens RI
Simon: b 2-13-1752 d 9-21-1821 m Levina Staples Pvt RI ★
Stephen: b 7-19-1736 d 2-28-1813 m Zelpha Angel Pvt MA
Stephen, Jr.: b 1750 d 1-16-1822 m (1) — Whipple (2)Lucina Paine Capt RI
Thomas: b 3-26-1752 d 8-8-1833 m (1)Lydia Gates (2)Mrs Woodward (3)Rhoda Merrill Sgt VT ★
Zebulon: b 4-26-1764 d 9-5-1851 m Lydia Russell Pvt CT ★

WHIPPS,
Benjamin: b 8- -1753 d 1840-5 m Susanna — Pvt MD

WHISTLER,
John: b 1756 d 9-3-1829 m Elizabeth Bishop Pvt PA

WHITAKER, (includes WHITACRE, WHITECAR, WHITEKER & WHITTAKER)
Aaron: b 1751 d 3-25-1833 m Martha Ann Roush Pvt PA
Abraham: b 9-19-1764 d p. 1840 m Betsy Whit Pvt CT ★
Abraham: b 1759 d 1819 m Cathrin Becker Pvt NY
Abraham: b c. 1751 d 11- -1814 m Susannah Humble Pvt VA
Alexander: b 1746 d 1824 m Hester White PS MD
Ambrose: b 12-15-1730 d 11-5-1796 m (1)Freelove Stratton (2)Ruth Harris (3)Rachel Leake QMDept NJ
Amos: b 1761 d 1845 m (1)Bathia Allen (2)Esther Ralph Pvt MA ★
Aquilla: b 1755 d 1824 m (1)Mary Kerkindall (2)Ruchamah — Pvt VA
Benjamin: b a. 1747 d 1792 m Adalicia Wilkins Wgn NJ
Edward: b 11-15-1725 d 1780 m Jacobia Hardenberg Capt PS NY
Edward: b 9-27-1741 d 12-1-1802 m Calatentia DuBois Lt NY
Elizabeth Ogden: b 4-9-1744 d 10-18-1833 m Squire Whitaker PS NY PA
Ephraim: b 2-19-1755 d 7-10-1846 m Hannah Stevenson Capt CT
Ezra: b 12-9-1751 d 1-14-1822 m Mary Wells Pvt MA
George: b 1745 d 1785 m Ruth Whitacre PS VA
Hudson: b 10-23-1757 d 7-5-1817 m Susannah Thomas Capt NC
James: b 12-22-1726 d 1788 m (1)Mary Saunders (2)Catharine Bee Tee Pvt MD
James: b 1-12-1756 d 5-12-1835 m Susanna Simonds Sol NY ★
James: b 1763 d 5-4-1842 m Susanna Beckham Pvt VA ★
John: b 5-21-1753 d 10-27-1833 m Nancy — Sgt MD W★
John: b 1744 d 10-1-1829 m Thankful Pierce Pvt NH
John: b 5-12-1747 d 7.20-1816 m Kitty Benton Col NC
John: b 1732 d p. 8-26-1781 m Olive Taylor CS PS NC
John: b c. 1760 d p. 1-31-1837 m Nancy — Pvt NC
John: b 5-2-1745 d 11- -1823 m (1)Elizabeth Hardy (2)Ferebee Pearson CS NC
John: b 1727 d 1826 m (1)Dinah Lewis (2)AM Pyle Pvt PA
John: b — d p. 2-13-1797 m Mary — PS VA
John: b 1759 d 1852 m Phoebe Baldwin Pvt VA

Jonathan: b 1731 d 1-11-1812 m Susannah White PS CT
Jonathan, Sr.: b 1724 d 6-17-1786 m Mary Miller Pvt NJ
Jonathan, Jr.: b 1758 d 7-13-1840 m Mary Mitchell Sgt NJ ★
Joseph: b 3-6-1755 d 7-8-1825 m Tabitha Davis Pvt NJ
Joseph: b — d 1790 m — Sol PA
Joseph: b a. 1760 d 1805 m Jane Wilson Pvt VA
Mark: b 1750 d 10- -1844 m — Pvt NC ★
Mark: b 4-8-1750 d 1842 m Catherine Boone PS NC
Matthew Cary: b 2-21-1762 d 6- -1814 m Elizabeth Ann Coffield
    Pvt NC
Nathaniel: b 2-22-1732 d 1-21-1795 m Sarah Smith PS MA
Nathaniel: b 6- -1758 d 10-25-1841 m (1)Hannah Drake (2)Ruth
    Haines Sgt NJ ★
Peter: b 10-11-1753 d 8-14-1843 m Mary Carpenter Pvt MA ★
Richard: b 6-6-1730 d p; 1785 m Patience Bowen Cpl MA
Richard: b 1762 d 8-28-1833 m Nancy Peets Pvt NC ★
Richard, Jr.: b c. 1752 d 1840 m (1)Rachel Bentley (2)Elizabeth Blair
    Pvt SC
Samuel: b 1753 d 1802 m Mary Graves Pvt GA
Squire: b 8-2-1742 d 1-31-1817 m Elizabeth Ogden Pvt PS NY
Stephen: b 1-10-1747 d 11-4-1827 m (1)Susan White (2)Ruth
    Conklin (3)Mary Cross (4)Agnes Patten Lt NJ
Thomas: b 4-28-1762 d 1814 m Mary Williams Pvt SC
Thomas: b c. 1740 d 1783 m Elizabeth — Pvt PA
Wm.: b 7-28-1750 d 7-22-1830 m Lydia Howe Drm MA
Wm.: b — d 1789 m (1)Mary — (2) — Wiggins PS SC
Willis: b 1748 d 6-17-1832 m Sarah Williams Capt SC

WHITALL,
Ann Cooper: b 4-23-1716 d 9-27-1797 m James Whitall PS NJ
James: b 9-4-1717 d 9-29-1808 m Ann Cooper PS NJ

WHITCOMB, (includes WHITCOM)
Abijah: b 6- -1751 d 5-17-1847 m (1)Mary Seaver (2)Susanna
    Warner Pvt NH
Abner: b 2-4-1733 d 1821 m (1)Sarah Jefts (3)Susannah Meads
    (4)Abigail Boynton MM MA
Anthony: b 6-17-1766 d 1807 m Lucy Wright Pvt VT
Asa: bpt 6-18-1719 d 3-16-1804 m (1)Eunice Sawyer (2)Betty Sawyer
    Col MA
Asa: b 2-29-1735 d 3-31-1812 m Joanna Raymond CS PS VT
Benjamin: b 12-27-1753 d 10-23-1828 m Sarah Rice Pvt MA
Benjamin: b 7-2-1737 d 7-22-1828 m Lydia Howe Maj NH ★
David: b 2-18-1749/50 d 8-30-1778 m Sarah — Cpl MA
Elihu: b 1760 d 3-17-1825 m Elizabeth Ruggles Sol MA
Elisha: b 10-18-1742 d 9-19-1814 m Joanna (Whitcomb) Capt NH
Ephraim: b c. 6-8-1743 d c. 1795 m Hannah Hoar 2Lt MA
Ephraim: b 7-22-1751 d p. 1819 m Sarah Longley Pvt MA ★
Ephraim: b 10-21-1750 d 7-30-1811 m Elizabeth Carter Sol NH
Hiram: b 2-25-1758 d 2-28-1836 m Sarah Dutton Pvt Tms CT ★
Jacob: b 9-13-1743 d 5-24-1823 m Olive Wetherbee MM NH
James, Sr.: b 11-1-1704 d 8-9-1782 m Hannah Graves PS MA
James, Jr.: b 7-4-1741 d 10-27-1790 m (1)Sarah Gates (2)Lucy
    Whitney Lt MA
Job: b 9- -1740 d 9-22-1813 m Keziah Wheelwright Pvt MA
Job: b 5-8-1724 d 3-2-1802 m Anna Skinner Sol CT
John, Sr.: b 2-20-1712 d 11-17-1785 m (1)Mary Carter (2)Rebecca
    Whitcomb BGen MA
John, Jr.: b 5-12-1760 d 12-3-1798 m Azubah (Whitcomb) Pvt MA
John: b 1-18-1711/12 d 5-18-1787 m Sarah Tower Pvt MA
John: b 1732 d 1809 m Hannah Nash Pvt MA
John: b 5-20-1759 d 1813 m Abigail Chapin Pvt MA
John: b 11-13-1731 d 3-31-1835 m Sarah Whitcomb Sgt NH ★
John: b 9-17-1761 d 1822 m Lydia Hayden Parmenter Pvt VT
John Skinner: b 6-10-1766 d 11-2-1838 m Sarah Marsh Pvt CT ★
Jonathan, Jr.: b 3-30-1754 d 2-21-1846 m (1)Sally Baker (2)Elizabeth
    Baker Pvt MA
Jonathan: b 12-23-1717 d 2-22-1790 m Sarah Tufts CS MA
Jonathan: b 1-14-1740 d 6-13-1792 m Dorothy Carter Capt NH
Joseph: b 3-31-1731 d p. 1790 m Elizabeth Wheelock Capt NH
Joshua: b 11-19-1734 d p. 1812 m Lucy Culver Sgt MA
Josiah: b 8-29-1761 d 1-20-1834 m Rebecca Chapin Pvt MA ★
Josiah: b 1762 d — m Miss Thayer Pvt NH
Lot: bpt 4-10-1746 d 5-30-1828 m Sarah Lincoln Cpl MA
Lot: b 5-2-1739 d 4-7-1797 m Lydia Nye Pvt PS VT
Moses: b 1739 d p. 1780 m Sarah Powers Sgt MA
Nathaniel: b 6-17-1762 d p. 1798 m Salome Snow Sol MA
Noah: b 1714 d 6-10-1798 m Mary Franklin Pvt MA
Philemon: b 10-29-1748 d 1-10-1824 m (1)Martha Sawyer (2)Mrs
    Amasa Aldrich PS NH
Reuben: b 2-2-1747 d 6- -1840 m Dinah Howe Pvt NH
Reuben: b 1756 d 11-9-1843 m Esther Bacon Pvt NH W★
Robert: b 5-1-1741 d 4-26-1817 m Eunice Sheldon Sgt CT
Scottoway: b 6-18-1739 d 7-28-1812 m Mary Winslow Lt MA
Silas: b 4-2-1742 d p. 1782 m — Pvt MA
Simon: b 9-19-1755 d 12-20-1824 m (1)Rachel Hebard (2)Abigail
    Hubbell Pvt NY
Thomas: b 10-4-1736 d 6-21-1824 m Anne Whitney Pvt NH ★
Thomas: b 6-3-1759 d 10-6-1828 m Betsey Bishop Pvt VT
Wm.: b 9-24-1710 d 12-5-1792 m Hannah Daby PS Pvt MA
Zelotes: b 1759 d 5-12-1813 m Sarah Parmenter Sol MA

WHITE,
Aaron: b 10-25-1723 d 1-19-1802 m Sarah Olmsted PS Sol CT
Abel: b 1758 d c. 1830 m Sarah Comfort Cpl VT
Abel: b 5-25-1760 d 10-29-1841 m Hannah Closson Pvt VT
Abijah: b 1-18-1763 d 1-27-1842 m Hannah Hall Pvt CT
Abner: b 1725 d p. 6-30-1794 m Ruth Brownell CS NY
Abraham: b 1745/6 d 6-18-1835 m — 1Lt MD
Abram: b 6-21-1762 d 6-22-1853 m (3)Mellicent Hopewell OrdISgt
    PA ★
Adonijah: b 10-29-1751 d 10-29-1837 m Hannah Kingsbury Cpl CT
    W★
Alexander: b 6-4-1752 d 1814/15 m Mary Clifford Capt NJ
Alexander: b 1748 d p. 1783 m Rachel Henderson Pvt PA CL
Aleander: b c. 1750 d p. 7-4-1819 m Elizabeth — Pvt SC
Ambrose: b 1754 d 6-2-1823 m Ann Jones 1Lt VA
Ambrose: b 1756 d a. 1839 m Cynthiana Green Pvt VA ★
Amos: b 11-20-1745 d 8-21-1825 m Sarah Griswold QM CT
Amos: b — d p. 1779 m Azuba Taft Pvt MA
Amos: b 1748 d 9-25-1819 m Mary Wells Pvt PA
Andrew: b c. 1722 d 1-29-1802 m Jean Herring Sol PA
Andrew: b c. 1755 d a. 10-6-1828 m Elizabeth — Pvt VA
Anthony, Sr.: b 3-20-1722 d 12-31-1790 m (1)Mrs King (2)Mrs
    Deborah Walker (3)Mary Ann Barton PS SC
Anthony, Jr.: b 12-30-1748 d 1799 m Hannah Barton QM SC
Anthony Walton: b 7-7-1750 d 2-10-1803 m Margaret Ellis ADC NJ
Antipas: b 3-12-1760 d 11-18-1832 m Lucinda Brewster Pvt MA ★
Archibald: b 1718 d 11-11-1800 m Susan Walker CS PS NC
Asa: b 11-6-1743 d 5- -1820 m (1)Mary Bingham (2)Hannah Cutler
    Sgt CT
Asa: b 4-25-1736 d 1818 m Lucy Humphrey Capt MA
Asa: b 1754/5 d p. 1798 m Mary Drake Pvt MA
Asa: b 6-2-1762 d 2-5-1847 m Lydia Hawes Pvt MA
Asaph: b 8-11-1747 d 9-18-1828 m (1)Lucretia Bingham (2)Martha
    — Lt MA
Barrett: b 7-22-1727 d 2-18-1782 m Elizabeth Starke PS VA
Benjamin: b 1746-50 d 4-24-1817 m Abigail Wilder Capt MA
Benjamin, Jr.: b 9-7-1754 d 7-12-1839 m Mary Chamberlin Sgt MA
Benjamin: b 11-14-1727 d 7-24-1804 m Elizabeth — Sol MA
Benjamin: b 4- -1747 d 10-20-1815 m Anna White Pvt MA
Benjamin: b 6-12-1756 d 1833 m Silence (Parker) Baker Pvt MA ★
Benjamin: b 1-23-1724 d 9-8-1783 m Mercy Thomas PS MA
Benjamin: b a. 1750 d p. 1782 m Hannah Sherburne PS MA
Benjamin: b c. 1760 d p. 1825 m Susan Bartee Pvt VA
Benjamin: b 1756 d 1830 m Martha Jobe Pvt VA
Buchminster: b 4-15-1759 d 10-9-1806 m Mercy Prouty Cpl MA
Caleb: b 8-19-1744 d 4-8-1840 m Amy Coleson Pvt MA ★
Carpus: b 1735 d 7- -1777 m Anna Delano Pvt MA
Charles: b 4-17-1758 d p. 1796 m Hannah Ricker Pvt MA
Charles: b 3-5-1749 d 7-15-1851 m Sarah Gray Pvt NH ★
Charles: b 9-5-1761 d 10-19-1854 m (1)Sarah Monroe (2)Charlotte
    Downs Pvt VA ★
Consider: b c. 1760 d 1-6-1837 m Sarah — Pvt CT ★
Cornelius, Sr.: b 1721 d 11-18-1787 m (1)Susanna Howell (2)Rachel
    Barney Hodges PS Capt MA
Cornelius, Jr.: b 1754 d 12-11-1806 m Abigail Leonard Pvt MA
Cornelius: b 10-8-1752 d 11-14-1820 m Abigail Thayer Cpl MA
Daniel: b 12-7-1749 d 9-1-1816 m Sarah Hale Lt CT
Daniel: b 4-14-1746 d p. 1788 m Mehitable Cummins PS CT
Daniel: b 9-7-1740 d 11-17-1815 m Sarah Goodrich 2Lt MA
Daniel: b 11-28-1752 d 9-15-1814 m Hannah Lamb Sol MA
Daniel: b 4-22-1760 d 12-10-1827 m Anna Williams Hall Pvt MA
Daniel: b 4-10-1760 d 6-4-1841 m Mary Hunt Pvt MA ★
Daniel: b 9-5-1726 d 12-15-1805 m Submit Morton PS MA
Daniel: b 1740 d 1818 m Elizabeth — Capt VA
Daniel: b 1737 d 1820 m Mary Marders Pvt VA
Daniel: b 1748 d 3-28-1830 m Susan Pettus Pvt VA
David: b 2-18-1748 d c. 1778 m Roxcellany Warner 1Lt MA
David: b 2-25-1753 d 1793 m Martha Cottle Pvt MA
David: b 12-7-1735 d 4-28-1816 m Mary Story Pvt MA
David: b c. 1735 d 1-3-1805 m Mary Crawford Capt PA
David: b 1754/5 d 3-11-1834 m Elizabeth Watts Pvt VA ★
Douglas: b 7-28-1748 d p. 1789 m Ruth Albee Pvt MA
Ebenezer: b 9-25-1752 d 1827 m Lydia Davis Cpl MA
Ebenezer: b 11-20-1726 d 3-10-1812 m Elizabeth Ellis Pvt MA
Ebenezer: b 1733 d 10-11-1817 m Sarah Church Pvt MA
Ebenezer: b 4-1-1761 d 9-17-1831 m Calista Partridge Pvt MA
Ebenezer: b 5-4-1762 d 6-26-1815 m Susanna Franklin Pvt MA
Ebenezer: b 3-3-1755 d 5-11-1823 m Lucretia Partridge Pvt MA
Ebenezer: b 9-3-1746 d 3-8-1827 m Helena Bartow Dr NY
Ebenezer: b 1723 d 2-11-1802 m — PS NY
Ebenezer: b 12-2-1731 d 7-24-1807 m (1)Hannah Merrill (2)Ruth
    Emerson Grd Sct VT
Edward: b 1733 d 1795 m Margaret — CS DE
Edward: b 2-12-1732 d 10-15-1795 m Rachael Baynard Pvt MD
Edward: b 12-18-1754 d 3-27-1826 m Mary Ann Benson Sol MD
Edward: b 11-27-1758 d 1-9-1812 m Mildred Scott Stubbs Lt MA
Edward: b 6-23-1719 d 11-30-1784 m Mehitable Breck Pvt MA
Edward: b 1746 d 5-18-1816 m Elizabeth — Pvt MA
Edward: b c. 1724 d p. 1792 m Rebecca Pelton Pvt NJ
Edward: b c. 1735 d — m Eliazabeth — Pvt SC
Edward: b 7-21-1749 d 12-9-1831 m Sarah Tourtelot Pvt VT
Edward: b 1751 d p. 8-8-1809 m (1)Pamela Singleton (2)Sarah
    Sidebottom Pvt VA

WHITE, contd.

Elihu: b 1734 d 12-23-1793 m Zeruiah Cole PS Lt MA
Elijah, Sr.: b 2-15-1719 d 5-18-1778 m Abigail Hurlburt PS CT
Elijah, Jr.: b 2-28-1748 d 12- -1804 m Elizabeth Arnold Pvt MA
Elijah: b 1740 d 11-16-1808 m (1)Rhoda (White) (2) Anna Wild Sgt MA
Elijah: b 8-15-1750 d 10-6-1827 m Beaulah Walker Pvt MA
Elijah: b 9-4-1762 d 11-5-1840 m Betsey Wiswell Pvt MA ★
Elijah: b 2-15-1761 d 7-22-1858 m Susannah Brame Pvt VA ★
Elisha: b 12-2-1762 d 5-31-1824 m Abigail Bates Pvt CT
Elisha: b 3-8-1753 d 7-28-1811 m Mary Corbett Pvt MA
Elisha, Sr.: b 3-8-1731 d p. 1776 m Alice Stearns PS MA
Elisha, Jr.: b 6-18-1759 d 6-14-1817 Deborah Hunt Fif MA
Elisha: b 3-15-1753 d 3-22-1833 m(1)Sarah Carter (2)Deborah Gilman Cpl MA
Enoch: b 2- -1747 d 1-10-1813 m Susannah Goodman Lt MA
Ephraim: b 1-3-1754 d 8-23-1842 m (1)Dorcas Richardson (2)Hope Bennett Sgt CT MA ★
Ephraim: b 1760 d 3-31-1838 m Mary Reeves Pvt NY
Ezekiel, Sr.: b 1-1-1722 d c. 1790 m Abigail Blanchard Pvt MA
Ezekiel, Jr.: b 5-6-1746 d 1-10-1821 m Sarah Vinton Cpl MA
Francis: b 6-29-1757 d 10-14-1839 m Annis Tuttle Pvt MA
Galen: b 8-20-1759 d 11-4-1833 m Mary Mildred Alexander Pvt VA ★
George: b 3-6-1746 d 1-16-1777 m Mary Benton Pvt CT
George, Sr.: b c. 1700 d 1788 m Sarah Bumpas PS CT
George: b c. 1746 d 5-9-1826 m (1)Lucy Thorne (2)Sarah Oliver Capt MA ★
George Jr.: bpt 10-19-1737 d p. 8-22-1804 m Patience — Capt NY
George: b 1722 d 5- -1792 m Susannah Read Sol NC
George: b c. 1740 d p. 8-18-1819 m Mary Earle Pvt MA
Giles: b 1752 d 4-21-1813 m Sarah Dodd Pvt MA
Godfrey: b 9-4-1760 d 3-25-1852 m Jane Ford Pvt RI ★
Haffield: b 1-3-1738 d 12-13-1818 m Lydia Masters Capt MA
Harmon: b 2-5-1753 d 10-15-1818 m Sarah Dean Sgt CT
Henry: b 1743 d 2-16-1823 m Esther White Lt MA
Henry: b 11-6-1753 d 2-9-1839 m Juliana Moore Pvt MA ★
Henry: b-31-1750 d 12-20-1840 m Ann Stephens Dr NY ★
Henry: b 6-11-1740 d 9-30-1787 m Francis — LCol SC
Henry: b 1734 d 12-20-1821 m Mariah Frances Barnett Pvt VA
Hugh: b 1733 d 1820 m Eunice Robinson Mus CT
Hugh, Jr.: b 1-16-1763 d 4-7-1827 m (1)Tryphena Lawrence (2)Susan Smith Pvt CT
Hugh: b 9-2-1749 d p. 11-16-1800 m Mrs Ann Rogers Reed Pvt MA
Hugh, Sr.: b 1-25-1733 d 4-16-1812 m (1)Mary Clark (2)Lois Davenport Cmsry CT
Hugh: b 1737 d 1822 m (1)Margaret Allison (2)Charlotte Weitzel Col PS PA
Ichabod: b 3-11-1761 d 3-10-1813 m Rhoda Hoag Pvt NY
Isaac, Jr.: b — d 9-28-1793 m Priscilla Moffett Pvt Sgt MA
Isaac: b 5-9-1745 d 4-21-1797 m Mehitabel Lane Lt MA
Isaac: b c. 1755 d 1821 m Sarah Vaughan Lt NC
Isaac: b c. 1750 d 1777 m Mary Anne — Sgt VA
Israel: b 3-7-1761 d 1-3-1816 m Sarah Slater Pvt PA
Jacob: b 7-14-1756 d 10-29-1797 m Esther Hoyt Pvt CT
Jacob: b — d 1800 m Elizabeth Gould Pvt VA
Jacob:b 1759 d 2-27-1805 m Nancy Walton Drm NC
Jacob: b 5-2-1759 d 7-20-1849 m (1)Josinah Mounts (2)Alcy — (3)Nancy Dews Capt PA
Jacob: b 1762 d 7-6-1833 m Mary Gyger Pvt PA
Jacob: b 10-20-1765 d 6-2-1832 m (1)Hannah Spiers (2)Nancy Oglesby Pvt VA
James: b 12-18-1755 d 4-1-1847 m Polly Farrington Pvt CT
James: b 1743 d 6-22-1823 m Sarah Mary Givens Capt NC
James: b 1747 d p. 5-10-1819 m Mary Lawson Capt NC
James: b c. 1760 d c. 1811 m Elizabeth Daves Sol NC
James: b 3-28-1744 d 11-25-1821 m Haudah Goodale Pvt VT
James: b 1746 d 7-12-1795 m Rachel McIlhaney Pvt VA
Jane Brown: b 1758 d 1841 m Wm. White PS SC
Jeremiah: b 10-11-1749 d p. 1790 m Jane Tirrell Sgt MA
Jeremiah: b c. 1740 d 5-19-1788 m Jane — 1Lt VA
Jeremiah: b c. 1727 d a. 4-25-1795 m Esther Watts CS VA
Jesse: b 6-12-1754 d 3-2-1830 m Anna Mason Sgt MA
Jesse: b c. 1755 d 1812 m Elizabeth Culin Sol NC
Jesse: b 1-21-1762 d 1840 m Elizabeth Wells Pvt SC
Jesse: b 1753 d 1839 m Elizabeth Brown Pvt VA
Joel: b 7-15-1755 d 1835 m Sarah Osborn Pvt Armr CT ★
Joel: b 4-6-1705 d 6-28-1789 m (1)Ruth — (2)Ruth Dart (3)Mrs Eunice Wolcott (4)Mrs Sarah Conant PS CT
Joel: b 10-20-1750 d 5-3-1826 m Sarah Osborn Pvt MA
Joel: b 7-30-1756 d 1822 m Margrett Shaw Pvt MA
John: b 10-21-1758 d 4-17-1845 m Priscilla Devol Sgt CT ★
John, Sr.: b 5-19-1722 d 11-24-1797 m Mary Dickerman Pvt CT
John, Jr.: b 1756 d 2-18-1830 m Anna Bostwick Pvt CT
John:b 4-9-1760 d 11-11-1838 m (1)Eunice Hedges (2)Sophia Buckley Pvt CT ★
John: b 10-20-1749 d 10-8-1823 m Barsheba Bunter Sol GA
John: b c. 1755 d 3- -1804 m Lucy Calhoun Pvt GA
John, Sr.: b 1725 d p. 1796 m Ann Burgess PS MD
John, Jr.: b 1759 d 10-21-1805 m Ursula Smith Pvt MD
John: b 10-14-1738 d 6-24-1791 m Mary Malcom Capt MA
John, Sr.: b 1741 d 2-23-1797 m Lois Wilder Capt MA
John 3d: b 11-30-1738 d 6-8-1812 m Lydia Jefts Capt MA

John: b 2-7-1720 d 7-11-1800 m (1)Miriam (Hoyt) Hazen (2)Mrs Elizabeth Haynes Capt MA
John: b 2-13-1729 d 4-3-1812 m Mercy Hathaway Sgt MA
John: b 12-23-1749 d 1-16-1834 m Martha Keith Sgt MA
John: b 7-19-1758 d 3-9-1847 m (1)Bethiah Braman (2)Henrietta Richardson Sgt MA ★
John: bpt 7-22-1739 d p. 1795 m Abigail McCord Lt MA
John: b 8- -1745 d 11-23-1822 m Mary Gray Cpl MA
John: b 4-7-1738 d p. 1796 m Sarah Carnahen Pvt Dr MA
John: b 4-27-1740 d 2-14-1797 m (1)Jane Stinson (2)Mary McCobb (3)Abigail Butler Pvt MA
John: b c. 1740 d p. 1779 m Hannah Dumbleton Pvt MA
John: b 2-23-1731 d 1809 m Susannah Eaton Pvt MA
John: b 1749 d 2-4-1828 m Susanna (White) Pierce Pvt MA
John: b 9-12-1756 d 10-15-1833 m Ruth Haskell Pvt MA
John: b 9-18-1757 d 12-21-1846 m Lucy Tucker Pvt MA ★
John: b c. 1760 d p. 1799 m (1)Mary Holland (2)Achsah Bigelow Pvt MA
John: b 12-26-1726 d 2-19-1800 m Elizabeth (Deane) Gilman (2)Sarah (LeBarron) Leonard PS MA
John: b 1719 d 1796 m Molly Wallace MM PS NH
John 3d: b 12-31-1740 d p. 1782 m Ruth Emery Lt NH
John: b 12-5-1742 d 1-11-1823 m Hannah Miller Cpl NH
John: b 1756 d 9-3-1832 m Nancy Robinson Pvt NH
John, Jr.: b 1733 d 12-8-1814 m Hannah — Capt NY
John: b 10-30-1754 d 12-30-1844 m Lydia Merrick PS NY ★
John: b 1736 d 1791 m Ann Colwell PS NY
John: b 1750 d a. 5-26-1801 m Agnes Mayfield Capt NC
John, Sr.: b 1730 d 1820 m Mary (Barker) Pvt NC
John: b c. 1747 d 1804 m Margaret — Sol NC
John: b c. 1736 d 1787 m Jane Paisley PS NC
John, Sr.: b 1726 d 8- -1806 m Mary Ann Patterson Maj PA
John: b c. 1750 d p. 3-8-1817 m Agnes Matthews Pvt PA
John: b 1759 d 8-9-1832 m Margaret Patton PS PA
John: b 1739 d 3-23-1835 m Elizabeth Gordon Pvt PA
John: b c. 1764 d 1809 m (1)Sarah Sutton (2)Mrs Rachel Carr (3)Mrs Mary Minton Benford Pvt PA
John: b 6-25-1759 d 7-8-1838 m Elizabeth Standley Gnr PA
John: b 1760 d 5-22-1822 m Ann Foster Pvt SC
John, Jr.: b 1752 d 8-25-1843 m Ann Bonar Lt CS VA
John: b 4-11-1715 d 10- -1799 m Catherine Evans Lt VA
John: b 3- -1756 d 6-12-1834 m Elizabeth Davenport Sgt VA ★
John: b 3-1-1751 d 10-16-1846 m Martha Woodson Fif VA ★
John: b 5-10-1760 d 8- -1818 m Eleanor Williams Pvt VA W★
John: b 1758 d p. 1840 m — Mills Pvt VA
John, Jr.: b 1764 d 1837 m Nancy Copely Pvt VA
John: b 4-7-1764 d 1-27-1849 m (1) — Tompkins (2)Elizabeth Estes Cav VA
John: b c. 1720 d p. 3-22-1782 m Mary — CS PS VA
John M: b 6-27-1743 d 2-6-1833 m Mildred Thornton Ballenger Capt VA
Jonathan: b 3-14-1739 d 7-25-1818 m Rebecca Haskell Sgt MA W★
Jonathan: b 1-29-1717 d 8-2-1789 m (1)Dorcas Alvord (2)Lydia Rugg PS MA
Joseph: b 8-19-1733 d 1776 m Ruth Churchill Cpl CT
Joseph: b 10-23-1748 d 12-8-1820 m Mary Brown Pvt CT W★
Joseph: b c. 1751 d p. 1810 m Betty Johnson Pvt CT
Joseph: b 9-26-1762 d 6-3-1832 m (1)Olive Holt (2)Deborah Holt Sol CT
Joseph: b 1720 d 4- -1796 m Mary Griffith 1Lt MD
Joseph, Sr.: b 11-1-1719 d 11-15-1780 m Patience Ball Capt MA
Joseph, Jr.: b 8-25-1751 d 7-15-1806 m Rebecca Hoar 2Lt MA
Joseph, Sr.: b 10-1-1706 d 1-28-1795 m Ruth Nash Matr MA
Joseph, Jr.: b 11-22-1742 d 7-18-1816 m Ruth Porter Sgt PS MA
Joseph: b 6-25-1738 d 2-5-1805 m Deborah Fish Pvt MA
Joseph: b 10-11-1739 d 12-31-1795 m Lucy — Pvt MA
Joseph: b 1761/62 d p. 1844 m Jane Copp Pvt MA ★
Joseph: b 1727 d 11-15-1805 m Mary Wilbean Chapman PS MA
Joseph: b 6-7-1746 d 4-15-1835 m Keziah Britton Sgt PS NH
Joseph: b 1758 d 1850 m Ann Alsop Arfr Sol NY ★
Joseph, Sr.: b c. 1724 d 1807 m Elizabeth White Sol NC
Joseph: b 6-1-1755 d 10-10-1840 m Mary — Sgt PA ★
Joseph: b 1741 d 12-14-1831 m Mary Hamilton Pvt PA
Joseph: b 1- -1763 d 7-3-1804 m Martha Elliott Capt SC
Joseph: b — d 1-7-1805 m Mary Fulton Pvt VA
Joseph: b c. 1750 d p. 8-13-1811 CS VA
Joshua: b 9-28-1718 d 9-28-1808 m Abthia Bryant Capt MA
Joshua: b 1735 d 1-1-1819 m Hannah Batson Pvt NH
Josiah: b 12-28-1730 d 1-1-1803 m Sarah McClure Capt MA
Josiah, Jr.: b 6-2-1741 d 1790 m Tabitha Carter Pvt MA
Josiah: b 3-13-1749 d 9- -1819 m Parnee Brooks Sol MA
Josiah: b 5-21-1741 d 12-1-1807 m Mary Stewart Cpl NH
Josiah: b c. 1750 d p. 1790 m Catherine McCool Pvt VA
Josiah: b 1-3-1714 d 9-1-1806 m (1)Deborah House (2)Mrs Elizabeth (3)Tabitha — Pvt VT
Justus: b 4-10-1751 d 4-15-1816 m Content Clark Pvt MA
Lawrence: b 1760 d 5-19-1842 m Eunice — Pvt CT
Lebbeus: b 6-10-1748 d 7-5-1779 m Abigail Weed Pvt CT
Lemuel: b 12-30-1758 d 8-7-1850 m Anna Brigham Pvt CT
Lemuel, Sr.: b 11-6-1736 d 5-4-1780 m Martha Loomis PS CT
Lemuel, Jr.: b 11-1-1762 d 12-8-1843 m Mary Wells Pvt CT
Lemuel: b 1751 d 2-11-1813 m Zelpha Bowdish Pvt VT
Lovell: b c. 1725 d 7-15-1801 m Sarah Thomas PS VA

Luke: b 12-8-1757 d 3-17-1837 m Eunice White Pvt MA
Luke: b c. 1750 d p. 1794 m Elizabeth Yokely Pvt PS NC
Luther: b 9-11-1749/50 d 7-4-1838 m (1)Sarah Bartlett (2)Mary
  Weldon Sgt MA
Major: b 10-4-1746 d p. 9-20-1811 m Zipporah Jarman Sol MD
Mark: b 4-12-1716 d 7-24-1798 m (1)Anna Chamberlain (2)Mary
  Reed MM MA
Matthew: b 6-30-1761 d 5-15-1823 m Esther Bailey Pvt CT W★
Media: b 1745-50 d c. 1804 m — Pvt NC
Micah: b 3-10-1758 d 11- -1841 m Sarah Mann Sgt MA ★
Moses: b 8-22-1727 d c. 1812 m Huldah Knowles Pvt CT
Moses: b 1757 d 11- -1783 m Melitta Porter Pvt CT
Moses: b 6-29-1756 d 5-28-1833 m Elizabeth Amelia Atlee Col MA
Moses: b 1750 d 2-10-1812 m Susannah Davis Sgt MA
Moses: b 6-22-1759 d p. 4-3-1833 m Dinah Stone Pvt MA ★
Moses: b 12-3-1759 d 10-10-1823 m Chloe Peck Pvt MA
Moses, Sr.: b c. 1715 d p. 6-4-1783 m Eleanor — PS NC
Moses, Jr.: b — d — m Mary Givens Sol NC
Moses: b 1749 d 8- -1794 m Sarah Poindexter Pvt VA
Nathan: b 2-10-1763 d p. 1793 m Elizabeth Sproat Cpl MA
Nathan: b 6-10-1755 d 1-27-1829 m (1)Eunice Chapin (2)Mrs
  Rebecca Baldwin Pvt MA
Nathan: b 1752 d 8-5-1834 m Elizabeth Fox Pvt VA★
Nathaniel: b 1725 d 3-21-1813 m Lydia Phelps Capt MA
Nathaniel: b 11-28-1749 d 10-15-1828 m Huldah Clark Sgt MA
Nathaniel, Sr.: b 10-4-1710 d 3-23-1787 m Martha Bascon PS MA
Nathaniel: b 4-10-1752 d 4-28-1809 m Rebeckah Ford Lt NH VT
Nathaniel: b 7-25-1759 d 1-24-1836 m (1)Hannah Finch (2)Priscilla
  Goldsberry Sgt NY ★
Nicholas: b 1753 d p. 1793 m Elinor Ryan Fennessy 2Lt FrA
Nicholas: b 5-9-1732 d 1802 m Mrs Sarah White Person Pvt PS VT
Nicholas: b 1759 d 1815 m Deborah Ford Pvt VT
Noah, Sr.: b 10-1-1724 d 3-3-1791 m Rebecca Trask Mus Pvt MA
Obadiah: b 1745/50 d p. 1790 m Rhoda Neville (Nevells) Pvt VA
Oliver: b 7-25-1764 d 3-16-1853 m — Pvt CT
Oliver: b 1724 d 6-28-1789 m (1)Elizabeth Carter (2)Abigail Selden
  Pvt MA
Patrick: b 1710 d 5-10-1792 m Jane (White) CS MA
Paul: b 12-1-1744 d 11- -1796 m (1)Mary Balkcom (2)Chloe
  Lesure Sol MA
Peter: b 12-6-1714 d 5-8-1782 m Jemima Taft Pvt MA
Peter: bpt 2-13-1729 d p. 1790 m Goodette Dekker Pvt NY
Peter: b c. 1758-60 d p. 1808 m Elizabeth Barheit Pvt NY
Philip: b 4-12-1760 d 10-17-1845 m Olive Rowley Pvt CT ★
Philip: b 7-28-1734 d 10-16-1822 m (1)Abigail Campbell (2)Mrs
  Sally Wood PS CT
Phillips: b 10-28-1729 d 8-11-1811 m (1)Ruth Brown (2)Sarah
  Dearborn PS NH
Phineas: b 6-26-1763 d 8-14-1841 m Jerusha Marsh Pvt VT
Potter: b 7-14-1769 d 9-9-1841 m Mary Jones Mrnr NGnr RI ★
Rand: b 10-5-1751 d 9-16-1809 m Mehitable Rice Pvt MA
Randolph: b c. 1755 d 9-7-1831 m Margaret Kincaid Pvt VA W★
Rawley: b 1746 d 9-15-1834 m (1)Maacah Spraggins (2)Ann
  Dunavant Dr VA
Richard: b 1760 d 5-24-1802 m Margaret Givens Pvt MD
Richard: b 4-27-1756 d 1849 m (1)Catey Oliver (2)Auney Wayt
  Lt VA ★
Richard: b 1762 d p. 1832 m Elizabeth Davis Smn VA ★
Richard P.: b 3-17-1758 d 1-17-1814 m Mary Meriwether Capt VA
Robert: b 1700 d a. 4- -1783 m Bethia Lovett Sol MA
Robert: b 8-25-1763 d — m Lydia Sibley Pvt MA
Robert: b 3-29-1759 d 11-2-1831 m Arabella Baker Capt VA
Royal: b 6-11-1754 d 5-1-1811 m Hannah Smith Pvt MA
Salmon: b 10-31-1731 d 6-21-1815 m Mary Wait Capt MA
Samuel: b 4-11-1714 d 6-4-1847 m Elizabeth Chandler Sol CT ★
Samuel: b — d 7-13-1839 m Susannah Hamilton Sgt MA
Samuel: b 4-12-1744 d 11-14-1818 m Priscilla Whitcomb Cpl MA
Samuel: b 1760 d 9-6-1830 m Eunice Eastman Pvt MA
Samuel: b 1730 d 4-26-1808 m Hannah Andrews Pvt MA
Samuel, Jr.: b 7-29-1750 d 1796 m Mary Williams Pvt MA
Samuel: b 9-15-1719 d 8-21-1801 m Sarah Brown PS VA
Samuel: b 1748 d 10- -1820 m Esther McKinley Pvt NC
Samuel: b 3-16-1759 d 11- -1841 m Jane Stuart Pvt VA
Seth, Jr.: b 4-18-1756 d 2-5-1837 m Jemima Keith Sol MA
Silas: b 5-18-1745 d 1802 m (1)Mary Birge (2)Hannah Scoville Cpl
  CT
Silas: b 10-16-1752 d 1-9-1835 m Bethiah Washburn Cpl MA
Silas: b c. 1737-40 d p. 1790 m Sarah Newsom Pvt NY
Simeon: b c. 1745 d 8-20-1820 m Hannah Hubbard Pvt MA
Sims: b 1738 d 8-12-1799 m Mary Wilkins Capt PS SC
Smith: b 10-9-1755 d 4-18-1823 m Eunice Albee Pvt MA
Solomon: b 4-28-1754 d 7-2-1838 m Esther Preble Pvt NH
Solomon: b 3-20-1739 d 10-8-1809 m Hannah Abbott Pvt PA
Stephen: b 5-12-1763 d 10-20-1860 m Abigail Kingsbury Matr MA
Stephen: b 11-25-1742 d 3-8-1846 m Miss Searcy Pvt NC ★
Stephen: b 7-19-1725 d p. 1-6-1812 m Ann Ross PS NC
Tarpley: b 1741/2 d 1811 m Elizabeth Divers Capt VA
Thaddeus: b 7-16-1759 d 9-25-1851 m Rebecca Gleason Pvt MA
Theophilus: b 4-10-1755 d 8-18-1842 m Mary Wilcox Pvt MA ★
Thomas: b 4- -1753 d 4- -1844 m Mary Ann Hunt Capt GA
Thomas: b 1758 d p. 1844 m Margarett Sympson Pvt MD ★
Thomas: b 12-26-1763 d 12-17-1843 m Sarah Small Pvt MD
Thomas: b c. 1750 d 8-6-1799 m Mary Wright Pvt MD

Thomas: b 9-15-1731 d p. 1778 m Deborah Nash Capt MA
Thomas, Jr.: b 9-4-1740 d 2-20-1814 m (1)Mindwell (White) Loomis
  (2)Elizabeth Morgan Lt MA
Thomas: b 7-20-1715 d 7-18-1795 m Mindwell Alvord Ens MA
Thomas, Sr.: b 4-21-1722 d p. 5- -1780 m Hannah Faulkner
  Pvt MA
Thomas: b 10-16-1735 d 10-2-1791 m Sarah Blair Pvt CS MA
Thomas: b 5-28-1748 d 3-28-1816 m Patience Leeds Sol Artl MA
Thomas, Sr.: b 7-27-1731 d 2-25-1822 m Abigail Muzzy Pvt MA
Thomas, Jr.: b 5-19-1746 d 8-20-1831 m (1)Mary French (2)Lucy
  Porter Pvt NH
Thomas: b 10-22-1740 d 1-3-1813 m Sarah — Capt NC
Thomas: b c. 1750 d p. 1790 m Elizabeth — Pvt NC
Thomas: b 9-11-1759 d 11-30-1834 m Cassandra Higgs Cpl NC ★
Thomas: b c. 1751 d 10-5-1832 m Elizabeth Lamb PS NC
Thomas: b a. 1750 d 1809-20 m Mary McCurdy Capt PA
Thomas: b 10-25-1751 d 1827 m (1)Mary VanDyke (2)Amy McGee
  Capt PA
Thomas: b 5-21-1755 d 5-27-1847 m Anna Bigger Capt PA
Thomas: b 1747 d 3-17-1838 m — Cpl PS PA ★
Thomas: b c. 1750-5 d 1816 m Jane Martin Pvt PA
Thomas: b 3-19-1739 d 9-13-1820 m Elizabeth Jones PS PA
Thomas: b 3-17-1754 d 9-10-1839 m Sarah Keys Capt VA
Thomas: b 5-15-1747 d p. 1779 m Betty Gilson Lt VA
Thomas: b 1755 d 1835 m Elizabeth Blackwell Lt VA
Thomas: b — d 9-4-1827 m Margaret — 1Lt VA
Thomas: b 1730 d 1795 m — Sykes Artl VA
Thomas: b c. 1745 d 1795-97 m Sarah Shelton Pvt VA
Thomas: b 3-15-1763 d p. 1804 m Jane Lusk Pvt VA ★
Thomas: b c. 1730 d p. 1797 m Anne — PS VA
Thomas Wells: b 8-12-1739 d 9-3-1815 m Naomi Wright Pvt CS MA
  VT
Tilley: b 9-3-1736 d 2-14-1810 m (1)Keturah Somes (2)Tamson
  Willey Pvt MA
Timothy: b 1761 d 2-24-1842 m Sarah Smith Cpl MA
Timothy, Jr.: b 10-29-1733 d 1803 m Lydia Main QM NH
Tobias: b 5-3-1753 d 6-14-1819 m Hannah Damon Pvt MA
Turner: b 12-4-1750 d p. 1790 m (1)Hannah Holbrook (2)Mrs Betsy
  Miles Pvt MA
Uriah: b 2- -1760 d 3-15-1846 m Orpha W — Pvt NY
Vassel: b 6-7-1761 d 12-1-1830 m Mary Kingsley Pvt MA ★
Walter: b 1748 d 1832 m (1)Sophia Brown (2)Esther Saunders Capt
  RI
Wm.: b 9-15-1758 d 7-19-1831 m Susanna Smith Pvt CT
Wm.: b 5-28-1759 d 4-28-1811 m (1)Elizabeth Crapper (2)Charlotte
  Cannon Sgt DE
Wm.: b c. 1760 d 1829 m Mary Early Sol GA
Wm.: b 1736 d 1780 m Elizabeth Smith 1Lt MD
Wm.: b c. 1743 d p. 1800 m Susanna Robinson Pvt MA
Wm.: b c. 1750 d 10-13-1781 m Lydia Bartlett Capt MA
Wm.: b 3-26-1737 d 11-7-1821 m Marcy Dresser Capt MA
Wm.: b 5-20-1744 d 2-16-1826 m (1)Esther Lynde (2)Mrs Elizabeth
  Browning Capt MA
Wm.: b 10-20-1763 d 9-22-1850 m Phoebe Edwards Pvt MA
Wm.: b 4-16-1721 d 5-30-1817 m Mercy Sears Matr MA
Wm.: b 2-22-1762 d 2- -1853 m Lydia — Pvt MA
Wm.: b 5- -1755 d 8-24-1838 m Jane Steele Pvt MA NH ★
Wm.: b 3-4-1740 d 11-9-1829 m (1)Mary Mills (2)Elizabeth Mitchell
  Maj NH
Wm.: b 1-7-1750 d 3-10-1837 m Betsey Shearer MM MA
Wm.: b 10-19-1728 d p. 1790 m Sarah Harris Pvt NY
Wm.: b 1756 d 8-24-1802 m Eunice (White) Pvt NY
Wm.: b 1754 d 1817 m Mary Ann Rogers Capt NC
Wm.: b 1715 d 1790 m Sarah Lucas Pvt PA
Wm.: b 2-4-1743 d 12-20-1813 m Ann Lowrey Sol PA
Wm.: b 3-24-1747 d 7-17-1836 m Mary Harrison Chp PA
Wm.: b 1753 d 11-18-1833 m Jane Brown Pvt SC
Wm.: b 1742 d 5-12-1827 m Eunice Rogers Lt VT
Wm.: b 3-11-1762 d 1-2-1850 m Jane Clemens 1Lt VT
Wm.: b 1743 d 1814 m Catherine (Chapman) Pendleton Capt VA
Wm.: b 12-22-1750 d 1806/7 m Dorothy Davis Pvt VA
Wm.: b c. 1755 d 7-6-1828 m Martha Watts Capt VA
Wm.: b 5-10-1756 d 2-20-1821 m Betsy Scott Wagerman Capt VA
Wm.: b 1745-50 d 1786 m Rachel Jacob Lt CS VA
Wm.: b 3-15-1751 d 12-2-1812 m Catherine Thomas 2Lt VA W★
Wm.: b c. 1762 d p. 1798 m Mary Johnson Pvt VA
Wm., Sr.: b c. 1720 d 1787 m (1)Ann — (2)Susannah Davis PS VA
Wm., Jr.: b 3-12-1751 d 7-10-1794 m Jane (White) PS NC
Wm. S: b 4- -1762 d 8- -1822 m Elizabeth Cowan Elliott Srgn Mte
  VA
Zebulon: b 7-20-1751 d 8-27-1835 m (1)Prudence Pitts (2)Mrs
  Sarah Everett 2Lt MA

WHITECOTTON,
James: b 1751 d p. 1840 m Ruth — Pvt VA ★

WHITEHALL,
Alexander: b 1750 d 1805 m Nancy — Capt NC

WHITEHEAD,
Aaron: b c. 1754 d 1809 m Achsah Halsey Pvt NJ
Benjamin: b 1760 d 7-25-1838 m Sarah Walker Sol VA
Benjamin: b 1740-50 d 1837 m Sarah — PS VA

WHITEHEAD, contd.
Daniel: b 6-1-1751 d 1-3-1824 m Sophia Mundy Matr NJ
David: b 2-27-1763 d 5-18-1845 m Judith Blackman Pvt CT
David: b 1726 d 4-22-1810 m Margaret Jewel Pvt NJ
Jehiel: b 7-28-1742 d 10-27-1794 m Elizabeth — Pvt CT
John: b — d 7-3-1783 m (1)Abigail Harrington (2)Mrs Anna Bond Lt MA
John: b 1760 d 1830 m Phoebe Turner Pvt NJ
John: b 10-13-1759 d 5-25-1847 m Margaret Cosman Pvt NY ★
John: b 1735 d 4- -1787 m Sarah Burch Sol VA
Nathaniel: b c. 1715 d p. 11-11-1776 m (1)Abigail Turney (2)Jemima Blackman Pvt CT
Onis: b 8-1-1741 d 7-4-1814 m Rebecca Condit Pvt NJ
Rahab Culpeper: b 1724 d 1815 m Nathan Whitehead PS NC
Robert: b 1755 d 1839 m Nancy McMullin Pvt VA
Timothy: b 1735 d 4- -1805 m — Pvt NJ
Wm.: b c. 1753 d 1837 m Sarah — Pvt GA
Wm.: b c. 1724 d 1816 m Sarah — Pvt NC
Wm.: b 1740 d 4- -1792 m Isable Dudly Cpl VA
Wm.: b 1740 d 1796 m (1)Patience Boykin (2)Mrs Clarissa (Boswell) Lamb PS VA

WHITEHILL,
David: b 5-24-1743 d 11-12-1809 m Rachael Clemson 2Capt PA
John: b 12-11-1729 d 9-16-1815 m Nancy Sanderson CS PS PA
Robert: b 7-24-1738 d 4-8-1813 m Eleanor Reed PS PA

WHITEHOUSE,
Daniel: b 1755 d 3-28-1835 m Martha Woodsum Pvt NH ★
Jonathan, Sr.: b 1720 d a. 2- -1791 m Elizabeth — PS VA

WHITELEY, see WHITLEY

WHITENAUGHT, (includes WHITENACK)
Andries: b c. 1744 d 1816 m (1)Catryna — (2)Mary Hageman Pvt NJ
John: b 8-23-1761 d 8-20-1828 m Gitty Stryker Pvt NJ

WHITESIDE, (includes WHITSETT & WHITESIDES)
Davis: b c. 1738 d 1780 m Eliza Johnson PS NC
John: b 12-8-1752 d 5-30-1841 m Margaret Robertson Capt NY ★
John: b 3-18-1748 d 3-18-1835 m (1)Eleanor Kelley (2)Sarah Cook Sol NC
John: b 1747 d 1815 m Judith Tolly Capt NC
John: b c. 1740 d p. 8-1-1804 m Catharine — Pvt VA
Phineas: b 6-31-1716 d 4-1-1793 m Ann Cooper PS NY
Robert: b 2-22-1743 d 1810 m Betsy Coffey Sol VA
Thomas: b 1758 d 4-17-1830 m Elizabeth Cramer Lt NY
Thomas: b c. 1736 d 1805 m Jean Porter Capt PS PA
Thomas: b — d c. 1821 m Mary Jenkins Sol PA
Wm., Sr.: b c. 1710 d p. 10-24-1777 m Elizabeth Stockton PS NC
Wm., Jr.: b 1747 d 1815 m Mary Booth Pvt NC
Wm.: b 1752 d 1840 m Hadessa Crawford Pvt PA
Wm.: b 8-20-1731 d 7-14-1811 m Ellen Menees Pvt VA

WHITFIELD,
Bryan: b 2-19-1754 d 6-23-1817 m (1)Nancy Bryan (2)Winifred Bryan Capt NC
Constantine: b 3-6-1728 d p. 10-28-1797 m Barbara Williams Sgt CS NC
John: b 1743 d 1-2-1832 m Milly Grimsley Sol NC
Joseph: b 1722 d c. 1790-1800 m Parnel Jenne Pvt MA
Luke: b 2-9-1719 d 12-2-1796 m Rachel Powell Capt SC
Matthew: b c. 1717 d p. 1785 m — Warren PS SC
Needham: b 2-20-1758 d 4-6-1812 m (1)Lucy Hatch (2)Betsey Hatch (3)Sallie Watkins (4)Mrs Penelope Burk PS NC
Thomas: b 1721 d 1781 m Mary — PS NC
Wm., Sr.: b 5-20-1715 d 3-31-1795 m Rachel Bryan PS NC
Wm., Jr.: b 6-1-1743 d 3- -1817 m (1)Hester Williams (2)Sallie (Oliver) Hurst (3)Hepsiba Hatch (4)Sarah Hatch Cmsry NC
Wm.: b 1759 d 1806 m Elizabeth — Sol NC
Wm.: b 1- -1751 d 1833 m Mary Towler Pvt VA ★

WHITFORD,
Christopher: b — d 10- -1811 m Sarah Howard Pvt RI W★
Constant: b 1760 d 9-15-1840 m (1)Martha Hunter (2)Rebecca — Pvt RI ★
David: b 10-31-1751 d a. 1790 m Lydia Sweet Pvt CT
George: b 1740 d p. 1786 m Hannah Wickes Pvt RI
Joshua: b 6-23-1731 d 9- -1813 m Prudence Burdick Ens CT
Peleg: b 3-11-1743 d 10-31-1831 m (1)Ruth Tibbits (2)Elizabeth Gardner Luther Pvt MA

WHITHAM,
Peregrine: b 1750 d 12-28-1799 m Elizabeth Rider PS MD
Wm.: b c. 1760 d 12- -1793 m (1)Augustine Haushing (2)Mary Chick Pvt MD

WHITING,
Aaron: b 2-2-1745 d 2-2-1837 m Mehetable Smith Ens MA
Abner: b 8-3-1760 d 5-30-1838 m Loacada Whiting Pvt MA
Allyn: b 6-23-1742 d 2-19-1818 m (1)Elizabeth Merry (2)Mrs Thankful (Sedgwick) Codwell Pvt CT

Amy Lathrop: b 9-8-1735 d 1-20-1815 m William Bradford Whiting PS CT
Asa: b 6-8-1731 d 12-22-1794 m Elizabeth Fisher Cpl MA
Benjamin: b 10-12-1731 d 4-9-1813 m Esther Merriman Ens CT
Caleb: bpt 8-19-1729 d 9-6-1819 m (1)Hannah Fairbanks (2)Hannah (Sibly) Southworth Maj MA
Caleb: b 3-9-1765 d 2-14-1825 m Elizabeth Walker Pvt MA
Comfort: b 9-15-1736 d 1-4-1830 m Mrs Grace (Liscom) McFadden Pvt MA
Cotton: b 10-27-1752 d 1815 m Susanna Holt Pvt MA
Daniel: b 2-5-1732/3 d 10-17-1806/7 m Mehitable Haven LCol MA
David: b 1752 d 4-5-1807 m Anna Bullard Sgt MA
Ebenezer: b 5- -1731 d 9-24-1817 m Eliza — Pvt MA
Elias: b 1-17-1753 d — m Polly Hall Pvt MA
Elijah: b 1759 d 5-22-1848 m Anna Faurote Sgt CT ★
Elizabeth Judson: b 1723 d 12-5-1793 m Samuel Whiting PS CT
Elkanah: b 7-4-1732 d 1-26-1802 m Margaret Gould Pvt MA
Enoch, Jr.: b 8-29-1733 d 6-21-1778 m Joanna Whiton Capt MA
Frederick Jones: b 7-5-1759 d 10-7-1804 m Rachel Starr Lt CT
Gamaliel: b 9-17-1727 d 11-27-1790 m Ann Gillett 2Lt MA
Henry: b 1730 d a. 5-2-1797 m Humphrey Ann Frances Toye Lt VA
Isaac: b 1766 d 1842 m Mary Cooley Pvt MA
Israel: b 9-20-1758 d 8-2-1840 m Hannah Stowell Pvt MA
Jacob: b 6-1-1762 d 1835 m (2)Dencea Sabin Pvt MA ★
John: b 11-6-1762 d 5-28-1835 m Nancy Welch Pvt CT ★
John, Sr.: b 11-23-1725/6 d 2-21-1820 m Sarah Foster PS CT
John, Jr.: b 7-24-1758 d 3-19-1830 m Sylvia Loomis Pvt CT
John: b 4-4-1761 d 2-29-1808 m Hannah Fairbanks Cpl MA
John: b 2-24-1760 d 9-3-1810 m Orpha Danforth Adj MA
John: b 1-25-1759 d 6-13-1846 m Margaret Fairbrother Pvt MA ★
John: b 1726 d — m Sarah Hunt Pvt NH
John: b 9- -1736 d 1810 m Mary Margaret — Pvt PA
John: b 1734 d p. 1791 m Mary Perrin Capt VA
John Lake: b 7-22-1755 d 1807 m Olive Wyman Pvt MA
Jonathan: b 5-1-1737 d 1-14-1797 m Rachel Smith Capt CT
Jonathan, Sr.: b 5-25-1726 d 10-11-1807 m (1)Elioenia Thurston (2)Mrs Hannah (Havens) Metcalf PS CS MA
Jonathan, Jr.: b 4-9-1757 d p. 1800 m (1)Sarah Whittier (2)Betsey Davis Pvt MA
Jonathan: b 8-1-1723 d 3-9-1804 m Rebecca Danforth Pvt MA
Joseph: b 1757 d 12-30-1820 m Nancy Buckingham Gunn Pvt CT
Joseph: b 4-19-1754 d p. 1791 m Abigail Alden Pvt MA
Joseph: b 6-16-1727 d 2- -1807 m Abigail Chamberlain PS NH
Lewis: b 8-18-1737 d 4-21-1827 m Betty Hancock Capt MA
Lydia Partridge: b 12-27-1728 d 10-4-1799 m Nathaniel Whiting PS MA
Matthew: b c. 1740-5 d c. 1800 m Elizabeth Robinson 2Lt VA
Nathan: b 12-22-1725 d 5-9-1790 m Mary Metcalf Lt MA
Nathaniel: b 2-2-1691 d 9-4-1779 m Margaret Mann PS MA
Oliver: b c. 4-17-1750 d 9-28-1829 m Martha Abbott Pvt NH
Samuel: b 8-15-1720 d 2-15-1803 m Elizabeth Judson Col CT
Samuel, Jr.: b 1744 d 1816 m Abigail Ferris SrgnMte CT
Samuel: b 12-10-1752 d 3-9-1835 m Mary Baker Sgt MA ★
Solomon: b 12-5-1724 d 10-15-1813 m Mary Campbell Pvt MA
Stephen: b 10-13-1722 d 1-14-1812 m (1)Mercy Campbell (2)Sarah Stodder Capt MA
Thomas: b 1712 d 1781 m (1)Elizabeth Beverly (2)Elizabeth Thurston (3)Elizabeth Sewall LCol PS VA
Timothy, Sr.: b 2-24-1732 d 7-12-1799 m Sarah Osgood SgtMaj MA
Timothy, Jr.: b 6-17-1758 d 1-12-1826 m (1)Abigail Kidder (2)Lydia Phelps Pvt MA ★
Wm.: b 12-16-1758 d 3-22-1849 m (1)Abigail Flower (2)Mrs Lucinda Whiting (3)Mrs Phebe Rich (4)Mrs Noble Pvt CT
Wm.: b 1-22-1704 d 1787 m Ann Raymond PS CS CT
Wm.: b 4-8-1730 d 12-8-1792 m Anna Mason PS Dr MA
Wm.: b 2-16-1757 d 3-11-1838 m Lois Andrews Pvt MA
Wm. Bradford: b 4-15-1731 d 10-13-1796 m (2)Amy Lathrop Col NY
Zachariah: b 12-19-1747 d 5-15-1814 m Kezia Wilder Lt MA
Zenas: b 10-1-1754 d p. 1790 m (1)Sarah Loring (2)Leah Loving (3)Mrs Phebe Raymond Pvt MA
Ziba: b 5-25-1764 d 1808 m Anna Bowers Pvt MA

WHITLATCH,
Wm.: b 4-20-1761 d 3-14-1846 m Nancy Veech Pvt PA MD ★

WHITLEDGE,
John: b c. 1734-8 d 10-11-1788 m (1)Alcey — (2)Francis Willis Capt VA
Wm., Jr.: b c. 1745 d p. 1810 m Sibby Whitledge PS VA

WHITLEY, (includes WHEATLEY, WHITELEY)
Alexander: b 12-23-1757 d 10-31-1834 m Peggy Stokes Sgt NC ★
Andrew: b 3-20-1750 d 7-7-1836 m Rubie Blodgett QM CT ★
George: b c. 1754 d 12-24-1828 m Mary Poor Pvt NC
John: b 1718 d 7-30-1786 m Submit Peck Cooke CS PS VT NH
John: b 1754 d 1-4-1832 m Betsy Cook Pvt VT ★
Joseph: b c. 1749 d 1818 m Sarah Stoppleton Pvt PS NC
Michael: b 1730 d 12- -1777 m Martha — Capt PA
Nathaniel: b 5-21-1752 d 7-26-1824 m (1)Vinal Bliss (2)Betsey Bailey Sgt NH
Samuel: b 3-2-1755 d 10- -1826 m Catherine Anglin Pvt GA W★
Solomon: b — d c. 1783 m Elizabeth Barnett PS VA

Wm.: b 1725 d 1780 m Mary Edwards Pvt GA
Wm.: b c. 1757 d a. 3-12-1816 m Sidney Glandon Lt MD
Wm.: b c. 1730 d 1791-1801 m Penelope Turner Sol VA
Wm.: b 8-14-1749 d 10-5-1813 m Esther Fuller Sol VA

WHITLOCK,
Daniel: b 1744 d p. 1796 m Ruth Scribner Pvt CT
Ephraim Lockhart: b 9-22-1755 d 9-22-1825 m Ann Tiebout Ens NJ
James: b 1737 d — m Hannah Herbert Maj NJ
James: b c. 1739 d p. 1788 m (1) — Messeroll (2)Jane Crusier Pvt NJ
James: b 1759 d 9-13-1823 m Phebe Green Pvt NJ ★
John: b 5-23-1733 d 2-13-1777 m Lydia Bowne Lt NJ
Nathan: b 5-24-1762 d 5-4-1853 m Mary Clinton Tms CT ★
Thaddeus: b 12-16-1757 d 11-30-1825 m Phebe Mead Pvt CT
Thaddeus: b 12-13-1749 d 2-12-1823 m Grace Burr Pvt NY

WHITMAN,
Abial: b 1758 d 8-8-1844 m Alice Dunham Pvt NH ★
Amos: b 2-17-1738 d 1791 m Anna Washburn Cpl MA
Benjamin: b 2-26-1758 d 8-21-1847 m Barbara Rounds Sgt RI VT ★
Charles: b 1731 d 12-10-1807 m (1)Anna Stevens (2)Catherine Davis (Swift) Pvt MA
Christian: b 1762 d 12-23-1827 m Hannah — Pvt PA
Daniel: b 7-16-1745 d 2-9-1829 m Martha Cole PS Pvt NH
Ebenezer: b 6-26-1713 d 8-20-1804 m Rebecca Paine Pvt MA
Ebenezer: b 12-6-1736 d 2-11-1786 m Abigail Freelove Pvt MA
Eleazer: b 9-5-1755 d 12-5-1846 m Mary Whitman Pvt MA
Ephraim: b 10- -1758 d 12-23-1838 m Mehitable Brown Pvt MA
Isaac: b 4-15-1751 d 11-17-1826 m Mary Nostrand Pvt NY
Isaac: b   -1750 d 3-20-1828 m Bathsheba Allen Pvt MA
Isaiah: b 6-5-1755 d 9-15-1843 m (2)Hannah Platt Brush Sol NY ★
Izra: b 1712 d 8-5-1797 m Betsy Haskell Pvt NY
Jacob: b 11-28-1753 d 12-29-1842 m Abigail Packard Pvt MA ★
Jacon: b 11-16-1716 d 5-10-1802 m Hannah Hartshorn PS RI
John: b c. 3-17-1735 d 7-26-1842 m Lydia Snow Lt MA
John: b 1734 d p. 1804 m Mary Kiblinger CS PS MA
Lemuel: b 4-24-1750 d c. 1821 m Mary Saxton Pvt MA
Matthew: b c. 1760 d 6-28-1836 m Katherine — Pvt VA ★
Nathaniel: b 1732 d 2- -1804 m Martha Smith 2Lt NY
Nicholas: b 1731 d 1803 m Mary House Pvt MA
Peter: b 5-4-1730 d 12-3-1801 m (1)Susannah Kieth (2)Sarah Wright Pvt MA
Samuel: b 7-26-1763 d 2-7-1810 m Abigail Abbott Ens CT
Samuel: b 10-7-1730 d 2-5-1824 m (1)Elizabeth Bonney (2)Mrs Sarah Waterman Pvt MA
Seth: b 1754 d 10-17-1783 m Eunice Bass Cpl MA
Simeon: b 1728 d 10-30-1811 m Martha Snow Sgt MA
Solomon, Sr.: b 4-20-1710 d 10-13-1803 m (1)Susanna Cole (2)Mrs Ruth (Hooker) Strong (3)Mrs Ruth (Hart) Wadsworth CS CT
Thomas: b 10-18-1751 d 6-27-1821 m Jemima Porter 2Lt MA
Thomas: b 1702 d 12-15-1788 m (1)Jemima Alden (2)Mrs Rebecca (Rickard) Allen Pvt MA
Zachariah: b 11-18-1722 d 1-14-1793 m Elizabeth Gates Pvt MA
Zachariah: b 1-25-1738 d 4-19-1819 m Abigail Kilborn Sgt MA
Valentine, Jr.: b 1745-7 d 7-12-1824 m Barbara Olin Pvt Smn RI

WHITMARSH,
Charles: b 6-12-1763 d 5-14-1821 m Anna Faxon Pvt MA
Ebenezer: b 1757 d 6-6-1827 m (1)Mary Humphrey (2)Mary Rich Pvt MA ★
Ezekiel: b 11-12-1747 d 2-19-1795 m Letitia Pratt Pvt MA
Jacob: b 1726 d 1-24-1803 m Hannah Shaw Pvt MA
Joseph: b 1749 d 5-29-1811 m Susannah Barton 1Lt RI
Micah: b 12-16-1749 d 12-29-1819 m Anna Arnold Capt RI W★
Thomas: b 1713 d p. 12-15-1779 m Elizabeth West Col NC

WHITMIRE,
Francis: b a. 1755 d 1832 m Catherine Rust Pvt PA
Frederick: b 1742 d c. 1832 m Phoebe Hagood Pvt SC

WHITMORE, (includes WHETMORE & WITMER)
Andrew: b 10-21-1760 d 3-31-1839 m Lucy Coulliard Pvt MA
Benjamin: b 10-22-1751 d 7-30-1848 m Sarah Thompson Pvt MA ★
Christopher, Sr.: b a. 1740 d p. 1789 m Eva Christina Fritzinger Pvt PA
Christopher, Jr.: b 12-13-1761 d 10-28-1825 m Hannah Reed Pvt PA
Daniel: b 12-25-1741 d 10-28-1824 m Robe Greene Pvt CT
Daniel: b 1741 d 5-7-1816 m (1)Sarah Hall (2)Rhoda Clapp LCol MA
David: b 10-18-1734 d 1-9-1828 m Lydia Giddings Pvt MA
David: b 12-15-1752 d 8-11-1835 m Esther Kendig Pvt PA
Edward: b 8-12-1763 d 11-15-1841 m Lydia Sampson Pvt MA
Francis: b 10-4-1714 d 4-27-1794 m Mary Hall PS ME
Francis: b c. 1720 d 5-31-1790 m Elizabeth — Capt PS CS VT
Herman: b 7-22-1753 d 1-5-1829 m Barbara Groff Pvt PA
Hezekiah: b 3-3-1756 d 2-27-1842 m Elizabeth Brainard Brooks Pvt CT ★
Isaac: b 3-3-1755 d 5-2-1847 m Rebecca Foster Pvt MA
Jabez: b 8-18-1766 d 12-5-1843 m Sally Roberts Drm CT
Jacob: b 9-6-1737 d 1798 m Hannah Brown Capt CT

John: b 1750 d 6-3-1817 m Elizabeth — Pvt PA
John: b a. 1749 d 5- -1793 m Mary Harmon PS PA
Joseph: b 7-19-1755 d 6-14-1841 m Abigail Babbidge Pvt MA ★
Joseph: b 9-9-1719 d 4-20-1805 m Mary Marion PS MA
Mathias: b 6-10-1757 d 5-5-1824 m Barbara — Pvt PA
Nathaniel: bpt 10-1-1738 d 8-24-1819 m Elizabeth Marsh Lt MA
Nathaniel: b 11-7-1753 d 11-17-1860 m Abigal Brooke Pvt MA
Oliver: b 2-4-1738 d 9-3-1819 m Abigail Hayden Sgt MA
Peter: b — d 4-19-1794 m Esther — Pvt PA
Peter, Jr.: b 2-16-1760 d 1-1-1828 m Anna Smith Pvt PA
Peter, Sr.: b 1737 d a. 8-3-1793 m Maria Solomana Matr PA
Peter, Jr.: b 1-11-1760 d 11-19-1835 m Mary Magdalene Overmyer Pvt PA
Samuel: b 1723 d 1804 m Hannah Hubbard Pvt CT
Samuel: b 7-4-1744 d 12-21-1808 m Mary Whitney Capt PS MA
Stephen: b 10-21-1739 d 10-15-1816 m Mary — (Whittemore) PS MA
Wm.: b 3-6-1752 d 1827 m Ruhamah Knight Pvt MA

WHITNER, (or WHITENER)
Benjamin: b 1749 d p. 2-18-1816 m (1)Magdalina Whistnant (2)Molley — PS Sol NC
Henry: b c. 1752 d 1811 m Catherine Shell Capt NC
Henry, Sr.: b 10-9-1717 d 7-31-1792 m Catherine Mull PS NC
Joseph: b 1757 d 4-12-1824 m Elizabeth Shackelford Pvt SC

WHITNEY,
Aaron: b 7-2-1740 d 4-13-1817 m (1)Anna Lawrence (2)Sarah Pollard Pvt MA
Aaron: b 7-31-1752 d 1791 m — Pvt MA
Abel: b 8-20-1734 d p. 1791 m Thankful Morton Cpl MA
Abijah: b 7-10-1754 d 5-24-1802 m Elizabeth Ellsworth Pvt NY
Abner: b 11-17-1744 d 1-6-1826 m Esther Jackson Ens MA
Abner, Sr.: b 1-21-1733/4 d 3-5-1802 m Sarah Hilton Pvt MA
Abraham: b 8-8-1716 d p. 1781 m Tabitha Allen Pvt MA
Abraham, Sr.: b 7-31-1724 d 4-3-1818 m Marcy Perry PS CS MA
Abraham, Jr.: b 1-7-1754 d 1814 m (1)Mehitable Ware (2)Sarah Whitman (3)Catherine Wood (4)Mrs Sarah (Conant) Jewell Pvt MA
Abraham: b 1752 d 1831 m Apphia Coombs Pvt MA ★
Abraham, Sr.: b 2-19-1710 d 5-19-1784 m Sarah Whitney PS MA
Abraham, Jr.: b 2-20-1748 d 1833 m Rebecca Dudley Pvt MA
Alexander: b 7-2-1751 d — m Lois Carroll Pvt PS NH
Amos: b 4-22-1752 d 1808 m (1)Anna Weston (2)Mary Smith Pvt MA
Andrew: b 3-29-1754 d 10-16-1818 m Lucy Miles Pvt MA
Asa: b 1743 d 8-10-1803 m (1)Sarah — (2)Hepsibath Watrous Armr CT
Benjamin: b 6-10-1753 d 1830 m — 2Lt MA
Benjamin: b 10-27-1741 d 9- -1821 m (1)Mary Turner (2)Rebecca Fitch (3)Ann Woods Sgt MA
Benjamin: b 5-22-1725 d 11-8-1797 m (1)Jane Brown (2)Mercy Hinkley Pvt MA
Benjamin: b 6-1-1750 d 1825 m Sarah Ketcham Pvt NY
Caleb: b 1750 d 10- -1822 m Sarah Trask Pvt MA ★
Caleb: b 4-2-1711 d 3-24-1777 m Hannah Cheney Pvt MA
Cornelius: b 7-5-1749 d 3-24-1833 m (1)Martha Graves (2)Elizabeth May Cpl CT
Cornelius: b 12-31-1753 d 11-6-1829 m Hetty Green Pvt CT W★
Daniel: b 5-10-1754 d 8-6-1826 m Hannah Selleck Pvt CT
Daniel: b 12-13-1733 d 4-6-1810 m Miriam Leland PS MA
Daniel, Sr.: b 2-26-1720 d 9-30-1782 m Dorothy Goss Pvt PS CS MA
Daniel, Jr.: b 12-11-1749 d 9-28-1805 m Sarah Durant Sgt MA
Daniel: b 9-15-1746 d 12-29-1809 m Catherine Stone Cpl MA
Daniel: b 9-26-1754 d 12-12-1834 m Abigail Stone Pvt MA
Daniel: b 11-18-1762 d 7-6-1838 m Louisa Stubbs Pvt MA
Daniel, Jr.: b 1-12-1745/6 d 6- -1784 m Martha Burt Pvt NY
Darling: b 9-25-1758 d 11-14-1834 m (1)Sarah Valentine (2)Catharine — Pvt CT
David: b 6-24-1721 d 4-16-1816 m Elizabeth Hyatt Mstr CT
David: b 10-4-1722 d 2-13-1802 m (1)Olive Sawyer (2)Mrs Sarah Wilder Rugg Hill Pvt MA
David: b 4-8-1732 d p. 1790 m (1)Hannah Brown (2)Abigail Knight (3)Rebecca Edgecomb Pvt MA ME
David: bpt 9-21-1746 d p. 1789 m Racheal Ransom Pvt MA
David Hyatt: b 8-25-1761 d 9-7-1834 m Nancy Raymond Pvt CT
Ebenezer: b 8-8-1742 d 4-2-1808 m Ruth Raymond Lt CT ★
Ebenezer: b 5-28-1762 d 3-31-1855 m (1)Rachel Penn Rawson (2)Lavina Burnham Potter Pvt MA
Elias, Sr.: b 11-14-1716 d 7-29-1810 m (1)Elizabeth Mellen (2)Elizabeth Boyden Pvt MA
Elias, Jr.: b 6-15-1750 d 5-22-1828 m Lucy Barnes Pvt MA
Elijah: b 7-8-1755 d 8-10-1842 m Lydia McElwaine Pvt VT MA ★
Elijah: b 1-15-1715 d a. 1790 m Hannah — PS MA
Elisha: b 2-27-1747 d 2-22-1807 m Eunice Farley Capt MA
Elisha: b 1747 d 7-4-1832 m Esther Clark Pvt MA ★
Elisha: b 10-6-1747 d 2-22-1807 m Abigail Dana 1Lt MA
Elnathan: b 3-28-1741 d 6-4-1820 m Mrs Lucy Allen Story Pvt MA
Enos: b 10-1-1761 d 10-8-1846 m (1)Eunice Avery (2)Mrs Mary Hiscox Pvt CT ★
Ephraim: b — d 9-16-1775 m Mary — Sol MA
Ephraim: b 5-13-1756 d 9-29-1827 m Jemima Whipple Pvt MA

WHITNEY, contd.

Ezekiel: b c. 1755 d c. 1853 m Patience Bailey Pvt CT ★
Ezekiel: b 4-12-1741 d 1801 m Catherine Draper Pvt MA
Ezra: b 2-22-1730 d 9-24-1804 m (1)Agnes Rossiter (2)Elizabeth —
    (3)Mercy Morse Lt MA
Henry: b 1735/6 d 2-19-1811 m Eunice Clark PS CT
Henry: b 12-31-1738 d c. 1788 m Hannah Tombs Pvt MA
Hezekiah: b c. 1742 d a. 4-7-1801 m Sarah Taylor Pvt CT
Hezekiah: b 12-26-1748 d 12-20-1827 m Olive Knight Pvt CT ★
Isaac: b 3-9-1720 d 1800 m (1)Sarah Crosby (2)Mrs Hannah Payne
    (3)Mrs Mary Walker Pvt MA
Isaiah: b 10-6-1751 d 3- -1835 m Mary Wheeler Cpl MA
Isaiah: b 11-28-1735 d 2-23-1817 m Persis Randall Pvt MA
Israel: b 6-22-1751 d 12-20-1826 m (1)Hannah Mead (2)Abigail
    Puffer Lt MA
Jabez: b 1-8-1750 d 1-30-1825 m (1)Experience Faribanks
    (2)Hannah Davis Pvt MA
Jacob: b 11-7-1756 d 10-12-1844 m Esther Wolcott QM Sgt MA
Jacob: b 3-25-1748 d 7-11-1825 m (1)Lois Hapgood (2)Mary Patch
    Pvt MA
James: b 8-10-1753 d 5-21-1841 m (1)Eunice Johnson (2)Mrs
    Rhoda Peet Pvt CT
James: b 10- -1755 d 6- -1800 m Susannah Hill Pvt MA
James: b c. 1740 d 1799 m Mary — Pvt PS NH
James: b 5-28-1751 d p. 1784 m Abigail — Pvt NY
James Rex: b 10-16-1760 d 2-4-1822 m Mary Allen Sgt NY
Jason: b 8-31-1729 d 6-23-1807 m (1)Elizabeth Beale (2)Mrs Lois
    (Fisher) Pratt Pvt MA
Jesse: b 11-24-1730 d 4-26-1815 m (1)Mary Cheney (2)Ruth Legg
    Wight (3)Abigail Rawson Lt MA
Jesse: b 3-18-1758 d 1-17-1832 m (1)Mary Sawyer (2)Mrs Charity
    Nowell Pvt MA ★
Joel: b 5-21-1743 d 1789 m Mary Weston Lt MA
Joel: b — d 1819 m Edia Holden Farwell Pvt NH
John: b 4-13-1754 d 9-8-1835 m (1)Amy Howd (2)Mrs Hannah
    (Lamphier) Chidsey Pvt CT ★
John: b 1754 d 1799 m Hannah Atherton Pvt MA
John: b 5-7-1749 d 1-21-1824 m Molly Corey Pvt MA ★
John: b 5-5-1751 d 9-19-1828 m Rachel Hiscock Pvt MA
John: b 10-3-1746 d 4-25-1802 m Sarah Atherton Pvt MA
John: b 4-15-1745 d 11-3-1829 m Mary Jones Pvt NH
John: b 4-21-1747 d 3- -1831 m (1)Rebecca Morehouse
    (2)Sarah (Osborn) Chapin Pvt NY
Jonas: b 7-2-1727 d 12-23-1791 m Zebudah Davis Pvt MA
Jonas: b 6-14-1751 d 4-28-1842 m Tamar Houghton PS VT NY
Jonathan: b 7-26-1737 d 8-22-1792 m Esther Parkhurst Capt MA
Jonathan: b 9-25-1734 d 1800 m Eunice Marshall Cpl MA
Jonathan: b 1736 d 11-20-1802 m (1)Mary Wyman (2)Lucy Smith
    Pvt MA
Jonathan: b 4-12-1743 d p. 5-11-1791 m Susanna Norcross Pvt MA
Jonathan: b 1745/6 d 1834 m Abigail Hennenway Pvt NH
Joseph: b 11-5-1743 d p. 1790 m Mary Lyon Sol CT
Joseph: b 2-28-1748 d 12-29-1813 m Abigail Barnard Pvt MA
Joseph: b 2-21-1716 d p. 1800 m (1)Mary Hastings (2)Mrs Anna
    (Palmer) Cpl PS NH
Joshua: b 11-27-1748 d 8-17-1793 m Hanna Green Pvt NY
Joshua: b 1-16-1745 d 8-8-1808 m Anna Ashley Lt CT
Joshua: b 3-25-1750 d 3-23-1821 m Sally Cochran Ens CT ★
Joshua: b 12-1-1724 d 1814 m — Pvt CT
Joshua: b 4-3-1737 d 5-7-1809 m (1)Mary Clarke (2)Abigail Wood
    Capt MA
Joshua: b 2-18-1754 d 7- -1812 m Vashti Knight Sgt MA
Joshua, Jr.: b 1758 d 12-8-1849 m (1)Esther Prouty (2)Electa
    Sawtell Pvt MA ★
Joshua: b 4-26-1754 d 2-2-1835 m Betty Wood Sgt NH W★
Josiah: b 8-8-1764 d 10-1-1850 m (1)Mary Smith (2)Sally Waterbury
    Pvt CT
Josiah, Sr.: b 9-11-1731 d 1-24-1806 m (1)Sarah Farr (2)Sarah
    Dwelly Col MA
Josiah, Jr.: b 2-25-1753 d 1-2-1827 m Anna Scollay 2Cpl MA
Josiah: b 11-22-1730 d 12-3-1800 m Sarah Lawrence Pvt MA
Josiah: b — d 12-10-1824 m Esther Weeks MM NY
Josiah Anson: b 1-18-1762 d 3-8-1813 m (1)Rebecca Olmstead
    (2)Sally Leet Pvt CT
Lemuel: b 1743 d 2-13-1813 m Thankful Griffith Pvt MA
Levi: b 12-5-1739 d 1-8-1809 m (1)Rebecca Clark (2)Mrs Lydia
    Randall Price Lt MA
Levi: b 6- 23-1751 d 1786 m (1)Sarah Lawrence (2)Hepsibeth Fay
    PS MA
Micah: b 6-4-1725 d 11-29-1791 m Lydia Mason Pvt MA
Micah: b 12-11-1752 d 6-19-1829 m Hannah Cobb Pvt MA
Moses: b 4-10-1755 d 4-10-1826 m (1)Hannah Palmer (2)Nancy
    Mann Tyler Sgt MA
Moses: b 10-17-1733 d 6-26-1810 m (1)Betty Hutchins (2)Martha
    Cunningham Pvt MA
Moses: b 3-17-1737 d 1820 m (1)Susanna Crockett (2)Molly Page
    (3)Mrs Abigail Kimball Pvt MA
Mose: b 1742 d 1824 m Sarah Gerry Pvt MA
Nathan: b 3-6-1723/4 d 10-28-1801 m Tabitha Bennett Pvt MA
Nathan: b 1-10-1706/7 d 1804 m (1)Lydia Young (2)Elizabeth
    Melcher PS MA ME
Nathaniel: b 12-12-1709 d p. 1790 m Hannah Day PS ME MA
Nathaniel: b 5-30-1749 d 6-4-1829 m Mary Houghton Lt VT

Nathaniel Ruggles: b 3-19-1759 d 12-17-1833 m Abigail Frothingham
    Pvt MA
Oliver: b 4-15-1744 d 1815 m Hannah Chase Pvt MA
Oliver: b 9-16-1764 d 1826 m Abigail Crampton Pvt VT
Peter: b 4-12-1738 d 6-19-1827 m Mercy Case Mid CT
Phineas: b 6-24-1740 d 1824 m Sarah Harrington Pvt MA
Phineas: b 7-3-1747 d 5-21-1830 m Keziah Fainsworth Cpl MA ★
Phinehas: b 1-16-1761 d p. 1795 m Elizabeth Rand Pvt MA
Reuben: b 2-21-1758 d 2-4-1823 m Lucy Fairbanks Pvt MA
Richard: b 7-31-1725 d 5-4-1798 m Mary Perry Sol MA
Richard: b 1743 d 1816 m (1)Sarah — (2)Hannah Holt Sgt NH
Salmon: b 2-16-1760 d 8-11-1844 m Hepsabeth Raymond Pvt MA
Samuel: b 12-13-1727 d c. 1775-8 m Hannah Judson Pvt CT
Samuel: b 2-17-1740/1 d 3-2-1820 m (1)Mariana Banks (2)Rebecca
    Banks Pvt CT
Samuel: b 10-12-1749 d 7-12-1832 m Mary St John Pvt MA
Samuel: b 5-23-1719 d 1-1-1782 m Abigail Fletcher Pvt MA
Samuel: b 8-5-1758 d 6-1-1831 m Mary Whitney Pvt MA
Samuel: b c. 1752 d c. 1837 m Hannah Thompson Pvt MA
Samuel: b 9-5-1734 d 5-29-1808 m Abigail Cutler PS MA
Samuel: b 9-23-1739 d 2-1-1811 m Phebe Harrington Pvt VT
Seth: b 1726 d 1807 m Sarah Mowor Moe PS NY
Silas: b 10-20-1752 d 11-14-1798 m Sarah Withington Pvt MA
Silas: b 2-26-1758 d 1838 m Patience Goodnow Pvt MA
Silas: b 1737 d 3-13-1813 m Jane Pearson Pvt VT
Stephen: b 4-23-1743 d 4-4-1833 m Relief Stearns Sgt MA
Stephen: b 5-1-1757 d 6-25-1806 mPersis Locke Pvt MA
Stephen: b 3-19-1755 d p. 6-8-1820 m Martha Irish Pvt RI ★
Thaddeus: b 7-10-1747 d 1832 m Temperance Hyde Pvt MA
Timothy: b 7-13-1744 d 6-15-1825 m (1)Anna Wood (2)Abigail
    Smith Mus CT
Uriah: b 11-12-1737 d 6- -1816 m (1)Sarah Platt (2)Martha (Hart)
    Owen Pvt CT
Urial: b 9-11-1757 d 11-10-1835 m Lydia Whitmore Pvt MA CL
Walter: b 2-3-1760 d 7-18-1846 m Anah Wells Cpl CT
Wm.: b 1753 d 6-24-1820 m Katherine Hall Ens CT
Wm.: b c. 1754 d 1-18-1810 m Ruth Rodman Pvt NY
Wm.: b 4-10-1736 d 7-10-1817 m Mary Mansfield Pvt PS MA
Wm. Clark: b 1762 d 10-26-1839 m Mary Thompson Pvt CT ★
Zachariah: b 8-7-1764 d 10-22-1849 m Elizabeth Seward Pvt MA

WHITON, (includes WHITIN)

Abijah: b 10-11-1756 d 12-1-1826 m Deborah Bates Sgt MA
Abraham: b 3-18-1729/30 d p. 1790 m Mary Ripley Pvt MA
Elias: b 6-10-1743 d 1778 m Sarah Blossom Capt MA
Elijah, Sr.: b 7-7-1714 d 8-20-1784 m (1)Priscilla Russ (2)Hannah
    Crocker PS CS CT
Elijah, Jr.: b 1747 d 5-5-1804 m Anna Brown Ens CT
Elijah, Jr.: b 2-5-1741/2 d 3-4-1814 m Lydia Lincoln Sgt MA
Elisha: b 11-3-1737 d 2-8-1819 m Jael Dunbar Pvt MA
Hezekiah: b 3-7-1757 d — m Mary Guild Pvt MA
Israel: b 9-3-1754 d 5-21-1819 m Dorothy Crosby Dr MA
James: b 12-18-1757 d 3-18-1823 m (1)Sarah Loomis (2)Abigail
    Seward Pvt CT
Joseph: b 11-9-1760 d 8-16-1828 m Amanda Garfield Pvt CT
Moses: b 3-3-1752 d 7-4-1823 m Martha Lincoln MM MA
Stephen: b 4-2-1752 d 7-3-1778 m Susanna Dana Pvt PA

WHITRIDGE,

Thomas, Jr.: b 9-30-1741 d 3-19-1813 m (1)Militiah Lawrence
    (2)Mrs Mercy Nye Cpl MA

WHITTEMORE,

Aaron: b 4-9-1746 d 5-1-1817 m Sarah Gilman Pvt NH
Abraham: bpt 3-7-1735/6 d p. 1800 m Hannah Floyd Pvt MA
Amos: b 2-9-1747 d 8-18-1827 m Molly Taylor Lt NH
Asa: b 11-10-1749 d 9-10-1821 m Lucy Muzzy MM MA
Edward Lloyd: b 11-13-1746 d p. 1790 m (1)Priscilla Bunker (2)Sarah
    Bassett (3)Mrs Hannah Bangs Pvt MA
James: b 12-16-1734 d 1811 m Dorothy Greene Lt MA
Jeremiah: b 8-16-1723 d 5-14-1803 m Mary Carter PS MA
Joel: b 1-23-1757 d p. 1810 m Catherine Green Pvt MA
Jonathan, Jr.: b 10-7-1737 d p. 1800 m Eunice Smith Pvt MA
Joseph: b 7-4-1736 d 5-4-1811 m Sarah Howe Lt CT
Joseph: b 2-27-1743 d 6-25-1821 m Rachel Waters 1Lt MA
Josiah: b 1749 d 4-11-1814 m (1)Lucy Snow (2)Martha (Parkhurst)
    Rider Pvt MA
Nathaniel: b 3-9-1756 d 6-9-1839 m (1)Lucy Harrington (2)Phoebe
    Waite (3)Joannah Hadley Pvt MA
Peter: b 4-2-1758 d 12-16-1836 m Elizabeth Baker Pvt NH
Reuben: b 4-29-1754 d 4-20-1832 m Abigail Watson Cpl MA
Samuel: b 7-27-1695 d 2-2-1793 m (1)Elizabeth Spring (2)Mrs Esther
    Prentice MM MA
Thomas: b 4-28-1755 d 8-28-1829 m (1)Lucy Snow (2)Hannah Sheldor
    Pvt MA

WHITTEN,

James: b 1-7-1759 d 3-15-1830 m Rebecca Cecil Sct VA
Joel: b 8-25-1764 d 7-31-1821 m Sarah Odle Sol PS SC
John: bpt c. 1712 d p. 4-16-1787 m Ruth Merrill PS MA
John: b 4-12-1760 d 2-8-1837 m Mary Reagan Matr VA
Phineas: b c. 1740 d — m Anna Joy PS MA ME
Richard: b 1763 d 4-11-1845 m Mercy Jose Pvt MA ★

Thomas: b 1749 d 1800 m Martha Paxon Pvt VA
Thomas, Sr.: b 1719 d 1785 m Elizabeth Cecil PS VA
Thomas, Jr.: b 1-23-1753 d 10-6-1841 m Elenor Cecil PS Ens VA ★

WHITTIER,
Benjamin: b 10-24-1736 d 11-11-1822 m Mary Joy Capt NH
Daniel: b 5-5-1753 d 12-3-1815 m (1)Polly Quimby (2)Sarah
　　(Severance) Whittier Pvt NH
Daniel Davies: b 4-21-1763 d 3-9-1831 m Hepzibah Black Pvt MA
David: b 9-17-1740 d 1815 m Abigail Morrel Capt MA
Francis: b 3-26-1737 d p. 1786 m Elizabeth — PS NH
Isaac: b 8-13-1754 d 2-9-1808 m Rhoda Sargent Pvt MA
Isaac: b 1736 d 9-6-1807 m Mary Blaisdell Pvt PS NH
John, Jr.: b 10-15-1743 d 2-23-1823 m Mehitabel Barker Pvt MA
Joseph: b 10-31-1755 d p. 1780 m Lydia Chandler Pvt PS NH
Nathaniel: b 2-23-1743 d 4-7-1798 m Elizabeth Prescott CS ME MA
Nathaniel: b 11-30-1751 d 12-30-1810 m Sarah Harvey PS NH
Richard, Sr.: b — d p. 10-23-1779 m Elizabeth Bodwell PS MA
Richard, Jr.: b 3-4-1753 d 3-30-1813 m Betsey Chase Ens MA
Thomas: b 9-9-1714 d p. 1797 m Susanna Warner Pvt MA
Wm.: b 4-25-1752 d 4-9-1814 m Elizabeth Hankerson 1Lt CS MA
Wm.: b 9-26-1752 d 8-25-1812 m Hannah Poor Pvt MA

WHITTINGTON,
Burrell: b 2-15-1750 d 6-28-1790 m Martha Wise Pvt SC
Cornelius: b 4-24-1750 d c. 1835 m Rebecca Gilliam Pvt SC ★
Faddy: b 2-12-1752 d 10- -1855 m Rebecca Roper Pvt NC ★
Francis, Sr.: b c. 1730 d 1786-90 m Elizabeth — PS SC
Francis, Jr.: b c. 1755 d p. 7-13-1816 m Patience — Pvt SC
Southey: b c. 1732 d 1785/6 m Esther Nairne PS MD
Wm.: b c. 1740 d p. 12-29-1815 m Priscilla Polk Cpl MD

WHITTLE,
Wm.: b 7-22-1764 d 2-17-1830 m Rachel Parker Pvt NH

WHITTLESEY,
Asaph: b 5-12-1753 d 7-3-1778 m Abigail Skeels Capt CT
Azariah: b 2-2-1741 d 4-9-1806 m Elizabeth Williams Mstr CT
Chauncey, Sr.: b 10-8-1717 d 7-24-1787 m (1)Elizabeth Whiting
　　(2)Martha Newton PS CT
Chauncey, Jr.: b 10-27-1746 d 3-14-1812 m Lucy Wetmore QM Gen
　　PS CT
David: b 9-18-1750 d 1-31-1825 m Martha Pomeroy Ens CT
Duren: b — d 3-27-1776 m X Pvt CT
Eliphalet, Sr.: b 5-10-1714 d 7-12-1786 m (1)Dorothy Kellogg (2)Mrs
　　Hannah Mollory PS CT
Eliphalet, Jr.: b 7-2-1748 d 1-25-1823 m Comfort Waller Pvt MA
Ezra: b 2-11-1738 d p. 1794 m Anne Pixley Capt MA
John: b 12-23-1741 d 3-22-1812 m Mary Beale Ens CT
John: b 1759 d 9-6-1781 m Lucy — Pvt CT
Joseph: b 5-20-1722 d 9-2-1806 m (1)Sarah Whittlesey (2)Lydia
　　Jones QM CT
Josiah: b 2-17-1714 d p. 1778 m Elizabeth Jackson Pvt NH
Lemuel: b 5-16-1740 d 8-30-1823 m Hannah Wells Lt CT
Martin: b 10-3-1737 d 5-29-1808 m Sarah Deming Sgt CT
Roger Newton: b 2-24-1754 d 3-15-1835 m Ann Woodruff Pvt CT

WHITTRIDGE, (or WHITTREDGE)
Livermore: b 2-13-1739 d 11-22-1803 m Lydia Herrick PS MA
Wm.: b 10-17-1731 d 1808 m Mary Saville Pvt MA
Wm.: b 2-7-1737 d 3-16-1804 m Mary (Herrick) Ellinwood Pvt MA

WHITWELL,
Samuel, Sr.: b 12-17-1717 d 6-18-1801 m (1)Elizabeth Kelsey
　　(2)Sarah Wood (3)Margaret Smith Pvt CS MA
Samuel, Jr.: b 1-12-1754 d 11-21-1791 m Lucy Tyler Dr MA

WHITWORTH,
Isaac: b c. 1749 d 11-5-1807 m — PS NC
John: b 3-9-1760 d 9-20-1837 m Elizabeth (Jones) Forsythe Pvt
　　NC ★

WIANT,
Yost: b 9-24-1747 d 12-9-1815 m Anna Barbara Roder Pvt PA

WIARD,
Seth: b 9-24-1748/9 d 12-19-1831 m (1)Dorcas Hopkins (2)Anna
　　Kellogg QM CT

WIBERT,
John: b 6-7-1760 d 2-21-1849 m Elizabeth Swartwout Pvt NY

WIBLE,
Frederick: b — d p. 8-7-1790 m — Pvt PA

WICKER,
David: b 6- -1732 d 4- -1803 m Ann Davis Pvt MA
Jacob: b 1-5-1723 d 3-9-1789 m Abiah Washburn Pvt MA
Thomas, Sr.: b 8-11-1717 d 1-7-1784 m Mary Hester PS NC
Thomas, Jr.: b 1754 d a. 8- -1832 m (1)Sally Tally (2)Esther —Sol
　　NC

WICKERSHAM,
Amos: b 1747 d 6-27-1821 m Elizabeth Hayes Pvt PA
Peter: b 1756 d 9-4-1841 m Mary Platter Pvt PA
Sampson: b 2-20-1751 d 11-22-1819 m (1)Elizabeth Jackson
　　(2)Elizabeth Sessenger Pvt PA
Wm., Jr.: b 7-20-1740 d 2-8-1822 m Elizabeth Pusey Pvt PA

WICKERT,
Jacob: b 4-20-1750 d 8-20-1838 m (1)Susannah Schlosser
　　(2)Christiana Rice Pvt PA

WICKES,
Alexander: b 1754 d 9-28-1841 m (1)Amy Thorpe (2)Anna Risley
　　(3)Sarah Homan Hudson Pvt CT ★
Daniel: b 6-7-1724 d 7-20-1784 m Rebecca Wood Pvt NY
Issac: b c. 1753-8 d p. 1810 m Elizabeth Valentine Slr NY
Josiah: b c. 1705 d 1799 m Mary Conklin PS NY
Lemuel: b 4-16-1743 d 8-18-1809 m Deborah Lupton 2Lt NY
Moses: b 1-21-1741 d c. 1819 m Mrs Sarah Blatchley Smith PS NY
Oliver: b 9-29-1757 d 6-22-1855 m (1)Abigail Greene (2)Mrs
　　Marguerite Littlefield Ens RI ★
Silas: b 9-10-1758 d 6-21-1838 m Elizabeth Rusco Pvt NY
Simon: b 1745 d 1814 m Mary Freeman Capt MD
Thomas: b 8-10-1744 d 11-30-1819 m Abigail Van Wyck PS Capt
　　NY
Thomas: b 1-28-1710 d a. 1785 m (1)Thankful Barton (2)Mrs
　　Elizabeth Williams (3)Sarah — PS RI
Wm.: b 2-25-1759 d 6-22-1839 m (1)Phebe Wick (2)Mary Ann Agnes
　　Kirts Cpl NJ ★
Zophar: b 10-9-1755 d 3-20-1841 m Jane Carpenter Lt NY ★

WICKHAM,
Hezekiah, Jr.: b 1756 d 10-2-1800 m (1)Lucretia Miller (2)Elizabeth
　　(Perrin) Buel Pvt CT
Samuel: b c. 1719/20 d c. 1776-90 m Abigail Howell PS NY
Stephen: b 10-17-1752 d 7-31-1810 m Margaret Reynolds Pvt NY
Thomas: b 11-20-1730 d 8-14-1790 m Mercy Huntting Mstr PS NY
Wm.: b c. 1735 d c. 1839 m Catherine — Sol NY

WICKISER,
Conrad: b c. 1753 d 6-17-1802 m Rosanna — Sol PA

WICKLEIN,
Adam: b c. 1750 d p. 7-25-1830 m Catherine — Sol PA

WICKLIFFE,
Arrington: b 1750 d 4- -1820 m Catharine Davis Pvt VA
Charles: b 1740 d 1816 m Lydia Hardin Sol PA VA
David: b 3-5-1755 d 1836 m Margaret Seaton Pvt VA ★
David: b 1723-25 d 1813 m Jane — PS VA

WICKWARE,
Grant: b 1760 d 4-21-1848 m Sarah Throop Pvt CT ★

WICKWIRE,
James: b 9-28-1759 d 9-4-1822 m Sarah Barnes Pvt CT ★
Joseph: b 6-22-1734 d 8-1-1822 m Martha Story Lt VT
Samuel: b 1738 d 2-11-1791 m Jane Brown Pvt CT

WIDGER,
Eli: b 5-15-1756 d 4-24-1848 m Lucy Green Slr CT ★

WIDRIG, (or WIDRICK)
George: b 1-15-1740 d 7-17-1830 m Nancy Sanford Pvt NY
Jacob: b 1754 d 1844 m Elizabeth Wrankle Pvt NY ★
Michael: b a. 1760 d — m Elizabeth Lints Pvt NY

WIEDER,
Adam: b 10-31-1721 d 7-16-1798 m Anna Margaret — PS PA
Michael: b 4-7-1763 d 8- -1804 m Eve Dorney Pvt PA

WIELAND, (or WILAND)
John: b 1755 d 1834 m Christina Oberlin Pvt PA

WIERMAN,
Benjamin: b c. 1746-56 d 10- -1811 m (1)Elizabeth Wierman
　　(2)Sarah Michel Pvt PA

WIESSMER,
Peter: b 1735 d p. 1790 m (1)Maria Graet (2)Maria Scherp (3)Rosina
　　Mesick 1Lt PS NY

WIGAL,
Phillip: b c. 1754 d a. 4-12-1815 m Barbara — Pvt PA

WIGFIELD,
Matthew: b c. 1735 d a. 8-23-1803 m Elizabeth — PS MD

WIGG,
Wm., Hazzard: b 11-24-1746 d 4-20-1798 m (2)Esther Hutson Maj
　　SC

WIGGIN,
Andrew 3d: b 5-5-1737 d 9-16-1778 m Mary (Jewett) Weeks PS NH
Benjamin: b 1751 d 2-16-1828 m Dorothy — Pvt MA ★
Benjamin: b 9-6-1756 d 10-17-1840 m Hannah Parsons Cpl NH ★
Bradstreet: b 4-18-1745 d p. 1790 m Judith Hard Pvt NH
Chase: b 9-1-1751 d 10-3-1850 m Molly Perkins Cpl NH
Chase: b 7-12-1730 d 9-3-1810 m Mary Perkins PS NH
David: b 11-16-1756 d 6- -1824 m (1)Hannah Rollins (2)Elizabeth Huntress Pvt NH
Elijah: b 1753 d 1808 m Abigail — Pvt NH
James: b 9-3-1760 d 1845 m Ruth Varney Pvt NH
John: b c. 1747 d p. 1830 m Eliz Durgin Pvt PS NH
Mark: b 10-25-1746 d 2-23-1821 m Betsy Brackett LCol NH
Nathan: b 10-22-1760 d 10-14-1847 m (1)Olive Weymouth (2)Mrs Elizabeth Miles Pvt NH ★
Simon: b 9-11-1731 d 10-11-1823 m Hannah Marble PS NH

WIGGINS,
Anon: b 4-2-1767 d 8-9-1851 m Catherine — Pvt NY
Blake Baker: b 1746 d 12-18-1809 m Sallie Lee PS NC
Edward: b 1739 d 1799 m Charity Preble Pvt PA
John: b c. 1726 d c. 1-8-1785 m (1)Mary Corey (2)Mary King Brown PS NY
John: b 1714 d 6-12-1794 m Elizabeth — Pvt PA
John: b c. 1723 d a. 7-16-1785 m Elizabeth (Wickens) PS VA
Jonathan: b 8-29-1763 d 12-6-1815 m Phebe Fordham Wgm NJ
Josiah: b a. 1742 d p. 1802 m Dorothy Frost Sgt NH
Thomas: d 9-28-1782 m Frances Brown LCol PS CS NC
Thomas: b c. 1730 d a. 1799 m (1)Tabitha — (2)Fannie Gresham PS NC
Wm., Jr.: b c. 1754 d c. 1830 m Sarah Lawrence Sol GA
Wm.: b 1748 d 1840 m Sarah — Pvt PA ★
Wm.: b 1740 d 1824 m Sarah Lamson Pvt VT
Winnifred: b 1741 d 1795 m Richard Hoskins PS NC

WIGGINTON, (or WIGINTON)
John: b — d p. 1788 m — Sol SC
Henry: b 11-19-1755 d 9-4-1842 m Nancy Vallandingham Pvt VA ★

WIGGLESWORTH,
Edward: bpt 12-6-1741 d 12-8-1826 m (1)Bridget Cogswell (2)Mrs Rebecca (Sanders) Babson Col MA
James, Sr.: b 1730 d p. 5-21-1810 m Mary Durrett PS VA
James, Jr.: b c. 1752 d 3-19-1825 m (1Mary Thomson (2)Priscilla Moore 2Lt VA

WIGHT,
Aaron: b 2-14-1742 d 2-8-1813 m (1)Mary Kittredge (2)Mary Haven (3)Jemima Rutter Dr MA
Aaron: b 10-31-1758 d 3-27-1837 m Priscilla Dorr Pvt RI
Abner: b 8-26-1756 d 10- -1844 m (2)Hulda Perrin Pvt MA
Daniel: b 3-22-1756 d p. 1824 m (1)Mrs Hannah Lyon (2)Mrs Mary (Mower) Wight Pvt MA ★
David: b 8-16-1733 d 9-8-1822 m Catherine Morse Pvt MA
Eliab: b 6-29-1760 d 10-4-1855 m Mrs Jemima Hawes Pvt MA ★
Henry: b 5-26-1752 d 8-12-1837 m (1)Alice Burrington (2)Clarissa Leonard Pvt MA
Joel: b 12-27-1741 d 2-19-1824 m Elizabeth Twitchell Pvt MA
John: bpt 11-7-1756 d 5- -1837 m (1)Hannah Parker (2)Oliver Westcott SgtMaj MA ★
John: b 3-29-1736 d 5-14-1814 m Elizabeth Reed Pvt NH
Joseph: b 12-17-1740 d 9-13-1809 m Judith Everett Cpl MA
Joseph, Jr.: b 8-10-1758 d 11-27-1846 m Olive Mann Cpl MA W★
Lemuel: b 9-16-1746 d 6-21-1821 m Elizabeth Ware Pvt MA
Moses: b 10-30-1745 d 3-4-1829 m Sarah Tolman Sgt MA
Nahum: b 5-15-1745 d 9-18-1834 m (1)Hannah Hill (2)Abigail Bullard Lt MA
Peter: b 5-21-1722 d 3-16-1800 m Mary Barber Pvt MA
Samuel: b 11-3-1711 d p. 1779 m Margaret Little Pvt MA
Seth, Jr.: b 1-20-1753 d 7-14-1799 m Mary Wight Pvt MA
Seth: b 1-1-1755 d 1822 m Lydia — Pvt MA
Simeon: b 3-20-1750 d 3-4-1777 m Margaret Smith Dr MA
Timothy: b 11-10-1741 d 1824/5 m (1)Mary Boyden (2)Sarah Fisher Cpl MA

WIGHTMAN, (includes WHITEMAN & WHITMAN)
Abraham, Jr.: b 5-16-1761 d 1826 m Catherine Randall Pvt CT
Benjamin: b 8-31-1755 d 6- -1829 m Esther Randall Pvt NY
Elisha: b 12-13-1728 d 10-16-1817 m Sybil Salisbury Sol RI
Henry: b 1726 d 5-14-1805 m Maria Scheuning Pvt NY
Henry: b — d p. 5- -1804 m Susannah — Sol VA
John: b 1750 d p. 1785 m Susannah — Pvt CT
Timothy: b 11-20-1719 d 11-14-1796 m (1)Jane Fish (2)Mary Stoddard PS CT
Ulrick Aron: bpt 3-31-1756 d 9-16-1805 m Balita Emerick Becker Pvt NY
Valentine: b 1747 d 10-12-1820 m Barbara Olin Capt RI

WIGNER,
Daniel: b 7-31-1755 d 1840 m — Pvt PA ★

WIGTON,
James: b a. 1750 d 7-3-1778 m Isabella Shannon Capt PA

John: b 1742 d 9-13-1793 m Margaret Cochran 1Lt PA
Samuel: b 1737 d 10-11-1812 m Elizabeth Hughes Lt PA
Thomas: b 1740 d 1820 m Elizabeth Gaylord PS PA

WIKOFF, (includes WYCKOFF)
Auke: b 10-29-1748 d 4-16-1820 m Sarah Schenck Col NJ
Cornelius: b 7-2-1760 d 8-27-1834 m Alice Conover Pvt CL ★
Garrett: b 9-22-1762 d 1-12-1838 m Rachel Crochsen Pvt NJ
Garret W: bpt 10-31-1730 d 4-10-1777 m Patience Williamson Pvt NJ
Jacob: b 11-3-1764 d p. 1833 m Susannah Allen Pvt NJ ★
Joachim: b 11-18-1749 d 5-18-1841 m Hannah Yerkese Pvt NJ ★
John: b 7-19-1747 d 8-2-1806 m (1)Aaltje Lane (2)Annatje — Pvt NJ
John: b 6-19-1754 d 1818 m Ursula Herriott Pvt NJ
John: b 1750 d c. 1816 m Martha Hynds Pvt NY
Joseph: b 1-5-1760 d 7-25-1810 m Keziah Foree Sol PA
Martin: b 6-20-1718 d 1803 m (1)Elizabeth Hubbard (2)Sarah Newell Sol NJ
Peter: b 3-19-1724 d 1-7-1807 m (1)Maria Dildyn (2)Jane Cornell (3)Rebecca Emans CS PA
Peter: b 3-21-1741 d 4-13-1803 m (1)Elizabeth Hampton (2)Sarah Lott Pvt NJ
Peter: b 5-15-1742 d 6-4-1813 m (1)Scytie Cornell (2)Jemima Veshtie Capt NJ
Peter, Jr.: bpt 1-22-1754 d 4-1-1809 m (1) — Vandervoorst (2) — Hageman Pvt NJ
Peter: bpt 1-22-1758 d 1840 m Catherine Van Etten Pvt NJ ★
Peter: b 3-28-1704 d 11-14-1776 m Sarah Amerman PS NJ
Peter: b 12-19-1748 d 9- -1825 m Lemma Lott QM NY
Peter: b 2-25-1734 d 4-1-1821 m Alice Longstreet Capt NJ
Samuel: b 6-10-1760 d 3-4-1842 m Maria Berger Pvt MD ★
Samuel: bpt 10-19-1732 d 4-24-1826 m Gertrude Shipman Pvt NJ
Simon: b 1730 d 1802 m Alche Van Doren PS NJ
Wm.: b 12-27-1761 d 4-2-1847 m Isabel Crownover Pvt NJ

WILBRAHAM,
Thomas: b c. 1750 d 1797 m Margaret Dismant Pvt PA

WILBUR,
Aaron, Sr.: b 5-24-1724 d 10- -1802 m Mary Church Capt PS RI
Aaron, Jr.: b 6-22-1753 d 7-21-1831 m Elizabeth Manchester Pvt 2Lt RI W★
Abijah: b 7-11-1743 d p. 2-22-1787 m (1)Rachel Wittam (2)Zilpha Leonard Pvt MA
Benjamin: b 10-22-1750 d 8-4-1841 m Betsey Hammond Ens MM VT
Christopher: b 1-7-1759 d 5- -1810 m Rachel Sayles Pvt RI
Daniel: b 4-26-1749 d 3-2-1821 m Mary Barnaby Sol MA
Daniel: b 6-1-1729 d 1803 m Mary Southworth PS RI
David: b 7-31-1740 d 9-13-1793 m (1)Mary Kirby (2) — Humphrey Pvt NY
Ebenezer: b 8-24-1762 d 1844 m Lydia Hollis Pvt MA
Elijah: b 1734 d 2-21-1797 m Phoebe Witherell Lt MA
Ephraim: b c. 1745 d 3-1-1814 m Hannah Field Pvt MA
George: b 9-2-1739 d 8-4-1803 m Lydia Shelley Pvt MA
George: b 9-23-1718 d 10- -1777 m (1)Rachel Sherman (2)Deborah Rundall PS VT
Gideon: b 8-20-1763 d 12-14-1843 m Huldah Gardner Pvt MA
Gideon: b 1742 d 1808 m Ruth Bathrick Pvt NY
Gideon: b 4-9-1766 d 7-6-1862 m Amelia Ismond Pvt NY
Holden: b 2-22-1762 d 11-5-1836 m (1)Ruth Tisdale (2)Mrs Polly Leonard Pvt MA
Ichabod: b 1762 d p. 1802 m Susanna Cooly Cpl NY
Jesse: b 1-28-1759 d 3-14-1853 m Abigail Gardner Pvt RI
John: b 10-18-1760 d 11-9-1846 m (1)Abigail Johnson (2)Mary — (3)Elizabeth Hulslander Pvt CT ★
John, Sr.: b 1-31-1733 d 8-24-1811 m Elizabeth Larrabie Pvt MA
John, Jr.: b 1-25-1762 d p. 1808 m Mary Jones Mte MA
John: b 3-24-1746 d 4-18-1836 m (2)Sarah — Sgt RI
John: b 5-4-1762 d 1-19-1851 m Mercy Greenhill Pvt RI ★
Joseph: b 1-26-1756 d 2-21-1793-96 m Elizabeth Herrick Sgt CT
Joseph: b 1733 d 11-15-1803 m (1)Mary Stearns (2)Silence Phillips Lt MA
Joseph: b 1719/20 d 6-27-1809 m (1)Susannah Leonard (2)Sarah West PS CS NH
Joseph: b 12-23-1751 d 2-2-1842 m (2)Elizabeth Kittrick Sgt NY ★
Joseph: b 9-23-1736 d p. 1778 m Sarah Hall Pvt RI
Joseph: b 6-26-1758 d 1-9-1838 m Hannah Brown Pvt RI
Joseph: b 12-26-1759 d 9-26-1830 m (1)Hannah — (2)Sally Burnett Pvt MA
Josiah: b 1752 d 1826 m Esther Burnham Pvt CT ★
Josiah: b 1717 d — m Jemima Wheeler Pvt NY
Nathaniel: b 1748 d p. 1790 m Deborah Aldrich Pvt PS NH
Peter: b 5-16-1740 d p. 1810 m — Freeman Pvt RI
Samuel: b 11-2-1739 d 10-27-1835 m (1)Mary Knight (2Wait Arnold Capt RI ★
Seth: b 3-29-1764 d 11-11-1806 m Rachel Shelly Pvt MA
Simeon: b 1739 d 9-20-1811 m Elizabeth White Pvt MA
Solomon: b 11-18-1758 d 3-13-1825 m Martha Presbrey Pvt MA
Wm.: b 3-28-1742 d 1-24-1822 m Sarah Sawyer Mstr CT

WILCHER,
Jeremiah: b c. 1760 d 1829 m Jane — Sol GA

WILCOX, (includes WILLCOCKS & WILLCOX)
Abel: b 3-13-1732 d 1-3-1807 m Mary Hull Sol CT
Abel, Sr.: b 6-22-1740 d 6-20-1809 m Susannah Hall Pvt MA
Abner: b 7-10-1748 d 1- -1837 m Deborah — Sgt NY
Amos: b 1726 d 1785 m Hannah Hoskins PS LCol CT
Benjamin: b 10-3-1742 d 3-20-1807 m (1)Lois — (2)Philena Rowe
  Pvt CT
Benjamin: b 9-24-1747 d 3-1-1816 m Patience Tucker Capt MA
Borden: b 2-3-1761 d 4-22-1848/9 m (1)Eleanor — (2)Mrs
  Eunice McCrillis Pvt Mrnr RI CT ★
Cook: b 4-28-1752 d 8-19-1830 m (1)Sarah Eslick (2)Mary Perry Ens
  RI
Daniel: b 2-26-1751 d 2-9-1839 m Alice Marsh Pvt CT
Daniel: b 1744 d 2-9-1836 m (1)Marcy Phelps (2)Mehitable Webster
  Pvt CT
Daniel: b 12-31-1715 d 7-29-1789 m Sarah White PS CT
David, Jr.: b — d 1826 m Mary Buell Drm CT
David: b 1759 d 1812 m Sally — Pvt NY
Edward: b 1760 d 1815 m Mary — Pvt PA
Eleazur: b 4-6-1749 d 6-23-1830 m Mary Mack PS NH
Eliab: b 2-23-1731/2 d 1-28-1810 m Jerusha Spencer Pvt CS NY
Elijah: b 1-14-1721 d 4-23-1809 m (1)Abigail Churchill (2)Mary
  Bushnell Pvt CT
Elijah, Jr.: b 1758 d p. 1826 m Mary French Sol CT MA ★
Eliphalet: b 8-30-1761 d 5-24-1839 m Abigail Shepherd Pvt CT
Elisha: b 11-25-1728/9 d 10-8-1812 m (1)Abigail Cornish (3)Esther
  — Pvt CT
Ephraim: b 5-26-1738 d 6-23-1816 m Diadama French Pvt VT
Ezra: b 1723 d 1786 m (1)Mary Humphrey (2)Mrs Rhoda Harris
  Pvt CT
Ezra: b 6-16-1753 d 4-1-1823 m Phebe Woodruff Pvt CT
Ezra: b 10-28-1728 d 3-14-1805 m Esther Meigs Pvt CT
Francis: b 1757 d 1847 m (1)Patty Worden (2)Hannah Wicks
  Pvt CT
Giles: b 11-23-1727 d 12-27-1783 m Lydia Ward Pvt CT
Hezekiah: b 12-25-1731 d 10-17-1819 m Hannah Parker Sol RI
Hiel: b 5-3-1734 d 12-5-1822 m Deborah Gillett Pvt NY
Isaac, Sr.: b c. 1735 d 1-26-1813 m Desire Crandall Pvt NY
Isaac, Jr.: b 1760 d p. 1797 m Nancy Newcomb Pvt NY
Isaac: b 12-30-1761 d 9- -1796 m Mary Crandell Pvt RI W★
Isaiah, Sr.: b c. 1740/1 d 3-3-1795 m Sarah Lewis PS RI
Isaiah, Jr.: b 1-31-1762/3 d 7-13-1844 m Mary Pendleton Pvt RI
Jacob: b 6-21-1758 d 11-3-1841 m Rachel Porter Sol CT
James: b 2-18-1764 d 1-23-1838 m Elizabeth Bradley Augur Pvt
  CT ★
James: b 7-19-1755 d 2-11-1839 m Eunice Vickery Sct VT
Jared: b 1753 d 1839 m Lydia Shepard Pvt MA ★
Jarius: b 1732 d 1807 m Mary Abbey Capt CT
Jehiel: b 1761 d 9-17-1848 m Clarissa Wilcox Pvt CT
Jeremiah: b a. 1760 d p. 1834 m — Sgt NY
Jesse: b 12-29-1762 d 7-5-1828 m (1)Nancy Pendleton (2)Mehitable
  Wilcox Pvt CT
Jesse: b 10-5-1744 d 3-13-1823 m Thankful Stevens Lt PS NH
Job: b 2-4-1743 d 11-1-1808 m Mary Gates Cpl RI
Joel: b 1763 d 1820 m Elizabeth Cowen Pvt CT ★
Joel: b 10-19-1746 d 3-13-1830 m Lydia — Pvt MA
John, Sr.: b 4-4-1732 d 7-9-1808 m Anne Stephens Pvt CT
John, Jr.: b 1-12-1762 d 11-10-1848 m Lois Augur Pvt CT ★
John: b 7- -1760 d 7-8-1812 m Margaret Kelsey Pvt CT
John: b 9-14-1745 d 12-16-1824 m Mary Kelsey Pvt MA
John, Jr.: b 1752 d 10-2-1819 m Mrs Polly (Maxwell) Line Pvt NJ
John: b 10-4-1756 d 1860 m Deborah Day Pvt NY
John: b 6-21-1728 d 1793 m Rebecca Butler PS NC
John, Jr.: b 3-7-1746/7 d p. 1790 m Jane Sherman Lt PS RI
John: b 1755 d 8-31-1827 m Catherine Woodward Pvt VT
John: b 1759 d 1839 m Nabbie Wilcox Pvt VT
Jonathan: b 1723 d 6-24-1776 m Rachel Tryon Pvt CT
Jonathan: b 3-13-1752 d 10-19-1818 m Elizabeth Todd Pvt CT
Joseph: b 8-27-1730 d 5-8-1804 m (1)Mary Burdick (2)Sarah Lewis
  Capt RI
Joseph: b 7-18-1758 d 7-11-1835 m Nanny Place Pvt RI W★
Josiah: b 3-13-1750 d 9-3-1835 m (1)Elizabeth Treat (2)Huldah
  Savage (3)Naomi Kirby Fif CT
Josiah: b 9-15-1753 d 3-3-1844 m Mrs Jemima Kelsey Pvt MA
Josiah: b 1762 d 1834 m Annie Noyes Pvt RI ★
Matthew: b 1751 d 11-2-1833 m (2)Rachel Tillotson Pvt CT
Moses: b 6-13-1745 d 1835 m Lydia Lancey Sol CT
Nathan: b 4-4-1730 d — m Tabitha Prosser Pvt CT
Nathan: b 11-5-1758 d 3-23-1813 m Elizabeth Elliott Pvt CT
Nathaniel: b 1-16-1759 d 2-14-1837 m Anna McGonigle Pvt NY ★
Obadiah: b 4-15-1719 d 8-27-1780 m Lydia (Wilcox) Pvt NH
Obadiah: b 7-24-1724 d 2-20-1810 m Sarah Talcott PS NH
Ozias: b 9-16-1730 d — m Mabel Gould QM CT
Phineas: b 1-14-1746/7 d c. 1791 m Cloe Dudley Sgt PS NH
Reuben: b 11-1-1762 d 12-10-1853 m Hannah Johnson Pvt CT ★
Robert: b 1753 d 10-11-1808 m Sarah Wilbur Pvt RI W★
Rufus: b 1760 d 1813 m Sarah Adams Pvt MA
Samuel: b 3-9-1720 d 2- -1802 m Elizabeth Swan Pvt CT
Samuel: b 6-6-1753 d 5-7-1835 m Sarah Gildersleeve Pvt CT
Samuel: b 1-2-1744 d 6-28-1827 m Lois Cogswell Capt MA
Samuel: b 8-22-1737 d 1-25-1811 m Geraldine Earle Pvt CT
Stephen: b 8-8-1762 d 9-15-1846 m Sabra Palmer OrdlSgt RI CT ★
Stephen: b 10-29-1746 d 12-21-1843 m Mary Kelsey Pvt MA

Sylvanus, Sr.: b 11-14-1733 d 7-5-1821-5 m (1)Christine Curtis
  (2)Sophia — Capt MA
Sylvanus, Jr.: b 5-26-1762 d 7-10-1846 m (1)Sarah Johnson
  (2)Sally Hamilton Cpl MA NY ★
Thomas: b 10-5-1720 d 11-9-1778 m Freelove Bradley PS CT
Thomas: b 6- -1741 d 12-19-1783 m Mary — Pvt NJ
Thomas: b 1760-3 d 1826 m Abigail Shipman Capt NY
Thomas: b 8-28-1757 d 5-26-1843 m Keziah Bennett Pvt RI ★
Tyler: b 1740 d 3-17-1809 m Deborah Russell Pvt NY
Uriah: b 3-13-1749 d 3-18-1822 m (1)Hannah Wright (2)Hannah
  Bartlett PS Lt NH
Wm., Sr.: b 4-1-1727 d 11-21-1775 m Lucy Case Lt CT
Wm., Jr.: b 1758 d 1827 m (1)Mercy Case (2)Anna Edgerton Moses
  Pvt CT
Wm.: b 11-30-1730 d p. 1775 m Mary Graves Sol CT
Wm.: b 9-2-1753 d 6-30-1807 m Mary Stevens Sgt MA W★
Wm.: b 1759 d 1835 m Hannah — Pvt MA
Wm.: b 1750 d 12-20-1826 m Elizabeth Ashfield Maj NY ★
Wm.: b 1750 d 1803 m Phebe Ashcraft Pvt VA

WILCOXSON, (includes WILCOXEN)
Daniel: b 3-13-1755 d 6-16-1837 m Nancy Faulknery Lt NC ★
Elnathan: b 8-4-1740 d 11-26-1840 m Sarah Wells Pvt CT
Ephraim John: b 11-15-1761 d 1-16-1838 m Mary Wheeler Pvt
  CT ★
Jesse: b 1-30-1738 d 12-11-1811 m Elizabeth Clagett Capt MD
John: b 8-30-1732 d 1799 m — PS MD
John: b c. 1720 d 1782 m Sarah Boone Sol VA
John: b 1756 d p. 1800 m Ruth — Pvt MD

WILD, (includes WILDE)
Benjamin: b 8-25-1747 d p. 1791 m Sarah Babbitt Sgt MA
Ebenezer: b 6-14-1757 d 12-4-1794 m Abigail Hayward Lt MA
Griffin: b 1738 d 1817 m Anna Bishop Pvt NY
John: b 6-3-1751 d 8-31-1831 m Jemima Spear Pvt MA
Jonathan: b 12-4-1759 d 8-11-1840 m Deborah Wild Pvt MA
Joseph: b 2-8-1738 d 10-30-1829 m Mehitable Doubleday 1Lt CL
Micah: b 5-20-1734 d p. 1790 m Deborah Hollis PS MA
Randall: b 3-8-1732 d 1780 m Jerusha Thayer Pvt MA
Samuel: b 6-28-1732 d p. 1790 m (1)Lydia Witherell (2)Marcy
  Pratt Pvt MA
Silas: b 3-8-1736 d 9-30-1807 m (1)Ruth Thayer (2)Sarah Kingman
  Capt MA
Thomas: b 7-1-1762 d 8-3-1848 m Anne Williams Pvt NY ★
Wm.: b 2-6-1721 d 4-12-1807 m Deborah Allen Pvt MA

WILDER,
Aaron: b 11-5-1754 d 7-13-1844 m Abigail Younglove Pvt CT ★
Abel: b 9-7-1741 d 1792 m Anna Butler Capt MA
Abel: b 1-16-1760 d 6-6-1806 m Hannah Green Pvt MA
Abel: b 2-16-1758 d 1831 m Relief Whitney Pvt MA
Abijah: b 11-28-1750 d 1-9-1835 m Sarah Ellis PS NH
Asa: b 10-16-1730 d 1780 m Lydia Rugg Lt MA
Asaph: b 7-20-1749 d 5-10-1799 m Olive Wilkinson Lt CT
Charles: b 6-14-1757 d 3-17-1838 m Sarah Spaulding Pvt CT ★
Cornelius: b 5-30-1752 d 2-15-1826 m (1)Elizabeth Hastings
  (2)Abigail Wilder Pvt MM MA
Daniel: b 5-17-1754 d 10-30-1838 m Nancy Star Pvt MA
Daniel Witherbee: b 1746 d 1834 m (1)Elizabeth Catlin Barnard
  (2)Sally Buck Pvt MA
David: b 3-30-1740 d 12-6-1815 m Lucy Joslin 1Maj MA
David: b 1705 d 11-17-1776 m Mrs Eunice Jennison PS MA
Edward: b 11-15-1751 d 11-2-1817 m Mary Hersey Sgt MA
Elijah: b 3-22-1757 d 1825-32 m Azubah Wells Pvt MA RI
Ephraim: b 7-8-1733 d 1-29-1805 m Lucretia Locke PS CS MA
Gamaliel: b 8-2-1743 d 1-9-1823 m Molly Warner Pvt CT
Gardner, Sr.: b 1711 d 4-24-1787 m Mary Phelps PS MA
Gardner, Jr.: b 6-9-1748 d 1807 m (1)Thankful Carter (2)Mrs Molly White
  Stearns Pvt MA
Isaac: b 6-21-1737 d 10-20-1810 m Letitia Chubbuck Smn CS MA
Jabez: b 3-14-1735/6 d p. 1790 m (1)Sarah Crocker (2)Martha
  Collamore Capt MA
Jacob: b 5-25-1754 d 10-10-1828 m Lydia Sawyer Cpl MA
Jacob: b 7-2-1757 d 7-19-1848 m Mary Wakefield Pvt MA ★
John: b 4-13-1713 d 4-30-1793 m Prudence Wilder Sol MA
John: b 8-5-1750 d 9-8-1776 m Abigail Kendall Pvt MA
Jonas: b 5-9-1731 d 2-4-1810 m Elizabeth — CS PS NH
Jonathan, Jr.: b 2-17-1743 d 5- -1798 m (1)Deborah Sawyer
  (2)Asenath — Sgt MA
Jonathan, Sr.: b 10-5-1710 d 1- -1794 m Zerviah Houghton Of PS
  MA
Joseph: b 4-15-1734 d 11-13-1820 m Elizabeth Heywood Pvt MA
Joshua: b 5-4-1759 d 3-4-1849 m (1)Lois Hawes (2)Mrs Dolly
  Stone Pvt VT
Josiah: b 1-6-1701 d — m Prudence Keyes PS MA
Jotham, Sr.: b 1710 d 5-25-1801 m Phebe Wheeler Pvt MA
Jotham, Jr.: b 2-10-1758 d 1811 m Lucy — Sol MA
Levi: b 4-2-1750 d 1-5-1793 m Sarah Stoddard Pvt MA
Moses: b 5-4-1736 d 3-30-1814 m (1)Submit Frost (2)Emma Forbush
  Cpl MA
Moses. J: b 1762 d 1839 m Priscilla Crowman Pvt NC
Nathan: b 5-3-1760 d p. 1795 m Susanna Sawyer Pvt MA

WILDER, contd.
Nathaniel: b 1743/4 d 3-3-1825 m (1)Mrs Priscilla Pratt Samson (2)Mrs Sarah (Wood) Tinkham Sgt MA
Nathaniel: b 5-23-1730 d 9-30-1777 m (1)Lydia Kendall (2)Lucy Knight Pvt NH
Oliver: b 11-17-1743 d 7-30-1813 m Mary Marks Cpl VT
Peter: b 5-25-1763 d *c.* 6-8-1853 m Freelove Russell Pvt MA ★
Peter: b 4-10-1761 d 4-25-1841 m Tamar Rice Pvt NH ★
Phineas: b 4-14-1730 d 8-14-1803 m (1)Lois Brown (2)Bridget Bayley Pvt MA
Reuben: b 6-19-1757 d 11-11-1832 m (1)Mary Pierce (2)Thankful Whitcomb Pvt MA ★
Sampson: b *c.* 1760 d *p.* 1840 m Sarah Barfield Pvt GA
Samuel: b 6-13-1745 d 10-22-1824 m Sarah Ballard 2Lt MA
Samuel: b 5-7-1739 d 5-9-1798 m (1)Dorothy Carter (2)Abigail (Carter) Fairbanks CS MA
Seth: b 2-3-1738 d *c.* 1814 m Miriam Beale Pvt MA
Shubael: b 8-14-1758 d 4-10-1840 m Sarah Wright Drm Maj MA
Silas: b 2-27-1747 d 11-19-1833 m Elizabeth Sawyer Sgt MA
Stephen: b 2-26-1747 d 10-9-1820 m (1)Betsey Sawyer (2)Patience Sargent Cpl MA
Theophilus, Sr.: b 3-12-1709/10 d 6-30-1787 m Mary Hersey Pvt MA
Theophilus, Jr.: b 5-16-1740 d 10-28-1821 m Lydia Cushing Capt PS MA
Thomas: b 9-23-1756 d 3-17-1835 m Tryphena Austin Pvt CT ★
Thomas, Jr.: b 1737 d 1802 m Abigail Carter Capt MA
Thomas, Sr.: b 9-13-1726 d *p.* 1784 m (1)Sarah Gardner (2)Olive Gardner Pvt MA
Thomas, Jr.: b 6-25-1757 d 9-15-1821 m Bethiah Gardner Pvt MA
Titus: b 12-4-1749 d 4-10-1837 m Mary Allen Pvt MA
Wm.: b *c.* 1753 d *a.* 4-19-1784 m Elizabeth Culpeper Sol GA
Wm.: b 1749 d *p.* 1825 m (2)Mary Wittington (3)Fanny — Sol GA
Wm.: b 5-5-1755 d 3-20-1816 m Relief Carter Lt MA
Zachariah: b 7-5-1756 d 11-1-1807 m Temperance Strong Pvt MA
Zenas: b 8-20-1752 d 8-24-1833 m Bathsheba (Wilder) Pvt MA

WILDERMAN,
George: b *c.* 1750 d 1821 m Patience Dorsey PS MD
Jacob: b *c.* 1720 d *p.* 3- -1778 m Elizabeth — PS MD

WILDERMUTH,
Wilhelm: b 9-7-1747 d 1816 m Maria Barbara Ebeling Pvt PA

WILDES,
Ezra: b 2-24-1758 d 12-17-1824 m (1)Polly Wright (2)Sally Phillips Pvt MA
Jacob: b 6-20-1762 d 1-16-1842 m Lydia Smith Pvt MA

WILDEY, (includes WILDE & WYLEY)
Thomas: b 1718 d 10-28-1776 m (1)Sarah Griffin (2)Nancy Smith (3)Juda Griffin Pvt NY

WILDMAN,
Comfort: b 1740 d 4-2-1782 m Rachel Rockwell Pvt CT
Jacob: b *c.* 1720 d *p.* 4-11-1795 m Elizabeth — PS VA
Matthew: b — d *p.* 1790 m Polly Reed Pvt CT

WILDRICK,
Michael: b 6-4-1753 d 4-1-1840 m (1) — Hawk (2)Mary Vass Ulp Pvt NJ ★

WILES,
Charles: b 1760 d 2-18-1837 m Catherine Meroe Sgt PA
Joseph Henry: b 1751 d 11-29-1831 m Mary Elizabeth — Pvt NY

WILEY,
Alexander: b 3-10-1758 d 5-2-1800 m Margaret Callahand Ens VA
Alexander: b *c.* 1754 d 1833 m Martha Noel Pvt VA ★
Andrew: b 1756 d 1836/7 m — Pvt VA ★
David: b 1748 d 10-17-1817 m Anne Gemmill Maj PA
George: b *c.* 1756 d *p.* 11-10-1805 m Frances Stanfield PS SgtMaj VA
Hillery: b 1759 d *a.* 1838 m Mary Kittrell Pvt NC
James: bpt 10-29-1738 d *p.* 3-9-1808 m Bathia (Frye) Johnson Sgt MA
James: b 1-24-1755 d 11-24-1823 m Mary Bryant Brown Pvt MA
Jonohn: b 3-17-1754 d 2-13-1844 m Dorothy Schuyler Pvt NJ W★
John: b 1748 d 1-29-1829 m Phoebe Halsted Capt NY
John: b 1738 d 12-25-1815 m Margaret Young Lt PA
John: b 11-10-1760 d 3-4-1797 m Hester Porter Lt PA
Joseph: b 1751 d 1811 m Miriam Evans Pvt PA
Levi: b 1744 d *p.* 1820 m Huldah Harding Pvt MA
Matthew: b 1751 d 3-12-1840 m Rebekah Nelson 1Lt PA
Nathaniel: b 4-11-1729 d 1822 m Mary Eaton Pvt MA
Oliver: b *c.* 1741 d 12- -1802 m Mary Shelby Capt NC
Robert: b *c.* 1745 d 11-17-1789 m Elizabeth Doughtery Pvt DE
Robert, Jr.: b *c.* 1740 d 1812 m — Pvt VA
Samuel: b 1758 d 1840 m Elizabeth Hull Pvt MA ★
Samuel: b 3-16-1757 d *p.* 1833 m Margaret Henderson Pvt PA ★
Thomas: b 1755 d 1825 m Mary — Pvt NC
Thomas: b *c.* 1753/4 d *p.* 1-26-1819 m Rebecca Lytle Pvt PA
Wm.: b 2-4-1758 d 5-21-1827 m Hannah Smith Pvt MA
Wm.: b 1742 d 1-12-1827 m Martha Harris Sol NC

Wm.: b 1762 d 10-12-1842 m Annie Shannon Vol NC
Wm.: b *c.* 1734 d *p.* 5-5-1782 m Eleanor — PS VA

WILFONG,
George: b 5-18-1740 d 11-3-1818 m Mrs Mary Poffle Mull Maj NC
John: b 4-8-1762 d 6-18-1838 m Hannah Sigmon Pvt SC ★

WILFORD,
Joseph: b 5-26-1755 d 11-26-1832 m Mercy Barker Sgt CT

WILGUS,
Wm.: b 8-20-1755 d 4-13-1817 m (1)Hannah Foster (2)Rhoda Herring Pvt NJ

WILHELM,
Henry: b 1756 d 1815 m Elizabeth — Pvt PA
Jacob: b 1739 d 10-17-1795 m Mary Elizabeth Haberstick Capt PA
Jacob Michael: b 1759 d 7-8-1834 m (1)Margaret — (2)Elizabeth Detrich Pvt PA

WILHOIT,
John: b 1732 d 1815 m (1) — Smith (2)Elizabeth Blankenbacker Pvt VA
John: b 2- -1742 d 1-1-1837 m Lucy Hancock Pvt VA ★
John: b *c.* 1715 d *a.* 10-4-1797 m Margaret Weaver PS VA
Lewis: b 1755 d 1830 m Mary Colvard Sol GA
Solomon: b *c.* 1750 d 1824 m (2)Catrana Maghee PS NC
Tobias: b 10-15-1750 d 2-7-1839 m Mary Shirley Pvt VA

WILKELOW,
John: b 1743 d 9-7-1817 m Jemima Trowbridge Pvt NY

WILKERSON, (includes WILKESON & WILKISON)
David: b *c.* 1764 d 6-13-1832 m (1)Elizabeth — (2)Sarah — Pvt VA
Francis: b 1760 d *p.* 1830 m Ursula Satterwhite Pvt NC ★
James: b 11-29-1758 d 12-4-1834 m Sarah Moore Pvt VA ★
John: b *a.* 1740 d 1799 m Mary Robinson Lt PA
John: b *c.* 1755 d 1824/5 m Suzanna Johnson Capt VA
John: b *c.* 1749 d 5-7-1818 m (2)Lydia Perrine Blanks Sol VA
Joseph: b 1757 d 10-7-1841 m Elizabeth Fowler Pvt VA ★
Nathan: b 1736 d 12-17-1807 m Ann Goble Lt NJ
Wm.: b 6- -1766 d 3-11-1857 m Sarah Fox Pvt MD
Wm.: b *c.* 1750 d 1797 m Sara — Sol GA

WILKES, (or WILKS)
John: b 1735 d 5-24-1793 m Remember Gurney Cpl MA
Samuel: b 10-24-1764 d 7-1-1837 m (1)Elizabeth Newman (2)Margaret Witt Pvt VA ★
Thomas: b 1759 d 3-16-1846 m Mary Frances Lester Pvt VA ★
Thomas: b *c.* 1707 d 3-18-1787 m Elizabeth Lowe PS MA

WILKIE,
Wm.: b 1734 d *p.* 12-14-1802 m Elizabeth — PS NC
Wm.: b 11-27-1753 d 10-21-1798 m Eleanor Ball Lt SC

WILKINS, (or WILKIN)
Amy Draper: b 1752 d 1839 m Caleb Wilkins PS PA
Andrew: b 1745 d 1811 m (1)Elizabeth Prescott (2)Elizabeth Green Sgt NH
Andrew: b 1761 d 9-10-1819 m Lucy Blanchard Pvt NH
Archelus, Sr.: b 6-23-1721 d *p.* 1790 m Rachel Case PS NH
Archibald, Sr.: b *c.* 1737 d 1799 m Ann Duncan Pvt PA
Archibald, Jr.: b 1760 d 1850 m Mary McMichael Pvt PA
Benjamin: bpt 11-25-1759 d 9-12-1821 m Sarah Wilkins Pvt MA
Benjamin: b 1745 d 2-9-1779 m Polly Barnes Lt SC
Bray, Sr.: b 4-20-1729 d 1775/6 m Lucy Wilkins MM Sgt NH MA
Bray, Jr.: b 4-27-1755 d *p.* 1795 m Lucy (French) Blanchard Pvt NH
Daniel: b 1751 d 1802 m Lucy — Pvt MD
Daniel: b *c.* 1743 d 7- -1776 m Tabitha Weston Capt NH
Douglas: b *c.* 1750 d *p.* 1786 m Tabitha Wyche Col CS VA
Elijah: b 1-8-1746 d 6-16-1806 m Mary Wheeler 2Lt MA
Enos: b 4-1-1741 d 8-13-1828 m Jemima Smith Pvt MA
Henry: b *c.* 1755 d 1802 m Ann T Drummond Capt VA
James: b 1734 d 1809 m Jean Rankin Maj PA
James: b 1746 d 1821 m Margaret — Pvt PA ★
Jason: b 2-10-1733 d 10-3-1804 m Sarah Bull Booth Capt NY
John: b 1698 d 2-9-1783 m Elisabeth Crawford PS NY
John, Sr.: b 6-1-1733 d 12-11-1809 m (1)Mary — (2)Katharine Rowan PS Capt PA
John, Jr.: b 12-23-1761 d 4-30-1816 m Catherine Stevenson SrgnMte PA
John: b *c.* 1740 d *p.* 1778 m Amy Haines Pvt PA
John: b *c.* 1755 d 1-8-1818 m (1)Rebecca Armitage (2)Catherine Edgar Pvt PA
John: b 1720 d 1796 m Elizabeth Haynie Col PS VA
John: b *c.* 1755 d *a.* 12-5-1803 m (2)Nancy — Pvt VA
John: b *c.* 1715 d 1775 m Judith — PS PA
John: b *c.* 1735 d *p.* 7-10-1792 m (1)Agnes Johnson (2)Smart Stockley PS VA
Jonathan: b 9-16-1748 d 4-16-1824 (1) — Towne (2)Lucy Whiting Mrnr Pvt MA ★
Josiah: b 7-1-1717 d 8-21-1783 m Lois Bush MM MA

Mathias: b 6- -1738 d 1803 m (1)Margaret Keller (2)Margaret Wilson PS VA
Reuben: b 12-23-1758 d 3-23-1811 m Mary Gardner Pvt MA W★
Robert Bradford: b 9-20-1755 d 8-20-1832 m (1)Elizabeth Stewart (2)Matilda Abbot Lt NH
Samuel: b 1-8-1742 d 12-27-1832 m Abigail Farwell CS PS NH
Stephen, Jr.: b 12-17-1736 d 8-27-1832 m Anna Berry Capt MA
Timothy, Sr.: b 7-3-1709 d 1791 m Anna Smith PS MA
Timothy, Jr.: b 9-14-1733 d 2-5-1820 m Mary Chamberlain Cpl MA
Uriah: b 11-22-1747 d 9-15-1833 m Phebe Russell Cpl MA W★
Uriah: b 10-5-1750 d p. 1790 m Rebecca — Pvt NH
Wm.: b 6-19-1737 d 8-21-1823 m Sarah Contant CS MD
Wm.: b 1-20-1720 d — m Elizabeth Rogers Pvt NY
Wm., Jr.: b 3-28-1753 d 2-28-1823 m Susannah Cranntz Pvt NY
Wm.: b 5-14-1746 d 4-2-1807 m Elizabeth Terrell Pvt NC
Wm.: b 1-25-1764 d 1860 m (1) — Ellison (2)Nancy J Sutfin Pvt NC ★
Wm.: b 1752 d 1-29-1826 m Elizabeth Montgomery Lt PA
Wm.: b c. 1740 d 4-2-1808 m Bridget — Pvt PA
Willie: b 2-1-1757 d 4-4-1815 m (2)Susan — PS VA
Zadock: b 1760 d 3-22-1832 m Abigail Berry Pvt MA

WILKINSON,
Amos: b 4- -1749 d 10-11-1833 m Mercy Carpenter Capt PA ★
Benjamin: b 9-23-1748 d p. 1-19-1810 m Anne — Pvt GA
Benjamin: b 11-1-1745 d 3-25-1818 m Hannah Staples Lt RI
Benning: b 1- -1764 d 10-20-1851 m Deborah Langley Pvt NH ★
Daniel, Jr.: b 1740 d 1-1-1787 m Anna Whipple Pvt RI W★
David: b 8-20-1763 d 12-10-1842 m Ruth Allen Sol MA
David: b 11-16-1707 d 1-31-1796 m Mary Arnold CS RI
Edward Mott: b 11-6-1765 d 12-4-1856 m Phoebe Freeman Pvt CT ★
Elisha: b 1763 d 1833 m Lucy Abernathy Sgt VA ★
Ichabod: b 11-4-1753 d 3- -1825 m Anna Taylor Pvt CT ★
Isarel: b 3-21-1711 d 4-30-1784 m Mary Aldrich PS RI
James: b 1757/8 d 12-28-1825 m (1)Anne Biddie (2)Celestine Charles Laveau Trudeau BGen MD
James: b 1735 d 11-25-1800 m Sarah Burnet Pvt NJ
James: b 7- -1763 d 4-4-1846 m (1)Nancy Stiles Pvt VA ★
James: b 1755 d p. 10-25-1844 m — Pvt VA ★
John: b 1744 d 11-3-1787 m Ann Douglas CS PS GA
John: b 1760 d 1825 m Elizabeth Murray Sgt MD
John: b 5- -1761 d 2-14-1847 m Patience Hathaway Pvt MA ★
John: b 1711 d 5-31-1782 m (1)Mary Lacey (2)Hannah Hughs LCol PA
John: b 5-9-1742 d 6-14-1802 m Content Moore Pvt NY
John: b 2-16-1753 d 12-26-1836 m Mary Mowry Dr RI ★
John: b 11-13-1758 d 1801 m Elizabeth Tower Pvt RI
John: b 1726 d 1-5-1806 m Leah Nieswanger Pvt VA
John: b 1757 d 1-3-1823 m Martha Rives Pvt VA
John: b — d p. 12-6-1814 m Lucretia — PS VA
Jonathan: b 9-7-1758 d 1-10-1837 m Lucy Hosford Strong Arfr CT ★
Joseph: b 3-11-1750 d 7-5-1814 m Mrs Elizabeth (Brownell) Peckham Pvt RI W★
Joseph: b c. 1732 d 8- -1789 m Mary — Sol VA
Morton: b c. 1742 d 11-22-1799 m Susanna Smith Col SC
Reuben: b 5-4-1754 d 2-26-1831 m Cynthia Pinney Pvt CT ★
Thomas: b 5-12-1745 d p. 1780 m Alice Pyle Pvt PA
Wm.: b 1753 d 1851 m Rachel Everson Pvt NY
Wm.: b 1758 d p. 1790 m Elizabeth Jackson Sol NC
Wm.: b a. 1740 d p. 1782 m Susan Toney Pvt PA
Wm. M.: b 2-12-1752 d 3-12-1799 m Ann Herbert Dent Capt MD

WILLARD, (or WILLIARD)
Aaron: b 1- -1701 d 5-27-1784 m Mary Wright Capt PS MA
Aaron: b 12-28-1749 d 1786 m Hannah Hamilton Cpl MA
Aaron: b 10-13-1757 d 5-20-1844 m (1)Catherine Gates (2)Mary Partridge Pvt MA
Aaron: b 1743 d 1-1-1817 m Mary Smead Lt VT
Amos: b 3-27-1751 d a. 1826 m Sybil Scott PS NH
Benjamin: b 4-30-1721 d p. 1780 m Hannah Godfrey Cpl MA
Daniel: b 4-22-1760 d 2-20-1814 m Sarah Silliman Pvt CT
Daniel 5th: b 2-25-1748 d 1790 m Abigail Bailey Pvt MA
Daniel: b 10-16-1755 d 9-25-1803 m Relief Phelps Pvt MA
Daniel, Jr.: b 1-6-1760 d 10-1-1838 m Lucy Bachelor Pvt MA
David: b 7-17-1741 d 4-18-1818 m Martha Sherlock Pvt MA
DeWalt: b 1739 d 10-7-1808 m Elizabeth Brandenburg Ens MD
Eli: b 7-4-1761 d 11-12-1841 m (1)Polly Cady (2)Polly Bliss (3)Salome La Count Pvt VT
Elias: b 2- -1759 d 12-16-1823 m Lois Stevens Pvt CT ★
Elias: b 6-24-1734 d p. 10-9-1813 m Rosanna Gumber 2Lt MD
Elias: b 3-29-1727 d 12-4-1794 m Ann Stanley QM MA
Elias: b 1-17-1756 d 3-20-1827 m Catherine Livingston Dr MA
Elijah: b 3-12-1751 d 8-19-1839 m (1)Mary Atherton (2)Phebe Archer (3)Betsy Knight PS Sol MA
Ephraim, Sr.: b 10-13-1726 d 10-8-1803 m Azubah Atherton 3Sgt MA
Ephraim, Jr.: b 3-2-1748 d 7-22-1821 m Lois Gary Pvt MA
Ezra: b 3-5-1761 d 4-14-1851 m Mary Kendall Pvt MA ★
Henry: b 5-13-1766 d 8-16-1850 m Sarah Wilder Pvt NH
Hezekiah: b 11-30-1740 d 5-29-1797 m Mary Winchel Sgt MA
Humphrey: b 11-29-1757 d 1846 m Hannah Wetherel Pvt MA ★
Isarel: bpt 3-23-1754 d 5-14-1821 m Susanna Longley Pvt MA

James: b 2-12-1749 d 5-23-1795 m Abigail Hayward Pvt MA
James: b 11-9-1763 d p. 1797 m Anna Hutchins Pvt VT
Jeremiah: b 11-29-1753 d 9-15-1810 m Bethiah Prescott Pvt MA
John: b 7-26-1739 d 7-3-1793 m Sarah Willard CS PS MA
Jonathan: b 7-2-1738 d 6-23-1833 m Lois Hooker Lt MA ★
Jonathan: b 3-23-1760 d 1828 m (1)Anna Goodnow (2)Esther Richardson Pvt MA
Jonathan: b 9-21-1745 d 8-29-1832 m (1)Betty Caswell (2)Catherine (Stevens) Stone Lt NH
Joseph: b 12-11-1741 d 2-13-1832 m Sarah Bigelow Pvt CT
Joseph: b 6-26-1750 d 10-30-1832 m Rachel Reeves Pvt CT ★
Joseph: b 4-27-1720 d 3-30-1799 m Hannah Rice Cmsry MA
Joseph: b 12-27-1741 d 9-24-1828 m Hannah Parker PS MA
Josiah: b 11-9-1749 d p. 1779 m Eunice Farnsworth Pvt MA
Josiah: b 3-23-1732 d c. 1815 m Dinah How 2Lt MA
Josiah: b 7-17-1756 d 3-6-1836 m Lurana Loomis Pvt MA
Lemuel: b 7-28-1725 d 10-18-1775 m Hannah Haskell Pvt MA
Lemuel: b 10-19-1751 d 3-21-1821 m Nabby Atherton Drm MA
Longley: b 3-22-1764 d 10-10-1848 m Deliverance Seaver Pvt NH ★
Moses: b 8-15-1738 d 8-17-1822 m Lydia Farwell Pvt NH
Nathaniel: b 4-3-1742 d 1- -1813 m Eunice Farwell Sgt MA
Nathaniel: b 2-28-1731/2 d p. 1795 m Elizabeth Haskell Pvt MA
Oliver: b 6-30-1759 d 1-13-1815 m Asenath Newell Pvt MA
Oliver: b 10-13-1741 d 4-20-1813 m Lucy Haskell Pvt MA
Oliver: b 3-6-1729/30 d 9-15-1810 m Thankful Doolittle Pvt VT
Peleg: b 4-5-1743 d p. 10-3-1798 m Hannah — Pvt MA
Reuben: b 11-14-1755 d 7-12-1823 m Catherine Parkhurst Pvt Capt MA
Rufus: b 5-29-1751 d c. 1813 m Parmelia Belding Pvt MA
Samuel: b 10-4-1761 d p. 1786 m (1)Prudence Rawson (2)Polly Willis Pvt MA
Samuel: bpt 1-24-1703 d 12-12-1792 m (1)Mary Lord (2)Dorothy Rogers PS MA
Samuel: b 11-28-1763 d 1802 m (1)Abigail Bellows (2)Joanna Putnam Pvt NH
Samuel: b 1745 d 1788 m Sarah Stark Capt VT
Simon: b 1-25-1745 d 1829 m Sarah Robbins Pvt CT
Simon: b c. 1755 d 1-28-1789 m Abigal Belden Pvt MA
Solomon: b 10-1-1755 d 4-4-1808 m Lydia Johnson CS MA
Wm.: b 11-30-1737 d 1786 m Mary Whittemore Pvt MA
Wm.: b 1755 d 11-9-1846 m Jane Cook Pvt VA ★

WILLAUER,
Adam: b c. 1740 d c. 1788 m Mary — 1Lt PA
John: b 1737 d 1797 m Anne Maria Linn Pvt PA
Peter: b 1759 d 6-11-1827 m Rebecca Geri Pvt PA

WILLCUTT,
Jesse, Sr.: b 2-25-1729 d 8-8-1815 m Lois Studley Pvt MA
Jesse, Jr.: b 3-26-1752 d 9-11-1834 m Katherine Beal Sgt MA ★
John: b 9-15-1746 d 5-11-1828 m Chloe Beal Pvt MA
Joseph: b 2-25-1717/8 d 8-7-1782 m (1)Rachel Phillips (2)Hannah James PS MA
Thomas: b 4-30-1760 d 7-14-1814 m Susannah Stodder Pvt MA

WILLETT,
Amos: b 1725 d 8-24-1791 m Elizabeth — Pvt NJ
Andrew: b 9-6-1743 d p. 1795 m Sibbel Hartshorn Lt MA
Augustine: b 1-9-1751 d 8-17-1825 m Elizabeth Hicks LCol PA
Benjamin: b 1744 d p. 8-22-1834 m Mary — Sol PS MD
Cornelius: b 1-15-1756 d 4-9-1843 m Nancy Whalen Sgt NJ
Edward: b 1761 d 7-3-1837 m Eleanor Fisher Ens MD
Hartshorne: b 1-1-1760 d 1841 m (1)Betsy Perrine (2)Polly Voorhees (3)Mrs Norfy Pvt NJ ★
Humphrey: b 1750 d 6-24-1827 m Margaret Williams Pvt NJ
James: b 6-20-1716/7 d 5-1-1792 m Ann Ridgway PS NJ
John: b 5-1-1727 d 7-3-1819 m Elizabeth Leffingwell PS CT
Ninian: b c. 1748 d p. 1790 m Ann Fleming PS MD
Samuel: b 7-18-1751 d 8-30-1843 m Elizabeth Anderson Sgt NJ ★
Samuel: b 5-19-1763 d 3-17-1830 m (1)Elizabeth Sperling (2)Martha Hooper Pvt NJ
Thomas: b 4-12-1762 d p. 1815 m Mary Allison Pvt PA
Wm.: b 1743 d 4-5-1785 m Mary — PS MD

WILLEY,
Abel: b 1-26-1745 d p. 1778 m Mercy Fowler Pvt NH
Abraham: b 5-11-1750 d 5-12-1841 m Susannah Beckwith Ens CT ★
Ahimaaz: b 1759 d 4-25-1831 m Jerusha Russel Pvt CT
Allen, Sr.: b 2-11-1730 d 5-8-1811 m Mary Fuller Pvt NH
Allen, Jr.: b 7-28-1760 d 4-3-1835 m Clo Frink Pvt NH
Barzilla: b 6-10-1764 d 5-23-1851 m Elizabeth McCough Drm Pvt CT ★
Ephraim: b 1762 d 4-2-1836 m Bethia Ackley Pvt MM VT ★
Joel: b 1750 d 4-30-1815 m Abigail Arnold Pvt MA
John: b 10-11-1732 d 12-26-1805 m Esther Comstock Capt CT
John: b 1741 d 7-28-1818 m Elizabeth Marshall Pvt CT
John: b 7-3-1757 d 4-3-1814 m Mary Griffith Pvt DE
John: b 9-20-1734 d p. 1782 m (1)Rachel Curtis (2)Mary — Capt RI
John, Jr.: b 1759-61 d 4-1-1833 m Elizabeth Bickford Pvt NH
Josiah: b 6-10-1762 d 1-19-1839 m Sally Drew Pvt NH ★
Nathan: b 1-1-1756 d 4-28-1807 m Priscilla Hadley Pvt MA
Robert: b 1760 d 6-21-1818 m Molly Denbow (Dinsmore) Pvt NH
Samuel, Jr.: b 1753 d 6-14-1844 m Elizabeth Glazier Pvt NH

WILLIAMS,

Aaron: b 2-5-1759 d 2-3-1830 m Mary Dodge Pvt NJ
Aaron: b 10-31-1757 d 1806 m Mary Newton Pvt NJ
Aaron: b 8-25-1735 d 6-11-1808 m Mary Lampman Pvt NY
Aaron: b 5-2-1753 d 3-10-1829 m Elizabeth Coe Pvt PA
Abel: b 12-8-1758 d 3-2-1842 m Sarah James Pvt PA
Abiel: b 1740 d 2-10-1830 m Zeruiah Staples Lt MA
Abraham: b 7-21-1726 d 5-19-1804 m Vesta Hunt Capt MA
Abraham: b 3-8-1727 d 8-12-1784 m Anne Breckminster PS MA
Abraham: b 2-10-1754 d 2-22-1796 m Abigail Freeman 1Lt MA
Abraham: b 10-27-1757 d 10-27-1837 m Lois — Pvt MA ★
Abraham: b 4-15-1695 d 7-10-1781 m (1)Prudence Howe
  (2)Elizabeth Brock (3)Elizabeth Bordman CS MA
Abraham: bpt 7-5-1746 d 12-19-1780 m Mary See Pvt NY
Absalom: b 1763 d 3-28-1836 m Ann Lukens Pitt Pvt PA
Amariah: b 2-9-1729 d 3-26-1802 m (1)Dinah Dimock (2)Mary
  Royce Capt CT
Andrew: b 1755 d p. 1785 m Jane Dill Cpl PA
Asa: b 3-2-1757 d 6-16-1834 m (1)Hannah Shepard (2)Prudence
  Pease Pvt CT ★
Asa: b 3-12-1757 d 3-20-1846 m Sylvia Peck Pvt MA
Asher: b c. 1755 d 12-18-1812 m Elizabeth Varguson Pvt CT
Barnett: b 1745 d p. 3-10-1795 m (1)Mary Pierce (2)Eliza Correl
  Pvt VA
Basil Lee: b c. 1734 d 12- -1799 m Arah Dorsey PS Pvt PA
Benjamin: b 5-26-1759 d c. 1852 m Elizabeth James Pvt CT ★
Benjamin, Jr.: b 1731 d — m Elizabeth Paine Sgt MA
Benjamin: b 8-27-1730 d p. 1802 m Elizabeth Boylston Pvt MA
Benjamin: b 1748 d 12-27-1776 m Sarah Wyman Pvt MA
Benjamin: b 6-20-1762 d 8-10-1828 m Mary Johnson Pvt MA ★
Benjamin: b 11-7-1695 d 11-10-1776 m (1)Susanna Howard
  (2)Abigail Parsons PS MA
Benjamin: b 1720 d 3-17-1784 m Anna — PS MA
Benjamin: b 10-25-1744 d 2-7-1835 m Hepzibath Brown Ens NH
Benjamin: b 11-30-1754 d 10-29-1814 m Ann Simpson Col NC
Benjamin: b 2-13-1760 d 7-14-1816 m Martha Ann Harris Sgt NC
Benjamin: b 1742 d 6-5-1835 m (1)Susanna Collins (2)Nancy
  Israel Pvt NC ★
Benjamin: b 1753 d 5-12-1823 m Tamar Wood Sol PA
Benjamin: b 12-30-1726 d p. 3-11-1785 m Mary Carr Sol VA
Burwell: b c. 1735-40 d p. 5-11-1816 m — PS NC
Caleb: b 4-12-1767 d 12-20-1854 m (1)Abigal Andrus (2)Eunice
  (Benson) Hathaway Tms CT ★
Caleb: b 6-5-1754 d 12-15-1830 m (1)Tabitha Fenner (2)Abby Dean
  Sol RI
Chaplin C.: b 1755 d 1780 m Susannah — Sol GA
Charles: b 1740 d 1782 m Susannah — Lt GA
Charles: b 1743 d 10-15-1826 m Ann Beckwith Sol PS MD
Charles: b c. 1740 d c. 1805 m Sally — Capt NC
Colden: b 2-27-1763 d 1-31-1832 m Mary Short Pvt NC
Cornelius: b 7-9-1750 d 7-25-1821 m (1)Anna Kelsey (2)Mrs
  Thankful (Sackett) Nash (3)Sarah E Kellogg Pvt NY
Daniel: b 11-1-1757 d 5-21-1844 m Asenath Day Pvt CT ★
Daniel: b 4-27-1759 d 8-12-1835 m Hannah Munson Pvt CT ★
Daniel: b 7-17-1728 d 9-26-1818 m Esther Avery Pvt MA
Daniel: b 2-2-1759 d 2-14-1846 m Lucretia Willard Pvt MA
Daniel: b 2-11-1752 d 12-6-1823 m Mary Jackson Capt NC
Daniel: b 1-5-1751 d 7-16-1831 m Sarah Nixon Capt NC ★
Daniel: b 4-12-1717 d 11-29-1794 m Jane Oldman PS PA
Daniel: b — d 11-19-1781 m X Capt SC
Daniel: b 1753-63 d 1820 m Violet Crouch Sol VA
Daniel: b 12-2-1755 d 1839 m Mary A Aldridge Pvt VA
David: b 10-15-1719 d 4-20-1800 m Elizabeth Dana Pvt CT
David: b 5-7-1744 d 6-6-1838 m Mindwell Sage Pvt CT
David: b 2-2-1756 d 10-13-1839 m Rachel Bidwell Pvt CT ★
David: b 2-21-1752 d 5-20-1837 m Lucy Walworth Pvt CT W★
David: b 7-24-1759 d 12-4-1836 m Sarah Hassell Pvt Mar MA ★
David: b 10-24-1746 d 1-28-1816 m Lois Webster Pvt MA
David: b 1757 d 8-1-1841 m Elizabeth C — Pvt NJ
David: b 10-21-1754 d 8-2-1831 m Nancy Benedict Pvt NY W★
David: b 1760 d 1834 m Martha Ivey Pvt NC
David: b 1763 d 5- -1832 m Mary James Pvt NC
David: b 1-27-1765 d 9-28-1830 m Eliz Anderson Pvt NC W★
David: b 1734 d 1812 m Anne (Williams) Pvt PA
David: b 1750 d 11-8-1831 m Nellie Williams Lt VA
Drury: b c. 1748/9 d c. 1805/6 m Tabitha Marshall PS VA
Dudley: b c. 1745 d 1792 m Elizabeth Meredith PS VA
Ebenezer: b 11-22-1723 d 1783 m Jerusha Porter Col CT
Ebenezer: b 2-4-1755 d 10-14-1835 m Esther Castle Sgt CT ★
Ebenezer: b 9-20-1759 d 4-8-1819 m Deborah Doane Pvt CT ★
Ebenezer: b 1-25-1744 d 11-17-1821 m Jerusha Pope Sgt MA
Ebenezer: b 10-14-1749 d 7-1-1847 m Sarah Stedman Lt MA ★
Ebenezer: b 1757 d 12-29-1841 m Catharine Jones Pvt VA ★
Edmund: b c. 1740 d 1795 m Lucretia Adams CS NC
Edward: b a. 1760 d 1800 m Margaret Williams Pvt MD
Edward: b 1760 d p. 1820 m Betsey Ross Pvt MD
Edward: b 1-28-1751 d 7-9-1820 m Sarah Lothrop Cpl MA
Edward: b 1761 d 1839-41 m Mary Barnes Sgt NC ★
Edward: b a. 1750 d p. 5-20-1799 m (1)Rebecca Houstes
  (2)Susannah — PS NC
Edward: b 1759 d 11-12-1821 m Priscilla T Beall Ens VA
Eleazer: b 1-27-1759 d 3-20-1814 m Mary Billings Sol CT

Eleazer: b 8-1-1730 d 9-24-1778 m Abby Prentice PS CT
Elias: b 2-10-1718 d 12-5-1798 m Prudence Robbins Capt CT
Elias: b c. 1750 d p. 1800 m (1)Elizabeth Van Zant (2)Ruth — Pvt NY
Elie: b 2-1-1750 d 12-28-1822 m Anna Barbara Grosh QM MD
Eliel: b 1-30-1746 d 8-2-1819 m Comfort Morton Cpl CT
Elihu: b c. 1730 d 1782 m Desire — Pvt CT
Elijah: b 2-14-1740 d p. 1790 m Elizabeth Bates Pvt MA
Elisha: b 12-14-1744 d 10-26-1825 m Lucy Denison Sgt CT
Elisha: b 8-24-1746 d 2-29-1832 m Deborah — Pvt MA
Elisha: b 1759 d p. 1832 m — Pvt VA ★
Elisha O.: b c. 1763 d 12-14-1805 m Harriet Beall Capt MD W★
Elisha Scott: b 10-7-1757 d 2-3-1845 m Abigail Livermore Adj CT ★
Ellis: b c. 1750 d 5-20-1821 m Jane Garrett Pvt PA
Elnathan: b 2-13-1729 d 10-23-1815 m Hannah Thorp PS Lt CT
Ennion: b 4-14-1752 d 2-14-1830 m (1)Catherine Leonard
  (2)Margaret Sims Maj PA
Enoch: b 9-20-1730 d 4-2-1805 m Hannah — Pvt PA
Enos: b 1751 d 3-8-1811 m Susanna Ogden Pvt NJ
Ephraim: b 5-31-1756 d 7-6-1804 m Hepzibah Phelps Sgt CT
Ephraim: b — d 1797 m Philey Colvin Pvt RI
Esau: b 1-3-1747 d 1798 m Mary Jones Ens MD
Ezekiel: b 5-4-1728 d 2-12-1818 m Prudence Stoddard CS CT
Francis: b 6- -1752 d 3-1-1833 m Rebecca Trager Sol MD ★
Frederick: b 1750 d p. 12-14-1793 m (1)Eleanor — (2)Jane —
  Sol GA
Frederick: b 10-28-1760 d 5-19-1829 m Mary Bailey Sgt CT
Frederick: b c. 1751 d c. 1821 m Miss Goff Pvt GA
Frederick: b 7-23-1743 d 2-18-1823 m Amy Williams Capt RI
Gabriel: b 1756 d 11-20-1827 m Margaret Lytton Sgt MD ★
George: b 1740 d 1819 m Mabel Perry Pvt GA
George: b 1717 d 12-5-1803 m (1)Sarah Hodges (2)Mary Dean Col
  MA
George: b 1744 d 1802 m Mercy Paull Sgt MA
George: b 1752 d 1825 m (1)Grace Adams (2)Mary Totman Cpl MA
George: b 2-10-1731 d 6-12-1797 m Lydia Pickering PS MA
George, Sr.: b 1732 d 1800 m (1)Martha Williams (2)Susanna Graham
  Pvt VA
George: b 4-8-1747 d 5- -1822 m ( )Mary Burk ( )Margaret Harless Pvt
  VA
Gideon: b 8-12-1746 d 1-22-1830 m Annah Burt Lt MA
Gilbert: b 1-20-1766 d 9-16-1805 m Lany Francisco Pvt NY
Hardin: b 4-27-1764/5 d 9-15-1837 m Jane Hart Spy NC ★
Henry: b 6-13-1716 d — m Mary Boardman Adj CT
Henry: b 1743 d 9-14-1821 m Jane Witherow Capt MD
Henry: b — d — m Mrs Bercount Pvt NJ
Henry: b 1-24-1759 d p. 1803 m Rachel Cessna Ens PA
Henry: b 7-20-1762 d 3-3-1850 m Martha Crandall Pvt RI ★
Henry: b 5-4-1741 d 10-8-1798 m Frankey Bagby 1Lt VA
Hubbard: b 12-2-1762 d 7-10-1833 m Mrs Nancy Jones Pvt VA
Humphrey: b 1748 d 1784 m Rebecca Renshaw Pvt PA
Ichabod: b 5-17-1756 d 9-29-1839 m Sarah — Pvt NY ★
Isaac: b 7-1-1729 d 12-1-1814 m Olive McCall Sol CT
Isaac 2d: b 3-23-1758 d 10-10-1844 m Phebe (Williams) Sol CT
Isaac: b 6-10-1744 d 12-5-1815 m Elizabeth Davis Lt MA
Isaac: b 1748 d 1817 m Hannah Miller Sgt MA
Isaac: b 1758 d 1836 m Hannah Mosher Pvt MA
Isaac: b 11-16-1722 d 1806 m Eunice Pierson Pvt NJ
Isaac: b 7-16-1737 d 9-25-1825 m Nancy Burke Pvt PA
Isaac: b 1751 d p. 1820 m Tabitha Gresham Pvt SC GA
Isaac: b 1749 d 1854 m Mary Anderson Pvt SC
Isarel: b 11-19-1763 d p. 1802 m (1)Temperance Holmes
  (2)Priscilla Howard Pvt MA
Jabez: b 6-21-1828 m Martha Jane Soverhill Pvt NJ
Jabez: b 6-10-1754 d 3-22-1838 m Lydia Tilmer Pvt RI
Jacob: b 4-28-1755 d 5-2-1829 m Hannah Sheple Pvt MA
Jacob: b 6-6-1758 d 10-22-1805 m Experience White Pvt MA
Jacob: b 1-10-1760 d 7-12-1814 m Joanna Dean (Williams) Pvt MA
Jacob: b 5-12-1747 d 7-6-1815 m Jane — Sol NY
Jacob: b 9-19-1732 d 8- -1781 m Chloe Wilder Pvt NC
Jacob: b 2-26-1751 d 7-12-1823 m Elizabeth Hampton Pvt PA
Jarius: b 11-25-1764 d 6-8-1841 m Hannah Morse Pvt MA
Jairus: b 3-15-1756 d 11-22-1835 m Lydia Condit Pvt NY
James: b 1756 d 6-11-1837 m (1)Elizabeth Watson (2)Eleanor
  Bernard Pvt DE
James: b 1757 d 1817 m Elizabeth Holloway Sol GA
James, Jr.: b 2- -1741 d 2-5-1826 m Susanna Shaw LCol MA
James: b 8-22-1759 d 6-14-1822 m Susanna Merrill Pvt MA
James: b 1-1-1703 d 6-10-1779 m Sarah Barney CS MA
James: b 4-13-1757 d 10-12-1844 m Mary Raymond Sgt NY
James: b 1725 d 12- -1804 m Mary Perry Pvt PA
James: b 1740 d 10-7-1780 m Mary Wallace Col PS SC
James: b a. 1756 d 11-8-1821 m Jemima Gunn Capt VA
James: b 1750 d 1794 m Elizabeth Blackburn Capt VA
James: b a. 1750 d 1821 m (1)Eleanor Green (2)Elizabeth Bruce
  Capt VA
James: b 4- -1762 d a. 10-21-1833 m Elizabeth — Pvt VA
James: b 5-13-1763 d 5-2-1851 m Kiziah Wilson Pvt VA ★
James: b 2-22-1759 d 7-11-1842 m Elizabeth Miller Pvt VA MD PA★
James M.: b 9-23-1763 d 1-12-1838 m Wilmoth Walker Pvt VA W★
Jarrett: b 7-31-1764 d 6-20-1833 m Ruth Ann Clemens Sgt PS MD
  PA ★
Jarrett: b c. 1755 d 1799 m (1)Elizabeth Phelps (2)Elizabeth
  Simmons Lt IL

Jarrett: b 1733 d *p.* 7-25-1824 m (1)Sally Lanier (2)Winifred — Lt VA
Jedediah: b 6-14-1748 d 11-24-1826 m (1)Abial Bail (2)Mrs Mercy Cleveland PS NH
Jehiel: b 6-30-1734 d 3-10-1814 m (1)Abiah — (2)Bethia Allen Sgt CT
Jehiel: b 2-16-1733 d 6-13-1810 m Ann Edwards PS CT
Jeremiah: b 12-31-1759 d 8-24-1842 m Mary Gaither Pvt MD ★
Jeremiah: b 2-14-1761 d 2-6-1845 m Mary Eurat Pvt PA ★
Jeremiah: b *c.* 1750 d 1-18-1831 m Nancy Jane Graham Capt SC
Jesse: b 6-9-1750 d 9-29-1835 m Rachel Gott Ens MD VA ★
Jesse: b 1750 d 1824 m Elizabeth Hucking Pvt VT
Job: b 7-21-1762 d 8-28-1827 m Alice Clark Pvt VT ★
John, Sr.: b 10-29-1715 d 8-25-1796 m Susannah Latham PS CT
John, Jr.: b 4-5-1739 d 9-6-1781 m Theoda Perkins Capt CT
John: b 12-23-1744 d 1811 m Keturah Randall Lt CT
John: b 12-3-1759 d 11-9-1848 m (1)Sarah Stark (2)Cathrine Morton Cpl CT ★
John: b 2-7-1747 d 4-9-1813 m Abigail Phelps Pvt CT
John: b 5-14-1714 d 3-21-1799 m Lydia Chesebrough CS CT
John: b 1755 d 1804 m Mercy Lee Sol CT
John: b *c.* 1732 d *p.* 5-22-1786 m (1)Sarah — (2)Agnes — Sol DE
John: b *c.* 1744 d 2-2-1837 m Margaret Taylor PS Capt MD
John: b *c.* 1730 d 1790 m — PS MD
John: b *c.* 1754 d 1792 m Mary — PS MD
John, Sr.: b 12-25-1719 d 2-8-1794 m (1)Anne Bird (2)Rebecca Winslow Pvt MA
John, Jr.: b 8-20-1750 d 9-26-1807 m (1)Polly Champney (2)Sarah Wheeler Sgt MA
John, 2d: b 1744 d 4-27-1821 m Huldah Whittaker Pvt MA ★
John: b 11-7-1758 d 12-13-1832 m Sarah Davis Pvt MA
John: b 5-13-1753 d *p.* 1791 m Nancy Brown Drm MA
John: b 5-27-1744 d 6-16-1809 m Mary Sumner MM MA
John: b 9-17-1712 d 4-9-1777 m (1)Elizabeth Williams (2)Mrs Bethia (Parker) Steadman PS MA
John: b 11-30-1756 d *p.* 1797 m (1)Alice Stevens (2)Rachel Cheney Pvt NH
John: b *c.* 1750 d — m Ann — Pvt NJ
John: bpt 4-12-1719 d 11-30-1780 m Cornelia Bogardus Capt PS NY
John: b 1756 d *c.* 1800 m Nancy — Pvt NY
John: b 2-28-1757 d 4-22-1832 m Mary Carl Randel Pvt NY
John: b 1752 d 7-22-1806 m Susanna Turner Dr NY
John: b 1765 d 1844 m Mary Donaldson Pvt NY ★
John: b *c.* 1745 d *p.* 1800 m Elizabeth Williamson LCol NC
John: b 1737 d 1- -1795 m Mrs Frances (Bustin) Slater Lt NC
John: b 1750 d 1802 m Sarah Lane Lt NC
John: b 1759 d 8-30-1833 m Judith King Pvt NC ★
John: b *c.* 1732 d 10- -1799 m Agnes (Bullock) Keeling PS NC
John: b 1738 d 4-24-1802 m Mary Wilson Capt PA
John: b 1705 d 1793 m Mary — Pvt PA
John: b 1731 d 5-27-1809 m Hannah Finch Pvt PA
John: b 1740 d 9- -1807 m Ruth — Pvt PA
John: b *c.* 1760 d 1793 m Mary Martin Pvt PA
John: b 11-11-1760 d 2-1-1838 m Sally Chadwick Pvt RI
John: b 12-27-1742 d *p.* 1842 m (1)Berthina Hopkins (2)Alice Hopkins (3)Elizabeth Smith PS RI
John: b *c.* 1730 d *p.* 7-24-1794 m (2)Anna Marie Miner Maj PS SC
John: b 11-4-1734 d 10-15-1824 m Cynthia Allen PS SC
John: b 8-29-1752 d 11-7-1835 m Abiah Morse Pvt VA ★
John: b 1742 d 1825 m Martha Chrisman Capt VA
John: b 1740 d 12- -1782 m Sarah Sullivan Lt VA
John: b 1760 d 8-12-1831 m Hannah Jane Smallett Pvt VA ★
John: b 1742 d *p.* 6-7-1830 m (1)Mary Ashby (2)Martha McMillian Pvt CS VA
John: b 1753 d 9-7-1833 m (2)Elizabeth (Sharon) Greene Pvt VA
John: b 1752 d 1830 m Eleanor Hite Sol VA
John: b 1747 d 4-30-1795 m Frances Hughes PS CS VA
John Chester: b *a.* 1750 d 5-19-1819 m Lucy Dickenson Maj MA
John Davis: b 12-25-1739 d 5-25-1807 m Hannah Davis PS MA
John Pugh: b *c.* 1738 d *p.* 1776 m Mary — Col NC
John Pugh: b 1750 d — m Jane Davis Capt NC
Jonas: b *c.* 1738 d *c.* 1783 m Eleanor Ward Pvt NY
Jonas: b 11-5-1754 d 7-25-1828 m Abigail Brewster PS NY
Jonas: b 4- -1723 d 11-20-1803 m Sarah Fleet PS NY
Jonathan: b 4-17-1764 d 3-11-1836 m (1)Frances Cowart (2)Sarah (Clark) Bond Sol CT
Jonathan: b 5-20-1741 d 2-16-1803 m Esther Wilmarth Pvt MA
Jonathan: b 8-21-1751 d 2-12-1837 m Phebe Reed Pvt MA
Jonathan: bpt 6-12-1763 d *c.* 1791 m Rachel Ridley Pvt MA
Jonathan: b *c.* 1744 d *p.* 1788 m Patience Chew Capt NJ
Jonathan: b 6- -1747 d 11-15-1838 m Mary Squire Pvt NJ ★
Jonathan: b 11-22-1749 d 12-23-1811 m Hannah Meeker Pvt NJ
Jonathan: b 1733 d 1801 m Eliza Ann Lewis Pvt VA
Joseph, Sr.: b 4-23-1723 d 1-10-1776 m (1)Hannah Lathrop (2)Eunice Wheeler Pvt CT
Joseph, Sr.: b *a.* 1749 d *p.* 1802 m Abigail — Capt CT
Joseph, Jr.: b 8-9-1765 d 3-18-1836 m Elizabeth Clark Pvt CT
Joseph: b 6-11-1744 d 11-11-1837 m (1)Mrs Mary Spelman (2)Eunice Ingraham Lt MA
Joseph: b 4-10-1708 d 5-26-1798 m (1)Martha Howell (2)Mrs Hannah Whiting Dudley PS MA
Joseph: b *c.* 1764 d 1847 m Sarah Williams Pvt NJ
Joseph: b 1762 d 12-3-1838 m Sarah Woodward Wgm NJ

Joseph: b 1757 d 8-2-1833 m Jane Sibley Pvt NY
Joseph: b 3-27-1748 d 8-11-1827 m Rebecca Lanier LCol PS NC
Joseph, Jr.: b 12-20-1759/60 d 12-27/28-1850 m Nannie Evins Lt NC ★
Joseph: b 1737 d 7-25-1825 m Martha Parrott Pvt NC
Joseph: b *c.* 1735 d *p.* 1788 m Pheba Little Pvt NC
Joseph: b *c.* 1756 d 1-9-1820 m Sarah Musick Pvt NC
Joseph: b 12-5-1725 d 1808 m Hannah Fuller Maj VT
Joseph: b 1732 d *a.* 11- -1810 m (2)Esther Hamilton Pvt VA
Joseph: b 1748 d 1830 m Catherine — PS VA
Joseph John: b 1730 d 1818 m (1)Rosannah Conner (2)Elizabeth Alston PS NC
Joshua: b 7-18-1749 d 4-3-1838 m (1)Dorothy Edgecombe (2)Priscilla Ruff (3)Hannah Hurlbut Sgt CT
Joshua: b 1756 d 1804 m Francis Calhoun Pvt GA
Joshua: b 1747 d *p.* 3-4-1833 m Bethia Clark Pvt MA ★
Joshua: b 1735 d 1790 m Sarah Higgins MM NJ
Joshua: b 1744 d 12-12-1825 m Mary Dill Capt PA
Joshua: b 1759 d 1823 m Lucinda Neal Sol VA
Josiah 2d: b 5-7-1725 d 2-7-1794 m Hannah Forbes Pvt MA
Josiah, 3d: b 4-19-1759 d 10-10-1789 m Hannah Kingman Pvt MA
Josiah: b *a.* 1712 d *p.* 1786 m Phoebe Rogers Pvt PS PA
Jotham: b 1751 d 9-20-1780 m Dorcas Baldwin Pvt NJ
Judah: b 12-14-1741 d 3-9-1807 m Mary Skinner Capt MA
Lawrence: b 2-28-1758 d 9-14-1834 m Mary — Sgt PS MD ★
Lemuel: b 5-2-1751 d 9-17-1820 m Anne Hilton Lt MA ★
Lemuel: b 8-3-1742 d 10-31-1833 m (1)Molly Jones (2)Abigail Briggs Pvt MA
Lewis: b *c.* 1740 d *p.* 1808 m Mary Hudson PS PA
Lewis, Sr.: b 1-21-1755 d 1-26-1836 m Sally Oslin Pvt VA
Lilburn: b 1748 d 7- -1794 m Mary Lee Thompson Capt MD
Luke: b 11-15-1722 d *p.* 2-19-1786 m Lucy — PS VA
Luke: b *a.* 1745 d *p.* 2-9-1810 m Catherine — PS VA
Matthew: b 1690 d 1-3-1814 m — Sol NJ
Membrance: b 1752 d 1802 m Mrs Nancy Brown Brunson Sol SC
Miles: b 1-6-1762 d 1-19-1838 m Elizabeth Darby Pvt NJ ★
Mordecai: b 6-6-1757 d 1812 m Rebecca Coates Pvt PA
Moses: b 7-11-1751 d 9-11-1814 m Mehitable Atwood Sol NH
Moses: b 1-8-1761 d 12-31-1821 m Martha Faulk Pvt SC W★
Nathan, Sr.: b *c.* 1735 d 5-10-1775 m Waittstill Davenport Capt CT
Nathan, Jr.: b 9-21-1760 d 3-14-1848 m Hannah Putnam Sgt NY MA ★
Nathan: b 11-4-1734 d 12-6-1789 m Sarah White Pvt MA
Nathan: b 1-2-1748 d 7-14-1823 m Abathia Harvey Pvt MA
Nathan: b 1758 d 11-2-1830 m Elizabeth Covode Pvt PA
Nathaniel: b 1735 d 2-15-1814 m Lois Sackett Pvt CT
Nathaniel: b 8-3-1757 d 8-18-1811 m Pardon (Monroe) Devolve Pvt CT
Nathaniel: b 3-20-1747 d 1799 m (1)Mrs Susannah Grey (2)Mehitable Preble Sgt MA
Nathaniel: b 3-29-1755 d 6-30-1829 m Lucilda Hodges Sgt MA
Nathaniel: b 1753 d 9-18-1823 m Lydia Leonard Cobb Cpl MA
Nathaniel: b 7-28-1723 d 2-16-1801 m Dorothy Stratton Pvt MA
Nathaniel: b 1757 d 2-15-1815 m Dinah Davis Pvt MA W★
Nathaniel: b 2-15-1721 d 11-27-1781 m Rachel Fleet PS NY
Nathaniel: b 1735 d 1796 m Sarah Averett Lt NC
Nathaniel, Jr.: b 10-5-1741 d 1-25-1805 m Mary Ann Williamson PS NC
Nimrod: b 1755 d 1816 m Mary Andrews Pvt NC
Nimrod: b *c.* 1750 d 2- -1820 m Christiana Griffin Pvt SC
Obadiah: b 3-21-1752 d 6- -1799 m Hannah Clifford Dr NH
Obed: b 1-1-1754 d 2-25-1832 m (1)Prudence Elizabeth Doolittle (2)Rhoda — Pvt CT ★
Osborn: b *c.* 1752 d 12-28-1819 m Elizabeth Magruder 1Lt MD ★
Oswald: b 10-16-1746 d 10-10-1831 m Mary Brattle Williams Lt MA
Othneil: b 3-24-1736 d 12-16-1782 m (1)Catharine Williams (2)Hannah Runnels Ens CT
Owen: b 6-21-1739 d 1817 m Martha Miller Pvt PS PA
Park: b 7-25-1755 d 12-9-1833 m Deborah Williams Drm CT
Peleg: b 3-26-1753 d 9-15-1823 m Margery Morgan Sgt CT
Peleg, Sr.: b 1719 d 1-31-1809 m (1)Mary Sheldon (2)Mrs Rebecca Thayer PS RI
Peleg, Jr.: b 1740 d 3-20-1821 m Sarah Wheeler 1Lt NH
Peter: b 3-17-1755 d 9-28-1837 m Mary Morgan Pvt MA
Philip: b 1717 d 1793 m (1)Hannah Crockah (2)Mrs Rachel Blush Drm CT
Philip: b *c.* 1745 d *p.* 1782 m — Hundley 1Lt PA
Phinehas: b 11-5-1734 d 12-28-1820 m Mary Field CS Capt VT
Ralph: b 1735 d 1806 m Ann Walker Capt NC
Rawling: b 3-20-1754 d 6-24-1827 m Rebecca Luttrell Pvt VA
Remembrance: b 1758 d 2-2-1843 m Eleanor — Pvt VA
Reuben: b 4-8-1737 d 11-5-1776 m Huldah Hubbell Sgt CT
Richard: b 1760 d 10- -1798 m Sally Young Pvt NY
Richard: b 10-16-1747 d 3- -1827 m Mrs Elizabeth (Andrews) Edwards Pvt NC
Richard: b 1726 d 5-6-1781 m Prudence Bales PS NC
Richard: b 1730 d 1812 m Rose Ann Hartzell Capt PA
Richard: b *c.* 1730-40 d *p.* 3-20-1795 m Margaret — PS VA
Robert: b 6-1-1759 d 8-6-1822 m Mrs Hanna (Newton) Singleton Fif CT ★
Robert: b 7-24-1753 d 11-16-1834 m (1)Bethiah Pearce (2)Hannah Jameson (3)Sarah Maxwell PM QM MA

WILLIAMS, contd.
Robert: b 8-25-1758 d 10-5-1840 m (1)Fanny Randolph (2)Nancy Haywood (3)Elizabeth Ellis Dr NC ★
Robert: b 1740 d 11-16-1834 m Sarah Lanier Pvt VA ★
Roger: b 2-9-1749 d 7-21-1835 m Cassie Ann Blair Pvt VA
Roger M: b c. 1764 d 12-29-1836 m (1)Catherine Quarles (2Mary Persell (Miller) Sgt VA
Rowland: b 1-3-1756 d 12-30-1813 m Nellie Banks Sol NC
Rufus: b c. 1750 d 7-3-1778 m Amy Jenkins Pvt CT
Rufus: b 11-6-1762 d 5-2-1831 m Ruth Chapman Pvt CT
Samuel: b 1734 d 5-28-1814 m Lois Avery Allyn Lt CT
Samuel: b 3-7-1726 d 7- -1778 m (1)Lois Scott (2)Huldah Warner Pvt CT
Samuel: b 8-20-1756 d 12-17-1828 m Hannah Gardiner Sol CT
Samuel: b 7-23-1742 d 5-9-1786 m Triphena Lyman LCol MA
Samuel: b 3-20-1747 d 7-7-1824 m Mercy Case Sgt MA
Samuel: b 1753 d 10- -1812 m Azubah Warner Sgt MA
Samuel: b 1730 d p. 1799 m Mercy Coombs Sgt MA
Samuel: b 1-22-1756 d 3-18-1834 m Nelle Wright Pvt MA ★
Samuel: b c. 1752 d 3-23-1799 m Lois — Pvt PS NH
Samuel: b c. 1757 d p. 1785 m Sobriety Bunker Pvt NH
Samuel: b 1733 d 1788 m (1)Mary Magdalene — (2)Hannah Isbell Capt NC
Samuel: b 1724 d 10-20-1801 m (2)Elenor — Pvt NJ
Samuel: b 7-6-1754 d 4-17-1824 m Eunice Pierson Pvt NJ W★
Samuel: b 3-23-1758 d c. 1833 m Mary Rebecca Harris OrdlSgt NC
Samuel: b c. 1754 d 1805 m Pheraby Ingram Pvt NC
Samuel: b 1759 d 1817 m Delilah — Pvt NC
Samuel: b 2-10-1753 d p. 3-16-1796 m Charity Alston Dawson PS NC
Samuel: b c. 1760 d p. 1796 m Elizabeth (Williams) Capt VT
Samuel: b c. 1750 d10- -1818 m (1)Sabina (Stuart) Wilson (2)Sallie Cox Ens VA
Samuel: b 1746 d 1823 m Susanna Ligon Ens VA
Seth: b 11-23-1746 d 10-18-1818 m Mary Snow Lt MA
Seth: b 12-13-1756 d 3-18-1817 m Susanna Fobes Pvt MA
Silas: b 2-4-1750 d 10-20-1843 m Mary Flynn Pvt CT
Silas: b 4-11-1764 d 1-7-1852 m Susanna Burr Pvt MA ★
Simeon: b 5-19-1750 d 3-24-1828 m Prudence Harding Sol CT
Simeon: b 2-21-1716 d 9-18-1794 m (1)Zipporah Crane (2)Waitstill Hodges PS MA
Simeon: b c. 1758 d p. 1826 m Mary Smith Pvt NJ
Simon: b 2-19-1729 d 11-10-1793 m Maria Floyd PS NH
Simon: b c. 1745 d p. 8-22-1808 m Ann — PS NC
Solomon: b 9-10-1754 d 7-6-1852 m Elizabeth Ashby Sgt CT ★
Solomon: b 7-25-1752 d 11-9-1834 m Mary Hooker Pvt CT
Solomon: b 1-4-1701 d 2-28-1776 m Mary Porter PS CT
Solomon: b 1752 d p. 1790 m Elizabeth — Cpl NC
Solomon: b c. 1730 d 8-23-1794 m Temperance Boddie Sol NC
Squire: b 5-20-1753 d 6-3-1840 m Anna Potter Pvt RI
Stephen: b 3-10-1737 d 9-15-1807 m (2)Sarah Nelson Pvt MA
Stephen: b 11-10-1752 d 12-25-1847 m Esther Leonard Pvt MA
Stephen: b 5-14-1693 d 6-10-1782 m (1)Abigail Davenport (2)Mrs Sarah Burt PS MA
Stephen: b 1760 d 1840 m Delilah Rhodes 1Sgt NC ★
Stephen: b 1745 d p. 1792 m Catherine Cole Lt SC
Stephen: b 11-8-1750 d p. 1800 m (1) — Hopkins (2)Pruda Howard Pvt VT
Thaddeus: b 3-21-1722 d 4-11-1796 m Frances Case PS PA
Thomas: b 1-25-1728 d 2-25-1806 m (1)Anna Hart Gates (2)Elizabeth (Sparrow) Fuller (3)Sarah Sparrow Lt CT
Thomas: b 1756 d 11-12-1839 m Elizabeth Robertson Sgt CT
Thomas: b 9-20-1721 d 9-6-1781 m Mercy Raymond Pvt CT
Thomas: b 11-12-1735 d 2-11-1819 m Rebecca Wells Dr PS CT
Thomas: b 1-25-1728 d 2-25-1806 m Ann Hart Pvt CT
Thomas: b 1748 d 1785 m Rachel Duckett LCol PS MD
Thomas: b 5-5-1746 d 7-10-1776 m Thankful Ashley LCol MA
Thomas: b 1-14-1754 d 7-31-1817 m Susanna Dana Sgt MA
Thomas: b 11-18-1732 d 1786/7 m Dorothy Tuxbury Pvt MA
Thomas: b 6-14-1756 d 6-21-1796 m Hannah Park Sol MA
Thomas: b 10-24-1757 d 11-17-1822 m Elizabeth Tolman Pvt MA
Thomas: b 2-12-1740 d 7-12-1830 m Dorcas Harrison Capt NJ
Thomas: b 10- -1755 d 9- -1859 m Polly McCabe Mil NY
Thomas: b 5-6-1745 d 1-25-1826 m Sarah Hubler Pvt PA ★
Thomas: b 7-20-1752 5-3-1817 m Chloe Ball Owsley Ens VA
Thomas Pool: b 2-2-1754 d 3-20-1817 m Elizabeth Pollock Sol NC
Thomas R.: b c. 1740 d 11- -1798 m Catherine Greenhill PS VA
Thomas S: b c. 1733 d 10- 1816 m Elizabeth Dawson Hartley Pvt PS VA
Timothy: b 12-25-1756 d 8-26-1811 m Jane Oakley PS NY
Tobias: b 1746 d 4-15-1834 m Jemima Williams Pvt NC ★
Uriah: b 1755 d 10-24-1834 m Joannah Stedman Sgt CT
Veach: b 4-23-1727 d 9-11-1804 m Lucy Wadsworth CS CT
Vincent: b 6-10-1745 d 6-16-1818 m (1)Elizabeth Van Meter (2)Eleanor Haggerty Pvt PS VA
Walter: b c. 1759 d a. 10-13-1812 m Ann McGill Sol VA MD
Wareham, Jr.: b 2-19-1759 d 1-10-1844 m Anna Stanton Pvt CT W★
Wm.: b c. 1749 d p. 1790 m — Capt PA
Wm.: b 6-10-1723 d 11-20-1785 m Martha (Williams) Pvt CT
Wm.: b 1747 d 1796 m Jerusha Gillett Pvt CT
Wm.: b 9-27-1762 d 4-1-1861 m Grace Robinson Pvt CT
Wm.: b 8-2-1762 d 11-5-1818 m (1)Lydia Williams (2)Lydia Loomis Sol CT

Wm.: b 2-16-1740 d 11-18-1814 m Mrs Prudence (Stanton) Fanning Capt CT
Wm.: b 4-8-1731 d 8-2-1811 m Mary Trumbull SDI CT
Wm.: b 5-1-1716 d 7-27-1801 m (1)Martha Wheeler (2)Mrs Mary Jewett CS PS CT
Wm.: b c. 1720 d a. 3-14-1788 m Volinda Lamar PS MD
Wm.: b 7-4-1762 d 4-12-1813 m Katherine Blanchard Lt MA
Wm.: b 11-18-1732 d 12-21-1812 m Lydia Hoyt Sgt MA
Wm.: b 6-10-1745 d 2-2-1800 m Phebe Nash Cpl MA
Wm.: b 11-11-1749 d 8-8-1834 m Hephza Sampson Sgt MA
Wm.: b 8-22-1731 d 8-1-1775 m Elizabeth Macpherson MM MA
Wm., Jr.: b 5-30-1754 d 1-9-1828 m Abigail Harris Pvt MA
Wm.: b 2-25-1758 d 8-13-1841 m Susanna Pond Pvt MA ★
Wm.: b 1711 d 6- -1788 m (2)Sarah Wells PS MA
Wm.: b c. 1715 d p. 4-19-1779 m (1)Neeltje Fynhout (2)Anna — Pvt NY
Wm.: b 11-19-1762 d 9-1-1848 m (1)Ruth Thomas (2)Honour Davis Pvt NY VA ★
Wm.: b 1740 d 7-31-1817 m Catherine Cooper Pvt NY
Wm.: b 1714-18 d 1778 m Mrs Elizabeth Whitmel Blount PS Col NC
Wm.: b 3-8-1760 d 1808 m (1)Ruina Webb (2)Elizabeth Kearney Lt NC
Wm.: b 12- -1747 d 6- -1820 m Anne — LCol PA
Wm.: b c. 1740 d c. 1815 m — PS PA
Wm.: b 3-15-1753 d 9-20-1831 m Lucy Horton Of SC W★
Wm.: b 1736 d 1822/3 m Zilpah Wilder Col VT
Wm.: b c. 1730 d c. 1780 m Lucy Terry 1Lt VA
Wm.: b 12-20-1760 d 2-18-1841 m (1)Elizabeth Daily (2)Margaret Plunket OrdlSgt VA ★
Wm.: b 9-17-1757 d 8-23-1832 m Mary Watts Pvt VA ★
Wm.: b c. 1749 d 1783 m Mrs Jemima Reeves Pvt VA
Wm.: b 1755 d 8-30-1808 m Barbara Steel Pvt VA
Wm.: b 1760 d 8-18-1846 m Susannah McDonald Pvt VA ★
Wm.: b 1710-13 d 1783 m Mary — PS VA
Willoughby: b c. 1756 d 6-6-1802 m Nancy Glasgow Cmsry NC
Zachariah: b 2-23-1760 d 5-29-1832 m Elizabeth Swartzlander Pvt PA
Zadcock: b c. 1740 d 1816-18 m Rachel Kent Pvt NJ
Zebedee: b 1732 d p. 1778 m Martha Olney Cpl RI

WILLIAMSON,
Abraham: b a. 1757 d 9-30-1829 m — Pvt NJ
Alden: b c. 1750 d 1816 m (1)Isabell Thompson (2)Polly Elizabeth Jackson Pvt VA
Anne Newton: b 3- -1738 d 1820 m Thomas Williamson PS NC
Charles: b 1748 d 1786 m Mary — PS Capt MD
Charles: b c. 1735 d 1816 m Lovey — CS PS VA
Cornelius: b — d c. 1-20-1808 m Statia Demott Pvt NJ
Cuthbert: b a. 1745 d p. 8-9-1811 m (1)Elizabeth Price (2)Susannah White Ens VA W★
David: bpt 7-13-1755 d p. 6-1-1814 m Submit Brown PS NY
David: b 1752 d 3-26-1809 m Polly Urie Col PA
David: b 10-31-1751 d 1803 m Elizabeth Johnson Lt PA
David: b 1748 d 1794 m Anne McCullough Sgt PA
Eleazer: b 7-13-1757 d 2-28-1839 m — McConnell Capt PA
Elijah: b 1754 d 9-29-1837 m Sarah Byrd Pvt SC ★
Elliott: b 1738 d 1818 m Deborah Echols Pvt PA
Garret: b 4-3-1758 d 2-18-1819 m Johanna Breese Sgt NJ W★
George: b 1-15-1754 d 10-10-1822 m Mary Foster PS CT
George: b 1738 d 1828 m Abigail Gordon Sol GA
George: b c. 1745 d 8- -1801 m (1)Moaning — (2)Mary Norwood Sol NC
George: b c. 1747 d 11-14-1824 m Anne — Capt VA
George: b 1752-57 d 1798/9 m Rebecca — Pvt VA
Henry: b 3-23-1751 d 11-29-1821 m Mary Marsh Pvt NC
Jacob: b 1756 d 10-17-1848 m Rachel Corwine Pvt NJ ★
Jacob: b 1-5-1759 d 7-17-1841 m (1)Hannah Ten Broeck (2)Martha (Baldwin) Suydam Pvt NJ ★
James: b 1752 d 4-9-1803 m Ann Ringgold Lt MD
James: b 1756 d a. 3-28-1840 m (1)Elizabeth Evans (2)Mrs Elizabeth Garrison 1Lt PA ★
James: b 1754 d 1818 m Jane McEwen 1Lt PA
Jedediah: bpt 5-8-1757 d 1-9-1837 m (1)Charity Mobrary (2)Sophia Satterly Pvt NY ★
Jeremiah: bpt 5-13-1733 d a. 7-30-1813 m Sarah — Pvt NY
Jese: b c. 1736 d 1801 m (1)Mary Person (2)Elizabeth Marable Capt VA
John: b 5-4-1748 d 3-3-1800 m Lucretia Tice Lt NJ
John: b c. 1758 d 2-19-1854 m Elizabeth Lavely Pvt NJ
John: b 7-21-1752 d 9-28-1844 m (1)Jemima — (2)Amy Borum Pvt NY ★
John: b 12-16-1764 d 8-7-1829 m Margaret Scott Cloyd Pvt NC
John, Sr.: b c. 1722 d c. 1791 m — Pvt PA
John: b 1755 d 8-22-1823 m Susanah Douglass PS PA
John: b 1748 d 6-26-1830 m — Capt SC
John: b a. 1740 d 10-9-1831 m Margaret (Leslie) Mitchell Pvt VA
John: b 10-27-1759 d 1-12-1849 m Cynthia Mountjoy Pvt VA ★
John: b 1-21-1726 d 11-11-1794 m Elizabeth Bulkley 1Lt PA
Joseph: b 1765 d 9-16-1812 m Martha Fuert Pvt NJ
Joseph: b 1755 d 1840 m (2)Mary Benn 2Lt PA ★
Joseph: b c. 1758 d p. 5-14-1823 m Mary — Pvt PA
Matthias, Sr.: b 1716 d 11-8-1807 m Susannah Halstead QMGen NJ
Matthias, Jr.: b c. 1750 d 1836 m Henrietta Levy Maj NJ

Micajah: b 1-28-1744 d 1795 m Sarah Gilliam LCol GA
Moses: b 1756 d c. 1809 m (2)Barbara Walters Pvt PA
Moses, Sr.: b 1723 d — m Jane Mills Pvt PS VA
Nicholas: b 10-8-1762 d 8-18-1856 m Alche Ditmars MM NJ
Nicholas: b 5-23-1761 d 1-11-1832 m Elizabeth Myer Cpl NY W★
Robert: b 1740 d 1807/8 m (1)Lucy Conyers (2)Sarah — Col GA
Samuel: b 1759 d 10-8-1815 m Annie Starr Pvt SC
Samuel: b 1745 d c. 9-1-1808 m (1)Sarah Claypole (2)Sarah Evans
    (3)Deborah Dickerson Ens PS VA
Sarah Gilliam: b — d p. 1796 m Micajah Williamson PS GA
Thomas: b 1736 d 4-16-1813 m Anne Newton Pvt NC
Thomas: b 1759 d 9-17-1832 m (1)Ruth Anderson (2)Mrs Rebecca
    (Bell) Brown Pvt PA
Thomas: b c. 1745 d 12-16-1804 m Elizabeth Hinds Capt PS SC
Thomas: b 1758 d c. 1828 m Martha Greives Sgt VA
Wm.: b c. 1745 d 1806 m Molly Terrill Pvt GA
Wm.: b 1716 d p. 9-7-1779 m Agnes — Capt NJ
Wm.: b — d c. 1808 m Lena Brewer OrdlSgt NJ W★
Wm.: b 4-6-1759 d 12-22-1835 m Helena Terhune Pvt NJ ★
Wm.: b 1762 d 3-17-1799 m Ann Suydam Pvt NJ
Wm.: b 9-23-1762 d 11-29-1839 m (1)Catherine Buford (2)Jane
    Smith (3)Hannah Johnson Pvt NC
Wm.: b 1745-50 d a. 8-20-1802 m Anne Maria — 2Lt PA
Wm.: b 6-20-1730 d 12-23-1799 m Sarah Janes Pvt VA
Wm.: b 1-10-1764 d 11-28-1852 m Rosanna — Pvt VA
Wynant: b c. 1757-8 d p. 1832 m (1)Martha Leonard (2)Lydia
    Ingraham Pvt MA

WILLIFORD, (includes WILLEFORD)
John: b 1757 d a. 6-6-1835 m — Sol NC
Jordan: b 5-30-1759 d 4-1-1855 m Charity Holloman Sgt VA ★
Nathan: b 9-15-1757 d 1-3-1842 m Martha Wood Lt SC ★

WILLING, (includes WILLEN & WILLIN)
Evans: b c. 1760 d a. 10-16-1819 m Mary — Pvt MD
James: b 1762 d 11-23-1802 m Ruth Miles Pvt MD
Thomas: b 12-19-1731 d 1-19-1821 m Ann McCall PS PA

WILLINGHAM,
John Baptist: b 1752 d 1799 m Mary — Pvt MD

WILLIS, (includes WYLLS & WYLLYS)
Andrew: b 1750 d 1796 m Sarah Pritchett Pvt MD
Benjamin: b 4-15-1764 d 7-12-1843 m Bridget Cole Sol NY
Caleb: b c. 1750 d p. 1794 m Phoebe Cobb Pvt MA
Charles: b 6-27-1753 d 1-14-1831 m Ann (Orcutt) Hewes Cpl MA
Charles: b 1728 d p. 1775 m Abigail Belknap PS MA
Daniel: b 2-28-1758 d 3-5-1824 m Agnes Carr Pvt CT ★
Daniel: b 1750 d 3- -1825 m Winneford — Pvt NC
David: b c. 1756 d 1845/6 m Mary Cook Ens VA
Ezra: b 10-28-1763 d 4-30-1818 m Susannah Haynes Cpl MA W★
Francis: b 1-5-1745 d 1-25-1829 m Elizabeth Edwards Capt VA
George: b 1754 d 1824 m Susanna Baker Sol VA
Henry: b c. 1758 d 9-25-1794 m (1)Anne Savage (2)Sarah F Williams
    2Lt VA
Henry: b 1740 d p. 1786 m — Sol VA
Hezekiah: b 10-12-1752 d 2-1-1835 m Abigail Healey Pvt MA W★
Hopestill: b 1-9-1747 d 3-14-1823 m Olive Smith Sgt MA
James: b 1761 d 7-17-1836 m Sarah Jackson Pvt MA
James: b — d 4-23-1802 m Mary Peters Lt NY
James: b 1755 d 1796 m Elizabeth Wilson PS NC
Jeduthan: b c. 1736 d 3-29-1820 m Sarah Bidwell Pvt CT
Joel: b c. 1756/7 d 6-10-1822 m (1)Amy — (2)Sarah — Sol NC
Joel: b a. 1740 d p. 1785 m Esther — Pvt PA
John: b c. 1745 d 1817 m Ann Short Pvt MD
John: b 2-16-1761 d 1840 m Mary Egerton Pvt MA
John: b 3-23-1741 d 4-1-1804 m Rachel Doremus Capt NJ
John: b a. 1759 d 4-22-1800 m Asenath Barnes Capt NC
John: b 1740 d 1816 m (2)Mary Jane Lewis Maj VA
John Whitaker: b c. 1758 d p. 1798 m Ann Beale Maj VA
Jonathan: b 1752 d 8-10-1842 m (1)Charlottte Saemie (2)Mrs
    Hannah Greeley Pvt NH
Joseph: b 1759 d 1-3-1842 m Grace — Pvt NJ ★
Joseph: b c. 1755 d 1813 m Mary Meldrum Pvt PA
Joseph: b 1752 d 1818 m Nancy — Pvt VA
Lewis: b 11-11-1734 d 1-15-1813 m (1)Mary Champe (2)Mrs Ann
    (Carter) Champe (3)Mrs Elizabeth Bromfield LCol VA
Lewis: b c. 1760 d 1817 m Edna Tillman Lt VA
Nathan: b 11-17-1738 d 1-24-1824 m (1)Martha Howard (2)Sarah
    White Pvt MA
Nathaniel: b 2-7-1755 d 4-1-1831 m (1)Lucy Douglas (2)Mary Cartwell
    PS MA
Richard: b c. 1740 d 1807 m Sybil Ranney Pvt NY
Richard: b 2-25-1746 d 12-25-1837 m Drusilla Pearson Pvt SC
Robert: b c. 1750 d 3- -1830 m (1)Sarah Gibson (2)Mrs Davis
    (3)Sarah — Pvt PA
Solomon: b 10-14-1731 d 12-10-1807 m Elizabeth Lathrop Col CT
Stoughton: b 3-28-1746 d p. 1820 m Mary Monk Pvt MA
Sylvanus: b 3-26-1756 d 8-18-1841 m Eunice Davidson Pvt CT ★
Thomas: b 2-2-1755 d 12-19-1838 m Ruth Williams Pvt CT ★
Thomas: b 10-10-1746 d 12-11-1836 m (1) — (2)Susannah
    Hewett (3)Sarah Dean Pvt MA

Wm.: b 3-27-1754 d 1793 m Phoebe Wilson Pvt NJ W★
Wm.: b 1727 d 9-25-1801 m (1)Betty Harlan (2)Hannah —
    Pvt PA
Wm.: b 1755 d 1827 m (1)Lucy — (2)Martha Middleton (3)Miney
    Winfree (4)Catherine Pond Sgt VA
Wm.: b 1730 d 1797 m Martha — Pvt VA
Wm.: b 1743 d 5-21-1838 m Elizabeth Garnett Pvt VA

WILLISTON,
Consider: b 8-3-1739 d 2-14-1794 m Rhoda King Lt CT
Ichabod: b 4-21-1750 d 11-5-1838 m Elizabeth Sanford Pvt RI ★
Israel: b 12-18-1744 d 2-3-1817 m Phoebe Chapin Lt MA
Thomas: b 8-11-1745 d 6-12-1810 m (1)Hannah Bowden (2)Elizabeth
    Smith Sgt Matr MA

WILLOUGHBY,
Alexander: b 2-19-1760 d 10-13-1842 m Elizabeth Rice Pvt VA ★
Andrew, Sr.: b 1717 d 8-27-1800 m Elizabeth Wallace CS PS VA
Bliss: b 2-22-1767 d 5-21-1849 m (1)Fanny Pattan Pvt CT ★
Bliss: b 12-10-1722 d 9-28-1807 m Rosanna Cole PS CS VT
Edlyne: b 1752 d 1839-41 m Eleanor Stark Pvt VA
Henry: b 1757 d 9- -1860 m Jennie Lipscomb Pvt VA ★
Jonas: b 12-24-1735 d 6-22-1834 m Azubah Wheeler Capt NH
Jonas: b 3-31-1737 d p. 1782 m Hannah Bates Pvt NH
Joseph: b 2-17-1739 d 7- -1810 m (1)Lois Ball (2)Mehitabel Rice
    (3)Annis Bates Ens VT
Samuel: b 2-24-1746 d 10-26-1832 m (1)Elizabeth — (2)Mary Gould
    Ens VT
Wm.: b 1756-9 d 1829 m — Pvt GA ★
Wm.: b 1736 d 1817 m Ruth Arnold Pvt NY

WILLS, (includes WILL)
Daniel: b 1-12-1747 d 9-19-1820 m Mary Magdalena Lora Capt PA
David: b c. 1745 d 1800 m Mary Strahan Pvt PA
Edward: b 1758 d 1820 m Sarah Vaughn Pvt VA
Elias: b 1730 d 10-3-1805 m Elizabeth — PS VA
Emanuel: b 1754/55 d 1810 m Sarah Fulgham Capt VA
Frederick William: b c. 1750 d 1795/6 m Frances Durret Cpl VA
George: b 5-3-1747 d 10-13-1828 m Susanna Hunsicker 1Lt PA
Heronimus: b — d p. 7-22-1828 m Maria Elizabeth — Sgt PA
James: b 1767 d 1815 m Hannah Jack Pvt PA
James: b 1758 d 10-12-1842 m (1)Mary Chamberlain (2)Polly
    Savage (3)Patty Hawes Pvt RI MA ★
James: b c. 1740 d 1820/1 m (1)Mary — (2)Mildred — PS VA
John: b 1740 d 1801 m Nancy Peebles Pvt PA
John: b c. 1745/6 d 1812-15 m Susanna Sherman Pvt PA
John: b 12-8-1742 d 4-7-1823 m Jane Tillery Pvt VA
Lawrence: b c. 1725 d 1784 m Ann Pryor CS VA
Lewis: b 10- -1744 d 3-5-1832 m (1)Catherine Dick (2)Ellen Martha
    King Pvt VA ★
Matthew, Sr.: b 1757 d 1814 m Martha Abney Pvt SC
Thomas: b 1738 d 1802 m Angelica Cary Capt VA
Wm.: b 4-16-1765 d 8-10-1834 m Mary Ballard Pvt VA ★

WILMARTH, (includes WILLMARTH)
Asa: b 4-27-1746 d 2-8-1830 m Chloe Peck Lt MA
Dan: b 12-16-1749 d 12-1-1845 m (1)Hannah Brown (2)Mrs Hannah
    Fuller Cpl MA
Ebenezer: b 6-4-1738 d 1-24-1828 m (1)Sarah Sweet (2)Molly Capron
    Pvt MA
Elisha: b 3-25-1738-40 d 1789 m Sarah Walker Sol MA
Ephraim: b 3-7-1752 d 3-3-1804 m Lucinda Worden Sgt VT
Gershom: b 8-5-1760 d 7-30-1841 m Sarah Stanton Pvt MA
John: b 7-10-1737 d 1786 m Jemima Bowen Pvt MA
Jonathan: b 11-16-1761 d 10- -1839 m Sarah Sheldon Pvt MA
Joseph: b 5-6-1751 d 8-15-1841 m Hannah Dryer Pvt MA
Joseph: b 3-19-1745/6 d 11-29-1827 m Hope Carpenter Capt MA
Moses: b 4-31-1732 d 11-16-1799 m Elizabeth Hodges Capt MA
Shubael: b 7-5-1739 d 10-30-1809 m Mary Bosworth Capt MA
Thomas, Sr.: b 1721 d 2-5-1793 m Hepzibah Claflin Pvt MA RI
Thomas, Jr.: b 8-3-1747 d 11-26-1779 m Martha Tiffany Sgt MA
Timothy, Sr.: b 5-15-1717 d 4-19-1781 m Mary Walker PS RI
Timothy, Jr.: b 12-3-1743 d 7-28-1815 m Thankful Steire Capt RI

WILMERTON,
John: b c. 1755 d 6- -1794 m Elizabeth Holman Sol VA

WILMORE,
John: b 5-15-1755 d 11- -1794 m Jane Campbell Pvt VA
John: b 1748 d 1779 m Mary Clayton Pvt VA

WILMOT,
Amos: b 2-29-1756 d 6-7-1809 m Sarah Hine Pvt CT
Amos: b 1749 d 10- -1805 m Mary Wortman Tms NJ
Asa: b 8-6-1752 d 1804 m Esther Curtis PS CT
Elijah: b 12-17-1742 d 1814 m Hannah Hine Sol CT
Elisha: b 3-12-1763 d p. 1798 m Hannah Gladding Pvt CT
John: b 12-21-1752 d 6-22-1807 m Ann — PS MD
Joseph: b 12-4-1745 d 12-6-1827 m Hannah Waterbury Sgt CT
Nathan: b 11-27-1741 d 1831 m Phoebe Ann Totten Pvt PS NY
Robert: b 12-25-1757 d 8-5-1839 m Priscilla Ridgley Dorsey Lt
    MD ★
Samuel: b 3-6-1742 d 3-4-1812 m Elizabeth Stores Capt CT

WILMOT, contd.
Thomas: b 1-6-1750 d 1-28-1816 m Elizabeth — Pvt CT
Timothy: b 1756 d 1-23-1825 m Mary Copp Bbd CT W★
Walter: b 1755 d 7- -1824 m Hannah Johnson Pvt CT ★

WILMOTH,
Thomas: b 1734 d 1-24-1823 m Nancy — Sol VA

WILSON, (includes WILLISON & WILLSON)
Aaron: b 3-19-1759 d 9-3-1847 m Dorcas Clark Pvt NH
Abiel: b 1753 d 2-16-1825 m (1)Hannah Cadwell (2)Anne (Olcott) Spencer Ens CT ★
Abner: b a. 1760 d p. 11-24-1787 m Lydia — Pvt PA
Albert: b 2-14-1755 d 11-13-1834 m Mary — Sgt NJ ★
Alexander: b 6-15-1761 d 9-17-1843 m Catharine Davison Pvt MA W★
Alexander, Sr.: b 5-5-1731 d 12- -1821 m Jane McKean PS CS NH
Alexander, Jr.: b 10-14-1764 d p. 1797 m Jean — Pvt NH
Alexander: b 10-4-1727 d 7-9-1815 m Deborah Gilmore Pvt PA
Alexander: b 1739 d 7- -1824 m Agnes Johnston Pvt PA
Alexander: b c. 1717 d 1798/9 m Mary Young Pvt PA
Amos: b 1-13-1726 d 5-14-1792 m (1)Zerviah Grant (2)Damaris Bailey Capt CT
Andrew: b 1730 d 3-4-1788 m Hester Bonham Cpl NJ
Andrew: b c. 1730 d 3-4-1788 m Hester Bonham Cpl NJ
Andrew: b 11-15-1757 d p. 1788 m Mary Margaret Tippy Pvt NJ
Andrew: b 1744 d 1-28-1804 m Agnes Hunter Pvt NY
Andrew: b c. 1740 d 1803 m Lillias Porter 2Lt PA
Andrew: b 1759 d c. 1800 m Rebecca McLane Pvt PA
Andrew: b 7-15-1761 d p. 1832 m Lily Porter Pvt VA ★
Archibald: b 6-13-1749 d 3-27-1814 m (1)Ann Claypool (2)Nancy Newman Capt VA
Asa: b 1763 d 9-1-1837 m Joanna Royce Pvt CT ★
Augustine: b 8-4-1755 d p. 12-29-1847 m — Ens NC ★
Azariah: b 10-1-1756 d 7-10-1793 m Sally Witherbee Pvt MA
Benjamin: b 4-30-1728 d p. 1790 m Sarah Allen Sgt MA
Benjamin: b 1734 d 1-6-1818 m Lydia Bancroft CS MA
Benjamin: b 1-6-1741 d 1-30-1805 m Dinah — Sol NY
Benjamin: b 5-6-1741 d 7-7-1809 m Mary Kniffin Tms NY
Benjamin: b 11-30-1747 d 12-2-1827 m (1)Anne Ruddle (2)Phebe Davisson Col VA
Benjamin: b c. 1745 d a. 8-16-1834 m Eleanor Wilson Pvt VA
Benjamin, Jr.: b 10-22-1759 d 9-8-1839 m Barbara Bullock Capt VA
Benjamin: b 12-26-1733 d 10-27-1814 m Anne Seay PS VA
Calvin: b 1755 d 5-20-1809 m Submit Denslow Pvt CT
Charles 2: b 1751 d 2-17-1826 m Ester Smith Sol PA
Charles: b 1759 d p. 6-5-1818 m Rachel Clarke 1Lt VA
Daniel: b 11-6-1745 d 11-13-1815 m Abigail Morse Pvt NH
Daniel: b 1755 d 1818 m Sarah Hopkins Sgt VA
Daniel Stephen: b 1-2-1757 d 5-25-1834 m Sabra Wilson Pvt CT ★
David: b 6-3-1745 d — m (1)Sarah Bolton (2)Martha Page Cpl MA
David: b 1742 d 4-10-1840 m Sallie McConnell Capt NC
David: b c. 1752 d p. 12-19-1803 m Jean — Capt NC
David: b 1759 d 3-3-1847 m Elizabeth Pennycoff Sol NC
David: b 6-8-1752 d 7-22-1846 m Jane Rowen Capt PA
David: b 12-25-1745 d 1780 m Mary Dickson Lt SC
David: b 4-11-1742 d 6-8-1812 m (2)Jane Morrow PS SC
David: b 1759 d 1830 m Elizabeth Wilson Ens VA
David: b c. 1758 d p. 12-17-1830 m Mary Tye Pvt VA
Ebenezer: b 5-16-1745 d — m Hannah Austin Pvt MA
Ebenezer: b 1746 d — m Phoebe Witt Pvt PS MA
Ebenezer: b 11-16-1754 d 9-1-1838 m Lydia Rowley Capt VT
Edward: b 7-6-1734 d 6-17-1816 m Lucy Francis Pvt MA
Edward: b 1759 d p. 1830 m Nancy Bullington Pvt VA ★
Eleanor: b c. 1724 d 1810 m Robert Wilson Sr PS NC
Eli: b 11-30-1740 d 7-21-1800 m Mindwell Scovell Lt CT
Eli B.: b c. 1755 d 5-11-1845 m Hannah Hempenstall Pvt VA ★
Elihu: b 8-26-1745 d c. 1800 m (1)Joanna Mitchell (2)Hannah Weeks Sgt NH MA
Elijah: b 6-23-1743 d 8-28-1830 m Lucy Chamberlain Pvt MA
Ephraim: b c. 2-14-1762 d 11-12-1839 m (1)Persis Gassett (2)Clarissa Gale Pvt Mrnr MA ★
Ephraim: b 7-18-1756 d 3-22-1850 m Elizabeth Wilson Pvt PA ★
Ezekiel: b 5-11-1744 d 1830 m (1)Sarah Turner (2)Sarah Joy Pvt VT
Francis: b 1740 d 2-7-1820 m Mary Hartwell Capt MA
George: b 1728 d 2- -1777 m Elizabeth Crawford McCreary LCol PA
George: b c. 1743 d 1818 m Isabelle Bennett Pvt PA
George: b 1752 d 5-31-1795 m Ann Richey Pvt SC
Gilbreath: b 1742 d 1834 m Christina Bothwell Pvt MD ★
Gittings: b 1-4-1750 d 1-18-1834 m Jane Rutledge 2Lt MD
Guile: b 1758 d 5-1-1829 m Ruth Ward Pvt MA
Henry: b 3-17-1729/30 d p. 1776 m Elizabeth Adams Matr Pvt MA
Henry: b 3-1-1754 d 11-1-1843 m Franky Faulkner Spy Sgt VA ★
Henry Wright: b 1725 d 1778 m (1)Anna Wilson (2)Agnes Lacy Dr VA
Hugh: b 6-15-1761 d 8-13-1845 m Sarah Craig Pvt PA
Hugh: b 9-27-1764 d 10-9-1845 m Catherine Irvine Pvt PA
Isaac: b 1758 d p. 1806 m Eleanor Decker Pvt NY
Isaac: b 1747 d 1823 m (1)Katie Griner (2)Sarah Neal PS NC
Isaac: b 10-22-1758 d 5-11-1841 m Sarah Kniver Pvt PA ★
Isaac: b 2-17-1752 d 8-22-1842 m Lydia Poole (Talbot) Sgt VT
Isaac: b 5-15-1735 d p. 1789 m Margaret Gordon Sgt VA
Isaac: b c. 1760 d 1827 m Jane Richardson Pvt VA

Israel: b 1758 d 1842 m Cynthia — Pvt NY ★
Jacob: b 1755 d 8-15-1833 m Ruth Knight Pvt CT ★
James: b 11-18-1764 d 4-30-1841 m Chloe Blake Roberts Pvt CT ★
James: b 6-1-1760 d 2-3-1818 m Elizabeth Veatch Pvt MD
James: b 6-10-1760 d 1-13-1834 m Mary Tilton Pvt MA
James: b 5-13-1733 d — m Eleanor Hopkins Pvt PS NH
James: b 4-24-1759 d 9-10-1821 m Mary Eaton Sol NH
James: b 1702/3 d 1788 m Martha Gage PS NH
James, Sr.: b c. 1730 d 4-16-1791 m Mary Shirley PS NH
James: b — d 1995 m Sarah Annan MM NJ
James: b 5-25-1747 d 4-6-1823 m Martha Hopkins Capt NY
James: b 1719 d 11-14-1795 m (1) — Wells (2)Sarah Campbell Cmsry NY
James: b 2-28-1756 d 9-28-1807 m Elizabeth Hoover Cpl NY ★
James: b c. 1743 d 2- -1792 m — Pvt NY
James: b c. 1730 d 3-1-1825 m (1)Sarah — (2)Mrs Elizabeth Ann (Gordon)(Pace) Woodward Capt NC
James: b c. 1738 d p. 11-9-1795 m Margaret — Pvt NC ★
James: b c. 1735 d 7- -1776 m (1) — Patton (2)Margaret (McKemy) Alexander PS NC
James: b a. 1761 d 1792 m Margaret Kerr Lt PA
James: b 1744 d 11-30-1835 m Martha Willock Ens PA
James: b 7-13-1743 d 6-8-1799 m Agnes Henderson PS Pvt PA
James: b 1740 d 1821 m Isabella Barr PS PA
James: b 1740 d 1790 m Mary Carmen Pvt PA
James: bpt 9-25-1742 d p. 1794 m Sarah Wallingsworth Shield Capt SC
James: b c. 1740-50 d 1-17-1781 m Martha Calhoun Sol SC
James, Jr.: b 1751 d 1828/9 m Susannah — Pvt SC
James: b 4-13-1753 d 9-17-1814 m Tabitha Beal Sol SC
James: b 1740 d 1824 m Martha Anderson CS Ens VA
James: b a. 1760 d 3- -1815 m Susannah — Pvt VA
James: b 12-10-1763 d 8-12-1829 m Agnes Pickett Pvt VA
James: b 1753 d 8-8-1839 m Catherine Collins Pvt VA ★
James: b 1757 d 9- -1811 m Mary — Sgt VA
James: b 1744 d 1814/15 m (1)Elizabeth Stephenson (2)Jean Baldwin CS VA
James: b 1715 d 1809 m Rebekah Wilson PS VA
James: b c. 1750 d a. 5- -1802 m Lydia — Sol VA
James: b 9-4-1742 d 11-18-1820 m (1)Mary Wilson (2)Mrs Elizabeth Boush CS VA
James Armstrong: b 1752 d 3-17-1788 m Margaret Miller Maj PA
James P.: b 1732 d 7-27-1791 m Martha Jamison Dr SC
James S: b 2-6-1765 d 1847 m Sarah Cox Pvt VA
Jared: b 6-17-1761 d 1844 m (1)Cate Lawrence (2)Caty Morse (3)Caroline Boyden Pvt MA ★
Jeremiah: b 12-24-1746 d 10-24-1833 m Eunice Whitcomb Pvt MA ★
Jeremiah, Sr.: b c. 1740 d p. 5-18-1815 m Catherine — Pvt VA
Jeremiah: b 12- -1758 d 3-4-1846 m Rhoda Sutton Pvt VA ★
Jesse: b 1740 d 1812 m (1)Ruth Merrill (2)Mary Hull Capt NH
Jesse: b c. 1760 d p. 1825 m (1)Elizabeth Chamness (2)Winnie Humphries Pvt NC
John: b 5-11-1749 d 9-13-1834 m Sarah Hughes Pvt Drm CT ★
John, Jr.: b 10-12-1756 d 12-21-1813 m Lydia Quintard Pvt CT
John: b 3-26-1760 d 12-1-1839 m Elizabeth Wilson (Davis) Drm CT
John: b c. 1757 d 1762 d 1-20-1849 m (1)Abigail Camden (2)Ruth Peck Pvt CT NY
John: b 11-7-1711 d 12-12-1799 m Abigail Stevens CS CT
John: b c. 1735 d 7-13-1781 m Susannah — Pvt DE
John: b 12-31-1756 d 2-15-1847 m Mary Roberson Capt GA
John: b 3-30-1739 d 9-5-1823 m Lydia Thatcher Pvt VA
John: b 1740 d 1800 m Alisanna Webster Pvt MD
John: b c. 1746 d p. 3-7-1805 m Susanna Gittings PS MD
John: b 10-29-1733 d 10- -1826 m Abigail Perry Sgt MA
John: b 10- -1740 d 8-28-1806 m Susannah Payne Pvt MA
John: b 10-16-1761 d 6-30-1842 m Catherine Law Pvt MA ★
John: b 4-16-1764 d 10-16-1847 m Mary Wheeler Pvt MA ★
John: b 7-24-1743 d 4-1-1812 m Jane Lynn Sgt PS NH
John: b 1729/30 d 8-2-1811 m (1)Margaret McFarland Pvt NH
John: b 6-23-1739 d 9-19-1804 m Agnes Grimes Pvt PS NH
John: b 1753 d 8-24-1814 m Mary Thomas Pvt NJ W★
John: b 1755 d 3-4-1841 m (2)Jane Thomspon Pvt Tms NJ ★
John: b 1755 d 9-5-1837 m Sarai Downs Pvt NJ
John: b c. 1744 d p. 1790 m Anna Kohn Capt NY
John: bpt 5-4-1722 d 1788/9 m Barbara Drippendorp Pvt NY
John: b 1726 d 1788 m Catherine Bogardus Pvt NY
John: b a. 1760 d p. 1781 m Mary Mercer Cpl NC
John, Sr.: b c. 1730 d p. 5-10-1800 m — Sol NC
John: b c. 1750 d a. 1802 m Lucy — Pvt NC
John: b 12-20-1760 d p. 4-6-1837 m Mary Barge Pvt NC ★
John: b 1742 d 1-4-1799 m Mary Wray PS NC
John: b 1742 d 3-3-1812 m Jane Nevin 1Lt PA
John: b 9-26-1751 d 9-11-1832 m Margaret Fleming 2Lt PA
John: b 1757 d p. 9-8-1827 m Martha McKee Sgt PA
John: b 10-1-1722 d 5-8-1812 m Ruth — Pvt PA
John: b 2-19-1730 d 3-24-1802 m Margaret Wilson Pvt PA
John: b 1747 d 5- -1808 m Elizabeth — Pvt PA
John: b 12-25-1748 d 4-26-1826 m Margaret Campbell Sol PA
John: b 2-22-1755 d 3-2-1822 m (1)Sarah Keen (2)Elizabeth Pile Bosn PA
John: b 1764 d 10-5-1836 m Nancy Foster Pvt PA ★
John, Sr.: b 1729 d 1803 m Margaret (Douglas) Carrigan Cmsry PA

John, Jr.: b 11-25-1761 d 1823 m Margaret Eckert PS PA
John: b c. 1740 d 10- -1808 m Susanna McClung Pvt PA
John: b 12-2-1728 d 1818 m (1)Mary Smith (2)Phoebe Dawson PS
 PA
John: b 1745 d 1-19-1823 m (1)Mary Lide (2)Charlotte Hicks
 Capt SC
John: b 9-22-1740 d 1-17-1833 m (1)Susannah Rutledge (2)Mrs
 Sarah Peele Pvt SC
John: b 6-10-1755 d 5-30-1849 m Elizabeth Pegg Pvt SC ★
John: b 3-18-1746 d 1793 m Ruth Joy Pvt VT
John:b 1740 d 5-21-1820 m Mary Lumpkin Col PS VA
John: b 1730 d 12-15-1779 m (1)Mary Ann Hooper (2)Margaret
 Bruce PS VA
John: b c. 1740 d 9-8-1781 m Ann — Lt VA
John: b 12-22-1733 d 5-28-1820 m Rebecca — Pvt VA ★
John: b 2-12-1755 d 7-24-1834 m Elizabeth Moore Pvt VA
John: b 4-12-1756 d 4-12-1827 m (1)Mrs Westfall (2)Mary
 Warthen Pvt VA
John: b 11-30-1756 d 10-26-1844 m — Pvt VA NC ★
John: b 6-16-1761 d 4-13-1809 m Susanna Kautzman Pvt VA
John: b c. 1735-38 d p. 12-17-1794 m Mary Israel PS VA
John: b 1739 d 1822 m Jane Pollock PS VA
John Gregg: b 2-19-1767/8 d 8-8-1855 m Sarah Newkirk Mus NY ★
John Overing: b 3-18-1756 d 5-19-1819 m Nancy Dench Pvt MA
Jonathan: b 12-25-1744 d 4-17-1837 m Anna Bowen Cpl CT ★
Jonathan: b 1735 d 4-19-1775 m Mrs Elizabeth (Stearns) Bacon
 Capt MA RI
Jonathan: b 4-7-1741 d 4-9-1830 m Lucy Blanding Pvt MA
Jonathan: b 2-17-1741 d 8-25-1830 m Ann Riddell Pvt NH
Joseph: b 1759 d p. 1840 m — VanDusen Pvt CT
Joseph: b c. 1750 d p. 7-19-1799 m Catharine Miller Pvt MD
Joseph: b 10-9-1759 d 5-17-1846 m (1)Elizabeth Caldwell (2)Margaret
 Johnson Pvt MA
Joseph: b 1-16-1762 d 6-3-1844 m Sarah Matthews Pvt MA
Joseph: b 8-27-1756 d 8-1-1821 m Lydia Waite Gnr MA
Joseph: b 1740 d p. 1790 m Elizabeth Rickey Slr Pvtr NY NJ
Joseph: b 1744 d 3-16-1826 m Mrs Mary Britton 1Lt PA
Joseph: b 1761 d 1831 m — Butler Pvt PA CL
Joseph: b 9-24-1763 d 4-14-1839 m Ann Wykoff Pvt PA
Joseph: b 1728 d p. 1789 m Martha Webster Pvt VA CL
Joseph: b 2-7-1745 d 3-18-1815 m Mary Carr Pvt VA CL
Joshua: b 1744 d 1823 m Dorothy Stevens Sol MA
Joshua: b 1762 d 2-25-1843 m Rebecca Spenser Pvt NH
Joshua: b 1-27-1759 d 9-17-1844 m Barbara Roper Pvt NC ★
Josiah: b 1746 d 1837 m Mary — Pvt VA
Lewis Feuilleteau: b 6- -1753 d 12-11-1804 m Margaret Hall
 Surgeon NJ
Malachi: b a. 1-10-1749/50 d a. 7-22-1794 m Ledy (Lydia) — PS VA
Mary: b c. 1745 d p. 1790 m Robert Wilson PS SC
Matthew: b 1741 d p. 10-7-1834 m Rachel — Pvt MD ★
Matthew: b 6-10-1721 d 9-27-1805 m Catherine Hubbard Pvt PA
Matthew: b c. 1730 d 1804 m Eleanor Mitchell Capt VA
Matthew: b c. 1758 d p. 1803 m — CS VA
Michael: b 2-22-1732 d 5-23-1829 m Martha — Sgt VT
Mindart: b 3-12-1758 d 4-9-1840 m Jannetie VanArsdalen Cpl NJ
Moore: b 3-25-1750 d p. 1840 m Christina Albright Pvt VA ★
Moses: b 9-11-1748 d 5-2-1837 m (1)Huldah Allen (2)Wealthy Ann
 Barnes Sgt CT ★
Moses: b 1740 d 1825 m Anna Stephens Sol VA
Nahum: b a. 1764 d 3-17-1817 m Experience — Pvt NY
Nathaniel: bpt 10- -1725 d 6-21-1802 m (1)Mary Silliman (2)Sarah
 Silliman Pvt CT
Nathaniel: b 1754 d 1796 m (1)Anne Broome (2)Margaret Parker
 Capt MD
Nathaniel: b 11-28-1740 d 10-28-1818 m (1)Anna Huston (2)Ann
 March 2Lt MA
Nathaniel: b 4-8-1711 d 8-19-1778 m Eunice Davenport PS MA
Nathaniel: b 11-9-1747 d 8-14-1825 m Abigail Earle Pvt MA
Nathaniel: b 6-24-1739 d 2-16-1819 m Elizabeth Barber Capt NH
Nathaniel: b 3-31-1743 d 3-21-1814 m Elizabeth — Pvt VA
Nathaniel: b 1-2-1755 d 5-31-1826 m Freelove Taylor Pvt RI ★
Nathaniel: b 1748 d 8-3-1818 m Eleanor Mitchell PS VA
Nehemiah: b 6-26-1751 d 1-24-1814 m Sarah Pierce Pvt CT
Nehemiah: b 5-13-1760 d 1827 m Polly Grover Pvt MA
Newhall: b 9-22-1755 d 9-22-1832 m Sarah Willson Cpl MA ★
Noah: b 12-2-1715 d 2-9-1796 m — PS CT
Noah: b 4- -1761 d 4-7-1844 m Mary Rowley Pvt MA ★
Oliver: b 1749 d 11-27-1812 m Sarah Heywood Sct ME
Peter: b 11-23-1746 d 8-1-1825 m (1) — Van Giesen (2)Catherine
 Duryea CS PS NJ
Peter: b 4-2-1750 d 7-30-1818 m Mary Cady Pvt NY
Peter: b 1730 d 1803 m Jane Galbraith Pvt PA
Peter: b 1764 d 1-20-1843 m Margaret Robinson Pvt PA
Peter: b 10-18-1749 d 4-26-1801 m Sally Ellis Lt PS VA
Richard: b 1762 d 1836 m Anna Dismuke OrdlSgt VA
Richard: b 11-12-1752 d 1-21-1827 m Priscilla Allen Cpl VA
Robert: b 1- -1756 d 1813 m Eunice Morehouse Pvt CT
Robert, Sr.: b c. 1718 d c. 1794 m Mary Douglass PS MD
Robert: b 1746 d 1-4-1797 m Sarah Felton Pvt MA
Robert: b 1737 d 12-25-1790 m Mary Hodge Maj NH
Robert: b 4-25-1733 d c. 6-14-1825 m Jane Thompson Capt PS NH
Robert: b 6-26-1759 d 10-17-1850 m (1)Margaret (Wilson) (2)Ann
 Wallace Pvt NH ★

Robert: b 7-30-1730 d 10-2-1791 m Jane Aiken PS CS NH
Robert: b 9-22-1736 d 2-25-1820 m Rachel D Hutchinson Lt NJ
Robert, Sr.: b 1747 d 9-1-1843 m — Pvt NJ ★
Robert: b a. 1747 d p. 1796 m Elenor Paulding Pvt NY
Robert: b 1717 d 9-4-1799 m Elizabeth Hindman PS NY
Robert, Sr.: b c. 1720 d p. 12-14-1793 m Eleanor — PS NC
Robert, Jr.: b 1760 d 1819 m Jane McDowell Pvt NC SC W★
Robert: b c. 1745 d p. 6-2-1797 m Mrs Elizabeth Johnson Pvt NC
Robert: b 7-6-1735 d 11-25-1783 m Elizabeth Grier Sub-Lt PS PA
Robert: b 11-10-1754 d 9-10-1835 m Jean Elliott Capt PA ★
Robert: b 1728 d 1781 m Ann Thompson Pvt PA
Robert: b 7- -1742 d 1812 m Esther Parks Pvt PA
Robert: b 1749 d 10-2-1824 m Sarah Friend Sol PA
Robert: b c. 1750 d 1824 m Sophia Burg Pvt PA
Robert: b 1752 d 1-24-1834 m Catherine Fischer Pvt PA
Robert: b 10-9-1737 d 3-4-1813 m Elizabeth McIlvain Pvt SC
Robert: b 1710 d a. 1785 m Mary Gordon PS SC
Robert: b 1727 d 11-11-1807 m Agnes Carnahan PS SC
Roger: b 12-26-1741 d 5-25-1825 m (1)Mary Frierson (2)Mrs Sarah
 Gordon Bradley (3)Mrs Anna Fitzpatrick Campbell PS QM SC
Russell, Sr.: b c. 1735 d p. 1806 m Susannah Rutherford Sol SC
Samuel: b 10-1-1761 d 4-11-1842 m Eleanor Lyon Pvt CT ★
Samuel: b c. 1762 d p. 4-7-1845 m (1) — (2)Nancy Shaw Sol GA
Samuel: b 7-29-1735 d 4-29-1790 m (1)Peggy Curtis (2) — Gale
 CS MD
Samuel: b 1742 d 1802 m Mary Lee PS MD
Samuel: b 1735 d 6-9-1780 m (1)Sarah Cown (2)Agnes Dunlap
 (3)Mary Hunter 2Lt MA
Samuel: b 3-26-1745 d — m — Pvt MA
Samuel: b 3- -1758 d 3-29-1844 m Rachel Locke Pvt MA
Samuel: b 1739 d 10-28-1806 m Sarah Newman Cpl NY
Samuel: b — d p. 1797 m — Pvt NC
Samuel, Jr.: b 10-16-1761 d 3-11-1847 m (1)Charity Rogers
 (2)Margaret Baldwin Pvt NY ★
Samuel, Sr.: b 1710 d 3-13-1778 m (1)Mary Winslow (2)Margaret
 Howard (3)Margaret Jack PS NC
Samuel: b 1761 d 2-19-1833 m Martha Dowell Pvt NC ★
Samuel: b 1736 d 4-7-1820 m Jane Vance Maj PA
Samuel: b c. 1750 d 1790 m Mary Hutchinson Ens PA
Samuel: b 1743 d 1819 m Martha Lowry Sgt PA
Samuel: b c. 1750 d c. 1824 m Elizabeth Morrow Pvt PA
Samuel: b c. 1753 d 1828 m (1)Chloe Reynolds (2)Mrs Mary
 Robbins Pvt VT
Samuel: b 1730 d 10-10-1744 d — m Mary Mathews Capt VA
Samuel: b 12-16-1760 d 9-19-1833 m Margaret Edmiston Pvt VA ★
Savil: b c. 1725 d a. 1-30-1787 m Susannah Chew CS NJ
Seth: b 4- -1724 d 5-14-1780 m Millicent Kingsbury Pvt MA
Solomon: b 9-26-1760 d 9-20-1840 m (1)Lucy Chandler (2)Rhoda
 Goddard Pvt MA
Stafford: b 1750 d 2-4-1833 m Agnes Boyle Pvt NJ
Supply: b 1-19-1750 d 1835 m (1)Susannah Cutter (2)Elizabeth
 (Woodbury) Batchelder Cpl NH
Thomas: b 10-25-1757 d 3-12-1856 m (1)Eunice Northrop (2)Sarah
 Monroe Sgt CT NY ★
Thomas: b 3-14-1722 d 2-26-1783 m Ann Dixon Sol DE
Thomas: b 4-5-1740 d p. 1797 m Elizabeth Hays Pvt MD
Thomas: b 1724 d 2-25-1799 m Elizabeth Hays PS PA
Thomas: b 3-12-1753 d 6-27-1830 m Ann Withrow Pvt NH
Thomas: b 1739 d 4-17-1826 m Elloner — Capt PA
Thomas: b c. 1745 d a. 4-11-1817 m Jean Swanzey Capt PA
Thomas: b 2-18-1733 d 1802 m Mary — 1Lt PA
Thomas: b 1-13-1753 d 1798 m Sarah Tomlinson Lt PA
Thomas: b 1750 d 1830 m Hannah Elrod Pvt PA
Thomas: b 1741 d 1825 m Agnes Murray Pvt PA
Thomas: b 1724 d 2-25-1799 m Elizabeth Hays PS PA
Thomas: b 8-18-1747 d 10-13-1834 m Mary Bosworth Pvt RI
Thomas: b — d 6-25-1812 m Mary Anderson Pvt VA
Thomas Branch: b 10-21-1730 d 1778 m (1)Elizabeth Finney
 (2)Judith Friend (3) — Booker LCol VA
Timothy: b 1728 d 12- -1785 m Rebecca Wyman Pvt MA
Valentine: b 1754 d 7-4-1833 m Amy VonSteinrod Pvt Grd NY ★
Violet: b 8-13-1741 d 12-13-1818 m John Davidson PS NC
Wadsworth: b a. 1742 d 1802 m Elinor Wilberforce PS MD
Wallis: b c. 1755 d p. 3-7-1846 m — Pvt VA ★
Walter: b c. 1741 d 1825 m Elizabeth — PS NJ
Wm.: b 1745 d 1828 m Hannah Backhouse SgtMaj DE
Wm.: b 1720 d 1780 m Cassandra Gover CS MD
Wm.: b 5-2-1762 d 7-11-1837 m (1)Margaret Boyer (2)Sarah
 Hardcastle Pearce Pvt MD ★
Wm.: b 5-8-1733 d 2-28-1778 m Hannah Fuller Pvt MA
Wm.: b 1750 d 1801 m Martha Clark Pvt MA
Wm.: b 12-19-1753 d 5-12-1824 m Phoebe Berry Pvt MA NH
Wm.: b 8-25-1753 d 11-23-1834 m Tina Autin Pvt NY ★
Wm.: b 1750 d 2-5-1841 m Elizabeth Caniff Lt NY ★
Wm.: b 6-15-1750/2 d 6-24-1836 m Esther Bowker Pvt NY ★
Wm.: b c. 1754 d 11- -1834 m Jane Cunningham Pvt NC
Wm.: b c. 1746 d p. 1790 m Nancy Green Sol NC
Wm.: b — d 1813 m Mary Scott Capt PA
Wm.: b 5-11-1746 d 12-14-1837 m Sarah Boileau 1Lt PA ★
Wm.: b 2- -1752 d 5- -1800 m Catherine Wilson Ens PA
Wm., Sr.: b c. 1725 d p. 1801 m — PS Pvt PA

WILSON, contd.
Wm.: b 1735 d 7-26-1814 m (1)Elizabeth Bruce (2)Timar Stanley Pvt PA
Wm.: b 11-7-1765 d 9-20-1834 m Sarah Riddle Pvt PA ★
Wm.: b 1752 d 3-27-1824 m Jane Martin Pvt PA ★
Wm.: b 4-17-1755 d 12-6-1821 m Esther Fickel Pvt PA
Wm.: b 1- -1758 d 6-25-1845 m Isabella Carr Pvt PA ★
Wm.: b — d p. 1780 m Elinor Johnson Pvt PA
Wm.: b 6-10-1760 d 6-8-1853 m Martha Scott Pvt PA
Wm.: b 2-15-1740 d 3-3-1793 m (1)Elizabeth Armstrong (2)Susanna (Ervin) Cooper Sol PS SC
Wm.: b c. 1746 d 3-8-1815 m Ann Butt Capt VA
Wm.: b 11-17-1745 d 5-25-1840 m Lucy Clarke Sgt VA ★
Wm., Sr.: b 1729 d 2-15-1777 m Hannah Stowe Pvt VA
Wm., Sr.: b 11-16-1722 d 1801 m Elizabeth Blackburn PS VA
Wm., Jr.: b 2-8-1754 d 1-1-1851 m Sarah Friend Pvt VA
Wm.: b 12-9-1750 d 1785 m Hannah McCarty Pvt VA
Wm., Jr.: b 1753 d 1833 m Rebecca Pettus Pvt VA
Willis: b c. 1740 d 1- -1800 m Sarah Blount Capt PS VA
Willis: b — d p. 1-11-1821 m Elizabeth (Trent) Black Lt VA
Zaccheus: b 1735-40 d 1824 m Lizzie (Conger) Ross PS NC

WILT, (includes WELTS & WILDT)
George: b 1748 d 1807 m Catherine Klein Pvt PA
Jacob: b 1762 d 6-13-1852 m Elizabeth Allen Pvt PA
John: b 4-6-1751 d p. 1806 m Rebecca Howes Pvt MA
John: b a. 1750 d 1824 m Mary — Pvt PA
Michael: b c. 1749 d p; 1794 m Margaret M Perr Pvt PA
Nicholas: b 1747 d 1817 m Ann Longanecker Pvt PA
Nicolas: b c. 1721/2 d 1786 m Maria Catherine — PS PA
Valentine: b a. 1796 d c. 1796 m Elizabeth Walter Pvt PA

WILTBANK,
John: b 1731 d 7-10-1792 m Mary Stockley Maj PS CS DE
Samuel: b 1754 d p. 1-20-1803 m Augusta Heverly Pvt DE

WILTSE, (includes WILLSE, WILLSEA, WILLSIE, WILLSEY, WILSEY, WILTSEE, WILTSEY & WILTSIE)
Abraham: b 12-2-1755 d 1840 m Seletje Lucky Sgt NY ★
Cornelius: b 5-29-1728 d 4-11-1802 m Hannah Filkin Sgt NY
Cornelius: b 1761 d 11-1-1828 m (1)Miss Bowers (2)Rachel Sparks Sgt NY
Cornelius: b 2-8-1724 d 1794 m Elizabeth Cornell Pvt NY
Daniel: b 2-24-1745 d 11-28-1832 m Rebecca Brown 1Lt NY
Gerardus: b 8-16-1737 d p. 1783 m Sarah Pinckney Pvt NY
Henry, Sr.: b 4-3-1702 d 11- -1794 m Pietronella DeBoog PS NY
Henry, Jr.: b 1736 d 1-28-1828 m (1)Phebe Wright (2)Elizabeth Waggoner Pvt NY
Henry: b 10-20-1751 d 1800 m — Pvt NY
Isaac: b 1757 d p. 1820 m Catherine — Pvt NY ★
Jacob, Sr.: b 9-6-1732 d p. 3-9-1791 m Catharine Cornell Sol NY
Jacob: bpt 10-30-1731 d 1800 m Amy Snyder 2Lt NY
Jacob, Jr.: b 7-31-1757 d 6-29-1834 m Bethiah Turner Sgt CL NY ★
James: b 9-13-1758 d 12-11-1844 m (1) — Willse (2)Mrs Dorothy Benson Hutchinson MM Sct NY
Johannes: b 6-30-1728 d 10-4-1796 m Eleanor Stockholm 1Lt NY
John: b 3-31-1748 d 7-26-1801 m (1)Anna Cary (2)Mary Catherine Conley Pvt NY
Lawrence: bpt 1718 d c. 1782/3 m Abigail Brower PS NY
Martin: b 7-8-1734 d 1815 m Anne Humphrey Pvt NY
Peter: b 2-12-1742 d p. 1788 m Margaret Little Pvt NY
Thomas: b 10-9-1745 d 11-6-1826 m (1)Elizabeth Cary (2)Mrs Eunice Brown Pvt NY
Thomas: b 10-2-1750 d 7-2-1821 m Mary — Pvt NY
Wm.: b 1732 d p. 11-22-1797 m (1)Maria Pinckney (2)Sarah Pinckney Pvt PS NY
Wm.: b 7-11-1751 d a. 3-30-1797 m Hannah Denny Pvt NY

WIMBERLY,
Ezekiel: b 1722 d 3-14-1809 m Mary Davis PS NC
John: b 10-1-1755 d 6-2-1835 m (1)Penelope Perry (2)Sally — Pvt NC
Lewis: b 1738 d 1818 m Martha Barbee PS NC

WIMBROUGH, (or WIMBOROUGH)
Richard: b 1762 d 6-25-1845 m Santer Hickman Pvt VA ★

WIMBROW,
Thomas P.: b c. 1760 d 3-28-1831 m Leah — Pvt MD ★

WIMBUSH, (includes WIMBISH)
James: b 1762 d 11-3-1835 m Lucy Hunt Pvt VA ★
John: b 1756 d 12-25-1818 m (1)Sarah McCraw (2)Nancy Williams Sgt VA
John: b 1755 d 1818 m Lucy Hunt CS VA
John: b — d a. 12-20-1802 m Mary Brady PS VA

WIMP,
John: b 1746 d 1824 m Rosina Kirkpatric Sgt PA

WIMSATT,
Robert: b 1742 d c. 1801 m Dorothy Abell Sol MD

WINAGLE,
Matthias: b 2-11-1749 d 1-8-1792 m Agnes Earley Pvt PA

WINANS, (includes WINNANTS)
Benjamin: b 1722 d 3-24-1793 m (1)Jane Wood (2)Abigail — Capt NJ
Craton: b 5-27-1756 d 1790 m Susanna Hopkins Sgt NJ
Elias: b 7-18-1742 d 2-12-1789 m Esther Perlee Lt NJ
Jacob: b 11-26-1725/6 d 1810 m (1)Rebecca Phoebe Clark (2)Rebecca Connot (3)Jemima Rae (4)Mary Mamie Gray (5)Hannah DeLong Adj PA
James: b 2-20-1744 d 11-5-1799 m (1)Elizabeth Clawson (2)Elizabeth Ross Pvt NJ
James, Sr.: b 2-17-1715 d 4-4-1795 m Sarah Reynolds PS NY
James, Jr.: b 3-14-1742 d 8-21-1803 m Johanna DeGraff Pvt NY
John: b 1750 d 2-2-1802 m Hannah — Pvt NJ
John: b 1745 d 7-19-1825 m Anna Margretha Minck Capt NY ★
John: b 8-29-1764 d 1-19-1841 m Catherine Waters Pvt NY ★
Lewis: b 1760 d 2-1-1825 m Sarah Halsey Pvt NJ
Lewis: b 1762 d 10-9-1826 m Martha Culver Pvt NY
Moses: b 11-9-1753 d 1-28-1822 m Ruth — Pvt NJ
Samuel: b 3-20-1746 d 5-6-1830 m Hannah Woodruff Pvt NJ
Silas: b 1760 d 9-25-1823 m Elizabeth Howe Matr NY ★
Wm.: b 10-23-1747 d 3-18-1821 m Mary — Pvt NY
Wynant: b a. 1725-30 d 1796 m Mary — Pvt NC

WINBORNE,
Henry: b c. 1720 d p. 1790 m Sarah Hare Pvt NC

WINBURGER, (or WINBIGLER)
George: b 1746 d p. 1796 m Margaret — Pvt MD

WINCH,
Caleb: b 9-26-1744 d 1826 m Mehitable Maynard Sgt MA
Ebenezer: b 2-12-1753 d 8-5-1831 m Esther Brinley Sgt MA
Jason: b 9-3-1746 d 7-2-1838 m Abigail Howe Sgt MA
Joseph: b 3-1-1733/34 d 4-7-1815 m Mary Beals Capt MA
Samuel: bpt 2-3-1760 d p. 1797 m Elizabeth Maynard Pvt NH
Silas: b 7-27-1744 d 9-19-1834 m Elizabeth Jones Pvt MA

WINCHELL, (includes WINCHEL)
Benjamin: b 6-10-1730 d 1812 m Lucy Bronson Lt MA
Dan: b 11-20-1736 d 1811 m Lois Curtis Pvt CT
Daniel: b 1758 d 1-7-1802 m Martha Bissell Pvt CT
Daniel: b 1761 d 1846 m Zelphia Virgil Pvt MA
Elijah: b 1741 d 1781 m Margaret Latimer Pvt NY
Elisha, Jr.: b 6-29-1757 d 12-10-1844 m Mindwell Hurlburt Pvt CT
James: b 1741 d 2-18-1778 m Mary Mills Pvt PS NY
James: b 2-18-1753 d 5-4-1840 m Mary Ferguson Sgt NY ★
Job: b a. 1752 d 1828 m (1)Sarah Kellogg (2)Sarah Hobbs 1Lt MA
John: b 5-2-1740 d 11-29-1791 m Ann Given PS MA
John: b 1760 d 9-14-1811 m Rachel Avery Pvt NY
Joseph: b — d a. 6-1-1790 m Laney Carner Sgt MA
Justice: b 7-12-1755 d 11-27-1823 m Hannah Taylor Pvt CT NY
Lemuel: b 1745 d 10-16-1827 m Susanna Fulver PS NY
Martin, Jr.: b 1739 d p. 1782 m Priscilla Dent Pvt CT
Robert Ruggles: b 1750 d 8- -1820 m Martha Hubbard SgtMaj MA
Samuel: b 2-8-1721 d p. 1779 m Sarah Burd Pvt MA
Wm.: b 11-3-1762 d 10-9-1839 m Elvira Moss Pvt CT

WINCHESTER,
Andrew: b 10-16-1750 d 5-1-1827 m Lydia Carver Pvt VT
Asa: b 1762 d 10-25-1831 m Sarah Adams Pvt VT ★
Benjamin: b 1744 d 1800-1810 m Bethia Benjamin Pvt CT
Benjamin: b 1-4-1760 d 8-24-1845 m (1)Abiah Alden (2)Bathsheba Alden Trask Pvt MA
Caleb: b 9-18-1734 d 6- -1816 m Anna Smith Pvt MA
Elhanan: b 2-29-1720 d 9-20-1810 m (2)Sarah Belcher (3)Lydia Jewett PS CS MA
Gulliver: b 1710 d — m Anna Hammond PS MA
Henry: b 5-25-1753 d 3-23-1834 m Lois Davis Phelps Sol MA
Jacob: b 11-6-1752 d 11-11-1805 m Anne Blunt 1Lt MD
Jacob Bancroft Parker: b 7-6-1762 d 8-24-1842 m Elizabeth Larned Pvt MA
James: b 2- -1752 d 7-26-1826 m Susan Black Capt MD
Jonathan: b 8-31-1755 d 1-16-1837 m Persis Whitmore Pvt MA
Jonathan: b 8-13-1756 d 3- -1839 m Eunice Smith Pvt NH
Joseph: b 1730 d 12-29-1803 m Lucy Harrington Sol VT
Lemuel: b 5-13-1740 d 1-17-1841 m (1)Lydia Flint (2)Mrs Margaret Smith Sgt PS NH ★
Richard: b 2-15-1755 d 10-14-1842 m Lydia Hodge Pvt CT ★
Samuel: b 3-11-1752 d 1-11-1823 m (1)Rebecca Chubb (2)Elizabeth Twist (3)Hannah Woods Pvt MA
Silas: b 9-5-1758 d 9-30-1838 m Sally King Pvt MA
Stephen: b 8-11-1723 d 7-8-1798 m (1)Beulah Trowbridge (2)Mrs Hannah (Hastings) Aspinwall Pvt MA
Wm.: b 12-22-1710 d 9-2-1790 m Lydia Richards PS MD
Wm.: b 4-25-1733 d 7-19-1807 m Hannah Parker Bancroft 1Lt MA

WINCK, (includes WINK)
Casper: b 1692 d 1788 m Gertrude Kemp PS PA
Dewait: b 2-12-1733 d p. 1790 m Margareth Reed PS Pvt PA
Jacob: b c. 1730 d 2-10-1806 m Elizabeth — PS PA

WINDECKER,
Frederick: b 1723 d 9-30-1808 m Barbara — Pvt NY

WINDER,
John: b 9-22-1736 d 4-5-1819 m Margaret Briggs Sol PA
John: b 1-19-1745 d 12-18-1822 m (1)Bette Jones (2)Susanna Harmanson Sol PA
Levin: b 9-4-1757 d 7-1-1819 m Mary Stoughton Sloss Maj MD
Wm.: b 3-16-1714 d 10-24-1792 m Esther Gillis CS MD

WINDHAM, (includes WINHAM)
Amos: b 11-11-1741 d a. 4-21-1798 m — Maj PS SC
George: b 1760 d 8-2-1831 m Mary Card Pvt MD ★

WINDLE,
David: b 2-18-1748 d 10-15-1819 m Abigail Kirk Pvt PA
Thomas: b 2-5-1734 d 1793 m Abigail Wickersham Pvt PA
Wm.: b 8-4-1739 d 5-26-1825 m Mary Jackson Pvt PA

WINDLEY,
Thomas: b 1743 d p. 5-5-1813 m Mary — Maj NC

WINE,
Jacob: b 1761 d 1814 m Mary Ann — Pvt VA CL

WINECOFF,
John Michael: b 1743 d 10- -1831 m Barbara Ann — Drm PS NC

WINEGAR, (includes WINGAR)
Garret: b 1737 d 9-11-1806 m Catherine Cown Pvt MA
John: b 1-14-1743 d 3-14-1798 m Elizabeth Doty CS MA
Samuel: b 3-27-1764 d p. 1833 m Martha Haskins Pvt Sct NY

WINES,
Barnabas, Sr.: b c. 1705 d 8-24-1784 m Bethiah Terrell Capt NY
Barnabus, Jr.: b 1739 d 12-21-1813 m Eunice Hallock Pvt NY
Thomas: b c. 1744 d 11-4-1794 m Eunice Case Pvt NY

WINFIELD, (includes WINGFIELD)
Abraham: b 8-25-1763 d 5-11-1813 m Margaret Quick Pvt NY
Abram: b 1765 d p. 1828 m Miss Miller Pvt NY ★
Charles: b 12-3-1728 d 1803 m Rachel Joyner Sol VA
Daniel: bpt 10-14-1759 d 1835 m Johanna Gross Pvt NY
David: b 8-10-1721 d 6-22-1806 m Engeltje Helm Sol NY
David, Jr.: bpt 9-25-1759 d 3-3-1839 m Syntye Van Vliet Pvt NY
Elias: bpt 10-10-1761 d 7-6-1817 m Maria Graham Pvt NY
Henry: b 2-22-1757 d 8-10-1840 m Mary Rogers Pvt NY ★
Jacob: b — d — m Katherine Helme Pvt NY
John, Jr.: b 7-20-1723 d 12-3-1793 m Frances Buck Sol GA
John, Jr.: b 9-9-1764 d 2-25-1853 m Jane VanNostrand Pvt NY
John: b 1756 d 1835 m Susan Lewis Pvt VA
John: b 1750 d 1804 m Margaret McFarland Pvt VA
John, Jr.: b c. 1759 d 1823 m Martha Hastings Tinsley Pvt VA
John: b 2-13-1742 d 1814 m Robina Langford PS VA
John, Sr.: b 1690 d 1785 m Sarah Garland PS VA
Joshua: b c. 1740 d p. 12-7-1796 m Mrs Rebecca Carloss 2Lt PS VA
Nathan: b c. 1750 d p. 11-4-1801 m Ann — Pvt VA
Peter: b — d a. 9-18-1788 m Lucretia Tucker PS VA
Robert: b c. 1744 d p. 3-26-1797 m Frances — PS VA
Simeon: b 2-2-1760 d 1832 m Marie Auer Cpl NY
Thomas: b 9-17-1745 d 7-24-1797 m Elizabeth Nelson Sol VA
Thomas: b 1733 d 1800 m Elizabeth Terrell PS VA
Wm.: b 6- -1754 d 10-20-1841 m Margaret Blain Pvt NY ★
Wm.: b 4- -1761 d 1847 m Elizabeth Davis Pvt VA

WINFREE, (includes WINFREY)
Jesse: b 1764 d c. 1810 m Frances Spencer Sol GA
John: b c. 1760 d 6- -1830 m Elizabeth Owen Pvt PS VA W★
Reuben: b a. 1744 d p. 1823 m Ann Scott Pvt VA
Valentine: b c. 1716 d 7-22-1796 m Martha — PS VA

WING,
Abraham: b 8-4-1721 d 5-3-1795 m Austis Wood PS NY
Allen: b 2-15-1745 d 8-28-1787 m Persis Allen Pvt MA
Bani: b 8-10-1763 d 4-2-1847 m (1)Lucy Eastman Clary (2)Thirza Flint Pvt MA
David: b 8-10-1732 d 1806 m Temperance Kelly Pvt MA
David: b 1735 d 5-10-1800 m Sarah — Pvt MA
David: b 11-21-1748 d p. 1813 m Mrs Dorcas Burdick Keech Pvt NY
Elisha: bpt 6-1-1755 d p. 1793 m Anna Boardman Pvt MA
Gideon: b 5-11-1744 d 2-21-1821 m Abigail Ripley Pvt VA W★
James: b 9-10-1756 d 8-11-1841 m Lydia Allis Cpl MA ★
James: b 11-18-1733 d 1-8-1791 m Ruth — PS MA
James: b 12-9-1756 d 1842 m Hannah Bowerman Mstr NY
John: b 4-11-1755/6 d 1-1-1832 m Mercy Almy 2Lt MA
John: b 9-25-1744 d 10-2-1826 m Margaret Look Cpl MA
John: b 5-17-1752 d 2-7-1823 m Margaret Buffam PS NH
Jonathan: b 4-18-1756 d p. 1823 m (1) — Lindsley (2)Irene Lindsley (3)Mrs Wetmore Ens MA
Jonathan: b 1746 d 6-12-1836 m Susannah Look Pvt MA
Joseph: b 10-21-1740 d 10-9-1826 m Rebecca Ashley Pvt MA
Lemuel: b 5-30-1756 d 6-6-1824 m (1)Thankful Swift (2)Mercy Gray Pvt MA

Moses: b 4-28-1760 d 10- -1809 m (2)Huldah Denslow Pvt CT
Moses: b 4-25-1759 d 7- -1837 m (1)Mary Chandler (2)Martha Maxim Srgn Mte MA
Nathaniel: b 6-21-1754 d 1-17-1842 m Mary Tobey Pvt MA
Noah: b 10-17-1757 d p. 1804 m Esther — Pvt MA
Paul: b 2-1-1760 d p. 3-4-1797 m Patience Trask Pvt MA
Samuel: b 10-24-1738 d 8-14-1777 m (1)Joanna Haskell (2)Mrs Lydia Moses Ens CT
Shubael: b 9-5-1738 d 1817 m Beaulah Weston Pvt MA
Simeon: b 11-15-1722 d 2-5-1794 m Mary Allen PS MA
Sylvanus: b 5-5-1738 d 11-21-1808 m Hannah T Wing Pvt MA
Thomas: b 1737 d p. 1793 m Phebe Ward Pvt CT

WINGATE, (includes WINGET)
Caleb: b 2-13-1744 d 2-13-1817 m (1) — (2)Sarah — Pvt PA
Daniel, Sr.: b 1-28-1722 d 1793 m Mary Frost PS NH
Daniel, Jr.: b 1755 d p. 1818 m Lydia White Pvt NH ★
David: b 1759 d 1819 m Lydia Tebbetts Sgt NH CL
Enoch: b 4-13-1753 d 8-4-1828 m Mary Meserve Sol NH
John: b 7-28-1739 d p. 1810 m Mary Philbrick CS PS Pvt NH
John: b 4-19-1754 d 9-16-1839 m Sarah Garland PS NH
John: b 1719 d — m Elizabeth Cushing CS NH
Joshua: b 8-2-1725 d 2-9-1796 m Abigail Roberts Col NH
Paine, Sr.: b 9-19-1703 d 2-19-1786 m Mary Balch PS MA
Paine, Jr.: b 5-14-1739 d 3-7-1838 m Eunice Pickering PS NH
Reuben: b c. 1765 d 1845 m (1)Mary — (2)Elizabeth — (3)Mary Rynearson Pvt PA
Samuel, Jr.: b 6-1-1749 d 9-24-1825 m Love Tibbetts PS NH
Wm.: b 7-9-1745 d 11-30-1821 m Mrs Mehetable Bradley Pvt MA
Wm.: b 11-8-1750 d 4-9-1830 m Deborah Buzzell Sgt PS NH

WINGO,
John W.: b 10-2-1761 d 1847 m (1)Frances Seay (2)Polly Seay Pvt VA ★
Wm.: b 1760 d p. 10-3-1833 m — Pvt VA

WINKELBLECK, (or WINKELPLECK)
John Leonard: bpt 5-9-1749 d p. 11-28-1795 m Elizabeth Herrold Sol PA

WINKLER,
Francis: b c. 1745 d p. 1799 m Maria Catherine Bott Ens PA

WINKLEY,
Francis: b 10-28-1733 d 10-9-1818 m Martha Hunking PS NH
John: b 2-9-1725/6 d 3-31-1811 m (2)Deborah Cain CS NH
Samuel: b 3-9-1731 d 11-29-1807 m Mary Brewster PS NH

WINKS,
Joseph: b c. 1740 d a. 1804 m (2)Elizabeth Marsh PS MD

WINLOCK,
Joseph: b 5-11-1758 d 3-28-1831 m Effie Stephenson Lt VA

WINN, (includes WINNE, WINNER, WINNIE, WYNN, WYNNE WYNNS)
Abraham: b 11-11-1738 d a. 2-21-1786 m Helletie Jerolman PS NJ
Benjamin: b 10-22-1759 d 1-28-1840 m Sarah Allen Pvt NA
Benjamin: b c. 1720 d p. 1780 m (1)Mary Baker (2)Margaret Pugh Col NC
Benjamin: b 12-21-1705 d 1797 m Rachel VanArnhem PS NY
Coenradt: b 11-19-1764 d p. 1808 m Jannetje Schoonmaker Pvt NY
Daniel: bpt 1-10-1739 d p. 1790 m Catharine Hooghteling Pvt NY
Daniel: b c. 1715 d 1799 m — PS VA
Franz, Jr.: b 9-22-1734 d 9-1-1797 m Anneke Viele Pvt NY
Isaac: b 8-24-1741 d 10-9-1807 m Mary — Pvt PA
Jacob: b 7-10-1758 d p. 1790 m Susanne Evertse Adj NY
Jeremiah: b 4-29-1749 d p. 1797 m Mehitable Buck Pvt MA
Jesse Durrett: b 4-13-1752 d 11-22-1823 m (1)Catherine Johnston (2)Mary Park (Gordon) Colbert PS VA
John, Sr.: b c. 1720 d 2-8-1781 m Sarah Ann Duval PS GA
John: b 1745 d 1812 m Elizabeth Schrembling Capt NY
John: b c. 1750 d p. 11-28-1796 m Anna — Sol NC
John: b c. 1720 d 4-19-1787 m Ann Pastorius Sgt PA
John: b c. 1732 d 7-16-1814 m (1)Dorothea Wright (2)Penelope Kirkland Col SC
John: b 1748 d 1820 m Ellen Hicks Pvt SC
John: b 1-9-1746 d 5-4-1820 m (1)Mary Lydall (2)Mrs Jane Childs Ens VA
John: b a. 1758 d 6-9-1802 m Mary Cox Pvt VA CL
John: b — d p. 11-4-1796 m (1)Agnes — (2)Susannah — PS VA
John: b c. 1740 d p. 1816 m Polly Lewis Sol VA
John, Sr.: b 1-20-1705 d 1789 m Mary — PS VA
John, Jr.: b 12-23-1751 d 1824 m Mary Bowles PS VA
John Danielse: bpt 11-17-1759 d 4-30-1837 m Agnieyje VanWie Sgt NY ★
Jonathan, Sr.: b c. 1710 d 4-17-1788 m Ann — Pvt PA
Jonathan, Jr.: b 10-28-1749 d 1817 m Lettia Hewitt PS PA
Jonathan: b 10-18-1767 d 1839 m (1)Margaret — (2)Sarah — Pvt PA
Joseph: b 7-3-1734 d 4-30-1817 m Betsey Poole Lt MA
Joseph: b 4-16-1760 d 9-16-1833 m Sarah Chase Pvt NH
Joseph: b 1745 d 1800 m Elizabeth — Capt PS VA
Joshua: b c. 1735 d 1805/6 m Elizabeth Appling Maj GA

WINN, contd.

Joshua: b 5-17-1747 d 10- -1817 m Hannah Wilson Pvt MA
Josiah: b c. 1755 d 1-27-1815 m Susanna Fortinbough Pvt NJ W★
Livinius: b 7-5-1745 d 3-29-1824 m Marytje Lansing Lt NY
Minor: b 1759 d 1820/21 m Mary Evans Lt SC
Minor: b 1730 d — m (1)Betty Withers (2)Eleanor — Lt VA
Owen: b c. 1750 d p. 9-8-1806 m Mary Cotton Pvt VA
Peter: b 1750 d 2-26-1824 m (1)Mary Farley (2)Ann Sumner Sol GA
Peter: b 1753 d p. 1797 m Charity Allen Pvt NY
Peter: b 1718 d 1790 m Susanna Vanderberg Capt NY
Peter: b c. 1725 d 7- -1782 m — PS NC
Peter J: b 12-27-1760 d p. 1817 m (1)Sarah Wolven (2)Grietje Wolven Pvt NY
Peter P: b — d p. 1779 m Catharine VanDenburg Pvt NY
Richard: b 1750 d 12-19-1818 m Priscilla McKinley Col SC
Robert: b 1742 d p. 4-23-1807 m Elizabeth — Pvt GA
Robert: b 1747 d 1815 m Mary Taylor PS MD
Robert: b 1749 d 12-1-1824 m Susanna Jordan Sol VA
Thomas: b 11-12-1733 d 9- -1782 m Margaret Coulton Lt PA
Thomas: b 12-27-1753 d 11-16-1824 m Elizabeth Dabney Anderson 1Lt VA
Thomas: b a. 1757 d 1797 m (1)Philadelphia Wynne (2)Lettice Wynne Pvt VA
Thomas: b 1728-30 d p. 11-16-1780 m Sarah — CS VA
Thomas, Sr.: b 1740 d 4-27-1807 m Mary Redding Col VA
Timothy, Sr.: b c. 7- -1712 d 3-2-1800 m Mary Bowers Capt CS MA
Timothy, Jr.: b 12-20-1740 d 3-31-1817 m (1)Sarah Reed (2)Mrs Mary Bridge Pvt PS MA
Warner: b 1-28-1747 d p. 4-13-1824 m Mary — Sol PA
Watkin William: b 9-30-1742 d a. 3-20-1821 m Ann VanPelt Capt PS CS NC
Wm.: b c. 1752 d p. 10-20-1823 m Ann Smallwood PS MD
Wm.: bpt 4-22-1716 d 11-18-1807 m Maria DeWandelaer Capt NY
Wm.: b c. 1755 d p. 1789 m Rosamond Hampton PS SC
Wm.: b 8-10-1729 d 7-8-1808 m (1)Cynthia Harmon (2)Phyllis Whitley (or Marr) PS VA
Wm. Smallwood: b 8-9-1751 d 2-7-1828 m Mildred Smallwood Pvt PS MD
Williamson: b 1760 d 1828/9 m Eleanor Magruder Pvt NC

WINSHIP,

Abel: b 8-30-1756 d 3-4-1844 m Elizabeth Ditson Pvt MA W★
Ebenezer: b 9-30-1735 d 1799 m (1)Elizabeth Raymond (2)Catherine Collard Capt CS MA
Isaac: b 6-8-1724 d 4-8-1783 m Hannah — Pvt MA
Jabez Lathrop: b 1752 d 1827 m Hannah Forsythe Pvt CT
John: b 5-12-1754 d 10-9-1822 m Deliverance Monroe Ens MA
Richard: b 11-30-1762 d 1838/39 m Sarah Terrel Pvt MA ★
Samuel: b 9-25-1712 d 2-16-1780 m (1)Hannah Loring (2)Abigail Crosby (3)Rebecca Johnson MM MA
Simon: b 11-2-1749 d 1-4-1813 m Johanna Abbott Pvt MA
Thomas: b 10-25-1729 d 8-4-1796 m (1)Sarah Godding (2)Sarah Harrington Pvt MA

WINSLOW,

Abner: b 5-17-1732 d 4-13-1803 m Rebecca Hathaway PS MA
Avery: b 4-1-1735 d 9-23-1810 m Jemima Simmons Pvt MA
Barnabas: b 3-12-1746 d 1- -1811 m (1)Deborah Glass (2)Deborah Bradford Pvt MA
Benjamin: b 6-19-1717 d 4-26-1796 m Hope Cobb Sgt MA
Benjamin: b 6-3-1758 d c. 1817 m (1)Rebecca Ellis (2)Prudence Albee Pvt MA
Benjamin: b p. 1733 d p. 12-10-1825 m Mary Valentine CS MA
Beverly: b 7-3-1734 d 7-12-1793 m Catharine Robinson Capt VA
Church: b c. 1765 d 1810 m Mary Gillett Pvt RI
Ebenezer: b 4-23-1761 d 3-4-1838 m Anna Frazier MM Pvt VT
Edward: b 1-3-1729 d 5-29-1803 m Eleanor Peirce Pvt MA
Ephraim: b 6-25-1727 d a. 1-17-1810 m Hannah Colcord Pvt NH
Ezra: b c. 1736 d c. 1796 m Rachel Fenno Sgt MA
George: b 9-28-1758 d 6-30-1836 m Sarah G Thomas Sgt MA ★
George: b 6-19-1728 d 4-4-1808 m Phebe Tisdale CS MA
James: b 1732 d 8-26-1805 m (1)Rhode Chase (2)Elizabeth Holmes Sgt MA
Job: b 7-10-1754 d 4-2-1839 m (1)Mary Atwood (2)Tamzon Westover 2Lt MA
John: b 9-29-1753 d 11-29-1819 m Ann Garnder PM Capt MA
Jonathan: b 1-1-1751 d 3-7-1826 m (1)Sybil Potter Pvt MA
Joseph: b 9-3-1753 d 9-28-1796 m Mercy Hunt Pvt MA
Joshua: b 6-1-1749 d 7-23-1788 Rhoda Phinney 2Lt MA
Kenelm: b 7-10-1752 d 2-13-1796 m Elizabeth Coles Pvt MA
Kenelm: b 12-11-1746 d p. 1788 m Damaris Wilder PS CS MA
Luther: b 1756 d 10-18-1823 m Kisiar — Pvt NH
Moses: b 1732 d 1815 m Jean Osborn PS NC
Nathan: b 3-14-1736 d 12-31-1820 m Eunice Mayo Pvt MA
Nathaniel: b 4-22-1730 d 1-6-1778 m Hannah Fitch PS CT
Nathaniel: b 10-6-1741 d 8-27-1808 m Sarah Hatch Maj MA
Nathaniel, Jr.: b 4-9-1761 d 4-30-1831 m (1)Joanna Kellogg (2)Anna Hannah Pvt MA
Nathaniel: b 8-18-1731 d 11-4-1803 m Thankful Randall Sol MA
Peter: b 1746 d 10-7-1780 m Mehetabel Babbitt Pvt MA
Prince: b 4-6-1737 d 1-6-1794 m Sarah Goodrich Sgt MA
Richard, Jr.: b 1-21-1739 d 5-2-1818 m Jane McCully Pvt MA

Samuel: b 7-28-1755 d 3-12-1850 m (1)Anna Ladd (2)Mrs Betsey Randall OrdlSgt NH ★
Shadrach: b 12-17-1750 d 2-1-1817 m Elizabeth Robbins SgnMte MA
Stephen: b 8-30-1746 d 2-12-1839 m Elizabeth West Pvt MA
Thomas: b 1704 d 4-10-1779 m Mehetable Winslow CS MA
Thomas: b 6-7-1711 d 3-14-1781 m Rebecca Ewer Pvt MA
Tisdale: b 4-8-1751 d p. 1792 m Jane Blackmore 1Lt MA
Wm.: b c. 1745 d 1827 m Hepsibah Hathaway Pvt MA
Zenas: b 10-30-1741 d 10-2-1829 m Abigail Clark LCol PS MA

WINSOR, (includes WINDSOR)

Abraham: b 8-7-1740 d 10-2-1813 m Roby Keech Capt RI
Abraham: b 10-4-1720 d 4-20-1798 m (1)Mary Smith (2)Sarah Smith PS RI
Amos: b 8-22-1742 d 1819 m Mary Bushee Lt Cav RI
Anan: b 6-21-1749 d 1820 m Amy Angell Ens RI
Isaac: b c. 1758 d p. 1-3-1817 m Nancy Riley Pvt PS MD
Isaac: b 8-21-1749 d 1-1-1805 m Amey Waterman Cav RI
John: b 1755 d 1-14-1831 m (2)Lydia Boardman Pvt NY ★
John: b c. 1750 d c. 1810 m — Pvt NC
Joshua: b 5-1-1749 d 11-7-1827 m Olive Thomas Pvt MA
Peter: b 8-21-1761 d 4-19-1845 m (1)Deborah Delano (2)Charlotte Delano Cpl MA
Stephen: b 12-14-1744 d 1-14-1820 m Mary Olney LCol RI
Wm.: b 6-30-1747 d 9-4-1844 m Phenia — Sol VA

WINSTEAD,

Mandley: b 10-29-1760 d 12-26-1846 m (1)Miss Tapp (2)Elizabeth Cox (3)Amy Hutcherson Pvt NC ★

WINSTON,

Abraham: b 1736 d 7-30-1814 m Rosannah — Sol NY
Alice Ann: b 8-8-1769 d 1-8-1813 m Henry Pendleton PS VA
Anthony: b c. 1710 d p. 11-14-1786 m Mary — PS NC
Anthony, Jr.: b 11-25-1750 d 12-20-1828 m Keziah Jones Capt PS VA
Anthony: b 3-22-1750 d p. 8-2-1832 m Mary Barrett Lt VA ★
Edmund: b 1745 d 1818 m (1)Alice Winston (2)Dorothea Dandridge (Henry) PS VA
Geddes: b 1720 d p. 1792 m Mary Jordon Sol VA
Isaac: b 4-22-1758 d 11-19-1835 m (1)Sarah Hill (2)Hannah Clark Ten Eyck Pvt MA ★
James: b 3-12-1752/3 d 7-17-1826 m Sarah Marks 1Lt VA
John: b 8-14-1757 d 4-28-1800 m Mary Johnson Maj VA
Joseph: b 6-17-1746 d 4-21-1815 m Minerva Lenior (or Lanier) Maj NC
Nathaniel: b 1758 d 2-26-1856 m — Pvt MA ★
Peter: b 11-14-1741 d 10-24-1784 m Elizabeth Povall PS VA
Wm.: b c. 1745 d 1804 m Rebecca Geddis Lt VA
Wm. Bobby: b 1758 d 2-6-1822 m (1)— Head (2) Nancy Ann Meriwether Sol VA
Wm. Overton: b 11-16-1747 d 12-11-1815 m (1)Joanna Robinson (2)Anne Kidley (Chamberlayne) Posey Capt VA

WINTER,

Christian: b 1757 d 11-6-1825 m Catherine Winter Pvt PA
Christopher: b 1752 d 3-13-1823 m Catherine Shaffer Pvt PA
David, Sr.: b a. 1762 d 8-24-1821 m Annie Cooper Pvt MA
Francis: b 12-3-1744 d 12- -1826 m Abigail Alden Chp MA
John: b 3-1-1756 d 6-19-1811 m Phebe Wright Pvt MA W★
John: b 7-25-1755 d 4-7-1821 m Ann Cyphers Ens NJ
Joseph: b 5-15-1748 d 4-20-1826 m Azubah Barton MM CT
Joseph: b 9-13-1757 d 12-2-1820 m Mary Prince Ens PS NY
Juvenil: b 3-18-1762 d 9-11-1841 m Amelia Heath Pvt CT
Moses: bpt 3-22-1724 d 4-22-1799 m Keziah Cady Pvt MA
Peter: b 9-4-1749 d — m — Pvt NJ ★
Wm., Jr.: b 1760 d 1787 m Catherine Hooe Capt MD
Wm.: b 3-28-1728 d p. 6-18-1794 m (1)Ann Boone (2)Eleanor Campbell Pvt PS PA

WINTERMUTE, (includes WINTERMUTH)

George: b 7-8-1748 d 1-8-1837 m (1)Anna Arason (2)Mrs Mary Ogden Shackelton Pvt NJ
Peter: b 3-20-1752 d 3-18-1830 m Esther Rhodes Pvt NJ

WINTERRODE,

John Jacob: b 4-20-1735 d 2-3-1797 m Ann Barbara — Pvt PA

WINTERS,

George: b c. 1731 d 1798 m Ann — PS MD
Jacob: b 1760 d 1827 m Mary — Pvt PA
John: b a. 1759 d p. 1776 m — Pvt PA
John: b 1744 d 3-10-1839 m Martha Jones Pvt PA
Moses: b 1758 d p. 1830 m Polly Preston Pvt NY
Moses: b — d p. 7-9-1798 m Elizabeth Head Sol NC
Thomas: b 1744 d 1839 m Mary Jone Pvt PA

WINTERSTEIN,

James: b 1-26-1740 d 2-28-1810 m Ariantee VanderBeek Pvt NJ

WINTON,

Nathan: b 2- -1760 d p. 1850 m Elizabeth Bradley Pvt CT

WIRE,
Nehemiah: b 4-24-1733 d 11-5-1793 m Clara Allen Pvt CT
Samuel: b 2-8-1763 d 12-24-1827 m Eunice Gould Sol CT

WISE,
Adam, Sr.: b 1718 d 6-9-1781 m (1)Marillias — (2)Catherine — PS PA
Adam, Jr.: b 4-5-1763 d 7-15-1842 m Barbara Zollers Pvt PA
Andrew: b 5-7-1748 d 3-4-1840 m Zeruah Hartman Pvt PA
Daniel: b 1755 d 2-13-1843 m Lydia Owens Pvt MA ★
Ebenezer: b 11-25-1751 d 2-4-1824 m Mary Hazeltine Pvt NH MA ★
Frederick: b 1753 d 1790 m Catherine Wise Pvt PA
George: b c. 1759 d 1810 m Mary — Pvt MD
Jacob: b 7-21-1750 d 7-24-1817 m Ann Bushy Pvt PA
Jacob: b 1759 d p. 9-24-1845 m (1)Harriet Blalock (2)Elizabeth — Pvt SC ★
Jacob: b 5-8-1750 d 8-18-1818 m Margaret Mumbaert Pvt VA
James: b — d 4- -1784 m Rebeckah Massie PS NC
John: b 12-12-1733 d 7-24-1800 m Anne Smith Cpl VA
Joseph: b 1745 d 1804 m Margaret (Patton) Pvt GA
Peter: b 3-8-1757/8 d 1820/1 m Mary Miller Pvt PA
Tully: b 6-8-1728 d 9-25-1777 m Susan Fultz Pvt VA
Tully: b 4-30-1758 d 4-16-1817 m Sarah Luker Sol VA
Tully Robinson: b c. 1720 d p. 4-30-1778 m Tahitha Douglas PS VA
Wm.: b 12-31-1755 d p. 5-13-1816 m Margaret — Pvt GA

WISEBURN,
Daniel: b c. 1760 d 1799 m Barbary — Sol FrA

WISECARVER, (or WISEGARVER)
George: b 1730 d p. 6- -1805 m Mary Elizabeth Steele Pvt PA
George: b 8-11-1756 d 1842 m — Orndoff Pvt VA ★

WISEMAN,
Caleb: b 12-29-1755 d 8-13-1835 m Katherine — Pvt PA ★
Isaac, Sr.: b 8-18-1738 d 5-3-1818 m Elizabeth Davis PS PA
Jacob: b c. 1730 d 1807 m Elizabeth — Pvt NC
John: b 8-18-1760 d 1-22-1842 m Sarah Greene PS PA
Joseph: b 3-29-1759 d 12-27-1836 m Elizabeth Bateman Pvt NC
Wm.: b 1741 d 1830 m (1)Mary Davenport (2)Lydia Bedford PS NC

WISENBAKER,
John: b c. 1754 d a. 8-23-1802 m (1)Ann Dasher (2)Mrs Mary Taylor PS GA

WISER,
George: b c. 1765 d 4-18-1846 m Mary — Pvt VA ★

WISEHART, (or WISEHARD)
Edward: b 1755/6 d 1804 m Julianna Grubb Pvt PA
Wm.: b c. 1750 d 1778 m Elizabeth Harrison Pvt NC
Wn.: b 9-17-1729 d 5-31-1814 m (1)Susan Lytle (2)Elizabeth Rhodes Ens PA

WISINGER,
Ludwick: b c. 1756/7 d 3- -1842 m Susan Miller Pvt MD ★

WISLER, (or WISSLER)
Andrew: b 1735 d 1802-4 m Anna Magdalena Groff Pvt PA
Michael: b 9-30-1756 d 9-14-1824 m Sophia Herblin Pvt PA ★

WISMER,
Abraham: b 11-5-1756 d 3-3-1844 m (1)Veronica Myers (2)Mary (Freed) Detweiler Pvt PA
Mark: b 1737 d 1831 m — Pvt PA

WISNER,
David: b 12-4-1758 d 6-18-1840 m (1)Sarah Blain (2)Deliverance Dowling Ens NY ★
Henry: b 7-11-1742 d 5-29-1812 m Susanna Goldsmith LCol NY
Henry, Sr.: b 1720 d 3-4-1790 m (1)Sarah Norton (2)Sarah (Cornell) Waters PS NY
Herny, Jr.: b 1741 d 4-11-1800 m Sarah Barnet PS NY
Jehiel: b 6-17-1762 d 1838 m (1)Rachel — (2)Sarah Ann Wiggins (3)Susanna Chandler Pvt NY ★
John, Sr.: b 1718 d 1778 ,m Anna — Capt NY
John, Jr.: b 1747 d 3-1-1811 m (1)Mary Thompson (2)Mrs Sarah Hall Capt NY
Samuel: b 1763 d 11-28-1848 m (2)Julaner Tedd Sgt NJ NY ★
Thomas: b c. 1738 d p. 1790 m — Winters Lt NY
Wm.: b 1746 d 1803 m Elizabeth Roe Pvt Sct PS NY

WISTAR,
John: b 1759 d 1815 m Charlotte Newbold Pvt PA

WISWALL, (or WISWELL)
Ebenezer: b 6-10-1722 d 3- -1809 m Irene Lane Pvt MA
Henry: b 8-24-1751 d 6-18-1814 m Joanna Thayer Pvt MA
Jeremiah: b 10-27-1725 d 1-26-1809 m (1)Elizabeth Murdock (2)Hannah Marean Capt MA
John: b 10-3-1753 d 12-28-1838 m (1)Esther Trowbridge (2)Lois Worsley Pvt MA
Jonathan: b 2-11-1737 d 1-17-1808 m Mary Daniels Lt MA

Masa: b 4-3-1762 d p. 1804 m Polly Heath Pvt MA
Noah: b 11-25-1727 d 8-10-1813 m (1)Hannah Hodges (2)Mary Pond Sgt PS MA
Noah: b 9-7-1699 d 6-13-1786 m (1)Thankful Fuller (2)Deliverance (Kendrick) Brown Pvt MA
Samuel: b 12-13-1761 d 2-14-1839 m Sallie or Salome Oakes Pvt VT ★
Samuel: b 1735 d 2-9-1810 m ( )Ruth — (2)Nancy Boyer Pvt VT
Thomas: b 1707 d c. 1790 m Sarah Daniell PS MA
Timothy: b 10-23-1741 d 3-29-1830 m Diadama Daniels Pvt MA

WITBECK, (or WHITBECK)
Gerrit Lucase: b 3-18-1752 d — m Emitje Perry PS NY
Isaac: bpt 6-4-1739 d 8-30-1793 m Jane Van Vechten PS NY
John: b 4-13-1747 d 2-10-1831 m Elizabeth Delamater Pvt NY
John A: b 1733 d 9-20-1786 m Aneka Bronk Capt NY
John L: b 6-5-1737 d p. 1800 m Cornelia Huyck Ens NY
Wm.: b 1-1-1755 d 12-31-1829 m Catherine DeForest Pvt NY

WITCHER, (or WHITCHER)
Chase: b 10-6-1753 d 2- -1836 m Hannah Morrill Pvt NH ★
Daniel: b 1746 d 1785 m Susanna — CS VA
Sargent: b 1755-60 d p. 1785 m Anna Clark Pvt NH
Wm., Sr.: b 1724 d 6-8-1808 m Anne — Maj PS VA

WITDERSTEIN,
John: b 7-12-1762 d 6-19-1835 m Margaret Kesler Pvt NY

WITHAM, (or WITHUM)
Andrew: b 1755 d 1-5-1840 m Lydia Grant Mar NH ★
Benjamin: bpt 3-28-1736 d 12-10-1814 m Ruth Ayer Pvt MA
Jedediah: b c. 1750 d 6-28-1778 m Hannah (Davis) Spinney Pvt MA
John: b p. 1753 d p. 1789 m Susanna Andrews Smn MA
Saunders: b 1737 d a. 1790 m Patience Harris Pvt Smn PS MA

WITHERBEE,
Thomas: b 1-12-1747 d 5-8-1828 m Relief Heuston Pvt MA
Zaccheus: b 12-27-1754 d 12-6-1796 m Sarah Snow Sgt MA

WITHERELL, (includes WETHERELL & WETHERILL)
Abijah: b 1756/6 d 3-16-1831 m Celia Bassett Sgt MA
Elisha: b 1760 d 5-12-1818 m Mary Bulkeley Pvt CT
George: b c. 1715 d p. 7-30-1804 m — PS NJ
James: b 6-16-1759 d 1-9-1838 m Amy Hawkins Adj MA
James: b 1754/5 d 3-16-1837 m (1)Susannah White (2)Priscilla Burt Pvt MA
John: b 1-25-1758 d 6-12-1854 m Mary Morrell Gerrish QM ME
John: b c. 1740 d p. 1790 m Anna Bolcom Drm Pvt MA
John: b 2-3-1730 d 1-15-1814 m Hannah — Col NJ
Josiah: b 3-12-1754 d 4-9-1840 m Lydia — Pvt MA
Obadiah: b 8-26-1748 d 12-15-1845 m Mary Bussell Lt MA ★
Samuel, Sr.: b 10-12-1736 d 9-24-1816 m — PS PA
Simeon: b a. 1757 d p. 1801 m Mary Pierce Pvt MA
Simeon: b 12-14-1748 d 2-9-1832 m Hannah Presho Lt VT
Solomon: b 9-6-1742 d 3-12-1826 m (1)Hepzibah Lincoln (2)Jerusha White (3)Anna Welsh Sgt MA
Solomon: b 10-25-1740 d p. 1790 m (1)Hannah Sweeting (2)Sarah Lincoln Ens MA
Thomas: b 10-16-1739 d 9-30-1817 m Rachel Fitz Randolph PS NJ

WITHERINGTON,
Daniel: b 2-4-1756 d p. 1840 m Mary Jones Pvt NC ★
Wm.: b 2-10-1741 d 9-22-1819 m Elizabeth — PS SC

WITHERS, (or WEATHERS)
Benjamin: b a. 1760 d 5- -1823 m Nancy Robinson Pvt VA
Elisha: b 8-10-1757 d 9-3-1840 m Sarah Gaskins Pvt NC W★
Enoch Keane: b 10-14-1760 d 1818 m Janet Chinn Adj VA
George: b c. 1745 d 1- -1795 m Mrs Ann Wilson Sharpless Pvt PA
George W: b 9-14-1747 d 5-23-1811 m Annie Kendig 2nd Lt PA
James: b c. 1752 d p. 3-25-1810 m Jemima — PS NC
James: b c. 1747 d 1791 m Elizabeth Rosser 2nd Lt VA
James: b c. 1748 d 1808 m Sarah Pickett Lt VA
James: b c. 1760 d 1840 m Nancy Hord Pvt VA
James: b 2-11-1716/7 d 1-9-1784 m (1)Catherine Barbee (2)Jemima Garner PS VA
John: b 1748 d p. 1790 m Mildred Horne Pvt NC
John: b 12-24-1729 d 12-24-1813 m Hannah Wilson Capt PA
John: b a. 1755 d p. 1800 m Frances Gray Lt SC
John: b 12-15-1738 d 6-12-1818 m (1)Hannah Routt (2)Dilly Allen Cpl VA
John, Sr.: b 1744/5 d p. 3-30-1827 m (1)Rosamond Duncan (2)Susanna Rosser PS VA
John Edmond: b c. 1738 d p. 1792 m Mary Wrenn Cpl VA
Spencer: b 1765 d 4-24-1843 m Ester (Potts) OrdlSgt VA ★
Thomas: b 2-15-1723 d 11-12-1794 m Elizabeth — Wgn VA
Wm.: b 1-4-1726 d 1-6-1804 m Elizabeth Barbey Lt VA
Wm.: b 1-31-1731 d 2-26-1816 m Priscilla Wright Lt VA
Wm.: b 3-21-1747 d 10-18-1821 m Hannah Rosser 2Lt VA
Wm.: b 1-20-1754 d 8- -1809 m Mary Withers Pvt VA
Willis: b 3-29-1759 d p. 10-1-1838 m —Terry Pvt NC ★

WITHERSPOON, (or WEATHERSPOON)
David: b 1732 d 1817 m Agnes Linn Lt NH
David: b 3-24-1760 d 4-21-1835 m (1)Elizabeth Bradley (2)Mary Story 2Lt SC ★
David: b 1738 d 1781 m (1)Janet Blakely (2)Jane Bryan Pvt SC
David: b 1758 d 5- -1828 m Elizabeth Gordon Lt NC
Gavin: b 1748 d 12- -1834 m (1)Elizabeth Dick (2)Mrs E Thompson Capt SC
Gavin: b 1747 d 5-18-1818 m (1)Esther Jane Witherspoon (2)Ann Witherspoon Sgt SC
James: b 1747 d 7-8-1838 m (1)Elizabeth Graham (2)Eliner Baird Black Capt NC
James: b 3-20-1759 d 9-29-1791 m Nancy White Capt SC
James: b 1741 d p. 1792 m (1)Jane Matthews (2)Ann Pressly (3)Jane Patterson (4)Eliza Raphiel (5)Elizabeth Bland Lt SC
John: b 2-5-1722 d 11-15-1794 m (1)Elizabeth Montgomery (2)Anne Marshall Dill SDI NJ
John: b 12-11-1756 d p. 3-4-1842 m (1)Margaret Carson Pvt NC ★
John: b 1726 d 11-7-1778 m Martha Pettigrew CS NC
John: b 10-14-1763 d 1-14-1839 m Elizabeth Shute Pvt NC ★
John, Sr.: b 1730 d 1805 m Mary Witherspoon Pvt SC
John, Jr.: b 1755 d 1827 m Rebecca (McBride) Ervin Lt SC
Mary: b 1764 d 6-11-1831 m Daniel Conyers PS SC
Wm.: b c. 1750 d 1818 m Mary Herkum Sol PS NC

WITHINGTON,
Ebenezer: b 10-19-1729 d 8-19-1806 m Mary Preston Capt MA
Francis: b 8-27-1739 d 8-18-1819 m (1)Rachel Mason (2)Elizabeth Townsend (3)Abigail Ramsdell Sol PS NH
Henry Bailey: b 8-4-1743 d 1-5-1836 m Sarah Bent Cpl MA
Hopestill: b 9-2-1707 d 12-28-1778 m Mary Baker Pvt MA
John: b 3-7-1717 d 1-16-1798 m (1)Martha Wentworth (2)Desire Liscom PS MA
Joseph Weeks: b 9-29-1759 d 5-13-1845 m Elizabeth White Pvt MA
Lemuel: b 10-25-1757 d 11-12-1847 m Anne Baker Fif MA
Peter: b 1-17-1733 d 5-11-1777 m Eve Albert Schepler Capt PA
Samuel: b 4-10-1720 d 10-29-1781 m Jane Kelton Lt MA
Wm.: b 1-17-1743 d 9- -1823 m Martha Locke Pvt MA

WITHROW, (or WITHEROW)
James: b 1746 d 12-6-1838 m Mary Bronson Lt NC ★
James: b 6-10-1764 d 1849 m — Pvt NC ★
John: b 1730 d 8-21-1794 m Margaret Barbour PS MD

WITHY, (includes WETHY, WITHEE & WITHEY)
James: b c. 1750 d p. 1790 m Sarah Claypoole Pvt NH
Jeduthan: b 10-3-1762 d 1845 m (2)Phoebe (Thorne) Comfort Pvt CT NY
Lemuel: b 6-6-1737 d p. 1790 m Mary Mulkins Ens CT
Zoe: b 4-22-1762 d 12-27-1840 m Sally Bettis Pvt NH ★

WITMAN, (or WITTMAN)
Christopher: b 1725 d 5- -1778 m Barbara — PS CS PA
George Adam: b — d p. 3-4-1806 m Margaret — PS PA
Wm.: b 1752 d 10-12-1808 m Catherine — Lt PA

WITMYER,
Simon: b 1730 d p. 9-10-1801 m Mary Klingenmyer CS PA

WITT, (includes DE WITT & WHITT)
Abner: b 3-27-1756 d 5-13-1812 m Molly Rowland Cpl MA
Artemus: b 1749 d 1823 m Eunice Peacock Sol NH
Benjamin: b 8-15-1750 d 4-17-1818 m Olivia Campbell Pvt MA
Burgess: b 1-12-1764 d 12-16-1843 m Elizabeth Mayo Pvt NC ★
Caleb: b 9-2-1762 d 1-20-1827 m Miriam Horner Pvt VA
David: b 1750 d — m Sally — PS VA
Elijah: b c. 1755 d 1806 m (1)— Hutchinson (2)Sally Batton Pvt NC
Elisha: b 9-18-1759 d 12-16-1835 m Phoebe Dodd Pvt VA
Ivory: b 10-20-1752 d 12-6-1820 m Abigail Montague Pvt MA
Jacob: b 11-15-1754 d 11-13-1835 m Eva Shultz Sgt PA ★
Jesse: b 5-11-1760 d 4-4-1852 m Ruth Whit Pvt NC
John, Jr.: b 1753 d 1825 m Elizabeth Luttrell Pvt VA
Jonathan: b 10-12-1758 d p. 1804 m Catherine — Sol VT
Joseph: b 1-2-1757 d 7-9-1839 m Lovisa Montague Pvt MA
Lewis: b c. 1748 d c. 1820 m Anne Mills MM VA
Littleberry: b 1755 d 1796 m Jenny Burnett Pvt VA
Robert: b 1760 d 1849 m Nancy Reese Pvt VA
Wm.: b 1756 d c. 1846 m Lettice Adkinson Pvt VA ★
Wm.: b c. 1765 d c. 1840 m Lucy Reeves PS VA
Zacchens: b 1757 d 7-2-1833 m Hannah Sawtelle Pvt NH

WITTER,
Asa: b 1744 d 1792 m Joanna Kinne PS CT
Ebenezer: b 11-30-1700 d 9-19-1789 m (1)Elizabeth Brown (2)Mary Avery Sol CT
Ebenezer: b 9-11-1732 d 8-22-1817 m (1)Amy Meach (2)Abigail Gier Capt CT
Ezra: b 1-4-1755 d p. 1800 m Patience — Pvt NY
Frederick: b 8-13-1752 d 12-6-1801 m Lydia Tyler Cpl CT
Isaac: b 1-10-1757 d 10-11-1843 m Margaret Owen Cook NY
James: b 6-11-1748 d p. 9-29-1788 m Frances Rivers Capt SC
Jonah: b 1758 d 1847 m Eunice Cady Pvt CT
Joseph: b 4-7-1762 d 1830 m Hannah Washburn Pvt MA

Josiah: b 2-21-1741 d c. 1818 m Mary Kimball Sgt CT
Josiah: b 1-25-1739 d 7-20-1828 m (1)Tacy Reynolds (2)Abigail Lawton Capt MA CT ★
Wm.: b 3-27-1707 d 9-9-1798 m (1)Mary Douglass (2)Zerviah Smith (3)Hannah Freeman (4)Mrs Elizabeth Bishop Lathrop (5)Mrs Elizabeth Draper PS CT

WIXOM,
Elijah, Sr.: b 1735 d 5-22-1805 m Mary — Pvt NY
Elijah, Jr.: b 1760 d 5-20-1826 m (1)Temperance Penny (2)Elizabeth Turner Pvt NY

WIXON,
Ebenezer: b a. 1752 d p. 1799 m Frances Gage Pvt NY
Solomon: b 8-10-1751 d 4-11-1813 m Mary Randall Sol NY

WODROW,
Andrew: b 11-14-1752 d 7- -1814 m Mary Ann Wilson LCol VA

WOFFORD,
James: b 1744 d 7-14-1815 m Katy Hoppock Pvt SC
John: b 1730 d 1812 m Eleanor Roland Pvt SC
Joseph: b 1743 d 1831 m Martha Llewellyn Capt SC
Wm.: b 10-25-1728 d 1823 m Sarah Cameron LCol CS PS SC

WOGAN,
Jacob: b a. 1749 d 5-29-1783 m Anne — Fif PA

WOHLGEMUTH,
John: b 11-27-1747 d 10-23-1812 m Mary Smith Sgt NY
Wm.: b 8-28-1763 d 3-26-1813 m Maria Countryman Cpl NY

WOHLPART, (includes WOHLFORD & WOLFORD)
George: b c. 1725 d a. 1-30-1794 m (1)Elizabeth Zimmerman (2)Elizabeth Bricker Pvt PA
Ludwick: b c. 1730 d 1810 m Anna Margaretha Hoeg Pvt PA
Peter: b c. 1750 d p. 1794 m Barbara Bricker Pvt PA

WOLCOTT, (includes WALCOTT & WALCUTT)
Alexander: b 1-7-1712 d 3-25-1795 m (1)Lydia Atwater (2)Mrs Mary Allyn (3)Mary Richards PS Dr CT
Benajah: b 1762 d 1832 m Elizabeth Bradley Pvt CT ★
Benjamin Stewart: b 7-27-1755 d 5-21-1824 m Marcy Dexter 1Lt RI
Christopher: b 10-1-1754 d 4-23-1821 m (1)Lucy Parsons (2)Amy Gillet Srgnmate CT
Elijah: b 1740 d 11-28-1823 m — Sgt CT
Elijah: b c. 1750 d 4-17-1813 m Mary Beecher Pvt CT W★
Elijah: b 1742 d 11-16-1829 m Dorcas Wright Pvt VT
Elisha: b 10-2-1755 d 1-17-1827 m Mary Welles Sol CT
Epaphras: b 5-2-1740 d 1-1-1825 m Mabel Burnham PS CT
Erastus, Sr.: b 9-21-1722 d 9-14-1793 m Jerusha (Wolcott) BG CT
Erastus, Jr.: b 1752 d 6-7-1797 m Chloe Bissell CS PS Capt CT
Frederick: b 11-2-1767 d 5-28-1837 m Elizabeth Huntington PS CT
Frederick: b 1-21-1740 d 12-27-1822 m Mary Taylor Pvt MA
George: b 1-18-1747 d 7-23-1809 m Elizabeth Nott Ens CT
Gideon: b 2-24-1750 d 12-22-1794 m Hannah Woodworth Sgt NY
Giles: b 7-16-1734 d 6-8-1819 m Sybil Alden Capt VT
Henry: b 5-15-1729 d 10-25-1813 m Dorcas Allen PS CT
Jabez: b c. 9-23-1711 d 11-27-1781 m Lydia Flint Pvt MA
Jabez: b 12-17-1756 d 8-19-1825 m Mary Baker Pvt MA
Jesse: b 2-27-1734 d 4-1-1800 m Rebecca Conant Pvt MA
John: b 1-24-1732 d 9-22-1811 m Sarah Gardner Cpl MA
John: b 6-14-1728 d 5-30-1807 m Rebecca Jones Capt MA
John: b 7-1-1759 d 1824 m Sarah — PS PA
Joseph: b c. 1755 d 1792 m Sarah Lothrop Fif CT W★
Joseph: b 1740 d 5-21-1808 m Elizabeth Bosworth Pvt MA
Josiah: b 9-17-1755 d 1-18-1838 m (1)Lydia Russell (2)Mrs Nancy (Williams) Higgins (3)Mrs Elizabeth Brown OrdlSgt CS CT ★
Justus: b 2-1-1735 d 4-29-1831 m (1)Rachel Bidwell (2)Mrs Edify Scott Pvt NY
Luke: b 1755 d p. 1790 m Mary Wheeler 1Lt NY
Moses: b 1759 d 3-6-1837 m (1)Olive Russell (2)Freelove Burton Pvt MA
Nathaniel: b 10-27-1741 d p. 1780 m Lydia Flint PS CT
Oliver: b 12-1-1726 d 12-1-1797 m Lorraine Collins SDI MajGen PS CT
Oliver: b 1-16-1761 d 8-10-1845 m Lydia Haynes Pvt MA
Roger: b 11-10-1737 d 1-18-1799 m Dorcas Burnham Ens CT
Roger: b 11- -1740 d 4- -1828 m (1)Mary Slater (2)Esther Wilson 1Lt NH
Samuel: b 4-4-1751 d 6-7-1813 m Jerusha (Wolcott) Cmsry CT
Samuel: b 11-15-1736 d 8-24-1824 m (1)Prudence Robbins (2)Mrs Elizabeth (Hinman) Beach Maj MA
Samuel: b 7-14-1752 d c. 1817 m (1)Mary — (2)Mrs Rhoda Brown Pvt MA
Samuel, Sr.: b 5-28-1727 d p. 1786 m Lucy Wright Sol VT
Silas: b 8-4-1755 d 6-4-1834 m Margaret Rowen Pvt PA ★
Simon: b 8-27-1733 d 7-2-1784 m Mary Gillett Capt CT
Simon: b 1747 d 1809 m Lucy Rodgers Dr CT
Solomon: b 6-21-1743 d 1-11-1811 m Sarah Wells Pvt CT
Solomon: b 9-1-1735 d 8-12-1829 m Abigail Hastings PS CT
Wm.: b 8-16-1730 d 2-25-1782 m Phebe Alling Cpl CT
Wm.: b 1-30-1754 d 3-11-1841 m (1)Rebecca Goodrich (2)Huldah Wells Pvt CT

Wm.: b 4-13-1761 d 6-23-1833 m Anna Macey Pvt MD ★
Wm.: b 7-21-1711 d 5-22-1799 m Abigail Abbott PS CT
Wm.: b 2-27-1745 d 11-25-1827 m Elizabeth Wetherbee Pvt MA
Wm.: b 1752 d 1834 m Sarah Wheeler Cpl NY
Wyatt: b 4-9-1739 d 7-28-1821 m Desire Saxton Sgt PS NY

WOLFE, (includes WOLF & WOLFF)
Adam: b 6- -1750 d 3-19-1835 m Maria Magdalena Schlegel Lt PA ★
Adam: b 12-15-1760 d 4-24-1845 m Rachel Oldham Pvt PA ★
Andrew: b — d p. 12-29-1804 m Margaret — Pvt PA
Anthony: b c. 1755 d 8-25-1810 m Mary Eldredge Pvt CT
Bernardt: b 1-1-1732 d 8-20-1792 m Anna Charlotte Bier Pvt PS PA
Christian: b 1744 d 9-10-1814 m Catherine Wolf Pvt PA
Daniel: b 8-25-1752 d 10-31-1794 m Catherine Smith Pvt PA
David: b c. 1754 d 12-22-1807 m Elizabeth — Pvt PA
Elias: b 6-24-1747 d 6-4-1827 m Barbara — Pvt PA
George, Sr.: b 1715 d 1790 m (1)Elizabeth — (2)Catherine Dierhamer Capt PA
George, Jr.: b 3-19-1737 d 11-5-1809 m Margaret — Pvt PA
George: b c. 1750 d 1809 m Catherine Schrower PS PA
George: b c. 1752 d 1839 m (1)Anna Maria — (2)Elizabeth Grove Pvt VA
George Wendell: b 3-16-1740 d 3-12-1826 m Anna Elizabeth Reid Pvt PA
Henry, Sr.: b 1724 d 11-16-1776 m Polly Seaburn Pvt PA
Henry, Jr.: b 1746 d 1821 m Elizabeth Mitchell Pvt PA
Henry: b 5-2-1762 d 1-18-1841 m Anna Dominy Pvt PA
Jacob: b 1745 d c. 1789 m Catherine Zook PS MD
Jacob: b 1751 d 3-4-1819 m Margaret Lepard Pvt NY
Jacob: b 1738 d 4-20-1835 m (1)Elizabeth Kline (2)Mrs Barbara Brightsel PS Pvt PA
Jacob: b 1740 d 11- -1786 m Anne Agatha — Pvt PA
Jacob: b 1740 d 1806 m Eva Krebsin Pvt PA
Jacob: b 4-4-1753 d 1838 m Christena King Pvt PA ★
Jacob: b c. 1760 d a. 1815 m Eleanor Gunsaulus Pvt PA
Jacob: b 6-5-1762 d 3-31-1830 m Cornelia Knight Pvt PA
Jacob: b 10-26-1734 d 12-15-1815 m Elizabeth — PS VA
John: b — d 1804 m Anna Maria Spangler Pvt PA
John Henry: b 12-4-1723 d 1-9-1809 m Anna Catherina Cammer Pvt PA
Jonas: b 12-27-1739 d p. 9-7-1787 m Appollonia Dick Lt PA
Lewis, Sr.: b 9-11-1752 d a. 8-1-1848 m Barbara — PS VA
Michael: b a. 1754 d c. 1825 m Margaret — Capt PA
Nicholas: b 1745 d 6-5-1817 m Frans (Wolf) Pvt PA
Peter: b 10-1-1724 d 2-27-1796 m Maria Elizabeth Haas PS PA
Peter: b 5-14-1757 d p. 1789 m Elizabeth Grove Pvt PA
Philip: b 1740 d 5-23-1817 m Elizabeth Files Sol NC
Philip: b 1755 d 4-25-1850 m Catherine — Pvt PA
Philip: b c. 1738 d 1823 m Maria Esther Burkhard Pvt PA
Sebastian: b c. 1740 d a. 10-30-1803 m (2)Katharine Cook 2Lt PA
Valentine: b 1-3-1742 d 10- -1781 m (1)Susannah — (2)Mary — Pvt PA

WOLFENBARGER, (or WOLFERSBERGER)
John: b c. 1724 d 11- -1788 m Hannah — PS VA
Philip: b 2-14-1739 d 7-14-1824 m (1)Margaret — (2)Charlotte — 1Lt PA

WOLFLEY, (or WOELFLEY)
John: b 3-30-1760 d 8- -1822 m (1)Elizabeth Haverling (2)Mrs Elizabeth Heintzelman McCartney Pvt PA
John Conrad: b 1732 d 1795 m Anna Catherine Shocky Pvt PS PA

WOLFSKILL,
Joseph: b c. 1730 d 1817 m X PS NC

WOLLERTON,
Charles: b c. 1705 d c. 5-13-1781 m Jane Chilcot Pvt PA

WOLVEN,
Adam: b — d 6-12-1811 m — Backer Sol NY
Hendricus: b 10-3-1740 d p. 1790 m Margrietjen Burhans PS NY
John: b 3-1-1743 d 9-26-1798 m Maritje Brink Pvt NY

WOMACK, (or WAMACK)
Abraham: b 4-22-1742 d 12-9-1804 m (1)Martha Mitchell (2)Martha — CS GA
Abraham: b 1726 d 5-6-1800 m Elizabeth — PS NC
Charles: b c. 1743 d a. 10-28-1811 m Agnes — 1Lt VA
David: b a. 1740 d p. 1804 m Mildred Pryor PS Sol NC
Jesse: b 1739 d 1815 m (1)Dorothy Prior (2)Phebe — Lt GA
Jesse: b 1744 d 8-2-1782 m Sarah Daniel Sol VA
John: b c. 1748 d 1827 m Mrs Lucy (Pryor) Tapley CS Sol NC
Massanello: b 5-24-1751 d a. 8-25-1837 m Elizabeth Venable Sgt Cmsry VA
Wm., Sr.: b 1710 d 9-26-1791 m Mary — PS VA

WOMBLE,
John: b 1756 d 1820 m (2)Catharine — Pvt NC ★

WOMELSDORF,
Daniel: b c. 1745 d c. 1800 m Anna Eva Weiser Capt PA

WOOD,
Aaron: b 5-4-1742 d 7-22-1818 m Freelove Mason Sgt MA
Aaron: b 10-3-1748/9 d 2-24-1812 m Dorothy Mead MM Pvt MA
Aaron: b 1762 d 1838 m (1)Mary Perkins (2)Olive Lamprey Pvt MA
Aaron: b 10-19-1762 d 7-4-1815 m (1)Lucy Jackson (2)Thier Bard Pvt MA
Aaron: b 1757 d 7-19-1834 m (1)Dorothea Moreland (2)Matilda Mayhew Pvt VA NC
Abel: b 12-22-1755 d 3-23-1846 m Phoebe Holden Pvt MA
Abijah: b 2-15-1754 d 7-24-1840 m Dorothy Wheeler Cpl MA
Abijah: b 3-22-1743 d 9-12-1819 m Esther Lewis Pvt MA
Abner: b 11-15-1744 d 10-18-1821 m Elizabeth Cross Capt CT ★
Abner: b 6-16-1758 d 9-22-1838 m Phoebe Potter Pvt RI ★
Abner: b 2.24-1731/2 d 5-10-1833 m Deborah Bearce Pvt MA
Abraham: b 7-30-1752 d 8-6-1804 m Lydia Johnson Drm MM MA
Abraham: b 12-25-1759 d 8-23-1842 m Phebe Irwin Pvt NY
Abraham: b 8-29-1762 d 8-30-1828 m Jane Gilbert Pvt NC
Amos: b 4-7-1756 d p. 1833 m Mercy Whiting Pvt MA ★
Andrew: b 1753 d 1787 m Mrs Elizabeth (Wood) Leister Sgt NY
Asa: b 8-4-1761 d 1-13-1844 m Hannah Dibble Pvt CT ★
Barnabas: b 7-26-1735 d 1808-10 m (1)Sibilla Darbee (2)Mary Alworth MM NY
Barnard: b c. 1758 d p. 1800 m Eleanor Codner Pvt RI
Barzillia: b 1754 d 12- -1831 m (1)Mary Shattuck (2)Anna Woodbury Pvt MA ★
Benjamin: b 6-23-1752 d 3-3-1828 m Tamar Warner Cpl CT
Benjamin: b 4-29-1751 d 4-4-1833 m Lucy Olds Pvt MA
Benjamin: b 12- -1755 d 1830 m Ruth Bailey Pvt MA
Benjamin: b 1740 d 1821 m Naomi Smith Ens RI
Benjamin: b c. 1760 d a. 12-8-1838 m Ailsey Abigail Duncan Pvt SC
Benjamin: b 4-30-1761 d 4-4-1829 m (1)Sarah Follice (2)Elizabeth Abbott Pvt VA
Bezaleel: b 1758 d 2-25-1818 m Mehitable Darby Pvt VT
Caldwell: b 1754 d 9-5-1845 rn Nancy Sublette Pvt VA ★
Caleb: b 1750 d 5-8-1789 m Huldah Greene Sol CT
Charles: b 6-27-1760 d 3- -1844 m Betsey Dewey Pvt Armr CT ★
Christopher: b 5-31-1763 d 12-21-1826 m Abigail Harrison Pvt NJ
Clement: b 1753 d 4/5-11-1823 m (1)Sarah Canfield (2)Mary — Ens NJ
Consider: b 1760 d 2-25-1822 m Mary Adams Pvt MA ★
Cornelius: b 1728 d 1798 m Sarah McCamley Pvt NY
Cornelius: b c. 1735 d p. 1816 m Mary Sharples Pvt PA
Daniel, Sr.: b 1726 d 12-1-1808 m Mary — PS CT
Daniel, Jr.: b 1752 d 9-21-1829 m (1)Wealthy Munrow (2)Mrs Lydia Lobdell Pvt PS CT
Daniel: b 7-13-1739 d 6-27-1819 m (1)Hannah Carleton (2)Mrs Mary Roberts (Plummer) Philpot Maj MA
Daniel: b 2-27-1749/50 d 5-23-1821 m Rebekah Ingalls Pvt MA
Daniel: b 3-10-1757 d p. 1790 m Meribah Hayward Sgt MA
Daniel: b 1754 d 12-23-1846 m (1)Mrs Perry (2) — (3)Sarah Barnes Pvt MA ★
Daniel: b — d p. 8-18-1832 m Hannah Barrett Pvt MA
Daniel: b 6-29-1751 d 10-3-1843 m (1)Mary Scofield (2)Catherine Crouse Dr Capt NY ★
Daniel B.: b 1757 d 3-15-1815 m Priscilla Farmer Sol VA
Daniel Smith: b 1741/2 d 2-8-1832 m (1)Mary Potter (2)Sarah Johnson Capt NJ
David: b 9-14-1759 d 10-25-1835 m (1)Rebecca King (2)Mrs Electa Hosmer Cpl CT ★
David: b 1738 d 9-28-1811 m Sarah Ingersoll Pvt CT
David: b 9-30-1719 d 6-4-1796 m Mary Hovey Lt MA
David: b 6-13-1746 d p. 1790 m Elizabeth Inman Pvt MA
David: b 8-11-1748 d 9-26-1835 m Molly Farnum Pvt MA
David: b 9-9-1748 d 3-2-1836 m Eleanor Cooley Pvt MA ★
David: b 12-19-1763 d 12-19-1846 m Princes Danks Pvt MA ★
David: b 1737 d 1813 m Mary Watson Pvt VA
Ebenezer: b 3-13-1736 d 2-13-1803 m Sally Bennett Pvt MA
Ebenezer: b 1-20-1754 d 12-28-1840 m Phebe Brooks Pvt MA ★
Ebenezer: b 1754 d 10-23-1831 m (1)Mary Hutchins (2)Celinda M S D Dart Pvt MA ★
Ebenezer: b 1760 d 11-18-1840 m Charity Miers Pvt NJ
Ebenezer: b 10-6-1729 d 4-18-1810 m (1)Christina Tremper (2)Margaret Hubbard CS PS NY
Ebenezer: b 11-15-1726 d — m Philippa Story Col PS VT
Edmond: b 1721 d 12-29-1805 m Patience Farnham Pvt MA
Edward: b a. 1760 d p. 1809 m Sarah — Pvt NH
Eleazer: b 1762 d 1845 m Patience Shaw Pvt MA
Elijah: b 12-23-1736 d 2-8-1788 m Isabel Wood Pvt MA
Elijah: b 5-15-1744 d 2-11-1810 m Mrs Mercy Lothrop PS NY
Eliphalet: b 6-4-1754 d 8- -1833 m Elizabeth Tilton Cpl MA
Enoch: b 12-24-1763 d 8-27-1847 m (1)Sibble Sprague (2)Elizabeth Taylor (3)Lydia Rockwell Pvt NY ★
Enos: b 2-23-1761 d 2-22-1851 m Asenath Hazen Cpl VT ★
Ephraim: b 8-1-1733 d 4-8-1814 m (1)Mary Heald (2)Mrs Millicent Barrett PS CS MA
Ephraim: b c. 1744 d 12-9-1831 m Sarah French Pvt MA
Ephraim: b 3-4-1762 d 12-5-1836 m Martha Jackman Pvt NH ★
Ephraim: b 11-20-1755 d 8-21-1830 m Esther Eastman Pvt NY
Ezekiel: b 10-29-1724 d 10-29-1781 m Mary Collins Dr MA
Ezekiel: b 2-5-1743/4 d 9-15-1811 m Sarah Albee PS MA
Ezra: b 3-15-1726 d 8-29-1815 m — Annah Chapin Col MA
George: b 6-3-1762 d 9- -1820 m Sarah Sartwell Pvt MA

WOOD, contd.

George: b 11-29-1753 d 8-22-1832 m (1)Elizabeth Whitman (2)Ann Corwine Matr PS PA
George: b 11-2-1730 d 6- -1820 m (1)Comfort Taylor (2)Desire Gray Lt RI
Gerad: b 1754 d 11- -1822 m Winifred Chunn Srgr Mte MD
Gideon: b 7-10-1759 d 4-6-1843 m Kezia Owen PS CT
Henry: b 1755 d 1843 m Nancy Scott Pvt MD
Henry: b 9-18-1757 d 6-18-1814 m Hannah Eldridge Capt NJ
Henry: b 1753 d p. 1832 m Nancy Butler Pvt NC ★
Henry: b 12-16-1756 d 6-12-1842 m (1)Susan Elizabeth Mayfield (2)Nancy Burns Pvt NC
Henry: b c. 1720 d p. 1796 m Elizabeth — PS NC
Hezekiah: b c. 1740 d 1801 m Deborah Cluckston Pvt CT
Hezekiah: b 7-1-1748 d 5-26-1811 m Lucy Treadway Cpl MA
Holland: b 1750 d 5-30-1835 m Abigail Cheney Sgt MA
Isaac: b 8-31-1743 d 12-16-1797 m Luranie Southworth Capt MA
Isaac: b 9-7-1746 d 1-5-1835 m Elizabeth Hartwell Ens PS NH
Isaac: b 6-16-1752 d 6-6-1839 m (1)Susannah — (2)Bathsheba Walker Lt RI ★
Isaac: b 7-5-1741 d 7-25-1813 m (1)Susan Grayson (2)— Tomlin Pvt VA
Isaac: b 12-26-1729 d 4-21-1803 m Rachel Ramey Sol PS VA
Israel: b 8-14-1738 d 4-6-1818 m Sarah Stevens Pvt MA
Israel: b 10-16-1744 d 11-13-1800 m Phebe Holt 1Lt MA
Israel: b c. 1758 d p. 8-1-1811 m Anna Randall Pvt NY
James: b 5-2-1751 d 5-16-1840 m Rebecca Humphrey Sol Pvt CT
James: b 3-12-1731/2 d 1793 m Achsah Phinney Pvt MA
James: b 11-4-1755 d 7-31-1838 m Elizabeth Buss Pvt MA ★
James: b 6-14-1746 d 9-24-1816 m Margaret Sharon Pvt VA
James, Sr.: b 1725 d 1779 m Martha Allen Mstr VA
Japhet: b 3-9-1768 d p. 2-4-1831 m Abigail Dailey Pvt MA ★
Jehu: b 5-17-1748 d 7-6-1783 m Mary Kinsey Reeve Capt NJ
Jeremiah: b 2-2-1755 d 8-25-1841 m Sarah Updike Pvt NJ
Jeremiah: b 11-17-1713 d 6-26-1797 m Mary — Pvt NY
Job: b 1750 d 3-14-1824 m Jane Campbell Matr NY RI W★
Job: b 7-31-1737 d p. 1781 m Theoda Walbridge Cpl VT
John: b 11-19-1729 d 8-31-1805 m Mary Chapin Capt CT
John, Jr.: b 1759/60 d 4-19-1832 m Abby Fish Sgt CT ★
John: b c. 1756 d 4-14-1833 m Abigail Church Pvt CT
John: b 6-22-1757 d 4-26-1845 m (1)Elizabeth Williams (2)Hester (Caulkins) Lee Pvt CT ★
John: b 11-29-1754 d 11-11-1832 m (1)Martha Ogle (2)Rachel (Greathouse) Bratton Ens MD W★
John: b 11-10-1757 d 12-6-1823 m Elizabeth Watson Drm Fif MD
John: b 1763 d 7-28-1843 m Elizabeth Sunderland Pvt MD
John: b 8-23-1740 d 10-19-1809 m Dorcas Smith Capt MA
John: b 2-29-1745 d 7-8-1812 m Lydia Hosmer Sgt MA
John: b 6-25-1731 d 2-12-1831 m Mary Parmer Cpl MA
John: b 3-12-1753 d 1-15-1832 m Susannah Temple Cpl MA ★
John: b 9-3-1747 d 5-4-1826 m Lucy Martin Pvt MA
John: b 4-29-1751 d 12-28-1830 m Lois Olds Pvt MA
John: b 7-3-1753 d 1- -1844 m — Pvt NJ ★
John: b 7-29-1738 d 8-19-1824 m Ann Reeves PS CS NJ
John: b 1743 d 8-4-1810 m (1)Hannah Hopkins (2)Hannah Carpenter Adj NY
John: b 12-10-1739 d 4-10-1806 m Rebecca Cain Capt NY
John: b — d 1804 m Sarah — Sgt NY
John: b c. 1755 d 1800 m Sarah Hulse Pvt NY
John: b 1763 d 1841 m Margaret Vander Worker Pvt NY
John: b c. 1740 d 10- -1784 m — Pvt PA
John: b 8-12-1759 d 6-12-1840 m Phoebe Arnold Pvt RI ★
John: b 1745 d 11- -1781 m Rebecca Berry Of SC
John: b 1732 d 1814 m Sarah Baker Pvt SC
John: b 1-6-1731/2 d 3-9-1810 m Hannah Richardson Pvt VT
John: b c. 1740 d p. 1-30-1799 m Hannah — Sgt VA
John: b 1763 d 4-23-1853 m — Ricks Smn VA
John: b 1725 d 1802 m Nancy Drury Pvt VA
John: b c. 1735 d 1816/17 m Maiden Seay Pvt VA
John: b 1757 d 1843 m Mary Terrill Pvt VA
John: b 6-5-1744 d 5-29-1829 m Margaret Robinson Pvt VA
John: b c. 1755 d p. 1836 m (1)Phebe Durham (2)Peggy Martin Pvt VA
Jonah: b 1761-5 d 1819 m Mary Dickson Pvt CT
Jonah: b 1742 d 1816 m Sarah Bryan Pvt NY
Jonas: b 1756 d — m Lois Howel MM NY
Jonathan, Sr.: b 9- -1730 d 12-15-1804 m Rachel Wood Capt MA
Jonathan, Jr.: b 3-25-1760 d 8-20-1814 m Martha White Fif Pvt MA
Jonathan: bpt 9-23-1716 d 6-9-1781 m Sarah Redington Pvt MA
Jonathan: b 8-3-1727 d 10-18-1797 m (1)Abigail Daby (2)Katharine Gardner Pvt MA
Jonathan: b 11-16-1738 d p. 1784/5 m Lillace Wood Pvt MA
Jonathan: b 6-13-1746 d 9-23-1823 m Mehitable Luther Pvt MA RI ★
Jonathan: b 1754 d 7-31-1826 m Grace Hastings Pvt NH
Jonathan: b 1-21-1741 d 1777 m Millicent Stretch Capt NJ
Jonathan: b 1729 d 1-4-1804 m Jerusha Halsey PS NJ
Jonathan: b 6-9-1752 d 6-11-1795 m (2)Jane Wilson Pvt NY
Jonathan: b 10-11-1755 d 12-22-1800 m Mary Durland Pvt NY
Jonathan: b 1745 d 11-13-1804 m Nancy (Davidson) Osborne Sol PS VA
Joseph: b 1-25-1755 d 8-4-1836 m Mary St John Pvt CT

Joseph, Sr.: b 1710 d 1782 m (1)Sarah Hodgson (2)Catherine Julian CS MD
Joseph: b c. 1710 d c. 1788 m Evaline Burgess PS MD
Joseph, Jr.: b 9-17-1743 d p. 1800 m Anne Reed Col MD
Joseph: b 9-24-1739 d 1-21-1808 m Mercy Blashfield 1Lt MA
Joseph: b 2-24-1761 d 4-17-1826 m Bethiah (Palmer) Gray Sgt MA ★
Joseph, Jr.: b 8-21-1755 d 8-7-1821 m Martha Willard Pvt MA
Joseph: b 1734 d 5-7-1801 m Mary Varnum Pvt MA
Joseph: b 1748 d 10-13-1820 m Miriam Collester Pvt MA
Joseph, Sr.: b 12-25-1724 d 11-2-1798 m Ann Palmer Pvt NH
Joseph, Jr.: b 11-8-1759 d 12-17-1859 m Sarah Gerrish Pvt NH
Joseph: b 1747 d 3- -1822 m Abigail Kitchel Fif Sol VT
Joseph: b — d p. 1781 m Elizabeth — PS VA
Joshua: b 1-26-1747 d p. 1789 m Mary Crane Pvt CT
Joshua: b 10-16-1727 d 12-3-1803 m (1)Elizabeth Campbell (2)Mrs Lucy Butler Capt MA
Josiah: b 3-9-1740 d c. 1792 m Ruth Thompson Pvt CT
Josiah: b c. 1737 d 11-3-1815 m Zipporah Wheelock Capt PS MA
Josiah, Jr.: b 1740 d 2-11-1824 m Salome Woods Pvt MA
Judah: b 1730 d 3-22-1783 m Hannah Porter Lt MA
Lashley: b c. 1740 d p. 8-15-1809 m — Lucas Capt VA MD
Leighton, Jr.: b c. 1746 d 3-9-1820 m Ann Blagrove CS VA
Lemuel: b 8-6-1761 d 7-4-1808 m Elizabeth Kundle Pvt CT W★
Levi: b 12-12-1755 d 8-10-1833 m Bethany Fuller Pvt MA
Mathew: b 12-20-1757 d 10-21-1839 m Margaret Moss Fif Maj VA
Moses: b 5-7-1748 d 1810 m Sarah Barker Pvt MA
Nathan: b 4-16-1761 d 11- -1832 m Lucy Johnson Pvt CT
Nathan: b 5-15-1735 d 3-23-1816 m Martha Farrington Sgt MA
Nathan, Sr.: b 3-24-1723 d 6-18-1777 m Rebecca Haines PS MA
Nathan, Jr.: b 11-7-1752 d 1-6-1841 m (1)Mehitable Cowey (2)Margaret Hadley Pvt MA
Nathan: b 9-16-1761 d 5-31-1839 m Zilpha Sprague Pvt NY
Nathan: b 8-16-1758 d 3-26-1830 m Susannah Dutton Pvt MA W★
Nathaniel, Sr.: b 1725 d 6-25-1803 m (1)Martha Tinkham (2)Mary Winslow Capt MA
Nathaniel, Jr.: b 4-6-1749 d 1825 m Desire Shaw 1Cpl MA
Nathaniel: b 5-23-1742 d 3- -1818 m Rhoda Brewer Lt MA
Nathaniel: b p. 7-14-1737 d 3-12-1776 m Abigail Carver Sgt MA
Nathaniel: b 11-19-1729 d 1813 m Miriam Wood Sgt VT
Nehemiah, Jr.: b 3-10-1766 d 11- -1849 m Sarah Brown Mil NY
Obadiah: b 8-19-1749 d 3-10-1818 m Jerusha Stedman Pvt CT
Oliver: b 4-11-1730 d 7-1-1816 m Lucy Hosmer Pvt MA
Peleg: b 4-10-1752 d 3-1-1825 m Esther Brush PS NY
Peter: b 6-23-1740 d 3-5-1820 m Sybil Howe CS MA
Peter: b 1-24-1749 d 9-15-1829 m Sarah Standish Tinkham Sol MA
Peyton: b 1750 d c. 1824 m Mercy Daniel Sol PS NC
Philip: b 4-29-1756 d 7-16-1845 m Eunice Pierce Pvt MA
Preserve: b 5- -1756 d 11-26-1806 m Mercy Benidict SrgnMte CT
Reuben: b 1742 d 3- -1801 m Jonothea — Pvt NJ
Reuben: b 2-21-1754 d 2-10-1836 m (1)Mary Ann Demming (2)Marcy Phillips Sgt RI
Richard: b 3-18-1727/8 d 5-1-1807 m (1)Hannah Davis (2)Mary (Stewart) Bacon PS NJ
Richard: b 1733 d 2-14-1810 m Joanna Wood Pvt NY
Robert: b 1717 d 10-15-1800 m Abigail Barber PS CT
Robert: b 8-12-1736 d 1792 m Catherine Dorsey Capt PS MD
Robert: b 8-9-1756 d 10-1-1831 m Eleanor Vansant Pvt PA
Robert: b 1756 d 12-3-1840 m Mary Green Pvt RI ★
Robert: b 7-27-1747 d 1801 m Comfort Welch PS VA
Samuel: b 4-3-1716 d 1-22-1807 m Jerusha Abbe Pvt CT
Samuel: b c. 1729 d p. 6- -1776 m Lydia Ripley Chp CT
Samuel: b 12-11-1750 d 6-17-1830 m Abiah Peirce Pvt MA
Samuel: b 1-26-1761 d 10-8-1828 m (1)Anna Calef (2)Huldah Cole Pvt MA
Samuel, Jr.: b 7-24-1748 d p. 1779 m Rebecca Brooks Pvt NH
Samuel: b 4-6-1765 d 5-11-1853 m Elizabeth Smith Pvt NY ★
Samuel: b 5-2-1737 d a. 8- -1800 m (1)Mary Robertson (2)Sarah Reives Sol NC
Samuel C.: b 3-15-1755 d 7-29-1837 m Elizabeth Sperry Pvt CT ★
Silas: b 5-23-1729 d 10-21-1806 m Priscilla Cobb Pvt MA
Silas: b 8-22-1753 d 1814 m Asenath Wood Sgt NH
Silvanus: b 1-27-1749 d 8-12-1840 m (2)Deborah Bruce Lt MA
Solomon: b 4-6-1750 d 8-17-1815 m Elizabeth Eason Capt GA
Solomon: b 5-14-1744 d 6-17-1822 m Hannah Fish MM Lt MA
Solomon: b 1756 d 6-5-1820 m Eunice Hall Pvt MA
Solomon: b 3-31-1762 d 2-26-1846 m Parthena Hutchins Pvt VT ★
Stephen: b 11-9-1732 d 10-9-1828 m Bethesda Kibby Pvt MA
Stephen: b 4-11-1751 d 6-9-1835 m Jemima Taft Pvt MA ★
Stephen: b 2-18-1741 d 3-30-1805-15 m Naomi Smith PS NY
Stephen: b 4-14-1749 d 12-27-1831 m Hannah Storrs Cpl VT
Theophilus: b a. 1756 d 1791-5 m Tabitha Wheeler Pvt NY
Thomas: b 1- -1755 d 4-1-1843 m Hannah Alden Pvt CT ★
Thomas: b 1-24-1720 d p. 1783 m Dinah Perry PS CT
Thomas: b 1753 d 1822 m Dorothy Carleton Sol MA
Thomas: b 9-9-1719 d 7-17-1811 m Mary Taylor Sgt MA
Thomas: b 3-17-1753 d 9-28-1824 m Lois Pratt Sgt MA ★
Thomas: b 2-24-1731 d 10-22-1817 m Sarah Thomas Pvt MA
Thomas: b 4-8-1744 d 6-13-1813 m (1)Allis Bailey (2)Mrs Sarah Wallingford Fif MA
Thomas, Sr.: b 3-11-1707/8 d p. 1792 m (1)Abigail Rand (2)Rebecca Osborn PS MA

Thomas, Jr.: b 3-22-1742 d 1-23-1814 m Mary Davenport Pvt MA
Thomas: b *c.* 1740 d *p.* 1790 m Rebecca Yerkes Sol PA
Thomas: b 1727 d 7- -1814 m (1)Mary Fisk (2)Susanna — Pvt RI
Thomas: b 3-3-1740 d 1799 m Katherine Carter SgtMaj VA
Thurston: b 1760 d 4-17-1838 m Katherine Beckwood Tms NY
Timothy: b 4-8-1757 d 9-10-1835 m Mrs Susanna (Warner) DeMilt Pvt CT
Timothy: b 3-2-1757 d 1848 m Esther Hustis Pvt NY ★
Timothy, Sr.: b *c.* 1702 d *a.* 5-6-1780 m Hannah Oldfield PS NY
Timothy, Jr.: b 1740 d *p.* 1790 m Petrenella Van Dyke Pvt NY
Titus: b 11-5-1756 d 1-30-1839 m Susanna — Pvt MA
Valentine: b 9-2-1724 d 3-13-1781 m Lucy Henry CS VA
Wm.: b *c.* 1750 d 11-2-1800 m Sarah Perkins Pvt CT
Wm., Sr.: b 8-31-1735 d 1810 m (1)Susanna How (2)Elizabeth Gale Pvt MA
Wm., Jr.: b 4-18-1764 d 2-2-1850 m Sally Andrews Sgt MA ★
Wm.: b 10-23-1760 d 5-6-1832 m Phebe Goulding Cpl MA W★
Wm.: b 10- -1755 d 8-17-1827 m Anna Soule Pvt MA
Wm.: b 1723 d 1794 m (1)Hannah Hicks (2)Susanna (Lombard) Stuart Pvt MA
Wm.: b 3-6-1752 d 1-14-1827 m Susannah Wright Pvt NH
Wm.: b 1737 d 4-26-1804 m Martha Kendrick Capt NC
Wm.: b 7-15-1751 d 9- -1837 m — Boggan Pvt NC ★
Wm.: b *c.* 1765 d 1824 m Ann Granberry Pvt NC
Wm.: b 12-28-1734 d 12-28-1806 m Margaret Mitchell Pvt PA
Wm., Jr.: b 7-21-1735 d 10-8-1812 m Elizabeth Gorton Pvt RI
Wm.: b 5-5-1748 d 7-11-1819 m Sarah Stark 2Lt VA
Wm.: b *a.* 1755 d 5-20-1820 m (1)Marther Glenn (2)Elizabeth Burke Ens VA
Zebedee: b 3-30-1732 d 6-6-1803 m Esther Hough Pvt MA
Zebedee: b 2-14-1745 d 7-11-1824 m Mary — Sol NC

WOODALL,
John: b 1-25-1734 d *a.* 1-8-1802 m Mary Everett Pvt MD
Wm.: b 5-7-1737 d 1780 m Mary Mann Capt MD

WOODBRIDGE,
Benjamin, Sr.: b 6-7-1711 d 1797 m Susanna Tappan PS ME
Benjamin, Jr.: bpt 9-30-1739 d 9-17-1817 m Ann Hodge Adj MA
Benjamin: b 1-7-1757 d 4-13-1846 m Martha Melende Pvt MA
Enoch: b 12-25-1750 d 4-1-1805 m Nancy Winchell Adj VT
Henry: b 1748 d 9-6-1781 m Michal Street Pvt CT
Howell: b 3-17-1746 d 6-13-1796 m Mary Plummer Col CT
Jahleel: b 1738 d 1796 m Lucy Edwards PS Capt of MM MA
John, Sr.: b 12-25-1702 d 9-10-1783 m (1)Tryhena Ruggles (2)Mrs Martha Strong PS MA
John, Jr.: b 7-24-1732 d 12-27-1782 m Mary Whitney Maj MA
Russell: b 5-8-1719 d 11-5-1782 m Anna Olmstead PS CT
Samuel: b 1732 d 7-4-1794 m Martha Olmstead Pvt CT
Samuel: b 8-21-1730 d 1804 m (1)Patience Locke (2)Abra Twombly Pvt MA
Theodore: b 1-10-1748 d 11-28-1806 m Esther Plummer Brig Maj CT
Theophilus: b 3-23-1754 d 11-8-1815 m Mary Noble Lt CT

WOODBURN,
George: b 9-15-1722 d *p.* 1782 m Mary Culver Pvt CT
John: b 4-25-1763/2 d 7-6-1823 m Nancy Whitman PS CT
Moses: b 10-2-1764 d 12-30-1836 m Asenath Wright CT ★

WOODBURY, (includes WOODBERRY)
Abel: b 10-20-1731 d 12- -1778 m Jerusha Day Capt PS MA
Bartholomew: b 11-10-1740 d 7-7-1819 m Ruth Greenwood Col MA
Benajah: b 2-21-1747 d 2-22-1802 m Abigail Stockwell Pvt MA
Benjamin: b 10- -1750 d 4-20-1809 m Zilla Dow Sgt NH
Benjamin: b 4-18-1699 d 8-22-1781 m Ruth Conant Pvt MA
Benjamin: b 2-5-1726 d 10-17-1793 m Hannah Putnam CS PS MA
Benjamin: b 10-31-1761 d 3-3-1849 m Rhoda Collins Pvt MA ★
Daniel: b 5-21-1753 d 11-5-1837 m Mrs Mehitable Bailey Pvt MA ★
Ebenezer: b 9-12-1760 d *p.* 1790 m Elizabeth Wheeler Pvt NH
Ebenezer: b 9-20-1760 d 1835 m Mrs Rebecca Parker Pomeroy Pvt NH ★
Elisha, Sr.: b 12-20-1735 d 4-28-1816 m (1)Elisabeth Peaslie (2)Sarah — (3)Rhoda Bidwell Capt NH
Ezekiel: b 12-4-1734 d 10-21-1821 m (2)Anna Hubbard Pvt MA
Gideon: b 8-31-1757 d 1- -1816 m Hannah Bisson Pvt MA
Issac, Jr.: b 2-17-1759 d 1-2-1845 m Anna E Kimball Pvt MA
Israel: b 4-13-1756 d 8-23-1847 m Anna Morgan Pvt MA
Israel: b 12-10-1759 d 10-16-1859 m Mehitable Hall Pvt NH
Jacob Brown: b 7-30-1756 d 2-17-1839 m Hannah Roberts Pvt PS MA ★
James: b 6-4-1738 d 3-3-1823 m Hannah Trask PS NH
James Hill: b 4-15-1758 d 3-11-1840 m Olive Corliss Pvt NH ★
Jesse: b 10-22-1762/3 d 10-6-1802 m Abigail Boutwell Pvt NH
John: b 9-26-1749 d 12-12-1831 m (1)Mary Chase (2)Esther Bixby Lt MA
John: b 6-30-1752 d 3-18-1821 m Mary Ward Pvt MA
John: b 1735 d 6-7-1806 m Joanna (Mitchell) Plummer Pvt MA
John: b 1757 d 1-20-1783 m Sarah Adams Pvt MA
John: b 5-14-1753 d 2-28-1829 m Elizabeth Sanborn PS NH
Jonathan: b 11-25-1740 d 3-2-1828 m Hannah Dudley Capt MA
Jonathan: b 4-6-1762 d 12-4-1827 m Hannah Woodbury Pvt MA
Jonathan: b 12-11-1713 d 9-5-1776 m Lydia Dodge Sol NH

Joseph: b 9-21-1741 d 2-3-1816 m (1)Huldah Putnam (2)Mrs Abiel Porter Pvt MA
Joshua: b 3-25-1723 d 4-15-1782 m Dorcas Parks Pvt MA
Josiah: b 1-18-1753 d 9-29-1808 m (1)Sarah Harmon (2)Mrs Sarah Brazill (3)Betsey Woodberry Pvt MA
Luke: b 11-25-1755 d 7-4-1845 m Charity Taylor Pvt MA ★
Luke: b 1751 d 3-6-1827 m Elizabeth Kemp Lt NH ★
Nathan: b 11-28-1759 d 1-16-1838 m Elizabeth Boyd Slr MA ★
Nathaniel: b 4-1-1720 d 12-23-1805 m Abigail Dike Pvt MA
Nathaniel: b 2-24-1715 d *p.* 1783 m Rebecca — PS NH
Nicholas: b 5-31-1743 d 7-14-1831 m (1)Elizabeth Smith (2)Mrs Sarah Clark Pvt MA
Peter, Sr.: b 5-20-1736 d 2-24-1806 m (2)Zerviah Greenwood Capt MA
Peter, Jr.: b 3-14-1755 d 5-7-1833 m Elizabeth Moody Pvt MA
Peter: b 6-20-1705 d 5-14-1755 m Hannah Batchelder Sgt MA
Peter: b 4-18-1724 d *p.* 1783 m Hannah White PS ME
Peter: b 3-28-1738 d 10-11-1817 m Elizabeth (Dodge) Rea Pvt PS NH
Richard, Sr.: b 1749/50 d *p.* 3-19-1808 m Elizabeth Bellune PS SC
Samuel: bpt 5-17-1724 d 7-24-1814 m (1)Christian Lovett (2)Rebecca Holden Pvt MA
Thomas: b 5-19-1743 d 1789 m Jane Homans Slr MA
Wm.: b 11-24-1758 d 10-11-1810 m Hannah Kelley Pvt NH
Zachariah: b 1-8-1730 d 2-8-1815 m ( )Hannah Corning (2)Louisa Chandler Sgt PS NH

WOODCOCK,
Benjamin: b 6-12-1707 d 10-25-1791 m Margaret White Pvt MA
David: b 6-4-1742 d 12-7-1790 m Abigail Holmes Sgt MA
John: b 6-15-1744 d 3-22-1822 m Elizabeth Capron Sgt MA
Jonathan: b 7-21-1729 d 1786-90 m Abagail Hill Pvt NH
Nathan: b 1-9-1737 d *c.* 1817 m Lovina Goodenowe PS NH
Nathaniel: b 1748-50 d 1- -1826 m Rebecca A Healey Pvt MA
Nehemiah: b 1737 d 3-10-1816 m Hannah Bristol Lt MA
Samuel J.: b 1755 d 10-21-1833 m Rhoda Bishop Sgt CT ★

WOODDELL,
James: b 1760 d 1819 m Elizabeth — Pvt PA
Joseph: b 1752 d 7-26-1834 m Elizabeth — 1Lt VA ★

WOODFIELD, (or WOODFILL)
Joseph: b 9-17-1754 d 9-20-1798 m Catherine Godschall Pvt PA

WOODFIN,
John, Sr.: b 1740 d 1805 m Polly James Pvt VA
Nicholas: b 8-2-1759 d 12-21-1832 m Hannah Mary Ashbrook Pvt VA

WOODFORD,
Bissel: b 4-10-1754 d 9-3-1835 m Delightful Thompson Pvt CT ★
Catesby: b 1738-41 d 10- -1791 m Mary Buckner PS VA
Dudley: b 1753 d 1803 m (1)Elizabeth Ford (2)Candace North Pvt CT
Ezekiel: b 1748 d 5-10-1820 m Anne Bishop Capt CT
Joseph, Sr.: b 1705 d 2-4-1783 m Sarah North PS CT
Joseph, Jr.: b 3-12-1732 d 1823 m (1)Elizabeth Hart (2)Eunice (Hart) Cowles Capt CT
Wm., Sr.: b 11-13-1722 d 3-26-1803 m Susanna Garrett Capt CT
Wm.: b 10-6-1734 d 11-13-1780 m Mary Thornton BGen VA
Wm., Jr.: b 1747 d — m Esther Wilcox Ens CT
Wm.: b *c.* 1730 d *c.* 1779 m Fanny — Pvt VA

WOODHOUSE,
Abijah: b 4-25-1762 d 6-2-1810 m Jane Deming Pvt CT
Henry: b 3-5-1761 d 10-6-1841 m Catharine Owen Cpl VT ★
John: b 10-1-1723 d 12-15-1786 m Anne Nott Lt CT
Jonathan: b *c.* 1750 d 1823 m (1)Anna Barnes Lt VA
Samuel: b 12-23-1756 d 9-6-1834 m Thankful B — Pvt CT ★
Wm.: b *c.* 1750 d *c.* 1783 m Susan Pallett Capt VA

WOODHULL,
Abigail Howell: b 9-16-1745 d 11-16-1829 m Ebenezer Woodhull PS NY
Ebenezer: b 5-24-1741 d 10-7-1803 m Abigail Howell Capt NY
Jesse: b 2-10-1735 d 2-4-1795 m Hester Dubois Col NY
John: b 1760 d 2-4-1805 m Catherine Smith Pvt NY
John: b 1-15-1719 d 1-3-1794 m Elizabeth Tangier Smith PS NY
John: b 2-24-1727 d 4-2-1808 m Frances Satterly PS NY
John: b 1-26-1744 d 12-22-1824 m Sarah Spofford Chp PA
Josiah: b 1733 d 11-9-1787 m Hannah Terry PS NY
Nathan: b 7-5-1720 d 10-27-1804 m (1)Joanna Mills (2)Elizabeth Smith Maj PS NY
Nathaniel: b 12-30-1722 d 9-20-1776 m Ruth Floyd BGen NY
Ruth Floyd: b 1732 d 1822 m Nathaniel Woodhull PS NY
Wm.: b 12-3-1741 d 10-24-1824 m Elizabeth Hedges PS NY
Zebulon: b 1-2-1737 d 5-14-1789 m (1)Wait Reeves (2)Martha Emmons PS NY

WOODIN, (includes WOODING)
Amos: b 3-29-1753 d 10-19-1843 m Mary Wilsey Sgt MA ★
Aner: b 1757 d 11-9-1834 m Ruth Foote Pvt CT ★
Darius: b 10-26-1757 d 1846 m Charlotte Thornton Pvt NY
James: b 1737 d 11- -1822 m Abbie Leonard Cpl Bbd MA

WOODIN, contd.
John: b a. 1750 d 1826 m Nancy Hood Pvt MD
Peter, Sr.: b 1732 d 1785 m Achsah — Lt MA
Peter, Jr.: b 1760 d 4-14-1854 m Ruth Curtis 2Lt MA
Reuben: b 1-3-1765 d 1-31-1822 m Patience Landers Pvt NY W★
Robert: b c. 1740 d a. 5-14-1796 m Mrs Elizabeth Hill Col VA
Samuel: b 7-2-1747 d 7-5-1779 m Elizabeth Punderson Pvt CT
Timothy: b 8-18-1742 d 5-15-1814 m (1) — Gregory (2)Anna Howe
    Pvt NY

WOODLE,
Wm.: b c. 1750 d 1826 m — Sol NC

WOODLEY,
Jacob: b 1724 d 11-13-1802 m Grace Loker CS VA

WOODLIFFE,
Augustine: b a. 1765 d a. 11-11-1819 m Milly — Pvt NC

WOODLING,
Andrew: b a. 1755 d p. 6-10-1809 m Catherina — Pvt PA
George: b 1-16-1761 d 1845 m Hannah Herb Pvt PA

WOODMAN,
Archelaus: b c. 8-18-1737 d p. 1790 m (1)Sarah Joy (2)Sarah
    Downer 1Lt NH
Benjamin: b 2-17-1743 d 8-14-1834 m Sally Bryant Pvt MA
Edward: b 12-25-1749 d 12-23-1820 m Sarah Stephens Pvt NC ★
Ephraim: b 1-7-1765 d 3-23-1828 m (1)Olive Bryant (2)Elizabeth
    Billings Pvt MA
James: b 6-24-1753 d 2-2-1842 m Mary Hancock Pvt MA
Jeremiah: b 1761 d 4-20-1841 m Mary Buzzell Pvt NH
John: b 4-24-1740 d 3-21-1808 m Sarah Page PS MA
John: b 10-4/5-1750 d 11-18-1828 m (1)Mary Bean (2)Dorcas
    (Foss) Elden Sgt NY
Jonathan: b c. 1730 d 4-15-1799 m Patience Chesley PS NH
Joseph: b 11-5-1747 d 8-3-1835 m Elizabeth Dole Pvt MA
Joseph: b 8-22-1748 d 9-28-1807 m Esther Whittemore Hall PS NH
Joshua: b 1-22-1720 d 1800 m Alice Stimson Pvt MA
Joshua: b 6-11-1736 d 8-13-1827 m Lois Woodman Capt NH
Joshua: b 10-25-1703 d 11-4-1778 m (1)Elizabeth Doe (2)Rachel
    — PS NH
Joshua: b 6-6-1708 d 4-4-1791 m Eunice Sawyer PS NH
Nathan: b 6-26-1726 d 1812 m Olive Gray Cpl MA
Nathaniel: b 2-22-1730 d 11-13-1821 m Anna Wheeler CS NH
Sylvester: b 3-23-1760 d 8-23-1835 m Merebah Brownell Pvt RI ★
Thomas: b 9-8-1750 d 4-14-1843 m (1)Lydia Drake (2)Anna Carr
    Pvt NH ★

WOODMANSEE,
David: b 11-14-1719 d 7-13-1799 m Penelope Warden CS NJ
Gideon: b 1758 d 4-11-1851 m Almy Carter Cpl MA
James: b 8-26-1732 d 1-29-1820 m Hannah Worden Lt NJ
Squire: b 4-17-1746 d 1843 m Annie Crawford Pvt MA RI ★

WOODRUFF, (includes WOODROOF)
Amos: b 1749 d 5-26-1835 m Phebe Hart Pvt CT
Benjamin: b 1715 d 3-9-1782 m Eunice Martin Sol CT
Benjamin: b 11-26-1744 d 10-18-1837 m (1)Phebe Pierson
    (2)Patience Lumm Sgt NJ ★
Benjamin: b 1763 d 9-19-1822 m Phebe Woodruff Pvt NJ
Daniel: b 1742 d 4-15-1812 m Mary Pierson Pvt NJ
David: b 1733 d 12-31-1786 m Esther Clark Lt CT
David: b 1746 d 7-29-1804 m Joanna Meeker Lt NJ
David: b 1737 d 1817 m Clary Powell Capt VA
Elias: b 3- -1739 d 5-1-1802 m Mary Joline Cmsry NJ
Elisha: b 3-14-1746 d p. 1794 m Anna Griswold Lt CT
Enoch: b 1742 d 3-5-1786 m Mary Treat Capt CT
Enos: b 1750 d 1820 m Charity Ogden Pvt NJ
Enos, Jr.: b 12- -1751 d 9-19-1805 m Mary Foster Ens NJ
Ephraim: b 1753 d 3-15-1827 m Mary Byram Lt NJ
Ezekiel, Jr.: b 9-13-1744 d 1-14-1802 m Sarah Dorrington 1Maj NJ
Gedor: b 7-20-1761 d 6-16-1842 m (1)Corinne North (2)Sarah
    Ingham Pvt CT ★
Gurdon: b 6- -1755 d 4-6-1830 m Anna Webster Pvt CT
Hawkins: b 10-20-1750 d 1-1-1813 m Lois Hill Pvt CT
Hezekiah Stites: b 6-28-1754 d 8-16-1842 m (1)Mary Blatchley
    (2)Mrs Elizabeth Dufford Dr NJ
Hunloke: b 10-23-1754 d 7-4-1811 m Maria Lansing Dr NY
Isaac: b 8-14-1722 d 10-17-1803 m Sarah — PS NJ
Jacob: b 2-2-1749 d 4-23-1813 m Anna Orton Sol CT
James: b 8-21-1749 d 4-3-1813 m (1)Lucy Morris (2)Sarah
    Bartholomew Sol CT
Jesse: b 5-20-1757 d 10-13-1826 m Esther Buchanan Pvt VA ★
John: b 9-28-1729 d 9-22-1799 m Hannah Lambert Capt CT
John: b 9-29-1757 d 2-16-1834 m Sarah Cole Sgt CT W★
John: b 1734 d 9- -1806 m Sarah Baker Pvt CT
John: b 10-8-1760 d 9-4-1835 m Sarah De Forest Pvt CT
John: b — d p. 12-20-1813 m Susanna Joslin Pvt NJ
Jonah: b 2-8-1747/8 d 3-29-1823 m Mary Olmstead Sgt CT
Jonah: b 1755 d 10-12-1831 m Mabel Adams Pvt CT
Jonathan: b 5-15-1744 d 1797 m Mary Hatfield Pvt NJ
Joseph: b 9-4-1753 d 2-25-1836 m (2)Abigail Smith Cpl CT ★

Joseph: b c. 1735 d 1- -1799 m Mary Forrester Sol GA
Joseph: b 1751 d 1817 m Anne Lindsay Pvt NC
Josiah: b c. 1740 d p. 1783 m Abigail Hart CS PS MA
Josiah, Sr.: b 1724 d 7-21-1790 m Patience Wade Pvt NJ
Josiah, Jr.: b 2-21-1762 d 7-22-1836 m (1)Esther Earl (2)Mrs Susan
    Richards Pvt PS NJ ★
Judah: b 12-30-1722 d 12-17-1799 m Eunice Judd Capt CT
Noah: b 1-15-1731 d 1-18-1790 m Mary Barnes Capt CT
Oliver: b 9-23-1750 d 1827 m Sarah Porter Pvt CT
Oliver: b 4-30-1755 d 12-24-1845 m Annis Knapp Pvt CT ★
Richard: b 1755 d p. 6-11-1789 m Susannah Hobbs Pvt VA
Robert: b 10-31-1757 d 7-14-1844 m Euphemia High Pvt NJ ★
Samuel, Sr.: b 10-3-1734 d 7-7-1816 m Ruth Lyman Pvt CT
Samuel, Jr.: b 2-19-1760 d 11-25-1850 m (1)Esther Sloper (2)Chloe
    Phelps Sol CT
Samuel: b 4-10-1759 d 3-21-1847 m Jemima Judd Pvt CT
Samuel: b c. 1720 d 1-1-1785 m Rachel — Cmsry NJ
Samuel: b 8-9-1750 d 2-16-1838 m Mary Johnston OrdlSgt PA ★
Selah: b 1761 d 11-17-1844 m Caroline Mygatt Pvt CT
Seth: b 7- -1741 d 10-7-1814 m Phebe Hains Ens NJ
Shubael: b 9-23-1763 d 5-22-1803 m Esther Dryer Pvt MA
Silas: b 1744 d 4-1-1829 m Hannah — Pvt NY
Solomon: b 1743 d 5-9-1796 m (1)Hannah Goodwin (2)Theodosia
    Merrill (3)Ruth Ensign Pvt CT
Solomon: b 10-30-1759 d 1-18-1811 m Susanna Nettleton Pvt CT
Stephen: b 1731 d 1789 m (2)Hannah Pangborn Pvt NJ
Thomas: b 1734 d 4-23-1805 m Mary Tyson Capt Adj NJ
Thomas: b 6-15-1722 d 4-2-1804 m Mary — PS NJ
Timothy: b a. 1760 d p. 1786 m Phebe Brown Pvt NJ
Wm.: b 11-9-1760 d 5-6-1813 m Ruth Porter Cpl CT
Wm.: b 1743 d 2-23-1811 m Mary — QM NJ

WOODS,
Abel: b 1754 d p. 4-21-1823 m Mary Bridge Pvt MA ★
Adam: b 8-12-1742 d 3-4-1826 m Ann Kavanaugh Sgt VA
Ahijah: b c. 1740 d 4-11-1828 m Mary Moreson Pvt VA
Alpheus: b 2-27-1727 d 12-12-1794 m Millicent Howe Sol PS MA
Amos: b 12-17-1748 d 11-28-1829 m Betsey Tarbell Pvt MA
Andrew, Sr.: b c. 1720 d 1781 m Martha Poage CS VA
Archibald: b 1-20-1749 d 12-13-1836 m (1)Mourning Harris Shelton
    (2)Dorcas Henderson Capt VA ★
Archibald: b 11-14-1764 d 10-26-1846 m Anne Poage Pvt VA
Daniel: b 4-16-1764 d 3-25-1842 m Ruhama Ely Pvt VT
David: b 12-31-1746 d 3-7-1793 m Deborah Swallow 2Lt MA
David: b 6-12-1720 d 4-2-1807 m Martha Wheeler Pvt MA
Dennis: b c. 1756 d 1799 m (2)Cizziah — PS GA
Ebenezer: b 12-19-1728 d p. 1-10-1781 m Eunice Boyden Col VT
Elisha: b 1-11-1759/60 d 2-21-1841 m Hannah Spencer Pvt MA ★
Francis: b 1742 d — m Rebecca Thompson Sgt MA
George: b a. 1733 d 1796 m (1)Jane McDowell (2)Phoebe Wolf Col
    PA
George: b c. 1739 d a. 8-24-1829 m Margaret Taylor Pvt PA
Henry, Sr.: b 9-4-1733 d 3-5-1804 m Deborah Parker LCol MA
Henry, Jr.: b 3-11-1757 d 9-2-1813 m Alice Fitch Pvt MA
Isaac: b 10-29-1725 d 1-25-1812 m (1)Tryphena Parker (2)Mrs Amy
    (Willard) Hazelton (3)Mary Woods Capt MA
James: b 1736 d 1823 m Catherine Allen Sol PS PA
James: b 1-21-1743 d 9-11-1823 m Mary Garland Col VA
James: b 1709 d a. 6-4-1781 m Barbara — PS VA
John: b 1752 d 10-21-1831 m Leanah Milton Pvt Sct GA
John: b 10-28-1761 d 10-21-1810 m Abagail Ely Sgt MA VT ★
John: b 1-12-1760 d 9-2-1819 m Sarah Stevenson Pvt PA ★
John: b 1751 d p. 4-19-1815 m Abbigail Estill Capt VA
John: b 2-19-1712 d 10-14-1791 m Susanna Anderson PS VA
John: b 1760 d 1800 m (2)Agnes Hairston Pvt VA
John French: b 8-9-1756 d 10-3-1818 m Mary Parker Pvt MA
Jonas: b 9-4-1759 d 11-25-1847 m Lydia Hobart Pvt NH
Jonathan: b c. 1750 d p. 1790 m Alice Parker Pvt VA
Jonathan: b 11-5-1761 d 2-1-1830 m Lydia Barr Pvt MA
Joseph: b 1721 d 1797 m Mary Sterling PS GA
Joseph: b 11-2-1758 d 7-16-1834 m Esther Newell Sgt MA ★
Joseph: b c. 1755 d 10-12-1807 m Keziah Goddard Cpl MA W★
Joseph: b 1-3-1754 d 5-11-1830 m Mary Waugh Pvt MA
Joseph: b c. 1740 d p. 1795 m Mary Apperson Pvt VA
Joseph: b 7-15-1723 d 2-14-1776 m Elizabeth Logan PS SC
Joseph: b 8-22-1745 d 1-16-1835 m Mary Hamilton Pvt VA
Levi: b 5-10-1753 d 1826 m Sibel Gilson Pvt MA
Matthew: b 2-6-1765 d 10-4-1826 m Margaret Faucette Capt NC
Michael: b 11-10-1735 d 1-27-1808 m (1)Jean Lackey (2)Margaret
    Trimble (3)Agnes Gilleland PS TN
Michael: b 1740 d p. 1800 m Hannah Wallace Capt VA
Moses: b 1750 d 5-3-1837 m (1)Keziah — (2)Hazadiah Spaulding
    Sgt MA ★
Nathaniel: b 6-3-1732 d 1776 m Anne Parker Pvt MA
Nehemiah: b 1732 d 1-10-1815 m Sarah Lakin Pvt NH
Richard: b 1715 d 1801 m (1)Margaret — (2)Elizabeth Ann Stuart
    PS VA
Robert: b 1720 d 1811 m Elizabeth Middleton Capt CS PS VA
Samson: b 1760 d 1826 m Alice Tarbell Pvt MA
Samuel: b 6-19-1722 d 11-8-1808 m (1)Tabitha Evelett (2)Abigail
    (Whitney) Underwood Pvt MA
Samuel: b 1-2-1759 d 3-28-1825 m (1)Elizabeth Woods (2)Mary
    (Peters) Buell Pvt MA ★

Samuel: b 5-1-1751 d 3-7-1813 m (1)Elizabeth Hemingway (2)Mrs Phebe Holton Pvt CS MA
Samuel: b 1740 d 1825 m Margaret Holmes Capt NC
Samuel: b 10-11-1758 d 12-5-1836 m Francis Sterrett Pvt PA
Samuel: b c. 1740 d p. 4-28-1802 m Elizabeth Wilson Pvt PA
Samuel, Sr.: b 1738 d 2-3-1826 m Margaret — Lt VA
Samuel: b 5-17-1727 d 1-10-1781 m (1)Mary Woods (2)Sarah Rice Cmsry PS VA
Seth: b 10-9-1738 d 3-10-1812 m Mary Beals Cpl MA
Solomon: b 8-29-1747 d 5-3-1783 m Mary Taylor 2Lt MA
Susannah Wallace: b 1719 d 1797 m William Woods PS VA
Thomas: b 12-10-1759 d 12-10-1833 m Anna — Pvt PA ★
Thomas: b 1730 d 10-19-1789 m Mary Scott Pvt PA
Thomas: b 12-13-1758 d 6-22-1834 m Loraine Byers Capt SC ★
Wm.: b 11-9-1734 d 1818 m Naomi Longley PS NH
Wm., Sr.: b 1723 d c. 1- -1799 m Mary Logan Pvt PS PA
Wm., Jr.: b 10-15-1755 d 6-5-1793 m Jean Ramsey Ens PA
Wm.: b 11-2-1715 d 4-12-1782 m Susanna Wallace PS VA
Wm.: b 1758 d 1808 m (1)Louisa Dabney (2)Martha Scott Pvt VA

WOODSIDE,
Archibald: b 4-28-1756 d 7-13-1844 m Elizabeth Gaily Pvt NC ★
John: b 1747 d 1810 m Helen Montgomery Ens PA
John: b 3-9-1760 d 9-11-1835 m Margaret McMullen Pvt PA
Wm.: b 10-11-1733 d 4-14-1801 m Elizabeth Hunter Pvt MA
Wm.: b 4-4-1758 d 8-23-1850 m Eleanor McKissick Pvt PA

WOODSON,
Allen: b c. 1762 d p. 1-21-1822 m Jane Taylor Pvt VA
Charles: b 3-30-1759 d 12-1-1830 m Judith Leake Capt VA
Charles: b c. 1710 d p. 7-10-1795 m (1)Mary Pleasants (2)Agnes (Parsons) Richardson PS VA
George: b 5-4-1747 d c. 10-12-1800 m Sarah Friend Capt PS VA
Hughes: b 1730 d 1810 m (2)Elizabeth Strange Capt VA
Jacob: b 5-11-1748 d 12-5-1839 m Elizabeth Morton Capt VA
John: b 1730 d 12-2-1789 m Dorothea Randolph PS Col VA
John, Sr.: b c. 1696 d 1790/1 m Mary Miller PS VA
John, Jr.: b 1-21-1734 d 8-8-1810 m (1)Joanna Booker (2)Betsey (Raine) Venable Pvt VA
John Stephen: b 8-17-1757 d 9-16-1833 m Nannie Woodson 2Lt VA
Joseph: b 1746 d 3- -1829 m Sarah Hughes Pvt VA
Joseph: b 9-7-1751 d p. 9-4-1838 m — Jones Pvt VA ★
Joseph: b 1749 d 1839 m Mildred Redford PS VA
Josiah: b 1-16-1758 d 1817 m Elizabeth Woodson Maj VA
Matthew: b 7-17-1731 d 10-23-1794 m Elizabeth LeVilliau Chp VA
Miller: b 1745 d 1830 m Mary B deGraffenreid Capt VA
Patrick: b — d a. 1-26-1824 m Nancy Cluff PS VA
Samuel: b 1752 d 1810 m Elizabeth Payne Capt VA
Tarleton: b 3-18-1754 d 2- -1818 m (1)Anne VanDerVeer (2)Ann Friend Maj VA
Tarleton: b 3-22-1758 d p. 1795 m Ann Shepherd Sgt VA
Tucker: b c. 1720 d 1795 m (1)Sarah Hughes (2)Mary Netherland CS VA
Wade N.: b 1-16-1763 d 4-8-1847 m (1)Mary Harris (2)Alice Chick Pvt VA ★

WOODSUM,
John: b 1759 d p. 1779 m Sarah Bryant Sol MA
Samuel: b 7-25-1756 d 6-30-1841 m Eunice Atkinson Pvt ME

WOODWARD, (includes WOODARD)
Abel: b 4-1-1736 d 12-31-1820 m Lucy S Atwood Sol CT
Abel: b 4-2-1727 d p. 1794 m (1)Mary Worcester (2)Elizabeth Tucker PS NH
Abijah: b 1-29-1748 d 2-23-1831 m Asenath Mead Pvt NY
Abishai: b 1752 d 1809 m Mary Spicer Pvt CT
Abner: b 6-10-1762 d 1-28-1840 m (1)Miriam Knowlton (2)Eunice Fuller Pvt CT
Ambrose: b 9-9-1743 d 3-18-1828 m Rachel Lincoln Pvt MA
Amos: b 8-19-1734 d 3-24-1818 m Anna Patten Pvt MA CT
Anthony, 2d: b c. 1739 d p. 8-26-1793 m Increase Dennis Sol NJ
Arunah: b 1753 d 1-1-1835 m Charlotte — Pvt VT
Asa: b 2-15-1760 d 8-30-1837 m (2)Ruth Joy Pvt VT ★
Benedict: b a. 1760 d 12-20-1813 m Elizabeth Clossom Pvt NY ★
Benjamin: b 10- -1758 d 1843 m Sarah Ann — Pvt VA ★
Benjamin T.: b 5-4-1759 d 9-24-1846 m Jane Cavan Pvt NY ★
Bezaleel: b 7-16-1745 d 8-28-1804 m Mary Wheelock Pvt CS PS VT
Cabel: b 2-6-1746 d 1-10-1825 m Rhoda — Pvt MA
Caleb: b c. 1751 d p. 12-13-1803 m Dorcas Woodard PS VA
Daniel: b 4-23-1759 d 11-11-1840 m Sybil Woodward Pvt MA
Daniel: b 5-10-1762 d 7-23-1814 m Olive Brown Pvt MA
Daniel: b 1760 d 9-20-1853 m Keziah Newton Sol MA
David: b 8-11-1752 d p. 1783 m Bathsheba Luscombe Pvt MA
David, Sr.: b 5-20-1725 d p. 1781 m Temperance Kilbourn Capt CS PS NH
Deliverance, Sr.: b 11-5-1713 d 7-3-1793 m Abigail Jewell CS NH
Ebenezer: b 1737 d 1789 m Mary Willis Cpl MA
Ebenezer: b 1751 d 2-8-1836 m (1)Patience Ormes (2)Molly Hayes Pvt CT ★
Ebenezer, 2d.: b 3-22-1749 d 3-24-1832 m Elizabeth Curtis Pvt VT W★
Eleazer: b 2-26-1747/8 d p. 1790 m Mary Collins Pvt CT

Eleazer: b 1-8-1738 d 12-19-1815 m Hannah Putnam PS NH
Elias: b 1741 d 4-10-1825 m Bethiah Clift Pvt QM CT
Eliphalet: b 5-28-1758 d 2-23-1826 m Martha Gage Pvt NH ★
Elisha: b 11-1-1754 d 5-2-1841 m Lucy Manson Pvt MA
Enos: b 1-31-1725 d 8-9-1803 m Mary Bennett Pvt PA
Ephraim: b 5-15-1753 d 10-4-1824 m Weltha Babbitt Cpl MA
George: b 1744 d 12-25-1817 m Margaret Mount CS NJ
Gideon: b 8-27-1759 d 4-29-1850 m Zeruah Tyler Pvt CT ★
Hezekiah: b 6-13-1763 d 5-21-1815 m Asenath Bradley Pvt CT
Isaac: b 3-20-1762 d 8-12-1819 m (1)Polly Brackett (2)Lucy Whitcomb Pvt MA
Jacob: b 5-28-1762 d 4-9-1849 m Mercy Tolman Pvt MA
James: b 3-29-1741 d 1-11-1812 m (1)Hannah Clark (2)Mrs Elizabeth Hale Poor CS Pvt PS NH
James: b 1-28-1737 d 4-10-1820 m Alice Thornberry Pvt PA
James: b 1755 d a. 9-4-1820 m (1)— (2)Mary — Sol SC
Jason: b 7-19-1753 d 7-15-1821 m Sarah Sumner Sol CT
Jesse: b 1762-4 d 3-21-1844 m Ruth Patten Pvt CT ★
Jesse: b 9-1-1764 d 9- -1820 m Mary Hayden Sol MD
John: b 7-11-1712 d 5-25-1791 m Mary Denison Sol CT
John: b 1742 d 1827 m Lydia Trowbridge Pvt CT
John: b 6-10-1755 d 2-20-1844 m Hannah Bicknell Arfr Sol CT ★
John: b 7-9-1752 d 10-17-1778 m Mary Lowell Capt MA
John: b 2-23-1717 d 12-10-1804 m Jane Torrey Pvt MA
John: b 6-30-1749 d 1808 m Lydia Martin Pvt PA
John: b c. 1747 d 1817 m Esther McDonald Capt SC
John: b 1760 d 1843 m (2)Lucy Washburn Pvt VT
John: b c. 1742 d 5-26-1817 m Nancy Ackiss Ens VA
Jonathan: b 5-1-1740 d 12-24-1840 m Sarah Reed Sol MA
Jonathan: b 8-8-1762 d 5-19-1843 m Rebecca Smith Pvt NH VT ★
Joseph: b 1745 d — m Temperance Fish Cpl CT
Joseph: b 1725/6 d 7-8-1814 m Elizabeth Perkins CS CT
Joseph: b 7-2-1729 d 2-2-1778 m Keziah Fisher Lt MA
Joseph: b 10-6-1754 d 5-13-1841 m Elizabeth Scharpe Sgt NY
Joseph: b 11-4-1737 d 5-31-1812 m Rebecca Martin Pvt PA
Joshua: b 4-11-1755 d 7-10-1844 m Experience Jerald Pvt CT ★
Joshua: b 1750 d 1796 m Sarah Clemons Pvt MA
Josiah: b 1760 d 3-28-1840 m Jane Tyler Pvt CT
Josiah: b 8-19-1746 d 2-25-1825 m Sarah Burt Pvt MA
Moses: b 3-30-1745 d 1818 m Abigail West Cnt CT
Moses: b 8-22-1749 d 9-30-1829 m Lydia Herrick Pvt CT
Moses: b 3-31-1740 d 1810 m (1)Eunice Wallis (2)Sarah Roberts (3)Elizabeth Mathews Capt PS NH
Nathan: b 1745 d 1800 m Prudence Briggs MM MA
Nathaniel: b 3-5-1743 d 7-22-1823 m (1)Elizabeth Withington (2)Elizabeth Darby Pvt MA
Nehemiah: b 1-28-1751 d 8-16-1834 m Lucy Rand Pvt RI ★
Noah: b 9-27-1737 d p. 1790 m Mary Fuller Pvt PS MA
Noah: b 1-24-1758 d 1-14-1818 m Delilah Bryant Sol NC
Oliver: b 10-1-1749 d 10-2-1842 m Thankful Brown Pvt CT ★
Peter: b 12-14-1752 d 8-27-1811 m Mary Fowler 1Lt CT
Philemon: b 8-24-1758 d p. 1795 m Rebecca Henley Sol VA
Rosewell: b 10-10-1750 d 9-5-1807 m Huldah Ruggles Pvt CT
Samuel: b 9-25-1742 d 12-2-1824 m (1)Deborah Jackson (2)Priscilla Jackson Sgt MA
Samuel: b 11-22-1749 d 10-21-1832 m (1)Mary Coombs (2)Ann Woodside Pvt MA
Samuel: b 10-9-1750 d 11-8-1815 m Sarah Barstow Pvt MA
Samuel: b 6-5-1742 d 1815 m Patience Alderman MM NY
Samuel: b 1750 d 1791 m Sarah Jackson Sol PA
Seth: b c. 1747 d 9-16-1829 m (1)Ruth Ayres (2)Elizabeth Barber Pvt MA
Stephen: b 6-16-1758 d 4-27-1819 m Elizabeth Morris Sol CT
Stephen: b 8-21-1754 d p. 1792 m Jemima Newton PS NH
Theodore: b 1760 d 1840 m Esther Stark Cpl VT ★
Thomas: b — d p. 1791 m Rachel Starr Capt SC
Thomas: b 4-9-1730 d 8-31-1777 m Mehitable Goldsmith Pvt CT
Thomas: b 2-19-1731 d 4- -1799 m Margaret Ijams PS MD
Thomas: b 1723 d 1785 m Elizabeth Kirk Sol PA
Thomas: b c. 1729 d 5-12-1779 m (1)Jemima Collins (2)Mrs Elizabeth Stokes May Capt SC
Thomas: b c. 1716 d 1791 m Mary — CS SC
Ward: b 4-16-1751 d 4-12-1810 m Rebecca Putnam Pvt CT
Wm., Jr.: b 1747 d 1807 m Jane Ridgely Pvt MD
Wm.: b 1750 d 1805 m Catherine Tate Pvt PA or CT
Wm.: b 1-16-1741 d — m Mary Pyle Pvt PA
Wm.: b 1762 d 7-23-1820 m Nancy Barrett Pvt SC
Wm.: b 1755 d p. 1785 m Olive Butt Pvt VA
Wm.: b a. 1761 d p. 1791 m X Pvt VA
Wm. Garrett: b 1725 d 8-22-1799 m (1)Dinah Warfield (2)Katherine — PS MD

WOODWELL,
Gideon: b 1720 d 8-24-1790 m (1)Hannah Woodwell (2)Martha Noyes (3)Ruth Goodwin Capt of MM MA

WOODWORTH,
Abel: b 6-6-1758 d p. 1833 m Esther Strong Sgt CT ★
Amos: b a. 1749 d p. 1791 m Eunice Newland Pvt NY
Asa: b 4-25-1744 d 3-16-1817 m Sarah Ford Capt CT
Benjamin: b 1751 d 8-5-1830 m Abigail Bryant Sgt MA
Caleb: b 8-8-1763 d 11-27-1810 m Rebecca Traver Pvt NY
Dyer: b 10-20-1757 d p. 9- -1838 m Ann — Pvt NY CT ★

WOODWORTH, contd.
Ephraim, Sr.: b 9-22-1732 d 7-30-1825 m Anna Moore Capt NY
Ephraim, Jr.: b 3-2-1755 d 3-5-1838 m Delight Rowley Pvt NY
Ezra: b 1763 d 1-8-1834 m Anna Woodworth Pvt CT ★
Gershom: b 9-16-1728 d 5-16-1810 m Rosanna Everts 1Lt NY
Gershom Evert: b 1759 d 1835 m (2)Phoebe Travers Sgt NY
Jabez: b 1759 d 5-12-1842 m Elizabeth Clark Pvt CT
James: b 10-11-1733 d 8-15-1812 m (1)Hannah Hockstone
  (2)Mehitable (Hyde) Phelps Sgt CT
James: b 6-17-1754 d 2-12-1830 m Ruth Staples Sgt MA ★
Jesse: b 12-3-1740 d p. 1790 m Mabel Otis Cav CT
John: b 1756 d 1825 m Eliza Mory Sgt VT
Jonathan: b 10-28-1738 d 9-5-1818 m Mercy Parker 2Lt CT
Joseph: b 5-29-1758 d 5-21-1841 m (1)Sally Gould (2)Weity Parks
  Couse Pvt CT ★
Joseph: b 10-18-1759 d 9-8-1824 m Sarah Harding Sol CT
Reuben: b 8-22-1733 d 6-11-1813 m Elizabeth McGee Pvt CT
Richard: b 1755 d 3-3-1843 m Sarah Ann Robinson Cpl PA ★
Robert: b 6-4-1746 d 2-8-1809 m Rachel Fitch Capt NY
Roger: b 1756 d 10-21-1834 m Lydia — Pvt CT ★
Roswell: b 1758 d 6-16-1812 m Phebe Parker Pvt CT W★
Samuel: b 8-20-1763 d 6-13-1854 m (2)Sallie Maria (Blowers)
  Wells Pvt CT ★
Selah: b 8-11-1750 d 10-25-1823 m Rebecca Dunham Pvt NY
Solomon: b 1743 d 7-2-1781 m Phebe Foote Capt NY
Stephen: b 11-26-1746 d 5-30-1822 m Eunice Lathrop Pvt CT
Sylvanus: b 1-2-1748 d 2-8-1793 m Tamesin Nevins Pvt CT
Timothy: b 1759 d 8-22-1839 m (1)Eunice Lyman (2)Lydia Dennett
  Pvt CT W★
Walter: b 1731 d 9-18-1805 m Rachel French Sol CT
Wm.: b 2-28-1752 d 2-13-1813 m Lydia Bacon Pvt CT
Wm.: b 1-4-1735 d 3-30-1814 m Mary Lott 1Lt NY
Wm. G.: b 10-13-1758 d 2-9-1839 m Sarah Thompson Sgt NY ★

WOODY,
John: b 1758 d 6-1-1840 m X Pvt NC ★
Jonathan: b 6-15-1756 d p. 12-10-1847 m Mary Lovell Pvt NC

WOOL,
Isaiah: b 9-4-1753 d 10-7-1794 m Margaret Whitlock Capt NY
James: b — d — m Mercy Brewster Pvt NY
Robert: b 1750 d 9-21-1826 m Elizabeth Douglass Pvt NY

WOOLARD,
John: b c. 1712 d 9-13-1800 m (1)Elizabeth Vines (2)Mrs Melvina
  Rebecca Fathered PS NC

WOOLAVER, (includes WALLABER)
Jacob: b 2-7-1761 d 12-4-1827 m Susanna Flagg Pvt NY W★
Peter: b 3-9-1732 d 11-17-1829 m Catharina Flack Drm NY

WOOLBRIGHT,
Jacob: b c. 1755 d 1832 m — Caldwell Sol VA MD

WOOLDRIDGE,
Edmund: b c. 1750 d 1791/2 m Elizabeth Watkins PS VA
Gibson: b c. 1755 d 10- -1816 m (1)Lucy B Hudspeth (2)Leah — CS
  PS NC
John: bpt 2-4-1759 d 9-29-1828 m Tabitha Pousland Pvt MA RI ★
John: b 1755 d 1826 m Mary Watkins Cpl VA
Josiah: b 11-15-1755 d 11-15-1837 m Martha Trabue Pvt VA ★
Simon: b c. 1753 d 1-29-1830 m Lucy Giles Wgn VA
Thomas: b 1756 d 1840 m (1)Sarah Ann Barnes (2)Mrs Agnes Kelley
  Pvt VA ★
Wm.: b c. 1728 d 7- -1798 m Sarah Flournoy Capt CS NC

WOOLEY,
Abraham: b — d 4- -1826 m Abigail — Capt NJ
Abraham: b c. 1725 d p. 1800 m Catherine Woodruff Pvt NJ
Asa: b 10-26-1760 d 12-1-1841 m Catherine Douglass Pvt NJ ★
Isaac: b 1760 d 4-17-1799 m Hannah — Pvt NJ
Jacob: b 1-27-1762 d 11-21-1829 m Hannah Thompson Pvt Fif NJ
  W★
Jared: b 10-12-1742 d 6-27-1827 m (1)Abigail — (2)Joanna Hulse
  Pvt NY
Jedediah: b 1747 d 9-11-1802 m Mary Remington Pvt NJ
John: b 11-13-1729 d 11-12-1816 m Mary Blodd Pvt MA
Jonathan: b 8-21-1758 d 7-21-1848 m (1)Lucinda Belding (2)Anna
  Gates Potter Pvt NH ★
Joseph: b 1740 d 1828 m Mary Toffey Pvt NY
Nathan: b 7-20-1757 d 12-30-1840 m Lucy Rood Pvt MA ★
Nathan: b 12-3-1733 d p. 1777 m Sarah Flagg PS NH
Stephen: b 2-1-1757 d 7-15-1848 m (1)Priscilla Stiles (2)Jane
  Cheney Pvt NJ W★
Thomas: b 1-3-1698 d 3- -1793 m Mary Chamberlain PS NH
Tilton: b 2- -1761 d 5-16-1834 m Deborah Almy Slocum Pvt NY
Wm.: b 1752 d p. 3-10-1785 m Charity White Sol NJ

WOOLFKILL,
John: b 6- -1752 d 7- -1839 m Agnes (Kunders) Conrad Pvt VA

WOOLFOLK,
John, Sr.: b 11-6-1727 d 1-18-1816 m (1)Elizabeth Wigglesworth
  (2)Mrs Sarah Partlow Lt VA

John, Jr.: b 9-9-1760 d 10-11-1842 m Elizabeth Lewis Sol VA
John George: b 10-1-1750 d 4-16-1819 m Elizabeth Powers
  Broadnax Pvt VA
Robert, Sr.: b c. 1728 d p. 10- -1788 m Ann George 1Lt VA
Robert, Jr.: b 4- -1756 d 8-18-1854 m Jane Peay OrdlSgt Wgm VA ★
Wm.: b a. 1750 d p. 1818 m — Noden Cnt VA

WOOLFORD,
James: b 1739 d 1811 m Mary Dieffenderfer Pvt MD
Levin: b a. 1751 d p. 4-17-1791 m (2)Mollie (Keene) Woolford 1Lt MD
Roger: b a. 1733 d a. 1790 m Elizabeth Jones PS MD
Stevens: b 1729 d 1800 m Elizabeth Whitely Capt MD
Thomas: b c. 1735 d p. 2-20-1794 m Betty — LCol MD
Thomas: b 1-10-1755 d 10-8-1841 m Elizabeth Brook Capt MD ★

WOOLHEATER,
Adam: b 6-10-1756 d p. 6-28-1838 m Cathrin Porter Pvt MD

WOOLLEN, (includes WOOLEN)
Edward: b c. 1745 d 1805 m Tabitha Cami PS MD
Richard: b 3-4-1700 d 3- -1784 m Elizabeth Buchanan PS MD
Wm.: b 1750 d 1831 m Mary Whiteley Pvt MD

WOOLSEY,
Daniel: b 1720 d 8- -1801 m Mary (VanVolzen) Ward Pvt NY
Daniel: b 11-25-1755 d 5-28-1845 m Ann Fuller Pvt NY ★
Gilbert: b c. 1735 d 1777-1790 m Prudence Bates Pvt CT
Henry: b c. 1730 d p. 1800 m Abigail — Pvt NY
John: b 3-22-1761 d 2-19-1850 m (1)Phebe Rogers (2)Elizabeth
  Schofield (3)Sarah Reed Fif CT ★
John, Sr.: b 1727 d 1805 m Elizabeth Haviland Pvt NY
Josiah: b 1738 d 12-3-1779 m Mary Owen Sol NY
Melancthon Lloyd: b 5-8-1758 d 6-29-1819 m Alida Livingston
  MajGen NY
Wm.: b 8- -1742 d 4- -1800 m Abigail Woolsey Ens NY

WOOLSON,
Isaac: b 11-11-1757 d 10-11-1820 m Marcy Nelson Pvt MA VT ★
Jonas, Jr.: b 6-16-1757 d 1804 m Elizabeth — Pvt NH

WOOLVERTON,
Charles: b 10-30-1741 d 9-18-1816 m Mary Drake PS NJ
Daniel: b 1739 d 4-10-1786 m Hannah Chamberlain Capt NJ
John: b 9-5-1755 d 12-10-1837 m Rachel Quimby Pvt NJ

WOOLWORTH,
Levi: b 6-9-1757 d 10-10-1836 m Elizabeth Prudence Rose Pvt CT ★
Phineas: b 11- -1754 d 1815 m Mercy Sheldon Pvt CT
Richard: b 3-1-1717 d 3-11-1802 m (1)Naomi Wright (2)Lois Colton
  CS MA

WOOSTER,
Benjamin: b 10-29-1762 d 2-18-1840 m (1)Sarah Harris (2)Sarah
  Cooper Pvt CT
David: b 3-2-1710 d 5-2-1777 m Mary Clap BGen CT
Ephraim: b 4-8-1755 d 8-27-1838 m Elizabeth Ann Mills Sgt CT ★
Ephraim: b 8-3-1753 d 5-5-1808 m Abigail Lyman Pvt CT
Henry: b 1737 d 1815 m Elizabeth Twitchell Pvt CT
John: b 12-22-1719 d 8-2-1804 m Eunice Hull PS CT
Joseph: b 10-2-1753 d 1-23-1839 m Charity Curtiss Sgt CT
Lemuel: b 6-23-1757 d 10-1-1832 m (1)Rebecca Gillett (2)Lavinia
  Judson Pvt CT ★
Nathan: b 8-4-1757 d 9-15-1820 m Diantha Blackman Pvt CT
Thomas: b 10-11-1724 d 12-9-1798 m Lois Hawkins Capt CT
Walter: b 7-7-1745 d 7-21-1829 m Ursula Beebe Sgt CT
Wm.: b 3-16-1750 d 9-14-1819 m Hannah Rider Pvt NY

WOOTEN, (includes WOOTTON & WOOTTON)
Jesse: b c. 1748-50 d 1806-8 m — Pvt NC
Joel: b c. 1754 d 1813 m Elizabeth Jordan Sol Arfr NC
John: b c. 1742 d 1794 m Anne Harris Pvt NC
Richard: b 1760 d 1- -1798 m Lucretia Cade Lt GA
Samuel: b 1725 d 1814 m Sarah — Pvt VA
Shadrach: b 1739 d 4-12-1812 m (1)Eiizabeth Allen (2)Mary
  Treadwill Ens NC
Thomas: b c. 1740 d 1808 m (?)Sarah Rabun ? (2)Mrs Tabitha Pope
  CS NC
Turner: b 1757 d 11-22-1833 m Nancy Roper Pvt VA ★
Wm.: b 2-14-1740 d 6- -1828 m Lucy Owen 2Lt VA

WORCESTER, (includes WORSTER)
Asa: b 1-27-1738 d 1817-8 m Anna Parker Pvt VT
Benjamin: b 8-8-1742 d 2-9-1821 m Molly Wood Pvt MA
Eldad: b 1-22-1763 d 5-5-1853 m Esther Brown Sol MA
Francis: bpt 8-13-1749 d 11-5-1836 m Mary Simmons Pvt MA
Francis, Sr.: b 3-30-1721 d 10-19-1800 m (1)Hannah Boynton
  (2)Mrs Elizabeth (Brown) Brown CS PS NH
Francis, Jr.: b 4-27-1758 d 9-28-1800 m Hannah Parker Pvt NH
Jesse: b 4-30-1761 d 1-20-1834 m Sarah Parker Pvt NH
John: b 8-11-1734 d 1813 m (1)Mary Muzzy (2)Rebecca White Pvt
  MA
John: b 1736-7 d 6-28-1830 m Sarah Thomas Pvt VA

Jonathan: b 9-23-1733 d 11- -1812 m (1)Lucy Green (2)Eunice Nutting Cpl MA
Moses: bpt 9-9-1744 d *p.* 8-21-1807 m (1)— (2)Mrs Susannah Nash Knowles Sgt MA
Noah, Sr.: b 10-4-1735 d 8-13-1817 m (1)Lydia Taylor (2)Hepzibar Sherwin Capt CS PS NH
* Noah, Jr.: b 11-25-1758 d 10-31-1837 m (1)Hannah Brown (2)Hannah Huntington FifMaj NH
Phillip: b 6-2-1757 d 11-25-1817 m Ann Rindge Fif MA
Samuel: b 10-19-1743 d 4-17-1812 m Nancy Wizel Pvt MA
Samuel: b 1-14-1759 d 3-28-1840 m Hannah Foster Pvt MA
Samuel: bpt 11-2-1718 d 1787 m Judith Hall PS ME
Thomas: b 1756 d 3-18-1822 m Susannah — Pvt MA
Wm.: b 2-4-1729 d *p.* 1781 m Dorcas Whiting Pvt MA
Wm.: b 1-28-1754 d 8-7-1842 m (1)Susannah Dickson (2)Eleanor Hurd Pvt MA ★

WORD,
Charles, Jr.: b 7-9-1740 d 10-17-1780 m Elizabeth Adams Pvt NC
Charles: b 9-12-1738 d 7-18-1778 m Mary Culver Fif VA CL
John: b 10-22-1738 d 8- -1821 m Fanny Collins Pvt VA
Thomas: b 2-4-1740 d *p.* 1800 m Frances Dickerson Adj Cav PS SC

WORDEN, (includes WORDIN)
Abial: b 5-12-1740 d — m — Cpl CT
Benjamin: b 1-24-1758 d 6-6-1830 m (2)Anne McCollar Pvt CT
Henry: b 7-10-1757 d 1797 m Sarah Irish Sgt CT
Ichabod: b 1-24-1761 d 11-1-1845 m Margaret Brown Pvt CT
Isaac: b *c.* 1753 d 4-18-1781 m Mary — Pvt CT
Jesse: b 4-25-1761 d 8-27-1843 m Ruth Dart Pvt CT RI ★
John: b 3-29-1739 d 1-6-1842 m (1)Johanna Stark (2)Mrs Ames Preston Pvt CT PA
John: b 9-14-1753 d *p.* 9- -1840 m Lucy Hale Pvt MA
Joseph: b *c.* 1745 d *p.* 1815 m Rachel Grant Pvt NY
Joseph: b 1753 d 1817 m Amy (or Anna) Lamb Cpl RI
Nathaniel: b 1735 d 10-17-1807 m Sarah Husted Pvt NY
Peter, Sr.: b 6-6-1728 d 2-21-1808 m Mercy Moon Pvt MA
Thomas: b 4-30-1754 d 2-2-1830 m Mary Curtis Pvt CT
Thomas: b 8-28-1765 d 5-6-1842 m (1)Mary Curtis (2)Clorinda Johnson (3)Jemima Stewart Pvt CT
Thomas: b 6-28-1759 d 11-5-1854 m Eunice Hale Sol MA ★
Walter: b 3-19-1757 d 9-20-1814 m Lucretia Hicks Pvt CT
Wm., Sr.: b 1733 d 10-27-1808 m Anna Odell Capt CT
Wm., Jr.: b 1760 d 4-15-1814 m Dorcas Cook Pvt CT

WORKIZER,
John: b 8-2-1760 d 6-25-1838 m (1)Mary E Turner (2)Sarah Rooke Pvt PA

WORKMAN,
Hugh: b 8-19-1759 d 1843 m Margaret — Pvt PA ★
Isaac: b 1742 d 11-29-1827 m (1)— (2)Lydia — PS MD
Jacob: b *c.* 1740 d *p.* 2-23-1821 m Elizabeth Wyckoff Pvt MD
John: b 1750 d *c.* 1830 m Fransina Duffel Pvt VA

WORKS, (includes WORK)
Asa: b 8-25-1763 d 1844 m Abigail Marks Pvt MA
Jacob: b 7- -1747 d 3-4-1825 m Margaret Clark Pvt MA
James: b 1743 d 8-3-1783 m Martha — Sgt CS MA
James: b 3-5-1751 d 1-17-1839 m Esther Stevens Cpl MA
John: b — d 11-27-1815 m Rachel Moore LCol PA
John: b 1762 d *p.* 1804 m Mary Brady Pvt PA
Joseph: b *a.* 1752 d 1-7-1809 m Agness Shearer Capt PA
Samuel: b 6-15-1754 d 7-19-1795 m Susannah Chandler Pvt NH
Samuel: b *a.* 1758 d 1816 m Jean McCune Pvt PA
Wm.: b 2-4-1760 d 8-1-1828 m Miriam Scroggs Pvt PA

WORLAND, (includes WARLAND)
John: b 1720 d 1790 m Mary — PS MD
Thomas: b 7-17-1757 d 8-27-1837 m Elizabeth Bell Sgt MA

WORLEY, (includes WERLEY & WERLINE)
Brice: b 1740 d 1809 m Martha Johnston Sol VA PA
Caleb: b *c.* 1730 d *c.* 1790 m (1)Patience — (2)Rebecca Allen PS VA
Daniel: b 1716 d 10-18-1803 m Mary Pennington Pvt PA
Ezekiel: b 1-5-1747 d 6-3-1836 m Narcissa Wallen Pvt PA
Francis: b — d 1786 m Ruth Collins Pvt PA
Johann Nicholas: b 8-27-1752 d 12-1-1831 m Margaretha Hantz Pvt PA
Michael: b — d 1804 m (1)— Kemp (2)Elizabeth Siegfried Pvt PA
Zachariah: b 6- -1762 d 10-27-1837 m (1)Lucy Kerr (2)Millie DeWitt Pvt VA W★

WORMAN,
George: b 1752 d 3-13-1824 m Catherine Yurts Pvt PS PA

WORMLEY,
Englehart: b 3-24-1755 d 8-28-1827 m Mary Elizabeth Rupley Pvt PA

WORMOUTH, (includes WARMUTH)
Peter: b *c.* 1722 d *p.* 1798 m Anna Feling Pvt NY

Thaddeus Hartridge: b 1761 d 12-31-1847 m (1)Winnie — (2)Polly Bower Sol VA ★
Wm.: b 11-7-1751 d *c.* 1791 m Regina Spraker Pvt NY

WORMSTED,
Robert: b 1754 d 10- -1782 m Martha Shepherd Sgt MA

WORMWOOD,
Amos: b 6-11-1759 d 2-18-1809 m Lydia Storer Sgt MA

WORRELL, (includes WORRALL)
Amos: b *c.* 1755 d 1812 m Lucy Whitlock PS NC
Benjamin: b *c.* 1748 d *p.* 1798 m Elinor Morris Pvt PA
Demas: b 2-2-1742/3 d 1-23-1825 m (1)Elizabeth Collom (2)Alice Yerkes Capt PA
Elisha: b *c.* 1755 d 8- -1824 m Ann Dicks Pvt PA
Isaac: b 8-16-1753 d 4-25-1825 m Elizabeth Rambo Capt PA
Isaiah: b *c.* 1732 d 8-26-1818 m Elizabeth Harper Sol PA
James: b 1732 d 12- -1801 m (1)Elizabeth — (2)Mrs Barbary Pennick Pvt PA
John: b 1724 d 1789 m Priscilla — Pvt NC
John: b 1-31-1758 d 5-1-1800 m Hannah Thatcher Pvt PA
Robert: b 8-22-1754 d 3-4-1841 m Catharine Keiter Pvt PA
Samuel: b *c.* 1735/6 d *a.* 1797 m Ellinor (Worrall) Pvt PA
Samuel: b 6-2-1754 d 2-14-1827 m Martha Gamble Pvt PA
Thomas: b 7-29-1728 d 2-3-1804 m Mary Pierce Pvt PA
Wm.: b 12-29-1730 d 1826 m Phoebe Grubb Pvt PA

WORSHAM,
Charles: b 7-22-1755 d 11-3-1841 m Polly Ellington Pvt VA ★
Daniel: b 11-19-1721 d *c.* 1-27-1803 m Mrs Elizabeth (Branch) Worsham Sgt VA
Henry: b 8-5-1727 d 2- -1789 m — Pvt VA
John: b 1731 d 1779 m Sophia Watkins CaptLt VA
Richard: b 1756 d 2-17-1826 m Mary Wingfield Lt VA ★
Wm.: b 1752 d 1813 m (1)Clarissa Walthall (2)Sarah M Gathright Lt VA

WORTH,
Christopher: b 10-28-1706 d 12-21-1804 m Dinah Paddock CS MA
John: bpt 11-25-1739 d 3-27-1778 m Abigail Swain PS MA
John: b 10-5-1745 d 10-17-1790 m Mary Bentley Pvt PA
Thomas: b *a.* 1752 d 1805-12 m Bathsheba — Pvt NC
Timothy: b 1739 d 5-31-1832 m Susannah Gove Pvt MA
Wm.: b 11-27-1694 d 10-16-1780 m Mary Butler PS MA

WORTHAM,
John: b *c.* 1750 d *p.* 1830 m Mary Marshall PS NC

WORTHEN, (includes WORTHAN & WORTHING)
Barnard: b 9-25-1744 d 7-13-1820 m (1)Dorothy Bagly (2)Mrs Susanna Dake Pvt MA
Benjamin: b 7-15-1753 d — m Betsey Bailey Pvt MA
Enoch: b 5-15-1750 d 12-4-1833 m Jemima Quimby Cpl NH
Ezekiel: b 3-18-1710 d 10-17-1783 m Hannah Currier PM PS Maj NH
Ezekiel: b 4-12-1739 d 1827 m Abigail Bartlett Lt PS NH
Ezekiel: b 1759 d *p.* 1790 m Lydia Silloway Pvt NH
Ezra: b 11-20-1738 d 12-7-1804 m Jerusha Bagley Lt MA
Isaac: b 3-4-1762 d 3-1-1841 m Judith C Currier Mar NH ★
Michael: b 1-6-1758 d 1-12-1841 m Dorothy Brown Pvt NH
Moses: b 7-4-1719 d 1787 m Abigail — Pvt NH
Samuel: b 1-15-1749 d 4-29-1824 m Hannah Ingalls Cpl NH
Samuel: b 4-26-1739 d 7-10-1815 m Doborah Johnson Pvt PS NH
Stephen: b 11-18-1753 d 4-27-1834 m Mary Hoyt Pvt Arfr MA

WORTHINGTON,
Asa: b 10-11-1755 d 11-13-1822 m Lovina Kellogg 3 Sgt CT
Brice Thomas Beale: b 11-2-1727 d *p.* 9-20-1793 m Ann Ridgely PS MD
Daniel: b 8-12-1733 d 2- -1830 m Margaret Parsons Pvt MA
David: b 7-19-1755 d 4-20-1818 m Affa Gilbert Pvt MA
Edward: b *c.* 1754 d *p.* 1804 m Mary — Capt VA IL
Elias: b 10-31-1722 d 9-23-1811 m Rhoda Chamberlain Col CT
Elijah: b 1-1-1736 d 7-15-1797 m Anna Lovet Lt CT MA
Eliphalet: b *c.* 1765 d *c.* 8-11-1825 m Mrs Meletiah (Packard) Bliss Pvt MA ★
Gad: b 6-11-1747-9 d 1-31-1812 m Rebecca Robbins Sgt CT
John: b 2-17-1744 d 4-10-1783 m Abigail Wright PS CT
Nicholas: b 3-29-1734 d 11-26-1793 m Catherine Griffith PS Col MD
Robert: b 1730 d 1779 m Margaret Mathis Sol VA
Samuel: b 11-19-1733 d 4-7-1815 m (1)Mary Tolley (2)Martha Garretson PS MD
Samuel: b 2-16-1729 d 12-17-1811 m Elizabeth Wells Pvt MA
Samuel: b 3- -1746 d 1-3-1821 m Elizabeth Carney PS VA
Thomas: b 5-2-1726 d 1796 m Hannah Duncan Pvt PA
Wm.: b 2- -1756 d 7-15-18-- m Ann Wilson 2Lt MD
Wm.: b 5-1-1761 d 1845 m Mary Mason Pvt PA ★
Wm.: b 4- -1762 d 1846 m (2)Martha Harris Pvt SC

WORTHLEY,
Daniel: b 1760 d 4-7-1820 m Dorcas Small Pvt MA W★

WORTHLEY, contd.
Jonathan: b 1752 d 1836 m Sarah Ordway Pvt PS NH
Thomas, Sr.: b 1694 d 1800 m (1)Mehitable Yarrow (2)Mrs
  Mehitable Ordway PS NH

WORTMAN,
Abraham: b 5- -1753 d 12-29-1835 m (1)Mary Gordon (2)Abigail
  Ponwort Pvt NJ ★
John: b 9-25-1757 d 5-19-1831 m Geertjie Metselaer Tms NJ
John: b 11-16-1730 d 8-25-1807 m (1)Sarah Tunis (2)Sarah Harriott
  Cpl NJ W★
Peter: b 1738 d 2-4-1816 m (1)Sarah VanNest (2)Catherine — Pvt
  NJ

WOTRING, (includes WOODRING)
Abraham, Sr.: b c. 1745 d 1809 m Anna Margaret Troxwell 2Lt PA
Abraham, Jr.: b 10-1-1749 d 1828 m Catharine Schuebley Ens PA
Nicholas: b 4- -1745 d 7-15-1818 m Margaret Frantz Cpl PA
Philip: b 1-9-1741 d 4-7-1819 m Mary Elizabeth — Pvt PA
Samuel: b 1745 d 1805 m Mary Barbara Hoffman Cpl PA

WOULDS,
James: b c. 1740 d a. 7-7-1785 m Alice — Ens PS MD

WREN,
James: b c. 1728 d 1815 m (1)Catherine Brent (2)Sarah — CS Capt
  VA
Wm.: b c. 1750 d p. 7-22-1813 m — PS VA

WRENKLE,
Lorentz: b a. 1747 d 8-6-1777 m Catherine — Pvt NY

WRIGHT,
Aaron: b 11-26-1755 d 4-2-1840 m (1)Hepsibah Merriam (2)Sarah
  Stratton Sgt MA ★
Aaron: b 11-3-1762 d 1-14-1829 m Mary Chamberlin Pvt MA
Aaron: b 1744 d 11-18-1816 m Jane Kennedy 2Lt PA W★
Abel: b 6-1-1747 d 6-9-1827 m (1)Mary Doane (2)Sybel — Lt NH
  VT ★
Abraham: b 7-13-1752 d 2-14-1814 m (1)Sarah Babcock (2)Phebe
  Burt Lt NY
Alexander: b 1-1-1746 d 5-25-1838 m Esther Silcox Pvt CS PA
Alexander: b 1758 d 8-19-1820 m (1)Ann Maxwell (2)Mary Patton
  Pvt VA
Amaziah: b 2-11-1739 d p. 1784 m Zeruiah Fitch Capt CT
Ambrose: b 4-26-1745 d 1-14-1805 m Anna Maria Gregory PS GA
Amos: b 1743 d 3-19-1825 m Dorcas Wright Cpl MA
Amos: b 7-26-1738 d 11-6-1792 m (1)Elizabeth — (2)Abigail Clark
  Pvt MA
Andrew: b 3-11-1763 d 3-8-1833 m Jerusha Benton Pvt MA ★
Andrew: b 12-25-1748 d 11-25-1816 m (1)Sarah S Wright (2)Lucy
  Childress Pvt VA W★
Asahel: b 1755 d 12-31-1833 m Rachel Searl Pvt MA
Asahel: b 2-26-1757 d 2-16-1834 m (1)Mary Worthington (2)Mrs
  Lydia Dutton Pvt MA
Ashael: b 9-16-1751 d 3-1-1850 m Rachel Rice Sgt Wgn MA ★
Ashbel: b 12-7-1758 d 8-31-1817 m Abigail Deming Pvt CT
Asher: b 5-9-1755 d 3-12-1833 m Beulah Strong Pvt CT
Azariah: b 3-7-1737 d 8-27-1811 m (1)Mary Safford (2)Miriam Hall
  2Lt VT
Benjamin: b 12-20-1760 d 2-29-1832 m Hester Chapman Mus Fif
  Maj CT
Benjamin: b 9-30-1760 d 1-20-1839 m Susannah Murray Pvt CT ★
Benjamin: b 1749 d 4-6-1824 m (1)Miriam Talbot (2)Abigail Davis
  Pvt MA
Benjamin: b 8-4-1759 d 1842 m Sybil Britt Pvt MA
Benjamin: b 10-21-1751 d 8-29-1833 m Betty Adams Cpl NH
Benjamin: b 1752 d 1842 m (1)Barbary Morgan (2)Patsey — Sol PS
  NC
Benjamin, Sr.: b 1-9-1714 d 1798 m Rachel Owen PS CS VT
Benjamin, Jr.: b 1736 d 1803 m Ann Reddington Lt VT
Bezaleel: b 2-29-1748 d 1822 m Mary Huested Pvt MA
Bledsoe: b c. 1751 d c. 10- -1835 m (2)Sarah Beasley Sol VA
Caleb, Sr.: b c. 1723/4 d 1-22-1815 m Sarah Strong Capt MA
Caleb, Jr.: b 4-24-1746 d 2-25-1817 m Elizabeth Stillman Sgt NY
Carmi: b 1753 d 9-7-1832 m Eunice Cooley Cpl MA★
Charles: b 9-17-1739 d 7-13-1820 m Ruth Smith Capt CT
Charles: b 1761 d 1-29-1821 m Betsey Barstow Pvt CT
Charles: b 1-5-1718/9 d 12-23-1793 m Ruth Boltwood PS VT
Constantine: b c. 1755 d 1824 m (1)Bethany Wroten (2)Nelly Hurst
  Sol MD
Dan: b 4-7-1757 d 9-10-1832 m Sarah Freeman Sol CT
Daniel: b 4-15-1759 d 4-12-1831 m Mabel Loveland Pvt CT
Daniel: b 3-21-1764 d 4-25-1838 m Sarah Wilkinson Pvt CT
Daniel: b 6-23-1723 d 1794 m (1)Lucy Steevens (2)Deborah — PS
  CT
Daniel: b 11-18-1755 d 12-26-1824 m Roxana Hunt Pvt MA
Daniel: b 1757 d 10-1-1822 m Patience Bill Pvt NH ★
Daniel: b c. 1744 d a. 4-26-1781 m (1)Keziah Sammis (2)Rachel
  Horton Pvt PS NY
Daniel: b 1-19-1752 d 3-16-1840 m Lovina Sutherland Pvt NY ★
Daniel: b 9-27-1759 d 5-24-1838 m Nancy Young Capt NC
Darius: b 5-21-1761 d 10-1-1846 m Lovisa Taylor Pvt MA W★

David: b 8-19-1735 d 5-22-1819 m Prudence Cummings Pvt MA
David, Jr.: b 12-1-1748 d 5-10-1824 m Elizabeth Cleaver Pvt NJ
David: b 1745 d 1833 m Margaret Woodhull Pvt NY
David: b c. 1754 d p. 3-13-1827 m Elizabeth Chamberline Hill Lt NC
David: b 3-14-1749 d 2-21-1822 m Hannah Bailey Ens VT
David: b 1750-60 d p. 1833 m (2)Mrs Nancy Turner (3)Sarah
  Talbot Capt VA
David, Jr.: b 1762 d 1823 m Jane — Sol VA
David, Sr.: b 1734 d 1799 m Margaret — PS VA
Delano: b 11-21-1760 d 2-22-1847 m Jemima Owen Pvt NH
Dudley: b 4-6-1717 d 6-11-1806 m Demise Loomis PS CT
Earl: b 6-10-1726 d 1810 m Esther Lewis Pvt NY
Ebenezer: b 1-14-1742 d 9-2-1808 m Grace Butler Lt CT
Ebenezer: b 2-22-1701 d 4-22-1786 m (1)Elizabeth Newcomb
  (2)Sarah Huntington (3)Mrs Mary Mason Huntington Pvt CT
Ebenezer: b 1-29-1733/4 d 10-2-1811 m Lucy Barrit Pvt MA
Ebenezer: b 5-22-1756 d 10-28-1798 m Martha Wellman Pvt NH
Ebenezer: b 2-3-1754 d 8-8-1834 m (1)Rebecca Stannard (2)Lois
  Smith Pvt VT
Edmund: b 7-26-1763 d 12-10-1837 m Mrs Mary (Keith) Pratt
  Pvt MA
Edward: b 3-10-1720/1 d 12-26-1803 m Tryphena Hines Fif MA
Edward, Jr.: b 1748 d 1831 m Chloe Pomeroy MM MA
Edward: b 1759 d 1849 m Abigail Wright Pvt PA
Edward: b 1735 d 1783 m Elizabeth Quagle Pvt PA
Eldad: b 1-9-1733 d 10-31-1822 m (1)Anna Taylor (2)Eunice
  Baldwin Capt MA
Eleazer: b 4-12-1741 d 1-1-1825 m Anna Marsh Pvt CT
Eleazer: b 8-3-1739 d p. 1786 m Hannah Pendleton Pvt MA
Elijah, Sr.: b 8-14-1730 d 12-23-1802 m Temperance Waters Capt
  CT
Elijah, Jr.: b 1759 d 2-28-1839 m Jane Richardson Pvt CT ★
Eliphaz: b 10-8-1738 d 12-26-1822 m Irene (Judd) Southmaid Sgt
  MA
Eliphaz: b 8-18-1749 d 12-10-1813 m Anna Mosely Sgt MA
Elisha: b 4-30-1760 d 11-4-1841 m Sarah Sears Sgt CT MA ★
Elisha: b 4-20-1741 d p. 1790 m Sarah Merriman Cpl MA
Elizur: b 6-30-1718/19 d 12-3-1787 m (1)Esther Williams (2)Hannah
  (Dix) Boardman Pvt CT
Elnathan: b 2-8-1717 d 3-30-1801 m Mary Hannum Pvt MA
Enoch: b 1720 d 1792 m Elizabeth — Pvt MA
Enoch: b 3-26-1763 d 5-7-1810 m Tryphena West Wgn MA
Enos: b 1-15-1755 d 5-30-1834 m Elizabeth — Pvt MA
Ephraim, Sr.: b 1712 d 1-25-1794 m Miriam Wright PS CS MA
Ephraim, Jr.: b 1-1-1747 d 3-31-1814 m Abigail Lyman Sol MA
Ephraim: b 1725 d 1775 m Abigail Whittemore Pvt MA
Ephraim: b 3-16-1735 d 3-29-1808 m (1)Lucretia Holdidge (2)Olive
  Reeves Pvt NY
Ezekiel: b 3-8-1757 d 12-1-1812 m Sarah Melvin Jewett Pvt MA
Freedom: b 7-3-1749 d 8- -1824 m (1)Anna Horton (2)Phebe
  Turner (3)Jerusha Sheldon Sol CT
Gabriel: a. 1747 d 1801 m Deborah Ball Pvt VA
George, Jr.: b 3-31-1761 d 7-21-1821 m Elizabeth Post Pvt CT
George: b c. 1766 d 1803 m Edie — Pvt SC
George: b 1761 d 2-26-1836 m Sallie Vorden Pvt VA ★
George: b 2-4-1756 d 1829 m Sophia Owens Sol VA
Henry: b 1732 d 10-12-1806 m Sarah Spalding Pvt MA
Henry: b c. 1750 d p. 1-7-1821 m Alice Mann Sol SC
Isaac: b 5-20-1760 d 11-21-1842 m Sarah Douglass Mus CT ★
Isaac: b 1-19-1762 d 1-23-1851 m (1)Peggy Wright (2)Mrs Anna
  Jackson Adkins Lt MD
Isaac: b 5-25-1761 d 1814 m Henrietta Dashield Pvt MD
Isaac: b 3-2-1760 d p. 1784 m Sarah Titus Pvt NY CL
Isaac: b 1731 d p. 2-7-1812 m Rebecca Thompson Sol PS NC
Isaiah: b 7-23-1750 d 2-17-1813 m Sarah Payne Pvt CT
Jabez: b 7-4-1737 d 3-21-1813 m Martha Baldwin Capt CT
Jacob: b 11-18-1759 d 5-13-1818 m (1)Milcah Cannon (2)Mollie
  (Hooper) Wallace Capt MD
Jacob: b c. 1748 d p. 1800 m Hannah Dart Pvt MA
Jacob: b 1758 d 7-10-1844 m (1)Patty Reed (2)Elizabeth (Howard)
  Davis Pvt MA ★
Jacob: b 1722 d 1777 m Elizabeth Haight Capt NY
Jacob: b 1753 d 12-12-1833 m Mary Griffin Capt NY
Jacob: b — d 1793 m Jane Roney Pvt PA
James: b 1740 d 10-20-1813 m Elizabeth Lee Pvt CT
James: b 1736 d 8-29-1793 m Ann — Capt MD
James: b 4-5-1739 d a. 10-28-1782 m Mary Hunt Pvt MA
James: b 9-25-1755 d 1839 m Charity Beck Lt NC
James: b c. 1710 d p. 1778 m Lucy Chitty PS NC
James: b c. 1742 d 1782 m Mary (Mitchell?) Capt VA
James: b 1754 d 6-24-1825 m Martha Hamilton Capt VA
James: b c. 1748 d 10-21-1814 m Sarah Park Pvt VA
James: b c. 1753 d 9-5-1845 m Frances Finney Pvt VA
James: b 1756/7 d 3-11-1823 m Margaret Young Sol VA
Jarrett: b 3-29-1758 d 12-20-1835 m Elizabeth Griffin Cpl VA ★
Jeremiah: b 1-13-1737 d p. 1790 m Hannah Brown Pvt CT
Jeremiah: b 3-29-1762 d 5-18-1833 m Mary Cunningham Lt VA ★
Jesse: b 8-11-1753 d 7-13-1827 m Lydia Parker Pvt MA
Job: b 10-2-1746 d 2-24-1830 m Sarah Stevens Capt CT
Job: b 8-16-1759 d 8-16-1844 m (1)Mary Olive (2)Peninah Trask
  Pvt CT NY ★
Joel: b 7-15-1752 d 2- -1839 m (1)Ruth Loomis (2)Elizabeth
  Perkins Pvt CT

Joel: b 1-28-1744 d 6-24-1796 m Ursula Moseley Sgt PS MA
John: b 7-8-1749 d 9-13-1786 m Martha Robbins Pvt CT
John: b 5-31-1709 d 11-12-1784 m Prudence Deming PS CT
John, Jr.: b 1-22-1743 d 7-29-1825 m (1)Lydia Mason (2)Sarah Case Pvt CT
John: b 1731 d 1809 m Elizabeth Wright Capt GA
John: b 1738 d *p.* 1813 m Jemima Hendon QM MD
John: b 8-12-1744 d 11-8-1805 m Ruth Robinson Capt MA
John: b 6-27-1756 d — m Hannah Walker Pvt MA
John, Jr.: b 4-10-1739 d *p.* 1781 m Phebe Tidd Pvt NH
John, Jr.: b 5-14-1748 d *p.* 1792 m (1)Hannah Butterfield (2)Zubiah Roby Sol NH
John: b 1746 d 5-29-1824 m Elizabeth Peck QM NJ
John: b 3-29-1729 d *a.* 6-19-1803 m Phebe Seaman Pvt PS NY
John: b 1744 d 11-24-1828 m Jane Montanye Pvt NY
John: b 4-15-1756 d 7-2-1839 m Tamar — Pvt NY
John, Sr.: b 12-5-1759 d 10-4-1844 m Penelope Clark Pvt NC ★
John, Jr.: b *c.* 1731 d 10-30-1789 m Ann Williams Pvt PS NC
John: b 10-25-1761 d 1839 m Phoebe — Pvt NC ★
John: b — d 8-26-1825 m Elizabeth — Sgt PA
John: b 1739 d 6-29-1820 m Elizabeth Hammond Pvt PA
John: b 1755 d 12-3-1836 m Jane — Pvt Wgn PA
John: b 1716 d *p.* 1790 m Rachel Wells Pvt SC
John: b 4-20-1743 d 9-10-1799 m Olive Partridge Lt VT
John: b *a.* 1757 d *c.* 1824 m Margaret McKittrick Sgt VA CL
John: b 1729 d 3-28-1831 m Bathsheba Starr Pvt VA
John: b 1740 d *p.* 9-26-1803 m Elizabeth Pate Pvt PS VA
John: b *c.* 1740 d 1803 m Nancy — Pvt VA
John: b 8-8-1767 d *p.* 1805 m Mary Kincannon Pvt VA
John: b 1754 d 3-10-1824 m Nancy Ann McCormack Pvt VA
John: b *c.* 1745 d 12- -1814 m — Sol VA
John: b *c.* 1760 d 1815 m Elizabeth Durrett Sol VA
John, Sr.: b *c.* 1710 d *p.* 6-1-1785 m Elizabeth Darnall CS VA
John Alverson: b *a.* 1750 d *p.* 1790 m — Willis Pvt VA CL
Jonathan: b 8-25-1746 d 4-15-1835 m (1)Leah Bissell (2)Triphena Tray (3)Thankful Landon Ens CT
Joseph: b 6-10-1721 d 8-24-1804 m Sarah Brewster Pvt MA
Joseph: b 2-28-1722 d 10-16-1815 m Rebecca Heywood Pvt MA
Joseph: b 9-25-1736 d 4-16-1813 m (1)Dorothy Heald (2)Hannah Kemp Pvt MA
Joseph: b 11-2-1746 d 12-17-1803 m Martha Eveleth MM MA
Joseph: b 1758 d 8-8-1825 m Elizabeth Parmeter Pvt MA ★
Joseph: b 1-13-1754 d 1- -1843 m — Pvt NC ★
Joseph: b 1744 d 1795 m Mary — Sol PS SC
Joseph: b 1742 d *p.* 2-21-1815 m Elizabeth Kemp PS Pvt VA
Joseph: b 1760 d *c.* 1835 m Nancy Bryant Pvt VA
Joseph: b — d *p.* 5-16-1804 m Frances — PS VA
Joshua: b 11-9-1758 d — m Susanna Pearsons Pvt MA
Joshua: b 5-19-1716 d 8-5-1776 m Abigail Richardson PS NH
Joshua: b 10-22-1748 d *c.* 1819 m Sarah Mitchell Pvt PA
Josiah: b 4-9-1752 d 1-2-1817 m (2)Susanna Pratt Lt VT
Josiah: b 7-31-1737 d 11-4-1783 m Dolly Shattuck Pvt MA
Josiah: b 7-16-1748 d 12-9-1832 m Mrs Mary Ruey Pvt MA
Jotham: b 1757 d — m Elizabeth Dusenberry Lt MA
Luther: b 11-15-1762 d 12-28-1834 m Lorenda Gibbs Pvt PS MA ★
Matthew: b 1740 d 1838 m Susann Lee Pvt MA
Moses: b 7-3-1732 d 12-20-1822 m Thankful Norton Pvt CT
Moses: b 1-10-1727 d *p.* 1786 m Hannah Knight Capt NY
Moses: b 1744-9 d 3- -1830 m Elizabeth Whitehead Pvt VA
Nathan: b 1735 d 3-22-1796 m Betsey Swift Pvt CT
Nathan: b 1749 d 5-14-1816 m Mary Whittemore Sgt MA
Nathan: b 11-7-1760 d 3-1-1836 m Mary Fulton Pvt SC ★
Nathaniel: b *c.* 1750 d 1783-1785 m Sophia Rutledge Lt MD
Nathaniel: b 3-29-1747 d 7-27-1828 m (1)Jemima Bartlett (2)Mary Page (3)Martha Conant Ens NH
Obadiah: bpt 2-24-1739 d 11-27-1815 m Sarah Adams PS CT
Oliver: b 1-16-1741 d 5-20-1820 m Lois Johnson Ens NH
Oliver: b 9-9-1758 d 9-3-1847 m Martha Dunster Pvt NH ★
Patrick: b *c.* 1750 d *a.* 2-3-1816 m Ann Rea Pvt PA
Pelatiah: b 1734 d 3-1-1800 m Alice Powers Pvt MA
Peter: b 11-19-1759 d 5-17-1850 m Esther Reed Pvt MA ★
Peter: b 7-9-1740 d 6-7-1821 m Elizabeth Baker PS Capt VT
Peter: b *c.* 1712 d 1793 m Jane Hughart PS VA
Philemon: b 9-2-1760 d 6-2-1839 m Abigail Wyman Sgt MA
Phineas: b 1762 d 12-25-1842 m Esther Dilno Pvt CT
Phineas: b 7-20-1710 d 8-25-1795 m Joanna Field Col MA
Phineas: b 8-8-1745 d 2-20-1814 m Lois Cadwell Sgt MA
Phineas: b 4-14-1751 d 9- -1829 m Esther Coates Cpl NH
Phineas: b 1752 d 5-6-1812 m Zilpah Cooper Cpl NH
Prudence Cummings: b 11-26-1740 d 12-2-1823 m David Wright PS MA
Reuben: b *c.* 1740 d *p.* 1804 m (1)Sarah Smith (2)Phebe Quinby Sgt CT
Reuben: b 7-9-1749 d 4-17-1841 m Martha Gridley Sgt CT ★
Reuben: b 1-28-1713 d 5-6-1798 m (1)Sarah Edwards (2)Hanna Wright Pvt MA VT NY
Reuben: b 11-13-1757 d 9-7-1822 m Eunice Smith Pvt MA
Reuben: b 1746 d 9-25-1796 m (1)— (2)Sarah — Pvt NY
Reuben: b 1758 d 1837 m Miss Finney Sol VA
Richard, Sr.: b *c.* 1730 d *p.* 9-3-1784 m Ann — Pvt NC
Richard, Jr.: b 7-4-1757 d *p.* 5-12-1833 m (1)Mary Morgan (2)Kara Kittreel Pvt NC

Robert: b 1737 d 5- -1818 m (1)Johannah Mosher (2)Mrs Elizabeth (Curry) Lee Pvt NY
Robert: b 12- -1762 d 10-23-1823 m Juda — Pvt NY ★
Robert: b 3-7-1762 d 3-24-1847 m Keziah Bibb Lt VA
Robert: b *c.* 1762 d *p.* 3-8-1852 m Agnes Durrett Pvt VA ★
Robert: b 1759 d 8-7-1831 m (1)Nancy Turner (2)Mary Goodwin Pvt VA W★
Robert: b 10-11-1760 d 12-6-1845 m (1)Janet Gault (2)Agnes Holmes Pvt PA ★
Robert: b 1736 d *p.* 5-29-1831 m Mary Fitzpatrick Pvt VA
Roderick: b 1754 d 4-18-1801 m Mary Edson Fif CT
Samuel: b *c.* 1751 d 1835 m (1)Ruth Kibbe (2)Azuba Gibbs Capt CT
Samuel: b 9-27-1752 d 3-12-1835 m Vienna Bond Pvt CT
Samuel: b 7-3-1757 d — m Charity Norton Pvt CT
Samuel: b 1738 d 5-4-1804 m Rebecca Bruce Capt GA
Samuel: b 9-16-1736 d 3-31-1817 m Plilena Bill Pvt MA
Samuel: b 9-27-1753 d 3-11-1814 m (1)Amelia — (2)Mary — Pvt NJ
Samuel: b 8-27-1761 d 7-5-1806 m Phoebe Cheesman Sgt NY W★
Samuel: b 8-7-1753 d 4-3-1837 m Sarah — Pvt NY
Samuel, Sr.: b 2-10-1745 d 8-9-1815 m (1)Susanna — (2) — (3)Mercy (Buell) McClaren Capt PS VT
Sarah Bowman: b 2-9-1741 d 1817 m George Wright Jr PS SC
Seth: b 1754 d 8-15-1822 m (1)Miriam — (2)Polly — Pvt MA
Seth: b 8-27-1754 d 12-20-1828 m Sarah Clark Pvt MA
Shadrach: b 4-19-1750 d 4-22-1816 m Prudence Floyd Capt GA
Silas: b 5-22-1752 d 5-27-1827 m Mercy Freeman Hayford Pvt MA W★
Silas: b 4-8-1742 d *p.* 1800 m Mary Crafts Capt CS NH
Simeon: b 10-18-1751 d 1848 m Freelove Foote Pvt VT
Simeon: b 7-26-1743 d 12-13-1786 m Sarah Shattuck Pvt VT
Solomon: b 10-25-1747 d *p.* 3-18-1818 m (1)Eunice Dewey (2)Ruth Williams McCall Sgt CT
Solomon: b *a.* 1755 d 7-9-1798 m Elizabeth — Pvt MD
Solomon: b 1748 d 1811 m Mrs Reynolds Pvt SC
Solmon: b 12-28-1763 d 3-24-1837 m Eunice Slafter Jewett Pvt VT
Stephen: b 5-24-1758 d 2-16-1857 m Sarah Prescott Drm Pvt MA
Stephen: b 7-31-1716 d 2-20-1791 m Miriam Sikes CS MA
Stephen: b 12-24-1763 d 12-25-1851 m Abby Conner Ens VA
Thaddeus: b 8-26-1763 d 3-31-1848 m (1)Mary Allen (2)Jane Gloyd Pvt MA ★
Thomas: b 6-19-1740 d *a.* 5-11-1787 m Mary — PS MD
Thomas: b 1743 d *p.* 4-5-1783 m Rachel Clayton Col MD
Thomas: b 10-28-1734 d 11-12-1813 m Elizabeth Walker Capt MA
Thomas: b 2-18-1758 d 6-22-1840 m Mary Clanton Pvt NC
Thomas: b 1760 d 5-15-1853 m Elizabeth Northrup Pvt PA
Thomas: b *c.* 1740 d *a.* 1-10-1820/21 m Elizabeth — PS SC
Thomas: b 9-29-1760 d 9-16-1852 m (1)Elizabeth Graves (2)Mary Rice Capt VA
Thomas: b *c.* 1745 d 1790/1 m Elizabeth McGehee PS VA
Thomas Martin: b 12-14-1750 d 5-22-1839 m Elizabeth Newton Cpl MA ★
Timothy: b — d — m Mehitable Brainerd Pvt CT
Timothy: b *c.* 1739 d 9-27-1821 m Sarah Satterwaite Pvt PA
Turbutt: b *a.* 1744 d 1783 m Elizabeth Evans PS MD
Uriah: b 12-8-1754 d 1840 m Eunice Jewett Pvt NH
Westwood: b 4-20-1757 d 4-9-1826 m Sarah Billings Pvt MA
Wm.: b 1716 d 10-11-1779 m Esther — PS MD
Wm.: b 1-10-1753 d *p.* 1786 m Sarah Lyons Lt NY
Wm.: b *c.* 1750 d 1822 m Elizabeth Furr Capt NC
Wm.: b 3-23-1761 d *p.* 1832 m Betsey Morgan Pvt NC ★
Wm.: b 1760 d 1809 m (1)Anne Blount (2)Mrs Allen (Davis) Jones (3)Martha A Crump Sol NC
Wm.: b 1748 d 6-7-1820 m Sarah Ann Osborn Pvt PA
Wm.: b 3-25-1762 d 10-27-1841 m (1)Margaret Philipps (2)Rhoda Wharton Pvt PA ★
Wm.: b *a.* 1744 d *p.* 1-7-1793 m Elizabeth Bartram CS PA
Wm.: b *a.* 1754 d 1828 m Mary Wright Cpl VA
Wm.: b 12-18-1751 d 1839 m Susanna Isabel Threlkeld Sgt PS VA ★
Wm.: b 11-1-1740 d 8-29-1806 m Elizabeth — Sgt VA
Wm.: b 1752 d 4-26-1838 m Elizabeth Woodson Sgt VA
Wm.: b 1758 d 9-4-1834 m (2)Milly Malone Yowell Pvt VA ★
Wm.: b 10-17-1765 d 1-14-1829 m Frances Riddle Pvt VA
Wm.: b 6- -1736 d 6-8-1795 m Mary Philpot Pvt VA
Winifield: b 1738 d 1783 m Hannah — Pvt NC
Zachariah: b 1762 d *p.* 7-25-1850 m Polly Hayes Sol NC

WRIGHTINGTON,
Henry: b 9- -1728 d — m Mary — Sol MA

WRITER,
Casper: b 1742 d 11-15-1842 m Eve Kortright PS NY

WUCHTER, (includes WOUGHTER)
John: b 1754/5 d 5-31-1816 m Margaret — Pvt PA
Martin: b 8-10-1763 d 2-19-1840 m Magdalena Ebert Pvt PA

WUNDER, (includes WONDER)
Andrew: b 1762 d 1846 m Catherine Swartz Pvt PA ★
George: b 9-9-1718 d 9-27-1803 m Dorethea Elizabeth — PS PA
Valentine: b 4-1-1758 d 11-20-1828 m (2)Mary Magdalena Smith Pvt PA

WUNDERLICH, (includes WONDERLEIGH, WONDERLICH & WONDERLY)
Daniel: b 8-27-1737 d 2-1-1799 m Eva Barbara Sichlein Pvt PA
John: b 4-14-1733 d 9-3-1818 m Maria Elizabeth Sickele Pvt PA
John 3d: b 11-11-1757 d 12-10-1829 m Anna Margaret Yetter Pvt PA

WYATT, (includes WIATT)
Benjamin: b — d 3-30-1851 m Mary Wyatt Pvt MA
Daniel: b 1745 d 1821 m Hannah Rodgers Pvt CS NH
Francis: b 1755 d 1824 m Elizabeth Hayden Pvt NC
George: bpt 11-5-1727 d 12-29-1800 m Sarah Stone Pvt MA
John: b 6-4-1748 d 6-17-1833 m Susan Summit Pvt VA ★
John: b 1756 d — m Mary Tremble Pvt VA
John: b 1730-40 d p. 1795 m Mary — PS VA
John Edward: b 12-5-1732 d 1-5-1805 m Mary Todd Pvt VA
Joshua: b 12-5-1756 d 5-13-1822 m Elizabeth Shaw Pvt MA
Lemuel: b 2-28-1724 d 3-18-1807 m Sarah Tillinghast PS RI
Nathaniel: b 1-5-1762 d 8-18-1824 m (1) — (2)Ann Brundage Pvt NY
Richard: b 1-1-1762 d 6-12-1845 m Nancy Ware Pvt VA
Samuel: b 3-25-1736 d 9-16-1810 m Elizabeth Sands Pvt NY
Simon: bpt 7-27-1760 d p. 1820 m Elizabeth Cross Matr MA ★
Spivy: b 1759/60 d p. 1832 m (1)Elizabeth Lewelling (2)Selah Ellis Sgt VA ★
Stukeley T: b 2-10-1758 d 11-6-1829 m Susannah Bailey Lt RI
Thomas: b c. 1755 d p. 1799 m Ann — Pvt MD
Thomas: b 7-18-1753 d 9-17-1830 m Nancy Ann — Pvt VA
Thomas Ballard: b 1755 d 1831 m Mary Susannah Needham Pvt VA
Wm., Jr.: b 1-22-1742 d 2-28-1815 m (1)Frances Newton (2)Elizabeth Snoew Sol VA
Wm.: b 3-14-1762 d 11-23-1825 m Mary A — Pvt VA
Wm.: b 1752 d 4-16-1800 m Catherine Julian PS VA

WYBORN,
Isaac: b 10-9-1739 d p. 1790 m Anna Whipple Pvt MA

WYCHE,
George: b 8-5-1746 d 2-10-1809 m Mary Peterson LCol CS GA
Peter: b 10-30-1748 d 12-10-1803 m Elizabeth Jenkins Pvt NC

WYER,
Edward: b 1762 d 5-5-1800 m Elizabeth Johnson Drm MA

WYETH,
Ebenezer: b 4-8-1727 d 8-4-1799 m Mary Winship Pvt MM MA
Joshua: b 10-6-1758 d 2- -1832 m (2)Mary Elizabeth Brewer Pvt PS PS MA ★
Noah: b 7-7-1742 d 9-11-1814 m Betty Fitch Pvt MA

WYGANDT, (includes WEYGANDT, WIGANT & WIGENT)
Cornelius, Sr.: b 3-7-1713 d 10-1-1799 m Maria Agneta Bechtel PS PA
Cornelius, Jr.: b c. 1740 d 1-11-1828 m Barbara Stecher Pvt PA
George Peter: b 1752 d 1818 m Eva Catharine Fehr Pvt PA
Jacob: b 12-13-1742 d 7-11-1828 m Catherine Nowlane Capt PA
James: b 1761 d p. 1846 m Charity — Pvt NJ
James: b 1760 d 1835 m Dolly Wigant Sol NJ
John: b 1745 d 8-18-1823 m Katharine Powell Sgt NY
John: b 1-9-1750 d 1-27-1830 m Elizabeth Smith Sgt PS NY
John: b 1740 d 12-15-1804 m Hannah Rider Pvt NY
John: b 1757 d p. 5-30-1823 m Mary Burr PS NY
Matthew: b 1747 d 1831 m Sarah Waring Lt NY
Michael: b 6-9-1723 d 9-10-1807 m Rebecca — Pvt NY
Michael: b 3-22-1763 d 3-21-1837 m Hannah Tooker Pvt NY
Thomas: b 8-16-1754 d 1823 m Elizabeth Bond Pvt PS NY

WYLE,
Luke: b a. 1730 d c. 1778 m Cassandra — Capt MD

WYLIE, (includes WYLLEY, WYLLIE, WYLLY, & WYLY)
Andrew: b c. 1760 d p. 1802 m — Cochrane Sol PA
Francis: b 8-12-1750 d 1-14-1843 m — Hamilton Pvt SC ★
James: b 12-19-1762 d 2-12-1850 m (1)Barbour — (2)Mary Whitenberger Pvt VA ★
John: b 1-16-1751 d 6-5-1795 m Deborah Allyn Ens CT
John: b 12- -1751 d 6-19-1838 m Mary Lermond Mstr MA
Richard: b 4-23-1744 d 10-11-1801 m (1)Mary Bryan (2)Mrs Mary Bryan Morel Col PS GA
Robert, Jr.: b 1747 d 6-7-1815 m Mary Kennedy Pvt MA
Robert: b c. 1751 d c. 1827 m (2)Mrs Mary McLaughlin Humphrey Sgt PA
Robert: b 1742 d 1831 m Jean Thompson Pvt PA
Samuel: b 1743 d 1777 m Margaret Beath Sgt MA
Samuel: b 1754 d 3-6-1814 m Flora Hutchinson Pvt PA
Thomas: b 1-10-1762 d 5-31-1846 m (1)Susannah Dawson (2)Naomi Rosenburg (3)Sara King Goldwire Dep QMGen GA
Thomas: b 1752 d 1802 m Elizabeth Irish Capt PA
Wm.: b a. 1762 d 1830 m Isabella Kelso Pvt SC

WYMAN,
Abijah: b 8-9-1745 d 11-24-1804 m (1)Bettie Stearns (2)Martha Stevens Capt MA
Abraham: b 4-2-1728 d c. 1803 m Dorothy Call PS MA

Asahel: b 2-20-1735 d p. 1784 m Rebecca Cummings Pvt MA
Daniel: b 1754 d 5-5-1832 m Ruth Wing Pvt MA
David: b 4-29-1762 d 8-8-1828 m Sarah Stedman Pvt MA ★
Elijah: b 10- -1747 d 8-21-1789 m Abigail Weatherby Sgt MA
Elijah: b 2-22-1727 d 7-9-1777 m Hulda Eames Pvt MA
Ezra: b 2-2-1737 d 5-25-1811 m Eunice Perkins Pvt MA
Francis: b 1- -1751 d 10-24-1815 m Lucy (Wyman) — Pvt MA
Henry: b 3-16-1742 d p. 1790 m Sarah Mason Pvt MA
Hezekiah: b 8-5-1720 d 9- -1779 m (1)Sarah Reed (2)Susanna Fowle Pvt MA
Hezekiah, Jr.: b 3-21-1747 d 12-31-1802 m Abigail Frost Pvt MA
Increase: b 6-4-1732 d p. 1784 m Catherine — Pvt MA
Isaac, Sr.: b 1-18-1724 d 3-31-1792 m Sarah Wells LCol NH
Isaac, Jr.: b 1755 d 4-8-1835 m Lucretia Hammond Sgt NH
James: b 9-9-1728 d 1783 m (1)Sarah Carter (2)Judith Richardson Pvt MA
James: b 6-18-1741 d 11-13-1822 m (1)Anna Porter (2)Lydia Simonds Sol CS MA
James: b 1-21-1757 d p. 1817 m (1)Mehetable Bacon (2)Mary Gill Pvt MA
Jesse: b 3-18-1737 d 3-8-1782 m Esther Burbeen Capt MA
John: b 10-19-1745 d 9-18-1813 m Hasadiah Bowder Sgt MA
John: b 1743 d 7-23-1828 m Hephzibah Oliver Lt RI MA
John: b 6-6-1733 d — m Mary Johnson Cpl MA
John: b 10-14-1760 d p. 1785 m Hepsibeth Melvin Pvt MA
John, Jr.: b 11-27-1763 d 3-26-1839 m Hannah Stiles Pvt MA
John: b c. 1763 d 1834 m Abigail Tipingwell Pvt MA ★
Jonas: b 9-9-1759 d 10-10-1818 m Lydia Chandler Pvt NH W★
Jonathan: b 10-5-1763 d p. 1794 m Ruby Richardson Pvt MA
Joseph, Sr.: b 1734 d p. 1790 m (1)Keziah Parker (2)Sarah Allen Pvt MA
Joseph, Jr.: b 4-3-1763 d 10-28-1841 m Betsy Whaley Pvt MA
Levi: b 2-26-1761 d 8-14-1851 m Dolly Wells Pvt NH
Nathan: b 7-5-1743 d 2-20-1809 m Hannah Dodge Pvt MA
Nathaniel: b 1735 d 12-31-1789 m Martha Campbell PS ME MA
Nehemiah: b 2-21-1762 d 1-1-1820 m Susanna Stearns Pvt MA
Paul: b 6-24-1735 d 3-9-1803 m Lucy White MM MA
Reuben: b 4-26-1738 d p. 1790 m Elizabeth Bancroft Pvt MA
Reuben: b 1764 d 1843 m Olive Wyman Pvt MA
Ross: b 8-16-1717 d 9-11-1808 m (1)Elizabeth Jefts (2)Dinah Taylor (3)Sarah Hagget Capt MA
Samuel: b 6-18-1731 d 5-17-1782 m (2)Mary Meriam Pvt MA
Samuel, Sr.: b 4-4-1717 d 6-14-1787 m Abigail Hartwell PS MA
Samuel, Jr.: b 3-24-1746 d 11-29-1789 m Catherine Fowle Pvt MA
Seth: b 3-27-1745 d 6-22-1825 m Sarah Wright Pvt MA ★
Seth: b 2-17-1750 d 4-11-1825 m Ruth Belknap Pvt MA
Seth: b 12-11-1751 d 3-7-1825 m (1)Annie Steward (2)Achsah Reed Pvt MA
Solomon: b 5-12-1744 d — m Eunice Pease Sgt MA
Thomas: b 4-5-1735 d 11-21-1776 m Hannah Baterick Pvt MA
Wm.: b 4-29-1730 d 3-3-1820 m Mary Griggs Capt MA
Wm.: b 11-30-1752 d 2-15-1809 m Mary Gibson Pvt MA
Wm.: b 4-16-1755 d 4-17-1829 m Anna Noyes Pvt MA
Wm.: b 9-5-1762 d 10-3-1857 m Mary Percy Pvt MA
Wm., Sr.: b c. 1730 d c. 1814 m Margaret Holmes Pvt VT
Wm., Jr.: b 6-16-1765 d 3-6-1842 m Malinda Eaton Pvt VT

WYMER, (includes WEIMER)
John: b 1740 d 1-24-1831 m Susanna — Cpl PA
Peter: b 1751 d 3-21-1817 m Catherine Lybrand Pvt PA

WYNKOOP, (includes WYNCOOP & WYNKEEP)
Adrian: b 1734 d 1818 m Sarah Randell Lt VA
Benjamin: b 9-17-1731 d 1782 m Grissel Frost Pvt CT
Cornelius: b 12-1-1754 d 2-20-1824 m (1)Elizabeth Covenhoven (2)Cornelia Van Pelt Ens PA
Cornelius: b 11-15-1732 d 8-6-1796 m Mary Catherina Ruehl Capt NY
Cornelius D: b 3-5-1734 d 12-4-1792 m (1)Leah De Bois (2)Anna Gansevoort Col NY
Cornelius E: b 3-4-1746 d 9-19-1795 m Cornelia Mancius Maj PS NY
Derrick D: b 2-23-1738 d 1-24-1837 m (1)Sarah Eltinge (2)Anna Eltinge PS NY
Dirck: b 10-15-1732 d 12-9-1796 m (1)Tiaatje Wynkoop (2)Sarah Smedes PS CS Sol NY
Evert: b 9-8-1743 d 4-6-1830 m Alice Meyer Lt NY
Evert: bpt 6-13-1731 d p. 1800 m Saartje Decker Pvt NY
Gerardus: b 9-30-1732 d 1812 m Elizabeth Bennett Lt PA
Henry: b 3-2-1737 d 3-25-1816 m (1)Susannah Wanshaer (2)Maria Cummings (3)Sarah Newkirk PS Maj CS PA
Hezekiah: bpt 6-3-1750 d 1837/8 m Maria Meyer Sgt NY ★
Jacobus: b 1721 d 5-4-1795 m Alida Meyers Capt NY
Petrus: b 8-4-1760 d 8-14-1828 m Helena Beer Ens NY
Tobias: b 4-28-1717 d 1786 m Leah Legg PS NY
Tobias, Jr.: b 8-13-1758 d 1827 m Jannetje Schermerhorn Ens NY
Wm.: b 3-4-1753 d — m Charity Schermerhorn Sol NY

WYSHAM.
John: b c. 1758 d 1798 m Ann Blackwell Sol MD

WYSONG,
Jacob: b 1757 d 9-7-1823 m Mary Byers DrmMaj PS VA W★

YADEN,
Joseph: b 12-17-1756 d 9-21-1843 m Mary Pennybacker Drm VA ★

YAKELY,
Henry: b 1755 d 1804 m Elizabeth Haines Pvt PA

YALE,
Amasa: b 9-12-1756 d 10-2-1797 m Sally Baxter Pvt CT
Amerton: b 6-27-1756 d 9-29-1807 m (1)Sarah Meriman (2)Mercy
   Scoville Pvt CT
Asahel: b 12-17-1764 d 2-6-1836 m Sarah Merriman Pvt CT
Daniel: b 7-24-1750 d 3-28-1834 m Phebe Mariams Pvt CT
Elihua: b 1747 d 5-12-1806 m Lucretia Stanley Capt CT
Elisha: b 8-29-1742 d 4-1-1825 m Rebecca North Lt PS CT
Job: b 2-17-1738 d 2-26-1799 m Elizabeth Hendrick 1Lt CT
Josiah: b 6-19-1752 d 5-13-1822 m Ruth Tracy Capt MA
Moses: b 10-19-1743 d 5-27-1813 m Lois Lyman Pvt VT
Nash: b 4-29-1744 d 9-30-1789 m Anna Coats Pvt CT
Nathaniel, 3d: b 9-16-1740 d 1776/7 m Huldah Foster Pvt CT
Nathaniel: b 6-28-1753 d 12-12-1814 m Hannah Scoville Pvt CT
Nathaniel: b 1-5-1720 d 1791-1800 m (1)Hannah Weeks (2)Mrs
   Abigail G Pratt Pvt MA
Nathaniel: b 1743 d 1814 m Esther Franklin Pvt NY
Samuel: b 8-18-1763 d 9-18-1810 m Eunice Paine Pvt CT
Stephen: b 10-17-1732 d 11-22-1799 m (1)Sarah Beadles (2)Phoebe
   Preston Hart Capt CT
Stephen: b 6-6-1749 d 9-3-1818 m Olive Clark Pvt CT
Street: b 1739 d — m Mary — Pvt CT
Theophilus: bpt 2-11-1762 d 1805 m Sarah Andrews PS CT
Thomas: b 11-16-1756 d 3-14-1833 m (1)Mary Couch (2)Phebe
   Butler Pvt CT
Thomas: b 3-23-1739 d 6-27-1811 m Mrs Elizabeth Riggs Mills PS CT
Uriah: b 4-12-1761 d 10-12-1833 m Eunice Merwin Pvt NY
Waitstill: b 7-19-1744 d 1-27-1820 m (1)Jemima — (2)Olive
   Boardman Pvt CT

YAMMELL,
John: b 1749 d 1827 m Margaret Mann PS MA

YANCEY, (includes YANCY)
Austin: b 8-29-1752 d p. 10-8-1833 m Sarah Garrison Pvt SC
Charles, Sr.: b 1714 d 1814 m — Dumas PS VA
Charles, Jr.: b 5-10-1741 d 1841 m Mary Crawford Capt VA
James: b 1712 d 1779 m Anna Thornton PS NC
James: b c. 1752 d p. 1787 m — Cudworth Cpl VA
Jeremiah: b 3-9-1745 d 11-3-1784 m Margaret Mullins PS VA
John: b 1753 d 1810 m Mary Hamlin QM VA
Layton: b 2- -1754 d 4-4-1813 m Frances Lewis Capt VA W★
Louis: b 1736 d 1819 m Mary Graves PS NC
Mary: b c. 1745 d p. 10-25-1790 m Richard Yancey PS VA
Mary Crawford: b 1742 d p. 1814 m Charles Yancey PS VA
Philemon: b 1755-8 d 5-25-1839 m Sarah Powers Pvt VA ★
Robert: b 1750 d 11-17-1824 m Elizabeth Holloway Capt PS VA ★
Robert: b 1748 d 1818 m — Holliday Capt VA
Thornton: b 1740 d 1799 m Elizabeth Mitchell 2Maj CS PS NC
Zachariah: b 1756 d 12-25-1852 m Elizabeth Mayes CS VA

YANDES,
Simon: b 1756 d p. 1790 m Catherine Rider Pvt PA

YANDLE,
Wm.: b 5-1-1742 d p. 1785 m — Wilson Sol NC

YANNEY,
Christian: b c. 1720 d — m Susannah Boshart Cpl NY
Henry: b 9-18-1749 d 3-1-1830 m Elizabeth Margaret Kline Sgt NY

YANT,
Philip: b 1747 d 12-27-1826 m Maria Magdalene Rerig Pvt PA

YANTIS,
Jacob: b c. 1750 d a. 6-10-1805 m Ruth Crisman Pvt PA

·YAPLE,
John Nicholas: b 1764 d 7-21-1845 m Catharine Akerly PS Pvt
   NY ★

YARBOROUGH,
Henry: b c. 1739 d p. 8-2-1793 m Elizabeth — PS NC
Wm.: b 1766 d 3-20-1859 m Rachel Shelby Pvt PA
Wm.: b c. 1753 d 5-6-1831 m Charlotte Burnes Pvt SC

YARD,
Archibald Wm.: b 1732 d 3-10-1810 m (1)Margaret — (2)Catherine
   Pearson PS NJ
Benjamin: b 1714 d 1808 m Ann Pierson PS NJ
George: b 11-5-1755 d 1837 m Catherine Stout Pvt NJ
Isaac: b 1732 d 1-1-1819 m Mary Ely Lt NJ

YARNALL,
Caleb: b 1-25-1759 d 10-4-1849 m (1)Phoebe Minshall (2)Mrs Ann
   F Dawson Pvt PA
George: b 11-12-1745 d p. 1809 m Lydia Ashton Pvt PA

John: b 2-8-1739 d 9-24-1799 m Elizabeth Newlin Pvt DE
Peter: b 2-17-1754 d 2-25-1798 m (1)Hannah Sharpless (2)Hannah
   (Haines) Thornton Dr DE

YARRINGTON,
Abel: b 12- -1739 d 6-29-1824 m Rebecca Keazer Pvt CT
Jonathan: b 1733 d 6-4-1782 m Sarah Smith Sol NY
Wm.: b 1-27-1735 d 10-28-1811 m Chloe Cleveland Cpl NY

YATES, (includes YEATES)
Amariah: b 2-28-1749 d 1813 m Margaret Thayer Pvt RI
Andrew: b c. 1740 d 1804 m X PS VA
Barzillia: b 10-12-1757 d 9-1-1841 m Mercy Thayer Sgt RI
Benjamin: b 4-3-1745 d 1-30-1849 m (2)Sarah Robinson Spy MD ★
Christopher: b 7-8-1737 d 1785 m Jannetje Bradt Col NY
Christopher Johannes: b 8-27-1736 d p. 1795 m Catherine Lansing
   Pvt NY
Christopher Peter: b 3-18-1750 d 1-20-1815 m (1)Rebecca Van
   Santford (2)Maria Frey (3)Rebecca Winne Maj NY
Evert: b 10-25-1764 d 1846 m Catharine Fonda Pvt NY
George: b c. 1727/8 d a. 12-11-1777 m Frances Lewis PS VA
George James: b 4-23-1748 d 1-16-1821 m Nancy Richards Capt
   MA
Jacob: b 3-28-1755 d 11-21-1831 m Elizabeth VanDenBerg Capt NY
James: b c. 1745 d p. 7-9-1806 m Avarilla Walston PS NC
Jasper: b 4-9-1745 d 3-14-1817 m Sarah Burd Capt PS PA
Jellis: b 4-22-1744 d 11-13-1812 m Anantje Bradt Lt NY
John: b 1-7-1755 d 4-4-1834 mMercy Hopkins Pvt MA ★
John: b 8-4-1763 d 12-16-1840 m Nancy — Pvt NY
John: b c. 1751 d p. 1-13-1846 m Elizabeth Chandler Lt VA ★
John G.: b 3-6-1735 d 10-20-1811 m Catlina Gelwey Pvt NY
Jonathan: b a. 1743 d a. 12-20-1787 m Elizabeth Bruce Maj PS MD
Joseph: b a. 1750 d 1778-83 m Sarah Atmar Pvt SC
Joshua: b 1-28-1741 d 5-6-1831 m Nancy Boilston PS MD
Michael: b c. 1725 d 1789 m Martha — PS VA
Michael, Jr.: b 6-20-1753 d p. 1800 m Mrs Ann Estes Butler Dr VA
Nicholas: b 12-20-1752 d 9-15-1795 m Rebecca Fonda Lt NY
Peter: b 1-8-1727 d 9-6-1807 m Sarah Vanalstyne Col NY
Peter W: bpt 8-23-1747 d 3-9-1826 m (1)Ann Mary Helmes (2)Mary
   TerBoss Pvt NY
Robert: b 3-17-1738 d 9-9-1801 m Jane VanNess PS NY
Thomas: b 1740 d 11-15-1815 m Mary Myers Capt MD
Thomas: b c. 1742 d 3-15-1834 m Rebecca Ragsdale Ens NC
Wm.: b 8-30-1732 d 1783 m Sarah Iszard PS NJ
Wm., Sr.: b 1727 d 1808 m Mary — Pvt NC
Wm.: b 1745-50 d 12-2-1789 m (1)Ann Isham Poythress (2)Elizabeth
   Booth LCol VA

YEAGER, (includes YAGER)
Adam, Jr.: b 5-9-1738 d 1812/3 m Juriah Berry Ens VA
Andrew: b 7-5-1730 d 8-15-1790 m Anna Barbara Schuster Pvt PA
Elisha: b 11-30-1761 d p. 1833 m (1)Mary Gibbs (2)Elizabeth Yager
   Pvt VA ★
Frederick: b 7-7-1748 d 1-29-1822 m Katherine Baum Ens PA
George: b 3-12-1761 d 1848 m (2)Mrs Margaret Davis Pvt PA
George: b 5-27-1718 d 8-27-1790 m Anna Maria — Pvt PA
John: b 7-2-1754 d 7-2-1819 m Catherine Pepperly Pvt PA
John: b 10-9-1721 d 4-6-1796 m Eve Elizabeth Schneider PS PA
John: b 10-5-1762 d 1-7-1833 m Phoebe Anise Hull Pvt VA
John: b c. 1750 d 1-3-1831 m — Pvt VA ★
John: b 9-15-1732 d 8-17-1826 m Mary Wilhoit Sol VA
Joseph: b 1739 d 2-2-1838 m Catherine — PS PA
Michael: b 6-29-1728 d 1794/5 m Elizabeth Manspeil PS VA
Philip: b 6-22-1753 d 9-3-1830 m Caty Kuhl Pvt NY
Solomon: b 11- -1759 d 10-27-1851 m (1)Elizabeth Broyles
   (2)Phebe Hamblen Pvt VA ★

YEAKLE, (includes YAGLEY & YEAKEL)
Abraham: b 1-14-1752 d 6-17-1841 m Sarah Wagner Pvt PA
George: b c. 1738 d a. 11-13-1784 m Anne Deppen PS PA
Jeremiah: b 4-9-1736 d 2-10-1818 m Susanna Weigner Pvt PA
John: b 1-1-1739 d 7-9-1801 m Anna Wiegner Pvt PA

YEALDHALL,
Samuel: b c. 1740 d a. 5-7-1808 m Frances Pumphrey PS MD

YEARGAN,
Benjamin: b 8-22-1759 d 3-22-1812 m Mrs Sarah Morgan Patterson
   SrgnMte QM NC

YEARY,
Henry, Sr.: b 1730 d 1799 m Elizabeth Croxstol PS VA
Henry, Jr.: b 1765 d 1840 m Martha Ball Pvt VA

YEASLEY, (includes YEISLEY)
George Adam: b 1753 d 11- -1825 m Christina — Pvt PA
Michael: b 5-12-1730 d 9-1-1808 m Catherine Welsh Nofsinger
   Entler Pvt PA

YEATER,
Andrew: b 1760 d 1829 m X Pvt PA

YEATMAN,
John: b 1742 d *a.* 3-26-1811 m Susannah Self PS VA
Thomas: b 2-1-1740 d *a.* 11-26-1810 m Frances Robinson Lt PS VA

YEATON,
Hopley: b 1740 d 5-12-1812 m (1)Comfort Marshall (2)Elizabeth
    Gerrish 3Lt NH
John: bpt 2-14-1741/2 d 10-28-1836 m Sarah Dyer Sgt MA
Johnathan: b 8-11-1757 d 10-25-1839 m (2)Jane Wood Pvt NH
Moses: b 10-13-1753 d 2-8-1842 m Sally Hill 2Lt Smn NH ★
Paul: b 1760 d 1856 m Mary Hussey Pvt NH
Philip: bpt 4-7-1728 d 3-29-1817 m Dorcas Smith Pvt MA
Richard: b *c.* 1737 d *a.* 9-8-1785 m Experience Pray Sgt NH
Samuel: b 1747 d 9-13-1820 m Margaret Snow Pvt NH
Wm.: b 7- -1756 d 1831 m Hannah Towle Lt NH

YELL,
Nathaniel: b 8-3-1742 d *p.* 11- -1780 m Mrs Mehitable Creesy Mrnr
    MA

YENTZER,
John: b 1753 d 2-8-1834 m Mary — Lt PA

YEOMANS, (includes YEAMANS, YEOMAN, & YOUMANS)
Benjamin: b 1-1-1750 d 3-5-1830 m Sarah Howell Capt NJ
Daniel: b 9-17-1747 d 8-15-1825 m Esther Sterling Pvt CT
Edward: b 7-18-1760 d 8-5-1840 m (1)Marcy Clark (2)Mrs Gratis
    Newell Pvt CT ★
Eliab: b 1735 d — m Catherine Wooley MM NY
Elijah: b 5-16-1756 d 1800 m Lydia Simmons Pvt CT
Ezekiel: b 1743 d 1802 m Mary — PS NY
Francis: b 3-10-1727 d 3-15-1819 m Margaret Galatin Sgt NY
Isaac: b 12-25-1751 d 5-11-1833 m Nancy Cockran Pvt NY ★
John: b 1755 d 7-12-1827 m Martha Congdon Lt MA
Jonas: b 5-18-1758 d 3-28-1850 m — Cpl NY ★
Jonathan: b 4-7-1734 d 10-10-1822 m Phebe — Sgt MA
Joshua: b 11-15-1752 d 8-8-1835 m Elizabeth Jones Cpl CT
Samuel: b *c.* 1747 d *p.* 1833 m Sabra Bromley OrdlSgt CT ★
Samuel: b 1758 d *p.* 1780 m Deborah Purdy Pvt NY
Solomon: b 1760 d *c.* 1840 m — Pvt NC ★
Stephen: b 1748 d 5-10-1829 m Abigail Fountain Pvt PS NY

YERDON,
Nicholas: b 5-7-1763 d 11-27-1839 m Catherine Hufnail Pvt NY

YERGER,
Adam: b 2-13-1752 d 4-16-1831 m (1)Elizabeth Newman (2)Margaret
    Kurtz Pvt PA
Andrew: b 11-12-1750 d 11-26-1817 m (1)Anna Stauffer (2)Philibina
    Reif Pvt PA
Peter: b 1737 d 1796 m Maria Barbara Roth Pvt PA

YERKES, (includes YERKS)
Anthony: b *c.* 1745 d *c.* 1804 m Mary Harper Pvt PA
Harman: b 1-18-1720 d 11-29-1804 m (1)Mary Stroud (2)Mrs Mary
    H Clayton (3)Mrs Elizabeth B Tompkins Pvt PA
James: bpt 5-3-1747 d 11- -1806 m Aeltje Yerks Pvt NY W★
John, Sr.: b 1724 d 1798 m Susannah Foseur Pvt PA
Jonathan: b 12-5-1759 d 3-27-1835 m Elizabeth Jarrett Pvt PA
Silas: b 2-15-1723 d 8-25-1795 m Hannah Dungan Pvt PA
Wm.: b 4-10-1725 d *a.* 1785 m (2)Catrina See Pvt NY

YETTER,
Martin: b 1-25-1736 d 4-20-1804 m Marie Magdalena — Pvt PA
Samuel: b *c.* 1760 d 1830 m Maria Yocum Sgt PA

YINGST, (includes YENGST)
Henry: b 5-20-1736 d *p.* 1781 m Catherine — Pvt PA
Peter: b 1758 d 1847 m Catherine Roland Pvt PA

YOCUM,
James: b 1753 d 2-21-1836 m Margaret Hendricks Pvt PA
John: b 2-14-1757 d 8-2-1844 m Mary Evans Pvt PA
John: b 9-25-1750 d 10-14-1823 m Hanna Bunn Pvt PA

YODER,
Abraham: b 12-19-1747 d 12-30-1820 m Maria — Pvt PA
Conrad: b *c.* 1735 d *a.* 1790 m (1)Christina Klein (2)— Seitz
    (3)Catherine Huffman PS NC
Daniel: b 4-22-1748 d 8-21-1820 m Margaret Oyster PS PA
Jacob: b 8-11-1758 d 4-7-1832 m Mary Mossman Pvt PA
John: b 1718 d 4-7-1812 m Catharine Oyster PS PA

YOHE,
Michael: b 3-31-1747 d 12-14-1833 m Mary Shouse Pvt PA

YOHN,
John: b *a.* 1755 d 4-29-1825 m (1)Maria Betz (2)Bandina Peters
    Vanderslice Pvt PA

YOHO,
Henry: b 1752 d 3-12-1845 m Catherine — Pvt Spy VA ★
Peter: b *c.* 1745 d 1817-28 m X Pvt PA

YONCE,
Peter: b *c.* 1757 d *p.* 1804 m (1)Elizabeth Keller (2)Clara — Pvt PA

YONKER,
George: b 2-16-1757 d 1853 m Rachel Schall Cpl NY

YORAN,
Jacob: b 1746 d *c.* 1798 m Catherine Hitcok Pvt NY

YORDAN,
John: b 7-10-1758 d 2-18-1840 m Magdalene Matlan Pvt NY ★

YORK, (includes YORKE)
Allen: b 1-1-1754 d 1835 m Zeruiah Wheeler Pvt CT
Amos: b 10-15-1730 d 11- -1778 m Lucretia Miner PS PA
Andrew: b 12-26-1742 d 3-23-1794 m Eleanor Cox QM NJ
Bell: b 1725 d 7- -1798 m Ruth Main Sol PS CT
Daniel: b 1730-5 d *p.* 1793 m Maria VanAken Pvt PS NY
Edward: b 9-20-1740 d 4-12-1791 m Sarah Stille Capt PA
Henry: b *c.* 1730 d *p.* 1805 m X PS NC
Isaac: b 8-15-1758 d 11- -1847 m Betsey Merservey Pvt MA
James: b 1760 d *c.* 1803 m Aletha Wright Pvt GA
Jeremiah: b 1-14-1765 d 5-26-1853 m Thankful Thurston Sol CT
Jeremiah: b 6-22-1762 d 9-10-1835 m (1)Sarah Hargass (2)Mrs Joanna
    Allsworth (3)Letitia Boyd Pvt VA ★
Jesse: b 8-1-1740 d 12-13-1808 m Annah Breed Sgt CT
John, Sr.: b 3-16-1716 d 5-12-1784 m Anna Brown PS CT
John, Jr.: b 7-30-1744 d 6-16-1820 m Keturah Brown Pvt CT
John: b 1749 d 1827 m Abigail Bean Sol MA
John: b *c.* 1751 d 1792 m Catherine — Pvt PS NC
Joshua: b 1-22-1756 d *p.* 1836 m Nancy McDaniel Pvt PA ★
Robert: b 5-29-1752 d 4-7-1817 m (1)Lydia — (2)Mary White Lt MA
Samuel, Sr.: b 10-13-1715 d 1808 m Joanna Skillings Pvt MA
Samuel, Jr.: b *c.* 1739 d 1798 m Hannah Hoyt Pvt MA
Solomon: b 6-12-1763 d 2-10-1825 m (1)Betty Babson (2)Mrs
    Patience Gott Campbell Pvt MA ★
Wm.: b 1755 d 2-1-1849 m (1)Lucy Hilliard (2)Betsey Choate Pvt NH
Wm. Ring: b 3-2-1757/8 d 1-16-1848 m (1)Mary Drinkwater (2)Mary
    Ridiout Pvt Mstr MA ★

YORKER,
Jacob: b 1760 d 1828 m Jane — Pvt NY

YOST,
Caspar: b 1748 d 1781/2 m Catharine Cole 2Maj PA
Daniel: b 9-14-1736 d 8-6-1812 m Elizabeth Spare Pvt PA
Henry: b 1749 d 1803 m Mary Mariah Wagnor Lt MD
Isaac: b 8-30-1756 d *p.* 2-11-1825 m Elizabeth — Sol PS PA
John: b 1743 d 1806 m Rebecca Waggoner PS MD
John: b — d *p.* 7-29-1801 m (1)Mollie Krause (2)Anna Maria
    Sieval Pvt PA
John: b 7-14-1726 d 3-10-1784 m Mary Foster Pvt PA
John: b *c.* 1740 d *p.* 1790 m X Pvt PA
John, Jr.: b *c.* 1750 d 1781 m Margaret — Pvt PA
Peter: b 1741 d 2-3-1811 m Mary Magdalene Shields Pvt NY
Philip: b 8-24-1757 d 8-28-1832 m Rosina Beringer Pvt PA

YOUKER, (includes JUNGKURTH)
Frederick: b 8-25-1748 d 3-10-1816 m Anna Barbara Sorber Lt PA
Jacob: b 10-26-1757 d 2- -1848 m (1)Magdalena Dussler (2)Margaret
    Mosher Pvt NY ★

YOUNG,
Aaron, Jr.: b 8-3-1746 d 1814 m Dorothy — Lt NH
Aaron: b 1756 d 1796 m Hannah James Pvt NJ
Abraham: b 10-16-1756 d 2-19-1829 m (1)Susanna Cummings
    (2)Susanna Purves (3)Rebecca Holmes Sgt MA ★
Alexander: b 10-14-1726 d 2-19-1800 m Martha Orr Pvt PA
Andrew: b — d *p.* 1778 m — PS MD
Andrew: b *a.* 1743 d 1807 m — Cox Pvt PA
Asa: b 3-7-1754 d 1-18-1808 m Nancy Clark Pvt RI
Asaph: b 6- -1750 d 5-20-1827 m Abigail Brooks Pvt CT
Baltzer: b 12-28-1760 d 9-8-1845 m Elizabeth Buss Sol MA
Barnabas: b 4-14-1757 d 6-11-1802 m Abigail Swett Bbd MA
Barney: b 8-28-1754 d 1-15-1833 m Elizabeth Rankins Pvt NY
Benjamin: b *c.* 1748 d 8-30-1831 m Waity Hill Pvt CT ★
Benjamin: b 1752 d 8-13-1828 m Mary Hodgson Sgt MD ★
Benjamin: b 7-5-1756 d 12-13-1848 m (1)Phoebe Allen (2)Rebecca
    Bickford Pvt NH
Caleb: b *a.* 1760 d 2-8-1841 m Miriam Webb Sgt NH
Calvin: b 6-18-1757 d 8-6-1806 m Eve Van Eps Pvt NY
Charles: b 1757 d *c.* 1848 m Catherine Elizabeth Kint Pvt PA ★
Christian: b 3-18-1764 d 5- -1849 m Nancy Humes Pvt VA
Christopher: b 3-3-1764 d 3-10-1843 m Mary Bonney Pvt MA
Conrad: b 1728 d 1825 m Madelina — Pvt PS PA
Daniel: b 9-7-1753 d 5-21-1790 m Mrs Mehitable Wheeler Mstr MA
Daniel: b 6-26-1760 d 5-25-1828 m Patty Wiley Pvt MA
Daniel: b 1744 d 10-17-1814 m (1)Abiah Sweezey (2)Mary Halsey
    PS NY
David: b 4-17-1754 d 1785 m Nancy Cruse Matr MD
David: b 5-15-1753 d 2-14-1826 m Elizabeth Clarke Pvt MA
David: b — d 1-15-1841 m Hannah Lombard Pvt MA

David: b *c.* 1750 d 1810 m Sarah Eastman PS NH
David: b *c.* 1750 d *p.* 1790 m — Searing Pvt NJ
Eleazer: b 9-21-1756 d 11-9-1845 m Hannah Bailey Pvt PS NH ★
Eli: b 10-1-1752 d 8-15-1843 m Cleopatra — Pvt CT ★
Elias: b 1762 d 9-6-1842 m Hannah Watson Pvt RI ★
Ephraim: b 10-26-1749 d 11-18-1793 m (1)Phoebe Cutler (2)Dinah (Lee)Cutler Pvt NJ
Esek: b 1748 d *p.* 1820 m Lydia — Pvt RI ★
Ezekiel: b 1736 d 1800 m Ruth — CS VA
Ezra: b 1731 d *p.* 1809 m Susanna Demeritt Sgt NH
Francis: b 10- -1742 d 8- -1822 m Jane Caruthers Sol NC
Francis: b 1735 d 12- -1794 m Elizabeth Bennett CS VA
Frederick: b 6-16-1756 d 9-20-1802 m Merip Major Pvt PA
George: b 1741 d 1814 m Elizabeth Shaffer Pvt MD
George: b 3-26-1755 d 1807 m Mary Helen — Pvt MD
George: b 5-1-1761 d 9-3-1849 m (1)Jane Orr (2)Mrs Mary Bowman Pvt NJ ★
George: b 1722 d 3-11-1799 m Maritje Emerich Pvt NY
George: b 12-5-1755 d 10-13-1833 m (1)Elizabeth McCrary (2)Ailsey Whitmore Pvt SC
George, Jr.: b *c.* 1755 d 1836-39 m Nancy Hampton Sol VA
Gideon: b 6-4-1738 d 1800 m Jemima Cilley Pvt MA
Gideon: b 3-9-1761 d 3-30-1847 m (1)Lydia Young (2)Elizabeth Mann Pvt MA ★
Gilbert: b 1-22-1752 d 1837 m Nancy Homan Pvt NJ
Guy: b 4-23-1749 d 3-4-1828 m (1)Dirke Winne (2)Maria Lansing Capt NY ★
Heman: b 5-24-1744 d *p.* 1790 m Phoebe Godfrey Sgt MA
Hendrick: b 1740 d 1809 m Maria (Fletcher) Lidger Pvt NY
Henry: b *c.* 1745 d 1790 m Lydia Ross Pvt MA
Henry: b 3-5-1746 d 11-6-1795 m Millicent Townsend Ens NJ
Henry: b 1739 d 1807 m Catherine Granger 1Maj NC
Henry: b *c.* 1758/9 d *p.* 1792 m Winifred Tucker Goodwyn Capt VA
Hiat: b 1739 d 10-10-1810 m Mary Hinckley Sgt MA
Isaac: b 9-23-1760 d *c.* 1837 m (1)Charity Hubbell (2)Elizabeth — Pvt CT ★
Isham: b 1-17-1760 d 4- -1837 m (1)Nancy Bailey (2) — Harvey Pvt NC GA ★
Jacob, Sr.: b *c.* 1725 d 1781 m Eleanor Tully PS MD
Jacob, Jr.: b *c.* 1750 d 1816/7 m Penelope Watt Pvt PS MD
Jacob: b 7-1-1759 d — m Hannah Martin Pvt NJ
Jacob: b 4-22-1736 d 6-10-1826 m Catharine — QM NJ
Jacob: b 1751 d 5-29-1833 m Tamer Warford Pvt NY
Jacob: b 1758-60 d *p.* 5-15-1816 m Magdaleen — PS NC
Jacob: b 10-3 1756 d 6-3-1843 m (1)Elizabeth Shafer (2)Anna Maria — Pvt PA W★
Jacob A.: b 4-6-1755 d 5-20-1833 m Eva Kneeshern Pvt NY
James: b 10-12-1745 d 6-8-1813 m Hannah Fuller Pvt CL
James: b 1-22-1753 d *c.* 9-18-1783 m (1)Elizabeth Lowrain (2)Ruth Halsey Pvt NJ
James: b 7-12-1756 d 8-9-1833 m Sarah (Cowell) Capt NY ★
James: b 3-22-1760 d 1-11-1850 m Maria Houghtaling Pvt NY
James: b — d *p.* 4-9-1816 m X Capt PA
James: b 4-17-1766 d 9-25-1836 m Nancy Smith Pvt PA
James, Sr.: b *c.* 1728 d 1787 m Elizabeth Ramsey Pvt PS PA
James: b 3-5-1760 d *p.* 1840 m (1) — (2)Mrs Simpson Sol PA ★
James: b 8-15-1750 d 9-17-1802 m Mary Thompson PS Lt SC
James: b *c.* 1759 d 1857 m Anna Foster Pvt SC
James: b 5-20-1762 d 3-3-1818 m Mary Kellough Pvt SC
James: *c.* 1732 d 1- -1782 m Anne — Sol VA
Jane: b *c.* 1759 d 5-21-1842 m Joseph Young PS NY W★
Jared: b 1762 d 1-10-1835 m X Pvt SC ★
Jeremiah: b 8-21-1754 d 3-29-1845 m Mary Saloma Strobeck Ens NY ★
Jesse: b 1-3-1751 d 9-2-1804 m Ruby Richardson Lt NH
Johann Heinrich: b 2-2-1751 d 8-10-1828 m Anna Maria Bastian Pvt PA
John: b 1728 d 1802 m Zerviah Huntington Pvt CT
John: b 3-6-1763 d 10-12-1839 m (1)Nabby Howe (2)Mrs Hannah Brown Pvt PA
John: bpt 2- -1748/9 d 12-17-1797 m (1)Elizabeth Bayley (2)Jonaca Webb Sgt NH
John: b 5-22-1739 d 2-28-1807 m (1)Margaret Conkey (2)Elizabeth Smith Dr PS NH
John: b *a.* 1726 d 1785 m (1)Susannah Gatchell (2)Theodora (Wheelock) Phelps PS NH
John: b 11-30-1750 d 2-16-1826 m Hanna Mitchell Cpl NJ
John: b 10-4-1752 d 9-7-1834 m (1)Elizabeth Parsons (2)Prudence Elliott Sgt NY
John: b 10-8-1759 d 7-1-1820 m Elizabeth Forney Cpl NC
John: b 1759 d 12-13-1837 m (1)Mary Rankin (2)Cynthia McCullough Pvt NC ★
John: b 7-14-1763 d 2-29-1844 m Margaret Galbraith Pvt NC
John: b 1742 d 8-19-1822 m (1)Eliza Taylor (2)Elizabeth Llewllyn Capt PA ★
John: b 1-2-1742 d 9-15-1829 m Eve — Ens PA
John: b 1-12-1750 d 1-8-1811 m Anna Lane Cpl PA
John: b 1758 d *p.* 4-10-1821 m Isabelle — Pvt PA
John: b 1746 d 2-13-1826 m Elizabeth Elder Pvt PA
John: b *c.* 1755 d 8-13-1842 m — Kelly Pvt PA ★
John: b *a.* 1753 d *a.* 1801 m Dorcas — Pvt PA
John: b 12-31-1760 d 11-15-1829 m Lamma Myres PS PA
John: b 1736 d 6-19-1820 m Rebecca Harding Dr RI ★

John: b *c.* 1746 d 10- -1840 m Mary Sarah Beckett Pvt SC
John: b 12-1-1762 d 4-14-1835 m Nancy Saumon Pvt SC
John: b 3-25-1737 d 12-5-1824 m (1)Mary White (2)Mary Setlington Capt VA
John: b 8- -1760 d 6-17-1850 m Keziah Tackett Townsend Spy VA ★
John: b 2-18-1760/1 d 7-5-1843 m (1)Sarah Rodgers (2)Margaret Rodgers Pvt VA ★
John: b 8-24-1764 d 3-25-1855 m Mary Moore PS VA
John: b 1732 d 7-11-1798 m (1)Mary Martin (2)Sarah Martin PS VA
John: b *c.* 1756 d 1828 m X PS VA
John Christian: b 1755 d 2-28-1835 m (1)Mary Elizabeth Ehle (2)Margaret Schunk Pvt VA
Jonas: b *c.* 1745 d 1799-1803 m Prudence Riggs Sol NJ
Jonathan: b 1-12-1756 d 3-27-1807 m Sarah Clifford Pvt NH
Jonathan: b 1739 d 1808 m Zerviah King PS NY
Joseph: b 1761 d 8- -1842 m Elizabeth Thorne Pvt CT
Joseph: b 1749 d 1-20-1834 m Elenor Dombalton Pvt MA ★
Joseph: b 9-25-1762 d *p.* 1812 m Anna Nickerson Pvt MA
Joseph, Sr.: b 8-24-1726 d 4-11-1806 m (1)Anna Folsom (2)Mary Foss Pvt NH
Joseph, Jr.: b 5-4-1754 d 7-6-1812 m Dorcas Margaretta Ewer Cpl NY
Joseph: b 7-16-1768 d 3-30-1850 m Eunice Priest Pvt NH
Joseph: b *c.* 1753 d 3-18-1830 m Jane Flint Pvt NY W★
Joseph: b 1- -1741 d 5-6-1817 m Keziah Alexander Sol NC
Joseph: b 1745/6 d 10-23-1823 m (1)Martha Miller (2)Agnes Woodburn Lt PA
Joshua: b 1739 d 1-8-1832 m Eleanor Whittam Sgt MA
Leonard: b 1-30-1745 d 10-2-1821 m (1)Mary Higgins (2)Elizabeth Doggett PS VA
Levi: b *a.* 1748 d *p.* 10- -1782 m Eunice — Sgt MA
Ludwig, Sr.: b 1729/30 d 1-10-1795 m Mary Magdeline Simmons PS MD
Marcus: b 1754 d *c.* 1839 m Rebecca Jahger Fif PA ★
Martin: b 1732 d *c.* 1777 m Margaret Ursula Winkler Pvt PA
Matthew: bpt 6-4-1745 d 6-17-1827 m Catharina — Pvt NY
Matthew: b *c.* 1735 d *a.* 8-10-1787 m — Pvt PA
Matthias: b 1760 d 8-1-1838 m Anna Barbara Christ Pvt MM MD ★
Michael: b 1753 d 1807 m Elizabeth Barnett Pvt PA
Morgan: b 1713 d 11-20-1792 m Elizabeth Mills Wgm NJ
Morgan: b 10- -1752 d 1-1-1844 m Elizabeth — Pvt NJ ★
Nathan: b 5-16-1742 d 3-5-1793 m Lydia Sears Pvt CT
Nathan: b 1712 d 5-22-1818 m Nancy Hogan Sgt VA ★
Nathaniel: b 10-7-1760 d 11-12-1739 m Chloe Cummings Pvt MA
Nicholas: b 1730 d *p.* 1790 m Rachel Bond Pvt PA
Noah: b 3-5-1752 d 1816 m Mary Chatful Pvt NJ
Notley: b 9-24-1736 d *p.* 3-14-1798 m Ellenor Digges PS MD
Othneil: b 1-29-1758 d 7-28-1846 m Esther Phillips Pvt RI ★
Peter: b 3-16-1731 d 7-11-1809 m (1)Mary Snyder (2)Elizabeth Hummer Cpl NJ
Peter: b 3-2-1756 d 2-14-1842 m Rachel Henry Tms Wgm NJ
Peter: b *c.* 1725 d 1800 m Margaretha Freemire Sol NY
Peter: b *c.* 1730 d 4- -1781 m X Pvt PS NY
Peter: b 1750 d 1795 m Margaret — Lt PA
Peter: b *c.* 1760 d *p.* 1803 m X Pvt VA
Peter Warren: b 1734 d 10-20-1820 m Margaret Servoss Lt NY
Philip: b 3-5-1744/5 d 11-2-1815 m (1)Azube Higgins (2)Anna Snow Pvt MA
Phillip: b 1766 d 7-1-1840 m Amelia (Youngs) Pvt NJ
Powell: b 12-3-1755/6 m Elizabeth Fishbaugh Pvt NJ
Richard 10-24-1753 d 3-23-1837 m Christine Sherman Sgt NY ★
Richard: b *c.* 1740 d 1815 m Mary Margaret Moore QM VA
Robert: b 2-12-1757 d 1-29-1840 m Sarah Briant Pvt NJ ★
Robert: b 1710-15 d *p.* 2-8-1792 m Mary — Sol CS NC
Robert: b 10-12-1722 d 1-16-1797 m Elizabeth Jourdan Pvt PA
Robert: b 1750 d 11-19-1824 m Bethinia York Pvt PA
Robert: b 1-16-1748 d 6-24-1814 m Martha Shields Pvt PA
Robert, Jr.: b 1755-60 d *a.* 1-29-1823 m Mary Coulter Pvt PA
Robert: b 3-4-1752 d 5-4-1790 m Judith Heath Tebbs Lt VA W★
Robert: b *c.* 1735 d *p.* 1804 m Jenny Morrison CS VA
Rufus: b 1748 d 8-24-1828 m Mehitable Tuthill PS NY
Samuel: b 3-14-1740 d 9-19-1810 m Lydia Drew Lt PS CT
Samuel: b 3-19-1756 d 2-27-1819 m Lydia Ames Pvt MA
Samuel, Sr.: b *c.* 1720 d 1793 m Rebecca Tate NC
Samuel: b 7-19-1747 d 8-20-1805 m Hannah Johnson Sgt NH
Samuel: b 5-7-1762 d 2-28-1841 m X Pvt VA PA
Samuel: b 7-6-1756 d 11-16-1847 m Amey Champlin Pvt RI ★
Solomon: b 12-26-1760 d 5-25-1849 m Abigail Bailey Pvt CT
Thomas: b 4-24-1734 d 9-11-1800 m Mary Davis Grd MA
Thomas: b 1745 d *p.* 1830 m Barbara Clingham Pvt PA
Thomas, Sr.: b 1-5-1732 d 7-9-1829 m (1)Judith Johnston (2)Lucy Ragsdale PS NC
Thomas: b *a.* 1746 d *c.* 1800 m Ann Potter Pvt PA
Thomas: b 1-17-1764 d 11-7-1848 m X Cav SC ★
Wm.: b 3-3-1759 d 8-8-1836 m Mary Manning Pvt CT W★
Wm., Sr.: b 1743 d 2-21-1776 m Sophia Box PS GA
Wm., Jr.: b *c.* 1754/5 d 1814 m Mary Henderson Sol GA
Wm.: b *c.* 1736 d *p.* 1- -1783 m Barbara Rittenhouse Pvt MD
Wm.: b *c.* 1706 d *p.* 3-20-1779 m Eleanor Birckhead PS MD
Wm.: b 1714 d *a.* 8-4-1795 m Jane Foster PS MA
Wm.: b 1741 d 4-16-1812 m Elizabeth Johnson Pvt MA
Wm.: b — d 3- -1798 m Sarah Sheppherd Pvt NJ
Wm.: b 1761 d *c.* 1837/8 m X Pvt NC

YOUNG, contd.
Wm.: b *a*. 1760 d 1805 m Catherine Etzler Lt PA
Wm.: b 10-1-1727 d *p*. 3-22-1779 m Margaret Scouller PS PA
Wm.: b 10-23-1743 d 12-27-1820 m Mary Elder Pvt PA
Wm.: b 7-21-1759 d 12-7-1826 m Mary Salmon Capt Lt SC ★
Wm.: b 6-7-1762 d 8-23-1831 m Frances Holloway Pvt SC
Wm.: b — d *p*. 9-22-1824 m Ellender — Sol SC
Wm.: b *c*. 1735 d 4- -1813 m Elizabeth — Lt VA
Wm.: b 1755 d *p*. 9-4-1833 m Sally Singleton Sgt VA ★
Wm.: b 1741 d 1793 m Caroline Walker Ens VA
Winthrop: b 1753 d 1-6-1832 m Mary Otis PS NH
Zebedee: b *c*. 1756 d *p*. 11-20-1801 m Jemima Whipple Pvt RI

YOUNGBLOOD, (includes JUNGBLUT)
Jacob: b 6- -1750 d *p*. 11-13-1832 m X Sgt SC
Johannes Willem: b 1730 d 3-5-1802 m Catherine Buchstaber Pvt
  NY
Peter: b *c*. 1750 d 9-10-1794 m (1)Susannah — (2)Mary Fenden
  Capt SC
Peter: b 1732 d 1788 m Susanna — Sol SC
Samuel: b — d *p*. 1812 m Jane — Pvt SC
Thomas: b 1740 d *p*. 3-28-1816 m Amy Hopkins Pvt SC

YOUNGER,
Joshua: b 5-11-1752 d 8-2-1834 m (1)Elizabeth Lee (2)Catherine
  Yoter Pvt VA ★

YOUNGLOVE,
David: b 7-2-1754 d 7-2-1797 m Nancy Failing Dr NY
Isaiah: b 4-8-1717 d 12-27-1798 m Mary Lucas PS NY
John: b 12-11-1756 d 7-13-1840 m Thankful Copeland Pvt CT
John: b 6-25-1743 d 2-3-1821 m Martha Perine PS 2Maj NY
Joseph: b 10-11-1741 d 3-30-1810 m Azubah Skinner QM NY
Samuel: b 4-15-1763 d 8-30-1846 m (1)Anna Keeler (2)Mary
  Youngs Sgt NY ★
Timothy: b 1733 d 12-31-1796 m Violet — 1Lt MA

YOUNGMAN,
Jabez: b 3-4-1764 d 4-30-1839 m Susannah Powers Pvt NH
John: b 1758 d 1813 m Abigail — Pvt MA NH
Nicholas: b 10-18-1723 d 9-14-1814 m (1)Mary Wright (2)Lydia
  Hobart Pvt NH

YOUNGS,
Abimael: b 6-28-1755 d 8-4-1828 m Mary (Tuthill) Harlow Pvt NY
Abraham: b *c*. 1724 d 7- -1807 m Hannah Hunt Pvt CT
Birdseye: b *c*. 1737 d *c*. 1798 m Rachel Strong 1Lt NY
Daniel: b 1-21-1748 d 11-5-1809 m Susanna Kelsey Capt NY
David: b 8-29-1745 d 8-31-1796 m (1)Elizabeth Tucker (2)Catherine
  Beers Sgt NJ
Eliphalet: b 3-16-1744 d 10-17-1785 m Martha Burnham Cpl CT
Henry: b 4-29-1765 d 12-10-1803 m Elizabeth Rumsey Pvt NY
Israel: b 11-11-1721 d 1-26-1786 m Jemima Brown PS NY
John Fitz: b *c*. 1745 d 12-24-1801 m Mehitable Wiggins Pvt PS NY
Joseph: b 6-9-1760 d 1842 m Elizabeth Peck Pvt CT ★
Joseph: b 1721 d 1815 m (1)Abigail Aldrich (2)Hannah Brown Pvt
  NY
Joseph: b 1732 d 1789 m (1)Deliverance Mills (2)Phebe Young
  (3)Isabel Berry PS NY
Nathan: b 1754 d 2-29-1816 m Mary Terry Pvt PS NY
Reuben: b 6-5-1725 d 12-16-1805 m Mercy — Pvt NY
Richard: b — d 1785 m Martha Webb Cpl CT
Samuel: b *c*. 1744 d 11-25-1823 m Malatiah Fuller Pvt CT
Samuel: b 9-30-1712 d 3-18-1798 m Rebecca Brown PS CT
Samuel: b 11-5-1753 d 11-2-1797 m Rebecca Brush PS NY
Silas, Sr.: b 10-25-1719 d 3-16-1796 m Martha Vail PS NY
Silas, Jr.: b 8-14-1748 d 12-28-1819 m Elizabeth Strong PS NY
Thomas, Sr.: b 1719 d 2-19-1793 m Rhoda Budd PS NY
Thomas, Jr.: b 1748 d 2-16-1816 m Lydia Tuthill PS NY

YOUNT, (includes YUND, YUNDT)
Andrew: b 7-24-1760 d 2-26-1841 m Barbara Dietrich Pvt PA
Daniel: b 7-28-1748 d *p*. 1790 m Anna Maria Hauerer Pvt PA
George: b 3-30-1744 d 4-13-1828 m Eva Catharine Knauss Pvt PA
Henry: b 1757 d 10-20-1822 m Mariann Waymire PS NC
Jacob: b 1752 d 1818 m Amarilla Killiam Sol NC
John: b 8-10-1756 d 4-7-1832 m Rachel Simone Pvt PA
Nicholas: b 3-3-1751 d 2- -1830 m (1)Elizabeth — (2)Theresa —
  Pvt PA

YOUSE,
John: b 10-16-1740 d 11-1-1812 m Catherine Smith Pvt PA
John: b 1747 d 2-22-1823 m Doratha — Pvt PA ★

YOUTZ,
Jacob: b *c*. 1750 d 1804/5 m Ruth Chrysman Pvt PA
Peter: b 1763 d 8-22-1821 m Elizabeth — Pvt PA

YOXTHEIMER,
Henry: b 1753 d *p*. 1832 m Maria — Pvt PA ★

YULE,
James: b 9-13-1755 d 3-30-1832 m Margaret Christman Ens MD

ZABRISKIE,
Christian: b 9-19-1754 d 9-26-1830 m Elizabeth Morgan PS NJ

ZACHARIAS,
Daniel, Jr.: b 5-26-1761 d 4-4-1827 m Elizabeth Reiff Pvt PA
Mathias: b 7-5-1757 d *p*. 1802 m Ann Stockslager Pvt PA

ZACHARY,
James: b *c*. 1730 d *a*. 3-8-1790 m Mary — Pvt GA SC
John: b 1748 d *p*. 1830 m Sarah Hay Sgt VA
Peter: b *c*. 1745 d 1797 m Mary — Sol VA

ZAHNISER,
Matthias: b 1749 d 4-28-1833 m Mary Lint Pvt PS PA

ZANE,
Ebenezer: b 10-7-1747 d 11-19-1812 m Elizabeth McCulloch Col
  PS VA
Elizabeth McCulloch: b 10-30-1748 d *p*. 12-9-1800 m Ebenezer Zane
  PS VA
Elizabeth: b 1766 d 1826-8 m (1)Ephraim McLaughin (2)Jacob Clark
  PS VA
Hester Scull: b 1740 d 4-27-1818 m Joel Zane PS DE
Isaac: b 1753 d 1816 m X PS VA
Jonathan: b 1749 d 1824 m Ann Mills PS VA
Silas: b *c*. 1751 d 1785 m (1)Mrs Katherine Ryan Capt VA
Wm.: b 2-16-1752 d 5- -1824 m Elizabeth Hillman PS NJ

ZARTMAN,
Alexander, Sr.: b 7-29-1731 d 12-2-1803 m Magdalena — Pvt PA
Alexander, Jr.: b 3-19-1756 d 3-23-1819 m Maria Barabara — Pvt
  PA
Henry: b 1750 d 1803 m Elizabeth Hauser PS PA
Jacob, Sr.: b *c*. 1723 d 1793 m Anna Margaretha Riehm Pvt PA
Jacob, Jr.: b 1754 d *p*. 1795 m Regina Fitler Pvt PA

ZECHMAN,
George: b 1752 d 10-26-1841 m Catharine — Pvt PS PA ★

ZEH, (includes ZEAH)
David: b 10-5-1755 d 7-3-1842 m Marua Schaeffer Pvt NY ★
Joost: b 12-28-1740 d 12-12-1823 m Anna Barbara Werner Pvt NY
Joost: b 9-4-1750 d *p*. 1793 m Christina Haines Pvt NY

ZEHMER,
Henry: b 9-13-1755 d 5-20-1810 m Anna Maria Schreiner Pvt PA

ZEILEY, (includes ZEILE & ZIELLEY)
John: b 4-19-1743 d 3-9-1825 m Elizabeth Eckerson Capt NY
Peter: b 10-16-1733 d 12-9-1806 m Cornelia Becker LCol NY
Peter W.: b 10-8-1711 d 6-7-1790 m Martie Eckerson PS NY

ZEITHEISER,
Hartman: b *c*. 1750 d 1830 m Elizabeth — Ens PA

**ZELLER, (includes ZELLAR, ZELLERS & ZOELLER, See also
  SELLERS)**
Andrew: b 8-15-1755 d 5-24-1839 m (1) — (2) — Fif PA
Frantz: b 4-11-1751 d 10-3-1821 m Elizabeth Aurand Sgt PA
George: b *c*. 1748 d 1805 m Maria Coleman Sgt PA
Heinrich: b *a*. 1713 d 1789 m Maria Margretta Rieth Pvt PA
John George: b *c*. 1730 d 1792 m Maria Barbara — PS PA
Peter: b *c*. 1730 d *p*. 1782 m Hannah Bassler Pvt PS PA

ZEPERNICK,
Frederick: b — d 1808 m Elizabeth — Pvt PA

ZERBE,
Christian: b 11-16-1750 d 8-6-1809 m Sophia Elizabeth Eva Maria
  Liecken Sol PA
Daniel: b *c*. 1757 d *p*. 1811 m Maria Wertz PS PA
George: b 4-24-1750 d 1-19-1814 m Barbara Sponchuchen PS PA
John: b 1735-8 d 1805 m Catherine Scheafer Pvt PA
Leonard: b 7-12-1745 d 8-20-1824 m Barbara Wenrick Ens PA
Michael: b 1744 d 1806 m Anna Maria Donmier Sgt PA
Phillip: b *c*. 1717 d 1790 m (1) — (2)Susannah — MM PA

ZERFASS,
Adam: b 1-25-1742 d *p*. 1800 m Mary Elizabeth Shafer Capt PA
John: b *a*. 1755 d *c*. 7-20-1824 m Susannah Hone Sol PA

ZERGER,
Jacob: b *c*. 1757 d *c*. 1815 m Margaret — Pvt PA

ZETTLER,
Daniel: b *c*. 1752 d *p*. 1784 m Hannah Dasher Sol GA

ZEVELY,
Henry: b 12-26-1736 d 5-16-1795 m — Enochs Sol NC

ZIEGLER, (includes ZEIGLER & ZIGLAR)
Andrew: b *c*. 1707 d *p*. 11-20-1794 m Elizabeth Kolb PS PA

Barnet: b 1740 d 1797 m Rosina — CS PA
Dilman: b c. 1734 d 1794 m Barbara — Pvt PA
Emanuel: b 12-22-1762 d 1854 m Julia Felser Pvt PA ★
Francis Ottomar: b 11-17-1750 d 9-17-1800 m Mary Frances Hook Col
  PA
George Phillip: b 8-4-1742 d 9-6-1804 m Eva Uhler Lt PA
John George: b — d p. 3-21-1795 m Anna Catherine Rau Pvt GA
Kilian: b 8-1-1742 d 10-17-1808 m Anna Maria Lischy Pvt PA
Leonard: b 1762 d 8-10-1849 m Nancy Zimmerman Pvt VA ★
Lucas: b 8-5-1744 d 11-4-1812 m (1)Salome Zettler (2)Ann Buntz PS
  GA
Michael: b 1747 d 1809 m (1)Martha Picot (2)Mrs Mary — Pvt SC
Peter: b 1760 d 4- -1819/20 m (1) — Dawson (2)Rebecca Roates
  Ens PA
Philip: b 1734 d p. 1785 m Regina Reguel Pvt PA

ZIMMER,
Adam: b 10-17-1749 d 6-26-1830 m Margaret Schaeffer Pvt NY
George: b 1765 d 8-5-1857 m Katherine Settle Vol NY
Jacob: b 10-16-1722 d 7- -1782 m Catherine Boter PS NY
Peter: b 2-9-1740 d 1797 m Elizabeth Casselman Cpl NY
Wm.: b 10-14-1753 d 10-17-1830 m Nancy Weidman Pvt NY

ZINN,
Henry: b 4- -1752 d 11-25-1837 m (1)Ann Gardner (2)Jane Dourbon
  Brown Pvt SC
Jacob: b 11-25-1749 d 5-20-1815 m Margaret Lutz Fif Drm PA
Jacob: b 1740 d 1815 m Susannah (Ardis) Edmonds Lt SC
John: b 6-21-1763 d 4- -17-1847 m (1)Elizabeth Kizer (2)Nancy
  Mullikin Pvt VA ★

ZINZINDORFER,
Martin: b 6- -1739 d 10-11-1784 m Hannah Binder Pvt PA

ZIRKLE, (includes CIRCLE)
Lewis: b 1738/9 d 1-22-1815 m Mary Magdalene Roush PS VA
Peter: b c. 1740 d 1818 m Fanny — Pvt VA

ZITTRAUER,
Ernest: b c. 1750 d 1817 m (1)Johannah Reitter (2)Anna Catherine
  Pvt GA

ZOLIKOFER, (includes ZOLLICOFER, ZOLLIKOFFER)
George: b 4-11-1738 d 1-4-1815 m Anna Lindsay Capt NC
John Conrad: b 4-13-1742 d 2- -1796 m Caroline Tribolett Capt NC

ZOLL,
Jacob: b 2-16-1743 d 11-16-1819 m Elizabeth Markle PS PA

ZOLLER,
Jacob: b — d 1777 m Elizabeth Moyer Pvt NY

ZOLLINGER,
Jacob: b 11-16-1753 d 4-6-1820 m Rosanna Sprecher Lt PA
Nicholas: b 1752 d c. 1832 m Barbara Miller 2Lt PA
Peter: b 12-22-1756 d 11-4-1842 m (1) — (2) — Capt PA ★

ZORN,
Christian: b 1739 d 12-31-1800 m (1)Elizabeth Debusin (2)Eve
  — Pvt PS PA

ZUBER, (or ZUBERS)
Abraham: b 1740-5 d 1802 m Mary Bartling Lt PA
John: b c. 1750 d c. 1850 m Elizabeth Volker Pvt SC

ZUBLY,
David: b c. 1730 d a. 4-16-1790 m Ann Meyer PS SC

ZUG, (includes ZOOK & ZUCK)
Christian: b c. 1730 d 1815 m Barbara Bollinger Pvt PA
Christian: b 4-20-1752 d 10-8-1826 m Magdalena Blank Pvt PA
Jacob: b 4- -1757 d 2- -1829 m (1)Gertrude Kenege (2)Mary
  Willauer Pvt PA

ZUMWALT, (includes SUMWALT)
Adam: b 1755/6 d 1834 m Mary Roth Pvt VA ★
Christopher: b 1750 d 1819 m Marilius — Pvt VA
George H.: b 3-31-1760 d 10-5-1835 m Mary Wirt Sol PA
George: b c. 1745 d p. 9-4-1815 m Mary — Pvt VA
John: b c. 1750 d a. 2-27-1821 m Elizabeth Conrad Sol VA

ZWINGLI,
George, Jr.: b 1755 d 1842 m X PS Capt MD
George, Sr.: b 1724 d 1800 m Margaretta Thomas PS MD